Pronunciation Symbols

Pronunciations are given using the International Phonetic Alphabet (IPA). The symbols used, with their values, are as follows:

Consonants

$b, d, f, h, k, l, m, n, p, r, s, t, v, w,$ and z have their usual English values. Other symbols are used as follows:

g	get	θ	thin	x	loch
j	yes	ð	this	tʃ	chip
ʃ	she	ŋ	ring	dʒ	jar
ʒ	vision				

Vowels

æ	cat	i:	see	əi	pipe
ɑr	arm	ɒ	hot	au	how
e	bed	ɔr	pore	ʌu	house
ə	ago	ʌ	run	ei	day
ɜr	her	ʊ	put	o:	no
ɪ	sit	u:	too	ɔi	boy
i	cozy	ai	my		

- In addition the following IPA symbols are used in the representation of foreign pronunciations:

ã	franglais
æ̃	Canadien
ɔ̃	Brayon

- The main or primary stress of a word is shown by ' preceding the relevant syllable; any secondary stress in words of three or more syllables is shown by , preceding the relevant syllable.

The Canadian Oxford Paperback Dictionary

Edited by
Alex Bisset

OXFORD
UNIVERSITY PRESS

OXFORD
UNIVERSITY PRESS

70 Wynford Drive, Don Mills, Ontario M3C 1J9
www.oupcan.com

Oxford University Press is a department of the Univesity of Oxford. It furthers the University's objective of excellence in research, scholarship, and education by publishing worldwide in

Oxford New York
Athens Auckland Bangkok Bogotá Buenos Aires Calcutta
Cape Town Chennai Dar es Salaam Delhi Florence Hong Kong Istanbul
Karachi Kuala Lumpur Madrid Melbourne Mexico City Mumbai
Nairobi Paris São Paulo Singapore Taipei Tokyo Toronto Warsaw

and associated companies in
Berlin Ibadan

Oxford is a trade mark of Oxford University Press in the UK and in certain other countries

Published in Canada
by Oxford University Press

Copyright © Oxford University Press Canada 2000

Canadian Cataloguing in Publication Data
Main entry under title:

The Canadian Oxford paperback dictionary

ISBN 0-19-541453-5

1. English language – Canada – Dictionaries.   2. English language – Dictionaries.
3. Canadianisms (English) – Dictionaries.*   I. Bisset, Alex, 1969–   .

PE3235.C36 2000   423   C00-930694-3

1 2 3 4 – 03 02 01 00

This book is printed on permanent (acid-free) paper ∞.

Printed in Canada

Guide to the Use of This Dictionary

The *Canadian Oxford Paperback Dictionary* is designed to be as straightforward and self-explanatory as possible and the use of special conventions has been kept to a minimum. The following notes will enable the reader to understand more fully the principles involved in assembling the information.

1. HEADWORD

The headword is printed in large bold roman type, or in large bold italic type if the word is originally a foreign word and not naturalized in English.

Order of headwords

● Strict alphabetical order is followed even when the headword consists of more than one word or of a hyphenated word.

● Capitalized headwords come before lower case headwords of the same spelling.

Form of headwords

● All compound nouns, adjectives, and adverbs, whether forming one word (such as **bathroom**, **newspaper**) or consisting of two or more words separated by a space or a hyphen (such as **serial number**, **drawing-room**) are listed as main entries.

Variant spellings

Variant spellings or forms are given at the main headword, in bold type in brackets before the definition, or are given their own headword entry and cross-reference when these are more than seven entries away from the main headword. The main headword represents the most common form in Canadian usage.

> **phony** *informal* (also **phoney**) ● *adj.* (**phonier, phoniest**) **1** sham; counterfeit; fake. **2** insincere. ● *n.* (*pl.* **-ies** or **-eys**) a phony person or thing. ◻ **phoniness** *n.*

> **artefact** *var. of* ARTIFACT.

> **artifact** *n.* a product of human art and workmanship. ◻ **artifactual** *adj.*

● If the variant spelling or form applies only to one sense or part of an entry it will appear at that sense or part of the entry.

> **alpine** ● *adj.* **1 a** of or relating to high mountains. **b** growing or found on high mountains, esp. above the timberline. **2** (**Alpine**) of or relating to the Alps. **3** of or relating to competitive downhill or slalom skiing. ● *n.* a plant native or suited to mountain districts.

> **Neanderthal** /niˈændɜr,θɒl, -,tɒl/ ● *adj.* **1** of or belonging to the type of human widely distributed in paleolithic Europe, with a retreating forehead and massive brow ridges. **2** (also **neanderthal**) *jocular* or *derogatory* **a** primitive, uncivilized, uncouth. **b** reactionary; extremely conservative. ● *n.* **1** a Neanderthal hominid. **2** (also **neanderthal**) *jocular* or *derogatory* **a** a primitive, uncivilized, or uncouth person. **b** a reactionary or extremely conservative person.

● Variant spellings chiefly restricted to certain parts of the English-speaking world are introduced by an appropriate restrictive label. Such labels indicate only that the variants are very infrequent in Canadian practice, not that they are unacceptable.

> **anaemia** etc. esp. *Brit. var. of* ANEMIA etc.

> **anemia** /əˈniːmiə/ *n.* a deficiency in the blood, usu. of red cells or their hemoglobin, resulting in pallor and weariness.

> **fibreglass** *n.* (also esp. *US* **fiberglass**) any material consisting of glass filaments woven into a textile or paper, or embedded in plastic etc., for use as a construction or insulation material.

Alternative names

Alternative names or forms are occasionally given at the main headword. They are also given their own headword entry and cross-reference when these are more than seven entries away from the main headword. Pronunciation, where appropriate, will be given at the cross-reference entry, not at the main headword. The main headword represents the most common form in Canadian usage.

Abbreviations

Many commonly used abbreviations are included at the main headword entry for the full form, in bold, preceded by 'Abbr.'. These and other abbreviations will also be found as entries, with a cross-reference from the abbreviation to the main entry. In cases where the abbreviation is significantly more common than the full form, however, the main entry is to be found at the the abbreviation.

CCF *abbr. Cdn hist.* Co-operative Commonwealth Federation. □ **CCFer** *n.*

Co-operative Commonwealth Federation *n. hist.* (in Canada) a progressive labour party formed in 1932, refounded as the NDP in 1961. Abbr.: **CCF**.

Registered Home Ownership Savings Plan *n. Cdn* = RHOSP.

RHOSP /ˈɑrhɒsp/ *abbr. Cdn* Registered Home Ownership Savings Plan, a tax-sheltered account in which a first-time homebuyer may save money for a down payment.

Homographs

Words that are significantly different in origin but spelled the same way (called homographs) are treated as separate headwords, distinguished by superscript numbers immediately following the headword.

butt[1] ● *v.* **1** *intr. & tr.* push or strike with the head or horns. **2** *intr.* (usu. foll. by *out*) project, jut. **3** *intr. & tr.* (usu. foll. by *against, on*) lie or place with one end flat against; abut. ● *n.* **1** a push or blow made with the head or horns. **2** (also **butt joint**) a simple joint in which two pieces of wood etc. are bonded without overlapping. □ **butt in 1** interrupt, meddle. **2** push into (a line of people) out of turn. **butt out** esp. *N Amer.* cease to interrupt or meddle.

butt[2] *n.* **1** (often foll. by *of*) an object of ridicule etc. (*the butt of his jokes*). **2 a** a mound behind a target to stop stray bullets etc. **b** (in *pl.*) a shooting range. **c** a target.

butt[3] ● *n.* **1** (also **butt end**) the thicker end, esp. of a tool or a weapon (*gun butt*). **2** *N Amer.* a cut of pork from the shoulder. **3 a** the stub of a cigar or a cigarette. **b** *slang* a cigarette. **4** esp. *N Amer. slang* the buttocks. **5** the trunk of a tree, esp. the part just above the ground. ● *v.tr. N Amer.* extinguish (a cigarette) by pressing it into an ashtray etc. □ **butt out** *N Amer.* **1** = BUTT *v.* **2** stop smoking, esp. permanently.

butt[4] *n.* **1** a large cask for wine or ale. **2** a former unit of measure equal to two hogsheads.

2. PRONUNCIATION

Guidance on the pronunciation of headwords is given only for difficult or rare words and for words with more than one possible pronunciation. In those cases where pronunciations are given, they are found immediately after the headword to which they apply, enclosed in oblique strokes //. The pronunciations given in this dictionary are based on thorough surveys of English-speaking Canadians from across the country.

● A pronunciation is not given for headwords consisting of more than one word where the separate words are listed elsewhere in the dictionary with their own pronunciation.

● In some cases, more than one pronunciation is given: that given first is generally the most common pronunciation in Canada, though there may in fact be little difference in the frequency of use of the given pronunciations.

● Guidance on the pronunciation of words printed in bold type within an entry (for example, in the derivatives list) is limited to cases in which the pronunciation is substantially different from that of the headword.

The International Phonetic Alphabet

Pronunciations are given using the International Phonetic Alphabet (IPA). The symbols used, with their values, are to be found on the inside front cover of this volume.

3. PART OF SPEECH

● A part of speech identifier, such as *n.* (= noun), *v.* (= verb), *adj.* (= adjective), is given for all main headwords.

● All derivatives are given a part of speech identifier. Phrases listed under a main headword are given a part of speech when necessary to aid clarity.

● When a headword has more than one part of speech, the treatment of successive parts of speech is introduced by ● in each case:

lack ● *n.* (usu. foll. by *of*) an absence, want, or deficiency. ● *v.tr.* be without or deficient in (*lacks courage*). □ **for lack of** owing to the absence of. **lack for** lack (*never lacks for odd jobs*).

● The following standard parts of speech are used (the abbreviation used is given in brackets):

adjective (*adj.*)
adverb (*adv.*)
conjunction (*conj.*)
interjection (*interj.*)
noun (*n.*)
preposition (*prep.*)
pronoun (*pron.*)
verb (*v.*)
verb, auxiliary (*v.aux.*)
verb, intransitive (*v.intr.*)
verb, reflexive (*v.refl.*)
verb, transitive (*v.tr.*)

• The following standard identifiers are used in place of a part of speech:

abbreviation (*abbr.*)
combining form (*comb.form*)
contraction (*contr.*)
prefix
suffix
symbol

The following additional explanations should also be noted (see also section 7 below):

• *attrib.* (= attributive) is used to describe an adjective placed in front of the word it modifies; *attrib.adj.* is used as a part of speech identifier for adjectives which can normally only be used attributively, as **breakneck** in *breakneck speed* or **consulting** in *consulting physician*.

• *attrib.* is also used to describe a noun which is placed before and used to modify another noun but where its function is not fully adjectival (e.g. **prize** in *a prize poem*; *the poem is prize* is not acceptable usage).

• *predic.* (= predicative) is used to describe an adjective placed in the predicate of a sentence (usually after a verb); *predic.adj.* is used as a part of speech identifier for adjectives which can normally only be used predicatively, as **asleep** in *she's asleep* (not *the asleep child*), or **bonkers** in *he's bonkers* (not *the bonkers character*).

• 'in *comb.*' (= in combination) refers to uses of words (especially adjectives) as an element joined usually by a hyphen with another word, as **bellied**, in *pot-bellied*, *yellow-bellied*, and so on.

4. INFLECTION

Inflection of words (i.e. plurals, past tenses, etc.) is given after the part of speech concerned:

> **char**[1] ● *v.tr. & intr.* (**charred, charring**) **1** make or become black by burning; scorch. **2** burn or be burned to charcoal. ● *n.* a charred substance.

> **safari** *n.* (*pl.* **-s**) **1** a hunting or scientific expedition, esp. in East Africa (*go on safari*). **2** a sightseeing trip esp. to see African animals in their natural habitat.

• The forms given are those normally in use in Canadian English. Variant forms with restricted distribution are identified by the appropriate label.

> **catalogue** (also esp. *US* **catalog**) ● *n.* **1** a complete list of items (e.g. articles for sale, books held by a library), usu. in alphabetical or other systematic order and often with a description of each. **2** an extensive list (*a catalogue of crimes*). ● *v.tr.* (**catalogues, catalogued, cataloguing**; *US* **catalogs, cataloged, cataloging**) **1** make a catalogue of. **2** enter in a catalogue. □ **cataloguer** *n.*

• Pronunciation of inflected forms is given when this differs significantly from the pronunciation of the headword. The designation '*pronunc.* same' denotes that the pronunciation, despite a change of form, is the same as that of the headword.

• The inflection of nouns, verbs, adjectives, and adverbs is given when it is irregular (as described below) or when, though regular, it may cause difficulty (as with forms such as **budgeted**, **coos**, and **taxis**).

Plurals of nouns

Nouns that form their plural regularly by adding -*s* (or -*es* when they end in -*s*, -*x*, -*z*, -*sh*, or soft -*ch*) receive no comment. Other plural forms are indicated, notably:

• nouns ending in -*i* or -*o*.

• nouns ending in -*y*.

• nouns ending in Latinate forms such as -*a* and -*um*.

• nouns with more than one plural form, e.g. **fish** and **aquarium**.

• nouns with plurals involving a change in the stem, e.g. **foot**, **feet**.

• nouns with a plural form identical to the singular form, e.g. **sheep**.

• nouns ending in -*ful*, e.g. **handful**.

Forms of verbs

The following forms are regarded as regular:

• third person singular present forms adding -*s* to the stem (or -*es* to stems ending in -*s*, -*x*, -*z*, -*sh*, or soft -*ch*).

• past tenses and past participles adding -*ed* to the stem, dropping a final silent *e* (e.g. **changed**, **danced**).

• present participles adding -*ing* to the stem, dropping a final silent *e* (e.g. **changing**, **dancing**).

Other forms are given, notably:

• doubling of a final consonant, e.g. **bat**, **batted**, **batting**.

• strong and irregular forms involving a change in the stem, e.g. **come**, **came**, **come**, and **go**, **went**, **gone**.

Comparative and superlative of adjectives and adverbs

• Words of one syllable adding -*er* or -*est* and those ending in silent *e* dropping the *e* (e.g. **braver**, **bravest**) are regarded as regular. Most one-syllable words have these forms, but participial adjectives (e.g. **pleased**) do not.

• Those that double a final consonant (e.g. **hot**, **hotter**, **hottest**) are given, as are two-syllable words that have comparative and superlative forms in -*er* and -*est* (of which very many are forms ending in *-y*, e.g. **happy, -ier, -iest**, and their negative forms, e.g. **unhappy, -ier, -iest**).

● It should be noted that specification of these forms indicates only that they are used; it is usually also possible to form comparatives with *more* and superlatives with *most* (as in *more happy, most unhappy*), which is the standard way of proceeding with adjectives and adverbs that cannot be inflected.

Adjectives in *-able* formed from transitive verbs

These are given as derivatives when there is sufficient evidence of their currency; in general they are formed as follows:

● Verbs drop silent final *-e* except after *c* and *g* (e.g. **achievable** but **exchangeable**).

● Verbs of more than one syllable ending in *y* (preceded by a consonant) change *y* to *i* (e.g. **enviable, fanciable**).

● A final consonant is often doubled as in normal inflection (e.g. **conferrable, regrettable**).

5. DEFINITION

Definitions are listed in a numbered sequence in order of comparative familiarity and importance, with the most current and important senses first. They are subdivided into lettered senses (**a, b,** etc.) when these are closely related or call for collective treatment.

pan¹ ● *n.* **1 a** a cooking vessel of metal, earthenware, heat-resistant glass, etc. **b** the contents of this. **2** a panlike vessel in which substances are heated etc. **3** any similar shallow container such as the bowl of a pair of scales. **4** *N Amer.* = ICE PAN. **5** a hollow in the ground. **6** a hard substratum of soil. **7 a** a metal drum in a steel band. **b** steel-band music and the associated culture. ● *v.* (**panned, panning**) **1** *tr. informal* criticize severely. **2 a** *tr.* wash (gold-bearing gravel) in a shallow pan. **b** *intr.* search for gold by panning gravel. **c** *intr.* (foll. by *out*) (of gravel) yield gold. □ **pan out** (of an action etc.) turn out well or in a specified way. □ **panful** *n.* (*pl.* **-fuls**). **panlike** *adj.*

6. ILLUSTRATIVE EXAMPLES

Many examples of words in use are given to support, and in some cases supplement, the definitions. These appear in italics in brackets. They are meant to amplify meaning and (especially when following a grammatical point) illustrate how the word is used in context.

7. GRAMMATICAL INFORMATION

Definitions are often accompanied by expla-nations in brackets of how the word or phrase in question is used in context. Often, the comment refers to words that usually follow (foll. by) or precede (prec. by) the word being explained.

pride ● *n.* **1 a** a feeling of elation or satisfaction at achievements or qualities or possessions etc. that do one credit. **b** (prec. by *the*; foll. by *of*) an object of this feeling (*the pride of the museum's collection*). **c** the foremost or best of a group. **2** a high or overbearing opinion of one's worth or importance. **3** knowledge of one's own worth or character; a sense of dignity and respect for oneself. **4** a group or company (of animals, esp. lions). ● *v.refl.* (foll. by *on, upon*) be proud of. □ **one's pride and joy** a thing of which one is very proud. **take pride** (or **a pride**) **in 1** be proud of. **2** maintain in good condition or appearance. □ **prideful** *adj.* **pridefully** *adv.*

● With verbs, the fact that a sense is transitive or intransitive can affect the construction. In the examples given below, prevail is intransitive (and the construction is *prevail on a person*) and urge is transitive (and the construction is *urge a person on*).

prevail *v.intr.* **1** (often foll. by *against, over*) be victorious or gain mastery. **2** be the more usual or predominant. **3** exist or occur in general use or experience; be current. **4** (foll. by *on, upon*) persuade.

urge ● *v.tr.* **1** (often foll. by *on*) drive, hasten, or impel with force or encouragement (*she urged her teammates on*). **2** encourage or entreat earnestly or persistently; exhort (*urged them to go*). **3** (often foll. by *on, upon*) advocate (an action or argument etc.) pressingly or emphatically (to a person). **4** advocate or recommend eagerly or insistently (*we urge caution; we urge that they should be cautious*). **5** present or state earnestly or insistently in argument, justification, or defence (*I must urge the seriousness of this problem*). ● *n.* a strong impulse, desire, or tendency. □ **urging** *n.*

● The formula (foll. by *to* + infin.) means that the word is followed by a normal infinitive with *to*, as in *want to leave* and *eager to learn*.

● The formula (foll. by *that* + clause) indicates the routine addition of a clause with *that*, as in *said that it was late*.

● 'pres. part.' and 'verbal noun' denote verbal forms in *-ing* that function as adjectives and nouns respectively, as in *set him laughing* and *tired of asking*.

8. USAGE

If the use of a word is restricted in any way, this is indicated by any of various labels printed in italics, as follows:

Geographical labels

● *Cdn* indicates that the use is found exclusively in Canadian English. To show that a use is restricted to a particular region or regions within Canada, any of the following labels may be included in addition to *Cdn: Alta., BC, Cape Breton, E Ont., Man., Maritimes, NB, Nfld, NS, PEI, North, NW Ont., NWT, Ont., Prairies, Que., Sask., S Ont., West,* and *Yukon.*

● *N Amer.* indicates that the use is found chiefly in Canada and the US but not in British English.

● *Brit.* indicates that the use is found chiefly in British English (and often also in Australian and New Zealand English and in other parts of the Commonwealth except Canada) but not in North American English.

● *US* indicates that the use is found chiefly in American English but not in Canadian or British English except as a conscious Americanism.

● Other geographical designations (e.g. *Austral., NZ, Scot., South Africa*) restrict uses to the areas named.

● These usage labels should be distinguished from comments of the type '(in the UK)' or '(in Canada)' preceding definitions, which indicate that the thing defined (usually an institution or organization) pertains only to the country named, and that the name given is used by all speakers of whatever nationality to denote the institution or organization.

> **FCC** *abbr.* (in Canada) Farm Credit Corporation.

Register labels

Levels of usage, or registers, are indicated as follows:

● *formal* indicates uses that are normally restricted to formal (esp. written) English, e.g. **commence**.

● *informal* indicates a use that is normally restricted to informal (esp. spoken) English.

● *slang* indicates a use of the most informal kind, unsuited to formal written English and often restricted to a particular social group.

● *coarse slang* indicates a slang use which is normally taboo.

● *dialect* indicates a word that is restricted to nonstandard or dialect use.

● *archaic* indicates a word that is now obsolete and found only in texts at least a century old, or in special contexts such as legal or religious use, or is used for special effect, e.g. **brimstone**.

● *dated* indicates a word from living memory that is no longer current, which may still be used occasionally by older generations, but would strike most people as old-fashioned, e.g. **beau**.

● *literary* indicates a word or use that is found chiefly in literature.

● *jocular* indicates uses that are intended to be humorous or playful.

● *derogatory* denotes uses that are intentionally disparaging.

● *offensive* denotes uses that cause offence, whether intentionally or not.

● *disputed* indicates a use that is disputed (and often regarded as erroneous or controversial). Often this is enough to alert the user to a danger or difficulty; when further explanation is needed a usage note (see note below) is used as well or instead. In using this label the editors are not passing judgment on disputed words and usages; they are merely indicating that these words and usages are in fact current, and warning that their use may provoke criticism.

● *hist.* (= historical) denotes a word or use that is confined to historical reference, normally because the thing referred to no longer exists.

● *proprietary* denotes a term that has the status of a trade mark (see Note on proprietary status, found at the end of this guide).

Subject labels

The many subject labels, e.g. *Law, Med., Math., Naut.,* show that a word or sense is current only in a particular field of activity.

Usage notes

These are added to give extra information not central to the definition, and to explain points of grammar and usage. They are introduced by the symbol ¶. The purpose of these notes is not to prescribe usage but to alert the user to a difficulty or controversy attached to a particular use.

9. IDIOMS AND PHRASAL VERBS

These are listed in alphabetical order after the treatment of the main senses, introduced by the symbol □. The words *a, the, one,* and *person* do not count for purposes of alphabetical order:

> **ask** *v.* **1** *tr.* call for an answer to or about (*ask him his name; ask a question of her*). **2** *tr.* seek to obtain from another person (*ask a favour of; ask to be allowed*). **3** *tr.* invite; request the company of (*must ask them over; asked her to dinner*). **4** *intr.* (foll. by *for*) seek to obtain, meet, or be directed to (*ask for a donation; asking for you*). □ **ask after** inquire about (esp. a person). **ask for it** *slang* invite trouble. **ask me another** *informal* I do not know. **for the asking** (obtainable) for nothing. **I ask you!** an exclamation of disgust, surprise, etc. **if you ask me** *informal* in my opinion. □ **asker** *n.*

They are normally defined under the first important word in the phrase, except when a later word is more clearly the key word or is the common word in a phrase with variants (in which case a cross-reference often appears at the entry for the first word):

yea ● *interj.* **1** yes. **2** = YAY[1]. ● *adv.* indeed, even (*ready, yea eager*). ● *n.* **1** the word 'yea'. **2** an affirmative answer or assent, esp. in voting. □ **the yeas have it** = THE AYES HAVE IT (*see* AYE[1]).

10. DERIVATIVES

Words formed by adding a suffix to another word are in many cases listed at the end of the entry for the main word, introduced in a separate section by the symbol □. In this position they are not given a definition since they can be understood from the sense of the main word.

zoology /zu:ˈɒlədʒi, zo:-/ *n.* the scientific study of animals, esp. with reference to their structure, physiology, classification, and distribution. □ **zoologist** *n.* **zoological** *adj.* **zoologically** *adv.*

When further definition is called for they are given main entries in their own right (e.g. **changeable**).

11. PREFIXES, SUFFIXES, AND COMBINING FORMS

A large selection of prefixes (**ex-**, **re-**, etc.), suffixes (**-ness**, etc.), and combining forms (such as **bio-** and **-aholic**) is given in the main body of the text.

● The pronunciation given for a prefix, suffix, or combining form is an approximate one for purposes of articulating and (in some cases) identifying the headword; pronunciation and stress may change considerably when they form part of a word.

● Some words beginning with the prefixes *in-*, *non-*, *re-*, and *un-* will be found at the bottom of the page on which they would normally appear, but with no definition given. These words are included for spelling purposes; their meanings are easily deducible by applying the prefix to the root word.

12. CROSS-REFERENCES

These are introduced by any of a number of reference types, as follows:

● '=' denotes that the meaning of the item at which the cross-reference occurs is the same as that of the item referred to.

● 'see' indicates that information will be found at the point referred to, and is widely used in the idiom sections of entries to deal with items that can be located at any of a number of words included in the idiom.

● 'see also' indicates that further information can be found at the point referred to.

● 'compare' denotes an item related or relevant to the one being consulted, and the reference often completes or clarifies the exact meaning of the item being treated.

● 'opp.' refers to a word or sense that is opposite to the one being treated, and again often completes or clarifies the sense.

● References of the kind '*pl.* of' (= plural of), '*past* of' (= past tense of), etc., are given at entries for inflections and other related forms.

● 'var. of' (= variant of) refers to a word that is the main headword form of one or more variant forms.

13. ABBREVIATIONS AND SYMBOLS

A complete list of the abbreviations commonly used in this dictionary can be found inside the back cover of this volume. Abbreviations in general use (such as 'etc.', 'i.e.') are explained in the dictionary itself.

Symbols used in the dictionary

¶ introduces notes on usage.

□ introduces defined phrases and idioms, or undefined derivatives formed by adding a suffix to the main word.

● introduces a new part of speech.

14. NOTE ON PROPRIETARY STATUS

This dictionary includes some words which have or are asserted to have proprietary status as trademarks or otherwise. Their inclusion does not imply that they have acquired for legal purposes a non-proprietary or general significance nor any other judgment concerning their legal status. In cases where the editors have some evidence that a word has proprietary status this is indicated in the entry for that word but no judgment concerning the legal status of such words is made or implied thereby.

Acknowledgements

Producing *The Canadian Oxford Paperback Dictionary* would not have been possible without the excellent foundation provided by *The Canadian Oxford Dictionary*. The unparalleled research into and analysis of Canadian English that has been carried on by Oxford University Press Canada over the past seven years has already produced two outstanding dictionaries, and it is my hope that *The Canadian Oxford Paperback Dictionary* will live up to the standards that these two dictionaries have set. I am especially grateful to my colleagues Katherine Barber, editor-in-chief of *The Canadian Oxford Dictionary*, and Robert Pontisso and Eric Sinkins, editors of *The Canadian Oxford Spelling Dictionary*, for their support, advice, and assistance. I am also indebted to my wife, Elizabeth, for her many years of encouragement, and to my daughter, Maggie, for the joy that she has brought to my life.

W.A.B.

Aa

A¹ *n.* (also **a**) (*pl.* **As** or **A's**) **1** the first letter of the alphabet. **2** *Music* the sixth note of the diatonic scale of C major. **3** the first hypothetical person or example. **4** the highest class or category (of academic marks etc.). **5** (usu. **a**) *Algebra* the first known quantity. **6** a human blood type of the ABO system. □ **from A to B** from one place to another. **from A to Z** over the entire range, completely.

A² *abbr.* (also **A.**) **1** ampere(s). **2** answer. **3** Associate of. **4** atomic (energy etc.). **5** alto. **6** analog (recording).

Å *abbr.* angstrom(s).

A1 *adj. informal* excellent; first-rate.

a¹ *indefinite article* (also **an** before a vowel) **1** (as an unemphatic substitute) one, some, any. **2** one like (*a Judas*). **3** one single (*not a thing*). **4** the same (*all of a size*). **5** in, to, or for each (*twice a year; $20 a person*).

a² *abbr.* are (metric unit).

AA *abbr.* **1** ALCOHOLICS ANONYMOUS. **2** a size of battery, having a voltage of 1.5 V. **3** *Sport* **a** a level of amateur competition. **b** *Baseball* a minor league directly below AAA. **4** a level of bond rating below AAA. **5** *Military* anti-aircraft. **6** (in Ontario) ADULT ACCOMPANIMENT.

AAA *abbr.* **1** a size of battery, having a voltage of 1.5 V. **2** Amateur Athletic Association. **3** *Sport* **a** a level of amateur sports competition. **b** *Baseball* a minor league directly below the major leagues. **4** the highest level of bond or credit rating.

aardvark *n.* a nocturnal, insectivorous, badger-sized mammal, *Orycteropus afer*, having large ears, a long snout, and a long extensile tongue, native to sub-Saharan Africa.

aardwolf *n.* (*pl.* **aardwolves**) an African mammal, *Proteles cristatus*, related to the hyena family, with grey fur and black stripes, that feeds on insects.

AB¹ *n.* a human blood type of the ABO system.

AB² *abbr.* **1** Alberta (in postal use). **2** *US* Bachelor of Arts. **3** *Baseball* (times) at bat. **4** able rating or seaman.

ab *n.* (usu. in *pl.*) *slang* an abdominal muscle.

aback *adv.* □ **take aback** surprise, disconcert.

abacus /'æbəkəs/ *n.* (*pl.* **abacuses**) an oblong frame with rows of wires or grooves along which beads are slid, used for calculating.

abalone /ˌæbə'loːni/ *n.* any mollusc of the genus *Haliotis*, with a shallow ear-shaped shell having respiratory holes, and lined with mother-of-pearl.

abandon ● *v.tr.* **1** give up completely or before completion. **2 a** forsake or desert (a person or a post of responsibility). **b** leave or desert (a motor vehicle or ship). **3 a** give up to another's control or mercy. **b** *refl.* yield oneself completely to a passion or impulse. ● *n.* lack of inhibition or restraint; reckless freedom of manner (*wild abandon*). □ **abandonment** *n.*

abandoned *adj.* **1 a** (of a person) deserted, forsaken. **b** (of a building, vehicle, etc.) left empty or unused. **2** (of a person or behaviour) unrestrained, profligate.

abase *v.tr. & refl.* humiliate or degrade (another person or oneself). □ **abasement** *n.*

abash *v.tr.* (usu. as **abashed** *adj.*) embarrass.

abate *v.* **1** *tr. & intr.* make or become less strong, severe,

intense, etc. **2** *tr. Law* **a** quash (a writ or action). **b** put an end to (a nuisance). □ **abatement** *n.*

abattoir /'æbəˌtwɑr/ *n.* a slaughterhouse.

abbé /æ'bei/ *n.* a francophone priest not belonging to a religious order.

abbess /'æbəs/ *n.* a woman who is the head of certain communities of nuns.

abbey *n.* (*pl.* **-eys**) **1** the building(s) occupied by a community of monks or nuns. **2** the community itself. **3** a church or house that was an abbey.

abbot *n.* a man who is the head of an abbey of monks.

abbreviate *v.tr.* shorten, esp. represent (a word etc.) by a part of it. □ **abbreviation** *n.*

ABC *n.* **1** the alphabet. **2** the rudiments of any subject. **3** an alphabetical guide.

abdicate *v.* **1** *intr. & tr.* give up or renounce (the throne). **2** *tr.* renounce (a responsibility, duty, etc.). □ **abdication** *n.* **abdicator** *n.*

abdomen *n.* **1** the part of the body containing the stomach, bowels, reproductive organs, etc. **2** *Zool.* the hinder part of an insect, crustacean, spider, etc.

abdominal /æb'dɒmɪnl/ ● *adj.* of or pertaining to the abdomen. ● *n.* (usu. in *pl.*) an abdominal muscle. □ **abdominally** *adv.*

abduct *v.tr.* carry off or kidnap (a person) illegally by force or deception. □ **abduction** *n.* **abductor** *n.*

Abegweit /'æbəgˌwɪt/ *n.* a member of an Algonquian band living on PEI.

Abenaki /æbə'næki/ ● *n.* **1** (*pl.* same or **-s**) a member of an Algonquian-speaking Aboriginal people of the eastern woodlands of N America, now living in S Quebec and Maine. **2** the language of the Abenaki. ● *adj.* of or relating to the Abenaki.

Aberdeen Angus *n.* a breed of hornless black beef cattle, with a compact and low-set body.

aberrant /ə'berənt/ *adj.* **1** esp. *Biol.* diverging from the normal type. **2** departing from an accepted standard. □ **aberrance** *n.* **aberrancy** *n.*

aberration /ˌæbə'reiʃən/ *n.* **1** a departure from what is normal or accepted or regarded as right. **2** a moral or mental lapse. **3** the apparent displacement of a celestial body caused by the observer's velocity.

abet *v.tr.* (**abetted**, **abetting**) (often in **aid and abet**) encourage or assist (esp. an offender or offence). □ **abetment** *n.* **abettor** *n.*

abhor /əb'hɔr/ *v.tr.* (**abhorred**, **abhorring**) detest; regard with disgust and hatred. □ **abhorrence** *n.*

abhorrent *adj.* **1** (often foll. by *to*) (of conduct etc.) inspiring disgust, repugnant; hateful, detestable. **2** (foll. by *to*) not in accordance with; strongly conflicting with (*abhorrent to the spirit of the law*).

abide *v.* (*past* **abided** or rarely **abode**) **1** *tr.* (usu. in *neg.* or *interrog.*) tolerate, endure (*can't abide him*). **2** *intr.* (foll. by *by*) **a** act in accordance with (*abide by the rules*). **b** remain faithful to (a promise).

abiding *adj.* enduring, permanent. □ **abidingly** *adv.*

ability *n.* (*pl.* **-ies**) **1** (often foll. by *to* + infin.) capacity or power. **2** cleverness, talent; mental power.

abject *adj.* **1** miserable, wretched (*abject poverty*). **2**

degraded, humble (*abject apology*). **3** despicable. □

abjection *n.* **abjectly** *adv.* **abjectness** *n.*

abjure /əb'dʒʊr/ *v.tr.* **1** renounce on oath (an opinion, cause, claim, etc.). **2** swear perpetual absence from (one's country etc.). □ **abjuration** *n.*

ablaze *predic.adj. & adv.* **1** on fire (*set it ablaze; the house was ablaze*). **2** (often foll. by *with*) glittering, glowing. **3** (often foll. by *with*) greatly excited.

able *adj.* (**abler, ablest**) **1** (often foll. by *to* + infin.; used esp. in *is able, will be able*, etc., replacing tenses of *can*) having the capacity or power (*was not able to come*). **2** having great ability; skilful. □ **ably** *adv.*

able-bodied *adj.* **1** not physically handicapped. **2** fit, healthy.

abled /'eibəld/ *adj.* able-bodied, not disabled (also in *comb.*: *differently abled*).

able seaman *n.* (also **Able Seaman**) a non-commissioned officer of the second-lowest rank in the Canadian Navy, ranking above Ordinary Seaman and below Leading Seaman. Abbr.: **AB**.

abloom *predic.adj.* blooming; in flower.

ablution /ə'blu:ʃən/ *n.* (usu. in *pl.*) **1** the ceremonial washing of parts of the body or sacred vessels etc. **2** *informal* the ordinary washing of the body.

ABM *abbr.* ANTI-BALLISTIC MISSILE.

Abnaki /æb'næki/ *var. of* ABENAKI.

abnegate /'æbnə,geit/ *v.tr.* **1** give up or deny oneself (a pleasure etc.). **2** renounce or reject (a right or belief). □ **abnegation** *n.* **abnegator** *n.*

abnormal *adj.* **1** deviating from what is normal or usual; exceptional. **2** relating to or dealing with what is abnormal. □ **abnormally** *adv.*

abnormality *n.* (*pl.* **-ies**) **1 a** an abnormal quality, occurrence, etc. **b** the state of being abnormal. **2** a physical irregularity.

ABO *adj.* designating or pertaining to the system in which blood is classified into four types based on the presence or absence of certain inherited antigens.

aboard ● *adv.* **1** on or into a ship, aircraft, train, etc. **2** onto a horse; on horseback. **3** in or into a group, team, etc. **4** *Baseball* on base. **5** *Naut.* alongside. ● *prep.* **1** on or into (a ship, aircraft, train, etc.). **2** on or onto (a horse). □ **all aboard!** a call that warns of the imminent departure of a ship, train, etc.

abode¹ *n.* a dwelling place; one's home.

abode² *past of* ABIDE.

aboiteau /,æbwʊ'to:/ *n.* (*pl.* **aboiteaux**) *Cdn* (*Maritimes*) *hist.* **1** a sluice gate in a dike, which allows flood water to flow out but does not allow sea water to enter. **2** the dike system containing such gates.

abolish *v.tr.* put an end to the existence or practice of (esp. a custom or institution). □ **abolishment** *n.*

abolition *n.* **1** the act or process of abolishing or being abolished. **2** (**Abolition**) **a** the abolition of slavery. **b** the abolition of capital punishment.

abolitionist *n.* a person who favours the abolition of a practice or institution. □ **abolitionism** *n.*

A-bomb *n.* = ATOMIC BOMB.

abominable *adj.* **1** detestable; morally reprehensible. **2** very bad or unpleasant. □ **abominably** *adv.*

abominable snowman *n.* a manlike or bearlike animal said to exist in the Himalayas.

abomination *n.* **1** an object of disgust. **2** an odious or degrading habit or act. **3** loathing.

Aboriginal (also **aboriginal**) ● *adj.* **1** (of peoples) inhabiting or existing in a land from the earliest times or from before the arrival of colonists. **2** of or relating to Aboriginal peoples. **3** of the Australian

Aboriginals. ● *n.* an Aboriginal inhabitant, esp. of Australia. □ **aboriginality** *n.*

Aboriginal rights *n.pl.* rights enjoyed by a people by virtue of the fact that their ancestors inhabited an area from time immemorial.

Aboriginal title *n.* the communal right of Aboriginal peoples to occupy and use the land inhabited by their ancestors from time immemorial.

aborigine /,æbə'rɪdʒini/ *n.* (usu. in *pl.*) **1** an Aboriginal inhabitant. **2** (usu. **Aborigine**) an Aboriginal inhabitant of Australia.

abort ● *v.* **1** *intr.* **a** (of a woman) undergo abortion; miscarry. **b** (of a fetus) suffer abortion. **2** *tr.* **a** effect the abortion of (a fetus). **b** effect abortion in (a mother). **3 a** *tr.* cause to end fruitlessly or prematurely. **b** *intr.* end unsuccessfully or prematurely. **4 a** *tr.* abandon or terminate (a space flight, computer application, etc.) before its completion, usu. because of a fault. **b** *intr.* terminate or fail to complete such an undertaking. **5** *Biol.* **a** *intr.* (of an organism) remain undeveloped; shrink away. **b** *tr.* cause to do this. ● *n.* **1** a prematurely terminated space flight or other undertaking. **2** the termination of such an undertaking.

abortifacient /ə,bɔrtɪ'feiʃənt/ ● *adj.* effecting abortion. ● *n.* a drug etc. that effects abortion.

abortion *n.* **1** the expulsion of a fetus (naturally or esp. by medical induction) from the womb before it is able to survive independently. **2** a stunted or deformed creature or thing. **3** the failure of a project or an action.

abortionist *n.* **1** a person who carries out abortions, esp. illegally. **2** a person who favours the legalization of abortion.

abortion pill *n.* a pill which induces an early abortion by preventing the implantation of the embryo.

abortive *adj.* **1** fruitless, unsuccessful, unfinished. **2** resulting in abortion. □ **abortively** *adv.*

abound *v.intr.* **1** be plentiful. **2** (foll. by *in, with*) be rich; teem or be infested.

about ● *prep.* **1 a** on the subject of (*a book about birds*). **b** relating to (*something funny about this*). **c** in relation to (*symmetry about a plane*). **d** so as to affect (*can do nothing about it*). **2** at a time near to (*come about four*). **3 a** in, around, surrounding (*a scarf about her neck*). **b** all around from a centre (*look about you*). **4** here and there in; at points throughout. **5** at a point or points near to (*fighting going on about us*). **6** carried with (*have no money about me*). **7** occupied with (*what's he about?*). ● *adv.* **1 a** approximately. **b** *informal* used to indicate understatement (*it's about time they came*). **2** here and there (*a lot of flu about*). **3** all around; in every direction (*look about*). **4** on the move; in action (*out and about*). **5** in partial rotation or alteration from a given position (*the wrong way about*). **6** in rotation or succession (*turn and turn about*). □ **be about to** be on the point of (doing something).

about-face (also **about-turn**) ● *n.* **1** a turn made so as to face the opposite direction. **2** a change of opinion or policy etc. ● *v.intr.* make an about-face. □

above ● *prep.* **1** over; on the top of; higher than; over the surface of (*above the din*). **2** more than (*above average*). **3** farther north than. **4** higher in rank, importance, etc., than (*above all*). **5 a** too great or good for (*is not above cheating*). **b** beyond the reach of; not affected by (*above suspicion*). ● *adv.* **1** at or to a higher point; overhead (*the floor above*). **2 a** upstairs. **b** upstream. **3** (of a text reference) further back on a page or in a book (*as noted above*). **4** higher than zero on the temperature scale (*forty above*). **5** on the upper side (*looks similar above and below*). **6** in addition (*over and above*). **7** *literary* in heaven. ● *adj.* mentioned earlier; preceding (*the above argument*). ● *n.* (prec. by *the*) what is mentioned above (*the above shows*). □ **above oneself** conceited, arrogant.

above board *adj. & adv.* (hyphenated when *attrib.*) without concealment; fair or fairly; open or openly.

above ground *adj. & adv.* (hyphenated when *attrib.*) not underground.

above-mentioned *adj.* mentioned earlier.

abracadabra ● *interj.* a supposedly magic word used by conjurors. ● *n.* **1** a spell or charm. **2** jargon or gibberish.

abrade *v.tr.* scrape or wear away by rubbing.

abrasion *n.* **1** the scraping or wearing away (of skin, rock, etc.). **2** a damaged area resulting from this.

abrasive ● *adj.* **1 a** tending to rub or graze. **b** capable of polishing by rubbing or grinding. **2** harsh or hurtful in manner. ● *n.* an abrasive substance.

abreast *adv.* **1** side by side and facing the same way. **2** (usu. foll. by *of*) well-informed, up to date (*abreast of all the changes*). **3** (foll. by *of*) alongside; parallel to.

abridge *v.tr.* **1** shorten (a book, film, etc.) by using fewer words or making deletions. **2** curtail (liberties, rights, etc.). **3** cut short. □ **abridgeable** *adj.* **abridgement** *n.* (also **abridgment**).

abroad *adv.* **1** in or to a foreign country or countries. **2** over a wide area; everywhere (*scatter abroad*). **3** at large; in circulation (*there is a rumour abroad*).

abrogate /ˈæbrəˌgeɪt/ *v.tr.* repeal or abolish (a law or custom). □ **abrogation** *n.* **abrogator** *n.*

abrupt *adj.* **1** sudden and unexpected; hasty. **2** (of speech, manner, etc.) uneven; curt. **3** steep, precipitous. □ **abruptly** *adv.* **abruptness** *n.*

ABS *abbr.* **1** anti-lock braking system. **2** acrylonitrile butadiene styrene, a hard, lightweight plastic.

abscess /ˈæbses/ *n.* a swollen area accumulating pus within a body tissue. □ **abscessed** *adj.*

abscond /əbˈskɒnd/ *v.intr.* depart hurriedly and furtively, esp. unlawfully or to avoid arrest.

absence *n.* **1** the state of being away from a place or person. **2** the time or duration of being away. **3** (foll. by *of*) the non-existence or lack of. □ **absence of mind** inattentiveness.

absent ● *adj.* **1 a** not present. **b** (foll. by *from*) not present at or in. **2** not existing. **3** inattentive to the matter in hand. ● *v.refl.* **1** stay away. **2** withdraw. □ **absently** *adv.* (in sense 3 of *adj.*).

absentee *n.* a person not present, esp. one who is absent from work or school.

absenteeism *n.* the practice of absenting oneself from work or school etc., esp. frequently or illicitly.

absentee landlord *n.* a landlord who leases a property while living elsewhere.

absent-minded *adj.* habitually forgetful or inattentive; with one's mind on other things. □ **absent-mindedly** *adv.* **absent-mindedness** *n.*

absinth /ˈæbsɪnθ/ *n.* **1** a shrubby plant, *Artemisia absinthium*, or its essence. **2** (usu. **absinthe**) a green aniseed-flavoured potent liqueur based on absinth and turning milky when water is added.

absolute ● *adj.* **1** complete, utter, perfect (*absolute bliss*). **2** unconditional, unlimited (*absolute authority*). **3** despotic; ruling arbitrarily or with unrestricted power (*an absolute monarch*). **4** (of a standard) universally valid; not relative or comparative. **5** *Grammar* **a** (of a construction) syntactically independent of the rest of the sentence, as in *dinner being over, we left the table*. **b** (of an adjective or transitive verb) used or

usable without an expressed noun or object, e.g. *the hungry; guns kill*. **6** (of a legal decree etc.) final. ● *n.* **1** a value, standard, etc., which is objective and universally valid, not subjective or relative. **2** (prec. by *the*) **a** *Philos.* that which can exist without being related to anything else. **b** *Theol.* God. □ **absoluteness** *n.*

absolutely *adv.* **1** completely, utterly, perfectly. **2** independently; in an absolute sense (*God exists absolutely*). **3** (foll. by *neg.*) (no or none) at all. **4** *informal* in actual fact; positively (*it absolutely exploded*). **5** *Grammar* in an absolute way, esp. (of a verb) without a stated object. **6** *informal* (used in reply) quite so; yes.

absolute majority *n.* **1** a majority over all others combined. **2** more than half.

absolute pitch *n.* *Music* the ability to recognize the pitch of a note or produce any given note.

absolute zero *n.* a theoretical lowest possible temperature, calculated as −273.15°C (or 0 K).

absolution *n.* **1** a formal release from guilt, obligation, or punishment. **2** an ecclesiastical declaration of forgiveness of sins or of the remission of penance. **3** forgiveness.

absolutism *n.* **1** the acceptance of or belief in absolute principles in political, philosophical, ethical, or theological matters. **2** the principle of absolute government. □ **absolutist** *n. & adj.*

absolve *v.tr.* **1** (often foll. by *from, of*) **a** set or pronounce free from blame or obligation etc. **b** acquit; pronounce not guilty. **2** pardon or give absolution for (a sin etc.). □ **absolver** *n.*

absorb *v.tr.* **1** include or incorporate as part of itself or oneself. **2** take in; suck up (liquid, heat, knowledge, etc.). **3** reduce the effect or intensity of; deal easily with (an impact, sound, difficulty, etc.). **4** consume (income, time, resources, etc.). **5** engross the attention of (*TV absorbs them completely*). □ **absorbable** *adj.* **absorbability** *n.* **absorber** *n.*

absorbed *predic.adj.* intensely engaged or interested.

absorbent ● *adj.* having a tendency to absorb. ● *n.* a substance that absorbs. □ **absorbency** *n.*

absorbing *adj.* engrossing; intensely interesting. □ **absorbingly** *adv.*

absorption *n.* **1** the process or action of absorbing or being absorbed. **2** disappearance through incorporation into something else. **3** mental engrossment. □ **absorptive** *adj.*

abstain *v.intr.* **1 a** (usu. foll. by *from*) restrain oneself; refrain from indulging in (*abstained from meat*). **b** refrain from drinking alcohol. **2** formally decline to use one's vote. □ **abstainer** *n.*

abstention *n.* the act or an instance of abstaining, esp. from voting.

abstinence /ˈæbstɪnəns/ *n.* the act of abstaining, esp. from food, drugs, or sexual activity. □ **abstinent** *adj.*

abstract ● *adj.* **1 a** to do with or existing in thought rather than matter, or in theory rather than practice; not tangible or concrete. **b** (of a word, esp. a noun) denoting a quality or condition or intangible thing rather than a concrete object. **2** (of art) achieving its effect by grouping shapes and colours in satisfying patterns rather than by the recognizable representation of physical reality or by telling a story. ● *v.* **1** *tr.* (often foll. by *from*) take out of; extract; remove. **2** *tr.* summarize (a book etc.). **3** *tr. & refl.* (often foll. by *from*) disengage (a person's attention etc.); distract. **4** *tr.* (foll. by *from*) consider abstractly or separately from something else. ● *n.* **1** a summary or statement of the contents of a book etc. **2** an abstract work of art. **3** an abstraction or abstract term. □ **in the abstract** in

theory rather than in practice. □ **abstractly** adv.
abstractor n. (in sense 2 of v.). **abstractness** n.
abstracted adj. inattentive to the matter in hand; preoccupied. □ **abstractedly** adv.
abstract expressionism n. a development of abstract art which aims at a subjective emotional expression of an ideal.
abstraction n. **1** the act or an instance of abstracting or taking away. **2 a** an abstract or visionary idea. **b** the formation of abstract ideas. **3 a** abstract qualities (esp. in art). **b** an abstract work of art. **4** absentmindedness.
abstractionism n. **1** the principles and practice of abstract art. **2** the pursuit or cult of abstract ideas. □ **abstractionist** n.
abstruse /əb'stru:s/ adj. hard to understand.
absurd /əb'sɜrd, -'zɜrd/ adj. **1** (of an idea, suggestion, etc.) wildly unreasonable, illogical, or inappropriate. **2** (of a person) unreasonable or ridiculous in manner. **3** ludicrous (an absurd situation). □ **absurdly** adv. **absurdity** n. (pl. **-ies**).
absurdist ● adj. pertaining to or characteristic of the theatre of the absurd. ● n. a writer of absurdist drama. □ **absurdism** n.
abundance n. **1** a very great quantity, usu. considered to be more than enough. **2** wealth.
abundant adj. existing or available in large quantities; plentiful. □ **abundantly** adv.
abuse ● v.tr. **1** misuse. **2** maltreat. **3** insult verbally. ● n. **1 a** incorrect or improper use (drug abuse). **b** an instance of this (an abuse of power). **2** unjust or corrupt practice (political abuses). **3** maltreatment of a person. **4** insulting language (a torrent of abuse). □ **abuser** n.
abusive adj. **1** involving maltreatment. **2** (of a person) tending to abuse others. **3** using or containing insulting language. **4** (of language) insulting. □ **abusively** adv. **abusiveness** n.
abut v. (**abutted, abutting**) **1** tr. (of buildings, sites, etc.) be located next to. **2** intr. (foll. by on, against) (of part of a building) touch or lean upon (another) with a projecting end or point. **3** intr. (foll. by onto, on) abut.
abutment n. **1** the lateral supporting structure of a bridge, arch, etc. **2** the point of junction between such a support and the thing supported.
abuzz predic.adj. **1** in a state of excitement or activity. **2** buzzing.
abysmal /ə'bɪzməl/ adj. **1** extremely bad. **2** profound, utter (abysmal ignorance). □ **abysmally** adv.
abyss /ə'bɪs/ n. **1** a deep or seemingly bottomless chasm. **2 a** an immeasurable depth (abyss of despair). **b** a catastrophic situation as contemplated or feared. **3** a vast difference (cultural abyss). **4** (prec. by the) hell.
Abyssinian ● n. **1** a native or inhabitant of Abyssinia (a former name for Ethiopia). **2** (in full **Abyssinian cat**) a breed of cat having a long slender body, long ears, and short brown hair. ● adj. of or pertaining to Abyssinia or its inhabitants.
AC abbr. **1** (also **ac**) ALTERNATING CURRENT. **2** before Christ.
Ac symbol actinium.
a/c abbr. **1** = ACCOUNT n. 2, 3. **2** = AIR CONDITIONING.
acacia /ə'keɪʃə/ n. **1** any usu. thorny leguminous tree or shrub of the genus Acacia with usu. yellow flowers. **2** (also **false acacia**) = LOCUST 4b.
academe /'ækə,di:m/ n. **1** the world of learning. **2** universities collectively.
academia /,ækə'di:miə/ n. the academic world.
academic ● adj. **1 a** scholarly; to do with learning. **b** of or relating to a scholarly institution (academic

dress). **2** abstract; theoretical; not of practical relevance. **3** Art conventional, over-formal. ● n. a teacher or scholar in a university or institute of higher education. □ **academically** adv.
academic freedom n. a scholar's freedom to express ideas without risk of official interference.
academician /,ækədə'mɪʃən, ə,kædə'mɪʃən/ n. **1** a member of an Academy. **2** an academic.
academics n.pl. (also treated as sing.) studies in the humanities or sciences.
academic year n. a period of nearly a year, from early September to the following summer, during which a school or university is in session.
academy n. (pl. **-ies**) **1** a place of study or training in a special field (military academy). **2** (usu. **Academy**) a society or institution of distinguished scholars, artists, etc. (Royal Academy). **3** a school (esp. in proper names). **4** N Amer. (prec. by the) academia.
Academy Award n. any of the annual awards of the Academy of Motion Picture Arts and Sciences.
Acadian ● n. **1** a native or inhabitant of the former French colony of Acadia, which at its greatest extent occupied the entire region between the St. Lawrence and the Atlantic. **2** esp. Cdn a francophone descendant of the early French settlers in Acadia. ● adj. of or relating to Acadians.
acanthus /ə'kænθəs/ n. any spiny-leaved Mediterranean plant or shrub of the genus Acanthus.
a cappella /,ɒ kə'pelə, ,æ kə'pelə/ adj. & adv. (of singing) unaccompanied.
accede /æk'si:d/ v.intr. (usu. foll. by to) **1** assent or agree (acceded to the request). **2** take office, esp. become monarch. **3** (foll. by to) formally subscribe to a treaty or other agreement.
accelerate v. **1** intr. **a** (esp. of a vehicle) move or begin to move more quickly. **b** (of a process) happen or reach completion more quickly. **2** tr. **a** cause to increase speed. **b** cause (a process) to happen more quickly. **3** tr. (often as **accelerated** adj.) hasten advancement in (a career, studies, etc.).
acceleration n. **1** the process or act of accelerating or being accelerated. **2** an instance of this. **3** the capacity of a vehicle etc. to gain speed. **4** the rate of change of velocity in terms of a unit of time.
accelerator n. **1** a device for increasing speed, esp. the pedal that controls the speed of a vehicle's engine. **2** Physics an apparatus for imparting high speeds to charged particles. **3** Chem. a substance that speeds up a chemical reaction.
accent n. **1** a particular mode of pronunciation, esp. one associated with a particular region or group. **2** prominence given to a syllable by stress or pitch. **3 a** mark on a letter or word to indicate pitch, stress, or the quality of a vowel. **4** (usu. foll. by on) emphasis (an accent on comfort). **5** (often attrib.) a distinctive or contrasting feature (blue with accents of red; accent colours). **6** Music emphasis on a particular note or chord. ● v.tr. **1** emphasize (a word or syllable). **2** write or print accents on (words etc.). **3** accentuate or enhance (esp. with a contrasting element). **4** Music play (a note etc.) with an accent.
accentuate v.tr. emphasize; make prominent. □ **accentuation** n.
accept v. **1** tr. & intr. consent to receive (a thing offered). **2** tr. & intr. give an affirmative answer to (an offer or proposal). **3** tr. **a** regard favourably; treat as welcome (his colleagues never accepted him). **b** approve for admission. **4** tr. **a** believe, receive, recognize (an explanation etc.) as adequate or valid. **b** be prepared to subscribe to (a belief, philosophy, etc.). **5** tr. receive

as suitable (*accepts traveller's cheques*). **6** *tr.* **a** tolerate; submit to (*accepted the umpire's decision*). **b** be willing to believe (*we accept that you meant well*). **7** *tr.* undertake (an office or responsibility).

acceptable *adj.* **1 a** worthy of being accepted. **b** pleasing, welcome. **2** adequate, satisfactory. **3** tolerable. □ **acceptability** *n.* **acceptably** *adv.*

acceptance *n.* **1** the act or fact of accepting or being accepted (*acceptance to university*). **2** willingness to receive (a gift, payment, duty, etc.). **3** an affirmative answer to an invitation or proposal. **4** (often foll. by *of*) a willingness to accept (conditions, a circumstance, etc.). **5 a** approval, belief (*found wide acceptance*). **b** willingness or ability to tolerate. □ **acceptant** /ək'septənt/ *adj.*

access ● *n.* **1** a way of approaching or reaching or entering. **2 a** (often foll. by *to*) the right or opportunity to reach or use or visit (*has access to secret files*). **b** *Law* the right of a parent who does not have legal custody of a child to visit the child and inquire about his or her welfare. **c** the condition of being readily approached; accessibility. **3** *Computing* the action or process of obtaining stored documents, data, etc. ● *v.tr.* gain access to (esp. data, a file, etc.).

accessible *adj.* (often foll. by *to*) **1** that can readily be reached, entered, or used. **2** (of a building) posing no obstacles to handicapped people. **3** (of a person) readily available. **4** easy to understand or appreciate. □ **accessibility** *n.* **accessibly** *adv.*

accession *n.* **1** entering upon an office (esp. the throne) or a condition (as adulthood). **2** (often foll. by *to*) a thing added, e.g. a book to a library.

accessorize *v.tr. & intr.* choose or wear accessories to suit (clothing etc.).

accessory ● *n.* (*pl.* **-ies**) **1** an additional or extra thing. **2** (usu. in *pl.*) **a** a small attachment or fitting. **b** a small item of (esp. a woman's) dress, e.g. shoes. **3** (often foll. by *to*) a person who helps in or knows the details of an (esp. illegal) act, esp. one (**accessory before the fact**) who encourages or assists another to commit a crime but is not present when the crime is committed, or one (**accessory after the fact**) who knowingly assists a criminal to escape. ● *adj.* additional; contributing or aiding in a minor way. □ **accessorial** /ˌækse'sɔriəl/ *adj.*

access road *n.* a road providing access to something, esp. a remote site, airport, highway, etc.

accident *n.* **1** an event that is without apparent cause, or is unexpected. **2** an unfortunate event, esp. one causing physical harm or damage, brought about unintentionally. **3** an automobile collision or crash. **4** the working of fortune (*accident accounts for much in life*). **5** *euphemism* an occurrence of involuntary urination or defecation. **6** an irregularity in structure. □ **by accident** unintentionally.

accidental ● *adj.* **1** happening by chance, unintentionally, or unexpectedly. **2** not essential to a conception; subsidiary. ● *n.* **1** *Music* a sign indicating a momentary departure from the key signature by raising or lowering a note. **2** something not essential to a conception. □ **accidentally** *adv.*

accident-prone *adj.* (of a person) subject to frequent accidents.

acclaim ● *v.tr.* **1** (often as **acclaimed** *adj.*) praise publicly; welcome or applaud enthusiastically. **2** hail as (*was acclaimed the winner*). **3** *Cdn Politics* elect without opposition. ● *n.* **1** public praise; applause. **2** a shout of acclaim. □ **acclaimer** *n.*

acclamation *n.* **1** *Cdn Politics* (esp. in **by acclamation**) the act or an instance of election by virtue of

being the sole candidate. **2** loud and eager assent to a proposal. **3** (usu. in *pl.*) shouting in a person's honour. **4** the act or process of acclaiming.

acclimate /'æklɪˌmeit, ə'klai-/ *v.tr. N Amer.* acclimatize. □ **acclimation** *n.*

acclimatize /ə'klaiməˌtaiz/ *v.* **1** *tr.* accustom to a new climate or to new conditions. **2** *intr.* become acclimatized. □ **acclimatization** *n.*

accolade /'ækəˌleid/ *n.* the awarding of praise; an acknowledgement of merit.

accommodate *v.tr.* **1** provide lodging or room for. **2** adapt, harmonize, reconcile.

accommodating *adj.* obliging, compliant. □ **accommodatingly** *adv.*

accommodation *n.* **1** (in *sing.* or *pl.*) temporary lodging, as at a hotel etc. **2** an adjustment or adaptation to suit a special or different purpose. **3** a convenient arrangement; a compromise.

accompaniment *n.* **1** *Music* an instrumental or orchestral part supporting or partnering a solo instrument, voice, or group. **2** an accompanying thing. **3** the act or fact of accompanying someone.

accompanist /ə'kʌmpənɪst/ *n.* a person who provides a musical accompaniment.

accompany *v.tr.* (**-ies, -ied**) **1** go with; escort. **2** (usu. in *passive*; foll. by *with, by*) **a** be done or found with; supplement. **b** have as a result. **3** *Music* support or partner with accompaniment.

accomplice *n.* a partner in a crime or wrongdoing.

accomplish *v.tr.* complete; succeed in doing.

accomplished *adj.* clever, skilled.

accomplishment *n.* **1** the fulfilment or completion (of a task etc.). **2** an acquired skill, esp. a social one. **3** a thing done; an achievement.

accord ● *v.* **1** *intr.* (often foll. by *with*) (esp. of a thing) be in harmony. **2** *tr.* **a** grant (permission, a request, etc.). **b** give (a welcome etc.). ● *n.* **1** agreement, consent. **2** harmony or correspondence in pitch, tone, colour, etc. **3** a formal act of agreement; a treaty. □ **of one's own accord** voluntarily. **with one accord** unanimously.

accordance *n.* □ **in accordance with** in a manner corresponding to.

according *adv.* **1** (foll. by *to*) **a** as stated by or in (*according to my sister*). **b** in a manner corresponding to; in proportion to (*lives according to her principles*). **2** (foll. by *as* + clause) in a manner or to a degree that varies as (*he pays according as he is able*).

accordingly *adv.* **1** as suggested or required by the (stated) circumstances. **2** consequently, therefore.

accordion *n.* **1** a musical instrument played by means of keys, buttons, and pleated bellows, which are expanded and contracted to force air through metal reeds. **2** (*attrib.*) having folds like the bellows of an accordion. □ **accordionist** *n.*

accost /ə'kɒst/ *v.tr.* approach and address (a person), esp. boldly.

account ● *n.* **1** a narration or description. **2 a** an arrangement at a financial institution for transactions, esp. for depositing and withdrawing money. **b** the assets credited by such an arrangement (*has a large account*). **c** an arrangement at a store etc. for buying goods or services on credit. **3** (often in *pl.*) a record or statement of money, goods, or services received or expended, with calculation of the balance. **4** a statement of the administration of money in trust. **5** (in *pl.*) the department of a firm etc. that deals with accounts. **6** a customer or client having an account with a firm. **7** counting, reckoning. ● *v.tr.* consider, regard as (*account it a* *misfortune).* □ **account for 1** serve as or provide an explanation or reason for. **2 a** give a reckoning of (money etc. entrusted). **b** answer for (one's conduct). **3** succeed in killing, destroying, or defeating. **4** supply or make up a specified amount or proportion of. **by all accounts** in everyone's opinion. **call to account** require an explanation from (a person). **give a good** (or **bad**) **account of oneself** make a favourable (or unfavourable) impression; be successful (or unsuccessful). **keep account of** keep a record of; follow closely. **leave out of account** fail or decline to consider. **of no account** unimportant. **on account 1** (of goods or services) to be paid for later. **2** (of money) in part payment. **on account of** because of. **on no account** under no circumstances; certainly not. **on one's own account** for one's own purposes; at one's own risk. **settle** (or **square**) **accounts with 1** receive or pay money etc. owed to. **2** have revenge on. **take account of** (or **take into account**) consider along with other factors.

accountable *adj.* **1** responsible; required to account for one's conduct. **2** understandable. □ **accountability** *n.* **accountably** *adv.*

accountancy *n.* the profession or duties of an accountant.

accountant *n.* a person whose profession is to keep or inspect financial accounts.

accounting *n.* **1** the process of or skill in keeping and verifying accounts. **2** *in senses of* ACCOUNT *v.*

account payable *n.* (*pl.* **accounts payable**) (usu. in *pl.*) an amount owed by a business to a supplier.

account receivable *n.* (*pl.* **accounts receivable**) (usu. in *pl.*) an amount owed by a customer to a business.

accoutre /ə'ku:tər/ *v.tr.* (also esp. *US* **accouter**) (usu. as **accoutred** *adj.*) equip, esp. with a special outfit.

accoutrement /ə'ku:trəmənt, -tərmənt/ *n.* (usu. in *pl.*) **1** equipment, trappings. **2** *Military* a soldier's outfit other than weapons and garments.

accredit *v.tr.* (**-credited, -crediting**) **1** officially recognize as meeting certain standards. **2** (foll. by *to*) attribute (a saying etc.) to (a person). **3** (foll. by *with*) credit (a person) with (a saying etc.). **4** (usu. foll. by *to* or *at*) send (an ambassador etc.) with credentials; recommend by documents as an envoy. **5** gain belief or influence for or make credible (an adviser, a statement, etc.). □ **accreditation** *n.*

accredited *adj.* **1** (of a person or organization) officially recognized. **2** (of a belief) orthodox.

accrete /ə'kri:t/ *v.* **1** *intr.* grow together or into one. **2** *intr.* (often foll. by *to*) form around or on, as around a nucleus. **3** *tr.* attract (such additions).

accretion *n.* **1** growth by organic enlargement. **2 a** the growing of separate things into one. **b** the product of such growing. **3 a** extraneous matter added to anything. **b** the adhesion of this. □ **accretive** *adj.*

accrue *v.* (**accrues, accrued, accruing**) (often foll. by *to*) **1** *intr.* come as a natural increase or advantage, esp. financial. **2** *tr.* esp. *N Amer.* accumulate (esp. interest). □ **accrual** *n.* **accrued** *adj.*

acct. *abbr.* account.

acculturate /ə'kʌltʃə,reit/ *v.* **1** *intr.* adapt to or adopt a different culture. **2** *tr.* cause to do this. □ **acculturation** *n.* **acculturative** *adj.*

accumulate *v.* **1** *tr.* **a** acquire an increasing number or quantity of. **b** produce or acquire (a resulting whole) in this way. **2** *intr.* grow numerous or considerable; form an increasing mass or quantity. □ **accumulator** *n.*

accumulation *n.* **1** the act or process of accumulat-

ing or being accumulated. **2** an accumulated mass. **3** the growth of capital by the continued addition of interest.

accuracy *n.* (*pl.* **-ies**) **1** the quality of being accurate. **2** exactness or precision.

accurate *adj.* **1** careful, precise; lacking errors. **2** conforming exactly with the truth or with a given standard. **3** able to reach a target or measure a quantity etc. with precision. □ **accurately** *adv.*

accursed /ə'kɜːsəd, ə'kɜːst/ *adj.* **1** lying under a curse; ill-fated. **2** (*attrib.*) detestable, annoying.

accusation *n.* **1** the act or process of accusing or being accused. **2** a statement charging a person with an offence or crime.

accusative ● *n.* the case of nouns, pronouns, and adjectives, expressing the object of an action or the goal of motion. ● *adj.* of or in this case.

accusatory *adj.* (of language, manner, etc.) of or implying accusation.

accuse *v.tr.* **1** (foll. by *of*) charge (a person etc.) with a fault or crime; indict. **2** lay the blame on. □ **accuser** *n.* **accusing** *adj.* **accusingly** *adv.*

accused ● *n.* (*pl.* same) a person charged with a crime. ● *adj.* charged with a crime, fault, etc.

accustom *v.tr. & refl.* (foll. by *to*) make (a person or thing or oneself) used to.

accustomed *adj.* **1** (usu. foll. by *to*) used to (*accustomed to hard work*). **2** customary, usual.

AC/DC ● *abbr.* alternating current/direct current (of an appliance etc. that can operate on either type of current). ● *adj. slang* bisexual.

ace ● *n.* **1 a** a playing card, domino, etc., with a single spot and generally having the value 'one' or in card games the highest value in each suit. **b** a single spot on a playing card etc. **2 a** a person who excels in some activity. **b** a fighter pilot who has shot down many enemy aircraft. **c** *Baseball* the best starting or relief pitcher on a team. **3 a** (in racquet sports, volleyball, etc.) a point scored on a service that an opponent fails to touch. **b** a service that achieves this. **4** *Golf* a hole in one. ● *v.tr.* **1** *N Amer. informal* achieve a high grade in (an exam etc.) (*she aced the course*). **2** *Tennis etc.* score an ace against (an opponent). **3** *Golf* complete (a hole) in one stroke. ● *adj.* (also *predic.* **aces**) *slang* excellent. □ **ace up one's sleeve** (or **in the hole**) something effective kept in reserve. **come up aces** *N Amer.* perform exceptionally well. **play one's ace** use one's best resource. **within an ace of** on the verge of.

acerbic /ə'sɜːbɪk/ *adj.* **1** biting in speech, manner, or temper. **2** sour; harsh-tasting. □ **acerbically** *adv.* **acerbity** *n.* (*pl.* **-ies**).

acetaminophen /ˌəsi:tə'mɪnəfən/ *n. N Amer.* a drug used to relieve pain and reduce fever.

acetate /'æsə,teit/ *n.* **1** a salt or ester of acetic acid, esp. the cellulose ester of acetic acid (CELLULOSE ACETATE) used to make textiles, plastics, etc. **2** a fabric made from cellulose acetate. **3** a disc coated with cellulose acetate, for direct recording by a cutting stylus; any direct-cut disc. **4 a** a clear plastic film of cellulose acetate, used for overhead transparencies etc. **b** a sheet of this.

acetic acid /ə'si:tɪk/ *n.* the clear liquid acid that gives vinegar its characteristic taste.

acetone /'æsə,to:n/ *n.* a colourless volatile liquid ketone valuable as a solvent for paints etc.

acetylene /ə'setə,li:n/ *n.* a colourless hydrocarbon gas, burning with a bright flame.

acetylsalicylic acid /æ'si:təl,sælə,sɪlɪk/ *n.* a drug used to relieve pain and reduce fever, the active ingredient in Aspirin. Abbr.: **ASA**.

ache ● *n.* **1** a continuous or prolonged dull pain. **2** mental distress. ● *v.intr.* **1** suffer from or be the source of an ache. **2** (foll. by *to* + infin.) desire greatly (*we ached to be at home again*). □ **achingly** *adv.*

achieve *v.* **1** *tr.* **a** reach or attain by effort (*achieved victory*). **b** acquire, gain, earn (*achieved notoriety*). **2** *tr.* accomplish or carry out (a feat or task). **3** *intr.* be successful; attain a desired level of performance. □ **achievable** *adj.* **achiever** *n.*

achievement *n.* **1** something achieved. **2 a** the act of achieving. **b** an instance of this. **3** *Psych.* performance in a standardized test.

Achilles heel /ə'kɪliːz/ *n.* a person's weak or vulnerable point.

Achilles tendon *n.* the tendon connecting the heel with the calf muscles.

achoo *interj.* (also **a-choo**) representing the characteristic sound of a sneeze.

achy *adj.* (**-ier, -iest**) full of or suffering from aches.

acid ● *n.* **1 a** any of a class of substances that liberate hydrogen ions in water, are usu. sour and corrosive, and have a pH of less than 7. **b** any compound or atom donating protons. **2** (in general use) any sour substance. **3** *slang* the drug LSD. ● *adj.* **1** sour. **2** biting, sharp (*an acid wit*). **3** *Chem.* having the essential properties of an acid. **4** (of precipitation) containing acids formed in the atmosphere from industrial waste gases. **5** (of a colour) intense, bright. □ **acidic** *adj.* **acidly** *adv.* (in sense 2 of *adj.*).

acid house *n.* (also **acid rock**) a kind of synthesized music with a simple repetitive beat, often associated with the taking of hallucinogenic drugs.

acidify *v.tr. & intr.* (**-ies, -ied**) make or become acid. □ **acidification** *n.*

acidity *n.* (*pl.* **-ies**) **1** an acid quality or state. **2** an excessively acid condition of the stomach.

acid jazz *n.* a form of jazz combining elements of jazz, funk, and sometimes other musical forms such as hip hop etc.

acidophilus /ˌæsɪ'dɒfɪləs/ *n.* a bacterium, *Lactobacillus acidophilus*, used to make yogourt and to supplement the intestinal flora.

acid rain *n.* acid formed in the atmosphere esp. from industrial waste gases and falling with rain.

acid test *n.* **1** a severe or conclusive test. **2** a test in which acid is used to test for gold etc.

ackee /'æki/ *n.* **1** a tropical evergreen tree, *Blighia sapida.* **2** the bland, leathery, red or yellow fruit of this tree, edible only when cooked.

acknowledge *v.tr.* **1 a** recognize; accept; admit the truth of. **b** recognize as (*acknowledged it to be a success*). **c** admit that something is so (*acknowledged that he was wrong*). **2** confirm the receipt of. **3 a** show that one has noticed (*acknowledged my arrival with a grunt*). **b** express appreciation of (a service etc.). **4** recognize the validity of (*the acknowledged king*).

acknowledgement *n.* (also **acknowledgment**) **1** the act or an instance of acknowledging. **2 a** a thing given or done in return for a service etc. **b** a letter confirming receipt of something. **3** (usu. in *pl.*) an author's statement of thanks to others.

acme /'ækmi/ *n.* the highest point or period (of achievement, success, etc.); the peak of perfection.

acne *n.* a skin condition, usu. of the face, characterized by red pimples. □ **acned** *adj.*

acolyte /'ækəˌlɔɪt/ *n.* **1** a person assisting a priest in a service or procession. **2** an assistant; a beginner.

aconite /'ækəˌnaɪt/ *n.* **1 a** any poisonous herbaceous plant of the genus *Aconitum*, esp. monkshood. **b** = ACONITINE. **2** = WINTER ACONITE. □ **aconitic** *adj.*

aconitine /ə'kɒnɪˌtiːn/ *n.* a poisonous alkaloid drug obtained from the aconite plant, esp. from the species *A. napellus*, formerly used as a sedative.

acorn *n.* the fruit of the oak, with a smooth nut in a rough cuplike base.

acorn squash *n.* N Amer. = PEPPER SQUASH.

acoustic ● *adj.* **1** relating to sound or the sense of hearing. **2** (of music, musicians, or musical instruments) not using electrical amplification (*acoustic guitar*). **3** (of building materials) used for soundproofing or modifying sound. ● *n.* **1** (usu. in *pl.*) the properties or qualities (esp. of a room or hall etc.) in transmitting sound (*good acoustics; a poor acoustic*). **2** (in *pl.*; usu. treated as *sing.*) the science of sound. □ **acoustical** *adj.* **acoustically** *adv.*

acoustic coupler *n.* Computing a modem which converts digital signals into audible signals and vice versa, so that the former can be transmitted and received over telephone lines.

acquaint *v.tr. & refl.* (usu. foll. by *with*) make (a person or oneself) aware of or familiar with. □ **acquainted with** having personal knowledge of.

acquaintance *n.* **1** a person one knows slightly. **2** the fact or process of being acquainted (*our acquaintance lasted a year*). **3** (usu. foll. by *with*) knowledge (of a person or thing). □ **make someone's acquaintance** first meet or introduce oneself to another person. □ **acquaintanceship** *n.*

acquaintance rape *n.* N Amer. = DATE RAPE.

acquiesce /ˌækwi'es/ *v.intr.* **1** (often foll. by *to*) agree, esp. tacitly. **2** (foll. by *in*) accept (an arrangement etc.). □ **acquiescence** *n.* **acquiescent** *adj.*

acquire *v.tr.* gain by and for oneself; obtain; come to possess. □ **acquirable** *adj.* **acquirement** *n.*

acquired immune deficiency syndrome *n.* see AIDS.

acquired taste *n.* **1** a liking gained by experience. **2** the object of such a liking.

acquisition *n.* **1** the act or an instance of acquiring. **2** something acquired, esp. if regarded as useful.

acquisitive *adj.* keen to acquire things. □ **acquisitively** *adv.* **acquisitiveness** *n.* **acquisitor** *n.*

acquit *v.* (**acquitted, acquitting**) **1** *tr.* (often foll. by *of*) declare not guilty. **2** *refl.* **a** conduct oneself or perform in a specified way (*acquitted ourselves well*). **b** (foll. by *of*) discharge (a duty etc.).

acquittal *n.* **1** the process of freeing or being freed from a charge, esp. by a judgment of not guilty. **2** performance of a duty.

acre *n.* **1** a measure of land, 4,840 sq. yds., 0.405 ha. **2** (in *pl.*) a large area. □ **acred** *adj.* (also in *comb.*).

acreage *n.* **1** a number of acres. **2** an extent of land, esp. farmland.

acrid /'ækrɪd/ *adj.* **1** bitterly pungent; corrosive. **2** bitter in manner etc. □ **acridity** *n.* **acridly** *adv.*

acrimonious *adj.* extremely bitter in manner or temper. □ **acrimoniously** *adv.*

acrimony /'ækrɪməni/ *n.* (*pl.* **-ies**) extreme bitterness of temper or manner; ill feeling.

acro *n.* a freestyle skiing event in which competitors perform choreographed acrobatic moves to music.

acrobat *n.* a person who performs feats of agility, esp. in a circus. □ **acrobatic** *adj.* **acrobatically** *adv.*

acrobatics *n.pl.* **1** the feats or skills of an acrobat. **2** (as *sing.*) the art of performing these. **3** a skill requiring dexterity (*mental acrobatics*).

acronym *n.* a word, usu. pronounced as such, formed from the initial letters of other words, e.g. *laser*, *NATO* (compare INITIALISM).

across ● *prep.* **1** to or on the other side of. **2** from one side to another side of (*stretched across the opening*). **3** at or forming an angle (esp. a right angle) with (*across his legs*). ● *adv.* **1** to or on the other side (*ran across*). **2** from one side to another (*stretched across*). **3** forming a cross (*with cuts across*). **4** (of a crossword clue or answer) read horizontally (*cannot do nine across*). **5** *Cdn* (*PEI*) in or to Nova Scotia or New Brunswick.

acrostic *n.* **1** a poem or other composition in which certain letters in each line form a word or words. **2** a word puzzle constructed in this way.

acrylic ● *adj.* **1** of material made with a synthetic polymer derived from acrylic acid. **2** (of paint) having acrylic resin as a vehicle. **3** *Chem.* of or derived from acrylic acid. ● *n.* **1** an acrylic fibre. **2** an acrylic paint. **3** a painting in acrylic paints.

acrylic acid *n.* a pungent liquid organic acid.

acrylic resin *n.* any of various transparent colourless polymers of acrylic acid.

act ● *n.* **1** a deed or action. **2** the process of doing something (*caught in the act*). **3 a** a piece of entertainment, usu. one of a series in a program. **b** the performer(s) of this. **4** a pretense. **5** a main division of a play or opera. **6 a** a written ordinance of a parliament etc. **b** a document attesting a legal transaction. **7** (often in *pl.*) the recorded decisions or proceedings of a committee, etc. ● *v.* **1** *intr.* behave (*see how they act under stress*). **2** *intr.* perform actions or functions; operate effectively; take action (*act as referee; the brakes failed to act*). **3** *intr.* exert energy or influence (*the medicine soon began to act*). **4** *intr.* **a** perform a part in a play, film, etc. **b** pretend. **c** embody or portray a character convincingly in a theatrical production. **5** *tr.* **a** perform the part of (*acted Othello*). **b** perform (a play etc.). **c** portray (an incident) by actions. **d** feign (*we acted indifference*). □ **act for** be the (esp. legal) representative of. **act on** (or **upon**) perform or carry out; put into operation. **act out 1** translate (ideas etc.) into action. **2** *Psych.* represent (one's subconscious desires etc.) in action. **act up** *informal* misbehave; give trouble. **get one's act together** *informal* become properly organized. **get in on the act** *informal* become a participant (esp. for profit). **a hard act to follow** *informal* a person or thing difficult to be more impressive or successful than. **put on an act** *informal* carry out a pretense.

acting ● *n.* **1** the art or occupation of performing parts in plays, films, etc. **2** in senses of ACT *v.* ● *attrib.adj.* serving temporarily or on behalf of another or others.

acting sub-lieutenant *n.* (also **Acting Sub-Lieutenant**) a commissioned officer ranking below Sub-Lieutenant in the Canadian Navy. Abbr.: **A/SLt**.

actinium /æk'tɪniəm/ *n.* a radioactive metallic element, occurring naturally in pitchblende.

action ● *n.* **1** the fact or process of doing or acting. **2** (also *attrib.*) forcefulness or energy as a characteristic (*a woman of action; action photograph*). **3** the exertion of energy or influence. **4** something done; a deed or act. **5 a** a series of events represented in a story, play, etc. **b** *informal* activity (*want some action*). **6 a** armed conflict (*killed in action*). **b** an occurrence of this, esp. a minor military engagement. **7 a** the way in which a machine, instrument, etc. works. **b** the mechanism that makes a musical instrument, gun, etc. work. **c** the mode or style of movement of an animal or human. **8** a legal process; a lawsuit (*bring an action*). **9** (in *imper.*) a word of command to begin, esp. used by a

film director etc. ● *v.tr.* bring a legal action against. □ **go into action** start work. **out of action** not working. **take action** act, esp. against something.

actionable *adj.* giving cause for legal action.

action central *n.* *N Amer.* a central location where much activity is concentrated.

action committee *n.* (also **action group** etc.) a body formed to take active steps, esp. in politics.

action figure *n.* a doll representing a person or fictional character capable of or known for vigorous action, e.g. a soldier, athlete, superhero, etc.

action film *n.* (also **action movie** etc.) a feature film containing a great deal of fast-moving (esp. violent) action.

action-packed *adj.* full of action or excitement.

action stations *n.pl.* positions taken up by troops etc. ready for battle.

activate *v.tr.* **1** make active; bring into action. **2** *Chem.* cause reaction in. **3** *Physics* make radioactive. □ **activation** *n.* **activator** *n.*

activated carbon *n.* (also **activated charcoal**, **active carbon**) carbon, esp. charcoal, treated to increase its adsorptive power.

active ● *adj.* **1 a** consisting in or marked by action; energetic (*an active life*). **b** able to move about or accomplish practical tasks. **2** working, operative (*an active volcano*). **3** not merely passive or inert (*active ingredients*). **4** radioactive. **5** of the form of a verb whose grammatical subject is the person or thing that performs the action, e.g. of the verbs in *guns kill*; *we saw him*. ● *n.* the active form or voice of a verb. □ **actively** *adv.* **activeness** *n.*

active duty *n.* *N Amer.* **1** = ACTIVE SERVICE. **2** active involvement in an organization or group.

active-matrix *n.* (*attrib.*) of or designating a form of liquid crystal display in which each pixel is controlled by its own transistor, thus improving contrast.

active service *n.* full-time service in the armed forces or police.

activewear *n.* clothing worn primarily during exercise or sports activities.

activism *n.* vigorous action to further a cause. □ **activist** *n.*

activity *n.* (*pl.* **-ies**) **1 a** the condition of being active or moving about. **b** the exertion of energy; vigorous action. **2** (often in *pl.*) a particular occupation or pursuit (*outdoor activities*). **3** = RADIOACTIVITY.

act of God *n.* a usu. disastrous event caused by uncontrollable natural forces.

actor *n.* **1** a person who acts a part in a play, film, etc. **2** a person whose profession is performing such parts. **3** a person who is skilled at portraying characters in theatrical productions. **4** a participant.

ACTRA /'æktrə/ *abbr.* Alliance of Canadian Cinema, Television and Radio Artists.

ACTRA Award *n.* *hist.* any of several annual awards presented from 1970–1985 by ACTRA to Canadian broadcast journalists, performers, and writers.

actress *n.* **1** a woman or girl who acts a part in a play, film, etc. **2** a woman or girl whose profession is performing such parts. **3** a woman who is skilled at embodying or portraying characters in theatrical productions.

actual *adj.* (usu. *attrib.*) existing in fact; real (often as distinct from ideal). ¶Redundant use, as in *tell me the actual facts*, is disputed, but common. □ **actualize** *v.tr.* **actualization** *n.*

actuality *n.* (*pl.* **-ies**) **1** reality; what is the case. **2** (in *pl.*) existing conditions.

actually *adv.* **1** as a fact, really. **2** as a matter of fact, even (strange as it may seem) (*he actually refused!*).

actuary /'æktʃʊeri/ *n.* (*pl.* **-ies**) an expert in statistics, esp. one who calculates insurance risks and premiums. □ **actuarial** *adj.* **actuarially** *adv.*

actuate /'æktʃʊ,eit/ *v.tr.* **1** communicate motion to (a machine etc.). **2** cause the operation of (a device etc.). **3** cause to act. □ **actuation** *n.* **actuator** *n.*

acuity /ə'kjuːiti/ *n.* (of the mind or the senses, esp. vision) sharpness, acuteness.

acumen /'ækjʊmən, ə'kjuːmən/ *n.* the ability to understand and judge things quickly and clearly.

acupressure *n.* = SHIATSU.

acupuncture *n.* a method (originally Chinese) of treating various conditions by pricking the skin with needles. □ **acupuncturist** *n.*

acute ● *adj.* **1** (of sensation or senses) keen, penetrating. **2** shrewd, perceptive (*an acute critic*). **3** (of a disease) coming sharply to a crisis; severe, not chronic. **4** (of a difficulty or controversy) critical, serious. **5 a** (of an angle) less than 90°. **b** sharp, pointed. **6** (of a sound) high, shrill. ● *n.* (in full **acute accent**) a mark (´) placed over letters in some languages to show pronunciation (e.g. *rosé*), etc. □ **acutely** *adv.* **acuteness** *n.*

acyclovir /ei'saiklovi:r/ *n.* an antiviral drug used to combat some types of herpes, esp. genital herpes.

AD *abbr.* (of a date) of the Christian era. ¶Strictly, AD should precede a date (e.g. AD 410), but uses such as *the tenth century* AD are well established.

ad *n. informal* an advertisement.

Ada /'eidə/ *n.* a programming language used esp. in real-time control situations.

adage /'ædidʒ/ *n.* a traditional maxim, a proverb.

adagio /ə'dæʒio:, -dʒio:/ *Music & Dance* ● *adv. & adj.* in slow time. ● *n.* (*pl.* **-os**) an adagio movement etc.

Adam[1] *n.* □ **not know a person from Adam** be unable to recognize the person in question.

Adam[2] *n. slang* the hallucinogenic drug MDMA.

adamant *adj.* stubbornly resolute; resistant to persuasion. □ **adamantly** *adv.*

Adam's apple *n.* a projection of the thyroid cartilage of the larynx, esp. as prominent in men.

adapt *v.* **1** *tr.* **a** (foll. by *to*) fit, adjust (one thing to another). **b** (foll. by *to, for*) make suitable for a purpose. **c** alter or modify (esp. a text). **d** arrange for broadcasting etc. **2** *intr. & refl.* (usu. foll. by *to*) become adjusted to new conditions. □ **adaptive** *adj.*

adaptable *adj.* **1** able to adapt oneself to new conditions. **2** that can be adapted. □ **adaptability** *n.* **adaptably** *adv.*

adaptation *n.* (also **adaption**) **1** the act or process of adapting or being adapted. **2** a thing made by adapting something else, esp. a text for production on radio etc. **3** *Biol.* the process by which an organism or species becomes suited to its environment.

adapter *n.* (also **adaptor**) **1 a** a device for making equipment compatible. **b** a device for changing voltage or current. **2** a device for connecting several electrical plugs to one socket. **3** a person who adapts.

ADC *abbr.* **1** AIDE-DE-CAMP. **2** analog-digital converter.

ADD *abbr.* ATTENTION DEFICIT DISORDER.

add *v.* **1** *tr.* join (one thing to another) as an increase or supplement. **2** *tr. & intr.* put together (two or more numbers) to find a number denoting their combined value. **3** *tr.* say in addition (*added a remark*). □ **add in** include. **add to** increase; be a further item among. **add up 1** find the total of. **2** (foll. by *to*) amount to;

constitute. **3** *informal* make sense; be understandable. □ **added** *adj.*

addendum /ə'dendəm/ *n.* (*pl.* **addenda** /-də/) **1** a thing (usu. something omitted) to be added, esp. (in *pl.*) as additional matter at the end of a book. **2** an appendix; an addition.

adder *n.* **1** any of a variety of non-venomous N American snakes, e.g. the hognose snake. **2** any of various small venomous snakes of Europe and Asia, esp. the common viper, *Vipera berus*.

addict ● *n.* **1** a person addicted to a habit, esp. one dependent on a (specified) drug. **2** *informal* an enthusiastic devotee of a sport or pastime (*film addict*). ● *v.tr. & refl.* (usu. in *passive*; usu. foll. by *to*) make addicted.

addicted *adj.* (often foll. by *to*) **1** dependent on as a habit; unable to do without (*addicted to heroin*). **2** devoted (*addicted to football*).

addiction *n.* the fact or process of being addicted, esp. the condition of taking a drug habitually and being unable to give it up without adverse effects.

addictive *adj.* (of a drug, habit, etc.) causing addiction or dependence.

add-in *n.* (usu. *attrib.*) a piece of computer hardware for installation into an existing system.

Addison's disease *n.* a disease characterized by progressive anemia and debility and brown discoloration of the skin.

addition *n.* **1** the act or process of adding or being added. **2** a person or thing added. □ **in addition** (often foll. by *to*) furthermore; as something added. □ **additional** *adj.* **additionally** *adv.*

additive ● *n.* a thing added, esp. a substance added to another so as to give it specific qualities (*food additive*). ● *adj.* characterized by addition.

addle ● *v.* **1** *tr.* muddle, confuse. **2** *intr.* (of an egg) become addled. ● *adj.* **1** muddled, unsound (*addlebrained*). **2** (of an egg) addled.

addled *adj.* **1** confused. **2** (of an egg) rotten.

add-on *n.* something added to an object or quantity.

address ● *n.* **1 a** the place where a person lives or an organization is situated. **b** particulars of this, esp. for postal purposes. **c** *Computing* the location of an item of stored information. **d** *Computing* the string of codes representing a person's location on an electronic mail network. **2** a discourse delivered to an audience. **3** skill, dexterity, readiness. **4** (in *pl.*) a courteous approach, courtship (*pay one's addresses to*). ● *v.tr.* **1** write the name and address of the intended recipient on (an envelope etc.). **2** direct in speech or writing (remarks, a protest, etc.). **3** speak or write to, esp. formally. **4** direct one's attention to (*addressed my concerns*). □ **address oneself to 1** speak or write to. **2** attend to. □ **addressable** *adj.* **addresser** *n.*

addressee *n.* the person to whom something (esp. a letter) is addressed.

adduce /ə'djuːs/ *v.tr.* cite as an instance or as evidence.

adenine /'ædə,niːn/ *n.* a purine derivative found in all living tissue as a component base of DNA or RNA.

adenoidal /,ædə'nɔidəl/ *adj. Med.* **1** suffering from enlarged adenoids. **2** (of the voice) having the nasal tones of a person with enlarged adenoids.

adenoids *n.pl.* a mass of lymphatic tissue between the back of the nose and the throat.

adept ● *adj.* (often foll. by *at, in*) highly gifted or skilled. ● *n.* a skilled performer; an expert. □ **adeptly** *adv.* **adeptness** *n.*

adequate *adj.* **1** sufficient, satisfactory. **2** barely sufficient. □ **adequacy** *n.* **adequately** *adv.*

à deux /æ'dɜː/ *adv. & adj.* for or between two people.

adhere *v.intr.* **1** (usu. foll. by *to*) (of a substance) stick fast to a surface, another substance, etc. **2** (foll. by *to*) behave according to; follow in detail (*adhered to our plan*). **3** (foll. by *to*) give support or allegiance.

adherent ● *n.* **1** a supporter of a party, person, etc. **2** a devotee of an activity. ● *adj.* **1** (foll. by *to*) faithfully observing a rule etc. **2** (often foll. by *to*) (of a substance) sticking fast. □ **adherence** *n.*

adhesion /əd'hiːʒən/ *n.* **1** the act or process of adhering. **2** the capacity of a substance to stick fast. **3** *Med.* an unnatural union of surfaces due to inflammation. **4** the maintenance of contact between the wheels of a vehicle and the road. **5** the giving of support or allegiance. ¶More common in physical senses, with *adherence* used in abstract senses (e.g. *adherence to principles*).

adhesive /əd'hiːsɪv, əd'hiːzɪv/ ● *adj.* sticky, enabling surfaces or substances to adhere to one another. ● *n.* an adhesive substance, esp. one used to stick others together. □ **adhesively** *adv.* **adhesiveness** *n.*

ad hoc /æd 'hɒk/ *adv. & adj.* for a particular (usu. exclusive) purpose (*an ad hoc committee*).

ad hominem /æd 'hɒmɪˌnem/ *adv. & adj.* **1** relating to or associated with a particular person. **2** appealing to the emotions and not to reason.

adieu ● *interj.* goodbye. ● *n.* (*pl.* **adieus** or **adieux** /ə'djuːz/) a goodbye (esp. in *bid adieu to*).

ad infinitum /æd ˌɪnfɪ'naɪtəm/ *adv.* forever.

adios *interj.* goodbye.

adipose tissue *n.* fatty connective tissue.

Adirondack chair *n. N Amer.* a slatted wooden lawn chair with a fan-shaped back and broad arms.

adjacent *adj.* (often foll. by *to*) **1** lying near or adjoining. **2** *Math.* (of angles) sharing a vertex and one common line. □ **adjacency** *n.*

adjective ● *n.* a word or phrase naming an attribute, added to or grammatically related to a noun to modify it or describe it. ● *adj.* additional; not standing by itself; dependent. □ **adjectival** /ˌædʒək'taɪvəl/ *adj.* **adjectivally** *adv.*

adjoin *v.tr.* be close to or joined with. □ **adjoining** *adj.*

adjourn *v.* **1** *tr.* **a** put off; postpone. **b** break off (a meeting, discussion, hearing, etc.) with the intention of resuming later. **2** *intr.* (of persons at a meeting) **a** break off proceedings and disperse. **b** (foll. by *to*) transfer the meeting to another place.

adjournment *n.* adjourning or being adjourned, esp. the postponement of a court case.

adjudge *v.tr.* **1** adjudicate (a matter). **2** consider. **3** pronounce judicially. **4** (foll. by *to*) award judicially.

adjudicate *v.* **1** *intr.* act as judge in a competition, court, etc. **2** *tr.* **a** decide judicially regarding (a claim etc.). **b** (foll. by *to be* + *n.* or *adj.*) pronounce. □ **adjudication** *n.* **adjudicative** *adj.* **adjudicator** *n.*

adjunct ● *n.* **1** (usu. foll. by *to*, *of*) something added to something else, and auxiliary to or dependent on it. **2** an assistant, esp. one with a temporary appointment only. **3** *Grammar* a word or phrase used to explain or amplify the predicate, subject, etc. ● *attrib.adj.* connected with in a subordinate or temporary capacity (*adjunct professor*).

adjust *v.* **1** *tr.* **a** arrange; put in the correct order or position. **b** regulate, esp. by a small amount. **2** *tr.* (usu. foll. by *to*) make suitable. **3** *tr.* assess (loss or damages). **4** *intr.* (usu. foll. by *to*) make oneself suited to. **5** *tr.* (foll. by *for*) alter (a statistic etc.) to allow for circumstances. □ **adjustable** *adj.* **adjustability** *n.* **adjuster** *n.* **adjustment** *n.*

adjutant /'ædʒətənt/ *n.* **1** *Military* an officer who assists superior officers by communicating orders, conducting correspondence, etc. **2** an assistant.

ad lib ● *v.intr.* (**ad libbed**, **ad libbing**) speak or perform without formal preparation; improvise. ● *adj.* improvised. ● *adv.* (also **ad libitum** /'lɪbɪtəm/) as one pleases, to any desired extent. ● *n.* something spoken or played extempore.

ADM *abbr. Cdn* Assistant Deputy Minister.

Adm. *abbr.* (preceding a name) Admiral.

adman *n.* (*pl.* **admen**) *informal* a person who produces advertisements commercially.

admin *informal* ● *n.* administration. ● *adj.* administrative.

administer *v.* **1** *tr.* attend to the running of (business affairs etc.); manage. **2** *tr.* **a** be responsible for the implementation of (the law, justice, punishment, etc.). **b** *Christianity* give out, or perform the rites of (a sacrament). **c** (usu. foll. by *to*) direct the taking of (an oath). **3** *tr.* **a** give, apply (medication etc.). **b** deliver (a rebuke etc.). **4** *tr.* have someone undergo (a test etc.). **5** *intr.* (foll. by *to*) provide what is necessary to satisfy (a person or their needs). **6** *intr.* act as administrator.

administrate *v.tr. & intr.* administer (esp. business affairs); act as an administrator.

administration *n.* **1 a** management of a business, institution, etc. **b** management of public affairs. **2** *N Amer.* those responsible for administering a business, institution, etc. **3** the government in power. **4** *N Amer.* the term of office of a government or political leader. **5** *Law* the management of another person's estate. **6** (foll. by *of*) **a** the administering of justice, an oath, etc. **b** application of medication etc.

administrative *adj.* concerning or relating to the management of affairs. □ **administratively** *adv.*

administrative assistant *n.* an office worker who assists an executive by handling routine administrative tasks.

administrator *n.* **1** a person who administers a business or public affairs. **2** *Computing* = SYSTEM ADMINISTRATOR. **3** *Law* a person appointed to manage the estate of a person who has died without a will. **4** a person who performs official duties in some sphere, e.g. in religion or justice. □ **administratorship** *n.*

administratrix /əd,mɪnɪ'streɪtrɪks/ *n. Law* a woman appointed to manage the estate of a person who has died without a will.

admirable *adj.* **1** deserving admiration. **2** excellent. □ **admirably** *adv.*

admiral *n.* **1** (also **Admiral**) **a** a naval officer of high rank, esp. (in Canada) the highest rank in the Maritime Command. **b** a rear admiral or vice admiral. **2** any of various butterflies (*red admiral*).

admiration *n.* **1** respect, warm approval. **2** an object of this. **3** pleased contemplation.

admire *v.tr.* **1** regard with approval, respect, or satisfaction. **2** express one's admiration of.

admirer *n.* **1** a person who admires, esp. a devotee of an able or famous person. **2** a person who is sexually attracted to another.

admiring *adj.* showing or feeling admiration. □ **admiringly** *adv.*

admissible *adj.* **1** worth accepting or considering. **2** *Law* allowable as evidence. **3** (foll. by *to*) capable of being admitted. □ **admissibility** *n.*

admission *n.* **1** an acknowledgement or confession. **2 a** the process or right of admitting. **b** a charge for this. **3** (in *pl.*) the department (of a university, hospital, etc.) responsible for admitting new students, patients, etc. **4** a person admitted to a hospital. ¶See ADMITTANCE.

admit v. (**admitted, admitting**) **1** tr. **a** (often foll. by to be, or that + clause) acknowledge; recognize as true. **b** accept as valid or true. **2** intr. (foll. by to) acknowledge responsibility for a deed, fault, etc. **3** tr. **a** allow (a person) entrance or access. **b** allow (a person) to be a member of (an institution, group, etc.) or to share in (a privilege etc.). **c** (of a hospital etc.) bring in (a person) for treatment. **4** tr. (of an enclosed space) have room for. **5** intr. (foll. by of) allow as possible (the law admits of many interpretations).

admittance n. the right or process of admitting or being admitted (no admittance except on business). ¶A more formal and technical word than admission.

admittedly adv. as an acknowledged fact (admittedly, there are problems).

admixture n. **1** a combination, esp. of disparate elements. **2** a thing added, esp. a minor ingredient. **3** the act of adding this.

admonish /æd'mɒnɪʃ/ v.tr. **1** reprove, esp. gently. **2** (foll. by to + infin.) urge. **3** (foll. by to + infin.) give advice to. **4** (foll. by of) warn. □ **admonition** /ˌædmə'nɪʃən/ n. **admonitory** /æd'mɒnɪˌtɔrɪ/ adj.

ad nauseam /'nɔːziˌəm, -zɪˌæm/ adv. to an excessive or disgusting degree.

ado n. fuss, busy activity; trouble, difficulty. □ **without further** (or **more**) **ado** immediately.

adobe /ə'doːbi/ n. **1** a sun-dried brick made from clay and straw (often attrib.: adobe house). **2** the clay used for making such bricks.

adolescent ● adj. **1** between childhood and adulthood. **2** of or characteristic of this age. ● n. an adolescent person. □ **adolescence** n.

Adonai /ˌædoː'naɪ/ n. Lord; a name of God used as a substitute for the Hebrew YHVH.

Adonis /ə'dɒnɪs/ n. a handsome young man.

adopt v.tr. **1** take into a relationship, esp. another's child as one's own. **2** choose to follow (a course of action etc.). **3** assume (adopt an air of indifference). **4** take over (an idea etc.) from another person. **5** choose as a candidate for office. **6** accept; formally approve (a recommendation, legislation, etc.). □ **adoptable** adj. **adoption** n.

adoptive attrib.adj. **1** related by adoption (adoptive parents). **2** (of a city, country, etc.) chosen as residence by one born elsewhere. □ **adoptively** adv.

adorable adj. **1** informal delightful, cute. **2** deserving adoration. □ **adorably** adv.

adore v.tr. **1** regard with honour and deep affection. **2** worship as divine. **3** informal like very much. □ **adoration** n. **adorer** n. **adoring** adj. **adoringly** adv.

adorn v.tr. **1** add beauty or lustre to; be an ornament to. **2** decorate. □ **adornment** n.

adrenal /ə'driːnəl/ adj. **1** of the adrenal glands. **2** at or near the kidneys.

adrenal gland n. either of two ductless glands above the kidneys, secreting adrenalin.

adrenalin /ə'drɛnəlɪn/ n. (also **adrenaline**) **1** a hormone secreted by the adrenal glands, affecting circulation and muscular action, and causing excitement and stimulation. **2** this substance used as a stimulant.

Adriatic /ˌeɪdrɪ'ætɪk/ adj. of or relating to the arm of the Mediterranean Sea between the Balkans and the Italian peninsula.

adrift adv. & predic.adj. **1** (of a boat etc.) drifting, esp. without direction. **2** away from the intended course,

amiss. **3** lacking purpose or guidance; detached (youth adrift in our cities). **4** informal unfastened.

adroit adj. **1** dexterous, skilful. **2** clever, astute. □ **adroitly** adv. **adroitness** n.

adsorb v.tr. (usu. of a solid) hold (molecules of a gas or liquid or solute) to its surface, causing a thin film to form. □ **adsorption** n. (also **adsorbtion**).

ADT abbr. Atlantic Daylight Time.

adulate /'ædjʊˌleɪt/ v.tr. flatter or praise obsequiously. □ **adulation** n. **adulator** n. **adulatory** adj.

adult ● adj. **1** mature, grown-up. **2** (attrib.) **a** of or for adults (adult education). **b** euphemism sexually explicit (adult films). ● n. **1** an adult person. **2** Law a person who has reached the age of majority. □ **adulthood** n.

Adult Accompaniment n. (in Ontario and the Maritimes) a film classification which requires viewers under 14 years of age to be accompanied by an adult. Abbr.: **AA**.

adulterant ● adj. used in adulterating. ● n. an adulterant substance.

adulterate ● v.tr. corrupt or debase (esp. foods) by adding other or inferior ingredients. ● adj. spurious, debased, counterfeit. □ **adulteration** n.

adultery n. (pl. -**ies**) **1** voluntary sexual intercourse between a married person and a person (married or not) other than his or her spouse. **2** an instance of this; an adulterous relationship. □ **adulterer** n. **adulteress** n. **adulterous** adj. **adulterously** adv.

adumbrate /'ædəmˌbreɪt/ v.tr. **1** outline or indicate faintly. **2** foreshadow. **3** overshadow. □ **adumbration** n.

advance ● v. **1** tr. & intr. move or put forward. **2** intr. make progress. **3** tr. **a** pay (money) before it is due. **b** lend (money). **4** tr. give active support to; promote. **5** tr. put forward (a claim or suggestion). **6** tr. cause (an event) to occur at an earlier date (advanced the meeting three hours). **7** tr. raise (a price). **8** intr. rise (in price). ● n. **1** an act of going forward. **2** progress. **3** a payment made before the due time. **4** a loan. **5** (esp. in pl.; often foll. by to) an amorous or friendly approach. **6** a rise in price. ● attrib.adj. done or supplied beforehand (advance warning). □ **advance on** approach threateningly. **in advance** ahead in place or time. □ **advancer** n.

advanced adj. **1** far on in progress. **2** ahead of the times. **3** highly developed, complex.

advanced green n. Cdn a flashing green traffic light in advance of the steady green light, indicating that oncoming traffic is halted.

advance man n. N Amer. a person who arranges security, publicity, etc. before the arrival of a touring politician etc.

advancement n. the progression or promotion of a person, cause, or plan.

advance poll n. Cdn an early poll for voters who expect to be absent from their riding on election day.

advantage /əd'væntɪdʒ/ ● n. **1** a beneficial feature; a favourable circumstance. **2** benefit, profit (is not to your advantage). **3** (often foll. by over) superiority in a particular respect. **4** Tennis the next point won after deuce. **5** Hockey numerical superiority over the opposing team, as on a power play (a two-man advantage). ● v.tr. **1** be beneficial or favourable to. **2** further, promote. □ **have the advantage of** be in a better position in some respect than. **take advantage of 1** make good use of (a favourable circumstance). **2** exploit or outwit (a person), esp. unfairly. **3** euphemism seduce. **to advantage** in a way which exhibits the merits (was seen to advantage). **turn to advantage** benefit from. □ **advantageous** /ˌædvən'teɪdʒəs/ adj. **advantageously** adv.

advantaged *adj.* having advantages; privileged.

Advent /'ædvent/ *n.* **1** *Christianity* the season before Christmas, including the four preceding Sundays. **2** *Christianity* the coming or Second Coming of Christ. **3** (**advent**) the arrival of esp. an important person etc.

Advent calendar *n.* a calendar for the month preceding Christmas, esp. with flaps or windows opened one each day to reveal a picture etc.

Adventist *n.* a member of a Christian group that believes in the imminent Second Coming of Christ. □ **Adventism** *n.*

adventitious /ˌædven'tɪʃəs/ *adj.* **1** accidental. **2** extrinsic. **3** *Biol.* formed accidentally or under unusual conditions. □ **adventitiously** *adv.*

adventure /əd'ventʃər/ ● *n.* **1 a** an unusual and exciting experience. **b** (*attrib.*) designating a type of tourism to exotic, esp. wilderness destinations usu. combined with hiking, canoeing, etc. **2** a daring enterprise; a hazardous activity. **3** enterprise (*the spirit of adventure*). **4** a commercial speculation. ● *v.intr.* **1** (often foll. by *into, upon*) dare to go or come. **2** (foll. by *on, upon*) dare to undertake. **3** incur risk; engage in adventure. □ **adventuresome** *adj.*

adventurer *n.* **1** a person who seeks adventure, esp. for gain or enjoyment. **2** a financial speculator.

adventuress *n.* **1** *derogatory* a woman who pursues financial gain or social advancement, esp. by sexual means. **2** a woman who engages in adventures.

adventurism *n.* a tendency to take risks, often imprudently, esp. in foreign policy. □ **adventurist** *n.*

adventurous *adj.* **1** rash, venturesome; enterprising. **2** characterized by adventures. □ **adventurously** *adv.* **adventurousness** *n.*

Advent wreath *n. Christianity* a wreath with four candles lit on successive Sundays in Advent.

adverb *n.* a word or phrase that modifies or qualifies another word (esp. an adjective, verb, or other adverb) or a word group, expressing a relation of place, time, cause, degree, etc. □ **adverbial** *adj. & n.*

adversarial *adj.* **1** involving conflict or opposition. **2** opposed, hostile.

adversary *n.* (*pl.* **-ies**) **1** an enemy. **2** an opponent in a sport or game; an antagonist.

adverse *adj.* **1** contrary, hostile. **2** hurtful, injurious. □ **adversely** *adv.* **adverseness** *n.*

adversity *n.* (*pl.* **-ies**) **1** the condition of adverse fortune (*courage in adversity*). **2** a misfortune.

advertise *v.* **1** *tr.* draw attention to or describe favourably (goods or services) in a public medium to promote sales. **2** *tr.* make generally or publicly known. **3** *intr.* (foll. by *for*) seek by public notice, esp. in a newspaper. **4** *tr.* (usu. foll. by *of*, or *that* + clause) notify. □ **advertiser** *n.*

advertisement *n.* **1** a public notice or announcement, esp. one advertising goods or services. **2** the act or process of advertising.

advertorial *n.* a newspaper etc. advertisement giving information about a product in the style of an editorial or objective journalistic comment.

advice *n.* **1** words offered as an opinion or recommendation about future action; counsel. **2** (often in *pl.*) information given; news, esp. communications from a distance. **3** formal notice of a transaction. □ **take advice 1** obtain advice, esp. from an expert. **2** act according to advice given.

advisable *adj.* (usu. *predic.*) to be recommended, sensible. □ **advisability** *n.* **advisably** *adv.*

advise *v.* **1** *tr. & intr.* give advice to. **2** *tr.* recommend;

offer as advice. **3** *tr.* (usu. foll. by *of*, or *that* + clause) inform, notify. **4** *intr.* (foll. by *with*) esp. *N Amer.* consult.

advised *adj.* **1** judicious (*ill-advised*). **2** deliberate, considered. **3** recommended. □ **advisedly** *adv.*

advisement *n. N Amer.* □ **take under advisement** reserve judgment while considering.

adviser *n.* (also **advisor**) a person who advises, esp. one appointed to do so and regularly consulted.

advisory ● *adj.* having the power to advise (*advisory board*). ● *n.* (*pl.* **-ies**) *N Amer.* an advisory statement, esp. a bulletin about bad weather.

advocacy /'ædvəkəsi/ *n.* **1** (usu. foll. by *of*) verbal support or argument for a cause, policy, etc. (often *attrib.*: *advocacy group*). **2** the function of an advocate.

advocate ● *n.* /'ædvəkət/ **1** (foll. by *of, for*) a person who supports or speaks in favour. **2** a person who pleads for another. **3** a lawyer. ● *v.tr.* /'ædvəˌkeit/ **1** recommend or support by argument (a cause, policy, etc.). **2** plead for, defend.

adze ● *n.* a tool for cutting away the surface of wood, like an axe with an arched blade at right angles to the handle. ● *v.tr.* dress or cut with an adze.

AECB *abbr.* (in Canada and the US) Atomic Energy Control Board.

Aegean /əˈdʒiːən/ *adj.* of or relating to the Aegean Sea or Islands.

aegis /'iːdʒɪs/ *n.* **1** auspices; control. **2** a protection; an impregnable defence.

aeon *var. of* EON.

aerate *v.tr.* **1** charge (a liquid) with a gas, esp. carbon dioxide, e.g. to produce effervescence. **2** introduce air into (soil etc.). **3** expose to the mechanical or chemical action of the air. □ **aeration** *n.* **aerator** *n.*

aerial ● *adj.* **1** by, from, or involving aircraft (*aerial photography*). **2 a** existing, moving, or happening in the air. **b** lofty or elevated. **c** of or in the atmosphere. **3 a** thin as air; ethereal. **b** immaterial, imaginary. **c** of air; gaseous. **4** designating events in freestyle skiing in which competitors leap off a ski jump and perform twists and flips in the air before landing. ● *n.* **1** = ANTENNA. **2** *Football* a pass thrown toward the opponent's end zone. **3** (in *pl.*) aerial events in freestyle skiing. □ **aeriality** *n.* **aerially** *adv.*

aerialist *n.* **1** a high-wire or trapeze artist. **2** a freestyle skier specializing in aerial events.

aerie /'eri, 'iːri/ *n.* **1** a nest of a bird of prey, esp. an eagle, built high up. **2** a high place or position.

aero /'ero:/ *attrib.adj. informal* aerodynamic.

aero- *comb. form* **1** relating to air or the atmosphere (*aerodynamics*). **2** relating to aircraft (*aerobatics*).

aerobat *n.* a pilot who performs aerobatics. □ **aerobatic** *adj.* **aerobatically** *adv.*

aerobatics *n.pl.* feats of expert and usu. spectacular flying and manoeuvring of aircraft.

aerobe /'ero:b/ *n.* a micro-organism usu. growing in the presence of air, or needing air for growth.

aerobic *adj.* **1** increasing or pertaining to oxygen consumption by the body (*aerobic exercise*). **2** of or relating to aerobics (*aerobic shoes*). **3** *Biol.* of or relating to aerobes. □ **aerobically** *adv.*

aerobics *n.pl.* exercises, esp. those done to music, designed to increase fitness by any maintainable activity that increases oxygen intake and heart rate.

aerodynamic *adj.* **1** of or relating to aerodynamics. **2** (of a vehicle etc.) designed to minimize drag. □ **aerodynamically** *adv.*

aerodynamics *n.pl.* (usu. treated as *sing.*) **1** the interaction between the air and solid bodies moving through it. **2** the study of this. □ **aerodynamicist** *n.*

aeronautics *n.pl.* (usu. treated as *sing.*) the science or practice of motion or travel in the air. □ **aeronautic** *adj.* **aeronautical** *adj.*

aerosol *n.* **1 a** a substance packed under pressure with a device for releasing it as a fine spray (usu. *attrib.*: *aerosol can*). **b** the container holding this. **2** a suspension of particles dispersed in air etc.

aerospace *n.* **1** the earth's atmosphere and outer space. **2 a** the technology of flight in the atmosphere and in space. **b** the industry concerned with this.

aesthete /'esθiːt/ *n.* a person who has or professes to have a special appreciation of beauty.

aesthetic /es'θetɪk/ ● *adj.* **1** concerned with beauty or the appreciation of beauty. **2** having such appreciation; sensitive to beauty. **3** in accordance with the principles of good taste. ● *n.* **1** (in *pl.*) the philosophy of the beautiful, esp. in art. **2** (in *pl.*) aesthetically pleasing elements. **3** a conception of what is beautiful or artistically valid (*a minimalist aesthetic*). □ **aesthetically** *adv.* **aestheticism** *n.*

aesthetician /ˌesθəˈtɪʃən/ *n.* **1** a person versed in or devoted to aesthetics. **2** a beautician.

AF *abbr.* **1** *Photog.* AUTOFOCUS. **2** AIR FORCE.

afar *adv.* at or to a distance. □ **from afar** from a distance.

AFC *abbr.* (in the US) American Football Conference.

affable *adj.* friendly, good-natured. □ **affability** *n.* **affably** *adv.*

affair *n.* **1** a concern; a matter to be attended to. **2 a** a celebrated or notorious happening or sequence of events. **b** a thing or event of a specified sort (*a black-tie affair*). **3** a romantic or sexual relationship between two people, esp. an adulterous one. **4** (in *pl.*) **a** ordinary pursuits of life. **b** business dealings. **c** matters or issues (*current affairs*).

affaire /æˈfer/ *n.* (usu. **l'affaire** /læˈfer/) (followed by a proper name) a controversy or notorious event involving the specified person (*l'affaire Ben Johnson*).

affect¹ *v.tr.* **1 a** produce an effect on; influence. **b** (of a disease etc.) attack. **2** move; touch the feelings of (*affected me deeply*). ¶*Affect* should not be confused with *effect* which means 'to bring about, to accomplish', e.g. *The government effected great changes*. Note also that *effect* is commonly used as a noun as well as a verb. □ **affecting** *adj.* **affectingly** *adv.*

affect² *v.tr.* **1 a** pretend to have or feel. **b** (foll. by *to* + infin.) pretend. **2** assume the character or manner of, usu. pretentiously. **3** show a preference or liking for, usu. ostentatiously.

affectation *n.* **1** an assumed or contrived manner of behaviour, esp. in order to impress. **2** (foll. by *of*) a studied display. **3** pretense.

affected *adj.* **1** in senses of AFFECT¹, AFFECT². **2** artificially assumed or displayed; pretended. **3** (of a person) artificial. □ **affectedly** *adv.*

affection *n.* **1** (often foll. by *for, toward*) goodwill; fond or kindly feeling. **2** a mental state; an emotion. **3** a mental disposition. **4** the act or process of affecting or being affected. **5** a disease; a diseased condition. □ **affectional** *adj.* (in sense 2). **affectionally** *adv.*

affectionate *adj.* loving, fond; showing love or tenderness. □ **affectionately** *adv.*

affective *adj.* **1** concerning the affections; emotional. **2** *Psych.* of feeling or mood (*affective disorders*). □ **affectivity** *n.*

affidavit /ˌæfɪˈdeɪvɪt/ *n.* a written statement confirmed by oath, for use as evidence in court.

affiliate ● *v.* (foll. by *to, with*) **1** *tr.* attach or connect (to a larger organization); adopt as a member, branch, etc. **2** *intr.* associate oneself with an organization etc. ●

n. an affiliated person or organization. □ **affiliated** *adj.* **affiliation** *n.*

affinity *n.* (*pl.* **-ies**) **1** (often foll. by *for, with, between*, or *to*) a spontaneous or natural liking for or attraction to a person or thing. **2** relationship other than by blood, esp. by marriage or adoption (*compare* CONSANGUINITY 1). **3** resemblance in structure between animals, plants, or languages. **4** a similarity of characters suggesting a relationship.

affinity card *n.* a credit card for which the issuer donates to a specified charity etc. a portion of the money spent using the card.

affirm *v.* **1** *tr.* assert strongly; state as a fact. **2** *intr.* **a** Law make an affirmation. **b** make a formal declaration. **3** *tr.* Law confirm, ratify (a judgment).

affirmation *n.* **1** the act or process of affirming or being affirmed. **2** *Law* a solemn declaration by a person who conscientiously declines to take an oath.

affirmative ● *adj.* **1** affirming; asserting that a thing is so. **2** (of a vote) expressing approval. ● *n.* **1** an affirmative statement, reply, or word. **2** (prec. by *the*) a positive or affirming position. ● *interj.* esp. *N Amer.* yes. □ **in the affirmative** with affirmative effect; so as to accept or agree to a proposal; yes. □ **affirmatively** *adv.*

affirmative action *n.* esp. *N Amer.* a policy to favour those who often suffer from discrimination, esp. in employment.

affix ● *v.tr.* **1** (usu. foll. by *to, on*) attach, fasten. **2** impress (a seal, stamp, etc.). **3** add in writing (a signature or postscript). ● *n.* **1** an appendage; an addition. **2** a prefix or suffix. □ **affixation** *n.*

afflict *v.tr.* distress with bodily or mental suffering. □ **afflicted with** suffering from. □ **afflictive** *adj.*

affliction *n.* **1** physical or mental distress, esp. pain or illness. **2** a cause of this.

affluence *n.* wealth.

affluent *adj.* **1** wealthy, rich. **2** abundant. **3** flowing freely or copiously. □ **affluently** *adv.*

afford *v.tr.* **1 a** have enough money, means, time, etc., for; be able to spare (*can afford $50; could not afford to worry about it*). **b** be in a position to do something (esp. without risk of adverse consequences) (*can't afford to let him think so*). **2** provide (*affords a view of the lake*). □ **affordability** *n.* **affordable** *adj.*

affray *n.* a public fight; riot.

affront ● *n.* an open insult. ● *v.tr.* **1** insult openly. **2** offend the modesty or self-respect of.

Afghan /'æfɡæn/ ● *n.* **1 a** a native or national of Afghanistan, a country in central Asia. **b** a person of Afghan descent. **2** the official language of Afghanistan. **3** (**afghan**) a knitted or crocheted woollen blanket or shawl. **4** (in full **Afghan coat**) a kind of sheepskin coat with the skin outside and usu. with a shaggy border. **5** (in full **Afghan hound**) a tall hunting dog with long silky hair. ● *adj.* of or relating to Afghanistan or its people or language.

Afghani /æfˈɡæni/ ● *n.* (*pl.* **-is**) = AFGHAN *n.* 1. ● *adj.* = AFGHAN *adj.*

aficionado /əfɪʃəˈnɒdoː, əˌfɪsjə-/ *n.* (*pl.* **-os**) a devotee, fan or enthusiast.

afield *adv.* **1** (esp. in **far afield**) away from home; to or at a distance. **2** in the field or the countryside.

afire *adv. & predic.adj.* **1** on fire. **2** intensely roused or excited. **3** glittering, glowing; coloured like fire.

aflame *adv. & predic.adj.* **1** in flames. **2** = AFIRE 2. **3** red as if on fire (*his cheeks were aflame*).

afloat *adv. & predic.adj.* **1** floating in water or air. **2** on board ship. **3** out of debt or difficulty. **4** in general circulation. **5** full of or covered with a liquid.

AFN *abbr.* (in Canada) ASSEMBLY OF FIRST NATIONS.

afoot *adv. & predic.adj.* **1** in operation; progressing. **2** stirring; on the move. **3** *N Amer.* **a** on foot (*they arrived afoot*). **b** on one's feet (*slow afoot*).

afore- *comb. form* before, previously (*aforementioned*).

aforethought *adj.* premeditated (*malice aforethought*).

afoul *adv.* esp. *N Amer.* (usu. in **run** or **fall afoul of**) into conflict or difficulty with.

afraid *predic.adj.* **1** alarmed, frightened. **2** unwilling or reluctant for fear of the consequences (*was afraid to go in*). □ **be afraid** admit or declare with (real or politely simulated) regret (*I'm afraid there's none left*).

A-frame *n.* **1** a frame (of a house etc.) having the shape of a capital letter A. **2** *N Amer.* an A-frame house. **3** *N Amer.* Forestry an A-shaped frame supporting running lines in high-lead logging.

afresh *adv.* anew; with a fresh beginning.

African ● *n.* **1** a native or inhabitant of Africa. **2** a person of African descent (esp. a dark-skinned person). ● *adj.* of or relating to Africa.

African-American *n.* an American citizen of black African origin or descent.

African-Canadian *n.* a Canadian citizen of black African origin or descent.

African elephant *n.* the elephant, *Loxodonta africana*, of Africa, larger than the Indian elephant.

African violet *n.* a plant of the genus *Saintpaulia*, with heart-shaped velvety leaves and blue, purple, pink, or white flowers, grown as a houseplant.

Afrikaans /ˌæfrɪˈkɑːns/ *n.* the language of the Afrikaner people developed from Dutch, an official language of the Republic of South Africa.

Afrikaner /ˌæfrɪˈkɑːnər/ *n.* an Afrikaans-speaking white South African, esp. one of Dutch descent.

Afro ● *adj.* **1** (also **afro**) (of a hairstyle) shaped into a wide curly or frizzy bush. **2** African. ● *n.* (*pl.* **-os**) an Afro hairstyle.

Afro- *comb. form* African (*Afro-Asian*).

Afro-American ● *adj.* of or relating to American blacks or their culture. ● *n.* an American black.

Afro-Asiatic ● *adj.* of or pertaining to a family of languages in N Africa and W Asia, including Arabic. ● *n.* the Afro-Asiatic language family.

Afro-Caribbean ● *n.* a person of African descent in or from the Caribbean. ● *adj.* of or relating to the Afro-Caribbeans or their culture.

Afrocentric *adj.* centred on Africa or on cultures of African origin, esp. N American black culture.

aft[1] *adv.* at or toward the stern of a ship or tail of an aircraft.

aft[2] *n.* *Cdn informal* afternoon (*I'll see you this aft*).

after ● *prep.* **1 a** following in time; later than. **b** *N Amer.* past the hour of (*a quarter after eight*). **2** in view of (something that happened shortly before) (*after your behaviour tonight what do you expect?*). **3** (with concessive force) in spite of (*after all my efforts*). **4** behind (*shut the door after you*). **5** in pursuit or quest of (*run after them; is after a job*). **6** about, concerning (*asked after her*). **7** in allusion to (*named her Patricia after her mother*). **8** in imitation of (a person, word, etc.) (*a painting after Rubens*). **9** next in importance to (*the best book on the subject after mine*). **10** according to (*after a fashion*). **11** dialect **a** to have just done (*I was after seeing him just last week*). **b** in the act of, on the point of (*he's after putting the kettle on*). ● *conj.* in or at a time later than that when (*left after they arrived*). ● *adv.*

1 later in time. **2** behind in place (*look before and after*). ● *adj.* **1** later, following (*in after years*). **2** *Naut.* nearer the stern (*after cabins*). □ **after all 1** in spite of all that has happened or has been said etc. **2** in spite of one's exertions, expectations, etc. (*so you went after all!*).

after you a formula used in offering precedence.

afterbirth *n.* the placenta and fetal membranes discharged from the uterus after childbirth.

afterburner *n.* an auxiliary burner in a jet engine to increase thrust.

after-care *n.* care of a patient after a stay in hospital or of a person on release from prison.

afterdeck *n.* *Naut.* the part of a ship's deck nearest the stern.

after-effect *n.* an effect that follows after an interval or after the primary action of something.

afterglow *n.* **1** a light or radiance remaining after its source has disappeared or been removed. **2** a period of happiness, fame, etc. immediately following a successful event.

after-hours *attrib.adj.* occurring or operating after the usual or legal operating hours (*an after-hours bar*).

afterlife *n.* **1** life after death. **2** life at a later time.

aftermarket *n.* **1** a market in spare parts and components. **2** *Stock Exch.* a market in shares after their original issue.

aftermath *n.* **1** consequences; after-effects. **2** the period immediately following an event.

afternoon ● *n.* **1** the time from noon to evening (also *attrib.: afternoon nap*). **2** a time compared with this, esp. the later part of something (*the afternoon of life*). ● *interj.* = GOOD AFTERNOON.

afternoon tea *n.* a light meal served in the afternoon, consisting of tea and usu. sandwiches, small cakes, etc.

aftershave *n.* an astringent lotion for use on the face after shaving.

aftershock *n.* **1** a lesser shock following the main shock of an earthquake. **2** an after-effect.

aftertaste *n.* **1** a taste remaining or recurring after eating or drinking. **2** a persistent feeling etc.

afterthought *n.* an item or thing that is thought of or added later.

afterwards *adv.* (also **afterward**) later.

afterword *n.* concluding remarks in a book, either by the author or by someone else.

AG *abbr.* **1** ATTORNEY GENERAL. **2** *Cdn* AUDITOR GENERAL.

Ag *symbol* the element silver.

ag *abbr.* esp. *N Amer. informal* agriculture, agricultural.

again *adv.* **1** another time; once more. **2** as in a previous position or condition (*quite well again*). **3** in addition (*as much again*). **4** further, besides (*again, what about the children?*). **5** on the other hand (*I might, and again I might not*). □ **again and again** repeatedly.

against *prep.* **1** in opposition to (*fight against the invaders; am against hanging*). **2** into collision or in contact with (*lean against the wall*). **3** to the disadvantage of (*her age is against her*). **4** in contrast to (*against a dark background*). **5** in anticipation of or preparation for (*protected against the cold*). **6** as a compensating factor to (*income against expenditure*). **7** in return for (*issued against payment of the fee*).

Aga Khan /ˌɑːɡə ˈkɑːn/ *n.* the hereditary spiritual leader of most of the Ismaili Muslims.

agape[1] /əˈgeɪp/ *adv. & predic.adj.* gaping, open-mouthed, esp. with wonder or expectation.

agape[2] /ˈæɡəˌpeɪ/ *n.* **1** a Christian feast in token of fellowship, esp. one held by early Christians in commemoration of the Last Supper. **2** *Theol.* Christian fellowship, esp. as distinct from erotic love.

agar /ˈeigɑr/ *n.* (also **agar-agar**) a gelatinous substance obtained from any of various kinds of red seaweed, and used as a thickener in food, a culture medium for bacteria, and a laxative.

agate /ˈægət/ *n.* **1** any of several varieties of hard usu. streaked chalcedony. **2** a coloured toy marble resembling this.

agave /əˈgeivi/ *n.* any plant of the genus *Agave*, with rosettes of succulent spiny leaves, and tall inflorescences, e.g. the century plant.

age ● *n.* **1 a** the length of time that a person or thing has existed or is likely to exist (*ten years of age*). **b** (*attrib.*) of the age of (*age ten*). **c** a particular point in or part of one's life, often as a qualification (*old age*). **2 a** *informal* (often in *pl.*) a long time (*waited for ages*). **b** a distinct period of the past (*Bronze Age; Middle Ages*). **c** a division of geological time, esp. a subdivision of an epoch. **d** a generation. **3** old age (*the wisdom of age*). ● *v.* (*pres. part.* **aging, ageing**) **1** *intr.* show signs of advancing age. **2** *intr.* grow old. **3** *intr.* (esp. of wine or cheese) mature. **4** *tr.* cause or allow to age. □ **of age** adult (esp. in law 18 and over, formerly 21 and over) (*come of age*).

aged *adj.* **1** /eidʒd/ **a** of the age of (*aged ten*). **b** that has been subjected to aging. **2** /ˈeidʒəd/ having lived long; old.

ageing *var. of* AGING.

ageism *n.* prejudice or discrimination on the grounds of age. □ **ageist** *adj. & n.*

ageless *adj.* **1** never growing or appearing old or outmoded. **2** eternal, timeless.

agency *n.* (*pl.* **-ies**) **1 a** an organization or business providing a (usu. specific) service (*advertising agency*). **b** esp. *N Amer.* a government office providing a specific service. **2** a person or business operating on behalf of another, esp. at a distance (*our Vancouver agency*). **3 a** the duty or function of an agent. **b** the office or place of business of an agent. **4** means; instrumentality. **5** active working or operation; action.

agenda *n.* (*pl.* **-s**) **1** a list of items of business to be considered at a meeting. **2** a series of things to be done (*on the agenda*). **3** a plan of action (*hidden agenda*). **4** *N Amer.* a book containing a calendar and usu. an address list etc., used to plan one's activities.

agent *n.* **1** a person who provides a specific service etc. (*insurance agent*). **2** a person who acts for another in business, politics, etc. **3** a person or company that represents an organization, company, or government in a particular territory. **4** a person or thing that exerts power or produces an effect. **5** a spy (*enemy agent*). **6** *Cdn* = INDIAN AGENT. □ **agentry** *n. N Amer.*

agent general *n.* (*pl.* **agents general**) the chief representative of a Canadian province or Australian state in a foreign country or region.

age of consent *n.* the age at which marriage or consent to sexual intercourse is valid in law.

age of discretion *n.* the esp. legal age at which a person is able to manage his or her own affairs.

Age of Reason *n.* **1** the late 17th and 18th c. in western Europe and N America, characterized by faith in human reason. **2** (usu. **age of reason**) the age at which a person is considered capable of making rational judgments.

age-old *adj.* having existed for a very long time.

Aggadah /əˈɡɒˈdə/ *n.* = HAGGADAH.

agglomerate ● *v.tr. & intr.* /əˈɡlɒmə,reit/ **1** collect into a mass. **2** accumulate in a disorderly way. ● *n.* /əˈɡlɒmərət/ **1** a mass or collection of things. **2** *Geol.* a

mass of large volcanic fragments bonded under heat (*compare* CONGLOMERATE *n.* 3). ● *adj.* /əˈɡlɒmərət/ collected into a mass. □ **agglomeration** *n.*

agglomerative *adj.*

agglutinate *v.* **1** *tr.* unite as with glue. **2** *tr. & intr. Biol.* cause or undergo adhesion (of bacteria, red blood cells, etc.). □ **agglutination** *n.*

aggrandize /əˈɡrændaiz/ *v.tr.* **1** increase the power, rank, or wealth of (a person or nation). **2** cause to appear greater or more important than is the case. □ **aggrandizement** /-daizmənt, -dɪzmənt/ *n.*

aggravate *v.tr.* **1** increase the gravity of (an illness, offence, etc.). **2** annoy, exasperate (a person). ¶Use in sense 2 is regarded by some as incorrect, but is common in informal use. □ **aggravation** *n.*

aggravated assault *n. Law* assault involving wounding, maiming, disfigurement or endangerment of the life of the victim.

aggregate ● *n.* **1** a collection of, or the total of, disparate elements. **2** pieces of crushed stone, gravel, etc. used in making concrete. **3 a** *Geol.* a mass of minerals formed into solid rock. **b** a mass of particles. ● *adj.* **1** (of disparate elements) collected into one mass. **2** constituted by the collection of many units into one body. ● *v.tr. & intr.* collect together; combine into one mass. □ **in the aggregate** as a whole. □ **aggregation** *n.*

aggression *n.* **1** the act or practice of attacking without provocation. **2** an unprovoked attack. **3** *Psych.* hostile or destructive tendency or behaviour.

aggressive *adj.* **1** of a person: **a** given to aggression; openly hostile. **b** forceful, assertive, energetic, enterprising (*aggressive salespeople*). **2** (of an act) offensive, hostile. **3** suggesting assertiveness or hostility (*aggressive shoulder pads*). **4** growing or multiplying rapidly (*a very aggressive ivy*). □ **aggressively** *adv.* **aggressiveness** *n.*

aggressor *n.* a person or country that attacks without provocation.

aggrieved *adj.* wronged; having a grievance.

aghast *predic.adj.* (often foll. by *at*) amazed; filled with dismay or consternation.

agile *adj.* **1** characterized by ease and grace of movement. **2** mentally acute. □ **agilely** *adv.* **agility** *n.*

aging ● *n.* **1** the process of growing old. **2** the act or process of causing to age or mature. ● *adj.* becoming or appearing older.

agism *var. of* AGEISM.

agitate *v.* **1** *tr.* disturb or excite (a person or feelings). **2** *intr.* (often foll. by *for, against*) stir up or attempt to stir up public interest or concern. **3** *tr.* shake or move, esp. briskly. □ **agitated** *adj.* **agitatedly** *adv.*

agitation *n.* **1** the act or process of agitating or being agitated. **2** mental anxiety or concern.

agitato /ˌædʒɪˈtɒto/ *adv. & adj. Music* in an agitated manner.

agitator *n.* **1** a person who agitates for or against a cause etc. **2** an apparatus for shaking or mixing liquid etc., esp. in a washing machine.

agitprop /ˈædʒɪt,prɒp/ *n.* **1** (**Agitprop**) *hist.* a Soviet agency for the dissemination of Communist political propaganda, esp. in literature, film, etc. **2** (also *attrib.*) political and usu. pro-communist propaganda.

aglet /ˈæɡlət/ *n.* **1** a plastic or metal tag attached to each end of a shoelace etc. **2** = AIGUILLETTE 1.

aglow *predic.adj.* glowing.

AGM *abbr.* **1** *Cdn, Brit., & Austral.* ANNUAL GENERAL MEETING. **2** air-to-ground missile.

agnolotti /ˌænjəˈlɒti/ n. half-moon shaped or triangular pasta filled with meat, cheese, etc.

agnostic /æɡˈnɒstɪk/ ● n. a person who believes that nothing is known, or can be known, of the existence or nature of God or of anything beyond material phenomena. ● adj. of or relating to agnostics or agnosticism. □ **agnosticism** n.

Agnus Dei /ˌæɡnʊs ˈdeɪi:, ˌænjʊs/ n. Christianity **1** a figure of a lamb bearing a cross or flag, as an emblem of Christ. **2 a** a prayer or hymn beginning with the words 'Lamb of God' said or sung before or during Communion in some Christian liturgies. **b** a musical setting of this.

ago adv. earlier, before the present.

agog predic.adj. eager; excited.

à gogo /əˈɡɒɡoː/ adv. informal in abundance (placed after noun: whisky à gogo).

agonize v. **1** intr. (often foll. by over) undergo (esp. mental) anguish. **2** tr. cause agony to. **3** intr. struggle, contend. □ **agonizing** adj. **agonizingly** adv.

agonized adj. characterized by or expressing agony (an agonized look; agonized breathing).

agony n. (pl. **-ies**) **1** extreme mental or physical suffering. **2** a severe struggle. **3** the struggle or suffering preceding death.

agoraphobia /ˌæɡərəˈfoʊbiə/ n. an abnormal fear of open spaces or public places. □ **agoraphobe** n. **agoraphobic** adj. & n.

agouti /əˈɡuːti/ n. (pl. **-s**) **1** any burrowing rodent of the genus Dasyprocta or Myoprocta of Central and S America, related to the guinea pig. **2** any animal whose fur has each hair banded dark and light.

agrarian /əˈɡreriən/ ● adj. **1** of or relating to the land or its cultivation. **2** relating to landed property. ● n. a person who advocates a redistribution of landed property.

agree v. (**agrees**, **agreed**, **agreeing**) **1** intr. hold a similar opinion. **2** intr. (often foll. by to, or to + infin.) consent (agreed to go). **3** intr. (often foll. by with) a become or be in harmony. **b** suit; be good for (caviar didn't agree with him). **c** Grammar have the same number, gender, case, or person as. **4** tr. consent to or approve of (terms, a proposal, etc.). **5** tr. bring (things, esp. accounts) into harmony. **6** intr. (foll. by on) decide by mutual consent. □ **agree to differ** leave a difference of opinion etc. unresolved. **be agreed** have reached the same opinion.

agreeable adj. **1** pleasant; enjoyable. **2** willing to agree (was agreeable to going). **3** (foll. by to) acceptable. □ **agreeableness** n. **agreeably** adv.

agreement n. **1** the act of agreeing. **2** mutual understanding. **3 a** an arrangement between parties as to a course of action etc. **b** a document outlining such an arrangement. **4** Grammar the condition of having the same number, gender, case, or person. **5** a state of being harmonious.

Agribition n. Cdn the annual agricultural exhibition in Regina, Saskatchewan.

agribusiness n. **1** agriculture conducted on strictly commercial principles, esp. using advanced technology. **2** an organization engaged in this. **3** the group of industries dealing with the produce of, and services to, farming.

agricultural representative n. Cdn (also informal **ag rep**, **ag representative**) an employee of an agriculture ministry who advises farmers in a particular region.

agriculture n. the science or practice of cultivating the soil and rearing animals. □ **agricultural** adj. **agriculturalist** n. **agriculturally** adv.

agri-food adj. esp. Cdn (of an industry) concerned with or involved in food production or processing.

agrimony /ˈæɡrɪˌmoʊni/ n. (pl. **-ies**) any herbaceous plant of the genus Agrimonia, with small yellow flowers.

agrochemical n. a chemical used in agriculture.

agroforestry n. agriculture in which there is integrated management of trees or shrubs along with conventional crops or livestock.

agronomy /əˈɡrɒnəmi/ n. the science of soil management and crop production. □ **agronomic** adj. **agronomical** adj. **agronomically** adv. **agronomist** n.

aground predic.adj. & adv. (of a ship) on or onto the bottom of shallow water.

ague /ˈeɪɡjuː/ n. **1** hist. a malarial fever, with cold, hot, and sweating stages. **2** a shivering fit. □ **agued** adj.

AH abbr. used to show the year in the Muslim calendar, calculated from the Hegira in AD 622.

ah interj. expressing surprise, pleasure, sudden realization, resignation, etc.

AHA abbr. ALPHA-HYDROXY ACID.

aha interj. expressing, surprise, triumph, irony, etc.

ahead adv. **1** further forward in space or time. **2** in the lead (ahead 3–1). **3** in the line of one's forward motion (construction ahead). **4** straight forwards. □ **ahead of 1** further forward or advanced than. **2** in the line of the forward motion of.

ahem interj. (not usu. clearly articulated) used to attract attention, gain time, or express disapproval.

ahistorical /ˌeɪhɪsˈtɔrɪkəl, -ˈtɒrɪkəl/ adj. (also **ahistoric**) not historic; unrelated to history. □ **ahistorically** adv. **ahistoricism** n.

AHL abbr. American Hockey League.

-aholic comb. form denoting addiction (workaholic).

Ahousat /əˈhaʊsæt/ n. (also **Ahousaht**) a member of the principal group of Nuu-chah-nulth, living on the west coast of Vancouver Island.

ahoy interj. Naut. a call used to hail a ship or to attract attention.

AI abbr. **1** Computing artificial intelligence. **2** artificial insemination.

AID abbr. **1** artificial insemination by donor. **2** Agency for International Development.

aid ● n. **1** help. **2** financial or material help, esp. given by one country to another. **3** a material source of help (teaching aid). **4** a person or thing that helps. ● v.tr. **1** help. **2** promote or encourage. □ **in aid of** in support of. **what's this** (or **all this**) **in aid of?** informal what is the purpose of this?

aide n. **1** an assistant. **2** an aide-de-camp.

aide-de-camp n. (pl. **aides-de-camp** pronunc. same) an officer acting as a confidential assistant to a senior officer.

AIDS n. (also **Aids**) acquired immune deficiency syndrome, a condition caused by a virus transmitted in the blood, marked by severe loss of resistance to infection and so ultimately fatal.

AIDS-related complex n. a set of symptoms (chronic illness, fever, weight loss, etc.) of a person infected with HIV, which seems to precede the full development of AIDS. Abbr.: **ARC**.

AIDS virus n. = HIV.

aiguillette /ˌeɪɡwiˈlet/ n. **1** a tagged point hanging from the shoulder on the breast of some uniforms. **2** a thin strip of meat, esp. poultry.

aikido /aiˈkiːdoː, ˈaikiˌdoː/ n. a Japanese form of self-defence and martial art, developed from ju-jitsu and involving holds and throws.

ail v. **1** tr. trouble or afflict in mind or body (*what ails him?*). **2** intr. be ill or in pain.

ailing adj. **1** ill, esp. chronically. **2** in poor condition (*the ailing economy*).

ailment n. an illness, esp. a minor one.

aim ● v. **1** intr. intend or try (*aim at winning; aim to win*). **2** tr. (usu. foll. by *at*) direct or point (a weapon, remark, etc.). **3** intr. take aim. **4** intr. (foll. by *at, for*) seek to attain or achieve. ● n. **1** a purpose, a design, an object aimed at. **2** the directing of a weapon, missile, etc., at an object. □ **take aim** direct a weapon etc. at an object.

aimless adj. without aim or purpose. □ **aimlessly** adv. **aimlessness** n.

ain't contraction informal **1** am not; are not; is not. **2** has not; have not. ¶Usually regarded as an uneducated use, and unacceptable in spoken and written English, except jocularly or in fixed informal phrases.

Ainu /'ainu:/ ● n. **1** (pl. same or **Ainus**) a member of the non-Mongoloid aboriginal inhabitants of the Japanese archipelago. **2** their language. ● adj. of or pertaining to the Ainu.

aïoli /ai'jo:li/ n. a garlic mayonnaise, originally a specialty of Provence.

air ● n. **1** an invisible gaseous substance surrounding the earth, a mixture mainly of oxygen and nitrogen. **2 a** the earth's atmosphere. **b** the free or unconfined space in the atmosphere (*in the open air*). **c** the atmosphere as a place where aircraft operate. **d** the atmosphere as a medium for transmitting radio waves. **3 a** a distinctive impression or characteristic (*an air of absurdity*). **b** one's manner or bearing, esp. a confident one (*a triumphant air*). **c** (esp. in pl.) an affected manner; pretentiousness (*gave himself airs*). **4** Music a tune or melody; a melodious composition. **5** a breeze or light wind. **6** N Amer. informal air conditioning. ● v. **1** tr. (usu. foll. by *out*) expose (a room etc.) to the open air; ventilate. **2** tr. hang (washed laundry etc.) to remove dampness. **3** tr. express publicly (an opinion, grievance, etc.). **4** tr. & intr. broadcast (a program). **5** tr. parade; show ostentatiously (esp. qualities). **6** refl. go out in the fresh air. □ **by air** by aircraft. **in the air** (of opinions or feelings) prevalent; gaining currency. **on** (or **off**) **the air** in (or not in) the process of broadcasting. **take the air** go out of doors. **up in the air 1** aloft. **2** uncertain, undetermined (*his fate is up in the air*). **walk on air** feel elated.

air ambulance n. an aircraft specially equipped for transporting the sick or injured to hospital by air.

air bag n. a safety device that fills with air on impact to protect the occupants of a vehicle in a collision.

air ball n. Basketball slang a shot which results in the ball missing the basket and backboard entirely.

air base n. a base for military aircraft.

air bed n. an inflatable mattress.

air bladder n. **1** a bladder or sac filled with air in fish or some plants (*compare* SWIM BLADDER). **2** any similar bladder or sac made of synthetic material.

airborne adj. **1** moving through or carried by the air (*airborne pollutants*). **2** (of aircraft) in the air; in flight. **3** (of military activity) involving paratroops.

air brake n. **1** a brake worked by air pressure. **2** a device on an aircraft to reduce its speed.

airbrush ● n. a device for spraying colour over a surface by means of compressed air, used by artists and to retouch photographs, esp. to conceal flaws. ● v.tr. **1** paint with an airbrush. **2** gloss over or hide.

air command n. **1** a major subdivision of an air force. **2** (**Air Command**) the official name for the Canadian air force.

air-conditioned adj. (of a room, building, etc.) equipped with air conditioning.

air conditioning n. **1** a system for lowering the temperature and humidity in a building or vehicle. **2** the apparatus for this. □ **air conditioner** n.

air-cool v.tr. cool (an engine etc.) by means of a current of air. □ **air-cooled** adj.

air corridor n. = CORRIDOR 5.

aircraft n. (pl. same) a machine capable of flight, esp. an airplane or helicopter.

aircraft carrier n. a warship that carries and serves as a base for airplanes.

aircrew n. **1** the crew of an aircraft. **2** (pl. **aircrews**) a member of such a crew.

air cushion n. **1** an inflatable cushion. **2** the layer of air supporting a hovercraft or similar vehicle.

airdrop ● v.tr. deliver (food, supplies, etc.) by parachute from an aircraft. ● n. a delivery in this way.

air-dry v.tr. & intr. dry (clothing, hair, etc.), or become dry, by exposure to air without added heat.

Airedale /'erdeil/ n. a large breed of terrier with a rough coat.

airfare n. the price paid by a passenger for transportation by air.

airfield n. an area of land where aircraft take off and land, are maintained, etc.

airflow n. a current of air, esp. that encountered by a moving aircraft or vehicle.

airfoil n. N Amer. a structure with curved surfaces, e.g. a wing, fin, or tailplane, designed to give lift in flight.

air force n. the branch of a nation's armed forces concerned with fighting or defence in the air.

airframe n. the body of an aircraft as distinct from its engine(s).

air freight ● n. the transport of goods by air. ● v.tr. (usu. **airfreight**) transport goods by air.

air freshener n. a fragrant spray or solid used to mask odours in a room, car, etc.

air gun n. a gun using compressed air to propel pellets etc.

airhead n. **1** a base for aircraft in enemy territory. **2** slang usu. derogatory a foolish person.

air hockey n. N Amer. a game in which players use hand-held paddles to direct a plastic disc supported on a cushion of air over an oblong surface, often a large table, into the opponent's goal.

air horn n. a horn which produces sound by compressed air.

airing n. **1** exposure to fresh air, esp. for exercise or an excursion. **2** exposure (of laundry etc.) to warm air. **3** public expression of an opinion etc.

air lane n. a path or course regularly used by aircraft.

airless adj. **1** stuffy; not ventilated. **2** without wind or breeze; still. □ **airlessness** n.

airlift ● n. the transport of troops and supplies by air. ● v.tr. transport in this way.

airline n. **1** an organization providing a regular public service of air transport on one or more routes. **2** (usu. **air line**) a hose supplying air, esp. to a diver.

airliner n. a large passenger aircraft.

airlock n. **1** a stoppage of the flow in a pump or pipe, caused by an air bubble. **2** a compartment with controlled pressure and parallel sets of doors, to permit movement between areas at different pressures.

airmail ● n. **1** a system of transporting mail by air. **2** mail carried by air. ● v.tr. send by airmail.

airman n. (pl. **-men**) **1** a pilot or member of the crew of an aircraft, esp. in an air force. **2** a member of an air force below commissioned rank.

air mass *n.* a very large body of air with a roughly uniform temperature and humidity.

air mattress *n.* an inflatable mattress for sleeping on or for floating on water.

Air Miles *n.pl. proprietary* a consumer incentive program in which participants collect credits redeemable for free air travel etc. on purchases.

airplane *n.* a powered heavier-than-air flying vehicle with fixed wings.

airplay *n.* broadcasting (of recorded music).

air pocket *n.* **1** an apparent vacuum in the air causing an aircraft to drop suddenly. **2** (in soil, a pipe, etc.) any bubble of air.

airport *n.* a complex of runways and buildings for the takeoff, landing, and maintenance of civil aircraft, with facilities for passengers.

air power *n.* the ability to defend and attack by means of aircraft, missiles, etc.

air pump *n.* a device for pumping air into or out of a vessel, room, etc.

air purifier *n.* a small electrical appliance which draws air through a filter to remove impurities.

air quality index *n.* a numerical indicator of the concentration of pollutants in the air.

air raid *n.* an attack by military aircraft (also *attrib.*: *air raid siren*).

air rifle *n.* a rifle using compressed air to propel pellets etc.

air sac *n.* an extension of the lungs in birds or the tracheae in insects.

air-sea rescue *n.* rescue from the sea by aircraft.

airship *n.* a powered balloon that can be steered, esp. one having a rigid elongated structure.

air show *n.* a public display of aircraft or aerobatics.

airsick *adj.* affected with nausea due to travel in an aircraft. □ **airsickness** *n.*

air space *n.* **1** (usu. **airspace**) the air available to aircraft to fly in, esp. the part subject to the jurisdiction of a particular country. **2** a space filled with (usu. trapped) air, as between two panes of glass etc. **3** *Law* the space above a piece of land or the buildings constructed on it, extending notionally indefinitely upwards.

airspeed *n.* the speed of an aircraft relative to the air through which it is moving (*compare* GROUNDSPEED).

airstream *n.* a current of air; an airflow.

air strike *n.* = AIR RAID.

airstrip *n.* a strip of ground suitable for the takeoff and landing of aircraft.

air terminal *n.* = TERMINAL *n.* 3.

airtight *adj.* **1** not allowing air to pass through. **2** without weakness (*an airtight argument*).

air time *n.* **1** time allotted for a broadcast, commercial, etc. **2** the starting time for a TV or radio program.

air-to-air *adj.* from one aircraft to another in flight.

air-to-ground *adj.* (also **air-to-surface**) from an aircraft in flight to the earth (*air-to-ground missile*).

air traffic control *n.* an airport department which controls air traffic by giving radio instructions to pilots concerning route, altitude, takeoff, and landing. □ **air traffic controller** *n.*

airwaves *n.pl.* radio waves used in broadcasting.

airway *n.* **1 a** a recognized route followed by aircraft. **b** (often in *pl.*) = AIRLINE 1. **2** *Med.* **a** the normal passage for air into the lungs. **b** a tubular device for assisting a patient's breathing.

airwoman *n.* (*pl.* **-women**) a woman pilot or member of the crew of an aircraft, esp. in an air force.

airworthy *adj.* (of an aircraft) fit to fly.

airy *adj.* (**-ier, -iest**) **1** well-ventilated, breezy. **2** flippant, superficial. **3 a** light as air. **b** graceful, delicate. **4** insubstantial, ethereal. □ **airily** *adv.* **airiness** *n.*

airy-fairy *adj. informal* **1** unrealistic, impractical, foolishly idealistic. **2** light and delicate.

aisle *n.* **1 a** a passage between rows of pews, seats, etc. **b** a passage between rows of shelves in a supermarket etc. **2** part of a church, esp. one parallel to and divided by pillars from the nave, choir, or transept. □ **aisled** *adj.*

aitch /eɪtʃ/ *n.* the letter H (*drop one's aitches*).

Aivilik /ˈaɪvɪlɪk/ *n.* a branch of the Iglulik Inuit of Canada's Arctic.

ajar[1] *adv. & predic.adj.* (of a door) slightly open.

ajar[2] *adv. & predic.adj.* out of harmony.

AK *abbr.* Alaska (in postal use).

AK-47 *n.* a Soviet-designed assault rifle, widely used by Communist and guerrilla armies.

a.k.a. *abbr.* also known as.

akee *var. of* ACKEE.

akimbo /əˈkɪmbo:/ *adv.* (of the arms) with hands on the hips and elbows turned outwards.

akin *predic.adj.* **1** related by blood. **2** (usu. foll. by *to*) of similar or kindred character.

Akita /əˈkiːtə/ *n.* a breed of Japanese dog, similar to a spitz.

AL *abbr.* **1** Alabama (in postal use). **2** *Baseball* American League.

Al *symbol* the element aluminum.

Ala. *abbr.* Alabama.

à la /ˈæ lə, ˈɑ lə/ *prep.* after the manner of (*à la russe*).

Alabaman ● *adj.* of or relating to the US state of Alabama. ● *n.* a resident or native of Alabama.

alabaster /ˈæləˌbæstər, ˌæləˈb-/ ● *n.* a translucent usu. white form of gypsum, often carved into ornaments. ● *adj.* **1** of alabaster. **2** like alabaster in whiteness or smoothness.

à la carte /ˈkɑrt/ *adv. & adj.* ordered as separately priced item(s) from a menu, not as part of a set meal.

alacrity /əˈlækrɪti/ *n.* speed or willingness.

à la king *adj.* (of poultry etc.) served in a creamy sauce with cooked mushrooms and pimento.

à la mode *adj.* **1** in fashion; fashionable. **2 a** *N Amer.* (of desserts) served with ice cream. **b** (of beef) braised in wine and served with vegetables.

Alar /ˈeɪlɑr/ *n. proprietary* a growth-regulating chemical sprayed on fruit trees to improve the quality of the crop.

alarm ● *n.* **1** a warning of danger etc. (*gave the alarm*). **2 a** a sound or device to warn, alert, or signal (*a burglar alarm*). **b** a buzzer etc. on a clock or watch. **c** (in full **alarm clock**) a clock with a device that can be made to sound at a certain time, usu. to rouse a person from sleep. **3 a** frightened expectation of danger or difficulty (*filled with alarm*). **b** worry, concern, uneasiness. ● *v.tr.* **1** frighten or disturb. **2** arouse to a sense of danger.

alarming *adj.* frightening. □ **alarmingly** *adv.*

alarmist ● *n.* a person given to spreading needless alarm. ● *adj.* creating needless alarm. □ **alarmism** *n.*

alas *interj.* an expression of regret, sorrow, etc.

Alaskan ● *adj.* of or relating to the US state of Alaska. ● *n.* a resident or native of Alaska.

Alaska Time /əˈlæskə/ *n.* a time zone covering most of Alaska, nine hours behind Greenwich Mean Time.

alb /ælb/ n. a white vestment reaching to the feet, worn by some Christian clergy.

albacore /'ælbə,kɔr/ n. **1** a long-finned tuna, *Thunnus alalunga*. **2** any of various other related fish.

Albanian ● n. **1 a** a native or national of Albania, a republic in SE Europe. **b** a person of Albanian descent. **2** the language of Albania. **●** adj. of or relating to Albania, its people, or its language.

albatross /'ælbə,trɒs/ n. **1** any of several large, long-winged, tube-nosed, stout-bodied birds of the family Diomedeidae, which come ashore only to nest. **2** a source of frustration or guilt; an encumbrance.

albeit /ɒl'biːət/ conj. though (*an improvement, albeit a modest one*).

Alberta Family Day n. the official name of FAMILY DAY.

Albertan ● adj. of or relating to Alberta. **●** n. a resident or native of Alberta.

albino /æl'baino:/ n. (pl. **-os**) **1** a person or animal having a congenital absence of pigment in the skin and hair (which are white), and the eyes (which are usu. pink). **2** a plant lacking normal colouring. □ **albinism** /'ælbɪ,nɪzəm/ n.

albite /'ælbəit/ n. a feldspar, usu. white, rich in sodium.

album n. **1** a blank book for the insertion of photographs, stamps, etc. **2 a** a disc or tape comprising several pieces of music. **b** an integral set of discs or tapes.

albumen /,æl'bjuːmɪn/ n. **1** egg white. **2** = ENDOSPERM.

albumin /,æl'bjuːmɪn/ n. any of a class of water-soluble proteins found in egg white, milk, blood, etc. □ **albuminous** adj.

albuminuria /,ælbjuːmɪ'njɜriə/ n. the presence of albumin in the urine, a symptom of kidney disease.

album-oriented rock n. a type of popular music in which a hard rock background is combined with softer, more melodic elements.

ALCB abbr. Alberta Liquor Control Board

alchemy /'ælkəmi/ n. (pl. **-ies**) **1** the medieval forerunner of chemistry, esp. seeking to turn base metals into gold or silver. **2** a miraculous transformation or the means of achieving this. □ **alchemic** adj. **alchemical** adj. **alchemist** n. **alchemize** v.tr.

alcohol n. **1** (in full **ethyl alcohol**) a colourless volatile inflammable liquid forming the intoxicating element in spirits etc., also used as a solvent, fuel, etc. **2** any liquor containing this. **3** any of a large class of organic compounds that contain one or more hydroxyl groups attached to carbon atoms.

alcoholic ● adj. of, containing, or caused by alcohol. **●** n. a person suffering from alcoholism.

Alcoholics Anonymous an organization of alcoholics who attempt to overcome their addiction by counselling and mutual support. Abbr.: **AA**.

alcoholism n. **1** addiction to the consumption of alcoholic liquor. **2** the diseased condition resulting from this.

alcool /'ælkuːl/ n. Cdn (esp. Que.) a colourless, unflavoured alcoholic spirit distilled from grains.

alcove n. **1** a recess, esp. in the wall of a room (*a dining alcove*). **2** an arbour or shady bower.

Ald. abbr. (preceding a name) Alderman etc.

aldehyde /'ældə,haid/ n. Chem. any of a class of compounds formed by the oxidation of alcohols.

al dente /æl 'dentei/ adj. (of pasta etc.) cooked so as to be still firm when bitten.

alder /'ɒldər/ n. any tree or shrub of the genus *Alnus*, related to the birch, with catkins and toothed leaves.

alderfly n. (pl. **-flies**) an insect of the genus *Sialis*, found near streams.

alderman /'ɒldərmən/ n. (pl. **-men**) N Amer. & Austral. a city councillor, esp. the elected representative of a district or ward. □ **aldermanic** /-'mænɪk/ adj.

Alderney /'ɒldɜrni/ n. a breed of small dairy cattle.

alderperson n. N Amer. = ALDERMAN.

alderwoman n. (pl. **-women**) N Amer. a female city councillor.

aldrin /'ældrɪn/ n. a white crystalline chlorinated hydrocarbon used as an insecticide.

ale n. N Amer. a type of beer fermented rapidly at high temperatures.

alehouse n. hist. a tavern.

aleph /'ɒlef/ n. the first letter of the Hebrew alphabet.

alert ● adj. **1** watchful or vigilant; ready to take action. **2** nimble (esp. of mental faculties); attentive. **●** n. **1** a call or alarm warning of an attack, storm, etc. **2** the duration of this. **●** v.tr. (often foll. by to) make alert; warn (*were alerted to the danger*). □ **on** (**the**) **alert** on the lookout against danger or attack. □ **alertly** adv. **alertness** n.

Aleut /'æljuːt, ə'luːt/ n. **1** (pl. same or **-s**) a member of an Aboriginal people living in the Aleutian Islands and SW Alaska. **2** the language of the Aleut. □ **Aleutian** /ə'luːʃən/ adj. & n.

alevin /'æləvɪn/ n. a very young fish, esp. a salmon or trout.

alewife n. (pl. **alewives**) **1** a fish of the herring family, *Alosa pseudoharengus*, found off the Atlantic coast of N America and in the Great Lakes. **2** any of several related fish.

Alexander n. a cocktail made with crème de cacao, sweet cream, and brandy or gin.

Alexandrian /,ælɛg'zændriən/ adj. **1** of or characteristic of Alexandria, the chief port of Egypt, historically a major centre of Hellenistic culture. **2 a** belonging to or akin to the schools of literature and philosophy of Alexandria. **b** derivative or imitative.

alexia /ə'lɛksiə/ n. the inability to understand written words or to read, as a result of brain disorder (compare DYSLEXIA). □ **alexic** adj.

alfalfa n. a leguminous plant, *Medicago sativa*, with clover-like leaves and flowers used for fodder.

alfalfa sprouts n.pl. fine young sprouts of alfalfa, eaten as a salad vegetable or garnish.

alfredo /æl'freido:/ adj. (often placed after noun) designating a sauce for pasta made of butter, cream, and Parmesan cheese (*fettucine alfredo*).

alfresco /æl'fresko:/ adv. & adj. (also **al fresco**) in the open air.

alga /'ælgə/ n. (pl. **algae** /'ældʒi, 'ælgi /) (usu. in pl.) **1** any of a large group of non-vascular, mainly aquatic cryptogams capable of photosynthesis, including seaweeds and many unicellular organisms. **2** (in full **blue-green algae**) = CYANOBACTERIA. □ **algal** adj.

algebra n. **1** the branch of mathematics that uses letters and other general symbols to represent numbers and quantities in formulas and equations. **2** a system of this based on given axioms (*linear algebra*). □ **algebraic** /,ældʒə'breɪɪk/ adj. **algebraical** adj. **algebraically** adv. **algebraist** n.

algicide /'ælgɪ,said/ n. a preparation for destroying algae.

Algonquian /æl'gɒŋkwiən, -kiən/ (also **Algonkian** /-kiən/) **●** n. **1** the largest Aboriginal language group in Canada, including Abenaki, Algonquin, Blackfoot, Cree, Maliseet, Mi'kmaq, and Ojibwa. **2** (pl. same or

-s) a member of any of the peoples speaking languages of this family, living in the Maritimes, Quebec, Ontario, the Prairies, and the eastern US. ● *adj.* of or relating to the Algonquian peoples or languages.

Algonquin /æl'goŋkwɪn, -kɪn/ ● *n.* **1** (also **Algonkin**) /-kɪn/ (*pl.* same or **-s**) a member of an Aboriginal people living along the Ottawa River and its tributaries. **2** (also **Algonkin**) the dialect of Algonquian spoken by the Algonquin. **3** a type of snowshoe with an upturned front and long tapering tail. ● *adj.* **1** of or relating to the Algonquin or their language. **2** = ALGONQUIAN. ¶The use of *Algonquin* to refer to the Algonquian peoples or their language is widespread but strictly incorrect.

algorithm /'ælgə͵rɪðəm/ *n.* **1** *Math.* a process or set of rules used for calculation or problem-solving, esp. with a computer. **2** the Arabic or decimal notation of numbers. □ **algorithmic** *adj.*

alias ● *adv.* also named or known as. ● *n.* **1** a false or assumed name. **2** *Computing* a command or address which substitutes for another, more complicated one. ● *v.tr. Computing* assign or use an alias.

aliasing *n.* the misidentification of a signal frequency, introducing distortion or error, esp. in a computer image.

alibi ● *n.* (*pl.* **alibis**) **1** a claim, or the evidence supporting it, that when an alleged act took place one was elsewhere. **2** *disputed* an excuse of any kind; a pretext or justification. ● *v.* (**alibis**, **alibied**, **alibiing**) *informal* **1** *tr.* provide an alibi or offer an excuse for (a person). **2** *intr.* provide an alibi.

Alice-in-Wonderland *adj.* fantastic, absurd.

alien ● *adj.* **1 a** (often foll. by *to*) unfamiliar; not in accordance or harmony; unacceptable or repugnant (*army discipline was alien to him*). **b** (often foll. by *from*) different or separated. **2** foreign (*alien powers*). **3** of or relating to beings supposedly from other worlds. **4** (of a plant) introduced from elsewhere and naturalized in its new home. ● *n.* **1** a foreigner, esp. one who is not a naturalized citizen of the country where he or she is living. **2** a being from another world. **3** an alien plant. □ **alienness** *n.*

alienable *adj.* *Law* able to be transferred to new ownership. □ **alienability** *n.*

alienate *v.tr.* **1 a** cause (a person) to become unfriendly or hostile. **b** (often foll. by *from*) cause (a person) to feel isolated or estranged from (friends, society, etc.). **2** *Law* transfer ownership of (property) to another person etc. □ **alienator** *n.*

alienated *adj.* **1** withdrawn in feeling or affection, isolated. **2** *Law* transferred to other ownership.

alienation *n.* **1** the act of estranging or state of estrangement in feeling or affection. **2** (in full **alienation effect**) *Theatre* a dramatic effect whereby an audience remains objective, not identifying with the characters or action of a play. **3** *Psych.* loss of mental faculties; insanity (*mental alienation*).

alight¹ *v.intr.* (*past* and *past part.* **alighted**) **1 a** (often foll. by *from*) descend from a vehicle. **b** dismount from a horse. **2** come to rest or settle; descend to earth from the air. **3** (foll. by *on*) find by chance; notice.

alight² *predic.adj.* **1** on fire; burning. **2** lighted up; excited (*eyes alight with expectation*).

align *v.tr.* **1** put in a straight line or bring into line (*the wheels need aligning*). **2** esp. *Politics* (usu. foll. by *with*) bring (oneself etc.) into agreement or alliance with (a cause, policy, party, etc.). □ **alignment** *n.*

alike ● *adv.* in a similar way or manner; equally (*all were treated alike*). ● *adj.* (usu. *predic.*) similar, like one another; indistinguishable.

alimentary /͵ælɪ'mentəri/ *adj.* of, relating to, or providing nourishment or sustenance.

alimentary canal *n.* the passage along which food passes from the mouth to the anus during digestion.

alimentation /͵ælɪmen'teɪʃən/ *n.* *formal* **1** feeding. **2** maintenance, support; supplying with the necessities of life.

alimony *n.* a husband's or wife's provision for a spouse or former spouse after they are separated or divorced. ¶In legal language, now replaced by *support* or *maintenance*.

A-line *adj.* (of a garment) having a fitted waist or shoulders and somewhat flared skirt.

aliphatic /͵ælɪ'fætɪk/ *adj.* *Chem.* of, denoting, or relating to organic compounds in which carbon atoms form open chains, not aromatic rings.

A-list *n.* a list of people or items of the highest importance.

alive *adj.* (usu. *predic.*) **1** living, not dead. **2 a** (of a thing) existing; continuing; in operation or action (*kept his interest alive*). **b** under discussion; provoking interest (*the topic is still very much alive*). **3** (of a person or animal) lively, active. **4** charged with an electric current; connected to a source of electricity. **5** (foll. by *to*) aware of; alert or responsive to. **6** (foll. by *with*) **a** swarming or teeming with. **b** full of. □ **alive and kicking** *informal* very active; lively. **alive and well** still alive or active (esp. despite contrary assumptions or rumours). □ **aliveness** *n.*

aliyah /͵bli:'b/ *n.* the migration of Jews to Israel.

alkali /'ælkə͵laɪ/ *n.* (*pl.* **alkalis**) **1 a** any of a class of bases that liberate hydroxide ions in water, usu. form caustic or corrosive solutions, and have a pH of more than 7. **b** any other substance with similar but weaker properties. **2** *N Amer.* a soluble salt or mixture of salts existing in excess in soil and damaging crops.

alkaline /'ælkə͵laɪn/ *adj.* **1** of, relating to, or having the nature of an alkali; rich in alkali. **2** *Chem.* having a pH above 7; basic. □ **alkalinity** /-'lɪnɪti/ *n.*

alkaline battery *n.* a dry cell with an alkaline electrolyte of potassium hydroxide, with more power and durability than conventional batteries.

alkaloid /'ælkə͵lɔɪd/ *n.* any of a series of nitrogenous organic compounds of plant origin, many of which are used as drugs, e.g. morphine, quinine, nicotine.

alkane /'ælkeɪn/ *n.* *Chem.* any of a series of saturated aliphatic hydrocarbons, including methane, ethane, and propane.

alky *n.* (*pl.* **-ies**) *slang* an alcoholic or drunkard.

alkyd /'ælkɪd/ *n.* any of the group of synthetic resins derived from various alcohols and acids, commonly used in paints etc.

alkyl /'ælkɪl/ *n.* (in full **alkyl radical**) *Chem.* any radical derived from an alkane by the removal of a hydrogen atom.

all ● *adj.* **1 a** the whole amount, quantity, or extent of (*all his life; we all know why; take it all*). **b** (with *pl.*) the entire number of (*all the others left*). **2** any whatever (*beyond all doubt*). **3** greatest possible (*with all speed*). ● *n.* **1 a** all the persons or things concerned (*all were present*). **b** everything (*that is all*). **2** (foll. by *of*) **a** the whole of (*take all of it*). **b** every one of (*all of us*). **c** as much as (*all of three feet tall*). **d** *informal* affected by; in a state of (*all of a dither*). ¶Use of the preposition *of* after *all* is sometimes criticized, esp. before mass nouns (as in *all of the bread*), but is perfectly idiomatic. **3** one's whole strength or resources (*gave her all*). ● *adv.* **1 a** entirely, quite (*all round the room*). **b** as an intensifier (*stop all this grumbling*). **2** *informal* very (*went all shy*). **3** (foll. by *the* + comparative) by so much; to that extent (*if they go, all the better*). **4** (in games) on both sides (*two all*). □ **all along** all the time (*he knew about it all along*). **all but** very nearly (*all but drowned*). **all for** strongly in favour of. **as all get-out** *N Amer. informal* to a high degree (*stubborn as all get-out*). **all in all** everything considered. **all one** (or **the same**) a matter of indifference (*it's all the same to me*). **all over 1** completely finished. **2** in or on all parts of (esp. the body) (*went hot and cold all over*). **3** *informal* typically (*that is you all over*). **4** *slang* effusively attentive to (a person). **all the same** nevertheless, in spite of this. **all set** *informal* ready to start. **all that** *informal* particularly; very (*wasn't all that difficult*). **all there** *informal* mentally alert. **all together** all at once; all in one place or in a group (*they came all together*) (compare ALTOGETHER). **all very well** an expression used to reject or to imply skepticism about a favourable or consoling remark. **at all** (with *neg.* or *interrog.*) in any way; to any extent (*did not swim at all*). **in all** altogether. **one and all** everyone.

Allah /ˈælə, ˈɒlə/ *n.* the name of the Supreme Being in Islam.

all-American ● *adj.* **1** (esp. of an athlete) chosen as one of the best in, or representing the whole of, the US. **2** truly, typically, or exclusively American. ● *n.* an all-American athlete.

all around ● *adj.* **1** (of a person) versatile. **2** comprehensive, affecting everything or everyone. ● *adv.* **1** for each person (*bought drinks all around*). **2** in all respects (*a good performance all around*).

allay /əˈleɪ/ *v.tr.* **1** diminish (fear, suspicion, etc.). **2** relieve or alleviate (pain, hunger, etc.).

all-Canadian ● *adj.* **1** (esp. of an athlete) chosen as one of the best in, or representing the whole of, Canada. **2** truly, typically, or exclusively Canadian. ● *n.* an all-Canadian athlete.

all-candidates meeting *n. Cdn* a public meeting held during an election campaign at which all the candidates for an electoral district present their platforms and answer questions from the audience.

all-clear *n.* a signal that danger or difficulty is over.

all-day *attrib.adj.* lasting throughout a day.

all-dressed *adj. Cdn* (*Que., NB, & E Ont.*) designating an item of food served with all the optional garnishes.

allée /ˈæˈleɪ/ *n.* a walk bordered by trees or clipped hedges in a garden or park.

allegation *n.* **1** an assertion or accusation, esp. an unproven one. **2** the act or an instance of alleging.

allege *v.tr.* **1** (often foll. by *that* + clause, or *to* + infin.) declare to be the case, esp. without proof. **2** advance as an argument or excuse. □ **alleged** *adj.*

allegedly *adv.* as is alleged or said to be the case.

allegiance *n.* **1** loyalty (to a person or cause etc.). **2** the duty of a subject to his or her sovereign or government.

allegorical *adj.* (also **allegoric**) consisting of or relating to allegory. □ **allegorically** *adv.*

allegorize /ˈæləɡəˌraɪz/ *v.tr.* treat as or by means of an allegory. □ **allegorization** *n.*

allegory *n.* (*pl.* **-ies**) **1** a story, play, poem, picture, etc., in which the meaning or message is represented symbolically. **2** the use of such symbols. **3** a symbol.

allegretto /ˌæləˈɡretoʊ/ *Music* ● *adv. & adj.* in a fairly brisk tempo. ● *n.* (*pl.* **-os**) an allegretto passage or movement.

allegro /əˈleɡroʊ/ *Music* ● *adv. & adj.* in a brisk tempo. ● *n.* (*pl.* **-os**) an allegro passage or movement.

allele /ˈæliːl/ *n.* one of the (usu. two) alternative

forms of a gene that occupy the same relative position on a chromosome. □ **allelic** /əˈliːlɪk/ *adj.*

alleluia ● *interj.* God be praised. ● *n.* **1** praise to God. **2** a song of praise to God.

allemande /ˈælmɑːnd/ *n.* **1 a** the name of several German dances. **b** the music for any of these, esp. as a movement of a suite. **2** a figure in square dancing in which dancers join arms or hands and make a full or partial turn.

all-embracing *adj.* including everything (*an all-embracing theory*).

Allen key *n.* (also **Allen wrench**) an L-shaped tool designed to fit into and turn an Allen screw.

Allen screw *n.* a screw with a hexagonal socket in the head.

allergen /ˈælərˌdʒən/ *n.* any substance that causes an allergic reaction. □ **allergenic** *adj.*

allergic *adj.* **1** (foll. by *to*) **a** having an allergy to. **b** *informal* having a strong dislike for (a person or thing). **2** caused by or relating to an allergy.

allergist /ˈælərˌdʒɪst/ *n.* a physician who specializes in the treatment of allergies.

allergy *n.* (*pl.* **-ies**) **1** a condition of reacting adversely to certain substances, esp. particular foods, pollen, fur, or dust. **2** *informal* an antipathy.

alleviate *v.tr.* lessen or make less severe (pain, suffering, a problem, etc.). □ **alleviation** *n.*

alley *n.* (*pl.* **-eys**) **1 a** a narrow street. **b** a narrow passageway or lane, esp. between or behind buildings. **2** a path or walk in a park or garden. **3** = BOWLING ALLEY. **4** *Baseball* the area between the outfielders in left-centre or right-centre field. **5** *Tennis* either of the two side strips of a doubles court. **6** (usu. **Alley**) an area known for a specified characteristic, esp. a street or lane with a concentration of similar businesses etc. (*Gourmet Alley*). □ **up one's alley** *informal* suited to one's tastes, interests, or abilities.

alley cat *n.* a stray cat in an urban area, often mangy or half wild.

alley-oop ● *interj.* encouraging or drawing attention to the performance of some physical, esp. acrobatic, feat. ● *n. Basketball* **1** (often *attrib.*) a high lob or pass caught by a leaping teammate. **2** a basket scored by the receiver of such a pass.

alleyway *n.* = ALLEY 1.

All Hallows *n.* = ALL SAINTS' DAY.

alliak /ˈæliæk/ *n.* = KOMATIK.

alliance *n.* **1 a** formal union or agreement to cooperate, esp. among nations with a specific goal. **b** a formal grouping of persons having a common aim. **c** the parties involved. **2** union through marriage. **3** a relationship resulting from an affinity in nature or qualities etc. (*the alliance between Church and State*). **4** (**Alliance**) = CHRISTIAN AND MISSIONARY ALLIANCE.

allied *adj.* **1 a** united or associated in an alliance. **b** (**Allied**) of or relating to the Allies. **2** connected or related (*studied medicine and allied subjects*).

Allies *n.pl.* **1** the nations allied against the Central Powers in World War I, primarily the British Empire, France, and the Russian Empire, and later the US. **2** the nations allied against the Axis powers in World War II, primarily the UK and the Commonwealth, France, and later the USSR, the US, and China.

alligator *n.* **1 a** a large reptile of the order Crocodylia of S America, China, and the southeastern US, with upper teeth that lie outside the lower teeth and a head broader and shorter than that of the crocodile. **2** any of several large members of the crocodile family. **3 a** the skin of such an animal or material resembling it. **b** (in *pl.*) shoes of this.

alligator clip *n.* a metal clip with teeth for gripping wires or other electrical connectors.

all-important *adj.* crucial; vitally important.

all in *adj.* (*predic.*) *informal* exhausted.

all-inclusive *adj.* including all or everything.

all-in-one ● *attrib.adj.* comprising all the necessary features in one indivisible unit. ● *n.* a garment combining parts usually worn separately, e.g. a corselette.

alliterate /əˈlɪtə,reɪt/ *v.* **1** *intr.* a contain alliteration. **b** use alliteration in speech or writing. **2** *tr.* **a** construct (a phrase etc.) with alliteration. **b** speak or pronounce with alliteration. ☐ **alliterative** /əˈlɪtərətɪv/ *adj.*

alliteration *n.* the occurrence of the same letter or sound at the beginning of adjacent or closely connected words (e.g. *cool, calm,* and *collected*).

allium /ˈælɪːəm/ *n.* any plant of the genus *Allium,* usu. bulbous and strong smelling, e.g. onion and garlic.

all-new *adj.* totally new.

all-night *attrib.adj.* lasting or remaining open throughout the night (*all-night café*).

all-nighter *n. informal* an event or task that continues throughout the night, esp. a study session before an examination.

allocate *v.tr.* assign, designate, or set aside for a specific purpose. ☐ **allocation** *n.* **allocator** *n.*

allopathy /əˈlɒpəθiː/ *n.* the treatment of disease by conventional means, i.e. with drugs having opposite effects to the symptoms (*compare* HOMEOPATHY). ☐ **allopathic** /ˌæləˈpæθɪk/ *adj.*

allophone /ˈælə,foːn/ *Cdn* (in Quebec) ● *n.* an immigrant whose first language is neither French nor English. ● *adj.* having a first language other than French, English, or an Aboriginal language.

allot *v.tr.* (**allotted, allotting**) **1** give or apportion to (a person) as a share or task; distribute officially to. **2** assign or allocate.

allotment *n.* **1** the action of allotting. **2** a share allotted. **3** a small piece of land.

all-out ● *attrib.adj.* total; unrestrained (*all-out war*). ● *adv.* (**all out**) with all one's strength; at full speed (*going all out*).

all-over *adj.* covering every part (*an all-over pattern*).

allow *v.* **1** *tr.* permit (a practice, a person to do something, a thing to happen, etc.). **2** *tr.* give or provide; permit (a person) to have (a limited quantity or sum). **3** *tr.* provide or set aside for a purpose; add or deduct in consideration of something (*allow 10% for inflation*). **4** *tr.* **a** admit, agree, concede (*he allowed that it was so*). **b** *informal* state the opinion that. **5** *refl.* permit oneself, indulge oneself in (conduct) (*allowed herself to be persuaded*). **6** *intr.* (foll. by *of*) admit of. **7** *intr.* (foll. by *for*) take into consideration or account; make addition or deduction corresponding to (*allowing for wastage*). ☐ **allowable** *adj.* **allowably** *adv.*

allowance ● *n.* **1 a** an amount or sum given to a person, esp. regularly for a stated purpose. **b** *N Amer.* an amount of money given regularly to a child. **2** an amount allowed in reckoning. **3** a deduction or discount (*an allowance for your trade-in*). **4** (foll. by *of*) tolerance of. **5** a portion of something, e.g. land or fabric, allowed for a specified purpose (*road allowance*). ● *v.tr.* **1** make an allowance to (a person). **2** supply in limited quantities. ☐ **make allowances** (often foll. by *for*) **1** take into consideration (mitigating circumstances). **2** look with tolerance upon, make excuses for (a person, bad behaviour, etc.).

alloy ● *n.* **1** a metallic substance made by combining two or more elements at least one of which is a metal, e.g. brass (a mixture of copper and zinc). **2** an inferior metal mixed esp. with gold or silver. ● *v.tr.* **1** mix (metals). **2** debase (a pure substance) by admixture.

all-points bulletin *n.* *US* a generally issued alert among police officers, esp. calling for the apprehension of a wanted person. ¶Not used in Canada.

all-purpose *adj.* suitable for many uses.

all right ● *adv.* **1** satisfactorily (*it worked out all right*). **2** as an intensifier (*that's the one all right*). ● *adj.* satisfactory; safe and sound. ● *interj.* expressing consent or assent to a proposal or order.

all round *var. of* ALL AROUND.

All Saints' Day *n.* a Christian festival in honour of the souls in heaven, celebrated on Nov. 1 in Western Churches and on the first Sunday after Pentecost in Eastern Churches.

allsorts *n.pl.* an assortment, esp. of licorice candies.

All Souls' Day *n.* Nov. 2, a Catholic holy day with prayers for the souls of the dead in purgatory.

allspice *n.* **1** the aromatic spice obtained from the ground berry of the pimento tree, *Pimenta dioica.* **2** the berry of this tree. **3** any of various other aromatic shrubs.

all-star ● *n.* **1** *Sport* a player chosen as among the finest in his or her league. **2** a superstar. ● *adj.* relating to or consisting of all-stars (*an all-star cast*).

all-terrain bicycle *n.* = MOUNTAIN BIKE. **Abbr.: ATB**.

all-terrain vehicle *n.* **1** a tank-like military vehicle with treads used to travel over rough terrain. **2** a rugged one-person vehicle with three or four wheels, designed for travel both on and off roads. **Abbr.: ATV**.

all-time *attrib.adj.* (of a record etc.) hitherto unsurpassed.

all told *adv.* in all; when everything is considered.

allude *v.intr.* (foll. by *to*) **1** refer, esp. indirectly, covertly, or briefly to. **2** *disputed* mention.

allure ● *v.tr.* attract, charm, or fascinate. ● *n.* attractiveness, personal charm, fascination. ☐ **allurement** *n.* **alluring** *adj.* **alluringly** *adv.*

allusion *n.* a reference, esp. a covert, passing, or indirect one. ¶Often confused with *illusion*.

allusive *adj.* **1** containing an allusion. **2** containing many allusions. ☐ **allusively** *adv.* **allusiveness** *n.*

alluvial /əˈluːvɪəl/ ● *adj.* of or relating to alluvium. ● *n.* alluvium, esp. containing a precious metal.

alluvial fan *n.* a fan-shaped deposit formed when a mountain river enters a large valley or plain.

alluvium /əˈluːviːəm/ *n.* (*pl.* **alluvia** /-viːə/ or **-s**) a deposit of usu. fine fertile soil left during a time of flood, esp. in a river valley or delta.

all-weather *attrib.adj.* suitable for use whatever the weather.

all-wheel drive *n.* *N Amer.* = FOUR-WHEEL DRIVE.

ally ● *n.* (*pl.* **-ies**) **1** a state formally co-operating or united with another for a special purpose, esp. by a treaty. **2** a person or organization that co-operates with or helps another. ● *v.tr.* (**-ies, -ied**) (often foll. by *with*) combine or unite in alliance.

alma mater /ˌælmə ˈmɒtər/ *n.* the university, school, or college which one attended.

almanac *n.* **1** an annual calendar of months and days, usu. with astronomical data and other information. **2** an annual book of general esp. statistical information.

almighty ● *adj.* **1** having complete power; omnipotent. **2** (**the Almighty**) God. **3** *slang* very great (*an almighty crash*). ● *adv. slang* extremely.

almond /ˈɒmənd, ˈɒl-/ *n.* **1** the oval nutlike seed (kernel) of the stone fruit from the tree *Prunus dulcis*.

2 the tree itself, of the rose family and allied to the peach and plum. **3** a very pale beige colour.

almond paste *n.* = MARZIPAN.

almost *adv.* all but; very nearly.

alms /ɒmz/ *n.pl.* charitable donations of money or food given to the poor.

almsgiving *n.* the giving of charitable donations. □ **almsgiver** *n.*

aloe /'æləʊ/ *n.* **1** any plant of the genus *Aloe*, including succulent herbs, shrubs, and trees. **2** (in *pl.*) (in full **bitter aloes**) a strong laxative obtained from the bitter juice of various species of aloe. **3** (in full **American aloe**) = CENTURY PLANT.

aloe vera /'vɛrə/ *n.* a succulent plant, *Aloe vera*, yielding a juice used in cosmetics and as a treatment for burns.

aloft *predic.adj. & adv.* **1** in the air; overhead. **2** upwards.

aloha ● *interj.* (in Hawaii and the S Pacific) a greeting or farewell; hello or good-bye. ● *adj.* reflecting characteristics considered typically Hawaiian, such as brightly coloured garments or a relaxed approach to life (*aloha shirt*).

alone ● *predic.adj.* **1 a** without others present. **b** without others' help. **c** lonely and isolated (*felt alone*). **2** (often foll. by *in*) standing by oneself in an opinion etc. (*was alone in thinking this*). ● *adv.* only, exclusively (*you alone can help me*). □ **go it alone** act by oneself without assistance. □ **aloneness** *n.*

along ● *prep.* **1** from one end to the other end of. **2** on or through any part of the length of (*walking along the road*). **3** beside or through the length of (*shelves stood along the wall*). **4** during the course of (*stop along the way*). ● *adv.* **1** onward; into a more advanced state (*getting along nicely*). **2** at or to a particular place; arriving (*I'll be along soon*). **3** in company with a person, esp. oneself (*bring a book along*). **4** beside or through part or the whole length of a thing. □ **along with** in addition to; together with.

alongside ● *adv.* (sometimes foll. by *of*) at or to the side. ● *prep.* **1** close to the side of; next to. **2** in close association with.

aloof ● *adj.* distant, unsympathetic. ● *adv.* away, apart (*he kept aloof*). □ **aloofly** *adv.* **aloofness** *n.*

aloud *adv.* audibly; not silently or in a whisper.

alpaca /æl'pækə/ *n.* **1** a S American mammal, *Lama pacos*, related to the llama, with long shaggy hair. **2** the wool from this animal. **3** fabric made from the wool, with or without other fibres.

alpha *n.* **1** the first letter of the Greek alphabet (*A*, α). **2** (*attrib.*) designating the first of a series or set. **3** *Astronomy* the chief star in a constellation. □ **alpha and omega** the beginning and the end.

alphabet *n.* **1** the set of letters used in writing a language (*the Russian alphabet*). **2** a set of symbols or signs representing letters. **3** the rudiments of a branch of knowledge etc.

alphabetical *adj.* (also **alphabetic**) **1** of or relating to an alphabet. **2** in the order of the letters of the alphabet. □ **alphabetically** *adv.*

alphabetize *v.tr.* arrange (words, names, etc.) in alphabetical order. □ **alphabetization** *n.*

alphabet soup *n.* **1** a soup containing letter-shaped pieces of pasta. **2** a jumble of words or letters.

alpha-hydroxy acid *n.* any of a class of aliphatic carboxylic acids containing a hydroxyl group, some of which are used in skin care preparations for their exfoliating properties. Abbr.: **AHA**.

alphanumeric *adj.* (also **alphanumerical**) containing both alphabetical and numerical symbols.

alpha test ● *n.* a preliminary test of computer software etc., usually carried out within the organization developing it (*compare* BETA TEST). ● *v.tr.* submit (a product) to an alpha test.

alpine ● *adj.* **1 a** of or relating to high mountains. **b** growing or found on high mountains, esp. above the timberline. **2** (**Alpine**) of or relating to the Alps. **3** of or relating to competitive downhill or slalom skiing. ● *n.* a plant native or suited to mountain districts.

alpine fir *n.* a tall and slender fir tree, *Abies lasiocarpa*, native to northwestern N America and growing at high altitudes.

already *adv.* **1** before the time in question. **2** as early or as soon as this (*already, at the age of six, he could play the piano*). **3** *N Amer.* used as an intensifier to express impatience etc. (*tell the story already!*).

alright *disputed var.* of ALL RIGHT.

ALS *abbr.* AMYOTROPHIC LATERAL SCLEROSIS.

Alsatian /æl'seɪʃən/ ● *adj.* of or relating to Alsace, a region of NE France. ● *n.* **1** a native or resident of Alsace. **2** a German dialect spoken in Alsace.

also *adv.* in addition; likewise; besides.

also-ran *n.* **1** a contestant not among the winners in a race, election, etc. **2** an undistinguished person.

Alt /ɒlt/ *n.* *Computing* a key on a computer keyboard which alters the function of another key pressed simultaneously.

Alta. *abbr.* Alberta.

Altaic /æl'teɪɪk/ ● *n.* a family of languages including Turkic and Mongolian. ● *adj.* denoting or pertaining to this family of languages or its speakers.

altar *n.* **1** a table or flat-topped block, often of stone, for sacrifice or offering to a deity. **2** *Christianity* a table on which bread and wine are consecrated in the Communion service. **3** *Christianity* the raised area in a church on which the altar, lecterns, pulpit, etc. are found. □ **lead to the altar** marry.

altar boy *n.* a boy who serves as a priest's assistant in a service.

altar call *n.* (esp. in pentecostal Christian worship) an invitation to members of a congregation to gather at the front of the sanctuary, esp. to make a public confession of faith or request special prayers etc.

altar girl *n.* a girl who serves as a priest's assistant in a service.

altarpiece *n.* a piece of art, esp. a painting, set above or behind an altar.

altar server *n.* a child or adult who serves as a priest's assistant in a service.

alter *v.* **1** *tr. & intr.* make or become different; change. **2** *tr.* modify the style or size of (clothing); tailor. **3** *tr.* castrate or spay. □ **alterable** *adj.* **alteration** *n.*

altercate *v.intr.* dispute hotly; wrangle.

altercation *n.* a heated argument or dispute.

alter ego *n.* (*pl.* **alter egos**) **1** an intimate and trusted friend. **2** a person's secondary personality.

alternate ● *v.* **1** *intr.* (often foll. by *with*) (of two things) succeed each other by turns. **2** *intr.* (foll. by *between*) change repeatedly (between two conditions). **3** *tr.* (often foll. by *with*) cause (two things) to succeed each other by turns (*we alternated criticism with reassurance*). ● *adj.* **1** (with noun in *pl.*) every other (*comes on alternate days*). **2** (of things of two kinds) each following and succeeded by one of the other kind (*alternate joy and misery*). **3** (of a sequence etc.) consisting of alternate things. **4** *Bot.* (of leaves etc.) placed alternately on the two sides of the stem. **5** = ALTERNATIVE. ● *n.* esp. *N Amer.* a person or thing that substitutes for another. □ **alternately** *adv.*

alternate angles *n.pl.* two angles, not adjoining one another, that are formed on opposite sides of a line that intersects two other lines.

alternating current *n.* an electric current that reverses its direction at regular intervals. Abbr.: **AC**.

alternation *n.* the action or result of alternating.

alternative ● *adj.* **1** (of one or more things) available or usable instead of another (*an alternative route*). ¶Use with reference to more than two options (e.g. *many alternative methods*) is common and acceptable. **2** (of two things) mutually exclusive. **3** of or relating to practices that offer a substitute for the conventional ones (*alternative medicine*). ● *n.* **1** any of two or more possibilities. **2** the freedom or opportunity to choose between two or more things (*I had no alternative but to go*). □ **alternatively** *adv.*

alternative dispute resolution *n.* (also **alternate dispute resolution**) *Law* a method of solving a dispute without resorting to litigation, e.g. mediation, arbitration, etc.

alternator *n.* a generator that produces an alternating current.

although *conj.* = THOUGH *conj.* 1-3.

altimeter /ˈæltɪmɪtər/ *n.* an instrument for showing height above sea or ground level, esp. in aircraft.

altiplano /ˌæltɪplæːno:/ *n.* the high tableland of central S America.

altitude *n.* **1** the height of an object in relation to a given point, esp. sea level or the horizon. **2** *Astronomy* the angular distance of a celestial body above the horizon. **3** *Geom.* the length of the perpendicular from a vertex to the opposite side of a figure. **4** a high or exalted position. □ **altitudinal** *adj.*

altitude sickness *n.* an illness caused by ascent to high altitude, characterized by nausea and exhaustion.

alto /ˈɒlto:, ˈælto:/ *n.* (*pl.* **-os**) **1** = CONTRALTO. **2 a** the highest adult male singing voice, above tenor. **b** a singer with this voice. **c** a part written for it. **3 a** (*attrib.*) denoting the member of a family of instruments pitched second- or third-highest. **b** an alto instrument, esp. an alto saxophone.

altogether *adv.* **1** totally, completely (*you are altogether wrong*). **2** on the whole (*altogether it had been a good day*). **3** in total (*there are six bedrooms altogether*). ¶Note that *all together* is used to mean 'all at once' or 'all in one place', as in *there are six bedrooms all together*. □ **in the altogether** *informal* naked.

altoist *n.* an alto saxophone player.

altruism /ˈɒltruːˌɪzəm, ˈæl-/ *n.* **1** regard for others as a principle of action. **2** unselfishness. □ **altruist** *n.* **altruistic** *adj.* **altruistically** *adv.*

alum¹ /ˈæləm/ *n.* **1** a double sulphate of aluminum and potassium, having astringent properties. **2** any of a group of compounds of double sulphates of a monovalent metal (or group) and a trivalent metal.

alum² /əˈlʌm/ *n.* *N Amer. informal* alumnus or alumna.

alumina /əˈluːmɪnə/ *n.* the compound aluminum oxide occurring naturally as corundum and emery.

aluminosilicate /əˌluːmɪno:ˈsɪlɪkeɪt/ *n.* a silicate containing aluminum, esp. a rock-forming mineral of this kind, e.g. a feldspar, a clay mineral.

aluminum /əˈluːmɪnəm/ *n.* (*Brit.* **aluminium** /ˌælju:ˈmɪnɪəm/) a silvery light and malleable metallic element resistant to tarnishing by air.

alumna /əˈlʌmnə/ *n.* (*pl.* **alumnae** /-nai, -ni/) **1** a female graduate of a specified university or school. **2** a woman who is a former member of a specified group or organization.

alumnus /əˈlʌmnəs/ *n.* (*pl.* **alumni** /-nai/) **1** a graduate of a specified university or other school. **2** a former member of a specified group or organization.

alvar /ˈælvɑr/ *n.* a low-lying area of flat, exposed limestone with shallow soil, covered with shrubs, native grasses, sedges, or wildflowers.

alveolar ridge *n.* the bony ridge behind the upper teeth.

alveolus /ˌælviˈoːləs, ælˈviːələs/ *n.* (*pl.* **alveoli** /-lai, -li/) **1** a small cavity, pit, or hollow. **2** any of the many tiny air sacs of the lungs which allow for rapid gaseous exchange. **3** the bony socket for the root of a tooth. **4** the cell of a honeycomb. □ **alveolar** *adj.*

always *adv.* **1** at all times; on all occasions. **2** whatever the circumstances (*I can always sleep on the floor*). **3** repeatedly; often (*they are always complaining*).

alyssum /əˈlɪsəm/ *n.* **1** (in full **sweet alyssum**) a low-growing widely-cultivated plant, *Lobularia maritima*, having very small white or purple flowers. **2** any plant of the genus *Alyssum*, widely cultivated and usu. having yellow or white flowers.

Alzheimer's disease /ˈɒlts,haimərz, ˈɒls-, ˈælts-, ˈæls-/ *n.* (also **Alzheimer's**) a serious disorder of the brain manifesting itself in premature senility.

AM *abbr.* **1 a** AMPLITUDE MODULATION. **b** the band of radio stations broadcasting with this system (often *attrib.*: *an AM radio*). **2** *US* Master of Arts.

Am *symbol* americium.

am *1st person sing. present of* BE.

a.m. *abbr.* before noon.

amalgam /əˈmælgəm/ *n.* **1** a mixture or blend. **2** an alloy of mercury with one or more other metals, used esp. for dental fillings.

amalgamate *v.* **1** *tr. & intr.* combine or unite to form one structure, organization, etc. **2** *intr.* (of metals) alloy with mercury. □ **amalgamation** *n.*

amandine /ˌæmɒnˈdiːn, -mən-/ *adj.* garnished with (usu. sliced) almonds (*green beans amandine*).

amaranth /ˈæməˌrænθ/ *n.* **1** any herbaceous plant of the genus *Amaranthus*, usu. having small green, red, or purple tinted flowers, some species of which are weeds, e.g. pigweed, with other species cultivated as grain crops or ornamentals. **2** an imaginary flower that never fades. **3** a purplish-red dye used esp. to colour foods.

amaretti /ˌæməˈreti/ *n.pl.* (also **amaretti cookies**) small, dry, Italian macaroons.

amaryllis /ˌæməˈrɪlɪs/ *n.* **1** a plant genus with a single species, *Amaryllis belladonna*, a bulbous lily-like plant native to South Africa with white or rose-pink flowers. **2** any of various related plants formerly of this genus now transferred to other genera, notably *Hippeastrum*.

amass *v.tr.* **1** gather or heap together. **2** accumulate (*riches etc.*). □ **amasser** *n.*

amateur /ˈæməˌtʃər, -ˌtər/ *n.* **1** (often *attrib.*) a person who engages in a pursuit, e.g. an art or sport as a pastime rather than a profession. **2** (*attrib.*) for or done by amateurs (*amateur athletics*). **3** an unskilful or inexperienced person. **4** (foll. by *of*) a person who is fond of (a thing). □ **amateurism** *n.*

amateurish *adj.* characteristic of an amateur, esp. unskilful or inexperienced. □ **amateurishly** *adv.* **amateurishness** *n.*

amatory /ˈæməˌtɔri/ *adj.* of or relating to sexual love or desire.

amautik /əˈmautɪk/ *n.* (also **amauti** /əˈmauti/) *Cdn* (*North*) **1** an Inuit woman's parka with a large hood in which a child may be carried. **2** the large hood of such a parka.

amaze v.tr. surprise greatly; overwhelm with wonder (was amazed to find them alive). ☐ **amazement** n.

amazing adj. **1** causing great surprise; overwhelming. **2** informal exceptional (an amazing book). ☐ **amazingly** adv. **amazingness** n.

Amazon n. **1** a member of a mythical race of female warriors which appears in many Greek legends. **2** (amazon) a very tall, strong, or athletic woman. ☐ **Amazonian** /ˌæməˈzoːnɪən/ adj.

ambassador n. **1** an accredited diplomat sent by a state on a mission to, or as its permanent representative in, a foreign country. **2** a representative or promoter of a specified thing (an ambassador of peace). ☐ **ambassadorial** adj. **ambassadorship** n.

ambassadress n. **1** a female ambassador. **2** an ambassador's wife.

amber ● n. **1 a** a yellowish translucent fossilized resin deriving from extinct (esp. coniferous) trees and used in jewellery. **b** the honey-yellow colour of this. **2** a yellow traffic light meaning caution. ● adj. made of or coloured like amber.

ambergris /ˈæmbərgrɪs, -ˌgriːs/ n. a strong-smelling waxlike secretion of the intestine of the sperm whale, found floating in tropical seas and used in perfume manufacture.

amberjack n. any large brightly-coloured marine fish of the genus Seriola found in tropical and subtropical Atlantic waters.

ambidextrous /ˌæmbɪˈdekstrəs/ adj. **1 a** (of a person) able to use the right and left hands equally well. **b** (of an object) suited for use with either the right or left hand (ambidextrous scissors). **2** working skilfully in more than one medium. **3** double-dealing; trying to please both parties.

ambience /ˈæmbiɑ̃s, ˌɑ̃mbiˈɑ̃s, ˈæmbiəns/ n. (also **ambiance**) the surroundings or atmosphere of a place; mood.

ambient /ˈæmbiənt/ adj. surrounding.

ambiguity n. (pl. **-ies**) **1 a** a double meaning which is either deliberate or caused by inexactness of expression. **b** an example of this. **2** an expression able to be interpreted in more than one way.

ambiguous adj. **1** having an obscure or double meaning. **2** difficult to classify. ☐ **ambiguously** adv. **ambiguousness** n.

ambition n. **1** (often foll. by to + infin.) the determination to achieve success or distinction, usu. in a chosen field. **2** the object of this determination.

ambitious adj. **1 a** full of ambition. **b** showing ambition. **2** (foll. by to + infin.) strongly determined. ☐ **ambitiously** adv. **ambitiousness** n.

ambivalence /æmˈbɪvələns/ n. (also **ambivalency**) the coexistence in one person of opposing emotions or attitudes towards the same object or situation. ☐ **ambivalent** adj. **ambivalently** adv.

amble ● v.intr. **1** walk at an easy pace. **2** (of a horse etc.) move by lifting the two feet on one side together. **3** ride an ambling horse; ride at an easy pace. ● n. an easy pace; the gait of an ambling horse.

amblyopia /ˌæmbliˈoːpiə/ n. impaired vision without obvious defect or change in the eye. ☐ **amblyopic** /-ˈɒpɪk/ adj.

ambrosia /æmˈbroːʒə/ n. **1** Gk & Rom. Myth the food of the gods. **2** anything very pleasing to taste or smell. **3** N Amer. a dessert of sliced oranges and shredded coconut, sometimes also with bananas or pineapple. ☐ **ambrosial** adj. **ambrosian** adj.

ambulance n. a vehicle specially equipped for conveying the sick or injured to and from a hospital.

ambulance chaser n. N Amer. informal derogatory a person who strives to profit from the misfortune of others, esp. a lawyer who specializes in actions for personal injuries.

ambulance technician n. Cdn (Que.) = PARAMEDIC.

ambulatory adj. **1 a** (of a patient) able to walk about; not confined to bed. **b** (of treatment) not confining a patient to bed. **2** of or adapted for walking. **3 a** movable. **b** not permanent.

ambush ● n. **1** a surprise attack by persons in a concealed position. **2 a** the concealment of persons to make such an attack. **b** the place where they are concealed. **c** the persons concealed. ● v.tr. **1** attack by means of an ambush. **2** lie in wait for.

ameba esp. US var. of AMOEBA.

ameliorate /əˈmiːliəˌreɪt/ v.tr. & intr. formal make or become better; improve. ☐ **amelioration** n. **ameliorative** adj. **ameliorator** n.

amen /ɑːˈmen, eɪ-/ ● interj. **1** uttered at the end of a prayer or hymn etc., meaning 'so be it'. **2** (foll. by to) expressing agreement or assent (amen to that). ● n. an utterance of 'amen' (sense 1).

amenable /əˈmiːnəbəl/ adj. **1** willing to co-operate; open to suggestion or influence. **2** (often foll. by to) (of a person) subject to the authority of (amenable to the law). **3** (foll. by to) (of a thing) answerable or liable. ☐ **amenability** n. **amenably** adv.

amend v.tr. **1** formally revise or alter (a constitution, legislation, etc.). **2** make minor improvements in (a text or a written proposal). **3** correct an error or errors in (a document). **4** make better; improve. ¶Often confused with emend, a more technical word used in the context of textual correction. ☐ **amendable** adj. **amender** n.

amending formula n. a prescribed method for amending a constitution specifying the proportions of various interested parties that must assent for an amendment to be passed.

amendment n. **1** a minor improvement in a document (esp. a legal or statutory one). **2** the process or an instance of altering a document. **3** an article officially supplementing a constitution. **4** the act or process of improving, esp. one's conduct.

amends n. ☐ **make amends** (often foll. by for) compensate or make up (for).

amenity n. (pl. **-ies**) **1** (usu. in pl.) a pleasant or useful feature. **2** pleasantness, agreeableness (of a place, person, etc.).

amenorrhea /eɪˌmenəˈriə/ n. (also **amenorrhoea**) Med. an abnormal absence of menstruation.

Amer. abbr. American.

American ● adj. **1** of, relating to, or characteristic of the US or its inhabitants. **2** (usu. in comb.) of or relating to the Americas (Latin-American). **3** designating plants or animals native to the Americas (American elk). ● n. **1** a native or citizen of the US. **2** (usu. in comb.) a native or inhabitant of the Americas (North Americans). **3** the English language as used in the US.

Americana n.pl. things pertaining to and typical of American culture, e.g. publications, artifacts, etc.

American aloe n. see CENTURY PLANT.

American dream n. (also **American Dream**) the traditional American belief that in the US success and material prosperity are available to all.

American eagle n. = BALD EAGLE.

American elm n. an elm, Ulmus americana, native to

eastern N America, cultivated as a shade tree, and particularly susceptible to Dutch elm disease.

American football *n.* a form of football played in the US between two teams of 11 players, played on a smaller field than Canadian football, with four downs and slightly different scoring rules.

American Indian *n.* **1** (also **North American Indian**) a member of a group of Aboriginal peoples of the western hemisphere, excluding the Inuit and Aleuts. **2** *Cdn* a member of these peoples who is a citizen or resident of the US.

Americanism *n.* **1 a** a word, sense, or phrase peculiar to or originating from the US. **b** a thing or feature characteristic of or peculiar to the US. **2** attachment to or sympathy for the US.

Americanize *v.* **1** *tr.* **a** make American in character. **b** naturalize as an American. **2** *intr.* become American in character. □ **Americanization** *n.*

American plan *n.* *N Amer.* a method of charging for a hotel room which includes meals (*compare* EUROPEAN PLAN, MODIFIED AMERICAN PLAN).

America's Cup *n.* an international yachting trophy, originally won by the schooner *America* in 1851, for which a competition is held every three or four years.

americium /ˌæməˈrɪʃɪəm/ *n.* an artificially made radioactive metallic element.

Amerindian *adj. & n.* (also **Amerind**) ● *adj.* of or relating to American Indians. ● *n.* an American Indian.

amethyst /ˈæməθɪst/ *n.* a precious stone of a violet or purple variety of quartz.

amiable /ˈeɪmɪəbəl/ *adj.* friendly and pleasant in temperament; likeable. □ **amiability** *n.* **amiably** *adv.*

amicable *adj.* showing or done in a friendly spirit (*an amicable meeting*). □ **amicability** *n.* **amicableness** *n.* **amicably** *adv.*

amid *prep.* (also **amidst**) **1** in the middle of. **2** in the course of.

amide /ˈæmaɪd, ˈeɪm-/ *n.* *Chem.* a compound formed from ammonia by replacement of one (or sometimes more than one) hydrogen atom.

amidships *adv.* (*N Amer.* also **amidship**) in or into the middle of a ship.

amigo *n.* (*pl.* **-os**) *N Amer.* *informal* (often as a form of address) a friend or comrade.

amine /ˈæmiːn, əˈmiːn/ *n.* *Chem.* a compound formed from ammonia by replacement of one or more hydrogen atoms by an organic radical or radicals.

amino /əˈmiːnəʊ/ *n.* (*attrib.*) *Chem.* of, relating to, or containing the monovalent group $-NH_2$.

amino acid /əˈmiːnəʊ, ˈæmənəʊ/ *n.* any of a group of organic compounds containing both the carboxyl (COOH) and amino (NH_2) group, occurring naturally in plant and animal tissues and forming the basic constituents of proteins.

Amish /ˈɒmɪʃ, ˈeɪ-/ *n.* (prec. by *the*; treated as *pl.*) the members of a strict Mennonite group whose communal farms are found in S Ontario and parts of the US, esp. Pennsylvania. ● *adj.* of, pertaining to, or characteristic of this group.

amiss ● *predic.adj.* wrong; out of order; faulty (*knew something was amiss*). ● *adv.* wrong; wrongly; inappropriately (*everything went amiss*). □ **take amiss** be offended by (*took my words amiss*).

amity /ˈæmɪti/ *n.* friendship; friendly relations.

ammeter /ˈæmɪtər/ *n.* an instrument for measuring electric current in amperes.

ammo /ˈæməʊ/ *n.* *informal* ammunition.

ammonia *n.* **1** a colourless strongly alkaline gas with a characteristic pungent smell. **2** a solution of ammonia gas in water.

ammonium /əˈməʊnɪəm/ *n.* the monovalent ion NH_4^+, formed from ammonia.

ammonium chloride *n.* the salt of ammonia and hydrogen chloride, used as an electrolyte in dry cells and as a constituent of soldering fluxes.

ammunition *n.* **1** a supply of projectiles (esp. bullets, shells, and grenades). **2** points used or usable to advantage in an argument.

amnesia /æmˈniːʒə/ *n.* a partial or total loss of memory. □ **amnesiac** /-zɪˌæk/ *n.* **amnesic** *adj. & n.*

amnesty ● *n.* (*pl.* **-ies**) **1** a general pardon, esp. for political offences. **2** a period during which people may admit an offence without fear of prosecution.

Amnesty International *n.* an independent international organization campaigning for the human rights of prisoners of conscience.

amnio *n.* *informal* = AMNIOCENTESIS.

amniocentesis /ˌæmnɪəʊsenˈtiːsɪs/ *n.* (*pl.* **-teses** /-siːz/) *Med.* the sampling of amniotic fluid by insertion of a hollow needle to determine the condition of an embryo.

amnion /ˈæmnɪən/ *n.* (*pl.* **amnia**) the innermost membrane that encloses the embryo of a reptile, bird, or mammal. □ **amniotic** *adj.*

amniotic fluid *n.* the fluid contained within the amnion, in which the fetus effectively floats.

amoeba /əˈmiːbə/ *n.* (*pl.* **-s** or **amoebae** /-biː/) any usu. aquatic protozoan of the genus *Amoeba*, esp. *A. proteus*, capable of changing shape. □ **amoebic** *adj.* **amoeboid** *adj.*

amok /əˈmʌk, əˈmɒk/ *adv.* □ **go** (or **run**) **amok 1** be out of control. **2** run about wildly in an uncontrollable violent rage.

among *prep.* (also **amongst**) **1** surrounded by; in the company of (*be among friends*). **2** in the number of (*among us were those who disagreed*). **3** an example of; in the class or category of (*is among the wealthiest people alive*). **4 a** between; within the limits of (collectively or distributively); shared by (*had $5 among us; divide it among you*). **b** by the joint action or from the joint resources of (*among us we can manage it*). **5** with one another; by the reciprocal action of. **6** as distinguished from; pre-eminent in the category of (*she is one among many*).

amoral /eɪˈmɒrəl, -ˈmɒrəl/ *adj.* **1** not concerned with or outside the scope of morality (*compare* IMMORAL). **2** having no moral principles. □ **amoralism** *n.* **amoralist** *n.* **amorality** *n.*

amorous /ˈæmərəs/ *adj.* **1** showing, feeling, or inclined to sexual love. **2** of or relating to sexual love. □ **amorously** *adv.* **amorousness** *n.*

amorphous /əˈmɔːfəs/ *adj.* **1** shapeless. **2** vague, ill-organized. **3** *Geol. & Chem.* non-crystalline; having neither definite form nor structure.

amortize /ˈæmɔːtaɪz, əˈmɔːr-/ *v.tr.* *Commerce* **1** gradually pay off (a debt) by money regularly put aside. **2** gradually write off the initial cost of (assets). □ **amortization** *n.*

amount ● *n.* a quantity, esp. the total of a thing or things in number, size, value, extent, etc. ● *v.intr.* (foll. by *to*) be equivalent to in number, size, significance, etc. (*amounted to $100; amounted to a disaster*). □ **any amount of** a great deal of. **no amount of** not even the greatest possible amount of.

amour /əˈmɔːr/ *n.* a love affair, esp. a secret one.

amoxicillin /əˌmɒksɪˈsɪlən/ *n.* (also **amoxycillin**) a broad spectrum semi-synthetic penicillin, closely related to ampicillin, used esp. for treating ear and upper respiratory infections.

amp¹ *n. Electricity* an ampere.

amp² *n. informal* an amplifier.

amp³ *n. informal* an amputee.

amperage /'æmpərɪdʒ/ *n.* the strength of an electric current in amperes.

ampere /'æmper/ *n.* the SI base unit of electric current. Symbol: **A**.

ampersand *n.* the sign & (= *and*).

amphetamine /æm'fetəmi:n/ *n.* a synthetic drug used esp. as a stimulant.

amphibian ● *adj.* **1** living both on land and in water. **2** of or relating to the class Amphibia. **3** (of a vehicle or airplane) able to operate on land and water. ● *n.* **1** any vertebrate of the class Amphibia, with a life history of an aquatic gill-breathing larval stage followed by a terrestrial lung-breathing adult stage, including frogs, newts, and salamanders. **2** (in general use) a creature living both on land and in water. **3** an amphibian vehicle or airplane.

amphibious *adj.* **1** living both on land and in water. **2** of or relating to or suited for both land and water. **3** *Military* **a** (of a military operation) involving forces landed from the sea. **b** (of forces) trained for such operations. **4** having a twofold nature; occupying two positions. □ **amphibiously** *adv.*

amphitheatre /'æmfɪˌθiːətər/ *n.* (also **-theater**) **1** an oval or circular building with seats rising in tiers around a central open space. **2** a piece of level ground surrounded naturally by rising slopes. **3** a large lecture theatre with seats rising in tiers. **4** a gallery in a theatre.

amphora /'æmfərə/ *n.* (*pl.* **amphorae** /-ˌriː/ or **-s**) a Greek or Roman vessel with two handles and a narrow neck.

ampicillin /ˌæmpɪ'sɪlən/ *n.* a semi-synthetic penicillin used esp. in treating infections of the urinary and respiratory tracts.

ample *adj.* (**ampler**, **amplest**) **1 a** plentiful, abundant, extensive. **b** *euphemism* large, stout. **2** enough or more than enough. □ **ampleness** *n.* **amply** *adv.*

amplifier *n.* an electronic device for increasing the strength of electrical signals, esp. for conversion into sound in stereo equipment etc.

amplify *v.* (**-ies**, **-ied**) **1** *tr.* increase the volume or strength of (sound, electrical signals, etc.). **2** *tr.* enlarge upon or add detail to (a story etc.). **3** *intr.* expand what is said or written. □ **amplification** *n.*

amplitude *n.* **1 a** *Physics* the maximum extent of a vibration or oscillation from the position of equilibrium. **b** *Electricity* the maximum departure of the value of an alternating current or wave from the average value. **2 a** spaciousness, breadth; wide range. **b** abundance.

amplitude modulation *n.* **1** variation of the amplitude of a radio or other wave as a means of carrying information such as an audio signal. **2** the system using such modulation. Abbr.: **AM**.

ampoule /'æmpjuːl/ *n.* (also esp. *US* **ampul** or **ampule** /'æmpuːl/) a small capsule in which measured quantities of liquids or solids are sealed ready for use.

amputate *v.tr.* cut off by surgical operation (a part of the body, esp. a limb), usu. because of injury or disease. □ **amputation** *n.* **amputator** *n.*

amputee *n.* a person who has lost a limb etc. by amputation.

amt. *abbr.* amount.

amuck /ə'mʌk/ *var. of* AMOK.

amulet /'æmjolət/ *n.* **1** an ornament or small piece of jewellery worn as a charm against evil. **2** something which is thought to give such protection.

amuse *v.* **1** *tr.* cause (a person) to laugh or smile. **2** *tr.* & *refl.* (often foll. by *with, by*) interest or occupy; keep (a person) entertained. □ **amusing** *adj.* **amusingly** *adv.*

amusement *n.* **1** something that amuses, esp. a pleasant diversion, game, or pastime. **2 a** the state of being amused. **b** the act of amusing. **3** a mechanical device, e.g. a merry-go-round, for entertainment at a fairground etc.

amusement arcade *n.* = ARCADE 3.

amusement park *n.* a commercially operated fairground with rides, e.g. Ferris wheel, roller coaster, etc., and booths for refreshments and games.

amyl /'eimail, 'æmɪl/ *n.* (used *attrib.*) *Chem.* the monovalent group C_5H_{11}-, derived from pentane.

amyotrophic lateral sclerosis /ˌæmaio:'troːfɪk/ *n.* a progressive degenerative disease of the central nervous system resulting in weakness and wasting of the muscles and ultimately death. Abbr.: **ALS**.

an *indefinite article* the form of the indefinite article (*see* A¹) used before words beginning with a vowel sound (*an egg; an hour; an MP*). ¶Now less often used before aspirated words beginning with *h* and stressed on a syllable other than the first (so *a hotel*, not *an hotel*).

Anabaptism *n.* the doctrine that baptism should only be administered to believing adults. □ **Anabaptist** *n.*

anabolic steroid *n.* any of a group of synthetic steroid hormones used to increase muscle size.

anachronism *n.* **1 a** the attribution of a custom, event, etc., to a period to which it does not belong. **b** a thing attributed in this way. **2 a** anything out of harmony with its period. **b** an old-fashioned or out-of-date person or thing. □ **anachronistic** *adj.* **anachronistically** *adv.*

anaconda *n.* a S American boa of the genus *Eunectes*, esp. the very large, semi-aquatic *E. murinus*, that kills its prey by constriction.

anaemia etc. esp. *Brit. var. of* ANEMIA etc.

anaerobe /'ænəˌroːb, ə'nero:b/ *n.* an organism that grows without air or requires oxygen-free conditions.

anaerobic /ˌænə'roːbɪk/ *adj.* **1** growing without air, or requiring oxygen-free conditions to live. **2** (of exercise) in which oxygen is used by the muscles faster than it can be supplied by the bloodstream.

anaesthesia /ˌænəs'θiːzɪə, -ʒə/ *n.* the absence of sensation, esp. artificially induced insensitivity to pain usu. achieved by the administration of gases or the injection of drugs.

anaesthesiology *var. of* ANESTHESIOLOGY.

anaesthetic ● *n.* a substance that produces insensibility to pain etc. ● *adj.* producing partial or complete insensibility to pain etc.

anaesthetist /ə'nesθətɪst, ə'niː-/ *n.* **1** *Cdn & Brit.* a medical doctor specializing in the administration of anaesthetics. **2** (usu. **anesthetist**) (in the US) a person other than a doctor, e.g. a nurse etc., who administers anaesthetics.

anaesthetize /ə'nesθəˌtaiz, ə'niː-/ *v.tr.* **1** administer an anaesthetic to. **2** deprive of physical or mental sensation. □ **anaesthetization** *n.*

anagram *n.* a word or phrase formed by rearranging the letters of another word or phrase. □ **anagrammatic** *adj.* **anagrammatical** *adj.*

anal *adj.* **1 a** relating to or situated near the anus. **b** (of sexual activity) involving the insertion of one partner's penis into the other's anus. **2** *Psych.* designating or pertaining to a stage of infantile psychosexual development that is thought to involve a preoccupation with the anus and defecation. **3** *informal* = ANAL-RETENTIVE. □ **anally** *adv.*

analgesia /ˌænəlˈdʒiːziə, -siə/ *n.* the absence or relief of pain.

analgesic ● *adj.* relieving pain. ● *n.* an analgesic drug.

analog *n.* **1** (also **analogue**) (*attrib.*) (of a watch, clock, etc.) that gives a reading by means of hands or a pointer rather than displayed digits (*compare* DIGITAL *adj.* 2). **2** (*attrib.*) (of a computer or electronic process) operating with signals or information represented by a continuously variable quantity, such as spatial position, voltage, etc. (*compare* DIGITAL *adj.* 3). **3** (*attrib.*) (of a recording or recording equipment) in which the signal corresponds to a physical variable, such as the groove on a phonograph record or magnetic particles on an audio cassette tape (*compare* DIGITAL *adj.* 4).

analogize /əˈnælədʒaɪz/ *v.* **1** *tr.* represent or explain by analogy. **2** *intr.* use analogy.

analogous /əˈnæləɡəs/ *adj.* (usu. foll. by *to*) partially similar or parallel; showing analogy. □ **analogously** *adv.*

analogue *n.* (*US* **analog**) an analogous or parallel thing.

analogy /əˈnælədʒi/ *n.* (*pl.* **-ies**) **1** (usu. foll. by *to*, *with*, *between*) correspondence or partial similarity. **2** *Logic* a process of arguing from similarity in known respects to similarity in other respects. **3** *Linguistics* the imitation of existing words in forming inflections or constructions of others, without the existence of corresponding intermediate stages. **4** *Biol.* the resemblance of function between organs essentially different. **5** an analogue. □ **analogical** *adj.*

anal-retentive *adj.* (of a person) excessively orderly and fussy.

analysand /əˈnælɪˌsænd/ *n.* a person undergoing psychoanalysis.

analysis /əˈnæləsɪs/ *n.* (*pl.* **analyses** /-ˌsiːz/) **1 a** a detailed examination of the elements or structure of a substance etc. **b** a statement of the result of this. **2** *Chem.* the determination of the constituent parts of a mixture or compound. **3** psychoanalysis. **4** *Math.* the use of algebra and calculus in problem-solving. □ **in the final** (or **last** or **ultimate**) **analysis** after all due consideration; in the end. □ **analytic** *adj.* **analytical** *adj.* **analytically** *adv.*

analyst *n.* **1** a person engaged or skilled in analysis. **2** a psychoanalyst.

analytic geometry *n.* (also **analytical geometry**) geometry involving the use of algebra, with points represented by a pair of numbers, and lines and curves represented by equations.

analyze *v.tr.* (also **analyse**) **1** examine in detail the constitution or structure of. **2** *Chem.* ascertain the constituents of (a sample of a mixture or compound). **3** examine critically (a book etc.) in order to bring out essential elements or structure. **4** resolve (a sentence) into its grammatical constituents. **5** psychoanalyze. □ **analyzable** *adj.* **analyzer** *n.*

anaphora /əˈnæfərə/ *n.* **1** *Rhetoric* the repetition of a word or phrase at the beginning of successive clauses. **2** *Grammar* the use of a word referring to or replacing a word used earlier in a sentence, to avoid repetition, e.g. *do* in *I like it and so do they.* □ **anaphoric** /ˌænəˈfɒrɪk/ *adj.*

anaphylaxis /ˌænəfɪˈlæksɪs/ *n.* (*pl.* **anaphylaxes** /-ksiːz/) *Med.* hypersensitivity of tissues to a dose of

antigen, as a reaction against a previous dose. □ **anaphylactic** *adj.*

anarchism *n.* the doctrine that government should be abolished. □ **anarchist** *n.* **anarchistic** *adj.*

anarchy /ˈænɑːki/ *n.* **1** disorder, esp. political or social. **2** lack of government in a society. □ **anarchic** /əˈnɑːkɪk/ *adj.* **anarchical** *adj.* **anarchically** *adv.*

anathema /əˈnæθəmə/ *n.* (*pl.* **-s**) **1** a detested thing or person. **2 a** a declaration of the Church, excommunicating a person or denouncing a doctrine. **b** a cursed thing or person. **c** a strong curse.

anathematize *v.tr. & intr.* curse.

anatomical /ˌænəˈtɒmɪkəl/ *adj.* (also **anatomic**) of or relating to anatomy. □ **anatomically** *adv.*

anatomize /əˈnætəˌmaɪz/ *v.tr.* **1** examine in detail. **2** dissect.

anatomy *n.* (*pl.* **-ies**) **1** the science of the bodily structure of animals and plants. **2** this structure. **3** *informal* a human body. **4** analysis. **5** the dissection of the human body, animals, or plants.

ancestor *n.* **1** any (esp. remote) person from whom one is descended. **2** an early type of animal or plant from which others have evolved. **3** an early prototype or forerunner. □ **ancestral** *adj.*

ancestral name *n.* (esp. among the Sne Nay Muxw) the personal name of an ancestor, conferred upon a child as a ceremonial name.

ancestry *n.* (*pl.* **-ies**) **1** lineage or descent. **2** ancestors collectively.

ancho chili /ˈæntʃoː/ *n.* esp. *N Amer.* **1** a large, fairly hot chili pepper, used (usu. dried) in traditional Mexican dishes. **2** the plant which bears this fruit.

anchor ● *n.* **1** a heavy metal weight used to moor a ship to the bottom of a river, lake, sea, etc. or a balloon to the ground. **2** a person or thing that gives stability or security. **3** the main announcer on a news or sports broadcast, who introduces the reports of other broadcasters. **4** a person who plays a crucial part, esp. at the back of a tug-of-war team. **5** a bolt or fitting for attaching something to a wall, floor, etc. **6** a store which is the principal tenant of a shopping centre. ● *v.* **1** *tr.* secure (a ship or balloon) by means of an anchor. **2** *tr.* fix firmly. **3** *intr.* cast anchor. **4** *intr.* be moored by means of an anchor. **5** *tr.* act as an anchor. □ **at anchor** moored by means of an anchor. **cast** (or **come to**) **anchor** let the anchor down. □ (in senses 3 & 4 of *n.*) **anchorman** *n.* (*pl.* **-men**). **anchorperson** *n.* **anchorwoman** *n.* (*pl.* **-women**).

anchorage *n.* **1** a place where a ship may be anchored. **2** the act of anchoring or lying at anchor. **3** something that provides security for something else.

anchorite *n.* **1** a hermit; a religious recluse. **2** a person of secluded habits. □ **anchoress** *n.*

anchoveta /ˌæntʃəˈvetə/ *n.* a small Pacific anchovy, *Cetengraulis mysticetus*, caught for use as bait, animal feed, or fertilizer.

anchovy /ˈæn.tʃoːvi, ˈæntʃə-, ænˈtʃoː-/ *n.* (*pl.* **-ies**) a small Mediterranean fish of the herring family, *Engraulis encrasicholus*, which has a rich flavour and is usu. eaten pickled or in pastes, sauces, etc.

anchylose etc. *var. of* ANKYLOSE etc.

ancien régime /ˌɑ̃sjɛ reiˈʒiːm/ *n.* (*pl.* **anciens régimes** *pronunc.* same) **1** the political and social system in France before the Revolution of 1789. **2** any superseded regime.

ancient *adj.* **1 a** of long ago. **b** of or pertaining to the world prior to the fall of Rome in 476. **2** having lived or existed long; very old. □ **the ancients 1** the people of ancient times, esp. the Greeks, Romans,

Hebrews, and Egyptians. **2** the writers of classical Greece or Rome.

ancient history *n.* **1** the history of the ancient civilizations of the Mediterranean area and the Near East before the fall of the Western Roman Empire in 476. **2** something already long familiar.

ancillary /æn'sɪləri / ● *adj.* **1** (of a person, activity, or service) providing essential support to a central service or industry. **2** associated, secondary. ● *n.* (*pl.* **-ies**) **1** an ancillary worker. **2** something which is ancillary; an auxiliary or accessory.

and *conj.* **1 a** connecting words, clauses, or sentences that are to be taken jointly. **b** implying progression (*better and better*). **c** implying causation (*do that and I'll hit you*). **d** implying great duration (*he cried and cried*). **e** implying a great number (*miles and miles*). **f** implying addition (*two and two are four*). **g** implying variety (*there are books and books*). **h** implying succession (*walking two and two*). **2** *informal* to (*try and open it*). **3** in relation to (*Canada and NATO*). □ **and/or** either or both of two stated possibilities.

Andalusian /ˌændəlu'siːən/ ● *adj.* of or relating to Andalusia in southern Spain, its inhabitants, or its language. ● *n.* **1** a native or inhabitant of Andalusia. **2** the variety of Spanish spoken in Andalusia.

andante /æn'dɒntei, -'dæntei / *Music* ● *adv.* & *adj.* in a moderately slow tempo. ● *n.* an andante passage or movement.

Andean /æn'diːən, 'ændiən/ *adj.* of or relating to the region of the Andes, a high mountain range in western S America.

androcentric /ˌændro'sentrɪk/ *adj.* male-centred. □ **androcentrism** *n.*

androgen /'ændrədʒən/ *n.* a male sex hormone or other substance capable of developing and maintaining certain male sexual characteristics. □ **androgenic** *adj.*

androgyne /'ændrə,dʒain/ ● *adj.* hermaphrodite. ● *n.* a hermaphrodite person.

androgynous /æn'drɒdʒɪnəs/ *adj.* **1** having both male and female characteristics; hermaphrodite. **2** not distinguishably male or female, esp. in appearance. **3** *Bot.* with stamens and pistils in the same flower or inflorescence. □ **androgyny** *n.*

android *n.* a robot with a human appearance.

androstenedione /ˌændro'stiːndaɪɒn/ *n.* a naturally occurring androgenic steroid often taken in concentrated form to elevate blood levels of testosterone.

anecdotal *adj.* **1** of, pertaining to, or consisting of anecdotes. **2** based on or consisting of incidental observations or reports rather than systematic research (*anecdotal evidence*). □ **anecdotalist** *n.*

anecdote *n.* a short account of an entertaining or interesting incident. □ **anecdotist** *n.*

anemia /ə'niːmiə/ *n.* a deficiency in the blood, usu. of red cells or their hemoglobin, resulting in pallor and weariness.

anemic *adj.* **1** relating to or suffering from anemia. **2** pale; lacking in vitality.

anemometer /ˌænə'mɒmɪtər/ *n.* an instrument for measuring the force of the wind.

anemone /ə'nemənɪ/ *n.* **1** any plant of the genus *Anemone*, related to the buttercup, with flowers of various vivid colours. **2** = PASQUE FLOWER.

anesthesia etc. *var.* of ANAESTHESIA etc.

anesthesiology *n.* US the science of administering anaesthetics. □ **anesthesiologist** *n.*

aneurysm /'ænju,rɪzəm/ *n.* (also **aneurism**) an excessive localized enlargement of a blood vessel.

anew *adv.* **1** again. **2** in a different way.

angakok /'æŋgəko:k/ *n.* *Cdn* (*North*) an Inuit shaman or healer.

angel *n.* **1 a** an attendant or messenger of God. **b** a conventional representation of this in human form with wings. **c** an attendant spirit (*guardian angel*). **d** *Christianity* a member of the lowest of the nine orders of angelic beings. **2 a** a very virtuous person. **b** an obliging person (*be an angel and answer the door*). **3** *N Amer.* = SNOW ANGEL. **4** *slang* a financial backer of an enterprise, esp. in the theatre. **5** *informal* an unexplained radar echo.

angel dust *n.* *slang* the hallucinogenic drug phencyclidine hydrochloride.

Angeleno /ˌændʒə'liːnoː/ *n.* (also **Los Angeleno**) esp. *US* a native or inhabitant of Los Angeles.

angelfish *n.* any of various fish, esp. *Pterophyllum scalare*, with large dorsal and ventral fins.

angel food cake *n.* (also esp. *Brit.* **angel cake**) a light, usu. tall and ring-shaped cake made of beaten egg whites, sugar, and flour.

angel hair *n.* **1** very fine spaghetti. **2** spun glass with very fine filaments forming a fluffy white material used esp. in Christmas decorations.

angelic *adj.* **1** like or relating to angels. **2** having characteristics attributed to angels, esp. sublime beauty, innocence, or goodness. □ **angelically** *adv.*

angelica /æn'dʒelɪkə/ *n.* **1** an aromatic umbelliferous plant, *Angelica archangelica*, used in cooking and medicine. **2** its candied stalks.

angel pie *n.* *N Amer.* a dessert consisting of a meringue base filled with custard and fruit and topped with whipped cream.

angelus /'ændʒələs/ *n.* *Catholicism* **1** a devotion commemorating the Incarnation, traditionally said at morning, noon, and sunset. **2** a bell announcing this.

anger ● *n.* extreme or passionate displeasure. ● *v.tr.* make angry; enrage.

angina /æn'dʒainə/ *n.* **1** (in full **angina pectoris** /'pektərɪs/) pain in the chest brought on by exertion, owing to an inadequate blood supply to the heart. **2** an attack of intense constricting pain often causing suffocation.

angiogram /ˌændʒiə'græm/ *n.* an X-ray made by angiography.

angiography /ˌændʒi'ɒgrəfi/ *n.* (*pl.* **-ies**) radiography of blood and lymph vessels, carried out after introduction of a radiopaque substance.

angioplasty /'ændʒiə,plæsti/ *n.* (*pl.* **-ies**) surgical repair of a damaged blood vessel.

angiosperm /'ændʒiə,spɜrm/ *n.* any plant producing flowers and reproducing by seeds enclosed within a carpel, including herbaceous plants, herbs, shrubs, grasses and most trees (opp. GYMNOSPERM).

angishore /'æŋəʃɔr/ *Cdn* (*Nfld & Maritimes*) *var.* of HANGASHORE.

Angle *n.* (usu. in *pl.*) a member of a tribe from Schleswig that settled in E Britain in the 5th c., giving their name to England. □ **Anglian** *adj.*

angle¹ ● *n.* **1 a** the space between two meeting lines or surfaces. **b** the inclination of two lines or surfaces to each other. **2 a** a corner. **b** a sharp projection. **3 a** the direction from which a photograph etc. is taken. **b** the aspect from which a matter is considered. **4** *Cdn* (*Nfld*) a curved inlet in a lake or pond. ● *v.* **1** *tr.* & *intr.* move or place obliquely. **2** *tr.* present (information) from a particular point of view. □ **angled** *adj.*

angle² *v.intr.* **1** (often foll. by *for*) fish with hook and line. **2** (foll. by *for*) seek an objective by devious or calculated means (*angled for an invitation*).

angle brackets *n.pl.* brackets in the form < >.

angle iron *n.* a piece of iron or steel with an L-shaped cross-section, used to strengthen a framework.

angle parking *n.* N *Amer.* parking of vehicles at an angle to the curb. □ **angle-park** *v.intr.*

angler *n.* **1** a person who fishes with a hook and line. **2** (in full **anglerfish**) any of various fishes that prey upon small fish, attracting them by filaments arising from the dorsal fin.

Anglican ● *adj.* of or relating to the Church of England or any Church in communion with it, e.g. the Anglican Church of Canada. ● *n.* a member of an Anglican Church. □ **Anglicanism** *n.*

anglicism /ˈæŋglɪˌsɪzəm/ *n.* **1** an English word, structure, etc. borrowed into another language. **2** a word or custom peculiar to England. **3** Englishness. **4** preference for what is English.

anglicize *v.tr.* make English in form or character.

Anglo *n.* (pl. **-os**) **1** Cdn *informal* an anglophone, esp. in Quebec. **2** US & Austral. an English-speaking person of British or northern-European origin (in the US esp. as distinct from Hispanic Americans).

Anglo- comb. form **1** English. **2** of English origin (*an Anglo-Canadian*). **3** English or British and.

Anglo-American ● *adj.* **1** of American and English (or British) descent. **2** English (or British) and American. ● *n.* an American of English (or British) descent.

Anglo-Canadian ● *adj.* **1** of or pertaining to English-speaking Canadians. **2** English (or British) and Canadian. ● *n.* **1** an English-speaking Canadian. **2** a Canadian of English descent.

Anglo-Catholic ● *adj.* of a High Church Anglican group which emphasizes its Catholic tradition. ● *n.* a member of this group. □ **Anglo-Catholicism** *n.*

Anglo-French ● *adj.* **1** English (or British) and French. **2** of Anglo-French. ● *n.* the French language as retained and separately developed in England after the Norman Conquest.

Anglo-Indian ● *adj.* **1** of or relating to England and India. **2** **a** of British descent or birth but living or having lived in India. **b** of mixed British and Indian parentage. **3** (of a word) adopted into English from an Indian language. ● *n.* an Anglo-Indian person.

Anglo-Irish ● *adj.* **1** of English descent living in Ireland. **2** English (or British) and Irish. **3** of the English language as spoken in Ireland. ● *n.* **1** the Anglo-Irish language. **2** an Anglo-Irish person.

Anglo-Latin ● *adj.* of Latin as used in medieval England. ● *n.* this form of Latin.

Anglo-Norman ● *adj.* **1** of the Normans in England after the Norman Conquest. **2** of the dialect of French used by them. **3** English and Norman. ● *n.* the Anglo-Norman dialect.

anglophile /ˈæŋgloˌfaɪl/ ● *n.* a person who is fond of or greatly admires England, the English, or English-speaking culture. ● *adj.* being or characteristic of an anglophile. □ **anglophilia** /ˈæŋgloˌfɪlɪə/ *n.*

anglophobia /ˌæŋgləˈfoːbiə/ *n.* intense hatred or fear of anglophones, the English, or England. □ **anglophobe** *n.* **anglophobic** *adj.*

anglophone esp. Cdn ● *adj.* English-speaking. ● *n.* an English-speaking person.

Anglo-Saxon ● *adj.* **1** of the English Saxons (as distinct from the Old Saxons, and from the Angles) before the Norman Conquest. **2** of the Germanic peoples (Angles, Saxons, and Jutes) who settled in Britain before the Norman Conquest. **3** of English descent. ● *n.* **1** an Anglo-Saxon person. **2** the Old English language. **3** *informal* plain (esp. crude) English.

Angolan /æŋˈgoːlən/ ● *n.* a native or inhabitant of Angola, a republic on the west coast of Africa. ● *adj.* of or relating to Angola or its people.

angora /æŋˈgɔrə/ *n.* **1** a fabric made from the hair of the angora goat or rabbit. **2** a long-haired variety of cat, goat, or rabbit.

angora wool *n.* a mixture of sheep's wool and angora rabbit hair.

angry *adj.* (**-ier**, **-iest**) **1** feeling or showing anger; extremely displeased or resentful. **2** (of a wound, sore, etc.) inflamed, painful. **3** suggesting or seeming to show anger (*an angry sky*). □ **angrily** *adv.*

angry young man *n.* **1** any of a group of young British writers of the 1950s who criticized the social conventions of the time. **2** any young person who disagrees vehemently with existing attitudes.

angst *n.* **1** anxiety. **2** a feeling of guilt or remorse.

angstrom /ˈæŋstrəm/ *n.* (also **ångström** /ˈɒŋ-/) a unit of length equal to 10^{-10} m, used esp. for electromagnetic wavelengths. Symbol: **Å**.

anguish *n.* severe misery or mental suffering.

anguished *adj.* suffering or expressing anguish.

angular *adj.* **1** a having angles or sharp corners. **b** (of a person) having sharp features; lean and bony. **c** awkward in manner. **2** forming an angle. **3** measured by angle (*angular distance*). □ **angularity** *n.* **angularly** *adv.*

Angus *n.* = ABERDEEN ANGUS.

anhydride /ænˈhaɪdraɪd/ *n.* Chem. a substance obtained by removing the elements of water from a compound, esp. from an acid.

aniline /ˈænɪˌliːn, -lɪn, -ˌlaɪn/ *n.* a colourless oily liquid, used in the manufacture of dyes, drugs, and plastics.

aniline dye *n.* **1** any of numerous dyes made from aniline. **2** any synthetic dye.

anima /ˈænɪmə/ *n.* Psych. **1** the inner personality (opp. PERSONA 1). **2** Jung's term for the feminine part of a man's personality (opp. ANIMUS 4).

animal ● *n.* **1** a living organism which feeds on organic matter, usu. one with specialized sense organs and nervous system, and able to respond rapidly to stimuli. **2** such an organism other than man. **3** a brutish or uncivilized person. **4** *informal* a person or thing of any kind (*there is no such animal*). ● *adj.* **1** characteristic of animals. **2** of animals as distinct from vegetables (*animal fat*). **3** characteristic of the physical needs of animals; carnal, sensual.

Animal Cracker *n.* proprietary (also **animal cookie**) N *Amer.* a small (usu. arrowroot) cookie in the shape of an animal, esp. a circus animal.

animal husbandry *n.* the science of breeding and caring for farm animals.

animalism *n.* **1** the nature and activity of animals. **2** the belief that humans are not superior to other animals. **3** concern with physical matters; sensuality. □ **animalistic** *adj.*

animality /ˌænɪˈmælɪtɪ/ *n.* **1** the animal world. **2** the nature or behaviour of animals.

animal magnetism *n.* power to attract others.

animal rights *n.* the right of animals to be free from abuse or exploitation by humans.

animate ● *adj.* **1** having life. **2** lively. ● *v.tr.* **1** enliven, make lively. **2** give life to. **3** produce (a film etc.) by animation. **4** inspire, actuate. **5** encourage.

animated *adj.* **1** lively, vigorous. **2** having life. **3** (of a

film etc.) using techniques of animation. □
animatedly adv.

animateur /ˌænɪmæˈtɜr/ n. a person who coordinates, or acts as a driving force behind, a cultural or other activity.

animation n. **1** vivacity, ardour. **2** the state of being alive. **3** Film the technique of filming successive drawings or positions of puppets to create an illusion of movement when the film is shown as a sequence.

animator n. **1** a person who makes animated films. **2** var. of ANIMATEUR.

animatronics /ˌænɪməˈtrɒnɪks/ n. the technique of constructing robots resembling animals, people, etc. which are programmed to perform lifelike movements to a soundtrack. □ **animatronic** adj.

anime /ˈænimei/ n. Japanese film and television animation, typically having a science-fiction theme and sometimes including violent or sexual material.

animism /ˈænɪˌmɪzəm/ n. **1** the attribution of a living soul to plants, inanimate objects, and natural phenomena. **2** the belief in a supernatural power that organizes and animates the material universe.□ **animist** n. **animistic** adj.

animosity n. (pl. **-ies**) a spirit or feeling of strong hostility.

animus /ˈænɪməs/ n. **1** a display of animosity. **2** ill feeling. **3** a motivating spirit or feeling. **4** Psych. Jung's term for the masculine part of a woman's personality (opp. ANIMA 2).

anion /ˈænˌaiən/ n. a negatively charged ion; an ion that is attracted to the anode in electrolysis (opp. CATION).□ **anionic** /ˌænaiˈɒnɪk/ adj.

anise /ˈænɪs/ n. **1** an umbelliferous plant, Pimpinella anisum, having aromatic seeds. **2** any of several trees and shrubs of the genus Illicium, which bear fruit with the odour of anise, esp. the star anise, I. verum.

aniseed /ˈænɪˌsiːd/ n. the seed of the anise, used to give liqueurs, candies, etc. a liquorice-like flavour.

Anishinabe /æˈnɪʃɪˌnɒbi/ (also **Anishnabe** /æˈnɪʃˌnɒbi/) ● n. (pl. same) **1** the preferred name for the Ojibwa and Cree, part of the Algonquian language group, living in northern Quebec, northern and central Ontario, Manitoba, Saskatchewan, and Alberta. **2** the Algonquian language of this people. ● adj. of or relating to this people or their culture.

ankh /æŋk/ n. a device consisting of a looped bar with a shorter crossbar, used in ancient Egypt as a symbol of life.

ankle n. **1** the joint connecting the foot with the leg. **2** the part of the leg between this and the calf.

ankle-biter n. N Amer. & Austral. slang a child.

ankle bone n. a bone forming the ankle.

ankle sock n. a short sock just covering the ankle.

anklet n. **1** an ornament or fetter worn around the ankle. **2** esp. US = ANKLE SOCK.

ankylose /ˈæŋkɪˌloz/ v.tr. & intr. (of bones or a joint) stiffen or unite by ankylosis.

ankylosis /ˌæŋkɪˈloːsɪs/ n. **1** the abnormal stiffening and immobility of a joint by fusion of the bones. **2** such fusion.□ **ankylotic** adj.

annal n. **1** the annals of one year. **2** a record of one item in a chronicle.

annalist n. a writer of annals.

annals n.pl. **1** a narrative of events year by year. **2** historical records. **3** (in proper names) a learned journal.

annatto /əˈnæto:/ n. **1** a tropical tree, Bixa orellana. **2** an orange-red dye obtained from the seed coat of this tree, used esp. as a food colouring.

anneal /əˈniːl/ ● v.tr. **1** heat (metal or glass) and allow it to cool slowly, esp. to toughen it. **2** toughen. ● n. treatment by annealing.□ **annealer** n.

annelid /ˈænəlɪd/ n. an animal of the phylum Annelida, members of which have bodies made up of annular segments.

annex ● n. **1** a separate or added building, esp. for extra accommodation. **2** an addition to a document. **3** N Amer. (now esp. in proper names) an area annexed to a city, usu. for housing development. ● v.tr. **1** add or append as a subordinate part. **2** incorporate (territory of another) into one's own. **3** add as a condition or consequence. **4** informal take without right. □ **annexation** n.

annexationism n. **1** a policy which favours annexation of territory. **2** Cdn any of several historical movements favouring Canadian political union with the US.□ **annexationist** n.

annihilate /əˈnaiəˌleit/ v.tr. **1** completely destroy. **2** defeat utterly; make insignificant or powerless. □ **annihilation** n.

anniversary n. (pl. **-ies**) **1 a** the yearly return of a date on which an event took place in a previous year. **b** the anniversary of a wedding. **2** the celebration of this.

Anno Domini /ˌæno: ˈdɒmɪˌni, ˈdɒmɪˌnai/ adv. in the year of the Christian era.

annotate v.tr. add explanatory notes to (a book, document, etc.). □ **annotatable** adj. **annotation** n. **annotative** adj. **annotator** n.

announce v.tr. **1** (often foll. by that) make publicly known. **2** make known the arrival or imminence of (a guest, dinner, etc.). **3** make known (without words) to the senses or the mind; be a sign of.

announcement n. a statement in written or spoken form that makes something known.

announcer n. a person who announces speakers, singers, programs, etc., esp. on radio or television.

annoy v.tr. **1** cause slight anger or mental distress to. **2** (in passive) be somewhat angry. **3** harass repeatedly. □ **annoyance** n. **annoyer** n. **annoying** adj.

annual ● adj. **1** reckoned by the year. **2** occurring every year. **3** living or lasting for one year. ● n. **1** a book etc. published once a year; a yearbook. **2** a plant that lives only for a year or less.□ **annually** adv.

annual allowable cut n. Cdn (BC) Forestry the volume of wood which may be cut each year in a specified area.

annual general meeting n. Cdn, Brit., & Austral. a yearly meeting of members or shareholders, esp. for holding elections and reporting on the year's events.

annualized adj. (of rates of interest, inflation, etc.) calculated on an annual basis, as a projection from figures obtained for a shorter period.

annual report n. a yearly report made by a company to its shareholders, containing the financial statements and a summary of the year's activities.

annuity n. (pl. **-ies**) **1** a yearly grant or allowance. **2** an investment of money entitling the investor to a series of equal annual sums. **3** a sum payable for a particular year.□ **annuitize** v.tr.

annul v.tr. (**annulled, annulling**) **1** declare (a marriage etc.) invalid. **2** cancel, abolish.□ **annulment** n.

annular /ˈænjʊlər/ adj. ring-shaped. □ **annularly** adv.

annulus /ˈænjʊləs/ n. (pl. **annuli** /-lai/) **1** a ring-shaped part. **2** the area between two concentric circles.

annunciate /əˈnʌnsiˌeit/ v.tr. proclaim.

annunciation n. **1** (**Annunciation**) Christianity **a** the announcing of the Incarnation, made by the angel Gabriel to Mary. **b** the festival commemorating this on 25 March. **2 a** the act or process of announcing. **b** an announcement.

annunciator *n.* **1** a device giving an audible or visible indication of which of several electrical circuits has been activated, of the position of a train, etc. **2** an announcer.

anode /'ænoʊd/ *n.* *Electricity* **1** the positive electrode in an electrolytic cell or electronic valve or tube. **2** the negative terminal of a primary cell such as a battery (*opp.* CATHODE). ☐ **anodal** *adj.* **anodic** /ə'nɒdɪk/ *adj.*

anodize /'ænə,daiz/ *v.tr.* coat (a metal, esp. aluminum) with a protective oxide layer by electrolysis. ☐ **anodizer** *n.*

anodyne /'ænə,dain/ ● *adj.* **1** able to relieve pain. **2** mentally soothing, esp. because innocuous. ● *n.* an anodyne drug or medicine.

anoint *v.tr.* **1** apply oil or ointment to, esp. as a religious ceremony, e.g. at baptism, or the consecration of a priest or king, or in ministering to the sick. **2** choose (a leader, successor, etc.) as though by anointing. **3** (usu. foll. by *with*) smear, rub.

anointing of the sick *n.* a rite of some Christian denominations (a sacrament in the Catholic Church) in which a gravely ill person is prayed for and anointed with oil as a sign of healing.

anomalous /ə'nɒmələs/ *adj.* having an irregular or deviant feature; abnormal. ☐ **anomalously** *adv.*

anomaly /ə'nɒməli/ *n.* (*pl.* **-ies**) **1** an anomalous circumstance or thing; an irregularity. **2** irregularity of motion, behaviour, etc.

anomie /'ænəmi/ *n.* (also **anomy**) lack of the usual social or ethical standards in an individual or group. ☐ **anomic** /ə'nɒmɪk/ *adj.*

anon. *abbr.* anonymous; an anonymous author.

anonymous *adj.* **1** of unknown name. **2** of unknown or undeclared source or authorship. **3** without character; featureless, impersonal. **4** (**Anonymous**) (placed after noun) designating a mutual support group in which the members do not have to reveal their names (*Alcoholics Anonymous*). ☐ **anonymity** /,ænə'nɪmɪti/ *n.* **anonymously** *adv.*

anorak /'ænə,ræk/ *n.* **1** a waterproof jacket of cloth or plastic, usu. with a hood and with drawstrings at the waist, cuffs, and hood. **2** a light jacket or cardigan with a drawstring waist.

anorexia /,ænə'reksiə/ *n.* **1** a lack or loss of appetite for food. **2** (in full **anorexia nervosa** /,nɜr'voʊsə/) a psychological illness, esp. in young women, characterized by an obsessive desire to lose weight by refusing to eat.

anorexic ● *adj.* **1** involving, producing, or characterized by a lack of appetite, esp. in anorexia nervosa. **2** extremely thin. ● *n.* a person with anorexia.

another ● *adj.* **1** an additional; one more (*have another cookie*). **2** a person like or comparable to (*another Olivier*). **3** a different (*quite another matter*). **4** some or any other (*will not do another man's work*). ● *pron.* **1** an additional one (*have another*). **2** a different one (*take this book and bring me another*). **3** some or any other one (*I love another*).

answer ● *n.* **1** something said or done to deal with or in reaction to a question, statement, or circumstance. **2** the solution to a problem. **3** (foll. by *to*) an equivalent or rival (*Quebec's answer to the Champs Elysées*). ● *v.* **1** *tr.* make an answer to (*answer me; answer my question*). **2** *intr.* (often foll. by *to*) make an answer. **3** *tr.* respond to the summons or signal of (*answer the door*). **4** *tr.* be satisfactory for (a purpose or need). **5** *intr.* (foll. by *for,*

to) be responsible (*you will answer to me for your conduct*). **6** *intr.* (foll. by *to*) correspond, esp. to a description. **7** *intr.* be satisfactory or successful. ☐ **answer back** answer a rebuke etc. impudently. **answer to the name of** be called.

answerable *adj.* **1** (usu. foll. by *to, for*) responsible. **2** that can be answered. ☐ **answerability** *n.*

answering machine *n.* a device which supplies a pre-recorded answer to a telephone call and allows the caller to record a message.

answering service *n.* a business that receives and answers telephone calls for its clients.

ant *n.* any small insect of a widely distributed hymenopterous family, wingless (except for males in the mating season), and living in complex social colonies. ☐ **have ants in one's pants** fidget, esp. because of nervousness or impatience.

antacid ● *n.* a substance that prevents or corrects acidity esp. in the stomach. ● *adj.* having these properties.

antagonism /æn'tægə,nɪzəm/ *n.* active opposition or hostility.

antagonist *n.* **1** an opponent or adversary. **2** a muscle, organism, or substance that partially or completely opposes the action of another. ☐ **antagonistic** *adj.* **antagonistically** *adv.*

antagonize *v.tr.* **1** evoke hostility or opposition or enmity in. **2** (of one force etc.) counteract or tend to neutralize (another). ☐ **antagonization** *n.*

Antarctic /ænt'ɑrktik, -'ɑrtik/ ● *adj.* of the south polar regions. ● *n.* these regions.

ante /'ænti/ ● *n.* **1** a stake put up by a player in poker etc. before receiving cards. **2** an amount to be paid in advance. ● *v.tr.* (**antes, anted**) **1** put up as an ante. **2** a bet, stake. **b** (foll. by *up*) pay. ☐ **up** (or **raise**) **the ante** increase what is at stake.

ante- *prefix* forming nouns and adjectives meaning 'before, preceding' (*antedate*).

anteater *n.* **1** any of several toothless mammals of the family Myrmecophagidae, having a long snout and sticky tongue, and feeding on ants and termites. **2** any animal resembling this, e.g. an aardvark.

antecedent /,ænti'si:dənt/ ● *n.* **1** a preceding thing or circumstance. **2** *Grammar* a word, phrase, clause, or sentence, to which another word (esp. a pronoun, usu. following) refers. **3** (in *pl.*) history or ancestry, esp. of a person. ● *adj.* **1** (often foll. by *to*) previous. **2** presumptive, a priori. ☐ **antecedence** *n.* **antecedently** *adv.*

antechamber /'ænti,tʃeimbər/ *n.* a small room leading to a main one.

antedate ● *v.tr.* /,ænti'deit/ **1** exist or occur at a date earlier than. **2** assign an earlier date to (a document, event, etc.), esp. one earlier than its actual date. ● *n.* /'ænti,deit/ a date earlier than the actual one.

antelope *n.* (*pl.* same or **-s**) **1** any of various deerlike ruminants of the family Bovidae, esp. abundant in Africa and typically tall, slender, graceful, and swift-moving with smooth hair and upward-pointing horns, e.g. gazelles. **2** *N Amer.* = PRONGHORN. **3** leather made from the skin of any of these.

antenna /æn'tenə/ *n.* **1** (*pl.* **antennas**) a metal rod or other structure by which signals are transmitted or received as part of a radio or television transmitting or receiving system. **2** (*pl.* **antennae** /-niː/) one of a pair of mobile appendages on the heads of insects, crustaceans, etc., sensitive to touch and taste.

anterior /æn'tiːriər/ *adj.* **1** nearer the front. **2** (often foll. by *to*) earlier, prior. ☐ **anteriority** /-ri'ɒriti, -ri'ɔriti/ *n.* **anteriorly** *adv.*

anteroom /'ænti,ru:m/ n. a small room leading to a main one, esp. one used as a waiting room.

anthem n. **1** a solemn song expressing loyalty etc., esp. = NATIONAL ANTHEM. **2** a short choral composition set to a passage of scripture and sung during church services. **3** a song adopted by a group as expressing their feelings, aspirations, etc.

anther n. Bot. the apical portion of a stamen containing pollen.

anthill n. **1** a moundlike nest built by ants or termites. **2** a community teeming with people.

anthologize v.tr. & intr. compile or include in an anthology.

anthology n. (pl. **-ies**) a published collection of poems, stories, songs, reproductions of paintings, etc. □ **anthologist** n.

anthracite /'ænθrə,sait/ n. coal of a hard variety burning with little flame and smoke.

anthrax n. a lethal disease of sheep and cattle caused by bacterial spores and transmissible to humans.

anthro n. N Amer. informal anthropology.

anthropocentric /,ænθrəpo:'sentrık, ,ænθrɒpo:-/ adj. regarding human beings as the centre of existence. □ **anthropocentrically** adv. **anthropocentrism** n.

anthropoid /'ænθrə,pɔid/ ● adj. **1** esp. Biol. of or relating to the primate suborder Anthropoidea (including humans, apes, and monkeys), esp. designating the larger apes. **2** resembling a human being in form. ● n. esp. Biol. a member of the suborder Anthropoidea, esp. an anthropoid ape.

anthropology /,ænθrə'pɒlədʒi/ n. **1** the study of human beings, esp. of their societies and customs. **2** the study of the structure and evolution of human beings as animals. □ **anthropological** adj. **anthropologist** n.

anthropomorphic /,ænθrəpə'mɔrfık/ adj. **1** of or characterized by anthropomorphism. **2** having or representing a human form. □ **anthropomorphically** adv.

anthropomorphism n. the attribution of human characteristics to a god, animal, or thing. □ **anthropomorphize** v.tr.

anti /'ænti, 'æntai/ ● prep. opposed to (is anti everything). ● n. (pl. **-s**) a person opposed to a particular policy etc.

anti- /'ænti, 'æntai/ prefix forming nouns and adjectives meaning: **1** opposed to; against (anticlerical). **2** preventing (antifreeze). **3** designed to destroy or render useless (anti-aircraft). **4** the opposite of (anticlimax). **5** rival (antipope). **6** unlike the conventional form (anti-hero).

anti-abortion adj. opposed to the practice of and legalization of medically induced abortion. □ **anti-abortionist** n.

anti-aircraft adj. (of a gun, missile, etc.) used to attack enemy aircraft.

antialiasing /,ænti'eiliəsıŋ/ n. the reduction or prevention of aliasing, esp. the smoothing of curved or inclined lines that appear artificially jagged in a computer image.

anti-ballistic missile n. a missile designed to intercept and destroy a ballistic missile. Abbr.: **ABM**.

antibiotic /,æntibai'ɒtık/ ● n. any of various substances, e.g. penicillin, produced by micro-organisms or made synthetically, that can inhibit or destroy susceptible micro-organisms, esp. disease-producing bacteria and fungi. ● adj. functioning as an antibiotic.

antibody n. (pl. **-ies**) any of various blood proteins produced in response to and then counteracting antigens.

antic ● n. **1** (usu. in pl.) absurd or foolish behaviour. **2** an absurd or silly action. ● adj. excited, agitated, frenzied.

anti-choice adj. opposed to the principle of allowing women to choose to have an abortion. ¶A derogatory synonym for PRO-LIFE.

Antichrist n. **1** an arch-enemy of Christ. **2** a postulated opponent of Christ expected by the early Church to appear before the end of the world.

anticipate v.tr. **1** foresee and deal with ahead of time. **2** disputed expect; regard as probable (did not anticipate any difficulty). **3** forestall (a person or thing). **4** look forward to (anticipate your next letter). □ **anticipator** n. **anticipatory** /æn'tısıpə,tɔri/ adj.

anticipation n. **1** the act or process of anticipating. **2** Music the sounding of one note of a chord before the rest of the chord.

anticlerical ● adj. opposed to the influence of the clergy, esp. in politics. ● n. an anticlerical person. □ **anticlericalism** n.

anticlimax n. a trivial conclusion to something significant or impressive, esp. where a climax was expected. □ **anticlimactic** adj. **anticlimactically** adv.

anticoagulant ● n. any drug or agent that retards or inhibits coagulation, esp. of the blood. ● adj. retarding or inhibiting coagulation.

anticonvulsant ● n. any drug or agent that prevents or reduces the severity of convulsions, esp. epileptic fits. ● adj. preventing or reducing convulsions.

antidepressant ● n. any drug or agent that alleviates depression. ● adj. alleviating depression.

antidote n. **1** a medicine etc. taken or given to counteract poison. **2** anything that counteracts something unpleasant or harmful. □ **antidotal** adj.

antifreeze n. a substance (usu. ethylene glycol) added to water to lower its freezing point, esp. in the radiator of a motor vehicle.

antigen /'æntıdʒən, -,dʒen/ n. a foreign substance, e.g. a toxin, which causes the body to produce antibodies. □ **antigenic** adj.

anti-gravity n. a hypothetical force opposing gravity.

anti-hero n. (pl. **-oes**) a central character in a story or drama who noticeably lacks conventional heroic attributes.

antihistamine /,ænti'hıstəmi:n, -mın/ n. a substance that counteracts the effects of histamine, used esp. in the treatment of allergies.

anti-inflammatory ● adj. reducing inflammation of body tissues and associated pain, swelling, etc. ● n. (pl. **-ies**) an anti-inflammatory drug or treatment, e.g. cortisone.

anti-knock adj. (of a compound added to fuel etc.) preventing premature combustion in an engine.

anti-lock brake n. an automobile brake which prevents skidding by alternately locking and freeing the wheels when applied suddenly.

antimatter n. Physics a hypothetical matter composed solely of antiparticles.

antimony /'æntı,mo:ni/ n. a brittle silvery-white metallic element used esp. in alloys.

anti-nuclear adj. opposed to the development of nuclear weapons or nuclear power.

antioxidant n. **1** a substance (e.g. vitamins C and E) that removes potentially damaging oxidizing agents in a living organism. **2** an agent that inhibits oxidation, esp. used to counteract deterioration of stored food products.

antiparticle *n. Physics* an elementary particle having the same mass as a given particle but opposite electric or magnetic properties.

antipasto /ˌæntiˈpæstoː/ *n.* (*pl.* **-os** or **antipasti** /-tiː/) **1** a cold appetizer preceding an Italian meal, usu. consisting of meat or fish and vegetables or fruit. **2** a mixture of pickled vegetables served as an appetizer.

antipathetic *adj.* (usu. foll. by *to*) having a strong aversion or natural opposition.

antipathy /ænˈtɪpəθi/ *n.* (*pl.* **-ies**) (often foll. by *to, for, between*) a strong or deep-seated aversion or dislike.

anti-personnel *adj.* (of a bomb, mine, etc.) designed to kill or injure people rather than to damage buildings or equipment.

antiperspirant ● *n.* a substance applied to the skin to prevent or reduce perspiration. ● *adj.* that acts as an antiperspirant.

antiphon /ˈæntɪˌfɒn/ *n.* **1** a hymn or psalm, the parts of which are sung or recited alternately by two groups. **2** a versicle or phrase from this. **3** a Biblical verse sung or recited at a specific moment in a Christian liturgy, e.g. at the beginning of the Mass or before Communion. **4** a response.

antiphonal /ænˈtɪfənəl/ ● *adj.* **1** sung or recited alternately by two groups. **2** responsive, answering. ● *n.* a collection of antiphons. □ **antiphonally** *adv.*

antipode /ˈæntɪˌpoːd/ *n.* the exact opposite.

antipodes /ænˈtɪpəˌdiːz/ *n.pl.* **1** places on opposite sides of the earth to each other. **2** (**Antipodes**) Australia and New Zealand. **3** (usu. foll. by *of*) the exact opposite. □ **antipodal** *adj.* **antipodean** *adj. & n.*

antipope *n.* a person set up as pope in opposition to one (held by others to be) canonically chosen.

antiproton *n. Physics* the negatively charged antiparticle of a proton.

antiquarian /ˌæntɪˈkweriən/ ● *adj.* **1** of or dealing in antiques or rare books. **2** of the study of antiquities. ● *n.* an antiquary. □ **antiquarianism** *n.*

antiquary /ˈæntɪˌkweri/ *n.* (*pl.* **-ies**) a student or collector of antiques or antiquities.

antiquated /ˈæntɪˌkweitəd/ *adj.* out of date.

antique ● *n.* an object of considerable age, esp. an item of furniture or the decorative arts having a high value. ● *adj.* **1** of or existing from an early date. **2** old-fashioned, archaic. **3** of ancient times. ● *v.* (**antiques, antiqued, antiquing**) **1** *tr.* give an antique appearance to (furniture etc.) by artificial means. **2** *intr.* (usu. as **antiquing** *n.*) shop for antiques.

antiquity *n.* (*pl.* **-ies**) **1** ancient times, esp. the period before the Middle Ages. **2** great age (*a city of great antiquity*). **3** (usu. in *pl.*) physical remains or relics from ancient times, esp. buildings and works of art. **4** (in *pl.*) customs, events, etc., of ancient times. **5** the people of ancient times regarded collectively.

anti-racism *n.* the policy or practice of opposing racism and promoting racial tolerance. □ **anti-racist** *n. & adj.*

anti-Semite /ˌæntiˈsemaɪt/ *n.* a person hostile to or prejudiced against Jews. □ **anti-Semitic** /-səˈmɪtɪk/ *adj.* **anti-Semitism** /-ˈsemɪˌtɪzəm/ *n.*

antiseptic ● *adj.* **1** counteracting sepsis esp. by preventing the growth of disease-causing micro-organisms. **2** sterile or free from contamination. **3** lacking character or emotion; dispassionate. ● *n.* an antiseptic agent. □ **antiseptically** *adv.*

antiserum *n.* (*pl.* **antisera**) a blood serum containing antibodies against specific antigens, injected to treat or protect against specific diseases.

anti-social *adj.* **1** opposed or contrary to normal social instincts or practices. **2** not sociable; unfriendly toward others.

antithesis /ænˈtɪθəsɪs/ *n.* (*pl.* **antitheses** /-ˌsiːz/) **1** (foll. by *of, to*) the direct opposite. **2** (usu. foll. by *of, between*) contrast or opposition between two things. **3** a contrast of ideas expressed by parallelism of strongly contrasted words.

antithetical /ˌæntɪˈθetɪkəl/ *adj.* (also **antithetic**) **1** contrasted, opposite. **2** connected with, containing, or using antithesis. □ **antithetically** *adv.*

antitoxin *n.* an antibody that counteracts a toxin. □ **antitoxic** *adj.*

antitrust *adj. US* (of a law etc.) opposed to or controlling trusts or other monopolies (see TRUST *n.* 9).

antitussive /ˈæntɪˌtʌsɪv/ *Pharm.* ● *adj.* suppressing coughing. ● *n.* an antitussive drug or treatment.

antivenin /ˌæntiˈvenin/ *n.* (also **antivenom** /-ˈvenəm/) an antiserum containing antibodies against specific poisons in the venom of esp. snakes, spiders, scorpions, etc.

antiviral *adj.* effective against viruses.

antler *n.* **1** each of the branched horns of a (usu. male) deer. **2** a branch of this. □ **antlered** *adj.*

antonym /ˈæntənɪm/ *n.* a word opposite in meaning to another, e.g. *bad* and *good* (opp. SYNONYM).

antsy *adj. N Amer. informal* agitated, impatient, or fidgety.

anus *n.* (*pl.* **anuses**) the excretory opening at the end of the alimentary canal.

anvil *n.* **1** a block (usu. of iron) with a flat top, concave sides, and often a pointed end, on which metals are worked in forging. **2** something that resembles an anvil in appearance or use.

anxiety *n.* (*pl.* **-ies**) **1** the state of being anxious. **2** concern about an imminent danger, difficulty, etc. **3** (usu. foll. by *to* + infin.) anxious desire. **4** a thing that causes anxiety. **5** *Psych.* a nervous disorder characterized by a state of excessive uneasiness.

anxious *adj.* **1** worried or troubled; uneasy in the mind. **2** causing or marked by anxiety (*an anxious moment*). **3** disputed (usu. foll. by *to* + infin.) earnestly desiring; eager (*anxious for you to succeed*). ¶Many claim that *anxious* should not be used to mean *eager*, but this use is well established, and standard since the 18th c. □ **anxiously** *adv.* **anxiousness** *n.*

any ● *adj.* **1** (with *interrog., neg.,* or conditional expressed or implied) **a** one, no matter which, of several (*cannot find any answer*). **b** some, no matter how much or many or of what sort (*do you have any sugar?*). **2** a minimal amount of (*hardly any difference*). **3** whichever is chosen (*any fool knows that*). **4 a** an appreciable or significant (*did not stay for any length of time*). **b** a very large (*has any amount of money*). ● *pron.* **1** any one (*did not know any of them*). **2** any number (*are any of them yours?*). **3** any amount (*is there any left?*). ● *adv.* (usu. with neg. or interrog.) at all, in some degree (*is that any good?; do not make it any larger*). □ **any time** (or **day** or **minute** etc.) **now** *informal* at any time in the near future.

anybody *n. & pron.* **1 a** a person, no matter who. **b** a person of any kind. **c** whatever person is chosen. **2** a person of importance (*he isn't anybody*).

anyhow *adv.* **1** anyway. **2** in a disorderly manner or state (*just does his work anyhow*).

anymore *adv.* (also **any more**) **1** any longer; to any further extent (*don't like you anymore*). **2** *N Amer. informal* nowadays (*almost everyone has a TV anymore*). ¶In Canada, the positive use of *anymore* is strongest in rural Southern Ontario. ¶Always written as two words when specifying quantity, as in *can't eat any more food*.

anyone *pron.* anybody. ¶Written as two words when specifying a numerical sense, as in *any one of us can*.

anyplace *adv. N Amer. informal* anywhere.

anything ● *pron.* **1** a thing, no matter which. **2** a thing of any kind. **3** whatever thing is chosen. ● *adv.* (usu. foll. by *like*) in any way whatsoever; at all (*doesn't sound anything like Mozart*). □ **anything but** not at all (*was anything but honest*). **like anything** *informal* with great vigour, intensity, etc.

any time *adv.* (also **anytime**) *esp. N Amer.* at any time.

anyway *adv.* **1** in any way or manner. **2** at any rate. **3** (also *N Amer. informal* **anyways**) in any case. **4** to resume (*anyway, as I was saying*).

anywhere ● *adv.* **1** in or to any place. **2** designating any quantity etc. within a specified range (*anywhere from $10 to $20.*) **3** to any extent (*is it anywhere near full?*). ● *pron.* any place (*anywhere will do*).

Anzac *n.* **1** *hist.* a soldier in the Australian and New Zealand Army Corps (1914–18). **2** any member of the armed services of Australia or New Zealand.

AOB *abbr.* any other business.

A-OK *abbr. N Amer. informal* excellent; in good order.

AOR *abbr. Music* ALBUM-ORIENTED ROCK.

aorta /eɪˈɔːrtə/ *n.* (*pl.* **aortas**) the main artery, giving rise to the arterial network through which oxygenated blood is supplied to the body from the heart. □ **aortic** *adj.*

AP *abbr.* AMERICAN PLAN.

A/P *abbr.* accounts payable.

apace *adv.* swiftly, quickly.

Apache /əˈpætʃi/ ● *n.* **1** (*pl.* same or **-s**) a member of an Aboriginal people living in the southwestern US, primarily in Arizona and New Mexico. **2** the Athapaskan language of the Apache. ● *adj.* of or relating to the Apache or their culture or language.

apart *adv.* **1** separately; not together (*keep your feet apart*). **2** into pieces (*came apart*). **3** to or on one side; aside (*set apart from the rest*). **4** to or at a distance (*ten kilometres apart*). **5** from one another (*can't tell the twins apart*). □ **apart from 1** except for. **2** in addition to (*apart from roses we grow irises*). □ **apartness** *n.*

apartheid /əˈpɑːrteɪt, -taɪd, -teɪt/ *n.* **1** *hist.* the South African policy of segregation and discrimination against non-whites. **2** segregation or discrimination in other contexts.

apartment *n.* **1** *N Amer.* **a** one or more rooms rented and used as a residence, esp. in a building with other similar dwellings. **b** = APARTMENT BUILDING. **2** (usu. in *pl.*) a room in a house.

apartment building *n.* (also **apartment block**, *esp. US* **apartment house**) a building other than a house divided into several apartments.

apartment hotel *n. N Amer.* a hotel with furnished suites of rooms including kitchens, for short-term or long-term rental.

apathetic /ˌæpəˈθetɪk/ *adj.* having or showing no emotion or interest. □ **apathetically** *adv.*

apathy /ˈæpəθi/ *n.* indifference.

apatite /ˈæpətaɪt/ *n.* a naturally occurring crystalline mineral of calcium phosphate and fluoride, used in the manufacture of fertilizers.

APB *abbr. US* ALL-POINTS BULLETIN.

APC *abbr.* ARMOURED PERSONNEL CARRIER.

ape ● *n.* **1** any of the various primates of the family Pongidae characterized by the absence of a tail, e.g. the gorilla, chimpanzee, or gibbon. **2** (in general use)

any monkey. **3** an imitator. **4** a clumsy, coarse, or stupid person. ● *v.tr.* imitate, mimic. □ **go ape** *slang* become crazy.

APEC /ˈeɪpek/ *abbr.* **1** Asia-Pacific Economic Co-operation Conference. **2** Atlantic Provinces Economic Council. **3** Alliance for the Preservation of English in Canada.

ape man *n.* any of various apelike primates held to be forerunners of present-day humans.

aperçu /ˌæperˈsuː/ *n.* **1** a summary or survey. **2** an insight.

aperitif /əˌperɪˈtiːf/ *n.* an alcoholic drink taken before a meal to stimulate the appetite.

aperture /ˈæpərˌtʃər/ *n.* **1** an opening; a gap. **2** a space through which light passes in an optical or photographic instrument.

Apex /ˈeɪpeks/ *n.* (also **APEX**) a system of reduced fares for scheduled airline flights when paid for before a certain period in advance of departure.

apex /ˈeɪpeks/ *n.* (*pl.* **apices** /ˈeɪpɪˌsiːz/ or **apexes**) **1** the highest point. **2** a climax; a high point of achievement etc. **3** the vertex of a triangle or cone. **4** a tip or pointed end.

Apgar score /ˈæpˌɡɑːr/ *n.* an evaluation of the condition of a newborn by allotting up to two points each for heart rate, breathing effort, muscle tone, response to stimulation, and colour.

aphasia /əˈfeɪʒə, -ziə/ *n. Med.* the loss of ability to understand or express speech, owing to brain damage. □ **aphasic** /əˈfeɪzɪk/ *adj. & n.*

aphid /ˈeɪfɪd, ˈæfɪd/ *n.* any small homopterous insect which feeds by sucking sap from leaves, stems, or roots of plants.

aphis /ˈeɪfɪs, ˈæfɪs/ *n.* (*pl.* **aphides** /-ˌdiːz/) an aphid, esp. of the genus *Aphis*.

aphorism /ˈæfəˌrɪzəm/ *n.* **1** a short pithy maxim. **2** a brief statement of a principle. □ **aphoristic** *adj.*

aphrodisiac /ˌæfrəˈdiːziæk, ˌæfrəˈdɪzi,æk/ ● *adj.* that arouses sexual desire. ● *n.* an aphrodisiac substance.

API *abbr. Computing* application program interface.

apiary /ˈeɪpiˌeri/ *n.* (*pl.* **-ies**) a place where bees are kept. □ **apiarist** *n.*

apical /ˈeɪpɪkəl, ˈæp-/ *adj.* of, at, or forming an apex.

apices *pl. of* APEX.

apiece *adv.* for each one; severally (*ten dollars apiece*).

aplenty *adv.* in great quantity (*bargains aplenty*).

aplomb /əˈplɒm/ *n.* assurance; self-confidence.

apnea /æpˈniːə/ *n.* (also *esp. Brit.* **apnoea**) *Med.* a temporary cessation of breathing.

apocalypse /əˈpɒkəlɪps/ *n.* **1** catastrophic destruction, esp. the end of the world. **2** a revelation, esp. of the end of the world.

apocalyptic /əˌpɒkəˈlɪptɪk/ *adj.* **1** of or resembling the Apocalypse. **2** revelatory, prophetic. □ **apocalyptically** *adv.*

Apocrypha /əˈpɒkrɪfə/ *n.pl.* **1** those books of the Septuagint version of the Hebrew Scriptures which were later rejected from the Jewish canon; most are considered canonical by the Catholic and Orthodox Churches, but are not included in the Protestant Bible. **2** (**apocrypha**) writings or reports not considered genuine.

apocryphal *adj.* **1** of doubtful authenticity. **2** invented, mythical (*an apocryphal story*). **3** of or belonging to the Apocrypha.

apogee /ˈæpəˌdʒiː/ *n.* **1** the point in a celestial body's orbit where it is furthest from the earth (opp. PERIGEE). **2** the highest or most distant point; maximum.

apolitical /ˌeipəˈlɪtɪkəl/ *adj.* **1** not interested in or concerned with politics. **2** without political bias.

Apollonian /ˌæpəˈloːniən/ *adj.* **1** of or relating to Apollo, the sun god and patron of music and poetry. **2** orderly, rational, self-disciplined.

apologetic ● *adj.* **1** regretfully acknowledging or excusing an offence or failure. **2** diffident. **3** of reasoned defence or vindication. ● *n.* (usu. in *pl.*) **1** a reasoned defence, esp. of Christianity. **2** the branch of theology concerned with this. □ **apologetically** *adv.*

apologia /ˌæpəˈloːdʒiə/ *n.* a formal defence of one's opinions or conduct.

apologist /əˈpɒlədʒɪst/ *n.* a person who defends something by argument.

apologize *v.intr.* make an apology; express regret.

apology *n.* (*pl.* **-ies**) **1** a regretful acknowledgement of an offence or failure. **2** an assurance that no offence was intended. **3** an explanation or defence. **4** (foll. by *for*) a poor or scanty specimen of (*this apology for a letter*).

apophthegm /ˈæpəˌθem, ˈæpəfˌθem/ *n.* a terse saying or maxim; an aphorism.

apoplectic /ˌæpəˈplektɪk/ *adj.* **1** of, causing, suffering, or liable to apoplexy. **2** *informal* enraged. □ **apoplectically** *adv.*

apoplexy /ˈæpəˌpleksi/ *n.* a sudden loss of consciousness, voluntary movement, and sensation caused by blockage or rupture of a brain artery; a stroke.

apostasy /əˈpɒstəsi/ *n.* (*pl.* **-ies**) **1** renunciation of a belief or faith, esp. religious. **2** abandonment of principles or of a party. **3** an instance of apostasy.

apostate /əˈpɒsteit/ ● *n.* a person who renounces a former belief etc. ● *adj.* engaged in apostasy. □ **apostatize** /-təˌtaiz/ *v.intr.*

a posteriori /ˌei pɒˌstiriˈɔrai/ ● *adj.* (of reasoning) inductive, empirical; proceeding from effects to causes. ● *adv.* inductively, empirically; from effects to causes (*opp.* A PRIORI).

apostle *n.* **1** (**Apostle**) **a** any of a group of followers of Christ made up of the twelve disciples and Paul and Barnabas, sent out to preach the gospel after the Resurrection. **b** the first successful Christian missionary in a country or to a people. **2** a leader or outstanding figure, esp. of a reform movement (*apostle of temperance*). **3** a messenger or representative. **4** one of the twelve administrative officials of Mormonism. □ **apostleship** *n.*

Apostles' Creed *n.* a Christian creed dating from the 4th c., traditionally ascribed to the Apostles, and now used in many Christian liturgies.

apostolate /əˈpɒstələt/ *n.* **1** the position or authority of an Apostle. **2** an organization dedicated to a religion or doctrine.

apostolic /ˌæpəˈstɒlɪk/ *adj.* **1** of or relating to the Apostles. **2** of the Pope regarded as the successor of St. Peter. **3** of the character of an Apostle.

Apostolic Fathers *n.pl.* the Christian leaders immediately succeeding the Apostles.

apostrophe¹ *n.* a punctuation mark used to indicate: **1** the omission of letters or numbers, e.g. *can't*; *he's*; *1 Jan. '97.* **2** the possessive case (e.g. *Dad's book*; *boys' coats*).

apostrophe² *n.* an exclamatory passage in a speech or poem, addressed to a person (often dead or absent) or thing. □ **apostrophize** *v.tr. & intr.*

apothecaries' measure *n.* (also **apothecaries' weight**) units of weight and liquid volume formerly used in pharmacy.

apothecary /əˈpɒθəˌkeri/ *n.* (*pl.* **-ies**) *hist.* a person licensed to dispense medicines and drugs.

apothegm *var. of* APOPHTHEGM.

apotheosis /əˌpɒθiˈoːsɪs/ *n.* (*pl.* **apotheoses** /-siːz/) **1** elevation to divine status; deification. **2** a glorification of a thing; a sublime example (*apotheosis of the dance*). **3** a deified ideal.

app *n.* esp. *N Amer. Computing informal* application.

app. *abbr.* **1** appendix. **2** appeal.

Appalachian /ˌæpəˈleiʃən/ ● *adj.* **1** of or relating to the Appalachian Mountains in the eastern US. **2** of or relating to the region or people of Appalachia in eastern N America. ● *n.* a native or inhabitant of Appalachia.

appall *v.tr.* (also **appal**) (**appalled, appalling**) greatly dismay or horrify.

appalling *adj. informal* shocking, unpleasant; bad. □ **appallingly** *adv.*

Appaloosa /ˌæpəˈluːsə/ *n.* a N American breed of horse, having dark spots on a light background.

apparat /ˌæpəˈræt/ *n.* the administrative system of a Communist party, esp. in a Communist country.

apparatchik /ˌæpəˈrætʃɪk/ *n.* **1 a** a member of a Communist apparat. **b** a Communist agent or spy. **2 a** a member of a political party in any country who executes policy; a zealous functionary. **b** an official of a public or private organization.

apparatus /ˌæpəˈrætəs, ˌæpəˈreitəs/ *n.* **1** the equipment needed for a particular purpose or function, esp. scientific or technical. **2** complex structure of an organization (*apparatus of government*). **3** *Anat.* the organs used to perform a particular process (*digestive apparatus*).

apparel *n.* clothing, dress.

apparent *adj.* **1** readily visible or perceivable. **2** seeming. □ **apparently** *adv.*

apparition /ˌæpəˈrɪʃən/ *n.* **1** a sudden or dramatic appearance, esp. of a ghost. **2** a visible ghost.

appeal ● *v.* **1** *intr.* make an earnest or formal request; plead (*appealed for calm*). **2** *intr.* (usu. foll. by *to*) be attractive or of interest; be pleasing. **3** *intr.* (foll. by *to*) resort to or cite for support. **4** *Law* **a** *intr.* (often foll. by *to*) apply (to a higher court) for a reconsideration of the decision of a lower court. **b** *tr.* refer to a higher court to review (a case). **c** *intr.* (foll. by *against*) apply to a higher court to reconsider (a verdict or sentence). **5** *tr. & intr.* request a review of (a decision) by an authority. ● *n.* **1** the act or an instance of appealing. **2** a formal or urgent request for public support, esp. financial, for a cause. **3** *Law* the referral of a case to a higher court. **4** attractiveness; appealing quality (*sex appeal*).

appealing *adj.* attractive, likeable. □ **appealingly** *adv.*

appear *v.intr.* **1** become or be visible. **2** be evident (*a new problem then appeared*). **3** seem; have the appearance of being (*appeared healthy*). **4** present oneself publicly or formally, esp. on stage or as the accused or counsel in a law court. **5** be published (*it appeared in the papers*).

appearance *n.* **1** the act or an instance of appearing. **2** an outward form as perceived (whether correctly or not), esp. visually. **3** a semblance (*gives the appearance of trying hard*). □ **keep up appearances** maintain an impression or pretense of affluence, virtue, etc. **make** (or **put in**) **an appearance** be present, esp. briefly. **to all appearances** as far as can be seen; apparently.

appearance notice *n. Cdn Law* a written form given by a police officer to an accused person at the scene of the crime, stating the date, time, and place that the accused must appear in court.

appease v.tr. **1** make calm or quiet, esp. conciliate (a potential aggressor) by making concessions. **2** satisfy (an appetite, scruples, etc.). □ **appeasement** n. **appeaser** n.

appellant / ə'pelənt / n. Law a person who appeals to a higher court.

appellate / ə'pelət / adj. Law (esp. of a court) concerned with or dealing with appeals.

appellation / ˌæpə'leɪʃən / n. formal a name or title; nomenclature.

appellation contrôlée / ˌæpela'sjɔ̃ ˌkɔ̃tro:'lei / n. a guarantee of the origin of a French wine (or other food) in conformity with statutory regulations.

append v.tr. (usu. foll. by to) attach, affix, add, esp. to a written document etc.

appendage n. **1** something attached; an addition. **2** Zool. a leg or other projecting part of an arthropod.

appendectomy n. (pl. **-ies**) the surgical removal of the appendix.

appendicitis n. inflammation of the appendix.

appendix n. (pl. **appendices** or **appendixes**) **1** Anat. a small outgrowth of tissue forming a tube-shaped sac attached to the lower end of the large intestine. **2** subsidiary matter at the end of a book or document.

appetite n. **1** a desire for food. **2** a natural desire to satisfy bodily needs, esp. for sexual activity. **3** (usu. foll. by for) an inclination or desire.

appetizer n. a small amount of food or drink which stimulates the appetite before a meal.

appetizing adj. pleasing; stimulating an appetite, esp. for food. □ **appetizingly** adv.

applaud v. **1** intr. to clap as an expression of strong approval or praise. **2** tr. express approval of (a person or action).

applause n. **1** clapping etc. as an expression of approbation. **2** emphatic approval.

apple n. **1** the fruit of a tree of the genus Malus, rounded in form and with a crisp flesh. **2** (in full **apple tree**) the tree bearing this. **3** N Amer. the most prominent part of the cheek, over the cheekbone and below the eye. **4** N Amer. slang derogatory an Aboriginal person who is seen (esp. by other Aboriginals) as part of the white establishment. □ **apples and oranges** irreconcilably different issues etc., esp. when in comparison. **apple of one's eye** a cherished person or thing. **upset the apple cart** spoil careful plans.

apple butter n. N Amer. a jam-like spread made from stewed spiced apples.

apple-cheeked adj. having round, rosy cheeks.

apple cider n. N Amer. see CIDER 1.

apple green ● n. a yellow-green colour like that of a green apple. ● adj. of this colour.

applejack n. N Amer. a spirit distilled from fermented apple juice.

apple pandowdy n. esp. US a baked pudding of sliced apples topped with a tea-biscuit crust.

apple pie n. **1** any of various pies with a filling of apples. **2** US (attrib.) embodying qualities thought to be American.

apple-pie order n. perfect order; extreme neatness.

applesauce n. **1** a purée of stewed apples, often served with pork or as a dessert. **2** N Amer. informal nonsense.

appliance n. **1** an electrical or gas-powered device or piece of equipment used for a specific task, esp. for

domestic tasks such as washing dishes etc. **2** a prosthetic or orthodontic device.

applicable adj. **1** that may be applied. **2** having reference; appropriate. □ **applicability** n. **applicably** adv.

applicant n. a person who applies for something.

application n. **1** the act or an instance of applying. **2** a formal request, usu. in writing, for employment, membership, etc. **3 a** relevance. **b** the use to which something can or should be put. **4** sustained or concentrated effort; diligence. **5** a task that a computer can be programmed to do.

applicator n. **1** a device for applying a substance to a surface. **2** a device to aid insertion of something, e.g. a tampon, into a body orifice. **3** a person who applies something, such as pesticide or paint.

applied adj. (of a subject of study) put to practical use as opposed to being theoretical (compare PURE adj. 9).

appliqué / 'æplɪkeɪ / ● n. ornamental work in which fabric is cut out and attached, usu. sewn, to the surface of another fabric to form pictures or patterns. ● adj. executed in appliqué. ● v.tr. (**appliqués, appliquéd, appliquéing**) decorate with appliqué; make using appliqué technique.

apply v. (**-ies, -ied**) **1** intr. (often foll. by for, to, or to + infin.) make a formal request for something to be done, given, etc. **2** intr. have relevance (does not apply in this case). **3** tr. **a** make use of as relevant or suitable; employ (apply the rules). **b** operate (apply the brake). **4** tr. (often foll. by to) **a** put or spread on (applied the ointment to the cut). **b** administer (applied common sense to the problem). **5** refl. devote oneself (applied myself to the task). □ **applier** n.

appoint v.tr. **1** assign a post or office to (appoint him treasurer). **2** (often foll. by for) fix, decide on (a time, place, etc.) (8:30 was the appointed time). **3** prescribe; ordain (the Bible as appointed to be read in churches). **4** Law **a** declare the destination of (property etc.). **b** declare (a person) as having an interest in property etc. (Jones was appointed in the will). □ **appointee** n.

appointed adj. equipped, furnished (well-appointed).

appointive adj. N Amer. depending on or filled by appointment (the Canadian Senate is appointive).

appointment n. **1** an arrangement to meet at a specific time and place. **2 a** a post or office available for applicants, or recently filled. **b** a person appointed. **3** (usu. in pl.) **a** furniture, fittings. **b** equipment.

apportion / ə'pɔrʃən / v.tr. (often foll. by to) share out; assign as a share. □ **apportionment** n.

apposite / 'æpəzɪt / adj. (often foll. by to) **1** apt; well chosen. **2** well expressed. □ **appositely** adv. **appositeness** n.

apposition n. **1** placing side by side; juxtaposition. **2** Grammar the placing of a word next to another, esp. the addition of one noun to another, in order to qualify or explain the first, e.g. William the Conqueror; my friend Sue. □ **appositive** / ə'pɒzɪtɪv / adj. & n.

appraisal n. the act or an instance of appraising.

appraise v.tr. **1** estimate the quality or worth of. **2** evaluate the price of (property, jewellery, etc.). **3** consider (a situation etc.) so as to make a judgment. □ **appraisable** adj. **appraisingly** adv.

appraiser n. a person who assesses the worth or value of something, esp. of property, jewellery, etc.

appreciable adj. large enough to be noticed; significant; considerable. □ **appreciably** adv.

appreciate v. **1** tr. **a** esteem highly; value. **b** be grateful for (we appreciate your sympathy). **c** be sensitive to (appreciate the nuances). **2** tr. (often foll. by that +

clause) understand; recognize (*I appreciate that I may be wrong*). **3 a** *intr.* (of property etc.) rise in value. **b** *tr.* raise in value. □ **appreciative** *adj.* **appreciatively** *adv.* **appreciativeness** *n.*

appreciation *n.* **1** favourable or grateful recognition. **2** an estimation or judgment; sensitive understanding of or reaction to (*a quick appreciation of the problem; music appreciation*). **3** an increase in value. **4** a (usu. favourable) review of a book, film, etc.

apprehend *v.tr.* **1** understand, perceive (*apprehend your meaning*). **2** seize, arrest (*apprehended the criminal*). **3** anticipate with uneasiness or fear (*apprehending the results*).

apprehensible *adj.* capable of being apprehended by the senses or the intellect. □ **apprehensibility** *n.*

apprehension *n.* **1** uneasiness; dread. **2** grasp, understanding. **3** arrest, capture (*apprehension of the suspect*). **4** an idea; a conception.

apprehensive *adj.* **1** (often foll. by *of, for*) uneasily fearful; dreading. **2** relating to perception by the senses or the intellect. □ **apprehensively** *adv.* **apprehensiveness** *n.*

apprentice ● *n.* **1** (often *attrib.*) a person who is learning a trade by being employed in it for an agreed period, usu. at lower wages than is normal for that trade. **2** a beginner; a novice. ● *v.* **1** *tr.* engage or bind as an apprentice (*was apprenticed to a builder*). **2** *intr.* N Amer. serve as an apprentice. □ **apprenticeship** *n.*

apprise *v.tr.* inform. □ **be apprised of** be aware of.

approach ● *v.* **1** *tr.* come near or nearer to (a place or time). **2** *intr.* come near or nearer in space or time (*the hour approaches*). **3** *tr.* make a tentative proposal or suggestion to (*approached me about a loan*). **4** *tr.* **a** be similar in character, quality, etc., to (*doesn't approach her for artistic skill*). **b** approximate to; be slightly less than (*a population approaching 5 million*). **5** *tr.* set about (a task etc.). **6** *intr.* (of an aircraft etc.) prepare to land. **7** *intr.* Golf play an approach shot. ● *n.* **1** an act or means of approaching (*made an approach; an approach lined with trees*). **2** an approximation (*an approach to an apology*). **3** a way of dealing with a person or thing (*needs a new approach*). **4** (usu. in *pl.*) a sexual advance. **5** the final part of a flight before landing. **6** Golf a stroke from the fairway to the green.

approachable *adj.* **1** friendly; easy to talk to. **2** able to be approached. □ **approachability** *n.*

approbation /ˌæprəˈbeɪʃən/ *n.* approval, consent. □ **approbative** /ˈæprəˌbeɪtɪv/ *adj.* **approbatory** *adj.*

appropriate ● *adj.* (often foll. by *to, for*) suitable or proper. ● *v.tr.* **1** take possession of, esp. without authority. **2** devote (money etc.) to special purposes. □ **appropriately** *adv.* **appropriateness** *n.* **appropriation** *n.* **appropriator** *n.*

approval *n.* **1** the act of approving. **2** a favourable opinion (*looked at him with approval*). □ **on approval** (of goods supplied) to be returned if not satisfactory.

approve *v.* **1** *tr.* confirm; declare acceptable. **2** *intr.* give or have a favourable opinion. **3** *tr.* commend (*approved the new hat*). □ **approve of 1** pronounce or consider good or satisfactory; commend. **2** agree to. □ **approvingly** *adv.*

approx. *abbr.* **1** approximate. **2** approximately.

approximate ● *adj.* **1** fairly correct or accurate (*an approximate guess*). **2** near or next (*your approximate neighbour*). ● *v.tr. & intr.* **1** (often foll. by *to*) bring or come near, esp. in quality, number, etc. (*approximates to the truth*). **2** estimate (*approximate the distance to be a kilometre*). □ **approximately** *adv.*

approximation *n.* **1** an act or instance of approximating or bringing close. **2** an estimate, guess, or result that is approximately correct, or close enough for a particular purpose.

appt. *abbr.* appointment.

appurtenance /əˈpɜːtɪnəns/ *n.* (usu. in *pl.*) a belonging; an appendage; an accessory.

APR *abbr.* annual or annualized percentage rate (esp. of interest on loans or credit).

Apr. *abbr.* April.

après-ski /ˌæpreɪˈskiː/ ● *n.* the evening, esp. its social activities, following a day's skiing. ● *attrib.adj.* (of clothes, drinks, etc.) appropriate to social activities following skiing.

apricot /ˈæprɪˌkɒt, ˈeɪp-/ ● *n.* **1 a** a juicy soft fruit, similar to but smaller than a peach, of an orange-yellow colour. **b** the tree, *Prunus armeniaca*, bearing it. **2** the ripe fruit's orange-yellow colour. ● *adj.* orange-yellow (*apricot dress*).

April *n.* the fourth month of the year.

April Fool *n.* a person successfully tricked on April 1.

April Fool's Day *n.* April 1, traditionally a day on which people play practical jokes on one another.

a priori /ˌeɪ praɪˈɔːraɪ/ ● *adj.* **1** (of reasoning) deductive; proceeding from causes to effects (opp. A POSTERIORI). **2** (of concepts, knowledge, etc.) logically independent of experience; not derived from experience (opp. EMPIRICAL). **3** not submitted to critical investigation (*an a priori conjecture*). ● *adv.* **1** in an a priori manner. **2** as far as one knows; presumptively.

apron *n.* **1 a** a garment worn to protect the front of a person's clothes from dirt or damage, fastened at the back. **b** a similar garment worn as part of official or ceremonial dress (*Freemason's apron*). **2** Theatre the part of a stage in front of the curtain. **3** the hard-surfaced area on an airfield used for manoeuvring or loading aircraft. □ **tied to a person's apron strings** dominated by or dependent on that person (usu. a woman). □ **aproned** *adj.*

apropos /ˌæprəˈpoʊ, ˈæprəˌpoʊ/ ● *adj.* to the point or purpose; appropriate (*her comment was apropos*). ● *prep. informal* (often foll. by *of*) with respect to; concerning (*apropos the meeting; apropos of the talk*). ● *adv.* **1** appropriately (*spoke apropos*). **2** by the way; incidentally (*apropos, she's not going*).

apse *n.* a large semicircular or polygonal recess, arched or with a domed roof, esp. at the eastern end of a church. □ **apsidal** /ˈæpsɪdəl/ *adj.*

apt *adj.* **1** appropriate, suitable. **2 a** having a tendency, inclined (*he is too apt to lose his temper*). **b** likely (*there is apt to be local interest*). **3** clever; quick to learn (*an apt pupil*). □ **aptly** *adv.* **aptness** *n.*

apt. *abbr.* N Amer. apartment.

aptitude *n.* **1** a natural propensity or talent. **2** ability to learn or understand; intelligence.

aptitude test *n.* a test designed to determine a person's aptitude for a particular task or occupation.

aqua /ˈækwə, ˈɒ-/ ● *n.* the colour aquamarine. ● *adj.* of this colour.

aquaculture /ˈækwəˌkʌltʃər, ˈɒkwə-/ *n.* the cultivation or rearing of fish or aquatic plants for human consumption. □ **aquaculturist** *n.*

aqualung /ˈækwəˌlʌŋ/ *n.* = SCUBA n. 1.

aquamarine /ˌækwəməˈriːn/ ● *n.* **1** a light bluish-green beryl. **2** its colour. ● *adj.* of this colour.

aquarium *n.* (*pl.* **-s** or **aquaria**) **1** a tank of water with transparent sides containing fish or other live aquatic animals and plants. **2** a building in which live aquatic animals are exhibited and studied.

Aquarius *n.* **1** a constellation between Pisces and Capricorn, traditionally regarded as contained in the figure of a water carrier. **2 a** the eleventh sign of the zodiac. **b** a person born when the sun is in this sign, usu. between Jan. 22 and Feb. 18. ☐ **Aquarian** adj. & n.

aquatic /əˈkwɒtɪk, əˈkwætɪk/ ● adj. **1** of or relating to water. **2** growing or living in or near water. **3** (of a sport) played in or on water. ● n. **1** an aquatic plant or animal. **2** (in pl.) aquatic sports.

aqueduct /ˈækwəˌdʌkt/ n. an artificial channel for conveying water, esp. in the form of a bridge supported by tall columns across a valley.

aqueous /ˈeikwiəs/ adj. **1** of, containing, or like water. **2** Chem. dissolved in water (aqueous formaldehyde). **3** Geol. created from sediments laid down in water (aqueous rocks).

aquifer /ˈækwɪfər/ n. Geol. a layer of permeable rock able to store significant quantities of water, through which groundwater moves.

AR abbr. Arkansas (in postal use).

Ar symbol argon.

A/R abbr. ACCOUNT RECEIVABLE.

Arab /ˈerəb, ˈærəb/ ● n. **1** a member of a Semitic people originally inhabiting Saudi Arabia and the neighbouring countries, now the Middle East generally. **2** = ARABIAN n. 2. ● adj. of Arabia in the Middle East or the Arabs.

arabesque /ˌærəˈbesk, ˌerə-/ n. **1** Dance & Figure Skating **a** a posture with one leg extended straight backwards and elevated (compare ATTITUDE 2c). **b** a position of the arms in which they are fully extended to the front or side, with the palms facing downwards. **2** a design of intertwined leaves etc.

Arabian ● adj. of or relating to Arabia (the Arabian desert). ● n. **1** a native of Arabia. ¶Now less common than **Arab** in this sense. **2** (in full **Arabian horse**) a breed of horse developed in Arabia, renowned for its speed, intelligence and mild disposition.

Arabian camel n. a domesticated camel with one hump, Camelus dromedarius, native to the deserts of N Africa and Arabia.

Arabic ● n. **1** the Semitic language of the Arabs, now spoken in much of N Africa and the Middle East. **2** = GUM ARABIC. ● adj. of or relating to Arabia.

arabica /əˈræbɪkə/ n. **1** coffee or coffee beans from the most widely grown species of coffee plant, Coffea arabica. **2** the plant itself.

Arabic numeral n. any of the numerals 0, 1, 2, 3, 4, 5, 6, 7, 8, and 9 (compare ROMAN NUMERAL).

Arabist /ˈerəbɪst, ˈærə-/ n. **1** a student of Arabic civilization, language, etc. **2** a supporter of Arab nationalism or political self-assertion.

arable /ˈerəbəl, ˈærə-/ ● adj. **1** (of land) plowed, or suitable for plowing and crop production. **2** that can be grown on arable land. ● n. arable land or crops.

arachnid /əˈræknɪd/ n. any arthropod of the class Arachnida, having four pairs of walking legs and characterized by simple eyes, e.g. spiders, scorpions, mites, and ticks.

arachnoid /əˈræknɔɪd/ ● n. Anat. (in full **arachnoid membrane**) one of the three membranes (see MENINGES) that surround the brain and spinal cord of vertebrates. ● adj. **1** Bot. covered with long cobweb-like hairs. **2** of or relating to arachnids.

arak /əˈræk/ n. a Middle Eastern alcoholic spirit, esp. distilled from coco sap or rice.

-arama /ərɑmə/ comb. form = -RAMA.

Aramaic /ˌerəˈmeɪk, ˌærə-/ ● n. a branch of the Semitic family of languages, esp. the language of Syria used as a lingua franca in the Near East from the 6th c. BC, later dividing into varieties. ● adj. of or in Aramaic.

Aran /ˈerən, ˈæ-/ adj. designating a type of thick knitwear with cable patterns and large diamond designs.

Arawak /ˈerəˌwæk, ˈærə-/ ● n. **1** (pl. same or **-s**) a member of the Aboriginal peoples of the Greater Antilles and northern and western S America, forced out of the Antilles by the Carib Indians shortly before the Spanish expansion into the Caribbean. **2** the family of their languages. ● adj. of the Arawak or their languages. ☐ **Arawakan** adj. & n.

arbiter /ˈɑrbɪtər/ n. **1** = ARBITRATOR. **2** (often foll. by of) a judge; an authority (arbiter of taste). **3** (often foll. by of) a person or organization having entire control of something (supreme arbiter of academic matters).

arbitrage /ˈɑrbɪˌtrɒʒ, -trɑdʒ/ n. the buying and selling of stocks or bills of exchange to take advantage of varying prices in different markets.

arbitrageur /ˌɑrbɪtrɒˈʒɜr/ n. (also **arbitrager** /ˈɑrbɪˌtrɒdʒɜr/) a person who engages in arbitrage.

arbitrary adj. **1** based on the unrestricted will of a person, not according to a scheme or plan; capricious. **2** established at random. **3** despotic. ☐ **arbitrarily** adv. **arbitrariness** n.

arbitration n. Law the hearing and resolution of a dispute by a referee, usu. chosen and agreed upon by all disputants, who has the power to impose a settlement. ☐ **arbitrate** v.tr. & intr.

arbitrator n. a person appointed to settle a dispute, usu. with the power to impose a settlement.

arbor[1] n. an axle or spindle on which something rotates, esp. one holding a cutter in machine tooling.

arbor[2] var. of ARBOUR.

Arbor Day n. (in Canada, the US, Australia, and other countries) a day dedicated annually to public tree planting.

arboreal /ɑrˈbɔriəl/ adj. of, living in, or pertaining to trees.

arboretum /ˌɑrbəˈriːtəm/ n. (pl. **-s** or **arboreta** /-tə/) a botanical garden devoted to trees.

arboriculture /ɑrˈbɔrɪˌkʌltʃər/ n. the cultivation of trees and shrubs. ☐ **arboricultural** adj.

arborio rice /ɑrˈbɔrio:/ n. a plump, short-grained rice, sticky when cooked, often used in risotto and other Italian dishes.

Arborite n. Cdn proprietary a plastic laminate used in countertops, tables, etc.

arborvitae /ˌɑrbərˈviːtai, -ˈvaiti/ n. any of the evergreen conifers of the genus Thuja, including the eastern white cedar and the western red cedar, native to N America and N Asia.

arbour n. (also **arbor**) a shady garden alcove with the sides and roof formed by trees or climbing plants.

arbutus /ɑrˈbjuːtəs/ n. **1** any evergreen tree or shrub of the genus Arbutus, having dark green leaves and clusters of small, fragrant, bell-shaped flowers, esp.: **a** A. menziesii, native to the Pacific coast of N America, with peeling red bark, the only broadleaf evergreen tree native to Canada. **b** A. unedo, native to S Europe, having strawberry-like berries. **2** N Amer. see TRAILING ARBUTUS.

ARC abbr. AIDS-RELATED COMPLEX.

arc ● n. **1** Geom. part of the circumference of a circle or any other curve. **2** any curved shape or course. **3** Electricity a luminous discharge between two electrodes. ● v.intr. (**arced; arcing**) form an arc.

ARCA abbr. Associate of the Royal Canadian Academy (of Arts).

arcade n. **1** Archit. a series of arches supporting or set along a wall. **2** a passageway lined with arches. **3** a public place containing coin-operated game machines. □ **arcaded** adj.

arcade game n. a coin-operated game machine, esp. a video game machine or a pinball machine.

Arcadian /ɑrˈkeidiən/ ● n. an idealized peasant or country dweller, esp. in poetry. ● adj. simple and poetically rural. □ **Arcadianism** n.

arcane adj. mysterious, secret; understood by few.

arcanum /ɑrˈkeinəm/ n. (pl. **arcana** /-nə/) (usu. in pl.) a mystery; a profound secret.

arch[1] ● n. **1 a** a curved structure spanning an opening, acting as a support for a bridge, roof, floor, etc. **b** an arch used in building as an ornament. **c** a monument whose principal feature is an arch. **2** something shaped like an arch, esp. the curved bony structure on the underside of the foot or the arrangement of teeth in the mouth. ● v. **1** tr. form into an arch (the cat arched its back). **2** tr. span like an arch. **3** intr. form an arch. □ **arched** adj.

arch[2] adj. self-consciously or affectedly playful or teasing. □ **archly** adv. **archness** n.

arch- comb. form **1** chief, superior (archbishop). **2** preeminent of its kind, extreme (arch-villain).

Archaean var. of ARCHEAN.

archaeology /ˌɑrkiˈɒlədʒi/ n. the study of human history and prehistory through the excavation of sites and the analysis of physical remains. □ **archaeological** adj. **archaeologist** n.

archaeopteryx /ˌɑrkiˈɒptərɪks/ n. the oldest known fossil bird, Archaeopteryx lithographica, from the Jurassic period, with teeth, feathers, and a reptilian tail.

archaic adj. **1 a** antiquated. **b** (of a word etc.) no longer in ordinary use, though retained for special purposes. **2** primitive. **3** (often **Archaic**) of an early period of art or culture, esp. the 7th and 6th c. BC in Greece. **4** (**Archaic**) of the period in N American societies between 6000 BC and 500 AD. □ **archaically** adv.

archaism /ˈɑrkeiˌɪzəm/ n. **1** the retention or imitation of the old or obsolete, esp. in language or art. **2** an archaic word or expression. □ **archaist** n.

archangel /ˈɑrk,eindʒəl/ n. **1** an angel of the highest rank. **2** Christianity a member of the eighth order of the nine ranks of heavenly beings.

archbishop n. the chief bishop of an ecclesiastical province.

archbishopric n. the office or diocese of an archbishop.

archdeacon n. an Anglican cleric ranking below a bishop, or a member of the clergy of similar rank in other Churches. □ **archdeaconry** n. (pl. **-ies**)

archdiocese n. the diocese of an archbishop. □ **archdiocesan** adj.

archduchess n. hist. the wife or daughter of an Austrian archduke.

archduke n. hist. a chief duke, esp. as the title of a prince of the Austrian Empire. □ **archducal** adj. **archduchy** n. (pl. **-ies**).

Archean /ɑrˈkiːən/ ● adj. of or relating to the earlier part of the Precambrian era, from about 4 billion to 2.5 billion years ago. ● n. this time.

arch-enemy n. (pl. **-ies**) **1** a chief enemy. **2** Satan.

archeology var. of ARCHAEOLOGY.

archeparch /ˈɑrtʃˈepɑrk/ n. an archbishop in an Eastern-Rite Church. □ **archeparchy** n.

archer n. a person who shoots with a bow and arrows.

archery n. shooting with a bow and arrows, esp. as a sport.

archetype n. **1 a** a prototype. **b** a typical specimen. **2** (in Jungian psychology) an inherited primitive mental image, supposed to be present in the collective unconscious. **3** a recurrent symbol or motif in literature etc. □ **archetypal** adj. **archetypical** adj.

Archimedean /ˌɑrkiˈmiːdiən/ adj. of or associated with the Greek mathematician Archimedes (d. 212 BC).

Archimedean screw n. (also **Archimedes' screw**) a device of ancient origin for raising water by means of a rotating spiral tube, or a rotating screw in an inclined cylinder.

Archimedes' principle /ˌɑrkiˈmiːdiːz/ n. the law that a body totally or partially immersed in a fluid is subject to an upward force equal in magnitude to the weight of the fluid it displaces.

archipelago /ˌɑrkiˈpeləgo/ n. (pl. **-os** or **-oes**) **1** a group of islands. **2** a sea with many islands.

architect n. **1** a person who designs buildings and supervises their construction. **2** (foll. by of) a person who brings about a specified thing (architect of economic reform). **3** a landscape architect.

architectonic /ˌɑrkitekˈtɒnik/ ● adj. **1** of or relating to architecture; suggesting architectural design or structure. **2** Metaphysics of or relating to the systematization of knowledge. ● n. (in pl.; usu. treated as sing.) **1** the scientific study of architecture. **2** the study of systematization of knowledge.

architecture n. **1** the art or science of designing and constructing buildings. **2** the style of a building as regards design and construction (Gothic architecture). **3** buildings or other structures collectively. **4** the structure or design of something (the architecture of the human body). **5** the conceptual structure of the various processing elements in a computer or computer system, e.g. memory organization, user interface, etc., and their interconnection. □ **architectural** adj. **architecturally** adv.

architrave /ˈɑrki,treiv/ n. (in classical architecture) a main beam resting across the tops of columns.

archive ● n. **1** (usu. in pl.) a collection of public, corporate or institutional documents or records. **2** (usu. in pl.) the place where these are stored. **3** Computing a store of (usu. large amounts of) data kept in machine-readable form but not necessarily on a disk. ● v.tr. **1** place or store in an archive. **2** Computing transfer (data) to a store of less frequently used files, e.g. from disk to tape. □ **archival** adj.

archivist /ˈɑrkɪvɪst/ n. a person who maintains and is in charge of archives.

archway n. **1** a vaulted passage. **2** an arched entrance.

arc lamp n. (also **arc light**) a light source using an electric arc between carbon electrodes and producing extremely intense white light.

arco /ˈɑrco/ Music ● adv. using a bow to sound the strings of a violin, double bass, etc. (compare PIZZICATO). ● adj. (of a note, passage, etc.) performed arco. ● n. (pl. **archi** /ˈɑrki/) a note etc. played arco.

ARCT abbr. (in Canada) Associateship Diploma of the Royal Conservatory of Toronto.

Arctic /ˈɑrktik, ˈɑrtik/ ● n. **1 a** the area north of the Arctic Circle. **b** an extremely cold, arid, treeless ecological zone including this and, in Canada, the shores of Hudson Bay, Ungava, and the Labrador coast. **2** (**arctic**) esp. US = ARCTIC BOOT. ● adj. **1 a** of the Arctic. **b** designating animals and plants of northern species. **2** (**arctic**) designed for use in arctic conditions (*arctic sleeping bag*). **3** (**arctic**) (esp. of weather) very cold.

arctic boot *n.* (in *pl.*) heavy felt-lined rubber-soled boots suitable for extremely cold weather.

Arctic char *n.* a freshwater fish of the north, *Salvelinus alpinus*, with pink flesh similar to salmon.

Arctic Circle *n.* the parallel of latitude 66°33′ north of the equator.

Arctic fox *n.* a small fox, *Alopex lagopus*, native to the Arctic, whose coat turns white or grey-blue in winter.

Arctic grayling *n.* a highly coloured grayling, *Thymallus arcticus*, abundant in N Canada.

Arctic ground squirrel *n.* a large squirrel, *Spermophilus parryii*, with a dappled greyish-brown coat, of N Canada and Asia.

Arctic hare *n.* a large hare, *Lepus arcticus*, whose coat is brown in summer and white in winter, inhabiting the tundra of Canada and Greenland.

Arctic haze *n.* a smog-like form of air pollution found in the Arctic, caused by pollutants originating at northern coal-based industrial centres.

Arctic loon *n.* a loon, *Gavia arctica*, inhabiting the circumpolar regions, esp. the Pacific coast of N America.

Arctic poppy *n.* (*pl.* **-ies**) any of several golden flowers of the north, including *Papaver radicatum* and *P. macounii*, with four large petals.

Arctic tern *n.* a tern, *Sterna paradisaea*, which breeds in the Arctic and migrates to the Antarctic.

Arctic willow *n.* any of several species of small shrubs native to the Arctic and cultivated as ornamentals, esp. *Salix arctica*.

arc welding *n.* a method of welding using an electric arc to melt metal.

ardent *adj.* **1** zealous, eager; fervent, passionate. **2** burning. □ **ardency** *n.* **ardently** *adv.*

ardour (also **ardor**) *n.* zeal, passion.

ardox nail *n.* *Cdn* a type of nail with a spiral shaft.

arduous *adj.* **1** hard to achieve, overcome or endure; laborious, strenuous. **2** steep, difficult (*an arduous path*). □ **arduously** *adv.* **arduousness** *n.*

are[1] *2nd sing. present & 1st, 2nd, 3rd pl. present of* BE.

are[2] /er, ɑr/ *n.* a metric unit of measure equal to 100 square metres. Abbr.: **a.**

area *n.* **1** the extent or measure of a surface (*over a large area*; *3 hectares in area*; *the area of a triangle*). **2** a region or tract (*the southern area*). **3** a space allocated for a specific purpose (*dining area*). **4** a part of something (*an area of the brain*). **5** the scope or range of an activity or study (*very knowledgeable in the area of botany*). **6** a sunken space in front of a building, usu. leading to the basement. □ **areal** *adj.*

area code *n.* *N Amer.* a three-digit prefix to local phone numbers used in making calls from one telephone area to another.

area municipality *n.* *Cdn* (*Ont.*) a local municipality within a larger regional municipality.

area rug *n.* *N Amer.* a rug covering part of a floor only, not extending to the walls.

areaway *n.* *N Amer.* = AREA 6.

areca /ˈærəkə, əˈriːkə/ *n.* any tropical palm of the genus *Areca*, native to Asia.

areca nut *n.* the seed of a species of areca, *A. catechu*.

arena *n.* **1** an enclosed building containing an open, usu. oblong central area (esp. an ice surface) for sports, entertainment, or recreation, surrounded by seats for spectators. **2** the central part of an amphitheatre, bullring, stadium, etc., in which the action

occurs. **3** a scene of conflict; a sphere of action or discussion (*the political arena*).

arena rock *n.* rock music as performed in arenas, characterized by extravagant lighting and staging.

aren't contraction **1** are not. **2** (in *interrog.*) am not (*aren't I coming too?*).

areola /əˈrɪələ/ *n.* (*pl.* **areolae** /-liː/) **1** *Anat.* a circular pigmented area, esp. that surrounding a nipple. **2** any of the spaces between lines on a surface, e.g. those between the veins of a leaf or an insect's wing.

arête /æˈret/ *n.* a sharp narrow mountain ridge formed by the meeting of adjacent glacial valleys.

arf *n.* *N Amer.* a representation of a dog's bark.

Argentine /ˌɑrdʒənˈtain/ (also **Argentinian** /-ˈtiniən/) ● *adj.* of or relating to Argentina in S America. ● *n.* **1** a native or national of Argentina. **2** a person of Argentine descent.

argentine /ˈɑrdʒən,tain, -,tiːn/ *adj.* of silver; silvery.

argh *interj.* expressing usu. feigned pain, disgust, or exasperation.

argillite /ˈɑrdʒɪl,əit/ *n.* a metamorphic rock of a softness between shale and slate, used in Haida sculpture.

argon *n.* an inert gaseous element, of the noble gas group, used in arc welding and semiconductor crystals, and to fill light bulbs and vacuum tubes.

argot /ˈɑrgoː, -gət/ *n.* the jargon of a group or class, formerly esp. of criminals.

arguable *adj.* **1** capable of being argued. **2** supportable by argument. **3** questionable, open to dispute. □ **arguably** *adv.*

argue *v.* (**argues, argued, arguing**) **1** *intr.* exchange views or opinions, especially heatedly or contentiously; quarrel. **2** *tr. & intr.* indicate; maintain by reasoning. **3** *intr.* provide reasons supporting or challenging something (*argued against the policy*). **4** *tr.* challenge, dispute (*argued the referee's call*). **5** *tr.* treat by reasoning (*argue the point*). **6** *tr.* persuade (*argued me into going*). **7** *tr.* suggest, indicate (*a twitch that argued anxiety*). □ **arguer** *n.*

argument *n.* **1** an exchange of views, esp. a contentious or prolonged one. **2** (often foll. by *for*, *against*) a reason advanced; a reasoning process (*an argument for conscription*). **3** a summary of the subject matter or line of reasoning of a book. **4** *Math.* an independent variable determining the value of a function. **5** *Computing* the part of a command specifying which file etc. the command is to be executed on.

argumentation *n.* **1** methodical reasoning. **2** debate or argument.

argumentative *adj.* **1** fond of arguing; quarrelsome. **2** using methodical reasoning. □ **argumentatively** *adv.* **argumentativeness** *n.*

argus /ˈɑrgəs/ *n.* **1** (**Argus**) a watchful guardian. **2** a butterfly having markings resembling eyes.

Argus-eyed *adj.* vigilant.

argyle /ˈɑrgail/ (also **argyll**) ● *adj.* designating a knitting pattern with diamonds of various colours on a single background colour. ● *n.* **1** this pattern. **2** (in *pl.*) socks in this pattern.

aria /ˈɑriə, ˈeriə, ˈæriə/ *n.* *Music* a long, accompanied song for solo voice in an opera, oratorio, etc.

Arian /ˈeriən, ˈæ-/ ● *n.* an adherent of the doctrines of the Alexandrian priest Arius (*c.*250–*c.*336), who denied the divinity of Christ. ● *adj.* of or concerning Arius or his doctrines. □ **Arianism** *n.*

arid /ˈerɪd, ˈærɪd/ *adj.* **1 a** (of ground, climate, etc.) extremely dry, parched. **b** too dry to support vegetation; barren. **2** emotionless, uninteresting (*arid writing*). □ **aridity** /ə'rɪdɪti / *n.* **aridly** *adv.*

Aries *n.* (*pl.* same) **1** a constellation between Pisces and Taurus, traditionally regarded as contained in the figure of a ram. **2 a** the first sign of the zodiac. **b** a person born when the sun is in this sign, usu. between 21 March and 19 April. □ **Arian** *adj. & n.*

arietta /,ɑri'etə, ,æ-, ,e-/ *n.* a shorter and simpler aria.

aright *adv.* rightly, correctly.

arioso /ɑri'o:so:, æri-, eri-/ *n.* **1** a recitative with expressive qualities similar to those of an aria. **2** a melodious passage at the beginning or end of an aria.

arise *v.intr.* (*past* **arose**; *past part.* **arisen**) **1** begin to exist; originate. **2** (usu. foll. by *from, out of*) result (*accidents can arise from carelessness*). **3** come to one's notice; emerge (*the question of payment arose*). **4** rise, esp. from a seated position or from sleep.

aristo /ə'rɪsto:/ *n.* (*pl.* **-os**) *informal* an aristocrat.

aristocracy *n.* (*pl.* **-ies**) **1 a** the nobility. **b** the nobility as a ruling class. **2 a** government by the nobility or a privileged group. **b** a state governed in this way. **3** (often foll. by *of*) the best representatives or upper echelons (*aristocracy of labour*).

aristocrat *n.* a member of the nobility.

aristocratic *adj.* **1** of or relating to the aristocracy. **2 a** grand; stylish. **b** distinguished in manners or bearing. □ **aristocratically** *adv.*

Aristotelian /,erɪstə'ti:liən, ,æri-, ə,rɪstə-/ ● *n.* a disciple or student of the Greek philosopher Aristotle (d. 322 BC). ● *adj.* of or concerning Aristotle or his ideas. □ **Aristotelianism** *n.*

arithmetic ● *n.* **1 a** the science of numbers. **b** one's knowledge of this (*have improved my arithmetic*). **2** the use of numbers; computation (*a problem involving arithmetic*). ● *adj.* (also **arithmetical**) of or concerning arithmetic. □ **arithmetician** /ə,rɪθmə'tɪʃən/ *n.*

arithmetic mean *n. Math.* **1** the central number in an arithmetic progression. **2** = AVERAGE *n.* 2.

arithmetic progression *n. Math.* **1** an increase or decrease by a constant quantity, e.g. 1, 2, 3, 4, etc., 9, 7, 5, 3, etc. **2** (also **arithmetic sequence**) a sequence of numbers showing this.

Ariz. *abbr.* Arizona.

Arizonan ● *adj.* of or relating to the US state of Arizona. ● *n.* a resident or native of Arizona.

Ark. *abbr.* Arkansas.

ark *n.* **1** = NOAH'S ARK **1. 2** = HOLY ARK. **3** (**Ark**) = ARK OF THE COVENANT. □ **out of the ark** *informal* very antiquated.

Arkansan ● *adj.* of or relating to the US state of Arkansas. ● *n.* a resident or native of Arkansas.

Ark of the Covenant *n.* (also **Ark of the Testimony**) the wooden chest which in Biblical times contained the tablets of the Law given to Moses by God, the Hebrews' most sacred symbol of God.

Ark of the Law *n.* = HOLY ARK.

arm[1] *n.* **1** each of the two upper limbs of the human body from the shoulder to the hand. **2 a** the forelimb of an animal. **b** the flexible limb of an invertebrate animal, e.g. an octopus. **3** the ability to throw (*that pitcher has an impressive arm*). **4 a** anything resembling an arm in function or in being attached to a larger mass or main stem (*an arm of the sea*). **b** the sleeve of a garment. **c** the side part of a chair etc., used to support a sitter's arm. **d** a large branch of a tree. **e** either of the pieces of an eyeglass frame that extend from the front backwards over the wearer's ears. **5** authority; power (*the long arm of the law*). □ **an arm**

and a leg a large sum of money. **arm in arm** (of two or more persons) with arms linked. **as long as your** (or **my**) **arm** *informal* very long. **at arm's length 1** as far as an arm can reach. **2** far enough to avoid undue familiarity or influence. **give one's right arm** sacrifice a great deal. **in arms** (of a baby) too young to walk. **in a person's arms** embraced. **on one's arm** supported by one's arm. **under one's arm** between the arm and the body. **within arm's reach** reachable without moving one's position. **with open arms** cordially. □ **armful** *n.* (*pl.* **-fuls**)

arm[2] ● *n.* **1** (usu. in *pl.*) **a** a weapon. **b** = FIREARM. **2** (in *pl.*) the military profession. **3** a branch of the military, e.g. infantry, cavalry, artillery, etc. **4** a subdivision of an organization, devoted to a specific function or jurisdiction. **5** (in *pl.*) heraldic devices (*coat of arms*). ● *v.tr. & refl.* **1** supply with weapons. **2** supply with tools or other requisites or advantages; equip (*armed with binoculars and a camera*). **3** make (a bomb etc.) able to explode. **4** activate (*armed the burglar alarm*). □ **in arms** armed. **lay down one's arms** cease fighting. **take up arms** begin fighting. **under arms** ready for war or battle. **up in arms** (usu. foll. by *against, about*) actively rebelling. □ **armless** *adj.*

armada /ɑr'mɒdə/ *n.* a fleet of warships.

armadillo *n.* (*pl.* **-os**) any nocturnal insect-eating mammal of the family Dasypodidae, native to S America and southern N America, with large claws for digging and a body covered in bony plates, often rolling itself into a ball when threatened.

Armageddon /,ɑrmə'gedən/ *n.* **1** *New Testament* **a** the last battle between good and evil before the Day of Judgment. **b** the place where this will be fought. **2** a vast and deadly armed conflict, esp. one causing the end of the world through nuclear destruction.

armament *n.* **1** (often in *pl.*) military weapons and equipment, esp. guns on a warship or missiles on an airplane. **2** the process of equipping for war. **3** a force equipped for war.

armamentarium /,ɑrməmən'teriəm/ *n.* (*pl.* **armamentaria** /-riə/) **1** the instruments, drugs, etc. available for medical use. **2** the resources available for a given task.

armature /'ɑrmə,tʃər/ *n.* **1 a** the rotating coil or coils of an electric motor or generator. **b** any moving part of an electrical machine in which a voltage is induced by a magnetic field. **2** a piece of soft iron placed in contact with the poles of a horseshoe magnet to preserve its power. **3** *Biol.* the protective covering of an animal or plant. **4** a metal framework on which a sculpture is moulded with clay etc.

arm band *n.* a band worn around the upper arm to hold up a shirt sleeve or for identification etc.

armchair *n.* **1** a usu. upholstered chair with side supports for the arms. **2** (*attrib.*) theoretical; not active or practical (*an armchair quarterback*).

armed *adj.* **1** equipped with or characterized by the use of weapons. **2** (foll. by *with*) equipped, provided or prepared. **3** (of a weapon etc.) activated.

armed forces *n.pl.* **1** (**Armed Forces**) the official name of the united military services in Canada. **2** (also **armed services**) the combined military services of a country or group of countries.

Armenian /ɑr'mi:niən/ ● *n.* **1 a** a native of the region or the republic of Armenia in the Caucasus. **b** a person of Armenian descent. **2** the language of the Armenians. ● *adj.* of or relating to Armenia, its language, or the Christian Church established there *c.*300.

armistice /ˈɑrmɪstɪs/ n. a cessation of hostilities by common agreement of the opposing sides; a truce.

Armistice Day n. the anniversary of the armistice of 11 Nov. 1918 (compare REMEMBRANCE DAY).

armload n. esp. N Amer. the quantity that can be carried in the arms; an armful.

armoire /ɑrmˈwɑr/ n. a large wardrobe or cupboard, esp. one that is ornate or antique.

armorial /ɑrˈmɔriəl/ adj. of or relating to heraldry or heraldic arms.

armour (also **armor**) ● n. **1** protective clothing, made of fabric, metal plates, etc., designed to deflect or absorb the impact of weapons, bullets, etc. **2 a** (in full **armour-plate**) a protective metal covering for an armed vehicle, ship, etc. **b** armoured fighting vehicles collectively. **3** a protective covering or shell on certain animals and plants. **4** heraldic devices. ● v.tr. provide with a protective covering.

armoured adj. (also **armored**) **1** equipped with a protective covering, esp. of metal (also attrib.: armoured car). **2** (of an infantry division etc.) equipped with tanks and other armoured vehicles.

armoured personnel carrier n. Military a tank-like vehicle used for transporting troops.

armourer n. (also **armorer**) **1** a maker or repairer of arms or armour. **2** an official in charge of a ship's or a regiment's arms.

armoury n. (also **armory**) (pl. **-ies**) **1** a place where arms are kept; an arsenal. **2** (in pl.) Cdn a place where militia units drill and train. **3** an array of weapons, defensive resources, usable material, etc.

armpit n. **1** the hollow under the arm at the shoulder. **2** N Amer. slang a place considered disgusting or contemptible (the armpit of the world).

armrest n. = ARM¹ 4c.

arms control n. international agreement to limit or reduce armaments.

arm's-length attrib.adj. **1** without friendliness or intimacy; at a distance. **2** (of institutional or commercial relations) with neither party controlled by the other.

arms race n. competition between nations in the development and accumulation of weapons.

arm-twisting n. persuasion by the use of moral pressure.

arm wrestling n. a trial of strength in which two people, with elbows on a tabletop, grip hands, with each trying to force the other's forearm down onto the table. □ **arm-wrestle** v.intr.

army n. (pl. **-ies**) **1** an organized force armed for fighting on land. **2** (usu. as **the Army**) the entire body of land forces of a country. **3** a very large number (an army of bureaucrats). **4** a body of people organized for a particular cause (Salvation Army).

army ant n. any of various tropical ants of the subfamily Dorylinae, which migrate in large columns and prey mainly on insects and spiders.

army fatigues n.pl. esp. N Amer. loose-fitting clothing, usu. khaki, olive drab, or camouflaged, of a sort worn by soldiers on field duty or when engaged in manual labour. ¶In the Canadian Forces, the word combat dress is used.

army surplus n. = SURPLUS n. 3.

army worm n. any of various moth or fly larvae occurring in destructive swarms.

aroma n. **1** a fragrance; a distinctive and pleasing smell, often of food. **2** a subtle pervasive quality.

aromatherapy n. the use of aromatic plant extracts and essential oils, esp. for relief of stress-related

symptoms. □ **aromatherapeutic** adj. **aromatherapist** n.

aromatic /ˌerəˈmætɪk/ ● adj. **1** fragrant, spicy; (of a smell) pleasantly pungent. **2** (of organic compounds) having an unsaturated ring, esp. containing a benzene ring. ● n. an aromatic substance. □ **aromatically** adv. **aromaticity** /ˌerəməˈtɪsɪti/ n.

arose past of ARISE.

around ● adv. **1** on every side; so as to surround. **2** in various places; here and there; at random (shop around). **3** informal **a** in existence; available (has been around for weeks). **b** near at hand (it's good to have you around). **4** with circular motion (wheels go around). **5** with return to the starting point or an earlier state (summer soon comes around again). **6 a** with rotation, or change to an opposite position (she turned around to look). **b** with change to an opposite opinion etc. (he came around to her point of view). **7** to, at, or affecting all or many points of a circumference or an area or the members of a company etc. (look around). **8** in every direction from a centre or within a radius (everyone for a mile around). **9** by a circuitous way (go the long way around). **10** to a place (come around to see us). **11** measuring a (specified distance) in girth. ● prep. **1** on or along the circuit of. **2** on every side of; enveloping. **3** here and there in or near (chairs around the room). **4** approximately at; at a time near to (come around four o'clock). **5** so as to encircle or enclose. **6** at or to points on the circumference of (sat around the table). **7** in various directions from or with regard to (towns around Calgary). **8** having as an axis of revolution or as a central point (turns around its centre of gravity; write a book around an event). **9 a** so as to double or pass in a curved course (go around the corner). **b** having passed in this way (be around the corner). **c** in the position that would result from this (find them around the corner). **10** so as to come close from various sides but not into contact. □ **have been around** informal be widely experienced, esp. sexually.

arouse v.tr. **1** induce; call into existence (esp. a feeling, emotion, etc.). **2** awake from sleep. **3** stir into activity. **4** stimulate sexually. □ **arousal** n.

arpeggio /ɑrˈpedʒio:/ n. (pl. **-os**) Music the notes of a chord played or sung in succession, either ascending or descending. □ **arpeggiated** adj.

arpent /ˈɑrpənt, ˈɑrpɑ̃/ n. Cdn hist. **1** an old French unit of land area equivalent to 3 420 square metres (about 1 acre), the standard measure of land in those areas settled during the French regime, in use until the 1970s. **2** a unit of linear measure equivalent to about 58 metres (190 ft.) used in New France.

arr. abbr. **1** Music arranged by. **2** arrives.

arrack /ˈærək/ var. of ARAK.

arraign /əˈreɪn/ v.tr. **1** call on (a person) to answer a criminal charge before a court; indict; accuse. **2** find fault with; call into question (an action or statement). □ **arraignment** n.

arrange v. **1** tr. put into the required order; classify. **2** tr. plan or provide for; cause to occur (arranged a meeting). **3** tr. settle beforehand the order or manner of. **4** tr. take measures; form plans (arrange to be there at eight). **5** intr. come to an agreement (arranged with her to meet later). **6** tr. **a** Music adapt (a composition) for performance with instruments or voices other than those originally specified. **b** adapt (a play etc.) for broadcasting. **7** tr. settle (a dispute etc.). □ **arrangeable** adj. **arranger** n. (esp. in sense 6).

arranged marriage n. a marriage planned and agreed to by the families or guardians of the couple concerned, rather than by the couple themselves.

arrangement *n.* **1** the act or process of arranging or being arranged. **2** the condition of being arranged; the manner in which a thing is arranged. **3** something arranged (*a flower arrangement*). **4** (in *pl.*) plans (*make arrangements*). **5** a setting of a piece of music for instruments or voices other than those for which it was first written. **6** settlement of a dispute etc.

arrant /ˈerənt/ *adj.* downright, utter, notorious (*arrant liar*). □ **arrantly** *adv.*

array ● *n.* **1** an imposing or well-ordered series or display. **2** an ordered arrangement, esp. of troops (*battle array*). **3** attire, dress; an outfit (*in fine array*). **4 a** *Math.* an arrangement of quantities or symbols in rows and columns; a matrix. **b** *Computing* an ordered set of related elements. ● *v.tr.* **1** deck, adorn. **2** set in order; marshal (forces).

arrears *n.pl.* an amount still outstanding or uncompleted, esp. a debt unpaid. □ **in arrears** behind in payments etc. □ **arrearage** *n.*

arrest ● *v.tr.* **1 a** seize (a person) and take into custody, esp. by legal authority. **b** seize (a ship) by legal authority. **2** stop or check (esp. a process or moving thing). **3 a** attract (a person's attention). **b** attract the attention of (a person). ● *n.* **1** the act of arresting or being arrested, esp. the legal seizure of a person. **2** a stoppage or checking of motion (*cardiac arrest*).

arresting *adj.* attracting attention; striking. □ **arrestingly** *adv.*

arrestor *n.* (also **arrester**) **1** a person who arrests someone or something. **2** something which arrests, esp. a device on an aircraft carrier for slowing an aircraft after landing.

arrhythmia /əˈrɪðmɪə/ *n.* *Med.* deviation from the normal rhythm of the heart. □ **arrhythmic** *adj.*

arrival *n.* **1 a** the act of arriving. **b** an appearance on the scene. **2** a person or thing that has arrived.

arrive *v.intr.* **1** reach a destination; come to the end of a journey or a specified part of a journey. **2** (foll. by *at*) reach (a conclusion, decision, etc.). **3** *informal* establish one's reputation or position. **4** (of a child) be born. **5** (of a thing) be brought (*the flowers have arrived*). **6** (of a time) come (*her birthday arrived at last*). **7** come on the scene (*CD-ROMs arrived in the late eighties*).

arriviste /ˌæriːˈviːst/ *n.* an ambitious or ruthlessly self-seeking person.

arrogant *adj.* unduly appropriating authority or importance; aggressively conceited or presumptuous; overbearing. □ **arrogance** *n.* **arrogantly** *adv.*

arrow *n.* **1** a sharp pointed wooden or metal stick shot from a bow. **2** a drawn or printed etc. representation of an arrow indicating a direction. □ **arrowy** *adj.*

arrowhead *n.* **1** the pointed end of an arrow. **2** an aquatic or marsh plant of the genus *Sagittaria*, bearing white flowers and arrowhead-shaped leaves. **3** a decorative device resembling an arrowhead.

arrowroot *n.* **1** a plant of the genus *Maranta*, esp. the Caribbean *M. arundinacea* with fleshy tuberous rhizomes. **2** pure edible starch prepared from the tubers of *M. arundinacea*, or other plants. **3** (in full **arrowroot cookie**) a cookie made with arrowroot flour.

arrow sash *n.* *Cdn hist.* = CEINTURE FLÉCHÉE.

arroyo /əˈrɔɪoː/ *n.* (*pl.* **-os**) esp. *US* a usu. dry channel or gully cut by a stream, esp. in arid regions.

arse *coarse slang* esp. *Brit.* & *Cdn* (esp. *Nfld*) *var. of* ASS².

arsehole *coarse slang* esp. *Brit. var. of* ASSHOLE.

arsenal *n.* **1** a store of weapons. **2** a government establishment for the storage and manufacture of weapons and ammunition. **3** a collection of items, methods, beliefs, etc. available for tackling a problem.

arsenic ● *n.* /ˈɑrsənɪk/ **1** a non-scientific name for arsenic trioxide, a highly poisonous white powdery substance used in weed killers, rat poison, etc. A brittle semi-metallic element, used in semiconductors and alloys. ● *adj.* /ɑrˈsɛnɪk/ of or concerning arsenic.

arsenic hour *n.* the period in the late afternoon when young children become particularly cranky and unmanageable.

arson *n.* the act of maliciously setting fire to property. □ **arsonist** *n.*

art *n.* **1 a** human creative skill or its application. **b** work exhibiting this. **2 a** (in *pl.*; prec. by *the*) the various branches of creative activity concerned with the production of imaginative designs, sounds, ideas, etc., e.g. painting, music, writing, etc. considered collectively. **b** any one of these branches. **3** creative activity, esp. painting and drawing, resulting in visual representation (*interested in music but not art*). **4** human skill or workmanship as opposed to the work of nature. **5** (often foll. by *of*) a skill, aptitude, or knack (*keeping people happy is quite an art*). **6** (in *pl.*) certain branches of (esp. university) study, esp. the fine arts and humanities, as distinguished from the sciences or technological subjects.

art deco *n.* the predominant decorative art style of the period 1910–30, characterized by precise and boldly delineated geometric motifs, shapes, and strong colours.

art director *n.* **1** the person in charge of the design and production of the costumes and decor for a motion picture. **2** the person in charge of the graphics, layout, etc. of a magazine.

artefact *var. of* ARTIFACT.

artemisia /ɑrtəˈmiːʒə, -ˈmiːʃə/ *n.* any of numerous aromatic or bitter-tasting plants of the genus *Artemisia*, of the composite family, which includes wormwood, etc.

arterial *adj.* **1 a** of or relating to an artery (*arterial disease*). **b** (of blood) oxygenated in the lungs and of a bright red colour. **2** (esp. of a road) main, important, esp. providing direct access to the centre of a city.

arteriole /ɑrˈtiːrɪˌoːl/ *n.* a small branch of an artery leading into capillaries.

arteriosclerosis /ɑrˌtiːrioːsklərˈoːsəs/ *n.* abnormal thickening and hardening of the walls of the arteries. □ **arteriosclerotic** /-ˈrɒtək/ *adj.*

artery *n.* (*pl.* **-ies**) **1** any of the muscular-walled tubes forming part of the blood circulation system of the body, carrying oxygen-enriched blood from the heart (*compare* VEIN). **2** a major road, railway, river, etc.

artesian well /ɑrˈtiːʒən/ *n.* a well bored perpendicularly, esp. through rock, into water-bearing strata lying at an angle, so that natural pressure produces a constant supply of water with little or no pumping.

art film *n.* a film aiming for aesthetic effect rather than commercial success.

art form *n.* **1** any medium of artistic expression. **2** an established form of composition, e.g. the novel, sonata, sonnet, etc.

artful *adj.* **1** skilful, clever. **2** crafty, deceitful. **3** characterized by skill or art. □ **artfully** *adv.* **artfulness** *n.*

art house *n.* (also **art theatre** etc.) a movie theatre specializing in alternative films, e.g. art films, foreign films, etc.

arthritis *n.* inflammation of a joint or joints. □ **arthritic** *adj.* & *n.*

arthropod /ˈɑrθrəˌpɒd/ *n.* *Zool.* any invertebrate animal of the phylum Arthropoda, with a segmented body, jointed limbs, and an external skeleton, e.g. an insect, spider, or crustacean.

arthroscopy /ɑr'θrɒskəpi/ n. (pl. **-ies**) Med. examination of, or surgery on, the interior of a joint by the insertion of an instrument called an arthroscope through a small incision. □ **arthroscopic** adj. **arthroscope** n.

artichoke n. **1** a plant native to the Mediterranean, Cynara scolymus, allied to the thistle (see also JERUSALEM ARTICHOKE). **2** = GLOBE ARTICHOKE.

article ● n. **1** a particular or separate thing, esp. one of a set (articles of clothing). **2** a piece of writing, complete in itself, in a newspaper, magazine, scholarly journal, etc. **3** a separate clause or portion of any document. **4** Grammar the definite or indefinite article. **5** (in pl.) the period of apprenticeship of a law student. ● v. **1** tr. bind by a written contract, esp. for a period of training. **2** intr. Cdn (of a law student) serve one's period of apprenticeship. □ **article of faith 1** a basic point of religious belief. **2** any firmly held belief. **genuine article** something authentic; not imitative.

articled clerk n. a law student who is articling.

articular /ɑr'tɪkjʊlər/ adj. of or relating to the joints.

articulate ● adj. **1** able to speak fluently and coherently. **2** (of sound or speech) having clearly distinguishable parts. **3** having joints. ● v. **1** tr. a pronounce (words etc.) clearly and distinctly. **b** express (an idea etc.) coherently. **2** intr. speak distinctly. **3** tr. (usu. in passive) connect by joints. **4** tr. mark with apparent joints. **5** intr. (often foll. by with) form a joint. □ **articulacy** n. **articulately** adv.

articulated adj. designating a vehicle consisting of two or more sections connected by a flexible joint (articulated bus).

articulation n. **1 a** the act of speaking. **b** articulate utterance; speech. **2 a** the act or a mode of jointing. **b** a joint, esp. that between two bones, or parts of an invertebrate exoskeleton.

artifact n. a product of human art and workmanship. □ **artifactual** adj.

artifice /'ɑrtəfɪs/ n. **1** a clever device; a contrivance. **2 a** cunning. **b** an instance of this. **3** skill, dexterity.

artificial adj. **1** produced by human skill or effort rather than originating naturally (an artificial lake; artificial flavours). **2** formed in imitation of something natural (artificial flowers). **3** affected, insincere (an artificial smile). **4** designating a device etc. that performs the functions of an organ, limb, etc. (artificial heart). □ **artificiality** n. **artificially** adv.

artificial ice n. **1** an ice surface in a skating rink kept frozen by cooling pipes running under the concrete base of the rink. **2** ice frozen by mechanical refrigeration.

artificial insemination n. the injection of semen into the vagina or uterus other than by sexual intercourse. Abbr.: **AI**.

artificial intelligence n. the field of study that deals with the capacity of a machine, esp. a computer, to simulate or surpass intelligent human behaviour. Abbr.: **AI**.

artificial language n. **1** a composite language, esp. for international use, made from the words and other elements in several languages, e.g. Esperanto. **2** a language invented for use by computers.

artificial life n. computer programs or systems which simulate the behaviour, population dynamics, or other characteristics of living organisms.

artificial respiration n. the restoration or initia-

tion of breathing by manual or mechanical or mouth-to-mouth methods.

artificial turf n. a synthetic surface used as a substitute for grass on sports fields etc.

artillery n. **1** large-calibre guns used in warfare on land. **2** a branch of the armed forces that uses these.

artisan /'ɑrtɪ,zæn, -sæn/ n. **1** a craftsperson specializing in decorative arts, esp. pottery, weaving, etc. **2** a skilled (esp. manual) worker. □ **artisanal** adj.

artist n. **1** a person who practises any of the fine arts, esp. painting, sculpting, etc. **2** a person who practises one of the performing arts. **3** a person who shows great skill and inspiration in a particular activity. **4** a habitual practiser of a specified (usu. reprehensible) activity (con artist). □ **artistry** n.

artiste /ɑr'tiːst/ n. **1** esp. Brit. a professional performer. **2** derogatory a person who cultivates a pretentiously artistic attitude or lifestyle.

artistic adj. **1** having natural skill in art. **2** made or done with art. **3** of art or artists. □ **artistically** adv.

artistic director n. the director of a performing arts organization in charge of programming and casting decisions etc.

artless adj. **1** guileless, ingenuous; without deceit. **2** without art or skill. **3** clumsy. □ **artlessly** adv.

art nouveau n. a European art style of the late 19th c. characterized by flowing lines and natural organic forms.

arts and crafts n.pl. decorative design and handicrafts.

artsie n. N Amer. slang **1** a student in an arts program at a university or college. **2** an artist or a person who is interested in the arts.

artsy adj. (also **arty**, derogatory **artsy-fartsy**) esp. N Amer. informal pretentiously or affectedly artistic.

artsy-craftsy adj. informal **1** having a liking for, or engaged in, handicrafts. **2** characterized by the presence of handicrafts.

artwork n. **1** a work of art. **2** the illustrations in a printed work. **3** prepared or camera-ready copy.

arugula /ə'ruːgələ/ n. a cruciferous plant, Eruca vesicaria sativa, having purple-veined pale yellow or white flowers and bitter leaves used in salads.

arum /'erəm/ n. **1** any plant of the European genus Arum, typically having a white spathe and arrow-shaped leaves. **2** any of various other plants of the family Araceae.

As symbol the element arsenic.

as ● adv. & conj. ... to the extent to which ... is or does etc. (I am as tall as he is; as recently as last week; it is not as easy as you think). ● conj. (with relative clause expressed or implied) **1** (with antecedent so) expressing result or purpose (came early so as to meet us; so good as to exceed all hopes). **2** (with antecedent adverb omitted) having concessive force (try as he might, he could not do it). **3** (without antecedent adverb) **a** in the manner in which (do as you like). **b** in the capacity or form of (I speak as your friend; as a matter of fact). **c** during or at the time that (came up as I was speaking). **d** for the reason that; seeing that (as you are here, we can talk). **e** for instance (port cities, as Vancouver). ● rel.pron. (with verb of relative clause expressed or implied) **1** that, who, which (I had the same trouble as you). **2** a fact that (he lost, as you know). □ **as and when** to the extent and at the time that (I'll do it as and when I want to). **as for** with regard to. **as from** on and after (a specified date). **as if!** indicating disbelief or disdain. **as if** (or **though**) as would be the case if (acts as if he were in charge; looks as though we've won). **as it is** (or **as is**) in the existing circumstances or state. **as it were** in a way; to a certain extent (*she is, as it were, infatuated*). **as of 1** = AS FROM. **2** as at (a specified time). **as to** with respect to; concerning (*said nothing as to money*). **as was** in the previously existing circumstances or state. **as yet** until now or a particular time in the past.

ASA *abbr. Cdn* ACETYLSALICYLIC ACID.

asana /ˈɒsənə/ *n.* any of various postures used in yoga.

ASAP *abbr.* as soon as possible.

asbestos /æzˈbestəs, æs-/ *n.* **1** a fibrous silicate mineral that is incombustible. **2** this used as a heat-resistant or insulating material.

asbestosis /ˌæzbeˈstoːsɪs, ˌæs-/ *n.* a lung disease resulting from the inhalation of asbestos particles.

ascend *v.* **1** *intr.* move upwards; rise. **2** *intr.* a slope upwards. **b** lie along an ascending slope. **3** *tr.* climb; go up. **4** *intr.* rise in rank or status. **5** *tr.* mount upon. **6** *intr.* (of sound) rise in pitch. **7** *tr.* go along (a river) to its source. □ **ascend the throne** become king or queen.

ascendancy *n.* (also **ascendency**) a superior or dominant condition or position.

ascendant ● *adj.* **1** rising. **2** *Astronomy* rising toward the zenith. **3** *Astrology* just rising above the eastern horizon. **4** predominant. ● *n. Astrology* the point of the ecliptic or sign of the zodiac which at a given moment (esp. at a person's birth) is just rising above the eastern horizon. □ **in the ascendant 1** supreme or dominating. **2** rising; gaining power or authority.

ascender *n.* **1** a a part of a letter that extends above the main part (as in *b* and *d*). **b** a letter having this. **2** a person or thing that ascends.

ascension *n.* **1** the act or an instance of ascending. **2** *Christianity* (**Ascension**) a the ascent of Christ into heaven on the fortieth day after the Resurrection. **b** (in full **Ascension Day**) the day on which Christians annually celebrate the Ascension, either the Thursday forty days after Easter, or the Sunday following this. □ **ascensional** *adj.*

ascent *n.* **1** the act or an instance of ascending. **2** a an upward movement or rise. **b** advancement or progress (*the ascent of man*). **3** a way by which one may ascend; an upward slope.

ascertain /ˌæsərˈteɪn/ *v.tr.* find out as a definite fact. □ **ascertainable** *adj.* **ascertainment** *n.*

ascetic /əˈsetɪk/ ● *n.* a person who practises severe self-discipline and abstains from all forms of pleasure, esp. for religious or spiritual reasons. ● *adj.* abstaining from pleasure. □ **ascetically** *adv.* **asceticism** /-tɪˌsɪzəm/ *n.*

ASCII /ˈæski/ *n. Computing* a standard code for storing and transmitting information.

ascorbic acid /əˈskɔrbɪk/ *n.* a vitamin found in citrus fruits and green vegetables, essential in maintaining healthy connective tissue.

ascot /ˈæskət, -kɒt/ (in full **ascot tie**) a broad necktie or scarf covering the area of an open neck or waistcoat.

ascribe *v.tr.* (usu. foll. by *to*) **1** attribute or impute. **2** regard as belonging. □ **ascribable** *adj.*

ascription *n.* the act or an instance of ascribing.

aseptic /eiˈseptɪk/ *adj.* **1** free from contamination caused by harmful bacteria, viruses, or other microorganisms. **2** (of a wound, instrument, or dressing) surgically sterile or sterilized. **3** (of a surgical method etc.) aiming at the elimination of harmful microorganisms, rather than counteraction (compare ANTISEPTIC).

asexual /eiˈsekʃʊəl, æ-/ *adj. Biol.* **1** without sex or sexual organs. **2** (of reproduction) not involving the fusion of gametes. **3** without sexuality. □ **asexuality** *n.* **asexually** *adv.*

ash¹ *n.* **1** a (often in *pl.*) the powdery residue left after the burning of any substance. **b** *Chem.* such residue used in chemical analysis, e.g. to assess mineral content (*low ash cat food*). **2** (in *pl.*) the remains of the human body after cremation or disintegration. **3** ashlike material thrown out by a volcano. **4** pale grey.

ash² *n.* **1** any forest tree of the genus *Fraxinus*, with silver-grey bark, compound leaves, and tough, flexible, pale wood. **2** the wood of the ash, used to make hockey sticks and implement handles. **3** an Old English runic letter, = æ.

ashamed *predic.adj.* **1** embarrassed or disconcerted by shame (*ashamed of having lied; ashamed to be seen with him*). **2** hesitant, reluctant (but usu. not actually refusing or declining) (*am ashamed to admit that I was wrong*). □ **ashamedly** *adv.*

ashen *adj.* **1** ash-coloured; deathly pale. **2** of or resembling ashes.

Ashkenazi /ˌæʃkəˈnɒzi/ *n.* (*pl.* **Ashkenazim** /-zɪm/) a Jew of central, northern, or eastern Europe, or of such ancestry (compare SEPHARDI). □ **Ashkenazic** *adj.*

ash-leaved maple *n.* (also **ash-leaf maple**) = MANITOBA MAPLE.

ashore *adv.* toward or on the shore or land.

ashram /ˈæʃrəm/ *n.* a place of religious retreat for Hindus; a hermitage.

ashtray *n.* a small receptacle for cigarette ash etc.

Ash Wednesday *n. Christianity* the first day of Lent, on which the foreheads of penitents are customarily marked with ashes.

ashy *adj.* (**-ier, -iest**) **1** = ASHEN. **2** covered with ashes.

Asiago /ˈɒsiˈɒɡo/ *n.* a hard light yellow cheese made from cow's milk.

Asian ● *n.* **1** a native of Asia. **2** a person of Asian descent. ● *adj.* of or relating to Asia or its people, customs, or languages.

Asiatic /ˌeiʃiˈætɪk, ˌeiz-/ ● *n. offensive* an Asian. ● *adj.* Asian.

A-side *n.* **1** the first side of a recording, esp. the side of a single featuring the music deemed by the producers to have the greater commercial potential. **2** the music on this side.

aside ● *adv.* **1** to or on one side; away. **2** out of consideration (placed after noun: *joking aside*). ● *n.* **1** words spoken in a play for the audience to hear, but supposed not to be heard by the other characters. **2** an incidental remark. □ **aside from** apart from. **set aside 1** put to one side. **2** keep for a special purpose or future use. **3** reject or disregard. **4** *Law* annul. **5** remove (land) from agricultural production for fallow, forestry, or other use. **take aside** engage (a person) esp. for a private conversation.

asinine /ˈæsɪˌnain/ *adj.* **1** stupid. **2** of or concerning asses; like an ass. □ **asininity** /-ˈnɪnɪti/ *n.*

ask *v.* **1** *tr.* call for an answer to or about (*ask him his name; ask a question of her*). **2** *tr.* seek to obtain from another person (*ask a favour of; ask to be allowed*). **3** *tr.* invite; request the company of (*must ask them over; asked her to dinner*). **4** *intr.* (foll. by *for*) seek to obtain, meet, or be directed to (*ask for a donation; asking for you*). □ **ask after** inquire about (esp. a person). **ask for it** *slang* invite trouble. **ask me another** *informal* I do not know. **for the asking** (obtainable) for nothing. **I ask you!** an exclamation of disgust, surprise, etc. **if you ask me** *informal* in my opinion. □ **asker** *n.*

askance /əˈskæns/ *adv.* sideways or squinting. □

look askance at regard with suspicion or disapproval.

askew ● *adv.* obliquely, crookedly; awry. ● *predic.adj.* oblique, crooked; awry.

asking price *n.* the price of an object set by the seller.

aslant ● *adv.* obliquely or at a slant. ● *prep.* obliquely across (*lay aslant the path*).

asleep *predic.adj. & adv.* **1 a** in or into a state of sleep. **b** inactive, inattentive (*the nation is asleep*). **2** (of a limb etc.) numb. **3** *euphemism* dead. □ **asleep at the switch** *N Amer.* inattentive.

A/SLt *abbr. Cdn* ACTING SUB-LIEUTENANT.

ASM *abbr.* air-to-surface missile.

asocial /eiˈsoːʃəl/ *adj.* **1** not social; anti-social. **2** inconsiderate of or hostile to others.

asp *n.* **1** a cobra, *Naja haje*, native to N Africa and Arabia. **2** either of two small vipers: **a** (in full **asp viper**) *Vipera aspis*, native to S Europe, resembling a small adder. **b** (in full **horned asp**) *Cerastes cornutus*, with a large head and two small horns above the eyes, found in the deserts of N Africa and SW Asia.

asparagus *n.* any plant of the genus *Asparagus*, esp. *A. officinalis* with edible young shoots.

asparagus fern *n.* a decorative fernlike plant, *Asparagus setaceus*, having feathery foliage used in flower arrangements.

aspartame /ˈæspərˌteim/ *n.* a very sweet low-calorie sugar substitute derived from amino acids.

aspect *n.* **1 a** a particular component or feature of a matter (*only one aspect of the problem*). **b** a particular way in which a matter may be considered. **2** a facial expression; an appearance or look (of a person or thing) (*a cheerful aspect*). **3** the side of a building or location facing a particular direction (*southern aspect*).

aspect ratio *n.* **1** the ratio of picture width to height on a movie screen, television set, etc. **2** *Aviation* the ratio of the span to the mean chord of an airfoil.

aspen *n.* any of several poplars characterized by leaves which tremble in the slightest wind, esp. *Populus tremuloides*, widely distributed across N America, and *P. tremula*, found in Europe.

asperity /əˈspɛrɪti/ *n.* (*pl.* **-ies**) **1** harshness or sharpness of temper or tone. **2** roughness. **3** a rough excrescence.

aspersion /əˈspɜrʒən/ *n.* a disparaging remark. □ **cast aspersions on** attack the reputation or integrity of.

asphalt /ˈæsfɒlt, ˈæʃ-/ ● *n.* **1** a dark bituminous pitch occurring naturally or made from petroleum. **2** a mixture of this with sand, gravel, etc., for surfacing roads etc. ● *v.tr.* surface with asphalt.

asphyxia /æsˈfiksiə/ *n.* a lack of oxygen in the blood, causing unconsciousness or death; suffocation.

asphyxiate *v.tr.* cause (a person) to have asphyxia, smother; suffocate. □ **asphyxiation** *n.*

aspic *n.* **1** a clear savoury jelly prepared from meat or fish stock, used as a garnish or glaze or combined with meat, vegetables, etc. in moulded dishes. **2** a dish of jelled tomato juice with vegetables etc.

aspidistra *n.* any plant of the genus *Aspidistra*, with broad tapering leaves, native to E Asia, esp. *A. lurida*, often grown as a houseplant.

aspirant /ˈæspɪrənt, əˈspaɪrənt/ ● *adj.* aspiring. ● *n.* a person who aspires.

aspirate /ˈæspɪrət/ *Phonetics* ● *adj.* **1** pronounced with an exhalation of breath. **2** blended with the sound of *h*. ● *n.* **1** a consonant pronounced in this way. **2** the sound of *h*. ● *v.* /-ˌreit/ **1 a** *tr.* pronounce with a breath.

b *intr.* make the sound of *h*. **2** *tr. Med.* draw (fluid) by suction from a vessel or cavity.

aspiration *n.* **1** a strong desire to achieve an end; an ambition. **2** the act or process of drawing breath. **3** the action of aspirating.

aspire *v.intr.* (usu. foll. by *to* or *after*, or *to* + infin.) have ambition or strong desire (*aspired to be prime minister*).

Aspirin *n.* (*pl.* same or **Aspirins**) *proprietary* **1** a white powder, acetylsalicylic acid, used to relieve pain and reduce fever. **2** a tablet of this.

aspiring *adj.* **1** desirous of attaining a specified position, career, etc. (*an aspiring actor*). **2** having strong desire for advancement; ambitious.

ass¹ ● *n.* **1 a** either of two kinds of four-legged long-eared mammal of the horse genus *Equus*, *E. africanus* of Africa and *E. hemionus* of Asia. **b** (in general use) a donkey. **2** a stupid person. □ **make an ass of** make (a person) look absurd or foolish.

ass² *n. coarse slang* **1** the buttocks. **2** the rectum. **3 a** sexual gratification. **b** *derogatory* a woman or women regarded as an object providing this.

assail *v.tr.* **1** make a strong or concerted attack on. **2** make a strong or constant verbal attack on (*was assailed with angry questions*). **3** make a resolute start on (a task). □ **assailable** *adj.*

assailant *n.* a person who attacks another, esp. physically.

Assam /æˈsæm/ a strong, dark brown tea from Assam in NE India.

assassin *n.* a killer, esp. of a political or religious leader.

assassinate *v.tr.* kill (esp. a political or religious leader) for political or religious motives. □ **assassination** *n.*

assault ● *n.* **1** a violent physical or verbal attack. **2 a** (in civil law) an act that threatens physical harm to a person. **b** (in criminal law) threatened or actual physical contact without consent. **c** = SEXUAL ASSAULT. **3** (*attrib.*) relating to or used in a military assault (*assault craft; assault troops*). **4** a vigorous start made to a lengthy or difficult task. **5** a final rush on a fortified place, esp. at the end of a prolonged attack. ● *v.tr.* **1** make an assault on. **2** sexually assault. □ **assault and battery** *Law* (in civil law) a threatening act that is followed by physical contact without consent, whether or not harm is caused. □ **assaulter** *n.* **assaultive** *adj.*

assault rifle *n.* a lightweight, automatic or semi-automatic military rifle using high-performance ammunition.

assay /əˈsei, ˈæsei/ ● *n.* a test to determine the composition of a substance, esp. the analysis of an ore or metal to determine its purity. ● *v.tr.* **1** analyze (a substance) to determine its composition or to ascertain the activity of certain substances in it. **2** determine the presence or activity of (a substance) by testing. **3** analyze or examine. **4** attempt or try.

assay office *n.* an establishment which analyzes metals, ores, etc. and is authorized to put hallmarks on precious metals.

assemblage *n.* **1** the act or an instance of bringing or coming together. **2** a collection of things or gathering of people. **3 a** the act or an instance of fitting together. **b** an object made of pieces fitted together. **4** a work of art made by grouping found or unrelated objects.

assemble *v.* **1** *tr. & intr.* gather together; collect. **2** *tr.* arrange in order. **3** *tr.* fit together the parts of (*assemble the bicycle*). **4** *tr. Computing* produce (a machine-coded form of a low-level symbolic code).

assembler *n.* **1** a person who assembles a machine or its parts. **2** *Computing* **a** a program for converting instructions written in low-level symbolic code into machine code. **b** the low-level symbolic code itself; an assembly language.

assembly *n.* (*pl.* **-ies**) **1** the act or an instance of assembling or gathering together. **2 a** a group of persons gathered together for a specific purpose. **b** a general gathering of the members of a school. **3** (also **Assembly**) a legislative council or deliberative body, esp.: **a** = GENERAL ASSEMBLY. **b** = HOUSE OF ASSEMBLY. **c** = LEGISLATIVE ASSEMBLY. **d** = NATIONAL ASSEMBLY. **4** the assembling of a machine or structure or its parts. **5** a number of component parts fitted together to form a whole. **6** *Military* a call to assemble, given by drum.

assembly language *n.* *Computing* a low-level language employing mnemonic symbols which correspond exactly to groups of machine instructions.

assembly line *n.* a sequence of machines and workers along which a product moves as it is assembled.

assemblyman *n.* (*pl.* **-men**) **1** a member of an (esp. legislative) assembly. **2** *Cdn hist.* (in PEI) one of the two representatives elected to the Legislative Assembly in each riding (compare COUNCILLOR 3).

Assembly of First Nations *n.* a national political organization officially representing status First Nations in Canada. Abbr.: **AFN.**

assent ● *v.intr.* (usu. foll. by *to*) **1** consent (*assented to my request*). **2** express agreement (*'That's true,' he assented*). ● *n.* **1** acceptance or agreement (*a nod of assent*). **2** consent or sanction, esp. official (*see also* ROYAL ASSENT). □ **assenter** *n.* (also **assentor**).

assert *v.* **1** *tr.* declare; state clearly (*assert one's beliefs*; *assert that it is so*). **2** *refl.* **a** (of a person) insist on one's rights or opinions; demand recognition. **b** (of a prevailing mood, tendency, etc.) become influential. **3** *tr.* make or enforce a claim to (*assert one's rights*).

assertion *n.* **1** a declaration; a forthright statement. **2** the act or an instance of asserting. **3** (also **self-assertion**) insistence on the recognition of one's rights or claims.

assertive *adj.* **1** tending to assert oneself; forthright, positive. **2** dogmatic. □ **assertively** *adv.* **assertiveness** *n.*

assess *v.tr.* **1** determine or estimate the size, quality, or extent of. **2** judge or evaluate. **3 a** estimate the value of (a property) for taxation. **b** fix the amount of (a tax etc.) and impose it on a person or community. **4** penalize or fine a specific amount (*assessed $100 in damages*). □ **assessable** *adj.* **assessment** *n.*

assessor *n.* **1** a person who makes assessments, esp. one who assesses taxes or estimates the value of property for taxation or insurance purposes. **2** a person called upon to advise a judge, committee of inquiry, etc., on technical questions.

asset *n.* **1 a** a useful or valuable quality. **b** a person or thing possessing such a quality or qualities (*is an asset to the company*). **2** (usu. in *pl.*) **a** property and possessions, esp. regarded as having value in meeting debts etc. **b** any possession having value.

asset-stripping *n.* the practice of taking over a company and selling off its assets to make a profit.

asshole *n.* *N Amer. coarse slang* **1** the anus. **2** a contemptible person.

assiduous *adj.* **1** persevering, hard-working. **2** attending closely. □ **assiduously** *adv.*

assign ● *v.tr.* **1** (usu. foll. by *to*) **a** allot as a share, responsibility, task, etc. (*assign homework*). **b** appoint to a position, task, etc. **2** fix (a time, place, etc.) for a specific purpose. **3** (foll. by *to*) ascribe or refer to (a

reason, date, etc.) (*assigned the manuscript to 1832*). **4** (foll. by *to*) transfer formally (esp. personal property) to (another). ● *n.* an assignee. □ **assignable** *adj.*

assignation /ˌæsɪgˈneɪʃən/ *n.* **1 a** an appointment to meet. **b** a secret appointment, esp. between illicit lovers. **2** the act or an instance of assigning or being assigned.

assignee *n.* **1** a person appointed to act for another. **2** a person to whom property or rights are legally transferred.

assignment *n.* **1** something assigned, esp. a task allotted to a person. **2** the act or an instance of assigning or being assigned. **3 a** a legal transfer. **b** the document effecting this.

assimilate *v.* **1** *tr.* **a** absorb and digest (food etc.) into the body. **b** absorb (information etc.) into the mind. **2** *tr.* absorb (people) into a larger group, esp. by causing a minority culture to acquire the characteristics of the majority culture. **3** *intr.* be absorbed into the body, mind, or a larger group. **4** *tr.* (usu. foll. by *to*, *with*) make similar to; cause to resemble. □ **assimilation** *n.* **assimilationism** *n.* **assimilationist** *n.* & *adj.* **assimilative** *adj.*

Assiniboine /əˈsɪnɪbɔɪn/ ● *n.* **1** (*pl.* same or **-s**) a member of an Aboriginal people living in S Saskatchewan and NE Montana. **2** the Siouan language of the Assiniboine. ● *adj.* of or relating to the Assiniboine.

assist ● *v.* **1** *tr.* help (a person, process, etc.). **2** *intr.* act as an assistant (*assisted in the ceremony*). **3** *Hockey* **a** *intr.* (usu. foll. by *on*) score an assist. **b** *tr.* set up (a goal scorer) with an assist. ● *n.* **1 a** *Hockey* a point awarded to up to two players who successively touch the puck with their stick immediately before a teammate scores a goal. **b** *Baseball* a fielder's action of helping to put out an opponent. **2** *N Amer.* an act of helping. □ **assistance** *n.* **assister** *n.*

assistant *n.* **1** a helper. **2** (often *attrib.*) a person who assists, esp. as a subordinate in a particular role.

assistant commissioner *n.* *Cdn* an officer ranking below deputy commissioner in the RCMP.

assistant director general *n.* *Cdn* an officer of the Sûreté du Québec ranking above chief inspector.

assistant professor *n.* *N Amer.* a university instructor ranking below an associate professor.

assisted suicide *n.* suicide effected with the assistance of another person, esp. the taking of lethal drugs, provided by a doctor for the purpose, by a patient considered incurable.

assize /əˈsaɪz/ *n.* *Cdn* (usu. in *pl.*) **1** a session of a court. **2** a trial or lawsuit held before a travelling judge.

ass-kissing *n.* (also **ass-licking**) *N Amer. coarse slang* obsequiousness for the purpose of gaining favour.

Assn. *abbr.* Association.

Assoc. *abbr.* (as part of a title etc.) **1** Association. **2** Associate. **3** Associated.

associate ● *v.* /əˈsoʊsiˌeɪt, -ʃiˌeɪt/ **1** *tr.* connect in the mind (*associate red with danger*). **2** *tr.* join or combine. **3** *refl.* make oneself a partner; declare oneself in agreement (*did not want to associate myself with the plan*). **4** *intr.* combine for a common purpose. **5** *intr.* (usu. foll. by *with*) meet frequently or have dealings. ● *n.* /əˈsoʊsiət, -ʃiət/ **1** a business partner or colleague. **2** a friend or companion. **3** a subordinate member of a body, institute, etc. **4** a thing connected with another. ● *adj.* /əˈsoʊsiˌət, -siət/ **1** joined in companionship, function, or dignity. **2** allied; in the same group or category. **3** of less than full status (*associate member*). □ **associateship** *n.*

associate professor *n.* *N Amer.* a university instructor ranking below a full professor.

association *n.* **1** a group of people or organizations united for a joint purpose. **2** the act or an instance of associating. **3** fellowship or companionship. **4** a mental connection between ideas. □ **associational** *adj.*

associative /ə'soːsiətɪv, ə'soː.ʃi-/ *adj.* **1** of or involving association. **2** *Math.* & *Computing* involving the condition that a group of quantities connected by operators (see OPERATOR 4) gives the same result whatever their grouping, as long as their order remains the same, e.g. $(a \times b) \times c = a \times (b \times c)$.

Assomption sash /ə,sʊmpʃən/ *n. Cdn hist.* = CEINTURE FLÉCHÉE.

assorted *adj.* **1** of various sorts put together; miscellaneous. **2** sorted into groups. **3** matched (*illassorted*; *poorly assorted*).

assortment *n.* a set of various sorts of things or people put together; a mixed collection.

Asst. *abbr.* Assistant.

assuage /ə'sweidʒ/ *v.tr.* **1** calm or soothe (a person, pain, etc.). **2** appease or relieve (an appetite or desire).

assume *v.tr.* **1** (often foll. by *that* + clause) take or accept as being true, without proof, for the purpose of argument or action. **2** simulate or pretend (*assumed an air of indifference*). **3** undertake (an office or duty). **4** a take on (an aspect, attribute, etc.) (*the problem assumed immense proportions*). **b** accept (another's responsibility etc.) as one's own (*assumed the company's debts*). **5** usurp, or seize (power etc.) (*assumed the presidency*). □ **assumable** *adj.*

assumption *n.* **1** the act or an instance of assuming. **2 a** the act or an instance of accepting without proof. **b** a thing assumed in this way. **3** arrogance. **4** *Catholicism* (**Assumption**) **a** the reception of the Virgin Mary bodily into heaven. **b** the feast day in honour of this (Aug. 15).

assurance *n.* **1** a positive declaration that a thing is true. **2** a solemn promise or guarantee. **3** certainty. **4** a self-confidence. **b** impudence.

assure *v.tr.* **1** (often foll. by *of*) **a** make (a person) sure; convince (*assured him of my sincerity*). **b** tell (a person) confidently (*assured them the bus went to Halifax*). **2 a** make certain of; ensure the happening etc. of (*will assure her success*). **b** make safe. □ **assurer** *n.*

assured *adj.* **1** certain, guaranteed. **2** self-confident. □ **rest assured** remain confident. □ **assuredly** *adv.*

Assyrian /ə'sɪriən/ ● *n.* **1** an inhabitant of Assyria, an ancient country in N Iraq. **2** the Semitic language of Assyria. ● *adj.* of or relating to Assyria.

AST *abbr.* Atlantic Standard Time.

astatine /'æstə,tiːn/ *n.* a radioactive element which occurs naturally and can be artificially made.

aster *n.* any composite plant of the genus *Aster*, with bright daisy-like flowers, e.g. the Michaelmas daisy.

asterisk ● *n.* a symbol (*) used in printing and writing to mark words etc. for reference, to stand for omitted matter, etc. ● *v.tr.* mark with an asterisk.

astern *adv.* (often foll. by *of*) *Naut.* & *Aviation* **1** aft; away to the rear. **2** backwards.

asteroid *n.* **1** any of the small planetary bodies revolving around the sun, mainly between the orbits of Mars and Jupiter. **2** a starfish. □ **asteroidal** *adj.*

asteroid belt *n.* the region between the orbits of Mars and Jupiter where most asteroids are found.

asthma /'æzmə/ *n.* a respiratory disorder, often provoked by allergy, causing wheezing and paroxysms of difficult breathing.

asthmatic /æz'mætɪk/ ● *adj.* relating to or suffering from asthma. ● *n.* a person suffering from asthma. □ **asthmatically** *adv.*

Asti /'æsti/ *n.* (*pl.* **Astis**) a sparkling white wine from NW Italy.

astigmatism /ə'stɪgmə,tɪzəm/ *n.* a defect in the eye or in a lens resulting in distorted images, as light rays are prevented from meeting at a common focus. □ **astigmatic** *adj.*

astilbe /ə'stɪlbi/ *n.* any plant of the genus *Astilbe*, with plumelike heads of tiny white, red, orange, or pink flowers.

Asti Spumante /spuː'mænti, -'mɒntei/ *n.* a light, sweet, sparkling form of Asti. ¶In 1994, Asti Spumante was officially renamed *Asti*.

astonish *v.tr.* amaze. □ **astonishing** *adj.* **astonishingly** *adv.* **astonishment** *n.*

astound *v.tr.* overcome with surprise or shock; amaze. □ **astounding** *adj.* **astoundingly** *adv.*

astral /'æstrəl/ *adj.* **1** of or connected with the stars. **2** consisting of stars; starry. **3** relating to or arising from a supposed ethereal existence, esp. of a counterpart of the body, associated with oneself in life and surviving after death. □ **astrally** *adv.*

astray *adv.* & *predic.adj.* **1** in or into error or sin (esp. *lead astray*). **2** out of the right way. □ **go astray 1** be lost or mislaid. **2** wander from the right way.

astride ● *prep.* with a leg on each side of; extending across. ● *adv.* with a leg on each side, or legs apart.

astringent /ə'strɪndʒənt/ ● *adj.* **1** causing the contraction of body tissues. **2** checking bleeding. **3 a** severe, austere. **b** sharp, caustic. ● *n.* an astringent substance or drug. □ **astringency** *n.*

astrochemistry *n.* the study of molecules and radicals in interstellar space.

astrolabe /'æstrə,leɪb/ *n.* an instrument, usu. consisting of a graduated disc and a pointer, formerly used to make astronomical measurements and as an aid in navigation.

astrology *n.* the study of the movements and relative positions of celestial bodies interpreted as an influence on human affairs. □ **astrologer** *n.* **astrological** *adj.* **astrologist** *n.*

astronaut *n.* **1** a person who is trained to travel in a spacecraft. **2** *Cdn (BC)* a (usu. Asian) immigrant to Canada who commutes back to Hong Kong, Taiwan, etc. frequently to work, while leaving dependents resident in Canada (also *attrib.*: *astronaut family*).

astronautics *n.* the science of space travel.

astronomical *adj.* (also **astronomic**) **1** of or relating to astronomy. **2** extremely large; too large to contemplate. □ **astronomically** *adv.*

astronomy *n.* the study of the universe and its contents beyond the bounds of the Earth's atmosphere. □ **astronomer** *n.*

astrophysics *n.* a branch of astronomy concerned with the physics and chemistry of celestial bodies. □ **astrophysical** *adj.* **astrophysicist** *n.*

Astroturf *n.* *proprietary* a synthetic surface used as a substitute for grass on sports fields etc.

astute *adj.* **1** shrewd; clever. **2** crafty. □ **astutely** *adv.* **astuteness** *n.*

asunder *adv. literary* apart.

ASW *abbr.* anti-submarine warfare.

asylum *n.* **1** sanctuary; protection, esp. for those pursued by the law (*seek asylum*). **2** = POLITICAL ASYLUM.

asymmetry /ei'sɪmətri, æ'sɪm-/ *n.* (*pl.* **-ies**) lack of symmetry. □ **asymmetric** /-'metrɪk/ *adj.* **asymmetrical** *adj.* **asymmetrically** *adv.*

asymptomatic /ei,sɪmptə'mætɪk/ *adj.* producing or showing no symptoms.

asynchronous /ei'sɪŋkrənəs/ *adj.* not synchronous. □ **asynchronously** *adv.*

AT *abbr.* ATLANTIC TIME.

At *symbol* astatine.

at *prep.* **1** expressing position, exact or approximate (*wait at the corner; at a distance*). **2** expressing a point in time (*went at dawn*). **3** expressing a point in a scale or range (*at boiling point; at her best*). **4** expressing engagement or concern in a state or activity (*at war; at work*). **5** expressing a value or rate (*sell at $10 each*). **6 a** with or with reference to; in terms of (*at a disadvantage; annoyed at losing; good at math*). **b** by means of (*drank it at a gulp*). **7** expressing: **a** motion towards (*arrived at the station; went at them*). **b** aim towards or pursuit of (physically or conceptually) (*aim at the target; laughed at us*). □ **at it 1** engaged in an activity; working hard (*let's get at it*). **2** *informal* repeating a habitual (usu. disapproved of) activity (*found them at it again*). **at that** moreover (*found one, and a good one at that*). **where it's at** *slang* the fashionable scene or activity.

atavism /'ætə,vɪzəm/ *n.* **1** a resemblance to remote ancestors rather than to parents in plants or animals. **2** reversion to an earlier type. □ **atavistic** *adj.*

ATB *abbr.* ALL-TERRAIN BICYCLE.

at-bat *n.* *Baseball* a turn at bat which results in the batter making either a hit or an out.

ATC *abbr.* AIR TRAFFIC CONTROL.

ate *past of* EAT.

atelier /,ætəl'jei/ *n.* a workshop or studio, esp. of an artist or designer.

a tempo *adv.* *Music* in the previous tempo.

Athanasian Creed /,æθə'neiʃən/ *n.* an affirmation of Christian faith formerly much used in the Western Church.

Athapaskan /,æθə'pæskən/ (also **Athabascan, Athabaskan** /-'bæ-/, **Athapascan**) ● *n.* **1** an Aboriginal language group of the subarctic regions of the NWT, the Yukon, northern BC, and the northern Prairie provinces. **2** (*pl.* same or **-s**) a member of any of the N American peoples speaking languages of this family. ● *adj.* of or relating to the Athapaskan peoples or their languages.

Atharva-Veda /ə,tɑrvə'veidə, -'vi:də/ *n.* an ancient collection of sacred Hindu hymns and incantations.

atheism /'eiθi,ɪzəm/ *n.* disbelief in the existence of God or gods. □ **atheist** *n.* **atheistic** *adj.*

Athenian /ə'θi:niən/ ● *n.* a native or inhabitant of ancient or modern Athens, a city in Greece. ● *adj.* of or relating to ancient or modern Athens.

atherosclerosis /,æθəro:sklə'ro:sɪs/ *n.* a form of arteriosclerosis characterized by the degeneration of the arteries because of the buildup of fatty deposits. □ **atherosclerotic** /-'rɒtɪk/ *adj.*

athlete *n.* **1** a person who trains to compete in sports and other exercises requiring physical skill, strength, and endurance. **2** a person with a natural talent for sports.

athlete's foot *n.* a fungal foot condition causing itching, flaking, and cracking of the skin, esp. between the toes.

athletic *adj.* **1** of or relating to athletes or athletics (*an athletic competition*). **2** muscular or physically fit. **3** active in, esp. skilled at, sports. □ **athletically** *adv.* **athleticism** *n.*

athletics *n.pl.* (usu. treated as *sing.*) competitive activities requiring physical skill and endurance.

athletic shoe *n.* a shoe designed for sports or recreation.

athletic supporter *n.* = JOCKSTRAP.

at-home ● *n.* a social reception in a person's home. ● *adj.* occurring in or remaining in the home.

-athon *comb. form* (also **-a-thon**) forming nouns denoting: **1** an extended event involving a single activity, usu. to raise money for a charity (*walkathon*). **2** an activity of abnormal length (*gab-a-thon*).

athwart ● *prep.* from side to side of. ● *adv.* across from side to side (usu. obliquely).

Atlantic *adj.* of or adjoining the Atlantic Ocean.

Atlanticist /æt'læntɪsɪst/ ● *adj.* advocating or favouring a close relationship between N America and Europe. ● *n.* a person who advocates or favours such a relationship.

Atlantic provinces *n.pl.* (also **Atlantic Canada**) New Brunswick, Nova Scotia, PEI, and Newfoundland (compare MARITIMES).

Atlantic puffin *n. see* PUFFIN.

Atlantic salmon *n.* a salmon, *Salmo salar*, of the coastal N Atlantic and its freshwater tributaries.

Atlantic Time *n.* the time in a zone including the Maritime provinces, parts of Labrador and E Quebec, and eastern Central and S America. **Atlantic Standard Time** is four hours behind GMT; **Atlantic Daylight Time** is three hours behind GMT.

atlas *n.* a book of maps or charts.

ATM *abbr.* AUTOMATED TELLER MACHINE.

atmosphere *n.* **1 a** the envelope of gases surrounding the earth, any other planet, or any substance. **b** the air in any particular place, esp. if unpleasant. **2 a** the pervading tone or mood of a place or situation, esp. with reference to the feelings or emotions evoked. **b** the feelings or emotions evoked by a work of art, a piece of music, etc. **3** *Physics* a unit of pressure equal to mean atmospheric pressure at sea level, 101.325 kilopascals.

atmospheric /,ætməs'fi:rɪk, -'ferɪk/ *adj.* **1** of, relating to, or occurring in the atmosphere. **2** possessing or evoking a particular or characteristic tone, mood, or set of associations.

atmospheric pressure *n.* the pressure exerted on the earth's surface by the weight of the air above it.

atmospherics *n.pl.* **1** electrical disturbance in the atmosphere, esp. caused by lightning. **2** interference with telecommunications caused by this. **3** = ATMOSPHERE 2.

atoll /'ætɒl/ *n.* a ring-shaped coral reef enclosing a lagoon.

atom *n.* **1 a** the smallest particle of a chemical element that can take part in a chemical reaction. **b** this particle as a source of nuclear energy. **2** *Cdn* **a** a level of children's sports, usu. involving children aged 9–11. **b** a player in this age group. **3** (often with *neg.*) a very small portion of a thing or quality (*not an atom of pity*).

atomic *adj.* **1** concerned with or using atomic energy or atomic bombs. **2** of or relating to an atom or atoms. □ **atomically** *adv.*

atomic age *n.* the current historical period, characterized by the use of atomic energy.

atomic bomb *n.* (also **atom bomb**) a bomb involving the release of energy by nuclear fission.

atomic energy *n.* energy obtained by nuclear fission or fusion.

atomicity /,ætə'mɪsɪti/ *n.* **1** the number of atoms in the molecules of an element. **2** the state or fact of being composed of atoms.

atomic number *n.* the number of protons in the nucleus of an atom, which is characteristic of a chemical element and determines its place in the periodic table. Symbol: Z.

atomic particle *n.* any one of the particles of which an atom is constituted.

atomic pile *n.* a nuclear reactor.

atomic theory *n.* **1** *Physics* the concept of an atom as being composed of elementary particles. **2** *Physics* the theory that all matter is made up of small indivisible particles called atoms, and that the atoms of any one element are identical in all respects but differ from those of other elements and unite to form compounds in fixed proportions. **3** *Philos.* atomism.

atomism *n. Philos.* the theory that all matter consists of tiny individual particles. □ **atomistic** *adj.*

atomize *v.tr.* **1** reduce to atoms or fine particles. **2** break up (a society etc.) into small constituent parts; fragment. □ **atomization** *n.*

atomizer *n.* an instrument for emitting liquids as a fine spray.

atonal /ei'to:nəl/ *adj. Music* not written in any key or mode. □ **atonality** *n.*

atone *v.intr.* (usu. foll. by *for*) make amends; expiate (for a wrong).

atonement *n.* **1** expiation; reparation for a wrong or injury. **2** (**Atonement**) *Christianity* the reconciliation of God and humanity, esp. the expiation by Christ of mankind's sin.

atop ● *prep.* on the top of. ● *adv.* on the top.

atrazine /'ætrəzi:n/ *n.* an agricultural herbicide used esp. to control annual weeds.

atrium /'eitriəm/ *n.* (*pl.* **-s** or **atria** /-triə/) **1 a** the central court of an ancient Roman house. **b** a central hall or court, often rising through several storeys, with galleries and rooms opening off it. **2** a cavity in the body, esp. one of two upper cavities of the heart, receiving blood from the veins. □ **atrial** *adj.*

atrocious *adj.* **1** very bad or unpleasant (*their manners were atrocious*). **2** extremely savage or wicked (*atrocious cruelty*). □ **atrociously** *adv.*

atrocity *n.* (*pl.* **-ies**) **1** an extremely wicked or cruel act, esp. one involving physical violence or injury. **2** extreme wickedness. **3** something that evokes outrage or disgust.

atrophy /'ætrəfi/ ● *v.* (**-ies, -ied**) **1** *intr.* waste away through undernourishment, ageing, or lack of use; become emaciated. **2** *tr.* cause to atrophy. ● *n.* the process of atrophying. □ **atrophic** /ə'trɒfɪk/ *adj.*

Atsina /æt'si:nə/ *n.* = Gros Ventre.

attaboy *interj.* esp. *N Amer.* expressing encouragement or admiration.

attach *v.* **1** *tr.* fasten, affix, join. **2** *tr.* (in *passive*; foll. by *to*) be very fond of or devoted to (*am attached to her*). **3** *tr.* attribute, assign (some function, quality, or characteristic) (*attaches great importance to it*). **4 a** *tr.* accompany; form part of (*no conditions are attached*). **b** *intr.* (foll. by *to*) be an attribute or characteristic (*great prestige attaches to the job*). **5** *refl.* take part in; join (*attached themselves to the expedition*). **6** *tr.* appoint for special or temporary duties. **7** *tr. Law* seize (a person or property) by legal authority. □ **attachable** *adj.*

attaché /ætæ'ʃei/ *n.* **1** a person appointed to an ambassador's staff, usu. with a special sphere of activity (*cultural attaché*). **2** *N Amer.* an attaché case.

attaché case *n.* a small flat rectangular case for carrying documents etc.; a briefcase.

attachment *n.* **1** a thing attached or to be attached, esp. to a machine, device, etc., for a special function. **2** affection, devotion. **3** a means of attaching. **4** the

act of attaching or the state of being attached. **5** legal seizure. **6** a temporary position in an organization.

attack ● *v.* **1** *tr.* act violently against. **2** *tr. Military* begin an offensive against. **3** *tr.* criticize adversely. **4** *tr.* act harmfully upon (*a virus attacking the nervous system*). **5** *tr.* vigorously apply oneself to; begin work on (*attacked his meal with gusto*). **6** *intr.* make an attack. **7** *intr.* be in a mode of attack. ● *n.* **1** the act or process of attacking. **2** an offensive military operation. **3** *Music* the action or manner of beginning a piece, passage, etc. **4** gusto, vigour. **5** a sudden occurrence of esp. an illness. **6** *Sport* **a** the players seeking to score goals etc. **b** the players seeking to score goals etc. □ **attacker** *n.*

attain *v.* **1** *tr.* arrive at; reach (a goal etc.). **2** *tr.* gain, accomplish (an aim, distinction, etc.). **3** *intr.* (foll. by *to*) arrive at by conscious development or effort. □ **attainable** *adj.* **attainability** *n.*

attainment *n.* **1** (often in *pl.*) something attained or achieved. **2** the act or an instance of attaining.

attempt ● *v.tr.* **1** (often foll. by *to* + infin.) seek to achieve or complete (a task or action) (*attempted the exercise; attempted to explain*). **2** seek to climb or master (a mountain etc.). ● *n.* an act of attempting; an endeavour. □ **attemptable** *adj.*

attend *v.* **1** *tr.* **a** be present at (*attended the meeting*). **b** go regularly to (*attend school*). **2** *intr.* **a** be present (*many members failed to attend*). **b** be present in a serving capacity; wait. **3 a** *tr.* escort, accompany (*she was attended by three bridesmaids*). **b** *intr.* (foll. by *on*) wait on; serve. **4** *intr.* **a** turn or apply one's mind; focus one's attention (*attend to what I am saying*). **b** (foll. by *to*) deal with (*shall attend to the matter myself*). **5** *tr.* (usu. in *passive*) follow as a result from (*the error was attended by serious consequences*). □ **attender** *n.*

attendance *n.* **1** the act of attending or being present. **2** the number of people present.

attendant ● *n.* a person employed to wait on others or provide a service (*flight attendant*). ● *adj.* **1** accompanying (*attendant circumstances*). **2** waiting on; serving (*ladies attendant on the queen*).

attendee *n.* a person who attends (a meeting etc.).

attention ● *n.* **1** the act or faculty of applying one's mind (*give me your attention*). **2 a** consideration. **b** care (*give special attention to your handwriting*). **3** (in *pl.*) **a** ceremonious politeness (*he paid his attentions to her*). **b** wooing, courting (*the subject of his attentions*). **4** a soldier's drill position, standing upright with feet together and arms stretched downwards (*stand at attention*). ● *interj.* **1** calling people to listen to an announcement etc. (*Attention, please!*). **2** ordering soldiers to come to attention.

attention deficit disorder *n. Psych.* a disorder esp. of children characterized by a short attention span and impulsiveness, often accompanied by hyperactivity. Abbr.: **ADD**.

attentive *adj.* **1** paying attention. **2** assiduously polite. □ **attentively** *adv.* **attentiveness** *n.*

attenuate ● *v.tr.* /ə'tenjʊ,eit/ **1** reduce in force, value, or virulence. **2** *Electricity* reduce the amplitude of (a signal or current). **3** make thin. ● *adj.* /ə'tenjʊət/ **1** slender. **2** tapering gradually. □ **attenuated** *adj.* **attenuation** *n.* **attenuator** *n.*

attest *v.* **1** *tr.* confirm the validity or truth of. **2** *tr.* be evidence or proof of. **3** *intr.* (foll. by *to*) bear witness to. □ **attestable** *adj.* **attestor** *n.*

attestation *n.* **1** the act of attesting. **2** a testimony.

attic *n.* **1** the highest storey of a house, usu. immediately under the beams of the roof. **2** a room in the attic area.

Attikamek /æ'tɪkə,mek/ ● *n.* **1** (*pl.* same or **-s**) a member of an Aboriginal people living in the upper St. Maurice River valley in Quebec. **2** the Algonquian language of this people. ● *adj.* of or relating to the Attikamek or their culture or language.

attire ● *v.tr.* (usu. as **attired** *adj.*) dress, esp. in fine clothes or formal wear. ● *n.* clothes, esp. fine or formal.

attitude *n.* **1 a** a settled opinion or way of thinking. **b** behaviour reflecting this (*I don't like his attitude*). **2 a** a bodily posture. **b** a pose adopted in a painting or a play, esp. for dramatic effect (*strike an attitude*). **c** *Dance* a pose in which the dancer stands on one leg, with the other raised and bent in front or behind. **3** *informal* an uncooperative or hostile disposition (*a teenager with attitude*). □ **attitudinal** *adj.*

attn. *abbr.* **1** attention. **2** for the attention of.

attorney *n.* (*pl.* **-eys**) **1** a person, esp. a lawyer, appointed to act for another in business or legal matters. **2** *US* a lawyer, esp. one representing a client in a law court.

Attorney General *n.* (*pl.* **Attorneys General**) **1** (in Canada) the minister of the Crown (federally and provincially) responsible for the administration of justice and also acting as legal adviser to the government. **2** a similar chief legal officer in other countries.

attract *v.* **1** *tr.* draw or bring to oneself or itself (*attracts many admirers*). **2** *tr.* & *intr.* be attractive to; fascinate (*opposites attract*). **3** *tr.* (of a magnet, gravity, etc.) exert a pull on (an object). □ **attractor** *n.*

attractant ● *n.* a substance which attracts something. ● *adj.* attracting.

attraction *n.* **1 a** the act or power of attracting (*the attraction of foreign travel*). **b** a person or thing that attracts by arousing interest (*the fair is a big attraction*). **2** *Physics* the force by which bodies attract or approach each other (*opp.* REPULSION).

attractive *adj.* **1** attracting or capable of attracting; interesting (*an attractive proposition*). **2** aesthetically pleasing or appealing. □ **attractively** *adv.* **attractiveness** *n.*

attribute ● *v.tr.* **1** regard as belonging or appropriate to (*a poem attributed to Shakespeare*). **2** ascribe to; regard as the effect of a stated cause (*delays were attributed to the traffic*). ● *n.* **1 a** a quality ascribed to a person or thing. **b** a characteristic quality. **2 a** a material object recognized as appropriate to a person, office, or status (*a sceptre is an attribute of majesty*). **3** an attributive adjective or noun. □ **attributable** *adj.* **attribution** *n.*

attributive *adj.* (of an adjective or noun) preceding the word described and expressing an attribute, as *old* in *the old dog* (but not in *the dog is old*) and *expiry* in *expiry date* (*opp.* PREDICATIVE). □ **attributively** *adv.*

attrition *n.* **1** *N Amer.* & *Austral.* reduction of a workforce by processes other than firing, as by non-replacement of employees who retire, die, etc. **2 a** the act or process of gradually wearing out, esp. by friction. **b** abrasion. □ **attritional** *adj.*

attune *v.tr.* (usu. foll. by *to*) adjust (a person or thing) to a situation.

ATV *abbr.* ALL-TERRAIN VEHICLE.

atypical /ˌeiˈtɪpɪkəl/ *adj.* not typical; not conforming to a type. □ **atypically** *adv.*

Au *symbol* the element gold.

auberge /oˈbɛrʒ/ *n.* an inn.

aubergine /ˈoːbɜrˌʒiːn/ *n.* a dark purple colour.

auburn *adj.* reddish brown (usu. of a person's hair).

au contraire *interj.* on the contrary; not true.

au courant /ˌoː kuːˈrɑ̃/ *predic.adj.* (usu. foll. by *with*, *of*) **1** aware of what is going on; well-informed. **2** trendy; fashionable.

auction ● *n.* a sale of goods, usu. in public, in which articles are sold to the highest bidder. ● *v.tr.* sell by auction. □ **at auction** in an auction sale.

auction block *n.* *N Amer.* a place or facility for the auction of goods. □ **on the auction block** available for auction or sale.

auctioneer *n.* a person who conducts auctions professionally, by calling for bids and declaring goods sold. □ **auctioneering** *n.*

auction house *n.* a company which specializes in sales by auction.

audacious *adj.* **1** daring, bold. **2** impudent. □ **audaciously** *adv.* **audaciousness** *n.* **audacity** *n.*

audible ● *adj.* capable of being heard. ● *n.* *Football* a play called by the quarterback at the line of scrimmage to replace one previously agreed on. □ **audibility** *n.* **audibleness** *n.* **audibly** *adv.*

audience *n.* **1 a** the assembled listeners or spectators at an event, esp. a stage performance etc. **b** the people addressed by a film, book, etc. **2** a formal interview with a person in authority.

audio *n.* (usu. *attrib.*) **1** sound or its (esp. electrical) reproduction. **2** equipment for electrical reproduction of sound, e.g. speakers etc. (*home audio*).

audio- *comb. form* hearing or sound.

audiophile *n.* a person who has a particularly strong interest in high-fidelity sound reproduction.

audio tape ● *n.* **1** a magnetic tape on which sound can be recorded. **2** a sound recording on tape. ● *v.tr.* (**audiotape**) record (sound, speech, etc.) on tape.

audiovisual *adj.* (esp. of teaching methods) using electrical equipment, e.g. projectors, tape recorders, etc., directed at the senses of sight and hearing.

audit ● *n.* **1** an official examination and verification of accounts. **2** a detailed examination or analysis, esp. to assess strengths and weaknesses (*environmental audit*). ● *v.tr.* & *intr.* (**audited, auditing**) **1** conduct an audit (of). **2** *N Amer.* attend (a class) informally, without working for credits.

audition ● *n.* **1** an interview for a role as a singer, actor, dancer, etc., consisting of a practical demonstration of suitability. **2** the power of hearing or listening. ● *v.* **1** *tr.* interview (a candidate at an audition). **2** *intr.* be interviewed at an audition.

auditor *n.* **1** a person who audits accounts. **2** *N Amer.* a person who audits a class. **3** a listener.

Auditor General *n.* (*pl.* **Auditors General**) *Cdn* the official responsible for auditing the accounts of a (federal or provincial) government's agencies, departments, and some Crown corporations, and presenting an annual report on government spending to the House of Commons or legislature.

auditorium *n.* (*pl.* **-s** or **auditoria**) **1** the part of a theatre etc. in which the audience sits. **2** *N Amer.* a building incorporating a large hall for public gatherings, performances, sports events, etc. **3** *N Amer.* a large room, esp. in a school, used for assemblies, theatrical performances, etc. and also usu. as a gymnasium.

auditory *adj.* **1** concerned with hearing. **2** received by the ear.

au fait /oː ˈfei/ *predic.adj.* (usu. foll. by *with*) having current knowledge; conversant (*fully au fait with the arrangements*).

au fond /oː ˈfɔ̃/ *adv.* basically.

Aug. *abbr.* August.

auger *n.* **1** a tool resembling a large corkscrew, for boring holes in wood, the ground, ice, etc. **2** a similar device enclosed in a cylinder for moving grain etc.

augment *v.tr. & intr.* make or become greater; increase or enhance. □ **augmenter** *n.*

augmentation *n.* **1** enlargement; growth; increase. **2** *Music* the lengthening of the time-values of notes in melodic parts.

au gratin /ˌoː ɡræˈtæ/ *adj. Cooking* cooked with a crisp brown crust usu. of bread crumbs or melted cheese.

augur ● *v.* **1** *intr.* **a** (of an event, circumstance, etc.) suggest a specified outcome (*augurs ill*). **b** portend, bode (*all augured well for our success*). **2** *tr.* **a** foresee, predict. **b** portend. ● *n. Rom. Hist.* a religious official who observed natural signs, interpreting these as an indication of divine approval or disapproval of a proposed action. □ **augural** *adj.*

augury *n.* (*pl.* **-ies**) **1** an omen; a portent. **2** the work of an augur; the interpretation of omens.

August *n.* the eighth month of the year.

august /ɒˈɡʌst/ *adj.* inspiring reverence and admiration; venerable, impressive. □ **augustly** *adv.* **augustness** *n.*

Augustan /ɒˈɡʌstən/ ● *adj.* **1** connected with, occurring during, or influenced by the reign of the Roman emperor Augustus (63 BC–AD 14), esp. as an outstanding period of Latin literature. **2** (of a literary period, esp. the 18th c. in England) characterized by a refined and classical style. ● *n.* a writer of the Augustan age of any literature.

Augustinian /ˌɒɡəˈstɪniən/ ● *adj.* **1** of or relating to St. Augustine of Hippo (354–430) or his doctrines. **2** belonging to a religious order observing a rule derived from St. Augustine's writings. ● *n.* **1** an adherent of the doctrines of St. Augustine. **2** a member of an Augustinian religious order.

au jus /oː ˈʒuː/ *adj.* (of meat, esp. roast beef) served with its natural juices.

auk *n.* any of various marine diving birds of the family Alcidae, with a heavy body, short wings, and black and white plumage, e.g. the guillemot.

auklet *n.* any of various small auks, chiefly of the N Pacific.

au naturel *predic.adj. & adv.* **1** naked. **2** in a natural, untouched, or unimproved state. **3** uncooked; (cooked) in the most natural or simplest way.

aunt /ænt, *Maritimes* ɒnt/ *n.* **1** the sister of one's father or mother. **2** an uncle's wife. **3** *informal* an unrelated woman friend of a child or children. □ **my** (or **my sainted** etc.) **aunt** *slang* an exclamation of surprise, disbelief, etc.

auntie /ˈænti, *Maritimes* ˈɒnti/ *n.* (also **aunty**) (*pl.* **-ies**) *informal* = AUNT.

au pair *n.* a young person from another country, esp. a woman, helping with housework etc. in exchange for room and board, esp. as a means of learning a language.

aura *n.* (*pl.* **auras**) **1** the distinctive atmosphere diffused by or attending a person, place, etc. **2** (in mystic or spiritualistic use) a supposed subtle emanation, visible as a sphere of white or coloured light, surrounding the body of a living creature. **3** a subtle aroma from flowers etc. □ **aural** *adj.*

aural *adj.* of or relating to or received by the ear. □ **aurally** *adv.*

aureole /ˈɔːriˌoːl/ *n.* **1** a halo or circle of light, esp. around the head or body of a portrayed religious figure. **2** a corona around the sun or moon.

Aureomycin /ˌɔːrioˈmaɪsɪn/ *n. proprietary* an antibiotic

of the tetracycline family used esp. to treat lung diseases.

au revoir *interj. & n.* goodbye (until we meet again).

auricula /ɔːˈrɪkjələ/ *n.* a primula, *Primula auricula*, with a dark purple outer ring and pale yellow centre.

aurora /əˈrɔːrə/ *n.* (*pl.* **-s** or **aurorae** /-riː/) **1** a luminous phenomenon, usu. of shimmering coloured streamers, seen in the upper atmosphere in high latitudes, and caused by the interaction of charged solar particles with atmospheric gases, under the influence of the earth's magnetic field. **2** *literary* the dawn. □ **auroral** *adj.*

aurora australis /ɒˈstrælɪs/ *n.* a southern occurrence of the aurora. *Also called* SOUTHERN LIGHTS.

aurora borealis /ˌbɔːriˈælɪs/ *n.* a northern occurrence of the aurora. *Also called* NORTHERN LIGHTS.

auscultation /ˌɒskəlˈteɪʃən/ *n.* the act of listening, esp. to sounds from the heart, lungs, etc., as a part of medical diagnosis. □ **auscultatory** /-ˈkʌltətɔːri/ *adj.*

auspice *n.* **1** (in *pl.*) patronage, support (*under the auspices of*). **2** a forecast.

auspicious *adj.* of good omen; favourable. □ **auspiciously** *adv.* **auspiciousness** *n.*

Aussie *informal* ● *n.* **1** an Australian. **2** Australia. ● *adj.* Australian.

austere *adj.* **1** severely simple. **2** morally strict. **3** harsh, stern. □ **austerely** *adv.*

austerity *n.* (*pl.* **-ies**) **1** sternness; moral severity. **2** frugality or money-saving practices. **3** (esp. in *pl.*) an austere practice (*the austerities of a monk's life*).

austral /ˈɒstrəl/ *adj.* **1** southern. **2** (**Austral**) of Australia or Australasia (*Austral English*).

Australian ● *n.* **1** a native or national of Australia, an island country and continent in the SW Pacific. **2** a person of Australian descent. ● *adj.* of or relating to Australia. □ **Australianism** *n.*

Australian crawl *n. Swimming* = CRAWL *n.* 3.

Australian Rules *n.* a form of football played with an oval ball on an oval field by teams of 18, having very few rules.

Australoid /ˈɒstrələɪd/ ● *adj.* of a race of peoples that diffused from Asia to Australia at a time of lower sea level. ● *n.* a person of Australoid ethnological type.

Australopithecus /ˌɒstrələˈpɪθɪkəs/ *n.* any extinct bipedal primate of the genus *Australopithecus* having apelike and human characteristics, or its fossilized remains. □ **australopithecine** /-ˌsiːn/ *n. & adj.*

Austrian ● *n.* **1** a native or national of Austria, a country in central Europe. **2** a person of Austrian descent. ● *adj.* of or relating to Austria.

Austrian pine *n.* a pine, *Pinus nigra*, native to Europe and W Asia, with a dense branch system, widely cultivated as an ornamental.

Austro- *comb. form* **1** Austrian; Austrian and (*Austro-Hungarian*). **2** Australian; Australian and (*Austronesian*).

Austronesian /ɒstroˈniːʒən/ ● *n.* a family of languages spoken widely in Malaysia, Indonesia, and other parts of SE Asia, and in the islands of the central and S Pacific. ● *adj.* of or relating to this language family.

autarky /ˈɒtɑːrki/ *n.* (*pl.* **-ies**) **1** self-sufficiency, esp. as an economic system. **2** a state etc. run according to such a system. □ **autarkic** *adj.* **autarkical** *adj.*

auteur /oːˈtɜːr/ *n.* a director who so greatly influences the films directed as to be able to rank as their author.

authentic *adj.* **1 a** of undisputed origin; genuine. **b** reliable or trustworthy. **2** *Music* performed on instruments dating from and with techniques typical of the same period as the piece performed. □

authentically *adv.* **authenticity** *n.*

authenticate *v.tr.* **1** establish the truth or genuineness of. **2** validate. □ **authentication** *n.*

author ● *n.* **1** a writer, esp. of books. **2** the originator of an event, a condition, etc. (*the author of all my woes*). ● *v.tr. disputed* be the author of. □ **authorial** *adj.*

authoress *n.* a female writer, esp. of books. ¶*Author* is now usu. preferred.

authoritarian ● *adj.* **1** favouring, encouraging, or enforcing strict obedience to authority, as opposed to individual freedom. **2** tyrannical or domineering. ● *n.* a person favouring absolute obedience to a constituted authority. □ **authoritarianism** *n.*

authoritative *adj.* **1** recognized as true or dependable. **2** (of a person etc.) commanding or self-confident. **3** official (*an authoritative document*). □ **authoritatively** *adv.* **authoritativeness** *n.*

authority *n.* (*pl.* **-ies**) **1 a** the power or right to enforce obedience. **b** (often foll. by *for*, or *to* + infin.) delegated power. **2** (esp. in *pl.*) a person or body having authority, esp. a police or government official. **3 a** an expert in a particular subject. **b** a book etc. that can supply reliable information. **4** considerable force or strength (*spoke with authority*). **5** testimony, evidence (*took it on their authority*).

authorize *v.tr.* **1** sanction formally. **2** (foll. by *to* + infin.) give authority. □ **authorization** *n.*

Authorized Version *n.* = KING JAMES VERSION.

authorship *n.* **1** the origin of a book or other written work (*of unknown authorship*). **2** the occupation of writing.

autism *n.* a mental condition, usu. present from childhood, characterized by complete self-absorption and a reduced ability to respond to or communicate with the outside world. □ **autistic** *adj.*

auto (*pl.* **-os**) *N Amer.* ● *n.* an automobile (usu. *attrib.*: *auto mechanic*). ● *adj.* automatic.

auto- *comb. form* **1** originating with, induced by, or pertaining to the self (*autobiography*). **2** self-operating; automatic (*autofocus*). **3** relating to automobiles or the automobile industry (*automaker*).

autobiography *n.* (*pl.* **-ies**) **1** a personal account of one's own life, esp. for publication. **2** this as a process or literary form. □ **autobiographer** *n.* **autobiographic** *adj.* **autobiographical** *adj.*

autochthonous /ɒ'tɒkθənəs/ *adj.* **1** *Geol.* (of a rock formation) originating in the place in which it is found. **2** indigenous.

autocracy /ɒ'tɒkrəsi/ *n.* (*pl.* **-ies**) **1** absolute government by one person. **2** the power exercised by such a person. **3** an autocratic country or society.

autocrat /'ɒtə,kræt/ *n.* **1** an absolute ruler. **2** a dictatorial person. □ **autocratic** *adj.* **autocratically** *adv.*

autodidact /,ɒto:'daɪdækt/ *n.* a self-taught person. □ **autodidactic** *adj.*

auto-eroticism *n.* (also **auto-erotism**) *Psych.* masturbation. □ **auto-erotic** *adj.*

autofocus *n.* a device for focusing a camera etc. automatically.

autogenic training /ɒtə'dʒenik/ *n.* a relaxation technique in which the patient learns a form of self-hypnosis and biofeedback as a way of managing stress.

autograph ● *n.* **1 a** a signature, esp. that of a celebrity. **b** handwriting. **2** a manuscript in an author's own handwriting. **3** a document signed by its author. ● *v.tr.* **1** sign (a photograph, autograph album, etc.). **2** write (a letter etc.) by hand.

autoimmune *adj.* (of a disease) caused by antibodies produced against substances naturally present in the body. □ **autoimmunity** *n.*

automaker *n.* a company which manufactures automobiles.

automata *pl. of* AUTOMATON.

automate *v.tr.* convert to or operate by automation (*the ticket office has been automated*).

automated teller machine *n.* an electronic machine which allows users to perform banking transactions by inserting an encoded plastic card.

automatic ● *adj.* **1** (of a machine, device, etc., or its function) working by itself, without direct human intervention. **2 a** done spontaneously, without conscious thought or intention (*an automatic reaction*). **b** necessary and inevitable (*an automatic penalty*). **3** *Psych.* performed unconsciously or subconsciously. **4 a** (of a firearm) that continues firing until the pressure on the trigger is released or the ammunition is exhausted. **b** (of a pistol) that fires each time the trigger is pulled, without requiring manual reloading. **5** (of a motor vehicle or its transmission) using gears that change automatically according to speed and acceleration. ● *n.* **1** an automatic device, esp. a gun or transmission. **2** a vehicle with automatic transmission. □ **automatically** *adv.* **automaticity** /,ɒtəmə'tɪsɪti/ *n.*

automatic pilot *n.* **1** a device for keeping an aircraft on a set course. **2** the state of a person doing something by routine or habit, without concentration.

automation *n.* **1** the use of automatic equipment to save mental and manual labour. **2** the state of being automated.

automatism /ɒ'tɒmə,tɪzəm/ *n.* **1** *Psych.* **a** the performance of actions unconsciously or subconsciously (*epileptic automatism*). **b** such action. **2** *Law* an involuntary action for which one is not held legally responsible. **2** unthinking routine.

automaton /ɒ'tɒmətɒn/ *n.* (*pl.* **automata** /-tə/ or **-s**) **1** a mechanism which operates with concealed motive power, esp. one simulating a living being. **2** a person who behaves without active intelligence or mechanically in a set pattern or routine.

automobile *n.* *N Amer.* a car (often *attrib.*).

automotive *adj.* concerned with motor vehicles.

autonomic nervous system /,ɒtə'nɒmɪk/ *n.* the part of the nervous system responsible for control of the bodily functions not consciously directed, e.g. heartbeat.

autonomous /ɒ'tɒnəməs/ *adj.* **1** having self-government. **2** acting or existing independently or having the freedom to do so. □ **autonomously** *adv.*

autonomy *n.* (*pl.* **-ies**) **1** the right of self-government. **2** personal freedom or independence. **3** freedom of the will. **4** a self-governing community. □ **autonomist** *n.*

Autopac *n.* *Cdn* (*Man.*) *proprietary* the vehicle insurance provided by the Manitoba government through Manitoba Public Insurance.

autopilot *n.* = AUTOMATIC PILOT.

autopsy *n.* (*pl.* **-ies**) **1** a post-mortem examination conducted to determine the cause of death. **2** a critical analysis of an event etc. after its completion.

autoroute /'ɒto:,ru:t/ *n.* an expressway in Quebec, France, and other French-speaking regions.

auto worker *n.* a labourer employed by an automobile manufacturer.

autumn n. **1** the third season of the year, associated with harvests and falling leaves, in the northern hemisphere from September to November and in the southern hemisphere from March to May. **2** Astronomy the period from the autumnal equinox to the winter solstice. **3** a time of maturity or incipient decay.

autumnal /ɒˈtʌmnəl/ adj. **1** of, characteristic of, or appropriate to autumn. **2** occurring in autumn (autumnal equinox). **3** maturing or blooming in autumn. **4** past the prime of life.

autumnal equinox n. (also **autumn equinox**) the equinox occurring on or about 22 Sept. in the northern hemisphere and on or about 21 March in the southern hemisphere.

auxiliary /ɒɡˈzɪljəri, -ˈzɪləri/ ● adj. **1** (of a person or thing) helpful, giving support. **2** (of services or equipment) subsidiary, additional. **3** (of a sailing vessel) equipped with an engine. ● n. (pl. **-ies**) **1** an auxiliary person or thing. **2** N Amer. a group of volunteers who assist a church, hospital, etc. with fundraising and other charitable activities. **3** (in pl.) Military foreign or allied troops in a belligerent nation's service. **4** Grammar an auxiliary verb.

auxiliary bishop n. Catholicism a bishop who assists a diocesan bishop.

auxiliary verb n. a verb used in forming tenses, moods, and voices of other verbs, e.g. will in she will go.

AV abbr. **1** AUDIOVISUAL. **2** AUTHORIZED VERSION.

avail ● v. **1** tr. help, benefit. **2** refl. (foll. by of) profit by; take advantage of. ● n. **1** (usu. in neg. phrases) use, profit (to no avail). **2** (in pl.) esp. Cdn proceeds or profits, esp. those produced by another person's labour (living off the avails of prostitution).

available adj. (often foll. by to, for) **1** capable of being used; at one's disposal; obtainable. **2** (of a person) a free for consultation or service. **b** presently uninvolved in a romantic relationship. □ **availability** n. **availableness** n. **availably** adv.

avalanche ● n. **1** a mass of snow, ice, rock, etc. tumbling rapidly down a mountainside. **2** a sudden appearance or arrival of anything in large quantities (faced with an avalanche of work). ● v. **1** intr. descend like an avalanche. **2** tr. carry down like an avalanche.

avant-garde /ˌævɒntˈɡɑrd/ ● n. pioneers or innovators esp. in art and literature. ● adj. (of ideas, works of art, etc.) experimental, progressive. □ **avant-gardism** n. **avant-gardist** n.

avarice /ˈævərɪs/ n. extreme greed for money or gain; cupidity. □ **avaricious** /ˌævəˈrɪʃəs/ adj. **avariciously** adv. **avariciousness** n.

avatar /ˈævəˌtɑr/ n. **1** Hinduism the descent of a deity or released soul to earth in bodily form. **2** incarnation; embodiment. **3** a manifestation or phase.

Ave. abbr. Avenue.

ave /ˈɒveɪ/ n. (in full **Ave Maria** /ˈɒveɪ məˈriːə/) = HAIL MARY 1.

avenge v.tr. **1** inflict retribution on behalf of (a person, a violated right, etc.). **2** take vengeance for (an injury). □ **be avenged** avenge oneself. □ **avenger** n.

avens /ˈævənz/ n. **1** any of various plants of the genus Geum. **2** = MOUNTAIN AVENS.

avenue n. **1 a** an urban road or street. **b** (in many N American grid-layout cities) a road running perpendicular to a street, esp. east-west (compare STREET 1d). **2** a road, driveway, or path with trees at regular intervals along its sides. **3** a way of approaching or dealing with something (explored every avenue to find an answer).

aver /əˈvɜr/ v.tr. (**averred**, **averring**) formal assert or affirm.

average ● n. **1 a** the usual amount, extent, or rate. **b** the ordinary standard. **2** the result of adding several amounts together and dividing the total by the number of amounts (the average of 4, 5, and 9 is 6). **3** Baseball = BATTING AVERAGE. **4** N Amer. the overall mean of a student's marks, expressed as a percentage, number, or letter grade (had an 82% average in Grade 12) (compare GRADE POINT AVERAGE). ● adj. **1** usual, ordinary. **2** estimated or calculated by average. ● v.tr. **1** amount on average to (the sale of the product averaged one hundred a day). **2** do on average (averages six hours' work a day). **3 a** estimate the average of. **b** estimate the general standard of. □ **average out** result in an average. **law of averages** the principle that if one of two extremes occurs the other will also tend to so as to maintain the normal average. **on average** as an average rate or estimate. □ **averagely** adv.

averse predic.adj. (foll. by to) opposed, disinclined (was not averse to helping me). ¶ Often confused with adverse.

aversion n. **1** (usu. foll. by to) a dislike or unwillingness (has an aversion to hard work). **2** an object of dislike (my pet aversion).

aversion therapy n. behaviour therapy designed to cause the patient to give up an undesirable habit by associating it with an unpleasant effect.

avert v.tr. **1** (often foll. by from) turn away (one's eyes or thoughts). **2** prevent or ward off (an undesirable occurrence). □ **avertible** adj.

Avesta /əˈvestə/ n. (usu. prec. by the) the sacred writings of Zoroastrianism (compare ZEND).

Avestan ● adj. of or relating to the Avesta. ● n. the ancient E Iranian language of the Avesta, closely related to Vedic Sanskrit.

avian /ˈeɪviən/ adj. of or relating to birds.

aviary /ˈeɪviˌeri/ n. (pl. **-ies**) a large enclosure or building for keeping birds.

aviation n. **1** the skill or practice of operating aircraft. **2** aircraft manufacture.

aviator n. an aircraft pilot.

avid adj. **1** eager or enthusiastic (an avid cyclist). **2** greedy. □ **avidity** n. **avidly** adv.

avocado n. (pl. **-os**) **1 a** (in full **avocado pear**) a pear-shaped fruit with rough leathery skin, a smooth oily edible flesh, and a large pit. **b** the tropical evergreen tree, Persea americana, native to Central America, bearing this fruit. **2** (also **avocado green**) the light green colour of the flesh of this fruit.

avocation /ˌævəˈkeɪʃən/ n. **1** a secondary activity undertaken in addition to one's main work. **2** informal a vocation or calling.

avoid v.tr. **1** keep away or refrain from (a thing, person, or action). **2** escape; evade. □ **avoidable** adj. **avoidably** adv. **avoidance** n. **avoider** n.

avoirdupois /ˌævərdəˈpɔɪz/ n. **1** (in full **avoirdupois weight**) a system of weights based on a pound of 16 ounces or 7,000 grains. **2** (usu. /ˌævwɑrduːˈpwɒ/) informal excess body weight.

avow v.tr. admit, confess. □ **avowal** n.

avowed /əˈvaʊd/ adj. admitted (the avowed author). □ **avowedly** /əˈvaʊədli/ adv.

avuncular /əˈvʌŋkjələr/ adj. **1** (of an older man, esp. in relation to younger people) benevolent and friendly. **2** of or pertaining to an uncle.

aw interj. N Amer. & Scot. expressing mild protest, entreaty, commiseration, disgust, or disapproval.

AWACS /ˈeɪwæks/ n. a long-range radar system for detecting enemy aircraft.

await v. **1** tr. wait for. **2** tr. (of an event or thing) be in store for (a surprise awaits you). **3** intr. wait.

awake ● v. (past **awoke**; past part. **awoken**) **1** intr. a cease to sleep. **b** become active. **2** intr. (foll. by to) become aware of. **3** tr. rouse from sleep. **4** tr. arouse; provoke (awoke our interest). ● predic.adj. **1** not asleep. **2** vigilant. **3** (foll. by to) aware of.

awaken v. **1** tr. & intr. = AWAKE v. **2** tr. (often foll. by to) make aware.

awakening ● n. an arousal from sleep, inaction, indifference, ignorance, etc. (a rude awakening). ● attrib.adj. incipient.

award ● v.tr. **1** give or order to be given as a prize, payment, or penalty (awarded them a trophy; was awarded damages). **2** grant, assign. ● n. **1** a prize or payment awarded. **2 a** a judicial decision. **b** the penalty awarded by a judicial decision. □ **awarder** n.

aware predic.adj. **1** (often foll. by of, or that + clause) conscious; not ignorant; having knowledge. **2** well-informed. ¶Attributive use in sense 2, as in a very aware person, is disputed. □ **awareness** n.

awash predic.adj. **1** (usu. foll. by in, with) overrun as if by a flood (the country is awash in natural resources). **2** level with the surface of water, so that it just washes over. **3** carried or washed by the waves; flooded.

away ● adv. **1** to or at a distance from the place, person, or thing in question (go away; give away). **2** towards or into non-existence (sounds die away; explain it away; idled their time away). **3** constantly, persistently, continuously (work away). **4** without delay (fire away!). **5** Baseball out (one away). **6** Cdn (Nfld & Maritimes) in a place other than the speaker's home province or Atlantic Canada in general (they're from away). ● adj. Sport played in an opponent's venue (away game). □ **away with** (as imper.) let us be rid of.

AWD abbr. ALL-WHEEL DRIVE.

awe ● n. a feeling of respect combined with fear or wonder (stand in awe of). ● v.tr. inspire with awe.

awe-inspiring adj. causing awe or wonder; amazing, magnificent.

awesome adj. **1** inspiring awe; dreaded. **2** slang excellent. □ **awesomely** adv. **awesomeness** n.

awestruck adj. (also **awestricken**) affected or overcome with awe.

awful adj. **1 a** unpleasant or horrible (awful weather). **b** poor in quality; very bad (awful handwriting). **c** informal (attrib.) excessive; large (an awful lot of money). **2** literary inspiring awe. □ **awfulness** n.

awfully adv. **1** in an unpleasant, bad, or horrible way. **2** informal very (she's awfully young). **3** literary reverently.

awhile adv. for an unspecified length of time.

awkward adj. **1** ill-adapted for use; unwieldy. **2** clumsy or bungling. **3 a** embarrassed or ill at ease (felt awkward in such company). **b** embarrassing (an awkward silence). **4** difficult to deal with (an awkward situation). □ **awkwardly** adv. **awkwardness** n.

awl n. a small pointed tool used for piercing holes, esp. in leather or wood.

awn n. a bristle-like projection growing from the grain sheath of barley, oats, and other grasses, or terminating a leaf etc. □ **awned** adj.

awning n. a sheet of canvas, plastic, etc. sloping outward from the top of a window, storefront, or doorway or suspended above a ship's deck or other area to provide protection from the sun or rain. □ **awninged** adj.

awoke past of AWAKE.

awoken past part. of AWAKE.

AWOL /'eiwɒl/ abbr. informal absent without leave.

awry ● adv. **1** crookedly or askew. **2** improperly or amiss. ● predic.adj. **1** crooked. **2** amiss or wrong. □ **go awry** go or do wrong.

aw-shucks adj. N Amer. informal marked by a self-deprecating, self-conscious, or shy manner.

axe ● n. **1** a chopping tool, usu. of iron with a steel edge and wooden handle. **2** the drastic cutting or elimination of expenditure, staff, etc. **3** dismissal, cancellation, etc. (he got the axe). **4** slang **a** an electric guitar used in jazz or rock music. **b** a saxophone used in jazz. ● v.tr. (**axing**) **1** cut (esp. costs or services) drastically. **2** remove or dismiss. □ **an axe to grind** private ends to serve.

Axel n. (also **axel**) Figure Skating a one-and-a half turn jump from the front outside edge of one skate to the back outside edge of the other.

axeman n. (pl. **-men**) **1** a person who works with an axe, esp. one who fells trees. **2** slang a jazz or rock guitarist.

axial /'æksiəl/ adj. **1** forming or belonging to an axis. **2** around an axis (axial rotation). □ **axially** adv.

axil /'æksɪl/ n. the upper angle between a leaf and the stem it springs from, or between a branch and trunk.

axilla /æk'sɪlə/ n. (pl. **axillae** /-li:/) **1** Anat. the armpit. **2** the corresponding part of a bird or other creature.

axiom /'æksiəm/ n. **1** an established or widely accepted principle. **2** esp. Geom. a self-evident truth.

axiomatic adj. **1** self-evident. **2** relating to or containing axioms. □ **axiomatically** adv.

axis n. (pl. **axes** /'æksi:z/) **1 a** an imaginary line about which a body rotates or about which a plane figure is conceived as generating a solid. **b** a line which divides a regular figure symmetrically. **2** Math. a fixed reference line for the measurement of coordinates etc. **3** Bot. the central column of an inflorescence or other growth. **4** Anat. the second cervical vertebra. **5** Physiol. the central part of an organ or organism. **6** an agreement or alliance between two or more countries forming a centre for an eventual larger grouping of nations sharing an ideal or objective. **7** (**the Axis**) **a** the alliance of Germany and Italy formed before and during the Second World War, later extended to include Japan and other countries. **b** these countries as a group.

axle n. a rod or spindle (either fixed or rotating) on which a wheel or group of wheels is fixed.

axon /'æksɒn/ n. Anat. & Zool. a long threadlike part of a nerve cell, conducting impulses from the cell body.

ayatollah /ˌaijə'tɒːlə/ n. a Shiite religious leader in Iran.

aye¹ /ai/ (also **ay**) ● adv. **1** archaic or Brit. yes. **2** (in voting) I assent. **3** (as **aye aye**) Naut. a response accepting an order. ● n. an affirmative answer or assent, esp. in voting. □ **the ayes have it** the affirmative votes are in the majority.

aye² /ei/ adv. archaic ever, always. □ **for aye** forever.

Ayrshire /'erʃir/ n. a hardy breed of dairy cattle, mainly white with spots of red or brown.

Ayurveda /aijər'veidə/ n. a form of traditional Hindu medicine using naturally based therapies. □ **Ayurvedic** adj.

AZ abbr. Arizona (in postal use).

azalea /ə'zeiliə/ n. any of various flowering deciduous shrubs of the genus Rhododendron, with pink, purple, white, or yellow flowers.

Azerbaijani /ˌæzərbai'dʒɒni/ ● n. **1** (also **Azeri** /ə'zeri/) a native or inhabitant of Azerbaijan, a country in the Caucasus. **2** the Turkic language of Azerbaijan. ● adj. of or pertaining to Azerbaijan or its people.

azimuth /ˈæzɪməθ/ *n.* **1** the angle between the most northerly point of the horizon and the point directly below a given celestial body, usu. measured clockwise using due north as the zero point. **2** the horizontal angle or direction of a compass bearing. **3** the angle of a recording head on a VCR in relation to the tape. □ **azimuthal** /-ˈmuːθəl/ *adj.*

AZT *n.* an antiviral drug used to treat HIV infection and AIDS.

Aztec ● *n.* **1** a member of the Aboriginal people dominant in central and southern Mexico before the Spanish conquest of 1519. **2** the language of the Aztecs. ● *adj.* of the Aztecs. *See also* NAHUATL.

azure /ˈæʒɪr, -zjɜr/ ● *n.* **1 a** a deep sky-blue colour. **b** *Heraldry* blue. **2** *literary* the clear sky. ● *adj.* **1** of the colour azure. **2** *Heraldry* blue.

Bb

B¹ *n.* (also **b**) (*pl.* **Bs** or **B's**) **1** the second letter of the alphabet. **2** *Music* the seventh note of the diatonic scale of C major. **3** the second hypothetical person or example. **4** the second highest class or category (of academic marks etc.). **5** *Math.* (usu. **b**) the second known quantity. **6** a human blood type of the ABO system. **7** designating the degree of softness of a pencil lead (*a 4B pencil is darker than a 2B pencil*).

B² *symbol* boron.

B³ *abbr.* (also **B.**) **1** Bachelor. **2** bel(s). **3** billion. **4** bishop. **5** Blessed. **6** bass.

b. *abbr.* **1** born. **2** billion.

B.A. *abbr.* **1** Bachelor of Arts. **2** (**BA**) BATTING AVERAGE.

Ba *symbol* the element barium.

baa ● *v.intr.* (**baas, baaed, baaing**) (esp. of a sheep) bleat. ● *n.* (*pl.* **baas**) the bleat of a sheep.

baba¹ /ˈbɒbə/ *n.* a small rich cake leavened with yeast, usu. soaked in rum-flavoured syrup.

baba² *n.* **1** (among people of E European descent) grandmother. **2** *informal* an old woman of E European descent.

baba³ *n.* **1** (among people of Indian descent) father. **2** (also **Baba**) a spiritual leader or holy man in India.

baba ghanouj /ˈbɒbə gəˌnuːʃ/ *n.* a dip, originally Middle Eastern, made from mashed baked eggplant, tahini, garlic and other seasonings.

babble ● *v.* **1** *intr.* **a** talk in an inarticulate or incoherent manner. **b** chatter excessively or irrelevantly. **c** (of a stream, bird, etc.) produce a succession of indistinct sounds. **2** *tr.* repeat foolishly. ● *n.* **1 a** incoherent speech. **b** foolish, idle, or childish talk. **2** the murmur of voices, water, etc.

-babble *comb. form* forming nouns denoting the jargon of a specified subject or group (*psychobabble*).

babbler *n.* **1** a chatterer. **2** a person who reveals secrets.

babe *n.* **1** a baby. **2** an innocent or helpless person. **3** esp. *N Amer. slang* a young and attractive person, esp. a woman. ¶Sometimes *offensive* when used of women. □ **babe in arms 1** a small baby, esp. one too young to walk. **2** an innocent or naive person.

babel /ˈbeɪbəl, ˈbæb-/ *n.* **1** a confused noise, esp. of voices. **2** a noisy assembly. **3** a scene of confusion.

babiche /bæˈbiːʃ/ *n. N Amer.* strips of rawhide or sinew used as laces, thread, webbing, etc., e.g. in snowshoes.

baboon *n.* **1** any of various African and Arabian monkeys of the genus *Papio*, having a long doglike snout and large teeth. **2** an ugly or uncouth person.

babushka /bəˈbuːʃkə/ *n.* **1** a kerchief tied under the chin. **2** an old Russian woman.

baby ● *n.* (*pl.* **-ies**) **1** a very young child, esp. one not yet able to walk. **2** an unduly childish person (*he's such a baby!*). **3** the youngest member of a family, team, etc. **4** (often *attrib.*) **a** a young or newly born animal. **b** a thing that is small of its kind (*baby corn*). **5** *slang* a young woman; a sweetheart (often as a form of address). ¶Often *offensive* if used to a stranger. **6** *slang* a person or thing regarded with affection or familiarity. **7** one's own responsibility, invention, concern, etc., regarded in a personal way. ● *v.tr.* (**-ies,**

-ied) **1** treat like a baby. **2** pamper. □ **throw out the baby with the bathwater** reject the essential with the inessential. □ **babyhood** *n.*

baby beef *n.* meat from young cattle older than those producing veal.

baby blue *n. & adj.* soft, pale blue.

baby blues *n.pl. informal* attractive blue eyes.

baby bonus *n. Cdn* family allowance or child tax benefit.

baby boom *n.* a temporary marked increase in the birth rate.

baby boomer *n.* a person born during a baby boom, esp. after the war of 1939–45.

baby boomlet *n.* a small baby boom, esp. that at the end of the 1980s.

baby bottle *n. N Amer.* a bottle with a rubber nipple for feeding babies and small toddlers.

baby bust *n.* a temporary marked decrease in the birth rate.

baby buster *n.* a person born during a baby bust, esp. in the late 1960s and early 1970s.

baby carriage *n.* (also **baby buggy**) *N Amer.* a four-wheeled carriage for a baby, pushed by a person.

baby doll *n.* **1** a doll resembling a baby. **2 a** (in *pl.*) (in full **baby doll pyjamas**) women's or girls' pyjamas consisting of a hip-length top of a delicate fabric and matching panties. **b** (in full **baby doll dress**) a short, loose-fitting, usu. sleeveless dress, extending to just below the buttocks.

baby fat *n.* the fatty tissue which gives babies and young children their characteristic plumpness, peaking at nine months of age and diminishing until about the age of seven.

baby food *n.* a light, usu. puréed diet for babies.

babyish *adj.* **1** childish, simple. **2** immature.

Babylon /ˈbæbɪˌlɒn/ *n.* **1** any magnificent and decadent city. **2** *derogatory* (among some blacks, esp. Rastafarians) **a** white society. **b** any representation of this, esp. the police.

Babylonian /ˌbæbɪˈloːniən/ ● *n.* **1** an inhabitant of the ancient city or kingdom of Babylon. **2** the language of the Babylonians. ● *adj.* of or relating to Babylon.

baby monitor *n.* an intercom which allows parents to listen to a baby while in another room.

baby oil *n.* a mineral oil used to soften skin, in massaging, and to remove makeup.

baby powder *n.* a usu. scented talcum powder used on babies' skin.

baby's breath *n. N Amer.* a plant of the pink family, *Gypsophila paniculata*, with tiny usu. white flowers, often used to ornament bouquets of larger flowers.

baby shower *n. N Amer.* a party given for a pregnant woman at which her female friends and relatives give her presents for the baby.

babysit *v.intr. & tr.* (**-sitting**; *past* and *past part.* **-sat**) look after a child or children while the parents are out. □ **babysitter** *n.* **babysitting** *n.*

baby talk *n.* childish talk used by or to young children.

baby tooth n. (pl. **teeth**) a tooth belonging to a person's first set of teeth, shed between the ages of five and thirteen.

baccala /bækə'lɒ, bʊkə'lɒ/ n. (also **bacalao** /bækə'lau/, **bacalhau** /bʊkə'ljau/) cod, esp. dried and salted.

baccalaureate /ˌbækə'lɔːriət/ n. **1** the university degree of bachelor. **2** an examination intended to qualify successful candidates for higher education.

baccarat /'bækəˌrɒ, ˌbækə'rɒ, bʊ-/ n. (also **baccara**) a card game similar to blackjack, in which players take turns betting against the dealer.

bacchanal /ˌbækə'nɒl, ˌbɒk-/ ● n. **1** a wild, drunken revelry. **2** a drunken reveller. ● adj. of or like Bacchus, the Greek or Roman god of wine, or his rites.

bacchanalia /ˌbækə'neɪliə, ˌbɒk-/ n.pl. a drunken revelry. □ **bacchanalian** adj. & n.

bachelor n. **1** an unmarried man. **2 a** (in full **bachelor's degree**) a degree awarded to someone who has completed undergraduate studies. **b** a person who has been awarded a bachelor's degree. **3** esp. Cdn = BACHELOR APARTMENT. □ **bachelorhood** n.

bachelor apartment n. **1** Cdn an apartment consisting of a single large room serving as bedroom and living room, with a separate bathroom. **2** any apartment occupied by a bachelor.

bachelorette n. **1** N Amer. a young unmarried woman. **2** Cdn a very small bachelor apartment.

bacillus /bə'sɪləs/ n. (pl. **bacilli** /-laɪ/) **1** any rod-shaped bacterium. **2** (usu. in pl.) any pathogenic bacterium.

bacillus thuringiensis /ˌθɜːrɪndʒi'ensɪs, θə,rɪndʒ-/ n. **1** a bacterium containing a glycoprotein that is toxic to insects but not to vertebrates. **2** a bacterial pesticide used against spruce budworm etc.

back ● n. **1 a** the rear surface of the human body from the shoulders to the hips. **b** the corresponding upper surface of an animal's body. **c** the spine. **2 a** any surface regarded as corresponding to the human back, e.g. of the head or a chair. **b** the part of a garment that covers the back. **3 a** the less active or visible or important part of something functional, e.g. of a piece of paper. **b** the side or part normally away from the spectator or the direction of motion or attention, e.g. of a car or room (stood at the back). **4 a** (in football etc.) a player positioned behind the front line of play. **b** this position. ● adv. **1** to the rear; away from what is considered to be the front. **2 a** in or into an earlier or normal position or condition (went back home). **b** in return (pay back). **3** in or into the past (back in June). **4** at a distance (stand back). **5** in check (hold him back). **6** N Amer. behind (five points back). ● v. **1** tr. a help with moral or financial support. **b** bet on the success of. **2** tr. & intr. (usu. foll. by up) move, or cause (a vehicle etc.) to move, backwards. **3** tr. **a** put or serve as a back, background, or support to. **b** Music accompany. **4** tr. lie at the back of (backed by steep cliffs). **5** intr. (of the wind) move round in a counter-clockwise direction. ● adj. **1** situated behind, esp. as remote or subsidiary (back street). **2** not current (back pay). **3** reversed, backward (back somersault). □ **at a person's back** in pursuit or support. **at the back of one's mind** remembered but not consciously thought of. **back and forth** to and fro. **back down** withdraw one's claim or point of view etc.; concede defeat in an argument etc. **(in) back of** N Amer. behind. **the back of beyond** a very remote or inaccessible place. **back off 1** draw back, retreat. **2** abandon one's intention, stand, etc. **back on to** have its back adjacent to. **back out** (often foll. by of) withdraw from a

commitment. **back up 1** give (esp. moral) support to. **2** Computing make a spare copy of (data, a disk, etc.). **3** (of water) accumulate behind an obstruction. **4** reverse (a vehicle) into a desired position. **5** N Amer. form a line of vehicles in congested traffic. **get** (or **put**) **a person's back up** annoy or anger a person. **get off a person's back** stop troubling a person. **go back on** fail to honour (a promise etc.). **in back** N Amer. informal in or at the back. **know like the back of one's hand** be entirely familiar with. **(flat) on one's back** injured or ill in bed. **pat** (or **slap** or **clap**) **on the back** a gesture of approval or congratulation. **pat** (or **slap** or **clap**) **a person on the back** congratulate a person. **put one's back into** approach (a task etc.) with vigour. **turn one's back on 1** abandon. **2** ignore. **with one's back to** (or **up against**) **the wall** in a desperate situation; hard-pressed. □ **backer** n. (in sense 1 of v.). **backless** adj.

backache n. a (usu. prolonged) pain in one's back.

back alley n. N Amer. **1** a passageway behind buildings. **2** the hidden aspects of something.

back bacon n. Cdn & Brit. round, lean bacon cut from the eye of a pork loin.

back bay n. Cdn a shallow bay off a lake.

backbench n. Cdn, Brit., Austral., & NZ **1** (often in pl.) a backbencher's seat. **2** the backbenchers' seats collectively. **3** (often attrib.) the backbenchers collectively.

backbencher n. Cdn, Brit., Austral., & NZ a member of a legislative assembly who is not a member of the cabinet, an opposition critic, or a party leader.

backbiting n. speaking maliciously of an absent person. □ **backbiter** n.

backboard n. **1** Basketball the vertical board to which the basket is attached. **2** (in pl.) Hockey the boards behind the net at each end of the rink. **3** a board placed at or forming the back of anything. **4** a board worn to support or straighten the back.

backbone n. **1** the spine. **2** the main support or most important element in a structure, organization, etc. **3** firmness of character.

back-breaker n. **1** an extremely arduous task. **2** N Amer. esp. Sport a decisive event or action, esp. one that ensures an opponent's defeat.

back-breaking adj. (esp. of manual work) very hard.

back burner n. **1** a position receiving little attention or low priority (the project has been put on the back burner). **2** a heating element at the rear of a stove. □ **back-burner** v.tr.

back cast n. N Amer. Angling the action of casting a line backwards before casting it into the water.

backcatcher n. Cdn = CATCHER 2.

back channel n. **1** Cdn a backwater or side channel of a river. **2** a person who acts as a secret intermediary in diplomatic negotiations. **3** (often attrib.) a secretive, covert action.

backcheck v.intr. Hockey (of a forward) return to the defensive zone and check attacking opponents. □ **backchecker** n. **backchecking** n.

back concession n. Cdn (Ont. & Que.) **1** a concession at some distance from a more heavily settled road or area. **2** (in pl.) rural areas.

backcountry n. N Amer., Austral., & NZ an area away from settled districts.

backcourt n. **1** Tennis the area between the baseline and the service line. **2** Basketball the half of the court which a team defends.

back crawl n. = BACKSTROKE 2.

backdate *v.tr.* **1** put an earlier date to (an agreement etc.) than the actual one. **2** make retrospectively valid.

back door ● *n.* **1** a door at the back of a house etc. **2** an alternative, usu. indirect or less conspicuous means of gaining an objective. ● *adj.* (**backdoor**) **1 a** secondary, alternative (*backdoor route*). **b** underhanded (*backdoor deal*). **2** *Basketball* involving a pass from the top of the key to a player who has just run to the side of the basket.

backdraft *n.* **1** a reverse draft of air or other gas. **2** the violent explosion occurring when air reaches an oxygen-starved fire.

backdrop *n.* **1** a painted cloth hung across the back of a stage as the principal part of the scenery. **2** the setting for an event or situation.

back eddy *n.* *Cdn* (esp. *BC*) **1** an area of water behind an obstruction in a watercourse in which the current is the reverse of the general direction of flow. **2** = BACKWATER 2.

back end *n.* **1** the rearmost part of something. **2** the final stage of a process, esp. the profits generated by a film etc., or the termination of an agreement (often *attrib.*: *back-end charges*). **3** *Computing* (often *attrib.*) the elements of a computer's architecture pertaining to data stored in a database (*compare* FRONT END 2).

backfat *n.* a layer of fat between the skin and muscle of animals, esp. along the back.

backfield *n.* *Football* **1** the area of play behind the line of scrimmage. **2** the players who line up in the backfield collectively, esp. the running backs and quarterback. ☐ **backfielder** *n.*

backfill ● *v.tr.* refill an excavated hole with the material dug out of it. ● *n.* excavated material used to refill an excavation.

backfire ● *v.intr.* **1** undergo a mistimed explosion, as in the cylinder or exhaust of an internal combustion engine. **2** (of a plan etc.) have the opposite effect to what was intended. ● *n.* **1** an instance of backfiring. **2** *N Amer.* a fire set deliberately to stop the advance of a forest fire or prairie fire.

backflip *n.* a backwards aerial somersault.

backgammon *n.* **1** a game for two played on a board with pieces moved according to throws of the dice. **2** the most complete form of win in this.

background *n.* **1** part of a scene, picture, or description, that serves as a setting to the chief figures or objects and foreground. **2** an inconspicuous or obscure position (*kept in the background*). **3** a person's education, knowledge, or social circumstances. **4** explanatory or contributory information or circumstances.

background music *n.* music intended as an unobtrusive accompaniment to some activity, or to provide atmosphere in a film etc.

backhand ● *n.* **1** (often *attrib.*) any arm motion performed with the arm initially across and in front of the torso, esp.: **a** *Tennis etc.* a stroke made with the back of the hand turned towards the opponent. **b** a blow made with the back of the hand. **2** *Hockey* (often *attrib.*) a shot or pass made by striking the puck with the back of the stick's blade. ● *v.tr.* strike with a backhand.

backhanded *adj.* **1** (of an arm motion) performed with the arm initially across the torso, or with the back of the hand (*backhanded catch*). **2** indirect; ambiguous (*a backhanded compliment*).

backhander *n.* a backhand shot, blow, stroke, etc.

backhoe *n.* a mechanical excavator which operates

by drawing toward itself a bucket attached to a hinged boom.

backing *n.* **1** support. **2** material used to form a back or support. **3** (often *attrib.*) musical accompaniment, esp. to a singer.

backlands *n.pl.* sparsely-settled areas.

back lane *n.* *Cdn & Brit.* = BACK ALLEY 1.

backlash *n.* **1** an excessive or marked adverse reaction. **2 a** a sudden recoil or reaction between parts of a mechanism. **b** excessive play between such parts.

backlight ● *n.* (also **backlighting**) light illuminating something (esp. a photographic subject or a computer screen) from behind. ● *v.tr.* (*past and past part.* **backlit** or **backlighted**) illuminate (esp. a photographic subject, a computer screen, etc.) from behind. ☐ **backlighting** *n.* **backlit** *adj.*

backlog ● *n.* an accumulation of uncompleted work etc. ● *v.* (**-logged**, **-logging**) **1** *tr.* overload (a system, process, etc.). **2** *intr.* accumulate unfinished tasks or unprocessed material.

back nine *n.* *Golf* the final nine holes on an 18-hole course.

back order *n.* a retailer's order yet to be filled by a supplier. ☐ **on back order** ordered by a retailer but not yet received from the supplier.

backpack ● *n.* a knapsack. ● *v.intr.* travel or hike with a backpack. ☐ **backpacker** *n.* **backpacking** *n.*

backpedal *v.intr.* (**-pedalled**, **-pedalling**) **1** pedal backwards on a bicycle etc. **2** reverse one's previous action or opinion. **3** walk or sprint backwards.

backrest *n.* a support for the back.

back road *n.* a little-used road or highway, esp. through the countryside.

backroom *n.* **1** a room at the back of a store, office, etc., usu. off limits to the public. **2** (usu. *attrib.*) a place where secret plans are made (*backroom deal*).

back-scratcher *n.* **1** a rod terminating in a clawed hand for scratching one's own back. **2** a person who performs services for another for mutual gain. ☐ **back-scratching** *n.*

back seat *n.* a seat at the back of a vehicle, airplane, etc. ☐ **take a back seat** occupy a subordinate place.

back-seat driver *n.* **1** a person who rides in the back seat of a car and gives unwanted advice to its driver. **2** a person who criticizes or attempts to control without responsibility.

backside *n.* *informal* the buttocks.

backslap *v.tr. & intr.* slap jovially on the back as an (often excessive) expression of camaraderie.

backslapping *adj.* **1** characterized by (excessive) displays of camaraderie. **2** vigorously hearty.

backslash *n.* a backward-sloping diagonal line (\\).

backslide *v.intr.* (*past and past part.* **-slid**) relapse into bad ways or error, esp. in ideology. ☐ **backslider** *n.*

backspace *v.intr.* move a typewriter carriage, cursor, etc. back one or more spaces. ● *n.* the key on a keyboard which performs this function.

backspin *n.* a backward spin imparted to a ball causing it to slow down or roll or bounce back on hitting a surface.

backsplash *n.* *N Amer.* a covering, usu. ceramic, behind a sink, counter, etc., to protect the wall.

backsplit *n.* *Cdn* a house with floors raised half a storey at the rear, having an upper and lower main floor and an upper and lower basement.

backstabber *n.* a person who betrays a friend or associate. ☐ **backstabbing** *n. & adj.*

backstage ● *adv.* **1** *Theatre* out of view of the audience, esp. in the wings or dressing rooms. **2** not known to the public. ● *adj.* concealed.

back stairs *n.pl.* **1** stairs at the back or side of a building. **2** (**backstairs**) (*attrib.*) denoting underhand or clandestine activity.

backstop ● *n.* **1** *Baseball* a catcher. **2** a goaltender. **3** *Sport* a wall, fence, etc. used to keep the ball in the playing area, esp. behind home plate in baseball. **4** a source of esp. financial support. ● *v.tr.* **1** *Sport* serve (a team) as goaltender, catcher, etc. **2** underwrite (a project, loan, company, etc.).

back street *n.* **1** a street in a quiet part of a city, away from the main streets. **2** (**backstreet**) (*attrib.*) denoting illicit or illegal activity.

backstroke *n. Swimming* **1** a stroke performed on the back. **2** such a stroke in which the arms are lifted alternately out of the water in a backward circular motion and the legs extended in a kicking action.

backswing *n. Sport* the upward or backward motion bringing a bat etc. into position for the swing.

back-to-back ● *adj. N Amer.* (of two events) consecutive (*back-to-back victories*). ● *adv.* (**back to back**) **1** with backs adjacent and opposite each other (*we stood back to back*). **2** *N Amer.* consecutively (*challenge two opponents back to back*).

back to front ● *adv.* **1** with the back at the front. **2** in disorder. ● *adj.* backwards.

back-to-nature *adj.* (*usu. attrib.*) applied to a movement or enthusiast for the reversion to a simpler, more natural way of life.

back-to-school *adj.* (*usu. attrib.*) pertaining to the start of a new school year (*back-to-school sale*).

back-to-work *attrib.adj.* denoting legislation etc. requiring striking workers to return to work.

backtrack *v.intr.* **1** retrace one's steps. **2** reverse one's previous action or opinion.

backup *n.* **1** moral or technical support (*called for extra backup*). **2 a** something kept in reserve, esp. for emergency replacement. **b** *Sport* (often *attrib.*) an alternate player (*a backup goalie*). **3** *Computing* (often *attrib.*) **a** the procedure for making security copies of data (*backup facilities*). **b** the copy itself (*made a backup*). **4** *N Amer.* a line of vehicles in congested traffic. **5** (*attrib.*) *N Amer.* designating a light, beeper, etc. activated when a vehicle is in reverse gear. **6** (often *attrib.*) musical accompaniment (*backup singers*).

backward ● *adv.* = BACKWARDS. ● *adj.* **1** directed to the rear or starting point (*a backward look*). **2** reversed. **3** mentally retarded or slow. **4** reluctant, shy, unassertive. **5** unsophisticated, underdeveloped. □ **backwardness** *n.*

backwards *adv.* **1** away from one's front (*lean backwards*). **2 a** with the back foremost (*walk backwards*). **b** in reverse of the usual way (*count backwards*). **3 a** into a worse state (*new policies are taking us backwards*). **b** into the past (*looked backwards*). **c** (of a thing's motion) back towards the starting point. □ **backwards and forwards** in both directions alternately; to and fro. **bend** (or **lean**) **over backwards** *informal* (often foll. by *to* + infin.) make every effort, esp. to be fair or helpful. **know backwards** be entirely familiar with.

backwash ● *n.* **1 a** a receding waves created by the motion of a ship etc. **b** a backward current of air created by a moving aircraft. **2** repercussions. **3** water pumped backwards through a swimming pool filter to clean it. **4** *slang* liquid which flows from the mouth back into the bottle etc. while one is drinking. **5** the motion of a receding wave. ● *v.tr.* clean (a swimming pool filter) with backwash.

backwater *n.* **1** stagnant water fed from a stream. **2** a place or condition remote from the centre of activity or thought.

backwoods *n.pl.* (often *attrib.*) **1** remote uncleared land. **2** any remote or sparsely inhabited region.

backwoodsman *n.* (*pl.* **-men**) **1** an inhabitant of backwoods. **2** an uncouth person.

backyard *n.* **1** *N Amer.* a piece of ground, usu. landscaped, behind a house and belonging to it. **2** a place near at hand (*not in my backyard*).

bacon *n.* cured meat from the back or sides of a pig. □ **bring home the bacon** *informal* **1** succeed in one's undertaking. **2** supply material provision or support.

bacteria *n.pl.* (*sing.* **bacterium**) any of various groups of unicellular micro-organisms lacking organelles and an organized nucleus, some of which can cause disease. □ **bacterial** *adj.*

bacteriology /bæk,ti:ri'ɒlədʒi/ *n.* the study of bacteria. □ **bacteriological** *adj.* **bacteriologically** *adv.* **bacteriologist** *n.*

Bactrian camel /'bæktriən/ *n.* a camel, *Camelus bactrianus*, native to central Asia, with two humps.

bad ● *adj.* (**worse**; **worst**) **1** inferior, inadequate, defective (*a bad driver*). **2 a** unpleasant, unwelcome (*bad news*). **b** unsatisfactory, unfortunate (*a bad business*). **3** harmful (*is bad for you*). **4** (of food) decayed, putrid. **5** *informal* ill, injured (*a bad leg*). **6** *informal* regretful, guilty, ashamed (*feels bad about it*). **7** serious, severe (*a bad headache*). **8 a** morally wicked or offensive (*bad language*). **b** naughty; badly behaved (*a bad child*). **9** worthless; not valid (*a bad cheque*). **10** (of a loan, debt, etc.) unlikely to be paid. **11** (**badder**, **baddest**) esp. *N Amer. slang* admirable, excellent. ● *n.* **1 a** ill fortune (*take the bad with the good*). **b** ruin; a degenerate condition (*go to the bad*). **2** the debit side of an account (*$500 to the bad*). **3** (as *pl.*; prec. by *the*) bad or wicked people. ● *adv. N Amer.* disputed badly. □ **from bad to worse** into an even worse state. **in a bad way** ill; in trouble. **not** (or **not so**) **bad** *informal* fairly good. **too bad** *informal* (of circumstances etc.) regrettable but now beyond helping. □ **badness** *n.*

bad apple *n.* **1** an apple that has gone bad. **2** *N Amer.* a member of an otherwise admirable group whose actions disgrace it.

badass *esp. N Amer. slang* ● *adj.* belligerent or intimidating; tough. ● *n.* a troublemaker.

bad blood *n.* ill feeling, animosity.

bad boy *n.* a man with a rebellious attitude.

bad breath *n.* unpleasant-smelling breath.

baddy *n.* (also **baddie**) (*pl.* **-ies**) *informal* a villain or criminal, esp. in a story, film, etc.

bade *see* BID.

bad faith *n.* intent to deceive.

bad form *n.* an offence against social conventions.

badge *n.* **1** a distinctive emblem worn as a mark of office etc. **2** any feature or sign which reveals a characteristic condition or quality.

badger ● *n.* an omnivorous grey-coated nocturnal mammal of the family Mustelidae, with a white stripe flanked by black stripes on its head. ● *v.tr.* pester, harass, tease.

bad guy *n. informal* a villain.

bad hair day *n.* a day when everything seems to be going wrong, typified by one's hair being unmanageable.

badinage /'bædɪˌnɑːʒ/ *n.* playful ridicule.

badlands *n.pl.* barren, strikingly-eroded tracts in arid areas, as along the Red Deer River in S Alberta.

badly *adv.* (**worse**; **worst**) **1** in a bad manner (*works* *badly*). **2** *informal* very much (*wants it badly*). **3** severely (*was badly defeated*).

B.Admin. *abbr.* Bachelor of Administration.

badminton *n.* a game in which players use racquets to hit a shuttlecock back and forth across a high net.

bad-mouth *v.tr. N Amer.* subject to malicious criticism.

bad news *n.* **1** unwelcome information. **2** *informal* an unpleasant or troublesome person etc.

bad-tempered *adj.* having a bad temper; irritable; easily annoyed. □ **bad-temperedly** *adv.*

baffle ● *v.tr.* **1** confuse or perplex (a person, one's faculties, etc.). **2 a** frustrate or hinder (plans etc.). **b** restrain or regulate the progress of (fluids, sounds, etc.). ● *n.* **1** (also **baffle plate**) a device used to restrain the flow of fluid, air, etc., through an opening, often found in microphones etc. to regulate the emission of sound. **2** a device used to impede or block access etc. □ **bafflement** *n.* **baffler** *n.* **baffling** *adj.* **bafflingly** *adv.*

bafflegab *n. N Amer.* official or professional jargon which confuses more than it clarifies.

bag ● *n.* **1** a receptacle of flexible material with an opening at the top. **2 a** (usu. in *pl.*) a piece of luggage (*put the bags in the trunk*). **b** a woman's handbag. **3** (in *pl.*; usu. foll. by *of*) *informal* a large amount; plenty. **4** *slang derogatory* a woman, esp. regarded as unattractive or unpleasant. **5** an animal's sac containing poison, honey, etc. **6** an amount of game or fish taken by a sportsman. **7** (usu. in *pl.*) baggy folds of skin under the eyes. **8** *slang* the scrotum. **9** *slang* a person's particular interest or preoccupation (*country music is not my bag*). **10** *Baseball* first, second, or third base. **11** an udder. ● *v.* (**bagged, bagging**) **1** *tr.* put in a bag. **2** *tr. informal* **a** attain, secure (*bagged three awards*). **b** apprehend (a criminal etc.). **c** shoot (game). **d** *informal* steal. **3 a** *intr.* hang loosely; bulge; swell. **b** *tr.* cause to do this. □ **bag and baggage** with all one's belongings. **bag of tricks** *informal* one's (usu. ingenious) resources or techniques (*flattery is in his bag of tricks*). **in the bag** *informal* as good as secured; achieved. **left holding the bag** *N Amer. informal* abandoned, left to face consequences alone. □ **bagful** *n.* (*pl.* **-fuls**).

bagel *n.* a chewy, ring-shaped bread roll that is simmered before baking.

baggage *n.* **1** suitcases, bags, etc. packed for travelling; luggage. **2** an encumbrance (esp. psychological). **3** the portable equipment of an army.

baggage claim *n. N Amer.* (in full **baggage claim area**) an area in an airport, railway station, etc. where passengers retrieve their checked baggage.

baggage handler *n.* a person whose job it is to load and unload luggage.

baggataway /bəˈgætəwei/ *n.* a forerunner of lacrosse played by the Aboriginal peoples of eastern N America.

Baggie *n. proprietary* a small bag made of clear plastic, used for storing sandwiches etc.

baggy *adj.* (**-ier, -iest**) **1** (of clothes) loosely fitting. **2** puffed out. □ **baggily** *adv.* **bagginess** *n.*

bag lady *n.* esp. *N Amer.* a homeless woman who carries her possessions around in shopping bags.

bagman *n.* (*pl.* **-men**) *Cdn* a political fundraiser.

bagpipe *n.* (usu. in *pl.*) a musical instrument consisting of a windbag connected to drone pipes which produce single sustained notes and a fingered melody pipe or 'chanter'. □ **bagpiper** *n.*

baguette /bæˈget/ *n.* a long narrow loaf of bread.

bah *interj.* an expression of contempt or disbelief.

Baha'i /bəˈhai/ *n.* (*pl.* **Baha'is**) a member of a monotheistic religion founded in Persia in 1863, emphasizing the unity of all religions, and world peace. □ **Baha'ism** *n.*

Bahamian /bəˈheimiən/ ● *n.* **1** a native or national of the Bahamas in the W Indies. **2** a person of Bahamian descent. ● *adj.* of or relating to the Bahamas.

Bahasa /bəˈhɒsə/ *n.* either of the forms of Malay spoken as the official languages of Indonesia or Malaysia.

bail[1] ● *n.* **1** money etc. required as security against the temporary release of a prisoner pending trial. **2** a person or persons giving such security. **3** (also **pretrial release** or **judicial interim release**) the temporary release of a prisoner who provides such security (*grant bail*). ● *v.tr.* **1** (usu. foll. by *out*) **a** release or secure the release of (a prisoner) on payment of bail. **b** release from a difficulty; come to the rescue of (esp. financially). **2** *Law* deliver (goods) in trust for a specified purpose. □ **jump** (or **skip** or *formal* **forfeit**) **bail** fail to appear for trial after being released on bail. **stand** (or **post**) **bail** (often foll. by *for*) act as surety (for an accused person). □ **bailable** *adj.*

bail[2] *v.tr.* **1** (usu. foll. by *out*) scoop water out of (a boat etc.). **2** scoop (water etc.) out. □ **bailer** *n.*

bail[3] *v.tr.* □ **bail out 1** make an emergency parachute jump from an aircraft. **2** desert a difficult situation.

bail bond *n.* the document executed to secure the release of a person awaiting trial.

bail bondsman *n.* (*pl.* **-men**) a person who posts bail for another, esp. as a business.

bailey *n.* (*pl.* **-eys**) **1** the outer wall of a castle. **2** a court enclosed by it.

bailiff *n.* **1** (in full **court bailiff**) an officer of the court who serves processes and enforces orders, esp. warrants authorizing the seizure of a debtor's goods. **2** (in full **private bailiff**) *Cdn* a person who repossesses property for private clients. **3** *N Amer.* an official in a court of law who keeps order, looks after prisoners, etc.

bailiwick *n.* **1** *Law* the district or jurisdiction of a sheriff or bailiff. **2** a person's sphere of operations or particular area of interest.

bailout *n.* a financial rescue.

bain-marie /ˌbæmæˈriː/ *n.* (*pl.* **bains-marie** *pronunc.* same) a cooking vessel containing hot water into which a second vessel containing a sauce etc. is placed so as to cook gently.

Bairam /baiˈræm, ˈbairæm/ *n.* either of two Muslim festivals, the **Lesser Bairam**, lasting one day, which follows the fast of Ramadan, and the **Greater Bairam**, lasting three days, seventy days later.

bait ● *n.* **1** food used to entice prey. **2** an allurement; something intended to tempt or entice. ● *v.* **1** *tr.* **a** harass or annoy (a person, community, etc.) (*red-baiting*). **b** torment (a chained animal). **2** *tr.* put bait on (a hook, trap, etc.) to entice a prey.

bait and switch *n.* (often *attrib.*) the practice of luring customers with a limited supply of bargains in order to sell them more expensive items.

baitcaster *n.* (also **baitcasting reel**) esp. *N Amer.* a fishing reel mounted on top of the rod, with an open rotating spool (compare SPINCASTER, SPINNING REEL).

baitcasting rod *n.* a fishing rod with eyes along the top and a finger grip, used with baitcasters and spincasters.

baitfish *n.* (*pl.* same or **-fishes**) any small fish eaten by larger fish, often used to lure game fish.

baize /beiz/ *n.* a coarse usu. green woollen material resembling felt used as a covering or lining, esp. on the tops of billiard tables and card tables.

Bajan /'beidʒən/ *n. & adj.* = BARBADIAN.

bake ● *v.* **1 a** *tr.* cook (food) by dry heat in an oven or on a hot surface, without direct exposure to a flame. **b** *intr.* undergo the process of being baked. **2** *intr. informal* **a** (usu. as **be baking**) (of weather etc.) be very hot. **b** (of a person) become hot. **3 a** *tr.* harden (clay etc.) by heat. **b** *intr.* (of clay etc.) be hardened by heat. **4 a** *tr.* (of the sun) affect by its heat, e.g. ripen (fruit). **b** *intr.* (e.g. of fruit) be affected by the sun's heat. ● *n.* **1** the act or an instance of baking. **2** (esp. in *comb.*) baked goods (*bake table*). **3** (in *comb.*) *N Amer.* a social gathering, esp. a picnic, at which baked food is eaten (*clambake*). **4** a baked dish, esp. a casserole (*sausage and rigatoni bake*).

bakeapple *n.* (also **baked-apple berry**) *N Amer.* (esp. *Nfld & Maritimes*) = CLOUDBERRY.

baked Alaska *n.* a dessert consisting of ice cream on a slab of cake, covered with meringue and browned quickly.

baked beans *n.pl.* dried white beans baked in a tomato sauce.

baked custard *n.* = CUSTARD 1.

Bakelite /'beikə,lɑit/ *n. proprietary* any of various thermosetting resins or plastics made from formaldehyde and phenol, used for cables, plates, etc.

Bake-Off *n. proprietary* a competition at which (esp. amateur) cooks prepare baked goods for judging.

baker *n.* **1** a person who bakes and sells bread, cakes, etc., esp. professionally. **2** an appliance or dish in which something is baked.

baker's dozen *n.* thirteen.

bakery *n.* (*pl.* **-ies**) a place where bread and cakes are made or sold.

bake sale *n. N Amer.* a sale of home-baked goods, usu. to raise money for a charity etc.

bakeshop *n. N Amer.* = BAKERY.

bakeware *n.* pans, pie plates, etc., used in baking.

baking powder *n.* a mixture of sodium bicarbonate and an acid such as cream of tartar, etc., used as leavening in baking.

baking sheet *n.* a large shallow pan, used for baking cookies, rolls, etc.

baking soda *n.* sodium bicarbonate used as an antacid, as a leavener in baked goods, or as a household cleaner and deodorizer.

baklava /'bækləvə, ˌbæklə'vɑ/ *n.* a rich sweet dessert of flaky pastry, honey, and nuts.

balaclava /ˌbælə'klɒvə/ *n.* a tight knitted garment for the whole head, with holes for the eyes and mouth.

balalaika /ˌbælə'laikə/ *n.* a guitar-like musical instrument having a triangular body and 2 to 4 strings, popular in Russia and other Slavic countries.

balance ● *n.* **1** an apparatus for weighing, esp. one with a central pivot, beam, and two scales. **2 a** a counteracting weight or force. **b** (in full **balance wheel**) the regulating device in a clock etc. **3 a** an even distribution of weight or amount. **b** stability of body or mind (*regained his balance*). **4** a preponderating weight or amount (*the balance of opinion*). **5 a** an agreement between or the difference between credits and debits in an account. **b** the amount of money held in a bank account at a given moment. **c** the difference between an amount due and an amount paid (*will pay the balance next week*). **d** an amount left over; the rest. **6** Art harmony of design and proportion. **7 a** the relative volume of various musical parts (*bad balance between violins and trumpets*). **b** the relative volume of two or more stereo speakers. **c** a dial on a stereo for adjusting this. ● *v.* **1** *tr.* (foll. by *with, against*) offset or compare (one thing) with

another. **2** *tr.* counteract, equal, or neutralize the weight or importance of. **3 a** *tr.* bring into or keep in equilibrium (*balanced a book on her head*). **b** *intr.* be in equilibrium (*balanced on one leg*). **4** *tr.* (usu. as **balanced** *adj.*) establish equal or appropriate proportions of elements in (*a balanced diet*). **5** *tr.* weigh (arguments etc.) against each other. **6 a** *tr.* compare and esp. equalize debits and credits of (an account) (*balance the budget*). **b** *intr.* (of an account) have credits and debits equal. □ **in the balance** uncertain; at a critical stage. **off balance 1** in danger of falling. **2** unprepared, confused. **on balance** all things considered. **strike a balance** choose a moderate course or compromise. □ **balanceable** *adj.* **balancer** *n.*

balance beam *n.* **1** a long narrow wooden beam on which female gymnasts perform feats of balance and agility. **2** the gymnastics event in which this is used.

balanced fund *n.* an investment fund comprising a mixture of stocks, bonds, and other investments such as money market funds.

balance of payments *n.* the difference in value between payments into and out of a country.

balance of power *n.* **1** a situation in which the chief nations of the world have roughly equal power. **2** the power held by a small group when larger groups are of equal strength.

balance of trade *n.* (also **trade balance**) the difference in value between imports and exports.

balance sheet *n.* **1** a written statement of the assets and liabilities of an organization on a given date. **2** an organization's financial state.

balancing act *n.* the dexterous handling of several different tasks simultaneously.

balata /'bælətə/ *n.* **1** any of several latex-yielding trees of Central America, esp. *Manilkara bidentata*. **2** the dried sap of this, used esp. in golf balls.

balcony *n.* (*pl.* **-ies**) **1** a usu. balustraded platform on the outside of a building, with access from an upper-floor window or door. **2** a projecting tier of seats above the main floor in a theatre. □ **balconied** *adj.*

bald *adj.* **1** (of a person) with the scalp wholly or partly lacking hair. **2** (of an animal, plant, etc.) not covered by the usual hair, feathers, leaves, etc. **3** (of a landscape) treeless. **4** with the surface worn away (*a bald tire*). **5 a** blunt, unelaborated (*a bald statement*). **b** undisguised (*the bald effrontery*). **6** meagre or dull (*a bald style*). **7** marked with white, esp. on the face (*a bald horse*). □ **balding** *adj.* (in senses 1 & 2). **baldish** *adj.* **baldly** *adv.* (in sense 5). **baldness** *n.*

bald eagle *n.* an eagle of N America (*Haliaeetus leucocephalus*), with large brown wings and body, a white head and a yellow bill, the emblem of the US.

balderdash *n.* senseless talk or writing; nonsense.

bald-faced *adj.* = BAREFACED.

baldheaded *adj.* having little or no hair on the head.

baldie *n. informal* a bald person.

baldpate *n.* **1** a baldheaded person. **2** a N American duck, *Anas americana*, the male having a white crown.

bale ● *n.* **1** a bundle of material tightly wrapped or bound (*a bale of hay*). **2** the quantity in a bale as a unit of measure. ● *v.tr.* make up into bales.

baleen /bə'li:n/ *n.* whalebone.

baleen whale *n.* any of various whales of the suborder Mysticeti, having plates of baleen fringed with bristles for straining plankton from the water.

baleful *adj.* **1** (esp. of a manner, look, etc.) gloomy, menacing. **2** harmful, malignant, destructive. □ **balefully** *adv.* **balefulness** *n.*

baler *n.* a machine for making bales of hay, straw, or other material.

baler twine *n. N Amer.* = BINDER TWINE.

balk / bɔk / (also esp. *Brit.* **baulk**) ● *v.* **1** *intr.* **a** refuse to go on. **b** (often foll. by *at*) hesitate. **2** *tr.* **a** thwart, hinder. **b** disappoint. **3** *tr.* **a** miss, let slip (a chance etc.). **b** ignore, shirk. **4** *intr. Baseball* commit a balk. ● *n.* **1** a hindrance; a stumbling block. **2** a rafter or beam used for building. **3** *Baseball* an illegal motion made by a pitcher which allows the baserunners to advance one base. □ **balker** *n.*

Balkan / 'bɒlkən / *adj.* of or relating to the people or nations of the Balkan Peninsula in SE Europe.

balkanize *v.tr.* divide (a country etc.) into smaller mutually hostile units. □ **balkanization** *n.*

balky *adj.* (also esp. *Brit.* **baulky**) (**-ier, -iest**) reluctant, perverse. □ **balkiness** *n.*

ball[1] ● *n.* **1** a solid or hollow sphere, esp. for use in a game. **2 a** any roughly spherical object resembling a ball. **b** a rounded part of the body (*ball of the foot*). **3** a game played with a ball, esp. baseball. **4** *Baseball* **a** a pitch that is out of the designated strike zone and is not swung at. **b** a pitched ball, or one which has been struck by the batter (*fair ball*). **5** (in *pl.*) *coarse slang* **a** the testicles. **b** (usu. as an exclamation of contempt) nonsense. **c** courage. ● *v.* **1** *tr.* squeeze or wind into a ball. **2** *intr.* (often foll. by *up*) form or gather into a ball or balls. **3** *tr. & intr.* esp. *N Amer. coarse slang* have sexual intercourse (with). □ **the ball is in your** etc. **court** you etc. must be next to act. **ball** (or **balls**) **up** *coarse slang* bungle; make a mess of. **on the ball** *informal* alert. **play ball** *informal* co-operate. **start** (or **keep**) **the ball rolling** begin (or maintain the momentum of) an activity.

ball[2] *n.* **1** a formal social gathering for dancing. **2** *informal* an enjoyable time (*have a ball*).

ballad *n.* **1** a poem or song narrating a popular story. **2** a slow sentimental or romantic song.

ballade / bæˈlɑːd / *n.* **1** a poem of one or more triplets of stanzas with a repeated refrain and an envoy. **2** *Music* a short lyrical piece, esp. for piano.

balladeer *n.* a singer or composer of ballads.

ball and chain *n.* **1** a heavy metal ball secured by a chain to the leg of a prisoner etc. to prevent escape. **2** *informal* **a** a severe hindrance. **b** *derogatory* a wife.

ball-and-socket joint *n.* a joint in which a rounded end lies in a concave cup or socket, allowing considerable freedom of movement.

ballast ● *n.* **1** any heavy material carried by a ship etc. to secure stability. **2** coarse stone etc. used to form the bed of a railway track etc. **3** any device used to stabilize the current in a circuit. **4** anything that affords stability or permanence. ● *v.tr.* **1** provide with ballast. **2** afford stability or weight to.

ball bearing *n.* **1** a bearing in which the two halves are separated by a ring of small metal balls which reduce friction. **2** one of these balls.

ballboy *n.* (in tennis, baseball, etc.) a boy who retrieves balls that go out of play during a game.

ball club *n.* a baseball team.

ballerina *n.* a female ballet dancer.

ballet *n.* **1 a** a theatrical style of dancing using set steps and techniques and characterized esp. by movement with the legs turned out in the hip sockets and by the women dancing on pointe. **b** a theatrical work using ballet abstractly or to tell a story. **c** a piece of music composed for a ballet. **d** a performance of ballet. **2** a company performing ballet. **3** = ACRO. □ **balletic** / bəˈletɪk / *adj.*

ball field *n. N Amer.* a baseball field.

ball game *n.* **1** any game played with a ball, esp. a game of baseball. **2** esp. *N Amer. informal* a particular affair or concern (*a whole new ball game*).

ballgirl *n.* (in tennis, baseball, etc.) a girl who retrieves balls that go out of play during a game.

ball hockey *n. Cdn* **1** a version of hockey played in a gymnasium or in an arena without ice, using a hard plastic ball in place of a puck. **2** a version of hockey, usu. without formal rules, played on a paved surface, using a tennis ball instead of a puck.

ballistic *adj.* **1** of or relating to projectiles. **2** moving under the force of gravity only. □ **go ballistic** esp. *N Amer. slang* become incensed or act in a hysterical manner. □ **ballistically** *adv.*

ballistic missile *n.* a missile which is initially powered and guided but falls under gravity on its target.

ballistic nylon *n.* a durable, tightly woven nylon used in bulletproof vests, luggage, etc.

ballistics *n.pl.* (usu. treated as *sing.*) the science of projectiles and firearms.

balloon ● *n.* **1** a small inflatable rubber pouch with a neck, used as a toy or as decoration. **2** a large bag inflated with hot air or gas to make it rise in the air, often carrying a basket for passengers. **3** an outline enclosing the words or thoughts of characters in a comic strip etc. **4** a window covering falling in wide, puffy bands (usu. *attrib.: balloon blind*). **5** *Med.* a tiny inflatable pouch attached to a catheter and used to dilate an artery etc. during angioplasty or other procedures. **6** a large globular drinking glass for brandy or wine. ● *v.* **1** *intr. & tr.* **a** swell out or cause to swell out like a balloon. **b** grow or increase dramatically (*the deficit has ballooned*). **2** *intr.* travel by balloon. □ **when the balloon goes up** *informal* when the action or trouble starts. □ **balloonist** *n.* **ballooning** *n. & adj.*

ballot ● *n.* **1** a system of secret voting, usu. by marking a paper with one's choice of candidate etc. **2 a** a single round of voting (*won on the second ballot*). **b** the total number of votes recorded in a ballot. **3** a paper or ticket etc. used in voting. **4** the drawing of lots. ● *v.* (**balloted, balloting**) **1** *intr.* (usu. as **balloting** *n.*) **a** vote by ballot. **b** draw lots for precedence etc. **2** *tr.* solicit votes from (*the union balloted its members*).

ballot box *n.* **1** a sealed box into which voters put completed ballots. **2** an election (*lost at the ballot box*).

ballpark *n. N Amer.* **1** a field or stadium designed for baseball. **2** (*attrib.*) *informal* approximate, rough. □ **in the ballpark** *informal* approximately correct.

ballplayer *n.* a player in a ball game, esp. baseball.

ballpoint *n.* (in full **ballpoint pen**) a pen in which the writing point is a tiny rotating ball which rolls ink from an internal cartridge onto the paper.

ballroom *n.* a large room or hall for dancing.

ballroom dancing *n.* formal or recreational social dancing for couples, including the foxtrot, waltz, tango, and rumba.

ballsy *adj.* (**-ier, -iest**) *slang* courageous, tough, gutsy.

ballyhoo ● *n.* **1** extravagant publicity; hype. **2** a confused state or commotion. ● *v.tr.* (**-hooed, -hooing**) **1** promote using sensational publicity or hype. **2** praise extravagantly. □ **ballyhooed** *adj.*

balm *n.* **1** an aromatic ointment for anointing, soothing, or healing. **2** a fragrant and medicinal exudation from certain trees and plants. **3** a healing or soothing influence or consolation. **4** = BALM OF GILEAD 1a. **5** any aromatic herb, esp. one of the genus *Melissa*. **6** a pleasant perfume or fragrance.

balm of Gilead *n.* **1 a** any of various evergreen trees of the genus *Commiphora*, of W Asia and N Africa. **b** a fragrant resin exuded by such a tree. **2** a frequently planted hybrid poplar. **3** a balsam fir, *Abies balsamea*.

balmy *adj.* **(-ier, -iest) 1** (of weather) warm. **2** mild and fragrant; soothing. **3** yielding balm. □ **balmily** *adv.* **balminess** *n.*

baloney *n.* **1** *N Amer.* = BOLOGNA. **2** *informal* nonsensical or absurd ideas.

balsa *n.* **1** (in full **balsa wood**) a tough lightweight wood used for making boats etc. **2** the tropical American tree, *Ochroma lagopus*, from which it comes.

balsam /ˈbɒlsəm/ *n.* **1** any of several aromatic resins, such as balm, obtained from various trees and shrubs and used as a base for certain fragrances and medical preparations. **2** an ointment, esp. one composed of a substance dissolved in oil or turpentine. **3** any of various trees or shrubs which yield balsam. **4** any of several flowering plants of the genus *Impatiens*. **5** a healing or soothing agent.

balsam fir *n.* **1** a N American fir, *Abies balsamea*. **2** any of several other firs of northwestern N America, esp. the alpine fir.

balsamic vinegar /bɒlˈsæmɪk/ *n.* an aged sweet red-wine vinegar made from white grapes.

Balt /bɒlt/ *n.* a native or inhabitant of one of the Baltic states.

Baltic ● *adj.* of or relating to the Baltic or the Baltic language group. ● *n.* **1** (**the Baltic**) **a** an almost landlocked sea of northern Europe. **b** the states bordering this sea. **2** an Indo-European branch of languages including Lithuanian and Latvian.

Baltimore oriole *n.* a bright orange and black N American oriole, *Icterus galbula galbula*.

baluster /ˈbæləstər/ *n.* each of a series of often ornamental short posts supporting a railing etc. ¶Often confused with *banister*.

balustrade /ˌbæləˈstreɪd/ *n.* a railing supported by balusters, esp. forming an ornamental parapet to a balcony, bridge, or terrace.

bam *interj.* **1** expressing the sound of a hard blow. **2** indicating suddenness.

bambino /bæmˈbiːnoː/ *n.* (*pl.* **-os** or **bambini** /-niː/) **1** *informal* a young (esp. Italian) child. **2** an image of the infant Jesus in a painting etc.

bamboo *n.* **1** a mainly tropical giant woody grass of the genus *Bambusa* and related genera. **2** its hollow jointed stem, used as building material etc.

bamboo curtain *n.* a political and economic barrier between China and non-Communist countries.

bamboo shoot *n.* a young shoot of bamboo, eaten as a vegetable.

bamboozle *v.tr. informal* **1** cheat, deceive, swindle. **2** mystify, perplex. □ **bamboozler** *n.*

ban ● *v.tr.* (**banned, banning**) forbid, prohibit, esp. formally. ● *n.* **1** a formal or authoritative prohibition. **2** a tacit prohibition by public opinion.

banal /bəˈnæl/ *adj.* trite, trivial, commonplace. □ **banality** *n.* (*pl.* **-ies**). **banally** *adv.*

banana *n.* **1** a long curved fruit with soft pulpy flesh and yellow skin when ripe, growing in clusters. **2** (in full **banana tree**) any of several tropical and subtropical treelike plants of the genus *Musa* bearing this fruit. *See also* TOP BANANA, SECOND BANANA.

banana belt *n. informal* a region having a relatively warm climate, esp. (for Canadians) the Niagara Peninsula or southern BC.

banana pepper *n.* a small, yellow hot pepper.

banana republic *n.* often *derogatory* a small tropical nation, esp. in Central or S America, economically dependent on fruit exports or similar trade.

bananas *predic.adj. informal* **1** crazy or angry. **2** extremely enthusiastic.

banana split *n.* a dessert consisting of a split banana, ice cream, sauce, whipped cream etc.

band¹ ● *n.* **1 a** a flat, thin strip or loop of material, e.g. paper, metal, or cloth, put around something esp. to hold it together or decorate it (*headband*). **b** a strip of material forming part of a garment (*waistband*). **2** a stripe of a different colour or material on an object. **3** any long and narrow strip or grouping (*band of thunderstorms*). **4 a** a range of frequencies or wavelengths in a spectrum (esp. of radio frequencies). **b** a range of values within a series. **5** a ring without a prominent precious stone. **6** a section of a phonograph record, usu. comprising a single song etc. **7** a loop of metal or plastic attached to the leg of a bird etc. for identification. **8** a belt connecting wheels or pulleys. ● *v.tr.* **1** put a band on, esp. attach an identification band to a bird etc. **2** mark with stripes. □ **banded** *adj.*

band² ● *n.* **1** an organized group of people having a common objective (*a band of protesters*). **2** (in Canada) an Indian community officially recognized as an administrative unit by the federal government. **3** *Anthropology* a basic organizational unit in nomadic societies, consisting of several families. **4 a** a group of musicians, esp. playing wind and percussion instruments (*brass band*). **b** a group of musicians playing jazz, rock, or pop music. **c** *informal* an orchestra. **5** *N Amer.* a herd or flock. ● *v.tr. & intr.* form into a group for a purpose (*band together*).

bandage ● *n.* **1** a strip of material for binding up a wound etc. **2** any piece of material used for binding or covering. ● *v.tr.* bind (a wound etc.) with a bandage.

Band-Aid *n.* **1** *proprietary* an adhesive bandage with a gauze pad for dressing small cuts etc. **2** (also **band-aid**) (often *attrib.*) a makeshift or temporary solution.

bandana *n.* (also **bandanna**) a coloured handkerchief or head scarf, usu. of cotton, and often having a figured design.

B & B *abbr.* **1** bed and breakfast. **2** *Cdn* bilingualism and biculturalism.

band council *n. Cdn* a local form of Aboriginal government, consisting of a chief and councillors who are elected for two or three year terms to carry on band business. □ **band councillor** *n.*

B and E *abbr. slang* BREAKING AND ENTERING.

bandeau /ˈbændoː, -ˈdoː/ *n.* (*pl.* **-s** or **-eaux** /-doːz/) **1** a band of material worn around the breasts, esp. as part of a swimsuit. **2** a narrow headband.

banding *n.* in senses of BAND¹ *v.*, BAND² *v.*

bandit *n.* **1** a robber; esp. a member of a gang; a gangster. **2** an outlaw. □ **banditry** *n.*

bandleader *n.* the leader of a band of musicians.

bandmaster *n.* the conductor of a band.

bandolier /ˌbændəˈliːr/ *n.* (also **bandoleer**) a belt or strap worn diagonally across the chest with loops or pockets for ammunition.

bandpass *n. Electronics* the range of frequencies (of sound, electrical signals, etc.) which are transmitted through a filter.

band saw *n.* an electric saw with a seamless toothed band which rotates clockwise around two wheels.

bandshell *n.* a bandstand in the form of a large concave shell with special acoustic properties.

bandstand *n.* **1** a covered outdoor platform for a band to play on, usu. in a park. **2** any stage or platform for a band.

B & W *abbr.* (of film etc.) black and white.

bandwagon *n.* **1** a wagon used for carrying a band in a parade etc. **2** (esp. in **jump** (or **climb**) **on the bandwagon**) a party, cause, or group that is fashionable or seems likely to succeed.

bandwidth *n.* the range of frequencies within a given band (see BAND¹ *n.* 4a).

bandy ● *adj.* (**-ier, -iest**) **1** (of the legs) curved so as to be wide apart at the knees. **2** (also **bandy-legged**) (of a person) bowlegged. ● *v.tr.* (**-ies, -ied**) **1** (often foll. by *about*) a pass (a story, rumour, etc.) to and fro. **b** throw or pass (a ball etc.) to and fro. **2** (often foll. by *about*) discuss disparagingly (*bandied her name about*). **3** (often foll. by *with*) exchange (blows, insults, etc.) (*don't bandy words with me*). ● *n.* **1** an early form of hockey played on a field or on ice with a ball and large curved sticks. **2** (*pl.* **-ies**) the curved stick used in this sport.

bane *n.* **1** the cause of ruin or trouble (*the bane of my existence*). **2** *literary* ruin; woe. **3** *archaic* (except in *comb.*) poison (*ratsbane*). □ **baneful** *adj.* **banefully** *adv.*

bang ● *n.* **1** a a loud sudden sound. **b** an explosion. **c** the firing of a gun. **2** a a sharp blow. **b** the sound of this. **3** *N Amer. informal* a thrill (*got a bang out of it*). **4** (in *pl.*) esp. *N Amer.* a fringe of hair cut across the forehead. **5** *coarse slang* an act of sexual intercourse. **6** *slang* an exclamation mark. ● *v.* **1** *tr. & intr.* strike or shut noisily (*banged the door shut; banged on the table*). **2** *tr. & intr.* make or cause to make the sound of a blow or an explosion. **3** *tr. esp. N Amer.* hit (hair) into bangs. **4** *tr. & intr. coarse slang* have sexual intercourse (with). ● *adv.* **1** with a bang or sudden impact. **2** *informal* exactly (*bang in the middle*). ● *interj.* indicating suddenness or swiftness. □ **bang on** *Cdn & Brit. informal* exactly right. **bang out** *informal* produce (a piece of work etc.) quickly and without attention to detail. **bang up** damage or injure. **bang for one's buck** *N Amer.* value for one's money. **with a bang 1** quickly and noisily. **2** with great commotion, publicity, success, etc.

bangbelly *n.* (*pl.* **-ies**) *Cdn* (*Nfld*) a pudding, cake, or pancake consisting of a dumpling-like mixture fried, baked, or stewed.

banger *n.* **1** a thing that makes a banging noise, e.g. a firecracker or device for scaring away birds etc. **2** (in *comb.*) *slang* an engine having a specified number of cylinders (*four-banger*).

Bangladeshi /ˌbæŋɡləˈdeʃi/ ● *n.* (*pl.* same or **-is**) a native or inhabitant of Bangladesh. ● *adj.* of or relating to Bangladesh or its people.

bangle *n.* a rigid bracelet, usu. without a clasp, worn around the arm or ankle.

bang-up *adj. N Amer. informal* first-class, excellent (*a bang-up job*).

banish *v.tr.* **1** formally expel (a person), esp. from a country. **2** dismiss from one's presence or mind. □ **banishment** *n.*

banister *n.* **1** the handrail at the side of a staircase. **2** (in *pl.*) a handrail and its supporting uprights. **3** (usu. in *pl.*) an upright supporting a handrail. ¶Often confused with *baluster*.

banjo *n.* (*pl.* **-os** or **-oes**) a four- or five-stringed musical instrument with a neck and head like a guitar and an open-backed body consisting of parchment stretched over a metal hoop.

bank¹ ● *n.* **1** the sloping ground bordering a body of water. **2** the area of ground alongside a river. **3** a slope or raised shelf of ground. **4** an underwater ridge of land (*Grand Banks*). **5** the slope built into a road etc., enabling vehicles to maintain speed around a curve. **6** the tilt of an aircraft etc. to one side during a turn. **7** a mass of cloud, fog, snow, etc. ● *v.* **1** *tr. & intr.* (often foll. by *up*) heap or rise into banks. **2** a

intr. (of a vehicle or aircraft) tilt to one side while rounding a curve. **b** *tr.* cause (a vehicle or aircraft) to do this. **3** *tr.* contain or confine within a bank or banks. **4** *tr.* build (a road etc.) higher at the outer edge of a bend to enable fast cornering. **5** *tr.* heap up (a fire) tightly so that it burns slowly. **6** *tr.* cause (a puck) to rebound off the boards of a hockey rink.

bank² ● *n.* **1** a a financial establishment which uses money deposited by customers for investment, pays it out when required, lends money at interest, etc. **b** a building in which this takes place. **2** a an institution which collects a product and stores it for future use (*food bank*). **b** a place where information is stored in a computer (*data bank*). **3** a the money etc. held by the banker in some games. **b** the banker or dealer in such games. **4** = PIGGY BANK. ● *v.* **1** *tr.* deposit (money etc.) in a bank. **2** *intr.* engage in business as a banker. **3** *intr.* (often foll. by *at, with*) keep money (at a bank). **4** *intr.* act as banker in a game. □ **bank on** rely on.

bank³ *n.* **1** a row of similar objects, esp. of keys, lights, or switches. **2** a tier of oars.

bankable *adj.* **1** acceptable at a bank. **2** reliable (*a bankable reputation*). **3** certain to bring in a profit.

bank barn *n. N Amer.* (esp. *Ont. & US Midlands*) a barn built into a hill with an entrance to the top storey on one side and to the lower storey on the other.

bank book *n.* = PASSBOOK.

bank card *n.* a plastic card with an encoded magnetic strip, used at automated teller machines.

bank draft *n.* an order for payment drawn by one bank on another.

banker¹ *n.* **1** a person who manages or owns a bank or group of banks. **2** a a keeper of the bank in some gambling games. **b** a card game involving gambling.

banker² *n.* **1** a fishing boat operating in the waters off Newfoundland, esp. the Grand Banks. **2** a Newfoundland fisherman.

banking¹ *n. Cdn* (*Nfld*) fishing for cod off the south-east coast of Newfoundland.

banking² *n.* **1** the business conducted by a bank. **2** the custom given to a bank by a customer.

bank machine *n.* = AUTOMATED TELLER MACHINE.

banknote *n.* a piece of paper money issued by a central bank, circulating as a nation's currency.

Bank of Canada *n.* the federally owned central bank which controls Canada's bank rate etc.

bank rate *n.* esp. *Cdn* the central bank's minimum interest rate on short-term loans to banks etc.

bankroll ● *n. N Amer.* **1** a roll of banknotes. **2** a sum of money; available funds. ● *v.tr.* esp. *N Amer. informal* support financially.

bankrupt ● *adj.* **1** a legally declared unable to pay debts; insolvent. **b** undergoing the legal process resulting from this. **2** (often foll. by *of*) exhausted or drained (of some quality etc.); deficient; lacking. ● *n.* **1** an insolvent debtor whose estate is administered and disposed of for the benefit of the creditors. **2** a person exhausted of or deficient in a certain attribute (*a moral bankrupt*). ● *v.tr.* make bankrupt. □ **bankruptcy** *n.* (*pl.* **-ies**)

banner ● *n.* **1** a large sign or strip of cloth etc. bearing a slogan or design. **2** a belief or principle serving as a rallying point. **3** (in full **banner headline**) a large newspaper headline, esp. one across the top of the front page. **4** a national flag. ● *attrib.adj. N Amer.* excellent, outstanding (*a banner year in sales*). □ **bannered** *adj.*

bannister *var. of* BANISTER.

bannock *n. Cdn* a bread similar to tea biscuits, made

of flour, water, and fat, sometimes leavened with baking powder, cooked on a griddle or over a fire.

banns *n.pl.* an oral or published notice announcing an intended marriage and giving the opportunity for objections.

banquet ● *n.* **1** an elaborate and extensive feast. **2** a dinner for many people followed by speeches in favour of a cause or in celebration of an event. ● *v.* (**banqueted, banqueting**) **1** *intr.* hold a banquet; feast. **2** *tr.* entertain with a banquet.

banquet hall *n.* **1** a room in which banquets are held. **2** a building containing one or more of these.

banquette /bæŋˈket/ *n.* an upholstered bench along a wall, esp. in a restaurant or bar.

banshee *n.* (in Gaelic mythology) a female spirit whose wailing warns of imminent death in a family.

bantam *n.* **1** any of several small breeds of domestic fowl, of which the rooster is very aggressive. **2** a small but aggressive person. **3** *Cdn* **a** a level of amateur sport, usu. involving children aged 13–15. **b** a player in this age group.

bantamweight *n.* **1** a weight class in certain sports between flyweight and featherweight, in the professional boxing scale not more than 118 lbs. (53 kg). **2** an athlete of this weight.

banter ● *n.* good-humoured teasing. ● *v.* **1** *tr.* ridicule in a good-humoured way. **2** *intr.* talk humorously or teasingly. ☐ **banterer** *n.*

Bantu /ˈbæntuː/ ● *n.* **1** a group of Niger-Congo languages spoken in equatorial and southern Africa, including Swahili, Xhosa, and Zulu. **2** (*pl.* same or **-s**) a member of the peoples speaking these languages. ● *adj.* of or relating to these languages or peoples.

banyan /ˈbænjən/ *n.* an Indian fig tree, *Ficus benghalensis*, the branches of which produce aerial roots to form new trunks.

baptism *n.* **1 a** a religious rite symbolizing admission to the Christian Church, involving sprinkling the forehead with water or total immersion and generally accompanied by naming. **b** the act of baptizing or being baptized. **2** any similar rite of initiation, purification, or naming. ☐ **baptismal** *adj.*

baptism of fire *n.* **1** initiation into battle. **2** a painful new undertaking or experience.

Baptist *n.* a member of a Protestant denomination advocating baptism by total immersion, esp. of adults, as a symbol of membership of and initiation into the Church.

baptistery /ˈbæptɪstri/ *n.* (also **baptistry**) (*pl.* **-ies**) **1** the part of a church used for baptism. **2** (in a Baptist church) a tank used for total immersion.

baptize *v.tr.* **1** administer baptism to. **2** give a name or nickname to.

bar¹ ● *n.* **1** a long rod or piece of rigid wood, metal, etc., esp. used as an obstruction, fastening, weapon, etc. **2 a** something resembling a bar in being (thought of as) straight, narrow, and rigid (*chocolate bar*). **b** a band of colour or light, esp. on a flat surface. **c** = CROSSBAR. **d** a metal strip below the clasp of a medal, awarded as an extra distinction. **e** a bank of sand etc. across the mouth of a river or harbour (*compare* SANDBAR). **f** a rail (*towel bar*). **3 a** a barrier of any shape. **b** a restriction (*a bar to promotion*). **c** *Law* a legal obstacle preventing an action or claim. **4 a** a counter in a pub, restaurant, or home across which alcohol or refreshments are served. **b** a room in a restaurant, hotel, etc. in which customers may sit and drink. **c** *N Amer.* an establishment serving alcoholic drinks; a pub. **5** a small shop, stall, department, etc. which specializes in a particular product (*gas bar*;

snack bar). **6 a** any of the sections of usu. equal time value into which a musical composition is divided by vertical lines across the staff. **b** = BAR LINE. **7 a** a rail in a law court separating the space occupied by the judge, lawyers, and parties to a case from the general public. **b** an enclosure in which an accused person stands before a court of law. **c** a rail marking the end of the chamber in the House of Commons. **8** *N Amer. Law* (prec. by *the*) **a** lawyers collectively. **b** the profession of lawyer. ● *v.tr.* (**barred, barring**) **1 a** fasten (a door, window, etc.) with a bar or bars. **b** (usu. foll. by *in, out*) shut or keep in or out. **2** obstruct, prevent (*bar her progress*). **3 a** (usu. foll. by *from*) prohibit, exclude (*bar them from attending*). **b** exclude from consideration (*compare* BARRING). **4** mark with stripes. **5** *Law* prevent or delay (an action) by legal obstacle. ● *prep.* except (*bar none*). ☐ **at (the) bar** (of a lawsuit, defendant, etc.) currently before the courts. **be called** (or **admitted**) **to the bar** be formally admitted into the legal profession. **behind bars** in prison.

bar² *n.* esp. *Meteorol.* a unit of pressure equal to 100 kilopascals.

barachois /ˈbɑːrəˌʃwɒ/ *n.* (also **barachois pond**) *Cdn* (*Nfld & Maritimes*) a shallow coastal lagoon or pond created by the formation of a sandbar a short distance offshore from a beach.

barb ● *n.* **1** a secondary backward-projecting point of an arrow, fish hook, etc., angled to make extraction difficult. **2** a deliberately hurtful remark. **3** a beard-like filament at the mouth of some fish, e.g. barbel and catfish. **4** any one of the fine hairlike filaments growing from the shaft of a feather, forming the vane. ● *v.tr.* furnish (an arrow, fish hook, etc.) with a barb or barbs.

Barbadian /bɑːrˈbeɪdiən/ ● *n.* **1** a native or national of Barbados. **2** a person of Barbadian descent. ● *adj.* of or relating to Barbados or its people.

barbarian ● *n.* **1** an uncultured or brutish person. **2** a member of a people regarded as uncivilized. ● *adj.* **1** rough and uncultured. **2** uncivilized.

barbaric *adj.* **1** brutal; cruel. **2** rough and uncultured. **3** primitive. ☐ **barbarically** *adv.*

barbarism *n.* **1 a** the absence of culture and civilized standards; ignorance and rudeness. **b** an example of this. **2** a word or expression not considered correct. **3** anything considered to be in bad taste.

barbarity *n.* (*pl.* **-ies**) **1** savage cruelty. **2** an example of this.

barbarize *v.tr. & intr.* make or become barbarous. ☐ **barbarization** *n.*

barbarous *adj.* **1** uncivilized. **2** cruel. **3** coarse and unrefined. ☐ **barbarously** *adv.* **barbarousness** *n.*

barbecue (also **barbeque**) ● *n.* **1 a** a meal, esp. of meat, cooked on an open fire or grill out of doors. **b** a party at which such a meal is cooked and eaten. **2 a** a metal appliance equipped with a grill on which meat etc. is cooked over charcoal or gas flame. **b** a fireplace, usu. of brick, containing a grill for cooking. ● *v.tr.* (**barbecues, barbecued, barbecuing**) cook (esp. meat) on a barbecue.

barbecue sauce *n.* a highly seasoned sauce, usu. tomato-based, used to baste barbecued meat.

barbed *adj.* **1** equipped with barbs. **2** (of a remark etc.) deliberately hurtful.

barbed wire *n.* wire bearing sharp pointed spikes close together and used in fencing, or in warfare as an obstruction.

barbel /ˈbɑːrbəl/ *n.* **1** any large European freshwater fish of the genus *Barbus*, with fleshy filaments hanging from its mouth. **2** such a filament growing from the mouth of any fish.

barbell *n.* a metal bar with a series of weighted discs at each end, used for weightlifting exercises.

barber ● *n.* a person who cuts men's hair and shaves or trims beards as an occupation; a men's hairdresser. ● *v.tr.* **1** cut the hair, shave or trim the beard of. **2** cut or trim (grass etc.) closely.

barber chair *n.* **1** a chair used by hairdressers, esp. one which can be raised or lowered. **2** *Cdn* a tree stump with a large splintered point of wood left above the undercut as a result of improper sawing.

barber pole *n.* a pole with spiral red and white stripes, hung outside a barbershop as a business sign.

barbershop *n.* esp. *N Amer.* **1** a shop where a barber works. **2** (also **barbershop quartet**) a style of close harmony singing for four male voices.

Barbie *n.* (also **Barbie doll**) **1** *proprietary* a doll representing a slim, fashionably dressed, attractive young woman. **2** a woman with similar characteristics, esp. (*derogatory*) an unintelligent one.

barbital /ˈbɑrbɪˌtɒl/ *n.* a long-acting hypnotic and sedative drug.

barbiturate /bɑrˈbɪtʃərət, -ˌreɪt/ *n.* any derivative of barbituric acid used in the preparation of sedative and sleep-inducing drugs.

barbituric acid /ˌbɑrbɪˈtʃʊrɪk, -ˈtjʊrɪk/ *n.* an organic acid from which various sedatives and sleep-inducing drugs are derived.

barbotte[1] /ˈbɑrbət/ *n.* (also **barbot**) *Cdn* (*Que.* & *Ont.*) a large catfish, esp. *Ictalurus punctatus*.

barbotte[2] /bɑrˈbɒt/ *n.* *Cdn* (esp. *Que.*) a gambling game similar to craps but played with three dice.

barbwire *N Amer. var. of* BARBED WIRE.

B.Arch. *abbr.* Bachelor of Architecture.

bar chart *var. of* BAR GRAPH.

bar code *n.* a code in the form of a pattern of stripes, used for identification by an optical scanner. □ **bar-coded** *adj.* **bar-coding** *n.*

bard *n.* **1** *hist.* a Celtic minstrel. **2** *literary* a poet. □ **the Bard** Shakespeare. □ **bardic** *adj.*

bare ● *adj.* **1** unclothed or uncovered. **2** without appropriate covering or contents: **a** (of a tree) leafless. **b** unfurnished; empty (*bare rooms*). **c** (of a floor) uncarpeted. **d** (of ground) without vegetation. **3** *N Amer.* (of a road etc.) clear of snow and ice. **4 a** undisguised (*the bare truth*). **b** unadorned (*bare facts*). **5** (*attrib.*) **a** scanty (*a bare majority*). **b** mere (*bare necessities*). ● *v.tr.* **1** uncover, unsheathe (*bared his teeth*). **2** reveal (*bared her soul*). □ **bare of** without. **lay bare** expose, reveal. **with one's bare hands** without using tools or weapons. □ **bareness** *n.*

bareback *adj. & adv.* on an unsaddled horse etc.

bareboat *n.* (usu. *attrib.*) a boat, esp. a sailboat, that is rented without a crew (*bareboat charter*).

bare bones *n.pl.* essential parts or components. □ **bare-bones** *adj.*

barefaced *adj.* undisguised; impudent (*barefaced lie*). □ **barefacedly** /berˈfeɪsədli/ *adv.* **barefacedness** *n.*

barefoot *adj. & adv.* (also **barefooted**) with nothing on the feet.

bare-handed *adj. & adv.* with bare hands.

bare-headed *adj. & adv.* without a covering for the head.

bare-knuckle *adj.* (also **bare-knuckled**) **1** *Boxing* without gloves; with bare fists. **2** without niceties (*bare-knuckle political campaign*).

barely *adv.* **1** only just; scarcely (*barely escaped*). **2** scantily (*barely furnished*).

barf *informal* ● *v.intr.* vomit or retch. ● *n.* **1** vomited food, etc. **2** an attack of vomiting. ● *interj.* expressing disgust (*I have to clean the fridge. Barf!*).

barfly *n.* (*pl.* **-flies**) *informal* a person who frequents bars.

bargain ● *n.* **1 a** an agreement on the terms of a transaction or sale. **b** this seen from the buyer's viewpoint (*a bad bargain*). **2** something acquired or offered cheaply. ● *v.intr.* (often foll. by *with*, *for*) discuss the terms of a transaction (*bargained for the table*). □ **bargain away** part with for something worthless (*bargained away the farm*). **bargain for** (or **on**) be prepared for; expect (*didn't bargain for bad weather*). **bargain on** rely on. **drive a hard bargain** pursue one's own profit in a transaction keenly. **into** (or **in**) **the bargain** moreover; in addition to what was expected. **make** (or **strike**) **a bargain** agree to a transaction. □ **bargainer** *n.*

bargain basement ● *n.* a store, or basement of a store, where bargains are available. ● *adj.* **1** inexpensive, cheap. **2** inferior, poor-quality.

bargaining chip *n.* something which can be used to advantage in negotiations.

bargaining table *n.* a table around which negotiations are conducted.

bargaining unit *n.* a group of workers united for the purpose of collective bargaining.

barge ● *n.* **1** a long flat-bottomed boat for carrying freight etc. **2** *Cdn* (*Nfld*) a large boat used to collect, hold, and process cod. **3** a long ornamental boat used for pleasure or ceremony. ● *v.* **1 a** *tr.* transport (goods) on a barge. **b** *intr.* travel by barge. **2** *intr.* (often foll. by *around*) lurch or rush clumsily about. **3** *intr.* (foll. by *in*, *into*) **a** intrude or interrupt rudely or awkwardly. **b** collide with (*barged into her*).

barge pole *n.* □ **would not touch with a barge pole** see TOUCH.

bargoon *n.* *Cdn slang* a bargain.

bar graph *n.* a graph using bars to represent quantity.

bar harbour *n.* *N Amer.* a harbour with an entrance that is partially obstructed by a sandbar.

bar-hop *v.intr.* *N Amer.* (**-hopped**, **-hopping**) *informal* go drinking in one bar after another.

baritone /ˈbɛrɪˌtoːn, ˈbærɪ-/ ● *n.* **1 a** the second-lowest adult male singing voice. **b** a singer with this voice. **c** a part written for it. **2 a** an instrument that is second-lowest in pitch in its family. **b** its player. ● *adj.* of the second-lowest range.

barium /ˈbɛriəm, ˈbæ-/ *n.* **1** a white reactive soft metallic element. **2** (usu. *attrib.*) a mixture of barium sulphate and water which is opaque to X-rays, given to patients requiring radiological examination of the stomach and intestines (*barium enema*).

bark[1] ● *n.* **1** the sharp cry of a dog, fox, etc. **2** a sound resembling this cry. ● *v.* **1** *intr.* (of a dog etc.) give a bark. **2** *tr.* & *intr.* speak or utter sharply or brusquely. **3** *intr.* cough fiercely. □ **one's bark is worse than one's bite** one is not as ferocious as one appears. **bark up the wrong tree** be on the wrong track; make an effort in the wrong direction.

bark[2] ● *n.* **1** the tough protective outer sheath of the trunks, branches, and twigs of trees or woody shrubs. **2** this material used for tanning leather or dyeing material. **3** *N Amer.* a type of flat usu. chocolate candy containing nuts. ● *v.tr.* **1** graze or scrape (one's shin etc.). **2** strip bark from (a tree etc.). **3** tan or dye (leather etc.) using the tannins found in bark. **4** *Cdn* (*Nfld*) boil (nets, sails, etc.) in an infusion of conifer buds and bark as a preservative.

bark[3] *n. literary* a ship or boat.

barkeep *n.* (also **barkeeper**) *N Amer. informal* a bartender.

barkentine *var. of* BARQUENTINE.

barker *n.* **1** a person who calls out loudly to attract customers to an auction, a stall at a fair, etc. **2** a dog etc. that barks persistently.

barley *n.* any of various hardy awned cereals of the genus *Hordeum*, widely used as food and in malt liquors and spirits such as whisky.

bar line *n. Music* a vertical line used to mark divisions between bars.

barmaid *n.* a female bartender.

barman *n.* (*pl.* **-men**) a male bartender.

bar mitzvah /bɑr ˈmɪtzvə/ *n.* **1** the religious initiation ceremony of a Jewish boy who has reached the age of 13. **2** the boy undergoing this ceremony.

barn *n.* **1** a large farm building for housing animals, storing grain, etc. **2** *derogatory* a large plain or unattractive building. **3** *N Amer.* a large shed for storing road or railway vehicles.

barnacle *n.* **1** any of various species of small marine crustaceans of the class Cirripedia which in adult form cling to rocks, ships' bottoms, etc. **2** a tenacious attendant or follower who cannot easily be shaken off. □ **barnacled** *adj.*

barnboard *n. N Amer.* wide unplaned softwood boards, used esp. for building barns.

barnburner *n. N Amer. informal* **1** something exciting or successful. **2** a lively or exciting esp. political speech (*delivered a two-hour barnburner*). **3** a game or competition that has a close result.

barn dance *n.* **1** an informal social gathering for dancing, originally in a barn. **2** a dance for a number of couples forming a line or circle.

barn owl *n.* an owl of the genus *Tyto*, esp. *T. alba*, which usu. has a white face and underside and frequently nests in farm buildings.

barn raising *n. N Amer.* a gathering of people to put up the framework of a neighbour's barn, usu. followed by a dance.

barnstorm *v.* **1** *N Amer.* **a** *intr.* make a rapid tour holding political meetings. **b** *tr.* visit (an area) to hold such meetings. **2** *intr. N Amer.* give informal flying exhibitions, esp. at country fairs etc.; do stunt flying. **3** *intr.* tour rural districts giving theatrical performances (formerly often in barns). **4** *intr.* (of a sports team) tour through an area playing exhibition games. □ **barnstormer** *n.*

barn swallow *n. N Amer.* the common swallow, *Hirundo rustica*, which builds mud nests on buildings.

barnyard *n.* **1** the usu. fenced area around a barn. **2** (*attrib.*) earthy, coarse (*barnyard humour*).

Barolo /bəˈroːloː/ *n.* (*pl.* **-os**) a full-bodied red Italian wine from the Barolo region of Piedmont in N Italy.

barometer *n.* **1** an instrument measuring atmospheric pressure, esp. in forecasting the weather and determining altitude. **2** anything which reflects changes in circumstances, opinions, etc. □ **barometric** /ˌbærəˈmetrɪk/ *adj.* **barometrical** *adj.* **barometry** *n.*

baron *n.* **1** a member of the lowest order of nobility in the United Kingdom or other countries. **2** an important businessman or other powerful or influential person (*timber baron*).

baroness *n.* **1** a woman holding the rank of baron either as a life peerage or as a hereditary rank. **2** the wife or widow of a baron.

baronet *n.* a member of the lowest hereditary titled British order, below a baron but above a knight.

baronial /bəˈroːnɪəl/ *adj.* of or befitting barons.

baroque /bəˈroːk/ ● *n.* **1** a style of architecture and decorative art of the late 16th to early 18th c., characterized by extensive ornamentation. **2** a style of music from the period 1600–1750, characterized by increasing complexity and emphasis on contrast. ● *adj.* **1** of or relating to this period or style. **2** highly ornate and complex.

barque *n.* **1** a sailing ship with the rear mast fore-and-aft-rigged and the remaining (usu. two) masts square-rigged. **2** *literary* any boat.

barquentine /ˈbɑrkən,tiːn/ *n.* a sailing ship with the foremast square-rigged and the remaining (usu. two) masts fore-and-aft-rigged.

barrack ● *n.* (usu. in *pl.*, often treated as *sing.*) **1** a building or complex used to house soldiers. **2** *Cdn* a building housing a local detachment of the RCMP. **3** any building used to accommodate large numbers of people. **4** a large building with a bleak or plain appearance. ● *v.tr.* place (soldiers etc.) in barracks.

barracuda *n.* (*pl.* same or **-s**) a large and voracious tropical marine fish of the family Sphyraenidae.

barrage ● *n.* **1** a concentrated artillery bombardment over a wide area. **2** a rapid succession of questions or criticisms. **3** an artificial barrier, esp. in a river. **4** a heat or deciding event in fencing, show jumping, etc. ● *v.tr.* subject to a barrage of artillery fire, questions, etc.

barre /bɑr/ *n.* a waist-level horizontal bar to help dancers keep their balance during some exercises.

barré /ˈbæreɪ/ *n. Music* a method of playing a chord on the guitar etc. with a finger laid across the strings at a particular fret, raising their pitch.

barred owl *n.* a large owl, *Strix varia*, with large brown vertical streaks on its breast, which inhabits the southern boreal forest of N America.

barrel ● *n.* **1** a cylindrical container usu. bulging out in the middle, made of wooden staves with metal hoops around them, or of plastic or metal. **2** the contents of this. **3** a measure of capacity, usu. varying from 30 to 40 imperial gallons (136 to 182 litres). **4** a unit of capacity for oil and petroleum products equal to 35 imperial gallons (about 159 litres). **5** the cylindrical body or trunk of an object, e.g. a pump, pen, etc. **6** the metal tube of a gun, through which the shot is discharged. **7** the fuel outlet from the carburetor on a gasoline engine. **8** the trunk of a horse etc. ● *v.* (**barrelled**, **barrelling**) **1** *tr.* put into a barrel or barrels. **2** *intr. N Amer. informal* move quickly. □ **barrel of fun** (or **laughs**) *informal* a great deal of fun. **over a barrel** *informal* in a helpless position.

barrel-chested *adj.* having a large rounded chest.

barrelhead *n.* the flat top of a barrel. □ **on the barrelhead** *N Amer.* immediately and up front.

barrelhouse *n.* **1** a disreputable or cheap bar. **2** (often *attrib.*) an unrestrained style of jazz music.

barrel-jumping *n. Cdn* a sport in which a skater jumps over a row of barrels lying on their sides.

barrel organ *n.* a mechanical musical instrument in which a rotating pin-studded cylinder acts on a series of pipe-valves, strings, or metal tongues.

barrel race *n. N Amer.* a women's rodeo event in which a mounted rider must navigate a triangular arrangement of three barrels and return to the starting line. □ **barrel racer** *n.* **barrel racing** *n.*

barrel roll *n.* an aerobatic manoeuvre in which an aircraft rolls once about its longitudinal axis.

barren ● *adj.* (**barrener**, **barrenest**) **1** a unable to bear young. **b** unable to produce fruit or vegetation. **2** meagre, unprofitable. **3** dull, unstimulating. ● *n.* **1** (in eastern N America) a tract of elevated flat land that supports shrubs and bushes but no trees. **2** *Cdn* (*NB* & *NS*) an expanse of marsh or muskeg. ☐ **barrenly** *adv.* **barrenness** *n.*

barren ground caribou *n.* a caribou, *R. tarandus groenlandicus*, native to the tundra of N Canada.

Barrens, the *n.pl.* (also **barrens**, **Barren Grounds**, **Barren Lands**) *Cdn* the treeless, sparsely populated region of N Canada, lying between Hudson Bay and Great Slave and Great Bear lakes.

barrette *n.* a bar-shaped clip or ornament for a woman's or girl's hair.

barricade ● *n.* a barrier, esp. one improvised across a street etc. ● *v.tr.* block with a barricade.

barrier *n.* **1** a fence or other obstacle that bars advance or access. **2** an obstacle or circumstance that keeps people or things apart, or prevents communication (*a language barrier*). **3** anything that prevents progress or success. **4** a gate at a parking garage etc., that controls access. **5** an exposed sandbar that parallels a coast, as on the north shore of PEI (*barrier island*). **6** *informal* = SOUND BARRIER. **7** something that prevents transmission of a substance.

barrier reef *n.* a coral reef separated from the shore by a broad deep channel.

barring *prep.* in the absence of (*barring complications*).

barrister *n.* (in full **barrister-at-law**) a lawyer who pleads cases before the courts. ¶All lawyers in Canadian common law provinces are both barristers and solicitors.

barrister and solicitor *n. Cdn* a lawyer.

barroom *n.* = BAR[1] 4b.

barrow[1] *n.* **1** = WHEELBARROW. **2** *Cdn* (*Nfld*) a flat, rectangular wooden frame with handles at both ends, used by two people to carry fish etc.

barrow[2] *n. Archaeology* a mound of earth constructed in ancient times to cover one or more burials.

bar stool *n.* a high, usu. cushioned stool for sitting at bars or counters.

bartender *n.* a person serving drinks at a bar. ☐ **bartend** *v.intr.* **bartending** *n.*

barter ● *v.* **1** *tr.* exchange (goods or services) without using money. **2** *intr.* make such an exchange. ● *n.* trade by exchange of goods. ☐ **barterer** *n.*

Bartlett pear *n.* esp. *N Amer.* a large, yellow, juicy variety of pear.

basal /'beisəl/ *adj.* **1** of, at, or forming a base. **2** fundamental.

basal metabolism *n.* the chemical processes occurring in an organism at complete rest.

basalt /'bæsɒlt/ *n.* a dark basic volcanic rock whose strata sometimes form columns. ☐ **basaltic** *adj.*

B.A.Sc. *abbr.* Bachelor of Applied Science.

base[1] ● *n.* **1 a** a part that supports from beneath or serves as a foundation for an object or structure. **b** a notional structure or entity on which something draws or depends (*power base*). **2** a principle or starting point. **3 a** a place from which an operation or activity is directed. **b** *Military* a military installation from which operations are conducted and where equipment and supporting facilities are concentrated. **4 a** a main or important ingredient of a mixture. **b** a substance, e.g. water, in combination with which pigment forms paint etc. **5** a substance used as a foundation for makeup. **6** *Chem.* a substance capable of combining with an acid to form a salt and water and usu. producing hydroxide ions when dis-

solved in water. **7** *Math.* a number in terms of which other numbers or logarithms are expressed. **8** *Archit.* the part of a column between the shaft and pedestal or pavement. **9** *Geom.* a line or surface on which a figure is regarded as standing. **10** *Surveying* a known line used as a geometrical base for trigonometry. **11** *Electronics* the middle part of a transistor separating the emitter from the collector. **12** *Linguistics* a root or stem as the origin of a word or a derivative. **13** *Baseball* one of the four stations that must be reached in turn when scoring a run. **14** *Bot.* & *Zool.* the end at which a part or organ is attached to the main part. ● *v.tr.* **1** found or establish (*a theory based on speculation*). **2** station (*troops were based in Cyprus*). ☐ **cover** (or **touch**) **all the bases** *N Amer. informal* deal with all the related details. **make it to** (or **reach** etc.) **first base** esp. *N Amer. informal* achieve the first step of an objective, plan, etc. **off base 1** *Baseball* not touching a base. **2** esp. *N Amer. informal* **a** mistaken. **b** unprepared, unawares. **touch base** esp. *N Amer. informal* contact or communicate (with someone).

base[2] *adj.* **1** lacking moral worth; cowardly, despicable. **2** menial. **3** not pure; alloyed. **4** (of a metal) low in value. ☐ **basely** *adv.* **baseness** *n.*

baseball *n.* **1** a game played with teams of nine in which a batter must hit a ball (thrown by the opposing team's pitcher) with a bat, and then complete a diamond-shaped circuit of four bases to score a run. **2** the ball used in this game.

baseball cap *n.* (also **baseball hat**) a cap with a rounded visor and soft, rounded crown, often with a crest on the front.

baseboard *n. N Amer.* a strip of wood along the bottom of a wall in a house.

baseboard heater *n. N Amer.* a heater attached to a wall near the floor, esp. one which provides heat by means of a radiant electric coil.

basehead *n. slang* a person who habitually takes freebased cocaine or crack.

base hit *n. Baseball* a hit that enables the batter to reach base without a fielder's error and without forcing out a runner already on base.

baseless *adj.* unfounded, groundless.

baseline *n.* **1** a line used as a base or starting point. **2** the area on a baseball diamond within which a runner must remain when running between bases. **3** (in tennis, basketball, etc.) the line marking each end of the court. **4** (usu. *attrib.*) a basic level or standard; something which serves as a basis (*baseline health study*). **5** a line which serves as the basis for subsequent surveying in a town or township.

baseman *n.* (pl. **-men**) (usu. in *comb.*) *Baseball* a player whose position is first, second, or third base.

basement *n.* **1** the lowest floor of a building, at least partly below ground level. **2** *N Amer. Sport informal* the lowest position in the standings.

basepath *n. Baseball* **1** the prescribed path for a baserunner extending between consecutive bases or between first or third base and home plate. **2** (in *pl.*) *informal* the aspect of the game concerned with running or stealing bases (*a disaster on the basepaths*).

baserunner *n. Baseball* a member of the batting team who is on base or running between bases. ☐ **baserunning** *n.*

bases *pl.* of BASE[1], BASIS.

base unit *n.* a unit (of measurement etc.) defined arbitrarily and not by combinations of other units.

bash ● *v.* **1** *tr.* **a** strike bluntly or heavily. **b** *informal* attack violently. **c** (often foll. by *in*, *down*, etc.) damage or break by striking forcibly. **2** *intr.* (foll. by *into*) collide with. **3** *tr.* (often as **bashing** *n.*) *informal* deride, criticize (*Toronto-bashing*). ● *n.* **1** a heavy blow. **2** *informal* a party or social event. □ **basher** *n.*

bashful *adj.* **1** shy, diffident, self-conscious. **2** sheepish. □ **bashfully** *adv.* **bashfulness** *n.*

bashing *n.* = GAY BASHING.

BASIC *n.* a computer programming language using familiar English words, designed for beginners and widely used on microcomputers.

basic ● *adj.* **1** forming or serving as a base. **2** fundamental. **3 a** simplest or lowest in level (*basic requirements*). **b** vulgar (*basic humour*). **4** *Chem.* having the properties of or containing a base. **5** *Geol.* (of volcanic rocks etc.) having less than 50 per cent silica. ● *n.* (usu. in *pl.*) the fundamental facts or principles. □ **basically** *adv.*

basic industry *n.* an industry of fundamental economic importance.

basic training *n.* a period of initial training in the police, armed forces, etc.

basil /'bæzəl, 'beiz-/ *n.* an aromatic herb of the genus *Ocimum*, esp. *O. basilicum* (in full **sweet basil**), whose leaves are used as a flavouring in savoury dishes.

basilica /bə'sɪlɪkə, bæ'zɪl-/ *n.* **1** an ancient Roman public hall with an apse and colonnades, used as a law court and place of assembly. **2** a similar building used as a Christian church. **3** a title of honour awarded to certain Catholic churches by the Pope.

basin *n.* **1 a** a wide shallow open container, esp. one for holding water. **b** a bathroom sink. **2** a hollow rounded depression. **3** any sheltered area of water where boats can moor safely. **4** a round valley. **5** an area drained by rivers and tributaries. □ **basinful** *n.* (*pl.* **-fuls**).

basis /'beisɪs/ *n.* (*pl.* **bases** /-siːz/) **1** the foundation or support of something, esp. an idea or argument. **2** the main or determining principle or ingredient (*on a purely friendly basis*). **3** the starting point for a discussion etc.

basis point *n.* *Finance* one-hundredth of one per cent.

bask *v.intr.* **1** sit or lie back lazily in warmth and light (*basking in the sun*). **2** (foll. by *in*) derive great pleasure (from) (*basking in glory*).

basket *n.* **1** a container made of interwoven cane etc. **2** a container resembling this. **3** the amount held by a basket. **4** *Basketball* **a** a net fixed on a ring attached to a backboard and raised usu. about 10 feet above the surface of the court. **b** a goal scored through this. **5** a group, category, or range (*a broad basket of goods and services*). □ **basketful** *n.* (*pl.* **-fuls**).

basketball *n.* **1** a game between two teams of five, in which goals are scored by throwing a ball through a basket suspended at either end of a court. **2** the ball used in this game.

basket case *n.* *informal* a person or thing that is incapacitated, esp. by emotional or mental disturbance or bankruptcy.

basketry *n.* **1** the art of making baskets. **2** baskets collectively.

basket sled *n.* (also **basket sleigh**) *Cdn* (*North*) a toboggan with runners and siderails.

basket weave *n.* a weave resembling that of a basket.

basketwork *n.* **1** material woven in the style of a basket. **2** the art of making this.

basmati /bæs'mæti/ *n.* a kind of rice with very long thin grains and a delicate fragrance.

Basque /bæsk, bʊsk/ ● *n.* **1** a member of a people inhabiting the western Pyrenees in N Spain and SW France. **2** the language of this people. ● *adj.* of or relating to the Basques or their language.

basque /bæsk/ *n.* a close-fitting bodice extending from the shoulders to the waist and often with a short continuation below waist level.

bas-relief /ˌbɑːrɪ'liːf, ˌbæs-/ *n.* sculpture or carving in which the figures project from the background.

bass¹ ● *n.* **1 a** the lowest adult male singing voice. **b** a singer with this voice. **c** a part written for it. **2** (also **bass line**) the lowest part in harmonized music. **3 a** an instrument that is the lowest in pitch in its family. **b** its player. **4 a** a bass guitar or double bass. **b** its player. **5** the low-frequency output of a radio etc., corresponding to the bass in music. ● *adj.* **1** lowest in musical pitch. **2** deep-sounding.

bass² *n.* (*pl.* same or **basses**) any of various edible freshwater and marine fishes of the families Serranidae and Centrarchidae, having spiny fins.

bass³ *n.* **1** = BAST. **2** *var.* of BASSWOOD.

bass clef *n.* *Music* a sign that indicates that the second highest line of the staff represents the F below middle C.

basset hound *n.* (also **basset**) a breed of hunting dog with a long body, short legs, and droopy ears.

bassinet *n.* a portable basket-like bed for a young baby, often with a hood.

bassist *n.* a person who plays a bass guitar or a double bass.

basso /'bæsoː/ *n.* (*pl.* **-os** or **bassi** /-siː/) a singer with a bass voice.

bassoon *n.* **1** a bass instrument of the oboe family, with a double reed. **2** its player. □ **bassoonist** *n.*

basso profundo /pro:'fondo:/ *n.* a bass singer with an exceptionally low range.

basswood *n.* **1** any of several trees of the linden family, esp. *Tilia americana*, native to the deciduous forests of eastern N America. **2** the wood of this tree, which is very soft and light.

bast /bæst/ *n.* the inner bark of lindens, or other flexible fibrous bark, used as fibre in matting etc.

bastard ● *n.* **1** a person born of parents not married to each other. ¶Offensive in other than legal or historical contexts. **2** *coarse slang* **a** an unpleasant or despicable person. **b** a person of a specified kind (*poor bastard; lucky bastard*). **3** *coarse slang* a difficult or awkward thing, undertaking, etc. ● *adj.* **1** born of parents not married to each other; illegitimate. **2** (of things) **a** unauthorized, counterfeit. **b** hybrid.

bastardize *v.tr.* **1** corrupt, debase. **2** declare (a person) illegitimate. □ **bastardization** *n.*

baste¹ *v.tr.* moisten (meat) with gravy, melted fat, etc. during cooking. □ **baster** *n.*

baste² *v.tr.* stitch loosely together in preparation for sewing; tack.

baste³ *v.tr.* beat soundly; thrash.

bastion *n.* **1** a projecting part of a fortification built at an angle to, or against the line of, a wall. **2** a thing regarded as protecting (*bastion of freedom*). **3** a natural rock formation resembling a bastion.

bat¹ ● *n.* **1** an implement with a rounded usu. wooden handle and a solid head with a flat or rounded surface, used for hitting a ball in various games, such as baseball. **2** an at-bat. **3** *Cdn* (*Nfld*) a pole 1.5–2.5 m (5–8 ft.) long, having an iron hook and spike on one end, used to kill seals and assist a sealer on the ice. ● *v.* (**batted**, **batting**) **1** *tr.* hit with or as with a bat. **2** *intr.* take a turn at batting. □ **bat around 1** discuss (an idea or proposal). **2** *Baseball* have an inning in which all nine players have an at-bat. **go to**

bat for N Amer. informal defend the interests of. **right off the bat** N Amer. immediately.

bat² n. any mouselike nocturnal mammal of the order Chiroptera, capable of flight by means of membranous wings extending from its forelimbs. □ **have bats in the belfry** be eccentric or crazy. **like a bat out of hell** very fast.

bat³ v.tr. (**batted, batting**) blink (one's eyelid); flutter (one's eyelashes). □ **bat an eye** (or **eyelash** or **eyelid**) informal show reaction or emotion.

bat boy n. Baseball a person who takes care of the bats etc. of a baseball team.

batch¹ • n. **1** a number of things or persons forming a group or dealt with together. **2** an instalment (have sent off the latest batch of proofs). **3** a quantity produced by one operation, or the amount of material necessary for this (a batch of doughnuts). **4** (attrib.) using or dealt with in batches, not as a continuous flow (batch production). **5** Computing a group of records processed as a single unit. • v.tr. arrange or deal with in batches.

batch² v.intr. & tr. N Amer., Austral., & NZ (esp. in **batch it**) live alone and keep house for oneself, esp. temporarily.

bateau /bæ'to:, 'bæto:/ n. Cdn hist. (pl. **batteaux** /-'to:, -'to:z/) a light, shallow-draft, flat-bottomed boat with pointed bow and stern, propelled by oars, poles, or sails, ōr drawn by horses.

bated adj. □ **with bated breath** very anxiously.

bath n. (pl. **baths** /ba:ðz, bæθs/) **1** the act or process of immersing the body for washing or therapy (have a bath). **2 a** = BATHTUB. **b** this with its contents (your bath is ready). **3 a** a vessel containing liquid in which something is immersed, e.g. a film for developing. **b** this with its contents. **4** esp. N Amer. = BATHROOM. **5** (usu. in pl.) a building with baths or a swimming pool. • v. Cdn & Brit. **1** tr. wash (esp. a person) in a bath. **2** intr. take a bath.

bathe v. **1** intr. swim. **2** intr. N Amer. wash oneself. **3** tr. immerse in or wash or treat with liquid esp. for cleansing or medicinal purposes. **4** tr. (of sunlight etc.) envelop. □ **bathing** n.

bather /'beɪðər/ n. a swimmer.

bathhouse n. **1** a building with baths for public use. **2** a building for changing one's clothes at a pool etc.

bathing suit n. a garment worn for swimming.

bathos /'beɪθɒs/ n. an unintentional lapse in mood from the sublime to the absurd or trivial; a commonplace or ridiculous feature offsetting an otherwise sublime situation. □ **bathetic** /bə'θetɪk/ adj.

bathrobe n. a loose usu. belted robe worn over nightwear, esp. one made of thick terry cloth.

bathroom n. **1** a room containing a bath and usu. other washing facilities. **2** esp. N Amer. a room containing a toilet or toilets. □ **go to the bathroom** N Amer. euphemism urinate or defecate.

bathroom tissue n. = TOILET PAPER.

bath towel n. a towel large enough to be suitable for drying oneself after bathing or showering.

bathtub n. a tub for bathing in.

bathtub race n. Cdn an event in which bathtubs are motorized and piloted across bodies of water.

bathwater n. the water in a bath.

batik /bə'ti:k/ • n. **1** a method (originally used in Java) of producing coloured designs on textiles by waxing the parts not to be dyed. **2** a piece of cloth treated in this way. • v.tr. (usu. as **batiked** adj.) produce coloured designs in this way.

bat mitzvah /bæt 'mɪtsvə/ n. **1** a religious initiation ceremony for a Jewish girl aged twelve years and one

day, regarded as the age of religious maturity. **2** the girl undergoing this ceremony.

baton n. **1** a thin stick used by a conductor to direct an orchestra, choir, etc. **2** a short stick or tube carried and passed on by the runners in a relay race. **3** a stick carried and twirled by a drum major or majorette. **4** a staff of office or authority. **5** a police officer's truncheon.

bâtonnier /bæton'jei/ n. (in Quebec) a president of a Bar Association.

bats predic.adj. slang crazy.

batsman n. (pl. **-men**) a person who bats or is batting, esp. in cricket.

batt n. **1** a sheet of usu. fibreglass insulation sized to fit between studs, joists, or rafters. **2** = BATTING 2.

battalion n. **1** a large body of soldiers ready for battle, esp. an infantry unit forming part of a brigade. **2** a large group of people pursuing a common aim or sharing a major undertaking.

batteau var. of BATEAU.

batten • n. **1** a long flat strip of wood or metal used to hold something in place. **2** Naut. **a** a thin, narrow strip of wood or plastic inserted in pockets in a sail to maintain its proper shape. **b** a strip of wood or metal for securing a tarpaulin over a ship's hatchway. • v.tr. strengthen, fasten, or secure with or as if with battens. □ **batten down the hatches 1** Naut. secure a ship's tarpaulins. **2** prepare for a difficulty or crisis.

batter¹ v. **1 a** tr. strike repeatedly with hard blows. **b** intr. (often foll. by against, at, etc.) strike repeated blows; pound heavily and insistently (batter at the door). **2** tr. (often in passive) **a** handle roughly, esp. over a long period. **b** censure or criticize severely.

batter² n. **1** a fluid mixture of flour, egg, and a liquid, used for coating food before frying. **2** a mixture of flour and other raw ingredients for a cake etc., more liquid than a dough.

batter³ n. a player batting, esp. in baseball.

batter⁴ • n. **1** a wall etc. with a sloping face. **2** a receding slope. • v.intr. have a receding slope.

battered¹ adj. (of a person, esp. a woman or child) subjected to repeated violence from a spouse etc.

battered² adj. coated in batter and deep-fried.

batterer n. a person who batters someone or something.

battering ram n. hist. a heavy beam, originally with an end in the form of a carved ram's head, used in breaching fortifications.

battery n. (pl. **-ies**) **1** a device, consisting of one or more cells, in which chemical energy is converted into electricity. **2** a set of similar units of equipment, esp. connected (a battery of clocks). **3** a usu. exhaustive series of tests. **4 a** a fortified emplacement for heavy guns. **b** an artillery unit of guns, personnel, and vehicles. **5** Law an act, including touching, inflicting unlawful personal violence on another person, even if no physical harm is done (see ASSAULT 2). **6** Baseball the pitcher and the catcher. □ **recharge one's batteries** restore one's strength, enthusiasm, etc.

batting n. **1** the action of hitting with a bat. **2** wadding of cotton, polyester, etc. prepared in sheets for use in quilts etc.

batting average n. Baseball a statistic indicating a batter's proficiency, calculated by dividing the number of hits by the number of at-bats.

batting cage n. a mesh enclosure in which baseball players can practise batting.

batting order n. the order in which baseball players take their turn at bat.

battle ● *n.* **1 a** a prolonged fight between large organized armed forces. **b** a fight or violent altercation between opposed groups. **2** a contest; a prolonged or difficult struggle (*a battle of wits*). ● *v.* **1** *intr.* struggle, strive; fight persistently (*battled for women's rights*). **2** *tr.* struggle against. **3** *tr. N Amer.* engage in battle with. □ **battle it out** fight to a conclusion. **half the battle** the key to the success of an undertaking. □ **battler** *n.*

battle-axe *n.* **1** a large axe used in ancient warfare. **2** (**battleaxe**) *informal* a formidable or domineering older woman.

battle cry *n.* **1** a rallying cry used in battle. **2** a rallying cry or slogan of a group of people.

battledress *n.* **1** attire worn for battle. **2** *hist.* a soldier's or airman's everyday khaki uniform.

battlefield *n.* **1** the piece of ground on which a battle is or was fought. **2** = BATTLEGROUND 1.

battleground *n.* **1** an area of disputation, contention, or hostility. **2** = BATTLEFIELD 1.

battlement *n.* (usu. in *pl.*) **1** an alternately high and low parapet along the top of a wall, as part of a fortification. **2** a section of roof enclosed by this. □ **battlemented** *adj.*

battle-scarred *adj.* (also **battle-weary**) *N Amer.* **1** (of a soldier) scarred or weary from battle. **2** (of a person, group of people, etc.) exhausted from activity, esp. of a particular kind (*battle-scarred government*). **3** (of a building, city, etc.) **a** damaged by war or violence. **b** *informal* worn out through use.

battleship *n.* a warship of the most heavily armed and armoured class.

battleship grey ● *adj.* of a drab, slightly bluish-grey colour (often used for warships to reduce their visibility). ● *n.* this colour.

batty *adj.* (**-ier, -iest**) *informal* crazy. □ **battily** *adv.* **battiness** *n.*

batwing *adj.* shaped like the wing of a bat.

bauble *n.* a showy trinket or toy of little value.

baud /bɔd/ *n.* (*pl.* same or **-s**) *Computing etc.* **1** a unit used to express the speed of electronic code signals, corresponding to one information unit per second. **2** (loosely) a unit of data-transmission speed of one bit per second.

Bauhaus /ˈbauhʌʊs/ *n.* **1** a German school of architectural design (1919–33). **2** its principles, based on functionalism and development of existing skills.

baulk esp. *Brit. var.* of BALK.

baulky esp. *Brit. var.* of BALKY.

bauxite /ˈbɔksʌɪt/ *n.* a claylike mineral containing varying proportions of alumina, the chief source of aluminum. □ **bauxitic** /-ˈsɪtɪk/ *adj.*

Bavarian /bəˈvɛrɪən/ ● *adj.* of or relating to Bavaria in Germany, its people, or their German dialect. ● *n.* **1** a native or inhabitant of Bavaria. **2** the Bavarian dialect.

Bavarian cream *n.* a usu. moulded dessert of flavoured whipped cream stiffened with gelatin.

bawdy ● *adj.* (**-ier, -iest**) humorously indecent. ● *n.* bawdy talk or writing. □ **bawdily** *adv.* **bawdiness** *n.*

bawdy house *n.* a brothel.

bawl *v.* **1** *tr.* speak or call out noisily. **2** *intr.* weep loudly. **3** *intr.* (of a cow, seal, etc.) cry out, wail. □ **bawl out** *informal* reprimand angrily. □ **bawler** *n.*

bawn *n. Cdn* (*Nfld*) **1** a meadow near a house etc. **2** a stretch of rocks on which salted cod are dried.

Bay *n. Cdn proprietary* the Hudson's Bay Company, or one of its posts or retail stores.

bay[1] *n.* **1** a body of water where the coastline curves inwards. **2** an indentation or recess in a range of hills etc. **3** *Cdn* (*Nfld*) (often *attrib.*) a large indentation on the coast, including several harbours, islands, etc.

bay[2] *n.* **1** (in full **bay laurel** or **bay tree**) a Mediterranean laurel, *Laurus nobilis*, having deep green leaves and purple berries. **2** = BAY LEAF. **3** (in *pl.*) a wreath made of bay leaves, for a victor or poet.

bay[3] *n.* **1** a space created by a window-line projecting outwards from a wall. **2** a recess; a section of wall between buttresses or columns, esp. in the nave of a church etc. **3** a compartment (*bomb bay*). **4** an area specially allocated or marked off (*loading bay*).

bay[4] ● *adj.* (esp. of a horse) dark reddish-brown. ● *n.* a bay horse with a black mane and tail.

bay[5] ● *v.* **1** *intr.* (esp. of a large dog) bark or howl loudly and plaintively. **2** *tr.* bay at. ● *n.* the sound of baying, esp. in chorus from hounds in close pursuit. □ **at bay 1** cornered, apparently unable to escape. **2** in a desperate situation. **bring to bay** gain on in pursuit; trap. **hold** (or **keep**) **at bay** hold off (a pursuer). **stand at bay** turn to face one's pursuers.

bayberry *n.* (*pl.* **-ies**) **1** any of various N American shrubs or small trees of the genus *Myrica*, having aromatic leaves and bearing berries covered in a wax coating. **2** the fruit of the bay tree, *Laurus nobilis*, a fragrant, oil-bearing Caribbean tree, *Pimenta acris*. **3** a fragrant, oil-bearing Caribbean tree, *Pimenta acris*.

bayfront *n. N Amer.* the shoreline of a bay.

bay leaf *n.* the aromatic (usu. dried) leaf of the bay tree, used in cooking (see BAY[2] 1).

bayman *n.* (*pl.* **-men**) **1 a** esp. *US* a person living near a bay. **b** *Cdn* (*Nfld*) an inhabitant of an outport, as opposed to someone living in a town. **2** (**Bay man**) *Cdn hist.* an employee of the Hudson's Bay Company.

bayonet ● *n.* **1** a stabbing blade attachable to the muzzle of a rifle. **2** an electrical or other fitting engaged by being pushed into a socket and twisted. ● *v.tr.* (**bayonetted, bayonetting**) stab with a bayonet.

bayou /ˈbaiu:/ *n.* a marshy offshoot of a river etc. in the southern US.

bay scallop *n.* **1** a scallop, *Aequipecten irradians*, of the Atlantic coast of Canada and New England. **2** the edible adductor muscle of this scallop.

bayside ● *adj.* situated at or near a (usu. specified) bay. ● *n.* (**Bayside**) *Cdn* the area around Hudson Bay (also *attrib.*: *Bayside post*).

Bay Street *n. Cdn* **1** a street in Toronto where the headquarters of many financial institutions are located. **2** the moneyed interests of Toronto, esp. as opposed to other regions of Canada (*Bay Street is nervous about the election*).

bay window *n.* a window, usu. with glass on three sides, projecting from an outside wall.

baywop *n. Cdn* (*Nfld*) *derogatory* = BAYMAN 1b.

bazaar *n.* **1** (esp. in the Middle East) a marketplace or shopping quarter. **2** a fundraising sale of various articles, esp. for charity. **3** a large store selling miscellaneous items. **4** a place where items of a specified sort are sold (*sex bazaars*).

bazooka *n.* **1** a tubular short-range rocket-launcher used against tanks. **2** a crude trombone-like musical instrument.

bazoom *n. slang* (usu. in *pl.*) a woman's breast.

bazz *v.tr. Cdn* (*Nfld*) throw (a stone, marble, etc.).

BB[1] *abbr.* double-black (pencil lead).

BB[2] *n.* a small pellet for shooting out of an air rifle etc.

B.B.A. *abbr.* Bachelor of Business Administration.

BBC *abbr.* British Broadcasting Corporation.

bbl. *abbr.* barrels (esp. of oil).

BBQ *abbr. informal* barbecue.

BBS *abbr.* bulletin-board service, a computerized system for the exchange of electronic messages etc.

BC *abbr.* **1** British Columbia. **2** (of a date) before Christ.

BCD *n. Computing* a code representing decimal numbers as a string of binary digits.

BCE *abbr.* before the Common Era. ¶Used to denote years before the traditional date of Christ's birth.

B.C.E. *abbr.* Bachelor of Civil Engineering.

B.C.L. *abbr.* **1** Bachelor of Canon Law. **2** Bachelor of Civil Law.

B.Com. *abbr.* (also **B.Comm.**) Bachelor of Commerce.

B.C.S. *abbr.* Bachelor of Computer Science.

B.D. *abbr.* Bachelor of Divinity.

bdrm *abbr.* bedroom.

B.E. *abbr.* **1** Bachelor of Education. **2** Bachelor of Engineering. **3** bill of exchange.

Be *symbol* beryllium.

be (*sing. present* **am**; **are**; **is**; *pl. present* **are**; *1st and 3rd sing. past* **was**; *2nd sing. past and pl. past* **were**; *present subj.* **be**; *past subj.* **were**; *pres. part.* **being**; *past part.* **been**) ● *v.intr.* **1** (often prec. by *there*) exist, live (*there is a house on the corner*). **2 a** occur; take place (*dinner is at eight*). **b** occupy a position in space (*he is in the garden*). **3** remain, continue (*let it be*). **4** linking subject and predicate, expressing: **a** identity (*she is the person*). **b** condition (*he is ill today*). **c** state or quality (*she is very kind*). **d** opinion (*I am against hanging*). **e** total (*two and two are four*). **f** cost or significance (*it is nothing to me*). ● *v.aux.* **1** with a past participle to form the passive voice (*it was done*; *it is said*). **2** with a present participle to form progressive tenses (*we are coming*). **3** with an infinitive to express duty or commitment, intention, possibility, destiny, or hypothesis (*they were never to meet again*). □ **be about** occupy oneself with (*is about her business*). **be at** occupy oneself with (*mice have been at the food*). **been** (or **been and gone**) **and** *slang* an expression of protest or surprise (*he's been and taken my car!*). **be off** *informal* go away; leave.

beach ● *n.* **1** a pebbly or sandy shore of a body of water, esp. a lake or ocean. **2** *Cdn* (*Nfld*) a stretch of shingle or smooth rocks used for drying salt cod. ● *v.tr.* run or haul up (a boat etc.) on to a beach.

beach ball *n.* a large lightweight inflated ball, esp. for games on the beach.

beachcomber *n.* **1** *Cdn* (*BC*) a person who earns a living by collecting logs that have broken loose from log booms. **2** a person who searches beaches for articles of value. **3** a long wave rolling in from the sea. □ **beachcomb** *v.intr. & tr.*

beached *adj.* (of a sea mammal etc.) stranded on the shore, esp. by the action of tides etc.

beachfront esp. *N Amer.* ● *n.* land that fronts onto a beach. ● *adj.* located on or overlooking a beach.

beach grass *n.* any of various grasses which grow on sand dunes, esp. marram.

beachhead *n.* **1** a fortified position established on a beach by landing forces. **2** an initial position from which one may advance.

beach volleyball *n.* a form of volleyball played by teams of two on a beach or other surface covered deeply with sand.

beacon *n.* **1** a fire or light set up in a high or prominent position as a warning etc. **2** a visible warning or guiding point or device, e.g. a lighthouse, navigation buoy, etc. **3** a radio transmitter whose signal helps fix the position of a ship, aircraft, etc.

bead ● *n.* **1 a** a small usu. rounded and perforated piece of glass, stone, etc., for threading with others to make jewellery, or sewing on to fabric, etc. **b** (in *pl.*) a string of beads. **c** (in *pl.*) a rosary. **2** a drop of liquid; a bubble. **3** a small knob in the foresight of a gun. **4** the inner edge of a pneumatic tire that grips the rim of the wheel. ● *v.* **1** *tr.* furnish or decorate with beads. **2** *tr.* string together. **3** *intr.* form or grow into beads. □ **draw a bead on** take aim at. □ **beaded** *adj.*

beading *n.* **1** decoration in the form of or resembling a row of beads, esp. lacelike looped edging. **2** the bead of a tire.

beadle *n.* **1** a ceremonial usher, mace-bearer, etc. in certain universities etc. **2** a Presbyterian church officer attending on the minister. **3** a layperson employed by a church, synagogue, etc., to perform various minor functions. □ **beadleship** *n.*

beadwork *n.* ornamental work with beads.

beady *adj.* (**-ier**, **-iest**) **1** (of the eyes) small, round, and bright. **2** covered with beads or drops. □ **beadily** *adv.* **beadiness** *n.*

beady-eyed *adj.* **1** with beady eyes. **2** observant.

beagle ● *n.* a short-legged breed of dog with a short black and white or brown and white coat. ● *v.intr.* (often as **beagling** *n.*) hunt with beagles.

beak *n.* **1 a** a bird's horny projecting jaws; a bill. **b** the similar projecting jaw of other animals, e.g. a turtle. **2** *slang* a hooked nose. **3** a spout. □ **beaked** *adj.* **beaky** *adj.*

beaker *n.* a lipped cylindrical glass vessel for scientific experiments.

be-all and end-all *n. informal* (often foll. by *of*) the whole being or essence.

beam ● *n.* **1** a long sturdy piece of metal or squared timber etc. spanning an opening or room, usu. to support the structure above. **2 a** a ray or shaft of light. **b** a directional flow of particles or radiation. **3** a bright look or smile. **4 a** a series of radio or radar signals as a guide to a ship or aircraft. **b** the course indicated by this (*off beam*). **5** the crossbar of a balance, from which the pans or weights are suspended. **6 a** a ship's breadth at its widest point. **b** *informal* (esp. in **broad in the beam**) the width of a person's hips. **7** (in *pl.*) the horizontal cross-timbers of a ship supporting the deck and joining the sides. **8** the side of a ship (*land on the port beam*). **9** = BALANCE BEAM. ● *v.* **1** *tr.* emit or direct (light, radio waves, etc.). **2** *intr.* **a** shine. **b** look or smile radiantly. □ **the beam in one's eye** a fault that is greater in oneself than in the person one is finding fault with. **off beam** *informal* mistaken.

beamed *adj.* having a beam or beams (*beamed ceiling*).

bean ● *n.* **1 a** any kind of leguminous plant with edible usu. kidney-shaped seeds in long pods. **b** one of these seeds. **2** a similar seed of coffee and other plants. **3** *N Amer. informal* the head. **4** (in *pl.*; with *neg.*) *N Amer. informal* anything at all (*doesn't know beans about it*). ● *v.tr. N Amer. informal* hit on the head. □ **full of beans** *informal* lively; in high spirits. **not a hill of beans** *N Amer. slang* an insignificant amount.

beanbag *n.* **1** a small bag filled with dried beans and used esp. in children's games. **2** a large cushion filled usu. with polystyrene beads and used as a seat.

beanball *n. Baseball* a pitch thrown at the batter's head.

bean-counter *n. informal derogatory* a person, esp. an accountant or bureaucrat, perceived as placing excessive emphasis on numbers, budgets, etc., esp. to the detriment of creativity. □ **bean-counting** *n.*

bean curd *n.* = TOFU.

beanery *n.* (*pl.* **-ies**) *N Amer. informal* a cheap restaurant.

beanie *n.* a skullcap, esp. of a sort worn formerly by small boys.

bean sprout *n.* (usu. in *pl.*) a sprout of a bean seed, esp. of the mung bean, eaten raw or cooked.

beanstalk *n.* the stem of a bean plant.

bear[1] *v.* (*past* **bore**; *past part.* **borne**, **born**) ¶In the passive *born* is used with reference to birth (e.g. *was born in July*), except for *borne* by foll. by the name of the mother (e.g. *was borne by Sarah*). **1** *tr.* carry, bring, or take (esp. visibly) (*bear gifts*). **2** *tr.* show; have as an attribute or characteristic (*bear marks of violence*). **3** *tr.* **a** produce, yield (fruit etc.). **b** give birth to (*has borne a son; was born last week*). **4** *tr.* **a** sustain (a weight, responsibility, cost, etc.). **b** stand, endure (an ordeal, difficulty, etc.). **5** *tr.* **a** tolerate (*can't bear her*). **b** admit of; be fit for (*does not bear repeating*). **6** *tr.* carry in thought or memory (*bear a grudge*). **7** *intr.* veer in a given direction (*bear left*). **8** *tr.* bring or provide (*bear him company*). **9** *refl.* behave (in a certain way). □ **bear arms 1** carry weapons; serve as a soldier. **2** wear or display heraldic devices. **bear away** (or **off**) win (a prize etc.). **bear down** exert downward pressure. **bear down on** approach rapidly or purposefully. **bear fruit** have results. **bear in mind** take into account having remembered. **bear on** (or **upon**) be relevant to. **bear out** support or confirm (an account or the person giving it). **bear up** raise one's spirits; not despair. **bear with** treat forbearingly; tolerate patiently. **bear witness** testify.

bear[2] *n.* **1** any large mammal of the family Ursidae, having thick fur and walking on its soles. **2** a rough, unmannerly, or uncouth person. **3** a person who sells shares hoping to buy them back later at a lower price. **4** (**the Bear**) *informal* Russia.

bearable *adj.* that may be endured or tolerated. □ **bearability** *n.* **bearableness** *n.* **bearably** *adv.*

bearberry *n.* (*pl.* **-ies**) **1** a small trailing evergreen shrub of the chiefly N American genus *Arctostaphylos*, esp. *A. uva-ursi*, with bright red astringent berries. **2** the berries of this plant.

beard ● *n.* **1** hair growing on the chin and lower cheeks of the face, esp. a man's face. **2** a similar tuft or part on an animal (esp. a goat). ● *v.tr.* oppose openly; defy. □ **bearded** *adj.* **beardless** *adj.*

bearded seal *n.* an Arctic seal, *Erignathus barbatus*, with a large mouth surrounded by beardlike bristles.

bearer *n.* **1** a person or thing that bears or carries. **2** a carrier of equipment on an expedition etc. **3** a person who presents a cheque or other order to pay money. **4** (*attrib.*) payable to the possessor (*bearer stock*).

bear hug *n.* a tight embrace.

bearing *n.* **1** a person's bodily attitude or outward behaviour. **2** (foll. by *on, upon*) relation or relevance to. **3** endurability (*beyond bearing*). **4** a part of a machine that supports a rotating or other moving part. **5** direction or position relative to a fixed point, measured esp. in degrees. **6** (in *pl.*) **a** one's position relative to one's surroundings. **b** awareness of this; a sense of one's orientation (*get one's bearings*). **7** *Heraldry* a device or charge. **8** = BALL BEARING.

bearish *adj.* **1 a** *Stock Exch.* causing, predicting, or associated with a fall in prices. **b** pessimistic. **2** like a bear, esp. in temper; rough, surly. □ **bearishly** *adv.*

Bear Lake *n.* = SAHTU DENE.

bear market *n.* a market with falling prices.

Béarnaise sauce */ˌbeɪərˈneɪz/ n.* a rich sauce containing egg yolks, butter, vinegar and tarragon.

bearpaw *n.* **1** the paw of a bear. **2** *Cdn* an almost circular, tailless type of snowshoe.

bearskin *n.* **1 a** the skin of a bear. **b** a rug etc. made

of this. **2** a tall furry hat worn ceremonially by some regiments.

beast *n.* **1** an animal other than a human being, esp. a wild quadruped. **2 a** a brutal person. **b** *informal* an objectionable or unpleasant person or thing. **3** (prec. by *the*) a human being's brutish or uncivilized characteristics (*saw the beast in her*). □ **the nature of the beast** the undesirable but unchangeable essential quality or character of the thing.

beastie *n. jocular* **1** a small animal. **2** a small malevolent creature.

beastly ● *adj.* (**-ier**, **-iest**) **1** *informal* objectionable, unpleasant. **2** like a beast; brutal. ● *adv. informal* very, extremely. □ **beastliness** *n.*

beast of burden *n.* an animal used for carrying loads.

beat ● *v.* (*past* **beat**; *past part.* **beaten**) **1** *tr.* **a** strike (a person or animal) persistently or repeatedly, esp. to harm or punish. **b** strike (a thing) repeatedly, e.g. to sound (a drum etc.). **2** *intr.* (foll. by *against, at, on*, etc.) **a** pound or knock repeatedly (*waves beat against the shore*). **b** = BEAT DOWN 3. **3** *tr.* **a** overcome; surpass; win a victory over. **b** complete an activity before (another person etc.). **c** be too hard for. **4** *tr.* mix or stir (ingredients) vigorously so as to incorporate air. **5** *tr.* (often foll. by *out*) fashion or shape (metal etc.) by blows. **6** *intr.* (of the heart etc.) pulsate rhythmically. **7** *tr.* (often foll. by *out*) **a** indicate (a tempo or rhythm) by gestures, tapping, etc. **b** sound (a signal etc.) by striking a drum or other means. **8 a** *intr.* (of a bird's wings) move up and down. **b** *tr.* cause (wings) to move in this way. **9** *tr.* make (a path etc.) by trampling. **10** *tr.* strike (bushes etc.) to rouse game. **11** *intr. Cdn* (*Nfld*) (of herd animals, esp. seals) migrate. ● *n.* **1 a** a main accent or rhythmic unit in music or verse. **b** the indication of rhythm by a conductor's movements (*watch the beat*). **c** (in popular music) a strong rhythm. **d** (*attrib.*) characterized by a strong rhythm (*beat music*). **2 a** a stroke or blow, e.g. on a drum. **b** a measured sequence of strokes (*the beat of the waves*). **c** a throbbing movement or sound (*the beat of his heart*). **3 a** a route or area allocated to a police officer, reporter, etc. **b** a person's habitual round. **4** *informal* = BEATNIK. ● *adj.* **1** (*predic.*) *informal* exhausted, tired out. **2** (*attrib.*) of the beat generation or its philosophy. □ **beat about** (often foll. by *for*) search (for an excuse etc.). **beat around the bush** discuss a matter without coming to the point. **to beat the band** in such a way as to defeat all competition. **beat one's breast** strike one's chest in anguish or sorrow. **beat the bushes** *N Amer.* search thoroughly (*beating the bushes for work*). **beat the clock** complete a task within a stated time. **beat down 1 a** bargain with (a seller) to lower the price. **b** cause a seller to lower (the price). **2** strike (a resisting object) until it falls. **3** (of the sun, rain, etc.) radiate heat or fall continuously and vigorously. **beat the drum for** publicize, promote. **beaten at the post** defeated at the last moment. **beat in** crush. **beat it** *informal* go away. **beat off** drive back (an attack etc.). **beat a retreat** withdraw. **beat time** indicate or follow a musical tempo with a baton or other means. **beat a person to it** arrive or achieve something before another person. **beat up** give a beating to, esp. with punches and kicks. (**it**) **beats me** I do not understand (it). **two hearts that beat as one** two people who are perfectly united in thought. □ **beatable** *adj.*

beaten *adj.* **1** outwitted; defeated. **2** exhausted; dejected. **3** (of gold or any other metal) shaped by a hammer. **4** (of a path etc.) much-used. □ **off the**

beaten track (or **path**) **1** in or into an isolated place. **2** unusual.

beater n. **1** an implement used for beating (e.g. eggs, a drum, etc.). **2** N Amer. informal an old or dilapidated vehicle. **3** a person who beats metal. **4** Cdn (Nfld) a young harp seal, about three to four weeks old.

beat generation n. the members of a movement of young people esp. in the 1950s who rejected conventional society in their dress, habits etc.

beatific /ˌbiːəˈtɪfɪk/ adj. **1** informal blissful (a beatific smile). **2** making blessed; imparting supreme happiness. □ **beatifically** adv.

beatification n. **1** Catholicism the act of formally declaring a dead person 'blessed', often a step towards canonization. **2** the act or fact of making or being blessed.

beatify /biːˈætɪˌfaɪ/ v.tr. (-**ies**, -**ied**) **1** Catholicism announce the beatification of. **2** make happy.

beating n. **1** a physical punishment or assault. **2** a defeat. □ **take some** (or **a lot of**) **beating** be difficult to surpass.

beatitude /biːˈætɪˌtuːd/ n. **1** blessedness. **2** (in pl.) the declarations of blessedness in Matthew 5:3–11.

beatnik n. a member of the beat generation.

beat-up adj. informal in a state of disrepair.

beau /boː/ n. (pl. **beaux** or **beaus** /boːz, boː/) esp. N Amer. dated or jocular an admirer; a boyfriend.

Beaufort scale /ˈboːfərt/ n. a scale of wind speed ranging from 0 (calm) to 12 (hurricane).

Beaujolais /ˈboːʒəˌleɪ/ n. a red or white burgundy wine from the Beaujolais district of France.

beaut /bjuːt/ n. esp. N Amer., Austral., & NZ informal an excellent or beautiful person or thing.

beauteous adj. literary beautiful.

beautician n. **1** a person who gives beauty treatment. **2** a person who runs a beauty salon.

beautiful adj. **1** delighting the aesthetic senses (a beautiful voice). **2** enjoyable (had a beautiful time). **3** excellent (a beautiful specimen). □ **beautifully** adv.

beautify v.tr. (-**ies**, -**ied**) make beautiful; adorn. □ **beautification** n. **beautifier** n.

beauty ● n. (pl. -**ies**) **1 a** a combination of qualities such as shape, colour, etc., that pleases the aesthetic senses, esp. the sight. **b** a combination of qualities that pleases the intellect or moral sense (the beauty of the argument). **c** something beautiful. **2 a** an excellent specimen (what a beauty!). **b** an attractive feature; an advantage (that's the beauty of the plan!). **3** a beautiful woman. ● interj. N Amer. expressing satisfaction etc. □ **beauty is only skin deep** a pleasing appearance is not a guide to character.

beauty contest n. (also **beauty pageant**) a competition in which participants, usu. women, are judged on their physical attractiveness.

beauty queen n. the woman judged most beautiful in a beauty contest.

beauty salon n. (also **beauty parlour**) an establishment in which beauty treatment, esp. hairdressing, is practised professionally.

beauty sleep n. sleep as contributing to one's beauty.

beauty spot n. **1** a place known for its beauty. **2** (also **beauty mark**) a small natural or artificial mark such as a mole on the face, considered to enhance another feature.

beauty treatment n. the use of cosmetics, hairdressing, etc. to enhance personal appearance.

beaux pl. of BEAU.

Beaver ● n. (pl. same or -**s**) **1** a member of an Aborigi-

nal people of the Peace River area of Alberta and BC. **2** the Athapaskan language of this people. ● adj. of or relating to the Beaver or their culture.

beaver ● n. (pl. same or **beavers**) **1 a** any large semi-aquatic broad-tailed rodent of the genus Castor, native to N America, Europe, and Asia, and able to gnaw down trees and build dams. **b** this as an emblem of Canada. **2 a** the soft, light brown fur of this animal. **b** (in full **beaver hat**) hist. a hat made from beaver wool. **3** (**Beaver**) a member of the youngest level (ages 5, 6, and 7) in Scouting. **4** Cdn hist. **a** = MADE BEAVER. **b** a coin used during the fur trade, having a value equal to one made beaver. **5** coarse slang the female genitals. ● v.intr. informal (usu. foll. by away) work hard.

beaver dam n. N Amer. a dam of mud and sticks built by beavers across a stream or river.

beaver house n. (also **beaver lodge**) N Amer. a den constructed by beavers from sticks and mud, usu. in a beaver pond.

beaver meadow n. N Amer. a flat, fertile, treeless area created by the silting up of a beaver pond.

beaver pond n. N Amer. a pool of water formed behind a beaver dam.

beaver tail n. **1** the broad, flat tail of a beaver. **2** N Amer. (attrib.) (usu. **beavertail**) having the round, broad shape of a beaver tail (beavertail snowshoe). **3** (**Beaver Tail**) Cdn (esp. E. Ont.) proprietary a flat oval of deep-fried dough served with various garnishes, esp. sugar and cinnamon.

beaver wool n. N Amer. the short smooth hair under the thick fur of a beaver pelt.

bebop /ˈbiːbɒp/ n. a type of jazz originating in the 1940s and characterized by complex harmony and rhythms. □ **bebopper** n.

becalmed adj. (of a sailing ship) deprived of wind and unable to move.

because conj. for the reason that; since. □ **because of** on account of; by reason of.

béchamel /ˈbeɪʃəˌmel/ n. = WHITE SAUCE.

beck n. a gesture requesting attention, e.g. a nod, wave, etc. □ **at a person's beck and call** having constantly to obey a person's orders.

beckon v. **1** tr. attract the attention of; summon by gesture. **2** intr. (usu. foll. by to) make a signal to attract a person's attention; summon a person by doing this. □ **beckoning** adj.

become v. (past **became**; past part. **become**) **1** intr. begin to be. **2** tr. **a** look well on; suit (blue becomes him). **b** befit (behaviour that becomes a professional). □ **become of** happen to (what will become of me?).

becoming adj. **1** flattering the appearance. **2** suitable; decorous. □ **becomingly** adv.

B.Ed. abbr. Bachelor of Education.

bed ● n. **1 a** a piece of furniture used for sleeping or resting on. **b** a mattress and covers. **2** any place used by a person or animal for sleep or rest. **3** a bed and associated facilities, esp.: **a** for a patient in a hospital. **b** for a guest in a hotel etc. **4** the act of or usual time for being in bed. **5** the use of a bed: **a** informal for sexual intercourse. **b** for rest. **6** a place where something is embedded. **7** a level surface or other base upon which something rests. **8** the body or floor of a truck. **9** a plot of land in which plants are grown. **10** the bottom of a lake, sea, or river. **11** a layer of oysters etc. congregated in a particular spot. ● v. (**bedded**, **bedding**) **1** tr. & intr. (usu. foll. by down) **a** put or go to bed. **b** settle, make oneself comfortable. **2** tr. informal have sexual intercourse with. **3** tr. (often foll. by out) plant in a garden bed. **4** tr. embed; fix firmly in something. **5 a** *tr.* arrange as a layer. **b** *intr.* be or form a layer. □ **bed of roses** a position of ease and luxury. **get up on the wrong side of the bed** be bad-tempered during the day. **go to bed 1** retire for the night. **2** (foll. by *with*) have sexual intercourse. **3** (of a publication) go to press. **be** (or **get**) **in bed with 1** have sexual intercourse with. **2** fraternize or consort with. **make the bed** tidy and arrange the covers of a bed after use. **make one's bed and lie in it** accept the consequences of one's actions. **put to bed 1** cause to go to bed. **2** make (a publication) ready for press. **take to one's bed** retire to bed because of illness.

bed and breakfast *n.* **1** accommodation and breakfast the next morning in a hotel etc. **2** an establishment providing this for one inclusive price.

bedbug *n.* any of several flat, wingless, bloodsucking insects of the genus *Cimex*, esp. *C. lectularius*, which infest beds and houses.

bedclothes *n.pl.* (also **bedcovers**) covers for a bed, such as sheets, blankets, etc.

bedding *n.* **1** the articles which compose a bed, esp. a mattress and bedclothes. **2** a layer of straw etc. on which livestock sleep. **3** a bottom layer.

bedding plant *n.* a plant, esp. an annual, suitable for a garden bed.

bedeck /bɪ'dek/ *v.tr.* adorn.

bedevil *v.tr.* (**bedevilled**, **bedevilling**) **1** plague; afflict. **2** confound; confuse. **3** possess as if with a devil; bewitch. □ **bedevilment** *n.*

bedfellow *n.* **1** a person who shares a bed with another. **2** an associate. □ **strange bedfellows** an oddly assorted group of persons, things, etc.

bedlam *n.* a scene of uproar and confusion.

bedlamer /'bedləmər/ *n. Cdn* (*Nfld*) a young harp seal.

bed linen *n.* sheets and pillowcases.

Bedouin /'beduːɪn/ *n.* (*pl.* same) **1** a member of an Arabic-speaking nomadic people inhabiting the desert regions of the Middle East, traditionally herders of camels, goats, and sheep. **2** a wanderer; a nomad. ● *adj.* **1** of or relating to the Bedouin. **2** wandering; nomadic.

bedpan *n.* a receptacle used by a bedridden patient for urine and feces.

bedraggled *adj.* **1** dishevelled. **2** dilapidated.

bedrest *n.* confinement of an invalid to bed.

bedridden *adj.* confined to bed by infirmity, esp. permanently.

bedrock *n.* **1** solid rock underlying loose superficial material, alluvial deposits, etc. **2** the underlying principles or facts of a theory, character, etc.

bedroll *n.* esp. *N Amer.* portable bedding rolled into a bundle.

bedroom *n.* **1** a room for sleeping in. **2** (*attrib.*) of or referring to sexual suggestiveness (*bedroom eyes*).

bedroom community *n.* (also **bedroom suburb**) *N Amer.* a residential suburb outside a larger city, inhabited largely by commuters.

bedsheet *n.* = SHEET[1] 1.

bedside *n.* **1** the space beside a bed. **2** (*attrib.*) of or relating to the side of a bed (*bedside table*).

bedside manner *n.* the manner of a doctor when attending a patient.

bedspread *n.* a top cover placed over a bed.

bedspring *n. N Amer.* **1** a set of springs contained in a mattress or box spring. **2** any of the individual springs.

bedstead *n.* a framework of wood or metal supporting the springs and mattress of a bed.

bedtime *n.* **1** the usual time for going to bed. **2** (*attrib.*) of or relating to bedtime (*bedtime story*).

Beduin *var. of* BEDOUIN.

bedwetting *n.* urination in bed while asleep. □ **bedwetter** *n.*

bee *n.* **1 a** a stinging hymenopterous insect of the genus *Apoidea*, which collects nectar and pollen, produces wax and honey, and lives in large communities. **b** a related insect of the family Apoidea, either social or solitary. **2** esp. *N Amer.* a social gathering at which communal work is performed (*quilting bee*). **3** a competition, e.g. in spelling, in which competitors take turns answering questions and are eliminated if their answers are incorrect. □ **a bee in one's bonnet** an obsession. **the bee's knees** *slang* something outstandingly good (*thinks he's the bee's knees*). **busy bee** a busy person.

beech *n.* **1** any large deciduous tree of the genus *Fagus*, growing in temperate regions and having smooth grey bark and glossy leaves. **2** (also **beechwood**) its wood. **3** any similar tree of the genus *Nothofagus* growing in Australasia and S America.

beechnut *n.* the small rough-skinned fruit of the beech tree.

beef ● *n.* **1** the flesh of a cow, steer, or bull used as food. **2** (*pl.* **beeves**) **a** a cow, steer, or bull raised for its meat. **b** its carcass. **3** *informal* muscle or flesh; strength, size, or power. **4** (*pl.* **beefs**) *slang* a complaint; a protest. ● *v.intr. slang* complain. □ **beef up** *slang* strengthen, reinforce, augment.

beefalo /'biːfəlo:/ *n.* (*pl.* same or **-oes**) a hybrid breed of bovine, usu. five-eighths buffalo and three-eighths domestic cow, raised for its meat.

beefburger *n.* = HAMBURGER 1, 2.

beefcake *n. informal* muscular male physique, esp. when prominently displayed in photographs etc.

beefsteak *n.* a slice of beef, usu. for grilling.

beefsteak tomato *n.* any of several large and firm varieties of tomato.

beef stroganoff *n. see* STROGANOFF.

beefy *adj.* (**-ier, -iest**) **1** like beef. **2** solid; muscular. □ **beefily** *adv.* **beefiness** *n.*

beehive *n.* **1** an artificial habitation for keeping bees, traditionally in the shape of a dome but now usu. a box containing the combs on wooden slides. **2** a busy place. **3** a woman's high cone-shaped hairstyle. **4** (*attrib.*) anything having a domed shape.

beehive burner *n. Cdn* (*BC*) a dome-shaped incinerator used to burn waste at a sawmill.

beekeeper *n.* a person who raises honeybees for their honey and beeswax. □ **beekeeping** *n.*

beeline *n.* a straight line between two places. □ **make a beeline for** hurry directly to.

been *past part. of* BE.

been there, done that *interj.* indicating that the speaker has already experienced something or is familiar with it, esp. to the point of boredom or complacency.

beep ● *n.* **1** a high-pitched noise, esp. one produced electronically. **2** the sound of a car horn. ● *v.* **1** *intr.* emit a beep. **2** *tr.* cause to beep. **3** *tr.* summon or alert by means of a beeping device.

beeper *n.* **1** *N Amer.* a small device which emits a high-pitched signal when the user is contacted, usu. by telephone. **2** anything that emits a beep.

beer *n.* **1 a** an alcoholic drink made from yeast-fermented malt etc., flavoured with hops. **b** a bottle, can, or glass of this. **2** any of several other carbonated drinks flavoured with plant extracts (*ginger beer*).

beer belly *n.* a protruding stomach caused by drinking large quantities of beer. □ **beer-bellied** *adj.*

beer cellar *n.* **1** an underground room for storing beer. **2** a pub located in a basement or cellar.

beer garden *n.* an outdoor garden with tables and chairs where beer is sold and consumed.

beer hall *n.* a large room where beer is sold and consumed.

beernut *n. N Amer.* a shelled roasted peanut with a crisp sweet coating.

beer parlour *n. Cdn* a room in a hotel or tavern where beer is served.

beer slinger *n. Cdn informal* a bartender. □ **beer slinging** *n.*

beery *adj.* (**-ier, -iest**) **1** showing the influence of drink in one's appearance or behaviour. **2** smelling or tasting of beer. □ **beerily** *adv.* **beeriness** *n.*

beeswax *n.* **1** the wax secreted by bees to make honeycombs. **2** this wax refined and used to make candles, ointments, polishes, etc. **3** *N Amer. informal* business (*mind your own beeswax*).

beet *n.* any plant of the genus *Beta*, esp. *B. vulgaris*, having an edible spherical dark red root used as a vegetable. *See also* SUGAR BEET.

beetle[1] ● *n.* **1** any insect of the order Coleoptera, with modified front wings forming hard protective cases closing over the back wings. **2** any similar, usu. black, insect. ● *v.intr. informal* scurry.

beetle[2] ● *n.* **1** a usu. wooden tool with a heavy head, used for ramming, crushing, driving wedges, etc. **2** a machine used for heightening the lustre of cloth by pressure from rollers. ● *v.tr.* **1** ram, crush, drive, etc., with a beetle. **2** finish (cloth) with a beetle.

beet red ● *n.* an extremely dark shade of red, esp. describing a deep blush. ● *adj.* of this colour.

beeves *pl. of* BEEF 2.

befall *v.* (*past* **befell**; *past part.* **befallen**) **1** *tr.* happen to (*a similar fate befell him*). **2** *intr.* happen (*so it befell*).

befit *v.tr.* (**befitted, befitting**) **1** be fitted or appropriate for; suit. **2** be incumbent on. □ **befitting** *adj.* **befittingly** *adv.*

befog *v.tr.* (**befogged, befogging**) **1** confuse; obscure. **2** envelop in fog.

before ● *conj.* **1** earlier than the time when. **2** rather than that (*would starve before she stole*). ● *prep.* **1 a** in front of. **b** ahead of (*crossed the finish line before him*). **c** under the impulse of (*recoiled before the attack*). **d** awaiting (*the future before them*). **2** earlier than; preceding. **3** rather than (*death before dishonour*). **4 a** in the presence of (*appear before the judge*). **b** for the attention of (*a plan put before the committee*). ● *adv.* **1 a** earlier than the time in question; already. **b** in the past (*happened long before*). **2** ahead (*go before*). **3** on the front (*hit before and behind*). □ **before God** a solemn oath meaning 'as God sees me'.

Before Christ *adv.* (of a date) reckoned backwards from the birth of Christ.

beforehand *adv.* in anticipation; in advance; in readiness (*had prepared the meal beforehand*).

befoul *v.tr.* **1** make foul or dirty. **2** degrade; defile.

befriend *v.tr.* be or become friendly with.

befuddle *v.tr.* **1** confuse. **2** make drunk. □ **befuddlement** *n.*

beg *v.* (**begged, begging**) **1 a** *intr.* (usu. foll. by *for*) ask for (esp. food, money, etc.) (*begged for alms*). **b** *tr.* ask for (food, money, etc.) as a gift. **c** *intr.* live by begging. **2** *tr.* & *intr.* (usu. foll. by *for*, or to + infin.) ask earnestly or

humbly (*please, I beg of you*). **3** *tr.* ask formally for (*beg leave*). **4** *intr.* (of a dog etc.) sit up with the front paws raised expectantly. **5** *tr.* take or ask leave (to do something) (*I beg to differ*). **6** *intr.* demand (*stories begging to be written*). □ **beg one's bread** live by begging. **beg off** decline to take part or attend. **beg a person's pardon** apologize. **beg the question 1** *disputed* pose the question. ¶This is now the more common use of the phrase, although many people object that the phrase should only be used in its original sense (sense 2 below). **2** assume the truth of an argument or proposition to be proved, without arguing it (*by spending so much on education in the fight against drugs we are begging the question of the effectiveness of education*, i.e. we are assuming that through education we can radically reduce drug-taking). **3** *informal* evade a difficulty; cause (*violence begets violence*). **go begging** (of a chance or a thing) not be taken; be unwanted.

beget *v.tr.* (**begetting**; *past* **begat**; **begot**; *past part.* **begotten**) **1** be the parent, esp. the father of. **2** give rise to; cause (*violence begets violence*). □ **begetter** *n.*

beggar ● *n.* **1** a person who begs, esp. one who lives by begging. **2** a poor person. **3** *informal* a person; a fellow (*poor beggar*). ● *v.tr.* **1** reduce to poverty. **2** exhaust the resources of (*beggar description*). □ **beggars can't be choosers** those without other resources must take what is offered.

beggar-thy-neighbour *n.* (also **beggar-my-neighbour**) **1** a card game in which a player seeks to capture an opponent's cards. **2** (*attrib.*) (of a policy) self-aggrandizing at the expense of competitors.

beggary *n.* extreme poverty.

begging bowl *n.* a bowl held out for food or alms.

begin *v.* (**beginning**; *past* **began**; *past part.* **begun**) **1** *tr.* start; perform the first part of. **2** *intr.* come into being; arise: **a** in time (*the strike began last week*). **b** in space (*our property begins beyond the river*). **3** *tr.* start at a certain time (*then began to feel ill*). **4** *intr.* be begun (*the meeting will begin at 7*). **5** *intr.* **a** start speaking ('No,' she began). **b** take the first step; be the first to do something (*who wants to begin?*). **6** *intr. informal* (usu. with *neg.*) show any attempt or likelihood (*can't begin to compete*). □ **begin at** start from. **begin on** (or **upon**) set to work at. **begin with** take (a subject, task, etc.) first or as a starting point. **to begin with** in the first place.

beginner *n.* a person beginning to learn a skill etc.

beginner's luck *n.* good luck supposed to attend a beginner at games etc.

beginning *n.* **1** the time or place at which anything begins. **2** a source or origin. **3** the first part. □ **the beginning of the end** the first clear sign of the end of something.

begonia /bɪˈɡoːnjə, -nɪə/ *n.* any plant of the genus *Begonia* with brightly coloured sepals and no petals, and often having brilliant glossy foliage.

begot *past of* BEGET.

begotten *past part. of* BEGET.

begrudge *v.tr.* **1** resent; be dissatisfied at. **2** envy (a person) the possession of. □ **begrudgingly** *adv.*

beguile /bɪˈɡaɪl/ *v.tr.* **1** charm; amuse. **2** divert attention pleasantly from (toil etc.). **3** (usu. foll. by *of, out of,* or *into*) delude; cheat (*beguiled him into paying*). □ **beguiler** *n.* **beguiling** *adj.* **beguilingly** *adv.*

beguine /bɪˈɡiːn/ *n.* **1** a popular dance of W Indian origin. **2** its rhythm.

begun *past part. of* BEGIN.

behalf *n.* □ **on behalf of** (also esp. *US* **in behalf of**) **1** in the interests of (a person, principle, etc.). **2** as representative of (*acting on behalf of my client*).

behave *v.* **1** *intr.* **a** act or react (in a specified way) (*behaved well*). **b** (esp. to or of a child) conduct oneself properly. **c** (of a machine etc.) work well (or in a specified way) (*the computer is not behaving today*). **2** *refl.* show good manners (*behaved herself*). □ **behave towards** treat (in a specified way).

behaviour *n.* (also **behavior**) **1 a** the way one conducts oneself; manners. **b** the treatment of others; moral conduct. **2** the way in which a vehicle, machine, chemical substance, etc., acts or works. **3** *Psych.* an observable pattern of actions (of a person, animal, etc.), esp. in response to a stimulus. □ **be on one's best behaviour** behave well.

behavioural *adj.* (also **behavioral**) of or relating to behaviour. □ **behaviouralist** *n.*

behavioural science *n.* the scientific study of human behaviour.

behaviourism *n.* (also **behaviorism**) *Psych.* **1** the theory that objective investigation of stimuli and responses is the only valid psychological method, and that psychological disorders are best treated by altering behaviour patterns. **2** such study and treatment in practice. □ **behaviourist** *n.*

behaviour therapy *n.* the treatment of neurotic symptoms by training the patient's reactions.

behead *v.tr.* cut off the head of (a person), esp. as a form of execution. □ **beheading** *n.*

behemoth /bə'hi:məθ, 'bɪə,məθ/ *n.* an enormous creature or thing.

behest *n.* a command; a request.

behind ● *prep.* **1 a** in, towards, or to the rear of. **b** on the farther side of (*behind the bush*). **c** hidden by (*something behind that remark*). **2 a** in the past in relation to (*trouble is behind me now*). **b** late in relation to (*behind schedule*). **3** inferior to; weaker than (*behind the others in math*). **4 a** in support of (*she's behind the idea*). **b** responsible for; giving rise to (*the reasons behind his resignation*). **5** in the tracks of; following. ● *adv.* **1 a** in or to or towards the rear; further back (*glance behind*). **b** on the further side (*a high wall with a field behind*). **2** remaining after departure (*stay behind*). **3 a** in arrears (*behind with the rent*). **b** late in accomplishing a task etc. (*working too slowly and getting behind*). **4** in an inferior position (*the team was two points behind*). **5** following (*her dog running behind*). ● *n.* *informal* the buttocks. □ **behind a person's back** without a person's knowledge. **behind the times** antiquated. **come from behind** win after trailing. **fall** (or **lag**) **behind** not keep up; begin to trail. **put behind one 1** refuse to consider. **2** get over (an unhappy experience etc.).

behold *v.tr.* (*past* and *past part.* **beheld**) *literary* **1** see, observe. **2** (*in imper.*) pay attention.

beholden *predic.adj.* (usu. foll. by *to*) under obligation.

beholder *n.* *literary* a person who beholds. □ **in the eye of the beholder** to be judged subjectively.

behoove /bi'hu:v/ *v.tr.* (also esp. *Brit.* **behove** /-'hoʊv/) *formal* **1** be incumbent on. **2** (usu. with *neg.*) befit (*it ill behooves him to protest*).

beige /beiʒ/ ● *n.* a very pale yellowish brown. ● *adj.* of this colour.

being *n.* **1** existence. **2** the nature or essence (of a person etc.) (*his whole being revolted*). **3** a human being. **4** anything that exists or is imagined.

bejesus *n.* (also **bejabbers**) *N Amer., Scot. & Irish* used as an intensifier (*beat the bejesus out of him*).

bejewelled *adj.* adorned with jewels.

bel *n.* a unit used in the comparison of power levels in electrical communication or intensities of sound, corresponding to an intensity ratio of 10 to 1.

belabour *v.tr.* (also **belabor**) **1** argue or elaborate (a

subject) in excessive detail. **2** attack verbally. **3** thrash; beat.

Belarussian /ˌbelə'rʌʃən/ ● *n.* **1** a native or national of Belarus. **2** the Slavic language of Belarus. ● *adj.* of or relating to Belarus, its people, or language.

belated *adj.* coming late or too late. □ **belatedly** *adv.* **belatedness** *n.*

belay /bi'lei/ (*past* and *past part.* **belayed**) ● *v.* **1** *tr.* secure (a rope) around a cleat, pin, rock, etc. **2** *tr. & intr.* (usu. in *imper.*) *Naut.* stop, halt (*belay there!*). ● *n.* **1** a spike of rock etc. used for belaying a rope in climbing. **2** an act of belaying.

bel canto *n.* **1** a lyrical style of operatic singing using a full rich broad tone and smooth phrasing. **2** (*attrib.*) (of a type of aria or voice) characterized by this.

belch ● *v.* **1** *intr.* emit gas noisily from the stomach through the mouth. **2** *tr.* **a** (of a chimney, volcano, etc.) send (smoke etc.) out or up. **b** gush forth. **c** utter forcibly. ● *n.* an act of belching.

beleaguer *v.tr.* **1** vex, harass. **2** lay siege to.

beleaguered *adj.* beset with difficulties.

belfry *n.* (*pl.* **-ies**) **1** a bell tower or steeple housing bells, esp. forming part of a church. **2** a space for hanging bells in a church tower.

Belgian /'beldʒən/ ● *n.* **1** a native or national of Belgium. **2** a person of Belgian descent. **3** a draft horse of a large, heavy, and short-legged breed of Flemish origin. ● *adj.* of or relating to Belgium.

Belgian endive *n.* *N Amer.* the white-leaved crown of the chicory plant, used in salads.

Belgian waffle *n.* a type of waffle with very deep indentations.

belie /bə'lai/ *v.tr.* (**belying**) **1** give a false notion of; fail to corroborate (*its appearance belies its age*). **2 a** fail to fulfill (a promise etc.). **b** fail to justify (a hope etc.).

belief *n.* **1 a** a firm opinion or conviction (*my belief is that he did it*). **b** an acceptance (of a thing, fact, statement, etc.) (*belief in the afterlife*). **c** a person's religion; religious conviction. **2** (usu. foll. by *in*) trust or confidence. □ **beyond belief** incredible. **to the best of my belief** in my genuine opinion.

believe *v.* **1** *tr.* accept as true or as conveying the truth. **2** *tr.* think, suppose (*I believe it's raining*). **3** *intr.* (foll. by *in*) **a** have faith in the existence of (*believes in God*). **b** have confidence in (*believes in alternative medicine*). **c** have trust in the advisability of (*believes in telling the truth*). **4** *intr.* have (esp. religious) faith. □ **believe one's eyes** (or **ears**) (usu. in *neg.*) accept that what one apparently sees or hears etc. is true. **believe it or not** *informal* it is true though surprising. **make believe** pretend. □ **believability** *n.* **believable** *adj.* **believably** *adv.*

believer *n.* **1** an adherent of a specified religion. **2** a person who believes, esp. in the efficacy of something (*a great believer in exercise*).

belittle *v.tr.* **1** make (a person, action, etc.) seem unimportant or worthless. **2** make small; dwarf. □ **belittlement** *n.* **belittler** *n.* **belittlingly** *adv.*

bell¹ ● *n.* **1 a** hollow usu. metal object in the shape of a deep upturned cup usu. widening at the lip, made to sound a clear musical note when struck. **2 a a** sound or stroke of a bell, esp. as a signal. **b** *Naut.* (prec. by a numeral) the time as indicated every half-hour of a watch by the striking of the ship's bell one to eight times. **3** anything that sounds like or functions as a bell, esp. an electronic device that rings etc. as a signal. **4 a** any bell-shaped object or part, e.g. of a musical instrument. **b** the corolla of a flower when bell-shaped. **5** *Music* (in *pl.*) a set of cylindrical metal tubes of different lengths, suspended in a frame and played by being struck with a hammer. **6** *Cdn* the dangling appendage under a moose's neck. ● *v.tr.* **1** provide with a bell or bells; attach a bell to. **2** (foll. by *out*) form into the shape of the lip of a bell. □ **bells and whistles** *informal* attractive but non-essential components; gimmicks. **bell the cat** attempt something daring or dangerous. **clear** (or **sound**) **as a bell** perfectly clear or sound. **ring a bell** *informal* revive a distant recollection; sound familiar. **saved by the bell** spared (from an unpleasant occurrence) at the last moment. **with bells on** enthusiastically.

bell² ● *n.* the cry of a stag or buck at rutting time. ● *v.intr.* make this cry.

Bella Bella /ˈbelə ˈbelə/ *n. & adj.* = HEILTSUK.

Bella Coola /ˌbelə ˈkuːlə/ *n. & adj.* = NUXALK.

belladonna *n.* **1** a poisonous plant, *Atropa belladonna*, with purple flowers and purple-black berries. **2** a drug prepared from its root and leaves.

bell-bottom *n.* **1** a wide flare below the knee of a trouser leg. **2** (in *pl.*) trousers with bell bottoms. □ **bell-bottomed** *adj.*

bellboy *n.* esp. *N Amer.* = BELLHOP.

bellcast *adj.* designating a style of roof typical of traditional architecture in Quebec, with gables having the shape of a squared-off bell.

belle /bel/ *n.* **1** a beautiful woman. **2** a woman recognized as the most beautiful (*the belle of the ball*).

belle époque /ˌbel eiˈpɒk/ *n.* the period of settled comfort and prosperity before the First World War.

belles lettres /bel ˈletr/ *n.pl.* (also treated as *sing.*) writings or studies of a purely literary nature, esp. essays and criticisms. □ **belletrism** /beˈletrɪzəm/ *n.* **belletrist** *n.* **belletristic** *adj.*

bellhop *n.* *N Amer.* a hotel employee who helps guests with luggage, shows them to rooms, etc.

bellicose /ˈbelɪˌkoːs/ *adj.* inclined to war or fighting; warlike. □ **bellicosity** /-ˈkɒsɪti/ *n.*

bellied *adj.* (in *comb.*) having a belly of a specified kind (*pot-bellied*).

belligerence /bəˈlɪdʒərəns/ *n.* **1** aggressive or warlike behaviour. **2** the status of a belligerent.

belligerent ● *adj.* **1** engaged in war or conflict. **2** given to repeated fighting. ● *n.* a nation or person engaged in war or conflict. □ **belligerently** *adv.*

bellman *n.* (*pl.* **-men**) *N Amer.* = BELLHOP.

bellow ● *v.* **1** *intr.* **a** emit a deep loud roar. **b** cry or shout with pain. **2** *tr.* utter loudly and usu. angrily. ● *n.* a bellowing sound.

bellows *n.pl.* (also treated as *sing.*) **1** a device with an air bag that emits a stream of air when squeezed, esp.: **a** (in full **pair of bellows**) a kind with two handles used for blowing air onto a fire. **b** a kind used in a harmonium or small organ. **2** an expandable component, e.g. joining a lens to a camera body.

bell pepper *n.* see PEPPER *n.* 2.

bell-ringing *n.* **1** the ringing of church bells. **2** *Cdn* the ringing of bells in a legislative assembly to summon members for a vote, esp. when provoked as a tactic for stalling debate.

bellwether *n.* **1** (often *attrib.*) a person, thing, or event which presages incipient change. **2** the leading sheep of a flock, on whose neck a bell is hung.

belly ● *n.* (*pl.* **-ies**) **1** the part of the human body below the chest, containing the stomach and bowels. **2** the stomach, esp. representing the body's need for food. **3** the front surface of the body from the waist to the groin. **4** the corresponding part or surface of the body of an animal. **5** a cavity or bulging part of anything. ● *v.tr. & intr.* (**-ies, -ied**) (often foll. by *out*)

swell or cause to swell; bulge. □ **belly up** approach closely (*bellied up to the bar*). **go belly up** esp. *N Amer.* fail; become bankrupt; die.

bellyache *informal* ● *n.* a stomach pain. ● *v.intr.* complain noisily or persistently. □ **bellyacher** *n.*

belly button *n.* *informal* the navel.

belly dance *n.* a woman's solo dance of Middle Eastern origin, involving the rippling of the abdominal muscles. □ **belly dancer** *n.* **belly dancing** *n.*

belly flop *informal* ● *n.* a dive into water in which the body lands with the belly flat on the water. ● *v.intr.* (**belly-flop**) (**-flopped, -flopping**) perform this dive.

bellyful *n.* (*pl.* **-fuls**) **1** enough to eat. **2** *informal* enough or more than enough of anything.

belong *v.intr.* **1** (foll. by *to*) **a** be the property of. **b** be rightly assigned to as a duty, right, part, member, characteristic, etc. **c** be a member of (a club, family, group, etc.). **2** have the right personal or social qualities to be a member of a particular group (*he's nice but just doesn't belong*). **3** (foll. by *in, under*) **a** be rightly placed or classified. **b** fit a particular environment. □ **belonging** *n.* **belongingness** *n.*

belongings *n.pl.* personal possessions or effects.

beloved ● *adj.* dearly loved. ● *n.* a dearly loved person.

below ● *prep.* **1** lower in position. **2** beneath the surface of; at or to a greater depth than (*head below water*; *below 50 metres*). **3** lower in rank, position, or importance than. **4** unworthy of. ● *adv.* **1** at or to a lower point or level. **2 a** on or to a lower floor or deck (*went below*). **b** downstream. **3** further down on a page or later in an article, book, etc. (*as noted below*). **4** on the lower side (*looks similar above and below*). **5** lower than zero on a temperature scale (*20 below*). **6** *literary* **a** on earth. **b** in hell.

belt ● *n.* **1** a flat encircling strip of leather, cloth, etc., worn around the waist or from the shoulder to the opposite hip to support clothes, tools, weapons, etc., or as a decorative accessory. **2 a** a belt worn as a sign of rank or achievement. **b** a belt of a specified colour indicating the wearer's level of proficiency in judo, karate, etc. (compare BLACK BELT). **3 a** a circular band of material used as a driving medium in machinery etc. **b** a conveyor belt. **c** a flexible strip for feeding a machine gun with ammunition. **4** a seat belt. **5** a strip of colour or texture etc. differing from that on either side. **6** a zone or region of distinct character or occupancy (*wheat belt*; *Bible belt*). **7** *informal* a heavy blow or stroke. **8** a strip of reinforcing material (esp. steel) placed beneath the tread of a tire for durability. **9** *informal* a drink. ● *v.* **1** *tr.* put a belt around. **2** *tr.* (often foll. by *on*) fasten with a belt. **3** *tr.* a beat with a belt. **b** *informal* hit hard. **4** *intr. informal* rush, hurry (usu. with compl.: *belted along*). **5** *tr.* drink quickly. □ **below the belt** unfair or unfairly. **belt out** *informal* sing or utter loudly and forcibly. **belt up** *informal* **1** be quiet. **2** put on a seat belt. **tighten one's belt** curtail expenditure. **under one's belt** **1** (of food or drink) consumed. **2** securely acquired (*has a degree under her belt*). □ **belter** *n.* (esp. in sense of *belt out*).

belted *adj.* **1** fastened or ornamented with a belt. **2** (of a tire) having a strip of reinforcing material beneath the tread.

belted kingfisher *n.* see KINGFISHER.

beltline *n.* **1** the waistline. **2** the area where the hood and doors of a car meet the windshield and windows.

beluga /bəˈluːɡə/ *n.* **1 a** a whale, *Delphinapterus leucas*, of the Arctic Ocean which is found as far south as the St. Lawrence estuary, and is white when adult. **2 a** a large kind of sturgeon, *Huso huso*, of the Caspian and Black Seas. **b** caviar obtained from it.

belying *pres. part.* of BELIE.

bemoan *v.tr.* **1** express regret or sorrow over; lament. **2** complain about.

bemuse *v.tr.* (usu. as **bemused** *adj.*) cause (often somewhat amused) puzzlement. □ **bemusedly** *adv.* **bemusement** *n.*

bench ● *n.* **1** a long seat, with or without a back, for several people. **2** a work table used by a carpenter etc., or in a laboratory. **3** (prec. by *the*) **a** the office or status of a judge. **b** the seat on which the judge or judges sit in court. **c** a court of law. **d** judges and magistrates collectively. **4** *Sport* **a** a seat used by players when not participating in a game. **b** the substitute players collectively. **5** *Parl.* a seat (*back bench*). **6 a** a bank or shelf of ground. **b** a level ledge in earthwork, masonry, etc. **c** esp. *Geomorph.* = BENCHLAND. ● *v.tr.* **1** *N Amer.* & *Austral. Sport* remove or retire (a player) to the bench esp. for poor performance. **2** exhibit (a dog etc.) at a show. □ **behind the bench** *Hockey* serving as a coach. **on the bench** serving as a judge or magistrate.

bench-clearing *n.* (esp. *attrib.*) *N Amer.* an incident in which an entire sports team leaves the players' bench and enters the playing area, usu. to engage in a brawl.

bencher *n.* **1** (in *comb.*) *Parl.* an occupant of a specified bench (*backbencher*). **2** *Cdn Law* a member of the regulating body of the law society in all provinces except New Brunswick.

benchland *n.* *N Amer.* a relatively narrow, naturally occurring terrace often backed by a steep slope.

benchmark ● *n.* **1** a surveyor's mark cut in a wall, post, etc., used as a reference point in measuring comparative elevations. **2** a standard or point of reference. **3** (in full **benchmark test**) a means of testing a computer, usu. by a set of programs run on a series of different machines. ● *v.tr.* test or check by comparison with a benchmark.

bench penalty *n.* (also **bench minor**) *Hockey* a minor penalty assessed to a team as a whole and served by a single player.

bench press ● *n.* an exercise in which a person lying face upwards on a bench with feet on the floor raises a barbell by extending both arms upward from the chest. ● *v.tr.* & *intr.* (usu. **bench-press**) raise (a weight) in a bench press.

benchwarmer *n.* *N Amer. informal* an athlete who routinely is not selected to play.

bend ● *v.* (*past* and *past part.* **bent**) **1 a** *tr.* force or adapt (esp. something straight) into a curve or angle. **b** *intr.* (of an object) be altered in this way. **2** *intr.* move or stretch in a curved course (*the road bends to the left*). **3** *intr.* & *tr.* (often foll. by *down*, *over*, etc.) incline or cause to incline from the vertical (*bent down to pick it up*). **4** *tr.* & *refl.* (foll. by *to*, *on*) direct or devote (oneself or one's attention, energies, etc.). **5** *tr.* turn (one's steps or eyes) in a new direction. **6** *tr.* (in *passive*; foll. by *on*) have firmly decided; be determined (*was bent on selling*). **7 a** *intr.* stoop or submit. **b** *tr.* force to submit. ● *n.* **1** a curve in a road or other course. **2** a departure from a straight course. **3** a bent part of anything. **4** (in *pl.*; prec. by *the*) *informal* = DECOMPRESSION SICKNESS. □ **bend one's elbow** drink alcohol. **bend someone's ear** importune someone with persistent talk; have a word with someone. **bend the rules** interpret or modify rules to suit oneself. **on bended knee** kneeling in reverence, supplication, or submission. **round the bend** *informal* crazy, insane. □ **bendable** *adj.*

bender *n.* **1** *slang* a wild drinking spree. **2** an instrument for bending (pipes etc.).

bendy *adj.* (**-ier**, **-iest**) *informal* capable of bending; soft and flexible. □ **bendiness** *n.*

beneath ● *prep.* **1** below, under. **2** not worthy of; too demeaning for (*it was beneath him to reply*). ● *adv.* below, under, underneath.

Benedictine /ˌbenəˈdɪktiːn/ ● *n.* **1** a monk or nun of an order following the rule of St. Benedict. **2** *proprietary* a liqueur of brandy and herbs, originally made by Benedictines in France. ● *adj.* of St. Benedict or the Benedictines.

benediction /ˌbenəˈdɪkʃən/ *n.* **1** the utterance of a blessing, esp. at the end of a religious service. **2** (**Benediction**) a chiefly Catholic service in which the congregation is blessed with the Host, usu. displayed in a monstrance. **3** the state of being blessed.

benefaction /ˌbenəˈfækʃən/ *n.* **1** a donation or gift. **2** an act of giving or doing good.

benefactor *n.* a person who gives support (esp. financial) to a person or cause. □ **benefactress** *n.*

benefice /ˈbenəfɪs/ *n.* **1** a position held by a member of the clergy that ensures an income or a specified property. **2** the income from such a position.

beneficent /bəˈnefɪsnt/ *adj.* doing good; generous, actively kind. □ **beneficence** *n.* **beneficently** *adv.*

beneficial *adj.* **1** advantageous; having benefits. **2** *Law* of, pertaining to, or having the use or benefit of property etc. □ **beneficially** *adv.*

beneficiary /ˌbenəˈfɪʃieri, -ˈfɪʃəri/ *n.* (*pl.* **-ies**) **1** a person who receives or is entitled to receive benefits, esp. under a will or life insurance policy. **2** a person who benefits from a particular event, action, etc.

benefit ● *n.* **1** a favourable or helpful factor or circumstance; advantage, profit. **2** (often in *pl.*) allowance of money etc. to which a person is entitled from a pension plan, government support programs, etc. (*employment insurance benefits*). **3** (often in *pl.*) an advantage other than salary associated with a job, e.g. dental coverage, life insurance, etc. **4** a public performance, sporting event, etc. held in order to raise money for a particular charity etc. ● *v.* (**benefited**, **benefiting**; also **benefitted**, **benefitting**) **1** *tr.* do good to; be of advantage to; improve. **2** *intr.* (often foll. by *from*, *by*) receive an advantage or gain. □ **the benefit of the doubt** assumption of a person's innocence, rightness, etc., rather than the contrary in the absence of proof.

benefit of clergy *n.* ecclesiastical sanction or approval (*marriage without benefit of clergy*).

benevolent /bəˈnevələnt/ *adj.* **1** wishing to do good; actively friendly and helpful. **2** charitable (*benevolent fund*). □ **benevolence** *n.* **benevolently** *adv.*

B.Eng. *abbr.* Bachelor of Engineering.

Bengali /benˈɡʊli, -ˈɡæli/ ● *n.* **1** a native of Bengal, a region in the northeast of the Indian subcontinent. **2** the language of this people, descended from Sanskrit. ● *adj.* of or relating to Bengal or its people.

Bengal tiger *n.* a tiger of a variety found in the Indian subcontinent, having unbroken stripes.

benighted *adj.* **1** intellectually or morally ignorant. **2** unfortunate. **3** overtaken by night or darkness.

benign /bəˈnaɪn/ *adj.* **1** gentle, mild, kindly. **2** fortunate, salutary. **3** (of climate etc.) mild, favourable. **4** *Med.* (of a disease, tumour, etc.) not malignant. □ **benignly** *adv.*

benjamina ficus /bendʒəˈmiːnə/ *n.* (also **Benjamin's fig**) = FICUS BENJAMINA.

Bennett buggy *n.* *Cdn hist.* an automobile hitched to horses or oxen, used during the Depression by owners who could no longer afford gasoline etc.

benny *n.* (*pl.* **-ies**) *slang* an amphetamine tablet, esp. as a stimulant.

benomyl /'benəmɪl/ *n.* a systemic fungicide used on fruit and vegetable crops.

bent¹ ● *v. past and past part. of* BEND *v.* ● *adj.* **1** curved or having an angle. **2** (foll. by *on*) determined to do or have. **3** *slang* homosexual. ● *n.* **1** an inclination or bias. **2** (foll. by *for*) a talent for something specified (*a bent for mimicry*). □ **bent out of shape** *N Amer. informal* upset or annoyed, esp. unreasonably so.

bent² *n.* **1 a** (also **bent grass**) any grass of the genus *Agrostis*, a hardy grass used esp. in golf courses. **b** any of various grasslike reeds, rushes, or sedges. **2** a stiff stalk of a grass usu. with a flexible base.

benthos /'benθɒs/ *n.* the flora and fauna at the bottom of a sea or lake. □ **benthic** *adj.*

bentonite /'bentə,naɪt/ *n.* a kind of highly absorbent clay having numerous uses, esp. as a filler.

benzene /'benziːn/ *n.* a colourless carcinogenic volatile liquid found in coal tar, petroleum, etc., and used as a solvent and in the manufacture of plastics etc.

benzene ring *n.* the hexagonal unsaturated ring of six carbon atoms in the benzene molecule.

benzodiazepine /'benzo,daɪ'æzepiːn/ *n.* any of a class of heterocyclic compounds used as tranquilizers, including Librium and Valium.

benzoic acid /ben'zo:ɪk/ *n.* a white crystalline substance used esp. as a food preservative.

benzoin /'benzo:ɪn/ *n.* **1** a fragrant gum resin obtained from various E Asian trees of the genus *Styrax*, and used in the manufacture of perfumes and incense. **2** the white crystalline constituent of this.

benzol /'benzɒl/ *n.* (also **benzole** /-zo:l/) benzene, esp. unrefined and used as a fuel.

Beothuk /bi'ɒθʊk/ (also **Beothuck**) ● *n.* **1** (*pl.* same or **-s**) a member of an Aboriginal people formerly inhabiting Newfoundland but extinct since the early 19th c. **2** the Algonquian language of this people. ● *adj.* of or relating to the Beothuk.

bequeath /bi'kwiːθ, bi'kwiːð/ *v.tr.* **1** leave (an estate or piece of property) to a person by will. **2** hand down to posterity. □ **bequeathal** *n.* **bequeather** *n.*

bequest *n.* **1** the act or an instance of bequeathing. **2** a thing bequeathed.

berate *v.tr.* scold, rebuke.

Berber /'bɜrbər/ ● *n.* **1** a member of the indigenous mainly Muslim Caucasian peoples of N Africa (now mainly in Morocco and Algeria) speaking related languages. **2** the Afro-Asiatic language or group of languages of these peoples. **3** (**berber**) a type of sturdy carpet having large tightly woven loops, and often having the appearance of tweed. ● *adj.* of the Berbers or their language.

bereave *v.tr.* (*past* and *past part.* **bereaved** or **bereft**) (usu. foll. by *of*) deprive of a relation, friend, etc., esp. by death. □ **bereavement** *n.*

bereaved *adj.* saddened by the death of a loved one.

bereft *adj.* (foll. by *of*) deprived (esp. of a non-material asset) (*bereft of hope*).

beret /bə'rei, be'rei/ *n.* a round brimless cap of felt or cloth that is close-fitting and lies flat on the head.

berg *n.* = ICEBERG.

bergamot /'bɜrgə,mɒt/ *n.* **1** a citrus tree, *Citrus bergamia*, bearing fruit similar to an orange, from the rind of which a fragrant essential oil is extracted. **2** the oil or essence itself, used esp. in perfumes, Earl Grey tea, etc. **3** any of several herbaceous plants of the mint family smelling like bergamot, esp.: **a** *N Amer.* (in full **wild bergamot**) a N American plant,

Monarda fistulosa, having purple or pink flowers. **b** a related plant, *Monarda didyma*, grown for its showy heads of scarlet flowers. **c** a Mediterranean mint, *Mentha citrata*, grown for its fragrance.

beriberi /,beri'beri/ *n.* a disease causing inflammation of the nerves due to a deficiency of vitamin B₁ (thiamine), mainly associated with rice-based diets.

berkelium /bər'kiːliəm, 'bɜrkliəm/ *n.* a radioactive metallic element produced by bombardment of americium.

berm *n.* **1 a** a flat strip of land, raised bank, or terrace bordering a river etc. **b** a narrow path or grass strip beside a road. **2** a narrow ledge, esp. in a fortification between a ditch and a parapet.

Bermuda shorts *n.pl.* (also **Bermudas**) knee-length shorts.

berried *adj.* **1** (of a plant) bearing berries (also in *comb.*: *yellow-berried*). **2** (of a lobster) egg-bearing.

berry *n.* (*pl.* **-ies**) **1** any small roundish juicy fruit without a stone. **2** *Bot.* a fruit with its seeds enclosed in pulp, e.g. the grape, gooseberry, tomato, etc. **3** any of various kernels or seeds, esp. of wheat etc. **4** an egg of a fish or lobster.

berry ground *n. Cdn* (*Nfld*) an elevated, treeless area where wild berries are found.

berrying *n.* gathering berries.

berserk *adj.* (esp. in **go berserk**) wild, frenzied.

berth ● *n.* **1** a fixed bunk on a ship, train, etc., for sleeping in. **2** a ship's place at a wharf. **3** room for a ship to swing at anchor. **4** sufficient room for a ship to manoeuvre. **5** *Sport* an opportunity for a team or athlete to compete (*a playoff berth*). **6** *informal* a situation or appointment. **7** the proper place for anything. **8** *Cdn Forestry* a specified area of timberland in which a company or individual is entitled to fell trees. **9** *Cdn* (*Nfld*) a particular area claimed by a boat on fishing grounds. ● *v.* **1** *tr.* moor (a ship) in its berth. **2** *tr.* provide a sleeping place for. **3** *intr.* (of a ship) come to its mooring place. □ **give a wide berth to** stay away from; avoid.

beryl /'berɪl/ *n.* **1** a kind of transparent precious stone, esp. pale green, blue, or yellow, and consisting of beryllium aluminum silicate. **2** a mineral species which includes this, emerald, and aquamarine.

beryllium /bə'rɪliəm/ *n.* a hard white metallic element used in light corrosion-resistant alloys.

B.E.S. *abbr.* Bachelor of Environmental Studies.

beseech *v.tr.* (*past* and *past part.* **besought** or **beseeched**) **1** (foll. by *for*, or *to* + infin.) entreat, implore. **2** ask earnestly for. □ **beseeching** *adj.* **beseechingly** *adv.*

beset *v.tr.* (**besetting**; *past* and *past part.* **beset**) **1** attack or harass persistently (*beset by worries*). **2** surround or hem in (a person etc.).

besetting *adj.* characteristic or predominant.

beside *prep.* **1** at the side of; near. **2** compared with. **3** irrelevant to (*beside the point*). □ **beside oneself** overcome with worry, anger, etc.

besides ● *prep.* **1** in addition to; as well as. **2** other than; apart from; except; excluding. ● *adv.* in addition; as well; moreover.

besiege *v.tr.* **1** lay siege to. **2** crowd around oppressively. **3** harass with requests. **4** assail, beset. □ **besieger** *n.*

besmirch *v.tr.* **1** soil, discolour. **2** dishonour; sully the reputation or name of.

besotted *adj.* **1** infatuated. **2** intoxicated, stupefied. **3** foolish, confused.

besought *past and past part. of* BESEECH.

bespeak *v.tr.* (*past* **bespoke**; *past part.* **bespoken** or as *adj.* **bespoke**) **1** suggest; be evidence of (*his gift bespeaks a kind heart*). **2** engage in advance.

bespectacled *adj.* wearing eyeglasses.

bespoke *adj.* **1** (of goods, esp. clothing) made to order. **2** (of a tailor etc.) making goods to order.

best ● *adj.* (*superlative of* GOOD) of the most excellent or outstanding or desirable kind. **●** *adv.* (*superlative of* WELL[1]) **1** in the best manner (*does it best*). **2** to the greatest degree (*like it best*). **3** most usefully (*is best ignored*). **●** *n.* **1** that which is best (*the best is yet to come*). **2** the chief merit or advantage (*brings out the best in him*). **3** (foll. by *of*) a winning majority of (a certain number of games etc. played) (*the best of five*). **4** a best performance recorded to date (*her personal best*). **●** *v.tr.* informal defeat, outwit, outbid, etc. □ **all the best** an expression of goodwill. **as best one can** (or **may**) as effectively as possible under the circumstances. **at best** on the most optimistic view. **at one's best** in peak condition etc. **at the best of times** even in the most favourable circumstances. **be for** (or **all for**) **the best** be desirable in the end. **the best of both worlds** the benefits of two different desirable outcomes, possibilities, etc., without having to choose between them. **the best part of** most of. **do** (or **give it**) **one's best** do all one can. **get the best of** defeat, outwit. **give a person one's best** express one's best wishes to a person. **had best** would find it wisest to. **make the best of** derive what limited advantage one can from (something unsatisfactory or unwelcome); put up with. **to the best of one's ability, knowledge,** etc. as far as one can do, know, etc. **with the best of them** as well as anyone.

best-before date *n.* the date marked on food showing the period after which it will deteriorate.

best bet *n.* the best option under the circumstances.

best buy *n.* the purchase giving the best value in proportion to its price; a bargain.

best friend *n.* a person's closest friend.

bestial /'bi:stiəl, 'bes-/ *adj.* **1** brutish, cruel, savage. **2** sexually depraved; lustful. **3** of or like a beast. □ **bestialize** *v.tr.* **bestially** *adv.*

bestiality /,bi:sti'æliti, ,best-/ *n.* (*pl.* **-ies**) **1** sexual intercourse between a person and an animal. **2** bestial behaviour or an instance of this.

best man *n.* the groom's chief attendant at a wedding.

bestow *v.tr.* confer (a gift, right, etc.). □ **bestowal** *n.*

bestride *v.tr.* (*past* **bestrode**; *past part.* **bestridden**) **1** sit astride on. **2** stand astride over. **3** dominate.

best-seller *n.* **1** a book or other item that has sold in large numbers. **2** the author of such a book etc. □ **best-selling** *adj.* **bestsellerdom** *n.*

bet ● *v.* (**betting**; *past* and *past part.* **bet** or **betted**) **1** *intr.* risk a sum of money etc. against another's on the basis of the outcome of an unpredictable event (esp. the result of a race, game, etc.). **2** *tr.* risk (an amount) on such an outcome or result (*bet $20 on a horse*). **3** *tr.* risk a sum of money against (a person). **4** *tr. informal* feel sure (*bet they've forgotten it*). **●** *n.* **1** the act of betting (*make a bet*). **2** the money etc. staked (*put a bet on*). **3** *informal* an opinion, esp. a quickly formed or spontaneous one (*my bet is that he won't come*). **4** *informal* a choice or course of action (*she's a good bet*). □ **you bet** you can be certain.

beta /'bi:tə/ *n.* **1** the second letter of the Greek alphabet (*B*, *β*). **2** (*attrib.*) designating the second of a series or set. **3** *Astronomy* the second brightest star in a constellation.

beta blocker *n.* a drug preventing stimulation of beta receptors.

beta carotene *n.* an isomer of carotene found in carrots etc., and converted in the body to vitamin A.

Betamax *n. proprietary* (also **Beta**) a standard format for video and videotapes using the whole area of the tape to record.

beta receptor *n.* one of two kinds of receptor in the sympathetic nervous system, which increase cardiac activity when stimulated.

beta test ● *n.* a test of computer hardware or software in the final stages of development, carried out by the users for whom it is intended (*compare* ALPHA TEST). **●** *v.tr.* (also **beta-test**) submit (a product) to a beta test.

beta version *n.* a version of a computer program or component used in beta testing.

betel /'bi:təl/ *n.* the leaf of the Asian evergreen climbing plant *Piper betle*, commonly chewed with parings of the areca nut in SE Asia.

betel nut *n.* = ARECA NUT.

bête noire /beit 'nwɑr/ *n.* (*pl.* **bêtes noires** *pronunc.* same) a person etc. one particularly dislikes or fears.

betide *v.tr.* happen to (*woe betide you if you do!*).

betoken *v.tr.* **1** be a sign of; indicate. **2** augur.

betray *v.tr.* **1** place (a person, one's country, etc.) in the hands or power of an enemy. **2** be disloyal to (another person, a person's trust, etc.). **3** reveal involuntarily or treacherously; be evidence of (*his shaking hand betrayed his fear*). **4** lead astray or into error. □ **betrayal** *n.* **betrayer** *n.*

betroth /bi'trəʊð/ *v.tr. formal* bind with a promise to marry. □ **betrothal** *n.*

betrothed /bi'trəʊð, -ðəd/ *formal* **●** *n.* the person to whom one is betrothed; one's fiancé or fiancée. **●** *adj.* engaged to be married.

better ● *adj.* (*comparative of* GOOD) **1** of a more excellent or outstanding or desirable kind. **2** partly or fully recovered from illness (*feeling better*). **●** *adv.* (*comparative of* WELL[1]) **1** in a better manner (*she sings better*). **2** to a greater degree (*like it better*). **3** more usefully or advantageously (*is better forgotten*). **●** *n.* **1** that which is better (*the better of the two*). **2** (usu. in *pl.*) one's superior in ability or rank (*take notice of your betters*). **●** *v.* **1** *tr.* improve on; surpass (*I can better his offer*). **2** *tr.* make better; improve. **3** *refl.* improve one's position etc. **4** *intr.* become better; improve. □ **better off** in a better (esp. financial) position. **better than** more than. **the better part of** most of. **the better to ...** so as to ... better (*the better to see*). **for better or for worse** whatever changes may take place; whatever happens. **get the better of** defeat, outwit; win an advantage over. **go one better 1** outbid etc. by one. **2** outdo another person. **had better** would find it wiser to. **no better than** merely. **no better than one should** (or **ought to**) **be** of doubtful moral character, esp. sexually promiscuous.

better half *n. informal jocular* one's spouse.

betterment *n.* making better; improvement.

betting *n.* **1** gambling by risking money on an unpredictable outcome. **2** the odds offered in this.

bettor *n.* a person who bets.

between ● *prep.* **1 a** at or to a point in the area or interval bounded by two or more other points in space, time, etc. **b** along the extent of such an area or interval (*are five houses between here and the main road*; *works best between five and six*). **2** separating, physically or conceptually (*the distance between here and Regina*; *the difference between right and wrong*). **3 a** by combining the resources of (*great potential between* *them).* **b** shared by; as the joint resources of (*$5 between them*). **c** by joint or reciprocal action (*an agreement between us*). ¶Use in sense 3 with reference to more than two people or things is established and acceptable (e.g. *relations between Canada, the US, and Mexico*). **4** to and from (*runs between Ottawa and Montreal*). **5** taking one and rejecting the other of (*decide between eating here and going out*). ● *adv.* (also **in between**) at a point or in the area bounded by two or more other points in space, time, sequence, etc. (*not fat or thin but in between*). □ **between ourselves** (or **you and me**) in confidence. **between times** occasionally.

bevel /'bevəl/ ● *n.* **1** a sloping surface or edge; a slope from the horizontal or vertical in carpentry etc. **2** (in full **bevel square**) an adjustable tool for marking angles in carpentry etc. ● *v.* (**bevelled, bevelling**) **1** *tr.* reduce (a square edge) to a sloping edge. **2** *intr.* slope at an angle; slant.

beverage *n.* a drink (*alcoholic beverages*).

beverage room *n. Cdn* a lounge, bar, etc. where alcoholic drinks are sold.

bevy /'bevi/ *n.* (*pl.* **-ies**) a group or company of any kind.

bewail *v.tr.* **1** greatly regret or lament. **2** wail over; mourn for. □ **bewailer** *n.*

beware *v.* (only in *imper.* or *infin.*) **1** *intr.* be cautious, take heed (*beware of the dog; beware that you don't fall*). **2** *tr.* be cautious of (*beware the Ides of March*).

bewilder *v.tr.* utterly perplex or confuse. □ **bewildered** *adj.* **bewilderedly** *adv.* **bewildering** *adj.* **bewilderingly** *adv.* **bewilderment** *n.*

bewitch *v.tr.* **1** enchant; greatly delight. **2** subject to the influence of magic or witchcraft. □ **bewitching** *adj.* **bewitchingly** *adv.* **bewitchment** *n.*

beyond ● *prep.* **1** at or to the further side of (*beyond the river*). **2** outside the scope, range, or understanding of (*beyond repair*). **3** more than. ● *adv.* **1** at or to the further side. **2** further on. ● *n.* (prec. by *the*) the unknown after death.

bezel /'bezəl/ *n.* **1** the sloped edge of a chisel. **2** the oblique faces of a cut gem. **3 a** a groove holding a watch glass or gem. **b** a rim holding a glass etc. cover, e.g. on a clock, navigational instrument, etc.

BF *abbr.* butterfat.

BFA *abbr.* Bachelor of Fine Arts.

BGen *abbr. Cdn* = BRIGADIER GENERAL.

BGH *abbr.* BOVINE GROWTH HORMONE.

B.G.S. *abbr.* Bachelor of General Studies.

Bhagavad-Gita /ˌbʌgəvʌd'giːtɑ/ *n.* the most famous religious text of Hinduism, an independent devotional work incorporated into the Mahabharata.

bhangra /'bæŋgrə/ *n.* a style of popular (esp. dance) music combining Punjabi folk music with rock or disco elements.

BHT *abbr.* butylated hydroxytoluene, an antioxidant used to retard rancidity in foods containing fats etc.

Bi *symbol* the element bismuth.

bi *n. & adj. informal* bisexual.

bi- *comb. form* forming nouns and adjectives meaning: **1** having two; a thing having two (*bilateral*). **2 a** occurring twice in every one or once in every two (*bi-weekly*). **b** lasting for two (*biennial*). **3** doubly; in two ways (*biconvex*). **4** *Chem.* a substance having a double proportion of the acid etc. indicated by the simple word (*bicarbonate*).

BIA *abbr. Cdn* **1** Business Improvement Association, a grouping of businesses which promotes commerce in a designated area and lobbies for the area's interests.

2 Business Improvement Area, the area served by a Business Improvement Association.

bi and bi *n. Cdn* bilingualism and biculturalism.

biannual *adj.* occurring, appearing, etc., twice a year (compare BIENNIAL). □ **biannually** *adv.*

bias ● *n.* **1** (often foll. by *towards, against*) a predisposition or prejudice. **2** a systematic distortion of a statistical result due to a factor not allowed for in its derivation. **3** a diagonal line or cut across the weave of a fabric. **4 a** the irregular shape given to a ball in lawn bowling. **b** the oblique course this causes it to run. **5** a steady voltage, magnetic field, etc., applied to an electronic system or device, esp. to minimize distortion in tape recording. ● *v.tr.* (**biased, biasing**) **1** influence (usu. unfairly); prejudice. **2** give a bias to.

biased *adj.* having a bias; prejudiced.

bias-ply *adj. N Amer.* (of a tire) having fabric layers with cords lying crosswise (compare RADIAL *adj.* 4).

biathlon /bai'æθlɒn/ *n. Sport* an athletic contest in cross-country skiing and shooting or in cycling and running. □ **biathlete** *n.*

bib *n.* **1** a piece of cloth or plastic fastened around the neck, esp. of a baby, to keep the clothes clean during a meal. **2** the top front part of an apron, overalls, etc. **3** a coloured patch on the chest of certain dogs, cats, etc. □ **best bib and tucker** best clothes.

bibb *n.* a mild and tender head lettuce with loose, dark green leaves.

Bible *n.* **1 a** the Christian scriptures consisting of the Old and New Testaments. **b** the Jewish scriptures. **c** (*also* **bible**) any copy of these. **d** a particular edition of the Bible (*New English Bible*). **2** (usu. **bible**) any authoritative book (*the gardener's bible*). **3** the scriptures of any non-Christian religion.

Bible belt *n.* esp. *N Amer.* any area known for its fundamentalist Christian beliefs.

Bible school *n.* **1** (also **Bible college**) a post-secondary institution offering courses in theology, esp. for evangelical Protestants. **2** *N Amer.* an organized course of study devoted to the Bible.

Bible-thumping *n. informal* aggressive fundamentalist preaching. □ **Bible-thumper** *n.*

Biblical *adj.* (also **biblical**) **1** of, concerning, or contained in the Bible. **2** resembling the language of the King James Bible. □ **biblically** *adv.*

bibliography *n.* (*pl.* **-ies**) **1 a** a list of the books referred to in a scholarly work, usu. printed as an appendix. **b** a list of the books of a specific author or publisher, or on a specific subject, etc. **2 a** the history or description of books, including authors, editions, etc. **b** any book containing such information. □ **bibliographer** *n.* **bibliographic** *adj.* **bibliographical** *adj.* **bibliographically** *adv.*

bibliophile /'bɪblioˌfaɪl/ *n.* a person who collects or is fond of books. □ **bibliophilic** /-'fɪlɪk/ *adj.*

bib overalls *n. N Amer.* loose-fitting pants with fabric extending up to cover the front torso, fastened around the neck or over the shoulders.

bicameral /bai'kæmərəl/ *adj.* (esp. of a parliament or legislative body) having two chambers.

bicarbonate /bai'kɑrbəneit, -nət/ *n.* **1** *Chem.* any acid salt of carbonic acid. **2** (in full **bicarbonate of soda**) = BAKING SODA.

bicentenary ● *n.* (*pl.* **-ies**) **1** a bicentennial. **2** a celebration of this. ● *adj.* of a bicentenary.

bicentennial esp. *N Amer.* ● *n.* a two-hundredth anniversary. ● *adj.* **1** lasting two hundred years or occurring every two hundred years. **2** of or concerning a bicentennial.

bicep /ˈbaisep/ n. informal a biceps muscle. ¶Although bicep is becoming more common in informal use, biceps remains standard as the singular noun.

biceps n. (pl. same) the flexor muscle at the front of the upper arm or at the back of the thigh.

bicker v.intr. quarrel pettily; wrangle. □ **bickerer** n.

bicolour ● adj. (also **bicoloured**) having two colours. ● n. a bicolour blossom or animal.

biconvex adj. (esp. of a lens) convex on both sides.

bicultural adj. having or involving two cultures, esp. (in Canada) English-Canadian and French-Canadian. □ **biculturalism** n.

bicuspid /baiˈkʌspɪd/ ● adj. having two cusps or points. ● n. **1** the premolar tooth in humans. **2** a tooth with two cusps.

bicycle ● n. a vehicle with two wheels held in a frame one behind the other, propelled by pedals and steered with handlebars attached to the front wheel. ● v.intr. ride a bicycle. □ **bicycler** n. **bicyclist** n.

bicycle shorts n.pl. **1** tight-fitting, thigh-length elastic shorts with a padded crotch, worn esp. by cyclists. **2** a tight-fitting undergarment extending from the waist to mid-thigh.

bid ● v. (**bidding**) **1** tr. & intr. (past and past part. **bid**) (often foll. by for, against) **a** (esp. at an auction) offer (a certain price) (did not bid for the vase; bid $100). **b** offer to do work etc. for a stated price. **2** tr. (past **bid**, **bade** /beid, bæd/; past part. **bid**, **bidden**) **a** command; order (bid the soldiers shoot). **b** invite (bade her start). **3** tr. (past **bade**, **bid**; past part. **bidden**, **bid**) utter (greeting or farewell) to (I bade him welcome). **4** (past and past part. **bid**) Cards a intr. state before play how many tricks one intends to make. **b** tr. state (one's intended number of tricks). ● n. **1** a (esp. at an auction) an offer (of a price) (a bid of $5). **b** an offer (to do work, supply goods, etc.) at a stated price; a tender. **2** Cards a statement of the number of tricks a player proposes to make. **3** an attempt; an effort (a bid for power). □ **bid fair to** seem likely to. (**make a**) **bid for** try to gain. □ **bidder** n.

biddable adj. obedient. □ **biddability** n.

bidding n. **1** the offers made for something being sold. **2** Cards the act of making a bid or bids. **3** a command, request, or invitation.

biddy n. (pl. **-ies**) slang derogatory a woman (old biddy).

bide v.intr. □ **bide one's time** await one's best opportunity.

bidet /biːˈdei/ n. a low oval bathroom fixture used for washing the genital and anal regions.

biennial /baiˈeniəl/ ● adj. **1** recurring every two years (compare BIANNUAL). **2** lasting two years. ● n. **1** Bot. a plant that takes two years to grow from seed to fruition and die (compare ANNUAL, PERENNIAL). **2** an event celebrated or taking place every two years. □ **biennially** adv.

bier n. a movable frame on which a coffin or a corpse is placed or taken to a grave.

biff slang ● n. a sharp blow. ● v.tr. strike (a person).

biffy n. (pl. **-ies**) N Amer. (esp. West) informal **1** an outhouse. **2** a toilet.

bifocal ● adj. having two focuses, esp. of a lens with a part for distant vision and a part for near vision. ● /ˈbaifoːkəl/ n. (in pl.) bifocal glasses.

bifold ● adj. designating a two-piece door which moves on tracks and folds along a hinge down the centre. ● n. a bifold door.

bifurcate /ˈbaifər,keit, baiˈfɜrkeit, -kət/ ● v.tr. & intr. divide into two branches; fork. ● adj. forked; branched. □ **bifurcation** n.

big ● adj. (**bigger**, **biggest**) **1** a of considerable size, amount, intensity, etc. **b** of a large or the largest size (big toe). **2** a significant; outstanding (my big chance). **b** famous, popular (a big celebrity). **3** a grown up (a big boy now). **b** elder (big sister). **4** informal **a** boastful (big words). **b** often ironic generous (big of him). **c** ambitious (big ideas). **d** (of a game etc.) well-played. **5** a advanced in pregnancy (big with child). **b** fecund (big with consequences). ● adv. informal in a big manner, esp.: **1** effectively (went over big). **2** boastfully (talk big). **3** ambitiously (think big). **4** to a considerable extent (win big). ● n. N Amer. (in pl.) the major baseball leagues. □ **be big on** be enthusiastic about. **come** (or **go**) **over big** make a great effect. **come up big** perform successfully when relied upon to do so. **in a big way 1** on a large scale. **2** informal with great enthusiasm, display, etc. **look** (or **talk**) **big** boast. **make it big** achieve great success. **too big for one's britches** (or **boots**) slang conceited. □ **biggish** adj. **bigness** n.

bigamy /ˈbɪɡəmi/ n. (pl. **-ies**) the crime of marrying when one is lawfully married to another person. □ **bigamist** n. **bigamous** adj.

big band n. a large jazz or swing orchestra.

big bang n. **1** Astronomy the violent explosion of all matter from a state of high density and temperature, postulated as the origin of the universe. **2** any sudden or dramatic beginning of drastic change.

Big Blue Machine n. Cdn the Ontario Progressive Conservative Party during the premiership of William Davis (1971–85).

Big Board n. US informal the New York Stock Exchange.

big box n. N Amer. a very large, warehouse-style store, often specializing in one kind of merchandise (e.g. books), usu. at lower prices than in other stores.

Big Brother n. **1** an all-powerful dictator or government which keeps the populace under close observation and strict control. **2** an adult who befriends a fatherless child, esp. through an agency. □ **Big Brotherism** n. (in sense 1).

big bucks n. N Amer. slang a great deal of money.

big business n. large commercial, industrial, or financial companies, esp. when having a significant social, economic, or political influence.

big C n. informal cancer.

big cat n. any of the larger members of the feline family, e.g. lions, leopards, tigers, etc.

big cheese n. informal a very important person.

big deal n. informal something important.

Bigfoot n. = SASQUATCH.

big game n. large animals hunted for sport.

biggie n. informal a very important person etc.

big government n. government characterized by large-scale participation in domestic affairs.

big gun n. informal **1** an important person, company, etc. **2** Sport a high-scoring player.

big hair n. informal a bouffant hairstyle with the hair standing upwards or outwards from the head.

big head n. informal a conceited person. □ **have a big head** be conceited. □ **big-headed** adj.

big heart n. a generous nature. □ **big-hearted** adj.

bighorn n. a N American sheep, Ovis canadensis, with large curving horns, esp. native to the Rockies.

big house n. (also **Big House**) **1** slang a prison. **2** N Amer. a communal dwelling, sometimes up to 18 m (60 ft.) in length, used by West Coast Aboriginal peoples, with a section for each family as well as a central common area. **3** Cdn hist. the residence of the chief trader at a fur-trading post.

bight /baɪt/ n. **1** a curve or recess in a coastline, river, etc. **2** a loop of rope.

big idea n. often ironic the important intention or scheme.

big kahuna n. N Amer. slang **1** an important person; a big shot. **2** anything very large, esp. a large wave.

big league N Amer. ● n. **1** the highest professional league in a sport, esp. baseball. **2** the highest class in any field (made it to the big leagues). ● adj. (**big-league**) first-class; worthy of being in the big leagues. □ **big-leaguer** n.

big lie n. esp. N Amer. an intentional distortion of facts, esp. by a politician, official body, etc.

big money n. **1** a great deal of money, esp. as pay or profit. **2** large corporations, the very wealthy, etc.

bigmouth n. a talkative or boastful person.

big name n. a famous person (often attrib.: big-name stars).

big one n. informal **1** a major event. **2** (also **Big One**) (usu. prec. by the) an anticipated massive earthquake along the San Andreas Fault in California. **3** a sum of money or a banknote representing it (fifty big ones).

bigot /ˈbɪɡət/ n. a person intolerant of another's beliefs, race, politics, etc. □ **bigoted** adj. **bigotry** n.

big picture n. (prec. by the) an issue etc. viewed or understood as a whole.

big screen n. **1** the screen in a movie theatre. **2** (usu. prec. by the) motion pictures collectively, esp. as seen in theatres (appearing on the big screen).

big shot n. informal **1** an important person, esp. in a corporation etc. **2** a pretentious person.

Big Sister n. an adult who befriends a motherless child, esp. through an agency.

big smoke n. informal (prec. by the) any large city.

big spender n. an extravagant person.

Big Three n. (usu. prec. by the) (in N America) the three largest automakers.

big-ticket attrib.adj. expensive (big-ticket items).

big time informal ● n. the highest level of success in a profession, esp. entertainment (dreams of the big time). ● adv. esp. N Amer. as an intensifier (lost big time). □ **big-time** adj. **big-timer** n.

big toe n. either of the innermost and largest toes.

big top n. **1** the main tent of a circus. **2** a circus. **3** a tent capable of holding a large gathering.

biguine var. of BEGUINE.

bigwig n. (N Amer. also **big wheel**) informal an important person.

bike informal ● n. a bicycle or motorcycle. ● v.intr. ride a bicycle or motorcycle.

biker n. **1** a cyclist, esp. a motorcyclist. **2** a member of a motorcycle gang.

bikeway n. N Amer. a transportation route reserved for or specially adapted for bicycles.

bikini n. **1** a two-piece bathing suit for women, the bottom half of which consists of skimpy briefs not reaching above the top of the pelvis. **2** a skimpy bathing suit for men, similar to the bottom half of a bikini. **3** = BIKINI BRIEFS. **4** (attrib.) designating the pubic hairline, esp. of a woman (bikini line). □ **bikinied** adj.

bikini briefs n.pl. (also **bikini underwear**) skimpy briefs.

bilateral /baɪˈlætərəl/ adj. **1** of, on, or with two sides. **2** affecting or between two parties, countries, etc. (bilateral negotiations). □ **bilaterally** adv.

bilateral symmetry n. a type of body arrangement in which there is only one plane along which an organism can be divided into two symmetrical halves.

Bildungsroman /ˈbɪldʊŋzroː,mɒn/ n. a novel dealing with one person's early life and development.

bile n. **1** a bitter greenish-brown alkaline fluid which aids digestion and is secreted by the liver and stored in the gallbladder. **2** bad temper; peevish anger.

bile duct n. the duct which conveys bile from the liver and the gallbladder to the duodenum.

bi-level ● adj. **1** having or functioning on two levels. **2** N Amer. designating a style of two-storey house in which the lower storey is partially sunk below ground level, and the main entrance is between the two storeys. ● n. N Amer. a bi-level house.

bilge /bɪldʒ/ n. **1 a** the lowest area inside a ship, where water collects. **b** the area on the outer surface of a ship's hull where the flat bottom meets the vertical side. **2** (in full **bilge water**) a filthy water that collects inside the bilge. **b** informal nonsense. ● v. **1** tr. stave in the bilge of (a ship). **2** intr. spring a leak in the bilge. **3** intr. swell out; bulge.

bilingual /baɪˈlɪŋɡwəl, baɪˈlɪŋɡjuːəl/ ● adj. **1** able to speak two languages, esp. fluently. **2** spoken or written in or involving two languages. ● n. a bilingual person. □ **bilingually** adv.

bilingualism n. **1** the ability to speak two languages, esp. (in Canada) English and French. **2** a policy promoting this among a population.

bilingualize v.tr. Cdn make bilingual.

bilious /ˈbɪljəs, ˈbɪlɪəs/ adj. **1** affected by a disorder of the bile. **2** bad-tempered. **3** of or like bile; nauseating (bilious haze). □ **biliously** adv. **biliousness** n.

bilk v.tr. informal **1** cheat. **2** avoid paying (a creditor or debt). □ **bilker** n.

bill[1] ● n. **1 a** a printed or written statement of charges for goods supplied or services rendered. **b** the amount owed; the cost of something (ran up a bill of $300). **2** = BILL OF EXCHANGE. **3** a draft of a proposed law. **4 a** a printed list, esp. a concert or theatre program. **b** the entertainment itself (double bill). **5** N Amer. a banknote (ten-dollar bill). **6** Cdn (Nfld) the share of a fishing or sealing season's profit paid as wages to each fisherman or sealer. **7 a** a poster; a placard. **b** = HANDBILL. ● v.tr. **1** present publicly (the trip was billed as a fact-finding tour). **2** invoice (bill me for the books). □ **billable** adj.

bill[2] ● n. **1** the beak of a bird, esp. when it is slender, flattened, or weak, or belongs to a web-footed bird or a bird of the pigeon family. **2** the muzzle of a platypus. **3** the long, pointed upper jaw of marlins, sailfish, etc. **4** N Amer. the visor on a baseball cap. **5** a narrow promontory. ● v.intr. (of doves etc.) stroke a bill with a bill. □ **bill and coo** exchange caresses. □ **billed** adj. (usu. in comb.).

billboard n. a large outdoor board for ads etc.

billet[1] ● n. **1 a** a place, esp. a private home, where a student, soldier, etc. is provided with accommodation, usu. without charge. **b** a written order requiring a householder to lodge the bearer. **2** informal a situation; a job. ● v. (**billeted**, **billeting**) **1** tr. (usu. foll. by on, in, at) arrange temporary free lodging for. **2** tr. (of a householder) provide with board and lodging. **3** intr. take lodging with a billet.

billet[2] n. **1** a thick piece of wood, esp. one cut for firewood. **2** a metal bar.

billet-doux /ˌbɪleɪˈduː, ˌbɪli-/ n. (pl. **billets-doux** /-ˈduːz/) often jocular a love letter.

billfish n. (pl. same or **-fishes**) any of various large marine game fishes of the family Istiophoridae, with long spearlike upper jaws.

billfold n. N Amer. a wallet for keeping paper money.

billiards n. **1 a** any of various games played on an oblong cloth-covered table, with a cue used to strike a number of balls. **b** a version of this using three balls, either with pockets around the edge of the table (**English billiards**) or without (**carom**, or **French billiards**). **2** (**billiard**) (in *comb.*) used in billiards.

billing *n.* **1** *in senses of* BILL[1] *v.* **2** placement in a list of performers (*received top billing*).

billion ● *n.* (*pl.* same or (in sense 2) **-s**) (in *sing.* prec. by *a* or *one*) **1** a thousand million (1,000,000,000 or 10⁹). **2** (in *pl.*) *informal* a very large number (*billions of years*). ● *adj.* that amount to a billion. □ **billionth** *adj. & n.*

billionaire *n.* a person possessing over a billion dollars, pounds, etc.

bill of exchange *n.* a written order to pay a sum of money on a given date to the drawer or to a payee.

bill of fare *n.* **1** a menu. **2** an offering of entertainment.

bill of health *n.* **1** *Naut.* a certificate regarding infectious disease on a ship or in a port at the time of sailing. **2** (**clean bill of health**) **a** such a certificate stating that there is no disease. **b** a declaration that a person or thing examined has been found to be free of illness or in good condition.

bill of lading *n.* a list of goods delivered to a carrier by a shipper, including a shipping agreement.

Bill of Rights *n. Law* (also **bill of rights**) a statement of the rights of a group of people.

bill of sale *n.* **1** a printed record of a purchase; a receipt. **2** a certificate of transfer of personal property, esp. as a security against debt.

billow ● *n.* **1** a wave. **2** a soft rising flow, as of smoke. **3** any large soft mass. ● *v.intr.* **1** (of the sea, smoke, etc.) rise in billows; surge. **2** (of sails etc.) swell or undulate, as in the wind. □ **billowy** *adj.*

billy *n.* (*pl.* **-ies**) (in full **billycan**) a tin or enamel pot with a lid and wire handle, for outdoor cooking.

billy club *n. N Amer.* a police officer's truncheon.

billy goat *n.* (also **billy** *pl.* **-ies**) a male goat.

bimah /'biːmə/ *n.* (also **bima**) a raised platform for readers in a synagogue.

bimbo *n.* (*pl.* **-os**) *slang usu. derogatory* **1** (also **bimbette**) a woman, esp. a young, sexually attractive, unintelligent one. **2** a person.

bimonthly ● *adj.* occurring every two months or twice a month. ● *adv.* every two months or twice a month. ● *n.* (*pl.* **-ies**) a periodical produced bimonthly. ¶Often avoided, because of the ambiguity of meaning, in favour of *biweekly* or *twice-monthly*.

bin ● *n.* **1** a large receptacle for storage or for depositing rubbish, recyclables, etc. **2** a partitioned stand for storing bottles of wine. **3** *slang* = LOONY BIN. ● *v.tr.* (**binned**, **binning**) *informal* store or put in a bin.

binary /'baɪnəri, -,neri/ ● *adj.* **1 a** dual. **b** of or involving a pair or pairs. **2** of the arithmetical system using 2 as a base. ● *n.* (*pl.* **-ies**) **1** something having two parts. **2** a binary star. **3** a binary number.

binary code *n. Computing* a coding system using the binary digits 0 and 1 to represent a letter, digit, or other character in a computer (*see* BCD).

binary compound *n. Chem.* a compound having two elements or radicals.

binary number *n.* (also **binary digit**) one of two digits (usu. 0 or 1) in a binary system of notation.

binary system *n.* **1** (also **binary star**) a system of two stars orbiting each other. **2** a system in which information can be expressed by combinations of the digits 0 and 1 (corresponding to 'off' and 'on').

binational *adj.* involving two nations.

bind ● *v.* (*past and past part.* **bound**) **1** *tr.* (often foll. by *to*, *on*, *together*) tie or fasten tightly, attach. **2** *tr.* restrain;

put in bonds. **3** *tr.* **a** esp. *Cooking* cause (ingredients) to cohere using another ingredient. **b** hold by chemical bonding; combine with. **4** *tr.* fasten or hold together as a single mass. **5** *tr.* compel; impose an obligation or duty on. **6** *tr.* **a** edge (fabric etc.) with braid etc. **b** fix together and fasten (the pages of a book) in a cover. **7** *tr.* constipate. **8** *tr.* ratify (a bargain, agreement, etc.). **9** *tr.* (in *passive*) be required by an obligation or duty (*am bound to answer*). **10** *tr.* (often foll. by *up*) **a** put a bandage or other covering around. **b** fix together with something put around (*bound her hair*). **11** *tr.* indenture as an apprentice. **12** *intr.* (of snow etc.) cohere, stick. **13** *intr.* be prevented from moving freely. ● *n.* **1** a difficult situation; a position that prevents free action. **2** *informal* a nuisance; a restriction. **3** = BINE. □ **bind over** *Law* order (a person) to do something, esp. keep the peace. **bind up** bandage.

binder *n.* **1** a detachable cover for sheets of paper, magazines, etc. **2** a substance that acts cohesively. **3** esp. *hist.* a machine for binding grain into sheaves. **4** a bookbinder.

binder twine *n.* a coarse twine used esp. to tie bales of hay, straw, etc.

binding ● *n.* **1** the strong covering of a book holding the sheets together. **2** the fastening attaching a boot to a ski. **3** a trim for binding raw edges of fabric. ● *adj.* **1** legally enforceable (*binding arbitration*). **2** causing or tending to cohere.

bindweed *n.* any of various twining plants of the morning glory family (Convolvulaceae), with funnel-shaped flowers.

bine *n.* **1** the twisting stem of a climbing plant, esp. the hop. **2** a flexible shoot.

bing *interj.* indicating a sudden action or event.

Bing cherry *n. N Amer.* a large, dark red cherry.

binge ● *n.* a period of uncontrolled indulgence in some activity, esp. eating or drinking. ● *v.intr.* (**bingeing** or **binging**; *past* and *past part.* **binged**) indulge in uncontrolled eating, drinking, shopping, etc. □ **binger** *n.*

bingo ● *n.* a game for any number of players, each having a card of squares with numbers, which are marked off as numbers are randomly drawn by a caller. ● *interj.* indicating a sudden action or event, or satisfaction, etc., as in winning at bingo.

binocular /bɪ'nɒkjʊlər, baɪ-/ ● *adj.* adapted for or using both eyes. ● *n.* /bɪ'nɒkjʊlər/ = BINOCULARS.

binoculars *n.pl.* an optical instrument with lenses for each eye, for viewing distant objects.

binomial /baɪ'noʊmiəl/ ● *n.* **1** an algebraic expression of the sum or the difference of two terms. **2** a two-part name, esp. in taxonomy. ● *adj.* consisting of two terms. □ **binomially** *adv.*

bio *n. informal* **1** *N Amer.* a biography. **2** biology.

bio- *comb. form* **1** life (*biography*). **2** of living beings (*biochemistry*). **3** biology (*biomedicine*).

bioaccumulate *v.intr.* (of poisons, chemicals, etc.) collect in animal tissue in progressively higher concentrations towards the top of the food chain.

biochem. /'baɪoʊ:,kem/ *abbr. & n.* biochemistry.

biochemistry *n.* the study of the chemical and physicochemical processes of living organisms. □ **biochemical** *adj.* **biochemist** *n.*

biocide /'baɪə,saɪd/ *n.* **1** a poisonous substance, esp. a pesticide, herbicide, etc. **2** the destruction of life.

biodegradable *adj.* capable of being decomposed by bacteria etc. □ **biodegradability** *n.*

biodegrade *v.intr.* decompose through the action of bacteria etc. □ **biodegradation** *n.*

biodiversity *n.* variety of species.

bioengineering *n.* **1** the application of engineering techniques to biological processes. **2** the use of artificial tissues, organs, or organ components to replace damaged or absent parts of the body, e.g. artificial limbs, pacemakers, etc. **3** the industrial use of biological processes. □ **bioengineer** *n. & v.*

bioethics *n.pl.* (treated as *sing.*) the ethics of medical and biological research and practice. □ **bioethical** *adj.* **bioethicist** *n.*

biofeedback *n.* the use of electronic monitoring of a normally automatic bodily function, e.g. temperature, in order to train a person to acquire voluntary control of it.

biogeography *n.* the scientific study of the geographical distribution of plants and animals. □ **biogeographic** *adj.* **biogeographical** *adj.*

biography *n.* (*pl.* **-ies**) **1 a** a written account of a person's life, usu. by another. **b** such writing as a branch of literature. **2** the course of a living (usu. human) being's life. □ **biographer** *n.* **biographic** *adj.* **biographical** *adj.*

biological ● *adj.* **1** (also **biologic**) of or relating to biology or living organisms. **2** (of a parent) involved in the procreation of the child in question, as opposed to its rearing. ● *n.* a biological product, esp. one used therapeutically or in biological control. □ **biologically** *adv.*

biological clock *n.* **1** an innate mechanism controlling the rhythmic physiological activities of an organism, e.g. sleep. **2** an innate mechanism regulating the aging process, esp. in relation to childbearing.

biological control *n.* the control of a pest by the introduction of a natural enemy.

biological weapon *n.* a weapon which unleashes toxins or harmful micro-organisms.

biology *n.* **1** the study of living organisms. **2** the plants and animals of an area. □ **biologist** *n.*

bioluminescence *n.* the emission of light by living organisms such as the firefly and glow-worm. □ **bioluminescent** *adj.*

biomass *n.* **1** the total quantity or weight of organisms in a given area or of a given species. **2** non-fossilized organic matter (esp. regarded as fuel).

biome /ˈbaɪoːm/ *n.* **1** a large, naturally-occurring community of flora and fauna adapted to the conditions in which they occur, e.g. tundra. **2** the geographical region containing such a community.

biomechanics *n.* the study of the mechanical laws relating to the movement or structure of organisms. □ **biomechanical** *adj.* **biomechanically** *adv.*

biomedicine *n.* the application of biology to clinical medicine. □ **biomedical** *adj.*

biometrics /ˌbaɪoˈmetrɪks/ *n.* (also **biometry** /baɪˈɒmɔtri/) the application of statistical analysis to biological investigation. □ **biometric** *adj.* **biometrical** *adj.* **biometrician** /ˌbaɪoˌmɔˈtrɪʃɔn/ *n.*

bionic *adj.* **1** having artificial body parts or the superhuman powers resulting from these. **2** relating to bionics. □ **bionically** *adv.*

bionics *n.pl.* (treated as *sing.*) the study of mechanical systems that function like living organisms or parts of living organisms.

biophysics *n.pl.* (treated as *sing.*) the science of the application of the laws of physics to biological phenomena. □ **biophysical** *adj.* **biophysicist** *n.*

biopic /ˈbaɪoːpɪk/ *n. informal* a biographical film.

biopsy /ˈbaɪɒpsi/ ● *n.* (*pl.* **-ies**) the removal and examination of tissue taken from a living body to discover the presence or extent of a disease. ● *v.tr.* (**-ies**, **-ied**) examine (tissue) for diagnostic purposes.

bioregion *n.* an area or region that constitutes a natural ecological community. □ **bioregional** *adj.*

BIOS /ˈbaɪoːs/ *abbr. Computing* firmware which controls many basic operations, such as booting.

biosphere /ˈbaɪɔˌsfiːr/ *n.* the regions of the earth's crust and atmosphere occupied by living organisms.

biota /baɪˈoːtɔ/ *n.* the animal and plant life of a region.

biotech /ˈbaɪoːtek/ *informal* ● *n.* biotechnology. ● *adj.* biotechnological.

biotechnology *n.* (*pl.* **-ies**) the exploitation of biological processes for industrial and other purposes, esp. genetic manipulation of micro-organisms. □ **biotechnological** *adj.*

biotic /baɪˈɒtɪk/ *adj.* **1** relating to life or to living things. **2** of biological origin.

biotin /ˈbaɪɔtɪn/ *n.* a vitamin of the B complex, found esp. in egg yolk, liver, and yeast, and involved in the metabolism of carbohydrates, fats, and proteins.

bipartisan *adj.* of or involving two (esp. political) parties. □ **bipartisanship** *n.*

bipartite /baɪˈpɑrtaɪt/ *adj.* **1** consisting of two parts. **2** shared by or involving two parties. **3** (of a contract, treaty, etc.) drawn up in two corresponding parts or between two parties.

biped ● *n.* a two-footed animal. ● *adj.* two-footed. □ **bipedal** *adj.* **bipedalism** *n.* **bipedality** *n.*

biphenyl /baɪˈfenɔl, -fiːnɔl/ *n. Chem.* a crystalline hydrocarbon containing two benzene rings.

biplane *n.* an early type of airplane having two sets of wings, one above the other (*compare* MONOPLANE).

bipolar *adj.* **1** having two poles or extremities. **2** characterized by two extremes. □ **bipolarity** *n.*

birch ● *n.* **1** any tree of the genus *Betula*, having thin peeling bark and slender branches, found predominantly in northern temperate regions. **2** (in full **birchwood**) the hard fine-grained pale wood of these trees. **3** (in full **birch rod**) a bundle of birch twigs used for flogging. ● *v.tr.* beat with a birch (in sense 3). ● *adj.* made of or derived from birch.

birchbark *n.* **1** the bark of *Betula papyrifera*, traditionally used by some Algonquian peoples to make canoes etc. **2** *N Amer.* such a canoe.

birch broom *n. Cdn* (*Nfld*) a broom made from birch twigs or whittled from a single stick of birch.

bird ● *n.* **1** a feathered, warm-blooded vertebrate of the class Aves, having a beak and wings, laying eggs, and usu. able to fly. **2** a game bird. **3** *informal* a person of a specified type (*a tough old bird*). **4** a shuttlecock. **5** *slang* **a** a booing etc. as an expression of disapproval. **b** *N Amer.* a gesture of contempt made by raising the middle finger. □ **a bird in the hand** something secured or certain. **the bird is** (or **has**) **flown** the prisoner etc. has escaped. **the birds and the bees** *euphemism* sexual activity and reproduction. **birds of a feather** people of like character. **for the birds** *informal* useless, not worth consideration. **have a bird** *N Amer. slang* become agitated (*Mom had a bird when I told her*). **eat like a bird** eat very small amounts. **a little bird** *informal* an unnamed informant.

bird bath *n.* a basin in a garden etc. with water for birds to bathe in.

birdbrain *n. informal* a silly or stupid person. □ **birdbrained** *adj.*

birdcage *n.* **1** a cage for birds usu. made of wire or cane. **2** an object of a similar design.

bird call *n.* **1** a bird's natural call. **2** an imitation of this. **3** an instrument imitating this.

bird course *n. Cdn derogatory slang* a university or high-school course requiring little work or ability.

bird dog *n.* **1** a hunting dog trained to retrieve birds. **2** *N Amer. informal* a scout for a sports team etc.

birder *n.* a birdwatcher.

bird feeder *n.* a raised platform or other receptacle for holding birdseed, erected to attract wild birds.

birdhouse *n.* a box designed to attract nesting birds.

birdie ● *n.* **1** *informal* a small bird. **2** *Golf* a score of one stroke under par at any hole. **3** a shuttlecock. **●** *v.tr.* (**birdies, birdied, birdieing**) *Golf* play (a hole) in one stroke under par.

birding *n.* birdwatching.

birdlife *n.* the birds of a region collectively.

bird of paradise *n.* **1** any bird of the family Paradiseidae found chiefly in New Guinea, the males having brilliantly coloured plumage. **2** a southern African plant with orange and blue flowers, *Strelitzia reginae*, cultivated for flower arrangements.

bird of prey *n.* a bird which hunts animals for food.

birdseed *n.* a blend of seed used in bird feeders etc.

bird's-eye maple *n.* the wood of the sugar maple used in panelling, cabinetmaking, etc., having a characteristic pattern of round black knots.

bird's-eye view *n.* **1** an overhead view (of a landscape etc.). **2** a general overview (of a subject etc.).

birdsong *n.* the musical call or sound of a bird.

birdwatcher *n.* a person who observes birds in their natural surroundings. □ **birdwatching** *n.*

Birkenstock /'bɜrkənstɒk/ *n. proprietary* a kind of flat-soled sandal with a contoured cork insole.

birl *v.tr. N Amer.* cause (a floating log) to rotate by using one's feet; spin. □ **birling** *n.*

birth ● *n.* **1** the emergence of a (usu. fully developed) infant or other young from the body of its mother. **2** the beginning or coming into existence of something (*the birth of socialism*). **3 a** origin, descent, ancestry (*of noble birth*). **b** high or noble birth; inherited position. **4** (*attrib.*) designating the parent who gave birth to or fathered a child (*birth mother*). **●** *v. N Amer.* **1** *tr.* give birth to. **2** *intr.* give birth. □ **give birth** bear a child etc. **give birth to 1** produce (young) from the womb. **2** cause to begin, found.

birth canal *n.* the canal comprising the cervix, vagina, and vulva, through which the fetus passes during delivery.

birth certificate *n.* an official document identifying a person by name and place and date of birth.

birth control *n.* the practice or methods of preventing pregnancy, esp. by contraception.

birth control pill *n.* an oral contraceptive containing progesterone and often estrogen, used to prevent ovulation.

birthdate *n.* one's date of birth.

birthday *n.* **1** the anniversary of a person's birth. **2** the day on which a person etc. was born. **3** the anniversary of the day on which something came into being (*July 1 is Canada's birthday*).

birthday suit *n. jocular* the bare skin; nakedness.

birthing *n.* the act or process of giving birth.

birthmark *n.* an unusual brown or red mark on one's body at or from birth.

birthplace *n.* **1** the place where a person was born. **2** a place of origin or commencement (*the birthplace of Confederation*).

birth rate *n.* the number of live births per thousand of population per year.

birthright *n.* a right of possession or privilege belonging to one from birth.

birthstone *n.* a gemstone popularly associated with the month of one's birth.

birth weight *n.* the weight of a baby at birth.

biscotti /bɪ'skɒti/ *n.pl. N Amer.* hard, dry, Italian cookies, usu. containing ground nuts.

biscuit ● *n.* **1** a dry, hard, flat, baked foodstuff (*dog biscuit*). **2** *N Amer.* = TEA BISCUIT. **3** fired unglazed pottery. **4** a light brown colour. **●** *adj.* biscuit-coloured. □ **have had the biscuit** *Cdn slang* be no longer good for anything; be done for.

bisect *v.tr.* **1** divide into two (strictly, equal) parts. **2** cut across. □ **bisection** *n.* **bisector** *n.*

bisexual ● *adj.* **1** sexually attracted to persons of both sexes. **2** *Biol.* having characteristics of both sexes. **3** of or concerning both sexes. **●** *n.* a bisexual person. □ **bisexuality** *n.*

bishop *n.* **1** a member of the highest rank of clerical hierarchy in some Christian denominations, usu. in charge of a diocese, and empowered to confer holy orders. **2** a chess piece which is moved diagonally and has the upper part shaped like a mitre.

bishopric /'bɪʃəprɪk/ *n.* **1** the office of a bishop. **2** a diocese.

bismarck /'bɪzmɑrk/ *n. N Amer.* **1** *Alta., Sask., & US Midwest* a sugar-coated jam-filled doughnut. **2** *Man.* a cream-filled doughnut, often with a chocolate glaze.

bismuth /'bɪzməθ/ *n.* **1** a brittle reddish-white metallic element, occurring naturally and used in alloys. **2** any compound of this used medicinally.

bison /'bɑɪsən, 'baɪzən/ *n.* (*pl.* same) either of two heavily built bovines of the genus *Bison*, *B. bison*, native to the N American plains, or *B. bonasus*, native to Europe, both having a high shoulder hump, shaggy hair, and a large head with short horns.

bisque¹ /bɪsk/ *n.* a rich soup usu. made from shellfish but also from game or vegetables.

bisque² *n.* **1** a variety of unglazed white porcelain used for statuettes etc. **2** = BISCUIT 4.

bistro /'biːstroː, 'bɪs-/ *n.* (*pl.* **-os**) a small restaurant.

bit¹ *n.* **1** a small piece or quantity. **2 a** a fair amount (*needed a bit of persuading*). **b** *informal* somewhat (*am a bit tired*). **c** (foll. by *of*) *informal* rather (*a bit of an idiot*). **3** a short time or distance (*wait a bit*). **4** a part, esp. of a film etc. (*I liked the bit where they fell in love*). **5** *N Amer. informal* a unit of 12 ¹⁄₂ cents (used only in even multiples). **6** (*attrib.*) relating to a minor speaking role in a film etc. (*bit part*). **7** *informal* a characteristic way of behaving (*the dog did its protective bit*). □ **bit by bit** gradually. **bit on the side** *slang* **1** a sexual relationship involving infidelity to one's partner. **2** the person with whom one is unfaithful. **bits and pieces** (or **bobs**) an assortment of small items. **do one's bit** *informal* make a useful contribution to an effort or cause. **not a bit** (**of it**) not at all. **to bits** into pieces.

bit² *past of* BITE.

bit³ ● *n.* **1** a metal mouthpiece on a bridle, used to control a horse. **2** a (usu. metal) tool or piece for boring or drilling. **3 a** the cutting or gripping part of a plane etc. **b** the cutting blade or edge of an axe etc. **4** the part of a key that engages with the lock lever. **●** *v.tr.* (**bitted, bitting**) **1** put a bit into the mouth of (a horse). **2** restrain. □ **chomp** (or **champ** or **chafe**) **at the bit** be restlessly impatient. **take the bit between** (or **in**) **one's teeth 1** take decisive personal action. **2** escape from control.

bit⁴ *n. Computing* a unit of information expressed as a choice between two possibilities; a 0 or 1 in binary code.

bitch ● *n.* **1** a female dog or other canine animal. **2** *offensive slang* a malicious, spiteful, or unpleasant woman. **3** *coarse slang* a very unpleasant or difficult thing or situation. ● *v.intr.* **1** (often foll. by *about*) speak scathingly. **2** complain. □ **bitchery** *n.*

bitchy *adj.* (**-ier, -iest**) *slang* spiteful; bad-tempered. □ **bitchily** *adv.* **bitchiness** *n.*

bite ● *v.* (*past* **bit**; *past part.* **bitten**) **1** *tr.* cut or puncture using the teeth. **2** *tr.* (foll. by *off*, *away*, etc.) detach with the teeth. **3** *tr.* wound with a sting, fangs, etc. **4** *intr.* **a** (of a wheel, screw, etc.) grip, penetrate. **b** Curling (of a rock) come to a stop. **5** *intr.* **a** (of fish) accept bait. **b** accept inducement or be taken in by a deception. **6** *intr.* have a (desired) adverse effect. **7** *tr.* (in *passive*) **a** take in; swindle. **b** (foll. by *by*, *with*, etc.) be infected by (enthusiasm etc.). **8** *intr.* (foll. by *at*) snap at. **9** *intr.* *N Amer. slang* be extremely bad or unpleasant (*this movie bites*). ● *n.* **1** an act of biting. **2** a wound or sore made by biting. **3 a** a mouthful of food. **b** a snack or light meal. **4** the taking of bait by a fish. **5** pungency (esp. of flavour). **6** incisiveness, sharpness. **7** a pithy quotation or excerpt (*sound bite*). **8** a portion exacted (*the tax bite*). **9** = OCCLUSION 3. □ **bite back** restrain (one's speech etc.). **bite the big one** *N Amer. slang* **1** die. **2** be very bad or unpleasant. **bite the bullet** *informal* behave bravely or stoically. **bite the dust** *slang* **1** die. **2** fail; break down. **bite the hand that feeds one** hurt or offend a benefactor. **bite a person's head off** *informal* respond fiercely or angrily. **bite one's tongue** refrain from speaking, esp. reluctantly. **bite off more than one can chew** take on a commitment one cannot fulfill. **once bitten twice shy** an unpleasant experience induces caution. **put the bite on** *N Amer. & Austral. slang* borrow or extort money from. **take a bite out of** *informal* reduce by a significant amount. **what's biting you?** *slang* what is annoying you? □ **biter** *n.*

bite-sized *adj.* (also **bite-size**) **1** small enough to be eaten in one mouthful. **2** very small or short.

biting *adj.* **1** that bites (*biting insects*). **2** stinging; intensely cold (*a biting wind*). **3** sharp; effective (*biting sarcasm*). □ **bitingly** *adv.*

bitmap *n.* *Computing* **1** a representation, e.g. of a computer memory, in which each item is represented by one bit. **2** a graphic display in which characters are formed by assigning a bit value to each individual pixel. □ **bitmapped** *adj.*

bitten *past part. of* BITE.

bitter ● *adj.* **1** having a sharp pungent taste. **2 a** caused by or showing mental pain or resentment (*bitter memories*). **b** painful or difficult to accept (*bitter disappointment*). **3** a virulent (*bitter animosity*). **b** piercingly cold. ● *n.* (in *pl.*) liquor with a bitter flavour (esp. of wormwood) used as an additive in cocktails. □ **to the bitter end** to the very end in spite of difficulties. □ **bitterly** *adv.* **bitterness** *n.*

bittern *n.* any of several marsh birds of the heron family, esp. of the genus *Botaurus*, with a booming call.

bitter pill *n.* something unpleasant that must be accepted or endured.

bittersweet ● *adj.* **1** sweet with a bitter aftertaste. **2** arousing pleasure tinged with pain or sorrow. ● *n.* **1 a** sweetness with a bitter aftertaste. **b** pleasure tinged with pain or sorrow. **2** any of several N American climbing vines of the genus *Celastrus*, esp. *C. scandens*. **3** = WOODY NIGHTSHADE.

bitty *adj.* (**-ier, -iest**) *N Amer. informal* very small.

bitumen /bɪˈtjuːmən, -ˈtuː-/ *n.* any of various tarlike mixtures of hydrocarbons derived from petroleum and used for road surfacing and roofing.

bituminous *adj.* of or containing bitumen.

bituminous coal *n.* a volatile form of coal burning with a smoky flame.

bivalent /baɪˈveɪlənt/ ● *adj.* **1** *Chem.* having a valence of two. **2** *Biol.* (of homologous chromosomes) associated in pairs. ● *n.* *Biol.* any pair of homologous chromosomes. □ **bivalence** *n.*

bivalve ● *n.* any of a group of aquatic molluscs of the class Bivalvia, with laterally compressed bodies enclosed within two hinged shells, e.g. oysters, mussels, etc. ● *adj.* **1** with a hinged double shell. **2** (of a seed capsule) having two valves.

bivouac /ˈbɪvʊˌwæk/ ● *n.* a temporary open encampment e.g. of soldiers. ● *v.intr.* (**bivouacked, bivouacking**) camp in a bivouac, esp. overnight.

biweekly ● *adv.* **1** every two weeks. **2** twice a week. ● *adj.* produced or occurring biweekly. ● *n.* (*pl.* **-ies**) a biweekly periodical. ¶See *bimonthly*.

biyearly ● *adv.* **1** every two years. **2** twice a year. ● *adj.* produced or occurring biyearly. ¶See *bimonthly*.

biz *n.* *informal* business.

bizarre *adj.* strange in appearance or effect; eccentric. □ **bizarrely** *adv.* **bizarreness** *n.*

bizarro *adj.* *N Amer. slang* bizarre.

B.J. *abbr.* Bachelor of Journalism.

Bk *symbol* berkelium.

bk. *abbr.* book.

BL *abbr.* **1** Bachelor of Law. **2** BILL OF LADING.

bl. *abbr.* **1** barrel. **2** black.

B.L.A. *abbr.* Bachelor of Landscape Architecture.

blab *v.* (**blabbed, blabbing**) **1** *intr.* **a** talk foolishly or indiscreetly. **b** reveal secrets. **2** *tr.* reveal (a secret etc.) by indiscreet talk. □ **blabby** *adj.*

blabber ● *n.* (also **blabbermouth**) a person who blabs. ● *v.intr.* (often foll. by *on*) talk foolishly or inconsequentially, esp. at length.

black ● *adj.* **1** very dark, having no colour from the absorption of all or nearly all incident light. **2** completely dark from the absence of a source of light (*black night*). **3** (also **Black**) **a** belonging or relating to any of various peoples having dark-coloured skin, esp. of African or Australian origin. **b** of or relating to black peoples or their culture (*black studies*). **4** (of the sky, a cloud, etc.) dusky; heavily overcast. **5** angry; threatening (*a black look*). **6** implying disgrace or condemnation (*in his black books*). **7** wicked, sinister (*black-hearted*). **8** gloomy, depressed (*a black mood*). **9** portending trouble or difficulty (*things looked black*). **10** (of hands etc.) dirty, soiled. **11** (of humour or its representation) with sinister as well as comic import (*a black comedy*). **12** (of coffee) without milk. **13** dark in colour as distinguished from a lighter variety (*black bear*; *black pine*). **14** *Cards* belonging to spades or clubs. ● *n.* **1** a black colour or pigment. **2** black clothes or material (*dressed in black*). **3 a** (in a game) a black piece etc. **b** the player using such pieces. **4** the absence of light on a stage or film set (*fade to black*). **5** the credit side of an account (*in the black*). **6** (also **Black**) a black person. ● *v.tr.* **1** make black (*blacked his face*). **2** polish with blacking. □ **black out 1 a** effect a blackout on. **b** undergo a blackout. **2** obscure windows etc. or extinguish all lights for protection esp. against an air attack. □ **blackish** *adj.* **blackly** *adv.* **blackness** *n.*

black and blue *adj.* discoloured by bruises.

black and white ● *n.* writing or printing (*in black and white*). ● *adj.* **1** (of film etc.) not in colour. **2**

consisting of extremes only, oversimplified (*interpreted the problem in black and white terms*).

black art *n.* = BLACK MAGIC.

black ash *n.* an ash of eastern N America, *Fraxinus nigra*, growing in swampy woodland.

blackball *v.tr.* **1** reject (a candidate) in a vote. **2** ostracize or exclude.

black bean *n.* **1** any of several leguminous plants of the genus *Phaseolus*. **2** the edible black seed of this plant. **3** a fermented soybean, used as flavouring in oriental cooking.

black bear *n.* either of two bears with black or blueblack fur, the American black bear *Ursus americanus* of N American forests, or the Asian black bear *Selenarctos thibetanus*.

black belt *n.* **1** a black belt worn by an expert in one of the martial arts. **2** a person qualified to wear this.

blackberry *n.* (*pl.* **-ies**) **1** any thorny shrub of the genus *Rubus*, esp. *R. fruticosus* and *R. allegheniensis*, bearing white or pink flowers. **2** a black fleshy edible fruit of this plant. **3** *Cdn* (*Nfld*) = CROWBERRY.

blackbird *n.* **1** *N Amer.* any of various birds of the subfamily Icterinae with mainly black plumage, esp. the red-winged blackbird and the grackle. **2** a common European thrush, *Turdus merula*.

black blizzard *n.* *Cdn* a dust storm of soil blown by high winds on the prairies.

blackboard *n.* a board with a smooth dark surface used in schools etc. for writing on with chalk.

black box *n.* **1** a flight recorder in an aircraft. **2** any complex piece of equipment, with contents which are mysterious to the user.

black bread *n.* a coarse dark type of rye bread.

black-capped chickadee *n.* see CHICKADEE.

black cherry *n.* **1** a cherry, *Prunus serotina*, of eastern N America, bearing dark, edible fruit. **2** this fruit.

blackcurrant *n.* **1** a widely cultivated shrub, *Ribes nigrum*, bearing flowers in racemes. **2** the small dark edible berry of this plant.

Black Death *n.* a pandemic of bubonic and pneumonic plague that killed perhaps one-third of the population of Europe in the mid-14th c. and resurfaced throughout the next few centuries.

black diamond *n.* **1** (in *pl.*) coal. **2** (*attrib.*) designating a particularly difficult ski run.

black duck *n.* a wild duck, *Anas rubripes*, predominantly dark brown with a purple patch on the wings, found throughout eastern Canada.

blacken *v.* **1** *tr. & intr.* make or become black or dark. **2** *tr.* speak evil of, defame (*blacken someone's character*).

blackened *adj.* (of food, esp. in Cajun dishes) cooked quickly over high heat; charred.

black English *n.* the form of English used by some N American blacks, esp. as an urban dialect.

black eye *n.* bruised or discoloured skin around the eye, esp. resulting from a blow.

black-eyed pea *n.* **1** a leguminous plant, *Vigna unguiculata* or *V. sinensis*, commonly grown for forage in the southern US. **2** the edible seed of this plant.

black-eyed Susan *n.* any of several plants having yellow flowers with dark centres, esp. *Thunbergia alata* and species of *Rudbeckia*.

blackface *n.* **1** facial makeup used by a non-black performer playing a black role. **2** a variety of sheep with a black face.

black flag *n.* a pirate's ensign.

blackfly *n.* (*pl.* **-flies**) *N Amer.* any of various gnatlike flies, esp. of the genus *Simulium*.

Blackfoot 1 (*pl.* same or **-feet**) a member of a group

of N American Aboriginal peoples comprising the Siksika, Blood, and Peigan, now largely found in S Alberta and Montana. **2** = SIKSIKA. **3** the Algonquian language of this people. ● *adj.* of or relating to the Blackfoot or their language.

Black Forest cake *n.* a layered chocolate cake with a filling of cherries and whipped cream.

Black Forest ham *n.* *N Amer.* a variety of sweetened and smoked ham.

black gold *n.* *informal* crude oil.

blackguard /'blægɑrd, -gərd, 'blæk,gɑrd / *n.* a scoundrel; an unscrupulous, unprincipled person.

blackhead *n.* a black-tipped plug of fatty matter in a skin follicle, esp. on the face.

black hole *n.* **1** a region of space having a gravitational field so intense that no matter and radiation can escape. **2** any inescapable void or place of confinement.

black ice *n.* thin hard transparent ice, esp. on a road surface or body of water.

blacking *n.* any black paste or polish, esp. for shoes.

blackjack ● *n.* **1 a** a card game in which players try to acquire cards with a face value exceeding the dealer's but no more than 21. **b** two cards totalling 21 in this game. **2** *N Amer.* a flexible bludgeon of leather-covered lead. **3** a shrubby oak of eastern N America, *Quercus marilandica*. **4** a pirates' black flag. ● *v.tr.* strike or beat with a blackjack.

blacklead /'blæk led / ● *n.* graphite. ● *v.tr.* polish with graphite.

blacklist ● *n.* a list of persons under suspicion, in disfavour, etc. ● *v.tr.* put the name of (a person) on a blacklist.

black locust *n.* a leguminous tree native to eastern N America, *Robinia pseudoacacia*, with pinnate leaves and black pods.

black magic *n.* magic involving supposed invocation of evil spirits.

blackmail ● *n.* **1 a** an extortion of payment in return for not disclosing discreditable information, a secret, etc. **b** any payment extorted in this way. **2** the use of threats or moral pressure. ● *v.tr.* **1** extort or try to extort money etc. from (a person) by blackmail. **2** threaten, coerce. □ **blackmailer** *n.*

black mark *n.* a mark of discredit.

black market *n.* an illicit traffic in officially controlled or scarce commodities. □ **black marketeer** *n.*

Black Mass *n.* **1** a travesty of the Mass said to be used in the cult of Satanism. **2** a requiem Mass in which the celebrant wears black vestments.

Black Muslim *n.* a follower of the Nation of Islam.

black nationalism *n.* a political and social movement originating in the US in the 1960s, advocating solidarity, pride, and self-government among blacks.

blackout *n.* **1** a temporary or complete loss of vision, consciousness, or memory. **2** a loss of power, radio reception, etc. **3** a compulsory period of darkness as a precaution against air raids. **4** a temporary suppression of the release of information, esp. from police or government sources. **5** a sudden darkening of a theatre stage. **6** *N Amer.* (often *attrib.*) a period in which discounts, esp. on airfare, do not apply.

black pepper *n.* a condiment made from the unripe ground or whole berries of *Piper nigrum*.

blackpoll *n.* (in full **blackpoll warbler**) a N American warbler, *Dendroica striata*, the male of which has a black crown in spring.

black powder *n.* = GUNPOWDER.

black power n. a movement in support of civil rights and political power for blacks.

black raspberry n. a N American raspberry, *Rubus occidentalis*, having black berries.

black robe n. *Cdn hist.* a Christian priest working as a missionary among Aboriginal peoples.

Black Rod n. (in full **Usher of the Black Rod**) (in Canada) the principal usher of the Senate, who summons the Commons to the Senate at the opening of Parliament. ¶Until 1997 the term in full was **Gentleman Usher of the Black Rod**.

black sheep n. *informal* an unsatisfactory member of a family, group, etc.; an outcast.

blackshirt n. a member of a militant fascist organization.

blacksmith n. **1** a smith who works in iron. **2** N Amer. = FARRIER 1. □ **blacksmithing** n.

black spot n. any of various diseases of plants causing the appearance of black spots.

black spruce n. a widely distributed spruce of Canada and the northeastern US, *Picea mariana*.

black squirrel n. a black phase of the grey squirrel.

blacktail n. (in full **blacktail deer, black-tailed deer**) = MULE DEER.

black tea n. tea that is fully fermented before drying.

blackthorn n. **1** a N American hawthorn, esp. *Crataegus calpodendron*. **2** a thorny European shrub, *Prunus spinosa*, bearing white-petalled flowers before small blue-black fruits. **3** a cudgel or walking stick made from the blackthorn.

black tie n. **1** a black bow tie worn with a tuxedo etc. **2** an occasion requiring that men wear a tuxedo (also attrib.: *black-tie dinner*) (compare WHITE TIE).

blacktop ● n. **1** a type of bituminous road-surfacing material; asphalt. **2** a road surfaced with this. ● v.tr. (**-topped, -topping**) surface with blacktop.

black walnut n. **1** a walnut tree, *Juglans nigra*, of the northeastern US and southern Canada, planted for its edible nut and as an ornamental. **2** the rich, dark brown wood of this tree, much prized in cabinetmaking. **3** the edible nut of this tree.

Black Watch n. **1** the Royal Highland Regiment of the Canadian Forces. **2** a very dark green and navy blue tartan.

black widow n. a venomous black spider of the genus *Latrodectus*, esp. *L. mactans*, the female of which usu. devours the male after mating.

bladder n. **1** any of various membranous sacs in some animals, containing urine (**urinary bladder**), bile (**gallbladder**), or air (**swim bladder**). **2** an inflated pericarp or vesicle in various plants. **3** anything inflated and hollow.

blade ● n. **1 a** the flat part of a knife, chisel, etc. that forms the cutting edge. **b** = RAZOR BLADE. **2** the flattened functional part of an oar, skate, hockey stick, etc. **3 a** the flat, narrow, usu. pointed leaf of grass and cereals. **b** the broad thin part of a leaf apart from the petiole. **4 a** a broad flat bone, esp. in the shoulder. **b** a cut of beef from behind the neck and above the shoulder. **5** a dashing, pleasure-seeking young man. ● v.intr. N Amer. = ROLLERBLADE v. □ **bladed** adj. (also in comb.). **blader** n. **blading** n.

blah informal ● n. **1** (also **blah-blah**) pretentious nonsense. **2** (in pl.) a general feeling of depression. ● adj. **1** dull, unexciting, bland. **2** lethargic, lacking in enthusiasm. ● interj. (usu. **blah blah blah**) indicating long-winded and tedious speech or writing.

blain n. an inflamed swelling or sore on the skin.

blam ● n. a loud sharp sound, as of a gunshot or an explosion. ● v.intr. (**blammed, blamming**) make such a loud sound.

blame ● v.tr. **1** assign fault or responsibility to. **2** (foll. by *on*) assign the responsibility for (an error or wrong) to a person etc. ● n. **1** responsibility for a bad result. **2** the act of blaming or attributing responsibility; censure (*she got all the blame*). ● adj. (also **blamed**) N Amer. informal damned, confounded. □ **be to blame** be responsible; deserve censure (*she is not to blame for the accident*). **have only oneself to blame** be solely responsible (for something one suffers). **I don't blame you** etc. I think your etc. action was justifiable. □ **blameable** adj. (also **blamable**).

blameless adj. innocent; free from blame. □ **blamelessly** adv. **blamelessness** n.

blameworthy adj. deserving blame. □ **blameworthiness** n.

blanch v. **1** tr. make white or pale by extracting colour. **2** intr. & tr. grow or make pale from shock, fear, etc. **3** tr. **a** peel (almonds etc.) by scalding. **b** immerse (vegetables or meat) briefly in boiling water. **4** tr. whiten (a plant) by depriving it of light.

bland adj. **1 a** mild, not irritating. **b** tasteless. **2** unstimulating, insipid. **3** expressionless, mild-tempered. □ **blandly** adv. **blandness** n.

blandish /'blændɪʃ/ v.tr. flatter; coax, cajole.

blandishment n. (usu. in pl.) flattery; cajolery.

blank ● adj. **1 a** (of paper) not written or printed on. **b** (of a document) with spaces left for a signature or details. **c** (of a tape, disk, etc.) containing no recorded sound etc. **d** (of a television screen etc.) not displaying any images, characters, etc. **2 a** not filled; empty (*a blank space*). **b** lacking contrast; sheer (*a blank wall*). **3 a** having or showing no interest or expression (*a blank face*). **b** void of incident or result. **c** puzzled, nonplussed. **d** having (temporarily) no knowledge or understanding (*my mind went blank*). **4** complete, downright (*a blank refusal*). **5** Curling (of an end) played without either rink scoring a point. **6** euphemism used in place of an adjective regarded as coarse or abusive. ● n. **1 a** a space left to be filled in a document. **b** a document having blank spaces to be filled. **2** (in full **blank cartridge**) a cartridge containing gunpowder but no bullet, used for training etc. **3** an empty space or period of time. **4 a** a coin disc before stamping. **b** a metal or wooden block before final shaping. **5 a** a dash written instead of a word or letter, esp. instead of an obscenity. **b** euphemism used in place of a noun regarded as coarse. **6** a blank domino or tile in some games. ● v.tr. **1** (usu. foll. by *off, out*) screen, obscure (*clouds blanked out the sun*). **2** N Amer. Sport defeat without allowing to score; shut out. **3** Curling play (an end) without either rink scoring a point. □ **draw a blank** elicit no response; fail. □ **blankly** adv. **blankness** n.

blank cheque n. **1** a cheque with the amount left for the payee to fill in. **2** informal unlimited freedom of action.

blanket ● n. **1** a large piece of woollen or other material used esp. as a bedcover. **2** (usu. attrib.) a type of woollen cloth similar to a woollen blanket (*blanket coat*). **3** a thick mass or layer that covers something (*blanket of fog*). **4** N Amer. (often attrib.) traditional Indian life or culture. ● adj. inclusive (*blanket condemnation*). ● v.tr. (**blanketed, blanketing**) **1** cover with or as if with a blanket (*snow blanketed the land*). **2** stifle; keep quiet (*blanketed all discussion*). □ **born on the wrong side of the blanket** illegitimate.

blanket coat n. esp. N Amer. a coat made from a

blanket or blanket cloth, esp. (in Canada) = HUDSON'S BAY BLANKET COAT.

blankety adj. (also **blankety-blank**) = BLANK adj. 6.

blank verse n. unrhymed verse, esp. iambic pentameters.

blare ● v. **1** intr. make a loud harsh sound (car horns blared). **2** tr. & intr. produce or utter (such sounds) loudly (the radio was blaring). ● n. a loud harsh sound.

blarney ● n. **1** cajoling talk; flattery. **2** nonsense. ● v. (**-eys, -eyed**) **1** tr. flatter (a person) with blarney. **2** intr. talk flatteringly.

blasé /blɒ'zei, 'blɒzei/ adj. **1** unimpressed or indifferent because of over-familiarity. **2** tired of pleasure; surfeited.

blaspheme /blæs'fiːm, 'blæs-/ v. **1** intr. swear or curse, making use of religious names etc. **2** tr. speak evil of; revile. □ **blasphemer** n.

blasphemy /'blæsfəmi/ n. (pl. **-ies**) **1** profane talk. **2** an instance of this. □ **blasphemous** adj.

blast ● n. **1** a strong gust of wind. **2 a** an explosion. **b** a destructive wave of highly compressed air spreading outwards from an explosion. **c** the quantity of explosive used in a blasting operation. **3** a single loud note emitted by a car horn, whistle, brass instrument, etc. **4** a gunshot. **5** informal a severe reprimand. **6** a strong current of air used in smelting etc. **7** informal a good time (was having a blast). **8** Sport a vigorous hit, throw, etc. ● v. **1** tr. blow up (rocks etc.) with explosives. **2** tr. create out of or from rocks etc. by blasting. **3** intr. & tr. make or cause to make a loud or explosive noise (blasted away on his trumpet). **4 a** tr. informal reprimand severely. **b** intr. exclaim vehemently or loudly. **5** informal **a** tr. shoot; shoot at. **b** intr. shoot. **6** tr. Sport hit or throw forcefully. **7** tr. destroy, ruin (blasted her hopes). **8** tr. wither, shrivel, or blight (a plant etc.) (blasted oak). **9** tr. strike with divine anger; curse. ● interj. expressing annoyance. □ **full blast** informal working at maximum speed etc. **blast from the past** informal a forcefully nostalgic event or thing. **blast off** (of a rocket etc.) take off from a launching site.

blasted adj. **1** (attrib.) damned; annoying (that blasted dog!). **2** (predic.) informal drunk.

blaster n. **1** in senses of BLAST v. **2** N Amer. = GHETTO BLASTER.

blast furnace n. a smelting furnace into which compressed hot air is driven.

blasthole n. a hole containing an explosive charge for blasting.

blast-off n. the launching of a rocket etc.

blat ● n. a loud discordant noise, e.g. the sounding of a horn. ● v.intr. (**blatted, blatting**) make a loud discordant sound.

blatant adj. **1** flagrant, unashamed. **2** offensively noisy or obtrusive. □ **blatancy** n. **blatantly** adv.

blather ● n. foolish chatter. ● v.tr. & intr. chatter foolishly. □ **blathering** n.

blaxploitation n. US informal (usu. attrib.) the exploitation of blacks, esp. as actors in films.

blaze¹ ● n. **1** a bright flame or fire. **2 a** a bright glaring light (the sun set in a blaze of orange). **b** a full light (a blaze of publicity). **3** a violent outburst (of passion etc.). **4 a** a glow of colour (roses were a blaze of scarlet). **b** a bright display (a blaze of glory). ● v.intr. **1** burn with a bright flame. **2** be brilliantly lighted. **3** be consumed with anger, excitement, etc. **4 a** show bright colours (blazing with jewels). **b** emit light (stars blazing). **5** esp. Sport move quickly. □ **blaze away** (often foll. by at) **1** fire continuously with rifles etc. **2** work enthusiastically. **blaze up 1** burst into flame. **2** burst out in anger. **go to blazes** informal go to hell.

like blazes informal **1** with great energy. **2** very fast. **what in blazes** informal what on earth.

blaze² ● n. **1** a white mark on an animal's face. **2** a mark made on a tree by slashing the bark, esp. to mark a route. ● v.tr. mark (a tree or a path) by chipping bark. □ **blaze a trail** (or **path**) **1** mark out a path or route. **2** be the first to do or study something.

blaze orange N Amer. ● adj. of a vivid orange colour (often used for hunting attire). ● n. this colour.

blazer n. **1** a jacket of a solid colour, often with a crest and patch pockets, worn as part of a uniform. **2** a plain jacket of a dark solid colour that is not part of a suit.

blazing adj. **1** in senses of BLAZE¹ v. **2** very hot (a blazing hot day). □ **blazingly** adv.

blazon ● v.tr. **1** (esp. in **blazon abroad**) proclaim. **2** Heraldry **a** describe or paint (arms). **b** inscribe or paint (an object) with arms, names, etc. ● n. a record or description, esp. of virtues etc.

bldg. abbr. building.

bleach ● v.tr. & intr. whiten by a chemical process or by exposure to sunlight. ● n. **1** a bleaching substance, esp. a solution of sodium hypochlorite used domestically for whitening laundry and as a disinfectant. **2** the process of bleaching.

bleacher n. **1** (usu. in pl.) esp. N Amer. **a** uncovered, tiered, inexpensive bench seating at a sports ground, stadium, etc. **b** a similar type of seating in a gymnasium etc. **2 a** a person who bleaches (esp. textiles). **b** a vessel or chemical used in bleaching.

bleak adj. **1** bare, exposed; windswept. **2** unpromising; dreary (bleak prospects). **3** cold or harsh (a bleak wind). □ **bleakly** adv. **bleakness** n.

bleary adj. (**-ier, -iest**) **1** (of the eyes or mind) dim; blurred. **2** indistinct. □ **blearily** adv. **bleariness** n.

bleary-eyed adj. having irritated, and unfocused eyes, esp. from lack of sleep or inebriation.

bleat ● v. **1** intr. (of a sheep, goat, calf, etc.) give its natural tremulous cry. **2** intr. & tr. (often foll. by out) speak or say feebly, foolishly, or plaintively. ● n. **1** the sound made by a sheep, goat, etc. **2** a weak, plaintive, or foolish exclamation, statement, etc. □ **bleater** n. **bleatingly** adv.

blech /blek/ interj. N Amer. expressing disgust.

bleed ● v. (past and past part. **bled**) **1** intr. emit blood. **2** tr. draw blood from surgically. **3** tr. extort money from. **4** intr. spend or lose money in large quantities. **5** intr. (of a plant) emit sap. **6** intr. **a** (of dye) come out in water. **b** (of colour) run. **7** tr. **a** allow (fluid or gas) to escape from a closed system through a valve etc. **b** treat (such a system) in this way. **8** intr. (often foll. by for) suffer wounds or violent death (bled for the Revolution). **9** Printing **a** intr. (of a printed area) be cut into when pages are trimmed. **b** tr. cut into the printed area of when trimming. **c** tr. extend (an illustration) to the cut edge of a page. ● n. **1** a draining of fluid or gas from a closed system. **2** (usu. in comb.) an act of bleeding (nosebleed). □ **bleed dry** (or **white**) drain (a person, country, etc.) of wealth etc. **one's heart bleeds** usu. ironic one is very sorrowful.

bleeder n. **1** a person or thing that bleeds. **2** informal a hemophiliac.

bleeding heart n. **1** informal a person perceived as overly sentimental, esp. in regard to social problems. **2** any of various plants, esp. Dicentra spectabilis, having heart-shaped pinkish-red flowers hanging from an arched stem.

bleep ● n. **1** an intermittent high-pitched sound made electronically. **2** this sound or the word itself used as a substitute for an expletive. ● v. **1** intr. & tr.

make or cause to make such a sound, esp. as a signal. **2** tr. (often foll. by *out*) substitute a bleep for.

blemish ● n. **1** a flaw or defect (*a blemish on her character*). **2** a mark on the skin, esp. a pimple, blackhead, scar, etc. ● v.tr. spoil the perfection of.

blend ● v. **1** tr. **a** mix (esp. sorts of coffee, spirits, etc.) together to produce a desired flavour etc. **b** produce by this method (*blended whisky*). **2** intr. form a harmonious compound; become one. **3** tr. & intr. mingle or be mingled (*her voice blends in with the others*). **4 a** tr. (often foll. by *in*) mix thoroughly. **b** tr. & intr. combine (ingredients) using an electric blender. **5** intr. (esp. of colours) a pass imperceptibly into each other. **b** go well together; harmonize. ● n. **1 a** a mixture, esp. of various sorts of coffee, spirits, etc. **b** a combination (of different abstract or personal qualities). **2** a word blending the sounds and combining the meanings of two others, e.g. *motel*.

blende / blend/ n. any naturally occurring metal sulphide, esp. zinc blende.

blender n. **1** an electric kitchen appliance with rotating blades, used for puréeing, liquefying, or finely chopping. **2** a person or thing that blends.

bless v.tr. (*past* and *past part.* **blessed**, *archaic* **blest**) **1 a** (of a priest etc.) pronounce words, esp. in a religious rite, to confer or invoke divine favour on. **b** bestow divine favour on (*bless this house*). **2 a** consecrate (esp. bread and wine). **b** sanctify. **3** call (God) holy; adore. **4** refl. make the sign of the cross. **5** attribute one's good fortune to (an auspicious time, one's fate, etc.); thank (*bless the day I met her*). **6** (usu. in *passive*; often foll. by *with*) make happy or successful (*blessed with children*; *they were truly blessed*). □ (**God**) **bless me** (or **my soul**) an exclamation of surprise, pleasure, indignation, etc. (**God**) **bless you!** **1** an exclamation of endearment, gratitude, etc. **2** an exclamation made to a person who has just sneezed. **I'm blessed** (or **blest**) an exclamation of surprise etc. **not have a penny to bless oneself with** be impoverished.

blessed / 'blesəd, blest/ adj. (also *archaic* **blest**) **1** sanctified, revered. **2** / blest/ often *ironic* fortunate (in the possession of) (*blessed with good health*). **3** *euphemism* cursed; damned (*blessed nuisance!*). **4** in paradise. **5** (**Blessed**) *Catholicism* a title given to a beatified person. **6** bringing happiness; blissful (*blessed ignorance*). □ **blessedly** adv.

blessedness / 'blesədnəs/ n. **1** happiness. **2** the enjoyment of divine favour.

blessing n. **1** the act of declaring, seeking, or bestowing (esp. divine) favour (*sought God's blessing*; *mother gave them her blessing*). **2** grace said before or after a meal. **3** a gift of a deity, nature, etc.; a thing one is glad of (*what a blessing he brought it!*). □ **blessing in disguise** an apparent misfortune that eventually has good results.

bleu / blø/ n. *Cdn* esp. *hist.* a Quebec supporter of a Conservative party.

blew *past of* BLOW[1].

blight ● n. **1** any plant disease caused by mildews, fungi, insects, etc. **2** any insect or parasite causing such a disease. **3** any obscure force which is harmful or destructive. **4** the act or state of deteriorating or being destroyed (*urban blight*). ● v.tr. **1** affect with blight. **2** harm, destroy. **3** spoil.

blimp n. **1** a small non-rigid airship. **2** an obese person. **3** a soundproof cover for a movie camera.

blind ● adj. **1** lacking the power of sight. **2 a** without foresight, discernment, or adequate information (*blind effort*). **b** (often foll. by *to*) unwilling or unable to appreciate (a factor, circumstance, etc.) (*blind to*

argument). **3** not governed by purpose or reason (*blind forces*). **4** reckless (*blind hitting*). **5** concealed, obscured (*blind corner*). **6 a** (of a door, window, etc.) walled up. **b** (of a street etc.) closed at one end. **7** (of flying) without direct observation, using instruments only. **8** (of a wall) having no windows. **9** (of a test or experiment) conducted in a way that does not allow the subject or examiner to prejudice the results. **10** *informal* drunk. ● v.tr. **1** deprive of sight, permanently or temporarily. **2** (often foll. by *to*) rob of judgment; deceive (*blinded them to the danger*). ● n. **1 a** a screen for a window, esp. on a roller, or with slats. **b** an awning over a store window. **2 a** something designed or used to hide the truth; a pretext. **b** a legitimate business concealing a criminal enterprise. **3** *N Amer.* a camouflaged shelter used for observing or hunting wildlife. **4** any obstruction to sight or light. ● adv. **1** *Aviation* using instruments only (*fly blind*). **2** without guidance (*buy it blind*). **3** to a great extent (*robbed them blind*). □ **blind as a bat** completely blind. **blind with science** overawe with a display of (often spurious) knowledge. **not a blind bit of** *informal* not the slightest amount of (*didn't do a blind bit of good*). **turn a blind eye to** pretend not to notice. □ **blindness** n.

blind alley n. a course of action leading nowhere.

blind date n. **1** a social engagement between two people who have not previously met. **2** either of the two people on a blind date.

blinder n. *informal* (usu. in *pl.*) *N Amer.* = BLINKER n. 1.

blindfold ● v.tr. **1** deprive (a person) of sight by covering the eyes, esp. with a tied cloth. **2** deprive of understanding; hoodwink. ● n. **1** a bandage or cloth used to blindfold. **2** any obstruction to understanding. ● adj. & adv. **1** with eyes bandaged. **2** without care or circumspection (*went into it blindfold*).

blinding ● n. the act of causing blindness. ● adj. **1** causing temporary or permanent inability to see (a *blinding snowstorm*). **2** dazzlingly bright. **3** extreme; severe (*blinding speed*). □ **blindingly** adv.

blindly adv. **1** without being able to see. **2** without understanding or thought (*plunged in blindly*).

blind man's bluff n. (also esp. *Brit.* **blind man's buff**) a game in which a blindfold player tries to catch others while being pushed about by them.

blind pig n. *N Amer. informal* an illegal bar.

blind side ● n. a direction in which one cannot see the approach of danger etc. ● v.tr. (usu. **blindside**) *N Amer.* **1** attack or strike on the blind side. **2** surprise, take unawares; take advantage of.

blind spot n. **1** *Anat.* the point of entry of the optic nerve on the retina, insensitive to light. **2** an area where vision is obscured or hindered, esp. that part of the road which a driver of a motor vehicle cannot see using mirrors. **3** an area in which a person lacks understanding or impartiality. **4** a point of unusually weak radio reception.

blind trust n. **1** a trust independently administering the private business affairs of a person in public office. **2** complete, unthinking faith.

blini / 'blini/ n. (*pl.* same or -**s**) an originally Russian pancake made from buckwheat flour and yeast.

blink ● v. **1** intr. & tr. shut and open the eyes quickly and usu. involuntarily. **2** intr. (often foll. by *at*) look with eyes opening and shutting, esp. in surprise or bewilderment. **3** tr. **a** (often foll. by *back*) prevent (tears) by blinking. **b** (often foll. by *away*, *from*) clear (dust etc.) from the eyes by blinking. **4 a** intr. shine with an unsteady or intermittent light. **b** tr. cause (a light) to flash briefly. **5** intr. back down in a confrontation. ● n. **1** an act of blinking. **2** a momen-

tary gleam or glimpse. ☐ **on the blink** *informal* out of order, esp. intermittently. **the blink of an eye** a very short time.

blinker ● *n.* **1** (usu. in *pl.*) either of a pair of screens attached to a horse's bridle to prevent it from seeing sideways. **2** a device that blinks, esp. a vehicle's turn signal. ● *v.tr.* obscure with blinkers.

blinkered *adj.* having narrow and prejudiced views.

blintz /blɪns/ *n.* (also **blintze**) (*pl.* **-es**) a thin pancake wrapped around a filling, usu. of cream cheese.

blip ● *n.* **1** a quick popping sound; a short bleep. **2** a small image of an object on a radar screen. **3** a temporary movement in statistics. ● *v.intr.* (**blipped, blipping**) **1** make a blip. **2** (of figures etc.) rise suddenly and temporarily.

bliss ● *n.* **1 a** perfect joy or happiness. **b** enjoyment; gladness. **2 a** the state of being in heaven. **b** a state of blessedness. ● *v.intr.* (foll. by *out*) esp. *N Amer. slang* reach a state of ecstasy.

blissed-out *adj.* esp. *N Amer. slang* in a state of bliss.

blissful *adj.* perfectly happy; joyful. ☐ **blissful ignorance** fortunate unawareness of something unpleasant. ☐ **blissfully** *adv.* **blissfulness** *n.*

blister ● *n.* **1** a small bubble on the skin filled with serum and caused by friction, burning, etc. **2** a similar swelling on any other surface. ● *v.* **1** *tr.* raise a blister on. **2** *intr.* come up in a blister or blisters. **3** *tr.* attack sharply (*blistered them with his criticisms*).

blistering *adj.* **1** very harsh (*a blistering attack on her character*). **2** very intense (*blistering sun*). **3** very fast (*a blistering shot*). ☐ **blisteringly** *adv.*

blithe /blaɪð, blaɪθ/ *adj.* (usu. *attrib.*) **1** happy, joyous. **2** careless, casual. ☐ **blithely** *adv.* **blitheness** *n.*

blither *var. of* BLATHER.

blithering *adj. informal* **1** senselessly talkative. **2 a** (*attrib.*) utter (*blithering idiot*). **b** contemptible.

blitz *informal* ● *n.* **1 a** an intensive or sudden (esp. aerial) attack. **b** *informal* any sudden or concentrated effort, esp. on a large scale (*publicity blitz*). **2** (**the Blitz**) the intensive German air raids on Britain in 1940. **3** *Football* a play in which one or more defensive backs charge the quarterback of the opposing team. ● *v.* **1** *tr.* attack, damage, or destroy by a blitz. **2** *intr. Football* charge into the offensive backfield.

blitzed *adj. slang* drunk.

blitzkrieg /ˈblɪtskriːg/ *n.* an intense military campaign intended to bring about a swift victory.

blizzard ● *n.* **1** a severe snowstorm with high winds. **2** *informal* a large amount of something (*a blizzard of paperwork*). ● *v.intr.* (of a snowstorm) attain blizzard conditions (*it's really blizzarding*).

bloat ● *v.tr. & intr.* inflate, swell. ● *n.* **1** an accumulation of gas in the stomach or abdomen. **2** the quality of something which has grown beyond manageable size (*administrative bloat*).

bloated *adj.* **1** swollen, puffed. **2** suffering from an excess of gas or water. **3** larger than necessary (*bloated bureaucracy*). **4** puffed up with pride or excessive wealth (*bloated plutocrat*).

blob *n.* **1** a small roundish mass; a drop of matter. **2** a drop of liquid. **3** a spot of colour. **4** *informal* a large shapeless person. ☐ **blobby** *adj.* (**-ier, -iest**)

bloc *n.* **1** a combination of nations, parties, groups, or people, formed to promote a particular purpose. **2** (**Bloc**) (in Canada) = BLOC QUÉBÉCOIS.

block ● *n.* **1** a solid hewn or unhewn piece of hard material, esp. of stone, wood, or ice. **2** a hollow usu. rectangular masonry building unit (*concrete block*). **3** a flat-topped block used as a base for chopping,

beheading, hammering on, etc. **4** = AUCTION BLOCK. **5 a** a large building, esp. when subdivided (*East Block*). **b** = CELLBLOCK. **6 a** an area bounded by (usu. four) streets. **b** *N Amer.* the length of one side of this, esp. as a measure of distance (*three blocks away*). **7 a** an obstruction. **b** anything preventing normal progress or operation (*writer's block*). **8** the metal casting containing the cylinders of an internal combustion engine. **9** a pulley or system of pulleys mounted in a case. **10** (in *pl.*) = BUILDING BLOCK. **11** a piece of wood or metal engraved for printing on paper or fabric. **12** *informal* the head (*knock his block off*). **13** a large quantity or allocation of things treated as a unit, esp. shares, seats in a theatre, etc. **14** *Computing* a collection of data that can be stored and processed as a single unit. **15** a pad of paper, esp. for drawing. **16** *Athletics* = STARTING BLOCK. **17** *Sport* an obstruction of an opponent or an opponent's play. **18 a** a tract of land offered to an individual settler by a government. **b** a large area of land. **19** a chock for stopping the motion of a wheel etc. ● *v.tr.* **1 a** obstruct (a passage etc.). **b** put obstacles in the way of (progress etc.). **2** *Sport* intercept (an opponent or the ball, puck, etc.) with one's body. ● *attrib.adj.* treating (many similar things) as one unit (*block booking*). ☐ **block in 1** sketch roughly; plan. **2** confine. **block out 1 a** shut out (light, noise, etc.). **b** exclude from memory, as being too painful. **2** sketch roughly; plan. **block up 1** confine; shut (a person etc.) in. **2** infill (a window, doorway, etc.) with bricks etc. **on the block** *N Amer.* = ON THE AUCTION BLOCK (see AUCTION BLOCK). ☐ **blocked** *adj.*

blockade ● *n.* **1** the surrounding or blocking of access to a place to prevent entry and exit of supplies etc. **2** anything that prevents access or progress. **3** obstruction or prevention of a physiological or mental function. ● *v.tr.* **1** subject to a blockade. **2** obstruct (a passage etc.). ☐ **run a blockade** enter or leave a blockaded port by evading the blockading force. ☐ **blockader** *n.*

blockade-runner *n.* a vessel etc. that attempts to pass through a blockade. ☐ **blockade-running** *n.*

blockage *n.* **1** an obstruction. **2** a blocked state.

block and tackle *n.* a system of pulleys and ropes, esp. for lifting.

blockbuster *n.* an extremely popular or financially successful film, book, etc.

block capitals *n.pl.* capital block letters.

blocker *n.* **1** a person or thing that blocks. **2** *Hockey* a glove with a rectangular pad worn by a goaltender to protect the hand which holds the stick. **3** *Football* a player whose role is to block the opponent's play. **4** a substance which prevents or inhibits a given physiological function.

blockhead *n.* a stupid person. ☐ **blockheaded** *adj.*

block heater *n. N Amer.* an electric heater used to warm the coolant and hence the engine block of a motor vehicle in winter, allowing for easier starting.

block letters *n.pl.* (esp. capital) letters written without serifs and separate from each other.

blocky *adj.* (**-ier, -iest**) like a block; solid, chunky.

Bloc Québécois *n.* a federal political party advocating Quebec separatism, founded in 1990.

bloke *n.* esp. *Brit. informal* a man, a fellow.

blond (also **blonde**) ● *adj.* **1** (of hair or the complexion) light-coloured; fair. **2** (of wood) of a light yellowish colour. ● *n.* a person with fair hair and skin. ¶The form *blonde* is more likely to be used of females than of males; *blond* can be used of both males and females. ☐ **blondish** *adj.* **blondness** *n.*

Blood *n.* **1** a member of an Aboriginal people of S Alberta. **2** the Algonquian language of the Blood.

blood ● *n.* **1** a usu. red liquid circulating in the arteries and veins of vertebrates that carries oxygen to and carbon dioxide from the tissues of the body. **2** a corresponding fluid in invertebrates. **3** bloodshed, esp. killing. **4** passion, temperament. **5** the blood as the vehicle of hereditary characteristics or relationship; family descent (*musical ability runs in their blood*). **6** a relationship; relations (*own flesh and blood*). ● *v.tr.* **1** give (a hound) a first taste of blood. **2** initiate (a person) by experience. □ **bad blood** ill feeling. **blood-and-thunder** (*attrib.*) *informal* sensational, melodramatic. **one's blood is up** one is in a fighting mood. **in one's blood** inherent in one's character. **make one's blood boil** infuriate one. **make one's blood run cold** horrify one. **new** (or **fresh**) **blood** new members admitted to a group, esp. as an invigorating force. **of the blood** royal. **out for a person's blood** set on getting revenge. **taste blood** be stimulated by an early success. **young blood 1** a younger member or members of a group. **2** a rake or fashionable young man.

blood bank *n.* **1** a place where supplies of blood or plasma for transfusion are stored. **2** any supply of blood for transfusions.

bloodbath *n.* a massacre.

blood blister *n.* a blister containing blood.

blood brother *n.* a brother by birth or by the ceremonial mingling of blood.

blood-curdling *adj.* horrifying.

blood donor *n.* a person who gives blood.

blood donor clinic *n. Cdn* a usu. temporary location where people can give blood.

blooded *adj.* **1** (in *comb.*) having blood or a disposition of a specified kind (*cold-blooded*). **2** (of horses etc.) of good pedigree.

blood feud *n.* a feud between families involving killing or injury.

blood group *n.* = BLOOD TYPE.

bloodhound *n.* a large hound of a breed used in tracking, having a very keen sense of smell.

bloodless *adj.* **1** without blood. **2** unemotional; cold. **3** pale. **4** without bloodshed. **5** feeble; lifeless. □ **bloodlessly** *adv.* **bloodlessness** *n.*

bloodletting *n.* **1** the removal of some of a person's blood for some purpose, esp. surgically or ritually. **2** bloodshed. **3** *informal* (in a workplace etc.) bitter quarrelling, esp. accompanied by reductions in staff.

bloodline *n.* (usu. in *pl.*) **1** (of animals) pedigree. **2** family; ancestry.

blood meal *n.* dried blood used for feeding animals and as a fertilizer.

blood money *n.* **1** money paid to the next of kin of a person who has been killed. **2** money paid to a hired murderer. **3** money paid for information about a murder or murderer.

blood poisoning *n.* a diseased state caused by the presence of micro-organisms or toxins in the body.

blood pressure *n.* the pressure of the blood in the circulatory system, often measured for diagnosis.

blood-red *adj.* red as blood.

blood relative *n.* (also **blood relation**) a relative by birth, not by marriage.

bloodshed *n.* **1** the spilling of blood. **2** slaughter.

bloodshot *adj.* (of an eyeball) tinged with blood.

blood sport *n.* sport, esp. hunting, involving the wounding or killing of animals.

bloodstain *n.* a discoloration caused by blood.

bloodstained *adj.* **1** stained with blood. **2** guilty of bloodshed.

bloodstream *n.* blood in circulation.

bloodsucker *n.* **1** an animal or insect that sucks blood. **2** an extortionist. □ **bloodsucking** *adj.*

blood sugar *n.* **1** the amount of glucose in the blood. **2** the glucose itself.

blood test *n.* (also **blood work**) a scientific examination of a blood sample, esp. for diagnosis, measurement of sugar or alcohol level, etc.

bloodthirsty *adj.* (**-ier, -iest**) **1** having a longing for blood (*bloodthirsty mosquitoes*). **2 a** eager to kill (*bloodthirsty killer*). **b** taking pleasure or showing interest in killing or violence (*bloodthirsty spectators*). **3** (of a film etc.) describing or depicting killing or violence. □ **bloodthirstily** *adv.* **bloodthirstiness** *n.*

blood transfusion *n.* the injection of a volume of blood, previously taken from a healthy person, into a patient.

blood type *n.* any one of the various types of human blood determining compatibility in transfusion.

blood vessel *n.* a vein, artery, etc. carrying blood.

bloody ● *adj.* (**-ier, -iest**) **1 a** of or like blood. **b** running or smeared with blood. **2 a** involving, loving, or resulting from bloodshed (*bloody battle*). **b** cruel (*bloody murderer*). **3** esp. *Cdn, Brit., Austral., & NZ informal* expressing annoyance or antipathy, or as an intensive (*a bloody shame*). **4** red. ● *adv. informal* as an intensive (*you can bloody well do it*). ● *v.tr.* (**-ies, -ied**) make bloody; stain with blood. □ **bloody murder** *N Amer.* vociferously (*screaming bloody murder*). □ **bloodily** *adv.* **bloodiness** *n.*

Bloody Caesar *n. Cdn* a drink composed of vodka and tomato clam cocktail, garnished with celery.

Bloody Mary *n.* (*pl.* **-ys**) a drink composed of vodka and tomato juice.

bloom ● *n.* **1 a** a flower, esp. one cultivated for its beauty. **b** the state of flowering (*in bloom*). **2** a state of perfection or loveliness (*in full bloom*). **3 a** (of the complexion) a flush; a glow. **b** a delicate powdery surface deposit on plums, grapes, leaves, etc., indicating freshness. **c** a cloudiness on a shiny surface. **4** a scum formed by the rapid proliferation of microscopic algae on water. ● *v.intr.* **1** bear flowers; be in flower. **2 a** come into, or remain in, full beauty. **b** flourish; be in a healthy, vigorous state. □ **take the bloom off** make stale.

bloomer *n.* **1** a plant that blooms (in a specified way) (*early autumn bloomer*). **2** *N Amer.* a person who develops or matures later (**late bloomer**) or earlier (**early bloomer**) than normal.

bloomers *n.pl.* **1** women's loose-fitting knee-length underpants. **2** *informal* any women's underpants.

blooming *adj.* flourishing; healthy.

bloop esp. *N Amer. Baseball* ● *v.tr.* hit (a ball) as a blooper. ● *n.* a blooper (also *attrib.*: *bloop single*).

blooper *n. informal* **1** an embarrassing blunder. **2** *Baseball* **a** a fly ball hit just beyond the infield. **b** a ball thrown high by the pitcher.

Bloquiste / blɔˈkiːst / *n. Cdn* a member of the BQ.

blossom ● *n.* **1** a flower or a mass of flowers, esp. of a fruit tree. **2** the stage or time of flowering (*the cherry tree in blossom*). **3** a promising stage (*the blossom of youth*). ● *v.intr.* **1** open into flower. **2** reach a promising stage; mature, thrive. □ **blossomy** *adj.*

blot ● *n.* **1** a spot or stain of ink etc. **2** a moral defect in an otherwise good character; a disgraceful act or quality. **3** any disfigurement or blemish. ● *v.* (**blotted, blotting**) **1 a** *tr.* spot or stain with ink; smudge. **b** *intr.* (of a pen, ink, etc.) make blots. **2** *tr.* a use blotting paper or other absorbent material to absorb (liquid), esp. by dabbing or pressing rather than rubbing. **b** (of blotting paper etc.) soak up (liquid). **3** tr. disgrace (*blotted her reputation*). □ **blot out 1 a** obliterate (writing). **b** obscure (a view, sound, etc.). **2** obliterate (from the memory) as too painful. **3** destroy.

blotch • n. **1** a discoloured or inflamed patch on the skin. **2** an irregular patch of colour. • v.tr. cover with blotches. □ **blotchy** adj. (**-ier, -iest**).

blotter n. **1** a sheet or sheets of blotting paper, usu. inserted into a frame. **2** N Amer. a record of arrests and charges in a police station.

blotting paper n. unsized absorbent paper used for soaking up excess ink.

blouse /blauz, blʌus/ • n. **1** a woman's or girl's lightweight upper garment, usu. with buttons and a collar. **2** a waist-length belted jacket worn as part of an airman's or soldier's uniform in some military forces. **3** a loose linen or cotton garment, usu. hanging above the knees and belted at the waist. • v.tr. make (a bodice etc.) loose like a blouse.

blow¹ • v. (past **blew**; past part. **blown**) **1 a** intr. (esp. of the wind or air) move along; act as an air current. **b** intr. be driven by an air current (*papers blew along the sidewalk*). **c** tr. drive with an air current (*blew the sign down*). **2 a** tr. send out (esp. air) by breathing (*blew smoke*). **b** intr. send a directed air current from the mouth. **3** tr. & intr. sound or be sounded by blowing. **4** tr. **a** direct an air current at (*blew the embers*). **b** (foll. by *off, away*, etc.) clear of by means of an air current (*blew the dust off*). **5** tr. (past part. **blowed**) slang curse, confound (*blow it!; I'll be blowed!*). **6** tr. **a** clear (the nose) of mucus by blowing. **b** remove contents from (an egg) by blowing through it. **7 a** intr. puff, pant. **b** tr. (esp. in passive) exhaust of breath. **8** slang **a** tr. depart suddenly from (*blew the town yesterday*). **b** intr. depart suddenly. **9** tr. & intr. explode or cause to explode. **10** tr. & intr. melt or cause to melt from overloading (*the fuse has blown*). **11** tr. make or shape (glass or a bubble) by blowing air in. **12** intr. (of a whale) eject air and water through a blowhole. **13** tr. informal **a** squander, spend recklessly (*blew $50 on a meal*). **b** spoil, bungle (an opportunity etc.) (*he's blown his chance*). **c** waste, esp. by incompetence (*blew a two-goal lead*). **d** reveal (a secret etc.) (*blew her cover*). **14** tr. (of flies) deposit eggs in. **15** tr. coarse slang fellate. • n. **1 a** an act of blowing. **b** informal a session of jazz playing (on any instrument). **2 a** a gust of wind or air. **b** N Amer. a storm. □ **blow away** slang **1** kill or destroy, esp. with a gun. **2** defeat soundly. **3** impress greatly. **blow a person's cover** reveal a person's secret identity. **blow the doors off something** N Amer. be outstandingly more successful than something. **blow in** informal arrive unexpectedly. **blow a kiss** pretend to place a kiss on one's hand and blow it to a distant person. **blow a person's mind** slang **1** impress a person greatly; overwhelm. **2** cause a person to have drug-induced hallucination. **blow off 1** remove or be removed by the force of an air current, esp. the wind. **2** remove by an explosive force, esp. a bomb or bullet. **3** N Amer. slang disregard. **4** N Amer. slang waste (time). **5** N Amer. slang fail to do (work) or attend (classes etc.). **blow out 1** extinguish (esp. a flame) by blowing. **2** send outwards by an explosion. **3** (of a tire) burst. **4** (of a fuse etc.) melt. **5** N Amer. slang **a** defeat convincingly. **b** render useless, break (*he blew out his knee*). **6** cause to lose strength by blowing (*the storm blew itself out*). **blow out of the water** N Amer. defeat overwhelmingly or completely. **blow over** (of trouble etc.) fade away without serious

consequences. **blow one's own horn** etc. praise oneself. **blow one's top** (or N Amer. **stack**) informal explode in rage. **blow up 1 a** shatter or destroy by an explosion. **b** explode, erupt. **2** inflate (a tire etc.). **3** informal **a** enlarge (a photograph). **b** exaggerate. **4** informal come to notice; arise. **5** informal lose one's temper.

blow² n. **1** a hard stroke with a hand or weapon. **2** a sudden shock or misfortune. □ **come to blows** end up fighting. **in** (or **at**) **one blow** in one operation. **strike a blow for** (or **against**) help (or oppose).

blow-by-blow attrib.adj. (of a description etc.) giving all the details in sequence.

blowdown n. N Amer. **1** the uprooting of trees by the wind. **2** a tree so felled.

blow-dried adj. **1** (of hair) dried with a blow-dryer. **2** (of a person) well-groomed and usu. superficially or pretentiously suave.

blow-dry • v.tr. arrange (the hair) while drying it with a hand-held dryer. • n. an act of doing this. □ **blow-dryer** n.

blower n. **1** in senses of BLOW¹ v. **2** a device for creating a current of air. **3** informal a telephone.

blowfish n. = PUFFERFISH.

blowfly n. (pl. **-flies**) any of various flies of the family Calliphoridae, which deposit their eggs on meat and carcasses, e.g. the bluebottle.

blowhard n. informal a boastful or pompous person.

blowhole n. **1** the nostril of a whale, on the top of its head. **2** a hole in ice through which seals or other animals breathe. **3** a vent for air, smoke, etc., in a tunnel etc. **4** a hole in a coastal rock or cliff through which jets of spray and water are intermittently forced upward.

blowing snow n. snow whipped up by the wind from accumulations on the ground.

blow job n. coarse slang an act of fellatio.

blown past part. of BLOW¹.

blowout n. **1** informal a burst tire. **2** N Amer. informal a game, election, etc. with a lopsided result. **3** informal an elaborate party or feast; an extravaganza. **4** N Amer. informal a sale in a retail store featuring drastic price reductions. **5** a rapid uncontrolled upward rush from an oil or gas well.

blowsy /ˈblauzi/ adj. (also **blowzy**) (**-ier, -iest**) **1** coarse and red-faced. **2** dishevelled, slovenly. □ **blowsily** adv. **blowsiness** n.

blowtorch n. a portable device which creates a very hot flame, used for welding etc.

blow-up • n. **1** an enlargement (of a photograph etc.). **2** an explosion. **3** N Amer. informal a quarrel. • attrib.adj. **1** inflatable. **2** enlarged (a *blow-up photograph*).

B.L.S. abbr. Bachelor of Library Science.

BLT n. N Amer. a bacon, lettuce, and tomato sandwich.

blubber • n. **1** an insulating layer of fat in whales, polar bears and other swimming mammals. **2** body fat. **3** a period of weeping. • v. **1** intr. weep loudly. **2** tr. sob out (words). □ **blubbery** adj.

bludgeon /ˈblʌdʒən/ • n. a club with a heavy end. • v.tr. **1** beat with a bludgeon. **2** coerce.

blue • adj. **1** having a colour between green and violet in the spectrum, like that of a clear sky. **2** sad, depressed; (of a state of affairs) gloomy, dismal (*feel blue*). **3** with bluish skin through cold, fear, etc. **4** having blue or a bluish shade as a distinguishing colour (*blue jay*). **5** pornographic (a *blue film*). **6** Cdn & Brit. politically conservative. • n. **1** a blue colour or pigment. **2** blue clothes or material (*dressed in blue*). **3** (also **Blue**) Cdn & Brit. a supporter of a Conservative party. **4** any of various small blue-coloured butter-flies of the family Lycaenidae. **5** a blue ball, piece, etc. in a game or sport. **6** (prec. by *the*) the clear sky. ● *v.tr.* (**blues, blued, bluing** or **blueing**) **1** make blue. **2** treat (laundry) with bluing. □ **until one is blue in the face** repeatedly and at great length until one becomes frustrated, angry, etc. **blue murder** = BLOODY MURDER (see BLOODY). **once in a blue moon** very rarely. **out of the blue** unexpectedly. **talk etc. a blue streak** esp. *N Amer.* speak etc. in a swift, continuous stream of words. □ **blueness** *n.*

blueback *n.* **1** any of several fishes, esp. two species of Pacific coast salmon: **a** *Cdn* a small or immature coho. **b** = SOCKEYE. **2** *Cdn* a very young hooded seal.

bluebell *n.* **1** = HAREBELL. **2** any of several Eurasian plants of the genus *Endymion*, esp. *E. nonscriptus*, with clusters of bell-shaped blue flowers on a stem arising from a rhizome. **3** any of several other plants with blue bell-shaped flowers, esp. of the genus *Mertensia*.

blueberry *n.* (*pl.* **-ies**) **1** any of several plants of the genus *Vaccinium*, cultivated for their edible fruit. **2** the small blue-black fruit of these plants.

blueberry buckle *n. Cdn* (*Maritimes*) a cake topped with blueberries and a crumbly topping.

bluebird *n.* any of various N American songbirds of the thrush family, esp. of the genus *Sialia*, the males having distinctive blue plumage on the back or head.

blue-black ● *n.* a black colour with a tinge of blue. ● *adj.* of this colour.

blueblood *n.* **1** *N Amer.* a wealthy or socially promi-nent person. **2** an aristocrat. **3** (**blue blood**) noble birth. □ **blue-blooded** *adj.*

blue book *n.* **1** (**Blue Book**) *Cdn* a report of esti-mated government expenditures tabled annually in the House of Commons. **2** *N Amer.* a reference book listing the market value of certain consumer items, esp. used cars. **3** a directory listing people considered socially important.

bluebottle *n.* any of several large blowflies with a metallic-blue body, esp. *Calliphora vomitoria*.

blue box *n. Cdn* a blue plastic box for the collection of recyclable household materials.

blue cheese *n.* any of several strong cheeses pro-duced with veins of blue mould, e.g. Roquefort.

blue chip ● *n.* a stock exchange investment consid-ered to be fairly reliable though not entirely without risk. ● *attrib.adj.* (usu. **blue-chip**) **1** (of an investment, company, etc.) reliable; consistently giving a good yield. **2** of the highest quality.

blue-collar *adj.* of or relating to manual or indus-trial labourers, usu. paid wages rather than salary (compare WHITE-COLLAR).

bluefin *n.* (in full **bluefin tuna**) the common tuna, *Thunnus thynnus*.

bluefish *n.* **1** a voracious blue-coloured marine food fish, *Pomatomus saltatrix*, inhabiting warmer waters of the Atlantic and Indian oceans. **2** = POLLOCK 1.

bluegill *n.* a small colourful N American freshwater sunfish, *Lepomis macrochirus*.

blue grama *n.* a grass of the shortgrass prairie, *Bouteloua gracilis*, also grown as an ornamental.

bluegrass *n.* **1** any of several bluish-green grasses of the genus *Poa*, esp. Kentucky bluegrass. **2** a kind of country music characterized by close harmony and virtuosic playing of banjos, guitars, fiddles, etc.

blue-green algae *n.pl.* = CYANOBACTERIA.

blue helmet *n. informal* a UN peacekeeping soldier.

blue heron *n.* = GREAT BLUE HERON.

blue ice *n. Cdn* a vivid blue ice formed when a large amount of water freezes quickly.

blue jay *n.* a crested jay of central and eastern N America, *Cyanocitta cristata*, having a large tail and blue, black, and white plumage.

blue jeans *n.pl.* pants made of blue denim. □ **blue-jeaned** *adj.*

blue line *n. Hockey* **1** one of the two lines on the ice surface between the centre and the goal. **2** a team's defencemen collectively.

blue mould *n.* a bluish fungus of the genus *Penicillium* growing on food (esp. cheeses) etc.

Bluenose *n.* (also **Bluenoser**) *Cdn informal* a Nova Scotian.

blue pages *n.pl. N Amer.* the pages of a telephone directory containing listings of government depart-ments and services.

blueprint ● *n.* **1** a photographic print of the final stage of engineering or other plans in white on a blue background. **2** a detailed plan, esp. in the early stages of a project or idea. ● *v.tr. N Amer.* plan, project; make a blueprint of (a building, etc.).

blue ribbon ● *n.* the highest honour in a competi-tion etc. ● *attrib.adj.* (usu. **blue-ribbon**) **1** of the highest quality. **2** (of a committee, jury, etc.) carefully or specially selected.

blue rinse ● *n.* a preparation for tinting grey hair. ● *adj.* (also **blue-rinse, blue-rinsed**) composed of or relating to esp. conservative elderly women.

blues *n.pl.* **1** (prec. by *the*) a bout of depression (*had a fit of the blues*). **2 a** (prec. by *the*; often treated as *sing.*) a melancholic musical style characterized by frequent blues notes and often in a twelve-bar sequence. **b** (*attrib.*) of or relating to such music (*the band played a blues number*). □ **bluesy** *adj.* (in sense 2).

blue-sky *adj.* not practical; unrealistic.

bluesman *n.* (*pl.* **-men**) a musician, esp. a profes-sional, who plays the blues.

blue spruce *n.* a N American spruce with bluish-green needles, *Picea pungens*.

bluestem *n.* any of several tall N American grasses of the genus *Andropogon*, growing in prairie regions.

blue water *n.* open sea.

blue whale *n.* a baleen whale, *Balaenoptera musculus*, the largest of all living animals.

blue-winged teal *n.* see TEAL *n.* 1.

bluey *adj.* = BLUISH.

bluff¹ ● *v.* **1** *intr.* make a pretense of strength or confidence to gain an advantage. **2** *tr.* mislead by bluffing. ● *n.* a show of confidence or assertiveness intended to deceive. □ **call a person's bluff** chal-lenge a person thought to be bluffing. □ **bluffer** *n.*

bluff² ● *n.* **1** a steep cliff or bank. **2** *Cdn* (*Prairies*) a grove or clump of trees, usu. poplars or willows. ● *adj.* **1** (of a person or manner) good-naturedly blunt, frank, hearty. **2** (of a cliff, or a ship's bows) having a vertical or steep broad front.

bluing *n.* a blue powder or liquid used to prevent white laundry from yellowing.

bluish *adj.* somewhat blue.

blunder ● *n.* a careless or foolish mistake, esp. an important one. ● *v.* **1** *intr.* make a blunder; act clumsily or ineptly. **2** *tr.* deal incompetently with; mismanage. **3** *intr.* move about blindly or clumsily; stumble. □ **blunderer** *n.* **blunderingly** *adv.*

blunt ● *adj.* **1** (of a knife, pencil, etc.) lacking in sharpness; having a worn-down point or edge. **2** (of a person or manner) direct, uncompromising, outspoken. **3** short and with a squared-off end (*blunt* fingers). ● *v.tr.* **1** make blunt or less sharp. **2** weaken or reduce the sensitivity of (the senses, one's feelings, etc.). □ **bluntly** *adv.* (in sense 2 of *adj.*). **bluntness** *n.*

blur ● *v.* (**blurred**, **blurring**) **1** *tr.* & *intr.* make or become unclear or less distinct. **2** *tr.* smear; partially efface. **3** *tr.* make (one's memory etc.) dim or less clear. ● *n.* something that appears or sounds indistinct or unclear. □ **blurry** *adj.* (**-ier, -iest**).

blurb ● *n.* a promotional (usu. complimentary) description, esp. printed on a book's jacket by its publisher. ● *v.intr.* & *tr.* print or utter a blurb.

blurt *v.tr.* (usu. foll. by *out*) utter abruptly, thoughtlessly, or tactlessly.

blush ● *v.intr.* **1 a** develop a pink tinge in the face from embarrassment or shame. **b** (of the face) redden in this way. **2** feel embarrassed or ashamed. **3** be or become red or pink. ● *n.* **1** the act of blushing. **2** a pink tinge. **3** *N Amer.* (also **blusher**) a cosmetic used to give a pinkish colour to the cheeks. **4** a fairly sweet, pale pink wine. □ **at first blush** on the first glimpse or impression.

bluster ● *v.intr.* **1** behave pompously and boisterously; utter empty threats. **2** (of the wind etc.) blow fiercely. ● *n.* **1** noisily self-assertive talk. **2** empty threats. □ **blusterer** *n.* **blustery** *adj.*

Blvd *abbr.* Boulevard.

BM *abbr.* **1** Bachelor of Medicine. **2** *informal* bowel movement.

B movie *n.* a film regarded as second-rate, esp. one which relies on stereotypes and formulas.

B.Mus. *abbr.* Bachelor of Music.

B.Mus.Ed. *abbr.* Bachelor of Music Education.

BMX *n.* **1** organized bicycle racing on a dirt track, esp. for youngsters. **2** the sturdy, manoeuvrable kind of bicycle used for this. **3** (*attrib.*) of or related to such racing or the equipment used (*BMX gloves*).

B.N. *abbr.* Bachelor of Nursing.

bn. *abbr.* billion.

BNA *abbr.* *hist.* British North America.

B.O. *abbr.* **1** *informal* BODY ODOUR. **2** BOX OFFICE.

boa *n.* **1** any of several large snakes of the subfamily Boinae, found mainly in warm regions, which crush and suffocate their prey. **2** any related snake which is similar in appearance, such as the python or anaconda. **3** a long thin scarf made of feathers or fur.

boa constrictor *n.* a large snake, *Constrictor constrictor*, native to tropical America and the West Indies, which crushes its prey.

boar *n.* **1** (in full **wild boar**) a tusked wild pig of Eurasia and Africa, *Sus scrofa*, from which domestic pigs are descended. **2** an uncastrated male pig. **3** its flesh. **4** a male guinea pig etc.

board ● *n.* **1 a** a flat thin piece of sawn timber, usu. long and narrow. **b** a material resembling this, made from compressed or synthetic fibres (*cardboard*). **c** a thin slab of wood or a similar substance, often with a covering, used for any of various purposes (*ironing board*; *notice board*). **d** thick stiff card used in bookbinding. **2** = CIRCUIT BOARD. **3** the provision of regular meals, usu. with accommodation, for payment. **4 a** the directors of a company or other organization. **b** a specially constituted administrative body. **5** *N Amer.* (in *pl.*) the wooden fencelike structure enclosing the ice surface of a skating rink. **6** (in *pl.*) *slang* skis. ● *v.* **1 a** *tr.* & *intr.* go on board (a ship, aircraft, etc.). **b** *tr.* force one's way on board (a ship etc.) in attack. **c** *intr.* receive passengers (*the plane is now boarding*). **d** *tr.* allow (passengers) on board; load (an airplane). **2 a** *intr.* receive regular meals, or meals and lodging, for payment. **b** *tr.* (often foll. by *out*) arrange accommodation away from home for (*boarded the dog*). **c** *tr.* provide (a lodger etc.) with regular meals. **3** *tr.* (usu. foll. by *up*) cover with boards; seal or close. **4** *tr. Hockey* bodycheck (an opponent) into the boards with excessive force. □ **across the board** general; generally; applying to all. **go by the board** be neglected, omitted, or discarded. **on board 1** on or in a ship, train, etc. **2** present and functioning as a member of a team, corporation, etc. **3** *Baseball* on base. **take on board** consider (a new idea etc.).

board and batten *n.* a siding of vertical boards with battens at the joints between the boards.

boarder *n.* **1** a person who boards, esp. a lodger or a pupil at a boarding school. **2** a person who boards a ship, esp. an enemy.

board foot *n. N Amer.* a unit of volume for lumber equal to one square foot of one-inch-thick board.

board game *n.* a game played on a board, usu. with special pieces, dice, etc.

boarding *n. Hockey* the infraction of bodychecking an opponent into the boards with excessive force.

boarding house *n.* an establishment providing board and lodging for paying guests.

boarding pass *n.* a pass which permits a passenger to board an airplane, usu. indicating the departure gate and seat number etc.

boarding school *n.* a school at which most or all pupils are resident during the school term.

board of control *n. Cdn* (in Ontario) an elected body in municipal government having executive powers, comprising the mayor and controllers elected on a city-wide basis rather than to represent wards.

board of education *n. N Amer.* (*Ont. & US*) **1** a body responsible for administering public schools within a stated jurisdiction. **2** the jurisdiction covered by such a board.

board of trade *n. N Amer.* a chamber of commerce.

boardroom *n.* a meeting room in which the directors of a company etc. convene.

boardsailing *n.* = WINDSURFING. □ **boardsailor** *n.*

boardwalk *n. N Amer.* a walkway of crosswise wooden boards, constructed esp. on sand etc.

boast ● *v.* **1** *intr.* declare one's achievements, possessions, or abilities with indulgent pride and satisfaction. **2** *tr.* own or have as something praiseworthy etc. ● *n.* **1** an act of boasting. **2** something one is proud of. □ **boaster** *n.* **boastingly** *adv.*

boastful *adj.* **1** given to boasting. **2** characterized by boasting. □ **boastfully** *adv.* **boastfulness** *n.*

boat ● *n.* **1** a small vessel propelled on water by an engine, oars, or sails. **2** (in general use) a ship of any size. **3** an elongated boat-shaped container for holding gravy, sauce, etc. ● *v.* **1** *intr.* travel or go in a boat, esp. for pleasure. **2** *tr.* catch (a fish) and bring it into a boat. □ **off the boat** often *offensive* recently arrived from a foreign country. **in the same boat** sharing the same (usu. adverse) circumstances.

boater *n.* **1** a person who boats, esp. as a recreation. **2** a flat-topped hardened straw hat with a brim.

boathouse *n.* a shed at the edge of a river, lake, etc., for housing boats.

boating *n.* the use of boats for recreation etc.

boatload *n.* **1** enough to fill a boat. **2** *informal* a large number of people.

boatman *n.* (*pl.* **-men**) a man who hires out boats or provides transport by boat.

boat people *n.pl.* refugees who have fled by sea.

boatswain /ˈbəʊsən/ *n.* a ship's officer in charge of equipment and the duties of the crew.

Bob *n.* □ **Bob's your uncle** *Cdn & Brit. slang* an expression of completion or satisfaction.

bob¹ ● *v.* (**bobbed, bobbing**) **1** *intr.* move quickly up and down, esp. on water. **2** *tr.* move (the body or part of it) up and down with a slight jerk. ● *n.* a jerking or bouncing movement, esp. upward. □ **bob for** try to catch (floating apples etc.) with the mouth alone, as a game. **bob up** come to the surface or reappear suddenly.

bob² ● *n.* **1** a woman's or child's hairstyle cut short and even all around. **2** a weight on a pendulum, plumb line, or kite tail. **3 a** a short runner on a sled etc. **b** = BOBSLED. **4** a horse's docked tail. **5** (also **bobber**) a float used in fishing to suspend a line or net at a fixed depth. ● *v.tr.* (**bobbed, bobbing**) cut (hair) short and even all around.

bobbin *n.* **1** a cylinder or cone holding thread, yarn, wire, etc., used esp. in weaving and machine sewing. **2** a spool or reel.

bobbin lace *n.* lace made by hand with thread wound on bobbins and worked on a pillow.

bobble¹ ● *v.* **1** *intr.* move with continual bobbing. **2** *tr. N Amer.* mishandle or fumble (a ball). ● *n. N Amer.* a mistake or error, esp. a fumble of a ball.

bobble² *n.* a small woolly or tufted ball as a decoration or trimming. □ **bobbled** *adj.*

bobby pin *n. N Amer., Austral., & NZ* a flat hairpin of metal bent double.

bobby socks *n.pl.* esp. *N Amer.* socks reaching just above the ankle, esp. worn by teenage girls in the 1940s.

bobby soxer *n.* esp. *N Amer.* an adolescent girl, esp. one of the 1940s, wearing bobby socks.

bobcat *n.* a small N American lynx, *Felis rufus*, with a spotted reddish-brown coat and a short tail.

bobolink *n.* a N American songbird, *Dolichonyx oryzivorus*, the male of which is black with yellow and white markings, and the female yellowish buff.

bobskate *n. N Amer.* a child's skate consisting of two parallel blades attached with straps to a shoe etc.

bobsled (also **bobsleigh**) ● *n.* a mechanically steered and braked sled for two or four people, used for racing down a steep ice-covered run with many turns. ● *v.intr.* (**-sledded, -sledding**) race in a bobsled. □ **bobsledder** *n.*

bobwhite *n.* any N American quail of the genus *Colinus*, esp. *C. virginianus*.

bocce /'bɒtʃə/ *n.* (also **boccie, bocci** /'bɒtʃi/) an Italian form of lawn bowling, usu. played on a narrow dirt-covered court.

bocconcini /bɒkɒntʃi:ni/ *n.* a mild Italian cheese similar to mozzarella, in the form of a small ball.

bod *n.* informal *N Amer.* a body (*has a gorgeous bod*).

bodacious /bo:'deɪʃəs/ *adj. N Amer. slang* **1** outstanding, excellent. **2** esp. *US (South)* audacious.

bode *v.tr.* portend, foreshow. □ **bode well** (or **ill**) show good (or bad) signs for the future. □ **boding** *n.*

Bodhisattva /ˌbo:di'sætvə/ *n.* in Mahayana Buddhism, a person who is able to reach nirvana but delays doing so through compassion for others.

bodice /'bɒdɪs/ *n.* **1** the part of a woman's dress or blouse (excluding sleeves) which is above the waist. **2** a woman's sleeveless garment, usu. laced in the front, worn over a blouse or dress.

bodied *comb. form* having a body of the specified shape, colour, character, etc. (*full-bodied*).

bodily ● *adj.* of or concerning the body. ● *adv.* **1** with the whole bulk; as a whole (*threw them bodily*). **2** in the body; as a person.

body *n.* (pl. **-ies**) **1 a** the physical structure of a person or an animal, whether dead or alive. **b** the torso apart from the head and the limbs. **c** a corpse. **2 a** the main or central part of a thing (*the body of the essay*). **b** the bulk or majority; the aggregate (*body of opinion*). **3 a** a group of persons regarded collectively, esp. as having a corporate function (*governing body*). **b** (usu. foll. by *of*) a collection (*body of facts*). **4** a quantity (*body of water*). **5** a piece of matter; a mass (*celestial body*). **6** *informal* a person. **7 a** a full or substantial quality of flavour, tone, etc., e.g. in wine, musical sounds, etc. **b** an appearance of fullness and usu. waviness of the hair. □ **in a body** all together. **keep body and soul together** keep alive, esp. barely. **over my dead body** *informal* entirely without my assent. **take the body** *Hockey* bodycheck.

body armour *n.* armour, esp. made of bulletproof etc. fabric.

body bag *n.* a bag for carrying a corpse from the scene of an accident, crime, battle, etc.

bodybuilding *n.* the practice of strengthening, shaping, and enlarging the muscles by lifting weights and systematic exercise. □ **bodybuilder** *n.*

bodycheck *Hockey* ● *n.* an instance of using one's body to hit or obstruct an opposing player. ● *v.tr.* hit or obstruct in this way.

body count *n.* a list or total of people killed, esp. in a military operation.

body double *n.* a stand-in for a film actor during stunt or nude scenes.

bodyguard *n.* a person or group of persons escorting and protecting another person.

body language *n.* the process of communicating through conscious or unconscious gestures and expressions.

body odour *n.* the smell of the human body, esp. when unpleasant.

body piercing *n.* the piercing of holes in parts of the body other than the earlobes.

body politic *n.* organized society; a people or nation regarded as a political entity.

body rub *n.* a massage, esp. one given for sexual stimulation.

body-rub parlour *n. Cdn* a place where body rubs and often other sexual services are provided.

body search *n.* a search of a person's entire body and clothing for a hidden weapon, drugs, etc.

body shop *n.* a shop or garage where repairs to the bodywork of vehicles are carried out.

bodysuit *n.* a close-fitting one-piece stretch garment worn esp. for sporting activities.

bodysurf *v.intr.* ride the crest of a wave without a surfboard. □ **bodysurfer** *n.* **bodysurfing** *n.*

body weight *n.* the weight of a person's body.

bodywork *n.* **1** the structure of a vehicle body. **2** the manufacture or repair of vehicle bodies.

Boer /bɔr, bo:r, bʊr/ ● *n.* a South African of Dutch descent. ● *adj.* of or relating to the Boers.

boff *v.tr. & intr. N Amer. slang* have sex (with).

boffo *adj. N Amer. slang* **1** (esp. of a film, theatrical performance, etc.) resoundingly successful; highly lucrative. **2** (of a person) very popular.

bog ● *n.* **1** wet spongy ground too soft to support any heavy body, composed largely of mosses, sedges, rushes, and decomposing plant matter. **2** a stretch of such ground. ● *v.tr. & intr.* (**bogged, bogging**) **1** make or become unable to proceed (*was bogged down in paperwork*). **2** sink into mud or wet ground. □ **boggy** *adj.* (**-ier, -iest**).

bogan /'bo:gən/ n. N Amer. (Maritimes & Maine) a stagnant backwater adjacent to a river, lake, etc.
bogey[1] /'bo:gi/ Golf ● n. (pl. **-eys**) **1** a score of one stroke over par at any hole. **2** (formerly) = PAR 3. ● v.tr. (**-eys, -eyed**) play (a hole) in one stroke over par.
bogey[2] n. (also **bogy**) (pl. **-eys** or **-ies**) **1** an evil or mischievous spirit. **2** an awkward or threatening thing or circumstance. **3** slang = BOOGER.
bogeyman /'bo:gi,mæn/ n. (pl. **-men**) an imaginary evil spirit, esp. invoked to frighten children.
boggle v. informal **1** intr. & tr. be or cause to be startled or baffled (the mind boggles; boggles the mind). **2** intr. (usu. foll. by at) hesitate, demur.
bogland n. an expanse of boggy land.
bogus adj. sham, fictitious, spurious. □ **bogusly** adv.
Bohemian /bo:'hi:miən/ ● n. **1** a native of Bohemia. **2** (also **bohemian**) a socially unconventional person, esp. an artist or writer. ● adj. **1** of or characteristic of Bohemia, a region of the Czech Republic, or its people. **2** (also **bohemian**) socially unconventional. □ **bohemianism** n. (in sense 2).
Bohemian waxwing n. a waxwing, Bombycilla garrulus, which breeds in northwestern N America and northern Eurasia and wanders widely in winter.
boho /'bo:ho:/ informal ● n. (pl. **-os**) = BOHEMIAN n. 2. ● adj. = BOHEMIAN adj. 2.
bohunk /'bo:hʌŋk/ n. N Amer. **1** derogatory an immigrant from central or SE Europe. **2** a rough or muscular person.
boil[1] ● v. **1** intr. **a** (of a liquid) start to bubble up and turn to vapour; reach a temperature at which this happens. **b** (of a vessel) contain boiling liquid (the kettle is boiling). **2 a** tr. bring (a liquid or vessel) to a temperature at which it boils. **b** tr. & intr. cook by boiling. **c** tr. subject to the heat of boiling water, e.g. to clean. **3** intr. **a** (of the sea etc.) undulate or seethe like boiling water. **b** be greatly agitated, esp. by anger. ● n. **1** the act or process of boiling; boiling point (bring to a boil). **2** N Amer. a party at which (a usu. specified) food is boiled and eaten (corn boil). □ **boil down 1** reduce volume by boiling. **2** reduce to essentials. **3** (foll. by to) amount to. **boil over 1** spill over in boiling. **2** lose one's temper; become overexcited.
boil[2] n. an inflamed pus-filled swelling caused by infection of a hair follicle etc.
boiled dinner n. N Amer. (Maritimes, Nfld, US North & US North Midlands) a dish of meat and vegetables, esp. beef brisket, potatoes, cabbage and root vegetables, stewed together in water.
boiler n. **1** a strong vessel for generating steam under pressure. **2** a tank for heating a hot-water supply. **3** a metal tub or other vessel used for boiling.
boilerplate n. **1** a piece of rolled steel for making boilers. **2** a standard form, computer subroutine, etc. which can easily be replicated. **3** N Amer. (often attrib.) hackneyed or predictable ideas, language, or writing.
boiler room n. a room with a boiler and other heating equipment.
boiling adj. (also **boiling hot**) informal very hot.
boiling point n. **1** the temperature at which a liquid starts to boil. **2** a state of high excitement or extreme agitation (tempers reached the boiling point).
boing /bɔiŋ/ (also **boing-boing**) ● n. a twanging sound, such as that of a compressed spring suddenly released. ● interj. indicating this sound.
boink N Amer. var. of BONK.
boisterous /'bɔistərəs/ adj. **1** rough; noisily

exuberant. **2** (of the sea, weather, etc.) stormy, rough. □ **boisterously** adv. **boisterousness** n.
boîte /bwɒt/ n. a bar or nightclub.
bok choy /bɒk'tʃɔi/ n. N Amer. a cabbage-like plant of the mustard family, Brassica chinensis, having dark green outer leaves, white stalks, and a yellow centre.
bold ● adj. **1** confidently assertive; adventurous, courageous. **2** forthright, impudent. **3** vivid, distinct, well-marked (bold colours). **4** (in full **boldface, boldfaced**) printed in a thick black typeface. ● n. (also **boldface**) bold type. ● v.tr. (also **boldface**) set in bold type. □ **as bold as brass** excessively bold or self-assured. **be** (or **make**) **so bold as to** presume to; venture to. □ **boldly** adv. **boldness** n.
bole n. the stem or trunk of a tree.
bolero /bə'lero:/ n. (pl. **-os**) **1** a a Spanish dance in simple triple time. **b** music for or in the time of a bolero. **2** a sleeved or sleeveless open jacket just reaching the waist.
Bolivian /bə'liviən/ ● adj. of or relating to Bolivia, a country in S America, or its people or culture. ● n. a native or inhabitant of Bolivia.
boll /bo:l/ n. a rounded capsule containing seeds, esp. cotton or flax.
boll weevil n. a small weevil of Mexico and the southern US, Anthonomus grandis, whose larvae destroy cotton bolls.
bolo n. (pl. **-os**) **1** a large and heavy knife, used esp. in the Philippines. **2** (in full **bolo tie**) N Amer. a necktie made of cord or thick string, fastened at the collar with a decorative clasp.
bologna /bə'lo:ni, -nə/ n. N Amer. a smoked luncheon meat made from finely minced pork and beef.
Bolognese /,bɒlə'neiz/ ● adj. **1** (**bolognese**) (placed after noun) designating a sauce for pasta made of ground beef, tomatoes, etc. **2** of or pertaining to Bologna, Italy. ● n. a resident of Bologna.
Bolshevik /'bo:lʃəvɪk/ ● n. **1** hist. a member of the radical faction of the Russian socialist party, which became the communist party in 1918. **2** a Russian communist. **3** (in general use) any revolutionary socialist. ● adj. **1** of or relating to the Bolsheviks. **2** communist. □ **Bolshevism** n. **Bolshevist** n.
bolster ● n. **1** a long, often cylindrical pillow or cushion. **2** a pad or support, esp. in a machine. ● v.tr. **1** support, reinforce (bolstered our morale). **2** support with a bolster or pillow; prop up. □ **bolsterer** n.
bolt ● n. **1** a sliding bar and socket used to fasten or lock a door, gate, etc. **2** a large usu. metal pin with a head, usu. riveted or used with a nut, to hold things together. **3** a discharge of lightning. **4** the sliding piece of the breech mechanism of a rifle. **5** a sudden escape or dash for freedom. **6** a roll of fabric, paper, etc. ● v. **1** tr. fasten or lock with a bolt. **2** tr. (foll. by in, out) keep (a person etc.) from leaving or entering by bolting a door. **3** tr. fasten together with bolts. **4** intr. a dash suddenly away, esp. to escape. **b** (of a horse) suddenly gallop out of control. **5** tr. gulp down (food or drink) hurriedly. **6** intr. (of a plant) run to seed. □ **bolt from** (or **out of**) **the blue** a complete surprise. **bolt upright** rigidly, stiffly. **shoot one's bolt** do all that is in one's power.
bolt-on ● adj. **1** able to be fastened or attached by bolts. **2** able to be added when required. ● n. a thing that can be bolted on.
bolus /'bo:ləs/ n. (pl. **boluses**) a soft ball, esp. of chewed food.
bomb ● n. **1 a** a container with explosive, incendiary material, smoke, or gas etc., designed to explode on impact or by means of a time-mechanism or remote-

control device. **b** an ordinary object fitted with an explosive device (*letter bomb*). **2** (prec. by *the*) the atomic or hydrogen bomb considered as a weapon with supreme destructive power. **3** *N Amer. informal* a bad failure (*her latest play is a real bomb*). **4** an aerosol can or its contents. **5** *N Amer. Sport* a long pass, kick, shot or hit. ● *v.* **1** *tr.* attack with bombs; drop bombs on. **2** *tr.* (foll. by *out*) drive (a person etc.) out of a building or refuge by using bombs. **3** *intr.* throw or drop bombs. **4** *intr. esp. N Amer. informal* (often foll. by *out*) fail badly. **5** *intr. informal* move or go very quickly.

bombard *v.tr.* **1** attack with a number of bombs etc. **2** (often foll. by *with*) subject to persistent questioning etc. **3** *Physics* direct a stream of high-speed particles at (a substance). □ **bombardment** *n.*

Bombardier /ˌbɒmbəˈdiːr, bɒmˈbɑrdjei/ *n. Cdn proprietary* an enclosed vehicle for travelling over snow or ice, driven by rear caterpillar treads and steered by front skis, and capable of carrying several passengers.

bombardier /ˌbɒmbərˈdiːr/ *n.* **1** *N Amer.* a member of a bomber crew responsible for sighting and releasing bombs. **2** *Cdn & Brit.* a non-commissioned officer in the artillery, of a rank equivalent to corporal.

bombast *n.* pompous or extravagant language. □ **bombastic** *adj.* **bombastically** *adv.*

bombe /bɒm/ *n.* a dome-shaped frozen dessert, usu. consisting of an outer layer of ice cream filled with custard, cake crumbs, or another type of ice cream.

bombé /ˈbɒmbei/ *adj.* (esp. of furniture) rounded.

bombed *adj. informal* **1** intoxicated. **2** subjected to bombing.

bombed-out *adj.* **1** (of a person) driven out by bombing. **2** (of a building etc.) rendered uninhabitable by bombing. **3** *slang* = BOMBED 1.

bomber *n.* **1** an aircraft equipped to carry and drop bombs. **2** a person using bombs, esp. illegally. **3** *Cdn* = WATER BOMBER.

bomber jacket *n.* a short leather or cloth jacket tightly gathered at the waist and cuffs.

bombproof *adj.* able to resist the effects of a bomb.

bombshell *n.* **1** an overwhelming surprise or disappointment. **2** an artillery bomb. **3** *informal* a very attractive woman.

bomb shelter *n.* a room or building built to withstand bombs, used as an air-raid shelter.

bomb squad *n.* a division of a police force etc. that defuses or safely detonates unexploded bombs.

bona fide /ˌbɒnə ˈfaid, ˌboːnə ˈfaidi/ ● *adj.* genuine; sincere. ● *adv. Law* in good faith.

bona fides /ˌboːnə ˈfaidiːz/ *n.* **1** esp. *Law* an honest intention; sincerity. **2** (as *pl.*) *informal* documentary evidence of acceptability (*his bona fides are in order*).

bonanza ● *n.* **1** a source of wealth or good fortune. **2** a large output (esp. of a mine). **3 a** prosperity; good luck. **b** a run of good luck. ● *adj.* greatly prospering or productive.

bon appétit /ˌbɒnæpeˈtiː/ *interj.* expressing a wish that someone will enjoy what they are about to eat.

bonbon /ˈbɒnbɒn/ *n.* a candy, esp. a fancy one.

bond ● *n.* **1 a** a thing that ties another down or together. **b** (usu. in *pl.*) a thing restraining bodily freedom (*broke his bonds*). **2** (often in *pl.*) **a** a uniting force (*sisterly bond*). **b** a restraint; a responsibility (*bonds of duty*). **3** a binding engagement (*my word is my bond*). **4** a certificate issued by a government or a public company promising to repay borrowed money at a fixed rate of interest at a specified time; a debenture. **5** adhesiveness. **6** *Law* a sum of money put up as recognizance, esp. as a guarantee of good conduct (*released on $50,000 bond*). **7** a strong force of attraction holding atoms together in a molecule or crystal. **8** = BOND PAPER. ● *v.* **1** *tr.* bind together with an adhesive. **2** *intr.* adhere; hold together. **3** *tr.* connect with a bond. **4** *tr.* place (goods) in bond. **5 a** *intr.* become emotionally attached. **b** *tr.* link by an emotional or psychological bond. □ **in bond** (of goods) stored in a bonded warehouse until the importer pays the duty owing. □ **bondable** *adj.*

bondage *n.* **1** slavery. **2** subjection to constraint, obligation, etc. **3** sado-masochistic practices, including the use of physical restraints.

bonded *adj.* **1** (of goods) in bond. **2** (of material) reinforced by or cemented to another. **3** (of a person's or company's behaviour or performance) secured by a deposit of money. **4** (of a debt) secured by bonds.

bonded warehouse *n.* a warehouse for the retention of imported goods until duty is paid.

bondholder *n.* a person holding a bond granted by a private person, company, or government.

bond paper *n.* high-quality writing paper, usu. containing cotton fibre.

bond store *n. Cdn (Nfld)* a liquor store.

bone ● *n.* **1** any of the pieces of hard tissue making up the skeleton in vertebrates. **2** (in *pl.*) **a** the skeleton, esp. as remains after death. **b** the body, esp. as a seat of intuitive feeling (*felt it in my bones*). **3 a** the material of which bones consist. **b** a similar substance such as ivory. **4** (also *attrib.*) a thing made of bone. **5** (in *pl.*) **a** the essential part of a thing (*the bare bones*). **6** (in *pl.*) **a** dice. **b** castanets. **7** a strip of stiffening in a corset etc. **8** a pale ivory colour. ● *v.tr.* **1** take out the bones from (meat or fish). **2** stiffen (a garment) with bone etc. □ **bone of contention** a source or ground of dispute. **bone up** (often foll. by *on*) *informal* study (a subject) intensively. **close to** (or **near**) **the bone 1** tactless to the point of offensiveness. **2** destitute; hard up. **have a bone to pick** (usu. foll. by *with*) have a cause for dispute (with another person). **jump a person's bones** *slang* have sexual intercourse with a person. **make no bones about 1** make no attempt to conceal; admit openly. **2** not hesitate (*made no bones about revealing her income*). **to the bone 1** to the bare minimum (*cut expenses to the bone*). **2** completely (*chilled to the bone*). **work one's fingers to the bone** work very hard, esp. thanklessly. □ **boneless** *adj.*

bone-chilling *adj.* **1** extremely cold. **2** frightening.

bone china *n.* fine china made of clay mixed with the ash from bones.

boned *adj.* **1** (in *comb.*) having bones of a specified sort (*fine-boned*). **2** (of meat or fish) having the bones removed. **3** (of a corset etc.) having bones as stays.

bone-dry *adj.* extremely dry.

bonefish *n.* any of several species of large game fish, esp. *Albula vulpes*, having many small bones.

bonehead *informal* ● *n.* a stupid person. ● *adj.* stupid. □ **boneheaded** *adj.*

bone marrow *n.* a soft substance in the cavities of bones, of importance in blood cell formation.

bone meal *n.* crushed or ground bones used esp. as a fertilizer.

boner *n. informal* **1** a stupid mistake. **2** *N Amer. coarse slang* an erection.

boneyard *n. informal* a cemetery.

bonfire *n.* a large open-air fire for burning rubbish, as part of a celebration, or as a signal.

Bonfire Night *n. Cdn (Nfld)* Nov. 5, on which people light very large bonfires of combustible items, e.g. oil barrels and tires, often on prominent heights.

bong¹ *n.* a low pitched sound as of a bell.

bong[2] *n.* a type of water pipe for smoking drugs.

bongo *n.* (*pl.* **-os**) either of a pair of small long-bodied drums usu. held between the knees and played with the fingers.

bonhomie /ˌbɒnɒˈmiː/ *n.* geniality.

bonito /bəˈniːtoː/ *n.* (*pl.* **-os**) any of various striped tuna, esp. *Sarda sarda* of the Atlantic and Mediterranean.

bonk ● *v.* **1** *tr.* hit resoundingly. **2** *intr.* bang; bump. **3** *tr.* & *intr. coarse slang* have sexual intercourse (with). ● *n.* an instance of bonking. □ **bonker** *n.*

bonkers *predic.adj. slang* crazy.

bon mot /bɒ̃ ˈmoː, bɒn-/ *n.* (*pl.* **bons mots** *pronunc.* same or /-moːz/) a witty saying.

bonnet *n.* **1 a** a woman's or child's hat tied under the chin and usu. with a brim framing the face. **b** *informal* any hat. **2** = WAR BONNET. **3** the cowl of a chimney etc. **4** a protective cap in various machines. □ **bonneted** *adj.*

bonsai /ˈbɒnsaɪ/ *n.* (*pl.* same) **1** the art of cultivating ornamental artificially dwarfed varieties of trees and shrubs. **2** a tree or shrub grown by this method.

bonspiel /ˈbɒnspiːl/ *n.* a curling tournament.

bonus *n.* (*pl.* **bonuses**) **1** an unsought or unexpected extra benefit. ¶The phrase *added bonus*, although common, is regarded as tautologous by some people and is to be avoided in formal usage. **2** an amount of money given in addition to normal pay, in recognition of exceptional performance etc.

bonusing *n. Cdn* an act of subsidizing something, esp. as an inducement for development etc.

bon voyage /ˌbɒ̃ vwʌˈjʒ, vɔɪˈjɒʒ/ *interj.* & *n.* an expression of good wishes to a departing traveller.

bony *adj.* (**-ier, -iest**) **1** (of a person) thin with prominent bones. **2** having many bones. **3** of or like bone. **4** (of a fish) having bones rather than cartilage.

boo ● *interj.* **1** an expression of disapproval or contempt. **2** a sound intended to surprise. ● *n.* an utterance of 'boo', esp. as an expression of disapproval or contempt made to a performer etc. ● *v.* (**boos, booed**) **1** *intr.* utter a boo or boos. **2** *tr.* jeer at (a performer etc.) by booing. □ **not say boo to a goose** remain silent, esp. from shyness or timidity.

boob *n.* **1** *slang* a foolish person. **2** *informal* a woman's breast.

booboo *n. informal* a mistake.

boob tube *n.* (usu. prec. by *the*) *N Amer. informal* television; a television set.

booby *n.* (*pl.* **-ies**) **1** = BOOB. **2** any of various seabirds of the genus *Sula*, related to the gannet.

booby prize *n.* a prize given to the least successful competitor in a contest.

booby trap ● *n.* **1** a trap intended to surprise someone as a practical joke. **2** *Military* an apparently harmless explosive device intended to kill or injure anyone touching it. ● *v.tr.* (usu. **booby-trap**) place a booby trap or traps in or on.

boodle *n. slang* money, esp. when gained or used dishonestly, e.g. as a bribe.

booger *n. N Amer. informal* a piece of dried nasal mucus.

boogeyman /ˈbʊgiˌmæn/ *var. of* BOGEYMAN.

boogie /ˈbʊgi, ˈbuːgi/ ● *v.intr.* (**boogies, boogied, boogying**) *informal* **1** dance enthusiastically to rock music. **2** move or go quickly (*let's boogie on out of here*). ● *n.* **1** (in full **boogie-woogie**) a style of playing blues or jazz on the piano, marked by a persistent bass rhythm. **2** *informal* a dance to rock music.

boo hoo ● *interj.* (also **boo hoo hoo**) expressing weeping. ● *n.* (**boo-hoo**) (*pl.* **boo-hoos**) loud sobbing;

bewailing. ● *v.intr.* (**boo-hoo**) (**boo-hoos, boo-hooed**) (esp. of a child) weep loudly.

book ● *n.* **1 a** a written or printed work consisting of pages glued or sewn together along one side and bound in covers. **b** a literary composition intended for publication. **2** a bound set of blank sheets for writing or keeping records in. **3** a set of tickets, cheques, etc., bound up together. **4** (in *pl.*) a set of records or accounts. **5** a main division of a literary work or the Bible. **6** a libretto etc. **7** a telephone directory (*my number's in the book*). **8** a record of bets made and money paid out at a race meeting by a bookmaker. **9** an imaginary record or list (*broke every rule in the book*). ● *v.* **1** *tr.* **a** engage (a seat etc.) in advance; make a reservation of. **b** engage (a guest etc.) for some occasion. **2** *tr.* **a** take the personal details of (an offender or rule-breaker). **b** enter in a book or list. **3** *tr.* issue a railway etc. ticket to. **4** *intr.* make a reservation (*no need to book*). □ **book off** *Cdn* stay home from work, esp. when sick. **booked up** with all places reserved. **bring to book** call to account. **by the book** according to the rules. **close the books** ensure that all pertinent information is entered at the end of an accounting period. **in a person's bad** (or **good**) **books** in disfavour (or favour) with a person. **in my book** in my opinion. **make book 1** give odds, take bets and pay out winnings. **2** bet. **off the books** unofficially, not appearing in payroll reports etc. **on the books 1** (of a rule, law, etc.) publicly recorded. **2** contained in a list of members etc. **throw the book at** *informal* charge or punish to the utmost. □ **booker** *n.*

bookbinder *n.* a person who binds books professionally. □ **bookbinding** *n.*

bookcase *n.* a set of shelves for books in the form of a cabinet.

book club *n.* a society which sells its members selected books on special terms.

bookend ● *n.* **1** one of a pair of props used to keep a row of books upright. **2** one of a pair of e.g. television commercials etc. situated at either end of something. **3** *Football* a player positioned at either end of a team's defensive line. ● *v.tr.* **1** serve as or provide with something which frames a larger item on either side. **2** (of two people) flank a (third) person.

bookie *n. informal* = BOOKMAKER.

bookish *adj.* **1** studious; fond of reading. **2** acquiring knowledge from books rather than practical experience. **3** (of a word, language, etc.) literary; not colloquial. □ **bookishly** *adv.* **bookishness** *n.*

bookkeeper *n.* a person who keeps accounts for a trader, a public office, etc. □ **bookkeeping** *n.*

booklet *n.* a small book consisting of a few sheets usu. with paper covers.

bookmaker *n.* a person who takes bets, calculates odds, and pays out winnings. □ **bookmaking** *n.*

bookmark ● *n.* **1** a strip of leather, card, etc., used to mark one's place in a book. **2** a tag or character which can be inserted by a user at a particular point in an electronic text, making it easier to return to that point. **3** an electronic reference to a particular Internet site, which a reader has chosen to store permanently in the browser software, so as to reconnect rapidly with it. ● *v.tr.* mark (a site) with a bookmark.

bookseller *n.* a person who sells books, esp. the proprietor of a bookstore.

bookshelf *n.* (*pl.* **-shelves**) **1** a single shelf for books, either attached to a wall or as part of a bookcase. **2** = BOOKCASE. **3** (*attrib.*) designating stereo equipment etc.

that is small enough to place on a bookshelf (*bookshelf speakers*).

bookstore *n.* (also **bookshop**) a store where books are sold.

book value *n.* the value of an asset as entered in business or other records (*opp.* MARKET VALUE).

bookworm *n.* **1** *informal* a person devoted to reading. **2** the larva of a moth or beetle which feeds on the paper and glue used in books.

Boolean /'buːlɪən/ *adj.* pertaining to a system in which logical propositions are manipulated using the operators 'and', 'or', and 'not'.

boom[1] ● *n.* **1** a deep resonant sound, as of a distant explosion or a bass drum. **2** the resonant cry made by some birds and animals, esp. the prairie chicken and bittern. **3** a period of prosperity or sudden activity in commerce. ● *v.* **1** *intr.* make a deep hollow resonant sound. **2** *tr.* (usu. foll. by *out*) speak or utter with a booming sound. **3** *intr.* be suddenly prosperous or successful. □ **booming** *adj.*

boom[2] ● *n.* **1 a** a movable arm used for lifting etc. **b** a movable arm supporting a camera, microphone, etc. **2 a** a barrier stretched across a river, harbour, etc. to obstruct navigation. **b** *N Amer.* a barrier of floating timber used to contain, restrain, or guide floating logs. **c** a similar barrier used to contain oil spills etc. on water. **3** *N Amer.* a raft of timber or logs fastened together for transportation on water. **4** a pivoted spar to which the foot of a sail is attached. ● *v.tr. N Amer.* **1** gather or confine (logs) in a boom. **2** move or transport (logs) by forming them into a boom.

boom box *n.* a large and powerful portable stereo.

boom chain *n. Cdn Forestry* a chain linking two boomsticks, used to hold booms of logs together.

boomer *n.* = BABY BOOMER.

boomerang ● *n.* **1** a curved flat hardwood projectile used by Australian Aboriginals to kill prey, and often of a kind able to return in flight to the thrower. **2** a plan etc. that backfires. ● *v.intr.* **1** act as a boomerang. **2** (of a plan etc.) backfire.

booming ground *n.* **1** *Cdn* a section of a lake, river, etc. where logs are collected into booms. **2** *N Amer.* the mating ground of the prairie chicken.

boomlet *n.* a small boom, as in business etc.

boomstick *n. N Amer. Forestry* one of the logs that surrounds a boom and holds it together.

boom town *n.* a town owing its origin, growth, or prosperity to a boom in some commodity or activity.

boomy *adj.* (**-ier, -iest**) **1** having a loud, deep, resonant sound. **2** of or relating to a boom in business etc.

boon[1] *n.* an advantage; a blessing.

boon[2] *adj.* close, intimate, favourite (*boon companion*).

boondocks *n.pl.* (also **boonies**) *N Amer. informal* rough or isolated country; backwoods.

boondoggle *n. N Amer. informal* ● *n.* **1** work of little or no value done merely to appear busy. **2** a government project with no purpose other than political patronage. ● *v.* **1** *tr.* deceive (a person etc.). **2** *intr.* do work for the purpose of appearing to be busy.

boor /'bʊər/ *n.* **1** a rude person. **2** a clumsy person. □ **boorish** *adj.* **boorishly** *adv.* **boorishness** *n.*

boost ● *v.tr.* **1** promote or increase the reputation of (a person, scheme, etc.) by praise or advertising. **2** increase or raise (*boost prices*). **3** push from below (*boosted me up the tree*). **4** raise the voltage in (a circuit etc.). **5** *N Amer.* recharge (a car battery). **6** *N Amer. slang* steal. **7** amplify (a radio signal). ● *n.* **1** a lift or push from below. **2** an improvement in spirits, confidence,

etc. **3** an increase (*a boost in popularity*). **4** *N Amer.* the action of recharging a car battery.

booster *n.* **1** a device for increasing electrical power or voltage. **2** an auxiliary engine or rocket used to give initial acceleration. **3** a dose of an immunizing agent increasing or renewing the effect of an earlier one (also *attrib.: booster shot*). **4** a person who boosts by helping or encouraging. **5** = BOOSTER SEAT.

booster cable *n. N Amer.* (usu. in *pl.*) = JUMPER CABLE.

boosterism *n. N Amer.* the tendency to praise, advertise, or promote oneself or one's own (town, country, product, etc.). □ **boosterish** *adj.*

booster seat *n.* a small seat placed on another seat, e.g. in a car or at a table, to elevate a toddler.

boot[1] ● *n.* **1** an outer covering for the foot usu. reaching above the ankle. **2** *informal* a kick. **3** (prec. by *the*) *informal* dismissal, esp. from employment (*gave them the boot*). ● *v.tr.* **1** kick. **2** (often foll. by *out*) dismiss (a person) forcefully. □ **die with one's boots on** die in action. **put the boots to** kick brutally. **to boot** as well; to the good. **you bet your boots** *informal* it is quite certain. □ **booted** *adj.*

boot[2] *Computing* ● *n.* the operation or procedure of booting a computer or an operating system. ● *v.* **1** *tr.* prepare (a computer) for operation by causing an operating system to be loaded into its memory. **2** *tr.* cause (an operating system) to be loaded in this way. **3** *tr.* (often foll. by *up*) load (a routine) into a computer's memory. **4** *intr.* (of a computer etc.) undergo booting. □ **bootable** *adj.*

boot camp *n. N Amer. informal* **1** a centre for basic military training. **2** a penal institution in which young, esp. first-time, offenders undergo rigorous exercise and work and military-style discipline.

booth *n.* (*pl.* **booths** /buːθs, buːðs/) **1** a small temporary structure or stall for the display or sale of goods, e.g. at an exhibition. **2** an enclosure or compartment for various purposes, e.g. voting. **3** a set of a table and benches in a restaurant etc.

bootie *n.* (also **bootee**) **1** a soft woollen or cloth shoe. **2** a woman's short boot.

bootleg ● *adj.* **1** (of alcoholic beverages, drugs, etc.) illicitly produced, transported, or sold. **2** (of a recording) made without authorization, e.g. by illicitly recording a live concert. **3** *Football* of or relating to a play in which a player feigns a pass to another player, then continues with the ball concealed near his hip. ● *n.* **1** something produced or sold illegally. **2** *Football* a bootleg play. ● *v.tr.* (**-legged, -legging**) make, distribute, or smuggle illicit goods (esp. alcohol). □ **bootlegger** *n.*

bootlicker *n. informal* a person who behaves obsequiously or servilely.

bootstrap ● *n.* **1** a loop at the back of a boot used to pull it on. **2** *Computing* the action of bootstrapping; a bootstrapping routine. ● *v.* **1** make one's way or get oneself into a new state using existing resources; modify or improve by making use of what is already present. **2** *Computing* = BOOT[2] *v.* □ **pull oneself up by one's bootstraps** better oneself by one's efforts.

booty *n.* **1** plunder gained by force or violence. **2** *informal* something gained or won.

booze *informal* ● *n.* **1** alcoholic drink. **2** a drinking bout. ● *v.intr.* drink alcoholic liquor, esp. excessively.

booze can *n. Cdn* an illegal bar, esp. one operating in a private home.

boozer *n. informal* a person who drinks alcohol, esp. to excess.

booze-up *n. slang* a drinking bout.

boozy *adj.* (**-ier, -iest**) *informal* **1** intoxicated; addicted to drink. **2** involving a great deal of alcoholic drink (*a boozy dessert*). □ **boozily** *adv.* **booziness** *n.*

bop[1] *informal* ● *n.* = BEBOP. ● *v.intr.* (**bopped**, **bopping**) **1** dance, esp. to pop music. **2** move, go. □ **bopper** *n.*

bop[2] *informal* ● *v.tr.* (**bopped**, **bopping**) hit, punch lightly. ● *n.* a light blow or hit.

borage /ˈbɔrədʒ, ˈbʌ-/ *n.* any plant of the genus *Borago*, esp. *B. officinalis*, with hairy leaves and bright blue flowers, sometimes used in salads etc.

borax /ˈbɔræks/ *n.* **1** a mineral salt occurring in alkaline deposits. **2** the purified form of this salt, used in making glass, as an antiseptic, and as a household cleanser.

Bordeaux /bɔrˈdoː/ *n.* (*pl.* same /-ˈdoːz/) any of various red, white, or rosé wines from the district of Bordeaux in SW France.

bordello /bɔrˈdelo/ *n.* (*pl.* **-os**) a brothel.

border ● *n.* **1** the edge or boundary of anything, or the part near it. **2 a** the line separating two areas, esp. countries. **b** the district on each side of this. **3** a distinct edging around anything, esp. for strength or decoration. **4** a long narrow bed of flowers or shrubs in a garden. ● *v.* **1** *tr.* be a border to. **2** *tr.* provide with a border. **3** *intr.* (usu. foll. by *on, upon*) **a** adjoin; be situated alongside. **b** come close to being (*this borders on madness*). □ **borderless** *adj.*

border collie *n.* a long-haired usu. black and white breed of dog, often used for herding sheep.

border crossing *n.* **1** a place at which one may officially cross an international border. **2** the act of passing through customs and immigration formalities when crossing a border.

borderline ● *n.* **1** a marginal position between two categories or qualities. **2** a line marking a boundary. ● *adj.* **1** on the borderline. **2** verging on each of two categories or conditions without clearly being identifiable as one or the other.

bore[1] ● *v.* **1** *tr.* make a hole in, esp. with a revolving tool. **2** *tr.* hollow out (a tube etc.). **3** *tr.* **a** make (a hole) by boring or excavation. **b** make (one's way) through a crowd etc. **4** *intr.* drill a well (for oil etc.). **5** *tr.* (of an animal) move by burrowing. ● *n.* **1** the hollow of a firearm barrel or of a cylinder in an internal combustion engine. **2** the diameter of this. **3** = BOREHOLE.

bore[2] ● *n.* a tiresome or dull person or thing. ● *v.tr.* cause to lose all interest by tedious talk or dullness. □ **bore a person to tears** cause (a person) intense boredom. □ **bored** *adj.*

bore[3] *n.* a high wave caused by rapidly rising tide entering a long shallow narrow inlet.

bore[4] *past of* BEAR[1].

boreal /ˈbɔrial/ *adj.* **1** of the North or northern regions. **2** of the north wind.

boreal forest *n.* the northernmost and coldest forest zone of the northern hemisphere, which forms a belt across N America, Europe, and Asia.

boredom *n.* the state of being bored.

borehole *n.* a deep narrow hole, esp. one made in the earth to find water, oil, etc.

borer *n.* **1** any of several worms, molluscs, insects, or insect larvae which bore into wood, other plant material, and rock. **2** a tool for boring.

boric acid /ˈbɔrɪk/ *n.* an acid derived from borax, used as a mild antiseptic and in the manufacture of heat-resistant glass and enamels.

boring *adj.* that makes one bored; uninteresting, tedious, dull. □ **boringly** *adv.* **boringness** *n.*

born *adj.* **1** existing as a result of birth. **2 a** being such or likely to become such by natural ability or quality

(*a born leader*). **b** having a specified destiny or prospect (*born to shop*). **3** (*in comb.*) of a certain status by birth (*Canadian-born; well-born*). **4** created or caused (*anger born of frustration*). □ **born and bred** by birth and upbringing. **in all one's born days** *informal* in one's life so far. **not born yesterday** *informal* not stupid; shrewd.

born-again *attrib.adj.* **1** of or relating to a Christian who has made a new or renewed commitment to esp. evangelical faith. **2** full of enthusiasm and esp. new-found zeal for a cause.

borne 1 *past part. of* BEAR[1]. **2** (*in comb.*) carried or transported by (*airborne*).

boron /ˈbɔrɒn/ *n.* a non-metallic brown amorphous or black crystalline element extracted from borax and boric acid and mainly used for hardening steel.

borrow *v.* **1 a** *tr.* acquire temporarily with the promise or intention of returning. **b** *intr.* obtain money in this way. **2** *tr.* use (an idea, invention, etc.) originated by another; plagiarize. **3** *tr. & intr.* (in subtraction) take (one) from a digit of the minuend in order to add it as 10 to the digit holding the next lower place. **4** *tr.* (of a language) adopt (a word form) from another language. □ **borrowed time** an unexpected extension, esp. before an imminent disaster. **borrow trouble** *N Amer.* go out of one's way to find trouble. □ **borrower** *n.* **borrowing** *n.*

borscht /bɔrʃt/ *n.* an originally Eastern European soup with various ingredients including beets and cabbage, and served with sour cream. □ **cheap like borscht** *Cdn informal* extremely cheap.

borzoi /ˈbɔrzɔi/ *n.* a breed of large Russian wolfhound with a narrow head and silky, usu. white, coat.

bo's'n *var. of* BOATSWAIN.

bosom /ˈbʊzəm/ *n.* **1 a** a person's breast or chest, esp. a woman's. **b** *informal* each of a woman's breasts. **c** the enclosure formed by a person's breast and arms. **2** an emotional centre, esp. as the source of an enfolding relationship (*in the bosom of one's family*). **3** the part of a woman's dress covering the breast.

bosom friend *n.* (also **bosom buddy**) a very close or intimate friend.

bosomy *adj.* (of a woman) having large breasts.

boss[1] ● *n.* **1** a person in charge of employees. **2** a person who controls or manages an organization, e.g. a political party, union, etc. **3** a person who asserts authority (*let them know who's boss*). ● *v.tr.* **1** (usu. foll. by *around*) treat domineeringly; give constant peremptory orders to. **2** be the master or manager of. ● *adj. slang* first-rate, excellent.

boss[2] *n.* a round knob, stud, or other protuberance, esp. on the centre of a shield or in ornamental work.

bossa nova /ˌbɒsə ˈnoːvə/ *n.* **1** a dance like the samba, originating in Brazil. **2** a piece of music for this or in its rhythm.

boss man *n.* a man in charge.

bossy *adj.* (**-ier**, **-iest**) *informal* domineering; tending to boss. □ **bossily** *adv.* **bossiness** *n.*

Boston baked beans *n. N Amer.* baked beans with salt pork and molasses.

Boston bluefish *n. Cdn* = POLLOCK 1.

Boston cream pie *n. N Amer.* a round, vanilla cake with a custard filling and chocolate icing.

Boston fern *n.* esp. *N Amer.* an ornamental fern, *Nephrolepis exaltata bostoniensis*.

Bostonian /bɒsˈtoːniən/ ● *n.* a native or inhabitant of Boston, Massachusetts. ● *adj.* of or relating to Boston.

Boston ivy *n. N Amer.* an ornamental climbing vine,

Parthenocissus tricuspidata, the leaves of which turn a vivid red in autumn.

Boston lettuce *n. N Amer.* a cultivated salad lettuce having a round head and soft pale leaves.

Boston States *n.pl. Cdn (Maritimes)* New England.

bosun (also **bo'sun**) *var. of* BOATSWAIN.

botanical ● *adj.* (also **botanic**) **1** of or relating to botany. **2** of, relating to, or derived from plants. ● *n.* a drug, insecticide, or cosmetic etc. derived from parts of a plant. □ **botanically** *adv.*

botanical garden *n.* (also **botanic garden**) a large garden in which plants are studied and displayed.

botany *n.* **1** the study of the physiology, genetics, ecology, and classification of plants. **2** the plant life of a particular area or time. □ **botanist** *n.*

botch *v.tr.* **1** bungle; do badly. **2** patch or repair clumsily. □ **botcher** *n.*

both ● *adj. & pron.* the two, not only one (*both girls; the girls are both here*). ● *adv.* with equal truth in two cases (*both the boy and his sister are here*). □ **have it both ways** alternate between two incompatible points of view to suit the needs of the moment.

bother ● *v.* **1** *tr.* **a** give trouble to; worry, disturb. **b** *refl.* (often foll. by *about*) be anxious or concerned. **2** *intr.* **a** worry or trouble oneself; go to an effort (*didn't bother to tell me*). **b** (foll. by *with*) be concerned. ● *n.* **1 a** a person or thing that bothers or causes worry. **b** a minor nuisance. **2** trouble, worry, fuss. ● *interj.* esp. *Brit.* expressing annoyance or impatience. □ **cannot be bothered** will not make the effort needed.

bothersome *adj.* causing bother; troublesome.

bo tree *n.* an Indian fig tree, *Ficus religiosa*, regarded as sacred by Buddhists.

botrytis /bəˈtraitis/ *n.* a fungus of the genus *Botrytis*, esp. *B. cinerea*, cultivated on the grapes used for certain wines. □ **botrytised** /bəˈtraitaizd/ *adj.*

bottle ● *n.* **1** a container, usu. of glass or plastic and with a narrow neck, for storing liquid, pills, etc. **2** the amount that will fill a bottle. **3** = BABY BOTTLE. **4** a (prec. by *the*) *informal* liquor or other alcoholic drink (*problems drove him to the bottle*). **b** a bottle of an alcoholic drink. **5** a metal cylinder for liquefied gas. ● *v.tr.* **1** put into bottles or jars. **2** (usu. foll. by *up*) **a** conceal or restrain for a time (esp. a feeling). **b** keep (people) contained or entrapped. □ **hit the bottle** *informal* drink heavily. **on the bottle** *informal* drinking (alcoholic drink) heavily. □ **bottleful** *n.* (*pl.* **-fuls**).

bottled *adj.* **1** (of a liquid) contained in a bottle. **2** (of a gas) compressed to a liquid and contained in a tank.

bottle-feed *v.tr.* (*past and past part.* **-fed**) feed (a baby) with milk by means of a bottle.

bottle green ● *n.* dark green. ● *adj.* (**bottle-green**) of this colour.

bottleneck *n.* **1** a point at which the flow of traffic, production, etc., is constricted. **2** a narrow place causing constriction. **3 a** a smooth cylinder worn on a guitarist's finger used to produce sliding effects on the strings. **b** the guitar style characterized by this.

bottlenose dolphin *n.* (also **bottlenosed dolphin**) any of several dolphins of the genus *Tursiops*, with an elongated beak.

bottler *n.* a person or company which bottles drinks.

bottom ● *n.* **1 a** the lowest point or part (*bottom of the stairs*). **b** the part on which a thing rests (*bottom of a saucepan*). **c** the underside. **d** the furthest or inmost part (*bottom of the garden*). **e** (in *pl.*) *N Amer.* = BOTTOMLAND. **2** *informal* the buttocks. **3** the seat of a chair. **4** the less honourable, important, or successful portion (*at the bottom of his class*). **5** the ground under the water of a lake etc. **6** the basis; the origin (*get to the*

bottom of the problem). **7** *Baseball* **a** the second half of an inning, in which the home team bats. **b** the lower third of a batting order. **c** the batters making up this part of the batting order. **8** (in *pl.*) the part of a two-piece garment, esp. pyjamas or a bathing suit, worn below the waist. **9** *Naut.* **a** the keel or hull of a ship. **b** a ship, esp. a cargo carrier. **10** staying power; endurance. ● *adj.* **1** lowest. **2** last (*got the bottom score*). ● *v.* **1** *tr.* provide with a bottom. **2** *intr.* (of a ship) reach or touch the bottom. **3** *tr.* find the extent or real nature of; work out. **4** *tr.* (usu. foll. by *on*) base (an argument etc.) (*bottomed on logic*). **5** *tr.* touch the bottom or lowest point of. □ **at bottom** basically, essentially. **be at the bottom of** be the cause of. **bet one's bottom dollar** *slang* be assured. **bottom falls out** collapse occurs. **bottom out** reach the lowest level. **bottoms up!** a toast made when drinking. **bottom up** upside down. **get to the bottom of** fully investigate and explain.

bottom-feeder *n. N Amer.* **1** a fish or other organism living and feeding near the bottom of a body of water. **2** *derogatory* a person who exploits or lives parasitically off others. □ **bottom-feeding** *adj.*

bottomland *n. N Amer.* low-lying, fertile land along a watercourse; a flood plain.

bottomless *adj.* **1** without a bottom. **2** very deep (*a bottomless pit*). **3 a** (of a supply etc.) inexhaustible. **b** (of drinks) refilled at no extra charge. **4** naked below the waist (*bottomless dancers*). **5** featuring bottomless dancers etc. (*a bottomless bar*).

bottom line *n.* **1** the last line of a set of accounts, showing the final profit or loss. **2** net profit or loss. **3** *informal* the deciding or crucial factor.

bottom-up *attrib.adj.* **1** proceeding from detail to general theory, or from the bottom upwards. **2** non-hierarchical.

botulism /ˈbɒtʃʊˌlɪzəm/ *n.* poisoning caused by a toxin produced by the bacillus *Clostridium botulinum* growing in poorly preserved food.

boudoir /ˈbuːdwɑr/ *n.* a woman's small private room or bedroom.

bouffant /buːˈfɒnt/ ● *adj.* (of a dress, hair, etc.) puffed out. ● *n.* a bouffant hairstyle.

bougainvillea /ˌbuːɡənˈvɪliə/ *n.* any widely cultivated tropical plant of the genus *Bougainvillaea*, with large coloured bracts (usu. purple, red, or white).

bough /bau/ *n.* a branch of a tree, esp. a main one.

bought *past and past part. of* BUY.

boughten /ˈbɔtən/ *adj. N Amer.* bought; not homemade. ¶This usage is more current in rural than in urban areas. Although this leads some to think it dialectal or ungrammatical, it has been used by such Canadian writers as Margaret Laurence.

bouillabaisse /ˈbuːjəˌbeis/ *n.* a rich, spicy fish stew, originally from Provence.

bouillon /ˈbuːjɔ̃, ˈbuːljɒn, ˈbʊljɒn/ *n.* a clear broth made by cooking meat or fish in water.

bouillon cube *n.* a cube of concentrated soup stock which dissolves in boiling water to make broth.

boulder *n.* a large stone, esp. one worn smooth.

boule /buːl/ *n.* (also **boules** *pronunc.* same) a French form of lawn bowling, played on rough ground with usu. metal balls.

boulevard /ˈbʊlə,vɑrd/ *n.* **1** *N Amer.* a broad urban road. **2** a broad street, esp. with rows of trees planted along it. **3** *N Amer.* (esp. *Cdn*) **a** a strip of grass or other vegetation between a sidewalk and a roadway. **b** a median in the centre of a road, separating opposite directions of traffic. □ **boulevarded** *adj.*

boulevardier /buːləvɑrˈdjei/ n. a man who lives luxuriously and frequents fashionable places.

bounce ● v. **1 a** intr. (of a ball etc.) rebound. **b** tr. cause to rebound. **c** tr. & intr. bounce repeatedly. **2 a** intr. (of light etc.) reflect. **b** tr. cause (light etc.) to reflect. **3** informal **a** intr. (of a cheque) be returned by a bank when there are insufficient funds to meet it. **b** tr. write or present a cheque for which there are insufficient funds. **c** tr. refuse to pay (the bank bounced my rent cheque). **4** intr. **a** (foll. by about, up) (of a person, dog, etc.) jump or spring energetically. **b** (foll. by in, out, etc.) rush noisily, angrily, enthusiastically, etc. **5** tr. informal **a** eject forcibly (from a bar etc.). **b** dismiss (from a job). **6** intr. Baseball hit a ground ball (bounced to the shortstop). **7** intr. (of an e-mail message) be returned to the sender. ● n. **1 a** rebound. **b** the power of rebounding (this ball has good bounce). **c** a springy quality (gives your hair bounce). **2** a boost or rise (a bounce in popularity). **3** informal **a** swagger, self-confidence. **b** liveliness. **4** slang an instance of luck (the bounces went our way). **5** slang an act of ejection or dismissal. □ **bounce back** regain one's good health, spirits, prosperity, etc. **bounce off the walls** N Amer. informal be extremely excited, agitated, etc.

bouncer n. **1** a person employed to eject troublemakers from a bar etc. **2** Baseball a high-bouncing ground ball. **3** a person or thing that bounces.

bouncing adj. **1** (esp. of a baby) big and healthy. **2** boisterous.

bouncy adj. (**-ier**, **-iest**) **1** (of a ball etc.) tending to bounce well. **2** cheerful and lively. **3** resilient, springy. □ **bouncily** adv. **bounciness** n.

bound[1] ● v. intr. **1 a** spring, leap (bounded out of bed). **b** walk or run with leaping strides. **2** (of a ball etc.) bounce. ● n. **1** a springy movement upwards or outwards; a leap. **2** a bounce.

bound[2] ● n. (usu. in pl.) **1** a limitation; a restriction (beyond the bounds of possibility). **2** a border of a territory; a boundary. ● v. tr. **1** (esp. in passive; foll. by by) set bounds to; limit (views bounded by prejudice). **2** be the boundary of. □ **in bounds** inside the part of a playing field, court, etc. in which play is conducted. **out of bounds 1** outside the part of a playing field, court, etc. in which play is conducted. **2** outside the area in which one is allowed to be according to regulations. **3** beyond what is acceptable; forbidden.

bound[3] adj. (usu. foll. by for or in comb.) moving in a specified direction or toward a specified goal.

bound[4] ● v. past and past part. of BIND. ● adj. **1** tied or secured with rope, cord, etc. **2** certain (the dictionary's bound to be a hit). **3** required; obligated (bound by the law). **4** (in comb.) constricted, prevented from advancing (snowbound). **5** (of the pages in a book etc.) held together by a binding. □ **bound up with** (or **in**) closely associated with.

boundary n. (pl. **-ies**) a line marking the limits of an area, territory, etc.

boundless adj. unlimited; immense (boundless enthusiasm). □ **boundlessly** adv. **boundlessness** n.

bounteous adj. literary **1** = BOUNTIFUL. **2** freely given (bounteous affection). □ **bounteously** adv.

bountiful adj. **1** generous, liberal, plentiful. **2** ample. □ **bountifully** adv.

bounty n. (pl. **-ies**) **1** liberality; generosity. **2** a gift or reward, made usu. by a government, esp.: **a** a sum paid for the killing of dangerous or undesirable animals. **b** a sum paid for bringing criminals to justice. **3** an abundance.

bounty hunter n. a person who pursues criminals or kills animals for a reward. □ **bounty hunting** n.

bouquet /buːˈkei, boː-/ n. **1** an arrangement of cut flowers, esp. bound together for carrying. **2** the scent of wine etc. **3** a favourable comment; a compliment.

bourbon n. whisky distilled from corn mash and rye.

bourgeois /bɔrˈʒwɒ, ˈbʊr-/ often derogatory ● adj. **1 a** conventionally middle class. **b** humdrum, unimaginative. **c** selfishly materialistic. **2** upholding the interests of the capitalist class. ● n. (pl. same) **1** a bourgeois person. **2** Cdn hist. = WINTERING PARTNER.

bourgeoisie /ˌbɔrʒwɒˈziː/ n. **1** the capitalist class. **2** the middle class.

bourguignon /ˈbɔrɡɪˌnjɔ̃/ adj. designating a sauce of red wine, beef stock, mushrooms, and onions.

bout n. (often foll. by of) **1 a** a limited period (of intensive work or exercise). **b** a drinking session. **c** a period (of illness) (a bout of the flu). **2 a** a wrestling or boxing match. **b** a fight. **c** a trial of strength.

boutique ● n. a small shop or department of a store selling specialized goods or services, esp. fashionable clothes or accessories. ● attrib.adj. designating products, services, etc. produced on a small scale and marketed to a specialized clientele.

boutonniere /ˌbuːtənˈiːr/ n. a flower or spray of flowers worn in a buttonhole or on a lapel.

bouzouki /buːˈzuːki/ n. a Greek form of mandolin.

bovine /ˈboːvain/ ● adj. **1** of or resembling oxen or cattle. **2** stupid, dull. ● n. a bovine animal.

bovine growth hormone n. a growth hormone of cattle, administered in genetically engineered form to dairy cows to increase production. Abbr.: **BGH**.

bow[1] /boː/ ● n. **1 a** a slip-knot with a double loop. **b** a ribbon, shoelace, etc., tied with this. **c** a decoration (on a gift, in the hair, etc.) in the form of a bow. **2 a** device for shooting arrows with a taut string joining the ends of a curved piece of wood etc. **3 a** a rod with horsehair stretched along its length, used for playing the violin, cello, etc. **b** a single stroke of a bow over strings. **4 a** a shallow curve or bend. **b** a rainbow. **5** N Amer. the frame or temple of a pair of eyeglasses. ● v. **1** tr. & intr. use a bow on (a violin etc.). **2** intr. curve outward like a bow.

bow[2] /bau/ ● v. **1** intr. **a** incline the head or upper body, esp. in greeting or acknowledgement of applause. **b** incline or bend downward. **2** intr. submit (bowed to the inevitable). **3** tr. cause to incline (bow your head). ● n. an inclining of the head or body in greeting, acknowledgement of applause, etc. □ **bow and scrape** be obsequious or fawning. **bow down 1** bend or kneel in submission or reverence. **2** (usu. in passive) crush under the weight of (was bowed down by the burden). **bow out 1** make one's exit (esp. formally). **2** retreat, withdraw; retire gracefully. **take a bow** acknowledge applause.

bow[3] /bau/ n. **1** (often in pl.) the front end of a boat. **2** = BOWMAN[2]. □ **shot across the bows** a warning.

bowdlerize /ˈbaudləˌraiz/ v. tr. expurgate (a book etc.) by removing or altering material considered improper or offensive. □ **bowdlerization** n.

bowel n. **1 a** the part of the alimentary canal below the stomach. **b** (usu. in pl.) the intestines. **2** (in pl.) the depths; the innermost parts (the bowels of the earth).

bowel movement n. **1** discharge from the bowels; defecation. **2** the feces discharged from the body.

bower[1] /ˈbauər/ n. **1** a secluded place, esp. in a garden, enclosed by foliage; an arbour. **2** a small hut providing shade in a park or garden. □ **bowery** adj.

bower[2] n. either of the two highest cards in euchre, the jack of trumps (**right bower**) and the other jack of the same colour (**left bower**).

bowhead /'bo:hed/ n. a large baleen whale, *Balaena mysticetus*, inhabiting Arctic waters.

bowhunt v.tr. & intr. hunt (game) with a bow and arrows. □ **bowhunter** n. **bowhunting** n.

bowing n. the manner of playing a violin etc. with a bow.

bowl¹ n. **1 a** a usu. round deep basin used for food or liquid. **b** the quantity (of soup etc.) a bowl holds. **c** the contents of a bowl. **2 a** any deep-sided container shaped like a bowl (*toilet bowl*). **b** the bowl-shaped part of a tobacco pipe, spoon, balance, etc. **3 a** esp. *N Amer.* a bowl-shaped natural basin. **b** a bowl-shaped structure, esp. an amphitheatre or stadium (*Hollywood Bowl*). **4** (also **bowl game**) *Football* a post-season game or tournament between leading football teams (*Super Bowl*). □ **bowlful** n. (*pl.* **-fuls**).

bowl² ● v. **1 a** tr. roll (a ball etc.) along the ground. **b** intr. play a game of bowling. **2** intr. go along rapidly by revolving, esp. on wheels. ● n. **1** a wooden or hard rubber ball used in lawn bowling. **2** (in *pl.*; usu. treated as *sing.*) = LAWN BOWLING. □ **bowl over 1** knock down. **2** *informal* **a** impress greatly. **b** overwhelm.

bow legs /bo:/ n.pl. legs which are curved so as to be wide apart below the knee. □ **bowlegged** adj.

bowler¹ n. a person who participates in bowling.

bowler² n. (in full **bowler hat**) a derby hat.

bowling n. a game in which players roll a ball toward an arrangement of usu. five or ten pins with the intent of knocking down as many as possible.

bowling alley n. **1** a long and narrow hardwood lane along which the ball is rolled in the game of bowling. **2** a building containing several of these.

bowman¹ n. (*pl.* **-men**) an archer.

bowman² n. (also **bowsman**) (*pl.* **-men**) the paddler or rower nearest the bow of a boat, esp. a canoe.

bowsprit /'bo:sprɪt/ n. *Naut.* a spar running out from a ship's bow to which the forestays are fastened.

bowstring n. the string of an archer's bow.

bow tie n. **1** a necktie in the form of a bow (BOW¹ n. 1). **2** something in the shape of a bow tie, esp. a form of pasta. □ **bow-tied** adj.

bow-wow ● interj. an imitation of a dog's bark. ● n. **1** informal a dog. **2** a dog's bark.

box¹ ● n. **1** a container, usu. with flat sides and of firm material such as wood or cardboard. **2** the amount that will fill a box. **3** a separate compartment for any of various purposes, esp.: **a** a private seating area for a small group in a theatre or sports stadium. **b** a stand for a witness or prisoner in a courtroom. **c** a stall for a horse in a stable. **4 a** a rectangular arrangement of people or things, e.g. of four hockey players on a power play. **b** an enclosed area or space. **5** an enclosure or receptacle for holding a specified item or items (*shoe box*). **6 a** a box, either at a post office or at the side of a road, where mail is delivered. **b** a compartment at a newspaper office for receiving replies to a private advertisement. **7** (prec. by *the*) informal television. **8 a** *N Amer.* = BOOM BOX. **b** any of various electric or electronic devices housed in a box. **9** *slang* a computer. **9** a space or area enclosed by a border on a printed sheet or computer screen. **10** a protective casing for a piece of a machine etc. **11** (prec. by *the*) any of several specially demarcated areas in various sports, esp.: **a** a *Hockey* the penalty box. **b** *Baseball* any of the areas designating the positions to be taken by the batter, pitcher, catcher, or coaches. **c** the enclosed area in which box lacrosse is played. ● v.tr. **1** put in or provide with a box. **2** (foll. by *in*, *up*, *out*) surround or confine (a person, vehicle, etc.); restrain from movement. **3** mix up. □ **boxful** n. (*pl.* **-fuls**). **boxlike** adj.

box² ● v. **1 a** tr. fight in a boxing match. **b** intr. participate in boxing. **2** tr. slap or punch (esp. a person's ear). ● n. a slap or punch, esp. on the ear.

box³ n. = BOXWOOD.

boxboard n. a lightweight cardboard used in packaging etc.

box canyon n. a narrow canyon with a flat bottom and vertical walls.

boxcar n. *N Amer.* an enclosed railway freight car, usu. having sliding doors on the sides.

box elder n. = MANITOBA MAPLE.

boxer n. **1** a person who participates in boxing, esp. for sport. **2** a breed of medium-size dog with a smooth brown coat and puglike face. **3** (in *pl.*) = BOXER SHORTS.

boxer shorts n. **1** men's loose-fitting underwear with an elasticized waistband. **2** men's or women's shorts of a similar design.

boxing n. the sport of fighting with the fists, esp. in padded gloves.

Boxing Day n. (in parts of the Commonwealth) a holiday celebrated on Dec. 26 or the first weekday after Christmas.

boxing glove n. each of a pair of heavily padded gloves used in boxing.

Boxing Week n. *Cdn* the week between Christmas and New Year's Day.

box lacrosse n. (also informal **boxla** /'bɒkslə/) *Cdn* a form of lacrosse played in an enclosed area (usu. a hockey rink without ice) by teams of six players.

box lunch n. *N Amer.* a cold meal packed in a box etc.

box number n. a number of a postal box etc.

box office n. **1** an office for booking seats and buying tickets at a theatre, cinema, stadium, etc. **2** the financial aspect of the arts and entertainment industry (often *attrib.*: *a box-office failure*).

box score n. *N Amer.* a table summarizing a baseball game etc., showing the score, names of players, their statistics, and other information.

box set n. a collection of several compact discs, cassettes, books, etc. sold together in a box.

box social n. *N Amer.* a fundraising event at which box lunches are auctioned to raise funds, often such that the purchaser shares the meal with the person who prepared it.

box spring n. *N Amer.* a rectangular wooden frame containing vertical springs and used as a support for a mattress.

box stall n. *N Amer.* an enclosed, usu. square stall in a barn, esp. for a horse.

boxwood n. **1** any small slow-growing evergreen tree or shrub of the genus *Buxus*, esp. *B. sempervirens*, having glossy dark green leaves and popular as hedging. **2** the hard wood of this, used for carving etc.

boxy adj. (**-ier**, **-iest**) resembling a box in shape.

boy ● n. **1** a male child or youth. **2** a young man, esp. regarded as not yet mature. **3** a son. **4** a male belonging to a specified group (*a country boy*). **5** (**the boys**) informal a group of men mixing socially. **6** (usu. as a form of address) a male animal (*Down, boy!*). ● interj. expressing pleasure, surprise, etc. □ **boys will be boys** such behaviour from young males is to be expected. □ **boyhood** n. **boyish** adj. **boyishly** adv. **boyishness** n.

boycott v.tr. **1** combine to coerce or punish (a person, company, etc.) by a systematic refusal of normal commercial or social relations. **2 a** refuse to handle or purchase (goods) to this end. **b** refuse to attend (a meeting etc.) with this aim. ● *n.* such a refusal.

boyfriend *n.* **1** a regular male companion or lover. **2** any male friend.

Boy Scout *n.* = SCOUT[1] 4.

boysenberry /'bɔizən,beri/ *n.* (*pl.* **-ies**) **1** a hybrid of several species of bramble. **2** the large red edible fruit of this plant.

boys in blue *n.pl. informal* police officers; the police.

boy toy *n. N Amer. slang derogatory* **1** an attractive young man who is the lover of an older person. **2** a woman considered to have an overtly sexual image.

boy wonder *n.* a very talented young man.

bozo *n.* (*pl.* **bozos**) *esp. N Amer. slang* a stupid or annoying person.

BP *abbr.* **1** boiling point. **2** blood pressure. **3** before the present (era).

B.P.E. *abbr.* Bachelor of Physical Education.

B.Phil. *abbr.* Bachelor of Philosophy.

bps *abbr. Computing* bits per second.

BQ *abbr.* (in Canada) BLOC QUÉBÉCOIS.

Br *symbol* bromine.

Br. *abbr.* **1** Brother. **2** Britain; British. **3** (also **BR**) bedroom.

bra *n.* (*pl.* **bras**) **1** an undergarment worn by women and adolescent girls to support the breasts. **2** *N Amer. & Austral.* a piece of vinyl etc. designed to fit over the front end of a car to protect the finish. □ **braless** *adj.*

brace ● *n.* **1 a** a device that clamps or fastens tightly. **b** a strengthening piece of iron or timber used in building. **2** (in *pl.*) *Cdn, Brit., Austral. & NZ* suspenders. **3** (in *pl.*) an orthodontic appliance consisting of metal wires and brackets worn on the teeth to straighten them. **4** a device to support an injured joint or other body part (*neck brace*). **5** (*pl.* same) a pair. **6** a large hand drill consisting of a crank handle and a chuck to hold a bit. **7** a rope attached to the yard of a ship for trimming the sail. **8 a** a connecting mark { or } used in printing. **b** *Music* a similar mark connecting staffs to be performed at the same time. ● *v.tr.* **1** fasten tightly, give firmness to. **2** make steady by supporting. **3** invigorate, refresh. **4** (often *refl.*) prepare for a shock etc.

bracelet *n.* **1** an ornamental band, hoop, or chain worn on the wrist, arm, or ankle. **2** a band or chain worn around the wrist for identification, esp. for medical purposes. **3** *slang* a handcuff.

bracing ● *adj.* invigorating, refreshing. ● *n.* a system or series of braces. □ **bracingly** *adv.*

bracken *n.* **1** a large branching fern, *Pteridium aquilinum*, having long coarse fronds. **2** a mass of such ferns.

bracket ● *n.* **1** a right-angled or other support attached to and projecting from a vertical surface. **2 a** shelf fixed with such a support to a wall. **3** each of a pair of marks () [] {} or <> used to enclose words or figures. **4** a group classified as containing similar elements or falling between given limits (*income bracket*). ● *v.tr.* (**bracketed**, **bracketing**) **1 a** link or couple (names, lines, etc.) with a brace. **b** imply a connection or equality between. **2 a** enclose in brackets as parenthetic or spurious. **b** *Math.* enclose in brackets as having specific relations to what precedes or follows. **3** enclose on either side.

brackish *adj.* (of water etc.) slightly salty. □ **brackishness** *n.*

bract *n.* a modified and often brightly coloured leaf, with a flower or an inflorescence in its axil.

brag ● *v.* (**bragged, bragging**) **1** *intr.* talk boastfully. **2** *tr.* boast about. ● *n.* **1** a boastful statement; boastful talk. **2** a card game like poker. □ **bragger** *n.*

braggingly *adv.* **braggy** *adj.* (**-ier, -iest**).

braggadocio /,brægə'doːtʃioː, -'doːʃio:/ *n.* empty boasting; a boastful manner of speech and behaviour.

Brahma /'brɒmə/ *n.* a breed of cattle from India, with a humped shoulder and neck.

Brahman /'brɒmən/ *n.* (also **brahman**) (*pl.* **-mans**) **1** (also **Brahmin** /-mɪn/) a member of the highest Hindu caste, whose members are traditionally eligible for the priesthood. **2** = BRAHMA. □ **Brahmanic** /-'mænɪk/ *adj.* **Brahmanical** *adj.*

Brahmanism *n.* the complex sacrificial pantheistic religion that emerged in post-Vedic India (*c.*900 BC), characterized by the caste system.

braid ● *n.* **1** a length of hair, straw, etc. in three or more interlaced strands. **2** a woven band of fabric or thread used for edging or trimming. ● *v.tr.* **1** plait or intertwine (hair, rope, etc.). **2** trim or decorate with braid. □ **braider** *n.*

braided *adj.* **1** intertwined in a braid. **2** (of a river) split by deposits into interconnected streams.

braiding *n.* **1** various types of braid collectively. **2** braided work.

Braille /breil/ ● *n.* a system of writing and printing for the blind, using patterns of raised dots. ● *v.tr.* print or transcribe in Braille.

brain ● *n.* **1** an organ of soft nervous tissue contained in the skull of vertebrates, functioning as the coordinating centre of sensation, and of intellectual and nervous activity. **2** (in *pl.*) the substance of the brain, esp. as food. **3 a** a person's intellectual capacity (*has a poor brain*). **b** (often in *pl.*) intelligence; high intellectual capacity (*has brains*). **4** *informal* an intelligent person. **5** (often in *pl.*; prec. by *the*) *informal* **a** the cleverest person in a group. **b** a person who originates a complex plan or idea (*the brains behind the robbery*). **6** an electronic device with functions comparable to those of a brain. ● *v.tr.* **1** dash out the brains of. **2** strike hard on the head. □ **on the brain** *informal* obsessively in one's thoughts.

brainchild *n.* (*pl.* **-children**) *informal* an idea, plan, etc. regarded as the result of a person's mental effort.

brain damage *n.* injury to the brain permanently impairing its functions. □ **brain-damaged** *adj.*

brain-dead *adj.* **1** having suffered brain death. **2** *informal derogatory* stupid.

brain death *n.* permanent cessation of the functions of the brain stem that control breathing etc., regarded as indicative of death.

brain drain *n. informal* the loss of skilled personnel by emigration.

brainless *adj.* stupid, foolish.

brainpower *n.* mental ability or intelligence.

brain scan *n.* a radiographic scan of the brain.

brain stem *n.* the central trunk of the brain, upon which the cerebrum and cerebellum are set, and which continues downwards to form the spinal cord.

brainstorm ● *n.* **1** a concerted intellectual treatment of a problem by discussing spontaneous ideas about it. **2** *N Amer.* = BRAINWAVE 2. **3** a violent or excited outburst often as a result of a sudden mental disturbance. **4** *informal* mental confusion. ● *v.intr. & tr.* seek solutions to a problem by discussing spontaneous ideas about. □ **brainstorming** *n.*

brainteaser *n.* *informal* a puzzle or problem.

brain trust *n.* esp. *N Amer.* a group of expert advisers.

brainwash *v.tr.* subject (a person) to a prolonged

process by which ideas other than and at variance with those already held are implanted in the mind. □ **brainwashing** n.

brainwave n. **1** (usu. in pl.) an electrical impulse in the brain. **2** informal a sudden bright idea.

brainy adj. (**-ier, -iest**) intellectually clever or active. □ **brainily** adv. **braininess** n.

braise v.tr. fry lightly and then stew slowly with a little liquid in a closed container.

brake¹ ● n. **1** (often in pl.) a device for stopping the motion of a mechanism, esp. a wheel or vehicle, or for keeping it at rest. **2** anything that has the effect of hindering or impeding. ● v. **1** intr. **a** apply a brake. **b** slow or come to a stop upon application of a brake. **2** tr. retard or stop with a brake. □ **put on the brakes** slow down.

brake² n. = BRACKEN.

brake drum n. a cylinder attached to a wheel, whose inner surface is gripped by brake shoes when drum brakes are applied.

brake fluid n. fluid used in a hydraulic brake system.

brake light n. (usu. in pl.) a red light at the rear of a motor vehicle, lit when the brakes are applied.

brakeman n. (pl. **-men**) N Amer. an employee on a train, responsible for maintenance on a journey.

brake pad n. **1** either of two metal pads which squeeze the disc when disc brakes are applied. **2** either of two pieces of hard rubber applied to the rim of a bicycle wheel as a brake.

brake shoe n. a long curved metal block which presses on the inside of a brake drum when drum brakes are applied.

bramble n. **1** any of various thorny shrubs bearing fleshy red or black berries, esp. the blackberry bush. **2** the edible berry of these shrubs. **3** any of various other shrubs with similar foliage, esp. a wild rose. □ **brambly** adj.

bran n. edible husks of grain separated from flour after grinding.

branch ● n. **1** a limb extending from a tree or bough. **2** a lateral extension or subdivision, esp. of a river, road, or railway (also attrib.: branch line). **3** a conceptual extension or subdivision, as of a family etc. **4** a local division or office etc. of a large business, bank, library, etc. ● v.intr. (often foll. by off) **1** diverge from the main part. **2** divide into branches. **3** (of a tree) bear or send out branches. □ **branch out** extend one's field of interest. □ **branched** adj. **branchlet** n. **branchy** adj. (**-ier, -iest**).

branch plant n. Cdn a factory etc. owned by a company based in another country (often attrib.: branch-plant economy).

brand ● n. **1 a** a particular make of goods. **b** an identifying trademark, label, etc. **2** (usu. foll. by of) a special or characteristic kind (brand of humour). **3** an identifying mark burned on livestock or (formerly) prisoners etc. with a hot iron. **4** an iron used for this. **5** a piece of burning, smouldering, or charred wood. **6** a stigma; a mark of disgrace. ● v.tr. **1** mark with a hot iron. **2** stigmatize; mark with disgrace (was branded for life). **3** impress unforgettably on one's mind. **4** assign a trademark or label to. □ **brander** n.

brandied adj. preserved or flavoured with brandy.

branding iron n. an iron used to brand livestock etc.

brandish v.tr. flourish as a threat or in display.

brand name n. (often attrib.) **1** a trade or proprietary name. **2** a product with a brand name.

brand new adj. completely or obviously new.

brandy n. (pl. **-ies**) a strong alcoholic spirit distilled from wine or fermented fruit juice.

brant n. N Amer. an Arctic goose, Branta bernicla, similar to the Canada goose but smaller and darker.

brash¹ adj. **1** vulgarly or ostentatiously self-assertive. **2** hasty, rash. **3** impudent. □ **brashly** adv. **brashness** n.

brash² n. loose broken rock or ice.

brass ● n. **1 a** yellow alloy of copper and zinc. **2 a** an ornament or other decorated piece of brass. **b** brass objects collectively. **3** Music brass wind instruments forming a band or a section of an orchestra. **4** (in full **top brass**) informal persons in authority or of high (esp. military) rank. **5** an inscribed or engraved memorial tablet of brass. **6** informal effrontery (then had the brass to demand money). ● adj. made of brass.

brass band n. a group of musicians playing brass instruments, sometimes also with percussion.

brass bed n. a bedstead with the head and usu. the foot of brass spindles.

brasserie /'bræsəri/ n. **1** a restaurant, originally one serving beer with food. **2** Cdn (Que.) a pub.

brassica /'bræsɪkə/ n. any cruciferous plant of the genus Brassica, having taproots and erect branched stems, including cabbage, broccoli, and turnip.

brassiere /brə'zɪːr/ n. = BRA 1.

brass knuckles n.pl. connected metal rings worn on the fingers to make punches more severe.

brass ring n. N Amer. noteworthy success, esp. as viewed as a reward for ambition, hard work, etc. (reach for the brass ring).

brass tacks n.pl. informal actual details; real business (get down to brass tacks).

brassy adj. (**-ier, -iest**) **1** impudent. **2** showy, pretentious. **3** loud and blaring. **4** of or like brass. □ **brassily** adv. **brassiness** n.

brat n. **1** usu. derogatory a child, esp. a badly behaved one. **2** a child brought up in a specified milieu (Forces brat). □ **brattish** adj. **brattiness** n. **bratty** adj.

brat pack n. slang a rowdy and ostentatious group of young celebrities, esp. film stars. □ **brat packer** n.

bratwurst /'brætwɜrst/ n. a type of small German pork sausage.

bravado /brə'vɒːdo/ n. a bold manner or a show of boldness intended to impress.

brave ● adj. **1** able or ready to face and endure danger, pain, adversity, etc. **2** literary splendid, spectacular (make a brave show). ● n. hist. a N American Aboriginal warrior. ● v.tr. defy; encounter bravely. □ **brave it out** behave defiantly under suspicion or blame. □ **bravely** adv. **braveness** n.

brave new world n. usu. ironic an era of supposed happiness brought on by technological or social developments.

bravery n. **1** brave conduct. **2** a brave nature.

bravo /'brɒvo, brɒ'vo/ ● interj. expressing approval of a performer etc. ● n. (pl. **-os**) a cry of bravo.

bravura /brə'vʊrə/ ● adj. requiring or displaying brilliant or virtuosic skill (a bravura performance). ● n. brilliant or virtuosic skill, esp. in artistic performance.

brawl ● n. **1** a rowdy fight, usu. involving several people. **2** a noisy quarrel. ● v.intr. fight or quarrel noisily or roughly. □ **brawler** n.

brawn n. **1** muscular strength. **2** muscle; lean flesh.

brawny adj. (**-ier, -iest**) muscular, strong.

bray ● n. **1** the cry of a donkey. **2** a sound like this cry, e.g. that of a harshly-played brass instrument, a laugh, etc. ● *v.* **1** *intr.* make a braying sound. **2** *tr.* utter harshly.

Brayon /breɪˈjɔ̃/ *Cdn* ● *n.* an inhabitant of the Madawaska region of New Brunswick. ● *adj.* denoting the Brayons, their mixed francophone and anglophone culture, etc.

braze¹ ● *v.tr.* solder with an alloy of copper and zinc at a high temperature. ● *n.* **1** a brazed joint. **2** the alloy used for brazing.

braze² *v.tr.* **1 a** make of brass. **b** cover or ornament with brass. **2** make hard like brass.

brazen ● *adj.* **1** (also **brazen-faced**) flagrant and shameless. **2** made of brass. **3** of or like brass, esp. in colour or sound. ● *v.tr.* (usu. in phr. **brazen it out**) face (censure) in a defiantly unrepentant manner. □ **brazenly** *adv.* **brazenness** *n.*

brazier¹ /ˈbreɪzɪər, -ʒər/ *n.* **1** *N Amer.* a charcoal grill for cooking. **2** a portable heater consisting of a pan or stand for holding lighted coals.

brazier² *n.* a worker in brass. □ **braziery** *n.*

Brazilian /brəˈzɪlɪən/ ● *adj.* of or relating to Brazil, a country in S America, or its people or culture. ● *n.* a native or inhabitant of Brazil.

Brazil nut /brəˈzɪl/ *n.* the large three-sided nut of the S American tree *Bertholletia excelsa*.

breach ● *n.* **1** (often foll. by *of*) the breaking of or failure to observe a law, contract, regulations, etc. **2 a** a breaking of relations; an estrangement. **b** a quarrel. **3 a** a broken state. **b** a gap, esp. one made by artillery in fortifications. ● *v.* **1** *tr.* break through; make a gap in. **2** *tr.* break (a law, contract, etc.). **3** *intr.* (of a whale) leap clear out of the water. □ **step into** (or **fill**) **the breach** give help in a crisis, esp. by replacing someone who has dropped out.

breach of the peace *n.* an infringement or violation of the public peace by any disturbance etc.

bread ● *n.* **1** baked food made of flour and a liquid and often leavened with yeast. **2 a** necessary food. **b** (also **daily bread**) one's livelihood. **3** *slang* money. ● *v.tr.* coat with bread crumbs for cooking. □ **bread and wine** the Eucharist. **break bread** share a meal. **know which side one's bread is buttered** (**on**) know where one's advantage lies. **take the bread out of a person's mouth** take away a person's living, esp. by competition etc.

bread and butter ● *n.* **1** bread spread with butter. **2** an essential element, esp. that which provides one's livelihood. ● *adj.* (usu. **bread-and-butter**) **1** designating something basic and fundamental to one's livelihood (*bread-and-butter concerns*). **2** commonplace, humdrum. **3** expressing gratitude, esp. for hospitality (*bread-and-butter letter*).

breadbasket *n.* **1** a basket for bread or rolls. **2 a** region producing much grain. **3** *slang* the abdomen or stomach.

breadboard *n.* a board for cutting bread on.

breadbox *n.* *N Amer.* a container in which bread is kept.

bread crumb *n.* **1** a very small fragment of bread. **2** (in *pl.*) bread crumbled for use in cooking.

bread flour *n.* flour, usu. milled from hard wheat, with a high proportion of gluten, for making bread.

breadfruit *n.* **1** a tropical evergreen tree, *Artocarpus altilis*, bearing edible usu. seedless fruit. **2** this fruit, which when roasted becomes soft like new bread.

breadknife *n.* (*pl.* **-knives**) a knife with a long serrated blade, for slicing bread.

breadline *n.* *N Amer.* a line of people waiting to receive free food.

bread stick *n.* a long, stick-like piece of crisp bread.

breadth *n.* **1** the distance or measurement from side to side of a thing. **2** a piece (of cloth etc.) of standard or full breadth. **3** extent, range. **4** freedom from limitations, esp. in opinion or interests.

breadwinner *n.* a person who earns the money to support a family. □ **breadwinning** *n.* & *adj.*

break ● *v.* (*past* **broke**; *past part.* **broken** or *archaic* **broke**) **1** *tr.* & *intr.* **a** separate into pieces under a blow or strain; shatter; fracture. **b** make or become inoperative, esp. from damage. **c** break a bone in or dislocate (part of the body). **d** break the skin of (the head or crown). **2 a** *tr.* cause or effect an interruption in (*broke the silence*). **b** *intr.* have an interval between spells of work (*let's break for coffee*). **3** *tr.* fail to observe or keep (a law, promise, etc.). **4 a** *tr.* & *intr.* make or become subdued or weakened (*broke his spirit*). **b** *tr.* weaken the effect of (a fall, blow, etc.). **c** *tr.* = BREAK IN 3c. **d** *tr.* defeat, destroy (*broke the enemy's power*). **e** *tr.* defeat the object of (a strike, e.g. by employing other personnel). **5** *tr.* surpass (a record). **6** *intr.* (foll. by *with*) quarrel or cease association with (another person etc.). **7** *tr.* **a** be no longer subject to (a habit). **b** (foll. by *of*) cause (a person) to be free of a habit (*broke them of their addiction*). **8** *tr.* & *intr.* reveal or be revealed; (cause to) become known (*the story broke on Friday*). **9** *intr.* **a** (of the weather) change suddenly, esp. after a hot spell. **b** (of waves) curl over and dissolve into foam. **c** (of the day) dawn. **d** (of clouds) move apart. **e** (of a storm) begin violently. **10** *tr.* *Electricity* disconnect (a circuit). **11** *intr.* **a** (of the voice) change with emotion. **b** (of a boy's voice) change in register etc. at puberty. **12** *tr.* **a** (often foll. by *up*) divide (a set etc.) into parts, e.g. by selling to different buyers. **b** change (a bill, etc.) for coins. **13** *tr.* ruin (an individual or institution) financially. **14** *tr.* penetrate a safe etc. by force. **15** *tr.* decipher (a code). **16** *tr.* make (a way, path, etc.) by separating obstacles. **17** *intr.* burst forth (*the sun broke through the clouds*). **18 a** *intr.* (usu. foll. by *free, loose, out*, etc.) escape from constraint suddenly. **b** *tr.* escape or emerge from (prison, bounds, cover, etc.). **19** *intr.* *Baseball* (of a pitch) curve or drop. **20** *intr.* *Billiards etc.* disperse the balls at the beginning of a game. **21** *tr.* bring an end to (an undecided condition, state of affairs, etc.) (*an effort to break the impasse*). **22** *tr.* (in golf, bowling, etc.) achieve or surpass (a noteworthy score) (*hopes to break 200*). **23** *tr.* *N Amer., Austral., & NZ* (often foll. by *in*) bring (virgin land) under cultivation. ● *n.* **1 a** an act or instance of breaking. **b** a point where something is broken; a gap. **2 a** an interval, an interruption; a pause in work. **b** a holiday (*spring break*). **3** a sudden dash (esp. to escape). **4** *informal* an instance of luck, esp. of a specified kind (*lucky break*). **5** *Sport* = BREAKAWAY 1. **6** *Billiards etc.* **a** a series of points scored during one turn. **b** the opening shot that disperses the balls. **7** *Electricity* a discontinuity in a circuit. □ **break away** make or become free or separate. **break the back of 1** overburden (a person). **2** exert (oneself) greatly. **3** do the hardest or greatest part of (a task). **4** *N Amer.* defeat, destroy, crush. **break the bank 1** exhaust all one's financial resources. **2** (in gaming) exhaust the bank's resources; win spectacularly. **break down 1 a** fail in mechanical action; cease to function. **b** (of human relationships etc.) fail, collapse. **c** fail in (esp. mental) health. **d** be overcome by emotion; collapse in tears. **2 a** demolish, destroy. **b** suppress (resistance). **c** force (a person) to yield under pressure. **3** analyze into components. **4** decompose. **break even** emerge from a transaction etc. with neither profit nor loss.

break a game (wide) open decisively turn a close game in one's favour with dramatic scoring. **break the ice 1** begin to overcome formality or shyness, esp. between strangers. **2** make a start. **break in 1** enter premises by force, esp. with criminal intent. **2** interrupt. **3 a** accustom to a habit etc. **b** wear etc. until comfortable. **c** accustom (a horse) to saddle and bridle etc. **break in on** disturb; interrupt. **break into 1** enter forcibly or violently. **2 a** suddenly begin, burst forth with (a song, laughter, etc.). **b** suddenly change one's pace for (a faster one). **3** interrupt. **break a leg** (as *interj.*) *Theatre slang* good luck. **break loose 1** escape from constraint or a fixed position suddenly. **2** (of a condition etc.) develop suddenly (*all hell broke loose*). **break new ground** innovate. **break of day** dawn. **break off 1** detach by breaking. **2** bring to an end. **3** cease talking etc. **break open** open forcibly. **break out 1** escape by force, esp. from prison. **2** begin suddenly; burst forth (*violence broke out*). **3** (usu. foll. by *in*) become covered in (a rash, pimples, etc.). **4** exclaim. **5 a** open up (a receptacle) and remove its contents. **b** remove (articles) from a place of storage. **break step** get out of step. **break (into) a sweat** begin sweating, esp. because of nervousness or physical exertion. **break trail** *N Amer.* **1** beat a path, e.g. through deep snow or undergrowth. **2** innovate. **break up 1** break into small pieces. **2** disperse; disband. **3 a** terminate a relationship. **b** cause to do this. **4** (of the weather) change suddenly (esp. after a fine spell). **5** (of a frozen body of water) break into blocks of ice at the spring thaw. **6** esp. *N Amer.* **a** upset or be upset. **b** excite or be excited. **c** convulse or be convulsed. **break wind** release gas from the anus. **give me a break** *N Amer. informal* expressing skepticism, exasperation, scorn, etc.

breakable ● *adj.* that may or is apt to be broken easily. ● *n.* (esp. in *pl.*) a breakable thing.

breakage *n.* **1 a** a broken thing. **b** damage caused by breaking. **2** an act or instance of breaking.

break and enter *n.* = BREAKING AND ENTERING.

breakaway ● *n.* **1** (also **break**) (in hockey etc.) a long rush towards the goal or net after having passed all defenders. **2** the act or an instance of breaking away or seceding. **3** a false start in a race. ● *attrib.adj.* **1** broken away or separated from a larger body (*breakaway republic*). **2** designed to break easily to prevent more serious damage (*breakaway mirrors*).

breakdancing *n.* an energetic style of (usu. solo) street dancing, frequently involving spinning on the back or head. □ **breakdance** *n. & v.* **breakdancer** *n.*

breakdown *n.* **1** a mechanical failure. **2** a loss of (esp. mental) health and strength. **3** a collapse or disintegration (*communication breakdown*). **4** chemical or physical decomposition. **5** a detailed analysis.

breaker *n.* **1** a person or thing that breaks something (*circuit breaker*). **2** a heavy wave that breaks. **3** *Cdn* (*Nfld*) a submerged rock with waves breaking above it. **4** a person who breaks in a horse. **5** *N Amer.* a breakdancer. **6** *N Amer.* a person who interrupts the conversation of others on a CB radio.

break-even ● *adj.* designating the point at which earnings equal expenditures. ● *n.* a break-even point.

breakfast ● *n.* the first meal of the day. ● *v.intr.* have breakfast. □ **eat for breakfast** *slang* destroy (something) or defeat (a person) easily.

breakfast nook *n.* a small area in or off a kitchen, with a table or counter and seating, designed for eating breakfast.

break-in *n.* **1** an illegal forced entry into premises,

esp. with criminal intent. **2** an illegal accessing of information from a computer.

breaking *adj.* (of news, events, etc.) happening, occurring, esp. at the moment (*late-breaking story*).

breaking and entering *n.* the illegal entering of a building with intent to commit an indictable offence.

breaking ball *n.* (also **breaking pitch**) *Baseball* a pitch that drops just before reaching the batter.

breaking-point *n.* the point of greatest strain, at which a thing breaks or a person gives way.

breakneck *attrib.adj.* (of speed) dangerously fast.

breakout *n.* **1** (in hockey etc.) a sudden offensive rush. **2** a forcible escape. **3** *N Amer.* an outbreak, esp. of pimples. **4** the breaking of a gathering into smaller groups for discussion (usu. *attrib.*: *breakout groups*).

break point *n.* **1** a place or time at which an interruption or change is made. **2** (usu. **breakpoint**) *Computing* a place in a computer program where the sequence of instructions is interrupted, esp. by another program. **3** *Tennis* **a** a point which would win the game for the player(s) receiving service. **b** the situation at which the receiver(s) may break service by winning such a point. **4** = BREAKING-POINT.

breakthrough *n.* **1** a major advance or discovery. **2** an act of breaking through an obstacle etc.

breakup *n.* **1** disintegration, collapse. **2** the termination of a relationship. **3** dispersal. **4** *Cdn* (also **spring breakup**) **a** the breaking of a frozen river etc. into blocks of ice at the spring thaw. **b** the time during which this happens.

breakwater *n.* a structure which breaks the force of waves, esp. at the entrance to a harbour.

bream *n.* (*pl.* same) **1** a carp-like freshwater fish of Europe, *Abramis brama*, with an arched back. **2** (in full **sea bream**) a similarly shaped marine fish of the family Sparidae. **3** *N Amer.* = BLUEGILL.

breast ● *n.* **1 a** either of two milk-secreting organs on the upper front of a woman's body. **b** a corresponding organ on females of other mammals, esp. primates. **c** the corresponding usu. rudimentary part of a man's body. **2 a** the upper front part of a human body; the chest. **b** the corresponding part of an animal. **3 a** portion of poultry cut from the breast. **4** the part of a garment that covers the breast. **5** the breast as a source of nourishment or emotion. ● *v.tr.* **1** face, meet in full opposition (*breast the waves*). **2** contend with. **3** reach the top of (a hill). □ **make a clean breast of** confess fully. □ **breasted** *adj.* (also in *comb.*).

breast-beating *n.* an ostentatious display of remorse, sorrow, etc.

breastbone *n.* a thin flat vertical bone and cartilage in the chest connecting the ribs.

breast-feed *v.* (*past* and *past part.* **-fed**) **1** *tr. & intr.* feed (a baby) from the breast. **2** *intr.* (of a baby) feed from the breast.

breast implant *n.* a small silicone-filled pouch surgically inserted in a breast to enlarge it.

breastplate *n.* a vestment or piece of armour covering the breast.

breaststroke *n.* *Swimming* a stroke performed by a swimmer floating face down, extending the joined hands outward from the chest to above the head and then sweeping them down on either side of the body, while the legs execute a frog kick.

breath *n.* **1 a** the air taken into or expelled from the lungs. **b** one respiration of air. **c** an exhalation of air that can be seen, smelled, or heard (*bad breath*). **2 a** a slight movement of air; a breeze. **b** a whiff of perfume etc. **3** a whisper, a murmur (esp. of a scandalous nature). **4** the power of breathing; life. □ **below** (or **under**) **one's breath** in a whisper. **breath of fresh air 1** a small amount of or a brief time in the fresh air. **2** a refreshing change. **catch one's breath 1** cease breathing momentarily in surprise, suspense, etc. **2** rest after exercise to restore normal breathing. **draw breath** breathe; live. **hold one's breath** cease breathing temporarily. **don't hold your breath** *informal* do not expect something to happen imminently. **in the same breath** (esp. of saying two contradictory things) within a short time. **out of breath** gasping for air, esp. after exercise. **take breath** pause for rest. **take one's breath away** astound; surprise; awe; delight. **waste one's breath** talk or give advice without effect.

breathable *adj.* **1** fit to be breathed. **2** (of textiles, clothing, etc.) allowing the passage of air and inhibiting condensation. □ **breathability** *n.*

Breathalyzer *n. proprietary* an instrument for measuring the amount of alcohol in the breath (and hence in the blood) of a driver. □ **breathalyze** *v.tr.*

breathe *v.* **1** *intr.* take air into and expel it from the lungs. **2** *intr.* be or seem alive (*is she breathing?*). **3** *tr.* **a** utter; say (esp. quietly). **b** express; display (*breathed defiance*). **4** *intr.* take breath, pause. **5** *tr.* **a** send out (as if) with exhaled air (*breathed a sigh of relief*). **b** take in (as if) with breathed air (*breathed the fumes*). **6** *intr.* (of wine, fabric, etc.) be exposed to fresh air. **7** *intr.* **a** (of textiles, clothing, etc.) allow the passage of air and inhibit condensation. **b** (of the skin) absorb oxygen and get rid of moisture. **8** *intr.* (of wind) blow softly. □ **breathe easy** (or **freely**) be relieved from tension, suspense, etc. **breathe down a person's neck** be close behind a person, esp. in mistrust or pursuit. **breathe** (**new**) **life into** invigorate; make lively. **breathe one's last** die. **not breathe a word of** keep quite secret.

breather /ˈbriːðər/ *n.* **1** *informal* a brief pause for rest. **2** a person or animal that breathes, esp. a specified substance or in a specified way (*heavy breathers*).

breathing *n.* the process of taking air into and expelling it from the lungs.

breathing hole *n.* a hole made by seals through the ice covering a body of water, used for breathing.

breathing space *n.* (also **breathing room**) **1** a pause or respite; a time to rest, recover, reconsider, etc. **2** a space or area which allows for easy movement, rest, etc. (*our breathing space in the city*).

breathless *adj.* **1** panting, out of breath. **2** holding the breath because of excitement, suspense, etc. **3** unstirred by wind; still. □ **breathlessly** *adv.* **breathlessness** *n.*

breath mint *n.* a usu. mint-flavoured lozenge for sweetening the breath.

breathtaking *adj.* awe-inspiring. □ **breathtakingly** *adv.*

breath test *n.* a test of a person's alcohol consumption using a Breathalyzer.

breathy *adj.* (**-ier, -iest**) (of a singing voice etc.) containing the sound of breathing. □ **breathily** *adv.* **breathiness** *n.*

B.Rec. *abbr.* Bachelor of Recreation.

breech *n.* **1 a** the part of a cannon behind the bore. **b** the back part of a rifle or gun barrel. **2** (*attrib.*) designating a birth in which the baby presents in the birth canal with the buttocks or feet foremost.

breeches *n.pl.* (also **pair of breeches** *sing.*) **1** short trousers, esp. fastened below the knee, now used esp. for riding or in court costume. **2** = BRITCHES.

breech-loader *n.* a gun loaded at the breech, not through the muzzle. □ **breech-loading** *adj.*

breed ● *v.* (*past* and *past part.* **bred**) **1** *tr.* & *intr.* bear, generate (offspring). **2** *tr.* propagate or cause to propagate; raise (livestock). **2** *tr.* **a** yield, produce; result in (*war breeds famine*). **b** spread (*discontent bred by rumour*). **4** *intr.* arise; spread (*disease breeds in the tropics*). **5** *tr.* bring up; train (*bred to the law*). **6** *tr. Physics* create (fissile material) by nuclear reaction. ● *n.* **1** a stock of animals or plants within a species, having a similar appearance, and usu. developed by deliberate selection. **2** a race; a lineage. **3** a sort, a kind. **4** *offensive* a person of mixed racial descent; a half-breed. □ **bred and born** = BORN AND BRED (see BORN). **bred in the bone** hereditary. □ **breeder** *n.*

breeding *n.* **1** the process of developing or propagating (animals, plants, etc.). **2** generation; childbearing. **3 a** upbringing or education. **b** behaviour, esp. good manners. **4** wealthy or aristocratic family background.

breeding ground *n.* **1** an area of land where an animal, esp. a bird, habitually breeds. **2** a thing that favours the development or occurrence of something, esp. something unpleasant.

breeze ● *n.* **1** a gentle wind. **2** *Meteorol.* a wind of 1.6–13.8 m/s (4–31 mph) and between force 2 and force 6 on the Beaufort scale. **3** a wind blowing from land at night or a large body of water during the day. **4** esp. *N Amer. informal* an easy task. ● *v.intr.* **1** (foll. by *in, out, along*, etc.) *informal* come or go in a casual or lighthearted manner. **2** (usu. foll. by *through*) emerge successfully and easily from (a test, competition, etc.).

breezeway *n. N Amer.* a covered passageway, as between a house and a garage.

breezy *adj.* (**-ier, -iest**) **1 a** windswept. **b** pleasantly windy. **2** *informal* lively; jovial. **3** *informal* careless (*breezy indifference*). □ **breezily** *adv.* **breeziness** *n.*

brekkie *n. Cdn, Brit., & Austral. slang* breakfast.

brethren *n.pl. see* BROTHER.

Breton /ˈbrɛtən/ ● *n.* **1** a native of Brittany, a region of NW France. **2** the Celtic language of Brittany. ● *adj.* of or relating to Brittany or its people.

brevity /ˈbrɛvɪti/ *n.* **1** economy of expression; conciseness. **2** shortness (of time etc.).

brew ● *v.* **1** *tr.* **a** make (beer etc.) by infusion, boiling, and fermentation. **b** make (tea, coffee, etc.) by infusion. **2** *intr.* undergo either of these processes (*the tea is brewing*). **3** *intr.* (of trouble, a storm, etc.) gather force; threaten (*mischief was brewing*). **4** *tr.* bring about; set in train; concoct (*brewed their fiendish scheme*). ● *n.* **1** an amount (of beer etc.) brewed at one time (*this year's brew*). **2** what is brewed (esp. with regard to its quality) (*a good strong brew*). **3 a** beer. **b** a serving of beer. **4** the action or process of brewing. **5** a mixture, esp. of disparate elements.

brewer *n.* a person or company that makes beer.

brewer's yeast *n.* a non-leavening dry yeast of the genus *Saccharomyces*, used in the fermentation of beer and wine, added to some foods as a nutritive agent.

brewery *n.* (*pl.* **-ies**) a place where beer etc. is brewed commercially.

brewis /ˈbruːz/ *n. Cdn (Nfld)* **1** a stew made of hardtack soaked in water and boiled. **2** = FISH AND BREWIS.

brewmaster *n. N Amer.* a master brewer.

brew pub *n.* a bar with on-site brewing facilities.

brewski *n.* (*pl.* **-is** or **-ies**) *N Amer. slang* a beer.

briar *var. of* BRIER.

bribe ● *n.* a sum of money or other reward offered or demanded in order to procure an (often illegal or dishonest) action or decision in favour of the giver. ●

v.tr. persuade (a person etc.) by means of a bribe (*bribed the guard*). □ **briber** *n.* **bribery** *n.*

bric-a-brac /'brɪkə‚bræk/ *n.* (also **bric-à-brac**) miscellaneous, often old, ornaments, trinkets, furniture, etc., of no great value.

brick ● *n.* **1 a** a small, usu. rectangular, block of fired or sun-dried clay, used in building. **b** the material used to make these. **c** a similar block of concrete etc. **2** a brick-shaped solid object (*a brick of ice cream*). **3** a white, smooth, firm cow's-milk cheese with a brick-like shape. ● *v.tr.* (foll. by *in*, *up*) close or block with brickwork. ● *adj.* **1** built of brick. **2** = BRICK RED *adj.* □ **like a ton of bricks** *informal* with crushing weight, force, or authority. **run into a brick wall** come up against an unsurmountable obstacle.

brickbat *n.* **1** a piece of brick, esp. when used as a missile. **2** an uncomplimentary remark.

bricklayer *n.* a worker who builds with bricks. □ **bricklaying** *n.*

brick red ● *n.* the dull red colour typical of bricks. ● *adj.* (hyphenated when *attrib.*) of this colour.

brickwork *n.* **1** construction using brick. **2** a wall, building, etc. made of brick.

brickyard *n.* a place where bricks are made.

bricolage /‚brɪkə'lɒʒ/ *n.* **1** construction or creation from whatever is immediately available for use. **2** something constructed or created in this way.

bridal *adj.* of or concerning a bride or a wedding.

bride *n.* a woman on her wedding day and for some time before and after it.

bridegroom *n.* a man on his wedding day and for some time before and after it.

bride price *n.* a payment of money or goods made to a bride or her parents by the groom or his parents.

bridesmaid *n.* **1** a girl or woman attending a bride on her wedding day. **2** *N Amer.* a person or group that never quite attains a desired goal.

bridge¹ ● *n.* **1 a** a structure carrying a road, path, railway, etc., across a stream, ravine, road, etc. **b** anything providing a connection between different things (*a bridge between cultures*). **2** the superstructure on a ship from which the captain and officers direct operations. **3 a** the upper bony part of the nose. **b** the central part of a pair of eyeglasses, which rests on this and connects the two lenses. **4** an upright piece of wood, metal, etc. on a violin, guitar, etc. over which the strings are stretched. **5** *Music* a transitional piece between main themes. **6** a dental structure used to cover a gap, joined to and supported by the teeth on either side. **7** *Billiards* a long stick with a structure at the end which is used to support a cue for a difficult shot. **b** a support for a cue formed by a raised hand. **8** = LAND BRIDGE. ● *v.tr.* **1 a** be a bridge over. **b** make a bridge over; span. **2** span as if with a structure (*bridged the gap between east and west*). □ **cross that bridge when one comes to it** deal with a problem when and if it arises.

bridge² *n.* a card game for four players derived from whist, in which one player's cards are exposed at a certain point and then played by his or her partner.

bridge-building *n.* **1** the activity of building bridges. **2** the promotion of friendly relations, esp. between countries. □ **bridge-builder** *n.*

bridgehead *n.* **1** a fortified position held on the enemy's side of a river or other obstacle. **2** an initial position established as a basis for advancing further.

bridge loan *n.* (*Cdn* also **bridge financing**) a short-term loan covering the interval between two transactions, e.g. the purchase of a second house before the closing of the sale of the first.

Bridge Mixture *n.* *N Amer.* *proprietary* (also **bridge mix**) an assortment of small chocolates with a variety of fillings, e.g. peanuts, raisins, jellies, etc.

bridgework *n.* **1** = BRIDGE¹ *n.* 6. **2** the art or process of building bridges.

bridle ● *n.* **1** the headgear used to control a horse, consisting of buckled leather straps, a metal bit, and reins. **2** a restraining thing or influence (*put a bridle on your tongue*). ● *v.* **1** *tr.* put a bridle on (a horse etc.). **2** *tr.* bring under control; curb. **3** *intr.* (often foll. by *up*) express offence, resentment, etc.

bridle path *n.* (also **bridleway**) a rough path or road fit only for riders or walkers, not vehicles.

brie /bri:/ *n.* a kind of ripened soft cheese with a white mould skin.

brief ● *adj.* **1** of short duration. **2** concise in expression. **3** abrupt, brusque. **4** short; scanty (*a brief halter top*). ● *n.* **1** (in *pl.*) close-fitting legless underpants. **2** *N Amer.* *Law* a written statement of the arguments for a case. **3** instructions given for a task, operation, etc. **4** esp. *Brit.* a set of instructions, as a job description etc. **5** a brief news article or summary. ● *v.tr.* instruct (an employee, participant, etc.) in preparation for a task; inform or instruct thoroughly in advance (compare DEBRIEF). □ **in brief** in short. □ **briefer** *n.* **briefly** *adv.* **briefness** *n.*

briefcase *n.* a flat rectangular case for carrying documents etc.

briefing *n.* **1** a meeting for giving information or instructions. **2** the information or instructions given. **3** the action of informing or instructing.

Brier *n.* the bonspiel for the Canadian men's national curling championship.

brier *n.* **1** any prickly bush esp. of a wild rose. **2** a white plant of the heath family, *Erica arborea*, native to S Europe. **3** a tobacco pipe made from its root.

Brig. *abbr.* BRIGADIER.

brig *n.* **1** a two-masted square-rigged ship. **2** a prison, esp. on a warship.

brigade ● *n.* **1** a subdivision of an army. **2** an organized or uniformed band of workers (*fire brigade*). **3** *informal* any group of people with a characteristic in common (*the couldn't-care-less brigade*). **4** *Cdn* *hist.* a group or fleet of canoes, bateaux, Red River carts, pack horses, etc., travelling together to the same trading post etc. ● *v.tr.* form into a brigade.

brigadier /‚brɪgə'dɪ:r/ *n.* (also **Brigadier**) (in the UK and *hist.* in the Canadian Army) **1** an officer commanding a brigade. **2** a staff officer of similar standing, above a colonel and below a major general.

brigadier general *n.* (also **Brigadier General**) (in the Canadian Army and Air Force and US Army, Air Force, and Marines) an officer ranking next above colonel.

brigand /'brɪgənd/ *n.* a member of a robber band living by pillage and plunder, usu. in wild terrain. □ **brigandage** *n.* **brigandry** *n.*

brigantine /'brɪgən‚ti:n/ *n.* a two-masted sailing ship with a square-rigged foremast and a fore-and-aft-rigged mainmast.

Brig. Gen. *abbr.* Brigadier General.

bright ● *adj.* **1 a** emitting or reflecting much light; shining. **b** full of light (*a bright apartment*). **2** (of colour) intense, vivid. **3** clever, talented, quick-witted. **4** cheerful, vivacious. **5** full of hope; promising (*a bright future*). ● *adv.* esp. *literary* brightly. ● *n.* (in *pl.*) **1** bright colours. **2** *N Amer.* headlights switched to high beam. □ **bright and early** very early in the morning. **bright-eyed and bushy-tailed** *informal* alert and

sprightly. **look on the bright side** be optimistic. □
brightly adv. **brightness** n.

brighten 1 make or become brighter. **2** make or
become more cheerful. □ **brightener** n.

bright lights n.pl. (prec. by the) the glamour and
excitement of the city.

brightwork n. polished metal or metal-like parts on
a car, boat, etc.

brilliance n. **1** great brightness. **2** outstanding talent or intelligence. □ **brilliancy** n.

brilliant adj. **1** very bright; sparkling. **2** outstandingly talented or intelligent. **3** showy. **4** informal excellent, superb. □ **brilliantly** adv.

brim ● n. **1** the edge or lip of a cup or other vessel, or
of a hollow. **2** the projecting edge of a hat. ● v.tr. & intr.
(**brimmed, brimming**) fill or be full to the edge. □
brim over overflow. □ **brimless** adj. **brimmed** adj.
(usu. in comb.).

brimful adj. (also **brim-full**) (usu. predic.; often foll. by
of) filled to the brim.

brimstone n. archaic the element sulphur.

brin n. Cdn (Nfld) burlap (brin bag).

brindled adj. (also **brindle**) (esp. of domestic animals)
brownish or tawny with streaks of other colour.

brine ● n. **1** water saturated or strongly impregnated
with salt. **2** sea water. ● v.tr. soak in or saturate with
brine.

brine shrimp n. a small crustacean of the genus
Artemia, used as food for aquarium fish.

bring v.tr. (past and past part. **brought**) **1** come carrying
or leading or accompanying. **2** cause to come or be
present (what brings you here?). **3** cause or result in (the
pills brought some relief). **4** be sold for; produce as
income. **5 a** make (a legal charge). **b** initiate (legal
action). **6** cause to become or to reach a particular
state (brought them to their senses). **7** adduce (evidence,
an argument, etc.). **8** make (something) move in the
direction or way specified. □ **bring about 1** cause to
happen. **2** turn (a ship) around. **bring back** call to
mind. **bring down 1** cause to fall. **2** lower (a price). **3**
informal make unhappy or less happy. **4** informal damage
the reputation of. **5** Cdn, Austral., & NZ esp. Parl. present
(a budget, law, report, etc.). **bring down the house**
get loud applause. **bring forth 1** give birth to. **2**
produce, emit, cause. **bring forward 1** move to an
earlier date or time. **2** transfer from the previous
page or account. **3** draw attention to; adduce. **bring
home to** cause to realize fully (brought home to me that
I was wrong). **bring in 1** introduce (legislation, a
custom, topic, etc.). **2** yield as income or profit. **bring
into play** cause to operate; activate. **bring low**
overcome. **bring off** achieve successfully. **bring on 1**
cause to happen or appear. **2** accelerate the progress
of. **bring out 1** emphasize; make evident. **2** publish.
bring over convert to one's own side. **bring round**
(or **around**) **1** restore to consciousness. **2** persuade.
bring tears to the eyes cause to weep. **bring
through** aid (a person) through adversity, esp.
illness. **bring to 1** restore to consciousness (brought
her to). **2** check the motion of. **bring to bear** (usu.
foll. by on) direct and concentrate (forces). **bring to
mind** recall; cause one to remember. **bring to pass**
cause to happen. **bring under** subdue. **bring up 1**
rear (a child). **2** call attention to. **3** vomit. **4** stop
suddenly. **bring on** (or **upon**) **oneself** be responsible for (something one suffers). □ **bringer** n.

brink n. **1** the extreme edge of land before a precipice,
river, etc., esp. when a sudden drop follows. **2** the
point or state very close to something unknown,

dangerous or exciting. □ **on the brink of** about to
experience or suffer; in imminent danger of.

brinkmanship n. (also **brinksmanship**) the art or
policy of pursuing a dangerous course to the brink of
catastrophe before desisting.

briny ● adj. (**-ier, -iest**) of brine or the sea; salty. ● n.
(prec. by the) slang the sea. □ **brininess** n.

brio / 'briːoː/ n. style, vigour, vivacity.

briquette /brɪˈket/ n. (also **briquet**) a block of compressed charcoal or coal dust etc. used as fuel.

brisk adj. **1** quick, lively, keen (a brisk pace). **2** cold but
pleasantly fresh. □ **briskly** adv. **briskness** n.

brisket n. **1** the breast of an animal. **2** a cut of beef
used esp. to make corned beef.

bristle ● n. **1** a short stiff hair, esp. one of those on an
animal's back. **2** this, or a synthetic substitute, used
in clumps to make a brush. ● v. **1 a** intr. (of the hair)
stand upright, esp. in anger or pride. **b** tr. make (the
hair) do this. **2** intr. show irritation or defensiveness. **3**
intr. (usu. foll. by with) be covered or abundant (in). □
bristly adj. (**-ier, -iest**).

bristol board n. a kind of fine smooth pasteboard.

Brit informal ● n. a British person. ● adj. British.

Brit. abbr. **1** British. **2** Britain.

Britannic adj. of Britain (Her Britannic Majesty).

britches n.pl. informal any pants, shorts, or underwear.
□ **too big for one's britches** more arrogant than
one's situation or knowledge allows.

Briticism /'brɪtɪˌsɪzəm/ n. a word or idiom used in
Britain but not in other English-speaking countries.

British ● adj. **1** of or relating to Great Britain or the
United Kingdom, or to its people or language. **2** of the
British Commonwealth or (formerly) the British
Empire (British subject). ● n. (prec. by the; treated as pl.)
the British people. □ **Britishness** n.

British Columbian ● adj. of or relating to British
Columbia. ● n. a resident or native of British
Columbia.

British connection n. Cdn hist. the relationship
that existed between Canada and Great Britain.

Britisher n. a British subject, esp. of British descent.
¶Not used in Britain.

Britishism var. of BRITICISM.

British thermal unit n. the amount of heat needed
to raise 1 lb. of water at maximum density through
one degree Fahrenheit. Abbr.: **BTU**.

Briton n. **1** a native or inhabitant of Great Britain or
(formerly) of the British Empire. **2** one of the people
of S Britain before the Roman conquest.

britpop n. British pop music of the nineties, showing
influences from a variety of British musical traditions and perceived as a reaction against American
grunge music.

brittle ● adj. **1 a** hard but easily broken; fragile. **b**
insecure; easily damaged (brittle nerves). **2** (of a sound)
unpleasantly hard and sharp (a brittle laugh). **3** (of a
person) lacking in warmth. ● n. a brittle candy made
from nuts and set melted sugar. □ **brittlely** adv.
brittleness n.

bro / broː / n. (pl. **bros**) N Amer. slang brother; buddy.

broach ● v. **1** tr. raise (a subject) for discussion. **2** tr.
pierce (a cask) to draw liquor. **3** tr. open and start
using the contents of (a box etc.). **4** tr. begin drawing
(liquor). **5** intr. (of a fish etc.) break the surface of the
water. ● n. a spit for roasting meat on.

broad ● adj. **1** large in extent from one side to the
other; wide. **2** (following a measurement) in breadth.
3 spacious or extensive (a broad plain). **4** full and clear
(broad daylight). **5** explicit, unmistakable (broad hint).

6 general; not taking account of detail (*in the broadest sense*). **7** of or including a great variety of people, things, or experiences (*a broad range of options*). **8** chief or principal (*the broad facts*). **9** tolerant, liberal (*take a broad view*). **10** somewhat coarse (*broad humour*). **11** (of speech) markedly regional (*a broad accent*). ● *n.* **1** the broad part of something (*broad of the back*). **2** *N Amer. slang offensive* a woman.

broadaxe *n.* a large axe with a broad blade, used esp. for shaping or trimming rather than felling.

broadband *n.* a transmission technique utilizing a wide range of frequencies, which enables information to be communicated simultaneously.

broad bean *n.* a kind of bean, *Vicia faba*, with pods containing large edible flat seeds.

broad-brush *attrib.adj.* as if painted with a broad brush; general (*adopted a broad-brush approach*).

broadcast ● *v.* (*past* **-cast** *or* **-casted**; *past part.* **-cast**) **1** *tr.* transmit (programs or information) by radio or TV. **b** disseminate (information) widely. **2** *intr.* undertake or take part in a radio or TV transmission. **3** *tr.* scatter (seed etc.) over a large area, esp. by hand. ● *n.* a radio or TV program or transmission. ● *adj.* **1** transmitted by radio or TV. **2 a** scattered widely. **b** (of information etc.) widely disseminated. ● *adv.* over a large area. □ **broadcaster** *n.* **broadcasting** *n.*

broadcloth ● *n.* **1** a closely woven fabric of wool, cotton, silk, or a mixture of the three. **2** a densely woven woollen cloth in a plain or twill weave and having a lustrous finish.

broaden *v.tr. & intr.* make or become broader.

broad jump *n. N Amer.* = LONG JUMP.

broadleaf ● *adj.* (also **broad-leaved**, **broad-leafed**) **1** designating any of a number of weeds, e.g. dandelion, having broad leaves. **2** (of a tree) deciduous and hard-timbered. ● *n.* (*pl.* **-leaves**) **1** a broadleaf weed. **2** a broadleaf tree.

broadloom *n.* carpet woven in broad widths. □ **broadloomed** *adj.*

broadly *adv.* in a broad manner; widely. □ **broadly speaking** disregarding minor exceptions.

broadsheet *n.* **1** a sheet of paper printed for posting or distribution, esp. for spreading information. **2** a newspaper with a large format.

broadside ● *n.* **1** the firing of all guns from one side of a ship. **2** a vigorous verbal onslaught. **3** the side of a ship above the water between the bow and quarter. **4** = BROADSHEET. ● *adv.* with the side turned towards a given object (*the car hit the wall broadside*). ● *adj.* sideways. ● *v.tr. N Amer.* run into or collide with on the side (*the truck broadsided the car*).

broad spectrum *adj.* **1** (of a drug) effective against a wide range of pathogens. **2** (of a sunscreen) effective against most wavelengths of sunlight. **3** having a wide range of applications.

brocade ● *n.* a rich fabric with a silky finish with a raised pattern, often with gold or silver thread. ● *v.tr.* (usu. as **brocaded** *adj.*) weave with this design.

broccoflower /'brɒkəflaur/ *n.* a hybrid vegetable, the result of a genetic cross between broccoli and cauliflower, resembling a green cauliflower that tastes like broccoli.

broccoli *n.* **1** a brassica, related to the cauliflower, with a loose cluster of usu. greenish flower buds. **2** the flower stalk and head used as a vegetable.

brochette /brɒ'ʃet, brə'ʃet/ *n.* a dish consisting of chunks of food, esp. meat, threaded on a skewer and grilled.

brochure *n.* a pamphlet or leaflet, esp. one giving descriptive information.

brogue[1] /broːg/ *n.* a marked accent, esp. Irish.

brogue[2] *n.* **1** a strong outdoor shoe with ornamental perforated bands. **2** a rough leather shoe.

broil *v.* esp. *N Amer.* **1** *tr.* cook by direct exposure to heat. **2** *tr. & intr.* make or become very hot.

broiler *n.* **1** *N Amer.* an appliance or the element in an oven used for broiling. **2** a young chicken raised for broiling or roasting. **3** *informal* a very hot day.

broiling *adj. N Amer.* very hot (*a broiling summer day*).

broke ● *v.* past of BREAK[1]. ● *predic.adj. informal* having no money; financially ruined. □ **go for broke** *slang* risk everything in a strenuous effort.

broken ● *v. past part. of* BREAK[1]. ● *adj.* **1 a** that has been broken. **b** out of order. **2** reduced to despair; beaten. **3** spoken falteringly and with many mistakes (*broken English*). **4** disturbed, interrupted (*broken time*). **5** uneven (*broken ground*). **6** trained, tamed (*broken to the saddle*). **7** (of a marriage, family, etc.) divided by separation or divorce. □ **brokenly** *adv.* **brokenness** *n.*

broken-down *adj.* **1** worn out by age, use, or ill-treatment. **2** out of order.

broken-hearted *adj.* overwhelmed with sorrow or grief. □ **broken-heartedness** *n.*

broker ● *n.* **1** an agent who buys and sells or acts for others; an intermediary. **2** a member of a stock exchange who deals in stocks and shares. ● *v.tr.* act as a broker; negotiate, esp. as an intermediary.

brokerage *n.* **1** the action or service of a broker. **2** a company providing such a service. **3** a broker's fee.

broking *n.* the action or service of a broker.

brome *n.* (also **brome grass**) any oatlike grass of the genus *Bromus* of the temperate zone.

bromide /'broːmaɪd/ *n.* **1** *Chem.* a compound of bromine with a less electronegative element or radical. **2** *Pharm.* a preparation of usu. potassium bromide, used as a sedative. **3** a trite remark.

bromine /'broːmiːn/ *n.* a dark liquid element with a choking irritating smell, used in the manufacture of chemicals for photography and medicine.

bronc *n. N Amer. informal* = BRONCO.

bronchial /'brɒŋkɪəl/ *adj.* of or relating to the bronchi or bronchioles.

bronchiole /'brɒŋkɪˌoːl/ *n.* any of the minute divisions of a bronchus. □ **bronchiolar** /-'oːlər/ *adj.*

bronchitis /brɒŋ'kaɪtɪs/ *n.* inflammation of the mucous membrane in the bronchial tubes. □ **bronchitic** /-'kɪtɪk/ *adj. & n.*

bronchodilator /ˌbrɒŋkoːdaɪ'leɪtər/ *n.* a substance which causes widening of the bronchi, used esp. to alleviate asthma.

bronchus /'brɒŋkəs/ *n.* (*pl.* **bronchi** /-kaɪ/) any of the major air passages of the lungs, esp. either of the two main divisions of the windpipe.

bronco *n.* (*pl.* **-os**) *N Amer.* a wild or half-tamed horse.

broncobuster *n. N Amer. informal* a person who breaks in horses. □ **broncobusting** *n.*

brontosaurus /ˌbrɒntə'sɔːrəs/ *n.* (*pl.* **-sauruses**) (also **brontosaur**) a large plant-eating dinosaur of the genus *Apatosaurus*, of the Jurassic and Cretaceous periods, with a long whip-like tail and trunklike legs.

bronze ● *n.* **1** any of a group of alloys of copper and tin. **2** its brownish colour. **3** a thing made of bronze, esp. as a work of art. **4** = BRONZE MEDAL. ● *adj.* made of or coloured like bronze. ● *v.* **1** *tr.* give a bronzelike surface to. **2** *tr. & intr.* make or become brown; tan. □ **bronzy** *adj.*

Bronze Age *n.* the period preceding the Iron Age, when weapons and tools were usu. made of bronze.

bronze medal n. a medal usu. awarded to a competitor who comes third (esp. in sport).

brooch n. an ornament fastened to clothing with a hinged pin.

brood ● n. **1** the young of an animal (esp. a bird) produced at one hatching or birth. **2** informal the children in a family. **3** a group of related things. **4** bee or wasp larvae. **5** (attrib.) kept for breeding (brood mare). ● v. **1** intr. (often foll. by on, over, etc.) worry or ponder (esp. resentfully). **2** tr. & intr. (of a bird) sit on eggs to hatch them. **3** intr. (usu. foll. by over) (of silence, a storm, etc.) hang or hover closely.

brooder n. **1** a heated device or structure for raising chicks etc. **2** a person who broods.

brooding adj. **1** (of a person) melancholy, glum. **2** (of a landscape etc.) sombre and giving the impression of hovering over the surroundings. □ **broodingly** adv.

broody adj. (-ier, -iest) **1** (of a hen) wanting to brood. **2** sullenly thoughtful or depressed. □ **broodily** adv.

brook¹ n. a small stream. □ **brooklet** n.

brook² v.tr. (usu. with neg.) tolerate, allow.

brookie n. N Amer. informal = BROOK TROUT.

brook trout n. a trout, Salvelinus fontinalis, found widely throughout eastern N America.

broom n. **1** a brush of bristles, straw, etc. on a long handle, used for sweeping. **2** any of various shrubs, esp. Cytisus scoparius, bearing bright yellow flowers.

broomball n. N Amer. a game similar to hockey in which players run rather than skate and use rubber brooms or broom handles to propel a ball, esp. a volleyball, into the goal. □ **broomballer** n.

broomstick n. the handle of a broom.

Bros. abbr. Brothers (esp. in the name of a company).

broth n. **1** a thin soup of meat or fish stock. **2** unclarified meat or fish stock.

brothel n. a house etc. where prostitution takes place.

brother ● n. **1** a man or boy in relation to other sons and daughters of his parents. **2 a** (often as a form of address) a close male friend or associate. **b** a male fellow member of a union etc. **3** (pl. also **brethren**) **a** a member of a male religious order, esp. a monk. **b** a fellow member of a religion, esp. the Christian Church. **c** an associate in a common cause, association, etc. **4** a fellow human being. ● interj. esp. N Amer. expressing mild deprecation or annoyance. □ **brotherly** adj. & adv. **brotherliness** n.

brotherhood n. **1 a** the relationship between brothers. **b** brotherly friendliness; companionship. **2 a** an association, society, or community of people linked by a common interest, religion, trade, etc. **b** its members collectively. **3** N Amer. (in proper names) a labour union. **4** community of feeling between all human beings.

brother-in-law n. (pl. **brothers-in-law**) **1** the brother of one's wife or husband. **2** the husband of one's sister. **3** the husband of one's sister-in-law.

brought past and past part. of BRING.

brouhaha /'bru:hɑ,hɑ/ n. **1** commotion, sensation; hubbub, uproar. **2** an instance of this.

brow n. **1** the forehead. **2** (usu. in pl.) an eyebrow. **3** the summit of a hill or pass. **4** the edge of a cliff, riverbank, etc. □ **browed** adj.

browbeat v.tr. (past **-beat**; past part. **-beaten**) intimidate; bully. □ **browbeater** n.

brown ● adj. **1** having the colour produced by mixing red, yellow, and black, as of dark wood or rich soil. **2** dark-skinned or suntanned. **3** (of bread) made from a dark flour, e.g. whole wheat. **4** (of species or varieties) distinguished by brown coloration. ● n. **1** a brown colour or pigment. **2** brown clothes or material (dressed in brown). **3** N Amer. = BROWN TROUT. **4** (in a game or sport) a brown ball, piece, etc. **5** brown bread. ● v.tr. & intr. make or become brown by cooking etc. □ **brownish** adj. **brownness** n. **browny** adj.

brown bag N Amer. ● n. a plain brown paper bag in which a lunch is packed and carried to work etc. ● v.tr. take (a packed lunch) to work, school, etc. □ **brown bagger** n.

brown bear n. a bear, Ursus arctos, of northern N America, Europe, and Asia, including the grizzly (U. arctos horribilis), kodiak (U. arctos middendorffi), and Siberian brown bear (U. arctos beringianus).

brown cow n. Cdn a cocktail of coffee liqueur and milk or cream.

browned off adj. Brit. & Cdn slang fed up.

brownie n. **1** (usu. **Brownie**; in full **Brownie Guide**) a member of the junior branch of the Guides. **2** a small square of rich, usu. chocolate, cake with nuts. **3** a benevolent elf said to haunt houses and do household work secretly.

brownie point n. informal a notional credit for something done to please or win favour.

browning n. Cdn & Brit. browned flour or any other additive used to colour gravy.

brown-noser n. esp. N Amer. a person who behaves obsequiously in the hope of advancement. □ **brown-nose** v.intr. **brown-nosing** n.

brownout n. esp. N Amer. a temporary reduction in electrical power, esp. for conservation.

brown owl n. **1** any of various owls, esp. the tawny owl. **2** (**Brown Owl**) Cdn an adult leader of a Brownie pack.

brown paper n. a coarse unbleached paper used esp. for wrapping.

brown rice n. unpolished rice with only the husk of the grain removed.

brownshirt n. **1** (**Brownshirt**) a member of an early Nazi militia, the Storm Troopers (German Sturmabteilung), whose violent intimidation of political opponents played a key role in Hitler's rise to power. **2** a fascist. □ **brown-shirted** adj.

brownstone n. N Amer. **1** a kind of reddish-brown sandstone used for building. **2** a building faced with this.

brown sugar n. **1** refined sugar to which molasses has been added. **2** unrefined or partially refined sugar.

brown trout n. a trout, Salmo trutta, native to Europe and W Asia and introduced into N America.

browse ● v. **1** intr. & tr. read or survey haphazardly. **2** intr. (often foll. by on) feed (on leaves, twigs, or scanty vegetation). **3** tr. crop and eat. **4** intr. & tr. Computing read or survey (data files etc.), esp. via a network. ● n. **1** twigs, young shoots, etc., as fodder for cattle etc. **2** an act of browsing.

brr interj. expressing cold or shivering.

bruise ● n. **1** an injury appearing as an area of discoloured skin on a human or animal body, caused by a blow or impact. **2** a similar area of damage on fruit etc. ● v. **1** tr. **a** inflict a bruise on. **b** hurt mentally. **2** intr. be susceptible to bruising. **3** tr. crush or pound.

bruiser n. informal **1** a large tough-looking person. **2** a professional boxer.

bruit /bru:t/ v.tr. (often foll. by abroad, about) spread (a report or rumour).

brunch ● *n.* a late-morning meal intended to combine breakfast and lunch. ● *v.intr.* eat brunch.

brunette ● *n.* a woman with dark brown hair. ● *adj.* (of a woman) having dark brown hair.

brunt *n.* the chief or initial impact of an attack etc.

bruschetta /ˌbruːˈʃetə, -ˈsketə/ *n.* slices of toasted bread drizzled with olive oil and usu. topped with diced tomatoes, garlic etc.

brush ● *n.* **1** an implement with bristles, wire, etc. set into a block or projecting from the end of a handle, for any of various purposes, esp. cleaning or scrubbing, painting, grooming, etc. **2** the application of a brush; brushing. **3 a** (usu. foll. by *with*) a short esp. unpleasant encounter (*a brush with the law*). **b** a skirmish. **4 a** the bushy tail of a fox. **b** a brushlike tuft. **5** either of a pair of thin sticks with long wire bristles for softly playing a drum etc. **6** esp. *N Amer.* & *Austral.* **a** undergrowth; small trees and shrubs. **b** *N Amer.* such wood cut and bundled as kindling. **c** land covered with brush. ● *v.* **1** *tr.* **a** sweep or scrub or put in order with a brush. **b** treat (a surface) with a brush so as to change its nature or appearance. **2** *tr.* **a** remove (dust etc.) with a brush. **b** apply (a liquid preparation) to a surface with a brush. **3** *tr.* & *intr.* graze or touch in passing. **4** *intr.* perform a brushing action or motion. □ **brush aside** dismiss or dispose of (a person, idea, etc.) curtly or lightly. **brush off** rebuff; dismiss abruptly. **brush over** paint lightly. **brush up** (usu. foll. by *on*) revive one's former knowledge of (a subject). □ **brushlike** *adj.* **brushy** *adj.*

brush cut *n. N Amer.* a very short haircut.

brushcutter *n.* a device with blades for cutting heavy undergrowth.

brushed *adj.* **1** swept or smoothed with a brush. **2** (of metallic surfaces) treated so as to be lustreless. **3** (of fabric) brushed so as to raise the nap.

brush fire *n. N Amer.* & *Austral.* **1** a fire in brush or scrub. **2** (often *attrib.*) a localized, small-scale flare-up or skirmish.

brushland *n. N Amer.* = BRUSH 6c.

brush-off *n.* a rebuff; an abrupt dismissal.

brush stroke *n.* **1** the trace of paint left on a painting by one application of a loaded brush. **2** a painter's style in this.

brushwork *n.* **1** manipulation of the brush in painting. **2** a painter's style in this.

brusque /brʌsk, brʊsk, bruːsk/ *adj.* abrupt in manner or speech. □ **brusquely** *adv.* **brusqueness** *n.*

Brussels sprouts *n.pl.* **1** a variety of cabbage, *Brassica oleracea gemmifera*, with small compact cabbage-like buds close together along a tall single stem. **2** these eaten as a vegetable.

brut /bruːt/ *adj.* (of wine) unsweetened; very dry.

brutal *adj.* **1** savagely or coarsely cruel. **2** harsh, merciless (*brutal cold*). **3** *N Amer. slang* very bad (*a brutal haircut*). □ **brutality** *n.* (*pl.* **-ies**). **brutally** *adv.*

brutalism *n.* **1** brutality. **2** a heavy plain style of architecture etc. □ **brutalist** *n. & adj.*

brutalize *v.tr.* **1** make brutal. **2** treat brutally. □ **brutalization** *n.*

brute ● *n.* **1 a** a brutal or violent person or animal. **b** *informal* an unpleasant person. **2** an animal as opposed to a human being. **3** a large and very strong person etc. ● *adj.* **1** unthinking; entirely physical (*brute strength*). **2** not possessing the capacity to reason. **3** animal-like, cruel. □ **brutish** *adj.*

BS *n. & v.* (**BS's**, **BS'd**, **BSing**) esp. *N Amer. slang* BULLSHIT. □ **BSer** *n.*

B.Sc. *abbr.* Bachelor of Science.

B.Sc. (Agr.) *abbr.* (also **B.S.A.**) Bachelor of Science in Agriculture.

B.Sc.F. *abbr.* Bachelor of Science in Forestry.

B.Sc.N. *abbr.* Bachelor of Science in Nursing.

B.Sc.O.T. *abbr.* Bachelor of Science in Occupational Therapy.

B.Sc.P.T. *abbr.* Bachelor of Science in Physiotherapy.

BSE *abbr.* **1** bovine spongiform encephalopathy, a usu. fatal virus disease of cattle involving the central nervous system and causing extreme agitation. **2** breast self-examination.

B-side *n.* **1** the second side of a recording, esp. the usu. less commercial side of a single. **2** the music on this side.

bsmt. *abbr.* basement.

B.S.N. *abbr.* Bachelor of Science in Nursing.

BST *abbr.* bovine somatotropin, a growth hormone occurring naturally in cows, sometimes added to cattle feed to boost milk production.

B.S.W. *abbr.* Bachelor of Social Work.

BT *abbr.* (also **Bt**) BACILLUS THURINGIENSIS.

B.T. *abbr.* Bachelor of Technology.

B.Th. *abbr.* Bachelor of Theology.

BTU *abbr.* (also **Btu**) BRITISH THERMAL UNIT.

BTW *abbr.* by the way.

bu. *abbr.* bushel(s).

bubba *n.* esp. *N Amer. slang* a conservative, blue-collar white male, esp. of the southern US.

bubbe /ˈbʊbə/ *n.* (also **bubbie** /ˈbʊbi/) a Jewish grandmother.

bubble ● *n.* **1 a** a thin sphere of liquid enclosing air etc. **b** an air-filled cavity in a liquid or a solidified liquid such as glass or amber. **2** the sound or appearance of boiling. **3** a transparent domed cavity. **4** a situation in which investments, sales, etc. increase rapidly and then collapse. ● *v.intr.* **1 a** rise in or send up bubbles. **b** become manifest; arise as if from a depth. **2** make the sound of boiling. **3** be exuberant with laughter, excitement, anger, etc.

bubble bath *n.* **1** a preparation for adding to bathwater to make it foam. **2** a bath with this added.

bubble gum *n.* **1** chewing gum that can be blown into bubbles. **2** *N Amer. slang derogatory* (often *attrib.*) bland, repetitive pop music intended to appeal esp. to children and young teenagers. **3** (often *attrib.*) a pink or purple colour like that of bubble gum.

bubblehead *n.* esp. *N Amer. slang* usu. *derogatory* a foolish or unintelligent person, esp. a woman. □ **bubbleheaded** *adj.*

Bubble Jet printer *n.* *proprietary* a type of ink-jet printer in which the ink is heated to boiling to produce a bubble.

bubbly ● *adj.* (**-ier**, **-iest**) **1** having or resembling bubbles. **2** exuberant. ● *n.* (*pl.* **-ies**) *informal* sparkling wine, esp. champagne.

bubo /ˈbjuːboː, ˈbuː-/ *n.* (*pl.* **-oes**) a swollen inflamed lymph node esp. in the armpit or groin.

bubonic plague /bjuːˈbɒnɪk, buː-/ *n.* a highly contagious bacterial disease characterized by fever, delirium, and the formation of buboes.

buccaneer *n.* **1** a pirate, esp. one who plundered the Spanish colonies of the Caribbean and S American coasts in the late 17th c. **2** an unscrupulous adventurer. □ **buccaneering** *n. & adj.*

buck¹ ● *n.* **1** (also *attrib.*) the male of various animals, esp. the deer. **2** a self-assured young man. ● *v.* **1** *intr.* **a** (of a horse) jump upwards with back arched and feet drawn together. **b** (of a vehicle etc.) move jerkily and with a strong up-and-down motion. **2** *tr.* (usu. foll. by *off*) throw (a rider etc.) in this way. **3** *tr.* esp. *N Amer.* **a** oppose, resist (*bucking the trend*). **b** make one's way with difficulty against (*bucking easterly winds*). **4** *tr.* Football charge into (an opponent's line) while carrying the ball. □ **buck for** *N Amer. informal* strive for (a promotion, advantage, etc.). **buck up** *informal* make or become more cheerful.

buck² *n.* **1** *N Amer., Austral. & NZ informal* a dollar. **2** *slang* an object placed as a reminder before a player whose turn it is to deal at poker. □ **buck-naked** *N Amer. slang* completely naked. **a fast** (or **quick**) **buck** easy money. **pass the buck** *informal* shift responsibility (to another).

buck³ *N Amer* ● *v.tr.* cut (a tree) into logs. ● *n.* a frame supporting wood for sawing.

buck and doe *n. Cdn* (*Ont.*) = STAG AND DOE.

buckaroo *n. N Amer.* a cowboy.

buckbrush *n. N Amer.* any of various shrubs, esp. the shrubby cinquefoil, *Potentilla fruticosa*, or *Symphoricarpos occidentalis* of the honeysuckle family.

bucker *n. N Amer.* **1** a horse or bull that bucks. **2** Forestry a person who cuts felled trees into logs for transporting.

bucket ● *n.* **1 a** a roughly cylindrical open container of metal, plastic, etc. with a handle, for carrying, drawing, or holding water etc. **b** the amount contained in this. **2** (in *pl.*) large quantities of liquid, esp. rain or tears (*wept buckets*). **3** the scoop of a backhoe etc. **4** one of a series of containers on a mechanical conveyor etc. ● *v.* (**bucketed, bucketing**) **1** *intr. & tr.* (often foll. by *along*) move or drive jerkily or bumpily. **2** *intr.* (often foll. by *down*) (of liquid, esp. rain) pour heavily. □ **bucketful** *n.* (*pl.* **-fuls**).

bucket seat *n.* a seat with a rounded back to fit one person, esp. in a car.

buckeye *n.* **1** any tree or shrub of the genus *Aesculus*, with large sticky buds and showy red or white flowers. **2** the shiny brown fruit of this plant.

buckle ● *n.* **1** a flat often rectangular frame with a hinged pin, for joining the ends of a belt etc. **2** a similarly shaped ornament on a shoe etc. ● *v.* **1** *tr.* (often foll. by *up, on*, etc.) fasten with a buckle. **2** *tr. & intr.* give way or cause to give way under longitudinal pressure. **3** *intr.* (often foll. by *under*) submit under pressure. □ **buckle down** make a determined effort. **buckle up** fasten one's seat belt.

bucko *n. slang* (*pl.* **-oes**) a swaggering or domineering fellow.

buck-passing *n.* the act of shifting responsibility to another person. □ **buck-passer** *n.*

bucksaw *n. N Amer.* a woodcutting saw having the blade set within an H-shaped upright frame.

buckshot *n.* a coarse lead shot used in shotgun shells.

buckskin *n.* **1 a** the skin of a male deer. **b** a usu. suede yellowish-tan leather made from this or sheepskin. **c** (in *pl.*) *N Amer.* clothing made from buckskin. **2** a thick smooth cotton or woollen cloth resembling buckskin.

bucktail *n. N Amer.* a fishing lure made of hairs from the tail of a deer etc.

buckthorn *n.* any thorny shrub or small tree of the genus *Rhamnus*, esp. *R. cathartica* with berries formerly used as a cathartic, and *R. purshiana*, source of cascara sagrada.

bucktooth *n.* (*pl.* **-teeth**) an upper front tooth that projects. □ **bucktoothed** *adj.*

buckwheat *n.* any cereal plant of the genus *Fagopyrum*, esp. *F. esculentum* with seeds used for fodder and for flour to make bread and pancakes.

bucolic /bju:ˈkɒlɪk/ ● *adj.* **1** of or pertaining to an idyllic life in the countryside. **2** of shepherds, pastoral. ● *n.* (usu. in *pl.*) a pastoral poem or poetry.

bud¹ ● *n.* **1 a** an immature knoblike shoot from which a stem, leaf, or flower develops. **b** a flower or leaf that is not fully open. **2** anything still undeveloped. ● *v.* (**budded, budding**) **1** *intr.* form a bud or buds. **2** *intr.* begin to grow or develop (*a budding actor*). **3** *tr. Hort.* graft a bud (of a plant) on to another plant. □ **in bud** having newly formed buds.

bud² *n. N Amer. informal* (as a form of address) = BUDDY.

Buddhism /ˈbuːdɪzəm, ˈbʊd-/ *n.* a widespread Asian religion or philosophy, founded by Gautama Buddha in India in the 5th c. BC, which teaches that elimination of the self and earthly desires is the highest goal. □ **Buddhist** *n. & adj.* **Buddhistic** *adj.*

buddleia /ˈbʌdlɪə/ *n.* any shrub of the genus *Buddleia*, with fragrant flowers attractive to butterflies.

buddy esp. *N Amer.* ● *n.* (*pl.* **-ies**) **1** *informal* a close friend or companion. **2** *informal* (esp. as a form of address) any male. ¶In Newfoundland and the Maritimes *buddy* is used to refer to an absent unspecified male (*there was a buddy coming down the road*). **3** a person's assigned or chosen companion for some activity, esp. a dangerous one. ● *v.intr.* (**-ies, -ied**) (often foll. by *up*) become friendly.

buddy movie *n.* (also **buddy film**) a film in which camaraderie between two characters of the same sex (usu. men) is a central theme.

budge *v.* **1** *intr.* **a** make the slightest movement. **b** change one's opinion (*he's stubborn, he won't budge*). **2** *tr.* cause or compel to budge (*nothing will budge him*).

budgerigar /ˈbʌdʒərɪˌgɑr/ *n.* (also *informal* **budgie**) a small Australian parakeet, *Melopsittacus undulatus*.

budget ● *n.* **1** a periodic (esp. annual) estimate of the revenue and expenditure of a country, organization, etc. **2** a similar estimate for a private individual or family, often over a short period. **3** (*attrib.*) inexpensive. **4** the amount of money needed or available (for a specific item etc.) (*a budget of $200*). ● *v.* (**budgeted, budgeting**) **1** *tr. & intr.* (often foll. by *for*) allow or arrange for in a budget (*have budgeted for a new car*). **2** *tr.* to plan the expenditure or allotment of (money, time, etc.). □ **on a budget** with a restricted amount of money. □ **budgetary** *adj.*

budworm *n.* **1** SPRUCE BUDWORM. **2** a larva destructive to the buds of plants.

buff ● *adj.* of a yellowish beige colour. ● *n.* **1** a yellowish beige colour. **2** *informal* an enthusiast or expert in a specified subject or activity (*film buff*). **3** a thick ox or buffalo leather of a dull yellow colour and velvety surface (also *attrib.*: *buff gloves*). ● *v.tr.* **1** polish (metal, fingernails, etc.). **2** make (leather) velvety like buff, by removing the surface. □ **in the buff** *informal* naked.

buffalo *n.* (*pl.* same or **-oes**) **1** esp. *N Amer.* the N American bison, *Bison bison*. **2** either of two species of ox, the Cape buffalo *Syncerus caffer*, native to Africa, or the water buffalo *Bubalus arnee*, native to Asia.

buffalo bean *n.* a leguminous plant of western N America, *Astragalus crassicarpus*, with yellow flowers and edible pods.

buffalo berry *n.* **1** a shrub of the N American genus *Shepherdia* of the oleaster family, esp.: **a** *S. argentea* (in full **silver buffalo berry**) found from BC to Manitoba. **b** *S. canadensis* (in full **Canada buffalo berry**) found in wooded areas across Canada. **2** the edible red or yellow fruit of these plants.

buffalo chip *n. N Amer.* **1** a piece of dried buffalo dung, esp. when used as fuel by early settlers on the Prairies. **2** (usu. in *pl.*) thickly cut french fries.

buffaloed *adj.* *N Amer. slang* overawed, outwitted.

buffalo grass *n.* a grass, *Buchloe dactyloides*, of the N American plains.

buffalo jump *n.* *N Amer. hist.* a cliff over which Plains Indians drove herds of buffalo to slaughter them.

buffalo pound *n.* *Cdn hist.* a sturdy corral or enclosure into which Plains Indians drove buffalo in order to slaughter them.

buffalo robe *n.* *N Amer.* **1** a lap robe, blanket, or rug made of the hairy hide of the N American bison. **2** clothing made from bison skins.

buffalo run *n.* *N Amer. hist.* **1** a buffalo hunt conducted on horseback. **2** a trail made by buffalo.

buffalo stone *n.* a small fossil found on the prairies, believed by Plains Aboriginal peoples to give their finders great power with the buffalo.

Buffalo wings *n.pl.* (also **Buffalo style chicken wings**) *N Amer.* deep-fried chicken wings coated in a spicy sauce and served with blue cheese dressing.

buffer[1] • *n.* **1** a device that protects against or reduces the effect of an impact. **2** a substance that maintains the hydrogen ion concentration of a solution when an acid or alkali is added. **3** (often *attrib.*) **a** a country or area between two potential belligerents, regarded as reducing the likelihood of open hostilities (*buffer zone*). **b** a person or thing that protects from the potentially damaging impact of one person, activity, etc. on another. **4** *Computing* an intermediate memory for the temporary storage of information during data transfers, e.g. before printing. • *v.tr.* **1** act as a buffer to. **2** *Chem.* treat with a buffer.

buffer[2] *n.* a device for buffing or polishing.

buffet[1] /'bʊfei, 'bʌfei, 'bɒfei/ *n.* **1 a** a meal consisting of several dishes set out from which guests serve themselves (*buffet lunch*). **b** a table or counter from which such meals are served. **c** a restaurant having such a table or counter. **2** a sideboard or cabinet for china, silverware, etc.

buffet[2] /'bʌfət/ • *v.* (**buffeted, buffeting**) **1** *tr.* **a** strike or knock repeatedly (*wind buffeted the trees*). **b** strike, esp. repeatedly, with the hand or fist. **2** *tr.* (usu. in *passive*) attack; plague (*buffeted by the recession*). **3 a** *intr.* struggle; fight one's way (*through difficulties etc.*). **b** *tr.* contend with (waves etc.). • *n.* **1** a blow, esp. of the hand or fist. **2** a shock. □ **buffeting** *n.*

buffoon *n.* **1** a jester; a mocker. **2** a stupid person. □ **buffoonery** *n.* **buffoonish** *adj.*

bug[1] • *n.* **1 a** *N Amer.* any small insect. **b** any of various insects with oval flattened bodies and mouthparts modified for piercing and sucking. **2** *informal* a microorganism, esp. a bacterium, or a disease caused by it. **3** *informal* a concealed microphone etc. used in electronic surveillance. **4** *informal* a mistake or malfunction in a computer program or system etc. **5** *informal* an obsession, enthusiasm, etc. • *v.* (**bugged, bugging**) **1** *tr.* *informal* annoy, bother. **2** *tr.* *informal* conceal a microphone in (a room etc.). **3** *intr.* (often foll. by *out*) *N Amer.* (of the eyes) bulge. □ **put a bug in a person's ear** *N Amer.* suggest something to a person, esp. confidentially.

bug[2] *v.intr.* *N Amer.* **1** (foll. by *off*) *informal* go away. **2** (foll. by *out*) esp. *Military slang* leave quickly.

bugaboo /'bʌɡəˌbuː/ *n.* **1** a bugbear. **2** an object of fear or anxiety.

bugbear *n.* **1** a cause of annoyance or anger. **2** an object of baseless fear.

bug-eyed *adj.* having bulging eyes.

bugger ¶Often considered a coarse or taboo word. • *n.* **1** *slang* **a** a person, esp. of a specified kind (*the old bugger*). **b** an unpleasant or awkward person or thing

(*the bugger won't fit*). **2** a person who commits buggery. • *v.tr.* **1** *slang* as an exclamation of annoyance (*bugger it*). **2** *slang* (often foll. by *up*) ruin; spoil (*really buggered it up*). **3** commit buggery with. • *interj.* expressing annoyance. □ **bugger about** (or **around**) (often foll. by *with*) **1** mess about. **2** mislead; persecute. **bugger off** esp. *Brit.* go away.

bugger all *n.* esp. *Brit. coarse slang* nothing.

buggery *n.* **1** anal intercourse. **2** = BESTIALITY 1.

buggy[1] *n.* (*pl.* **-ies**) **1** a light horse-drawn vehicle for one or two people. **2** a small, sturdy, esp. open, automobile (*dune buggy*). **3** *N Amer.* = BABY BUGGY (see BABY CARRIAGE). **4** *N Amer.* = SHOPPING CART.

buggy[2] *adj.* (**-ier, -iest**) **1** infested with bugs. **2** (of software) having programming errors. **3** *N Amer. slang* mad or crazy.

bugle /'bjuːɡəl/ • *n.* **1** a brass instrument like a small trumpet, used esp. for military signals. **2** the call of a bull elk at rutting time. • *v.* **1** *intr.* sound a bugle. **2** *tr.* sound (a note etc.) on a bugle. **3** *intr.* (of a bull elk etc.) make a loud bellowing call. □ **bugler** *n.*

build • *v.* (*past* and *past. part.* **built**) **1** *tr.* **a** construct (a house, vehicle, fire, etc.) by putting parts or material together. **b** commission, finance, and oversee the building of (*built two new hospitals*). **2** *tr.* (often foll. by *up*) establish, develop, or accumulate gradually (*built the business up from nothing*). **b** (often foll. by *on*) base (hopes, theories, etc.). **3** *intr.* (of sounds etc.) become more intense. • *n.* **1** the proportions of esp. the human body. **2** a style of construction; a make. □ **build in** (or **into**) **1** incorporate as part of a structure. **2** integrate as part of a plan, policy, activity, etc. **build on 1** add (an extension etc.). **2** make further advances after achieving (a success etc.). **build up 1** increase in size or strength. **2** praise; boost. **3** gradually become established.

builder *n.* a person who builds, esp. a contractor for building houses etc. **2** a substance added to a soap or detergent to increase its efficiency.

building *n.* **1** a permanent fixed structure forming an enclosure and providing protection from the elements etc. **2** the constructing of such structures.

building block *n.* **1** a basic component or element (*the building blocks of DNA*). **2** a block of stone or other material used in building. **3** one of a set of wooden or plastic cubes etc. that fit together, as a child's toy.

building code *n.* the body of regulations governing standards of construction.

buildup *n.* **1** a favourable description in advance. **2** a gradual approach to a climax or maximum (*the buildup was slow but sure*). **3** an accumulation.

built • *v.* *past* and *past part.* of BUILD. • *adj.* **1** having a specified build (*sturdily built*). **2** produced by building. **3** *slang* (of a woman) having large breasts.

built-in • *adj.* **1** forming an integral part of a structure (*a built-in flash*). **2** inherent, integral, innate (*a built-in bias*). • *n.* a built-in cabinet, appliance, etc.

built-up *adj.* **1** (of a locality) densely covered by houses etc. **2** increased in height etc. by the addition of parts. **3** composed of separately prepared parts.

bulb *n.* **1 a** the globular underground organ of an onion, lily, etc., which contains the following year's bud and scale leaves that serve as food reserves. **b** a plant grown from this, e.g. a daffodil. **2** = LIGHT BULB. **3** any object or part shaped like a bulb.

bulbous /'bʌlbəs/ *adj.* **1** shaped like a bulb. **2** having a bulb or bulbs. **3** growing from a bulb.

Bulgarian /bʌl'ɡɛriən/ • *n.* **1 a** a native or national of Bulgaria, a country in SE Europe. **b** a person of

Bulgarian descent. **2** the language of Bulgaria. ● *adj.* of or relating to Bulgaria or its people or language.

bulge ● *n.* **1 a** a convex part of an otherwise flat or flatter surface. **b** an irregular swelling; a lump. **2** *informal* a temporary increase in quantity or number. ● *v.* **1** *intr.* swell outwards. **2** *intr.* be full or replete. **3** *tr.* swell (a bag, cheeks, etc.) by stuffing. □ **bulgingly** *adv.* **bulgy** *adj.*

bulgur /ˈbʌlɡər/ *n.* (also **bulgar**, **bulghur**) a cereal food of whole wheat partially boiled then dried.

bulimia /buːˈliːmiə/ *n.* **1** (in full **bulimia nervosa**) an emotional disorder in which bouts of extreme overeating are followed by self-induced vomiting, purging, or fasting. **2** insatiable overeating. □ **bulimic** *adj. & n.*

bulk ● *n.* **1 a** size; magnitude (esp. large). **b** a large mass, body, or person. **c** a large quantity. **2** a large shape, body, or person (*jacket barely covered his bulk*). **3** (usu. prec. by *the*; treated as *pl.*) the greater part or number. **4** roughage. **5** cargo, esp. unpackaged. ● *v.* **1** *intr.* seem, as regards size or importance (*bulks large in his reckoning*). **2** *tr.* make (a substance) seem bulkier. **3** *tr.* combine (consignments of a commodity) together. ● *attrib.adj.* pertaining to material bought, sold, handled, etc. in bulk. □ **in bulk 1** loose, not packaged. **2** in large quantities. **bulk up** increase in bulk or mass.

bulk carrier *n.* (also **bulker**) a ship that carries cargo in bulk.

bulkhead *n.* an upright partition separating the compartments in a ship, aircraft, vehicle, etc.

bulk mail *n.* a category of mail for mailing out large numbers of identical items at a reduced rate.

bulky *adj.* (**-ier, -iest**) **1** taking up much space, large. **2** awkwardly large. □ **bulkily** *adv.* **bulkiness** *n.*

bull¹ ● *n.* **1 a** an uncastrated male bovine animal. **b** the male of various other large animals, e.g. whale, elephant, moose. **2** a person who buys shares hoping to sell them at a higher price later (*compare* BEAR²). **3** *slang* = BULLSHIT. **4** *N Amer. slang* a policeman. ● *adj.* **1** like that of a bull (*bull neck*). **2** (in comb.) *N Amer.* Forestry chief or head. ● *v.* **1** *tr. & intr.* act or treat violently. **2** *Stock Exch.* **a** *intr.* speculate for a rise. **b** *tr.* produce a rise in the price of (stocks, etc.). □ **bull in a china shop** a reckless or clumsy person. **take the bull by the horns** meet a difficulty boldly. **bull through** *N Amer.* force through with great effort.

bull² *n.* a papal edict.

bull³ *n.* an expression containing a contradiction in terms or implying ludicrous inconsistency.

bullcook *n.* *N Amer.* a person who performs various chores in a logging camp etc. (e.g. chopping wood, cleaning bunkhouses, etc.).

bulldog *n.* **1** a sturdy, powerful breed of dog with a large head, protruding lower jaw, and smooth hair. **2** a tenacious and courageous person.

bulldogging *n.* *N Amer. slang* = STEER WRESTLING. □ **bulldogger** *n.*

bulldoze *v.tr.* **1** clear with a bulldozer. **2** *informal* **a** intimidate. **b** make (one's way) forcibly.

bulldozer *n.* **1** a powerful tractor with a broad curved vertical blade at the front for clearing ground. **2** a forceful and domineering person.

bullet *n.* **1** a projectile of lead etc. for a rifle, revolver, etc. **2** *Printing* a small usu. solid circle used to introduce and emphasize an item in a list etc.

bulletin *n.* **1** a short official account, statement, or broadcast report of news. **2** a regular list of information etc. issued by an organization or society.

bulletin board *n.* **1** *N Amer.* a board for displaying notices. **2** a system for storing information in a com-

puter so that any authorized user can access and add to it from a remote terminal or personal computer.

bulletproof ● *adj.* **1** impenetrable by bullets (*bulletproof vest*). **2** unassailable, safe from criticism etc. (*financially bulletproof*). ● *v.tr.* make bulletproof.

bullfight *n.* a sport of baiting and (usu.) killing bulls as a public spectacle, esp. in Spain. □ **bullfighter** *n.* **bullfighting** *n.*

bullfrog *n.* any of several frogs with bellowing calls, esp. the largest N American frog, *Rana catesbeiana*.

bullhead *n.* **1** any N American freshwater catfish of the genus *Ictalurus* having a large head with several barbels. **2** any of various northern fishes of the family Cottidae with large heads bearing spines.

bullheaded *adj.* obstinate; impetuous; blundering. □ **bullheadedly** *adv.* **bullheadedness** *n.*

bullhorn *n.* an electronically amplified megaphone.

bullion /ˈbʊliən/ *n.* a metal (esp. gold or silver) in bulk before coining, or valued by weight.

bullish *adj.* **1 a** *Stock Exch.* causing or associated with a rise in prices. **b** aggressively optimistic. **2** like a bull. □ **bullishly** *adv.* **bullishness** *n.*

bull market *n.* a market with shares rising in price.

bullock *n.* = STEER².

bullpen *n.* **1** *Baseball* **a** an area where pitchers, esp. relief pitchers, warm up. **b** the relief pitchers on a team. **2** a large cell in which prisoners are held temporarily, in a courthouse, police station, or jail.

bull riding *n.* *N Amer.* a rodeo event in which a rider attempts to remain on a bucking bull for eight seconds while holding onto a rope tied around the animal's middle with one hand. □ **bull rider** *n.*

bullring *n.* an arena for bullfights.

bull's eye *n.* **1 a** the centre of a target. **b** a shot, dart, etc. hitting this. **2** a hemisphere or thick disc of glass in a ship's deck or side to admit light. **3** a small circular window. **4 a** a hemispherical lens. **b** a lantern fitted with this. **5** an accurate guess etc.

bullshit *coarse slang* ● *n.* (often as *interj.*) nonsensical, foolish, or deceptive talk or writing. ● *v.intr.* (**-shitted**, **-shitting**) talk nonsense; bluff. □ **bullshitter** *n.*

bull snake *n.* a large yellowish-brown N American constricting snake of the genus *Pituophis*.

bull terrier *n.* a stocky, short-haired breed of dog that is a cross between a bulldog and a terrier.

bull trout *n.* *N Amer.* = DOLLY VARDEN 1.

bullwhip esp. *N Amer.* ● *n.* a whip with a long heavy lash. ● *v.tr.* thrash with such a whip.

bully¹ ● *n.* (*pl.* **-ies**) a person who uses strength or power to coerce others by fear. ● *v.tr.* (**-ies, -ied**) **1** persecute or oppress by force or threats. **2** (foll. by *into* + verbal noun) pressure or coerce (a person) to do something (*bullied him into agreeing*).

bully² *interj.* *slang* (foll. by *for*) expressing admiration or approval, or *ironic* (*bully for you!*).

bully³ *n.* (*pl.* **-ies**) (also **bully boat**) *Cdn* (*Nfld*) a two-masted decked boat used for fishing on the coasts of NE Newfoundland and Labrador.

bully boy *n.* a young bully, esp. a hired ruffian.

bulrush *n.* **1** any rushlike water plant of the genus *Scirpus*, esp. *S. lacustris*, used for weaving. **2** a tall water plant, *Typha latifolia*, having a brown cigar-shaped flower head. **3** *Bible* a papyrus plant.

bulwark /ˈbʊlwərk, -wɔːk/ *n.* **1** a defensive wall, esp. of earth. **2** a person, principle, etc., that acts as a defence. **3** (usu. in *pl.*) a ship's side above deck.

bum¹ *n.* *Cdn, Brit., Austral., & NZ informal* the buttocks.

bum² ● *n.* **1** a street person or vagrant. **2** a lazy or irresponsible person. **3** *N Amer.* an obnoxious person.

4 *N Amer.* a person who devotes a lot of time to a specified activity (*beach bum*). ● *v.* (**bummed**, **bumming**) **1** *intr.* (often foll. by *around*) loaf or wander around. **2** *tr.* acquire by begging. **3** *tr. N Amer.* (foll. by *out*) disappoint. ● *attrib.adj.* **1** malfunctioning (*a bum knee*). **2** worthless (*a bum cheque*). **3** unfair, disappointing (*a bum deal*). □ **on the bum** vagrant, begging. **give a person the bum's rush** *N Amer.* **1** forcibly eject. **2** abruptly dismiss.

bumble *v.intr.* **1** (often as **bumbling** *adj.*) act ineptly; blunder. **2** (foll. by *on*) speak in a rambling incoherent way. **3** make a buzz or hum. □ **bumbler** *n.*

bumblebee *n.* any large hairy bee of the genus *Bombus* with a loud buzz, common in temperate regions.

bumbleberry pie *n.* *Cdn* a pie with a filling of mixed berries, e.g. blackberries, raspberries, blueberries, strawberries, etc.

bummed *adj. N Amer.* (also **bummed out**) disappointed.

bummer *n. N Amer. informal* **1** an unpleasant occurrence. **2** an idler.

bump ● *n.* **1** a dull-sounding blow or collision. **2** a swelling or dent caused by this. **3** an uneven patch on a road, field, etc. ● *v.* **1 a** *tr.* hit or come against with a bump. **b** *intr.* (of two objects) collide. **2** *intr.* (foll. by *against, into*) hit with a bump; collide with. **3** *tr.* (often foll. by *against, on*) hurt or damage by striking (*bumped my head on the ceiling*). **4** *intr.* (usu. foll. by *along*) move or travel with much jolting (*bumped along the road*). **5** *tr. N Amer.* displace, e.g. from a job (by seniority) or airline reservation. □ **bump and grind** move (one's hips etc.) to music, esp. as part of an erotic dance. **bump into** *informal* meet by chance. **like a bump on a log** *N Amer.* inertly. **bump off** *slang* murder. **bump up** *informal* increase (prices etc.).

bumper *n.* **1** a horizontal bar or strip fixed across the front or back of a motor vehicle to reduce damage in a collision or as a trim. **2** (usu. *attrib.*) an unusually large or fine example (*a bumper crop*). □ **bumper to bumper 1** (of traffic) backed up. **2** *N Amer.* (of automobile insurance etc.) covering the entire vehicle from one bumper to the other.

bumper car *n.* each of a number of small electrically-driven cars in an enclosure at an amusement park etc., driven around and bumped into each other.

bumper sticker *n. N Amer.* a sticker with a slogan etc. to be displayed on a vehicle's bumper.

bumpkin *n.* an unsophisticated and socially inept rural person.

bumptious /'bʌmpʃəs/ *adj.* offensively conceited. □ **bumptiously** *adv.* **bumptiousness** *n.*

bumpy *adj.* (**-ier, -iest**) **1** having many bumps (*a bumpy road*). **2** affected by bumps (*a bumpy ride*). □ **bumpily** *adv.* **bumpiness** *n.*

bum rap *n.* **1** imprisonment on a false charge. **2** a false accusation.

bum steer *n.* false information.

bun *n.* **1** *N Amer.* a small unsweetened bread roll. **2** a small sweetened bread roll or cake, often with dried fruit. **3** (in *pl.*) *N Amer. informal* the buttocks. **4** hair worn in a tight coil at the back of the head. □ **have a bun in the oven** *slang* be pregnant.

bunch ● *n.* **1** a cluster of things growing or fastened together. **2** a collection; a set or lot. **3** *informal* a group; a gang. **4** *informal* a large amount; lots (*a bunch of ideas*; *thanks a bunch*). ● *v.* **1** *tr.* make into a bunch or bunches; gather into close folds. **2** *intr.* form into a group or crowd. □ **buncher** *n.* **bunchy** *adj.*

bunchberry *n.* (*pl.* **-ies**) a dwarf dogwood, *Cornus canadensis*, or its red fruit.

bunch grass *n.* any of various N American grasses that grow in clumps.

bundle ● *n.* **1** a collection of things tied or fastened together. **2** a set of nerve fibres etc. banded together. **3** *informal* a large amount of money. ● *v.tr.* **1** (usu. foll. by *up*) tie in or make into a bundle. **2** (usu. foll. by *into*) throw or push, esp. quickly or confusedly (*bundled the papers into the drawer*). **3** (usu. foll. by *out, off, away*, etc.) send (esp. a person) away hurriedly or unceremoniously (*bundled them off the premises*). **4** dress (*bundled them into their snowsuits*). **5** (in *passive*) sell as a unit (*software bundled with the computer*). □ **be a bundle of nerves** (or **prejudices** etc.) be extremely nervous (or prejudiced etc.). **bundle up** dress warmly or cumbersomely. □ **bundler** *n.*

Bundt pan *n. N Amer.* proprietary a tube pan with fluted sides used for baking cakes.

bung ● *n.* a stopper for closing a hole in a container, esp. a cask. ● *v.tr.* stop with a bung. □ **bunged up** *informal* **1** *N Amer.* damaged; malfunctioning. **2** closed, blocked. **3** constipated.

bungalow *n.* **1** a one-storeyed house. **2** *Cdn* (*Cape Breton*) a summer cottage, esp. a modest one.

bungee cord *n.* **1** strong elasticized cord or cable. **2** a piece of this, usu. with a hook on each end and used esp. for securing baggage etc.

bungee jump *v.intr.* jump from a height, as from a bridge or crane, while attached to it by a bungee cord. □ **bungee jumper** *n.* **bungee jumping** *n.*

bungle ● *v.* **1** *tr.* blunder over, mismanage, or fail at (a task). **2** *intr.* work badly or clumsily. ● *n.* a bungled attempt; bungled work. □ **bungler** *n.*

bunion /'bʌnjən/ *n.* a swelling on the foot, esp. at the first joint of the big toe.

bunk¹ ● *n.* **1** a simple bed, esp. one of two or more arranged on top of one another. **2** *N Amer.* a large trough for feeding cattle in a feedlot etc. ● *v.intr.* sleep in or lie on a bunk or improvised bed. □ **bunk down** go to bed.

bunk² *n. slang* nonsense, humbug.

bunk bed *n.* each of two or more beds one above the other, forming a unit.

bunker ● *n.* **1** a large container or compartment for storing fuel. **2** *Military* a reinforced underground shelter. **3** a hollow filled with sand, used as an obstacle in a golf course. ● *v.tr.* **1** fill the fuel bunkers of (a ship etc.). **2** (usu. in *passive*) **a** trap in a bunker (in sense 3). **b** bring into difficulties.

bunkhouse *n.* **1** a house where workers etc. are lodged. **2** *Cdn* = BUNKIE.

bunkie *n. Cdn* a small outbuilding on the property of a summer cottage providing extra sleeping accommodation for guests.

bunny *n.* (*pl.* **-ies**) **1** *informal* a rabbit. **2** *derogatory* (usu. in *comb.*) a young, attractive woman, esp. one who is sexually available, involved in a particular activity (*ski bunny*). **3** *N Amer.* (*attrib.*) designating an easy hill for beginner skiers (*bunny hill*).

bunny hug *n. Cdn* (*Sask.*) a hooded sweatshirt.

Bunsen burner *n.* a small adjustable gas burner used in scientific work as a source of great heat.

bunt ● *v.* **1** *tr. & intr.* push with the head or horns; butt. **2** *Baseball* **a** *tr.* strike or tap (the ball) with the bat without swinging. **b** *intr.* bunt the ball. ● *n.* **1** an act of bunting. **2** a bunted ball. □ **bunter** *n.*

bunting *n.* **1 a** flags and other decorations. **b** a loosely-woven fabric used for these. **2** (also **bunting bag**) *N Amer.* a snug, hooded sleeping bag for infants.

3 any of numerous seed-eating birds related to the finches and sparrows.

buoy /bɔɪ, 'buːi/ ● n. **1** an anchored float serving as a navigation mark or to show reefs etc. **2** a lifebuoy. ● v.tr. **1** (usu. foll. by up) **a** keep afloat. **b** sustain the courage or spirits of (a person etc.); uplift, encourage. **2** mark with a buoy or buoys.

buoyancy /'bɔɪənsi/ n. **1** the capacity to be buoyant. **2** resilience; recuperative power. **3** cheerfulness.

buoyant adj. **1 a** able to keep afloat or rise to the top of a liquid or gas. **b** (of a liquid or gas) able to keep something afloat. **2** lighthearted. □ **buoyantly** adv.

buppie n. informal a black yuppie.

bur var. of BURR n. 1-3.

burb n. N Amer. informal (usu. in pl.) = SUBURB.

burble ● v.intr. **1** make a murmuring noise. **2** speak ramblingly. ● n. **1** a murmuring noise. **2** rambling speech. □ **burbler** n.

burbot /'bɜːbət/ n. a freshwater fish, Lota lota, of the cod family, with a broad head and barbels.

burden ● n. **1** a load, esp. a heavy one. **2** an oppressive duty, obligation, expense, emotion, etc. **3** a ship's carrying capacity. **4 a** the refrain or chorus of a song. **b** the chief theme or gist of a speech, book, poem, etc. ● v.tr. load with a burden; encumber, oppress. □ **burden of proof** the obligation to prove one's case. □ **burdensome** adj.

burdock n. any plant of the genus Arctium, with prickly flowers and docklike leaves.

bureau /'bjʊərəʊ/ n. (pl. **-s**) **1 a** Cdn & Brit. a writing desk with drawers and usu. an angled top opening downwards to form a writing surface. **b** N Amer. a chest of drawers. **2 a** an office or business with a specified function. **b** a government department.

bureaucracy /bjʊˈrɒkrəsi/ n. (pl. **-ies**) **1 a** government by central administration. **b** a nation or organization so governed. **2** the officials of such a government, esp. regarded as oppressive and inflexible. **3** conduct typical of such officials.

bureaucrat /'bjʊərəˌkræt, -rə,kræt/ n. **1** an official in a bureaucracy. **2** an inflexible, insensitive administrator. □ **bureaucratic** adj. **bureaucratically** adv.

bureaucratese /ˌbjʊərəˌkræˈtiːz/ n. a style of language believed to be characteristic of bureaucrats, marked by jargon, abstractions, circumlocution, etc.

bureaucratize /bjʊˈrɒkrəˌtaɪz/ v.tr. govern by or transform into a bureaucratic system. □ **bureaucratization** n.

burg n. N Amer. informal a town or city.

burgeon /'bɜːdʒən/ v.intr. begin to grow rapidly; flourish. □ **burgeoning** adj.

burger n. **1** informal a hamburger. **2** (in comb.) a kind of hamburger or variation of it (cheeseburger; fishburger).

burgher /'bɜːgər/ n. N Amer. a middle-class inhabitant of a (usu. specified) city or town.

burglary n. (pl. **-ies**) **1** entry into a building illegally with intent to commit theft, do bodily harm, or do damage. **2** an instance of this. ¶In Canadian law, now replaced by BREAKING AND ENTERING. □ **burglar** n.

burgle v.tr. & intr. (also N Amer. **burglarize**) commit burglary.

burgundy ● n. (pl. **-ies**) **1** (also **Burgundy**) **a** the wine (usu. red) of Burgundy. **b** a similar wine from another place. **2** the reddish purple colour of burgundy wine. ● adj. of this colour.

burial n. **1** the burying of a dead body. **2** a funeral.

burial ground n. a cemetery.

burl n. **1** N Amer. a flattened knotty growth on a tree. **2** = BURR n. 6. **3** a knot or lump in wool or cloth.

burlap n. **1** coarse canvas esp. of jute used for sacking etc. **2** a similar lighter material for use in dressmaking or furnishing.

burlesque /bɜːˈlesk/ ● n. **1 a** comic imitation, esp. in parody of a dramatic or literary work. **b** a performance or work of this kind. **c** bombast, mock-seriousness. **2** N Amer. a variety show, often including striptease. ● adj. of or in the nature of burlesque. ● v.tr. (**-lesques**, **-lesqued**, **-lesquing**) make or give a burlesque of.

Burlington bun n. Cdn (NS) = JELLY DOUGHNUT.

burly adj. (**-ier**, **-iest**) big and strong. □ **burliness** n.

Burmese /bɜːˈmiːz/ ● n. (pl. same) **1 a** a native or national of Burma (now Myanmar) in SE Asia. **b** a person of Burmese descent. **2** a member of the largest ethnic group of Burma. **3** the language of this group. ● adj. of or relating to Burma or its people.

burn ● v. (past and past part. **burned** or **burnt**) **1** tr. & intr. be or cause to be consumed or destroyed by fire. **2** intr. a blaze or glow with fire. **b** be in the state characteristic of fire. **3** tr. & intr. be or cause to be injured or damaged by fire or great heat or by radiation. **4** tr. & intr. use or be used as a source of heat, light, or other energy (the lights burned all night). **5** tr. & intr. char or scorch in cooking. **6** tr. produce (a hole, a mark, etc.) by fire or heat. **7** tr. colour, tan, or parch with heat or light. **8** tr. & intr. put or be put to death by fire. **9** tr. brand. **b** (foll. by in) imprint by burning. **10** tr. & intr. make or be hot, give or feel a sensation or pain of or like heat. **11** tr. & intr. make or be passionate; feel or cause to feel great emotion (burn with shame). **12** intr. slang drive fast. **13** tr. N Amer. informal anger, irritate. **14** intr. (of acid etc.) gradually penetrate (into) causing disintegration. **15** tr. metabolize in the body (burn calories). **16** tr. & intr. cause or feel a sharp sensation (the alcohol burned in her throat). **17** tr. informal swindle or cheat. **18** tr. Computing copy data onto (a compact disc). **19** tr. Curling touch (a rock in play) with one's foot, broom, etc. **20** tr. & intr. Cdn (Nfld) freeze (a part of the body) in extreme cold; suffer frostbite. ● n. **1 a** a mark or injury caused by burning. **b** a mark or injury caused by friction or abrasion (razor burn). **2** N Amer., Austral., & NZ **a** an area of forest destroyed by a forest fire. **b** a forest area cleared by intentional burning. □ **burn one's bridges** (or **boats**) commit oneself irrevocably. **burn the candle at both ends** exhaust one's strength or resources by undertaking too much. **burn down 1 a** destroy (a building) by burning. **b** (of a building) be destroyed by fire. **2** burn less vigorously as fuel fails. **burn one's fingers** or **get one's fingers burned** suffer for meddling or rashness. **burn a hole in one's pocket** (of money) be quickly spent. **burn low** (of fire) be nearly out. **burn the midnight oil** read or work late into the night. **burn off 1** remove by fire. **2** expend (burn off energy). **burn out 1** be reduced to nothing by burning. **2** fail or cause to fail by burning. **3** esp. N Amer. suffer physical or emotional exhaustion. **4** consume the contents of by burning. **5** make (a person) homeless by burning his or her house. **burn up 1** get rid of by fire. **2** begin to blaze. **3** N Amer. slang be or make furious. **have money to burn** have more money than one needs.

burner n. **1** a person or thing that burns. **2 a** the part of a gas stove etc. that emits and shapes the flame. **b** N Amer. the heating element of an electric stove. **3** a furnace, esp. of a specified kind (oil burner).

burnet / 'bɜːnət / n. any plant of the genus *Sanguisorba* of the rose family, with pink or red flowers.

burning adj. **1** ardent, intense (*burning desire*). **2** hotly discussed, exciting (*burning question*). **3** flagrant (*burning shame*). □ **burningly** adv.

burning bush n. any of various shrubs with red fruits or red autumn leaves, esp. of the genus *Euonymus*.

burnish ● v.tr. polish by rubbing. ● n. a polished lustre. □ **burnisher** n.

burnout n. **1** physical or emotional exhaustion, esp. caused by stress. **2** depression, disillusionment.

burnt ● v. past and past part. of BURN. ● adj. **1** marked or affected by burning or as if burning. **2** (of a pigment) made darker by burning.

burnt offering n. an offering burned on an altar as a sacrifice.

burnt-out adj. **1** physically or emotionally exhausted. **2** destroyed by burning so that only a shell remains.

burnt sienna n. a dark reddish-orange colour.

burp ● v. **1** intr. belch. **2** tr. make (a baby) belch, usu. by patting its back. ● n. a belch.

burr ● n. **1 a** a prickly clinging seed-case or flower head. **b** any plant producing these. **2** a rough edge left on cut or punched metal, paper, etc. **3** a surgeon's or dentist's small drill. **4** a whirring sound. **5** a rough sounding of the letter *r*. **6** a swirled pattern in the grain of wood (also attrib.: *burr walnut*). ● v. **1** tr. pronounce with a burr. **2** intr. speak indistinctly. **3** intr. make a whirring sound. □ **burr under** (or **in**) **one's saddle** N Amer. an esp. persistent source of irritation.

burrito / bəˈriːtəʊ / n. (pl. **-os**) N Amer. a tortilla rolled around a spicy filling of meat, beans, etc.

burro n. (pl. **-os**) esp. US a small donkey used as a pack animal.

burrow ● n. a hole etc. dug by a small animal as a dwelling. ● v. **1** intr. make or live in a burrow. **2** tr. make (a hole etc.) by digging. **3** intr. hide oneself. **4** intr. (foll. by *into*) investigate, search. □ **burrower** n.

bursar n. a treasurer or other financial officer, esp. of a university or college.

bursary n. (pl. **-ies**) Cdn a financial award to a university student made primarily on the basis of financial need or some other criterion in addition to academic merit.

burst ● v. (past and past part. **burst**) **1 a** intr. break suddenly and violently apart by expansion of contents or internal pressure. **b** tr. cause to do this. **c** tr. send (a container etc.) violently apart. **2 a** tr. open forcibly. **b** intr. come open or be opened forcibly. **3 a** intr. (usu. foll. by *in*, *out*) make one's way suddenly, dramatically, or by force. **b** tr. break away from or through (*the river burst its banks*). **4** intr. (usu. foll. by *with*) have in abundance (*bursting with flavour*). **5** intr. appear or come suddenly (*the sun burst out*). **6** intr. (foll. by *into*) give sudden expression to (*burst into tears*). **7** intr. be as if about to burst because of effort, excitement, etc. **8** tr. suffer bursting of (*burst a blood vessel*). ● n. **1** the act of or an instance of bursting; a split. **2** a sudden issuing forth (*burst of flame*). **3** a sudden outbreak (*burst of applause*). **4 a** a short sudden effort; a spurt. **b** a gallop. **5** an explosion. □ **bursting at the seams** full to overflowing. **burst out 1** suddenly begin (*burst out laughing*). **2** exclaim.

bury v.tr. (**-ies, -ied**) **1** place (a dead body) in the earth, in a tomb, or in the sea etc. **2** lose by death (*has buried three children*). **3 a** put under ground (*bury alive*). **b** hide (treasure, a bone, etc.) in the earth. **c** cover up; submerge. **4 a** put out of sight (*buried his face in his hands*). **b** consign to obscurity (*the idea was buried*). **c** put away; forget. **5** involve deeply (*buried herself in her work*). □ **bury the hatchet** cease to quarrel.

bus ● n. (pl. **buses**) **1** a large motor vehicle designed to carry several passengers, esp. one serving the public on a fixed route or as a chartered service. **2** informal a car, airplane, etc., functioning like a bus. **3** Computing a defined set of conductors carrying data and control signals within a computer. ● v. (**buses, bused, busing**) **1** intr. go by bus. **2** tr. N Amer. transport by bus. **3** tr. N Amer. carry or remove (dishes etc.) in a cafeteria; clear (a table etc.) of dishes.

busboy n. N Amer. a waiter's assistant who clears tables etc.

busby / 'bʌzbi / n. (pl. **-ies**) a tall fur hat worn by hussars etc.

bus depot n. N Amer. a bus station.

bush¹ ● n. **1** a shrub or clump of shrubs with stems of moderate length. **2** a thing resembling this, esp. a clump of hair or fur. **3** Cdn a woodlot. **4** (esp. in N and S America, Australia, and Africa) a wild uncultivated district; woodland or forest. **5** (attrib.) (of a plant) shaped like a bush (*bush beans*). ● v.intr. (usu. foll. by *out*) branch or spread like a bush.

bush² ● n. **1** a metal lining for a round hole enclosing a revolving shaft etc. **2** a sleeve providing electrical insulation. ● v.tr. provide with a bush.

bush camp n. Cdn the living quarters, offices, etc., of a mining or lumbering operation in the bush.

bush country n. a wooded wilderness area.

bushcraft n. N Amer. the knowledge or experience needed to survive in the bush.

bushed adj. **1** (predic.) informal tired out. **2** forested; wooded. **3** Cdn informal (of a person) **a** living in the bush. **b** crazy; insane (due to isolation).

bushel n. **1** (in Canada and other Commonwealth countries) a measure of capacity for grain, fruit, etc., equal to 8 imperial gallons or 36.4 litres. **2** (in the US) a similar unit of measure equal to 64 US pints or 35.24 litres. □ **bushelful** n. (pl. **-fuls**)

bush farm n. Cdn hist. a farm in the bush, esp. one that has not been completely cleared of trees.

bush fever n. Cdn any of various disorders caused by protracted isolation in the bush.

bushing n. = BUSH² n.

bush jacket n. Cdn = LUMBERJACK JACKET.

bushland n. = BUSH¹ 4.

bush league N Amer. ● n. = MINOR LEAGUE. ● adj. (also **bush-league**) inferior, unsophisticated.

bushlot n. Cdn = WOODLOT.

bushman n. (pl. **-men**) **1** a person who lives or gains his livelihood in the bush, e.g. a logger. **2** (**Bushman**) **a** a member of an aboriginal people in southern Africa. **b** the language of this people.

bush pilot n. N Amer. a pilot who flies small aircraft into isolated areas.

bush plane n. N Amer. a small plane used for flying into isolated areas, usu. equipped with floats or skis.

bush road n. Cdn a usu. dirt road through a bush.

bushwhack v. **1** intr. N Amer., Austral., & NZ **a** clear a way through underbrush, dense vegetation, etc. **b** clear land in bush country and establish a settlement. **2** tr. N Amer. ambush.

bushwhacker n. N Amer., Austral., & NZ **1** a person who clears land in bush country and settles there. **2** a person who hikes in bush country.

bushworker n. Cdn a logger; a person who works in the bush. □ **bush work** n.

bushy adj. (**-ier, -iest**) **1** growing thickly like a bush.

2 having many bushes. **3** covered with bush. □ **bushily** adv. **bushiness** n.

business n. **1** one's regular occupation, profession, or trade. **2** a thing that is one's concern (none of your business). **3 a** a task or duty. **b** a reason for coming (what is your business?). **4** serious work or activity (get down to business). **5** derogatory a matter (sick of the whole business). **6** a thing or series of things needing to be dealt with. **7** volume of trade (did a lot of business). **8 a** a company etc. **b** commercial enterprises collectively. **9** patronage (take my business elsewhere). **10** N Amer. euphemism (esp. of pets) an occurrence of defecation or urination. □ **business as usual** an ongoing, unchanging state of affairs, esp. in adversity. **has no business** has no right. **in business 1** engaged in commercial activity. **2** able to begin operations. **the business end** informal the functional part of a tool or device. **in the business of** engaged in. **like nobody's business** informal extraordinarily. **make it one's business to** undertake to. **mean business** be in earnest. **mind one's own business** not meddle. **on business** with purpose relating to one's regular occupation. **send a person about his or her business** dismiss a person.

business administration n. a program of study at a university or college which trains students for managerial positions in businesses etc.

business card n. a card printed with one's name and professional details.

business class n. a more expensive class of seating than economy class in an aircraft, typically offering roomier seating, better food, and other advantages.

business cycle n. recurring periods of increased and decreased economic activity.

business day n. a day on which a business is open to the public.

business hours n.pl. the hours during which stores or offices are open to the public.

businesslike adj. efficient, systematic, practical.

businessman n. (pl. **-men**) a male business person.

business person n. (pl. **business people**) a person engaged in commerce, esp. at a senior level.

business studies n.pl. training in economics, management, etc.

businesswoman n. (pl. **-women**) a female business person.

busk v.intr. perform (esp. music) for voluntary donations, usu. in the street. □ **busker** n. **busking** n.

bus lane n. a lane on a road reserved for use by buses.

busload n. the number of people travelling in a bus.

buss N Amer. informal ● n. a kiss. ● v.tr. kiss.

bus shelter n. a shelter from rain etc. at a bus stop.

bus station n. a place in a city or town where intercity buses depart and arrive.

bus stop n. **1** a regular stopping place of a bus. **2** a sign marking this.

bust¹ n. **1 a** the human chest, esp. that of a woman. **b** the circumference of the body at bust level (a 36-inch bust). **c** the part of a woman's garment fitting over the bust (too small in the bust). **2** a sculpture of a person's head, shoulders, and chest.

bust² informal ● v. (past and past part. **busted** or **bust**) **1** tr. & intr. burst, break. **2** tr. esp. N Amer. **a** raid, search. **b** arrest. **3** tr. N Amer. tame (esp. broncos). ● n. **1** a failure. **2** a sudden economic downturn. **3** a police raid. **4** esp. N Amer. **a** punch; a hit. ● adj. **1** (also **busted**) broken, burst, collapsed. **2** bankrupt. □ **bust a gut 1** become overwrought, upset, etc. **2** exert oneself exceedingly. **bust up 1** bring or come to collapse;

explode. **2** (of esp. a married couple) separate. **go bust** become bankrupt.

bustard n. any large terrestrial bird of the family Otididae, with long neck, long legs, and stout tapering body.

buster n. **1** a person or thing that busts. **2** informal fellow (used esp. as a disrespectful form of address). **3** (in comb.) something that eradicates an undesirable or unpleasant phenomenon.

bustier /ˈbʌstiˌeɪ/ n. a woman's form-fitting, sleeveless, and often strapless bodice or top, sometimes laced at the front.

bustle ● v. **1** intr. (often foll. by about) **a** work etc. showily, energetically, and officiously. **b** hasten (bustled about the kitchen). **2** tr. make (a person) hurry or work hard. **3** intr. (often foll. by with) (of a place) be full of activity. ● n. excited activity. □ **bustler** n.

bust-up n. **1** a quarrel. **2** a marital separation or other breakup. **3** a collapse.

busty adj. (**-ier, -iest**) (of a woman) having a prominent bust. □ **bustiness** n.

busy ● adj. (**-ier, -iest**) **1** (often foll. by in, with, at, or pres. part.) occupied or engaged in work etc. with the attention concentrated (was busy packing). **2** full of activity (a busy evening). **3** (of a street etc.) having heavy traffic. **4** (of patterns etc.) overwhelmed by an excess of detail, variety, etc. (a very busy print). **5** employed continuously; unresting (busy as a bee). **6** esp. N Amer. (of a telephone line) already in use. ● v.tr. (**-ies, -ied**) (refl.) keep busy; occupy (busied herself with the accounts). □ **busily** adv. **busyness** n.

busybody n. (pl. **-ies**) **1** an overly inquisitive or meddlesome person. **2** a mischief-maker.

busy signal n. N Amer. a sound indicating that a telephone line is in use.

but ● conj. **1 a** nevertheless, however (tried hard but did not succeed). **b** on the other hand (I am old but you are young). **2** except, other than, otherwise than (what could we do but run?). **3** without the result that (it never rains but it pours). **4** prefixing an interruption to the speaker's train of thought (the weather is ideal - but is that a cloud on the horizon?). ● prep. except; apart from; other than. ● adv. **1** only; no more than; only just (is but a child). **2** introducing emphatic repetition; definitely (want to see nobody, but nobody). ● rel.pron. who not; that not (there is not a man but feels pity). ● n. an objection (ifs and buts). ● v.tr. (in phr. **but me no buts**) do not raise objections. □ **but for** without the help or hindrance etc. of (but for you I'd be rich by now). **but one** (or **two** etc.) excluding one (or two etc.) from the number (last but one). **but that** (prec. by neg.) that (I don't deny but that it's true). **but that** (or informal **what**) other than that; except that (who knows but that it is true?). **but then** (or **yet**) however, on the other hand.

butane /ˈbjuːteɪn, bjuːˈteɪn/ n. a hydrocarbon of the alkane series used in liquefied form as fuel.

butch slang ● adj. masculine; tough-looking. ● n. **1** (often attrib.) **a** a mannish woman. **b** a mannish lesbian. **2** a tough, usu. muscular, youth or man.

butcher ● n. **1 a** a person whose trade is dealing in meat. **b** a person who slaughters animals for food. **2** a person who kills or has people killed indiscriminately or brutally. ● v.tr. **1** slaughter or cut up (an animal) for food. **2** kill (people) wantonly or cruelly. **3** ruin (a job etc.) through incompetence.

butcher block n. N Amer. laminated strips of hardwood used to make countertops and similar surfaces.

butchery n. (pl. **-ies**) **1** needless or cruel slaughter (of people). **2** a butcher's trade.

butler n. the principal male servant of a household, usu. in charge of serving meals and receiving visitors.

butt[1] ● v. **1** intr. & tr. push or strike with the head or horns. **2** intr. (usu. foll. by out) project, jut. **3** intr. & tr. (usu. foll. by against, on) lie or place with one end flat against; abut. ● n. **1** a push or blow made with the head or horns. **2** (also **butt joint**) a simple joint in which two pieces of wood etc. are bonded without overlapping. □ **butt in 1** interrupt, meddle. **2** push into (a line of people) out of turn. **butt out** esp. N Amer. cease to interrupt or meddle.

butt[2] n. **1** (often foll. by of) an object of ridicule etc. (the butt of his jokes). **2 a** a mound behind a target to stop stray bullets etc. **b** (in pl.) a shooting range. **c** a target.

butt[3] ● n. **1** (also **butt end**) the thicker end, esp. of a tool or a weapon (gun butt). **2** N Amer. a cut of pork from the shoulder. **3 a** the stub of a cigar or a cigarette. **b** slang a cigarette. **4** esp. N Amer. slang the buttocks. **5** the trunk of a tree, esp. the part just above the ground. ● v.tr. N Amer. extinguish (a cigarette) by pressing it into an ashtray etc. □ **butt out** N Amer. **1** = BUTT v. **2** stop smoking, esp. permanently.

butt[4] n. **1** a large cask for wine or ale. **2** a former unit of measure equal to two hogsheads.

butte /bjuːt/ n. a high isolated hill with steep sides and a flat top, esp. in western N America.

butt-ending n. Hockey the infraction of jabbing an opponent with the butt of the stick. □ **butt-end** v.tr.

butter ● n. **1 a** a pale yellow edible fatty substance made by churning cream and used as a spread or in cooking. **b** a substance of a similar consistency or appearance (peanut butter). **2** excessive flattery. ● v.tr. spread, cook, or serve with butter. □ **butter up** informal flatter excessively. **look as if butter wouldn't melt in one's mouth** seem demure or innocent, probably deceptively.

butterball n. **1** a piece of butter shaped into a ball. **2** N Amer. slang a plump person, animal, etc.

buttercream n. a mixture of butter, sugar, etc. used as a filling or icing for a cake.

buttercup n. any of various plants of the genus Ranunculus, bearing usu. yellow cup-shaped flowers.

buttercup squash n. N Amer. a winter squash, a variety of Cucurbita maxima, with dark green skin.

butterfat n. the natural fats derived from milk, consisting mainly of glycerides. Abbr.: **BF**.

butterfingers n. informal a clumsy person prone to drop things. □ **butterfingered** adj.

butterflied adj. (of shrimp, a steak, etc.) sliced down the centre and spread apart.

butterfly ● n. (pl. **-flies**) **1** any diurnal insect of the order Lepidoptera, with knobbed antennae, a long thin body, and four usu. brightly coloured wings erect when at rest. **2** a showy or frivolous person. **3** (in pl.) informal a nervous sensation felt in the stomach. **4** a swimming stroke in which with both arms are lifted out of the water and the legs are kept together while kicking. **5** Hockey a kneeling position assumed by a goaltender in which the lower legs are spread apart to cover the bottom part of the goal. **6** Cdn a social dance in which trios of people alternate between promenading slowly around the dance floor and whirling each other in circles. ● v.tr. (**-flies**; **-flying**; past **-flied**) slice (meat, shrimp, etc.) down the centre and spread apart before cooking.

butterfly net n. a fine net on a ring attached to a pole, used for catching butterflies.

butterhead n. (also **butter lettuce**) any of several varieties of lettuce having soft and tender leaves and crisp hearts, e.g. bibb or Boston lettuce.

buttermilk n. **1** a slightly acid liquid left after churning butter. **2** a dairy product prepared commercially by adding bacterial culture to milk.

butternut n. **1** a deciduous, eastern N American tree of the walnut family, Juglans cinerea, having light grey bark and soft wood. **2** the oily nut of this tree. **3** the soft, light brown wood of this tree. **4** N Amer. a light brownish-grey colour.

butternut squash n. N Amer. a pear-shaped variety of winter squash with light yellowish-brown skin.

butterscotch n. **1** a brittle candy made from butter, brown sugar, etc. **2** the flavour of this.

butter tart n. Cdn a tart with a filling of butter, eggs, brown sugar, and usu. raisins.

buttery adj. like, containing, or spread with butter. □ **butteriness** n.

buttock n. (usu. in pl.) **1** each of two fleshy protuberances on the lower rear part of the human trunk. **2** the corresponding part of an animal.

button ● n. **1** a small disc or knob sewn on to a garment, either to fasten it by being pushed through a buttonhole, or as an ornament. **2 a** a knob on a piece of mechanical or electronic equipment which performs a particular function when pressed. **b** a small box depicted on a computer screen, representing a function which can be selected by clicking with a mouse. **3** N Amer. a usu. round badge bearing a slogan etc. fastened to the clothing with a pin. **4** a small round object resembling a button (often attrib.: button nose). **a** a bud. **b** a button mushroom. **6** Curling the four-foot circle in the centre of the house. **7** Fencing a knob covering the point of a foil to make it harmless. ● v. **1** tr. & intr. = BUTTON UP 1. **2** tr. supply with buttons. □ **button it** informal cease talking. **button one's lip** informal remain silent. **button up 1** fasten with buttons. **2** informal become silent. **3** informal complete (a task etc.) satisfactorily. **on the button** esp. N Amer. informal exactly on target. **push a person's buttons** esp. N Amer. informal exploit a person's fears, emotions, prejudices, etc. **push** (or **press** or **hit**) **the right buttons** play expertly on a person's emotions so as to elicit a desired response. □ **buttoned** adj. **buttonless** adj.

button-down adj. **1** (of a collar) having the points buttoned to the shirt. **2** (of a shirt) having a button-down collar.

buttoned-down adj. (also **buttoned-up**) informal **1** formal and inhibited in manner. **2** conservative.

buttonhole ● n. a loop or slit made in a garment through which a button may be passed for fastening. ● v.tr. **1** informal accost and detain (a reluctant listener). **2** make buttonholes in.

button mushroom n. a young unopened mushroom.

buttonwood n. = SYCAMORE 1.

buttress ● n. **1** a projecting support of stone or brick etc. built against a wall. **2** a source of help or support. **3** a projecting portion of a hill or mountain. ● v.tr. (often foll. by up) **1** support with a buttress. **2** provide with support (a claim buttressed by facts).

buxom /ˈbʌksəm/ adj. **1** (of a woman) having large breasts. **2** (of a woman) plump and healthy-looking.

buy ● v. (**buys**, **buying**; past and past part. **bought**) **1** tr. **a** purchase. **b** serve to obtain (money can't buy happiness). **2** tr. **a** procure (the loyalty etc.) of a person by bribery, promises, etc. **b** win over (a person) in this way. **3** tr. get by sacrifice, great effort, etc. (bought with our sweat). **4** tr. informal accept, believe in (bought my story). **5** *intr.* be a buyer for a store etc. (*buys for a furniture chain*). ● *n. informal* a purchase (*a good buy*). ☐ **buy in 1** buy a stock of. **2** withdraw (an item) at auction because of failure to reach the reserve price. **buy into 1** obtain a share in (an enterprise) by payment. **2** *informal* accept (a line of reasoning etc.). **buy it** (*N Amer.* also **buy the farm**) (usu. in *past*) *slang* be killed. **buy off 1** get rid of (a claim, a claimant, a blackmailer) by payment. **2** bribe. **buy oneself out** (or **off**) obtain one's release (esp. from the armed services) by payment. **buy out** pay (a person, company, etc.) to give up an ownership, interest, etc. **buy time** delay an event, conclusion, etc., temporarily. **buy up 1** buy as much as possible of. **2** absorb (another firm etc.) by purchase.

buyback *n.* the purchase of a thing (esp. stock in a company) after having sold it.

buyer *n.* **1** a purchaser, a customer. **2** a person who selects and purchases stock for a store etc.

buyer's market *n.* (also **buyers' market**) an economic position in which goods are plentiful and cheap and buyers have the advantage over sellers.

buyout *n.* the purchase of a controlling share in a company etc.

buzz ● *n.* **1** the humming sound of an insect or a machine etc. **2** the sound of a buzzer. **3 a** a confused low sound as of people talking; a murmur. **b** a stir; hurried activity (*a buzz of excitement*). **c** *informal* a rumour. **d** *informal* publicity, esp. created by word of mouth. **4** *slang* a telephone call (*give me a buzz*). **5** *slang* a thrill; a feeling of mild intoxication, esp. from drink or drugs. **6** (also **buzz cut**) *N Amer. slang* a very short haircut. ● *v.* **1** *intr.* make a humming sound. **2 a** *tr.* & *intr.* signal or call with a buzzer. **b** *tr. informal* telephone. **3** *intr.* **a** (often foll. by *about*) move or hover busily. **b** (of a place) have an air of excitement or purposeful activity. **4** *tr. informal* throw hard. **5** *tr. Aviation informal* fly fast and very close to (another aircraft, the ground, etc.). ☐ **buzz off** *slang* go or hurry away. ☐ **buzzy** *adj.* (**-ier, -iest**).

buzzard *n.* **1** any of a group of predatory birds of the hawk family, esp. of the genus *Buteo*, with broad wings well adapted for soaring flight. **2** *N Amer.* = TURKEY VULTURE. **3** *slang* an old person.

buzzbait *n.* a fishing lure with a spinning spoon-shaped blade which emits vibrations.

buzzed *adj. slang* intoxicated.

buzzer *n.* an electromagnetic device that makes a buzzing noise. ☐ **at the buzzer** *N Amer.* at the end of a game etc. (*scored at the buzzer*).

buzz saw *n. N Amer.* a circular saw.

buzzword *n.* **1** a fashionable piece of jargon, esp. one that sounds technical. **2** a catchword or slogan, esp. one of little exact meaning.

BVM *abbr.* Blessed Virgin Mary.

by ● *prep.* **1** near, beside, in the region of (*stand by the door*). **2** through the agency, means, instrumentality, or causation of (*a play by Shakespeare*; *went by bus*; *divide four by two*). **3** not later than; as soon as (*by next week*). **4** a past, beyond (*drove by the church*). **b** via (*went by Montreal*). **5** in the circumstances of (*by day*). **6** to the extent of (*missed by a foot*). **7** according to; using as a standard or unit (*judge by appearances*; *paid by the hour*). **8** with the succession of (*worse by the minute*; *one by one*). **9** concerning (*all right by me*). **10** used in mild oaths (*by God*). **11** placed between specified lengths in two directions (*three feet by two*). **12** avoiding, ignoring (*passed us by*). **13** (esp. in names of compass points) inclining to (*northeast by north*). ● *adv.* **1** near (*lives close by*). **2** aside; in reserve (*put $5 by*). **3** past (*they marched*

by). ☐ **by and by** before long; eventually. **by and large** on the whole, everything considered. **by the by** (or **bye**) incidentally, parenthetically. **by oneself 1 a** unaided. **b** without prompting. **2** alone.

by-blow *n.* **1** an incidental blow not at the main target. **2** an illegitimate child.

by-boat *n.* (also **bye-boat**) *Cdn hist.* a small fishing boat used by Europeans who travelled to the Maritimes to fish in the summer.

bycatch *n.* fish of species other than that being fished for, caught in nets and usu. discarded.

bye¹ *n.* the status of an unpaired competitor in a tournament, who proceeds to the next round as if having won.

bye² *interj.* (also *informal* **bye-bye**) = GOODBYE.

bye-bye *n.* (also **bye-byes**) (a child's word for) sleep.

by-election *n. Cdn, Brit., Austral., & NZ* an election held in a single constituency to fill a vacancy arising during a government's term of office.

bygone ● *attrib.adj.* past, antiquated (*bygone years*). ● *n.* (in *pl.*) past events, esp. offences. ☐ **let bygones be bygones** forgive and forget.

bylaw *n.* **1** a rule made by a society etc. for its members. **2** *Cdn, Brit., & Austral.* a law made by a body subordinate to a legislature, esp. a municipal government.

byline *n.* **1** a line in a newspaper naming the writer of an article. **2** *Soccer* the goal line or touchline.

BYO *abbr. informal* (also **BYOB**) bring your own (bottle of liquor), e.g. to a social gathering (*the party was BYO*).

bypass ● *n.* **1** a road passing around a town or its centre to provide an alternative route for through traffic. **2** a secondary channel or pipe etc. to allow a flow when the main one is closed or blocked. **3** *Med.* **a** an alternative passage for diverting blood or other fluids around an obstruction or away from a particular area during surgery. **b** = CORONARY BYPASS. ● *v.tr.* **1** avoid; go around. **2** provide with a bypass.

by-product *n.* **1** an incidental product made in the manufacture of something else. **2** a secondary result.

bystander *n.* a person who is present but does not take part; a spectator or passive witness.

byte *n. Computing* a group of usu. eight binary digits, often used to represent one character.

byway *n.* **1** a minor road. **2** a minor activity.

byword *n.* **1** a person or thing cited as a notable example (*is a byword for luxury*). **2** a familiar saying.

by-your-leave *n.* a request for permission or an expression of apology for taking a liberty.

Byzantine /ˈbɪzənˌtiːn, -tain/ ● *adj.* **1** of or relating to the ancient Greek city of Byzantium. **2** (of a political situation etc.) **a** extremely complicated. **b** inflexible. **c** carried on by underhand methods. **3** (of art etc.) of a highly decorated style developed in the Byzantine Empire. ● *n.* a citizen of Byzantium.

Cc

C¹ *n.* (also **c**) (*pl.* **Cs** or **C's**) **1** the third letter of the alphabet. **2** *Music* the first note of the diatonic scale of C major. **3** the third hypothetical person or example. **4** the third highest class or category (of academic marks etc.). **5** *Math.* (usu. **c**) the third known quantity. **6** (as a Roman numeral) 100. **7** (also ©) copyright. **8** a size of battery, having a voltage of 1.5 V.

C² *symbol* the element carbon.

C³ *abbr.* (also **C.**) **1** Cape. **2** Conservative. **3** Celsius, Centigrade. **4** coulomb(s). **5** *Cdn* Commons.

C⁴ *n.* *Computing* a programming language combining the features of high-level and assembly languages.

c. *abbr.* **1** century; centuries. **2** chapter. **3** cent(s). **4** cold. **5** cubic. **6** centi-. **7** cup(s).

c. *abbr. circa*.

CA *abbr.* **1** (in Canada and Scotland) = CHARTERED ACCOUNTANT. **2** California (in postal use).

Ca *symbol* the element calcium.

Ca. *abbr.* California.

ca. *abbr. circa*.

CAA *abbr.* Canadian Automobile Association.

CAAT *abbr.* (in Canada) College of Applied Arts and Technology.

cab ● *n.* **1** a taxi. **2** the driver's compartment in a truck, train, tractor, crane, etc. ● *v.intr.* travel by taxi.

cabal /kə'bæl/ *n.* **1** a secret intrigue or conspiracy. **2** a political clique or faction.

cabana /kə'bænə/ *n.* *N Amer.* a cabin or other shelter, esp. at a beach or swimming pool.

cabane à sucre /kə'bæn æ ,su:krə/ *n.* (*pl.* **cabanes à sucre** *pronunc.* same) *Cdn* (*Que.*) = SUGAR SHACK.

cabaret /'kæbə,rei/ *n.* **1** a nightclub or restaurant, esp. one in which entertainment is provided while guests eat or drink. **2** the entertainment provided.

cabbage *n.* any of several cultivated varieties of *Brassica oleracea*, with a head of thick green or purple leaves eaten as a vegetable.

cabbage roll *n.* (usu. in *pl.*) *N Amer.* a boiled cabbage leaf wrapped around a filling of rice and usu. ground meat and baked, usu. with tomato sauce.

cabbala /kə'bʊlə, 'kæbələ/ *n.* **1** mystic interpretation; any esoteric doctrine or occult lore. **2** (**Cabbala**) *var.* of KABBALAH 1. □ **cabbalism** *n.* **cabbalist** *n.* **cabbalistic** *adj.*

cabbie *n.* (also **cabby**) (*pl.* **-ies**) *informal* a taxi driver.

Cabernet /'kæbər,nei/ *n.* **1** a variety of black grape (esp. **Cabernet Franc** /frã/ or **Cabernet Sauvignon** /,so:vi'njõ/) used in winemaking. **2** a vine on which these grow. **3** a wine made from these.

cabin *n.* **1 a** a small shelter or house, esp. of wood. **b** *N Amer.* a summer cottage. **2** a room or compartment in an aircraft or ship for passengers or crew. **3** a driver's cab.

cabin crew *n.* the crew members on an airplane attending to passengers and cargo.

cabinet *n.* **1 a** a cupboard or case with drawers, shelves, etc., for storing or displaying articles. **b** a piece of furniture housing a stereo, television set, etc. **2** (also **Cabinet**) **a** (in Canada, the UK, etc.) a committee of senior ministers responsible for controlling government policy. **b** (in the US) a body of advisers to the President, composed of the heads of the executive departments of the government.

cabinetmaker *n.* a person skilled in making furniture and light woodwork. □ **cabinetmaking** *n.*

cabinet minister *n.* a member of a cabinet.

cabinet order *n.* *Cdn* = ORDER-IN-COUNCIL.

cabinetry *n.* cabinets or fine woodwork collectively.

cabin fever *n.* *N Amer.* a condition characterized by lassitude, irritability, anxiety, etc. resulting from long confinement indoors, esp. during the winter.

cable ● *n.* **1** a thick rope of wire or hemp. **2** an encased group of insulated wires for transmitting electricity or electrical signals. **3** = CABLE TELEVISION. **4** = CABLEGRAM. **5 a** *Naut.* the chain of an anchor. **b** (in full **cable length**) a unit of measure, equal to one-tenth of a nautical mile (185 m) or 100 fathoms in Canadian and British use, and 120 fathoms in the US. **6** (in full **cable stitch**) a knitted stitch resembling twisted rope. ● *v.* **1 a** *tr.* transmit (a message) by cablegram. **b** *tr.* inform (a person) by cablegram. **c** *intr.* send a cablegram. **2** *tr.* furnish or fasten with a cable or cables. □ **cabling** *n.*

cable car *n.* a small passenger car (often one of a series) suspended on an endless cable and drawn up and down a mountain etc. by an engine at one end.

cablegram *n.* a telegraph message sent by undersea cable etc.

cable-knit ● *adj.* (of a knitted garment) having a design of cables. ● *n.* a cable-knit garment.

cable television *n.* (also **cable TV, cablevision**) a broadcasting system with signals transmitted and received by cable (as opposed to antenna), allowing subscribers access to a large number of channels.

caboodle *n.* □ **the whole (kit and) caboodle** *informal* the whole lot (of persons or things).

caboose *n.* **1** *N Amer.* a railway car, usu. at the end of the train, for housing the crew etc. **2** *Cdn* a portable wooden cabin, esp. one on runners which can be pulled over snow.

cabriole /'kæbri,o:l/ *n.* a kind of ornamental and curved leg characteristic of 18th-c. furniture.

caca /'kækæ/ *n.* *slang* **1** excrement. **2** nonsense.

cacao /kə'kæo:, -'keio:/ *n.* (*pl.* **-os**) **1** a seed pod from which cocoa and chocolate are made. **2** a small widely cultivated evergreen tree, *Theobroma cacao*, bearing these.

cacciatore /,kætʃə'tɔri/ *adj.* cooked with tomatoes, mushrooms, and herbs (*chicken cacciatore*).

cache /kæʃ/ ● *n.* **1** a hiding place. **2** *Cdn* (*North*) a place, structure, or device used for storing food, supplies, equipment, etc. **3** the contents of a cache. **4** an auxiliary computer memory from which high-speed retrieval is possible. ● *v.tr.* (**cached, caching**) put in a cache.

cachet /kæ'ʃei, 'kæʃei/ *n.* **1** a distinguishing mark or seal. **2** prestige.

cackle ● *n.* **1** a clucking sound as of a hen or a goose. **2** a loud silly laugh. **3** noisy inconsequential talk. ● *v.*

1 *intr.* emit a cackle. **2** *intr.* talk noisily and inconsequentially. **3** *tr.* utter or express with a cackle.

cacophony /kə'kɒfəni/ *n.* (pl. **-ies**) **1** a harsh discordant mixture of sound. **2** dissonance; discord. □ **cacophonous** *adj.*

cactus /'kæktəs/ *n.* (pl. **cacti** /-tai/ or **cactuses**) **1** any succulent plant of the family Cactaceae, found in arid regions, having a thick fleshy stem, usu. spines but no leaves, and brilliantly coloured flowers. **2** any of various other succulent or spiny plants.

CAD *abbr.* **1** computer-aided design. **2** Canadian dollars.

cad *n.* a person who behaves dishonourably.

cadaver /kə'dævər/ *n.* a corpse, esp. for dissection.

cadaverous *adj.* **1** corpselike. **2** deathly pale or gaunt.

caddis fly *n.* (pl. **caddis flies**) any small hairy-winged nocturnal insect of the order Trichoptera, living near water.

caddisworm *n.* (also **caddis**) a larva of the caddis fly, living in water and making protective cylindrical cases from bits of sand, wood, leaves, etc.

caddy¹ *n.* (pl. **-ies**) **1** a small container, sometimes with subdivisions, for holding small items. **2** a small container for tea leaves.

caddy² (also **caddie**) ● *n.* (pl. **-ies**) a person who assists a golfer by carrying clubs etc. ● *v.intr.* (**caddies**, **caddied**, **caddying**) act as a caddy.

cadence /'keidəns/ *n.* **1** a fall in pitch of the voice, esp. at the end of a phrase or sentence. **2** intonation, tonal inflection. **3** *Music* the resolution at the end of a musical phrase. **4** rhythm; the measure or beat of sound or movement. □ **cadenced** *adj.*

cadenza /kə'denzə/ *n.* a virtuosic passage for a solo voice or instrument, usu. near the close of an aria or a concerto movement, sometimes improvised.

cadet *n.* **1 a** a member of a corps receiving elementary military or police training, esp. for the rank of an officer. **b** (in Canada) a member of a paramilitary organization for young people aged 12 to 18, run by the reserve forces of the army, navy, or air force. **2** an apprentice. **3** a younger son.

cadge *v.* **1** *tr.* get or seek by begging or scrounging. **2** *intr.* beg or scrounge. □ **cadger** *n.*

cadmium /'kædmiəm/ *n.* a soft bluish-white metallic element occurring naturally with zinc ores, and used in the manufacture of solders and in electroplating.

cadre /'kædrə, 'kædrei, 'kɒd-/ *n.* **1** a small, usu. exclusive group with a common objective, etc. **2 a** a group of activists in a communist or revolutionary party. **b** a member of such a group. **3** a permanent establishment of trained soldiers, etc. that can be enlarged when necessary.

caecum *var. of* CECUM.

Caenozoic /ˌsiːnəˈzoʊɪk/ *var. of* CENOZOIC.

Caesar /'siːzər/ *n.* **1** the title of the Roman emperors, esp. from Augustus to Hadrian. **2** an autocrat. **3** *N Amer.* = CAESAR SALAD. **4** *Cdn* = BLOODY CAESAR.

Caesarean /səˈzɛriən/ (also **Caesarian**) ● *adj.* **1** of Julius Caesar or the Caesars. **2** (of a birth) effected by Caesarean section. ● *n.* a Caesarean section.

Caesarean section *n.* an operation for delivering a child by cutting through the wall of the abdomen and uterus.

Caesar salad *n.* a salad of romaine lettuce tossed usu. with Parmesan cheese, garlic croutons, bacon bits, and a dressing of oil, lemon juice, raw egg, etc.

caesium *var. of* CESIUM.

CAF *abbr.* **1** CANADIAN ARMED FORCES. **2** cost and freight.

caf *n.* (also **caff**) *informal Cdn* a cafeteria.

café /kæ'fei/ *n.* **1** a restaurant serving coffee and light meals. **2** *N Amer.* a bar or nightclub.

café au lait /o: 'lei/ *n.* **1** strong coffee with a roughly equal portion of hot milk, usu. served in a large mug or bowl. **2** the colour of this.

cafeteria *n.* **1** a restaurant in which customers collect their meals on trays at a counter and usu. pay before sitting down to eat. **2** a lunch room in a school, office, etc.

caffeinated /'kæfineitəd/ *adj.* containing caffeine.

caffeine /kæ'fiːn/ *n.* an alkaloid drug with stimulant action found in coffee, tea, chocolate, cola, etc.

caftan *n.* **1** an ankle-length tunic, usu. belted at the waist, worn by men in E Europe and the Middle East. **2 a** a woman's long loose dress. **b** a loose shirt or top.

cage ● *n.* **1** a structure of bars, wires, wood, etc. used as a place of confinement for birds or animals. **2** any similar framework, esp.: **a** an enclosed platform used as an elevator, esp. in a mine. **b** a protective structure of strong metal bars built into the body of an automobile. **3** a system of netting or mesh strung around a metal framework, esp.: **a** a hockey net. **b** = BATTING CAGE. **4** a wire face mask attached to a helmet, e.g. of a baseball catcher or goaltender. **5** *informal* a jail or prison camp. ● *v.tr.* place or keep in a cage.

cagey *adj.* (also **cagy**) (**-ier, -iest**) *informal* cautious and uncommunicative; wary. □ **cagily** *adv.* **caginess** *n.* (also **cageyness**).

cahoots *n.pl.* □ **in cahoots** (often foll. by *with*) *slang* in collusion.

caiman /'keimən/ *n.* any of various Central and S American alligator-like reptiles, esp. of the genus *Caiman.*

Cain *n.* □ **raise Cain** *informal* make a disturbance; create trouble.

Cainozoic /ˌkainəˈzoʊɪk/ *var. of* CENOZOIC.

cairn *n.* a mound of rough stones as a monument.

caisse populaire /ˌkes pʊpjuːˈlɛr/ *n. Cdn* (in Quebec and other francophone communities) a co-operative financial institution similar to a credit union.

cajole /kəˈdʒoʊl/ *v.* (often foll. by *into*) **1** *tr.* persuade by flattery, deceit, etc. **2** *intr.* use cajolery. □ **cajolery** *n.*

Cajun /'keidʒən/ ● *n.* **1** a descendant of the French-speaking settlers who were expelled from Acadia in the mid-18th c., living esp. in S Louisiana. **2** the French patois of the Cajuns. ● *adj.* **1** of or relating to the Cajuns or their language. **2** designating a type of cooking originating among Cajuns, characterized esp. by the use of strong seasonings.

cake ● *n.* **1** a baked sweet food usu. containing flour, eggs, sugar, and often fat and leavening. **2** any of several other foods in a flat round shape (*fish cake*). **3** a flattish compact mass (*a cake of soap*). ● *v.* **1** *tr. & intr.* form into a compact mass. **2** *tr.* (usu. foll. by *with*) cover (with a hard or sticky mass) (*caked with mud*). □ **have one's cake and eat it (too)** *informal* enjoy two mutually exclusive alternatives. **a piece of cake** *informal* something easily achieved. **a slice of the cake** a share of assets or benefits.

cake doughnut *n. N Amer.* a doughnut made from a cake-like batter.

cakewalk *n. informal* an easy task.

Cal. *abbr.* California.

cal *abbr. & n.* (often in *comb.* or *attrib.*) large calorie (*see* CALORIE 1) (*low-cal*).

calabash /'kæləˌbæʃ/ *n.* **1 a** an evergreen tree, *Crescentia cujete*, native to tropical America, bearing fruit in the form of large gourds. **b** a gourd from this tree.

2 the shell of this or a similar gourd used as a vessel for water, to make a tobacco pipe, etc.

calabogus *Cdn var. of* CALLIBOGUS.

calamari /kælə'mɑri/ *n.* the flesh of the squid when used as food.

calamary /'kæləmeri/ *n.* (*pl.* **-ies**) a squid with a long, tapering, horny, internal shell, esp. one of the common genus *Loligo*.

calamata *var. of* KALAMATA.

calamine /'kælə,main/ *n.* **1** a pink powder consisting of zinc carbonate and a small quantity of ferric oxide used as a lotion or ointment, e.g. for sunburn, insect bites, or rashes. **2** an ore of zinc, esp. zinc carbonate.

calamity /kə'læmiti/ *n.* (*pl.* **-ies**) **1** a disaster, a great misfortune. **2** a adversity. **b** deep distress. □ **calamitous** *adj.* **calamitously** *adv.*

calcareous /kæl'keriəs/ *adj.* of or containing calcium carbonate; chalky.

calcify /'kælsə,fai/ *v.tr. & intr.* (**-ies, -ied**) **1** harden or become hardened by deposition of calcium salts; petrify. **2** convert or be converted to calcium carbonate. **3** make or become inflexible or rigid. □ **calcification** *n.*

calcine /'kælsain, -sɪn/ *v.* **1** *tr.* **a** reduce, oxidize, or desiccate by strong heat. **b** burn to ashes. **c** reduce to calcium oxide by roasting or burning. **2** *intr.* undergo any of these. □ **calcination** *n.*

calcite /'kælsəit/ *n.* natural crystalline calcium carbonate.

calcium *n.* a soft greyish-white metallic element occurring in limestone, etc., and in animal bones and teeth, and whose ions and salts are essential to life.

calcium carbonate *n.* a white insoluble solid occurring naturally as chalk, limestone, and marble, used in the manufacture of lime and cement.

calcium oxide *n.* = LIME[1] *n.* 1.

calcium phosphate *n.* a white insoluble powder, the main constituent of animal bones and used as a fertilizer and food additive.

calcium sulphate *n.* a white crystalline solid occurring esp. as gypsum.

calculable /'kælkjʊləbəl/ *adj.* able to be calculated or estimated. □ **calculability** *n.*

calculate *v.* **1** *tr.* ascertain or determine by using mathematics or one's judgment. **2** *tr.* intend or design for a particular purpose (*his speech was calculated to stir up the crowd*). **3** *intr.* (foll. by *on*) rely or depend on.

calculated *adj.* **1** done with awareness of the likely consequences (*a calculated risk*). **2** (foll. by *to* + infin.) designed or suitable. □ **calculatedly** *adv.*

calculating *adj.* (of a person) shrewd, scheming.

calculation *n.* **1** the act or process of calculating. **2** a result obtained by calculating. **3** a reckoning or forecast.

calculator *n.* **1** a device (esp. a small electronic one) used for making mathematical calculations. **2** a person or thing that calculates. **3** a set of tables used in calculation.

calculus /'kælkjʊləs/ *n.* (*pl.* **calculi** /-,lai/ or **calculuses**) **1** *Math.* **a** a particular method of calculation or reasoning (*calculus of probabilities*). **b** the infinitesimal calculi of integration or differentiation (*see* INTEGRAL CALCULUS, DIFFERENTIAL CALCULUS). **2 a** *Med.* a stone or concretion of minerals formed within the body, esp. in the kidney or gallbladder. **b** = TARTAR 1.

caldera /kæl'derə, kɒl-/ *n.* a large volcanic crater, esp. one whose breadth greatly exceeds that of the vent or vents within it, created by a volcanic explosion.

calèche /kə'leʃ/ *n. Cdn* a two-wheeled one-horse vehicle, commonly used in tourist areas of Quebec.

Caledonian /,kælə'do:niən/ *adj.* **1** of or relating to Scotland. **2** *Geol.* of a mountain-forming period in NW Europe in the Paleozoic era.

calendar *n.* **1** a system by which the beginning, length, and subdivisions of the year are fixed. **2** a chart or series of pages showing the days, weeks, and months of a particular year, or giving special seasonal information. **3** a timetable or program of appointments, special events, etc. **4** *Cdn* a book containing a list of courses offered at a university or college, along with general information on registration etc. **5** a list or register, esp. of canonized saints, cases for trial, etc.

calendar month *n.* = MONTH 1a.

calendar year *n.* = YEAR 2.

calender ● *n.* a machine in which cloth, paper, etc., is pressed by rollers to glaze or smooth it. ● *v.tr.* press in a calender.

calf[1] *n.* (*pl.* **calves**) **1** a young bovine animal. **2** the young of other animals, e.g. elephant, whale, and seal. **3** = CALFSKIN. **4** *Naut.* a floating piece of ice detached from an iceberg. □ **in calf** (of a cow) pregnant. □ **calfhood** *n.* **calflike** *adj.*

calf[2] *n.* (*pl.* **calves**) the fleshy hind part of the human leg below the knee. □ **-calved** *adj.* (in *comb.*).

calf roping *n. N Amer.* a rodeo event in which contestants on horseback chase and lasso a calf before dismounting and tying its legs. □ **calf roper** *n.*

calfskin *n.* the hide of a calf, esp. as leather used in bookbinding and shoemaking.

Calgarian /kæl'geriən/ ● *n.* a native or inhabitant of Calgary, Alberta. ● *adj.* of or relating to Calgary.

calibrate *v.tr.* **1** mark (a gauge) with a standard scale of readings. **2** correlate the readings of (an instrument) with a standard. **3** determine the calibre of (a gun). **4** determine the correct capacity or value of.

calibration *n.* **1** the act or process of calibrating something. **2** each of a set of graduations on an instrument etc.

calibre *n.* (esp. *US* **caliber**) **1 a** the internal diameter of a gun or tube. **b** the diameter of a bullet or shell. **2** strength or quality of character; ability, importance (*we need someone of your calibre*).

calico ● *n.* (*pl.* **-oes** or **-os**) *N Amer.* a cotton fabric with a printed pattern. ● *adj.* **1** made of calico. **2** *N Amer.* **a** (of an animal etc.) having irregular patches of colours, mottled. **b** (of a domestic cat) having a coat with patches of orange tabby, black, and white.

Calif. *abbr.* California.

Californian ● *adj.* of or relating to the US state of California. ● *n.* a resident or native of California.

californium /,kælə'fɔrniəm/ *n.* a radioactive metallic element produced artificially from curium.

caliper ● *n.* (usu. *in pl.*) **1** an instrument with two pivoting bowed legs for measuring the diameter of convex bodies (**outside calipers**), or with outturned points for measuring internal dimensions (**inside calipers**). **2** the part of an automobile or bicycle brake assembly which houses the pads and grips the disc or wheel. ● *v.tr.* measure with calipers.

caliph /'keilif, 'kæl-/ *n. hist.* the chief Muslim civil and religious ruler, regarded as the successor of Muhammad. □ **caliphate** *n.*

calisthenics /,kælɪs'θeniks/ *n.pl.* gymnastic exercises to achieve bodily fitness and grace of movement. □ **calisthenic** *adj.*

Cal-Ital /kælɪ'tæl/ *adj.* (of cuisine) combining Californian and Italian elements.

calk esp. US var. of CAULK[1],[2].

call ● *v.* **1 a** *intr.* (often foll. by *out*) cry, shout. **b** *intr.* (of a bird or animal) emit its characteristic note or cry. **c** *tr. N Amer.* attract (a bird etc.) by mimicking its sound. **2** *tr.* communicate or converse with by telephone or radio. **3** *tr.* **a** bring to one's presence by calling; summon. **b** arrange for (a person or thing) to come or be present (*called a taxi*). **4** *intr.* (often foll. by *at, in, on*) pay a brief visit (*call on me*). **5** *tr.* **a** order to take place; fix a time for (*called a meeting*). **b** direct to happen (*called a stop to it*). **6 a** *intr.* require one's attention or consideration (*duty calls*). **b** *tr.* urge, invite, nominate (*call to the bar*). **7** *tr.* name; describe as (*call her Liz*). **8** *tr.* consider; regard or estimate as (*I call that silly*). **9** *tr.* rouse from sleep (*call me at 8*). **10** *intr.* guess the outcome of tossing a coin etc. **11** *intr.* (foll. by *for*) order, require (*called for silence*). **12** *tr.* read out (a list of names to determine those present). **13** *intr.* (foll. by *on, upon*) appeal to; request or require (*called on us to be quiet*). **14** *tr. Sport* (of an umpire or referee) **a** rule; assess (*called a penalty*). **b** officiate (a game). **15** *Cards tr.* specify (a suit or contract) in bidding. **16** *tr. N Amer.* (foll. by *on*) **a** require (of someone) proof or support for a statement (*they called him on the numbers he presented*). **b** criticize, condemn (*called them on their behaviour*). ● *n.* **1 a** a shout or cry; an act of calling. **2 a** the characteristic cry of a bird or animal. **b** an imitation of this. **c** an instrument for imitating it. **3** a brief visit (*paid them a call*). **4 a** an act of telephoning. **b** a telephone conversation. **5 a** an invitation or summons to appear or be present. **b** an appeal or invitation (from a specific source or discerned by a person's conscience etc.) to follow a certain profession, set of principles, etc. **6** a duty, need, or occasion (*no call to be rude; no call for violence*). **7** (foll. by *for, on*) a demand (*not much call for it these days*). **8 a** *Sport* a ruling made by an official. **b** a decision (*you make the call*). **9** a signal on a bugle etc.; a signalling whistle. **10** *Stock Exch.* an option of buying stock at a fixed price at a given date. **11** *Cards* **a** a player's right or turn to make a bid. **b** a bid made. □ **call away** divert, distract, summon elsewhere. **call down 1** invoke. **2** reprimand. **call forth** elicit. **call in 1** withdraw from circulation. **2** seek the advice or services of. **call in** (or *into*) **question** dispute; doubt the validity of. **call into play** make use of. **call a person names** abuse a person verbally. **call off 1** cancel (an arrangement etc.). **2** order (an attacker or pursuer) to desist. **3** *N Amer.* chant (the directions) for a square dance etc. **call of nature** a need to urinate or defecate. **call out** CALL *v.* 1a. **2** summon (troops etc.) to action. **3** order (workers) to strike. **call the shots** (or **tune**) be in control. **call to mind** recollect; cause one to remember. **call to order 1** request to be orderly. **2** declare (a meeting) open. **call up 1** reach by telephone. **2** imagine, recollect. **3** summon, esp. to serve in the army. **4** *Sport* promote (a player) to the major leagues. **on** (or **at**) **call 1** (of a doctor etc.) available if required but not formally on duty. **2** (of money lent) repayable on demand.

calla /'kælə/ *n.* **1** (in full **calla lily**) *Zantedeschia aethiopica*, with an esp. white funnel-shaped spathe and a yellow spadix. **2** (in full **wild calla**) = WATER ARUM.

callback *n.* an instance of calling back, e.g. by a salesperson or service person, or for a job interview.

call box *n. N Amer.* a direct telephone line, e.g. for reporting emergencies to the police.

call display *n. Cdn* = CALLER ID.

caller *n.* **1** a person who calls, esp. one who pays a visit or makes a telephone call. **2** a person who announces something, esp. the directions in a square dance or the numbers in a bingo game.

caller ID *n.* (also **caller identification**) a telephone service which displays the number of an incoming caller on a screen on the subscriber's telephone.

call forwarding *n. N Amer.* a service which allows users to have telephone calls automatically forwarded to another line.

call girl *n.* a female prostitute who accepts appointments by telephone.

callibogus /ˌkælə'bo:gəs/ *n. Cdn* (esp. *Nfld*) a beverage made from spruce beer, rum, and molasses.

calligraphy /kə'lɪgrəfi/ *n.* **1** handwriting, esp. when fine or pleasing. **2** the art of stylized or beautiful handwriting. □ **calligrapher** *n.* **calligraphic** *adj.*

call-in *n.* = PHONE-IN.

calling *n.* **1** a profession or occupation. **2** an inwardly felt call or summons; a vocation.

calling card *n.* **1** a small card with one's name and often address and telephone number, presented when visiting. **2** (**Calling Card**) *proprietary* a credit card issued by a telephone company allowing a customer to charge long-distance calls to an account. **3** a distinctive mark or feature.

calliope /kə'laɪəpi/ *n. N Amer.* a keyboard instrument resembling an organ, with a set of steam whistles producing musical notes.

calliper var. of CALIPER.

callisthenics var. of CALISTHENICS.

call letters *n.pl. N Amer.* the letters identifying a radio or television station.

call number *n.* the cataloguing numbers and letters assigned to a book or other item in a library.

callous ● *adj.* **1** unfeeling, insensitive. **2** (of skin) hardened or hard. ● *n.* = CALLUS 1. □ **calloused** *adj.* **callously** *adv.* (in sense 1 of *adj.*). **callousness** *n.*

call-out *n.* a paid duty or service performed by a worker or police officer, esp. outside of normal business hours.

callow *adj.* inexperienced, immature. □ **callowly** *adv.* **callowness** *n.*

call sign *n.* **1** a conventional signal identifying a particular radio transmitter. **2** a name by which a person communicating by radio, esp. an aircraft pilot, is identified.

call to arms *n.* **1** an instance of calling up for active military service. **2** an instance of inciting or encouraging people to vigorous, usu. defensive action.

call-up *n.* **1** the act or process of calling up, esp. being summoned to the army or promoted to the major leagues. **2** a person who is called up.

callus *n.* (*pl.* **calluses**) **1** a hard thick area of skin or tissue. **2** a hard tissue formed around bone ends after a fracture. **3** *Bot.* a new protective tissue formed over a wound. □ **callused** *adj.*

call waiting *n.* a telephone service which alerts subscribers that a second call is coming through and allows the user to switch between the two calls.

calm /kɒm, kɒlm/ ● *adj.* **1** tranquil, quiet, windless (*a calm sea*). **2** (of a person or disposition) settled; not agitated (*remained calm*). **3** self-assured, confident (*his calm assumption that we would wait*). ● *n.* **1** stillness, serenity. **2 a** a period without wind or storm. **b** *Meteorol.* absence of wind, force 0 on the Beaufort scale. **3** (in *pl.*) an area, esp. of the sea, with predominantly calm weather. ● *v.tr. & intr.* (often foll. by *down*) make or become calm. □ **calmly** *adv.* **calmness** *n.*

caloric /kə'lɒrɪk/ *adj.* of heat or calories.

calorie *n.* a unit of quantity of heat: **1** (in full **large calorie**) the amount needed to raise the temperature of 1 kilogram of water through 1°C, often used to measure the energy value of foods. **2** (in full **small calorie**) the amount needed to raise the temperature of 1 gram of water by 1°C.

calorific /ˌkælə'rɪfɪk/ *adj.* **1** producing heat. **2** pertaining to or high in calories. □ **calorifically** *adv.*

calorimeter /ˌkælə'rɪmɪtər/ *n.* any of various instruments for measuring quantity of heat, esp. to find calorific values. □ **calorimetric** *adj.*

calumet /'kælju,met/ *n.* a N American Aboriginal tobacco pipe with a clay bowl and long reed stem, smoked esp. as a sign of peace.

calumny /'kæləmni/ ● *n.* (*pl.* **-ies**) **1** slander; malicious representation. **2** an instance of this. ● *v.tr.* (**-ies**, **-ied**) slander. □ **calumnious** /kə'lʌmniəs/ *adj.*

Calvados /'kælvə,dɒs/ *n.* (also **calvados**) a French apple brandy.

Calvary *n.* the place where Christ was crucified.

calve *v.* **1** *a intr.* give birth to a calf. **b** *tr.* (esp. in *passive*) give birth to (a calf). **2** *tr. & intr.* (of an iceberg) break off or shed (a mass of ice).

calves *pl.* of CALF[1], CALF[2].

Calvinism *n.* the theology of John Calvin (1509–64) or his followers. □ **Calvinist** *n.* **Calvinistic** *adj.*

calypso /kə'lɪpso:/ *n.* (*pl.* **-os**) **1** a kind of West Indian music in syncopated African rhythm, usu. improvised on a topical theme. **2** a song in this style. **3** an orchid found across Canada and parts of the US, *Calypso bulbosa*, with pink, slipper-shaped flowers.

calyx /'keilɪks, 'kæl-/ *n.* (*pl.* **calyces** /-lɪ,siːz/ or **calyxes**) **1** *Bot.* the sepals collectively, forming the protective layer of a flower in bud. **2** *Biol.* any cuplike cavity or structure.

CAM *abbr.* computer-aided manufacturing.

cam *n.* a projection on a rotating part in machinery, shaped to impart reciprocal or variable motion to the part in contact with it.

camaraderie /ˌkɒmə'rɒdəri, ˌkæmə'ræd-, ˌkæmə'rɒd-/ *n.* mutual trust and sociability among friends.

camas /'kæməs/ *n.* any of several N American plants of the lily family, esp. *Camassia quamash*, the bulbs of which were a staple of Aboriginal diet.

camber ● *n.* **1** the slightly convex or arched shape of the surface of a road, ship's deck, aircraft wing, etc. **2** a slight sideways inclination of the wheels of a motor vehicle. ● *v.* **1** *intr.* (of a surface) have a camber. **2** *tr.* give a camber to; build with a camber.

cambium /'kæmbiəm/ *n.* (*pl.* **cambia** /-biə/ or **-s**) *Bot.* a cellular plant tissue responsible for the increase in girth of stems and roots. □ **cambial** *adj.*

Cambodian /kæm'boːdiən/ ● *n.* **1 a** a native or national of Cambodia in SE Asia. **b** a person of Cambodian descent. **2** the Khmer language. ● *adj.* of or relating to Cambodia or its people.

camboose *n. Cdn hist.* **1** (in full **camboose shanty**) a large wooden cabin with a central fireplace, serving as a winter shelter in a logging camp. **2** an open fireplace or cooking stove.

Cambrian /'kæmbriən, 'keim-/ *adj.* **1** Welsh. **2** of or relating to the first period of the Paleozoic era, lasting from about 590 to 505 million years BP.

camcorder *n.* a portable video camera which records picture and sound on a video cassette.

came *past of* COME.

camel *n.* **1** either of two kinds of large cud-chewing mammals having slender legs and one hump (**Arabian camel**, *Camelus dromedarius*) or two humps (**Bactrian camel**, *C. bactrianus*). **2** a fawn colour.

camel hair *n.* (also **camel's hair**) **1 a** the hair of a camel. **b** a fabric made of this. **2** a fine soft hair used in artists' brushes.

camellia /kə'miːliə/ *n.* any evergreen shrub of the genus *Camellia*, native to E Asia, with shiny leaves and red, pink, or white roselike flowers.

Camembert /'kæməm,ber/ *n.* a kind of soft creamy cheese, usu. with a strong flavour.

cameo *n.* (*pl.* **-os**) **1** a small piece of hard stone or coral carved in relief with a background of a different colour. **2 a** a small character part in a play or film, usu. brief and played by a distinguished actor or actress. **b** a short descriptive literary sketch etc.

camera *n.* **1** an apparatus for taking photographs, either for still photographs or for motion-picture film. **2** a piece of equipment which forms an optical image and converts it into electrical impulses for video transmission or storage. □ **in camera 1** privately. **2** *Law* in a judge's private room. **on** (or **off**) **camera** (esp. of an actor or actress) being (or not being) filmed or televised at a particular moment.

cameraman *n.* (*pl.* **-men**) a camera operator, esp. a male one.

camera operator *n.* (also **cameraperson** *pl.* **-persons**) a person who operates a film or television camera, esp. professionally.

camera-ready *adj. Printing* (of copy etc.) in a form suitable for immediate photographic reproduction.

camerawoman *n.* (*pl.* **-women**) a female camera operator.

camera work *n.* the technique of using cameras in films or television.

cami /'kæmi/ *n. informal* = CAMISOLE.

camisole /'kæmə,soːl/ *n.* **1** a woman's waist-length sleeveless undergarment with shoulder straps. **2** a similar outer garment.

camo /'kæmo:/ *n. slang* **1** = CAMOUFLAGE. **2** (*pl.* **-os**) camouflage clothing.

camomile /'kæmə,mail/ *n.* any of various aromatic plants of the composite family, esp. *Chamaemelum nobilis* and plants of the genera *Anthemis* and *Matricaria*, with daisy-like flowers.

camouflage ● *n.* **1 a** the disguising of military vehicles, personnel, artillery, and installations, etc. by painting or covering them to make them blend with their surroundings. **b** such a disguise or uniform etc. **2** the natural colouring of an animal which enables it to blend in with its surroundings. **3** a misleading or evasive precaution or expedient. ● *v.tr.* **1** hide or disguise by means of camouflage. **2** conceal or disguise (a flaw, emotion, etc.).

camp[1] ● *n.* **1** temporary overnight lodging in tents etc. in the open. **2** temporary accommodation of various kinds, usu. consisting of huts or tents, for detainees, homeless persons, etc. **3 a** a complex of buildings for holiday accommodation, usu. with extensive recreational facilities. **b** a summer holiday program for children, offering various recreational or educational activities. **c** a place where such a program is offered. **d** *N Amer.* (*N Ont., Maritimes, US Northeast & Gulf States*) a summer cottage. **4** *N Amer.* a place of accommodation for workers at a particular place of employment (*logging camp*). **5 a** a place where troops are lodged or trained. **b** the military life. **6** an ancient fortified site or its remains. **7** the adherents of a particular party or doctrine regarded collectively (*the Conservative camp was crushed*). **8** = TRAINING CAMP. ● *v.intr.* **1** set up or spend time in a camp (in senses 1 and 5 of *n*.). **2** (often foll. by *out*) lodge in temporary quarters or in the open. □ **camping** *n.*

camp² *informal* ● *adj.* **1** effeminate. **2** homosexual. **3** done in an exaggerated way for effect. ● *n.* a camp manner or style. ● *v.intr. & tr.* behave or do in a camp way. □ **camp it up** overact; behave affectedly. □ **campy** *adj.* (**-ier, -iest**). **campily** *adv.* **campiness** *n.*

campaign ● *n.* **1** an organized course of action for a particular purpose, esp. to arouse public interest. **2 a** a series of military operations in a definite area or to achieve a particular objective. **b** military service in the field (*on campaign*). ● *v.intr.* conduct or take part in a campaign. □ **campaigner** *n.*

campaign trail *n.* the series of public appearances, speeches, etc. made by a candidate in the course of a political campaign.

campanula /kæm'pænjʊlə/ *n.* any plant of the genus *Campanula*, with bell-shaped flowers.

camper *n.* **1** a person who camps out as a recreation, or lives temporarily at a camp. **2** a vehicle or trailer equipped for camping.

campesino /kæmpə'si:no:/ *n.* (*pl.* **-s**) (in Central or S America) a farmer or peasant.

campfire *n.* an outdoor fire in a camp etc.

camp follower *n.* **1** a civilian, esp. a prostitute, who provides services to personnel in a military camp. **2** a disciple or adherent, esp. a hanger-on.

campground *n.* an area with facilities for camping.

camphor /'kæmfər/ *n.* a white translucent crystalline volatile substance with an aromatic smell and bitter taste, used to make celluloid and in medicine.

camphor tree *n.* a tree of the laurel family, *Cinnamomum camphora*, which is native to E Asia and the major source of natural camphor.

campion /'kæmpiən/ *n.* **1** any plant of the genus *Silene*, with usu. pink or white flowers with notched petals. **2** any of several similar cultivated plants of the genus *Lychnis*.

camp meeting *n. N Amer.* an evangelical Christian worship service held outdoors or in a tent, often lasting several days.

camp-out *n. N Amer.* an instance of camping out.

campsite *n.* any place used for camping.

camp stove *n.* a portable cooking stove used by campers etc., usu. using naphtha as fuel.

campus *n.* (*pl.* **campuses**) **1 a** the grounds of a university or college. **b** *N Amer. & Austral.* one of several local branches of a large university. **2** (often *attrib.*) a university or college (*campus newspaper*).

campylobacter /,kæmpələ:'bæktər/ *n.* a bacterium of the genus *Campylobacter*, occurring in unpasteurized dairy products, poultry, and other foods, capable of causing food poisoning in humans.

camshaft *n.* a shaft with one or more cams attached.

Can. *abbr.* Canada; Canadian.

can¹ *v.aux.* (*3rd sing. present* **can**; *past* **could**) **1 a** be able to; know how to (*I can run fast; can you speak French?*). **b** be potentially capable of (*you can do it if you try*). **2** be permitted to (*can we go to the party?*).

can² ● *n.* **1** a metal vessel for liquid. **2** a metal container in which food or drink is hermetically sealed to enable storage over long periods. **3** a bin or other similar receptacle (*garbage can*). **4** (prec. by *the*) *slang* **a** a prison. **b** *N Amer.* a washroom or toilet. **5** *N Amer.* the buttocks. ● *v.tr.* (**canned, canning**) **1** put or preserve in a can or jar. **2** *N Amer. informal* **a** cease, end.

b remove. **c** fire, dismiss. **3** record on film or tape for future use. □ **can it** *N Amer. informal* be quiet. **in the can** *informal* completed, ready. □ **canner** *n.*

Canada *n. N Amer.* (usu. in *pl.*) a Canada goose.

Canada Day *n.* the annual holiday commemorating the creation of the Dominion of Canada on 1 July 1867 (formerly called DOMINION DAY).

Canada dogwood *n.* = BUNCHBERRY.

Canada Games *n.pl.* a national sports competition, with events divided into summer and winter sports, held in Canada every four years since 1967.

Canada goose *n.* a wild goose native to N America, *Branta canadensis*, with a brownish-grey back, black head and neck, and white cheeks and breast.

Canada jay *n.* = GREY JAY.

Canada lynx *n.* a larger subspecies of lynx, often classified separately as *Felis canadensis*, found in northern N America.

Canada poplar *n.* = CAROLINA POPLAR.

Canadarm *n. proprietary* a type of mechanical arm on a space shuttle's cargo bay, used for releasing, retrieving, and repairing satellites etc.

Canada thistle *n. N Amer.* a perennial thistle with pink or purple flowers, *Cirsium arvense*, native to Europe and now a flourishing weed in N America.

Canada violet *n.* a violet, *Viola canadensis*, of eastern N America, bearing flowers with white petals tinged with purple on the back.

Canada yew *n.* = GROUND HEMLOCK.

Canadian ● *n.* **1** a native or inhabitant of Canada. **2** (in *pl.*) *informal* the Canadian national championships in a given sport. ● *adj.* of or relating to Canada or its people. □ **Canadianness** *n.*

Canadiana *n.* things pertaining to and typical of Canadian culture, e.g. publications, artifacts, etc.

Canadian Armed Forces *n.* an unofficial name for the Canadian Forces.

Canadian canoe *n.* a small, lightweight two-person canoe, usu. about 6 m (20 ft.) long.

Canadian English *n.* the English language as it is spoken and written by anglophone Canadians.

Canadian football *n.* a form of football played on a field 110 by 65 yards in which teams of 12 players attempt to throw, carry, or kick an oval ball across their opponents' goal line.

Canadian Forces *n.* the official name of the Canadian military, comprised of the former army, navy, and air force.

Canadian French *n.* the French language as it is spoken and written by francophone Canadians.

Canadianism *n.* **1 a** a word or expression originating in Canada. **b** an English or French word or expression used only in Canada. **2** loyalty or devotion to Canada. **3 a** the state of being Canadian. **b** Canadian character or spirit.

Canadianist *n.* a specialist in Canadian studies.

Canadianize *v.tr.* make or become Canadian in content, ownership, etc. □ **Canadianization** *n.*

Canadian whisky *n.* = RYE 2a.

Canadien /,kænæ'djæ̃/ *n.* a French Canadian.

Canadienne /,kænæ'djen/ *n.* a French-Canadian woman or girl.

Canajun /,kə'neidʒən/ (also **Canajan**) *Cdn jocular* ● *adj.* typically or purely Canadian. ● *n.* **1** a Canadian. **2** Canadian English, esp. as allegedly spoken by unsophisticated Canadians.

canal *n.* **1** an artificial waterway for inland navigation or irrigation. **2** any of various tubular ducts or passages in a plant or animal body.

Can-Am *Cdn* ● *adj.* designating an event, esp. a sporting event, for Canadian and American participants. ● *n.* a Can-Am event.

canapé /ˈkænəpeɪ/ *n.* **1** a cracker or small piece of bread with a savoury food on top, often served as an hors d'oeuvre. **2** a sofa.

canard /kəˈnɑːrd/ *n.* **1** an unfounded rumour or story. **2** an extra surface attached to a boat etc. for added stability or control.

canary ● *n.* (*pl.* **-ies**) **1** any of various small finches of the genus *Serinus*, esp. *S. canaria*, a songbird native to the Canary Islands, of which wild varieties are green and the numerous cage varieties usu. bright yellow. **2** (in full **canary yellow**) a bright yellow colour. ● *adj.* having a bright yellow colour.

cancan *n.* a lively stage dance with high kicking, usu. performed by women holding up the front of their long ruffled skirts.

cancel ● *v.* (**cancelled, cancelling**) **1** *tr.* **a** announce that (something already arranged and decided upon) will not be done or take place; call off. **b** discontinue (an arrangement in progress) (*cancel my subscription*). **2** *tr.* obliterate or delete (writing etc.). **3** *tr.* mark or pierce (a cheque, stamp, etc.) so that it may not be used again. **4** *tr.* annul; make void; abolish. **5** (often foll. by *out*) **a** *tr.* (of one factor or circumstance) neutralize or counterbalance (another). **b** *intr.* (of two factors or circumstances) neutralize each other. **6** *tr. Math.* strike out (an equal factor) on each side of an equation or from the numerator and denominator of a fraction. ● *n.* **1** an order revoking a previous one. **2** the cancellation of a postage stamp. □ **canceller** *n.*

cancellation *n.* **1** the act or an instance of cancelling or being cancelled. **2** something that has been cancelled, esp. a booking or reservation. **3** the marks made by cancelling, esp. a stamp.

cancer *n.* **1 a** any malignant growth or tumour from an abnormal and uncontrolled division of body cells. **b** a disease characterized by this. **2** an evil influence or corruption spreading uncontrollably. **3** (**Cancer**) a constellation between Gemini and Leo, regarded as contained in the figure of a crab. **4** (**Cancer**) **a** the fourth sign of the zodiac. **b** a person born when the sun is in this sign, usu. between June 21 and July 22. □ **Cancerian** /kænˈseriən, -ˈsiːriən/ *n. & adj.* (in sense 4). **cancerous** *adj.*

CanCon *n.* (also **Cancon**) *Cdn informal* Canadian content, esp. with reference to quotas in broadcasting.

CanCult *n.* (also **Cancult**) *Cdn informal* Canadian culture.

candela /kænˈdiːlə, -ˈdelə/ *n.* the SI unit of luminous intensity.

candelabra /ˌkændəˈlæbrə, -lɒb-/ *n.* (also **candelabrum** *pl.* **candelabra**) a large branched candlestick or lampholder.

candid ● *adj.* **1** frank; not hiding one's thoughts. **2** (of a photograph) taken informally, usu. without the subject's knowledge. ● *n.* a candid photograph. □ **candidly** *adv.* **candidness** *n.*

candida /kænˈdiːdə, ˈkændɪdə/ *n.* **1** any yeastlike parasitic fungus of the genus *Candida*, esp. *C. albicans*, causing thrush. **2** = CANDIDIASIS.

candidate *n.* **1** a person who seeks or is nominated for an office, award, etc. **2** a person or thing likely to gain some distinction or position. **3** a person entered for an examination. □ **candidacy** *n.*

candidiasis /ˌkændɪˈdaɪəsɪs/ *n.* an infection with candida, esp. causing oral or vaginal thrush.

candied *adj.* **1** (esp. of fruit) preserved by being coated or impregnated with sugar. **2** cooked with a large quantity of sugar (*candied parsnips*).

candle ● *n.* **1** a cylinder or block of wax or tallow with a central wick that is burned for light. **2** = VOTIVE CANDLE 1. ● *v.* **1** *tr.* test (an egg) for freshness by holding it to the light. **2** *intr.* esp. *Cdn* (of ice) deteriorate into candle ice. □ **cannot hold a candle to** is much inferior to.

candlefish *n.* *N Amer.* = EULACHON.

candle holder *n.* = CANDLESTICK.

candle ice *n.* (also **candled ice**) esp. *Cdn* ice which has deteriorated into untapered, candle-like icicles before breaking up.

candlelight *n.* light provided by candles (also *attrib.*: *candlelight dinner*). □ **candlelit** *adj.*

Candlemas *n.* *Christianity* (in some churches) a feast with blessing of candles (2 Feb.), commemorating the Purification of the Virgin Mary and the presentation of Christ in the Temple.

candlestick *n.* a holder for one or more candles.

candlewick *n.* **1** a thick soft cotton yarn. **2** material made from this, with a tufted pattern.

can-do *attrib.adj. informal* displaying enthusiasm, confidence, and efficiency (*can-do attitude*).

candour *n.* (also **candor**) candid behaviour or action; frankness.

CANDU *n.* (also **Candu**) (*pl.* **-s**) a nuclear reactor using easily replaceable fuel bundles and a heavy water cooling and moderating system.

C. & W. *abbr.* country and western.

candy *n.* (*pl.* **-ies**) **1** esp. *N Amer.* **a** a confection with a high proportion of sugar, often also including chocolate, nuts, etc. **b** such confections collectively. **2** sugar crystallized by repeated boiling and slow evaporation.

candy apple *n.* *N Amer.* an apple covered with a hard, usu. bright red, sugar glaze and impaled on a stick.

candy-apple red *N Amer.* ● *n.* a bright, glossy red. ● *adj.* of this colour.

candy-ass *n.* *N Amer. slang* a timid or cowardly person. □ **candy-assed** *adj.*

candy bar *n.* esp. *US* = CHOCOLATE BAR.

candy cane *n.* a hard, thin, striped candy with a curved end resembling a walking stick, often eaten at Christmastime.

candy floss *n.* *Cdn & Brit.* a fluffy mass of spun sugar wrapped around a stick.

candy stripe *n.* a pattern consisting of stripes (usu. red or pink) on a white background.

candystriper *n.* *N Amer.* a usu. young volunteer at a hospital.

cane ● *n.* **1 a** the hollow jointed stem of giant reeds or grasses. **b** the solid stem of slender palms. **2** = SUGAR CANE. **3** a raspberry cane. **4** material of cane used for wickerwork etc. **5 a** a cane used as a walking stick or a support for a plant or an instrument of punishment. **b** any slender walking stick. ● *v.tr.* **1** beat with a cane. **2** weave cane into (a chair etc.). □ **caning** *n.*

cane sugar *n.* sugar obtained from sugar cane.

canine ● *adj.* **1** of a dog or dogs. **2** of or belonging to the family Canidae, including dogs, wolves, etc. ● *n.* **1** a dog. **2** (in full **canine tooth**) a pointed tooth between the incisors and premolars.

canister *n.* **1** a container, esp. one of a set, for holding flour, sugar, coffee, tea, etc. **2 a** a cylinder of shot, tear gas, etc., that explodes on impact. **b** such cylinders collectively. **3** a metallic cylindrical container for storing toxic waste etc.

canker ● *n.* **1 a** a destructive fungus disease of trees and plants. **b** an open wound in the stem of a tree or plant. **2** an ulcerous ear disease of animals, esp. cats and dogs. **3** (also **canker sore**) an ulceration esp. on the lips or the inside of the mouth. **4** a corrupting influence. ● *v.tr.* **1** consume with canker. **2** corrupt. □ **cankerous** *adj.*

CanLit *abbr. Cdn informal* Canadian literature.

cannabis /ˈkænəbɪs/ *n.* **1** any hemp plant of the genus *Cannabis*, esp. Indian hemp. **2** a preparation of parts of this used as an intoxicant or hallucinogen.

canned *adj.* **1** supplied in a can (*canned peas*). **2** prerecorded (*canned laughter; canned music*). **3** *informal* drunk. **4** *informal* (of a speech etc.) prepared in advance to suit many different occasions.

cannelloni /ˌkænəˈloːni/ *n.pl.* tubes or rolls of pasta stuffed with meat or a vegetable mixture.

canner *n.* **1** a large cooking vessel in which jars of preserves are immersed to be sterilized. **2** *Cdn* (*Maritimes*) a lobster designated for canning because it is too small for the market. **3** a person who preserves food by canning (*home canners*).

cannery *n.* (*pl.* **-ies**) a factory where food is canned.

cannibal ● *n.* **1** a person who eats human flesh. **2** an animal that feeds on flesh of its own species. ● *adj.* of or like a cannibal. □ **cannibalism** *n.* **cannibalistic** *adj.* **cannibalistically** *adv.*

cannibalize *v.tr.* use (a machine etc.) as a source of spare parts for others. □ **cannibalization** *n.*

canning *n.* the process of preserving food in cans or hermetically sealed glass jars.

cannon ● *n.* **1** (*pl.* same or **-s**) a large gun installed on a carriage or mounting. **2** a similar device for discharging a specific substance (*water cannon*). **3** an automatic aircraft gun firing shells. ● *v.intr.* (usu. foll. by *against, into*) collide heavily or obliquely.

cannonball ● *n.* **1** a large usu. metal ball fired by a cannon. **2** *Cdn* (*BC*) a cannonball-like weight tied to commercial fishing lines to control depth and angle. **3** *N Amer.* a jump (into a swimming pool etc.) with the knees clasped close to the chest. ● *v.intr.* move with the speed and force of a cannonball.

cannon bone *n.* the tube-shaped bone between the hock and fetlock of a horse etc.

cannot *v.aux.* can not.

cannula /ˈkænjələ/ *n.* (*pl.* **cannulae** /-liː/ or **-s**) *Med.* a small tube inserted into the body to allow fluid to enter or escape.

canny *adj.* (**-ier**, **-iest**) **1 a** shrewd. **b** thrifty. **c** cautious. **2** sly, drily humorous. □ **cannily** *adv.* **canniness** *n.*

canoe ● *n.* a small narrow boat with pointed upcurved ends usu. propelled by paddling (also *attrib.*: *canoe trip*). ● *v.* (**canoes**, **canoed**, **canoeing**) **1** *intr.* travel in a canoe. **2** *tr.* paddle a canoe on or along (a lake, river, etc.). □ **canoeist** *n.* **canoeing** *n.*

canoe-camping *n. Cdn* camping in which campgrounds are reached by canoe. □ **canoe camper** *n.*

canoeman *n.* (*pl.* **-men**) esp. *Cdn* **1** *hist.* a voyageur. **2** a canoeist.

can of worms *n. informal* a complicated problem.

canola /kəˈnoːlə/ *n.* any of several varieties of rapeseed low in erucic acid, producing an oil used in cooking (also *attrib.*: *canola oil*).

canon *n.* **1 a** a general law, rule, principle, or criterion. **b** a church decree or law. **2 a** a member of a cathedral chapter. **b** a member of certain Roman Catholic orders. **3 a** a collection or list of sacred books etc. accepted as genuine. **b** the recognized genuine works of a particular author, composer, etc.; a list of these. **c** a collection or list of books generally regarded as most important in a given field (*the literary canon*). **4** *Music* a piece with different parts taking up the same theme successively, either at the same or at a different pitch.

canonical /kəˈnɒnɪkəl/ *adj.* (also **canonic**) **1 a** according to or ordered by canon law. **b** included in the canon of Scripture. **2** authoritative, standard, accepted. **3** of a cathedral chapter or a member of it. **4** *Music* in canon form. □ **canonically** *adv.*

canonical hours *n.pl. Christianity* **1** the times fixed for a formal set of prayers. **2** the offices appointed for these times, e.g. matins, vespers, compline, etc.

canonize *v.tr.* **1 a** declare officially to be a saint, usu. with a ceremony. **b** regard as a saint. **2 a** admit to the canon of Scripture. **b** accept as canonical. **3** sanction by Church authority. □ **canonization** *n.*

canon law *n.* ecclesiastical law.

can opener *n.* a device for opening cans of food etc.

canopy ● *n.* (*pl.* **-ies**) **1 a** a covering hung or held up over a throne, bed, person, etc. **b** the sky. **c** an overhanging shelter. **2** *Archit.* a rooflike projection over a niche etc. **3** the uppermost layers of foliage etc. in a forest. **4 a** the expanding part of a parachute. **b** the cover of an aircraft's cockpit. ● *v.tr.* (**-ies**, **-ied**) (usu. in *passive*) cover with a canopy.

canot du maître /kæˌnoːduːˈmetrə/ *n. Cdn hist.* the largest birchbark canoe of the fur trade, up to 12 m (40 ft.) long, used between the St. Lawrence River and Lake Superior.

canot du nord /kæˌnoːduːˈnɔr/ *n. Cdn hist.* a birchbark canoe of the fur trade, about 9 m (30 ft.) long, used on the rivers and lakes northwest of Lake Superior.

cant¹ *n.* **1** insincere pious or moral talk. **2** ephemeral or fashionable catchwords. **3** language peculiar to a class, profession, sect, etc.; jargon.

cant² *n.* **1 a** a slanting surface, e.g. of a bank. **b** a bevel of a crystal etc. **2** an oblique push or movement that upsets or partly upsets something. **3** a tilted or sloping position. **4** a partly trimmed log. ● *v.* **1** *tr.* push or pitch out of level; tilt. **2** *intr.* take or lie in a slanting position. **3** *tr.* impart a bevel to.

can't *contraction* can not.

cantaloupe /ˈkæntəˌloːp/ *n.* (also **cantaloup**) a small round variety of melon with orange flesh.

cantankerous *adj.* bad-tempered, quarrelsome. □ **cantankerously** *adv.* **cantankerousness** *n.*

cantata /kænˈtɑːtə, -tɒtə/ *n. Music* a short narrative or descriptive composition with vocal solos and usu. chorus and orchestral accompaniment.

canteen *n.* **1** a soldier's or camper's water flask. **2 a** a restaurant for employees in an office or factory etc. **b** a shop selling provisions or liquor in a barracks or camp. **3** a case or box of cutlery. **4** a set of eating or drinking utensils.

canter ● *n.* a gentle gallop. ● *v.* **1** *intr.* (of a horse or its rider) go at a canter. **2** *tr.* make (a horse) canter.

cant hook *n.* an iron hook at the end of a long handle, used for rolling logs.

canticle *n.* a song or chant with a Biblical text.

cantilever bridge *n.* a bridge made of cantilevers projecting from the piers and connected by girders.

canto *n.* (*pl.* **-os**) a division of a long poem.

Cantonese ● *adj.* of Canton (Guangzhou), a city in S China, or the Cantonese dialect of Chinese. ● *n.* (*pl.* same) **1** a native of Canton. **2** the dialect of Chinese spoken in SE China and Hong Kong.

cantor /ˈkæntɜr, -tɔr/ *n.* **1** the leader of the singing in a church. **2** a person employed to sing the solo prayers in a synagogue.

Canuck *informal* ● *n.* a Canadian. ● *adj.* Canadian.

canvas *n.* **1 a** a strong coarse kind of cloth usu. made from cotton or other coarse yarn and used for sails, tents, sturdy bags, etc. and as a surface for oil painting. **b** a piece of this. **2** a painting on canvas, esp. in oils. **3** an open kind of canvas used as a basis for tapestry and embroidery. □ **under canvas 1** in a tent or tents. **2** with sails spread.

canvasback *n.* a wild duck, *Aythya valisineria*, of N America, the male of which has back feathers the colour of unbleached canvas, and a chestnut head and neck.

canvass ● *v.* **1 a** *intr.* solicit votes, charitable donations, support, custom, etc., esp. by going door to door. **b** *tr.* solicit votes etc. from (people). **c** *tr.* visit (a building, area, etc.) in order to do this. **2** *tr.* **a** ascertain opinions of. **b** discuss thoroughly. **3** *tr.* propose (an idea or plan etc.). ● *n.* the process of or an instance of canvassing. □ **canvasser** *n.*

canyon *n.* **1** a deep gorge, often with a stream or river. **2** a street hemmed in by tall buildings (*the canyons of downtown Toronto*). □ **canyonland** *n.*

CAO *abbr.* Chief Administrative Officer.

cap ● *n.* **1 a** a close-fitting brimless head covering, often of a soft material and usu. with a visor (*baseball cap*). **b** a head covering worn in a particular profession (*nurse's cap*). **c** an academic mortarboard or soft hat. **2 a** a cover like a cap in shape or position (*kneecap*). **b** a device to seal a bottle or protect the point of a pen etc. **c** the top of a bird's head. **3** = CROWN *n.* 9b. **4** the pileus of a mushroom or toadstool. **5** a small amount of explosive powder contained in metal or paper and exploded by striking, used esp. in toy guns. ● *v.tr.* **6** (**capped, capping**) **1 a** put a cap on. **b** cover the top or end of. **c** set a limit to (*rate-capping*). **d** seal (a well) to prevent or control the loss of gas or oil. **2 a** lie on top of; form the cap of. **b** surpass, excel. **c** serve as a final climax or culmination to; complete (*capped the season with a shutout*). □ **cap in hand** humbly. **if the cap fits** = IF THE SHOE FITS (see SHOE). **set one's cap at** try to attract as a suitor. □ **capped** *adj.* (also in *comb.*). **capping** *n.*

cap. *abbr.* **1** capital. **2** capital letter. **3** capitalization.

capability *n.* (*pl.* **-ies**) **1** (often foll. by *of*, *for*, *to*) ability, power; the condition of being capable. **2** an undeveloped or unused faculty.

capable *adj.* **1** competent, able, gifted. **2** (foll. by *of*) **a** having the ability or fitness or necessary quality for. **b** susceptible or admitting of (explanation or improvement etc.). □ **capably** *adv.*

capacious /kəˈpeɪʃəs/ *adj.* roomy; able to hold much.

capacitor /kəˈpæsɪtər/ *n.* a device of one or more pairs of conductors used to store an electric charge.

capacity ● *n.* (*pl.* **-ies**) **1 a** the power of containing, receiving, experiencing, or producing. **b** the maximum amount that can be contained or produced etc. **c** the volume, e.g. of the cylinders in an internal combustion engine. **2 a** mental power. **b** a faculty or talent. **3** a position or function (*in my capacity as a critic*). **4** legal competence. **5** *Electricity* capacitance. ● *attrib.adj.* filling all available space (*capacity crowd*). □ **to capacity** fully; using all resources (*working to capacity*). □ **capacitative** *adj.* (also **capacitive**) (in sense 5).

cape *n.* **1** a sleeveless cloak. **2** a short sleeveless cloak as a fixed or detachable part of a longer cloak or coat. **3** a headland or promontory. □ **caped** *adj.*

Cape Ann *n.* *Cdn* (*Nfld*) a broad-brimmed rain hat with an extended back flap.

Cape Bretoner *n.* a resident or native of Cape Breton.

Cape Breton pork pie *n.* *Cdn* a date-filled tart with short pastry.

Cape Cod *n.* a style of rectangular house, usu. one-and-a-half storeys, with a steeply gabled roof (also *attrib.*: *Cape Cod house*).

Cape Island boat *n.* (also **Cape Islander**) *Cdn* a boat used by inshore fishermen esp. in Nova Scotia, with a high prow and a low stern.

capelin *var. of* CAPLIN.

caper[1] ● *v.intr.* jump or run about playfully. ● *n.* **1** a playful jump or leap. **2 a** a fantastic proceeding; a prank. **b** *informal* any (esp. disreputable) activity or occupation. □ **cut a caper** (or **capers**) act friskily.

caper[2] *n.* **1** a bramble-like S European shrub, *Capparis spinosa*. **2** (in *pl.*) its flower buds cooked and pickled for use as flavouring esp. for a savoury sauce.

capiche /kəˈpiːʃ/ *interj.* *N Amer. slang* understand?

capicollo /ˌkæpiˈkoːloː/ *n.* (also **capicolla** /-lə/) spicy Italian cured pork shoulder butt, usu. served in thin slices.

Capilano /ˌkæpiˈlænoː/ *n.* a part of the Squamish Aboriginal group, currently residing in the North Vancouver area.

capillary /kəˈpɪləri/ ● *adj.* **1** of or like a hair. **2** (of a tube) of hairlike internal diameter. **3** of one of the delicate ramified blood vessels intervening between arteries and veins. ● *n.* (*pl.* **-ies**) **1** a capillary tube. **2** a capillary blood vessel.

capital ● *n.* **1** the city or town in a country, province, etc. at which the principal government institutions (the legislature, judiciary, administrative headquarters) are located. **2** the most noteworthy place for a specified quality (*sunshine capital*). **3 a** the money or other assets with which a company starts in business. **b** accumulated wealth, esp. as used in further production. **c** money invested or lent at interest. **4** the holders of wealth as a class; capitalists. **5** a capital letter. **6** the head or cornice of a pillar or column. ● *adj.* **1 a** principal; most important; leading. **b** *informal* excellent, first-rate. **2 a** involving or punishable by death (*capital punishment; a capital offence*). **b** (of an error etc.) vitally harmful; fatal. **3** (of letters of the alphabet) large in size and of the form used to begin sentences and names etc. ● *interj.* expressing approval or satisfaction. □ **make capital out of** use to one's advantage. **with a capital —** emphatically such (*art with a capital A*). □ **capitally** *adv.*

capital gain *n.* a profit from the sale of investments or property.

capital gains tax *n.* a tax levied on the profit from the sale of investments or property.

capital goods *n.pl.* goods, esp. machinery etc., used or to be used in producing commodities.

capital-intensive *adj.* requiring much use of capital.

capitalism *n.* **1 a** an economic system in which the production and distribution of goods depend on invested private capital and profit-making. **b** the possession of capital or wealth. **2** the dominance of private owners of capital and of production for profit.

capitalist ● *n.* **1** a person using or possessing capital; a rich person. **2** an advocate of capitalism. ● *adj.* of or favouring capitalism. □ **capitalistic** *adj.*

capitalize *v.* **1** *tr.* **a** convert into or provide with capital. **b** calculate or realize the present value of an income. **c** reckon (the value of an asset) by setting future benefits against the cost of maintenance. **2** *tr.* **a** write (a letter of the alphabet) as a capital. **b** begin (a word) with a capital letter. **3** *intr.* (foll. by *on*) use to one's advantage; profit from. □ **capitalization** *n.*

capital sum *n.* a lump sum of money, esp. payable to an insured person.

capitulate /kə'pɪtʃʊˌleɪt/ *v.intr.* surrender, esp. on stated conditions. □ **capitulator** *n.*

capitulation *n.* **1** the act of capitulating; surrender. **2** a statement of the main divisions of a subject. **3** an agreement or set of conditions.

caplet *n.* an oblong medicinal tablet, usu. coated.

caplin /'kæplɪn, 'keɪplɪn/ *n.* a small smeltlike fish, *Mallotus villosus*, of the N Atlantic, used as food and as bait for catching cod etc.

cap'n /kæpn/ *n. slang* captain.

capo[1] /'keɪpo:/ *n.* (in full **capo tasto** /'tæsto:/) (*pl.* **capos** or **capo tastos**) *Music* a device secured across the neck of a fretted instrument to raise equally the tuning of all strings by the required amount.

capo[2] /'kæpo:/ *n.* (*pl.* **-s**) esp. *N Amer.* the head of a crime syndicate, esp. the Mafia, or one of its branches.

capon /'keɪpɒn/ *n.* a cockerel castrated and fattened for eating.

capote /kə'pɒt/ *n.* (also **capot**) *hist.* a long coat with a hood, esp. (in Canada) tied with a colourful sash.

capper *n.* **1** *informal* an event etc. that surpasses or completes others. **2** a device etc. that applies caps.

cappuccino /ˌkæpə'tʃi:no/ *n.* (*pl.* **-os**) espresso coffee with milk made frothy with pressurized steam.

capri /kə'pri:/ *n.* (*pl.* **-s**) (usu. *attrib.*) women's close-fitting, tapered pants or leggings extending to just above the ankles (*capri tights*).

caprice /kə'pri:s/ *n.* **1 a** an unaccountable or whimsical change of mind or conduct. **b** a tendency to this. **2** a work of lively fancy in painting, music, etc.

capricious /kə'prɪʃəs, -prɪʃ-/ *adj.* **1** guided by or given to caprice. **2** irregular, unpredictable. □ **capriciously** *adv.* **capriciousness** *n.*

Capricorn *n.* **1** a constellation between Sagittarius and Aquarius, regarded as contained in the figure of a goat's horns. **2 a** the tenth sign of the zodiac. **b** a person born when the sun is in this sign, usu. between Dec. 22 and Jan. 19. □ **Capricornian** *n. & adj.*

caprock *n.* **1** a hard rock or stratum overlying a salt dome or a deposit of oil, gas, coal, etc. **2** a hard rock or stratum at the top of a hoodoo, butte, etc.

caps. *abbr.* capital letters.

capsicum /'kæpsɪkəm/ *n.* **1** any plant of the genus *Capsicum*, having edible capsular fruits containing many seeds, esp. *C. annuum*, varieties of which yield paprikas, green or red peppers, chilies, and cayenne pepper. **2** the fruit of any of these plants.

capsize *v.* **1** *tr.* upset or overturn (a boat). **2** *intr.* be capsized.

capstan /'kæpstən/ *n.* **1** a thick revolving cylinder with a vertical axis, for winding an anchor cable or a halyard etc. **2** a revolving spindle on a tape recorder, that guides the tape past the head.

capstone *n.* **1 a** a stone which caps a structure. **b** = CAPROCK. **2** a culmination or highest point.

capsule *n.* **1** a small soluble case of gelatin enclosing a dose of medicine and swallowed with it. **2** (in full **space capsule**) a detachable compartment of a spacecraft or nose cone of a rocket. **3** a membranous or fibrous envelope around an organ, joint, etc. **4 a** a dry fruit that releases its seeds when ripe. **b** the spore-producing part of mosses. **5** a concise or highly condensed report (also *attrib.*: *a capsule review*). □ **capsular** *adj.* **capsulated** *adj.*

Capt *abbr.* Captain.

captain ● *n.* **1 a** a chief or leader. **b** the leader of a team, esp. in sports. **c** a powerful or influential person (*captain of industry*). **2 a** the person in command of a ship. **b** the pilot of a civil aircraft. **3** (also **Captain**) **a** (in Canada, the US, and the UK) an officer in land-based forces ranking below major and above lieutenant. **b** (in Canada and the US) an officer in the air force ranking below major and above lieutenant. **c** (in Canada, the US, and the UK) a naval officer ranking above commander. **d** (in some Canadian police forces) an officer ranking above lieutenant and below inspector. **4 a** a foreman. **b** *N Amer.* a supervisor of waiters or bellboys. **5 a** a great soldier or strategist. **b** an experienced commander. ● *v.tr.* be captain of; lead. □ **captaincy** *n.* (*pl.* **-ies**)

caption ● *n.* **1** a title or brief explanation appended to an illustration, cartoon, etc. **2** wording appearing on a cinema or television screen as part of a film or broadcast. ● *v.tr.* provide with a caption.

captivate *v.tr.* **1** overwhelm with charm or affection. **2** fascinate. □ **captivatingly** *adv.* **captivation** *n.*

captive ● *n.* **1** a person or animal that has been taken prisoner or confined. **2** a person or thing that is dominated. ● *adj.* **1 a** taken prisoner. **b** kept in confinement or under restraint. **2 a** unable to escape. **b** in a position of having to comply (*captive audience*). **3** of or like a prisoner (*captive state*). □ **captivity** *n.*

captive breeding *n.* a program of breeding animals held in captivity. □ **captive-bred** *adj.*

Capt(N) *abbr. Cdn* captain (in the Navy).

captor *n.* a person who takes or holds (a person etc.) captive.

capture ● *v.tr.* **1 a** take prisoner. **b** seize as a prize. **c** obtain by force or trickery. **2** win control of (something) (*captured our imagination*). **3** portray or preserve faithfully, esp. in permanent form (*captured their adventure on film*). **4** *Physics* absorb (a subatomic particle). **5** (in board games) make a move that secures the removal of (an opposing piece) from the board. **6** cause (data) to be stored in a computer. ● *n.* **1** the act of capturing. **2** a thing or person captured.

Capuchin /'kæpjuːtʃɪn, -puːʃɪn, -juː-/ *n.* **1** a Franciscan friar of a branch established in 1529 to re-emphasize the ideals of poverty and austerity. **2** (**capuchin**) any monkey of the genus *Cebus* of S America, with cowl-like fur on its head.

car *n.* **1** a road vehicle with an enclosed passenger compartment, powered by an internal combustion engine; an automobile. **2** a wheeled vehicle, esp. of a specified kind (*cable car*). **3** *N Amer.* a railway vehicle for carrying passengers or freight. **4** the passenger compartment of an elevator, balloon, etc. **5** *N Amer.* = STREETCAR. □ **carful** *n.* (*pl.* **-fuls**)

carabiner /ˌkærə'bɪnər, 'kærə-/ *n.* a clip with a spring latch used for securing a rope in climbing or mountaineering.

carafe /kə'ræf/ *n.* **1** a wide-mouthed glass container for beverages, esp. water or wine. **2** the contents of a carafe. **3** an insulated, decorative jug for serving beverages, esp. coffee.

caragana /ˌkærə'gænə, 'kærə-/ *n.* any Asian leguminous shrub of the genus *Caragana*.

carambola /ˌkærəm'boːlə, 'kærə-/ *n.* **1** a small tree, *Averrhoa carambola*, native to SE Asia, bearing golden-yellow ribbed fruit. **2** this fruit.

caramel /'kerə‚mel, 'karməl/ • n. **1** sugar or syrup heated until it turns brown, then used as a flavouring, garnish, or colour. **2** a kind of soft candy made with sugar, butter, milk, etc. **3** the light brown colour of caramel. • adj. **1** flavoured with caramel. **2** of the light brown colour of caramel.

caramelize /'kerəmə‚laiz, 'kærə-, 'karmə-/ v. **1** a tr. convert (sugar or syrup) into caramel. **b** intr. be converted into caramel. **2** tr. coat or cook (food) with caramelized sugar or syrup. ☐ **caramelization** n.

carapace /'kerə‚peis, 'kærə-/ n. **1** the hard upper shell of a turtle or a crustacean. **2** something serving as a shell or protection.

Caraquet /'karə‚ket/ n. Cdn a small variety of edible oyster found in the waters off New Brunswick.

carat /'kerət, 'kæ-/ n. **1** a unit of weight for precious stones, equivalent to 200 milligrams. **2** var. of KARAT.

caravan n. **1** a company of people with vehicles or pack animals travelling together, esp. across a desert. **2** N Amer. a covered motor vehicle with living accommodations. **3** a covered cart or carriage.

caraway /'kerə‚wei/ n. **1** an umbelliferous plant, *Carum carvi*, bearing clusters of tiny white flowers. **2** (also **caraway seed**) the fruit of the caraway plant used as flavouring and as a source of oil.

carb n. informal a carburetor.

carbide n. **1** a binary compound of carbon with a lower or comparable electronegativity. **2** a very hard material made of cobalt or nickel and carbides of metals such as tungsten and tantalum, used in the cutting parts of tools.

carbine /'karbain/ n. a short firearm, usu. a rifle, originally for cavalry use.

carbo n. N Amer. slang carbohydrate.

carbohydrate n. **1** any of a large group of energy-producing organic compounds containing carbon, hydrogen, and oxygen, e.g. starch, glucose, and other sugars. **2** (usu. in pl.) a foodstuff that is high in carbohydrates, e.g. bread, sweets, pasta, etc.

carbo-loading n. N Amer. the practice of eating large amounts of carbohydrate, esp. before a sporting event to improve stamina. ☐ **carbo-load** v.intr.

car bomb n. a terrorist bomb concealed in or under a parked car.

carbon n. **1** a non-metallic element occurring naturally as diamond, graphite, and charcoal, and in all organic compounds. **2 a** = CARBON COPY 1. **b** = CARBON PAPER. **3** a rod of carbon in an arc lamp.

carbon-12 n. a carbon isotope of mass 12.

carbon-14 n. a long-lived radioactive carbon isotope of mass 14, used in radiocarbon dating.

carbonaceous /‚karbə'neiʃəs/ adj. **1** consisting of or containing carbon. **2** of or like coal or charcoal.

carbonara /‚karbə'narə/ adj. designating a sauce for pasta made of eggs, cream, Parmesan cheese, and pieces of bacon (*linguine carbonara*).

carbonate • n. Chem. a salt of carbonic acid. • v.tr. **1** impregnate (a liquid) with carbon dioxide to produce effervescence. **2** convert into a carbonate. ☐ **carbonation** n.

carbonated adj. (of a beverage) having an effervescent quality due to carbon dioxide.

carbon copy n. **1** a copy made with carbon paper. **2** an exact duplicate (*is a carbon copy of his father*).

carbon dating n. (also **carbon-14 dating**) = RADIOCARBON DATING.

carbon dioxide n. a colourless odourless gas occurring naturally in the atmosphere and formed by respiration.

carbon fibre n. a thin strong crystalline filament of carbon used as strengthening material in plastic etc.

carbonic acid /kar'bɒnɪk/ n. a very weak acid formed from carbon dioxide dissolved in water.

Carboniferous /‚karbə'nɪfərəs/ adj. **1** (**carboniferous**) producing carbon or coal. **2** of or relating to a period of the Paleozoic era, lasting from about 360 to 286 million years BP, between the Devonian and the Permian. • n. this geological period.

carbonize v.tr. **1** convert into carbon by heating. **2** reduce to charcoal or coke. **3** coat with carbon. ☐ **carbonization** n.

carbon monoxide n. a colourless odourless toxic gas formed by the incomplete burning of carbon.

carbon paper n. a thin carbon-coated paper placed between two ordinary sheets of paper so that what is written or typed on the top sheet will be reproduced on the bottom sheet.

carbon steel n. a steel with properties dependent on the percentage of carbon present.

carbon tetrachloride n. a colourless volatile liquid used as a refrigerant and in dry cleaning.

carbonyl /'karbə‚nɪl/ n. (used attrib.) Chem. the divalent radical CO.

carborundum /‚karbə'rʌndəm/ n. a compound of carbon and silicon used esp. as an abrasive.

carboxyl /kar'bɒksɪl/ n. Chem. the monovalent acid radical (-COOH), present in most organic acids. ☐ **carboxylic** adj.

carburetor /'karbə‚reitər, 'karbjʊreitər/ n. (also **carburettor**) an apparatus for controlling the mixture of gasoline and air in an internal combustion engine.

carcass n. **1** the dead body of an animal, esp. one slaughtered for its meat. **2** the bones of a cooked bird. **3** informal a human body, living or dead. **4** the skeleton or framework of a building etc. **5** worthless remains.

carcinogen /kar'sɪnədʒən/ n. any substance that produces cancer. ● **carcinogenic** adj. **carcinogenicity** /-'nɪsɪti/ n.

carcinoma /‚karsɪ'no:mə/ n. (pl. **-s** or **carcinomata** /-tə/) a cancer, esp. one arising in epithelial tissue.

card[1] • n. **1** thick stiff paper or thin pasteboard. **2 a** a flat piece of this, esp. for writing or printing on. **b** = POSTCARD. **c** a card used to send greetings, issue an invitation, etc. (*birthday card*). **d** = CALLING CARD 1. **e** = BUSINESS CARD. **f** a card with a photograph of a sports figure etc., collected as part of a set. **g** a card indicating membership or entitling admission. **3 a** = PLAYING CARD. **b** a similar card in a set designed for a particular game. **c** (in pl.) card playing; a card game. **d** a specified advantageous usu. political factor (*politicians will play the crime card yet again*). **4 a** a program of events at a race, boxing match, etc. **b** a scorecard. **c** a list of holes on a golf course, on which a player's scores are entered. **5** informal an amusing person (*he's a real card!*). **6** a printed or written notice or advertisement. **7** a small rectangular piece of plastic issued by a bank or other institution with personal (often machine-readable) data on it (*credit card*; *health card*). **8** Computing **a** = PUNCH CARD. **b** a circuit board. ● v.tr. **1** affix to a card. **2** write on a card, esp. for indexing. **3** demand identification from (a person). **4** Cdn (in passive) (of an amateur athlete) receive government funding to pursue one's training. ☐ **card up one's sleeve** a plan in reserve. **in the cards** possible or likely. **play one's cards right** (or **well**) act carefully; carry out a scheme successfully. **put** (or **lay**) **one's cards on the table** reveal one's resources, intentions, etc.

card² ● *n.* **1** a machine through which fibre is fed past a series of wire teeth to align and disentangle the fibre before spinning. **2** a toothed instrument or wire brush for raising the nap on cloth. ● *v.tr.* prepare (fibre) with a card. □ **carder** *n.*

cardamom /'kɑrdəməm/ *n.* (also **cardamon** /-mən/) **1** an aromatic SE Asian plant, *Elettaria cardamomum*. **2** the seed capsules of this used as a spice.

cardboard ● *n.* pasteboard or stiff paper, esp. for making cards or boxes. ● *adj.* **1** made of cardboard. **2** flimsy, insubstantial, artificial.

card-carrying *attrib.adj.* **1** registered as a member (e.g. of a union). **2** devoted to a specified party or cause.

card catalogue *n.* a file of cards which serves as an index to the holdings of a library.

carded *adj.* *Cdn* (of an amateur athlete) receiving government funding to pursue training.

card game *n.* a game in which playing cards are used.

cardholder *n.* a person who has a specific card, esp. a credit card.

cardiac ● *adj.* **1** of or relating to the heart. **2** of or relating to the part of the stomach nearest the esophagus. ● *n.* a person with heart disease.

cardiac arrest *n.* a sudden cessation of the heartbeat.

cardigan *n.* a knitted jacket or sweater fastening down the front, usu. with long sleeves.

cardinal ● *n.* **1** (as a title **Cardinal**) a leading dignitary of the Catholic Church, one of the college electing the Pope. **2** a N American songbird, *Cardinalis cardinalis*, the males of which have scarlet plumage. ● *adj.* **1** chief, fundamental; on which something hinges (*a cardinal rule*). **2** deep scarlet in colour.

cardinal humour *n.* see HUMOUR *n.* 5.

cardinal number *n.* a number denoting quantity (one, two, three, etc.), as opposed to an ordinal number (first, second, third, etc.).

cardinal point *n.* one of the four main points of the compass: north, south, east, west.

cardinal sin *n.* **1** a deadly sin. **2** an action perceived as unforgivable.

card index *n.* an index in the form of a file with each item entered on a separate card. □ **card-index** *v.tr.*

cardio *n.* *slang* **1** cardiovascular exercise. **2** cardiovascular fitness.

cardiogram *n.* = ELECTROCARDIOGRAM.

cardiograph *n.* = ELECTROCARDIOGRAPH. □ **cardiographer** *n.* **cardiography** *n.*

cardiology *n.* the branch of medicine concerned with diseases and abnormalities of the heart. □ **cardiologist** *n.*

cardiomyopathy /ˌkɑrdioːˈmaiˈɒpəθi/ *n.* (*pl.* **-ies**) *Med.* chronic disease of the heart muscle.

cardiopulmonary *adj.* of the heart and lungs.

cardiopulmonary resuscitation *n.* a series of emergency techniques used to revive a patient whose heart has stopped, including artificial respiration and heart massage. Abbr.: **CPR**.

cardiovascular *adj.* of or relating to the heart and blood vessels.

card sharp *n.* (also *N Amer.* **card shark**) a person who professionally or habitually cheats at card games. □ **card-sharp** *v.intr.*

card table *n.* a square table for playing card games, esp. one with folding legs.

care ● *n.* **1** a process of looking after or providing for someone or something; the provision of what is needed for health or protection (*child care; skin care*). **b** *Cdn* & *Brit.* protective custody or guardianship provided by a child welfare agency for a child whose parents are deemed unable to provide proper care (*was taken into care*). **2** serious attention or thought in doing something properly or avoiding damage to something (*handle with care*). **3** a troubled state of mind arising from worry or anxiety. **4** maintenance (*car care*). **5** a matter of concern; something to be done or seen to. ● *v.intr.* **1 a** (usu. foll. by *about, for, whether*) feel concern or interest. **b** have an objection; mind (*she won't care if we leave early*). **2** feel liking, affection, regard, or deference (*don't care for jazz*). **3** wish or be willing (*do not care to be seen with him*). **4** in conventional polite offers, esp. of food or drink (*care for a cup of tea?*). □ **care for 1** provide for or look after, esp. an old or sick person. **2** love or be very fond of. **care of** at the address of (*sent it care of his sister*). **for all one cares** *informal* denoting a lack of interest or concern (*I could be dying for all you care*). **have a care** take care; be careful. **I** (etc.) **couldn't** (or *N Amer. disputed* **could**) **care less** *informal* an expression of complete indifference. **take care 1** be careful. **2** (foll. by *to* + *infin.*) not fail or neglect. **3** a conventional expression of good wishes on parting etc. **take care of 1** look after; keep safe. **2** deal with. **3** dispose of. **who cares?** no one cares; I don't care.

careen *v.* **1** *intr.* *N Amer.* rush headlong; hurtle unsteadily. **2 a** *intr.* tilt; lean over. **b** *tr.* cause to do this.

career ● *n.* **1 a** one's advancement through life, esp. in a profession. **b** the progress through history of a group or institution. **2** a profession or occupation, esp. as offering advancement. **3** swift course; impetus (*in full career*). ● *adj.* **1** (*attrib.*) **a** pursuing or wishing to pursue a career (*career woman*). **b** working permanently in a specified profession (*career diplomat*). **2** (*attrib.*) *Sport* **a** (of a statistic etc.) accumulated over one's career (*scored 500 career goals*). **b** constituting a high point in one's career (*a career game*). ● *v.intr.* **1** move or swerve about wildly. **2** go swiftly.

careerist *n.* a person predominantly concerned with personal advancement. □ **careerism** *n.*

career path *n.* a recognized pattern of advancement within a job or profession.

carefree *adj.* free from anxiety or responsibility. □ **carefreeness** *n.*

careful *adj.* **1** painstaking, thorough. **2** cautious. **3** done with care and attention. **4** showing care or concern for. □ **carefully** *adv.* **carefulness** *n.*

caregiver *n.* **1** a parent or guardian who cares for a child. **2** a person who cares for a sick or elderly person. **3** a person employed to look after a child. □ **caregiving** *n.*

careless *adj.* **1** not taking care or paying attention. **2** unthinking, insensitive. **3** done without care; inaccurate. **4** lighthearted. **5** (foll. by *of*) not concerned about. □ **carelessly** *adv.* **carelessness** *n.*

care package *n.* **1** a parcel of food, clothing, or other staple items sent to the needy in a foreign country. **2** a parcel of luxuries (esp. homemade foods) sent to a person who is living away from home.

caress ● *v.tr.* **1** touch or stroke gently or lovingly. **2** treat fondly or kindly. ● *n.* a loving or gentle touch or kiss. □ **caressingly** *adv.*

caret /'kɑrət/ *n.* a mark (ˆ) indicating a proposed insertion in printing or writing.

caretaker *n.* **1** a custodian or janitor. **2** = CAREGIVER. **3** (*attrib.*) exercising temporary authority (*caretaker government*). □ **caretaking** *n.*

careworn *adj.* showing the effects of prolonged worry.

cargo *n.* (*pl.* **-oes** or **-os**) goods carried on a ship, aircraft, or other vehicle.

Carib /'kerɪb/ ● *n.* **1** an aboriginal inhabitant of the southern W Indies or the adjacent coasts. **2** the language of this people. ● *adj.* of this people.

Caribbean /ˌkerə'biːən, kə'rɪbiən/ ● *n.* the part of the Atlantic between the southern W Indies and Central America. ● *adj.* **1** of or relating to this region or its people. **2** of the Caribs or their language.

cariboo *rare var. of* CARIBOU.

caribou *n.* (*pl.* same) **1** any of several subspecies of reindeer (*Rangifer tarandus*) inhabiting N Canada and Alaska, esp. the woodland or barren ground caribou. **2** the meat or hide of this animal. **3** *Cdn* (esp. *Que.*) a beverage made from red wine and whisky blanc.

Caribou Inuit *n.* an inland Inuit people formerly inhabiting the Barrens and relying almost entirely on caribou for food and clothing.

caricature ● *n.* **1** a grotesque usu. comic representation of a person by exaggeration of characteristic traits, in a picture, writing, etc. **2** a ridiculously poor or absurd imitation or version. ● *v.tr.* make or give a caricature of. □ **caricatural** *adj.* **caricaturist** *n.*

caries /'keriːz/ *n.* (*pl.* same) decay and crumbling of a tooth or bone.

carillon /'kerələn, -ɒn/ *n.* **1** a set of bells sounded either from a keyboard or mechanically. **2** a tune played on bells.

caring *adj.* compassionate or considerate, esp. towards other people. □ **caringly** *adv.*

cariole *var. of* CARRIOLE.

carjacking *n.* the hijacking of a car or its passengers. □ **carjack** *v.tr.* **carjacker** *n.*

carload *n.* **1** the quantity of freight that can be shipped in a railway car. **2** *N Amer.* the number of people that can travel in an automobile.

carmaker *n.* = AUTOMAKER.

Carmelite /'kɑrmə,laɪt/ ● *n.* **1** a member of an order of mendicant friars, founded in the 12th c. **2** a nun of an order modelled on this order of friars. ● *adj.* of or relating to the Carmelites.

carminative /kɑr'mɪnətɪv, 'kɑr-/ ● *adj.* relieving flatulence. ● *n.* a carminative drug.

carmine /'kɑrmaɪn/ ● *adj.* of a vivid crimson colour. ● *n.* this colour.

carnage *n.* the killing of many people, animals, etc., usu. with much bloodshed.

carnal /'kɑrnəl/ *adj.* **1** of the body or flesh; worldly. **2** sensual, sexual. □ **carnality** /-'næləti/ *n.* **carnalize** *v.tr.* **carnally** *adv.*

carnation ● *n.* **1** any of several cultivated varieties of the clove pink (see CLOVE[1] 2), with variously coloured showy flowers. **2** this flower. **3** a rosy pink colour. ● *adj.* of this colour.

carnival *n.* **1 a** the festivities usual during the period before Lent in some countries. **b** any festivities, esp. those occurring during a regular season (*winter carnival*). **2** *N Amer.* a travelling fair with exhibits, games, rides, and other amusements. **3** merrymaking, revelry. **4** *Cdn Figure Skating* a non-competitive performance given by the members of a figure skating club. □ **carnivalesque** *adj.*

carnivore *n.* **1 a** any mammal of the order Carnivora (cats, dogs, bears, seals, etc.) with powerful jaws and teeth adapted for stabbing, tearing, and eating flesh. **b** any other flesh-eating mammal. **2** any insect-eating plant. **3** a person who eats (esp. large amounts of) meat; a non-vegetarian.

carnivorous *adj.* **1** (of an animal) feeding on flesh. **2** (of a plant) digesting trapped insects or other animal substances. **3** of or relating to the order Carnivora. **4** (of a person) not vegetarian.

carob /'kerəb, 'kær-/ *n.* **1** (in full **carob tree**) an evergreen tree, *Ceratonia siliqua*, native to the Mediterranean, bearing edible pods. **2** its bean-shaped edible seed pod. **3** the powdered pulp of these pods, used esp. as a substitute for chocolate.

carol ● *n.* a joyous song or hymn, esp. one celebrating Christmas. ● *v.* (**carolled, carolling**) **1** *intr.* sing carols, esp. outdoors at Christmas. **2** *tr. & intr.* sing joyfully. □ **caroller** *n.*

Carolina poplar *n.* a hybrid between a European poplar and the N American eastern cottonwood.

Carolinian /ˌkerə'lɪniən, ˌkær-/ ● *adj.* **1** of or relating to a forest region extending from S Ontario to N and S Carolina, characterized by broadleaf deciduous trees such as the tulip tree and magnolia. **2** of or relating to the states of S or N Carolina. ● *n.* a native or inhabitant of S or N Carolina.

carom /'kerəm, 'kær-/ *N Amer.* ● *n.* **1** *Billiards* a shot in which the cue ball strikes two other balls in succession. **2** an instance of striking and rebounding. ● *v.intr.* **1** *Billiards* make a carom. **2** (usu. foll. by *off*) strike and rebound.

carotene /'kerə,tiːn, 'kær-/ *n.* any of several orange-coloured plant pigments found in carrots, tomatoes, etc., acting as a source of vitamin A.

carotid /kə'rɒtɪd/ ● *n.* each of the two main arteries carrying blood to the head and neck. ● *adj.* of or relating to either of these arteries.

carouse /kə'rauz/ ● *v.intr.* **1** participate in a noisy or lively drinking party. **2** drink heavily. ● *n.* a noisy or lively drinking party. □ **carouser** *n.*

carousel *n.* **1** *N Amer.* **a** a large revolving device in a playground, for children to ride on. **b** a merry-go-round. **2** a rotating delivery or conveyor system, esp. for passengers' luggage at an airport. **3** a rotating tray for holding specific objects, esp. on a slide projector or compact disc player.

carp[1] *n.* (*pl.* same) any freshwater food fish of the family Cyprinidae, esp. *Cyprinus carpio*, having large scales and barbels on either side of its mouth.

carp[2] *v.intr.* find fault; complain pettily. □ **carper** *n.*

carpaccio /kɑr'pætʃio/ *n.* a thin strip of marinated raw meat, esp. beef, as an appetizer.

carpal ● *adj.* of or relating to the bones in the wrist. ● *n.* any of the bones forming the wrist.

carpal tunnel syndrome *n.* a painful disorder of the hand caused by compression of a major nerve in the wrist, often brought about by overexertion.

car park *n. Cdn, Brit., Austral., & NZ* = PARKING LOT.

carpel *n. Bot.* the female reproductive organ of a flower, consisting of a stigma, style, and ovary.

carpenter ● *n.* a person skilled in woodwork, esp. of a structural kind. ● *v.* **1** *intr.* do carpentry. **2** *tr.* make by carpentry. **3** *tr.* construct; fit together.

carpentry *n.* **1** the work or occupation of a carpenter. **2** woodwork constructed by a carpenter.

carpet ● *n.* **1 a** a thick fabric for covering a floor or stairs. **b** a piece of this fabric. **2** an expanse or layer resembling a carpet in being smooth, soft, bright, or thick (*carpet of violets*). ● *v.tr.* (**carpeted, carpeting**) cover with or as with a carpet. □ **call** (or **have up**) **on the carpet** reprimand; reprove. **sweep under the carpet** conceal (a problem or difficulty) in the hope that it will be forgotten.

carpet bag n. a travelling bag of a kind originally made of carpet-like material.

carpetbagger n. **1** esp. N Amer. a political candidate in an area where the candidate has no local connections. **2** an unscrupulous opportunist.

carpet bombing n. the dropping of a large number of bombs uniformly over an area.

carpet bowling n. Cdn an indoor game similar to lawn bowling, played with either round balls or asymmetrical bowls.

carpeting n. **1** material for carpets. **2** carpets collectively.

car phone n. a cellular telephone for use in a vehicle.

car pool n. N Amer. an arrangement between people to travel together in a single vehicle, usu. with each member taking a turn at driving the others. □ **carpool** v.intr. **carpooler** n. **carpooling** n.

carport n. a shelter with a roof and open sides for a car, usu. beside a house.

carpus /'kɑrpəs/ n. (pl. **carpi** /-paɪ/) the small bones between the forelimb and metacarpus in terrestrial vertebrates, forming the wrist in humans.

carrageen /'kerə,giːn, 'kærə-/ n. (also **carragheen**) an edible purplish-red seaweed, Chondrus crispus, of the northern hemisphere.

carrageenan /,kerə'giːnən, kærə-/ n. (also **carrageenin**) a mixture of polysaccharides extracted from carrageen or similar seaweed and used as a gelling, thickening, and emulsifying agent in food products.

carrel /'kerəl, 'kær-/ n. a small cubicle or desk with high sides in a library, designed for individual study.

carriage n. **1** a wheeled passenger vehicle, esp. one with four wheels and pulled by horses. **2** = BABY CARRIAGE. **3 a** the conveying of goods. **b** the cost of this. **4** the part of a machine (e.g. a typewriter) that carries other parts into the required position. **5** = GUN CARRIAGE. **6** one's bearing or deportment.

carriage return n. = RETURN n. 7.

carriage trade n. the wealthy clients or customers of a business.

Carrier ● n. **1** a member of an Athapaskan people inhabiting the BC interior. **2** the Athapaskan language of this people. ● adj. of or relating to this people.

carrier n. **1** a person or thing that carries or in which something is carried. **2** a person or company undertaking to convey goods or passengers for payment. **3** a part of a bicycle etc. for carrying luggage or a passenger. **4** a person who delivers newspapers, flyers, etc. **5** a person or animal that may transmit a disease or a hereditary characteristic without suffering from or displaying it. **6** = AIRCRAFT CARRIER. **7** a substance used to support or convey a pigment, a catalyst, radioactive material, etc. **8** Physics a mobile electron or hole that carries a charge in a semiconductor. **9** (in full **carrier wave**) a high-frequency electromagnetic wave modulated in amplitude or frequency to convey a signal.

carrier pigeon n. a homing pigeon trained to carry messages tied to its neck or leg.

carriole /'keri,oːl, 'kæ-/ n. **1** a small open carriage for one person. **2** a covered light cart. **3** Cdn hist. **a** a horse-drawn sleigh with seats for a driver and often one or more passengers. **b** (North) a type of dogsled designed to carry a passenger or load in the front, with a rear platform for the driver to stand on.

carrion n. **1** dead putrefying flesh. **2** something vile or filthy.

carrot n. **1 a** an umbelliferous plant, Daucus carota, with a tapering orange-coloured root. **b** this root as a vegetable. **2** a means of enticement or persuasion.

carrot-and-stick n. (attrib.) designating an approach etc. combining rewards for desirable behaviour and punishment for undesirable behaviour.

carrot cake n. a cake containing grated carrots and spices, typically served with cream cheese icing.

carry ● v. (**-ies**, **-ied**) **1** tr. support or hold up, esp. while moving. **2** tr. convey with one from one place to another. **3** tr. have on one's person (I never carry money). **4** tr. conduct or transmit (carries electric current). **5** tr. take (a process etc.) to a specified point (carry into effect; carry a joke too far). **6** tr. (foll. by to) continue or prolong (carry modesty to excess). **7** tr. involve, imply; have as a feature or consequence (carries a two-year guarantee). **8** tr. (in calculations) transfer (a figure) to a column of higher value. **9 a** refl. conduct oneself in a specified way, esp. in reference to one's bearing (carries herself with pride). **b** tr. hold (a part of the body) in a specified way (carries his head low). **10** tr. **a** (of a newspaper or magazine) publish; include in its contents, esp. regularly. **b** (of a radio or television station) broadcast, esp. regularly. **11** tr. (of a retailing outlet) keep a regular stock of (particular goods for sale). **12** tr. make regular payments towards (a mortgage, loan, etc.). **13** intr. **a** (of sound, esp. a voice) be audible at a distance. **b** (of a missile) travel, penetrate. **14** tr. (of a gun etc.) propel a specified distance. **15** tr. **a** win victory or acceptance for (a proposal etc.). **b** win acceptance from (carried the audience with them). **c** win, capture (a prize, a fortress, etc.). **d** N Amer. win (a constituency) in an election. **e** Golf cause the ball to pass beyond (a bunker etc.). **16** intr. Football attempt to gain yardage by rushing with the ball. **17** tr. **a** endure the weight of; support (columns carry the dome). **b** be the chief cause of the effectiveness of; be the driving force in. **18** tr. be pregnant with (is carrying twins). **19** tr. **a** (of a motive, money, etc.) cause or enable (a person) to go to a specified place. **b** (of a journey) bring (a person) to a specified point. **20** tr. sing (a tune) on pitch. ● n. (pl. **-ies**) **1** an act of carrying. **2** Golf the distance a ball travels before reaching the ground. **3** a portage between rivers etc. **4** the range of a gun etc. **5** Football an instance of rushing with the ball. □ **carry all before one** overcome all opposition. **carry away 1** remove. **2** inspire; affect emotionally or spiritually. **3** deprive of self-control (got carried away). **carry back** take (a person) back in thought to a past time. **carry the can** Cdn & Brit. informal bear the responsibility or blame. **carry the day** be victorious or successful. **carry forward** transfer to a new page or account. **carry it off** (or **carry it off well**) do well under difficulties. **carry off 1** take away, esp. by force. **2** win (a prize). **3** (esp. of a disease) kill. **4** render acceptable or passable. **carry on 1** continue (carry on eating). **2** engage in (a conversation or a business). **3** informal behave strangely or excitedly. **4** (often foll. by with) informal flirt or have a love affair. **5** advance (a process) by a stage. **carry out 1** put (ideas, instructions, etc.) into practice. **2** perform or conduct (an investigation, test, etc.). **carry over** be temporarily suspended and resumed later; postpone. **carry through 1** complete successfully. **2** bring safely out of difficulties. **carry weight** be influential or important. **carry with one** remember; bear in mind.

carryall n. N Amer. a large bag or case for carrying things.

carrying capacity n. **1** the capacity of something, e.g. a vehicle, to hold passengers or cargo. **2** the maximum population of a certain species that can be supported by a given environment.

carrying charge *n.* **1** the interest on a loan etc. **2** an unproductive expense, e.g. for goods stored.

carrying-on *n.* (also **carryings-on** *n.pl.*) **1** a state of excitement or fuss. **2** a questionable piece of behaviour. **3** a flirtation or love affair.

carry-on ● *adj.* (of a suitcase etc.) suitable for carrying onto an airplane, bus, etc., rather than loading as checked baggage. ● *n.* a carry-on suitcase.

carry-over *n.* **1** something retained or carried over. **2** the act of retaining something or carrying something over.

car seat *n.* **1** a portable chair that fastens to the seat of a car and is used for securing young children. **2** the seat of a car.

cart ● *n.* **1** a strong vehicle with two or four wheels for carrying loads, drawn by a horse, ox, etc. **2** a light vehicle for pushing or pulling by hand (*shopping cart*). **3** a light vehicle with two wheels for driving in, drawn by a single horse. **4** = GOLF CART. ● *v.tr.* **1** convey in or as in a cart. **2** *informal* carry (esp. a cumbersome thing) with difficulty or over a long distance (*carted it home*). □ **cart off** remove, esp. by force. **put the cart before the horse 1** reverse the proper order or procedure. **2** take an effect for a cause. □ **carter** *n.*

cartful *n.* (*pl.* **-fuls**).

cartage *n.* **1** the act of carting or conveying goods. **2** the price paid for carting.

carte blanche /kɑrt 'blɑ̃ʃ/ *n.* complete freedom to act as one thinks best.

cartel *n.* **1** a group of manufacturers or suppliers who collude to maintain prices at a high level, and control production, marketing, etc. **2** a political combination between parties. □ **cartelize** *v.tr. & intr.*

Cartesian /kɑr'ti:ʒən, -i:ʒən/ ● *adj.* of or relating to the French philosopher René Descartes (1596–1650), his philosophy, or his mathematical methods. ● *n.* a follower of Descartes.

Cartesian coordinates *n.pl.* a system for locating a point by reference to its distance from two or three axes intersecting at right angles.

Carthusian /kɑr'θju:ziən, -'θu:ʒən/ ● *n.* a Christian monk or nun of a strictly contemplative order founded in France in 1084, leading a hermitic way of life remarkable for its austerity and self-denial. ● *adj.* of or relating to the Carthusians.

cartilage /'kɑrtəlɪdʒ/ *n.* a firm, elastic, semi-opaque connective tissue of the vertebrate body; gristle. □ **cartilaginous** /-'lædʒɪnəs/ *adj.*

cartography *n.* the science or practice of map drawing. □ **cartographer** *n.* **cartographic** *adj.* **cartographical** *adj.*

carton *n.* **1** a light cardboard or plastic box or container. **2** the contents of a carton.

cartoon ● *n.* **1** a humorous drawing in a newspaper, magazine, etc., esp. as a topical comment. **2** = COMIC STRIP. **3** a filmed sequence of drawings using the technique of animation. **4** an artist's full-size preliminary design for a painting, tapestry, mosaic, etc. ● *v.* **1** *tr.* draw a cartoon of. **2** *intr.* draw cartoons. □ **cartoonist** *n.* **cartoon-like** *adj.*

cartoonish *adj.* resembling a comic cartoon or its style, esp. by showing simplification or exaggeration of some features. □ **cartoonishly** *adv.*

cartoony *adj.* resembling a comic cartoon.

cartridge *n.* **1** a case containing a charge of propelling explosive for firearms or blasting, with a bullet or shot if for small arms. **2** a spool of film, magnetic tape, etc., in a sealed container ready for insertion

into a particular mechanism. **3** a container of ink, toner, etc., for insertion in a pen, printer, photocopier, etc.

cartwheel ● **1** the (usu. spoked) wheel of a cart. **2** a circular sideways handspring with the arms and legs extended. ● *v.intr.* **1** perform cartwheels. **2** turn end over end.

carve *v.* **1** *tr.* produce or shape (a statue etc.) by cutting into a hard material. **2** *tr.* **a** cut patterns, designs, letters, etc. in (hard material). **b** (foll. by *into*) form a pattern, design, etc., from (*carved it into a bust*). **c** (foll. by *with*) cover or decorate (material) with figures or designs cut in it. **3** *tr. & intr.* cut (meat etc.) into slices for eating. **4** *tr.* cut (a way, passage, etc.). □ **carved in stone** (of a decision etc.) unchangeable. **carve out 1** take from a larger whole. **2** establish (a career etc.) purposefully (*carved out a name for themselves*). **carve (out) a niche** establish oneself in a particular area of a market etc. in order to excel. **carve up 1** divide into several pieces; subdivide (territory etc.). **2** cut (a person) with a knife. □ **carver** *n.*

carving *n.* a carved object, esp. as a work of art.

carving knife *n.* a knife with a long blade, for carving meat.

car wash *n.* a business or building with equipment for washing cars.

CAS *abbr.* (in Canada) CHILDREN'S AID SOCIETY.

casaba /kə'sɑbə/ *n.* a type of melon, *Cucumis melo inodorus*, having a yellow wrinkled skin and whitish flesh.

Casanova /ˌkæsə'no:və/ *n.* a man notorious for seducing women.

CASBY /'kæzbi/ *n.* (*pl.* **-IES**) (in Canada) any of several awards presented annually to Canadian popular music performers; voting is conducted by ballot among the general public.

cascade ● *n.* **1** a small waterfall, esp. forming one in a series or part of a large broken waterfall. **2 a** a succession of electrical devices or stages in a process. **b** a rapid sequence of events. **3** a quantity of material etc. draped in descending folds. **4** a process of disseminating information from senior to junior levels in an organization. **5** a thing that falls or hangs in a way suggestive of a waterfall (*cascades of blond hair*). ● *v.intr.* fall in or like a cascade.

cascara /kæs'kɑrə/ *n.* (in full **cascara sagrada** /səg'rɑdə/) the dried bark of the western N American buckthorn, *Rhamnus purshiana*, used as a purgative.

case[1] *n.* **1** an instance of something occurring. **2** a state of affairs, hypothetical or actual. **3** the position or circumstances in which one is (*in your case*). **4 a** an instance of a person receiving professional guidance, e.g. from a doctor or social worker. **b** this person or the circumstances involved. **5** a matter under official investigation, esp. by the police. **6** *Law* **a** a cause or suit for trial. **b** a statement of the facts or evidence for a trial etc. **7 a** the sum of the arguments on one side, esp. in a lawsuit (*that is our case*). **b** a set of arguments, esp. in relation to persuasiveness (*have a good case*). **c** a valid set of arguments (*have no case*). **8** *Grammar* **a** the relation of a word to other words in a sentence. **b** a form of a noun, adjective, or pronoun expressing this. □ **as the case may be** according to the situation. **get off** (or **on**) **one's case** *N Amer.* stop (or start) harassing one. **in any case** whatever the truth is; whatever may happen. **in case 1** in the event that; if. **2** lest; in provision against a stated or implied possibility (*take an umbrella in case it rains*). **in case of** in the event of. **in the case of** as regards. **in**

no case under no circumstances. **in that case** if that is true; should that happen. **is** (or **is not**) **the case** is (or is not) so.

case² ● *n.* **1** a container or covering serving to enclose, hold, or contain. **2** a container with its contents. **3** an outer protective covering. **4** an item of luggage, esp. a suitcase. ● *v.tr.* **1** enclose in a case. **2** (foll. by *with*) surround. **3** *slang* reconnoitre (a house etc.), esp. with a view to robbery. □ **have got it cased** have got everything under control.

case-harden *v.tr.* **1** harden the surface of, esp. give a steel surface to (iron) by carbonizing. **2** make callous. □ **case-hardened** *adj.*

case history *n.* information about a person for use in professional treatment, e.g. by a doctor.

casein /'keisi:n, 'keisii:n/ *n.* **1** the main protein in milk, esp. in coagulated form as in cheese. **2** this protein used in making plastics, etc.

case law *n.* the law as established by the outcome of former cases (compare COMMON LAW, STATUTE LAW).

caseload *n.* the cases with which a doctor etc. is concerned at one time.

casement *n.* a window or part of a window hinged vertically to open like a door.

case study *n.* **1** an attempt to understand a person, institution, etc., from collected information. **2** a record of such an attempt. **3** the use of a particular instance as an exemplar of general principles.

casework *n.* social work concerned with individuals, esp. involving understanding of the client's family and background. □ **caseworker** *n.*

cash ● *n.* **1** money in coins or banknotes, as distinct from cheques, money orders, or payment on credit. **2** (also **cash down**) money given as full payment at the time of purchase, as distinct from credit. **3** *informal* money. **4** *Cdn informal* = CASH REGISTER. ● *v.tr.* give or obtain cash for (a note, cheque, etc.). □ **cash in 1** obtain cash for. **2** *informal* (usu. foll. by *on*) profit (from); take advantage (of). **3** (in full **cash in one's chips**) *informal* die. **cash out** count and check cash takings at the end of a day's business.

cash and carry ● *adj.* (of a store, sale, etc.) operated on a system of cash payments and with no delivery available. ● *n.* a store where this system operates.

cash bar *n.* a bar at a special function at which guests buy drinks rather than having them provided free (compare OPEN BAR).

cash box *n.* a box for storing money used in sales, usu. having a tray divided into compartments.

cash card *n.* = BANK CARD.

cash cow *n.* *informal* a business, product, or operation that provides a steady and abundant cash flow.

cash crop *n.* a crop produced for sale. □ **cash cropper** *n.* **cash cropping** *n.*

cash desk *n.* *Cdn & Brit.* a counter in a store where goods are paid for.

cash dispenser *n.* = AUTOMATED TELLER MACHINE.

cashew /'kæʃu:, kæ'ʃu:/ *n.* **1** a bushy evergreen tree, *Anacardium occidentale*, native to Central and S America, bearing kidney-shaped nuts attached to fleshy fruits. **2** the edible nut of this tree.

cash flow *n.* the movement of money as affecting liquidity or as a measure of profitability.

cashier¹ *n.* **1** a person handling customer payments in a store. **2** a person in charge of a bank's or company's cash.

cashier² *v.tr.* dismiss from service, esp. from the armed forces with disgrace.

cashless *adj.* (of a society, economic system, etc.) functioning without cash, all financial transactions being executed electronically or by credit card.

cash machine *n.* = AUTOMATED TELLER MACHINE.

cashmere *n.* **1** a fine soft wool, esp. that of a Kashmir goat. **2** a material made from this.

cash on delivery *n.* a system of paying the carrier for goods when they are delivered.

cash register *n.* a machine in a store etc. with a drawer for money, recording the amount of each sale, totalling receipts, etc.

cashspiel /'kæʃspi:l/ *n. Cdn* a bonspiel in which curlers compete for cash prizes.

cash-strapped *adj.* extremely short of money.

casing *n.* **1** a protective or enclosing cover or shell. **2** the material for this.

casino *n.* (*pl.* **-os**) a room or building for gambling.

cask *n.* **1** a large barrel-like container made of wood, metal, or plastic, esp. one for alcoholic liquor. **2** its contents. **3** its capacity. **4** *Cdn* (*Nfld*) a wooden container for shipping dried and salted cod, containing four hundredweight (about 200 kg).

casket *n.* **1** esp. *N Amer.* a coffin. **2** a small often ornamental box or chest for jewels, letters, etc.

Cassandra /kə'sændrə/ *n.* a prophet of disaster, esp. one who is disregarded.

cassava /kə'spvə/ *n.* **1 a** any plant of the genus *Manihot*, esp. the cultivated varieties *M. esculenta* (**bitter cassava**) and *M. dulcis* (**sweet cassava**), having starchy tuberous roots. **b** the roots themselves. **2** a starch or flour obtained from these.

casse-croûte /kæs'kru:t/ *n. Cdn* (*Que.*) a snack bar.

casserole *n.* **1** a covered dish, usu. of earthenware or glass, in which food is cooked, esp. in an oven. **2** food cooked in a casserole, esp. a savoury dish combining meat or fish, vegetables, pasta, sauce, etc.

cassette *n.* a sealed case containing a length of tape, ribbon, etc., ready for insertion in a machine, esp.: **1** a length of magnetic tape wound onto spools, ready for insertion in a tape recorder. **2** a length of photographic film, ready for insertion in a camera.

cassia /'kæsiə, 'kæʃə/ *n.* **1** any plant of the genus *Cassia*, esp. one yielding senna. **2 a** (in full **cassia bark**) the cinnamon-like bark of *Cinnamomum cassia* used as a spice. **b** (in full **cassia tree**) this tree.

cassis /kæ'si:s/ *n.* a syrupy blackcurrant liqueur.

cassock *n.* a close-fitting garment with sleeves, fastened at the neck and reaching to the heels, worn under a surplice, alb, etc. by some clerics etc.

cassoulet /'kæsu,lei/ *n.* a stew of beans with pork, mutton, and either duck or goose.

cast ● *v.* (*past* and *past part.* **cast**) **1** *tr.* throw, esp. deliberately or forcefully. **2** *tr.* (often foll. by *on, over*) **a** direct or cause to fall (one's eyes, light, a shadow, a spell, etc.). **b** express (doubts, aspersions, etc.). **3** *tr.* throw out (a fishing line) into the water. **4** *tr.* let down (an anchor etc.). **5** *tr.* **a** throw off, get rid of. **b** shed (skin etc.) esp. in the process of growth. **6** *tr.* record, register, or give (a vote). **7** *tr.* **a** shape (molten metal or plastic material) in a mould. **b** make (a product) in this way. **8** *intr.* (of dogs etc.) search for a scent. **9 a** *tr.* (usu. foll. by *as*) assign (a theatrical performer) to the role of a particular character. **b** allocate roles in (a play, film, etc.). **c** *intr.* select performers for the roles in (a play, film, etc.). **10** *tr. Cdn* (*Nfld*) catch (caplin) using a cast net. ● *n.* **1 a** the throwing of a missile etc. **b** the distance reached by this. **2** a throw or a number thrown at dice. **3** a throw of a net, fishing line, etc. **4** *Fishing* **a** that which is cast, esp. the line with hook, fly, etc. **b** a place for casting (*a good cast*). **5 a** an object of metal, clay, etc., made in a mould. **b** a moulded mass of solidified material, esp. plaster protecting a broken limb. **6** the performers taking part in a play, film, etc. **7** form, type, or quality (*cast of mind*). **8** a tinge or shade of colour. **9 a** a mass of earth excreted by a worm. **b** a mass of indigestible food thrown up by a hawk etc. □ **cast about** (or **around** or **round**) make an extensive search (actually or mentally) (*cast about for a solution*). **cast adrift** leave to drift. **cast ashore** (of waves etc.) throw to the shore. **cast aside** give up using; abandon. **cast away 1** reject. **2** (in *passive*) be shipwrecked (compare CASTAWAY). **cast down** depress, deject (compare DOWNCAST). **cast in stone** (of a decision etc.) irrevocably set. **cast loose** detach; detach oneself. **cast one's mind back** think back; recall an earlier time. **cast a wide net** (or **one's net wide**) cover a wide field of supply, activity, inquiry, etc. **cast off 1** abandon. **2** *Knitting* take the stitches off the needle by looping each over the next to finish the edge. **3** *Naut.* **a** set a ship free from a quay etc. **b** loosen and throw off (rope etc.). **cast on** *Knitting* make the first row of loops on the needle. **cast out** expel. **cast up 1** (of water) deposit (something) on the shore. **2** add up (figures etc.).

castanets *n.pl.* a pair of shell-shaped pieces of wood or ivory clicked together with the fingers, esp. as a rhythmic accompaniment to Spanish dance.

castaway ● *n.* **1** a shipwrecked person. **2** an outcast; a drifter. **3** a castoff. ● *adj.* **1** shipwrecked. **2** rejected.

caste /kæst/ *n.* **1** any of the Hindu hereditary classes whose members have no social contact with other classes, but are socially equal with one another and often follow the same occupations. **2** a more or less exclusive social class. **3** a system of such classes. **4** the position it confers. **5** *Zool.* a form of social insect having a particular function. □ **lose caste** descend in the social order. □ **casteism** *n.*

caster *n.* **1** a person who casts. **2** a small swivelled wheel (often one of a set) fixed to a leg (or the underside) of a piece of furniture. **3** a small container with holes in the top for sprinkling the contents (*sugar caster*). □ **castered** *adj.* (in sense 2).

castigate *v.tr.* rebuke or punish severely.

Castilian /kəˈstɪlɪən/ ● *n.* **1** a native of Castile in Spain. **2** the language of Castile, standard spoken and literary Spanish. ● *adj.* of or relating to Castile.

casting *n.* **1** an object made by casting, esp. of molten metal. **2** the action of allocating roles to performers. **3** the list of roles with the performers assigned to them. **4** the action of throwing out a fishing line into the water.

casting director *n.* a director responsible for assigning roles in a film, play, etc.

cast iron ● *n.* a hard alloy of iron, carbon, and silicon cast in a mould. ● *adj.* (also **cast-iron**) **1** made of cast iron. **2** hard, unchallengeable, unchangeable.

castle ● *n.* **1 a** a large fortified building or group of buildings; a stronghold. **b** a formerly fortified mansion. **2** *Chess* = ROOK[2]. ● *v. Chess* **1** *intr.* make a special move (once only in a game on each side) in which the king is moved two squares along the back rank and the nearer rook is moved to the square passed over by the king. **2** *tr.* move (the king) by castling. □ **castles in the air** (or **in Spain**) a visionary unattainable scheme; a daydream.

cast net *n.* *Fishing* a net thrown out and immediately drawn in.

cast-off ● *adj.* abandoned, discarded. ● *n.* (**castoff**) a cast-off person or thing.

castor[1] *var. of* CASTER 2,3.

castor[2] *n.* (also **castoreum** /kæsˈtɔːrɪəm/) a pungent, bitter-tasting, reddish-brown substance obtained from two perineal sacs of the beaver, formerly used in medicine and perfumes.

castor gras /grɒ/ *n.* *hist.* a beaver pelt used as clothing to soften it and to allow the long hairs to fall out, valuable during the fur trade.

castor oil *n.* an oil from the seeds of a plant, *Ricinus communis*, used as a purgative and lubricant.

castrate *v.tr.* **1** remove the testicles of; geld. **2** deprive of vigour or power. □ **castration** *n.*

casual ● *adj.* **1** accidental; due to chance. **2** not regular or permanent; temporary, occasional (*casual work*). **3 a** unconcerned, uninterested (*was very casual about it*). **b** made or done without great care or thought (*a casual remark*). **c** acting carelessly or unmethodically. **4** (of clothes) informal. **5** (of sexual activity) happening between individuals who are not regular or established sexual partners. ● *n.* **1** a casual worker. **2** (usu. in *pl.*) casual clothes or shoes. □ **casually** *adv.* **casualness** *n.*

casualty *n.* (*pl.* **-ies**) **1** a person killed or injured in a war or accident. **2** a thing lost or destroyed. **3** an accident, mishap, or disaster.

CAT *abbr. Med.* COMPUTERIZED AXIAL TOMOGRAPHY.

Cat *n.* *proprietary* = CATERPILLAR 2b.

cat *n.* **1** a small soft-furred four-legged domesticated animal, *Felis catus*. **2** any wild animal of the genus *Felis*, e.g. a lion, tiger, or leopard. **3** a catlike animal of any other species (*civet cat*). **4** *informal* a malicious or spiteful woman. **5** *slang* **a** a person; a fellow (*cool cat*). **b** a jazz enthusiast. **6** = CATFISH. **7** *Cdn* (*Nfld*) a young or newborn seal; a pup. □ **cat got your tongue?** *informal* don't you have anything to say? **cat's whiskers** (or **pyjamas** or **meow** or *Cdn* **ass**) *informal* an excellent person or thing. **first** (or **last**) **kick at the cat** one's first (or last) opportunity to do something. **let the cat out of the bag** reveal a secret, esp. involuntarily. **like a cat on a hot tin roof** (or **on hot bricks**) very agitated or agitatedly. **put** (or **set**) **the cat among the pigeons** cause trouble. **rain cats and dogs** rain very hard.

catabolism /kəˈtæbəˌlɪzəm/ *n.* the breakdown of complex molecules in living organisms to form simpler ones with the release of energy; destructive metabolism. □ **catabolic** /ˌkætəˈbɒlɪk/ *adj.*

cataclysm /ˈkætəˌklɪzəm/ *n.* **1 a** a violent, esp. social or political, upheaval or disaster. **b** a great change. **2** a great flood or deluge. □ **cataclysmic** *adj.* **cataclysmically** *adv.*

catacomb *n.* (often in *pl.*) **1** an underground cemetery, esp. a Roman subterranean gallery with recesses for tombs. **2** a cellar.

Catalan /ˈkætəlæn/ ● *n.* **1** a native of Catalonia in Spain. **2** the language of Catalonia. ● *adj.* of or relating to Catalonia or its people or language.

catalepsy /ˈkætəˌlɛpsɪ/ *n.* a state of trance or seizure with loss of sensation and consciousness accompanied by rigidity of the body. □ **cataleptic** *adj.* & *n.*

catalogne /ˌkætəˈlɒnjə/ *n.* *Cdn* (*Que.*) a kind of weaving using rags as the weft and widely spaced threads as the warp.

catalogue (also esp. *US* **catalog**) ● *n.* **1** a complete list of items (e.g. articles for sale, books held by a library), usu. in alphabetical or other systematic order and often with a description of each. **2** an extensive list (*a catalogue of crimes*). ● *v.tr.* (**catalogues**, **catalogued**, **cataloguing**; *US* **catalogs**, **cataloged**, **cataloging**) **1** make a catalogue of. **2** enter in a catalogue. □ **cataloguer** *n.*

catalpa /kəˈtælpə/ *n.* any tree of the genus *Catalpa*, with heart-shaped leaves, trumpet-shaped flowers, and long pods, planted as ornamentals.

catalysis /kə'tælɪsɪs/ n. (pl. **catalyses** /-,si:z/) the acceleration of a reaction by a catalyst.

catalyst n. **1** Chem. a substance that increases the rate of a reaction without itself undergoing any permanent chemical change. **2** a person or thing that precipitates a change.

catalytic /,kætə'lɪtɪk/ adj. Chem. relating to or involving catalysis. □ **catalytically** adv.

catalytic converter n. a device fitted in the exhaust system of some motor vehicles which converts pollutant gases into less harmful ones.

catalyze /'kætə,laɪz/ v.tr. (also **catalyse**) produce (a reaction) by catalysis.

catamaran /,kætəmə'ræn/ n. **1** a boat with twin hulls in parallel. **2** a raft of yoked logs or boats. **3** Cdn (Nfld) a heavy sled used for hauling wood.

catamount n. **1** a lynx, leopard, cougar, or similar cat. **2** a wild quarrelsome person.

cat and mouse n. a situation in which two opposing parties engage in prolonged wary manoeuvres (also attrib.: playing a cat-and-mouse game).

catapult ● n. **1** hist. a military machine worked by a lever and ropes for hurling large stones etc. **2** a mechanical device for launching a glider, an aircraft from the deck of a ship, etc. ● v. **1** intr. move suddenly and unexpectedly from one state or situation to another. **2** tr. **a** hurl from or launch with a catapult. **b** fling forcibly. **3** intr. leap or be hurled forcibly.

cataract n. **1 a** a large waterfall or cascade. **b** a downpour; a rush of water. **2 a** a disease in which the lens of the eye becomes cloudy, causing partial or total blindness. **b** an area clouded in this way.

catarrh /kə'tɑr/ n. **1** inflammation of the mucous membrane of the nose, air passages, etc. **2** a watery discharge in the nose or throat due to this. □ **catarrhal** adj.

catastrophe n. **1** a great and usu. sudden disaster. **2** the denouement of a tragedy. **3** a disastrous end; ruin. □ **catastrophic** adj. **catastrophically** adv.

catatonia /,kætə'to:niə/ n. **1** schizophrenia with intervals of catalepsy and sometimes violence. **2** catalepsy.

catatonic /,kætə'tɒnɪk/ ● adj. **1** affected by catatonia. **2** inert or unemotional, as if affected by catatonia. ● n. a person affected by catatonia.

catbird n. any of various birds with a characteristic mewing cry, esp. the N American songbird Dumetella carolinensis, having slate-coloured plumage. □ **catbird seat** a position of power or prominence.

cat burglar n. a burglar who enters by climbing to an upper storey.

catcall ● n. a shrill whistle of disapproval made at sports events, concerts, etc. ● v. **1** intr. make a catcall. **2** tr. make a catcall at.

catch ● v. (past and past part. **caught**) **1** tr. **a** lay hold of so as to restrain or prevent from escaping; capture in a trap, in one's hands, etc. **b** (also **catch hold of**) get into one's hands so as to retain, operate, etc. (caught hold of the handle). **2** tr. detect or surprise (a person, esp. in a wrongful or embarrassing act) (caught me in the act). **3** tr. intercept and hold (a moving thing) in the hands etc. (a bowl to catch the drips). **4** tr. **a** contract (a disease) by infection or contagion. **b** acquire (a quality or feeling) from another's example (caught her enthusiasm). **5** tr. **a** reach in time and board (an airplane, bus, etc.). **b** be in time to see etc. (a person or thing about to leave or finish) (if you hurry you'll catch them). **6** tr. **a** attend (catch a movie tonight). **b** meet with

(catch you later). **7** tr. apprehend (do you catch my meaning?). **8** tr. (of an artist etc.) reproduce faithfully. **9 a** intr. become fixed or entangled; be checked (the bolt caught). **b** tr. cause to do this (caught the kite in a tree). **c** tr. (often foll. by on) hit, deal a blow to (caught him on the nose). **10** tr. draw the attention of; captivate (caught my eye). **11** intr. **a** begin to burn. **b** (of an engine) start. **12** tr. capture and absorb or reflect (light) (catch some sun). **13** tr. be the recipient of (catch hell). **14** tr. (often foll. by up) reach or overtake (a person etc. ahead). **15** tr. check suddenly (caught her breath). **16** tr. (foll. by at) grasp or try to grasp. **17** refl. stop (oneself) just in time (caught myself before I said it). **18** intr. Baseball play as catcher. ● n. **1 a** an act of catching. **b** Baseball a chance or act of catching the ball. **2 a** an amount of a thing caught, esp. of fish. **b** a thing or person caught or worth catching, esp. in marriage. **3** a game in which a ball is thrown back and forth between two or more players. **4 a** a question, trick, etc., intended to deceive, incriminate, etc. **b** an unexpected or hidden difficulty or disadvantage. **5** a device for fastening a door, window, bag, etc. **6** a check or impediment in the voice, breath, throat, etc. **7** a snag in a sweater etc. **8** a fragment of a song. **9** Music a round, esp. with words arranged to produce a humorous effect. □ **catch-as-catch-can 1** a style of wrestling with few holds barred. **2** a situation where there are no rules; a free-for-all. **catch it** slang be punished or in trouble. **catch on** informal **1** (of a practice, fashion, etc.) become popular. **2** (of a person) understand what is meant. **catch out 1** detect in a mistake etc. **2** take unawares; cause to be bewildered or confused. **catch up 1 a** (often foll. by with) reach a person etc. ahead (caught up with us). **b** (often foll. by with, on) make up arrears (of work etc.). **2** snatch or pick up hurriedly. **3** (often in passive) **a** involve; entangle (caught up in intrigue). **b** fasten up (hair caught up in a ribbon).

Catch-22 n. (often attrib.) a dilemma or circumstance from which there is no escape because of mutually conflicting or dependent conditions.

catch-all n. (often attrib.) a thing designed to be all-inclusive.

catch-and-release n. (often attrib.) N Amer. a method of sport fishing in which anglers release fish immediately after catching them.

catch basin n. **1 a** a storm sewer or artificial pond for catching excess rainwater. **b** a receptacle to trap debris before it enters a storm sewer. **2** an area or organization which attracts people of a specific kind.

catcher n. **1** a person or thing that catches. **2** Baseball the fielder positioned behind home plate.

catching adj. **1 a** (of a disease) infectious. **b** (of a practice, habit, etc.) likely to be imitated. **2** attractive; captivating.

catchment n. **1** the act or process of collecting water. **2** a place where water is collected; a reservoir. **3** (in full **catchment area**) **a** the area from which rainfall flows into a river etc. **b** the area served by a school, hospital, etc.

catchphrase n. a phrase or slogan in frequent use.

catch-up n. (often attrib.) the act of attempting to reach someone or something which is ahead. □ **play catch-up** N Amer. & Austral. attempt to overtake an opponent or competitor.

catchword n. **1** a word or phrase in common (often temporary) use; a topical slogan. **2** a word placed so as to draw attention. **3** Theatre an actor's cue.

catchy adj. (**-ier, -iest**) **1** (of a tune, phrase, etc.) easy to remember. **2** capable of snaring or entrapping; deceptive. □ **catchily** adv. **catchiness** n.

catechetical /ˌkætəˈketɪkəl/ adj. (also **catechetic**)
1 of or by oral teaching. **2** according to the catechism
of a Christian religion. **3** consisting of or proceeding
by question and answer.

catechism /ˈkætəˌkɪzəm/ n. **1 a** a summary of the
principles of a Christian religion in the form of
questions and answers. **b** a book containing this. **2** a
series of questions put to anyone.

catechist /ˈkætəkɪst/ n. a teacher giving oral instruction in Christianity by means of a catechism.

catechize /ˈkætəˌkaiz/ v.tr. **1** instruct by means of
question and answer, esp. from a catechism. **2** put
questions to; examine. □ **catechizer** n.

catechumen /ˌkætəˈkjuːmən/ n. a Christian convert
under instruction before baptism.

categorical adj. unconditional, absolute; explicit,
direct (a categorical refusal). □ **categorically** adv.

categorize v.tr. place in a category or categories. □
categorization n.

category n. (pl. **-ies**) **1** a class or division. **2** Philos. **a**
one of a possibly exhaustive set of classes among
which all things might be distributed. **b** any relatively fundamental philosophical concept.

cater v. **1** a intr. (often foll. by for) provide food, drink,
etc. for a reception etc. **b** tr. N Amer. provide food for (a
party etc.). **2** intr. **a** (foll. by to, for) provide for; meet the
needs of. **b** (foll. by to) pander to (one's whims etc.). □
caterer n. **catering** n.

caterpillar n. **1 a** the larva of a butterfly or moth. **b**
(in general use) any similar larva of various insects. **2**
(often attrib.) **a** an endless articulated steel tread passing around the wheels of a tractor etc. for travel on
rough ground. **b** (**Caterpillar**) proprietary a vehicle
equipped with these treads.

caterwaul ● v.intr. make the shrill howl of a cat. ● n. a
caterwauling noise.

cat fight n. **1** a dispute in which the participants are
spiteful and unrestrained. **2** a malicious fight or
dispute between women. **3** a fight between cats.

catfish n. (pl. same) any of numerous fishes of the
order Siluriformes, usu. inhabiting fresh water and
having whisker-like barbels around the mouth.

catgut n. a material made from the twisted intestines of a sheep, horse, or other animal, and used to
make the strings of musical instruments, racquets,
and surgical sutures.

catharsis /kəˈθɑːrsɪs/ n. (pl. **catharses** /-siːz/) **1** a
release or relieving of emotions, esp. through drama
or art. **2** Psych. the process of freeing and eliminating
repressed emotion. **3** Med. purgation.

cathartic /kəˈθɑːrtɪk/ ● adj. **1** effecting catharsis. **2**
purgative. ● n. a cathartic drug. □ **cathartically** adv.

cathedral n. the principal church of a diocese, containing the bishop's throne.

cathedral ceiling n. N Amer. a high usu. sloping or
vaulted ceiling, esp. one with exposed rafters, e.g. in
the entryway or living room of a house.

catheter /ˈkæθətər/ n. Med. a tube for insertion into a
body cavity or blood vessel for introducing or removing fluid etc.

cathode /ˈkæθoːd/ n. Electricity **1** the negative electrode in an electrolytic cell or electronic valve or
tube. **2** the positive terminal of a primary cell such as
a battery (opp. ANODE). □ **cathodic** /kəˈθɒdɪk/ adj.

cathode ray n. a beam of electrons emitted from
the cathode of a high-vacuum tube.

cathode ray tube n. a high-vacuum tube in which
cathode rays produce a luminous image on a fluorescent screen, used in televisions etc. Abbr.: **CRT**.

catholic ● adj. **1** (**Catholic**) of the Roman Catholic
religion. **2** pertaining to the ancient Church before
the great schism between East and West, or the
Western Church after the schism and before the
Reformation, or to any Church standing in historical
continuity with it. **3** all-embracing; of wide sympathies or interests (has catholic tastes). **4** of interest or
use to all; universal. ● n. (**Catholic**) a Roman
Catholic. □ **Catholicism** /kəˈθɒlɪˌsɪzəm/ n.

cation /ˈkætˌaiən, -aiən/ n. a positively charged ion; an
ion that is attracted to the cathode in electrolysis
(opp. ANION). □ **cationic** adj.

catkin n. a spike of usu. downy or silky unisexual
flowers hanging from a willow, hazel, or other tree.

catlike adj. **1** like a cat. **2** stealthy.

cat litter n. granular absorbent material, usu. clay,
for lining a box for a cat to urinate and defecate in
indoors.

catnap ● n. a short sleep. ● v.intr. (**catnapped**,
catnapping) have a catnap.

catnip n. a white-flowered herb of the mint family,
Nepeta cataria, having a smell attractive to cats.

CAT scan n. a medical examination using an X-ray
apparatus which produces a series of detailed cross-
sectional pictures of internal organs, esp. the brain. □
CAT scanner n.

cat's cradle n. a child's game in which a loop of
string is held between the fingers and patterns are
formed.

catskinner n. N Amer. the operator of a vehicle
equipped with caterpillar treads.

cat's-paw n. **1** a person used as a mere instrument
by another. **2** a slight breeze rippling the surface of
an area of water.

catsuit n. a close-fitting garment with trouser legs,
covering the body from neck to feet.

catsup /ˈkætsəp/ esp. US var. of KETCHUP.

cattail n. N Amer. = BULRUSH 2.

cattle n.pl. large ruminant animals with horns and
cloven hoofs, e.g. cows, bison, and buffalo, esp. of the
genus Bos.

cattle guard n. N Amer. a ditch covered by metal bars
spaced so as to allow vehicles and pedestrians to pass
over but not cattle or other animals.

cattleman n. (pl. **-men**) N Amer. a person who tends or
rears cattle.

cat train n. Cdn (North) a series of linked freight-
carrying sleds hauled over snow by a tractor
equipped with caterpillar treads.

catty adj. (**-ier, -iest**) **1** sly, spiteful; deliberately
hurtful. **2** catlike. □ **cattily** adv. **cattiness** n.

catwalk n. **1** a narrow footway along a bridge, above
a theatre stage, etc. **2** a narrow platform along which
models walk during a fashion show.

Caucasian /kɒˈkeiʒən/ ● adj. **1** of or relating to the
white or light-skinned race of humans originally
inhabiting Europe, N Africa, and the Middle East. **2** of
or relating to the Caucasus or its its people. **3** of or
relating to the non-Indo-European languages of this
region, e.g. Georgian. ● n. a Caucasian person.

caucus n. (pl. **caucuses**) **1** N Amer. & NZ **a** the
members of a legislative assembly belonging to a
particular party. **b** a subgroup of these comprising
the members from a particular region. **c** a closed-
door meeting of either of these groups to discuss
policy etc. **2** a group sharing common political goals,
esp. a faction within a larger group. **3** a usu. secret
meeting of a small group of people to discuss matters
concerning a larger group.

caudal /ˈkɒdəl/ adj. **1** of or like a tail. **2** of the posterior part of the body.

caught past and past part. of CATCH.

caul n. **1 a** the inner membrane enclosing a fetus. **b** part of this occasionally found on a child's head at birth, thought to bring good luck. **2 a** the omentum. **b** the omentum of cattle, pigs, and other animals used as food.

cauldron n. **1 a** a large deep bowl-shaped vessel for boiling over an open fire. **b** an ornamental vessel resembling this. **2** a volatile or chaotic situation.

cauliflower n. **1** a variety of cabbage with a large white flower head of immature buds in its centre. **2** the flower head eaten as a vegetable.

caulk[1] /kɔk/ ● v.tr. **1** fill (a seam, crack, etc.) with a watertight or airtight material. **2** make something watertight or airtight by this method. ● n. (also **caulking**) a substance used to caulk. □ **caulker** n.

caulk[2] /kɒk, kɔk/ N Amer. ● n. **1** a small spike fitted to the sole of a boot to resist slipping. **2** (in full **caulk boot**) a boot equipped with such spikes, used esp. by loggers. ● v.tr. furnish (a boot) with caulks.

causal adj. **1** of, forming, or expressing a cause or causes. **2** relating to, or of the nature of, cause and effect. □ **causally** adv.

causality n. **1** the relation of cause and effect. **2** the principle that everything has a cause.

causation n. **1** the act of causing or producing an effect. **2** = CAUSALITY.

causative adj. **1** acting as cause. **2** (foll. by of) producing; having as effect. **3** Grammar expressing cause. □ **causatively** adv.

cause ● n. **1 a** that which produces an effect, or gives rise to an action, phenomenon, or condition. **b** a person or thing that occasions something. **c** a reason or motive; a ground that may be held to justify something (no cause for complaint). **2** a reason adjudged adequate (he was asked to show cause why he shouldn't be held in contempt of court). **3** a principle, belief, or purpose which is advocated or supported (faithful to the cause). **4 a** a matter to be settled at law. **b** an individual's case offered at law. **5** the side taken by any party in a dispute. ● v.tr. **1** be the cause of, produce, make happen (caused a commotion). **2** induce (caused me to smile; caused it to be done). □ **cause and effect 1** a cause and the effect it produces; the doctrine of causation. **2** the operation or relation of a cause and its effect. **in the cause of** to maintain, defend, or support (in the cause of justice). **make common cause with** join the side of.

'cause conj. & adv. informal = BECAUSE.

cause célèbre /ˌkɒz seˈleb, koːz, sei-, -lebrə/ n. (pl. **causes célèbres** pronunc. same) a lawsuit or other affair that attracts much attention.

causeway n. **1** a raised road or track across low or wet ground or water. **2** a raised path by a road.

caustic ● adj. **1** capable of burning or corroding organic tissue. **2** sarcastic, biting. **3** strongly alkaline. ● n. a caustic substance. □ **caustically** adv. **causticity** n.

caution ● n. **1** attention to safety; prudence, carefulness. **2** a warning. **3** Cdn, Brit., & Austral. Law a warning to an arrested person that his or her statements may be used as evidence in court. **4** informal an amusing or surprising person or thing. ● v. **1** tr. & intr. (often foll. by against, or to + infin.) warn or admonish. **2** tr. Cdn, Brit., & Austral. Law issue a caution to. □ **throw caution to the wind** act imprudently or rashly, esp. intentionally.

cautionary adj. giving or serving as a warning.

cautious adj. careful, prudent. □ **cautiously** adv. **cautiousness** n.

cavalcade n. a procession of riders, vehicles, etc.

cavalier /ˌkævəˈliːr/ ● n. **1** a gallant or fashionable man, esp. escorting a woman. **2** hist. (**Cavalier**) a supporter of Charles I in the English Civil War (1642–9). ● adj. offhand, haughtily careless in manner, supercilious. □ **cavalierly** adv.

cavalry n. (pl. **-ies**) (usu. treated as pl.) **1** soldiers on horseback. **2** soldiers in armoured vehicles.

cave ● n. **1** a large natural underground hollow, esp. with a roughly horizontal opening. **2** a cellar for storing wine etc. ● v.intr. explore caves, esp. interconnecting or underground. □ **cave in 1 a** (of a wall, earth over a hollow, etc.) subside, collapse. **b** cause (wall, earth, etc.) to do this. **2** yield or submit under pressure; give up. □ **cavelike** adj.

caveat /ˈkævɪˌæt/ n. a warning or proviso.

caveat emptor /ˈemptɔr/ n. the principle that the buyer alone is responsible if dissatisfied.

cave-in n. a collapse, submission, etc.

caveman n. (pl. **-men**) **1** a prehistoric human, esp. one using a cave as shelter. **2** a crude person.

cavern n. an underground hollow; a vast cave.

cavernous adj. of or resembling a cavern in size or appearance (a cavernous hall). □ **cavernously** adv.

caviar n. the pickled roe of sturgeon or other large fish, eaten as a delicacy.

cavil /ˈkævəl/ ● v.intr. (**cavilled, cavilling**) (usu. foll. by at, about) carp. ● n. a trivial objection.

caving n. the exploration of caves as a sport or recreation.

cavity n. (pl. **-ies**) **1** a hollow within a solid body. **2** a decayed part of a tooth.

cavort v.intr. prance; jump, dance, or behave excitedly or happily.

CAW abbr. Canadian Auto Workers.

caw ● n. the harsh cry of a crow, raven, etc. ● v.intr. utter this cry.

cayenne /kaiˈen, ˈkaien, keiˈen, ˈkeien/ n. (in full **cayenne pepper**) a pungent red powder obtained from the ground fruit and seeds of various capsicums, used as a seasoning.

cayman var. of CAIMAN.

Cayuga /keiˈuːgə/ n. **1** a member of an Iroquoian people originally inhabiting central New York State, now living mainly on the Six Nations reserve near Brantford, Ont. **2** the Iroquoian language of this people. □ **Cayugan** adj.

cayuse /ˈkaiuːs, ˈkei-/ n. N Amer. **1** a feral or domesticated mustang or pony in the west, esp. one tamed by Aboriginal peoples. **2** informal a horse.

CB abbr. citizens' band (radio).

CBA abbr. **1** Canadian Bar Association. **2** Canadian Booksellers' Association. **3** Canadian Basketball Association.

CBC abbr. Canadian Broadcasting Corporation.

CBD abbr. CENTRAL BUSINESS DISTRICT.

CC abbr. Companion of the Order of Canada.

cc ● abbr. (also **c.c.**) **1** cubic centimetre(s). **2** carbon copy. ● n. (pl. **cc's**) a cubic centimetre.

CCD abbr. CHARGE-COUPLED DEVICE.

CCF abbr. Cdn hist. CO-OPERATIVE COMMONWEALTH FEDERATION. □ **CCFer** n.

CD[1] abbr. **1** Civil Defence. **2** Corps Diplomatique.

CD[2] n. a compact disc.

Cd symbol cadmium.

cd abbr. candela.

CD-I abbr. compact disc-interactive.

CDIC abbr. Canada Deposit Insurance Corporation.

Cdn. abbr. Canadian.

Cdr abbr. COMMANDER.

Cdre. abbr. Commodore.

CD-ROM abbr. compact disc read-only memory (for storage and retrieval of text or data on a computer).

CDT abbr. Central Daylight Time.

CD video n. a system of simultaneously reproducing high-quality sound and video pictures from a CD.

CE abbr. **1** civil engineer. **2** Common Era.

Ce symbol cerium.

cease v.tr. & intr. stop; bring or come to an end (ceased to exist). □ **without cease** continually, unrelentingly.

ceasefire n. Military **1** an order to stop firing. **2** a period of truce; a suspension of hostilities.

ceaseless adj. without end; not ceasing. □ **ceaselessly** adv.

cecum /ˈsiːkəm/ n. (pl. **ceca** /-kə/) a pouch-like cavity at the junction of the small and large intestines.

cedar n. **1** any evergreen conifer of the genus *Cedrus*, native to the region from the E Mediterranean to central Asia, having tufts of short needles and cones of papery scales. **2** any of various similar conifers yielding timber, including species of arborvitae, cypress, and juniper. **3** (in full **cedarwood**) the fragrant durable wood of any cedar tree, often used to line closets etc. □ **cedary** adj.

cedar shake n. N Amer. a type of shingle made from cedar, with at least one face split rather than sawn.

cedarstrip n. Cdn (usu. attrib.) a technique for making boats, esp. canoes, consisting of long strips of cedar.

cedar swamp n. N Amer. an area of swamp or bog in which cedars are the predominant trees.

cedar waxwing n. (also **cedar bird**) a N American waxwing, *Bombycilla cedrorum*, having brownish plumage with red-tipped wings and a yellow belly and tail tip.

cede v.tr. **1** give up one's rights to or possession of. **2** transfer possession of.

cedilla /səˈdɪlə/ n. **1** a mark written under the letter *c* in French and Portuguese to show that it is sibilant (as in *façade*). **2** a similar mark under *c* or *s* to distinguish voiceless from voiced consonants in modern Turkish.

CEF abbr. hist. Canadian Expeditionary Force.

CEGEP /ˈsiːdʒep, ˈseɪʒep/ abbr. (also **Cegep**) (in Quebec) Collège d'enseignement général et professionnel, a post-secondary educational institution offering two-year programs for preparation for university and three-year training programs in professions and trades.

ceilidh /ˈkeɪli/ n. **1** a party featuring traditional Scottish or Irish music, dancing, songs, and stories. **2** a concert at which traditional Scottish music and dancing are performed.

ceiling n. **1 a** the upper interior surface of a room or other similar compartment. **b** the material forming this. **2** an upper limit on prices, wages, performance, etc. **3** Aviation the maximum altitude a given aircraft can reach. **4** the altitude of the base of a cloud layer. □ **ceilinged** adj. (in comb.).

ceiling fan n. a fan suspended from a ceiling, having long blades to circulate air.

ceinture fléchée /sætuːr fleɪˈʃeɪ/ n. (pl. **ceintures fléchées** pronunc. same) Cdn hist. a long, brightly coloured sash woven with an arrow-shaped pattern and worn around the waist, esp. by voyageurs.

cel /sel/ n. a transparent sheet of celluloid etc. which

can be drawn on and used in combination with others in the production of animated films.

celadon /ˈselə,dɒn/ • n. **1** a pale greyish shade of green. **2** a grey-green glaze used on some pottery or porcelain. • adj. of a grey-green colour.

celeb /səˈleb/ n. informal a celebrity.

celebrant /ˈseləbrənt/ n. **1** a person who performs a rite, esp. a priest who officiates at the Eucharist. **2** a person participating in a celebration. **3** a person who celebrates or praises someone or something.

celebrate v. **1** tr. mark (a festival or special event) with festivities etc. **2** intr. engage in festivities, usu. after a special event etc. **3** tr. perform publicly and duly (a religious ceremony etc.). **4 a** tr. officiate at (the Eucharist). **b** intr. officiate, esp. at the Eucharist. **5** tr. make publicly known; extol, praise widely. □ **celebration** n. **celebrator** n. **celebratory** adj.

celebrated adj. publicly honoured, widely known.

celebrity n. (pl. **-ies**) **1** a well-known person. **2** fame. □ **celebrityhood** n.

celery n. an umbelliferous plant, *Apium graveolens*, with closely packed leaf stalks used as a vegetable.

celestial adj. **1** heavenly; divinely good or beautiful; sublime. **2 a** of the sky; of that part of the sky commonly observed in astronomy etc. **b** of heavenly bodies. □ **celestially** adv.

celestial equator n. the great circle of the sky in the plane perpendicular to the earth's axis.

celestial sphere n. an imaginary sphere of which the observer is the centre and in which celestial objects are represented as lying.

celiac /ˈsiːliˌæk/ adj. **1** of or pertaining to the abdominal cavity. **2** afflicted with celiac disease.

celiac disease n. a digestive disorder of the small intestine, causing chronic failure to digest food properly unless gluten is excluded from the diet.

celibate /ˈselɪbət/ • adj. **1** committed to abstention from sexual relations and from marriage, esp. for religious reasons. **2** abstaining from sexual relations. • n. a celibate person. □ **celibacy** n.

cell n. **1** a small room, esp. in a prison or monastery. **2** a compartment, e.g. in a honeycomb. **3** a small group operating as a local branch of a political movement, esp. of a subversive kind. **4** Computing a location or address where a piece of information is stored, esp. in a spreadsheet or database. **5** the local area covered by one of the short-range radio transmitters in a cellular telephone system. **6** Biol. **a** the basic structural and functional unit of an organism, usu. microscopic, consisting of cytoplasm and a nucleus enclosed in a membrane. **b** an enclosed cavity in an organism etc. **7** Electricity **a** a battery or other device for generating electricity or producing electrolysis from chemical energy. **b** = SOLAR CELL. **8** an atmospheric mass with roughly uniform properties (high-pressure cell).

cellar • n. **1** a room below ground level in a house, often used for storage of food and wine. **2** a stock of wine in a cellar (has a good cellar). **3** N Amer. Sport informal = BASEMENT 2. • v.tr. store or put in a cellar.

cellblock n. one of several sections of cells into which a large prison is divided.

cello /ˈtʃeloʊ/ n. (pl. **-os**) the second-largest instrument of the violin family, held upright on the floor between the knees of the seated player. □ **cellist** n.

Cellophane /ˈseləˌfeɪn/ n. proprietary a thin transparent packaging material made from viscose.

cellular • adj. **1 a** of or having small compartments or cavities. **b** porous. **2** of or consisting of biological cells. **3** (of a fabric etc.) having an open texture. **4** (of a plant) having no distinct stem, leaves, etc. **5** (of a telephone system) using a number of short-range radio transmitters to cover a large area, the signal being switched from one transmitter to the next as the user travels. ● *n.* **1** a cellular telephone. **2** a cellular telephone system.

cellular telephone *n.* (also **cellphone, cellular phone**) a portable telephone which operates by means of a cellular network.

cellulite *n.* fatty tissue regarded as causing a dimpled or lumpy texture on the hips and thighs.

celluloid /'seljə,lɔɪd/ ● *n.* **1** a transparent flammable plastic made from camphor and nitrocellulose. **2** motion-picture film. ● *adj.* **1** made of celluloid. **2** relating to film or motion pictures.

cellulose /'seljə,lo:s, -,lo:z/ *n.* **1** *Biochem.* a carbohydrate forming the main constituent of the cell walls of plants, used in the production of textile fibres. **2** a compound of this (esp. cellulose acetate or nitrocellulose) in solution, used as a base for paints etc.

cellulose acetate *n.* an insoluble compound derived from cellulose, used to make lacquers, textiles, etc.

Celsius *adj.* of or denoting a temperature on the Celsius scale, with 0° as the freezing point of water and 100° as the boiling point.

Celt /kelt, selt/ *n.* a member of a group of W European peoples, including the pre-Roman inhabitants of Britain and Gaul and their descendants, esp. in Ireland, Wales, Scotland, Cornwall, Brittany, etc.

Celtic ● *adj.* of or relating to the Celts. ● *n.* a group of languages spoken by Celtic peoples, including Gaelic, Welsh, Cornish, Manx, and Breton.

cement ● *n.* **1 a** a powdery substance made by calcining lime and clay, mixed with water to form mortar or used in concrete. **b** concrete. ¶The use of *cement* to mean *concrete* rather than the binding substance in concrete has been criticized, but *Cement* is the older word, and in non-technical use such uses as *cement floor* or *cement sidewalk* are unambiguous. **2** any substance that hardens on setting. **3** a uniting factor or principle. **4** a substance for filling cavities in teeth. ● *v.tr.* **1 a** unite with or as with cement. **b** establish or strengthen (a friendship etc.). **2** line or cover with cement.

cement mixer *n.* a machine (usu. with a revolving drum) for mixing cement with water.

cemetery *n.* (*pl.* **-ies**) a place where people are buried.

cenotaph /'senə,tæf/ *n.* a tomblike monument, esp. a war memorial, to a person or persons whose bodies are interred elsewhere.

Cenozoic /,si:nə'zo:ɪk, ,sen-/ *adj.* of, relating to, or denoting the most recent geological era, following the Mesozoic and lasting from about 65 million years ago to the present day (compare MESOZOIC, PALEOZOIC).

cens /sãs/ *n.* (*pl.* same) *Cdn hist.* a token payment made to a seigneur by a habitant, reaffirming the feudal nature of the land tenure.

censer /'sensər/ *n.* a vessel in which incense is burned, esp. during a religious ceremony etc.

censitaire /sãsi'ter/ *n. Cdn hist.* a tenant on a seigneury.

censor /'sensər/ ● *n.* an official authorized to examine printed matter, films, news, etc., before public release, and to suppress any parts on the grounds of obscenity, threats to security, etc. ● *v.tr.* **1** act as a censor of. **2** make deletions or changes in. □ **censorial** /-'sɔːrɪəl/ *adj.* **censorship** *n.*

censorious /sen'sɔːrɪəs/ *adj.* severely critical; quick or eager to criticize. □ **censoriousness** *n.*

censure ● *v.tr.* criticize harshly; reprove. ● *n.* harsh criticism; expression of disapproval.

census *n.* (*pl.* **censuses**) an official count of a population or of a class of things, often with various statistics noted.

cent *n.* **1 a** a monetary unit in various countries, equal to one-hundredth of a dollar or other decimal currency unit. **b** a coin of this value. **2** *informal* a very small sum of money. **3** *see* PER CENT.

cent. *abbr.* century.

centaur /'sentɔːr/ *n. Gk Myth.* a creature with the head, arms, and torso of a man and the body and legs of a horse.

centenary /sen'tenəri, -ti'nɛəri/ ● *n.* (*pl.* **-ies**) **1** a centennial. **2** a celebration of this. ● *adj.* of or relating to a centenary.

centennial /sen'tenɪəl/ *esp. N Amer.* ● *n.* a hundredth anniversary. ● *adj.* **1** lasting for a hundred years or occurring every hundred years. **2** of or concerning a centennial; in Canada, esp. of Confederation, in 1967.

center etc. *var. of* CENTRE etc.

centi- *comb. form* **1** one-hundredth, esp. of a unit in the metric system (*centimetre*). **2** hundred. Abbr.: **c.**

centigrade /'sentɪ,greɪd/ *adj.* **1** = CELSIUS. **2** having a scale of a hundred degrees.

centigram *n.* a metric unit of mass, equal to one-hundredth of a gram.

centilitre *n.* (also esp. *US* **centiliter**) a metric unit of capacity, equal to one-hundredth of a litre.

centimetre *n.* (also esp. *US* **centimeter**) a metric unit of length, equal to one-hundredth of a metre (0.394 in.).

centimetre-gram-second system *n.* the system using the centimetre, gram, and second as basic units of length, mass, and time.

centipede *n.* any arthropod of the class Chilopoda, with a wormlike body of many segments each with a pair of legs.

central ● *adj.* **1** of, at, or forming the centre. **2** from the centre. **3** chief, essential, most important. **4** *attrib.adj.* denoting a house's heating, air conditioning, or vacuum system in which the rooms are connected via pipes, ducts, or tubes to a single source of heat, cool air, or suction. ● *n. N Amer. informal* a place with a high concentration of a specified thing etc. (*cowboy central*). □ **centrality** *n.* **centrally** *adv.*

Central America *n.* the southernmost part of N America, linking the continent to S America. □ **Central American** *n. & adj.*

central bank *n.* a national bank issuing currency etc.

central business district *n.* the area of a town or city where business, shopping, administrative, and entertainment facilities are most densely located.

Central Canada *n.* see CENTRAL PROVINCES.

Central Intelligence Agency *n.* a US federal agency responsible for coordinating government intelligence activities. Abbr.: **CIA**.

centralism *n.* a system that centralizes (esp. an administration). □ **centralist** *n.*

centralize *v.* **1** *tr. & intr.* bring or come to a centre. **2** *tr.* **a** concentrate (administration) at a single centre. **b** subject (a state) to this system. □ **centralization** *n.* **centralizer** *n.*

central nervous system *n. Anat.* the complex of nerve tissues that controls the activities of the body, in vertebrates the brain and spinal cord.

central planning *n.* the complete planning of an

economy by a central authority which controls all prices, wages, and production.

central processing unit n. (also **central processor**) the part of a computer which controls the system and performs arithmetical and logical operations on data. Abbr.: **CPU**.

Central provinces n.pl. Ontario and Quebec.

Central Time n. the time in a zone including Saskatchewan, Manitoba, and the central US states. **Central Standard Time** is six hours behind GMT; **Central Daylight Time** is 5 hours behind GMT.

centre (also **center**) ● n. **1** the middle point, esp. of a line, circle, or sphere, equidistant from the ends or from any point on the circumference or surface. **2** a pivot or axis of rotation. **3 a** a place or group of buildings forming a central point in a district, city, etc., or a main area for an activity (town centre). **b** a place or group of buildings with a specified function (detention centre). **c** (with preceding word) a piece or set of equipment for a number of connected functions (entertainment centre). **4** a point of concentration or dispersion; a nucleus or source. **5** a political party or group holding moderate opinions. **6** the filling in a chocolate etc. **7** Sport the middle player in a line or group in some games, esp.: **a** (in hockey) the forward who takes faceoffs at centre ice. **b** (in football) the offensive lineman who snaps the ball to the quarterback, punter, etc. **c** (in basketball) the forward who plays near the net. **8** Sport a pass from the side to the centre of the playing area, esp. in the offensive zone. **9** (attrib.) of or at the centre. ● v. **1** intr. (foll. by in, on, around) have as its main centre or focus. **2** tr. place in the centre. **3** tr. mark with a centre. **4** tr. (foll. by in etc.) concentrate. **5** tr. Sport pass (the ball, puck, etc.) from the side to the centre of the playing area, esp. in the offensive zone. **6** tr. Hockey be a centreman for (two wingers) or on (a line) (centres the checking line). □ **centred** adj. (often in comb.). **centredness** n. (usu. in comb.). **centremost** adj. **centric** adj. **centrical** adj. **centricity** n.

centreboard n. a retractable keel on a sailboat.

centre field n. Baseball **1** the part of the outfield between left field and right field. **2** the position of the player who covers this area. □ **centre fielder** n.

centrefold n. **1** a centre spread of a magazine laid out as a unit, often with a portion that folds out. **2** a usu. naked or scantily clad model pictured on such a spread.

centre ice n. the central area of a rink, esp. the spot where faceoffs take place at the start of each period and after every goal.

centreman n. (pl. **-men**) = CENTRE n. 7a.

centre of attention n. a person or thing that draws general attention.

centre of gravity n. **1** a point from which the weight of a body or system may be considered to act. **2** the point or object of greatest importance etc.

centrepiece n. **1** an ornament for the middle of a table. **2** a principal item.

centre stage ● n. **1** the central, most prominent area on a theatrical stage. **2** the most prominent position. ● adv. in or into this position.

centrifugal /,sen'trɪfjəgəl, sentrɪ'fju:gəl/ adj. moving or tending to move from a centre.

centrifugal force n. an apparent force that acts outwards on a body moving about a centre.

centrifuge /'sentrɪ,fju:dʒ/ ● n. a machine with a rapidly rotating device designed to separate liquids from solids or other liquids. ● v.tr. **1** subject to the

action of a centrifuge. **2** separate by centrifuge. □ **centrifugation** /-fju'geɪʃən/ n.

centripetal /sen'trɪpətəl/ adj. moving or tending to move towards a centre.

centripetal force n. the force acting on a body in circular motion directing it towards the centre of rotation.

centrist n. Politics a person who holds moderate views. □ **centrism** n.

centurion /sen'tʃɜrɪən, -'tʃʊrɪən/ n. the commander of a century in the ancient Roman army.

century n. (pl. **-ies**) **1 a** a period of one hundred years. **b** any of the centuries reckoned from the supposed date of the birth of Christ. ¶In older use, the twentieth century was reckoned from 1901–2000. In modern use it is often reckoned as 1900–1999. **2** Sport **a** a score etc. of a hundred, esp. a hundred runs by one batsman in cricket. **b** a group or total of a hundred (first to reach the century mark this season). **3** a company in the ancient Roman army, originally of 100 men.

century home n. Cdn (also **century house**) **1** a house which is about one hundred years old. **2** any house designed or decorated in century-old styles.

century plant n. a plant, Agave americana, flowering once in many years and yielding sap from which tequila is distilled.

CEO abbr. = CHIEF EXECUTIVE OFFICER.

cep /sep/ n. an edible mushroom, Boletus edulis, with a stout stalk and brown smooth cap.

cephalic /sə'fælɪk/ adj. of or in the head.

cephalopod /'sefələ,pɒd/ n. any mollusc of the class Cephalopoda, having a well-developed head surrounded by tentacles, e.g. octopus, squid, etc.

cephalosporin /,sefələ:'spɔrɪn/ n. any of a class of semi-synthetic antibiotics derived from a mould of the genus Cephalosporium.

ceramic ● adj. **1** designating or pertaining to hard brittle substances produced by the process of strong heating of a non-metallic mineral, esp. clay. **2** of or relating to pottery. ● n. **1** a ceramic article or product. **2** a substance, esp. clay, used to make ceramic articles.

ceramics n.pl. **1** ceramic products. **2** (usu. treated as sing.) the art of making ceramic articles.

cereal ● n. **1** (usu. in pl.) **a** any kind of grain used for food. **b** any grass producing this, e.g. wheat, corn, rye, etc. **2** a breakfast food made from a cereal. ● adj. of edible grain or products of it.

cerebellum /,serə'beləm/ n. (pl. **-s** or **cerebella** /-lə/) the part of the brain at the back of the skull in vertebrates, which coordinates and regulates muscular activity. □ **cerebellar** adj.

cerebral /sə'ri:brəl, 'serəbrəl/ adj. **1** of the brain. **2** intellectual, not emotional. □ **cerebrally** adv.

cerebral cortex n. the intricately folded outer layer of the cerebrum.

cerebral hemisphere n. each of the two halves of the vertebrate cerebrum.

cerebral palsy n. a condition marked by weakness and impaired coordination of the limbs, esp. caused by damage to the brain before or at birth.

cerebrospinal /sə'ri:bro:'spaɪnəl/ adj. of the brain and spine.

cerebrospinal fluid n. a clear fluid surrounding the brain and spinal cord. Abbr.: **CSF**.

cerebrum /sə'ri:brəm, 'serə-/ n. (pl. **cerebra** /-brə/) the principal part of the brain in vertebrates, located in the front area of the skull, which integrates complex sensory and neural functions.

ceremonial ● *adj.* **1** concerning or used in ritual or ceremony. **2** formal (*a ceremonial bow*). ● *n.* **1** a system of rites etc. to be used esp. at a formal or religious occasion. **2** one of these rites. □ **ceremonially** *adv.*

ceremonious *adj.* behaving or performed in a formal, ritualistic, or elaborate way. □ **ceremoniously** *adv.* **ceremoniousness** *n.*

ceremony *n.* (*pl.* **-ies**) **1** a formal religious or public rite, observance, or occasion, esp. celebrating a particular event or anniversary. **2** formalities, esp. of an empty or ritualistic kind. **3** excessively polite behaviour (*bowed with great ceremony*). □ **stand on ceremony** insist on the observance of formalities. **without ceremony** informally.

cerise /sə'riːz, -'riːs/ ● *adj.* of a dark clear red. ● *n.* this colour.

cerium /'sɪːrɪəm/ *n.* a silvery metallic element occurring naturally in various minerals and used in the manufacture of lighter flints.

cert *n. slang* (esp. **dead cert**) **1** an event or result regarded as certain to happen. **2** a racehorse etc. regarded as certain to win.

cert. *abbr.* **1** certificate. **2** certified.

certain ● *adj.* **1 a** confident, convinced (*certain that I put it here*). **b** indisputable; known for sure (*it is certain that he is guilty*). **2 a** that may be relied on to happen (*it is certain to rain*). **b** destined (*certain to become a star*). **3** definite, unfailing, reliable (*a certain indication of the coming storm*). **4** (of a person, place, etc.) that might be specified, but is not (*a certain lady*). **5** some though not much (*a certain reluctance*). **6** (of a person, place, etc.) existing, though probably unknown to the reader or hearer (*a certain John Smith*). ● *pron.* (as *pl.*) some but not all (*certain of them*). □ **for certain** without doubt. **make certain** = MAKE SURE (see SURE).

certainly *adv.* **1** undoubtedly, definitely. **2** confidently. **3** yes; by all means.

certainty *n.* (*pl.* **-ies**) **1 a** an undoubted fact. **b** a certain prospect (*his return is a certainty*). **2** an absolute conviction (*has a certainty of his own worth*). **3** a thing or person that may be relied on (*a certainty to win*). □ **for a certainty** beyond the possibility of doubt.

certifiable *adj.* **1** able or needing to be certified. **2** *informal* insane.

certificate ● *n.* a formal document attesting a fact, esp. birth, marriage, or death, a medical condition, a level of achievement, a fulfillment of requirements, ownership of shares, etc. ● *v.tr.* (esp. as **certificated** *adj.*) provide with or license or attest by a certificate. □ **certification** *n.*

certified cheque *n.* a cheque the validity of which is guaranteed by a bank.

certified general accountant *n. Cdn* an accountant authorized to sign audit statements.

certified management accountant *n.* (in Canada) an accountant qualified to manage the finances of an organization for internal purposes.

certify *v.tr.* (**-ies, -ied**) **1** make a formal statement of; attest; attest to. **2 a** declare by certificate that a person is qualified or competent (*certified as a bookkeeper*). **b** declare by certificate that something has met esp. safety standards (*the car has been certified*). **3** officially declare insane (*he should be certified*).

certitude *n.* **1** a feeling of absolute certainty or conviction. **2** a belief held with absolute certainty.

cerulean /sə'ruːlɪən/ *literary* ● *adj.* deep blue like a clear sky. ● *n.* this colour.

cervical *adj.* **1** of or relating to the neck (*cervical vertebrae*). **2** of or relating to the cervix (*cervical cancer*).

cervical cap *n.* a contraceptive device consisting of a small cap of a rubber-like plastic placed over the cervix to prevent the passage of sperm.

cervical collar *n.* a band worn round the neck to support it after whiplash injuries etc.

cervical screening *n.* examination of a large number of apparently healthy women for cervical cancer.

cervix *n.* (*pl.* **cervices** /'sɜːvɪˌsiːz/) *Anat.* **1** the narrow lower part of the uterus, extending into the vagina. **2** the neck.

Cesarean (also **Cesarian**) *var. of* CAESAREAN.

cesium /'siːzɪəm/ *n.* a soft silver-white element occurring naturally in a number of minerals, and used in photoelectric cells.

cessation /se'seɪʃən/ *n.* a ceasing.

cession /'seʃən/ *n.* **1** (often foll. by *of*) the ceding or giving up (of rights, property, and esp. of territory). **2** the territory etc. so ceded.

cesspit *n.* **1** a pit for the disposal of refuse. **2** = CESSPOOL.

cesspool *n.* **1** an underground container for the temporary storage of liquid waste or sewage. **2** a centre of corruption, depravity, etc.

cetacean /sə'teɪʃən/ ● *n.* any marine mammal of the order Cetacea with a streamlined hairless body and dorsal blowhole for breathing, including whales, dolphins, and porpoises. ● *adj.* of cetaceans.

ceviche /se'viːtʃeɪ/ *n.* a Latin American dish of raw fish or seafood marinated in lime or lemon juice, usu. garnished and served as an appetizer.

Ceylon satinwood *n. see* SATINWOOD 1.

Ceylon tea *n.* a Pekoe tea produced in Sri Lanka.

CF *abbr.* **1** cystic fibrosis. **2** Canadian Forces.

Cf *symbol* californium.

cf. *abbr.* compare.

CFA *abbr. Cdn* (*Maritimes & Nfld*) COME FROM AWAY.

CFB *abbr.* Canadian Forces Base.

CFC *abbr.* chlorofluorocarbon, any of various usu. gaseous compounds of carbon, hydrogen, chlorine, and fluorine, used in refrigerants etc. and thought to be harmful to the ozone layer in the earth's atmosphere.

CFL *abbr.* Canadian Football League.

CFO *abbr.* CHIEF FINANCIAL OFFICER.

CFR *abbr.* Canadian Finals Rodeo.

CFS *abbr.* **1** Canadian Forces Station. **2** CHRONIC FATIGUE SYNDROME.

cfs *abbr.* cubic feet per second.

cg *abbr.* centigram(s).

CGA *abbr.* **1** (in Canada) CERTIFIED GENERAL ACCOUNTANT. **2** colour graphics adapter, a general-purpose adapter for personal computers, generating a 320 by 200 pixel, four-colour screen, largely superseded (*compare* EGA, VGA).

CGIT *abbr. Cdn* Canadian Girls in Training.

CGS *abbr.* Chief of General Staff.

CGT *abbr.* capital gains tax.

ch. *abbr.* **1** church. **2** chapter. **3** channel.

Chablis /ʃæ'bliː, ʃə-, 'ʃæbli/ *n.* (*pl.* same /-liːz/) **1** a dry white wine from N Burgundy. **2** *N Amer. & Austral.* any dry white wine.

cha-cha (also **cha-cha-cha**) ● *n.* **1** a ballroom dance with a Latin-American rhythm. **2** music for or in the rhythm of a cha-cha. ● *v.intr.* (**cha-chas, cha-chaed** or **cha-cha'd, cha-chaing**) dance the cha-cha.

chador /'tʃʌdər/ *n.* a large piece of cloth worn in some countries by Muslim women, wrapped around the body to leave only the face exposed.

chafe /tʃeif/ ● v. **1** tr. & intr. make or become sore or damaged by rubbing. **2** tr. rub (esp. the skin to restore warmth or sensation). **3** tr. & intr. make or become annoyed; fret (they chafed at the delay). ● n. **1 a** an act of chafing. **b** a sore resulting from this. **2** a state of annoyance.

chafer n. any of various large slow-moving beetles of the family Scarabaeidae, esp. the cockchafer.

chaff /tʃæf/ ● n. **1** the husks of grain etc. separated from the seed by winnowing or threshing. **2** chopped hay and straw used as fodder. **3** lighthearted joking; banter. **4** worthless things; rubbish. **5** strips of metal foil released in the air to obstruct radar detection. ● v.tr. & intr. tease; banter. □ **separate the wheat from the chaff** distinguish good from bad. □ **chaffy** adj.

chafing dish n. a dish supported on a stand and heated from below by an alcohol burner.

chagrin /ʃə'grɪn/ ● n. acute vexation or mortification. ● v.tr. affect with chagrin.

chain ● n. **1 a** a connected flexible series of esp. metal links. **b** something resembling this (a human chain). **2** (in pl.) **a** fetters used to confine prisoners. **b** any restraining force. **3** a sequence, series, or set (chain of events; mountain chain). **4** a group of associated hotels, stores, newspapers, etc., esp. with the same owners or management. **5** a badge of office in the form of a chain worn around the neck (mayoral chain). **6** Surveying **a** a jointed measuring line consisting of one hundred linked metal rods. **b** its length (66 ft., approx. 20 m). **7** Chem. a group of (esp. carbon) atoms bonded in sequence in a molecule. **8** a figure in a quadrille or similar dance. **9** (in pl.) a set of linked chains fastened around a vehicle's tires to prevent skidding in snow. **10** a chain for fastening a door to its jamb as a security device. ● v. **1** tr. (often foll. by up) secure or confine with a chain. **2** tr. confine or restrict (a person). **3** tr. & intr. Computing link (a file etc.) or be linked with another by the inclusion in each item of an address by which a successor may be located.

chain gang n. a team of convicts chained together and forced to work in the open air.

chain letter n. one of a sequence of letters the recipient of which is requested to send copies to a specific number of other people.

chain-link adj. made of wire in a diamond-shaped mesh (chain-link fence).

chain of command n. a hierarchical arrangement in an organization by which orders are carried out.

chain reaction n. **1** Physics a self-sustaining nuclear reaction, esp. one in which a neutron from a fission reaction initiates a series of these reactions. **2** Chem. a self-sustaining molecular reaction in which intermediate products initiate further reactions. **3** a series of events, each caused by the previous one.

chainsaw ● n. a motor-driven saw with teeth on an endless chain. ● v.tr. (**-sawed**, **-sawing**) cut with a chainsaw.

chain-smoke v.tr. & intr. smoke (cigarettes etc.) continually, esp. lighting each from the stub of the last one smoked. □ **chain-smoker** n. **chain-smoking** n.

chain store n. one of a series of stores owned by one company and selling the same sort of goods.

chair ● n. **1** a separate seat for one person, of various forms, usu. having a back. **2 a** a professorship. **b** a seat of authority, esp. on a board of directors. **c** a position as a musician in an orchestra. **3 a** a chairperson. **b** the seat or office of a chairperson (will you take the chair?). ● v.tr. **1** act as chairperson of or

preside over (a meeting). **2** install in a chair, esp. as a position of authority. □ **take a chair** sit down.

chairlift n. a series of chairs on an endless cable for carrying passengers up and down a mountain etc.

chairman n. (pl. **-men**) **1** a person chosen to preside over a meeting. **2** the permanent president of a committee, a board of directors, a company, etc. **3** (**Chairman**) (since 1949) the leading figure in the Chinese Communist Party. **4** a master of ceremonies. □ **chairmanship** n.

chairperson n. (pl **-s** or **-people**) a chairman or chairwoman (used as a neutral alternative).

chairwoman n. (pl. **-women**) a female chairperson.

chaise longue /ʃeiz 'laʊndʒ, -lɒŋ/ n. (pl. **chaise longues** or **chaises longues**) (also **chaise**, **chaise lounge**) a chair with an extended seat on which to rest the legs.

chakra /'tʃʌkrə/ n. (in yoga) each of the seven centres of spiritual power in the human body.

chalcedony /kæl'sedəni/ n. a type of quartz occurring in several different forms, e.g. agate etc.

Chaldean /kæl'diːən/ ● n. **1 a** a native of ancient Chaldea or Babylonia. **b** the language of the Chaldeans. **2** an astrologer. **3** a member of an Eastern Catholic sect in Iran etc. ● adj. **1** of or relating to ancient Chaldea or its people or language. **2** of or relating to astrology. **3** of the Chaldean Church.

chalet n. **1** a style of wooden house, typical of the European Alps, having a steeply pitched roof with very deep overhanging eaves. **2** the main building at a ski resort, usu. with rental facilities and a restaurant. **3** Cdn (Que.) a holiday cottage.

chalice n. Christianity a wine cup used in the Eucharist.

chalk ● n. **1 a** a white soft earthy limestone (calcium carbonate) formed from the skeletal remains of sea creatures. **2 a** a similar substance (calcium sulphate), sometimes coloured, used for writing or drawing. **b** a piece of this. **3** a series of strata consisting mainly of chalk. **4** Billiards a small blue chalk-like cube, rubbed againt the tip of a pool cue to reduce slippage. ● v.tr. rub, mark, draw, or write with chalk. □ **chalk and talk** traditional teaching methods (employing blackboard, chalk, and interlocution). **chalk out** sketch or plan a thing to be accomplished. **chalk up 1** (foll. by to) attribute, charge (chalk it up to my upbringing). **2** register (a point scored, a success, etc.).

chalkboard n. N Amer. = BLACKBOARD.

chalky adj. (**-ier**, **-iest**) **1** abounding in chalk. **2** white as chalk. **3** having the consistency of chalk. □ **chalkiness** n.

challah /'hɒlə/ n. (pl. **-s** or **challoth**) a loaf of white leavened egg bread, often braided, traditionally baked to celebrate the Jewish Sabbath.

challenge ● n. **1 a** a summons to take part in a contest or a trial of strength etc. **b** a summons to prove or justify something. **2 a** a demanding or difficult task. **b** a difficult but stimulating task. **3** Law an objection made to a jury member. **4** a call to respond, esp. a sentry's call for a password etc. **5** an invitation to a sporting contest, esp. one issued to a reigning champion. ● v.tr. **1** (often foll. by to + infin.) **a** invite to take part in a contest, game, debate, duel, etc. **b** invite to prove or justify something. **2** dispute, deny (I challenge that remark). **3** stretch, stimulate (challenges him to produce his best). **4** (of a sentry) call to respond. **5** claim (attention, etc.). **6** Law object to (a jury member, evidence, etc.). □ **challengeable** adj. **challenger** n.

challenged adj. **1** (often in comb.) disabled (physically *challenged*). **2** (in *comb.*) *jocular* not having a specified quality, e.g. *vertically challenged* for *short*.

challenging *adj.* stimulatingly difficult.

chamber *n.* **1 a** a hall used by a legislative or judicial body. **b** the body that meets in it. **c** any of the houses of a parliament. **2** (in *pl.*) a judge's room used for hearing cases not needing to be taken in court. **3** *Music* (*attrib.*) of or for a small group of instruments. **4** an enclosed space in machinery etc. (esp. the part of a gun that contains the cartridge or shell). **5 a** a cavity in a plant or in the body of an animal. **b** a compartment in a structure. **6** a space, cavity, or room constructed for a specific purpose. □ **chambered** *adj.*

chamberlain /ˈtʃeimbərlin/ *n.* an officer managing the household of a sovereign or a great noble.

chambermaid *n.* **1** a housemaid at a hotel etc. **2** *N Amer.* a housemaid.

chamber of commerce *n.* an association to promote local commercial interests.

chamber pot *n.* a receptacle for urine etc., used in a bedroom.

chambré /ˈʃɑbrei/ *adj.* (of red wine) brought to room temperature.

chameleon /kəˈmiːliən/ *n.* **1** any of a family of small lizards having protruding eyes and the power of changing colour. **2** a variable or inconstant person or thing. □ **chameleonic** /-ˈbnik/ *adj.*

chamfer /ˈtʃæmfər/ ● *v.tr.* bevel symmetrically (a right-angled edge or corner). ● *n.* a bevelled surface at an edge or corner.

chamois *n.* **1** /ˈʃæmwɪ/ (*pl.* same /-wɒz/) an agile goat-antelope, *Rupicapra rupicapra*, native to the mountains of Europe and Asia. **2** /ˈʃæmi/ (*pl.* same /-iːz/) (in full **chamois leather**) a soft pliable leather from sheep, goats, deer, etc. **b** a piece of this for polishing etc.

chamomile *var. of* CAMOMILE.

champ¹ *n.* informal a champion.

champ² *n. & v.* = CHOMP.

champagne *n.* **1 a** a white sparkling wine from Champagne in NE France. **b** a similar wine from elsewhere. ¶Use in sense b is strictly incorrect. **2** a pale cream or straw colour.

champion ● *n.* **1** (often *attrib.*) a person (esp. in a sport or game), animal, etc., that has defeated or surpassed all rivals in a competition etc. **2** a person who fights or argues for a cause or on behalf of another person. ● *v.tr.* support the cause of, defend, argue in favour of. ● *adj.* informal first-class, splendid.

championship *n.* **1** (often in *pl.*) a contest for the position of champion in a sport etc. **2** the position of champion over all rivals. **3** the advocacy or defence (of a cause etc.).

chance ● *n.* **1 a** a possibility. **b** (often in *pl.*) probability (*chances are that you will be promoted*). **2** a risk (*take a chance*). **3 a** an unplanned occurrence (*just a chance that they met*). **b** the absence of design or discoverable cause (*leave nothing to chance*). **4** an opportunity (*didn't have a chance to speak to him*). **5** the way things happen; fortune; luck (*leave it to chance*). **6** (often **Chance**) the course of events regarded as a power; fate. ● *adj.* fortuitous, accidental (*a chance meeting*). ● *v.* **1** *tr.* informal risk (*we'll chance it and go*). **2** *intr.* happen without intention (*I chanced to find it*). □ **by any chance** as it happens; perhaps. **by chance** without design; unintentionally. **chance on** (or **upon**) happen to find, meet, etc. **no chance** there is no possibility of that. **on the chance** (often foll. by *of*, or *that* + clause) in view of the possibility. **stand a chance** have a prospect of success etc. **take a chance** (or

chances) behave riskily; risk failure. **take a** (or **one's**) **chance on** (or **with**) consent to take the consequences of; trust to luck.

chancel *n.* a part of some (esp. Anglican) churches, located near the altar, which is usu. separated from the nave by steps or enclosed by a screen.

chancellor *n.* **1** a state or legal official of various kinds. **2** the head of the government in Germany and Austria. **3** *Cdn & Brit.* the non-resident honorary head of a university.

chancery /ˈtʃɑːnsəri/ *n.* (*pl.* **-ies**) **1** an office attached to an embassy or consulate. **2** the administrative office of a Catholic diocese. **3** a public record office.

chancre /ˈʃæŋkər/ *n.* a hard, painless ulcer developing as the primary lesion of syphilis and certain other infectious diseases.

chancy *adj.* (**-ier**, **-iest**) subject to chance; risky.

chandelier *n.* an ornamental branched hanging support for several light bulbs or candles. □ **chandeliered** *adj.*

chandler /ˈtʃændlər/ *n.* **1** a dealer of supplies or goods for a specific purpose, esp. of boating supplies. **2** a person who makes or sells items of tallow or wax.

change ● *n.* **1 a** the act or an instance of making or becoming different. **b** an alteration or modification. **2 a** money given in exchange for money in larger units or a different currency. **b** money returned as the balance of that given in payment. **c** coins. **d** *N Amer.* a relatively small amount of something, esp. money (*$10 million and change*). **3** a new experience; variety (*time for a change*). **4 a** the substitution of one thing for another; an exchange (*change of scene*). **b** a set of clothes etc. put on in place of another. **5** (in full **change of life**) *informal* menopause. **6** (of the moon) arrival at a fresh phase, esp. at the new moon. ● *v.* **1** *tr.* & *intr.* undergo, show, or subject to change; make or become different. **2** *tr.* **a** take or use another instead of; go from one to another (*changed the tire; changed his doctor; changed trains*). **b** give up or get rid of in exchange (*changed the car for a van*). **3** *tr.* **a** give or get change in smaller denominations for (*can you change a twenty?*). **b** exchange (a sum of money) for (*changed our dollars for pounds*). **4** *tr.* & *intr.* put fresh clothes or coverings on (*change the baby; changed into something more comfortable*). **5** *tr.* give and receive, exchange (*changed places with her*). **6** *intr.* change trains etc. (*changed at Montreal*). **7** *intr.* (of the voice) become deeper in tone. **8** *tr.* (of the moon) arrive at a fresh phase, esp. become new. □ **change of air** a different climate; variety. **change colour** blanch or flush. **change gear** engage a different gear in a vehicle. **change hands 1** pass to a different owner. **2** substitute one hand for another. **change of heart** a conversion to a different view. **change over** change from one system or situation to another. **change the subject** begin talking of something different, esp. to avoid embarrassment. **change one's tune 1** voice a different opinion from that expressed previously. **2** change one's style of language or manner, esp. from an insolent to a respectful tone. □ **changeful** *adj.* **changer** *n.*

changeable *adj.* **1** irregular, inconstant. **2** that can change or be changed. □ **changeability** *n.* **changeableness** *n.* **changeably** *adv.*

changeless *adj.* unchanging. □ **changelessly** *adv.*

changeling *n.* a child or thing believed to have been secretly substituted for another.

changeover *n.* the act or process of changing over.

change room *n.* (also **changing room**) a room

where people may change their clothes, esp. before and after physical activity.

change table *n.* (also **changing table**) a table designed for use in changing a baby's diaper.

changeup *n. Baseball* a slow pitch, thrown with the motions of a fastball, to deceive the batter.

Changing of the Guard *n.* **1** a ceremonial replacement of one body of guards by another, esp. at parliament buildings etc. **2** a profound change in management, approach, etc.

channel ● *n.* **1 a** a length of water wider than a strait, joining two larger areas. **b** the bed of a river, stream, or other watercourse. **c** the navigable part of a waterway. **d** (**the Channel**) the English Channel. **2** a medium of communication; an agency for conveying information (*through the usual channels*). **3 a** a band of frequencies used in radio and television transmission, esp. as used by a particular station. **b** a service or station using this. **4** the course in which anything moves; a direction. **5** a tubular passage for liquid. ● *v.tr.* (**channelled, channelling**) **1** guide or convey through or as if through a channel (*channelled them through customs*). **2** direct (funds, energy, emotions, etc.) toward a goal. **3** act as a medium for (a spirit). **4** form channels in; groove.

channel cat *n.* (in full **channel catfish**) a large edible freshwater catfish, *Ictalurus punctatus*, of central N America.

channel changer *n.* a remote control for changing a television set.

channel surfing *n. N Amer. informal* the act of flipping from one television channel to another in rapid succession using a remote. □ **channel surfer** *n.*

chanson /ʃãˈsɔ̃/ *n.* a French song, usu. sung by a solo singer with minimal accompaniment and characterized by political or social commentary.

chansonnier /ˌʃãsɔnˈjei/ *n.* a singer of chansons.

chansonnière /ˌʃãsɔnˈjer/ *n.* a female singer of chansons.

chant ● *n.* **1 a** a spoken singsong phrase, esp. one performed in unison by a crowd etc. **b** a repetitious singsong way of speaking. **2** *Music* **a** a short musical passage in two or more phrases used for singing unmetrical words, e.g. psalms. **b** the psalm etc. so sung. **c** a song, esp. monotonous or repetitive. **3** a musical recitation, esp. of poetry. ● *v.tr. & intr.* **1** intone monotonously or repetitiously, esp. in a singsong voice. **2** sing or intone (a psalm etc.).

chanter *n.* **1** a person who chants. **2** the pipe of a bagpipe, on which the melody is played.

chanterelle /ˌtʃæntəˈrel/ *n.* an edible fungus, *Cantharellus cibarius*, with a yellow funnel-shaped cap.

chanteuse /ʃɒnˈtɜːz/ *n.* a female singer of popular songs.

Chantilly /ʃænˈtɪli, ʃãtiːˈjiː/ *n.* **1** a delicate kind of bobbin lace. **2** sweetened or flavoured whipped cream.

chanty *var. of* SHANTY[2].

Chanukah *var. of* HANUKKAH.

chaos *n.* **1** utter confusion. **2** the formless matter supposed to have existed before the creation of the universe. □ **chaotic** *adj.* **chaotically** *adv.*

chaos theory *n.* the theory that small changes in the physical world can eventually have unpredictable and potentially major consequences.

chap[1] *n. informal* a man; a boy; a fellow.

chap[2] ● *v.* (**chapped, chapping**) **1** *intr.* (esp. of the skin) crack in fissures, esp. because of exposure and

dryness. **2** *tr.* (of the wind, cold, etc.) cause to chap. ● *n.* (usu. in *pl.*) a crack in the skin.

chap[3] *n.* the lower jaw or half of the cheek, esp. of a pig as food.

chap. *abbr.* chapter.

chaparajos /ˌʃæpəˈreioːs, ˌtʃæp-/ *n.pl. N Amer.* = CHAPS.

chaparral /ˌʃæpəˈræl, ˌtʃæp-/ *n. N Amer.* dense tangled brush; undergrowth.

chapati /tʃəˈpɒti, -ˈpæti/ *n.* (also **chapatti**) (*pl.* **-is**) a flat thin Indian cake of unleavened wheat bread.

chapbook *n.* a small and often self-published booklet of poetry, stories, etc.

chapel *n.* **1** *Christianity* **a** a small sanctuary within a larger church or cathedral. **b** a place of worship attached to a hospital, school, etc. **c** any other place of worship that is neither a parish church nor a cathedral. **2** a chapel service. **3** a funeral home, or the room in a funeral home in which funerals are held.

chaperone (also **chaperon**) ● *n.* **1** a person who supervises young people on trips, etc. **2** a person who ensures that no improper behaviour occurs on a date, at a dance, etc. **3** esp. hist. a person, esp. an older woman, who ensures propriety by accompanying a young unmarried woman on social occasions. ● *v.tr.* act as a chaperone to.

chapfallen *adj.* dispirited, dejected.

chaplain *n.* a member of the clergy attached to a private chapel, institution, ship, regiment, etc. □ **chaplaincy** *n.* (*pl.* **-ies**)

chapped *adj.* (esp. of the lips) dry and cracking.

chappie *n. informal* = CHAP[1].

chaps /tʃæps, ʃæps/ *n.pl. N Amer.* **1** thick leather leggings worn by western riders over trousers as protection against thorns etc. **2** similar protective leather leggings worn by loggers.

Chap Stick *n. N Amer. proprietary* a soothing, wax-like balm applied to chapped lips, usu. in a tube.

chapter *n.* **1** a main division of a book, treatise, etc. **2** *N Amer.* a local branch of a society. **3** a period of time (in a person's life etc.). **4 a** the canons of a cathedral or other religious community. **b** a meeting of these. **5** an Act of Parliament numbered as part of a session's proceedings. □ **chapter and verse** an exact reference or authority.

char[1] ● *v.tr. & intr.* (**charred, charring**) **1** make or become black by burning; scorch. **2** burn or be burned to charcoal. ● *n.* a charred substance.

char[2] *n.* (also **charr**) (*pl.* same) **1** a small trout of the genus *Salvelinus*, esp. the Arctic char. **2** a Dolly Varden trout or brook trout.

character *n.* **1** the collective qualities or characteristics, esp. mental and moral, that distinguish a person or thing. **2** moral strength (*has a weak character*). **3** reputation (*a blot on her character*). **4** distinctive or unusual features (*a house with character*). **5 a** a person in a novel, play, etc. **b** a part played by a performer; a role. **6** (*attrib.*) **a** designating an acting role requiring strong delineation of individual and esp. eccentric character, or an actor who plays such roles. **b** designating roles in dramatic ballets, or the artists performing them, which require more acting than dancing. **7** *informal* a person, esp. an eccentric or outstanding individual (*he's a real character*). **8 a** a printed or written letter or symbol. **b** *Computing* any of a group of symbols representing a letter etc. **9** a characteristic (esp. of a biological species). □ **in** (or **out of**) **character** consistent (or inconsistent) with a person's character. □ **characterful** *adj.* **characterless** *adj.*

character assassination *n.* a malicious attempt to harm or destroy a person's good reputation.

characteristic ● *adj.* typical, distinctive. ● *n.* a characteristic feature or quality. □ **characteristically** *adv.*

characterize *v.tr.* **1 a** describe or portray the character of. **b** (foll. by as) describe as. **2** be characteristic of. □ **characterization** *n.*

charade /ʃəˈreɪd/ *n.* **1 a** (usu. in *pl.*, treated as *sing.*) a game of guessing a word from a written or acted clue given for each syllable and for the whole. **b** one such clue. **2** an absurd pretense.

charbroil *v.tr.* cook (meat etc.) on a grill over a charcoal fire. □ **charbroiled** *adj.*

charcoal ● *n.* **1** an amorphous form of carbon consisting of a porous black residue from partially burnt wood, bones, etc. **2** a piece of this, or a pencil made from it, used for drawing. **3** a drawing in charcoal. **4** (in full **charcoal grey**) a dark grey colour. ● *adj.* (in full **charcoal grey**) dark grey.

chard *n.* (in full **Swiss chard**) a kind of beet, *Beta vulgaris*, with edible white leaf stalks and green blades.

Chardonnay /ˈʃɑːdəˌneɪ/ *n.* **1** a variety of white grape used in winemaking. **2** a dry white wine made from Chardonnay grapes.

charge ● *v.* **1** *tr.* **a** ask (an amount) as a price (*charge $5 a ticket*). **b** ask (a person) for an amount as a price (*you forgot to charge me*). **2** *tr.* **a** (foll. by *to, up to*) debit the cost of to (a person or account) (*charge it to my account*). **b** debit (a person or an account) (*bought a new car and charged the company*). **3** *tr.* **a** (often foll. by *with*) accuse (of an offence) (*charged him with theft*). **b** (foll. by *that* + clause) make an accusation that. **4** *tr.* **a** (foll. by *to* + infin.) instruct or command. **b** (of a judge) instruct (a jury). **5** *tr.* (foll. by *with*) entrust with. **6 a** *intr.* make a rushing attack. **b** *tr.* make a rushing attack on; throw oneself against. **7** (often foll. by *up*) **a** *tr.* give an electric charge to (a body). **b** *tr.* store energy in (a battery). **c** *intr.* (of a battery etc.) receive and store energy. **8** *tr.* (often foll. by *with*) load or fill (a vessel, gun, etc.) to the full or proper extent. **9** *tr.* (usu. as **charged** *adj.*) **a** (foll. by *with*) saturated with (*air charged with vapour*). **b** (usu. foll. by *with*) pervaded (with strong feelings etc.) (*atmosphere charged with emotion*). ● *n.* **1 a** a price asked for goods or services. **b** a financial liability or commitment. **2 a** an accusation, esp. against a prisoner brought to trial. **b** a judge's instructions to a jury. **3 a** a task, duty, or commission. **b** care, custody, responsible possession. **c** a person or thing entrusted. **d** the congregation(s) for which a minister is responsible. **4 a** an impetuous rush or attack, esp. in a battle. **b** the signal for this. **5** the appropriate amount of material to be put into a receptacle, mechanism, etc. at one time, esp. of explosive for a gun. **6 a** a property of matter that is a consequence of the interaction between its constituent particles and exists in a positive or negative form, causing electrical phenomena. **b** the quantity of this carried by a body. **c** energy stored chemically for conversion into electricity. **d** the process of charging a battery. **7** esp. *N Amer. informal* a thrill. **8** a burden or load. **9** *Heraldry* a device; a bearing. □ **charge up 1** recharge (a battery etc.). **2** (usu. as **charged up** *adj.*) excite. **free of charge** at no cost. **in charge** having command. **put a person on a charge** charge a person with a specified offence. **return to the charge** begin again, esp. in argument. **take charge** (often foll. by *of*) assume control or direction. □ **chargeable** *adj.*

charge card *n.* a credit card, esp. one which must be paid in full when a statement is issued.

charge-coupled device *n.* a light-sensitive grid on a silicon chip which creates digital signals from images, used in video recorders, photocopiers, etc.

chargé d'affaires /ˌʃɑːʒeɪ dæˈfeːr/ *n.* (also **chargé**) (*pl.* **chargés d'affaires** *pronunc.* same) **1** an ambassador's deputy. **2** an envoy to a country to which an ambassador has not been sent.

charger *n.* **1** an apparatus for charging a battery. **2** a cavalry horse. **3** a person or thing that charges.

charging *n. Hockey* an illegal play involving an attack of more than two steps against a member of the opposing team in order to take him or her out of play.

chariot *n. hist.* a two-wheeled vehicle drawn by horses, used in ancient warfare and racing.

charioteer *n.* a chariot driver.

charisma *n.* **1 a** the ability to inspire followers with devotion and enthusiasm. **b** an attractive aura; great charm. **2** (*pl.* **charismata** /kəˈrɪzmətə/) a divinely conferred power or talent.

charismatic ● *adj.* **1** having charisma; inspiring enthusiasm. **2** (of Christian worship) characterized by spontaneity, ecstatic utterances, etc. ● *n.* a Christian who emphasizes charismatic worship and experiences. □ **charismatically** *adv.*

charitable *adj.* **1** generous in giving to those in need. **2** of, relating to, or connected with a charity or charities. **3** apt to judge favourably of persons, acts, and motives. □ **charitableness** *n.* **charitably** *adv.*

charity *n.* (*pl.* **-ies**) **1 a** a voluntary giving to those in need. **b** the help, esp. money, so given. **2 a** an organization for helping those in need. **b** a non-profit organization. **3 a** kindness, benevolence. **b** tolerance in judging others. **c** love of one's fellow humans.

charlatan /ˈʃɑːlətən/ *n.* a person falsely claiming a special knowledge or skill. □ **charlatanism** *n.*

Charleston /ˈtʃɑːlstən/ ● *n.* a fast dance of the 1920s, in which the knees are turned inwards and the legs kicked sideways. ● *v.intr.* dance the Charleston.

charley horse *n. N Amer.* cramp or soreness in a muscle, esp. in the leg.

charlotte *n.* any of various desserts consisting of a filling of fruit, custard, cream, etc. encased in strips of bread, sponge cake, etc.

charm ● *n.* **1 a** the power or quality of giving delight or arousing admiration. **b** fascination, attractiveness. **c** (usu. in *pl.*) an attractive or enticing quality. **2** a trinket on a bracelet etc. **3** an object, act, or word(s) supposedly having occult or magic power; a spell. **b** a thing worn to avert evil etc. **4** *Physics* a property of matter manifested by some quarks and other subatomic particles. ● *v.tr.* **1** delight, captivate. **2** influence or protect as if by magic (*leads a charmed life*). **3 a** gain by charm (*charmed agreement out of him*). **b** influence by charm (*charmed her into consenting*). **4** cast a spell on, bewitch. □ **like a charm** perfectly, wonderfully. □ **charmer** *n.*

charming *adj.* **1** delightful, attractive, pleasing. **2** (often as *interj.*) *ironic* expressing displeasure or disapproval. □ **charmingly** *adv.*

charmless *adj.* lacking charm; unattractive.

charnel house *n.* a house or vault in which dead bodies or bones are piled.

Charolais /ˈʃærəˌleɪ/ *n.* (*pl.* same) a breed of large white beef cattle.

charr *var.* of CHAR².

chart ● *n.* **1** information in the form of a table, graph, etc. **2** a geographical map or plan, esp. for navigation. **3** (usu. in *pl.*) a listing of the most popular songs, albums, etc., for a given period. **4** a record of medical information concerning a patient. ● *v.* **1** *tr.* make a chart of; map. **2** *tr.* outline, plan (*chart a new course*). **3** *tr.* trace systematically (*charted its progress*). **4** *intr.* (of a recording or an artist) appear on the charts.

chartbuster *n. informal* a best-selling popular song, album, artist, etc.

charter ● *n.* **1 a** a written grant of rights by the sovereign or legislature, esp. the creation of a university etc. **b** a written constitution or description of an organization's functions etc. **2** (**the Charter**) (in Canada) the Canadian Charter of Rights and Freedoms. **3 a** the hiring of an aircraft etc. for a special purpose (also *attrib.*: *charter flight*). **b** a contract for this. **c** the aircraft etc. chartered. ● *v.tr.* **1** grant a charter to. **2** hire (an aircraft etc.). □ **charterer** *n.*

charter community *n. Cdn* (*NWT*) a small municipality having some by-law authority and at least 25 residents who are eligible to vote.

chartered accountant *n.* a person trained and licensed to practise accounting. Abbr.: **CA**.

chartered bank *n.* (in Canada) a large, privately-owned bank chartered by Parliament and operating under the provisions of the Bank Act.

charter member *n.* an original member.

charter school *n. N Amer.* a publicly funded school run by parents, teachers, and members of the business community, operating by contract or charter to the local school board or government.

chartreuse /ʃɑrˈtrɜːz/ ● *n.* **1** (**Chartreuse**) *proprietary* a pale green or yellow liqueur of brandy and aromatic herbs etc. **2** a pale yellowish green. ● *adj.* pale yellowish-green.

chary /ˈtʃeri/ *adj.* (**-ier, -iest**) (often foll. by *of*) **1** cautious, wary. **2** sparing; ungenerous (*chary of giving praise*). □ **charily** *adv.* **chariness** *n.*

chase ● *v.* **1** *tr.* pursue in order to catch. **2** *tr.* **a** (foll. by *from, out of, to,* etc.) force to leave. **b** (foll. by *away*) dispel (*chase away all fears*). **3** *intr.* **a** (foll. by *after*) hurry in pursuit of (a person). **b** (foll. by *around* etc.) *informal* act or move about hurriedly. **4** *tr.* (usu. foll. by *up, down*) *informal* make efforts to find or obtain quickly. **5** *tr. informal* **a** try to attain. **b** court persistently and openly. ● *n.* **1** the act or an instance of pursuing. **2** (prec. by *the*) hunting, esp. as a sport. **3** an animal etc. that is pursued. **4** = STEEPLECHASE. □ **give chase** pursue a person, animal, etc.; hunt.

chaser *n.* **1** a person or thing that chases. **2** *informal* a drink taken after another of a different kind, e.g. beer after hard liquor. **3** *N Amer.* a logger who unhooks logs at a landing. **4** a horse for steeplechasing.

chasm /ˈkæzəm/ *n.* **1** a deep fissure or opening in the earth, rock, etc. **2** a wide difference of feeling, interests, etc.; a gulf. □ **chasmic** *adj.*

Chassid (also **Chasid**) *var. of* HASID.

chassis /ˈtʃæsi, ˈʃæsi/ *n.* (*pl.* same / -siːz/) **1** the basic frame of a motor vehicle, trailer, etc., including the engine, wheels, and other mechanical parts, but not the body. **2** the frame of a stereo, television set, etc.

chaste *adj.* **1** abstaining from extramarital, or from all, sexual intercourse. **2** (of behaviour, speech, etc.) pure, virtuous, decent. **3** (of artistic etc. style) simple, unadorned. □ **chastely** *adv.* **chasteness** *n.*

chasten *v.tr.* **1** (esp. as **chastening** *adj.*, **chastened** *adj.*) subdue, humble (*a chastening experience*; *chastened by his failure*). **2** discipline, punish. □ **chastener** *n.*

chastise *v.tr.* **1** rebuke or reprimand severely. **2** punish, esp. by beating. □ **chastisement** *n.*

chastity *n.* **1** being chaste. **2** sexual abstinence; virginity. **3** simplicity of style or taste.

chat[1] ● *v.intr.* (**chatted, chatting**) talk in a light familiar way. ● *n.* **1** informal conversation or talk. **2** an instance of this. □ **chat up** *informal* chat to, esp. flirtatiously or with an ulterior motive.

chat[2] *n.* **1** any of various small birds with harsh calls, esp. a N American warbler of the genus *Granatellus* or *Icteria*. **2** a Eurasian thrush of the genus *Saxicola*.

château /ʃæˈtoː, ˈʃætoː/ *n.* (*pl.* **châteaux** /-toːz/) **1** a French country house or castle, often giving its name to wine made in its neighbourhood. **2** *hist.* (in French Canada) the residence of a seigneur or a governor.

Château Clique *n. Cdn hist.* a name given to the governing class of Lower Canada.

Château style *n. Cdn* a style of architecture derived from the French château, characterized by steep, often copper-covered, roofs and round towers, used esp. in building railway hotels in the early 20th c.

chatelaine /ˈʃætəˌleɪn/ *n.* the mistress of a large house.

chat line *n.* a telephone or e-mail service which enables users to exchange casual conversation, either individually or by means of a conference line, with other subscribers or with employees of the service.

chat show *n.* = TALK SHOW.

chattel *n.* (usu. in *pl.*) **1** a movable possession; any possession or piece of property other than real estate or a freehold. **2** a slave. □ **goods and chattels** personal possessions.

chattel mortgage *n. N Amer.* a loan in which movable possessions (e.g. equipment or appliances) are used as security.

chatter ● *v.intr.* **1** talk quickly, incessantly, trivially, or indiscreetly. **2** (of an animal) emit short quick sounds. **3** (of the teeth) click repeatedly together (usu. from cold). **4** (of a tool) rattle from vibration. ● *n.* **1** chattering talk or sounds. **2** the vibration of a tool. □ **chatterer** *n.* **chattery** *adj.*

chatterbox *n.* a talkative person.

chattering classes *n.pl. usu. derogatory* the educated members of the middle and upper classes who consider themselves politically liberal and socially aware.

chatty *adj.* (**-ier, -iest**) **1** fond of chatting; talkative. **2** *informal* and lively (*a chatty letter*). □ **chattily** *adv.* **chattiness** *n.*

chauffeur /ʃoˈfər, ˈʃoː-/ *n.* a person employed to drive a limousine or other automobile. ● *v.tr.* **1** drive (a car) as a chauffeur. **2** transport by car.

chauffeuse /ʃoˈfɜːz/ *n.* a female chauffeur.

chauvinism *n.* **1** exaggerated or aggressive patriotism. **2** prejudice against or lack of consideration for those of a different sex, class, nationality, culture, etc. (*male chauvinism*).

chauvinist *n.* a person who exhibits chauvinism. □ **chauvinistic** *adj.* **chauvinistically** *adv.*

cheap ● *adj.* **1** low in price, inexpensive; worth more than its cost (*a cheap holiday*; *cheap labour*). **2** charging low prices; offering good value (*a cheap restaurant*). **3** of poor quality; inferior (*cheap housing*). **4** *N Amer. informal* (of a person) careful with money. **5 a** requiring little effort or acquired by discreditable means (*talk is cheap*). **b** contemptible, despicable (*a cheap joke*). **c** ashamed; of low esteem (*made us feel cheap*). **d** unwarranted, uncalled for (*a cheap penalty*). ● *adv.* inexpensively (*got it cheap*). □ **dirt cheap** very inexpensive. **on the cheap** inexpensively. □ **cheapish** *adj.* **cheaply** *adv.* **cheapness** *n.*

cheapen *v.tr. & intr.* make or become cheap or cheaper.

cheapo (also **cheapie**) *informal* ● *adj.* inexpensive or of low quality. ● *n.* **1** something inexpensive or of low quality. **2** a stingy person.

cheap shot *n. N Amer.* **1** a malicious or cruel comment directed at a defenceless person. **2** *Sport* an illegal attack on an unsuspecting player.

cheapskate *n. informal* a stingy person; a miser.

cheat ● *v.* **1** *tr.* **a** (often foll. by *into*, *out of*) deceive or trick (*cheated him out of his savings*). **b** (foll. by *of*) deprive of (*cheated of a chance to reply*). **2** *intr.* gain unfair advantage by deception or breaking rules, esp. in a game or examination. **3** *tr.* avoid (something undesirable) by luck or skill (*cheated fate*). **4** *tr. & intr.* esp. *N Amer.* (usu. foll. by *on*) be sexually unfaithful to. ● *n.* **1** a person who cheats. **2** a trick, fraud, or deception. **3** an act of cheating. □ **cheatingly** *adv.*

cheater *n.* **1** a person who cheats. **2** (in *pl.*) *N Amer. slang* eyeglasses.

Chechen /ˈtʃetʃən/ ● *n.* **1** a member of a Muslim people of the Chechen Republic, an autonomous republic in SE Russia. **2** the Caucasian language of this people. ● *adj.* of or relating to this people.

check ● *v.* **1** *tr. & intr.* **a** examine the accuracy, quality, or condition of; inspect. **b** (often foll. by *that* + clause) make sure; verify (*checked the train times*). **c** search (*checked the house*). **2** *tr.* **a** stop or slow the motion of; curb, restrain (*checked his anger*). **b** find fault with; rebuke. **3** *tr. Hockey* **a** physically obstruct the progress of (an opponent). **b** cause (an opponent) to lose possession of the puck. **4** *tr. Chess* move a piece into a position that directly threatens (the opposing king). **5** *tr.* (often foll. by *off*) make a mark next to an item to indicate that it has been dealt with, chosen, or verified. **6** *tr. N Amer.* deposit (a coat, luggage, etc.) for temporary storage or dispatch. ● *n.* **1** a means or act of testing or ensuring accuracy, quality, satisfactory condition, etc. **2** a measure or policy to ensure against fraud or abuse (*checks and balances*). **3 a** a stopping or slowing of motion; a restraint on action. **b** a rebuff or rebuke. **c** a person or thing that restrains. **4** *Hockey* an instance of checking an opponent. **5** *Chess* **a** the exposure of a king to direct attack from an opposing piece. **b** (also as *interj.*) an announcement of this by the attacking player. **6** *N Amer.* = CHECK MARK. **7 a** a pattern of small squares or intersecting lines. **b** fabric having this pattern. **8** esp. *US var. of* CHEQUE etc. **9** *N Amer.* a bill in a restaurant. **10** a ticket used to claim an item which has been temporarily stored. **11** a crack or flaw in timber. ● *interj. N Amer.* expressing assent or agreement. □ **check in 1** arrive or register at a hotel, airport, etc. **2** record the arrival of. **check into 1** register one's arrival at (a hotel etc.). **2** investigate. **check (up) on 1** examine carefully or in detail; ascertain the truth about. **2** keep a watch on (a person, work done, etc.). **check out 1** leave a hotel etc. after paying the appropriate fees. **2 a** investigate; examine for authenticity or suitability. **b** *informal* look at; give consideration to (*check out that outfit*). **3** (of two or more items, accounts, etc.) agree or correspond when compared. **4** *N Amer. informal* die. **check over** examine for errors; verify. **in check** under control, restrained.

checker[1] *n.* **1** a person or thing that verifies or examines. **2** esp. *US* a cashier in a supermarket or store. **3** *Hockey* a forward whose role is primarily defensive. **4** any player who checks an opponent.

checker[2] ● *n.* **1** (often in *pl.*) a pattern of squares, often alternately coloured. **2 a** (in *pl.*; usu. treated as *sing.*) *N Amer.* a game for two, played on a checkerboard, in which players attempt to capture their opponent's pieces. **b** one of the small round pieces used in this game. ● *v.tr.* **1** mark with a checkered pattern. **2** diversify with a different colour etc.

checkerboard *n.* **1** a board with a pattern of squares of alternating colours, used in checkers. **2** something with a pattern resembling this.

checkered *adj.* (also **checked**) **1** marked with a pattern of small squares, often of alternating colours. **2** having undergone varied fortunes; having discreditable episodes (*a checkered career*).

checkered flag *n. Motorsport* a flag with a black and white checkered pattern, displayed to drivers or riders at the moment of finishing a race.

check-in *n.* **1** the act of registering one's arrival at a hotel, airport, etc. (often *attrib.*: *check-in counter*). **2** the place where one registers arrival at a hotel etc.

checklist *n.* an inventory or other (usu. complete) list of items for comparison or verification.

check mark *n. N Amer.* a mark placed beside an item to indicate that it has been dealt with, chosen, etc.

checkmate ● *n.* **1** *Chess* a check from which a king cannot escape, indicating that the game is over. **b** (also as *interj.*) an announcement of this. **2** a final defeat or deadlock. ● *v.tr.* **1** *Chess* put into checkmate. **2** defeat; frustrate.

checkout *n.* **1** an act of registering one's departure from a hotel etc. **2** a counter at which goods are paid for in a supermarket or store.

checkpoint *n.* a place, esp. a roadblock or manned entrance, where documents, vehicles, etc. are officially inspected.

checkroom *n. N Amer.* a room where coats, luggage, etc. may be temporarily deposited for a fee.

checks and balances *n.pl.* (esp. in the US) constitutional means of limiting or counteracting the wrongful use of governmental or administrative power, esp. in the form of guarantees and counterbalancing influences.

checkstop *n. Cdn (Alta.)* a roadside checkpoint where drivers are randomly tested with a Breathalyzer.

checkup *n.* a thorough examination, esp. of a person's general medical condition.

cheddar *n.* (also **Cheddar**) any of several firm varieties of cheese ranging in colour from white to orange and becoming increasingly strong with age.

cheder /ˈxeidər, ˈhei-/ *n.* a school for Jewish children in which Hebrew and religious knowledge are taught.

cheechako /tʃiˈtʃæko:/ *n. N Amer.* a newcomer or tenderfoot, esp. in the Yukon and Alaska.

cheek ● *n.* **1 a** the side of the face below the eye. **b** the side wall of the mouth. **c** *Cdn* the edible tender flesh around the mouth of a fish, esp. cod. **2 a** impertinent speech. **b** impertinence; cool confidence (*had the cheek to ask*). **3** *slang* either of the buttocks. **4 a** either of the side posts of a door etc. **b** either of the jaws of a vise. ● *v.tr.* speak impertinently to. □ **cheek by jowl** close together; side by side; intimate. **turn the other cheek** accept attack etc. meekly; refuse to retaliate.

cheekbone *n.* the bone below the eye that forms the prominent part of the cheek.

-cheeked *comb. form* having cheeks of a specified kind.

cheeky *adj.* (**-ier**, **-iest**) impertinent, impudent. □ **cheekily** *adv.* **cheekiness** *n.*

cheep ● *n.* the weak shrill cry of a young bird. ● *v.intr.* make such a cry.

cheer ● *n.* **1 a** a shout of encouragement or applause.

b an organized chant or other series of actions performed by cheerleaders or by a crowd at a sporting event etc. **2** mood, disposition (*full of good cheer*). **3** cheerfulness, gladness. **4** food and drink (*Christmas cheer*). ● *interj.* (in *pl.*) an informal drinking toast. ● *v.* **1** *tr.* **a** applaud with shouts. **b** (usu. foll. by *on*) urge or encourage. **2** *intr.* shout for joy. **3** *tr.* (usu. foll. by *up*) make or become less depressed. □ **three cheers** three successive hurrahs for a person etc.

cheerful *adj.* **1** in good spirits, noticeably happy. **2** bright, pleasant (*a cheerful room*). **3** willing, not reluctant. □ **cheerfully** *adv.* **cheerfulness** *n.*

cheerleader *n.* **1** a person who leads a crowd in formal cheers at a sporting event. **2** a person who rouses his or her colleagues into action. □ **cheerleading** *n.*

cheerless *adj.* gloomy, dreary, miserable. □ **cheerlessly** *adv.* **cheerlessness** *n.*

cheery *adj.* (**-ier, -iest**) lively; in good spirits; genial, cheering. □ **cheerily** *adv.* **cheeriness** *n.*

cheese ● *n.* **1** a food made from the curds of milk separated from the whey, often coagulated by rennet and pressed into a solid mass. **2** a complete cake of this with rind. **3** (also **big cheese**) *slang* an important person. ● *v.tr. slang* (foll. by *off*) bore or exasperate. □ **say cheese** smile for a photograph.

cheeseboard *n.* **1** a board or tray from which cheese is served. **2** a selection of cheeses.

cheeseburger *n.* a hamburger with melted cheese.

cheesecake *n.* **1** a rich sweet cake made with cream cheese or cottage cheese. **2** *informal* the portrayal of women in a sexually provocative manner in photographs.

cheesecloth *n.* thin loosely woven cloth resembling gauze.

cheese cutter *n.* **1** any of various utensils used for slicing cheese with a blade or by pulling a wire through it. **2** *Cdn* (*Que. & E Ont.*) *slang* = BOBSKATE.

cheesy *adj.* (**-ier, -iest**) **1** like cheese in taste, smell, appearance, etc. **2** *slang* inferior in quality, cheap. **3** *slang* unsophisticated, corny. □ **cheesiness** *n.*

cheetah *n.* a spotted feline native to the plains of Africa and SW Asia, *Acinonyx jubatus*, the world's fastest-running land animal.

chef *n.* a cook, esp. the chief cook in a restaurant.

chef de mission / ˈʃef ˌdə mɪˈsjɔ̃/ *n.* (*pl.* **chefs de mission**) the person in charge of a sports delegation, esp. a national team attending international games.

chef's knife *n.* a large kitchen knife having a long, gently curved, triangular pointed blade.

chela[1] /ˈkiːlə/ *n.* (*pl.* **chelae** /-liː/) a prehensile claw of crabs, lobsters, scorpions, etc.

chela[2] /ˈtʃeɪlə/ *n.* (in Hinduism) a disciple or pupil.

chem *n. N Amer. informal* a chemistry class or course.

chem. *abbr.* **1** chemical. **2** chemistry. **3** chemist.

chemical ● *adj.* of, made by, or employing chemistry or chemicals. ● *n.* a distinct substance obtained by or used in a chemical process. □ **chemically** *adv.*

chemical bond *n.* = BOND *n.* 7.

chemical engineering *n.* the science of the utilization of chemical processes in manufacturing and industry. □ **chemical engineer** *n.*

chemical reaction *n.* a process whereby compounds or elements undergo a change in structure and form new compounds.

chemical warfare *n.* the military deployment of chemical weapons.

chemical weapon *n.* a weapon that depends for its

effect on the release of a toxic or noxious substance, e.g. poison gas.

chemise /ʃəˈmiːz/ *n.* a woman's loose-fitting undergarment or dress hanging straight from the shoulders.

chemist *n.* a scientist trained in chemistry.

chemistry *n.* (*pl.* **-ies**) **1** the study of the elements, the compounds they form, and the reactions they undergo. **2 a** the chemical constituents or properties of a substance or organism. **b** the elements that make up an emotional process etc. (*the chemistry of fear*). **3** *informal* the interaction, attraction, or rapport existing among two or more people.

chemo /ˈkiːmoʊ/ *n. N Amer. informal* = CHEMOTHERAPY.

chemotherapy /ˌkiːmoʊˈθerəpi/ *n.* the treatment of disease, esp. cancer, by use of chemical substances. □ **chemotherapeutic** *adj.* **chemotherapist** *n.*

chenille /ʃəˈniːl/ *n.* **1** a velvety cord or yarn surrounded with pile, used in trimming furniture, bedspreads, or clothing. **2** fabric made from this.

Chenin Blanc /ˌʃenɪn ˈblɒŋk/ *n.* **1** a variety of white grape used to make wine with a distinctive flowery taste. **2** a wine made from this.

cheque *n.* **1** a written order to a bank to pay the stated sum from the drawer's account to a specified person or company. **2** the printed form on which such an order is written.

cheque book *n.* a book of forms for writing cheques and recording the transactions of an account.

chequebook journalism *n.* the payment of large sums by a news medium for exclusive rights to material for (esp. personal or scandalous) stories.

chequer etc. esp. *Brit. var.* of CHECKER[2].

chequing account *n. N Amer.* a bank account against which cheques may be written.

cherish *v.tr.* **1** protect or tend to lovingly. **2** hold dear, cling to (emotions, memories, etc.).

Cherokee /ˈtʃerəki/ ● *n.* (*pl.* same or **-s**) **1** a member of an Iroquoian people now living esp. in Oklahoma and N Carolina. **2** the language of this people. ● *adj.* of or relating to the Cherokee.

cheroot /ʃəˈruːt/ *n.* a cigar with both ends open.

cherry ● *n.* (*pl.* **-ies**) **1 a** a small soft round fruit, usu. red when ripe, with a single stone in its centre. **b** any of several trees of the genus *Prunus* bearing this fruit or grown for its ornamental flowers. **2** (also **cherrywood**) the reddish wood of a cherry tree. **3** *N Amer. slang* **a** virginity. **b** a virgin. **4** *N Amer. slang* the red light on the roof of a police car. ● *adj.* of a light red colour. □ **bowl of cherries** a consistently pleasurable experience (*life is not a bowl of cherries*).

cherry brandy *n.* a dark red liqueur of brandy in which cherries have been steeped.

cherry-pick *v.tr. & intr. N Amer.* **1** select only those items which are desirable or require little effort. **2** select items individually from various places, esp. to obtain the best value.

cherry picker *n.* **1** a crane with an articulated arm and a bucket for raising and lowering workers, firefighters, etc. **2** *Cdn* (*BC*) a tractor-like machine with a crane for retrieving logs lost along a road etc.

cherrystone *n.* (also **cherrystone clam**) a small edible northern quahog clam.

cherry tomato *n.* a small red or yellow variety of tomato.

chert /tʃɜrt/ *n.* a flintlike form of quartz. □ **cherty** *adj.*

cherub /ˈtʃerəb/ *n.* **1** (*pl.* **cherubim** /-bɪm/) **a** *Bible* a supernatural being resembling a winged lion with a human face. **b** *Christianity* a member of the second order of the nine ranks of heavenly beings. **2** (*pl.* **cherubs**) *Art* a representation of a winged child or the head of a winged child. **3** (*pl.* **cherubs**) a beautiful or innocent child.

Cheshire /ˈtʃeʃər, ˈtʃeʃɪːr/ *n.* a kind of firm crumbly cheese resembling cheddar.

Cheshire cat *n.* an imaginary cat with a broad fixed inexplicable grin. □ **grin like a Cheshire cat** smile with a broad, contented grin as if highly amused or knowing a secret.

chess *n.* a game for two, played on a chessboard with 16 pieces each, in which players attempt to place their opponent's king in checkmate.

chessboard *n.* a board with a pattern of squares of alternating colours, used in the game of chess.

chessman *n.* (*pl.* **-men**) any of the 32 pieces used in the game of chess.

chest *n.* **1 a** the part of a human or animal body enclosed by the ribs. **b** the upper front surface of the body; the breast. **2** a large strong box, esp. for storage or transport of items. **3** a small cabinet for toiletries, medicines, etc. □ **get a thing off one's chest** *informal* disclose a fact, secret, etc., to relieve one's anxiety about it. **play** (**one's cards, a thing,** etc.) **close to one's chest** *informal* be cautious or secretive about.

-chested *comb. form* having a chest of a specified kind.

chesterfield *n.* **1** *Cdn* any couch or sofa. **2** a padded sofa with arms the same height as the back.

chestnut ● *n.* **1** any of several trees of the genus *Castanea* of the beech family, bearing flowers in catkins and nuts enclosed in a spiny fruit, esp.: **a** *C. dentata* of N America. **b** *C. sativa* of Eurasia. **2** the large edible nut of any of these trees. **3** the heavy wood of any of these trees. **4** = HORSE CHESTNUT. **5** a horse of a reddish-brown or yellowish-brown colour. **6** *informal* a stale joke or anecdote. **7** a reddish-brown colour. ● *adj.* reddish brown.

chest of drawers *n.* a piece of furniture consisting of a set of drawers in a frame.

chesty *adj.* (**-ier, -iest**) **1** *informal* having a large chest or prominent breasts. **2** *N Amer. slang* arrogant.

Chetnik /ˈtʃetnɪk/ *n.* a member of a Serbian nationalist and anti-Communist guerrilla force which operated during both World Wars and re-emerged in the late 1980s.

chèvre /ˈʃevr/ *n.* a French variety of goat's-milk cheese.

chevron /ˈʃevrən, -rɒn/ *n.* **1** a badge in a V shape on the sleeve of a uniform indicating rank or length of service. **2** an ornamental representation of this. **3** any V-shaped line or stripe.

chevy *var. of* CHIVVY.

chew ● *v.* **1** *tr. & intr.* work (food etc.) between the teeth; crush or indent with the teeth. **2** *tr.* (often foll. by *up*) shred, mangle, mutilate, or otherwise damage (*the car chewed up the road*). **3** *tr.* (foll. by *on* or *over*) think about, meditate on, discuss. **4** *intr.* use chewing tobacco, esp. habitually. ● *n.* **1** an act of chewing. **2** something intended for chewing, esp. tobacco or candy. □ **chew the cud 1** (of an animal) ruminate. **2** reflect, ponder. **chew the fat** (or **rag**) *slang* chat; converse informally. **chew out** *N Amer. informal* reprimand harshly. □ **chewable** *adj.* **chewer** *n.*

chewing gum *n.* flavoured and sweetened gum, esp. chicle, for chewing.

chewing tobacco *n.* flavoured tobacco designed for chewing rather than smoking.

chewy *adj.* (**-ier, -iest**) **1** needing much chewing. **2** suitable for chewing. □ **chewiness** *n.*

Cheyenne /ʃaɪˈæn, -ˈen/ ● *n.* **1** (*pl.* same or **-s**) a member of an Algonquian people now inhabiting Oklahoma and Montana. **2** the language of this people. ● *adj.* of or relating to the Cheyenne.

chez /ʃeɪ/ *prep.* at the house or home of.

chi /kaɪ/ *n.* the twenty-second letter of the Greek alphabet (*X*, χ).

ch'i /ˈtʃiː/ *n.* (also **chi**) *var. of* QI.

Chianti /kiˈænti/ *n.* (*pl.* **Chiantis**) a dry usu. red Italian wine.

chiaroscuro /kiˌɑrəˈskuːroː, -skjɑro/ *n.* **1** the treatment of light and shade in drawing and painting. **2** a monochrome print or woodcut. **3** any contrast of light and dark.

chic ● *adj.* (**chicer, chicest**) stylish, elegant (in dress or appearance). ● *n.* stylishness, elegance. □ **chicly** *adv.* **chicness** *n.*

Chicana /tʃɪˈkɒnə, -ˈkænə/ *n.* esp. *US* a female American of Mexican origin.

chicanery /ʃɪˈkeɪnəri/ *n.* (*pl.* **-ies**) **1** clever but misleading talk; a false argument. **2** deception.

Chicano /tʃɪˈkɒnoː, -ˈkænoː/ *n.* (*pl.* **-os**) esp. *US* an American, esp. a male, of Mexican origin.

chi-chi /ˈʃiːʃiː/ *adj.* **1** (of a thing) ostentatiously stylish. **2** (of a person or behaviour) fussy, affected.

chick *n.* **1** a young or newly hatched bird, esp. a chicken. **2** *slang* often *offensive* a young woman. **3** a child. □ **neither chick nor child** no children at all.

chickadee *n.* any of various small N American birds of the titmouse family, esp. the black-capped chickadee, *Parus atricapillus*, with a distinctive dark-crowned head.

Chickasaw /ˈtʃɪkəˌsɒ/ *n.* **1** a member of a Muskogean people now living in Oklahoma. **2** the language spoken by this people and the Choctaw.

chicken ● *n.* **1** any of several varieties of domestic fowl raised for their flesh or eggs, esp. a young one. **2** the flesh of the chicken prepared as food. **3** *Cdn* (*BC & Prairies*) = PRAIRIE CHICKEN. **4** *informal* a cowardly person. **5** *informal* a contest in which participants attempt dangerous or reckless feats, usu. to see which one will yield first. ● *adj. informal* cowardly. ● *v.intr.* (foll. by *out*) *informal* withdraw from some activity through fear or lack of nerve. □ **count one's chickens (before they are hatched)** be overoptimistic.

chicken-and-egg *adj.* of or pertaining to the unresolved question as to which of two things caused the other.

chicken coop *n.* a coop for keeping poultry in.

chicken feed *n.* **1** food for domestic fowl. **2** *informal* a small amount of money.

chicken-hearted *adj.* (also **chicken-livered**) easily frightened; lacking nerve or courage.

chicken pox *n.* an infectious disease, esp. of children, with a rash of small blisters.

chickenshit *N Amer. coarse slang* ● *adj.* **1** petty, trivial. **2** cowardly. ● *n.* **1** trivialities, petty concerns; nonsense. **2** a coward.

chicken wire *n.* a light wire netting with a hexagonal mesh.

chick flick *n. informal* a movie that is perceived or marketed to appeal esp. to women, usu. featuring strong female characters and themes of romance, relationships, and female solidarity.

chickpea *n.* **1** a leguminous plant, *Cicer arietinum*, with short swollen pods containing yellowish-brown pea-shaped seeds. **2** this seed used as a vegetable.

chickweed *n.* any of several plants of the genera

Cerastium and *Stellaria*, esp. *S. media*, a common weed with slender stems and tiny white flowers.

chicle /ˈtʃɪkəl, -liː/ *n.* the milky juice of the sapodilla tree, used in the manufacture of chewing gum.

chicory *n.* (*pl.* **-ies**) **1** a blue-flowered plant, *Cichorium intybus*, cultivated for its salad leaves and its root. **2** its root, roasted and ground as a substitute for or an additive to coffee.

chide *v.tr. & intr.* (*past* **chided** or **chid**; *past part.* **chided** or **chidden**) **1** scold, rebuke. **2** compel by chiding; goad. □ **chider** *n.* **chidingly** *adv.*

chief ● *n.* **1 a** a leader or ruler. **b** the head of a tribe, clan, or Aboriginal band. **c** the leader of a Canadian Aboriginal community under the band council system. **2** the head of a police or fire department etc.; the highest official. ● *adj.* **1** first in position, importance, influence, etc. (*chief engineer*). **2** prominent, leading. □ **-in-chief** (in *comb.*) principal, head (*editor-in-chief*). □ **chiefdom** *n.*

chief electoral officer *n.* *Cdn* an official appointed to oversee the conduct of federal, provincial, and territorial elections.

chief executive *n.* **1** = CHIEF EXECUTIVE OFFICER. **2** *US* the governor of a state or (**Chief Executive**) the president of the US.

chief executive officer *n.* the highest-ranking executive of a corporation or other institution.

Chief Factor *n.* *Cdn hist.* (in the fur trade) the senior officer overseeing a major trading post and its surrounding district.

chief financial officer *n.* the senior executive in charge of financial affairs for a corporation etc.

chief inspector *n.* (in the Sûreté du Québec) an officer ranking above inspector.

chief justice *n.* (also **chief judge**) (in Canada, the US, and several Commonwealth countries) the presiding judge of the Supreme Court or of a court which has several judges.

chiefly *adv.* above all; mainly but not exclusively.

Chief of Defence Staff *n.* **1** (in Canada) the senior military official responsible for the control and administration of the Canadian Forces. **2** the senior military official of some other countries.

chief of police *n.* (in some municipal police forces and the Royal Newfoundland Constabulary) the highest ranking police officer.

chief of staff *n.* **1** the senior staff officer of a branch of the armed forces. **2** the head of any government staff, esp. the adviser to a prime minister etc.

chief operating officer *n.* the senior executive in charge of directing the operations of a corporation etc.

chief petty officer *n.* (also **Chief Petty Officer**) **1** *Cdn* (in the Canadian navy) an officer of either of two ranks: chief petty officer first class, the highest non-commissioned rank, or chief petty officer second class, ranking next below it. **2** an officer of the highest non-commissioned rank in other navies.

chief superintendent *n.* (in the OPP and RCMP) an officer ranking above superintendent.

chieftain *n.* the leader of a tribe or clan; chief. □ **chieftaincy** *n.* (*pl.* **-ies**). **chieftainship** *n.*

chief warrant officer *n.* (also **Chief Warrant Officer**) (in the Canadian Army and Air Force) the highest-ranking non-commissioned officer.

chiffon /ʃəˈfɒn/ ● *n.* a light diaphanous fabric of silk, nylon, etc. ● *adj.* **1** made of chiffon. **2** (of a pie filling, dessert, etc.) light in texture.

chiffon cake *n.* a light-textured cake made from a

batter of flour, sugar, oil, and egg yolks folded into beaten egg whites, usu. baked in a tube pan.

chiffon pie *n.* a pie with a jelled filling into which beaten egg whites have been folded.

chigger *n.* **1** the larva of any of various mites, several of which are parasitic. **2** = CHIGOE.

chigoe *n.* a tropical flea, *Tunga penetrans*, the pregnant females of which burrow beneath the skin of humans and animals and cause painful sores.

chihuahua /tʃəˈwɒwɒ/ *n.* a very small breed of dog with smooth hair, large eyes, and prominent ears.

Chilcotin /tʃɪlˈkoːtən/ *var. of* TSILHQOT'IN.

child *n.* (*pl.* **children**) **1 a** a young human being below the age of puberty. **b** an unborn or newborn human being. **2** one's son or daughter (at any age). **3** (foll. by *of*) a descendant, adherent, or product of (*children of Israel*; *child of the TV generation*). **4** a childish person. □ **childless** *adj.* **childlessness** *n.*

child abuse *n.* maltreatment of a child, esp. by beating, neglect, or sexual molestation.

child-bearing ● *n.* the act of giving birth to a child. ● *adj.* of, relating to, or suitable for the bearing of a child or children (*women of child-bearing age*).

child benefit *n.* *Cdn* = CHILD TAX BENEFIT.

childbirth *n.* the act of giving birth to a child.

child care *n.* **1** the care and rearing of a child or children. **2** = DAYCARE.

childhood *n.* the state or period of being a child.

childish *adj.* **1** of, like, or proper to a child. **2** immature, silly. □ **childishly** *adv.* **childishness** *n.*

childlike *adj.* **1** of or resembling a child (*a childlike appearance*). **2** having the qualities of a child, esp. positive ones such as innocence or frankness.

childproof ● *adj.* **1** unable to be damaged, operated, or opened by a child (*childproof locks*). **2** designed so as to be safe for young children (*a childproof kitchen*). ● *v.tr.* render childproof.

children *pl. of* CHILD.

Children's Aid Society *n.* (also **Children's Aid**) (in Canada) an organization to provide assistance or guardianship for homeless or abused children.

child's play *n.* an easy task.

child support *n.* money paid to a divorced spouse or guardian for the support of one's children.

child tax benefit *n.* (in Canada) a federal government program providing tax-free monthly payments to low- and moderate-income families with children under 18 years of age.

Chilean /ˈtʃɪliən, tʃɪˈleɪən/ ● *n.* **1** a native or national of Chile, a country on the west coast of S America. **2** a person of Chilean descent. ● *adj.* of Chile.

chili *n.* (*pl.* **-ies**) (also **chile**) **1** (in full **chili pepper**) the small hot-tasting red pod of a capsicum, often dried and ground and used as a seasoning and in several spices. **2 a** = CHILI CON CARNE. **b** a spicy meatless dish made usu. with chilies or chili powder, cooked tomatoes, beans, and onions.

chili con carne /kɒn ˈkɑrni/ *n.* a spicy dish of chopped or ground meat, chilies or chili powder, and usu. cooked tomatoes, beans, and onions.

chili dog *n.* *N Amer.* a hot dog garnished with chili con carne.

chili powder *n.* a hot condiment made usu. with cayenne or dried chilies, garlic, cumin, etc.

chili sauce *n.* a spicy sauce made with tomatoes, chilies, and spices.

Chilkat /ˈtʃɪlkæt/ *n.* a member of a subdivision of the Tlingit people inhabiting the Alaskan coast.

Chilkat blanket *n.* a pentagonal ceremonial blanket worn by W Coast Aboriginal peoples, woven from mountain goat hair and shredded cedar bark.

chill ● *n.* **1 a** an unpleasant cold sensation; lowered body temperature. **b** a feverish cold (*catch a chill*). **2** unpleasant coldness (of air, water, etc.). **3 a** a depressing influence (*cast a chill over*). **b** a feeling of fear or dread accompanied by coldness. **4** coldness of manner. ● *v.* **1** *tr. & intr.* make or become cold. **2** *tr.* depress, dispirit. **3** *tr.* cool (food or drink); preserve by cooling. **4** *intr.* esp. *N Amer. slang* **a** (often foll. by *out*) relax, settle down. **b** loiter, hang out. ● *adj.* chilly. □ **take the chill off** warm slightly. □ **chiller** *n.* **chillingly** *adv.*

Chilliwack /'tʃɪlə,wæk/ *n.* **1** a member of a Salishan people, a division of the Halkomelem, living in part of the Fraser River valley in BC. **2** the Halkomelem language of these people.

chilly *adj.* (**-ier, -iest**) **1** (of the weather or an object) somewhat cold. **2** (of a person or animal) feeling somewhat cold; sensitive to the cold. **3** unfriendly; unemotional. □ **chilliness** *n.*

chime ● *n.* **1 a** a set of bells. **b** the series of sounds given by this. **c** (in *pl.*) a musical instrument comprising a set of attuned bells or bars. **d** (often in *pl.*) a doorbell. **2** agreement, correspondence, harmony. ● *v.* **1 a** *intr.* (of bells) ring. **b** *tr.* sound (a bell or chime) by striking. **2** *tr.* (of a clock or bell) indicate (the hour) by chiming. **3** *intr.* (usu. foll. by *together, with*) be in agreement, harmonize. □ **chime in 1** interject a remark. **2** join in harmoniously. **3** (foll. by *with*) agree with. □ **chimer** *n.*

chimera /kai'mi:rə, ki-/ (also **chimaera**) *n.* **1 a** *Gk Myth* a fire-breathing female monster with a lion's head, a goat's body, and a serpent's tail. **b** any mythical beast with parts taken from various animals. **2** a fantastic or grotesque product of the imagination. **3** any cartilaginous fish of the family Chimaeridae, typically having erect pointed fins and a long tail. □ **chimeric** /-'merɪk/ *adj.* **chimerical** *adj.*

chimichanga /,tʃimi'tʃæŋɡə/ *n.* a tortilla wrapped around a filling of meat etc. and deep-fried.

chimney *n.* (*pl.* **-eys**) **1** a vertical shaft conducting smoke or combustion gases etc. up and away from a fire, furnace, etc. **2** the part of this which projects above a roof. **3** a glass tube protecting the flame of a lamp. **4** a narrow vertical crack in a rock face, often used by mountaineers to ascend.

chimney sweep *n.* a person whose job is removing soot from inside chimneys.

chimp *n. informal* = CHIMPANZEE.

chimpanzee *n.* a Central and W African anthropoid ape of the genus *Pan*, of which there are two species, *P. troglodytes*, and the pygmy chimpanzee, *P. paniscus*.

chin *n.* the front of the lower jaw. □ **chin up** *informal* cheer up. **keep one's chin up** *informal* remain cheerful, esp. in adversity. **take it on the chin 1** suffer a severe blow from (a misfortune etc.). **2** endure courageously. □ **-chinned** *adj.* (in *comb.*).

china ● *n.* **1** a kind of fine white or translucent ceramic or porcelain. **2** things made from ceramic, esp. household tableware or figurines. ● *adj.* made of china.

china cabinet *n.* a large piece of furniture with shelves and often glass doors, used for holding china.

Chinaman *n.* (*pl.* **-men**) usu. *offensive* a native of China. □ **the Chinaman's** *Cdn* (*Prairies*) = CHINESE CAFÉ.

China tea *n.* smoke-cured tea from a small-leaved tea plant grown in China.

Chinatown *n.* a district of any non-Chinese city in which the population is predominantly Chinese.

chinch¹ /tʃɪntʃ/ *n.* (in full **chinch bug**) a small insect of tropical and N America, *Blissus leucopterus*, that destroys both of grasses and grains.

chinch² /tʃɪnʃ/ *var. of* CHINSE.

chinchilla /tʃɪn'tʃɪlə/ *n.* **1 a** a small rodent of the genus *Chinchilla*, esp. *C. laniger*, native to S America, having soft silver-grey fur and a bushy tail. **b** its highly valued fur. **2** a breed of cat or rabbit having silver-grey fur resembling that of a chinchilla.

Chinese ● *adj.* of or relating to China, a country in E Asia, its people, or its language. ● *n.* **1** the Sino-Tibetan language of China, having several dialects including Mandarin and Cantonese. **2** (*pl.* same) **a** a native or national of China. **b** a person of Chinese descent.

Chinese cabbage *n.* **1** a vegetable, *Brassica pekinensis*, resembling lettuce. **2** = BOK CHOY.

Chinese café *n. Cdn* (*Prairies*) a café in a small town, operated by a Chinese proprietor and serving Chinese and other food.

Chinese checkers *n.* a game for two to six players played with marbles on a star-shaped board, with players attempting to move all of their marbles from one point to the opposite one.

Chinese lantern *n.* **1** a collapsible paper lantern. **2** a Eurasian plant, *Physalis alkekengi*, bearing white flowers and globular orange fruits enclosed in an orange-red papery calyx.

Chinese New Year *n.* the celebration of the New Year in the Chinese calendar, observed officially for a month starting in late January or early February.

ching *n.* an abrupt ringing sound, esp. one made by a cash register.

Chink *n. slang offensive* a Chinese person.

chink¹ ● *n.* **1** a fissure or crack. **2** a narrow opening or slit that admits light. ● *v.tr.* esp. *N Amer.* fill (a crack or opening) with a sealant etc. □ **chink in one's armour** a vulnerability or weakness. □ **chinking** *n.*

chink² ● *v.* **1** *intr.* make a slight ringing sound, as of glasses or coins striking together. **2** *tr.* cause to make this sound. ● *n.* this sound.

chin music *n. slang* **1** esp. *US* idle talk or chatter. **2** *Baseball* a pitch thrown near a batter's head. **3** *Cdn* (*Nfld*) sung or hummed music as accompaniment to a dance.

chino /'tʃi:no:/ *n.* (*pl.* **-os**) **1** a cotton twill fabric, usu. khaki-coloured. **2** (in *pl.*) trousers made from this.

chinoiserie /ʃi:n,wɒzə'ri:/ *n.* **1** the imitation of Chinese motifs and techniques in painting and in decorating furniture. **2** an object or objects in this style.

Chinook /ʃə'nʊk/ *n.* **1** a member of a Pacific Coast Aboriginal people formerly living along the Columbia River in Oregon and Washington. **2** the language of this people.

chinook *n.* **1 a** a warm dry wind which blows east of the Rocky Mountains, often causing significant temperature increases in winter. **b** a warm wet southerly wind west of the Rocky Mountains. **2** (in full **chinook salmon**) a large silver-coloured salmon with black spots, *Oncorhynchus tshawytscha*, native to the N Pacific and introduced into the Great Lakes and elsewhere.

chinook arch *n. Cdn* a bow-shaped cloud formation bordering an expanse of clear sky, visible on the western Prairies before or during a chinook wind.

Chinook Jargon *n.* a pidgin composed largely of Chinook, Nuu-chah-nulth, English, and French, formerly used by traders in the N Pacific coast of N America.

chinse /tʃɪns/ *v.tr. N Amer. (Maritimes & New England)* fill (the seams or spaces) in a boat, cabin, etc.

chintz /tʃɪns/ • *n.* a cotton fabric, usu. multicoloured and often with a flower pattern, with a glazed finish. • *adj.* made from or upholstered with this fabric.

chintzy *adj.* (**-ier, -iest**) **1** resembling, pertaining to, or decorated with chintz. **2** cheap; of poor quality. **3** *N Amer.* contemptible. **4** *N Amer.* stingy, miserly. □ **chintzily** *adv.* **chintziness** *n.*

chin-up *n. N Amer.* an exercise involving raising oneself with one's arms by pulling against a horizontal bar fixed above one's head.

chinwag *informal* • *n.* a talk or chat. • *v.intr.* (**-wagged, -wagging**) chat or gossip.

chip • *n.* **1 a** a small piece removed by or in the course of chopping, cutting, or breaking, esp. from hard material such as wood or stone. **b** the place from which such a chip has been removed. **2** *N Amer.* **a** (in full **potato chip**) a wafer-thin slice of potato deep-fried until crisp and eaten as a snack. **b** a similarly thin and crisp food (*nacho chips*). **3** a small piece of chocolate etc. used in baking. **4** *Cdn & Brit.* = FRENCH FRY. **5** a piece of dried bovine dung, esp. when used as fuel. **6** a counter used in some gambling games to represent money. **7** = MICROCHIP. **8** (also **chip shot**) *Sport* a short shot, kick, or pass with the ball travelling in an arc. • *v.* (**chipped, chipping**) **1** *tr.* (often foll. by *off, away*) cut or break (a piece) from a hard material. **2** *intr.* (often foll. by *at, away at*) cut pieces off (a hard material) to alter its shape, break it up, etc. **3** *intr.* (of stone, china, etc.) be susceptible to being chipped (*will chip easily*). **4** *tr. & intr. Sport* strike or kick (the ball) so that it travels in a short arc. **5** *tr.* cut (potatoes) into chips. □ **chip in** *informal* contribute (money etc.). **a chip off the old block** a child who resembles a parent, esp. in character. **a chip on one's shoulder** a disposition or inclination to feel resentful or aggrieved. **let the chips fall where they may** whatever the consequences. **when the chips are down** when the situation becomes difficult or critical.

chipboard *n.* = PARTICLEBOARD.

Chipewyan /tʃɪpə'waiən/ • *n.* **1** a member of an Athapaskan people inhabiting much of the northern Prairie provinces and the subarctic NWT. **2** the language of this people. • *adj.* of or relating to this people.

chipmunk *n.* any ground squirrel of the genus *Tamias* or *Eutamias*, having alternate light and dark stripes along the back.

chipotle /tʃɪ'potlei/ *n.* a hot red pepper, usu. smoked, commonly used in Mexican cooking.

Chippendale *adj.* **1** (of furniture) designed or made by the English cabinetmaker Thomas Chippendale (1718–79). **2** in the ornately elegant style of Chippendale's furniture, characterized by curved legs, Chinese or Gothic motifs, and carving.

chipper[1] *adj. informal* cheerful and lively.

chipper[2] *n.* a person or tool that chips timber.

Chippewa /'tʃɪpə,wɒ/ *n. & adj.* = OJIBWA. ¶*Chippewa* is normally used to refer only to the Ojibwa living to the east, south, and southwest of the Great Lakes.

chippy *adj.* (**-ier, -iest**) *Cdn informal* **1** short-tempered or irritable. **2** *Hockey* characterized by rough or dirty play. □ **chippiness** *n.*

chip set *n. Computing* a set of integrated circuits that when connected together form a single block.

chip wagon *n. Cdn* a mobile roadside stand or vehicle selling french fries etc.

chiropody /ʃɪ'rɒpədi, kɪ-/ *n.* esp. *Cdn & Brit.* = PODIATRY. □ **chiropodist** *n.*

chiropractic /,kairo'præktɪk/ *n.* the diagnosis and manipulative treatment of mechanical disorders of the joints, esp. of the spinal column. □ **chiropractor** /'kairo:-/ *n.*

chirp • *v.* **1** *intr.* (usu. of small birds, grasshoppers, etc.) emit a short sharp high-pitched note. **2** *tr. & intr.* speak or utter in a lively or cheerful way. • *n.* a chirping sound. □ **chirper** *n.*

chirpy *adj.* (**-ier, -iest**) *informal* cheerful, lively. □ **chirpily** *adv.* **chirpiness** *n.*

chirrup /'tʃɪrəp/ • *v.intr.* (**chirruped, chirruping**) (esp. of small birds) chirp, esp. repeatedly; twitter. • *n.* a chirruping sound. □ **chirrupy** *adj.*

chisel • *n.* a hand tool with a squared bevelled blade for shaping wood, stone, or metal. • *v.tr. & intr.* (**chiselled, chiselling**) **1** cut or shape with or as if with a chisel. **2** *slang* **a** cheat, swindle. **b** obtain by swindling. □ **chiseller** *n.*

chiselled *adj.* (of facial features, etc.) finely shaped.

chit[1] *n.* (usu. **a chit of a girl**) **1** *derogatory* or *jocular* a young and inexperienced girl or woman. **2** a young child.

chit[2] *n.* a voucher or note specifying a sum owed, esp. for food or drink.

chit-chat *informal* • *n.* light conversation; gossip. • *v.intr.* (**-chatted, -chatting**) talk informally; gossip.

chitin /'kaitɪn/ *n.* a polysaccharide forming the major constituent in the exoskeleton of arthropods and in the cell walls of fungi. □ **chitinous** *adj.*

chitter esp. *N Amer.* • *v.intr.* (of a bird, squirrel, etc.) make a twittering or chattering sound. • *n.* a twittering or chattering sound.

chivalrous /'ʃɪvəlrəs/ *adj.* **1** (usu. of a male) gallant, honourable, courteous. **2** involving or showing chivalry. □ **chivalrously** *adv.*

chivalry *n.* **1** the medieval knightly system with its religious, moral, and social code. **2** the combination of qualities expected of an ideal knight, esp. courage, honour, courtesy, justice, and readiness to help the weak. **3** a man's courteous behaviour, esp. towards women. □ **chivalric** *adj.*

chive *n.* (usu. in *pl.*) a small plant, *Allium schoenoprasum*, having purple-pink flowers and dense tufts of long tubular leaves which are used as a herb.

chivvy /'tʃɪvi/ *v.tr.* (**-ies, -ied**) (also **chivy, chevy** /'tʃevi/) harass, nag.

chlamydia /klə'mɪdiə/ *n.* **1** (*pl.* **chlamydiae** /-di,i:/) any parasitic bacterium of the genus *Chlamydia*, some of which cause diseases such as trachoma and psittacosis. **2** a sexually transmitted infection caused by *C. trachomatis*, often leading to urethritis or pelvic inflammatory disease.

chloride *n. Chem.* any compound of chlorine with another element or group.

chlorinate *v.tr.* **1** treat (esp. water) with chlorine, esp. to disinfect. **2** *Chem.* cause to react or combine with chlorine. □ **chlorination** *n.* **chlorinator** *n.*

chlorine *n.* a poisonous greenish-yellow gaseous element of the halogen group occurring naturally esp. as sodium chloride in salt, sea water, rock salt, etc., and used for purifying water, bleaching, etc.

chlorofluorocarbon /,klɔːrə'flʊərəʊ,kɑːbən/ *see* CFC.

chloroform /'klɔːrə,fɔːm/ • *n.* a colourless volatile sweet-smelling liquid used as a solvent and formerly used as a general anaesthetic. ● *v.tr.* render (a person) unconscious with this.

chlorophyll /ˈklɔrəfɪl/ *n.* the green pigment found in most plants, responsible for light absorption to provide energy for photosynthesis.

chock ● *n.* **1** a block or wedge of wood used to prevent a wheel etc. from moving. **2** a strong metal eye or hook on a ship's deck through which a line may be passed or secured. ● *v.tr.* fit or make fast with chocks. ● *adv.* as closely or tightly as possible.

chockablock *adj. & adv.* crammed close together; crammed full (*a street chockablock with cars*).

chock full *predic.adj. & adv.* crammed full or close together (*a cupboard chock full of clothes*).

chocoholic *n.* (also **chocaholic**) *informal* a person very fond of eating chocolate.

chocolate ● *n.* **1 a** an edible paste or solid made from cacao seeds by roasting, grinding, etc., often combined with flavourings, sugar, cream, etc. **b** a candy made of or coated with this. **c** a drink made by mixing chocolate with (usu. hot) milk or water. **2** (also **chocolate brown**) a dark brown colour. ● *adj.* **1** made from or flavoured with chocolate. **2** (also **chocolate brown**) dark brown. □ **chocolatey** *adj.* (also **chocolaty**).

chocolate bar *n.* a bar of sweetened chocolate or chocolate-coated caramel, nuts, etc.

chocolate milk *n.* milk flavoured with chocolate.

Choctaw /ˈtʃɒktɔ/ *n.* **1** (*pl.* same or **-s**) **a** a member of a Muskogean people originally resident in Mississippi and Alabama, and subsequently in Oklahoma. **b** the language spoken by this people and the Chickasaw. **2** *Figure Skating* (*pl.* **-s**) a step from one edge of a skate to the other edge of the other skate in the opposite direction (*compare* MOHAWK 2).

choice ● *n.* **1 a** an act or instance of choosing between alternatives. **b** a thing or person chosen (*a good choice*). **c** one of two or more possibilities from which one may choose. **2** a range from which to choose. **3** the best or preferred item (*the critics' choice*). **4** the power or opportunity to choose (*what choice do I have?*). **5** the right of a woman to choose to have an abortion. ● *adj.* **1** of superior quality; carefully chosen. **2** designating a grade of canned fruits and vegetables between standard and fancy, where slight variation in size, colour, or maturity is allowed but the produce is almost free from blemishes and other defects. □ **by choice** because one has chosen (*here by choice*). **of choice** preferred (*method of choice*). **of one's choice** that one has chosen (*the restaurant of your choice*). □ **choicely** *adv.* **choiceness** *n.*

choir *n.* **1** a group or company of singers. **2 a** the part of a church in which the choir sings. **b** in some cathedrals and other (esp. Anglican) churches, the area between the altar and the nave lined on either side with benches, used by the choir and clergy (*compare* CHANCEL). **3** *Music* a group of instruments of one family playing together.

choirboy *n.* a boy who sings in esp. a church choir.

choirgirl *n.* a girl who sings in esp. a church choir.

choir loft *n.* *N Amer.* a balcony in a church in which the choir sings.

choirmaster *n.* the director of esp. a church choir.

choir stall *n.* = STALL¹ *n.* 4.

choke ● *v.* **1** *tr.* hinder or impede the breathing of, esp. by constricting the windpipe or (of gas, smoke, etc.) by being unbreathable. **2** *intr.* suffer a hindrance or stoppage of breath (*choked on a piece of food*). **3** *tr. & intr.* (often foll. by *up*) make or become speechless from emotion. **4** *tr.* retard the growth of or kill (esp. plants)

by the deprivation of light, air, nourishment, etc. **5** *tr.* (often foll. by *back*) suppress (emotions) with difficulty. **6** *tr. & intr.* (often foll. by *up*) block or clog (a passage, tube, etc.). **7** *intr.* esp. *Sport informal* fail to perform effectively when under pressure. **8** *tr.* enrich the fuel mixture in (an internal combustion engine) by reducing the intake of air. ● *n.* **1** an instance of choking. **2** the valve in the carburetor of an internal combustion engine that controls the intake of air, esp. to enrich the fuel mixture. □ **choke down** swallow with difficulty. **choke off** impede or stop.

chokeberry *n.* (*pl.* **-ies**) **1** any N American shrub of the genus *Aronia* of the rose family. **2** its scarlet berry-like fruit.

choke chain *n.* (also **choke collar**) a chain looped round a dog's neck to exert control by pressure on its windpipe when the dog pulls.

chokecherry *n.* (*pl.* **-ies**) **1** any of several N American cherry trees, esp. *Prunus virginiana*. **2** the astringent fruit of this tree.

choked *adj.* clogged or plugged (*a snow-choked road*).

choker *n.* **1** a close-fitting necklace or ornamental neckband. **2** a clerical or other high collar. **3** *N Amer.* a heavy cable with a hook used for gripping and hauling logs. **4** a competitor that fails to perform effectively under pressure.

chokerman *n.* (*pl.* **-men**) (also **chokersetter**) *N Amer.* a person who attaches chokers to logs.

cholecalciferol /ˌkɒlɪkælˈsɪfəˌrɒl/ *n.* one of the D vitamins, produced by the action of sunlight on a cholesterol derivative widely distributed in the skin.

cholera /ˈkɒlərə/ *n.* an infectious and often fatal disease of the small intestine caused by the bacterium *Vibrio cholerae*, resulting in severe vomiting and diarrhea.

cholesterol /kəˈlestəˌrɒl/ *n.* a sterol found in most body tissues, including the blood, where high concentrations promote arteriosclerosis.

chomp ● *v. tr. & intr.* munch or chew noisily. **2** *tr.* (of a horse etc.) work (the bit) noisily between the teeth. ● *n.* a chewing noise or motion.

choose *v.* (*past* **chose**; *past part.* **chosen**) **1** *tr.* select from a number of alternatives. **2** *intr.* (usu. foll. by *between, from*) take or select one or another. **3** *tr.* decide, be determined (*chose to stay behind*). **4** *intr.* like, prefer (*do as you choose*). □ **cannot choose but** must. **nothing** (or **little**) **to choose between** little or no difference between. □ **chooser** *n.*

choosy *adj.* (**-ier**, **-iest**) *informal* demanding; fussy. □ **choosily** *adv.* **choosiness** *n.*

chop¹ ● *v.tr.* (**chopped**, **chopping**) **1 a** (usu. foll. by *off, down*, etc.) cut or fell by a blow, usu. with an axe or other blade. **b** make or prepare by cutting into large pieces (*chop firewood*). **2** (often foll. by *up*) cut (esp. meat or vegetables) into small pieces. **3** strike (esp. a ball) with a short downward stroke or blow. **4** *informal* remove; reduce by (*chopped $5,000 from the budget*). ● *n.* **1** a cutting blow, esp. with an axe. **2** a thick slice of meat (esp. pork or lamb) usu. including a rib. **3** a short downward stroke or blow in tennis, baseball, boxing, etc. **4** the broken motion of water, usu. owing to the action of the wind against the tide. **5** *Cdn, Brit.,* & *Austral.* (prec. by *the*) *informal* **a** dismissal from employment. **b** the action of killing or being killed. □ **chop logic** argue pedantically.

chop² *n.* (usu. in *pl.*) **1** the jaw or mouth. **2** *Music informal* technical facility or virtuosity on a wind instrument. □ **bust one's chops** *N Amer. slang* exert oneself. **bust someone's chops** *N Amer. slang* nag or criticize.

chopped liver n. N Amer. **1** a dish of cooked esp. chicken liver, chopped with onions, hard-boiled eggs, and seasonings. **2** slang a person or thing regarded as of insignificant worth or interest.

chopper • n. **1** a person, tool, or piece of machinery that chops. **2** informal a helicopter. **3** Baseball a high-bouncing ground ball. • v.tr. & intr. informal transport or travel by helicopter.

chopping block n. a block of wood on which logs etc. are chopped with an axe or on which food is cut with a knife. □ **on the chopping block** vulnerable to imminent removal, elimination, etc.

choppy adj. (**-ier, -iest**) **1** (of a body of water) with a rough surface of small, irregular waves. **2** disjointed (the movie's editing was choppy). **3** jerky, not fluid (choppy stride). □ **choppily** adv. **choppiness** n.

chopstick n. each of a pair of small thin sticks of wood or plastic etc., held both in one hand as eating utensils, originally in the Far East.

chop suey n. a Chinese-style dish usu. consisting of meat, bean sprouts, bamboo shoots, and onions.

choral adj. of, for, or sung by a choir or chorus.

chorale /kɔrˈæl/ n. (also **choral**) **1 a** a stately and simple hymn tune. **b** a harmonized version of this. **2** esp. US a choir.

chord¹ • n. a group of (usu. three or more) notes sounded together, as a basis of harmony. • v.intr. play a chord, esp. on a guitar etc. □ **chordal** adj.

chord² n. **1** Math. a straight line joining the extremities of an arc. **2** Aviation the width of an airfoil from leading to trailing edge. **3** Anat. var. of CORD. **4** Engin. one of the two principal members, usu. horizontal, of a truss. □ **strike** (or **touch**) **a chord** evoke some reaction in a person, esp. elicit sympathy.

chore n. **1 a** a routine task, esp. a domestic one. **b** N Amer. (in pl.) the routine daily tasks of a farm. **2** any tedious or unpleasant piece of work.

chorea /kəˈriə/ n. Med. a disorder characterized by jerky involuntary movements affecting esp. the shoulders, hips, and face.

choreograph /ˈkɔriəˌɡræf/ v.tr. **1** compose the choreography for (a ballet etc.). **2** arrange or direct, esp. something involving large numbers of people and complicated interactions. □ **choreographer** n.

choreography n. (pl. **-ies**) **1** the design or arrangement of a staged dance, figure skating, etc. **2** the sequence of steps and movements in dance or figure skating. **3** the written notation for this. □ **choreographic** adj. **choreographically** adv.

chorion /ˈkɔriən/ n. the outermost membrane surrounding an embryo of a mammal, reptile, or bird. □ **chorionic** /-ˈɒnɪk/ adj.

chorionic gonadotropin n. see HUMAN CHORIONIC GONADOTROPIN.

chorionic villus sampling n. a procedure for obtaining information about a fetus in which a sample of tissue is taken from the villi of the chorion.

chorister /ˈkɔrɪstər/ n. **1** a member of a choir. **2** a choirboy.

chorizo /tʃəˈriːzoː/ n. (pl. **-os**) a type of sausage containing pork, garlic, and hot spices.

chortle • v.intr. chuckle gleefully. • n. a gleeful chuckle.

chorus • n. (pl. **choruses**) **1** a group (esp. a large one) of singers; a choir. **2** a piece of music composed for a choir. **3** the refrain or the recurring part of a popular song. **4** any simultaneous utterance by many persons etc. (a chorus of disapproval). **5** a group of singers or dancers performing in concert in a musical comedy, opera, etc. **6** (in Greek tragedy) **a** a group of performers who comment together in voice and movement on the main action. **b** an utterance of the chorus. **7** (in Elizabethan drama) **a** a character who speaks the prologue and other linking parts of the play. **b** the part spoken by this character. • v.tr. & intr. (of a group) speak or utter simultaneously. □ **in chorus** (uttered) together; in unison.

chorus line n. a group of esp. female singers and dancers performing in a musical comedy, cabaret act, etc., often dancing together in a long line.

chose past of CHOOSE.

chosen • v. past part. of CHOOSE. • adj. **1** selected or preferred. **2** destined by God for salvation.

chosen people n. a people believing themselves to have been specially chosen by God for salvation, esp. the Jews.

choux pastry /ʃuː/ n. a pastry made of flour, water, butter, and eggs, which when cooked forms a hollow round puff, used in cream puffs etc.

chow slang • n. food. • v.intr. N Amer. (foll. by down) eat.

chow chow n. **1** (also **chow**) a breed of dog developed in China, with a thick coat, compact body, and a bluish-black tongue. **2** a relish of pickled chopped mixed vegetables.

chowder n. N Amer. a thick soup, usu. containing fish, clams, corn, or potatoes.

chowderhead n. N Amer. informal a stupid person.

chow mein /ˈmeɪn/ n. a Chinese-style dish of fried noodles with chopped meat etc. and vegetables.

chrism /ˈkrɪzəm/ n. a consecrated mixture of oil and balsam used for anointing in rites of the Catholic and Orthodox Churches.

Chrissake /ˈkraɪseɪk/ n. & interj. (also **Chrissakes**) informal (for) Christ's sake (see SAKE¹).

Christ • n. **1** the title, also now treated as a name, given to Jesus of Nazareth, believed by Christians to have fulfilled the Old Testament prophecies of a coming Messiah. **2** the Messiah as prophesied in the Old Testament. **3** an image or picture of Jesus. • interj. taboo slang expressing surprise, anger, etc. □ **Christlike** adj.

Christ child n. (prec. by the) Jesus as a child or baby.

christen /ˈkrɪsən/ v.tr. **1** admit (a person) to the Christian Church by baptism. **2** give a Christian name to (a person) at baptism. **3** name and dedicate (a ship, a bell, etc.) by a ceremony analogous to baptism. **4** give a name to a thing; call. **5** informal use for the first time. □ **christener** n. **christening** n.

Christendom /ˈkrɪsəndəm/ n. **1** Christians worldwide, regarded as a collective body. **2** hist. the countries occupied by Christians, esp. in the Middle Ages.

Christian • adj. **1** pertaining to Christ or his teachings. **2** believing in or adhering to the teachings of Christianity. **3** showing the qualities associated with Christianity. **4** (of a person) kind, fair, decent. • n. **1 a** a person who has received Christian baptism. **b** an adherent of Christianity. **2** a person exhibiting Christian qualities. □ **Christianize** v.tr. & intr. **Christianization** n. **Christianly** adv.

Christian and Missionary Alliance n. an evangelical Protestant movement founded in New York in the late 19th c., stressing Christ as saviour and actively promoting missionary work.

Christian Brothers n.pl. (in full **Brothers of the Christian Schools**) a Catholic religious congregation involved in education, esp. of the poor.

Christian Democrat n. a member of any of various moderate European political parties having a Catholic base. □ **Christian Democratic** adj.

Christian era *n.* the era reckoned from the traditional date of Christ's birth.

Christianity *n.* **1** the religion based on the doctrines of Christ and his disciples, encompassing the Catholic, Protestant, and Orthodox faiths. **2** the state of being a Christian; Christian quality or character. **3** = CHRISTENDOM.

Christian name *n.* esp. *Brit.* = FIRST NAME.

Christian Reformed *adj.* of or pertaining to a Calvinist denomination whose adherents are primarily of Dutch origin.

Christian Science *n.* the beliefs and practices of the Church of Christ, Scientist, which holds that God and his spiritual creation are the only ultimate reality, and that healing can be effected through prayer. □ **Christian Scientist** *n.*

Christie *n.* (*pl.* **-ies**) *Skiing* a sudden turn in which the skis are kept parallel, used for changing direction or stopping quickly.

Christly *adj.* **1** Christlike. **2** *Cdn & US* (*New England*) *slang* used as an intensifier (*I hate that Christly dog!*).

Christmas *n.* (*pl.* **Christmases**) **1** (also **Christmas Day**) *Christianity* the annual festival of Christ's birth, celebrated by Western churches on Dec. 25, and by most Eastern churches on Jan. 7. **2** the season in which this occurs. □ **Christmasy** *adj.*

Christmas box *n.* *Cdn* (*Nfld*) a Christmas present.

Christmas cake *n.* *Cdn & Brit.* a rich fruitcake eaten at Christmas.

Christmas card *n.* a card sent with greetings at Christmas.

Christmas cracker *n.* a small tube wrapped in decorated paper gathered at both ends, usu. containing a paper hat, small toy, etc., which pops when the ends are pulled to open it, usu. at a Christmas dinner.

Christmas Eve *n.* the day or the evening before Christmas Day.

Christmas lights *n.pl.* a string of small, usu. coloured light bulbs, used esp. at Christmas to decorate houses, trees, etc.

Christmas pudding *n.* a rich steamed pudding eaten at Christmas, made with flour, suet, dried fruit, spices, etc.

Christmas rose *n.* a winter-blooming evergreen, *Helleborus niger*, with white flowers.

Christmas spirit *n.* a mood of joy and generosity, held to be prevalent at Christmas.

Christmas stocking *n.* a stocking hung by children at Christmas to be filled with small gifts.

Christmastime *n.* (also **Christmastide**) the Christmas season.

Christmas tree *n.* **1** an evergreen or artificial tree set up with decorations at Christmas. **2** *Cdn* a Christmas party. **3** a system of pipes and valves which controls the pressure of an oil or natural gas well.

Christy *var.* of CHRISTIE.

chromatic /kro'mætɪk/ *adj.* **1** of or produced by colour; in (esp. bright) colours. **2** *Music* **a** of or having notes not belonging to a diatonic scale (*chromatic chord*). **b** (of a scale) ascending or descending by semitones. **c** (of an instrument) capable of producing all the tones of the chromatic scale.

chromatography /ˌkro:mə'tɒgrəfi/ *n.* *Chem.* the separation of the components of a mixture by slow passage through or over a material which adsorbs them differently. □ **chromatograph** *n.* **chromatographic** *adj.*

chrome *n.* chromium, esp. as plating on the trimmings of a car etc.

chromed *adj.* **1** plated with chromium. **2** trimmed with chrome.

chrome-moly /'mɒli/ *n.* a strong but light steel alloy of chromium and molybdenum.

chrome steel *n.* a hard fine-grained steel containing much chromium and used for tools etc.

chromium /'kro:miəm/ *n.* a hard white metallic element, occurring naturally and used in alloys and as a shiny decorative electroplated coating.

chromosome /'kro:mə,so:m/ *n.* *Biochem.* one of the threadlike structures, usu. found in the cell nucleus, that carry the genetic information in the form of genes. □ **chromosomal** *adj.*

chronic *adj.* **1** persisting for a long time (usu. of an illness or a personal or social problem). **2** having a chronic complaint. **3** *informal* habitual, inveterate (*a chronic liar*). □ **chronically** *adv.*

chronic fatigue syndrome *n.* a disease characterized by extreme fatigue, poor coordination, giddiness, depression, and general malaise, the cause of which is unknown. Abbr.: **CFS**.

chronicle ● *n.* **1** a register of events in order of their occurrence. **2** a narrative, a full account. ● *v.tr.* record (events) in the order of their occurrence. □ **chronicler** *n.*

chronograph /'krɒnə,græf, 'kro:nə-/ *n.* **1** an instrument for recording time with great accuracy. **2** a stopwatch. □ **chronographic** *adj.*

chronological /ˌkrɒnə'lɒdʒɪkəl/ *adj.* **1** (of a number of events) arranged or regarded in the order of their occurrence. **2** of or relating to chronology. **3** of or relating to time. □ **chronologically** *adv.*

chronology *n.* (*pl.* **-ies**) **1 a** the arrangement of events, dates, etc. in the order of their occurrence. **b** a table or document displaying this. **2** the study of historical records to establish the dates of past events. □ **chronologist** *n.* **chronologize** *v.tr.*

chronometer /krə'nɒmɪtər/ *n.* a time-measuring instrument, esp. one keeping accurate time at all temperatures and used in navigation.

chrysalis /'krɪsəlɪs/ *n.* (*pl.* **chrysalises** or **chrysalides** /krɪ'sælɪ,di:z/) **1 a** a quiescent pupa of a butterfly or moth. **b** the hard outer case enclosing it. **2** a preparatory or transitional state.

chrysanthemum /krɪ'sænθəməm/ *n.* any composite plant of the genus *Chrysanthemum*, having brightly coloured flowers.

chthonic /'kθɒnɪk, 'θɒnɪk/ *adj.* of, relating to, or inhabiting the underworld.

chub[1] *n.* any of various fishes with short, thick, rounded bodies and large heads, esp. any of several species of the carp family in N America.

chub[2] *n.* a short, fat sausage.

chubby *adj.* (**-ier, -iest**) plump and rounded (esp. of a person etc.). □ **chubbily** *adv.* **chubbiness** *n.*

chuck[1] ● *v.tr.* **1** *informal* a fling or throw carelessly or with indifference. **b** discard. **2** *informal* (often foll. by *in*) give up; reject (*chucked my job*). **3** touch playfully, esp. under the chin. ● *n.* a playful touch under the chin. □

chuck out *informal* **1** expel (a person) from a gathering etc. **2** get rid of, discard.

chuck[2] *n.* **1** a cut of beef extending from the neck to the sixth rib. **2** a device for holding e.g. a bit in a drill. **3** *N Amer. informal* food, provisions.

chuck[3] *n.* *N Amer.* (*BC, Alaska, & US Northwest*) *informal* a large body of water (*compare* SALTCHUCK).

chuckle ● *v.intr.* laugh quietly or inwardly. ● *n.* a quiet or suppressed laugh. □ **chuckler** *n.*

chuckwagon *n.* **1** a wagon carrying provisions,

cooking utensils, etc., as used on a ranch, esp. covered with a canvas supported by hoops. **2** a small cart resembling this, used in chuckwagon races.

chuckwagon dinner *n.* *N Amer.* an informal meal in the style of those served from chuckwagons, usu. consisting of beef, potatoes, baked beans, etc.

chuckwagon race *n.* *N Amer.* a rodeo event in which chuckwagons pulled by teams of four horses race on an oval course.

chuff *v.intr.* **1** (of a steam engine etc.) move with a regular sharp puffing sound. **2** make a sound like a puffing steam engine.

chug *N Amer.* ● *v.* (**chugged, chugging**) **1** *intr.* emit a regular muffled explosive sound, as of an engine running slowly. **2** *intr.* move with this sound. **3** *intr.* move slowly but steadily. **4** *tr. & intr.* (also **chugalug**) *slang* drink (a beer etc.) in large gulps without pausing. ● *n.* a chugging sound.

chum¹ ● *n.* informal a close friend. ● *v.intr.* (often foll. by *with, around*) associate with as a friend.

chum² *N Amer.* ● *n.* **1** refuse from fish. **2** chopped fish used as bait. ● *v.* **1** *intr.* fish using chum. **2** *tr.* bait (a fishing place) using chum.

chum³ *n.* (also **chum salmon**) a salmon, *Oncorhynchus keta*, of the N American Pacific coast.

chummy informal ● *adj.* (**-ier, -iest**) intimate, friendly, sociable. ● *n.* *Cdn (Nfld)* a person, usu. male, not known to the speaker (*chummy slipped on the ice*). □ **chummily** *adv.* **chumminess** *n.*

chump *n.* informal a gullible or foolish person.

chunk¹ ● *n.* **1** a thick solid slice or piece of something firm or hard. **2** a substantial amount or piece. ● *v.* **1 a** *tr.* tear or cut into chunks (*chunked tuna*). **b** *intr.* break into chunks. **2** *tr.* *Psych.* (of the mind) group items of information together to be remembered as a unit.

chunk² ● *v.* **1** *intr.* make a muffled metallic sound. **2** *tr.* cause to make this sound. ● *n.* this sound.

chunky *adj.* (**-ier, -iest**) **1** containing or consisting of chunks. **2** thick and solid. **3** (of clothes) made of a thick material. **4** stocky. □ **chunkiness** *n.*

chuppah /ˈxʊpə/ *n.* (also **chuppa**) a canopy beneath which Jewish marriage ceremonies are performed.

church *n.* **1** a building for public (usu. Christian) worship. **2** a meeting for public worship in such a building (*met after church*). **3** (**Church**) the body of all Christians. **4** (also **Church**) an organized Christian group of any time, country, or distinct principles of worship (*the medieval Church; Church of Scotland*). **5** (also **Church**) institutionalized religion as a political or social force (*Church and State*). □ **poor as a church mouse** exceedingly poor. □ **churchly** *adj.*

churchgoer *n.* a person who goes to church, esp. regularly. □ **churchgoing** *n. & adj.*

churchman *n.* (*pl.* **-men**) a male member of the clergy or of a church.

Church of Christ, Scientist *n.* the official name of the Christian Science Church.

Church of England *n.* an English branch of the Western Church, which has retained episcopacy but rejected the Pope's supremacy.

Church of Jesus Christ of Latter-day Saints *n.* the official name of the Mormon Church.

Church of Scotland *n.* the official (Presbyterian) Church in Scotland.

church school *n.* **1** a school founded by or associated with a church. **2** = SUNDAY SCHOOL.

church union *n.* *Cdn* the merger, in 1925, of Canadian Methodist and Congregationalist Churches together with the majority of Canadian Presbyterians to form the United Church of Canada.

churchwarden *n.* *Anglicanism* either of two elected lay representatives of a parish.

churchwoman *n.* (*pl.* **-women**) a woman member of the clergy or of a church.

churchy *adj.* **1** obtrusively or intolerantly devoted to the Christian Church or opposed to religious dissent. **2** like a church. □ **churchiness** *n.*

churchyard *n.* the enclosed ground around a church, esp. as used for burials.

churl *n.* an ill-mannered person.

churlish *adj.* surly; mean. □ **churlishly** *adv.* **churlishness** *n.*

churn ● *n.* a machine for making butter by agitating milk or cream. ● *v.* **1** *tr.* agitate (milk or cream) in a churn. **2** *tr.* produce (butter) in this way. **3** *tr.* (usu. foll. by *up*) cause distress to; upset, agitate. **4** *intr.* (esp. of a liquid) move about violently (*my stomach churned*). **5** *tr.* (often foll. by *up*) agitate or move (liquid, soil, etc.) vigorously. **6** *tr.* (of a broker) buy and sell (a client's investments) frequently in order to earn more commission. □ **churn out** produce routinely or mechanically, esp. in large quantities.

chute¹ *n.* **1** a sloping or vertical channel, tube, or slide, with or without water, for conveying things to a lower level. **2** a slide into a swimming pool. **3 a** a pen from which an animal is released to begin a race, rodeo event, etc. **b** a narrow passage or enclosure for sheep or cattle. **4** *Cdn* a rapid.

chute² *n.* informal a parachute. □ **chutist** *n.*

chutney *n.* (*pl.* **-eys**) a spicy condiment made of fruits or vegetables, vinegar, sugar, etc.

chutzpah /ˈhʊtzpə, hʌts-, xuːts-, -pʊ/ *n.* *slang* **1** shameless audacity; cheek. **2** boldness.

CI *abbr.* *Cdn* Collegiate Institute.

Ci *abbr.* curie.

CIA *abbr.* CENTRAL INTELLIGENCE AGENCY.

ciao /tʃaʊ/ *interj.* informal **1** goodbye. **2** hello.

CIAU *abbr.* Canadian Inter-university Athletic Union.

cicada /sɪˈkeɪdə, -ˈkɒdə/ *n.* any transparent-winged large insect of the family Cicadidae, the males of which make a loud, shrill chirping sound.

CIDA /ˈsiːdə/ *abbr.* Canadian International Development Agency.

cider *n.* **1** *N Amer.* an unfermented drink made from apple juice. **2** (also **hard cider**) an alcoholic drink made from fermented apple juice.

cider vinegar *n.* vinegar made from fermented apple juice.

c.i.f. *abbr.* cost, insurance, freight.

cigar *n.* a cylinder of tobacco rolled in tobacco leaves for smoking. □ **close but no cigar** *N Amer.* (of an attempt etc.) almost but not quite successful.

cigarette *n.* (*US* also **cigaret**) **1** a thin cylinder of finely-cut tobacco rolled in paper for smoking. **2** a similar cylinder containing a narcotic or medicated substance.

cilantro /sɪˈlæntro/ *n.* fresh coriander, used as a herb.

cilia /ˈsɪlɪə/ *n.pl.* (*sing.* **cilium** /-ɪəm/) **1** short minute hairlike vibrating structures on the surface of some cells, causing currents in the surrounding fluid. **2** eyelashes. □ **ciliary** /ˈsɪlɪeri/ *adj.* **ciliated** *adj.*

ciliate /ˈsɪlɪeɪt/ ● *adj.* having cilia. ● *n.* a protozoan with cilia, of the phylum Ciliophora.

C.-in-C. *abbr.* commander-in-chief.

cinch ● *n.* **1** informal **a** a sure thing; a certainty. **b** an easy task. **2** a firm hold. **3** esp. *N Amer.* a girth for a saddle or pack. ● *v.tr.* **1 a** tighten as with a cinch (*cinched at the waist with a belt*). **b** secure a grip on. **2** *slang* make certain of. **3** esp. *N Amer.* put a cinch on.

cinchona /sɪŋ'koːnə/ *n.* **1** any evergreen tree or shrub of the genus *Cinchona*, native to S America, with fragrant flowers and yielding cinchona bark. **2** the bark of this tree, containing quinine.

cinder *n.* **1** the residue of coal or wood etc. that has stopped giving off flames but still has combustible matter in it. **2** slag. **3** (in *pl.*) ashes. □ **burned to a cinder** made useless by burning. □ **cindery** *adj.*

cinder block *n. N Amer.* a block made of cinders mixed with sand and cement, the standard block used in building warehouses etc. (also *attrib.*: *cinder-block house*).

Cinderella *n.* **1** (often *attrib.*) a person or thing of unrecognized or disregarded merit or beauty, esp. that achieves success in the end (*Cinderella team*). **2** a neglected or despised member of a group.

cinema *n.* **1** motion pictures collectively. **2** the production of films as an art or industry.

cinematic *adj.* **1** having the qualities characteristic of the cinema. **2** of or relating to the cinema. □ **cinematically** *adv.*

cinematography /ˌsɪnəmə'tɒɡrəfi/ *n.* the art or technique of shooting motion pictures, involving the choice of film, camera, lens, lighting, camera angle, etc. □ **cinematographer** *n.* **cinematographic** *adj.*

cinéma-vérité /ˌsɪneˌmə veri'tei/ *n. Film* **1** the art or process of making realistic (esp. documentary) films which avoid artificiality and artistic effect. **2** such films collectively.

Cineplex *n. N Amer.* proprietary a movie theatre comprising several separate cinemas.

cinnamon *n.* **1** an aromatic spice from the peeled, dried, and rolled bark of a SE Asian tree. **2** any tree of the genus *Cinnamomum*, esp. *C. zeylanicum*, yielding the spice. **3 a** yellowish-brown. **b** reddish-brown.

cinnamon bun *n.* (also **cinnamon roll**) *N Amer.* a baked spiral of cinnamon- and sugar-sprinkled dough, often glazed and with raisins.

cinnamon stick *n.* a stick-like roll of cinnamon bark.

cinquefoil /'sɪŋkfɔɪl/ *n.* any plant of the genus *Potentilla*, with compound leaves of usu. five leaflets.

cipaille /si'pai/ *n. Cdn* a deep pie with alternating layers of meat and pastry.

cipher ● *n.* **1 a** a secret or disguised system of writing; a code. **b** a message etc. written in this way. **c** the key to it. **2** the arithmetical symbol (0) denoting no amount but used to occupy a vacant place in decimal etc. numeration (as in 12.05). **3** a person or thing of no importance. **4** the interlaced initials of a person etc.; a monogram. **5** any Arabic numeral. ● *v.tr.* **1** put into secret writing. **2** (usu. foll. by *out*) work out by arithmetic; calculate.

circa *prep.* (preceding a date) about, approximately.

circle ● *n.* **1 a** a round plane figure whose circumference is everywhere equidistant from its centre. **b** the line enclosing a circle. **2** a thing, group, etc. shaped or arranged roughly in a circle. **3** a ring. **4** a circular route. **5** persons grouped round a centre of interest. **6** a group of people having similar interests, characteristics, etc. (*circle of friends; in scientific circles*). **7** a period or cycle (*the circle of the year*). **8 a** an unbroken sequence of reciprocal cause and effect. **b** an action and reaction that intensify each other. **c** the fallacy of proving a proposition from another which depends on the first for its own proof. **9** = FACEOFF CIRCLE. **10** (among N American Aboriginal peoples) a meeting for prayer, healing, etc. in which the partici-

pants gather in a circle. ● *v.* **1** *intr.* (often foll. by *round*, *about*) move in a circle. **2** *tr.* **a** move in or form a circle around. **b** draw a circle around. □ **circle back** move in a wide loop towards the starting point. **circle the wagons** *N Amer.* (of a group) unite in defence of a common interest. **come full circle** return to the starting point. **go round in circles** make no progress despite effort. **run round in circles** *informal* be fussily busy with little result.

circlet *n.* **1** a small circle. **2** a circular band made of precious metal, flowers, etc., worn around the head.

circuit *n.* **1** a line or course enclosing an area; the distance around. **2** a standard series of events or places visited by a judge, group of athletes, preacher, etc. (*circuit court*). **3** *Electricity* **a** the path of a current. **b** the apparatus through which a current passes.

circuit board *n.* a thin rigid board containing an electric circuit.

circuit breaker *n.* an automatic device for stopping the flow of current in an electrical circuit, usu. as a safety measure, e.g. when the circuit is overloaded.

circuit court *n.* (in Canada) a province's superior court travelling to different communities to sit.

circuitous /sər'kjuːɪtəs/ *adj.* **1** indirect (and usu. long). **2** going a long way around. □ **circuitously** *adv.* **circuitousness** *n.*

circuit rider *n. N Amer. hist.* a person, esp. a Methodist preacher, who travels from community to community to preach, work, etc.

circuitry *n.* (*pl.* **-ies**) **1** a system of electric circuits. **2** the equipment forming this.

circular ● *adj.* **1 a** having the form of a circle. **b** moving or taking place along a circle (*circular tour*). **2** *Logic* (of reasoning) depending on the conclusion for proof. **3** (of a letter or advertisement etc.) printed for distribution to a large number of people. ● *n.* a circular leaflet etc. □ **circularity** *n.* **circularly** *adv.*

circular saw *n.* a power saw with a rapidly rotating toothed disc.

circulate *v.* **1** *intr.* go round from one place or person etc. to the next and so on; be in circulation. **2** *intr.* (of blood, sap, etc.) flow through a body, tree, etc. **3** *tr.* **a** cause to go around; put into circulation. **b** give currency to (a report etc.). **4** *intr.* be actively sociable at a party, gathering, etc. □ **circulator** *n.*

circulation *n.* **1 a** movement to and fro, or from and back to a starting point, esp. of a fluid in a confined area or circuit. **b** the movement of blood from and to the heart. **c** a similar movement of sap etc. **2 a** the transmission or distribution (of news or information or books etc.). **b** the number of copies sold, esp. of journals and newspapers. **3 a** currency, coin, etc. **b** the movement or exchange of this in a country etc. □ **in** (or **out of**) **circulation** participating (or not participating) in activities etc.

circulatory /'sɜːrkjʊlə,tɔri/ *adj.* of or relating to the circulation of blood or sap.

circum- *comb. form* around, about (*circumlocution*).

circumcise *v.tr.* **1** cut off the foreskin of, as a Jewish or Muslim rite or a surgical operation. **2** cut off the clitoris (and sometimes the labia) of, usu. as a religious rite.

circumcision *n.* **1** the act or rite of circumcising or being circumcised. **2** (**Circumcision**) *Christianity* (in the Anglican and formerly in the Catholic Church) the feast of the Circumcision of Christ, Jan. 1.

circumference *n.* **1** the enclosing boundary, esp. of a circle. **2** the distance around. □ **circumferential** /ˌsɜːkəmfə'renʃəl/ *adj.* **circumferentially** *adv.*

circumflex ● *n.* (in full **circumflex accent**) a

mark (ˆ or ⌒) placed over a vowel in some languages to indicate a contraction, length, or a special quality. ● *adj. Anat.* curved, bending around something else (*circumflex nerve*).

circumlocution /ˌsɜːkəmləˈkjuːʃən/ *n.* **1 a** a round-about expression. **b** evasive talk. **2** the use of many words where fewer would do; verbosity. □ **circumlocutional** *adj.* **circumlocutionary** *adj.* **circumlocutory** /-ˈlɒkjʊˌtɔri/ *adj.*

circumnavigate *v.tr.* sail or fly round (esp. the world). □ **circumnavigation** *n.* **circumnavigator** *n.*

circumpolar *adj.* **1** around or near one of the earth's poles. **2** *Astronomy* (of a star or motion etc.) above the horizon at all times in a given latitude.

circumscribe *v.tr.* **1** (of a line etc.) enclose or outline. **2** lay down the limits of; confine, restrict. **3** *Math.* draw (a figure) around another, touching it at points but not cutting it. □ **circumscribable** *adj.* **circumscriber** *n.* **circumscription** *n.*

circumspect *adj.* wary, cautious; taking everything into account. □ **circumspection** *n.*

circumstance *n.* **1 a** a fact, occurrence, or condition, esp. (in *pl.*) the time, place, manner, cause, occasion etc., or surroundings of an act or event. **b** (in *pl.*) the external conditions that affect or might affect an action. **2** (often foll. by *that* + clause) an incident, occurrence, or fact, as needing consideration (*the circumstance that he left early*). **3** (in *pl.*) one's state of financial or material welfare (*in reduced circumstances*). **4** ceremony, fuss (*pomp and circumstance*). **5** full detail in a narrative (*told it with much circumstance*). □ **in** (or **under**) **the** (or **these**) **circumstances** the state of affairs being what it is. **in** (or **under**) **no circumstances** not at all; never.

circumstantial *adj.* **1** given in full detail (*a circumstantial account*). **2** (of evidence, a legal case, etc.) tending to establish a conclusion by inference from known facts hard to explain otherwise. **3 a** depending on circumstances. **b** adventitious, incidental. □ **circumstantiality** *n.*

circumvent *v.tr.* **1 a** evade (a difficulty); find a way around. **b** baffle, outwit. **2** entrap (an enemy) by surrounding. □ **circumvention** *n.*

circus *n.* (*pl.* **circuses**) **1 a** a travelling show of performing animals, acrobats, clowns, etc. **b** a performance given by them. **2** *informal* a situation characterized by lively and chaotic activity. **3** *Rom. Hist.* **a** a rounded or oval arena with tiers of seats, for equestrian and other sports and games. **b** a performance given there.

ciré /ˈsiːreɪ/ ● *n.* a fabric with a smooth shiny surface obtained esp. by waxing and heating. ● *adj.* having such a surface.

cirque /sɜːk/ *n.* a large bowl-shaped hollow of glacial origin at the head of a valley or on a mountainside.

cirrhosis /sɪˈrəʊsɪs/ *n.* a chronic disease of the liver caused by alcoholism, hepatitis, etc. in which much of the liver is replaced by fibrous tissue.

cirriped /ˈsɪrɪˌped/ *n.* (also **cirripede** /-ˌpiːd/) any marine crustacean of the class Cirripedia, having a valved shell and usu. sessile when adult.

cirrostratus /ˌsɪrəʊˈstrɑːtəs/ *n. Meteorol.* cloud forming a thin, fairly uniform layer at high altitude.

cirrus /ˈsɪrəs/ *n.* **1** *Meteorol.* **a** clouds formed at high altitudes as delicate white wisps. **b** a cloud of this type. **2** *Bot.* a tendril. **3** *Zool.* a long slender filamentary appendage. □ **cirrose** *adj.* **cirrous** *adj.*

CIS *abbr.* Commonwealth of Independent States.

cisco /ˈsɪskoʊ/ *n.* (*pl.* **-oes**) any of various N American freshwater salmonid whitefish of the genus *Coregonus*.

Cistercian /sɪsˈtɜːʃən/ ● *n.* a monk or nun of an order founded in 1098 as a stricter branch of the Benedictines. ● *adj.* of the Cistercians.

cistern /ˈsɪstɜːn/ *n.* **1** a tank or reservoir for storing water. **2** a fluid-filled cavity in an organism or cell.

citadel *n.* **1** a fortress, usu. on high ground protecting or dominating a city. **2** a meeting hall of the Salvation Army. **3** a position viewed as unassailable (*the citadels of the avant-garde*).

citation *n.* **1** the act of citing something from a book or other source. **2** a passage cited. **3** a summons to appear in court. **4** *Military* a commendation in an official dispatch. **5** a descriptive announcement of an award (*received a citation for bravery*).

cite *v.tr.* **1** mention as an example or to support an argument. **2** quote (a passage, book, or author). **3** *Military* commend in an official dispatch. **4** summon to appear in a law court. □ **citable** *adj.*

CITES /ˈsaɪtiːz/ *abbr.* Convention on International Trade in Endangered Species.

citified /ˈsɪtɪˌfaɪd/ *adj.* usu. *derogatory* city-like or urban in appearance or behaviour.

citizen *n.* **1** a member of a nation or Commonwealth, either native or naturalized (*Canadian citizen*). **2** (usu. foll. by *of*) an inhabitant of a city or town. **3** a member of society, esp. as regards one's contribution to it (*our company is a good corporate citizen*).

citizenry *n.* citizens collectively.

citizens' band *n.* a system of local intercommunication by individuals on special radio frequencies.

citizenship *n.* **1** the fact of being a citizen of a country. **2** the qualities considered desirable in a person as a member of society (*citizenship award*).

Citizenship Court *n. Cdn* a federal court operating under the Department of the Secretary of State, for awarding Canadian citizenship.

citrate /ˈsɪtreɪt/ *n.* a salt or ester of citric acid.

citric *adj.* derived from citrus fruit.

citric acid *n.* a sharp-tasting water-soluble organic acid found in the juice of lemons etc.

citron *n.* **1** a shrubby tree, *Citrus medica*, bearing large lemon-like fruits with thick fragrant peel. **2** this fruit. **3** the candied peel of this, used in baking etc.

citronella /ˌsɪtrəˈnelə/ *n.* **1** any fragrant grass of the genus *Cymbopogon*, native to S Asia. **2** the scented oil from these, used in insect repellent and perfume etc.

citrus *n.* (*pl.* same) **1** any tree or shrub of the genus *Citrus*, including citron, lemon, lime, orange, and grapefruit. **2** (in full **citrus fruit**) fruit from such a tree. □ **citrous** *adj.* **citrusy** *adj.*

city *n.* (*pl.* **-ies**) **1 a** a large town. **b** (in Canada) a municipality with a large population or area or combination of the two. **c** the people of a city. **d** the government, administration, or employees of a city. **2** (*attrib.*) of or relating to a city (*city parks*). **3** *informal* (as an intensifier) a person, place, state of affairs, etc., characterized by the specified quality or action (*when the teacher called my name, it was panic city!*).

city block *n.* the area bounded by four city streets.

city council *n.* the elective governing body of a city. □ **city councillor** *n.*

city editor *n. N Amer.* the editor dealing with local news in a newspaper or magazine.

city father *n.* (usu. in *pl.*) any of the prominent citizens or esp. elected officials of a city.

cityfied *var.* of CITIFIED.

city hall n. N Amer. **1** the central administrative offices of a municipality. **2** municipal government. **3** bureaucracy (you can't fight city hall).

city manager n. N Amer. an official directing the administration of a city.

city planner n. = URBAN PLANNER. □ **city planning** n.

cityscape n. **1** a view of a city (actual or depicted). **2** city scenery.

city slicker n. usu. derogatory **1** a person with a sophistication often attributed to city-dwellers. **2** a slick untrustworthy person.

city state n. esp. hist. a city that with its surrounding territory forms an independent state.

city-wide adj. occurring throughout or open to an entire city (city-wide elections).

civet /'sɪvət/ n. **1** (in full **civet cat**) any of several carnivorous mammals of the Asian and African family Viverridae, esp. Viverra civetta of central Africa. **2** a strong musky perfume obtained from the anal glands of these animals.

civic adj. **1** of a city; municipal. **2** of or proper to citizens (civic virtues). **3** of citizenship; civil.

civic centre n. **1** a building or building complex containing municipal offices and sometimes other public buildings such as a library, auditorium, etc. **2** a public facility containing an arena, theatre, etc.

civic holiday n. Cdn a holiday that is commonly observed but not legislated, esp. the first Monday in August, observed as a holiday in all of Canada except Quebec and PEI.

civics n.pl. (usu. treated as sing.) **1** the study of the rights and duties of citizenship. **2** N Amer. the study of government, esp. as taught in schools.

civil adj. **1** of or belonging to citizens. **2** of ordinary citizens and their concerns, as distinct from military or naval or ecclesiastical matters. **3** polite, obliging, not rude. **4** Law relating to civil law. **5** of or relating to the state (civil authorities). **6** (of the length of a day, year, etc.) fixed by custom or law, not natural or astronomical. **7** Cdn (Nfld) (of the weather or sea) calm.

civil aviation n. non-military, esp. commercial aviation.

civil code n. a comprehensive legislative enactment of private law, based on Roman and Napoleonic civil law. ¶In Canada, only Quebec has a civil code.

civil defence n. the organization and training of civilians for the protection of lives and property during and after attacks in wartime.

civil disobedience n. the refusal to comply with certain laws or to pay taxes etc. as a peaceful form of political protest.

civil engineer n. an engineer who designs or maintains roads, dams, etc. □ **civil engineering** n.

civilian ● n. a person not in the armed services or the police force. ● adj. of or for civilians.

civility n. (pl. **-ies**) **1** politeness. **2** an act of this.

civilization n. **1** an advanced stage or system of social development. **2** those peoples of the world regarded as having this. **3** a people or nation (esp. of the past) regarded as an element of social evolution (the Inca civilization). **4** the act or process of making or becoming civilized. **5** informal inhabited or usu. urban areas, esp. as opposed to wilderness.

civilize v.tr. **1** bring out of a barbarous or primitive stage of society. **2** enlighten; refine and educate.

civilized adj. **1** having an advanced and organized state of human social development. **2** having high moral standards (no civilized country should permit such terrible injustice). **3** having or showing good behaviour

or manners (behave in a civilized way). **4** having characteristics considered typical of a sophisticated society, esp. comfort, politeness, orderliness, lack of aggression, etc. (afternoon tea is a very civilized custom).

civil law n. **1** law concerning private rights (opp. CRIMINAL LAW). **2** a system of law, based on Roman law, in which laws are codified in statutes (opp. COMMON LAW 1). ¶In Canada, sense 2 applies only in Quebec.

civil liberty n. (often in pl.) freedom of action and speech subject to the law. □ **civil libertarian** n.

civil marriage n. a marriage solemnized as a civil contract without religious ceremony.

civil rights n.pl. the rights of citizens to political and social freedom and equality.

civil servant n. a member of the civil service.

civil service n. the permanent professional branches of government administration, excluding military and judicial branches and politicians.

civil war n. a war between citizens of the same country.

CJ abbr. chief justice.

CKC abbr. Canadian Kennel Club.

Cl symbol chlorine.

cl abbr. centilitre(s).

clack ● v. **1** intr. make a sharp sound as of hard objects struck together. **2** tr. cause (a thing) to make a clacking sound, as by hitting it in something. **3** intr. chatter, esp. loudly. ● n. a clacking sound. □ **clacker** n.

clad¹ adj. **1** clothed (often in comb.: leather-clad; scantily clad). **2** provided with cladding.

clad² v.tr. (**cladding**; past and past part. **cladded** or **clad**) provide with cladding.

cladding n. a covering or coating on a structure or material etc.; siding.

claim ● v.tr. **1** demand as one's due or property. **2** submit a request for payment under an insurance policy. **3 a** represent oneself as having or achieving (claim victory; claim accuracy). **b** profess (claimed to be the owner). **c** assert, contend (claim that one knows). **4** have as an achievement or a consequence (the fire claimed many victims). **5** (of a thing) deserve (one's attention etc.). ● n. **1 a** a demand or request for something considered one's due (lay claim to; put in a claim). **b** an application for compensation under the terms of an insurance policy. **2** (foll. by to, on) a right or title to a thing (his only claim to fame). **3** a contention or assertion. **4** a thing claimed. **5** a statement of the novel features in a patent. **6** Mining a piece of land allotted or taken. □ **claimable** adj.

claimant n. a person making a claim, esp. in a lawsuit or for a government benefit.

clairvoyance n. **1** the supposed faculty of perceiving things or events in the future or beyond normal sensory contact. **2** exceptional insight.

clairvoyant /klɛr'vɔɪənt/ ● n. a person having clairvoyance. ● adj. having clairvoyance.

clam ● n. **1** any bivalve mollusc, esp. the edible N American hard or round clam (Venus mercenaria) or the soft or long clam (Mya arenaria). **2** informal a shy or withdrawn person. ● v.intr. (**clammed, clamming**) **1** dig for clams. **2** (foll. by up) informal refuse to talk. □ **happy as a clam** extremely happy.

Clamato /klə'mætoʊ/ n. N Amer. proprietary a type of tomato clam cocktail.

clambake n. N Amer. **1** a seaside picnic at which clams etc. are baked and eaten. **2** informal any social gathering.

clamber /'klæmbər, 'klæmər/ v.intr. climb with hands and feet, esp. with difficulty or laboriously.

clam juice n. a stock made by boiling clams in water.

clammer n. (also **clam digger**) a person who digs for clams, esp. for a living.

clammy adj. (**-ier, -iest**) **1** cold and damp or slimy. **2** (of weather) cold and damp. □ **clammily** adv. **clamminess** n.

clamour (also **clamor**) ● n. **1** loud or vehement shouting or noise. **2** a protest or complaint. **3** an appeal or demand. ● v. **1** intr. make a clamour. **2** tr. utter with a clamour. □ **clamour for** demand insistently. □ **clamorous** adj. **clamorously** adv.

clamp ● n. **1** a device for strengthening other materials or holding things together. **2** a device for immobilizing an illegally parked car. ● v.tr. **1** strengthen or fasten with a clamp. **2** place or hold firmly. **3** immobilize (an illegally parked car) by fixing a clamp to one of its wheels. □ **clamp down 1** (often foll. by on) be rigid in enforcing a rule etc. **2** (foll. by on) try to suppress. □ **clamper** n. (in sense 3 of v.).

clampdown n. severe restriction or suppression.

clamshell n. **1** the shell of a clam. **2** a container or tool having a hinge along one side.

clan n. **1** the basic social and political organization of many Aboriginal societies, consisting of a number of related groups and families, often sharing a common symbol or totem. **2** a group of families in the Scottish Highlands with a common ancestor. **3** a large, close-knit family. **4** a group with a strong common interest.

clandestine /klæn'destɪn, -tɪn/ adj. surreptitious. □ **clandestinely** adv. **clandestinity** /-'tɪnɪti/ n.

clang ● n. a loud resonant metallic sound as of a bell etc. ● v. **1** intr. make a clang. **2** tr. cause to clang.

clangour /'klæŋgər/ n. (also **clangor**) **1** a prolonged or repeated clanging noise. **2** an uproar or commotion. □ **clangorous** adj. **clangorously** adv.

clank ● n. a sound as of heavy pieces of metal meeting or a chain rattling. ● v. **1** intr. make a clanking sound. **2** tr. cause to clank. **3** intr. move with a clanking sound. □ **clankingly** adv. **clanky** adj.

clannish adj. usu. derogatory **1** (of a family or group) tending to hold together. **2** of or like a clan. □ **clannishly** adv. **clannishness** n.

clap[1] ● v. (**clapped, clapping**) **1 a** intr. strike the palms of one's hands together as a signal or repeatedly as applause. **b** tr. strike (the hands) together in this way. **2** tr. applaud or show one's approval of (esp. a person) in this way. **3** tr. (of a bird) flap (its wings) audibly. **4** tr. put or place quickly or with determination (clapped a tax on books). **5** tr. (foll. by on) slap (a person) encouragingly on (the back, shoulder, etc.). ● n. **1** the act of clapping, esp. as applause. **2** an explosive sound, esp. of thunder. **3** a slap, a pat. □ **clap eyes on** informal see.

clap[2] n. coarse slang venereal disease, esp. gonorrhea.

clapboard /'klæpbɔrd, 'klæbərd/ n. N Amer. **1** (also attrib.) a siding material consisting of a series of horizontal boards with edges overlapping to keep out the rain etc. **2** one of these boards. □ **clapboarded** adj.

clapper n. the tongue or striker of a bell.

claptrap n. insincere or pretentious talk, nonsense.

claret /'klerət, klæ-/ ● n. **1** red wine, esp. from Bordeaux. **2** a deep purplish red. ● adj. claret-coloured.

clarified butter n. butter from which the milk solids have been removed, leaving pure butterfat.

clarify v. (**-ies, -ied**) **1** tr. & intr. make or become clearer.

2 tr. **a** free (liquid, butter, etc.) from impurities or solid matter. **b** make transparent. **c** purify. □ **clarification** n. **clarifier** n.

clarinet n. **1 a** a woodwind instrument with a single-reed mouthpiece, a cylindrical tube with a flared end, holes, and keys. **b** its player. **2** an organ stop with a quality resembling a clarinet. □ **clarinetist** n. (also esp. Brit. **clarinettist**).

clarion ● n. a clear rousing sound. ● adj. clear, loud, and stimulating (a clarion call for action).

clarity n. the state or quality of being clear, esp. of sound or expression.

clash ● n. **1 a** a loud jarring sound as of metal objects being struck together. **b** a collision, esp. with force. **2 a** a conflict or disagreement. **b** a discord of colours etc. ● v. **1 a** intr. make a clashing sound. **b** tr. cause to clash. **2** intr. collide. **3** intr. (often foll. by with) **a** come into conflict or be at variance. **b** (of colours) be discordant. **c** coincide inconveniently. □ **clasher** n.

clasp ● n. **1 a** a device with interlocking parts for fastening. **b** a buckle or brooch. **c** a metal fastening on a book cover. **2 a** an embrace; a person's reach. **b** a grasp or handshake. ● v. **1** tr. fasten with or as with a clasp. **2** tr. **a** grasp, hold closely. **b** embrace, encircle. **3** intr. fasten a clasp. □ **clasp hands** shake hands with fervour or affection. **clasp one's hands** interlace one's fingers. □ **clasper** n.

class ● n. **1** any set of persons or things grouped together, or graded or differentiated from others (economy class; Mozart is in a different class from his contemporaries). **2 a** a division or order of society (professional classes). **b** a caste system, a system of social classes. **3** informal distinction or high quality in appearance, behaviour, etc. **4 a** a group of students taught together. **b** the occasion when they meet. **c** their course of instruction. **5** N Amer. all the students of an educational institution graduating in a given year (the class of 1999). **6 a** a series of exercises performed regularly by dancers to warm up their bodies and improve their technique. **b** the group of dancers engaged in this. **7** Biol. a grouping of organisms, the next major rank below a division or phylum. ● v.tr. assign to a class or category. ● adj. excellent; of high quality. □ **in a class of its** (or **one's**) **own** (also **in a class by oneself** or **itself**) unequalled.

class act n. a person or thing regarded as elegant or first-rate in quality, performance, etc.

class action n. N Amer. a single legal action brought on behalf of all members of a group with a common interest or grievance.

class-conscious adj. aware of and reacting to social divisions or one's place in a system of social class. □ **class-consciousness** n.

classic ● adj. **1 a** of the first class; of acknowledged excellence. **b** remarkably typical; outstandingly important (a classic case). **2 a** of ancient Greek and Latin literature, art, or culture. **b** (of style in art, music, etc.) simple, harmonious, well-proportioned; in accordance with established forms (compare ROMANTIC). **3** (of clothes) made in a simple elegant style not much affected by changes in fashion. ● n. **1 a** a classic writer, artist, work, or example, esp. one of lasting value. **2 a** an ancient Greek or Latin writer. **b** (in pl.) the study of ancient Greek and Latin literature and history. **3** a follower of classic models. **4** a garment in classic style. **5** (usu. in pl.) a piece of classical music (the concert featured light classics).

classical adj. **1 a** of ancient Greek or Latin literature or art. **b** (of language) having the form used by the ancient standard authors (classical Hebrew). **c** based on the study of ancient Greek and Latin (a *classical education*). **d** learned in classical studies. **2 a** (of music) seen as serious or conventional esp. as opposed to folk, rock, pop, jazz, etc. **b** of the period from *c.*1750–1800 (compare ROMANTIC 4). **3** designating or pertaining to a form or period of an art etc. regarded as representing the height of achievement; in a long-established style of acknowledged excellence. **4** established and widely accepted (*classical economic theory*). **5** in or following the restrained style of classical antiquity (compare ROMANTIC). ☐ **classicality** n. **classically** adv.

classical college n. Cdn (Que.) = COLLÈGE CLASSIQUE.

classical guitar n. an acoustic guitar with a hollow waisted body, a 12-fretted neck, and six strings, usu. played by plucking or strumming with the fingers, and used esp. for classical and folk music.

classicism /'klæsɪ,sɪzəm/ n. **1** the following of a classic style. **2 a** classical scholarship. **b** the advocacy of a classical education. ☐ **classicist** n.

classified ● adj. **1** arranged in classes or categories. **2** (of information etc.) designated as officially secret. **3** (of newspaper advertisements) arranged in columns according to various categories. ● n. (usu. in pl.) a classified advertisement.

classify v.tr. (**-ies**, **-ied**) **1 a** arrange in classes or categories. **b** assign (a thing) to a class or category. **2** designate as officially secret or not for general disclosure. ☐ **classifiable** adj. **classification** n. **classificatory** adj. **classifier** n.

classism n. discrimination on the grounds of social class. ☐ **classist** adj. & n.

classless adj. making or showing no distinction of classes (*classless society*). ☐ **classlessness** n.

classmate n. a fellow member of a class.

classroom n. a room in which a class is taught.

class struggle n. (also **class war**, **class warfare**) conflict between social classes.

classy adj. (**-ier**, **-iest**) **1** of high quality; expensive and stylish (a *classy sports car*). **2** distinguished or admirable, esp. by being dignified, gracious, etc. ☐ **classily** adv. **classiness** n.

clastic /'klæstɪk/ adj. Geol. designating a rock composed of broken pieces of older rocks.

clatter ● n. **1** a rattling sound as of many hard objects struck together. **2** noisy talk; chatter. ● v. **1** intr. **a** make a clatter. **b** fall or move etc. with a clatter. **2** tr. cause (plates etc.) to clatter.

clause n. **1** a distinct part of a sentence, including a subject and predicate. **2** a single statement in a law, contract, or insurance policy.

claustrophobia /,klɒstrə'fəʊbɪə/ n. an abnormal fear of confined places.

claustrophobic adj. **1** suffering from claustrophobia. **2** inducing claustrophobia. ☐ **claustrophobically** adv.

clavicle /'klævɪkəl/ n. the collarbone.

claw ● n. **1 a** a pointed horny nail on an animal's or bird's foot. **b** a foot armed with claws. **2** the pincers of a shellfish. **3** a device for grappling, holding, etc. ● v. **1** tr. & intr. scratch, tear, or pull (a person or thing) with or as with claws. **2** tr. proceed by or as if by using one's hands or claws (*clawing her way to the top*). **3** tr. make by or as if by clawing (*clawed a hole in the earth*). ☐ **claw back** Cdn & Brit. **1** regain laboriously or gradually. **2** recover (money paid out) from another source (e.g. by taxation). ☐ **clawed** adj. (also in comb.). **clawless** adj.

clawback n. Cdn & Brit. **1** the act of clawing back. **2** money recovered in this way.

claw foot n. a foot of a table, bathtub, etc., shaped like a bird's or animal's claw. ☐ **claw-footed** adj.

clay n. **1** a stiff tenacious fine-grained earth, which becomes plastic when water is added and is used for making bricks, pottery, ceramics, etc. **2** literary the substance of the human body. **3** = CLAY PIGEON. ☐ **clayey** adj. **clayish** adj. **claylike** adj.

claymation n. a type of animation using clay sculptures rather than drawings.

clay pigeon n. a breakable disc thrown up from a trap as a target for shooting.

CLC abbr. Canadian Labour Congress.

clean ● adj. **1** (often foll. by of) free from dirt or contaminating matter. **2** clear; unused or unpolluted (*clean air*). **3** free from obscenity or indecency. **4** attentive to personal hygiene and cleanliness. **5** even; straight; free from roughness (a *clean edge*). **6** unobstructed; without difficulty (a *clean getaway*). **7 a** (of a ship etc.) streamlined, smooth. **b** well-formed, slender and shapely (*the car has clean lines*). **8** adroit, skilful (*clean fielding*). **9** legible; having few corrections (*clean copy*). **10** Sport fair; played without fouls. **11 a** free from ceremonial defilement or from disease. **b** (of food) not prohibited. **12 a** free from any record of a crime, offence, etc. (a *clean driver's licence*). **b** informal above suspicion. **c** informal not carrying a weapon or incriminating material. **13** faultless (a *clean triple Axel*). **14** informal free from or cured of addiction to drugs. **15** (of a taste etc.) sharp, fresh, distinctive. ● adv. **1** completely, outright, simply (*clean forgot*). **2** in a clean manner. ● v. **1** tr. (also foll. by of) & intr. make or become clean. **2** tr. eat all the food on (one's plate). **3** tr. Cooking remove the innards of (fish or fowl). **4** tr. Weightlifting raise (a weight) from the floor to shoulder level in a single movement. ● n. the act or process of cleaning or being cleaned (*give it a clean*). ☐ **clean down** clean by brushing or wiping. **clean out 1** clean thoroughly. **2** slang empty or deprive (esp. of money). **clean up 1 a** clear (a mess) away. **b** put (things) tidy. **c** make (oneself) clean. **2** restore order or morality to. **3** slang **a** acquire as gain or profit. **b** make a gain or profit. **clean up one's act** begin to behave responsibly or soberly. **come clean** informal own up; confess everything. **clean hands** freedom from guilt. **make a clean job of** informal do thoroughly. ☐ **cleanable** adj. **cleanish** adj. **cleanness** n.

clean break n. a quick and final separation.

clean-cut adj. **1** sharply outlined. **2** (of a person) clean and tidy.

cleaner n. **1** a person employed to clean the interior of a building. **2** (usu. in pl.) a commercial establishment for cleaning clothes. **3** a device or substance for cleaning. ☐ **take to the cleaners** slang **1** defraud or rob (a person) of all his or her money. **2** criticize severely.

cleaning lady n. a woman paid to clean the interior of a building.

cleanly[1] /'kli:nli/ adv. **1** in a clean way. **2** efficiently; without difficulty.

cleanly[2] /'klɛnli/ adj. (**-ier**, **-iest**) habitually clean; with clean habits. ☐ **cleanliness** n.

cleanout n. N Amer. **1** the act or an instance of cleaning out. **2** an opening for cleaning something out.

clean room n. a room free from dust and bacteria, used for medical purposes or the assembly of products such as computer parts.

cleanse v.tr. **1** usu. formal make clean. **2** (often foll. by of) purify from sin or guilt.

cleanser *n.* something that cleans, esp. an abrasive or disinfectant product for cleaning the skin etc.

clean-shaven *adj.* without a beard, whiskers, etc.

clean sheet *n.* (also **clean slate**) freedom from commitments or imputations.

cleansing *n.* the purging of 'undesired' social or ethnic groups from an area (*ethnic cleansing*).

cleanup *n.* **1** an act of cleaning up. **2** *Baseball* the fourth position in the batting order.

clear ● *adj.* **1** free from dirt or contamination. **2** (of weather, the sky, etc.) not dull or cloudy. **3 a** transparent. **b** lustrous, shining; free from obscurity. **4** (of soup) not containing solid ingredients. **5 a** distinct, easily perceived by the senses. **b** unambiguous, easily understood (*make oneself clear*). **c** manifest; not confused or doubtful (*clear evidence*). **6** that discerns or is able to discern readily and accurately (*clear thinking*). **7** (usu. foll. by *about*, *on*, or *that* + clause) confident, certain. **8** (of a conscience) free from guilt. **9** (of a road etc.) unobstructed. **10 a** net, without deduction (*a clear $1000*). **b** complete (*three clear days*). **11** (often foll. by *of*) unencumbered by debt, commitments, etc. **12** (foll. by *of*) not obstructed by. **13** (of timber) free from knots (*clear pine*). **14** (of skin) not marked by pimples or other blemishes. ● *adv.* **1** clearly (*speak loud and clear*). **2** completely (*got clear away*). **3** apart, out of contact (*stand clear of the doors*). **4** (often foll. by *to*) *N Amer.* all the way. ● *v.* **1** tr. make or become clear. **2 a** tr. (often foll. by *of*) free from prohibition or obstruction. **b** tr. & intr. make or become empty or unobstructed. **c** tr. free (land) for cultivation or building by cutting down trees etc. **d** tr. cause people to leave (a room etc.). **3** tr. (often foll. by *of*) show or declare (a person) to be innocent. **4** tr. approve (a person) for special duty, access to information, etc. **5** tr. pass over or by safely or without touching. **6** tr. make (an amount of money) as a net gain or to balance expenses. **7** tr. pass (a cheque) through a clearing house. **8** tr. pass through (a customs office etc.). **9** tr. remove (an obstruction, unwanted object, etc.). **10** tr. & intr. *Sport* send (the ball, puck, etc.) out of one's defensive zone. **11** intr. (often foll. by *away*, *up*) (of physical phenomena) disappear, gradually diminish (*my cold has cleared up*). □ **clear the air 1** make the air less sultry. **2** disperse an atmosphere of suspicion, tension, etc. **clear away 1** remove completely. **2** remove the remains of a meal from the table. **clear the decks** prepare for action, esp. fighting. **clear off 1** get rid of. **2** *informal* go away. **clear out 1** empty. **2** remove. **3** *informal* go away. **clear one's throat** cough slightly to make one's voice clear. **clear up 1** tidy up. **2** solve (a mystery etc.). **3** (of weather) become fine. **clear the way 1** remove obstacles. **2** stand aside. **clear a thing with** get approval or authorization for a thing from (a person). **in the clear** free from suspicion or difficulty. **out of a clear blue sky** as a complete surprise. □ **clearly** *adv.* **clearness** *n.*

clearance *n.* **1** the act or an instance of clearing. **2** clear space between two objects or two parts in machinery etc. **3** special authorization or permission (esp. for an aircraft to take off or land, or for access to information etc.). **4** (also **clearance sale**) a sale to get rid of stock. **5** the removal of buildings, persons, etc., so as to clear land. **6 a** the clearing of a person, ship, etc., by customs. **b** a certificate showing this. **7** the clearing of cheques.

clear-cut ● *adj.* **1** sharply defined. **2** completely evident. **3** of or relating to a method of logging in which all of the trees in an area of forest are har-

vested at the same time. ● *n.* an area of forest that has been clear-cut. ● *vtr.* log (an area of forest) by cutting down all of the trees. □ **clear-cutter** *n.* **clear-cutting** *n.*

clear-eyed *adj.* **1** having clear or bright eyes. **2** perceptive; discerning.

Clear Grit *n.* *Cdn hist.* a member or supporter of the Clear Grit Party, a liberal reform party in Upper Canada during the 1840s and 1850s.

clear-headed *adj.* **1** able to think clearly. **2** (of an idea, argument, etc.) reasoned; well-thought-out.

clearing *n.* **1** *in senses of* CLEAR *v.* **2 a** an area in a forest cleared of trees. **b** an area of a forest naturally devoid of trees. **3** *Cdn* a settlement in the bush.

clearing house *n.* **1** a bankers' establishment where cheques and bills from member banks are exchanged, so that only the balances need be paid in cash. **2** an agency for collecting and distributing information, materials, etc.

clearing pass *n.* *Hockey* a forward pass intended to move the puck out of the defending team's end.

cleat *n.* **1** a metal or wooden fitting with two projecting horns, fastened to a flagpole, boat, etc., around which a rope may be made fast. **2 a** a projecting piece on the bottom or side of a shoe or boot, to improve grip. **b** (in *pl.*) *N Amer.* a pair of shoes or boots with these, esp. for playing field sports. **3** a projecting piece on a spar, gangway, etc., to improve footing. **4** a piece of metal, wood, etc. attached to something to provide strength or hold it in place.

cleavage *n.* **1** the hollow between a woman's breasts, esp. as exposed by a low-cut garment. **2** a division or splitting. **3** the splitting of rocks, crystals, etc., in a preferred direction.

cleave[1] *v.* (*past* **cleaved** *or* **clove** *or* **cleft**; *past part.* **cloven** *or* **cleft** *or* **cleaved**) **1 a** tr. chop or break apart, split, esp. along the grain or the line of cleavage. **b** intr. come apart in this way. **2** tr. make one's way through (air or water). □ **cleavable** *adj.*

cleave[2] *v.intr.* (*past* **cleaved**) (foll. by *to*) *literary* adhere.

cleaver *n.* a tool for cleaving, esp. a broad-bladed knife used for cutting meat.

clef *n.* *Music* any of several symbols placed at the beginning of a staff, indicating the pitch of the notes written on it.

cleft ● *adj.* split, partly divided. ● *n.* a split or fissure; a space or division made by cleaving.

cleft lip *n.* a congenital split in the upper lip.

cleft palate *n.* a congenital split in the roof of the mouth.

clematis /ˈklemətɪs, kləˈmætɪs/ *n.* any erect or climbing plant of the genus *Clematis*, bearing white, pink, or purple flowers and feathery seeds.

clement /ˈklemənt/ *adj.* **1** mild, temperate (*clement weather*). **2** merciful. □ **clemency** *n.*

clementine /ˈklemənˌtaɪn, -ˌtiːn/ *n.* a small citrus fruit, thought to be a hybrid between a tangerine and sweet orange.

clench ● *v.tr.* **1** close (the teeth or fingers) tightly. **2** grasp firmly. **3** = CLINCH *v.* 4. ● *n.* **1** a clenching action. **2** a clenched state.

clerestory /ˈklɪərˌstɔːri, -ˌstɒri/ *n.* (*pl.* **-ies**) **1 a** an upper row of windows in a cathedral or large church, above the level of the aisle roofs. **b** the section of wall containing such windows. **2** a similar wall or row of windows in other types of buildings.

clergy *n.* (*pl.* **-ies**) (usu. treated as *pl.*) **1** (usu. prec. by *the*) the body of all persons ordained for religious duties, esp. in the Christian church. **2** a number of such persons. **3** a member of the clergy.

clergyman *n.* (*pl.* **-men**) an esp. male member of the clergy.

clergyperson *n.* (*pl.* **-persons**) a member of the clergy.

Clergy Reserves *n. Cdn hist.* crown lands set aside during the settlement of Upper and Lower Canada, the revenue from which was to be used to support Protestant clergy.

clergywoman *n.* (*pl.* **-women**) a female member of the clergy.

cleric *n.* a member of the clergy.

clerical *adj.* **1** of the clergy. **2** of or done by an office clerk or secretary. □ **clericalism** *n.* **clericalist** *n.*

clerical collar *n.* a stiff upright white collar fastening at the back, worn by the clergy in some Christian denominations.

clerk ● *n.* **1** a person employed in an office, bank, store, etc., to keep records, accounts, etc. **2** *N Amer.* a salesperson or assistant in a store or hotel. **3** a secretary, agent, or record-keeper of a municipal government (*town clerk*). **4** *Law* **a** an officer of a court who keeps records, issues subpoenas and other court documents, etc. **b** *Cdn* a judge's research assistant. **c** see ARTICLED CLERK. **5** (in full **clerk of session**) (in Presbyterian and United churches) an elder elected to serve as a congregation's primary officer. **6** a senior official in a legislative assembly. ● *v.intr.* work as a clerk. □ **clerkly** *adj.* **clerkship** *n.*

Clerk of the House *n. Cdn & Brit.* the chief administrative officer and procedural adviser of the House of Commons.

Clerk of the Privy Council *n. Cdn* the senior public servant in charge of the Privy Council Office.

clever *adj.* (**cleverer, cleverest**) **1** quick to understand and learn. **2** skilful, dexterous. **3** (of the doer or the thing done) ingenious, cunning. **4** witty (*clever dialogue*). □ **cleverly** *adv.* **cleverness** *n.*

clevis /ˈklɛvɪs/ *n.* **1** a U-shaped piece of metal at the end of a beam for attaching tackle etc. **2** a connection in which a bolt holds one part that fits between the forked ends of another.

CLGA *abbr.* Canadian Ladies' Golf Association.

cliché /kliːˈʃeɪ, ˈkliː-/ *n.* a hackneyed phrase, opinion, or thing.

clichéd /kliːˈʃeɪd, ˈkliː-/ *adj.* hackneyed; full of clichés.

click ● *n.* **1** a slight sharp sound as of a switch being operated. **2** a sharp non-vocal suction, used as a speech sound in some languages. **3** *Computing* an instance of clicking a button on a mouse. ● *v.* **1 a** *intr.* make a click. **b** *tr.* cause (one's tongue, heels, etc.) to click. **2** *intr. informal* **a** become clear or understandable (*when I saw them it all clicked*). **b** be successful, secure one's object. **c** (foll. by *with*) become friendly, esp. with a person of the opposite sex. **d** come to an agreement. **3** *tr. & intr. Computing* **a** press (one of the buttons on a mouse). **b** select (an item represented on the screen, a particular function, etc.) by so doing. □ **click in** *N Amer. informal* (of a system) become active or effective. □ **clickable** *adj.* (in sense 3 of v.) **clicker** *n.*

client *n.* **1** a person using the services of a lawyer, architect, social worker, or other professional person. **2** a customer or patron. **3** *Computing* a terminal or workstation that is connected to a server.

clientele /ˌkliːɒnˈtɛl, ˌkliːɒnˈtɛl/ *n.* **1** clients collectively. **2** the customers or patrons of a store etc.

client-server *n. Computing* (*attrib.*) designating a type of system in which a server distributes files and databases to clients.

cliff *n.* a steep rock face. □ **clifflike** *adj.* **cliffy** *adj.*

cliff-hanger *n.* **1** a story etc. with a strong element of suspense; a suspenseful ending to an episode of a serial. **2** a game or situation in which the outcome is uncertain until the very end. □ **cliff-hanging** *adj.*

cliffside ● *n.* the face of a cliff. ● *adj.* situated or occurring beside a cliff (*cliffside restaurant*).

clifftop *n.* the top of a cliff.

climactic *adj.* of or forming a climax.

climate *n.* **1** the prevailing weather conditions of an area. **2** a region with particular weather conditions. **3** the prevailing trend of opinion or public feeling. □ **climatic** *adj.*

climate control *n.* a system for regulating the humidity and temperature of air through heating and air conditioning. □ **climate-controlled** *adj.*

climatology /ˌklaɪməˈtɒlədʒi/ *n.* the scientific study of climate. □ **climatological** *adj.* **climatologist** *n.*

climax ● *n.* **1** the event or point of greatest intensity or interest. **2** orgasm. **3** *Ecology* a state of equilibrium reached by a plant community (also *attrib.*: *climax community*). ● *v.tr. & intr. informal* bring or come to a climax.

climb ● *v.* **1** *tr. & intr.* (often foll. by *up*) ascend, mount, go or come up, esp. by using one's hands. **2** *intr.* (of a plant) grow up a wall, trellis, etc. by clinging with tendrils or by twining. **3** *intr.* make progress from one's own efforts, esp. in social rank, intellectual or moral strength, etc. **4** *intr.* (of an aircraft, the sun, etc.) go upwards. **5** *intr.* slope upwards. **6** *intr.* (of numbers etc.) increase. ● *n.* **1** an ascent by climbing. **2 a** a place, esp. a hill, climbed or to be climbed. **b** a recognized route up a mountain etc. □ **climb down 1** descend with the help of one's hands. **2** withdraw from a stance taken up in argument, negotiation, etc. **climb the walls** *N Amer.* go crazy; become frantic. □ **climbable** *adj.*

climbdown *n.* a withdrawal from a position taken up in argument, negotiation, etc.

climber *n.* **1** a mountaineer. **2** a climbing plant. **3** a person with strong social etc. aspirations.

climbing skins *n.pl.* strips of fur etc. strapped to the bottom of skis to give traction when climbing slopes.

clime *n. literary* **1** a region. **2** a climate.

clinch ● *v.* **1** *tr.* confirm or settle (an argument, bargain, etc.) conclusively. **2** *tr. Sport* secure (a position on a team, in league standings, etc.). **3** *intr. Boxing & Wrestling* (of participants) become too closely engaged. **4** *intr. informal* embrace. ● *n.* **1 a** a clinching action. **b** a clinched state. **2** *informal* an (esp. amorous) embrace. **3** *Boxing & Wrestling* an action or state in which participants become too closely engaged.

clincher *n. informal* **1** a person or thing that clinches. **2** a remark or argument that settles a matter conclusively. **3** *Sport* a game or match that clinches a player's or team's position in standings etc.

cline *n.* **1** a continuum with an infinite number of gradations. **2** *Biol.* the graded sequence of differences within a species etc.

cling ● *v.intr.* (*past* and *past part.* **clung**) **1** (foll. by *to, onto, on*) hold on tightly. **2** (foll. by *to*) become attached to; stick closely to (*the smell clings to one's clothes*). **3** (foll. by *to*) refuse to abandon; remain persistently or stubbornly attached to (a belief, power, hope, possessions, etc.). **4** be emotionally dependent on (a person); stay too close to (a person) (*clung to me all evening*). **5** stay close to (something) (*don't cling to the curb*). ● *n.* **1** the adhering together of separate objects (*static cling*). **2** = CLINGSTONE (also *attrib.*: *cling peach*). □ **clingingly** *adv.*

clingstone *n.* a variety of peach or nectarine in which the flesh adheres to the stone.

clingy *adj.* (**-ier, -iest**) liable to cling. □ **clinginess** *n.*

clinic *n.* **1** a place or occasion for giving medical or dental treatment or advice (*fertility clinic*). **2** *N Amer.* a group of doctors or dentists sharing the same building and working together. **3** a gathering at a hospital bedside for the teaching of medicine or surgery. **4** *N Amer.* a conference or short course on a particular subject (*golf clinic*). **5** see BLOOD DONOR CLINIC. **6** see LEGAL CLINIC.

clinical *adj.* **1** *Med.* **a** of or for the treatment of patients. **b** taught or learned at the hospital bedside. **c** based on the observed symptoms. **d** involving the study or care of actual patients (*clinical trials*). **2** dispassionate, coldly detached. **3** (of a room, building, etc.) bare, functional. □ **clinically** *adv.*

clinical medicine *n.* medicine dealing with the observation and treatment of patients.

clinician /klɪˈnɪʃən/ *n.* a doctor having direct contact with and responsibility for patients, as opposed to one doing research.

clink ● *n.* **1** a sharp ringing sound. **2** *slang* prison. ● *v.* **1** *intr.* make a clink. **2** *tr.* cause (glasses etc.) to clink.

clinker *n.* **1** a mass of slag or lava. **2** a stony residue from burnt coal. **3** *N Amer. informal* a mistake or blunder.

clip¹ ● *n.* **1** a device for holding things together or for attachment to an object as a marker, esp. a paper clip or a device worked by a spring. **2** a piece of jewellery fastened by a clip. **3** a set of attached cartridges for a firearm. ● *v.tr.* (**clipped, clipping**) **1** attach with a clip. **2** grip tightly. **3** surround closely.

clip² ● *v.* (**clipped, clipping**) **1** *tr.* cut with shears or scissors, esp. cut short or trim (hair, wool, fingernails, etc.). **2** *tr.* trim or remove the hair or wool of. **3** *tr. informal* hit smartly. **4** *tr.* curtail, diminish, cut short. **5** *tr.* cut (an article, coupon, etc.) from a newspaper etc. **6** *tr.* cut the wings of (a bird) so that it is unable to fly. **7** *tr. & intr. Football* block (a member of the opposing team) illegally from behind. **8** *tr. slang* swindle, rob. ● *n.* **1** an act of clipping, esp. shearing or hair-cutting. **2** *informal* a smart blow, esp. with the hand. **3** a short sequence from a film, video, etc. **4** *informal* (in phr. **at a fair clip**, etc.) speed, esp. rapid. □ **clip a person's wings** prevent a person from pursuing ambitions or acting effectively. □ **clippable** *adj.*

clip art *n.* artwork, either published in printed form or included as part of computer software, that can be copied into reports, advertisements, etc.

clipboard *n.* **1** a small board with a spring clip for holding papers etc. and providing support for writing. **2** a feature of some computer programs which allows the temporary storage of extracted text, so that it can be edited etc. before being inserted or saved into another file.

clip-clop ● *n.* a sound such as the beat of a horse's hooves. ● *v.intr.* (**-clopped, -clopping**) make such a sound.

clip-on ● *adj.* attached by a clip. ● *n.* a thing (e.g. a necktie, earring) that attaches by a clip.

clipper *n.* **1** a person or thing that clips. **2** (usu. in *pl.*) any of various instruments for clipping hair, fingernails, hedges, etc. **3** a fast sailing ship, esp. one with raking bows and masts.

Clipper chip *n.* an encryption system for digital telecommunication proposed as a compulsory universal standard, which would enable law enforcement agencies to decipher communications when necessary.

clipping *n.* **1** a short piece clipped or cut from a newspaper, magazine, etc. **2** (usu. in *pl.*) small pieces of grass etc. produced by clipping or mowing.

clique /kliːk/ *n.* a small exclusive group of people. □ **cliquey** *adj.* **cliquish** *adj.* **cliquishness** *n.*

clit *n. coarse slang* = CLITORIS.

clitoris /ˈklɪtərɪs/ *n.* a small erectile part of the female genitals at the upper end of the vulva. □ **clitoral** *adj.*

cloaca /kloʊˈeɪkə/ *n.* (*pl.* **cloacae** /-siː/) the genital and excretory cavity at the end of the intestinal canal in birds, reptiles, etc. □ **cloacal** *adj.*

cloak ● *n.* **1** an outdoor overgarment, usu. sleeveless, hanging loosely from the shoulders. **2** a covering (*cloak of snow*). **3** something which conceals (*a cloak of secrecy*). ● *v.tr.* **1** cover with a cloak. **2** cover over (*hills cloaked in trees*). **3** conceal, disguise. □ **under the cloak of** using as a pretext.

cloak-and-dagger *adj.* involving or characteristic of plot and intrigue, esp. espionage.

cloakroom *n.* a room where outdoor clothes or luggage may be left by visitors, clients, etc.

clobber *v.tr. informal* **1 a** hit repeatedly; beat up. **b** strike with great force. **2** defeat. **3** criticize severely.

cloche /klɒʃ, kloʊʃ/ *n.* **1** (in full **cloche hat**) a woman's close-fitting bell-shaped hat. **2** a small translucent cover for protecting or forcing outdoor plants.

clock ● *n.* **1** an instrument for measuring time, indicating hours, minutes, etc., by hands on a dial or by displayed figures. **2** any measuring device resembling a clock, e.g. a speedometer or stopwatch. **3** a downy seed head, esp. that of a dandelion. ● *v.tr.* **1** (often foll. by *up*) attain or register (a stated time, distance, or speed, esp. in a race). **2** time (a race) with a stopwatch. **3** measure the speed of (*was clocked at 95 mph*). □ **against the clock 1** against time taken as an element in competitive sports etc. (*ran against the clock*). **2** hurriedly and with time running out (*I'm working against the clock*). **clean someone's clock** *N Amer. informal* beat someone soundly. **clock in** register one's arrival at work, esp. by means of an automatic recording clock. **clock out** register one's departure similarly. **round** (or **around**) **the clock** all day and (usu.) night. **turn** (or **put**) **the clock back** (or **turn back the clock**) return to an earlier time. **watch the clock** be a clock-watcher. □ **clocker** *n.*

clockmaker *n.* a person who makes and repairs clocks and watches. □ **clockmaking** *n.*

clock radio *n.* a combined radio and clock, which can be set so the radio will come on at a desired time.

clock-watcher *n.* a person who keeps a close watch on the passage of time, esp. so as not to exceed minimum working hours. □ **clock-watching** *n.*

clockwise *adj. & adv.* in a curve corresponding in direction to the movement of the hands of a clock.

clockwork *n.* **1** a mechanism like that of a mechanical clock, with a spring and gears. **2** (*attrib.*) **a** driven by clockwork. **b** regular, mechanical. □ **like clockwork** smoothly, regularly, automatically.

clod *n.* **1** a lump of earth, clay, etc. **2** *informal* a silly or foolish person.

clodhopper *n.* **1** (usu. in *pl.*) *informal* a large heavy shoe. **2** an unsophisticated person.

clog ● *n.* **1** a shoe with a thick wooden sole. **2** *N Amer.* an encumbrance or impediment (*a clog in the drain*). ● *v.tr. & intr.* (**clogged, clogging**) (often foll. by *up*) block or become blocked so as to hinder free passage, action, or function.

cloister ● *n.* **1** a covered walk, often with a wall on one side and a colonnade open to a quadrangle on the other, esp. in a convent, monastery, or cathedral. **2 a** a convent or monastery. **b** life in a convent or monastery. **3** a place or the state of seclusion. ● *v.tr.* seclude or shut up in or as if in a convent etc.

cloistered *adj.* **1** secluded, sheltered. **2** living in a convent or monastery, esp. in an order whose members have little or no contact with the outside world.

clomp *var. of* CLUMP *v.* 2.

clone ● *n.* **1 a** a group of organisms produced asexually from one stock or ancestor. **b** one such organism. **2** a person or thing regarded as identical with another. **3** a microcomputer designed to simulate another, more expensive, model. ● *v.tr.* propagate as a clone. □ **clonal** *adj.*

clonk ● *n.* an abrupt heavy sound of impact. ● *v.* **1** *intr.* make such a sound. **2** *tr. informal* hit.

clop ● *n.* the sound made by a horse's hooves. ● *v.intr.* (**clopped, clopping**) make this sound.

close¹ ● *adj.* **1** (often foll. by *to*) situated at only a short distance or interval. **2 a** having a strong or immediate relation or connection (*close relatives*). **b** in intimate friendship or association (*we're very close*). **c** corresponding almost exactly (*close resemblance*). **d** fitting tightly. **e** (of hair etc.) short, near the surface. **3** in or almost in contact (*close proximity*). **4** dense, compact, with no or only slight intervals (*close formation; close thicket*). **5** in which competitors are almost equal (*close contest*). **6** leaving no gaps or weaknesses, rigorous (*close reasoning*). **7** concentrated, searching (*close attention*). **8** (of air etc.) stuffy or humid. **9** closed, shut. **10** limited or restricted to certain persons etc. (*close corporation*). **11 a** hidden, secret, covered. **b** secretive. **12** (of a danger etc.) directly threatening, narrowly avoided. **13** niggardly. **14** narrow, confined, contracted. **15** under prohibition; not readily available. ● *adv.* **1** (often foll. by *by, on, to, upon*) at only a short distance or interval (*live close by; close to home*). **2** closely, in a close manner (*shut close*). □ **closely** *adv.* **closeness** *n.*

close² ● *v.* **1 a** *tr.* shut (a lid, box, door, eye, etc.). **b** *intr.* be shut. **c** *tr.* prevent access to (a room, region, bridge, etc.) (*closed the border to tourists*). **2 a** *tr. & intr.* bring or come to an end (*closed the debate*). **b** *intr.* finish speaking (*closed with prayer*). **c** *tr. & intr.* settle or finalize (a deal, offer, etc.). **3 a** *intr.* (of a business, school, etc.) cease work or business temporarily (*the store closes at six*). **b** *tr.* temporarily cease work or business at (a business, school, etc.). **4** *tr. & intr.* cease or cause to cease the operation of (an office, business, etc.). **5** *tr.* withdraw all the money from (a bank account etc.). **6** *tr.* remove from use or stop using (a room, bed, etc.) (*the hospital closed 100 beds*). **7 a** *intr.* (of a group of people) come close to or surround someone or something. **b** *tr. & intr.* draw near to or come within striking distance of (a person or thing). **8** *intr.* (of stocks etc.) be at a particular price at the close of a day's trading. **9** *tr.* make (an electric circuit etc.) continuous. ● *n.* a conclusion, an end. □ **close down 1** discontinue (or cause to discontinue) business, esp. permanently. **2** (of a broadcasting station) end transmission esp. until the next day. **close one's eyes to** pay no attention to. **close in 1** come nearer. **2** (of days) get successively shorter with the approach of the winter solstice. **close off** prevent access to by covering or blocking the means of entrance. **close out** *N Amer.* discontinue, terminate, dispose of (a business). **close ranks 1** (esp. of soldiers) move closer together. **2** establish or maintain solidarity. **close up 1** shut,

esp. temporarily. **2** (of groups of people) move closer. **3** block up. **4** (of an aperture) grow smaller.

close call *n.* a narrow escape.

close-cropped *adj.* (of hair etc.) cut very short.

closed *adj.* **1** not giving access; shut. **2** (of a store etc.) having ceased business temporarily. **3** (of a society, system, etc.) self-contained; not communicating with others. **4** *Cdn* (of a mortgage etc.) that may not be paid off before the stated term without a financial penalty. **5** (of a sport etc.) restricted to specified competitors etc.

closed caption ● *n.* one of a series of captions to a television program, accessible through a decoder. ● *v.tr.* provide (a program) with these. □ **closed-captioned** *adj.* **closed-captioning** *n.*

closed-circuit *adj.* (of television) transmitted by wires to a restricted set of receivers.

closed custody *n. Cdn =* SECURE CUSTODY.

closed door ● *n.* an obstacle, impasse, or restriction. ● *adj.* (usu. **closed-door**) private; not open to the public (*closed-door meeting*). □ **behind closed doors** privately; in secret.

closed shop *n.* **1** a place of work etc. where all employees must belong to an agreed labour union (*opp.* OPEN SHOP). **2** this system.

close-fitting *adj.* (of a garment) fitting close to the body.

close harmony *n.* harmony in which the notes of the chord are close together.

close-knit *adj.* (also **closely-knit**) tightly bound or interlocked; closely united in friendship.

close-mouthed *adj.* reticent.

close quarters ● *n.pl.* a cramped place (*live in very close quarters*). ● *adj.* (usu. **close-quarter**; also **close-quarters**) (of battle etc.) involving direct and close combat. □ **at close quarters** very close together.

closer *n.* **1** a person or thing that closes. **2** *Baseball* a relief pitcher brought in by a team with a lead to pitch the final innings.

close-set *adj.* separated only by a small interval or intervals.

close shave *n. informal* a narrow escape.

closet ● *n.* **1** a cupboard or recess, esp. one used for hanging clothes. **2** a small or private room. **3** (*attrib.*) secret, covert (*closet leftist*). ● *v.tr.* (**closeted, closeting**) shut away, esp. in private conference or study. □ **in the closet 1** keeping one's homosexuality from public knowledge. **2** hidden from public scrutiny. **out of the closet 1** into the open; into public scrutiny. **2** having publicly declared one's homosexuality.

closeted *adj.* secret, covert (*a closeted lesbian*).

close-up *n.* **1** a photograph etc. taken at close range and showing the subject on a large scale. **2** an intimate description.

closing *n.* **1** an act or the process of closing. **2** the end or conclusion, e.g. of a speech. **3** the final phase of a transaction, esp. of buying or selling real estate. **4** something that closes; a fastener.

closing time *n.* the time at which a bar, store, etc., ends business.

closure *n.* **1** the act or process of closing. **2** a closed condition. **3** something that closes or seals. **4** *Parl.* a procedure for ending a debate and taking a vote. **5** conclusion (*catching her murderer will give her family a sense of closure*).

clot ● *n.* **1** a thick mass of coagulated liquid, esp. of blood. **2** a mass of material stuck together. ● *v.tr. & intr.* (**clotted, clotting**) form into clots.

cloth n. (pl. **cloths** /klɒθz, klɒðz/) **1** woven or felted material. **2** a piece of this. **3** a piece of cloth for a particular purpose; a tablecloth, dishcloth, etc. **4 a** profession or status, esp. of the clergy, as shown by clothes. **b** (prec. by the) the clergy (man of the cloth). **5** (in full **cloth-bound**) (of a book) bound with cloth rather than paper.

clothe v.tr. (past and past part. **clothed** or formal **clad**) **1** put clothes on; provide with clothes. **2** cover as with clothes or a cloth. **3** (foll. by with) endue (with qualities etc.).

clothes n.pl. **1** garments worn to cover the body. **2** bedclothes.

clothes horse n. **1** a frame for airing washed clothes. **2** informal a person who has many, esp. fashionable, clothes.

clothesline n. a rope or wire etc. on which washed clothes are hung to dry.

clothes moth n. any moth of the family Tineidae, with a larva destructive to wool, fur, etc.

clothespin n. N Amer. a clip or forked device for securing clothes to a clothesline.

clothier /ˈkloːðiːɜr/ n. a maker or seller of clothes, esp. men's clothes.

clothing n. clothes collectively.

cloud ● n. **1** a visible mass of condensed watery vapour floating in the atmosphere high above the general level of the ground. **2** a mass of smoke or dust. **3 a** a hazy area in the night sky produced by the light of distant stars. **b** a region of dust, gas, etc., in deep space appearing lighter or darker owing to the reflection, absorption, etc. of light. **4** (foll. by of) a great number of insects, birds, etc., moving together. **5 a** a state of gloom, trouble, or suspicion. **b** a frowning or depressed look (a cloud on his brow). **6** a local dimness or a vague patch of colour in or on a liquid or a transparent body. ● v. **1** tr. cover or darken with clouds or gloom or trouble. **2** intr. (often foll. by over, up) become overcast or gloomy. **3** tr. **a** make unclear (prejudice clouded the issue). **b** make unreliable; distort (alcohol clouded his judgment). **4** tr. variegate with vague patches of colour. □ **in the clouds 1** unreal, imaginary, mystical. **2** (of a person) abstracted, inattentive. **on cloud nine** informal extremely happy. **under a cloud** out of favour, discredited, under suspicion. **with one's head in the clouds** daydreaming, unrealistic. □ **cloudless** adj. **cloudlessly** adv. **cloudlet** n.

cloudberry n. (pl. **-ies**) a low-growing plant of the raspberry family, Rubus chamaemorus, with a white flower and an edible amber fruit.

cloudburst n. a sudden violent rainstorm.

cloud cover n. **1** a canopy of clouds. **2** the extent of this canopy.

cloudy adj. (**-ier, -iest**) **1 a** (of the sky) covered with clouds. **b** (of weather) characterized by clouds. **2** not transparent; unclear. □ **cloudily** adv. **cloudiness** n.

clout ● n. **1** a heavy blow. **2** informal influence. ● v.tr. hit hard. □ **clouter** n.

clove[1] n. **1 a** a dried flower bud of a tropical plant, Syzygium aromaticum, used as a pungent aromatic spice. **b** this plant. **2** (in full **clove pink**) a clove-scented pink, Dianthus caryophyllus, the original of the carnation and other double pinks.

clove[2] n. any of the small bulbs making up a compound bulb of garlic, shallot, etc.

clove[3] past of CLEAVE[1].

cloven adj. split, partly divided.

cloven hoof n. (also **cloven foot**) the divided hoof of ruminant quadrupeds (e.g. oxen, sheep, goats).

clover n. any leguminous fodder plant of the genus Trifolium, having dense flower heads and leaves each consisting of usu. three leaflets. □ **in clover** in ease and luxury.

cloverleaf n. (pl. **-s**) a junction of roads intersecting at different levels with connecting sections forming the pattern of a four-leaf clover.

clown ● n. **1** a comic entertainer, esp. in a circus, usu. with traditional costume and makeup. **2** a silly, foolish, or playful person. ● v. **1** intr. (often foll. by around) behave like a clown; act foolishly or playfully. **2** tr. perform (a part, an action, etc.) like a clown. □ **clownish** adj. **clownishly** adv. **clownishness** n.

cloy v.tr. (usu. foll. by with) satiate or sicken with an excess of sweetness, richness, etc.

cloying adj. **1** extremely sweet. **2** excessively sentimental. □ **cloyingly** adv.

CLSC n. Cdn (in Quebec) a provincially funded community health care clinic.

club ● n. **1** a heavy stick with a thick end, used as a weapon etc. **2** a stick or bat used in a game to strike a ball, esp. one with a head used in golf. **3 a** a playing card of a suit denoted by a black trefoil. **b** (in pl.) this suit. **4** an association of persons united by a common interest, usu. meeting periodically for a shared activity (bridge club). **5** an organization or premises offering members social amenities, meals, temporary accommodation, etc. **6** an organization or premises having athletic and exercise facilities (health club). **7** an organization offering members certain benefits (book club). **8** a group of persons, nations, etc., having something in common. **9** a sports team and its administrative staff. **10** a bar or nightclub. ● v. (**clubbed, clubbing**) **1** tr. beat with or as with a club. **2** intr. (foll. by together, with) combine for joint action, esp. making up a sum of money for a purpose. **3** tr. contribute (money etc.) to a common stock. **4** intr. visit nightclubs etc. □ **join** (or **welcome to**) **the club** you're not the only one to feel that way.

clubber n. **1** a member of a club. **2** a person who frequents nightclubs.

clubbing n. the practice of frequenting nightclubs.

clubby adj. (**-ier, -iest**) **1** sociable; friendly. **2** cliquish; tending to exclude others. **3** typical of a social club, esp. in sumptuous decor etc. □ **clubbiness** n.

club foot n. a congenitally deformed foot, usu. turned downward and inward so that one walks on the outer edge of the foot. □ **club-footed** adj.

clubhouse n. **1** the premises used by a club. **2** N Amer. the dressing room of an esp. baseball team.

clubland n. nightclubs collectively.

club sandwich n. (Cdn also **clubhouse sandwich**) a sandwich usu. consisting of two layers of bacon, lettuce, tomato, mayonnaise, and chicken or turkey served between three slices of toast or bread.

club soda n. N Amer. = SODA 2.

cluck ● n. **1** a guttural cry like that of a hen. **2** slang a silly or foolish person (dumb cluck). ● v.intr. **1** (of a hen) emit a cluck or clucks. **2** (of a person) make a clucking sound with the tongue. **3** (also **cluck-cluck**) express annoyance, disapproval, etc. by making a similar noise.

clue ● n. **1** a fact or idea that serves as a guide, or suggests a line of inquiry, in a problem or investigation. **2** a piece of evidence etc. in the detection of a crime. **3** a verbal formula serving as a hint as to what is to be inserted in a crossword. ● v.tr. (**clues, clued, cluing** or **clueing**) provide a clue to. □ **clue in** informal inform. **not have a clue** informal be ignorant or incompetent.

clueless *adj. informal* ignorant, stupid. □ **cluelessly** *adv.* **cluelessness** *n.*

clump ● *n.* **1** (foll. by *of*) a cluster or compact group of things or people, esp. of trees, hair, buildings, etc. **2** an agglutinated mass or lump. **3** a dull thudding sound. ● *v.* **1 a** *intr.* form a clump. **b** *tr.* heap or plant together. **2** *intr.* walk with heavy steps. **3** *tr. informal* hit. □ **clumpy** *adj.* (**-ier, -iest**).

clumper *n.* (also **clumpet** /ˈklʌmpət/) *Cdn* (*Maritimes & Nfld*) a large floating chunk of ice.

clumsy *adj.* (**-ier, -iest**) **1** not graceful in movement or shape; awkward. **2** done without skill or ease (*a clumsy forgery*). **3** tactless (*a clumsy apology*). **4** (of tools, furniture, etc.) difficult to use or move; not well designed. □ **clumsily** *adv.* **clumsiness** *n.*

clung *past and past part. of* CLING.

clunk ● *n.* a dull sound as of thick pieces of metal striking. ● *v.* **1** *intr.* make such a sound. **2** *intr.* (often foll. by *along*) move or progress clumsily. **3** *tr.* hit hard so as to make a clunking sound. □ **clunking** *adj.*

clunker *n.* *N Amer. informal* **1** a dilapidated automobile or machine. **2** a failure; flop.

clunky *adj.* (**-ier, -iest**) *informal* **1** *N Amer.* awkward or clumsy. **2** *N Amer.* not sleekly designed (*a clunky station wagon*). **3** tending to make clunking sounds.

cluster ● *n.* **1** a close group or bunch of similar things growing together. **2** a close arrangement or group of people, animals, faint stars, etc. ● *v.* **1** *tr.* bring into a cluster or clusters. **2** *intr.* be or come into a cluster or clusters. **3** *intr.* (foll. by *around*) gather.

cluster bomb *n.* an anti-personnel bomb spraying smaller bombs or shrapnel when detonated.

clutch[1] ● *v.* **1** *tr.* **a** seize eagerly. **b** grasp tightly. **2** *intr.* (foll. by *at*) snatch suddenly. ● *n.* **1** a tight grasp. **2** (in *pl.*) power or control (*in his clutches*). **3 a** (in a motor vehicle) a device for connecting and disconnecting the engine to the transmission. **b** the pedal operating this. **c** an arrangement for connecting or disconnecting working parts of a machine. **4** *N Amer.* a decisive or crucial situation (*came through in the clutch*). **5** = CLUTCH BAG. ● *attrib.adj. N Amer. Sport slang* **1** occurring at a decisive time (*a clutch home run*). **2** (of a person) performing well at crucial times.

clutch[2] *n.* **1 a** a set of eggs to be hatched at one time. **b** the brood resulting from this. **2** a group of people or of similar items.

clutch bag *n.* (also **clutch purse**) a handbag without a handle or strap.

clutter ● *n.* **1** a crowded and untidy collection of things. **2** an untidy state. ● *v.tr.* (often foll. by *up, with*) crowd untidily, fill with clutter.

cluttered *adj.* crowded so as to cause confusion, esp. with many small objects.

Clydesdale *n.* a draft horse of a heavy powerful breed, usu. dark-coloured with thick white hair on the lower legs.

CM *abbr.* Member of the Order of Canada.

Cm *symbol* curium.

cm *abbr.* centimetre(s).

CMA *abbr.* **1** Canadian Medical Association. **2** (in Canada) CERTIFIED MANAGEMENT ACCOUNTANT.

Cmdr *abbr.* COMMANDER.

Cmdre *abbr.* COMMODORE.

CMHC *abbr.* Canada Mortgage and Housing Corp.

CMM *abbr.* (in Canada) Commander of the Order of Military Merit.

CMV *abbr.* CYTOMEGALOVIRUS.

CNE *abbr.* Canadian National Exhibition.

C-note *n. N Amer. slang* a one-hundred-dollar bill.

CNS *abbr.* CENTRAL NERVOUS SYSTEM.

CO *abbr.* **1** Commanding Officer. **2** Colorado (in postal use).

Co *symbol* cobalt.

Co. *abbr.* **1** company. **2** county. □ **and Co.** *informal* and the rest of them; and similar things.

c/o *abbr.* care of.

co- *prefix* added to: **1** nouns, with the sense 'joint, mutual, common' (*co-pilot*). **2** adjectives and adverbs, with the sense 'jointly, mutually' (*co-dependent*). **3** verbs, with the sense 'together with another or others' (*co-operate*).

co-accused *n.* a person who is accused of a crime jointly with another or others.

coach ● *n.* **1** a bus which is comfortably equipped for longer journeys. **2 a** a person who trains or instructs a sports team or athlete. **b** a private tutor. **c** a person who teaches an actor, singer, etc. in specific aspects of their art. **3** *N Amer.* economy class seating in an aircraft, train, etc. **4** a four-wheeled carriage, usu. closed and drawn by one or more horses. ● *adv. N Amer.* in economy class seating. ● *v.* **1 a** *tr.* train or instruct (a student, sports team, etc.) as a coach. **b** *intr.* work as a coach. **c** *tr.* give hints to; prime with facts. **2** *intr.* travel by coach. □ **coachable** *adj.* **coaching** *n.*

coach house *n.* a building designed to hold horse-drawn coaches or carriages.

coachman *n.* (*pl.* **-men**) the driver of a horse-drawn carriage.

coady /ˈkoːdi/ *n. Cdn* (*Nfld*) a thick sweetened sauce, usu. made from boiled molasses.

coagulant *n.* a substance that produces coagulation.

coagulate /koˈægjʊˌleɪt/ *v.tr. & intr.* **1** change from a fluid to a solid or semi-solid state. **2** clot, curdle. **3** set, solidify. □ **coagulation** *n.*

coal *n.* **1 a** a hard black or blackish rock, mainly carbonized plant matter, found in underground seams and used esp. as a fuel. **b** a piece or pieces of this for burning. **2** (in *pl.*) burning or charred pieces of coal, wood, etc. in a fire. **3** = CHARCOAL 1. □ **coals to Newcastle** something brought or sent to a place where it is already plentiful. **rake** (or **haul**) **over the coals** reprimand severely.

coal-black *adj.* completely black.

coalesce /ˌkoʊəˈlɛs/ *v.intr.* **1** come together and form one whole. **2** combine in a coalition. □ **coalescence** *n.* **coalescent** *adj.*

coalfield *n.* an extensive area with strata containing coal.

coal-fired *adj.* heated or powered by coal.

coalition *n.* **1** a temporary alliance for combined action, esp. of distinct parties forming a government. **2** fusion into one whole. □ **coalitionist** *n.*

coal oil *n. N Amer. dated* kerosene or petroleum.

coal tar *n.* a thick black viscid liquid distilled from coal and used as a source of benzene and many other organic chemicals.

coarse *adj.* **1 a** rough or loose in texture or grain; made of large particles. **b** (of a person's features) rough or large. **2** lacking refinement or delicacy; crude, obscene (*coarse humour*). □ **coarsely** *adv.* **coarseness** *n.*

coarsen *v.tr. & intr.* make or become coarse.

coast ● *n.* **1 a** the border of the land near the sea; the seashore. **b** (**the Coast**) *N Amer.* the Pacific coast of N America. **2** a run, usu. downhill, in or on a vehicle without the use of power. ● *v.intr.* **1** ride or move, usu. downhill, without use of power. **2** make progress without much effort. □ **the coast is clear** there is no danger of being observed or caught. □ **coastal** *adj.*

coastal boat *n. Cdn (Nfld)* a boat carrying supplies, mail, and some passengers to outports.

coaster *n.* **1** a small tray or mat for a bottle or glass. **2** *N Amer.* **a** a sled or toboggan. **b** a roller coaster. **3** a ship that travels along the coast from port to port.

coast guard *n.* **1** (also **Coast Guard**) **a** (in Canada) an organization whose responsibilities include rescue at sea or on major lakes, icebreaking, maintaining aids to navigation, and resupply of remote northern settlements. **b** a similar organization in another country. **2** a member of a coast guard.

coastline *n.* the line of the seashore, esp. with regard to its shape (*a rugged coastline*).

Coast Salish *n.* = SNE NAY MUXW.

coast-to-coast *adj. & adv.* **1** across a continent or island. **2** *Basketball* from one end of the court to the other while in possession of the ball.

Coast Tsimshian *n.* **1** a member of a part of the Tsimshian linguistic group living on the NW coast of BC. **2** the language of these people.

coat ● *n.* **1** an outer garment with sleeves and often extending below the hips; an overcoat or jacket. **2** **a** an animal's fur, hair, etc. **b** *Physiol.* a structure, esp. a membrane, enclosing or lining an organ. **c** a skin, rind, or husk. **d** *Bot.* a layer of a bulb etc. **3** **a** a layer or covering. **b** a covering of paint etc. laid on a surface at one time. ● *v.tr.* **1** (usu. foll. by *with*, *in*) apply a coat of paint etc. to; provide with a layer or covering. **2** (of paint etc.) form a covering over.

coat check *n. N Amer.* a place at a theatre, restaurant, etc. where patrons may leave their coats, bags, etc. with an attendant.

coated *adj.* **1** covered with a coat of some substance. **2** (also in *comb.*) having a coat of a specified sort. **3** (of paper) treated with a coating of clay to provide a glazed surface.

coat hanger *n.* = HANGER 2.

coating *n.* **1** a thin layer or covering. **2** a substance used for covering in a thin layer.

coat of arms *n.* a shield or other arrangement of the heraldic bearings of a person, family, government, etc.

coat rack *n. N Amer.* a stand with hooks or a long pole on which to hang coats, hats, etc.

coattail *n.* each of the flaps extending below the waist from the back of a tailcoat. □ **(riding) on the coattails of** undeservedly benefiting from (another's success).

co-author ● *n.* an author who collaborates with another on a book or article. ● *v.tr.* be a co-author of.

coax¹ *v.tr.* **1** (usu. foll. by *into*, or *to* + infin.) persuade gradually by flattery or by continued patient trial. **2** (foll. by *out of*) obtain by coaxing. **3** manipulate (a thing) carefully or slowly. □ **coaxer** *n.* **coaxing** *n.*

coax² /ˈkoʊæks/ ● *adj.* = COAXIAL. ● *n.* coaxial cable.

coaxial /koʊˈæksiəl/ *adj.* **1** having a common axis. **2** *Electricity* (of a cable or line) transmitting (telephone, telegraph, television, or radio signals) by means of two concentric conductors separated by an insulator.

cob *n.* **1** the cylindrical centre of an ear of corn, to which the rows of kernels are attached. **2** a sturdy horse with short legs. **3** a male swan.

cobalt /ˈkoʊbɒlt/ *n.* a silvery-white magnetic metallic element occurring as a mineral in combination with sulphur and arsenic, and used in many alloys.

cobalt-60 *n.* a long-lived radioisotope of cobalt, used as a radioactive tracer and in cancer therapy.

cobalt blue ● *n.* **1** a pigment containing a cobalt salt. **2** the deep blue colour of this. ● *adj.* (hyphenated when *attrib.*) of this colour.

cobalt bomb *n.* **1** a container of cobalt-60 or other radioisotope used in the treatment of cancer. **2** a hydrogen bomb designed to disperse radioactive cobalt.

cobble¹ ● *n.* a small stone, larger than a pebble, rounded by the action of water. ● *v.tr.* (esp. as **cobbled** *adj.*) pave with cobblestones.

cobble² *v.tr.* **1** mend or patch up (esp. shoes). **2** (often foll. by *together*) join or assemble roughly.

cobbler *n.* **1** a person who mends shoes, esp. professionally. **2** a baked dessert of fruit topped with a tea-biscuit crust. **3** an iced drink of wine etc., sugar, and lemon (*sherry cobbler*).

cobblestone *n.* a small rounded stone used for paving.

COBOL /ˈkoʊbɒl/ *n. Computing* a programming language designed for use in commerce.

cobra *n.* any of a number of venomous Asian and African snakes esp. of the genus *Naja*, which can dilate their necks to form a hood when excited.

cobweb *n.* **1** **a** a fine network of threads spun by a spider from a liquid secreted by it, used to trap insects etc. **b** the thread of this. **2** anything compared with a cobweb, esp. in flimsy texture. **3** a trap or insidious entanglement. **4** (in *pl.*) a state of mental inertia (*a walk will clear the cobwebs*). □ **cobwebbed** *adj.* **cobwebby** *adj.*

coca /ˈkoʊkə/ *n.* **1** a S American shrub, *Erythroxylum coca*. **2** its dried leaves, chewed as a stimulant.

cocaine *n.* a white crystalline alkaloid derived from coca leaves, used as a local anaesthetic or in various forms as a narcotic with euphoric effects.

co-chair ● *n.* (also **co-chairman**, **co-chairperson**) a person who chairs a committee jointly with another or others. ● *v.tr.* act as a co-chair for.

cochlea /ˈkɒkliə/ *n.* (*pl.* **cochleae** /-kli,iː/) the spiral cavity of the internal ear, in which the sensory reception of sound occurs. □ **cochlear** *adj.*

cock ● *n.* **1** **a** a male bird, esp. of a domestic fowl; a rooster. **b** the male of certain sea creatures, e.g. the lobster or clam. **2** = WOODCOCK. **3** *coarse slang* the penis. ¶Usually considered a taboo word. **4** **a** a firing lever in a gun which can be raised to be released by the trigger. **b** the cocked position of this (*at full cock*). **5** *Curling* the position at the end of the rink at which rocks are aimed. **6** a tap or valve controlling flow. **7** *Brit. & Cdn (Nfld) slang* (usu. **old cock** as a form of address) a friend; a fellow. ● *v.tr.* **1** raise or make upright or erect. **2** turn or move (the eye or ear) attentively or knowingly. **3** set aslant, or turn up the brim of (a hat). **4** raise the cock of (a gun). □ **at half cock** only partly ready.

cockade *n.* a rosette etc. worn in a hat as a badge of office etc. or as part of a uniform. □ **cockaded** *adj.*

cock-a-doodle-doo *n.* a rooster's crow.

cockamamie *adj.* (also **cockamamy**) *N Amer. informal* ridiculous or incredible (*a cockamamie theory*).

cockapoo *n.* a breed of dog obtained by crossing a cocker spaniel and a poodle.

cockatiel /ˌkɒkəˈtiːl/ *n.* (also **cockateel**) a small delicately coloured crested Australian parrot, *Nymphicus hollandicus*.

cockatoo *n.* any of several parrots of the subfamily Cacatuinae, having powerful beaks and erectile crests.

cockchafer /ˈkɒk,tʃeifɜr/ *n.* a large nocturnal beetle,

Melolontha melolontha, which feeds on leaves and whose larva feeds on roots of crops etc.

cocked hat *n.* a hat with the brim permanently turned up in two or usu. three places. □ **knock into a cocked hat** defeat utterly.

cockerel *n.* a young rooster.

cocker spaniel *n.* a small breed of spaniel with a silky coat and long drooping ears.

cockeyed /ˈkɒkaid/ *adj. informal* **1** crooked, askew, not level. **2** (of a scheme etc.) absurd, not practical. **3** drunk. **4** squinting.

cockfight *n.* a fight between pitted cocks, often fitted with metal spurs, usu. with spectators betting on the outcome. □ **cockfighting** *n.*

cockle[1] *n.* **1** any edible mollusc of the genus *Cardium*, having a chubby ribbed bivalve shell. **2** its shell. □ **warm the cockles of one's heart** make one contented; be satisfying.

cockle[2] *n.* any of various plants, esp. the corn cockle, of the genus *Agrostemma*.

cockney ● *n.* (*pl.* **-eys**) **1** a native of the East End of London, England. **2** the dialect or accent typical of this area. ● *adj.* of or characteristic of cockneys or their dialect or accent.

cockpit *n.* **1 a** a compartment for the pilot (and crew) of an aircraft or spacecraft. **b** a similar compartment for the driver in an automobile. **c** a space for the helmsman in some small yachts. **d** the space in which the paddler sits in a kayak. **2** an arena of war or other conflict. **3** a place where cockfights are held.

cockroach *n.* any of various flat brown insects, typically a stout-bodied scavenger resembling a beetle, with hardened forewings; esp. the large dark brown *Blatta orientalis* and *Periplaneta americana*, which infest households, warehouses, etc.

cocksucker *n. coarse slang* **1** a person who performs fellatio. **2** a contemptible person. □ **cocksucking** *n. & adj.*

cocksure *adj.* **1** presumptuously or arrogantly confident. **2** (foll. by *of*, *about*) absolutely sure. □ **cocksurely** *adv.* **cocksureness** *n.*

cocktail *n.* **1** a usu. alcoholic drink made by mixing various spirits, fruit juices, etc. **2** (*attrib.*) **a** denoting a small item of food served as an hors d'oeuvre etc. (*cocktail wiener*). **b** denoting a place or occasion where drinks are served (*cocktail party*). **3** a dish of mixed ingredients (*fruit cocktail*). **4** any hybrid mixture.

cocktail dress *n.* a usu. short evening dress suitable for wearing on a semiformal occasion.

cocktail lounge *n.* a room in a restaurant, hotel, etc. where alcoholic drinks are served.

cocktail party *n.* a social event, usu. held in the early evening, at which cocktails and refreshments are served.

cocky *adj.* (**-ier**, **-iest**) **1** conceited, arrogantly confident. **2** saucy, impudent. □ **cockiness** *n.*

coco /ˈkoːkoː/ *n.* (also **cocoa**, **coconut palm**) (*pl.* **cocos** or **cocoas**) a tall tropical palm tree, *Cocos nucifera*, bearing coconuts.

cocoa /ˈkoːkoː/ *n.* **1** a powder made from crushed cacao seeds, often with other ingredients. **2** a drink made from this powder and hot water or milk.

cocoa bean *n.* a cacao seed.

cocoa butter *n.* a fatty substance obtained from cocoa beans, used in confectionery, cosmetics, etc.

co-conspirator *n.* a fellow conspirator.

coconut *n.* (also **cocoanut**) **1** a large oval brown seed of the coco, with a hard shell and edible white fleshy lining enclosing a milky juice. **2** (in full

coconut palm) = COCO. **3** the edible white fleshy lining of a coconut.

coconut milk *n.* **1** the white milky liquid found inside the coconut. **2** a coconut-flavoured liquid obtained by soaking grated coconut in water.

coconut oil *n.* the liquid or semi-solid oil obtained from the flesh of the coconut, used as an ointment or in foods.

cocoon ● *n.* **1 a** a silky case spun by many insect larvae for protection as pupae. **b** a similar structure made by other animals. **2** anything which encloses or protects like a cocoon. **3** a protective covering sprayed on metal equipment to prevent corrosion. ● *v.* **1** *tr. & intr.* wrap in or form a cocoon. **2** *tr.* spray with a protective coating.

cocooning *n. N Amer.* the practice of spending one's leisure time in the home rather than by going out. □ **cocooner** *n.*

COD *abbr.* **1** *N Amer.* collect on delivery. **2** cash on delivery.

cod *n.* (*pl.* same) any large marine food fish of the family Gadidae, esp. *Gadus morhua*.

coda /ˈkoːdə/ *n.* **1** *Music* the concluding passage of a piece or movement, usu. forming an addition to the basic structure. **2** the concluding section of a dance, drama, or literary work. **3** a concluding event or series of events.

coddle *v.tr.* **1** treat indulgently or over-attentively. **2** cook (an egg) in water below boiling point.

code ● *n.* **1 a** a pre-arranged system of words, letters, numbers, signals, or symbols, used to represent others for brevity or to ensure secrecy. **b** any similar system used for conveying specific information with arbitrarily assigned symbols (*postal code*). **c** = GENETIC CODE. **2 a** a set of instructions written in a programming language. **b** the language itself. **c** = BAR CODE. **3 a** a systematic collection of statutes. **b** a set of rules on any subject (*dress code*). **4 a** the prevailing morality of a society or class (*code of honour*). **b** a person's standard of moral behaviour. ● *v.* **1** *tr.* put (a message, program, etc.) into code. **2** *intr.* (foll. by *for*) *Biochem.* be the genetic code for (an amino acid etc.). □ **bring up to code** *N Amer.* renovate an older building to make it conform to revised, more stringent building code regulations. □ **coder** *n.*

codec /ˈkoːdek/ *n.* a device that converts an analog signal into an encoded digital form, and decodes digital signals into analog form, used in telephone systems and in video systems for computers.

co-defendant *n.* a joint defendant.

codeine /ˈkoːdiːn/ *n.* an alkaloid derived from morphine and used to relieve pain.

code name *n.* a name used for secrecy or convenience instead of the usual name. □ **code-name** *v.tr.*

cod end *n.* the narrow-necked bag at the end of a trawl net etc.

codependent ● *adj.* emotionally or psychologically dependent on supporting or caring for another person, esp. a person with an addiction or illness. ● *n.* a codependent person. □ **codependency** *n.*

code-sharing *n.* the practice of two airlines using the same identifying code letters or flight numbers for connecting services. □ **code-share** *v.intr.*

codex /ˈkoːdeks/ *n.* (*pl.* **codices** /-dəˌsiːz, ˈkɒd-/) an ancient manuscript text in book form.

codfish *n.* = COD.

codger *n.* (usu. in **old codger**) *informal* a person, esp. an old or strange one.

codicil /ˈkoːdəsɪl, ˈkɒd-/ *n.* an addition explaining, modifying, or revoking a will or part of one.

codify /'kɒdɪˌfaɪ, 'kɒd-/ *v.tr.* (**-ies, -ied**) arrange (laws etc.) systematically into a code. □ **codification** *n.* **codifier** *n.*

codling[1] *n.* (also **codlin**) **1** any of several varieties of apple having a long tapering shape, used for cooking. **2** (also **codling moth**) a small moth, *Carpocapsa pomonella*, the larva of which feeds on apples.

codling[2] *n.* a small codfish.

cod-liver oil *n.* an oil pressed from the fresh liver of cod or related fishes, rich in vitamins D and A.

cod tongue *n.* *Cdn* (*Nfld*) the tongue of a codfish, fried in pork fat and eaten as a delicacy.

cod trap *n.* *Cdn* a device used for inshore fishing, consisting of a long net along which fish are guided into a box-shaped trap.

coed *informal* ● *adj.* **1** coeducational. **2** open to both males and females. ● *n.* *N Amer. dated* a female student at a coeducational institution.

co-edit *v.tr.* edit jointly with another or others. □ **co-editor** *n.*

coeducation *n.* the education of male and female students together. □ **coeducational** *adj.*

coefficient *n.* **1** *Math.* a quantity placed before and multiplying an algebraic expression (e.g. 4 in $4x^y$). **2** *Physics* a multiplier or factor that measures some property (*coefficient of expansion*).

coelenterate /siːˈlɛntəˌreɪt/ *n.* any marine animal of the phylum Coelenterata with a simple tube-shaped or cup-shaped body, e.g. jellyfish and corals.

coeliac *var. of* CELIAC.

coenzyme *n.* *Biochem.* a non-proteinaceous compound that assists in the action of an enzyme.

coerce /kəʊˈɜːs/ *v.tr.* (often foll. by *into*) persuade or restrain (a person) by force (*coerced me into signing*).

coercion /kəʊˈɜːʃən/ *n.* **1** the act or process of coercing. **2** government by force. □ **coercive** *adj.* **coercively** *adv.* **coerciveness** *n.*

coeval /kəʊˈiːvəl/ ● *adj.* **1** having the same age or date of origin. **2** living or existing at the same epoch. **3** having the same duration. ● *n.* a coeval person, a contemporary. □ **coevally** *adv.*

coexist *v.intr.* (often foll. by *with*) **1** exist together (in time or place). **2** (esp. of nations) exist in mutual tolerance though professing different ideologies etc. □ **coexistence** *n.* **coexistent** *adj.*

co-extensive *adj.* extending over the same space, time, or limits.

coffee ● *n.* **1 a** a drink made from the roasted and ground beanlike seeds of a tropical shrub of the genus *Coffea*. **b** a cup of this. **c** = INSTANT COFFEE. **2 a** the shrub yielding these seeds. **b** these seeds raw, or roasted and ground. **3** the pale brown colour of coffee mixed with milk. ● *adj.* **1** of the colour of coffee mixed with milk. **2** flavoured with coffee. □ **wake up and smell the coffee** become aware of (usu. unpleasant) realities.

coffee bean *n.* the beanlike seed of the coffee shrub, esp. when roasted but not ground.

coffee break *n.* a short break from work during which food or drink may be consumed.

coffee cake *n.* *N Amer.* a type of cake or sweet bread topped or filled with cinnamon sugar, often containing nuts or raisins.

coffee house *n.* **1** a place serving coffee and other refreshments. **2** a form of entertainment, usu. jazz or folk music or poetry readings etc., performed cabaret-style.

coffee klatch /klætʃ/ *n.* (also **coffee klatsch**)

N Amer. an informal gathering for conversation at which coffee is served, esp. one involving women.

coffee maker *n.* a device for making coffee.

coffee pot *n.* a tall covered pot with a handle and spout, in which coffee is made or served.

coffee shop *n.* a small informal restaurant, esp. in an office building, serving simple meals and beverages.

coffee table *n.* a small low oblong table.

coffee-table book *n.* a large lavishly illustrated book suitable for prominent display.

coffer *n.* **1** a box, esp. a large strongbox for valuables. **2** (in pl.) a treasury or store of funds. **3** *Archit.* a sunken panel in a ceiling, soffit, etc. □ **coffered** *adj.*

coffin *n.* a long narrow usu. wooden box in which a corpse is buried or cremated.

co-founder *n.* a person who founds an institution etc. jointly with another or others. □ **co-found** *v.tr.*

cog *n.* **1 a** each of a series of teeth on the edge of a wheel or shaft transferring motion by engaging with another series. **b** (in full **cogwheel**) a wheel or shaft furnished with these. **2** a person who plays a minor or routine role in an organization. □ **cogged** *adj.*

cogeneration *n.* the use of otherwise wasted energy for heating or generating electricity.

cogent /'kəʊdʒənt/ *adj.* (of arguments etc.) convincing, compelling. □ **cogency** *n.* **cogently** *adv.*

cogitate /'kɒdʒəˌteɪt/ *v.tr. & intr.* ponder, meditate. □ **cogitation** *n.* **cogitative** *adj.* **cogitator** *n.*

cognac /'kɒnjæk, 'kɔːn-/ *n.* a high-quality brandy, properly that distilled in Cognac in W France.

cognate ● *adj.* **1** (of a word) having the same linguistic family or derivation (as another); representing the same original word or root (e.g. English *father*, German *Vater*, Latin *pater*). **2** related to or descended from a common ancestor. ● *n.* **1** a cognate word. **2** a relative. □ **cognately** *adv.*

cognition *n.* **1** the mental faculties of perception, thought, reason, and memory. **2** a perception, sensation, notion, or intuition.

cognitive *adj.* **1** of or pertaining to cognition. **2** based on or pertaining to empirical knowledge. □ **cognitively** *adv.*

cognizance /'kɒgnɪzəns, 'kɒn-/ *n.* **1** knowledge or awareness; perception, notice. **2** the sphere of one's observation or concern. **3** *Law* the right of a court to deal with a matter. □ **take cognizance of** notice or take account of, esp. officially.

cognizant /'kɒgnɪzənt, 'kɒn-/ *adj.* (foll. by *of*) having knowledge or being aware of.

cognoscenti /ˌkɒɡnəˈʃɛnti, -sɛnti/ *n.pl.* connoisseurs; discerning experts.

cogwheel *n.* = COG 1b.

cohabit *v.intr.* (**cohabited, cohabiting**) **1** live together amicably. **2** live together in a sexual and romantic relationship without marriage. □ **cohabitant** *n.* **cohabitation** *n.* **cohabiter** *n.*

cohere *v.intr.* **1** (of parts or a whole) stick together, remain united. **2** (of reasoning etc.) be logical or consistent.

coherent *adj.* **1** (of a person) able to speak intelligibly and articulately. **2** (of speech, an argument, etc.) logical and consistent; easily followed. **3** cohering; sticking together. **4** *Physics* (of waves) having a constant phase relationship. □ **coherence** *n.* **coherency** *n.* **coherently** *adv.*

cohesion *n.* **1 a** the act or condition of sticking together. **b** a tendency to cohere. **2** *Chem.* the force with which molecules cohere. □ **cohesive** *adj.* **cohesively** *adv.* **cohesiveness** *n.*

coho *n.* (in full **coho salmon**) (*pl.* same or **-os**) a silver salmon, *Oncorhynchus kisutch*, of the N Pacific.

cohort *n.* **1** *N Amer.* a companion or colleague. **2 a** a group of persons with a common demographic or statistical characteristic. **b** persons banded or grouped together, esp. in a common cause. **3** a band of warriors.

co-host ● *n.* a person who hosts (esp. a broadcast) jointly with another or others. ● *v.tr.* act as a co-host for (a broadcast, competition, conference, etc.).

coif¹ /kɔif/ *n.* a close-fitting cap, esp. as worn by nuns under a veil.

coif² /kwɒf/ ● *n.* esp. *N Amer.* a hairstyle. ● *v.tr.* (**coiffed, coiffing**) (usu. as **coiffed** *adj.*) arrange or style (hair).

coiffure /kwɒˈfjʊr/ ● *n.* a hairstyle. ● *v.tr.* style (hair), often in a specified way. □ **coiffured** *adj.*

coil ● *n.* **1** anything arranged in a joined sequence of concentric circles. **2** a length of rope, a spring, etc., arranged in this way. **3** a single turn of something coiled. **4** a lock of hair twisted and coiled. **5** an intrauterine contraceptive device in the form of a coil. **6 a** = INDUCTION COIL. **b** any helix of wire through which electric current passes, as in a transformer or electromagnet. **7** a length of wire, piping, etc., wound in circles or spirals. ● *v.* **1** *tr.* arrange in a series of concentric loops or rings. **2** *tr. & intr.* twist or be twisted into a circular or spiral shape. **3** *intr.* move sinuously.

coil spring *n.* a helical spring, having the form of a cone or a cylinder.

coin ● *n.* **1** a piece of flat usu. round metal stamped and issued by a government as money. **2** metal money collectively. **3** *slang* money, wealth (*they've got coin*). ● *v.tr.* **1** invent or devise (esp. a new word or phrase). **2** make (metal) into coins. **3** make (coins) by stamping. □ **coin money** *informal* make a large amount of money quickly. **the other side of the coin 1** the opposite view of the matter. **2** an apparently contrasting aspect of a situation. **to coin a phrase** *ironic* introducing a banal remark or cliché.

coinage *n.* **1** the act or process of coining. **2 a** coins collectively. **b** a system or type of coins in use. **3 a** an invention, esp. of a new word or phrase. **b** a newly invented word or phrase.

coincide *v.intr.* **1** occur at or during the same time. **2** occupy the same portion of space. **3** (often foll. by *with*) be in agreement.

coincidence *n.* **1** a remarkable concurrence of events or circumstances without apparent causal connection. **2 a** the fact of occurring or being together. **b** an instance of this.

coincident *adj.* **1** occurring together in space or time. **2** (foll. by *with*) in agreement; harmonious.

coincidental *adj.* **1** in the nature of or resulting from a coincidence. **2** happening or existing at the same time. □ **coincidentally** *adv.*

coin-op *n.* **1** a coin-operated machine, esp. a computer video game. **2** a laundromat.

coin-operated *adj.* (of a machine) automatically activated when the user inserts a coin or coins.

Cointreau /ˈkwɒntrəʊ/ *n.* *proprietary* a colourless orange-flavoured liqueur.

coitus /ˈkɔitəs, ˈkɔːɪt-/ *n.* (also **coition** /kəʊˈɪʃən/) *Med.* sexual intercourse. □ **coital** *adj.* **coitally** *adv.*

coitus interruptus /ˌɪntəˈrʌptəs/ *n.* intercourse in which the penis is withdrawn before ejaculation.

cojones /kəˈhoːneɪs/ *n.pl.* *N Amer.* *coarse slang* **1** testicles. **2** courage, guts.

Coke *n.* *proprietary* Coca-Cola, a cola soft drink.

coke¹ ● *n.* **1** a solid substance left after the gases have been extracted from coal, used as fuel and in metallurgy. **2** a residue left after incomplete combustion of petroleum. ● *v.tr.* convert (coal) into coke.

coke² *slang* ● *n.* cocaine. ● *v.tr.* (usu. foll. by *up*; usu. in *passive*) drug (esp. oneself) with cocaine.

cokehead *n.* *slang* a person addicted to or habitually using cocaine.

Col *abbr.* (also **Col.**) COLONEL.

col. *abbr.* column.

COLA /ˈkoːlə/ *abbr.* *N Amer.* cost-of-living adjustment.

cola *n.* **1** any small tree of the genus *Cola*, native to W Africa, bearing seeds containing caffeine. **2** a sweet carbonated drink usu. flavoured with cola seeds.

colander *n.* a perforated metal or plastic container, used to strain off liquids.

colby *n.* a mild, soft-textured cheese resembling cheddar.

cold ● *adj.* **1** of or at a low or relatively low temperature. **2** not heated; cooled after being heated. **3** (of a person) feeling cold. **4** lacking ardour, friendliness, or affection. **5** depressing, uninteresting (*cold facts*). **6 a** dead. **b** *informal* unconscious. **7** *informal* at one's mercy (*had me cold*). **8** sexually frigid. **9** *N Amer. Sport* not performing well. **10** (of a scent in hunting) having become weak. ● *n.* **1 a** the prevalence of a low temperature, esp. in the atmosphere. **b** cold weather; a cold environment (*went out into the cold*). **2** an infection in which the mucous membrane of the nose and throat becomes inflamed, causing runny nose, sneezing, sore throat, coughing, etc. ● *adv.* **1** completely, entirely (*cold sober*). **2** unrehearsed, without preparation. □ **cold (hard) cash** cash, esp. in large quantities and as opposed to credit. **in cold blood** without feeling or passion; deliberately, ruthlessly. **out in the cold** ignored, neglected. **throw** (or **pour**) **cold water on** be discouraging or depreciatory about. □ **coldly** *adv.* **coldness** *n.*

cold-blooded *adj.* **1** having a body temperature varying with that of the environment (e.g. of fish). **2** callous; deliberately cruel. □ **cold-bloodedly** *adv.* **cold-bloodedness** *n.*

cold call *n.* an unsolicited sales call to a prospective customer by phone or in person. □ **cold-call** *v.tr. & intr.*

cold chisel *n.* a steel chisel suitable for cutting unheated metal.

cold-cock *v.tr.* *N Amer. slang* punch or strike (a person) in the head, esp. to render unconscious.

cold cuts *n.pl.* slices of cold cooked meats.

cold deck *n.* *N Amer.* Forestry a pile of logs intended to be moved or processed at a later time.

cold draw *n.* Curling a shot in which a rock is curled into the house without touching another rock.

cold feet *n.pl.* *informal* loss of nerve or confidence.

cold fish *n.* a person, little moved by emotions, regarded as hard and unfeeling.

cold frame *n.* a box-shaped frame with a glass top, placed over plants to protect them from the weather.

cold front *n.* the forward edge of an advancing mass of cold air.

cold-hearted *adj.* lacking affection or warmth. □ **cold-heartedly** *adv.* **cold-heartedness** *n.*

cold shoulder ● *n.* a show of intentional unfriendliness. ● *v.tr.* (**cold-shoulder**) be deliberately unfriendly to.

cold snap *n.* (also **cold spell**) a sudden brief spell of cold weather.

cold sore *n.* inflammation and blisters in and around the mouth, caused by a virus infection.

cold storage *n.* **1** storage in a refrigerator or other cold place for preservation. **2** a state in which something (esp. an idea) is put aside temporarily.

cold sweat *n.* a state of sweating due to fear or illness.

cold turkey *informal* ● *n.* **1** abrupt withdrawal from addictive drugs. **2** the symptoms of this. ● *adv.* abruptly. □ **go cold turkey** cease (esp. an addictive habit) completely and abruptly.

cold war *n.* **1** a state of prolonged hostility between nations short of armed conflict, often consisting of threats, violent propaganda, and subversive political activities. **2** (**Cold War**) relations of this nature between the Soviet Union and the US and their respective allies in the decades following the Second World War. □ **Cold Warrior** *n.*

cole *n.* any of various brassicas, esp. cabbage or rape.

Coleman stove *n.* *N Amer.* *proprietary* a camp stove.

coleslaw *n.* a salad of shredded raw cabbage with a dressing and often other vegetables.

colic /ˈkɒlɪk/ *n.* **1** severe spasmodic abdominal pain. **2** a condition in young babies characterized by long, loud crying. □ **colicky** *adj.*

coliform /ˈkɒləfɔrm/ ● *adj.* of or pertaining to a group of bacteria typified by *Escherichia coli*, which inhabit the large intestine of humans and animals and when present in water indicate fecal contamination. ● *n.* a bacillus of this group.

coliseum *n.* a large amphitheatre, stadium, arena, etc.

colitis /kəˈlaɪtɪs/ *n.* inflammation of the colon lining.

coll. *abbr.* **1** college. **2** collection.

collaborate *v.intr.* (often foll. by *with*) **1** work jointly, esp. in a literary or artistic production. **2** co-operate traitorously with an enemy. □ **collaboration** *n.* **collaborationist** *n. & adj.* **collaborative** *adj.* **collaboratively** *adv.* **collaborator** *n.*

collage ● *n.* **1 a** a form of art in which various materials (e.g. photographs) are arranged and assembled or glued to a backing. **b** a work of art done in this way. **2** a literary, musical, or cinematic work involving the juxtaposition of several genres or elements. **3** a collection of unrelated things. ● *v.tr.* (**collaged**, **collaging**) arrange in a collage. □ **collagist** *n.*

collagen /ˈkɒlədʒən/ *n.* a protein found in animal connective tissue, yielding gelatin on boiling.

collapse ● *n.* **1** the tumbling down or falling in of a structure or hollow body; caving in. **2** a sudden failure or breakdown of a plan, undertaking, organization, etc. **3** a physical or mental breakdown. ● *v.* **1 a** *intr.* undergo or experience a collapse. **b** *tr.* cause to collapse. **2** *intr.* *informal* sit or lie down and relax, esp. after prolonged effort (*collapsed into a chair*). **3 a** *intr.* (of furniture etc.) be foldable and capable of storage in a small space. **b** *tr.* fold (furniture) in this way. □ **collapsible** *adj.*

collar ● *n.* **1** the part of a shirt, dress, coat, etc., that goes around the neck, either upright or folded over. **2 a** a band of linen, lace, or other material encircling the neck or forming the upper part of a garment. **b** = CLERICAL COLLAR. **c** a band worn around the neck for a specific purpose (*cervical collar*). **3** a band put around the neck of a dog or other animal, esp. in order to control or identify it. **4** a band or ring fastened over a pipe, rod, etc. in order to restrain or connect. **5** a coloured marking resembling a collar around the neck of a bird or animal. **6** *Cdn* (*Nfld*) a rope or chain with a looped end used to moor a boat. ● *v.tr.* **1** seize (a

person) by the collar or neck. **2** furnish with a collar. **3** capture, apprehend, arrest. **4** *informal* accost and detain (a reluctant listener etc.). □ **collared** *adj.* (also in *comb.*). **collarless** *adj.*

collarbone *n.* either of the two curved bones joining the breastbone and the shoulder blade.

collard *n.* (also **collards**, **collard greens**) *N Amer.* a variety of cabbage without a distinct heart.

collate *v.tr.* **1** sort or arrange (pages) in the correct order. **2** (in bookbinding) verify the order of (sheets) by their signatures. **3** analyze and compare (texts, statements, etc.) to identify points of agreement and difference. **4** assemble from different sources.

collateral ● *n.* **1** security pledged as a guarantee for repayment of a loan. **2** a person having the same ancestry as another but by a different line. ● *adj.* **1** descended from the same ancestors but by a different line. **2** side by side; parallel. **3 a** additional but subordinate. **b** contributory; corroborating. **c** connected but aside from the main subject, course, etc. □ **collateralize** *v.tr.* **collaterally** *adv.*

collateral damage *n.* destruction or injury to civilians as the unintended or unexpected result of a military attack.

collation *n.* **1** the act or an instance of collating. **2** a light informal meal.

colleague *n.* a person with whom one works, esp. in a profession or business.

collect[1] ● *v.* **1** *tr. & intr.* bring or come together; assemble, accumulate. **2** *tr.* systematically seek and acquire (e.g. books, stamps) as a continuing hobby. **3 a** *tr.* demand or obtain (taxes, contributions, payment due, etc.) from a person or persons. **b** *intr.* (often foll. by *on*) receive a payment. **4** *tr.* come for and take away (*garbage is collected once a week*). **5 a** *refl.* regain control of oneself esp. after a shock. **b** *tr.* concentrate (one's energies, thoughts, etc.). **6** *tr.* receive (an award, prize, etc.). ● *adj. & adv.* *N Amer.* (of a telephone call, parcel, etc.) to be paid for by the recipient.

collect[2] /ˈkɒlekt/ *n.* a short prayer of the Anglican and Roman Catholic Churches, esp. one assigned to a particular day or season.

collected *adj.* **1** calm and cool; not perturbed or distracted. **2** (esp. of literary works) gathered together in one place or publication. □ **collectedly** *adv.*

collectible (also esp. *Brit.* **collectable**) ● *adj.* **1** worth collecting. **2** able to be collected. ● *n.* an item sought by collectors.

collection *n.* **1** the act or process of collecting or being collected. **2** any group of things systematically assembled, esp.: **a** specimens or collectibles acquired by a specialist or hobbyist. **b** the holdings of a museum, library, etc. **c** a book of short stories, poems, or essays, or a recording including several songs or compositions. **d** a line of fashionable clothes, cosmetics, furniture etc. offered by a designer or retail store. **3** (foll. by *of*) an accumulation; a mass or pile (*a collection of dust*). **4 a** the collecting of money, esp. in church or for a charitable cause. **b** the amount collected. **5** the regular removal of mail, garbage, etc. for dispatch or disposal.

collective ● *adj.* **1** formed by or constituting a collection. **2** taken as a whole; aggregate (*our collective opinion*). **3** of or from several or many individuals; common (*collective memory*). **4** of or pertaining to a union of workers (*collective bargaining*). ● *n.* **1 a** a co-operative enterprise. **b** its members. **c** (in full **collective farm**) (in communist countries) the state-owned holdings of several farmers run as a joint enterprise. **2** (in full **collective noun**) a noun that is grammatically singular and denotes a collection or number of individuals (e.g. *assembly*, *family*, *troop*). □ **collectively** *adv.* **collectiveness** *n.*

collective agreement *n.* an agreement between a union and employer reached by collective bargaining.

collective bargaining *n.* the process by which wages etc. for all members of a bargaining unit are negotiated between the union and an employer.

collective memory *n.* the memory of a group of people, often passed from one generation to the next.

collective ownership *n.* the ownership of land and means of production by a number of people for their common benefit.

collective unconscious *n.* (in Jungian theory) the part of the unconscious mind derived from ancestral memory and experience common to all humans.

collectivism *n.* the theory and practice of the collective ownership of land and the means of production. □ **collectivist** *n.* **collectivistic** *adj.*

collectivity *n.* **1** a group or community of people bound together by common beliefs or interests. **2** collective quality.

collectivize *v.tr.* organize on the basis of collective ownership. □ **collectivization** *n.*

collector *n.* **1** a person who collects, esp. things of interest as a hobby. **2** a person who collects due payments etc. (*tax collector*; *ticket collector*). **3** a thing that collects, esp. solar energy or heat. **4** *Cdn* a lane running parallel to the express lanes of a freeway affording access between it and other roads. **5** *Cdn* (*Nfld*) (in full **collector boat**) a boat which gathers catches of cod from several locations and transports them to a single location for processing.

collector's item *n.* a valuable object, esp. one of interest to collectors.

college *n.* **1** an establishment for further or higher education: **a** an institution within a university, usu. with residence facilities and curricular autonomy but without degree-granting privileges. **b** a faculty within a university. **c** a school for specialized professional education (*business college*). **d** = COMMUNITY COLLEGE. **e** *Cdn* = CEGEP. **f** *N Amer.* post-secondary education in general. **2** the buildings or premises of a college. **3** the students and teachers in a college. **4** an organized body of persons with shared functions and privileges (*College of Physicians*). □ **give a thing the (old) college try** *N Amer.* put forth one's best effort despite the unlikelihood of success.

collège classique /kɒˈleʒ klæˈsiːk/ *n.* (*pl.* **collèges classiques**) *Cdn hist.* (in Quebec) a private school offering a four-year secondary education and a four-year post-secondary program leading to a BA, with the curriculum emphasizing classics, literature, philosophy, and religion.

College of Cardinals *n.* a body comprising all the cardinals of the Roman Catholic Church, which elects and advises the Pope.

collegial /kəˈliːdʒəl, -dʒiəl/ *adj.* **1** characterized by collaboration among colleagues. **2** pertaining to or involving a body of colleagues. **3** of or pertaining to a college. □ **collegiality** /-dʒiˈælɪti/ *n.* **collegially** *adv.*

collegiate ● *adj.* **1** of or pertaining to colleges or universities (*collegiate sports*). **2** constituted of or belonging to colleges. ● *n.* *Cdn* (in full **collegiate institute**) (in some provinces) a public secondary school, originally one having specialist teachers and a prescribed classical curriculum.

collide *v.intr.* (often foll. by *with*) **1** strike together with an abrupt or violent impact. **2** be in conflict.

collie *n.* a sheepdog of a breed originating in Scotland, with a long pointed nose and long hair.

collier /ˈkɒlɪər/ *n.* **1** a coal miner. **2 a** a ship transporting coal. **b** a member of its crew.

colliery /ˈkɒlɪəri/ *n.* (*pl.* **-ies**) a coal mine.

Collins *n.* an iced drink made of gin or whisky etc. with soda water, lemon or lime juice, and sugar.

collision *n.* **1** a violent impact of a moving body, esp. a vehicle, with another object. **2** the clashing of opposed interests or considerations. **3** *Physics* the action of particles striking or coming together.

collision course *n.* a course or action that is bound to cause a collision or conflict.

collocate *v.tr.* **1** place together or side by side. **2** arrange; set in a particular place.

collocation *n.* **1** the action of collocating or state of being collocated. **2** *Linguistics* **a** the (esp. habitual) juxtaposition or association of a word with other words. **b** the words so juxtaposed.

colloid /ˈkɒlɔɪd/ *n.* **1** *Chem.* **a** a substance consisting of ultramicroscopic particles. **b** a mixture of such a substance uniformly dispersed through a second substance esp. to form a viscous solution. **2** *Physiol.* a gelatinous substance in the body, esp. present in the thyroid gland or in diseased tissue. □ **colloidal** *adj.*

colloquial /kəˈloʊkwɪəl/ *adj.* belonging to or proper to ordinary or familiar conversation. ¶*Colloquial* designates words or usages appropriate to a familiar or informal, rather than a formal, style of speech or writing. □ **colloquially** *adv.*

colloquialism *n.* **1** a colloquial word or phrase. **2** the use of colloquialisms.

colloquium /kəˈloʊkwɪəm/ *n.* (*pl.* **colloquia** /-kwɪə/) an academic conference focused on a specific topic.

collude /kəˈluːd/ *v.intr.* conspire together for a fraudulent or underhanded purpose; connive, plot.

collusion /kəˈluːʒən/ *n.* **1** a secret agreement, esp. for a fraudulent purpose. **2** *Law* such an agreement between ostensible opponents in a lawsuit. □ **collusive** *adj.*

Colo. *abbr.* Colorado.

cologne /kəˈloʊn/ *n.* a dilute solution of alcohol and a concentrate of perfume.

colon[1] *n.* a punctuation mark (:) with several uses: **1** to introduce a quotation or a list of items. **2** to separate clauses when the second expands or illustrates the first. **3** between numbers in a statement of proportion (10:1). **4** to separate hour from minutes in rendering the time (9:30). **5** in Biblical references to separate chapter and verse (*John 3:16*).

colon[2] *n.* the lower part of the large intestine, from the cecum to the rectum. □ **colonic** /kəˈlɒnɪk/ *adj.*

colonel *n.* (also **Colonel**) **1** (in Canada and the US) an officer in the armed forces ranking above a lieutenant colonel. **2** a lieutenant colonel.

colonial ● *adj.* **1 a** of or relating to a colony or colonies. **b** (of mentalities, attitudes etc.) typical of people living in a colony or former colony, esp. in their dependence on and admiration for the mother country or other dominant culture. **2** of or relating to the period of a nation's history during which it was under the rule of a mother country. **3** of or relating to the Thirteen Colonies (the British colonies in N America that became the founding states of the US in 1776). **4** (of architecture or furniture) built, designed in, or in a style characteristic of a colonial period. **5** (of plants or animals) living in colonies. ● *n.*

1 a person inhabiting a colony. **2** a house built in colonial style. □ **colonially** *adv.*

colonialism *n.* **1** a policy of acquiring or maintaining colonies. **2** the exploitation or subjugation of a people by a larger or wealthier power. □ **colonialist** *n. & adj.*

Colonial Office *n. hist.* the British government department in charge of colonies.

Colonial Secretary *n. hist.* the British government minister in charge of the Colonial Office.

colonist *n.* a settler in or inhabitant of a colony.

colonist car *n. Cdn hist.* a railway car furnished with slatted wooden platforms for sitting or sleeping and equipped with a small stove.

colonize *v.* **1** *tr.* **a** establish a colony or colonies in (a country or area). **b** settle as colonists. **2** *intr.* establish or join a colony. **3** *tr.* (of one country, society, etc.) impose its culture on (another). **4** *tr.* (of plants, animals, and micro-organisms) become established (in an area). □ **colonization** *n.* **colonizer** *n.*

colonnade /ˌkɒləˈneɪd/ *n.* a row of columns, esp. supporting a roof etc. □ **colonnaded** *adj.*

colonoscope /kəˈlɒnəskoʊp/ *n.* an illuminated fibre-optic tube introduced through the anus and used to examine the colon, remove polyps, or obtain tissue specimens. □ **colonoscopic** *adj.* **colonoscopy** *n.*

colony *n.* (*pl.* **-ies**) **1 a** a group of people who settle in a new territory (whether or not already inhabited) and form a community connected with a mother country. **b** the territory of such settlers. **2** any country or area subject to the colonial rule of another. **3** a group of people of common nationality, religion, or (esp. artistic) occupation inhabiting a particular area in a city. **4 a** a group which is segregated from a larger population, either freely or through expulsion (*nudist colony*). **b** the territory occupied by such a group. **5** a community of Hutterites. **6** *Bot. & Zool.* a collection of plants or animals connected, in contact, or living close together.

color etc. *var. of* COLOUR etc.

Colorado potato beetle *n.* a yellow and black striped beetle, *Leptinotarsa decemlineata*, the larva of which is highly destructive to the potato plant.

Colorado spruce *n.* = BLUE SPRUCE.

coloration *n.* (also **colouration**) **1** colouring; a scheme or method of applying colour. **2** the natural (esp. variegated) colour of living things or animals.

coloratura /ˌkʌlərəˈtʊərə, -ˈtjʊərə, kɒl-/ *n.* **1** elaborate ornamentation of a vocal melody with runs and trills. **2** a singer (esp. a soprano) skilled in this method of singing.

colossal *adj.* of immense size, scope, extent, or amount; huge, gigantic. □ **colossally** *adv.*

colossus /kəˈlɒsəs/ *n.* (*pl.* **colossi** /-saɪ/) **1** a gigantic person, building, etc. **2** a statue much bigger than life-size. **3** an extremely powerful person etc.

colostomy /kəˈlɒstəmi/ *n.* (*pl.* **-ies**) *Med.* an operation on the colon to make an opening in the abdominal wall to provide an artificial anus.

colostrum /kəˈlɒstrəm/ *n.* the fluid secreted from the mammary glands in the first few days after giving birth, rich in protein and antibodies.

colour (also **color**) ● *n.* **1 a** the sensation produced on the eye by rays of light when resolved as by a prism etc. into different wavelengths. **b** the perception of colour by the eye; a system of colours. **2** one, or any mixture, of the constituents into which light can be separated as in a spectrum or rainbow, sometimes including (loosely) black and white. **3** a colouring substance, e.g. a paint or pigment. **4** the use of all colours, not only black and white, in photography, television, etc. **5** *N Amer.* analysis, trivia, statistics, etc. provided by a sports broadcaster as a supplement to the play-by-play (also *attrib.*: *colour commentary*). **6 a** pigmentation of the skin, esp. as determined by race or ethnicity. **b** a skin colour or race other than white. **7** ruddiness of complexion (*a healthy colour*). **8** quality, mood, or variety in music, literature, speech, etc.; distinctive character or timbre. **9** (in *pl.*) appearance or aspect (*her true colours*). **10** (in *pl.*) **a** a coloured ribbon or uniform etc. worn to signify membership in a particular school, club, team, or group. **b** the flag of a regiment or ship. **c** a national flag. **11** (in *pl.*) coloured clothing (*wash the colours separately*). **12** a show of reason; a pretext (*under colour of*). ● *v.* **1** *tr. & intr.* apply colour to, esp. by painting or dyeing or with coloured pens or pencils. **2** *tr.* influence (*coloured by experience*). **3** *tr.* misrepresent, exaggerate, esp. with spurious detail (*a highly coloured account*). **4** *intr.* take on colour; blush. □ **of colour** not Caucasian. **show one's true colours** reveal one's true character or intentions. **under false colours** deceitfully.

colourable *adj.* (also **colorable**) **1** plausible. **2** counterfeit. □ **colourably** *adv.*

colouration *var. of* COLORATION.

colour-blind *adj.* **1** unable to distinguish certain colours. **2** (of a company, project, etc.) characterized by or displaying freedom from racial bias. □ **colour-blindness** *n.*

colour code ● *n.* the use of colours as a standard means of identification. ● *v.tr.* (**colour-code**) identify by means of a colour code. □ **colour-coded** *adj.* **colour-coding** *n.*

coloured (also **colored**) ● *adj.* **1** having colour(s). **2** (also **Coloured**) *offensive* **a** wholly or partly of non-white descent. **b** of or relating to coloured people. ● *n.* (also **Coloured**) *offensive* a coloured person. **2** (in *pl.*) = COLOUR *n.* 11.

colourfast *adj.* (also **colorfast**) dyed in colours that will not fade or be washed out. □ **colourfastness** *n.*

colourful *adj.* (also **colorful**) **1** having much or varied colour; bright. **2** full of interest; vivid, lively. □ **colourfully** *adv.* **colourfulness** *n.*

colour graphics adapter *n. see* CGA 2.

colouring *n.* (also **coloring**) **1** the act or process of using colour(s). **2** the style in which a thing (e.g. a painting) is coloured. **3 a** facial complexion. **b** natural colour (e.g. of a bird). **4** an artificial colouring agent; a pigment. **5** false appearance.

colouring book *n.* a book of outline drawings to be coloured with crayons etc., usu. by children.

colourist *n.* (also **colorist**) **1** a person who uses colour, esp. with great skill. **2** a hairdresser who dyes or colours hair. □ **colouristic** *adj.*

colourize *v.tr.* (also **colorize**) colour (a black and white film etc.) by means of a computer. □ **colourization** *n.*

colourless *adj.* (also **colorless**) **1** without colour. **2** lacking character or interest. **3** dull or pale in hue. **4** neutral, impartial, indifferent. □ **colourlessly** *adv.*

colour of right *n. Cdn* the right of ownership of a thing.

colour scheme *n.* an arrangement or planned combination of colours, esp. in interior design.

colourway *n.* (also **colorway**) a colour scheme.

colt *n.* **1** a young uncastrated male horse, usu. less than four years old. **2** a young or inexperienced person. □ **coltish** *adj.*

colter *var. of* COULTER.

coltsfoot *n.* (*pl.* **-s**) a composite herbaceous plant, *Tussilago farfara*, with large leaves and yellow flowers.

columbine /ˈkɒləm,baɪn/ *n.* any wild or cultivated plant of the genus *Aquilegia*.

column *n.* **1** an upright cylindrical pillar often slightly tapering and usu. supporting an entablature or arch, or standing alone as a monument. **2** a structure or part shaped like a column. **3** a vertical cylindrical mass of liquid or vapour. **4 a** a vertical division of a page, chart, etc., containing a sequence of figures or words. **b** the figures or words themselves. **5** a part of a newspaper regularly devoted to a particular subject. **6** an arrangement of troops in successive lines, with a narrow front. □ **columnar** /kəˈlʌmnər/ *adj.* **columned** *adj.*

columnist *n.* a journalist contributing a regular column to a newspaper, magazine, etc.

coma *n.* (*pl.* **-s**) a prolonged deep unconsciousness, caused esp. by severe injury or excessive use of drugs.

comatose /ˈkoʊmə,toʊs/ *adj.* **1** in a coma. **2** drowsy, sleepy, lethargic.

comb ● *n.* **1** a toothed strip of rigid material for tidying and arranging the hair, or for keeping it in place. **2** a device or part of a machine having a similar design or purpose. **3 a** the red fleshy crest of a fowl, esp. a rooster. **b** an analogous growth in other birds. **4** a honeycomb. ● *v.tr.* **1** arrange or tidy (the hair) by drawing a comb through. **2** search (a place) thoroughly. □ **comb out 1** tidy and arrange (hair) with a comb. **2** remove with a comb. □ **combed** *adj.*

combat ● *n.* **1** a fight, struggle, or contest. **2** an armed encounter with enemy forces (also *attrib.*: *combat zone*). ● *v.* (**-batted, -batting** or **-bated, -bating**) **1** *intr.* engage in combat. **2** *tr.* engage in combat with. **3** *tr.* oppose; strive against.

combatant /ˈkɒmbætənt, kəm-, ˈkɒmbætənt, ˈkʌm-/ ● *n.* a person engaged in fighting. ● *adj.* **1** fighting. **2** for fighting.

combat boot *n.* a heavy, laced, close-fitting leather boot reaching above the ankle, with a thick sole.

combat dress *n.* = BATTLEDRESS.

combative /ˌkɒmˈbætɪv, kəm-/ *adj.* ready or eager to fight; pugnacious. □ **combativeness** *n.*

comber *n.* a long curling wave; a breaker.

combi /ˈkɒmbi/ *n.* a machine, appliance, etc. with a combined function or mode of action (often *attrib.*).

combination *n.* **1** the act or an instance of combining; the process of being combined. **2** a combined state (*in combination with*). **3** a combined set of things or people. **4** a sequence of numbers or letters used to open a combination lock. **5** (*in pl.*) a single undergarment for the body and legs. **6** *Math.* a selection of a given number of elements from a larger number of elements, without regard to the order of the elements chosen (*compare* PERMUTATION). □ **combinatory** /ˈkɒmbɪnətəri/ *adj.*

combination lock *n.* a lock that can be opened only by a specific sequence of movements.

combine ● *v.* **1** *tr. & intr.* join together; unite for a common purpose. **2** *tr.* possess (qualities usually distinct) together (*combines charm and authority*). **3 a** *intr.* coalesce in one substance. **b** *tr.* cause to do this. **c** *intr.* form a chemical compound. **4** *intr.* co-operate. **5** *tr. & intr.* harvest (crops etc.) by means of a combine. ● *n.* **1** a combination of esp. commercial interests to control prices etc. **2** a self-propelled machine that reaps and threshes in one operation. □ **combinable** *adj.* **combiner** *n.*

combined *adj.* **1** united; joined together (*combined*

choirs). **2** (of an action, etc.) performed by a group acting together (*combined effort*).

combining form *n. Grammar* a linguistic element used in combination with another element to form a word, e.g. *bio-* = life, *-graphy* = writing.

combo *n.* (*pl.* **-os**) *informal* **1** a small jazz or dance band. **2** any combination (*seafood combo*).

combust *v.* **1** *tr.* subject to combustion. **2** *intr.* undergo combustion.

combustible ● *adj.* **1** capable of or used for burning. **2** excitable; easily irritated. ● *n.* a combustible substance. □ **combustibility** *n.*

combustion *n.* **1** burning; consumption by fire. **2** *Chem.* the development of light and heat from the chemical combination of a substance with oxygen.

combustion chamber *n.* a space in which combustion takes place, e.g. in an engine.

come ● *v.intr.* (*past* **came**; *past part.* **come**) **1** move, be brought towards, or reach a place thought of as near or familiar to the speaker or hearer. **2** reach or be brought to a specified situation or result (*came into prominence*). **3** reach or extend to a specified point (*comes within a mile of us*). **4** traverse or accomplish (*have come a long way*). **5** occur, happen; become present instead of future (*how did you come to break it?*). **6** take or occupy a specified position in space or time (*it comes on the third page*). **7** become perceptible or known (*came into sight*; *comes as a surprise*). **8** be available (*it comes in three sizes*). **9** become (*the handle has come loose*). **10** (foll. by *of*) **a** be descended from (*comes of a rich family*). **b** be the result of (*that comes of complaining*). **11** (foll. by *from*) **a** originate in; have as its source. **b** have as one's home. **12** *informal* play the part of; behave like. **13** *coarse slang* have an orgasm. **14** (in *subj.*) *informal* when a specified time is reached (*come the revolution*). **15** (as *interj.*) expressing caution or reserve (*come, it can't be that bad*). ● *n. coarse slang* ejaculated semen. □ **as ... as they come** typically or supremely so (*is as tough as they come*). **come about** happen; take place. **come across 1** be effective or understood. **2** *slang* (foll. by *with*) hand over what is wanted. **3** meet or find by chance. **come again** *informal* **1** make a further effort. **2** (as *imper.*) what did you say? **come along 1** arrive, appear. **2** make progress; move forward. **3** (as *imper.*) hurry up. **come and go 1** pass to and fro; be transitory. **2** pay brief visits. **come apart** fall or break into pieces, disintegrate. **come at 1** reach, discover; get access to. **2** attack (*came at me with a knife*). **come away 1** become detached or broken off (*came away in my hands*). **2** (foll. by *with*) be left with a feeling, impression, etc. (*came away with many misgivings*). **come back 1** return. **2** recur to one's memory. **3** become fashionable or popular again. **4** *N Amer.* reply, retort. **come before 1** be dealt with by (a judge etc.). **2** have greater importance than. **come between 1** interfere with the relationship of. **2** separate; prevent contact between. **come by 1** pass; go past. **2** call on a visit (*why not come by tomorrow?*). **3** acquire, obtain (*came by a new bicycle*). **come down 1** come to a place or position regarded as lower. **2** lose position or wealth (*has come down in the world*). **3** be handed down by tradition or inheritance. **4** be reduced; show a downward trend (*prices are coming down*). **5** (foll. by *against, in favour of*) reach a decision or recommendation. **6** (foll. by *to*) signify or betoken basically; be dependent on (a factor) (*it comes down to cost*). **7** (foll. by *on*) criticize harshly; rebuke, punish. **8** (foll. by *with*) begin to suffer from (a disease). **9** (of rain) fall heavily. **10** (of a decision, budget, etc.) be announced or delivered.

come for 1 come to collect or receive. **2** = COME AT 2. **come forward 1** advance. **2** offer one's help, services, etc. **come in 1** enter a house or room. **2** take a specified position in a race etc. (*came in third*). **3** become fashionable or seasonable. **4 a** have a useful role or function. **b** prove to be (*came in handy*). **c** have a part to play (*where do I come in?*). **5** be received (*more news has just come in*). **6** begin speaking, esp. in radio transmission. **7** be elected; come to power. **8** (foll. by *for*) receive (usu. something unwelcome) (*came in for much criticism*). **9** (foll. by *on*) join (an enterprise etc.). **10** (of a tide) turn to high tide. **11** (of a train, ship, or aircraft) approach its destination. **come into 1** see senses 2, 7 of *v*. **2** receive, esp. as heir. **come off 1** *informal* (of an action) succeed; be accomplished. **2** fare; turn out (*came off badly*). **3** be detached or detachable (from). **4** fall (from). **5** be reduced or subtracted from (*$5 came off the price*). **come off it** (as *imper.*) *informal* an expression of disbelief or refusal to accept another's opinion, behaviour, etc. **come on 1** continue to come. **2** advance, esp. to attack. **3** make progress; thrive (*is really coming on*). **4** begin (*I've got a cold coming on*). **5** appear on the stage, field of play, etc. **6** be heard or seen on television, on the telephone, etc. **7** arise to be discussed. **8** (as *imper.*) expressing encouragement. **9** = COME UPON. **10** (foll. by *to*) make sexual advances to. **11** (of a light, appliance, etc.) start functioning. **come out 1** emerge; become known (*it came out that he had left*). **2** appear or be published. **3 a** declare oneself; make a decision (*came out in favour of joining*). **b** openly declare that one is a homosexual. **4 a** be satisfactorily visible in a photograph etc., or present in a specified way (*the dog didn't come out*). **b** (of a photograph) be produced satisfactorily or in a specified way (*they all came out well*). **5** (of a stain etc.) be removed. **6** make one's debut on stage or in society. **7** (foll. by *in*) be covered with (*came out in a rash*). **8** (of a problem) be solved. **9** (foll. by *with*) declare openly; disclose. **come over 1** come from some distance or nearer to the speaker (*come over here*). **2** change sides or one's opinion. **3 a** (of a feeling etc.) overtake or affect (a person). **b** *informal* feel suddenly (*came over faint*). **4** appear or sound in a specified way (*the ideas came over clearly*). **5** affect or influence (*what came over her?*). **come round 1** pay an informal visit. **2** recover consciousness. **3** be converted to another person's opinion. **4** (of a date or regular occurrence) recur; be imminent again. **come through 1** be successful; survive. **2** survive or overcome (a difficulty). **3** provide support, assistance, etc. when needed. **come to 1** recover consciousness. **2** reach in total; amount to. **3** *refl.* **a** recover consciousness. **b** stop being foolish. **4** reach a particular (usu. bad) situation or state of affairs (*what is the world coming to?*). **come to hand** become available; be recovered. **come to nothing** have no useful result in the end; fail. **come to pass** happen, occur. **come to rest** cease moving. **come to that** *informal* in fact; if that is the case. **come under 1** be classified as or among. **2** be subject to (influence or authority). **come up 1** come to a place or position regarded as higher. **2** attain wealth or position (*come up in the world*). **3 a** (of an issue, problem, etc.) arise; present itself; be mentioned or discussed. **b** (of an event etc.) occur, happen (*coming up next*). **4** (often foll. by *to*) **a** approach a person, esp. to talk. **b** approach or draw near to a specified time, event, etc. (*coming up to eight p.m.*). **5** (foll. by *to*) match (a standard etc.). **6** (foll. by *with*) produce (an idea etc.), esp. in response to a challenge. **7** (of a plant etc.) spring up out of the ground. **come**

up against be faced with or opposed by. **come upon 1** meet or find by chance. **2** attack by surprise. **come what may** no matter what happens. **have it coming to one** *informal* be about to get one's deserts. **how come?** *informal* why? **if it comes to that** in that case. **not know if one is coming or going** be confused from being very busy. **to come** future; in the future (*the year to come; still to come*). **where a person is coming from** a person's meaning, intention, or personality.

comeback *n.* **1** a return to a previous (esp. successful) state. **2** *informal* a retaliation or retort.

comedian *n.* **1** a humorous entertainer on stage, television, etc. **2** an actor in comedy. **3** a person who behaves comically.

comedienne /kə,mi:di'en/ *n.* a female comedian.

comedown *n.* **1** a loss of status; decline or degradation. **2** a disappointment.

comedy *n.* (*pl.* **-ies**) **1 a** a play, film, etc., of an amusing or satirical character, usu. with a happy ending. **b** the dramatic genre consisting of works of this kind. **2** an amusing or farcical incident or series of incidents in everyday life. **3** humour, esp. in a work of art etc. □ **comedic** /kə'mi:dɪk/ *adj.*

comedy of errors *n.* **1** a comedy in which the humour derives from mistaken identities, misunderstandings, etc. **2** any event made laughable by an accumulation of mistakes.

come from away *n. Cdn* (Maritimes & Nfld) a person who is not from the Atlantic region generally.

come-hither *attrib.adj. informal* enticing, flirtatious.

comely *adj.* (**-ier**, **-iest**) (esp. of a person) pleasant to look at. □ **comeliness** *n.*

come-on *n. informal* **1** a gesture, remark, description, etc. intended to attract or persuade. **2** a remark or behaviour intended to allure someone sexually.

comer *n.* **1** a person who comes, esp. as an applicant, participant, etc. **2** *informal* a person likely to be a success. □ **all comers** any applicants (with reference to a position etc. that is unrestricted in entry).

comet *n.* a hazy object usu. with a nucleus of ice and dust surrounded by gas and with a tail pointing away from the sun, moving about the sun in an eccentric orbit. □ **cometary** *adj.*

comeuppance *n. informal* one's deserved fate or punishment (*got his comeuppance*).

comfort ● *n.* **1** consolation; relief in affliction. **2 a** a state of physical well-being; being comfortable. **b** (usu. in *pl.*) things that make life easy or pleasant. **3** a cause of satisfaction. **4** a person who consoles or helps one. ● *v.tr.* **1** soothe in grief; console. **2** make comfortable. □ **comforting** *adj.* **comfortingly** *adv.*

comfortable *adj.* **1** giving ease (*a comfortable pair of shoes*). **2** free from discomfort; at ease. **3** *informal* having an adequate standard of living. **4** having no qualms (*did not feel comfortable about refusing him*). **5** with a wide margin (*a comfortable win*). □ **comfortableness** *n.* **comfortably** *adv.*

comforter *n.* **1 a** one who comforts. **b** (**Comforter**) *Christianity* the Holy Spirit. **2** *N Amer.* a warm quilt.

comfort food *n.* food, esp. rich in carbohydrates, which provides comfort as well as nourishment.

comfortless *adj.* **1** dreary, cheerless. **2** without comfort.

comfort zone *n.* **1** the range of temperature and relative humidity within which people, animals, etc. feel comfortable. **2** = PERSONAL SPACE. **3** a range of action, behaviour, etc. with which a person feels comfortable, often complacently so.

comfrey /'kʌmfri/ *n.* (*pl.* **-eys**) any of various herbs of the genus *Symphytum*, esp. *S. officinale* having large hairy leaves and clusters of usu. white or purple bell-shaped flowers.

comfy /'kʌmfi/ *adj.* (**-ier**, **-iest**) *informal* comfortable.

comic ● *adj.* **1** (often *attrib.*) of, or in the style of, comedy (*a comic actor*; *comic opera*). **2** causing or meant to cause laughter; funny. ● *n.* **1** a professional comedian. **2 a** (**comics**) a section of a newspaper containing comic strips. **b** = COMIC BOOK.

comical *adj.* causing laughter. □ **comically** *adv.*

comic book *n.* a book or magazine containing a single narrative told through comic strips.

comic opera *n.* **1** an opera with much dialogue, usu. with humorous treatment. **2** this genre.

comic relief *n.* **1** comic episodes in a play etc. intended to offset more serious portions. **2** the relaxation of tension etc. provided by such episodes.

comic strip *n.* a horizontal series of drawings in a comic book, newspaper, etc., usu. telling a story.

coming ● *attrib.adj.* **1** approaching, next (*this coming Sunday*). **2** of potential importance (*a coming entrepreneur*). ● *n.* arrival; approach. □ **coming and going** (or **comings and goings**) activity, esp. intense.

comingle *var. of* COMMINGLE.

coming of age *n.* the reaching of adulthood.

comma *n.* **1** a punctuation mark (,) indicating a pause between parts of a sentence, or dividing items in a list, a string of figures, etc. **2** (in full **comma butterfly**) a butterfly, *Polygonia c-album*, with a white comma-shaped mark on the underside of the hindwing.

command ● *v.* **1** *tr.* give formal orders or instructions to (*commands us to obey*; *commands that it be done*). **2** *tr.* & *intr.* have authority or control over. **3** *tr.* **a** restrain, master. **b** gain the use of; have at one's disposal or within reach (skill, resources, etc.) (*commands an extensive knowledge of history*). **4** *tr.* deserve and get (sympathy, respect, etc.). **5** *tr.* dominate (a strategic position) from a superior height; look down over. ● *n.* **1** an authoritative order; an instruction. **2** mastery, control, possession (*good command of languages*). **3** the exercise or tenure of authority, esp. naval or military (*has command of this ship*). **4** *Military* **a** *Cdn* one of the three divisions of the Canadian Forces (*Air Command*). **b** a body of troops etc. (*Bomber Command*). **c** a district under a commander (*Western Command*). **5** *Computing* **a** an instruction causing a computer to perform one of its basic functions. **b** a signal initiating such an operation. □ **at** (or **by**) **a person's command** following a person's request. **in command of** commanding; having under control. **under command of** commanded by.

commandant /,komən'dænt, -'dɒnt, 'kɒm-/ *n.* a commanding officer, esp. of a particular force etc.

command economy *n.* an economy, e.g. that of Cuba, which relies on the direction of a central governing body.

commandeer *v.tr.* **1** seize (men or goods) for military purposes. **2** take possession of without authority.

commander *n.* a person who commands, esp. (also **Commander**) a naval officer next in rank below captain. Abbr.: **Cdr.** □ **commandership** *n.*

commander-in-chief *n.* (*pl.* **commanders-in-chief**) the supreme commander, esp. of a nation's forces.

commanding *adj.* **1** dignified, exalted, impressive. **2** (of a hill or other high point) giving a wide view. **3** (of an advantage, a position, etc.) controlling; superior (*a commanding lead*). □ **commandingly** *adv.*

commanding officer *n.* (also **Commanding Officer**) the officer in command of a military unit, formation, or force. Abbr.: **CO.**

commandment *n.* a divine command.

commando *n.* (*pl.* **-os**) *Military* **1** a group of soldiers specially trained for carrying out quick attacks in enemy areas. **2** a member of such a group. **3** (*attrib.*) of or concerning a commando (*a commando operation*).

command post *n.* the headquarters of a military unit.

comme ci, comme ça /kɒm,si: kɒm'sɒ/ *adv.* & *adj.* so-so; neither good nor bad.

commemorate *v.tr.* **1 a** preserve in memory by some celebration. **b** (of a stone, plaque, etc.) be a memorial of. **2** celebrate in speech or writing. □ **commemorative** *adj.* **commemorator** *n.*

commemoration *n.* **1** an act of commemorating. **2** a service or part of a service in memory of a person, an event, etc.

commence *v.tr.* & *intr.* *formal* begin.

commencement *n.* *formal* **1** a beginning. **2** esp. *N Amer.* a ceremony for the conferral of diplomas.

commend *v.tr.* **1** (often foll. by *to*) entrust, commit (*commends his soul to God*). **2** praise. **3** recommend. **4** (*refl.*) find favour with (*this approach commended itself to the politicians*). □ **commendation** *n.*

commendable *adj.* praiseworthy. □ **commendably** *adv.*

commensurable /kə'menʃərəbəl, -sjərəbəl/ *adj.* **1** (often foll. by *with*, *to*) measurable by the same standard. **2** (foll. by *to*) proportionate to. **3** *Math.* (of numbers) in a ratio equal to the ratio of integers. □ **commensurability** *n.* **commensurably** *adv.*

commensurate /kə'mensərət, -ʃərət, -sjərət/ *adj.* **1** (usu. foll. by *with*) having the same size, duration, etc. **2** (often foll. by *to*, *with*) proportionate. **3** at a level appropriate to (*salary commensurate with qualifications*). □ **commensurately** *adv.*

comment ● *n.* **1 a** a remark. **b** criticism; gossip (*his behaviour aroused much comment*). **c** the action of responding to questions (*refused comment*). **d** commentary (*news and comment*). **2 a** an explanatory note (e.g. on a written text). **b** written criticism or explanation (e.g. of a text). **3** (of a play, book, etc.) a critical illustration; a parable (*her art is a comment on society*). ● *v.intr.* **1** (often foll. by *on*, *upon*, or *that* + clause) make (esp. critical) remarks. **2** (often foll. by *on*, *upon*) write explanatory notes. □ **no comment** *informal* I decline to answer your question.

commentary *n.* (*pl.* **-ies**) **1** a set of explanatory or critical notes on a text etc. **2** a descriptive spoken account (esp. on radio or television) of an event or a performance as it happens. **3** something that serves to illustrate or exemplify something (*a sad commentary on our society*).

commentator *n.* **1** a person who provides a commentary on an event etc. **2** the writer of a commentary. **3** a person who writes or speaks on current events.

commerce *n.* **1** financial transactions, esp. the buying and selling of merchandise, on a large scale. **2** social intercourse (*the daily commerce of gossip*).

commercial ● *adj.* **1** of, engaged in, or concerned with, commerce. **2** of or relating to the production of esp. foodstuffs on an industrial scale. **3** (of radio or TV broadcasting) funded by the revenue from broadcast advertising. **4** (of an airline, aircraft, vehicle, etc.) engaged in, used by, or suitable for business or commerce; not private or governmental (*commercial flight*). **5** of, relating to, or suitable for office buildings etc. (*commercial land*). **6** usu. *derogatory* having profit as a primary aim rather than artistic etc. value. ● *n.* a TV or radio advertisement. □ **commercially** *adv.*

commercial bank *n.* a privately-owned bank that provides a wide range of financial services to businesses and the general public.

commercial break *n. N Amer.* an interruption in a program for the broadcasting of commercials.

commercialism *n.* **1** the principles and practice of commerce. **2** (esp. excessive) emphasis on financial profit as a measure of worth.

commercialize *v.tr.* **1** exploit or spoil for the purpose of gaining profit. **2** make commercial. □ **commercialization** *n.* **commercialized** *adj.*

commercial paper *n.* **1** a corporate promissory note, usu. unsecured and for a short term. **2** *N Amer.* any negotiable paper, such as bills of exchange.

commie *n. & adj. slang derogatory* communist.

commingle /kə'mɪŋɡəl/ *v.tr. & intr.* mingle together.

commiserate /kə'mɪzə,reit/ *v.intr.* (usu. foll. by *with*) express or feel pity. □ **commiseration** *n.* **commiserative** *adj.* **commiserator** *n.*

commish *n. N Amer. informal* a commissioner, esp. a commissioner of a professional sports league.

commissary /'kɒmɪsɜri, kə'mɪs-/ *n.* (*pl.* **-ies**) **1** a deputy or delegate. **2** a representative or deputy of a bishop. **3** *N Amer.* a store for the sale of food and other goods, esp. to soldiers etc.

commission ● *n.* **1 a** the authority to perform a task or certain duties. **b** a person or group entrusted esp. by a government with such authority. **c** an instruction, command, or duty given to such a group or person. **2** an order for something, esp. a work of art, to be produced specially. **3** *Military* **a** a warrant conferring the rank of officer. **b** the rank so conferred. **4 a** the authority to act as agent for a company etc. in trade. **b** a percentage paid to the agent or sales representative from the profits of goods etc. sold, or business obtained. **c** the pay of a commissioned agent. **5** the act of committing (a crime, sin, etc.). **6** the office or department of a commissioner. **7** *hist.* the government of Newfoundland, consisting of a governor and six commissioners, appointed by the Crown 1934–1949. ● *v.tr.* **1** authorize or empower by a commission. **2 a** give (an artist etc.) a commission for a piece of work. **b** order (a work) to be written (*commissioned a play*). **3 a** *Military* appoint (an officer) by means of a commission. **b** prepare (a ship) for active service. **4** bring (a machine, equipment, etc.) into operation. □ **in commission** (of a warship etc.) manned, armed, and ready for service. **out of commission** not in service, not in working order.

commissioner *n.* **1** a person appointed, esp. by a commission, to perform a specific task. **2** a person appointed as a member of a commission. **3** a representative of the supreme authority in a district, department, etc. **4** (in the OPP and RCMP) the highest ranking officer. **5** *N Amer.* a person appointed by an athletic league or association to carry out various administrative and judicial functions (*baseball commissioner*).

Commissioner for Oaths *n.* a person, e.g. a lawyer, MP, MLA or MPP, etc., authorized to administer oaths and take affidavits.

commit *v.* (**committed, committing**) **1** *tr.* (usu. foll. by *to*) entrust or consign for: **a** safekeeping. **b** treatment, usu. destruction (*committed the book to the flames*). **2** *tr.* perpetrate (esp. a crime or blunder) (*commit murder*). **3** *tr.* pledge, involve, or bind (esp.

oneself) to a certain course or policy (*does not like committing herself*). **4** *intr.* (usu. foll. by *to*) pledge or engage oneself firmly (*we expect you to commit to the project*). **5** *tr.* consign (a person) to a mental hospital, prison, etc., by or as if by legal authority. **6** *tr. Politics* refer (a bill etc.) to a committee. □ **commit to memory** memorize. □ **committable** *adj.*

commitment *n.* **1** the process or an instance of committing oneself. **2** an engagement or (esp. financial) obligation that restricts freedom of action. **3** the state of being committed.

committal *n.* **1** the act of committing a person to an institution, esp. prison or a mental hospital. **2** the burial of a dead body.

committed *adj.* **1** having a strong dedication to a cause or belief. **2** obliged (to take a certain action).

committee *n.* **1** a body of persons elected or appointed for a specific function by, and usu. out of, a larger body. **2** (also **parliamentary committee**) (in the Commonwealth) such a body drawn from the upper or lower houses of a legislature, appointed to consider the details of a proposed bill after its second reading (also *attrib*). **3** = COMMITTEE OF THE WHOLE.

committee of the whole *n.* **1** a committee comprising all the members of a legislative body or other organization. **2** (in full **Committee of the Whole House**) (in the Commonwealth) the entire House of Commons when sitting as a committee to discuss the details of a proposed bill.

commode /kə'moːd/ *n.* **1** a chest of drawers. **2 a** a bedside table with a cupboard containing a chamber pot. **b** a chamber pot concealed in a chair with a hinged cover. **3** *N Amer. informal* a toilet or bathroom.

commodification /kə,mɒdɪfɪ'keɪʃən/ *n.* the action of turning something into or treating something as a (mere) commodity. □ **commodify** *v.tr.* (**-ies, -ied**).

commodious /kə'moːdiəs/ *adj.* roomy and comfortable. □ **commodiously** *adv.* **commodiousness** *n.*

commodity *n.* (*pl.* **-ies**) **1** an article that can be bought and sold, esp. a product as opposed to a service. **2** any of several raw or partially processed materials, e.g. grain or metals. **3** a useful thing.

commodore *n.* **1** (also **Commodore**) (in Canada and the UK, and formerly also in the US) a naval officer ranking above captain and below rear admiral. **2** the commander of a squadron or other group of vessels smaller than a fleet.

common ● *adj.* (**commoner, commonest**) **1 a** occurring often (*a common mistake*). **b** ordinary; of ordinary qualities; without special rank or position (*the common people*). **2 a** shared by, coming from, or done by, more than one (*common knowledge*). **b** belonging to, open to, or affecting, the whole community or the public (*common land*). **3** *derogatory* low-class; vulgar. **4** of the most familiar type (*common loon*). **5** *Math.* belonging to two or more quantities (*common denominator*). ● *n.* **1** (**the Commons**) = HOUSE OF COMMONS. **2** a piece of land set aside for public use, esp. as a park or recreation area in a city or town. **3** (in *pl.*) **a** the common people as opposed to those in authority. **b** the common people viewed as forming part of a political system, esp. as opposed to those of aristocratic status. **4** (in *pl.*) provisions or rations of food. □ **common** or **garden** *informal* ordinary. **in common 1** in joint use; shared. **2** of joint interest (*have little in common*). **in common with** in the same way as. **short commons** insufficient food. □ **commonly** *adv.* **commonness** *n.*

commonality n. (pl. **-ies**) **1** the sharing of an attribute. **2** a common occurrence.

common carrier n. **1** a person or company undertaking to transport any goods or person in a specified category. **2** N Amer. a company providing public telecommunications services.

common denominator n. **1** Math. a common multiple of the denominators of several fractions. **2** a common feature of members of a group.

commoner n. one of the common people, as opposed to the aristocracy.

Common Era n. = CHRISTIAN ERA.

common ground n. a point or argument accepted by both sides in a dispute.

common law n. (usu. hyphenated when attrib.) **1** law derived from custom and judicial precedent rather than statutes (compare CASE LAW, STATUTE LAW). **2 a** (usu. attrib.) denoting a relationship between cohabiting partners, recognized as a marriage in some common law jurisdictions but not brought about by a civil or ecclesiastical ceremony. **b** a common-law spouse.

Common Market n. the European Economic Community.

common noun n. (also **common name**) Grammar a name denoting a class of objects or a concept as opposed to a particular individual, e.g. boy, beauty.

commonplace • adj. lacking originality; trite. • n. **1 a** an everyday saying; a platitude. **b** an ordinary topic of conversation. **2** anything usual or trite. □ **commonplaceness** n.

common room n. a room in a college etc. which students and staff may use for relaxation or work.

common salt n. = SALT n. 1.

common seal n. a seal with a mottled grey coat, Phoca vitulina, of N Atlantic and N Pacific coasts.

common sense • n. sound practical sense, esp. in everyday matters. • adj. = COMMONSENSICAL.

commonsensical adj. possessing or marked by common sense.

common share n. (also **common stock**) N Amer. an ordinary capital share in a company, yielding a flexible dividend (compare PREFERRED SHARE).

common weal /ˌwiːl/ n. common well-being; the general good.

commonwealth n. **1 a** a community of people viewed as a political entity in which everyone has an interest. **b** any aggregate of persons or nations united by some common factor. **2** (**Commonwealth**) **a** (in full **the Commonwealth of Nations**) an international association comprising members of the former British Empire which acknowledge the British sovereign as official head of state. **b** hist. the republican period of government in Britain 1649–60.

Commonwealth Games n.pl. a sports competition including teams from all Commonwealth countries, held every four years.

commotion n. **1 a** a confused and noisy disturbance or outburst. **b** loud and confusing noise. **2** a civil insurrection.

communal adj. **1** relating or belonging to a community; for common use (communal bathroom). **2** of or relating to a commune. **3** of or relating to ethnic or religious groups within a larger community (communal violence). □ **communality** /ˌkɒmjəˈnæləti/ n. **communally** adv.

communalism n. **1** a principle of political organization based on federated communes. **2** the principle of communal ownership etc. **3** excessive devotion to

one's own ethnic or religious community as opposed to society in general. □ **communalist** n.

commune[1] /ˈkɒmjuːn/ n. **1** a group of people, not necessarily related, sharing living accommodation and possessions, esp. as a political act. **2** a communal settlement esp. for the pursuit of shared interests.

commune[2] /kəˈmjuːn/ v.intr. **1** (usu. foll. by with) **a** speak confidentially and intimately. **b** feel in close touch. **2** N Amer. Christianity receive Holy Communion.

communicable adj. (esp. of a disease) able to be passed on. □ **communicability** n.

communicant n. **1** Christianity a person who receives Holy Communion, esp. regularly. **2** a person who imparts information.

communicate v. **1** tr. **a** transmit or pass on (information) by speaking, writing, or other means. **b** transmit (heat, motion, etc.). **c** pass on (an infectious illness). **d** impart (feelings etc.) non-verbally (communicated his affection). **2** intr. succeed in conveying information, evoking understanding, etc. (she communicates well). **3** intr. (often foll. by with) share a feeling or understanding; relate socially. **4** intr. (often foll. by with) (of a room etc.) have a common connecting door. **5** Christianity **a** tr. administer Holy Communion to. **b** intr. receive Holy Communion. □ **communicator** n. **communicatory** adj.

communication n. **1 a** the act of communicating, esp. imparting news. **b** an instance of this. **c** the information etc. communicated. **2** a means of connecting different places, such as a door, passage, road, or railway. **3** social contact; routine exchange of information. **4** (in pl.) **a** the science and practice of transmitting information esp. by electronic or mechanical means. **b** a field of study encompassing writing and broadcasting skills as they apply to media and business. **c** the function of communicating information to the public by a company, organization, etc. (also attrib.: communications officer).

communications satellite n. (also **communication satellite**) an artificial satellite used to relay telephone, television, or radio signals.

communicative adj. **1** open, talkative, informative. **2** ready to communicate. **3** designating styles of teaching, esp. of a second language, that emphasize the communication of meaning in real-life situations.

communion n. **1** an instance of sharing, esp. thoughts or feelings; fellowship (their minds were in communion). **2** participation; a sharing in common (communion of interests). **3** (also **Communion**) Christianity **a** (in full **Holy Communion**) the Eucharist. **b** participation in the Communion service. **c** (attrib.) of or used in the Communion service (Communion table). **4** fellowship, esp. between branches of the Catholic Church. **5** a body or group within the Christian faith (the Anglican communion).

communiqué /kəˌmjuːnəˈkei, kəˈmjuːnəˌkei/ n. an official communication, esp. a news report.

communism n. **1** a system of society with property vested in the community and each member working for the common benefit according to his or her capacity and receiving according to his or her needs. **2** (usu. **Communism**) **a** the movement or political party advocating such a system, esp. as derived from Marxism and seeking the overthrow of capitalism by a proletarian revolution. **b** the communistic form of society established in the 20th c. in the former USSR and elsewhere. **3** = COMMUNALISM.

communist • n. **1** a person advocating or practising communism. **2** (**Communist**) a member of a Communist Party. ● *adj.* **1** of or relating to communism (*a communist play*). **2** (**Communist**) of or relating to Communism. ☐ **communistic** *adj.*

communitarian /kə,mju:nɪˈtɛrɪən/ ● *n.* a member of a community practising co-operation and some communism. ● *adj.* of or relating to such a community. ☐ **communitarianism** *n.*

community *n.* (*pl.* **-ies**) **1 a** all the people living in a specific locality. **b** a specific locality, including its inhabitants. **c** *Cdn* (*Nfld & PEI*) a small incorporated municipality. **2** a body of people having a religion, profession, etc., in common (*the immigrant community*). **3** fellowship of interests etc.; similarity (*community of intellect*). **4** joint ownership or liability (*community of goods*). **5** (prec. by *the*) the public. **6** *Ecology* a group of animals or plants living or growing together in the same area. **7** (*attrib.*) = COMMUNITY ACCESS (*community channel*).

community access *n.* (usu. *attrib.*) *Cdn* = PUBLIC ACCESS.

community care *n.* public health care emphasizing the treatment of long-term patients in their communities rather than in hospitals or institutions.

community centre *n.* a place providing social and recreational facilities for a neighbourhood.

community college *n.* esp. *N Amer.* a post-secondary educational institution offering training esp. in specific employment fields.

community hall *n. Cdn* a hall maintained by a community for holding suppers, dances, wedding receptions, etc.

community service *n.* work, esp. voluntary and unpaid, or stipulated by a community service order, in the community.

community service order *n.* an order for a convicted offender to perform a period of unpaid work in the community.

community spirit *n.* a feeling of belonging to a community, expressed in mutual support etc.

community worker *n.* a person who works in a community to promote its welfare, either as a paid social worker or volunteer. ☐ **community work** *n.*

commutable /kəˈmju:təbəl/ *adj.* **1** convertible into money; exchangeable. **2** *Law* (of a punishment) able to be commuted. **3** within commuting distance.

commute ● *v.* **1** *intr.* travel to and from one's daily work, esp. from suburbs to the centre of a city by car or public transit. **2** *tr. Law* (often foll. by *to*) change (a judicial sentence etc.) to another less severe. **3** *tr.* (often foll. by *into*, *for*) **a** change (one kind of payment) for another. **b** make a payment etc. to change (an obligation etc.) for another. **4** *tr.* **a** exchange; interchange (two things). **b** change (to another thing). ● *n.* **1** an act of commuting. **2** a distance travelled by a commuter.

commuter ● *n.* a person who travels some distance to work, esp. from suburbs to the centre of a city by car or public transit. ● *adj.* **1** relating to or for the use of commuters. **2** of or relating to a flight, aircraft, or airline that flies comparatively short distances, usu. between small communities.

Comox /ˈko:mɒks/ *n.* **1** a member of an Aboriginal group, part of the Salishan linguistic group, living on Vancouver Island. **2** the language of this people.

comp *n. informal* **1** a competition. **2** a complimentary ticket, pass, etc. **3** a comprehensive examination. **4** composition. **5** compensation (*worker's comp*).

compact[1] ● *adj.* **1** closely or neatly packed together. **2** (of a piece of equipment, a room, etc.) well-fitted and practical though small. **3** (of style etc.) con-

densed; brief. **4** (esp. of the human body) small but well-proportioned. **5** *N Amer.* designating a car larger than a subcompact and smaller than a mid-size. ● *v.tr.* **1** join or press firmly together. **2** condense. **3** (usu. foll. by *of*) compose; make up. ● *n.* **1** a small, flat case for face powder, a mirror, pills, etc. **2** an object formed by compacting powder. **3** *N Amer.* a compact car. ☐ **compaction** *n.* **compactly** *adv.* **compactness** *n.* **compactor** *n.* (also **compacter**).

compact[2] *n.* an agreement or contract between two or more parties.

compact disc *n.* a disc on which information or sound is recorded digitally and reproduced by reflection of laser light.

compact fluorescent *n.* a low-wattage energy-efficient fluorescent light bulb with a standard screw-in base, designed to replace a regular incandescent bulb.

companion ● *n.* **1 a** (often foll. by *in*, *of*) a person who accompanies, associates with, or shares with, another. **b** a person employed to live with and assist another. **2** a handbook or reference book on a particular subject. **3** a thing that matches another. **4** (**Companion**) a member of the highest grade of the Order of Canada. ● *v.* **1** *tr.* accompany. **2** *intr. literary* (often foll. by *with*) be a companion.

companionable *adj.* agreeable as a companion; sociable. ☐ **companionability** *n.* **companionably** *adv.*

companionship *n.* good fellowship; friendship.

company *n.* (*pl.* **-ies**) **1 a** a number of people assembled; a crowd; an audience. **b** guests or a guest. **2** companionship, esp. of a specific kind (*do not care for their company*). **3 a** a commercial business. **b** (usu. **Company**) the partner or partners not named in the title of a firm (*Smith and Company*). Abbr.: **Co. 4 a** a group of performers. **b** the organization to which they belong, including administrators, fundraisers, etc. **5** a subdivision of an infantry battalion usu. commanded by a major or a captain. **6** a group of Guides. **7** *Cdn* the Hudson's Bay Company. ☐ **be in good company** discover that one's companions, or better people, have done the same as oneself. **in company** not alone. **in company with** together with. **keep company** (often foll. by *with*) associate habitually. **keep a person company** accompany a person; be sociable. **part company 1** separate (*parted company until the weekend*). **2** (often foll. by *with*) **a** cease to associate. **b** differ, disagree.

company car *n.* a car provided by a company for the business and usu. private use of an employee.

company store *n. N Amer.* a store operated by a company, esp. in an isolated area, for the sale of goods to its employees, usu. as a monopoly.

company town *n. N Amer.* a town, esp. in an isolated area, that is dependent upon one company, e.g. a mine, for all or almost all of its employment etc.

comparable /ˈkɒmpərəbəl, kəmˈpɛrəbəl/ *adj.* (often foll. by *to*, *with*) **1** fit to be compared; worth comparing. **2** able to be compared. **3** similar. ☐ **comparability** *n.* **comparably** *adv.*

comparative /kəmˈpɛrətɪv, -ˈpærətɪv/ ● *adj.* **1** perceptible by comparison; relative (*in comparative comfort*). **2** estimated by comparison (*the comparative merits of the two ideas*). **3** (esp. of sciences etc.) of or involving comparison (*comparative anatomy*). **4** *Grammar* (of an adjective or adverb) expressing a higher degree of a quality, but not the highest possible (e.g. *braver*, *more fiercely*). ● *n. Grammar* **1** the comparative expression or form of an adjective or adverb. **2** a word in the comparative. □ **comparatively** adv.

compare ● v. **1** tr. (usu. foll. by to) express similarities in; liken (compared the landscape to a painting). **2** tr. (often foll. by to, with) estimate the similarity or dissimilarity of; assess the relation between (compared radio with television; that lacks quality compared to this). ¶In current use to and with are generally interchangeable, but with often implies a greater element of formal analysis. **3** intr. (often foll. by with) bear comparison (compares favourably). **4** intr. (often foll. by with) be equal or equivalent to. **5** tr. form the comparative and superlative degrees of (an adjective or an adverb). ● n. literary comparison (beyond compare). □ **compare notes** exchange ideas or opinions.

comparison n. **1** the act or an instance of comparing. **2** a simile or semantic illustration. **3** capacity for being likened; similarity (there's no comparison). **4** Grammar the positive, comparative, and superlative forms of adjectives and adverbs. □ **bear** (or **stand**) **comparison** (often foll. by with) be able to be compared favourably. **beyond comparison 1** totally different in quality. **2** greatly superior; excellent. **in comparison with** compared to.

compartment ● n. **1** a space within a larger space, separated from the rest by partitions, e.g. in a ship, wallet, desk, etc. **2** an area of activity etc. kept apart from others in a person's mind. ● v.tr. put into compartments. □ **compartmentation** n.

compartmental adj. consisting of or relating to compartments or a compartment.

compartmentalize v.tr. divide into compartments or categories. □ **compartmentalization** n.

compass ● n. **1** (in full **magnetic compass**) an instrument showing the direction of magnetic north and bearings from it. **2** (often in pl.) an instrument for taking measurements and describing circles, with two legs connected at one end by a movable joint. **3** a circumference or boundary. **4** area, extent; scope (e.g. of knowledge or experience) (beyond my compass). **5** the range of tones of a voice or a musical instrument. ● v.tr. literary **1** hem in. **2** grasp mentally. **3** contrive, accomplish. **4** go around.

compassion n. pity inclining one to be merciful etc.

compassionate adj. sympathetic, pitying. □ **compassionately** adv.

compatible ● adj. **1** (often foll. by with) **a** able to coexist; well-suited; mutually tolerant (a compatible couple). **b** consistent (their views are not compatible with their actions). **2** (of equipment etc.) capable of being used in combination. ● n. (usu. in comb.) Computing a piece of equipment that can use software etc. designed for another brand of the same equipment. □ **compatibility** n. **compatibly** adv.

compatriot n. **1** a native or inhabitant of one's own country or region. **2** an associate, colleague, or peer.

compel v.tr. (**compelled**, **compelling**) **1** force, constrain (compelled them to admit it). **2** bring about (an action) by force (compel submission).

compelling adj. arousing strong interest, attention, conviction, or admiration. □ **compellingly** adv.

compendium /kəmˈpendiəm/ n. (pl. **-s** or **compendia** /-diə/) **1** a collection of detailed items of information, esp. in a book. **2 a** a summary or abstract of a larger work. **b** an abridgement.

compensate v. (often foll. by for) **1** tr. recompense (a person) (compensated her for her loss). **2** intr. make amends (compensated for the insult). **3** tr. counterbalance. **4** intr. Psych. offset a disability or

frustration by development in another direction. □ **compensator** n. **compensatory** adj.

compensation n. **1 a** the act of compensating. **b** the process of being compensated. **2** something, esp. money, given as a recompense. **3** N Amer. a salary or wages. **4** Psych. **a** an act of compensating. **b** the result of compensating.

compete v.intr. **1** (often foll. by with, against a person, for a thing) strive for superiority or supremacy. **2** (often foll. by in) take part (in a contest etc.).

competence n. (also **competency** pl. **-ies**) **1 a** (often foll. by for, or to + infin.) ability; the state of being competent. **b** an area in which a person is competent; a skill. **2** an income large enough to live on, usu. unearned. **3** Law the legal capacity (of a court, a magistrate, etc.) to deal with a matter.

competent adj. **1 a** adequately qualified or capable (not competent to drive). **b** effective (a competent swimmer). **2** Law (of a judge, court, or witness) legally qualified or qualifying. □ **competently** adv.

competition n. **1** (often foll. by for) the act or an instance of competing or contending with others (for supremacy, a position, a prize, etc.). **2** an event or contest in which people compete. **3 a** the people competing against a person. **b** the opposition they represent. **c** products in the same category as another sold in the marketplace (the dictionary outsold the competition). **4** Biol. interaction between organisms etc. that share a limited environmental resource.

competitive adj. **1** involving, offered for, or by competition. **2** (of prices etc.) low enough to compare well with those of rival products etc. **3** (of a person) having a strong urge to win; keen to compete. □ **competitively** adv. **competitiveness** n.

competitor n. **1** a person who competes. **2** a rival, esp. in business or commerce.

compilation n. **1 a** the act of compiling. **b** the process of being compiled. **2** something compiled, esp. a book etc. composed of separate articles etc.

compile v.tr. **1 a** collect (material) into a list, volume, etc. **b** make up (a volume etc.) from such material. **2** Computing produce (a machine-coded form of a high-level program). **3** Sport accumulate (a large number of) (compiled a score of 160).

compiler n. **1** Computing a program for translating a high-level programming language into machine code. **2** a person who compiles.

complacency n. (pl. **-cies**) (also **complacence**) **1** smug self-satisfaction. **2** tranquil pleasure.

complacent adj. **1** smugly self-satisfied. **2** calmly content. □ **complacently** adv.

complain v.intr. **1** express dissatisfaction (is always complaining). **2** (foll. by of) announce that one is suffering from (an ailment) (complained of a headache). □ **complainer** n. **complainingly** adv.

complainant n. Law a plaintiff in certain lawsuits.

complaint n. **1** an act of complaining. **2** a grievance. **3** an ailment or illness. **4** N Amer. Law the plaintiff's case in a civil action.

complement ● n. **1 a** something that completes. **b** one of a pair, or one of two things that go together. **2** (often **full complement**) the full number needed to crew a ship, operate a factory, etc. **3** Grammar a word or phrase added to a verb to complete the predicate of a sentence. **4** Geom. the amount by which an angle is less than 90°. ● v.tr. **1** complete. **2** form a complement to (the scarf complements her dress). ¶Often confused with compliment.

complementarity n. (pl. **-ies**) a complementary relationship or situation.

complementary *adj.* **1** completing; forming a complement. **2** (of two or more things) complementing each other. ¶Often confused with *complimentary*.
complementary angle *n.* either of two angles making up 90°.
complete ● *adj.* **1** having all its parts (*the set is complete*). **2** finished (*my task is complete*). **3** of the maximum extent or degree (*a complete surprise*). **4** *Football* (of a forward pass) caught by the receiver. ● *v.tr.* **1** finish. **2 a** make whole or perfect. **b** make up the amount of (*completes the quota*). **3** fill in the answers to (a questionnaire etc.). **4** *Football* make or execute (a forward pass) successfully. □ **complete with** having (as an important accessory) (*comes complete with instructions*). □ **completed** *adj.* **completely** *adv.* **completeness** *n.* **completer** *n.* **completion** *n.*
complex ● *n.* **1** a building, network, etc. made up of related parts (*arts complex*). **2** *Psych.* a related group of usu. repressed feelings or thoughts which cause abnormal behaviour or mental states (*inferiority complex*). **3** (in general use) a preoccupation or obsession (*has a complex about punctuality*). **4** *Chem.* a compound in which molecules or ions form coordinate bonds to a metal atom or ion. ● *adj.* **1** consisting of related parts; composite. **2** complicated (*a complex problem*). □ **complexity** *n.* (*pl.* **-ies**). **complexly** *adv.*
complexion *n.* **1** the natural colour, texture, and appearance of the skin, esp. of the face. **2** an aspect; a character (*puts a different complexion on the matter*). □ **complexioned** *adj.* (also in comb.).
compliance *n.* **1** the act or an instance of complying. **2** unworthy acquiescence. □ **in compliance with** according to (a wish, command, etc.).
compliant *adj.* disposed to comply; yielding, obedient. □ **compliantly** *adv.*
complicate *v.tr. & intr.* make or become difficult, confused, or complex.
complicated *adj.* complex; intricate.
complication *n.* **1 a** an involved or confused condition or state. **b** a complicating circumstance; a difficulty. **2** *Med.* a secondary disease or condition aggravating a previous one.
complicity *n.* partnership in a crime or wrongdoing. □ **complicit** *adj.* **complicitous** *adj.*
compliment ● *n.* **1 a** a spoken or written expression of praise. **b** an act or circumstance implying praise (*their success was a compliment to their efforts*). **2** (in *pl.*) **a** formal greetings, esp. as a written accompaniment to a gift etc. (*with the compliments of the management*). **b** praise (*my compliments to the cook*). ● *v.tr.* **1** (often foll. by *on*) congratulate; praise. **2** (often foll. by *with*) present as a mark of courtesy (*complimented her with his attention*). ¶Often confused with *complement*. □ **compliments of 1** given free of charge (*won a book, compliments of OUP*). **2** usu. *ironic* thanks to (*a 75-cent surcharge, compliments of the Minister of Finance*). **pay a compliment to** praise. **return the compliment 1** give a compliment in return for another. **2** retaliate or recompense in kind.
complimentary *adj.* **1** expressing a compliment; praising. **2** (of a service, goods, theatre ticket, etc.) provided free of charge. ¶Often confused with *complementary*. □ **complimentarily** *adv.*
compline /ˈkɒmplɪn, -plaɪn/ *n.* *Christianity* **1** the last of the canonical hours of prayer, said before retiring at night. **2** the service taking place during this.
comply *v.intr.* (**-ies**, **-ied**) (often foll. by *with*) act in accordance (with a wish, command, regulation, etc.).
component ● *n.* a part of a larger group or system. ●

adj. being part of a larger whole (*component parts*). □ **componential** *adj.* **componentry** *n.*
comport /kəmˈpɔːt/ *v.refl.* *literary* conduct oneself; behave. □ **comportment** *n.*
compose *v.* **1 a** *tr.* construct or create (a work of art, esp. literature or music). **b** *intr.* compose music. **2** *tr.* (often in *passive*) constitute; make up (*the committee is composed of workers and managers*). **3** *tr.* put together to form a whole, esp. artistically; order; arrange (*composed the group for the photographer*). **4** *tr.* (often *refl.*) calm; settle (*composed himself*). **5** *tr.* *Printing* **a** set up (type) to form words and blocks of words. **b** set up (a manuscript etc.) in type.
composed *adj.* calm, unruffled. □ **composedly** *adv.*
composer *n.* a person who composes (esp. music).
composite ● *adj.* **1** made up of various parts; blended. **2** (esp. of a synthetic building material) made up of recognizable constituents. **3** of the plant family Compositae. ● *n.* **1** a thing made up of several parts or elements. **2** a synthetic building material. **3** any plant of the family Compositae, having a head of many small flowers forming one bloom, e.g. the daisy or the dandelion.
composite high school *n.* *Cdn* (*Alta.*) (also **composite school**) a secondary school offering vocational and academic courses.
composite index *n.* a stock market index based on the performance of a selection of stocks.
composition *n.* **1 a** the act of putting together; formation or construction. **b** something so composed; a mixture. **c** the constitution of such a mixture; the nature of its ingredients (*the powers and composition of the Senate*). **2 a** a literary or musical work. **b** the act or art of producing such a work. **c** a piece of writing assigned as an exercise. **d** the craft of writing (*taught grammar and composition*). **e** an artistic arrangement (of parts of a picture, subjects for a photograph, etc.). **3** (often *attrib.*) a compound artificial substance, esp. one serving the purpose of a natural one. **4** the setting up of type. **5** *Grammar* the formation of words into a compound word. □ **compositional** *adj.* **compositionally** *adv.*
compositor *n.* a person who sets up type or text for printing.
compost ● *n.* a mixture of decomposing vegetable matter, table scraps, manure, etc., used to fertilize soil. ● *v.* **1** *tr.* treat (soil) with compost. **2** *tr. & intr.* make (manure, vegetable matter, etc.) into compost. **3** *intr.* degrade into compost. □ **compostable** *adj.*
composter *n.* (also **compost bin**) a container for table scraps etc. used to create compost.
compost heap *n.* (also **compost pile**) a layered structure of garden refuse, soil, etc., which decays to become compost.
composure *n.* a tranquil manner; calmness.
compote /ˈkɒmpəʊt, -pɒt/ *n.* **1** fruit preserved or cooked in syrup. **2** a bowl supported on a stem for serving this.
compound[1] ● *n.* **1** a mixture of two or more things, qualities, etc. **2** (also **compound word**) a word made up of two or more existing words. **3** *Chem.* a substance formed from two or more elements chemically united in fixed proportions. ● *adj.* **1 a** made up of several ingredients. **b** consisting of several parts. **2** combined; collective. **3** *Zool.* consisting of individual organisms. **4** *Biol.* consisting of several or many parts. **5 a** (of a noun) that is a compound. **b** (of a verb tense) formed using an auxiliary verb. ● *v.* **1** *tr.* mix or combine (ingredients, ideas, motives, etc.) (*grief compounded with fear*). **2** *tr.* increase or complicate (diffi-

culties etc.) (*anxiety compounded by discomfort*). **3** *tr.* make up (a composite whole). **4** *tr. Law* **a** condone (a liability or offence) in exchange for money etc. **b** forbear from prosecuting (an indictable offence) from private motives. **5** *intr.* (usu. foll. by *with, for*) *Law* come to terms with a person, for forgoing a claim etc. for an offence. **6** *tr.* combine (words or elements) into a word. **7** *tr. & intr.* increase by compound interest.

compound² *n.* an enclosed area, as for a prison etc.

compound eye *n.* an eye consisting of numerous visual units, as found in insects and crustaceans.

compound fracture *n.* a fracture involving the exposure of the bone through a skin wound.

compound interest *n.* interest payable on capital and its accumulated interest (compare SIMPLE INTEREST).

compound leaf *n.* a leaf consisting of several or many leaflets.

compound lens *n.* = LENS 2.

compound sentence *n.* a sentence with more than one independent clause, joined by a coordinating conjunction, and having no subordinate clauses.

comprehend *v.tr.* **1** grasp mentally; understand (a person or a thing). **2** include; take in.

comprehensible *adj.* **1** that can be understood; intelligible. **2** that can be included or contained. □ **comprehensibility** *n.* **comprehensibly** *adv.*

comprehension *n.* **1** the act or capability of understanding, esp. writing or speech. **2** inclusion.

comprehensive ● *adj.* **1** complete; including all or nearly all elements, aspects, etc. **2** of or relating to understanding (*the comprehensive faculty*). **3** (of motor vehicle insurance) providing complete protection. ● *n.* (in full **comprehensive examination**) a test of one's learning or proficiency in all aspects, elements, etc. of a subject. □ **comprehensively** *adv.* **comprehensiveness** *n.*

comprehensive high school *n. Cdn* a secondary school offering both vocational and academic courses.

comprehensive land claim *n. Cdn* a land claim made on a usu. large area of land which was never ceded or surrendered by treaty or purchase.

compress ● *v.tr.* **1** squeeze together. **2** bring into a smaller space or shorter extent. **3** *Computing* condense (data etc.) for easier handling, storage, etc. ● *n.* a cloth or icepack etc. pressed onto part of the body to relieve inflammation etc. □ **compressibility** *n.* **compressible** *adj.* **compressive** *adj.*

compressed air *n.* air at more than atmospheric pressure.

compression *n.* **1** the act of compressing or being compressed. **2** the reduction in volume (causing an increase in pressure) of the fuel mixture in an internal combustion engine before ignition.

compressor *n.* an instrument or device for compressing, esp. a machine used for increasing the pressure of air or other gases.

comprise *v.tr.* **1** include; comprehend. **2** consist of, be composed of (*the book comprises 350 pages*). **3** make up, compose (*the essays comprise his total work*). ¶Such uses as *The panel is comprised of five individuals* or *Women comprise a large proportion of the sample* are strongly opposed by some, who prefer *The panel is composed* (or *made up*) *of five individuals* or *Women constitute* (or *make up*) *a large proportion of the group*. The disputed uses are very common, however, and considered unobjectionable by many.

compromise ● *n.* **1** the settlement of a dispute by mutual concession (*reached a compromise*). **2** (often foll. by *between*) an intermediate state between conflicting opinions, actions, etc., reached by mutual concession or modification (*a compromise between ideals and practicality*). ● *v.* **1** *intr.* settle a dispute by mutual concession. **2** *tr.* bring into disrepute or danger esp. by indiscretion or folly (*compromised our relationship*). □ **compromiser** *n.*

comptroller /kənˈtroʊlər, kɒmp-/ *n.* (also **controller**) an official or executive in charge of financial affairs.

compulsion *n.* **1** the action of compelling; an obligation. **2** *Psych.* an irresistible urge to a form of behaviour, esp. against one's conscious wishes.

compulsive *adj.* **1** resulting or acting from, or as if from, compulsion (*a compulsive gambler*). **2** *Psych.* resulting or acting from compulsion against one's conscious wishes. □ **compulsively** *adv.* **compulsiveness** *n.*

compulsory ● *adj.* **1** required by law or a rule. **2** essential; necessary. ● *n.* (also **compulsory figure**) one of a number of specified figures that must be performed as a component of a competition, e.g. in figure skating or synchronized swimming. □ **compulsorily** *adv.* **compulsoriness** *n.*

compunction *n.* (usu. with *neg.*) **1** an uneasy conscience; a feeling of remorse. **2** a scruple.

computational *adj.* **1** of or pertaining to computing. **2** using computers to assist in analysis.

compute *v.* **1** *tr.* (often foll. by *that* + clause) reckon or calculate (a number, an amount, etc.). **2** *intr.* make a reckoning, esp. using a computer. **3** *intr. informal* make sense (*it doesn't compute*). □ **computability** *n.* **computable** *adj.* **computation** *n.* **computing** *n.*

computer *n.* **1** an electronic device for storing and processing data (usu. in binary form), according to instructions given to it in a variable program. **2** a person who computes or makes calculations.

computerese *n.* the jargon associated with computers.

computer game *n.* **1** a game played on a computer, esp. one involving graphics and operating in real time. **2** a software package for such a game.

computer graphics *n.* **1** visual images produced or modified by means of a computer. **2** the use of a computer to generate and manipulate these.

computerize *v.* **1 a** *tr.* equip with a computer; install a computer in. **b** *intr.* equip oneself with computers. **2** *tr.* store, process, perform, or produce by computer. □ **computerization** *n.* **computerized** *adj.*

computerized axial tomography *n.* tomography in which the X-ray scanner makes many sweeps of the body and the results are processed by computer to give a cross-sectional image. Abbr.: **CAT.**

computer language *n.* any of numerous systems of rules, words, and symbols for writing computer programs or representing instructions etc.

computer-literate *adj.* familiar with the operation of computers. □ **computer literacy** *n.*

computer science *n.* the study of the principles and use of computers.

computer virus *n.* a hidden code within a computer program intended to corrupt a system or destroy data stored in it.

comrade *n.* **1 a** a workmate, friend, or companion. **b** (also **comrade-in-arms**) a fellow soldier etc. **2** a fellow socialist or communist (often as a form of address). □ **comradely** *adj.* **comradeship** *n.*

con¹ *informal* ● *n.* **1** a swindle in which the swindler first gains the victim's confidence (also *attrib.*: *con man*). **2** a deceiving comment, action, etc. ● *v.tr.* (**conned, conning**) **1** swindle (*conned them out of their money*). **2** deceive (*you can't con me: you're not really* *sick!*). **3** (foll. by *into*) persuade after dishonestly gaining trust (*readers are conned into buying trash*).

con² ● *n.* (usu. in *pl.*) a reason against. ● *prep. & adv.* against (*compare* PRO²).

con³ *n.* slang a convict.

Con. *abbr.* (also **Conc.**) *Cdn* (esp. *Ont.*) = CONCESSION 4.

con artist *n.* **1** a swindler. **2** a person skilled at deception.

concatenate /kənˈkætɪˌneɪt/ ● *v.tr.* link together (a chain of events, things, etc.). ● *adj.* joined; linked. □ **concatenation** *n.*

concave *adj.* having an outline or surface curved like the interior of a circle or sphere (*compare* CONVEX). □ **concavely** *adv.* **concavity** *n.* (*pl.* -ies).

conceal *v.tr.* **1** (often foll. by *from*) keep secret (*concealed her motive from him*). **2** not allow to be seen; hide (*concealed the letter*). □ **concealment** *n.*

concealer *n.* **1** a cosmetic which covers blemishes and dark spots on the skin, esp. the circles under the eyes. **2** a person or thing that conceals.

concede *v.tr.* **1 a** admit to be true (*conceded that his work was poor*). **b** admit defeat in. **2** (often foll. by *to*) grant, yield, or surrender (a right, a privilege, points or a start in a game, etc.). **3** *Sport* allow an opponent to score (a goal) or to win (a match), etc.

conceit *n.* **1** excessive pride in oneself or one's powers, abilities, etc. **2 a** a far-fetched comparison, esp. as a stylistic affectation; a convoluted or unlikely metaphor. **b** a fanciful notion.

conceited *adj.* full of conceit; vain. □ **conceitedly** *adv.* **conceitedness** *n.*

conceivable *adj.* capable of being grasped or imagined. □ **conceivability** *n.* **conceivably** *adv.*

conceive *v.* **1 a** *intr.* become pregnant. **b** *tr.* become pregnant with (a child). **2** *tr.* (usu. in *passive*) **a** devise, compose, formulate (a plan etc.). **b** apprehend, understand, perceive. **3** *tr.* develop (an emotion, feeling, etc.). □ **conceive of** form in the mind; imagine.

concentrate ● *v.* **1** *intr.* (often foll. by *on, upon*) focus all one's attention or mental ability. **2** *tr.* **a** bring toward or collect at a centre (*industry is concentrated in the east*). **b** cause to converge or be focused on (*such things concentrate the mind*). **3** *tr.* increase the strength of (a liquid etc.) by removing water or any other diluting agent. **4** *tr.* bring (ore etc.) to a state of greater purity by mechanical means. ● *n.* **1** a concentrated substance. **2** a concentrated form of esp. food. □ **concentrative** *adj.* **concentrator** *n.*

concentrated *adj.* **1** (of an emotion etc.) intense, strong. **2** increased in strength or value by concentrating (*concentrated orange juice*). **3** wholly directed toward one thing (*a concentrated effort*).

concentration *n.* **1 a** the act or power of concentrating (*needs to develop concentration*). **b** an instance of this (*interrupted my concentration*). **2** something concentrated (*a concentration of resources*). **3** something brought together; a gathering. **4** (often in *pl.*) the weight of substance in a given weight or volume of material.

concentration camp *n.* a camp for the detention or extermination of political prisoners, internees, etc., esp. one run by Nazi Germany.

concentric *adj.* (esp. of circles) having a common centre. □ **concentrically** *adv.* **concentricity** *n.*

concept *n.* **1** a general notion; an abstract idea. **2 a** an idea, theme or design, esp. as the basis for development or execution. **b** the product of this (*a new concept in swimwear*). **3** an idea or mental picture of a group or class of objects formed by combining all their aspects.

conception *n.* **1** the act or an instance of conceiving; the process of being conceived. **2** an idea or plan, esp. as being new or daring. **3** an understanding (*his conception of God was simplistic*). □ **no conception of** an inability to imagine.

conceptual *adj.* of mental conceptions or concepts. □ **conceptually** *adv.*

conceptual art *n.* art which emphasizes the process of producing art and the ideas conveyed rather than the art object produced.

conceptualism *n.* **1** *Philos.* the theory that universals exist, but only as concepts in the mind. **2** = CONCEPTUAL ART. □ **conceptualist** *n.*

conceptualize *v.tr.* form a concept or idea of. □ **conceptualization** *n.*

concern ● *v.tr.* **1 a** be relevant or important to (*this concerns you*). **b** relate to; be about. **2** (usu. *refl.*) interest or involve oneself (*don't concern yourself with my problems*). **3** worry, affect (*it concerns me that he is always late*). ● *n.* **1 a** anxiety, worry. **b** solicitude, interest in others' well-being (*known for his warmth and concern*). **2 a** a matter of interest or importance to one, esp. causing anxiety. **b** (usu. in *pl.*) affairs, private business (*meddling in my concerns*). **3** a business (*quite a prosperous concern*). □ **have a concern in** have an interest or share in. **have no concern with** have nothing to do with. **to whom it may concern** to those who have a proper interest in the matter (as an address to the reader of a reference etc.).

concerned *adj.* **1** involved, interested (*the people concerned*). **2** troubled, anxious (*concerned about him*). □ **as** (or **so**) **far as I am concerned** as regards my interests. □ **concernedly** *adv.*

concerning *prep.* about, regarding.

concert *n.* **1 a** a musical performance of usu. several separate compositions. **b** a public performance of a variety of entertainments, e.g. music, dancing, comedy skits, etc. **c** (*attrib.*) performing in concerts, esp. as a professional soloist (*concert pianist*). **2** agreement, accordance, harmony. **3** a combination of voices or sounds. □ **in concert 1** (often foll. by *with*) acting jointly and accordantly. **2** (*predic.*) (of a musician) in a performance.

concerted *adj.* **1** combined together; jointly arranged or planned. **2** serious (*a concerted effort*).

concert-goer *n.* a person who often goes to concerts.

concert hall *n.* **1** an auditorium in which concerts are performed. **2** a building enclosing this.

concertina /ˌkɒnsərˈtiːnə/ *n.* a musical instrument held in the hands and stretched and squeezed like bellows, having reeds and a set of buttons at each end to control the valves.

concertmaster *n.* esp. *N Amer.* the principal first-violin player in an orchestra.

concerto /kənˈtʃɛrtoʊ/ *n.* (*pl.* -os or **concerti** /-tiː/) *Music* a composition for a solo instrument or instruments accompanied by an orchestra.

concert pitch *n.* **1** *Music* the international pitch standard used for tuning musical instruments, with the A above middle C at 440 Hz. **2** a state of unusual readiness, efficiency, and keenness (for action etc.).

concession *n.* **1 a** the act or an instance of conceding. **b** a thing conceded. **2 a** a right or privilege granted by a government (*tax concessions*). **b** the right to use land or other property, granted esp. by a government or local authority, esp. for a specific use. **c** the right, given by a company, to sell goods, esp. in a particular territory. **d** the land or property used or given. **3** *N Amer.* a booth or stand in a stadium, theatre, etc., where esp. refreshments and souvenirs are sold. **4** *Cdn* **a** (*Ont.* & *Que.*) a tract of surveyed farmland, itself further divided into lots. **b** esp. *Ont.* a rural road separating concessions.

concession line *n.* *Cdn* (*Ont.*) **1** a surveying line separating concessions. **2** (also **concession road**) = CONCESSION 4b.

concessive *adj.* **1** of or tending to concession. **2 a** (of a preposition or conjunction) introducing a phrase or clause which might be expected to preclude the action of the main clause, but does not (e.g. *in spite of*, *although*). **b** (of a phrase or clause) introduced by a concessive preposition or conjunction.

conch /kɒntʃ, kɒŋk/ *n.* (*pl.* **conches** /ˈkɒntʃəz/ or **conchs** /kɒŋks/) **1** a thick heavy spiral shell, occasionally bearing long projections, of various marine gastropod molluscs of the family Strombidae. **2** any of these gastropods.

concierge /kɔ̃siˈerʒ, kɒn-/ *n.* **1** (esp. in France) a person in charge of the entrance of a building, often also serving as a caretaker. **2** a hotel employee responsible for attending to special needs of guests, making taxi reservations, etc.

conciliate *v.* **1** *intr.* attempt to settle an esp. labour dispute by hearing all disputants and recommending solutions. **2** *tr.* make calm and co-operative; pacify. **3** *tr.* gain (esteem or goodwill). □ **conciliative** *adj.* **conciliator** *n.* **conciliatory** *adj.*

conciliation *n.* **1** *Law* the hearing and attempted resolution of a dispute by an appointed conciliator. **2** the use of conciliating measures; reconciliation.

concise *adj.* (of speech, writing, style, or a person) brief but comprehensive in expression. □ **concisely** *adv.* **conciseness** *n.*

conclave /ˈkɒnkleiv/ *n.* **1** a private meeting. **2** *Catholicism* **a** the assembly of cardinals for the election of a pope. **b** the meeting place for a conclave.

conclude *v.* **1** *tr. & intr.* bring or come to an end. **2** *tr.* infer (from given premises). **3** *tr.* settle, arrange (a treaty etc.). **4** *tr.* state in conclusion.

conclusion *n.* **1** a final result; a termination. **2** a judgment reached by reasoning. **3** the summing-up of an argument, book, etc. **4** a settling; an arrangement (*the conclusion of peace*). **5** *Logic* a proposition that is reached from given premises; the last part of a syllogism. □ **in conclusion** to conclude.

conclusive *adj.* decisive, convincing. □ **conclusively** *adv.* **conclusiveness** *n.*

concoct *v.tr.* **1** make by combining elements not usually mixed together, esp. from what is available. **2** invent (a story, a lie, etc.). □ **concoction** *n.*

concomitant /kɒnˈkɒmɪtənt/ ● *adj.* going together; associated (*concomitant circumstances*). ● *n.* an accompanying thing. □ **concomitantly** *adv.*

concord *n.* **1** agreement or harmony between people or things. **2** a treaty. **3** *Music* a chord that is satisfactory in itself, not requiring resolution.

concordance ● *n.* **1** agreement. **2 a** a book containing an alphabetical list of the important words used in a book or by an author, usu. with citations of the passages concerned. **b** an alphabetized list of all the words in a text or group of texts, usu. with some accompanying text. ● *v.tr.* make a concordance to (a book etc.). □ **concordancing** *n.*

concordant *adj.* **1** (often foll. by *with*) agreeing, harmonious. **2** *Music* in harmony.

Concord grape *n.* a variety of dark purple grape, a cultivated variety of the fox grape, used esp. for making juice, jelly, etc.

concourse *n.* **1** an open central area in a large public building, airport, etc. **2** *N Amer.* an indoor shopping area, often on the lowest (usu. underground) level of an office building etc. **3** a crowd. **4** a coming together; a gathering (*a concourse of ideas*).

concrete ● *adj.* **1 a** existing in a material form; real. **b** specific, definite (*a concrete proposal*). **2** *Grammar* (of a noun) denoting a material object as opposed to an abstract quality, state, or action. ● *n.* (often *attrib.*) a durable building material made from a mixture of gravel, sand, cement, and water, which forms a stone-like mass on hardening. ● *v.* **1** *tr.* **a** cover with concrete. **b** embed in concrete. **2 a** *tr. & intr.* form into a mass; solidify. **b** *tr.* make concrete instead of abstract. □ **concretely** *adv.* **concreteness** *n.*

concretion /kənˈkriːʃən/ *n.* **1 a** a hard solid concreted mass. **b** the forming of this by coalescence. **2** *Med.* a stony mass formed within the body. **3** a small round mass of rock particles embedded in limestone or clay.

concubine /ˈkɒŋkjʊˌbaɪn, ˈkɒn-/ *n.* (among polygamous peoples) a secondary wife.

concur *v.intr.* (**concurred, concurring**) **1** happen together; coincide. **2** (often foll. by *with*) **a** agree in opinion. **b** express agreement. **3** combine together for a cause; act in combination.

concurrent *adj.* **1** (often foll. by *with*) **a** existing or in operation at the same time. **b** existing or acting together. **2** *Math.* (of three or more lines) meeting at or tending toward one point. **3** agreeing, harmonious. □ **concurrence** *n.* **concurrently** *adv.*

concuss /kənˈkʌs/ *v.tr.* **1** subject to concussion. **2** shake violently. □ **concussive** *adj.*

concussion *n.* **1** *Med.* a violent injury to the brain caused by shaking or jarring, usu. accompanied by loss of consciousness. **2** violent shaking.

condemn *v.tr.* **1** express utter disapproval of; censure. **2 a** find guilty; convict. **b** (usu. foll. by *to*) sentence to (a punishment, esp. death). **c** show or suggest one's guilt (*his looks condemn him*). **3** pronounce (a building etc.) unfit for use or habitation. **4** (usu. foll. by *to*) doom or assign (to something unwelcome or painful). **5** pronounce incurable. □ **condemnation** *n.* **condemnatory** *adj.*

condensation *n.* **1** the act of condensing. **2** any condensed material (esp. water on a cold surface). **3** an abridgement. **4** *Chem.* the combination of molecules with the elimination of water etc.

condensation trail *n.* = CONTRAIL.

condense *v.* **1** *tr.* make denser or more concentrated. **2** *tr.* express in fewer words; make concise. **3** *tr. & intr.* reduce or be reduced from a gas or solid to a liquid.

condensed milk *n.* milk thickened by evaporation and sweetened, usu. tinned.

condenser *n.* **1** an apparatus or vessel for condensing vapour. **2** a person or thing that condenses.

condescend *v.intr.* **1** usu. *ironic* be gracious enough (to do a thing) esp. while showing one's sense of dignity or superiority (*condescended to attend the meeting*). **2** (foll. by *to*) *derogatory* behave as if one is on equal terms with (an inferior), usu. while maintaining an attitude of superiority. □ **condescending** *adj.* **condescendingly** *adv.*

condescension *n.* **1** a condescending manner. **2** an act or instance of condescending.

condiment *n.* a spice or foodstuff used in small quantities to enhance the flavour of other foods, e.g. salt and pepper, vinegar, etc.

condition ● *n.* **1** something upon the fulfillment of which something else depends. **2 a** the state of being or fitness of a person or thing (*in good condition*). **b** an ailment or abnormality (*a heart condition*). **3** (in *pl.*) circumstances, esp. those affecting the functioning or existence of something (*working conditions*). **4** *Grammar* a clause expressing a condition. ● *v.tr.* **1 a** bring into a good or desired state or condition. **b** make fit. **2** teach or accustom to adopt certain habits etc. (*conditioned by society*). **3** govern, determine (*his behaviour was conditioned by his drunkenness*). **4 a** impose conditions on. **b** be essential to (*the two things condition each other*). **5** apply conditioner to (hair, the skin, etc.). ☐ **in** (or **out of**) **condition** in good (or bad) condition. **in no condition to** certainly not fit to. **on condition that** with the stipulation that. ☐ **conditioned** *adj.*

conditional ● *adj.* **1** (often foll. by *on, upon*) dependent; not absolute; containing a condition or stipulation (*a conditional offer*). **2** (of a clause, sentence, mood, proposition etc.) expressing a condition on which something depends, e.g. the first clause in *if she wins, we will be rich*. ● *n.* **1** esp. *Grammar & Logic* a word, clause, proposition, etc., expressing or including a condition. **2** *Grammar* the conditional mood. ☐ **conditionality** *n.* **conditionally** *adv.*

conditional discharge *n.* an order made by a criminal court whereby an offender will not be sentenced for an offence unless a further offence is committed within a stated period.

conditioned reflex *n.* (also **conditioned response**) a reflex response to a non-natural stimulus, established by training.

conditioner *n.* a substance or device that improves the condition of something, esp. the hair.

conditioning ● *n.* **1** the act of bringing a person, animal, or thing into good condition. **2** degree of fitness, esp. aerobic capacity. **3** the training or accustoming of a person or animal to give conditioned responses. ● *adj.* that conditions.

condo *n.* (*pl.* **-os**) *N Amer. informal* = CONDOMINIUM 1.

condolence *n.* (often in *pl.*) an expression of sympathy (*my condolences on your loss*).

condom *n.* **1** a rubber sheath worn on the penis during sexual intercourse as a contraceptive or to prevent infection. **2** (in full **female condom**) a plastic sheath inserted into the vagina prior to intercourse to prevent pregnancy or infection.

condominium *n.* **1** *N Amer.* **a** an apartment building, office building, or townhouse complex containing units which are individually owned. **b** a unit in such a building or complex. **2** the joint control of a country's affairs by other countries.

condone *v.tr.* **1** forgive or overlook (an offence or wrongdoing). **2** approve or sanction, usu. reluctantly.

condor *n.* **1** (in full **Andean condor**) a large vulture, *Vultur gryphus*, of S America, having black plumage with a white neck ruff and a fleshy wattle on the forehead. **2** (in full **California condor**) a small vulture, *Gymnogyps californianus*, of California.

conducive *adj.* contributing or helping (toward something) (*not conducive to negotiation*).

conduct ● *n.* **1** behaviour; way of acting. **2** the action or manner of directing or managing (business, war, etc.). ● *v.* **1** *tr.* direct or manage (business etc.). **2** *tr.* carry out or administer (*conduct an investigation*). **3 a** *tr. & intr.* be the conductor of (an orchestra, choir, etc.). **b** *tr.* direct the performance (of a piece of music). **4** *tr.* *Physics* transmit (heat, electricity, etc.) by conduction. **5** *refl.* behave (*conducted himself appropriately*). **6** *tr.* lead or guide (a person or persons).

conductance *n. Physics* the power of a specified material to conduct electricity. Symbol: **G**.

conduction *n.* **1 a** the transmission of heat through a substance from a region of higher to a region of lower temperature. **b** the transmission of electricity through a substance by the application of an electric field. **2** the conducting of liquid through a pipe etc.

conductive *adj.* having the property of conducting (esp. heat, electricity, etc.).

conductivity *n.* the conducting power of a specified material.

conductor *n.* **1** a person who directs the performance of an orchestra or choir etc. **2** *Physics* **a** a thing that conducts or transmits heat or electricity. **b** = LIGHTNING ROD. **3 a** a person who collects fares in a bus etc. **b** *N Amer.* a person in charge of a train.

conduit /ˈkɒndʊɪt, -djʊɪt/ *n.* **1** a channel or pipe for conveying liquids. **2** a person, organization, etc. through which anything is conveyed (*a conduit for information*). **3 a** a tube or trough for protecting insulated electric wires. **b** a length or stretch of this.

cone *n.* **1** a solid figure with a circular (or other curved) plane base, tapering to a point. **2** a thing of a similar shape, solid or hollow. **3** the reproductive structure of conifers and related plants, often woody and cone-shaped. **4 a** a conical wafer for holding ice cream. **b** = ICE CREAM CONE. **5** any of the minute cone-shaped structures in the retina.

coneflower *n.* any of several N American plants belonging to the genus *Rudbeckia* and related genera of the composite family, having flowers with cone-like centres. *See also* PURPLE CONEFLOWER.

coney *var.* of CONY.

confab *informal* ● *n.* /ˈkɒnfæb/ a conversation. ● *v.intr.* /kənˈfæb/ (**-fabbed, -fabbing**) confabulate.

confabulate /kənˈfæbjʊˌleɪt/ *v.intr.* converse, chat. ☐ **confabulation** *n.*

confection *n.* **1** a sweet dessert or candy. **2** anything regarded as over-elaborate or contrived.

confectionary ● *n. var.* of CONFECTIONERY 1. ● *adj.* of or like confections.

confectioner *n.* a maker or retailer of confectionery.

confectionery *n.* **1 a** candy and other sweets. **b** a candy factory or store. **c** *N Amer.* a corner store. **2** the art or business of making candy or sweets.

confederacy *n.* (*pl.* **-ies**) **1 a** a league or alliance of persons, states, etc. **b** *N Amer.* (usu. **Confederacy**) a league or alliance of Aboriginal peoples (*the Iroquois Confederacy*). **2** a league for an unlawful or evil purpose; a conspiracy.

confederate ● *adj.* **1** esp. *Polit.* allied; joined by an agreement or treaty. **2** (**Confederate**) of or relating to the Confederate States in the US Civil War. **3** *Cdn* (*Nfld*) of or relating to the political movement which supported the union of Newfoundland and Canada. ● *n.* **1** (**Confederate**) a supporter of the Confederate States. **2** *Cdn* (*Nfld*) (**Confederate**) a supporter of the political union of Newfoundland and Canada. **3** an accomplice, esp. in criminal activity. ☐ **confederated** *adj.*

confederation *n.* **1 a** a union or alliance of peoples, countries, unions, etc. **b** (**Confederation**) (in Canada) the federal union of provinces and territories forming Canada, originally including Ontario, Quebec, New Brunswick, and Nova Scotia and subsequently expanded. **c** (**Confederation**) (in Newfoundland) the political union of Newfoundland and Canada. **2** the act or an instance of confederating. **3** (**Confederation**) (also **Confederation Day**) **a** (in Canada) the date of the creation of the Dominion of Canada, 1 July 1867. **b** (in

Newfoundland) the date of the political union of Newfoundland and Canada, 31 March 1949.

confederationist *Cdn esp. hist.* ● *n.* a supporter of Confederation. ● *adj.* of or relating to a political movement supporting Confederation.

confer *v.* **(-ferred, -ferring) 1** *tr.* (often foll. by *on, upon*) grant or bestow (a title, degree, favour, etc.). **2** *intr.* (often foll. by *with*) consult. □ **conferral** *n.*

conference ● *n.* **1** a meeting for discussion or presentation of information, esp. a regular one held by an association or organization. **2** the linking of several telephones, computer terminals, etc., so that each user may communicate with the others simultaneously (also *attrib.: conference call*). **3** a division within a sports league. **4 a** an assembly which discusses church issues, formulates policy, etc. **b** a group of churches whose representatives meet regularly in such an assembly. **5** an association of nations etc. for a specified purpose. **6** consultation, discussion. ● *v.intr.* (usu. as **conferencing** *n.*) take part in a conference or conference call. □ **in conference** engaged in discussion.

confess *v.* **1** *tr. & intr.* acknowledge or admit (a fault, wrongdoing, etc.). **2** *tr.* admit reluctantly; concede (*I confess I have my doubts*). **3 a** *tr. & intr.* declare (one's sins) to a priest. **b** *tr.* (of a priest) hear the confession of.

confession *n.* **1 a** confessing or acknowledgement of a fault, wrongdoing, crime, etc. **b** an instance of this. **c** a thing confessed. **2 a** the act of a penitent declaring sins to a priest to obtain absolution. **b** that part of the public litany in some Christian churches in which a general acknowledgement of sinfulness is made. **3** (in full **confession of faith**) a formal declaration of one's religious beliefs.

confessional ● *n.* **1** an enclosed stall in a church in which a priest hears confessions. **2** the practice of confession. ● *adj.* **1** of or relating to confession. **2** denominational. ¶In Canada, *confessional* is used in sense 2 primarily in Quebec and Newfoundland.

confessor *n.* **1** a priest who hears confessions and gives counsel. **2** a person who makes a confession. **3** a person who avows a religion in the face of its suppression, but does not suffer martyrdom.

confetti /kən'feti/ *n.* small bits of paper, usu. coloured, thrown on festive occasions, esp. at the bride and groom at weddings.

confidant /ˌkɒnfɪ'dɒnt, 'kɒnfɪˌdɒnt, -dænt/ *n.* a person to whom secrets, problems, etc. are confided.

confidante /ˌkɒnfɪ'dɒnt, 'kɒnfɪˌdɒnt, -dænt/ *n.* a woman to whom secrets, problems, etc. are confided.

confide *v.* **1** *tr.* tell (a secret etc.) in confidence. **2** *intr.* (foll. by *in, to*) take (a person) into one's confidence; talk confidentially. **3** *tr. literary* (foll. by *to*) entrust (an object of care, a task, etc.) to. □ **confidingly** *adv.*

confidence *n.* **1** firm trust; faith. **2 a** belief in one's own abilities. **b** assurance or certainty. **3 a** something told confidentially. **b** the telling of private matters with mutual trust. **4** *Parl.* (often *attrib.*) majority support for a government, policy, etc. expressed by a legislature. □ **in confidence** as a secret. **take into one's confidence** confide in.

confidence game *n. N Amer.* a swindle in which the victim is persuaded to trust the swindler.

confidence man *n.* a man who robs by means of a confidence game.

confident *adj.* **1** feeling or showing confidence; self-assured, bold (*a confident air*). **2** assured, trusting (*confident that he will come*). □ **confidently** *adv.*

confidential *adj.* **1** spoken, written or kept in confidence. **2** indicating private intimacy (*a confiden-*

tial tone). **3** entrusted with secrets (*confidential secretary*). □ **confidentiality** *n.* **confidentially** *adv.*

configuration *n.* **1 a** an arrangement of parts or elements in a particular form or figure. **b** the form, shape, or figure resulting from such an arrangement. **2** *Computing* **a** the interrelating or interconnecting of a computer system or elements of it so that it will accommodate a particular specification. **b** an instance of this. □ **configurational** *adj.*

configure *v.tr.* **1** put together in a certain configuration; fashion. **2** interconnect or interrelate (a computer system or elements of it) so as to fit it for a designated task. □ **configurable** *adj.*

confine ● *v.tr.* (often foll. by *to*) **1** (also *refl.*) keep or restrict (within certain limits etc.) (*confine your remarks to ten minutes*). **2** hold captive; imprison. **3** oblige (a person) to remain indoors, in bed, etc., through illness, bad weather, etc. ● *n.* (usu. in *pl.*) a limit or boundary (*within the confines of the town*).

confinement *n.* **1** the act or an instance of confining; the state of being confined. **2** *dated* the time of a woman's giving birth.

confirm *v.tr.* **1** provide support for the truth or correctness of; make definitely valid. **2** establish more firmly (power, possession, etc.). **3** (foll. by *in*) encourage (a person) in (an opinion etc.) (*his conduct confirmed me in my view of him*). **4** ratify (a treaty, possession, title, etc.). **5** administer the religious rite of confirmation to. □ **confirmatory** *adj.*

confirmation *n.* **1** the act or an instance of confirming; the state of being confirmed. **2 a** a religious rite confirming a baptized person as a full member of the Christian Church. **b** a ceremony in which a young person is formally confirmed as an adult member of the Jewish faith.

confirmed *adj.* **1** firmly settled in some habit or condition (*a confirmed bachelor*). **2** genuine; valid (*confirmed reservations*).

confiscate *v.tr.* **1** take or seize by authority. **2** appropriate to the public treasury (by way of a penalty). □ **confiscation** *n.* **confiscator** *n.*

confit /kɔ'fiː, kən-/ *n.* pork, duck, goose, turkey, etc., cooked slowly in its own fat, and preserved by storing in the fat.

conflagration *n.* a great and destructive fire.

conflate *v.tr.* blend or fuse together. □ **conflation** *n.*

conflict ● *n.* **1 a** a state of opposition or hostilities. **b** a fight or struggle. **2** (often foll. by *of*) **a** the clashing of opposed principles etc. **b** an instance of this. **c** a difficulty caused by the occurrence of two events at the same time. **3** *Psych.* **a** the opposition of incompatible wishes or needs in a person. **b** an instance of this. **c** the distress resulting from this. ● *v.intr.* **1** clash; be incompatible. **2** (often foll. by *with*) struggle; contend. □ **in conflict** conflicting. □ **conflictual** *adj.*

conflicting *adj.* not compatible; contradictory (*conflicting opinions*).

conflict of interest *n.* (*pl.* **conflicts of interest**) the situation of a politician, corporate officer, etc., whose private interests might benefit from his or her public actions or influence.

conflict resolution *n.* the process of solving disputes.

confluence *n.* **1** the place where two rivers etc. meet. **2** a coming together (*a confluence of ideas*).

conform *v.* **1** *intr.* (usu. foll. by *to*) comply with; comply with general custom. **2** *intr.* (foll. by *to, with*) be in accordance with; comply with (*conform to safety standards*). **3** *tr.* (often foll. by *to*) form according to a pattern; make similar.

conformance n. = CONFORMITY 1, 2.

conformation n. the way in which a thing is formed; shape, structure.

conformist • n. **1** a person who conforms to an established practice; a conventional person. **2** a person who conforms to the practices of an established church, esp. the Church of England. • adj. (of a person) conforming to established practices; conventional. □ **conformism** n.

conformity n. **1** (often foll. by to, with) action or behaviour in accordance with established practice; compliance. **2** (often foll. by to, with) correspondence in form or manner; likeness, agreement. **3** compliance with the practices of an established church, esp. the Church of England.

confound v.tr. **1** throw into perplexity or confusion (his behaviour confounded me). **2** mix up; confuse (in one's mind) (she confounded fact with fiction). **3** damn (used in mild imprecations) (confound it!).

confounded adj. informal damned.

confront v.tr. **1 a** face in hostility or defiance. **b** face up to and deal with (a problem, difficulty, etc.). **2** (of a difficulty etc.) present itself to (countless obstacles confronted us). **3** (foll. by with) bring (a person) face to face with (a circumstance); esp. by way of accusation (confronted them with the evidence). **4** meet or stand facing. □ **confrontation** n. **confrontational** adj.

Confucianism /kən'fju:ʃənɪzəm/ n. a system of philosophical and ethical teachings founded by Confucius in China in the 6th c. BC. □ **Confucian** n. & adj. **Confucianist** n. & adj.

confuse v.tr. **1** disconcert, perplex, bewilder. **2** mix up in the mind; mistake (one for another). **3** make indistinct (confuses the issue). **4** throw into disorder. □ **confusing** adj. **confusingly** adv.

confused adj. **1** perplexed; bewildered. **2** unclear; indistinct (confused thinking). **3** (esp. of an elderly person) mentally infirm. **4** disorderly (a confused jumble of clothes). □ **confusedly** adv.

confusion n. **1 a** the act of confusing (the confusion of fact and fiction). **b** a misunderstanding. **2 a** a confused state; disorder (trampled in the confusion of battle). **b** (foll. by of) a disorderly jumble (a confusion of ideas). **3** a riot or similar disturbance (confusion broke out).

conga • n. **1** a Latin-American dance of African origin, usu. performed by people in a single line, one behind another, who take three steps forward and then kick. **2** (also **conga drum**) a tall, narrow, low-toned drum beaten with the hands. • v.intr. (**congas**, **congaed**, **congaing**) perform the conga.

congeal v.intr. & tr. **1** make or become semi-solid by cooling. **2** (of blood etc.) coagulate. **3** (of ideas etc.) make or become fixed. □ **congealed** adj.

congenial /kən'dʒi:niəl/ adj. **1** (of a person, character, etc.) pleasant because akin to oneself in temperament or interests. **2** (of a place, activity, etc.) suited or agreeable. □ **congeniality** n.

congenital adj. **1** (esp. of a disease, defect, etc.) existing from birth. **2** having a specified nature deeply ingrained as if from birth (a congenital liar). □ **congenitally** adv.

congest v.tr. (esp. as **congested** adj.) **1** affect with congestion (congested lungs). **2** obstruct, block (congested streets). □ **congestive** adj.

congestion n. **1** abnormal accumulation of blood or mucus in a part of the body. **2** crowding or obstruction, esp. of traffic.

conglomerate • n. **1** a number of things or parts forming a heterogeneous mass. **2** a group or corporation formed by the merging of separate and diverse

firms. **3** Geol. a rock made up of small stones held together (compare AGGLOMERATE n. 2). • adj. **1** gathered into a rounded mass. **2** Geol. of or forming a conglomerate. • v.tr. & intr. collect into a coherent mass. □ **conglomeration** n.

Congolese /ˌkɒŋgə'li:z/ • adj. of or relating to Congo (formerly Zaire), the Republic of the Congo, or the region surrounding the Congo River. • n. **1** a native or resident of any of these regions. **2** any of the Bantu languages spoken by the Congolese people.

congrats n.pl. & interj. informal congratulations.

congratulate /kən'grætʃə,leit, -'græd ʒ-/ v.tr. & refl. (often foll. by on, upon) **1** tr. express pleasure at the happiness or good fortune or excellence of (a person). **2** refl. think oneself fortunate or clever. ¶ Although the second pronunciation is very common, some people look upon its use unfavourably. □ **congratulator** n. **congratulatory** adj.

congratulation n. **1** the act or an instance of congratulating. **2** (also as interj.; usu. in pl.) an expression of this (congratulations on winning!).

congregate v.intr. & tr. collect or gather into a crowd or mass.

congregation n. **1 a** a body assembled for religious worship. **b** a body of persons regularly attending a particular church etc. **2** the process of congregating; collection into a crowd or mass. **3** a crowd or mass gathered together. **4** Catholicism a body of persons obeying a common religious rule.

congregational adj. **1** of a congregation. **2** (**Congregational**) of Congregationalism.

Congregationalism n. a system of ecclesiastical organization whereby individual churches are largely self-governing. □ **Congregationalist** n.

congress n. **1** (**Congress**) **a** the national legislative body of the US, comprising the House of Representatives and the Senate. **b** this body during any two-year term. **2** the national legislative body in some other countries. **3** a formal meeting of delegates for discussion. **4** a society or organization. □ **congressional** adj.

congressman n. (pl. **-men**) a member of the US Congress, esp. of the House of Representatives.

congressperson n. (pl. **-persons** or **-people**) a member of the US Congress, esp. of the House of Representatives.

congresswoman n. (pl. **-women**) a female member of the US Congress, esp. of the House of Representatives.

congruence n. (also **congruency**) **1** agreement, consistency. **2** Math. the state of being congruent.

congruent adj. **1** (often foll. by with) suitable, agreeing. **2** Math. (of figures) coinciding exactly when superimposed. □ **congruently** adv.

congruous adj. suitable, agreeing; fitting. □ **congruity** /-'gru:ɪti/ n. **congruously** adv.

Conibear /'kɒnɪbər/ n. (in full **Conibear trap**) N Amer. a trap with a trigger mechanism designed to kill an animal instantly.

conic adj. of, pertaining to, or resembling a cone.

conical adj. cone-shaped. □ **conically** adv.

conifer /'kɒnɪfər, 'kəʊnɪ-/ n. any evergreen tree of a group usu. bearing cones, including pines, yews, cedars, and redwoods. □ **coniferous** /kə'nɪfərəs/ adj.

conjectural adj. based on, involving, or given to conjecture. □ **conjecturally** adv.

conjecture • n. **1** the formation of an opinion on incomplete information; guessing. **2** an opinion or conclusion reached in this way. • v.tr. & intr. guess.

conjoin *v.tr. & intr.* join, combine.

conjoined twins *n.pl.* twins joined at any part of the body and sometimes sharing organs etc.

conjugal /'kɒndʒʊgəl/ *adj.* of marriage or the relation between husband and wife. □ **conjugality** *n.*

conjugate ● *v.* **1** *tr.* Grammar inflect (a verb) in its various forms of voice, mood, tense, number or person. **2** *intr. Biol.* **a** unite sexually. **b** (of gametes) become fused. ● *adj.* **1** joined together, esp. as a pair. **2** Grammar derived from the same root. ● *n.* a conjugate word or thing. □ **conjugative** *adj.*

conjugation *n.* **1** Grammar a system of verbal inflection. **2** the act or an instance of conjugating.

conjunction *n.* **1** Grammar a word used to connect clauses or sentences or words in the same clause (e.g. *and*, *but*, *if*). **2 a** the action of joining; the condition of being joined. **b** an instance of this. **3 a** a combination (of events or circumstances). **b** a number of associated persons or things. **4** the alignment of two bodies in the solar system so that they have the same longitude as seen from the earth. □ **in conjunction with** together with.

conjunctiva /ˌkɒndʒʌŋk'taɪvə, kən'dʒʌŋktɪvə/ *n.* (pl. **-s** or **conjunctivae** /-viː/) *Anat.* the mucous membrane that covers the front of the eye and lines the inside of the eyelids. □ **conjunctival** *adj.*

conjunctive ● *adj.* **1** serving to join; connective. **2** Grammar of the nature of a conjunction. ● *n.* Grammar a conjunctive word.

conjunctivitis /kənˌdʒʌŋktɪ'vaɪtɪs/ *n.* inflammation of the conjunctiva.

conjuncture *n.* a combination of events; a state of affairs.

conjure *v.* **1** *tr.* cause to appear or disappear as if by magic. **2** *intr.* perform tricks which are seemingly magical. **3** *tr.* call upon (a demon, spirit, etc.) to appear. **4** *tr.* evoke. □ **conjure up 1** bring into existence or cause to appear as if by magic. **2** cause to appear to the eye or mind; evoke.

conjuring *n.* the performance of seemingly magical tricks, esp. by rapid movements of the hands.

conjuror *n.* (also **conjurer**) a performer of conjuring tricks.

conk[1] *v.intr. informal* □ **conk out 1** (of a machine etc.) break down. **2** (of a person) become exhausted and give up. **3** (of a person) fall asleep.

conk[2] *slang* ● *n.* **1** the head. **2** a blow, esp. on the nose or head. ● *v.tr.* hit, esp. on the head.

con man *n.* = CONFIDENCE MAN.

Conn. *abbr.* Connecticut.

connect *v.* **1** *tr.* (often foll. by *to*, *with*) join (one thing with another). **b** *tr.* join (two things). **c** *intr.* be joined or joinable (*the two parts do not connect*). **2** *tr.* (often foll. by *with*) associate mentally or practically (*never connected her with the theatre*). **3** *intr.* (foll. by *with*) (of an airplane etc.) be synchronized at its destination with another airplane etc., so that passengers can transfer. **4** *tr.* put into communication by telephone. **5** *tr.* meet; establish contact (*let's try to connect next week*). **6** *tr.* a join (a house etc.) to a source of electricity, gas, water, etc. **b** hook up (a phone, television, etc.) to a telecommunications system. **7 a** *tr.* (usu. in *passive*; foll. by *with*) unite or associate with others in relationships etc. (*he is connected with the mayor's office*). **b** *intr.* establish a rapport based on common interests, opinions etc. **8** *intr.* form a logical sequence; be meaningful (*the two ideas do not connect*). **9** *intr. informal* hit or strike effectively (*connect with the ball*). □ **connector** *n.*

connected *adj.* **1** joined in sequence. **2** (of ideas etc.)

coherent. **3** related or associated. □ **connectedly** *adv.* **connectedness** *n.*

connecting rod *n.* the rod between the piston and the crankshaft etc. in an internal combustion engine or between the wheels of a locomotive.

connection *n.* **1 a** the act of connecting; the state of being connected. **b** an instance of this. **2** the point at which two things are connected. **3 a** a thing or person that connects; a link (*cannot see the connection between the two ideas*). **b** a telephone link (*got a bad connection*). **c** an electronic link to computer networks, electronic mail, etc. (*a connection to the Internet*). **4** arrangement or opportunity for catching a connecting airplane etc.; the airplane etc. itself (*missed the connection*). **5** Electricity **a** the linking up of an electric current by contact. **b** a device for effecting this. **6** (often in *pl.*) a relative or associate, esp. one with influence (*has connections at city hall*; *a business connection*). **7** slang a supplier of narcotics. □ **in connection with** with reference to. **in this** (or **that**) **connection** with reference to this (or that).

connective ● *adj.* serving or tending to connect. ● *n.* something that connects. □ **connectivity** *n.*

connective tissue *n.* a fibrous tissue that supports, binds, or separates more specialized tissue and organs of the body.

conner *n.* (also **connor**) *Cdn* (*Nfld*) a saltwater bottom-feeding fish, *Tautogolabrus adspersus*, found commonly around rocks and wharves.

connive *v.intr.* **1** (often foll. by *with*) conspire. **2** (foll. by *at*) disregard or tacitly consent to (a wrongdoing). □ **connivance** *n.* **conniver** *n.* **conniving** *adj. & n.*

connoisseur /ˌkɒnə'sɜr, -'sʊr/ *n.* (often foll. by *of*, *in*) an expert judge in matters of taste (*a connoisseur of fine wine*). □ **connoisseurship** *n.*

connotation *n.* **1** that which is implied by a word etc. in addition to its literal or primary meaning. **2** the act of connoting or implying.

connote *v.tr.* **1** (of a word etc.) imply in addition to the literal or primary meaning. **2** (of a fact) imply as a consequence or condition. **3** mean, signify. □ **connotative** *adj.*

conquer *v.* **1 a** *tr.* overcome and control (an enemy or territory) by military force. **b** *intr.* be victorious. **2** *tr.* overcome by effort (*conquered his fear*). **3** *tr.* climb (a mountain) successfully. **4** *tr.* gain the admiration, love, etc. of. □ **conquerable** *adj.* **conqueror** *n.*

conquest *n.* **1** the act or an instance of conquering; the state of being conquered. **2 a** a conquered territory. **b** something won. **3** a person whose affection or favour has been won. **4** (**the Conquest**) the British conquest of French N America in 1763.

conquistador /kɒn'kwɪstə,dɔr/ *n.* (pl. **conquistadores** /-rez/ or **-s**) a conqueror, esp. one of the 16th-c. Spanish conquerors of Mexico and Peru.

Cons. *abbr.* Conservative.

consanguinity /ˌkɒnsæn'ɡwɪnɪti/ *n.* **1** relationship by descent from a common ancestor; blood relationship. **2** close connection or association.

conscience *n.* **1** a moral sense of right and wrong esp. as felt by a person and affecting behaviour. **2** an inner feeling as to the goodness or otherwise of one's behaviour (*my conscience is clear*). □ **in all** (or **good** or **all good**) **conscience** honestly; fairly; in such a way that one's conscience is clear. **on one's conscience** causing one feelings of guilt.

conscientious *adj.* (of a person or conduct) diligent and scrupulous. □ **conscientiously** *adv.* **conscientiousness** *n.*

conscientious objector *n.* a person who for reasons of conscience objects to conforming to a requirement, esp. that of military service.

conscious ● *adj.* **1** awake and aware of one's surroundings and identity. **2** aware, knowing (*conscious of his inferiority*). **3** (of actions, emotions, etc.) realized or recognized by the doer; intentional (*made a conscious effort not to laugh*). **4** (in *comb.*) aware of; concerned with (*appearance-conscious*). ● *n.* (prec. by *the*) the conscious mind. □ **consciously** *adv.*

consciousness *n.* **1** the state of being conscious (*lost consciousness*). **2** awareness of one's existence; self-consciousness. **3 a** awareness, perception (*had no consciousness of being ridiculed*). **b** (in *comb.*) awareness of, concern with (*class-consciousness*). **4** the totality of the thoughts and feelings of a person or group, esp. relating to a particular sphere (*moral consciousness*).

consciousness-raising *n.* the activity of increasing esp. social or political awareness.

conscript ● *v.tr.* enlist by conscription. ● *n.* a person enlisted by conscription.

conscription *n.* compulsory enlistment for military service.

consecrate *v.tr.* **1** make or declare sacred; dedicate formally to a religious or divine purpose. **2** (in Christian belief) make (bread and wine) into the body and blood of Christ. **3** (foll. by *to*) devote (one's life etc.) to (a purpose). **4** ordain (esp. a bishop) to a sacred office. □ **consecrated** *adj.* **consecration** *n.*

consecutive *adj.* **1 a** following continuously, in uninterrupted sequence. **b** in unbroken or logical order. **2** *Grammar* expressing consequence. □ **consecutively** *adv.* **consecutiveness** *n.*

consensual *adj.* of or by consent or consensus.

consensus *n.* (often foll. by *of*) **1 a** general agreement (of opinion etc.). **b** an instance of this. **2** (*attrib.*) majority view (*consensus politics*).

consent ● *v.intr.* (often foll. by *to*) express willingness, give permission, agree. ● *n.* voluntary agreement, permission, compliance.

consenting adult *n.* an adult who consents to something, esp. a sexual act.

consequence *n.* **1** the result or effect of an action or condition. **2 a** importance (*it is of no consequence*). **b** social distinction (*persons of consequence*). □ **in consequence** as a result. **face** (or **take**) **the consequences** accept the results of one's choice or action.

consequent *adj.* **1** (often foll. by *on*, *upon*) following as a result or consequence. **2** logically consistent.

consequential *adj.* **1** following as a result or consequence. **2** resulting indirectly (*consequential damage*). **3** (of a person) self-important. □ **consequentiality** *n.* **consequentially** *adv.*

consequently *adv.* & *conj.* as a result; therefore.

conservancy *n.* (*pl.* **-ies**) **1** a body concerned with the preservation of natural resources. **2** conservation; official preservation (of forests etc.).

conservation *n.* preservation, esp. of the natural environment.

conservation area *n.* an area containing a noteworthy environment and specially protected by law against undesirable changes.

conservationist *n.* a supporter or advocate of environmental conservation.

conservatism *n.* **1** any of several political philosophies, esp. one opposing radical reform, placing value in established institutions, and subjugating individual freedom to order, rank, security, and the good of the community, or one promoting individu-

alism and non-intervention by the state. **2** opposition to change.

conservative ● *adj.* **1 a** averse to rapid change. **b** (of taste etc.) moderate, avoiding extremes. **2** (of an estimate etc.) purposely low; moderate, cautious. **3 a** (**Conservative**) of or characteristic of a Conservative party. **b** espousing the tenets of political conservatism. **4** tending to conserve. ● *n.* **1** a conservative person. **2** (**Conservative**) a supporter or member of a Conservative party. □ **conservatively** *adv.*

Conservative Judaism *n.* a branch of Judaism allowing only minor changes in traditional ritual etc.

Conservative Party *n.* **1** a Canadian political party, officially named the Progressive Conservative Party. **2** a similar party elsewhere.

conservator /kən'sɜrvətər, 'kɒnsər,veitər/ *n.* a person who preserves something, esp. in a museum etc.

conservatory *n.* (*pl.* **-ies**) **1** esp. N Amer. a school of esp. classical music or other arts. **2** a greenhouse. **3** a glassed-in sunroom attached to a house.

conserve ● *v.tr.* **1** store up; keep from harm, damage, or depletion, esp. for later use. **2** preserve (food, esp. fruit), usu. with sugar. ● *n.* a jam-like mixture, often of several fruits.

consider *v.* **1** *tr.* & *intr.* contemplate mentally, esp. in order to reach a conclusion. **2** *tr.* & *intr.* examine the merits of (a course of action, a candidate, claim, etc.). **3** *tr.* give attention to. **4** *tr.* take into account. **5** *tr.* (foll. by *that* + clause) have the opinion. **6** *tr.* believe; regard as (*consider it settled*). **7** *tr.* show thoughtfulness for (*consider his feelings*). **8** *tr.* look at. □ **all things considered** taking everything into account.

considerable *adj.* **1** enough in amount or extent to need consideration. **2** much; a lot of (*considerable pain*). **3** notable, important. □ **considerably** *adv.*

considerate *adj.* thoughtful towards other people. □ **considerately** *adv.*

consideration *n.* **1** careful thought. **2** thoughtfulness for others. **3** a fact or a thing taken into account in deciding or judging something. **4** compensation; a payment or reward. **5** *Law* (in a contractual agreement) anything given or promised or forborne by one party in exchange for the promise or undertaking of another. □ **in consideration of** in return for; on account of. **take into consideration** include as a factor, reason, etc.; make allowance for. **under consideration** being considered.

considered *attrib.adj.* formed after careful thought (a *considered opinion*).

considering *prep.* **1** in view of; taking into consideration (*considering their youth*). **2** (without compl.) *informal* all in all (*not so bad, considering*).

consign /kən'sain/ *v.tr.* (often foll. by *to*) **1** deliver to a person's possession or trust. **2** assign; commit decisively or permanently (*consigned to years of misery*). **3** transmit or send (goods), usu. by a public carrier. □ **consignee** /ˌkɒnsai'niː, kən,sai'niː/ *n.* **consignor** *n.*

consignment *n.* **1** the act or an instance of consigning; the process of being consigned. **2** a batch of goods consigned. **3** (*attrib.*) designating a store selling goods on consignment. □ **on consignment** (of goods) held in trust to be sold for the owner.

consist *v.intr.* **1** (foll. by *of*) be composed; have specified ingredients or elements. **2** (foll. by *in*, *of*) have its essential features as specified (*its beauty consists in the use of colour*). **3** (usu. foll. by *with*) harmonize; be consistent.

consistency *n.* (*pl.* **-ies**) **1** the degree of firmness or viscosity, esp. of thick liquids. **2** the state of being consistent; conformity with other or earlier attitudes, practice, etc. **3** the state or quality of holding or sticking together and retaining shape.

consistent *adj.* (usu. foll. by *with*) **1** compatible or in harmony; not contradictory. **2** (of a person) constant to the same principles of thought or action. **3** tending to maintain a constant level of success. □ **consistently** *adv.*

consolation *n.* **1** the act or an instance of consoling; the state of being consoled. **2** a consoling thing, person, or circumstance. □ **consolatory** *adj.*

consolation prize *n.* a prize given to a competitor who just fails to win a main prize.

console[1] *v.tr.* comfort, esp. in disappointment or grief. □ **consolable** *adj.* **consolingly** *adv.*

console[2] *n.* **1** a panel or unit accommodating a set of switches, controls, etc. **2** a cabinet for television or radio equipment etc. **3** *Music* a cabinet with the keyboards, stops, pedals, etc., of an organ.

consolidate *v.* **1** *tr. & intr.* make or become strong or solid. **2** *tr.* reinforce or strengthen (one's position, power, etc.). **3** *tr.* combine (territories, companies, debts, etc.) into one whole. □ **consolidated** *adj.* **consolidation** *n.* **consolidator** *n.*

consolidated revenue fund *n. Cdn* a federal or provincial government fund into which all revenue (taxes, tariffs, charges, etc.) is paid and from which all government expenditures are made.

consolidated school *n. Cdn* a school replacing several smaller schools in a district.

consommé /ˈkɒnsəˌmei, ˌkɒnsəˈmei/ *n.* a clear soup made with meat stock.

consonance *n.* agreement, harmony.

consonant ● *n.* **1** a speech sound in which the breath is at least partly obstructed, and which to form a syllable must be combined with a vowel. **2** a letter or letters representing this. ● *adj.* (foll. by *with*, *to*) consistent; in agreement or harmony.

consort[1] ● *n.* **1 a** a wife or husband, esp. of royalty (*prince consort*). **b** a partner, companion, associate, etc. **2** a ship sailing with another. ● *v.* **1** *intr.* (usu. foll. by *with*, *together*) **a** keep company; associate. **b** harmonize. **2** *tr.* class or bring together.

consort[2] *n.* a group of musicians, esp. playing early music (*recorder consort*).

consortium /kənˈsɔːtiəm, -ˈsɔːʃəm/ *n.* (*pl.* **consortia** /-tiə/ or **consortiums**) an association, esp. several large companies in a joint venture.

conspicuous *adj.* **1** clearly visible; striking to the eye; attracting notice. **2** remarkable of its kind. □ **conspicuously** *adv.* **conspicuousness** *n.*

conspicuous consumption *n.* ostentatious acquisition and display of expensive goods.

conspiracy *n.* (*pl.* **-ies**) **1** a secret plan to commit a crime or do harm. **2** the act of conspiring.

conspiracy theory *n.* a belief that some covert but influential agency or organization is responsible for an unexplained event.

conspirator *n.* a person who takes part in a conspiracy.

conspiratorial *adj.* **1** pertaining to or characteristic of a conspirator or conspiracy. **2** suggestive of a conspirator (*conspiratorial whispers*). □ **conspiratorially** *adv.*

conspire *v.intr.* **1** combine secretly to plan and prepare an unlawful or harmful act. **2** (often foll. by *against*, or *to* + infin.) (of events or circumstances) seem to be working together, esp. disadvantageously.

Const. *abbr.* constable.

constable *n.* **1** (in Canada, the UK, Australia, NZ, etc.) a police officer of the lowest rank. **2** an officer of the peace, as a bailiff etc., with minor judicial duties.

constabulary /kənˈstæbjuːˌleri/ *n.* (*pl.* **-ies**) a police force (*Royal Newfoundland Constabulary*).

constancy *n.* **1** the quality of being unchanging and dependable; faithfulness. **2** endurance.

constant ● *adj.* **1** continuous (*needs constant attention*). **2** occurring frequently (*constant complaints*). **3** unchanging (*speed remained constant*). **4** faithful, dependable. ● *n.* **1** anything that does not vary. **2** *Math.* a component of a relationship between variables that does not change its value. **3** *Physics* **a** a number expressing a relation, property, etc., and remaining the same in all circumstances. **b** such a number that remains the same for a substance in the same conditions. □ **constantly** *adv.*

constellation *n.* **1 a** a group of fixed stars whose outline is traditionally regarded as forming a particular figure. **b** one of eighty-eight sections based on these into which the sky has been divided. **2** a group of associated persons, ideas, etc.

consternation *n.* anxiety or dismay causing mental confusion.

constipate *v.tr.* (usu. in *passive*) **1** cause constipation in. **2** obstruct abnormally. □ **constipated** *adj.*

constipation *n.* **1** irregularity and difficulty in defecating. **2** abnormal lack of efficacy or ease.

constituency *n.* (*pl.* **-ies**) **1** a body of voters in a specified area who elect a representative member to a legislative body. **2** the area represented in this way. **3** a body of customers, supporters, etc.

constituent ● *adj.* **1** composing or helping to make up a whole. **2** able to make or change a (political etc.) constitution (*constituent assembly*). **3** appointing or electing. ● *n.* **1** a member of a constituency (esp. political). **2** a component part.

constitute *v.tr.* **1** be the components or essence of; make up, form. **2 a** be equivalent or tantamount to (*constitutes an official warning*). **b** formally establish (*does not constitute a precedent*). **3** give legal or constitutional form to; establish by law.

constitution *n.* **1** the act or method of constituting; the composition (of something). **2 a** the body of fundamental principles or established precedents according to which a state or other organization is acknowledged to be governed. **b** a (usu. written) record of this. **3** a person's physical state as regards vitality, health, strength, etc. **4** a person's mental or psychological makeup.

constitutional ● *adj.* **1** of, consistent with, authorized by, or limited by a political constitution (*constitutional monarchy*). **2** inherent in, stemming from, or affecting the physical or mental constitution. ● *n.* a walk taken regularly to maintain or restore good health. □ **constitutionality** *n.* **constitutionalize** *v.tr.* **constitutionally** *adv.*

constitutionalism *n.* **1** a constitutional system of government. **2** the adherence to or advocacy of such a system.

constitutionalist ● *n.* **1** a proponent of constitutional government. **2** an expert in constitutional matters. ● *adj.* of or pertaining to a constitution.

constitutive *adj.* **1** component. **2** essential. **3** able to form or appoint. □ **constitutively** *adv.*

constrain *v.tr.* (usu. in *passive*) **1** restrict severely as regards action, behaviour, etc. **2** compel; urge irresistibly or by necessity. **3** imprison.

constrained *adj.* **1** in senses of CONSTRAIN *v.* **2** forced; not natural (*a constrained manner*).

constraint n. **1** the act or result of constraining or being constrained. **2** something that constrains; a limitation on motion or action. **3** the restraint of natural feelings or their expression; a constrained manner.

constrict v. **1** tr. & intr. make or become narrow or tight. **2** tr. & intr. Biol. contract. **3** tr. restrict, obstruct. □ **constriction** n. **constrictive** adj.

constrictor n. any snake (esp. a boa) that kills by coiling around its prey and compressing it.

construct ● v.tr. **1** make by fitting parts together; build, form (something physical or abstract). **2** Math. draw or delineate, esp. accurately to given conditions (construct a triangle). ● n. a thing constructed, esp. by the mind. □ **constructor** n.

construction n. **1** the act or a mode of constructing. **2 a** a thing constructed. **b** repair or building work on a stretch of road. **3** the building industry. **4** an interpretation or explanation (put a strict construction on the law). **5** the manner in which something is arranged; structure. **6** Grammar an arrangement of words according to syntactical rules. □ **constructional** adj. **constructionally** adv.

construction holiday n. Cdn (Que.) a holiday for construction workers during the last two weeks of July, taken as a holiday by many other Quebecers.

construction paper n. N Amer. a heavy, usu. coloured paper used for making posters and crafts.

construction worker n. an esp. manual labourer who constructs buildings, roadways, etc.

constructive adj. **1** of construction. **2** helpful, tending to construct (constructive criticism). **3** belonging to the structure of a building. □ **constructively** adv. **constructiveness** n.

constructivism n. an originally Russian artistic movement in which assorted (usu. mechanical or industrial) objects are combined into non-representational and mobile structural forms. □ **constructivist** n.

construe v.tr. (**construes**, **construed**, **construing**) **1** interpret (words or actions). **2** (often foll. by with) combine (words) grammatically ('rely' is construed with 'on'). **3** analyze the syntax of (a sentence). **4** translate word for word. □ **construable** adj. **construal** n.

consul n. **1** an official appointed by a nation to live in a foreign city and protect the interests of the nation's citizens in the region and promote trade. **2** hist. either of two annually elected chief magistrates in ancient Rome. □ **consular** adj.

consulate n. **1** the building officially used by a consul. **2** the office or period of office of a consul.

consult v. **1** tr. seek information or advice from (a person, book, watch, etc.). **2** intr. (often foll. by with) refer to a person for advice, an opinion, etc. **3** tr. seek permission or approval from (a person) for a proposed action. **4** tr. take into account; consider (feelings, interests, etc.). □ **consultative** adj.

consultancy n. (pl. **-ies**) the professional practice or position of a consultant.

consultant n. a person who gives professional advice or services in a specialized field, esp. on a freelance basis.

consultation n. **1** a meeting arranged to consult (esp. with a physician). **2** the act or an instance of consulting.

consulting attrib.adj. giving professional advice to others working in the same field (consulting physician).

consumable ● adj. that can be consumed; intended

for consumption. ● n. (usu. in pl.) a commodity that is eventually used up, worn out, or eaten.

consume v.tr. **1** eat or drink. **2** use up (time, energy, resources, etc.). **3** completely destroy; reduce to nothing or to tiny particles (fire consumed the building). **4** (esp. in passive) engage the full attention of, engross (consumed with rage). □ **consumingly** adv.

consumer ● n. **1** a person who consumes, esp. one who uses a product. **2** a purchaser of goods or services. ● attrib.adj. intended for use by consumers, esp. domestically, rather than in business or manufacturing (consumer goods).

consumer confidence n. consumers' willingness to spend.

consumerism n. **1** the protection or promotion of consumers' interests. **2** preoccupation with consumer goods and their acquisition. **3** the promoting of consumer spending for the economic benefit of society. □ **consumerist** adj. & n.

consumer price index n. esp. N Amer. an index of price changes for consumer goods and services, expressed as a percentage of the prices in a base year.

consumer society n. (also **consumer culture**) a society in which the marketing and consumption of goods and services is an important social and economic activity.

consummate ● v.tr. /ˈkɒnsəˌmeɪt, -sjə-/ **1** complete; make perfect. **2 a** make (a marriage) legally complete by having sex. **b** give sexual expression to (love, a non-marital union, etc.). ● adj. /ˈkɒnsəmət, kənˈsʌmət/ **1** complete, perfect, of the highest level (consummate artistry). **2** perfectly skilled (a consummate general). □ **consummately** adv. **consummation** n.

consumption n. **1** the act or an instance of consuming; the process of being consumed. **2** hist. any disease causing wasting of tissues, esp. pulmonary tuberculosis. **3** an amount consumed. **4** the purchase and use of goods etc. □ **consumptive** adj.

cont. abbr. **1** contents. **2** continued.

contact ● n. **1 a** the state or condition of touching, meeting, or communicating. **b** the first interaction between Europeans and Aboriginal peoples in parts of the world colonized by Europeans. **2** a person who is or may be communicated with for information, supplies, assistance, etc. **3** Electricity **a** a connection for the passage of a current. **b** a device for providing this. **4** a person likely to carry a contagious disease through being associated with an infected person. **5** (usu. in pl.) informal a contact lens. ● adj. caused by touching (contact dermatitis). ● v.tr. **1** get into communication with (a person). **2** begin correspondence or personal dealings with.

contact cement n. an instantly-bonding adhesive applied to both surfaces to be bonded.

contact lens n. a small glass or plastic lens placed directly on the eyeball to correct vision.

contact sport n. a sport in which participants come into bodily contact with one another.

contagion n. **1 a** the communication of disease from one person to another by bodily contact. **b** a contagious disease. **2** a contagious or harmful influence. **3** moral corruption, esp. when widespread.

contagious adj. **1 a** (of a person) likely to transmit disease by contact. **b** (of a disease) transmitted in this way. **2** (of emotions, reactions, etc.) likely to affect others (contagious enthusiasm). □ **contagiously** adv.

contain v.tr. **1** hold or be capable of holding within itself; include, comprise. **2** (of measures) consist of or be equal to (a metre contains 100 centimetres). **3** prevent (an enemy, costs, etc.) from moving, spreading, or increasing. **4** restrain (oneself, one's feelings, etc.).

contained *adj.* **1** included, enclosed, held. **2** restrained, showing self-restraint, reserved.

container *n.* **1** a vessel, box, etc., for holding particular things. **2** a large boxlike receptacle of standard design for the transport of goods, esp. one readily transferable between forms of transport.

containerize *v.tr.* **1** pack in or transport by container. **2** adapt to transport by container. □ **containerization** *n.*

container ship *n.* a ship designed to carry goods stored in containers.

containment *n.* **1** *in senses of* CONTAIN *v.* **2** the action or policy of preventing the expansion of a hostile country or influence.

contaminant *n.* something which contaminates.

contaminate *v.tr.* **1** make impure by contact or mixture; pollute. **2** infect. **3** introduce radioactivity into (a substance where it is harmful or undesirable). □ **contamination** *n.* **contaminator** *n.*

cont'd *abbr.* continued.

contemplate *v.* **1** *tr.* look at or consider in a calm, reflective manner. **2** *tr.* regard (an event) as possible. **3** *tr.* intend; have as one's purpose. **4** *intr.* meditate. □ **contemplation** *n.*

contemplative ● *adj.* of or given to (esp. religious) contemplation. ● *n.* a person whose life is devoted to contemplation, esp. a monk or nun of a cloistered order devoted to prayer. □ **contemplatively** *adv.*

contemporaneous *adj.* (usu. foll. by *with*) **1** existing or occurring at the same time. **2** of the same period. □ **contemporaneity** *n.* **contemporaneously** *adv.*

contemporary ● *adj.* **1** living or occurring at the same time. **2** approximately equal in age. **3** (of styles etc.) following the latest ideas or fashion. **4** living or existing at the present. ● *n.* (*pl.* **-ies**) **1** a person or thing living or existing at the same time as another. **2** a person of roughly the same age as another. □ **contemporarily** *adv.* **contemporariness** *n.*

contempt *n.* **1** a feeling that a person or a thing is beneath consideration or worthless, or deserving scorn or extreme reproach. **2** the condition of being held in contempt. **3** (in full **contempt of court**) disobedience to or disrespect for a court of law and its officers. □ **beneath contempt** utterly despicable. **hold in contempt** despise.

contemptible *adj.* deserving contempt; despicable. □ **contemptibility** *n.* **contemptibly** *adv.*

contemptuous *adj.* (often foll. by *of*) showing contempt; insolent. □ **contemptuously** *adv.*

contend *v.* **1** *intr.* (usu. foll. by *with*) strive, fight. **2** *intr.* compete (*contending emotions*). **3** *tr.* (usu. foll. by *that* + clause) assert, maintain.

contender *n.* an esp. serious challenger or competitor.

content[1] ● *predic.adj.* **1** (often foll. by *with*) satisfied; adequately happy. **2** (foll. by *to* + infin.) willing. ● *v.tr.* (usu. *refl.* or in *passive*; often foll. by *with*, or *to* + infin.) make content; satisfy. ● *n.* a contented state. □ **to one's heart's content** to the full extent of one's desires.

content[2] *n.* **1** (usu. in *pl.*) what is contained in something. **2 a** the amount of a substance contained (*sodium content*). **b** the proportion of a specified feature present (*Canadian content*). **3** the substance or material dealt with (in a speech, work of art, etc.) as distinct from its form or style. **4** the capacity or volume of a thing. **5** (in *pl.*) (in full **table of**

contents) a list of the titles of chapters etc. given at the front of a book, periodical, etc.

contented *adj.* happy, satisfied. □ **contentedly** *adv.* **contentedness** *n.*

contention *n.* **1** a point contended for in an argument. **2 a** a dispute or argument. **b** rivalry, competition. □ **in contention** competing, esp. with a good chance of success. **out of contention** having lost any chance of succeeding.

contentious *adj.* **1** argumentative. **2** controversial. □ **contentiously** *adv.* **contentiousness** *n.*

contentment *n.* satisfied, tranquil happiness.

contest ● *n.* **1 a** a competition, raffle, draw, etc. **b** a process of contending. **2** a dispute; a controversy. ● *v.tr.* **1** challenge or dispute (a decision etc.). **2** debate (a statement etc.). **3** contend or compete for (a prize, parliamentary seat, etc.). □ **no contest** indicating a clearly undisputed winner in some supposed competition. □ **contestable** *adj.* **contested** *adj.*

contestant *n.* a person who takes part in a contest or competition.

contestation *n.* **1** an act or instance of disputation. **2** an assertion contended for.

context *n.* **1** the parts of something written or spoken that immediately precede and follow a word or passage and clarify its meaning. **2** the circumstances relevant to something under consideration. □ **in context** with the surrounding words or circumstances (*must be seen in context*). **out of context** without the surrounding words or circumstances and so not fully understandable. □ **contextual** *adj.* **contextualize** *v.tr.* **contextualization** *n.* **contextually** *adv.*

contiguous /kən'tɪgjʊəs/ *adj.* (usu. foll. by *with*, *to*) **1** touching, adjoining, in contact. **2** neighbouring, in close proximity. **3** esp. *US* used in reference to the continental US, excluding Alaska and Hawaii. □ **contiguity** /ˌkɒntɪ'gjuːɪti/ *n.* **contiguously** *adv.*

continent[1] *n.* **1** any of the main continuous expanses of land (Europe, Asia, Africa, N and S America, Australia, Antarctica). **2** (**the Continent**) the mainland of Europe as distinct from the British Isles. **3** continuous land.

continent[2] *adj.* **1** able to control movements of the bowels and bladder. **2** exercising self-restraint, esp. sexually. □ **continence** *n.* **continently** *adv.*

continental ● *adj.* **1** of or characteristic of a continent. **2 a** (**Continental**) of or relating to mainland Europe. **b** (of cooking etc.) reflecting the traditions of various European countries. ● *n.* an inhabitant of mainland Europe. □ **continentally** *adv.*

continental breakfast *n.* a light breakfast of coffee, rolls, etc.

continental divide *n.* the boundary between separate drainage basins on a continent, esp. (**Continental Divide**) the N American watershed formed by the Rocky Mountains.

continental drift *n.* the theory that the continents are slowly moving relative to each other over the surface of the earth.

continentalism *n.* N Amer. the belief that Canada and the US should pursue greater economic, political, and cultural co-operation, esp. in contrast to nationalistic policies. □ **continentalist** *n.* & *adj.*

continental shelf *n.* a gently sloping, shallow marine platform between the shore of a continent and the deeper ocean.

contingency *n.* (*pl.* **-ies**) **1** a possible future event or circumstance regarded as potentially able to influence present action. **2** a thing dependent on an uncertain event. **3** uncertainty of occurrence. **4** one thing incident to another.

contingency plan *n.* a plan designed to take account of a possible future event or circumstance.

contingent ● *n.* **1** a group with common origins, interests, etc. representing a larger body. **2** a force contributed to form part of an army or navy. ● *adj.* **1** (usu. foll. by *on*, *upon*) conditional, dependent (on an uncertain event or circumstance). **2** associated with or dependent upon something else for existence or occurrence. **3** incidental. **4** that may or may not occur. **b** fortuitous.

continual *adj.* **1** constantly or frequently recurring. **2** ongoing; always happening. ¶See CONTINUOUS. □ **continually** *adv.*

continuance *n.* **1** a state of continuing in existence or operation. **2** the duration of an event or action. **3** *N Amer. Law* an adjournment or postponement of proceedings to a future date.

continuation *n.* (often foll. by *of*) **1 a** the act or an instance of continuing. **b** the process of being continued. **2** a part that continues something else.

continue *v.* (**continues, continued, continuing**) **1** *tr.* persist in, maintain, not stop (an action etc.). **2 a** *tr. & intr.* resume or prolong (a narrative, journey, etc.). **b** *intr.* recommence after a pause (*we'll continue shortly*). **3** *tr.* be a sequel to. **4** *intr.* **a** remain in existence or unchanged. **b** remain in a specified state (*the weather will continue cold*). **5** *tr. N Amer. & Scot. Law* adjourn (proceedings) until some future date.

continuing education *n.* **1** instruction intended esp. for adult, part-time students. **2** courses given to update participants in a particular field of study.

continuity *n.* (*pl.* **-ies**) **1 a** the state of being continuous. **b** an unbroken succession. **c** a logical sequence. **2 a** the detailed and self-consistent scenario of a film or broadcast. **b** the maintenance of consistency or of a continuous flow of action in a film sequence. **3 a** the linking of broadcast items. **b** the music, commentary, etc. introducing or providing linkage between items in a broadcast.

continuous *adj.* **1** unbroken, uninterrupted. ¶*Continuous* refers to something which is non-stop; *continual* refers to something happening repeatedly, but with intervals in between. **2** (often foll. by *with*) connected throughout in time or space. **3** *Grammar* = PROGRESSIVE *adj.* **6**. **4** (of paper etc.) designating a folded stack or roll perforated to form separate sheets. □ **continuously** *adv.* **continuousness** *n.*

continuum /kən'tɪnjʊəm/ *n.* (*pl.* **continua** /-jʊə/) anything seen as having a continuous structure without perceptibly distinct parts.

contort *v.* **1** *tr.* twist or force out of normal shape. **2** *intr.* become twisted, distorted, or forced out of shape. □ **contorted** *adj.*

contortion *n.* **1** the act or process of twisting. **2** a twisted state, esp. of the face or body. **3** a thing or idea distorted by a twisting of character, meaning, context, etc. (*the verbal contortions of the politician*).

contortionist *n.* an entertainer who adopts contorted postures.

contour ● *n.* **1** an outline, esp. representing or bounding the shape of something with a curving form. **2** the outline of a natural feature, e.g. a coast or mountain mass. **3** = CONTOUR LINE. **4** the defining traits of a person's character, a society, etc., perceived as a linkage of common, delimiting characteristics. ● *v.tr.* **1** mark with contour lines. **2** construct (a road etc.) according to the outline of the land.

contoured *adj.* **1** designed or shaped to fit a specific form (*contoured seats*). **2** furnished with contour lines.

contour line *n.* **1** a line on a map joining points of equal altitude. **2** a line in a painting etc. joining points or enclosing an area of similar colour etc.

contour map *n.* a map marked with contour lines to depict the relief of the land.

contra- *comb. form* against, opposite (*contradict*).

contraband ● *n.* **1** anything that has been smuggled, imported, or exported illegally. **2** prohibited trade; smuggling. **3** (in full **contraband of war**) goods forbidden to be supplied by neutrals to belligerents. ● *adj.* **1** forbidden to be imported or exported (at all or without payment of duty). **2** concerning traffic in contraband (*contraband trade*). **3** forbidden.

contraception *n.* the use of contraceptives.

contraceptive ● *adj.* preventing pregnancy. ● *n.* a device, drug, etc. preventing conception.

contract ● *n.* **1** a written or spoken agreement between two or more parties, intended to be enforceable by law. **2** a document recording this. **3** marriage regarded as a legal arrangement. **4** *Bridge etc.* a commitment to win the number of tricks bid. **5** *informal* a criminal arrangement for someone to be killed in exchange for money. ● *v.* **1** *tr. & intr.* **a** make or become smaller. **b** draw together (muscles, the brow, etc.) or be drawn together. **2 a** *intr.* (usu. foll. by *with*) make a contract. **b** *intr.* (usu. foll. by *for*, or *to* + infin.) enter formally into a business or legal arrangement. **c** *tr.* (often foll. by *out*) arrange (work) to be done by contract. **d** *tr.* place under a contract. **3** *tr.* catch or develop (a disease). **4** *tr.* form or develop (a friendship, habit, etc.). **5** *tr.* enter into (marriage). **6** *tr.* incur (a debt etc.). **7** *tr.* shorten (a word) by combination or elision.

contract bridge *n.* the most common form of bridge, in which only tricks bid and won count.

contractile /kən'træktaɪl/ *adj.* capable of or producing contraction.

contraction *n.* **1** an act or instance of contracting. **2 a** a shortening or tensing of a muscle in response to a nerve impulse. **b** (usu. in *pl.*) the tensing of the uterine muscles esp. during labour. **3** shrinking. **4 a** shortening of a word by combination or elision. **b** a contracted word or group of words.

contractor *n.* a person who undertakes a contract, esp. to provide materials, conduct building operations, etc.

contractual *adj.* of, in the nature of, or secured by a contract. □ **contractually** *adv.*

contradict *v.* **1** *tr.* affirm the contrary of (a statement etc.). **2 a** *tr.* deny or express the opposite of a statement made by (a person). **b** *intr.* make a contradictory statement. **3** *tr.* be in opposition to or in conflict with (*evidence contradicted our theory*).

contradiction *n.* **1 a** denial; statement of the opposite. **b** an instance of this. **2** an inconsistency between statements, qualities, etc. **3** a person or thing characterized by conflicting qualities. □ **contradiction in terms** a self-contradictory statement or group of words.

contradictory *adj.* **1** expressing a denial or opposite statement. **2** (of statements etc.) mutually opposed or inconsistent. **3** (of a person) inclined to contradict. □ **contradictorily** *adv.*

contradistinction *n.* difference made apparent by contrast (*in contradistinction to*).

contrail *n.* a visible stream of water droplets or ice crystals occurring in the exhaust of an aircraft etc.

contraindicate *v.tr. Med.* (usu. in *passive*) cause (a medication, course of treatment, etc.) to be inappropriate. □ **contraindication** *n.*

contralto /kən'trɒlto: -ælto:/ *n.* (pl. **-os**) **1 a** the lowest female singing voice. **b** a singer with this voice. **2** a part written for contralto.

contraption *n.* often *derogatory* or *jocular* a machine, esp. a strange, improvised, or particularly intricate one.

contrapuntal /ˌkɒntrəˈpʌntəl/ *adj. Music* of, pertaining to, or of the nature of counterpoint.

contrarian ● *n.* a person who opposes or rejects majority opinions, attitudes, etc., esp. in economic matters. ● *adj.* going against popular opinion or current practice. □ **contrarianism** *n.*

contrary ● *adj.* **1** (usu. foll. by *to*) opposed in nature or tendency. **2** mutually opposed. **3** (of a wind) unfavourable, impeding. **4** opposite in position or direction. **5** /kən'treri/ *informal* perverse, wilful. ● *n.* (pl. **-ies**) (usu. prec. by *the*) the opposite. ● *adv.* (foll. by *to*) in opposition or contrast (*contrary to expectations*). □ **on the contrary** intensifying a denial of what has just been implied or stated. **to the contrary** to the opposite effect. □ **contrarily** *adv.* **contrariness** *n.*

contrast ● *n.* **1 a** a juxtaposition or comparison showing striking differences. **b** a difference so revealed. **2** (often foll. by *to*) a thing or person having qualities noticeably different from another. **3** the degree of difference between tones in a television picture or a photograph. ● *v.* (often foll. by *with*) **1** *tr.* compare or set together so as to reveal a difference. **2** *intr.* have or show a difference on comparison. □ **contrasting** *adj.* **contrastingly** *adv.*

contravene *v.tr.* **1** infringe, violate (a law, standards, guidelines, etc.). **2** (of things) conflict with.

contravention *n.* **1** infringement, violation, opposition. **2** an instance of this. □ **in contravention of** infringing, violating (a law etc.).

contribute /kən'trɪbju:t, *disputed* 'kɒntrɪ,bju:t/ *v.* (often foll. by *to*) **1** *tr.* give (money, an idea, help, etc.) toward a common purpose. **2** *intr.* help to bring about a result etc. (*contributed to their downfall*). **3** *tr. & intr.* supply (an article etc.) for publication with others in a journal etc. □ **contributing** *adj.* **contributor** *n.*

contribution *n.* **1** the act of giving or contributing. **2** something given, esp. money. **3** an article etc. furnished to a publication.

contributory *adj.* **1** contributing to a result; partly responsible for. **2** operated by means of contributions (*contributory pension scheme*).

contributory negligence *n.* failure on the part of an injured party to take adequate precautions to prevent accident or injury.

contrite *adj.* penitent. □ **contritely** *adv.*

contrition *n.* the condition of being distressed in mind for some fault or injury done, usu. with resolution to make amends.

contrivance *n.* **1 a** a device made for a particular purpose. **b** an obviously artificial construction or presentation of parts or details. **2** an elaborate act or plan, esp. a deceitful one. **3** inventive capacity.

contrive *v.tr.* **1 a** devise. **b** plan or make resourcefully or with skill. **2 a** manage (*contrived to make matters worse*). **b** plot or scheme.

contrived *adj.* so obviously planned as to seem unnatural or forced (*the plot seemed contrived*).

control ● *n.* **1** the power of directing, command. **2** the power of restraining, esp. self-restraint. **3 a** a means of restraint; a check. **b** prevention of the spread or proliferation of something (*disease control*).

4 (usu. in *pl.*) a means of regulating prices etc. **5 a** a device or switch used to control something (also *attrib.*: *control panel*). **b** (usu. in *pl.*) the switches etc. by which an aircraft or car is controlled. **6** (in full **control key**) *Computing* a key which is held down while another key is depressed, altering the function of the latter. **7** a person or group that checks, monitors, or controls something. **8 a** a standard of comparison for checking the results of a survey or experiment. **b** a person or thing acting as such a standard. ● *v.tr.* (**controlled, controlling**) **1** dominate or have command of. **2** regulate or exert control over. **3** curb, restrain, or hold in check (*control yourself*). **4** serve as a standard of comparison for a test, study, etc. **5** check, verify. □ **in control** (often foll. by *of*) directing an activity. **out of control** no longer subject to containment, restraint, or guidance. **under control** being controlled; in order. □ **controllable** *adj.* **controllability** *n.*

control freak *n. informal* a person with a near obsessive desire for order and control of self, others, surroundings, etc.

control group *n.* a group forming the standard of comparison in an experiment.

controlled-release *adj.* (of a substance, esp. a drug) activated gradually or at predetermined intervals over a period of time.

controlled substance *n.* (also **controlled drug**) any addictive or behaviour-altering substance the possession of which is restricted by law, e.g. cocaine.

controller *n.* **1** a person or device that regulates, directs, or controls. **2** = COMPTROLLER. **3** *Cdn* (in Ontario) a member of a board of control.

controlling interest *n.* ownership of sufficient stock in a company to enable a shareholder to exert control over policy, management, etc.

controlling shareholder *n.* an individual who owns a sufficient number of shares in a company to have a controlling interest in it.

control tower *n.* a tall structure at an airport etc. from which air traffic is controlled.

controversial *adj.* **1** causing or subject to dispute or debate. **2** fond of debate, argument, or controversy. □ **controversialist** *n. & adj.* **controversially** *adv.*

controversy /ˈkɒntrə,vɜrsi, kən'trɒvərsi/ *n.* (pl. **-ies**) a prolonged argument or dispute, esp. when conducted publicly and over a matter of opinion.

controvert *v.tr.* **1** dispute, deny, oppose. **2** argue about; discuss. □ **controverted** *adj.*

conundrum /kə'nʌndrəm/ *n.* **1** a riddle, esp. one with a pun in its answer. **2** a hard or puzzling question or issue.

convalesce /ˌkɒnvə'les/ *v.intr.* recover one's health after illness or medical treatment.

convalescent ● *adj.* **1** recovering from an illness. **2** pertaining to convalescents. ● *n.* a person recovering from an illness or injury. □ **convalescence** *n.*

convection *n.* **1** transference of heat in a gas or liquid by upward movement of the heated and less dense medium. **2** *Meteorol.* the atmospheric process of air transfer, esp. of hot air upward. □ **convective** *adj.*

convection oven *n.* an oven with a fan that continually and uniformly circulates heated air to decrease cooking time.

convector *n.* a heating appliance that circulates warm air by convection.

convene *v.* **1** *tr.* **a** call or arrange (a meeting etc.). **b** call together (people) for a meeting. **2** *intr.* assemble or meet together, esp. for a common purpose. **3** *tr.* summon (a person) before a tribunal. □ **convenor** n. (also **convener**).

convenience n. **1** the quality of being convenient. **2** freedom from difficulty or trouble. **3** an accommodation or advantage (*your help was a great convenience*). **4** any thing, esp. an installation or device, that saves or simplifies effort. **5** a convenient time or place. □ **at your convenience** at a time or place that suits you. **at your earliest convenience** as soon as you can.

convenience store n. a small, conveniently located store with extended opening hours.

convenient adj. **1** (often foll. by *for, to*) **a** serving one's comfort, interests, or needs. **b** easily accessible. **c** suitable. **d** free of trouble or difficulty. **2** available or occurring at a suitable time or place (*will try to find a convenient moment*). **3** well situated for some purpose. □ **conveniently** adv.

convent ● n. **1** a religious community, esp. of nuns, under vows. **2** the premises occupied by this. **3** (in full **convent school**) a school attached to and run by a convent. ● adj. of or associated with a convent.

convention n. **1 a** general agreement, esp. on social behaviour etc. by implicit consent of the majority. **b** a custom or customary practice, esp. an artificial or formal one. **2 a** a formal assembly or conference for a common purpose. **b** N Amer. an assembly of the delegates of a political party to select candidates for office. **3 a** a formal agreement. **b** an agreement between nations, somewhat less formal than a treaty.

conventional adj. **1** depending on or according with convention. **2** (of a person) conforming to social conventions. **3 a** usual (*conventional office attire*). **b** traditional, normal (in opposition to recent inventions etc.) (*conventional or microwave ovens*). **4** not spontaneous, sincere, or original. **5** (of weapons or power) non-nuclear. **6** Art following accepted models, traditions, etc. instead of directly imitating nature or working out original ideas. □ **conventionality** n. **conventionalize** v.tr. **conventionally** adv.

conventional wisdom n. a common body of accumulated opinion etc. on a certain subject.

conventioneer n. N Amer. a person attending a convention.

converge v.intr. **1 a** (often foll. by *on*) come together from several diverse points toward a common point. **b** (of ideas) move toward a common conclusion, opinion, etc. **2** (of lines) tend to meet at a point. **3** (foll. by *on, upon*) approach from different directions.

convergence n. the action, fact, or property of converging. □ **convergent** adj. **convergency** n.

conversant adj. (usu. foll. by *with*) well experienced or acquainted with a subject etc. □ **conversancy** n.

conversation n. **1** the informal exchange of ideas by spoken words. **2** an instance of this. □ **make conversation** talk politely.

conversational adj. **1** of conversation. **2** fond of or skilled in conversation. **3** informal in style; typical of conversation. □ **conversationally** adv.

conversationalist n. a person who is fond of or excels at conversing.

converse[1] /kən'vɜrs/ v.intr. (often foll. by *with*) engage in conversation.

converse[2] /'kɒnvɜrs/ ● adj. opposite, contrary, reversed. ● n. something that is opposite or contrary. □ **conversely** /kən'vɜrsli/ adv.

conversion n. **1 a** the act or an instance of changing one's beliefs, opinions, etc. **b** the process of having one's beliefs changed, esp. in religion. **c** the turning of sinners to God. **2** an adaptation of a building for new purposes. **3 a** the changing of funds from one

currency to another. **b** the changing of units, measurements, etc. from one system or expression to another. **4** alteration to a car, rifle, etc. to enhance its performance. **5 a** the physical transformation of something from one substance, state, etc. to another (*conversion of food into energy*). **b** the transformation of fertile into fissile material in a nuclear reactor. **6** Sport the scoring of additional points in certain sports, e.g. by a successful kick in football. **7** Computing **a** the adaptation of software designed for one system to another system. **b** the transfer or copying of data from one storage medium to another.

convert ● v. **1** tr. (usu. foll. by *into*) change in form, character, or function. **2 a** intr. change beliefs, opinions, etc. **b** tr. cause (a person) to change beliefs, opinion, party, etc. **3** tr. change (stocks, units in which a quantity is expressed, etc.) into others of a different kind. **4** tr. make structural alterations in (a building) so as to serve a new purpose. **5** tr. & intr. Football complete (a touchdown) by kicking a goal or crossing the goal line. **6** intr. be converted or convertible (*the sofa converts into a bed*). **7** tr. Computing **a** adapt (software) from one system to another. **b** transfer or copy (data) from one storage medium to another. ● n. **1** (often foll. by *to*) a person who has been converted to a different belief, opinion, etc. **2** Cdn Football the scoring of points after a touchdown by kicking the ball between the uprights (for one point) or by carrying or passing the ball over the defending team's goal line (for two points).

converter n. **1** a person or thing that converts. **2 a** an electrical apparatus for the interconversion of alternating current and direct current. **b** an apparatus for converting a signal from one frequency to another. **c** an auxiliary apparatus that allows a television or radio to pick up channels for which it was not originally designed. **3** = CATALYTIC CONVERTER.

convertible ● adj. **1** that may be converted. **2** (of currency, bonds, etc.) that may be converted into other forms, esp. into gold or US dollars. **3** (of a car) having a folding or detachable roof. **4** Cdn designating a mortgage which may not be paid off before the stated term without a financial penalty, but which may be converted to a longer term without penalty. ● n. **1** a car with a folding or detachable roof. **2** bonds or securities which can be readily changed to common stock. □ **convertibility** n.

convex adj. having an outline or surface curved like the exterior of a circle or sphere (*compare* CONCAVE). □ **convexity** n. **convexly** adv.

convey v.tr. **1** communicate (an idea, meaning, etc.). **2** transport or carry (goods, passengers, etc.). **3** Law transfer the title to (property). □ **conveyable** adj.

conveyance n. **1 a** the act or process of carrying. **b** the communication (of ideas etc.). **c** transmission. **2 a** means of transport; a vehicle. **3** Law **a** the transfer of property from one owner to another. **b** a document effecting this.

conveyor n. (also **conveyer**) **1** a person or thing that conveys. **2** (in full **conveyor belt**) a flexible, endless belt moving on rollers used to convey articles or materials.

convict ● v.tr. (often foll. by *of*) declare guilty, esp. by the verdict of a jury or the decision of a judge. ● n. **1** a person found guilty of a criminal offence. **2** a person serving a prison sentence.

conviction n. **1 a** the act or process of proving or finding guilty. **b** an instance of this (*has two previous convictions*). **2** a firm belief or opinion. **3** a feeling of one's own sinfulness.

convince v.tr. persuade (a person) to believe, realize, or agree. □ **convincer** n. **convincible** adj.

convinced adj. firmly persuaded (a convinced pacifist).

convincing adj. **1** persuading by argument or evidence (a convincing case). **2 a** plausible or seeming worthy of belief (a convincing message). **b** leaving no margin of doubt, substantial (a convincing victory). □ **convincingly** adv.

convivial /kən'vɪvɪəl/ adj. **1 a** (of a person) friendly, fond of good company. **b** sociable and lively (convivial banter). **2** festive (a convivial atmosphere). □ **conviviality** n. **convivially** adv.

convocation n. **1** N Amer. a formal assembly at a university or college for graduation ceremonies. **2** a large, formal gathering of people. **3** Cdn Law a meeting of the elected governing officials of a provincial law society.

convoke v.tr. formal call (people) together to a meeting etc.; summon to assemble.

convoluted adj. **1** (of style, meaning, etc.) complicated, difficult to comprehend (a convoluted plot). **2** coiled, twisted. □ **convolutedly** adv.

convolution n. **1** a complex or confused condition or issue. **2** coiling or twisting. **3** a coil or twist.

convoy ● n. **1** a group of ships travelling together or under escort. **2** a supply of provisions etc. under escort. **3** a group of vehicles travelling on land together or under escort. **4** the act of travelling or moving in a group or under escort. ● v.tr. **1** (of a warship) escort (a merchant or passenger vessel). **2** escort, esp. with armed force. □ **in convoy** under escort with others; as a group.

convulse v. **1** intr. **a** move violently or uncontrollably. **b** contort. **2 a** tr. cause to laugh uproariously. **b** intr. laugh wildly. **3 a** tr. disturb greatly. **b** intr. be agitated. **4 a** tr. affect with convulsions; cause to twist or contort. **b** intr. be affected with convulsions.

convulsion n. **1** (usu. in pl.) violent irregular motion of a limb or limbs or the body caused by involuntary contraction of muscles. **2** a violent natural disturbance, esp. an earthquake. **3** violent social or political agitation. **4** (in pl.) uncontrollable laughter.

convulsive adj. **1** of the nature of, characterized by or affected with convulsions. **2** producing convulsions. □ **convulsively** adv.

cony n. (pl. **-ies** or **-eys**) **1** a rabbit. **2** its fur.

COO abbr. CHIEF OPERATING OFFICER.

coo ● n. a soft murmuring sound like that of a dove. ● v. (**coos, cooed**) **1** intr. make the sound of a coo. **2** intr. & tr. talk or say in a soft or amorous voice.

cook ● v. **1 a** tr. prepare (food) by heating it. **b** intr. prepare food for consumption (loves to cook). **2** intr. (of food) undergo cooking. **3** tr. informal falsify or alter (accounts etc.) (cooked the books). **4** tr. slang ruin, spoil. **5** intr. N Amer. informal **a** perform music with excitement or inspiration. **b** perform or proceed well. **6** intr. (as **be cooking**) informal be happening or about to happen (what's cooking?). ● n. a person who cooks, esp. professionally or in a specified way (a good cook). □ **cook a person's goose** ruin a person's chances. **cook up** informal invent or concoct (a story, excuse, etc.). **cook with gas** N Amer. informal proceed rapidly.

cookbook n. N Amer. a book containing recipes and other information about cooking.

cooker n. a container or device for cooking food.

cookery n. (pl. **-ies**) the art or practice of cooking.

cookhouse n. **1** a building used for cooking, esp. on a ranch, logging camp, etc. **2** a ship's galley.

cookie[1] n. N Amer. **1** a small sweet biscuit. **2** slang a person (one tough cookie). □ **toss** (or **lose**) **one's**

cookies slang vomit. **the way the cookie crumbles** informal how things turn out.

cookie[2] n. **1** a cook, esp. in a work camp or in the military. **2** a cook's assistant in a work camp.

cookie cutter n. N Amer. **1** a stamp for cutting cookie dough into a particular shape. **2** (often attrib.) denoting something mass-produced or lacking any distinguishing characteristics (cookie-cutter novels).

cookie jar n. N Amer. **1** a container for cookies. **2** a reserve of good things, usu. off-limits (caught with their hands in the cookie jar).

cookie sheet n. N Amer. a flat metal tray on which cookies etc. are baked.

cooking n. **1** the art or process by which food is prepared for consumption. **2** (attrib.) suitable for or used in cooking (cooking apple; cooking utensils).

cooking oil n. vegetable oil used in cooking.

cook-off n. N Amer. a cooking competition in which competitors assemble to prepare their entries.

cookout n. N Amer. a gathering with an open-air cooked meal.

cookstove n. N Amer. an esp. wood-burning stove used for cooking.

cooktop n. N Amer. a cooking unit consisting of burners or elements, esp. built into a countertop.

cookware n. utensils for cooking, esp. pans etc.

cool ● adj. **1** of or at a fairly low temperature, moderately cold (a cool day). **2** suggesting or achieving coolness (cool clothes). **3** calm, unexcited. **4** lacking zeal or enthusiasm. **5** unfriendly. **6** informal **a** excellent, esp. appealing to youth. **b** (of a person, style, etc.) following the latest fashions; hip. **c** considered socially acceptable by a group (esp. youth). **7** calmly audacious (a cool customer). **8** (prec. by a) informal at least (cost me a cool thousand). ● n. **1** coolness. **2** cool air; a cool place. **3** slang calmness, composure (lose one's cool). ● v.tr. & intr. (often foll. by down, off) make or become cool. □ **cool as a cucumber** completely unruffled. **cool it** informal relax, calm down. **cool out** informal relax, calm down. □ **coolish** adj. **coolly** adv. **coolness** n.

coolant n. a cooling agent, esp. fluid, to remove heat from an engine etc.

cooler n. **1** N Amer. an insulated, usu. portable container for keeping drinks etc. cool. **2** a vessel in which a thing is cooled. **3** a mixture of wine or spirits and soda water, often with a fruit flavour. **4** slang prison or a prison cell.

cool-headed adj. not easily excited.

coolie n. (pl. **-ies**) an unskilled, low paid labourer in or from India, China, or other Asian countries.

cooling-off period n. an interval to allow for a change of mind before commitment to action.

coon n. **1** N Amer. a raccoon. **2** slang offensive a black person. □ **a coon's age** a long time.

coonshit n. □ **a pinch of coonshit** Cdn coarse slang a negligible or contemptible quantity (not worth a pinch of coonshit; don't care a pinch of coonshit).

coonskin n. **1** the skin of a raccoon. **2** a cap etc. made of this.

coop ● n. **1** a cage or pen for confining poultry. **2** a small place of confinement, esp. a prison. ● v.tr. **1** put or keep (a fowl) in a coop. **2** (often foll. by up) confine (a person) in a small space. □ **fly the coop** N Amer. informal leave abruptly.

co-op n. informal **1** a co-operative business or store. **2** N Amer. a co-operative housing complex.

cooper n. a maker or repairer of casks, barrels, etc.

co-operate v.intr. (also **cooperate**) **1** (often foll. by *with*) work or act together, esp. agreeably. **2** (of things) concur in producing an effect. □ **co-operator** *n.*

co-operation *n.* (also **cooperation**) **1** working together to the same end. **2** the formation and operation of co-operatives.

co-operative (also **cooperative**) ● *adj.* **1** characterized by co-operation, esp. rather than competition (*a co-operative venture*). **2** willing to co-operate. **3** (of a farm, store, or other business, or a society owning such businesses) owned and run jointly by its members, with profits shared among them. **4** *N Amer.* designating a type of non-profit housing where the housing complex is jointly owned by the occupants, who pay rent on their individual unit to cover costs but cannot sell their unit. ● *n.* a co-operative farm, society, business, or housing complex. □ **co-operatively** *adv.* **co-operativeness** *n.*

Co-operative Commonwealth Federation *n.* *hist.* (in Canada) a progressive labour party formed in 1932, refounded as the NDP in 1961. Abbr.: **CCF**.

co-opt *v.tr.* **1 a** absorb into a larger (esp. political) group. **b** take over, adopt. **2** appoint to membership of a body by invitation of the existing members. □ **co-optation** *n.* **co-option** *n.* **co-optive** *adj.*

coordinate (also **co-ordinate**) ● *v.* **1** *tr.* bring (various parts, movements, activities, etc.) into a proper or required relation to ensure harmony or effective operation etc. **2** *intr.* work or act together effectively. **3** *tr.* make coordinate. ● *adj.* **1** equal in rank or importance. **2** in which the parts are coordinated; involving coordination. **3** *Grammar* (of parts of a compound sentence) equal in status. ● *n.* **1** *Math.* each of a set of magnitudes used to fix the position of a point, line, or plane. **2** a person or thing equal in rank or importance. **3** (in *pl.*) matching items of clothing. □ **coordinately** *adv.* **coordinator** *n.*

coordinated *adj.* **1** put together so as to ensure efficient functioning. **2** matching (*colour-coordinated*). **3** able to move various parts of the body in harmony (*Katherine's not very coordinated*).

coordinate geometry *n.* = ANALYTIC GEOMETRY.

coordinating conjunction *n.* any of a number of conjunctions (*and, or, but, nor, yet, for, so, whereas*) which can join independent clauses.

coordination *n.* **1** the harmonious or effective working together of different parts. **2** the arrangement of parts etc. into an effective relation. **3** the ability to control one's movements properly or effectively, esp. of one part of the body in conjunction with another (*hand-eye coordination*).

coot *n.* **1** any dark grey or black marsh bird of the genus *Fulica*, e.g. the American coot, *F. americana*, with the upper mandible extended backwards to form a white plate on the forehead. **2** a scoter. **3** *derogatory* a stupid person, esp. an elderly person.

cootie *n.* *slang* a body louse.

cop *informal* ● *n.* a police officer. ● *v.tr.* (**copped**, **copping**) **1** catch or arrest (an offender). **2** receive, suffer. **3** take, seize, win. □ **cop out 1** withdraw; give up an attempt. **2** go back on a promise. **3** escape. **cop an attitude** *N Amer.* assume an esp. arrogant posture, attitude, etc. **cop a plea** *N Amer.* plea bargain.

copayment *n.* *N Amer.* a payment made by a beneficiary (esp. for health services) in addition to that made by an insurer.

cope¹ *v.intr.* **1** (foll. by *with*) deal effectively or contend successfully with a person or task. **2** deal with a situation or problem (*could no longer cope*).

cope² *n.* *Christianity* a long cloaklike vestment worn by a priest or bishop in ceremonies and processions.

Copernican system /kəˈpɜːrnɪkən/ *n.* (also **Copernican theory**) the theory that the planets (including the earth) move around the sun.

copier *n.* a machine or person that copies (esp. documents).

co-pilot *n.* a second pilot in an aircraft.

coping *n.* the action of dealing with difficult circumstances (also *attrib.*: *coping mechanism*).

copious *adj.* **1** abundant, plentiful. **2** producing much. **3** providing much information. □ **copiously** *adv.* **copiousness** *n.*

copolymer *n.* *Chem.* a polymer with units of more than one kind. □ **copolymerize** *v.tr. & intr.*

cop-out *n.* a cowardly or feeble evasion.

copper¹ ● *n.* **1** a malleable red-brown natural metallic element, used esp. as an electrical conductor and in alloys. **2** a copper or bronze coin, esp. a penny. **3** any of various butterflies with copper-coloured wings. ● *adj.* made of or coloured like copper.

copper² *n.* *slang* a police officer.

copperhead *n.* a venomous but rarely fatal viper, *Agkistrodon contortrix*, native to N America.

Copper Inuit *n.pl.* an Inuit people living along the Coppermine River in the NWT.

coppery *adj.* of or like copper, esp. in colour.

coprocessor *n.* a microprocessor providing additional functions to supplement a primary processor.

co-produce *v.tr.* produce (a play, film, broadcast, etc.) jointly with another producer. □ **co-producer** *n.* **co-production** *n.* **co-product** *n.*

cops and robbers *n.* a children's game in which the participants stalk, chase, and pretend to shoot each other as police officers and criminals.

copse /kɒps/ *n.* a small wood or thicket.

cop shop *n.* *informal* a police station.

Copt *n.* **1** a native Egyptian in the Hellenistic and Roman periods. **2** a Christian of the Coptic Church.

'copter *n.* *informal* a helicopter.

Coptic ● *n.* the language of the Copts, now used only in the Coptic Church. ● *adj.* of or relating to the Copts.

Coptic Church *n.* the native Church of Egypt, isolated from the rest of Christendom since 451.

copula /ˈkɒpjʊlə/ *n.* (*pl.* **copulas**) *Logic & Grammar* a connecting word, esp. parts of the verbs *be*, *seem*, etc., connecting a subject and predicate. □ **copular** *adj.*

copulate *v.intr.* (often foll. by *with*) have sexual intercourse.

copulation *n.* **1** sexual union. **2** a grammatical or logical connection.

copulative *adj.* **1** serving to connect. **2** *Grammar* **a** (of a word) that connects words or clauses linked in sense. **b** connecting a subject and predicate. **3** relating to sexual union. □ **copulatively** *adv.*

copy ● *n.* (*pl.* **-ies**) **1** a thing made to imitate or be identical to another. **2** a single specimen of a publication or issue. **3 a** matter to be printed. **b** material for a newspaper or magazine article (*scandals make good copy*). **c** the text of an advertisement. **4** a model to be copied. ● *v.* (**-ies, -ied**) **1** *tr.* make a copy of. **b** (often foll. by *out*) transcribe. **2** *intr.* make a copy, esp. clandestinely. **3** *tr.* (foll. by *to*) send a copy of (a letter) to a third party. **4** *tr.* do the same as; imitate.

copycat *n.* *informal* a person who copies another, esp. slavishly (also *attrib.*: *copycat remark*).

copy-edit *v.tr.* edit (copy) for printing.

copy editor *n.* a person who edits copy, esp. to correct grammatical, stylistic, or punctuation errors.

copyist *n.* **1** a person who makes (esp. written) copies. **2** an imitator.

copyright ● *n.* the exclusive legal right granted for a specified period to an author, designer, etc., or another appointed person, to print, publish, perform, film, or record original literary, artistic, or musical material. ● *adj.* (of such material) protected by copyright. ● *v.tr.* secure copyright for (material).

copywriter *n.* a person who writes or prepares copy (esp. of advertising material) for publication. □ **copywriting** *n.*

coquette /ko:'ket/ *n.* a woman who flirts. □ **coquettish** *adj.* **coquettishly** *adv.*

coral ● *n.* **1 a** a hard calcareous substance secreted by various marine polyps for support and habitation, and occurring in both single specimens and vast accumulations. **b** any of these usu. colonial organisms. **2** a reddish-pink colour. ● *adj.* **1** of a reddish-pink colour. **2** made of coral.

coral reef *n.* (also **coral island**) a reef (or island) formed by the growth of coral.

corbel ● *n.* **1** a projection of stone, timber, etc., jutting out from a wall to support a weight. **2** a short timber laid longitudinally under a beam to help support it. ● *v.tr. & intr.* (**corbelled**, **corbelling**) (foll. by *out*, *off*) support or project on corbels.

cord ● *n.* **1 a** long thin flexible material made from several twisted strands, esp. thicker than string and finer than rope. **b** a piece of this. **2** a structure in the body resembling a cord (*spinal cord*). **3 a** ribbed fabric, esp. corduroy. **b** (in *pl.*) corduroy pants. **c** a cordlike rib on fabric. **4** an insulated electric cable bringing power to appliances etc. **5** a measure of cut wood (usu. 128 cu. ft., 3.6 cubic metres). ● *v.tr.* fasten or bind with cord. □ **cordlike** *adj.*

corded *adj.* **1** (of cloth) ribbed. **2** provided with cords. **3** (of muscles) standing out like taut cords.

cordial /'kɔrdʒəl, -diəl/ ● *adj.* **1** heartfelt, sincere. **2** warm, friendly. ● *n.* **1** a fruit-flavoured drink. **2** a comforting or pleasant-tasting medicine. □ **cordiality** /kɔrdi'ælɪti/ *n.* **cordially** *adv.*

cordillera /kɔr'dɪlərə, ˌkɔrdɪ'ljerə/ *n.* a system or group of usu. parallel mountain ranges together with intervening plateaux etc., esp. as a major continental feature. □ **cordilleran** *adj.*

cordless *adj.* (of an electrical appliance, telephone, etc.) working from an internal source of energy etc. (esp. a rechargeable battery).

cordon ● *n.* **1** a line or circle of police, soldiers, guards, etc., esp. preventing access to or from an area. **2** an ornamental cord or braid. ● *v.tr.* (often foll. by *off*) enclose or separate with a rope, police, etc.

cordon bleu /ˌkɔrdɒn 'blʊ, ˌkɔrdɔ̃/ *Cooking* ● *adj.* **1** of the highest class. **2** designating a type of chicken or veal dish consisting of a cutlet of meat stuffed with ham and Swiss cheese, breaded and shallow fried. ● *n.* a cordon bleu cook.

Cordura /kɔr'dʊrə/ *n. proprietary* a tough nylon fabric used in bags, boots, etc.

corduroy *n.* **1** a thick cotton fabric with velvety ribs. **2** (in *pl.*) corduroy pants.

corduroy road *n.* esp. *hist.* a road made of tree trunks laid across muddy or swampy ground.

cordwood *n.* wood that is or can be measured in cords.

core ● *n.* **1** the hard central part of various fruits, containing the seeds. **2** (often *attrib.*) the central or most important part of anything (*core curriculum*). **3** the central part of the earth, esp. that within the mantle, with a radius of 3 500 km (2,200 miles). **4** (in full **core lanes**) *Cdn* the express lanes on a highway, usu. separated from the collector lanes. **5** the central part of a nuclear reactor, containing the fissile material. **6** the inner strand of an electric cable, rope, etc. **7** a piece of soft iron forming the centre of an electromagnet or induction coil. **8** an internal mould filling a space to be left hollow in a casting. **9** the central part cut out (esp. of rock etc. in boring). ● *v.tr.* remove the core from. □ **corer** *n.*

-core *comb. form* designating types of usu. abrasive popular music (*grindcore*).

coreopsis /ˌkɔri'ɒpsɪs, kɒ-/ *n.* (*pl.* same) any composite plant of the genus *Coreopsis*, having rayed usu. yellow flowers.

corgi /'kɔrgi/ *n.* (*pl.* **corgis**) (in full **Welsh corgi**) a short-legged breed of dog with a foxlike head.

coriander /ˌkɔri'ændər/ *n.* **1** a plant, *Coriandrum sativum*, with leaves used for flavouring and small round aromatic fruits. **2** (also **coriander seed**) the dried fruit used for flavouring curries etc.

Corinthian /kə'rɪnθiən/ ● *adj.* **1** of ancient Corinth in S Greece. **2** *Archit.* of an order characterized by ornate decoration and flared capitals with rows of acanthus leaves. ● *n.* a native of Corinth.

cork ● *n.* **1** the buoyant light brown bark of the cork oak. **2** a bottle stopper of cork or other material. **3** a float of cork used in fishing etc. **4** *Bot.* a protective layer of dead cells immediately below the bark of woody plants. **5** (*attrib.*) made of cork. ● *v.tr.* (often foll. by *up*) **1** stop or confine. **2** restrain (feelings etc.). **3** *Baseball* hollow out and fill (a bat) with cork illicitly to make it lighter. **4** blacken with burnt cork. □ **put a cork in it** *slang* shut up; be quiet. □ **corklike** *adj.*

corkboard *n. N Amer.* **1** board made of compressed cork. **2** a piece of this for posting bulletins etc.

cork boot *n. Cdn* (*BC*) a logger's boot with spiked soles.

corked *adj.* **1** stopped with a cork. **2** (of wine) spoiled by a decayed cork. **3** blackened with burnt cork.

corker *n. informal* **1** an excellent or astonishing person or thing. **2** something that puts an end to a discussion etc.

corking *adj. informal* strikingly impressive or excellent.

cork oak *n.* a S European oak, *Quercus suber*, from which cork is obtained.

corkscrew ● *n.* **1** a spirally twisted steel device for extracting corks from bottles. **2** (often *attrib.*) a thing with a spiral shape. ● *v.tr. & intr.* twist.

corky *adj.* (**-ier**, **-iest**) **1** corklike. **2** (of wine) corked.

corm *n.* an underground swollen stem base of some plants, e.g. gladiolus.

cormorant /'kɔrmərənt/ *n.* any diving, fish-eating water bird of the family Phalacrocoracidae, having lustrous black plumage.

corn[1] ● *n.* **1 a** a cereal plant, *Zea mays*, yielding large, edible, usu. yellow grains set in rows on a cob. **b** the cob or grains of this. **2 a** any cereal before or after harvesting, esp. the chief crop of a region. **b** a grain or seed of a cereal plant. **3** *informal* something corny or trite. ● *v.tr.* preserve (meat) with brine.

corn[2] *n.* a small area of horny usu. tender skin esp. on the toes, extending into subcutaneous tissue.

cornball *adj. N Amer.* = CORNY 1.

corn boil *n. N Amer.* a social gathering at which corn on the cob is boiled and eaten.

cornbread *n.* bread, esp. a quick bread, made from cornmeal.

corn broom *n. Curling* a straw broom.

corn chip *n. N Amer.* = TORTILLA CHIP.

corncob n. the cylindrical centre of an ear of corn, to which rows of grains are attached.

corncob pipe n. a tobacco pipe with a bowl made from a hollowed-out corncob.

corn cockle n. see COCKLE² 1.

corncrib n. a ventilated building for storing ears of corn.

cornea /'kɔːnɪə/ n. the transparent circular part of the front of the eyeball. □ **corneal** adj.

corn earworm n. **1** a moth, *Heliothis armigera* or *H. zea*, whose larvae are a pest of cultivated plants, esp. of corn in N America. **2** a larva of this moth.

corned beef n. **1** N Amer. beef brisket cured in brine and boiled. **2** low quality beef preserved in brine and saltpetre, chopped and pressed and packaged in tins.

corner ● n. **1** a place where converging sides or edges meet. **2** a projecting angle, esp. where two streets meet. **3** the internal space or recess formed by the meeting of two sides, esp. of a room. **4** a difficult position, esp. one from which there is no escape (*driven into a corner*). **5** a secluded or remote place. **6** a region or quarter, esp. a remote one (*from the four corners of the earth*). **7** the action or result of buying or controlling the whole available stock of a commodity, thereby dominating the market. **8** *Boxing & Wrestling* **a** an angle of the ring, esp. one where a contestant rests between rounds. **b** a contestant's supporters offering assistance at the corner between rounds. ● v. **1** tr. force (a person or animal) into a difficult or inescapable position. **2** tr. **a** establish a corner in (a commodity). **b** dominate (dealers or the market) in this way. **3** intr. (esp. of or in a vehicle) go around a corner. □ **in a person's corner** esp. N Amer. supporting a person. **just around the corner** informal very near, imminent. **turn a** (or **the**) **corner** pass from one situation to another, particularly making a decisive change for the better.

cornerback n. *Football* a defensive player or position covering the sideline behind the line of scrimmage.

cornerstone n. **1 a** a stone in a projecting angle of a wall. **b** a foundation stone. **2** an indispensable part or basis of something.

corner store n. a small local convenience store, esp. at a street corner.

cornet n. **1** a brass instrument resembling a trumpet but shorter and wider. **2** its player. □ **cornetist** n.

cornfield n. a field in which corn is being grown.

cornflake n. **1** (in pl.) a breakfast cereal of toasted flakes made from ground corn. **2** a flake of this.

corn flour n. flour made from corn.

cornflower n. any herbaceous plant of the genus *Centaurea*, esp. *C. cyanus*, with deep-blue flowers.

cornice /'kɔːnɪs/ n. **1** a moulding around the wall of a room just below the ceiling. **2** a horizontal moulded projection crowning a building etc.

Cornish ● adj. of or relating to Cornwall in SW England. ● n. **1** the ancient Celtic language of Cornwall. **2** a small, heavy breed of chicken used esp. in crossbreeding to produce roasting chickens.

Cornish hen n. = Rock CORNISH.

cornmeal n. meal made from corn.

corn on the cob n. corn cooked and eaten from the corncob.

corn pone n. US a simple cornbread.

corn roast n. N Amer. a party at which corn on the cob is cooked and eaten.

cornrow n. (usu. in pl.) each of a series of small tight braids made close to the head.

cornsilk n. the threadlike styles on an ear of corn.

corn snow n. *Skiing* a soft surface layer of coarse granular snow, formed during cold nights after warm days.

cornstalk n. N Amer. the stalk of a corn plant.

cornstarch n. esp. N Amer. purified starch from corn, used as a thickener and as an absorbent powder.

corn syrup n. N Amer. glucose syrup, esp. when made from corn flour.

cornucopia /ˌkɔːnjʊˈkoːpɪə/ n. **1 a** a symbol of plenty consisting of a goat's horn overflowing with flowers, fruit, and grain. **b** an ornamental vessel shaped like this. **2** an abundant supply.

corny adj. (**-ier, -iest**) **1** informal **a** trite. **b** feebly humorous. **c** sentimental. **d** old-fashioned; out of date. **2** of or abounding in corn. □ **corniness** n.

corolla /kəˈrɒlə, -roːlə/ n. *Bot.* a whorl or whorls of petals forming the inner envelope of a flower.

corollary /kəˈrɒlərɪ/ ● n. (pl. **-ies**) **1 a** a proposition that follows from (and is often appended to) one already proved. **b** an immediate deduction. **2** (often foll. by *of*) a natural result. ● adj. **1** supplementary, associated. **2** (often foll. by *to*) forming a corollary.

corona¹ /kəˈroːnə/ n. (pl. **coronae** /-niː/ or **coronas**) **1 a** a small circle of light round the sun or moon. **b** the rarefied gaseous envelope of the sun, seen as an irregularly shaped area of light around the moon's disc during a total solar eclipse. **2** *Bot.* a crownlike outgrowth from the inner side of a corolla.

corona² n. a long cigar with straight sides.

coronary ● adj. **1** of or relating to the heart. **2** of or relating to the coronary arteries. **3** (of blood vessels, nerves, etc.) resembling or encircling like a crown. ● n. (pl. **-ies**) (in full **coronary thrombosis**) a blockage of blood flow to the heart caused by a blood clot in a coronary artery.

coronary artery n. either of two arteries supplying blood to the heart.

coronary bypass n. a surgical procedure to relieve obstruction of the coronary arteries by creating an additional channel connecting the aorta to a point beyond the obstruction.

coronation n. the act or ceremony of crowning a sovereign or a sovereign's consort.

coroner n. a public official responsible for investigating violent, suspicious, or accidental deaths, and certifying deaths occurring outside hospital.

coronet n. **1** a small crown (esp. as worn, or used as a heraldic device, by a peer or peeress). **2** a circlet of precious materials, esp. as a woman's headdress or part of one. □ **coroneted** adj.

Corp. abbr. **1** N Amer. Corporation. **2** Corporal.

corpora pl. of CORPUS.

corporal¹ n. **1 a** (in the Canadian army and air force) a non-commissioned officer ranking above private. **b** (in the UK and hist. in Canada) a non-commissioned army or air force officer ranking next below sergeant. **2** (in some Canadian municipalities, the RCMP, and SQ) a police officer ranking below sergeant.

corporal² adj. of or relating to the human body (*compare* CORPOREAL). □ **corporality** n. **corporally** adv.

corporal punishment n. punishment inflicted on the body, esp. by beating.

corporate adj. **1** of or relating to business corporations (*corporate responsibility*). **2** forming a corporation (*corporate body*). **3** forming one body of many individuals. □ **corporately** adv.

corporate raider n. a person who mounts an unwelcome takeover bid by buying up a company's shares on the stock market, esp. one who makes a practice of doing so.

corporate welfare bum *n. Cdn slang derogatory* **1** a business perceived to be exploiting tax loopholes etc. or to be benefiting unduly from government subsidies or tax breaks. **2** a person who directs such a business.

corporation *n.* **1** a group of people authorized to act as an individual and recognized in law as a single entity, esp. in business. **2** the legal entity which carries on the business of a municipality.

corporatism *n.* a political ideology or system, esp. associated with fascist states, in which business, industry, labour, etc. are organized as corporate entities. ☐ **corporatist** *adj.*

corporeal *adj.* **1** bodily, physical, material, esp. as distinct from spiritual (compare CORPORAL[2]). **2** *Law* consisting of material objects (*corporeal property*). ☐ **corporeality** *n.* **corporeally** *adv.*

corps /kɔr/ *n.* (*pl.* **corps** /kɔrz/) **1** *Military* **a** a body of troops with special duties (*intelligence corps*). **b** a main subdivision of an army in the field, consisting of two or more divisions. **2** a body of people engaged in a special activity (*press corps*). **3** = CORPS DE BALLET.

corps de ballet /ˌkɔr də bæˈleɪ/ *n.* the group of dancers of the lowest rank in a ballet company.

corpse *n.* a dead (usu. human) body.

corps sergeant major *n.* (in the RCMP) an officer ranking above sergeant major and below inspector.

corpulent /ˈkɔrpjʊlənt/ *adj.* portly; fat. ☐ **corpulence** *n.* **corpulency** *n.*

corpus *n.* (*pl.* **corpora** /ˈkɔrpərə/ or **corpuses**) **1** a body or collection of writings, esp. by one author. **2** *Linguistics* a body of spoken or written material taken as a representative sample of a language, on which a linguistic analysis is based. **3** *Anat.* any of various masses of tissue in the body that have a distinct structure or function.

Corpus Christi /ˈkrɪsti/ *n. Christianity* a feast commemorating the Eucharist, observed the Thursday after Trinity Sunday or the next Sunday.

corpuscle /ˈkɔrpʌsəl/ *n.* a minute body or cell in an organism, esp. (in *pl.*) the red or white cells in the blood of vertebrates. ☐ **corpuscular** /kɔrˈpʌskjʊlər/ *adj.*

corpus luteum /ˈluːtiəm/ *n.* (*pl.* **corpora lutea**) *Anat.* a hormone-secreting mass of tissue that develops in the ovary after discharge of an ovum, remaining in existence only if pregnancy has begun.

corral ● *n. N Amer.* **1** a pen for horses etc. **2** a trap for capturing wild animals or fish. ● *v.tr.* (**corralled**, **corralling**) **1** drive or keep in or as in a corral (*he corralled us into the living room*). **2** *N Amer. informal* capture; get (*corralled some new members for the team*).

correct ● *adj.* **1** true, right, accurate. **2** (of conduct etc.) proper, right. **3** in accordance with good standards of taste etc. ● *v.* **1** *tr.* set right; amend (an error, omission, etc., or the person responsible for it). **2** *tr.* mark the errors in (written or printed work etc.). **3** *tr.* substitute the right thing for (the wrong one). **4** *tr.* **a** admonish or rebuke (a person). **b** punish (a person or fault). **5** *tr.* counteract (a harmful quality, ailment, etc.). **6** *tr.* adjust (an instrument etc.) to function accurately or accord with a standard. **7** *intr.* (of stock prices) stabilize, esp. after a sharp decline or increase. ☐ **correct for** adjust or recalculate (statistical data etc.) to compensate for a deviant factor. ☐ **correctable** *adj.* **correctly** *adv.* **correctness** *n.* **corrector** *n.*

correction *n.* **1 a** the act or process of correcting. **b** an instance of this. **2** a thing substituted for what is wrong. **3** *N Amer.* (usu. **corrections**) **a** the treatment of convicted offenders through incarceration, parole, etc. **b** the system which oversees such treatment.

correctional *adj.* **1** *N Amer.* of or pertaining to the corrections system (*correctional facility*). **2** of or pertaining to correction.

correction fluid *n.* a usu. white liquid that is painted over a typed or written error.

correction line *n. Cdn* (*Prairies*) *Surveying* **1** one of a set of parallel lines of latitude 24 miles apart along which correction is made for the discrepancy between straight surveying lines and northward-converging meridians. **2** a jog in a road where it intersects one of these lines.

corrective ● *adj.* serving or tending to correct or counteract something undesired or harmful. ● *n.* (usu. foll. by *to*) something, e.g. a theory or practice, that corrects or counteracts a tendency viewed as harmful. ☐ **correctively** *adv.*

correlate ● *v.* /ˈkɔrəˌleɪt, ˈkɒ-/ **1** *intr.* (foll. by *with*, *to*) have a mutual relation. **2** *tr.* (usu. foll. by *with*) bring into a mutual relation; establish the likely relation between. ● *n.* /ˈkɔrəˌlət, ˈkɒr-, -leɪt/ each of two related or complementary things (esp. so related that one implies the other).

correlation *n.* **1** a mutual relation between two or more things (*a correlation between smoking and cancer*). **2** the act or process of correlating. **3** *Statistics* a interdependence of variable quantities. **b** a quantity measuring the extent of this.

correlative /kəˈrelətɪv/ ● *adj.* **1** (often foll. by *with*, *to*) having a mutual relation; corresponding. **2** *Grammar* (of words) corresponding to each other and regularly used together (as *neither* and *nor*). ● *n.* a correlative word or thing. ☐ **correlatively** *adv.*

correspond *v.intr.* **1 a** (usu. foll. by *to*) be analogous or similar. **b** (usu. foll. by *to*) match; agree in amount, position, etc. (*my tally corresponds with yours*). **c** (usu. foll. by *with*, *to*) be in harmony or agreement. **2** (usu. foll. by *with*) communicate by interchange of letters.

correspondence *n.* **1** (usu. foll. by *with*, *to*, *between*) agreement, similarity, or harmony. **2 a** a communication by letters. **b** letters sent or received.

correspondence course *n.* a course of study conducted by mail.

correspondent *n.* **1** a person employed to contribute material for publication in a periodical or for broadcasting (*a CBC correspondent*). **2** a person who writes letters to a person or newspaper, esp. regularly. **3** a person or firm having regular business relations with another, esp. in another country.

corresponding *adj.* **1** identical; equivalent (*of corresponding height*). **2** analogous in position, purpose, etc. **3** belonging together as a unit (*a skirt with its corresponding jacket*). **4** handling correspondence (*corresponding secretary*). ☐ **correspondingly** *adv.*

corridor *n.* **1** a passage from which doors lead into rooms. **2** a passage in a railway car from which doors lead into compartments. **3** a densely populated belt of land with major overland and air transportation routes (*the Quebec-Windsor corridor*). **4 a** a strip of territory that runs through that of another state and secures access to the sea or some desired part. **b** a right-of-way reserved for utilities (*hydro corridor*). **5** a route to which aircraft are restricted, esp. over a foreign country. **6** an extent of land characterized by a specific activity, e.g. wildlife migration.

corridors of power *n.pl.* the upper echelons of

government, business, etc., where power and influence are considered to reside.

corroborate *v.tr.* confirm or give support to (a statement or belief, or the person holding it), esp. in relation to witnesses in a law court. □ **corroboration** *n.* **corroborative** *adj.*

corrode *v.* **1 a** *tr.* wear away, esp. by chemical action. **b** *intr.* be worn away; decay. **2** *tr.* destroy gradually (*corroded his self-esteem*). □ **corroded** *adj.*

corrosion *n.* **1** the process of corroding, esp. of a rusting metal. **2** damage caused by corroding.

corrosive ● *adj.* **1** tending to corrode or consume. **2** destructive; wearing (*the corrosive effects of famine*). ● *n.* a corrosive substance. □ **corrosively** *adv.* **corrosiveness** *n.*

corrugate *v.* **1** *tr.* form into alternate ridges and grooves, esp. to strengthen. **2** *tr.* & *intr.* contract into wrinkles or folds. □ **corrugation** *n.*

corrugated *adj.* formed into alternate ridges and grooves, esp. to strengthen (*corrugated cardboard*).

corrupt ● *adj.* **1** influenced by or using bribery or fraudulent activity. **2** morally depraved; wicked. **3** (of a text, language, etc.) harmed (esp. made suspect or unreliable) by errors or alterations. **4** (of a computer disk or program) contaminated with errors; unusable. ● *v.* **1** *tr.* & *intr.* make or become corrupt or depraved. **2** *tr.* affect or harm by errors or alterations. □ **corrupter** *n.* **corruptible** *adj.* **corruptly** *adv.*

corruption *n.* **1** use of corrupt practices, esp. bribery or fraud. **2** moral deterioration, esp. widespread. **3 a** irregular alteration (of a text, language, etc.) from its original state. **b** an irregularly altered form of a word. **4** decomposition.

corsage /kɔr'sɒʒ/ *n.* an arrangement of flowers worn by a woman at the front of a dress below the shoulder, or at the waist or wrist.

corselette /ˌkɔrsə'let/ *n.* a woman's foundation garment combining corset and bra.

corset *n.* **1** a closely-fitting undergarment worn by women to shape and support the torso. **2** a similar garment worn by men and women because of injury, weakness, or deformity. □ **corseted** *adj.*

Corsican /'kɔrsɪkən/ ● *adj.* of or relating to Corsica, an island off the west coast of Italy. ● *n.* **1** a native of Corsica. **2** the Italian dialect of Corsica.

cortège /kɔr'teʒ/ *n.* **1** a procession, esp. for a funeral. **2** a train of attendants.

cortex /'kɔrteks/ *n.* (*pl.* **cortices** /-tɪˌsiːz/) **1** the outer part of an organ, esp. of the brain (**cerebral cortex**) or kidneys (**renal cortex**). **2** *Bot.* **a** an outer layer of tissue immediately below the epidermis. **b** bark. □ **cortical** *adj.*

corticosteroid /ˌkɔrtɪkoʊ'steroɪd/ *n.* (also **corticoid**) **1** any of a group of steroid hormones produced in the adrenal cortex and concerned with regulation of salts and carbohydrates, inflammation, and sexual physiology. **2** an analogous synthetic steroid.

cortisone /'kɔrtɪˌzoʊn/ *n.* a steroid hormone produced by the adrenal cortex or synthetically, used medicinally esp. against inflammation and allergy.

Cortland *n. N Amer.* a red variety of apple.

corundum /kə'rʌndəm/ *n.* extremely hard crystallized alumina, used esp. as an abrasive, and varieties of which, e.g. ruby, are gemstones.

corvée /'kɔrveɪ/ *n. hist.* **1** a day's work of unpaid labour due to a feudal lord from a vassal. **2** labour enforced by statute, esp. on road maintenance etc.

corvette *n.* a small naval escort vessel.

corymb /'kɔrɪmb, 'kɒr-, -ɪm/ *n. Bot.* a flat-topped clus-ter of flowers with the flower stalks proportionally longer down the stem.

cos /kɒs/ *n.* = ROMAINE.

Cos. /koːz/ *abbr.* Companies.

Cosa Nostra /ˌkoːzə 'nɒstrə/ *n.* a US criminal organization resembling and related to the Mafia.

co-sign *v.tr.* & *intr.* sign (a document, esp. a cheque, lease, etc.) jointly with another. □ **co-signer** *n.*

cosine /'koːsaɪn/ *n. Math.* the ratio of the side adjacent to an acute angle (in a right-angled triangle) to the hypotenuse.

cosmetic ● *adj.* **1** intended to adorn or beautify the body, esp. the face. **2** intended to improve only appearances (*a cosmetic change*). **3** (of surgery) aimed at improving, restoring, or modifying the appearance. ● *n.* (often in *pl.*) a cosmetic preparation, esp. for the face. □ **cosmetically** *adv.*

cosmetic bag *n. Cdn* a usu. zippered bag with a waterproof lining, for storing cosmetics etc.

cosmic *adj.* **1** of the universe or cosmos, esp. as distinct from the earth. **2** of or for space travel. **3** immeasurably vast. □ **cosmically** *adv.*

cosmic dust *n.* small particles of matter distributed throughout space.

cosmic rays *n.pl.* (also **cosmic radiation** *n.*) radiation from outer space that reaches the earth from all directions, usu. with high energy and penetrative power.

cosmogony /kɒz'mɒɡəni/ *n.* (*pl.* **-ies**) **1** a theory or account of the origin of the universe. **2** the study of the origin of the universe. □ **cosmogonic** /-mə'ɡɒnɪk/ *adj.* **cosmogonical** *adj.* **cosmogonist** *n.*

cosmology /kɒz'mɒlədʒi/ *n.* **1** the study of the origin and development of the universe. **2** an account or theory of the origin of the universe. □ **cosmological** *adj.* **cosmologist** *n.*

cosmonaut *n.* a Russian or *hist.* Soviet astronaut.

cosmopolitan ● *adj.* **1 a** of or from or knowing many parts of the world. **b** consisting of people from many or all parts. **2 a** free from national limitations or prejudices. **b** sophisticated; worldly. **3** *Ecology* (of a plant, animal, etc.) widely distributed. ● *n.* a cosmopolitan person. □ **cosmopolitanism** *n.*

cosmos[1] /'kɒzmoːs, -məs/ *n.* **1** the universe, esp. as a well-ordered whole. **2** an ordered system of ideas etc.

cosmos[2] *n.* any composite plant of the genus *Cosmos*, bearing single dahlia-like blossoms of various colours frequently grown in gardens.

Cossack /'kɒsæk/ ● *n.* **1** a member of a people living on the northern shores of the Black and Caspian seas, originally famous for their military skill. **2** a member of a Cossack military unit. ● *adj.* of, relating to, or characteristic of the Cossacks.

cossack *n. Cdn* (*Nfld*) a hooded pullover made of animal skin, swanskin, canvas, or calico.

cosset /'kɒsət/ *v.tr.* (**cosseted, cosseting**) (usu. in *passive*) pamper.

cost ● *v.* (*past* and *past part.* **cost**) **1** *tr.* be obtainable for (a sum of money); have as a price. **2** *tr.* **a** involve as a loss or sacrifice (*it cost him his life*). **b** necessitate or involve the expenditure of (time, trouble, etc.) **3** *tr.* (*past* and *past part.* **costed**) fix or estimate the cost or price of. **4** *informal* **a** *tr.* be costly to (*that ring will cost you*). **b** *intr.* be costly. ● *n.* **1** what a thing costs; the price paid or to be paid. **2** a loss or sacrifice; an expenditure of time, effort, etc. **3** (in *pl.*) **a** expenses for running a home or business (*cutting costs*). **b** legal expenses, esp. those allowed in favour of the winning party or against the losing party in a suit. □ **at all costs** (or **at any cost**) no matter what the cost or risk may be. **at cost** at the initial cost; at cost price. **at the cost of** at the expense of losing or sacrificing. **cost a person dear** (or **dearly**) involve a person in a high cost or a heavy penalty. **to a person's cost** with loss or disadvantage to a person.

co-star ● n. **1** a film, television, or stage star appearing with another or other stars of equal importance. **2** a film, television, or stage star whose status in a production is slightly below that of a star. ● v. (**-starred, -starring**) **1** intr. take part as a co-star. **2** tr. (of a production) include as a co-star.

Costa Rican /ˌkɒstə ˈriːkən/ ● adj. of or relating to Costa Rica, a republic in Central America, or its people. ● n. a native or inhabitant of Costa Rica.

cost-benefit adj. assessing the relation between the cost of an operation and the value of the resulting benefits (cost-benefit analysis).

cost-conscious adj. aware of cost or costs.

cost-cutting n. the cutting of costs (often attrib.).

cost-effective adj. effective or productive in relation to its cost. □ **cost-effectively** adv. **cost-effectiveness** n.

costing n. (often in pl.) **1** the determination of the cost of producing or undertaking something. **2** the cost so arrived at.

costly adj. (**-ier, -iest**) **1** costing much; expensive. **2** involving great loss or sacrifice (a costly mistake). **3** of great value. □ **costliness** n.

cost of living n. the level of prices esp. of the basic necessities of life (often attrib.: cost-of-living index).

cost price n. the price paid for a thing by a person who later sells it.

costume ● n. **1** a style or fashion of dress, esp. that of a particular place, time, nationality, or class. **2** an ensemble of unusual or period clothes worn at Halloween etc. (often attrib.: costume party). **3** clothing for a particular activity (riding costume). **4** a theatrical performer's clothes for a part. ● v.tr. (esp. in passive or adj.) provide with a costume. □ **costuming** n.

costume jewellery n. relatively inexpensive jewellery made of metal, wood, plastic, etc., often set with artificial or semi-precious stones.

cosy var. of COZY.

cot n. N Amer. a small folding or portable bed.

cotangent n. Math. the ratio of the side adjacent to an acute angle (in a right-angled triangle) to the opposite side.

coterie /ˈkoʊtəri/ n. a group of people who associate closely; clique.

Côtes du Rhône /ˌkoːtduːˈroːn/ n. a light red wine produced in the southern Rhone valley in France.

cotoneaster /kəˌtoʊniːˈæstər/ n. any shrub of the genus Cotoneaster, bearing usu. bright red berries.

cottage ● n. **1** N Amer. a dwelling used for vacation purposes, usu. located in a rural area near a lake or river (also attrib.: cottage country). **2** Cdn (Que.) a small, two-storey house in the city. ● v.intr. N Amer. vacation at a cottage. □ **cottagey** adj. **cottaging** n.

cottage cheese n. soft white cheese made from skimmed milk curds.

cottage country n. Cdn an area in which there are many cottages.

cottage garden n. an informal garden well-stocked with colourful traditional hardy plants.

cottage hospital n. Cdn (Nfld) a small hospital with non-specialist medical services.

cottage industry n. a business activity partly or wholly carried on at home.

cottager n. N Amer. a person vacationing at or living in a cottage.

cottage roll n. Cdn a pickled, boneless, prepared ham from the pork butt.

cotter n. **1** a bolt or wedge for securing parts of machinery etc. **2** (in full **cotter pin**) a split pin that opens after passing through a hole.

cotton ● n. **1** a soft white fibrous substance covering the seeds of certain plants. **2 a** (in full **cotton plant**) such a plant, esp. any of the genus Gossypium. **b** cotton plants cultivated as a crop. **3** thread or cloth made from the fibre. ● v.intr. N Amer. take a liking to (a person). □ **cotton on** (often foll. by to) informal begin to understand. □ **cottony** adj.

cotton batting n. N Amer. (Cdn also **cotton batten**) fluffy cotton wadding used for crafts, first aid, etc.

cotton candy n. N Amer. candy floss.

cotton gin n. a machine for separating cotton from its seeds.

cotton grass n. a sedge of the genus Eriophorum, with fruiting heads of long white cottony hairs.

cotton-pickin' adj. (also **cotton-picking**) esp. US slang damned (you're a cotton-pickin' liar!).

cottontail n. a rabbit of the N American genus Sylvilagus, most species of which have a white fluffy underside to the tail.

cottonwood n. any of several poplars, native to N America, having seeds covered in white cottony hairs.

cotyledon /ˌkɒtɪˈliːdən/ n. an embryonic leaf in seed-bearing plants.

couch¹ ● n. **1** an upholstered piece of furniture for several people; a sofa. **2** a long padded seat with a headrest at one end, esp. one on which a psychiatrist's or doctor's patient reclines during examination. ● v.tr. **1** (foll. by in) (usu. in passive) express in words of a specified kind (couched in simple language). **2** cause (an animal) to lie down.

couch² n. (in full **couch grass**) any of several grasses of the genus Agropyron, esp. A. repens, having long creeping roots.

couch potato n. esp. N Amer. slang a person who spends much leisure time watching television.

cougar n. N Amer. a moderately large carnivorous mammal of the cat family, Felis concolor, with a tawny or greyish coat and long black-tipped tail, found in parts of N and S America.

cough ● v.intr. **1** expel air from the lungs with a sudden sharp sound produced by abrupt opening of the glottis, to remove an obstruction or congestion. **2** (of an engine, gun, etc.) make a similar sound. ● n. **1** an act of coughing. **2** a condition of the respiratory organs causing coughing. **3** a tendency to cough. □ **cough up** (also **cough out**) **1** eject by coughing. **2** slang bring out or hand over (money or information) reluctantly. **3** N Amer. slang yield or eject (cough up the puck). □ **cougher** n.

cough drop n. a medicated lozenge to relieve a cough.

cough syrup n. (also **cough medicine**) a liquid medicine to relieve a cough.

could v.aux. (3rd. sing. **could**) past of CAN¹, used esp.: **1 a** in reported speech (she said she could come). **b** to express the conditional mood (he could have been on time if he had left earlier). **2** to express a question or polite request (could you please come?). **3** to express probability (that could be right). **4** to ask permission (could I leave?). **5** to offer a suggestion, advice, etc. (you could try looking it up). **6** to express habitual action (when I was a child, I could not play hockey).

couldn't contraction could not.

coulee /'ku:li/ n. N Amer. (West) a deep ravine with steep sides, formed by heavy rain or melting snow.

coulis /'ku:li/ n. (pl. same) a purée of fruit, tomatoes, etc., thin enough to pour.

coulomb /'ku:lɒm/ n. Electricity the SI unit of electric charge, equal to the quantity of electricity conveyed in one second by a current of one ampere. Symbol: **C**.

coulter /'ko:ltər/ n. a vertical cutting wheel or blade fixed in front of a ploughshare.

Coun. abbr. Cdn & Brit. Councillor.

council n. **1 a** an advisory, deliberative, or administrative body of people formally constituted and meeting regularly. **b** a meeting of such a body. **2** the elected administrative body of a municipality. **3** a body of persons chosen as advisers (Privy Council). **4** an ecclesiastical assembly. **5** = GENERAL COUNCIL.

councillor n. **1** esp. Cdn & Brit. an elected member of a municipal council. **2** a member of a council. **3** Cdn hist. (in PEI) one of the two representatives elected to the Legislative Assembly in each riding (compare ASSEMBLYMAN 2). □ **councillorship** n.

counsel ● n. **1** advice, esp. formally given. **2** consultation, esp. to seek or give advice. **3** (pl. same) a lawyer; a body of these advising in a case. **4** a plan of action. ● v.tr. **(counselled, counselling) 1** (often foll. by to + infin.) advise (a person). **2 a** give advice to (a person) on social or personal problems, esp. professionally. **b** assist or guide (a person) in resolving personal difficulties. **3** (often foll. by that) recommend (a course of action). □ **keep one's own counsel** not confide in others. **take counsel** (usu. foll. by with) consult.

counselling n. **1** the act or process of giving counsel. **2** the process of assisting and guiding clients, esp. by a trained person on a professional basis, to resolve esp. personal, social, or psychological problems and difficulties (compare COUNSEL v. 2a).

counsellor n. (also **counselor**) **1** a person who gives counsel; an adviser. **2** a person trained to give guidance on personal, social, or psychological problems. **3** N Amer. any of the supervisors of a children's camp.

count¹ ● v. **1** tr. determine the total number or amount of. **2** intr. repeat numbers in ascending order; conduct a reckoning. **3 a** tr. (often foll. by in) include in one's reckoning or plan (you can count me in). **b** intr. be included in a reckoning or plan. **4** tr. consider (a person or thing) to be (lucky etc.) (count yourself lucky). **5** intr. (often foll. by for) have value; matter (that try doesn't count). **6** intr. depend or rely on (I'm counting on you). ● n. **1 a** the act of counting; a reckoning (after a count of fifty). **b** the sum total of a reckoning (pollen count). **2** Law each charge in an indictment (guilty on ten counts). **3** a count of up to ten seconds by a referee when a boxer is knocked down. **4** Politics the act of counting the votes after an election. **5** one of several points under discussion (you're wrong on three counts). **6** Baseball the number of balls and strikes called against a batter during a single at-bat. □ **count against** be reckoned to the disadvantage of. **count one's blessings** be grateful for what one has. **count one's chickens (before they're hatched)** be over-optimistic or hasty in anticipating good fortune. **count the cost 1** consider the risks before taking action. **2** suffer the consequences of a careless or foolish action. **count the days (or hours** etc.) be impatient. **count down** recite numbers backwards to zero, esp. as part of a rocket-launching procedure. **count on (or upon) 1** depend on, rely on; expect confidently. **2** make allowance for. **count on (the fingers of) one hand** reckon as no more than five. **count out 1** count while taking

from a stock. **2** complete a count of ten seconds over (a fallen boxer etc.), indicating defeat. **3** (in children's games) select (a player) for dismissal or a special role by use of a counting rhyme etc. **4** informal exclude from a plan or reckoning (count me out). **count sheep** imagine sheep jumping over a fence and count them, to combat insomnia. **count up** find the sum of. **down** (or **out**) **for the count 1** Boxing defeated by being unable to rise within ten seconds. **2** informal a defeated or demoralized. **b** soundly asleep. **keep count** take note of how many there have been etc. **lose count** fail to take note of the number etc. **not counting** excluding from the reckoning. **stand up and be counted** state publicly one's support. **take the count** Boxing be defeated.

count² n. (in some countries) a noble corresponding in rank to an English earl.

countable adj. **1** that can be counted. **2** Grammar (of a noun) that can form a plural or be used with the indefinite article.

countdown n. **1 a** the act of counting down, esp. at the launching of a rocket etc. **b** the procedures carried out during this time. **2** the final moments before any significant event.

countenance /'kauntənəns/ ● n. **1 a** the face. **b** the facial expression. **2** composure. **3** favour; moral support. ● v.tr. **1** give approval to (an act etc.) (cannot countenance this). **2** encourage (a person or a practice).

counter¹ n. **1 a** a long flat-topped fixture in a store, bank, etc., across which business is conducted with customers. **b** a similar structure used for serving food etc. in a cafeteria or bar. **c** N Amer. a flat surface in a kitchen, usu. on top of a low cabinet, at a height suitable for working standing up, on which food is prepared. **2 a** a small disc or other object used for keeping score etc., esp. in some board games. **b** a token representing a coin. **c** something used in bargaining; a pawn. **3** an apparatus used for counting. **4** Physics an apparatus used for counting individual ionizing particles etc. **5** a person or thing that counts. □ **over the counter** by ordinary retail purchase, without a prescription or permit etc. **under the counter** (esp. of the sale of scarce goods) surreptitiously, esp. illegally.

counter² ● v. **1** tr. **a** oppose, contradict (countered our proposal with their own). **b** meet by a countermove. **2** intr. **a** make a countermove. **b** make an opposing statement. **3** intr. Boxing give a return blow while parrying. ● adv. **1** in the opposite direction. ● contrary (counter to my wishes). ● adj. **1** opposed; opposite. **2** duplicate; serving as a check. ● n. **1** a parry; a countermove. **2** something opposite or opposed. □ **act** (or **go) counter to** disobey (instructions etc.). **run counter to** act contrary to.

counter- comb. form denoting: **1** retaliation, opposition, or rivalry (counter-threat). **2** opposite direction (counter-current). **3** correspondence, duplication, or substitution (counterpart; countersign).

counteract v.tr. **1** hinder or oppose by contrary action. **2** neutralize. □ **counteraction** n.

counter-argument n. an argument in reply to or opposition to another.

counterattack ● n. an attack in reply to an attack by an enemy or opponent. ● v.tr. & intr. attack in reply.

counterbalance ● n. **1** a weight balancing another. **2** an argument, force, etc., balancing another. ● v.tr. act as a counterbalance to.

counterclaim ● n. **1** a claim made against another claim. **2** Law a claim made by a defendant in a suit against the plaintiff. ● *v.tr. & intr.* make a counterclaim (for).

counter-clockwise *N Amer.* ● *adv.* in a curve opposite in direction to the movement of the hands of a clock. ● *adj.* moving counter-clockwise.

counterculture *n.* a culture having values or lifestyles that are in opposition to those of the current accepted culture. □ **countercultural** *adj.*

counterfeit /ˈkaʊntɜrfɪt / ● *adj.* **1** (of money etc.) made in imitation; not genuine; forged. **2** (of a claimant etc.) pretended. ● *n.* a forgery; an imitation. ● *v.tr.* **1 a** imitate fraudulently (money, documents, recordings, etc.); forge. **b** make an imitation of. **2** simulate (feelings etc.) (*counterfeited interest*). **3** resemble closely. □ **counterfeiter** *n.* **counterfeiting** *n.*

counter-insurgency *n.* (usu. *attrib.*) action against insurrection (*counter-insurgency operations*).

counter-intelligence *n.* action taken to frustrate enemy spying.

counterintuitive *adj.* contrary to intuition.

counterirritant *n.* **1** *Med.* something used to produce surface irritation of the skin, thereby counteracting more painful symptoms. **2** anything resembling a counterirritant in its effects. □ **counterirritation** *n.*

counterman *n.* (*pl.* **-men**) *N Amer.* a person who works behind a counter, e.g. in a cafeteria or diner.

countermeasure *n.* an action taken to counteract a danger, threat, etc.

countermove ● *n.* a move or action in opposition to another. ● *v.intr.* make a countermove.

counteroffensive *n.* **1** *Military* an attack made against an attacking force. **2** any attack made from a defensive position.

counterpart *n.* **1 a** a person or thing extremely like another. **b** a person or thing forming a natural complement or equivalent to another. **2** one of two copies of a legal document.

counterpoint ● *n.* **1 a** the art or technique of setting, writing, or playing a melody or melodies in conjunction with another, according to fixed rules. **b** a melody played in conjunction with another. **2** a contrasting element, theme, etc. **3** contrast. ● *v.tr.* **1** *Music* add counterpoint to. **2** set (an argument, theme, etc.) in contrast to (a main element).

counterpoise ● *n.* **1** a force etc. equivalent to another on the opposite side. **2** a state of equilibrium. **3** a counterbalancing weight. ● *v.tr.* **1** counterbalance. **2** compensate. **3** bring into or keep in equilibrium.

counterproductive *adj.* having the opposite of the desired effect.

counterpunch ● *n.* a punch or attack given in return; a boxer's counter. ● *v.intr.* make a counterpunch or counterpunches. □ **counterpuncher** *n.*

counter-reformation *n.* **1** (**Counter-Reformation**) *hist.* the reform of the Catholic Church in the 16th and 17th c. in response to the Reformation. **2** a reformation running counter to another.

counter-revolution *n.* a revolution opposing a former one or reversing its results. □ **counter-revolutionary** *adj. & n.* (*pl.* **-ies**).

countersign ● *v.tr.* add a signature to (a document previously signed by oneself or another). ● *n.* a sign or signal used in response to another, esp. a watchword or password spoken to a person on guard. □ **counter-signature** *n.*

countersink ● *v.tr.* (*past* and *past part.* **-sunk**) **1** enlarge and bevel (the rim of a hole) so that a screw or bolt can be inserted flush with the surface. **2** sink (a

screw etc.) in such a hole. ● *n.* a tool used to countersink a hole.

counter-tenor *n.* **1 a** an adult male alto singing voice. **b** a singer with this voice. **2** a part written for counter-tenor.

counterterrorism *n.* measures to combat terrorism.

countertop *n.* esp. *N Amer.* the flat working surface of a counter, esp. in a kitchen.

countervail ● *v.* **1** *tr.* counterbalance. **2** *tr. & intr.* (often foll. by *against*) oppose forcefully and usu. successfully. ● *n.* *Cdn* a countervailing duty.

countervailing duty *n.* a tax put on imports to offset a subsidy in the exporting country or a tax on similar goods not from abroad.

counterweight *n.* a counterbalancing weight.

countess *n.* **1** the wife or widow of a count or an earl. **2** a woman holding the rank of count or earl.

countless *adj.* too many to be counted.

countrified *adj.* often *derogatory* rural or rustic.

country *n.* (*pl.* **-ies**) **1** the territory of a nation with its own government; a nation. **2** (often *attrib.*) **a** a rural districts as opposed to cities or towns (*a country girl*). **b** styles of clothing, fabric, furnishing, etc. supposed to be typically rural, usu. inspired by historical fashions. **3** the land of a person's birth or citizenship. **4** a territory marked by some particular characteristic (*maple country*). **5** an area of interest or knowledge. **6** a region associated with a particular person, esp. a writer or painter (*Leacock country*). **7** a national population, esp. as voters. **8 a** = COUNTRY AND WESTERN. **b** = NEW COUNTRY. **9** *Cdn* (*Nfld*) **a** the thin strip of settlements along the coast. **b** the interior of Newfoundland and Labrador. □ **across country** not keeping to roads. **by a country mile** *N Amer.* informal by a great extent. **go** (or **appeal**) **to the country** *Cdn & Brit.* test public opinion by dissolving Parliament and holding a general election.

country and western *n.* a style of music combining elements of British folk music as preserved in the rural or southern areas of N America, cowboy songs, and other styles of popular music, often dealing with themes of lost love.

country bumpkin *n.* = BUMPKIN.

country club *n.* a suburban sport and social club, with facilities for golf and usu. tennis, etc.

country elevator *n.* *Cdn* (*Prairies*) a grain elevator equipped to unload grain from trucks, store it, and load it into rail cars.

countryfied *var. of* COUNTRIFIED.

country food *n.* *Cdn hist.* game, fish, or other foods that can be obtained while in the bush.

country house *n.* **1** a usu. large house in the country, esp. the residence of a wealthy person. **2** *Cdn* (*Que.*) a summer cottage.

country kitchen *n.* *N Amer.* a large airy kitchen, usu. with pine or oak kitchen cabinets.

countryman *n.* (*pl.* **-men**) **1** a person living in a rural area. **2 a** (also **fellow-countryman**) a person of one's own country or region. **b** (often in *comb.*) a person from a specified country or region.

country marriage *n.* *Cdn hist.* a common-law marriage between a fur trader of European descent and an Aboriginal or Metis woman.

country music *n.* **1** = COUNTRY AND WESTERN. **2** = NEW COUNTRY.

country rock *n.* a blend of rock music with country and western.

countryside n. **1 a** a rural area. **b** rural areas in general. **2** the inhabitants of a rural area.

country store n. N Amer. a rural general store.

countrywide adj. extending throughout a nation.

country wife n. Cdn hist. the Indian or Metis common-law wife of a fur trader.

countrywoman n. (pl. **-women**) **1** a woman living in a rural area. **2 a** a person of one's own country or region. **b** (often in comb.) a person from a specified country or region.

county n. (pl. **-ies**) any of the territorial divisions of some countries or provinces, for electoral, judicial, or local government purposes.

county council n. the elected governing body of an administrative county. □ **county councillor** n.

county seat n. (also **county town**) the administrative capital of a county.

coup /kuː/ n. **1** a notable or successful stroke or move. **2** = COUP D'ÉTAT. **3** (among Plains Indian peoples) the act of touching an enemy in battle and escaping, considered a heroic act. □ **count coup** (among Plains Indian peoples) perform a coup or recount having done so.

coup de grâce /ˌkuː də ˈgrɒs/ n. (pl. **coups de grâce** pronunc. same) a finishing stroke, esp. to kill a wounded animal or person.

coup d'état /ˌkuː deɪˈtɒ/ n. (pl. **coups d'état** pronunc. same) a violent or illegal seizure of power.

coupe[1] /kuːp/ n. a two-door car with a hard roof, esp. one seating only two persons.

coupe[2] n. **1** a shallow glass or dish used for serving fruit, ice cream, etc. **2** fruit etc. served in this.

couple ● n. **1** (usu. foll. by of; often treated as sing.) **a** two (a couple of girls). **b** about two (a couple of hours). ¶The use of couple without a following of, as in they'd had a couple beers, is highly informal and should be avoided in writing. **2** (often treated as sing.) **a** two people who are romantically involved. **b** a pair of partners in dancing, figure skating, etc. ● v. **1** tr. fasten or link together; connect (esp. railway cars etc.). **2** tr. (often foll. by together, with) associate in thought or speech (high unemployment coupled with inflation). **3** tr. & intr. (often foll. by with, up (with)) bring or come together as companions or partners. **4** intr. copulate.

coupler n. **1** a person or thing that couples or links things together. **2** = COUPLING 1. **3** a transformer used for connecting electric circuits.

couplet n. two successive lines of verse, usu. rhyming and of the same length.

coupling n. **1 a** a link connecting railway cars etc. **b** a device for connecting parts of machinery. **2** a thing that couples or links things together. **3** the act of a person that couples.

coupon /ˈkuːpɒn, ˈkjuː-/ n. **1** a certificate entitling the bearer to a discount on a purchase etc. **2** a form in a newspaper, magazine, etc., which may be filled in and sent as an application for a purchase, information, etc. **3** a voucher given with a retail purchase, a certain number of which entitle the holder to a discount, premium, etc. **4** a detachable portion of a bond etc. which is given up in return for a payment of interest. **5** a detachable ticket entitling the holder to a ration of food etc., esp. in wartime.

courage n. the ability to disregard fear; bravery. □ **courage of one's convictions** the courage to act on one's beliefs. **lose courage** become less brave. **pluck up** (or **take**) **courage** muster one's courage.

courageous adj. brave, fearless. □ **courageously** adv. **courageousness** n.

coureur de bois /ˌkʊrɜr də ˈbwɒ/ n. Cdn hist. (pl. **coureurs de bois** pronunc. same) a French or Metis fur trader, esp. one employed by the Hudson's Bay or North West Companies.

courier ● n. **1** a person or company hired to convey documents, packages etc. from sender to recipient. **2** a person who transports drugs, arms, etc. illegally, esp. from one country to another. **3** a special messenger. ● v.tr. ship (a package etc.) by courier.

course ● n. **1** a continuous onward movement or progression. **2 a** a line along which a person or thing moves; a direction taken (the course of the river). **b** a correct or intended direction or line of movement. **c** the direction taken by a ship or aircraft. **3 a** the ground on which a race (or other sport involving extensive linear movement) takes place. **b** a series of fences, hurdles, or other obstacles to be crossed in a race etc. **c** = GOLF COURSE. **4 a** a series of lectures, lessons, etc., in a particular subject. **b** a book for such a course (A Modern French Course). **5** any of the successive parts of a meal. **6** a sequence of medical treatment etc. (a course of antibiotics). **7** a line of conduct. **8** a continuous horizontal layer of brick, stone, shingles, etc., in a building. **9** a channel in which water flows. ● v. **1** intr. (esp. of liquid) run, esp. fast (blood coursed through her veins). **2** tr. & intr. **a** use (hounds) to hunt. **b** pursue (hares etc.) in hunting. □ **the course of nature** ordinary events or procedure. **in the course of** during. **in the course of time** as time goes by; eventually. **of course** naturally; as is or was to be expected; admittedly. **on** (or **off**) **course** following (or deviating from) the desired direction or goal. **run** (or **take**) **its course** (esp. of an illness) complete its natural development.

coursebook n. a book designed for use on a particular course of study.

courser n. **1** literary a swift horse. **2** a dog used in coursing.

courseware n. material (esp. computer programs) designed for use in an educational or training course.

coursework n. the work done during a course of study, esp. when counting towards a student's grade.

court ● n. **1** (in full **court of law**) **a** an assembly of a judge or judges and other persons acting as a tribunal in civil and criminal cases. **b** a regular session of a court. **c** a courtroom or courthouse. **2 a** a demarcated quadrangular area for playing certain games (tennis court). **b** a subdivision of this area. **3 a** a small enclosed street adjoining a larger one. **b** (in proper names) a large house, apartment building, street, etc. **c** = ATRIUM 1b. **4 a** the establishment, retinue, and courtiers of a sovereign. **b** a sovereign and his or her councillors, constituting a ruling power. **c** a sovereign's residence. **d** an assembly held by a sovereign. **5** attention paid to a person whose favour, love, or interest is sought (paid court to her). **6** (in Presbyterian and United churches) any of several governing bodies made up of clergy and elders, e.g. sessions etc. ● v.tr. **1** a try to win the affection or favour of (a person). **b** pay amorous attention to (courting couples). **2** seek to win (applause, fame, etc.). **3** invite (misfortune) by one's actions (courting disaster). □ **go to court** take legal action. **hold court** preside (esp. pompously) over a group of attendants, admirers, etc. **in court** appearing as a party or an advocate in a court of law. **out of court 1** (of a plaintiff) not entitled to be heard. **2** (of a settlement) arranged before a hearing or judgment can take place.

courteous adj. polite, kind, or considerate in manner. □ **courteously** adv. **courteousness** n.

courtesan /ˌkɔːtɪˈzæn, ˈkɔːt-/ n. hist. **1** a prostitute, esp. one with wealthy or upper-class clients. **2** the mistress of a wealthy man.

courtesy n. (pl. **-ies**) **1** courteous behaviour; good manners. **2** a courteous act. □ **by courtesy** by favour, not by right. **by courtesy of** with the formal permission of (a person etc.). **courtesy of** thanks to.

courtesy title n. a title held by courtesy, usu. having no legal validity.

courthouse n. a building in which a judicial court is held.

courtier n. a person who attends or frequents a sovereign's court.

courtly adj. (**-ier, -iest**) **1** polished or refined in manners. **2** obsequious. □ **courtliness** n.

courtly love n. the conventional medieval tradition of knightly love for a lady, and the etiquette used in its (esp. literary) expression.

court martial ● n. (pl. **courts martial**) a judicial court for trying members of the armed services. ● v.tr. (**court-martial**) (**-martialled, -martialling**) try by a court martial.

Court of Appeal n. a court of law hearing appeals against judgments in lower courts, esp. (in Canada) the highest appeal court in a province or territory.

court of first instance n. a court of primary jurisdiction.

court order n. a direction by a court or judge, usu. requiring a person to do or not do something.

court reporter n. N Amer. **1** an official stenographer in a law court. **2** a journalist who reports on trials, etc.

courtroom n. the place or room in which a court of law meets.

courtship n. **1 a** a courting, esp. with intent to marry. **b** the behaviour of male and female animals, birds, etc. prior to and during mating. **c** a period of courtship. **2** an attempt, often protracted, to gain advantage by flattery, attention, etc.

court shoe n. N Amer. an athletic shoe with a non-marking sole, worn esp. when playing sports on a wooden floor, such as squash or racquetball.

court tennis n. N Amer. a type of tennis played on an indoor walled court.

courtyard n. an area enclosed by walls or buildings, often opening off a street.

couscous /ˈkuːskuːs/ n. **1** a type of N African pasta in granules made from crushed durum wheat. **2** a dish of this, often with meat or fruit added.

cousin n. **1 a** (also **first cousin**) the child of one's uncle or aunt. **b** any other relative with whom one shares a common ancestor; a second cousin, etc. **c** a person who is married to one's cousin. **2** a person or thing related to another by common features etc. **3** (usu. in pl.) applied to the people of kindred races or nations (our American cousins).

couth /kuːθ/ jocular ● adj. cultured; well-mannered. ● n. good manners; cultured behaviour.

couture /kuːˈtʃʊr, -tuːr, -tjuːr/ ● n. **1** the design and manufacture of fashionable clothes. **2** = HAUTE COUTURE. ● adj. (of clothing) highly fashionable.

couturier /kuːˈtʊriˌei/ n. a person who designs and oversees the making of high-fashion clothes.

couturière /kuːˌtʊriˈer/ n. a woman who designs and oversees the making of high-fashion clothes.

covalence /koˈveilns/ n. (also **covalency**) **1** the linking of atoms by a covalent bond. **2** the number of pairs of electrons an atom can share with another.

covalent adj. **1** relating to, designating, or character-ized by chemical bonds. **2** formed by sharing of electrons usu. in pairs by two atoms in a molecule (covalent bond). □ **covalently** adv.

cove n. **1** a small, esp. sheltered, bay or other indentation in the shoreline of an ocean, lake, river, etc. **2** a sheltered recess.

covenant ● n. **1** an agreement; a contract. **2** Law **a** a contract drawn up under a seal. **b** a clause of a covenant. **3** (**Covenant**) Bible an agreement between God and a person, nation, etc. See also ARK OF THE COVENANT. ● v.tr. & intr. agree, esp. by legal covenant.

cover ● v. **1** tr. (often foll. by with) protect or conceal by means of a cloth, lid, etc. **2** tr. **a** extend over; occupy the whole surface of (covered in dirt). **b** (often foll. by with) strew thickly or thoroughly (covered the floor with straw). **c** be a covering to (the blanket scarcely covered her). **3** tr. protect; clothe. **4** tr. include; comprise; deal with (the talk covered recent discoveries). **5** tr. travel (a specified distance). **6** tr. Journalism **a** report (events, a meeting, etc.). **b** investigate as a reporter. **7** tr. be enough to defray (expenses, a bill, etc.) ($20 should cover it). **8 a** refl. take precautionary measures so as to protect oneself (had covered myself by saying I might be late). **b** intr. (foll. by for) deputize or stand in for (a colleague etc.) (will you cover for me?). **9** tr. Military **a** aim a gun etc. at. **b** (of a fortress, guns, etc.) command (a territory). **c** stand behind (a person in the front rank). **d** protect (an exposed person etc.) by being able to return fire. **10** tr. Sport **a** esp. Baseball stand behind (another player) to stop any missed balls. **b** (in hockey, football, etc.) keep close to so as to prevent the free movement of (a player of the other side). **c** defend (an area of a field or court, a base, etc.). **11** tr. perform or record a cover (of a song etc.). ● n. **1** something that covers or protects, esp.: **a** a lid. **b** the binding of a book, magazine, etc. **c** either board or sheet of this. **d** an envelope or the wrapper of a parcel (under separate cover). **e** a stamped envelope of interest to stamp collectors. **f** (in pl.) bedclothes. **2** a hiding place; a shelter. **3** woods or undergrowth sheltering game or covering the ground. **4 a** a pretense; a screen (under cover of humility). **b** a spy's pretended identity or activity, intended as concealment. **c** Military a supporting force protecting an advance party from attack. **5 a** funds, esp. obtained by insurance, to meet a liability or secure against a contingent loss. **b** the state of being protected (third party cover). **6** = COVER CHARGE. **7** a recording or performance of a previously recorded song etc., made esp. to take advantage of the original's success (also attrib.: cover version). □ **break cover** (of an animal, esp. game, or a hunted person) leave a place of shelter, esp. vegetation. **cover in** provide with a roof etc. **cover one's tracks** conceal evidence of what one has done. **cover up 1** completely cover or conceal. **2** conceal (circumstances etc., esp. illicitly). **3** assist in a deception (refused to cover up for them). **from cover to cover** from beginning to end of a book etc. **take cover** use a natural or prepared shelter against an attack.

coverage n. **1** an area or an amount covered. **2** the amount of press etc. publicity received by a particular story, person, etc. **3** a risk covered by an insurance policy. **4** an area reached by a particular broadcasting station or advertising medium.

coverall n. esp. N Amer. (usu. in pl.) a one-piece garment worn over other clothing to protect it.

cover charge n. an extra charge levied per head in a restaurant, nightclub, etc.

cover crop n. a crop grown between main crops for the protection and enrichment of the soil.

covered *adj.* **1** provided with a lid. **2** provided with a covering. **3 a** enclosed (*covered bridge*). **b** (of a ship) decked. **4** thickly laid over or enveloped (*snow-covered hills*). **5** insured. **6** wearing a hat, veil, etc.

covered wagon *n.* *N Amer.* a large wagon with an arched canvas roof, used by pioneers for travel westward across the prairies.

cover girl *n.* a female model whose picture appears on magazine covers etc.

covering *n.* anything that covers something else for protection, concealment, etc.

covering letter *n.* (*N Amer.* also **cover letter**) a letter which accompanies a résumé, package, etc.

coverlet *n.* a bedspread.

cover-point *n.* **1** *Hockey hist.* a player who stands just in front of point to prevent the puck from coming near the goal. **2** *Lacrosse* a player positioned just in front of point.

cover story *n.* **1** a story in a magazine that is illustrated or advertised on the front cover. **2** an invented story intended to mislead or to conceal one's true actions, motives, etc.

covert /ˈkoːvərt, koːˈvɜrt, kʌ-/ • *adj.* secret or disguised (*covert operations*). • *n.* /ˈkoːvərt/ a shelter, esp. a thicket or wooded area which hides game. □ **covertly** *adv.*

cover-up *n.* **1** an act of concealing circumstances, esp. illicitly. **2** any loose outer garment worn over a bathing suit, exercise clothes, etc.

cover version *n.* = COVER *n.* 7.

covet *v.tr.* (**coveted, coveting**) **1** desire wrongfully or inordinately, esp. something belonging to another person. **2** long for or desire greatly, but not inappropriately (*we covet your prayers*). □ **coveted** *adj.*

covetous *adj.* (usu. foll. by *of*) **1** greedy, wrongfully eager to possess something. **2** greatly desirous (of something). □ **covetously** *adv.* **covetousness** *n.*

covey /ˈkʌvi/ *n.* (*pl.* **-eys**) **1** a brood of game birds, as partridges, ptarmigan, etc. **2** a small party or group of people or things.

cow¹ *n.* **1 a** a fully grown female of any bovine animal, esp. of the genus *Bos*, used as a source of milk and beef. **b** a domestic bovine animal (regardless of sex or age). ¶It is considered incorrect by many people to call a male bovine a *cow*. **c** a female domestic bovine animal which has borne a calf (*compare* HEIFER). **2** the female of other large animals, esp. the moose, elephant, whale, and seal. **3** *derogatory slang* a woman, esp. a coarse or unpleasant one. □ **have a cow** *N Amer. slang* become angry, hysterical, excited, etc. **till the cows come home** *informal* an indefinitely long time. □ **cowlike** *adj.*

cow² *v.tr.* (usu. in *passive*) intimidate, frighten, or browbeat into submission (*cowed by the threats*).

cowabunga *interj.* *slang* expressing delight or satisfaction, or as a call to action.

coward *n.* a person with little courage who shows shameful fear in the face of danger, pain, etc.

cowardice *n.* lack of courage.

cowardly *adj.* **1** of or like a coward; lacking courage. **2** (of an action) done against a person who cannot retaliate. □ **cowardliness** *n.*

cowbell *n.* **1** a bell worn round a cow's neck for easy location of the animal. **2** a similar bell used as a percussion instrument.

cowberry *n.* (*pl.* **-ies**) **1** an evergreen shrub, *Vaccinium vitis-idaea*, bearing red berries. **2** this berry.

cowbird *n.* any of several N American orioles, esp.

the brown-plumaged *Molothrus ater*, which lays its eggs in other birds' nests.

cowboy *n.* **1** a person who herds and tends cattle, esp. in western N America. **2** *informal* **a** a person who acts outside of established rules, conventions, etc. **b** an unscrupulous or reckless person, esp. an unqualified one.

cowboy boot *n.* a square-heeled boot with a pointed toe, extending to midcalf and usu. with decorative tooling or stitching.

cowboy hat *n.* a hat, usu. of felt, with a high crown and broad brim.

cowboying *n.* *N Amer.* the job, skills, etc. of a cowboy.

cowboys and Indians *n.* a children's game in which the participants imitate the supposed actions of cowboys and Indians in conflict.

cowcatcher *n.* *N Amer.* a metal frame at the front of a locomotive for pushing aside obstacles on the line.

cower *v.intr.* crouch or shrink back, esp. in fear.

cowgirl *n.* a woman who herds and tends cattle.

cowhand *n.* *N Amer.* a person who tends cattle.

cowhide *n.* **1 a** a cow's hide. **b** leather made from this. **2** a leather whip made from cowhide.

Cowichan /ˈkauwɪtʃən/ • *n.* (*pl.* same) **1** a member of an Aboriginal people living on SE Vancouver Island. **2** the language of this people, a dialect of Halkomelem. • *adj.* of or relating to this people.

Cowichan sweater *n.* *Cdn* a handspun, heavy-knit pullover sweater made by the Cowichan.

cowl *n.* **1 a** the hood of a monk's habit. **b** a loose hood. **c** a monk's hooded habit. **d** a cloak with wide sleeves worn by members of Benedictine orders. **2** the hood-shaped covering of a chimney or ventilating shaft. **3** (also **cowling**) the removable cover of a vehicle or aircraft engine. □ **cowled** *adj.*

cowlick *n.* a projecting lock of hair, esp. at the crown or forehead.

co-worker *n.* a person who works with another.

cow-pie *n.* (also **cow patty, cow pat**) a flat, round piece of cow dung.

cowpoke *n.* (also **cowpuncher**) *N Amer.* = COWBOY 1.

cowpox *n.* a contagious disease of cows, of which the virus was formerly used in vaccination against smallpox.

co-write *v.tr.* (*past* **-wrote**; *past part.* **-written**) write (something) together with another person. □ **co-writer** *n.*

cowslip *n.* **1** a primula, *Primula veris*, with fragrant yellow flowers and growing in pastures. **2** = SHOOTING STAR 2.

cowtown *n.* a town or city in a cattle area of western N America, esp. one involved in the cattle industry.

cox • *n.* a coxswain, esp. of a racing boat. • *v.* **1** *intr.* act as a cox. **2** *tr.* act as cox for. □ **coxless** *adj.*

coxcomb *n.* an ostentatiously conceited man; a dandy or fop. □ **coxcombry** /ˈkɒkskəmri/ *n.* (*pl.* **-ies**).

coxswain /ˈkɒksən, -sweɪn/ *n.* **1** a person who steers, esp. in a rowboat. **2** the senior petty officer in a small ship.

coy *adj.* (**coyer, coyest**) **1** artfully or affectedly shy, esp. in a provocative manner. **2** irritatingly reticent (*always coy about his age*). □ **coyly** *adv.* **coyness** *n.*

coydog *n.* *N Amer.* a hybrid of a coyote and a dog.

coyote /kaɪˈoːti, ˈkaɪoːt/ *n.* **1** a wolflike wild dog, *Canis latrans*, native to N America, noted for its cunning. **2** a hero and trickster figure in N American Aboriginal folklore.

coz¹ *n.* *N Amer. informal* cousin.

coz² *conj.* *slang* because.

cozy ● *adj.* (**-ier, -iest**) **1** comfortable, warm, or snug. **2** intimate and friendly (*a cozy restaurant*). **3** beneficial or opportune, esp. for insidious purposes (*a cozy contract*). **4** *derogatory* complacent. ● *n.* (*pl.* **-ies**) a cover to keep something hot, esp. a teapot. □ **cozy up to** (**-ies, -ied**) *N Amer. informal* **1** ingratiate oneself with. **2** snuggle up to. □ **cozily** *adv.* **coziness** *n.*

CP *abbr.* **1** Canadian Pacific (Railway etc.). **2** Canadian Press. **3** *Med.* cerebral palsy. **4** Communist Party.

cp. *abbr.* compare.

CPI *abbr.* Consumer Price Index.

cpi *abbr.* characters per inch.

Cpl *abbr.* (also **Cpl.**) corporal[1].

CPO *abbr.* chief petty officer.

CPP *abbr.* Canada Pension Plan.

CPR *abbr.* **1** cardiopulmonary resuscitation. **2** Canadian Pacific Railway.

CPR strawberries *n.pl. Cdn informal jocular* prunes or dried apples.

CPS *abbr.* Canadian Parks Service.

cps *abbr.* (also **c.p.s.**) **1** *Computing* characters per second. **2** cycles per second.

CPU *abbr. Computing* central processing unit.

Cr *symbol* chromium.

Cr. *abbr.* **1** creditor. **2** credit. **3** Crescent. **4** Creek.

crab[1] ● *n.* **1 a** any of numerous ten-footed crustaceans having the first pair of legs modified as pincers. **b** the flesh of a crab, esp. *Cancer pagurus*, as food. **2** (in full **crab louse**) (often in *pl.*) a parasitic louse, *Phthirus pubis*, infesting hairy parts of the body and causing extreme irritation. ● *v.intr.* (**crabbed, crabbing**) **1** fish for crabs. **2** move sideways, esp. with short, abrupt movements. □ **crablike** *adj.*

crab[2] *n.* **1** (in full **crabapple**) a small, sour apple. **2** (in full **crab tree** or **crabapple tree**) any of several trees of the genus Malus bearing this fruit. **3** a bad-tempered person.

crab[3] *v.tr. & intr.* (**crabbed, crabbing**) *informal* find fault, criticize; grumble.

crabbed /ˈkræbd/ *adj.* **1** (of handwriting) cramped and hard to decipher. **2** = crabby. **3** perverse (*crabbed view of democracy*). **4** difficult to understand (*crabbed construction of the law*). □ **crabbedly** /ˈkræbidli:/ *adv.*

crabber *n.* **1** a person who fishes for crabs. **2** a boat used in crab fishing.

crabby *adj.* (**-ier, -iest**) surly, irritable, or morose. □ **crabbily** *adv.* **crabbiness** *n.*

crabgrass *n. N Amer.* any of several creeping grasses infesting lawns, esp. of the genus *Digitaria*.

crabmeat *n.* = crab[1] 1b.

crack ● *n.* **1 a** a sudden sharp or explosive noise (*the crack of a whip*). **b** (in a voice) a sudden harshness or change in pitch. **2** a sharp blow. **3 a** a narrow opening formed by a break. **b** a partial fracture, with the parts still joined. **c** a chink. **4** *informal* a joke or gibe; a witty or cutting remark. **5** *informal* **a** an attempt (*I'll have a crack at it*). **b** an opportunity (*a crack at the job*). **6** (in full **crack cocaine**) *slang* a potent, highly addictive hard crystalline form of cocaine broken into small pieces and inhaled or smoked for its stimulating effect. **7** the exact moment (*the crack of dawn*). ● *v.* **1** *tr. & intr.* break without a complete separation of the parts. **2** *intr. & tr.* make or cause to make a sudden sharp or explosive sound. **3** *intr. & tr.* break or cause to break with a sudden sharp sound. **4** *intr. & tr.* break down, esp. under severe pressures, e.g. torture. **5** *intr.* (of the voice, esp. of an adolescent boy or a person under strain) change tone, break, become harsh. **6** *tr.* **a** decipher, find a solution to (a problem, code, etc.). **b**

break into or force open (*cracked the safe*). **7** *tr.* tell (a joke etc.) in a jocular way. **8** *tr. informal* hit sharply or hard (*cracked her head on the ceiling*). **9** *tr. Chem.* decompose (heavy oils) by heat and pressure with or without a catalyst to produce lighter hydrocarbons (such as gasoline). **10** *tr.* gain access to (*crack the job market*). **11** *tr.* **a** open (a bottle) (*crack a beer*). **b** open slightly (*crack open the window*). ● *attrib.adj. informal* excellent; first-rate (*a crack shot*). □ **crack a book** *informal N Amer.* study or research. **crack down on** *informal* take severe measures against. **crack a smile** *informal* begin to smile. **crack the whip** *informal* exercise authority. **crack up** *informal* **1** suffer a mental or emotional breakdown. **2** burst into laughter suddenly. **3** cause to break into laughter (*cracked me up*). **crack wise** *N Amer. informal* make wisecracks. **get cracking** *informal* begin promptly and vigorously. **have a crack at** *informal* attempt. **not all it's cracked up to be** *informal* not all a thing seems to be. □ **cracky** *adj.*

crackdown *n. informal* enforcement of severe or measures (esp. against lawbreakers, activists, etc.).

cracked *adj.* **1** having cracks. **2** *informal* (usu. *predic.*) eccentric, mad, or crazy. **3** damaged, injured, or impaired (*cracked hands*). **4** varying or broken in tone, e.g. voice or sounds (*a cracked voice*).

cracked wheat *n.* wheat that has been crushed into small pieces.

cracker *n.* **1 a** a thin, dry biscuit often eaten with cheese. **b** *N Amer.* a cookie (*a graham cracker*). **2** a paper cylinder both ends of which are pulled, esp. at Christmas, making a sharp noise and releasing a small toy etc. **3** a firework exploding with a sharp noise. **4** *Computing* a hacker who wilfully damages or destroys the information or systems accessed.

crackerjack *esp. N Amer. slang* ● *adj.* exceptionally fine or expert. ● *n.* an exceptionally fine thing etc.

crackers *predic.adj. slang* **1** crazy. **2** wildly enthusiastic (*crackers over the new film*).

crackhead *n. N Amer. slang* a habitual user of crack cocaine.

crack house *n. N Amer.* a gathering place where crack cocaine is bought, sold, or used.

crackie *n. Cdn (Nfld)* a small, yappy dog of mixed breed.

crackle ● *v.intr.* make a repeated slight cracking sound (*the radio crackled*). ● *n.* **1** such a sound. **2 a** paintwork, china, or glass decorated with a pattern of minute surface cracks. **b** the smooth surface of such paintwork etc. □ **crackly** *adj.*

crackling *n.* the crisp skin of roast pork.

crackpot *slang* ● *n.* an eccentric or impractical person. ● *adj.* bizarre, unworkable (*a crackpot scheme*).

crack the whip *n. N Amer.* a skating game in which participants form a line and, by skating rapidly then changing directions abruptly, attempt to fling the end skaters off.

crack-up *n. informal* **1** a mental breakdown. **2** a car crash. **3** a collapse or disintegration.

cracky *n.* □ **by cracky** *interjection* expressing determination, assertiveness, etc. (*we'll go, by cracky*).

cradle ● *n.* **1 a** a baby's bed with high sides, esp. one mounted on rockers. **b** a place in which a thing begins, esp. a civilization etc., or is nurtured in its infancy. **2** a framework resembling a cradle, esp.: **a** one on which a ship etc. rests during construction or repairs. **b** one on which a worker is suspended to work on a ceiling, a ship, the vertical side of a building, etc. **c** the part of a telephone on which the receiver rests when not in use. ● *v.tr.* **1 a** hold, contain, or shelter as if in a cradle (*cradled his head in her arms*). **b** support, rock, or move gently as though in a cradle (*cradled on the waves*). **2** *Lacrosse* carry (the ball) in the stick's net, esp. when running with it. □ **from the cradle** from infancy (*a socialist from the cradle*). **from (the) cradle to (the) grave** from infancy till death. **rob the cradle** become romantically involved with someone much younger.

cradleboard *n.* (among some N American Aboriginal peoples) a board to which an infant is strapped.

cradle-to-grave *adj.* from birth to death.

craft ● *n.* **1 a** (esp. in *comb.*) a trade or an art (*statecraft*; *the craft of pottery*). **b** (usu. in *pl.* or *attrib.*) the product of such skill. **2** skill, esp. in practical arts. **3** the activity of producing handiwork. **4 a** a trade union, guild or company. **b** the members of such an association. **5** (*pl.* **craft**) **a** a boat or vessel. **b** an aircraft or spacecraft. **6** cunning or deceit. ● *v.tr.* make, fashion, or hone in a skilful way (*crafted a poem*).

crafter *n. N Amer.* = CRAFTSPERSON.

craft shop *n.* **1** a small store in which handicrafts, usu. made locally, are sold. **2** (also **craft store**) a store in which craft supplies are sold.

craftsman *n.* (*pl.* **-men**) **1** a skilled worker who has usu. completed a period of apprenticeship or training. **2** a person who practises a handicraft.

craftsmanship *n.* **1** the quality of execution in a thing made. **2** skilled workmanship.

craftsperson *n.* (*pl.* **-people**) a person who practises a handicraft, esp. a highly skilled artisan.

craftswoman *n.* (*pl.* **-women**) **1** a skilled female worker who has usu. completed a period of apprenticeship or training. **2** a woman who practises a handicraft.

crafty *adj.* (**-ier**, **-iest**) cunning, artful, wily. □ **craftily** *adv.* **craftiness** *n.*

crag *n.* a steep or rugged rock.

craggy *adj.* (**-ier**, **-iest**) **1** (of a landscape) having crags. **2** (esp. of a person's face) rugged; angular, with sharply defined features, e.g. jutting cheekbones etc.

cram *v.* (**crammed**, **cramming**) **1** *tr.* a fill to bursting; stuff (*the room was crammed*). **b** (foll. by *in*, *into*) force (a thing) into (*cram the books into the bag*). **2** *tr. & intr.* prepare for an examination by intensive study. **3** *tr. & intr. informal* eat greedily. □ **cram in** push in to bursting point (*crammed in another five people*).

cramp ● *n.* **1** a painful involuntary contraction of a muscle or muscles from the cold, exertion, etc. **2** = WRITER'S CRAMP. **3** esp. *N Amer.* (usu. in *pl.*) a painful muscle contraction in the abdomen, uterus, etc., esp. preceding or accompanying menstruation. ● *v.* **1** *tr.* affect with a cramp or cramps. **2** *tr.* confine, restrict, or hamper (energies etc.). **3** *intr.* (usu. foll. by *up*) become stiff or incapacitated because of a cramp. □ **cramp a person's style** prevent a person from acting freely or naturally. □ **crampy** *adj.*

cramped *adj.* **1** (of handwriting) small, tightly packed, and difficult to read. **2** uncomfortably limited or restricted in space (*cramped quarters*).

crampon /'kræmpɒn/ *n.* (usu. in *pl.*) a spiked iron plate fixed to a boot for walking on ice, climbing, etc.

cranberry *n.* (*pl.* **-ies**) **1** any of several evergreen shrubs of the genus *Vaccinium*, esp. *V. macrocarpon* of eastern N America, grown commercially for its red acid fruit, and *V. oxycoccos* and *V. vitis-idaea*, yielding smaller fruit. **2** a berry from this used for a sauce and in cooking.

crane ● *n.* **1** a machine for moving heavy objects, usu. by suspending them from a projecting beam. **2 a** any tall wading bird of the family Gruidae, with long

legs, long neck, and straight bill. **b** = GREAT BLUE HERON. **3** a trolley with a long boom supporting a platform on which a camera can be mounted. ● *v.tr. & intr.* stretch out (one's neck) in order to see.

cranesbill *n.* any of various herbaceous plants of the genus *Geranium*, having beaked fruits.

cranial /'kreiniəl/ *adj.* of or relating to the skull.

cranial nerve *n.* each of twelve pairs of nerves which originate directly in the brain, not from the spinal cord, and which reach the external surface of the body through natural skull apertures.

cranium /'kreiniəm/ *n.* (*pl.* **-s** or **crania** /-niə/) **1** the skull of a vertebrate. **2** the part of the skeleton that encloses the brain.

crank[1] ● *n.* part of an axle or shaft bent at right angles for converting reciprocal into circular motion and vice versa. ● *v.tr.* **1** cause to move by means of a crank. **2** start (an engine etc.), esp. by turning a crank. □ **crank out** *informal* produce quickly in a mechanical or mass-produced fashion (*cranks out pulp novels*). **crank up 1** start, turn on, or power up (a machine, appliance, etc.) (*crank up the engine*). **2** *informal* increase (speed, sound, etc.) (*crank up the volume*). **3** stimulate, stir up, or produce (*crank up enthusiasm*). **turn one's crank** *slang* please, appeal to, or excite one's interest.

crank[2] ● *n.* **1** an eccentric person, esp. one obsessed by a particular theory. **2** *N Amer.* a bad-tempered person. ● *adj.* of, by, or pertaining to an eccentric or unbalanced person (*crank theories*).

crankbait *n. N Amer.* a plug type fishing lure which dives beneath the surface when retrieved.

crank call *n.* a harassing telephone call usu. made by young people as a prank.

crankcase *n.* a metal covering enclosing an engine's crankshaft, connecting rods, etc.

crankshaft *n.* a shaft driven by one or more cranks.

cranky *adj.* (**-ier**, **-iest**) **1** esp. *N Amer.* bad-tempered. **2** working badly. □ **crankily** *adv.* **crankiness** *n.*

cranny *n.* (*pl.* **-ies**) a small narrow opening or hole; a chink, crevice, or crack (*nooks and crannies*).

crap[1] *coarse slang* ● *n.* **1 a** feces. **b** an act of defecation. **2** nonsense or falsehood (*he talks crap*). **3** something without value (*the poetry was crap*). **4** garbage, litter, refuse (*pick up that crap*). ● *v.intr.* (**crapped**, **crapping**) defecate. □ **cut the crap** *slang* get to the point; stop evading the issue. **give a crap** *slang* care, be concerned about (*I don't give a crap*).

crap[2] *n. N Amer.* **1** (in *pl.*) a gambling game in which two dice are thrown with the aim of scoring 7 or 11 on a first throw or any score but 7 on a second throw. **2** a losing score of 2, 3, or 12 on a first throw in craps. □ **crap out** *N Amer.* **1** make a losing throw while shooting craps. **2** *informal* **a** fail. **b** withdraw from a game etc. **shoot craps** play craps.

crape *n.* **1** CREPE. **2** a fabric, usu. of black silk or imitation silk, formerly used for mourning clothes.

crappie *n.* a N American freshwater sunfish of the genus *Pomoxis*.

crappy *adj.* (**-ier**, **-iest**) *slang* **1** markedly inferior. **2** disgusting, unfair, nasty (*a crappy comment*).

crapshoot *n. N Amer. slang* a gamble, risk, or highly uncertain venture. □ **crapshooter** *n.*

crash ● *v.* **1** *intr. & tr.* make or cause to make a loud smashing noise. **2** *tr. & intr.* throw, move, drop, or fall with a loud smashing noise. **3** *intr. & tr.* **a** collide or cause or cause (a vehicle) to collide violently with another vehicle, obstacle, etc. **b** overturn or cause to overturn (a vehicle) at high speed. **4** *intr. & tr.* fall or cause (an aircraft) to fall violently to the land or water. **5** *intr.* (usu. foll. by *into*) collide violently. **6** *intr.* undergo financial ruin (*the market crashed*). **7** *tr.* *informal* enter without permission (*crashed the party*). **8** *intr.* *informal* be heavily defeated (*crashed to a 4–0 defeat*). **9** *intr.* *Computing* (of a machine or system) fail suddenly. **10** *tr.* *informal* pass (a red traffic light etc.). **11** *intr.* (often foll. by *out*) *slang* a sleep, esp. in an improvised setting. **b** stay somewhere temporarily. **12** *intr.* *slang* experience depression, exhaustion, etc. as the effects of cocaine etc. wear off. ● *n.* **1 a** a loud and sudden smashing noise. **b** an instance of noisily breaking or falling to pieces (esp. of china, glass, etc.). **2 a** a violent collision, esp. of one vehicle with another or with an object. **b** the violent fall of an aircraft to the land or water. **3** a sudden collapse of the stock market etc. **4** *Computing* a sudden failure which puts a system out of action. **5** (*attrib.*) marked by an urgent and concentrated effort, esp. for immediate results etc. (*a crash course*). **6** a dramatic decrease in numbers. □ **crash and burn** *informal* ● *v.intr.* collapse or fail utterly. ● *n.* (usu. *attrib.*) a complete and often spectacular failure (*crash and burn programming*).

crashing *adj.* *informal* overwhelming (*a crashing bore*).

crash-land *v.* **1** *intr.* (of an aircraft or pilot) make an emergency landing, usu. with damage to the craft. **2** *tr.* cause to crash-land. □ **crash landing** *n.*

crash test ● *v.tr.* assess and evaluate (a product, usu. a vehicle) for safety and reliability under severe conditions often including collisions etc. ● *n.* such a test.

crass *adj.* **1** boorish, unsubtle (*crass materialism*). **2** insensitive, rude, vulgar (*a crass remark*). **3** extreme (*crass stupidity*). □ **crassly** *adv.* **crassness** *n.*

crate ● *n.* **1** a case or box, often of slatted wood, for packing, shipping, or storing esp. fragile goods for transportation. **2** *slang* an old airplane or other vehicle. ● *v.tr.* pack in a crate.

crater ● *n.* **1** the mouth of a volcano. **2** a bowl-shaped cavity, esp. that made by the explosion of a bomb. **3** a hollow with a raised rim on the surface of a planet or moon, caused by the impact of a meteorite. ● *v.tr. & intr.* make a crater or craters in. □ **cratered** *adj.*

cravat /krə'væt/ *n.* a scarf worn inside an open-necked shirt, esp. by men.

crave *v.* **1** *tr.* a long for. **b** beg for. **c** need desperately. **2** *intr.* (foll. by *for*) long for; beg for. □ **craver** *n.*

craven ● *adj.* (of a person, behaviour, etc.) cowardly, obsequious. ● *n.* a cowardly person. □ **cravenly** *adv.* **cravenness** *n.*

craving *n.* (usu. foll. by *for*) a strong desire or longing.

craw *n.* the crop of a bird or insect. □ **stick in one's craw** *informal* be difficult to accept.

crawfish *n.* (*pl.* same) a large marine spiny lobster.

crawl ● *v.intr.* **1** move slowly, esp. on hands and knees. **2** (of an insect, snake, etc.) move slowly with the body close to the ground etc. **3** move or progress slowly. **4** (often foll. by *to*) *informal* behave obsequiously or ingratiatingly. **5** (often foll. by *with*) be or seem to be covered or filled with crawling or moving things, people etc. (*crawling with shoppers*). **6** (esp. of the skin) feel a creepy sensation. **7** swim with a crawl stroke. ● *n.* **1** an act of crawling. **2** a slow rate of movement. **3** a high-speed swimming stroke with alternate overarm movements and rapid straight-legged kicks. **4 a** (usu. in *comb.*) *informal* a leisurely journey between places of interest (*culture-crawl*). **b** = PUB-CRAWL. □ **crawly** *adj.* (in senses 5, 6 of *v.*).

crawler *n.* **1** a person or thing that crawls, esp. a baby or an insect. **2** a tractor moving on an endless chain. **3** *N Amer.* (usu. in *pl.*) a baby's overall for crawling in; rompers. **4** *N Amer.* (also **night crawler**) *informal* an earthworm.

crawl space *n.* a low, constricted space, usu. in a house, for storage or to gain access to wiring etc.

crayfish *n.* (*pl.* same) **1** a small lobster-like freshwater crustacean. **2** a crawfish.

crayon ● *n.* a stick or pencil of coloured wax etc. used for drawing. ● *v.* **1** *tr.* draw or colour (a picture) with crayons. **2** *intr.* draw or colour with crayons.

craze ● *v.tr.* (usu. in *passive*) make insane (*crazed with grief*). ● *n.* **1** a usu. temporary enthusiasm (*a craze for hula hoops*). **2** the object of this (*the dinosaur craze*).

crazed *adj.* **1** mentally impaired, insane. **2** (usu. in *comb.*) manic, wildly enthusiastic (*dance-crazed teens*).

crazy ● *adj.* (**-ier**, **-iest**) **1** *informal* (of a person, action, etc.) **a** mentally unstable, insane. **b** foolish, impractical. **2** *informal* (usu. foll. by *about*) extremely enthusiastic. **3** *slang* **a** exciting, wild (*a crazy party*). **b** excellent. ● *n.* (*pl.* **-ies**) *slang* (usu. in *pl.*) a person who is wild, eccentric, unbalanced, etc. □ **like crazy** = LIKE MAD (see MAD). □ **crazily** *adv.* **craziness** *n.*

crazy eights *n.* (treated as *sing.*) *N Amer.* a card game, usu. played by children, in which a player plays a card of the same suit or denomination as the preceding one, with eight being a wild card.

crazy quilt *n.* **1** a patchwork quilt made of material of various shapes, sizes, and colours. **2** an apparently random collection (e.g. of laws, districts, etc.).

creak ● *n.* a harsh scraping or squeaking sound. ● *v.intr.* **1** make a creak. **2 a** move with a creaking noise. **b** move slowly or stiffly. **c** show weakness or frailty under strain. □ **creakingly** *adv.*

creaky *adj.* (**-ier**, **-iest**) **1** creaking or liable to creak. **2 a** stiff or frail (*creaky joints*). **b** (of a practice, institution, etc.) decrepit, dilapidated, outmoded. □ **creakily** *adv.* **creakiness** *n.*

cream ● *n.* **1 a** the fatty content of milk which gathers at the top and can be made into butter by churning. **b** this eaten (often whipped) with a dessert, as a cake filling, etc. **2** (usu. prec. by *the*) the best or choicest part of something, esp. an elite group of people. **3** a creamlike preparation, esp. a cosmetic (*hand cream*). **4** a very pale yellow or off-white colour. **5 a** a filling, dessert, etc. with a creamy consistency. **b** a soup or sauce containing milk or cream. **c** a full-bodied mellow sweet sherry. **d** a sandwich cookie with a cream filling. **e** a chocolate-covered, usu. fruit-flavoured, fondant. ● *v.* **1** *tr.* **a** take the cream from (milk). **b** (usu. foll. by *off*) take the best or a specified part from. **2** *tr.* work (butter, esp. with sugar etc.) to a creamy consistency. **3** *tr.* treat (the skin etc.) with cosmetic cream. **4** *tr.* add cream to (coffee etc.). **5** *intr.* (of milk or any other liquid) form a cream or scum. **6** *tr.* *N Amer.* *informal* defeat decisively (esp. in a game etc.). **7** *tr.* esp. *N Amer.* *slang* **a** hit (*creamed him with my purse*). **b** beat thoroughly. ● *adj.* pale yellow; off-white.

cream cheese *n.* a soft, rich, spreadable, and unripened cheese made from milk or cream.

creamed *adj.* **1** prepared in a cream sauce. **2** (of honey) whipped or churned. **3** (of cottage cheese) having the curds combined with milk.

creamer *n.* **1** esp. *N Amer.* a jug or container for cream. **2 a** a non-dairy product used as a substitute for cream or milk in coffee or tea. **b** a small, single-serving container of this. **3** a small, single-serving container of cream for use in coffee or tea.

creamery *n.* (*pl.* **-ies**) a factory producing butter or cheese.

cream of tartar *n.* purified and crystallized potassium hydrogen tartrate, used esp. as a leavener.

cream pie *n.* *N Amer.* a pie with a custard-like filling, often with a whipped cream topping.

cream puff n. **1** a ball-shaped pastry shell filled with whipped cream etc. **2** informal a weak, ineffectual person. **3** slang (also attrib.) a car etc. maintained in excellent condition.

cream sauce n. **1** a sauce containing a high proportion of cream. **2** a white sauce made from milk and thickened with butter and flour.

cream soda n. a vanilla-flavoured soft drink.

creamy adj. (**-ier, -iest**) like cream in taste, colour, or consistency. □ **creamily** adv. **creaminess** n.

crease ● n. **1 a** a line in paper etc. caused by folding etc. **b** a vertical line pressed into trousers with an iron. **c** a fold or wrinkle. **2** a marked area in front of the goal in hockey or lacrosse into which the puck or ball must precede the players. ● v. **1** tr. make creases in (material). **2** intr. become creased.

create v.tr. **1** cause to exist; make (something) new or original. **2** have as a result; produce (a feeling etc.).

creation n. **1 a** the act of creating. **b** an instance of this. **c** something created. **2 a** (usu. **the Creation**) the creating of the universe regarded as an act of God. **b** (usu. **Creation**) everything so created; the universe. **3** a product of human intelligence, esp. of imaginative thought or artistic ability.

creationism n. Theol. a theory attributing all matter, biological species, etc., to separate acts of creation, esp. according to a literal interpretation of Genesis, rather than to evolution. □ **creationist** n. & adj.

creative adj. **1** of or involving the skilful and imaginative use of something to produce e.g. a work of art. **2** able to create things, usu. in an imaginative way. **3** inventive. □ **creatively** adv. **creativity** n.

creative writing n. the writing of fiction, plays, etc.

creator n. **1** one who creates. **2** (**the Creator**) God.

creature n. **1 a** an animal, as distinct from a human being. **b** any living being (we are all God's creatures). **2** a person of a specified kind. **3** a person owing status to and obsequiously subservient to another. **4** anything created; a creation. **5** a person whose character is defined by a specified influence (creatures of our culture). □ **creature of habit** a person set in an unvarying routine. □ **creaturely** adj.

creature comforts n.pl. material comforts such as good food, warmth, etc.

crèche /kreʃ, kreɪʃ/ n. N Amer. = NATIVITY SCENE.

cred n. informal credibility (street cred).

credence /'kriːdəns/ n. **1** belief. **2** believability. □ **give credence to 1** believe. **2** (also **lend credence to**) support or reinforce the believability of it.

credential n. (usu. in pl.) **1** evidence of a person's achievements or trustworthiness, usu. in the form of references etc. **2** a letter or letters of introduction. □ **credentialed** adj.

credibility n. **1** the condition of being credible or believable. **2** reputation, status.

credible adj. **1** (of a person or statement) believable or worthy of belief. **2** (of a threat etc.) convincing. □ **credibly** adv.

credit ● n. **1** (usu. of a person) a source of honour, pride, etc. (is a credit to the school). **2** the acknowledgement of merit. **3** a good reputation. **4 a** acknowledgement of competence (give me some credit!). **b** something believable or trustworthy (that statement has credit). **5 a** a person's financial standing; the sum of money at a person's disposal in a bank etc. **b** the power to obtain goods etc. before payment. **6** (usu. in pl.) **a** an acknowledgement of a contributor's services to a film, television program, etc., usually listed at the beginning or end. **b** a film or television program etc. in which a person has participated. **7** a reputa-

tion for solvency and honesty in business. **8 a** (in bookkeeping) the acknowledgement of being paid by an entry on the credit side of an account. **b** the sum entered. **c** the credit side of an account. **d** = TAX CREDIT. **9** N Amer. **a** official recognition that a student has completed a course meeting the requirements of a diploma or degree. **b** a value ascribed to a credit course (needed three credits). ● v.tr. (**credited, crediting**) **1** (foll. by with; usu. in passive) ascribe (often without certainty) an accomplishment to (was credited with the discovery). **2** believe (cannot credit it). **3** (usu. foll. by to, with) enter on the credit side of an account. □ **do credit to** (or **do a person credit**) enhance the reputation of a person. **get credit for** be given credit for. **give a person credit for 1** enter (a sum) to a person's credit. **2** ascribe (a good quality) to a person. **give credit to** believe. **on credit** with an arrangement to pay later. **take credit (for)** accept praise or commendation, esp. for something one is not responsible for. **to one's credit** in one's praise, commendation, or defence.

creditable adj. (often foll. by to) **1** bringing credit or honour. **2** that can be credited (tax-creditable). □ **creditability** n. **creditably** adv.

credit card n. a card issued by a bank or business authorizing the obtaining of goods on credit.

credit course n. N Amer. a course taken for credit towards a degree, diploma, etc.

Créditiste /kredi'tiːst/ n. Cdn a member or supporter of the Quebec wing of the Social Credit Party.

credit line n. = LINE OF CREDIT.

creditor n. **1** a person to whom a debt is owing. **2** a person or company that gives credit for money or goods (compare DEBTOR).

credit rating n. an estimate of one's suitability to receive credit.

credit union n. a banking co-operative offering financial services to members.

creditworthy adj. considered suitable to receive commercial credit. □ **creditworthiness** n.

credo /'kriːdoː, 'kreɪ-/ n. (pl. **-os**) **1** a set of principles held by a specified group, esp. as a philosophy. **2** (**Credo**) a creed, esp. the Apostles' or Nicene creed.

credulous adj. **1** too ready to believe; gullible. **2** (of behaviour) showing such gullibility. □ **credulity** /krə'djuːlɪti/ n. **credulously** adv. **credulousness** n.

Cree ● n. (pl. same or **Crees**) **1** a member of a part of the Algonquian linguistic family, living from the west coast to the Rocky Mountains, and forming the largest Aboriginal group in Canada. **2** the language of this people. ● adj. of or relating to the Cree.

creed n. **1** a set of principles or opinions, esp. as a philosophy of life. **2 a** (often **the Creed**) a brief formal summary of Christian doctrine. **b** the Creed as part of the Mass.

Creek ● n. **1** a member of a N American Aboriginal confederacy of the Muskogee and some other peoples. **2** the Muskogean language of the Muskogee. ● adj. of or relating to this people.

creek /kriːk, krɪk/ n. N Amer., Austral., & NZ a tributary of a river; a stream or brook. □ **up the creek** slang **1** in difficulties or trouble. **2** crazy.

creel n. **1** a large wicker basket for fish. **2** an angler's fishing basket.

creep ● v.intr. (past and past part. **crept**) **1** move with the body prone and close to the ground; crawl. **2** (often foll. by in, out, up, etc.) come, go, or move slowly and stealthily or timidly. **3** enter slowly (into a person's affections, life, awareness, etc.) (a feeling crept over her). **4** informal act abjectly or obsequiously in the hope of advancement. **5** (of a plant) grow along the ground or up a wall by means of tendrils etc. **6** (as **creeping** adj.) developing slowly and steadily (*creeping inflation*). **7** (of the flesh) feel as if insects etc. were creeping over it, as a result of fear, horror, etc. ● n. **1 a** the act of creeping. **b** an instance of this. **2** (in pl.; prec. by *the*) informal a nervous feeling of revulsion or fear. **3** informal an unpleasant or obnoxious person. □ **creep up on** approach (a person) stealthily or unnoticed.

creeper n. **1** any climbing or creeping plant. **2** any bird that climbs. **3** slang a soft-soled shoe.

creeping charlie n. a common Eurasian plant of the mint family, *Glechoma hederacea*, naturalized in N America, with bluish-purple flowers.

creepy adj. (**-ier**, **-iest**) **1** informal having or producing a creeping of the flesh (*I feel creepy*; *a creepy film*). **2** given to creeping. □ **creepily** adv. **creepiness** n.

creepy-crawly informal ● n. (pl. **-ies**) an insect, worm, etc. ● adj. creeping and crawling.

cremate /'kri:meit, kri:'meit, krə-/ v.tr. burn (a corpse etc.) to ashes, esp. ceremonially. □ **cremation** n.

crematorium /ˌkri:mə'tɔriəm/ n. (pl. **crematoria** or **-s**) a building in which corpses are cremated.

creme /kri:m/ n. **1** a creamy substance used as a filling etc., not containing real cream (*creme-filled cookies*). **2** a toiletry, cosmetic product, or ointment having the consistency of cream.

crème brûlée /ˌkrem bru:'lei/ n. a baked custard topped with caramelized sugar.

crème caramel /kerə'mel, kərə-, kærə-/ n. a baked custard cooked in a caramel-coated dish, usu. inverted so that the caramel forms a sauce.

crème de cacao /kə'kau, kə'keiɔ:/ n. a chocolate-flavoured liqueur.

crème de la crème n. the best part; the elite.

crème de menthe /'mãt, 'menθ/ n. a mint-flavoured liqueur.

crème fraîche /'freʃ/ n. heavy cream thickened by slight fermentation, with a tart taste.

Creole /'kri:o:l/ ● n. **1 a** a descendant of European (esp. Spanish) settlers in the W Indies or Central or S America. **b** a white descendant of French settlers in the southern US. **c** a person of mixed European and black descent. **2 a** a language formed from the contact of a European language (esp. English, French, or Portuguese) with another (esp. African) language. **b** (usu. **creole**) a former pidgin that has become the sole or native language of a community. ● adj. **1** of or relating to a Creole or Creoles. **2** (usu. **creole**) of Creole origin or production.

creosote ● n. **1** (in full **creosote oil**) a dark brown oil distilled from coal tar, used as a wood preservative. **2** a colourless fluid distilled from wood tar, used as an antiseptic. ● v.tr. treat with creosote.

crepe /kreip, krep/ n. **1** a woven or knitted fabric with a wrinkled surface. **2** a thin pancake, usu. with a savoury or sweet filling. **3** (also **crepe rubber**) a very hard-wearing wrinkled sheet rubber used for the soles of shoes etc. **4** (in full **crepe paper**) thin crinkled paper.

crepe Suzette /su:'zet/ n. (pl. **crepes Suzette** pronunc. same) a crepe in an orange sauce, flamed in alcohol at the table.

crept past and past part. of CREEP.

Cres. abbr. Crescent.

crescendo /krə'ʃendo/ ● n. (pl. **-dos**, **-di** /-i:/) **1** Music a passage gradually increasing in loudness. **2** a progress towards a climax (*a crescendo of emotions*). **b** a climax (*reached a crescendo then died away*). ● adv. & adj.

with a gradual increase in loudness. ● v.intr. (**-oes**, **-oed**) increase gradually in loudness or intensity.

crescent ● n. **1** the curved sickle shape of the waxing or waning moon. **2** anything of this shape. **3** a curving street. **4** a crescent-shaped item of food, esp. a bread roll or cookie. **5 a** the crescent-shaped emblem of Islam or Turkey. **b** (**the Crescent**) the world or power of Islam. ● adj. **1** increasing. **2** crescent-shaped.

cresol /'kri:sɒl/ n. any of three isomeric phenols present in creosote and used as disinfectants.

cress n. any of various cruciferous plants usu. with pungent edible leaves, e.g. watercress.

crest ● n. **1 a** a comb or tuft of feathers, fur, etc. on a bird's or animal's head. **b** something resembling this, esp. a plume of feathers on a helmet. **c** a helmet; the top of a helmet. **2** the top of something, esp. of a wave etc. **3** Heraldry **a** a device above the shield and helmet of a coat of arms. **b** such a device reproduced on writing paper or on a seal, signifying a family. **4** a shield or coat of arms (*our school crest*). **5 a** a line along the top of the neck of some animals. **b** the hair growing from this; a mane. **6** the highest level reached by a river in flood. ● v. **1** tr. reach the crest of (a hill, wave, etc.). **2** tr. a provide with a crest. **b** serve as a crest to. **3** intr. (of a wave) form into a crest. **4** intr. (of a river in flood) reach its highest level. □ **the crest of a wave** the most favourable moment in one's progress. □ **crested** adj. (also in comb.).

crestfallen adj. **1** dejected, dispirited. **2** with a fallen or drooping crest.

Cretaceous /krɪ'teiʃəs/ ● adj. **1** (**cretaceous**) of the nature of chalk. **2** of or relating to the last period of the Mesozoic era, lasting from about 144 to 65 million years BP, between the Jurassic and Tertiary periods. ● n. this geological era or system.

Cretan /kri:tən/ ● n. a native of Crete, an island SE of the Greek mainland. ● adj. of or relating to Crete or the Cretans.

cretin /'kretin, 'kri:-/ n. **1** a person who is deformed and mentally retarded as the result of a thyroid deficiency. **2** informal derogatory a stupid person. □ **cretinism** n. **cretinize** v.tr. **cretinous** adj.

cretons /krə'tɔ̃/ n.pl. Cdn (Que.) a spread of shredded pork cooked with onions in pork fat.

crevasse /krə'væs/ n. a deep open crack, esp. in a glacier.

crevice n. a narrow opening or fissure, esp. in a rock or building etc.

crew[1] ● n. (often treated as pl.) **1 a** a group of people operating a ship, aircraft, train, etc. **b** such a group as distinguished from the captain or officers. **c** a body of people working together; a team. **2** informal a company of people. ● v.tr. & intr. supply or act as a crew or member of a crew (for).

crew[2] past of CROW[2].

crewcut n. a very short haircut; a brush cut.

crewman n. (pl. **-men**) a member of a crew.

crewneck n. **1** a close-fitting round neckline, esp. on a sweater. **2** a sweater etc. with a crewneck.

crib ● n. **1** a bed for a baby or young child, having barred sides. **2** a barred container or rack for animal fodder. **3** informal **a** a sheet of notes, answers to questions, etc. used surreptitiously by students as an aid in an exam etc. **b** plagiarized work etc. **4** (also **cribbing**) heavy crossed timbers used in foundations in loose soil, to support a pier, to form a dam, etc. **5 a** informal cribbage. **b** (in cribbage) a set of cards discarded by the players and used by the dealer. ● v.tr. & intr. (**cribbed**, **cribbing**) **1** informal copy (another person's work) unfairly or without acknowledgement. **2** confine in a small space. **3** *informal* pilfer, steal. □ **cribber** *n.*

cribbage *n.* a card game in which the dealer may score from the cards in the crib (see CRIB *n.* 5b), esp. using pegs in a board for keeping score.

crib death *n.* N *Amer.* = SUDDEN INFANT DEATH SYNDROME.

crick ● *n.* a sudden painful stiffness in the neck or the back etc. ● *v.tr.* produce a crick in (the neck etc.).

cricket[1] *n.* any of various grasshopper-like insects of the family Gryllidae, the males of which produce a characteristic chirping sound.

cricket[2] ● *n.* a game played on a field with two teams of 11 players taking turns to bowl at a wicket defended by a batting player of the other team. ● *v.intr.* (**cricketed, cricketing**) play cricket. □ **cricketer** *n.*

cri de cœur /ˌkriː də ˈkɜr/ *n.* (*pl.* **cris de cœur** *pronunc.* same) a passionate appeal or protest.

cried *past and past part.* of CRY.

crier *n.* **1** a person who cries. **2** an officer who makes public announcements in a public place etc.

crime *n.* **1 a** an offence punishable by law. **b** illegal acts as a whole (*resorted to crime*). **2** an evil act. **3** a shameful act (*a crime to waste it*).

crime fighter *n.* a person who fights crime. □ **crime-fighting** *n.*

crime scene *n.* N *Amer.* the place where a crime has been committed.

crime wave *n.* a sudden increase in crime.

criminal ● *n.* a person who has committed a crime or crimes. ● *adj.* **1** of, involving, or concerning crime (*criminal records*). **2** having committed (and usu. been convicted of) a crime. **3** *Law* relating to or expert in criminal law rather than civil or political matters (*criminal lawyer*). **4** scandalous, deplorable. □ **criminality** *n.* **criminally** *adv.*

Criminal Code *n.* a federal statute embodying most of Canada's criminal law and specifying criminal procedures and sentencing options.

criminal harassment *n.* Cdn the criminal offence of stalking.

criminalize *v.tr.* **1** turn (an activity) into a criminal offence by making it illegal. **2** turn (a person) into a criminal, esp. by making his or her activities illegal. □ **criminalization** *n.*

criminal law *n.* law concerned with the prosecution of crime (*opp.* CIVIL LAW 1).

criminal negligence *n.* Cdn Law an offence involving a wanton or reckless disregard for the lives or safety of others.

criminology /ˌkrɪmɪˈnɒlədʒi/ *n.* the scientific study of crime. □ **criminological** *adj.* **criminologist** *n.*

crimp ● *v.tr.* **1** compress into small folds or ridges. **2** make narrow wrinkles or flutings in; corrugate. **3** make waves in (the hair) with a hot iron. ● *n.* a crimped thing or form. □ **put a crimp in** N *Amer.* *informal* thwart; interfere with. □ **crimper** *n.*

crimson ● *adj.* of a rich deep red inclining to purple. ● *n.* this colour. ● *v.tr. & intr.* make or become crimson.

cringe ● *v.intr.* **1** contract the muscles of the body involuntarily; shrink back in fear, apprehension, or disgust. **2** feel excessively embarrassed. **3** (often foll. by *to*) behave obsequiously. ● *n.* the act or an instance of cringing. □ **cringer** *n.*

crinkle ● *n.* **1** a wrinkle or crease in paper, cloth, etc. **2** fabric with a wrinkled surface. ● *v.* **1** *intr.* form crinkles. **2** *tr.* form crinkles in. □ **crinkly** *adj.*

crinkle-cut *adj.* (of vegetables) cut with wavy edges.

crinoline /ˈkrɪnəlɪn/ *n.* **1** a stiffened or hooped petti-

coat worn to make a skirt stand out. **2** a stiff fabric used for linings, hats, etc.

cripes *interj.* *slang* expressing surprise, anger, etc.

cripple ● *n.* a person who is permanently impaired in movement, esp. one unable to walk normally. ● *v.tr.* **1** make a cripple of; lame. **2** disable, impair. **3** weaken or damage seriously (*crippled by lack of funding*). □ **crippled** *adj.* **crippling** *adj.* **cripplingly** *adv.*

crisis *n.* (*pl.* **crises** /ˈkraɪsiːz/) **1** a time of danger or great difficulty. **2** the turning point, esp. of a disease. **3** a decisive moment.

crisis centre *n.* a place offering immediate counselling, treatment, etc. to people who are victims of sexual assault, physical abuse, etc.

crisis management *n.* **1** the practice of taking managerial action only when a crisis has developed. **2** the management of a crisis situation.

crisp ● *adj.* **1** hard but brittle. **2** (of air or weather) dry and cold. **3** (of a style or manner) brisk and decisive, esp. dismissive. **4** (of pictures etc.) clear and distinct. **5** (of cloth etc.) slightly stiff. **6** (of hair) closely curling. **7** (of fruit or vegetables) firm and fresh. **8** invigorating to the sense of smell or taste. ● *n.* **1** a baked dessert made of fruit topped with a crumbly mixture of flour, oats, butter, and sugar. **2** a thing overdone in roasting etc. (*burned to a crisp*). **3** a crisp cookie. ● *v.tr. & intr.* **1** make or become crisp. **2** curl in short stiff folds or waves. □ **crisply** *adv.* **crispness** *n.*

crispbread *n.* **1** a thin crisp biscuit of crushed rye etc. **2** these collectively.

crisper *n.* a compartment in a refrigerator for storing fruit and vegetables.

Crispin *n.* a large yellow or greenish-yellow cooking and eating apple.

crispy *adj.* (**-ier, -iest**) **1** crisp, brittle. **2** curly. **3** brisk. □ **crispiness** *n.*

criss-cross ● *v.* **1 a** *tr. & intr.* cross or intersect repeatedly. **b** *intr.* move crosswise. **2** *tr.* mark or make with a criss-cross pattern. ● *n.* **1** a pattern of crossing lines. **2** the crossing of lines or currents etc. ● *adj.* crossing; in cross lines (*criss-cross marking*). ● *adv.* crosswise; at cross purposes.

crit *n.* *informal* **1** = CRITICISM 2. **2** = CRITIQUE.

criterion *n.* (*pl.* **criteria**) a principle or standard that a thing is judged by. ¶The plural form of *criterion*, *criteria*, is often used incorrectly as the singular.

critic *n.* **1** a person who censures. **2 a** a person who reviews, analyzes, or judges the merits of literary, artistic, theatrical, or musical works etc., esp. regularly or professionally. **b** a person who writes or broadcasts reviews of restaurants, wine, etc. **3** a person engaged in textual criticism. **4** Cdn a member of an opposition party monitoring and criticizing a specific government ministry (*finance critic*).

critical *adj.* **1 a** making or involving adverse or censorious comments or judgments. **b** expressing or involving criticism. **c** involving judgment or discernment (*use your critical sense*). **2** skilful at or engaged in criticism. **3** providing textual criticism (*a critical edition of Milton*). **4 a** of or at a crisis; involving risk or suspense (*in critical condition*). **b** decisive, crucial (*of critical importance; at the critical moment*). **5 a** *Math.* & *Physics* marking transition from one state etc. to another (*critical angle*). **b** (of a nuclear reactor) maintaining a self-sustaining chain reaction. □ **criticality** *n.* (in sense 5). **critically** *adv.*

critical mass *n.* **1** the amount of fissile material needed to maintain a nuclear chain reaction. **2** the amount of anything required to achieve a desired effect (*a critical mass of volunteers*).

criticism n. **1 a** finding fault; censure. **b** a statement or remark expressing this. **2 a** the work of a critic. **b** an article, essay, etc., expressing or containing an analytical evaluation of something.

criticize v.tr. & intr. **1** find fault with; censure. **2** discuss critically. □ **criticizer** n.

critique ● n. a critical essay or analysis; an instance or the process of formal criticism. ● v.tr. (**critiques, critiqued, critiquing**) discuss critically.

critter n. informal an animal, insect, etc.

croak ● n. **1** a deep hoarse sound as of a frog or a raven. **2** a sound resembling this. ● v. **1 a** intr. utter a croak. **b** tr. utter with a croak or in a dismal manner. **2** slang **a** intr. die. **b** tr. kill.

croaker n. **1** an animal that croaks. **2** any fish of the family Sciaenidae, which make sounds using the swim bladder as a resonating chamber.

croaky adj. (**-ier, -iest**) (of a voice) croaking; hoarse. □ **croakily** adv. **croakiness** n.

Croatian /kro:'eiʃən/ (also **Croat** /'kro:æt/) ● n. **1 a** a native or inhabitant of Croatia, a country in SE Europe. **b** a person of Croatian descent. **2** the language of the Croatians, a form of Serbo-Croat written in the Roman alphabet. ● adj. of or relating to Croatia, the Croatians, or their language.

croc n. informal a crocodile.

crochet /kro:'ʃei, 'kro:-/ ● n. **1** a handicraft in which yarn is made up into a patterned fabric by means of a small slender hooked rod. **2** work made in this way. ● v. (**crocheted** /-ʃeid/; **crocheting** /-ʃeiŋ/) **1** tr. make by crocheting. **2** intr. do crochet.

crock n. **1** an earthenware pot or jar. **2** a broken piece of earthenware. **3** esp. N Amer. informal (also **crock of shit** coarse slang) something untrue, deceitful, etc. (their story was just a crock).

crocked adj. N Amer. slang drunk.

crockery n. earthenware or china dishes, plates, etc.

Crock-Pot n. proprietary a slow cooker.

crocodile n. **1** any of a group of large tropical and subtropical amphibious reptiles with thick scaly skin, a long tail, and long jaws (sometimes treated as a family, Crocodylidae) related to alligators. **2** leather from its skin, used to make bags, shoes, etc.

crocodile tears n. **1** insincere grief. **2** tears shed without feeling any real sorrow, pain, etc.

crocus n. (pl. **crocuses**) **1** any plant of the genus Crocus, growing from a corm and having brilliant usu. yellow or purple flowers. **2** see PRAIRIE CROCUS.

Crohn's disease /'kro:nz/ n. a chronic inflammatory disease of the intestines, esp. the colon and ileum, causing ulcers and fistulae.

croissant /krwɒ'sɑ̃, krwə-/ n. a rich, flaky, crescent-shaped bread roll.

crokinole /'kro:kə,no:l/ n. esp. Cdn a game in which wooden discs are flicked across a round wooden board towards its centre.

Cro-Magnon /kro:'mægnɒn, -'mægnən/ ● adj. of a tall broad-faced European race of late paleolithic times. ● n. a Cro-Magnon person.

crone n. a withered old woman.

crony n. (pl. **-ies**) often derogatory a close friend or companion.

cronyism n. N Amer. the appointment of friends to political posts without due regard to qualifications.

crook n. **1 a** informal a criminal. **b** a swindler. **2** the hooked staff of a shepherd or bishop. **3 a** a bend, curve, or hook. **b** anything hooked or curved. ● v.tr. & intr. bend, curve. ● adj. crooked.

crooked adj. (**crookeder, crookedest**) **1 a** not

straight or level; bent, curved, twisted. **b** deformed, bent with age. **2** informal dishonest. □ **crookedly** adv. **crookedness** n.

croon ● v.tr. & intr. hum or sing in a low subdued voice, esp. sentimentally. ● n. such singing. □ **crooner** n.

crop ● n. **1 a** the produce of cultivated plants, esp. cereals. **b** the season's total yield of this (a good crop). **2** a group or an amount produced or appearing at one time (this year's crop of students). **3** the stock or handle of a whip. **4 a** a style of hair cut very short. **b** the cropping of hair. **5** Zool. **a** the pouch in a bird's gullet where food is prepared for digestion. **b** a similar organ in other animals. ● v. (**cropped, cropping**) **1** tr. a cut off. **b** (of animals) bite off (the tops of plants). **2** tr. **a** cut (hair, edges of a book, a dog's ears, etc.) short. **b** trim (a photograph) to fit a space. **3** tr. gather or reap (produce). **4** tr. (foll. by with) sow or plant (land) with a crop. **5** intr. (of land) bear a crop. □ **crop out** Geol. appear at the surface. **crop up 1** (of a subject, circumstance, etc.) appear or come to one's notice unexpectedly. **2** Geol. = CROP OUT.

crop-dusting n. the sprinkling of powdered insecticide or fertilizer on crops, esp. from the air. □ **crop-duster** n.

cropland n. land on which crops are grown.

cropper n. □ **come a cropper** slang **1** fail badly. **2** fall heavily.

croquet /kro:'kei, 'kro:-/ n. a game played on a lawn, in which mallets are used to drive wooden balls through a series of hoops.

crosier var. of CROZIER.

cross ● n. **1** an upright post with a transverse bar, as used in antiquity for crucifixion. **2 a** (**the Cross**) in Christianity, the cross on which Christ was crucified. **b** a representation of this as an emblem of Christianity. **c** = SIGN OF THE CROSS. **3** a staff surmounted by a cross. **4 a** a thing or mark shaped like a cross, esp. a figure made by two short intersecting lines (+ or x). **b** a monument in the form of a cross, esp. on a tomb. **5** a cross-shaped decoration awarded for personal valour. **6 a** an intermixture of animal breeds or plant varieties. **b** an animal or plant resulting from this. **7** (foll. by between) a mixture or compromise of two things. **8** Boxing a blow with a crosswise movement of the fist. **9** a trial or affliction; something to be endured. ● v. **1** tr. (often foll. by over; also intr.) go across or to the other side of (a road, river, sea, etc.). **2 a** intr. intersect or be across one another (the roads cross near the bridge). **b** tr. place crosswise (cross one's legs). **3** tr. draw a line or lines across (cross your t's). **4** tr. (foll. by off, out) cancel or obliterate or remove from a list with lines drawn across. **5** tr. (often refl.) make the sign of the cross on or over. **6** intr. **a** pass in opposite or different directions. **b** (of letters between two correspondents) each be dispatched before receipt of the other. **c** (of telephone lines) become wrongly interconnected so that intrusive calls can be heard. **7** tr. **a** cause to interbreed. **b** cross-fertilize (plants). **8** tr. slang cheat; double-cross. ● adj. **1** (often foll. by with) peevish, angry. **2** (usu. attrib.) transverse; reaching from side to side. **3** (usu. attrib.) intersecting. **4** (usu. attrib.) contrary, opposed, reciprocal. □ **at cross-purposes** misunderstanding or conflicting with one another. **bear one's cross** accept trials and misfortunes stoically. **cross one's fingers** (or **keep one's fingers crossed**) **1** put one finger across another as a sign of hoping for good luck. **2** trust in good luck. **cross the floor** Cdn & Brit. join the opposing side in a legislature, leadership convention, etc. **cross one's heart** make a solemn pledge, esp.

by crossing one's front. **cross one's mind** (of a thought etc.) occur to one, esp. transiently. **cross over 1** pass over (a street, boundary, etc.). **2** move from one culture or artistic style to another. **cross paths** (or **cross one's path**) encounter or meet. **cross swords** (often foll. by *with*) encounter in opposition; have an argument or dispute. **cross wires** (or **get one's wires crossed**) **1** become wrongly connected by telephone. **2** have a misunderstanding. □ **crossly** *adv.* **crossness** *n.*

crossbar *n.* a horizontal bar between two upright bars, e.g. on a bicycle or hockey net.

crossbeam *n.* a transverse beam in a structure.

crossbill *n.* any finch of the genus *Loxia*, having a bill with crossed mandibles for opening pine cones.

crossbones *n.* a representation of two crossed thigh bones, usu. under the figure of a skull, as an emblem of piracy or death.

cross-border *adj.* passing, occurring, or performed across a border between two countries.

crossbow *n.* a bow fixed across a wooden stock, with a groove for an arrow and a mechanism for drawing and releasing the string.

crossbreed ● *n.* **1** a breed of animals or plants produced by crossing different breeds. **2** an individual animal or plant of a crossbreed. ● *v.tr.* (*past* and *past part.* **-bred**) produce or modify by crossing different breeds.

cross-check ● *v.tr.* **1** check by a second or alternative method, or by several methods. **2** (in hockey and lacrosse) obstruct (an opponent) by holding one's stick horizontally in both hands and thrusting it at their body. ● *n.* an instance of cross-checking.

cross-country ● *adj. & adv.* **1** across fields or open country (*cross-country running*). **2** across a country (*a cross-country train trip*). ● *adj.* of or designating the sport of skiing across the countryside using long, narrow skis. ● *n.* (*pl.* **-ies**) a cross-country sport or race.

cross-cultural *adj.* of or relating to different cultures or comparison between them. □ **cross-culturally** *adv.*

cross-current *n.* **1** a current in a body of water flowing across the main current. **2** (often in *pl.*) a conflicting tendency or movement.

crosscut ● *v.* **1** *tr.* cut across (a piece of wood etc). **2** *intr.* switch back and forth between two or more sequences or shots in a film so they appear to be taking place at the same time. ● *adj.* cut across the main grain or axis. ● *n.* a diagonal cut, path, etc.

crosscut saw *n.* a saw for cutting across the grain of wood.

cross-dressing *n.* the practice of wearing the clothes of the opposite sex. □ **cross-dress** *v.intr.* **cross-dresser** *n.*

crosse /krɒs/ *n.* (in women's field lacrosse) the stick.

cross-examine *v.tr.* **1** examine (a witness in a law court) esp. to check, extend, or discredit testimony already given. **2** interrogate with minute and persistent questioning. □ **cross-examination** *n.* **cross-examiner** *n.*

cross-eyed *adj.* (as a disorder) having one or both eyes turned permanently inwards towards the nose.

cross-fertilization *n.* **1** fertilization from one of a different species. **2** fruitful interchange of ideas, information, etc. □ **cross-fertilize** *v.tr.*

crossfire *n.* **1** lines of gunfire crossing one another simultaneously from different positions. **2 a** attack or criticism from several sources at once. **b** a lively or combative exchange of views etc.

cross fox *n.* a yellowish N American variety of the red fox with a cross-shaped patch across the shoulders.

cross-grained *adj.* **1** (of timber) having a grain that runs across the regular grain. **2** perverse, intractable.

crosshair *n.* a fine wire at the focus of an optical instrument for use in measurement.

cross-hatch *v.tr.* shade with intersecting sets of parallel lines. □ **cross-hatching** *n.*

cross-ice *adj.* (of a pass in hockey, ringette, etc.) shot from one side of the rink to the other.

crossing *n.* **1** a place where things (esp. roads) cross. **2** a place at which one may cross a street, railway tracks, etc. **3** a journey across water. **4** *Biol.* mating.

crossing guard *n.* *N Amer.* a person who escorts pedestrians, usu. children, safely across a busy intersection or crosswalk.

crossing over *n.* an exchange of genes between homologous chromosomes (compare RECOMBINATION).

cross-legged *adj.* with one leg crossed over the other.

Cross of Valour *n.* Canada's highest award for bravery, given to civilians and military personnel who perform selfless acts of courage in the face of extreme danger.

crossover ● *n.* **1** a point or place of crossing from one side to the other. **2** the process of crossing over, esp. from one style or genre of music etc. to another. ● *adj.* **1** having a part that crosses over. **2** that crosses over, esp. from one style or genre to another.

crosspatch *n.* *informal* a bad-tempered person.

crosspiece *n.* a transverse beam or other component of a structure etc.

cross-pollinate *v.tr. & intr.* **1** pollinate (a plant) from another. **2** blend together (styles of music, ideas, etc.) □ **cross-pollination** *n.*

cross-refer *v.intr.* (**-referred**, **-referring**) refer from one part of a book, article, etc., to another.

cross-reference ● *n.* a reference from one part of a book, article, etc., to another. ● *v.tr.* provide with cross-references.

cross rib *n.* a cut of beef from the front part of the ribs, below the blade.

crossroad *n.* **1** *N Amer.* a road that crosses a main road or connects two main roads. **2** = CROSSROADS.

crossroads *n.pl.* (treated as *sing.*) **1** an intersection of two or more roads. **2** a critical turning point.

cross-section *n.* **1 a** a cutting of a solid at right angles to an axis. **b** a plane surface produced in this way. **c** a representation of this. **2** a representative sample, esp. of people. **3** *Physics* a quantity expressing the probability of interaction between particles. □ **cross-sectional** *adj.*

cross-stitch ● *n.* **1** a stitch formed of two stitches crossing each other. **2** needlework done using this stitch. ● *v.tr.* sew or embroider with cross-stitches.

cross street *n.* a street crossing another or connecting two streets (*turn at the next cross street*).

crosstalk *n.* unwanted transfer of signals between communication channels.

crosstown *N Amer.* ● *adj.* **1** extending across or following a route across a town or city. **2** coming from the other side of a town or city, esp. in reference to two competing sports teams in the same town (*crosstown rivals*). ● *adv.* **1** across a town or city. **2** to a rival team in the same city (*was traded crosstown*).

cross-train *v.* **1** *tr.* train in two or more sports to improve performance, esp. in one's main sport. **2** *tr. &*

intr. train (an employee etc.) in more than one skill. □ **cross-trainer** *n.* **cross-training** *n.*

crosswalk *n.* *N Amer. & Austral.* a pedestrian crossing.

crossways *adv.* = CROSSWISE *adv.*

crosswind *n.* a wind blowing across one's direction of travel.

crosswise *adj. & adv.* **1** across; transverse or transversely. **2** in the form of a cross; intersecting.

crossword *n.* (also **crossword puzzle**) a puzzle of a grid of squares and blanks into which words crossing vertically and horizontally have to be filled from clues.

crostini /krɒ'sti:ni/ *n.pl.* small pieces of toasted bread topped with vegetables etc., served as an appetizer.

crotch *n.* **1** the place where the legs join the trunk of the human body. **2** the part of a pair of pants, underwear, etc. where the two legs or panels join. **3** a fork of a tree or bough.

crotchety /'krɒtʃəti/ *adj.* peevish, irritable. □ **crotchetiness** *n.*

crouch *v.intr.* stoop low with the legs bent close to the body, esp. for concealment, or (of an animal) before pouncing; be in this position. ● *n.* an act of crouching; a crouching position.

croup¹ /kru:p/ *n.* an inflammation of the larynx and trachea in children, with a hard cough and difficulty in breathing. □ **croupy** *adj.*

croup² *n.* the rump or hindquarters esp. of a horse.

croupier /'kru:pi:ər, -i:,ei/ *n.* the person in charge of a gaming table, raking in and paying out money etc.

crouton /'kru:tɒn/ *n.* a small cube of fried or toasted bread used as a garnish for soups, salads, etc.

Crow ● *n.* (*pl.* same or **Crows**) **1** a member of an Aboriginal people living in southern Montana. **2** the Siouan language of this people. ● *adj.* of or relating to this people or their culture or language.

crow¹ *n.* **1** any large black bird of the genus *Corvus*, having a powerful black beak, e.g. the omnivorous common crow of N America, *C. brachyrhynchos*. **2** any similar bird of the family Corvidae, e.g. the raven or magpie. **3** *slang derogatory* a woman, esp. an old or ugly one. □ **as the crow flies** in a straight line. **eat crow** *N Amer. informal* be forced to admit a mistake.

crow² ● *v.intr.* **1** (*past* **crowed** or **crew**) (of a rooster) utter its characteristic loud cry. **2** (usu. foll. by *over*, *about*) express gleeful satisfaction; swagger; boast. ● *n.* **1** the cry of a rooster. **2** a happy or triumphant cry uttered by a person.

crowbar *n.* an iron bar with a flattened end, used as a lever.

crowberry *n.* (*pl.* **-ies**) **1** a heathlike evergreen shrub *Empetrum nigrum*, bearing black berries. **2** the flavourless edible berry of this plant.

crowd ● *n.* **1** a large number of people gathered together, usu. without orderly arrangement. **2** a mass of spectators; an audience. **3** *informal* a particular company or set of people (*the crowd from sales*). **4** (*prec.* by *the*) the mass or multitude of people (*go along with the crowd*). **5** a large number of things. ● *v.* **1** *intr.* **a** come together in a crowd. **b** force one's way (*we crowded into the bar*). **2** *tr.* **a** (foll. by *into*) force or compress into a confined space (*crowded the children into the gym*) **b** (often foll. by *with*; usu. in *passive*) fill or make abundant with (*was crowded with tourists*). **3** *tr.* **a** (of a number of people) come aggressively close to. **b** *informal* harass or pressure (a person). **4** *tr.* *N Amer. informal* approach (a specified age, time, etc.) closely (*must be crowding fifty*). □ **crowd out** exclude by crowding. □ **crowded** *adj.* **crowdedness** *n.*

crowd-pleaser *n.* *informal* an event, person, or thing,

esp. a song, movie, poem, etc., that is well-received by an audience. □ **crowd-pleasing** *adj.*

crowfoot *n.* **1** = BUTTERCUP. **2** a grass widely naturalized in N America, *Dactyloctenium aegyptium*.

crown ● *n.* **1** a monarch's ornamental and usu. jewelled headdress. **2** (**the Crown**) **a** the monarch, esp. as head of state. **b** the power or authority residing in the monarchy. **3 a** a wreath of leaves or flowers etc. worn on the head, esp. as an emblem of victory. **b** an award or distinction gained by a victory or achievement, esp. in sport. **4** a crown-shaped thing, esp. a device or ornament. **5** the top part of a thing, esp. of the head or a hat. **6 a** the highest or central part of an arched or curved thing (*crown of the road*). **b** a thing that completes or forms the summit. **7 a** the part of a plant just above and below the ground. **b** the leaves and upper branches of a tree. **8** the upper part of a cut gem above the girdle. **9 a** the part of a tooth projecting from the gum. **b** an artificial replacement or covering for this. **10** = CROWN ATTORNEY. ● *v.tr.* **1** put a crown on (a person or a person's head). **2** invest (a person) with a royal crown or authority. **3** (often in *passive*) be a crown to; encircle or rest on the top of (*the hill was crowned with an oak tree*). **4 a** (often as **crowning** *adj.*) be or cause to be the consummation, reward, or finishing touch to (*the crowning glory*). **b** bring (efforts) to a happy issue. **5** fit a crown to (a tooth). **6** *slang* hit on the head. **7** promote (a piece in checkers) to king.

Crown attorney *n.* (also **Crown counsel**, **Crown prosecutor**) *Cdn* a lawyer who conducts prosecutions of indictable offences on behalf of the Crown.

crown colony *n.* (*pl.* **-ies**) a colony controlled by a foreign monarchy.

Crown corporation *n.* *Cdn* a corporation owned by the federal or provincial governments.

crown jewel *n.* **1** (in *pl.*) the regalia and other jewellery worn by a sovereign on certain state occasions. **2** the most valuable or beautiful possession, feature, etc. (*the crown jewel of my record collection*).

crown land *n.* (in Canada and other Commonwealth nations) land owned by federal or provincial or state governments.

crown of thorns *n.* **1** a starfish, *Acanthaster planci*, which has spines on its upper surface and feeds on coral polyps. **2** a plant, *Euphorbia milli*, with very thorny stems and small flowers surrounded by showy bracts, often grown as a houseplant.

crown prince *n.* a male heir to a sovereign throne.

crown princess *n.* **1** the wife of a crown prince. **2** a female heir to a sovereign throne.

Crown reserve *n.* *Cdn hist.* a portion of land reserved for the Crown as a source of revenue free from the control of the colonial legislature.

Crown witness *n.* *Cdn* a witness called to testify by the Crown.

Crow rate *n.* *Cdn hist.* a reduced rate for shipping grain or flour by rail from Western to Eastern Canada.

crow's feet *n.pl.* wrinkles at the outer corner of a person's eye.

crow's nest *n.* a barrel etc. fixed at the masthead of a sailing vessel as a shelter for a lookout man.

crozier /'kro:ʒər, -ziər/ *n.* **1** a hooked staff carried by a bishop as a symbol of pastoral office. **2** the curled tip of a young plant, esp. a fern.

CRS *abbr.* computer reservation system.

CRT *abbr.* cathode ray tube.

CRTC *abbr.* Canadian Radio-television and Telecommunications Commission.

cruces pl. of CRUX.

crucial adj. **1** decisive, critical. **2** very important. □ **cruciality** n. (pl. **-ies**). **crucially** adv.

crucible /ˈkruːsəbəl/ n. **1** a container in which metals etc. are heated. **2** a severe test or trial.

crucifer /ˈkruːsəfər/ n. **1** a cruciferous plant. **2** a person carrying a processional cross or crucifix.

cruciferous adj. of the family Cruciferae, having flowers with four petals arranged in a cross.

crucifix n. a model or image of a cross with a figure of Christ on it.

crucifixion n. **1 a** crucifying or being crucified. **b** an instance of this. **2** (**Crucifixion**) **a** the crucifixion of Christ. **b** a representation of this.

cruciform ● adj. cross-shaped (esp. of a church with transepts). ● n. a cross.

crucify v.tr. (**-ies, -ied**) **1** put to death by fastening to a cross. **2 a** cause extreme pain to. **b** persecute; torment. **c** criticize or punish harshly. **3** slang defeat thoroughly in an argument, game, etc.

crud n. slang **1** a deposit of dirt, grease, encrusted food, etc. **2** an unpleasant person. **3** something of little value (who wrote this crud?). □ **cruddy** adj.

crude ● adj. **1 a** in the natural or raw state; not refined (crude oil). **b** rough, unpolished; lacking finish. **2 a** offensive, indecent (a crude gesture). **b** (of an action or statement or manners) rude, blunt. **3 a** Statistics (of figures) not adjusted or corrected. **b** rough (a crude estimate). ● n. unrefined petroleum. □ **crudely** adv. **crudeness** n. **crudity** n. (pl. **-ies**).

crudités /ˌkruːdɪˈteɪ, -diː-/ n.pl. an hors d'oeuvre of mixed raw vegetables often served with a sauce into which they are dipped.

cruel adj. (**crueller, cruellest**) **1** causing pain or suffering, esp. deliberately (a cruel remark). **2** indifferent to or gratified by another's suffering. **3** merciless; harsh; unrelentingly severe (cruel fate). □ **cruelly** adv. **cruelness** n.

cruelty n. (pl. **-ies**) **1** a cruel act or attitude; indifference to another's suffering. **2** a succession of cruel acts; a continued cruel attitude (suffered cruelty). **3** Law physical or mental harm inflicted (whether or not intentional), esp. as a ground for divorce.

cruelty-free adj. (of cosmetics etc.) produced without involving cruelty to animals.

cruise ● v. **1** intr. make a journey aboard ship calling at a series of ports usu. according to a predetermined plan, esp. for pleasure. **2** intr. sail about without a precise destination. **3** intr. **a** (of a motor vehicle or aircraft) travel at a moderate or economical speed. **b** (of a vehicle or its driver) travel at random, esp. slowly. **4** intr. achieve an objective, win a race etc., with ease. **5** intr. & tr. slang walk or drive about (the streets etc.) in search of a sexual (esp. homosexual) partner. **6** tr. & intr. N Amer. inspect an area of forest to estimate the volume of timber on it. ● n. **1** a cruising voyage on board a ship, esp. as a holiday (also attrib.: cruise ship). **2** the act or an instance of cruising. **3** N Amer. a survey or estimate of the volume of timber in an area. □ **cruisin' for a bruisin'** N Amer. slang heading for trouble or a beating.

cruise control n. a device on some motor vehicles that can be set to maintain a predetermined constant speed without use of the accelerator pedal.

cruise missile n. a missile able to fly at a low altitude and guide itself by reference to the features of the region it crosses.

cruiser n. **1** a warship of high speed and medium armament. **2** N Amer. a police patrol car. **3** N Amer. a

person who estimates the volume of timber in an area of forest.

cruiserweight n. esp. Brit. = LIGHT HEAVYWEIGHT.

cruller /ˈkrʌlər, ˈkruː-, ˈkrʊ-/ n. N Amer. a small, sweet cake made of a rich dough twisted and deep-fried.

crumb ● n. **1 a** a small fragment, esp. of bread. **b** a small particle; bit (a crumb of sympathy). **2** the soft inner part of a loaf of bread or a cake. **3** slang an objectionable person. ● v.tr. **1** cover with bread crumbs. **2** break into crumbs.

crumble ● v. **1** tr. & intr. break or fall into crumbs or fragments. **2** intr. (of power, a reputation, etc.) gradually disintegrate. ● n. **1** = CRISP n. 1. **2** a crumbly or crumbled substance.

crumbly adj. (**-ier, -iest**) consisting of, or apt to fall into, crumbs or fragments. □ **crumbliness** n.

crumby adj. (**-ier, -iest**) **1** like or covered in crumbs. **2** = CRUMMY adj.

crummy ● adj. (**-ier, -iest**) informal **1** dirty, squalid (a crummy apartment). **2** inferior, worthless. **3** sick or depressed (I feel crummy). ● n. (pl. **-ies**) N Amer. an old or converted vehicle for transporting loggers from their camp to work. □ **crummily** adv. **crumminess** n.

crumpet n. a small, round, sponge-like yeast cake resembling an English muffin, eaten toasted.

crumple ● v.tr. & intr. **1** crush or become crushed into a compact mass or irregular creases (crumpled the paper into a ball). **2** intr. collapse, give way (she crumpled to the floor). ● n. a crease or wrinkle. □ **crumply** adj.

crumple zone n. a part of a motor vehicle, esp. the extreme front and rear, designed to crumple easily in a crash and absorb impact.

crunch ● v. **1** tr. **a** crush noisily with the teeth. **b** grind (gravel, dry snow, etc.) under foot, wheels, etc. **2** intr. (often foll. by along, through) make a crunching sound in walking, moving, etc. **3** tr. informal process (large amounts of numbers or data) esp. by computer. ● n. **1** crunching; a crunching sound. **2** crunchiness (nuts add crunch to a salad). **3** informal a shortage or reduction (housing crunch). **4** informal a decisive event or moment. **5** N Amer. (often in pl.) a half sit-up, in which a person raises the upper body a few centimetres off the ground rather than sitting up fully. □ **cruncher** n.

crunchy ● adj. (**-ier, -iest**) hard and crispy. ● n. (pl. **-ies**) something that crunches when eaten. □ **crunchily** adv. **crunchiness** n.

crusade ● n. **1** (usu. **Crusade**) any of several medieval military expeditions made by Europeans to recover the Holy Land from the Muslims. **2** a vigorous campaign in favour of a cause. ● v.intr. engage in a crusade. □ **crusader** n.

crush ● v. **1** tr. compress with force or violence, so as to break, bruise, etc. **2** tr. reduce to powder by pressure. **3** tr. crease or crumple by rough handling. **4** tr. defeat or subdue completely. **5** tr. (usu. in passive) humiliate; disappoint; upset (I was crushed by his comment). **6** intr. advance in large numbers (the crowd crushed into the stadium). ● n. **1** an act of crushing. **2** a crowded mass of people. **3** informal **a** (usu. foll. by on) a (usu. passing) infatuation. **b** the object of an infatuation. □ **crushable** adj. **crusher** n. **crushing** adj. (esp. in sense 4 of v.). **crushingly** adv.

crust ● n. **1 a** the hard outer part of a loaf of bread. **b** a slice of bread from the end of the loaf. **c** a hard dry scrap of bread. **2 a** the pastry covering of a pie, tart, etc. **b** the bottom, usu. of pastry, of a pie, tart, pizza, etc. **3** a hard casing of a softer thing, e.g. a harder layer over soft snow. **4** Geol. the outer portion of the earth. **5 a** a coating or deposit on the surface of anything. **b** a hard dry formation on the skin, a scab. ● *v.tr. & intr.* **1** cover or become covered with a crust. **2** form into a crust. ☐ **crustal** *adj.* (in sense 4 of *n.*).

crustacean /krʌˈsteiʃən/ ● *n.* any arthropod of the class Crustacea, having a hard shell and usu. aquatic, e.g. the crab, lobster, and shrimp. ● *adj.* of or relating to crustaceans. ☐ **crustaceous** *adj.*

crusted *adj.* having a crust.

crusty *adj.* (**-ier, -iest**) **1** having a crisp crust (*a crusty loaf*). **2** irritable, curt. **3** hard, crustlike (*a crusty scab*). ☐ **crustily** *adv.* **crustiness** *n.*

crutch *n.* **1** a support for a lame person, usu. with a crosspiece at the top fitting under the armpit. **2** any support or prop (*alcohol is a crutch for many people*).

crux *n.* (*pl.* **cruxes** or **cruces** /ˈkruːsiːz/) **1** the decisive point at issue. **2** a difficult matter; a puzzle.

cry ● *v.* (**cries, cried**) **1** *intr.* (often foll. by *out*) make a loud or shrill sound, esp. to express pain, grief, etc., or to appeal for help. **2 a** *intr.* shed tears; weep. **b** *tr.* shed (tears). **3** *tr.* (often foll. by *out*) say or exclaim loudly or excitedly. **4** *intr.* (of an animal, esp. a bird) make a loud call. ● *n.* (*pl.* **cries**) **1** a loud inarticulate utterance of grief, pain, fear, joy, etc. **2** a loud excited utterance of words. **3** an urgent appeal or entreaty. **4** a period of weeping. **5 a** public demand; a strong movement of opinion. **b** a watchword or rallying call. **6** the natural utterance of an animal, esp. of birds. **7** the call of a street vendor etc. ☐ **cry one's eyes** (or **heart**) **out** weep bitterly. **cry from the heart** a passionate appeal or protest. **cry off** *informal* withdraw from a promise or undertaking. **cry out for** demand as a self-evident requirement or solution. **cry up** praise, extol. **a far cry 1** a long way. **2** a very different thing. **for crying out loud** *informal* an exclamation of surprise or annoyance. **in full cry** (esp. of hounds) in keen pursuit.

crybaby *n.* (*pl.* **-ies**) **1** a person, esp. a child, who cries frequently. **2** a whiny or self-pitying person.

crying *attrib.adj.* (of an injustice or other evil) flagrant, demanding redress (*a crying shame*).

cryogenics /ˌkraioˈdʒɛniks/ *n.* **1** the branch of physics dealing with the production and effects of very low temperatures. **2** = CRYONICS. ☐ **cryogenic** *adj.* **cryogenically** *adv.*

cryonics /kraiˈɒniks/ *n.* the practice or technique of deep-freezing human corpses for possible revival in the future. ☐ **cryonic** *adj.* **cryonicist** *n.*

crypt *n.* an underground room or vault, esp. one beneath a church, used usu. as a burial place.

cryptic *adj.* **1 a** obscure in meaning. **b** (of a crossword clue etc.) indicating the solution in a way that is not obvious. **c** secret, mysterious, enigmatic. **2** (of coloration etc.) serving to camouflage an animal in its natural environment. ☐ **cryptically** *adv.*

cryptogam /ˈkriptəˌgæm/ *n.* a plant that has no true flowers or seeds, e.g. ferns. ☐ **cryptogamic** *adj.*

cryptography /krɪpˈtɒɡrəfi/ *n.* the art of writing or solving codes and ciphers. ☐ **cryptographer** *n.* **cryptographic** *adj.* **cryptographically** *adv.*

crystal ● *n.* **1 a** a clear transparent mineral, esp. quartz. **b** a piece of this. **2 a** highly transparent glass, usu. containing lead oxide. **b** articles made of this, such as glassware and ornaments. **3** the glass over a watch face. **4** a crystalline piece of semiconductor. **5** *Chem.* **a** an aggregation of molecules with a definite internal structure and the external form of a solid enclosed by symmetrically arranged plane faces. **b** a solid whose constituent particles are symmetrically arranged. ● *adj.* (usu. *attrib.*) made of, like, or clear as

crystal. ☐ **crystal clear 1** unclouded, transparent. **2** readily understood.

crystal ball *n.* a glass globe used in crystal gazing.

crystal gazing *n.* the process of concentrating one's gaze on a crystal ball supposedly in order to obtain a picture of future events etc. ☐ **crystal gazer** *n.*

crystalline /ˈkristəˌlain, -ˌliːn/ *adj.* **1** of, like, or clear as crystal. **2** *Chem. & Geol.* having the structure and form of a crystal. ☐ **crystallinity** /-ˈlɪnti/ *n.*

crystalline lens *n.* a transparent lens enclosed in a membranous capsule behind the iris of the eye.

crystallize *v.* **1** *tr. & intr.* form or cause to form crystals. **2** (often foll. by *out*) **a** *intr.* (of ideas or plans) become definite. **b** *tr.* make definite. **3** *tr. & intr.* coat or impregnate or become coated or impregnated with sugar (*crystallized fruit*). ☐ **crystallization** *n.*

crystallography /ˌkristəˈlɒɡrəfi/ *n.* the science of crystal form and structure. ☐ **crystallographer** *n.* **crystallographic** *adj.*

CS *abbr.* **1** Civil Service. **2** Christian Science.

Cs *symbol* cesium.

c/s *abbr.* cycles per second.

CSA *abbr.* Canadian Standards Association.

CSB *abbr.* Canada Savings Bond.

CSC *abbr.* Correctional Service of Canada.

C-section *n.* *N Amer.* = CAESAREAN SECTION.

CSF *abbr. Med.* cerebrospinal fluid.

CSIS /ˈsiːsɪs/ *abbr.* Canadian Security Intelligence Service.

CSJ *abbr.* Catholicism Congregation of St. Joseph.

CSR *abbr.* customer service representative.

CST *abbr.* Central Standard Time.

Cst. *abbr. Cdn* Constable.

CT *abbr.* **1** Connecticut (in postal use). **2** *Med.* computerized tomography. **3** CENTRAL TIME.

ct. *abbr.* carat.

CTC *abbr.* Canadian Transport Commission.

Ctrl. *abbr. Computing* Control key.

CT scan *n.* = CAT SCAN.

CTV *abbr.* Canadian Television Network Limited.

Cu *symbol* the element copper.

cu. *abbr.* cubic.

cub ● *n.* **1** the young of a fox, bear, lion, etc. **2** (**Cub**) a member of the junior level (ages 8, 9, and 10) in Scouting. **3** (in full **cub reporter**) *informal* a young or inexperienced newspaper reporter. ● *v.tr. & intr.* (**cubbed, cubbing**) give birth to (cubs).

Cuban /ˈkjuːbən/ ● *adj.* of or relating to Cuba, an island republic in the Caribbean, or its people. ● *n.* a native or national of Cuba.

cubby *n.* (*pl.* **-ies**) **1** a very small room. **2** a snug or confined space.

cubbyhole *n.* **1** a very small room. **2** a small compartment.

cube ● *n.* **1** a solid contained by six equal squares. **2** a cube-shaped block. **3** the product of a number multiplied by its square. ● *v.tr.* **1** find the cube of (a number). **2** cut (food etc.) into small cubes.

cube van *n.* (also **cube truck**) *Cdn* a truck resembling a van at the front, with a taller and wider cube-like storage compartment behind.

cubic *adj.* **1** cube-shaped. **2** of three dimensions. **3** involving the cube (and no higher power) of a number (*cubic equation*). **4** designating a volume equal to that of a cube whose edge is a specified unit of linear measure (*cubic yard*).

cubicle *n.* a small partitioned space, esp. screened for privacy.

cubism n. a style and movement in art, esp. painting, in which objects are represented as an assemblage of geometrical forms. □ **cubist** n. & adj. **cubistic** adj.

cuckold /ˈkʌkoːld/ ● n. a man whose wife is unfaithful. ● v.tr. make a cuckold of.

cuckoo /ˈkuːkuː, ˈkʊku/ ● n. **1** any of various birds of the family Cuculidae, e.g. the black-billed cuckoo *Coccyzus erythropthalmus* or yellow-billed cuckoo *C. americanus* of N America, with brown backs and white underparts, or the Eurasian grey or brown speckled bird, *Cuculus canorus*, which leaves its eggs in the nests of small birds and has a distinctive two-note call. **2** *informal* a crazy or foolish person. ● *predic.adj.* *informal* crazy, foolish.

cuckoo clock n. a clock that strikes the hour with a sound like a cuckoo's call, usu. with the emergence on each note of a mechanical cuckoo.

cucumber n. **1** a long green fleshy fruit eaten esp. as a salad vegetable or pickled. **2** the climbing plant, *Cucumis sativus*, yielding this fruit.

cucurbit /kjuːˈkɜrbɪt/ n. = GOURD 1b.

cud n. **1** half-digested food returned from the first stomach of ruminants to the mouth for further chewing. **2** any substance, e.g. tobacco, used by a person to keep in the mouth and chew. □ **chew the cud** reflect meditatively, ruminate.

cuddle ● v. **1** tr. hold in an affectionate embrace, hug. **2** intr. nestle together, lie close and snug. ● n. an instance of cuddling. □ **cuddler** n.

cuddly adj. (**-ier, -iest**) **1** pleasant to cuddle. **2** (of a person) plump. □ **cuddliness** n.

cuddy n. (pl. **-ies**) (in full **cuddy cabin**) a room in a ship, esp. a shelter or locker in the bow of a small boat.

cudgel /ˈkʌdʒəl/ ● n. a short thick stick used as a weapon. ● v.tr. (**cudgelled, cudgelling**) beat with a cudgel. □ **cudgel one's brains** think hard about a problem. **take up the cudgels** (often foll. by *for*) make a vigorous defence.

cue¹ ● n. **1** something said or done on stage which serves as a signal for another performer or technician to speak, enter, or execute an action. **2 a** a stimulus to perception, understanding, etc. **b** a signal for action. **c** a hint on how to behave in particular circumstances. **3** a facility for or an instance of cueing audio equipment. ● v.tr. (**cues, cued, cueing** or **cuing**) **1** give a cue to. **2** put (a piece of audio equipment, esp. a record player or tape recorder) in readiness to play a particular part of the recorded material. □ **cue in** 1 insert a cue for. **2** give information to. **on cue** at the correct moment. **take one's cue from** follow the example or advice of.

cue² Billiards etc. ● n. a long straight tapering rod for striking the ball. ● v. (**cues, cued, cueing** or **cuing**) **1** tr. strike (a ball) with a cue. **2** intr. use a cue.

cue ball n. Billiards etc. the usu. white ball that is to be struck with the cue.

cue card n. a small card from which a person giving a speech, a television presenter, etc. reads lines.

cuff¹ ● n. **1 a** the end part of a sleeve. **b** the part of a glove covering the wrist. **2** N Amer. the lower turned up end of a pant leg. **3** (in pl.) informal handcuffs. **4** the inflatable band which is wound around a limb when blood pressure is measured. **5** a muscle ringing a joint (*rotator cuff*). ● v.tr. **1** provide (a garment) with a cuff or cuffs. **2** informal put handcuffs on. □ **off-the-cuff** informal without preparation, extempore. **shoot one's cuffs** make the cuffs of one's shirt visible by pulling them out beyond the cuffs of one's jacket. □ **cuffed** adj. (also in comb.).

cuff² ● v.tr. strike with an open hand. ● n. such a blow.

cufflink n. a device of two joined studs etc. to fasten the sides of a cuff together.

Cuisinart /ˈkwiːzənˌɑrt/ n. proprietary an electric food processor.

cuisine /kwɪˈziːn/ n. a style or method of cooking, esp. of a particular country or establishment.

cuke n. N Amer. informal a cucumber.

cul-de-sac /ˈkʌldəˌsæk, ˈkʊl-/ n. (pl. **cul-de-sacs** or **culs-de-sac** pronunc. same) **1** a street or passage closed at one end. **2** a route or course leading nowhere; a position from which one cannot escape.

culinary /ˈkʌlɪˌneri, ˈkjuː-, ˈkʊ-/ adj. of or for cooking.

cull ● v.tr. **1** select, choose, or gather from a large quantity or amount (*knowledge culled from books*). **2** pick or gather (flowers, fruit, etc.). **3** select (animals) according to quality, esp. poor or surplus specimens for killing. **4** N Amer. remove (timber) as being inferior. ● adj. rejected as being surplus or inferior (*cull apples*). ● n. **1** an act of culling. **2** an animal or animals culled. **3** an item picked out as being surplus or inferior. □ **culler** n.

culm /kʌlm/ n. Bot. the stem of a plant, esp. of grasses.

culminate v. **1** intr. (usu. foll. by *in*) reach its highest or final point (*the antagonism culminated in war*). **2** tr. bring to its highest or final point. **3** intr. (of a celestial object) reach its greatest altitude, be on the meridian. □ **culmination** n.

culottes /kuːˈlɒts, ˈkuː-/ n.pl. a woman's garment that hangs like a skirt but has separate legs, like trousers.

culpable /ˈkʌlpəbəl/ adj. deserving blame. □ **culpability** n. **culpably** adv.

culprit n. **1** a person accused of or guilty of an offence. **2** a person or thing held responsible for something (*smoking is often the culprit in heart disease*).

cult n. **1 a** a system of religious worship esp. as expressed in ritual. **b** a religious sect considered to be unorthodox or anti-social. **c** the members of such a sect. **2 a** devotion or homage to a person or thing (*the cult of aestheticism*). **b** a popular fashion esp. followed by a specific section of society. **3** (attrib.) denoting a person or thing popularized in this way (*cult film*). □ **cultic** adj. **cultish** adj. **cultishness** n. **cultism** n. **cultist** n.

cultivar n. a plant variety produced by cultivation.

cultivate v.tr. **1 a** prepare and use (soil etc.) for crops or gardening. **b** break up (the ground) with a cultivator. **c** remove weeds using a cultivator or hoe. **2 a** raise or produce (crops). **b** culture (bacteria etc.). **c** raise or produce (mussels, pearls, etc.). **3 a** make (the mind, feelings, etc.) more educated and sensitive. **b** pay attention to or nurture (a person or a person's friendship). **4** try to acquire or develop (a talent, attitude, manner, etc.). □ **cultivation** n.

cultivated adj. **1** (of a person, manners, etc.) having or showing education and good taste; refined. **2 a** (of land) used for growing crops. **b** (of plants) grown on farms etc. **3** (of mussels, pearls, etc.) grown in farms.

cultivator n. **1 a** a mechanical implement for breaking up the ground and uprooting weeds. **b** a two- or three-pronged hand tool used for weeding and loosening soil. **2** a person or thing that cultivates.

cultural adj. **1** of or relating to artistic or intellectual activity seen as cultivating the mind. **2** of or pertaining to culture in a society or civilization. □ **culturally** adv.

cultural imperialism n. the increasing influence in one country of the culture of another.

cultural sovereignty n. Cdn the power of a country

to maintain independence in its cultural activities from another, culturally dominant, nation.

culture ● *n.* **1 a** the arts and other manifestations of human intellectual achievement regarded collectively (*a city lacking in culture*). **b** a refined understanding of this; intellectual development (*a person of culture*). **2 a** the customs, civilization, and achievements of a particular time or people (*Mi'kmaq culture*). **b** the mode of behaviour within a particular group (*corporate culture*). **3** improvement by mental or physical training. **4 a** the cultivation of plants; the rearing of bees, silkworms, etc. **b** the cultivation of the soil. **5** a quantity of micro-organisms and the nutrient material supporting their growth. ● *v.tr.* maintain (bacteria etc.) in conditions suitable for growth.

cultured *adj.* **1** having refined taste and manners and a good education. **2** caused to develop by artificial means or in an artificial nutrient medium.

cultured pearl *n.* a pearl formed by an oyster after the insertion of a foreign body into its shell.

culture shock *n.* the feeling of disorientation experienced by a person suddenly subjected to an unfamiliar culture or way of life.

culvert *n.* **1** an underground channel carrying water across a road etc. **2** a channel for an electric cable.

cum[1] *prep.* (usu. in *comb.*) with, combined with, also used as (*a farmhouse-cum-museum*).

cum[2] *coarse slang* ● *n.* = COME *n.* ● *v.intr.* (*past* **came**; *pres. part.* **cumming**; *past part.* **cum**) = COME *v.* 13.

cumbersome *adj.* inconvenient in size, weight, or shape; unwieldy. □ **cumbersomely** *adv.*

cumbia /'kʊmbɪə/ *n.* **1** a form of dance music originating in Colombia. **2** a dance resembling the fandango performed to this music.

cumin /'kʌmɪn, kju:-/ *n.* **1** an umbelliferous plant, *Cuminum cyminum*, bearing aromatic seeds. **2** these seeds used as flavouring, esp. in curry powder.

cummerbund *n.* a wide, often horizontally pleated sash worn around the waist, esp. with a tuxedo.

cumulative *adj.* **1 a** increasing or increased in amount, force, etc., by successive additions (*cumulative evidence*). **b** formed by successive additions (*learning is a cumulative process*). **2** *Stock Exch.* (of shares) entitling holders to arrears of interest before any other distribution is made. □ **cumulatively** *adv.* **cumulativeness** *n.*

cumulonimbus /ˌkju:mjʊlo'nɪmbəs/ *n.* a cumulus cloud developed to a great height and producing rain or hail; a thundercloud (also *attrib.*).

cumulus /'kju:mjʊləs/ *n.* **1** clouds formed in rounded masses heaped on each other above a flat base. **2** a cloud of this type (also *attrib.*).

cuneiform /kju:'neɪəˌfɔrm, -'ni:ə-, 'kju:nɪ-/ ● *adj.* **1** wedge-shaped. **2** of, relating to, or using the wedge-shaped writing impressed usu. in clay in ancient Babylonian etc. inscriptions. ● *n.* cuneiform writing.

cunnilingus /ˌkʌnɪ'lɪŋgəs/ *n.* oral stimulation of the female genitals.

cunning ● *adj.* (**cunninger, cunningest**) **1 a** skilled in ingenuity or deceit. **b** selfishly clever or crafty. **2** ingenious (*a cunning device*). **3** *N Amer.* attractive, quaint. ● *n.* **1** craftiness; skill in deceit. **2** skill, ingenuity. □ **cunningly** *adv.* **cunningness** *n.*

cunt *n. coarse slang* **1** the female genitals. **2** *offensive* a woman. **3** *offensive* an unpleasant or stupid person. ¶A highly taboo word.

cup ● *n.* **1** a small bowl-shaped container, often with a handle, for drinking from. **2 a** its contents (*a cup of tea*). **b** *N Amer.* a measure of capacity esp. in cooking, equal to eight fluid ounces (237 ml). **3** a cup-shaped

thing, esp. the calyx of a flower or the socket of a bone. **4** an ornamental cup-shaped trophy as a prize for victory or prowess, esp. in a sports contest. **5** one's fate or fortune (*a bitter cup*). **6** either of the two cup-shaped parts of a brassiere. **7** the chalice used or the wine taken at the Eucharist. **8** *Golf* the hole on a putting green or the metal container in it. **9** the hard protective shell in a jockstrap. **10** a shallow bowl-shaped cooking utensil (*muffin cups*). ● *v.tr.* (**cupped, cupping**) **1** form (esp. one's hands) into the shape of a cup. **2** take or hold as in a cup. □ **one's cup of tea** *informal* what interests or suits one. **in one's cups** while drunk; drunk. □ **cupful** *n.* (*pl.* **-fuls**).

cupboard *n.* a recess or piece of furniture with a door and (usu.) shelves, in which things are stored.

cupcake *n.* **1** a small cake baked in a cup-shaped mould. **2** a term of endearment.

CUPE /'kju:pi/ *abbr.* Canadian Union of Public Employees.

cupidity /kju:'pɪdɪti/ *n.* greed for gain; avarice.

cupola /'kju:pələ/ *n.* **1 a** a rounded dome forming a roof or ceiling. **b** a small rounded dome adorning a roof. **2** a revolving dome protecting mounted guns in a fort or on a warship etc. □ **cupolaed** *adj.*

CUPW /ˌkʌp'dʌbəlju:/ *abbr.* Canadian Union of Postal Workers.

cur *n.* **1** a worthless or snappy dog. **2** a contemptible person.

curable *adj.* that can be cured. □ **curability** *n.*

curaçao /ˌkjɜrə'so:, ˌkjʊrə-/ *n.* (also **curaçoa** /-'so:ə/) (*pl.* **-os** or **curaçoas**) a liqueur of spirits flavoured with the peel of bitter oranges.

curare /kjʊ'rɑri, kʊ-/ *n.* a resinous bitter substance prepared from S American plants of the genera *Strychnos* and *Chondodendron*, paralyzing the motor nerves, formerly used to poison arrows by Aboriginals of S America, and as a muscle relaxant in surgery.

curate[1] /'kjʊrət, 'kjɜrət/ *n.* **1** *Catholicism* the priest of a parish in continental Europe. **2** a member of the clergy assisting a parish priest. □ **curate's egg** a thing that is partly good and partly bad.

curate[2] /'kjʊreɪt, 'kjɜreɪt/ *v.* **1** *tr.* act as curator of (a museum, exhibits, etc.); look after and preserve. **2** *tr.* select, organize, and present items for (an exhibition, film festival, etc.). **3** *intr.* perform the duties of a curator. □ **curation** *n.*

curative ● *adj.* tending or able to cure (esp. disease). ● *n.* a curative medicine or agent.

curator *n.* **1** an employee of a museum etc. responsible for the collections. **2** a person who curates an exhibition. **3** *Cdn* (*Que.*) = PUBLIC CURATOR. □ **curatorial** /ˌkjɜrə'tɔriəl, ˌkjʊrə-/ *adj.* **curatorship** *n.*

curb ● *n.* **1** the raised, usu. concrete border along the side of a street etc. **2** a check or restraint. **3** a strap etc. fastened to the bit and passing under a horse's lower jaw, used as a check. **4** an enclosing border or edging such as the frame around the top of a well or a fender around a hearth. ● *v.tr.* **1** restrain. **2** have (one's dog) defecate by the curb rather than on the sidewalk. **3** put a curb on (a horse).

curbside *n. N Amer.* **1** the area adjacent to a curb, often where garbage etc. is placed for collection (often *attrib.*: *curbside recycling*). **2** (*attrib.*) **a** denoting a transaction conducted outside an office or usual place of business. **b** denoting an opinion etc. made by an amateur or untrained person (*curbside comments*).

curbstone *n. N Amer.* a stone or portion of concrete forming a curb.

curd *n.* (often in *pl.*) a coagulated substance formed by the action of acids on milk, which may be made into cheese or eaten as food. □ **curdy** *adj.*

curd cheese *n.* a soft smooth cheese made from skimmed milk curds.

curdle *v.tr. & intr.* make into or become curds. □ **make one's blood curdle** fill one with horror.

cure ● *v.* **1** *tr.* (often foll. by *of*) restore (a person or animal) to health. **2** *tr.* eliminate (a disease, evil, etc.). **3** *tr.* preserve (meat, fruit, tobacco, or skins) by salting, drying, etc. **4 a** *tr.* vulcanize (rubber). **b** *tr.* harden (concrete or plastic). **c** *intr.* (of glue, caulking, etc.) set, harden. **5** *intr.* effect a cure. **6** *intr.* undergo a process of curing. ● *n.* **1** restoration to health. **2** a means of curing a disease. **3** a course of medical or healing treatment. **4 a** the office or function of a curate. **b** a parish or other sphere of spiritual ministration. **5 a** the process of curing rubber or plastic. **b** (with qualifying *adj.*) the degree of this. **6** the process of curing meat, fruit, etc. □ **curer** *n.*

curé /kjʊ'reɪ/ *n.* a parish priest in Quebec, France etc.

cure-all *n.* a panacea; a universal remedy.

curettage /kjʊ'retɪdʒ, -rɪ'tɒdʒ/ *n.* the use of or an operation involving the use of a curette.

curette /kjʊ'ret/ ● *n.* a surgeon's small scraping instrument. ● *v.tr. & intr.* clean or scrape with a curette.

curfew *n.* **1 a** a regulation restricting or forbidding the public circulation of people, esp. requiring people to remain indoors between specified hours, usu. at night. **b** a requirement that one be home etc. by a certain time. **2** the hour designated as the beginning of such a restriction. **3** a daily signal indicating this. **4** the ringing of a bell at a fixed evening hour. □ **break curfew** fail to observe a curfew.

Curia /'kjɜːrɪə, 'kjʊ-/ *n.* (also **curia**) the papal court; the government departments of the Vatican.

curie /'kjʊri/ *n.* **1** a unit of radioactivity, corresponding to 3.7×10^{10} disintegrations per second. **2** a quantity of radioactive substance having this activity.

curio *n.* (*pl.* **-os**) a rare or unusual object or person.

curiosity *n.* (*pl.* **-ies**) **1** an eager desire to know; inquisitiveness. **2** strangeness. **3** a strange, rare, or interesting object or thing.

curious *adj.* **1** eager to learn; inquisitive. **2** strange, surprising, odd. □ **curiously** *adv.* **curiousness** *n.*

curium /'kjʊrɪəm/ *n.* an artificially made radioactive metallic element.

curl ● *v.* **1** *tr. & intr.* (often foll. by *up*) **a** bend or coil into a spiral. **b** form or make something form into a curved shape, esp. so that the edges are rolled up. **2** *intr.* move in a spiral form (*smoke curling upwards*). **3 a** *intr.* (of the upper lip) be raised slightly on one side as an expression of contempt or disapproval. **b** *tr.* cause (the lip) to do this. **4 a** *intr.* play curling. **b** *tr.* play (a game of curling). ● *n.* **1** a lock of curled hair. **2** anything spiral or curved inwards. **3 a** a curling movement or act. **b** the state of being curled. **4** an exercise in which part of the body (e.g. the arms, legs, or abdomen) is curled and then released. □ **curl up 1** lie or sit with the knees drawn up. **2** *informal* writhe with embarrassment or horror. **make a person's hair curl** *informal* shock or horrify a person.

curler *n.* **1** a pin or roller etc. for curling the hair. **2** a player in the game of curling.

curlew *n.* (*pl.* same or **-s**) any wading bird of the genus *Numenius*, possessing a usu. long slender down-curved bill.

curlicue /'kɜːlɪ,kjuː/ *n.* a decorative curl or twist.

curling *n.* **1** in senses of CURL *v.* **2** a game played on ice, in which large round stones are slid across the surface towards a mark.

curling iron *n.* a device consisting of a barrel and a hinged clamp, heated so that hair can be twisted into curls around it.

curly *adj.* (**-ier**, **-iest**) **1** having or arranged in curls. **2** moving in curves. □ **curliness** *n.*

curly endive *n.* = ENDIVE 2.

curmudgeon /kɜː'mʌdʒən/ *n.* a bad-tempered person. □ **curmudgeonly** *adj.*

currant *n.* **1** a dried fruit of a small seedless variety of grape grown in California and the Middle East and much used in cooking. **2 a** any of various shrubs of the genus *Ribes* producing red, white, or black berries. **b** a berry of these shrubs.

currency *n.* (*pl.* **-ies**) **1 a** the money in general use in a country. **b** any other commodity used as a medium of exchange. **2** the condition of being current; prevalence, e.g. of words or ideas. **3** the time during which something is current.

current ● *adj.* **1** belonging to the present time; happening now (*current events*). **2** (of money, opinion, a rumour, a word, etc.) in general circulation or use. ● *n.* **1** a body of water, air, etc., moving in a definite direction, esp. through a stiller surrounding body. **2 a** an ordered movement of electrically charged particles. **b** a quantity representing the intensity of such movement. **3** (usu. foll. by *of*) a general tendency or course (of events, opinions, etc.).

current account *n.* **1** the part of a country's balance of payments account that records non-capital transactions. **2** a bank account from which money may be drawn without notice.

current affairs *n.pl. esp. Cdn & Brit.* (also esp. *N Amer.* **current events**) matters of public interest in progress.

currently *adv.* at the present time; now.

curriculum /kə'rɪkjʊləm/ *n.* (*pl.* **curricula** /-lə/) **1** the subjects that are studied or prescribed for study in a school, school board, etc. **2** any program of activities. □ **curricular** *adj.*

curriculum vitae /'viːtaɪ/ *n.* (*pl.* **curricula vitae** or **vitarum**) a brief account of one's education, qualifications, and previous occupations. Abbr.: **c.v.**

curry[1] ● *n.* (*pl.* **-ies**) a dish of meat, vegetables, etc., cooked in a highly spiced sauce, usu. served with rice. ● *v.tr.* (**-ies**, **-ied**) prepare or flavour with hot-tasting spices (*curried beef*).

curry[2] *v.tr.* (**-ies**, **-ied**) **1** groom with a curry comb. **2** treat (tanned leather) to improve its properties. **3** thrash. □ **curry favour** ingratiate oneself.

curry comb *n.* a hand-held metal serrated device for grooming horses.

curry powder *n.* a preparation of turmeric, cumin, and other spices for making curry.

curse ● *n.* **1** a solemn utterance intended to invoke a supernatural power to inflict destruction or punishment on a person or thing. **2** the evil supposedly resulting from a curse. **3** a violent exclamation of anger; a profane oath. **4** a thing that causes evil or harm. **5** (prec. by *the*) *slang* menstruation; a menstrual period. **6** a sentence of excommunication. ● *v.* **1** *tr.* **a** utter a curse against. **b** (in *imper.*) may God curse. **2** *tr.* (usu. in *passive*; foll. by *with*) afflict with (*cursed with blindness*). **3 a** *intr.* utter expletive curses; swear. **b** *tr.* feel or express negative thoughts about (*cursed my luck*). **4** *tr.* excommunicate.

cursed /'kɜːrsəd, kɜːrst/ *adj.* damnable, abominable. □ **cursedly** *adv.* **cursedness** *n.*

curses *interj.* expressing annoyance.

cursive ● *adj.* (of writing) done with joined characters. ● *n.* cursive writing. □ **cursively** *adv.*

cursor *n. Computing* a movable indicator on a computer screen identifying a particular position in the display, esp. the position that the program will operate on with the next keystroke.

cursor key *n.* one of usu. four keys grouped together on a computer keyboard, used to move the cursor vertically or horizontally.

cursory *adj.* hasty, hurried; superficial (*a cursory examination*). □ **cursorily** *adv.* **cursoriness** *n.*

curt *adj.* noticeably or rudely brief. □ **curtly** *adv.* **curtness** *n.*

curtail *v.tr.* cut short; reduce; terminate esp. prematurely (*curtailed his visit*). □ **curtailment** *n.*

curtain ● *n.* **1** a piece of cloth etc. hung up as a screen, usu. movable sideways or upwards, esp. at a window or between the stage and auditorium of a theatre. **2** *Theatre* the rise or fall of the stage curtain at the beginning or end of an act or scene. **3** a partition or cover. **4** (in *pl.*) *slang* the end. **5** any concentration of something forming a barrier (*curtain of fog*). ● *v.tr.* **1** furnish or cover with a curtain or curtains. **2** (foll. by *off*) shut off with a curtain or curtains. □ **curtained** *adj.* **curtainless** *adj.*

curtain call *n.* an appearance by a performer or performers to take a bow at the end of a performance.

curtain rod *n.* a rod from which a curtain is suspended.

curtain wall *n.* **1** *Fortification* the plain wall of a fortified place, connecting two towers etc. **2** *Archit.* a piece of plain wall not supporting a roof.

curtsy (also **curtsey**) ● *n.* (*pl.* **-ies** or **-eys**) a woman's or girl's formal greeting or salutation made by bending the knees and lowering the body. ● *v.intr.* (**-ies, -ied** or **-eys, -eyed**) make a curtsy.

curvaceous /kɜrˈveɪʃəs/ *adj. informal* (esp. of a woman) having a shapely figure with voluptuous breasts and hips.

curvature /ˈkɜrvətʃər/ *n.* **1** the act or state of curving. **2** a curved form. **3** *Math.* **a** the deviation of a curve from a straight line, or of a curved surface from a plane. **b** the quantity expressing this.

curve ● *n.* **1** a line or surface having along its length a regular deviation from being straight or flat, as exemplified by the surface of a sphere or lens. **2** a curved form or thing. **3** a curved line on a graph. **4** (also **curveball**) **a** *Baseball* a ball pitched so that it curves away from the side from which it was thrown. **b** something unexpected or unsettling. **5 a** a curved line on a graph illustrating a tendency. **b** a tendency which could be plotted on a graph as a curve. ● *v.tr. & intr.* **1** bend or shape so as to form a curve. **2** move or send along a curved path. □ **curved** *adj.*

curvy *adj.* (**-ier, -iest**) **1** having many curves. **2** (of a woman's figure) shapely. □ **curviness** *n.*

cushion ● *n.* **1** a pad or bag of cloth etc. stuffed with a mass of soft material and used as a soft support for sitting etc. **2** a means of protection against shock, jarring, etc. **3** a buffer of savings, time, etc. or (in sports) a comfortable lead in score meant to mitigate the effects of difficulty, possible future distress, etc. **4** a body of air supporting a hovercraft etc. ● *v.tr.* **1** provide or protect with a cushion or cushions. **2** provide with a defence; protect. **3** mitigate the adverse effects of (*cushioned the blow*). □ **cushioned** *adj.* **cushioning** *n.* **cushiony** *adj.*

Cushitic /kʊˈʃɪtɪk/ ● *n.* an Afro-Asiatic language family of NE Africa, including Somali. ● *adj.* designating, of, or pertaining to this group.

cushy *adj.* (**-ier, -iest**) *informal* **1** (of a job etc.) easy and pleasant. **2** *N Amer.* (of a seat, surroundings, etc.) soft, comfortable. □ **cushiness** *n.*

cusp *n.* **1** an apex or peak. **2** the horn of a crescent moon etc. **3** *Math.* the point at which two arcs meet from the same direction terminating with a common tangent. **4** *Bot.* a pointed end, esp. of a leaf. **5** a cone-shaped prominence on the surface of a tooth, esp. a molar or premolar. **6** a pocket or fold in a valve of the heart. □ **on the cusp** (usu. foll. by *of*) *N Amer.* at a point marking a change in condition etc. (*on the cusp of burnout*). □ **cusped** *adj.*

cuss *informal* ● *n.* **1** an obscene or profane expression. **2** usu. *derogatory* a strange and obstinate person or creature (*a tenacious cuss*). ● *v.* **1** *intr.* swear, use profanity. **2** *tr.* swear at.

cussed /ˈkʌsəd/ *adj. informal* awkward and stubborn. □ **cussedly** *adv.* **cussedness** *n.*

custard *n.* **1** (also **baked custard**) a baked dish made with milk and eggs, usu. sweetened. **2** (*N Amer.* **custard sauce**) a sweet sauce or filling of sweetened, flavoured milk, thickened with eggs or cornstarch. □ **custardy** *adj.*

custodial *adj.* **1** relating to legal custody or guardianship. **2** of or pertaining to the work of a caretaker or janitor. **3** of or pertaining to imprisonment or forcible institutionalization (*a custodial sentence*).

custodian *n.* **1** *N Amer.* a person responsible for maintaining a building etc.; a caretaker or janitor. **2** a person who has custody of and responsibility for another person, a thing, etc. □ **custodianship** *n.*

custody *n.* **1 a** legal guardianship, esp. of a minor. **b** safekeeping, protective care. **2** (often prec. by *in* or *into*) the charge or keeping of the police; imprisonment (*remains in custody*). □ **take into custody** arrest.

custom ● *n.* **1 a** the usual way of behaving or acting (*a slave to custom*). **b** a particular, established way of behaving. **2** *Law* established usage having the force of law. **3 a** habitual business patronage. **b** regular dealings or customers. **4** (in *pl.*; also treated as *sing.*) **a** a duty levied on certain imported and exported goods. **b** the official department that administers this. **c** the area at an airport, border, etc. where customs officials deal with incoming goods, baggage, etc. ● *adj.* CUSTOM-MADE.

customary *adj.* **1** usual, commonly done. **2** *Law* in accordance with custom rather than common law or statute. □ **customarily** *adv.*

customer *n.* **1** a person who buys goods or services from a store or business. **2** a person one has to deal with (*one tough customer*).

customize *v.tr.* make to order or modify according to individual requirements. □ **customizable** *adj.* **customization** *n.* **customized** *adj.*

custom-made *adj.* (also **custom-built** etc.) made to an individual customer's order or specifications.

customs house *n.* (also **custom house**) the government office at an airport, border, etc. at which customs duties are levied.

customs union *n.* a group of countries with an agreed common tariff, and usu. free trade with each other.

cut ● *v.* (**cutting**; *past* and *past part.* **cut**) **1** *tr. & intr.* penetrate or wound with a sharp-edged instrument. **2** *tr. & intr.* (often foll. by *into*) divide or be divided with a knife etc. **3** *tr.* **a** trim or reduce the length of (hair, a hedge, etc.) by cutting. **b** divide (what grows) with an edged instrument to take the part detached; mow (grass), hew (timber), etc. **4** *tr.* (foll. by *loose, open,* etc.)

make loose, open, etc. by cutting. **5** *tr.* (esp. as **cutting** *adj.*) cause sharp physical or mental pain to (*a cutting remark*; *a cutting wind*). **6** *tr.* (often foll. by *back* or *down*) **a** reduce (wages, time, etc.). **b** reduce or cease (services etc.). **7** *tr.* **a** shape or fashion (a gem, key, etc.) by cutting. **b** make (a path, tunnel, etc.) by removing material. **8** *tr.* perform, execute, make (*cut a caper*). **9** *tr. & intr.* cross, intersect (*the line cuts the circle at two points*). **10** *intr.* (foll. by *across*, *through*, etc.) pass or traverse, esp. in a hurry or as a shorter way (*cut across the grass*). **11** *tr.* renounce (a connection). **12** *tr.* esp. *N Amer.* deliberately fail to attend (a class etc.). **13** *Cards* **a** *tr.* divide (a pack) into two parts. **b** *intr.* select a dealer etc. by dividing the pack. **14** *Film* **a** *tr.* edit (a film or tape). **b** *intr.* (often in *imper.*) stop filming or recording. **c** *intr.* (foll. by *to*) go quickly to (another shot). **15** *tr.* switch off (an engine etc.). **16** *tr.* esp. *N Amer.* dilute, adulterate. **17 a** *tr.* remove (lines etc.) from a text; edit, abridge. **b** *tr. Computing* remove (information, esp. text) for placing elsewhere in a file etc. **18** *tr.* dissolve, clean away (*cut the grease*). **19** *intr.* swerve sharply; make a sudden turn or change in direction (*cut left*). ● *adj.* **1** divided or separated into pieces. **2** *Art* made, fashioned, etc. by cutting, grinding, etc. (*cut glass*). **3** lowered or reduced (*cut-price competitors*). ● *n.* **1** an act of cutting. **2** a division or wound made by cutting. **3** a stroke with a knife, sword, whip, etc. **4 a** a reduction (in prices, wages, etc.). **b** a cessation (of a power supply etc.). **5 a** an abrupt transition between film shots, achieved by splicing two distinct shots together. **b** a single song, piece, etc. on an album, CD, etc. **6** a wounding remark or act. **7** the way or style in which a garment, the hair, etc., is cut. **8** a piece of meat cut from a carcass. **9** *informal* a share of profits. **10** *Sport* an exclusion from a team, tournament, etc. **11 a** a railway cutting. **b** a passage cut through rock or gravel in building a road, canal, etc. **12** a quantity of a crop, esp. timber, cut in a season. □ **a cut above** *informal* noticeably superior to. **be cut out** be suited (*was not cut out to be a teacher*). **cut across 1** transcend or take no account of (normal limitations etc.) (*their concerns cut across normal rivalries*). **2** see sense 10 of *v.* **cut and dried 1** completely decided; prearranged; inflexible. **2** (of opinions etc.) ready-made, lacking freshness. **cut and thrust** a lively interchange of argument etc. **cut back 1** reduce (expenditure etc.). **2** prune (a tree etc.). **cut both ways 1** serve both sides of an argument etc. **2** (of an action) have both good and bad effects. **cut a corner** go across and not around a corner. **cut corners** do a task etc. perfunctorily or incompletely, esp. to save time or money. **cut down 1 a** bring or throw down by cutting. **b** kill, disable; defeat, ruin (*cut down in battle*). **2** see sense 6 of *v.* **3** reduce the length of. **4** (often foll. by *on*) reduce one's consumption (*try to cut down on beer*). **cut a person down to size** *informal* ruthlessly expose the limitations of a person's importance, ability, etc. **cut one's eye teeth** attain experience and some sophistication. **cut from the same cloth** of the same nature; alike. **cut in 1** interrupt. **2** pull in too closely in front of another vehicle (esp. having passed it). **3** give a share of profits etc. to (a person). **4** connect (a source of electricity, etc.). **5** join in a card game by taking the place of a player who cuts out. **6** interrupt a dancing couple to take over from one partner. **cut into 1 a** make a cut in. **b** divide. **2** interfere with and reduce (*cuts into my free time*). **cut it** *N Amer. informal* function or perform adequately (*couldn't cut it in the big leagues*). **cut it out** (usu. in *imper.*) *informal* stop doing something. **cut**

loose 1 begin to act freely. **2** see sense 4 of *v.* **cut one's losses** (or **a loss**) abandon an unprofitable enterprise before losses become too great. **cut the mustard** esp. *N Amer.* slang reach the required standard. **cut no ice** *slang* **1** have no influence or importance. **2** achieve little or nothing. **cut off 1** remove (an appendage) by cutting. **2 a** (often in *passive*) bring to an abrupt end or (esp. early) death. **b** intercept, interrupt; prevent from continuing (*cut off supplies*). **c** interfere with the progress of, esp. by abruptly pulling one's vehicle into another's lane of traffic. **d** disconnect (esp. a person engaged in a telephone conversation). **3 a** prevent from travelling or venturing out (*was cut off by the snow*). **b** (as **cut off** *adj.*) isolated, remote. **4** disinherit. **cut out 1** remove from the inside by cutting. **2** make by cutting from a larger whole. **3** omit; leave out (*cut him out of our loop*). **4** *informal* stop doing or using (something) (*cut out chocolate*; *let's cut out the arguing*). **5** cease or cause to cease functioning (*the engine cut out*). **cut short 1** interrupt; terminate prematurely (*cut short his visit*). **2** make shorter or more concise. **cut a** (or **the**) **rug** *N Amer. slang* dance. **cut** (**a person**) **some slack** *N Amer. slang* allow an individual some leeway in conduct, performance, etc. **cut one's teeth on** acquire initial practice or experience from (something). **cut a tooth** have it appear through the gum. **cut to the bone 1** reduce (expenditures) to a minimum. **2** chill thoroughly. **cut to the chase** *N Amer.* come to the point. **cut up 1** cut into pieces. **2** slash, wound, etc. (*we were all cut up and bruised*). **3** (usu. in *passive*) distress greatly (*was very cut up about it*). **4** criticize severely. **5** *N Amer.* behave in a comical or unruly manner. **make the cut** *informal* **1** be selected for a team, short list, etc. **2** achieve a specified status, condition, etc.

cut-and-paste *n.* the process of assembling text by adding or combining sections from other texts.

cutaneous /kju:'teiniəs/ *adj.* of the skin.

cutaway *adj.* **1** (of a diagram etc.) with some parts left out to reveal the interior. **2** (of a coat) with the front below the waist cut away.

cutback *n.* an instance or the act of cutting back, esp. a reduction in expenditure.

cutbank *n. N Amer.* a steep cliff or riverbank resulting from erosion.

cut-down *adj.* that has been reduced, esp. in length.

cute *adj. informal* **1** esp. *N Amer.* **a** attractive. **b** quaintly or affectedly attractive. **c** endearing, charming. **2** clever, ingenious. □ **cutely** *adv.* **cuteness** *n.*

cutesy *adj.* dainty or quaint to an affected degree.

cut glass *n.* glass with patterns and designs cut or ground on it.

cuticle /'kju:tikəl/ *n.* **1** the dead skin at the base of a fingernail or toenail. **2** the outer cellular layer of a hair. **3** the epidermis. **4** *Bot. & Zool.* the outer layer of an organism, esp. a protective often waxy layer covering the epidermis of a plant or invertebrate.

cutie *n. slang* an attractive person, esp. a woman.

cutie-pie *n.* **1** *informal* darling, sweetheart. **2** an attractive person, animal, etc.

cutlass *n.* a short sword with a slightly curved blade, esp. of the type formerly used by sailors.

cutlery *n.* knives, forks, and spoons for use at table.

cutlet *n.* **1** a small, thin piece of boneless veal etc. usu. served fried. **2** a flat patty of ground meat or nuts and breadcrumbs etc.

cutline *n.* **1** a caption to an illustration. **2** a line marked on wood etc. that indicates where a cut should be made. **3** *Cdn* a line cut through the bush, e.g. as a survey line, etc.

cut-off *n.* **1** the point at which something is cut off. **2** a device for stopping a flow. **3** (in *pl.*) esp. *N Amer.* shorts, esp. made from cut-down jeans. **4** (often *attrib.*) a time or point of demarcation after which some action is no longer possible, effective, etc. (*cut-off date*). **5** *Baseball* (usu. *attrib.*) the interception by an infielder of a ball thrown from outfield, e.g. to relay the ball to home plate. **6** *N Amer.* a road to a specific town etc. which turns off a larger thoroughfare.

cut-out ● *n.* **1 a** a figure cut out of paper etc. **b** a person, personality, etc. so little differentiated from the majority that it seems of a piece with it. **2** a device for automatic disconnection, release of exhaust gases, etc. ● *adj.* of or like a cut-out (in sense 1).

cutover ● *adj.* (of timberland etc.) having had the saleable timber felled and removed. ● *n.* cutover land.

cut-rate *adj.* (also **cut-price**) selling or sold at a reduced price.

cutter *n.* **1** a person or thing that cuts, esp. a person who takes measurements and cuts cloth, as a tailor, etc. **2** *Naut.* **a** a small, fast sailing ship. **b** a small, lightly armed government vessel (*a Coast Guard cutter*). **3** *N Amer.* a light horse-drawn sleigh.

cutthroat ● *n.* **1** a murderer. **2** (also **cutthroat trout**) a species of trout, *Salmo clarki*, with an orange or red mark under the jaw. ● *adj.* (of competition) ruthless and intense.

cutting ● *n.* **1** a piece or section cut from something. **2** a piece cut from a plant for propagation. **3** an excavated channel through high ground for a railway or road. **4** *N Amer. Forestry* **a** a stand of timber. **b** the site of a logging operation. ● *adj.* causing sharp physical or mental pain (*a cutting remark*).

cutting edge ● *n.* **1** an edge that cuts. **2** the forefront of a movement etc. ● *attrib.adj.* (**cutting-edge**) pioneering, innovative.

cutting horse *n.* *N Amer.* a saddle horse trained to separate individual cows, calves, etc. from a herd.

cuttlefish *n.* (also **cuttle**) any of various marine cephalopods of the genus *Sepia* or order Sepioidea, having an elongated body with an undulating lateral fin, ten arms, an internal shell, and the habit of ejecting a black fluid when alarmed.

cut-up *n.* esp. *N Amer.* a person who plays the fool; a prankster.

cutworm *n.* any of various caterpillars that eat through young plants level with the ground.

cuvée /kju:'vei/ *n.* a blend or batch of wine.

cuz *var. of* COZ¹,².

CV *abbr.* (in Canada) CROSS OF VALOUR.

c.v. *abbr.* CURRICULUM VITAE.

CVS *abbr.* CHORIONIC VILLUS SAMPLING.

C.V.S.M. *abbr.* Canadian Volunteer Service Medal.

CWAC /kwæk/ *abbr. hist.* **1** Canadian Women's Army Corps. **2** a member of this.

CWB *abbr.* Canadian Wheat Board (see WHEAT BOARD).

CWL *abbr.* Catholic Women's League.

CWO *abbr.* CHIEF WARRANT OFFICER.

CWS *abbr.* Canadian Wildlife Service.

cwt. *abbr.* hundredweight.

cyan /'saiæn/ ● *adj.* of a greenish-blue. ● *n.* a greenish-blue colour.

cyanide /'saiə,naid/ *n.* any of the highly poisonous salts or esters of hydrocyanic acid.

cyanobacteria /,saiæ,no:bæk'ti:riə/ *n.pl.* (*sing.* **-bacterium** /-riəm/) any prokaryotic organisms of the division Cyanobacteria, found in many environments and capable of photosynthesizing.

cyber- *comb. form* of computers, esp. pertaining to artificial intelligence or virtual reality.

cybernetics /,saibər'netiks/ *n.pl.* (usu. treated as *sing.*) the science of communications and automatic control systems in both machines and living things. □ **cybernetic** *adj.* **cybernetician** /-'tiʃən/ *n.* **cyberneticist** /-sist/ *n.*

cyberpunk *n.* **1** a style of science fiction featuring urban counterculture in a world of high technology and virtual reality. **2** *Computing slang* a highly proficient hacker.

cyberspace *n.* **1** the forum in which the global electronic communications network operates. **2** *Computing* the electronic realm in which virtual reality is experienced.

cyborg /'saibɔrg/ *n.* a person whose physical abilities are extended beyond normal human limitations by machine technology (as yet undeveloped).

cycad /'saikæd/ *n.* any of the palmlike plants of the order Cycadales inhabiting tropical and subtropical regions and often growing to a great height.

cyclamen /'sikləmən/ *n.* **1** any plant of the genus *Cyclamen*, having pink, red, or white flowers with reflexed petals, often grown as a houseplant. **2** the shade of colour of the red or pink cyclamen flower.

cycle ● *n.* **1 a** a recurrent series or period (of events, phenomena, etc.). **b** the time needed for one such series or period. **2 a** *Physics etc.* a recurrent series of operations or states. **b** *Electricity* = HERTZ. **3** a series of songs, poems, etc., usu. on a single theme. **4** a bicycle, tricycle, or similar machine. **5** *Computing* **a** (in full **cycle time**) the time required for one cycle of the memory system. **b** a set of operations which is repeated regularly and in the same sequence. ● *v.intr.* **1** ride a bicycle etc. **2** move in cycles.

cyclic *adj.* **1 a** recurring or revolving in cycles. **b** belonging to a chronological cycle. **c** of, pertaining to, or characterized by cycles. **2** *Chem.* with constituent atoms forming a ring. **3** of a cycle of songs etc. **4** *Bot.* (of a flower) with its parts arranged in whorls. **5** *Math.* of a circle or other closed curve.

cyclical ● *adj.* = CYCLIC 1. ● *n.* (usu. in *pl.*) industries, companies, etc. that are heavily dependent on global economic circumstances for their success. □ **cyclically** *adv.*

cycling *n.* **1** travelling or touring on a bicycle etc. **2** the sport of bicycle racing, usu. on a lightweight bicycle with low handlebars. **3** the act of moving in cycles.

cyclist *n.* a rider of a bicycle.

cycloalkane /,saiklo:'ælkein/ *n.* *Chem.* a saturated cyclic hydrocarbon.

cyclone *n.* **1 a** a system of winds rotating inwards to an area of low barometric pressure; a depression. **b** a tornado. **2 a** a wind system of this kind formed in localized areas over tropical oceans, sometimes developing into a hurricane or typhoon. **b** such a wind system having hurricane-force winds, originating in the Indian Ocean. **3** a centrifugal machine for separating solids. □ **cyclonic** *adj.*

cyclopedia /,saiklə'pi:diə/ *n.* (also **cyclopaedia**) an encyclopedia. □ **cyclopedic** *adj.*

Cyclops /'saiklops/ *n.* (*pl.* same or **Cyclopses** or **Cyclopes** /sai'klo:pi:z/) (in Greek mythology) a member of a race of one-eyed giants.

cyclosporin /saiklə'spɔrin/ *n.* a peptide drug used to prevent the rejection of grafts and transplants.

cyl. *abbr.* CYLINDER.

cylinder n. **1 a** a uniform solid or hollow body with straight sides and a circular section. **b** a thing of this shape, e.g. a container for liquefied gas. **2** a cylinder-shaped part of various machines, esp. a piston chamber in an engine. **3** a hollow metal roller used in printing for inking the type, carrying the type or printing surface, etc. **4** the rotating part of a revolver which houses the cartridge chambers. □ **firing** (or **hitting** etc.) **on all cylinders** working at peak efficiency and capacity. □ **cylindrical** adj.

cylinder head n. the end cover of a cylinder in an internal combustion engine, against which the piston compresses the cylinder contents.

cymbal n. a musical instrument consisting of a concave brass or bronze plate, struck with another or with a stick etc. to make a ringing sound.

cynic ● n. **1** a person with little faith in human goodness who sarcastically doubts or despises sincerity and merit. **2** (**Cynic**) one of a school of ancient Greek philosophers founded by Antisthenes (c. 445–365 BC), marked by a belief in self-control as the essence of virtue and an ostentatious contempt for ease and pleasure. ● adj. (**Cynic**) of the Cynics. □ **cynicism** n.

cynical adj. **1** of or characteristic of a cynic; incredulous of human goodness. **2** (of behaviour etc.) disregarding normal standards, esp. of morality. **3** sneering, mocking, sarcastic. □ **cynically** adv.

cypher var. of CIPHER.

cypress /'saiprəs/ n. **1** any coniferous tree of the genus *Cupressus* or *Chamaecyparis*, with hard wood and dark foliage. **2** the wood of this tree.

Cypriot /'sɪprɪət/ (also **Cypriote** /-o:t/) ● n. a native or national of Cyprus, an island in the E Mediterranean south of Turkey. ● adj. of Cyprus.

Cyrillic /sɪ'rɪlɪk/ ● adj. denoting the alphabet derived from Greek, adapted by the Slavic peoples, and now used esp. for Russian. ● n. this alphabet.

cyst n. **1** Med. an abnormal sac containing fluid, pus, etc. **2** Biol. **a** a hollow organ, bladder, etc., in an animal or plant, containing a liquid secretion. **b** a cell or cavity enclosing reproductive bodies, an embryo, parasite, micro-organism, etc.

cystic adj. **1** characterized by, of the nature of, or having a cyst. **2** of the urinary bladder or gallbladder.

cystic fibrosis n. a hereditary disease of the exocrine glands characterized by abnormal mucus production which affects esp. the lungs, pancreas, and gastrointestinal tract. Abbr.: **CF.**

cytology /sai'tɒlədʒi/ n. the microscopic study of cells, esp. to detect and identify disease. □ **cytological** adj. **cytologically** adv. **cytologist** n.

cytomegalovirus /ˌsaito:'megələ:ˌvairəs/ n. Med. a kind of herpesvirus which usually produces very mild symptoms in an infected person but may cause severe neurological damage in the newborn and in people with weakened immune systems. Abbr.: **CMV.**

cytoplasm /'saito:ˌplæzəm/ n. the protoplasmic content of a cell apart from its nucleus. □ **cytoplasmic** adj.

cytotoxic /ˌsaito:'tɒksɪk/ adj. toxic to living cells. □ **cytotoxicity** n.

czar /zar/ n. **1** hist. the title of the former emperor of Russia. **2** a person with great authority.

czarina /zar'i:nə/ n. hist. the title of the former empress of Russia.

Czech /tʃek/ ● n. **1** a native or national of the Czech Republic or hist. Czechoslovakia. **2** the Slavic language spoken in the Czech Republic or hist. Czechoslovakia. ● adj. **1** of or relating to the Czech Republic or hist. Czechoslavakia. **2** of or relating to the Czech language.

Czechoslovak /ˌtʃekə'slo:væk/ (also **Czechoslovakian**) ● n. a native or national of Czechoslovakia, a former state in central Europe. ● adj. of or relating to Czechoslovaks or Czechoslovakia.

Dd

D¹ *n.* (also **d**) (*pl.* **Ds** or **D's**) **1** the fourth letter of the alphabet. **2** *Music* the second note of the diatonic scale of C major. **3** the fourth hypothetical person or example in a series etc. **4** the fourth class or category (of academic marks etc.) denoting a barely acceptable quality. **5** *Math.* the fourth known quantity, group, section, etc. **6** (as a Roman numeral) 500. **7** a size of battery, having a voltage of 1.5 V.

D² *symbol* **1** deuterium. **2** *Physics* density.

D³ *abbr.* (also **D.**) **1** a government department (*DND*). **2** Doctor. **3** *US* Democrat. **4** dimension (*3-D*). **5** digital (recording).

d.¹ *abbr.* **1** died. **2** departs. **3** delete. **4** daughter. **5** diameter. **6** depth.

d.² *symbol* deci-.

'd *v.* (usu. after pronouns) had, would (*I'd*; *he'd*).

DA *abbr.* *US* district attorney.

D/A *abbr.* *Computing* digital to analog.

da *abbr.* deca-.

dab ● *v.* (**dabbed, dabbing**) **1** *tr.* press (a surface) briefly with a cloth etc., without rubbing, esp. in cleaning or to apply a substance. **2** *tr.* press (a cloth etc.) lightly on a surface. **3** *tr.* (foll. by *on*) apply (a substance) by dabbing a surface. **4** *intr.* (usu. foll. by *at*) pat; tap. ● *n.* **1** a brief application of a cloth, sponge, etc. to a surface without rubbing. **2** a small amount of something (*a dab of paint*). □ **smack dab** *adv.* *N Amer. informal* exactly, directly. □ **dabber** *n.*

dabble *v.intr.* **1** (usu. foll. by *in, at*) take a casual or superficial interest or part (in a subject or activity). **2** splash, play, move the feet, hands, etc. about in (usu. a small amount of) liquid. **3** (of a duck) feed in shallow water with splashing and quick bill movements. □ **dabbler** *n.*

DAC *abbr.* = DIGITAL TO ANALOG CONVERTER.

dachshund /'dækshənt, dɒk-/ *n.* a breed of dog with short legs and a long body.

Dacron *n. proprietary* a polyester used as fabric.

dad *n. informal* father.

Dada /'dɒdɒ/ *n.* an early 20th-c. movement in art, literature, music, and film, repudiating and mocking artistic and social conventions. □ **Dadaism** *n.* **Dadaist** *n. & adj.* **Dadaistic** *adj.*

dada /'dædæ/ *n. informal* father.

daddy *n.* (*pl.* **-ies**) *informal* **1** father. **2** the oldest or supreme example (*had a daddy of a headache*).

daddy-long-legs *n.* *N Amer.* any of various arachnids of the family Opilionidae, with very long thin legs, found in humus and on tree trunks.

dado /'deidoʊ/ *n.* (*pl.* **-os**) **1** the lower part of the wall of a room when distinct from the upper part. **2** *N Amer.* a rectangular slot or groove in a board etc.

daemon /'diːmən/ *n.* **1** *var. of* DEMON 5. **2** *Computing* in some operating systems, an unseen program that controls a peripheral device.

daemonic *var. of* DEMONIC.

daffodil *n.* **1 a** a bulbous plant, *Narcissus pseudonarcissus*, with a yellow trumpet-shaped crown. **b** any of various other large-flowered plants of the genus *Narcissus*. **c** a flower of any of these plants. **2** a pale-yellow colour.

daffy *adj.* (**-ier, -iest**) *slang* **1** silly, foolish, crazy. **2** (foll. by *about*) fond of; infatuated with. □ **daffily** *adv.* **daffiness** *n.*

dagger *n.* **1** a short stabbing weapon with a pointed and edged blade. **2** = OBELUS. □ **look daggers at** glare angrily or venomously at.

dahlia /'deiliə/ *n.* any composite garden plant of the genus *Dahlia*, of Mexican origin, cultivated for its many-coloured single or double flowers.

daikon /'daikɒn, -ən/ *n.* a long, thin, white oriental radish.

daily ● *adj.* **1** done, produced, or occurring every day or every weekday. **2** constant, regular. **3** calculated, measured, etc. by the day (*a daily quota*). ● *adv.* **1** every day; from day to day. **2** constantly. ● *n.* (*pl.* **-ies**) *informal* a daily newspaper. □ **dailiness** *n.*

dainty ● *adj.* (**-ier, -iest**) **1** delicately pretty. **2** delicate of build or in movement. **3** (of food) delicious or pleasing to the palate. **4** (of a person) possessing delicate taste, perception, and sensibility. ● *n.* (*pl.* **-ies**) **1** a choice morsel; a delicacy. **2** *Cdn* (*Prairies & NW Ont.*) (*in pl.*) fancy cookies, cakes, etc. served at social gatherings. □ **daintily** *adv.* **daintiness** *n.*

daiquiri /'dækəri/ *n.* (*pl.* **daiquiris**) a cocktail of rum, sugar, and lime or lemon juice, etc.

dairy *n.* (*pl.* **-ies**) **1** a building or room for the storage, processing, and distribution of milk and its products. **2** a store where milk and milk products are sold. **3** milk and milk products. **4** (*attrib.*) **a** of, containing, or concerning milk and its products. **b** used for or relating to the production of dairy products (*dairy cow*). **5** *Cdn* (*Cape Breton*) a convenience store.

dairy farm *n.* a farm which produces milk or milk products. □ **dairy farmer** *n.* **dairy farming** *n.*

dairying *n.* the business of producing, storing, and distributing milk and its products.

dais /'deiəs, 'deiɪs/ *n.* a low platform, usu. at the end of a room and used to support a table, throne, etc.

daisy *n.* (*pl.* **-ies**) **1** a small composite plant, *Bellis perennis*, bearing flowers each with a yellow disc and white rays. **2** any other plant with daisy-like flowers, esp. the larger ox-eye daisy. □ **pushing up the daisies** *slang* dead and buried.

daisy chain ● *n.* **1** a string of daisies threaded together. **2** a group of several connected things, events, etc. ● *v.tr.* (**daisy-chain**) esp. *Computing* link (several pieces of hardware, etc.) together in succession. □ **daisy-chained** *adj.*

Dakota /dəˈkoʊtə/ ● *n.* **1** a member of a N American Aboriginal people inhabiting the upper Mississippi and Missouri river valleys. **2** the Siouan language of this people. ● *adj.* of or relating to the Dakota.

dal /dɒl/ *n.* **1** a kind of lentil or split pea, a common foodstuff in India. **2** a dish made with this.

dale *n.* a valley, esp. in Northern England.

dalliance /'dæliəns/ *n.* **1** a leisurely or frivolous passing of time. **2** a casual love affair.

Dall sheep /dɒl/ *n.* (also **Dall's sheep**) a white

thinhorn sheep, *Ovis dalli dalli*, of the mountains of NW Canada and Alaska.

dally¹ *v.intr.* (**-ies, -ied**) **1** waste time, esp. frivolously. **2** (often foll. by *with*) play about; flirt, treat frivolously. □ **dally away** waste or fritter (time etc.).

dally² *N Amer.* (*West*) ● *n.* a loop of rope wound around a saddle horn etc. to act as a brake. ● *v.tr. & intr.* (**-ies, -ied**) loop (a rope) around a saddle horn etc.

Dalmatian *n.* a breed of large dog having white, short hair with dark spots.

dam¹ ● *n.* **1** a barrier constructed to hold back water and raise its level, forming a reservoir or preventing flooding. **2** = BEAVER DAM. **3** anything functioning as a dam does. ● *v.tr.* (**dammed, damming**) **1** provide or confine with a dam. **2** (often foll. by *up*) block up; hold back; obstruct.

dam² *n.* the female parent of an esp. four-footed domestic animal.

damage ● *n.* **1** harm or injury impairing the value or usefulness of something, or the health or normal function of a person. **2** (in *pl.*) *Law* a sum of money claimed or awarded in compensation for a loss or an injury. **3** (*prec. by the*) *informal* cost (*what's the damage?*). ● *v.tr.* **1** inflict damage on. **2** (esp. as **damaging** *adj.*) detract from the reputation of (*a damaging admission*). □ **damaged** *adj.* **damagingly** *adv.*

damage control *n.* **1** action taken to alleviate the effects of damage after an accident, negative publicity, etc. **2** the taking of such action.

damage deposit *n.* a sum of money given as a deposit against possible future damage to something rented or leased.

damask /ˈdæməsk/ ● *n.* **1 a** a figured woven fabric (esp. silk or linen) with a pattern visible on both sides. **b** twilled table linen with woven designs shown by the reflection of light. **2** a tablecloth made of this material. ● *adj.* made of or resembling damask. ● *v.tr.* **1** weave with figured designs. **2** ornament.

damask rose *n.* an old sweet-scented variety of rose, with very soft velvety petals.

dame *n. N Amer. slang offensive* a woman.

dammit *interj.* damn it.

damn ● *v.* **1** *tr. & intr.* curse (a person or thing). **2** *tr.* doom to hell; cause the damnation of. **3** *tr.* condemn, censure. **4** *tr.* **a** (often as **damning** *adj.*) (of a circumstance, piece of evidence, etc.) show or prove to be guilty; bring condemnation upon. **b** be the ruin of. **5** *tr.* used when swearing at a person or thing (*damn you!*). ● *n.* **1** an uttered curse. **2** *slang* a negligible amount (*not worth a damn*). ● *interj.* expressing emphatic annoyance, frustration, etc. ● *adj. & adv. informal* = DAMNED. □ **damn fool** *informal* foolish, stupid (*that's a damn fool idea*). **damn near** (also **damned near**) *informal* almost (*damn near died*). **damn well** *informal* (as an emphatic) simply (*damn well do as I say*). **damn with faint praise** commend so unenthusiastically as to imply disapproval. **I'll be** (or **I'm) damned if** *informal* I certainly do not, will not, etc. **not give a damn** not care at all. **well I'll be** (or **I'm) damned** *informal* exclamation of surprise, dismay, etc. □ **damningly** *adv.*

damnable *adj.* annoying. □ **damnably** *adv.*

damnation ● *n.* condemnation to eternal punishment, esp. in hell. ● *interj.* expressing anger or annoyance.

damned *informal* ● *adj.* damnable, infernal, unwelcome. ● *adv.* extremely (*damned hot*). □ **damned if you do and damned if you don't** unable to win approval no matter what one does.

damnedest *adj. informal* most surprising or extraordi-

nary (*the damnedest thing you ever saw*). □ **do one's damnedest** do one's utmost.

damp ● *adj.* slightly wet; moist. ● *n.* **1** diffused moisture in the air, on a surface, or in a solid, esp. as a cause of inconvenience or danger. **2** dejection; discouragement. ● *v.tr.* **1** make damp; moisten. **2** (often foll. by *down*) **a** take the force or vigour out of (*damp one's enthusiasm*). **b** make flaccid or spiritless. **c** make (a fire) burn less strongly by reducing the flow of air to it. **3** reduce or stop the vibration of (esp. the strings of a musical instrument). □ **damp off** (of a plant) die from a fungus attack in damp conditions. □ **damply** *adv.* **dampness** *n.*

dampen *v.* **1** *v.tr. & intr.* make or become damp. **2** *tr.* make less forceful or vigorous. □ **dampener** *n.*

damper *n.* **1** a person or thing that discourages, or tempers enthusiasm. **2** a device that reduces shock or noise. **3** a movable metal plate in a flue to control the draft, and so the rate of combustion. **4** *Cdn* (*Nfld*) a round lid or cover placed over an opening on the cooking surface of a wood or coal etc. stove. **5** a pad silencing a piano string except when removed by means of a pedal or by the note's being struck. □ **put a damper on** take the vigour or enjoyment out of.

damsel *n. archaic or jocular* a young unmarried woman.

damselfly *n.* (*pl.* **-flies**) any of various insects of the order Odonata, like a dragonfly but with its wings folded over the body when resting.

dance ● *v.* **1** *intr.* move about rhythmically alone or with a partner or in a group, usu. in fixed steps or sequences to music, for pleasure, as entertainment, or as a ritual. **2** *intr.* move in a lively way; skip or jump about. **3** *tr.* **a** perform (a specified dance or form of dancing). **b** perform (a specified role) in a ballet etc. **4** *intr.* move up and down (on water, in the field of vision, etc.). **5** *tr.* move (esp. a child) up and down. ● *n.* **1** a sequence of steps or bodily motions etc., usu. performed to music. **2** the act or an instance of dancing. **3** a social gathering for dancing. **4** the art of dancing. **5** a piece of music having a rhythm or style that is suitable for a particular dance. **6** a dancing or lively motion. **7** a formal or stylized pattern of movements etc. performed by an animal or bird. **8** = ICE DANCING. □ **dance to a person's tune** accede obsequiously to a person's demands and wishes. □ **danceable** *adj.* **dancey** *adj.*

dance band *n.* a band that plays music that is especially suitable for dancing to.

dance floor *n.* a usu. uncarpeted area for dancing.

dance hall *n.* **1** a public establishment for dancing. **2** an uptempo usu. electronic style of popular music, originating in the dance halls of Jamaica, derived from reggae and elements of rap and ragga.

dancer *n.* **1** a person who performs a dance. **2** a person whose profession is dancing.

dancing girl *n.* a girl or woman who performs esp. erotic or music hall dances.

D. and C. *n.* an operation in which the cervix is dilated and the uterine lining scraped off with a curette.

dandelion *n.* a composite plant, *Taraxacum officinale*, with jagged leaves and a large bright yellow flower on a hollow stalk, followed by a globular head of seeds with downy tuft.

dander¹ *n. informal* temper, anger, indignation. □ **get one's dander up** lose one's temper; become angry.

dander² *n.* dandruff, esp. in the hair of animals.

dandle *v.tr.* **1** dance (a child) on one's knees or in one's arms. **2** pamper, pet.

dandruff n. **1** dead skin in small scales among the hair. **2** the condition of having this.

dandy ● n. (pl. **-ies**) **1** a man unduly devoted to style, smartness, and fashion in dress and appearance. **2** informal an excellent thing. ● adj. (**-ier, -iest**) esp. N Amer. informal very good of its kind; splendid, first-rate. □ **dandyish** adj. **dandyism** n.

Dane n. **1** a native or national of Denmark, a country in Scandinavia. **2** hist. a Viking invader of England in the 9th–11th c.

dang adj. & interj. N Amer. informal = DAMN.

danger n. **1** liability or exposure to harm. **2** a thing that causes or is likely to cause harm. **3** an unwelcome possibility (the danger that people will do nothing). □ **in danger of** likely to incur or to suffer from.

dangerous adj. involving or causing danger. □ **dangerously** adv. **dangerousness** n.

dangle v. **1** intr. be loosely suspended, so as to be able to sway to and fro. **2** tr. hold or carry loosely suspended. **3** tr. hold out (a hope, temptation, etc.) enticingly. □ **dangler** n. **dangly** adj.

dangling adj. (of a participle in an absolute clause or phrase) having no expressed subject, but having an implicit subject that is different than the subject of the clause modified, e.g. talking in while talking on the cellphone, the car ran into the ditch.

Danish ● adj. of or relating to Denmark, a country in Scandinavia, or the Danes. ● n. **1** the Danish language. **2** (prec. by the; treated as pl.) the Danish people. **3** (in full **Danish pastry**) a baked good of sweet, flaky bread topped with icing, fruit, etc.

Danish blue n. a soft white cheese with blue veins.

dank adj. disagreeably damp and cold. □ **dankly** adv. **dankness** n.

daphne /'dæfni/ n. any flowering shrub of the genus Daphne, e.g. D. laureola, with small yellow flowers.

dapper adj. **1** neat and precise, esp. in dress or movement. **2** sprightly. □ **dapperly** adv. **dapperness** n.

dapple ● v. **1** tr. mark with spots or rounded patches of colour or shade. **2** intr. become marked in this way. ● n. **1** a dappled effect. **2** a dappled animal, esp. a horse. □ **dappled** adj.

dapple grey ● adj. (of an animal's coat) grey or white with darker spots. ● n. a dapple grey horse.

dare ● v.tr. **1** (3rd sing. present **dares** or sometimes **dare**) (foll. by infin. with or without to) venture (to); have the courage or impudence (to) (if they dare to come; how dare you?). **2** defy or challenge (a person) (I dare you to own up). **3** literary attempt; take the risk of (dared their anger). ● n. **1** an act of daring. **2** a challenge, esp. to prove courage. □ **I dare say 1** (often foll. by that + clause) it is probable. **2** probably; I grant that much (I dare say, but you are still wrong).

daredevil ● n. a recklessly daring person. ● adj. recklessly daring. □ **daredevilry** n.

daring ● n. adventurous courage. ● adj. adventurous, bold; prepared to take risks. □ **daringly** adv.

Darjeeling /dɑr'dʒiːlɪŋ/ n. the high-quality tea grown in the area around Darjeeling in NE India.

dark ● adj. **1** with little or no light. **2** of a deep or sombre colour. **3** (of a person) with deep brown or black hair, complexion, or skin. **4** gloomy, dismal (dark thoughts). **5** evil, sinister (dark deeds). **6** sullen, angry (a dark mood). **7** remote, mysterious, little-known (the dark and distant past). **8** ignorant, unenlightened. ● n. **1** absence of light. **2** nightfall (after dark). **3** a dark area or colour, esp. in painting. □ **in the dark 1** with little or no light. **2** lacking information. □ **darkish** adj. **darkly** adv. **darkness** n.

Dark Ages n.pl. (also **Dark Age**) (prec. by the) **1 a** the period of western European history between the fall of the Roman Empire and the high Middle Ages, c.500–1100. **b** a similar period in the history of Greece and other Aegean countries from the end of the Bronze Age until the beginning of the historical period. **2** any period of supposed unenlightenment.

dark chocolate n. esp. N Amer. sweet or semi-sweet chocolate made without the addition of milk.

darken v. **1** tr. make dark or darker. **2** intr. become dark or darker. □ **darken a door** appear at a place (I'll never darken this door again!). □ **darkener** n.

dark glasses n.pl. eyeglasses with dark lenses.

dark horse n. a little-known person who is unexpectedly successful or prominent.

darkroom n. a room for developing photographic work, with normal light excluded.

darling ● n. **1** (often as a form of address) a beloved or lovable person or thing. **2** a favourite. **3** informal a pretty or endearing person or thing. ● adj. **1** beloved, lovable. **2** favourite. **3** informal charming or pretty.

darn[1] ● v.tr. mend (esp. knitted material, or a hole in it) by interweaving yarn across the hole with a needle. ● n. a darned area in material. □ **darner** n.

darn[2] v.tr., interj., adj., & adv. informal = DAMN.

darndest adj. (also **darnedest**) = DAMNDEST.

darned adj. & adv. informal = DAMNED.

darnel n. any of several grasses of the genus Lolium of Europe and N Africa and naturalized in N America, planted as pasture grasses or to stabilize soil.

darning n. **1** the action of a person who darns. **2** things to be darned.

darning needle n. **1** a long needle with a large eye, used in darning. **2** N Amer. a dragonfly.

darn tootin' N Amer. informal ● interj. indicating fervent agreement. ● adv. & adj. used as an intensifier (darn tootin' I mind!). □ **you're darn tootin'** you're right.

dart ● n. **1** a small pointed missile thrown or fired as a weapon. **2 a** a small pointed missile with a feather or plastic flight, used in darts. **b** (in pl.; usu. treated as sing.) an indoor game in which such darts are thrown at a circular target to score points. **3** a sudden rapid movement. **4** a stitched tapered tuck for shaping a garment. ● v. **1** intr. (often foll. by out, in, past, etc.) move or go suddenly or rapidly. **2** tr. throw (a missile). **3** tr. direct suddenly (a glance etc.).

dartboard n. a circular board marked with numbered segments, used as a target in darts.

darter n. **1** any large water bird of the genus Anhinga, having a narrow head and long thin neck. **2** any of various small quick-moving freshwater fish of the family Percidae, native to N America.

Darwinian /dɑr'wɪniən/ ● adj. **1** of or relating to Charles Darwin's (1809–92) theory of the evolution of species by natural selection. **2** characterized by ruthless competition for survival. ● n. an adherent of Darwin's theory. □ **Darwinism** n. **Darwinist** n.

dash ● v. **1** intr. rush hastily or forcefully. **2** tr. strike or fling with great force, esp. so as to shatter. **3** tr. frustrate, daunt, dispirit (dashed their hopes). **4** tr. informal (esp. **dash it** or **dash it all**) = DAMN v. **1**. **5** tr. splash or splatter. ● n. **1** a rushing movement; a sudden advance. **2** a horizontal stroke in writing or printing to mark a pause or break in sense or to represent omitted letters or words. **3** a small amount of something (a dash of salt). **4** impetuous vigour or the capacity for this. **5** showy appearance or behaviour. **6** esp. N Amer. a short race; a sprint. **7** the longer signal of the two used in Morse code (compare DOT n. **3**). **8** = DASHBOARD. □ **cut a dash** make a brilliant show. **dash down** (or **off**) write or finish hurriedly.

dashboard n. the surface below the windshield of a motor vehicle or aircraft, containing instruments and controls.

dasher n. N Amer. (in full **dasher board**) one of the boards surrounding a hockey rink.

dashing adj. **1** spirited, lively. **2** attractive in a lively or stylish way. □ **dashingly** adv.

dastardly /ˈdæstərdli/ adj. despicable.

DAT abbr. digital audio tape.

data /ˈdeɪtə, ˈdeɪtə/ n. **1** quantities or characters operated on by a computer. **2** (treated as sing.) a body or series of facts; information. **3** (treated as pl.) facts, statistics. **4** pl. of DATUM. ¶In scientific writing, data is almost always treated as a plural, but the singular use is standard in all other levels of writing.

database n. (also **data bank**) an organized store of data, esp. one that may be accessed by a computer.

datable adj. that can be dated (to a particular time).

data glove n. Computing a device worn like a glove and containing sensors linked to a representation of a hand in a computer display, allowing the manual manipulation of images in virtual reality.

data link n. a telecommunications link over which data may be transmitted.

data processing n. a series of operations on data, esp. by a computer, to retrieve or classify etc. information. □ **data processor** n.

date[1] ● n. **1** a day of the month, esp. specified by a number. **2** a particular day or year, esp. when a given event occurred. **3** a statement (usu. giving the day, month, and year) in a document or inscription etc., of the time of composition or publication. **4 a** a social engagement, often of a romantic nature, with one other person. **b** N Amer. a person with whom one has a social engagement (my date is picking me up). **5** the period to which a work of art etc. belongs. **6** the time when an event happens or is to happen. **7** (in pl.) the dates of a person's birth and death, usu. in years (Laurier's dates are 1841–1919). ● v. **1** tr. mark with a date. **2** tr. **a** assign a date to (an object, event, etc.). **b** (foll. by to) assign to a particular time, period, etc. **3 a** tr. make or go out on a date with (a person). **b** intr. go out on a date or dates (they are now dating regularly). **4** intr. (often foll. by from, back to, etc.) have its origins at a particular time. **5** intr. become evidently out of date (a design that does not date). **6** tr. indicate or expose as being out of date (that hat really dates you). □ **to date** until now. **up to date** (attrib. **up-to-date**) meeting or according to the latest requirements, knowledge, or fashion; modern. □ **dating** n.

date[2] n. **1** a dark oval single-stoned fruit. **2** (in full **date palm**) the tall tree Phoenix dactylifera, native to W Asia and N Africa, bearing this fruit.

datebook n. N Amer. an appointment diary.

dated adj. **1** old-fashioned. **2** marked with a date.

dateline ● n. **1** (**Date Line**) the line from north to south partly along the meridian 180° from Greenwich, to the east of which the date is a day earlier than it is to the west. **2** a line at the head of a dispatch or special article in a newspaper showing the date and place of writing. ● v.tr. (usu. in passive) provide (a newspaper story) with a dateline.

date rape n. the rape of a girl or woman by a person with whom she is on a date.

date square n. Cdn (often in pl.) a dessert consisting of date filling spread on an oatmeal base and covered with a crumble topping, served cut into squares.

dative /ˈdeɪtɪv/ Grammar ● n. the case of nouns and pronouns (and words in agreement with them) indicating an indirect object. ● adj. of or in the dative.

datum /ˈdeɪtəm, ˈdeɪtəm/ n. (pl. **data**) **1** a piece of information. **2** a thing known or granted; an assumption or premise from which inferences may be drawn. **3** a fixed starting point of a scale etc. (datum line). **4** see also DATA.

daub ● v.tr. & intr. **1** tr. spread (paint, plaster, or some other thick substance) crudely or roughly on a surface. **2** tr. coat or smear (a surface) with paint etc. **3 a** tr. & intr. paint crudely or unskilfully. **b** tr. lay (colours) on crudely and clumsily. ● n. **1** paint or other substance daubed on a surface. **2** plaster, clay, etc., for coating a surface, esp. mixed with straw and applied to laths or wattles to form a wall.

daughter n. **1** a girl or woman in relation to either or both of her parents. **2** a female descendant. **3** (foll. by of) a female member of a family, nation, etc. **4** (foll. by of) a woman who is regarded as the spiritual descendant of a person or thing. **5** a product or attribute personified as a daughter in relation to its source. **6** Biol. a cell etc. formed by the division etc. of another. □ **daughterly** adj.

daughter-in-law n. (pl. **daughters-in-law**) the wife of one's son.

daunt v.tr. discourage, intimidate. □ **daunting** adj.

dauntless adj. intrepid, persevering.

davit /ˈdævɪt, ˈdeɪvɪt/ n. a small crane on a ship, esp. one of a pair for suspending or lowering a lifeboat.

Davy Jones n. slang **1** (in full **Davy Jones's locker**) the bottom of the sea, esp. regarded as the grave of those drowned. **2** the evil spirit of the sea.

dawdle ● v. **1** intr. **a** walk or move slowly. **b** delay; waste time. **2** tr. (foll. by away) waste (time). ● n. the act or an instance of dawdling. □ **dawdler** n.

dawn ● n. **1** the first light of day; daybreak. **2** the beginning or incipient appearance of something. ● v.intr. **1** (of a day) begin; grow light. **2** begin to appear or develop; become visible. **3** (often foll. by on, upon) begin to become evident or understood (by a person).

dawning n. **1** daybreak. **2** a beginning.

day n. **1** the time between sunrise and sunset. **2 a** a period of 24 hours as a unit of time, esp. from midnight to midnight, corresponding to a complete revolution of the earth on its axis. **b** a corresponding period on other planets. **3** the time in a day during which work or another activity is engaged in (an eight-hour day). **4** daylight (clear as day). **5 a** (also pl.) a period of the past or present (the modern day; the old days). **b** (prec. by the) the present time (the issues of the day). **6** the lifetime of a person or thing, esp. regarded as useful or productive (in my day things were different). **7** a point of time (will do it one day). **8 a** the date of a specific festival. **b** a day associated with a particular event or purpose (payday; Christmas day). **9** a particular date; a date agreed on. □ **all in a** (or **the**) **day's work** part of normal routine. **any day** at any time; under any conditions (my dog can beat yours any day!). **any day now** in the immediate future (could happen any day now). **at the end of the day** in the final reckoning, when all is said and done. **call it a day** end a period of activity, esp. content that enough has been done. **day after day** without respite. **day and night** all the time. **day by day** gradually. **day in, day out** routinely, constantly. **day of rest** the Sabbath. **from day one** from the beginning. **if one is a day** adding emphasis to an estimate of a person's age (he must be sixty if he's a day). **not one's day** a day of successive misfortunes for a person. **one of these days** before very long. **one of those days** a day when things go badly. **that will be the day** *informal* that will never happen. **this day and age** the present time or period. **win the day** be successful.

daybed *n.* a piece of furniture that can be used as a couch in the daytime and as a bed at night, usu. a single bed with a frame around three sides serving as a back and arms.

daybook *n.* **1** an appointment diary. **2** an account book in which a day's transactions are entered, for later transfer to a ledger.

daybreak *n.* the first appearance of morning light.

day camp *n. N Amer.* a camp which children attend during the day, usu. only on summer weekdays.

daycare *n.* **1** the supervision of young children during the working day by people other than their parents. **2** the care provided by a day centre. **3** *N Amer., Austral., & NZ* (in full **daycare centre**) a place where daycare is provided.

day centre *n.* a place providing care for the elderly or handicapped during the day.

daydream ● *n.* a pleasant fantasy or reverie. ● *v.intr.* indulge in this. □ **daydreamer** *n.* **daydreaming** *n. & adj.* **daydreamy** *adj.*

Day-Glo ● *n. proprietary* a make of fluorescent paint or other colouring. ● *adj.* coloured with or like this.

day job *n.* a job with regular daytime hours, esp. as opposed to artistic pursuits (*don't quit your day job*).

daylight *n.* **1** the light of day. **2** dawn (*before daylight*). **3 a** openness, publicity. **b** open knowledge. **4** a visible gap or interval (*I see daylight around the door frame*). □ **see daylight** begin to understand.

daylights *n.pl. informal* senses or wits (*scared the daylights out of me*; *beat the living daylights out of him*).

daylight saving *n.* (also **daylight savings**) the achieving of longer evening daylight, esp. in summer, by setting the time an hour ahead.

daylight time *n.* (also **daylight saving time**) esp. *N Amer.* time as adjusted for daylight saving.

day lily *n.* any plant of the genus *Hemerocallis*, whose flowers last only a day.

daylong *adj.* lasting for a day.

day nursery *n.* = DAYCARE 3.

Day of Atonement *n.* = YOM KIPPUR.

day off *n.* a day's holiday from work.

Day of Judgment *n.* = JUDGMENT DAY.

day of reckoning *n. see* RECKONING.

day pack *n.* a small backpack for use on one-day hikes or for carrying books etc.

day pass *n.* **1** a certificate etc. entitling a person to unlimited use of a transit system, amusement park, etc. throughout a given day. **2** a permit allowing a jailed offender to leave prison for a day.

day release *n. Cdn* release of a jailed offender during the day or for a short period of time, e.g. to attend school or for employment.

day school *n.* a school not providing boarding.

daytime *n.* the part of the day when there is natural light.

Daytimer *n. N Amer. proprietary* an appointment diary.

day-to-day *adj.* **1** involving daily routine. **2** planning for only one day at a time.

day trader *n. Stock Exch.* a person who tries to make quick profits by buying extremely volatile stocks and holding them for a very short time, usu. less than a full day. □ **day trading** *n.*

day trip *n.* a trip or excursion completed in one day.□ **day tripper** *n.*

daze ● *v.tr.* stupefy, bewilder. ● *n.* a state of confusion or bewilderment. □ **dazed** *adj.* **dazedly** *adv.*

dazzle ● *v.tr.* **1** blind temporarily or confuse the sight of by an excess of light. **2** impress or overpower (a person) with knowledge, ability, or any brilliant display or prospect. ● *n.* bright confusing light. □ **dazzled** *adj.* **dazzlement** *n.* **dazzler** *n.* **dazzling** *adj.* **dazzlingly** *adv.*

dB *abbr.* decibel(s).

DBS *abbr.* **1** direct-broadcast satellite. **2** direct broadcasting by satellite.

DC *abbr.* **1** (also **d.c.**) direct current. **2** District of Columbia.

D.C.L. *abbr.* Doctor of Civil Law.

D.D. *abbr.* Doctor of Divinity.

D-Day *n.* **1** the day (6 June 1944) on which Allied forces invaded N France to begin the liberation of W Europe. **2** the day on which an important operation is to begin or a change to take effect.

ddC *abbr.* dideoxycytidine, a drug for use against HIV.

ddI *abbr.* dideoxyinosine, a drug for use against HIV.

D.D.S. *abbr.* Doctor of Dental Surgery.

DDT *abbr.* dichlorodiphenyltrichloroethane, a colourless chlorinated hydrocarbon used as an insecticide, now banned in many countries.

DE *abbr.* Delaware (in postal use).

de- *prefix* added to verbs and their derivatives to form verbs and nouns implying removal or reversal (*decentralize*; *de-ice*; *demoralization*).

DEA *abbr.* (in Canada) Department of External Affairs (until 1994).

deacon ● *n.* **1** (in churches with a hierarchy) a minister of the third order, below bishop and priest. **2** (in some Protestant Churches) a layperson elected or appointed to assist the minister, manage the congregation's secular affairs, etc. ● *v.tr.* appoint or ordain as a deacon. □ **deaconate** /di'ækənət / *n.*

deaconess *n.* **1** a laywoman with functions similar to a deacon's. **2** = DIACONAL MINISTER.

deactivate *v.tr.* make inactive or less reactive. □ **deactivation** *n.* **deactivator** *n.*

dead ● *adj.* **1** no longer alive. **2** *informal* extremely tired or unwell. **3** affected by loss of sensation; numb (*my fingers are dead*). **4** (foll. by *to*) unappreciative or unconscious of; insensitive to. **5 a** no longer effective or in use; obsolete, extinct. **b** no longer functioning. **6** (of a fire etc.) no longer burning. **7** inanimate. **8 a** lacking force or vigour; dull, lustreless, muffled. **b** (of sound) not resonant. **9 a** quiet; lacking activity. **b** motionless, idle. **10 a** (of a microphone, telephone, etc.) not transmitting any sound, esp. because of a fault. **b** (of a circuit, conductor, etc.) carrying or transmitting no current (*a dead battery*). **11 a** (of the ball etc. in a game) out of play. **b** (of play) suspended. **12** abrupt, complete, exact, unqualified, unrelieved (*in dead silence*; *dead certainty*). **13** without spiritual life or energy. ● *adv.* **1** absolutely, exactly, completely (*dead on target*; *dead ahead*; *dead last*). **2** *informal* very, extremely (*dead broke*). ● *n.* (prec. by *the*) **1** (treated as *pl.*) those who have died. **2** a time of silence or inactivity (*the dead of night*). □ **dead drunk** so drunk as to be immobile or insensible. **dead from the neck up** *informal* stupid. **dead in the water** *N Amer.* **1** (of a ship etc.) motionless, esp. as a result of damage, malfunction, etc. **2** not progressing or functioning (*the economy is dead in the water*). **dead to the world** *informal* fast asleep; unconscious. **play dead** pretend to be dead by lying still. **stop dead in one's tracks** stop abruptly and decisively. **wouldn't be caught** (or **seen**) **dead in** (or **with**) *informal* shall have nothing to do with; shall refuse to wear etc. □ **deadness** *n.*

dead air *n.* **1** a pause in a radio etc. transmission during which the speakers are silent etc. **2** air trapped for insulating purposes, as in layers of clothing.

deadbeat *n.* **1 a** someone who avoids paying debts. **b** (in full **deadbeat dad** or **deadbeat father**) a man who avoids paying child support. **2** a worthless sponging idler; a loafer.

deadbolt *n.* esp. *N Amer.* a bolt engaged by turning a knob or key, rather than by spring action.

dead cert *n.* see CERT.

dead duck *n.* slang **1** a person in a hopeless position. **2** an unsuccessful or useless person or thing.

deaden *v.* **1** *tr. & intr.* deprive of or lose vitality, force, brightness, sound, etc. **2** *tr.* (foll. by *to*) make insensitive. □ **deadener** *n.*

dead end ● *n.* **1 a** a closed end of a road, passage, etc. **b** a street or road with a dead end. **2** (often, with hyphen, *attrib.*) a situation offering no prospects of progress or advancement (*dead-end job*). ● *v.intr.* (**dead-end**) *N Amer.* (of a road or progress, development, etc.) come to an end.

deadfall *n. N Amer.* **1** a trap in which a raised weight is made to fall on and kill esp. large game. **2** a tangled mass of fallen trees, branches, etc. **3** a dead tree that has fallen to the ground.

deadhead ● *n.* **1** a faded flower head. **2** a useless or unenterprising person. **3** *N Amer.* a sunken or submerged log, esp. one that is a hazard to boats. ● *v.tr.* remove deadheads from (a plant).

dead heat *n.* **1** a race in which two or more competitors finish at exactly the same time. **2** a situation in which all participants, competitors, etc. receive the same number of votes etc. **3** the result of such a competition.

dead horse *n.* □ **flog** (or **beat**) **a dead horse** waste energy on something unalterable.

dead language *n.* a language no longer commonly spoken, e.g. Latin.

dead letter *n.* **1** a law or practice no longer observed or recognized. **2** an undeliverable piece of mail.

deadline *n.* a time limit for the completion of an activity etc.

deadlock ● *n.* **1** a situation, esp. involving opposing parties, in which no progress can be made. **2** a type of lock requiring a key to open or close it. ● *v.tr. & intr.* bring or come to a standstill. □ **deadlocked** *adj.*

deadly ● *adj.* (**-ier, -iest**) **1 a** causing or able to cause fatal injury or serious damage. **b** poisonous. **2** intense, extreme (*deadly dullness*). **3** (of an aim etc.) extremely accurate or effective. **4** deathlike (*deadly gloom*). **5** *informal* dreary, dull. **6** implacable. ● *adv.* **1** like death; as if dead (*deadly faint*). **2** extremely, intensely (*deadly serious*). □ **deadliness** *n.*

deadly nightshade *n.* = BELLADONNA 1.

deadly sin *n.* a sin regarded as leading to damnation, esp. pride, covetousness, lust, gluttony, envy, anger, or sloth.

deadman's float *n.* a prone floating position, with arms extended forwards and legs backwards.

dead march *n.* a funeral march.

dead meat *n. N Amer. informal* a person or thing that is doomed or finished (*if they don't come, we're dead meat*).

dead-on *adj.* **1** exactly right. **2** perfectly on target.

deadpan ● *adj. & adv.* with a face or manner lacking all expression or emotion. ● *v.tr. & intr.* (**-panned, -panning**) say in a deadpan manner.

dead set *adj.* (foll. by *against*) fiercely opposed.

dead weight *n.* **1 a** an inert mass. **b** a heavy weight or burden. **2** a debt not covered by assets. **3** the total weight carried on a ship.

deadwood *n. informal* one or more useless or unprofitable people or things.

deaf *adj.* **1** wholly or partly without hearing. **2** (foll. by *to*) refusing to listen or comply. **3** insensitive to harmony, rhythm, etc. (*tone-deaf*). □ **deaf as a post** completely deaf. **fall on deaf ears** be ignored. **turn a deaf ear** (usu. foll. by *to*) be unresponsive. □ **deafly** *adv.* **deafness** *n.*

deafen *v.tr.* **1** (often as **deafening** *adj.*) overpower with sound. **2** deprive of hearing by noise, esp. temporarily. □ **deafeningly** *adv.*

deal ● *v.* (*past* and *past part.* **dealt**) **1** *intr.* (foll. by *with*) **a** take measures concerning (a problem, person, etc.), esp. in order to put something right. **b** do business with; associate with. **c** discuss or treat (a subject). **2** *intr.* (foll. by *in*) to sell or be concerned with commercially (*deals in insurance*). **3** *tr.* (often foll. by *out, round*) distribute or apportion to several people etc. **4** *tr. & intr.* distribute (cards) to players for a game or round. **5** *tr.* cause to be received; administer (*deal a heavy blow*). **6** *tr.* (foll. by *in*) *informal* include (a person) in an activity (*deal me in*). ● *n.* **1** (usu. **a good** or **great deal**) *informal* **a** a large amount (*a great deal of trouble*). **b** to a considerable extent (*is a good deal better*). **2** an agreement, esp. in business on certain terms for buying or doing something. **3** a specified form of treatment given or received (*got a fair deal*). **4 a** the distribution of cards by dealing. **b** a player's turn to do this (*it's my deal*). **c** the round of play following this. **d** a set of hands dealt to players. □ **it's a deal** *informal* expressing assent to an agreement.

de-alcoholized *adj.* (of an alcoholic drink) having had all or almost all alcohol removed.

dealer *n.* **1** a person etc. dealing in (esp. retail) goods (*car dealer*). **2** the player dealing at cards. **3** a person who deals in illegal drugs. □ **dealership** *n.* (in sense 1).

dealings *n.pl.* contacts or transactions.

dealt *past* and *past part.* of DEAL.

dean *n.* **1 a** the head of a university faculty or department. **b** a college or university official with disciplinary and advisory functions. **2** the head of the chapter of a cathedral. **3** the most senior or most prominent of a particular category or body of people.

dear ● *adj.* **1 a** beloved or much esteemed. **b** as a merely polite or ironic form (*my dear man*). **2** used as a formula of address, esp. at the beginning of letters. **3** (often foll. by *to*) precious; much cherished. **4** (usu. in *superlative*) earnest, deeply felt. **5 a** high-priced relative to its value. **b** having high prices. **c** (of money) available as a loan only at a high rate of interest. ● *n.* (esp. as a form of address) dear person. ● *adv.* at a high price or great cost (*will cost you dear*). ● *interj.* expressing surprise, dismay, pity, etc. □ **dear** (**only**) **knows** heaven knows.

dearie *n.* (esp. as a form of address) usu. *jocular* or *ironic* my dear. □ **dearie me!** *interj.* expressing surprise, dismay, etc.

dearly *adv.* **1** affectionately, fondly (*love her dearly*). **2 a** earnestly; keenly. **b** very much, greatly (*would dearly love to go*). **3** at a high price or great cost.

dearth /dɜrθ/ *n.* a scarcity or lack.

death *n.* **1** the final cessation of vital functions in an organism; the ending of life. **2** the event that terminates life. **3 a** the fact or process of being killed or killing (*stone to death*). **b** the fact or state of being dead (*eyes closed in death*). **4 a** the destruction or permanent cessation of something (*was the death of our hopes*). **b**

informal something terrible or appalling. **5** (usu. **Death**) a personification of death, esp. as a destructive power, usu. represented by a skeleton. □ **at death's door** close to death. *adj.* **be the death of 1** cause the death of. **2** be very harmful to. **catch one's death** *informal* catch a serious chill etc. **do to death 1** kill. **2** overdo. **fate worse than death** *informal* a disastrous misfortune or experience. **like death warmed over** *slang* very tired or ill. **put to death** kill or cause to be killed. **to death** to the utmost, extremely (*bored to death*). □ **deathless** **deathlessness** *n.* **deathlike** *adj.*

deathbed *n.* a bed as the place where a person is dying or has died (also *attrib.*: *deathbed conversion*). □ **on one's deathbed** near death.

death blow *n.* **1** a blow or other action that causes death. **2** an event or circumstance that abruptly ends an activity, enterprise, etc.

death camp *n.* a prison camp in which many people die or are put to death.

death certificate *n.* an official statement of the cause and date and place of a person's death.

death knell *n.* **1** the tolling of a bell to mark a person's death. **2** an event that heralds the end or destruction of something.

deathly ● *adj.* (**-ier, -iest**) suggestive of death (*deathly silence*). ● *adv.* **1** in a deathly way (*deathly pale*). **2** extremely (*deathly ill*).

death metal *n.* a form of heavy metal music whose lyrics deal esp. with death, violence, and Satanism.

death penalty *n.* punishment by being killed.

death rate *n.* the number of deaths per thousand of population per year.

death row *n.* a prison block or section for prisoners sentenced to death, esp. in the US.

death sentence *n.* **1** a judicial sentence of punishment by death. **2** a situation implying imminent or premature death (*cancer is not a death sentence*).

death squad *n.* an armed paramilitary group formed to kill political enemies etc.

death star *n.* *Cdn* a satellite transmitting television signals directly to consumers' homes, esp. considered as a threat to cable television providers.

death toll *n.* the number of people killed in an accident, battle, etc.

death trap *n.* *informal* a dangerous or unhealthy building, vehicle, etc.

death wish *n.* a desire (usu. unconscious) for the death of oneself or another.

deb /deb/ *n.* *informal* a debutante.

debacle /deiˈbɒkəl, -ˈbækəl, də-/ *n.* **1 a** an utter failure or disaster. **b** a sudden collapse or downfall. **2 a** confused rush or rout; a stampede. **3 a** a breakup of ice in a river, with resultant flooding. **b** a sudden rush of water carrying stone and other debris.

debark¹ /diːˈbɑːrk, dɪ-/ *v.tr. & intr.* = DISEMBARK.

debark² /diːˈbɑːrk/ *v.tr.* remove bark from (a tree etc).

debase *v.tr.* **1** lower in quality, value, or character. **2** depreciate (coin) by alloying etc. □ **debasement** *n.*

debatable *adj.* **1** questionable; subject to dispute. **2** capable of being debated. □ **debatably** *adv.*

debate ● *v.* **1** *tr. & intr.* discuss or dispute about (an issue, proposal, etc.) esp. formally in a legislative assembly, public meeting, etc. **2 a** *tr.* consider, ponder (a matter). **b** *tr.* consider different sides of a question. **3** *tr.* engage in a debate with (someone). ● *n.* **1** a formal discussion on a particular matter, esp. in a legislative assembly etc. **2** argument, discussion (*open to debate*). **3** a contest in which the affirmative and negative

sides of a question are presented by opposing speakers. □ **debater** *n.*

debauch /dəˈbɒtʃ/ ● *v.tr.* **1** corrupt morally. **2** cause to indulge in immoral or excessive sexual activity or drinking. **3** seduce (a woman). ● *n.* **1** a bout of sensual indulgence. **2** debauchery. □ **debauched** *adj.*

debauchery *n.* (*pl.* **-ies**) **1** excessive sensual indulgence. **2** an instance of this.

debenture /dəˈbentʃər/ *n.* a sealed bond issued by a corporation or company in respect of a long-term (esp. fixed-interest) loan.

debilitate /dəˈbɪlɪˌteɪt/ *v.tr.* enfeeble, enervate. □ **debilitating** *adj.* **debilitation** *n.*

debility *n.* (*pl.* **-ies**) **1** feebleness, esp. of health. **2** a disability or handicap.

debit ● *n.* **1** an entry in an account recording a sum owed or paid out. **2** the sum recorded. **3** the total of such sums. **4** the debit side of an account. ● *v.tr.* (**debited, debiting**) **1** (foll. by *against, to*) enter (an amount) on the debit side of an account. **2** (foll. by *with*) enter (a person) on the debit side of an account.

debit card *n.* a card enabling the holder to pay for purchases electronically by transferring funds from a bank account.

debonair /ˌdebəˈner/ *adj.* **1** carefree, cheerful. **2** suave, self-assured. **3** having pleasant manners.

debone *v.tr.* remove the bones from (poultry etc.).

debrief *v.tr.* discuss a completed mission, undertaking, or event with (a person). □ **debriefing** *n.*

debris *n.* **1** scattered fragments, esp. of something wrecked or destroyed. **2** *Geol.* an accumulation of loose material, e.g. from rocks or plants.

debt *n.* **1** a sum of money owed. **2** a state of obligation to pay something owed (*out of debt*). **3** gratitude for kindness, help, influence etc. **4** *archaic* sin (*forgive us our debts*). □ **in a person's debt** under an obligation to a person.

debtor *n.* a person, country, etc. that owes a debt.

debug *v.tr.* (**debugged, debugging**) **1** identify and remove defects from (a machine, computer program, etc.). **2** trace and remove concealed listening devices from (a room etc.). □ **debugging** *n.*

debugger *n.* *Computing* a program for debugging.

debunk *v.tr.* *informal* **1** show the good reputation or aspirations of (a person, institution, etc.) to be spurious. **2** expose the falseness of (a claim etc.). □ **debunker** *n.*

debut /deiˈbjuː, ˈdeɪ-/ ● *n.* **1** the first public appearance of a person in a specified role, esp. a performer. **2** the first appearance of a young woman of marriageable age in fashionable society. ● *adj.* first; inaugural (*their debut album*). ● *v.tr.* make a debut.

debutante /ˈdebjuːˌtɒnt, ˈdeɪ-/ *n.* (also **débutante**) a (usu. wealthy) young woman making her social debut.

Dec. *abbr.* December.

deca- /ˈdekə/ *comb. form* (also **dec-** before a vowel) **1** having ten. **2** tenfold. **3** ten, esp. of a metric unit (*decagram*).

decade /ˈdekeɪd, deˈkeɪd/ *n.* **1** a period of ten years. **2** a set, series, or group of ten. **3** /ˈdekəd/ *Catholicism* a set of ten Hail Marys as part of the rosary.

decadence *n.* **1** moral or cultural deterioration, esp. after a peak or culmination of achievement. **2** decadent behaviour; a state of decadence.

decadent /ˈdekədənt/ ● *adj.* **1 a** in a state of moral or cultural deterioration; showing or characterized by decadence. **b** of a period of decadence. **2** self-indulgent. **3** (of food, esp. dessert) very rich or sweet. ● *n.* a decadent person. ☐ **decadently** *adv.*

decaf *informal* ● *n.* decaffeinated coffee. ● *adj.* decaffeinated.

decaffeinate *v.tr.* **1** remove the caffeine from. **2** reduce the quantity of caffeine in (usu. coffee). ☐ **decaffeinated** *adj.* **decaffeination** *n.*

decal /'di:kæl, 'dekæl, 'dekəl/ *n.* a picture or design transferred from specially prepared paper to the surface of glass, plastic, etc.

decamp *v.intr.* **1** depart suddenly. **2** break up a camp.

decant /dɪ'kænt/ *v.tr.* gradually pour off (liquid, esp. wine or a solution) from one container to another, esp. without disturbing the sediment.

decanter *n.* a stoppered glass container into which wine or spirit is decanted.

decapitate /di'kæpɪ,teit/ *v.tr.* remove the head or top of. ☐ **decapitation** *n.*

decathlon /də'kæθlɒn/ *n.* an athletic contest in which each competitor takes part in ten events. ☐ **decathlete** /-li:t/ *n.*

decay ● *v.* **1** *a intr.* rot, decompose. **b** *tr.* cause to rot or decompose. **2** *intr. & tr.* decline or cause to decline in quality, power, energy, beauty, etc. **3** *intr. Physics* **a** (of a substance etc.) undergo change by radioactivity. **b** undergo a gradual decrease in magnitude of a physical quantity. ● *n.* **1** a rotten or ruinous state; a process of wasting away. **2** decline in health, quality, etc. **3** *Physics* **a** change into another substance etc. by radioactivity. **b** a decrease in the magnitude of a physical quantity, esp. the intensity of radiation.

decease *formal esp. Law* ● *n.* death. ● *v.intr.* die.

deceased ● *adj.* dead. ● *n.* (usu. prec. by *the*) a person who has died, esp. recently.

deceit *n.* **1** the act or process of deceiving, esp. by concealing the truth. **2** a dishonest trick or stratagem. **3** willingness to deceive.

deceitful *adj.* **1** (of a person) using deceit, esp. habitually. **2** (of an act, practice, etc.) intended to deceive. ☐ **deceitfully** *adv.* **deceitfulness** *n.*

deceive *v.* **1** *tr.* make (a person) believe what is false; mislead purposely. **2** *tr.* be unfaithful to, esp. sexually. **3** *intr.* use deceit. ☐ **be deceived** be mistaken or deluded. **deceive oneself** persist in a mistaken belief. ☐ **deceivable** *adj.* **deceiver** *n.*

decelerate /di'selə,reit/ *v.* **1** *intr.* move more slowly, slow down. **2** *tr.* diminish the speed of; cause to go slower. ☐ **deceleration** *n.* **decelerator** *n.*

December *n.* the twelfth month of the year.

decency *n.* (*pl.* **-ies**) **1** correct and tasteful standards of behaviour as generally accepted. **2** conformity with current standards of behaviour. **3** avoidance of obscenity. **4** (in *pl.*) the requirements of correct behaviour.

decent *adj.* **1** conforming with current standards of behaviour or propriety. **2** respectable. **3** satisfying a fair standard; acceptable. **4** kind, obliging, generous (*was decent enough to apologize*). **5** *informal* sufficiently clothed to see visitors (*are you decent?*). ☐ **decently** *adv.*

decentralize *v.tr.* **1** transfer (powers, functions, etc.) from a central to a regional or local authority, division, etc. **2** reorganize (a centralized institution, organization, etc.) on the basis of greater local or regional autonomy. ☐ **decentralist** *n. & adj.* **decentralization** *n.* **decentralized** *adj.*

decentre *v.tr.* (also esp. *US* **decenter**) remove the centre from.

deception *n.* **1** the act or instance of deceiving; the process of being deceived. **2** a thing that deceives.

deceptive *adj.* apt to deceive; easily mistaken for something else or as having a different quality. ☐ **deceptively** *adv.* **deceptiveness** *n.*

decertify *v.tr. & intr.* (**-ies, -ied**) revoke or renounce certification of (a person or thing, esp. a union) (*union members have voted to decertify*). ☐ **decertification** *n.*

deci- /'desɪ/ *comb. form* one-tenth, esp. of a unit in the metric system (*decimetre*).

decibel /'desɪbəl, -,bel/ *n.* **1** a unit (one-tenth of a bel) used in the comparison of two power levels relating to electrical signals or sound intensities, one of the pair usually being taken as a standard. Abbr.: **dB**. **2** *informal* a degree of noise.

decide *v.* **1** **a** *intr.* (often foll. by *on, about*) come to a resolution as a result of consideration. **b** *tr.* have or reach as one's resolution about something (*decided to stay*). **2** *tr.* resolve or settle (a question, dispute, etc.). **b** cause (a person) to reach a resolution (*was unsure about going but the weather decided me*). **3** *intr.* (usu. foll. by *between, for, against, in favour of,* or *that* + clause) give a judgment concerning a matter. ☐ **decidable** *adj.*

decided *adj.* **1** (usu. *attrib.*) definite, unquestionable (*a decided difference*). **2** (of a person, esp. as a characteristic) having clear opinions, resolute.

decidedly *adv.* undoubtedly, undeniably.

decider *n.* **1** a game, race, etc., to decide between competitors finishing equal in a previous contest. **2** any person or thing that decides.

deciduous /dɪ'sɪdʒʊəs, -djʊəs/ *adj.* **1** (of a tree) shedding its leaves annually. **2** (of leaves, horns, teeth, etc.) shed periodically. ☐ **deciduousness** *n.*

decigram /'desɪ,græm/ *n.* a metric unit of mass, equal to 0.1 gram.

decilitre /'desɪ,li:tər/ *n.* (also esp. *US* **deciliter**) a metric unit of capacity, equal to 0.1 litre.

decimal ● *adj.* **1** (of a system of numbers, measures, etc.) based on the number ten, in which the smaller units are related to the principal units as powers of ten (units, tens, hundreds, thousands, etc.). **2** of tenths or ten; reckoning or proceeding by tens. ● *n.* (also **decimal fraction**) a fraction whose denominator is a power of ten, esp. when expressed positionally by units to the right of a decimal point. ☐ **decimally** *adv.*

decimal place *n.* the position of a digit to the right of a decimal point.

decimal point *n.* a period placed before a numerator in a decimal fraction.

decimate /'desɪ,meit/ *v.tr.* **1** destroy a large proportion of. ¶Now the usual sense, although some still consider this an inappropriate use. **2** kill or remove one in every ten of. ☐ **decimation** *n.*

decimetre /'desɪ,mi:tər/ *n.* (also esp. *US* **decimeter**) a metric unit of length, equal to 0.1 metre.

decipher *v.tr.* **1** succeed in understanding (anything obscure or unclear). **2** convert (a text written in cipher) into an intelligible script or language. ☐ **decipherable** *adj.*

decision *n.* **1** the act or process of deciding. **2** a conclusion or resolution reached, esp. as to future action, after consideration. **3** *Baseball* a win or loss credited to a pitcher. **4** *Boxing* a victory determined by points. **5** **a** the settlement of a question. **b** a formal judgment.

decisive *adj.* **1** that decides an issue; conclusive. **2** able to decide quickly and effectively. ☐ **decisively** *adv.* **decisiveness** *n.*

deck ● *n.* **1 a** a platform in a ship covering all or part of the hull's area at any level and serving as a floor. **b** the accommodation on a particular deck of a ship. **2** anything compared to a ship's deck. **3** a component that carries a particular recording medium (such as a disc or tape) in sound-reproduction equipment. **4** *N Amer.* a pack of cards. **5** *N Amer.* a level unroofed area, usu. of wooden planks, adjoining a house. **6** the flat, usu. concrete area surrounding a swimming pool. **7** *N Amer.* a pile of logs ready for hauling, milling, etc. ● *v.tr.* **1** (often foll. by *out*) decorate, adorn. **2** furnish with or cover as a deck. **3** *slang* knock (a person) to the ground. □ **below deck** (or **decks**) in or into the space below the main deck. **on deck 1** in the open air on a ship's main deck. **2** (esp. of a batter in baseball) next in line.

deck chair *n.* a folding chair of wood and canvas, of a kind used on deck on passenger ships.

-decker *comb. form* having a specified number of decks or layers (*double-decker*).

deckhand *n.* a person employed in cleaning and odd jobs on a ship's deck.

deck shoe *n.* a shoe resembling a moccasin with rubber soles, leather uppers, and laces, usu. having a second lace looped around the heel.

declaim /dɪˈkleɪm/ *v.* **1** *intr. & tr.* speak or utter rhetorically or affectedly. **2** *intr.* practise oratory or recitation. **3** *intr.* (foll. by *against*) protest forcefully. **4** *intr.* deliver an impassioned speech. □ **declaimer** *n.*

declamation /ˌdɛkləˈmeɪʃən/ *n.* **1** the act or art of declaiming. **2** a rhetorical exercise or set speech. **3** an impassioned speech; a harangue. □ **declamatory** /dɪˈklæməˌtɔːri/ *adj.*

declaration *n.* **1** the act or process of declaring. **2 a** a formal, emphatic, or deliberate statement or announcement. **b** a statement asserting or protecting a legal right. **3** a written public announcement of intentions, terms of an agreement, etc. **4** *Law* **a** a plaintiff's statement of claim. **b** an affirmation made instead of taking an oath.

declarative /dɪˈklɛrətɪv/ ● *adj.* **1** of the nature of, or making, a declaration. **2** *Grammar* (of a sentence) that takes the form of a simple statement. ● *n.* a declarative sentence.

declare *v.* **1** *tr.* announce openly or formally (*declare war*). **2** *tr.* pronounce (a person or thing) to be something (*declared him to be an imposter*). **3** *tr.* (often foll. by *that* + clause) assert emphatically. **4** *tr.* acknowledge possession of (dutiable goods, taxable income, etc.). **5** *tr. Cards* **a** (also *intr.*) name (the trump suit etc.). **b** reveal that one holds (certain combinations of cards etc.) for scoring. **6** *tr.* (of things) make evident, prove. **7** *intr.* (often foll. by *for*, *against*) take the side of one party or another. **8** *intr. N Amer.* announce oneself to be a candidate (for some electoral race). □ **declare oneself** reveal one's intentions or identity. **well, I declare** (or **I do declare**) an exclamation of incredulity, surprise, or vexation. □ **declaratory** *adj.* **declarer** *n.*

declared *adj.* **1** that has been declared or made known. **2** (of a person) admitted, professed.

declaw /diːˈklɔː/ *v.tr.* **1** remove the claws from (a cat). **2** remove the force, vigour, or influence from.

declension /dɪˈklɛnʃən/ *n.* **1** *Grammar* **a** the variation of the form of a noun, pronoun, or adjective, by which its grammatical case, number, and gender are identified. **b** the class in which a noun etc. is put according to the exact form of this variation. **c** the entire set of inflected forms of a noun etc. **2** deterioration, declining.

declination /ˌdɛklɪˈneɪʃən/ *n.* **1** the angular distance of a star etc. north or south of the celestial equator. **2**

Physics the angular deviation of a compass needle from true north. **3** a downward bend or turn.

decline ● *v.* **1** *intr.* deteriorate; lose strength or vigour. **2 a** *tr.* reply with formal courtesy that one will not accept (an invitation, honour, etc.). **b** *tr.* refuse, esp. formally and courteously. **c** *tr.* turn away from (a challenge, battle, discussion, etc.). **d** *intr.* give or send a refusal. **3 a** *intr.* slope downwards or bend down. **b** *tr.* bend (something) down. **4** *tr. Grammar* state the forms of (a noun, pronoun, or adjective) corresponding to cases, number, and gender. **5** *intr.* **a** diminish in numbers or size. **b** decrease in price etc. ● *n.* **1 a** a decrease in numbers, rates, etc. **b** gradual loss of vigour or excellence. **2** decay, deterioration. **3** a fall in price or value. □ **on the decline** in a declining state; falling off. □ **declinable** *adj.* **decliner** *n.*

Deco /ˈdekoʊ/ *n.* (also **deco**) (usu. *attrib.*) = ART DECO.

decode *v.tr.* **1** convert (a coded message) into intelligible language. **2** analyze to extract meaning from (written or spoken communication etc.) (*compare* ENCODE 2). **3** *Electronics* convert or unscramble (a coded signal) into an accessible format.

decoder *n.* **1** a person or thing that decodes (texts etc.). **2** an electronic device for analyzing stereophonic signals and feeding separate amplifier channels. **3** (in full **decoder box**) an electronic device connected to a television to unscramble encoded transmissions, esp. cable programs.

decolonize *v.tr.* (of a state) withdraw from (a colony), leaving it independent. □ **decolonization** *n.*

decolorize *v.tr.* (also *Cdn* **decolourize**) remove the colour from. □ **decolorization**. **decolorizing** *adj.*

decommission *v.tr.* **1** close down (a nuclear reactor etc.). **2** take (a ship or aircraft) out of service.

decompose *v.* **1 a** *intr.* decay, rot. **b** *tr.* cause to decay. **2** *tr.* separate (a substance, light, etc.) into its elements or simpler constituents. **3** *intr.* disintegrate; break up. □ **decomposable** *adj.* **decomposition** *n.*

decompress *v.* **1** *tr.* **a** subject to decompression. **b** relieve or reduce the compression on. **2** *tr.* restore (computer files compacted for storage or distribution) to normal size. **3** *intr. N Amer. informal* calm down, relax. □ **decompressor** *n.*

decompression *n.* **1** the process of relieving or reducing pressure. **2** a gradual reduction of air pressure on a person who has been subjected to high pressure (esp. underwater). **3** a sudden reduction of air pressure in an aircraft etc. to the ambient external pressure. **4** the act or process of restoring compacted computer files to their normal size.

decompression chamber *n.* a chamber in which atmospheric pressure can be raised or lowered, e.g. for subjecting a person to decompression.

decompression sickness *n.* a disorder, esp. of deep-sea divers, caused by nitrogen bubbles forming in the tissues from a too rapid decompression and characterized by pain, paralysis, etc.

decongestant ● *adj.* that relieves (esp. nasal) congestion. ● *n.* a medicinal agent that relieves nasal congestion.

deconstruct *v.tr.* **1** subject to deconstruction. **2** undo the construction of, take to pieces. □ **deconstructive** *adj.*

deconstruction *n.* **1** a method of critical analysis aiming to expose unquestioned metaphysical assumptions and internal inconsistencies in (esp. philosophical and literary) language and texts. **2** a movement begun in the 1960s propounding such strategies. □ **deconstructionism** *n.* **deconstructionist** *adj. & n.*

decontaminate *v.tr.* remove contamination or the risk of it from (an area, person, etc.) affected by radioactivity, infectious disease, harmful chemicals, etc. ☐ **decontamination** *n.*

decontextualize *v.tr.* study or treat (a word, text etc.) in isolation from its context. ☐ **decontextualization** *n.* **decontextualized** *adj.*

decor /'deikɔr, dəˈkɔr/ *n.* **1** the overall effect, style, etc. of the decorations and furnishings of a room etc. **2** the furnishing and decoration of a room etc.

decorate *v.tr.* (often foll. by *with*) **1** make (something) more attractive by adding colour, adornments, etc. **2** provide (a room or building) with new paint, wallpaper, etc. **3** invest (a person) with a medal, military decoration, etc. ☐ **decorated** *adj.*

decoration *n.* **1** the process or art of decorating. **2** a thing that decorates or serves as an ornament. **3** a medal etc. conferred and worn as an honour.

decorative /'dekrətɪv/ *adj.* **1** serving to decorate. **2** ornamental rather than operational. ☐ **decoratively** *adv.* **decorativeness** *n.*

decorative art *n.* (usu. in *pl.*) an art form embracing the applied arts as well as the creation of objects which are purely for decoration.

decorator *n.* **1** an interior decorator. **2** a person who decorates (a cake etc.). **3** (*attrib.*) chosen or fashioned to contribute to a plan of interior design.

decorous /'dekərəs/ *adj.* respecting good taste or propriety. ☐ **decorously** *adv.* **decorousness** *n.*

decorum /dɪˈkɔrəm/ *n.* **1** seemliness, propriety. **2** a behaviour required by politeness or decency. **b** (usu. in *pl.*) the accepted customs of polite society.

decouple *v.tr.* make separate or independent. ☐ **decoupled** *adj.* **decoupling** *n.*

decoy ● *n.* /'diːkɔi/ **1 a** a person or thing used to mislead or to lure an animal or person into a trap or danger. **b** a bait or enticement. **2** a bird or animal, or an imitation of one, used to attract others. **3** *Military* an aircraft, missile, etc. used to distract the enemy, mislead radar, etc. ● *v.tr.* /dɪˈkɔi, 'diːkɔi/ (often foll. by *into, out of*) allure or entice, esp. by means of a decoy.

decrease ● *v.tr. & intr.* make or become smaller, fewer, weaker, less, etc. ● *n.* **1** the act or an instance of decreasing. **2** the amount by which a thing decreases. ☐ **decreasingly** *adv.*

decree ● *n.* **1** an official order issued by a legal authority. **2** a judgment or decision of certain law courts. ● *v.tr. & intr.* (**decrees**, **decreed**, **decreeing**) order by or as if by decree.

decrepit /dɪˈkrepɪt/ *adj.* **1** weakened or worn out by age and infirmity. **2** worn out by long use; dilapidated. ☐ **decrepitude** *n.*

decriminalize *v.tr.* make, or treat (an action etc.) as no longer criminal; legalize (esp. a drug, its possession, or use). ☐ **decriminalization** *n.*

decry *v.tr.* (**-ies, -ied**) denounce or disparage openly.

decrypt *v.tr.* decipher or decode. ☐ **decryption** *n.*

dedicate *v.tr.* **1** (foll. by *to*) **a** devote (esp. oneself) to a noble task or purpose. **b** commit, contribute, or set apart (resources etc.) for a particular cause or effort. **2** (foll. by *to*) **a** inscribe or address (one's own book, music, etc.) to a patron or friend as a compliment, mark of respect, etc. **b** request (a song or video) to be played on the radio or television as a greeting or token of affection for a friend. **3** (often foll. by *to*) consecrate with solemn rites (a building etc.) to a god, saint, sacred purpose, etc. **4 a** formally open (a building etc.) to the public. **b** devote (a monument etc.) to the memory of someone deceased etc.

dedicated *adj.* **1** (of a person) devoted to an aim or

vocation; having single-minded loyalty or integrity. **2** (of equipment etc.) designed, manufactured, or installed so as to be available only for a particular purpose or a particular category of user. **3** solemnly or formally set apart for a specific use or purpose.

dedication *n.* **1** the act or an instance of dedicating; the process or state of being dedicated. **2** the words or inscription with which a book etc. is dedicated. **3** the devoting (of a person's time etc.) to the pursuit of a purpose. **4** a formal ceremony commemorating a public opening of a building, monument, etc.

deduce /dɪˈduːs, -ˈdjuːs/ *v.tr.* (often foll. by *from*) infer; draw as a logical conclusion. ☐ **deducible** *adj.*

deduct *v.tr.* (often foll. by *from*) subtract, take away, withhold (an amount, portion, etc.).

deductible ● *adj.* that may be deducted, esp. from tax to be paid or taxable income. ● *n. N Amer.* a sum payable by an insured party in the event of a claim, the insurer paying the amount by which the claim exceeds this sum. ☐ **deductibility** *n.*

deduction *n.* **1 a** the act or process of deducting. **b** an amount deducted. **c** an allowable amount, expense, etc. deducted from taxable income. **2 a** the inferring of particular instances from a general law (compare INDUCTION 3a). **b** a conclusion deduced.

deductive *adj.* of or reasoning by deduction. ☐ **deductively** *adv.*

dee *n.* the letter D.

deed ● *n.* **1** a thing done; an act. **2** a brave, skilful, or conspicuous act. **3** actual fact or performance, often as contrasted with words. **4** *Law* a written or printed document under seal often used for a legal transfer of ownership and bearing the disposer's signature. ● *v.tr. N Amer.* convey or transfer by legal deed.

deejay *n. informal* a disc jockey.

deem *v.tr.* regard, consider, judge.

de-emphasize *v.tr.* reduce emphasis on. ☐ **de-emphasis** *n.*

deep ● *adj.* **1 a** extending far down from the top (*deep water*). **b** extending far in from the surface or edge (*deep wound*). **2** (*predic.*) **a** extending to or lying at a specified depth (*water 6 feet deep; ankle-deep*). **b** in a specified number of ranks one behind another (*six deep*). **3** situated far down, back, or in (*a cabin deep in the bush*). **4** coming or brought from far down or in (*deep breath*). **5** low-pitched, full-toned, not shrill (*deep voice*). **6 a** (of a condition, quality, state, etc.) intense, profound, extreme (*deep sleep*). **b** (of a colour) vivid, darkly hued (*a deep red*). **c** mysterious or obscure (*a deep secret*). **7** heartfelt, absorbing (*deep affection*). **8** (*predic.*) fully absorbed or overwhelmed (*deep in debt*). **9** profound, penetrating, not superficial (*deep thinker*). **10** *Baseball* relatively far in or into the outfield (*deep right field*). **11** *Sport* far into usu. the opposing team's territory. **12** (of prices, discounts, etc.) significantly larger than customary or expected. **13** cunning or secretive (*a deep one*). ● *n.* **1** (prec. by *the*) *literary* the sea. **2** *Naut.* a deep part of the sea, esp. below 3000 fathoms or approx. 6000 metres. **3** an abyss, pit, or cavity. **4** the most intense part (of the night, the winter), when the cold, dark, etc. are at their most intense. ● *adv.* **1** deeply (*dig deep*). **2** far down, in, on, or back (*lived deep in the bush*). **3** for an extended period, long (into) (*read deep into the night*). **4 a** *Baseball* relatively farther than usual in the outfield (*play deep*). **b** *Sport* far into usu. the other team's territory (*deep in the end zone*). ☐ **go off the deep end** *informal* **1** go crazy. **2** lose control and give way to anger or emotion. **3** act without due regard to common sense, moderation, etc. **in deep** inextricably involved in or committed (usu. to something complicated or unpleasant). **jump** (or **be thrown**) **in at the deep end** face (or be made to face) a difficult problem, undertaking, etc., with little experience of it. □ **deeply** *adv.* **deepness** *n.*

deep-dish esp. *N Amer.* ● *n.* **1** (usu. *attrib.*) a baking pan or dish with high sides and a flat bottom (*deep-dish pizza*). **2** something shaped like this (*a deep-dish satellite*). ● *adj.* **1** (of a pie) not having a bottom crust. **2** serious, staunch, ardent (*a deep-dish conservative*).

deep ecology *n.* an approach to environmentalism that considers humanity and the natural world to be inextricably interconnected. □ **deep ecologist** *n.*

deepen *v.tr. & intr.* **1** make or become deep or deeper. **2** make or become more serious, intense, or severe.

deep-freeze ● *n.* **1** a refrigerator in which food can be quickly frozen and kept for long periods at a very low temperature. **2** a suspension of activity. **3** *N Amer.* a period of very cold weather. ● *v.tr.* (**-froze, -frozen**) freeze or store (food) in a deep-freeze.

deep-fry *v.tr.* (**-fries, -fried**) fry (food) in an amount of oil or fat sufficient to cover it. □ **deep-fried** *adj.*

deep fryer *n.* (also **deep fat fryer**) a deep, heavy pan or appliance capable of holding 3-4 cm of hot fat in which food is immersed for frying.

deep pocket *n.* esp. *N Amer. informal* (usu. in *pl.*) substantial financial resources (*we need backers with deep pockets*). □ **deep-pocketed** *adj.*

deep-rooted *adj.* **1** (esp. of convictions) firmly established. **2** having long roots (*deep-rooted grasses*).

deep sea *n.* (often, with hyphen, *attrib.*) the deeper parts of the ocean (*deep-sea diving*).

deep-seated *adj.* (of emotion, disease, etc.) firmly established, profound.

deep-set *adj.* **1** (of the eyes) set deeply in the sockets. **2** firmly fixed or established (*deep-set differences*).

deep-six *v.tr. N Amer. slang* **1** defeat throughly, destroy completely (*deep-sixed her opponent*). **2** abandon, dispose of, discard (*deep-sixed the proposal*).

Deep South *n.* the southeast section of the US, esp. the states of South Carolina, Georgia, Alabama, Mississippi, and Louisiana.

deep space *n.* (often *attrib.*) = SPACE *n.* 3a.

deepwater *n.* (often *attrib.*) water of great depth.

deer *n.* (*pl.* same) any four-hoofed grazing animal of the family Cervidae, the males of which usu. have deciduous branching antlers, or of the related families Tragulidae and Moschidae (lacking horns).

deer fly *n.* any bloodsucking fly of the genus *Chrysops.*

deer mouse *n.* any mouse of the genus *Peromyscus*, esp. *P. maniculatus*, common throughout N America.

deerskin ● *n.* leather from a deer's skin. ● *adj.* made from a deer's skin.

DEET *n.* esp. *N Amer.* N,N-diethyl-meta-toluamide, the active ingredient in many insect repellents.

def *adj.* esp. *N Amer. slang* excellent.

deface *v.tr.* **1** spoil the appearance of; disfigure. **2** make illegible. □ **defacement** *n.* **defacer** *n.*

de facto /di: 'fækto:, dei/ ● *adj.* that exists or is such in fact, whether legally acknowledged or not (*a de facto ruler*). ● *adv.* in fact, whether by right or not (*compare* DE JURE).

defamation /ˌdefəˈmeiʃən, ˌdiːf-/ *n.* **1** the act of defaming or the fact of being defamed. **2** *Law* the offence of bringing a person into disrepute by making false statements. □ **defamatory** /dɪˈfæmətəri/ *adj.*

defame /dɪˈfeim/ *v.tr.* attack the good reputation of; speak ill of. □ **defamer** *n.*

defang *v.tr.* **1** extract the fangs of (a snake etc.). **2** render harmless.

default ● *n.* **1 a** failure to fulfill an obligation, esp. to appear, pay, or act in some way. **b** *Sport* failure to compete in or finish a game, contest, etc. **2** (often *attrib.*) a pre-selected option adopted by a computer program when no alternative is specified by the user. ● *v.* **1** *intr.* **a** *Law* (often foll. by *on* or *in*) fail to fulfill an obligation, esp. to pay money or to appear in a law court. **b** *Sport* fail to appear for or complete a game, contest, etc. **2** *tr. Law* declare (a party) in default and give judgment against (that party). **3** *tr.* lose by default. □ **by default 1** because of absence or failure to act. **2** because of a lack of opposition. **in default** guilty of default. **in default of** because of the absence of. **win by default** win because an opponent is absent. □ **defaulted** *adj.* **defaulter** *n.*

defeat ● *v.tr.* **1** overcome in a battle or other contest. **2** frustrate, thwart. **3** reject (a motion etc.) by voting. ● *n.* **1** the act or process of defeating or being defeated. **2** a state or instance of being defeated.

defeatism *n.* **1** excessive readiness to accept defeat. **2** conduct conducive to this. □ **defeatist** *n. & adj.*

defecate /ˈdefəˌkeit/ *v.intr.* discharge feces from the body. □ **defecation** *n.*

defect ● *n.* **1** a shortcoming, failing, or imperfection. **2** lack of something essential or required. ● *v.intr.* abandon one's country or cause in favour of another. □ **defector** *n.* **defection** *n.*

defective *adj.* **1** having a defect or defects; faulty. **2** (usu. foll. by *in*) lacking, deficient. □ **defectively** *adv.* **defectiveness** *n.*

defence *n.* (also **defense**) **1** the act of defending from or resisting attack. **2 a** a means of resisting attack. **b** (in *pl.*) something that protects, e.g. fortifications. **3** the military resources of a country. **4 a** a justification, vindication. **b** a speech or piece of writing used to this end. **c** the act of defending a thesis or dissertation. **5 a** the defendant's case in a lawsuit. **b** the counsel for the defendant. **6** *Sport* **a** the role of defending one's goal etc. against attack. **b** the plays, moves, or tactics aimed at such resistance. **c** the players in a team who perform this role. **7** = DEFENCE MECHANISM. □ **defenceless** *adj.* **defencelessly** *adv.* **defencelessness** *n.*

defenceman *n.* (*pl.* **-men**) a player in a defensive position in hockey or lacrosse.

defence mechanism *n.* **1** a usu. unconscious mental process to avoid conscious conflict or anxiety. **2** the body's reaction against disease organisms.

defend *v.* **1** *tr. & intr.* (often foll. by *against*, *from*) resist an attack made on; protect (a person or thing) from harm or danger. **2 a** *tr.* speak or write in favour of. **b** *tr.* present (a thesis or dissertation) orally to examiners and answer questions, challenges etc. **c** *intr.* make such a presentation. **3** *tr. & intr.* conduct the case for (a defendant in a lawsuit). **4** *Sport* **a** *tr. & intr.* protect (a goal etc.); resist an attack on (the goal etc.). **b** *tr.* compete to retain (a title) in a contest. □ **defendable** *adj.* **defender** *n.*

defendant *n.* a person etc. sued or accused in court.

defense *var. of* DEFENCE.

defensible *adj.* **1** justifiable. **2** that can be easily defended. □ **defensibility** *n.* **defensibly** *adv.*

defensive *adj.* **1** done or intended for defence or to defend. **2** (of a person or attitude) self-protective. **3** *Sport* (of players) primarily concerned with preventing the other team from scoring. □ **on the defensive 1** expecting criticism. **2** in an attitude or position of defence. ☐ **defensively** *adv.* **defensiveness** *n.*

defensive back *n. Football* **1** a player in charge of covering esp. the receivers in the defensive backfield, usu. a cornerback or safety. **2** this position.

defensive zone *n. Sport* the end of the field, court, or rink in which one's goal etc. is to be defended.

defer *v.* (**deferred, deferring**) **1** *tr.* put off to a later time. **2** *intr.* (foll. by *to*) yield or make concessions in opinion or action. ☐ **deferment** *n.* **deferral** *n.*

deference /ˈdefərəns/ *n.* **1** courteous regard, respect. **2** respectful compliance with the advice or wishes of another (*pay deference to*). ☐ **in deference to** out of respect for; in response to. ☐ **deferential** *adj.* **deferentially** *adv.*

defiance *n.* **1 a** open disobedience, bold resistance. **b** open disregard, contempt. **2** a challenge to fight or maintain a cause, assertion, etc. ☐ **in defiance of** disregarding; in conflict with.

defiant *adj.* **1** showing defiance. **2** openly disobedient. ☐ **defiantly** *adv.*

defibrillation /ˌdiːfɪbrɪˈleɪʃən/ *n. Med.* the application of an electric shock to the heart to stop fibrillation and encourage the resumption of coordinated contractions. ☐ **defibrillator** *n.*

deficiency *n.* (*pl.* **-ies**) **1** the state or condition of being deficient. **2** (usu. foll. by *of*) a lack or shortage. **3** a thing lacking or a defect. **4** the amount by which a thing, esp. revenue, falls short.

deficient *adj.* **1** (usu. foll. by *in*) incomplete, not having enough of a specified quality or ingredient. **2** insufficient in quantity, force, etc.

deficit *n.* **1** the amount by which a thing (esp. a sum of money) is too small. **2** an excess of liabilities or expenditures over assets or income in a given period, esp. a fiscal year. **3** a deficiency (*sleep deficit*).

deficit financing *n.* financing of (esp. government) spending by borrowing.

deficit spending *n.* spending, esp. by the government, financed by borrowing.

defile[1] /dəˈfaɪl/ *v.tr.* **1** make dirty or foul; pollute. **2** corrupt morally. **3** make unfit for ritual or ceremonial use. **4** violate the chastity of; deflower. ☐ **defilement** *n.* **defiler** *n.*

defile[2] /dəˈfaɪl, ˈdiːfaɪl/ *n.* a gorge or narrow passage.

define *v.tr.* **1** give the exact meaning of (a word etc.). **2** describe or explain the scope, essential qualities, etc. of (*define one's position*). **3** make clear, esp. in outline (*well-defined image*). **4** determine or indicate the boundary or extent of. ☐ **definable** *adj.* **definer** *n.*

defined *adj.* **1** having a definite or specified outline or form. **2** clearly marked; definite.

definite ● *adj.* **1** having exact and discernible limits. **2** clearly defined; precise and explicit. ¶See the note at *definitive*. **3** certain, sure. ● *n.* a definite thing, esp. (*Grammar*) a noun denoting a definite thing or object. ☐ **definiteness** *n.*

definite article *n. Grammar* the word (*the* in English) preceding a noun and implying a specific or known instance e.g. *the book on the table; the art of government*.

definitely ● *adv.* **1** in a definite manner. **2** certainly; without doubt (*they were definitely there*). ● *interj. informal* yes, certainly.

definition *n.* **1 a** the act or process of defining. **b** a statement of the meaning of a word or the nature of a thing. **2 a** the degree of distinctness in outline of an object or image (esp. of an image produced by a lens or shown in a photograph or on a film etc.). **b** the distinctness of the outline of a muscle. **3 a** making or

being distinct in outline. **b** definiteness, precision, exactitude. ☐ **by definition** self-evidently.

definitive *adj.* **1** (of an answer, verdict, etc.) conclusive, decisive, final. ¶Often confused with *definite*, which does not have connotations of authority and conclusiveness. **2** (of an edition etc.) most complete, reliable, and authoritative. ☐ **definitively** *adv.*

deflate *v.* **1 a** *tr.* let air or gas out of (a tire, balloon, etc.). **b** *intr.* be emptied of air or gas. **2 a** *tr.* cause to lose confidence or conceit. **b** *intr.* lose confidence. **3** *tr. Econ.* subject (a currency or economy) to deflation. **4** *tr.* reduce the importance of, depreciate. ☐ **deflated** *adj.* **deflator** *n.*

deflation *n.* **1** the act, process, or state of deflating or being deflated. **2** a policy or process of reducing economic activity and the inflation of currency. ☐ **deflationary** *adj.*

deflect *v.* **1** *tr. & intr.* bend or turn aside from a straight course or intended purpose. **2** *tr.* redirect (criticism etc.) from the intended target. ☐ **deflector** *n.*

deflection *n.* **1 a** the action of turning, or the state of being turned, from a straight line or course. **b** the amount of such deviation. **2** *Physics* the displacement of a pointer on an instrument from its zero position.

deflower *v.tr.* **1** deprive (esp. a woman) of virginity. **2** ravage, spoil. **3** strip of flowers.

defogger *n. N Amer.* a device in vehicles for clearing condensation, frost, and ice from windshields etc.

defoliate *v.tr.* remove leaves from, esp. as a military tactic. ☐ **defoliant** *n. & adj.* **defoliation** *n.*

deforest *v.tr.* clear of forests or trees. ☐ **deforestation** *n.* **deforested** *adj.*

deform *v.* **1** *tr.* mar the beauty or excellence of; disfigure, deface. **2** *tr.* spoil the form or shape of; misshape. **3** *intr.* undergo deformation; be deformed. ☐ **deformable** *adj.* **deformed** *adj.*

deformation *n.* **1 a** the action or result of marring the appearance, excellence, etc.; disfigurement, defacement. **b** alteration of a form for the worse; the action or result of misshaping. **2** *Physics* **a** (often foll. by *of*) change in shape, configuration, or structure. **b** a quantity representing the amount of this change.

deformity *n.* (*pl.* **-ies**) **1** the state of being deformed; ugliness. **2** a malformation, esp. of body or limb.

defraud *v.tr.* (often foll. by *of*) take or withhold rightful property, status, etc. from (a person) by fraud; cheat. ☐ **defrauder** *n.*

defray *v.tr.* provide money to pay (a cost or expense).

defrost ● *v.* **1** *tr.* free (the interior of a refrigerator) of excess frost. **b** remove frost or ice from (esp. the windshield of a motor vehicle). **2** *tr.* thaw (frozen food). **3** *intr.* become unfrozen. ● *n. N Amer.* **1** a device for defrosting, esp. one that stops ice forming on a windshield. **2** the setting on an appliance which causes defrosting. ☐ **defroster** *n.* **defrosting** *n.*

deft /deft/ *adj.* neatly skilful or dexterous; adroit. ☐ **deftly** *adv.* **deftness** *n.*

defunct *adj.* **1** no longer existing. **2** no longer used or in fashion.

defuse *v.tr.* **1** remove the fuse from. **2** reduce the tension or potential danger in (a crisis etc.).

defy *v.tr.* (**-ies, -ied**) **1** resist (an authority etc.) openly; refuse to obey. **2** (of a thing) resist completely (*defies solution*). **3** (foll. by *to* + infin.) challenge (a person) to do or prove something. **4** challenge the power of (esp. something immutable) (*defying the laws of gravity*).

deg. *abbr.* degree.

degenerate ● *adj.* **1 a** degenerated or characterized by degeneration. **b** having lost the qualities that are normal, desirable, or proper to the kind. **c** fallen from former excellence, esp. physical or moral. **2** *Biol.* having changed to a lower type. ● *n.* **1 a** a person of debased physical or mental condition. **b** a sexual deviate. **2 a** a person or thing which has lost, or become degenerate in, the qualities considered proper to its race or kind. **b** a degenerate specimen. ● *v.intr.* (often foll. by *into*) **1** lose, or become deficient in, the qualities proper to one's kind. **2** deteriorate physically, mentally, or morally. **3 a** revert to a lower type; gradually change into something inferior. **b** (of an organ or tissue) deteriorate to a simpler structure or less active form. □ **degeneracy** *n.*

degeneration *n.* **1 a** the process of becoming degenerate. **b** the state of being degenerate. **2** *Med.* morbid deterioration of tissue or change in its structure.

degenerative *adj.* **1** of or tending to degeneration. **2** (of disease) characterized by progressive, often irreversible deterioration.

degradation *n.* **1 a** an action that humiliates or lowers a person in social position, status, etc. **b** moral or intellectual debasement. **2** reduction in strength, amount, or other measurable property.

degrade *v.* **1** *tr.* lower in character or quality; debase. **2** *tr.* reduce to a lower rank, esp. as a punishment. **3** *tr.* bring into dishonour or contempt. **4** *intr.* deteriorate. □ **degradability** *n.* **degradable** *adj.*

degraded *adj.* **1 a** lowered in rank, position, reputation, etc.; debased. **b** diminished in quality or value. **2** (of soil etc.) differing from its natural or primary state as a result of cultivation, erosion, etc.

degrading *adj.* humiliating. □ **degradingly** *adv.*

degrease *v.tr.* remove unwanted grease or fat from. □ **degreaser** *n.*

degree *n.* **1** a stage in an ascending or descending scale, series, or process. **2** a stage in intensity or amount (*to a high degree*). **3** relative condition (*each is good in its degree*). **4** an academic rank conferred by a college or university after completion of a course or as an honour. **5** *Math.* a unit of measurement of angles, one-ninetieth of a right angle. Symbol: ° (as in 45°). **6** a unit of latitude or longitude used to define points on the earth's surface. Symbol: °. **7** *Physics* a unit in a scale of temperature, hardness, etc. Symbol: °. **8** *Med.* any of three grades (first, second, third) used to categorize burns according to their severity. **9** a grade of crime or criminality (*first-degree murder*). **10** a step in direct genealogical descent. **11** *Grammar* any of three stages (positive, comparative, superlative) in the comparison of an adjective or adverb. **12** *Music* the classification of a note by its position in the scale. **13** *Math.* the highest power of unknowns or variables in an equation etc. (*equation of the third degree*). **14** a unit of measurement of alcohol content. Symbol: °. □ **by degrees** a little at a time; gradually. **to a degree** somewhat.

dehorn *v.tr.* remove the horns from (an animal).

dehumanize *v.tr.* **1** deprive of human characteristics. **2** make impersonal or machine-like. □ **dehumanization** *n.*

dehumidify *v.tr.* (**-ies, -ied**) remove moisture from (esp. air). □ **dehumidification** *n.* **dehumidifier** *n.*

dehydrate *v.* **1** *tr.* a remove water from (esp. foods for preservation). **b** make dry, esp. make (the body) deficient in water. **2** *intr.* lose water. □ **dehydrated** *adj.* **dehydration** *n.* **dehydrator** *n.*

de-ice *v.tr.* **1** remove ice from. **2** prevent the formation of ice on.

de-icer *n.* a device or substance for removing ice from a windshield, aircraft, etc.

deify /'di:ə,fai, 'deiə-/ *v.tr.* (**-ies, -ied**) **1** make a god of. **2** regard or worship as a god. □ **deification** *n.*

deign /dein/ *v.intr.* (foll. by to + infin.) think fit; condescend (*she deigned to grace us with her presence*).

de-index *v.tr.* cancel the indexation of (pensions or other benefits). □ **de-indexation** *n.*

deindustrialize *v.tr.* make less industrial. □ **deindustrialization** *n.* **deindustrialized** *adj.*

de-ink *v.tr.* remove ink from (paper), esp. in recycling.

deinstitutionalize *v.tr.* **1** remove from an institution or from the effects of institutional life. **2** make less institutional; reorganize on more individual lines. □ **deinstitutionalization** *n.* **deinstitutionalized** *adj.*

deionize *v.tr.* remove the ions or ionic constituents from (water, air, etc.). □ **deionization** *n.* **deionized** *adj.* **deionizer** *n.*

deism /'di:ɪzəm/ *n.* belief in the existence of a supreme being arising from reason rather than revelation (compare THEISM). □ **deist** *n.* **deistic** *adj.*

deity /'di:ɪti, 'deiɪ-/ *n.* (*pl.* **-ies**) **1** a god or goddess. **2** divine status, quality, or nature. **3** (**the Deity**) the Creator, God.

déjà vu /,deiʒɑ 'vu:, -ʒɒ-/ *n.* **1** an illusory feeling of having already experienced a present situation. **2** something tediously familiar.

deject *v.tr.* (usu. as **dejected** *adj.*) make sad or dispirited. □ **dejectedly** *adv.* **dejection** *n.*

de jure /di 'dʒɔri, dei 'jorei/ ● *adj.* rightful (compare DE FACTO). ● *adv.* rightfully; by right.

deke *N Amer.* esp. *Hockey slang* ● *n.* a fake shot or movement done to draw a defensive player out of position and thus create a better opportunity to score. ● *v.* **1** *tr. & intr.* deceive (a defensive player) with a fake shot or movement. **2** *intr.* (foll. by *around*) avoid (an obstacle) or evade (an issue) (*ran across the road, deking around the cars*). **3** *intr.* move or go quickly; dart, dash (*deked in and out of the crowd*).

Del. *abbr.* the US state of Delaware.

Delaware ● *n.* **1** a member of an Aboriginal people formerly inhabiting the Delaware river basin in the northeastern US, some of whom moved north and now live near London, Ont. **2** the Algonquian language of this people. ● *adj.* of or relating to this people.

delay ● *v.* **1** *tr.* postpone; defer. **2** *tr.* make late (*was delayed at the doctor's office*). **3** *intr.* loiter; procrastinate (*don't delay!*). ● *n.* **1** the act or an instance of delaying; the process of being delayed. **2** time lost by inaction or the inability to proceed.

delayed-action *attrib.adj.* (esp. of a bomb, camera, etc.) operating some time after being primed or set.

delayed penalty *n.* *Hockey* **1** a penalty which the referee has signalled, but for which play has not yet been stopped. **2** the interval between the signalling of the penalty and the stopping of play.

delectable ● *adj.* **1** (of food) delicious. **2** delightful, pleasant. ● *n.* *N Amer.* (in *pl.*) delicious food or dishes, esp. desserts. □ **delectably** *adv.*

delegacy /'deləgəsi/ *n.* (*pl.* **-ies**) **1** a system of delegating. **2 a** an appointment as a delegate. **b** a body of delegates; a delegation.

delegate ● *n.* **1** a person chosen or elected to represent others at a conference, convention, etc. **2** a member of a committee. ● *v.tr.* **1** (often foll. by *to*) commit (authority, power, etc.) to an agent or deputy.

b entrust (a task) to another person. **2** send or authorize (a person) as a representative.

delegate-general n. (pl. **delegates-general**) Cdn (Que.) the chief representative of the province of Quebec in a foreign country or region.

delegation n. **1** a body of delegates. **2** the act or process of delegating or being delegated.

delete ● v.tr. **1** remove or obliterate (written or printed matter). **2** remove (an item) from a catalogue, so that it is no longer offered for sale. ● n. (in full **delete key**) Computing a key which is held down in order to remove characters from a document, screen display, etc. □ **deletion** n.

deleterious /,delə'ti:riəs/ adj. harmful (to the mind or body) (deleterious effects). □ **deleteriously** adv.

deli /'deli/ n. (pl. **delis**) informal a delicatessen.

deliberate ● adj. **1 a** intentional; done on purpose. **b** fully considered; not impulsive. **2** slow in deciding; cautious. **3** (of movement etc.) slow and careful. ● v. **1** intr. think carefully; take counsel (the jury deliberated for an hour). **2** tr. consider, discuss carefully (deliberated the question). □ **deliberately** adv. **deliberateness** n. **deliberator** n.

deliberation n. **1** careful consideration. **2** (often in pl.) formal debate or discussion, as of a committee, jury, etc. **3 a** caution and care. **b** (of movement) slowness or ponderousness.

deliberative adj. of, characterized by, or appointed for the purpose of, deliberation or debate. □ **deliberatively** adv. **deliberativeness** n.

delicacy n. (pl. **-ies**) **1** (esp. in craftsmanship or natural beauty) fineness or intricacy of structure or texture. **2** a choice or expensive food. **3** the quality of requiring discretion or sensitivity (a situation of some delicacy). **4** susceptibility to injury or disease. **5 a** consideration for the feelings of others. **b** avoidance of immodesty or vulgarity. **6** (esp. in a person or an instrument) accuracy of perception.

delicate adj. **1 a** fine in texture or structure; soft, slender, or slight. **b** of exquisite quality or workmanship. **c** (of a colour) subtle or subdued. **d** (of a flavour or scent) subtle; faint. **2 a** not robust; easily damaged. **b** (of a person) susceptible to illness. **3 a** requiring careful handling; tricky (a delicate situation). **b** (of an instrument) highly sensitive. **4** deft (a delicate touch). **5** (of a person) avoiding the immodest or offensive. **6** (esp. of actions) considerate. □ **delicately** adv. **delicateness** n.

delicatessen n. **1** a place selling cooked meats, cheeses, and unusual or foreign prepared foods. **2** (often attrib.) such foods collectively.

delicious ● adj. **1** highly delightful and enjoyable to the taste or sense of smell. **2** entertaining; very enjoyable (delicious gossip). ● n. (**Delicious**) N Amer. a slightly elongated, sweet, red or yellow variety of eating apple. □ **deliciously** adv. **deliciousness** n.

delight ● n. **1** great pleasure. **2** something giving pleasure. ● v. **1** tr. (often foll. by with) please greatly (delighted with the result). **2** intr. take great pleasure; be highly pleased (they delight in humiliating us). □ **delighted** adj. **delightedly** adv.

delightful adj. causing great delight; pleasant, charming. □ **delightfully** adv. **delightfulness** n.

delimit v.tr. (**delimited**, **delimiting**) **1** determine the limits of. **2** fix the territorial boundary of; demarcate. □ **delimitation** n.

delineate /də'lini,eit/ v.tr. **1** trace out by lines; trace or serve as the outline of. **2** represent by drawing; portray; draw in fine detail. **3** sketch out; outline. **4**

describe or portray in words; express (delineated her character). □ **delineation** n. **delineator** n.

delinquency n. (pl. **-ies**) **1** minor crime such as vandalism, esp. when committed by young people (juvenile delinquency). **2** wickedness (moral delinquency). **3** neglect of one's duty. **4** a minor offence.

delinquent ● n. an offender (juvenile delinquent). ● adj. **1** guilty of a minor crime or a misdeed. **2** failing in one's duty. **3** N Amer. in arrears (a delinquent loan). □ **delinquently** adv.

deliquesce /,delə'kwes/ v.intr. **1** become liquid, melt. **2** Chem. dissolve in water absorbed from the air. □ **deliquescent** adj.

delirious adj. **1** affected with delirium; temporarily or apparently mad; raving. **2** wildly excited, ecstatic. **3** (of behaviour) betraying delirium or ecstasy. □ **deliriously** adv.

delirium n. **1** an acutely disordered state of mind involving incoherent speech, hallucinations, and frenzied excitement, occurring in intoxication, fever, etc. **2** great excitement, ecstasy.

delirium tremens /'tremenz/ n. a psychosis of chronic alcoholism with tremors and hallucinations.

deliver v. **1** tr. **a** distribute (letters, parcels, ordered goods, etc.) to the addressee or the purchaser. **b** (often foll. by to) hand over (delivered the boy safely to his teacher). **2** tr. (also refl.) utter or recite (an opinion, verdict, speech, etc.). **3** tr. give forth or produce (this printer delivers high-quality printouts). **4** tr. **a** give birth to (delivered a girl). **b** assist at the birth of (delivered six babies). **c** assist in giving birth (delivered the patient successfully). **5** tr. launch or aim (a blow, ball, or attack). **6** tr. (often foll. by from) save, rescue, or set free (delivered from his enemies). **7** tr. (often foll. by up, over) abandon; resign; hand over (delivered his soul up to God). **8** intr. informal (often foll. by on) provide what is expected or what one has promised. **9** tr. cause (a substance, data, etc.) to be conveyed (deliver the medication intravenously). **10** tr. present or render (an account). **11** tr. Law hand over formally (esp. a sealed deed to a grantee). □ **deliver the goods** informal carry out one's part of an agreement. □ **deliverability** n. **deliverable** adj. **deliverer** n.

deliverance n. the act or an instance of rescuing; the process of being rescued.

delivery n. (pl. **-ies**) **1 a** the delivering of letters, goods, etc. (also attrib.: delivery man). **b** a regular distribution of letters, goods, etc. **c** something delivered. **2 a** the process of childbirth. **b** an act of this. **3 a** the uttering of a speech etc. **b** the manner or style of such a speech (a measured delivery). **4 a** an act of throwing, esp. of a baseball. **b** the style of such an act (a good delivery). **5** provision, esp. of services (health care delivery systems). **6** the act of giving or surrendering. **7** Law **a** the formal handing over of property. **b** the transfer of a deed to a grantee or a third party. □ **take delivery of** receive (something purchased).

dell n. a small usu. wooded hollow or valley.

delphinium /del'finiəm/ n. any garden plant of the genus Delphinium, of the buttercup family, with tall spikes of usu. blue flowers.

delt n. slang a deltoid muscle.

delta n. **1** a triangular tract of deposited earth, alluvium, etc., at the mouth of a river, formed by its diverging outlets. **2** the fourth letter of the Greek alphabet (Δ, δ). **3** (attrib.) designating the fourth of a series or set. **4** Math. an increment of a variable. **5** Astronomy the fourth brightest star in a constellation. □ **deltaic** /del'teiik/ adj.

deltoid /'deltɔid/ ● n. (in full **deltoid muscle**) a

thick muscle covering the shoulder joint and used for raising the arm away from the body.

delude v.tr. (also refl.) deceive or mislead. □ **deluder** n.

deluge /ˈdeljuːʒ, -juːdʒ/ ● n. **1** a great flood. **2** a great outpouring (of words, paper, etc.). **3** a heavy fall of rain. **4** (**the Deluge**) the Biblical Flood. ● v.tr. **1** (usu. foll. by with) inundate with a great number or amount (deluged with complaints). **2** flood.

delusion n. **1** a false belief or impression. **2** Psych. this as a symptom or form of mental disorder. □ **delusional** adj.

delusions of grandeur n.pl. a false idea of oneself as being important, noble, famous, etc.

deluxe adj. **1** of a superior kind. **2** luxurious or sumptuous.

delve v.intr. **1** (often foll. by in, into) **a** make a laborious search in documents etc.; research. **b** search energetically. **2** literary dig. □ **delver** n.

demagogue /ˈdeməgɒg/ n. **1** a leader or orator who tries to win support by inflaming people's emotions and prejudices. **2** hist. a leader of the people, esp. in ancient times. □ **demagogic** /-ˈgɒdʒɪk, -ˈgɒgɪk/ adj. **demagoguery** /-ˈgɒgəri/ n. **demagogy** /-ˈgɒgʒi, -ˈgɒgi/ n.

demand ● n. **1** an insistent and peremptory request. **2** the desire of purchasers or consumers for a commodity (demand for CD players has increased). **3** an urgent claim or requirement. ● v.tr. **1** (often foll. by of, from, or to + infin., or that + clause) ask for (something) insistently and urgently (demanded to know the answer; demanded five dollars). **2** require or need (a task demanding skill). **3** insist on being told ("What do you want?" she demanded). □ **in demand** sought after. **on demand** as soon as a demand is made (a cheque payable on demand). □ **demander** n.

demanding adj. **1** requiring skill, effort, etc. **2** hard to satisfy; exacting. □ **demandingly** adv.

demarcation /ˌdiːmɑːˈkeɪʃən/ n. **1** separation or distinction (a line of demarcation). **2** a boundary or limit. **3** the act of marking a boundary or limits. □ **demarcate** v.tr. **demarcator** n.

demean v.tr. lower the dignity of; debase (his behaviour demeaned the profession.). □ **demeaning** adj.

demeanour n. (also **demeanor**) outward behaviour or bearing.

demented adj. **1** mad; crazy. **2** suffering from dementia. □ **dementedly** adv. **dementedness** n.

dementia /dəˈmenʃə, -ʃiə/ n. Med. a chronic or persistent disorder of the mental processes marked by memory disorders, personality changes, impaired reasoning, etc., due to brain disease or injury.

demerit n. **1** a quality or action deserving blame; a fault. **2** N Amer. a mark given to an offender, esp. in a school or the armed forces or for traffic offences.

Demerol /ˈdemərɒl/ n. proprietary a brand of meperidine.

demigod n. **1 a** a partly divine being. **b** the offspring of a god or goddess and a mortal. **2** informal a person of compelling beauty, powers, or personality.

demilitarize v.tr. remove a military organization or forces from (a zone etc.). □ **demilitarization** n.

demineralize v.tr. remove minerals from (water etc.). □ **demineralization** n. **demineralized** adj.

demise ● n. **1** death (left a will on her demise). **2** termination or failure (the demise of the business). **3** Law conveyance or transfer (of property, a title, etc.) by demising. ● v.tr. Law **1** convey or grant (an estate) by will or lease. **2** transmit (a title etc.) by death.

demitasse /ˈdemiˌtæs/ n. **1** a small cup used to serve strong coffee. **2** a serving of coffee in such a cup.

demo n. (pl. **-os**) informal **1** = DEMONSTRATION 1, 2. **2** (attrib.) demonstrating the capabilities of a group of musicians, computer software, etc. (demo disc).

demob /diːˈmɒb/ Cdn, Brit., & Austral. dated ● v.tr. (**demobbed, demobbing**) demobilize. ● n. demobilization.

demobilize v.tr. **1** disband (troops, ships, etc.). **2** release from a mobilized state or from service in the armed forces. □ **demobilization** n.

democracy n. (pl. **-ies**) **1 a** a form of government in which the power resides in the people and is exercised by them either directly or by means of elected representatives. **b** a state so governed. **2** any organization governed on democratic principles. **3** a classless and tolerant form of society.

democrat n. **1** an advocate of democracy. **2** (**Democrat**) (in the US) a member or supporter of the Democratic Party. **3** (in full **democrat wagon**) N Amer. hist. a light wagon seating two or more people and usu. drawn by two horses.

democratic adj. **1** of, like, practising, advocating, or constituting democracy or a democracy. **2** favouring social equality. **3** (**Democratic**) (in the US) of the Democratic Party. □ **democratically** adv.

Democratic Party n. one of the two main US political parties, considered to support social reform and international commitment.

democratize /dəˈmɒkrəˌtaɪz/ v.tr. make (a state, institution, etc.) democratic. □ **democratization** n.

demodulate v.tr. Physics extract (a modulating signal) from its carrier. □ **demodulation** n.

demographics n.pl. population statistics, esp. those showing average age, income, marital status, etc.

demography /dəˈmɒgrəfi/ n. the study of the statistics of births, deaths, disease, etc., as illustrating the conditions of life in communities. □ **demographer** n. **demographic** adj. **demographical** adj. **demographically** adv.

demolish v.tr. **1 a** pull down (a building). **b** completely destroy or break. **2** refute (an argument, theory, etc.). **3** overthrow (an institution). **4** jocular eat up completely and quickly. □ **demolisher** n. **demolition** n. **demolitionist** n.

demolition derby n. N Amer. a competition in which drivers crash old cars into each other, the winner being the last vehicle still running.

demon n. **1** an evil spirit, esp. one thought to possess a person. **2** (often attrib.) a forceful, fierce, or skilful performer. **3** an evil passion or habit (the demon drink). **4** a cruel or destructive person. **5** an inner or attendant spirit (the demon of creativity). □ **a demon for work** informal a person who works strenuously.

demoniac /dəˈmoːniˌæk, ˈdiːməˌnaiæk/ ● adj. = DEMONIC. ● n. a person possessed by an evil spirit. □ **demoniacal** /ˌdiːməˈnaiəkəl/ adj. **demoniacally** adv.

demonic /dəˈmɒnɪk/ adj. **1** of or like demons. **2 a** supposedly possessed by an evil spirit. **b** of or concerning such possession. **3** fiercely energetic or frenzied. **4** having or seeming to have supernatural genius or power. □ **demonically** adv.

demonize v.tr. **1** make into or like a demon. **2** represent as a demon. □ **demonization** n.

demonology n. (pl. **-ies**) **1** the study of demons. **2** belief in demons. **3** a group of persons or things regarded as evil. □ **demonological** adj. **demonologist** n.

demonstrable adj. able to be shown or logically proved. □ **demonstrability** n. **demonstrably** adv.

demonstrate v. **1** tr. describe and explain (a scientific theory, machine, etc.) with the help of examples, experiments, practical use, etc. **2** tr. **a** logically prove the truth of (our findings demonstrate a link between diet and cancer). **b** be proof of the existence of. **3** tr. make known by outward indications; show evidence of (feelings etc.). **4** intr. take part in or organize a public demonstration. **5** intr. act as a demonstrator.

demonstration n. **1 a** a practical exhibition or explanation of something by experiment or example in order to teach or inform. **b** a practical display of a piece of equipment etc. to show how it works and its capacity. **2** a public meeting, march, etc., for a political or moral purpose. **3** proof provided by logic, argument, etc. **4** (foll. by of) **a** the outward showing of feeling etc. **b** an instance of this. **5** a show of military force. □ **demonstrational** adj.

demonstrative ● adj. **1** given to or marked by an open expression of feeling, esp. of affection (a very demonstrative person). **2** (usu. foll. by of) logically conclusive; giving proof (the work is demonstrative of their skill). **3** serving to point out or exhibit; illustrative. **4** Grammar (of an adjective or pronoun) indicating the person or thing referred to, e.g. this, that, those. ● n. a demonstrative adjective or pronoun. □ **demonstratively** adv. **demonstrativeness** n.

demonstrator n. **1** a person who takes part in a political demonstration etc. **2 a** a person who demonstrates, esp. machines, equipment, etc., to prospective customers. **b** a machine etc., esp. a car, used for such demonstrations.

demoralize v.tr. destroy (a person's) morale; make hopeless. □ **demoralization** n. **demoralizing** adj. **demoralizingly** adv.

demote v.tr. reduce to a lower rank or class. □ **demotion** n.

demotic /də'mɒtɪk/ ● n. **1** the popular colloquial form of a language. **2** a popular simplified form of ancient Egyptian writing. **3** a popular written or spoken form of modern Greek. ● adj. **1** (esp. of language) popular, colloquial, or vulgar. **2** of or concerning the ancient Egyptian or modern Greek demotic.

demur /də'mɜr/ ● v.intr. (**demurred**, **demurring**) raise scruples or objections. ● n. (also **demurral** /dɪ'mʌrəl/) (usu. in neg.) **1** an objection (agreed without demur). **2** the act or process of objecting.

demure /də'mjʊr/ adj. (**demurer**, **demurest**) **1** quiet and reserved. **2** affectedly shy and quiet; coy. **3** (of attire) modest. □ **demurely** adv. **demureness** n.

demystify v.tr. (**-ies**, **-ied**) clarify (obscure beliefs or subjects etc.); simplify. □ **demystification** n.

demythologize v.tr. **1** remove mythical elements from (a legend, famous person's life, etc.). **2** reinterpret what some consider to be the mythological elements in (the Bible).

den ● n. **1** a wild animal's lair. **2** a room in a home serving as an informal place for reading, pursuing a hobby, etc. **3** a place of crime or vice (opium den). ● v.intr. live in or as if in a den.

denationalize v.tr. **1** transfer (a nationalized industry etc.) from public to private ownership. **2 a** deprive (a nation) of its status or characteristics as a nation. **b** deprive (a person) of nationality or national characteristics. □ **denationalization** n.

denaturalize v.tr. **1** change the nature or properties of; make unnatural. **2** deprive of the rights of citizenship. **3** = DENATURE 2. □ **denaturalization** n.

denature v.tr. **1** change the properties of (a protein etc.) by heat, acidity, etc. **2** make (alcohol) unfit for drinking esp. by the addition of another substance. **3** change the essential nature of (a person, a literary work, etc.). □ **denaturant** n. **denatured** adj.

dendrite /'dendrəɪt/ n. **1 a** a stone or mineral with natural treelike or mosslike markings. **b** such marks on stones or minerals. **2** a branching process of a nerve cell conducting signals to a cell body.

Dene /'deneɪ/ n. a member of a group of Aboriginal peoples of the Athapaskan linguistic family, living esp. in the Canadian north.

dengue /'dengɪ/ n. an infectious viral disease of the tropics causing a fever and acute pains in the joints.

deniable adj. that may be denied. □ **deniability** n.

denial n. **1** the act or an instance of denying. **2** a refusal of a request or wish. **3** a statement that a thing is not true; a rejection. **4** a disavowal or disowning; refusal to recognize. **5** = SELF-ABNEGATION. **6** Psych. the usu. subconscious suppression of an unacceptable truth or emotion. □ **in denial** in a state in which one suppresses (usu. unconsciously) a painful or unacceptable wish or experience etc.

denier[1] /di:'naɪr/ n. a person who denies something.

denier[2] /'denjər/ n. a unit of weight by which the fineness of silk, rayon, or nylon yarn is measured.

denigrate /'denɪˌgreɪt/ v.tr. defame or disparage the reputation of (a person). □ **denigration** n. **denigrator** n. **denigratory** /-'greɪtərɪ/ adj.

denim /'denəm/ n. **1** (often attrib.) a usu. blue hard-wearing cotton twill fabric used for jeans, overalls, etc. **2** (in pl.) informal jeans, overalls, etc. made of this.

denizen /'denɪzən/ n. **1** (usu. foll. by of) an inhabitant or occupant. **2** a person who frequents a certain place. **3** a naturalized foreign word, animal, or plant.

denominate v.tr. **1** give a name to. **2** call or describe (a person or thing) as. **3** (in passive; usu. foll. by in) express in a specified monetary unit.

denomination n. **1** a religious sect or body with a distinctive name and organization. **2** a class of units within a range or sequence of numbers, weights, money, etc. **3 a** a name or designation, esp. a characteristic or class name. **b** a class or kind having a specific name. **4** the rank of a playing card within a suit, or of a suit relative to others.

denominational adj. **1** of or relating to a particular denomination. **2** (of education) according to the principles of a religious denomination. □ **denominationalism** n. **denominationalist** n.

denominator n. Math. the number below the line in a vulgar fraction; a divisor.

denotation n. **1** the meaning or signification of a term, as distinct from its implications or connotations. **2** the act of denoting or indicating. **3** a mark, sign, etc. that serves to denote something. **4** a term used to denote something; a designation.

denote v.tr. **1** be a sign of; indicate (the arrow denotes direction). **2** (usu. foll. by that + clause) mean, convey. **3** stand as a name for; signify.

denouement /ˌdeɪnuː'mɑ̃/ n. (also **dénouement**) **1** the final unravelling of a plot or complicated situation. **2** the final scene in a play, novel, etc., in which the plot is resolved.

denounce v.tr. **1** accuse publicly; condemn. **2** inform against. □ **denouncer** n.

de novo /diː 'noʊvoː, deɪ/ adv. starting again; anew.

dense adj. (**denser**, **densest**) **1** closely compacted in substance; thick (dense fog). **2** crowded together. **3** informal stupid. □ **densely** adv. **denseness** n.

density n. (pl. **-ies**) **1** the degree of compactness of a substance. **2** Physics degree of consistency measured by the quantity of mass per unit volume. **3** a crowded state. **4** stupidity.

dent ● *n.* **1** a slight mark or hollow in a surface made by, or as if by, a blow with a hammer etc. **2** a noticeable effect (*lunch made a dent in our funds*). ● *v.tr.* **1** mark with a dent. **2** have (esp. an adverse) effect on.

dental *adj.* **1** of or relating to the teeth. **2** of or relating to dentistry.

dental floss *n.* a strong, soft thread used to clean between the teeth.

dental surgeon *n.* a dentist.

denticare /'dentə,ker/ *n. Cdn* a plan for providing dental care funded by some provincial governments.

dentine /'denti:n/ *n.* a hard dense bony tissue forming the bulk of a tooth.

dentist *n.* a person who is qualified to treat the diseases and conditions that affect the mouth, jaws, teeth, etc., esp. the repair and extraction of teeth and the insertion of artificial ones. □ **dentistry** *n.*

denture *n.* an artificial replacement for one or more teeth attached to a removable plate or frame.

denude /dɪ'nu:d, -'nju:d/ *v.tr.* **1** make naked or bare. **2** (foll. by *of*) **a** strip of clothing, a covering, etc. **b** deprive of a possession or attribute. **3** *Geol.* lay (rock or a formation etc.) bare by removing what lies above.

denunciation *n.* **1** the act of denouncing (a person, policy, etc.); public condemnation. **2** an instance of this. □ **denunciate** *v.tr.* **denunciator** *n.* **denunciatory** *adj.*

Denver *n.* (in full **Denver sandwich**) *N Amer.* (*West*) a sandwich containing an omelette made with ham, onions, and sometimes green pepper.

deny /dɪ'naɪ, də'naɪ/ *v.tr.* (**-ies, -ied**) **1** declare untrue or non-existent (*denied the charge; denied that it is so*). **2** repudiate or disclaim (*denied his faith*). **3** (often foll. by *to*) refuse (a person or thing, or something to a person) (*denied her the satisfaction*). **4** refuse access to (a person sought). □ **deny oneself** be abstinent.

deodorant *n.* (often *attrib.*) a substance sprayed or rubbed on to the body or sprayed into the air to remove or conceal unpleasant smells.

deodorize *v.tr.* remove or destroy the smell of. □ **deodorization** *n.* **deodorizer** *n.*

Deo gratias /,deɪo: 'grætsɪəs/ *interj.* thanks be to God.

deoxygenate *v.tr.* remove oxygen, esp. free oxygen, from. □ **deoxygenated** *adj.* **deoxygenation** *n.*

deoxyribonucleic acid /,di:ɒksɪ,raɪbo:nu:'kleɪk, -nju:'kleɪɪk/ *n. see* DNA.

depanneur /,depə'nɜr/ *n.* (also **dep** /dep/) *Cdn* (*Que.*) a convenience store.

depart *v.* **1** *intr.* **a** (usu. foll. by *from*) go away; leave (*the train departs from this platform*). **b** (usu. foll. by *for*) start; set out (*buses depart for Hamilton every hour*). **2** *intr.* (usu. foll. by *from*) diverge; deviate (*departs from standard practice*). **3 a** *intr.* leave by death; die. **b** *tr. formal or literary* leave by death (*departed this life*).

departed ● *adj.* bygone. ● *n.* (prec. by *the*) euphemism a particular dead person or dead people.

department *n.* **1** a separate part of a complex whole, esp.: **a** a branch of municipal, provincial, or federal administration. **b** a branch of study and its administration at a university, school, etc. **c** a specialized section of a large store. **d** a subdivision of a company or organization. **2** *informal* an area of special expertise. □ **departmentalize** *v.tr.* **departmentalization** *n.*

department store *n.* a large store stocking many varieties of goods in different departments.

departure *n.* **1** the act or an instance of departing. **2**

(often foll. by *from*) a deviation (from the truth, a standard, etc.). **3** (often *attrib.*) the starting of a train, an aircraft, etc. on a journey. **4** a new course of action or thought.

depend *v.intr.* **1** (often foll. by *on, upon*) be controlled or determined by. **2** (foll. by *on, upon*) **a** be unable to do without (*depends on her mother*). **b** rely on (*I'm depending on you to come*). **3** (foll. by *on, upon*) be grammatically dependent on. □ **depending on** according to. **depend upon it!** you may be sure! **it** (or **it all** or **that**) **depends** expressing uncertainty or qualification in answering a question.

dependable *adj.* reliable. □ **dependability** *n.* **dependably** *adv.*

dependant *n.* a person who relies on another esp. for financial support.

dependence *n.* **1** the state of being dependent, esp. on financial or other support. **2** reliance; trust; confidence. **3** the state of being dependent on a drug, physically or psychologically.

dependency *n.* (*pl.* **-ies**) **1** a country or province controlled by another. **2** anything subordinate or dependent. **3** the fact or condition of being dependent on another for financial or emotional support. **4** the state of being dependent on drugs.

dependent ● *adj.* **1** (usu. foll. by *on*) depending, conditional. **2** unable to do without (esp. a drug). **3** maintained at another's cost. **4** *Math.* (of a variable) having a value determined by that of another variable. **5** *Grammar* (of a clause, phrase, or word) subordinate to a sentence or word. ● *n. var. of* DEPENDANT. □ **dependently** *adv.*

depersonalization *n.* esp. *Psych.* the loss of one's sense of identity.

depersonalize *v.tr.* **1** make impersonal. **2** deprive of personality.

depict *v.tr.* **1** represent in a drawing or painting etc. **2** portray in words; describe. □ **depiction** *n.*

depilate /'depɪ,leɪt/ *v.tr.* remove the hair from. □ **depilation** *n.*

depilatory /də'pɪlə,tɔri/ ● *adj.* that removes unwanted hair. ● *n.* (*pl.* **-ies**) a depilatory substance.

deplane *v.* esp. *N Amer.* **1** *intr.* disembark from an airplane. **2** *tr.* remove from an airplane.

deplete *v.tr.* (esp. in *passive*) **1** reduce in numbers or quantity. **2** empty out; exhaust (*their energies were depleted*). □ **depleter** *n.* **depletion** *n.*

deplorable *adj.* **1** exceedingly bad (*a deplorable meal*). **2** that can be deplored. □ **deplorably** *adv.*

deplore *v.tr.* **1** grieve over; regret. **2** be scandalized by; find exceedingly bad. □ **deploringly** *adv.*

deploy *v.* **1** *tr.* bring or send (armaments, armed forces, etc.) into position for action. **2** *Military* **a** *tr.* cause (troops) to spread out from a column into a line. **b** *intr.* (of troops) spread out in this way. **3** *tr. & intr.* move into a position for effective action (*the air bags deploy automatically*). **4** *tr.* use (talents, arguments, stylistic devices, etc.) effectively. □ **deployment** *n.*

depolarize *v.tr. Physics* reduce or remove the polarization of. □ **depolarization** *n.*

depoliticize *v.tr.* **1** make (a person, an organization, etc.) non-political. **2** remove from political activity or influence. □ **depoliticization** *n.*

depopulate *v.* **1** *tr.* reduce the population of. **2** *intr.* decline in population. □ **depopulation** *n.*

deport *v.tr.* **1 a** expel (an immigrant or foreigner) from a country, e.g. for criminal activity. **b** exile (a native) to another country. **2** *refl.* conduct (oneself) or behave (in a specified manner). □ **deportation** *n.*

deportee *n.* a person who has been or is being deported.

deportment *n.* bearing, demeanour, or manners, esp. of a cultivated kind.

depose *v.* **1** *tr.* remove (esp. a ruler) from office. **2** *intr. Law* (usu. foll. by *to*, or *that* + clause) bear witness, esp. on oath in court.

deposit ● *n.* **1 a** a sum of money placed or kept in an account in a bank. **b** anything stored or entrusted for safekeeping, usu. in a bank. **2 a** a sum payable as a first instalment on an item bought, or as a pledge for a contract. **b** a returnable sum payable on the short-term rental of a car etc. **c** a sum payable for a refillable bottle, refunded when the empty bottle is returned. **d** = DAMAGE DEPOSIT. **3** *Cdn & Brit.* a sum of money deposited by an election candidate and forfeited if he or she fails to receive a certain proportion of the votes. **4 a** a natural layer or accumulation of sand, rock, minerals, etc. **b** a layer of precipitated matter on a surface, e.g. scale in a kettle. ● *v.tr.* (**deposited**, **depositing**) **1 a** put or lay down in a (usu. specified) place. **b** (of water, wind, etc.) leave (matter etc.) lying in a displaced position. **2 a** store or entrust for keeping. **b** pay (a sum of money) into a bank account. **3** pay (a sum) as a first instalment or as a pledge for a contract. **4** insert (coins) in a vending machine etc. □ **on deposit** (of money) placed in a bank account.

deposition /ˌdepəˈzɪʃən, ˌdiːp-/ *n.* **1** the act or an instance of depositing. **2** *Law* **a** the process of giving sworn evidence; allegation. **b** an instance of this. **c** evidence given under oath; a testimony. **3** the act or an instance of deposing.

depositor *n.* a person who deposits money etc.

depot /ˈdiːpoː, ˈdepoː/ *n.* **1** a storehouse. **2 a** *N Amer.* = BUS DEPOT. **b** a building for the servicing, parking, etc. of esp. buses, trains, or trucks. **3** *Military* **a** a storehouse for equipment etc. **b** the headquarters of a regiment. **c** a military establishment at which recruits or other troops are assembled.

deprave *v.tr.* corrupt, esp. morally. □ **depraved** *adj.*

depravity /dɪˈprævɪti/ *n.* (*pl.* **-ies**) **1** moral corruption; wickedness. **2** a wicked act.

deprecate /ˈdeprɪˌkeɪt/ *v.tr.* **1** express disapproval of or a wish against (a plan, proceeding, purpose, etc.); deplore; plead earnestly against (*deprecate hasty action*). **2** express disapproval of (a person), reprove. **b** = DEPRECIATE 2. ¶Although sense 2b has been traditionally considered incorrect, it is not incorrect in such combinations as *self-deprecating* etc., which are far more common than *self-depreciating* etc. It is rarely used in this sense outside of these combinations, and may be considered incorrect if it is. □ **deprecatingly** *adv.* **deprecation** *n.* **deprecator** *n.* **deprecatory** /-ˈkeɪtəri/ *adj.*

depreciable /dɪˈpriːʃəbəl/ *adj. N Amer.* **1** capable of depreciating. **2** able to be depreciated for tax purposes.

depreciate /dɪˈpriːʃiˌeɪt/ *v.* **1** *tr. & intr.* diminish in value (*the car has depreciated*). **2** *tr.* disparage; belittle. ¶See Usage Note at DEPRECATE. **3** *tr.* reduce the purchasing power of (money). □ **depreciatory** *adj.*

depreciation /dɪˌpriːʃiˈeɪʃən, -siˈeɪʃən/ *n.* **1** the amount of wear and tear (of a property etc.) for which a reduction may be made in a valuation, an estimate, or a balance sheet. **2** *Econ.* a decrease in the value of a currency. **3** belittlement.

depredation /ˌdeprəˈdeɪʃən/ *n.* (usu. in *pl.*) **1** the act of despoiling, ravaging, or plundering. **2** an instance or instances of this.

depress *v.tr.* **1** push or pull down; lower. **2** make dispirited or dejected. **3** *Econ.* reduce the activity of (esp. trade). □ **depressing** *adj.* **depressingly** *adv.*

depressant ● *adj.* **1** that depresses. **2** *Med.* sedative. ● *n.* **1** *Med.* an agent, esp. a drug, that sedates. **2** an influence that depresses.

depressed *adj.* **1** dispirited or miserable. **2** *Psych.* suffering from depression. **3** suffering from economic hardship. **4** pressed down; having a flattened or hollowed surface. **5** (of the price of a commodity etc.) persistently lower than normal.

depression *n.* **1 a** *Psych.* a state of extreme dejection or morbidly excessive melancholy; a mood of hopelessness and feelings of inadequacy, often with physical symptoms such as loss of appetite, insomnia, etc. **b** a reduction in vitality, vigour, or spirits. **2 a** a long period of financial and industrial decline; a slump. **b** (**the** (**Great**) **Depression**) the depression which began in 1929 and lasted throughout most of the 1930s. **3** *Meteorol.* a lowering of atmospheric pressure, esp. the centre of a region of minimum pressure or the system of winds around it. **4** a sunken place or hollow on a surface. **5 a** a lowering or sinking. **b** the act or an instance of pressing down.

depressive ● *adj.* **1** tending to depress. **2** *Psych.* involving or characterized by depression. ● *n.* *Psych.* a person suffering from depression.

depressor *n.* **1 a** a muscle that causes the lowering of some part of the body. **b** a nerve that lowers blood pressure. **2** *Med.* an instrument for pressing down an organ etc. (*tongue depressor*).

depressurize *v.* **1** *tr.* cause a drop in the pressure of the gas inside (a container), esp. to the ambient level. **2** *intr.* lose air pressure. □ **depressurization** *n.*

deprive *v.tr.* (usu. foll. by *of*) dispossess; stop from enjoying. □ **deprivation** *n.*

deprived *adj.* **1** (of a child etc.) suffering from the effects of a poor or loveless home. **2** (of an area) having inadequate housing, facilities, employment, etc. **3** suffering from a deprivation.

Dept. *abbr.* Department.

depth *n.* **1 a** deepness. **b** the measurement from the top down, from the surface inwards, or from front to back. **2** difficulty. **3 a** wisdom. **b** intensity of emotion etc. (*the poem has little depth*). **4** an intensity of colour, darkness, etc. **5** (in *pl.*) **a** deep water, a deep place; an abyss. **b** a low, depressed state. **c** the lowest or inmost part. **6** the middle (*in the depth of winter*). □ **in depth** comprehensively, thoroughly, or profoundly. **out of one's depth 1** in water over one's head. **2** engaged in a task or on a subject too difficult for one.

depth charge *n.* an explosive device that detonates under water, esp. for dropping on a submarine etc.

depth finder *n.* an instrument used for measuring the depth of water by radar, ultrasound, etc.

depth sounder *n.* an instrument used for measuring the depth under a ship by ultrasound.

deputation /ˌdepjuˈteɪʃən/ *n.* a group of people appointed to represent others; a delegation.

depute /dɪˈpjuːt/ *v.tr.* (often foll. by *to*) **1** appoint as a deputy. **2** delegate (a task, authority, etc.).

deputize /ˈdepjuˌtaɪz/ *v.* **1** *tr.* esp. *N Amer.* appoint (a person) as a deputy. **2** *intr.* (usu. foll. by *for*) act as a deputy or understudy. □ **deputization** *n.*

deputy *n.* (*pl.* **-ies**) a person appointed or delegated to act for another or others (also *attrib.*: *deputy manager*).

deputy chief *n.* **1** (in municipal police forces) an officer ranking above staff superintendent and below chief of police. **2** (in the Royal Newfoundland Constabulary) an officer ranking above superintendent and below chief.

deputy commissioner n. (in the OPP and RCMP) an officer ranking below commissioner.

deputy director n. (in Quebec) a municipal police officer ranking above inspector and below director.

deputy minister n. Cdn the senior civil servant in a government department or ministry. Abbr.: **DM**.

deputy returning officer n. an official in charge of a polling station. Abbr.: **DRO**.

derail v. **1** tr. cause (a train etc.) to leave the rails. **2** intr. (of a train) leave the rails. **3** tr. obstruct the progress of (a person, plan, etc.). □ **derailment** n.

derailleur /di:'reilər/ n. a bicycle gear in which the ratio is changed by switching the line of the chain while pedalling so that it jumps to a different sprocket.

derange v.tr. **1** throw into confusion; cause to act irregularly. **2** (esp. as **deranged** adj.) make insane. **3** disturb; interrupt. □ **derangement** n.

Derby /'dɑrbi/ n. (pl. **-ies**) **1 a** /'dɑrbi/ an annual horse race run at Epsom Downs, near London, England. **b** any of several other important annual horse races. **2** (**derby**) a sporting contest or race open to all who wish to participate. **3** (**derby**) N Amer. a man's hard felt hat with a round dome-shaped crown.

deregulate v.tr. remove regulations or restrictions from. □ **deregulation** n. **deregulator** n.

derelict /'derəlıkt/ ● adj. **1** (esp. of property) ruined; dilapidated. **2** N Amer. negligent (of duty etc.). **3** abandoned, ownerless. ● n. **1** a social outcast; a person without a home, job, or property. **2** abandoned property, esp. a ship.

dereliction /,derı'lıkʃən/ n. **1** (usu. foll. by of) a neglect; failure to carry out one's obligations (dereliction of duty). **b** an instance of this. **2** the act or an instance of abandoning or being abandoned.

deride v.tr. be scornful of; mock. □ **derider** n.

de rigueur /də rı'gɜr/ predic.adj. required by custom or etiquette (evening dress is de rigueur).

derision /də'rıʒən/ n. ridicule; mockery.

derisive /də'raisıv/ adj. = DERISORY. □ **derisively** adv.

derisory /də'raisəri/ adj. **1** scoffing; scornful. **2** so small or unimportant as to be ridiculous.

derivation n. **1** the act or an instance of deriving or obtaining from a source; the process of being derived. **2 a** the formation of a word from another word or from a root. **b** a derivative. **c** the tracing of the origin of a word. **d** a statement or account of this. **3** extraction, descent. **4** Math. a sequence of statements showing that a formula, theorem, etc., is a consequence of previously accepted statements.

derivative ● adj. derived from another source; not original. ● n. **1** something derived from another source, esp.: **a** a word derived from another or from a root (e.g. quickly from quick). **b** Chem. a chemical compound that is derived from another. **2** Math. a quantity measuring the rate of change of another. **3** Finance an arrangement or instrument (such as a future, option, or warrant) whose value derives from and is dependent upon the value of an underlying variable asset, such as a commodity, currency, or security. □ **derivatively** adv.

derive /də'raiv/ v. **1** tr. (usu. foll. by from) get, obtain, or form. **2** intr. (foll. by from) arise from, originate in, be descended or obtained from (happiness derives from many things). **3** tr. gather or deduce. **4** tr. **a** trace the descent of (a person). **b** show the origin of (a thing). **5** tr. (usu. foll. by from) show or state the origin or

formation of (a word etc.). **6** tr. Math. obtain (a function) by differentiation. □ **derivable** adj.

dermatitis /,dɜrmə'taitıs/ n. skin inflammation.

dermatology /,dɜrmə'tɒlədʒi/ n. the study of the diagnosis and treatment of skin disorders. □ **dermatologic** adj. **dermatological** adj. **dermatologically** adv. **dermatologist** n.

dermis /'dɜrmıs/ n. **1** (in general use) the skin. **2** Anat. the thick layer of living tissue below the epidermis. □ **dermal** adj. **dermic** adj.

derogatory /də'rɒgətəri/ adj. (often foll. by to) involving disparagement or discredit; insulting, depreciatory (made a derogatory remark).

derrick n. **1** a kind of crane for moving or lifting heavy weights, having a movable pivoted arm. **2** the framework over an oil well or similar excavation, holding the drilling machinery.

derrière /,deri'er/ n. informal the buttocks.

derring-do /,derıŋ'du:/ n. literary jocular heroic courage or action.

derris /'derıs/ n. **1** any woody tropical climbing leguminous plant of the genus Derris, bearing leathery pods. **2** an insecticide made from the powdered root of some kinds of derris.

dervish n. a member of any of several Muslim fraternities vowed to poverty and austerity.

DES abbr. Computing Data Encryption Standard.

descant n. /'deskænt/ an independent soprano melody usu. sung or played above a basic melody.

descend v. **1** tr. & intr. go or come down (a hill, stairs, etc.). **2** intr. (of a thing) pass from a higher to lower position in space; fall (rain descended heavily). **3** intr. slope downwards (fields descended to the beach). **4** intr. (usu. foll. by on) **a** make a sudden attack. **b** informal make an unexpected and usu. unwelcome visit. **5** tr. & intr. (usu. foll. by from, to) **a** (often in passive) originate with or derive from (a progenitor or predecessor). **b** (of property, qualities, rights, etc.) be passed by inheritance. **6** intr. (foll. by to) come down mentally or morally; stoop to something unworthy (descend to violence). **7** intr. Music (of sound) become lower in pitch; go down (the scale). **8** intr. (usu. foll. by to) proceed (in discourse or writing) to what follows, esp. from the general (to the particular). **9** tr. move downstream along (a river etc.) to the sea etc.

descendant n. (often foll. by of) **1** a person or animal descended from another. **2** something deriving from or following after the form, function, or style of another, earlier structure, model, etc.

descent n. **1 a** the act of descending. **b** an instance of this. **c** a downward movement, esp. of an airplane. **2 a** a way or path etc. by which one may descend. **b** a downward slope. **3 a** lineage, family origin. **b** the transmission of qualities, property, privileges, etc. by inheritance. **4** a fall or decline to a lower state or condition. **5** a sudden violent attack.

descramble v.tr. convert or restore (an electronic signal) to intelligible form, esp. through an electronic device. □ **descrambler** n.

describe v.tr. **1 a** portray in words; give a detailed or graphic account of. **b** (foll. by as) assert to be; call (described him as an agitator). **2 a** mark out or draw (esp. a geometrical figure) (described a triangle). **b** move in (a specified way, esp. a curve) (described a parabola). □ **describable** adj. **describer** n.

description n. **1 a** the act or an instance of describing; the process of being described. **b** a spoken or written representation (of a person, object, or event). **2** a sort, kind, or class (no food of any description). □

answers (or **fits**) **the description** has the qualities specified.

descriptive *adj.* **1** serving or seeking to describe. **2** describing or classifying without expressing feelings or judging (*a purely descriptive account*). **3** *Linguistics* describing a language without comparing, endorsing, or condemning particular usage, vocabulary, etc. **4** *Grammar* (of an adjective) describing a quality of the noun, rather than its relation, position, etc., e.g. *blue* as distinct from *few*. □ **descriptivism** *n.* **descriptivist** *n. & adj.* (both in sense 3). **descriptively** *adv.* **descriptiveness** *n.*

desecrate /'desə,kreit/ *v.tr.* **1** violate (a venerated place or thing) with violence, profanity, etc. **2** deprive (a church etc.) of sanctity. □ **desecration** *n.*

desegregate *v.tr.* abolish racial segregation in (schools etc.) or of (people etc.). □ **desegregation** *n.*

desensitize *v.tr.* **1** reduce or destroy the sensitivity of (photographic materials, an allergic person, etc.). **2** reduce or eliminate emotional responses to, esp. through repeated exposure (*desensitized to violence*). □ **desensitization** *n.* **desensitizer** *n.*

desert[1] /də'zɜrt/ *v.* **1** *tr.* abandon, give up, leave without intention of returning. **2** *tr.* forsake or abandon (a cause, person, etc., esp. one having a claim on a person) (*deserted his wife and children*). **3** *tr.* (of a power or faculty) fail (someone) (*his presence of mind deserted him*). **4** *tr. & intr. Military* run away from or forsake (one's duty etc.). □ **deserter** *n.* **desertion** *n.*

desert[2] /'dezərt/ ● **1** *n.* a dry, barren area of land, often sand-covered, characteristically desolate, with little fresh water and scanty vegetation. **2** an uninteresting or intellectually barren place, subject, etc. (*a cultural desert*). ● *adj.* uninhabited, desolate.

desert[3] /də'zɜrt/ *n.* (usu. in *pl.*) **1** acts or qualities deserving reward or punishment. **2** just reward or punishment (*just deserts*).

desert boot *n.* an ankle-high suede boot with laces.

deserted *adj.* empty, abandoned (*a deserted house*).

desertification /də,zɜrtɪfɪ'keɪʃən/ *n.* the transformation of fertile land into a desert or arid waste.

desert island *n.* a remote (usu. tropical) island presumed to be uninhabited.

deserve *v.tr.* (often foll. by *to* + infin.) be entitled to or worthy of (a reward, punishment, etc.). □ **deserved** *adj.* **deservedly** /də'zɜrvədli/ *adv.* **deservedness** *n.*

deserving *adj.* meritorious, worthy. □ **deserving of** showing conduct or qualities worthy of (praise, blame, help, etc.). □ **deservingly** *adv.* **deservingness** *n.*

desiccant /'desɪkənt/ *n. Chem.* a drying or desiccating agent.

desiccate /'desɪ,keit/ *v.tr.* **1** remove the moisture from, dry (esp. food for preservation). **2** deprive (land, plants, etc.) thoroughly of moisture. □ **desiccation** *n.* **desiccative** /-kətɪv/ *adj.*

desiccated *adj.* **1 a** deprived or freed of moisture. **b** (of food) dried for preservation. **2** (of a person, text, etc.) deprived of energy or feeling.

desideratum /də,zɪdə'rætəm, də,sɪd-/ *n.* (*pl.* **-rata** /-tə/) something lacking but needed and desired.

design ● *n.* **1** a preliminary plan or sketch for the making or production of a building, machine, garment, etc. **2 a** the art of planning and creating something in accordance with appropriate functional and aesthetic criteria. **b** the selection and arrangement of artistic or functional elements making up a work of art, machine, etc. **c** = INTERIOR DESIGN. **3 a** the general arrangement or layout of a product. **b** an example or a completed version of a sketch, concept, or pattern. **c** an established version of a product (*one of our most popular designs*). **4** a motif or pattern of lines, shapes, etc. **5 a** a plan, purpose, or intention. **b** a plot, scheme, or intrigue. ● *v.* **1** *tr.* **a** make drawings and plans for the construction or production of (a building, machine, garment, etc.). **b** plan and execute (a structure, work of art, etc.), skilfully or artistically. **2** *tr.* **a** intend (something) for a specific purpose. **b** form a plan or scheme of; contrive (*designed an attack*). **3** *intr.* be a designer of works of art, buildings, garments, etc. □ **by design** on purpose. **have designs on 1** have one's sights set on. **2** hope to establish a romantic or sexual relationship with. **3** plan to attack or appropriate.

designate ● *v.tr.* /'dezɪg,neit/ **1** (often foll. by *as*) appoint to an office or function. **2** mark or point out clearly (*designate the boundaries*). **3** (often foll. by *as*) give a name or title to (*was designated Athlete of the Year*). **4** serve as the name or distinctive mark of. ● *adj.* /'dezɪgnət/ (placed after noun) appointed to a position but not yet officially occupying it (*bishop designate*). □ **designated** *adj.* **designator** *n.*

designated driver *n. N Amer.* a person who abstains from alcohol at a social gathering so as to be fit to drive others home.

designated hitter *n. Baseball* a non-fielding player named before the start of a game to bat for the pitcher anywhere in the batting order. Abbr.: **DH**.

designation *n.* **1** a name, description, or title. **2** the act or process of designating. **3** the appointment or nomination of a (person, city, etc.) to (a particular office, status, etc.).

designed *adj.* **1** planned, intended. **2** outlined, formed, or framed according to some design.

designer *n.* **1 a** a person who makes artistic designs or plans for construction, e.g. for clothing, machines, theatre sets. **b** an interior designer. **2** (*attrib.*) **a** (of clothing etc.) bearing the name or label of a famous designer (*designer jeans*). **b** (of ideas, objects, etc.) being or seeming fashionable or trendy (*designer beers*). **c** (of chemicals etc.) designed for a specific purpose or function (*designer herbicides*).

designer drug *n.* **1** a drug synthesized to mimic a legally restricted or prohibited drug without being subject to such restriction. **2** a specially formulated drug designed to be highly effective against a precisely targeted disease, chemical process, etc.

designing *adj.* crafty, artful, or scheming.

desirable *adj.* **1 a** worth having or doing; choice, excellent (*desirable accommodations*). **b** worthwhile, advisable (*a desirable law*). **2** arousing sexual desire; very attractive. □ **desirability** *n.* **desirably** *adv.*

desire ● *n.* **1 a** an unsatisfied longing or craving. **b** an expression of this or a request (*expressed a desire to rest*). **2** sexual appetite. **3** something desired. ● *v.tr.* **1 a** (often foll. by *to* + infin., or *that* + clause) long for, crave. **b** feel sexual desire for. **2** request (*desires tea*).

desirous *predic.adj.* (usu. foll. by *of*) having desire, wishful, wanting (*desirous of doing well*).

desist /də'sɪst/ *v.intr.* (often foll. by *from*) cease or abstain.

desk *n.* **1** a piece of furniture with a flat or sloped writing surface, often having drawers or compartments. **2** a service counter in a library, hotel, etc. at which a specific function is performed (*information desk*). **3** a section of an office, e.g. of a newspaper, that handles a particular matter, topic, etc. (*the sports desk*). **4** a music stand, esp. shared by two orchestra members. **5** (*attrib.*) **a** designating an item designed for use at a desk (*a desk dictionary*). **b** designating something done or someone working at a desk (a desk job).

desk clerk n. N Amer. the person on duty at the reception desk of a hotel.

desktop n. **1** the working surface of a desk. **2** (attrib.) of a size and nature suitable for use on a desk, esp. designating or pertaining to a microcomputer. **3** a desktop computer.

desktop publishing n. the design and production of high-quality printed matter using a desktop computer and a laser printer.

desolate ● adj. **1** (of a person) forlorn, wretched, and usu. solitary (was left desolate and weeping). **2 a** (of a building or place) uninhabited, ruined, neglected, barren (desolate Arctic wastes). **b** dismal, depressing (desolate prospects). ● v.tr. depopulate or devastate, lay waste to. □ **desolately** adv.

desolated adj. **1** made wretched or forlorn (desolated by grief). **2** made barren or uninhabitable.

desolation n. **1** loneliness, grief, or wretchedness, esp. caused by desertion. **2 a** the act of desolating. **b** the process or act of being desolated. **3** a neglected, ruined, barren, or empty region, place, etc.

despair ● n. the complete loss or absence of hope. ● v.intr. (often foll. by of) lose or be without hope (despaired of ever seeing her again). □ **be the despair of** be the cause of despair by badness or unapproachable excellence (he's the despair of his parents). □ **despairing** adj. **despairingly** adv.

despatch esp. Brit. var. of DISPATCH.

desperado /ˌdespəˈrɒdo:/ n. (pl. **-oes** or N Amer. **-os**) esp. hist. a desperate or reckless person, esp. a person ready for any deed of lawlessness or violence.

desperate adj. **1** reckless from despair, esp. to the point of violence or lawlessness. **2 a** extremely grave, critical, or serious (a desperate situation). **b** undertaken as a last resort, esp. as staking all on a small chance (a desperate remedy). **3** extreme, excessive (desperate poverty). **4** (usu. foll. by for) needing or desiring very much. □ **desperately** adv. **desperateness** n. **desperation** n.

despicable adj. vile, deserving to be despised, morally contemptible. □ **despicably** adv.

despise v.tr. look down on (someone etc.) as inferior, worthless, or contemptible. □ **despised** adj.

despite prep. notwithstanding; in spite of.

despoil v.tr. **1** spoil, destroy, make useless. **2** literary (often foll. by of) plunder, rob, deprive by force or violence (despoiled her of her inheritance).

despondent /dəˈspɒndənt/ adj. characterized by loss of courage or enthusiasm; dejected. □ **despondency** n. **despondently** adv.

despot n. **1** an absolute ruler. **2** a tyrant or oppressor. **3** any person in authority who acts like a tyrant. □ **despotic** adj. **despotically** adv.

despotism n. **1 a** the exercise of absolute political authority or rule, esp. by a despot. **b** a political system under the control of a despot. **2** tyranny.

dessert n. a sweet food eaten at the end of a meal.

dessert wine n. a sweet wine usu. served with or following a dessert.

destabilize v.tr. **1** deprive of stability. **2** subvert or undermine (a government, economy, etc.), so as to make it politically unstable. □ **destabilization** n.

destination n. **1** a place to which a person or thing is going, the intended end of a journey. **2** the end or purpose for which a person or thing is destined.

destine /ˈdestɪn/ v.tr. (in passive, often foll. by to, for, or

to + infin.) set apart for or devote to a particular purpose, activity, etc.

destined adj. **1** having a future decided or planned beforehand, esp. by fate or as if by fate (destined for greatness). **2** bound (for a certain place) (destined for PEI).

destiny n. (pl. **-ies**) **1 a** fate or the predetermined course of events. **b** (often **Destiny**) the power or agency that supposedly predetermines events etc. **2** what is destined to happen to a particular person etc. (it was their destiny to be rejected).

destitute adj. completely impoverished; without food, shelter, etc. □ **destitution** n.

destreaming n. Cdn the reversal of the practice of categorizing students into formal academic divisions based on their perceived ability. □ **destream** v.tr.

destroy v.tr. **1** demolish, pull or break down; shatter, smash to pieces. **2** put an end to or do away with (destroyed his confidence). **3** kill (esp. a sick or savage animal). **4** make useless, spoil utterly. **5** utterly discredit or ruin financially, professionally, or in reputation. **6** defeat, annihilate (destroyed the enemy).

destroyer n. **1** a person or thing that destroys. **2** a small, lightly armoured and heavily armed warship.

destruct ● v.tr. destroy (one's own rocket etc.) deliberately, esp. for safety reasons. ● n. **1** an act of destructing. **2** (attrib.) designating something capable of causing the destruction of itself, some other object, etc. (destruct mechanism).

destructible adj. able or liable to be destroyed. □ **destructibility** n.

destruction n. **1** the act or an instance of destroying; the process of being destroyed. **2** the fact or condition of being destroyed; ruin. **3** a cause of ruin; something that destroys.

destructive adj. **1** (often foll. by to, of) destroying or tending to destroy (destructive behaviour). **2** negative in attitude or criticism; refuting without suggesting, helping, amending, etc. (destructive criticism). □ **destructively** adv. **destructiveness** n.

desultory /ˈdesəlˌtɔri/ adj. **1** going constantly from one subject to another, esp. digressively and unmethodically. **2** disconnected, random, or occasional. □ **desultorily** adv. **desultoriness** n.

Det. abbr. Detective.

detach /dəˈtætʃ/ v.tr. **1** (often foll. by from) unfasten and remove; disconnect or disengage. **2** Military separate and send off (a part from a main body, e.g. a ship, regiment, officer, etc.) for a particular purpose, separate mission, etc. □ **detachable** adj.

detached adj. **1** impartial, unemotional (a detached viewpoint). **2** esp. Cdn & Brit. (esp. of a house) separate, not joined to another or others.

detachment n. **1 a** a state of aloofness from or indifference to other people, public opinion, etc. **b** disinterested independence of judgment; objectivity. **2 a** the act or process of detaching or being detached. **b** an instance of this. **3** Military **a** the action of separating a number of troops etc. from a main military body for a particular purpose. **b** a separate group or unit of an army etc. used for such a purpose. **4** Cdn the office or headquarters of a police district patrolled by the RCMP, OPP, etc.

detail ● n. **1 a** a small or subordinate particular. **b** such a particular, considered (ironically) to be unimportant (the truth of the statement is just a detail). **2 a** small items or particulars (esp. in an artistic work) regarded collectively (has an eye for detail). **b** the treatment of them (the detail was insufficient). **3** (often in pl.) a number of particulars or an aggregate of small items (*filled in the details on the form*). **4 a** a minor decoration on a building, in a picture, etc. **b** a small part of a picture etc. shown alone or considered in isolation. **5** *Military* **a** the distribution of detailed orders for the day, ranging from general to specific directives. **b** a small detachment of soldiers etc. for special duty. **c** this special duty (*kitchen detail*). ● *v.tr.* **1** relate or describe minutely, give particulars of (*detailed the plans*). **2** *Military* assign for special duty. **3** decorate (a carving, car, etc.) with intricate drawings or designs. □ **go into detail** give all the items or particulars. **in detail** item by item, minutely.

detailed *adj.* **1** (of a picture, story, etc.) having many details. **2** related or described minutely, itemized (*a detailed list*). **3** thorough in handling of details.

detailing *n.* the treatment of detail in a work of art, building, design, etc.

detain *v.tr.* **1** keep in confinement or under restraint as a prisoner, esp. without charge. **2** delay or keep (someone) waiting. □ **detainment** *n.*

detainee *n.* a person detained in custody, esp. for political reasons.

detect *v.tr.* **1** discover or perceive the existence or presence of. **2 a** discover the real (esp. hidden or disguised) character of. **b** discover (crime etc.). □ **detectable** *adj.* **detectably** *adv.*

detection *n.* **1 a** the act or an instance of detecting. **b** the process of being detected. **2** the work of a detective.

detective *n.* **1** (often *attrib.*) a person, esp. a member of a police force, employed to investigate crime (*police detective*; *detective agency*). **2** (in Canadian police forces with a detective branch) an officer ranking above constable and below detective sergeant. **3** (*attrib.*) designating a type of fiction describing crime and the detection of criminals (*compare* MYSTERY 5).

detective chief superintendent *n.* (in the OPP) an officer ranking above detective superintendent.

detective inspector *n.* (in the OPP) an officer ranking above sergeant major.

detective sergeant *n.* **1** (in Canadian police forces with a detective branch) an officer ranking above detective and below inspector with the equivalent rank of staff sergeant. **2** (in the OPP) an officer ranking above senior constable.

detective staff sergeant *n.* (in the OPP) an officer ranking above detective sergeant.

detective superintendent *n.* (in the OPP) an officer ranking above detective inspector.

detector *n.* a device which detects something liable to escape observation or indicates something out of the ordinary (*smoke detector*; *lie detector*).

détente /dei'tãt/ *n.* an easing of strained relations esp. between nations.

detention *n.* **1** an act or an instance of detaining or being detained. **2 a** the fact of being kept in school after hours as a punishment. **b** an instance of this. **3** the state of imprisonment or confinement, esp. of a criminal or political offender. **4** (*attrib.*) designating a place where people are held in detention.

detention centre *n.* **1** an institution for the short-term detention of criminals, esp. young offenders. **2** a camp or centre, esp. one established during or after a war, to house refugees, prisoners of war, etc.

deter *v.tr.* (**deterred, deterring**) **1** (often foll. by *from*) discourage or prevent (a person) through fear or dislike of the consequences. **2** discourage, check, or prevent (a thing, process, etc.). □ **determent** *n.*

detergent ● *n.* **1** a water-soluble cleansing agent which combines with impurities and dirt to make

them more soluble, and differs from soap in not forming a scum with the salts in hard water. **2** any additive with a similar action, e.g. holding dirt in suspension in lubricating oil. ● *adj.* cleansing, esp. in the manner of a detergent.

deteriorate *v.tr. & intr.* make or become worse or lower in quality, character, etc. □ **deterioration** *n.*

determinant ● *n.* a determining factor, element, word, etc. ● *adj.* serving to determine or define.

determinate *adj.* **1** limited in time, space, or character. **2** of definite scope or nature. □ **determinacy** *n.*

determination *n.* **1** firmness of purpose. **2 a** the process of deciding, determining, or calculating. **b** the result of such consideration. **3 a** the conclusion of a dispute by the decision of a judge or an arbitrator. **b** the decision so reached.

determine *v.* **1** *tr.* find out or establish precisely. **2** *tr.* decide or settle (*determined who should go*). **3** *tr.* be a decisive factor in regard to (*demand determines supply*). **4** *intr. & tr.* make or cause (a person) to make a decision (*we determined to go at once*). **5** *tr.* fix or define the position of. □ **determinable** *adj.*

determined *adj.* showing determination; resolute, unflinching. □ **determinedly** *adv.*

determinism *n. Philos.* the doctrine that all events, including human action, are determined by causes regarded as external to the will. □ **determinist** *n.* **deterministic** *adj.* **deterministically** *adv.*

deterrent ● *n.* **1** a thing or factor that deters (someone). **2** military strength or combat capability, esp. nuclear, intended to deter an enemy from attack. ● *adj.* tending to deter. □ **deterrence** *n.*

detest *v.tr.* hate, loathe. □ **detester** *n.*

detestable *adj.* deserving to be detested; intensely hateful. □ **detestably** *adv.*

detonate *v.* **1** *tr.* set off (an explosive charge). **2** *intr.* (of an explosive charge) be set off, explode. □ **detonative** *adj.* **detonator** *n.*

detonation *n.* **1** the act or process of detonating. **2** a violent explosion.

detour ● *n.* a divergence from a direct or intended route, esp. one that avoids a blocked road etc. ● *v.intr. & tr.* make or cause to make a detour.

detox esp. *N Amer. informal* ● *n.* **1** = DETOXIFICATION. **2 a** a detoxification clinic, program, etc. **b** = DRUNK TANK. ● *v.* **1** *tr.* subject (an alcoholic or drug addict) to detoxification. **2** *intr.* **a** (of a person) subject oneself to detoxification. **b** recover temporarily from the effects of alcohol or drugs.

detoxification *n.* **1 a** the act of depriving of poisonous qualities, esp. the elimination of poison from the body. **b** the state of being detoxified. **2** the supervised withdrawal of drugs etc. from an addict.

detoxification centre *n.* (also **detox centre**) a (usu. residential) centre for the treatment of alcoholism or drug abuse.

detoxify *v.tr.* (**-ies, -ied**) **1** subject (an alcoholic or drug addict) to detoxification. **2** remove the poison from (something).

detract *v.* (foll. by *from*) **1** *intr.* **a** take something away from. **b** diminish or belittle. **2** *tr.* take away (something) so as to diminish the whole, esp. an achievement. ¶*Detract* does not mean *distract*; uses such as *Nothing will detract their attention from the issue* are incorrect. □ **detraction** *n.*

detractor *n.* a person who disparages or belittles another's achievements, merits, etc.

detriment *n.* **1** harm, damage, disadvantage. **2**

something causing this. □ **to the detriment of** to the disadvantage of.

detrimental *adj.* harmful, damaging, or causing loss. □ **detrimentally** *adv.*

detritus /dəˈtraɪtəs/ *n.* **1** matter produced by erosion, such as gravel, silt, etc. **2** debris of any kind. **3** the organic litter produced by decomposing leaves etc.

deuce[1] /duːs, djuːs/ *n.* **1** the two in dice or playing cards. **2 a** *Sport* two points, goals, runs, etc. **b** *Tennis* the score of 40 all, at which two consecutive points are needed to win. **3** *informal* the number two as an identifying feature for various items.

deuce[2] *n. informal* the Devil, used esp. as an exclamation of surprise or annoyance (*who the deuce are you?*). □ **a** (or **the**) **deuce of a** a very bad or remarkable (*a deuce of a problem*). **the deuce to pay** trouble to be expected.

deuterium /duːˈtɪəriəm, ˌdjuː-/ *n.* a stable isotope of hydrogen with a mass about double that of the usual isotope.

Deutschmark /ˈdɔɪtʃmɑːk/ *n.* (also **Deutsche Mark** /ˈdɔɪtʃə mɑːk/) the chief monetary unit of Germany.

devalue *v.tr.* (**devalues, devalued, devaluing**) **1** reduce the value of (a person, thing, etc.). **2** reduce the value of (a currency) in relation to other currencies or to gold (*opp.* REVALUE 2). □ **devaluation** *n.*

devastate *v.tr.* **1** lay waste; cause great destruction to. **2** (often in *passive*) overwhelm with shock or grief; upset deeply. □ **devastation** *n.* **devastator** *n.*

devastating *adj.* crushingly effective; overwhelming. □ **devastatingly** *adv.*

develop *v.* (**developed, developing**) **1** *tr. & intr.* **a** make or become bigger or fuller. **b** bring or come to an active or visible state (*symptoms developed rapidly*). **c** bring or come into existence (*a crisis developed*). **2 a** *tr.* elaborate more fully and systematically the details of (a thought, argument, plot, etc.) **b** *intr.* (of a thought, argument, plot, etc.) unfold in this way. **3** *tr. & intr.* **a** grow or cause to grow to maturity or to a more advanced state (*some teens develop early*). **b** (of organisms) evolve or progress from a simpler or lower to a higher or more complex type. **4** *tr.* begin to exhibit or suffer from (*developed an infection*). **5** *tr.* **a** make (a tract of land) suitable for new purposes, esp. residential, industrial, etc. **b** realize the resource potential of (a site or property) by mining etc. **6** *tr.* create or design (a program, product, etc.). **7** *tr.* treat (photographic film etc.) chemically to make the latent image visible. □ **developable** *adj.*

developer *n.* **1** a person or company that develops land, esp. a speculative builder. **2** a chemical agent for developing photographs. **3** a person or thing which develops (a product etc.).

developing country *n.* a country that is becoming economically more advanced and industrialized.

development *n.* **1 a** the act or an instance of developing; the process of being developed. **b** *Business* the process of working up (an idea, product, etc.) for marketing etc. **2 a** a stage of growth or advancement. **b** a full-grown state. **3** a significant change in a course of action, events, circumstances, etc. (*the latest developments*). **4** the process of developing a photograph. **5** a developed tract of land, esp. a new housing area. **6** industrialization or economic advancement of a country or area.

developmental *adj.* pertaining to the process of achieving physical, mental, or social maturity (*developmental delays*). **2** of or pertaining to development. □ **developmentally** *adv.*

development bank *n.* a regional multilateral organization designed to contribute to the economic development and social progress of its members.

deviant /ˈdiːviənt/ ● *adj.* deviating or divergent, esp. from normal social standards. ● *n.* a person who or thing which deviates from the normal, esp. from normal social or sexual practices. □ **deviance** *n.*

deviate ● *v.intr.* /ˈdiːviˌeɪt/ (often foll. by *from*) **1** turn aside or diverge (from a course of action, rule, truth, norm, etc.). **2** digress. ● *n.* /ˈdiːviət/ a deviant, esp. a sexual pervert. ● *adj.* /ˈdiːviət/ = DEVIANT *adj.*

deviation *n.* **1 a** a divergence from a course, method, rule, or norm. **b** an instance of this. **2** *Statistics* the amount by which a single measurement differs from the mean. **3** the deflection of a compass needle caused by local deposits of iron, regional magnetic disturbances, etc. □ **deviational** *adj.*

device *n.* **1 a** a thing made or adapted for a particular purpose, esp. a mechanical contrivance. **b** an explosive contrivance, esp. a nuclear bomb. **2** a plan, scheme, or trick. **3 a** an emblematic or heraldic design. **b** an artistic drawing, design, pattern, etc. **4** any literary technique deliberately employed to achieve a specific effect, e.g. figures of speech etc. □ **leave a person to his or her own devices** leave a person to do as he or she wishes.

devil ● *n.* **1** (usu. **the Devil**) (in Christian and Jewish belief) the supreme spirit of evil; Satan. **2** an evil spirit; a superhuman malignant being. **3 a** a wicked or cruel person. **b** a mischievously energetic, clever, or self-willed person. **4** *informal* a person or animal (*lucky devil*). **5** fighting spirit, mischievousness (*the devil is in him tonight*). **6** *informal* something difficult or awkward (*this door is a devil to open*). **7** (**the devil, the Devil**) *informal* used as an exclamation of surprise or annoyance (*who the devil are you?*). ● *v.tr.* (**devilled, devilling**) *N Amer.* harass; worry. □ **between the devil and the deep blue sea** in a dilemma. **a devil of** *informal* a considerable, difficult, or remarkable. **the devil to pay** trouble to be expected. **go to the devil 1** be damned. **2** (in *imper.*) used to express anger or annoyance. **like the devil** with great energy. **speak of the devil** said when a person appears just after being mentioned.

devilled *adj.* (of eggs, ham, etc.) prepared with spicy seasonings.

devil-may-care *adj.* cheerful and reckless (*a devil-may-care manner*).

devilry *n.* (also **deviltry**) (*pl.* **-ies**) **1 a** wickedness; reckless mischief. **b** an instance of this. **2 a** black magic. **b** devil worship.

devil's advocate *n.* **1** a person who supports an opposing or unpopular view in order to provoke argument or discussion. **2** *Catholicism* the official whose function is to argue the case against beatification or canonization of a candidate.

devil's club *n.* *N Amer.* a prickly shrub of the aralia family, *Oplopanax horridus*.

devil's food cake *n.* *N Amer.* a chocolate cake with a reddish tinge.

devil's paintbrush *n.* *N Amer.* an orange-flowered hawkweed, *Hieracium aurantiacum*.

devious *adj.* **1** (of a person, plan etc.) not straightforward or sincere; underhand. **2** winding; circuitous. □ **deviously** *adv.* **deviousness** *n.*

devise /dəˈvaɪz/ ● *v.tr.* **1** plan or invent by careful thought. **2** *Law* leave (real estate) by the terms of a will (*compare* BEQUEATH). ● *n.* *Law* **1** the act or an instance of devising real estate. **2** a devising clause in a will. □ **devisable** *adj.* **deviser** *n.*

devitalize v.tr. take away strength and vigour from. □ **devitalization** n.

devoid /dəˈvɔɪd/ predic.adj. (foll. by of) totally lacking.

devolution /ˌdevəˈluːʃən, ˌdiː-/ n. 1 the delegation of power, esp. by central government to local or regional administration. 2 a descent or passing on through a series of stages. b descent by natural or due succession from one to another of property or qualities. 3 the transfer of an unexercised right to an ultimate owner. 4 Biol. degeneration. □ **devolutionism** n. **devolutionist** n.

devolve v. 1 (foll. by on, upon, etc.) a tr. pass (work or duties) to (a deputy etc.). b intr. (of work or duties) pass to (a deputy etc.). 2 intr. (foll. by on, to, upon) Law (of property etc.) descend or fall by succession to. □ **devolvement** n.

Devonian /dəˈvoʊniən/ ● adj. of or relating to the fourth period of the Paleozoic era, from about 408 to 360 million years BP, between the Silurian and Carboniferous periods. ● n. this period or system.

devote v.tr. & refl. (foll. by to) apply or give over (resources etc. or oneself) to (a particular activity or purpose or person) (devoted my time to reading).

devoted adj. very loving or loyal (a devoted husband). □ **devotedly** adv. **devotedness** n.

devotee /ˌdevəˈtiː, ˌdiː-/ n. 1 (usu. foll. by of) a zealous enthusiast or supporter. 2 a zealously pious or fanatical person.

devotion n. 1 (usu. foll. by to) enthusiastic attachment or loyalty (to a person or cause); great love. 2 a religious worship. b (in pl.) prayers. c devoutness; religious fervour.

devotional ● adj. of, pertaining to, or characterized by (esp. religious) devotion. ● n. (often in pl.) a short religious service. □ **devotionalism** n.

devour v.tr. 1 eat hungrily or greedily. 2 consume destructively; waste; destroy (devouring the world's resources). 3 take in greedily with the eyes or ears (devoured book after book). 4 (usu. in passive) absorb the attention of (devoured by anxiety). □ **devourer** n.

devout adj. 1 earnestly religious. 2 earnestly sincere (devout hope). □ **devoutly** adv. **devoutness** n.

dew /duː, djuː/ ● n. 1 atmospheric vapour condensing in small drops on cool surfaces at night. 2 beaded or glistening moisture resembling this, e.g. tears. ● v.tr. (usu. in passive) wet with or as with dew.

dewater /diːˈwɒtər/ v.tr. remove water from (sludge, a tunnel etc.); drain.

dewberry n. (pl. **-ies**) 1 a bluish fruit like the blackberry. 2 any of various shrubs of the genus Rubus bearing this.

dewdrop n. a drop of dew.

Dewey Decimal Classification /ˈduːi, ˈdjuːi/ n. (also **Dewey decimal system** informal) a decimal system of library classification.

dewlap n. 1 a loose fold of skin hanging from the throat of cattle, dogs, etc. 2 similar loose skin round the throat of an elderly person.

DEW Line n. N Amer. a network of radar stations stretching along the Arctic coast from Alaska to Baffin Island, built in the 1950s to provide advance warning of an aircraft or missile attack.

deworm /diːˈwɜrm/ v.tr. rid (a dog, cat, etc.) of worms. □ **dewormer** n.

dew point n. the temperature at which dew forms.

dew worm n. = EARTHWORM.

dewy adj. (**-ier**, **-iest**) 1 a wet with dew. b moist as if with dew (a dewy complexion). 2 = DEWY-EYED. 3 of or like dew. □ **dewily** adv. **dewiness** n.

dewy-eyed adj. innocently trusting; naive.

dexterity /dekˈsterəti/ n. 1 manual or manipulative skill or adroitness; good physical coordination. 2 mental adroitness or skill; cleverness.

dexterous /ˈdekstrəs/ adj. (also **dextrous**) having or showing dexterity. □ **dexterously** adv. **dexterousness** n.

dextromethorphan /ˌdekstroməˈθɔrfən/ n. a cough suppressant acting by making the cough centre in the brain less sensitive to incoming stimuli.

dextrorotatory /ˌdekstroroˈteɪtəri/ adj. Chem. having the property of rotating the plane of a polarized light ray to the right (compare LEVOROTATORY).

dextrose /ˈdekstros, -oːz/ n. a dextrorotatory form of glucose.

DFO abbr. Cdn Department of Fisheries and Oceans.

DH ● n. DESIGNATED HITTER. ● v. (**DHs, DHed**) 1 intr. act as a designated hitter. 2 tr. use (a player) as a designated hitter (the Jays DHed him last night). ● abbr. Skiing DOWNHILL.

dhal /dɒl/ var. of DAL.

dharma /ˈdɑrmə/ n. 1 (in Hinduism) the eternal law of the cosmos, inherent in the nature of things, upheld (but not created or controlled) by the gods; in the context of individual action, it denotes the social rules codified in the law books. 2 (in Buddhism) the true doctrine as preached by the Buddha.

dhoti /ˈdoːti/ n. (pl. **dhotis**) the loincloth worn by male Hindus.

dhow /dau/ n. a lateen-rigged Arab ship used on the E African, Arabian, and Indian coasts.

DHS abbr. Cdn District High School.

dia. abbr. diameter.

diabetes /ˌdaɪəˈbiːtiːz, -tɪs/ n. 1 any disorder of the metabolism characterized by excessive thirst and the production of large amounts of urine. 2 (in full **diabetes mellitus**) the commonest form of diabetes in which sugar and starch are not properly absorbed from the blood, characterized by thirst, emaciation, and excessive excretion of urine with glucose.

diabetic /ˌdaɪəˈbetɪk/ ● adj. 1 of or relating to or having diabetes. 2 for use by diabetics. ● n. a person suffering from diabetes.

diabolical /ˌdaɪəˈbɒlɪkəl/ adj. (also **diabolic**) 1 of the Devil. 2 devilish; inhumanly cruel or wicked. 3 fiendishly clever, cunning, or annoying. □ **diabolically** adv.

diaconal /daɪˈækənəl, diː-/ adj. 1 of a deacon or deaconess. 2 of or relating to a diaconal minister.

diaconal minister n. Cdn (in Presbyterian and United churches) a layperson belonging to a religious order who is employed by a congregation etc. to work with children, youth, the elderly, etc.

diacritic /ˌdaɪəˈkrɪtɪk/ ● n. a sign, e.g. an accent, cedilla, etc. used to indicate different sounds or values of a letter. ● adj. = DIACRITICAL.

diacritical ● adj. distinguishing; distinctive. ● n. (in full **diacritical mark** or **sign**) = DIACRITIC.

diadem /ˈdaɪədem/ n. a crown or headband worn as a sign of sovereignty.

diagnose /ˈdaɪəɡnoːs, -ˌnoːz, ˌdaɪəɡˈnoːs, -ˈnoːz/ v. 1 tr. make a diagnosis of (a disease, mechanical fault, etc.) from its symptoms. 2 intr. identify or distinguish by diagnosis. □ **diagnosable** adj.

diagnosis /ˌdaɪəɡˈnoːsɪs/ n. (pl. **diagnoses** /-ˌsiːz/) 1 a the identification of an illness or disease by means of a patient's symptoms. b an instance or formal statement of this. **2** a conclusion reached from analysis of a problem or situation.

diagnostic /ˌdaiəg'nɒstɪk/ ● *adj.* of or assisting diagnosis. ● *n.* a distinctive symptom or characteristic; a specific trait. □ **diagnostically** *adv.* **diagnostician** /-nɒ'stɪʃən/ *n.*

diagnostics *n.* **1** (treated as *pl.*) *Computing* programs and other mechanisms used to detect and identify faults in hardware or software. **2** (treated as *sing.*) the science or study of diagnosing disease.

diagonal ● *adj.* **1** crossing a straight-sided figure from corner to corner. **2** oblique. ● *n.* a line joining two non-adjacent corners. □ **diagonally** *adv.*

diagram ● *n.* **1** a drawing showing the general scheme or outline of an object and its parts. **2** a graphic representation of the course or results of an action or process. **3** *Math.* a figure made of lines used in proving a theorem etc. ● *v.tr.* (**diagrammed**, **diagramming**) represent by means of a diagram. □ **diagrammatic** *adj.* **diagrammatically** *adv.*

dial ● *n.* **1** the face of a clock or watch, marked to show the hours etc. **2** a similar flat plate marked with a scale for measuring weight, volume, pressure, consumption, etc., indicated by a pointer. **3** a movable disc on a telephone which is rotated for each digit of a number being called. **4 a** a rotating knob or button on a radio or television set for selecting wavelength or channel. **b** a similar selecting device on other equipment, e.g. a washing machine. **5** television or radio broadcasting (*a new program on the dial*). ● *v.* (**dialed, dialing; dialled, dialling**) **1** *tr. & intr.* make a telephone call to (a person or number) (*dialed 911*). **2** *tr.* (often foll. by *up*) (of a modem) connect with (another modem). **3** *tr.* measure, indicate, or regulate by means of a dial.

dialect *n.* **1** a form of speech peculiar to a particular region. **2** a subordinate variety of a language with non-standard vocabulary, pronunciation, or grammar. □ **dialectal** *adj.* **dialectological** *adj.* **dialectology** *n.* **dialectologist** *n.*

dialectic /ˌdaiə'lektɪk/ *Philos.* ● *n.* **1 a** the art of critically investigating the truth of opinions; the testing of truth by discussion. **b** logical disputation or argument. **2 a** the philosophy of metaphysical contradictions and their solutions. **b** the existence or action of opposing forces or tendencies in society etc. ● *adj.* **1** of, pertaining to, or of the nature of logical disputation. **2** fond of or skilled in logical disputation.

dialectical *adj.* of dialectic or dialectics. □ **dialectically** *adv.*

dialectical materialism *n.* the Marxist theory that political and historical events are due to a conflict of social forces caused by man's material needs.

dialectics *n.* (treated as *sing.* or *pl.*) = DIALECTIC *n.* 1.

dialer *n.* (also **dialler**) **1** an electronic device which dials phone numbers automatically. **2** a person who dials a telephone.

dialogic /ˌdaiə'lɒdʒɪk/ *adj.* (also **dialogical**) of, pertaining to, or of the nature of dialogue.

dialogue (*US* also **dialog**) ● *n.* **1 a** a conversation between two or more people. **b** conversation in written form, esp. between characters in a novel, play, etc. **2 a** discussion or diplomatic contact between representatives of different nations, blocs, etc. **b** the exchange of proposals, valuable or constructive communication, etc. between different groups. **3** a conversation; a talk. ● *v.intr.* take part in a dialogue; converse.

dial tone *n.* an uninterrupted telephone tone indicating that a caller may start to dial.

dial-up *adj.* pertaining to or designating a data transmission link that uses the telephone system.

dialysis /dai'æləsɪs/ *n.* (*pl.* **dialyses** /-ˌsiːz/) **1** *Chem.* the separation of particles in a liquid by differences in their ability to pass through a membrane into another liquid. **2** the purification of blood, e.g. of a person with inadequately functioning kidneys, by this technique.

diam. *abbr.* diameter.

diameter *n.* **1 a** a straight line passing from side to side through the centre of a body or figure, esp. a circle or sphere. **b** the length of this line. **2** a transverse measurement; width, thickness.

diametrical *adj.* **1** of or along a diameter. **2** (of opposition, difference, etc.) complete. □ **diametrically** *adv.*

diamond /'daimənd, 'daiə-/ ● *n.* **1 a** a usu. colourless or lightly tinted precious stone of great brilliance and hardness, used in jewellery and for cutting and abrading. **b** a piece of jewellery set with one or more diamonds. **2** a rhombus placed with its diagonals horizontal and vertical. **3** *Baseball* **a** the space delimited by the bases. **b** the entire field. **4 a** a playing card of a suit denoted by a red rhombus. **b** (in *pl.*) this suit. ● *adj.* **1** made of or set with diamonds or a diamond. **2** rhombus-shaped.

diamond anniversary *n.* the 60th (or 75th) anniversary of a wedding, graduation, etc.

diamondback *n.* **1** an edible freshwater terrapin, *Malaclemys terrapin*, native to N America, with lozenge-shaped markings on its shell. **2** any rattlesnake of the genus *Crotalus*, native to N America, with diamond-shaped markings.

diamond in the rough *n.* *N Amer.* **1** an uncut diamond. **2** a person, place, or thing of intrinsic but unrefined worth.

diamond willow *n.* *N Amer.* **1** a willow found across Canada with a diamond pattern in the bark and wood caused by fungi. **2** (often *attrib.*) the timber from such a willow.

diaper /'dəipər, 'daiə-/ ● *n.* *N Amer.* a piece of folded cloth or disposable absorbent material wrapped around a baby's bottom to absorb and retain urine and feces. ● *v.tr.* *N Amer.* put a diaper on (a baby).

diaper rash *n.* *N Amer.* redness and irritation of a baby's skin around the genitals or buttocks, caused by persistent contact with wet diapers.

diaphanous /dai'æfənəs/ *adj.* **1** (of fabric etc.) light and delicate, and almost transparent. **2** vague.

diaphragm /'daiəˌfræm/ *n.* **1** (in mammals) a muscular, dome-shaped partition which separates the thorax from the abdomen, and whose contraction leads to expansion of the lungs in respiration. **2** a thin, dome-shaped device of rubber placed over the cervix before intercourse to prevent conception. **3** a vibrating disc or cone producing sound waves, e.g. in telephone receivers, loudspeakers, etc. **4** a thin sheet of material used as a partition, esp. in a tube or pipe. **5** a device for varying the effective aperture of the lens in a camera etc. **6** a partition in animal and plant tissues.

diarist /'daiərɪst/ *n.* a person who keeps a diary.

diarrhea /ˌdaiə'riːə/ *n.* (also esp. *Brit.* **diarrhoea**) **1** a condition of excessively frequent and loose bowel movements. **2** watery or semi-liquid feces characteristic of this condition. □ **diarrheal** *adj.*

diary *n.* (*pl.* **-ies**) **1** a daily written record of events, feelings, or thoughts. **2** a book for this or for noting future engagements, usu. printed and with a calendar and other information.

Diaspora /dai'æspərə/ n. **1** (prec. by *the*) **a** the dispersion of the Jews among the Gentiles mainly in the 8th–6th c. BC. **b** Jews dispersed in this way. **c** (also *attrib.*) Jews or Jewish communities outside the state of Israel. **2** (also **diaspora**) **a** any group of people similarly dispersed. **b** their dispersion.

diatom /'daiətəm/ n. a microscopic unicellular alga with a siliceous cell wall.

diatomaceous earth /daiətə'meiʃəs/ n. a soft, fine-grained deposit composed of fossil diatoms, used as a filter, filler, etc., in various manufacturing processes, and as an insecticide in gardening.

diatonic adj. Music **1** (of a scale, interval, etc.) involving only notes proper to the prevailing key without chromatic alteration. **2** (of a melody or harmony) constructed from such a scale.

diatribe n. a forceful verbal attack.

diazepam /dai'æzə,pæm/ n. a tranquilizing muscle-relaxant drug with anticonvulsant properties used to relieve anxiety, tension, etc. (*compare* VALIUM).

diazinon /dai'æzənɒn/ n. an insecticide derived from pyrimidine.

dibber n. (also **dibble**) a hand-held tool with a pointed end, used for making holes in the ground for seeds or young plants.

dibs n.pl. N Amer. slang a first claim or option to use or have something (*I have dibs on that book*).

dice ● n.pl. **1 a** small cubes usu. made of plastic or wood, marked on each side with 1–6 spots, used in games and gambling. **b** (treated as *sing.*) one of these cubes (see DIE²). **2** a game played with one or more such cubes. **3** food cut into small cubes for cooking. ● v. **1** tr. cut (food) into small cubes. **2** intr. **a** play or gamble with dice. **b** take great risks, gamble (*dicing with death*). □ **no dice** slang no success or luck.

dicer n. **1** a manual or electrical appliance for dicing vegetables etc. **2** a person who plays or gambles with dice.

dicey adj. (**dicier, diciest**) slang risky; uncertain.

dichotomy /dai'kɒtəmi/ n. (pl. **-ies**) **1 a** a division into two, esp. a sharply defined one. **b** the result of such a division (*dichotomy between rich and poor*). **2** binary classification. **3** Bot. & Zool. repeated bifurcation. □ **dichotomize** v.tr. **dichotomous** adj.

dick¹ coarse slang ● n. **1 a** the penis. **b** a stupid, annoying boy or man; a jerk. **2** very little; nothing (*he knows dick about that*). ● v.intr. N Amer. (often foll. by *around*) waste time; fool around.

dick² n. esp. N Amer. slang a detective.

dickens n. (usu. prec. by *how, what, why*, etc., *the*) informal (esp. in exclamations) deuce; the Devil (*what the dickens are you doing here?*).

Dickensian /də'kenzi:ən/ ● adj. **1** of or relating to Charles Dickens (1812–70) or his work. **2** resembling or reminiscent of the situations, poor social conditions, or comically repulsive characters described in Dickens's work. ● n. an admirer or student of Dickens or his work. □ **Dickensianly** adv.

dicker esp. N Amer. ● v.intr. bargain; haggle. ● n. a deal, a barter.

dickhead n. coarse slang a stupid or obnoxious person, esp. a man; an idiot.

dickie n. (also **dickey**) (pl. **-ies** or **-eys**) a false shirt front.

dicot /'daikɒt/ n. = DICOTYLEDON.

dicotyledon /,daikɒtə'li:dən/ n. any flowering plant having two cotyledons. □ **dicotyledonous** adj.

dicta pl. of DICTUM.

Dictaphone /'dɪktə,foːn/ n. proprietary a machine for recording and playing back dictated words.

dictate ● v. **1** tr. say or read aloud (words to be written down or recorded). **2 a** tr. prescribe or lay down authoritatively (terms, things to be done, etc.). **b** intr. lay down the law; give orders. ● n. (usu. in pl.) an authoritative instruction (*dictates of conscience*).

dictation n. **1 a** the saying of words to be written down or recorded. **b** an instance of this, esp. as a school exercise. **c** the material that is dictated. **2 a** authoritative prescription. **b** an instance of this.

dictator n. **1** a ruler with unrestricted authority, esp. one who suppresses or succeeds a democratic government. **2** a person with supreme authority in any sphere. **3** a domineering person.

dictatorial /,dɪktə'tɔːriəl/ adj. **1** of or like a dictator. **2** imperious; overbearing. □ **dictatorially** adv.

dictatorship n. **1** a state ruled by a dictator. **2 a** the position, rule, or period of rule of a dictator. **b** rule by a dictator.

diction n. **1** the manner of enunciation in speaking etc. **2** the choice of words or phrases in speech etc.

dictionary n. (pl. **-ies**) **1** a book that lists (usu. in alphabetical order) and explains the words of a language or gives equivalent words in another language. **2** a reference book on any subject, the items of which are arranged in alphabetical order.

dictum /'dɪktəm/ n. (pl. **dicta** /-tə/ or **dictums**) **1** a formal utterance or pronouncement. **2** a saying or maxim. **3** Law = OBITER DICTUM.

did past of DO¹.

didactic /dai'dæktɪk, də-/ adj. **1** meant to instruct (*didactic poetry*). **2** (of a person) tediously pedantic. □ **didactically** adv. **didacticism** /-tə,sɪzəm/ n.

diddle v. informal **1** tr. cheat, swindle. **2** tr. have sexual intercourse with (a person). **3** intr. (often foll. by *with*) adjust; toy with (*diddled with the controls*). **4** intr. N Amer. waste time. □ **diddler** n.

diddly n. (also **diddley**) = DIDDLY-SQUAT.

diddly-squat n. (also **diddley-squat**) N Amer. slang **1** (with neg.) anything, the least bit (*doesn't mean diddly-squat to me*). **2** nothing at all.

didn't contraction did not.

die¹ v. (**dies, died, dying**) **1** intr. (often foll. by *of*) (of a person, animal, or plant) cease to live; expire (*died of hunger*). **2** intr. **a** come to an end, cease to exist, fade away (*the project died within six months*). **b** cease to function; break down (*the engine died*). **c** (of a flame) go out. **3** intr. (foll. by *on*) die or cease to function while in the presence or charge of (a person). **4** intr. (usu. foll. by of, from, with) be exhausted or tormented (*nearly died of boredom*). **5** intr. informal be overcome with embarrassment, laughter, etc. (*nearly died when she said that*). **6** tr. suffer (a specified death) (*died a natural death*). □ **be dying** wish for longingly or intently (*am dying to see you*). **die away** become weaker or fainter to the point of extinction. **die back** (of a plant) decay from the tip towards the root. **died and gone to heaven** informal having reached a state of supreme bliss. **die down** become less loud or strong. **die hard** die reluctantly, not without a struggle (*old habits die hard*). **die off 1** die one after another until few or none are left. **2** fade away gradually. **die out** become extinct, cease to exist. **never say die** keep up courage, not give in. **to die for** (predic.) informal extremely good or desirable (*chocolate to die for*).

die² n. **1** sing. of DICE n. 1a. ¶*Dice* is now standard in general use in this sense. **2** (pl. **dies**) **a** an engraved device for stamping a design on coins, medals, etc. **b**

a device for stamping, cutting, or moulding material into a particular shape. **c** an internally threaded hollow tool for cutting a screw thread. □ **as straight** (or **true**) **as a die 1** quite straight. **2** entirely honest or loyal. **the die is cast** an irrevocable step has been taken.

dieback *n.* the progressive dying back of a shrub or tree shoot owing to disease or unfavourable conditions.

die-casting *n.* the process or product of casting from metal moulds. □ **die-cast** *v.tr.*

dieffenbachia /ˌdiːfənˈbækiə/ *n.* any tropical American evergreen plant of the genus *Dieffenbachia*, of the arum family, often grown as a houseplant and having poisonous sap which can cause loss of the power of speech or death.

diehard ● *n.* a conservative or stubborn person. ● *adj.* **1** resolutely opposing change. **2** staunchly loyal (*a diehard fan*).

dieldrin /diˈeldrɪn/ *n.* a crystalline insecticide produced by the oxidation of aldrin.

die-off *n.* a sharp decline in a natural population, due to some factor other than human intervention.

diesel /ˈdiːzəl/ *n.* **1** (in full **diesel engine**) an internal combustion engine in which the heat produced by the compression of air in the cylinder ignites the fuel. **2** a vehicle driven by a diesel engine. **3** = DIESEL FUEL. □ **dieselize** *v.tr.* **dieselization** *n.*

diesel-electric ● *n.* a vehicle driven by the electric current produced by a diesel-engined generator. ● *adj.* of or powered by this means.

diesel fuel *n.* (also **diesel oil**) a heavy petroleum fraction used as fuel in diesel engines.

diet[1] ● *n.* **1** the kinds of food that a person or animal habitually eats. **2** a special course of food to which a person is restricted, esp. for medical reasons or to control weight. **3** a regular occupation or series of activities to which one is restricted or which form one's main concern, usu. for a purpose (*a diet of light reading and fresh air*). ● *v.intr.* (**dieted, dieting**) restrict oneself to small amounts or special kinds of food, esp. to control one's weight. ● *adj.* suitable for consumption by someone on a special (esp. calorie-reduced) diet (*diet pop*). □ **dieter** *n.*

diet[2] *n.* a legislative assembly in certain countries, e.g. Japan.

dietary *adj.* of, relating to, or provided by diet.

dietary fibre *n.* the part of a foodstuff that cannot be digested or absorbed; roughage.

dietetic /ˌdaɪəˈtetɪk/ *adj.* **1** of or relating to diet. **2** (of foodstuffs, etc.) suitable for a specific (esp. calorie-reduced) diet (*dietetic candies*). □ **dietetically** *adv.*

dietetics *n.pl.* (usu. treated as *sing.*) the scientific study of diet and nutrition.

dietitian *n.* (also **dietician**) an expert in dietetics.

diff *n.* N Amer. informal difference (*what's the diff?*).

differ *v.intr.* **1** (often foll. by *from*) be unlike or distinguishable. **2** (often foll. by *with*) disagree; be at variance (with a person). □ **differing** *adj.*

difference *n.* **1** the state or condition of being different or unlike. **2** a point in which things differ; a distinction. **3** a degree of unlikeness. **4 a** the quantity by which amounts differ (*make up the difference*). **b** the remainder left after subtraction. **5 a** a disagreement, quarrel, or dispute. **b** the grounds of disagreement (*put aside their differences*). □ **make a** (or **all the** etc.) **difference** (often foll. by *to*) have a significant effect or influence (on a person, situation, etc.). **make no difference** (often foll. by *to*) have no effect (on a

person, situation, etc.). **with a difference** having a new or unusual feature.

different *adj.* **1** (often foll. by *from, than*) unlike, distinguishable in nature, form, or quality (from another). ¶*Different from* is generally regarded as the most acceptable collocation, but *than* is well established, esp. when followed by a clause, e.g. *I am a different person than I was a year ago*. **2** distinct, separate; not the same one (as another). **3** *informal* unusual (*wanted to do something different*). □ **differently** *adv.* **differentness** *n.*

differential ● *adj.* of, exhibiting, or depending on a difference. ● *n.* **1** a difference between individuals or examples of the same kind. **2** *Math.* **a** an infinitesimal difference between successive values of a variable. **b** a function expressing this as a rate of change with respect to another variable. **3** (in full **differential gear**) a gear allowing power to be divided between two axles in line with one another and able to rotate at different speeds, e.g. when a vehicle corners. □ **differentially** *adv.*

differential calculus *n.* the part of calculus that deals with derivatives and differentiation (*compare* INTEGRAL CALCULUS).

differential equation *n.* an equation involving differentials among its quantities.

differentiate *v.* **1** *tr.* constitute a difference between or in. **2 a** *tr.* find differences (between). **b** *intr.* (often foll. by *between*) find differences; discriminate. **3** *tr.* & *intr.* make or become different in the process of growth or development. **4** *tr. Math.* transform (a function) into its derivative. □ **differentiated** *adj.* **differentiation** *n.* **differentiator** *n.*

differently abled *adj. euphemism* disabled.

difficult *adj.* **1 a** needing much effort or skill. **b** troublesome, perplexing. **2 a** not easy to please or satisfy. **b** uncooperative. **3** characterized by hardships or problems (*a difficult period in her life*).

difficulty *n.* (pl. **-ies**) **1** the state or condition of being difficult. **2 a** a difficult thing. **b** (often in *pl.*) a cause of distress or hardship (*financial difficulties*). □ **make difficulties** be intransigent or unaccommodating. **with difficulty** not easily.

diffident /ˈdɪfɪdənt/ *adj.* **1** shy, lacking self-confidence. **2** hesitant or reserved. □ **diffidence** *n.* **diffidently** *adv.*

diffract /dɪˈfrækt/ *v.tr. Physics* (of the edge of an opaque body, a narrow slit, etc.) break up (a beam of light) into a series of dark or light bands or coloured spectra. □ **diffraction** *n.*

diffuse ● *adj.* /dɪˈfjuːs/ **1** (of light, inflammation, etc.) spread out, diffused, not concentrated. **2** (of prose, speech, etc.) not concise; long-winded, verbose. ● *v.tr. & intr.* /dɪˈfjuːz/ **1** disperse or be dispersed from a centre. **2** spread or be spread widely; reach a large area. **3** *Physics* (esp. of fluids) intermingle by diffusion. □ **diffused** *adj.* **diffusely** *adv.* **diffuseness** *n.* **diffusible** *adj.* **diffusive** /dɪˈfjuːsɪv/ *adj.*

diffuser *n.* (also **diffusor**) **1** a person or thing that diffuses, esp. a device for diffusing light. **2** a duct for broadening an airflow and reducing its speed.

diffusion /dɪˈfjuːʒən/ *n.* **1** the act or an instance of diffusing; the process of being diffused. **2** *Physics* & *Chem.* the interpenetration of substances by the natural movement of their particles. **3** the spread of elements of culture etc. to another region or people.

dig ● *v.* (**digging**; *past* and *past part.* **dug** /dʌg/) **1** *intr.* break up and remove or turn over soil, ground, etc., with a tool, one's hands, (of an animal) claws, etc. **2** *tr.* **a** break up and displace (the ground etc.) in this way.

b (foll. by *up*) break up the soil of (a piece of land) (*dug up the lawn and planted flowers*). **3** *tr.* make (a hole, grave, tunnel, etc.) by digging. **4** *tr.* (often foll. by *up, out*) **a** obtain or remove by digging or by an action similar to digging (*dug the puck out of the corner*). **b** find or discover after searching. **5** *tr. & intr.* excavate (an archaeological site). **6** *tr. dated slang* like, appreciate, or understand. **7** *tr. & intr.* (often foll. by *in, into*) thrust or poke into or down into (*dug its teeth into my leg*). **8** *intr.* make one's way by digging (*dug through the mountainside*). ● *n.* **1** the act or an instance of digging. **2** a thrust or poke (*a dig in the ribs*). **3** *informal* (often foll. by *at*) a pointed or critical remark. **4** an archaeological excavation. **5** (in *pl.*) *informal* lodgings. ☐ **dig deep 1** draw on one's innermost resources (*dug deep to finish the race*). **2** give generously from one's financial resources (*dug deep to help the flood victims*). **dig in one's heels** be obstinate. **dig in** *informal* begin eating. **dig (oneself) in 1** prepare a defensive trench or pit. **2** establish one's position. **dig one's own grave** do something which causes one's own failure or ruin.

Digby chicken *n.* (also **Digby chick**) *Cdn* (*Maritimes*) a dried or cured herring.

digest ● *v.* /dai'dʒest, də-/ **1** *tr. & intr.* assimilate (food) in the stomach and bowels. **2** *intr.* (of food) undergo digestion. **3** *tr.* understand and assimilate mentally. **4** *tr.* **a** reduce to a systematic or convenient form; classify; summarize. **b** think over; arrange in the mind. ● *n.* /'daidʒest/ **1** a regular or occasional synopsis of current literature or news. **2** a methodical summary esp. of a body of laws. ☐ **digester** *n.* **digestible** *adj.* **digestibility** *n.*

digestif /ˌdiːʒes'tiːf/ *n.* something which promotes good digestion, esp. a drink taken after a meal, e.g. a liqueur or brandy.

digestion *n.* **1** the process of digesting. **2** the capacity to digest food (*has weak digestion*).

digestive ● *adj.* **1** of or relating to digestion. **2** aiding or promoting digestion. ● *n.* **1** a substance that aids digestion. **2** (in full **digestive cookie** or **digestive biscuit**) *Cdn & Brit.* a usu. round semi-sweet whole wheat cookie. ☐ **digestively** *adv.*

digger *n.* **1** a person who digs. **2** a tool or machine for digging, e.g. a mechanical excavator. **3** a miner. **4** *N Amer. informal* a person who works diligently, esp. a hockey player etc.

digit *n.* **1** any numeral from 0 to 9, esp. when forming part of a number. **2** each of a series of these representing increasingly higher powers of ten in a decimal-based numeral (*a six-digit income*). **3** a finger, thumb, or toe.

digital ● *adj.* **1** of or relating to a numerical digit or digits. **2** (of a clock, watch, etc.) that gives a reading by means of displayed digits instead of hands. **3 a** (of a computer) operating on data represented as a series of usu. binary digits or in similar discrete form. **b** of or relating to computers (*the digital age*). **4 a** (of a recording) with sound information represented in digits for more reliable transmission. **b** (of a recording medium) using this process. **5** of or relating to a finger or fingers. ● *n.* a digital device, esp. a watch or clock (*bought a digital*). ☐ **digitalize** *v.tr.* **digitally** *adv.*

digital audio tape *n.* magnetic tape on which sound is recorded digitally. Abbr.: **DAT**.

digitalis /ˌdɪdʒɪ'tælɪs/ *n.* a drug prepared from the dried leaves of foxgloves and containing substances that stimulate the heart muscle.

digital to analog converter *n.* a device for converting digital values to analog form.

digitize *v.tr.* convert (data etc.) into digital form. ☐ **digitization** *n.* **digitizer** *n.*

dignified *adj.* **1** having or expressing dignity. **2** noble or stately in appearance or manner. ☐ **dignifiedly** *adv.*

dignify *v.tr.* (**-ies, -ied**) **1** give dignity or distinction to. **2** give a pretentious name to (something unworthy or unimportant) (*it is a misnomer to dignify such works with the term Art*). **3** represent or treat as worthy (*will not dignify you with an answer*).

dignitary /'dɪɡnə.teri/ *n.* (pl. **-ies**) a person holding high rank or office.

dignity *n.* (pl. **-ies**) **1** a composed and serious manner or style. **2** the state of being worthy of honour or respect. **3** worthiness, excellence. **4** a high or honourable rank or position. **5** high regard or estimation. ☐ **beneath one's dignity** not considered worthy enough for one to do. **stand on one's dignity** insist (esp. by one's manner) on being treated with due respect.

digraph /'daigræf/ *n.* a group of two letters representing one sound, as in *ph* and *ey*.

digress /dai'gres/ *v.intr.* depart from the main subject temporarily in speech or writing. ☐ **digresser** *n.* **digression** *n.* **digressive** *adj.* **digressively** *adv.*

digs *n.pl.* see DIG *n.* 5.

Dijon mustard *n.* a mild mustard paste using brown and black varieties of seed blended with white wine.

dike[1] ● *n.* **1** a long wall etc. built to prevent flooding. **2** a ditch or artificial watercourse. **3 a** a low wall, esp. of turf. **b** a causeway. **4** a barrier or obstacle; a defence. ● *v.tr.* provide or defend with a dike or dikes.

dike[2] *var. of* DYKE[2].

dilapidate /dɪ'læpɪ.deit/ *v.intr. & tr.* fall or cause to fall into disrepair or ruin. ☐ **dilapidated** *adj.* **dilapidation** *n.*

dilatation *n.* **1** the widening or expansion of a hollow organ or cavity. **2** the process of dilating.

dilatation and curettage *n.* = D. AND C.

dilate /dai'leit/ *v.* **1** *tr. & intr.* make or become wider or larger (esp. of an opening in the body) (*dilated pupils*). **2** *intr.* (often foll. by *on, upon*) speak or write at length. ☐ **dilatable** *adj.* **dilation** *n.*

dilatory /'dɪlətəri/ *adj.* given to or causing delay. ☐ **dilatorily** *adv.* **dilatoriness** *n.*

dildo *n.* (pl. **-os**) an object shaped like an erect penis and used for sexual stimulation.

dilemma /dɪ'lemə/ *n.* **1** a situation in which a choice has to be made between two equally undesirable alternatives. **2** a state of indecision between two alternatives. **3** a difficult situation. ¶Although some people feel that usage in sense 3 is incorrect, it is widespread and perfectly acceptable.

dilettante /ˌdɪlə'tɒnt, 'dɪlə-, -'tænti/ ● *n.* (pl. **dilettantes** or **dilettanti** /-ti/) **1** a person who studies a subject or area of knowledge superficially. **2** a person who enjoys the arts. ● *adj.* trifling, not thorough; amateurish. ☐ **dilettantism** *n.*

diligence /'dɪlɪdʒəns/ *n.* **1** careful and persistent application or effort. **2** industriousness.

diligent *adj.* **1** careful and steady in application to one's work or duties. **2** showing care and effort. ☐ **diligently** *adv.*

dill *n.* **1** an umbelliferous herb, *Anethum graveolens*, with yellow flowers and aromatic seeds. **2** the leaves or seeds of this plant used for flavouring etc.

dill pickle *n.* a pickled cucumber flavoured with dill.

dillweed *n.* the leaves of the dill plant used as a seasoning.

dilly *n.* (*pl.* **-ies**) esp. *N Amer. informal* a remarkable or excellent person or thing.

dilly-dally *v.intr.* (**-ies, -ied**) *informal* **1** dawdle, loiter. **2** vacillate.

dilute / dai'luːt, dɪ- / ● *v.tr.* **1** reduce the strength of (a fluid) by adding water or another solvent. **2** weaken or reduce the strength or forcefulness of, esp. by adding something. ● *adj.* (also / 'dai-/) **1** (esp. of a fluid) diluted, weakened. **2** (of a colour) washed out; low in saturation. **3** *Chem.* (of a substance) in solution (*dilute sulphuric acid*). □ **diluted** *adj.* **dilution** *n.*

dim ● *adj.* (**dimmer, dimmest**) **1 a** only faintly luminous or visible; not bright. **b** obscure; ill-defined. **2** not clearly perceived or remembered. **3** *informal* stupid; slow to understand. **4** (of the eyes) not seeing clearly. **5** *N Amer.* not likely to succeed or happen (*a dim chance*). ● *v.* (**dimmed, dimming**) **1** *tr. & intr.* make or become dim or less bright. **2** *tr. N Amer.* lower the beam of (a vehicle's headlights) to reduce dazzle. □ **take a dim view of** *informal* **1** disapprove of. **2** feel gloomy about. □ **dimly** *adv.* **dimness** *n.*

dime *n. N Amer.* **1** a ten-cent coin. **2** a small amount of money. □ **a dime a dozen** very cheap or commonplace. **on a dime** *N Amer. informal* **1** within a small area or short distance. **2** quickly, instantly.

dimenhydrinate / ˌdaimen'haidrɪneit / *n.* a medication used to counter nausea and vomiting and prevent motion sickness.

dimension / dɪ'menʃən, dai-/ ● *n.* **1** a measurable extent of any kind, as length, breadth, depth, area, and volume. **2** (in *pl.*) size, scope, extent. **3** an aspect or facet of a situation, problem, etc. **4** *Algebra* one of a number of unknown or variable quantities contained as factors in a product (x^3, x^2y, *xyz*, *are all of three dimensions*). □ **dimensional** *adj.* (also in *comb.*). **dimensionality** *n.* (*pl.* **-ies**). **dimensionally** *adv.* **dimensionless** *adj.*

dimer *n. Chem.* a compound consisting of two identical molecules linked together.

dime store *n. N Amer.* **1** = FIVE-AND-DIME STORE. **2** (**dime-store**) (*attrib.*) **a** bought at a dime store. **b** cheap, of poor quality (*dime-store psychology*).

diminish *v.* **1** *tr. & intr.* make or become smaller or less. **2** *tr.* lessen the reputation or influence of (a person). □ **law of diminishing returns** the fact that an increase in expenditure, investment, taxation, etc., beyond a certain point ceases to produce a proportionate yield. □ **diminishment** *n.*

diminished *adj.* reduced; made smaller or less.

diminuendo / dɪˌmɪnju:'endo: / *Music* ● *n.* (*pl.* **-os**) **1** a gradual decrease in loudness. **2** a passage to be performed with such a decrease. ● *adv. & adj.* with a gradual decrease in loudness.

diminution / ˌdɪmɪ'nju:ʃən / *n.* **1** the act or an instance of diminishing. **2** the amount by which something diminishes.

diminutive / dɪ'mɪnjʊtɪv / ● *adj.* **1** remarkably small; tiny. **2** *Grammar* (of a word or suffix) implying smallness, either actual or imputed in token of affection, scorn, etc. (e.g. *-let, -kins*). ● *n.* a diminutive word or suffix. □ **diminutiveness** *n.*

dimmer *n.* (in full **dimmer switch**) a device for varying the brightness of an electric light.

dimorphic / dai'mɔːfɪk / *adj.* (also **dimorphous** / dai'mɔːfəs /) *Biol., Chem.,* & *Geol.* exhibiting, or occurring in, two distinct forms. □ **dimorphism** *n.*

dimple ● *n.* **1** a small hollow or dent in the flesh, esp. in the cheeks or chin. **2** a round depression, e.g. in a golf ball. ● *v.* **1** *intr.* produce or show dimples. **2** *tr.* produce dimples in (a cheek etc.). **3** *tr.* make a dent or depression in (a piece of sheet metal, the surface of a body of water, etc.). □ **dimpled** *adj.* **dimply** *adj.*

dim sum / dɪm 'sʌm / *n.* an assortment of small Chinese dumplings with various savoury fillings.

dim-wit *n. informal* a stupid person. □ **dim-witted** *adj.*

din ● *n.* a prolonged loud and distracting noise. ● *v.* (**dinned, dinning**) **1** *tr.* (foll. by *into*) instill (something) by constant repetition. **2** *intr.* make a din.

dinar / 'di:nɑr / *n.* **1** a monetary unit of Yugoslavia and Bosnia-Herzegovina. **2** the chief monetary unit of certain countries of the Middle East and N Africa.

dine *v.* **1** *intr.* eat dinner. **2** *tr.* give dinner to. □ **dine out 1** dine away from home. **2** (foll. by *on*) be entertained to dinner etc. on account of (one's ability to relate an interesting event, story, etc.). □ **dining** *n.*

diner *n.* **1** a person who dines, esp. in a restaurant serving short-order food. **2** *N Amer.* a small restaurant. **3** = DINING CAR.

dinette / dai'net / *n.* **1** a small room or part of a room used for eating meals. **2** *N Amer.* a set of a table and chairs for this.

ding[1] ● *v.intr.* make a ringing sound. ● *n.* a ringing sound, as of a bell.

ding[2] *N Amer. informal* ● *n.* a dent (*has a ding in the fender*). ● *v.tr.* **1** make a dent in (*dinged my car*). **2** hit. **3** charge (esp. an excessive amount).

ding-a-ling ● *n.* **1** the sound of a bell or bells. **2** *N Amer. informal* a crazy or stupid person (*he's a real ding-a-ling*). ● *adj.* crazy, eccentric (*what a ding-a-ling idea*).

dingbat *n. informal N Amer.* & *Austral.* a stupid or eccentric person.

ding-dong ● *n.* **1** the sound of alternate chimes, as of two bells. **2** *N Amer.* a crazy or stupid person. ● *adj.* crazy (*a ding-dong idea*).

dinger *n. Baseball slang* a home run.

dinghy / 'dɪŋi, 'dɪŋgi / *n.* (*pl.* **-ies**) any of various small boats, esp. an inflatable boat for emergency use.

dingo *n.* (*pl.* **-oes**) a wild or half-domesticated Australian dog, *Canis dingo*.

dingy / 'dɪndʒi / *adj.* (**-ier, -iest**) **1** dirty-looking. **2** drab, dull-coloured. **3** not bright; lacking light. □ **dingily** *adv.* **dinginess** *n.*

dining car *n.* a railway car equipped as a restaurant.

dining hall *n.* a hall in which meals are eaten.

dining room *n.* a room in which meals are eaten.

dining table *n.* (also **dining-room table**) a table on which meals are served or eaten.

dink[1] *n. N Amer. slang* **1** the penis. **2** a foolish, stupid, or obnoxious person.

dink[2] *n.* (also **dinky**; *pl.* **-ies**) *slang* **1** a well-off young working couple with no children. **2** either partner of this.

dinky *adj.* (**-ier, -iest**) *informal N Amer.* trifling, insignificant.

dinner *n.* **1** the main meal of the day. **2** a formal meal, often in honour of a person or event. □ **done like dinner** *Cdn* & *Austral. informal* utterly defeated.

dinner guest *n.* a person invited to dinner as a guest.

dinner jacket *n.* a man's short usu. black formal jacket for evening wear. □ **dinner-jacketed** *adj.*

dinner party *n.* a party to which guests are invited to eat dinner together.

dinner plate *n.* a large plate used for eating the main course of a dinner.

dinner theatre *n. N Amer.* **1** a theatre in which dinner, included in the price of the ticket, is served usu. before the performance. **2** the type of theatre performed in such a place.

dinnertime *n.* the time at which dinner is customarily eaten.

dinnerware *n.* dishes used for eating from, e.g. plates, bowls, etc.

dino /'daino:/ *n.* (*pl.* **-os**) *informal* a dinosaur (also *attrib.*).

dinoflagellate /daino:'fladʒəleit/ *n.* a unicellular aquatic organism with two flagella, of a group variously classed as algae and protozoa.

dinosaur *n.* **1** an extinct reptile of the Mesozoic era, often of enormous size. **2 a** a person or thing that has not adapted to new conditions. **b** a person or thing that is large or unwieldy.

dint ● *n.* a dent. ● *v.tr.* mark with dints. □ **by dint of** by force or means of.

diocesan /dai'bsIsən, -zən/ ● *adj.* of or concerning a diocese. ● *n.* the bishop of a diocese.

diocese /'daiəsi:s/ *n.* a district under the pastoral care of a bishop.

diode /'daio:d/ *n.* *Electronics* **1** a semiconductor allowing the flow of current in one direction only and having two terminals. **2** a thermionic valve having two electrodes.

Dionysiac /ˌdaiə'ni:si͵æk/ *adj.* (also **Dionysian**) wildly sensual; unrestrained.

diorama /ˌdaiə'ræmə/ *n.* **1** a scenic painting in which changes in colour and direction of illumination simulate a sunrise etc. **2** a representation of a scene with three-dimensional figures, often against a painted background. **3** a small-scale model or film set.

dioxide /dai'ɒksaid/ *n.* *Chem.* an oxide containing two atoms of oxygen which are not linked together.

dioxin *n.* *Chem.* any of a class of cyclic compounds produced as chemical by-products, esp. the highly toxic tetrachlorodibenzoparadioxin (TCDD).

DIP /dɪp/ *n.* a form of integrated circuit consisting of a small plastic or ceramic slab with two parallel rows of pins.

dip ● *v.* (**dipped, dipping**) **1** *tr.* put or let down briefly into liquid etc.; immerse. **2** *intr.* **a** go below a surface or level. **b** (of a level of income, activity, etc.) decline slightly, esp. briefly. **3** *intr.* take or have a downward slope (*the road dips*). **4** *intr.* go under water and emerge quickly. **5** *intr.* (foll. by *into*) **a** read briefly from (a book etc.). **b** take a cursory interest in (a subject). **6** (foll. by *into*) **a** *intr.* put a hand, ladle, etc., into a container to take something out. **b** *tr.* put (a hand etc.) into a container, pocket, etc. to do this. **c** *intr.* spend from or make use of one's resources (*dipped into our savings*). **7** *tr. & intr.* lower or be lowered, esp. in salute. **8** *tr.* (often foll. by *up, out of*) remove or scoop up (liquid, grain, etc., or something from liquid). ● *n.* **1** an act of dipping or being dipped. **2** a liquid into which something is dipped. **3** a brief swim. **4** a brief downward slope, followed by an upward one, in a road etc. **5** a usu. thick sauce into which food is dipped before eating. **6** *N Amer.* an item of food, esp. a sandwich, served with a dipping sauce (*beef dip*). **7** *N Amer.* an ice cream cone dipped in melted chocolate etc. **8** a depression or hollow. **9** *Astronomy & Surveying* the apparent depression of the horizon from the line of observation, due to the curvature of the earth. **10 a** the angle made with the horizontal at any point by the earth's magnetic field. **b** the downward inclination of a magnetic needle. **11** *N Amer. slang* a foolish or bumbling person.

diphtheria /dɪf'θi:riə, dɪp-/ *n.* an acute infectious bacterial disease with inflammation of a mucous membrane esp. of the throat, resulting in the formation of a false membrane causing difficulty in breathing and swallowing.

diphthong /'dɪfθɒŋ, dɪp-/ *n.* **1** a speech sound in one syllable in which the articulation begins as for one vowel and moves as for another (as in *coin*, *loud*, and *side*). **2 a** a digraph representing the sound of a diphthong or single vowel (as in *feat*). **b** a compound vowel character; a ligature (as *æ*).

Dipl. *abbr.* Diploma.

diploid /'dɪplɔid/ *Biol.* ● *adj.* (of an organism or cell) having two complete sets of chromosomes per cell. ● *n.* a diploid cell or organism.

diploma *n.* **1** a certificate awarded for passing an examination, completing a course of study, etc. **2** the qualification conferred with a diploma.

diplomacy *n.* **1 a** the management of international relations by negotiation. **b** expertise in this. **2** skill or tact in dealing with people etc.

diplomat *n.* **1** a person engaged by a government to conduct official negotiations with other countries; a member of a diplomatic service. **2** a tactful person.

diplomatic *adj.* **1 a** of or involved in diplomacy. **b** skilled in diplomacy. **2** tactful; skilful in personal relations. □ **diplomatically** *adv.*

diplomatic corps *n.* the body of diplomats representing other countries at a seat of government.

diplomatic immunity *n.* the exemption of diplomatic staff abroad from arrest, taxation, etc.

diplomatic recognition *n.* see RECOGNITION 5.

diplomatic service *n.* the branch of a national government concerned with the official representation of a country abroad.

dipole /'daipo:l/ *n.* **1** *Physics* two equal and oppositely charged or magnetized poles separated by a distance. **2** *Chem.* a molecule in which a concentration of positive charges is separated from a concentration of negative charges. **3** (also **dipole antenna**) an antenna composed of two equal straight rods mounted in line with one another and having an electrical connection in the centre. □ **dipolar** *adj.*

dipper *n.* **1** any of several stocky short-tailed songbirds constituting the genus *Cinclus* and family Cinclidae, which habitually bob up and down, frequent fast-flowing streams, and swim and walk under water to feed, esp. *C. mexicanus* of western N America, or *C. cinclus* of Eurasia. **2** a ladle. **3** *N Amer.* an item of food suitable for dipping, e.g. a potato chip, a raw vegetable, etc. **4** *Cdn* (*Nfld & PEI*) a small, lidless saucepan with a long handle.

dippy *adj.* (**-ier, -iest**) *informal* foolish or unintelligent.

dipstick *n.* **1** a graduated rod for measuring the depth of a liquid, esp. in a vehicle's engine. **2** a chemically sensitive stick or strip of paper etc. dipped into a liquid (esp. a urine sample) for diagnostic purposes. **3** *slang* a foolish or inept person; an idiot.

dipsy-doodle esp. *Cdn slang* ● *v.intr.* esp. *Hockey* evade the defending team by using feints, dekes, swerving motions, and finesse in stickhandling etc. ● *n.* **1** an evasive movement of this type. **2** a tactic designed to confuse, evade, or outwit opponents or competitors.

dipterous /'dɪptərəs/ *adj.* **1** of or relating to the insect order Diptera, whose members have two membranous wings, the hindwings being reduced to balancing organs, e.g. houseflies, mosquitoes, etc. **2** *Bot.* having two wing-like appendages.

dire *adj.* **1 a** calamitous, dreadful (*in dire straits*). **b** ominous (*dire warnings*). **2** urgent (*in dire need*).

direct /dɪ'rekt, dai-/ ● *adj.* **1 a** extending or moving in a straight line or by the shortest route; not crooked or circuitous. **b** (of a journey) not involving any changes of airplane, train, etc. **2 a** straightforward; going straight to the point. **b** frank; not ambiguous. **3**

without intermediaries or the intervention of other factors (*the direct result*; *direct sunlight*). **4** (of descent) lineal, not collateral. **5** exact, complete, greatest possible (esp. where contrast is implied) (*the direct opposite*). **6** (of a quotation, translation, etc.) literal; word for word. ● *adv.* **1** in a direct way or manner; without an intermediary or intervening factor (*buy direct from the manufacturer*). **2** by a direct route (*send it direct to head office*). ● *v.* **1** *tr.* guide, esp. with advice. **2** *tr.* control the movement of (*directing traffic*). **3** *tr.* administer, oversee. **4** *tr.* (foll. by *to* + infin., or *that* + clause) give a formal order or command to. **5** *tr.* (foll. by *to*) **a** address or give indications for the delivery of (a letter etc.). **b** tell or show (a person) the way to a destination. **6** *tr.* (foll. by *at*, *to*, *towards*) **a** point, aim, or cause (a blow or missile) to move in a certain direction. **b** aim or address (one's attention, energies, communication, etc.). **7 a** *tr.* & *intr.* supervise the performing, staging, etc., of (a film, play, etc.). **b** *tr.* supervise the performance of (an actor etc.). **8** *tr.* & *intr.* Music **a** conduct (a group of musicians, esp. singers). **b** guide the performance of (a group of musicians), esp. while performing oneself. □ **directness** *n.*

direct access *n.* = RANDOM ACCESS.

direct action *n.* action such as a strike or sabotage directly affecting the community and meant to reinforce demands on a government, employer, etc.

direct current *n.* an electric current flowing in one direction only. Abbr.: **DC**, **d.c.**

direct debit *n.* *Cdn* & *Brit.* an arrangement, authorized by the holder of an account in a bank etc., for the regular debiting of the account at the request of the payee.

direct deposit *n.* *N Amer.* the electronic transfer of money from one bank account to another.

direct dialing *n.* the facility of dialling a long-distance telephone number without making use of the operator. □ **direct-dial** *v.intr.* & *tr.* & *attrib.adj.*

direction *n.* **1** the act or process of directing. **2** (usu. in *pl.*) an order or instruction, esp. each of a set guiding use of equipment etc. **3 a** the course or line along which a person or thing moves or looks, or which must be taken to reach a destination. **b** (in *pl.*) guidance on how to reach a destination. **c** the point to or from which a person or thing moves or looks. **4** the tendency taken by events, research, etc. □ **sense of direction** the ability to know without guidance the direction in which one is or should be moving. □ **directionless** *adj.*

directional *adj.* **1** of or indicating direction. **2** *Electronics* **a** concerned with the transmission of radio or sound waves in a particular direction. **b** (of equipment) designed to receive radio or sound waves most effectively from a particular direction or directions and not others. □ **directionally** *adv.*

direction finder *n.* a device for determining the source of radio waves, esp. as an aid in navigation.

direct payment *n.* payment by means of a debit card, in which funds are transferred electronically from the cardholder's bank account to the account of a merchant etc.

directive ● *n.* a general instruction from an authority. ● *adj.* serving to direct.

directly *adv.* **1** without delay. **b** presently, shortly. **2** exactly (*directly opposite*). **3** in a direct manner.

direct mail *n.* advertising material sent unsolicited through the mail to usu. large numbers of prospective customers or donors. □ **direct mailing** *n.*

direct marketing *n.* selling goods or services by dealing directly with consumers rather than through retailers. □ **direct marketer** *n.*

direct object *n.* the primary object of the action of a transitive verb.

director *n.* **1** a person who directs, controls, or manages something, esp. an institution or a major division of a company. **2** a member of the board which governs the affairs of a company etc. **3** a person who directs a film etc., esp. professionally. **4** a conductor, esp. of a choir or band etc. of which the director is a performing instrumentalist. **5** (in Quebec municipal police forces) the highest ranking officer. □ **directorial** *adj.* **directorship** *n.* (esp. in sense 2).

directorate /dɪˈrektərət, daɪ-/ *n.* **1** a government agency or subdivision of a ministry with a specific responsibility. **2** a board of directors. **3** the office of director.

director general *n.* (*pl.* **directors general**) **1** the chief executive of an organization, especially a public one. **2** *Cdn* **a** a rank in the civil service immediately below assistant deputy minister. **b** a person holding this rank. **3** (in the SQ) the highest ranking officer.

directory *n.* (*pl.* **-ies**) **1 a** a book listing alphabetically or thematically a particular group of individuals (e.g. telephone subscribers) or organizations with various details. **b** *N Amer.* a large board listing names of departments, individuals, etc. and giving their location, esp. in a building complex, department store, etc. **2** a computer file listing other files or programs etc.

direct proportion *n.* a relation between quantities whose ratio is constant.

direct speech *n.* words actually spoken, not reported in the third person.

direct tax *n.* a tax paid directly to the government, e.g. income tax or property tax.

dirge /dɜrdʒ/ *n.* **1** a lament for the dead, esp. as part of a funeral service. **2** any mournful song or lament.

dirigible /ˈdɪrɪdʒɪbəl, dɪˈrɪdʒ-/ ● *n.* an airship. ● *adj.* capable of being steered or guided.

dirt *n.* **1** unclean matter that soils. **2 a** earth, soil. **b** earth, gravel, etc., used to make a surface for a road etc. (usu. *attrib.*: *dirt road*). **3 a** obscene or foul language. **b** information, especially of a scandalous nature; gossip. **4** excrement (*dog dirt*). **5** a person or thing considered worthless. □ **do a person dirt** *slang* harm or injure a person's reputation maliciously. **eat dirt** suffer insults, humiliation, etc. without retaliating. **hit the dirt** *N Amer.* **1** drop to the floor, ground, etc. **2** *Baseball slang* slide into base. **treat like dirt** treat (a person) contemptuously; abuse.

dirt bike *n.* a motorcycle designed for use on dirt roads and in cross-country racing.

dirt cheap *adj.* & *adv.* informal extremely cheap.

dirt poor *adj.* very poor.

dirt road *n.* *N Amer.* a road of packed earth, gravel, etc. with an unsealed surface.

dirt track *n.* **1** a rudimentary road or trail made of packed earth. **2** a course made of rolled gravel, soil, etc., for motorcycle racing or horse racing.

dirty ● *adj.* (**-ier**, **-iest**) **1** soiled, unclean. **2** causing one to become dirty; producing dirt (*a dirty job*). **3** pertaining to or obsessed with sexual activity; obscene (*dirty joke*; *dirty mind*). **4** unpleasant, nasty. **5** dishonest, dishonourable, unfair (*dirty play*). **6** (of weather) rough, squally. **7** (of a colour) not pure or clear, dingy. ● *adv.* informal in a malicious, unfair, or underhanded manner (*fight dirty*). ● *v.tr.* & *intr.* (**-ies**, **-ied**) make or become dirty. □ **dirty one's hands** (or

get one's hands dirty) *informal* acquire practical experience, esp. as opposed to theoretical knowledge. **do the dirty on** *informal* play a mean trick on. **talk dirty** *informal* use obscene language. □ **dirtily** *adv.* **dirtiness** *n.*

dirty laundry *n.* (also **dirty linen**) intimate secrets, esp. of a scandalous nature. □ **wash** (or **air**) **one's dirty laundry** (or **linen**) **in public** be indiscreet about one's domestic quarrels etc.

dirty look *n. informal* a look of disapproval, disgust, etc.

dirty thirties *n.* esp. *Cdn informal* **1** the Great Depression of the 1930s. **2** the years of drought coinciding with this on the Prairies.

dirty trick *n.* **1** a spiteful and underhanded act. **2** (in *pl.*) underhanded political activity, esp. to discredit an opponent. □ **dirty-trickster** *n.*

dirty word *n.* **1** an offensive or indecent word. **2** a word for something which is disapproved of.

dirty work *n.* unpleasant, difficult, or illegal activity.

dis / dɪs / *US slang* • *v.tr.* (**dissed**, **dissing**) put (a person etc.) down; bad-mouth. • *n.* a disrespectful attitude.

disability *n.* (*pl.* **-ies**) **1 a** a physical or mental handicap, either congenital or caused by injury, disease, etc. **b** the condition of having such a handicap. **2** a lack of some asset, quality, or attribute, that prevents one's doing something. **3** incapacity created or recognized by the law.

disable *v.tr.* **1** render unable to function. **2** deprive of an ability. □ **disablement** *n.*

disabled *adj.* **1** having reduced physical or mental abilities, esp. through injury or disease. **2** for the use of people with physical disabilities (*disabled parking space*). **3** made incapable of action or use.

disabled list *n. Baseball* a list of injured players who are unable to play, usu. for a specified length of time.

disabuse / dɪsəˈbjuːz / *v.tr.* **1** (foll. by *of*) free from a mistaken idea. **2** disillusion.

disaccharide / daɪˈsækəraɪd / *n. Chem.* a sugar whose molecule contains two linked monosaccharides.

disadvantage • *n.* **1** an unfavourable circumstance or condition. **2** damage to one's interest or reputation. • *v.tr.* cause disadvantage to. □ **at a disadvantage** in an unfavourable position or aspect.

disadvantaged *adj.* suffering from social or economic deprivation or discrimination.

disadvantageous *adj.* involving disadvantage or discredit. □ **disadvantageously** *adv.*

disaffected *adj.* **1** alienated and discontented, esp. with regard to authority. **2** disloyal. □ **disaffectedly** *adv.*

disaffection *n.* **1** discontentedness, esp. with political or social structures. **2** disloyalty. **3** (usu. foll. by *with*) disenchantment; loss of affection or respect.

disaggregate *v.tr.* separate into component parts; cease to treat as aggregated. □ **disaggregation** *n.*

disagree *v.intr.* (**-agrees**, **-agreed**, **-agreeing**) (often foll. by *with*) **1** hold a different opinion. **2** quarrel. **3** (of factors or circumstances) not correspond. **4** have an adverse effect upon (a person's health, digestion, etc.). □ **disagreement** *n.*

disagreeable *adj.* **1** unpleasant, not to one's liking. **2** quarrelsome. □ **disagreeably** *adv.*

disallow *v.tr.* **1** refuse to allow or accept as valid; prohibit. **2** annul (a statute) passed by a lower legislative body. □ **disallowance** *n.*

disappear *v.intr.* **1** cease to be visible; pass from sight.

2 cease to exist or be in circulation or use. **3** (of a person or thing) go missing. □ **disappearance** *n.*

disappoint *v.* **1 a** *tr.* fail to fulfill a desire or expectation of (a person). **b** *intr.* fail to live up to expectations. **2** *tr.* frustrate (hopes etc.). □ **disappointing** *adj.* **disappointingly** *adv.*

disappointed *adj.* frustrated or saddened by not having one's expectation etc. fulfilled in some regard (*disappointed with you*). □ **disappointedly** *adv.*

disappointment *n.* **1** an event, thing, or person that disappoints. **2** a feeling of distress, vexation, etc., resulting from this.

disapprove *v.* **1** *intr.* (usu. foll. by *of*) have or express an unfavourable opinion. **2** *tr.* withhold approval from; express disfavour of. □ **disapproval** *n.* **disapproving** *adj.* **disapprovingly** *adv.*

disarm *v.* **1** *tr.* deprive of a weapon or weapons. **2 a** *intr.* (of a nation) reduce the size, armament, etc. of one's armed forces. **b** *tr.* cause (a nation) to do this. **3** *tr.* remove the fuse from (a bomb etc.). **4** *tr.* deprive of the power to injure. **5** *tr.* pacify or allay the hostility or suspicions of; mollify; placate. **6** *tr.* deactivate (an alarm system etc.). □ **disarmer** *n.*

disarmament *n.* the reduction by a nation of its military forces and weapons.

disarming *adj.* reducing suspicion, anger, hostility, distrust, etc. (*a disarming smile*). □ **disarmingly** *adv.*

disarrange *v.tr.* bring into disorder.

disarray *n.* (often prec. by *in*, *into*) deprive, confusion.

disassemble *v.tr.* take (a machine etc.) to pieces. □ **disassembly** *n.*

disassembler *n. Computing* a program for converting machine code into assembly language.

disassociate *v.tr.* & *intr.* = DISSOCIATE. □ **disassociation** *n.*

disaster *n.* **1** a great or sudden misfortune. **2 a** a complete failure. **b** a person or enterprise ending in failure. □ **disastrous** *adj.* **disastrously** *adv.*

disaster area *n.* **1 a** an area affected by a natural disaster, e.g. flooding etc. **b** *US* such an area that is officially declared eligible for emergency relief funds and services from the government. **2** a place characterized by extreme disorderliness or misfortune.

disavow / dɪsəˈvaʊ / *v.tr.* disclaim knowledge of, responsibility or support for, or belief in. □ **disavowal** *n.*

disband *v.* **1** *tr.* break up the organization of (a group etc.). **2** *intr.* cease to work or act together; disperse.

disbar *v.tr.* (**disbarred**, **disbarring**) deprive (a lawyer) of the right to practise. □ **disbarment** *n.*

disbelief *n.* **1** lack of belief. **2** astonishment.

disbelieve *v.* **1** *tr.* be unable or unwilling to believe (a person or statement). **2** *intr.* have no faith. □ **disbeliever** *n.* **disbelievingly** *adv.*

disburse / dɪsˈbɜːrs / *v.tr.* expend (money). □ **disbursal** *n.* **disbursement** *n.* **disburser** *n.*

disc *n.* (also **disk**) **1 a** a flat thin circular object. **b** a round flat or apparently flat surface. **2** (in full **intervertebral disc**) a layer of cartilage between vertebrae. **3** a sound or video recording in the form of a disc. **4** the close-packed cluster of tubular florets in the centre of a composite flower. **5** *var. of* DISK *n.*

discard • *v.* **1** *tr.* reject or get rid of as unwanted or superfluous. **2 a** *tr.* remove or put aside (a playing card) from one's hand. **b** *tr.* play (a card) from a remaining suit when not following suit or trumping. **c** *intr.* discard a playing card. • *n.* **1** a rejected or abandoned item or person. **2** a discarded playing card.

disc brake *n.* a brake employing the friction of pads against a disc which is attached to the wheel.

discern /dɪˈsɜrn/ *v.tr.* **1** perceive through the senses, esp. by sight. **2** recognize or detect (*failed to discern her potential*). □ **discernible** *adj.* **discernibly** *adv.*

discerning *adj.* having or showing good judgment, taste, or insight. □ **discerningly** *adv.*

discernment *n.* **1** good judgment or insight. **2** the act or an instance of discerning.

discharge ● *v.* **1** *tr.* **a** let go, release, esp. from a duty, commitment, or period of confinement. **b** relieve (a bankrupt) of residual liability. **2** *tr.* dismiss from office, employment, etc. **3** *tr.* **a** fire (a gun etc.). **b** (of a gun etc.) fire (a bullet etc.). **4 a** *tr. & intr.* pour out or cause to pour out; emit (pus, liquid, etc.). **b** *intr.* (foll. by *into*) (of a river etc.) flow into (esp. a large body of water). **5** *tr.* **a** carry out, perform (a duty or obligation). **b** relieve oneself of (a financial commitment). **6** *tr. Physics* release an electrical charge from. **7** *tr.* **a** remove cargo from (a ship etc.). **b** unload (a cargo) from a ship. ● *n.* **1** the act or an instance of discharging; the process of being discharged. **2** a dismissal, esp. from the armed services. **3 a** a release, exemption, acquittal, etc. **b** a written certificate of release etc. **4** an act of firing a gun etc. **5 a** an emission (of pus, liquid, etc.). **b** the liquid or matter so discharged. **6** (usu. foll. by *of*) **a** the payment (of a debt). **b** the performance (of a duty etc.). **7** *Physics* **a** the release of a quantity of electric charge from an object. **b** a flow of electricity through the air or other gas esp. when accompanied by the emission of light. **c** the conversion of chemical energy in a cell into electrical energy.

disciple /dɪˈsaɪpəl/ *n.* **1** a follower or pupil of a leader, philosophy, etc. **2 a** one of the personal followers of Jesus during his lifetime, esp. one of the Apostles. **b** a professed Christian. □ **discipleship** *n.*

disciplinarian *n.* a person who practises or upholds firm discipline (*a strict disciplinarian*).

disciplinary *adj.* of, promoting, or enforcing discipline.

discipline ● *n.* **1 a** training, esp. of the mind and character, aimed at producing self-control, obedience, orderly conduct, etc. **b** the result of such training; ordered behaviour, e.g. of schoolchildren, soldiers, etc. (*poor discipline in the ranks*). **2** a system of rules used to maintain control over people, e.g. prisoners, military personnel, etc. **3** a branch of instruction or learning (*the scientific disciplines*). **4** punishment. ● *v.tr.* **1** punish, reprimand. **2** train to be obedient, self-controlled, skilful, etc.

disc jockey *n.* a person who introduces and plays recorded music on a radio program, at a dance, etc.

disclaim *v.tr.* deny or disown (*disclaim responsibility*).

disclaimer *n.* **1** a renunciation or disavowal, esp. of responsibility. **2** *Law* an act of repudiating another's claim or renouncing one's own.

disclose *v.tr.* **1** make known; reveal (*disclosed the truth*). **2** expose to view. □ **discloser** *n.*

disclosure *n.* **1** the act or an instance of disclosing; the process of being disclosed. **2** a revelation.

disc number *n. Cdn hist.* a number used in an identification system introduced in 1940 by the federal government in order to identify individual Inuit.

disco *informal* ● *n.* (*pl.* **-os**) **1** a place or event at which recorded popular music is played for dancing, often with elaborate lighting and other special effects. **2** = DISCO MUSIC. ● *v.intr.* (**-oes, -oed**) dance to disco music.

discography /dɪsˈkɒɡrəfi/ *n.* (*pl.* **-ies**) **1** a descriptive catalogue of sound recordings, esp. of a particular performer or composer. **2** a musician's recordings considered collectively. □ **discographer** *n.* **discographical** *adj.*

discolour *v.tr. & intr.* (also **discolor**) spoil or cause to spoil the colour of; stain; tarnish. □ **discoloration** *n.* (also **discolouration**).

discombobulate /ˌdɪskəmˈbɒbjʊˌleɪt/ *v.tr. N Amer. jocular* disturb; disconcert. □ **discombobulation** *n.*

discomfit /dɪsˈkʌmfɪt/ *v.tr.* (**discomfited, discomfiting**) disconcert, embarrass, or throw into confusion. □ **discomfiture** *n.*

discomfort ● *n.* **1 a** a lack of ease; slight pain. **b** mental uneasiness (*she felt some discomfort about taking drugs*). **2** a lack of comfort. ● *v.tr.* make uneasy, disturb.

discompose *v.tr.* disturb the composure of; agitate; disturb. □ **discomposure** *n.*

disco music *n.* a style of dance music characterized by a strong, repetitive rhythm, and the use of electronic instrumentation, popular esp. in the 1970s.

disconcert /ˌdɪskənˈsɜrt/ *v.tr.* (esp. in *passive*) disturb the composure of; agitate; fluster (*disconcerted by his expression*). □ **disconcertedly** *adv.* **disconcerting** *adj.* **disconcertingly** *adv.*

disconnect ● *v.* **1 a** *tr.* detach or separate something connected (*disconnected my phone; disconnect the hose*). **b** *intr.* become detached. **2** *tr.* detach (a customer) from a network of services, e.g. telephone, cable television, electricity, etc. **3** *tr.* interrupt (a telephone connection) (*I was on hold and then disconnected*). **4** *tr.* (usu. in *passive*; often foll. by *from*) break a connection between (people, actions, etc.). ● *n.* an act or instance of disconnecting. □ **disconnection** *n.*

disconnected *adj.* **1** (of speech, writing, argument, etc.) incoherent and illogical. **2** not connected. □ **disconnectedly** *adv.* **disconnectedness** *n.*

disconsolate /dɪsˈkɒnsələt/ *adj.* **1** without consolation or comfort; unhappy. **2** (of a place, thing, etc.) causing or showing a complete lack of comfort; cheerless, miserable. □ **disconsolately** *adv.*

discontent ● *n.* lack of contentment; dissatisfaction. ● *adj.* dissatisfied.

discontented *adj.* dissatisfied. □ **discontentedly** *adv.* **discontentedness** *n.*

discontinue *v.* (**-continues, -continued, -continuing**) **1** *intr. & tr.* cease or cause to cease to exist or be made (*that model has been discontinued*). **2** *tr.* give up, cease from (*the doctor recommended discontinuing antidepressants*). **3** *tr.* cease subscribing to or paying for (a newspaper, service, etc.). □ **discontinuance** *n.* **discontinuation** *n.*

discontinuous *adj.* lacking continuity in space or time; intermittent. □ **discontinuity** *n.* (*pl.* **-ies**) **discontinuously** *adv.*

discord *n.* **1** disagreement; strife. **2** a harsh or unpleasing clashing of sounds; a confused noise. **3** *Music* **a** a lack of harmony between notes sounding together. **b** an unpleasing or unfinished chord needing to be completed by another. **c** any interval except unison, an octave, a perfect fifth and fourth, a major and minor third and sixth, and their octaves. **d** a single note dissonant with another.

discordant /dɪsˈkɔrdənt/ *adj.* **1** not in accord; incongruous. **2** (of sounds) not in harmony; dissonant. □ **discordance** *n.* **discordancy** *n.* **discordantly** *adv.*

discotheque /ˈdɪskəˌtek/ *n.* = DISCO 1.

discount ● *n.* **1** a deduction from a bill or amount due given esp. for prompt or advance payment or to a special category of buyers. **2** a deduction from the face value of a bond, treasury bill, promissory note, or other bill of exchange when it is purchased before its maturity date. ● *v.tr.* **1** disregard as being unreliable or unimportant (*discounted his story*). **2 a** detract from; lessen; deduct (esp. an amount from a bill etc.). **b** reduce in price. **3** buy or sell (a bill of exchange before its maturity date) at a price less than its face value. ● *adj.* **1** selling goods at less than the normal retail price (*discount store*). **2** sold at less than the normal retail price (*discount fares*). ☐ **at a discount** below the nominal or usual price (compare PREMIUM). ☐ **discountable** *adj.* **discounter** *n.*

discount rate *n.* esp. *US* the interest rate set by the central bank on short-term loans to banks etc. *Compare* BANK RATE.

discourage *v.tr.* **1** deprive of courage, confidence, or enthusiasm. **2** (usu. foll. by *from*) dissuade (*discouraged him from going*). **3** oppose or deter (*the police presence is designed to discourage drug use*). ☐ **discouragement** *n.* **discouraging** *adj.* **discouragingly** *adv.*

discourse ● *n.* **1** conversation; talk. **2** a formal discussion of a subject in speech or writing. **3** the body of statements, analysis, etc., both written and spoken, concerning a specific subject, esp. as typified by recurring terms and concepts (*feminist discourse*). ● *v.* **1** *intr.* talk; converse. **2** *intr.* (usu. foll. by *of*, *on*, *upon*) speak or write learnedly or at length (on a subject).

discourteous *adj.* impolite; rude. ☐ **discourteously** *adv.* **discourteousness** *n.*

discourtesy *n.* (pl. **-ies**) **1** bad manners; rudeness. **2** an impolite act or remark.

discover *v.tr.* **1 a** find out or become aware of, whether by research or searching or by chance (*discovered a new entrance*). **b** be the first to find or find out (*discovered insulin*). ¶The use of the words *discover* and *discovery* in reference to Europeans' first contact with Aboriginal peoples in other continents is widely considered to be offensive to Aboriginal peoples. **2** (in show business) find and promote as a new singer, actor, etc. ☐ **discoverable** *adj.* **discoverer** *n.*

discovery *n.* (pl. **-ies**) **1 a** the act or process of discovering or being discovered. **b** an instance of this. **2** a person or thing discovered. **3** *Law* the compulsory disclosure, by a party to an action, of facts etc. on which the other party wishes to rely.

Discovery Day *n.* (in the Yukon) a statutory holiday observed on the third Monday in August, commemorating the discovery of gold in the Klondike on August 17, 1896.

discovery well *n.* the first productive well drilled in an oil exploration area.

discredit ● *n.* **1** harm to reputation (*brought discredit on the enterprise*). **2** a person or thing causing such harm (*he is a discredit to his family*). **3** lack of credibility or doubt (*has fallen into discredit*). ● *v.tr.* (**-credited**, **-crediting**) **1** harm the good reputation of. **2** take away the credibility of or destroy confidence in (an effort, a person, etc.). ☐ **discredited** *adj.*

discreditable *adj.* shameful; bringing discredit. ☐ **discreditably** *adv.*

discreet *adj.* (**discreeter**, **discreetest**) **1 a** circumspect in speech or action, esp. to avoid social embarrassment. **b** tactful, trustworthy. **2** unobtrusive. ☐ **discreetly** *adv.* **discreetness** *n.*

discrepancy /dɪsˈkrepənsi/ *n.* (pl. **-ies**) **1** (often foll. by *between*) difference; failure to correspond; inconsistency. **2** an instance of this.

discrete *adj.* **1** separate or individually distinct (*a series of discrete events*). **2** discontinuous; consisting of distinct or individual parts. **3** *Math.* specified only for

a distinct set of points (*discrete variables*). ☐ **discretely** *adv.* **discreteness** *n.*

discretion /dɪˈskreʃən/ *n.* **1** the quality of being discreet; tact, circumspection. **2** ability to discern what is right, advisable, etc., esp. as regards a person's own conduct. **3** the freedom to act and think as one wishes, usu. within legal limits (*it is within his discretion to leave*). *See also* AGE OF DISCRETION. **4** *Law* a court's freedom to decide a sentence etc. ☐ **at one's discretion** as one pleases. **at the discretion of** (to be settled or disposed of) according to the judgment or choice of (a person). **discretion is the better part of valour** wise caution is better than brave foolhardiness. **use one's discretion** act according to one's own judgment.

discretionary *adj.* (usu. *attrib.*) used, adopted, etc. when considered necessary (*discretionary powers*).

discriminate /dɪˈskrɪmɪ,neɪt/ *v.* **1** *intr.* (often foll. by *between*) make or see a distinction; differentiate. **2** *intr.* (usu. foll. by *against*) make a distinction, esp. unjustly and on the basis of race, age, sex, etc. **3** *tr.* (usu. foll. by *from*) make, discern, or constitute a difference in or between (*many things discriminate one person from another*). **4** *intr.* observe distinctions carefully; have good judgment. **5** *tr.* mark as distinctive; be a distinguishing feature of. ☐ **discriminately** /-nətli/ *adv.* **discriminative** /-nətɪv/ *adj.* **discriminator** *n.* **discriminatory** /-nətəri/ *adj.*

discriminating *adj.* **1** able to discern, esp. distinctions. **2** having good taste. **3** (usu. in *predic.*) practising or evincing racial, sexual, etc. discrimination. ☐ **discriminatingly** *adv.*

discrimination *n.* **1** (often foll. by *against*) an act, instance, policy, etc. of unfavourable treatment based on prejudice, esp. regarding race, age, or sex. **2** good taste or judgment in artistic matters etc. **3** the power of observing differences. **4** a distinction made with the mind or in action.

discursive /dɪˈskɜːsɪv/ *adj.* **1** rambling, digressive; passing indiscriminately from subject to subject. **2** *Philos.* proceeding by argument or reasoning (opp. INTUITIVE). ☐ **discursively** *adv.* **discursiveness** *n.*

discus /ˈdɪskəs/ *n.* (pl. **discuses**) **1** a heavy thick-centred disc thrown in ancient Greek games. **2** a similar disc thrown in modern field events. **3** the sport of discus throwing.

discuss *v.tr.* **1** hold a conversation about. **2** debate or examine by argument. ☐ **discussable** *adj.*

discussion *n.* **1** a conversation or exchange of views, esp. on specific subjects; informal debate. **2** an examination by argument, written or spoken.

disdain ● *n.* (often foll. by *for*) a feeling or attitude of scorn or contempt. ● *v.tr.* **1** treat or regard (a person, idea, etc.) with scorn or contempt. **2** think oneself superior to; reject (*disdained answering*). ☐ **disdainful** *adj.* **disdainfully** *adv.*

disease *n.* **1 a** an unhealthy condition of the body or mind; illness, sickness. **b** a particular kind of disease with special symptoms or location (*Crohn's disease*). **2** a corresponding physical condition of plants. **3** a deranged, depraved, or morbid condition (of society etc.) (*disease of materialism*).

diseased *adj.* **1** affected with disease. **2** abnormal, disordered.

disembark *v.intr.* & *tr.* leave or remove from a ship, aircraft, train, etc. ☐ **disembarkation** *n.*

disembody *v.tr.* (**-ies**, **-ied**) (esp. as **disembodied** *adj.*) separate or free from the body or a concrete form (*disembodied voices*). ☐ **disembodiment** *n.*

disembowel *v.tr.* (**-embowelled**, **-embowelling**)

remove the bowels or entrails of. □ **disembowelled** *adj.* **disembowelment** *n.*

disempower *v.tr.* remove the power to act from (a person, group, etc.). □ **disempowered** *adj.* **disempowerment** *n.*

disenchant *v.tr.* disillusion; free from enchantment. □ **disenchanted** *adj.* **disenchantment** *n.*

disenfranchise *v.tr.* **1** deprive (a person) of the right to vote. **2** deprive of or exclude from anything viewed as a right or privilege. □ **disenfranchised** *adj.* **disenfranchisement** *n.*

disengage *v.* **1 a** *tr.* detach, free, loosen, or separate (parts etc.) (*disengaged the clutch*). **b** *refl.* detach oneself; get loose. **c** *intr.* become detached. **2** *tr. Military* remove (troops) from a battle or a battle area.

disengaged *adj.* uncommitted, withdrawn.

disengagement *n.* **1 a** the act of disengaging. **b** an instance of this. **2** detachment; freedom from ties. **3** the dissolution of a relationship, esp. of an engagement to marry.

disentangle *v.* **1** *tr.* **a** extricate; free from complications, difficulties, etc. **b** unravel, untwist; bring out of a tangled state. **2** *intr.* become disentangled. □ **disentanglement** *n.*

disequilibrium *n.* (*pl.* **-a**) a lack or loss of equilibrium, stability, or balance.

disestablish *v.tr.* **1** deprive (a Church) of a state connection and support. **2** depose from an official position. **3** terminate the establishment of. □ **disestablishment** *n.*

disfavour (also **disfavor**) ● *n.* **1** disapproval or dislike. **2** the state of being disliked (*fell into disfavour*). ● *v.tr.* regard or treat with disfavour.

disfigure *v.tr.* spoil the appearance or beauty of; deface, deform. □ **disfiguration** *n.* **disfigured** *adj.* **disfigurement** *n.*

disfranchise *var. of* DISENFRANCHISE.

disgorge *v.tr.* **1** vomit or eject (matter) from the throat or stomach. **2** discharge the contents of; empty (*the boat disgorged passengers onto the pier*). **3** surrender, esp. what has been wrongly appropriated.

disgrace ● *n.* **1** the loss of reputation; shame, ignominy. **2** a person or thing that brings dishonour or shame (*the bus service is a disgrace*). ● *v.tr.* **1** bring shame or discredit on or be a disgrace to. **2** degrade from a position of honour; dismiss from favour. □ **in disgrace** having lost respect or reputation; out of favour. □ **disgraceful** *adj.* **disgracefully** *adv.*

disgruntled /dɪsˈɡrʌntəld/ *adj.* discontented; irritated, annoyed. □ **disgruntlement** *n.*

disguise ● *v.tr.* **1 a** (often foll. by *as*) alter the appearance, dress, mannerisms, etc. of (a person) so as to conceal true identity. **b** alter so as to make unrecognizable (*disguised his voice*). **2** misrepresent or cover up (*disguised their intentions*). ● *n.* **1** a garment, style, manner, etc. assumed as a means of concealment or deception. **2** the act, practice, or an instance of concealing reality under a false appearance. □ **in disguise 1** wearing a concealing costume etc. **2** appearing to be the opposite (*a blessing in disguise*). □ **disguised** *adj.*

disgust ● *n.* (usu. foll. by *at, for*) **1** repugnance; strong and instinctive aversion to something that is physically loathsome, morally offensive, etc. **2** a strong distaste for a food, drink, medicine, etc.; nausea. ● *v.tr.* **1** offend the sensibilities or principles of (*their behaviour disgusts me*). **2** excite physical nausea and loathing in. □ **in disgust** as a result of disgust (*left in disgust*). □ **disgustedly** *adv.*

disgusting *adj.* arousing disgust; sickening, repulsive. □ **disgustingly** *adv.* **disgustingness** *n.*

dish ● *n.* **1 a** a shallow, usu. flat-bottomed container made of glass, ceramic, metal, etc., used for holding or serving food. **b** the food served in a dish (*a dish of ice cream*). **c** food prepared in a particular way (*an Italian dish*). **2** (in *pl.*) dirty plates, cutlery, pots, etc. after a meal. **3 a** a dish-shaped receptacle, object, or cavity. **b** = SATELLITE DISH. ● *v.* **1** *tr.* put (food) into a dish for serving. **2** *tr.* make concave or dish-shaped. **3** *informal* **a** *tr.* gossip about (someone). **b** *intr.* gossip. □ **dish it out** *N Amer. informal* deal out punishment, criticism, etc. **dish out** *informal* deal out, distribute, esp. roughly or indiscriminately. **dish up 1** serve or prepare to serve (food). **2** *informal* seek to present (facts, argument, etc.) attractively. **dish the dirt** (often foll. by *on*) *informal* spread scandal or gossip. □ **dishlike** *adj.*

disharmony *n.* (*pl.* **-ies**) **1** a lack of harmony or agreement; discord. **2** something discordant.

dishcloth *n.* a cloth for washing dishes etc.

dishearten *v.tr.* cause to lose courage, confidence, hope, etc.; make despondent. □ **disheartening** *adj.* **dishearteningly** *adv.* **disheartenment** *n.*

dished *adj.* **1** dishlike or concave (*a dished face*). **2** (of vehicle wheels) angled so as to be closer to each other at the bottom than at the top.

dishevelled /dɪˈʃevəld/ *adj.* (of the hair, clothes, appearance, etc.) disordered, unkempt, untidy.

dishonest *adj.* (of a person, act, or statement) fraudulent or insincere. □ **dishonestly** *adv.*

dishonesty *n.* (*pl.* **-ies**) **1** a lack of honesty, esp. a willingness to cheat, steal, lie, or act fraudulently. **2** a dishonest or fraudulent act.

dishonour (also **dishonor**) ● *n.* **1** a state of shame, disgrace, or ignominy. **2** something that causes shame or disgrace (*a dishonour to his profession*). ● *v.tr.* **1** disgrace (*dishonoured his name*). **2** treat without honour or respect. **3** (often in *passive*) refuse to accept or pay (a cheque or a bill of exchange).

dishonourable *adj.* (also **dishonorable**) **1** ignominious; causing disgrace. **2** (of a person) unprincipled; having no sense of honour. □ **dishonourableness** *n.* **dishonourably** *adv.*

dish soap *n. Cdn* = DISHWASHING LIQUID.

dishtowel *n.* a thin towel for drying dishes, etc.

dishwasher *n.* **1** a machine for washing dishes. **2** a person who washes dishes. □ **dishwashing** *n.*

dishwashing liquid *n. N Amer.* (also **dishwashing detergent**) a liquid detergent used for hand-washing of dishes.

dishwater *n.* **1** water in which dishes have been washed. **2** *informal* (often *attrib.*) something weak, diluted, or resembling dishwater.

disillusion ● *n.* disenchantment, freedom from illusions. ● *v.tr.* deprive of belief in an illusion or ideal. □ **disillusionment** *n.*

disincentive ● *n.* **1** something that tends to discourage a particular action etc. **2** *Econ.* a source of discouragement to productivity or progress. ● *adj.* tending to discourage.

disinclination *n.* unwillingness or reluctance.

disincline *v.tr.* (usu. foll. by *to* + infin. or *for*) make unwilling or reluctant. □ **disinclined** *adj.*

disinfect *v.tr.* cleanse (a wound, room, etc.) of infection by destroying germs, esp. with a disinfectant. □ **disinfection** *n.*

disinfectant ● *n.* a usu. commercially produced chemical liquid or spray that destroys germs etc. ● *adj.* of disinfectants or causing disinfection.

disinformation n. deliberately false information, esp. as supplied by governments, the military, etc.

disingenuous adj. insincere; lacking in frankness. □ **disingenuously** adv. **disingenuousness** n.

disinherit v.tr. (**disinherited, disinheriting**) reject as one's heir; deprive of the right of inheritance.

disintegrate v. **1** tr. & intr. **a** separate into component parts or fragments. **b** lose or cause to lose cohesion or unity. **2** Physics **a** intr. (of a nucleus, particle, or radioactive substance) undergo disintegration. **b** tr. cause (a substance, atom, or nucleus) to undergo disintegration. **3** intr. informal deteriorate mentally or physically. □ **disintegrator** n.

disintegration n. **1** the act, process, or an instance of disintegrating. **2** Physics the process in which an atomic nucleus changes into another nuclide by emitting one or more particles or splitting into smaller nuclei.

disinter /ˌdɪsɪn'tɜr/ v.tr. (**disinterred, disinterring**) **1** exhume; remove or dig up from the ground. **2** bring (a secret etc.) out of obscurity or concealment.

disinterest n. **1** impartiality. **2** disputed lack of interest. ¶The use of disinterest to mean 'lack of interest' is sometimes objected to, but it is in this sense that it is most commonly found and the alternative uninterest is rare. The phrase lack of interest avoids both ambiguity and accusations of incorrect usage.

disinterested adj. **1** unbiased, impartial; not influenced by one's own advantage (a disinterested critic). **2** disputed uninterested, unconcerned. ¶Disinterested is commonly used to mean 'uninterested', but this is regarded by some as incorrect. □ **disinterestedly** adv. **disinterestedness** n.

disinvest v. **1** intr. (often foll. by from) reduce or withdraw financial investment from a place, company, etc. **2** tr. reduce or withdraw (investments or assets).□ **disinvestment** n.

disjoint ● v.tr. **1** take apart at the joints. **2 a** disturb the working, connection, or arrangement of (a system etc.). **b** dislocate or disturb (a pattern etc.).

disjointed adj. (of speech, writing, etc.) incoherent, rambling; not properly connected. □ **disjointedly** adv. **disjointedness** n.

disk ● n. (also **disc**) **1 a** (in full **magnetic disk**) a computer storage device consisting of a rotatable disc or discs with a magnetic coating. **b** (in full **optical disk**) a smooth non-magnetic disc with large storage capacity for data recorded and read by laser, esp. a CD-ROM. **2** var. of DISC. **3** N Amer. & NZ **a** = DISKER. **b** a circular steel blade on a disker. ● v.tr. till (soil) with a disker. □ **diskless** adj.

disk drive n. Computing a device that can store and retrieve data from rotating magnetic or optical disks.

disker n. (also **disk harrow**) N Amer. a harrow using sharp, curved disks to till land, remove weeds, etc.

diskette n. = FLOPPY n.

disk jockey var. of DISC JOCKEY.

dislike ● v.tr. have an aversion or objection to; not like. ● n. **1** a feeling that something is distasteful, unpleasant, objectionable, etc. **2** an object of dislike. □ **dislikable** adj. (also **dislikeable**).

dislocate v.tr. **1** disturb the normal connection of (esp. a joint in the body). **2** disorder or disrupt (affairs etc.) from their natural course. **3** displace or put (a thing) out of its proper relative position.

dislocation n. **1** the act or result of dislocating, esp. the displacement of a bone from its natural position. **2** a disordered state.

dislodge v.tr. & intr. remove from or leave an established or fixed position.

disloyal adj. (often foll. by to) **1** not loyal; unfaithful. **2** untrue to one's allegiances; treacherous to one's government etc. □ **disloyally** adv. **disloyalty** n.

dismal adj. **1** causing or showing gloom; cheerless, miserable. **2** dreary or sombre (dismal brown walls). **3** informal feeble or inept (a dismal performance). □ **dismally** adv. **dismalness** n.

dismantle v.tr. **1 a** take apart; disassemble (dismantle a faulty motor). **b** end (a system, organization, etc.) in a gradual and planned way (dismantled apartheid). **2** deprive of defences or equipment. **3** (often foll. by of) strip of covering or protection. □ **dismantler** n.

dismay ● n. **1** keenly felt disappointment. **2** discouragement, despair, or faintness of heart. **3** consternation or anxiety. ● v.tr. **1** discourage or reduce to despair. **2** fill with consternation or anxiety. □ **dismaying** adj. **dismayingly** adv.

dismember v.tr. **1** tear or cut the limbs from. **2** divide up (a country etc.). □ **dismemberment** n.

dismiss v. **1 a** tr. send away; cause (a person) to leave one's presence. **b** tr. disband (an assembly or army). **c** intr. (of an assembly etc.) disperse; break ranks. **2** tr. discharge from employment, office, etc., esp. dishonourably. **3** tr. banish (a thought, feeling, etc.) from the mind; treat as unworthy of consideration. **4** tr. treat (a subject) summarily (dismissed his application). **5** tr. Law refuse further hearing to (a case); send out of court. □ **dismissal** n. **dismissible** adj.

dismissive adj. disdainful; tending to dismiss from consideration. □ **dismissively** adv. **dismissiveness** n.

dismount ● v. **1 a** intr. alight from a horse, bicycle, etc. **b** tr. (usu. in passive) throw from a horse; unseat. **2** tr. take (a mechanism) from its framework; take apart. ● n. an act or method of dismounting (from a horse, parallel bars, etc.).

disobedient adj. disobeying; rebellious, rule-breaking. □ **disobedience** n. **disobediently** adv.

disobey v. **1** tr. fail or refuse to obey (orders, rules, a person, etc.); disregard. **2** intr. be disobedient or show disobedience. □ **disobeyer** n.

disorder ● n. **1** confusion, disarray; lack of order or regular arrangement. **2** a disturbance or commotion, esp. a breach of public order. **3** Med. an ailment or disturbance of the normal state of body or mind. ● v.tr. **1** disarrange; throw (a situation etc.) into confusion. **2** Med. upset the health or proper function of the body or mind. □ **disordered** adj.

disorderly adj. **1** unruly, riotous. **2** Law contrary to public order or morality. **3** marked by lack of order or regularity; untidy. □ **disorderliness** n.

disorganize v.tr. destroy the system, order, or organization of; throw into confusion. □ **disorganization** n. **disorganized** adj.

disorient v.tr. **1** confuse (a person) as to his or her whereabouts or bearings. **2** confuse (a person) as to what is true, correct, etc. □ **disorientation** n.

disown v.tr. **1** refuse to acknowledge (a person) as one's own or as connected with oneself. **2** repudiate or disclaim (an idea, intention, result, etc.).

disparage /dɪ'sperɪdʒ/ v.tr. **1** vilify or speak slightingly or critically of (a person, idea, etc.). **2** bring discredit or reproach upon (a person). □ **disparagement** n. **disparaging** adj. **disparagingly** adv.

disparate /'dɪsprət/ adj. essentially different in kind; without comparison or relation. □ **disparately** adv. **disparity** /dɪ'sperɪti/ n.

dispassionate *adj.* calm, impartial; free from the influence or effect of strong emotion. □ **dispassion** *n.* **dispassionately** *adv.* **dispassionateness** *n.*

dispatch ● *v.tr.* **1** send off to a destination or for a purpose. **2** kill, execute. **3** perform (business, a task, etc.) promptly; finish off. **4** *informal* eat (food, a meal, etc.) quickly. ● *n.* **1** the act or an instance of sending (a messenger, letter, etc.). **2** the act or an instance of killing; execution. **3 a** an official written message on state or esp. military affairs. **b** a report sent in by a newspaper's correspondent, usu. from a foreign country. **c** any written message requiring fast delivery. **4** promptness, efficiency (*done with dispatch*).

dispatcher *n.* a person who coordinates the departure of taxis, buses, trains, etc.

dispel *v.tr.* (**dispelled, dispelling**) dissipate; disperse; scatter.

dispensable *adj.* **1** unnecessary or expendable. **2** capable of being dispensed or administered. □ **dispensability** *n.*

dispensary *n.* (*pl.* **-ies**) **1** a place in a clinic, pharmacy, etc. where medicines are dispensed. **2** a public or charitable institution offering medical advice and the dispensing of medicines.

dispensation /ˌdɪspenˈseɪʃən, -pən-/ *n.* **1** the act or an instance of dispensing or distributing. **2 a** (usu. foll. by *from*) an exemption from a religious or legal observance, penalty, etc. **b** an instance of this. **3 a** the ordering or management of the world by Providence. **b** a specific example of such ordering (of a community, a person, etc.). **4** any established or prevailing system (of administration, government, etc.) under which one lives or works.

dispense *v.* **1** *tr.* distribute or deal out as a share from a common stock. **2** *tr.* administer (a sacrament, justice, etc.). **3** *tr.* make up and give out (medicine etc.) according to a doctor's prescription. **4** *tr.* (usu. foll. by *from*) grant (a person) a dispensation from an esp. religious obligation. **5** *intr.* (foll. by *with*) **a** do without; render needless (*dispense with formalities*). **b** give exemption from (a rule).

dispenser *n.* **1** an automatic machine that dispenses an item or a specific amount of something, e.g. soap etc. **2** a person who dispenses something.

disperse *v.* **1 a** *tr.* drive, throw, send, or scatter in different directions. **b** *intr.* become scattered, dispelled, or dissipated (*the clouds dispersed*). **2 a** *intr.* (of people in a crowd etc.) separate and go different ways. **b** *tr.* cause to do this. **3** *tr.* (usu. in *passive*) place or station at widely separated points. **4** *tr.* distribute or put (books, currency, etc.) into circulation, esp. from a main source or centre. **5** *tr. Chem.* distribute (small particles) uniformly in a medium. **6** *tr. Physics* separate (white light) into its coloured constituents. □ **dispersal** *n.* **disperser** *n.* **dispersive** *adj.*

dispersion /dɪˈspɜːrʒən/ *n.* **1** the act or an instance of dispersing or being dispersed. **2** *Statistics* the degree to which a set of observed values are spread over a range. **3** (**the Dispersion**) = DIASPORA 1.

dispirit *v.tr.* discourage; lower the morale of. □ **dispirited** *adj.* **dispiritedly** *adv.* **dispiritedness** *n.* **dispiriting** *adj.* **dispiritingly** *adv.*

displace *v.tr.* **1 a** replace (a thing) with another. **b** supplant or take the place of (a person), esp. in some official capacity (*moderates have displaced the extremists on the committee*). **2** move or shift from its accustomed place. **3** force (a person) to leave his or her home, country, etc., esp. because of military or political pressures. □ **displacer** *n.*

displaced person *n.* esp. *hist.* a refugee or person

forced to leave his or her home country because of war, persecution, etc. Abbr.: **DP.**

displacement *n.* **1 a** the act of displacing or the process of being displaced. **b** an instance of this. **2** *Physics* the amount by which anything is displaced, esp. the amount of a fluid displaced by a solid floating or immersed in it. **3** *Psych.* **a** the substitution of one idea or impulse for another. **b** the unconscious transfer of strong unacceptable emotions from one object to another. **4** *Geol.* the relative movement on either side of a fault plane.

display ● *v.tr.* **1** expose to view; show, exhibit. **2** show ostentatiously. **3** allow to appear; reveal, betray (*displayed his ignorance*). **4** spread out, unfold to view (*the flag should be properly displayed*). **5** show (data, images, etc.) on a computer screen etc. ● *n.* **1** the act or an instance of displaying. **2 a** an exhibition or show. **b** a presentation (of merchandise etc.) designed to show the product to advantage. **3** ostentation; flashiness. **4** the distinct behaviour of some birds and fish, used esp. to attract a mate. **5 a** the presentation of data, images, etc. on a computer screen etc. **b** the information so presented.

display case *n.* a usu. clear glass case for displaying items for observation or inspection.

displease *v.tr.* make indignant or angry; offend. □ **be displeased** (often foll. by *at, with*) be indignant or dissatisfied. □ **displeasing** *adj.*

displeasure *n.* disapproval; dissatisfaction; anger.

disposable ● *adj.* **1** intended to be used once and then thrown away (*disposable diapers*). **2** that can be thrown away or disposed of safely (*disposable alkaline batteries*). **3** (esp. of financial assets) accessible; available for use. ● *n.* a thing designed to be thrown away after one use. □ **disposability** *n.*

disposable income *n.* **1** income available after taxes, expenses, etc. for spending, saving, or investment. **2** the total amount of money at the disposal of consumers in a country, community, etc.

disposal *n.* **1** the act or an instance of getting rid of something. **2** the arrangement or placing of something. **3** control or management (of a person, business, etc.). **4** (esp. as **waste disposal**) the disposing of garbage. □ **at one's disposal 1** available for one's use. **2** subject to one's orders or decisions.

dispose *v.* **1** *tr.* make willing; incline (*was disposed to release them*). **2** *tr.* place suitably or in order (*disposed the pictures in sequence*). **3** *intr.* determine the course of events. □ **dispose of 1** settle or deal conclusively with (an issue, opponent, etc.). **b** get rid of. **c** finish (a task etc.). **d** kill. **2** sell (property etc.). **3** prove (a claim, an argument, an opponent, etc.) to be incorrect. **4** *informal* consume (food). □ **disposer** *n.*

disposed *adj.* (usu. foll. by *to*, or *to* + infin.) **1** inclined, prepared, or in the mood (to do something etc.). **2** having a specified mental inclination (usu. in *comb.*: *ill-disposed*). **3** subject, liable, or having a physical inclination to.

disposition *n.* **1 a** temperament or character, esp. as displayed in dealings with others (*a gentle disposition*). **b** (often foll. by *to*) a natural tendency or inclination (*a disposition to overeat*). **2 a** a condition or arrangement of affairs, esp. for a particular purpose. **b** spatial arrangement or relative position, esp. of constituent parts. ¶*Disposition* is the noun corresponding to the verb *dispose* 'arrange', whereas *disposal* corresponds to the verb *dispose of* 'get rid of'. **3** (usu. in *pl.*) **a** *Military* the stationing of troops ready for attack or defence. **b** preparations, plans. **4 a** a bestowal by deed or will (*the* *disposition of the estate*). **b** control; the power of disposing. **5** the action of ordering or regulating by esp. divine right or power.

dispossess *v.tr.* **1** dislodge; oust (a person) from a dwelling etc. **2** (usu. foll. by *of*) deprive of possessions, status, rights, etc. **3** alienate, disenfranchise, or estrange. □ **dispossessed** *adj.* **dispossession** *n.*

disproportion *n.* **1** a lack of proportion. **2** an instance of this. □ **disproportional** *adj.* **disproportionality** *n.* **disproportionally** *adv.*

disproportionate *adj.* **1** lacking proportion. **2** relatively too large or small etc. □ **disproportionately** *adv.* **disproportionateness** *n.*

disprove *v.tr.* prove false; refute. □ **disprovable** *adj.*

disputable *adj.* open to question; contentious.

disputant *n.* a person who disputes or argues, esp. one who engages in public debate or disputation.

disputation *n.* **1** a the act or an instance of disputing or debating. **b** an argument; a controversy. **2** a formal debate. □ **disputatious** *adj.* **disputatiously** *adv.* **disputatiousness** *n.*

dispute ● *v.* **1** *intr.* (usu. foll. by *with*, *against*) **a** debate, argue. **b** quarrel. **2** *tr.* discuss, esp. heatedly (*disputed whether it was true*). **3** *tr.* question the truth, correctness, or validity of (a statement, alleged fact, etc.). **4** *tr.* contend for; strive to win (*disputed the crown*). ● *n.* **1** a controversy; a debate. **2** a quarrel. **3** a disagreement between management and employees, esp. one leading to industrial action. □ **beyond** (or **without**) **dispute** certainly; indisputably. **in dispute** being argued about. □ **disputed** *adj.*

disqualification *n.* **1** a the act or an instance of disqualifying. **b** the state of being disqualified. **2** something that disqualifies.

disqualify *v.tr.* (**-ies, -ied**) **1** (often foll. by *from*) bar from a competition or pronounce ineligible as a winner because of an infringement of the rules etc. **2** (often foll. by *for*, *from*) make or pronounce ineligible or unsuitable (*his age disqualifies him for the job*). **3** (often foll. by *from*) deprive of legal capacity, power, or right (*disqualified from practising as a doctor*).

disquiet ● *v.tr.* worry; trouble; deprive of peace. ● *n.* anxiety, unrest. □ **disquieting** *adj.*

disquisition /ˌdɪskwɪˈzɪʃən/ *n.* a long or elaborate treatise or discourse on a subject.

disregard ● *v.tr.* **1** pay no attention to; ignore. **2** treat as of no importance. ● *n.* (often foll. by *of*, *for*) **1** indifference; neglect. **2** lack of regard or respect.

disrepair *n.* the state of being in poor condition, esp. due to neglect (*in disrepair*).

disreputable *adj.* **1** discreditable; of bad reputation. **2** not respectable in appearance; shabby; untidy. □ **disreputableness** *n.* **disreputably** *adv.*

disrepute /ˌdɪsrəˈpjuːt, -rɪ-/ *n.* a lack of good reputation or respectability (*fall into disrepute*).

disrespect ● *n.* a lack of respect or courtesy. ● *v.tr. informal* have or show no respect or reverence for. □ **disrespectful** *adj.* **disrespectfully** *adv.*

disrobe *v.tr. & intr.* undress; divest of a garment.

disrupt *v.tr.* **1** interrupt the flow or continuity of (a meeting, speech, etc.); bring disorder to. **2** separate forcibly; shatter. □ **disruption** *n.* **disruptive** *adj.* **disruptively** *adv.* **disruptiveness** *n.*

diss *var. of* DIS.

dissatisfy *v.tr.* (**-ies, -ied**) make discontented; fail to satisfy. □ **dissatisfaction** *n.* **dissatisfactory** *adj.*

dissect /daiˈsekt, dɪ-/ *v.tr.* **1** cut into pieces. **2** cut up (a plant or animal) to examine its parts, structure, etc.,

or (a corpse) for a post mortem. **3** analyze; criticize or examine in detail. □ **dissection** *n.*

dissemble /dɪˈsembəl/ *v.* **1** *intr.* conceal one's motives; talk or act hypocritically. **2** *tr.* **a** disguise or conceal (a feeling, intention, act, etc.). **b** simulate (*dissembled grief in public*). □ **dissemblance** *n.* **dissembler** *n.* **dissemblingly** *adv.*

disseminate /dɪˈsemɪˌneɪt/ *v.tr.* scatter about, spread (esp. ideas) widely. □ **dissemination** *n.* **disseminator** *n.*

disseminated *adj. Med.* spread through an organ or the body.

dissension *n.* disagreement giving rise to discord.

dissent ● *v.intr.* (often foll. by *from*) **1** think differently, disagree; express disagreement. **2** differ in religious opinion, esp. from the doctrine of an established or orthodox church. ● *n.* **1** a a difference of opinion. **b** an expression of this. **2** the refusal to accept the doctrines of an established or orthodox church. □ **dissenter** *n.* **dissenting** *adj.* **dissentingly** *adv.*

dissertation /ˌdɪsərˈteɪʃən/ *n.* a detailed discourse on a subject, esp. one submitted in partial fulfillment of the requirements of a doctorate.

disservice *n.* an unhelpful or injurious act, esp. done when trying to help.

dissident ● *adj.* disagreeing, esp. with an established government, system, etc. ● *n.* a dissident person. □ **dissidence** *n.*

dissimilar *adj.* (often foll. by *to*) unlike, not similar. □ **dissimilarity** *n.* (*pl.* **-ies**). **dissimilarly** *adv.*

dissipate *v.* **1** a *tr.* cause (a cloud, vapour, fear, darkness, etc.) to disappear or disperse. **b** *intr.* disperse, scatter, disappear. **2** *intr. & tr.* break up; bring or come to nothing. **3** *tr.* squander or fritter away (money, energy, etc.). □ **dissipative** *adj.*

dissipated *adj.* given to dissipation, dissolute.

dissipation *n.* **1** intemperate, dissolute, or debauched living. **2** (usu. foll. by *of*) wasteful expenditure. **3** scattering, dispersion, or disintegration. **4** a frivolous amusement.

dissociate /dɪˈsoʊsiˌeɪt, -ʃiˌeɪt/ *v.* **1** *tr. & intr.* (usu. foll. by *from*) disconnect or become disconnected; separate (*dissociated her from their guilt*). **2** *tr. Chem.* decompose, esp. reversibly. **3** *tr. Psych.* cause (a person's mind) to develop more than one centre of consciousness. □ **dissociate oneself from 1** declare oneself unconnected with. **2** decline to support or agree with (a proposal etc.). □ **dissociative** *adj.*

dissociation *n.* **1** the act or an instance of dissociating. **2** *Psych.* the state of suffering from multiple personality disorder.

dissolute /ˈdɪsəˌluːt/ *adj.* lax in morals; licentious.

dissolution *n.* **1** disintegration; decomposition. **2** (usu. foll. by *of*) the undoing or relaxing of a bond, esp.: **a** a marriage. **b** a partnership. **c** an alliance. **3** the dismissal or dispersal of an assembly, esp. of a parliament at the end of its term. **4** death. **5** bringing or coming to an end; fading away. **6** dissipation; debauchery.

dissolve ● *v.* **1** *tr. & intr.* make or become liquid, esp. by immersion or dispersion in a liquid. **2** *intr. & tr.* disappear or cause to disappear gradually. **3 a** *tr.* dismiss or disperse (an assembly, esp. parliament). **b** *intr.* (of an assembly) be dissolved. **4** *tr.* annul or put an end to (a partnership, marriage, etc.). **5** *intr.* (of a person) become enfeebled or emotionally overcome. **6** *intr.* (often foll. by *into*) change gradually (from one film or video image into another). ● *n.* the act or process of dissolving a film or video image. □ **dissolvable** *adj.*

dissonant /'dısənənt/ adj. **1** discordant. **2** incongruous; clashing. □ **dissonance** n.

dissuade /dı'sweid/ v.tr. (often foll. by from) discourage (a person); persuade against (dissuaded him from continuing). □ **dissuader** n. **dissuasion** n. **dissuasive** adj. **dissuasively** adv.

dissymmetry n. (pl. **-ies**) **1 a** lack of symmetry. **b** an instance of this. **2** symmetry as of mirror images or the left and right hands (esp. of crystals with two corresponding forms). □ **dissymmetric** adj. **dissymmetrical** adj.

distal /'dıstəl/ adj. situated away from the centre of the body or point of attachment. □ **distally** adv.

distance ● n. **1** the condition of being far off; remoteness. **2 a** a space or interval between two things. **b** the length of this (a distance of twenty kilometres). **3** a distant point or place (came from a distance). **4** the avoidance of familiarity; aloofness; reserve. **5** a remoter field of vision (saw him in the distance). **6** an interval of time (can't remember what happened at this distance). **7 a** the full length of a race etc. **b** Boxing the scheduled length of a fight. ● v.tr. (often refl.) **1** place far off (distanced herself from them). **2** leave far behind in a race or competition. □ **at a distance** far off. **go the distance 1** Boxing complete a fight without being knocked out. **2** complete, esp. a hard task; endure an ordeal. **keep one's distance** maintain one's reserve. **within hailing distance** not far; close enough to be called to. **within walking distance** near enough to walk to.

distance education n. (also **distance learning**) education by correspondence course or from broadcasts, telephone tutorials, etc.

distance runner n. an athlete who competes in long- or middle-distance races.

distant adj. **1 a** far away in space or time. **b** (usu. predic.) at a specified distance (three miles distant from them). **2** remote or far apart in position, time, resemblance, etc. (a distant relative). **3** not intimate; reserved; cool. **4** remote; abstracted (a distant stare). **5** faint, vague (a distant memory). □ **distantly** adv.

distant early warning n. N Amer. see DEW LINE.

distaste n. (usu. foll. by for) dislike; repugnance; aversion. □ **distasteful** adj. **distastefulness** n.

distemper¹ ● n. **1** a kind of paint using glue or size instead of an oil base, for use on walls or for scene painting. **2** a method of painting using this. ● v.tr. paint (walls etc.) with distemper.

distemper² n. **1 a** (also **canine distemper**) a disease of dogs, causing fever, coughing, and catarrh. **b** (also **feline distemper**) a usu. fatal viral disease of cats, causing fever, vomiting, and diarrhea. **c** a disease of various other animals. **2** uneasiness.

distempered adj. disordered, disturbed; uneasy.

distend v.tr. & intr. swell out by pressure from within (distended stomach). □ **distension** n.

distill v. (also **distil**) (**distilled**, **distilling**) **1** tr. Chem. purify (a liquid) by vaporizing it with heat, then condensing it with cold and collecting the result. **2** tr. **a** Chem. extract the essence of (a plant etc.) usu. by heating it in a solvent. **b** extract the essential meaning or implications of (an idea etc.). **3** tr. make (whisky, essence, etc.) by distilling raw materials. **4** tr. & intr. come as or give forth in drops; exude.

distillate /'dıstılət, -leit, -'stıl-/ n. a product of distillation.

distillation n. **1** the process of distilling or being distilled (in various senses). **2** something distilled.

distiller n. a person who distills, esp. a manufacturer of alcoholic liquor.

distillery n. (pl. **-ies**) a place where liquor is distilled.

distinct adj. **1** (often foll. by from) **a** not identical; separate; individual. **b** different in kind or quality; unlike. **2 a** clearly perceptible; plain. **b** clearly understandable; definite. **3** unmistakable, decided (a distinct impression). □ **distinctly** adv. **distinctness** n.

distinction n. **1 a** the act or an instance of discriminating or distinguishing. **b** the difference made by distinguishing. **2 a** something that differentiates, e.g. a mark, name, or title. **b** the fact of being different. **3** special consideration or honour. **4** distinguished character; excellence; eminence (a film of distinction). **5** a grade in an examination etc. denoting great excellence (passed with distinction).

distinctive adj. distinguishing, characteristic. □ **distinctively** adv. **distinctiveness** n.

distinguish v. **1** tr. **a** see or point out the difference of; draw distinctions (cannot distinguish one from the other). **b** constitute such a difference (this distinguishes us from the competition). **c** draw distinctions between; differentiate. **2** tr. be a mark or property of; characterize. **3** tr. discover by listening, looking, etc. (could distinguish two voices). **4** tr. (usu. refl.; often foll. by by) make prominent or noteworthy (distinguished herself by winning). **5** intr. (foll. by between) make or point out a difference between. □ **distinguishable** adj.

distinguished adj. **1 a** of high standing. **b** eminent; famous. **2** having a distinguished air, features, manner, etc.

distort v. **1 a** tr. & intr. put out of shape; make or become crooked or unshapely. **b** tr. distort the appearance of, esp. by curved mirrors, imperfect lenses, etc. **2** tr. misrepresent (motives, facts, statements, etc.). **3** tr. Electronics change the form of (a signal) during transmission or amplification. □ **distorted** adj. **distortedly** adv. **distortedness** n.

distortion n. **1** the act or an instance of distorting; the process of being distorted. **2** Electronics a change in the form of a signal during transmission etc. usu. with some impairment of quality. **3** the characteristic fuzzy sound of electric guitars in some forms of popular music, e.g. heavy metal.

distract v.tr. **1** (often foll. by from) draw away the attention of (a person, the mind, etc.). **2** bewilder; perplex. **3** amuse, esp. in order to take the attention from pain or worry. □ **distractible** adj.

distracted adj. **1** mad or angry (distracted with worry). **2** inattentive. □ **distractedly** adv.

distraction n. **1 a** the act of distracting, esp. the mind. **b** something that distracts; an interruption. **2** a relaxation from work; an amusement. **3** a lack of concentration. **4** perplexity. **5** frenzy; madness. □ **to distraction** almost to a state of madness.

distraught /dı'strɔt/ adj. very worried, upset, etc.

distress ● n. **1** severe trouble, anxiety, sorrow, etc. **2** Med. the state of an organ etc. that is not functioning normally or adequately. ● v.tr. **1** subject to distress; exhaust, afflict. **2** cause anxiety to; make unhappy; vex. **3** scratch or mark (clothing, furniture, etc.) to simulate the effects of age and wear. □ **in distress 1** suffering or in danger. **2** (of a ship, aircraft, etc.) in danger or damaged. □ **distressful** adj. **distressing** adj. **distressingly** adv.

distressed adj. **1** suffering from distress. **2** impoverished. **3** (of furniture, leather, etc.) having simulated marks of age and wear.

distress signal n. (also **distress call**) a signal from a ship etc. in danger.

distributary n. (pl. **-ies**) a branch of a river that does not return to the main stream (as in a delta).

distribute *v.tr.* **1** give shares of; deal out. **2** spread or disperse throughout a region; scatter. **3** divide into parts; arrange; classify. **4** supply (goods etc.) to customers. □ **distributable** *adj.*

distributed computing *n.* computing using a client-server system.

distribution *n.* **1** the act or an instance of distributing; the process or state of being distributed. **2 a** the dispersal of goods etc. among consumers, brought about by commerce. **b** the extent to which different groups, classes, or individuals share in the total production or wealth of a community. **3** *Statistics* the way in which a characteristic is spread over members of a class. □ **distributional** *adj.*

distributive ● *adj.* **1** of, concerned with, or produced by distribution. **2** *Logic & Grammar* (of a pronoun etc.) referring to each individual of a class, not to the class collectively, e.g. *each*, *either*. **3** *Math.* governed by or stating the condition that when an operation is performed on two or more quantities already combined by a second operation, the result is the same as when it is performed on each quantity individually and the products then combined. □ **distributively** *adv.*

distributor *n.* **1** a person or thing that distributes. **2** an agent who supplies goods. **3** *Electricity* a device in an internal combustion engine for passing the current to each spark plug in turn.

district *n.* **1** (often *attrib.*) a territory marked off for special administrative purposes. **2** an area which has common characteristics (*the wine-growing district*).

district attorney *n.* (in the US) the prosecuting officer of a district. Abbr.: **DA.**

district municipality *n. Cdn* (*BC*) a municipality having more than 800 hectares of land and an average density of less than five people per hectare.

distrust ● *n.* a lack of trust; doubt; suspicion. ● *v.tr.* have no trust or confidence in; doubt. □ **distruster** *n.* **distrustful** *adj.* **distrustfully** *adv.*

disturb *v.tr.* **1** break the rest, calm, order, or quiet of; interrupt. **2** agitate; worry, unsettle (*your story disturbs me*). **3** move from a settled position, disarrange (*the papers had been disturbed*). □ **disturber** *n.* **disturbing** *adj.* **disturbingly** *adv.*

disturbance *n.* **1** the act or an instance of disturbing; the process of being disturbed. **2** a tumult; an uproar. **3** agitation; worry. **4** an interruption. **5** *Meteorol.* a low-pressure feature.

disturbed *adj.* **1** *in senses of* DISTURB. **2** emotionally or mentally unstable or abnormal.

disulphide /daiˈsʌlfaid/ *n.* (*N Amer.* also **disulfide**) a binary chemical containing two atoms of sulphur in each molecule.

disuse ● *n.* **1** lack of use or practice; discontinuance. **2** a disused state. ● *v.tr.* cease to use. □ **fall into disuse** cease to be used.

ditch ● *n.* **1** a long narrow excavated channel esp. for drainage. **2** a watercourse, stream, etc. ● *v.* **1** *intr.* make or repair ditches. **2** *tr.* provide with ditches; drain. **3** *tr. informal* **a** get rid of. **b** cease consorting with (esp. a lover etc.). **c** abandon. **4** *tr.* **a** bring (an aircraft) down on water in an emergency. **b** drive (a vehicle) into a ditch. **5** *intr.* (of an aircraft) make a forced landing on water. □ **ditcher** *n.*

dither /ˈdɪðər/ ● *v.intr.* hesitate; be indecisive. ● *n. informal* **1** a state of agitation or apprehension. **2** a state of hesitation; indecisiveness. □ **ditherer** *n.* **dithery** *adj.*

dithering *n.* **1** *in senses of* DITHER *v.* **2** *Computing* a method of creating apparently smooth gradations of shade or continuous tones by gradually spacing single-tone pixels (*compare* GREY-SCALE). □ **dithered** *adj.*

Ditidaht /ˈdɪtidɒt/ *n.* = NITINAT.

ditto ● *n.* (*pl.* **-os**) **1** (in accounts, inventories, lists, etc.) the aforesaid, the same. ¶Often represented by double quotation marks under the word or sum to be repeated. **2** *informal* (replacing a word or phrase to avoid repetition) the same (*came in late last night and ditto the night before*). **3** a similar thing; a duplicate. ● *v.tr.* (**-oes**, **-oed**) repeat (another's action or words).

ditty *n.* (*pl.* **-ies**) a short simple song.

ditz *n. N Amer.* a ditzy person.

ditzy *adj.* (also **ditsy**) *N Amer. informal* (usu. of a woman) silly or foolish.

diuretic /ˌdaijʊˈretɪk/ ● *adj.* causing increased output of urine. ● *n.* a diuretic drug or substance.

diurnal /daiˈɜːnəl/ *adj.* **1** of or during the day; not nocturnal. **2** daily; of each day. **3** *Astronomy* occupying one day. **4** (of animals) active in the daytime. **5** (of plants) open only during the day. □ **diurnally** *adv.*

Div. *abbr.* **1** Division. **2** Divinity.

diva /ˈdiːvə/ *n.* (*pl.* **divas**) a great or famous woman singer; a prima donna.

divalent /daiˈveilənt/ *adj. Chem.* having a valence of two; bivalent. □ **divalence** *n.* **divalency** *n.*

divan /dɪˈvæn/ *n.* **1** a backless sofa. **2** a bed consisting of a base and mattress, usu. with no board at either end.

dive ● *v.* (*past* **dived**; *N Amer.* also **dove**) **1** *intr.* plunge (esp. headfirst) into water. **2** *intr.* **a** (of an aircraft) plunge steeply downwards at speed. **b** (of a submarine) submerge. **c** plunge downwards, drop. **3** *intr.* (foll. by *into*) *informal* **a** put one's hand into (a pocket, handbag, vessel, etc.) quickly and deeply. **b** occupy oneself suddenly and enthusiastically with (a subject, meal, etc.). **4** *tr.* (foll. by *into*) plunge (a hand etc.) into. **5 a** *intr.* swim underwater, esp. with scuba equipment. **b** *tr.* swim underwater to explore (a body of water, sunken ship, etc.). **6** (in hockey etc.) fall deliberately in an attempt to draw a penalty on one's opponent. ● *n.* **1** an act or instance of diving; a plunge. **2 a** the submerging of a submarine. **b** the steep descent of an aircraft. **3** a sudden darting movement. **4** *informal* a seedy, rundown nightclub, bar, etc. **5 a** *Boxing slang* a pretended knockout (*took a dive in the second round*). **b** (in hockey, soccer, etc.) a deliberate fall in an attempt to draw a penalty on one's opponent. □ **dive in** *informal* help oneself (to food).

dive-bomb *v.tr.* **1** (of an aircraft) bomb (a target) while diving towards it. **2** (of a bird, insect, etc.) descend rapidly from a height to attack something. □ **dive-bomber** *n.*

diver *n.* **1** a person who dives. **2** any of various diving birds, esp. of the family Gaviidae; a loon.

diverge *v.* **1** *intr.* **a** proceed in a different direction or in different directions from a point. **b** take a different course or different courses (*their interests diverged*). **2** *intr.* **a** (often foll. by *from*) depart from a set course (*diverged from his parents' wishes*). **b** differ markedly in opinion. **3** *tr.* cause to diverge; deflect.

divergent *adj.* **1** diverging. **2** *Psych.* (of thought) tending to reach a variety of possible solutions when analyzing a problem. □ **divergence** *n.* **divergency** *n.*

diverse /daiˈvɜːs, ˈdai-, dɪ-/ *adj.* unlike in nature or qualities; varied. □ **diversely** *adv.*

diversify *v.* (**-ies**, **-ied**) **1** *tr.* make diverse; vary; modify. **2** *tr.* spread (investment, efforts, etc.) over several enterprises or products, esp. to reduce the risk of loss. **3** *intr.* (often foll. by *into*) esp. *Business* (of a

firm etc.) expand the range of products handled. □
diversification n.

diversion n. **1 a** the act of diverting; deviation. **b** an
instance of this. **2 a** the diverting of attention
deliberately. **b** a stratagem for this purpose (created a
diversion). **3** a recreation or pastime, esp. as diverting
the mind from preoccupation or boredom. **4** an artificial watercourse created to divert the flow of water
from one body to another or to provide drainage. □
diversionary adj.

diversity /dai'vɜrsiti, di-/ n. (pl. **-ies**) **1** the condition
or quality of being diverse; variety. **2** a variety.

divert /dai'vɜrt, di-/ v.tr. **1** (often foll. by from, to) **a** turn
aside from a direction or course; deflect. **b** draw the
attention of; distract. **2** (often as **diverting** adj.)
entertain; amuse. □ **divertingly** adv.

divest /dai'vest/ v. **1** tr. & intr. sell off (a subsidiary
company, investments, etc.). **2** tr. (usu. foll. by of; often
refl.) unclothe; strip (divested himself of his jacket). **3** tr.
deprive, dispossess; free, rid (must divest ourselves of
such prejudices). □ **divestiture** n. **divestment** n.

divide ● v. **1** tr. & intr. (often foll. by in, into, up) separate
or be separated into parts; break up; split. **2** tr. & intr.
(often foll. by up) distribute; deal; share (divided it up
between them). **3** tr. **a** cut off; separate; part (divide the
sheep from the goats). **b** mark out into parts (a ruler
divided into centimetres). **c** specify different kinds of,
classify (people can be divided into two types). **4** tr. cause
to disagree; set at variance (opinions are divided). **5**
Math. **a** tr. find how many times (a number) contains
another (divide 20 by 4). **b** intr. (of a number) be contained in (a number) without a remainder (4 divides
into 20). **c** intr. be susceptible of division (10 divides by
2 and 5). **d** tr. find how many times (a number) is
contained in another (divide 4 into 20). **6** intr. Math. do
division. **7** Parl. **a** intr. (of a legislative assembly etc.)
part into two groups for voting (the House divided). **b** tr.
so divide (a Parliament etc.) for voting. ● n. **1 a** a
dividing or boundary line; a gulf (the divide between
rich and poor). **b** a separation (the cultural divide). **2** (also
Divide; usu. prec. by the) an esp. continental
watershed. □ **divided against itself** consisting of
opposing factions.

divided highway n. N Amer. a highway with a
median strip etc. separating opposing traffic.

dividend n. **1 a** a sum of money to be divided among
a number of persons, esp. that paid by a company to
shareholders. **b** a similar sum payable to members of
a co-operative, to creditors of an insolvent estate, etc.
c an individual's share of a dividend. **2** Math. a number to be divided by a divisor. **3** a benefit from any
action (their long training paid dividends).

divider n. anything which divides a whole into sections, esp. an insert in a binder, notebook, etc., or a
screen etc., dividing a room into two parts.

dividing line n. a real or notional line between
sharply contrasted things, characteristics, etc.

divination /ˌdɪvɪ'neɪʃən/ n. **1** supposed insight into
the future etc. gained by supernatural means. **2 a** a
skilful and accurate forecast. **b** a good guess.

divine ● adj. (**diviner, divinest**) **1 a** of, from, or like
God or a god. **b** devoted to God; sacred (divine service).
2 a more than humanly excellent, gifted, or
beautiful. **b** informal excellent; delightful. ● v. **1** tr.
discover by guessing, intuition, inspiration, or magic.
2 tr. foresee, predict, conjecture. **3** intr. practise
divination. ● n. **1** a cleric, usu. an expert in theology.
2 (**the Divine**) providence or God. □ **divinely** adv.
divineness n. **diviner** n.

diving n. **1** in senses of DIVE. **2** the sport of performing
dives, esp. with elaborate twists etc. of the body.

diving board n. an elevated board projecting over
water, used for diving from.

diving duck n. a duck that habitually dives for food,
esp. one of the tribe Aythyini.

diving suit n. a suit worn while diving, esp. a watertight one with a helmet and an air supply.

divinity n. (pl. **-ies**) **1** the state or quality of being
divine. **2 a** a god; a divine being. **b** (as **the Divinity**)
God. **3** the study of religion; theology. **4** N Amer. (also
divinity fudge) a type of fudge made with beaten
egg whites and nuts.

divisible /dɪ'vɪzəbəl/ adj. **1** capable of being divided,
physically or mentally. **2** (foll. by by) Math. containing
(a number) a number of times without a remainder.

division n. **1** the act or an instance of dividing; the
process of being divided. **2** Math. the process of dividing one number by another. **3** disagreement or discord (division of opinion). **4** Parl. the separation of
members of a legislative body into two sets for counting votes for and against. **5** one of two or more parts
into which a thing is divided. **6** a major unit of
administration or organization, esp.: **a** a group of
army brigades or regiments. **b** Cdn an administrative
unit of a police force. **c** Sport a grouping of teams or
athletes within a league etc. **d** = SCHOOL DIVISION. **7** a
district defined for administrative purposes. **8 a** Bot. a
major taxonomic grouping. **b** Zool. a subsidiary category between major levels of classification. □
divisional adj. **divisionally** adv. **divisionary** adj.

Divisional Court n. Cdn (in Ontario) a court consisting of tribunals of three judges of the Ontario Court,
which hears appeals from lower provincial courts
and provincial administrative tribunals.

division of labour n. the specialization of workers
in the process of production or any other economic,
domestic, etc. activity.

division of powers n. (in Canada) the separation of
governmental responsibilities and privileges into
federal and provincial jurisdictions.

division sign n. the sign (÷), placed between two
numbers to indicate that the one preceding the sign
is to be divided by the one following it.

divisive /dɪ'vɪsɪv, dɪ'vaɪsɪv, -zɪv/ adj. causing
disagreement. □ **divisively** adv. **divisiveness** n.

divisor /dɪ'vaɪzər/ n. **1** a number by which another is
to be divided. **2** a number that divides another without a remainder.

divorce ● n. **1 a** the legal dissolution of a marriage
(also attrib.: divorce court). **b** a legal decree of this. **2 a**
severance or separation (a divorce between thought and
feeling). ● v. **1 a** tr. (usu. as **divorced** adj.) (often foll. by
from) legally dissolve the marriage of (a divorced couple).
b intr. separate by divorce (they divorced last year). **c** tr.
end one's marriage with (divorced him). **2** tr. (often foll.
by from) detach, separate (divorced from reality).

divorcee /ˌdɪvɔr'si:/ n. a divorced person, esp. a
divorced woman.

divulge /dai'vʌldʒ, di-/ v.tr. disclose; reveal (a secret
etc.). □ **divulgence** n.

divvy informal ● v.tr. (**-ies, -ied**) (often foll. by up) share
out; divide. ● n. (pl. **-ies**) a distribution.

Diwali /di:'wɒli/ n. a Hindu festival held in October or
November honouring the goddess of prosperity, during which gifts are exchanged and lamps lit.

Dixie /'dɪksi/ n. the southern states of the US.

Dixieland n. **1** = DIXIE. **2** a kind of jazz with a strong
two-beat rhythm and collective improvisation.

DIY abbr. do-it-yourself. □ **DIYer** n.

dizzy ● *adj.* (**-ier, -iest**) **1 a** giddy, unsteady. **b** feeling confused. **c** *informal* scatterbrained. **2** causing giddiness (*dizzy heights*). ● *v.tr.* (**-ies, -ied**) **1** make dizzy. **2** bewilder. □ **dizzily** *adv.* **dizziness** *n.* **dizzying** *adj.* **dizzyingly** *adv.*

DJ ● *n.* a disc jockey. ● *v.intr.* (**DJed, DJing**) act as a disc jockey.

DJIA *abbr.* Dow-Jones Industrial Average.

DL *abbr.* Baseball DISABLED LIST.

dl *abbr.* decilitre(s).

D.Litt. *abbr.* Doctor of Letters.

DM *abbr.* **1** *Cdn* Deputy Minister. **2** (also **D-mark**) Deutschmark. **3** dextromethorphan.

dm *abbr.* decimetre(s).

DMD *abbr.* **1** (**D.M.D.**) Doctor of Dental Medicine. **2** DUCHENNE MUSCULAR DYSTROPHY.

D.Min. *abbr.* Doctor of Ministry.

DMs *abbr.* Doctor Martens.

D.Mus. *abbr.* Doctor of Music.

DNA *abbr.* deoxyribonucleic acid, the self-replicating material which is present in nearly all living organisms, esp. as a constituent of chromosomes, and is the carrier of genetic information.

DNA fingerprinting *n.* = GENETIC FINGERPRINTING.

DND *abbr.* (in Canada) Dept. of National Defence.

DNR *abbr.* do not resuscitate.

do¹ ● *v.* (*3rd sing. present* **does**; *past* **did**; *past part.* **done**) **1** *tr.* perform, carry out, achieve, complete (*work etc.*). **2** *tr.* **a** produce, make (*she was doing a painting*). **b** provide (*do you do lunches?*). **3** *tr.* bestow, grant; have a specified effect on (*a walk would do you good*; *do me a favour*). **4** *intr.* act, behave, proceed (*do as I do*). **5** *tr.* work at, study; be occupied with (*what does your mother do?*; *we're doing Chaucer*). **6 a** *intr.* be suitable or acceptable; suffice (*a sandwich will do*). **b** *tr.* satisfy; be suitable for (*will do me nicely*). **7** *tr.* deal with; put in order (*I must do my hair before we go*). **8** *intr.* **a** fare; get on (*he did badly in the test*). **b** perform, work (*could do better*). **9** *tr.* **a** solve; work out (*we did the puzzle*). **b** (*prec. by* can *or* be able to) be competent at (*I never could do grammar*). **10** *tr.* **a** traverse (a certain distance) (*we did fifty miles today*). **b** travel at a specified speed (*he was doing about eighty*). **11** *tr.* *informal* **a** act or behave like (*did a Houdini*). **b** play the part of (*she was asked to do hostess*). **12** *intr.* *informal* finish (*I'm done in the bathroom*). **13** *tr.* produce or give a performance of (*we've never done 'Pygmalion'*). **14** *tr.* cook (*the potatoes aren't done yet*). **15** *intr.* be in progress (*what's doing?*). **16** *tr.* *informal* visit; see the sights of (*we did all the art galleries*). **17** *tr.* *informal* **a** (often as **done** *adj.*) exhaust; tire out (*the climb has completely done me*). **b** beat up, defeat, kill. **c** ruin (*now you've done it*). **18** *tr.* *slang* **a** rob (*did a bank in Sarnia*). **b** swindle (*I was done at the market*). **19** *tr.* *slang* undergo (a specified term of imprisonment) (*he did two years for fraud*). **20** *tr.* *coarse slang* have sexual intercourse with. **21** *tr.* *slang* take (a drug). **22** have (a meal) as a social or business engagement (*let's do lunch!*). ● *v.aux.* **1 a** (except with *be, can, may, ought, shall, will*) in questions and negative statements (*do you understand?*). **b** (except with *can, may, ought, shall, will*) in negative commands (*don't be silly*). **2** *ellipt.* or in place of verb or verb and object (*you know her better than I do*). **3** forming emphatic present and past tenses (*I do want to*; *they did go*). **4** in inversion for emphasis (*did she but know it*). ● *n.* (*pl.* **dos** *or* **do's**) **1** *informal* an elaborate event, party, or operation. **2** *informal* a hairdo. **3** *euphemism* excrement. □ **be to do with** be concerned or connected with. **do away with** *informal* **1** abolish. **2** kill. **do battle** enter into combat. **do down** *informal* **1** cheat, swindle. **2** get the better of; overcome. **do for 1** be satisfactory or suffi-

cient for. **2** *informal* (esp. as **done for** *adj.*) destroy, ruin, kill (*he knew he was done for*). **3** *informal* act as housekeeper for. **do in 1** *slang* **a** kill. **b** ruin, do injury to. **2** *informal* exhaust, tire out. **do it** *informal* have sexual intercourse. **do nothing for** *informal* **1** detract from the appearance or quality of (*does nothing for our reputation*). **2** fail to impress or excite (*he does nothing for me*). **do or die** persist regardless of danger. **do a person out of** *informal* unjustly deprive a person of; swindle out of. **do over 1** *N Amer. informal* do again. **2** *slang* attack; beat up. **3** *informal* redecorate, refurbish. **dos and don'ts** rules of behaviour. **do something for (or to)** *informal* enhance the appearance or quality of (*that carpet does something for the room*). **do up 1** fasten, secure. **2** *informal* **a** refurbish, renovate. **b** adorn, dress up. **3** *slang* **a** ruin, get the better of. **b** beat up. **do well for oneself** prosper. **do well out of** profit by. **do with** (*prec. by* could) would be glad to have; would profit by (*I could do with a rest*). **do without** manage without; forgo (*did without supper*). **have** (or **be**) **nothing to do with 1** have no connection or dealings with. **2** be no business or concern of (*the decision has nothing to do with him*). **have to do** (or **something to do**) with be connected with.

do² /doː/ *n.* Music **1** (in tonic sol-fa) the first and eighth note of a major scale. **2** the note C in the fixed-do system.

DOA *abbr.* dead on arrival (at hospital etc.).

doable /ˈduːəbəl/ *adj.* able to be done; practical.

D.O.B. *abbr.* date of birth.

Doberman /ˈdoːbərmən/ *n.* (in full **Doberman pinscher** /ˈpɪnʃər/) a breed of large dog with a smooth coat, frequently used as a guard dog.

dobro /ˈdɒbroː/ *n.* a type of acoustic guitar with steel resonating discs inside the body under the bridge.

DOC *abbr.* Denominazione di Origine Controllata or Denominação de Origem Controlada; a guarantee of the origin of an Italian or Portuguese wine etc. in conformity with statutory regulations.

doc *n.* *informal* **1** doctor. **2** buddy, fellow (*what's up, doc?*). **3** documentary. **4** *Computing* document.

docile /ˈdɒsaɪl, ˈdoː-/ *adj.* submissive, easily managed. □ **docilely** *adv.* **docility** /-ˈsɪlɪti/ *n.*

dock¹ ● *n.* **1** *N Amer.* a ship's berth, a wharf. **2** an artificially enclosed body of water for the loading, unloading, and repair of ships. **3** (in *pl.*) a range of docks with wharves and offices; a dockyard. **4** *N Amer.* = LOADING DOCK. **5** = DRY DOCK. ● *v.* **1** *tr.* & *intr.* bring or come into a dock. **2 a** *tr.* join (spacecraft) together in space. **b** *intr.* (of spacecraft) be joined.

dock² *n.* the enclosure for the accused in a criminal court. □ **in the dock** on trial.

dock³ *n.* any of various plants of the genus *Rumex*, with a spike of many small, green flowers.

dock⁴ ● *v.tr.* **1 a** cut short (an animal's tail). **b** cut short the tail of. **2 a** (often foll. by *from*) deduct (a part) from wages, supplies, etc. **b** reduce (wages etc.) in this way. ● *n.* the solid bony part of an animal's tail.

docket *n.* *N Amer.* **1** a list of causes for trial or persons having causes pending. **2** a list of things to be done.

dockside *n.* (often *attrib.*) the area immediately adjacent to a dock.

dockyard *n.* an area with docks and equipment for building and repairing ships.

Doc Martens *var. of* DOCTOR MARTENS.

doctor ● *n.* **1 a** a qualified practitioner of medicine; a physician or surgeon. **b** *N Amer.* (esp. as an honorific) a qualified dentist, veterinarian, optometrist, or chiropractor. **2** a person who holds a doctorate. **3** *informal* a person who carries out repairs. ● *v.* *informal* **1**

a *tr.* treat medically. **b** *intr.* (esp. as **doctoring** *n.*) practise as a physician. **2** *tr.* castrate or spay. **3** *tr.* patch up (machinery etc.); mend. **4** *tr.* adulterate. **5** *tr.* tamper with, falsify. □ **what the doctor ordered** *informal* something beneficial or desirable.

doctoral *adj.* of or relating to a doctorate.

doctor-assisted suicide *n.* suicide as committed with the help of a doctor.

doctorate *n.* the highest university degree in any faculty.

Doctor Martens /ˈdɒktər ˈmɑrtɪnz/ *n.pl.* proprietary a type of heavy usu. laced boot or shoe with a cushioned sole.

Doctor of Philosophy *n.* **1** a doctorate awarded in the humanities, social sciences, pure sciences, etc. **2** a person holding such a degree. Abbr.: **Ph.D.**

doctrinaire /ˌdɒktrɪˈnɛr/ ● *adj.* seeking to apply a theory or doctrine in all circumstances without regard to practical considerations; theoretical and impractical. ● *n.* a pedantic theorist.

doctrinal /dɒkˈtrainəl, ˈdɒktrɪnəl/ *adj.* of, relating to, or concerned with a doctrine or doctrines. □ **doctrinally** *adv.*

doctrine /ˈdɒktrɪn/ *n.* **1** what is taught; a body of instruction. **2 a** a principle of religious or political etc. belief. **b** a set of such principles; dogma.

docudrama /ˈdɒkjʊˌdræmə/ *n.* a dramatized television film based on real events.

document ● *n.* **1** a piece of written or printed matter that provides a record or evidence of events, an agreement, ownership, identification, etc. **2** *Computing* a file, esp. a text file. ● *v.tr.* **1** prove by or provide with documents or evidence. **2** record in a document. **3** provide (a monograph etc.) with citations or references to support statements made. □ **documental** *adj.* **documenter** *n.*

documentarian *n.* **1** (also **documentarist**) a director or producer of documentaries. **2** a photographer specializing in producing a factual record.

documentary /ˌdɒkjʊˈmɛntəri/ ● *n.* (pl. **-ies**) a film or broadcast program based on real events, places, or circumstances and usu. intended primarily to record or inform. ● *adj.* **1** consisting of documents (*documentary evidence*). **2** providing a factual record or report.

documentation *n.* **1** the provision of documents. **2** the preparation or use of documentary evidence or authorities. **3** documents produced as evidence or proof of something. **4** a collection of documents relating to a process or event, esp. the written specification and instructions accompanying a computer program.

dodder *v.intr.* tremble or totter, esp. from age. □ **dodderer** *n.* **doddering** *adj.* **doddery** *adj.*

dodecagon /doˈdɛkəgɒn/ *n.* a plane figure with twelve sides.

dodecahedron /ˌdoʊdɛkəˈhiːdrən/ *n.* (pl. **-hedrons** or **-hedra** /-drə/) a solid figure with twelve faces.

dodge ● *v.* **1** *intr.* (often foll. by *about*, *around*) move quickly to one side or quickly change position, to elude a pursuer, blow, etc. **2** *tr.* evade by cunning or trickery (*dodged paying the fare*). **b** elude (a pursuer, opponent, blow, etc.) by a sideways movement etc. ● *n.* **1** a quick movement to avoid or evade something. **2** a clever trick or expedient.

dodger *n.* **1** a person who dodges, esp. an artful or elusive person. **2** a screen on a ship's bridge etc. as protection from spray etc.

dodo /ˈdoʊdoʊ/ *n.* (pl. **-os** or **-oes**) **1** any large flightless bird of the extinct family Raphidae, native to Mauritius. **2** an old-fashioned, stupid, or inactive

person. □ **as dead as the** (or **a**) **dodo 1** completely or unmistakably dead. **2** entirely obsolete.

DOE *abbr.* Department of the Environment.

doe *n.* a female deer, reindeer, hare, or rabbit.

doe-eyed *adj.* (esp. of a woman) having large gentle dark eyes.

doer /ˈduːər/ *n.* **1** a person who does something. **2** a person who acts rather than merely talking etc.

does *3rd sing. present of* DO[1].

doesn't *contraction* does not.

doff *v.tr. literary* take off (one's hat, clothing).

dog ● *n.* **1** any four-legged flesh-eating animal of the genus *Canis*, of many breeds domesticated and wild. **2** the male of these animals. **3** *informal* **a** a despicable person. **b** a person of a specified kind (*a lucky dog*). **c** *slang* an unattractive person, esp. a woman. **4** a mechanical device for gripping. **5** *N Amer. slang* something of poor quality, e.g. an ill-performing stock, a bad movie, etc. **6** *N Amer. euphemism* God (*dog knows we've seen enough*). **7** *slang* (usu. in *pl.*) a foot (*my dogs are aching*). **8** = HOT DOG *n.* 1. ● *v.tr.* (**dogged**, **dogging**) follow closely and persistently; pursue, track. □ **die like a dog** die miserably or shamefully. **dog in the manger** a person who prevents others from using something, although that person has no use for it. **dog it** esp. *N Amer. informal* act lazily; idle, shirk. **dog's age** *N Amer. informal* a long time. **dog's breakfast** *informal* a mess. **a dog's life** a miserable or wretched existence (*it's a dog's life*). **the dogs of war** *literary* the havoc accompanying war. **go to the dogs** *informal* deteriorate, be ruined. **not a dog's chance** *informal* no chance at all. **put on the dog** *N Amer. informal* behave pretentiously. **sick as a dog** *N Amer.* very ill. **work like a dog** *N Amer.* work very hard. □ **doggish** *adj.* **doglike** *adj.*

dogan /ˈdoʊgən/ *n. Cdn slang offensive* a Roman Catholic, esp. an Irish Roman Catholic.

dog collar *n.* **1** a collar for a dog. **2 a** *informal* a clerical collar. **b** a straight high collar. **3** a jewelled band worn around the neck.

dog days *n.pl.* **1** the hottest period of the year. **2** *informal* a period of inactivity, lethargy, etc.

dog-eared *adj.* (of a book etc.) with the corners worn or battered with use.

dog-eat-dog *adj. informal* (usu. *attrib.*; not hyphenated when *predic.*) ruthlessly competitive (*the dog-eat-dog world of business*; *it's dog eat dog out there*).

dogfight ● *n.* **1** a fight between dogs. **2** a close combat between fighter aircraft. **3** a violent and confused fight. ● *v.intr.* take part in a dogfight.

dogfish *n.* (pl. same or **dogfishes**) any of various small sharks esp. of the families Scyliorhinidae, Squalidae, and Triakidae.

dogged /ˈdɒgəd/ *adj.* tenacious; grimly persistent. □ **doggedly** *adv.* **doggedness** *n.*

doggerel /ˈdɒgərəl/ *n.* poor or trivial verse.

doggone /ˈdɒgɒn/ *esp. N Amer. slang* ● *adj. & adv.* damned. ● *interj.* expressing annoyance.

doggy ● *adj.* **1** of or like a dog. **2** devoted to dogs. ● *n.* (also **doggie**) (pl. **-ies**) a little dog; a pet name for a dog. □ **dogginess** *n.*

doggy bag *n.* a bag given to a customer in a restaurant or a guest at a party etc. for putting leftovers in to take home.

doghouse *n. N Amer.* a shelter for a dog. □ **in the doghouse** *informal* in disgrace or disfavour.

dogie /ˈdoʊgi/ *n. N Amer.* (*West*) a motherless or neglected calf.

dogleg ● *n.* a sharp bend like that in a dog's hind leg.

● adj. (also **doglegged**) bent sharply. ● v.intr. (**-legged**, **-legging**) bend sharply.

dogma /'dɒgmə/ n. **1** a belief or set of beliefs held by an authority or group, which others are expected to accept without argument. **2** an arrogant declaration of opinion.

dogmatic /dɒg'mætɪk/ adj. **1 a** (of a person) given to asserting or imposing personal opinions; arrogant. **b** intolerantly authoritative. **2 a** of or in the nature of dogma; doctrinal. **b** based on a priori principles, not on induction. □ **dogmatically** adv.

dogmatics n. **1** the study of religious dogmas; dogmatic theology. **2** a system of dogma.

dogmatism /'dɒgmə,tɪzəm/ n. a tendency to be dogmatic. □ **dogmatist** n. **dogmatize** v.

dog meat n. **1** the flesh of a dog. **2** meat to be used as food for dogs. **3** N Amer. informal a person who is defeated etc. (touch that and you're dog meat!).

do-gooder n. a person who actively tries to help others, esp. one considered unrealistic or officious. □ **do-good** adj. & n. **do-goodery** n. **do-goodism** n.

dog-paddle ● n. an elementary swimming stroke with short quick movements of the arms and legs beneath the body. ● v.intr. swim using this stroke.

Dogrib ● n. **1** a member of a Dene Aboriginal people living along the north shore of Great Slave Lake. **2** the Athapaskan language of this people. ● adj. of or relating to this people or their language.

dog salmon n. = CHUM³.

dogsled ● n. a sled designed to be pulled by dogs. ● v.intr. travel by dogsled. □ **dogsledding** n.

dog's tooth n. (in full **dog's tooth violet**) any plant of the genus Erythronium, often with speckled leaves, e.g. E. americanum of eastern N America and E. grandiflorum of western N America.

dog tag n. **1** a tag attached to a dog's collar, giving an identification number, the dog's name, the owner's phone number, or vaccination information. **2** N Amer. slang a soldier's metal identity tag.

dog team n. a team of dogs for pulling a dogsled.

dog-tired adj. utterly exhausted.

dogtrot n. a gentle easy trot.

dogwood n. **1** any of various shrubs or small trees of the genus Cornus, including the flowering dogwoods, C. florida of eastern N America and C. nuttallii of western N America, and the low-growing bunchberry C. canadensis. **2** any of various similar trees. **3** the wood of the dogwood.

doh var. of DO².

DOHC abbr. (of an automobile engine etc.) double overhead camshaft.

doily n. (pl. **-ies**) a small ornamental mat of paper, lace, etc., e.g. on a table, or on a plate for cookies, sandwiches, etc. □ **doilied** adj.

doing n. **1** an action; the performance of a deed (it was my doing). **2** activity, effort (it takes a lot of doing).

do-it-yourself ● adj. (of work, esp. building, decorating, etc.) done or to be done by an amateur at home. ● n. such work. □ **do-it-yourselfer** n.

dojo /'doːdʒoː/ n. (pl. **-os**) **1** a room or hall in which judo and other martial arts are practised. **2** a mat on which judo etc. is practised.

Dolby /'doːlbi/ n. proprietary an electronic noise reduction system used esp. in tape recording to reduce hiss.

doldrums /'doːldrəmz, dɒl-/ n.pl. (usu. prec. by the) **1** low spirits; a feeling of boredom or depression. **2** a period of inactivity or state of stagnation. **3** an equatorial ocean region of calms, sudden storms, and light unpredictable winds.

dole ● n. **1** (usu. prec. by the) informal benefit claimable by the unemployed from the government. **2 a** charitable distribution. **b** a charitable (esp. sparing) gift of food, clothes, or money. ● v.tr. (usu. foll. by out) deal out sparingly. □ **on the dole** informal receiving government unemployment benefits.

doleful adj. **1** mournful, sad. **2** dreary, dismal. □ **dolefully** adv. **dolefulness** n.

doll ● n. **1** a usu. small model of a human figure, usu. a child or woman, esp. for use as a toy. **2** informal **a** a pretty but silly young woman. **b** a young woman. **c** an attractive person. **d** a helpful or kind person. **e** an affectionate or familiar form of address. ● v.tr. & intr. (foll. by up) dress up smartly. □ **doll-like** adj.

dollar n. **1** the chief monetary unit of Canada, the US, Australia, and certain other countries. **2** money available to be spent (the spectator dollar). □ **bet dollars to doughnuts** N Amer. maintain as a certainty.

dollar amount n. the cost or value of something in dollars.

dollar store n. N Amer. a store selling low-priced, often discontinued or remaindered, items.

dollhouse n. N Amer. (also **doll's house**) **1** a miniature toy house for dolls. **2** a very small house.

dollop ● n. **1** a shapeless lump of something soft, esp. food. **2** something added as if in dollops (a dollop of morality). ● v.tr. (**dolloped**, **dolloping**) (usu. foll. by out) serve out in large shapeless quantities.

dolly ● n. (pl. **-ies**) **1** a child's name for a doll. **2** a small four-wheeled cart for moving appliances, boxes, etc. **3** a movable platform for a movie or video camera. ● v. (**-ies**, **-ied**) **1** tr. (foll. by up) dress up smartly. **2** intr. (foll. by in, up) move a motion picture camera in or up to a subject, or out from it.

Dolly Varden n. **1** a brightly spotted char, Salvelinus malma, of western N America. **2** a woman's large hat with one side drooping and a floral trimming.

dolomite /'dɒlə,maɪt/ n. a mineral or rock of calcium magnesium carbonate. □ **dolomitic** /,dɒlə'mɪtɪk/ adj.

dolphin n. any of various porpoise-like sea mammals of the family Delphinidae having a slender beaklike snout.

dolt n. a stupid person. □ **doltish** adj.

Dom /dɒm/ n. a title prefixed to the names of some Catholic dignitaries and monks.

-dom suffix forming nouns denoting a class of people (or the attitudes etc. associated with them) regarded collectively (officialdom).

domain /də'meɪn/ n. **1** an area under one rule; a realm. **2** an estate or lands under one control. **3** a sphere of control or influence. **4** Math. the set of possible values of an independent variable. **5** (also **domain name**) the parts of an e-mail address following the @ symbol.

dome ● n. **1 a** a rounded vault as a roof, with a circular, elliptical, or polygonal base; a large cupola. **b** the revolving openable hemispherical roof of an observatory. **2** N Amer. a stadium with a domed roof. **3 a** a natural vault or canopy (of the sky, trees, etc.). **b** the rounded summit of a hill etc. **4** a dome-shaped landform or underground structure. **5** N Amer. a raised, glassed-in area of the roof of a railway car, allowing passengers a full view of surrounding scenery. **6** slang the head. ● v.tr. (usu. as **domed** adj.) cover with or shape as a dome. □ **dome-like** adj.

domestic ● adj. **1** of the home, household, or family affairs. **2 a** of or within one's own country, not foreign or international. **b** homegrown or homemade. **3** (of an animal) kept by or living with human beings. **4** fond of home life. ● *n.* a household servant. ☐ **domestically** *adv.*

domesticate *v.tr.* **1** tame (an animal) to live with humans. **2** accustom to home life and management. **3** naturalize (a plant etc.). ☐ **domestication** *n.*

domesticated *adj.* **1** (of an animal or plant) kept by humans for work, food, or companionship; not wild. **2** (of a person) skilled at and fond of household tasks such as cooking, cleaning, sewing, etc.

domesticity /ˌdoːmə'stɪsɪti, ˌdɒm-/ *n.* **1** the state of being domestic. **2** domestic or home life.

domestic violence *n.* violent acts occurring within a household.

domicile ● *n.* a dwelling place; one's home. ● *adj.* (usu. as **domiciled** *adj.*) establish or settle in a place.

dominant ● *adj.* **1** dominating, prevailing, most influential. **2** (of a high place) prominent, overlooking others. **3 a** (of an allele) expressed even when inherited from only one parent. **b** (of an inherited characteristic) appearing in an individual even when its allelic counterpart is also inherited (*compare* RECESSIVE *adj.* 1). **4 a** designating the predominant species in a plant or animal community. **b** (of an animal) allowed priority in access to food, mates, etc. by others of its species because of success in previous aggressive encounters. **5** *Music* based on or pertaining to the dominant. ● *n.* **1 a** a dominant trait or gene. **b** an individual having such a trait or gene. **2** a predominant species of a plant or animal community. **3** a dominating feature, individual, group, etc. **4** *Music* the fifth note of the diatonic scale of any key. ☐ **dominance** *n.* **dominantly** *adv.*

dominate *v.tr. & intr.* **1** have a commanding influence on; exercise control over. **2** (of a person, sound, event, etc.) be the most influential or conspicuous factor in. **3** (of a building etc.) have a commanding position over; overlook. ☐ **dominating** *adj.* **dominator** *n.*

domination *n.* **1** command, control. **2 a** the act or an instance of dominating. **b** the process of being dominated.

dominatrix /dɒmə'neɪtrɪks/ *n.* (*pl.* **dominatrices** /-trɪsiːz/) a woman who is domineering, esp. a dominant woman in sado-masochistic sexual activities.

domineer *v.intr.* (often foll. by *over*) behave in an arrogant and overbearing way.

domineering *adj.* overbearing; offensively assertive or dictatorial. ☐ **domineeringly** *adv.*

Dominican¹ /də'mɪnɪkən/ ● *adj.* **1** of or relating to the mendicant Order of Friars Preaching, devoted to preaching and the study of theology. **2** of or relating to either of the two female religious orders founded on Dominican principles. ● *n.* a Dominican friar, nun, or sister.

Dominican² ● *n.* **1** a native or an inhabitant of the island of Dominica in the W Indies. **2** a native or an inhabitant of the Dominican Republic. ● *adj.* **1** of or pertaining to Dominica. **2** of or pertaining to the Dominican Republic, a country in the Caribbean, on the island of Hispaniola.

dominion *n.* **1** sovereign authority; control. **2** the territory of a sovereign or government; a domain. **3** the title of each of the self-governing territories of the Commonwealth. **4** *hist.* **a** (**the Dominion**) *informal* Canada. **b** *Cdn* (*Nfld*) Newfoundland as a self-governing part of the Commonwealth prior to 1949.

Dominion Day *n. hist.* = CANADA DAY.

domino /'dɒmɪˌnoː/ *n.* (*pl.* **-oes**) **1 a** any of 28 small oblong tiles, marked with 0–6 dots on each half. **b** (in *pl.*, usu. treated as *sing.*) a game played with these. **2** a

country etc. perceived as being one in a series and so likely to succumb to circumstances or crises affecting a similar country etc.

domino effect *n.* the effect of one event triggering a succession of other events, like a falling domino at the beginning of a line of upended dominoes.

don¹ /dɒn/ *n.* **1** (**Don**) **a** a Spanish title prefixed to a man's forename. **b** a Spanish gentleman; a Spaniard. **2** an Italian title of respectful address, esp. to a priest. **3** *Cdn* a senior person in a university residence, usu. responsible for the students and community life. **4** *N Amer.* a high-ranking member of the Mafia.

don² *v.tr.* (**donned, donning**) put on (clothing).

donair /doː'ner/ *n. N Amer.* spiced lamb cooked on a spit, served in slices, and usu. rolled in pita bread.

donate *v.tr.* give or contribute (money etc.), esp. voluntarily, to a fund or institution. ☐ **donator** *n.*

donation *n.* **1** the act or an instance of donating. **2** something, esp. an amount of money, donated.

done ● *v. past part. of* DO¹. ● *adj.* **1** finished, completed. **2** *informal* socially acceptable (*the done thing*). **3 a** (often with *in*) *informal* tired out. **b** (often with *up*) fixed up or made more attractive (*the motel was newly done up*). **4** (of food) cooked sufficiently. ☐ **be done with** have or be finished with. **done for** *informal* **1** in serious trouble. **2** finished, destroyed. **have done with** be rid of or have finished dealing with.

doneness *n.* the degree to which food is cooked.

dong ● *n.* **1** the deep sound of a large bell. **2** esp. *N Amer. coarse slang* the penis. ● *v.intr.* make the deep sound of a large bell.

Don Juan /dɒn 'wɒn, 'hwɒn/ *n.* a man with a reputation for seducing women; a rake, a libertine.

donkey *n.* (*pl.* **-eys**) **1** a domestic ass. **2** *informal* a stupid or foolish person. **3** (in full **donkey engine**) a small auxiliary engine.

donna /'dɒnə/ *n.* **1** an Italian, Spanish, or Portuguese lady. **2** (**Donna**) the courtesy title of such a lady.

donnybrook *n.* a scene of uproar; a brawl.

donor *n.* **1** a person who gives or donates something, e.g. to a charity. **2** a person who provides blood for a transfusion, an organ or tissue for transplant, etc.

do-nothing ● *n.* a person who does little or nothing. ● *adj.* characterized by doing or accomplishing little or nothing (*a do-nothing government*).

don't ● *contraction* do not. ● *n.* a prohibition; an injunction not to do something (*dos and don'ts*).

donut esp. *N Amer. var. of* DOUGHNUT.

doodad *n. N Amer.* something not readily nameable, esp. a gadget or ornament of an unnecessary kind.

doodle ● *v.* **1** *intr. & tr.* scribble or draw, esp. absentmindedly. **2** *intr. & tr.* play idly on a musical instrument. **3** *intr. N Amer.* waste time. ● *n.* a figure drawn absentmindedly. ☐ **doodler** *n.* **doodling** *adj.*

doo-doo *n. slang* **1** excrement. **2** serious trouble (*we're in deep doo-doo*).

doofus /'duːfəs/ *n.* (*pl.* **-fuses**) a stupid or inept person; an idiot.

doohickey *n.* (*pl.* **-eys**) *N Amer. informal* an unspecified object or small device, esp. a mechanical one.

doom ● *n.* **1 a** a grim fate or destiny. **b** impending death, disaster, or ruin. **2** the Last Judgment. ● *v.tr.* (usu. foll. by *to*) condemn or destine to some fate (*doomed to destruction*).

doom and gloom *n.* a general feeling of despair and pessimism.

doomed *adj.* consigned to misfortune or destruction.

doomsayer *n.* a person who predicts disaster, esp. of a political or economic nature. ☐ **doomsaying** *n.*

doomsday n. **1** the day of the Last Judgment. **2** any day of decisive judgment or final dissolution. **3** (also attrib.) projected time of destruction of the world, esp. by nuclear means (doomsday weapons). □ **till doomsday** forever.

doomsday clock n. **1** a symbolic clock created to measure the world's proximity to the final midnight of nuclear destruction. **2** this image applied to an imminent crisis of significant proportion.

doomsday cult n. a cult which believes that the end of the world is imminent, esp. one whose members commit mass suicide on a chosen date.

doomy adj. **1** portending, suggesting, or predicting doom. **2** ominous, gloomy (doomy music).

door n. **1 a** a hinged, sliding, or revolving barrier for closing and opening an entrance to a building, room, cupboard, etc. **b** this as representing a house etc. (lives two doors away). **2 a** an entrance or an exit; a doorway. **b** a means of access or approach. **c** (prec. by the) the entrance to a theatre, club, etc. at which admission must be paid or tickets shown. **3** something resembling a door in its movement or function, e.g. a lid, valve, or cover. **4** either of the two boards or metal plates attached to the ends of a trawl net. □ **close** (or **shut**) **the door to** (or **on**) exclude the opportunity for. **lay something at a person's door** impute something reprehensible etc. to a person. **leave the door open** ensure that an option remains available. **lie at a person's door** be the fault or responsibility of a person. **open the door to** create an opportunity for. **out of doors** outside the house, esp. in or into the open air. □ **doorless** adj.

doorbell n. a bell or buzzer connected to a door, rung by visitors to signal their arrival.

do-or-die attrib.adj. denoting a determination not to be deterred by any danger or difficulty, esp. in a desperate situation or circumstance.

doored adj. (also in comb.) having a door or doors.

door frame n. the structure into which a door fits.

doorknob n. **1** a usu. round handle on a door which is turned to open or close the door. **2** N Amer. slang an idiot; a stupid person.

doorman n. (pl. **-men**) an attendant at the entrance to a hotel etc. who assists those entering or leaving.

doormat n. **1** a mat at an entrance to a building for wiping mud etc. from the shoes. **2** a passive, submissive person.

doornail n. □ **dead as a doornail** completely or unmistakably dead.

doorpost n. (also **door jamb**) each of the uprights of a door frame.

door prize n. N Amer. something awarded as a prize at a gathering, usu. through a draw.

doorstep n. a step leading up to the outer door of a house etc. □ **on one's** (or **the**) **doorstep** very close.

doorstop n. **1** a weight or wedge placed under a door to keep it open. **2** a device fixed to the ground or wall to prevent a door from opening too widely.

door-to-door ● adj. **1 a** (of selling etc.) done systematically, covering each house on a street etc. **b** (of a salesperson etc.) working in this manner. **2** (of journeys, deliveries, etc.) direct. ● adv. (**door to door**) calling at each house in turn (travelled door to door).

doorway n. **1** an entryway to a room, building, etc., esp. one closed or opened by a door. **2** a means or medium of approach or access (a doorway to freedom).

doo-wop n. (often attrib.) a style of singing, originated by American rhythm-and-blues groups of the 1950s, in which nonsense phrases are used as the main line or as harmony. □ **doo-wopper** n.

doozy n. (also **doozie, doozer**) (pl. **-ies**) N Amer. slang something amazing, remarkable, or incredible.

dope ● n. **1 a** slang a narcotic drug. **b** a drug taken by an athlete or given to a horse etc. to affect performance. **2** slang a silly or stupid person. **3** slang essential facts, details, or information about a subject, esp. of a kind not generally divulged (the inside dope). **4** N Amer. a thick liquid, cream, or gel used as a lubricant, repellent, etc. (bug dope). **5** a substance added to gasoline etc. to increase its effectiveness. ● v. **1 a** tr. administer stimulating or stupefying drugs to (an athlete, horse, etc.). **b** intr. take addictive drugs. **2** tr. doctor or treat (a substance) with an adulterant. **3** tr. smear, daub. **4** tr. informal (foll. by out) work out, infer, or find out by calculation or surmise (doped out the plans). ● adj. slang excellent, outstanding. □ **doped up** slang heavily under the influence of drugs. □ **doper** n.

dopey adj. (also **dopy**) (**dopier, dopiest**) informal **1** stupid, silly. **2 a** half asleep. **b** stupefied by or as if by a drug. □ **dopily** adv. **dopiness** n.

doping n. Sport the use of any substance, foreign or natural to the body, to artificially enhance competition performance.

Doppler effect /'dɒplər/ n. Physics an increase (or decrease) in the frequency of sound, light, or other waves as the source and observer move toward (or away) from each other.

doré /dɔr'ei/ n. Cdn the walleye, Stizostedion vitreum.

dork n. slang **1** a socially awkward, often stupid person. **2** the penis. □ **dorky** adj.

dorm n. informal dormitory.

dormant adj. **1 a** lying inactive as in sleep; sleeping. **b** Biology alive but with development suspended (dormant fruit trees). **2** (of a volcano etc.) temporarily inactive. **3** (of potential faculties etc.) latent or not in current operation (dormant talent). □ **dormancy** n.

dormer n. **1** (in full **dormer window**) a projecting upright window in a sloping roof. **2** the projecting construction which supports the window.

dormitory /'dɔrmɪtɔri/ n. (pl. **-ies**) **1** N Amer. a university or college residence. **2** a large room containing beds, esp. in a school or other institution. **3** a small town or suburb from which people travel to work in a city etc. (also attrib.: dormitory suburb).

dormouse n. (pl. **dormice**) any small mouselike hibernating rodent of the family Gliridae, having a long bushy tail.

dorsal /'dɔrsəl/ adj. Anat., Zool., & Bot. **1** of, on, or near the back (dorsal fin). **2** ridge-shaped. □ **dorsally** adv.

Dorset /'dɔrsət/ n. a member of an Aboriginal people living in the eastern Arctic c. 1000 BC–AD 1000, whose culture was displaced by that of the Inuit.

dory[1] n. (pl. **-ies**) any of various marine fish having a compressed body and flat head, used as food.

dory[2] n. (pl. **-ies**) N Amer. a small flat-bottomed fishing boat with high sides.

doryman n. (pl. **-men**) Cdn a person who fishes from a dory.

DOS /dɒs/ n. an operating system for microcomputers.

dosage n. **1** the size of a dose of medicine etc. **2** the giving of medicine in doses.

dose ● n. **1** an amount of a medicine or drug taken or recommended to be taken at one time. **2** a quantity of something administered or allocated, e.g. work, praise, etc. **3** the amount of ionizing radiation to which a person or thing is exposed. **4** slang a bout of gonorrhea or syphilis. ● v.tr. **1** treat (a person or animal) with doses of medicine. **2** divide into, or administer in, doses.

do-si-do /ˌdoːsiˈdoː/ (also **do-se-do**) (pl. **-os**) ● n. a square dance figure in which two dancers pass around each other back to back and return to their original positions. ● v.intr. perform a do-si-do.

dossier /ˈdɒsiˌeɪ/ n. a set of documents, esp. a collection of information about a person, event, or subject.

DoT abbr. (also **DOT**) (in Canada) Dept. of Transport.

dot ● n. **1 a** a small spot, speck, or mark. **b** such a mark written or printed as part of an *i* or *j*, as a diacritical mark, as one of a series of marks to signify omission, or as a period. **c** a decimal point. **d** a period used in an electronic mail address or file name. **2** Music **a** a point placed after a note or rest to lengthen it by half as much again. **b** a point placed over a note to indicate that it is to be performed staccato. **3** the shorter signal of the two used in Morse code (compare DASH n. 7). **4** a tiny or apparently tiny object (a dot on the horizon). **5** a small amount (a dot of icing). **6 a** a pointlike element of a television picture. **b** the area of phosphor on the inside of a television tube corresponding to this. ● v.tr. (**dotted, dotting**) **1 a** mark with a dot or dots. **b** place a dot over (a letter). **2** Music mark (a note or rest) to show that the time value is increased by half. **3** occur singly throughout (an area) or over (a surface). □ **dot the i's and cross the t's** informal **1** be minutely accurate or emphasize details. **2** add the final touches to a task, exercise, etc. **on the dot** exactly on time.

dot-com n. **1** designating an email address ending in .com. **2** a company or Web site that conducts business on the Internet; e-commerce.

dote v.intr. (foll. by on, upon) be foolishly or excessively fond of. □ **doter** n. **doting** adj. **dotingly** adv.

dot matrix printer n. Computing a printer that creates each character from an array of dots usu. formed by transferring ink by mechanical impact.

dotted line n. a line of dots or dashes on a document, esp. to indicate the space left for a signature. □ **sign on the dotted line** agree fully or formally.

dotty adj. (**-ier, -iest**) informal **1** silly or confused, esp. due to old age. **2** eccentric. **3** absurd. **4** (foll. by about, over) infatuated with. □ **dottily** adv. **dottiness** n.

double ● adj. **1 a** consisting of two usu. equal parts or things. **b** consisting of two identical parts. **2** twice as much or many (double the number; double thickness). **3** having twice the usual size, quantity, strength, value, etc. (double whisky). **4 a** designed or suitable for two people (double bed). **b** (of bedding) suitable for a double bed. **5 a** having some essential part double (double-axle trailer). **b** (of a flower) having more than one circle of petals. **6 a** having two different roles, interpretations, applications, etc. (double meaning). **b** characterized by duplicity, falsity, or deceitfulness (leads a double life). **7** Music lower in pitch by an octave (double bassoon). **8** Figure Skating & Dance (of a jump, pirouette, etc.) involving two revolutions. ● adv. **1** at or to twice the amount, extent, etc. (counts double). **2** two at once or two together (sleep double). ● n. **1 a** a double quantity or thing; twice as much or many. **b** informal an alcoholic drink with a double measure of liquor. **2 a** a counterpart of a person or thing. **b** a person who looks exactly like another. **3** (in pl.) Sport (in tennis, badminton, etc.) a game between two pairs of players. **4** Baseball a successful hit which allows a player to get to second base safely. **5** Figure Skating & Dance a double jump, pirouette, etc. **6** Darts **a** a hit on the narrow ring enclosed by the two outer circles of a dartboard, scoring double. **b** the ring itself. **7 a** = UNDERSTUDY. **b** an actor who takes two parts in the same performance. **c** = BODY DOUBLE. **8** a double room

in a hotel, residence, etc. **9** Bowling two strikes in a row. ● v. **1** tr. & intr. make, become, or amount to twice as much or many. **2 a** tr. fold or bend (paper, cloth, etc.) over on itself so as to bring the two parts into contact. **b** intr. become folded. **3 a** tr. (of an actor) play (two parts) in the same piece. **b** intr. (often foll. by for) be an understudy, body double, etc. **c** intr. (usu. foll. by as) perform or function in an additional capacity. **4** intr. turn sharply in flight or pursuit; take a tortuous course. **5** Music **a** intr. (often foll. by on) play two or more musical instruments (the clarinetist doubles on tenor sax). **b** tr. add the same note in a higher or lower octave to (a note). **6** intr. move at twice the usual speed, esp. march at double time. **7** Baseball **a** intr. make a double. **b** tr. cause (a baserunner) to advance through a double. **c** tr. (usu. foll. by in) cause (a run) to score by hitting a double. **d** tr. tag out (a baserunner) as the second action of a double play. **8** (foll. by up) **a** intr. bend or curl up. **b** tr. cause to do this, esp. by a blow. **c** intr. be overcome with pain or laughter. **d** tr. & intr. share or assign to a room, quarters, etc., with another or others. □ **on** (or **at**) **the double** running, hurrying, or in double time. **bent double** folded, stooping. **double back** take a new direction opposite to the previous one. **double or nothing** a gamble in which the player either gains twice the bet or loses everything. **see double** perceive or seem to perceive two images of one object. □ **doubleness** n. **doubler** n. **doubly** adv.

Double-A = AA 2, 3, 4.

double-action adj. **1** (of a firearm) needing only a single pull of the trigger to cock and fire the weapon. **2** (of a fishing reel) having a spool that turns twice for every turn of the handle.

double agent n. a person who purports to spy for one country or organization while actually working for a hostile or rival one.

double-barrelled adj. **1** (of a gun) having two barrels. **2** very powerful, persuasive, or vehement. **3** twofold or serving a double purpose.

double bass n. **1** the largest and lowest-pitched instrument of the violin family. **2** a player of this instrument.

double bed n. a bed suitable for two people, esp. one measuring 137×190 cm ($53 \frac{1}{2} \times 75$ inches).

double bill n. two films, plays, etc. presented to an audience one after the other in the same program.

double bind n. a dilemma; a situation in which either of two possible courses will be wrong.

double-blind ● adj. designating a test or experiment in which neither the tester nor the subject has knowledge of identities or other factors that might lead to bias. ● n. such a test or experiment.

double-bogey Golf ● n. (pl. **-eys**) a score of two strokes over par on a hole. ● v.tr. & intr. (**-eys, -eyed**) complete (a hole) in two strokes over par.

double boiler n. a saucepan with a detachable upper compartment heated by boiling water in the lower one.

double bond n. a pair of bonds between two atoms in a molecule.

double-book v.tr. accept two reservations simultaneously for (the same seat, room, etc.), esp. to ensure that at least one will be used.

double-breasted adj. (of a coat etc.) having a substantial overlap of material at the front which crosses the body and is usu. fastened with two rows of buttons.

double-check v.tr. verify twice or in two ways.

double-click v. **1** intr. press and release the button of a mouse twice in quick succession to activate a program etc. **2** *tr.* click on (an icon etc.) in this way.

double-cross ● *v.tr.* deceive or betray (a person one is supposedly helping). ● *n.* an act of doing this.

double date ● *n.* a date on which two couples go together. ● *v.intr.* go on a double date.

double-dealing ● *n.* deceit, esp. in business. ● *adj.* deceitful or practising deceit. ☐ **double-deal** *v.intr.*

double-decker *n.* **1** a bus having an upper and lower deck. **2** *informal* anything consisting of two layers, e.g. a sandwich.

double density *adj. Computing* designating a storage device, esp. a disk, having twice the basic capacity.

double-digit *adj.* equal in quantity, rate, etc. to a number, esp. a percentage, between 10 and 99.

double-dip ● *adj.* having two downward movements, each followed by an upward one (*double-dip recession*). ● *n. N Amer.* an ice cream cone with two scoops.

double-dipping *n. N Amer.* **1** the practice of commuting an occupational pension to a lump sum and then drawing a government pension that would not otherwise be due. **2** the practice of receiving an income from two jobs, esp. a pension from a former job and a salary from a current one. ☐ **double-dipper** *n.*

double door *n.* (usu. in *pl.*) **1** a pair of doors side by side in one opening, meeting in the middle. **2** two doors situated one close behind the other.

double duty *n.* a twofold function or role.

double-edged *adj.* **1** having two functions or (often contradictory) applications, interpretations, etc. **2** (of a knife etc.) having two cutting edges.

double entendre / ɒn'tɒndrə / *n.* **1** a word or phrase open to two interpretations, one usu. risqué or indecent. **2** humour using such words or phrases.

double exposure *n. Photog.* the action or result of exposing the same frame, plate, etc. on two separate occasions, either accidentally or deliberately.

double figures *n.pl.* the numbers from 10 to 99.

double glazing *n.* two layers of glass with a space between them, designed to reduce loss of heat and exclude noise. ☐ **double-glazed** *adj.*

double-headed *adj.* having a double head or two heads.

doubleheader *n.* **1** *N Amer.* two games etc. in succession between the same or different opponents, esp. on the same day. **2** two events, occurrences, etc. happening one after the other.

double helix *n.* a pair of parallel helices with a common axis, esp. in the structure of DNA.

double minor *n. Hockey* two minor penalties, imposed for a single offence considered to be severe but accidental, served sequentially.

double negative *n.* a negative statement containing two negative elements, e.g. *didn't say nothing.* ¶Considered ungrammatical in standard English.

double-park *v.tr. & intr.* park (a vehicle) alongside one that is already parked parallel to a curb etc.

double play *n. Baseball* a play in which two runners are put out.

double-quick *adj. & adv.* very quick or quickly.

double room *n.* a room in a hotel with two beds, usu. double or queen size.

double-sided *adj.* **1** that can be used on both sides. **2** having two sides. **3** (of a text) printed etc. on both sides of a sheet of paper. ☐ **double-sidedness** *n.*

double space *v.tr. & intr.* type or format (a text) with every other line left empty. ☐ **double-spaced** *adj.*

doublespeak *n.* = DOUBLE-TALK.

double standard *n.* a rule etc. applied more strictly to some people than to others (or to oneself).

double star *n.* two stars actually or apparently very close together.

doublet / 'dʌblət / *n.* **1** *hist.* a man's short close-fitting jacket, with or without sleeves. **2** either of a pair of similar things.

double take *n.* a delayed and usu. contradictory reaction to an occurrence or situation immediately after one's first reaction.

double takeout *n. Curling* a shot which hits and knocks out of the house two of an opponent's rocks.

double-talk ● *n.* **1** language or talk that is usu. deliberately ambiguous or misleading. **2** meaningless gibberish. ● *v.* **1** *tr.* persuade (a person) through double-talk. **2** *intr.* engage in double-talk. ☐ **double-talking** *adj.*

double-team *v. N Amer.* **1** *tr. Basketball etc.* block (an opposing player) with two players. **2** *intr.* bring double pressure to bear on a person. ☐ **double-teaming** *n.*

doublethink *n.* **1** the mental capacity to accept as equally valid two entirely contradictory opinions or beliefs, esp. as a result of political indoctrination. **2** the practice of doing this.

double time ● *n.* **1** a rate of pay equal to twice the standard rate, usu. given for working extra on holidays etc. **2** *Military* a marching pace in which approximately twice as many steps per minute are made as in slow time. ● *v.intr.* (also **double-time**) march in double time.

double vision *n.* the simultaneous perception of two images of one object.

double whammy *n. informal* a twofold blow or setback.

double-wishbone suspension *n.* a suspension system for a vehicle on a chassis resembling two wishbones joined at the open ends.

doubt ● *n.* **1** a feeling of uncertainty; an undecided state of mind. **2** (often foll. by *of, about*) an inclination to disbelieve (*have one's doubts about*). **3** an uncertain state of affairs. **4** a lack of full proof or clear indication (*benefit of the doubt*). ● *v.* **1** *tr.* feel uncertain or undecided about. **2** *tr.* hesitate to believe or trust (a person, claim, etc.). **3** *intr.* have doubts or be undecided in opinion or belief. ☐ **beyond (a) doubt** certainly. **beyond a shadow of a doubt** definitely, absolutely. **give (a person) the benefit of the doubt 1** assume innocence rather than guilt, esp. when the evidence is conflicting. **2** incline to a more favourable or kindly decision, estimate, etc. **in doubt 1** (of a person) in a state of mental uncertainty or indecision. **2** (of an issue etc.) open to question, not certainly known or decided. **no doubt** in all likelihood or certainly. **without (a) doubt** unquestionably. ☐ **doubter** *n.* **doubtingly** *adv.*

doubtful *adj.* **1** feeling doubt, uncertainty, or misgivings; unsure or guarded in one's opinion. **2** causing doubt; ambiguous; uncertain in meaning etc. **3** (of a person) unreliable, of dubious character (*a doubtful ally*). ☐ **doubtfully** *adv.* **doubtfulness** *n.*

doubtless *adv.* (often qualifying a sentence) **1** certainly, without doubt. **2** probably, in all likelihood. ☐ **doubtlessly** *adv.*

douche / duːʃ / ● *n.* **1 a** a jet of liquid applied to part of the body, esp. the vagina, for cleansing or medicinal purposes. **b** the application of this. **2** a device for producing such a jet. ● *v.* **1** *tr.* treat with a douche. **2** *intr.* use a douche. ☐ **douching** *n.*

dough *n.* **1 a** a thick mixture of flour, water, etc. for baking into bread, pastry, etc. **b** any soft, pasty mass. **2** *slang* money.

doughnut *n.* **1** a small spongy cake of sweetened and deep-fried dough, usu. ring-shaped, or spherical with a jam or cream filling. **2** any of various circular objects with a hole in the middle. □ **do doughnuts** *N Amer. slang* (of a driver) cause a car to spin in wide circles by slamming on the brakes, esp. for fun.

doughty /'dauti/ *adj.* (**-ier, -iest**) fearless, valiant. □ **doughtily** *adv.* **doughtiness** *n.*

doughy *adj.* (**-ier, -iest**) **1** having the form or consistency of dough. **2** pale and sickly in colour.

Douglas fir *n.* (also **Douglas pine** or **Douglas spruce**) **1** any large conifer of the genus *Pseudotsuga*, of western N America. **2** the wood of this tree.

Doukhobor /'du:kəbɔr/ *n.* a member of an orig. Russian Christian sect similar to the Society of Friends.

dour /daur, dɔr/ *adj.* severe, stern, or sullenly obstinate in manner or appearance. □ **dourly** *adv.* **dourness** *n.*

douse /daus/ *v.tr.* **1 a** (often foll. by *with*) drench or wet thoroughly with a liquid. **b** immerse or plunge (a person, thing, etc.) vigorously into water or other liquid. **2 a** extinguish (a light, fire, etc.). **b** suppress (a feeling) or put an end to (an activity).

dove[1] *n.* **1** any bird of the family Columbidae, with short legs, small head, and large breast. **2** a gentle or innocent person. **3 a** a person who believes in a policy of negotiation and conciliation rather than warfare or confrontation (compare HAWK[1] 2). **b** a symbol of innocence, harmlessness, or peace. **4** (**Dove**) Christianity a representation of the Holy Spirit. **5** a soft grey colour. □ **dovelike** *adj.* **dovish** *adj.*

dove[2] *N Amer. past and past part.* of DIVE.

Dover sole *n.* **1** a European sole much prized as a food fish. **2** a mottled brown flatfish, *Microstomus pacificus*, of the N Pacific.

dovetail ● *n.* **1** a joint formed by one or more tenons in the shape of a dove's spread tail, fitting into the mortises of corresponding shape. **2** a tenon or mortise of such a joint. ● *v.* **1** *tr.* join together by means of a dovetail. **2** *tr. & intr.* (often foll. by *into, with*) fit together or become adjusted perfectly, so as to form a compact or harmonious whole.

dowager /'dauədʒər/ *n.* **1** a widow with a title or property derived from her late husband (*Queen dowager*). **2** *informal* a dignified elderly woman.

dowdy /'daudi/ ● *adj.* (**-ier, -iest**) **1** (of clothes) unfashionable; unattractively dull. **2** (of a person, esp. a woman) frumpy; unattractively dressed. ● *n.* (*pl.* **-ies**) a dowdy woman. □ **dowdily** *adv.* **dowdiness** *n.*

dowel /'dauəl/ ● *n.* a headless peg of wood, metal, or plastic for holding together components of a structure. ● *v.tr.* (**dowelled, dowelling**) fasten with a dowel or dowels. □ **dowelled** *adj.*

dowelling *n.* cylindrical rods for cutting into dowels.

dower *n.* a widow's share for life of her husband's estate.

dowitcher /'dautʃər/ *n.* any N American wading bird of the genus *Limnodromus*, related to sandpipers and having a long, straight bill.

Dow–Jones Average *n.* proprietary an index of the average level of share prices on the New York Stock Exchange at any time, based on the daily price of a selection of representative stocks.

down[1] ● *adv.* **1** into or toward a lower place, esp. to the ground (*fall down*). **2** in a lower place or position. **3** to or in a more southerly place (*drove down from Ottawa to Toronto*). **4 a** in or into a low or weaker position or condition (*down with a cold*). **b** in a position of lagging or loss (*we were down by three*). **c** (of a

computer system) out of action or unavailable for use (esp. temporarily). **5** from an earlier to a later time (*customs handed down*). **6** to a finer or thinner consistency or a smaller amount or size (*grind down*; *water down*). **7** lower in price or value (*gas is down*). **8** into a more settled state (*calm down*). **9** in writing; in or into recorded or listed form (*copy it down*). **10** (of part of a larger whole) paid; dealt with (*no money down*; *three down, six to go*). **11** inclusively of the lower limit in a series (*read down to the third paragraph*). **12** (as *interj.*) lie down, put (something) down, etc. **13** (of a crossword clue or answer) read vertically (*five down*). **14** downstairs, esp. after rising (*is not down yet*). **15** swallowed (*could not get the pill down*). **16** Football (of the ball) not in play. **17** Cdn (Nfld) heading north along the coast of Newfoundland and Labrador. ● *prep.* **1** downwards along, through, or into. **2** from top to bottom of. **3** along (*walk down the road*). **4** at or in a lower part of (*situated down the river*). ● *adj.* **1** directed downwards. **2** depressed; in low spirits. ● *v.tr. informal* **1** knock, shoot or bring down (*downed the plane*). **2** defeat (a team, player, etc.) (*the Leafs downed the Canadiens*). **3** swallow (a drink), esp. quickly. ● *n.* **1** Football any of a fixed number of attempts (3 in Canadian football, 4 in American football) to advance the ball a total of 10 yards. **2** an act of putting down (esp. an opponent in wrestling). **3** a reverse of fortune (*ups and downs*). □ **be down on** *informal* disapprove of; show animosity toward. **be down to 1** be attributable to. **2** be the responsibility of. **3** have used up everything except (*down to their last nickel*). **down for the count** (of a boxer) knocked unconscious. **2** completely defeated. **down in the dumps** depressed; in low spirits. **down on one's luck** *informal* **1** temporarily unfortunate. **2** dispirited by misfortune. **down the road** (or **line**) esp. *N Amer. informal* in the future; later on. **down tools** *informal* cease work, esp. to go on strike. **down to the wire** *informal* right up to the very last minute or the very end. **down with** *interj.* expressing strong disapproval or rejection of a specified person or thing. **when you get** (or **come**) (**right**) **down to it** in the final analysis.

down[2] *n.* **1 a** small soft feathers that cover and insulate the entire body of a young bird. **b** small soft feathers that lie between and beneath the surface feathers of an adult bird. **c** such feathers, usu. from ducks and geese, used to fill pillows etc. **2** fine soft hair esp. on the face. **3** short soft hairs on some leaves etc. **4** a fluffy substance, e.g. thistledown.

down[3] *n.* **1** (usu. in *pl.*) an area of open rolling land. **2** (usu. **the Downs**) undulating chalk and limestone uplands esp. in S England. **3** (in *pl.*) *N Amer.* often used in the names of racetracks (*Assiniboia Downs*).

down-and-dirty *adj.* esp. *N Amer. informal* **1** nasty; unprincipled. **2** unpretentious; natural.

down-and-out ● *adj.* **1** penniless; destitute. **2 a** Boxing unable to resume the fight. **b** (of a team, business etc.) out of the running; no longer successful. ● *n.* (also **down-and-outer**) a destitute and often homeless person.

down-at-the-heels *adj.* (also **down-at-the-heel**, **down-at-heel(s)**) **1 a** (of a person) shabby; slovenly. **b** (of a neighbourhood, building, etc.) rundown; dilapidated. **2** (**down-at-heel**) (of shoes) with the heels worn down.

downbeat ● *n.* Music **1** an accented beat, usu. the first of the bar. **2** a downward movement of a conductor's stick or hand indicating such a beat. ● *adj.* pessimistic; gloomy.

downcast *adj.* **1** (of eyes) looking downwards. **2** (of a person) dejected.

downdraft *n.* a downward current of air.

downer *n. slang* **1** a depressant or tranquilizing drug, esp. a barbiturate. **2 a** a depressing person or experience. **b** a depressed mood or state.

downfall *n.* **1 a** a fall from prosperity or power. **b** the cause of this. **2** a sudden heavy fall of rain, snow, etc.

downfield *adv. esp. N Amer.* in or to a position nearer to the opponents' end of a football, soccer, etc. field.

down-filled *adj.* stuffed or insulated with down.

downgrade ● *v.tr.* **1** make lower in rank or status (*downgraded the company's credit rating*). **2** speak disparagingly of. ● *n.* **1** an instance of downgrading or being downgraded (in sense 1 of *v.*). **2** esp. *N Amer.* a downward gradient, esp. on a railway or road. ● *adv.* downhill. □ **on the downgrade** *N Amer.* in decline.

downhearted *adj.* dejected; in low spirits.

downhill ● *adv.* in a descending direction, esp. toward the bottom of an incline. ● *attrib.adj.* **1** sloping down; descending. **2** declining; deteriorating. **3 a** designating skiing performed on a mountain or steep slope. **b** of or pertaining to downhill racing (*downhill champion*). ● *n. Skiing* a downhill race on a steep track marked by poles set at least 8 m apart, through which the skier has to pass. □ **go downhill** *informal* decline, deteriorate (in health, state of repair, etc.). □ **downhiller** *n. Skiing.*

down-home *attrib.adj. esp. N Amer.* unpretentious; unaffected (*down-home hospitality*).

down in the mouth *adj. informal* unhappy; dejected.

down-island *Cdn (BC)* ● *adv.* to or in a more southerly part of Vancouver Island. ● *adj.* directed southwards on Vancouver Island (*a down-island tour*).

downlink ● *n.* a communications link for signals coming from a satellite to earth. ● *v.tr.* provide with or send by a downlink.

download ● *v.tr.* **1** *Computing* copy or transfer (software or data) from one storage device or computer to another (esp. a smaller remote one). **2** *Cdn* shift or relegate responsibilities or costs for (a program) from one level of government to a lower one. ● *n.* a transfer of data (often *attrib.*: *download utilities*). □ **downloadable** *adj.*

down-market *adj. & adv. informal* relating to or directed toward the less affluent sector of the market.

down payment *n.* a partial payment made at the time of purchase.

downplay *v.tr.* minimize the importance of.

downpour *n.* a heavy fall of rain.

downrigger *n.* a trolling rig consisting of a cable attached underneath a boat to a fishing line, used to troll live bait at or near the bottom of a body of water.

downright ● *adv.* thoroughly; completely; positively (*downright rude*). ● *adj.* **1** utter; complete (*a downright lie*). **2** (of a person's speech or behaviour) straightforward; blunt.

downriver ● *adv.* at or towards a point nearer the mouth of a river. ● *adj.* situated or occurring downriver.

downscale *N Amer.* ● *adj.* at the lower end of a scale, esp. a social or economic scale (*a downscale neighbourhood*). ● *v.tr.* reduce or restrict in size or scale.

downshift ● *v.intr.* **1** change to a lower gear in a motor vehicle. **2** slow down; become less busy. ● *n.* an act or instance of downshifting.

downside *n.* **1** the negative aspect of something; a

disadvantage or drawback. **2** a downward movement of share prices etc. (also *attrib.*: *downside risk*).

downsize *v.tr. & intr. esp. N Amer.* **1** reduce in size (*downsize the deficit*). **2** (often euphemistic) lay off or fire (workers). □ **downsizing** *n.*

downslope ● *adv.* at or towards a lower point on a slope. ● *adj.* caused by, occurring, or acting on a downward slope (*downslope winds*). ● *n.* a downward slope.

downspout *n. N Amer.* a pipe to carry rainwater from an eavestrough to a drain or to ground level.

Down's syndrome *n.* (also **Down syndrome**) a congenital form of mental retardation due to a chromosome defect, in which the affected individual has a flattened facial profile, weak muscles, etc.

downstage *adj. & adv.* at or to the front of the stage.

downstairs ● *adv.* **1** down a flight of stairs. **2** to or on a lower floor. ● *adj.* situated downstairs. ● *n.* the main floor or basement of a house etc.

downstream ● *adv.* in the direction of the flow of a stream etc. ● *adj.* situated or occurring downstream.

downstroke *n.* a downward stroke, esp. of a machine part or a pen on paper.

downswing *n.* **1** a downward trend, esp. in economic conditions. **2** the downward movement of a golf club etc. when a player is about to hit the ball.

downtime *n.* **1** time during which a machine, esp. a computer, is unavailable for use, usu. as a result of malfunction or regular preventive maintenance. **2** time not spent working; leisure or recovery time.

down-to-earth *adj.* practical; realistic.

downtown *N Amer.* ● *adj.* being or located in the central part of a town or city, esp. the business district (*downtown Victoria*). ● *n.* a downtown area. ● *adv.* in or into a downtown area. □ **downtowner** *n.*

downtrodden *adj.* oppressed; badly treated.

downturn *n.* a decline, esp. in economic or business activity.

down under (also **Down Under**) *informal* ● *adv.* in or to Australia or New Zealand. ● *n.* Australia or New Zealand.

downward ● *adv.* (also **downwards**) **1** toward a lower place or position. **2** toward something which is lower in order, inferior, or less important. **3** onward from an earlier to a later time. ● *adj.* directed, moving, extending, pointing, or leading downward. □ **downwardly** *adv.*

downwind ● *adv.* in the direction toward which the wind is blowing. ● *adj.* occurring or situated downwind.

downy *adj.* (**-ier, -iest**) **1** of, like, or covered with down. **2** soft and fluffy. □ **downiness** *n.*

downy woodpecker *n.* a small black and white N American woodpecker, *Picoides pubescens*.

dowry /ˈdaʊəri/ *n.* (*pl.* **-ies**) property or money brought by a bride to her husband at marriage.

dowse¹ /daʊz/ *v.intr.* search for underground water or minerals by holding a Y-shaped stick or rod which dips abruptly when over the right spot. □ **dowser** *n.*

dowse² *var. of* DOUSE.

doxy /ˈdɒksi/ *n.* (*pl.* **-ies**) *slang* **1** a lover or mistress. **2** a prostitute.

doyen /ˈdɔɪən, dɔɪˈɛn, ˈdwʌjɑ̃/ *n.* the most senior or prominent male member of a body of people.

doyenne /dɔɪˈɛn, dwʌˈjɛn/ *n.* the most senior or prominent female member of a body of people.

doz. *abbr.* dozen.

doze ● *v.intr.* sleep lightly; be half asleep. ● *n.* a short light sleep. □ **doze off** fall lightly asleep.

dozen n. **1** (prec. by a or a number) (pl. **dozen**) twelve, regarded collectively (a dozen eggs). **2** a set or group of twelve. **3** informal about twelve; a fairly large indefinite number (several dozen people). **4** (in pl.; usu. foll. by of) informal very many (dozens of mistakes). □ **by the dozen** in large quantities. □ **dozenth** adj.

dozer /'do:zər/ n. informal = BULLDOZER.

dozy adj. (**-ier, -iest**) **1** drowsy; tending to doze. **2** Brit. & Cdn informal slow-witted or lazy. □ **doziness** n.

DP abbr. **1** DATA PROCESSING. **2** hist. DISPLACED PERSON. **3** Baseball double play.

D.Phil. abbr. Doctor of Philosophy.

dpi abbr. Computing dots per inch.

DPT abbr. diphtheria, pertussis, tetanus.

Dr. abbr. **1** Doctor. **2** Drive.

drab ● adj. (**drabber, drabbest**) **1** of a dull brownish colour. **2** lacking brightness or colour; dreary. **3** dull; uninteresting (a drab novel). ● n. drab colour. □ **drably** adv. **drabness** n.

drachma /'drækm ə/ n. (pl. **drachmas** or **drachmae** /-mi:/) **1** the chief monetary unit of Greece. **2** a silver coin of ancient Greece.

draconian /drə'ko:ni:ən, drei-/ adj. (also **draconic** /-'konik/) very harsh or severe (esp. of laws).

draft ● n. **1 a** a preliminary written version of a speech, document, book, etc. (also attrib.: draft statement). **b** a sketch or drawing of something to be constructed. **2** a current of air in a confined space, e.g. a room or chimney. **3** N Amer. a system of selection by which sports teams acquire the rights to esp. unsigned players (also attrib.: draft pick). **4** esp. US compulsory military service. **5** = DRAFT BEER. **6 a** a single act of drinking. **b** the amount drunk in this. **c** a dose of liquid medicine. **7 a** a written order for payment of money by a bank. **b** the drawing of money by means of this. **8** Naut. the depth of water needed to float a ship. **9** an act or the action of pulling something along, esp. a vehicle or farm implement. **10 a** the drawing in of a fishing net. **b** the fish taken at one drawing. **c** Cdn (Nfld) a measure of dried cod equalling two quintals (101.6 kg). ● v.tr. **1** prepare a draft of (a speech, document, etc.). **2** (usu. in passive) **a** N Amer. acquire the rights to esp. unsigned sports players. **b** esp. US conscript for military service. **3** select for any special duty or purpose. ● adj. (of an animal) used for pulling a cart, plow, etc. (draft horses). □ **on draft** (of beer etc.) ready to be drawn from a keg; not bottled or canned. □ **draftee** n. (in senses 3 and 4 of n.). **drafter** n. (in senses 1 and 4 of n.).

draft beer n. beer drawn from a keg; not bottled etc.

draft dodger n. a person who evades compulsory military service, esp. in the US. □ **draft dodging** n.

draftsman n. (pl. **-men**) **1** a person who makes drawings, plans, or sketches. **2** a person who drafts documents, esp. legal or parliamentary ones.

drafty adj. (**-ier, -iest**) (of a room etc.) letting in sharp currents of air. □ **draftily** adv. **draftiness** n.

drag ● v. (**dragged, dragging**) **1** tr. pull along with effort or difficulty. **2 a** tr. allow (one's feet etc.) to trail along the ground. **b** intr. trail along the ground (your coat is dragging). **c** intr. (of time etc.) go or pass slowly or tediously. **3 a** intr. (usu. foll. by for) use grapnels, nets, or drags (to find a drowned person or lost object). **b** tr. search the bottom of (a river etc.) with grapnels, nets, or drags. **4** tr. (often foll. by to) informal persuade (a person) to come or go somewhere unwillingly. **5** intr. (often foll. by on) continue at tedious length. **6** tr. Computing move (a window, icon, etc.) from one place to another on a screen, esp. by using a mouse. **7** intr. (foll. by on, at) draw on (a cigarette etc.). ● n. **1** Physics the force resisting the motion of a body through a liquid or gas. **2** informal a boring or dreary person, duty, performance, etc. **3** slang clothes usually worn by the opposite sex (in drag). **4** slang a draw on a cigarette etc. **5** N Amer. slang influence, pull. **6** an obstruction to progress. **7** an apparatus for dredging or removing drowned persons etc. from under water. **8** = DRAGNET 1. **9** an act of dragging. □ **drag one's feet** (or **heels**) be deliberately slow or reluctant to act. **drag in** introduce (a subject) irrelevantly. **drag out** protract. **drag up** informal deliberately mention (an unwelcome subject).

drag and drop n. a software technique for moving objects on the screen using a mouse.

dragger n. N Amer. a trawler. □ **draggerman** n.

dragnet n. **1** a net drawn through water or across ground to trap fish or game. **2** a systematic hunt for criminals etc.

dragon n. **1** a mythical monster like a reptile, usu. able to breathe out fire. **2** a fierce person, esp. a woman. **3** (in full **flying dragon**) a lizard, Draco volans, with a long tail and membranous wing-like structures. **4** an esp. newly industrialized Asian country with a powerful economy.

dragon boat n. a long wooden boat with a carved dragon's head on its prow and dragon's tail at its stern, propelled by 22 paddlers and used in races.

dragonfly n. (pl. **-ies**) any of various insects of the order Odonata, having a long body and two unequal pairs of large wings usu. spread while resting.

dragoon /drə'gu:n/ ● n. **1** hist. a mounted infantryman armed with a carbine. **2** (often **Dragoon**) a member of any of several cavalry (now armoured) regiments (Royal Canadian Dragoons). ● v.tr. **1** (foll. by into) coerce into doing something, esp. by use of strong force. **2** persecute, esp. with troops.

drag queen n. slang a male homosexual transvestite.

drag race n. a race between cars starting from a standstill. □ **drag racer** n. **drag racing** n.

dragster n. a car built or modified for drag races.

drag strip n. N Amer. a straight stretch of road built or used for drag races.

drain ● v. **1** tr. draw off liquid from, esp.: **a** make (land etc.) dry by providing an outflow for moisture. **b** (of a river) carry off the superfluous water of (a district). **c** remove purulent matter from (an abscess). **2** tr. **a** draw off (liquid), esp. by a pipe (drain the sink). **b** remove liquid from (drain the vegetables). **3** intr. (often foll. by away, off, through) flow or trickle away. **4** intr. (of dishes, cutlery, etc.) become dry as liquid flows away. **5** tr. (often foll. by of) exhaust or deprive (a person or thing) of strength, resources, property, etc. **6** intr. gradually disappear or fade (my hope drained away). **7** tr. a drink (liquid) to the dregs. **b** empty (a glass etc.) by drinking. ● n. **1 a** a channel, conduit, or pipe carrying off liquid, esp. an artificial conduit for water or sewage. **b** a tube for drawing off the discharge from an abscess etc. **2** a constant outflow or expenditure (a drain on my resources). □ **down the drain** informal lost, wasted.

drainage n. **1** the process or means of draining (the land has poor drainage). **2** a system of drains, artificial or natural. **3** what is drained off, esp. sewage.

drainage basin n. the area of land drained by a river and its tributaries.

drainer n. a device for draining; anything on which things are put to drain.

drainpipe n. a pipe for carrying off water, sewage, etc., from a building.

drake n. a male duck.

DRAM *abbr. Computing* dynamic random access memory.

dram *n.* **1** a small drink of spirits. **2** one-sixteenth of an ounce in avoirdupois weight (1.77 grams).

drama /'drɑːmə, 'drɒmə/ *n.* **1** a play for acting or broadcasting. **2 a** plays as a branch of literature and a performing art. **b** the art of acting. **3** an exciting or emotional event, set of circumstances, etc. **4** dramatic quality (*the drama of the situation*).

dramatic /drə'mætɪk/ *adj.* **1 a** of drama or the study of drama. **b** of acting. **2** (of an event, circumstance, etc.) sudden and exciting or unexpected. **3** vividly striking. **4** (of a gesture etc.) theatrical; overdone; absurd. □ **dramatically** *adv.*

dramatics *n.pl.* (often treated as *sing.*) **1** the production and performance of plays. **2** exaggerated or showy behaviour.

dramatist /'dræmətɪst/ *n.* a writer of dramas.

dramatize *v.* **1** *tr.* adapt (a novel, incident, etc.) to form a dramatic work, esp. a play or film. **2** *tr. & intr.* express or react to (something) in a dramatic way. □ **dramatization** *n.*

dramaturgy *n.* **1** the art of theatrical production; the theory of dramatics. **2** the application of this. □ **dramaturgic** *adj.* **dramaturgical** *adj.* **dramaturgically** *adv.*

drank *past of* DRINK.

drape *v.tr.* **1** hang, cover loosely, or adorn with cloth etc. **2** arrange (clothes or hangings) carefully in folds. **3** place or hang loosely or casually. ● *n.* **1** esp. N Amer. (often in *pl.*) a curtain or drapery. **2** a piece of drapery. **3** the way in which a garment or fabric hangs.

drapery *n.* (*pl.* **-ies**) **1** clothing or hangings arranged in folds. **2** (often in *pl.*) a curtain or hanging. **3** the arrangement of clothing in sculpture or painting.

drastic *adj.* having a strong or far-reaching effect; severe. □ **drastically** *adv.*

drat *informal* ● *v.tr.* (**dratted, dratting**) (usu. as an exclamation) curse, confound (*drat the thing!*). ● *interj.* expressing anger or annoyance. □ **dratted** *adj.*

draught /drɑːft/ esp. Brit. var. of DRAFT *n.* 2, 5, 6, 8, 9, 10 & *adj.*

draughtsman *n.* (*pl.* **-men**) esp. Brit. var. of DRAFTSMAN.

draughty esp. Brit. var. of DRAFTY.

Dravidian /drə'vɪdɪən/ ● *n.* **1** a member of a dark-skinned aboriginal people of S India and Sri Lanka (including the Tamils). **2** any of the group of languages spoken by this people. ● *adj.* of or relating to this people or group of languages.

draw ● *v.* (*past* **drew**; *past part.* **drawn**) **1** *tr.* pull or cause to move toward or after one. **2** *tr.* pull (a thing) up, over, or across. **3** *tr.* pull (curtains etc.) open or shut. **4** *tr.* take (a person) aside, esp. to talk to. **5** *tr.* attract; bring to oneself or to something; take in (*drew a deep breath; drew large crowds*). **6** *tr.* trace (a line, mark, or figure). **7 a** *tr.* produce (a picture) by tracing lines and marks. **b** *tr.* represent (a thing) by this means. **c** *intr.* make a drawing. **8** *tr.* frame (a document) in due form; compose. **9** *intr.* make one's or its way, proceed, move, come (*drew near the bridge; draw to a close*). **10** *intr.* (foll. by *at, on*) inhale smoke from (a cigarette, pipe, etc.). **11** *tr.* take out; remove (a gun from a holster, etc.) **12** *tr.* obtain or take from a source (*draw a salary; draw inspiration*). **13** *tr. & intr.* finish (a contest or game) with neither side winning. **14** *tr.* infer, deduce (a conclusion). **15** *tr.* **a** elicit, evoke. **b** bring about, entail (*draw criticism; drew a penalty*). **c** (foll. by *to* + infin.) induce (a person) to do something. **16** *tr.* haul up (water) from a well. **17** *tr.* cause (blood) to flow from an incision. **18** *tr.* obtain (beer etc.) from a keg. **19** *tr.* extract a liquid essence from. **20 a** *tr.* obtain by lot (*drew the winner*). **b** *intr.* draw lots. **21** *intr.* (foll. by *on*) make a demand on a person, a person's skill, memory, imagination, etc. **22** *tr.* write out (a bill, cheque, or draft). **23** *tr.* formulate or perceive (a comparison or distinction). **24** *tr.* (of a ship) require (a specified depth of water) to float in. **25** *tr.* *Curling* slide (a rock) so that it stops in the target area without striking another rock. ● *n.* **1** an act of drawing. **2 a** a person or thing that draws customers, attention, etc. **b** the power to attract attention. **3** the drawing of lots, esp. a raffle or lottery. **4** a drawn game; a tie. **5** a suck on a cigarette etc. **6** the act of removing a gun from its holster in order to shoot. **7** *Football* a play in which the quarterback hands the ball off to a running back who is running toward the line of scrimmage. **8** *Curling* a shot in which the rock stops within the target area without striking another rock. **9** *N Amer.* (*West*) a shallow valley; ravine. □ **draw back** withdraw from an undertaking. **draw fire** (also **draw heat**) attract hostility, criticism, etc. **draw in 1 a** (of successive days) become shorter because of the changing seasons. **b** (of a day) approach its end. **c** (of successive evenings or nights) start earlier because of the changing seasons. **2** persuade to join, entice. **3** (of a train, bus, etc.) arrive at a station. **draw the line** set a limit (of tolerance etc.). **draw off 1** drain away (liquid). **2** withdraw (troops). **draw on 1** utilize. **2** put (gloves, boots, etc.) on. **draw out 1** remove; pull out (*drew out a gun*). **2** prolong. **3** elicit. **4** induce to talk. **5** (of successive days) become longer because of the changing seasons. **6** (of a train, bus, etc.) leave a station etc. **draw up 1** compose or draft (a document etc.). **2** (of a vehicle) come to a halt. **3** make (oneself) stand straight. **4** (foll. by *with, to*) gain on or overtake. **quick on the draw** quick to act or react.

drawback *n.* a disadvantage.

drawbridge *n.* a bridge hinged at one end so that it may be raised to prevent passage or to allow ships etc. to pass.

drawdown *n.* **1** a lowering of the water level in a lake, pond, etc. **2** a withdrawal of oil from a reservoir. **3** an act of raising money through loans; borrowing. **4** a reduction or withdrawal, esp. of troops.

drawer /drɔːr/ *n.* **1** a boxlike storage compartment without a lid, sliding in and out of a frame, table, etc. (*chest of drawers*). **2** (in *pl.*) **a** *hist.* or *jocular* underpants. **b** *slang* pants or trousers. **3** /'drɔːr/ a person or thing that draws, esp.: **a** a person who draws a cheque etc. **b** a person who draws pictures.

drawing *n.* **1 a** the art of representing objects by line, using pencil, pen, etc., rather than paint. **b** a picture done in this way. **2** a sketch, diagram, etc.

drawing board *n.* a board on which paper is placed for drawing plans etc. □ **back to the drawing board** back to begin afresh (after failure).

drawing card *n.* N Amer. a performer, show, attraction, etc. that draws a large audience.

drawing-room *n.* a room, esp. in a large private house, in which people relax and guests are received and entertained.

drawknife *n.* a knife with a handle at each end at right angles to the blade, drawn toward the user to remove wood from a surface.

drawl ● *v.* **1** *intr.* speak with drawn-out vowel sounds. **2** *tr.* utter in this way. ● *n.* a drawling utterance or way of speaking.

drawn ● *v.* past part. of DRAW. ● *adj.* looking strained from fear, anxiety, or pain.

drawn-out *adj.* = LONG-DRAWN-OUT.

draw play n. = DRAW n. 7.

drawstring n. a string that can be pulled to tighten the mouth of a bag, the waist of a garment, etc.

dray n. a low cart without sides used esp. formerly by brewers for carrying heavy loads.

dread ● v.tr. **1** fear greatly. **2** shrink from; look forward to with great apprehension or fear (I dread going to the dentist). ● n. **1 a** a great fear or apprehension. **b** an object of fear or apprehension. **2 a** slang a Rastafarian. **b** (in pl.) = DREADLOCKS. ● adj. dreaded.

dreaded adj. **1** regarded with fear, apprehension, or awe. **2** informal regarded with mock fear.

dreadful adj. **1** terrible; causing great fear or suffering. **2** troublesome, disagreeable; very bad. □ **dreadfully** adv. **dreadfulness** n.

dreadlocks n.pl. **1** a Rastafarian hairstyle in which the hair is twisted into tight braids or ringlets hanging down on all sides. **2** hair dressed in this way. □ **dreadlocked** adj.

dream ● n. **1 a** a series of pictures or events occurring in the mind during sleep. **b** the act or time of seeing this. **c** (in full **waking dream**) a similar experience of one awake. **2** a daydream or fantasy. **3** an ideal, aspiration, or ambition. **4** a beautiful or ideal person or thing. **5** a state of mind without proper perception of reality (lives in a dream). ● v. (past and past part. **dreamt** or **dreamed**) **1** intr. experience a dream. **2** tr. imagine in or as if in a dream. **3** (usu. with neg.) **a** intr. (foll. by of) contemplate the possibility of, have any conception or intention of (would not dream of upsetting them). **b** tr. (often foll. by that + clause) think of as a possibility (never dreamt that he would come). **4** tr. (foll. by away) spend (time) unprofitably. **5** intr. be unrealistic or unpractical. **6** intr. fall into a reverie. ● adj. ideal (dream house). □ **a dream come true** an ideal or desired situation or thing. **dream in colour** (or **Technicolour**) Cdn be wildly unrealistic. **dream up** imagine, invent. **like a dream** informal easily, effortlessly. □ **dreamer** n. **dreamless** adj. **dreamlessly** adv. **dreamlike** adj.

dreamboat n. informal a very attractive or ideal person, esp. of the opposite sex.

dream catcher n. a webbed hoop believed by some woodland Aboriginal groups to protect a person from bad dreams.

dreamland n. **1** an ideal or imaginary land. **2** sleep.

dreamscape n. a dreamed or dreamlike scene.

dream team n. N Amer. slang **1** a team, real or hypothetical, composed of the top players in a given sport. **2** a group of people considered to be the stars of their field, discipline, etc.

dream world n. a state of mind distanced from reality.

dreamy adj. (**-ier, -iest**) **1** given to daydreaming; fanciful; unpractical. **2** dreamlike; vague; misty. **3** informal very attractive or ideal, esp. to the opposite sex. **4** informal delightful; marvellous (a dreamy house). **5** full of dreams. □ **dreamily** adv. **dreaminess** n.

dreary adj. (**-ier, -iest**) dismal, dull, gloomy. □ **drearily** adv. **dreariness** n.

dreck /drek/ n. slang **1** garbage; worthless junk. **2** a person or thing having no redeeming qualities.

dredge¹ ● v. **1** tr. **a** (often foll. by up) bring up (lost or hidden material) as if with a dredge (don't dredge all that up again). **b** (often foll. by up, out) bring up or clear (mud etc.) from a river, harbour, etc. with a dredge. **2** tr. clean (a harbour, river, etc.) with a dredge. **3** intr. use a dredge. ● n. an apparatus used to scoop up objects or to clear mud etc. from a river or sea floor.

dredge² v.tr. coat (food) with flour, sugar, etc.

dredger n. **1** a dredge. **2** a boat containing this.

dreg n. **1** (usu. in pl.) **a** a sediment; grounds, lees, etc. **b** a worthless part; refuse (the dregs of humanity). **2** a small remnant (not a dreg). □ **drink to the dregs** consume leaving nothing (drank life to the dregs).

drench ● v.tr. **1** wet thoroughly. **2** saturate; soak (in liquid). **3** cover thoroughly all over (sunlight drenched the garden). ● n. a soaking; a downpour.

dress ● v. **1 a** tr. clothe; array. **b** intr. wear clothes of a specified kind or in a specified way (dresses well). **2** intr. **a** put on clothes. **b** put on formal or evening clothes, esp. for dinner. **3** tr. decorate or adorn. **4** tr. **a** treat (a wound) with ointment etc. **b** apply a dressing to (a wound). **5** tr. trim, comb, brush, or smooth (the hair). **6** tr. **a** add a dressing to (a salad etc.). **b** clean and prepare (poultry etc.) for cooking or eating. **7** tr. prepare and finish the surface of (fabric, stone, pelts, etc.). **8** tr. groom (a horse). ● n. **1** a one-piece woman's garment consisting of a bodice and skirt. **2** clothing, esp. a whole outfit etc. (fussy about his dress). **3** formal or ceremonial costume (evening dress). **4** an external covering (birds in their winter dress). □ **dress down** informal **1** dress informally. **2** reprimand or scold.

dress for success wear expensive, tailored clothes in the workplace in order to cultivate a professional image (also attrib.: a dress-for-success suit). **dress up 1** dress (oneself or another) in good clothes, esp. for a special occasion. **2** (esp. of a child) dress in a costume or in special clothes for entertainment. **3** decorate; make more attractive. **4** disguise (unwelcome facts) by embellishment.

dressage /drəˈsɒʒ/ n. **1** the training of a horse in obedience and deportment, esp. for competition. **2** the execution by a horse of precise movements in response to its rider.

dress code n. a set of rules specifying the required manner of dress at a school, office, club, etc.

dresser¹ n. **1** N Amer. a chest of drawers. **2** a sideboard with shelves above for displaying plates etc.

dresser² n. **1** a person who assists theatrical performers to put on and remove costumes. **2** a person who dresses elegantly or in a specified way.

dressing n. **1** in senses of DRESS v. **2 a** a sauce for salads, esp. a mixture of oil, vinegar etc. (French dressing). **b** N Amer. = STUFFING 2. **3 a** a bandage for a wound. **b** ointment etc. used to dress a wound. **4** compost etc. spread over land (top dressing).

dressing-down n. informal a severe reprimand.

dressing gown n. a loose usu. belted robe worn over nightwear or while resting.

dressing room n. a room in a sports stadium, theatre, etc. where athletes or theatrical performers change into their uniforms or stage clothes.

dressing table n. a piece of furniture with a flat top, an upright mirror, and usu. drawers underneath, for use while applying makeup etc.

dressmaker n. a person who makes clothes professionally. □ **dressmaking** n.

dress rehearsal n. the final rehearsal of a play etc., with the performers in costume.

dress shirt n. **1** N Amer. a man's long-sleeved shirt, usu. worn with a tie. **2** a man's usu. starched white shirt worn with evening dress.

dress uniform n. formal military dress worn on ceremonial occasions.

dress-up n. the action of dressing up, either more formally or in costume.

dressy adj. (**-ier, -iest**) **1** (of clothes etc.) suitable for a formal occasion. **2** (of an occasion or place) requiring formal dress or one's best clothes (*a dressy restaurant*). **3** stylish; elegant. □ **dressiness** *n.*

drew past of DRAW.

dribble ● *v.* **1** *intr.* allow saliva to flow from the mouth. **2** *intr. & tr.* flow or allow to flow in drops or a trickling stream. **3** *tr. & intr.* **a** (in basketball) bounce (the ball), either to move forward or to prepare for a pass. **b** (esp. in soccer and field hockey) advance (the ball) with slight touches of the feet or stick. **4** *intr.* move with little momentum (*the puck dribbled into the net*). ● *n.* **1** the act or an instance of dribbling. **2** a small trickling stream. **3** a small amount. □ **dribbler** *n.* **dribbly** *adj.*

dribs and drabs *n.pl. informal* small scattered amounts (*did the work in dribs and drabs*).

dried past and past part. of DRY.

drier[1] *comparative of* DRY.

drier[2] *var. of* DRYER.

driest *superlative of* DRY.

drift ● *n.* **1 a** slow movement or variation. **b** such movement caused by a slow current. **2** the intention, meaning, scope, etc. of what is said etc. **3** a large mass of snow, sand, etc., accumulated by the wind. **4 a** a ship's deviation from its course, due to currents. **b** an aircraft's deviation due to side winds. **c** a projectile's deviation due to its rotation. **5** = CONTINENTAL DRIFT. ● *v.* **1** *intr.* be carried by or as if by a current of air or water. **2** *intr.* move or progress passively, casually, or aimlessly (*friends drifted apart*). **3 a** *tr. & intr.* pile or be piled by the wind into drifts. **b** *tr.* cover (a field, a road, etc.) with drifts. **4** *tr.* (of a current) carry. □ **drift off** fall asleep, esp. gradually.

drifter *n.* **1** an aimless or rootless person. **2** a boat used for drift net fishing.

drift net *n.* a large net for herrings etc., kept upright by weights and floats, and allowed to drift with the tide. □ **drift netter** *n.* **drift netting** *n.*

driftwood *n.* wood floating on, or driven ashore by, water.

drill[1] ● *n.* **1 a** a tool or machine with a usu. detachable revolving pointed end, used for boring cylindrical holes, sinking wells, etc. **b** a dentist's rotary tool for cutting away part of a tooth etc. **2 a** instruction or training in military exercises. **b** rigorous discipline or methodical instruction, esp. when learning or performing tasks. **c** a rehearsal of the routine procedure to be followed in an emergency (*fire drill*). **d** a routine or exercise. **3** *informal* a recognized procedure (*you know the drill*). ● *v.* **1** *tr. & intr.* **a** (of a person or a tool) make a hole with a drill through or into (wood, metal, etc.). **b** make (a hole) with a drill. **2** *tr. & intr.* esp. *Military* subject to or undergo discipline by drill. **3** *tr.* impart (knowledge etc.) by a strict method or by repetition, etc. **4** *tr. slang* **a** shoot with a gun. **b** punch or hit (a person) sharply (*drilled me one in the stomach*). **c** cause (a ball etc.) to move rapidly (*drilled the puck down the ice*). □ **driller** *n.*

drill[2] ● *n.* **1** a machine used for making furrows, sowing, and covering seed. **2** a small furrow for sowing seed in. **3** a ridge with such furrows on top. **4** a row of plants so sown. ● *v.tr.* **1** sow (seed) with a drill. **2** plant (the ground) in drills.

drill[3] *n.* a coarse twilled cotton or linen fabric.

drilling platform *n.* = PLATFORM 9.

drilling rig *n.* a structure with equipment for drilling an oil well etc.

drily *var. of* DRYLY.

drink ● *v.* (*past* **drank**; *past part.* **drunk**) **1 a** *tr.* swallow (a liquid). **b** *tr.* swallow the liquid contents of (a vessel). **c** *intr.* swallow liquid (*drank from the stream*). **2** *intr.* take

alcohol, esp. to excess. **3** *tr.* (of a plant, porous material, etc.) absorb (moisture). **4** *refl.* bring (oneself etc.) to a specified condition by drinking. **5** *tr.* (usu. foll. by *away*) spend (wages etc.) on drink (*drank away her money*). **6** *tr.* wish (a person's good health, luck, etc.) by drinking (*drank his health*). ● *n.* **1 a** a liquid for drinking. **b** a draft or specified amount of this (*had a drink of milk*). **2 a** alcoholic liquor. **b** a portion, glass, etc. of this. **c** excessive indulgence in alcohol (*drink is his vice*). **3** (**the drink**) *informal* a body of water. □ **drink deep** take a large draft or drafts. **drink in** listen to or watch closely or eagerly (*drank in every word*). **drink off** drink the whole (contents) of at once. **drink to** toast; wish success to. **drink a person under the table** remain sober longer than one's drinking companion. **drink up** drink the whole of; empty. **in drink** drunk. □ **drinkable** *adj.* **drinkability** *n.*

drinker *n.* **1** a person who drinks (something). **2** a person who drinks alcohol, esp. to excess.

drinking box *n. Cdn* a small plasticized cardboard carton of juice etc. packaged with a straw.

drinking water *n.* water pure enough for drinking.

drip ● *v.* (**dripped, dripping**) **1** *intr. & tr.* fall or let fall in drops. **2** *intr.* (often foll. by *with*) be so wet as to shed drops (*dripped with blood*). ● *n.* **1 a** the act or an instance of dripping. **b** a drop of liquid. **c** a sound of dripping. **2** *informal* a stupid, dull, or ineffective person. **3** *Med.* = DRIP-FEED. **4** (*attrib.*) pertaining to coffee made by pouring boiling water through ground coffee in a paper filter. □ **dripping wet** very wet. **dripping with** full of or covered with.

drip-dry ● *v.* (**-dries, -dried**) **1** *intr.* (of fabric etc.) dry crease-free when hung up to drip. **2** *tr.* leave (a garment etc.) hanging up to dry. ● *adj.* able to be drip-dried.

drip-feed ● *v.tr.* (*past* and *past part.* **-fed**) feed intravenously in drops. ● *n.* **1** the continuous intravenous introduction of fluid into the body. **2** the fluid so introduced. **3** the apparatus used to do this.

dripping *n.* (often in *pl.*) **1** fat melted from roasted meat and used for cooking. **2** water, oil, wax, etc., dripping from anything.

drippy *adj.* (**-ier, -iest**) **1** tending to drip. **2** *informal* (of a song etc.) sloppily sentimental. **3** (of a person) ineffectual; lacking character. □ **drippily** *adv.* **drippiness** *n.*

drive ● *v.* (*past* **drove**; *past part.* **driven**) **1** *tr.* urge in some direction, esp. forcibly (*drove back the wolves*). **2** *tr.* **a** (usu. foll. by *to* + infin., or *to* + verbal noun) compel or constrain forcibly (*was driven to complain*). **b** (often foll. by *to*) force into a specified state (*drove him mad*). **c** (often *refl.*) urge to overwork (*drives herself too hard*). **3** *tr. & intr.* **a** operate and direct the course of (a vehicle, locomotive, etc.). **b** convey or be conveyed in a vehicle. **c** be licensed or competent to drive (a vehicle). **4** *tr.* (of wind, water, etc.) carry along, propel, send, or cause to go in some direction. **5** *tr.* (often foll. by *into*) force (a stake, nail, etc.) into place by blows. **6** *tr.* effect or conclude forcibly (*drove a hard bargain*). **7** *tr.* (of steam or other power) set or keep (machinery) going. **8** *intr.* (usu. foll. by *at*) work hard; dash, rush, or hasten. **9** *tr. Sport* hit or kick (the ball, puck, etc.) forcefully. **10** *tr. Baseball* (often foll. by *in*) **a** cause the advance of (a baserunner) by a base hit or sacrifice fly. **b** cause (a run) to be scored by a base hit or sacrifice fly. **11** *tr. & intr. Golf* strike (a ball) with a driver from the tee. **12** *tr. N Amer. & NZ* float (timber) down a river etc. ● *n.* **1** an act of driving in a motor vehicle; a journey or excursion in such a vehicle. **2 a** the capacity for achievement; motivation and energy. **b** *Psych.* an inner urge to attain a goal or satisfy a need (*sex drive*). **3 a** a street or road, esp. a curving one. Abbr.: **Dr. b** = DRIVEWAY. **4** *Military* a forceful advance or attack. **5** an organized effort to achieve a usu. charitable purpose (*a famine-relief drive*). **6 a** the act or an instance of driving a puck, ball, etc. **b** the flight of the puck or ball etc. so driven. **c** *Football* a series of plays that advances the ball towards the opposing end of the field, often resulting in a touchdown or field goal. **d** *Golf* a shot, made esp. from the tee with a driver, intended to travel a great distance. **7 a** the transmission of power to machinery, the wheels of a motor vehicle, etc. (*front-wheel drive*). **b** the position of a steering wheel in a motor vehicle (*left-hand drive*). **c** the gear position or function in an automatic transmission which imparts forward motion. **8** *Computing* a device that can store and retrieve data on disks or tape. **9** an act of impelling (cattle, game, etc.) (*cattle drive*). **10** *Cdn* = LOG DRIVE. □ **drive at** seek, intend, or mean (*what is she driving at?*). **drive out** take the place of; oust; exorcise, cast out (evil spirits etc.). □ **driveability** *n.* (also **drivability**). **driveable** *adj.* (also **drivable**).

drive-by ● *attrib.adj.* (of a crime etc.) carried out from a moving vehicle. ● *n.* (*pl.* **-bys**) a drive-by shooting.

drive-in ● *attrib.adj.* (of a movie theatre, restaurant, etc.) that can be visited without getting out of one's car. ● *n.* such a movie theatre, restaurant, etc.

drivel /'drɪvəl/ ● *n.* silly nonsense; twaddle. ● *v.* (**drivelled, drivelling**) **1** *intr.* talk foolishly. **2** *intr.* run at the mouth or nose. □ **driveller** *n.* **drivelling** *adj.*

driven ● *v. past part. of* DRIVE. ● *adj.* **1** (of snow) piled into drifts or made smooth by the wind. **2** urged onward, impelled, forced. **3** (of a person) showing intensity or compulsion in behaviour. **4** (in *comb.*) having as the chief reason or determinant the thing specified (*market-driven*). **5** (in *comb.*) controlled by the means specified (*menu-driven*). □ **white** (or **pure**) **as driven snow** immaculately white or pure.

driver *n.* **1** (often in *comb.*) a person who drives a vehicle. **2** *Golf* a club with a flat face and wooden head, used for driving from the tee. **3** *Computing* a program that controls the operation of a device. **4** a person who herds or drives a usu. specified type of animal. □ **in the driver's seat** in charge. □ **driverless** *adj.*

driver's licence *N Amer.* a licence permitting a person to drive a motor vehicle.

driveshaft *n.* a rotating shaft that transmits power esp. to the differential in a motor vehicle.

drive shed *n. Cdn* (esp. *Ont.*) a large shed used for storing farm machinery, vehicles, etc.

drive-through esp. *N Amer.* ● *attrib.adj.* **1** designating a restaurant etc. which has a window at which customers are served without leaving their cars. **2** (of a place, facility, etc.) suitable for driving through. ● *n.* a place where drive-through service is offered.

drivetrain *n.* the powertrain of an automobile.

driveway *n.* **1** a paved or gravelled parking area leading to a garage or house. **2** a private road or lane leading to a house, barn, etc.

driving *adj.* **1** moving rapidly, esp. before the wind (*a driving rain*). **2** energetic (*a driving rhythm*). **3** used when driving a motor vehicle (*driving gloves*).

driving range *n. Golf* an area for practising drives.

driving shed *n. Cdn* (esp. *Ont.*) = DRIVE SHED.

driving test *n.* an official test of a motorist's competence which must be passed to obtain a driver's licence.

drizzle ● *n.* **1** very fine rain. **2** esp. *Cooking* fine drops;

a fine trickle. ● *v.* **1** *intr.* (esp. of rain) fall in very fine drops (*it's drizzling again*). **2** *tr.* esp. *Cooking* **a** sprinkle in fine drops or a thin trickle. **b** pour a liquid in a fine stream over (a food). □ **drizzly** *adj.*

Dr. Martens *var. of* DOCTOR MARTENS.

DRO *abbr.* DEPUTY RETURNING OFFICER.

droll /droʊl/ *adj.* **1** quaintly amusing. **2** strange; odd.

drone ● *n.* **1** a non-working male of the honeybee, whose sole function is to mate with fertile females. **2** an idler. **3** a deep humming sound. **4** a monotonous speech or speaker. **5 a** a pipe, esp. of a bagpipe, sounding a continuous note of fixed low pitch. **b** the note emitted by this. **6** a remote-controlled pilotless aircraft or missile. ● *v.* **1** *intr.* make a deep humming sound. **2** *intr. & tr.* speak or utter monotonously. **3 a** *intr.* be idle. **b** *tr.* (often foll. by *away*) idle away (one's time etc.).

drool ● *v.intr.* **1** have saliva coming out of the mouth; slobber. **2** (often foll. by *over*) show much pleasure or infatuation. ● *n.* saliva.

droop ● *v.* **1** *intr. & tr.* hang or allow to hang down; languish, decline, or sag, esp. from weariness. **2** *intr.* **a** (of the eyes) look downwards. **b** (of the sun) sink. **3** *intr.* lose heart; be dejected; flag. ● *n.* **1** an instance of drooping. **2** a loss of spirit or enthusiasm. □ **drooping** *adj.* **droopingly** *adv.*

droopy *adj.* (**-ier, -iest**) **1** drooping. **2** dejected, gloomy. □ **droopily** *adv.* **droopiness** *n.*

drop ● *n.* **1 a** a small round or pear-shaped portion of liquid that hangs or falls or adheres to a surface. **b** a very small amount of usu. drinkable liquid (*just a drop left*). **c** a glass etc. of alcoholic liquor (*take a drop with us*). **2 a** an abrupt fall or slope. **b** the amount of this. **c** an act of falling or dropping. **d** a reduction in prices, temperature, etc. **e** a deterioration or worsening (*a drop in status*). **3** something resembling a drop, esp.: **a** a pendant or earring. **b** a crystal ornament on a chandelier etc. **c** (often in *comb.*) a candy or lozenge (*cough drop*; *lemon drop*). **4** something that drops or is dropped, esp. *Theatre* a painted curtain or scenery. **5** *Med.* **a** the smallest separable quantity of a liquid. **b** (in *pl.*) liquid medicine to be measured in drops (*eye drops*). **6** a minute quantity. **7 a** the act of dropping people, supplies, etc. by parachute. **b** a descent by parachute. **c** the persons or supplies dropped. **8** *informal* a delivery. **9** *slang* **a** a hiding place for stolen or illicit goods. **b** a secret place where documents etc. may be left or passed on in espionage. **10** (*attrib.*) (of a part of a garment) set lower than normal (*drop waist*). ● *v.* (**dropped, dropping**) **1** *intr. & tr.* fall or let fall in drops. **2** *intr. & tr.* fall or allow to fall. **3 a** *intr. & tr.* sink or cause to sink or fall to the ground, onto a chair etc., from exhaustion, a blow, a wound, etc. **b** *intr.* die. **4 a** *intr. & tr.* cease or cause to cease; lapse or let lapse; abandon (*drop everything and come*). **b** *tr.* informal cease to associate with. **5** *tr.* set down (a passenger etc.) (*drop me at the station*). **6** *tr. & intr.* utter or be uttered casually (*dropped a hint*). **7** *tr.* send casually (*drop me a postcard*). **8 a** *intr. & tr.* fall or allow to fall in direction, amount, condition, degree, pitch, etc. (*dropped her voice*; *the wind dropped*). **b** *intr.* (of a person) jump down lightly; let oneself fall. **c** *tr.* remove (clothes, esp. trousers) rapidly, allowing them to fall to the ground. **9** *tr.* informal lose (money). **10** *tr.* esp. *N Amer.* dismiss (a person) from a team etc. **11** *tr. slang* take (a drug, esp. an illegal drug) orally. **12** *tr.* omit (a letter, syllable, etc.) in speech. **13** *tr. Sport* lose (a game, point, match, etc.). **14** *tr.* deliver (supplies etc.) by parachute. **15** *tr. Football* **a** send (a ball) by a drop kick. **b** score (a goal) by a drop kick. **16** *tr.* set (a part of a garment) in a lower position than is normal. ☐ **at the drop of a hat** given the slightest excuse. **drop anchor** anchor ship. **drop away** decrease or depart gradually. **drop back** (or **behind** or **to the rear**) fall back; get left behind. **drop back into** return to (a habit etc.). **drop the ball** N Amer. make a mess of something; fumble. **drop a brick** informal make an indiscreet or embarrassing remark. **drop dead 1** die suddenly, usu. from a heart attack or stroke. **2** slang an exclamation of intense scorn. **drop in** (or **by**) informal call casually as a visitor. **a drop in the ocean** (or **a bucket**) a very small amount, esp. compared with what is needed or expected. **drop into** informal **1** call casually at (a place). **2** fall into (a habit etc.). **drop it!** slang stop that! **drop names** = NAME-DROP. **drop off 1** decline gradually. **2** informal fall asleep. **3** = sense 5 of v. **4** leave or deposit (something) at an assigned place. **drop out** informal cease to participate, esp. in a race, a course of study, or in conventional society. **fit** (or **ready**) **to drop** extremely tired. **have the drop on** informal have the advantage over. **have had a drop too much** informal be slightly drunk. **one's jaw drops** one shows sudden surprise, dismay, or disappointment. ☐ **droplet** n.

drop cloth n. N Amer. a sheet of cloth or plastic used to protect furniture, floors, etc. when painting.

drop-dead attrib.adj. (also **drop-dead gorgeous** attrib. & predic.adj.) slang stunningly beautiful.

drop-down adj. designating a menu or list that appears below a heading when the heading is selected with a mouse.

drop-in ● adj. **1** (of a place or function) at which one can turn up informally, without prior appointment or referral (drop-in centre). **2** designed to drop into position. ● n. informal **1** esp. N Amer. a place or function at which one can turn up informally, without prior appointment or referral. **2** an unexpected visitor or visit.

drop kick ● n. **1** Football etc. a kick made by dropping the ball and kicking it on the bounce. **2** a movement in which a wrestler jumps into the air and kicks his or her opponent with both feet simultaneously, then drops onto one side. ● v. **1** tr. kick (a ball, a field goal, etc.) by means of a drop kick. **2** intr. make a drop kick.

drop-off n. **1 a** an act of dropping off or delivering something or someone. **b** a place where this can be done. **2** a decline, a decrease (a drop-off in sales). **3** N Amer. a sheer downward slope.

dropout n. **1** informal a person who has dropped out of society. **2** a person who leaves school before completing the program.

drop pass n. a backwards pass of a ball or puck, often executed without turning or looking around.

dropped adj. in a lower position than usual (dropped waist).

dropper n. **1** a device for administering liquid, esp. medicine, in drops. **2** a person or thing that drops.

droppings n.pl. **1** the dung of animals or birds. **2** something that falls or has fallen in drops.

dropsy n. (pl. **-ies**) = EDEMA.

dross / drɒs / n. **1** material without value or worth. **2 a** the scum separated from metals in melting. **b** foreign matter mixed with anything; impurities.

drought / draʊt / n. **1** the continuous absence of rain; dry weather. **2** the prolonged lack of something.

drove[1] past of DRIVE.

drove[2] n. **1 a** a large number (of people etc.) moving together; a crowd; a multitude; a shoal. **b** (in pl.) a great number (people arrived in droves). **2** a herd or flock being driven or moving together.

drover n. a person who drives herds to market; a cattle dealer. ☐ **drove** v.tr. **droving** n.

drown v. **1** tr. & intr. kill or be killed by submersion in liquid. **2** tr. submerge; flood; drench (drowned the fields in six feet of water). **3** tr. (often foll. by in) deaden (grief etc.) with drink (drowned his sorrows). **4** tr. **a** (often foll. by out) make (a sound) inaudible by means of a louder sound. **b** overcome by superior strength. ☐ **like a drowned rat** informal extremely wet and bedraggled.

drowse ● v. **1** intr. be dull and sleepy or half asleep. **2** tr. (often foll. by away) pass (the time) in drowsing. ● n. a condition of sleepiness.

drowsy adj. (**-ier, -iest**) **1** half asleep; dozing. **2** making one feel sleepy. **3** sluggish. ☐ **drowsily** adv. **drowsiness** n.

drub v.tr. (**drubbed, drubbing**) **1** thump; belabour. **2** beat in a fight. **3** (usu. foll. by into, out of) beat (an idea, attitude, etc.) into or out of a person. **4** defeat soundly. **5** criticize or reprimand harshly. ☐ **drubbing** n.

drudge ● n. a person who does heavy, unpleasant, or menial work. ● v.intr. (often foll. by at) work slavishly at heavy, unpleasant, or menial tasks. ☐ **drudgery** n.

drug ● n. **1** a medicinal substance. **2** a narcotic, hallucinogen, or stimulant, esp. one causing addiction. ● v.tr. (**drugged, drugging**) **1** add a drug to (food or drink). **2 a** administer a drug to. **b** stupefy with a drug. ☐ **drugless** adj.

drug addict n. a person who is addicted to a drug.

druggie n. informal a drug addict.

druggist n. esp. N Amer. a pharmacist.

druggy adj. (**-ier, -iest**) informal of or associated with narcotic drugs.

drugstore n. N Amer. a pharmacy that also sells cosmetics, household items, soft drinks, snacks, etc.

Druid / ˈdruːɪd / n. **1** an ancient Celtic priest, magician, or soothsayer of Gaul, Britain, or Ireland. **2** a member of a Welsh etc. Druidic order. ☐ **Druidic** adj. **Druidical** adj. **Druidism** n.

drum ● n. **1 a** a percussion instrument made of a hollow cylinder or hemisphere covered at one or both ends and sounded by striking. **b** (often in pl.) a drummer or a percussion section (the drums are playing too loud). **c** a sound made by or resembling that of a drum. **2** something resembling a drum in shape, esp.: **a** a cylindrical container or receptacle for oil, etc. **b** a cylinder or barrel in machinery on which something is wound etc. **3** the membrane of the middle ear; the eardrum. **4** (in full **drum fish**) any marine fish of the family Sciaenidae, having a swim bladder that produces a drumming sound. ● v. (**drummed, drumming**) **1** intr. & tr. play on a drum. **2** tr. & intr. beat, tap, or thump (knuckles, feet, etc.) continuously (on something) (drummed on the table). **3** intr. (of a bird or an insect) make a loud, hollow noise with quivering wings. ☐ **drum into** drive (a lesson) into (a person) by persistence. **drum up** summon, gather, or call up (drum up some support).

drumbeat n. a stroke or the sound of a stroke on a drum.

drum brake n. a brake in which shoes on a vehicle press against the drum on a wheel.

drum dance n. a dance, performed to an accompaniment of drumming, combining traditional Inuit dancing with Scottish and French-Canadian jigs and reels.

drumhead n. the skin or membrane of a drum.

drum kit n. a set of drums, cymbals, etc.

drumlin n. Geol. a long oval mound of glacial till.

drum machine n. an electronic device that imitates the sound of percussion instruments.

drum major n. the leader of a marching band.

drum majorette n. esp. N Amer. a member of a female baton-twirling parading group.

drummer n. **1** a person who plays a drum or drums. **2** esp. N Amer. informal a sales representative.

drum roll n. a rapid succession of notes on a drum.

drumstick n. **1** a stick used for beating a drum. **2** the lower joint of the leg of a cooked chicken etc.

drunk ● adj. **1** rendered incapable by alcohol. **2** (often foll. by with) overcome or elated with joy, success, power, etc. ● n. **1** a habitually drunk person. **2** slang a drinking bout; a period of drunkenness.

drunkard /'drʌŋkərd/ n. a person who is drunk, esp. habitually.

drunk driving n. the act of driving a vehicle with an excess of alcohol in the blood. □ **drunk driver** n.

drunken adj. (usu. attrib.) **1** = DRUNK. **2** caused by or exhibiting drunkenness (a drunken brawl). **3** fond of drinking. □ **drunkenly** adv. **drunkenness** n.

drunken driving n. = DRUNK DRIVING. □ **drunken driver** n.

drunk tank n. N Amer. slang a prison cell where persons arrested for drunkenness are detained, esp. overnight.

drupe /druːp/ n. any fleshy or pulpy fruit enclosing a stone containing one or a few seeds, e.g. a plum.

drupelet /'druːplət/ n. (also **drupel** /'druːpəl/) a small drupe usu. in an aggregate fruit, e.g. a raspberry.

druthers /'drʌðərz/ n. N Amer. informal preference, choice; one's way (if I had my druthers).

Druze /druːz/ n. (often attrib.) a member of a political or religious sect linked with Islam and living near Mt. Lebanon (Druze militia).

dry ● adj. (**drier; driest**) **1** free from moisture, not wet, esp.: **a** with any moisture having evaporated, drained, or been wiped away. **b** (of the eyes) free from tears. **c** (of a climate etc.) with insufficient rainfall; not rainy (a dry spell). **d** (of a river, well, etc.) dried up; not yielding water. **e** (of a liquid) having disappeared by evaporation etc. **f** not connected with or for use without moisture (dry shampoo). **2** (of wine etc.) not sweet (dry sherry). **3 a** meagre, plain, or bare (dry facts). **b** uninteresting; dull (dry as dust). **4** (of a sense of humour, a joke, etc.) subtle, ironic, and quietly expressed. **5 a** (of a country, legislation, etc.) prohibiting the sale of alcoholic drink. **b** (of a person) abstaining from alcohol or drugs. **6 a** (of toast, bread, etc.) without butter, margarine, etc. **b** (of bread, rolls, etc.) stale. **7** (of provisions, groceries, etc.) solid, not liquid. **8** (of a person etc.) impassive, unsympathetic. **9** (of a cow etc.) not yielding milk. **10** informal **a** thirsty (feel dry). **b** causing thirst (this is dry work). **11** N Amer. (of beer) having little or no aftertaste, due to longer brewing. **12** (of weather, a climate, etc.) not humid. ● v. (**dries, dried**) **1** tr. & intr. make or become dry by wiping, evaporation, draining, etc. **2** tr. (usu. as **dried** adj.) preserve (food etc.) by removing the moisture (dried fruit). **3** intr. (often foll. by up) Theatre informal forget one's lines. ● n. (pl. **dries**) **1** the process or an instance of drying. **2** (prec. by the) a dry place (come into the dry). **3 a** dry ginger ale. **b** dry wine, sherry, etc. □ **come up dry** N Amer. be unsuccessful. **dry out 1** become fully dry. **2** (of a drug addict, alcoholic, etc.) undergo treatment to cure addiction. **dry up 1** make utterly dry. **2** (of moisture) disappear utterly. **3** (of a well etc.) cease to yield water. **4** informal (esp. in imper.) cease talking. **5** disappear or cease (the market dried

up). **go dry** enact legislation for the prohibition of alcohol. □ **dryable** adj. **dryish** adj. **dryness** n.

dry battery n. a battery consisting of dry cells.

dry cell n. a galvanic cell in which the electrolyte is absorbed in a solid and cannot be spilled.

dry clean v.tr. & intr. clean (clothes etc.), or be cleanable, with organic solvents without using water. □ **dry cleaner** n. **dry cleaning** n.

dry cough n. a cough not producing phlegm.

dry-cure v.tr. cure (meat etc.) without pickling in liquid. □ **dry-cured** adj.

dry dock n. an enclosure for the building or repairing of ships, from which water can be removed.

dryer n. (also **drier**) **1** a machine or apparatus for drying the hair, laundry, etc. **2** a substance mixed with oil paint or ink to promote drying.

dry-eyed adj. not weeping.

dry fly ● n. an artificial fly which floats on the water (often attrib.: dry-fly anglers). ● v.intr. (usu. **dry-fly**) (**-flies, -flied**) fish by such a method.

dry goods n.pl. **1** N Amer. fabrics, clothing, etc. **2** Cdn & Brit. solid as opposed to liquid foodstuffs.

dry ice n. **1** solid carbon dioxide, which passes directly from solid to vapour at −78.5°C and is used as a refrigerant and to create theatrical effects of fog. **2** the fog produced in this way.

dryland n. **1** (**dry land**) land as opposed to the sea, a river, etc. **2** (also in pl.) esp. N Amer. an area or land where rainfall is low (also attrib.: dryland farming). **3** (also in pl.) esp. N Amer. a surface not covered by snow or ice as used for training by skiers, skaters, etc. (also attrib.: dryland training).

dryly adv. **1** (said) in a dry manner; humorously. **2** in a dry way or condition.

dry measure n. a measure of capacity for dry products such as grains etc.

dry-roasted adj. (esp. of nuts etc.) roasted by a process using little or no oil or liquid. □ **dry-roast** v.tr.

dry rot n. **1** a decayed state of wood in poorly ventilated conditions, caused by certain fungi. **2** these fungi.

dry run n. informal a rehearsal.

dry spell n. **1** a period of dry weather. **2** a period of unproductiveness.

dry suit n. a close-fitting waterproof rubber suit worn esp. when skin diving (compare WETSUIT).

drywall esp. N Amer. ● n. prefabricated sheets of plaster sandwiched between heavy paper, used for interior walls. ● v.tr. install drywall (on a wall etc.). □ **drywaller** n. **drywalling** n.

dry well n. **1** a well, drilled for oil, water, gas, etc., that is unproductive. **2** N Amer. an underground chamber used for draining off grey water etc.

DSC abbr. Distinguished Service Cross.

D.Sc. abbr. Doctor of Science.

DSM abbr. Distinguished Service Medal.

DSP abbr. digital signal processing or processor.

DT abbr. (also **DT's**) DELIRIUM TREMENS.

DTP abbr. DESKTOP PUBLISHING.

dual /'duːəl, 'djuːəl/ ● adj. **1** of two; twofold. **2** divided in two; double (dual ownership). **3** Grammar (in some languages) denoting two persons or things. ● n. (also **dual number**) a dual form of a noun, verb, etc. □ **duality** /-'ælɪti/ n. **dualize** v.tr. **dually** adv.

dual citizenship n. the status of a person who is a citizen of more than one country concurrently.

dualism n. **1** the state of being twofold; duality. **2** Philos. the theory that in any domain of reality there are two independent underlying principles, e.g.

mind and matter, form and content. **3** *Theol.* **a** the theory that the forces of good and evil are equally balanced in the universe. **b** the theory of the dual (human and divine) personality of Christ. □ **dualist** *n.* **dualistic** *adj.* **dualistically** *adv.*

dual-purpose *adj.* **1** (of a vehicle) usable for passengers or goods. **2** (of a farm animal) able to be used for two purposes, e.g. (of a cow) providing both meat and milk.

dub[1] /dʌb/ *v.tr.* (**dubbed, dubbing**) **1** confer an order of knighthood upon (a person) by the ritual touching of the shoulder with a sword. **2** give (a person or thing) a name, nickname, or title. **3** dress (an artificial fishing fly). **4** smear (leather) with grease.

dub[2] (**dubbed, dubbing**) ● *v.tr.* **1** provide (a film etc.) with an alternative soundtrack, esp. in a different language. **2** add (sound effects or music) to a film or a broadcast. **3** combine (soundtracks) into one. **4** transfer or make a copy of (a tape or disc). ● *n.* a dubbed tape etc.

dub[3] *v.intr.* (**dubbed, dubbing**) *slang* (foll. by *in, up*) pay up; contribute money.

dub[4] *n.* **1** (also **dub music**) a remixed version of a piece of recorded (esp. reggae) music, usu. with the melodic line removed and special effects added. **2** (also **dub poetry**) a kind of performance poetry in Jamaican (or black English) vernacular.

dubbing *n.* an alternative soundtrack to a film etc.

dubious /'du:biəs, 'dju:biəs/ *adj.* **1** hesitating or doubting (*dubious about going*). **2** of questionable value or truth (*a dubious claim*). **3** unreliable; suspicious (*dubious company*). **4** of doubtful result (*a dubious undertaking*). □ **dubiously** *adv.* **dubiousness** *n.*

ducal /'du:kəl, 'dju:-/ *adj.* of or pertaining to a duke.

ducat /'dʌkət/ *n.* **1** *hist.* any of various gold or silver coins, formerly current in most European countries. **2** a ticket, esp. for admission, a train, bus, etc.

Duchenne muscular dystrophy /du:'ʃein/ *n.* a severe form of muscular dystrophy caused by a genetic defect and usu. affecting boys. Abbr.: **DMD**.

duchess /'dʌtʃəs/ *n.* (as a title usu. **Duchess**) **1** a duke's wife or widow. **2** a woman holding the rank of duke in her own right.

duchy /'dʌtʃi/ *n.* (*pl.* **-ies**) a dukedom or the territory of a duke or duchess.

duck[1] *n.* **1 a** any of various swimming birds of the family Anatidae, esp. the domesticated form of the mallard or wild duck. **b** the female of this (*opp.* DRAKE). **c** the flesh of a duck as food. **2** esp. *N Amer.* a fellow, individual, etc., esp. a somewhat eccentric one (*he's an odd duck*). □ **like a duck to water** adapting very readily. **like water off a duck's back** *informal* (of remonstrances etc.) producing no effect.

duck[2] ● *v.* **1** *intr.* & *tr.* plunge, dive, or dip under water and emerge (*ducked him in the pond*). **2 a** *intr.* stoop suddenly or move quickly, esp. as an evasive measure (*ducked out of sight*). **b** *tr.* bob, jerk down, or lower (esp. the head) momentarily. **3** *tr.* & *intr.* *informal* (often foll. by *out*) avoid or dodge; withdraw (from) (*ducked out of the engagement*). ● *n.* **1** a quick swim or plunge into water etc. **2** a quick lowering of the head, rapid evasive movement, etc.

duck[3] *n.* **1** a strong untwilled linen or cotton fabric used for the outer clothing of sailors, small sails, etc. **2** (in *pl.*) trousers made of this (*white ducks*).

duckbill ● *n.* **1** (also **duck-billed platypus**) = PLATYPUS. **2** (also **duck-billed dinosaur**) = HADROSAUR. ● *adj.* (also **duck-billed**) having the spatulate shape of a duck's bill.

duckish *n.* Cdn (*Nfld*) (also *attrib.*) dusk, twilight, or the time between sunset and dark.

duckling *n.* **1** a young duck. **2** its flesh as food.

duck soup *n.* *N Amer. slang* **1** an easy task. **2** an easily or thoroughly beaten or defeated person.

ducktail *n.* esp. *N Amer. slang* a haircut with the hair on the nape of the head shaped like a duck's tail. □ **ducktailed** *adj.*

duck-walk ● *n.* a waddle or a walk in a squatting position. ● *v.intr.* walk in a squatting position.

duckweed *n.* any of various plants, esp. of the genus *Lemna*, growing on the surface of still water.

ducky ● *n.* (*pl.* **-ies**) (in full **rubber ducky**) a toy duck made of plastic, rubber, etc. ● *adj.* sweet, fine, splendid.

duct *n.* **1** a channel or tube for conveying air, fluid, cable, etc. **2 a** a tube or passage in the body conveying fluids or secretions such as tears, lymph, etc. **b** *Bot.* any of the vessels of the vascular tissue of plants, containing air, water, etc. □ **ducted** *adj.*

ductile /'dʌktaɪl/ *adj.* **1** (of a substance) flexible, pliant, malleable. **2** (of a material, esp. metal) pliable. **3** (of a person) docile, tractable, open to persuasion. □ **ductility** /-'tɪlɪti/ *n.*

ducting *n.* **1** a system of ducts. **2** material, esp. tubing or piping, in the form of a duct or ducts.

ductless *adj.* lacking or not using a duct or ducts, esp. of a gland secreting directly into the bloodstream.

duct tape *n.* *N Amer.* tape of plastic-backed webbed cloth, used for household repairs. □ **duct-tape** *v.tr.*

ductwork *n.* a system of ducts.

dud *n.* *slang* (also *attrib.*) **1** a useless, unsuccessful, ineffectual, or unsatisfactory person or thing (*a box office dud*). **2** a shell etc. that fails to explode. **3** a dishonoured cheque. **4** (in *pl.*) clothes.

dude *N Amer. slang* ● *n.* **1** a fellow or person. **2** a person, usu. male, fastidiously concerned with clothes, appearance, etc. **3** a city dweller, esp. one vacationing on a ranch in western Canada or the US; a tenderfoot. ● *v.refl.* & *tr.* (usu. foll. by *up*, usu. in *passive*) dress or fix up, esp. ostentatiously. □ **dudette** *n.*

dude ranch *n.* *N Amer.* a cattle ranch converted to a vacation resort for tourists, featuring riding, camping, barbecues, etc.

due /du:, dju:/ ● *adj.* **1** (*predic.*) owing or payable as a debt or an obligation (*our thanks are due to him; $500 was due*). **2** (often foll. by *to*) belonging to or incumbent upon (a person) by right, by duty, or as a necessity (*his due reward*). **3** proper, sufficient, or adequate (*due consideration*). **4** (*predic.*; foll. by *to*) attributable or ascribable to (a cause, an agent, etc.) (*death was due to cardiac arrest*). **5** (*predic.*) expected or intended to arrive or appear at a certain time (*a train is due at 7:30*). **6** scheduled or under an obligation or agreement to do something (*due to speak tonight*). ● *n.* **1** a thing which is owed to a person legally or morally (*a fair hearing is my due*). **2** (in *pl.*) **a** what a person owes, esp. obligations, responsibilities, etc. **b** an obligatory and legally demandable payment, toll, or charge, esp. the membership fees for a club etc. (*union dues*). ● *adv.* (of a point of the compass) exactly, directly (*went due east*). □ **due to** *disputed* because of, owing to (*was late due to an accident*) (*compare* sense 4 of *adj.*). ¶The use of *due to* to mean 'because of' as in the example *He was late due to an accident* is regarded as unacceptable by some people, though the usage is very well established. **fall** (or **become**) **due** (of a bill etc.) be immediately payable. **give a person his or her due** treat a person fairly or with justice. **in due course** (or **time**) **1** at about the appropriate time. **2** in the natural order. **pay one's dues 1** fulfill one's obligations. **2** undergo hardships to succeed or gain experience.

due date n. **1** the date on which payment of a bill etc. falls due. **2** the date, in a pregnancy, on which a child is predicted to be born. **3** the date on which a library book, rented item, etc. must be returned.

duel /'du:əl, 'dju:əl/ ● n. **1** hist. a private fight between two people, pre-arranged and fought with deadly weapons, usu. to settle a point of honour. **2** any contest between two people, parties, causes, animals, etc. (a duel of wits). ● v.intr. (**duelled, duelling**) fight a duel or duels. ☐ **dueller** n. **duellist** n.

due process n. (in full **due process of the law**) the administration of justice through the courts in accordance with established rules and principles.

duet /du:'et, dju:'et/ ● n. **1** Music a performance by two voices, instrumentalists, etc. **2** a composition for two performers. ● v.intr. (usu. foll. by with) (**dueted, dueting**) perform a duet. ☐ **duettist** n.

duff[1] n. Brit., Cdn (Maritimes), & US (New England) a boiled pudding.

duff[2] n. N Amer. the decaying vegetable matter which covers the forest ground.

duff[3] n. N Amer. & Scot. buttocks (get off your duff).

duffer n. slang **1** a person, often elderly, without practical ability. **2** a person who is incapable, inefficient, or useless in his or her business, occupation, or sport.

duffle n. (also **duffel**) **1** a coarse, closely woven, woollen cloth with a thick nap. **2** N Amer. a sportsman's or camper's equipment, food, clothing, etc. **3** (in full **duffle bag**) a large, cylindrical canvas bag closed by a drawstring and carried over the shoulder.

dufus var. of DOOFUS.

dug[1] past and past part. of DIG.

dug[2] n. **1** the udder, breast, teat, or nipple of a female animal. **2** slang (usu. in pl.) the breast of a woman.

dugout n. **1 a** N Amer. Sport a low shelter at the side of a baseball diamond etc. with seating for the team manager, trainer, players, etc. **b** a roofed shelter, esp. for troops in trenches. **2 a** esp. N Amer. a rough shelter hollowed out in a bank or hillside, usu. roofed with turf, canvas, etc. **b** Cdn (Prairies) a large hole in the ground used to catch and hold rain, spring runoff, etc. **3** a canoe made from a hollowed out tree trunk.

duh /də/ interj. indicating stupidity.

du jour /du: ʒʊr/ adj. (placed after noun) of the day; trendy or fashionable.

duke /du:k, dju:k/ ● n. **1** (as a title usu. **Duke**) **a** a person holding the highest hereditary title of the nobility and ranking next below a prince, esp. in Britain. **b** a sovereign prince ruling a duchy or small nation, esp. in certain European countries. **2** (usu. in pl.) slang **a** the hand or fist (put up your dukes!). **b** the verdict in a boxing match. ● v.tr. N Amer. slang (usu. foll. by out) fight, esp. with the fists (they decided to duke it out).

dukedom n. **1** a duchy or the territory ruled by a duke. **2** the rank of duke.

dulcimer /'dʌlsɪmər/ n. **1** a musical instrument with strings stretched over a trapezoidal sounding board or box, played by being struck with hammers. **2** a zither-like folk instrument with three or four strings, played by plucking or strumming.

dull ● adj. **1** uninteresting, tedious, or boring. **2** (of the weather) cloudy, overcast, gloomy. **3 a** (esp. of a knife-edge etc.) blunt. **b** (of colour, light, or taste) not bright, vivid, or keen. **4** (of a pain etc.) usu. prolonged and indistinct, not acute (a dull ache). **5** slow to understand, not quick-witted. **6** (of a trade, goods, etc.) sluggish or stagnant, slow-moving or not easily

saleable. **7** (of a person, animal, etc.) listless, depressed. **8** (of the ears, eyes, etc.) without keen perception. **9** (of sound) indistinct, muffled, not clear or loud (a dull thud). ● v.tr. & intr. make or become dull. ☐ **dull the edge of** blunt or make less sensitive, interesting, effective, amusing, etc. ☐ **dulled** adj. **dullish** adj. **dullness** n. (also **dulness**). **dully** /'dʌli, 'dʌli/ adv.

dulse /dʌls/ n. an edible seaweed, Rhodymenia palmata, with red wedge-shaped fronds.

duly /'du:li, 'dju:li/ adv. **1** in due manner, order, form, or time. **2** correctly, properly, fitly, or sufficiently.

dumb ● adj. **1 a** (of a person) unable to speak, usu. because of a congenital defect or deafness; mute. **b** (of an animal) naturally unable to speak (our dumb friends). **2** temporarily silenced by surprise, shyness, grief, etc. (struck dumb by this revelation). **3** persistently taciturn or reticent, esp. insultingly (dumb insolence). **4** (of an action, expression, etc.) performed or made without speech. **5** informal esp. N Amer. stupid, ignorant, foolish. **6** (of a computer terminal etc.) not programmable, able only to transmit data to or receive data from a computer (opp. INTELLIGENT 3b). **7** (of missiles etc.) firing in a straight line until hitting something (opp. SMART 7b). ● v.tr. N Amer. slang (usu. foll. by down) reduce or adapt (a text etc.) to a lower level of understanding. ☐ **dumbly** adv. **dumbness** n.

dumb-ass n. N Amer. slang (also attrib.) a thoroughly stupid or foolish person.

dumbbell n. **1** a short bar with a weight at each end, used for exercise, muscle building, etc. **2** slang a stupid person or a fool.

dumbfound v.tr. (also **dumfound**) (usu. in passive) astonish, strike dumb, or confound.

dumbo /'dʌmbo:/ n. (pl. **-os**) slang a stupid person.

dumbstruck adj. greatly shocked or surprised and so lost for words.

dummy ● n. (pl. **-ies**) **1** a model of a human being, esp.: **a** a ventriloquist's doll. **b** a figure used to model clothes in a store window etc. **c** a target used for firearms practice. **d** a mannequin used in crash tests for vehicles etc. **2** (often attrib.) an imitation, representation, or counterfeit of an object used to replace or resemble a real or normal one, as in a display etc. **b** a prototype. **3 a** informal a stupid person. **b** derogatory a mute person. **4 a** a figurehead present only for appearances or a person taking no significant part in an activity. **b** a person who is merely a tool for another, buying etc. on another's behalf. **5** Cdn & Brit. a soother, pacifier, or rubber nipple for a baby to suck on. **6** Bridge **a** the partner of the declarer, whose cards are exposed after the first lead. **b** this player's hand. **7** Military a blank round of ammunition. **8** (in full **dummy instruction**) Computing a sequence of data inserted into an instruction stream that merely occupies space and is not intended for execution. ● adj. **1** of or pertaining to a dummy, imitation, or copy. **2** sham, counterfeit, fictitious (a dummy corporation). ☐ **dummy up** N Amer. slang refuse to talk, keep quiet, give no information.

dump ● n. **1 a** (in full **garbage dump**) a place for depositing garbage. **b** a heap or pile of garbage, waste material, etc. **c** N Amer. informal a large deposit of something (a fresh dump of snow). **2** informal a shabby, unpleasant, or dreary place. **3** Military a temporary store of ammunition, provisions, etc. deposited for later use. **4 a** an accumulated pile of ore, earth, etc. from mining operations. **b** the place where this is deposited. **5 a** a printout or listing of stored data, esp. of the complete contents of a computer memory. **b** a periodic record of the state of a disk, made on magnetic tape in order to protect against accidental overwriting or mechanical failure. **6** (in full **log dump**) a place where logs are piled such as on a riverbank, near a road or railway, etc., in preparation for being moved to the mill. **7** esp. *N Amer. slang* an act of defecation. ● *v.tr.* **1 a** throw (a thing) down carelessly, clumsily, or unceremoniously. **b** throw down in or as in a lump or mass (*the storm dumped 15 cm of snow*). **c** fling abruptly out of a craft, esp. into water (*the wind came up and dumped us into the drink*). **2 a** empty or tip out (garbage etc.), esp. from a container. **b** discard or dispose of (garbage, hazardous waste, etc.). **3** *informal* **a** abandon or desert (a person, issue, etc.) (*they dumped her at the hospital and left*). **b** cast aside or transfer (difficulties etc.), usu. hastily and irresponsibly (*she dumped her work on me*). **c** abruptly end a relationship with (a person), usu. less than amicably (*she dumped him*). **4** *Econ.* **a** put (goods) on the market in large quatities and at low prices. **b** send (goods unsaleable at a high price in the home market) to a foreign market for sale at a low price, to keep up the price at home, and to capture a new market. **5** *Computing* **a** copy (stored data) to a different location, esp. to an external storage medium from an internal one, e.g. to check a program or safeguard data. **b** reproduce the contents of (a store) externally. **6 a** *Sport* beat (another team etc.) decisively. **b** *Boxing* lose (a match) intentionally. □ **dump on** esp. *N Amer.* **1** criticize severely, treat with scorn or contempt, or defeat heavily. **2** thwart (*fate dumped on my plans*). **take a dump** *N Amer. slang* defecate.

dump-and-chase *adj. Cdn Hockey* designating a strategy of play in which a player shoots the puck far down the ice and then chases after it.

dumper *n.* **1** *N Amer.* a large metal bin for garbage. **2 a** a person or company that dumps garbage etc., esp. one that disposes of toxic waste covertly or illegally. **b** a thing that dumps or disposes of garbage etc. □ **into the dumper** *N Amer. informal* into a dire state or condition (*the market went into the dumper*).

dumping *n.* **1** the practice of discarding garbage, hazardous waste, etc., esp. covertly or illegally. **2** the practice of dumping goods (see DUMP v. 4).

dumping ground *n.* **1** = DUMP 1a. **2** a catch-all category, institution, etc. used for something unclassified or as a place of last resort for those considered undesirable (*a dumping ground for criminals*).

dumpling *n.* **1 a** a small piece of dough, sometimes with a filling, boiled in water or in stew. **b** a dessert consisting of apple or other fruit enclosed in dough and baked. **2** *informal* a small fat person.

dumps *n.pl. informal* a state of depression, melancholy, or low spirits (*down in the dumps*).

Dumpster *n. proprietary* a very large garbage container, usu. emptied by being mechanically lifted onto a truck.

dump truck *n.* a usu. open topped truck with a body that tilts or opens at the back for unloading.

dumpy *adj.* (**-ier, -iest**) short, rounded, and stout. □ **dumpiness** *n.*

dun¹ ● *adj.* dull greyish-brown. ● *n.* **1** a dun colour. **2** a dun horse. **3 a** any of various dusky coloured flies, esp. mayflies. **b** a dark fishing fly resembling this.

dun² ● *n.* **1** a debt collector or an importunate creditor. **2** a demand for money, esp. in payment of a debt. ● *v.tr.* (**dunned, dunning**) **1** make repeated and persistent demands upon, esp. for money owed. **2** bother, pester, assail constantly.

dunce *n.* a person slow at learning.

dunderhead *n.* a ponderously stupid person.

dune /du:n, dju:n/ *n.* a ridge of loose sand etc. formed by the wind, esp. beside the sea or in a desert.

dune buggy *n.* a low, lightweight motor vehicle with wide tires for recreational driving on sand.

dung *n.* the excrement of animals; manure.

dungaree /ˌdʌŋɡəˈriː/ *n.* **1** a coarse, hard-wearing cotton fabric, often blue. **2** (in pl.) trousers, esp. jeans, made of dungaree or similar material. **3** trousers with a bib, esp. as worn by children.

dung beetle *n.* any of various beetles which lay their eggs in dung or roll up balls of dung for their larvae to feed on.

Dungeness crab /ˈdʌŋɡənəs/ *n. N Amer.* **1** a Pacific coast crab, *Cancer magister*, of considerable economic value. **2** this eaten as a dish.

dungeon *n.* a strong underground cell for prisoners.

dunk ● *v.tr.* **1** dip (bread, a biscuit, etc.) into soup, coffee, etc. while eating. **2 a** immerse, dip (*was dunked in the river*). **b** *Christianity slang* baptize. **3** *Basketball* shoot (the ball) down through the hoop by jumping so that the hands are above the ring. ● *n.* **1** (in full **dunk shot** or **slam dunk**) *Basketball* a shot made by jumping and pushing the ball down through the basket from above. **2** *N Amer.* an act or instance of immersing oneself in a lake etc. □ **dunker** *n.*

dunlin /ˈdʌnlɪn/ *n.* a long-billed holarctic sandpiper, *Calidris alpina*, the male of which has a reddish back and a black patch on the front.

Dunne-Za /ˌdʌnəˈzɒ/ *n.* = BEAVER.

dunno /dəˈnoʊ/ *interj. informal* (I) do not know.

duo /du:o, ˈdju:o:/ *n.* (pl. **-os**) **1** a pair of actors, entertainers, etc. (*a comedy duo*). **2** *Music* a duet.

duodenum /ˌdu:oˈdi:nəm, ˌdju:o:-, ˌdu:ˈɒdənəm/ *n.* the first part of the small intestine immediately below the stomach. □ **duodenal** *adj.*

duopoly /du:ˈɒpəli, dju:-/ *n.* (pl. **-ies**) *Econ.* a condition in which a particular market is controlled or dominated by only two suppliers, individuals, etc. □ **duopolist** *n.* **duopolistic** *adj.*

Duo-Tang /ˈdu:oʊtæŋ, dju:-/ *n. Cdn proprietary* a report folder of cardboard, having three flexible metal fasteners to insert through the holes of looseleaf paper.

dupe¹ /du:p, dju:p/ ● *n.* a person who is deluded or deceived by another. ● *v.tr.* deceive, mislead, make a dupe of, or gull (a person). □ **dupable** *adj.* **dupery** *n.*

dupe² *slang* ● *n.* a duplicate, esp. a duplicate negative made from a positive print. ● *adj.* duplicate (*dupe transparencies*). □ **duper** *n.* **duping** *n.*

duple /ˈdu:pəl, ˈdju:-/ *adj.* double, twofold.

duple time *n. Music* two beats to the bar.

duplex /ˈdu:pleks, ˈdju:-/ ● *n.* (pl. **-es**) **1** esp. *N Amer.* (also *attrib.*) **a** = SEMI-DETACHED. **b** a residential building divided into two apartments, esp. a two-storey dwelling with a separate apartment on each floor. **2** the capacity of a computer etc. to send and receive data simultaneously along a communications link such as a telephone etc. ● *adj.* **1** twofold, having two parts, or combining two elements, esp. with similar functions. **2** *Computing* (of a circuit) allowing the transmission or reception of signals in opposite directions simultaneously over a single channel etc. (opp. SIMPLEX 2). ● *v.tr.* **1** make (a cable, system, etc.) capable of transmitting in two directions simultaneously. **2** make (a building etc.) duplex. □ **duplexed** *adj.* **duplexing** *n.*

duplicate ● *adj.* /ˈdu:plɪkət, ˈdju:plɪkət/ **1** copied or exactly like something already existing (in any number of copies). **2 a** paired, double, or having two corresponding parts, examples, etc. **b** doubled or consisting of twice the number or quantity. ● *n.* /'dju:plɪkət, 'dju:plɪkət/ **1** one of two or more things exactly alike, so that each is a double of some original. **2** *Law* a second copy of a letter or document, having equal legal force of the original. **3** (in full **duplicate bridge** or **whist**) a form of bridge or whist in which the same hands are played successively by different players. ● *v.tr.* /'du:plɪ‚keɪt, 'dju:plɪ‚keɪt/ **1** multiply by two; double. **2 a** make or be an exact copy of. **b** make or supply copies of (*duplicated the leaflet for distribution*). **3** repeat (an action etc.), esp. unnecessarily. □ **in duplicate** consisting of two exact copies. □ **duplication** *n.*

duplicator *n.* a thing that duplicates, esp. a machine for making copies of a document, leaflet, slide, etc.

duplicity /du:'plɪsɪti, dju:-/ *n.* (*pl.* **-ies**) **1** the quality or practice of being two-faced, deceitful in manner or conduct, or double-dealing. **2** the state or quality of being double or twofold, esp. physically, psychologically, etc. □ **duplicitous** *adj.*

durable /'dʊərəbəl, 'djʊr-/ *adj.* capable of lasting or able to withstand change, decay, or wear. □ **durability** *n.*

dura mater /‚dʊərə 'meɪtər/ *n.* (also **dura**) the tough outermost membrane enveloping the brain and spinal cord (*see* MENINGES).

duration /dʊ'reɪʃən, djʊ-/ *n.* the time during which something lasts or continues. □ **for the duration 1** for a very long time. **2** until the end of a particular activity. □ **durational** *adj.*

duress /dʊ'res, djʊ'-, 'dʊ-, 'djʊ-/ *n.* **1 a** compulsion, constraint, esp. imprisonment, threats, or violence (*under duress*). **b** *Law* such constraint illegally used to force a person to act against his or her will. **2** forcible restraint, confinement, or imprisonment.

during *prep.* **1** throughout the whole continuance, course, or duration of (an activity, event, etc.) (*read during the meal*). **2** within, in the course of, or at some point in the duration of (a specified period of time).

durum /'dʊərəm, 'djʊərəm/ *n.* a kind of wheat, *Triticum durum*, having hard seeds and yielding a flour used in the manufacture of pasta.

dusk *n.* **1** the darker stage of twilight in the evening. **2** = NIGHTFALL. **3** shade, shadow, gloom.

dusky *adj.* (**-ier, -iest**) **1** shady, shadowy, dim. **2** somewhat dark in colour. **3** (of a complexion) swarthy, dark hued. □ **duskily** *adv.* **duskiness** *n.*

dust ● *n.* **1 a** finely powdered earth, dirt, etc., lying on the ground or on surfaces and blown about by the wind. **b** fine powder of any material (*sawdust*). **c** any substance pulverized. **d** a cloud of finely powdered earth or of other fine particles floating in the air. **2** that to which anything is reduced by disintegration or decay, esp. a dead person's remains. **3** an act of dusting (*give the table a dust*). ● *v.* **1** *tr. & intr.* clear (furniture etc.) of dust etc. by wiping, brushing, etc. **2** *tr.* **a** sprinkle (the skin, a plant, a cake, etc.) with powder, dust, sugar, etc. **b** sprinkle or strew (sugar, powder, etc.). **3** *tr.* make dusty. **4** *tr. slang* **a** beat, vanquish, win a victory over. **b** esp. *US* kill. **5** *tr.* apply a dust-like chemical to an object, esp. as a means of discovering fingerprints. □ **dust off 1** remove the dust from (an object on which it has long been allowed to settle). **2** use, apply, or enjoy again after a long period of neglect. **eat (a person's) dust 1** fall far behind. **2** an expression of contempt or dismissal (*Eat my dust!*). **in the dust 1** humiliated. **2** far behind or much inferior. **3** abandoned. **not see a person for dust** find that a person has made a hasty departure. **shake the dust off** (or **from**) **one's feet** depart indignantly or disdainfully. **throw dust**

in a person's eyes mislead a person by misrepresentation or by diverting attention from a point. **when the dust settles** when things quieten down or clear. □ **dustless** *adj.*

dustball *n.* *N Amer. informal* (also **dust bunny** *pl.* **-ies**) a clump of dust, lint, etc. found indoors, esp. in corners, under furniture, etc.

dust bowl *n.* an arid or unproductive dry region.

dust devil *n.* a small whirlwind common in dry regions which becomes visible as it whips up dust, debris, leaves, etc.

duster *n.* **1 a** a cloth, brush, etc. for dusting surfaces. **b** a person who dusts. **c** a device for sifting or applying dust. **2** a short, light, usu. cotton bathrobe or item of sleepwear, esp. for women. **3** *Baseball* = BEANBALL.

dusting *n.* **1** the action of removing dust. **2** the action of sprinkling with dust, powder, etc. (*cropdusting*). **3** a very thin layer of dust, powder, snow, etc.

dust jacket *n.* a removable, usu. decorated paper cover used to protect a book from dirt etc.

dustpan *n.* a small pan into which dust etc. is brushed from the floor.

dust storm *n.* a strong wind storm, raising and carrying clouds of dust or sand.

dust-up *n.* *informal* a fight, quarrel, or disturbance.

dusty *adj.* (**-ier, -iest**) **1 a** full of or covered with dust. **b** of the nature of or resembling dust. **2** (of a topic etc.) uninteresting, unsatisfactory. **3** (of a colour) dull or muted (*dusty rose*). □ **dustily** *adv.* **dustiness** *n.*

Dutch ● *adj.* of, relating to, or associated with the Netherlands. ● *n.* **1** the language of the Netherlands. **2** (prec. by *the*; treated as *pl.*) the people of the Netherlands or their descendants. □ **go Dutch** share expenses equally.

Dutch elm disease *n.* a disease affecting elms caused by the fungus *Ceratocystis ulmi*.

Dutchie *n.* *N Amer.* a usu. square, raised, glazed doughnut containing raisins.

Dutchman *n.* (*pl.* **-men**) **1 a** a native or national of the Netherlands. **b** a person of Dutch descent. **2** a Dutch ship. **3** *N Amer. slang* a German.

Dutch oven *n.* **1** a covered container, casserole, or cooking pot for braising etc. **2** a metal cooking utensil with an open side which is turned towards a fire.

Dutch Reformed Church *n.* a Christian denomination based upon the teachings of Dutch Calvinists.

Dutchwoman *n.* (*pl.* **-women**) **1** a woman who is a native or national of the Netherlands. **2** a woman of Dutch descent.

dutiable /'du:ti:əbl, 'dju:-/ *adj.* liable to customs taxes or other duties.

dutiful *adj.* **1** doing or observant of one's duty. **2** (of a response, action, etc.) characteristic of, resulting from, or expressing a sense of duty. □ **dutifully** *adv.* **dutifulness** *n.*

duty /'du:ti, dju:-/ *n.* (*pl.* **-ies**) **1 a** a moral or legal obligation or responsibility (*his duty to report it*). **b** the binding force of what is morally right (*sense of duty*). **c** the action or behaviour due by moral or legal obligation (*do one's duty*). **2** payment due to the public revenue and enforced by law or custom, esp.: **a** that levied on the import, export, manufacture, or sale of goods. **b** that levied on the transfer of property, licences, the legal recognition of documents, etc. (*probate duty*). **3 a** an action required by a person's business, occupation, or function (*his duties as caretaker*). **b** the performance of or engagement in the activities required by a person's occupation etc. **c** *Military* active service in armed forces of one's country.

4 (attrib.) **a** (of a person) having specific duties or being on duty (duty officer). **b** (of an accessory, post, etc.) for use by an individual while on duty (duty station). **c** (of a visit, call, or other undertaking) done as a duty rather than as a pleasure. □ **(above and) beyond the call of duty** much more than expected by obligation. **do duty for** serve as or pass for (something else). **duty bound** morally or legally obliged by duty. **on** (or **off**) **duty** engaged (or not engaged) in one's work.

duty-free ● adj. (of goods etc.) exempt from payment of customs and excise duties, esp. as a small personal allowance on entering or re-entering a country. ● n. (in full **duty-free shop**) a shop at an airport etc. at which duty-free goods can be bought.

duvet /'du:vei/ n. a quilt, filled with down or a synthetic fibre with a high loft, used instead of an upper sheet and blankets.

DVA abbr. (in Canada) Department of Veterans Affairs.

DVD n. proprietary a digital recording medium similar in appearance to a CD but with much increased storage capacity, capable of storing a full-length feature film.

DVE abbr. digital video effects.

DVI abbr. digital video interaction.

D.V.M. abbr. Doctor of Veterinary Medicine.

dwarf ● n. (pl. **dwarfs** or **dwarves**) **1 a** a person of abnormally small stature, esp. one with a normalsized head and body but short limbs. **b** (also attrib.) an animal or plant much below the ordinary size for the species. **2** any of a mythological race of diminutive beings, figuring esp. in Scandinavian folklore, who are typically skilled in mining and metalworking and often possess magical powers. **3** (in full **dwarf star**) a small, dense star with low to average luminosity. ● v.tr. **1** stunt or restrict the growth or development of (a thing etc.). **2** cause (something similar or comparable) to seem small or insignificant. □ **dwarfed** adj. **dwarfish** adj. **dwarfishness** n. **dwarf-like** adj.

dwarf birch n. any of several shrubby birches of N America, esp. Betula pumila, growing in wet places across Canada and the northern US.

dwarfism n. the condition of being a dwarf.

dweeb n. a nerd, esp. a studious or boring person. □ **dweebish** adj. **dweeby** adj. (-ier, -iest).

dwell v.intr. (past and past part. **dwelt** or **dwelled**) **1 a** literary (usu. foll. by in, at, near, on, etc.) live, reside. **b** continue for a time in a place, state, or condition. **2** (of a machine part) pause slightly during the working of the machine. □ **dwell on** (or **upon**) spend time on; write, brood, or speak at length on (a specified subject) (always dwells on his grievances). □ **dweller** n.

dwelling n. (also **dwelling place**) a house or place of residence.

dwindle v.intr. **1** become gradually reduced in size or quantity. **2** degenerate, decline, or diminish in quality, value, or importance. □ **dwindling** adj.

DX abbr. distance, esp. used for short-wave radio reception.

DX coding n. proprietary an electronic system which uses optical, electrical, and mechanical encoding to read the pattern on film and automatically select the appropriate film type, speed, etc.

Dy symbol dysprosium.

dye ● n. **1 a** a substance used to change the colour of hair, fabric, wood, etc. **b** a colour produced by this. **2** (in full **dyestuff**) a substance yielding a dye, esp. for colouring materials in solution. ● v. (**dyeing**) **1** tr. impregnate with dye. **2** tr. make (a thing) a specified

colour with dye. **3** intr. take colour in the process of dyeing.

dyed-in-the-wool adj. **1** unchangeable, inveterate. **2** (of a fabric) made of yarn dyed in its raw state.

dyer n. a person who dyes cloth etc.

dying ● adj. **1** connected with, or at the time of, death (her dying words). **2** about to die (a dying art). **3** coming to an end (the dying days of the age of sail). ● n. the act or process of ceasing to live, function, etc. □ **to one's dying day** for the rest of one's life.

dyke¹ var. of DIKE¹.

dyke² n. slang a lesbian.

dynamic ● adj. **1** energetic; active. **2** (also **dynamical**) Physics **a** concerning motive force (opp. STATIC). **b** concerning force in actual operation. **3** (also **dynamical**) of or concerning dynamics. **4** Music relating to the volume of sound. **5** Philos. relating to dynamism. **6** Computing (of memory etc.) depending on an applied voltage to refresh it periodically. ● n. **1** an energizing or motive force. **2** Music = DYNAMICS 3. □ **dynamically** adv.

dynamics n.pl. **1** (usu. treated as sing.) **a** Mech. the branch of mechanics concerned with the motion of bodies under the action of forces (compare STATICS). **b** the branch of any science in which forces or changes are considered (aerodynamics; population dynamics). **2** the motive forces, physical or moral, affecting behaviour and change in any sphere. **3** the varying degree of volume of sound in musical performance. □ **dynamicist** /-SIST/ n. (in sense 1a).

dynamism /'daɪnə,mɪzəm/ n. **1** energizing or dynamic action or power. **2** Philos. the theory that phenomena of matter or mind are due to the action of forces (rather than to motion or matter). □ **dynamist** n.

dynamite ● n. **1** a high explosive consisting of nitroglycerine mixed with an absorbent. **2** a potentially dangerous person etc. **3** slang a narcotic, esp. heroin. **4** informal a powerful or impressive person or thing. ● v.tr. charge or shatter with dynamite. ● adj. informal excellent or powerful. □ **dynamiter** n.

dynamo /'daɪnə,moʊ/ n. (pl. **-os**) **1** a machine converting mechanical into electrical energy, esp. by rotating coils of copper wire in a magnetic field. **2** informal an energetic person.

dynasty /'daɪnəsti/ n. (pl. **-ies**) **1** a line of hereditary rulers. **2** a succession of leaders in any field. □ **dynastic** /-'næstɪk/ adj.

dysentery /'dɪsənteri, -tri/ n. a disease with inflammation of the intestines, causing severe diarrhea with blood and mucus.

dysfunction /dɪs'fʌŋkʃən/ n. an abnormality or impairment of function. □ **dysfunctional** adj.

dyslexia /dɪs'leksiə/ n. an abnormal difficulty in reading and spelling, caused by a condition of the brain. □ **dyslexic** adj. & n.

dyspepsia /dɪs'pepsiə/ n. indigestion.

dyspeptic ● adj. **1** of or relating to dyspepsia. **2** illtempered. ● n. a person suffering from dyspepsia.

dysplasia /dɪs'pleɪʒə, -ziə/ n. Med. abnormal growth of tissues etc. □ **dysplastic** /-'plæstɪk/ adj.

dysprosium /dɪs'proʊziəm/ n. a naturally occurring soft metallic element, used as a component in certain magnetic alloys.

dystopia /dɪs'toʊpiə/ n. a nightmare vision of society, often as one dominated by a totalitarian state (opp. UTOPIA). □ **dystopian** adj. & n.

dystrophy /'dɪstrəfi/ n. impaired nourishment of an organ or part of the body. See also MUSCULAR DYSTROPHY.

Ee

E¹ *n.* (also **e**) (*pl.* **Es** or **E's**) **1** the fifth letter of the alphabet. **2** the third note of the scale of C major.

E² *abbr.* (also **E.**) **1** East, Eastern. **2** (also **e**) *slang* **a** the drug ecstasy. **b** a tablet of this. **3** emissivity.

E³ *symbol Physics* energy ($E = mc^2$).

e *symbol Math.* the base of natural logarithms, equal to approx. 2.71828.

e- /i, e/ *comb. form* electronic (*e-file*).

ea. *abbr.* each.

each ● *adj.* every one of two or more persons or things, regarded separately. ● *pron.* each person or thing. □ **each and every** every single.

each other *pron.* one another.

eager *adj.* **1** full of keen desire, enthusiastic. **2** keen, impatient, strongly desirous (*eager to learn*). □ **eagerly** *adv.* **eagerness** *n.*

eager beaver *n. informal* a very diligent person.

eagle ● *n.* **1 a** any of various large birds of prey of the family Accipitridae, with keen vision and powerful flight. **b** a figure of an eagle, esp. as a symbol of the US, or formerly as a Roman or French ensign. **2** *Golf* a score of two strokes under par at any hole. ● *v.tr. Golf* play (a hole) in two strokes less than par.

eagle eye *n.* keen sight. □ **eagle-eyed** *adj.*

eaglet /'i:glət/ *n.* a young eagle.

ear¹ *n.* **1 a** the organ of hearing and balance in humans and vertebrates, esp. the external part of this. **b** an organ sensitive to sound in other animals. **2** the faculty for discriminating sounds (*an ear for music*; *plays by ear*). **3** an ear-shaped thing, esp. the handle of a jug. **4** listening, attention. □ **all ears** listening attentively. **bring about one's ears** bring down upon oneself. **give ear to** listen to. **have a person's ear** receive a favourable hearing. **have** (or **keep**) **an ear to the ground** be alert to rumours or the trend of opinion. **in one ear and out the other** heard but disregarded or quickly forgotten. **out on one's ear** dismissed ignominiously. **up to one's ears** (often foll. by *in*) *informal* deeply involved or occupied. □ **eared** *adj.* (also in *comb.*). **earless** *adj.*

ear² *n.* the seed-bearing head of a cereal plant.

earache *n.* a (usu. prolonged) pain in the ear.

eardrum *n.* the membrane separating the outer ear and middle ear and transmitting vibrations resulting from sound waves to the inner ear.

earflap *n.* a flap attached to the side of a hat or cap, used for covering the ear in cold weather.

earful *n.* (*pl.* **-fuls**) *informal* **1** a copious or prolonged amount of talking. **2** a strong reprimand.

earl *n.* a British nobleman ranking between a marquess and a viscount (*compare* COUNT²). □ **earldom** *n.*

Earl Grey *n.* a type of tea flavoured with bergamot.

earlobe *n.* the lower soft external part of the ear.

early ● *adj.* (**-ier**, **-iest**) **1** happening before the due, usual, or expected time. **2 a** not far on in the day or night, or in time (*early evening*; *at the earliest opportunity*). **b** prompt (*early payment appreciated*). **3 a** not far on in a period, development, or process of evolution; being the first stage (*early Canadian painting*; *in her early thirties*). **b** of the distant past (*early man*). **c** not far on in a sequence or serial order (*the early chapters*). **4 a** of childhood, esp. the preschool years. **b** (of a piece of writing, music, etc.) immature, youthful (*an early work*). **5** flowering, ripening, etc., before other varieties. ● *adv.* before the due, usual, or expected time. □ **at the earliest** not before (*Monday at the earliest*). **early days yet** (or **still early days**) early in time for something to happen (*should save for retirement, but it's early days yet*). **early** (or **earlier**) **on** at an early (or earlier) stage. □ **earliness** *n.*

early bird *n. informal* a person who arrives, gets up, etc. early or earlier than others. □ **the early bird gets the worm** *informal* the person who seizes the earliest opportunity will be successful.

early music *n.* medieval, Renaissance, and baroque music, esp. as played on period instruments.

early retirement *n.* retirement from one's occupation before the statutory retirement age, esp. on advantageous financial terms.

early warning *n.* advance warning of an imminent (esp. nuclear) attack.

earmark ● *n.* an identifying mark or distinguishing characteristic. ● *v.tr.* set aside for a special purpose.

earmuff *n.* (usu. in *pl.*) either of a pair of ear coverings connected by a band across the top of the head, and worn to protect the ears from the cold.

earn *v.* **1** *tr. & intr.* **a** obtain (income) in the form of money in return for labour or services. **b** (of capital invested) bring in as interest or profit. **2** *tr.* **a** deserve; be entitled to; obtain as the reward for hard work or merit. **b** incur (a reproach, reputation, etc.). **3** *tr. Baseball* score (a run) without any error on the fielding side. □ **earned** *adj.* **earner** *n.*

earned income *n.* income derived from wages etc.

earned run *n. Baseball* a run that is not the result of an error or passed ball.

earned run average *n.* the average number of earned runs scored against a pitcher in every nine innings pitched.

earnest ● *adj.* **1** serious in intention; not trifling. **2** zealous or intense. **3** resulting from or displaying sincere conviction. ● *n.* **1** seriousness. **2** money paid as an instalment, esp. to confirm a contract etc. **3** a token or foretaste. □ **in earnest** serious(ly), not joking(ly); with determination. □ **earnestly** *adv.* **earnestness** *n.*

earnings *n.pl.* money earned.

EARP *abbr.* (in Canada) Environmental Assessment and Review Process.

earphone *n.* **1** each of a pair of receivers attached to each other so that they fit over the ears, used for listening to a radio, stereo, etc. **2** a similar device with a receiver that fits inside one ear.

earpiece *n.* **1** the part of a telephone etc. held to the ear during use. **2** the part of a pair of glasses, a helmet, etc., that fits over the wearer's ear.

ear-piercing ● *adj.* loud and shrill. ● *n.* the piercing of the ears to allow the wearing of earrings.

earplug *n.* either of two pieces of soft material placed in the ears to keep out cold air, water, or noise.

earring *n.* a piece of jewellery worn in or on (esp. the lobe of) the ear.

earshot *n.* the distance over which something can be heard (*within earshot; out of earshot*).

ear-splitting *adj.* excessively loud.

earth *n.* **1** (also **Earth**) the planet on which we live. **2** the inhabitants of this planet. **3 a** dry land; the ground (*fell to earth*). **b** the material that makes up the earth's surface; dirt, soil. **4** the present abode of mankind, as distinct from heaven or hell; the world. **5** the hole of a badger, fox, etc. **6** (prec. by *the*) *informal* a huge amount (*cost the earth*). **7** any of several metallic oxides that are stable, dry, and lacking in taste and odour, e.g. alumina, zirconia, etc. □ **come back** (or **down**) **to earth** return to realities. **gone to earth** in hiding. **on earth** *informal* **1** existing anywhere (*the happiest person on earth*). **2** as an intensifier (*what on earth?*).

earthbound *adj.* **1** attached to the earth or earthly things. **2** moving toward the earth.

earthen *adj.* **1** made of earth. **2** made of baked clay.

earthenware *n.* pottery, vessels, etc., made of clay fired to a porous state which can be made impervious to liquids by the use of a glaze.

earthling *n.* an inhabitant of the earth, esp. as regarded in fiction by outsiders.

earthly *adj.* **1** of the earth or human life on earth; terrestrial. **2** (usu. with *neg.*) *informal* remotely possible or conceivable (*is no earthly use*). □ **earthliness** *n.*

earth mother *n.* **1** *Myth* a spirit or deity symbolizing the earth. **2** a sensual and maternal woman.

earthmover *n.* a vehicle or machine for moving earth. □ **earthmoving** *n.*

earthquake *n.* **1** a convulsion of the superficial parts of the earth due to the release of accumulated stress as a result of faults in strata or volcanic action. **2** a severe disturbance, disruption, or upheaval.

earth science *n.* any of various sciences concerned with the earth or part of it, or its atmosphere (e.g. geology, meteorology). □ **earth scientist** *n.*

earth-shattering *adj.* (also **earth-shaking**) having a traumatic effect. □ **earth-shatteringly** *adv.*

earth tone *n.* any of several rich brown colours.

earth tremor *n.* = TREMOR *n.* 3.

earthward ● *adv.* (also **earthwards**) toward the earth. ● *adj.* moving or directed toward the earth.

earthwork *n.* **1** an artificial bank of earth in fortification or road-building etc. **2** the process of excavating soil in civil engineering work.

earthworm *n.* any of various annelid worms, esp. of the genus *Lumbricus* or *Allolobophora*, living and burrowing in the ground.

earthy *adj.* (**-ier, -iest**) **1** of or like earth or soil. **2** somewhat coarse or crude; unrefined (*earthy humour*). □ **earthily** *adv.* **earthiness** *n.*

earwax *n.* a waxy secretion produced by the ear.

earwig *n.* any small elongate insect of the order Dermaptera, with a pair of terminal appendages in the shape of forceps.

ease ● *n.* **1** absence of difficulty; effortlessness. **2** freedom or relief from pain, anxiety, trouble, embarrassment, constraint, etc. **3** freedom from toil; leisure (*a life of ease*). ● *v.* **1** *tr.* relieve from pain or anxiety etc. (*eased my mind*). **2** *intr.* (often foll. by *off, up*) **a** become less painful or burdensome. **b** relax; begin to take it easy. **c** slow down; moderate one's behaviour, habits, etc. **3** *intr. Meteorol.* become less severe (*the wind will ease tonight*). **4 a** *tr.* relax; slacken; make a less tight fit. **b** *tr. & intr.* move or be moved carefully into place (*eased it into the hole*). **5** *intr.* (often foll. by *off*) *Stock Exch.* (of shares etc.) descend in price or value. □ **at ease 1** free from anxiety or constraint. **2** *Military* **a** in a relaxed attitude, with the feet apart. **b** the order to stand in this way. **at one's ease** free from embarrassment, awkwardness, or undue formality.

easel *n.* a standing frame, usu. of wood, for supporting an artist's work, a blackboard, etc.

easement *n. Law* a right-of-way or a similar right over another's land.

easily *adv.* **1** without difficulty. **2** by far (*easily the best*). **3** very probably (*it could easily snow*).

east ● *n.* **1 a** the point of the horizon where the sun rises at the equinoxes (cardinal point 90° to the right of north). **b** the compass point corresponding to this. **c** the direction in which this lies. **2** (usu. **the East**) **a** the regions or countries lying to the east of Europe. **b** *hist.* the former Communist States of E Europe. **3** the eastern part of a country, town, etc. ● *adj.* **1** toward, at, near, or facing east. **2** coming from the east (*east wind*). ● *adv.* **1** toward, at, or near the east. **2** (foll. by *of*) further east than.

eastbound *adj. & adv.* travelling or leading eastwards.

East End *n.* **1** the eastern part of London, England, to the north of the Thames. **2** (also **east end**) the eastern part of any city or town.

Easter *n.* **1** (also **Easter Day** or **Easter Sunday**) a Christian festival (held on a variable Sunday in March or April) commemorating Christ's resurrection. **2** the season in which this occurs, esp. the weekend from Good Friday to Easter Monday.

Easter Bunny *n.* a rabbit popularly said to bring candy to children at Easter.

Easter egg *n.* an artificial (usu. chocolate) or decorated egg given at Easter, esp. to children.

Easter lily *n.* esp. *N Amer.* **1** a cultivated variety of *Lilium longiflorum*, a white-flowered lily native to Japan, sold as a houseplant at Easter. **2** any of various spring-flowering lilies or similar plants, esp. species of the dog's tooth violet *Erythronium*.

easterly ● *adj. & adv.* **1** in an eastern position or direction. **2** (of a wind) blowing from the east. ● *n.* (pl. **-ies**) a wind blowing from the east.

Easter Monday *n.* the Monday after Easter.

eastern *adj.* **1** of or in the east; inhabiting the east. **2** lying or directed toward the east. **3** (**Eastern**) of or in the Far East or Middle East. **4** (**Eastern**) of or pertaining to that branch of the Christian Church which developed in the territories formerly part of the Eastern Roman Empire. □ **easternmost** *adj.*

Eastern Church *n.* **1** the Orthodox Church. **2** any other Christian Church observing a liturgical rite based on that of the Orthodox Church, but in communion with the Catholic Church.

easterner *n.* a native or inhabitant of the east.

eastern hemisphere *n.* the half of the earth containing Europe, Asia, Africa, and Australia.

Eastern rite *n.* a Christian Church observing a liturgical rite based on the Eastern tradition, esp. one in communion with the Catholic Church.

Eastern Time *n.* the time in a zone including most of Ontario and Quebec as well as the eastern US. **Eastern Standard Time** is five hours behind GMT; **Eastern Daylight Time** is four hours behind GMT.

East Indian ● *adj. N Amer.* of or pertaining to the Indian subcontinent or its indigenous peoples or their descendants. ● *n.* a person descended from the indigenous peoples of the Indian subcontinent. ¶The term *South Asian* is now often preferred.

Eastmain Cree /ˈiːstˌmeɪn/ *n.* a member of a Cree

people living at the mouth of the Eastmain River on the shore of James Bay.

east-northeast *n.* the direction or compass point midway between east and northeast.

east-southeast *n.* the direction or compass point midway between east and southeast.

eastward ● *adj. & adv.* (also **eastwards**) toward the east. ● *n.* an eastward direction or region. □ **eastwardly** *adj. & adv.*

easy ● *adj.* (**-ier, -iest**) **1** not difficult; achieved without great effort. **2 a** free from discomfort, anxiety, pain, etc. **b** comfortably off, affluent (*easy circumstances*). **3** free from embarrassment, awkwardness, constraint, etc.; relaxed and pleasant (*an easy manner*). **4** compliant, obliging; easily persuaded (*easy prey*). **5** (of a person) promiscuous; sexually available. **6** moderate (*an easy pace*). **7** (of a slope) gentle, gradual; not steep. **8** loosely fitting. **9** *Stock Exch.* (of goods, money on loan, etc.) not much in demand. **10** (of credit) obtainable without stringent requirements of the borrower. ● *adv.* with ease; in an effortless or relaxed manner. ¶The use of *easy* as an adverb is usually restricted to set phrases such as *easy does it* and *take it easy*. Outside of such expressions, the adverb *easily* is more standard. ● *interj.* go carefully; move gently. □ **easy come easy go** *informal* what is easily got is soon lost or spent. **easy does it** *informal* go carefully. **easy on the eye** (or **ear** etc.) *informal* pleasant to look at (or listen to etc.). **go easy** (foll. by *with*, *on*) be sparing or cautious. **I'm easy** *informal* I have no preference. **stand easy!** *Cdn & Brit. Military* permission to a squad standing at ease to relax their attitude further. **take it easy 1** proceed gently or carefully. **2** relax; avoid overwork. **3** (often as *interj.*) calm down. □ **easiness** *n.*

easy-care *adj.* (esp. of synthetic fabrics) simple to wash, dry, etc.; serviceable.

easy chair *n.* a large comfortable chair, usu. an armchair.

easygoing *adj.* relaxed in manner.

easy listening *n.* (often *attrib.*) music that appeals to conventional tastes and is not loud, raucous, etc.

easy money *n.* money got without effort.

eat *v.* (*past* **ate**; *past part.* **eaten**) **1 a** *tr.* take into the mouth, chew, and swallow (food). **b** *intr.* consume food; take a meal. **c** *tr.* devour; feed destructively on (*the mosquitoes will eat you alive*). **2** *intr.* (foll. by (*away*) *at*, *into*) **a** destroy gradually, esp. by corrosion, erosion, disease, etc. **b** begin to consume or diminish (resources etc.). **3** *tr.* *informal* trouble, vex (*what's eating you?*). **4** *tr.* *informal* (of a machine etc.) cause (something) to disappear or be destroyed by absorbing it into its workings (*the bank machine ate my card*). □ **eat one's hat** *informal* admit one's surprise in being wrong (only as a proposition unlikely to be fulfilled: *I'll eat my hat if that's true*). **eat one's heart out** suffer from excessive longing or envy. **eat out** have a meal away from home, esp. in a restaurant. **eat out of a person's hand** be entirely submissive to a person. **eat up 1** eat or consume completely. **2** use or deal with rapidly or wastefully (*eats up gasoline*; *eats up the miles*). **3** encroach upon or annex (*eating up the neighbouring municipalities*). **4** absorb, preoccupy (*eaten up with pride*). **5** *informal* receive (something presented) with vigorous enjoyment. **6** consume; use up (*this project is eating up a lot of my time*). **eat one's words** admit that one was wrong. □ **eater** *n.*

eatable ● *adj.* that is in a condition to be eaten (*compare* EDIBLE). ● *n.* (usu. in *pl.*) food.

eatery *n.* esp. *N Amer.* (*pl.* **-ies**) *informal* a restaurant.

eating *adj.* **1** suitable for eating (*eating apple*). **2** used for eating (*eating place*). **3** of or relating to the process of eating (*eating disorders*).

eat-in kitchen *n.* esp. *N Amer.* a kitchen large enough that meals may be eaten in it.

eats *n.pl.* *informal* food.

eau de cologne /ˌoː də kəˈloːn/ *n.* = COLOGNE.

eau de toilette /ˌoː də twʌˈlet/ *n.* (*pl.* **eaux de toilette**) a dilute form of perfume that is somewhat stronger than eau de cologne.

eaves *n.pl.* the underside of a projecting roof.

eavesdrop *v.intr.* (**-dropped, -dropping**) listen secretly to a conversation. □ **eavesdropper** *n.*

eavestrough *n.* (also **eavestroughing**) *N Amer.* (esp. *Cdn*) a shallow trough attached to the eaves of a building to collect runoff from the roof.

ebb ● *n.* **1** the movement of the tide out to sea (also *attrib.*: *ebb tide*) (opp. FLOOD *n.* 3). **2** a flowing away; decline or decay. ● *v.intr.* (often foll. by *away*) **1** (of tidewater) flow out to sea. **2** decline; run low (*his life was ebbing away*). □ **at a low ebb** in a poor condition or state of decline. **ebb and flow** a continuing process of decline and upturn in circumstances. **on the ebb** in decline.

Ebola /ɪˈboːlə/ *n.* a tropical African virus that causes a severe, infectious, generally fatal hemorrhagic disease in humans (also *attrib.*: *Ebola virus*; *Ebola fever*).

ebony /ˈebəni/ ● *n.* (*pl.* **-ies**) **1** a heavy hard dark wood used for furniture. **2** any of various trees of the genus *Diospyros* producing this. ● *adj.* **1** made of ebony. **2** black like ebony.

ebullient /ɪˈbʌliənt, ɪˈbɒliənt/ *adj.* exuberant, high-spirited. □ **ebullience** *n.* **ebulliently** *adv.*

EC *abbr.* **1 a** European Community. **b** European Commission. **2** executive committee.

eccentric /ɪkˈsentrɪk, ek-/ ● *adj.* **1** odd or capricious in behaviour or appearance; whimsical. **2 a** not placed or not having its axis etc. placed centrally (*compare* CONCENTRIC). **b** (often foll. by *to*) (of a circle) not concentric (to another). **c** (of an orbit) not circular. ● *n.* an eccentric person. □ **eccentrically** *adv.* **eccentricity** /-ˈtrɪsɪti/ *n.* (*pl.* **-ies**).

ecclesiastic /ɪˌkliːziˈæstɪk/ ● *n.* a member of the Christian clergy. ● *adj.* = ECCLESIASTICAL.

ecclesiastical *adj.* of or relating to the Christian Church or the clergy. □ **ecclesiastically** *adv.*

ECE *abbr.* **1** early childhood education. **2** early childhood educator.

ECG *abbr.* **1** electrocardiogram. **2** electrocardiograph.

echelon /ˈeʃəˌlɒn, ˈeɪʃəˌlɔ̃/ *n.* **1** (often in *pl.*) a level or rank in an organization, in society, etc.; those occupying it. **2** *Military* a formation of troops, ships, aircraft, etc., in parallel rows with the end of each row projecting further than the one in front.

echidna /ɪˈkɪdnə/ *n.* any of several egg-laying pouch-bearing mammals native to Australia and New Guinea, with a covering of spines.

echinacea /ˌekɪˈneɪʃə/ *n.* **1** a plant of the genus *Echinacea*, of eastern N America, esp. the purple coneflower, *E. purpurea*. **2** a preparation made from the roots of an echinacea plant, used as a herbal remedy.

echinoderm /ɪˈkaɪnəˌdɜrm, ˈekɪn-/ *n.* any marine invertebrate of the phylum Echinodermata, usu. having a spiny skin, e.g. starfish and sea urchins.

echo ● *n.* (*pl.* **-oes**) **1 a** the repetition of a sound by the reflection of sound waves. **b** the secondary sound produced. **2** a reflected radio or radar beam. **3** a close imitation or repetition of something already done. **4** a person who slavishly repeats the words or opinions of another. **5** (often in *pl.*) circumstances or events reminiscent of or remotely connected with earlier ones. ● *v.* (**-oes, -oed**) **1** *intr.* **a** (of a place) resound with an echo. **b** (of a sound) be repeated; resound. **2** *tr.* repeat (a sound) by an echo. **3** *tr.* repeat or imitate the words, opinions, or actions of (a person). **4** *tr. & intr.* (of a computer system) send a copy of (an input signal) back to its source for display; cause (a keyed character) to appear on a screen as it is keyed.

echocardiogram /ˌekoˈkɑrdɪəˌgræm/ *n.* a tracing or image obtained by echocardiography. Abbr.: **ECG**.

echocardiography /ˌekoˌkɑrdɪˈɒgrəfi/ *n.* the use of ultrasound to investigate cardiac action. □ **echocardiograph** *n.* **echocardiographer** *n.* **echocardiographic** *adj.*

echolocation *n.* the location of objects by reflected sound. □ **echolocate** *v.tr.*

echo sounder *n.* a sounding apparatus for determining the depth of water beneath a ship by measuring the time taken for an echo to be received.

eclair /eɪˈkleər, ɪˈkleər/ *n.* an elongated cream puff filled with cream or custard esp. with chocolate icing.

eclampsia /ɪˈklæmpsɪə/ *n.* a condition involving convulsions leading to coma, occurring esp. in pregnancy.

éclat /eɪˈklɑ/ *n.* **1** brilliant display; dazzling effect. **2** social distinction; universal approbation.

eclectic /ɪˈklektɪk/ ● *adj.* **1** deriving ideas, tastes, style, etc., from various sources. **2** *Philos. & Art* selecting one's beliefs etc. from various sources; attached to no particular school of philosophy. ● *n.* an eclectic person. □ **eclectically** *adv.* **eclecticism** /-ˌsɪzəm/ *n.*

eclipse /ɪˈklɪps/ ● *n.* **1** the obscuring of the reflected light from one celestial body by the passage of another between it and the eye or between it and its source of illumination. **2** a deprivation of light or the period of this. **3** a rapid or sudden loss of importance or prominence, esp. in relation to another or a newly-arrived person or thing. ● *v.tr.* **1** (of a celestial body) obscure the light from or to (another). **2** deprive of prominence or importance; outshine, surpass. □ **in eclipse** surpassed; in decline.

ecliptic /ɪˈklɪptɪk/ *n.* the sun's apparent path among the stars during the year.

eco /ˈeko/ *n. informal* ecology (also *attrib.*: *eco freak*).

eco- /ˈiːko/ *comb. form* ecology, ecological.

ecocide *n.* destruction of the environment.

ecol. *abbr.* **1** ecology. **2** ecological.

eco-label *n.* a label identifying manufactured products that satisfy certain environmental conditions. □ **eco-labelling** *n.*

E. coli *var. of* ESCHERICHIA COLI.

ecology *n.* **1** the branch of biology dealing with the relations of organisms to one another and to their physical surroundings. **2** (in full **human ecology**) the study of the interaction of people with their environment. □ **ecological** *adj.* **ecologically** *adv.* **ecologist** *n.*

e-commerce *n.* business transactions conducted over the Internet.

econ. *abbr.* **1** economics. **2** economic.

econometrics /ɪˌkɒnəˈmetrɪks/ *n.pl.* (usu. treated as *sing.*) the branch of economics dealing with the application of mathematics, esp. statistics, to economic data. □ **econometric** *adj.* **econometrician** /-məˈtrɪʃən/ *n.*

economic /ˌekəˈnɒmɪk, ˌiːk-/ *adj.* **1 a** of, pertaining to, or concerned with economics. **b** relating to the wealth of a community or nation. **c** relating to the

management of finances. **2 a** maintained for profit or on a business footing (*an economic rent*). **b** paying at least the expenses of its operation or use (*not economic to run buses on Sunday*). **3** (of a subject etc.) practical or studied from an utilitarian or material standpoint (*economic geography*). **4** = ECONOMICAL.

economical *adj.* **1** thrifty, careful in the use of resources. **2** cheap. **3** = ECONOMIC. □ **economical with the truth** discreditably reticent. □ **economically** *adv.*

economic growth *n.* the rate of expansion of the national income, esp. the growth of output of goods and services per capita over a stated time.

economic indicator *n.* a statistical measure indicating the relative strength or weakness of selected variables such as output, inflation, debt burden, foreign investment, etc. in a given nation or region.

economics *n.pl.* (treated as *sing.*) **1 a** the social science of the production and distribution of wealth in theory and practice. **b** the application of this discipline to a particular subject or sphere. **2 a** the condition of a country etc. as regards material prosperity. **b** the financial considerations attaching to a particular activity, commodity, etc.

economist *n.* **1** an expert in or student of economics. **2** a person who manages financial or economic matters.

economize *v.* **1** *intr.* reduce expenses, or make savings in or on a commodity etc. **2** *tr.* (foll. by *on*) use sparingly, make a saving in, or spend less on (a thing). □ **economizer** *n.* **economizing** *n.*

economy /ɪˈkɒnəmi/ *n.* (pl. **-ies**) **1 a** the wealth and resources of a community, esp. in terms of the production and consumption of goods and services. **b** a particular kind of this (*a capitalist economy*). **c** the administration or condition of an economy. **2 a** frugality or the careful management of resources. **b** (often in *pl.*) an act, instance, or means of saving or reducing expenditure. **3** sparing or careful use of resources etc. (*economy of language*). **4** the cheapest class of some service or product, esp. of air travel. **5** (*attrib.*) (of a product) offering the customer the best value for money spent, esp. a large quantity for a proportionally lower cost.

economy class *n.* (also *attrib.*) the cheapest class of air travel, hotel accommodation, etc.

economy of scale *n.* (pl. **-ies**) (usu. in *pl.*) proportionate savings gained by using larger quantities.

ecosystem *n.* a biological community of interacting organisms and their environment.

eco-terrorism /ˈiːkoˌterərɪzəm/ *n.* **1** violence carried out to further environmentalist ends. **2** politically motivated damage to the natural environment. □ **eco-terrorist** *n.*

ecotourism *n.* tourism to areas of ecological interest, esp. having minimum adverse impact. □ **ecotour** *n.* **ecotourist** *n.*

ecstasy /ˈekstəsi/ *n.* (pl. **-ies**) **1** an overwhelming feeling of joy or rapture. **2 a** *Psych.* a pathological state of absorption and unresponsiveness. **b** a sort of trance or rapture such as is supposed to accompany religious, prophetic, or mystical inspiration. **c** a frenzy of poetic inspiration. **3** *slang* a powerful stimulant and hallucinatory drug (see MDMA). □ **in ecstasies** filled with pleasure.

ecstatic /ɪkˈstætɪk/ ● *adj.* **1** in a state of ecstasy. **2** very enthusiastic or excited. **3** of the nature of, characterized by, or producing ecstasy; sublime. ● *n.* a person subject to spells of usu. mystical ecstasy. □ **ecstatically** *adv.*

ECT *abbr.* ELECTROCONVULSIVE THERAPY.

ectoderm /ˈektoˌdɜːm/ *n.* the outermost layer of an embryo in early development, giving rise to epidermis and neural tissue. □ **ectodermal** *adj.*

ectopic /ˈektɒpɪk/ *adj. Med.* occurring in an abnormal place or position.

ectopic pregnancy *n.* a pregnancy in which the fertilized ovum is implanted somewhere other than in the uterus, e.g. in a Fallopian tube.

ectoplasm /ˈektoˌplæzəm/ *n.* the dense, clear, outer layer of the cytoplasm in some cells (*compare* ENDOPLASM). □ **ectoplasmic** *adj.*

ECU /ˈekjuː, ˈiː-, ˈeɪ-, -kuː/ *n.* (also **ecu, Ecu**) (*pl.* same or **-s**) = EUROPEAN CURRENCY UNIT.

ecumenical /ˌekjuːˈmenɪkəl, ˌiːk-/ *adj.* **1 a** of or representing the whole Christian world. **b** of or representing Christians of several denominations. **2** seeking or promoting worldwide Christian unity that transcends doctrinal differences. □ **ecumenically** *adv.* **ecumenism** /eˈkjuːməˌnɪzəm, ˈekjuː-/ *n.*

ecumenical council *n.* any of the various general councils of the early church or of the modern Catholic Church, whose decisions are considered authoritative.

eczema /ˈeksɪmə, ekˈziːmə/ *n.* non-infectious, superficial inflammation of the skin, usu. with itching and discharge from blisters.

ed *n. informal* education (*driver ed*).

ed. *abbr.* **1** edited by. **2** (*pl.* **eds.**) edition. **3** (*pl.* **eds.**) editor. **4** education (*B.Ed.*). **5** educated.

Edam /ˈiːdəm, -dæm/ *n.* a mild, round, pressed Dutch cheese, usu. pale yellow with a red rind.

Ed.D. *abbr. N Amer.* Doctor of Education.

eddy ● *n.* (*pl.* **-ies**) **1** a circular or contrary movement of water causing a small whirlpool. **2** a movement of wind, fog, or smoke resembling this. **3** a usu. relatively insignificant trend, mood, etc. going contrary to prevailing currents of thought, attitudes, etc. ● *v.tr. & intr.* (**-ies, -ied**) whirl around in an eddy or eddies.

edelweiss /ˈeɪdəlˌvaɪs/ *n.* an alpine plant, *Leontopodium alpinum*, with woolly white bracts around the flower heads, growing in rocky places.

edema /ɪˈdiːmə/ *n.* a condition in which an excess of watery fluid collects in the cavities or tissues of the body.

Eden /ˈiːdən/ *n.* (also **Garden of Eden**) **1** a paradise or a delightful abode. **2** a state of supreme happiness. **3** the abode of Adam and Eve in the Biblical account of the Creation. □ **Edenic** /ɪˈdenɪk/ *adj.*

edge ● *n.* **1** a boundary line or margin of an area or surface. **2 a** the edging of a garment, curtain, etc. **b** a narrow surface or side of a thin object, esp. each of the three surfaces of a book not protected by the binding. **3** a line along which two surfaces of a solid intersect. **4 a** the sharpened side of the blade of a cutting instrument etc. **b** the sharpness given a blade by whetting. **5 a** the area close to a steep drop. **b** the brink, verge, or crest of a bank, precipice, or sharply pointed ridge. **6** the inner or outer side of the blade of a skate. **7 a** (as a personal attribute) incisiveness, excitement. **b** an advantage, superiority. ● *v.* **1** *tr. & intr.* move gradually or furtively towards an objective. **2** *tr.* **a** provide with an edge or border. **b** form a border to. **c** trim the edge of. **3** *tr.* sharpen or give an edge to (a knife, tool, etc.). **4** *tr. N Amer.* defeat by a small margin. **5** *tr. Sport* tilt or incline (a ski or skate) sideways to make one edge dig into the snow or ice. □ **have the** (or **an**) **edge on** (or **over**) have a slight advantage over. **on edge 1** tense and restless or irritable. **2** eager, excited. **on the edge of** almost involved in or

affected by. **set a person's teeth on edge** (esp. of a taste or sound) cause a person acute irritation or discomfort, as if eating sour fruit. **take the edge off** dull, weaken; make less effective or intense. □ **edgeless** *adj.*

edged *adj.* **1** (usu. in *comb.*) **a** having an edge or border, esp. of a specified kind. **b** having a cutting edge. **2** (of a tone, comment, etc.) sarcastic, acerbic.

edger *n.* a tool for making, trimming, or finishing an edge, e.g. of a flower bed.

edgewise *adv.* (also esp. *Brit.* **edgeways**) **1** with the edge forward, uppermost, or towards the viewer. **2 a** sideways. **b** edge to edge. □ **get a word in edgewise** contribute to a conversation when the dominant speaker pauses briefly.

edging *n.* **1** something forming an edge, border, or fringe on a garment, curtain, flower bed, etc. **2** the process of making an edge. **3** *Skiing* the tilting or angling of a ski so that it cuts into the snow.

edgy *adj.* (**-ier, -iest**) **1** irritable, nervously anxious. **2 a** sharp-edged, not smooth. **b** (of humour, writing, etc.) characterized by sharp observation or wit. **3** *slang* unconventional, on the cutting edge. □ **edgily** *adv.* **edginess** *n.*

EDI *abbr.* ELECTRONIC DATA INTERCHANGE.

edible /ˈedɪbəl/ ● *adj.* fit or suitable to be eaten. ● *n.* (in *pl.*) things that may be eaten, food. □ **edibility** *n.*

edict /ˈiːdɪkt/ *n.* an order proclaimed by authority, esp. a proclamation having the force of law.

edification *n.* mental or moral enlightenment.

edifice /ˈedɪfɪs/ *n.* **1** a building, esp. a large, imposing, or stately one. **2** a complex organizational or conceptual structure.

edify /ˈedɪˌfaɪ/ *v.tr.* (**-ies, -ied**) (of a circumstance, experience, etc.) instruct and improve morally or intellectually. □ **edifying** *adj.* **edifyingly** *adv.*

edit ● *v.tr.* (**edited, editing**) **1 a** assemble, prepare, or modify (written material, esp. the work of another or others) for publication. **b** prepare an edition of (an author's work, a musical score, etc.), esp. by researching manuscripts. **2** be in overall charge of the content and arrangement of (a newspaper etc.). **3** prepare (a film, tape, etc.) by rearrangement, cutting, or collation of recorded material to form a unified sequence. **4 a** prepare (data) for processing by a computer. **b** alter (text entered in a word processor etc.). **5 a** reword, revise, or alter (a text etc.) to correct, alter the emphasis, etc. **b** (foll. by *out*) remove (part) from a text etc. ● *n.* **1 a** the action or process of editing. **b** an act, instance, or piece of editing. **2** an edited item. □ **editable** *adj.*

edition *n.* **1 a** a form or version of a book etc. at its first publication and after each revision or change of format (*paperback edition*). **b** one copy of a book in a particular form (*a first edition*). **2** a whole number of similar copies of a book, newspaper, etc. issued at one time. **3** a particular version or instance of a broadcast, esp. of a regular program or feature. **4** a person or thing similar to or resembling another.

editor *n.* **1 a** a person who edits material for publication or broadcasting. **b** the head of a department at a publishing house. **2** a person who selects or commissions material for publication. **3 a** a person in charge of the running and contents of a newspaper etc. **b** a person who oversees one particular section of a newspaper etc. (*sports editor*). **4** a person who cuts and edits film, videotape, sound tracks, etc. **5** a computer program enabling the user to write or alter programs, text, or other information. **6** a machine used to edit film, videotape, etc. □ **editorship** *n.*

editorial ● *adj.* **1 a** of or concerned with editing or editors. **b** of or pertaining to an editorial. **2** written or approved by an editor. **3** distinguished from news and advertising matter (*editorial content*). ● *n.* **1** a newspaper article written by, on behalf of, or under the direct responsibility of an editor, esp. one giving an opinion on a topical issue. **2** a broadcast statement expressing the opinions of a station owner, manager, etc. □ **editorialist** *n.* **editorially** *adv.*

editorialize *v.* **1** *intr.* write editorials or comment editorially. **2** *tr.* add editorial comment to.

editor-in-chief *n.* (*pl.* **editors-in-chief**) the chief editor of a publication, magazine, etc.

Edmontonian ● *n.* a native or inhabitant of Edmonton. ● *adj.* of or relating to Edmonton.

EDP *abbr.* electronic data processing.

EDT *abbr.* Eastern Daylight Time.

educate /ˈedʒʊˌkeɪt, -djʊ-/ *v.tr. & intr.* **1** give intellectual, moral, and social instruction to, esp. as a formal and prolonged process. **2** provide education for. **3** (often foll. by *in*, or *to* + infin.) train or instruct for a particular purpose. **4** instruct, advise, or give information to. □ **educable** /-kəbəl/ *adj.* **educative** /-kətɪv/ *adj.*

educated *adj.* **1** having had an education, esp. to a higher level than average. **2** characterized by or displaying cultivated taste, learning, culture, etc. **3** based on experience or study (*an educated guess*).

education *n.* **1 a** the act or process of educating or being educated. **b** systematic instruction, schooling, or training, including the whole course of such instruction received by a person. **2** a particular kind of or stage in education (*a classical education*). **3** pedagogical theory or the art and science of teaching.

educational *adj.* **1** of, pertaining to, or concerned with education. **2** conducive to education or having the power to educate. □ **educationally** *adv.*

educator *n.* **1** a person who teaches, educates, or is in the business of education, e.g. a principal etc. **2** an educational specialist.

edutainment *n.* entertainment with an educational aspect.

Edwardian ● *adj.* of, characteristic of, or associated with the reign of Edward VII of England (1901–10). ● *n.* a person belonging to this period.

-ee *suffix* forming nouns denoting: **1** the person affected directly or indirectly by the verbal action (*addressee*; *employee*). **2** a person concerned with or described as (*absentee*).

EEC *abbr.* European Economic Community.

EEG *abbr.* **1** ELECTROENCEPHALOGRAM. **2** ELECTROENCEPHALOGRAPH(Y).

eel *n.* any of various snakelike fishes of the genus *Anguilla*, members of which spend most of their lives in fresh water but breed in warm deep oceans. □ **eel-like** *adj.* **eely** *adj.*

eelgrass *n.* **1** any marine plant of the genus *Zostera*, esp. *Z. marina*, with long ribbon-like leaves. **2** any submerged freshwater plant of the genus *Vallisneria*.

eensy *adj.* (also **eensy-weensy**) esp. *N Amer. informal* tiny.

eerie *adj.* (**eerier**, **eeriest**) inspiring unease or fear. □ **eerily** *adv.* **eeriness** *n.*

eff *slang euphemism* (often foll. by *off*) = FUCK (in expletive use). □ **effing** *adj.*

efface /ɪˈfeɪs/ *v.* **1** *tr.* **a** rub or wipe out. **2** *tr.* **a** cause to disappear entirely or remove all traces of. **b** obliterate or wipe out (a memory, mental impression, etc.). **3** *tr.* utterly surpass, outshine, or eclipse.

effect ● *n.* **1** the result or consequence of an action

etc. **2** efficacy (*the drug had little effect*). **3** an impression produced on a spectator, hearer, etc. (*my words had no effect*). **4** (in *pl.*) (in full **personal effects**) property, luggage, etc. **5** (in *pl.*) = SPECIAL EFFECTS. **6** a scientific phenomenon, often named after its discoverer (*greenhouse effect*). **7** the state of being operative (*came into effect last year*). ● *v.tr.* **1** bring about (an event or result) or accomplish (an intention or desire). **2** cause to exist or occur. □ **bring into effect** accomplish, realize. **for effect** for the sake of making an impression. **give effect to** make operative or put into force. **in effect 1** virtually, for practical purposes. **2** in fact, in reality. **take effect** prove successful, come into force, or become operative. **to the effect that** to that end, with that significance, or the general substance or gist being. **to that effect** having that result or implication. ¶See Usage Note at AFFECT[1].

effective *adj.* **1 a** having a definite or desired effect. **b** efficient. **2** impressively powerful in effect. **3 a** actual, existing in fact rather than officially or theoretically (*took effective control in their absence*). **b** actually usable, realizable, or equivalent in its effect (*effective money*). **4** coming into operation. □ **effectively** *adv.* **effectiveness** *n.* **effectivity** *n.*

effectual *adj.* **1** effective, efficacious, or capable of producing the intended result or effect. **2** (of a legal document) valid, binding. □ **effectually** *adv.*

effeminate /ɪˈfemɪnət/ *adj.* **1** (of a man) feminine in appearance or manner; unmasculine. **2** characterized by or proceeding from weakness, delicacy, etc. □ **effeminacy** *n.* **effeminately** *adv.*

effervesce /ˌefərˈves/ *v.intr.* bubble or give off bubbles of gas, e.g. as a result of chemical reaction.

effervescent *adj.* **1** bubbly, fizzy. **2** (of a person) showing great enthusiasm, excitement, etc.; lively, energetic, and vivacious. □ **effervescence** *n.*

effete /ɪˈfiːt/ *adj.* decadent, degenerate, ineffectual, esp. as a result of overrefinement.

efficacious /ˌefɪˈkeɪʃəs/ *adj.* (of a thing) producing or sure to produce the desired effect; effective. □ **efficaciously** *adv.* **efficacy** /ˈefɪkəsɪ/ *n.*

efficiency *n.* (*pl.* **-ies**) **1 a** the state or quality of being efficient. **b** effectiveness, competence, or the ability to accomplish or fulfill what is intended. **c** an action aimed at achieving greater efficiency (*administrative efficiencies*). **2** *Mech. & Physics* the ratio of useful work performed to the total energy expended or heat taken in. **3** (in full **efficiency unit**) *Cdn* a hotel room etc. with limited washing and cooking facilities.

efficient /ɪˈfɪʃənt/ *adj.* **1** productive with minimum waste or effort. **2** (of a person) capable, acting effectively. **3** characterized by high or specified efficiency (*energy-efficient*). □ **efficiently** *adv.*

effigy /ˈefɪdʒɪ/ *n.* (*pl.* **-ies**) **1** (also *attrib.*) a representation of a person in the form of a sculptured figure, dummy, etc. **2** a crude representation of a person, esp. for ridicule etc. □ **burn in effigy** subject a usu. crude image of a person to a punishment desired for the person represented, e.g. burning.

effluent /ˈefluːənt/ *n.* **1** sewage or industrial waste discharged into a body of water. **2** a stream or lake flowing from a larger body of water.

effluvium /ɪˈfluːvɪəm/ *n.* (*pl.* **effluvia** /-vɪə/) **1** (usu. in *pl.*) waste material or refuse, esp. when transported by water. **2** an unpleasant odour or exhaled substance.

effort *n.* **1** strenuous physical or mental exertion. **2** a vigorous or determined attempt. **3** a force applied to a thing in motion along the direction of motion. **4** *informal* an achievement, accomplishment, or result of any concentrated or special activity (*not bad for a first effort*). **5** an undertaking engaged in by a group to support some specific action, end, goal, etc. (*the war effort*). □ **effortful** *adj.* **effortfully** *adv.*

effortless *adj.* easy, requiring no effort. □ **effortlessly** *adv.* **effortlessness** *n.*

effrontery /ɪˈfrʌntərɪ/ *n.* (*pl.* **-ies**) shameless insolence or impudent audacity.

effusion /ɪˈfjuːʒən/ *n.* **1 a** a copious outpouring. **b** something poured forth. **2** usu. *derogatory* **a** an unrestrained flow of speech or writing. **b** a literary composition or speech regarded as an excessive outpouring of emotion etc. **3 a** an escape of blood, pus, etc. into a body cavity. **b** accumulation of fluid in a body cavity.

effusive *adj.* gushing, demonstrative, exuberant (*effusive praise*). □ **effusively** *adv.* **effusiveness** *n.*

e.g. *abbr.* for example.

egalitarian /ɪˌɡælɪˈtɛrɪən/ ● *adj.* **1** of or relating to the principle of equal rights and opportunities for all. **2** advocating this principle. ● *n.* an advocate or supporter of egalitarian principles. □ **egalitarianism** *n.*

egg¹ *n.* **1 a** the more or less spheroidal reproductive body produced by females of animals such as birds, reptiles, fish, etc. and enclosed in a protective layer, shell, or firm membrane. **b** the egg of a domestic fowl, esp. of a hen, used for food. **c** material from inside an egg, esp. in or as food. **2** (also **egg cell**) an ovum, female gamete, or reproductive cell in animals and plants. **3** *informal* a person, usu. of a specified character (*a bad egg*). **4** anything resembling or imitating an egg, esp. in shape or appearance. □ **have** (or **put**) **all one's eggs in one basket** *informal* risk everything on a single venture. **lay an egg** *N Amer.* (of a performer, performance, etc.) fail badly. **teach one's grandmother to suck eggs** (usu. in *neg.*) presume to instruct a person in something already known. **walk on eggs** or **eggshells** see EGGSHELL. **with egg on one's face** *informal* in a condition of looking foolish or being embarrassed or humiliated by the turn of events. □ **eggy** *adj.* (**-ier, -iest**).

egg² *v.tr.* (foll. by *on*) urge, incite, provoke, or tempt.

egg beater *n.* **1** a small hand-operated rotary beater, used for beating eggs, whipping cream, etc. **2** *N Amer. slang* a helicopter.

egghead *n.* *informal* a person regarded as intellectual.

eggnog *n.* a thick drink, served hot or cold, consisting of beaten eggs, milk or cream, sugar, flavourings, and usu. rum or brandy.

eggplant *n.* esp. *N Amer.* **1** a tropical plant, *Solanum melongena*, having erect or spreading branches bearing white or purple egg-shaped fruit. **2** this fruit eaten as a vegetable.

egg roll *n.* a deep-fried appetizer consisting of a filling of vegetables, meat, etc. wrapped in egg dough.

eggs Benedict *n.* a dish consisting of poached eggs on a slice of ham on toast with hollandaise sauce.

eggshell ● *n.* **1** the thin shell or external covering of a bird's egg. **2** anything very fragile. ● *adj.* **1 a** having a delicacy like that of an eggshell. **b** (of china) of extreme thinness, fragility, and delicacy. **2** (of paint or finish) having the slight sheen or pale colour of a bird's egg. □ **walk on eggshells** walk warily or proceed cautiously.

egg white *n.* albumen or the translucent viscous fluid surrounding the yolk of an egg, which turns white when cooked.

egg yolk *n.* the yellow, internal part of a bird's egg.

ego /ˈiːɡoʊ/ *n.* (*pl.* **-os**) **1** *Metaphysics* oneself or the conscious, thinking subject. **2** *Psych.* **a** that part of

the mind which has a sense of individuality and is most conscious of self. **b** the part of the mind which, according to Sigmund Freud (1856–1939), mediates between the id and the superego and deals with external reality. **3 a** a person's self-esteem. **b** self-importance, egotism, conceit.

egocentric /ˌiːɡoʊˈsɛntrɪk/ ● *adj.* **1** *Psych.* & *Philos.* understanding the self as the centre of all experience with everything being considered only in relation to the self. **2** self-centred, egotistic. ● *n.* an egocentric person. □ **egocentricity** /-ˈtrɪsɪtɪ/ *n.*

egoism /ˈiːɡoʊˌɪzəm/ *n.* **1** an ethical theory that regards self-interest as the foundation of morality. **2** systematic self-centredness. **3** = EGOTISM. □ **egoist** *n.* **egoistic** *adj.* **egoistical** *adj.* **egoistically** *adv.*

egomania /ˌiːɡoʊˈmeɪnɪə/ *n.* obsessive self-love or self-centredness. □ **egomaniac** *n.* **egomaniacal** *adj.*

egotism /ˈiːɡəˌtɪzəm/ *n.* **1** the practice of continually talking about oneself. **2** an exaggerated opinion of oneself. **3** extreme selfishness. □ **egotist** *n.* **egotistic** *adj.* **egotistical** *adj.* **egotistically** *adv.*

ego trip *informal* ● *n.* an action or activity performed or indulged in to draw attention to one's abilities, for vanity's sake, etc. ● *v.intr.* (**ego-trip**) (**-tripped, -tripping**) indulge in an ego trip. □ **ego-tripper** *n.*

egregious /ɪˈɡriːdʒəs/ *adj.* gross, flagrant, shocking, or outstandingly bad (*egregious folly*). □ **egregiously** *adv.* **egregiousness** *n.*

egret /ˈiːɡrət/ *n.* any of various herons of the genus *Egretta* or *Bulbulcus*, usu. having long white feathers in the breeding season.

Egyptian ● *n.* **1** a native of ancient or modern Egypt or a national of the Arab Republic of Egypt. **2** the Hamitic language used in ancient Egypt until the 3rd c. AD. Compare COPTIC. ● *adj.* of or relating to ancient or modern Egypt, a country in NE Africa, or Egyptian or Egyptians. □ **Egyptianism** *n.*

Egyptology /ˌiːdʒɪpˈtɒlədʒɪ/ *n.* the study of the language, history, and culture of ancient Egypt. □ **Egyptologist** *n.*

eh *interj.* *informal* **1** inviting assent (*nice day, eh?*). **2** *Cdn* ascertaining the comprehension, continued interest, agreement, etc. of the person or persons addressed (*it's way out in the suburbs, eh, so I can't get there by bike*). ¶This is the only usage of *eh* that can be categorized as peculiarly Canadian, all other uses being common among speakers in other Commonwealth countries and to a lesser extent in the United States. **3** expressing inquiry or surprise. **4** asking for something to be repeated or explained.

EI *abbr.* *Cdn* employment insurance.

Eid /iːd/ *n.* **1** (in full **Eid ul-Fitr** /iːdəlˈfɪtrə/) a Muslim festival celebrating the end of Ramadan. **2** (in full **Eid ul-Adha** /iːduːlˈʊdə/) a Muslim festival marking the culmination of the annual pilgrimage to Mecca.

eider /ˈaɪdər/ *n.* any large northern sea duck of the genera *Somateria* and *Polysticta*, esp. the common eider, *S. mollisima*, the male of which is largely black and white and the female dull brown, or the king eider.

eight ● *n.* **1 a** one more than seven. **b** a symbol or figuring representing this (8, viii, VIII). **2** the eighth of a set or series with numbered members (*chapter eight*). **3** = FIGURE EIGHT. **4 a** a size etc. denoted by eight. **b** a shoe, garment, etc. of such a size. **5** eight o'clock. **6** a playing card with eight pips or spots. ● *adj.* one more than seven.

eight ball *n.* *N Amer.* **1** a variety of pool in which the winner is the first side to sink all seven of its own balls (either the striped ones or those in solid colours) and then sink the eight ball. **2** the black ball, numbered eight, in this. □ **behind the eight ball 1** in a difficult situation, at a disadvantage. **2** baffled, stymied.

eighteen ● *n.* **1 a** one more than seventeen. **b** a symbol for this (18, xviii, XVIII). **2** the eighteenth of a set or series with numbered members (*chapter eighteen*). **3** a size etc. denoted by eighteen. **4** a set or team of eighteen individuals. ● *adj.* one more than seventeen. □ **eighteenth** *adj., n., & adv.*

eighteen-wheeler *n. N Amer. informal* a large transport truck having eighteen wheels.

eighth ● *n.* **1 a** the position in a sequence corresponding to the number 8. **b** something occupying this position, usu. identified contextually as the day of the month or, following a proper name, a person, esp. a monarch or pope. **2** one of eight equal parts of a thing. **3** *Baseball* the eighth inning. ● *adj.* next in order after the seventh, being number eight in a series. ● *adv.* eighthly. □ **eighthly** *adv.*

eighth note *n. esp. N Amer. Music* a note having the time value of an eighth of a whole note and represented by a large dot with a hooked stem.

eighth rest *n. N Amer. Music* a rest having the time value of an eighth note.

800 number *n. N Amer.* a toll-free telephone number with an 800- or 888- prefix, used to provide free long-distance service to customers.

eighty ● *n. (pl.* **-ies)** **1 a** the product of eight and ten. **b** a symbol for this (80, lxxx, LXXX). **2** (in *pl.*) the numbers from 80 to 89, esp. the years of a century or of a person's life. ● *adj.* that amount to eighty. □ **eighty-first, -second,** etc. the ordinal numbers between eightieth and ninetieth. **eighty-one, -two,** etc. the cardinal numbers between eighty and ninety. □ **eightieth** *adj., n., & adv.*

eighty-six *v.tr. N Amer. slang* reject, discard, dismiss or destroy (a thing, person, idea, etc.).

einsteinium /ain'stainiəm/ *n.* a radioactive metallic element produced artificially from plutonium.

either /'aiðər, 'iːðər/ ● *adj. & pron.* **1** one or the other of two (*either book*). **2** each of two (*on either side of the road*). ● *adv. & conj.* **1** as one possibility (*is either black or white*). **2** as one choice or alternative (*either come in or go out*). **3** (with *neg.* or *interrog.*) **a** any more than the other (*I didn't like it either*). **b** moreover (*there is no time to lose, either*). □ **either way** in either case or event.

either-or ● *n.* an unavoidable choice between alternatives. ● *adj.* involving such a choice.

ejaculate ● *v.* /ɪ'dʒækjʊˌleit/ **1** *intr.* forcefully eject semen on achieving orgasm. **2** *tr.* a forcefully eject (semen). **b** suddenly eject (any matter) from the human, animal, or plant body. **3** *tr.* utter (words) suddenly; exclaim. ● *n.* /ɪ'dʒækjʊlət/ semen that has been ejaculated from the body. □ **ejaculation** *n.* **ejaculatory** *n.* **ejaculatory** /ɪ'dʒækjʊlə'tɔri/ *adj.*

eject ● *v.* **1** *tr.* **a** send or drive out precipitately or by force. **b** compel to leave, esp. a place or sporting event. **2 a** *tr.* cause (the pilot etc.) to be propelled from an aircraft or spacecraft in an emergency. **b** *intr.* be ejected in this way. **3** *tr.* cause to be removed or drop out, e.g. a disk or tape from a machine, a spent cartridge from a gun. ● *n.* (often *attrib.*) a device, computer command, etc. which causes something to be ejected (*eject button*). □ **ejectable** *adj.* **ejector** *n.*

ejection *n.* **1 a** the act or an instance of ejecting. **b** the process of being ejected. **2** an emergency procedure in which a pilot is catapulted out of and away from an aircraft.

eke /iːk/ *v.tr.* □ **eke out 1** contrive to make (a livelihood) or support (an existence). **2** (foll. by *with, by*) **a** supplement, make up for deficiencies in. **b** cause to last longer by economical use or by expedients.

EKG *abbr. N Amer.* **1** electrocardiogram. **2** electrocardiograph.

elaborate ● *adj.* /ɪ'læbərət/ **1** carefully or minutely worked out. **2** highly developed or complicated. **3** ostentatious, showy. ● *v.* /ɪ'læbəˌreit/ **1 a** *tr.* work out or explain in detail. **b** *tr. & intr.* go into the specifics or details of a situation, matter, etc. (*I need not elaborate*). **c** *intr.* (foll. by *on*) explain in detail. **2** *tr.* produce or develop (a thing) by effort or labour, esp. fashion (a product of art, craft, etc.) from raw material. **3** *tr.* (of nature or a natural agency) produce (a substance etc.) from its elements or sources. □ **elaborately** *adv.* **elaborateness** *n.* **elaboration** *n.*

élan /ei'lɑ̃/ *n.* style, vivacity, energy arising from enthusiasm.

elapse *v.intr.* (of time) pass by.

elastic /ɪ'læstɪk, i-/ ● *adj.* **1** able to resume its normal bulk or shape spontaneously after contraction, dilatation, or distortion. **2** flexible; adaptable (*elastic rules*). **3** springy. **4** (of a person or feelings) not permanently or easily depressed; buoyant. ● *n.* **1** elastic cord or fabric, usu. woven with strips of rubber. **2** esp. *N Amer.* (also **elastic band**) = RUBBER BAND. □ **elastically** *adv.* **elasticity** /-'tɪsɪti/ *n.*

elasticized *adj.* **1** (of a fabric) made elastic by weaving with rubber thread. **2** (of part of a garment, esp. a waistline, neckline, or cuff) made stretchy by the insertion of elastic in a casing.

elate /ɪ'leit, i-/ *v.tr.* make very happy or proud; fill with joy. □ **elated** *n.* **elatedly** *adv.* **elation** *n.*

elbow ● *n.* **1 a** the joint between the forearm and the upper arm. **b** the part of the sleeve of a garment covering the elbow. **2** an elbow-shaped bend or corner. **3** a short piece of pipe bent at a right angle. **4** a push with an elbow. ● *v.tr.* (foll. by *aside, out,* etc.) **1** thrust or jostle (a person or oneself). **2** make (one's way) by thrusting or jostling. □ **at one's elbow** close at hand. **elbow to elbow** sitting or standing close together. **give a person the elbow** *informal* dismiss or reject a person. **out at (the) elbows 1** (of a coat etc.) worn out; shabby. **2** (of a person) ragged, poor. **up to the elbows** *informal* busily engaged (in).

elbow grease *n. informal* hard manual work, esp. vigorous polishing or cleaning.

elbowing *n. Hockey* the illegal action of fouling an opponent with an elbow.

elbow room *n.* **1** adequate space to move or work in. **2** freedom from restriction; opportunity.

ELCIC *abbr.* Evangelical Lutheran Church in Canada.

elder¹ ● *attrib.adj.* (of two indicated persons, esp. when related) senior; of a greater age (*elder brother*). ● *n.* (often prec. by *the*) **1 a** the older or more senior of two indicated (esp. related) persons (*is my elder by ten years*). **b** (**Elder**) a title to distinguish between related persons of renown (*Pliny the Elder*). **2** (in *pl.*) **a** persons of greater age or seniority (*respect your elders*). **b** persons venerable because of age and wisdom (*the village elders*). **3** an official in the Presbyterian, United, or Mormon Churches who assists in the administration and government of the Church.

elder² *n.* any shrub or tree of the genus *Sambucus*, with white flowers and usu. blue-black or red berries.

elderberry *n. (pl.* **-ies)** the edible berry of the elder, esp. common elder (*Sambucus nigra*).

elderly *adj.* (of a person) rather old; past middle age. □ **elderliness** *n.*

elder statesman *n.* an older experienced person, esp. a politician, whose advice is often sought.

eldest ● *adj.* first-born or oldest surviving (member of a family, son, daughter, etc.). ● *n.* (often prec. by *the*) the eldest of three or more indicated.

El Dorado /ˌeldəˈrɑːdoː/ *n.* (*pl.* **-os**) **1** a fabled city or country abounding in gold, formerly believed to exist upon the Amazon. **2** (usu. **Eldorado**) a place of great abundance or opportunity.

elect ● *v.tr.* **1** choose (a person) by vote. **2** (usu. foll. by *to* + infin.) choose (a thing, a course of action, etc.) in preference to an alternative (*the principles they elected to follow*). **3** *Theol.* (of God) choose (persons) in preference to others for salvation. ● *adj.* **1** chosen. **2** select, choice. **3** *Theol.* chosen by God. **4** (in *comb.*, after a noun designating office) chosen but not yet in office (*president-elect*). ● *n.* (prec. by *the*; treated as *pl.*) **1** a specially chosen group of people; an elite. **2** *Theol.* those chosen by God for salvation. □ **electability** *n.* **electable** *adj.*

election *n.* **1** selection by vote (of candidates for a position. **2** the act or an instance of electing. **3** *Theol.* the doctrine of Calvin (see CALVINISM) that God chooses some people for salvation without relation to their faith or good works.

electioneer *v.intr.* **1** take part in an election campaign. **2** seek election by currying favour with voters. □ **electioneering** *n.*

elective ● *adj.* **1** (of an office or its holder) filled or appointed by election. **2** (of a body of people) having the power to elect (*an elective assembly*). **3** (of a surgical operation etc.) optional; not urgently necessary. **4** (of a course of study etc.) chosen by the student; optional. ● *n.* esp. *N Amer.* an elective course of study.

elector *n.* a person who has the right to vote.

electoral *adj.* relating to electors or elections. □ **electorally** *adv.*

electorate *n.* the body of persons entitled to vote in a country or constituency.

electric ● *adj.* **1** of, worked by, or charged with electricity. **2** producing or capable of generating electricity. **3 a** (of a musical instrument) amplified electronically. **b** (of an album etc.) performed using electronically amplified instruments. **4** causing or charged with sudden and dramatic excitement (*the atmosphere was electric*). ● *n.* **1** an electric car, train, etc. **2** (in *pl.*) electrical appliances or circuitry.

electrical *adj.* **1** of or concerned with or of the nature of electricity. **2** operating by electricity. □ **electrically** *adv.*

electrical engineering *n.* the branch of engineering that deals with the utilization of electricity, esp. electric power. □ **electrical engineer** *n.*

electrical storm *n.* a thunderstorm.

electrical tape *n. N Amer.* an adhesive tape used to cover exposed electrical wires etc.

electric blue ● *n.* a steely or brilliant light blue. ● *adj.* of this colour.

electric chair *n.* **1** a chair used for capital punishment by electrocution. **2** (usu. prec. by *the*) execution by this method.

electric eel *n.* an eel-like freshwater fish, *Electrophorus electricus*, native to S America, which possesses electric organs and can give a severe electric shock.

electric fence *n.* (also **electric fencing**) a fence (often consisting of a single strand of wire) which gives a mild electric shock to an animal touching it.

electric field *n.* a region in which an electric charge experiences a force, usu. because of a distribution of other charges.

electric guitar *n.* a guitar in which the vibrations of the strings are converted by a pickup into electrical signals and amplified by an independent amplifier and speaker.

electrician /ˌiːlekˈtrɪʃən, ˌel-, ɪˌlek-/ *n.* a person who installs or maintains electrical equipment.

electrician's tape *n. N Amer.* = ELECTRICAL TAPE.

electricity /ˌiːlekˈtrɪsɪti, ˌel-, ˌɪl,ek-/ *n.* **1** a form of energy resulting from the existence of charged particles (electrons, protons, etc.), either statically as an accumulation of charge or dynamically as a current. **2** the branch of physics dealing with electricity. **3** a supply of electric current for heating, lighting, etc. **4** excitement, tension.

electric organ *n.* **1** an organ in certain fishes able to produce an electrical discharge for stunning prey or sensing the surroundings, or as a defence. **2** *Music* an electrically operated organ.

electric ray *n.* any ray of the family Torpedinidae, as the Atlantic torpedo ray, *Torpedo nobiliana*, which possess electric organs and can give an electric shock.

electric shaver *n.* (also **electric razor**) an electrical device for shaving, with oscillating or rotating blades behind a metal guard.

electric shock *n.* **1** the effect of a sudden discharge of electricity on a person or animal, usually with stimulation of the nerves and contraction of the muscles. **2** = SHOCK TREATMENT 1.

electric storm *var. of* ELECTRICAL STORM.

electrify *v.tr.* (**-ies, -ied**) **1** charge with electricity; pass an electric current through. **2** convert (machinery or the place or system employing it) to the use of electric power. **3** cause dramatic or sudden excitement in. □ **electrification** *n.* **electrifier** *n.*

electro *n.* (*pl.* **-os**) **1** = ELECTROPLATE *n.* **2** (also *attrib.*) a style of dance music with a fast electronic beat backed by a synthesizer.

electro- *comb. form* of, relating to, or caused by electricity (*electromagnet*).

electroacoustic *adj.* **1** involving the direct conversion of electrical into acoustic energy or vice versa. **2** (of music) performed or composed with the creative use of electronic equipment.

electrocardiogram *n.* a chart or record produced by an electrocardiograph, used in the diagnosis of heart disease.

electrocardiograph *n.* an instrument that records or displays the electric activity of the heart by means of electrodes attached to the skin. Abbr.: **ECG, EKG.** □ **electrocardiographic** *adj.* **electrocardiographically** *adv.* **electrocardiography** *n.*

electrochemistry *adj.* the branch of science that deals with the relations between electrical and chemical phenomena. □ **electrochemical** *adj.* **electrochemically** *adv.* **electrochemist** *n.*

electroconvulsive therapy *n.* a method of treating certain mental illnesses in which an electric current is passed through the brain so as to produce a convulsion. Abbr.: **ECT.**

electrocute *v.tr.* (usu. in *passive*) cause the death of (a person or animal) by means of an electric current. □ **electrocution** *n.*

electrode *n.* a conductor through which electricity enters or leaves an electrolyte etc.

electroencephalogram /ɪˌlektroʊenˈsefələˌgræm/ *n.* a chart or record produced by an electroencephalograph. Abbr.: **EEG.**

electroencephalograph *n.* an instrument that records or displays the electrical activity of the brain, using electrodes attached to the scalp. Abbr.: **EEG.** □ **electroencephalography** n.

electrologist /ɪlekˈtrɒlədʒɪst/ n. N Amer. a person trained to remove excess body or facial hair using electrolysis.

electrolysis /ˌɪlekˈtrɒləsɪs/ n. **1** chemical decomposition produced by passing an electric current through an electrolyte. **2** the removal of excess hair by passing an electric current through the root. □ **electrolytic** /ɪˌlektrəˈlɪtɪk/ adj. **electrolytical** adj. **electrolytically** adv.

electrolyte /ɪˈlektrəˌlɒɪt/ n. **1** a liquid, esp. that present in a battery, which contains ions and can be decomposed by electrolysis. **2** (usu. in pl.) the ionized or ionizable constituents of a living cell, blood, etc.

electrolyze /ɪˈlektrəˌlɑɪz/ v.tr. subject to or treat by electrolysis. □ **electrolyzer** n.

electromagnet n. a piece of soft iron that becomes magnetic when an electric current is passed through the coil surrounding it.

electromagnetic adj. having both an electrical and a magnetic character or properties.

electromagnetic field n. a field of force created by changing electric and magnetic fields.

electromagnetic radiation n. a kind of radiation including visible light, radio waves, gamma rays, X-rays, etc., in which electric and magnetic fields vary simultaneously.

electromagnetism n. **1** the magnetic forces produced by electricity. **2** the study of this.

electromechanical adj. relating to the application of electricity to mechanical processes, devices, etc.

electromotive force n. a difference in potential that tends to give rise to an electric current. Abbr.: **emf, EMF.**

electron n. a stable subatomic particle with a charge of negative electricity, found in all atoms and acting as the primary carrier of electricity in solids.

electronegative adj. (of an element) tending to acquire electrons in chemical reactions. □ **electronegativity** n.

electronic /ˌɪlekˈtrɒnɪk, ˌiː-, ˌel-/ adj. **1 a** produced by or involving the flow of electrons. **b** of or relating to electrons or electronics. **2** (of a device) using electronic components. **3** using the electronic transmission or storage of information, as by computer (electronic text). **4 a** (of music) produced by electronic means and usu. recorded on tape. **b** (of a musical instrument) producing sounds by electronic means. □ **electronically** adv.

electronic bulletin board n. = BBS.

electronic data interchange n. a computer protocol for the exchange of electronic information, used by banks, businesses, etc. for invoicing, ordering, etc. Abbr.: **EDI.**

electronic mail n. **1** messages distributed by electronic means esp. from one computer system to one or more recipients. **2** the electronic mail system.

electronic publishing n. the publishing of books etc. in machine-readable form rather than on paper.

electronics n.pl. **1** (treated as sing.) a branch of physics and technology concerned with the behaviour and movement of electrons in a vacuum, gas, semiconductor, etc. **2** the circuits used in this. **3** (treated as pl.) electronic devices.

electron lens n. a device for focusing a stream of electrons by means of electric or magnetic fields.

electron microscope n. a microscope with high magnification and resolution, employing electron beams in place of light and using electron lenses.

electron volt n. a unit of energy equal to the work done on an electron in moving it through a potential difference of one volt. Abbr.: **eV.**

electrophoresis /ɪˌlektrəˌfəˈriːsɪs/ n. the movement of charged particles in a fluid or gel under the influence of an electric field. □ **electrophoretic** /-fəˈretɪk/ adj.

electroplate ● v.tr. coat (a utensil etc.) by electrolytic deposition with chromium, silver, etc. ● n. electroplated articles.

electropositive adj. **1** electrically positive. **2** (of an element) tending to lose electrons in chemical reactions.

electroshock ● n. = ELECTROCONVULSIVE THERAPY. ● adj. (of medical treatment) by means of electric shocks. ● v.tr. **1** treat (a patient) with electroconvulsive therapy. **2** kill (an animal) with an electric current.

electrostatic adj. relating to stationary electric charges or electrostatics. □ **electrostatically** adv.

electrostatics n.pl. (treated as sing.) the study of stationary electric charges or fields as opposed to electric currents.

electrotherapy n. the treatment of diseases by the use of electricity. □ **electrotherapeutic** adj. **electrotherapeutical** adj. **electrotherapist** n.

elegant adj. **1** tasteful, stylish, and refined in appearance. **2** showing refined grace in movement (an elegant dancer). **3** (of a mode of life etc.) of refined luxury. **4** ingeniously simple and satisfying (an elegant solution). □ **elegance** n. **elegantly** adv.

elegiac /ˌelɪˈdʒɑɪək/ adj. **1** of, pertaining to, or used for an elegy (elegiac metre). **2** mournful; melancholy. □ **elegiacally** adv.

elegy /ˈelədʒi/ n. (pl. **-ies**) (in modern literature) a poem of serious reflection, typically a lament for the dead. □ **elegist** n. **elegize** v.tr. & intr.

element n. **1** a component part or group; a contributing factor or thing. **2** Chem. & Physics any of the hundred or so substances that cannot be resolved by chemical means into simpler substances, each consisting of atoms with the same atomic number. **3** a resistance wire that heats up in an electric heater, stove, kettle, etc. **4** (in pl.) weather, esp. wind and storm. **5** (in pl.) the rudiments of learning or of a branch of knowledge. **6** (in pl.) the bread and wine of the Eucharist. **7** Math. & Logic an entity that is a single member of a set. □ **in** (or **out of**) **one's element** in (or out of) one's accustomed or preferred surroundings. **reduced to its elements** analyzed.

elemental ● adj. **1** essential; basic (elemental truths). **2** of the forces of nature, esp. seen as powerful and uncontrolled. **3** pertaining to chemical elements. **4** (of a chemical element) uncompounded. **5** of the four elements. ● n. an entity or force thought to be physically manifested by occult means.

elementary adj. **1 a** dealing with or arising from the simplest facts of a subject; rudimentary, introductory. **b** simple. **2** N Amer. of or pertaining to elementary school. **3** Chem. not decomposable. □ **elementarily** adv. **elementariness** n.

elementary particle n. a subatomic particle, esp. one not known to be decomposable into simpler particles.

elementary school n. N Amer. a school offering primary education, usu. for the first six or eight grades and also usu. including kindergarten.

elephant n. (pl. **-s** or same) the largest living land animal, of which two species survive, the larger African (*Loxodonta africana*) and the smaller Indian (*Elephas maximus*), both with a trunk and long tusks.

elephantiasis /ˌeləfən'taɪəsɪs/ n. gross enlargement of the body, esp. the limbs, due to lymphatic obstruction by a parasite transmitted by mosquitoes.

elephantine /'eləfən,tain, -,tiːn, ,elə'fæn-/ adj. **1** of or pertaining to elephants. **2 a** huge. **b** unwieldy.

elephant seal n. either of two very large seals of which the males have inflatable snouts.

elev. abbr. elevation.

elevate v.tr. **1** raise above the usual level or position (*elevate your heart rate with exercise*). **2** raise in status, rank or importance; promote. **3** turn or direct upwards (one's eyes, a gun, etc.). **4** raise morally or intellectually (*elevate the level of discussion*). **5** raise the spirits of; elate, exhilarate. **6** raise (a railway, highway, etc.) above ground level. □ **elevatory** adj.

elevation n. **1** the process, state, or fact of elevating or being elevated. **2** the height above a given level, esp. sea level. **3** a high place or position. **4 a** a drawing or diagram made by projection on a vertical plane. **b** an exterior face of a building or structure. **5 a** the capacity of a dancer to attain height in jumps. **b** the height attained in a jump. **6** the angle with the horizontal, esp. of a gun or of the direction of a celestial object. □ **elevational** adj.

elevator n. **1** N Amer. a platform or compartment housed in a shaft for raising and lowering persons or things to different floors of a building etc. **2** N Amer. (in full **grain elevator**) a tall building, typically having several cylindrical concrete silos or (on the prairies) a box-shaped wooden construction with a pitched roof, incorporating an elevating device which conveys grain from an unloading platform to bins where it is sorted, stored and cleaned before onward shipment. **3** the movable part of a tailplane for changing the pitch of an aircraft. **4** a device for hoisting or raising something from a lower level to a higher one. **5** something which elevates, esp. a muscle that raises a limb.

elevator manager n. Cdn (also esp. hist. **elevator agent**) an employee of a grain-handling company who receives, grades, and ships grain at a grain elevator and issues to the farmer a ticket negotiable for payment.

eleven ● n. **1 a** one more than ten. **b** a symbol for this (11, xi, XI) **2 a** a group of eleven persons or things. **b** the eleventh of a set or series (*page eleven*). **3 a** a size etc. denoted by eleven. **b** a shoe, garment, etc. of such a size. **4** eleven o'clock. ● adj. that amount to eleven.

eleventh ● n. **1** the position in a sequence corresponding to the number 11 in the sequence 1–11. **2** the eleventh person or thing of a category, series, etc. **3** one of eleven equal parts of a thing. ● adj. that is the eleventh. ● adv. in the eleventh place. □ **the eleventh hour** the last possible moment.

ELF abbr. extremely low frequency.

elf n. (pl. **elves**) **1** a mythological being, esp. one that is small and mischievous. **2** a small person. □ **elfish** adj. **elvish** adj.

elfin adj. **1** of elves; elflike. **2** diminutive, delicate, and full of strange charm.

elicit /ɪ'lɪsɪt, i-/ v.tr. (**elicited**, **eliciting**) draw out or forth; evoke (an admission, response, etc.). □ **elicitation** n. **elicitor** n.

elide /ɪ'laɪd, i-/ v.tr. **1** omit (a vowel, consonant, or syllable) by elision. **2** pass over in silence; ignore.

eligible adj. **1** (often foll. by *for*) fit or entitled to be chosen for a position, award, etc. **2** meeting specified preconditions (*eligible to receive EI benefits*). **3** desirable

or suitable, esp. as a partner in marriage. □ **eligibility** n. **eligibly** adv.

eliminate v.tr. **1** remove, get rid of. **2** exclude from consideration; ignore as irrelevant. **3** exclude from further participation in a competition etc. by defeat. **4** slang murder cold-bloodedly. **5** discharge (waste matter) from the body. □ **eliminable** adj. **elimination** n. **eliminative** adj. **eliminator** n.

ELISA /ɪ'laɪzə/ n. a diagnostic technique for determining the amount of protein or other antigen in a blood sample by means of an enzyme-catalyzed colour change.

elision /ɪ'lɪʒən, i-/ n. **1** the omission of a vowel, consonant, or syllable in pronouncing (as in *I'm*, *let's*). **2** the omission of a passage in a book etc.

elite /ɪ'liːt, ei-/ ● n. **1** (prec. by *the*) the best or choice part of a larger body or group. **2** a class or group of persons possessing wealth, power, prestige, etc. (*the ruling elite*). ● adj. of or belonging to an elite.

elitism n. **1** advocacy of or reliance on leadership or dominance by a select group. **2** a sense of belonging to an elite. □ **elitist** n. & adj.

elixir /ɪ'lɪksər, i-/ n. **1 a** a preparation supposedly able to change metals into gold. **b** (in full **elixir of life**) a preparation supposedly able to prolong life indefinitely. **2** a supposed remedy for all ills.

Elizabethan /ɪ,lɪzə'biːθən, i-/ ● adj. **1** of, belonging to, or characteristic of the period of Elizabeth I (reigned 1558–1603). **2** of or belonging to the UK during the reign of Elizabeth II of England (1952–). ● n. **1** (usu. in pl.) a person, esp. a poet or dramatist, of the time of Elizabeth I. **2** a person of the time of Elizabeth II.

elk n. (pl. same or **-s**) **1** N Amer. a wapiti. **2** (**Elk**) a member of the Benevolent and Protective Order of Elks, a social and charitable organization.

elkhound n. a large Scandinavian hunting dog with a shaggy coat.

ell n. **1** an extension of a building etc. which is at right angles to the main part. **2** a short piece of pipe bent at a right angle.

ellipse /ɪ'lɪps, i-/ n. a regular oval, traced by a point moving in a plane so that the sum of its distances from two other points is constant, or resulting when a cone is cut by an oblique plane which does not intersect the base (compare HYPERBOLA).

ellipsis /ɪ'lɪpsɪs, i-/ n. (pl. **ellipses** /-siːz/) **1** the omission from a sentence of words needed to complete the construction or sense. **2** the omission of a sentence at the end of a paragraph. **3** a set of three dots etc. indicating an omission.

ellipsoid ● n. a solid of which all the plane sections normal to one axis are circles and all the other plane sections are ellipses. ● adj. (also **ellipsoidal**) having the nature or shape of an ellipsoid.

elliptic /ɪ'lɪptɪk, i-/ adj. (also **elliptical**) **1** of, relating to, or having the form of an ellipse or ellipsis. **2** (of writing or speech) very concise, often so as to be obscure or cryptic. □ **elliptically** adv.

elm n. **1** any tree of the genus *Ulmus*, esp. the American elm, *U. americana*, with asymmetrical toothed leaves. **2** (in full **elmwood**) the wood of the elm.

El Niño /el'niːnjoʊ/ n. an irregularly occurring southward current in the equatorial Pacific Ocean, associated with weather changes and ecological change.

elocution /ˌelə'kjuːʃən/ n. **1** the art of clear and expressive speech, esp. of distinct pronunciation and articulation. **2** a particular style of speaking. □ **elocutionary** adj. **elocutionist** n.

elongate /iː'lɒŋ,geit, 'iː-/ ● v. **1** tr. lengthen, prolong.

2 *intr. Bot.* grow, become longer; have a slender or tapering form. ● *adj. Bot. & Zool.* long in proportion to width. □ **elongated** *adj.*

elongation *n.* **1** the act or an instance of lengthening; the process of being lengthened. **2** a part of a line etc. formed by lengthening.

elope /ɪˈloːp, i-/ *v.intr.* run away secretly with a lover, esp. to get married. □ **elopement** *n.* **eloper** *n.*

eloquence /ˈeləkwəns/ *n.* **1** fluent and effective use of language. **2** the quality of being eloquent; eloquent language. **3** rhetoric.

eloquent *adj.* **1** possessing or showing eloquence. **2** clearly expressive or indicative (*an eloquent performance*). □ **eloquently** *adv.*

else *adv.* **1** besides; in addition (*nowhere else; who else*). **2** instead; other, different (*what else could I say?; someone else*). □ **or else 1** otherwise; if not (*run, or else you will be late*). **2** *informal* a warning or threat of the consequences should a previously expressed order, expectation, etc. not be carried out or realized (*clean up your room, or else!*).

elsewhere *adv.* in or to some other place.

ELT *abbr.* EMERGENCY LOCATOR TRANSMITTER.

elucidate /ɪˈluːsɪˌdeɪt, i-/ *v.tr.* throw light on; explain, clarify. □ **elucidation** *n.*

elude /ɪˈluːd, i-/ *v.tr.* **1** escape adroitly from (a danger, difficulty, pursuer, etc.); dodge. **2** avoid compliance with (a law, request, etc.) or fulfillment of (an obligation). **3** (of a fact, solution, etc.) escape from or baffle (a person's memory or understanding). □ **eluder** *n.* **elusion** *n.*

elusive /ɪˈluːsɪv, i-/ *adj.* **1** difficult to find or catch; tending to elude. **2** difficult to remember or recall. **3** (of an answer etc.) avoiding the point raised; seeking to elude. □ **elusively** *adv.* **elusiveness** *n.*

elves *pl. of* ELF.

Elysium /ɪˈlɪziəm, ɪˈlɪʒ-, ɪˈliː-/ *n.* **1** (also **Elysian Fields**) (in Greek mythology) the abode of the blessed after death. **2** a place or state of ideal happiness. □ **Elysian** *adj.*

EM *abbr.* ELECTROMAGNETIC.

em /em/ *n.* **1** a unit of horizontal measurement in typesetting, usually equal to the width of capital M. **2** a unit of measurement equal to 12 points.

'em /əm/ *pron. informal* them (*let 'em all come*).

emaciate /ɪˈmeɪsiˌeɪt, i-/ *v.tr.* (esp. as **emaciated** *adj.*) make abnormally thin or feeble. □ **emaciation** *n.*

e-mail ● *n.* **1** = ELECTRONIC MAIL. **2** a message sent by e-mail (*received 5 e-mails*). ● *v.tr.* **1** send e-mail to (a person). **2** send by e-mail.

emanate /ˈeməˌneɪt/ *v.* **1** *intr.* (usu. foll. by *from*) issue, originate (from a source). **2** *tr.* emit; send forth.

emanation *n.* **1** the act or process of emanating. **2** something that emanates from a source (esp. of virtues, qualities, etc.). □ **emanative** *adj.*

emancipate /ɪˈmænsəˌpeɪt, i-/ *v.tr.* **1** free from restraint, esp. legal, social, or political. **2** free from slavery. □ **emancipation** *n.* **emancipator** *n.* **emancipatory** /ɪˈmænsəpəˌtɔri/ *adj.*

emancipated *adj.* **1** not inhibited by moral or social convention. **2** liberated, as from slavery.

emasculate ● *v.tr.* /ɪˈmæskjʊˌleɪt, i-/ **1** deprive of force or vigour; make feeble or ineffective. **2** castrate. ● *adj.* /ɪˈmæskjʊlət/ **1** deprived of force or vigour. **2** castrated. □ **emasculation** *n.*

embalm /emˈbɑm, ɪm-/ *v.tr.* **1** preserve (a corpse) from decay by means of arterial injection of a preservative, e.g. formaldehyde. **2** keep (a place etc.) unchanged. □ **embalmer** *n.*

embankment *n.* an earth or stone bank for keeping back water, or for carrying a road or railway.

embargo ● *n.* (*pl.* **-oes**) **1** an order prohibiting ships from entering or leaving a country's ports, usu. issued in anticipation of war. **2** an official, usu. temporary, suspension of commerce or other activity. **3** a prohibition (*an embargo on discussion*). ● *v.tr.* (**-oes**, **-oed**) **1** place (ships, trade, etc.) under embargo. **2** seize (a ship, goods) for state service.

embark *v.* **1** *tr. & intr.* put or go on board a ship or aircraft (to a destination). **2** *intr.* (foll. by *on, upon*) engage in an activity or undertaking. □ **embarkation** *n.* (in sense 1).

embarrass *v.tr.* **1** cause (a person) to feel awkward or self-conscious or ashamed. **2** (as **embarrassed** *adj.*) encumbered with debts. □ **embarrassedly** *adv.* **embarrassingly** *adv.*

embarrassment *n.* **1 a** a feeling of awkward confusion, shame, or self-consciousness. **b** a cause of this (*their behaviour is an embarrassment*). **2** a state of financial difficulty; shortage of money.

embassy /ˈembəsi/ *n.* (*pl.* **-ies**) **1 a** the residence or offices of an ambassador. **b** the ambassador and staff attached to an embassy. **2** a deputation or mission to a foreign country.

embattled *adj.* **1** involved in a conflict or difficult undertaking. **2** prepared or arrayed for battle.

embayment *n.* **1** a bay. **2** a recess like a bay.

embed *v.tr.* (**-bedded**, **-bedding**) (usu. in *passive*) **1** fix firmly in a surrounding mass (*embedded in concrete*). **2** fix (an idea, attitude, etc.) firmly within a structure. □ **embeddedness** *n.* **embedment** *n.*

embellish *v.tr.* **1** beautify, adorn. **2** add interest to (a narrative) with fictitious additions. □ **embellisher** *n.* **embellishment** *n.*

ember /ˈembər/ *n.* (usu. in *pl.*) **1** a small piece of glowing coal or wood in a dying fire. **2** an almost extinct residue of a past activity, feeling, etc.

embezzle *v.tr. & intr.* divert (money etc.) fraudulently to one's own use in violation of trust. □ **embezzlement** *n.* **embezzler** *n.*

embitter *v.tr.* **1** (usu. as **embittered** *adj.*) make (a person or feeling) intensely hostile, bitter, or discontented. **2** make more bitter or painful.

emblazon /emˈbleɪzən, ɪm-/ *v.tr.* **1** (usu. in *passive*) (foll. by *with*) inscribe a conspicuous design, logo, slogan, etc. on (a surface). **2** (foll. by *on*) inscribe (such a design) on a surface.

emblem *n.* **1** a symbol or representation typifying or identifying an institution, quality, etc. **2** a heraldic device or symbolic object as a distinctive badge. □ **emblematic** *adj.*

embody *v.tr.* (**-ies**, **-ied**) **1** give a concrete or discernible form to (an idea, concept, etc.). **2** (of a thing or person) be an expression of (an idea etc.). **3** express tangibly (*courage embodied in heroic actions*). **4** form into a body. **5** include, comprise. **6** provide (a spirit) with bodily form. □ **embodiment** *n.*

embolden *v.tr.* (usu. in *passive*) make bold; encourage.

embolism /ˈembəˌlɪzəm/ *n.* an obstruction of any artery by a clot of blood, air bubble, etc.

emboss *v.tr.* (usu. as **embossed** *adj.*) **1** carve or mould in relief. **2** form figures etc. so that they stand out on (a surface). **3** make protuberant. □ **embosser** *n.* **embossing** *n.*

embrace ● *v.* **1 a** *tr.* hold (a person) closely in the arms, esp. as a sign of affection. **b** *intr.* (of two people) hold each other closely. **2** *tr.* clasp, enclose. **3** *tr.* accept eagerly (an offer, opportunity, etc.). **4** *tr.* adopt (a course of action, doctrine, cause, etc.). **5** *tr.* include,

comprise. 6 *tr.* take in with the eye or mind. ● *n.* an act of embracing.

embroider *v.* **1 a** *tr. & intr.* decorate (cloth etc.) with needlework. **b** *tr.* create (a design) in this way. **2** *tr.* embellish (a narrative etc.) with fictitious additions.

embroidery *n.* (*pl.* **-ies**) **1** the art of embroidering. **2** embroidered work. **3** unnecessary or extravagant ornament. **4** fictitious additions to (a story etc.).

embroil *v.tr.* **1** (often foll. by *in*) involve (a person, company, etc.) in conflict or difficulties. **2** bring (affairs) into a state of confusion.

embryo /'embriːəʊ/ *n.* (*pl.* **-os**) **1 a** an unborn or unhatched offspring. **b** a human offspring in the first eight or twelve weeks from conception. **2** a rudimentary plant contained in a seed. **3** a thing in a rudimentary stage. □ **in embryo** undeveloped. □ **embryonal** /em'braɪənəl/ *adj.* **embryonic** /ˌembri'ɒnɪk/ *adj.*

embryology /ˌembri'ɒlədʒi/ *n.* the study of embryos. □ **embryological** *adj.* **embryologist** *n.*

embryo transfer *n.* **1** the removal of an embryo from a superior cow, sow, etc. and its replacement inside an inferior one, performed to increase the potential number of offspring from superior livestock. **2** the transfer of a human embryo from one female, or from storage, to another for gestation.

emcee *informal* ● *n.* a master of ceremonies. ● *v.* (**emcees**, **emceed**) **1** *intr.* act as master of ceremonies. **2** *tr.* act as master of ceremonies for.

em dash *n.* a long dash (—) used in punctuation.

emend *v.tr.* edit (a text etc.) to remove errors etc. □ **emendation** /ˌiːmen'deɪʃən/ *n.*

emerald ● *n.* **1** a bright green precious stone, a variety of beryl. **2** (in full **emerald green**) the colour of this. ● *adj.* (in full **emerald green**; sometimes hyphenated when *attrib.*) bright green.

emerge[1] *v.intr.* (often foll. by *from*) **1** come up or out into view, esp. when formerly concealed. **2** come up out of a liquid. **3** (of facts, circumstances, etc.) come to light, become known, esp. as a result of inquiry etc. **4** become recognized or prominent (*emerged as a contender*). **5** (of a question, difficulty, etc.) become apparent. **6** survive an ordeal etc. with a specified result (*emerged unscathed*). □ **emergence** *n.*

emerge[2] *n. Cdn slang* = EMERGENCY 4.

emergency *n.* (*pl.* **-ies**) **1** a sudden state of danger, conflict, etc., requiring immediate action. **2 a** a medical condition requiring immediate treatment. **b** a patient with such a condition. **3** (*attrib.*) characterized by or for use in an emergency. **4** *N Amer.* (often *attrib.*) a section of a hospital for handling emergencies.

emergency brake *n. N Amer.* a brake on a car etc., usu. hand-operated, used to stop it if the main brakes fail, and to prevent it from rolling while parked.

emergency locator transmitter *n.* a radio transmitter on an aircraft activated automatically by the inertia of impact and serving as a homing beacon for searching aircraft. Abbr.: **ELT**.

emergency room *n. N Amer.* = EMERGENCY 4.

emergent /ɪ'mɜːdʒənt/ *adj.* **1** becoming apparent; emerging. **2** (of a nation) newly formed or made independent.

emeritus /ɪ'merɪtəs/ *adj.* **1** retired and retaining one's title as an honour (*emeritus professor*; *professor emeritus*). **2** honourably discharged from service.

emery /'eməri/ *n.* **1** a coarse rock of corundum and magnetite or hematite used for polishing metal or other hard materials. **2** (*attrib.*) covered with emery.

emery board *n.* a strip of thin wood or board coated with emery or another abrasive, used as a nail file.

emery cloth *n.* (also **emery paper**) emery-covered cloth or paper, used to polish or clean metals etc.

emetic /ɪ'metɪk/ ● *adj.* that causes vomiting. ● *n.* an emetic medicine.

EMF *abbr.* **1** (usu. **emf**) electromotive force. **2** electromagnetic field(s).

emigrant ● *n.* a person who emigrates. ● *adj.* emigrating.

emigrate /'emɪˌgreɪt/ *v.intr.* leave one's own country to settle in another. □ **emigration** *n.*

émigré /'emɪˌgreɪ/ *n.* an emigrant, esp. an exile.

eminence *n.* **1** recognized superiority. **2** (**Eminence**) a title used in addressing or referring to a cardinal (*His Eminence*). **3** an important person.

éminence grise /ˌeɪmiːnɑ̃s 'griːz/ *n.* (*pl.* **éminences grises** *pronunc.* same) a person who exercises power or influence without holding office.

eminent *adj.* **1** distinguished, notable. **2** (of qualities) remarkable in degree. □ **eminently** *adv.*

emir /e'mɪːr/ *n.* a title of various Muslim rulers, esp. in the Middle East.

emirate /'emərət, -ˌreɪt/ *n.* the rank, domain, or reign of an emir.

emissary /'emɪˌseri/ *n.* (*pl.* **-ies**) a person sent on a special (usu. diplomatic) mission.

emission *n.* **1** the process or an act of emitting. **2** a thing emitted, as exhaust, radiation, fluid, etc.

emissive *adj.* having the power to radiate light, heat, etc. □ **emissivity** /ˌiːmɪ'sɪvɪti/ *n.*

emit *v.tr.* (**emitted**, **emitting**) **1 a** send out (heat, light, exhaust, etc.). **b** discharge from the body. **2** give forth (a sound).

emitter *n.* something which emits, esp. a region in a transistor producing carriers of current.

Emmenthal /'emən,tɒl/ *n.* (also **-tal**, **-taler** /-'tɒlɜr/, **-thaler**) a kind of hard yellow Swiss cheese with many large holes in it, similar to Gruyère.

Emmy *n.* (*pl.* **Emmys**) (in the US) a prize awarded annually to an outstanding television program or performer.

emollient /ɪ'mɒliənt, e-/ ● *adj.* **1** that softens or soothes the skin. **2** soothing. ● *n.* an emollient agent.

emote *v.intr. informal* show excessive emotion. □ **emoter** *n.*

emoticon /ɪ'məʊtɪˌkɒn, i-/ *n.* a (usu. sideways) representation of a facial expression constructed out of keyboard characters, added to an esp. e-mail message to help establish the tone, e.g. :-(representing a sad face.

emotion *n.* **1** a strong mental or instinctive feeling such as love, sorrow, etc. **2** emotional intensity or sensibility (*he spoke with emotion*). □ **emotionless** *adj.*

emotional *adj.* **1** of or relating to the emotions. **2 a** (of a person) liable to excessive emotion. **b** showing strong emotion, esp. by weeping. **3** expressing or based on emotion. **4** likely to excite emotion. □ **emotionalism** *n.* **emotionality** *n.* **emotionalize** *v.tr.* **emotionally** *adv.*

emotive *adj.* **1** of or characterized by emotion. **2** tending to excite emotion. **3** arousing feeling; not purely descriptive. □ **emotively** *adv.*

empathize *v.intr.* exercise empathy.

empathy /'empəθi/ *n.* the power of identifying oneself mentally with (and so fully comprehending) a person or object of contemplation. □ **empathetic** /-'θetɪk/ *adj.* **empathetically** *adv.* **empathic** /em'pæθɪk/ *adj.* **empathically** *adv.*

emperor *n.* **1** the male sovereign of an empire. **2** a male sovereign of higher rank than a king.

emphasis /'emfəsɪs/ n. (pl. **emphases** /-,siːz/) **1** special importance or prominence (emphasis on economy). **2** stress laid on a word or words to indicate special meaning or importance. **3** vigour or intensity of expression, feeling, action, etc.

emphasize v.tr. **1** bring (a thing, fact, etc.) into special prominence; put emphasis or stress on. **2** lay stress on (a word in speaking).

emphatic /em'fætɪk, ɪm-/ adj. **1** (of language, tone, or gesture) forcibly expressive. **2** of words: **a** bearing the stress. **b** used to give emphasis. **3** expressing oneself with emphasis. **4** (of an action or process) forcible, significant. □ **emphatically** adv.

emphysema /,emfɪ'ziːmə, -'siː-/ n. **1** enlargement of the air sacs of the lungs causing breathlessness. **2** a swelling caused by the presence of air in the connective tissues of the body.

empire n. **1** an extensive group of states or countries under a single supreme authority, esp. an emperor. **2** supreme dominion. **3** a large commercial organization etc. owned or directed by one person or group. **4** (**the Empire**) hist. **a** the British Empire. **b** the Holy Roman Empire. **5** a type or period of government in which the sovereign is called emperor. **6** (attrib.) **a** denoting a style of dress with a waistline under the bust and often a low neckline (empire waist). **b** (**Empire**) denoting a neoclassical style of furniture, often with Egyptian motifs. **7** (**Empire**) a red, sweet and tart eating apple, with characteristics of both McIntosh and Delicious apples.

empire builder n. a person who deliberately acquires extra territory, authority, etc. esp. unnecessarily. □ **empire building** n.

empirical /em'pɪrɪkəl, ɪm-/ adj. (also **empiric**) **1** based or acting on observation or experiment, not on theory. **2** Philos. regarding sense data as valid information. **3** deriving knowledge from experience alone. □ **empirically** adv.

empiricism /em'pɪrɪsɪzəm, ɪm-/ n. Philos. the theory that all knowledge is derived from sense-experience. □ **empiricist** n. & adj.

emplace v.tr. put into a specified position; situate.

emplacement n. **1** the act or an instance of putting in position. **2** a platform or defended position where a gun is placed for firing. **3** situation, position.

employ ● v.tr. **1** use the services of (a person) in return for payment. **2** use (a thing, time, energy, strategy, etc.) esp. to good effect. **3** (often foll. by in) keep (a person) occupied. ● n. the state of being employed, esp. for wages. □ **in the employ of** employed by. □ **employer** n.

employable ● adj. **1** qualified for employment and available for work. **2** usable. ● n. an employable person. □ **employability** n.

employee n. a person employed for wages or salary.

employment n. **1** the act of employing or the state of being employed. **2** the prevalence or proportion of this in a given area (politicians promising full employment). **3** a person's regular trade or profession.

employment insurance n. Cdn a federal government program providing payments to eligible unemployed people, funded by tax revenues and contributions by employers and workers. Abbr.: **EI**.

emporium /em'pɔːriəm, ɪm-/ n. (pl. **emporia** /-riə/ or **-ums**) **1** a specialized retail store etc. (perfume emporium). **2** a large retail store selling a wide variety of goods. **3** a centre of commerce, a market.

empower v.tr. (foll. by to + infin.) **1** authorize, license. **2** give power to; make able. **3** provide with the means,

opportunity, etc. necessary for independence, self-assertion, etc. □ **empowerment** n.

empress /'emprəs/ n. **1** the wife or widow of an emperor. **2** a female sovereign of an empire. **3** a female sovereign of higher rank than a queen.

empty ● adj. (**-ier, -iest**) **1** containing nothing. **2** (of a house etc.) unoccupied or unfurnished. **3** (of a transport vehicle etc.) without a load, passengers, etc. **4 a** meaningless, insincere (empty threats). **b** without substance or purpose (an empty existence). **5** informal hungry. **6** (foll. by of) devoid, lacking. **7** Math. & Logic (of a class or set) containing no members or elements. **8** (of a piece of land) without structures, crops, etc. (empty lot). **9** Hockey (of a net) left unguarded while a team substitutes an extra attacker for its goaltender. ● v. (**-ies, -ied**) **1** tr. a make empty; remove the contents of. **b** deprive of certain contents (emptied the room of its chairs). **2** tr. (often foll. by into) transfer (the contents of a container). **3** intr. become empty. **4** intr. (of a river) discharge itself (into the sea etc.). ● n. (pl. **-ies**) informal a container (esp. a bottle) left empty of its contents. □ **run on empty** continue to function though having exhausted all one's resources, sustenance, etc. □ **emptily** adv. **emptiness** n.

empty-handed adj. (usu. predic.) **1** bringing or taking nothing. **2** having achieved or obtained nothing. □ **empty-handedly** adv.

empty nest n. esp. N Amer. a household where the parents alone remain after the children have grown up and left home. □ **empty nester** n.

empty-netter n. (in full **empty-net goal**) Hockey a goal scored into an empty net.

EMS abbr. **1** EUROPEAN MONETARY SYSTEM. **2** Computing Expanded Memory Specification. **3** emergency medical services.

EMU /iːem'juː, 'iːmjuː/ abbr. economic and monetary union (of the EC); European monetary union.

emu /'iːmjuː/ n. a large shaggy flightless Australian bird, Dromaius novaehollandiae, related to the ostrich and capable of running at high speed.

emulate /'emjʊ,leɪt/ v.tr. **1** try to equal or excel. **2** imitate zealously. **3** rival. **4** Computing reproduce the function or action of (a different computer or software system). □ **emulation** n. **emulator** n.

emulsifier n. any substance that stabilizes an emulsion, esp. a food additive used to stabilize processed foods.

emulsify /ɪ'mʌlsɪ,faɪ/ v.tr. (**-ies, -ied**) convert into an emulsion. □ **emulsification** n.

emulsion /ɪ'mʌlʃən/ n. **1** a fine dispersion of one liquid in another, esp. as paint, medicine, etc. **2** a mixture of a silver compound suspended in gelatin etc. for coating plates or films. □ **emulsive** adj.

en n. a unit of measurement equal to half an em.

enable v.tr. **1** (foll. by to + infin.) give (a person etc.) the means or authority to do something. **2** make possible. **3** esp. Computing make (a device) operational.

enabler n. a person or thing which enables, esp. a person who helps others to achieve their potential or develop skills.

enabling adj. (of legislation) empowering a person or body to take certain action.

enact v.tr. **1 a** establish (a law, legal penalty, etc.). **b** make (a bill etc.) law. **2** play (a part or scene on stage or in life). □ **enaction** n. **enactment** n. **enactor** n.

enamel ● n. **1** a glasslike opaque or semi-transparent coating on metallic or other hard surfaces for ornament or as a preservative lining. **2 a** a smooth hard coating. **b** a paint that dries to give a smooth hard coat. **3** the hard glossy natural coating over the crown of a tooth. **4** painting done in enamel. ● *v.tr.* (**enamelled**, **enamelling**) **1** inlay or encrust (a metal etc.) with enamel. **2** portray (figures etc.) with enamel.

enamour /ɪˈnæmər, e-/ *v.tr.* (also **enamor**) (usu. in *passive*; foll. by *of*) **1** inspire with love or liking. **2** charm, delight.

encamp *v.tr. & intr.* **1** settle in a military camp. **2** lodge in the open in tents.

encampment *n.* **1** a place where troops etc. are encamped. **2** the process of setting up a camp.

encapsulate /enˈkæpsʊˌleɪt, -ˈkæpsjʊ-/ *v.tr.* **1** enclose in or as in a capsule. **2** summarize; express the essential features of. □ **encapsulation** *n.*

encase *v.tr.* **1** put into a case. **2** surround as with a case.

encephalic /ˌensəˈfælɪk, ˌenk-/ *adj.* of or relating to the brain.

encephalitis /enˌsefəˈlaɪtɪs, enˌkef-/ *n.* (*pl.* **-litides** /-ˈlɪtɪdiːz/) inflammation of the brain.

encephalitis lethargica /ləˈθɑːrdʒɪkə/ *n.* an infectious encephalitis caused by a virus, with headache and drowsiness leading to coma.

encephalomyelitis /enˌsefəloˌmaɪəˈlaɪtɪs, enˌkef-/ *n.* inflammation of the brain and spinal cord, esp. due to viral infection.

encephalopathy /enˌsefəˈlɒpəθi, enˌkef-/ *n.* (*pl.* **-ies**) disease of the brain. □ **encephalopathic** *adj.*

enchant *v.tr.* (usu. in *passive*) **1** delight. **2** bewitch. □ **enchantedly** *adv.* **enchanting** *adj.* **enchantingly** *adv.* **enchantment** *n.*

enchanter *n.* a person who enchants, esp. by supposed use of magic. □ **enchantress** *n.*

enchilada /ˌentʃɪˈlɒdə/ *n.* a tortilla with chili sauce and usu. a filling, esp. meat. □ **the whole enchilada** *N Amer.* a thing in its entirety.

encircle *v.tr.* **1** (usu. foll. by *with*) surround, encompass. **2** form a circle around.

encl. *abbr.* **1** enclosed. **2** enclosure.

enclave /ˈɒnkleɪv, ˈen-/ *n.* **1** a portion of territory of one state surrounded by territory of another or others, as viewed by the surrounding territory. **2** a group of people who are culturally, intellectually, or socially distinct from those surrounding them.

enclose *v.tr.* **1 a** surround with a wall, fence, etc. **b** shut in on all sides. **2** fence in (common land) so as to make it private property. **3** put in a receptacle (esp. in an envelope together with a letter). **4** esp. *Math.* bound on all sides; contain. **5** hem in on all sides.

enclosure *n.* **1** the act of enclosing, esp. of common land. **2** an enclosed space or area. **3** a thing enclosed with a letter. **4** an enclosing fence etc.

encode *v.tr.* **1** put (a message etc.) into code or cipher. **2** *Linguistics* convert ideas into linguistic expression (compare DECODE 2). **3** (of a gene or stretch of nucleic acid) specify the genetic code for (a protein or peptide). □ **encoder** *n.*

encomium /enˈkoːmiəm/ *n.* (*pl.* **-s** or **encomia** /-miə/) a formal or high-flown expression of praise.

encompass *v.tr.* **1** surround or form a circle about. **2** contain, include comprehensively.

encore /ˈɒŋkɔr, ˈɒn-/ ● *n.* **1** a call by an audience or spectators for the repetition of an item, or for a further item. **2** such an item. **3** a repetition of an event. ● *interj.* (also /-ˈkɔr/) again, once more.

encounter ● *v.tr.* **1** meet, come across, esp. by chance or unexpectedly. **2** meet as an adversary. ● *n.* **1** a meeting by chance. **2** a meeting in conflict. **3** a

sexual liaison or meeting. **4** an instance of exposure to something, esp. for the first time.

encourage *v.tr.* **1** give courage, confidence, or hope to. **2** (foll. by *to* + infin.) urge, advise. **3** stimulate by help, reward, etc. **4** promote or assist (an enterprise, opinion, etc.). □ **encouragement** *n.* **encourager** *n.* **encouraging** *adj.* **encouragingly** *adv.*

encroach *v.intr.* **1** (foll. by *on*, *upon*) intrude, esp. on another's territory or rights. **2** advance gradually beyond due limits. □ **encroachment** *n.*

encrust *v.* **1** *tr.* cover with a crust. **2** *tr.* overlay with an ornamental crust of precious material.

encrypt *v.tr.* **1** convert (data) into code, esp. to prevent unauthorized access. **2** conceal by this means. □ **encryption** *n.*

encumber *v.tr.* **1** be a burden to. **2** hamper, impede. **3** burden (a person or estate) with debts, esp. mortgages. **4** fill or block (a place).

encumbrance *n.* **1** a burden. **2** an impediment. **3** a mortgage or other charge on property. **4** an annoyance.

encyclical /enˈsɪklɪkəl/ ● *n.* a papal letter addressed to bishops and all members of the Catholic Church. ● *adj.* (of a letter) for wide circulation.

encyclopedia *n.* a book or set of books, usu. arranged alphabetically, giving information on many subjects or on many aspects of one subject.

encyclopedic *adj.* **1** of or resembling an encyclopedia, esp. in embracing all branches of learning. **2** (of knowledge etc.) comprehensive.

end ● *n.* **1 a** the extreme limit or the point beyond which a thing does not continue. **b** either of the two extremities of a line or of the greatest dimension of any object. **c** the furthest, most remote point imaginable (*to the ends of the earth*). **d** a part of a town originally situated on the outskirts (*the North End*). **2** an extreme part of a thing or the surface bounding a thing at either extremity (*put a nail in one end*). **3 a** the conclusion of an action, state, process, etc. (*no end to his misery*). **b** the latter or final part. **c** death, destruction, downfall (*met an untimely end*). **d** a result or outcome. **e** an ultimate state or condition. **4 a** an aim or thing one seeks to attain (*will do anything to achieve his ends*). **b** the purpose or object for which a thing exists. **5** a remnant, fragment, or piece left over. **6** (prec. by *the*) *informal* the limit of endurability. **7** the part or share, esp. of an enterprise or activity, with which a person is concerned (*no problem at my end*). **8** one half or side of a rink, court, or playing field, esp. the part occupied by either of two opposing teams or players. **9** *Curling* one of the frames of a game during which each player on both teams delivers two rocks. **10** *N Amer. Football* **a** the lineman positioned furthest from centre. **b** the position occupied by this player. ● *v.* **1** *tr. & intr.* bring or come to an end. **2** *tr.* conclude, destroy, put an end to, cause to cease. **3** *intr.* (foll. by *in*) lead to, have as a result or conclusion (*will end in tears*). **4** *intr.* (foll. by *by* or *up*) do, achieve, or come eventually to, esp. some specified state (*ended up making a fortune*). **5** *intr.* (of a portion of space, an object, etc.) terminate or have its end or extremity. **6** *tr.* surpass, outdo, (*war to end all wars*). □ **at an end** exhausted or completed. **at the end of one's rope** (or **tether**) having reached the limits of one's patience, resources, abilities, etc. **change ends** *Sport* switch from occupying one half of a rink, field, or court to the other, and change the direction of play. **come to a bad end** meet with ruin or disgrace. **come to an end** cease to exist. **end it** (**all**) *informal* commit suicide. **end of the road 1** the terminus of a road, path, etc. **2** the point at which a hope or endeavour has been abandoned. **end of the world 1** a calamitous matter or situation. **2** the cessation of life on earth. **end-on** with the end facing one, or with the end adjoining the end of the next object. **end to end 1** lengthwise, with the ends in contact. **2** from one end to another. **from end to end** from one end to the other or throughout the length of something. **in the end** finally, ultimately, in the long run. **keep one's end up** do one's part, hold one's own, or sustain one's part in an undertaking or performance, esp. despite difficulties. **make ends meet** live within one's income. **no end** *informal* to a great extent, very much. **no end of** *informal* much or many of (*no end of trouble*). **on end 1** in an upright position. **2** consecutively or continuously (*for three weeks on end*). **put an end to 1** stop (an activity etc.). **2** abolish, destroy.

endanger *v.tr.* **1** place in danger. **2** jeopardize the continuance of (a species etc). □ **endangerment** *n.*

endangered species *n.* **1** a species in danger of extinction, esp. when formally designated as such by a government, environmental protection agency, etc. **2** a category of person, phenomenon, etc., which is in danger of disappearing.

endear *v.tr.* make dear to or beloved by.

endearing *adj.* inspiring or manifesting affection. □ **endearingly** *adv.*

endearment *n.* **1** an expression of love fondness such as a pet name, caress, etc. **2** fondness, affection.

endeavour (also **endeavor**) ● *v.intr.* try earnestly. ● *n.* **1** an undertaking or effort directed to attain an object. **2** an earnest or strenuous attempt.

endemic /en'demɪk, ɪn-, ən-/ ● *adj.* **1** (of a disease, condition, etc.) of common occurrence or habitually present in a certain area as a result of permanent local factors. **2** (of a plant or animal) native and usu. restricted to a certain country or area. ● *n.* an endemic disease, plant, or animal. □ **endemically** *adv.* **endemism** /'endə,mɪzəm/ *n.*

ending *n.* **1** an instance of termination, conclusion, or completion. **2** an end or final part, esp. of a literary work, metrical line, or piece of music. **3** an inflected final part of a word.

endive /'endaɪv/ *n.* **1** N *Amer.* = BELGIAN ENDIVE. **2** a curly-leaved plant, *Cichorium endivia*, used in salads.

endless *adj.* **1** infinite, without end, eternal. **2** continual, incessant. **3** *informal* (of a number, quality, etc.) innumerable, unlimited (*drank endless cups of coffee*). **4** (of a belt, chain, etc.) made in the form of a loop, having the ends joined, for continuous action over wheels etc. □ **endlessly** *adv.* **endlessness** *n.*

end line *n.* **1** *Sport* a boundary line marking the end of the field, court, etc. **2** a line forming a conclusion.

endnote *n.* a note, similar to a footnote, printed at the end of a book, chapter, article, etc.

endocarp /'endo,kɑrp/ *n.* the innermost layer of the pericarp of a fruit, which lines the seed chamber.

endocrine /'endo,krain, -,krɪn/ ● *adj.* **1** (of a gland) secreting directly into the blood. **2** of or pertaining to such glands or their secretions. ● *n.* an endocrine gland, e.g. the thyroid, adrenal, or pituitary gland.

endocrinology /,endo:krɪ'nɒlədʒi/ *n.* the branch of medicine that deals with the structure and physiology of endocrine glands and hormones. □ **endocrinological** *adj.* **endocrinologist** *n.*

end of steel *n.* (also **end of the steel**) N *Amer.* **1** a terminus or the limit to which a railway extends. **2** the farthest extent to which tracks have been laid.

endogenous /en'dɒdʒɪnəs/ *adj.* **1** growing or ori-ginating from within. **2 a** having a cause inside the body or self. **b** not attributable to any external or environmental factor. □ **endogenously** *adv.*

endometriosis /,endo:miː'triˈoːsɪs/ *n.* a condition in which endometrial tissue grows in the pelvic cavity, resulting in pelvic pain and the formation of cysts.

endometrium /,endo:'miːtriəm/ *n.* (*pl.* **-tria**) the mucous membrane lining the uterus. □ **endometrial** *adj.*

endoplasm /'endo:,plæzəm/ *n.* the inner, usu. granular, fluid of the cytoplasm of some cells, e.g. amoebae (*compare* ECTOPLASM 1). □ **endoplasmic** *adj.*

endorphin /en'dɔrfɪn/ *n.* any of a group of peptide neurotransmitters occurring naturally in the brain and having pain-relieving properties.

endorse *v.tr.* **1 a** declare one's approval of (a candidate etc.). **b** confirm (a statement or opinion). **2 a** sign on the back of (a cheque) either as payee or to make (it) payable to someone other than the stated payee. **b** sign (a bill) to accept responsibility for paying it. □ **endorsable** *adj.*

endorsement *n.* **1** (*Cdn* also **endorsation**) **a** the act or an instance of endorsing. **b** approval, acceptance, support. **2** (in full **product endorsement**) a recommendation of a product or service, esp. in exchange for remuneration, which can be cited in advertising material. **3** something with which a document etc. is endorsed, esp. a signature or comment.

endoscope /'endo:,sko:p/ *n.* a flexible instrument, consisting of illuminated optical tubes, for viewing the internal cavities or hollow organs of the body. □ **endoscopic** /-'skɒpɪk/ *adj.* **endoscopically** *adv.* **endoscopist** /en'dɒskəpɪst/ *n.* **endoscopy** /en'dɒskəpi/ *n.*

endoskeleton /'endo:,skelətən/ *n.* an internal skeleton as found in vertebrates. □ **endoskeletal** *adj.*

endosperm /'endo:,spɜrm/ *n.* nutritive material surrounding the germ in some plant seeds.

endothermic /,endo:'θɜrmɪk/ *adj.* **1** occurring or formed with the absorption of heat. **2** dependent on or capable of internal generation of heat.

endotoxin /'endo:tɒksɪn/ *n.* a toxin present inside a bacterial cell and released when the cell disintegrates. □ **endotoxic** *adj.*

endow *v.tr.* **1 a** bequeath or give a permanent income to (a person, institution, etc.). **b** establish (an academic chair, annual prize, etc.) by providing the funds needed to maintain it. **2** enrich, provide, or invest with (a quality, ability, etc.). □ **endowed** *adj.*

endowment *n.* **1** the act or an instance of endowing. **2** assets, esp. property or income, with which a person or body is endowed. **3** (usu. in *pl.*) a skill, talent, etc. with which a person is endowed. **4** (*attrib.*) denoting forms of life insurance involving payment by the insurer of a fixed sum on a specified date or on the death of the insured person, whichever is earlier.

endpaper *n.* a usu. blank leaf of paper at the beginning and end of a book, fixed to the inside cover.

end point *n.* **1** a point at the end of a line. **2** the final stage of a process.

end product *n.* the final product, esp. of a manufacturing process, radioactive decay series, etc.

end result *n.* the final outcome.

end run *n.* N *Amer.* **1** *Football* an attempt by a player to run with the ball round the flank of his own team. **2** an evasive tactic, esp. in war or politics.

end table *n.* a small, low table usu. placed at an end of a couch, beside a chair, etc.

endue /ɪn'djuː, en-, ən-/ *v.tr.* (foll. by *with*) invest or provide (a person) with qualities, powers, etc.

endurance *n.* **1** the fact, habit, or power of enduring something unpleasant (*beyond endurance*). **2 a** the ability of a person or thing to last, hold out, or withstand prolonged strain (*endurance test*). **b** the ability of a metal or other substance to withstand the repeated applications of stress. **3** the act of enduring. **4** a thing which is endured.

endure *v.* **1** *tr.* **a** (of a person) undergo (a difficulty, hardship, etc.), esp. without giving way. **b** (of a thing) withstand (strain, pressure, etc.) without being damaged, compromised, etc. **2** *tr.* **a** tolerate (a person) (*cannot endure him*). **b** (esp. with *neg.*; foll. by *to* + infin.) bear. **3** *intr.* remain in existence, last, persist. **4** *tr.* submit to, experience without resisting. □ **endurability** *n.* **endurable** *adj.* **enduring** *adj.* **enduringly** *adv.*

end-user *n.* (often *attrib.*) **1** the person etc. who is the intended ultimate recipient or user of a product. **2** *Computing* the final destination of information transferred within a system, e.g. an operator, program, etc.

endways *adv.* (also **endwise**) **1** with its end uppermost, foremost, or towards the viewer. **2** end to end. **3** lengthwise.

end zone *n.* *N Amer.* *Football* the rectangular area between the goal line and the end line at the end of the field into which the ball must be carried or passed to score a touchdown.

ENE *abbr.* east-northeast.

enema /'enɪmə/ *n.* (*pl.* **-s**) **1** the injection of liquid or gas into the rectum or colon, esp. to expel the contents. **2** a fluid so injected. **3** a syringe or other appliance used for this purpose.

enemy *n.* (*pl.* **-ies**) **1 a** a person or group actively nursing hatred for or seeking to harm another person, group, or cause. **b** (usu. foll. by *of*, *to*) an adversary or opponent. **2 a** an armed foe, esp. another nation. **b** the hostile army or military force of a nation opposing or at war with one's own. **c** a member of such a force. **d** a hostile ship, aircraft, etc. **3** a thing that harms, injures, or is prejudicial to another. **4** (*attrib.*) of or belonging to an enemy. □ **be one's own worst enemy** have the habit of bringing trouble upon oneself by one's own actions or behaviour.

energetic *adj.* **1** having much energy or being strenuously active. **2** forcible, vigorous. **3** powerfully operative or effective. □ **energetically** *adv.*

energize *v.tr.* **1** infuse energy or vigour into (a person, work, movement, etc.). **2** provide energy for the operation of (a device), esp. by means of an electrical current. □ **energized** *adj.* **energizer** *n.*

energy *n.* (*pl.* **-ies**) **1 a** a person's force, vigour, or capacity for and tendency to strenuous activity. **b** force or vigour of expression. **2** (in *pl.*) individual powers in use (*devote your energies to this*). **3** *Physics* **a** the quantity of work a system is capable of doing, usu. measured in joules. **b** this ability provided in a readily utilized form, such as an electric current or piped gas. **c** resources that can be drawn on for this purpose. **4** a latent capacity to produce an effect.

enervate /'enərˌveɪt/ *v.tr.* deprive of vigour, vitality, or strength, mentally, morally, or physically. □ **enervating** *adj.* **enervation** *n.*

enfant terrible /ˌɑ̃fɑ̃ teˈriːbl/ *n.* (*pl.* **enfants terribles** *pronunc.* same) a person whose behaviour, ideas, etc. annoy, shock, or embarrass those with more conventional attitudes or opinions.

enfeeble *v.tr.* weaken, make feeble. □ **enfeebled** *adj.*

enfold *v.tr.* **1** (usu. foll. by *in*, *with*) wrap up, envelop, or enclose. **2** clasp, embrace, encompass, or encircle.

enforce *v.tr.* **1** compel performance or observance of (a law etc.). **2** (foll. by *on*, *upon*) produce or impose (an action, conduct, one's will) by force. **3** urge, press home, or persist in (a demand or argument). □ **enforceable** *adj.* **enforceability** *n.*

enforcement *n.* the act or an instance of enforcing, esp. the process of compelling observance of a law, regulation, etc.

enforcer *n.* **1** a person, organization, etc. that enforces something. **2** *N Amer.* *Hockey* a highly aggressive player whose fighting and intimidation skills serve to protect other players on his team. **3** *slang* a person who imposes his will on others by violence and intimidation, esp. as a member of a criminal group.

enfranchise /ɪnˈfræntʃaɪz, en-, ən-/ *v.* **1** *tr.* grant (a person) the rights of a citizen, esp. the right to vote. **2** *intr.* *Cdn* give up one's status as an Indian. □ **enfranchisement** *n.*

Eng. *abbr.* **1 a** English. **b** England. **2 a** Engineering. **b** Engineer.

engage *v.* **1** *tr.* arrange to employ or hire (a person). **2** *tr.* **a** (usu. in *passive*) be occupied or have a social or business engagement arranged (*sorry, I'm otherwise engaged tomorrow*). **b** attract and hold fast (a person's attention, interest, etc.). **c** draw into a conversation. **3 a** *tr.* (usu. foll. by *to* + infin.) bind by a legal or moral obligation, esp. by promise or contract. **b** *intr.* (foll. by *that* + clause or *to* + infin.) enter into a contract or pledge oneself. **4** *tr.* book, reserve, or secure for one's own use (a room, seat, etc.). **5 a** *tr.* bring (a component) into operation (*engage the clutch*). **b** *tr. & intr.* (usu. foll. by *with*) (of parts of a machine etc.) interlock or fit together to prevent or transmit movement. **c** *tr.* cause (gears, cogs, etc.) to do this. **6 a** *tr.* enter into combat with or attack (an enemy etc.). **b** *tr.* bring (forces) into battle. **c** *intr.* (usu. foll. by *with*) (of troops etc.) come into combat. **7** *intr.* take part in or be occupied by (a thing).

engagé /ɑ̃ˈɡæʒeɪ / ● *adj.* (of a writer, artist, etc.) showing social, moral, or political commitment. ● *n.* *Cdn hist.* (also **engage**) a boatman, originally usu. French-Canadian, hired by a trader, explorer, or fur company to work the inland trade.

engaged *adj.* **1** under a promise to marry. **2** (of a person) occupied, busy. **3** concerned, committed, actively participating in issues etc. (*an engaged, professional historian*). **4** (of gears etc.) in operation. **5** (of a baby's head) descended into the mother's pelvic area in the final weeks of pregnancy.

engagement *n.* **1** the act or state of engaging or being engaged. **2** an appointment with another person. **3** a betrothal. **4** an encounter between hostile forces. **5** a moral commitment or obligation. **6** a period or position of employment, esp. for a set term. **7** the period during which a theatrical performance is being produced at a given location.

engagement ring *n.* a usu. diamond ring given by a man to a woman when they promise to marry.

engaging *adj.* pleasing, attractive, charming. □ **engagingly** *adv.* **engagingness** *n.*

Engelmann spruce *n.* a spruce of the Rocky Mountains, *Picea engelmannii*.

engender *v.tr.* **1** give rise to; bring about (a feeling etc.). **2** beget or produce.

engine *n.* **1** a machine for producing energy of motion from some other form of energy, esp. heat that the machine itself generates. **2 a** a railway locomotive. **b** = FIRE ENGINE. **c** a stationary steam engine. **3** (foll. by *of*) a thing that is an agent or instrument of a desired end or achievement (*the engine of progress*). □ **engined** *adj.* (also in *comb.*).

engine block *n.* *N Amer.* the metal casting housing the cylinders etc. of an internal combustion engine.

engineer ● *n.* **1** a person qualified in any branch of engineering, esp. as a qualified professional. **2** = CIVIL ENGINEER. **3 a** a person who designs or makes engines. **b** a technician, mechanic, or other person who is in charge of or maintains an engine or other machine. **4** *N Amer.* a person who drives an engine, esp. a railway locomotive. **5** a soldier in a division of an army that specializes in engineering and the design as well as construction of military works. **6** (foll. by *of*) a skilful or artful plotter. ● *v.* **1** *tr.* arrange, contrive, or bring about, esp. artfully. **2** *tr.* design, make, or build as an engineer. **3** *tr.* deliberately alter or modify some specific aspect of a particular model, substance, etc., e.g. genes.

engineering *n.* **1** the application of science for directly useful purposes, as construction, propulsion, communication, or manufacture. **2** the work done by or the occupation of an engineer. **3** the action of working artfully to bring something about. **4** a field of study or activity concerned with deliberate alteration or modification in some particular area (*genetic engineering*).

engine room *n.* a room containing engines, esp. a ship's engines.

English ● *adj.* **1** of or relating to England, its language, its people, or their descendants. **2** *Cdn* of or relating to English-speaking Canadians. ● *n.* **1** the language descended from that of the Germanic invaders of England in the 5th c. and now used in many varieties in the British Isles, Canada and other Commonwealth countries, the US, and often internationally. **2** (prec. by *the*; treated as *pl.*) **a** the people of England. **b** English-speaking people. **3** English language or literature as a subject to be studied. □ **Englishness** *n.*

English Canada *n.* *Cdn* the areas of Canada where English-speaking Canadians predominate, as distinct from French Canada and esp. Quebec.

English Canadian ● *n.* **1** an English-speaking Canadian. **2** a Canadian of English descent. ● *adj.* (**English-Canadian**) of, by, or pertaining to English Canada or English Canadians.

English cucumber *n.* *N Amer.* a long, thin-skinned, seedless variety of cucumber.

English ivy *n.* an ivy with many cultivated varieties, *Hedera helix*, grown both in gardens as climbers and ground cover and as houseplants.

Englishman *n.* (*pl.* **-men**) a man who is English by birth, descent, or naturalization.

English muffin *n.* *N Amer.* a small, round, flat, yeast bread, usu. served split and toasted.

English walnut *n.* the common walnut tree, *Juglans regia*, native to Europe and Asia.

Englishwoman *n.* (*pl.* **-women**) a woman who is English by birth, descent, or naturalization.

engorge *v.tr.* **1** (in *passive*) be filled to excess. **2** *Med.* be congested with fluid, esp. with blood. **3** devour greedily or swallow up. □ **engorged** *adj.*

engrain *var. of* INGRAIN.

engrained *var. of* INGRAINED.

engrave *v.tr.* **1** inscribe, cut, or carve (a text or design) on a hard surface. **2** inscribe or ornament (a surface) with incised marks. **3 a** cut or produce (a design) for printing by removing parts of the surface of a plate or block. **b** produce (a representation of such a picture, lettering, etc.) from such a surface. **4** impress deeply or indelibly on a person's memory etc. □ **engraved** *adj.* **engraver** *n.*

engraving *n.* **1** a print made from an engraved plate. **2** the process or art of cutting a design etc. on metal, stone, etc. **3** an engraved design or inscription.

engross *v.tr.* **1** (of an object of thought or feeling) fully occupy (the mind, affections, etc.). **2** (usu. in *passive*; usu. foll. by *with*) absorb the whole attention of (a person). □ **engrossing** *adj.* (in sense 1). **engrossment** *n.*

engulf *v.tr.* **1** flow over and swamp or swallow up as in a gulf, abyss, etc. **2** overwhelm, engross, or affect powerfully. □ **engulfment** *n.*

enhance *v.tr.* **1 a** heighten or intensify (qualities, powers, value, etc.). **b** exaggerate or make (a colour etc.) appear greater or brighter, esp. by contrast. **c** raise (a price) or increase (a cost). **2 a** improve (a thing), esp. in quality or utility. **b** add on to or provide (a computer etc.) with more advanced or sophisticated features. □ **enhancement** *n.* **enhancer** *n.*

enigma /ɪ'nɪgmə, en-, ən-/ *n.* **1 a** a puzzling or unexplained thing. **b** a person who baffles others' conjecture as to his or her character, identity, etc. **2** a riddle or paradox, usu. involving metaphor. □ **enigmatic** /,enɪg'mætɪk/ *adj.* **enigmatical** *adj.* **enigmatically** *adv.*

enjoin *v.tr.* **1** (foll. by *to* + infin.) command, order, or call upon (a person). **2** (often foll. by *on*) impose or prescribe (an action or conduct). **3** *Law* (usu. foll. by *from*) prohibit or restrain (a person) by an injunction.

enjoy *v.* **1** *tr.* take delight or pleasure in. **2** *tr.* have the use or benefit of (something pleasant or advantageous). **3** *tr.* experience (*enjoy good health*). **4** *intr.* esp. *N Amer.* have an enjoyable experience. □ **enjoy oneself** experience pleasure. □ **enjoyable** *adj.* **enjoyableness** *n.* **enjoyably** *adv.* **enjoyment** *n.*

enlarge *v.* **1 a** *tr. & intr.* make or become larger or wider. **b** *tr.* make more comprehensive or increase in range or scope. **2 a** *tr.* describe in greater detail. **b** *intr.* (usu. foll. by *upon*) write or speak at great length or in detail. **3** *tr.* produce an enlargement of (a photographic negative). □ **enlarged** *adj.*

enlargement *n.* **1 a** an act or instance of increasing in size, extent, or scope. **b** the state of being enlarged. **2** *Photog.* a print that is larger than the negative from which it is produced.

enlarger *n.* an apparatus for producing photographic enlargements.

enlighten *v.tr.* **1** (often foll. by *on*) instruct or inform (about a subject). **2** free from prejudice or superstition. **3** give spiritual knowledge or insight to (a person). □ **enlightened** *adj.* **enlightening** *adj.*

enlightenment *n.* **1 a** the act or an instance of enlightening. **b** the state of being enlightened. **2** (**the Enlightenment**) the 18th-c. philosophical movement in Europe in which reason and individualism were emphasized at the expense of tradition. **3** *Buddhism* a state of pure and unqualified knowledge and intuitive insight.

enlist *v.* **1** *intr. & tr.* enrol in the armed forces. **2** *tr.* engage or secure (a person etc.) as a means of help or support. □ **enlistment** *n.*

enliven *v.tr.* **1** animate, invigorate, give fuller life or spirit to. **2** make cheerful or relieve the monotony or dreariness of (a picture etc.). □ **enlivening** *adj.*

en masse /ɑ̃ 'mæs/ *adv.* all together or as a group.

enmesh *v.tr.* catch or entangle in or as in a net.

enmity /'enmɪti/ *n.* (*pl.* **-ies**) **1** the condition of being an enemy or a state of mutual hostility. **2** a feeling of hostility, hatred, or ill-will.

ennoble *v.tr.* **1** refine, dignify, or elevate in nature, character etc. **2** give the rank of noble to (a person). □ **ennoblement** *n.* **ennobling** *adj.*

ennui / ɒˈnwiː / *n.* boredom or mental weariness from lack of occupation or interest.

enology *N Amer. var. of* OENOLOGY.

enormity *n.* (*pl.* **-ies**) **1** monstrous wickedness (*recognized the enormity of his crime*). **2** an act of extreme wickedness. **3** *disputed* great size, enormousness, or daunting magnitude. ¶Though regarded as incorrect by many people, this use of *enormity* is well established and has been in continuous use since the 18th c. **4** a serious irregularity or a gross error.

enormous *adj.* huge, very great, excessive in size or intensity. □ **enormously** *adv.* **enormousness** *n.*

enough ● *adj.* as much or as many as required. ● *n.* as much as is needed or that which is sufficient. ● *adv.* **1** sufficiently, adequately, or to the required degree (*are you warm enough?*). **2** fairly, tolerably, or passably (*she sings well enough*). **3** very, fully, quite (*oddly enough*). ● *interj.* that is enough (in various senses, esp. to put an end to an action, thing said, etc.). □ **enough is enough** stop, no more. **enough said** no more need be said. **have enough to do** (**to achieve something**) have no easy task. **have had enough of** be satiated with, tired of, or want no more of.

enquire *var. of* INQUIRE.

enquiry *var. of* INQUIRY.

enrage *v.tr.* (often foll. by *at, by, with*) make furious or very angry. □ **enraged** *adj.*

enrapture *v.tr.* entrance, delight intensely, or inspire with poetic fervour.

enrich *v.tr.* **1 a** make wealthy or wealthier. **b** endow with mental or spiritual wealth. **2 a** enhance, heighten or make (a thing) richer in quality, colour, flavour, etc. **b** fertilize or make (soil or land) more productive. **c** improve the nutritive quality of (food) by adding vitamins etc. **3** add something valuable or worthwhile to the contents of (a collection, book, etc.). **4** *N Amer.* make (a course or program of study) more challenging, esp. by adding coursework etc., which is not part of the standard curriculum. **5** increase the proportion of a particular constituent in (a substance), esp. enrich uranium with isotope U-235. □ **enriched** *adj.* **enriching** *adj.* **enrichment** *n.*

enrol *v.* (also **enroll**) (**enrolled, enrolling**) **1** *intr.* **a** enter one's name on a list or register, esp. as a commitment to membership of a society, class, etc. **b** join, esp. as a member, student, etc. **2** *tr.* **a** write the name of (a person) on a list for membership etc. **b** (usu. foll. by *in*) incorporate (a person) as a member of a society etc. □ **enrollee** *n.*

enrolment *n.* (also **enrollment**) **1 a** the act or an instance of enrolling. **b** the state of being enrolled. **2** *N Amer.* the number of persons enrolled, esp. at a school, university, etc.

en route / ɑ̃ ˈruːt / *adv.* on or along the way.

ensconce / ɪnˈskɒns, en-, ən-/ *v.tr.* (usu. *refl.* or in *passive*) establish or settle comfortably or safely.

ensemble / ɒnˈsɒmbəl / *n.* **1 a** a thing viewed as the sum of its parts. **b** the general effect of this. **2** an outfit or a set of clothes that harmonizes and is worn together. **3** a group of actors, dancers, etc. who perform together in a production, esp. the supporting members as opposed to the stars or principals. **4 a** a group of singers or musicians, esp. a small group of soloists, who perform together. **b** a piece of music sung or played by the whole group of musicians rather than by soloists. **c** the manner in which this is performed.

enshrine *v.tr.* **1** enclose in or as in a shrine. **2** integrate (a right, principle, etc.) into a law, constitution, etc. so as to preserve it perpetually. **3** contain or embody in a way that preserves, protects, or cherishes. □ **enshrinement** *n.*

ensign /ˈensain, -sən/ *n.* **1** a military or naval standard, esp. a flag flown at the stern of a vessel to show its nationality. **2** each of three such standards with the union flag in the corner (*see also* RED ENSIGN).

ensilage /ˈensilidʒ, ˈɪn-/ *n.* **1** the process of preserving green crops in a silo or pit without having dried them. **2** the material resulting from this.

enslave *v.tr.* **1** make (a person) completely subject to or dominated by habit, superstition, passion, etc. **2** reduce (a person) to slavery or deprive (a person) of political freedom. □ **enslavement** *n.*

ensnare *v.tr.* entrap, entangle in difficulties, or catch in or as in a snare.

ensue *v.intr.* **1** be subsequent or happen afterwards. **2** occur as a result or consequence. □ **ensuing** *adj.*

ensuite /ɑ̃ˈswiːt/ *Cdn & Brit.* ● *adv.* forming a single unit, with one room leading into another. ● *adj.* (of a room) immediately adjoining or forming part of the same set. ● *n.* an ensuite room, esp. a bathroom.

ensure *v.tr.* **1** (often foll. by *that* + clause) make certain the occurrence of (an event, situation, outcome, etc.). **2** (usu. foll. by *to, for*) secure (a thing for a person etc.). **3** (usu. foll. by *against*) make safe from a risk etc. **4** esp. *N Amer.* = INSURE 1-3.

ENT *abbr. Med.* ear, nose, and throat.

entablature /ɪnˈtæblətʃər, en-/ *n.* the upper part of a classical building supported by columns etc.

entail *v.tr.* **1** necessitate as a consequence, have as an inevitable accompaniment, or involve unavoidably (*entails much effort*). **2** *Law* bequeath (property etc.) so that it remains within a family. □ **entailment** *n.*

entangle *v.tr.* **1** cause to get caught in something that is tangled or that impedes movement or extrication. **2** interlace or cause to become tangled so that separation is difficult. **3 a** involve (a person) in difficulties, doubtful undertakings, etc. **b** involve (a person) in a compromising relationship etc. **4** make (a thing) tangled, complicated, or intricate.

entanglement *n.* **1** the act or condition of entangling or being entangled. **2 a** a thing that entangles. **b** a complication or embarrassment. **3** an extensive barrier, esp. one made of stakes and interlaced barbed wire, designed to obstruct an enemy's movements. **4** a compromising, esp. amorous, relationship.

entente /ɒnˈtɒnt/ *n.* **1** = ENTENTE CORDIALE. **2** a group of nations in such a relation. **3** an agreement to co-operate between esp. opposing parties.

entente cordiale /ɑ̃ˌtɑ̃t kɔrdiˈæl/ *n.* (*pl.* **ententes cordiales**) a friendly understanding between nations.

enter ● *v.* **1 a** *intr.* (often foll. by *into*) go or come in. **b** *tr.* go or come into (a place etc.). **c** *tr.* come or pass into (a certain condition). **2** *tr.* **a** pierce, penetrate, or go through (*a bullet entered his chest*). **b** (of a male) have sexual intercourse with. **3** *tr.* **a** write or record (particulars) in a list, register, account book, etc. **b** input (data) into a computer or issue (a command) to a computer program. **4 a** *intr.* register or announce oneself as a competitor. **b** *tr.* become a competitor in (an event). **c** *tr.* submit (an animal etc.) for judging in a competition. **5** *tr.* **a** enrol as or become a member of (a society, school, etc.). **b** procure admission into a society etc. for (a person). **6** *tr.* introduce, make known, or present (a matter etc.) for consideration (*entered a* *protest*). **7** *tr.* put into an official record, esp. record in due form in a court of law, deliberative body, etc. **8** *intr.* (foll. by *into*) **a** engage in (conversation, relations, an undertaking, etc.). **b** subscribe to or bind oneself by (an agreement etc.). **c** form part of (one's calculations, plans, etc.). **9** *intr.* (foll. by *on*, *upon*) **a** begin, undertake, or begin to deal with (a subject). **b** assume the functions of (an office). **10** *intr.* come on stage (as a direction: *enter Macbeth*). • *n.* the key on a computer keyboard or button on a computer window which when pressed or clicked instructs the computer to execute a command or enters a blank line into a text. □ **enterer** *n.*

enteric /en'terik/ • *adj.* of or occurring in the intestines. • *n.* (in full **enteric fever**) typhoid fever.

enteritis /entə'raitıs/ *n.* inflammation of the small intestine, often causing diarrhea.

enterprise *n.* **1** an undertaking, esp. a bold or difficult one. **2** (as a personal attribute) readiness to engage in such undertakings (*discouraged individual enterprise*). **3** a business. **4** businesses collectively. **5** activity undertaken with an economic or commercial end in view. □ **enterpriser** *n.*

enterprising *adj.* **1** ready to engage in enterprises. **2** imaginative, energetic. □ **enterprisingly** *adv.*

entertain *v.* **1** *tr.* amuse; occupy agreeably. **2 a** *tr.* receive or treat as a guest. **b** *intr.* receive guests (*they entertain a great deal*). **3** *tr.* give attention or consideration to (an idea, feeling, or proposal).

entertainer *n.* a person who entertains, esp. professionally on stage etc.

entertaining *adj.* amusing. □ **entertainingly** *adv.*

entertainment *n.* **1** the act or an instance of entertaining; the process of being entertained. **2** a public performance or show. **3** diversions or amusements for guests etc. **4** amusement (*much to my entertainment*). **5** hospitality.

entertainment centre *n.* **1 a** a combination of components such as a television, VCR, stereo console, etc. **b** a large shelving unit to hold these. **2** a place offering entertainment.

enthrall *v.tr.* (also **enthral**) (**-thralled**, **-thralling**) **1** captivate. **2** enslave. □ **enthralling** *adj.*

enthrone *v.tr.* (usu. in *passive*) **1** install (a king, bishop, etc.) on a throne, esp. ceremonially. **2** exalt. □ **enthronement** *n.*

enthuse *v.intr. & tr. informal* **1** be or make enthusiastic. **2** (often foll. by *about*) speak enthusiastically.

enthusiasm *n.* **1 a** strong interest or admiration. **b** great eagerness. **2** an object of enthusiasm. □ **enthusiast** *n.* **enthusiastic** *adj.* **enthusiastically** *adv.*

entice /ın'təis, en-, ən-/ *v.tr.* (often foll. by *from*, *into*, or *to* + infin.) attract by the offer of pleasure or reward. □ **enticement** *n.* **enticing** *adj.* **enticingly** *adv.*

entire *attrib.adj.* **1** whole, complete. **2** not broken or decayed. **3** unqualified, absolute (*an entire success*). **4** in one piece; continuous.

entirely *adv.* **1** wholly, completely (*entirely exhausted*). **2** solely, exclusively (*entirely for my benefit*).

entirety /ın'tairəti, ın'tairti, en-, ən-/ *n.* (pl. **-ies**) **1** completeness. **2** (usu. foll. by *of*) the sum total. □ **in its entirety** in its complete form; completely.

entitle *v.tr.* **1** give (a person etc.) a just claim or right. **2** give (a book etc.) the title of.

entitlement *n.* **1** something to which a person is entitled, esp. a social benefit. **2** the fact of being entitled or qualified.

entity /'entıti/ *n.* (pl. **-ies**) **1** a thing with distinct

existence, as opposed to a quality or relation. **2** a thing's existence regarded distinctly.

entomb *v.tr.* **1** place in or as in a tomb. **2** serve as a tomb for. □ **entombment** *n.*

entomology /entə'mɒlədʒi/ *n.* the study of the forms and behaviour of insects. □ **entomological** *adj.* **entomologist** *n.*

entourage /ˌɒntʊ'rɒʒ/ *n.* **1** people attending an esp. important person. **2** surroundings.

entr'acte /'ɒntrækt/ *n.* **1** an interval between two acts of a play. **2** a piece of music or a dance performed during this.

entrails /'entreilz/ *n.pl.* **1** the intestines of a person or animal. **2** the internal organs. **3** the innermost parts.

entrain[1] *v.tr.* **1** (of a fluid) carry (particles etc.) along in its flow. **2** incorporate or trap (air) in concrete etc. **3** bring on as a consequence. □ **entrainment** *n.*

entrain[2] *v.* **1** *intr.* go on board a train. **2** *tr.* put (a person or thing) on board a train.

entrance[1] /'entrəns/ *n.* **1** the act or an instance of coming or going in. **2 a** a door, passage, etc., by which one enters. **b** a point of entering something (*the entrance to the harbour*). **3** the right or privilege of admission (also *attrib.: university entrance exam*). **4** the moment, or point in the script, when an actor, dancer, etc. comes on stage. **5** *Music* = ENTRY 8.

entrance[2] /ın'træns/ *v.tr.* (usu. in *passive*) **1** enchant, delight. **2** put into a trance. **3** (often foll. by *with*) overwhelm with strong feeling. □ **entrancement** *n.* **entrancing** *adj.* **entrancingly** *adv.*

entranceway *n.* a passage or hallway at the entrance to a building etc.

entrant *n.* **1** a person who enters a competition; a candidate in an examination etc. **2** a person who enters a school, profession, etc. or becomes a member of an organization etc. **3** a company, product, etc. which enters a new market, field, etc.

entrap *v.tr.* (**entrapped**, **entrapping**) **1** catch in or as in a trap. **2** (often foll. by *into* + verbal noun) beguile or trick (a person).

entrapment *n.* **1** the act or an instance of entrapping; the process of being entrapped. **2** *Law* inducement to commit a crime, esp. by the authorities to secure a prosecution.

entreat *v.tr.* **1** (foll. by *to* + infin.) ask (a person) earnestly. **2** ask earnestly for (a thing).

entreaty *n.* (pl. **-ies**) an earnest plea; a supplication.

entree /'ɒntrei, 'ɑ:trei/ *n.* **1** esp. *N Amer.* the main dish of a meal. **2** the right or privilege of admission, esp. to an exclusive group.

entrench *v.* **1** *tr.* establish firmly (in a defensible position, in office, etc.). **2** *tr.* surround (a post, army, town, etc.) with a trench as a fortification. **3** *tr.* safeguard (rights etc.) by constitutional provision; provide for the legal or political perpetuation of. **4** *intr.* entrench oneself. **5** *intr.* (foll. by *upon*) encroach, trespass. □ **entrench oneself** adopt a well-defended position. □ **entrenchment** *n.*

entrenched *adj.* (of an attitude etc.) not easily modified.

entrepreneur /ˌɒntrəprə'nɜr/ *n.* a person who starts or organizes a commercial enterprise, esp. one involving financial risk. □ **entrepreneurial** /-'nɜriəl, -'njʊriəl/ *adj.* **entrepreneurialism** *n.* (also **entrepreneurism**). **entrepreneurship** *n.*

entropy /'entrəpi/ *n.* **1** *Physics* a measure of the unavailability of a system's thermal energy for conversion into mechanical work. Symbol: **S**. **2** *Physics* a measure of the disorganization or degradation of the universe. **3** a measure of the rate of transfer of information in a message etc. □ **entropic** /-'trɒpɪk/ adj. **entropically** adv.

entrust v.tr. **1** give responsibility for (a person or a thing) to a person in whom one has confidence. **2** assign responsibility for a thing to (a person).

entry n. (pl. **-ies**) **1** the act or an instance of coming or going in. **2** a place of entrance; a door, gate, etc. **3** liberty to go or come in. **4** an actor's entrance on stage. **5** an item entered in a diary, list, account book, etc. **6 a** a word, phrase, abbreviation, etc. entered in a dictionary, encyclopedia, etc. **b** this and its accompanying definition or explanation. **7 a** a person or thing competing in a race, contest, etc. **b** a list of competitors. **8** the start or resumption of a performer's part in a musical composition. **9** the act of entering (data etc.) into a file, database, etc.

entry draft n. N Amer. a draft of players, esp. juniors, whose rights are not owned by any team.

entry form n. an application form for a competition.

entry-level attrib.adj. **1** N Amer. (of employment) suitable for inexperienced applicants. **2** relatively unsophisticated and low in cost (entry-level computers).

entryway N Amer. = ENTRANCEWAY.

entwine v.tr. **1** twine together (a thing with or around another). **2** interweave.

enumerate /ɪ'nju:mə,reit, ɪ'nu:-/ v. **1** tr. specify (items); mention one by one. **2** Cdn **a** tr. enter (a person's name) on a list of voters for an election. **b** tr. prepare the voters list for (an area), usu. by conducting a house-to-house survey. **c** intr. conduct such a survey. **3** tr. count; establish the number of. □ **enumeration** n. **enumerative** adj.

enumerator n. **1** a person who enumerates. **2** a person employed in census taking. **3** Cdn a person employed to conduct a survey to register voters.

enunciate /ɪ'nʌnsi,eit/ v. **1** tr. & intr. pronounce (words) clearly. **2** tr. express (a proposition or theory) in definite terms. **3** tr. proclaim. □ **enunciation** n. **enunciative** /-siətɪv/ adj.

envelop /ɪn'veləp/ v.tr. (**enveloped, enveloping**) **1** (often foll. by in) **a** wrap up or cover completely. **b** make obscure; conceal (was enveloped in mystery). **2** Military completely surround (an enemy).

envelope /'envə,ləʊp, 'ɒn-/ n. **1** a folded paper container, usu. with a sealable flap, for a letter etc. **2** a wrapper or covering. **3** the structure within a balloon or airship containing the gas. **4** Bot. any enveloping structure esp. the calyx or corolla (or both). □ **push** (or **push the edge of**) **the envelope** N Amer. go to the greatest length that an activity allows.

enviable /'enviəbəl/ adj. (of a person or thing) exciting or likely to excite envy. □ **enviably** adv.

envious /'enviəs/ adj. (often foll. by of) feeling or showing envy. □ **enviously** adv.

environ /ɪn'vairən, en-, ən-/ v.tr. encircle, surround (esp. hostilely or protectively).

environment n. **1** the physical surroundings, conditions, circumstances, etc., in which a person lives, works, etc. (a smoke-free work environment). **2** the area surrounding a place. **3 a** external conditions as affecting plant and animal life. **b** (usu. **the environment**) the totality of the physical conditions on the earth or a part of it, esp. as affected by human activity. **4** Computing the overall structure within which a user, computer, or program operates. **5** a large artistic creation intended to be experienced with several senses while one is surrounded by it. □ **environmental** adj. **environmentally** adv.

environmentalist n. **1** a person who is concerned with or advocates the protection of the environment.

2 a person who considers that environment has the primary influence on the development of a person or group. □ **environmentalism** n.

environmentally friendly adj. (also **environment-friendly**) not harmful to the environment.

environs /ɪn'vairənz, 'envirənz/ n.pl. a surrounding district, esp. around an urban area.

envisage /ɪn'vɪzədʒ, en-, ən-/ v.tr. **1** have a mental picture of (a thing or conditions not yet existing). **2** contemplate or conceive, esp. as possible or desirable.

envision v.tr. envisage, visualize.

envoy /'ɒnvɔi, 'en-/ n. a messenger or representative, esp. on a diplomatic mission.

envy ● n. (pl. **-ies**) **1** a feeling of discontented or resentful longing aroused by another's better fortune etc. **2** the object or ground of this feeling (their house is the envy of the neighbourhood). ● v.tr. (**-ies, -ied**) feel envy of (a person, circumstances, etc.).

enzyme /'enzaɪm/ n. a protein produced by living cells and functioning as a catalyst in a specific biochemical reaction. □ **enzymatic** adj. **enzymatically** adv. **enzymology** n.

Eocene /'i:o,si:n/ ● adj. of or denoting the second epoch of the Tertiary period, between the Paleocene and the Oligocene, lasting from about 54.9 to 38 million years BP. ● n. this epoch or system.

eon /'i:ɒn/ n. **1** a very long or indefinite period. **2** Astronomy a billion years. **3** the largest division of geological time, composed of two or more eras.

eosin /'i:o:sɪn/ n. a red fluorescent dye used esp. as a stain in optical microscopy.

EP abbr. **1** (used of the speed of a videotape) extended play, allowing six hours of material to be recorded on a standard tape. **2** electroplate. **3** N Amer. EUROPEAN PLAN. **4** extreme pressure (used in grading lubricants).

EPA abbr. US Environmental Protection Agency.

eparchy n. (pl. **-ies**) a diocese in an Eastern-Rite church.

epaulette /,epə'let, 'epə,let/ n. (also **epaulet**) a decoration on the shoulder of a coat etc., esp. on a uniform.

épée /ei'pei/ n. Fencing a sharp-pointed duelling sword, often used with the end blunted. □ **épéeist** n.

ephedra /ɪ'fedrə/ n. an evergreen shrub with trailing stems and scalelike leaves.

ephedrine /'efədrɪn/ n. an alkaloid drug found in some ephedras, causing constriction of the blood vessels and widening of the bronchial passages, used to relieve asthma, hay fever, colds, etc.

ephemera /ɪ'femərə, ɪ'fi:m-/ n. (pl. **-s** or **ephemerae** /-,ri:/) **1** a winged insect of the genus Ephemera or the order Ephemeroptera, a mayfly. **2** = EPHEMERON.

ephemeral adj. **1** lasting or of use for only a short time; transitory. **2** lasting only a day. **3** (of an insect, flower, etc.) lasting a day or a few days.

ephemeron /ɪ'femərən, ɪ'fi:m-/ n. **1** (pl. **ephemera** /-rə/) (usu. in pl.) **a** a thing (esp. a printed item) of short-lived interest or usefulness. **b** a short-lived thing. **2** (pl. **-s**) = EPHEMERA 1.

epic ● n. **1** a long poem narrating the adventures or deeds of one or more heroic or legendary figures. **2** an imaginative work of any form, embodying a nation's conception of its past history. **3** a book or film based on an epic narrative or heroic in type or scale. **4** a subject fit for recital in an epic. ● adj. **1** of or like an epic. **2** grand, heroic. **3** impressive in scope, grandeur, etc. □ **epical** adj. **epically** adv.

epicentre /'epɪ,sentər/ n. (also esp. US **epicenter**) **1**

Geol. the point at which an earthquake reaches the earth's surface. **2** the centre or heart of something.

epicure /ˈepɪˌkjʊər/ *n.* a person with refined tastes, esp. in food and drink. ☐ **epicurism** *n.*

epicurean /ˌepɪkjʊˈriːən/ ● *n.* **1** = EPICURE. **2** (**Epicurean**) a disciple or student of the Greek philosopher Epicurus (341–270 BC). ● *adj.* **1** characteristic of an epicure. **2** (**Epicurean**) of or concerning Epicurus or his ideas. ☐ **Epicureanism** *n.*

epidemic ● *n.* **1** a widespread occurrence of a disease in a community at a particular time. **2** a wide prevalence of something usu. undesirable. ● *adj.* **1** in the nature of an epidemic (*compare* ENDEMIC). **2** widespread; prevalent.

epidemiology /ˌepɪdiːmiˈɒlədʒi/ *n.* the study of the incidence and distribution of diseases, and of their control and prevention. ☐ **epidemiologic** *adj.* esp. *N Amer.* **epidemiological** *adj.* **epidemiologically** *adv.* **epidemiologist** *n.*

epidermis /ˌepɪˈdɜːmɪs/ *n.* **1** the outer cellular layer of the skin. **2** *Bot.* the outer layer of cells of leaves, stems, roots, etc. ☐ **epidermal** *adj.* **epidermic** *adj.*

epidural /ˌepɪˈdʒʊərəl, -ˈdjʊərəl, -ˈdj-/ ● *adj.* **1** on or around the dura mater. **2** (of an anaesthetic) introduced into the space around the dura mater of the spinal cord. ● *n.* an epidural anaesthetic, used esp. in childbirth to produce loss of sensation below the waist.

epiglottis /ˌepɪˈɡlɒtəs/ *n.* a flap of cartilage at the root of the tongue, which is depressed during swallowing to cover the windpipe.

epigram /ˈepɪˌɡræm/ *n.* **1** a short witty poem. **2 a** a saying or maxim, esp. a proverbial one. **b** a pointed remark or expression, esp. a witty one. **3** the use of concise witty remarks. ☐ **epigrammatic** *adj.* **epigrammatically** *adv.*

epigraph *n.* **1** a quotation at the beginning of a chapter, book, etc. **2** an inscription on a statue, building, tomb, coin, etc.

epilepsy /ˈepɪˌlepsi/ *n.* a condition in which a person has attacks of disordered brain function, usu. causing loss of awareness or consciousness and sometimes convulsions (*compare* GRAND MAL, PETIT MAL).

epileptic ● *adj.* of or relating to epilepsy. ● *n.* a person with epilepsy.

epilogue /ˈepəˌlɒɡ/ *n.* **1** the concluding part of a literary work. **2** a speech or short poem addressed to the audience by an actor at the end of a play.

epinephrine /ˌepɪˈnefrɪn/ *n.* *Biochem.* = ADRENALIN.

epiphany /eˈpɪfəni, ɪˈpɪf-/ *n.* (*pl.* **-ies**) **1** (**Epiphany**) a Christian festival observed on Jan. 6 or the following Sunday, in the Orthodox Church commemorating the baptism of Jesus and in the Western Church the manifestation of Jesus to the Magi. **2** a manifestation of a god or demigod. **3** a sudden and important manifestation or realization.

epiphyte /ˈepɪˌfaɪt/ *n.* a plant growing but not parasitic on another, e.g. a moss. ☐ **epiphytic** /ˌepɪˈfɪtɪk/ *adj.*

episcopacy /ɪˈpɪskəpəsi/ *n.* (*pl.* **-ies**) **1** government of a Church by bishops. **2** = EPISCOPATE.

episcopal /ɪˈpɪskəpəl/ *adj.* **1** of a bishop or bishops. **2** (of a Church) constituted on the principle of government by bishops. **3** (**Episcopal**) of or relating to the Episcopal Church. ☐ **episcopalism** *n.*

Episcopal Church *n.* the Anglican Church in the US and Scotland.

episcopalian /ɪˌpɪskəˈpeɪliən/ ● *adj.* **1** of or advocating government of a Church by bishops. **2** of or belonging to an episcopal Church or (**Episcopalian**) the Episcopal Church. ● *n.* **1** an adherent of

episcopacy. **2** (**Episcopalian**) a member of the Episcopal Church. ☐ **episcopalianism** *n.*

episcopate /ɪˈpɪskəpət/ *n.* **1** the office or tenure of a bishop. **2** (prec. by *the*) the bishops collectively.

episiotomy /eˌpɪziːˈɒtəmi, eˌpɪz-/ *n.* (*pl.* **-ies**) a surgical cut made at the opening of the vagina during childbirth, to aid delivery.

episode *n.* **1** one event or a group of events as part of a sequence. **2** each of the parts of a serial story or broadcast. **3** an incident or set of incidents in a narrative. **4** an incident that is distinct but contributes to a whole (*a romantic episode in her life*). **5** *Music* a passage containing distinct material or introducing a new subject.

episodic /ˌepɪˈsɒdɪk/ *adj.* **1** in the nature of an episode. **2** sporadic; occurring at irregular intervals. **3** (of a novel, play, film, etc.) made up of unconnected episodes. ☐ **episodically** *adv.*

epistemic /ˌepɪˈstiːmɪk, -ˈstemɪk/ *adj.* *Philos.* relating to knowledge or to the degree of its validation.

epistemology /ɪˌpɪstɪˈmɒlədʒi/ *n.* the theory of knowledge, esp. with regard to its methods and validation. ☐ **epistemological** *adj.* **epistemologically** *adv.* **epistemologist** *n.*

epistle /ɪˈpɪsəl/ *n.* **1** *formal* or *jocular* a letter, esp. a long one on a serious subject. **2** (**Epistle**) **a** any of the letters of the apostles in the New Testament. **b** an extract from an Epistle read in a church service. **3** a literary work in the form of a letter or series of letters.

epitaph /ˈepɪˌtæf/ *n.* words written in memory of a person who has died, esp. as a tomb inscription.

epithelium /ˌepɪˈθiːliəm/ *n.* (*pl.* **-s** or **epithelia** /-liə/) the tissue forming the outer layer of the body surface and lining many hollow structures. ☐ **epithelial** *adj.*

epithet /ˈepɪˌθet/ *n.* **1** an adjective or other descriptive word expressing a quality or attribute, esp. used with or as a name. **2** such a word as a term of abuse.

epitome /ɪˈpɪtəmi/ *n.* **1 a** a typical example of a person or thing embodying a particular quality, class, etc. **b** a thing representing another in miniature. **2** a summary, abstract, or condensed account of a written work.

epitomize /ɪˈpɪtəˌmaɪz/ *v.tr.* **1** typify or be a perfect example of (a quality etc.). **2** summarize, give a condensed account of, or make an epitome of (a work). ☐ **epitomization** *n.*

epoch /ˈepɒk, ˈiːpɒk, ˈepək/ *n.* **1** a period of history or of a person's life marked by notable events. **2** the beginning of an era. **3** a division of geological time, esp. a subdivision of a period corresponding to a set of strata. **4** the point in time at which a particular phenomenon takes place, esp. an arbitrarily fixed date relative to which planetary or stellar measurements are expressed. ☐ **epochal** /ˈepəkəl/ *adj.*

eponym /ˈepənɪm/ *n.* **1** a person (real or imaginary) after whom a discovery, invention, place, institution, etc. is named or thought to be named. **2** the name given. ☐ **eponymous** /ɪˈpɒnɪməs/ *adj.*

epoxide /ɪˈpɒksaɪd/ *n.* a compound containing an oxygen atom bonded in a triangular arrangement to two carbon atoms.

epoxy /ɪˈpɒksi/ ● *adj.* relating to or derived from an epoxide, esp. designating epoxy resins and the substances made from them. ● *n.* (*pl.* **-ies**) (in full **epoxy resin**) a synthetic thermosetting resin containing epoxy groups or a substance made from them and used as a coating, adhesive, etc. ● *v.tr.* (**-ies**, **-ied**) secure (two materials) with epoxy glue etc.

epsilon /'epsɪ,lɒn/ n. the fifth letter of the Greek alphabet (E, ε).

Epsom salts /'epsəm/ n. (as *sing.* or *pl.*) a preparation of hydrated magnesium sulphate used medicinally as an anti-inflammatory, purgative, etc.

EQ *abbr. Electronics* equalization.

equable /'ekwəbəl/ *adj.* **1** not easily disturbed or angered. **2** (of motion, temperature, etc.) uniform, moderate, free from fluctuation or variation (*an equable climate*). □ **equability** *n.* **equably** *adv.*

equal ● *adj.* **1** (often foll. by *to, with*) **a** identical in amount, size, number, value, intensity, etc. **b** on the same level in rank, power, excellence, etc. **2** evenly proportioned or balanced (*an equal contest*). **3** having the same rights or status (*human beings are essentially equal*). **4** uniform in operation, application, or effect. ● *n.* a person or thing equal to another, esp. in rank, status, or characteristic quality. ● *v.tr.* (**equalled**, **equalling**) **1** be equal to in number, quality, etc. **2** match, rival, or achieve something that is equal to (an achievement) or to the achievement of (a person). □ **be equal to** have the ability or resources for.

equality n. (*pl.* **-ies**) **1** the condition of being equal in quantity, magnitude, value, intensity, etc. **2** the condition of having equal rank, power, excellence, etc. with others. **3** *Math.* an equation or symbolic expression of the fact that two quantities are equal.

equality rights *n.pl. Cdn* the rights guaranteed in section 15 of the Canadian Charter of Rights and Freedoms to equal treatment for all before and under the law regardless of race, national or ethnic origin, colour, religion, sex, age, or disability.

equalization payment n. (also **equalization grant**) *Cdn* an unconditional transfer by the federal government of funds from general revenues to a poorer province to ensure that all provinces provide comparable levels of service and taxation.

equalize v. **1** *tr. & intr.* make or become equal. **2** *tr.* render (a process, condition, etc.) uniform, esp. by compensating for (an inequality, imbalance, etc.). **3** *Electricity* **a** *tr.* correct or modify (a signal) with an equalizer. **b** *intr.* compensate for (an imbalance) by means of an equalizer. □ **equalization** n.

equalizer n. **1** a thing that makes disparities equal. **2** *Electricity* a network designed to modify a frequency response, esp. in such a way as to compensate for distortion. **3** a goal, run, etc. that equalizes the score in a game. **4** *slang* a weapon, esp. a gun.

equally *adv.* **1** in an equal manner (*treated them all equally*). **2** to an equal degree (*is equally important*). ¶In sense 2, construction with *as* (*equally as important*) is often found, but is considered incorrect by some people. **3** in equal shares or amounts.

equal opportunity n. **1** the opportunity or right to be considered for employment or promotion without discrimination on the grounds of race, gender, disability, etc. **2** (often *attrib.*) the practice or policy of not discriminating in this way.

equal pay n. the policy of giving the same rate of pay for a particular job, similar work, or work of equal value, regardless of the gender of the person doing it.

equal sign n. (also **equals sign**) the symbol =, used to indicate mathematical or other equality.

equanimity /,ekwə'nɪmɪti, ,iːk-/ n. (*pl.* **-ies**) mental composure, evenness of temper, esp. in misfortune. □ **equanimous** /ɪ'kwænɪməs/ *adj.*

equate v. **1** *tr.* (usu. foll. by *to, with*) **a** treat or regard as equal or equivalent. **b** associate strongly; establish a clear link between. **2** *intr.* (foll. by *with*) **a** be equal or equivalent to. **b** agree or correspond. **3** *tr.* esp. *Math.* state the equality of (a thing) with or to another.

equation n. **1 a** the action of making equal or equating. **b** the state of being equal or in equilibrium. **2 a** a statement that two mathematical expressions are equal (indicated by the sign =). **b** the relationship between factors to be taken into account when considering a matter. **3** a formula indicating a chemical reaction by means of the symbols for the elements or compounds involved in it.

equator n. **1 a** an imaginary line around the earth or other body, equidistant from the poles and marking the division between the northern and southern hemispheres. **b** the irregular line, passing around the earth near the geographical equator, on which the earth's magnetic field is horizontal. **2** *Astronomy* = CELESTIAL EQUATOR. **3** a circle on any spherical body that divides it into two equal parts, esp. one equidistant from the two poles of rotation.

equatorial /,ekwə'tɔriəl, ,iːk-/ *adj.* **1 a** of or pertaining to an equator, esp. that of the earth. **b** situated on, occurring near, or being characteristic of the earth's equator or equatorial regions. **2** (of the orbit of a satellite) lying in the plane of the equator.

equestrian /i'kwestriən/ ● *adj.* **1 a** of or relating to horses and horseback riding. **b** skilled in horseback riding. **2 a** on horseback. **b** (of a portrait or statue) representing a person on horseback. ● *n.* a person who is skilled at horseback riding.

equestrienne /i,kwestri'en/ n. a woman who is skilled at horseback riding.

equidistant /,ekwɪ'dɪstənt, 'iːkwi-/ *adj.* separated by an equal distance or equal distances.

equilateral /,ekwɪ'lætərəl, 'iːkwi-/ *adj.* having all its sides equal in length.

equilibrate /ɪ'kwɪlɪ,breit, ,iːkwɪ'laibreit/ v. **1** *tr.* cause (two things) to come or stay in equilibrium. **2** *intr. & tr.* balance or be in equilibrium. **3** *intr.* approach a state of equilibrium. □ **equilibration** n.

equilibrium /,iːkwɪ'lɪbriəm, 'ekwɪ-/ n. (*pl.* **equilibria** /-riə/ or **-s**) **1** a condition of balance between opposing physical forces. **2** a state of mental or emotional equanimity. **3** a state in which the influences or processes to which a thing is subject cancel one another and produce no overall change or variation. **4** *Econ.* a situation in which supply and demand are matched and prices stable.

equine /'ekwain, 'iːk-/ ● *adj.* of, like, or affecting a horse or horses. ● *n.* a horse.

equinox /'ekwɪ,nɒks, 'iːk-/ n. either of the two occasions in the year when the sun crosses the celestial equator and day and night are of equal length throughout the world.

equip *v.tr.* (**equipped**, **equipping**) **1** supply, fit out, or provide with what is needed. **2** (usu. in *passive*) provide with the mental, emotional, or physical abilities or resources needed for a task etc.

equipment n. **1** tools, articles, clothing, etc. used or required for a particular purpose. **2** intellectual or physical resources. **3** the process of equipping or being equipped.

equitable /'ekwɪtəbəl/ *adj.* **1** just or characterized by fairness or equity. **2** *Law* **a** (of a right, claim, etc.) valid or recognized in equity as distinct from common law. **b** pertaining to equity. □ **equitableness** n. **equitably** *adv.*

equity n. (*pl.* **-ies**) **1** fairness, impartiality, even-handedness. **2** the recourse to general principles of justice to correct or supplement common and statute law, esp. to provide remedies not otherwise available.

3 a (in full **equity capital**) the issued share capital of a company. **b** the shareholders' interest in a company. **c** (in *pl.*) the common shares of a company which pay relatively low, profit-related dividends rather than fixed interest. **4 a** the excess of assets over financial liabilities. **b** (in full **equity of redemption**) the net value of a mortgaged property after deducting any charges and claims against it. **5** (**Equity**) (in full **Actors' Equity Association**) a union for actors, dancers, and other performers.

equivalent /ɪˈkwɪvələnt/ ● *adj.* **1** (often foll. by *to*) equal in value, amount, importance, etc. **2** corresponding or having the same relative position or function. **3** having the same result or effect. ● *n.* an equivalent thing, amount, etc. □ **equivalence** *n.* **equivalency** *n.* **equivalently** *adv.*

equivocal /ɪˈkwɪvəkəl/ *adj.* **1** (of a word, expression, etc.) ambiguous or capable of more than one interpretation. **2** (of evidence, signs, etc.) of uncertain or doubtful significance. **3** (of a person, condition, tendency, etc.) questionable, suspect, of doubtful merit or character. □ **equivocally** *adv.*

equivocate /ɪˈkwɪvəˌkeɪt/ *v.intr.* hedge, prevaricate, or use ambiguous words and expressions to mislead. □ **equivocation** *n.*

ER *abbr.* N Amer. EMERGENCY ROOM (*see* EMERGENCY 4).

Er *symbol* erbium.

er *interj.* expressing the inarticulate sound made by a speaker who hesitates or is uncertain what to say.

-er[1] *suffix* forming nouns from nouns, adjectives, and many verbs, denoting: **1 a** a person involved with or in something, esp. as an occupation or profession (*executioner*). **b** an animal or thing that does a specified action or activity (*computer*; *eye-opener*). **2 a** a person who or thing which has or is, esp. a specified attribute, form, or nature (*foreigner*; *four-wheeler*). **b** a thing suitable for a specified function (*broiler*). **3 a** person or thing belonging to or connected with (*airliner*; *old-timer*; *whaler*). **4** a person belonging to, originating from, or resident in a specified place or group (*Newfoundlander*; *fifth-grader*).

-er[2] *suffix* forming the comparative of adjectives (*wider*; *hotter*) and adverbs (*faster*).

ERA *abbr.* **1** (also **era**) EARNED RUN AVERAGE. **2** US Equal Rights Amendment, a proposed constitutional amendment prohibiting discrimination on the basis of gender.

era /ˈɛrə, ˈiːrə/ *n.* **1 a** a system of numbering years from a particular, noteworthy event. **b** a period of years so numbered (*the Christian era*). **2 a** a usu. lengthy period of history characterized by a particular state of affairs, series of events, etc. (*the pre-Roman era*). **b** a date or period to which an event, item, etc. is assigned. **3** a date or event marking the beginning of a distinctive period. **4** a major division of geological time that is a subdivision of an eon.

eradicate /ɪˈrædɪˌkeɪt/ *v.tr.* **1** get rid of, remove or destroy completely. **2** uproot, root out, or pull out by the roots. □ **eradication** *n.* **eradicator** *n.*

erase *v.tr.* **1** rub out or obliterate (something written, typed, drawn, etc.). **2** remove all traces of, esp. from one's memory or mind. **3** remove recorded material from (a magnetic tape or medium). **4** Computing overwrite selected data with input representing an absence of data to give the impression that the original material has been removed. □ **erasable** *adj.*

eraser *n.* a thing that erases, esp. a piece of rubber or plastic used for removing pencil and ink marks.

erasure /ɪˈreɪʃər/ *n.* **1** an act or instance of erasing. **2** a word etc. that has been erased. **b** a place or mark where a letter, word, etc. has been erased.

erbium /ˈɜrbiəm/ *n.* a soft, silvery metallic element occurring naturally and used in special alloys.

ere /ɛr/ *prep. & conj. literary* or *archaic* before (of time) (*ere noon*; *ere they come*).

erect ● *adj.* **1 a** upright, vertical, not bending or stooping. **b** (of an optical image) having the same orientation as the subject, not inverted. **2** (of the penis, clitoris, or nipples) enlarged and firm, esp. in sexual excitement. **3 a** (of hair) bristling, standing up from the skin. **b** (of an animal's tail or ears) standing out stiffly from the body. ● *v.tr.* **1** raise or set in an upright position. **2** build. **3** establish, devise, or form (a theory, conclusion, etc.). □ **erector** *n.*

erectile /ɪˈrektaɪl/ *adj.* **1** that can be erected or become erect. **2** (of tissue or an organ) able to become erect when suitably stimulated.

erection *n.* **1 a** the act or an instance of erecting. **b** the state of being erected. **2 a** thing that is erected or built. **3 a** an erect state of an organ, esp. of the penis. **b** an occurrence of this.

ergo /ˈɛrɡoː, ˈɜr-/ *adv.* therefore.

ergonomics /ˌɜrɡəˈnɒmɪks/ *n.* (treated as *sing.* or *pl.*) the field of study that deals with the relationship between people and their working environment, esp. as it affects efficiency and safety. □ **ergonomic** *adj.* **ergonomically** *adv.* **ergonomist** /ɜrˈɡɒnəmɪst/ *n.*

ergot /ˈɜrɡət/ *n.* **1 a** a disease of rye and other cereals caused by the fungus *Claviceps purpurea*. **2 a** this fungus. **b** a preparation or extract of this fungus, used medicinally for the alkaloids they contain, esp. to induce labour.

ericaceous /ˌɛrɪˈkeɪʃəs/ *adj.* **1** of or relating to the plant family Ericaceae, which includes heathers, azaleas, and rhododendrons. **2** (of compost) suitable for ericaceous and other lime hating plants.

ERM *abbr.* EXCHANGE RATE MECHANISM.

ermine /ˈɜrmɪn/ *n.* (*pl.* same or **-s**) **1** a flesh-eating mammal, *Mustela erminea*, of the weasel family, having brown fur in the summer turning mainly white in the winter, with the tail remaining black-tipped. **2 a** the white fur of an ermine as used in clothing, often with the black tails displayed for the sake of effect. **b** a symbol of purity or honour, esp. with reference to the use of ermine in the robes of judges and peers. □ **ermined** *adj.*

erode *v.tr. & intr.* **1** wear away (esp. soil or rock), destroy or be destroyed gradually. **2** make or become gradually diminished in value etc. □ **eroded** *adj.*

erogenous /ɪˈrɒdʒɪnəs/ *adj.* (esp. of a part of the body) sensitive to sexual stimulation (*erogenous zone*).

eros /ˈɛroːs/ *n.* **1** earthly, romantic, or sexual love. **2** *Psych.* **a** the libido. **b** the urge towards self-preservation (*opp.* THANATOS).

erosion /ɪˈroːʒən/ *n.* **1** the wearing away of the earth's surface by wind, water, or glacial action. **2 a** the act or an instance of eroding. **b** the process of being eroded. □ **erosional** *adj.* **erosive** *adj.*

erotic /ɪˈrɒtɪk/ *adj.* **1** of or pertaining to sexual love. **2** tending to arouse sexual desire or excitement. □ **erotically** *adv.*

erotica *n.* intentionally erotic literature or art.

eroticism *n.* **1 a** erotic nature or character. **b** sexual excitement. **2** the use of or response to erotic images or stimulation.

eroticize *v.tr.* **1** make erotic or endow with an erotic quality. **2** stimulate sexually. □ **eroticized** *adj.*

erotomania /ɪˌrɒtəˈmeɪniə/ *n.* **1** an obsessive erotic desire, esp. with fantasies, delusions, etc. **2** an excessive, but not pathological, preoccupation with sexual passion. □ **erotomaniac** n.

err /er, ɜr/ v.intr. **1** be mistaken or incorrect. **2** do wrong, go morally astray, sin. □ **err on the side of** act with a specified bias (errs on the side of generosity).

errand /ˈerənd/ n. **1** a short trip, often on another's behalf, to buy or deliver something, take a message, etc. **2** the object of such a journey. □ **errand of mercy** a journey to give help, relieve suffering etc.

errant /ˈerənt/ adj. **1 a** erring, doing wrong, deviating from an accepted standard. **b** erratic or breaking with the dominant pattern, movement, etc. (soaked by an errant wave). **2** literary or archaic travelling in search of adventure (knight errant).

erratic /ɪˈrætɪk/ ● adj. **1** inconsistently variable in conduct, opinions, etc. **2** irregular or uncertain in movement, esp. having no fixed course or direction. **3** (of a boulder etc.) differing from surrounding rock and believed to have been brought from a distance by glacial action. ● n. a large block of rock carried by a glacier and deposited some distance from where it was formed. □ **erratically** adv.

erratum /ɪˈrætəm/ n. (pl. **errata** /-tə/) **1** an error in a printed or written text, esp. one noted in a list appended to a book or published in a subsequent issue of a journal. **2** (in pl.) a list of corrected errors attached to a book etc.

erroneous /ɪˈroːniəs/ adj. incorrect, containing or arising from an error. □ **erroneously** adv.

error n. **1** a mistake. **2** the condition of being wrong in conduct or judgment (led into error). **3** a wrong opinion or judgment. **4** the amount by which something is incorrect or inaccurate in a calculation or measurement. **5** Baseball a fielder's misplay, such as a fumble or wild throw, allowing a batter to reach base, a runner to advance, etc. □ **errorless** adj.

error message n. a message occurring on a computer screen or printout reporting an error.

ersatz /ˈerzæts, ˈɜr-/ ● adj. imitation (esp. of inferior quality). ● n. an ersatz thing.

erstwhile /ˈɜrstwaɪl/ adj. former, previous.

erucic acid /ɪˈruːsɪk/ n. a solid, unsaturated fatty acid present in mustard seeds and rape seeds.

erudite /ˈeruːˌdaɪt, ˈerjʊˌdaɪt/ adj. **1** (of a person) learned, scholarly. **2** (of writing etc.) showing great learning. □ **eruditely** adv. **erudition** /-ˈdɪʃən/ n.

erupt v.intr. **1** break out or burst forth suddenly or dramatically. **2** (of a volcano) become active and eject lava etc. **3 a** (of a rash, boil, etc.) appear on the skin. **b** (of the skin) produce a rash, pimples, etc. **4** (of the teeth) break through the gums in normal development. □ **eruption** n. **eruptive** adj.

erythema /ˌerɪˈθiːmə/ n. a superficial reddening of the skin, usu. in patches, as a result of injury or irritation. □ **erythematous** /-ˈθiːmətəs/ adj.

erythrocyte /ɪˈrɪθroʊˌsaɪt/ n. one of the principal cells in the blood of vertebrates, containing the pigment hemoglobin and transporting oxygen and carbon dioxide to and from the tissues.

erythromycin /ɪˌrɪθroʊˈmaɪsɪn/ n. an antibiotic isolated from Streptomyces erythreus, similar in its effects to penicillin.

Es symbol einsteinium.

Esc abbr. Computing escape (key).

escalate /ˈeskəˌleɪt/ v. **1** intr. & tr. increase or develop (usu. rapidly) by stages. **2** tr. cause (an action, activity, or process) to become more intense. □ **escalating** adj. **escalation** n.

escalator n. a moving staircase consisting of an endless chain of steps on a circulating belt.

escapade /ˈeskəˌpeɪd, ˌeskəˈpeɪd/ n. a daring, reckless, or adventurous act.

escape ● v. **1** intr. (often foll. by from) break free or free oneself by fleeing or struggling. **2** intr. (of a gas, liquid, etc.) leak or seep out from a container or pipe etc. **3** intr. get off safely or succeed in avoiding danger, punishment, etc. **4** tr. get completely free of (a person, grasp, etc.). **5** tr. avoid or elude (a commitment, danger, etc.). **6** tr. elude the notice or memory of (nothing escapes you). **7** tr. (of words etc.) be uttered inadvertently by. ● n. **1** the act or an instance of escaping or avoiding danger, injury, etc. **2** the state or fact of having escaped (was a narrow escape). **3** (often attrib.) a possibility or means of escaping (escape hatch). **4** a leakage of gas etc. **5** a temporary relief from reality or worry. **6** (in full **escape key**) Computing a key which either ends the current operation or changes the function of other keys pressed subsequently. □ **escapable** adj. **escaper** n.

escapee /ɪˈskeɪpiː, ɪskeɪˈpiː/ n. a person, esp. a prisoner, who has escaped.

escapism n. the tendency to seek distraction and relief from reality, esp. in the arts or through fantasy. □ **escapist** n. & adj.

escargot /eskarˈgoː, esˈkar-/ n. (pl. **escargots** pronunc. same) a snail as an item of food.

escarpment n. a long, steep-sided ridge, esp. one at the edge of a plateau or separating areas of land at different heights.

eschatology /ˌeskəˈtɒlədʒi/ n. (pl. **-ies**) the branch of theology concerned with last things, e.g. death, judgment, heaven, and hell. □ **eschatological** adj.

Escherichia coli /ˌeʃəˈrɪkiːə ˈkoːlaɪ/ n. (also **E. coli**) a species of bacillus which normally inhabits the large intestine and, under certain conditions, becomes pathogenic, esp. when transferred to other sites such as the urinary tract.

eschew /esˈtʃuː/ v.tr. literary carefully or deliberately avoid, abstain from, or shun. □ **eschewal** n.

escort ● n. **1 a** one or more persons, vehicles, ships, etc. accompanying another, esp. for protection, security, or as a mark of rank or status. **b** the protection or company of an escort. **2** a person accompanying a person of the opposite sex socially. **3** (also attrib.) **a** a usu. young, attractive person legitimately employed to provide another with entertainment etc. **b** euphemism a prostitute. ● v.tr. accompany for protection, guidance, courtesy, etc.

escutcheon /ɪˈskʌtʃən/ n. **1** a shield or emblem bearing a coat of arms. **2** the protective plate around a keyhole, door handle, tap, etc. **3** the middle part of a ship's stern where the name is placed. □ **blot on the escutcheon** a disgrace to the family name.

ESE abbr. east-southeast.

esker /ˈeskər/ n. a long, narrow ridge, usu. of sand and gravel, deposited in a river valley by a stream flowing under a former glacier or ice sheet.

Eskimo /ˈeskɪˌmoː/ ● n. (pl. same or **-os**) **1** a member of an Aboriginal people inhabiting N Canada, Alaska, Greenland, and E Siberia. **2** the language of this people. ● adj. of or relating to the Eskimos or their language. ¶In Canada, the word Eskimo has been superseded by Inuit with reference to the people and Inuktitut with reference to their language.

Eskimo dog n. N Amer. a sturdy dog with webbed feet and slanting eyes, used for pulling sleds etc.

Eskimo roll n. a complete revolution in a kayak, from upright to capsized to upright.

ESL abbr. English as a second language.

ESN abbr. electronic serial number.

esophagus /iː'sɒfəgəs/ n. (pl. **esophagi** /-dʒaɪ/ or **-guses**) the gullet or the part of the alimentary canal from the mouth to the stomach.

esoteric /ˌesəʊ'terɪk, ˌiː-/ adj. (of a doctrine, field of study, mode of speech, etc.) intended only for, or intelligible only to, the initiated or those with special knowledge. □ **esoterically** adv. **esotericism** n.

ESP abbr. extrasensory perception.

espalier /ə'spæljər/ ● n. **1** a latticework or framework of stakes along which the branches of a tree or shrub are trained to grow flat against a wall etc. **2** a tree or shrub trained in this way. ● v.tr. train (a plant, shrub, etc.) as an espalier. □ **espaliered** adj.

especial adj. **1** notable, pre-eminent, or exceptional. **2** individual; attributed or belonging chiefly to one person or thing (your especial charm).

especially adv. **1** chiefly, pre-eminently. **2** particularly or much more than in other cases.

Esperanto /ˌespə'ræntəʊ/ n. an artificial language invented in 1887 based on roots common to the chief European languages with endings standardized.

espionage /'espiəˌnɒʒ/ n. the practice of spying or of using spies, esp. to obtain secret information.

esplanade /ˌesplə'nɒd, -'neɪd, 'esp-/ n. **1** a level, open space along a waterfront, where people may walk or drive. **2** a level space separating a fortress from the town that it commands.

espousal /e'spauzəl/ n. (foll. by of) the action or an act of espousing a cause.

espouse /ɪ'spauz/ v.tr. adopt or support (a cause etc.).

espresso /e'spresəʊ/ n. (pl. **-os**) strong, concentrated, black coffee made by forcing steam through ground coffee beans.

esprit /e'spriː, 'espri/ n. **1** wit. **2** spirit, liveliness.

esprit de corps /e'spri də 'kɔr/ n. loyalty and devotion to, as well as regard for the honour and interests of, a group to which one belongs.

Esquimalt /es'kwaimɒlt/ n. a member of a Salishan Aboriginal group living near Esquimalt, BC.

ess n. the letter S.

-ess suffix forming nouns denoting females (actress; lioness; goddess). ¶For nouns designating women, those ending in -er, -or, etc. which are not gender specific, where such exist, are now often preferred.

essay ● n. /'eseɪ/ **1 a** a written composition, usu. short and in prose, on any subject. **b** a short, coherent composition in any medium (photo essay). **2** (often foll. by at, in) formal an attempt. ● v.tr. /e'seɪ/ formal attempt, try. □ **essayist** n. **essayistic** adj.

essence n. **1 a** the indispensable quality or element identifying a thing or determining its character. **b** the intrinsic nature or quality of something. **2 a** an extract of a plant, drug, etc. usu. obtained by distillation and containing all the source's important qualities in concentrated form. **b** a perfume or scent, esp. as an alcoholic solution of volatile substances. **3** Philos. an abstract reality underlying a phenomenon or all phenomena. □ **in essence** fundamentally. **of the essence** very important, indispensable.

Essene /'esiːn, e'siːn/ n. a member of an ancient Jewish ascetic sect who lived communally.

essential ● adj. **1** absolutely necessary; indispensable. **2** fundamental, basic (essential principles). **3** of or constituting the essence of a person or thing. **4** (of an amino acid or a fatty acid) required by a living organism for normal growth, but not produced by the organism and therefore required in the diet. ● n. (esp. in pl.) a basic or indispensable element or thing. □ **essentiality** /ɪˌsenʃi'ælɪti/ n. **essentially** adv.

essential element n. any of various chemical elements, such as calcium, magnesium, etc., required by living organisms for normal growth.

essentialism n. the belief that things have a set of characteristics which make them what they are, and that the task of science and philosophy is their discovery and expression. □ **essentialist** n. & adj.

essential oil n. a volatile oil having the odour of the plant etc. from which it is extracted.

EST abbr. **1** Eastern Standard Time. **2** electroshock treatment.

est. abbr. **1** established. **2** estimate. **3** estimated.

-est suffix forming the superlative of adjectives (nicest; happiest) and adverbs (soonest).

establish v.tr. **1** found or consolidate (a business, system, etc.) on a permanent basis. **2** (foll. by in) settle (a person or oneself) in some capacity (we are now established in our new house). **3** (esp. as **established** adj.) achieve permanent acceptance for (a custom, belief, practice, institution, etc.). **4 a** validate; place beyond dispute (a fact etc.). **b** find out; ascertain. **5** (of a person) gain recognition and acceptance (established herself as an expert). **6** bring about; achieve (establish contact). **7** enact; decree in law. **8** (in a novel, film, etc.) make a (character, setting, etc.) plausible and convincing (the first soliloquy establishes him as an evil character). □ **established** adj. **establisher** n.

established church n. a religious denomination recognized by a national government as its nation's official church.

establishment n. **1** the act or an instance of establishing; the process of being established. **2 a** a business organization or public institution. **b** a place of business. **3 a** the staff or equipment of an organization. **b** a household. **4** any organized body permanently maintained for a purpose. **5** a church system organized by law. **6 a** (also **Establishment**) the group in a society exercising authority or influence, and seen as resisting change. **b** any influential or controlling group.

estate n. **1** a property consisting of an extensive area of land usu. with a large house. **2** Law **a** the interest that a person has in land or other property. **b** all of a person's assets and liabilities, esp. at death. **3** a property where grapes, rubber, tea, etc., are cultivated. **4** (in full **estate of the realm**) esp. hist. an order or class forming (or regarded as) a part of the body politic, consisting of the first estate (the clergy), the second estate (the aristocracy), and the third estate (the commons).

Estates General n. the legislative body in France before 1789, representing the three estates.

esteem /ɪ'stiːm/ ● v.tr. **1** (usu. in passive) have a high regard for; greatly respect. **2** formal consider, deem (esteemed it an honour). ● n. high regard. □ **esteemed** adj.

ester /'estər/ n. any of a class of organic compounds produced by replacing the hydrogen of an acid by an alkyl, etc. group, many of which occur naturally as oils and fats.

esthete etc. var. of AESTHETE etc.

estimable /'estɪmbəl/ adj. worthy of esteem.

estimate ● n. /'estɪmət/ **1** a judgment or calculation of the approximate cost, value, size, etc. of something. **2** an appraisal of the character or qualities of a person or thing. **3** a price specified as that likely to be charged for work to be undertaken. ● v.tr. /'estɪmeɪt/ **1** form an approximate idea or rough calculation of (a number, size, etc.). **2** fix (a price etc.) by estimate. **3** form an opinion of. □ **estimated** adj. **estimative** adj. **estimator** n.

estimation n. **1** the process or result of estimating. **2** judgment or opinion of worth (*in my estimation*).

Estonian /ɪˈstoːnɪən/ ● n. **1 a** a native of Estonia, a country in the Baltics. **b** a person of Estonian descent. **2** the Finno-Ugric language of Estonia. ● adj. of or relating to Estonia or its people or language.

estrange /ɪˈstreɪndʒ/ v.tr. (usu. in *passive*; often foll. by *from*) cause (a person or group) to become unfriendly or distant; alienate. □ **estrangement** n.

estranged adj. (of a husband or wife) no longer living with his or her spouse.

estrogen /ˈestrədʒən/ n. **1** any of various steroid hormones developing and maintaining female characteristics of the body. **2** this produced artificially for use in oral contraceptives etc. □ **estrogenic** adj.

estrus /ˈestrəs/ n. a recurring period of sexual receptivity in many female mammals; heat.

estuary /ˈestʃuːˌeri/ n. (pl. **-ies**) the tidal mouth of a large river, where the tide meets the stream. □ **estuarine** /-ˌraɪn/ adj.

ET abbr. **1** EASTERN TIME. **2** extraterrestrial.

ETA abbr. estimated time of arrival.

eta /ˈeɪtə, ˈiːtə/ n. the seventh letter of the Greek alphabet (*H*, η).

et al. /et ˈæl/ abbr. and others.

etc. abbr. = ET CETERA.

et cetera /et ˈsetərə, ˈsetrə/ adv. (also **etcetera**) **1 a** and the rest; and similar things or people. **b** or similar things or people. **2** and so on.

etch ● v. **1 a** tr. engrave (metal, glass, or stone) by coating it with a protective layer, drawing on this with a needle, and then covering with acid or other corrosive that attacks the parts the needle has exposed. **b** tr. engrave (a plate) in this way in order to print from it. **2** intr. practise this craft. **3** tr. engrave by any method. **4** tr. (foll. by *on*, *upon*) impress deeply (esp. on the mind). ● n. the action or process of etching.

etching n. **1** a print made from an etched plate. **2** the art of producing these plates.

eternal adj. **1** existing always; without an end or beginning in time. **2** essentially unchanging; enduring (*eternal truths*). **3** *informal* seeming not to cease (*your eternal nagging*). □ **the Eternal** God. □ **eternalize** v.tr. **eternally** adv.

eternity n. (pl. **-ies**) **1** infinite or unending (esp. future) time. **2** *Theol.* the condition into which the soul enters at death; the afterlife. **3** the quality, condition, or fact of being eternal. **4** (often prec. by *an*) a very long time. **5** (in *pl.*) eternal truths.

ethane /ˈeθeɪn, ˈiːθ-/ n. a colourless odourless gaseous hydrocarbon of the alkane series, occurring in natural gas.

ethanol /ˈeθəˌnɒl/ n. *Chem.* = ALCOHOL 1.

ether /ˈiːθər/ n. **1 a** a colourless volatile organic liquid used as an anaesthetic or solvent. **b** any of a class of organic compounds with a similar structure to this, having an oxygen joined to two alkyl etc. groups. **2** the clear sky; the upper regions of air beyond the clouds. **3** a medium formerly assumed to permeate space and fill the gaps between particles of matter.

ethereal /ɪˈθiːriəl/ adj. **1** light, airy. **2** of unearthly delicacy and refinement (*ethereal music*). **3** heavenly, celestial. **4** *Chem.* of or relating to ether. □ **ethereality** /-ˈæliti/ n. **ethereally** adv.

Ethernet n. a system of communication for local area networks by coaxial cable that prevents simultaneous transmission by more than one station.

ethic ● n. a set of moral principles, esp. those of a specified religion, school of thought, etc. (*the Puritan ethic*). ● adj. = ETHICAL.

ethical adj. **1** relating to morals, esp. as concerning human conduct. **2** morally correct; honourable. □ **ethicality** /-ˈkæliti/ n. **ethically** adv.

ethicist /ˈeθɪsɪst/ n. a person who studies ethics and makes recommendations about ethical dilemmas.

ethics n.pl. **1** (usu. treated as *sing.*) the science of morals in human conduct. **2 a** (treated as *pl.*) moral principles; rules of conduct. **b** (often treated as *pl.*) a set of these (*medical ethics*). **3** (treated as *pl.*) moral correctness (*the ethics of his decision*).

Ethiopian /ˌiːθiˈoːpiən/ ● n. **1** a native or national of Ethiopia, a country in NE Africa. **2** a person of Ethiopian descent. ● adj. **1** of or relating to Ethiopia. **2** of or designating a biogeographical region comprising Africa south of the Sahara.

ethnic ● adj. **1** (of a population group) sharing a distinctive cultural and historical tradition, often associated with race, nationality, or religion. **2** relating to race or culture (*ethnic group*). **3** (of clothes, music, etc.) characteristic of or influenced by the traditions of a particular people or culture, esp. a minority within another culture or one regarded as exotic. **4** denoting origin by birth or descent rather than nationality (*ethnic Turks*). ● n. esp. *N Amer.* & *Austral.* a member of an (esp. minority) ethnic group. □ **ethnically** adv. **ethnicity** n.

ethnical adj. relating to ethnology.

ethnic cleansing n. *euphemism* the mass expulsion or extermination of people from opposing ethnic or religious groups within a certain area.

ethnic minority n. a (usu. identifiable) group differentiated from the main population of a community by racial origin or cultural background.

ethnobotany /ˌeθnoːˈbɒtəni/ n. **1** the traditional knowledge of a people concerning plants and their uses. **2** the study of such knowledge. □ **ethnobotanical** adj. **ethnobotanist** n.

ethnocentric /ˌeθnoːˈsentrɪk/ adj. **1** evaluating other races and cultures by criteria specific to one's own. **2** believing in the inherent superiority of one's own race or culture. □ **ethnocentrically** adv. **ethnocentricity** n. **ethnocentrism** n.

ethnocultural /ˌeθnoːˈkʌltʃərəl/ adj. pertaining to or having a particular ethnic group.

ethnography /eθˈnɒɡrəfi/ n. the scientific description of human races and cultures. □ **ethnographer** n. **ethnographic** adj. **ethnographical** adj. **ethnographically** adv.

ethnohistory n. the branch of knowledge that deals with the history of races and cultures, esp. non-Western ones. □ **ethnohistorian** n. **ethnohistoric** adj. **ethnohistorical** adj. **ethnohistorically** adv.

ethnology /eθˈnɒlədʒi/ n. the branch of knowledge that deals with the characteristics of different peoples and the differences and relationships between them. □ **ethnologic** adj. **ethnological** adj. **ethnologically** adv. **ethnologist** n.

ethnomusicology n. the study of the music of one or more (esp. non-European) cultures. □ **ethnomusicological** adj. **ethnomusicologist** n.

ethology /iːˈθɒlədʒi/ n. **1** the science of animal behaviour. **2** the science of character formation in human behaviour. □ **ethological** adj. **ethologically** adv. **ethologist** n.

ethos /ˈiːθɒs, ˈiːθoːs/ n. the characteristic spirit or attitudes of a community, people, or system, or of a literary work etc.

ethyl /ˈeθɪl/ n. (attrib.) the monovalent radical derived from ethane by removal of a hydrogen atom.

ethylene /ˈeθəˌliːn/ n. a gaseous hydrocarbon occurring in natural gas and crude oil, and used in the manufacture of polyethylene.

ethylene glycol n. a colourless viscous liquid used as an antifreeze and in the manufacture of polyesters.

etiology /ˌiːtiˈɒlədʒi/ n. **1** Med. the causation of diseases and disorders, esp. of a specific disease, as a subject of investigation. **2** the study of causation. **3** the assignment of a cause or reason. □ **etiologic** adj. **etiological** adj. **etiologically** adv.

etiquette /ˈetɪˌkət, -ˌket/ n. **1** the conventional rules of social or official behaviour. **2 a** the customary behaviour of members of a profession, sports team, etc. towards each other. **b** the unwritten code governing this (medical etiquette).

Etruscan /ɪˈtrʌskən/ ● adj. of ancient Etruria in W Italy, esp. its pre-Roman civilization. ● n. **1** a native of Etruria. **2** the language of Etruria.

-ette /et/ suffix forming nouns meaning: **1** small (kitchenette). **2** imitation or substitute (leatherette). **3** female (usherette). ¶The use of the suffix -ette to indicate a feminine role or identity may be offensive.

étude /eiˈtuːd, -ˈtjuːd, ˈei-/ n. a short musical composition or exercise, usu. for one instrument, designed to improve the technique of the player.

etymologize v.tr. trace the etymology of (a word).

etymology /ˌetɪˈmɒlədʒi/ n. (pl. **-ies**) **1 a** the historically verifiable sources of the formation of a word and the development of its meaning. **b** an account of these. **2** the branch of linguistics concerned with etymologies. □ **etymological** adj. **etymologically** adv. **etymologist** n.

EU abbr. European Union.

Eu symbol europium.

eucalyptus /ˌjuːkəˈlɪptəs/ n. (also **eucalypt**) (pl. **eucalyptuses** or **eucalypti** /-tai/ or **eucalypts**) **1** any tree of the genus Eucalyptus, native to Australasia, cultivated for its timber and for the oil from its leaves. **2** (in full **eucalyptus oil**) the essential oil from eucalyptus leaves, used esp. in medicinal preparations, perfumes, etc.

eucaryote var. of EUKARYOTE.

Eucharist /ˈjuːkərɪst/ n. **1** (in the Catholic, Anglican and Orthodox churches) the sacrament commemorating the Last Supper, in which bread and wine are consecrated and consumed. **2** the consecrated elements, esp. the bread (receive the Eucharist). □ **Eucharistic** adj. **Eucharistical** adj.

Eucharistic minister n. Catholicism a layperson assisting in the distribution of the Eucharist during Mass, during home visitations to the sick, etc.

euchre /ˈjuːkər/ ● n. **1** a card game for two to four players in which the highest cards are the joker (if used), the jack of trumps, and the other jack of the same colour in a pack with the lower cards removed, the aim being to win at least three of the five tricks played. **2** an instance of euchring or being euchred. ● v.tr. **1** (in euchre) prevent (a bidder) from winning three or more tricks, thereby scoring points oneself. **2** N Amer., Austral., & NZ slang deceive, outwit. **3** Cdn, Austral., & NZ slang (usu. in passive) ruin, finish, foil (if we miss the bus, we're euchred!).

Euclidean /juːˈklɪdiən/ adj. (also **Euclidian**) of the Greek mathematician Euclid (c.300 BC), esp. the system of geometry based on his principles.

eugenics /juːˈdʒenɪks/ n.pl. (treated as sing.) the science of improving the (esp. human) population by controlled breeding for desirable inherited characteristics. □ **eugenic** adj. **eugenicist** n.

eukaryote /juːˈkeriˌoːt/ n. an organism consisting of a cell or cells in which the genetic material is DNA in the form of chromosomes contained within a distinct nucleus (compare PROKARYOTE). □ **eukaryotic** /-ˈɒtɪk/ adj.

eulachon /ˈjuːləkɒn/ n. a small oily food fish, Thaleichthys pacificus, of the Pacific coast of N America, belonging to the smelt family.

eulogize /ˈjuːləˌdʒaiz/ v.tr. **1** praise in speech or writing. **2** compose or deliver a funeral oration in praise of a person. □ **eulogist** n. **eulogistic** adj.

eulogy /ˈjuːlədʒi/ n. (pl. **-ies**) **1 a** a speech or writing in praise of a person, esp. a person who has recently died. **b** N Amer. a funeral oration in praise of a person. **2** an expression of praise.

eunuch /ˈjuːnək/ n. **1** a castrated man, esp. (hist.) one employed at an oriental harem or court. **2** a person lacking effectiveness (political eunuch).

euonymus /juːˈɒnɪməs/ n. any tree or shrub of the genus Euonymus, e.g. the burning bush.

euphemism /ˈjuːfəˌmɪzəm/ n. **1** a mild or vague expression substituted for one thought to be too harsh or direct, e.g. pass away for die. **2** the use of such expressions. □ **euphemistic** adj. **euphemistically** adv. **euphemize** v.tr. & intr.

euphonium /juːˈfoːniəm/ n. a brass wind instrument of the tuba family, used esp. in brass bands.

euphony /ˈjuːfəni/ n. (pl. **-ies**) **1 a** pleasantness of sound, esp. of a word or phrase; harmony. **b** a pleasant sound. **2** the tendency to make a phonetic change for ease of pronunciation.

euphorbia /juːˈfɔrbiə/ n. any plant of the genus Euphorbia, including spurges and poinsettia.

euphoria /juːˈfɔriə/ n. **1** an intense feeling of wellbeing and excitement, esp. one based on over-confidence or over-optimism. **2** a mood marked by such a feeling, as symptomatic of drug use or mental illness. □ **euphoric** adj. **euphorically** adv.

Eurasian ● adj. **1** of mixed European and Asian parentage. **2** of Europe and Asia. ● n. a Eurasian person.

eureka /joˈriːkə, jə-/ ● interj. I have found it! (announcing a discovery etc.). ● n. a fortunate discovery.

eurhythmic etc. var. of EURYTHMIC etc.

Euro n. the European currency unit adopted by the European Union.

Euro- comb. form Europe, European.

Eurobond n. an international bond issued outside the country in whose currency its value is stated.

Euro-Canadian ● adj. pertaining to Canadians of European origin or descent. ● n. a Canadian of European origin or descent.

Eurocentric adj. **1** having or regarding Europe as its centre. **2** presupposing the supremacy of Europe and Europeans. □ **Eurocentricity** n. **Eurocentrism** n.

European ● adj. **1** of or in Europe. **2 a** descended from natives of Europe. **b** originating in or characteristic of Europe. **3 a** happening in or extending over Europe. **b** concerning Europe as a whole rather than its individual countries. **4** of or relating to the European Union. ● n. **1** a native or inhabitant of Europe. **2** a person descended from natives of Europe. **3** a white person, esp. in a country with a predominantly non-white population. □ **Europeanize** v.tr. & intr. **Europeanization** n.

European Community n. an economic and political association of certain European countries, incorporated since 1993 in the European Union.

European Currency Unit *n.* a notional unit of currency used within the European Monetary System and in trading Eurobonds. Abbr.: **ECU**.

European Economic Community *n.* an institution of the European Union, an economic association of western European countries.

European Monetary System *n.* a monetary system inaugurated by the European Community in 1979 to coordinate and stabilize the exchange rates of the currencies of member countries, as a prelude to monetary union. Abbr.: **EMS**.

European Parliament *n.* the principal representative and consultative body of the European Union.

European plan *n. N Amer.* a system of charging for a hotel room only without meals. Abbr.: **EP**.

European Union *n.* an economic and political association of certain European countries as a unit with internal free trade and common external tariffs.

europium /joˈroːpiəm/ *n.* a soft silvery metallic element occurring naturally in small quantities.

Euro-skeptic *n.* a person skeptical about the benefits of closer ties within the European Union.

eurythmic /joˈrɪðmɪk, jə-/ *adj.* **1** of or in harmonious proportion (esp. of architecture). **2** involving eurythmics (*eurythmic dancing*).

eurythmics *n.pl.* (also treated as *sing.*) harmony of bodily movement, esp. as developed with music and dance into a system of education.

eurythmy /joˈrɪðmi/ *n.* = EURYTHMICS.

euthanasia /ˌjuːθəˈneɪʒə/ *n.* an act of painlessly killing a person or animal suffering from an incurable condition. □ **euthanize** *v.tr.*

eutrophic /juːˈtrɒfɪk, -ˈtroːfɪk/ *adj.* (of a lake etc.) rich in nutrients and therefore supporting a dense plant population, which kills animal life by depriving it of oxygen. □ **eutrophicate** *v.tr.* **eutrophication** *n.* **eutrophy** /ˈjuːtrəfi/ *n.*

eV *abbr.* electron volt.

evacuate /ɪˈvækjuːˌeit, i-/ *v.* **1** *tr.* **a** remove (people) from a place of danger to stay elsewhere for the duration of the danger. **b** *tr.* empty (a place) in this way. **c** *intr.* depart, leave. **2** *tr.* produce a vacuum in (a vessel etc.). **3** *tr.* (of troops) withdraw from (a place). **4** *tr.* **a** empty (the bowels or other bodily organ). **b** discharge (feces etc.). □ **evacuation** *n.*

evacuee /ɪˌvækjuːˈiː, i-/ *n.* a person evacuated from a place of danger.

evade *v.tr.* **1 a** escape from, avoid (pursuers, arrest, etc.) esp. by guile or trickery. **b** avoid doing (one's duty etc.). **c** avoid giving a direct answer to. **2 a** fail to pay (tax due). **b** defeat the intention of (a law etc.), esp. while complying with its letter. **3** (of a thing) elude or baffle (a person). □ **evadable** *adj.* **evader** *n.*

evaluate *v.tr.* **1** assess, appraise (*evaluate the situation*). **2 a** find or state the number or amount of. **b** find a numerical expression for. □ **evaluation** *n.* **evaluative** /-ətɪv/ *adj.* **evaluator** *n.*

evanescent /ˌevəˈnesənt/ *adj.* (of an impression or appearance etc.) quickly fading; having no permanence. □ **evanescence** *n.*

evangelical /ˌiːvænˈdʒelɪkəl, ˌev-/ ● *adj.* (also **evangelic**) **1** of or according to the teaching of the gospel or the Christian religion. **2** of or denoting a branch of Protestant Christianity emphasizing the authority of Scripture, personal conversion, and the doctrine of faith in the Atonement. **3** zealously advocating a cause. ● *n.* a person who believes in evangeli-

cal doctrines or belongs to an evangelical church. □ **evangelicalism** *n.* **evangelically** *adv.*

evangelism /ɪˈvændʒəˌlɪzəm, i-/ *n.* **1** the preaching or promulgation of the Christian gospel. **2** zealous advocacy of a cause or doctrine.

evangelist *n.* **1** a preacher of the Christian gospel. **2** a person, esp. a layperson, engaged in itinerant Christian missionary work. **3** a zealous advocate of a cause etc. **4** (**Evangelist**) any of the writers of the four Gospels.

evangelistic *adj.* **1** of or relating to evangelists or evangelism. **2** of or relating to the four Evangelists.

evangelize *v.* **1** *tr. & intr.* preach the Christian gospel to. **2** *tr.* convert (a person) to Christianity. **3** *intr.* try to win support for a cause (*evangelize about forest conservation*). □ **evangelization** *n.* **evangelizer** *n.*

evaporate /ɪˈvæpəˌreit, i-/ *v.* **1** *intr.* turn from solid or liquid into vapour. **2** *intr. & tr.* lose or cause to lose moisture by evaporation. **3** *intr. & tr.* disappear or cause to disappear (*our courage evaporated*). □ **evaporation** *n.* **evaporative** /-rətɪv/ *adj.* **evaporator** *n.*

evaporated milk *n.* thick unsweetened milk, usu. bought in tins, which has had some of its liquid removed by evaporation.

evasion /ɪˈveiʒən, i-/ *n.* **1** the act or a means of evading a duty, question, etc. **2 a** a subterfuge or prevaricating excuse. **b** an evasive answer.

evasive *adj.* **1** seeking to evade something. **2** not direct in one's answers etc. **3** enabling or effecting evasion (*evasive action*). **4** (of a person) tending to evasion; habitually practising evasion. □ **evasively** *adv.* **evasiveness** *n.*

eve *n.* **1** the evening or day before a church festival or any date or event (*Christmas Eve*). **2** the time just before anything (*the eve of the election*). **3** evening.

even[1] ● *adj.* (**evener**, **evenest**) **1** level; flat and smooth. **2 a** (of an action, movement, etc.) uniform; constant; free from fluctuations (*an even pace*). **b** equal in number, amount, value, score, etc. **c** equally balanced. **3** (usu. foll. by *with*) in the same plane or line. **4 a** (of a person's temper etc.) equable, calm. **b** (of conduct, laws, etc.) equal, just, impartial. **5 a** (of a number such as 4, 6) divisible by two without a remainder. **b** bearing such a number (*no parking on even dates*). **c** not involving fractions; exact (*in even dozens*). **6 a** (of a person) neither owing money nor owed; square (*give me $10 and we're even*). **b** (of accounts, affairs, etc.) having no balance of debt on either side. **7** (of a chance, bet, etc.) as likely to succeed as not; fifty-fifty. ● *adv.* **1** used to invite comparison of the stated assertion, negation, etc., with an implied one that is less strong or remarkable (*never even opened [let alone read] the letter*). **2** used to introduce an extreme case (*even you must realize it*). **3** used to add force to a more exact or precise version of a word, phrase, etc. (*it's an unattractive building, even ugly*). ● *v.tr. & intr.* (often foll. by *up*) make or become even. □ **even as** at the very moment that. **even now 1** now as well as before. **2** at this very moment. **even out 1** become level or regular (*prices should even out shortly*). **2** spread (payments, work, etc.) evenly over a period of time or among a number of people. **even so 1** notwithstanding that; nevertheless. **2** quite so. **3** in that case as well as in others. **even though** despite the fact that. **even up** cause (an account, score, etc.) to become even or equal. **get** (or **be**) **even with** have one's revenge on. □ **evenly** *adv.* **evenness** *n.*

even[2] *n. archaic* or *literary* evening.

even-handed *adj.* impartial, fair. □ **even-handedly** *adv.* **even-handedness** *n.*

evening ● *n.* **1** the end part of the day, esp. from about 6 p.m., or sunset if earlier, to bedtime (*this evening*; *evening meal*). **2** an outing or party of a specified type, happening in the evening (*a theatre evening*). **3** *literary* a time compared with this, esp. the last part of a person's life. ● *interj.* = GOOD EVENING.

evening dress *n.* **1** (also **evening clothes**, **evening wear**) clothes worn for formal occasions in the evening. **2** = EVENING GOWN.

evening gown *n.* a woman's long formal dress.

evening primrose *n.* any plant of the genus *Oenothera*, esp. the eastern N American *O. biennis*, with yellow flowers, from whose seeds an oil is extracted for medicinal use.

evensong *n.* a service of evening prayer, esp. that of Anglican churches.

even-steven *adj.* (also **even-Steven**) *informal* **1** having no balance of debt on either side. **2** (of a game etc.) equal; tied.

even strength *n.* *Hockey* a situation where both teams have the same number of players on the ice (also *attrib.*: *even-strength goal*).

event *n.* **1** a thing that happens or takes place, esp. one of importance. **2 a** the fact of a thing's occurring. **b** a result or outcome. **3** an item in a sports program, or the program as a whole (*the giant slalom event*). □ **in any event** (or **at all events**) whatever happens. **in the event** as it turns (or turned) out. **in the event of** if (a specified thing) happens. **in the event that** if it happens that.

eventful *adj.* marked by many events or incidents, esp. noteworthy ones (*an eventful career*). □ **eventfully** *adv.* **eventfulness** *n.*

eventing /ˈiːvɛntɪŋ/ *n.* participation in horse trials, esp. cross-country, dressage, and show jumping.

eventless *adj.* without noteworthy events.

eventual *adj.* occurring or existing in due course or at last; ultimate. □ **eventually** *adv.*

eventuality *n.* (*pl.* **-ies**) a possible event or outcome.

ever *adv.* **1** at all times; always (*ever hopeful*; *ever after*). **2** at any time (*have you ever been to Paris?*; *as good as ever*). **3** as an emphatic word: **a** in any way; at all (*how ever did you do it?*; *when will they ever learn?*). **b** (prec. by *as*) in any manner possible (*be as quick as ever you can*). **c** *N Amer. informal* really (*did she ever feel like an idiot*). **4** (in *comb.*) constantly (*ever-present*). **5** (foll. by *so*, *such*) very; very much (*thanks ever so much*). **6** (foll. by comparative) constantly, increasingly (*grew ever larger*). □ **did you ever?** *informal* did you ever hear or see the like? **ever since** throughout the period since.

everbearing *adj.* (of a plant) bearing (fruit) continuously throughout the growing season.

evergreen ● *adj.* **1** always green or fresh. **2** (of a plant) retaining green leaves or needles throughout the year. ● *n.* an evergreen plant (*compare* DECIDUOUS 1).

everlasting ● *adj.* **1** lasting forever. **2** lasting for a long time, esp. so as to become unwelcome. **3** (of flowers) keeping their shape and colour when dried. ● *n.* **1** eternity. **2 a** any of various plants, chiefly of the composite family, with flowers of papery texture that retain their shape and colour after being dried, esp. a helichrysum. **b** (in full **everlasting pea**) a leguminous plant, *Lathyrus latifolius*, with large flowers, naturalized in N America. □ **everlastingly** *adv.* **everlastingness** *n.*

evermore *adv.* forever; always.

evert /ɪˈvɜːrt/ *v.tr. Physiol.* turn (an organ etc.) outwards or inside out. □ **eversible** *adj.* **eversion** *n.*

every *adj.* **1** each single (*heard every word*). **2** each at a specified interval in a series (*take every third one*; *every four days*). **3** all possible; the utmost degree of (*has every prospect of success*). □ **every bit as** *informal* (in comparisons) quite as (*every bit as good*). **every now and again** (or **now and then**) from time to time. **every other** each second in a series (*every other day*). **every so often** at intervals; occasionally. **every time** *informal* **1** without exception. **2** without hesitation. **every which way** *N Amer. informal* **1** in all directions. **2** in a disorderly manner.

everybody *pron.* every person.

everyday *adj.* **1** occurring every day. **2** suitable for or used on ordinary days (*everyday dishes*). **3** commonplace, usual (*everyday life*).

Everyman *n.* the ordinary man or human being.

everyone *pron.* every person; everybody. ¶Note that *every one* is used to refer to each person or thing in a given group, as in *every one of them has arrived*. □ **everyone who is anyone** (also **everybody who is anybody**) every person who is important etc.

everything *pron.* **1** all things; all the things of a group or class. **2** a great deal (*he owes her everything*). **3** the essential consideration (*speed is everything*). □ **have everything** *informal* possess every attraction, advantage, etc.

everywhere *adv.* (also *N Amer. informal* **everyplace**) in every place.

Everywoman *n.* the ordinary or typical woman.

evict /ɪˈvɪkt/ *v.tr.* expel (a tenant) from a property by legal process. □ **eviction** *n.* **evictor** *n.*

evidence ● *n.* **1** (often foll. by *for*, *of*) the available facts, circumstances, etc. supporting or otherwise a belief, proposition, etc., or indicating whether or not a thing is true or valid. **2** *Law* **a** information given personally or drawn from a document etc. and tending to prove a fact or proposition. **b** statements or proofs admissible as testimony in a law court. **3** a sign or indication (*evidence of hard work*). **4** clearness, obviousness. ● *v.tr.* (usu. in *passive*) be evidence of; demonstrate (*is very popular, as evidenced by the large turnout*). □ **call in evidence** *Law* summon (a person) as a witness. **in evidence** noticeable, conspicuous.

evident *adj.* plain or obvious (visually or intellectually); manifest.

evidential /ˌɛvɪˈdɛnʃəl/ *adj.* of or providing evidence.

evidentiary /ˌɛvɪˈdɛnʃəri/ *adj.* = EVIDENTIAL.

evidently *adv.* **1** plainly, obviously. **2** (qualifying a whole sentence) it is plain that; it would seem that (*evidently, we're too late*). **3** (said in reply) so it appears.

evil ● *adj.* **1** morally bad; wicked. **2** harmful or tending to harm, esp. intentionally or characteristically. **3** disagreeable or unpleasant (*an evil smell*). **4** unlucky; causing misfortune (*evil days*). ● *n.* **1** a moral force regarded as the source of harm or human wickedness, esp. as opposed to goodness. **2** a manifestation of this, esp. in people's actions; wickedness. **3** something that is morally wrong, harmful, or undesirable. □ **speak evil of** slander. □ **evilly** *adv.*

evildoer *n.* a person who does evil. □ **evildoing** *n.*

evil eye *n.* a gaze or stare superstitiously believed to be able to cause material harm.

evil one *n.* the embodiment of evil in certain religious beliefs, esp. (in Christianity) Satan.

evince /ɪˈvɪns/ *v.tr.* **1** indicate or make evident. **2** show that one has (a quality). □ **evincible** *adj.*

eviscerate /ɪˈvɪsəˌreɪt/ *v.tr. formal* **1** disembowel. **2** empty or deprive of essential contents. □ **evisceration** *n.*

evocation /ˌɛvəˈkeɪʃən/ *n.* **1** the act or an instance of evoking. **2** (esp. in civil law systems) the transfer of a legal case to a higher court.

evocative /ɪˈvɒkətɪv/ adj. tending to evoke (esp. feelings or memories). □ **evocatively** adv. **evocativeness** n.

evoke /ɪˈvoːk/ v.tr. **1** inspire or draw forth (memories, a response, etc.). **2** summon, call up (a spirit etc.).

evolution /ˌevəˈluːʃən, -ˈljuːʃən, ˌiːvə-/ n. **1** gradual development, esp. from a simple to a more complex form. **2 a** the development of an animal or plant, or part of one, from a rudimentary to a mature state. **b** a process by which different kinds of organism come into being by the differentiation and genetic mutation of earlier forms over successive generations, viewed as an explanation of their origins. **3** the appearance or presentation of events etc. in due succession (*the evolution of the plot*). □ **evolutionarily** adv. **evolutionary** adj.

evolutionist /ˌevəˈluːʃənɪst, ˌiːv-/ n. a person who believes in evolution as explaining the origin of species. □ **evolutionism** n. **evolutionistic** adj.

evolve /ɪˈvɒlv, iː-/ v. **1 a** intr. & tr. develop or come forth gradually. **b** intr. (of an organism, part or feature) come into being through evolutionary development. **c** tr. (usu. in passive) produce or develop in the course of evolution. **2** tr. work out or devise (a theory etc.).

ewe /juː/ n. a female sheep.

ewer /ˈjuːər/ n. a large pitcher or water jug with a wide mouth.

ex¹ n. informal a former spouse, lover, etc.

ex² ● abbr. example. ● n. Cdn exhibition.

ex³ prep. **1** (of goods) without charges to the purchaser until removed from (*ex warehouse*). **2** (of stocks or shares) without, excluding (*ex dividend*).

ex- prefix forming nouns from titles of office, status, etc., meaning 'formerly' (*ex-convict*; *ex-wife*).

exacerbate /ekˈsæsərˌbeɪt, ɪg-/ v.tr. **1** make worse. **2** irritate (a person). □ **exacerbation** n.

exact ● adj. **1** accurate; correct in all details. **2** precise. **3** rigorous; strict. **4** (of a scientific method, instrument, etc.) not allowing vagueness or uncertainty. ● v.tr. (often foll. by from, of) **1** demand and enforce payment of (money, fees, etc.) from a person. **2 a** demand; insist on. **b** (of circumstances) require urgently. □ **exactitude** n. **exactness** n.

exacting adj. **1** making great demands. **2** calling for much effort. □ **exactingly** adv. **exactingness** n.

exaction n. **1** the act or an instance of exacting; the process of being exacted. **2 a** an illegal or exorbitant demand; an extortion. **b** a sum or thing exacted.

exactly adv. **1** accurately, precisely; in an exact manner (*worked it out exactly*). **2** in exact terms (*exactly when did it happen?*). **3** (said in reply) quite so; I agree completely. □ **not exactly** informal by no means.

exactor /ɪgˈzæktər/ n. Cdn a bet on the first- and second-place finishers in a race, specifying their order of finish.

exactor box n. Cdn a bet on three or more horses in one race, specifying the first- and second-place finishers, not specifying their order of finish.

exaggerate v. **1** tr. & intr. give an impression of (a thing), esp. in speech or writing, that makes it seem larger or greater etc. than it really is. **2** tr. enlarge or alter beyond normal or due proportions (*exaggerated politeness*). □ **exaggerated** adj. **exaggeratedly** adv. **exaggeration** n. **exaggerative** adj. **exaggerator** n.

exalt /ɪgˈzɒlt/ v.tr. **1** raise in rank or power etc. **2** praise highly. **3** (usu. as **exalted** adj.) make lofty or noble (*an exalted style*). □ **exaltedly** adv.

exaltation /ˌegzɒlˈteɪʃən/ n. **1** the act or an instance of exalting; the state of being exalted. **2** elation; rapturous emotion.

exam n. = EXAMINATION 3, 4.

examination n. **1** the act or an instance of examining; the state of being examined. **2** a detailed inspection. **3 a** the testing of the proficiency or knowledge of students or other candidates for a qualification by oral or written questions. **b** a test of this kind. **4** an instance of examining or being examined medically. **5** Law the formal questioning of the accused or of a witness in court.

examination for discovery n. (pl. **examinations for discovery**) Cdn Law a pretrial meeting to disclose the evidence that will be presented at a civil trial.

examination-in-chief n. (pl. **examinations-in-chief**) Cdn & Brit. Law an examination in a court made by the party that called the person to give evidence.

examination paper n. **1** the printed questions in an examination. **2** a candidate's set of answers.

examine v.tr. **1** inquire into the nature or condition etc. of. **2** look closely or analytically at. **3** test the proficiency of, esp. by examination (see EXAMINATION 3). **4** check the health of (a patient) by inspection or experiment. **5** Law formally question (the accused or a witness) in court. □ **examinee** n. **examiner** n.

example n. **1** a thing characteristic of its kind or illustrating a general rule. **2** a person, thing, or piece of conduct, regarded in terms of its fitness to be imitated (*you are a bad example*). **3** a circumstance or treatment seen as a warning to others; a person so treated (*shall make an example of you*). **4** a problem or exercise designed to illustrate a rule. □ **for example** by way of illustration.

exasperate /ɪgˈzæspəˌreɪt/ v.tr. **1** (often as **exasperated** adj. or **exasperating** adj.) irritate intensely. **2** make (a pain, ill feeling, etc.) worse. □ **exasperatedly** adv. **exasperatingly** adv. **exasperation** n.

ex cathedra /ˌeks kəˈθiːdrə/ adj. & adv. with full authority (esp. of a papal pronouncement, implying infallibility as doctrinally defined).

excavate v.tr. **1 a** make (a hole or channel) by digging. **b** dig out material from (the ground). **2** reveal or extract by digging. **3** Archaeology dig systematically into the ground to explore (a site). □ **excavation** n. **excavator** n.

exceed v. **1** tr. be greater or more numerous than (*the price must not exceed $20*). **2** tr. go beyond what is allowed, necessary, or advisable (*exceeded the speed limit*). **3** tr. surpass, excel (a person or achievement). **4** intr. be pre-eminent; be greater or better.

exceeding adj. **1** surpassing in amount or degree. **2** pre-eminent.

exceedingly adv. **1** very; to a great extent. **2** surpassingly, pre-eminently.

excel v. (**excelled, excelling**) (often foll. by in, at) **1** tr. be superior to. **2** intr. be pre-eminent or the most outstanding (*excels at games*). □ **excel oneself** surpass one's previous performance.

excellence n. **1** the quality of being excellent; great merit. **2** the activity etc. in which a person excels.

Excellency n. (pl. **-ies**) (usu. prec. by Your, His, Her, Their) a title used in addressing or referring to certain high officials, e.g. governors general, ambassadors, and (in some countries) senior Church dignitaries.

excellent adj. extremely good; pre-eminent. □ **excellently** adv.

except ● v.tr. (often as **excepted** adj. placed after object) exclude from a general statement, condition, etc. (*excepted her from the amnesty*; *present company excepted*). ● *prep.* (also **excepting**) (often foll. by *for*) not including; other than (*all here except for Liz*). ● *conj.* (usu. foll. by *that*) with the exception; only.

exception *n.* **1** the act or an instance of excepting; the state of being excepted (*made an exception in my case*). **2** a thing that has been or will be excepted. **3** an instance that does not follow a rule. □ **take exception** (often foll. by *to*) **1** object; make objections to. **2** be offended (by); be resentful (about). **with the exception of** except; not including.

exceptionable *adj.* open to objection. ¶See Usage Note at UNEXCEPTIONABLE. □ **exceptionably** *adv.*

exceptional *adj.* **1** forming an exception. **2** unusual; not typical (*exceptional circumstances*). **3** unusually good; outstanding. ¶See Usage Note at UNEXCEPTIONABLE. **4** (of a schoolchild) having mental or physical disabilities. □ **exceptionally** *adv.*

excerpt /'eksɜrpt, 'egz-/ ● *n.* a short extract from a book, film, piece of music, etc. ● *v.tr.* **1** take an excerpt or excerpts from (a book etc.). **2** take (an extract) from a book etc. □ **excerption** *n.*

excess /ɪk'ses, 'ekses/ ● *n.* **1** the state or an instance of exceeding. **2** the amount by which one quantity or number exceeds another. **3** exceeding a proper or permitted limit. **4 a** the overstepping of the accepted limits of moderation, esp. intemperance in eating or drinking. **b** (in *pl.*) outrageous or immoderate behaviour. **5** an extreme or improper degree or extent (*an excess of cruelty*). ● *attrib.adj.* (usu. /'ekses/) exceeding a set or limited amount or number; extra (*excess weight*). □ **in** (or **to**) **excess** exceeding the proper amount or degree. **in excess of** more than; exceeding.

excess baggage *n.* **1** baggage exceeding a weight allowance and liable to an extra charge. **2** something perceived as superfluous and burdensome.

excessive *adj.* **1** too much or too great. **2** more than what is normal or necessary. □ **excessively** *adv.* **excessiveness** *n.*

exch. *abbr.* exchange.

exchange ● *n.* **1** the act or an instance of giving one thing and receiving another in its place. **2 a** the giving of money for its equivalent in the money of the same or another country. **b** the fee or percentage charged for this. **3** a place where telephone calls are connected between different lines. **4** a place where commodities, securities, etc. are bought and sold. **5** a place where an item may be exchanged for another similar item (*needle exchange*). **6** a system of settling debts between persons (esp. in different countries) without the use of money, by bills of exchange. **7 a** a short conversation, esp. a disagreement or quarrel. **b** a sequence of letters between correspondents. **8** a reciprocal visit between two people or groups from different regions or countries (also *attrib.: exchange student*). ● *v.* **1** *tr.* (often foll. by *for*) give or receive (one thing) in place of another. **2** *tr.* give and receive as equivalents (e.g. things or people, blows, information, etc.); give one and receive another of. **3** *tr.* substitute an equivalent item for (one purchased and returned). **4** *intr.* (often foll. by *with*) make an exchange. □ **in exchange** (often foll. by *for*) as a thing exchanged (for). □ **exchangeability** *n.* **exchangeable** *adj.* **exchanger** *n.*

exchange rate *n.* the value of one currency in terms of another.

Exchange Rate Mechanism *n.* a system for allowing the value of participating currencies to fluctuate to a defined degree in relation to each other so as to control exchange rates within the European Monetary System.

excise[1] /'eksaiz/ ● *n.* **1 a** a duty or tax levied on goods and commodities produced or sold within the country of origin. **2** a tax levied on certain licences. ● *v.tr.* **1** charge excise on (goods). **2** force to pay excise.

excise[2] /ek'saiz/ *v.tr.* **1** remove (a passage of a book etc.). **2** cut out by surgery. □ **excision** /-'sɪʒən/ *n.*

excitable *adj.* **1** (esp. of a person) easily excited. **2** (of an organism, tissue, etc.) responding to a stimulus, or susceptible to stimulation. □ **excitability** *n.* **excitably** *adv.*

excite *v.tr.* **1 a** rouse the feelings or emotions of (a person). **b** bring into play; rouse up (feelings, faculties, etc.). **c** arouse sexually. **2** bring about (an action or active condition). **3** promote the activity of (an organism, tissue, etc.) by stimulus. **4** *Electricity* **a** cause (a current) to flow in the winding of an electromagnet. **b** supply a signal. **5** *Physics* **a** cause the emission of (a spectrum). **b** cause (a substance) to emit radiation. **c** put (an atom etc.) into a state of higher energy. □ **excitation** /,eksaɪ'teɪʃən, -sɪ-/ *n.* **excitatory** *adj.* **excitedly** *adv.* **excitement** *n.* **exciter** *n.* (esp. in senses 4, 5). **exciting** *adj.* **excitingly** *adv.*

exclaim *v.intr.* & *tr.* cry out suddenly, esp. in anger, surprise, pain, etc.

exclamation *n.* **1** the act or an instance of exclaiming. **2** a sudden impassioned or emphatic utterance.

exclamation mark *n.* (*N Amer.* also **exclamation point**) a punctuation mark (!) indicating an exclamation.

exclamatory /ɪk'sklæmə,tɔri/ *adj.* of or serving as an exclamation.

exclude /ek'sklu:d/ *v.tr.* **1** shut or keep out (a person or thing) from a place, group, privilege, etc. **2** expel and shut out. **3** remove from consideration. **4** prevent the occurrence of; make impossible.

exclusion *n.* **1** the act or an instance of excluding. **2** the state of being excluded. □ **to the exclusion of** so as to exclude. □ **exclusionary** *adj.*

exclusion order *n.* **1** *Cdn & Brit.* an official order preventing a person (esp. a criminal) from entering a country. **2** *Cdn* an order made by a judge to clear spectators, reporters, etc. from a courtroom.

exclusive ● *adj.* **1** excluding other things. **2** (*predic.*; foll. by *of*) not including; except for. **3** tending to exclude others, esp. socially; select. **4** catering for few or select customers; high-class. **5 a** (foll. by *to*) (of a commodity) not obtainable elsewhere. **b** (of a newspaper article) not published elsewhere. **6** (*predic.*; foll. by *to*) restricted or limited to; existing or available only in. **7** employed or followed or held to the exclusion of all else (*exclusive rights*). ● *n.* an article or story published by only one newspaper or periodical. □ **exclusively** *adv.* **exclusiveness** *n.* **exclusivity** *n.*

exclusivism *n.* a policy or doctrine of (esp. national, racial, or religious) exclusiveness. □ **exclusivist** *adj.* & *n.*

excommunicate *Christianity* ● *v.tr.* /,ekskə'mju:nɪ,keit/ officially exclude (a person) from participation in the sacraments, or from formal communion with the Church. ● *adj.* /,ekskə'mju:nɪkət/ excommunicated. ● *n.* /,ekskə'mju:nɪkət/ an excommunicated person. □ **excommunication** *n.*

ex-con /eks'kɒn/ *n.* *informal* an ex-convict; a former inmate of a prison.

excoriate /eks'kɔri,eit/ *v.tr.* **1** censure severely. **2 a**

remove part of the skin of (a person etc.) by abrasion. **b** strip or peel off (skin). □ **excoriation** *n.*

excrement /ˈekskrəmənt/ *n.* feces.

excrescence /ɪkˈskresəns/ *n.* **1** an abnormal or morbid outgrowth on the body or a plant. **2** an ugly addition.

excreta /ekˈskriːtə, ɪk-/ *n.pl.* waste discharged from the body, esp. feces and urine.

excrete *v.tr.* (of an animal or plant) separate and expel waste matter as a result of metabolism. □ **excretion** *n.* **excretive** *adj.* **excretory** *adj.*

excruciating /ɪkˈskruːʃiˌeɪtɪŋ/ *adj.* (of physical or mental pain) intense, acute. □ **excruciatingly** *adv.*

exculpate /ˈekskʌlˌpeɪt/ *v.tr. formal* **1** free from blame. **2** (foll. by *from*) clear (a person) of a charge. □ **exculpation** *n.* **exculpatory** /-ˈkʌlpəˌtɔːri/ *adj.*

excursion *n.* **1** a short journey, esp. one made by a group of people together for pleasure. **2** a group of people making such a trip. **3** a trip at a reduced rate, e.g. on a train, ship, etc. (also *attrib.*: *excursion fare*). **4** a digression or diversion. □ **excursionist** *n.*

excuse ● *v.tr.* **1** attempt to lessen the blame attaching to (a person, act, or fault). **2** (of a fact or circumstance) serve in mitigation of (a person or act). **3** obtain exemption for (a person or oneself). **4** a (foll. by *from*) release (a person) from a duty etc. **b** allow (a person) to leave. **5** overlook or forgive (a fault or offence). **6** (foll. by *for*) forgive (a person) for a fault. **7** not insist upon (what is due). **8** *refl.* apologize for leaving. ● *n.* **1** a reason put forward to mitigate or justify an offence, fault, etc. **2** an apology (*made my excuses*). **3** *informal* (foll. by *for*) a poor or inadequate example of (*a poor excuse for a novel*). □ **be excused** be allowed to leave a room etc., e.g. to go to the lavatory. **excuse me 1** a polite apology for an interruption etc., or for disagreeing. **2** a polite formula used when trying to make one's way through a crowd etc. □ **excusable** *adj.* **excusably** *adv.*

exec /egˈzek, ɪg-/ *informal* ● *n.* an executive. ● *adj.* executive.

execute *v.tr.* **1 a** carry out a sentence of death on (a condemned person). **b** kill as a political act. **2** carry into effect, perform (a plan, duty, command, operation, etc.). **3 a** carry out a design for (a product of art or skill). **b** perform (a musical composition, dance, etc.). **4** make (a legal instrument) valid by signing, sealing, etc. **5** put into effect (a judicial sentence, the terms of a will, etc.). **6** *Computing* run or process (a command, program, file, etc.). □ **executable** *adj.*

execution *n.* **1** the carrying out of a sentence of death. **2** the act or an instance of carrying out or performing something. **3** technique or style of performance in the arts, esp. music.

executioner *n.* an official who carries out a sentence of death.

executive ● *n.* **1** a person or body with managerial or administrative responsibility in a business organization etc. **2** the branch of a government concerned with executing laws. **3** the person or persons in whom is vested the supreme executive authority of a country or state. ● *adj.* **1 a** designating the branch of government that deals with putting into effect laws and judicial sentences. **b** of or pertaining to the executive of a government. **2 a** concerned with administration or management. **b** relating to, designed for, or used by executives (*executive suite*). **3** *informal* exclusive; of the finest quality (*executive homes*). □ **executively** *adv.*

executive assistant *n.* a clerical assistant to an executive of a corporation etc.

executive council *n. Cdn* **1** a provincial or territorial cabinet. **2** *hist.* (in colonial government) a body of advisers appointed by the governor.

executive director *n. N Amer.* a person employed by a non-profit organization to oversee operations and management and implement the policy decisions of the board of directors.

executive federalism *n. Cdn* the practice of establishing Canadian constitutional, social, and economic policy at meetings of First Ministers and cabinet ministers, esp. behind closed doors.

executive officer *n.* **1** the second-in-command in naval units and some military units. **2** a senior executive in a corporation etc.

executive order *n. US* a regulation issued by the president, governor, etc., and having the force of law.

executive producer *n.* the person who oversees the financial aspects of the production of a film.

executive secretary *n.* a secretary to a business executive.

executor /ɪgˈzekjʊtər/ *n.* a person appointed by a testator to carry out the terms of his or her will.

executrix /ɪgˈzekjʊtrɪks/ *n.* (*pl.* **-trices** /-ˈtraisiːz/ or **-trixes**) a woman appointed by a testator to carry out the terms of his or her will.

exegesis /ˌeksɪˈdʒiːsɪs/ *n.* (*pl.* **exegeses** /-siːz/) critical explanation of a text, esp. of Scripture. □ **exegetic** /-ˈdʒetɪk/ *adj.* **exegetical** *adj.*

exemplar /ɪgˈzemplər, -plɑr/ *n.* **1** a model or pattern. **2** a typical instance of a class of things.

exemplary /ɪgˈzempləri/ *adj.* **1** fit to be imitated; outstandingly good. **2 a** serving as a warning. **b** *Law* (of damages) exceeding the amount needed for simple compensation. **3** illustrative, representative. □ **exemplarily** *adv.* **exemplariness** *n.*

exemplify /ɪgˈzemplɪˌfai/ *v.tr.* (**-ies**, **-ied**) **1** illustrate by example. **2** be an example of. **3** *Law* make an attested copy of (a document) under an official seal. □ **exemplification** *n.*

exempt ● *adj.* **1** free from an obligation or liability etc. imposed on others. **2** (foll. by *from*) not liable to. ● *n.* a person who is exempt, esp. from payment of tax. ● *v.tr.* (foll. by *from*) free from an obligation, esp. one imposed on others. □ **exemption** *n.*

exercise ● *n.* **1** activity requiring physical effort, done esp. as training or to sustain or improve health. **2** mental or spiritual activity, esp. as practice to develop a skill. **3** (often in *pl.*) a particular task or set of tasks devised as exercise, practice in a technique, etc. **4 a** the use or application of a mental faculty, right, etc. **b** practice of an ability, quality, etc. **5** (often in *pl.*) military drill or manoeuvres. **6** (foll. by *in*) a process directed at or concerned with something specified (*was an exercise in public relations*). **7** *N Amer.* (usu. in *pl.*) a formal or traditional routine or ceremony (*opening exercises*). ● *v.* **1** *tr.* use or apply (a faculty, right, influence, restraint, etc.). **2** *tr.* perform (a function). **3 a** *intr.* take (esp. physical) exercise; do exercises. **b** *tr.* provide (an animal) with exercise. **c** *tr.* train (a person). **4** *tr.* **a** tax the powers of. **b** perplex, worry. □ **exercise in futility** an activity which proves to be absolutely futile. **the object** (or **point**) **of the exercise** the essential purpose of an action or procedure. □ **exercisable** *adj.* **exerciser** *n.*

exercise bike *n.* a stationary apparatus used for physical exercise, in which a person can sit and pedal against resistance, like a cyclist.

exercise book *n.* **1** a book containing exercises. **2** esp. *Cdn & Brit.* a book for writing school work, notes, etc., in.

Exercycle /'eksər,saikəl/ n. proprietary = EXERCISE BIKE.

exert /ɪg'zɜrt/ v.tr. **1** bring to bear (a quality, force, influence, etc.). **2** refl. (often foll. by for, or to + infin.) use one's efforts or endeavours; strive.

exertion n. **1** the act of exerting. **2** strenuous physical activity.

exfoliate /eks'fo:li,eit/ v. **1** intr. (of bone, the skin, a mineral, etc.) come off in scales or layers. **2 a** tr. shed (material) in scales or layers. **b** tr. & intr. cause (the skin etc.) to shed flakes or scales. **3** intr. (of a tree) throw off layers of bark. □ **exfoliation** n.

exhalation /,ekshə'leiʃən/ n. **1 a** an expiration of air. **b** a puff of breath. **2** a mist, vapour. **3** an emanation or effluvium.

exhale /eks'heil, ɪgz-/ v.tr. & intr. **1** breathe out (esp. air or smoke) from the lungs. **2** give off or be given off in vapour.

exhaust ● v.tr. **1** consume or use up the whole of. **2 a** (often as **exhausted** adj. or **exhausting** adj.) use up the strength or energy of; tire out. **b** drain (soil) of nutritive ingredients. **3** study or expound on (a subject) completely. ● n. **1** expelled waste air or other gases etc., esp. those produced by an engine after combustion. **2** (also **exhaust pipe**) the pipe or system by which these are expelled. **3** the process of expulsion of these gases. □ **exhaustible** adj. **exhaustingly** adv.

exhaustion n. **1** the act or an instance of draining a thing of a resource or emptying it of contents; the state of being depleted or emptied. **2** a total loss of strength or vitality.

exhaustive adj. **1** thorough, comprehensive. **2** tending to exhaust a resource. □ **exhaustively** adv.

exhibit ● v.tr. (**exhibited, exhibiting**) **1** show or reveal publicly (for amusement, in competition, etc.). **2 a** show, display. **b** manifest (a quality). **3** submit for consideration. ● n. **1** a thing or collection of things forming part or all of an exhibition. **2** a document or other item or object produced in a law court as evidence.

exhibition n. **1** a display (esp. public) of works of art, industrial products, etc. **2** Cdn a large regional fair, esp. with amusements, agricultural exhibits, and craft displays, usu. lasting for an extended period. **3** a world's fair. **4** the act or an instance of exhibiting; the state of being exhibited. **5** N Amer. Sport (attrib.) denoting games whose outcomes do not affect the teams' standings, esp. those played before the start of a regular season. □ **make an exhibition of oneself** behave so as to appear ridiculous.

exhibitionism n. **1** a tendency towards display or extravagant behaviour. **2** Psych. a mental condition characterized by the compulsion to display one's genitals indecently in public. □ **exhibitionist** n. **exhibitionistic** adj. **exhibitionistically** adv.

exhibitor n. a person who provides an item or items for an exhibition.

exhilarate /ɪg'zɪlə,reit, eg-/ v.tr. (often as **exhilarating** adj. or **exhilarated** adj.) affect with great liveliness or joy; raise the spirits of. □ **exhilaratingly** adv. **exhilaration** n.

exhort /ɪg'zɔrt, eg-/ v.tr. (often foll. by to + infin.) urge or advise strongly or earnestly. □ **exhortation** n.

exhume /eks'u:m, ɪgz-, egz-/ v.tr. **1** dig out, unearth (esp. a buried corpse). **2** disinter, bring to light (esp. something lost). □ **exhumation** n.

exigency /'eksɪdʒənsi, ɪg'zɪdʒ-, eg-/ n. (pl. **-ies**) (usu. in pl.) an urgent need or demand.

exile /'egzail, 'eks-/ ● n. **1** expulsion, or the state of being expelled, from one's native land or home, esp.

for political reasons. **2 a** long absence from home, esp. as constrained by circumstances. **b** exclusion from a group, accustomed place, etc. **3** a person expelled or long absent from his or her native country, home, etc. **4** (also **Babylonian exile, Exile**) the captivity of the Jews in Babylon in the 6th c. BC. ● v.tr. (foll. by from) **1** officially expel (a person) from his or her native country or town etc. **2** exclude (a person or thing) from a group etc.

exist v.intr. **1** be real or actual; have being. **2 a** have being under specified conditions. **b** (foll. by as) exist in the form of (sports teams exist solely as public relations vehicles). **3** (of circumstances etc.) occur; be found. **4** live with no pleasure under adverse conditions (felt he was merely existing). **5** continue in being; maintain life (can hardly exist on this salary). **6** be alive, live. □ **existing** adj.

existence n. **1** the fact or condition of being or existing. **2** the manner of one's existing or living, esp. under adverse conditions. **3** all that exists.

existent adj. existing, actual, current.

existential /,egzɪ'stenʃəl, eks-/ adj. **1** of or relating to existence. **2** concerned with existence, esp. with human existence as viewed by existentialism.

existentialism n. a theory emphasizing the existence of the individual person as a free and responsible agent isolated in an otherwise deterministic world. □ **existentialist** n. & adj.

exit ● n. **1** a passage or door by which to leave a room, building, etc. **2** the act of going out. **3** the act of departing from or ceasing to participate or engage in. **4** a place where vehicles can leave a highway or major road. **5** the departure of an actor from the stage. ● v. (**exited, exiting**) **1 a** intr. go out of a room, building, etc. **b** tr. leave (a building, room, etc.). **2** tr. & intr. esp. N Amer. leave (a vehicle) leave (a highway or major road). **3** intr. (as a stage direction) (an actor) leaves the stage (exit Macbeth). **4** tr. & intr. terminate (a computer session, program, etc.).

exit permit n. (also **exit visa** etc.) authorization to leave a particular country.

exit poll n. an unofficial poll in which voters leaving a polling station are asked how they voted.

exocrine /'ekso:,krain/ adj. (of a gland) secreting through a duct (compare ENDOCRINE 1).

exodus /'eksədəs/ n. **1** a mass departure of people. **2** (**Exodus**) the departure of the Israelites from Egypt.

exogenous /ek'spdʒənəs/ adj. growing or originating from outside. □ **exogenously** adv.

exonerate /ɪg'zɒnə,reit/ v.tr. (often foll. by from) **1** free or declare free from guilt, blame, etc. **2** release from a duty etc. □ **exoneration** n.

exorbitant /ɪg'zɔrbɪtənt/ adj. (of a price etc.) grossly excessive. □ **exorbitance** n. **exorbitantly** adv.

exorcise /'ekso:r,saiz, -ər-/ v.tr. (also **-ize**) **1 a** endeavour to expel (a supposed evil spirit) by religious ceremonies, prayers, etc. **b** free (a person or place) of a supposed evil spirit. **2 a** remove (a malignant influence). **b** free (a person or place) of a malignant influence. □ **exorcism** n. **exorcist** n.

exoskeleton n. a rigid external covering for the body in certain animals, esp. arthropods, providing support and protection. □ **exoskeletal** adj.

exotic ● adj. **1** introduced from or originating in or existing in a foreign or distant place (exotic birds). **2** attractively or remarkably strange or unusual; bizarre. ● n. an exotic person or thing. □ **exotically** adv. **exoticism** n.

exotica n.pl. remarkably strange or rare things.

exotic dancer n. = STRIPPER 1.

exp. *abbr.* **1** expiry. **2** experience(d). **3** *Computing* expansion. **4** experimental. **5** *Photography* exposure.

expand *v.* **1** *tr. & intr.* increase in size, scope, or importance. **2** *intr.* (often foll. by *on*) give a fuller description or account. **3** *intr.* become more genial or effusive; discard one's reserve. **4** *tr.* a set or write out in full (something condensed or abbreviated). **b** *Math.* rewrite (a product, power, or function) as a sum. **5** *tr. & intr.* spread out flat. □ **expandability** *n.* **expandable** *adj.* **expander** *n.* **expanding** *adj.*

expanse *n.* **1** a wide continuous area or extent of land, space, etc. **2** an amount of expansion.

expansion *n.* **1** the act or an instance of expanding; the state of being expanded. **2** enlargement of the scale or scope of (esp. commercial) operations. **3** increase in the amount of a state's territory or area of control. **4** an increase in the volume of fuel etc. on combustion in the cylinder of an engine. **5** a an enlarged portion. **b** something formed by the expansion of a thing. **6** *N Amer. Sport* (often *attrib.*) the addition of new teams to a league (*expansion team*). □ **expansionary** *adj.*

expansion card *n.* (also **expansion board**) a circuit board that can be inserted in a computer to give extra facilities.

expansion draft *n.* *N Amer. Sport* a draft in which expansion teams select available players from existing teams' rosters.

expansionism *n.* a policy or theory advocating esp. territorial expansion. □ **expansionist** *n.*

expansion slot *n.* a place in a computer where an expansion card can be added.

expansive /ɪkˈspænsɪv, ek-/ *adj.* **1** able or tending to expand. **2** extensive, wide-ranging. **3** (of a person, feelings, or speech) effusive, open. □ **expansively** *adv.* **expansiveness** *n.*

expat /ˈekspæt/ *n. & adj. informal* = EXPATRIATE.

expatriate ● *adj.* /eksˈpeɪtrɪət, -ˈpætrɪət/ **1** living abroad, esp. for a long period. **2** expelled from one's country, home, etc.; exiled. ● *n.* /eksˈpeɪtrɪət, -ˈpætrɪət/ an expatriate person. ● *v.tr.* /eksˈpeɪtriˌeit, -ˈpætriˌeit/ **1** expel or remove (a person) from his or her native country, home, etc. **2** *refl.* withdraw (oneself) from one's citizenship or allegiance. □ **expatriation** *n.*

expect *v.tr.* **1** a regard as likely; assume as a future event or occurrence. **b** look for as appropriate or one's due (from a person) (*I expect co-operation*). **c** foresee or look forward to the arrival of (*expecting guests*). **2** *informal* think, suppose. **3** be pregnant with (*expecting twins*). □ **be expecting** *informal* be pregnant. □ **expectable** *adj.*

expectancy *n.* (*pl.* **-ies**) **1** a state of expectation. **2** what can reasonably be expected (*life expectancy*).

expectant *adj.* **1** revealing expectation. **2** (of a mother or father) expecting the birth of a child. □ **expectantly** *adv.*

expectation *n.* **1** the state or an instance of expecting or looking forward. **2** something expected or hoped for.

expectorant /ekˈspektərənt/ ● *adj.* causing the coughing out of phlegm etc. ● *n.* an expectorant medicine.

expedient /ɪkˈspiːdɪənt, ek-/ ● *adj.* **1** advantageous (in general or to a definite purpose); advisable on practical rather than moral grounds. **2** suitable, appropriate. ● *n.* a means of attaining an end; a resource. □ **expedience** *n.* **expediency** *n.* **expediently** *adv.*

expedite /ˈekspəˌdaɪt/ *v.tr.* **1** assist the progress of;

hasten (an action, process, etc.). **2** accomplish (esp. business) quickly.

expediter *n.* (also **expeditor**) **1** an employee responsible for ensuring that work is done efficiently and on schedule. **2** *Cdn* = OUTFITTER 1.

expedition *n.* **1** a journey or voyage for a particular purpose, esp. tourism, exploration, or scientific research. **2** the personnel or ships etc. undertaking this. **3** promptness, speed.

expeditionary *adj.* of or used in an expedition, esp. a military expedition to a foreign country.

expeditious /ˌekspəˈdɪʃəs/ *adj.* **1** acting or done with speed and efficiency. **2** conducive to speedy performance. □ **expeditiously** *adv.*

expel *v.tr.* (**expelled, expelling**) (often foll. by *from*) **1** compel the departure of (a person) from a school etc. **2** force out or eject (a substance from the body etc.). **3** order or force to leave a building etc.

expend *v.tr.* spend or use up (money, energy, etc.).

expendable ● *adj.* **1** that may be sacrificed or dispensed with, esp. to achieve a purpose. **2 a** not regarded as worth preserving or saving. **b** unimportant, insignificant. **3** not normally reused. ● *n.* an expendable person or thing. □ **expendability** *n.* **expendably** *adv.*

expenditure *n.* **1** the process or an instance of spending or using up. **2** a thing (esp. a sum of money) expended.

expense /ɪkˈspens, ek-/ *n.* **1** cost incurred; payment of money. **2** (usu. in *pl.*) **a** costs incurred in doing a particular job etc. (*will pay your expenses*). **b** an amount paid to reimburse this (*offered me $120 per day expenses*). **3** a thing that is a cause of much expense (*the house is a real expense*). ● *v.tr.* write off (an expense, loss, etc.) for tax purposes. □ **at the expense of** so as to cause loss or damage or discredit to (something). **at a person's expense 1** causing a person to suffer injury, ridicule, etc. **2** with costs paid by a person.

expense account *n.* a list of an employee's expenses to be reimbursed by the employer.

expensive *adj.* **1** costing much. **2** charging high prices. **3** causing much expense (*has expensive tastes*). □ **expensively** *adv.* **expensiveness** *n.*

experience ● *n.* **1** actual observation of or practical acquaintance with facts or events. **2** knowledge or skill resulting from this. **3 a** an event regarded as affecting one (*an unpleasant experience*). **b** the fact or process of being so affected (*learned by experience*). **4** the events that have taken place within the knowledge of an individual, a community, etc. (*the Canadian experience*). ● *v.tr.* **1** have experience of; undergo. **2** feel or be affected by (an emotion etc.). □ **experiencer** *n.*

experienced *adj.* **1** having had much experience. **2** skilled from experience (*an experienced driver*).

experiential /ɪkˌspiːrɪˈenʃəl, ek-/ *adj.* **1** involving or based on experience. **2** denoting a philosophical view that treats all knowledge as based on experience. □ **experientially** *adv.*

experiment ● *n.* **1** a procedure undertaken to make a discovery, test a hypothesis etc., or demonstrate a known fact. **2** (often foll. by *in, with*) a procedure or course of action tentatively adopted without being sure that it will achieve its purpose. ● *v.intr.* (often foll. by *on, with*) make an experiment. □ **experimentation** *n.* **experimenter** *n.*

experimental *adj.* **1** based on or making use of experiment (*experimental psychology*). **2 a** used in experiments (*experimental animal*). **b** serving or resulting from (esp. incomplete) experiment; tentat⸱⸱⸱

provisional. **3** based on experience, not on authority or conjecture. □ **experimentally** *adv.*

experimental farm *n.* (also **experimental station**) *Cdn* an agricultural research centre, esp. one established through Agriculture Canada.

experimentalism *n.* **1** the empirical approach in philosophy or science. **2** the use of experiment or innovation in the arts. □ **experimentalist** *n.*

expert ● *adj.* **1** (often foll. by *at*, *in*, *on*) having special knowledge or skill in a subject. **2** involving or resulting from this (*expert advice*). ● *n.* (often foll. by *at*, *in*) a person having special knowledge or skill. □ **expertly** *adv.* **expertness** *n.*

expertise *n.* expert skill, knowledge, etc.

expert system *n.* a computer program into which has been incorporated the knowledge of experts on a particular subject so that non-experts can use it for making decisions, evaluations, or inferences.

expert witness *n.* an expert called on to provide specialized information at a trial, inquest, etc.

expiate /ˈekspiˌeit/ *v.tr.* **1** pay the penalty for (wrongdoing). **2** make amends for. □ **expiation** *n.*

expiration *n.* **1** expiry. **2** breathing out.

expire *v.* **1** *intr.* (of a period of time, validity, etc.) come to an end. **2** *intr.* (of a document, authorization, etc.) cease to be valid; become void. **3** *intr.* (of a person) die. **4** *tr. & intr.* exhale (air etc.) from the lungs. □ **expiratory** *adj.* (in sense 4).

expiry *n.* (*pl.* **-ies**) **1** the end of the validity or duration of something. **2** death.

explain *v.* **1** *tr. & intr.* make (something) clear or intelligible with detailed information etc. **2** *tr.* say by way of explanation. **3** *tr.* account for (one's conduct, a phenomenon, etc.). □ **explain away** minimize the significance of (a difficulty or mistake) by providing reasons for it. **explain oneself** **1** make one's meaning clear. **2** give an account of one's motives or conduct. □ **explainable** *adj.* **explainer** *n.*

explanation *n.* **1** the act or an instance of explaining. **2** a statement or circumstance that explains something. **3** a declaration made with a view to mutual understanding or reconciliation.

explanatory *adj.* serving to explain.

expletive /ˈeksplətiv, ikˈspliːtəv, ek-/ *n.* an oath, swear word, or other expression, used in an exclamation.

explicable /ekˈsplikəbəl, ik-, ˈek-/ *adj.* that can be explained.

explicate /ˈekspliˌkeit/ *v.tr.* **1** make clear, explain. **2** develop the meaning or implication of (an idea, principle, etc.). □ **explication** *n.*

explicit *adj.* **1** expressly stated or conveyed, leaving nothing merely implied; stated in detail. **2** (of knowledge, a notion, etc.) definite, clear. **3** expressing views unreservedly; outspoken. **4** describing or representing nudity or intimate sexual activity. □ **explicitly** *adv.* **explicitness** *n.*

explode *v.* **1 a** *intr.* (of gas, gunpowder, a bomb, etc.) expand suddenly, burst, or fly into pieces with a loud noise owing to a release of internal energy. **b** *tr.* cause (a bomb etc.) to explode. **2** *intr.* give vent suddenly to emotion, esp. anger. **3** *intr.* increase suddenly or rapidly, esp. in size, numbers, amount, etc. **4** *intr.* appear suddenly and with great impact. **5** *tr.* show (a theory etc.) to be false or baseless.

exploit ● *n.* a bold or daring feat. ● *v.tr.* **1** make use of (a resource etc.); derive benefit from. **2** usu. *derogatory* utilize or take advantage of (esp. a person) for one's own ends. □ **exploitability** *adj.* **exploitable** *adj.* **exploitation** *n.* **exploitative** *adj.* **exploiter** *n.* **exploitive** *adj.*

exploratory *adj.* **1** (of discussion etc.) preliminary, serving to establish procedure etc. **2** involving exploration or investigation (*exploratory surgery*).

explore *v.* **1** *tr. & intr.* travel extensively (through a country etc.) in order to learn or discover about it. **2 a** *tr. & intr.* inquire (into); investigate thoroughly. **b** *intr.* experiment, try something new (in music etc.). **3** *tr. Surgery* examine (a part of the body) in detail. **4** *intr.* search for new deposits of minerals, oil, etc. □ **exploration** *n.* **explorer** *n.*

explosion *n.* **1** the act or an instance of exploding. **2** a loud noise caused by something exploding. **3 a** a sudden outburst of noise. **b** a sudden outbreak of feeling, esp. anger. **4** a rapid or sudden increase in numbers, size, or amount.

explosive ● *adj.* **1** able or tending or likely to explode. **2 a** highly controversial. **b** (of a situation etc.) dangerously tense. **3** rapid, sudden; violent (*explosive growth*). **4** (of an athlete) characterized by bursts of energy. ● *n.* an explosive substance. □ **explosively** *adv.* **explosiveness** *n.*

Expo *n.* (also **expo**) (*pl.* **-os**) **1** a large international exhibition. **2** an exhibition for a specific industry or with a specific theme (*bridal expo*).

exponent /ikˈspoːnənt, ek-/ ● *n.* **1** a person who favours or promotes an idea etc. **2** a representative or practitioner of an activity, profession, etc. **3** a person who explains or interprets something. **4** a type or representative. **5** *Math.* a raised symbol or expression beside a numeral indicating how many times it is to be multiplied by itself, e.g. $2^3 = 2 \times 2 \times 2$. ● *adj.* that sets forth or interprets.

exponential /ˌekspəˈnentʃəl/ ● *adj.* **1** *Math.* of or indicated by a mathematical exponent. **2** (of an increase etc.) more and more rapid. ● *n. Math.* an exponential quantity. □ **exponentially** *adv.*

export ● *v.tr.* **1** send out (goods, services, etc.) to another country, esp. for sale. **2** disseminate (a trend, ideology, etc.) into another country. **3** *Computing* transmit (data) from a system for use elsewhere. ● *n.* **1** the process of exporting. **2 a** an exported article or service. **b** (in *pl.*) an amount exported (*exports exceeded $50m.*). **3** (*attrib.*) suitable for export, esp. of better quality. □ **exportable** *adj.* **exporter** *n.*

expose *v.tr.* **1** remove the covering from or leave uncovered or unprotected. **2** (foll. by *to*) **a** cause to be liable to or in danger of. **b** subject, introduce, or lay open to (an influence etc.). **3** subject (a film) to light, esp. by operation of a camera. **4** reveal the identity or fact of (esp. a person or thing disapproved of or guilty of crime etc.). **5** disclose; make public. **6** exhibit, display. **7** leave (a person) in the open to die. □ **expose oneself** display one's body, esp. the genitals, publicly and indecently. □ **exposer** *n.*

exposé /ˌekspoːˈzei/ *n.* **1** the act or an instance of revealing something discreditable. **2** an orderly statement of facts.

exposed *adj.* **1** (foll. by *to*) open to; unprotected from (*exposed to the east*). **2** vulnerable, risky.

exposition *n.* **1** the action or process of stating or describing, in speech or writing; a detailed statement or description. **2** an explanation or commentary. **3** *Music* the part of a movement, esp. in sonata form, in which the principal themes are first presented. **4** a large public exhibition. **5 a** the act or an instance of exposing or being exposed. **b** *Catholicism* the act or an instance of exposing the Host or a relic.

expositor /ikˈspɒzitər, ek-/ *n.* **1** an expounder or interpreter. **2** someone who describes something in detail; a narrator. □ **expository** *adj.*

exposure n. **1** (foll. by *to*) **a** the act or condition of exposing or being exposed (to cold, danger, radiation, an influence, etc.). **b** the duration or extent of this condition. **2** the physical condition resulting from being exposed to the elements, esp. in severe conditions (*died from exposure*). **3** the revelation of an identity or fact, esp. when concealed or likely to find disapproval. **4** *Photog.* **a** the action of exposing a film etc. to the light. **b** the duration of this action. **c** the extent to which the film is exposed (dependent on shutter speed and aperture). **d** an area of film etc. so exposed. **5** the way in which something is situated in relation to compass direction, wind, sunshine, etc. **6** publicity; presence in the public eye.

expound v. **1** a tr. set out in detail (a doctrine, theory, etc.). **b** intr. (foll. by *on*) explain, discuss at length. **2** tr. explain or interpret (esp. a religious text). □ **expounder** n.

express[1] v.tr. **1** a represent or make known (thought, feelings, etc.) in words or by gestures, conduct, etc. **b** manifest, indicate, betoken. **2** refl. say what one thinks or means. **3** esp. *Math.* represent by symbols. **4** squeeze out (liquid or air). □ **expressible** adj.

express[2] • attrib.adj. **1** a operating at high speed. **b** (of a train, bus, elevator, etc.) making relatively few stops before reaching its destination. **c** (of a road, lane, etc.) designed for express traffic. **2** definitely stated, not merely implied. **3** done, made, or sent for a special purpose. **4** (of messages or goods) delivered immediately or rapidly. • adv. **1** at high speed. **2** by express courier or train. • n. **1** an express train, bus, etc. **2** (in company names) a courier. • v.tr. send by express courier or delivery. □ **expressly** adv. (in sense 2 of adj.).

expression n. **1** the act or an instance of expressing. **2** a word or phrase expressed, esp. a common saying or figure of speech. **3** *Math.* a collection of symbols expressing a quantity. **4** a person's facial appearance or intonation of voice, esp. as indicating feeling. **5** depiction of feeling, movement, etc., in art. **6** conveying of feeling in the performance of a piece of music. **7** the appearance in a phenotype of a character or effect attributed to a particular gene. □ **expressionless** adj. **expressionlessly** adv. **expressionlessness** n.

expressionism n. (also **Expressionism**) a style of painting, music, drama, etc., in which an artist or writer seeks to express emotional experience rather than impressions of the external world. □ **expressionist** n. & adj. **expressionistic** adj.

expressive adj. **1** full of expression (*an expressive look*). **2** (foll. by *of*) serving to express (*words expressive of contempt*). □ **expressively** adv. **expressiveness** n. **expressivity** n.

expresso /ek'spreso/ var. of ESPRESSO.

expressway n. *N Amer.* & *Austral.* a highway for fast-moving traffic, esp. in urban areas, with limited access and a median dividing opposing traffic.

expropriate /eks'pro:pri,eit/ v.tr. **1** (esp. of the state) **a** take away (property) from its owner. **b** deprive (a person) of property. **2** use or claim (another's ideas etc.) as one's own. □ **expropriation** n.

expulsion n. the act or an instance of expelling; the process of being expelled. □ **expulsive** adj.

expunge /ɪk'spʌndʒ, ek-/ v.tr. **1** erase, remove (esp. a passage from a book or a name from a list). **2** wipe out, annihilate, destroy.

expurgate /'ekspər,geit/ v.tr. **1** remove matter thought to be objectionable from (a book etc.). **2** remove (such matter).

exquisite /ek'skwɪzɪt, 'ekskwɪzɪt/ adj. **1** extremely beautiful or pleasing. **2** acute; keenly felt (*exquisite pleasure*). **3** keen; highly sensitive or discriminating (*exquisite taste*). □ **exquisitely** adv. **exquisiteness** n.

ex-service adj. **1** having formerly been a member of the armed forces. **2** relating to former members of the armed forces. □ **ex-serviceman** n. (pl. **-men**). **ex-servicewoman** n. (pl. **-women**).

ext. abbr. **1** extension. **2** exterior. **3** external. **4** extra.

extant /'ekstənt, ek'stænt, ɪk'st-/ adj. (esp. of a document, species, etc.) still existing, surviving.

extempore /ɪk'stempəri, ek-/ adj. & adv. without preparation.

extemporize /ɪk'stempə,raiz, ek-/ v.tr. & intr. compose or produce (music, a speech, etc.) without preparation; improvise. □ **extemporization** n.

extend v. **1** tr. & intr. lengthen or make larger in space or time. **2** tr. stretch or lay out at full length. **3** intr. & tr. (foll. by *to*, *over*) reach or be or make continuous over a certain area. **4** a intr. have a certain scope (*the permit does not extend to camping*). **b** tr. increase the scope or range of application of (*extend their control over the region*). **5** tr. **a** offer (an invitation, hospitality, kindness, etc.). **b** accord, grant (financial credit). **6** tr. (usu. refl. or in *passive*) tax the powers of (an athlete, student, performer, etc.) to the utmost. □ **extendable** adj. **extendability** n. **extensible** adj. **extensibility** n.

extended family n. **1** one's family including or esp. one's grandparents, aunts, uncles, cousins, etc. **2** such a group living in the same household or near each other.

extender n. **1** a person or thing that extends. **2** a substance added to paint, ink, glue, etc., to dilute its colour or increase its bulk.

extension n. **1** the act or an instance of extending; the process of being extended. **2** prolongation; enlargement. **3** a part enlarging or added on to a main structure, building, room, etc. **4** an additional part of anything. **5** a a subsidiary telephone on the same line as the main one. **b** its number. **6** an additional period of time, esp. extending allowance for a project etc. **7** extramural instruction by a university or college (*extension course*). **8** extent, range. **9** *N Amer.* an extension cord. **10** *Computing* a string of letters after a period in a file name, often identifying the file as belonging to a certain category.

extension cord n. *N Amer.* an electrical cable attached to the cord of an appliance etc., so that it can be plugged into a distant outlet.

extensive adj. **1** covering a large area in space or time. **2** having a wide scope; far-reaching, comprehensive (*extensive knowledge*). **3** *Agriculture* involving cultivation from a large area, with a minimum of special resources (*compare* INTENSIVE adj. 3). □ **extensively** adv. **extensiveness** n.

extensor n. (in full **extensor muscle**) a muscle that extends or straightens out part of the body.

extent n. **1** the space over which a thing extends. **2** the width or limits of application; scope (*to the full extent of their power*). **3** the whole of a space or area of a specified kind (*the extent of the ocean*).

extenuate /ɪk'stenjʊ,eit, ek-/ v.tr. (often as **extenuating** adj.) lessen the seeming seriousness of (guilt or an offence) by reference to some mitigating factor. □ **extenuatingly** adv. **extenuation** n.

exterior • adj. **1** a of or on the outer side (*opp.* INTERIOR). **b** (foll. by *to*) situated on the outside of (a building etc.). **c** coming from without. **d** intended for the outside or outer surfaces. **2** *Film* outdoor. • n. **1**

the outward aspect or surface of a building etc. **2** the outward or apparent behaviour or demeanour of a person. **3** *Film* an outdoor scene. □ **exteriority** *n.*

exterminate /ɪk'stɜrmɪ,neɪt, ek-/ *v.tr.* **1** destroy utterly (esp. something living). **2** get rid of; eliminate (a pest, disease, etc.). □ **extermination** *n.* **exterminator** *n.* **exterminatory** *adj.*

external ● *adj.* **1 a** of or situated on the outside or visible part (*opp.* INTERNAL). **b** coming or derived from the outside or an outside source. **2** relating to a country's foreign affairs. **3** outside the conscious subject (*the external world*). **4** (of medicine etc.) for use on the outside of the body. **5** pertaining to or consisting of outward acts or observances. **6** pertaining to a device that is subsidiary or peripheral to a computer system (*external modem*). ● *n.* (in *pl.*) **1** the outward features or aspect. **2** external circumstances. **3** inessentials. □ **externally** *adv.*

external affairs *n.pl.* **1** a country's international affairs. **2** (treated as *sing.*) the government department concerned with international affairs.

externality *n.* (*pl.* **-ies**) **1 a** the quality of being external. **b** *Philos.* the fact of existing outside the perceiving subject. **2** an external or outward object, feature, characteristic, circumstance, etc. **3** *Econ.* a side effect or consequence, esp. of an industrial or commercial activity, which affects other parties without this being reflected in the cost or price of the goods or services involved.

externalize *v.tr.* **1** treat (a fact, responsibility, etc.) as existing or occurring outside of oneself or in the external world. **2** *Psych.* attribute (one's own feelings etc.) to others, the external environment, etc. **3** give external form to. □ **externalization** *n.*

external relations *n.pl.* **1** = EXTERNAL AFFAIRS. **2** = PUBLIC RELATIONS.

extinct *adj.* **1 a** (of a species, language, etc.) no longer surviving in the world at large or in a specific locale. **b** (of a family) having no living descendant. **2 a** (of fire etc.) extinguished or no longer burning. **b** (of a volcano) no longer erupting. **3** (of life, hope, etc.) terminated, quenched. **4** (of an office, job, etc.) discontinued, obsolete, or no longer used.

extinction *n.* **1** the act or process of making or becoming extinct. **2** the state or fact of being extinct. **3** total destruction or annihilation.

extinguish /ɪk'stɪŋgwɪʃ/ *v.tr.* **1** quench, put out, or cause (a flame, light, etc.) to die out. **2** exterminate (*a program to extinguish disease*). **3** terminate, put an end to, or obscure utterly (a feeling, quality, etc.). **4 a** abolish or wipe out (a debt), esp. by full payment. **b** *Law* nullify or render void (a right, claim, etc.). □ **extinguishable** *adj.* **extinguishment** *n.*

extinguisher *n.* a device used for extinguishing, esp. a fire extinguisher.

extirpate /'ekstɜr,peɪt/ *v.tr.* **1** kill all the members of (a race, nation, etc.) or make (a species) extinct locally, but not globally. **2** do away with as such (a specified category or grouping of people). **3** root out or destroy completely (a vice or other immaterial thing). □ **extirpation** *n.*

extol /ɪk'sto:l/ *v.tr.* (**extolled, extolling**) praise enthusiastically.

extort *v.tr. & intr.* obtain (esp. money) by force, threats, persistent demands, etc. □ **extortion** *n.* **extortioner** *n.* **extortionist** *n.*

extortionate /ɪk'stɔrʃənət/ *adj.* **1** (of a price etc.) exorbitant or grossly excessive. **2** using or given to extortion. □ **extortionately** *adv.*

extra ● *adj.* additional; more than is usual or neces-

sary or expected. ● *adv.* **1** more than the usual, specified, or expected amount. **2** additionally. ● *n.* **1** an extra or additional thing. **2** a thing for which an extra charge is made. **3** a person engaged temporarily to fill out a scene in a film or play, esp. as one of a crowd. **4** a special issue of a newspaper etc.

extra- *comb. form* **1** outside, beyond. **2** beyond the scope of.

extra-base hit *n. Baseball* a base hit that allows a batter safely to reach more than one base.

extra-billing *n.* Cdn the practice of a doctor charging patients fees in excess of what provincial health insurance will pay.

extracellular *adj.* situated or taking place outside a cell or cells. □ **extracellularly** *adv.*

extract ● *v.tr.* **1** remove or take out (a tooth etc.) from a containing body or cavity, usu. with some degree of effort, force, dexterity, etc. **2** obtain (money, information, etc.) with difficulty or against a person's will. **3** obtain (a natural resource) from the earth. **4** take (a part) from a whole, esp. select or reproduce (a passage of writing, music, etc.) for quotation or performance. **5** obtain (constituent elements, juices, etc.) from a thing or substance by chemical or physical means such as pressure, distillation, etc. **6** derive (happiness, pleasure, amusement, etc.) from a specified source or situation. **7** draw out (the sense of something), deduce (a principle) etc. ● *n.* **1** an excerpt or short passage taken from a book, piece of music, etc. **2** a preparation containing the active principle of a substance in concentrated form (*vanilla extract*). □ **extractable** *adj.* **extractability** *n.*

extraction *n.* **1** the act or process of extracting or being extracted. **2** an instance of extracting, esp. the removal of a tooth. **3** origin, lineage, descent (*of Scottish extraction*).

extractive *adj.* of, involving, or concerned with the extraction of natural resources or products, esp. non-renewable ones.

extractor *n.* **1** a machine that extracts one thing from another, e.g. juice from fruit, water from wet laundry, etc. **2** the part of a breech-loading firearm which removes the cartridge. **3** a tool or instrument for loosening or removing tight-fitting parts etc.

extracurricular *adj.* **1** (of an activity or subject of study) not included in the normal curriculum. **2** outside the normal routine, job expectations, etc. **3** *informal* extramarital.

extradite *v.tr.* **1** hand over (a person accused or convicted of a crime) to the foreign country etc. in which the crime was committed. **2** obtain the extradition of (a person) from another country.

extradition /ˌekstrə'dɪʃən/ *n.* the surrender or delivery of a person into the jurisdiction of another country in order that he or she may be tried by a country for crimes committed there.

extra end *n. Curling* an additional end played to break a tie at the completion of regular play.

extramarital *adj.* involving or constituting a usu. sexual relationship between a married person and someone other than his or her spouse.

extramural *adj.* **1 a** (of courses etc.) taught or conducted off the premises of a university, college, or school. **b** (of instructors, researchers, etc.) working or located off the premises of a university, college, etc. **2** (of activities, work, etc.) additional to normal teaching or studies, esp. for non-resident students, or not done as part of one's official, paid duties. **3** outside the walls or boundaries of a town or city.

extraneous /ɪk'streɪniəs/ *adj.* **1** of external origin or added from without. **2** (often foll. by *to*) separate from or foreign to the object or body to which it is attached or which contains it. **3** irrelevant, unnecessary, or not part of the matter at hand. ☐ **extraneously** *adv.* **extraneousness** *n.*

extraordinaire /ˌekstrɔːrdɪˈner/ *adj.* (placed after noun) **1** remarkable, outstanding. **2** (of a person) unusually active or successful in a specified respect.

extraordinary /ekˈstrɔːrdɪneri, ˌekstrəˈɔːrd-/ *adj.* **1** unusual, remarkable, or out of the regular course or order. **2** exceeding what is usual in amount, degree, extent, or size, esp. to the point of provoking astonishment, admiration, or disapproval. **3** (of an official etc.) additional to regular staff or specially employed. ☐ **extraordinarily** *adv.* **extraordinariness** *n.*

extrapolate /ekˈstræpəˌleɪt/ *v.tr. & intr.* **1 a** infer more widely from a limited range of known facts. **b** predict on the basis of known facts or observed events. **2** *Math. & Philos.* **a** assume the continuance of a known trend in inferring or estimating an unknown value. **b** extend (a range of values, a curve, etc.) on the assumption that the trend exhibited inside the given part is maintained outside of it (*compare* INTERPOLATE 3). ☐ **extrapolation** *n.*

extrasensory *adj.* regarded as derived by means other than the known senses, e.g. by telepathy, clairvoyance, etc.

extrasensory perception *n.* the supposed ability to perceive outside, past, or future events without the use of known senses. Abbr.: **ESP.**

extraterrestrial ● *adj.* **1** existing or occurring beyond the earth or its atmosphere. **2** (in science fiction) from outer space. ● *n.* (in science fiction) a being, esp. an intelligent one, from outer space.

extraterritorial *adj.* **1** situated or (of laws etc.) valid outside a country's territory. **2** (of an ambassador etc.) free from the jurisdiction of the territory of residence. ☐ **extraterritoriality** *n.*

extravagance /ekˈstrævəgəns/ *n.* **1 a** prodigality, wastefulness, or excessive spending or use of resources. **b** a purchase or payment difficult to justify except as a whim or indulgence. **2 a** lack of moderation in behaviour. **b** an immoderate statement, action, or quality.

extravagant *adj.* **1** immoderate, excessive, or wasteful in use of resources, esp. money. **2** exorbitant or costing much. **3 a** (of ideas, speech, or behaviour) going beyond what is reasonable, usual, or justifiable (*extravagant claims*). **b** astonishingly elaborate or ostentatious. ☐ **extravagantly** *adv.*

extravaganza /ɪkˌstrævəˈgænzə/ *n.* **1** an event, festival, etc. featuring elaborate and colourful spectacle, massive participation, lavish expenditure, etc. **2** a fanciful literary, dramatic, etc. composition.

extra-virgin *adj.* (of olive oil) made from the first pressing, cold pressed, and thus of high quality.

extreme ● *adj.* **1 a** reaching a high or the highest degree or being exceedingly great or intense (*in extreme danger*). **b** (of a case, circumstance, etc.) having some feature or characteristic in the utmost degree. **2 a** severe, stringent, lacking restraint or moderation (*extreme measures*). **b** (of a person, opinion, etc.) going to great lengths, advocating severe and drastic measures, or being immoderate in opinion. **3 a** outermost, furthest from the centre (*the extreme edge*). **b** situated at either end. **c** last, utmost, very far advanced in any direction. **4** *Politics* radical or being on the far left or right of a party. **5** designating sports performed in a hazardous environment, involving a high physical risk (*extreme skiing*). ● *n.* **1**

(often in *pl.*) one or other of two things as remote or as different as possible in position, nature, or condition. **2** a thing at either end of anything. **3** the highest degree, the greatest length, or the most extreme measure of anything. ☐ **go to extremes** take an extreme course of action. **go to the other extreme** take a diametrically opposite course of action. **in the extreme** to an extreme degree. ☐ **extremely** *adv.*

extreme unction *n.* the former name for the sacrament of anointing the sick, esp. those thought to be near death.

extremist ● *n.* **1** a person who holds extreme opinions and advocates extreme measures. **2** a person who tends to go to extremes. ● *adj.* of or pertaining to extremists or extremism. ☐ **extremism** *n.*

extremity *n.* (*pl.* **-ies**) **1** the very end or terminal portion of anything. **2** (in *pl.*) the outermost parts of the body, esp. the hands and feet. **3** a condition of extreme adversity or difficulty.

extricate /ˈekstrɪˌkeɪt/ *v.tr.* (often foll. by *from*) free or disentangle (esp. a person) from a constraint or difficulty. ☐ **extricable** *adj.* **extrication** *n.*

extrinsic /ekˈstrɪnsɪk/ *adj.* **1** not inherent, intrinsic, or essential (*opp.* INTRINSIC). **2** (often foll. by *to*) (of a cause or influence) extraneous, lying outside, not part of. **3** due to external circumstances. ☐ **extrinsically** *adv.*

extrovert /ˈekstrəˌvɜrt/ ● *n.* **1** *Psych.* a person whose thoughts and interests are predominantly concerned with things outside the self. **2** an outgoing or sociable person (*compare* INTROVERT). ● *adj.* typical or characteristic of an extrovert. ☐ **extroversion** *n.* **extroverted** *adj.*

extrude *v.* **1** *tr.* (foll. by *from*) thrust, force out, or expel. **2** *tr.* shape (metal, plastics, etc.) by forcing through a die. **3** *intr.* protrude. ☐ **extruded** *adj.* **extruder** *n.* **extrusion** *n.* **extrusive** *adj.*

exuberant /ɪgˈzuːbərənt, -juː/ *adj.* **1** (of people or their actions) lively, high-spirited, effusive in display of feelings. **2** (of speech, writing, etc.) copious, diffuse, lavishly ornamented. **3** (of a plant etc.) prolific, growing luxuriously. ☐ **exuberance** *n.* **exuberantly** *adv.*

exude /ɪgˈzjuːd, -zuːd/ *v.* **1** *tr. & intr.* (of a liquid, moisture, etc.) ooze out, escape or cause to escape gradually. **2** *tr.* give off (moisture, a smell, etc.) in this way. **3** *tr.* **a** (of a person) display (a quality, emotion etc.) freely or abundantly (*exuded charm*). **b** (of a place) have a strong atmosphere of. ☐ **exudation** *n.*

exult /ɪgˈzʌlt/ *v.* **1** *intr.* (often foll. by *over*) have a feeling of triumph (over a person). **2** *intr.* be elated or greatly joyful. **3** *tr.* say exultingly. ☐ **exultation** *n.* **exultant** *adj.* **exultantly** *adv.* **exultingly** *adv.*

exurb /ˈeksɜːrb/ *n.* a town or community beyond the suburbs of a large city. ☐ **exurban** /ekˈsɜːrbən/ *adj.*

-ey *suffix var. of* -Y¹,².

eye ● *n.* **1 a** the organ of sight in humans and other animals. **b** the light-detecting organ in some invertebrates. **2** the eye characterized by the colour of the iris (*has blue eyes*). **3** the region of the face around the eye (*eyes red from weeping*). **4** a glass or plastic ball resembling an eye or serving as an artificial eye. **5** (in *sing.* or *pl.*) **a** a sight or the faculty of sight. **b** perception (*see it through a woman's eyes*). **6** a particular visual faculty or talent for appreciation, judgment, etc., either in general or with some specific reference (*an eye for detail*). **7** (in *sing.* or *pl.*) a look, gaze, or glance, esp. as indicating the disposition of the viewer (*a jaundiced eye*). **8 a** close attention, regard, observation, or supervision. **b** the imagined organ of sight as attributed to the heart, mind, etc. (*in my mind's eye*). **9** a person or animal etc. that sees on behalf of another (*she is my eyes*). **10 a** a thing resembling the eye in appearance, shape, function, or relative position. **b** a mark or spot resembling an eye, occurring on eggs, insect wings, etc. (*compare* EYELET *n.* 3). **c** the leaf bud of a potato. **11** the centre of something circular. **12** the centre of a vortex or eddy, esp. the relatively calm region at the centre of a storm or hurricane. **13** an aperture in an implement, esp. a needle, for the insertion of something, e.g. thread. **14** a ring or loop for a bolt or hook etc. to pass through. **15** the main mass of lean meat in a cut of meat, esp. beef (*eye of round*). ● *v.tr.* (**eyes**, **eyed**, **eyeing** or **eying**) **1** watch or observe closely, esp. admiringly or with curiosity or suspicion. **2** ogle or look at (a person) amorously or with sexual interest. □ **all eyes 1** watching intently. **2** general attention (*all eyes were on us*). **before a person's** (or **a person's very**) **eyes** right in front of a person. **catch a person's eye** attract a person's attention or interest. **close one's eyes to** ignore, refuse to recognize or consider. **an eye for an eye** retaliation in kind. **eyes front** (or **left** or **right**) *Military* a command to turn the head in the direction stated. **have an eye for** be capable of perceiving or appreciating. **have one's eye on** wish or plan to procure. **have eyes bigger than one's stomach** wish or expect to eat more than one can. **have eyes for** be interested in (*had eyes for no other*). **have an eye to** have as one's objective or prudently consider. **hit a person** (**right**) **between the eyes** *informal* be very obvious or impressive. **in the eyes** (or **eye**) **of** in the view or opinion of (*in the eyes of the law*). **keep an eye on 1** pay close attention to (a person). **2** look after or take care of (a child etc.). **keep an eye open** (or **out**) (often foll. by *for*) watch carefully. **keep one's eyes open** (or **peeled** or **skinned**) watch out or be on the alert. **lower one's eyes** look modestly or sheepishly down or away. **make eyes** (or **sheep's eyes**) (foll. by *at*) look amorously or flirtatiously at. **my eye** *slang* nonsense. **one in the eye** (foll. by *for*) a disappointment or setback, esp. for someone regarded as deserving it. **open a person's eyes** be enlightening or revealing to a person. **raise one's eyes** look upwards. **see eye to eye** (often foll. by *with*) be in full agreement. **set eyes on** see or catch sight of (a person etc.). **take one's eyes off** (usu. in *neg.*) stop watching or stop paying attention to (*I can't take my eyes off you*). **under the eye of** under the supervision or observation of. **up to the** (or **one's**) **eyes in 1** inundated with or deeply engaged or involved in (a thing) (*up to the eyes in work*). **2** to the utmost limit (*mortgaged up to the eyes*). **with one's eyes open** deliberately or with full awareness. **with one's eyes shut** (or **closed**) **1** easily or with little effort. **2** unobservant or without awareness (*goes around with his eyes shut*). **with an eye to** with a view to or prudently considering. **with one eye on** directing one's attention partly to. □ **eyed** *adj.* (also in *comb.*). **eyeless** *adj.* **eyelike** *adj.*

eyeball ● *n.* the firm white sphere of the eye within the eyelids and socket. ● *v.tr. N Amer. slang* look or stare at. □ **eyeball-to-eyeball** *informal* confronting or encountering closely. **to** (or **up to**) **the eyeballs** *informal* to a great extent.

eyebolt *n.* a bolt or bar with an eye at the end for a hook, ring, etc.

eyebrow *n.* the line, usu. arched, of short hair growing along the ridge above each eye socket. □ **raise eyebrows** cause surprise, disbelief, or disapproval.

raise one's eyebrows (or **an eyebrow**) show surprise, disbelief, or mild disapproval.

eyebrow pencil *n.* a cosmetic pencil for drawing lines to accentuate the eyebrows.

eye-catcher *n.* a person or thing which catches the eye, through attractiveness, uniqueness, etc. □ **eye-catching** *adj.*

eye contact *n.* the state or practice of looking directly into another person's eyes while he or she is looking into one's own.

eye doctor *n.* **1** an ophthalmologist. **2** an optometrist.

eyedropper *n.* = DROPPER 1.

eyeful *n.* (*pl.* **-fuls**) *informal* **1** a complete view or a good look at something. **2** a visually striking scene or thing, esp. an attractive person. □ **get an eyeful** take a good, long look.

eyeglass *n.* **1** (in *pl.*) esp. *N Amer.* a pair of lenses, in a frame resting on the nose and ears, used to correct defective eyesight or protect the eyes. **2** a lens for correcting or assisting defective sight.

eyelash *n.* a hair, or one of the rows of hairs, growing on the edge of the eyelid.

eyelet *n.* **1** a small hole in paper, leather, cloth, etc., for string or rope etc. to pass through. **2** a metal ring reinforcement for this. **3** a small eye, esp. a small mark on a butterfly's wing (*compare* EYE *n.* 10b). **4 a** a form of decoration in embroidery, composed of usu. round eyelets finished along the edge, which produces an open work effect. **b** a lightweight fabric having numerous small embroidered holes in a decorative pattern.

eye level *n.* (often *attrib.*) the height of the eyes or the level seen by the eyes looking straight ahead (*eye-level grill*).

eyelid *n.* either of the upper or lower folds of skin that meet when the eye is closed.

eyeliner *n.* a cosmetic applied as a line around the eye, usu. next to the lashes, to accentuate the eyes.

eye-opener *n.* *informal* a thing or experience that enlightens, surprises, etc. □ **eye-opening** *adj.*

eye patch *n.* a pad or piece of material worn to shield or protect an injured eye.

eyepiece *n.* the lens or lenses at the end of telescope etc. to which the eye is applied and through which an image is viewed or magnified.

eye-popping *adj.* surprising, astonishing, esp. visually spectacular. □ **eye-popper** *n.*

eyeshadow *n.* a coloured cosmetic applied to the eyelids, around the eyes, etc. to enhance the eyes.

eyesight *n.* the faculty or power of seeing.

eye socket *n.* the orbit of the eye.

eyesore *n.* a visually offensive thing, esp. a building.

eye strain *n.* fatigue of the muscles of the eyes, esp. from excessive or incorrect use.

eye tooth *n.* one of the canine teeth, esp. in the upper jaw. □ **would give one's eye teeth for** would make any sacrifice to obtain.

eyewear *n.* glasses, contact lenses, goggles, etc. worn on the eyes.

eyewitness ● *n.* a person who has seen a thing done or happen and can testify to it from his or her own observation. ● *v.tr.* be an eyewitness to (an event).

eyrie *var. of* AERIE.

e-zine *n.* a magazine or fanzine published in electronic format.

Ff

F¹ *n.* (also **f**) (*pl.* **Fs** or **F's**) **1** the sixth letter of the alphabet. **2** *Music* the fourth note of the diatonic scale of C major. **3** the lowest category of academic mark, denoting a failing grade.

F² *abbr.* (also **F.**) **1** Fahrenheit. **2** female. **3** a fine, moderately soft pencil lead, between B and H. **4** *Physics* force. **5** (in Ontario) FAMILY 8.

F³ *symbol* fluorine.

f *abbr.* (also **f.**) **1** female. **2** *Grammar* feminine. **3** (*pl.* *ff.*) following page etc. **4** *Music* forte. **5** (*pl.* *ff.*) folio. **6** frequency. **7** *Math.* function. **8** from.

FA *abbr.* **1** *slang* = FUCK ALL. **2** fine arts.

fa /fɒ/ *n. Music* **1** (in tonic sol-fa) the fourth note of a major scale. **2** the note F in the fixed-do system.

fab *adj. informal* fabulous, marvellous.

Fabian /'feibiən/ ● *n.* a member or supporter of the Fabian Society, a socialist organization founded in England in 1884 to promote cautious and gradual political change. ● *adj.* **1** relating to or characteristic of the Fabians. **2** employing a cautiously persistent and dilatory strategy to wear out an enemy (*Fabian tactics*). ☐ **Fabianism** *n.*

fable ● *n.* **1 a** a tale, esp. with animals as characters, conveying a moral. **b** a fictitious narrative, esp. a supernatural one. **2** (*collect.*) myths and legendary tales. **3** a false statement or lie. **4** a thing falsely claimed to exist or having no existence outside popular legend etc. ● *v.tr.* describe fictitiously.

fabled *adj.* **1** famous, legendary. **2** celebrated in fable.

fabric *n.* **1 a** a woven, knitted, or felted material; a textile. **b** the texture of this. **c** something resembling this. **2** a structure or framework, esp. the walls, floor, and roof of a building. **3** the essential structure or essence of a thing (*the fabric of society*).

fabricate *v.tr.* **1** construct or manufacture, esp. from prepared components. **2** invent or concoct (a story, evidence, etc.). **3** forge (a document). ☐ **fabrication** *n.* **fabricator** *n.*

fabric softener *n.* *N Amer.* a liquid added to the wash or a sheet placed in the dryer when doing laundry to soften clothes, reduce static, etc.

fabrique /fæ'bri:k/ *n. Cdn* (*Que.*) *hist.* a vestry or local parish body responsible for the maintenance, management, etc. of church property.

fabulous *adj.* **1** incredible, exaggerated, astonishing (*fabulous wealth*). **2** excellent, marvellous, terrific (*a fabulous dancer*). **3** celebrated in fable. **b** legendary, mythical. ☐ **fabulously** *adv.* **fabulousness** *n.*

FAC *abbr. Cdn* Firearms Acquisition Certificate.

facade /fə'sɒd/ *n.* **1** the face of a building, esp. its principal front. **2** an outward appearance or front, esp. a deceptive one.

face ● *n.* **1** the front of the head from the forehead to the chin. **2 a** the expression of the facial features (*had a happy face*). **b** a distorted look, grimace, etc. intended to express a usu. negative emotion. **3** calm, cool audacity or effrontery. **4** the surface of a thing, esp. as regarded or approached, esp.: **a** the visible part of the earth, a celestial body, etc. **b** a principal side, often vertical or steeply sloping, presented by an object, esp. the front of a mountain or cliff etc. **c** *Mining* the end of a tunnel at which work is progressing or the principal surface from which coal etc. is being removed. **d** *Math.* each surface of a solid. **e** the facade of a building. **f** the plate of a clock or watch bearing the digits, hands, etc. **5 a** the acting, striking, or working surface of an implement, tool etc. **b** the marked or picture side of a playing card. **c** either side of a coin, but esp. the side bearing the effigy. **6** = TYPEFACE. **7 a** the outward appearance, aspect, or semblance, esp. of an immaterial thing (*the unacceptable face of capitalism*). **b** pretense, outward show (*put a good face on the matter*). **8** a person, esp. conveying some quality or association (*some younger faces*). **9** esteem, respectable reputation (*a loss of face*). **10** makeup, cosmetics (*I have to put on my face*). **11** the inscribed side of a document etc. ● *v.* **1** *tr. & intr.* look or be positioned towards or in a certain direction. **2** *tr.* (of an engraving, illustration, etc.) stand on the opposite page to (*facing page 20*). **3** *tr.* **a** (often foll. by *down*) confront, meet resolutely or defiantly (*face one's critics*). **b** meet bravely and boldly or not shrink from. **c** recognize, consider seriously, or accept the inevitability of (an idea etc.) (*face the facts*). **4** *tr.* confront, present itself to (a person etc.) (*the problem that faces us*). **5** *tr.* **a** cover the surface of (a thing) with a coating, extra layer, etc. **b** put a facing on (a garment). **6** *intr. & tr.* turn or cause to turn in a certain direction (*right face*). **7** *Lacrosse* ● *intr.* start or restart play by placing the ball between the sticks of the two opposing players. **b** *tr.* place (the ball) in this way to start or restart play. ☐ **face a charge** (or **charges**) be forced to appear in court accused of something. **face down** (or **downwards**) with the face or surface turned towards the ground, floor, etc. **face off** *Hockey & Lacrosse* start or restart play by a faceoff. **2** assume a confrontational attitude; contend or compete against. **face up** (or **upwards**) with the face or surface turned upwards to view. **face up to** confront, accept bravely, or stand up to. **have the face** be shameless enough. **in one's face 1** directly at or straight against one. **2** confronting or irritatingly present. **in face** (or **the face**) **of 1** despite. **2** when confronted by. **3** in the presence of. **let's face it** *informal* we must be honest or realistic about it. **look a person in the face** confront a person with a steady gaze, implying courage, defiance, etc. **on the face of it** apparently, superficially, or obviously. **set one's face against** oppose or resist with determination. **the face of the earth 1** the surface of the earth. **2** anywhere. **to a person's face** openly in a person's presence. ☐ **facing** *adj.* (also in *comb.*).

face card *n.* a playing card, other than a joker or a tarot, bearing the representation of a human figure, e.g. the king, queen, or jack.

face cloth *n. Cdn & Brit.* a small cloth, usu. of terry, for washing one's face, hands, etc.

faced *adj.* (also in *comb.*) **1** having a face or expression of a specified kind. **2** having a surface of a specified kind (*marble-faced houses*).

faceless adj. **1** anonymous or purposely not identifiable. **2** with an individual identity, lacking an individualized character. **3** without a face.

facelift n. **1** cosmetic surgery to remove wrinkles etc. by tightening the skin of the face. **2** a procedure to improve the appearance of a thing, esp. the refacing or redecoration of a building.

face mask n. **1** any covering or device to shield or protect the face, usu. covering the whole face, nose and mouth, or nose and eyes. **2** (also **facial mask**) a preparation beneficial to the complexion, spread over the face and removed when dry.

faceoff n. **1** *Hockey & Lacrosse* the action of starting or restarting play by dropping or placing the puck or ball between two opposing players' sticks. **2** a direct confrontation.

faceoff circle n. each of five circles on a hockey rink, roughly 9 m in diameter, where faceoffs may be taken, including one at centre ice and two in each end situated to the left and right of the net.

face paint n. paint for applying to the face. □ **face painter** n. **face painting** n.

faceplate n. **1** an enlarged end or attachment on the end of a mandrel of a lathe to which work may be attached for being faced or made flat. **2** a plate protecting a piece of machinery. **3** the transparent window corresponding to the visor in protective headgear, esp. of a diving or space suit.

face powder n. a cosmetic powder for reducing the shine on the face.

facet /'fæsət/ n. **1** a particular aspect of a thing. **2 a** one side of a many sided body, esp. when flat and smooth. **b** any of the cut and polished faces of a cut gem. **3** one segment of a compound eye. □ **faceted** adj. (also in comb.). **faceting** n.

facetious /fə'si:ʃəs/ adj. **1** not intended seriously or literally; ironic. **2** characterized by flippant or inopportune humour. **3** (of a person) intending to be amusing, esp. inopportunely. □ **facetiously** adv.

face to face ● adv. closely or directly viewing, confronting, etc. ● attrib.adj. (**face-to-face**) with the people involved facing each other or in each other's presence (*face-to-face discussions*).

face value n. **1** the value printed or stamped on money or postage stamps. **2** the superficial appearance or implication of a thing. □ **take at face value** assume (a thing, person, etc.) is genuinely what it, he, she, etc. appears to be.

facia var. of FASCIA 3.

facial /'feiʃəl/ ● adj. of or for the face. ● n. a beauty treatment for the face. □ **facially** adv.

facile /'fæsail, -si:l/ adj. **1** usu. derogatory **a** easily obtained or achieved and so not highly valued. **b** (of speech, writing, etc.) easily produced, but superficial or of poor quality. **2** (of a person) fluent, glib, saying or doing things easily. □ **facilely** adv. **facileness** n.

facilitate /fə'sɪlɪˌteɪt/ v.tr. make (an action, result, etc.) easier, less difficult, or more easily achieved. □ **facilitation** n. **facilitative** adj.

facilitator n. **1** a person or thing that facilitates. **2** a person who encourages discussion and other activity without directing it or controlling it actively.

facility /fə'sɪlɪti/ n. (pl. **-ies**) **1 a** fluency, dexterity, or ease of speech, action, etc. **b** absence of difficulty or the fact or condition of being easy or easily done. **2** (esp. in pl.) the physical means, equipment, resources, or opportunity required to do something. **3** N Amer. a building designed for a specific purpose. **4** euphemism (pl.) a toilet or washroom.

facing n. **1 a** an esp. interior layer of material covering part of a garment etc. for contrast or strength. **b** (in pl.) the contrasting cuffs, collar, etc. of a military or military-style jacket. **2** a layer of brick etc. which forms the face of a building, wall, etc.

facsimile /fæk'sɪmɪli/ ● n. **1** (often attrib.) an exact copy, esp. of writing, printing, a picture, etc. (*facsimile edition*). **2 a** (often attrib.) production of an exact copy of a document etc. by electronic scanning and transmission of the resulting data (*see also* FAX). **b** a copy produced in this way. **3** something that resembles something else strongly. ● v.tr. (**facsimiled**, **facsimileing**) make a facsimile of. □ **in facsimile** as an exact copy.

fact n. **1** a thing that is known to have occurred, exist, or be true. **2** a thing that is believed or claimed to be true. **3** *Law* (usu. in pl.) a piece of evidence, an item of verified information, or events and circumstances as distinct from their legal interpretation. **4** truth, reality. □ **before** (or **after**) **the fact** before (or after) the occurrence of a pertinent event. **facts and figures** precise information, details, etc. **hard fact** (or **facts**) **1** inescapable truth (or truths). **2** concrete evidence. **in** (or **in point of**) **fact 1** in reality. **2** (in summarizing) in short. **the fact of the matter** the truth.

fact-finding ● n. the discovery and establishment of the facts of an issue. ● adj. **1** engaged in the finding out of facts. **2** (of a committee etc.) set up to discover and establish the facts of an issue. □ **fact-finder** n.

faction n. **1** a small, organized, and self-interested or turbulent group of people within a larger one, esp. in politics. **2** a state of dissension within an organization.

factional adj. **1** of or characterized by faction. **2** belonging to a faction. □ **factionalism** n.

fact of life n. **1** something, esp. unpleasant, that cannot be ignored and must be accepted. **2** (in pl.; usu. prec. by *the*) information about sexual functions and practices, esp. as given to children and teenagers.

factoid /'fæktɔɪd/ ● n. **1** an assumption or speculation that is reported and repeated so often that it becomes accepted as fact. **2** N Amer. a brief or trivial item of news or information. ● adj. being or having the character of a factoid; containing factoids.

factor ● n. **1** a circumstance, fact, or influence contributing to a result. **2** *Math.* a whole number etc. that when multiplied with another produces a given number or expression. **3** *Biol.* a gene etc. determining hereditary character. **4** (foll. by identifying number) any of several substances in the blood which contribute to coagulation (*factor VIII*). **5 a** a business agent or a merchant buying and selling on commission. **b** an agent or a deputy. **6** a company that buys a manufacturer's invoices and takes responsibility for collecting the payments due on them. **7** Cdn hist. an employee of the Hudson's Bay Company, ranking higher than a chief trader, in charge of a trading post. ● v.tr. *Math.* resolve into factors or express as a product of factors. □ **factor in** introduce as a factor. **factor out** exclude from an assessment.

factory n. (pl. **-ies**) **1** a building or buildings containing equipment for manufacturing or processing. **2** Cdn hist. a main trading post, esp. a large centre for the transshipment of furs (*York Factory*).

factory outlet n. a store in which factory-made goods, often surplus stock, are sold directly by the manufacturer to consumers at discount prices.

factory ship n. a fishing ship with facilities for immediate processing of the catch.

fact sheet *n.* a paper on which facts relevant to an issue are set out briefly.

factual /'fæktʃʊəl/ *adj.* **1** based on, concerned with, or of the nature of fact or facts. **2** actual, true. □ **factuality** *n.* **factually** *adv.*

faculty *n.* (*pl.* **-ies**) **1** an aptitude or ability for a particular activity. **2** (often in *pl.*) an inherent mental or physical power. **3 a** a group of university departments concerned with a major division of knowledge (*faculty of arts*). **b** *N Amer.* the teaching staff of a university or college.

fad *n.* a craze or something briefly but enthusiastically taken up, esp. by a group. □ **faddish** *adj.* **faddishly** *adv.* **faddishness** *n.* **faddism** *n.*

fade ● *v.* **1** *intr.* & *tr.* lose or cause to lose colour. **2** *intr.* lose freshness or strength. **3** *intr.* **a** (of colour, light, etc.) disappear gradually; grow pale or dim. **b** (of sound) grow faint. **4** *intr.* (of a feeling etc.) diminish. **5** *intr.* (foll. by *away*, *out*) (of a person etc.) disappear or depart gradually. **6** *tr.* (foll. by *in*, *out*) *Film & Broadcasting* **a** cause (a picture) to come gradually in or out of view on a screen, or to merge into another shot. **b** make (the sound) more or less audible. **7** *intr.* (of a radio signal) vary irregularly in intensity. **8** *intr.* (of a brake) temporarily lose effectiveness. ● *n.* the action or an instance of fading. □ **do a fade** *slang* depart. **fade away** *informal* languish, grow thin. □ **fadeless** *adj.* **fader** *n.* (in sense 6 of *v.*).

fadeaway *n.* **1** *Baseball* = SCREWBALL 1. **2** *Basketball* a shot made while the shooter jumps or falls away from the basket (also *attrib.*: *fadeaway jump shot*).

fade-in *n.* *Film & Broadcasting* the action or an instance of fading in a picture or sound.

fade-out *n.* **1** *Film & Broadcasting* the action or an instance of fading out a picture or sound. **2** *informal* a gradual reduction, disappearance, etc.

faeces etc. *var. of* FECES etc.

fag¹ *n.* *N Amer. slang offensive* a male homosexual. □ **faggy** *adj.* **(-ier, -iest)**

fag² *n.* esp. *Brit. informal* **1** a piece of drudgery; a wearisome or unwelcome task. **2** a cigarette.

faggot *n.* **1** *N Amer. slang offensive* a male homosexual. **2** (also **fagot**) **a** a bundle of sticks or twigs bound together as fuel. **b** a bundle of iron rods for heat treatment. **c** a bunch of herbs. □ **faggoty** *adj.*

fah *var. of* FA.

Fahrenheit /'færən,haɪt/ *adj.* of or measured on a scale of temperature on which water freezes at 32° and boils at 212° under standard conditions.

fail ● *v.* **1** *intr.* not succeed (*failed to qualify*). **2 a** *tr.* & *intr.* be unsuccessful in (an examination, test, course, interview, etc.); be rejected as a candidate. **b** *tr.* (of a commodity etc.) not pass (a test of quality). **c** *tr.* reject (a candidate etc.); declare unsuccessful. **3** *intr.* be unable to; neglect to; choose not to (*I fail to see the reason*; *he failed to appear*). **4** *tr.* disappoint; let down; not serve when needed. **5** *intr.* (of supplies, crops, etc.) be or become lacking or insufficient. **6** *intr.* become weaker; cease functioning; break down (*her health is failing*). **7** *intr.* **a** (of an enterprise) collapse; come to nothing. **b** become bankrupt. ● *n.* a failure in an examination or test. □ **without fail** for certain, whatever happens.

failed *adj.* **1** unsuccessful; not good enough (*a failed actor*). **2** deficient; broken down (*a failed battery*).

failing ● *n.* a fault or shortcoming; a weakness, esp. in character. ● *prep.* in default of; in the absence of (*failing a reconciliation, they will divorce*).

fail-safe *adj.* **1** reverting to a safe condition in the event of a breakdown etc. **2** totally reliable or safe.

failure *n.* **1** lack of success; failing. **2** an unsuccessful person, thing, or attempt. **3** non-performance, non-occurrence. **4** breaking down or ceasing to function (*heart failure*). **5** a cessation in the existence or availability of something. **6** bankruptcy, collapse.

faint ● *adj.* **1 a** indistinct, pale, dim. **b** (of a sound) not clearly perceived. **2** (of a person) weak or giddy; inclined to faint. **3** slight, remote, inadequate (*a faint chance*). **4** feeble, half-hearted (*faint praise*). **5** timid (*a faint heart*). ● *v.intr.* **1** lose consciousness. **2** become faint. ● *n.* a sudden loss of consciousness. □ **not have the faintest** *informal* have no idea. □ **faintly** *adv.* **faintness** *n.*

faint-hearted *adj.* cowardly, timid.

fair¹ ● *adj.* **1** just, unbiased, equitable; in accordance with the rules. **2** blond; light or pale in colour or complexion. **3 a** of (only) moderate quality or amount; average. **b** considerable, satisfactory (*a fair chance of success*). **4 a** (of weather) fine and dry. **b** (of the wind) favourable. **c** (of the sky) clear; cloudless. **5** clean, clear, unblemished (*fair copy*). **6** beautiful, attractive. **7** *Baseball* (of a batted ball) that lands or is caught within the legal area of play. **8 a** specious (*fair speeches*). **b** complimentary (*fair words*). ● *adv.* **1** in a fair manner (*play fair*). **2** exactly, completely (*was hit fair on the jaw*). **3** *dialect* really; thoroughly (*was fair exhausted*). ● *v.tr.* make (the surface of a ship, aircraft, etc.) smooth and streamlined. □ **fair and square 1** exactly. **2** straightforward, honest, above-board. **a fair deal** equitable treatment. **fair enough** *informal* that is reasonable or acceptable. **fair name** a good reputation. **the fair sex** *dated* or *jocular* women. **fair's fair** *informal* all involved should act fairly. **fair shake** (also **fair crack**) *informal* a fair opportunity; an equal chance. **in a fair way to** likely to. **no fair** *N Amer. informal* (that is) unfair. □ **fairish** *adj.* **fairness** *n.*

fair² *n.* **1** a usu. annual exhibition of produce, livestock, crafts, etc., held esp. in rural areas in conjunction with a travelling midway (*fall fair*). **2** an exhibition, esp. to promote particular products (*trade fair*). **3** a periodical gathering for the sale of goods, often with entertainments.

fair game *n.* a thing or person one may legitimately pursue, exploit, etc.

fairground *n.* (usu. in *pl.*) a place where a fair is held.

fair-haired *adj.* **1** having fair hair. **2** *N Amer.* favoured; favourite (*he's her fair-haired boy now*).

fairing *n.* a streamlining structure added to a ship, aircraft, vehicle, etc.

Fair Isle *n.* (also *attrib.*) a knitwear design with multicoloured stitches usu. radiating outward from the neckline.

fairly *adv.* **1** in a fair manner; justly. **2** moderately, acceptably (*fairly good*). **3** to a noticeable degree (*fairly narrow*). **4** used as an intensifier (*fairly glowed*). □ **fairly and squarely** = FAIR AND SQUARE (*see* FAIR¹).

fair-minded *adj.* just, impartial. □ **fair-mindedly** *adv.* **fair-mindedness** *n.*

fair play *n.* reasonable treatment or behaviour.

fairway *n.* **1** the part of a golf course between a tee and its green, kept free of rough grass. **2** a navigable channel; a regular course or track of a ship.

fair-weather *adj.* (of a person) tending to be unreliable in times of difficulty (*fair-weather friend*).

fairy ● *n.* (*pl.* **-ies**) **1** a small imaginary being with magical powers. **2** *slang derogatory* a male homosexual. ● *adj.* **1** of or relating to fairies. **2** fairy-like; delicate, small. □ **fairy-like** *adj.*

fairy godmother *n.* a person who provides unexpected help.

fairyland n. **1** the imaginary home of fairies. **2** an enchanted region.

fairy tale ● n. (also **fairy story**) **1** a tale about fairies. **2** an incredible story; a fabrication. ● adj. **(fairy-tale) 1** of or relating to fairy tales. **2** resembling a fairy tale. **3** highly unlikely.

fait accompli /ˌfeit ə'kɒmpliː, ə'kɔpliː/ n. a thing that has been done and is past arguing or altering.

faith n. **1** complete trust or confidence. **2** firm belief, esp. without logical proof. **3 a** a system of religious belief. **b** belief in God or religious doctrines. **c** spiritual apprehension of divine truth apart from proof. **d** things believed or to be believed. **4** duty or commitment to fulfill a trust, promise, etc. (keep faith). **5** (attrib.) concerned with a supposed ability to cure by faith rather than treatment (faith healing).

faithful adj. **1** showing faith. **2** loyal, trustworthy, constant. **3** remaining sexually loyal to one's spouse, lover, etc. **4** accurate; true to fact (a faithful account). **5 a (the Faithful)** the believers in a religion, esp. Muslims and Christians. **b (the faithful)** the loyal adherents of a political party. □ **faithfully** adv. **faithfulness** n.

faithless adj. **1** false, unreliable, disloyal. **2** without religious faith. □ **faithlessly** adv. **faithlessness** n.

fajita /fə'hiːtə/ n. (usu. in pl.) a dish consisting of small strips of grilled spiced beef or chicken rolled in a tortilla and garnished with fried chopped vegetables, cheese, and usu. guacamole, salsa, and sour cream.

fake ● n. **1** a thing or person that is not genuine. **2** a trick. **3** Sport a movement intended to deceive an opponent. ● adj. counterfeit; not genuine. ● v. **1** tr. make (a false thing) appear genuine; forge, counterfeit. **2** tr. make a pretense of having (a feeling, illness, etc.). **3** intr. pretend; fake something. **4** tr. & intr. Sport deceive (an opponent) by a misleading movement. □ **fake out** N Amer. slang deceive or trick (a person etc.). □ **faker** n. **fakery** n.

fakir /'feikiːr, fə'kiːr/ n. a Muslim or (rarely) Hindu religious mendicant or ascetic.

falafel /fe'lɒfəl/ n. **1** a spicy fried patty made of ground chickpeas or beans. **2** these served in a pita.

falcon /'fɒlkən, 'fæl-/ n. any diurnal bird of prey of the family Falconidae, having long pointed wings, sometimes trained to hunt small game for sport.

falconer n. **1** a keeper and trainer of hawks. **2** a person who hunts with hawks.

falconry n. the breeding and training of hawks; the sport of hawking.

fall ● v. (past **fell**; past part. **fallen**) **1** intr. **a** go or come down freely; descend rapidly from a higher to a lower level. **b** drop or be dropped. **2** intr. **a** (often foll. by over) cease to stand; come suddenly to the ground from loss of balance etc. **b** collapse forwards or downwards esp. of one's own volition (fell into my arms). **3** intr. become detached and descend or disappear. **4** intr. take a downward direction: **a** (of hair, clothing, etc.) hang down. **b** (of ground etc.) slope. **c** (foll. by into) (of a river etc.) discharge into. **5** intr. **a** find a lower level; sink lower. **b** subside, abate. **6** intr. (of the voice, a musical note, etc.) become lower or quieter. **7** intr. (of a barometer, thermometer, etc.) show a lower reading. **8** intr. occur; become apparent or present (darkness fell). **9** intr. decline, diminish (standards have fallen). **10** tr. N Amer., Austral., & NZ cut down (a tree etc.). **11** intr. **a** (of the face) show dismay or disappointment. **b** (of the eyes or a glance) look downwards. **12** intr. **a** lose power or status (the government will fall). **b** lose esteem, moral integrity, etc. **13** intr. commit sin; yield to temptation. **14** intr. take or have a particular direction

or place (his eye fell on me). **15** intr. (of speech) issue forth (the bad news fell from her lips). **16** intr. **a** find a place; be naturally divisible (the subject falls into three parts). **b** (foll. by under, within) be classed among. **17** intr. occur at a specified time (Easter falls early this year). **18** intr. come by chance or duty (it fell to me to answer). **19** intr. **a** pass into a specified condition (fell ill). **b** become (fall asleep). **20** intr. **a** (of a position etc.) be overthrown or captured; succumb to attack. **b** be defeated; fail. **21** intr. die (fall in battle). **22** intr. (foll. by on, upon) **a** attack. **b** meet with. **c** embrace or embark on avidly. **23** intr. (foll. by to + verbal noun) begin (fell to wondering). **24** intr. collapse or sink (too much sugar will make the cake fall). **25** intr. (foll. by to) lapse, revert (revenues fall to the Crown). ● n. **1** the act or an instance of falling; a sudden rapid descent. **2** (also **Fall**) N Amer. autumn. **3** that which falls or has fallen, e.g. snow, rocks, etc. **4** the recorded amount of rainfall etc. **5** a decline or diminution. **6** overthrow, downfall (the fall of Rome). **7 a** succumbing to temptation. **b (the Fall)** in Christian and Jewish theology, the lapse into a sinful state and the origin of the human condition (of suffering, toil, death, and sinfulness) resulting from the first act of disobedience by Adam and Eve. **8 a** (of material, land, light, etc.) a downward direction; a slope. **b** a downward difference in height. **9** (esp. in pl.) a waterfall, cataract, or cascade. **10** Music a cadence. **11 a** Wrestling a match or part of a match. **b** Wrestling a throw which keeps the opponent on the ground for a specified time. **c** a controlled act of falling, esp. as a stunt or in judo etc. □ **fall apart** (or **to pieces**) **1** break into pieces. **2** (of a situation etc.) disintegrate; be reduced to chaos. **3** lose one's capacity to cope. **fall away 1** (of a surface) incline abruptly. **2** become few or thin; gradually vanish. **3** desert, revolt; abandon one's principles. **fall back** retreat. **fall back on** have recourse to in difficulty. **fall behind 1** be outstripped by one's competitors etc.; lag. **2** be in arrears. **fall down** (often foll. by on) informal fail; perform poorly; fail to deliver (payment etc.). **fall for** informal **1** be captivated or deceived by. **2** admire; yield to the charms or merits of. **fall afoul** (or **foul**) **of** come into conflict with; quarrel with. **fall in 1 a** take one's place in military formation. **b** (as interj.) the order to do this. **2** collapse inwards. **fall into line 1** take one's place in the ranks. **2** conform or collaborate with others. **fall into place** begin to make sense or cohere. **fall in with 1** meet by chance. **2** agree with; accede to; humour. **3** coincide with. **fall off 1** (of demand etc.) decrease, deteriorate. **2** withdraw. **fall out 1** quarrel. **2** (of the hair, teeth, etc.) become detached. **3** Military come out of formation. **4** result; come to pass; occur. **fall out of** gradually discontinue (a habit etc.). **fall over oneself** informal **1** be eager or competitive. **2** be awkward, stumble through haste, confusion, etc. **fall short 1** be or become deficient or inadequate. **2** (of a missile etc.) not reach its target. **fall short of** fail to reach or obtain. **fall through** fail; come to nothing. **fall to** begin an activity, e.g. eating or working. **take the fall** N Amer. informal receive blame or punishment, esp. in the place of someone else.

fallacy /'fæləsi/ n. (pl. **-ies**) **1** a mistaken belief, esp. based on unsound argument. **2** faulty reasoning; misleading or unsound argument. □ **fallacious** /fə'leiʃəs/ adj.

fallback ● n. **1** a reserve; something that may be used in an emergency. **2** a falling back or reduction. ● attrib.adj. reserve, emergency (fallback plan).

fallen ● v. past part. of FALL. ● adj. **1** having fallen or dropped from a higher place, value, etc. (*fallen leaves*). **2** (*attrib.*) having lost one's honour or reputation. **3** killed in war. □ **fallenness** *n.*

faller *n.* **1** a person, animal, or thing that falls, esp. a person or animal in a race. **2** *N Amer., Austral.*, & *NZ* a logger who cuts down trees.

fall guy *n. slang* **1** an easy victim. **2** a scapegoat.

fallible /'fælɪbəl/ *adj.* **1** capable of making mistakes. **2** liable to be erroneous. □ **fallibility** *n.* **fallibly** *adv.*

falling *n.* the felling of trees for timber.

falling-out *n.* a quarrel.

fall-off *n.* a decrease, deterioration, withdrawal, etc.

Fallopian tube /fə'lo:piən/ *n.* either of two tubes in female mammals along which ova travel from the ovaries to the uterus.

fallout *n.* **1** radioactive debris caused by a nuclear explosion or accident. **2** the adverse side effects of a situation etc.

fallow /'fælo:/ ● *adj.* **1 a** (of land) plowed and harrowed but left unsown for a year. **b** uncultivated. **2** (of an idea etc.) potentially useful but not yet in use. **3** inactive. ● *n.* fallow or uncultivated land. ● *v.tr.* break up (land) to destroy weeds.

fall supper *n. Cdn* = FOWL SUPPER.

false ● *adj.* **1** not according with fact; wrong, incorrect. **2 a** spurious, sham, artificial (*false teeth*; *false modesty*). **b** acting as such; appearing to be such, esp. deceptively (*a false lining*). **3** illusory; not actually so (*a false economy*). **4** improperly so called (*false acacia*). **5** deceptive (*false advertising*). **6** (foll. by *to*) deceitful, treacherous, or unfaithful. **7** fictitious or assumed (*a false name*). **8** unlawful (*false imprisonment*). ● *adv.* in a false manner (*play someone false*). □ **falsely** *adv.* **falseness** *n.* **falsity** *n.* (*pl.* -**ies**).

false acacia *n.* = LOCUST 4b.

false alarm *n.* **1** an alarm given needlessly, either intentionally or in error. **2** a situation in which danger threatens but never materializes.

falsehood *n.* **1** the state of being false or untrue. **2** a false or untrue thing. **3** the act of lying.

false memory syndrome *n.* apparent memory of an event, esp. childhood sexual abuse, that did not occur, created by psychological techniques such as hypnosis, dream interpretation, etc. Abbr.: **FMS**.

false pretences *n.pl.* misrepresentations made with intent to deceive (*sold under false pretences*).

false start *n.* **1** an invalid or disallowed start in a race. **2** an unsuccessful attempt to begin something.

falsetto /fɒl'seto:/ *n.* (*pl.* -**os**) **1** a method of voice production used by male singers, esp. tenors, to sing notes higher than their normal range. **2** a singer using this method.

falsify *v.tr.* (-**ies**, -**ied**) **1** fraudulently alter or make false (a document, evidence, etc.). **2** misrepresent. **3** show to be false. **4** disappoint (a hope, fear, etc.). □ **falsifiable** *adj.* **falsifiability** *n.* **falsification** *n.*

falter *v.* **1** *intr.* stumble, stagger; go unsteadily. **2** *intr.* waver; lose courage. **3** *tr.* & *intr.* stammer; speak hesitatingly. **4** *intr.* show loss of momentum, energy, or functioning (*the economy was faltering*). □ **falterer** *n.* **falteringly** *adv.*

fame *n.* **1** renown; the state of being famous. **2** reputation.

famed *adj.* (foll. by *for*) famous; much spoken of.

familial /fə'mɪlɪəl/ *adj.* of, occurring in, or characteristic of a family or its members.

familiar ● *adj.* **1 a** (often foll. by *to*) well known; no longer novel. **b** common, usual; often encountered or experienced. **2** (foll. by *with*) knowing a thing well or

in detail (*am familiar with all the problems*). **3** (often foll. by *with*) **a** well acquainted (with a person); in close friendship. **b** sexually intimate. **4** excessively informal; impertinent. **5** unceremonious, informal. ● *n.* **1** a close friend or associate. **2** (in full **familiar spirit**) a demon supposedly attending and obeying a witch etc. **3** *Catholicism* a person rendering certain services in a pope's or bishop's household. □ **familiarly** *adv.*

familiarity *n.* (*pl.* -**ies**) **1** the state of being well known. **2** (foll. by *with*) close acquaintance. **3** a close relationship. **4 a** sexual intimacy. **b** (in *pl.*) acts of physical intimacy. **5** familiar or informal behaviour, esp. excessively so.

familiarize *v.tr.* **1** (foll. by *with*) make (a person) conversant or well acquainted. **2** make (a thing) well known. □ **familiarization** *n.*

family *n.* (*pl.* -**ies**) **1** a group of people related by blood, legal or common-law marriage, or adoption. **2 a** the members of a household, esp. parents and their children. **b** a person's children. **c** a person's spouse and children. **d** (*attrib.*) serving the needs of families (*family doctor*). **3 a** all the descendants of a common ancestor. **b** a race or group of peoples from a common stock. **4** all the languages ultimately derived from a particular early language, regarded as a group. **5** a brotherhood of persons or nations united by political or religious ties. **6** a group of objects distinguished by common features. **7** *Biol.* a group of related genera of organisms within an order in taxonomic classification. **8** *Cdn* (*Ont.*) a classification code indicating that a film is considered appropriate for viewing by people of all ages. Abbr.: **F.** □ **in the family way** *informal* pregnant.

family allowance *n. Cdn hist.* a universal monthly payment made by the federal government to mothers of children under 18.

Family Compact *n. Cdn* **1** a name given to the ruling class in Upper Canada in the early 19th c., esp. to the members of the legislative and executive councils. **2** any influential clique or faction.

Family Court *n. Cdn* (in Nova Scotia) a court which has jurisdiction over some aspects of family law, including custody and support payments etc., and also serves as a youth court.

Family Day *n.* the third Monday in February, a statutory holiday in Alberta.

family farm *n.* a farm that is owned and operated by a family, esp. one that has been handed down from one generation to another. □ **family farmer** *n.*

family law *n.* the part of the legal system that deals with matters affecting families, e.g. divorce etc.

family man *n.* a man having a wife and children, esp. one fond of family life.

family planning *n.* the planning of the number of children, etc. in a family by using birth control.

family room *n. N Amer.* a room in a house used by family members for relaxation etc.

family therapy *n.* a form of psychotherapy for the members of a family, aimed at improving communication and relationships. □ **family therapist** *n.*

family tree *n.* a chart showing relationships and lines of descent.

famine *n.* **1** extreme scarcity of food. **2** a shortage of something specified (*a labour famine*).

famish *v.tr.* & *intr.* (usu. in *passive*) **1** reduce or be reduced to extreme hunger. **2** *informal* feel very hungry. □ **famished** *adj.*

famous *adj.* **1** (often foll. by *for*) celebrated; well known. **2** *informal* excellent. **3** notorious. □ **famous last words** (an ironic comment on or rejoinder to) an overconfident or boastful assumption that may well be proved wrong by events. □ **famousness** *n.*

famously *adv.* **1** *informal* excellently. **2** notably.

fan¹ ● *n.* **1** an apparatus, usu. with rotating blades, giving a current of air for ventilation etc. **2** a device, usu. folding and forming a semicircle when spread out, for agitating the air to cool oneself. **3** anything spread out like a fan, e.g. a bird's tail or kind of ornamental vaulting. **4** = ALLUVIAL FAN. ● *v.* (**fanned, fanning**) **1** *tr.* **a** blow a current of air on, with or as with a fan. **b** agitate (the air) with a fan. **2** *tr.* (of a breeze) blow gently on; cool. **3** *tr.* sweep away by or as by the wind from a fan. **4** *intr.* & *tr.* (usu. foll. by *out*) spread out in the shape of a fan. **5** *intr.* (often foll. by *on*) *Hockey* miss or make only partial contact with the puck while attempting to pass or shoot etc. **6** *Baseball* **a** *tr.* (of a pitcher) strike out (a batter). **b** *intr.* (of a batter) strike out. **7** *tr.* make more ardent (*fanned her desire*). □ **fan the flames of** increase the intensity of (*fanned the flames of nationalism*). □ **fan-like** *adj.*

fan² *n.* a devotee or admirer of a particular activity, performer, etc. (*hockey fan*).

fanatic ● *n.* **1** a person filled with excessive and often misguided enthusiasm for something. **2** *informal* a person who is devoted to a hobby, pastime, sport, etc. (*curling fanatic*). ● *adj.* excessively enthusiastic. □ **fanatical** *adj.* **fanatically** *adv.* **fanaticism** *n.*

fan belt *n.* a belt that drives a fan to cool the radiator in a motor vehicle.

fancier *n.* **1** a connoisseur or follower of some activity or thing. **2** a breeder of a certain type of animal etc.

fanciful *adj.* **1** existing only in the imagination or fancy. **2** indulging in fancies; whimsical, capricious. **3** (of things) designed or decorated in an odd but creative manner. □ **fancifully** *adv.* **fancifulness** *n.*

fan club *n.* an organized group of a person's admirers.

fancy ● *n.* (*pl.* **-ies**) **1** an individual taste or inclination. **2** a caprice or whim. **3** a thing favoured, e.g. a horse to win a race. **4** an arbitrary supposition. **5 a** the faculty of using imagination or of inventing imagery. **b** a mental image. **6** delusion; unfounded belief. ● *adj.* (usu. *attrib.*) (**-ier**, **-iest**) **1 a** elaborate; not plain. **b** of high quality or very expensive. **2** capricious, whimsical, extravagant. **3** based on imagination, not fact. **4 a** (of foods etc.) of fine quality. **b** designating a grade of canned fruits and vegetables that are of the highest quality, as nearly perfect as possible, and uniform in colour and size. ● *v.tr.* (**-ies, -ied**) **1** (foll. by *that* + clause) be inclined to suppose; rather think. **2** *informal* have an unduly high opinion of (oneself, one's ability, etc.). **3** select (a horse, team, etc.) as the likely winner. **4** (in *imper.*) an exclamation of surprise (*fancy their doing that!*). **5** picture to oneself; conceive, imagine. □ **catch** (or **take**) **the fancy of** please; appeal to. **fancy up** *informal* make more fancy, elegant, etc. **take a fancy to** become (esp. inexplicably) fond of. □ **fancily** *adv.*

fancy footwork *n.* **1** skilful or agile use of the feet, esp. in sports, dancing, etc. **2** agility in negotiation, evasion, etc.

fancy-free *adj.* (often in phr. **footloose and fancy-free**) without (esp. emotional) commitments.

fancy-pants *adj.* *N Amer.* *informal* hotshot.

fandango /fænˈdæŋɡo/ *n.* (*pl.* **-oes** or **-os**) **1 a** a lively Spanish dance for two in triple time, usu. accompanied by castanets and guitars. **b** the music for this. **2** nonsense, tomfoolery.

fandom /ˈfændəm/ *n.* the world of fans and enthusiasts, esp. of fans of science fiction magazines and conventions.

fanfare *n.* **1** a short showy or ceremonious sounding of trumpets, bugles, etc. **2** an elaborate display; a burst of publicity.

fanfold *adj.* = CONTINUOUS 4.

fang *n.* **1** a sharply pointed canine tooth, e.g. of a dog or wolf. **2 a** the tooth of a venomous snake, by which poison is injected. **b** the biting mouthpart of a spider. **3** the root of a tooth or its prong. □ **bare one's fangs** show oneself ready for confrontation. □ **fanged** *adj.* (also in *comb.*). **fangless** *adj.*

fan hitch *n.* *Cdn* (*North*) a method of harnessing sled dogs, with the lead dog on a long trace and the other dogs arranged in a fan-shaped pattern on either side.

fan mail *n.* letters from fans to the person they admire.

fanny *n.* (*pl.* **-ies**) *N Amer.* *slang* the buttocks.

fanny pack *n.* *N Amer.* a small pouch for money or other valuables, worn on a belt around the waist etc.

fan palm *n.* a palm tree with fan-shaped leaves.

fantail *n.* **1** a pigeon with a broad-shaped tail. **2** a fan-shaped tail or end. **3** the fan of a windmill. **4** the projecting part of a boat's stern. □ **fantailed** *adj.*

fantasia /fænˈteɪʒə, -ziə/ *n.* a musical or other composition free in form and often in improvisatory style, or which is based on several familiar tunes.

fantasist /ˈfæntə,sɪst/ *n.* **1** a writer of fantasies. **2** a person who fantasizes.

fantasize /ˈfæntə,saiz/ *v.* **1** *intr.* **a** daydream about something one wishes to happen. **b** indulge in a sexual fantasy. **2** *tr.* imagine; create a fantasy about.

fantastic *adj.* (also **fantastical**) **1** *informal* excellent, extraordinary. **2** *informal* very large; lavish (*a fantastic increase in salary*). **3** extravagantly fanciful. **4** capricious, eccentric. **5** grotesque or quaint in design etc. **6** existing only in the imagination; unreal or impossible. □ **fantasticality** *n.* **fantastically** *adv.*

fantasy /ˈfæntəsi, -zi/ *n.* (*pl.* **-ies**) **1** the faculty of inventing images, esp. extravagant or visionary ones. **2** a sequence of mental images developed in the imagination and arising from conscious or unconscious wishes or attitudes, esp. involving sexual relations. **3** a whimsical speculation. **4** a fantastic invention or composition; a fantasia. **5** a genre of imaginative fiction involving fantastic stories, often in a magical pseudo-historical setting.

fantasyland *n.* an imaginary world where all fantasies are fulfilled.

fanzine /ˈfænziːn/ *n.* a magazine for fans, esp. those of science fiction, sport, or popular music.

FAO *abbr.* Food and Agriculture Organization (of the United Nations).

FAQ *n.* a text file containing a list of 'frequently asked questions' and answers relating to a particular subject, esp. one giving basic information on a topic to users of an Internet newsgroup.

far (**further, furthest** or **farther, farthest**) ● *adv.* **1** at or to or by a great distance (*far away*; *far off*). **2 a** a long way (off) in space or time (*travelling far*; *talked far into the night*). **3** to a great extent or degree; by much (*far better*; *far too early*). **4** much or many (*we need far more than that*). ● *adj.* **1** situated at or extending over a great distance in space or time; remote (*a far country*). **2** more distant (*the far end*). **3** extreme (*far left*). □ **as far as** to the distance of (a place). **2** to the extent that (*as far as I'm concerned*). **by far** by a great amount. **far and away** by a very large amount. **far and near** everywhere. **far and wide** over a large area. **far be it from me** (foll. by *to* + infin.) I am reluctant to (esp.

express criticism etc.). **far from** very different from being; tending to the opposite of (*the problem is far from being solved*). **go far 1** achieve much. **2** contribute greatly. **3** be adequate. **go too far** go beyond the limits of what is reasonable, polite, etc. **how far** to what extent. **so far 1** to such an extent or distance; to this point. **2** until now. **so** (or **in so**) **far as** (or **that**) to the extent that. **so far so good** progress has been satisfactory up to now.

faraway *adj.* **1** remote; long-past. **2** (of a look) dreamy. **3** (of a voice) sounding as if from a distance.

farce *n.* **1 a** a coarsely comic dramatic work based on improbable events. **b** this branch of drama. **2** absurdly futile proceedings; pretense, mockery.

farcical /ˈfɑrsɪkəl/ *adj.* **1** extremely ludicrous or futile. **2** of or like farce.

fare ● *n.* **1 a** the price a passenger has to pay to be conveyed by bus, airplane, etc. **b** a passenger paying to travel in a public vehicle, esp. a taxi. **2** a range of food provided by a restaurant etc. **3** something presented to the public, esp. for entertainment (*typical Hollywood fare*). ● *v.intr.* **1** progress; get on (*how did you fare?*). **2** happen; turn out.

Far East *n.* China, Japan, and other countries of E Asia. □ **Far Eastern** *adj.*

fare-thee-well *n.* (also **fare-you-well**) = FAREWELL.

farewell ● *interj.* goodbye, adieu. ● *n.* **1** leave-taking, departure (also *attrib.*: *farewell party*). **2** parting good wishes.

far-fetched *adj.* (of an idea, explanation, etc.) strained, unconvincing, improbable.

far-flung *adj.* **1** extending far; widely distributed. **2** remote; isolated (*far-flung northern communities*).

far gone *adj.* **1** *informal* in an advanced state of drunkenness, illness, etc. **2** long ago; past (*those days are far gone*).

farm ● *n.* **1** an area of land, and the buildings on it, used for growing crops, rearing animals, etc. (also *attrib.*: *farm machinery*). **2** a place or establishment for breeding a particular type of animal, growing fruit, etc. (*fish farm*). **3** a place for the storage of oil or oil products. ● *v.* **1 a** *tr.* use (land) for growing crops, rearing animals, etc. **b** *intr.* be a farmer; work on a farm. **2** *tr.* breed (fish etc.) commercially. **3** *tr.* (often foll. by *out*) **a** delegate or subcontract (work) to others. **b** contract (the collection of taxes) to another for a fee. **c** arrange for (a person, esp. a child) to be looked after by another. □ **farmer** *n.* **farming** *n.*

farmer's sausage *n. Cdn* seasoned pork sausage in a casing but not in links, esp. of German origin.

farmhand *n.* **1** a worker on a farm. **2** *N Amer. informal* a player on a farm team, esp. one who has just been called up to the major leagues.

farmhouse *n.* a dwelling (esp. the main one) attached to a farm.

farmland *n.* land used or suitable for farming.

farmstead *n.* a farm and its buildings as a unit.

farm team *n. N Amer.* (also **farm club**) a minor-league sports team affiliated with and serving as a source of players for a major-league team.

farmyard *n.* a yard or enclosure attached to a farmhouse.

Far North *n.* (in Canada) the Arctic and sub-Arctic regions of the country.

faro /ˈfero:/ *n.* a gambling card game in which bets are placed on the order of appearance of the cards.

far-off *adj.* remote; distant (*a far-off battlefield*).

far-out *adj. slang* **1** unconventional; avant-garde. **2** excellent.

farrago /fəˈrɑːgo:/ *n.* (*pl.* **-os** or **-oes**) a hodgepodge.

far-reaching *adj.* **1** extending widely. **2** having important consequences or implications.

farrier /ˈfærɪər/ *n.* **1** a smith who shoes horses. **2** a person who treats the disease and injuries of horses.

farrow ● *n.* a litter of pigs. ● *v.tr. & intr.* (of a sow) give birth to (pigs). □ **farrowing** *n.*

Farsi /ˈfɑrsi:/ *n.* the modern Persian language.

far-sighted *adj.* **1** having foresight, prudent. **2** esp. *N Amer.* able to see distant things more clearly than those close by. □ **far-sightedly** *adv.* **far-sightedness** *n.*

fart *coarse slang* ● *v.intr.* **1** emit intestinal gas from the anus. **2** (foll. by *about*, *around*) behave foolishly; waste time. ● *n.* **1** an emission of intestinal gas from the anus. **2** an annoying or unpleasant person.

farther *var. of* FURTHER *adv.* 1, *adj.* 1.

farthest *var. of* FURTHEST.

farthing *n. hist.* (in the UK) a coin and monetary unit worth a quarter of an old penny.

Far West *n.* (in Canada) **1** *hist.* the regions west of Ontario, sequentially Manitoba, Saskatchewan, Alberta, and British Columbia, as settlement advanced westward. **2** the area west of the Prairies.

FAS *abbr.* FETAL ALCOHOL SYNDROME.

fascia /ˈfeiʃə, ˈfæ-, -iə/ *n.* (*pl.* **fascias** or **fasciae** /-ʃiː/) **1** a flat horizontal band of wood, aluminum, etc. around the edge of a roof, often to which eavestroughs are attached. **2** /ˈfæʃə/ *Anat.* a thin sheath of fibrous tissue. **3** *Zool. & Bot.* a stripe or band of colour.

fascinate *v.tr.* **1** capture the interest of; attract irresistibly. **2** deprive of the power of escape or resistance; transfix. □ **fascinated** *adj.* **fascinating** *adj.* **fascinatingly** *adv.* **fascination** *n.*

Fascism /ˈfæʃizəm/ *n.* **1** *hist.* the totalitarian principles and organization of the extreme right-wing nationalist movement in Italy (1922–43). **2** (also **fascism**) **a** any similar nationalist and authoritarian movement, esp. German National Socialism. **b** *derogatory* any system of extreme right-wing or authoritarian views. □ **Fascist** *n. & adj.* **Fascistic** *adj.*

fashion ● *n.* **1** the current popular custom or style, esp. in dress or social conduct (also *attrib.*: *fashion designer*). **2** a manner or style of doing something (*in a peculiar fashion*). **3** (in *comb.*) in a specified manner (*walk crab-fashion*). **4** appearance; characteristic form. **5** fashionable society (*a woman of fashion*). ● *v.tr.* make into a particular or the required form. □ **after** (or **in**) **a fashion** as well as is practicable, though not satisfactorily. **in** (or **out of**) **fashion** fashionable (or not fashionable) at the time in question.

fashionable *adj.* **1** following, suited to, or influenced by the current fashion. **2** characteristic of or favoured by those who are leaders of social fashion (*a fashionable resort*). □ **fashionability** *n.* **fashionableness** *n.* **fashionably** *adv.*

fashion house *n.* a business where high-quality clothes are designed, displayed, and sold.

fashion plate *n.* a person who consistently dresses in the current fashion.

fashion victim *n.* a slavish follower of.

fast¹ ● *adj.* **1 a** rapid, quick-moving. **b** happening quickly (*a fast trip*). **2** capable of high speed. **3** enabling or causing or intended for high speed (*the fast lane*). **4** (of a clock etc.) showing a time ahead of the correct time. **5** (of a racetrack, ice surface, field, etc.) producing or allowing quick movement. **6 a** (of a photographic film) needing only a short exposure. **b** (of a lens) having a large aperture. **7 a** firmly fixed or attached. **b** secure; firmly established (*a fast* *friendship*). **8** (of a colour) not fading in light or when washed. **9** (of a person, lifestyle, etc.) immoral, dissipated. ● *adv.* **1** quickly; in quick succession. **2** firmly, fixedly, tightly, securely (*stand fast*). **3** soundly, completely (*fast asleep*). **4** in a dissipated manner; extravagantly (*live fast, die young*). **5** close, immediately (*fast on their heels*). □ **pull a fast one** *informal* try to deceive or gain an unfair advantage.

fast² ● *v.intr.* abstain from all or some kinds of food or drink, esp. as a religious observance or in preparation for medical tests etc. ● *n.* an act or period of fasting.

fast and furious ● *adv.* **1** rapidly. **2** eagerly, uproariously. ● *adj.* **1** rapid, fast-paced (*a fast and furious game*). **2** (of a party, music, etc.) lively, energetic.

fastball *n.* **1** a baseball pitch thrown at or near a pitcher's maximum speed. **2** *Cdn* = FAST PITCH.

fast break *n.* (in basketball etc.) a swift attack from a defensive position (often *attrib.*: *fast-break offence*).

fast-breeder *n.* (also **fast-breeder reactor**) a reactor using fast neutrons to produce the same fissile material as it uses.

fasten *v.* **1** *tr.* **a** make or become fixed or secure. **b** secure as a means of connection (a clasp, button, tie, etc.). **2** *tr.* lock securely; shut in. **3** *tr.* (foll. by *on*, *upon*) direct (a look, thoughts, etc.) fixedly or intently. **4** *tr.* (foll. by *on*, *upon*) fix (a nickname or imputation etc.). **5** *intr.* (foll. by *on*, *upon*) **a** take hold of (*fasten on an idea*). **b** single out (*he fastened on me*). **6** *intr.* become closed or attached (*this dress fastens in the back*). □ **fastener** *n.*

fastening *n.* a fastener.

fast food *n.* food that is wholly or partially prepared for quick sale or serving, esp. in a snack bar or restaurant (also *attrib.*: *fast-food chain*).

fast-forward ● *n.* **1** a control on a tape or video player for advancing the tape rapidly. **2** = CUE¹ *n.* 3. ● *adj.* designating such a control. ● *v.tr.* advance (a tape) rapidly, sometimes while simultaneously playing it at high speed.

fastidious /fæ'stɪdɪəs/ *adj.* **1** overly scrupulous in matters of taste, cleanliness, propriety, etc.; fussy. **2** easily disgusted; squeamish. □ **fastidiously** *adv.* **fastidiousness** *n.*

fast lane *n.* **1** a traffic lane on a highway etc. used by high-speed vehicles as a driving lane and by other vehicles as a passing lane. **2** a means or route of rapid progress. **3** a hectic, highly pressured lifestyle.

fastness *n.* **1** a stronghold or fortress. **2** the state of being secure. **3** the capacity of a dye to remain permanent and not fade or wash out.

fast neutron *n.* a neutron with high kinetic energy, esp. one released in nuclear fission and not slowed by a moderator etc.

fast pitch *n.* *N Amer.* a variety of the game of softball, featuring fast underhand pitching.

fast-talk esp. *N Amer. informal* ● *v.tr.* persuade by rapid or deceitful talk. ● *n.* (**fast talk**) such talk. □ **fast talker** *n.* **fast-talking** *adj.*

fast track ● *n.* a route, course, method, etc., which provides for more rapid results than usual (also *attrib.*: *fast-track executive*). ● *v.* (**fast-track**) **1** *tr.* give priority to; treat as urgent (*fast-track the proposal*). **2** *intr.* advance quickly (*fast-track through the ranks*). □ **fast-tracker** *n.*

fat ● *n.* **1 a** any of a group of natural esters of glycerol and various fatty acids found in the adipose tissue of animals and in some plants. **b** animal or vegetable tissue containing this. **c** fat from animals or plants, purified and used for cooking. **2** excessive presence of fat in a person or animal. **3** excess; surplus (*trim the fat in the budget*). ● *adj.* (**fatter**, **fattest**) **1** (of a person or animal) having excessive fat. **2** (of an animal) plump; well fed. **3** containing much fat. **4** greasy, oily. **5** (of land etc.) fertile, rich; yielding abundantly. **6 a** thick (*a fat book*). **b** substantial as an asset or opportunity (*a fat cheque*). **7** *informal ironic* very little; not much (*fat chance*). ● *v.tr.* & *intr.* (**fatted**, **fatting**) make or become fat. □ **the fat is in the fire** trouble is imminent. **kill the fatted calf** celebrate, esp. at a prodigal's return. **live off** (or **on**) **the fat of the land** have the best of everything. □ **fatly** *adv.* **fatness** *n.*

fatal *adj.* **1** causing or ending in death. **2** (often foll. by *to*) destructive; ruinous; ending in disaster (*made a fatal mistake*). **3** fateful, decisive. □ **fatally** *adv.*

fatalism *n.* **1** the belief that all events are predetermined and therefore inevitable. **2** a submissive attitude to events as being inevitable. □ **fatalist** *n.* **fatalistic** *adj.* **fatalistically** *adv.*

fatality *n.* (*pl.* **-ies**) **1 a** an occurrence of death by accident or in war etc. **b** a person killed in this way. **2** fatal influence; deadliness (*the fatality of certain diseases*). **3** a predestined liability to disaster. **4** subjection to or the supremacy of fate.

fatback *n.* *N Amer.* a strip of fat and fat meat, usu. salt-cured, from the upper part of a side of pork.

fat cat *n.* *slang derogatory* a wealthy person, esp. a complacent one who lives off the proceeds of other people's labour (also *attrib.*: *fat-cat lawyers*).

fate ● *n.* **1** a power regarded as predetermining events unalterably. **2 a** the future regarded as determined by such a power. **b** an individual's appointed lot. **c** the ultimate condition or end of a person or thing (*sealed our fate*). **3** death, destruction. ● *v.tr.* (usu. in *passive*) preordain (*was fated to win*).

fated *adj.* **1** decreed, determined or controlled by fate. **2** doomed to destruction.

fateful *adj.* **1** important, decisive; having far-reaching consequences. **2** controlled as if by fate. **3** causing or likely to cause disaster. **4** prophetic.

fathead *n.* *informal* a stupid person. □ **fatheaded** *adj.*

father ● *n.* **1 a** a man in relation to a child or children born from his fertilization of an ovum. **b** a man who has care of a child, esp. by adoption or remarriage. **2** any male animal in relation to its offspring. **3** (usu. in *pl.*) a progenitor or forefather. **4** (also **Father**) an originator, designer, or early leader. **5** (**Fathers**) (also **Fathers of the Church**) early Christian theologians whose writings are regarded as especially authoritative. **6** (also **Father**) (often as a title or form of address) a priest. **7** (**the Father**) (in Christian belief) the first person of the Trinity. **8** (**Father**) a venerable person, esp. as a title in personifications (*Father Time*). **9** (usu. in *pl.*) the leading men or elders in a city or state (*city fathers*). ● *v.tr.* **1** beget; be the father of. **2** behave as a father towards. **3** bring (a scheme etc.) into existence. **4** appear as or admit that one is the father or originator of. □ **fatherhood** *n.* **fatherless** *adj.* **fatherlessness** *n.*

father figure *n.* an older man who is respected like a father; a trusted leader.

father-in-law *n.* (*pl.* **fathers-in-law**) the father of one's husband or wife.

fatherland *n.* one's native country.

fatherly *adj.* **1** like or characteristic of a father in affection, care, etc. (*fatherly concern*). **2** of or proper to a father. □ **fatherliness** *n.*

Father of Confederation *n.* *Cdn* any of the delegates who represented colonies of British North

America at the three conferences which led to Confederation in 1867.

Father's Day n. a day (usu. the third Sunday in June) established for a special tribute to fathers.

Father Time n. = TIME n. 3b.

fathom /'fæðəm/ ● n. (pl. often **fathom** when prec. by a number) a measure of six feet (1.8 m), esp. used in taking depth soundings. ● v.tr. **1** grasp or comprehend (a problem). **2** measure the depth of (water) with a sounding line. □ **fathomless** adj.

fatigue ● n. **1 a** extreme tiredness after physical or mental exertion. **b** an activity that causes fatigue. **c** a state of indifference brought about by excessive appeals to one's generosity, compassion, etc. (donor fatigue). **2** weakness in materials, esp. metal, caused by repeated variations of stress. **3** a reduction in the efficiency of a muscle, organ, etc., after prolonged activity. **4** (in pl.) = ARMY FATIGUES. **5 a** a non-military duty in the army, often as a punishment. **b** (in full **fatigue-party**) a group of soldiers ordered to do fatigues. **c** (in pl.) clothing worn for such a duty. ● v.tr. (**fatigues, fatigued, fatiguing**) cause fatigue in.

fats n. slang offensive (as a term of address) a fat person.

fatso n. (pl. **-os**) slang offensive a fat person.

fatten v. **1** tr. make fat (esp. animals for slaughter). **2** intr. grow or become fat. **3** tr. fertilize, enrich (soil).

fattening adj. (of foods) high in calories.

fatty ● adj. (**-ier, -iest**) **1** consisting of or containing fat. **2** marked by abnormal deposition of fat. **3** like fat; oily, greasy. ● n. (pl. **-ies**) slang offensive a fat person (esp. as a nickname). □ **fattiness** n.

fatty acid n. any of a class of organic compounds consisting of a hydrocarbon chain and a terminal carboxyl group, esp. those occurring as constituents of lipids.

fatuous /'fætʃʊəs/ adj. vacantly silly; purposeless, idiotic. □ **fatuously** adv. **fatuousness** n.

fatwa /'fætwɑ/ n. (in Islamic countries) a ruling on a religious matter given by a mufti.

faucet n. N Amer. = TAP¹ 1.

fault ● n. **1** a defect or imperfection of character or of structure, appearance, etc. **2** a transgression, offence, or thing wrongly done. **3** responsibility for wrongdoing, error, etc. (it's your own fault). **4** a defect regarded as the cause of something wrong (the fault lies in the method). **5** a break or other defect in an electric circuit. **6** Geol. an extended break in the continuity of strata or a vein. **7 a** Tennis etc. a service of the ball not in accordance with the rules, esp. one which falls outside prescribed limits. **b** (in show jumping) a penalty point incurred for an error in performance. ● v. **1** tr. find fault with; blame. **2** tr. Geol. break the continuity of (strata or a vein). **3** intr. commit a fault. **4** intr. Geol. show a fault. □ **at fault** guilty; to blame. **find fault** (often foll. by with) make an adverse criticism; complain. **to a fault** (usu. of a commendable quality etc.) excessively (generous to a fault).

fault-finding n. continual criticism.

faultless adj. without fault; free from defect or error. □ **faultlessly** adv. **faultlessness** n.

fault line n. Geol. the line of intersection of a fault with the earth's surface or with a horizontal plane.

fault plane n. Geol. the surface of a fault fracture along which the rock masses on either side have been displaced.

fault-tolerant adj. Computing of or relating to a computer system that is capable of providing either full functionality or reduced functionality after a failure has occurred. □ **fault tolerance** n.

faulty adj. (**-ier, -iest**) having faults; imperfect, defective. □ **faultily** adv. **faultiness** n.

fauna n. the animal life of a particular region, geological period, or environment. □ **faunal** adj.

faux /fo/ adj. false, imitation (faux fur).

faux pas /fo: 'pʊ/ n. (pl. same /'pʊz/) **1** a tactless mistake; a blunder. **2** a social indiscretion.

fava bean /'fævə/ n. = BROAD BEAN.

fave n. & adj. slang = FAVOURITE.

favela /fə'velə/ n. a Brazilian shack, slum, or shantytown.

favour (also **favor**) ● n. **1** an act of kindness beyond what is due or usual. **2** esteem, liking, approval, goodwill; friendly regard (look with favour on). **3** partiality; too lenient or generous treatment. **4** a small gift, such as a noisemaker or paper hat, often given to guests at a party. **5** a thing given or worn as a mark of favour or support, e.g. a badge or a knot of ribbons. **6** (usu. in pl.) sexual relations, esp. as offered by a woman. ● v.tr. **1** regard or treat with favour or partiality. **2** give support or approval to; promote, prefer. **3** facilitate, help (a process etc.) (the wind favoured their sailing). **4** tend to confirm (an idea or theory). **5** (foll. by with) oblige (favour me with a reply). **6** avoid putting too much strain on (an injured limb etc.) **7** resemble in features (she favours her mother). □ **find favour** be liked; prove acceptable. **in favour 1** meeting with approval. **2** (foll. by of) in support of. **b** to the advantage of. **in one's favour** to a person's advantage. **out of favour** lacking approval.

favourable adj. (also **favorable**) **1** approving. **2** giving consent (a favourable answer). **3** promising, auspicious (a favourable recovery). **4** (often foll. by to) helpful, suitable (favourable legislation). **5** well-disposed; propitious. □ **favourableness** n. **favourably** adv.

favoured adj. (also **favored**) **1** treated with preference or partiality (the favoured daughter). **2** having special advantages (the favoured caste).

favourite (also **favorite**) ● adj. preferred to all others (my favourite book). ● n. **1** a specially favoured person or thing. **2** a competitor thought most likely to win.

favourite son n. N Amer. a person in the public eye who has endeared himself particularly to his province or state, or hometown.

favouritism n. (also **favoritism**) the unfair favouring of one person or group at the expense of another.

fawn¹ ● n. **1** a young deer in its first year. **2** a light yellowish brown. ● adj. of this colour.

fawn² v.intr. **1** (often foll. by on, over, upon) (of a person) behave in an obsequious manner; affect a cringing pleasure or fondness. **2** (of an animal, esp. a dog) show affection or pleasure. □ **fawning** adj. **fawningly** adv.

fax ● n. **1** facsimile transmission (see FACSIMILE n. 2). **2 a** a copy produced or message sent by this. **b** a machine for transmitting and receiving these. ● v.tr. transmit (a document) in this way.

faze v.tr. (often as **fazed** adj.) informal disconcert, perturb, disorient.

FBDB abbr. Cdn Federal Business Development Bank.

FBI abbr. (in the US) Federal Bureau of Investigation.

FCC abbr. (in Canada) Farm Credit Corporation.

FD abbr. Cdn forest district.

FDA abbr. (in the US) Food and Drug Administration.

Fe symbol the element iron.

fealty /'fi:əlti/ n. (pl. **-ies**) **1** hist. **a** a feudal tenant's or vassal's fidelity to a lord. **b** an acknowledgement of this. **2** allegiance.

fear ● n. **1** an unpleasant emotion caused by exposure to danger, expectation of pain, etc. **2** a cause of fear. **3** (often foll. by *of*) dread or fearful respect (towards) (*had a fear of heights*). **4** anxiety for the safety of (*in fear of their lives*). **5** danger; likelihood (of something unwelcome). ● *v.* **1 a** *tr.* feel fear about or towards (a person or thing). **b** *intr.* feel fear. **2** *intr.* (foll. by *for*) feel anxiety or apprehension about (*feared for my life*). **3** *tr.* apprehend; have uneasy expectation of (*fear the worst*). **4** *tr.* (usu. foll. by *that* + clause) apprehend with fear or regret (*I fear that you are wrong*). **5** *tr.* **a** (foll. by to + infin.) hesitate. **b** (foll. by verbal noun) shrink from; be apprehensive about (*he feared meeting his ex-wife*). **6** *tr.* show reverence toward. □ **for fear of** (or **that**) to avoid the risk of (or that). **never fear** there is no danger of that. **without fear or favour** impartially. **fearful** *adj.* **1** (usu. foll. by *of*, or *that* + clause) afraid. **2** terrible, awful. **3** *informal* extremely unwelcome or unpleasant. □ **fearfully** *adv.* **fearfulness** *n.*

fearless *adj.* without fear; courageous, brave. □ **fearlessly** *adv.* **fearlessness** *n.*

fearsome *adj.* **1** frightening, dreadful. **2** inspiring awe or admiration (*fearsome dedication*). □ **fearsomely** *adv.* **fearsomeness** *n.*

feasibility study *n.* a study of the practicability of a proposed project.

feasible *adj.* **1** practicable; easily or conveniently done. **2** likely, probable (*a feasible explanation*). ¶Although there is a tradition of opposition to sense 2, it is widely used and is considered acceptable. □ **feasibility** *n.* **feasibly** *adv.*

feast ● *n.* **1 a** a large or sumptuous meal. **b** a banquet for many guests, often with entertainment. **2** a gratification to the senses or mind. **3 a** an annual religious celebration. **b** a day dedicated to a particular saint. ● *v.* **1** *intr.* partake of a feast; eat and drink sumptuously. **b** enjoy; take pleasure in (*feast on movies*). **2** *tr.* a regale. **b** pass (time) in feasting. □ **feast one's eyes on** take pleasure in beholding. **feast or famine** either too much or too little.

feast day *n.* a day on which a feast (esp. a religious one) is held.

feat *n.* a noteworthy act or achievement.

feather ● *n.* **1** any of the appendages growing from a bird's skin, consisting of a partly hollow horny stem fringed with fine strands. **2** one or more of these as decoration etc. (also *attrib.: a feather boa*). **3** a piece or pieces of feather attached to the base of an arrow to direct its flight. **4** something resembling a feather, as a tuft of hair standing upright on a person's head. ● *v.* **1** *tr.* cover or line with feathers. **2** *tr. Rowing* turn (an oar) so that it passes through the air edgewise. **3** *tr. Aviation & Naut.* cause (propeller blades) to rotate in such a way as to lessen the air or water resistance. **4** *intr.* float, move, or wave like feathers. **5** *intr.* (of ink, lipstick, etc.) break into tiny feather-like lines when applied to a surface. **6** *tr.* execute (a pass) or pass (a puck, ball, etc.) lightly or gracefully. □ **a feather in one's cap** an achievement to be proud of. **feather one's nest** make oneself richer, more comfortable, etc. usu. at someone else's expense. **in fine** (or **high**) **feather** *informal* in good spirits. **ruffle** (**a person's**) **feathers** disturb or annoy (a person). □ **feathered** *adj.* (also in *comb.*). **featherless** *adj.* **feathery** *adj.*

feather bed ● *n.* **1** a bed with a mattress stuffed with feathers. **2** something (esp. a job, situation, etc.) comfortable or easy. ● *v.tr.* (**featherbed**) (**-bedded, -bedding**) provide with (esp. financial) advantages.

feathering *n.* **1** bird's plumage. **2** the feathers of an arrow. **3** a feather-like structure in an animal's coat.

featherweight *n.* **1 a** a weight in certain sports

intermediate between bantamweight and lightweight, in the amateur boxing scale 54–57 kg, but differing for professionals and wrestlers (also *attrib.: featherweight championship*). **b** a boxer etc. of this weight. **2** (also *attrib.*) a very light person or thing. **3** (usu. *attrib.*) trifling or unimportant.

feature ● *n.* **1** a distinctive or characteristic part of a thing. **2** (usu. in *pl.*) a distinctive part of the face, esp. with regard to shape and visual effect. **3** something offered for sale as a special. **4** a distinctive or regular article in a newspaper or magazine. **5 a** (in full **feature film**) a full-length film intended as the main item in a movie theatre program. **b** a broadcast or part of a broadcast devoted to a particular topic. ● *v.* **1** *tr.* **a** make a special display or attraction of; give special prominence to. **b** include as a characteristic part. **2** *tr. & intr.* have as or be an important actor, participant, or topic in a film, broadcast, etc. **3** *intr.* be a feature or special attraction. □ **featured** *adj.* (also in *comb.*). **featureless** *adj.*

feature-length *adj.* of the length of a typical feature film or program, usu. at least an hour long.

Feb. *abbr.* February.

febrile /ˈfiːbraɪl, ˈfeb-/ *adj.* of or relating to fever.

February /ˈfebrʊeri, ˈfebjʊeri, -uːeri/ *n.* (*pl.* **-ies**) the second month of the year, containing 28 days, except in a leap year when it has 29. ¶Although there is a tradition of opposition to the second pronunciation, it is used by educated speakers.

feces /ˈfiːsiːz/ *n.* waste matter discharged from the bowels. □ **fecal** /ˈfiːkəl/ *adj.*

feckless *adj.* **1** feeble, ineffective. **2** unthinking, irresponsible. □ **fecklessly** *adv.* **fecklessness** *n.*

fecund /ˈfiːkənd, ˈfek-/ *adj.* **1** fertile; highly productive of offspring, fruit, etc. **2** intellectually prolific or creative. □ **fecundity** /fɪˈkʌndɪti/ *n.*

fed[1] *past and past part.* of FEED.

fed[2] *n. slang* **1** *Cdn & Austral.* (in *pl.*) the federal government. **2** *US* (also **Fed**) a federal official, esp. a member of the FBI. **3** *US* (**Fed**) (prec. by *the*) **a** = FEDERAL RESERVE SYSTEM. **b** = FEDERAL RESERVE BOARD.

federal *adj.* **1** of a system of government in which power is divided between a central government and several regional ones. **2** relating to or affecting such a federation. **3** of or relating to the central government as distinguished from the separate units constituting a federation (*federal laws*). □ **federalize** *v.tr.* **federalization** *n.* **federally** *adv.*

Federal Court of Canada *n. Cdn* a court with jurisdiction to hear civil and criminal cases referred by federal boards, or tribunals, and to rule on constitutional questions referred by the Attorney General.

federalism *n.* **1** a federal system of government. **2** advocacy of a federal system of government; in Canada esp. support of Confederation in opposition to Quebec separatism. □ **federalist** *n. & adj.*

Federal Reserve Bank *n.* (in the US) each of twelve regional banks which regulate and serve the member banks of the Federal Reserve System.

Federal Reserve Board *n.* (in the US) the board regulating the Federal Reserve System.

Federal Reserve System *n.* (in the US) the national banking system with central cash reserves available to twelve major regional banks.

federate ● *v.tr. & intr.* (esp. as **federated**) organize or be organized on a federal basis. ● *adj.* having a federal organization. □ **federative** *adj.*

federation *n.* **1** a federal group of provinces, states, etc. **2** a federated society or group. **3** the act or an instance of federating.

fedora /fə'dɔrə/ n. a low soft felt hat with a crown creased lengthwise.

fed up adj. informal (often foll. by with) discontented or bored, esp. from a surfeit of something.

fee n. **1** a payment made to a professional person or a professional or public body in exchange for advice or services. **2** money paid as part of a special transaction, for a privilege, admission to a society, etc. (enrolment fee). **3** (in pl.) money paid (esp. to a school or university) for tuition. **4** Law an inherited estate, unlimited (**fee simple**) or limited (**fee tail**) as to the category of heir.

feeble adj. **1** weak, infirm. **2** lacking energy, force, or effectiveness. **3** dim, indistinct. **4** deficient in character or intelligence. □ **feebleness** n. **feebly** adv.

feeble-minded adj. **1** unintelligent. **2** mentally deficient. □ **feeble-mindedness** n.

feed ● v. (past and past part. **fed**) **1** tr. **a** supply with food. **b** put food into the mouth of. **2** tr. give as food, esp. to animals. **3** tr. serve as food for. **4** intr. (usu. foll. by on) (esp. of animals, informal of people) take food; eat. **5** tr. nourish; make grow. **6 a** tr. maintain a supply of raw material, fuel, etc., to (a fire, machine, etc.). **b** tr. (foll. by into) supply (material) to a machine etc. **c** intr. (often foll. by into) (of a river, road etc.) flow or merge into another. **d** tr. insert further coins into (a meter) to continue its function, validity, etc. **7** intr. (foll. by on) **a** be nourished by. **b** derive benefit from. **8** tr. relay or supply electrical signals or power to, esp. as part of a larger network or system. **9** tr. Sport send a pass to (a player). **10** tr. gratify, seek to satisfy (an appetite, passion, etc.). **11** intr. (of plants) take nutrients from the soil. ● n. **1 a** food, esp. for farm animals; fodder. **b** an amount of such food. **2** the act or an instance of feeding; the giving of food. **3** informal a meal. **4** a locally broadcast radio or television program transmitted by satellite or network to a larger audience. □ **off one's feed** slang having no appetite.

feedback n. **1** information about the result of an experiment, performance, etc.; response. **2** Electronics **a** the return of a fraction of the output signal from one stage of a circuit, amplifier, etc., to the input of the same or a preceding stage. **b** a signal so returned.

feeder n. **1** a person who supplies food for another person, an animal, etc. **2** a person, plant, or animal that eats in a specified manner (the baby is a good feeder). **3** a receptacle from which animals may feed. **4** N Amer. an animal being fattened for market (usu. attrib.: feeder steers). **5** a tributary stream. **6** a branch road, bus route, airline, etc., linking outlying districts with a main transportation system. **7** a school, sports team, etc. which supplies students, players, etc. to a larger or more senior school or team. **8 a** a main carrying electricity to a distribution point. **b** an electrical connection between an antenna and a transmitter or receiver of electromagnetic waves. **9** a person or apparatus which supplies material to a machine (an automatic paper feeder).

feed grain n. wheat etc. grown for animal food.

feeding frenzy n. **1** an instance of ravenous eating by a group of animals. **2** informal competitive, unscrupulous behaviour, esp. as exhibited by journalists covering a sensational story.

feedlot n. a farming operation where livestock are fed or fattened.

feedstock n. raw material to supply a machine or industrial process.

fee-for-service adj. of or designating an approach to the delivery of medical services in which physicians are paid a designated amount for each service provided rather than by salary.

feel ● v. (past and past part. **felt**) **1 a** tr. examine or search by touch. **b** intr. have the sensation of touch (was unable to feel). **2 a** tr. perceive, discover, or ascertain by handling or touching (could feel the heat). **b** tr. have a sensation of (felt that it was cold). **c** intr. (often foll. by for) grope about, search in, esp. by touch. **3** tr. **a** undergo, experience (shall feel my anger). **b** exhibit or be conscious of (an emotion, sensation, conviction, etc.). **4 a** intr. have a specified feeling or reaction (felt strongly about it). **b** tr. be physically or emotionally affected or injured by (felt the rebuke deeply). **5** tr. (foll. by that + clause) have a vague impression or conviction that. **6** tr. consider, think (felt it useful to go). **7** intr. seem, give an impression of being, or be perceived as (feels chilly). **8** intr. be conscious of being, regard oneself as (feel happy). **9** intr. (foll. by for) have pity or compassion for. **10** tr. (often foll. by up) slang fondle for sexual gratification. ● n. **1** the act or an instance of feeling or testing by touch. **2 a** a physical or mental sensation. **b** the sensation characteristically produced by an object, situation, etc. **3 a** a sensitive appreciation or an easy understanding of something (a feel for languages). **b** a sense of familiarity, competence, or comfort with something (haven't got the feel of this car yet). □ **feel free** (often foll. by to + infin.) not be reluctant or hesitant. **feel like 1** feel as though or similar to. **2** desire (a thing) or have an inclination towards (doing a thing). **feel no pain** slang be very drunk. **feel out** investigate cautiously. **feel up to** feel capable or be ready to face or deal with. **feel one's way** proceed carefully or act cautiously. **make one's influence** (or **presence** etc.) **felt** use one's authority, power, or strong personality for visible effect or to assert one's influence over others, proceedings, etc.

feeler n. **1** an organ in certain animals for testing things by touch or for searching for food. **2** a tentative proposal or suggestion, esp. to elicit a response or test opinion (put out feelers). **3** a person or thing that feels, tries, or tests.

feel-good adj. informal caused, causing, or characterized by positive feelings.

feeling ● n. **1 a** a sense of touch or the capacity to feel. **b** a physical sensation. **2 a** (often foll. by of) a particular emotional reaction (a feeling of despair). **b** (in pl.) emotional susceptibilities or sympathies (hurt my feelings; had strong feelings about it). **3** a particular and usu. intuitive sensitivity, aptitude, or appreciation (had a feeling for literature). **4 a** an opinion, notion, or belief not based solely on reason. **b** a vague, often irrational, awareness or sensation. **c** attitude or sentiment (the general feeling was against it). **5** the capacity or readiness to feel, esp. sympathy or compassion. **6 a** the general emotional effect produced on a hearer, spectator, etc. by a work of art, piece of music, etc. **b** emotional sensibility in artistic execution (played with feeling). ● adj. **1** sensitive, sympathetic, compassionate. **2** showing emotion. **3** sentient or capable of sensation. □ **feelingly** adv.

feet pl. of FOOT.

feign /fein/ v. **1** tr. simulate or pretend to be affected by (feign madness). **2** tr. allege or maintain fictitiously. **3** intr. indulge in pretense. □ **feigned** adj.

feint /feint/ ● n. **1** a sham move, attack, blow, etc. to divert attention or fool an opponent or enemy. **2** an assumed appearance or pretense. ● v.intr. make a feint.

feisty adj. (**-ier**, **-iest**) N Amer. informal **1** spirited, energetic, forceful, or exuberant, esp. when faced with opposition. **2** touchy, irritable, quarrelsome. □

feistily adv. **feistiness** n.

felafel /fe'lɒfəl/ var. of FALAFEL.

feldspar n. any of a group of aluminum silicates of potassium, sodium, or calcium, which are the most abundant minerals in the earth's crust.

felicitate v.tr. formal (usu. foll. by on) congratulate (a person). □ **felicitation** n. (usu. in pl.).

felicitous adj. **1** (of a name, expression, etc.) strikingly apt. **2 a** pleasing, delightful. **b** happy, showing or marked by great happiness. □ **felicitously** adv. **felicitousness** n.

felicity n. (pl. **-ies**) **1** happiness, bliss. **2** a cause or source of happiness. **3 a** a capacity for appropriate expression. **b** an appropriate or well-chosen phrase. **4** a stroke of fortune or a fortunate trait.

feline ● adj. **1** of or relating to the cat family Felidae. **2** catlike, esp. in beauty or slyness. ● n. any member of the cat family.

fell[1] past of FALL v.

fell[2] ● v.tr. **1** cut down (esp. a tree). **2** strike or knock down (a person or animal). **3** stitch down (the edge of a seam) so that it lies flat over the outer edge, leaving a smooth surface. ● n. an amount of timber cut in one season.

fell[3] adj. literary **1** fierce, ruthless, cruel. **2** terrible, destructive. □ **at** (or **in**) **one fell swoop** in a single (originally deadly) action or effort.

fella n. (also **fellah**) informal = FELLOW 1, 2.

fellatio /fə'leɪʃɪəʊ/ n. oral stimulation of the penis. □ **fellate** v.tr.

feller[1] n. = FELLOW 1, 2.

feller[2] n. a person or thing that fells something, esp. trees as timber.

feller-buncher n. a large machine used to shear trees just above ground level and pile them.

fellow n. **1** informal a man or boy. **2** (usu. in pl.) **a** a companion, associate, or comrade (were separated from their fellows). **b** a contemporary. **3** a partner, counterpart, or match; the other of a pair. **4** one of the same class or an equal in rank, ability, or kind. **5 a** an elected graduate receiving a stipend for a period of research. **b** a member of the governing body in some universities. **6** a member of a learned society. **7** (attrib.) belonging to the same class or activity (fellow Canadian). **8** derogatory a person regarded with contempt.

fellowship n. **1** companionship or friendly association with others. **2 a** a group of people or a society sharing a common interest or aim, e.g. a religious group, fraternity, or guild. **b** membership in such a group or society. **3 a** an award of money to a graduate student in return for some research, teaching, etc. **b** a post as a fellow in a college etc.

fellow-traveller n. **1** a person who travels with another. **2** a person who sympathizes with, but is not a member of, a particular party or movement, esp. the Communist party.

felon /'felən/ n. a person who has been convicted of a felony.

felonious /fə'ləʊnɪəs/ adj. **1** Law of or involving a felony. **2** (of a person) that has committed felony.

felony n. (pl. **-ies**) a (usu. violent) crime.

felquiste /fel'kiːst/ n. Cdn hist. a member of the FLQ.

felt[1] ● n. **1** a fabric made of wool, fur, or other fibrous material consolidated by heat and mechanical action so that the fibres are matted together. **2 a** a piece of felt. **b** something made of felt. **3** a heavy layer of material, usu. matted and fibrous, used in construc-

tion for roofing, insulation, etc. ● v. **1** tr. **a** make into felt or bring to a felt-like consistency. **b** mat or press together. **2** tr. cover with felt. **3** intr. become matted. □ **felted** adj. **felting** n. **felty** adj.

felt[2] past and past part. of FEEL.

felt pen n. a pen with a writing tip made of felt etc.

felt tip n. (often attrib.) **1** the writing point of a felt pen. **2** a felt pen. □ **felt-tipped** adj.

fem. abbr. feminine.

female ● adj. **1** of the sex that can bear offspring or produce eggs. **2** (of a plant, flower, etc.) bearing fruit or having pistils, but lacking stamen. **3** of or consisting of women, girls, or female animals. **4** (of a screw, socket, etc.) manufactured hollow or moulded to receive a corresponding, inserted, male part. ● n. a female person, animal, or plant. □ **femaleness** n.

female condom n. = CONDOM 2.

feminazi /'femɪˌnɒtsi, -ˌnætsi/ n. esp. US derogatory a radical feminist.

feminine ● adj. **1** of, pertaining to, or characteristic of women. **2** having qualities associated with women. **3** womanly, effeminate. **4** Grammar of or denoting the gender to which belong words classified as female on the basis of sex or some arbitrary distinction, such as form. ● n. **1** Grammar a feminine gender or word. **2** feminine qualities collectively. □ **femininely** adv. **femininity** n.

feminism n. **1** the advocacy of equality of the sexes, esp. through the establishment of the political, social, and economic rights of women. **2** the movement associated with this. □ **feminist** n. & adj.

feminize v. **1** tr. & intr. make or become feminine or female. **2** tr. make characteristic of or associated with women. **3** tr. Med. induce female physiological characteristics in. □ **feminization** n. **feminized** adj.

femme /fem/ n. slang a lesbian taking a traditionally feminine role in a relationship.

femme fatale /ˌfæm fæ'tæl/ n. (pl. **femmes fatales** pronunc. same) a woman to whom a person feels irresistibly attracted, usu. with dangerous or unhappy results.

femur /'fiːmər/ n. (pl. **-s** or **femora** /'femərə/) **1** Anat. the thigh bone in vertebrates, the thick bone between the hip and the knee. **2** the third articulated segment of the leg in insects and some other arthropods. □ **femoral** /'femərəl/ adj.

fen n. **1** a tract of low land covered wholly or partially with shallow water or subject to flooding. **2** wet land with alkaline, neutral, or slightly acid peaty soil.

fence ● n. **1** a barrier, railing, or other upright structure enclosing an area of ground, esp. to control access to or from a field, yard, etc. **2** a large, upright obstacle for a horse to jump over. **3** a person or establishment that deals in stolen goods. ● v. **1 a** tr. surround, divide, etc. (a thing) with a fence. **b** intr. build a fence or fences. **2** tr. **a** (foll. by in) surround or enclose (a person, thing, etc.) with a fence. **b** (foll. by off) separate (one area from another) (fenced off one end of the garden). **3** tr. (foll. by out) keep out or exclude with or as with a fence. **4** tr. & intr. deal in (stolen goods). **5** intr. practise the art or sport of fencing. **6** intr. **a** engage in skilful argument. **b** (foll. by with) evade answering (a person or question). □ (**sit**) **on the fence** (remain) neutral or undecided in a dispute etc.; (be) uncommitted. □ **fencer** n.

fenceline n. N Amer. **1** the continuous extent of fence encompassing a piece of land, esp. on a farm or ranch. **2** the line or boundary marked by a fence.

fence post n. a post that supports a fence.

fence-sitter *n.* a person who remains neutral or uncommitted on an issue. □ **fence-sitting** *n. & adj.*

fencing *n.* **1** a set or extent of fences. **2** material for making fences. **3** the action of putting up a fence. **4** the practice or sport of engaging in combat with swords, esp. according to a set of rules using foils, épées, or sabres to score points.

fend *v.* **1** *intr.* (foll. by *for*) support, take care of, or look after (esp. oneself). **2** *tr.* (usu. foll. by *off*) ward off (an attack), keep (a thing) away, or defend from (a threat etc.).

fender *n.* **1** *N Amer.* **a** the mudguard or area around the wheel well of a motor vehicle. **b** *disputed* the bumper of a motor vehicle. **c** the mudguard of a bicycle etc. **2** *Naut.* a piece of rubber etc. hung over a vessel's side to protect it against chafing or impact. **3** a low frame bordering a fireplace to keep in falling coals etc. **4** any thing used to keep something off, prevent a collision, etc. □ **fenderless** *adj.*

fender-bender *n. N Amer. slang* a usu. minor collision between vehicles.

feng shui /ˈfɛŋ ʃuːi, ˈfʌŋ/ *n.* (in Chinese thought) a system of good and evil influences in the natural surroundings, considered when siting or designing buildings etc.

Fenian /ˈfiːnɪən/ ● *n.* a member of the Irish Republican Brotherhood, a militant 19th-c. nationalist organization founded among the Irish in the US, whose members encouraged revolutionary activity and aimed for the overthrow of the British government in Ireland. ● *adj.* of or relating to the Fenians.

fennel *n.* **1** a yellow-flowered fragrant umbelliferous plant, *Foeniculum vulgare*, with fragrant seeds and fine leaves used as flavouring. **2** the seeds of this. **3** (in full **sweet fennel**) a variety of this, *azoricum*, with swollen leaf bases eaten as a vegetable.

feral /ˈfiːrəl, ˈferəl/ *adj.* **1 a** (of animals) belonging to or forming a wild population ultimately descended from individuals which escaped from captivity or domestication. **b** born in the wild of such an animal. **2** (of an animal or plant) wild, untamed, uncultivated. **3** brutal, savage, fierce.

ferment ● *n.* **1** social, political, etc. excitement, tumult, or unrest. **2 a** the action or process of fermenting. **b** a substance, e.g. yeast, that causes fermenting. ● *v.* **1** *intr. & tr.* undergo or subject to fermentation. **2** *tr.* excite, stir up, foment. □ **fermentable** *adj.* **fermented** *adj.* **fermenter** *n.*

fermentation *n.* the anaerobic breakdown of a substance by micro-organisms such as yeasts and bacteria, esp. of sugar to ethyl alcohol in making beers, wines, and spirits. □ **fermentative** *adj.*

fermium /ˈfɜːmɪəm/ *n.* a radioactive metallic element produced artificially.

fern *n.* any flowerless plant of the order Filicales, reproducing by spores and usu. having feathery fronds. □ **ferny** *adj.*

ferocious *adj.* **1** fierce, savage, or wildly cruel or destructive. **2** esp. *N Amer. informal* (as an intensifier) very great, extreme. □ **ferociously** *adv.*

ferocity *n.* (*pl.* **-ies**) **1** the quality or state of being ferocious. **2** a fierce or savage act.

ferret ● *n.* a small half-domesticated animal of the weasel family, *Mustela putorius furo*, kept as a pet or (in Europe) used to catch rabbits, rats, etc. ● *v.* **1 a** *tr.* (foll. by *out*) search out (secrets, criminals, etc.). **b** *intr.* search or rummage about. **2** *intr. & tr.* hunt with ferrets.

ferric *adj.* **1** of or containing iron. **2** of or containing iron in a trivalent form (compare FERROUS).

Ferris wheel *n.* a fairground ride consisting of a large, upright wheel revolving on a fixed axle, with seats suspended from its rims.

ferrite /ˈferaɪt/ *n. Chem.* **1** a compound, often with magnetic properties, formed from ferric oxide and a basic oxide or from ferric hydroxide and a base. **2** an allotrope of pure iron occurring in low carbon steel.

ferrous *adj.* **1** (of an alloy etc.) containing iron in significant quantities. **2** *Chem.* of or containing iron in a divalent form (compare FERRIC).

ferrule /ˈferuːl/ *n.* **1** a usu. metal ring or cap strengthening the end of a stick or tube. **2** a band strengthening or forming a joint.

ferry ● *n.* (*pl.* **-ies**) **1** (in full **ferry boat**) a boat which conveys passengers, vehicles, etc. across water as a regular service. **2** the service itself or the place where it operates. ● *v.* (**-ies**, **-ied**) **1** *tr. & intr.* convey or go in a boat etc. across water. **2** *tr.* transport from one place to another, esp. as a regular service.

fertile /ˈfɜːtaɪl, -təl/ *adj.* **1** (of soil) fruitful or rich in the materials needed to produce and support vegetation. **2 a** (of a human being, animal, or plant) able to produce offspring. **b** producing many offspring. **c** (of a seed, egg, etc.) capable of becoming a new individual. **3 a** (of the mind) inventive, full of or able to produce new ideas. **b** conducive to creativity, productivity, etc. (*a fertile field for research*). **4** (of nuclear material) able to become fissile by the capture of neutrons.

fertility *n.* **1** the quality of being fertile. **2** the actual number of live births.

fertilization *n.* **1** *Biol.* the fusion of male and female gametes during sexual reproduction to form a zygote. **2 a** the act or an instance of fertilizing. **b** the state or process of being fertilized.

fertilize *v.tr.* **1 a** make fertile or productive. **b** enrich (soil, plants, etc.), esp. with minerals, nutrients, etc. **2** cause to develop a new individual by introducing male reproductive material.

fertilizer *n.* a chemical or natural substance added to soil to make it more fertile.

fervent *adj.* ardent, impassioned, intense (*fervent love*). □ **fervency** *n.* **fervently** *adv.*

fervid *adj.* ardent, intense. □ **fervidly** *adv.*

fervour *n.* (also **fervor**) vehemence, passion, zeal.

fescue /ˈfeskjuː/ *n.* any grass of the genus *Festuca*, valuable for lawns, pasture, and fodder.

fess *v.intr.* (usu. foll. by *up*) *informal* confess.

fest *n.* **1** a festival or special occasion. **2** (in *comb.*) an activity of a specified type engaged in by a group of people (*gabfest*).

fester *v.* **1** *tr. & intr.* make or become infected and filled with pus. **2** *intr.* (of feelings, thoughts, etc.) become more bitter and angry. **3** *intr.* rot, stagnate.

festival ● *n.* **1** a day or period of celebration, religious or secular. **2** a series of performances of music, drama, films, etc. (*film festival*). ● *attrib.adj.* of or concerning a festival.

festival of lights *n.* **1** = HANUKKAH. **2** = DIWALI.

festive *adj.* **1** of or characteristic of a feast or festival. **2** joyous, cheerful. □ **festively** *adv.* **festiveness** *n.*

festive season *n.* (usu. prec. by *the*) a designated time for festivities, esp. Christmastime.

festivity *n.* (*pl.* **-ies**) **1** (often in *pl.*) a celebration. **2** rejoicing, merriment.

festoon ● *n.* **1** a garland of flowers, leaves, ribbons, etc. hung in a curve as a decoration. **2** something hanging in a downward curve. ● *v.tr.* (often foll. by *with*) **1** adorn with or form into festoons. **2** decorate elaborately. **3** drape with cloth, wires, etc. hanging in festoon-like curves. □ **festoonery** *n.*

feta /ˈfetə/ *n.* a very soft, white cheese made from ewe's milk or goat's milk, originally from Greece.

fetal /fiːtəl/ *adj.* **1** of or pertaining to a fetus. **2** being a fetus (*fetal lambs*).

fetal alcohol syndrome *n.* a syndrome of birth defects caused by alcohol consumption during pregnancy, including facial abnormalities, impaired mental and physical development, etc. Abbr.: **FAS**.

fetal position *n.* a curled position of the body, with the head and legs pulled in towards the torso, resembling that of a fetus in the uterus.

fetch ● *v.tr.* **1 a** go for and bring back (a person or thing) (*fetch a doctor*). **b** cause to come (*fetched a crowd of 15,000*). **c** Computing retrieve (a file etc.). **2** sell for (a price); realize (a profit) (*fetched $10*). **3** *informal* (usu. with recipient stated) give (a blow, slap, etc.) (*fetched him a slap on the face*). ● *n.* **1** an act of fetching, retrieving, bringing from a distance, etc. **2** a game, usu. played with a dog, in which a person throws a ball etc. and the dog retrieves it. □ **fetch and carry** run backwards and forwards with things or be a mere servant. **fetch up** *informal* arrive, come to rest.

fetching *adj.* attractive. □ **fetchingly** *adv.*

fete /feit/ ● *n.* **1** a festival, fair, or great entertainment. **2** a saint's day. ● *v.tr.* honour or entertain (a person) lavishly and in a special way.

Fête nationale /fet næsjʊˈnæl/ *n.* (in full **Fête nationale du Québec**) (in Quebec) the official name for the holiday celebrated on June 24, formerly (and commonly still) called St. Jean Baptiste Day.

fetid /ˈfetɪd, ˈfiː-/ *adj.* stinking or foul smelling.

fetish *n.* **1** *Psych.* a part of the body, object, action, etc. acting as a focus for sexual desire. **2 a** an inanimate object reverenced as having inherent magical powers or as being inhabited by a spirit. **b** an object, principle, etc. evoking irrational, even obsessive, devotion or respect. □ **fetishism** *n.* **fetishist** *n.* **fetishistic** *adj.*

fetishize *v.tr.* **1** make a fetish of. **2** overvalue or pay undue respect to. □ **fetishization** *n.*

fetlock *n.* the part of a horse's leg between the cannon bone and the pastern, forming a projection above and behind the hoof where a tuft of hair often grows.

fetter ● *n.* **1** a shackle or bond, esp. one put on the feet to limit movement. **2** (in *pl.*) captivity or bondage. **3** a restraint, check, or anything that confines, impedes, etc. ● *v.tr.* **1** bind with fetters etc. **2** restrict, impede, or hinder in any way.

fettle ● *n.* condition, state, or form (in *fine fettle*). ● *v.tr.* trim or clean (the rough edge of a metal casting, pottery before firing, etc.). □ **fettler** *n.*

fettuccine /fetəˈtʃiːni/ *n.* (also **fettucini**) pasta made in ribbons.

fetus *n.* (*pl.* **fetuses**) the unborn offspring of a mammal from the stage of development where the main features of an adult can be recognized.

feud ● *n.* **1** a prolonged mutual hostility, esp. between two families, tribes, etc., with murderous assaults in revenge for a previous injury (*a family feud*). **2** a prolonged or bitter quarrel or dispute. ● *v.intr.* conduct or participate in a feud.

feudal *adj.* of, according to, or resembling the feudal system. □ **feudalism** *n.*

feudal system *n.* the social system in medieval Europe whereby a vassal held land from a superior in exchange for allegiance and service.

fever *n.* **1 a** an abnormally high body temperature, often as a sign of illness. **b** any of various diseases characterized by this (*scarlet fever*). **2** intense nervous excitement or agitation.

fevered *adj.* **1** affected by or suffering from a fever. **2** highly excited (*a fevered imagination*).

feverfew *n.* an aromatic bushy plant, *Tanacetum parthenium*, with feathery leaves and white daisy-like flowers, formerly used to reduce fever.

feverish *adj.* **1 a** having symptoms like those of a fever. **b** of the nature or indicative of a fever. **2** excited, hectic, or restless. **3** (of a place) infested by or conducive to fever. □ **feverishly** *adv.* **feverishness** *n.*

fever pitch *n.* a state of extreme excitement.

fèves au lard /ˈfevoːlɑr/ *n.* *Cdn* (*Que.*) baked beans with pork.

few ● *adj.* not many. ¶See LESS. ● *pron.* (as *pl.*) **1** (prec. by *a*) some, but not many (*a few of his friends*). **2** a small number, not many (*few are chosen*). **3** (prec. by *the*) **a** the minority. **b** the elect. □ **every few** once in every small group of (*every few days*). **few and far between** neither numerous nor frequent. **have a few** *informal* take several alcoholic drinks. **no fewer than** as many as (a specified number). **quite** (or **not**) **a few** a considerable number. **some few** some but not at all many.

fey *adj.* **1 a** having a strange, almost otherworldly, whimsical charm. **b** clairvoyant. **2** usu. *ironic* or *derogatory* (of a person, behaviour, etc.) affected.

fez /fez/ *n.* (*pl.* **fezzes**) a red brimless felt cap with a flat top and tassel, worn by men in some Muslim countries.

ff *abbr.* Music fortissimo.

ff. *abbr.* **1** and the following (pages, lines, etc.). **2** folios.

fiancé /ˌfiɒnˈsei, fiˈɒnsei, -ɑ̃-/ *n.* a man to whom one is engaged to be married.

fiancée /fiˈɒnsei, fiˈɑ̃sei/ *n.* a woman to whom one is engaged to be married.

fiasco *n.* (*pl.* **-os**) a complete and ridiculous failure.

fiat /ˈfiːæt, ˈfaiæt/ *n.* **1** a formal authorization. **2** a decree or order.

fib ● *n.* a trivial lie, esp. about something unimportant. ● *v.intr.* (**fibbed**, **fibbing**) tell a fib. □ **fibber** *n.*

fibre *n.* (also esp. *US* **fiber**) **1** *Biol.* **a** a thread-like element in plant tissue, esp. an elongated cell with thick walls and no protoplasm. **b** any thread-like structure forming part of the muscular, nervous, connective, or other tissue in an animal body. **2 a** a thread or filament forming part of a textile. **b** any material consisting of animal, vegetable, or synthetic fibres, esp. a substance that can be spun, woven, or felted. **3** a thread formed from glass, metal, etc. **4 a** the texture or structure of a thing. **b** the essence of a person's character (*lacks moral fibre*). **5** = DIETARY FIBRE. □ **fibred** *adj.* (also in *comb.*). **fibreless** *adj.*

fibreboard *n.* (also esp. *US* **fiberboard**) a building material made of wood or other plant fibres compressed into boards.

fibreglass *n.* (also esp. *US* **fiberglass**) any material consisting of glass filaments woven into a textile or paper, or embedded in plastic etc., for use as a construction or insulation material.

fibre optics *n.pl.* **1** transmission of information, by means of infrared light signals, along a thin glass fibre. **2** (treated as *pl.*) the fibres etc. so used. □ **fibre optic** *adj.*

fibril /ˈfaibrɪl/ *n.* **1** a small or delicate fibre, esp. a constituent strand of an animal, vegetable, or synthetic fibre. **2** the ultimate subdivision of a fibre.

fibrillate v.intr. **1** (of a muscle, esp. in the heart) undergo a quivering movement or contract irregularly fibril by fibril. **2** (of a fibre) split up into fibrils. □ **fibrillation** n.

fibrin /ˈfaibrɪn/ n. an insoluble protein formed during blood clotting from fibrinogen. □ **fibrinous** adj.

fibrinogen /faiˈbrɪnədʒən/ n. a soluble blood plasma protein which produces fibrin when acted upon by the enzyme thrombin.

fibroblast /ˈfaibroːblæst/ n. Anat. a cell producing collagen fibres in connective tissue.

fibroma /faiˈbroːmə/ n. (pl. **-s** or **fibromata** /-mətə/) a fibrous tumour.

fibrosis /faiˈbroːsis/ n. Med. a thickening and scarring of connective tissue, usu. as a result of injury.

fibrositis /ˌfaibrəˈsəitis/ n. (also **fibromyalgia**) an inflammation of fibrous connective tissue, usu. rheumatic and painful.

fibrous adj. consisting of or like fibres. □ **fibrously** adv. **fibrousness** n.

fibula /ˈfɪbjʊlə/ n. (pl. **fibulae** /-ˌliː/ or **-s**) the smaller and outer of the two bones between the knee and the ankle in terrestrial vertebrates. □ **fibular** adj.

fiche /fiːʃ/ n. (pl. same or **-s**) a microfiche.

fickle adj. inconstant, changeable, esp. in loyalty. □ **fickleness** n.

fiction n. **1** an invented idea or statement or narrative; an imaginary thing. **2** literature, esp. novels, describing imaginary events and people. **3** a conventionally accepted falsehood (polite fiction). **4** the act or process of inventing imaginary things. **5** = LEGAL FICTION. □ **fictional** adj. **fictionality** n. **fictionally** adv. **fictionalization** n. **fictionalize** v.tr. **fictionalizer** n.

fictitious adj. **1** imaginary, unreal. **2** counterfeit; not genuine. **3** (of a name or character) assumed. **4** of or in novels. **5** regarded as what it is called by a legal or conventional fiction. □ **fictitiously** adv.

fictive /ˈfɪktɪv/ adj. **1** creating or created by imagination. **2** not genuine.

ficus /ˈfiːkəs, ˈfaikəs/ n. (pl. same) a tree or shrub of the large genus Ficus (mulberry family), including the fig and the rubber plant.

Ficus benjamina /bendʒəˈmiːnə/ n. (pl. same) a tropical tree with drooping branches, frequently grown as a houseplant.

fiddle ● n. **1** a stringed instrument played with a bow, esp. a violin. **2** informal an instance of cheating or fraud. ● v. **1** intr. **a** (often foll. by with, at) play restlessly. **b** (often foll. by about) move aimlessly. **c** act idly or frivolously. **d** (usu. foll. by with) tinker; make minor adjustments (esp. in an attempt to make improvements). **2** tr. slang **a** cheat, swindle. **b** falsify. **c** get by cheating. **3 a** intr. play the fiddle. **b** tr. play (a tune etc.) on the fiddle. □ **as fit as a fiddle** in very good health. **play second fiddle** take a subordinate role.

fiddlehead n. N Amer. the young, curled, edible frond of certain ferns.

fiddlehead green n. Cdn (usu. in pl.) = FIDDLEHEAD.

fiddler n. **1** a person who plays a fiddle. **2** any N American crab of the genus Uca, the male having one of its claws held in a position like a violinist's arm.

fiddlesticks interj. expressing scorn etc.

fiddling ● n. **1** the action of playing a fiddle, esp. in folk music. **2** the action of tinkering or playing with something. ● adj. **1** petty, trivial. **2** that fiddles.

fiddly adj. (**-ier, -iest**) informal intricate, awkward, or tiresome to do or use.

fidelity n. **1** (often foll. by to) faithfulness, loyalty. **2** sexual faithfulness to one's spouse, lover, etc. **3** strict conformity to truth or fact. **4** exact correspondence to the original. **5** precision in reproduction of sound (high fidelity).

fidget ● v. **1** (**fidgeted, fidgeting**) **1** intr. move or act restlessly or nervously, usu. while maintaining basically the same posture. **2** intr. be uneasy, worry. **3** tr. make (a person) uneasy or uncomfortable. ● n. **1 a** person who fidgets. **2** (usu. in pl.) a bodily uneasiness seeking relief in spasmodic movements; such movements. **b** a restless mood. □ **fidgety** adj.

fiduciary /fiˈduːʃəri, fiˈdjuː-/ ● adj. **1 a** of or relating to a trust, trustee, or trusteeship. **b** held or given in trust. **2** (of a paper currency) depending for its value on public confidence or securities. ● n. (pl. **-ies**) a trustee.

fief /fiːf/ n. **1** a piece of land held under the feudal system or in fee. **2** a person's sphere of operation or control.

fiefdom n. a fief.

field ● n. **1 a** an area of open land, esp. one used for pasture or crops. **b** (attrib.) grown in a field, as opposed to in a greenhouse etc. (field tomatoes). **2** a piece of land for a specified purpose, esp. an area marked out for games (football field). **3 a** the participants in a contest or sport. **b** all the competitors in a race or all except those specified. **4** an area rich in some natural product (gas field). **5** an expanse of ice, snow, sea, sky, etc. **6 a** a battlefield. **b** the scene of a campaign. **c** (attrib.) (of artillery etc.) light and mobile for use on campaign. **7** an area of operation or activity; a subject of study (outstanding in her field). **8 a** the region in which a force is effective (magnetic field). **b** the force exerted in such an area. **9** a range of perception (field of vision). **10** Math. a system subject to two operations analogous to those for the multiplication and addition of real numbers. **11** (attrib.) **a** (of an animal or plant) found in the countryside, wild (field mouse). **b** carried out or working in the natural environment, not in a laboratory etc. (field test). **12** the background of a picture, coin, flag, etc. **13** Computing a part of a record, representing an item of data. **14** N Amer. = FIELD ICE. ● v. **1** Baseball **a** intr. act as a fielder. **b** tr. stop (and return) (the ball). **2** tr. **a** select (a team or individual) to play in a game. **b** deploy (an army). **c** propose (a candidate). **3** tr. deal with (a succession of questions etc.). □ **in the field 1** on a military campaign. **2** working etc. away from one's laboratory, headquarters, etc. **play the field** informal avoid exclusive attachment to one person or activity etc. **take the field 1** begin a campaign. **2** (of a sports team) go on to a playing field to begin a game.

field corn n. N Amer. corn grown for use as a grain or animal feed.

field day n. **1** wide scope for action or success; a time occupied with exciting events (anglers are having a field day). **2** Military an exercise, esp. in manoeuvring. **3** a day spent in exploration, scientific investigation, etc., in the natural environment. **4** N Amer. a day at which an entire school competes in outdoor track and field events.

fielder n. Baseball etc. **1** a player who fields the ball. **2** a member (other than the pitcher) of the side that is fielding, esp. an outfielder.

fielder's choice n. Baseball a fielder's attempt to put out a baserunner rather than the batter, thus allowing the batter to reach base safely.

field event n. (usu. in pl.) an athletic event that

involves jumping or throwing something (e.g. a shot or javelin), and is not performed on a running track.

field goal n. **1** Football a goal scored by a drop kick or place kick from the field. **2** Basketball a goal scored when the ball is in normal play.

field guide n. a book for the identification of birds, flowers, etc., in the field.

field hockey n. a game played between two teams on a field with curved sticks and a small hard ball.

field ice n. N Amer. a large flat area of floating ice.

field lacrosse n. a type of lacrosse played on an open field with teams of ten men or twelve women.

field mouse n. any of various mice inhabiting fields.

field of vision n. all that comes into view when the eyes are turned in some direction.

field party n. (pl. **-ies**) Cdn a large outdoor party held in an open field.

fieldstone n. unfinished stone, esp. when used as a building material.

field test ● v.tr. test (a device) in the environment in which it is to be used. ● n. a test of a device etc. in the environment in which it is to be used.

field trial n. **1** a test or competition between gun dogs to determine their ability to perform in actual hunting conditions. **2** = FIELD TEST n.

field trip n. **1** a school trip, e.g. to a museum, a park, etc., to gain knowledge or experience away from the classroom. **2** a research trip to study something at first hand.

fieldwork n. **1** the practical work of a surveyor, collector of scientific data, sociologist, etc., conducted in the natural environment rather than a laboratory, office, etc. **2** a temporary fortification. □ **fieldworker** n.

fiend n. **1 a** an evil spirit, a demon. **b** (prec. by the) the Devil. **2 a** a very wicked or cruel person. **b** a person causing mischief or annoyance. **3** (with a qualifying word) informal **a** a devotee (fitness fiend). **b** an addict (dope fiend). □ **fiendlike** adj.

fiendish adj. **1** like a fiend; extremely cruel or unpleasant. **2** extremely difficult. □ **fiendishly** adv. **fiendishness** n.

fierce adj. (**fiercer, fiercest**) **1** vehemently aggressive or frightening in temper or action, violent. **2** eager, intense, ardent. **3** unpleasantly strong or intense; uncontrolled (fierce heat). □ **something fierce** slang to a great degree (I miss him something fierce). □ **fiercely** adv. **fierceness** n.

fiery adj. (**-ier, -iest**) **1** consisting of or flaming with fire. **2** like fire in appearance; bright red. **3 a** hot as fire. **b** acting like fire; producing a burning sensation. **4 a** flashing, ardent (fiery eyes). **b** eager, pugnacious, spirited, irritable (fiery temper). **5** (of gas, a mine, etc.) inflammable; liable to explosions.

fiesta n. **1** a holiday or festivity. **2** a religious festival in Spanish-speaking countries.

fife n. a kind of small shrill flute used with the drum in military music.

fifteen ● n. **1** one more than fourteen. **2** a symbol for this (15, xv, XV). **3** a size etc. denoted by fifteen. **4** a team of fifteen players, esp. in rugby. ● adj. that amount to fifteen. □ **fifteenth** adj. & n.

fifth ● n. **1** the position in a sequence corresponding to that of the number 5 in the sequence 1-5. **2** something occupying this position. **3** the fifth person etc. in a race or competition. **4** any of five equal parts of a thing. **5** Music **a** an interval or chord spanning five consecutive notes in the diatonic scale (e.g. C to G). **b** a note separated from another by this

interval. **6** Baseball the fifth inning. ● adj. that is the fifth. ● adv. fifthly. □ **take the Fifth** (in the US) exercise the right guaranteed by the Fifth Amendment. □ **fifthly** adv.

Fifth Amendment n. an amendment to the US constitution which states that no person may be compelled to give testimony that might incriminate himself or herself.

fifth column n. a group working for an enemy within a country at war etc. □ **fifth columnist** n.

fifth estate n. any group viewed as being separate from the traditional four estates of the nobility, clergy, commons, and the press, e.g. the electronic media, labour unions, etc.

fifth-generation adj. denoting a proposed new class of computer employing artificial intelligence.

fifth wheel n. **1** an extra wheel for a four-wheeled vehicle. **2** a superfluous person or thing. **3** N Amer. a coupling between a vehicle used for towing and a trailer. **4** (in full **fifth wheel trailer**) N Amer. a camper-trailer.

fifty ● n. (pl. **-ies**) **1** the product of five and ten. **2** a symbol for this (50, l, L). **3** (in pl.) the numbers from 50 to 59, esp. the years of a century or of a person's life. **4** a set of fifty persons or things. **5** a fifty-dollar bill etc. ● adj. that amount to fifty. □ **fifty-first, -second**, etc. the ordinal numbers between fiftieth and sixtieth. **fifty-one, -two**, etc. the cardinal numbers between fifty and sixty. □ **fiftieth** adj., n., & adv. **fiftyfold** adj. & adv.

fifty-fifty ● adj. equal, with equal shares or chances (on a fifty-fifty basis). ● adv. equally, half and half (go fifty-fifty).

fig n. **1** a soft pear-shaped fruit with many seeds, eaten fresh or dried. **2** (in full **fig tree**) any deciduous tree of the genus Ficus, esp. F. carica, having broad leaves and bearing figs. □ **not care** (or **give**) **a fig** not care at all.

fig. abbr. **1** figure. **2** figurative. **3** figuratively.

figgy duff n. Cdn (Nfld) a type of boiled pudding containing raisins.

fight ● v. (past and past part. **fought**) **1** intr. (often foll. by against, with) **a** contend or struggle in war, battle, a fist fight, etc. **b** argue or quarrel. **2** tr. contend with (an opponent) in this way. **3** tr. take part or engage in (a battle, war, duel, etc.). **4** tr. **a** contend about (an issue, election, etc.). **b** maintain (a lawsuit, cause, etc.) against an opponent. **5** intr. campaign or strive determinedly to achieve something. **6** tr. strive to overcome (disease, fire, fear, etc.). **7** tr. make (one's way) by fighting. ● n. **1 a** a combat between two or more persons, animals, or parties. **b** a boxing match. **c** a battle. **d** an argument. **2** a conflict or struggle; a vigorous effort in the face of difficulty. **3** power or inclination to fight (has no fight left). □ **fight back 1** counterattack. **2** (also **fight down**) suppress (one's feelings, tears, etc.). **fight for 1** fight on behalf of. **2** fight to secure (a thing). **fight off** repel with effort. **fight out** (usu. **fight it out**) settle (a dispute etc.) by fighting. **fight shy of** avoid; be unwilling to approach (a person, task, etc.). **make a fight of it** (or **put up a fight**) offer resistance.

fighter n. **1** a person or animal that fights. **2** a fast military aircraft designed for attacking other aircraft. **3** a person with great determination, etc.

fighter bomber n. an aircraft serving as both fighter and bomber.

fighting chance n. an opportunity of succeeding by great effort.

fighting words *n.pl. informal* words likely to provoke a fight or indicating a willingness to fight.

figment *n.* a thing existing only in the imagination.

Fig Newton *n. N Amer. proprietary* a small rectangular plain cookie with a filling of mashed figs, raisins, etc.

figural /ˈfɪɡjʊrəl/ *adj.* **1** figurative. **2** consisting of figures or shapes.

figuration /ˌfɪɡjʊˈreɪʃən/ *n.* **1 a** the act of formation. **b** a mode of formation; a form. **c** a shape or outline. **2 a** ornamentation by designs. **b** *Music* ornamental patterns of scales, arpeggios, etc., often derived from an earlier motif. **3** allegorical representation.

figurative *adj.* **1 a** metaphorical, not literal. **b** metaphorically so called. **2** containing or using many figures of speech. **3** of pictorial or sculptural representation. **4** emblematic, serving as a type. □ **figuratively** *adv.* **figurativeness** *n.*

figure ● *n.* **1 a** the external form or shape of a thing. **b** bodily shape, esp. of a woman (*has a very nice figure*). **2** a person as seen in outline but not identified. **3** a character or personage, esp. an important or well-known one (*a public figure*). **4** appearance as giving a certain impression (*cut a poor figure*). **5 a** a representation of the human form in drawing, sculpture, etc. **b** an image or likeness. **c** an emblem or type. **6 a** a numerical symbol, esp. any of the ten in Arabic notation. **b** a number so expressed. **c** an amount of money, a value (*cannot put a figure on it*). **d** (in *pl.*) arithmetical calculations. **7** any printed or written character that is not a letter. **8** *Geom.* a two-dimensional space enclosed by a line or lines, or a three-dimensional space enclosed by a surface or surfaces; any of the classes of these, e.g. the triangle, the sphere. **9** a diagram or illustrative drawing. **10** a decorative pattern. **11 a** a division of a set dance, an evolution. **b** (in skating) a prescribed pattern of movements from a stationary position. **12** *Music* a short succession of notes producing a single impression, a brief melodic or rhythmic formula out of which longer passages are developed. **13** (in full **figure of speech**) a recognized form of rhetorical expression giving variety, force, etc., esp. metaphor or hyperbole. ● *v.* **1** *intr.* appear or be mentioned, esp. prominently (*figures significantly in the book*). **2** *tr.* represent in a diagram or picture. **3** *tr.* imagine; picture mentally. **4** *tr.* **a** embellish with a pattern (*figured satin*). **b** *Music* embellish with figures. **5** *tr.* mark with numbers or prices. **6 a** *tr.* calculate. **b** *intr.* do arithmetic. **7** *tr.* be a symbol of, represent typically. **8** esp. *N Amer.* **a** *tr.* understand, ascertain, consider. **b** *intr. informal* be likely or understandable (*that figures*). □ **figure on** *N Amer.* count on, expect. **figure out 1** work out by arithmetic or logic. **2** estimate. **3** understand. **go figure** *N Amer.* it escapes explanation.

figure eight *n.* (usu. hyph. when *attrib.*) **1** the shape of the number eight. **2** something with this shape.

figurehead *n.* **1** a nominal leader or head without real power. **2** a carving at a ship's prow.

figure skate *n.* a type of skate having a fairly long, narrow blade with toe picks, used in figure skating.

figure skating *n.* a type of ice skating in which the skater combines a number of movements including steps, jumps, turns, etc. □ **figure skater** *n.*

figurine *n.* a small moulded or carved figure.

Fijian /fiːˈdʒiːən/ ● *adj.* of or relating to Fiji, a country in the S Pacific, its people, or language. ● *n.* **1** a native or national of Fiji. **2** the Austronesian language of this people.

filagree *var. of* FILIGREE.

filament *n.* **1** a slender threadlike body or fibre (esp.

in animal or vegetable structures). **2** a conducting wire or thread with a high melting point in an electric bulb or thermionic valve, heated or made incandescent by an electric current. **3** *Bot.* the part of the stamen that supports the anther. □ **filamentary** *adj.* **filamented** *adj.* **filamentous** *adj.*

filbert *n.* **1** any of various shrubs or small trees of the genus *Corylus*, esp. the cultivated hazel, *Corylus maxima*, bearing edible ovoid nuts. **2** this nut.

filch *v.tr.* pilfer, steal. □ **filcher** *n.*

file¹ ● *n.* **1** a folder, box, etc., for holding loose papers, esp. arranged for reference. **2** a set of papers kept in this. **3** *Computing* a collection of (usu. related) data stored under one name. **4** *Cdn* issues and responsibilities in a specified area, considered collectively (*the unity file*). ● *v.tr.* **1** place (papers) in a file or among (esp. public) records. **2** submit (a petition for divorce, an application for a patent, etc.) to the appropriate authority. **3** (of a reporter) send (a story, information, etc.) to a newspaper. □ **file away** place in a file, or make a mental note of, for future reference. **on file** in a file or filing system. □ **filer** *n.*

file² ● *n.* a line of persons or things one behind another. ● *v.intr.* walk in a file. □ **file off** (or **away**) *Military* go off by files.

file³ ● *n.* a tool with a roughened surface or surfaces, usu. of steel, for smoothing or shaping wood, fingernails, etc. ● *v.tr.* smooth or shape with a file. □ **file away** remove (roughness etc.) with a file. □ **filer** *n.*

filé /fiˈleɪ, ˈfiːleɪ/ *n.* pounded or powdered sassafras leaves used to flavour and thicken soup, esp. gumbo.

file name *n.* a string of characters that is used to identify a file to the operating system of a computer.

file server *n. Computing* a device which manages shared access to centralized files in a network.

filet /fiˈleɪ, ˈfiːlət/ *n.* **1** a kind of net or lace with a square mesh. **2** a fillet of meat or fish.

filet mignon /fiˈleɪ miːnˈjɔ̃/ *n.* a small tender piece of beef from the end of the tenderloin.

filial /ˈfɪlɪəl/ *adj.* **1** of or due from a son or daughter. **2** *Biol.* bearing the relation of offspring.

filibuster ● *n.* esp. *N Amer.* the obstruction of progress in a legislative assembly, esp. by prolonged speaking. ● *v.* **1** *intr.* act as a filibuster. **2** *tr.* act in this way against (a motion etc.). □ **filibusterer** *n.*

filigree *n.* **1** ornamental work of gold or silver or copper as fine wire formed into delicate tracery. **2** anything delicate resembling this. □ **filigreed** *adj.*

filing¹ *n.* (usu. in *pl.*) a particle rubbed off by a file.

filing² *n.* **1** the act of placing something in a file. **2** the act of submitting a petition, application, etc.

filing cabinet *n.* (*N Amer. also* **file cabinet**) a piece of furniture with drawers for storing documents.

Filipina /ˌfɪlɪˈpiːnə/ ● *n.* a woman or girl who is a native or national of the Philippines, a country in SE Asia. ● *adj.* who is a Filipina.

Filipino /ˌfɪlɪˈpiːnoʊ/ ● *n.* (*pl.* **-os**) a native or national of the Philippines, a country in SE Asia. ● *adj.* of or relating to the Philippines or the Filipinos.

fill ● *v.* **1 a** *tr. & intr.* (often foll. by *with*) make or become full. **b** *intr.* (of the eyes) brim with tears. **2** *tr.* occupy completely; spread over or through; pervade. **3** *tr.* **a** block up (a cavity or hole in a tooth) with cement, amalgam, gold, etc. **b** drill and put a filling into (a decayed tooth). **4** *tr.* appoint a person to hold (a vacant post). **5** *tr.* hold (a position); discharge the duties of (an office). **6** *tr.* esp. *N Amer.* supply (a prescription, order for goods, etc.). **7** *tr.* occupy (vacant time). **8** *intr.* (of a sail) be distended by wind. **9** *tr.* (usu. as **filling** *adj.*) (esp. of food) satisfy, satiate. **10** *tr.* satisfy, fulfill (a need or requirement). **11** *tr.* insert a filling into (a doughnut etc.). ● *n.* **1** (prec. by possessive) as much as one wants or can bear (*eat your fill*). **2** material used for filling something, esp. earth etc. used to fill a hole or raise the level of the ground. □ **fill the bill** = FIT THE BILL (see FIT¹). **fill in 1** add information to complete (a form, document, blank cheque, etc.). **2 a** complete (a drawing etc.) within an outline. **b** fill (an outline) in this way. **3** fill (a hole etc.) completely. **4** (often foll. by *for*) act as a substitute. **5** occupy oneself during (time between other activities). **6** *informal* inform (a person) more fully. **fill out 1** enlarge to the required size. **2** become enlarged or plump. **3** *N Amer.* fill in (a document etc.). **fill up 1** make or become completely full. **2** fill the fuel tank of (a car etc.). **3** provide what is needed to occupy vacant parts or places or deal with deficiencies in.

filler *n.* **1** material or an object used to fill a cavity or increase bulk. **2** an item filling space in a newspaper etc. **3** a person or thing that fills.

filles du roi /ˌfiː dʊ ˈrwɑ/ *n.pl. Cdn hist.* women of marriageable age sent from France to New France under royal direction between 1663–73 to be married to the men then living in the colony.

fillet /ˈfilət/ ● *n.* **1** (also /fiˈleɪ/) **a** a fleshy boneless piece of meat from near the loins or the ribs. **b** (in full **fillet steak**) the undercut of a sirloin. **c** a boned longitudinal section of a fish. **2 a** a headband, ribbon, string, or narrow band, for binding the hair or worn around the head. **b** a band or bandage. **3 a** a thin narrow strip of anything. **b** a raised rim or ridge on any surface. ● *v.tr.* (**filleted, filleting**) **1** (also /fiˈleɪ/) **a** remove bones from (fish or meat). **b** divide (fish or meat) into fillets. **2** bind or provide with a fillet or fillets. **3** encircle with an ornamental band.

fill-in *n.* a person or thing put in as a substitute or to fill a vacancy.

filling *n.* any material that fills or is used to fill, esp.: **1** a piece of material used to fill a cavity in a tooth. **2** the edible substance between the slices of bread in a sandwich or enclosed by pastry in a pie, etc.

filling station *n.* = GAS STATION.

fillip ● *n.* **1** something that adds interest or excitement. **2** a stimulus or incentive. **3 a** a sudden release of a finger or thumb when it has been bent and checked by a thumb or finger. **b** a slight smart stroke given in this way. ● *v.* (**filliped, filliping**) **1** *tr.* stimulate. **2** *tr.* strike slightly and smartly. **3** *tr.* propel (a coin, marble, etc.) with a fillip. **4** *intr.* make a fillip.

fill-up *n.* **1** a thing that fills something up. **2** the act of filling up a fuel tank etc.

filly *n.* (*pl.* **-ies**) **1** a young female horse, usu. before it is four years old. **2** *informal offensive* a girl or young woman.

film ● *n.* **1** a thin coating or covering layer. **2** *Photog.* a strip or sheet of plastic or other flexible base coated with light-sensitive emulsion for exposure in a camera, either as individual visual representations or as a sequence of images which form the illusion of movement when shown in rapid succession. **3 a** a representation of a story, episode, etc., on a film, with the illusion of movement. **b** a story represented in this way. **c** (in *pl.*) the cinema industry. **4** a slight veil or haze etc. **5** a dimness or morbid growth affecting the eyes. ● *v.* **1 a** *tr.* make a photographic film of (a scene, person, etc.). **b** *tr. & intr.* make a cinema or television film of (a book etc.). **c** *intr.* be (well or ill) suited for reproduction on film. **2** *tr. & intr.* cover or become covered with or as with a film.

film clip *n.* = CLIP² *n.* 3.

filmgoer *n.* a person who frequents the cinema.

filmic *adj.* of or relating to films or cinematography.

filmmaker *n.* a director or producer of films. □ **filmmaking** *n.*

filmography /filˈmɒɡrəfi/ *n.* (*pl.* **-ies**) a list of films by one director etc. or on one subject.

film star *n.* a celebrated actor or actress in films.

film strip *n.* a series of transparencies in a strip for projection.

filmy *adj.* (**-ier, -iest**) **1** thin and translucent. **2** covered with or as with a film.

filo *var. of* PHYLLO.

Filofax /ˈfaɪloʊˌfæks/ *n. proprietary* a portable loose-leaf datebook including pages for addresses, notes, etc.

filter ● *n.* **1** a porous device for removing impurities or solid particles from a liquid or gas passed through it. **2** = FILTER TIP. **3** a screen or attachment for absorbing or modifying light, X-rays, etc. **4** a device for suppressing electrical or sound waves of frequencies not required. ● *v.intr. & tr.* **1** pass or cause to pass through a filter. **2** (foll. by *through, into,* etc.) make way gradually. **3** (foll. by *out*) leak or cause to leak. □ **filter out** remove (impurities etc.) by means of a filter.

filter paper *n.* porous paper for filtering.

filter tip *n.* **1** a filter attached to a cigarette for removing impurities from the inhaled smoke. **2** a cigarette with this. □ **filter-tipped** *adj.*

filth *n.* **1** repugnant or extreme dirt. **2** vileness, corruption, obscenity. **3** foul or obscene language.

filthy ● *adj.* (**-ier, -iest**) **1** extremely dirty. **2** obscene. **3** vile. ● *adv.* **1** filthily (*filthy dirty*). **2** *informal* extremely (*filthy rich*). □ **filthily** *adv.* **filthiness** *n.*

filtrate ● *n.* filtered liquid. ● *v.tr.* filter. □ **filtration** *n.*

fin *n.* **1** an organ on various parts of the body of many aquatic vertebrates and some invertebrates, including fish and cetaceans, for propelling, steering, and balancing (*dorsal fin*). **2** a small projecting surface or attachment on an aircraft, rocket, or car for ensuring aerodynamic stability. **3** an underwater swimmer's flipper. **4** a finlike projection on the keel of a boat etc., used to increase stability. **5** a finlike projection on any device, for improving heat transfer etc. □ **finned** *adj.* (also in *comb.*).

finagle /fiˈneɪɡəl/ *v.intr. & tr. informal* act or obtain dishonestly. □ **finagler** *n.*

final ● *adj.* **1** situated at the end, coming last. **2** conclusive, decisive, unalterable, putting an end to doubt. **3** concerned with the purpose or end aimed at. ● *n.* **1** (usu. in *pl.*) the last or deciding heat or game in sports or in a competition. **2** the edition of a newspaper published latest in the day. **3** (usu. in *pl.*) the last examination in an academic course. □ **finally** *adv.*

finale *n.* **1 a** the last movement of an instrumental composition. **b** a piece of music closing an act in an opera. **2** the close of a drama etc. **3** a conclusion.

finalist *n.* a competitor in the final of a competition etc.

finality *n.* (*pl.* **-ies**) **1** the quality or fact of being final. **2** the belief that something is final. **3** a final act, state, or utterance.

finalize *v.tr.* **1** put into final form. **2** complete; bring to an end. **3** approve the final form or details of. □ **finalization** *n.*

final solution *n.* the policy under the German Nazi regime of exterminating European Jews.

finance /ˈfaɪnæns, fɪ-/ ● *n.* **1** the management of money. **2** monetary support for an enterprise. **3** (in *pl.*) the money resources of a country, company, or person. ● *v.tr.* provide capital for (a person, purchase, or enterprise), esp. as a loan.

finance company *n.* a company that provides money to consumers for purchasing goods on credit.

financial ● *adj.* of or pertaining to revenue or money matters. ● *n.* (in *pl.*) shares in companies dealing in money. □ **financially** *adv.*

financial institution *n.* an organization, e.g. a bank, that collects funds from individuals, other organizations, or government agencies and invests these funds or lends them to borrowers.

financial instrument *n.* a formal financial document.

financial year *n. Cdn & Brit.* = FISCAL YEAR.

financier /faɪnæn'sɪːr, ˌfiː-/ *n.* a person who is concerned with or skilled in finance, esp. on a large scale.

financing *n.* an act, instance, or the process of obtaining or providing funds, capital, etc. for an investment, purchase, etc.

finback *n.* (also **finback whale**) a large baleen whale, *Balaenoptera physalus*, which has a prominent dorsal fin.

finch *n.* any small seed-eating passerine bird of the family Fringillidae (esp. one of the genus *Fringilla*), including crossbills and canaries.

find ● *v.tr.* (*past* and *past part.* **found**) **1 a** discover or attain by or as if by search or effort. **b** become aware of. **c** gain or recover the use of (*I found my tongue*). **2 a** get possession of by chance (*found a treasure*). **b** obtain, receive (*found acceptance*). **c** make up, arrange to have, or succeed in obtaining (*can't find time to read*). **d** summon up (*found courage to protest*). **3 a** seek out and provide (*will find you a book*). **b** supply, furnish (*each finds his own equipment*). **4** ascertain by study, calculation, or inquiry. **5 a** perceive or experience (*find no sense in it*). **b** (often in *passive*) discover to be present (*the word is not found in Shakespeare*). **c** learn or prove (a thing) to be through experience, trial, etc. (*finds it too cold*). **6** *Law* (of a jury, judge, etc.) authoritatively decide and declare (a person) to be innocent, guilty, etc., or (an issue, offence, etc.) to be that specified (*found him guilty*). **7** reach by a natural or normal process (*water finds its own level*). ● *n.* **1** a discovery of treasure, minerals, etc. **2** a thing or person discovered, esp. when of value. □ **find against** *Law* decide against (a person), judge to be guilty. **find for** *Law* decide in favour of (a person), judge to be innocent. **find God** experience religious conversion. **find one's feet 1** become able to walk or get the use of one's feet. **2** grow in ability or confidence, develop one's powers, acquire knowledge or capability in a new job, etc. **find it in one's heart** (foll. by *to* + infin.) prevail upon oneself, be willing. **find oneself 1** discover that one is (*found herself agreeing*). **2** discover and attain one's special place, power, or vocation. **find out 1** discover or detect (a wrongdoer etc.). **2** (often foll. by *about*) get information (*find out about airfares*). **3** discover (*find out where we are*). **4** (often foll. by *about*) discover the truth, a fact, etc. **find one's way 1** (often foll. by *to*) manage to reach a place. **2** (often foll. by *into*) be brought or get.

finder *n.* **1 a** a person who finds. **b** a device which finds something, esp. an instrument for determining or discerning something (*fish finder*). **2** the viewfinder of a camera. □ **finders keepers** *informal* whoever finds a thing is entitled to keep it.

fin de siècle /ˌfæ̃ də 'sjɛkl/ ● *n.* the end of a century or the moods, attitudes, etc. characteristic of such a

time. ● *adj.* **1** characteristic of the end of the 19th c., esp. in world-weariness, decadence, or sophistication. **2** decadent. **3** designating or characteristic of the end of a century.

finding *n.* **1** (often in *pl.*) a result or conclusion of an official inquiry. **2** a verdict of a court or jury.

fine¹ ● *adj.* **1** of superior quality. **2 a** excellent, admirable, or of striking merit (*a fine painting*). **b** highly accomplished or very skilful (*a fine skier*). **c** honourable, noble, virtuous, or morally upright (*a fine young man*). **d** good, enjoyable, satisfactory, or acceptable (*that will be fine*). **e** fortunate (*has been a fine day for him*). **3 a** clear, pure, refined, or free from dross or impurity. **b** (of gold or silver) containing a high, usu. specified proportion of pure metal. **4 a** handsome, beautiful. **b** imposing, dignified (*a fine figure of a man*). **c** large, of a good size (*fine buildings*). **5** well, in good health or spirits (*I'm fine, thank you*). **6** (of weather, a day, etc.) free from rain or fog, esp. bright and clear with sunshine. **7 a** extremely thin or slender (*a fine thread*). **b** (of a weapon, tool, etc.) having a sharp point or edge (*a fine blade*). **c** in small particles. **d** worked in thin, delicate thread. **e** (esp. of print) small. **f** (of a pen) having a narrow point or tip. **8** (of a person) fastidious, dainty, characterized by or affecting refinement. **9** (of speech, writing, etc.) elegant, ornate, or affected. **10 a** capable of delicate perception or discrimination (*a fine eye for detail*). **b** subtle or perceptible only with difficulty (*a fine distinction*). **11 a** delicately beautiful or exquisitely fashioned (*fine crystal*). **b** (of feelings) refined, elevated. **12** *ironic* difficult, inopportune, inconvenient, etc. (*a fine mess*). ● *adv. informal* very well (*suits me fine*). □ **cut** (or **run**) **it fine** allow very little margin of time, room for error, etc. **fine and dandy** *informal* **1** great, first-rate. **2** (of a person) very well. **not to put too fine a point on it** to speak bluntly. □ **finely** *adv.* **fineness** *n.*

fine² ● *n.* a sum of money exacted as a penalty for an offence. ● *v.tr.* impose a fine upon or punish (a person) by a fine (*fined him $50*). □ **in fine** to sum up; in short.

fine art *n.* **1 a** (in *pl.*) those arts appealing to the intellect or the sense of beauty, as literature, music, and esp. painting, sculpture, and architecture. **b** any one of these arts. **2** a high accomplishment or a thing requiring a high degree of skill.

fine-grained *adj.* **1** having a fine grain. **2** consisting of very small particles.

fine print *n.* the information in legal documents etc. which is often printed in small type and contains important details that are easy to overlook.

finer points *n.pl.* details or aspects recognized and appreciated only by those who are very familiar with a thing, field, etc.

finery *n.* showy or elegant dress or decoration.

finesse ● *n.* **1** skill in dealing with people or situations cleverly or tactfully. **2** delicacy, refinement, or discrimination. **3** subtle or delicate manipulation. **4** artfulness or cunning, esp. in strategy etc. ● *v.* **1** *intr. & tr.* use or achieve by finesse. **2** *tr.* evade or trick by finesse.

finest ● *adj. superlative of* FINE¹ *adj.* ● *n. N Amer.* the police of a specified city (*Ottawa's finest*).

fine-tooth comb *n.* (also **fine-toothed comb**) a comb with narrow, close-set teeth. □ **go over with a fine-tooth comb** check or search thoroughly.

fine-tune *v.tr.* make small adjustments to in order to obtain the best results. □ **fine tuning** *n.*

finger ● *n.* **1** any of the terminal members of the hand, including or excluding the thumb. **2** the part of a glove etc. intended to cover a finger. **3** an object, structure, item of food, etc. shaped like a finger. **4** the breadth or length of a finger as a rough unit of measurement. ● *v.tr.* **1** touch, feel, or turn about with the fingers. **2** *Music* **a** play (a passage) with fingers used in a particular way. **b** play upon (an instrument) with the fingers. **c** mark (music) with signs showing which fingers are to be used. **3** select, identify, or indicate (a person or thing) for a specific purpose etc. **4** *slang* **a** inform on or identify (a criminal) to the police. **b** indicate (a victim) or supply (information) to criminals. □ **give (a person) the finger** *slang* make an obscene gesture with the middle finger raised as a sign of contempt. **have a finger in the pie** be concerned, esp. officiously, in a matter. **lay a finger on** touch however slightly. **point a** (or **the**) **finger at** (**someone**) **1** accuse or identify as responsible. **2** throw scorn on. **put one's finger on** point to or identify with precision (a cause of trouble etc.). **put the finger on** *slang* inform against (a person), identify (an intended victim), etc. **twist** (or **wrap**) **around one's finger** (or **little finger**) **1** persuade (a person) without difficulty. **2** dominate (a person) completely.

fingerboard *n.* a piece of wood on a guitar, violin, etc. where the strings are pressed against the neck of the instrument with the fingers to vary the tone.

fingered *adj.* (usu. in *comb.*) having fingers of a specified kind or number.

finger food *n.* food so served that it can be eaten conveniently without cutlery.

finger hole *n.* one of a series of holes in a wind instrument which are opened and closed by the fingers in playing.

fingering *n.* **1** a manner or technique of using the fingers in playing a musical instrument, in typing, etc. **2** the marking or numbers on a musical score indicating this.

fingerling *n.* a parr or any very young fish.

fingernail *n.* the nail at the tip of each finger.

finger paint ● *n.* a thick, jellylike paint that can be applied with the fingers, esp. for use by children. ● *v.intr.* apply such paint. □ **fingerpainting** *n.*

finger pointing *n.* an act of accusing or blaming.

fingerprint ● *n.* **1** an impression made on a surface by the fingertips, esp. as used for identifying individuals. **2** any distinctive characteristic, sign, pattern etc. definitively identifying a particular person, substance, action, etc. ● *v.tr.* record the fingerprints, DNA pattern, etc. of (a person).

fingertip ● *n.* the tip of a finger. ● *adj.* (of controls etc.) that can be controlled by a light movement of the fingers. □ **at one's fingertips** readily accessible. **by one's fingertips** barely.

finial /ˈfɪnɪəl/ *n.* **1** an ornament finishing off the apex of a roof, pediment, etc. **2** an ornamental knob on the top of a piece of furniture, stairpost, etc.

finicky *adj.* **1** fastidious. **2** needing much attention to detail.

finish ● *v.* **1 a** *tr.* (often foll. by *off*) complete; come or bring to an end. **b** *intr.* cease or come to an end of a task, activity, etc. **c** *tr.* (often foll. by *off*) provide with an ending. **2** *tr.* **a** (usu. foll. by *off*) *informal* kill, destroy, or reduce to utter exhaustion or helplessness. **b** (often foll. by *off*, *up*) consume or go through the whole or the remainder of (food, drink, paint, etc.). **3** *intr.* **a** *Sport* come to the end of a course or race, esp. in a particular condition or place. **b** (foll. by *up* + *in*, *by*) end in something, end by doing something (*the plan finished up in the garbage*). **4** *tr.* **a** complete the manufacture of (cloth, woodwork, etc.) by surface treatment. **b** apply varnish, paint, etc. to (wood). **c** put the final touches to. **5** *tr.* **a** make perfect or highly accomplished (*finished manners*). **b** complete or perfect the education of a person, esp. a girl and esp. in the social graces. **6 a** *tr.* complete the fattening of (cattle etc.) for sale or slaughter. **b** *intr.* (of cattle etc.) reach an intended market weight. **7** *tr.* (foll. by *with*) **a** have no more to do with, be no longer busy with or using (a thing) (*I'm finished with the phone*). **b** end one's association or connection with (a person, organization, etc.). ● *n.* **1 a** the end, last part, or last stage of a thing. **b** the point at which a race, hunt, or other contest or event ends. **c** a conclusive defeat of one person or party by another (*fight to the finish*). **2** a method, material, or texture used for surface treatment of wood, cloth, etc. **3** a thing which finishes or gives completeness or perfection to something.

finished *adj.* **1 a** ended, completed, or brought to a conclusion. **b** having passed through the final stage of manufacture or elaboration (*the finished product*). **2** ruined, doomed, or no longer effective (*finished as a politician*). **3** consummate, accomplished, or highly proficient. **4** (of cattle) appropriately fattened for market or slaughter. **5** (of part of a building, esp. a basement) having the walls and ceiling covered with drywall, panelling, etc.

finisher *n.* **1** a person who finishes something, esp. a race, contest, or similar event. **2** a worker or machine performing the final operation in a process.

finishing stroke *n.* a final and usu. fatal stroke.

finishing touch *n.* (usu. in *pl.*) a last action, added effect, or final detail completing and enhancing a piece of work, production, etc.

finish line *n.* a line which indicates the end of a race.

finite /ˈfaɪnaɪt/ *adj.* **1 a** having bounds, ends, or limits. **b** having an existence subject to limitations and conditions. **2** *Math.* **a** (of a line) having two ends. **b** (of a numerical quality) neither infinitely large nor infinitesimally small. **c** corresponding to and represented by a finite number or a finite number of items. **3** *Grammar* (of a part of a verb) limited by number and person. □ **finitely** *adv.*

fink *N Amer. slang* ● *n.* **1** an unpleasant person. **2** an informer. ● *v.intr.* **1** (foll. by *on*) inform on. **2** (foll. by *out*) back out of something or let a person down.

Finn *n.* **1** a native or national of Finland, a country on the Baltic Sea. **2** a person of Finnish descent.

Finnic /ˈfɪnɪk/ *adj.* of or pertaining to the Finns, or the group of people ethnically allied to the Finns.

Finnish /ˈfɪnɪʃ/ ● *adj.* of, pertaining to, or characteristic of Finland, the Finns, or their language. ● *n.* the language of the Finns.

Finno-Ugric /ˌfɪnoˈuːgrɪk, -ˈjuːgrɪk/ ● *adj.* belonging to the group of Uralic languages including Finnish, Estonian, Lapp, and Hungarian. ● *n.* this group.

fiord *n. var. of* FJORD.

fir *n.* **1** (in full **fir tree**) any evergreen coniferous tree, esp. of the genus *Abies*, with needles borne singly on the stems. **2** the wood of the fir.

fire ● *n.* **1 a** the state or process of combustion, in which substances combine chemically with oxygen, manifested as a hot, bright, shifting body of gas or as incandescence. **b** the flame or incandescence so produced. **2** a conflagration or destructive burning, esp. of a large area or mass (*forest fire*). **3** fuel in a state of combustion or a mass of burning material in a grate, furnace, etc. **4** the action of firing guns etc. **5 a** zeal, fervour, enthusiasm. **b** liveliness of imagination or poetic inspiration. **c** a vehement or burning passion or emotion. **6** burning heat, fever. **7** luminosity or a glowing or flashing appearance resembling that of fire. ● *v.* **1** *tr.* discharge (a gun etc.). **b** *tr.* throw, eject, or propel (a projectile) from or as from a gun etc. **c** *intr.* (often foll. by *at, into, on*) shoot or discharge a gun or other firearm. **d** *intr.* (of a gun etc.) go off. **e** *tr.* produce or deliver (a broadside, salute, etc.) by discharge of guns. **2** *tr.* light (gunpowder), let off (a firework), or explode (a mine). **3** *tr.* (often foll. by *off*) deliver or utter (a speech, questions, etc.) in rapid succession or in a sharp, explosive manner (*fired insults at us*). **4** *tr.* dismiss (an employee) from a job. **5** *tr.* set fire to with the intention of damaging or destroying. **6** *intr.* (of an explosive etc.) catch fire or be ignited. **7** *intr.* (of an internal combustion engine, or a cylinder in one) undergo ignition of its fuel. **8** *tr.* supply (a furnace, engine, boiler, or power station) with fuel. **9** *tr.* **a** inspire, inflame, or stimulate (the imagination). **b** fill (a person) with enthusiasm. **10** *tr.* **a** subject to the action or effect of fire. **b** bake or dry (pottery, bricks, etc.). **11** (in *imper.*) begin shooting weapons. □ **catch fire 1** begin to burn. **2 a** (of an idea, trend, etc.) become popular. **b** (of an individual) become motivated, enthusiastic. **fight fire with fire** use similar strategies, methods, etc. as one's opponent does. **fire and brimstone 1** the torments of hell. **2** preaching etc. emphasizing eternal damnation. **fire away** *informal* begin or go ahead. **fire up 1** *informal* **a** stimulate, fill with enthusiasm, or excite. **b** start up (an engine etc.). **2** show sudden anger. **fired-up 1** (of an engine etc.) started. **2** (of a person) highly motivated or enthused. **light a fire under** *N Amer.* cause to work faster, decide rapidly, etc. **on fire 1** burning. **2** excited. **set fire to** (or **set on fire**) ignite, kindle, cause to burn. **set the world on fire** do something remarkable or sensational. **take fire 1** catch fire. **2** become enthused, dynamic, energetic, etc. **under fire 1** being shot at. **2** being rigorously criticized or questioned. □ **fireless** *adj.*

fire alarm *n.* a device for giving warning of fire.

firearm *n.* (usu. in *pl.*) a portable gun of any sort, e.g. a pistol, rifle, etc.

fireball *n.* **1** a large, bright meteor. **2 a** a ball of flame or fire. **b** a ball of flame resulting from a nuclear explosion. **3 a** a very energetic person. **b** a person with a fiery temper. **4** lightning appearing as a glowing ball.

fireballer *n. Baseball slang* a pitcher known for throwing hard fastballs. □ **fireballing** *adj.*

firebomb ● *n.* an incendiary bomb, esp. a Molotov cocktail. ● *v.tr.* attack or destroy with a firebomb.

firebox *n.* **1** an enclosed space in which a fire is made in a fireplace, stove, etc. **2** the fuel chamber of a steam engine or boiler.

firebrand *n.* **1** a person who or a thing which kindles strife, inflames passion, causes trouble, etc. **2** a piece of burning wood.

firebreak *n.* an obstacle, usu. a strip of land cleared or plowed, designed to stop fire from spreading in a forest, on grasslands, etc.

fire-breathing *adj.* **1** (of a person) having an aggressive manner. **2** (of a dragon etc.) capable of breathing fire.

fire brigade *n.* esp. *Brit.* an organized body of firefighters.

fire chief *n. N Amer.* the officer in charge of a fire department.

firecracker *n.* esp. *N Amer.* a small firework that explodes with a cracking noise.

fire department *n. N Amer.* a usu. municipal authority in charge of preventing and fighting fires.

fire drill *n.* a rehearsal of the procedures to be used in case of fire.

fire engine *n.* = FIRE TRUCK.

fire-engine red ● *adj.* of a deep vibrant red. ● *n.* this colour.

fire escape *n.* an emergency staircase etc., esp. on the outside of a building, for use during a fire.

fire extinguisher *n.* a portable apparatus for discharging chemicals, water, etc. to put out a fire.

firefight *n.* a skirmish or battle involving the exchange of gunfire.

firefighter *n.* a person whose job is to extinguish fires, esp. a member of a fire department. □ **firefighting** *n. & adj.*

firefly *n.* (*pl.* **-flies**) any soft-bodied beetle of the family Lampyridae, emitting phosphorescent light.

fire hall *n. Cdn* a fire station.

firehose *n.* a heavy-duty hose used esp. by firefighters in extinguishing fires.

fire hydrant *n.* a pipe, usu. on the side of the street, with a valve for drawing water from a main to which a firehose can be attached.

firelight *n.* light from a fire or fires.

fireman *n.* (*pl.* **-men**) **1** a firefighter. **2** a stoker or person who tends a furnace or the fire of a steam engine, steamship, etc.

fire marshal *n. N Amer.* **1** a public official charged with investigating suspicious fires, enforcing fire regulations, etc. **2** a person responsible for evacuating people from a building in case of fire.

firepit *n.* a pit dug into the ground or made from stones etc. in which a fire is made and maintained.

fireplace *n.* **1** a place for a domestic fire, esp. a partially enclosed place at the base of a chimney. **2** a structure surrounding this or the area in front of it.

firepower *n.* **1** the destructive capacity of guns, missiles, a military force, etc. **2** financial, intellectual, physical, or emotional strength.

fireproof ● *adj.* able to resist fire or great heat. ● *v.tr.* make fireproof. □ **fireproofing** *n.*

fire-resistant *adj.* **1** almost completely non-flammable. **2** = FIRE-RETARDANT. □ **fire-resistance** *n.*

fire-retardant *adj.* capable of slowing or stopping the spread of fire.

fire sale *n.* **1** a sale, usu. at low prices, of goods remaining after a fire. **2** a sale of anything at a remarkably low price.

fireside ● *n.* **1** the area around a fireplace. **2** a person's home or home life. ● *adj.* **1** situated beside or pertaining to a domestic fire or fireplace. **2** intimate or relaxed, esp. designating an informal political talk broadcast to the nation (*fireside chat*).

fire station *n.* a building where fire trucks and firefighters are housed.

firestorm *n.* **1** an intense conflagration into which surrounding air is drawn with great force, esp. resulting from incendiary or nuclear bombing. **2** an intense and forceful response (*a political firestorm*).

fire truck *n. N Amer.* a heavy vehicle carrying equipment for fighting fires.

fire-wagon *n. Sport slang* (*attrib.*) (in hockey) a dramatic manner of play which emphasizes offensive teamwork, heavy checking, hard passing, and speed.

firewall *n.* **1** a fireproof wall to prevent the spread of fire. **2** *Computing* a system designed to control the passage of information between networks.

firewater *n. informal* strong alcoholic liquor.

fireweed *n.* any of several plants that spring up on

burnt land, esp. the willow herb, *Epilobium angustifolium*.

firewood *n.* wood prepared or suitable for use as fuel.

firework *n.* **1 a** a device containing chemicals that burn or explode spectacularly. **b** (in *pl.*) a colourful and spectacular display of such devices. **2** (in *pl.*) **a** an outburst of passion, esp. anger. **b** an impressive display of wit, brilliance, or skill.

firing *n.* **1** the discharge of guns etc. **2** the action of subjecting something to heat or fire, esp. the process which hardens clay into pottery etc.

firing line *n.* **1** the front line in a battle, nearest the enemy. **2** the forefront of or leading part in an activity, controversy, etc. □ **on the firing line** subject to challenge, criticism, blame, etc. because of one's responsibilities or position.

firing range *n.* = RANGE 5.

firing squad *n.* a group of soldiers detailed to shoot a condemned person.

firm¹ ● *adj.* **1 a** hard, resistant to pressure or impact, or of solid or compact structure. **b** securely fixed, stable; not easily moved. **c** steady or controlled, not shaking or wavering (*a firm voice*). **2 a** (of a person, opinion, etc.) resolute, determined, not easily swayed or shaken (*firm belief*). **b** steadfast, constant (*a firm friend*). **c** unassailable (*firm evidence*). **3 a** (of an offer etc.) not liable to cancellation after acceptance. **b** (of a decree, law, etc.) established, immutable. **4** *Commerce* (of prices or goods) maintaining their level or value. ● *adv.* firmly (*stand firm*). ● *v.tr. & intr.* make or become firm, secure, compact, or solid. □ **a firm hand** strong discipline or control. **firm up 1** work to tone and improve the condition of the muscles, voice, etc. **2** put (a thing) in final, fixed form, tidying up details etc. **3** strengthen, reinforce (standing, credibility, etc.). **4** become firm. □ **firmly** *adv.* **firmness** *n.*

firm² *n.* **1** a partnership or company for carrying on a business. **2** the name under which the business of a commercial enterprise is transacted.

firmament *n.* *literary* the arch or vault of the skies.

firmware *n.* *Computing* a permanent kind of software programmed into the read-only memory in certain types of computers.

first ● *adj.* **1 a** earliest or preceding all others in time, order, or experience. **b** coming next after a specified or implied time (*shall take the first bus*). **2** foremost in position, rank, or importance (*first mate*). **3** *Music* denoting one of two or more parts for the same instrument or voice, often the highest or more prominent of the two. **4** most willing or likely (*should be the first to admit it*). **5** basic or evident (*first principles*). ● *n.* **1** (prec. by *the*) the first part, the beginning, or the person or thing first mentioned or occurring. **2** the first occurrence of something notable. **3** the first day of a month. **4** first gear. **5 a** first place in a race. **b** the winner of this. **c** = FIRST DOWN. **d** the first inning. **e** *Baseball* = FIRST BASE. ● *adv.* **1** before any other person or thing in time, rank, serial order, etc. (*first of all*). **2** before another specified or implied thing, time, event, etc. (*do this first*). **3** for the first time. **4** rather or in preference to something else (*I'd die first*). □ **at first** at the beginning. **at first hand** gained or coming directly from the original source. **first off** *N Amer. informal* at first, first of all. **first things first** the most important things before any others. **from the first** from the beginning. **from first to last** throughout. **in the first place** as the first consideration.

first aid *n.* help given to a sick or injured person until proper medical treatment is available.

first base *n.* *Baseball* **1** the first of the bases that must be touched to score a run. **2** the position of the player covering this base and the area of the infield surrounding it. □ **get to first base** *N Amer. informal* make a successful start; achieve the first step of an undertaking. □ **first baseman** *n.*

first-born ● *adj.* eldest. ● *n.* a person's eldest child.

first class ● *n.* **1** a set of persons grouped together as the best. **2** the most comfortable and costly seating in an airplane, train, etc. **3** the class of mail given priority in handling. ● *adj.* (**first-class**) **1** belonging to, achieving, or travelling by, etc. the first class. **2** very good; of the best quality. ● *adv.* by the best or quickest form of transport or mail (*send it first class*).

first-come, first-served *n.* a system of providing service to people strictly in the order in which they arrive, apply, etc.

first contact *n.* the first interaction between colonizers and an Aboriginal people.

first cousin *n. see* COUSIN.

first-degree *adj.* **1 a** designating the most serious category of crime. **b** (of murder) premeditated and without mitigating circumstances. **2** denoting the least serious category of burn, those that affect only the surface of the skin, causing reddening.

first down *n.* *Football* **1** the first of three attempts (four attempts in American football) to advance the ball ten yards. **2** the achievement of an advance of ten or more yards, by which the offensive team is entitled to a new series of downs.

first edition *n.* **1** the first printed form in which a book etc. is published. **2** the whole number of copies in this form. **3** one copy in this form.

first floor *n.* **1** *N Amer.* the floor on the ground level. **2** esp. *Brit.* the floor above the ground floor.

first fruit *n.* (usu. in *pl.*) **1** the first results of work etc. **2** the first agricultural produce of a season, esp. as offered to God.

first gear *n.* the lowest gear on a car, bicycle, etc.

first generation *adj.* **1 a** designating the offspring born to immigrants once they have settled in their adopted country. **b** designating the immigrants themselves. **2** of or belonging to an initial model, program, period, etc.

first-hand *adj. & adv.* direct, from the original source or personal experience.

first lady *n.* **1** the leading woman in some specified activity or profession (*the first lady of Canadian theatre*). **2** (**First Lady**) (in the US) the wife of the President.

first language *n.* a person's native language.

first light *n.* the time when light first appears in the morning; daybreak.

first line *n.* **1** the preliminary effort, resources, etc. ready for immediate use or action (*first line of defence*). **2** (often *attrib.*) the thing, treatment, group of people, etc., which is most advanced or of the highest quality.

first love *n.* **1 a** the first time one falls in love. **b** the emotion felt then. **2** the first person with whom one falls in love. **3** a person's favourite occupation, possession, etc. (*her first love is the theatre*).

firstly *adv.* in enumerating topics, arguments, etc.) in the first place, first (compare FIRST *adv.*).

first mate *n.* (on a merchant ship) the officer second-in-command to the master.

First Meridian *n.* *Cdn* the north-south line, 97 degrees 27 minutes west, from which land in the prairies is surveyed.

First Minister *n.* *Cdn* **1** the prime minister of Canada. **2** the premier of a province.

first mortgage n. the mortgage having priority over all similar mortgages on the same property.

first name n. a person's personal or given name.

First Nation n. Cdn an Indian band, or an Indian community functioning as a band but not having official band status. ¶The term First Nations does not include the Inuit or Metis.

first officer n. **1** the mate on a merchant ship. **2** the second-in-command to the captain on an aircraft.

first past the post adj. Cdn & Brit. **1** winning a race etc. by being the first to reach the finish line. **2** (of an electoral system) selecting a candidate or party by simple majority.

First Peoples n.pl. the Aboriginal peoples of a particular country or region etc. ¶In Canada, the term First Peoples includes Indians, Inuit, and Metis.

first principle n. a fundamental axiom, assumption, etc. seen as underlying a given theory or procedure, esp. in mathematics, science, etc.

first-rate adj. **1** of the highest class, excellent. **2** informal very well (feeling first-rate).

first reading n. the first of three successive occasions on which a bill must have been presented to a legislature before it becomes law.

first refusal n. see REFUSAL.

first-run adj. designating the initial period in which a film, movie, etc. is first shown publicly.

first-string ● n. Sport the primary and usu. starting line of a team, composed of the best players. ● adj. of or like the best of a series, team, etc. □ **first-stringer** n.

first team n. a lineup of first-string players.

first thing informal ● n. (usu. prec. by the) the most elementary thing, aspect, etc. of something (doesn't know the first thing about it). ● adv. **1** before anything else (we must establish a budget first thing). **2** very early in the morning (first thing tomorrow).

first-time buyer n. a person seeking to buy a home who has not previously owned one.

first-timer n. a person who does or is something for the first time.

First World n. the developed countries apart from the former Communist bloc.

firth n. an estuary or narrow inlet of the sea.

fiscal adj. **1** of or related to public revenue, usu. taxes. **2** esp. N Amer. pertaining to financial matters. **3** N Amer. designating a fiscal year (fiscal 1998). □ **fiscally** adv.

fiscal year n. a period of twelve months over which annual accounts and taxes are calculated.

fish ● n. (pl. same or **fishes**) **1** a vertebrate cold-blooded animal with gills and fins living wholly in water. **2** any animal living wholly in water, e.g. cuttlefish, shellfish, jellyfish. **3** the flesh of fish as food. **4** Cdn (Nfld) cod. ● v. **1** intr. **a** try to catch fish, esp. with a line or net. **b** Cdn (Nfld) engage in sea fishery, esp. for cod, as opposed to freshwater angling. **2** tr. fish for (a certain kind of fish) or in (a certain stretch of water). **3** intr. (foll. by for) **a** search, grope, or feel for in water or a concealed place. **b** try to obtain or elicit by indirect means or artifice (fishing for compliments). **4** tr. (foll. by up, out, etc.) retrieve with careful or awkward searching. □ **a big fish in a small** (or **little**) **pond** a comparatively significant figure in a small group, community, etc. **drink like a fish** drink excessively. **fish or cut bait** N Amer. act on or disengage from a matter, an issue, etc. **fish out** depopulate (a lake, area of ocean, etc.) through excessive fishing. **fish out of water** a person in an unfamiliar, unsuitable, or unwelcome environment or situation. **other** (or

plenty more etc.) **fish in the sea** other people or things as good as the one that has failed or been lost. **other fish to fry** other matters to attend to. □ **fishability** n. **fishable** adj. **fishlike** adj.

fish and brewis n. Cdn (Nfld) a dish of salt cod and hardtack soaked in water and then fried and garnished with fried salt pork.

fish and chips n.pl. fish fried in batter and served with french fries.

fishboat n. Cdn (esp. BC) = FISHING BOAT.

fishbowl n. **1** a usu. round glass bowl for keeping pet fish in. **2** a place, situation, etc. in which one's life and activities are carefully and usu. publicly observed, commented upon, etc.

fish cake n. a small patty of flaked or minced fish and mashed potato, usu. coated in batter or bread crumbs and fried.

fish camp n. N Amer. (esp. North) a camp used as a base by a group engaged in fishing, sometimes run as a business with rudimentary lodging, supplies, etc.

fisher n. **1 a** a large N American arboreal carnivore of the weasel family, Martes pennanti, valued for its fur. **b** the pelt of such an animal. **2** a fisherman, either professional or recreational.

fisherman n. (pl. **-men**) a person who catches fish as a livelihood or for sport.

fishery n. (pl. **-ies**) **1 a** a fish hatchery or place where fish are reared. **b** a fishing ground or area where fish are caught. **2** the occupation or industry of catching or rearing fish.

fish eye n. **1** (in full **fish-eye lens**) a very wide-angle lens with a field of vision covering up to 180°, the scale being reduced towards the edges. **2** an eye of or like that of a fish.

fish farm n. a place where fish are bred for food. □ **fish farmer** n. **fish farming** n.

fish finder n. a device equipped with sonar to locate schools of fish in a body of water.

fish flake n. Cdn (Nfld) a rack on which to dry fish, usu. consisting of a framework of poles covered with spruce boughs to allow free air circulation.

fish fry n. N Amer. a usu. outdoor social gathering at which fish are cooked and eaten

fish hook n. a barbed hook for catching fish.

fish hut n. Cdn a small, portable shack placed over a hole in the ice of a lake to protect a person ice fishing.

fishing n. the catching of fish as food or as a job, sport, or hobby.

fishing boat n. any watercraft used for fishing.

fishing camp n. N Amer. **1** = FISHING LODGE. **2** = FISH CAMP.

fishing derby n. N Amer. a fishing competition, usu. for money or prizes, in which participants try for the largest catch in a variety of fish categories.

fishing expedition n. **1** a usu. extended fishing trip. **2** a search or investigation undertaken with the hope, though not the stated purpose, of discovering information.

fishing hole n. **1** a favoured spot in a lake, on a river, etc. for catching fish. **2** an opening cut in lake or river ice for ice fishing.

fishing line n. a long thread of nylon etc. to which a baited hook, sinker, float, etc., are attached, used with a fishing rod for catching fish.

fishing lodge n. N Amer. an establishment, usu. by a lake, providing accommodation, equipment, etc. for sport fishermen.

fishing rod n. (also **fishing pole**) a long, tapering, usu. jointed rod to which a fishing line and usu. a reel are attached.

fishing stage n. Cdn (esp. Nfld) a shed near the shoreline for gutting, heading, salting, etc. fish before they are dried on flakes.

fishing station n. Cdn a small sheltered cove from which fishing is undertaken on a seasonal basis, esp. in Newfoundland.

fishing trip n. a vacation with sport fishing as the primary intended activity.

fish ladder n. a series of pools built like steps to enable fish to ascend a fall or dam to reach their spawning grounds.

fishmonger n. a person who sells fish.

fishnet n. **1** (often attrib.) an open, meshed fabric or a garment made of it. **2** a net for catching fish.

fish pond n. **1** a pond or pool in which fish are kept. **2** N Amer. an attraction at a fair etc. where contestants use a rod and line to attempt to extract a prize etc. from a pool, enclosure, etc.

fish sauce n. a spicy condiment made from fermented anchovies, used in oriental cuisine.

fish stick n. a small, oblong piece of flaked or minced fish coated in batter etc. and fried.

fish store n. **1** a store selling fish. **2** Cdn (Nfld & Maritimes) a building where offshore fisherman store dried cod ready for collection or export.

fishtail ● v.intr. move the tail of a vehicle from side to side. ● n. a device etc. shaped like a fish's tail.

fishway n. Cdn a lock built to aid fish in passing a waterfall etc. on their way upstream to spawn.

fishy adj. (**-ier, -iest**) **1 a** of or like fish, esp. in smell or taste. **b** (of an eye) dull, vacant looking. **c** consisting of fish (a fishy repast). **2** slang of dubious character, questionable, suspect. □ **fishily** adv. **fishiness** n.

fissile /ˈfisail/ adj. **1** capable of undergoing nuclear fission. **2** cleavable, inclined or tending to split.

fission ● n. **1** Physics the spontaneous or impact-induced splitting of a heavy atomic nucleus, accompanied by a release of energy. **2** Biol. the division of a cell or organism into new cells or organisms as a mode of reproduction. **3** the action of splitting or dividing into pieces. ● v.intr. & tr. undergo or cause to undergo fission. □ **fissionable** adj.

fission bomb n. an atomic bomb.

fissure ● n. **1** an opening, usu. long and narrow, made by cracking, splitting, or separation of esp. rock or ice. **2** a division or split. ● v.tr. & intr. split or crack.

fist n. a tightly closed hand. ● v.tr. **1** strike with the fist. **2** clench (the hand, the fingers) into a fist. □ **fisted** adj. (also in comb.).

fist fight n. a fight with bare fists. □ **fist fighting** n.

fistful n. (pl. **-fuls**) **1** a quantity held in a fist. **2** a large quantity.

fistula /ˈfistjʊlə/ n. (pl. **-s** or **-lae** /-ˌliː/) an abnormal or surgically made passage between a hollow organ and the body surface or between two body organs.

fit¹ ● adj. (**fitter, fittest**) **1 a** (usu. foll. by for, or to + infin.) well adapted or suited. **b** (foll. by to + infin.) qualified, competent, worthy. **c** (foll. by for, or to + infin.) in a suitable condition, ready. **d** (foll. by for) good enough (fit for a king). **2** in good health or athletic condition, esp. having excellent cardiovascular function. **3** proper, becoming, right (it is fit that). ● v. (foll. by or (esp. in senses 1, 4, 6, and 7) **fit, fitting**) **1 a** tr. & intr. be of the right shape and size for (my shoes don't fit). **b** tr. adjust (an object) to the contours of its receptacle or counterpart (fitted shelves into the alcove). **c** intr. (often foll. by in, into) (of a component) be

correctly positioned (that piece fits here). **d** tr. find room for (can't fit another person). **2** tr. (foll. by for, or to + infin.) **a** make suitable; adapt. **b** make ready or competent (her education fitted her for the job). **3** tr. (usu. foll. by with) supply, furnish (fitted the boat with a new rudder). **4** tr. fix in place (fit a lock on the door). **5** tr. try clothing on (a person) in order to adjust it to the right size and shape (fitted me for a new suit). **6** tr. be in harmony with, befit, become (the punishment fits the crime). **7** tr. be suitable for (this fits our needs). ● n. **1** the way in which a garment, component, etc., fits (a tight fit). **2** suitability, compatibility (a perfect fit between the employee and the job). ● adv. (foll. by to + infin.) informal in a suitable manner, appropriately (was laughing fit to bust). □ **fit the bill** be suitable or adequate. **fit in 1** (often foll. by with) be (esp. socially) compatible or accommodating (doesn't fit in with the group). **2** find space or time for (an object, engagement, etc.) (fitted me in at the last minute). **fit out** (or **up**) (often foll. by with) equip. **see** (or **think**) **fit** (often foll. by to + infin.) decide or choose (a specified course of action). □ **fitly** adv.

fit² n. **1** a sudden seizure of epilepsy, hysteria, apoplexy, fainting, etc., with unconsciousness or convulsions. **2** a sudden brief attack of an illness or of symptoms (fit of coughing). **3** a sudden short bout or burst (fit of giggles). **4** an attack of strong feeling (fit of rage). **5** a capricious impulse (a fit of generosity). □ **by** (or **in**) **fits and starts** spasmodically. **give a person a fit** informal surprise or outrage him or her. **have** (or **throw**) **a fit** informal be greatly surprised or outraged.

fitful adj. active or occurring spasmodically or intermittently. □ **fitfully** adv. **fitfulness** n.

fitness n. **1** the quality or state of being physically fit (also attrib.: fitness program). **2** the quality of being suitable, qualified, or morally fit for something.

fitted adj. made or shaped to fill a space or cover something closely or exactly (fitted sheet).

fitter n. **1** a person who supervises the cutting, fitting, altering, etc. of garments or shoes. **2** a person who fits together and adjusts machine etc. parts.

fitting ● n. **1** the process or an instance of having a garment etc. fitted. **2** (usu. in pl.) decorative metal handles, corners, etc., on furniture, bathtubs, etc. **3** a small standard part or component. ● adj. proper, becoming, right. □ **fittingly** adv. **fittingness** n.

fitting room n. a room in a store or in a dressmaker's premises etc. where garments are tried on.

five ● n. **1** one more than four. **2** a symbol for this (5, v, V). **3** a size etc. denoted by five. **4** a set or team of five persons or things. **5** five o'clock. **6** a five-dollar bill etc. **7** a card with five pips. ● adj. that amount to five.

five-and-a-half n. Cdn (Que.) an apartment having three bedrooms, kitchen, living room, and bath.

five-and-dime store n. (also **five-and-dime, five-and-ten**) N Amer. **1** hist. a store where all the articles were originally priced at five or ten cents. **2** a store selling a wide variety of inexpensive household and personal goods.

five-a-side ● adv. Hockey with one player short on each side as a result of penalties. ● adj. designating soccer played with five players on each team. ● n. a game of five-a-side soccer.

fivefold adj. & adv. **1** five times as much or as many. **2** consisting of five parts. **3** amounting to five.

Five Nations n.pl. hist. the Seneca, Cayuga, Onondaga, Oneida, and Mohawk, who formed the League of the Iroquois in the 16th c.

five-pin bowling n. Cdn a variety of bowling in

which players have three chances to knock down five pins, each of different scoring value, using a smaller ball than in 10-pin bowling.

fiver *n. informal N Amer.* a five-dollar bill.

five senses *n.pl.* (prec. by *the*) sight, hearing, smell, taste, and touch.

five-star *adj.* (of a hotel, restaurant, etc.) given five stars in a grading, esp. where this indicates the highest quality.

five-year plan *n.* **1** (in the former USSR) a government plan for economic development over five years. **2** a similar plan in another country etc.

fix ● *v.* **1** *tr.* repair. **2** *tr.* put in order, adjust. **3** *tr.* make firm or stable; fasten, secure. **4** *tr.* decide, settle, specify (a price, date, etc.). **5** *tr.* implant (an idea or memory) in the mind. **6** *tr.* **a** (foll. by *on, upon*) direct steadily, set (one's eyes, gaze, attention, or affection). **b** attract and hold (a person's attention, eyes, etc.). **c** (foll. by *with*) single out with one's eyes etc. **7** *tr.* place definitely or permanently; establish, station. **8** *tr.* determine the exact nature, position, etc., of; refer (a thing or person) to a definite place or time. **9** *a tr.* make (eyes, features, etc.) rigid. **b** *intr.* (of eyes, features, etc.) become rigid. **10** *tr. N Amer. informal* prepare (food or drink). **11** *a tr.* deprive of fluidity or volatility. **b** *intr.* lose fluidity or volatility. **12** *tr. informal* punish or deal with (a person). **13** *tr. informal* **a** secure the support of (a person) fraudulently, esp. by bribery. **b** arrange the result of (a race, match, etc.) fraudulently (*the competition was fixed*). **14** *tr.* make (a pigment, photographic image, etc.) fast or permanent. **15** *tr.* (of a plant or micro-organism) assimilate (nitrogen or carbon dioxide) by forming a non-gaseous compound. **16** *tr.* castrate or spay (an animal). **17** *tr.* allocate or determine the incidence of (a responsibility, liability etc.). **18** *intr. N Amer.* (foll. by *to* + infin.) prepare; plan. ● *n.* **1** *informal* a position hard to escape from; a dilemma or predicament. **2** *informal* a repair, esp. to a computer program. **3 a** the act of finding one's position by bearings or astronomical observations. **b** a position found in this way. **4** *slang* **a** a dose of a narcotic drug to which one is addicted. **b** anything which one craves and enjoys immensely (*sugar fix*). **5** *informal* a clear understanding (*get a fix on her mood*). □ **be fixed** (usu. foll. by *for*) be disposed or affected (regarding) (*how is he fixed for money?*). **fix up 1** arrange, organize, prepare. **2** upgrade, improve. **3** (often foll. by *with*) provide (a person) (*fixed me up with a job*). □ **fixable** *adj.* **fixedly** /ˈfɪksɪdlɪ/ *adv.* **fixedness** *n.*

fixate *v.* **1** *intr.* (foll. by *on, upon*) be or become obsessed with. **2** *tr. Psych.* **a** (usu. in *passive*; often foll. by *on, upon*) cause (a person) to acquire an abnormal attachment to persons or things (*was fixated on his son*). **b** arrest (part of the libido) at an immature stage, causing such attachment. **3** *tr. & intr.* direct one's gaze on.

fixation *n.* **1** *Psych.* the act or an instance of being fixated. **2** an obsession. **3** fixing or being fixed. **4** coagulation. **5** the process of assimilating a gas to form a solid compound.

fixative ● *n.* a substance used to set or fix colours, hair, specimens, etc. ● *adj.* tending to fix or secure.

fixed-do *attrib.adj.* applied to a system of sight-singing in which C is called 'do', D is called 're', etc., irrespective of the key in which they occur.

fixed income *n.* income from a pension, investment, etc. that is set at a particular figure and does not rise with the rate of inflation (also *attrib.*: *fixed-income securities*).

fixed link *n. Cdn & Brit.* a permanent means of transit between two geographical areas separated by water.

fixed star *n.* a star so far from the earth that it appears motionless.

fixed-wing *adj.* designating aircraft of the conventional type, as opposed to helicopters etc.

fixer *n.* **1** a person or thing that fixes. **2** *Photog.* a substance used for fixing a photographic image etc. **3** *informal* a person who makes arrangements, esp. of an illicit kind.

fixing *n.* **1** (in *pl.*) *N Amer.* **a** the necessary ingredients for a dish, meal, etc. **b** appropriate trimmings etc. for a dish. **2** apparatus or equipment.

fix-it *n.* **1** the action or an act of fixing something (usu. *attrib.*: *fix-it project*). **2** a handyperson (esp. as a pseudo-surname: *Mr. Fix-It*).

fixity *n.* **1** a fixed state. **2** stability; permanence.

fixture *n.* **1 a** something fixed or fastened in position (*a light fixture*). **b** (usu. *predic.*) *informal* a person or thing confined to or established in one place (*he's a permanent fixture here*). **2** (in *pl.*) *Law* articles attached to a house or land and regarded as legally part of it.

fizz ● *v.intr.* **1** make a hissing or spluttering sound. **2** (of a drink) make bubbles; effervesce. ● *n.* **1** a hissing or spluttering sound. **2** effervescence. **3** *informal* excitement, energy (*the band lacks fizz*).

fizzle ● *v.intr.* **1** make a feeble hissing or spluttering sound. **2** (often foll. by *out*) end feebly. ● *n.* **1** a feeble hissing or spluttering sound. **2** a failure, a fiasco.

fizzy *adj.* (**-ier, -iest**) effervescent. □ **fizziness** *n.*

fjord /fiːˈɔːd, fjɔːd, ˈfiːɔːd/ *n.* a long, narrow, and deep inlet of sea between high cliffs.

FL *abbr.* Florida (in postal use).

fl. *abbr.* fluid.

Fla. *abbr.* Florida.

flab *n. informal* fat; flabbiness.

flabbergast /ˈflæbərˌɡæst/ *v.tr.* (esp. as **flabbergasted** *adj.*) overwhelm with astonishment.

flabby *adj.* (**-ier, -iest**) **1** (of flesh etc.) hanging down; limp; flaccid. **2** (of a person) having soft loose fatty flesh; overweight. **3** (of character etc.) feeble; lacking vigour. □ **flabbily** *adv.* **flabbiness** *n.*

flaccid /ˈflæsɪd, ˈflæksɪd/ *adj.* **1** (of flesh etc.) lacking stiffness; hanging or lying loose; limp. **2** relaxed, drooping. **3** lacking vigour; feeble (*flaccid prose*).

flack[1] *N Amer. slang* ● *n.* a publicist. ● *v.* **1** *intr.* act as a publicist. **2** *tr.* promote (a product, event, etc.).

flack[2] *var. of* FLAK.

flag[1] ● *n.* **1 a** a piece of cloth, usu. oblong or square, attachable by one edge to a pole or rope and used as a country's emblem or as a standard, signal, etc. **b** a small toy, device, etc., resembling a flag. **c** a piece of cloth raised, dropped, waved, etc., to indicate the start or finish of a race, to signal a penalty, etc. **2** a device that is raised to indicate that a taxi is for hire. **3** the tail of an animal, esp. a deer or setter. ● *v.* (**flagged, flagging**) **1** *intr.* **a** grow tired; lose vigour; lag. **b** hang down; droop; become limp. **2** *tr.* **a** place a flag on or over. **b** mark out with or as if with a flag or flags. **3** *tr.* (often foll. by *that*) **a** inform (a person) by flag signals. **b** communicate (information) by flagging. □ **flag down** signal to (a vehicle or driver) to stop. **keep the flag flying** continue the fight. **put the flag out** celebrate victory, success, etc. **wave the flag 1** make a display of one's patriotism. **2** (foll. by *for*) assert one's allegiance to (a cause etc.). **wrap oneself in the flag** assert one's allegiance to one's country. □ **flagger** *n.*

flag² ● *n.* = FLAGSTONE. ● *v.tr.* (**flagged**, **flagging**) pave with flagstones.

flag³ *n.* **1** any plant with a bladed leaf (esp. several of the genus *Iris*) growing on moist ground. **2** the long slender leaf of such a plant.

Flag Day *n. Cdn* Feb. 15, the anniversary of the adoption of the Maple Leaf flag in 1965.

flagellate¹ /ˈflædʒəˌleɪt/ *v.tr.* scourge, flog. □ **flagellation** *n.*

flagellate² /ˈflædʒələt, -ˌleɪt/ ● *adj.* (also **flagellated**) having flagella. ● *n.* a protozoan having one or more flagella.

flagellum /fləˈdʒeləm/ *n.* (*pl.* **flagella** /-lə/) **1** *Biol.* a long lash-like appendage found esp. on microscopic organisms. **2** *Bot.* a runner; a creeping shoot.

flagging¹ *adj.* losing vigour, vitality, etc.

flagging² *n.* paving of flagstones.

flagon /ˈflægən/ *n.* **1** a large bottle in which wine etc., is sold. **2 a** a large vessel usu. with a handle, spout, and lid, to hold wine etc. **b** a similar vessel used to hold the wine of the Eucharist.

flagpole *n.* a pole on which a flag may be hoisted. □ **run something up the flagpole** test (an idea etc.).

flagrant *adj.* (of an offence or an offender) glaring; notorious. □ **flagrancy** *n.* **flagrantly** *adv.*

flagship *n.* **1** a ship, esp. in a fleet or squadron, having an admiral on board. **2** something considered a leader or superior example of its kind.

flagstone *n.* **1** a flat usu. rectangular stone slab used for paving. **2** (in *pl.*) a pavement made of these. □ **flagstoned** *adj.*

flag-waving ● *n.* an excessive display of patriotism. ● *adj.* behaving in this manner. □ **flag-waver** *n.*

flail ● *n.* a threshing tool consisting of a wooden staff with a short heavy stick swinging from it. ● *v.* **1** *tr.* beat or strike with or as if with a flail. **2** *tr. & intr.* wave or swing wildly or erratically. **3** *intr.* (often foll. by *about, around*) **a** a move with one's limbs swinging wildly, usu. in desperation. **b** attempt desperately but unsuccessfully to find a direction to follow.

flair *n.* **1** special talent, aptitude, or ability (*a flair for languages*). **2** an instinct for selecting or performing what is excellent, useful, etc. **3** originality; stylishness of dress, manner, etc.

flak *n.* **1** anti-aircraft fire. **2** adverse criticism; hostile reaction.

flake¹ ● *n.* **1 a** a small thin light piece of snow. **b** a similar piece of another material, esp. one that has peeled or split off a surface or object (*paint flakes*). **2** a thin stratum or lamina. **3** (in *pl.*) any of various kinds of flaked breakfast cereal, esp. cornflakes. **4** a natural division of the flesh of some fish. **5** *N Amer. slang* a crazy or eccentric person. ● *v.tr. & intr.* **1** (often foll. by *away, off*) take off, shed, or come away in flakes. **2** separate or form into flakes. □ **flake out** *informal* fall asleep or drop from exhaustion; faint.

flake² *n.* a stage for drying fish etc.

flaky *adj.* (**-ier**, **-iest**) (also **flakey**) **1** of or like flakes; separating easily into flakes. **2** *N Amer. slang* crazy, eccentric. □ **flakily** *adv.* **flakiness** *n.*

flambé ● /ˈflɒmbeɪ, flɒmˈbeɪ, flæm-/ *adj.* (of food) covered with alcohol and set alight briefly. ● *v.tr.* /flɒmˈbeɪ/ (**flambés**, **flambéed**, **flambéing**) cover (food) with alcohol and set alight briefly.

flamboyant *adj.* **1** (of a person, behaviour, etc.) ostentatious; showy. **2** floridly decorated. **3** gorgeously coloured. □ **flamboyance** *n.* **flamboyancy** *n.* **flamboyantly** *adv.*

flame ● *n.* **1 a** ignited gas (*the fire burned with a steady flame*). **b** one portion of this (*the flame flickered and died*). **c** (usu. in *pl.*) visible combustion (*burst into flames*). **2 a** a bright light; brilliant colouring. **b** a brilliant orange-red colour. **3 a** strong passion, esp. love (*fan the flame*). **b** *informal* a boyfriend or girlfriend. **4** *slang* an angry message of censure or disparagement sent by one user of a computer network to another. ● *v.* **1** *intr. & tr.* (often foll. by *out, up*) emit or cause to emit flames. **2** *intr.* (often foll. by *out, up*) **a** (of passion, anger, etc.) break out. **b** (of a person) become angry. **3** *intr.* shine or glow like flame (*leaves flamed in the autumn sun*). **4 a** *tr.* censure or disparage (a user of a computer network) via electronic mail. **b** *intr.* engage in such behaviour. **5** *tr.* subject to the action of flame. □ **go up in flames** be consumed by fire. □ **flameless** *adj.* **flamelike** *adj.*

flamenco /fləˈmeŋkoː/ *n.* (*pl.* **-os**) **1** a style of music played (esp. on the guitar) and sung by Spanish gypsies. **2** a strongly rhythmical dance performed to this music.

flame-proof *adj.* **1** (esp. of a fabric) treated so as to be non-flammable. **2** (of cookware) that can be used in the oven or on a cooking element.

flame-thrower *n.* a weapon that projects a stream of burning fuel.

flaming *adj.* **1** emitting flames. **2** very hot; fiery. **3** *informal* **a** passionate; intense (*a flaming argument*). **b** expressing annoyance, or as an intensifier (*that flaming dog*). **4** bright-coloured. **5** *slang* (of a homosexual, esp. a man) flamboyant; conspicuously effeminate.

flamingo *n.* (*pl.* **-os** or **-oes**) any tall long-necked web-footed wading bird of the family Phoenicopteridae, with a crooked bill and pink, scarlet, and black plumage.

flammable *adj.* easily set on fire; highly combustible. ¶*Flammable* is often preferred because *inflammable* can be mistaken for a negative (the true negative being *non-flammable*). □ **flammability** *n.*

flan *n.* an open pastry or sponge pie case containing a fruit, jam or savoury filling.

flange /flændʒ/ ● *n.* a projecting flat rim, collar, or rib, used for strengthening or attachment, or (on a wheel) maintaining position on a rail. ● *v.tr.* (esp. as **flanged**) provide with a flange. □ **flangeless** *n.*

flank ● *n.* **1 a** the fleshy or muscular part of the side of a person or animal between the ribs and the hip. **b** a cut of meat, esp. beef, from the underside of an animal between the ribs and the hind legs (*flank steak*). **2** the side of a mountain, building, etc. **3** the right or left side of an army or other body of persons. ● *v.tr.* **1** (often in *passive*) be situated at both sides of. **2** *Military* **a** guard, strengthen, or defend on the flank. **b** menace or attack the flank of.

flanker *n.* **1 a** a fortification for protecting or menacing the flank. **b** one of a detachment of soldiers sent to guard the flanks of a military formation. **2** anything that flanks another thing. **3** (in football) an offensive player who lines up to the outside of an end.

flannel *n.* **1** any of various loose-textured soft woollen or synthetic fabrics of plain or twilled weave and slightly napped on one side. **2** = FLANNELETTE. **3** (in *pl.*) flannel garments, esp. trousers.

flannelette *n.* a napped cotton fabric imitating the texture of flannel, used for sheets, pyjamas, etc.

flap ● *v.* (**flapped**, **flapping**) **1 a** *tr.* move (wings, the arms, etc.) up and down when flying, or as if flying. **b** *intr.* (of wings, the arms, etc.) move up and down; beat. **2 a** *intr.* (esp. of curtains, loose cloth, etc.) swing or sway about; flutter, esp. with accompanying noise. **b** *tr.* cause to swing or sway about, flutter or flop, esp.

with accompanying noise. **3** *tr.* (usu. foll. by *away, off*) strike with something broad; drive. **4** *intr. informal* be agitated or panicky (*she is easily flapped*). ● *n.* **1 a** a piece of cloth, wood, paper, etc. hinged or attached by one side only and often used to cover a gap, e.g. the folded part of an envelope or book jacket, the cover of a pocket, etc. **2** one up-and-down motion of a wing, an arm, etc. **3** *informal* **a** a state of agitation; panic (*don't get into a flap*). **b** trouble, confrontation. **4** a hinged or sliding section of an aircraft wing used to control lift. **5** a light blow with something broad.

flapjack *n.* *N Amer.* a pancake.

flapper *n.* **1** a person or thing that flaps. **2** *hist.* a fashionable and unconventional young woman of the 1920s.

flare ● *v.* **1** *intr. & tr.* burn or cause to burn suddenly with a bright unsteady flame. **2** *intr.* burst into anger etc.; burst forth. **3** *intr. & tr.* widen or cause to widen gradually towards the top or bottom (*flared trousers*). ● *n.* **1 a** a dazzling irregular flame or light, esp. in the open air. **b** a sudden outburst of flame. **2 a** a bright flame used as a signal of distress etc. **b** a device that produces such a flame. **c** a flame dropped from an aircraft to illuminate a target etc. **3** *Astronomy* a sudden burst of radiation from a star. **4** a sudden outburst of emotion etc. **5 a** a gradual widening, esp. of a skirt or trousers. **b** (in *pl.*) wide-bottomed pants, esp. popular during the late 1960s and 1970s. □ **flare up 1** burst into a sudden blaze. **2** become suddenly angry or active.

flare-up *n.* an outburst of flame, anger, activity, a disease, etc.

flash ● *v.* **1** *intr. & tr.* emit or reflect or cause to emit or reflect light briefly, suddenly, or intermittently; gleam or cause to gleam. **2** *intr.* break suddenly into flame; give out flame or sparks. **3** *tr.* send or reflect like a sudden flame or blaze (*his eyes flashed fire*). **4** *intr.* **a** burst suddenly into view or perception (*flashed into my mind*). **b** move swiftly. **5 a** *tr.* send (news etc.) by radio, television, etc. **b** *intr. & tr.* (of a message, image, etc.) show or be shown briefly on a television or movie screen. **c** *tr.* signal to (a person) by shining lights or headlights briefly. **6** *tr.* *informal* **a** show or display briefly (*flashed an identification card*). **b** show or display ostentatiously (*flashed her engagement ring*). **7** *intr. slang* (esp. of a man) expose one's genitals briefly and indecently. ● *n.* **1** a sudden bright light or flame, e.g. of lightning. **2** a very brief time; an instant (*in a flash*). **3 a** a brief, sudden burst of feeling (*a flash of hope*). **b** a sudden display (*of wit, understanding, etc.*). **4** = NEWS FLASH. **5** *Photog.* (also **flash gun**) a device producing a flash of intense light, used for photographing by night, indoors, etc. **6** *Cdn & Brit.* a coloured patch of cloth on a uniform etc. as a distinguishing emblem. **7** vulgar display, ostentation. **8** a bright patch of colour. **9** = HOT FLASH. ● *adj. informal* gaudy; vulgar (*a flash car*). □ **flash in the pan** a promising start followed by failure.

flashback *n.* **1** a scene in a film, novel, etc. set in a time earlier than the main action. **2** *Psych.* a vivid, often recurrent remembrance of a usu. distressing event from the past.

flashbulb *n.* a bulb producing a flash of light used for photography under conditions of low light.

flasher *n.* **1** *slang* a person, esp. a man, who indecently exposes himself. **2 a** an automatic device for switching lights rapidly on and off. **b** a sign or signal, e.g. hazard lights on a vehicle, using this device. **3** a person or thing that flashes.

flash flood *n.* a sudden flood due to heavy rain etc.

flashing *n.* a usu. metallic strip used to prevent water penetration at the junction of a roof with a wall etc.

flashlight *n.* a portable, battery-powered light.

flash memory *n.* *Computing* a type of memory that retains data in the absence of a power supply.

flashpoint *n.* **1** the temperature at which vapour from oil etc. will ignite in air. **2** the point at which anger, indignation, etc. becomes uncontrollable. **3** a place or situation which has the potential to explode into sudden violence.

flashy *adj.* (**-ier, -iest**) showy; gaudy. □ **flashily** *adv.* **flashiness** *n.*

flask *n.* **1 a** a narrow-necked bulbous bottle used in chemistry. **b** a similarly shaped bottle used for storing oil, wine, etc. **2** = HIP FLASK.

flat¹ ● *adj.* (**flatter, flattest**) **1 a** a horizontally level (*a flat roof*). **b** even; smooth; unbroken; without projection or indentation (*a flat stomach*). **c** with a level surface and little depth; shallow (*a flat heel*). **d** spread out on a single plane; extending at full length. **2** unqualified; downright (*a flat refusal*). **3 a** dull; lifeless; monotonous (*spoke in a flat tone*). **b** without energy; dejected. **c** (of a joke etc.) trite; not funny. **4** (of a drink etc.) lacking in flavour, stale; esp. having lost effervescence. **5** (of a tire) punctured; deflated. **6** *Music* **a** below true or normal pitch. **b** (of a key) having a flat or flats in the signature. **c** (as **B flat** etc.) a semitone lower than B etc. **7** not proportional or variable (*flat fee*). **8** (of a painting, photograph, etc.) **a** lacking contrast. **b** lacking perspective. **9 a** (of paint etc.) not glossy; matte. **b** (of a tint) of uniform depth and shade. **10** (of a market, prices, etc.) inactive; sluggish. ● *adv.* **1** lying at full length; spread out, esp. on another surface (*lay flat on the floor*). **2** *informal* **a** completely, absolutely (*flat broke*). **b** exactly (*in five minutes flat*). **3** *Music* below the true or normal pitch. ● *n.* **1** the flat part of anything; something flat. **2** (usu. in *pl.*) **a** a level ground, esp. a plain or swamp. **b** nearly level ground over which the tide flows or which is covered by shallow water (*mud flats*). **3** *Music* **a** a note lowered a semitone below natural pitch. **b** the sign (♭) indicating this. **4** *informal* a flat tire. **5** a woman's shoe with a low heel or no heel. **6** *N Amer.* a shallow box or container for growing seedlings or shipping produce etc. **7** *Theatre* a flat section of scenery mounted on a frame. ● *v.tr.* (**flatted, flatting**) **1** make flat, flatten (esp. in technical use). **2** *N Amer. Music* make (a note) flat. □ **fall flat** fail to live up to expectations; not win applause. **flat out 1** at top speed. **2** using all one's strength, energy, or resources. **3** directly, bluntly (*told me flat out*). □ **flatly** *adv.* **flatness** *n.* **flattish** *adj.*

flat² *n.* one or more rooms, usu. on one floor, rented and used as a residence.

flatbed *n.* (in full **flatbed trailer** or **flatbed truck**) a trailer or truck, the body of which is an open platform without raised sides or ends.

flatbread *n.* any of various flat, thin, often unleavened breads.

flatcar *n.* a railway car without a roof or raised sides, used for carrying freight.

flatfish *n.* (*pl.* same or **flatfishes**) any marine fish of various families having an asymmetric appearance with both eyes on one side of a flattened body.

flat foot *n.* (usu. in *pl.*) a foot with a less than normal arch.

flat-footed *adj.* **1** having flat feet. **2** *informal* clumsy, awkward (*flat-footed prose*). **3** *informal* unprepared; off guard (*was caught flat-footed*). **4** *informal* downright, positive. □ **flat-footedly** *adv.* **flat-footedness** *n.*

flat-head ● *n.* any marine fish of the family Platycephalidae, having a flattened body with both eyes on the top side. ● *adj.* (of a screw etc.) having a flat head.

flatland *n.* (often in *pl.*) a region of flat land. □ **flatlander** *n.*

flat race *n.* a horse race over level ground, as opposed to a steeplechase etc. □ **flat racing** *n.*

flatten *v.* **1** *tr. & intr.* make or become flat. **2** *tr. informal* knock down. □ **flatten out** bring an aircraft parallel to the ground.

flatter *v.* **1** *tr.* compliment unduly; overpraise, esp. for gain or advantage. **2** *tr.* (usu. *refl.*; usu. foll. by *that* + clause) please, congratulate, or delude (oneself etc.) (*I flatter myself that I can sing*). **3** *tr.* **a** (of a colour, a style, etc.) make (a person) appear to the best advantage (*that blouse flatters you*). **b** (esp. of a portrait, a painter, etc.) represent too favourably. **4** *tr.* gratify the vanity of; make (a person) feel honoured. **5** *tr.* inspire (a person) with hope, esp. unduly (*was flattered into thinking himself invulnerable*). **6** *intr.* use flattery. □ **flatterer** *n.* **flattering** *adj.* **flatteringly** *adv.*

flattery *n.* (*pl.* **-ies**) **1** exaggerated or insincere praise. **2** the act or an instance of flattering.

flatulent /ˈflætjʊlənt/ *adj.* **1 a** causing formation of gas in the alimentary canal. **b** caused by or suffering from this. **2** (of speech etc.) inflated, pretentious. □ **flatulence** *n.* **flatulently** *adv.*

flatware *n.* N Amer. domestic cutlery.

flatwater *n.* N Amer. slowly moving water, as in a river etc. (also *attrib.*: *flatwater canoeing*).

flatworm *n.* any worm of the phylum Platyhelminthes, having a flattened body and no body cavity or blood vessels, including tapeworms, flukes, etc.

flaunt *v.tr. & intr.* **1** (often *refl.*) display ostentatiously (oneself or one's finery); show off; parade (*flaunted his gold cufflinks*). ¶*Flaunt* should not be confused with *flout*. **2** wave or cause to wave proudly (*flaunted the banner*). ● *n.* an act or instance of flaunting.

flautist /ˈflɔːtɪst, ˈflaʊ-/ *n.* a flute player. ¶Although some believe that this is the only correct form of the noun, *flutist* is more common in N American English and is perfectly acceptable.

flavour (also **flavor**) ● *n.* **1 a** a distinctive or characteristic taste. **2** an indefinable characteristic quality (*a romantic flavour*). **3** (usu. foll. by *of*) a slight admixture of a quality. **4** esp. N Amer. = FLAVOURING. ● *v.tr.* give flavour to; season. □ **flavour of the month** (or **week**) a temporary trend or fashion. □ **flavourful** *adj.* **flavourless** *adj.*

flavouring *n.* (also **flavoring**) a substance used to flavour food or drink.

flaw ● *n.* **1** an imperfection; a weakness (*pride was his flaw*). **2** a crack or chip in china, weaving defect in cloth etc. **3** *Law* an invalidating defect in a legal matter. ● *v.tr. & intr.* crack; damage; spoil. □ **flawed** *adj.* **flawless** *adj.* **flawlessly** *adv.* **flawlessness** *n.*

flax *n.* **1 a** any of various plants of the genus *Linum*, esp. the blue-flowered *L. usitatissimum*, cultivated for its textile fibre and its seeds (see LINSEED). **b** a plant resembling this. **2** dressed or undressed flax fibres.

flaxen *adj.* **1** of flax. **2** (of hair) pale yellow.

flaxseed *n.* the seed of flax; linseed.

flay *v.tr.* **1** strip the skin or hide off, esp. by beating. **2** criticize severely. **3** peel off (skin, bark, peel, etc.). **4** strip (a person) of wealth by extortion or exaction.

flea *n.* a small wingless jumping insect of the order Siphonaptera, feeding on human and other blood. □ **a flea in one's ear** a sharp reproof.

fleabane *n.* any of various composite plants of the genus *Inula* or *Erigeron*, supposed to drive away fleas.

flea-bitten *adj.* **1** bitten by or infested with fleas. **2** shabby.

flea collar *n.* an insecticidal collar for pets.

flea market *n.* a usu. outdoor market with individual vendors selling second-hand goods, antiques, discontinued merchandise, produce, etc.

fleck ● *n.* **1** a small patch of colour or light. **2** a small particle or speck, esp. of dust. ● *v.tr.* variegate.

fledge *v.* **1** *intr.* (of a bird) grow feathers. **2** *tr.* bring up (a young bird) until it can fly. **3** *tr.* deck or provide with feathers or down. **4** *tr.* provide (an arrow) with feathers.

fledged *adj.* **1** able to fly. **2** independent; mature.

fledgling ● *n.* **1** a young bird. **2** an inexperienced person. ● *adj.* young or new; inexperienced.

flee *v.* (*past* and *past part.* **fled**) **1** *intr.* (often foll. by *from*, *before*) run or hurry away; escape (esp. from danger, threat, etc.). **2** *tr.* run away from; leave abruptly; shun (*fled the room*; *fled her advances*). **3** *intr.* vanish; pass away (*all hope had fled*).

fleece ● *n.* **1 a** the woolly covering of a sheep or similar animal. **b** the amount of wool sheared from a sheep at one time. **2** a soft warm fabric with a pile, used in nightwear and athletic wear and for lining coats etc. **3** something resembling a fleece. ● *v.tr.* **1** (often foll. by *of*) strip (a person) of money, valuables, etc.; swindle. **2** remove the fleece from (a sheep etc.); shear. □ **fleeced** *adj.* (also in *comb.*).

fleecy *adj.* (**-ier**, **-iest**) of or like a fleece.

fleet¹ *n.* **1 a** a number of warships under one commander-in-chief. **b** (prec. by *the*) all the warships and merchant ships of a nation. **2** a number of ships, aircraft, buses, trucks, taxis, etc. operating together or owned by one proprietor.

fleet² *adj. literary* swift; nimble. □ **fleetness** *n.*

fleeting *adj.* transitory; brief. □ **fleetingly** *adv.*

Fleming /ˈflemɪŋ/ *n.* **1** a native of medieval Flanders, a region in the SW part of the Low Countries. **2** a member of a Flemish-speaking people inhabiting N and W Belgium (see also WALLOON).

Flemish /ˈflemɪʃ/ ● *adj.* of or relating to Flanders. ● *n.* **1** the West Germanic language of Flanders, comprising a group of Dutch dialects, now one of the two official languages of Belgium. **2** (**the Flemish**) (*pl.*) Flemings.

flense /flens/ *v.tr.* **1** remove the blubber or skin from (a whale or seal). **2** strip off (skin). □ **flenser** *n.*

flesh *n.* **1 a** the soft, esp. muscular, substance between the skin and bones of an animal or a human. **b** plumpness; fat (*has put on flesh*). **2** the body as opposed to the mind or the soul, esp. considered as sinful. **3** the pulpy substance of a fruit or a plant. **4 a** the visible surface of the human body with reference to its colour or appearance. **b** = FLESH COLOUR. □ **flesh out** make or become substantial. **in the flesh** in bodily form, in person. **make a person's flesh creep** frighten or horrify a person, esp. with tales of the supernatural etc. **sins of the flesh** unchastity. **the way of all flesh** experience common to all humankind. □ **fleshless** *adj.*

flesh and blood ● *n.* **1** the body or its substance. **2** humankind. **3** human nature, esp. as being fallible. ● *adj.* actually living, not imaginary or supernatural. □ **one's own flesh and blood** near relatives.

flesh colour *n.* a light brownish pink. □ **flesh-coloured** *adj.*

flesh-eating disease *n.* a disease in which bodily tissue is rapidly destroyed by streptococcal bacteria.

fleshed adj. (usu. in comb.) having flesh of a usu. specified kind (an orange-fleshed melon).

fleshly adj. (-ier, -iest) 1 (of desire etc.) bodily; lascivious; sensual. 2 mortal, not divine. 3 worldly.

flesh side n. the side of a hide that adjoined the flesh.

fleshy adj. (-ier, -iest) 1 plump, fat. 2 (of plant or fruit tissue) pulpy. 3 like flesh.

fleur-de-lys /ˌflɜːdəˈliː, ˌflɜːdəˈliːs/ n. (also **fleur-de-lis**) (pl. **fleurs-** pronunc. same) 1 a figure of a lily composed of three petals bound together near their bases, used as a symbol of Quebec and in the former royal arms of France. 2 the flag of the province of Quebec. 3 the iris flower.

flew past of FLY¹.

flex ● v.tr. & intr. 1 bend (a joint, limb, etc.) or be bent. 2 move (a muscle) or (of a muscle) be moved to bend a joint. ● n. 1 the act or an instance of flexing. 2 flexibility; pliability (has a great deal of flex). □ **flex one's muscle(s)** assert one's strength or power.

flexible adj. 1 able to bend without breaking; pliable; pliant. 2 willing or disposed to yield to influence or persuasion or to adapt to circumstances; not rigid. 3 adaptable; versatile; variable (flexible hours). 4 (of a person) able to bend, twist, and contort the limbs and torso easily and to a greater degree than average. □ **flexibility** n. **flexibly** adv.

flexor n. (in full **flexor muscle**) a muscle that bends part of the body (compare EXTENSOR).

flex-time n. 1 a system of working a set number of hours with the starting and finishing times chosen within agreed limits by the employee. 2 the hours worked in this way.

flick ● n. 1 a a light, sharp, quickly retracted blow with a whip etc. b the sudden release of a bent finger or thumb, esp. to propel a small object. 2 a sudden movement or jerk. 3 a quick turn of the wrist in playing games, esp. in throwing or striking a ball. 4 a slight, sharp sound. 5 informal a cinema film. ● v. 1 tr. strike, move, or remove with a rapid action of the fingers (flicked away the dust). 2 tr. give a flick with (a whip, towel, etc.). 3 tr. activate (a light, electrical appliance etc.) by flicking a switch (flicked on the lights). 4 intr. & tr. move rapidly, esp. back and forth. □ **flick through** 1 turn over (cards, pages, etc.). 2 a turn over the pages etc. of, by a rapid movement of the fingers. b look cursorily through (a book etc.).

flicker¹ ● v.intr. 1 (of light) shine unsteadily or fitfully. 2 (of a flame) burn unsteadily. 3 a (of an eyelid, a video image, etc.) quiver; vibrate. b (of the wind) blow lightly and unsteadily. 4 (of hope etc.) increase and decrease unsteadily and intermittently. ● n. 1 a flickering movement or light. 2 a brief period of hope, recognition, etc. □ **flicker out** die away after a final flicker. □ **flickery** adj.

flicker² n. any woodpecker of the genus Colaptes, native to N America.

flier var. of FLYER.

flight¹ n. 1 a the act or manner of flying through the air. b the swift movement or passage of a projectile etc. through the air. 2 a a journey made through the air or in space. b a scheduled journey made by an airline. c a unit of two or more military aircraft. 3 a a flock or large body of birds, insects, etc., esp. when migrating. b a migration. 4 (usu. foll. by of) a series, esp. of stairs between floors, or of hurdles across a race track. 5 an extravagant soaring, a mental or verbal excursion or sally (of wit etc.) (a flight of fancy). 6 the trajectory and pace of a ball in games. 7 the distance that a bird, aircraft, or missile can fly. □ **in**

the first (or **top**) **flight** taking a leading place. **take** (or **wing**) **one's flight** fly.

flight² n. 1 a the act or manner of fleeing. b a hasty retreat. 2 the selling of currency, investments, etc. in anticipation of a fall in value (capital flight). □ **put to flight** cause to flee. **take** (or **take to**) **flight** flee.

flight attendant n. an airline employee who serves meals etc. during a flight.

flight crew n. a team of people who ensure the effective operation and safety of an aircraft flight.

flight deck n. 1 the deck of an aircraft carrier used for takeoff and landing. 2 the part of an aircraft where the pilot, navigator, etc. perform their duties.

flight feather n. any of the large feathers in a bird's wing, supporting it in flight.

flightless adj. (of a bird etc.) naturally unable to fly.

flight path n. the planned course of an aircraft or spacecraft.

flight plan n. Aviation the pre-arranged plan for a particular flight, specifying the route etc.

flight recorder n. a device in an aircraft to record technical details during a flight, that may be used in the event of an accident to discover its cause.

flighty adj. (-ier, -iest) 1 frivolous, fickle, changeable. 2 crazy. □ **flightily** adv. **flightiness** n.

flim-flam n. 1 a trifle; nonsense; idle talk. 2 a deception or swindle. □ **flim-flammer** n.

flimsy adj. (-ier, -iest) 1 lightly or carelessly assembled; easily damaged (a flimsy structure). 2 (of an excuse etc.) unconvincing (a flimsy pretext). 3 (of clothing) thin (a flimsy blouse). □ **flimsily** adv.

flinch ● v.intr. 1 draw back in pain or expectation of a blow; wince. 2 (often foll. by from) give way; shrink, turn aside (flinched from your duty). ● n. an act or instance of flinching. □ **flinchingly** adv.

fling ● v. (past and past part. **flung**) 1 tr. throw or hurl (an object) forcefully. 2 refl. a (usu. foll. by into) rush headlong (into a person's arms etc.). b (usu. foll. by into) embark wholeheartedly (on an enterprise). c (usu. foll. by on) throw (oneself) on a person's mercy etc. 3 tr. utter (words) forcefully. 4 tr. (usu. foll. by out) suddenly spread (the arms). 5 tr. (foll. by on, off) put on or take off (clothes) carelessly or rapidly. 6 intr. go angrily or violently; rush (flung out of the room). 7 tr. put or send suddenly or violently (was flung into jail). 8 tr. (foll. by away) discard or put aside thoughtlessly or rashly. ● n. 1 an act or instance of flinging; a throw; a plunge. 2 a period of indulgence or wild behaviour. 3 any of various energetic, whirling, Scottish dances, esp. the Highland fling. 4 an attempt or trial (have a fling at writing a novel).

flint n. 1 a a hard grey stone of nearly pure silica occurring naturally as nodules or bands in chalk. b a piece of this esp. as flaked or ground to form a primitive tool or weapon. 2 a piece of hard alloy of rare-earth metals used to give an igniting spark in a lighter etc. 3 a piece of flint used with steel to produce fire. 4 anything hard and unyielding. □ **flinty** adj. (-ier, -iest). **flintily** adv. **flintiness** n.

flip ● v. (**flipped, flipping**) 1 a tr. flick or toss (a coin etc.) with a quick movement so that it spins in the air. b intr. decide or settle a question, tie, etc. by flipping a coin. c intr. (often foll. by for) settle a question with (a person) in this way. 2 a tr. turn (a small object) over. b intr. (of an object) turn over. c intr. perform a somersault. 3 tr. cause (something) to move with a flick of the fingers. 4 a tr. turn (a page in a book) with a flick of the fingers. b intr. move through a book etc. by flipping. c intr. (of pages) flip over (pages flipping in the breeze). d tr. open (a book, box, etc.) with a brisk movement of the fingers. **5** *N Amer.* **a** *tr.* change or switch (the channel on a television etc.), esp. by using a remote control. **b** *intr.* (often foll. by *through, past,* etc.) move from one channel to another. **6** *tr.* **a** move (a switch etc.) with a flick of the fingers. **b** (usu. foll. by *on, off*) turn (a light, an appliance, etc.) on or off by flipping a switch (*flip on the TV*). **7** *tr. N Amer.* resell (real estate, stocks, etc.), esp. to make a large profit. **8** *intr. slang* **a** become suddenly excited or enthusiastic. **b** = FLIP OUT. **9** *intr.* move about with sudden jerks. **10** *intr.* **a** make a fillip or flicking noise with the fingers. **b** (foll. by *at*) strike smartly at. ● *n.* **1** an act of flipping over. **2 a** a smart light blow; a flick. **b** the action or an instance of activating a switch etc. with a flip. **3** a somersault. **4** *Figure Skating* a jump in which the skater takes off from the back inside edge of one skate, using the toe of the second foot to provide momentum, goes through one or more counter-clockwise rotations, and lands on the second foot. **5** *N Amer.* the act or an instance of flipping real estate, stocks, etc. **6** = FLIP SIDE. **7** (*attrib.*) *Hockey* designating a type of pass or shot in which the puck is propelled a few inches above the surface of the ice so as to be above the blade of an opponent's stick (*flip shot*). ● *adj. informal* glib; flippant. □ **flip one's lid** (*N Amer.* also **wig**) *slang* = FLIP OUT. **flip out** *N Amer.* **1** lose self-control; become enraged. **2** become insane.

flip-flop ● *n.* **1** esp. *N Amer.* an abrupt reversal of policy. **2** a usu. rubber sandal with a thong between the big and second toe. **3** esp. *N Amer.* a backward somersault. **4** a repeated flapping sound. ● *v.intr.* (**-flopped**, **-flopping**) make a flip-flop. ● *adv.* in a flapping manner.

flippant *adj.* treating serious things lightly; disrespectful. □ **flippancy** *n.* **flippantly** *adv.*

flipper *n.* **1** a broadened limb of a seal, penguin, etc., used in swimming. **2** a flat rubber etc. attachment worn on the foot for underwater swimming. **3** a person or thing that flips. **4** *N Amer.* = SPATULA 1c. **5** a remote control for a television etc.

flip side *n. informal* **1** = B-SIDE. **2** the reverse or opposite of a person or thing.

flirt ● *v.* **1** *intr.* (usu. foll. by *with*) show sexual interest in (a person) without any serious intent. **2** *intr.* (usu. foll. by *with*) **a** superficially interest oneself (with an idea etc.). **b** come close to; have a brush with (danger etc.) (*flirting with disaster*). ● *n.* **1** a person who indulges in flirting. **2** a quick movement; a sudden jerk. □ **flirtation** *n.* **flirtatious** *adj.* **flirtatiously** *adv.* **flirtatiousness** *n.* **flirty** *adj.* (**-ier, -iest**).

flit ● *v.intr.* (**flitted, flitting**) **1** move lightly, softly, or rapidly. **2** fly lightly; make short flights (*flitted from branch to branch*). ● *n.* an act of flitting. □ **flitter** *n.*

flitter *v.intr.* flit about; flutter.

float ● *v.* **1** *intr. & tr.* **a** rest or move or cause (a buoyant object) to rest or move on the surface of a liquid without sinking. **b** get afloat or set (a stranded ship) afloat. **2** *intr.* move with a liquid or current of air; drift (*the clouds floated high up*). **3** *intr. informal* a move in a leisurely or casual way. **b** (often foll. by *before*) hover before the eye or mind (*the prospect of lunch floated before them*). **4** *intr.* (often foll. by *in*) move or be suspended freely in a liquid or a gas. **5** *intr.* be free from attachment, commitment, etc. **6** *tr.* **a** bring (a company, scheme, etc.) into being; launch. **b** offer (stock, shares, etc.) on the stock market. **7** *Business* **a** *intr.* (of currency) be allowed to have a fluctuating exchange rate. **b** *tr.* cause (currency) to float. **c** *tr. & intr.* (of an interest rate) fluctuate or be allowed to fluctuate according to market conditions. **8** *tr.* arrange (a loan);

arrange a loan for (someone). **9** *tr.* (of water etc.) support; bear along (a buoyant object). **10** *intr. & tr.* put forward (an idea, proposal, etc.); circulate. **11** *tr.* waft (a buoyant object) through the air. ● *n.* **1** a thing that floats, esp.: **a** a raft. **b** a buoyant piece of cork or plastic attached to a fishing line as an indicator of a fish biting. **c** a buoyant object supporting the edge of a fishing net. **d** the hollow or inflated part or organ supporting a fish etc. in the water; an air bladder. **e** a hollow structure fixed underneath an aircraft enabling it to float on water. **f** a floating device on the surface of water, fuel, etc., controlling the flow. **g** *N Amer.* a floating platform attached to a bank, dock, etc., and used as a landing for boats or float planes. **2** a vehicle carrying a display in a parade etc. **3 a** *Cdn & Brit.* a sum of money used to provide change at the beginning of a period of selling in a store etc. **b** a small sum of money for minor expenditure; petty cash. **4** a soft drink with a scoop of ice cream floating in it. **5** a tool used for smoothing plaster etc.

floatation *var. of* FLOTATION.

floatbase *n. Cdn* a place on a river, lake, etc. where float planes dock.

float camp *n. Cdn* (*BC*) a log raft supporting the living quarters etc. of a coastal logging crew.

floater *n.* **1** a person or thing that floats. **2** a voter who is undecided or may change allegiance from one party to another. **3** a person who frequently changes occupation etc.

floathouse *n. N Amer.* (*BC, US Northwest, & Alaska*) a house constructed on a log raft, usu. built so that it can be towed from one mooring to another.

floating *adj.* **1 a** supported on water. **b** in or on a ship or boat (*a floating disco*). **2 a** not settled in a definite place. **b** fluctuating; variable (*floating rates*). **3** (of an internal organ) not in its proper position. □ **floatingly** *adv.*

floating point *n. Computing* a decimal etc. point that does not occupy a fixed position in the numbers processed.

floating rib *n.* any of the lower ribs, which are not attached to the breastbone.

float plane *n.* an airplane equipped with floats instead of wheels, so that it can land on water.

flock¹ ● *n.* **1 a** a number of animals of one kind, esp. birds, feeding or travelling together. **b** a number of domestic animals, esp. sheep, goats, or geese, kept together. **2** a large crowd of people. **3 a** a Christian congregation or body of believers, esp. in relation to one priest or minister. **b** a family of children, a number of pupils, etc. ● *v.intr.* **1** congregate; mass. **2** (usu. foll. by *to*) move in great numbers; troop.

flock² *n.* **1** a lock or tuft of wool, cotton, etc. **2 a** (also in *pl.*) material for quilting and stuffing made of wool refuse or torn-up cloth. **b** powdered wool or cloth, applied to wallpaper, fabrics etc. to form a raised velvetlike pattern. □ **flocked** *adj.* **flocking** *n.*

floe *n.* a sheet of floating ice.

floe edge *n. N Amer.* the limit of landfast ice.

flog *v.* (**flogged, flogging**) **1** *tr.* **a** beat with a whip, stick, etc. (as a punishment or to urge on). **b** make work through violent effort (*flogged the engine*). **2** *tr. slang* **a** sell, esp. by aggressive effort. **b** publicize; promote. □ **flog to death** *informal* talk about or promote at tedious length. □ **flogger** *n.* **flogging** *n.*

flood ● *n.* **1 a** an overflowing or influx of water beyond its normal confines, esp. over land. **b** the water that overflows. **2 a** an outpouring of water; a torrent (*a flood of rain*). **b** something resembling a torrent (*a flood of memories*). **3** the inflow of the tide (also *attrib.*: *flood tide*) (*opp.* EBB *n.* 1). **4** *informal* a floodlight. **5** (**the Flood**) any universal flood as described by various ancient religious traditions, esp. the one recorded in the Bible as occurring in the time of Noah. ● *v.* **1** *tr.* **a** cover with or overflow in a flood (*flooded the basement*). **b** overflow as if with a flood (*a market flooded with imports*). **2** *tr.* irrigate (*flooded the fields*). **3** *tr.* deluge (a burning house, a mine, etc.) with water. **4** *intr.* arrive in great quantities (*complaints flooded in*). **5** *intr.* become inundated (*the bathroom flooded*). **6** *tr.* overfill (a carburetor) with fuel. **7** *tr.* (of rain etc.) fill (a river) to overflowing. **8** *tr.* N Amer. build up (the surface of a skating rink etc.) by covering it with water and allowing it to freeze. □ **flooding** *n.*

flood control *n.* the technique or an act of preventing or controlling floods by means of dams, artificial channels, dikes, etc.

floodgate *n.* **1** a gate opened or closed to admit or exclude water, esp. the lower gate of a lock. **2** (usu. in *pl.*) a restraint, or check holding back tears, rain, etc.

floodlight ● *n.* **1** a large powerful light (usu. one of several) to illuminate a building, playing field, stage, etc. **2** the illumination so provided. ● *v.tr.* (*past* and *past part.* **-lit**) illuminate with floodlights.

flood plain *n.* a relatively flat plain along the bank of a river etc., that is naturally subject to flooding.

flood tide *n.* **1** the inflow or rising of the tide. **2** a sudden influx of something.

flood water *n.* the water left by flooding.

floodway *n.* N Amer. a channel for diverting flood waters away from a city etc.

floor ● *n.* **1** **a** the lower surface of a room. **b** the boards etc. of which it is made. **2 a** the bottom of the sea, a lake, a cave, a cavity, etc. **b** any level area. **3** all the rooms etc. on the same level of a building; a storey (*the sixth floor*). **4 a** (in a legislative assembly) the part of the house in which members sit and from which they speak. **b** the right to speak next in debate (*gave her the floor*). **5** *Stock Exch.* the large central hall where trading takes place. **6** the minimum of prices, wages, etc. ● *v.tr.* **1** furnish with a floor. **2** bring to the ground; knock (a person) down. **3** *informal* confound, baffle (*was floored by the puzzle*). **4** *informal* get the better of; overcome. **5** N Amer. push (the accelerator pedal of a motor vehicle) all the way to floor, to gain maximum power or speed. □ **from the floor** (of a speech etc.) given by a member of the audience, not by those on the platform etc. **take the floor 1** begin to dance on a dance floor etc. **2** speak in a debate.

floorboard *n.* **1** (usu. in *pl.*) a long wooden board used for flooring. **2** N Amer. the floor of a car etc.

floor covering *n.* carpeting, tiles, linoleum, etc. used for covering floors.

floor hockey *n.* N Amer. a form of hockey played on an indoor floor, usu. using plastic sticks and a plastic puck or ball.

flooring *n.* the materials with which a floor is made or covered.

floor-length *adj.* reaching to the floor.

floor plan *n.* **1** a diagram of the rooms etc. on one storey of a building. **2** the arrangement of rooms in a house, apartment, etc.

floozie *n.* (also **floozy**) (*pl.* **-ies**) *informal* a disreputable or promiscuous girl or woman.

flop ● *v.intr.* (**flopped**, **flopping**) **1** sway about heavily or loosely (*hair flopped over her face*). **2** move in an ungainly way. **3** sit, kneel, lie, or fall awkwardly or suddenly (*flopped down on to the bench*). **4** *slang* (esp. of a play, film, book, etc.) fail. **5** *slang* sleep. **6** make a dull sound of a soft body landing, or of a flat thing

slapping water. ● *n.* **1 a** a flopping movement. **b** the sound made by it. **2** *informal* a failure.

-flop *comb. form* Computing floating-point operations per second (*megaflop*).

flophouse *n.* esp. N Amer. informal a cheap boarding house, esp. one used by vagrants, transients, etc.

floppy ● *adj.* (**-ier**, **-iest**) tending to flop; not firm or rigid. ● *n.* (*pl.* **-ies**) (in full **floppy disk**) Computing a flexible removable magnetic disk for the storage of data. □ **floppily** *adv.* **floppiness** *n.*

flora *n.* **1** the plants of a particular region, geological period, or environment. **2** a catalogue of the plants of a defined area, with descriptions of them, comments on the more unusual species, etc. **3** (in full **intestinal flora**) symbiotic bacteria normally present in the gut.

floral ● *adj.* **1** of, made of, or pertaining to flowers (*floral arrangement*). **2** decorated with or depicting flowers (*floral print*). **3** of flora or floras. ● *n.* **1** a print, pattern, fabric, etc. with a floral design. **2** a perfume scent of or like that of flowers. □ **florally** *adv.*

Florentine /ˈflɒrənˌtiːn, -tain, ˈflɔːr-/ ● *adj.* **1 a** of or relating to Florence in Italy. **b** denoting the art, styles, etc. developed in Renaissance Florence. **2** (**florentine** /-ˌtiːn/) (of a dish) served on a bed of spinach. ● *n.* **1** a native or inhabitant of Florence. **2** /-ˌtiːn/ a thin cookie containing nuts and candied fruit and coated on one side with chocolate.

floret /ˈflɒrɪt/ *n.* **1** each of the small flowers making up a composite flower head. **2** /flɒrˈet/ any of the segments into which a head of broccoli etc. may be divided. **3** a tiny blossom or flowering plant.

florid /ˈflɒrɪd, ˈfloʊ-/ *adj.* **1** (of a person's complexion) ruddy or flushed. **2** (of a book, work of art, etc.) elaborately ornate, ostentatious, or showy. □ **floridly** *adv.*

Florida room *n.* N Amer. a sunroom, usu. only partly insulated, enclosed in glass on three sides.

florist *n.* **1** a person who retails flowers and ornamental plants. **2** a person who grows flowers.

floss ● *n.* **1 a** the rough silk enveloping a silkworm's cocoon. **b** the silk down in corn and certain other plants. **2** untwisted silk or fine cotton thread used in embroidery. **3** = DENTAL FLOSS. ● *v.tr. & intr.* clean between (the teeth) with dental floss. □ **flossing** *n.*

flotation *n.* **1** the process of launching or financing a commercial enterprise, esp. by selling shares. **2** capacity to float. **3 a** the action or process of floating in a liquid etc. **b** the condition of keeping afloat.

flotilla /floʊˈtɪlə/ *n.* **1** a fleet of boats or small ships. **2** a small fleet of warships.

flotsam *n.* **1** wreckage of a ship or its cargo found floating on the water. **2** (in full **flotsam and jetsam**) **a** odds and ends, various unimportant items. **b** people who have been rejected by society.

flounce[1] ● *v.intr.* go or move in an agitated or exaggerated manner, usu. in impatience or anger. ● *n.* a sudden jerk, or movement of the body or limbs, usu. as an expression of annoyance, impatience, or disdain.

flounce[2] ● *n.* a frill or wide ornamental strip of material gathered and sewn to a skirt, dress, etc., so that its lower edge hangs full and free. ● *v.tr.* adorn or trim with a flounce or flounces. □ **flounced** *adj.* **flouncy** *adj.*

flounder[1] ● *v.intr.* **1** struggle or show confusion in thoughts, words, or actions. **2** manage something badly or with difficulty. **3** move or struggle clumsily or with difficulty through mud, snow, etc. ● *n.* an act or instance of floundering.

flounder² *n.* (*pl.* same or **-s**) any flatfish of the family Pleuronectidae or Bothidae, esp. those used for food.

flour ● *n.* **1** a fine powder obtained by grinding grain, esp. wheat, used for making bread, cakes, etc. **2** a fine powder made from other foodstuffs, e.g. potatoes, nuts, etc. ● *v.tr.* sprinkle or cover with flour. □ **floured** *adj.* **floury** *adj.* (**-ier, -iest**).

flourish /ˈflɜːrɪʃ, ˈflʌrɪʃ/ ● *v.* **1** *intr.* **a** (of a plant, tree, etc.) grow vigorously, thrive. **b** prosper, be successful. **c** be in one's prime or at the height of one's fame or excellence. **d** be in good health. **2** *intr.* spend one's life or be active during a specified period (*flourished in the Middle Ages*). **3** *tr.* show ostentatiously (*flourished his cheque book*). **4** *tr.* wave (a weapon, one's limbs, etc.) vigorously. ● *n.* **1** an ostentatious gesture with a weapon, a hand, etc. **2** an ornamental curving decoration of handwriting. **3** a florid verbal expression or rhetorical embellishment. **4** *Music* **a** a fanfare played by brass instruments. **b** an ornate musical passage. **c** an extemporized addition played esp. at the beginning or end of a composition. □ **flourishing** *adj.*

flout ● *v.tr.* express contempt or disrespect for (the law, rules, etc.) by openly refusing to heed or obey (*flouted convention by shaving her head*). ¶*Flout* should not be confused with *flaunt*. ● *n.* a mocking speech or act.

flow ● *v.intr.* **1** glide along as a stream (*the Red River flows through Winnipeg*). **2 a** (of a liquid, esp. water) spring or well up, gush out. **b** (of blood, tears, etc.) be spilled. **3** (of blood, money, electric current, etc.) circulate. **4** (of people or things) move freely and continuously (*traffic flowed past*). **5** (of talk, literary style, etc.) proceed easily and smoothly. **6** (of a garment, hair, etc.) hang easily or gracefully, or lie in undulating folds. **7** (often foll. by *from*) result from or be caused by (*his failure flows from his shyness*). **8** (esp. of the tide) come in, rise and advance. **9** (of wine etc.) be poured out copiously or unstintingly. ● *n.* **1 a** a flowing movement in a stream. **b** the quantity that flows; the rate of flowing (*a sluggish flow*). **c** a flowing liquid (*couldn't stop the flow*). **d** the act or fact of flowing. **2** any continuous movement, outpouring, etc. that resembles the flow of a river and denotes a copious supply (*a continuous flow of complaints*). **3** the incoming or rise of a tide or a tidal river. □ **go with the flow** *informal* be relaxed and not resist the tide of events.

flow chart *n.* (also **flow diagram**) **1** a diagram showing the movement, development, or action of things or persons through the different stages or processes of a series. **2** a graphic representation of a computer program in relation to its sequence of functions (as distinct from the data it processes).

flower ● *n.* **1** the part of a plant from which the fruit or seed is developed, esp. the reproductive organ containing one or more pistils or stamens or both, and usu. a corolla and calyx. **2** a blossom and usu. its stem considered independently of the growing plant, esp. as used in groups for decoration or as a mark of honour or respect. **3** a flowering plant, esp. one cultivated for its flowers. **4 a** the prime or most active or vigorous period in a person's life. **b** the finest embodiment of a quality etc. **c** the pick or choicest person, thing, etc. of a number of persons, things, etc. **5** (of a plant) the state of being in bloom (*the milkweed was in flower*). ● *v.* **1** *intr.* (of a plant) produce flowers; bloom or blossom. **2** *intr.* **a** develop into. **b** reach a peak, be in or attain one's fullest perfection, highest stage of development, etc. **3** *tr.* cause or allow (a plant) to flower. □ **flowerless** *adj.*

flower arrangement *n.* **1** the art of arranging flowers in vases etc. for artistic effect. **2** a bouquet of flowers so arranged. □ **flower arranging** *n.*

flowerbearer *n. Cdn* a person, often a child, who follows the pallbearers in a funeral procession, carrying wreaths of flowers.

flower bed *n.* a plot of soil where flowers are grown.

flower box *n.* a rectangular container filled with soil in which flowers, herbs, etc. are grown, usu. on a balcony or windowsill.

flower child *n.* a hippie, esp. in the late 1960s, who advocated a simple idealistic lifestyle based on love and peace.

flowered *adj.* **1** (usu. in *comb.*) having flowers of a specified quality. **2** decorated with flowers or a flower pattern.

flower girl *n.* a child bridesmaid.

flowering *adj.* **1** (of a plant) capable of producing flowers, esp. having showy flowers in contrast to a similar plant with the flowers inconspicuous or absent (*flowering dogwood*). **2** (of a plant) in bloom.

flowerpot *n.* **1** a container made of clay or plastic for growing plants in. **2** *Cdn* a tall column or island of rock formed by water erosion, often with vegetation on the top, found esp. in the Bay of Fundy and Georgian Bay.

flower power *n.* the ideas of the flower children regarded as an instrument for changing the world.

flowery *adj.* **1** decorated with flowers or floral designs. **2** (of literary style, manner of speech, etc.) high-flown, ornate. **3** full of flowers (*a flowery meadow*). **4** of, like, or reminiscent of flowers (*a flowery scent*). □ **floweriness** *n.*

flowing *adj.* **1 a** (of language, style, etc.) coming easily and smoothly. **b** (of manner or demeanour) easy, graceful, smooth. **2** (of a line, curve, etc.) smoothly continuous, not rigid or abrupt. **3** (of hair, a garment, a sail, etc.) unconfined, streaming, hanging loosely, easily, and gracefully. **4 a** gliding or running along. **b** brimming, abundant, or copious. □ **flowingly** *adv.*

flown *past part. of* FLY¹.

fl. oz. *abbr.* fluid ounce.

FLQ *abbr.* (in Canada) FRONT DE LIBÉRATION DU QUÉBEC.

FLQ crisis *n.* = OCTOBER CRISIS.

flu *n.* influenza. □ **flu-like** *adj.*

flub *N Amer. informal* ● *v.tr. & intr.* (**flubbed, flubbing**) botch, bungle, or perform badly. ● *n.* a slip-up or something badly or clumsily done.

fluctuate *v.intr.* **1** (of a price, rate, etc.) rise and fall or change irregularly. **2** (of an attitude or state) vacillate or change continually. □ **fluctuation** *n.*

flue *n.* **1** a duct for the passage of smoke, waste gases, etc. in a chimney. **2 a** a channel for conveying heat, esp. a hot-air passage in a wall. **b** a tube for heating water in some kinds of boiler.

flue gas *n.* (also *attrib.*) any mixture of gases from flues, esp. of chemical or smelting factories.

fluency *n.* (*pl.* **-ies**) **1** a ready command of words or of a specified foreign language. **2** a smooth, easy flow of words, wit, etc., esp. in speech or writing.

fluent *adj.* **1 a** (of speech or literary style) flowing naturally and readily. **b** able to speak a language easily and without hesitation (*is fluent in German*). **c** articulate, able to speak quickly and easily. **2** (of movement, etc.) easy and graceful. □ **fluently** *adv.*

fluff ● *n.* **1** soft, light, feathery material coming off blankets etc. **2** a piece of downy material, esp. a soft mass of fur or feathers. **3** *informal* a mistake or error made in speaking, delivering theatrical lines, playing a game, etc. **4** a trifle; something unimportant, insubstantial, or insignificant. **5** *slang* offensive (esp. in phr. **bit** or **piece of fluff**) a woman regarded as an object of sexual desire. ● *v.tr. & intr.* **1** (often foll. by *up*) make or become fluffy; shake into or become a soft, fluffy mass. **2** *informal* blunder or make a mistake, esp. in a game or performance (*fluffed his opening line*).

fluffy *adj.* (**-ier, -iest**) **1** of or like fluff. **2** covered in fluff; downy. **3** light and airy (*fluffy mashed potatoes*). **4** lacking depth, seriousness, or substance. □ **fluffily** *adv.* **fluffiness** *n.*

flugelhorn /ˈfluːɡəlˌhɔːn/ *n.* a valved brass wind instrument with a cup-shaped mouthpiece and a conical bore, like a cornet but with a broader tone.

fluid ● *n.* **1** a substance, esp. a gas or liquid, lacking definite shape and capable of flowing and yielding to the slightest pressure. **2** a liquid constituent or secretion of a living organism. ● *adj.* **1** able to flow and alter shape freely. **2** changing readily, not settled or stable (*the situation is fluid*). **3** (of a clutch, coupling, etc.) operating by means of a liquid, esp. using a liquid to transmit power. **4** (of speech etc.) fluent. **5** (of movement) smoothly flowing. □ **fluidity** *n.* **fluidly** *adv.*

fluid mechanics *n.* the branch of mechanics that deals with the flow of fluids and the way they respond to and exert forces.

fluid ounce *n.* a unit of capacity equal to one-twentieth of an imperial pint (approx. 28.4 ml), or (in the US) equal to one-sixteenth of a pint (approx. 29.6 ml).

fluke¹ *n.* a piece of luck, an unexpected success, or an unlikely but usu. fortunate chance occurrence.

fluke² *n.* **1** any parasitic flatworm of the class Digenea or Monogenea. **2** a flatfish, esp. a flounder.

fluke³ *n.* **1** a broad triangular plate on the arm of an anchor. **2** the barbed head of a lance, harpoon, etc. **3** either of the two lobes of a whale's tail.

flume *n.* **1** an artificial channel conveying water etc. for industrial use, esp. for the transport of logs or timber. **2** a deep, narrow channel or ravine with a stream running through it. **3** a water chute or waterslide at an amusement park or swimming pool.

flummox /ˈflʌməks/ *v.tr. informal* bewilder, disconcert.

flung *past and past part. of* FLING.

flunk *v. N Amer. informal* **1** *tr.* **a** (of a student) fail (an examination, course, etc.). **b** (of a teacher) fail (a student etc.). **2** *intr.* (often foll. by *out*) fail utterly and quit or be dismissed from school etc.

flunky *n.* (also **flunkey**) (*pl.* **-ies** or **-eys**) usu. derogatory **1** a person who performs menial tasks. **2** an obsequious, fawning person. **3** a footman.

fluoresce /flɔˈres/ *v.intr.* be or become fluorescent or exhibit fluorescence.

fluorescence /flɔˈresəns/ *n.* **1** the visible or invisible radiation produced from certain substances as a result of incident radiation of a shorter wavelength as X-rays, ultraviolet light, etc. **2** the property of absorbing light of short (invisible) wavelength and emitting light of longer (visible) wavelength.

fluorescent ● *adj.* **1** (of a substance) of, having, or showing fluorescence. **2** (of colours) very bright and glowing, similar to colours produced by fluorescence. ● *n.* (in full **fluorescent light, fluorescent bulb**, etc.) a light or bulb radiating largely by fluorescence, esp. one in which phosphor on the inside surface of a tube is made to fluoresce by ultraviolet radiation from mercury vapour.

fluoridate /ˈflɔrɪˌdeɪt/ *v.tr.* add traces of fluoride to (drinking water etc.) to reduce or prevent tooth decay. □ **fluoridated** *adj.* **fluoridation** *n.*

fluoride /ˈflɔraɪd/ *n.* a binary compound of fluorine, esp. as used to prevent tooth decay.

fluorine /ˈflɔriːn/ *n.* a naturally-occurring, poisonous, pale yellow gaseous element.

fluorocarbon /ˌflɔroˈkɑːbən/ *n.* a synthetic, chemically stable compound formed by replacing one or more of the hydrogen atoms in a hydrocarbon with fluorine atoms.

fluoxetine /fluˈɒksətiːn/ *n.* an organic compound used (orally, as the hydrochloride) as an antidepressant (compare PROZAC).

flurry ● *n.* (*pl.* **-ies**) **1** a short, usu. localized shower of snow. **2** a sudden burst of intense activity. **3** a number of things happening or arriving at once (*a flurry of penalties*). ● *v.* (**-ies, -ied**) **1** *tr.* agitate or confuse by haste or noise. **2** *intr.* move in a flustered, agitated manner. □ **flurried** *adj.*

flush¹ ● *v.* **1** *intr.* **a** (of the face) redden because of a rush of blood to the skin (*he flushed with embarrassment*). **b** glow with a warm colour, light, etc. (*sky flushed pink*). **2** *tr.* **a** cleanse (a toilet, drain, etc.) by a rushing flow of water. **b** (often foll. by *away, down*) dispose of (an object) in this way. **c** (often foll. by *out*) remove by a sudden rush of water or other liquid. **3** *Computing* cleanse, dump, or erase (a buffer etc.). ● *n.* **1 a** a flow of blood to the face, neck, etc. that causes red colouring. **b** a glow of light or colour. **2 a** a sudden rush of water, esp. as caused for a specific purpose. **b** the cleansing of a toilet, drain, etc. by flushing (also *attrib.*: *flush toilet*). **3** a rush of emotion, elation, etc., esp. as produced by a victory, success, etc. (*the flush of triumph*). **4** a sudden abundance or rush (*a flush of interest*). **5** the freshness and vigour of youth or a beginning, or the best and most fully developed stage (*in the full flush of success*). □ **flushable** *adj.* **flusher** *n.* **flushing** *n.*

flush² ● *adj.* **1 a** (often foll. by *with*) completely level, even, or continuous with another surface. **b** (of a vessel's deck) continued on one level from stem to stern. **2** (usu. *predic.*) *informal* **a** having plenty of something, esp. money. **b** (of money) abundant, plentiful. **3** (of text) even or level with the margin, neither indented nor protruding. ● *v.tr.* **1** make (surfaces) level. **2** fill in (a joint) level with a surface.

flush³ *n.* a hand of cards all of one suit, esp. in poker.

flush⁴ *v.* **1** *tr.* cause (esp. a game bird) to fly up suddenly, esp. from undergrowth. **2** *intr.* (of a bird) fly up and away, esp. from undergrowth. □ **flush out** force or drive (a person) out of a hiding place etc.

flushed *adj.* (often foll. by *with*) glowing or blushing, esp. with emotion, excitement, etc.

fluster ● *v.tr.* **1** make or become nervous, confused, agitated, etc. **2** *intr.* bustle. ● *n.* a nervous or agitated state (*always in a fluster*). □ **flustered** *adj.*

flute ● *n.* **1 a** a high-pitched woodwind instrument of metal or wood, having holes along it, stopped by the fingers or keys. **b** any of various wind instruments resembling a flute. **c** a flute player. **2 a** *Archit.* an ornamental vertical groove in a column. **b** a narrow, furrow-like frill on a dress etc. **c** any similar cylindrical groove. **3** a tall narrow wineglass, used esp. for sparkling wine. ● *v.* **1** *tr.* make, shape, or carve flutes or grooves in a thing as decoration. **2** *intr.* play the flute. **3** *intr.* speak, sing, or whistle in a flutelike way. □ **fluted** *adj.* **flutelike** *adj.* **fluting** *n.*

flutist *n. N Amer.* a flute player. ¶ See FLAUTIST.

flutter ● *v.* **1** *intr.* flap the wings lightly and quickly in flying or trying to fly. **b** *tr.* flap (the wings) in this way. **2** *intr.* fall with a quivering motion (*leaves fluttered to the ground*). **3** *intr. & tr.* move or cause to move in a quick, irregular way (*the wind fluttered the flag*). **4** *intr.* hover or move about aimlessly and restlessly. **5** *intr.* (of a pulse or heartbeat) beat feebly or irregularly, esp. because of nervous excitement. **6** *intr.* tremble with excitement or agitation. ● *n.* **1 a** the act of fluttering. **b** an instance of this. **2** tremulous excitement or agitation (*was in a flutter*). **3** an abnormally rapid but regular heartbeat. **4** *Electronics* a rapid variation in the pitch or loudness of a sound, not audible as such, but heard as distortion, esp. in a recording. **5** a vibration. □ **flutterer** *n.* **fluttering** *adj. & n.* **fluttery** *adj.*

flux ● *n.* **1 a** a process of flowing or flowing out. **b** the flowing in of the tide. **2** a stream or flood, esp. of people, talk, etc. **3** continuous change. **4 a** a substance mixed with a metal etc. to promote fusion. **b** a substance used to make colour fusible in enamelling, pottery, etc. **5** *Physics* the rate of flow of any fluid across a given area. **b** the amount of fluid crossing an area in a given time. **6** *Physics* the amount of radiation or particles incident on an area in a given time. **7** *Electricity.* the total electric or magnetic field passing through a surface. ● *v.* **1** *tr. & intr.* make or become fluid. **2** *tr.* treat or heat with a fusing flux.

flux density *n.* the quantity of magnetic, electric, etc. flux passing through a unit of area.

fly¹ ● *v.* (**flies**; *past* **flew**; *past part.* **flown**) **1** *intr.* move through the air with wings. **2** (of an aircraft or its occupants) **a** *intr.* travel through the air or through space. **b** *tr.* traverse (a region or distance) by flying (*flew the Vancouver-Victoria route*). **3 a** *tr. & intr.* control or pilot the flight of (esp. an aircraft). **b** *tr.* transport in an aircraft. **4 a** *tr.* cause to fly or remain aloft (*fly a kite*). **b** *intr.* (of a flag, hair, etc.) wave or flutter. **c** *tr.* set or keep (a flag) flying. **5** *intr.* pass or rise quickly through the air or over an obstacle. **6** *intr.* **a** go, move, or travel quickly. **b** (of time) pass swiftly. **7** *intr.* **a** flee. **b** *informal* depart hastily. **8** *intr.* **a** be forced or driven off or away suddenly and quickly (*sent me flying*). **b** (of a door, window, etc.) be thrown suddenly (open, up, etc.). **9** *intr.* (foll. by *at*) **a** hasten or spring violently. **b** attack or criticize fiercely. **10** *tr.* flee from, escape in haste. **11** *intr. Baseball* (*past & past part.* **flied**) hit a fly ball. **12** *intr. N Amer. informal* meet with approval, acceptance, success, etc. (*the plan will fly*). **13** *intr.* (of snow) fall, esp. for the first time in the winter (*before the snow flies*). ● *n.* (*pl.* **-ies**) **1 a** a zippered or buttoned opening, esp. from the waist to the crotch at the front of a pair of trousers. **b** a flap on a garment, esp. trousers, to contain or cover such a fastening. **2 a** a flap of material at the entrance of a tent. **b** an extra layer of fabric placed on top of a tent to repel moisture. **3** (in *pl.*) the space above a theatre stage which is behind the proscenium, into which scenery is raised. **4** the act or an instance of flying. **5** a flywheel or other similar speed-regulating device in clockwork and machinery. **6** *Baseball* a fly ball. **7 a** the breadth of a flag from the staff to the end (*compare* HOIST *n.* 3a). **b** the part of the flag which is furthest from the staff (*compare* HOIST *n.* 3b). □ **fly high 1** be happy, enthusiastic, etc. **2** excel, prosper. **3** pursue a high ambition. **fly in the face of** disregard, defy, or oppose rashly something that is generally accepted, e.g. an opinion, decision, facts, etc. **fly into a rage** (or **temper** etc.) become suddenly or violently angry. **fly off the handle** *informal* lose one's temper suddenly and unexpectedly. **fly the coop** *informal* escape or leave without warning, esp. a domestic or work situation, one's responsibilities or obligations, etc. **on the fly 1** quickly, esp. while on the go or in the midst of doing something else. **2** (of something hit or thrown) while

still flying through the air, before touching the ground (*caught it on the fly*).

fly² ● *n.* (*pl.* **flies**) **1** any insect of the order Diptera with two usu. transparent wings. **2** any other winged insect, e.g. a firefly or mayfly. **3** a natural fly or an imitation of this consisting of a hook with silk and feathers etc., used as bait in fishing. □ **catch flies** *informal* have one's mouth open for a prolonged time for no reason; breathe with one's mouth open. **fly in the ointment** a minor irritation that spoils an otherwise satisfactory situation or occasion. **fly on the wall** an unnoticed observer. **like flies** in large numbers or quantities. **no flies on** *informal* nothing to diminish (a person's) astuteness. **not hurt a fly** be kind, gentle, and unwilling to injure, offend, or cause unhappiness.

fly-away *adj.* **1** (of hair, a garment, etc.) loose, streaming, or tending to fly out or up. **2** (of a person, action, etc.) sudden, impulsive, volatile, or flighty.

fly ball *n.* *Baseball* a ball hit up into the air with the result that it is easily caught.

fly boy *n.* *slang* a member of the air force, esp. a pilot.

flyby *n.* (*pl.* **-bys**) **1** a flight past a position, esp. the approach of a spacecraft to a planet etc. for observation. **2** an often low-level, ceremonial procession, usu. in formation, of aircraft.

fly-by-night ● *adj.* **1** unreliable or dishonest. **2** superficial, short-lived. ● *n.* (also **fly-by-nighter**) an untrustworthy, dishonest, or unreliable person, esp. one who shirks debts.

fly cast *v.intr. N Amer.* fish with a rod and artificial flies rather than live bait, using a whip-like motion to cast the line. □ **fly caster** *n.* **fly casting** *n.*

flycatcher *n.* any of various birds catching flying insects esp. in short flights from a perch, esp. of the families Muscicapidae, Tyrannidae (**tyrant flycatcher**), and Monarchidae (**monarch flycatcher**).

flyer *n.* *informal* **1 a** a pilot or aviator. **b** a person who flies in an aircraft as a passenger, esp. on a commercial carrier (*frequent flyer*). **2** *N Amer.* a small advertising leaflet that is widely distributed. **3** a thing, creature, etc. that flies or is carried through the air. **4** *N Amer.* a risk, esp. a speculative investment. **5** a fast-moving animal or vehicle. **6** an ambitious or outstanding person (*high flyer*).

fly-fish *v.intr.* fish with an artificial fly as bait. □ **fly fisher** *n.* **fly fisherman** *n.* **fly-fishing** *n.*

fly-in ● *n.* **1** the action or an act of travelling or delivering goods etc. by air to a specific and usu. remote place. **2** a service etc. provided for people who arrive by air. ● *adj.* **1** of or for people arriving by air, esp. in a remote region (*fly-in canoe trips*). **2** accessible only by plane, helicopter, etc. (*fly-in lodge*).

flying ● *adj.* **1** that flies or flies about (*flying saucer*). **2** fluttering, waving, or hanging loose in the air etc. **3** hasty, brief (*a flying visit*). **4** designed for rapid movement. **5** passing or travelling swiftly (*a flying puck*). **6** (of an animal) able to make very long leaps by using wing-like membranes etc. (*flying squirrel*). **7** *Figure Skating* designating a spin which the skater commences with a vigorous leap through the air. ● *n.* the action of guiding, piloting, or travelling in an aircraft or spacecraft. □ **with flying colours** with distinction.

flying buttress *n.* a buttress, usu. on an arch, which slants upwards to a wall from a pier or other support.

flying fish *n.* any of various tropical fishes of the family Exocoetidae, capable of gliding above the water by means of wing-like pectoral fins.

flying saucer *n.* any unidentified, esp. circular, flying object, popularly supposed to have come from outer space.

flying start *n.* **1** a start (of a race etc.) in which the starting point is passed at full speed. **2** a vigorous start giving an initial advantage.

fly-leaf *n.* (*pl.* **-leaves**) a blank page at the beginning or end of a book.

flyline *n.* **1** a type of line used in fly fishing. **2** *Cdn* a point or height above which flies do not normally fly.

fly-out *adj. N Amer.* indicating services etc. that require flying out of a relatively easily accessible area into a remote region (*fly-out Arctic char fishing*).

flyover *n.* **1** *N Amer.* a flight of aircraft, usu. at low level, for observation, as part of a military display, etc. **2** (also **flypast**) a ceremonial flight of aircraft past a person or a place.

fly rod *n.* a very light, flexible rod designed for use in fly casting. □ **fly rodding** *n.*

fly swatter *n.* a device for killing flies by hitting them, usu. a piece of plastic attached to a long handle.

flytrap *n.* **1** any of various plants that catch flies, esp. the Venus flytrap. **2** a trap in which to catch flies.

flyway *n.* **1** the regular line of flight followed by a migrating bird. **2** a vast area occupied by bird populations containing both winter and breeding grounds linked by migratory routes.

flyweight *n.* **1** a weight in certain sports intermediate between light flyweight and bantamweight, in the amateur boxing scale 48-51 kg but differing for professionals and wrestlers. **2** an athlete of this weight.

flywheel *n.* a heavy wheel on a revolving shaft used to regulate machinery or accumulate power.

FM *abbr.* **1** FREQUENCY MODULATION. **2** radio stations broadcast using this.

Fm *symbol* fermium.

FMS *abbr.* FALSE MEMORY SYNDROME.

f-number *n. Photog.* the ratio of the focal length to the effective diameter of a lens, e.g. *f*5, indicating that the focal length is five times the diameter.

foal ● *n.* the young of a horse or related animal. ● *v.intr.* (of a mare etc.) give birth to a foal. □ **foaling** *n.*

foam ● *n.* **1** a mass of small bubbles formed on or in liquid by agitation, fermentation, etc. **2** a froth of saliva or sweat. **3** rubber (in full **foam rubber**) or plastic (in full **foam plastic**) solidified in a lightweight cellular mass with many small gas bubbles. **4** any of various chemical substances forming a thick mass of bubbles and used for various purposes (*shaving foam*). **5** *literary* the sea. ● *v.intr.* **1** emit foam; froth. **2** be very angry, rage. **3** (of a vessel) be filled and overflow with foam. □ **foam at the mouth** be very angry. □ **foaming** *adj.* **foamless** *adj.* **foam-like** *adj.* **foamy** *adj.* (**-ier, -iest**).

fob¹ *n.* **1** (in full **fob chain**) a chain attached to a watch for carrying in a waistcoat or waistband pocket. **2** a small pocket for carrying a watch. **3** a tab or ornament on a key ring.

fob² *v.tr.* (**fobbed, fobbing**) □ **fob off 1** (often foll. by *with* a thing) deceive into accepting something inferior. **2** (often foll. by *on to* a person) palm or pass off (an inferior thing).

f.o.b. *abbr.* free on board, i.e. transported to the ship and loaded without the buyer paying extra.

focaccia /fə'kætʃə/ *n.* a type of flat Italian bread usu. topped with herbs etc.

focal *adj.* of, at, or in terms of a focus.

focal length *n.* **1** the distance between the centre of a mirror or lens and its focus. **2** the equivalent distance in a compound lens or telescope.

focal point *n.* = FOCUS *n.* 1a, 3.

fo'c's'le *var. of* FORECASTLE.

focus ● *n.* (*pl.* **focuses** or **foci** /'fo:sai/) **1** *Physics* **a** point at which rays or waves (of light, heat, sound, etc.) meet after reflection or refraction, or from which divergent rays or waves appear to proceed. **b** the distance from a lens etc. to this point (*compare* FOCAL LENGTH). **2 a** *Optics* the point at which an object must be situated for an image of it given by a lens or mirror to be well defined (*bring into focus*). **b** the adjustment of the eye or a lens necessary to produce a clear image (*the binoculars were not in focus*). **c** a state of clear definition (*the photograph was out of focus*). **3** the centre of interest, activity, or greatest energy (*focus of attention*). **4** *Math.* one of a number of points from which the distances to any point of a given curve or solid obey a simple arithmetic relation. **5** *Med.* the primary or principal site of an infection, malignant growth, or other disease. **6** *Geol.* the place of origin of an earthquake, storm, volcanic eruption, etc. ● *v.* (**focused, focusing** or **focussed, focussing**) **1** *tr.* bring into focus, etc. **2 a** *tr.* adjust the focus of (a lens, the eye, etc.). **b** *intr.* focus the eye, a lens, etc. **3** *tr. & intr.* (often foll. by *on*) concentrate or be concentrated on. **4** *intr.* treat with something in the form of a spray, esp. an insecticide. □ **in a fog** puzzled; at a loss. □ **focuser** *n.*

focus group *n.* a representative selection of people surveyed for their opinions on products etc.

fodder *n.* **1** dried hay or straw etc. for cattle etc. **2 a** something that feeds or stimulates (creativity etc.). **b** people viewed as dispensable commodities.

foe *n.* an enemy or opponent.

foetid *var. of* FETID.

foetus esp. *Brit. var. of* FETUS.

fog ● *n.* **1 a** a thick cloud of water droplets or smoke suspended in the atmosphere at or near the earth's surface restricting or obscuring visibility. **b** any abnormal darkened state or obscurity in the atmosphere. **c** an opaque mass of smoke etc. (*insecticide fog*). **2** *Photog.* cloudiness on a developed negative etc. obscuring the image. **3** a state of confusion, uncertainty, perplexity, etc. ● *v.* (**fogged, fogging**) **1** *tr.* envelop or cover with fog or condensed vapour. **b** bewilder (a person), confuse (an idea), etc. **2** *intr.* become covered with fog or condensed vapour. **3** *tr. Photog.* cause cloudiness on (a negative etc.). **4** *intr.* treat with something in the form of a spray, esp. an insecticide. □ **in a fog** puzzled; at a loss. □ **fogged** *adj.* **fogger** *n.* **fogging** *n.*

fogbound *adj.* **1** completely shrouded in dense fog. **2** unable to leave a place because of fog.

fogey /'fo:gi/ *n.* (also **fogy**) (*pl.* **-eys** or **-ies**) a person with old-fashioned ideas which he or she is unwilling to change. □ **fogeydom** *n.* **fogeyish** *adj.* **fogeyism** *n.*

foggy *adj.* (**-ier, -iest**) **1** (of the atmosphere) thick or obscured with fog. **2** vague, confused, unclear. **3** (of a photograph) cloudy, obscured by a deposit of silver etc. □ **not have the foggiest** *informal* have no idea at all. □ **foggily** *adv.* **fogginess** *n.*

foghorn *n.* **1** a deep sounding instrument for warning ships in fog. **2** *informal* a penetrating voice.

fog lamp *n.* a headlight for improving visibility in fog.

foible /'fɔibəl/ *n.* a minor weakness or idiosyncrasy.

foie gras /fwʌ 'grʌ/ *n.* the liver of fattened geese or ducks eaten as a delicacy, esp. in the form of a pâté.

foil[1] *v.tr.* frustrate, baffle, defeat.

foil[2] *n.* **1 a** metal hammered or rolled into a thin sheet. **b** a sheet of this, or of tin amalgam, attached to mirror glass as a reflector. **c** aluminum foil (*cover with foil*). **d** a leaf of foil placed under a precious stone etc. to brighten or colour it. **2** a person or thing that enhances the qualities of another by contrast.

foil[3] *n.* a light blunt-edged sword with a button on its point used in fencing.

foil[4] *n.* = HYDROFOIL.

foist *v.tr.* (foll. by (*off*) *on*, (*off*) *upon*) impose (an unwelcome person or thing) on.

folate /'fɒleɪt/ *n.* a salt or ester of folic acid.

fold[1] ● *v.* **1** *tr.* **a** bend or close (a flexible thing) over upon itself. **b** (foll. by *back*, *over*, *down*) bend a part of (a flexible thing) in the manner specified (*fold down the flap*). **2** *intr.* become or be able to be folded. **3** *tr.* (foll. by *away*, *up*) make compact by folding. **4** *tr.* **a** bring together and cross or intertwine (the arms, legs, etc.). **b** (of a bird, insect, etc.) bring (the wings) together from an extended position. **5** *intr. informal* (often foll. by *up*) **a** collapse, disintegrate. **b** (of an enterprise) fail; go bankrupt. **c** close. **6** *tr. & intr.* lay (one's cards) face down on the table etc., so as to withdraw from play. **7** *tr.* (foll. by *in*) mix (an ingredient with others) using a gentle cutting and turning motion. **8** *tr. literary* embrace (*folded him to her breast*). **9** *tr.* (foll. by *about*, *around*) clasp (the arms). **10** *tr.* (often foll. by *in* etc.) wrap, envelop. ● *n.* **1** the act or an instance of folding. **2** a line made by or for folding. **3** a folded part. **4** a hollow among hills. **5** *Geol.* a curvature of strata. □ **foldable** *adj.* **folding** *adj.*

fold[2] ● *n.* **1** = SHEEPFOLD. **2** a body of believers or members of a Church. **3** a community or group of people sharing a way of life, values, etc. (*welcomed her back into the fold*). ● *v.tr.* enclose (sheep) in a fold.

-fold *suffix* forming adjectives and adverbs from cardinal numbers, meaning: **1** in an amount multiplied by (*repaid tenfold*). **2** consisting of so many parts (*threefold blessing*).

foldaway *adj.* adapted or designed to be folded away.

fold-down *adj.* designed to be folded down for use.

folder *n.* **1** a folding cover or holder for loose papers. **2** a folded leaflet. **3** *Computing* a directory in a computer system in which files may be accumulated.

fold-out ● *n.* an oversize page in a book etc. to be unfolded by the reader. ● *attrib.adj.* designed to be unfolded for use (*a fold-out bed*).

foley /'fəʊli/ *n.* (*attrib.*) designating sound effects in a motion picture etc. recorded separately from the shooting of the image and subsequently matched with it on the sound track (*foley artist*).

foliage /'fəʊliədʒ/ *n.* **1** leaves. **2** a design in art resembling leaves. □ **foliaged** *adj.*

foliage plant *n.* a plant grown for its leaves, esp. as opposed to one grown for its flowers etc.

foliate ● *adj.* /'fəʊliət/ **1** leaflike. **2** having leaves. **3** (in *comb.*) having a specified number of leaflets (*trifoliate*). ● *v.* /'fəʊliˌeɪt/ *intr. Geol.* (usu. as **foliated** *adj.*) split into laminae. □ **foliation** *n.*

folic acid /'fɒlɪk, 'fəʊlɪk/ *n.* a vitamin of the B complex, found in leafy green vegetables and liver, deficiency of which causes pernicious anemia.

folio /'fəʊliəʊ/ ● *n.* (*pl.* **-os**) **1** a leaf of paper etc., esp. one numbered only on the front. **2** a page number of a book. **3** a sheet of paper folded once making two leaves of a book. **4** a book made of such sheets. ● *adj.* (of a book) made of folios, of the largest size.

folk *n.* (*pl.* **folk** or **folks**) **1** (treated as *pl.*) people in general or of a specified class (*townsfolk*; *just regular folks*). **2** (in *pl.*) (usu. **folks**) one's parents or relatives. **3** (treated as *sing.*) a people. **4** (treated as *sing.*) *informal* = FOLK MUSIC. **5** (*attrib.*) of popular origin; traditional (*folk art*; *folk dance*; *folk tale*).

folk hero *n.* a person perceived as a hero by the common people.

folkie *informal* ● *n.* a devotee of folk music; a folksinger. ● *attrib.adj.* of or relating to folk music.

folkish *adj.* of the common people; unsophisticated.

folklore *n.* **1** the traditional beliefs, stories, customs, etc. of a people. **2** the study of these. **3** popular fantasy or belief. □ **folkloric** *adj.* **folklorist** *n.*

folk medicine *n.* medicine of a traditional kind, employing herbal remedies etc.

folk music *n.* **1** traditional music as made by the common people of a region etc. and transmitted orally. **2** contemporary music composed in this style.

folk-rock *n.* folk music incorporating the stronger beat of rock music and using electric instruments. □ **folk-rocker** *n.*

folksinger *n.* a singer of folk songs. □ **folksinging** *n.*

folk song *n.* **1** a song having a tune and lyrics that have been handed down esp. orally from one generation to the next in a particular region. **2** a song written in this style.

folksy *adj.* (**-ier**, **-iest**) **1** friendly, sociable, informal. **2 a** having the characteristics of folk art etc. **b** ostensibly or artificially folkish. □ **folksiness** *n.*

folkways *n.pl.* the traditional behaviour of a people.

folky *adj.* (**-ier**, **-iest**) **1** = FOLKSY **2**. **2** = FOLKISH.

follicle *n.* **1** *Anat.* a small secretory cavity, sac, or gland, esp. (in full **hair follicle**) the gland or cavity at the root of a hair. **2** a single-carpelled dry fruit opening on one side only to release its seeds. □ **follicular** *adj.*

follow *v.* **1** *tr.* or (foll. by *after*) *intr.* go or come after (a person or thing proceeding ahead). **2** *tr.* go along (a route, path, etc.). **3** *tr. & intr.* come after in order or time. **4** *tr.* take as a guide or leader. **5** *tr.* conform to. **6** *tr.* practise (a trade or profession). **7** *tr.* undertake (a course of study etc.). **8** *tr.* understand the meaning or tendency of (a speaker or argument). **9** *tr.* maintain awareness of the current state or progress of (events etc. in a particular sphere). **10** *tr.* (foll. by *with*) provide with a sequel or successor. **11** *intr.* happen after something else; ensue. **12** *intr.* **a** be necessarily true as a result of something else. **b** (foll. by *from*) be a result of. **13** *tr.* strive after; aim at; pursue (*followed fame and fortune*). □ **follow one's nose** trust to instinct. **follow on** continue. **follow out** carry out; adhere precisely to (instructions etc.). **follow suit 1** play a card of the suit led. **2** conform to another person's actions. **follow through 1** continue (an action etc.) to its conclusion. **2** *Sport* continue the movement of a stroke after the ball etc. has been struck or thrown. **follow up 1** (foll. by *with*) pursue, develop, supplement. **2** make further investigation of.

follower *n.* **1** an adherent or devotee. **2** a person or thing that follows. **3** a mechanical part whose motion or action is derived from that of another part to which force is applied.

following ● *prep.* as a sequel to. ● *n.* **1** a body of adherents or devotees. **2** that which follows (*see the following*). ● *adj.* that follows or comes after.

follow-on *adj.* **1** following or coming after as the next step in a progression. **2** continuing.

follow-the-leader *n.* a game in which players must do as the leader does.

follow-through *n.* the act or an instance of following through.

follow-up *n.* a subsequent or continued action, measure, experience, etc.

folly *n.* (*pl.* **-ies**) **1** foolishness; lack of good sense. **2** a foolish act, behaviour, idea, etc. **3** an ornamental building, usu. a tower or mock Gothic ruin. **4** (in *pl.*) **a** revue with glamorous female performers, esp. scantily clad. **b** the performers in such a revue.

foment /fo:'ment/ *v.tr.* instigate or stir up (trouble, sedition, etc.). □ **fomentation** *n.* **fomenter** *n.*

fond *adj.* **1** (foll. by *of*) having affection or a liking for. **2** affectionate, loving (*a fond farewell*). **3** doting; indulgent (*a fond parent*). **4** (of hopes, dreams, etc.) cherished but not likely to be realized (*has fond hopes of becoming prime minister*). □ **fondly** *adv.* **fondness** *n.*

fondant /'fɒndənt/ *n.* **1** a creamy, thick paste made of sugar and water, used as an icing or filling. **2** a candy made of or filled with this paste.

fondle *v.tr.* **1** touch or stroke lovingly; caress. **2** sexually molest (a person) by touching etc.

fondue *n.* **1** a dish of flavoured melted cheese into which cubes of bread are dipped. **2** any other dish in which pieces of food are dipped into hot oil or sauce.

font[1] *n.* **1** a receptacle in a church for baptismal water. **2** the reservoir for oil in a lamp.

font[2] *n.* **1** a selection of type of one face and size. **2** a set of letters, numbers, and symbols of a unified design and given size that may be displayed on a computer screen or printed out.

fontanelle /ˌfɒntə'nel/ *n.* a membranous space in an infant's skull at the angles of the parietal bones.

fontina /fɒn'tiːnə/ *n.* a mild, semi-soft to firm, pale yellow cow's milk cheese.

food *n.* **1** any substance that can be taken into the body to maintain life and growth; nourishment (also *attrib.*: *food grain*; *food fish*). **2** solid nourishment, as opposed to drink. **3** nutriment absorbed by a plant from the earth or air. **4** a particular kind of food (*cat food*; *snack food*). **5** ideas as a resource for or stimulus to mental work (*food for thought*).

food bank *n.* *N Amer.* a charitable institution which provides food to the needy.

food chain *n.* a hierarchy of organisms in which each feeds on those below and is the source of food for those above.

food colouring *n.* any of various edible dyes used to colour food.

food court *n.* an area, esp. in a shopping mall, with a variety of fast-food stalls surrounding a shared area with tables and chairs.

foodie *n.* *informal* a person who is interested in esp. exotic or trendy food; a gourmet.

foodland *n.* *Cdn* farmland; land that is or may be used for the production of food.

food poisoning *n.* illness due to bacteria or other toxins in food.

food processor *n.* a domestic kitchen appliance for chopping, grating, slicing, blending, or mixing foods.

foodstuff *n.* any substance suitable as food.

food web *n.* *Ecology* the system of interdependent food chains in a community.

fool ● *n.* **1** a person who acts unwisely or imprudently; a stupid person. **2** a dupe. ● *v.* **1** *tr.* deceive so as to cause to appear foolish. **2** *tr.* (foll. by *into* + verbal noun, or *out of*) trick; cause to do something foolish. **3** *tr.* play tricks on; dupe. **4** *intr.* act in a joking, frivolous, or teasing way. ● *adj.* *N Amer. informal* foolish, silly. □ **act** (or **play**) **the fool** behave in a silly way. **fool around 1** behave in a playful or silly way. **2 a** engage in sexual activity. **b** engage in adulterous sexual activity. **3**

waste time. **fool with** handle idly; play with carelessly. **make a fool of** make (a person or oneself) look foolish; trick or deceive. **no** (or **nobody's**) **fool** a shrewd or prudent person.

foolery *n.* (*pl.* **-ies**) **1** foolish behaviour. **2** a foolish act.

foolhardy *adj.* (**-ier, -iest**) rashly or foolishly bold; reckless. □ **foolhardily** *adv.* **foolhardiness** *n.*

foolish *adj.* lacking good sense or judgment; unwise. □ **foolishly** *adv.* **foolishness** *n.*

foolproof *adj.* (of a procedure etc.) so straightforward or simple as to be incapable of misuse or mistake.

foolscap /'fuːlskæp, 'fuːl-/ *n.* a type of legal-sized writing paper, usu. lined.

fool's gold *n.* iron pyrites.

foot ● *n.* (*pl.* **feet**) **1 a** the lower extremity of the leg below the ankle. **b** the part of a sock etc. covering the foot. **2 a** the lower or lowest part of anything, e.g. a mountain, a page, stairs, etc. **b** the lower end of a table. **c** the end of a bed where the user's feet normally rest. **d** a part of a chair, appliance, etc. on which it rests. **3** the base, often projecting, of anything extending vertically. **4** a step, pace, or tread; a manner of walking (*fleet of foot*). **5** (*pl.* **feet** or **foot**) a unit of linear measure equal to 12 inches (30.48 cm). **6** *Prosody* **a** a group of syllables (one usu. stressed) constituting a metrical unit. **b** a similar unit of speech etc. **7** the locomotive or adhesive organ of invertebrates. **8** the part by which a petal is attached. ● *v.tr.* **1** (usu. as **foot it**) a traverse (esp. a long distance) by foot. **b** dance. **2** pay (a bill). □ **at a person's feet** as a person's disciple or subject. **feet of clay** a fundamental weakness in a person otherwise revered. **get off on the wrong** (or **right**) **foot** make a bad (or good) start. **get one's feet wet** begin to participate. **have one's** (or **both**) **feet on the ground** be practical. **have a foot in the door** have a prospect of success. **have one foot in the grave** be near death or very old. **my foot!** *interj.* expressing strong contradiction. **not put a foot wrong** make no mistakes. **off one's feet** so as to be unable to stand, or in a state compared with this (*was rushed off my feet*). **on foot** walking, not driving or riding etc. **on one's feet 1** standing. **2** completely recovered from an illness or time of trouble. **3** in motion (*fast on one's feet*). **put one's best foot forward** make every effort; proceed with determination. **put one's feet up** *informal* take a rest. **put one's foot down** *informal* **1** be firmly insistent or repressive. **2** accelerate a motor vehicle. **put one's foot in one's mouth** (also **put one's foot in it**) *informal* commit a blunder or indiscretion. **set foot in** (or **on**) enter; go into. **think on one's feet** think or react rapidly under stress etc. **under foot 1** on the ground. **2** in the way. □ **footed** *adj.* (also in *comb.*). **footless** *adj.*

footage *n.* **1** length or distance in feet. **2** an amount of film made for showing, broadcasting, etc.

foot-and-mouth disease *n.* a contagious viral disease of cattle etc., characterized by ulceration of the hoofs and around the mouth.

football ● *n.* **1** any of several games in which each of two teams attempts to move a ball across the other's goal line, esp.: **a** *Cdn* = CANADIAN FOOTBALL. **b** *US* = AMERICAN FOOTBALL. **2** a large inflated ball of a kind used in these. **3** a topical issue or problem that is the subject of continued argument or controversy. ● *v.intr.* play football. □ **footballer** *n.*

footbed *n.* an insole used for cushioning or to provide a better fit.

footboard *n.* **1** a board to support the feet or a foot. **2** an upright board at the foot of a bed.

footbridge *n.* a bridge for use by pedestrians.

foot-dragging *n.* deliberate slowness or reluctance to act or proceed. □ **foot-dragger** *n.*

footer *n.* **1** (in *comb.*) a person or thing of so many feet in length or height (*six-footer*). **2** a line or block of text appearing at the foot of each page of a document etc.

footfall *n.* the sound of a footstep.

footgear *n.* = FOOTWEAR.

foothill *n.* (often in *pl.*) any of the low hills at the base of a mountain or mountain range.

foothold *n.* **1** a place, esp. in climbing, where a foot can be supported securely. **2** a secure initial position.

footing *n.* **1** a foothold; a secure position (*lost her footing*). **2** the basis on which an enterprise is established or operates; the position or status of a person in relation to others (*on an equal footing*). **3** (usu. in *pl.*) the part of a foundation resting directly on the earth.

footlights *n.pl.* a row of lights along the front of a stage at the level of the performers' feet.

footloose *adj.* (often in phr. **footloose and fancy-free**) free to go where or act as one pleases.

footman *n.* (*pl.* **-men**) a liveried servant attending at the door, at table, or on a carriage.

footnote ● *n.* **1** a note at the foot of a page referring to a marked part of the text on the page. **2** an event, comment, etc. that is added or subordinated to something more central or important (*a footnote to history*). ● *v.tr.* supply with a footnote or footnotes.

footpad *n.* **1** *hist.* an unmounted highwayman. **2** one of the pads on the sole of an animal's foot.

footpath *n.* a path for walking along.

foot-pound *n.* (*pl.* **foot-pounds**) the amount of energy required to raise 1 lb. a distance of 1 foot.

footprint *n.* **1** the impression left by a foot or shoe. **2** the area over which an aircraft is audible, a broadcast can be received, etc. **3** the surface area taken up by something, such as a computer etc.

foot race *n.* a race run between competitors on foot.

footrest *n.* a support for the feet or a foot.

footsie *n.* *informal* □ **play footsie with a person** touch or caress a person's feet lightly with one's own feet, usu. under a table, as a playful expression of affection or sexual interest.

foot soldier *n.* **1** a soldier who fights on foot; an infantry soldier. **2** a person who works for a cause at the basic level rather than in the leadership.

footstep *n.* **1** a step taken in walking. **2** the sound of this. **3** a footprint. □ **follow** (or **tread**) **in a person's footsteps** do as another person did.

footstool *n.* a stool for resting the feet on when sitting.

footwear *n.* anything worn on the feet.

footwork *n.* the use of the feet, esp. skilfully, in sports, dancing, etc.

foo yong /fuːˈjɒŋ/ *n.* a Chinese dish or sauce made with eggs mixed and cooked with other ingredients.

fop *n.* an affectedly elegant or fashionable man; a dandy. □ **foppish** *adj.*

for ● *prep.* **1** in the interest or to the benefit of; intended to go to (*these flowers are for you*; *wish to see it for myself*). **2** in defence, support, or favour of (*fight for one's rights*). **3** suitable or appropriate to (*a dance for beginners*). **4** with reference to; regarding; so far as concerns (*don't care for him*; *MP for Winnipeg North*). **5** representing or in place of (*here for my uncle*). **6** in exchange against (*swapped it for a bigger one*). **7 a** as the price of (*give me $5 for it*). **b** at the price of (*bought it for $20*). **c** to the amount of (*a bill for $100*). **8** as the penalty of (*fined them heavily for it*). **9** in requital of (*that's for upsetting my sister*). **10** as a reward for (*here's $10 for your trouble*). **11 a** with a view to; in the hope or quest of; in order to get (*go for a walk*; *run for a doctor*). **b** on account of (*could not speak for laughing*). **12** corresponding to (*word for word*). **13** to reach; in the direction of; towards (*left for Fredericton*). **14** conducive or conducively to; in order to achieve (*take the pills for a sound night's sleep*). **15** so as to start promptly at (*the meeting is at seven-thirty for eight*). **16** through or over (a distance or period); during (*sang for two hours*). **17** in the character of; as being (*knew it for a lie*; *I for one refuse*). **18** because of; on account of (*could not see for tears*). **19** in spite of; notwithstanding (*for all your fine words*). **20** considering or making due allowance with regard to (*good for a beginner*). ● *conj.* because, since, seeing that. □ **o** (or **oh**) **for** I wish I had.

forage /ˈfɒrɪdʒ, ˈfɒ-/ ● *n.* **1** food for cattle, etc., esp. hay or grass. **2** the act or an instance of searching for food. ● *v.* **1** *intr.* go searching; rummage (esp. for food). **2** *tr.* collect food from; ravage. **3** *tr.* **a** get by foraging. **b** supply with food. □ **forager** *n.*

foramen /fɒˈreɪmən/ *n.* (*pl.* **foramina** /-ˈræmɪnə/ or **-s**) *Anat.* an opening, hole, or passage, esp. in a bone.

foray ● *n.* **1** a sudden attack; a raid or incursion. **2** a brief, vigorous attempt to be involved in a different activity, profession, etc. ● *v.intr.* make or go on a foray.

forb *n.* any herbaceous plant other than a grass.

forbear[1] *v.intr.* & *tr.* (*past* **forbore**; *past part.* **forborne**) (often foll. by *from*, or *to* + infin.) *literary* abstain or desist (from) (*could not forbear from speaking out*).

forbear[2] *var. of* FOREBEAR.

forbearance *n.* patient self-control; tolerance.

forbid *v.tr.* (**forbidding**; *past* **forbade** /fɔˈbeɪd, -ˈbæd/ or **forbad** /-ˈbæd/; *past part.* **forbidden**) **1** order not (*I forbid you to go*). **2** refuse to allow (*I forbid it*). **3** refuse a person entry to. □ **God** (or **heaven**) **forbid** may it not happen! □ **forbidden** *adj.*

forbidding *adj.* uninviting, repellent, stern.

force ● *n.* **1** power; exerted strength or impetus; intense effort. **2** coercion or compulsion, esp. with the use or threat of violence. **3 a** military strength. **b** (in *pl.*) troops; fighting resources. **c** (**Forces**) = CANADIAN FORCES (also *attrib.*: *Forces lawyer*). **d** an organized body of people, esp. soldiers, police, or workers. **4** binding power; validity. **5** effect; precise significance (*the force of their words*). **6 a** mental or moral strength; influence (*force of habit*). **b** vividness of effect (*described with much force*). **7** *Physics* **a** an influence tending to cause the motion of a body. **b** the intensity of this equal to the mass of the body and its acceleration. **8** a person or thing regarded as exerting influence (*a force for good*). **9** *Baseball* = FORCEOUT. ● *v.* **1** *tr.* constrain (a person) by force or against his or her will. **2** *tr.* make a way through or into by force; break open by force. **3** *tr.* (usu. with *prep.* or *adv.*) drive or propel violently or against resistance. **4** *tr.* (foll. by *on*, *upon*) impose or press (on a person) (*forced their views on us*). **5** *tr.* **a** cause or produce by effort (*forced a smile*). **b** attain by strength or effort (*forced an entry*). **c** make (a way) by force. **6** *tr.* strain or increase to the utmost. **7** *tr.* artificially hasten the development or maturity of (a plant). **8** *tr.* seek or demand quick results from; accelerate the process of (*force the pace*). **9** *refl.* rape (*forced himself on her*). **10** *tr.* *Baseball* **a** cause (a runner) to be put out in a forceout. **b** cause (a runner or run) to score or be scored, esp. by walking a batter with the bases full. □ **by force of** by means of. **force a person's hand** make a person act prematurely or unwillingly. **force the issue** render an immediate decision necessary. **in force 1** valid, effective. **2** in great strength or numbers. **join forces** combine efforts.

forced *adj.* **1** compelled, imposed, or obtained by force (*forced labour*). **2** produced or maintained with effort (*a forced smile*). **3** required by emergency or necessity (*forced landing*). **4** produced or supplied by artificial means (*forced air*). **5** (of a plant, crop, etc.) made to bear, or produced, out of the proper season.

force-feed *v.tr* (*past* and *past part.* **-fed**) **1** force (a person or animal) to take food. **2** compel (a person) to absorb or assimilate propaganda, opinions, etc.

force field *n.* (in science fiction) an invisible barrier of force.

forceful *adj.* **1** vigorous, powerful. **2** (of speech) compelling. ☐ **forcefully** *adv.* **forcefulness** *n.*

forceout *n. Baseball* (also **force play**) a play in which a runner is put out after being forced (by another runner) to advance when he or she cannot do so safely.

forceps *n.* (*pl.* same) surgical pincers, used for grasping and holding.

forcible *adj.* **1** done by or involving force (*forcible confinement*). **2** forceful. ☐ **forcibly** *adv.*

ford ● *n.* a shallow place where a river or stream may be crossed by wading or in a vehicle. ● *v.tr* cross (water) at a ford.

fore ● *adj.* situated in front. ● *n.* the front part, esp. of a ship; the bow. ● *interj. Golf* a warning to a person in the path of a ball. ☐ **come to the fore** take a leading part. **to the fore** in front; conspicuous.

fore and aft ● *adv.* at both front and rear; going from front to rear. ● *adj.* (**fore-and-aft**) **1** (of a sail or rigging) set lengthwise, not on the yards. **2** backwards and forwards. **3** *N Amer.* (*BC* & *US Northwest*) designating a logging road constructed of logs laid end to end.

forearm¹ *n.* **1** the part of the arm from the elbow to the wrist or the fingertips. **2** the corresponding part in a foreleg or wing.

forearm² *v.tr* prepare or arm beforehand.

forebear *n.* (also **forbear**) (usu. in *pl.*) an ancestor.

forebode *v.tr* **1** betoken; be an advance warning of (an evil or unwelcome event). **2** have a presentiment of (usu. evil).

foreboding ● *n.* an expectation of trouble or evil; a presage or omen. ● *adj.* threatening, esp. evil. ☐ **forebodingly** *adv.*

forecast ● *v.tr* (*past* and *past part.* **-cast** or **-casted**) predict; estimate or calculate beforehand. ● *n.* a calculation or estimate of something future, esp. coming weather. ☐ **forecaster** *n.* **forecasting** *n.*

forecastle /'fo:ksəl/ *n.* (also **fo'c'sle**) *Naut.* the forward part of a ship where the crew has quarters.

forecheck *v.intr Hockey* (of a player or team) play an aggressive style of defence, checking opposing players before they can organize an attack. ☐ **forechecker** *n.* **forechecking** *n.*

foreclose *v.* **1** *tr.* & *intr.* (foll. by *on*) stop (a mortgage) from being redeemable or (a mortgagor) from redeeming, esp. as a result of defaults in payment. **2** *tr.* exclude, prevent. **3** *tr.* shut out. ☐ **foreclosure** *n.*

foredeck *n.* **1** the deck at the forward part of a ship. **2** the forward part of the deck.

forefather *n.* (usu. in *pl.*) **1** an ancestor. **2** a member of a past generation of a family or people.

forefinger *n.* the finger next to the thumb.

forefoot *n.* (*pl.* **-feet**) **1** either of the front feet of an animal. **2** the front part of the human foot.

forefront *n.* **1** the foremost part. **2** the leading position.

forego¹ *v.tr* & *intr.* (**-goes**; *past* **-went**; *past part.* **-gone**) precede in place or time. ☐ **foregoer** *n.*

forego² *var. of* FOREGO.

foregoing *adj.* preceding; previously mentioned.

foregone ● *v. past part. of* FOREGO¹. ● *attrib.adj.* previous, preceding, completed.

foregone conclusion *n.* an easily foreseen or predictable result.

foreground ● *n.* **1** the part of a view, esp. in a picture, that is nearest the observer. **2** the most conspicuous position. ● *v.tr* place in the foreground; make prominent.

forehand *n.* **1** *Tennis etc.* **a** a stroke played with the palm of the hand facing the opponent. **b** (*attrib.*) (also **forehanded**) of or made with a forehand. **2** the part of a horse in front of the seated rider.

forehead *n.* the part of the face above the eyebrows.

foreign *adj.* **1** of or from or situated in or characteristic of a country or a language other than one's own. **2** dealing with other countries (*foreign service*). **3** of another district, society, etc. **4** (often foll. by *to*) unfamiliar, strange, uncharacteristic. **5** coming from outside (*a foreign body*). ☐ **foreigner** *n.* **foreignness** *n.*

foreign affairs *n.pl.* the activities and interests of a nation that involve its relations with other nations.

foreign aid *n.* money, food, etc. given or lent by one country to another.

foreign exchange *n.* **1** the currency of other countries. **2** dealings in these.

foreign legion *n.* a body of foreign volunteers in a modern, esp. the French, army.

foreign minister *n.* (also **foreign secretary**) esp. *Brit.* a government minister in charge of his or her country's relations with other countries.

foreign service *n. N Amer.* = DIPLOMATIC SERVICE.

foreknow *v.tr.* (*past* **-knew**; *past part.* **-known**) know beforehand. ☐ **foreknowledge** *n.*

foreleg *n.* each of the front legs of a quadruped.

forelimb *n.* any of the front limbs of an animal.

forelock *n.* a lock of hair growing just above the forehead. ☐ **touch** (or **tug** etc.) **one's forelock** defer to a person of higher social rank.

foreman *n.* (*pl.* **-men**) **1** a worker with supervisory responsibilities. **2** the member of a jury who presides over its deliberations and speaks on its behalf.

foremast *n.* the forward (lower) mast of a ship.

foremost ● *adj.* **1** the chief or most notable. **2** the most advanced in position; the front. ● *adv.* in the first place (*first and foremost*).

foremother *n.* a female ancestor or predecessor.

forename *n.* a first name.

forensic /fə'rensɪk/ ● *adj.* **1** of or used in connection with courts of law, esp. in relation to crime detection (*forensic evidence*). **2** of or employing forensic science. ● *n.* (usu. in *pl.*) **1** forensic science. **2** a forensic science department, esp. as part of a police force. ☐ **forensically** *adv.*

forensic accounting *n.* the use of accounting skills to investigate fraud, embezzlement, etc. and to prepare an analysis of financial information suitable for use in litigation. ☐ **forensic accountant** *n.*

forensic science *n.* the application of biochemical and other scientific techniques to the investigation of crime.

foreordain *v.tr.* predestine; ordain beforehand. □ **foreordination** *n.*

forepart *n.* the foremost part; the front.

foreperson *n.* **1** a worker with supervisory responsibilities. **2** the member of a jury who presides over its deliberations and speaks on its behalf.

foreplay *n.* stimulation preceding sexual intercourse.

forequarters *n.pl.* the front legs and adjoining parts of a quadruped.

forerun *v.tr.* (**-running**; *past* **-ran**; *past part.* **-run**) **1** go before. **2** indicate the coming of; foreshadow.

forerunner *n.* **1** a predecessor. **2** an advance messenger.

foresail *n. Naut.* the principal sail on a foremast.

foresee *v.tr.* (*past* **-saw**; *past part.* **-seen**) see or be aware of beforehand. □ **foreseeable** *adj.* **foreseeability** *n.*

foreshadow *v.tr.* be a warning or indication of (a future event). □ **foreshadowing** *n.*

foreshore *n.* the part of the shore between high- and low-water marks, or between the water and cultivated or developed land.

foreshorten *v.tr.* show or portray (an object) with the apparent shortening due to visual perspective. □ **foreshortening** *n.*

foreshow *v.tr.* (*past part.* **-shown**) **1** foretell. **2** foreshadow, portend, prefigure.

foresight *n.* **1** regard or provision for the future. **2** the process of foreseeing. **3** the front sight of a gun. □ **foresighted** *adj.* **foresightedly** *adv.*

foreskin *n.* the fold of skin over the end of the penis.

forest ● *n.* **1 a** a large area covered chiefly with trees and undergrowth. **b** the trees growing in such an area. **2** a large number or dense mass of vertical objects (*a forest of tall buildings*). ● *v.tr.* **1** plant with trees. **2** convert into a forest. □ **not see the forest for the trees** be unable to perceive or understand the overall situation because one is preoccupied with details. □ **forested** *adj.* **forestland** *n.*

forestall *v.tr.* **1** act in advance of in order to prevent. **2** anticipate (the action of another, or an event).

forestation *n.* the establishing of a forest.

forestay *n. Naut.* a stay from the head of the foremast to the ship's deck to support the foremast.

forester *n.* **1** a person in charge of a forest or skilled in forestry. **2** a person or animal living in a forest. **3** (**Forester**) a member of the Independent Order of Foresters, a fraternal organization.

forest fire *n.* an uncontrolled fire in a forest.

forest floor *n.* the ground in a forest, specifically the layer of more or less decayed organic debris forming the upper soil of a forest.

forest green ● *n.* a dark green colour. ● *adj.* of this colour.

forest ranger *n.* esp. *N Amer.* an official who patrols, manages, and protects a public forest.

forestry *n.* the science and practice of planting, caring for, and managing forests.

foretaste *n.* a small experience of something before it actually happens; a sample in anticipation.

foretell *v.tr.* (*past and past part.* **-told**) tell of or presage (an event etc.) before it takes place. □ **foreteller** *n.*

forethought *n.* **1** care or provision for the future. **2** previous thinking or devising.

forever ● *adv.* **1** for all future time; in perpetuity. **2** continually, persistently (*is forever complaining*). **3** *informal* for an extremely long time (*talked on the phone forever*). ● *n. informal* an extremely long time.

forevermore *adv. an emphatic form of* FOREVER *adv.* **1**.

forewarn *v.tr.* warn beforehand.

forewent *past of* FOREGO[1],[2].

forewing *n.* either of the two front wings of a four-winged insect.

forewoman *n.* (*pl.* **-women**) **1** a female worker with supervisory responsibilities. **2** a woman who presides over a jury and speaks on its behalf.

foreword *n.* introductory remarks at the beginning of a book, often by a person other than the author.

forfeit /ˈfɔːfɪt/ ● *n.* **1** a penalty for a breach of contract or neglect; a fine. **2 a** a trivial fine for a breach of rules in clubs etc. or in games. **b** (in *pl.*) a game in which forfeits are exacted. **3** something surrendered as a penalty. **4** the process of forfeiting. **5** *Law* property or a right or privilege lost as a legal penalty. ● *adj.* lost or surrendered as a penalty. ● *v.tr.* (**forfeited**, **forfeiting**) lose the right to, be deprived of, or have to pay as a penalty (*forfeited their deposit*; *had to forfeit the game*). □ **forfeitable** *adj.* **forfeiter** *n.* **forfeiture** *n.*

forgave *past of* FORGIVE.

forge[1] *v.tr.* **1** write (a document or signature) in order to pass it off as written by another. **2** create or devise (an alliance, bond, etc.). **3** shape (esp. metal) by heating in a fire and hammering. ● *n.* **1** a blacksmith's workshop. **2** a furnace or hearth for melting or refining metal. □ **forger** *n.*

forge[2] *v.intr.* move forward gradually or steadily. □ **forge ahead 1** take the lead in a race. **2** move forward or make progress rapidly.

forgery *n.* (*pl.* **-ies**) **1 a** the act or an instance of forging, counterfeiting, or falsifying a document etc. **b** the crime of forgery. **2** a forged or spurious thing, esp. a document or signature.

forget *v.* (**forgetting**; *past* **forgot**; *past part.* **forgotten** or **forgot**) **1** *tr. & intr.* lose the remembrance of; not remember. **2** *tr.* inadvertently omit to bring or mention or attend to. **3** *tr. & intr.* put out of mind; cease to think of (*forgive and forget*). ¶The past participle *forgot*, though in use in N America, is much less frequent than *forgotten*, and is considered incorrect by many people. □ **forget (about) it!** *informal* take no more notice of it; there is no need for apology or thanks. **forget oneself 1** neglect one's own interests. **2** act unbecomingly or unworthily. □ **forgettable** *adj.*

forgetful *adj.* **1** apt to forget; absent-minded. **2** (often foll. by *of*) forgetting, neglectful. □ **forgetfully** *adv.* **forgetfulness** *n.*

forget-me-not *n.* **1** any plant of the genus *Myosotis*, esp. *M. sylvatica* with small yellow-eyed bright blue flowers. **2** *N Amer.* any of several Rocky Mountain plants of the genus *Eritrichium* of the borage family.

forging *n.* **1** an act or instance of forging (see FORGE[1]). **2** the process of forging metal. **3** a forged piece of metal etc.

forgive *v. tr. & intr.* (*past* **forgave**; *past part.* **forgiven**) **1** cease to feel angry or resentful towards; pardon (an offender or offence). **2** remit or let off (a debt or debtor). □ **forgivable** *adj.* **forgiveness** *n.*

forgiving *adj.* **1** inclined readily to forgive. **2** tolerant; accepting of differences in ability etc. (*is forgiving of beginners*). □ **forgivingly** *adv.*

forgo *v.tr.* (**-goes**; *past* **-went**; *past part.* **-gone**) **1** abstain from; go without; relinquish. **2** omit or decline to take or use (a pleasure, advantage, etc.).

forgot *past of* FORGET.

forgotten *past part. of* FORGET.

fork ● *n.* **1** a (usu. metal) implement with two or more prongs used for holding or transferring food. **2** a similar much larger instrument used for digging, lifting, etc. **3** any pronged device or component (*tuning fork*). **4** a forked support for a bicycle wheel. **5 a** a divergence of anything, e.g. a stick or road, or *N Amer.* a river, into two parts. **b** the place where this occurs. **c** either of the two parts (*take the left fork*). **d** *N Amer.* a major tributary of a river. **e** *N Amer.* (in *pl.*) the confluence of two rivers and the surrounding area (*the forks of the Red and the Assiniboine*). **6** a flash of forked lightning. ● *v.* **1** *intr.* form a fork or branch by separating into two parts. **2** *intr.* take one or other road etc. at a fork. **3** *tr.* dig or lift etc. with a fork. □ **fork out** (or **up**) *informal* hand over or pay, usu. reluctantly. **fork over** *informal* = FORK OUT. **2** turn over (soil etc.) with a fork. □ **forked** *adj.* (also in *comb.*). **forkful** *n.*

forkball *n.* *Baseball* a pitch in which the ball is held with the thumb, index finger, and middle finger spread.

forked lightning *n.* a lightning flash in the form of a zigzag or branching line.

forklift (in full **forklift truck**) ● *n.* a vehicle with a horizontal fork in front for lifting and carrying loads. ● *v.tr.* pile or move (loads) with a forklift.

forlorn *adj.* **1** sad and abandoned or lonely. **2** in a pitiful state; of wretched appearance. **3** hopeless, forsaken. □ **forlornly** *adv.* **forlornness** *n.*

form ● *n.* **1 a** a shape; an arrangement of parts. **b** the outward aspect (esp. apart from colour) or shape of a body. **2** a person or animal as visible or tangible (*the familiar form of the mailman*). **3** the mode in which a thing exists or manifests itself (*detergent in liquid form*). **4 a** a species, kind, or variety (*different forms of government*). **b** an artistic or literary genre (*sonnet form*). **5 a** a printed document with blank spaces for information to be inserted. **b** a regularly drawn document. **6** a customary method; what is usually done (*common form*). **7** a set order of words; a formula. **8** behaviour according to a rule or custom. **9** (prec. by *the*) correct procedure (*knows the form*). **10 a** (of an athlete, horse, etc.) condition of health and training. **b** *Racing* details of previous performances. **11** general state or disposition (*was in great form*). **12** formality or mere ceremony. **13** *Grammar* **a** one of the ways in which a word may be spelled or pronounced or inflected. **b** the external characteristics of words apart from meaning. **14 a** arrangement and expression of ideas esp. in the arts. **b** style in literary or musical composition. **15** *Philos.* the essential nature of a species or thing. **16** a mould, frame or block in or on which something is shaped. ● *v.* **1** *tr.* make or fashion into a certain shape or form. **2** *intr.* take a certain shape; be formed. **3** *tr.* be the material of; make up or constitute (*forms part of the structure*). **4** *tr.* train or instruct. **5** *tr.* develop or establish as a concept, institution, or practice (*form an idea; formed an alliance*). **6** *tr.* (foll. by *into*) embody, organize. **7** *intr.* come into existence; take shape or develop. **8** *tr. & intr.* (often foll. by *up*) esp. *Military* bring or be brought into a certain arrangement or formation. **9** *tr.* construct (a new word) by derivation, inflection, etc. □ **formable** *adj.*

formal ● *adj.* **1** used or done or held in accordance with rules, convention, or ceremony. **2** ceremonial; required by convention (*a formal call*). **3** precise or symmetrical (*a formal garden*). **4** prim or stiff in manner. **5** perfunctory, having the form without the spirit. **6** valid or correctly so called because of its form; explicit and definite (*a formal agreement*). **7** in accordance with recognized forms or rules. **8** (of education) officially given at a school, university, etc.

9 of or concerned with (outward) form or appearance, esp. as distinct from content or matter. ● *n.* *N Amer.* **1** a dance or other social occasion to which evening dress is worn. **2** an evening gown. □ **formally** *adv.*

formaldehyde /fɔr'mældə,haid, fər-/ *n.* a colourless, pungent, toxic gas used as a disinfectant and preservative and in the manufacture of resins.

formalism *n.* **1 a** excessive adherence to prescribed forms. **b** the use of forms without regard to inner significance. **2** *derogatory* an artist's concentration on form at the expense of content. □ **formalist** *n.*

formality *n.* (*pl.* **-ies**) **1 a** a formal or ceremonial act, requirement of etiquette, regulation, or custom (often with an implied lack of real significance). **b** a thing done simply to comply with a rule. **2** the rigid observance of rules or convention. **3** ceremony; elaborate procedure. **4** precision of manners.

formalize *v.tr.* **1** give definite shape or legal formality to. **2** make ceremonious, precise, or rigid. □ **formalization** *n.*

formal wear *n.* clothes customarily worn on formal occasions, e.g. tails, tuxedos, or evening dresses.

format ● *n.* **1** the shape and size of a book, periodical, etc. **2** the style or manner of an arrangement, design or procedure. **3** a defined structure for holding data etc. in a record for processing or storage. ● *v.tr.* (**formatted, formatting**) **1** arrange or put into a format. **2** prepare (a storage medium) to receive data.

formation *n.* **1** the act or an instance of forming; the process of being formed. **2** a thing formed. **3** a structure or arrangement of parts. **4** a particular arrangement, e.g. of troops, aircraft in flight, etc. **5** *Geol.* an assemblage of rocks or series of strata having some common characteristic.

formative *adj.* **1** serving to form or fashion; of formation. **2** having an important and lasting influence upon (a person's character etc.). □ **formatively** *adv.*

former¹ ● *attrib.adj.* **1** of or occurring in the past or an earlier period (*in former times*). **2** having been previously (*her former husband*). ● *n.* (prec. by *the*) the first or first mentioned of two (opp. LATTER *n.*).

former² *n.* a person or thing that forms.

formerly *adv.* in the past; in former times.

form-fitting *adj.* = CLOSE-FITTING.

Formica /fɔr'maikə/ *n.* *proprietary* a hard durable plastic laminate used for working surfaces etc.

formidable /fɔr'midəbəl, 'fɔr-/ *adj.* **1** inspiring fear or dread. **2** inspiring respect or awe. **3** likely to be hard to overcome, resist, or deal with. □ **formidableness** *n.* **formidably** *adv.*

formless *adj.* shapeless; without determinate or regular form. □ **formlessly** *adv.* **formlessness** *n.*

form letter *n.* a standardized letter to deal with frequently occurring matters.

formula *n.* (*pl.* **formulas** or (esp. in senses 1, 2) **formulae** /ˈfɔrmjʊ,li:/) **1** a set of chemical symbols showing the constituents of a substance and their relative proportions. **2** a mathematical rule expressed in symbols. **3 a** a fixed form of words, esp. one used on social or ceremonial occasions. **b** a rule unintelligently or slavishly followed; an established or conventional usage (also *attrib.*: *formula fiction*). **c** a fixed form of words as a definition or an enunciation of a principle or religious doctrine, esp. a statement or method intended to reconcile different aims or opinions. **4** a method or set of principles by which parties involved in negotiation arrive at a solution (compare AMENDING FORMULA). **5 a** a list of ingredients; a recipe. **b** *N Amer.* an infant's liquid food preparation, given as a substitute for breast milk. □ **formulaic** /-'leɪɪk/ *adj.*

Formula One *n.* the form of racing on the Grand Prix circuit, for open-wheeled, single-seater cars.

formulate *v.tr.* **1** express in a formula. **2** express clearly and precisely. **3** devise, create (*formulate a plan*). □ **formulation** *n.* **formulator** *n.*

fornicate *v.intr.* (of people not married or not married to each other) have sexual intercourse. □ **fornication** *n.* **fornicator** *n.*

for-profit *adj.* designating an institution run with the aim of making a profit, esp. one providing public service; private (*for-profit child care*).

forsake *v.tr.* (*past* **forsook**; *past part.* **forsaken**) **1** give up; break off from; renounce. **2** withdraw one's help, friendship, or companionship from; desert, abandon. □ **forsakenness** *n.* **forsaker** *n.*

forsythia /fɔr'sɪθɪə/ *n.* an ornamental shrub bearing yellow flowers in early spring.

fort *n.* **1** a fortified building or position. **2** *N Amer. hist.* a trading post, originally fortified.

forte /'fɔrteɪ / ● *n.* **1** a person's strong point; a thing in which a person excels. **2** *Music* a passage to be performed loudly. ● *adj.* performed loudly. ● *adv.* loudly.

fortepiano /,fɔrtəpi'æno:, -'pjæno:/ *n.* (*pl.* **-os**) = PIANOFORTE (esp. with reference to an instrument of the 18th to early 19th c.)

forth *adv.* (only in set phrases and after certain verbs, esp. *bring*, *come*, *go*, and *set*) **1** forward; into view. **2** onward in time (*from this time forth*; *henceforth*). **3** forwards. **4** out from a starting point (*set forth*). □ **and so forth** and so on; and the like.

forthcoming *adj.* **1 a** about or likely to appear or become available. **b** approaching. **2** produced when wanted (*no reply was forthcoming*). **3** (of a person) informative, responsive. □ **forthcomingness** *n.*

forthright ● *adj.* **1** direct and outspoken; straightforward. **2** decisive, unhesitating. ● *adv.* /fɔrθ'rəit/ in a direct manner; bluntly. □ **forthrightly** *adv.* **forthrightness** *n.*

forthwith /fɔrθ'wɪθ, -'wɪð/ *adv.* immediately.

fortification *n.* **1** the act or an instance of fortifying; the process of being fortified. **2** *Military* **a** the art or science of fortifying. **b** (usu. in *pl.*) defensive works fortifying a position.

fortify *v.tr.* (**-ies**, **-ied**) **1** provide or equip with defensive works so as to strengthen against attack. **2** strengthen or invigorate mentally or morally; encourage. **3** strengthen the structure of. **4** strengthen (wine) with alcohol. **5** increase the nutritive value of (food, esp. with vitamins).

fortissimo /fɔr'tɪsɪ,mo:/ *Music* ● *adj.* performed very loudly. ● *adv.* very loudly.

fortitude *n.* moral strength or courage, esp. in the endurance of pain or adversity.

fortnight *n.* a period of two weeks. □ **fortnightly** esp. *Brit. adj., adv. & n.* (*pl.* **-ies**).

Fortran /'fɔrtræn/ *n.* (also **FORTRAN**) *Computing* a high-level programming language used esp. for scientific calculations.

fortress *n.* **1** a military stronghold, esp. a strongly fortified town fit for a large garrison. **2** any place or source of refuge or protection.

fortuitous /fɔr'tu:ɪtəs, -'tju:-/ *adj.* due to or characterized by chance, esp. lucky chance. □ **fortuitously** *adv.* **fortuitousness** *n.*

fortunate *adj.* **1** favoured by fortune; lucky, prosperous. **2** auspicious, favourable.

fortunately *adv.* **1** luckily, successfully. **2** (qualifying a whole sentence) it is fortunate that.

fortune *n.* **1 a** chance or luck as a force in human affairs. **b** a person's destiny or future; fate. **2** (**Fortune**) this force personified, often as a deity. **3** (in *sing.* or *pl.*) luck (esp. favourable) that befalls a person or enterprise. **4** good luck. **5** prosperity; a prosperous condition. **6** great wealth; a huge sum of money. □ **make a** (or **one's**) **fortune** acquire wealth or prosperity. **tell a person's fortune** make predictions about a person's future.

fortune cookie *n. N Amer.* a small cookie containing a slip of paper printed with a prediction, joke, etc., served esp. in Chinese restaurants.

fortune teller *n.* a person who claims to predict future events in a person's life. □ **fortune-telling** *n.*

forty ● *n.* (*pl.* **-ies**) **1** the product of four and ten. **2** a symbol for this (40, xl, XL). **3** (in *pl.*) the numbers from 40 to 49, esp. the years of a century or of a person's life. ● *adj.* that amount to forty. □ **forty-first, -second**, etc. the ordinal numbers between fortieth and fiftieth. **forty-one, -two**, etc. the cardinal numbers between forty and fifty. □ **fortieth** *adj., adv. & n.* **fortyfold** *adj. & adv.* **fortyish** *adj.*

forty-five *n.* **1** (also **45**) a small phonograph record played at 45 rpm. **2** (also **.45**) *N Amer.* a .45 calibre revolver. **3** *N Amer.* (*Maritimes & New England*) a card game for two to six players in which the player or side first reaching forty-five points wins.

forty-ninth parallel *n.* the parallel at 49° north, esp. as forming the boundary between Canada and the US west of Lake of the Woods.

forty-ouncer *n.* (also *Cdn slang* **forty-pounder**) a forty-ounce bottle of liquor.

forum *n.* **1** a place of or meeting for public discussion. **2** a periodical, television program, etc. giving an opportunity for discussion. **3** a court or tribunal.

forward ● *adj.* **1** directed or moving towards a point in advance, onward, towards the front (*a forward movement*). **2 a** situated in front; near or at the front. **b** *Naut.* belonging to the forepart of a ship. **3** bold in manner; presumptuous. **4** *Business* **a** relating to future produce, delivery, etc. (*forward contract*). **b** prospective; advanced; with a view to the future (*forward planning*). **5** advanced; progressing towards or approaching maturity or completion. ● *n.* an attacking player positioned near the front of a team in hockey, soccer, etc. ● *adv.* **1 a** to the front; into prominence (*come forward*). **b** into a position for consideration or discussion (*bring forward a proposal*). **2** in advance; ahead (*sent them forward*). **3** onward so as to make progress (*not getting any further forward*). **4** towards the future; continuously onward (*from this time forward*). **5** (also **forwards**) **a** towards the front in the direction one is facing. **b** in the normal direction of motion or of traversal. **c** with continuous forward motion (*backwards and forwards*). **6** *Naut. & Aviation* in, near, or towards the bow or nose. ● *v.tr.* **1** send (a letter etc.) on to a further destination. **2** help to advance; promote. **3** advance (a videotape etc.) forward. □ **forwarder** *n.* **forwardly** *adv.* **forwardness** *n.* (esp. in sense 3 of *adj.*).

forward-looking *adj.* (also **forward-thinking**) progressive; favouring change.

forward pass *n.* **1** *Football* a pass thrown from behind the line of scrimmage towards the opponent's goal. **2** *Hockey etc.* a pass towards the opponent's goal. □ **forward passing** *n.*

forwent *past of* FORGO.

fossil ● *n.* **1** the remains or impression of a prehistoric plant or animal, usu. petrified while embedded in rock, amber, etc. **2** *informal* an antiquated or unchanging person or thing. ● *adj.* **1** of or like a fossil. **2** out of date. □ **fossilize** *v.tr. & intr.* **fossilization** *n.*

fossil fuel *n.* a natural fuel such as coal or gas formed in the geological past from the remains of living organisms.

foster ● *v.tr.* **1 a** promote the growth or development of. **b** encourage or harbour (a feeling). **2** bring up (a child that is not one's own by birth). **3** cherish; have affectionate regard for (an idea, scheme, etc.). ● *adj.* **1** having a family connection by fostering and not by birth (*foster child*). **2** involving or concerned with fostering a child (*foster home*).

fought *past and past part.* of FIGHT.

foul ● *adj.* **1** offensive to the senses; loathsome, stinking. **2** dirty, soiled, filthy. **3 a** revolting, disgusting. **b** angry or disagreeable (*in a foul mood*). **4 a** containing or charged with noxious matter (*foul air*). **b** clogged, choked. **5** morally offensive (*foul language*). **6 a** unfair; against the rules of a game etc. (*by fair means or foul*). **b** *Baseball* of or relating to a foul ball or foul line. **7** (of the weather) wet, rough, stormy. ● *n.* **1** *Sport* a violation of the rules. **2** a collision or entanglement, esp. in riding, rowing, or running. ● *adv.* **1** unfairly; contrary to the rules. **2** *Baseball* outside the foul lines (*hit the ball foul*). ● *v.* **1** *tr. & intr.* make or become foul or dirty. **2** *tr.* make dirty with excrement. **3** *Baseball* **a** *tr.* hit (a pitched ball) foul. **b** *intr.* hit a foul ball. **4** *Sport* **a** *tr.* commit a foul against (a player). **b** *intr.* commit a foul. **5 a** *tr.* (often foll. by *up*) cause (an anchor, cable, etc.) to become entangled or muddled. **b** *intr.* become entangled. **6** *tr. & intr.* be or become jammed or clogged. **7** *tr.* (usu. foll. by *up*) *informal* spoil or bungle. **8** *tr.* run foul of; collide with. □ **cry foul** protest. **foul off** hit (a pitch or the ball) foul. **foul one's** (**own**) **nest 1** bring discredit on one's family etc. by one's actions. **2** speak disparagingly of one's family etc. **foul out 1** *Baseball* (of a batter) be made out by hitting a foul ball which is caught on the fly by a member of the opposing team. **2** *Basketball* be put out of the game for exceeding the permitted number of fouls. □ **foulness** *n.*

foul ball *n.* *Baseball* a ball struck so that it falls outside the foul lines.

foul line *n.* **1** *Baseball* either of the straight lines extending from home plate and marking the limit of the playing area within which a ball is deemed to be fair. **2** *Basketball* a line on the court 15 ft. (4.6 m) from the backboard, from which free throws are made.

foul-mouthed *adj.* using obscene and offensive language.

foul play *n.* **1** *Sport* unfair play. **2** treacherous or violent activity, esp. murder.

foul-up *n.* a muddled or bungled situation.

found¹ *past and past part.* of FIND.

found² *v.* **1** *tr.* **a** establish (esp. with an endowment). **b** originate or initiate (an institution, society, etc.). **2** *tr.* be the original builder or begin the building of (a town etc.). **3** *tr.* lay the base of (a building etc.). **4** (foll. by *on*, *upon*) **a** *tr.* construct or base (a story, theory, rule, etc.) according to a specified principle or ground. **b** *intr.* have a basis in.

found³ *v.tr.* **1** melt and mould (metal or glass). **2** make by founding. □ **founder** *n.*

foundation *n.* **1 a** the solid ground or base, natural or artificial, on which a building rests. **b** (usu. in *pl.*) the lowest load-bearing part of a building, usu. below ground level. **2** a body or ground on which other parts are overlaid. **3** a basis or underlying principle; groundwork. **4 a** the act or an instance of establishing or constituting (esp. an endowed institution) on a permanent basis. **b** an institution, e.g. a monastery, college, or hospital, maintained by an endowment. **c** an organization with a permanent fund devoted to financing research, the arts, and other charitable causes. **d** a fund devoted to the permanent maintenance of an institution or organization; an endowment. **5** (in full **foundation garment**) a woman's supporting undergarment, e.g. a bra, girdle, etc. **6** a cosmetic in liquid or powdered form applied to the face as a base for other makeup and to even out skin tone. □ **foundational** *adj.*

foundation stone *n.* **1** a stone laid with ceremony to celebrate the founding of a building. **2** the main ground or basis of something.

founder¹ *n.* a person who founds an institution etc.

founder² *v.intr.* **1** (of a ship) fill with water and sink. **2** (of a plan etc.) fail. **3** (of earth, a building, etc.) fall down or in, give way. **4** (of a horse or its rider) fall to the ground, fall from lameness, stick fast in mud etc.

found-in *n.* *Cdn* a person arrested for being discovered in a bawdy house, an illegal bar, etc.

founding father *n.* (also **Founding Father**) a person associated with the founding of something.

foundling *n.* an abandoned infant of unknown parentage.

found object *n.* an object found or picked up at random and presented as a rarity or a work of art.

foundry *n.* (*pl.* **-ies**) **1** a factory where metal is melted and moulded into various objects. **2** the art or business of casting metal.

fount *n.* a spring or fountain (*a fount of knowledge*).

fountain *n.* **1 a** a jet or jets of water made to spout for ornamental purposes. **b** a structure built for such a jet or jets to rise and fall in. **2** a structure for the public supply of drinking water. **3** a natural spring of water. **4** a source (in physical or abstract senses). **5** = SODA FOUNTAIN. **6** a reservoir for oil, ink, etc.

fountainhead *n.* **1** the headwaters or source of a stream etc. **2** an original source, esp. of information.

fountain of youth *n.* a legendary spring said to restore to health and youth anyone who drank of it.

fountain pen *n.* a pen with a reservoir or cartridge holding ink.

four ● *n.* **1** one more than three. **2** a symbol for this (4, iv, IV). **3** a size etc. denoted by four. **4** a set or team of four persons or things. **5** four o'clock. **6** a card with four pips. ● *adj.* that amount to four. □ **on all fours** on hands and knees.

four-and-a-half *n.* *Cdn* (*Que.*) an apartment having two bedrooms, kitchen, living room, and bath.

four-by-four *n.* (also **4 × 4**) **1** an automotive vehicle, esp. a truck, with four-wheel drive. **2** a piece of wood measuring four inches by four in cross-section.

four-colour *adj.* (of a printing or photographic process) involving the principle in which three primary colours and black are used in combination to produce almost any other colour.

four-eyes *n.* *slang* a person wearing glasses. □ **four-eyed** *adj.*

fourfold *adj. & adv.* **1** four times as much or as many. **2** consisting of four parts. **3** amounting to four.

4-H club *n.* *N Amer.* a club for the instruction of young people in citizenry and agriculture.

four-leaf clover *n.* (also **four-leaved clover**) a clover leaf with four leaflets, thought to bring good luck.

four-letter word *n.* any of several short words referring to sexual or excretory functions, regarded as coarse or offensive.

four on the floor *n. N Amer. slang* a four-speed manual gearshift mounted on the floor of an automobile etc.

fourplex *n. N Amer.* a residential building divided into four self-contained apartments.

four-poster *n.* (in full **four-poster bed**) a bed with a post at each corner supporting a canopy.

foursome *n.* **1** a group of four persons. **2** a golf match between two pairs with partners playing the same ball.

four-square *adj.* **1** solidly based. **2** steady, resolute; forthright. **3** square-shaped.

four-star *adj.* (of a hotel, restaurant, etc.) given four stars in a grading in which this denotes the highest standard or the next standard to the highest.

four-stroke ● *attrib.adj.* **1** (of an internal combustion engine) having a cycle of four strokes (intake, compression, combustion, and exhaust). **2** (of a vehicle) having a four-stroke engine. ● *n.* a four-stroke engine or vehicle.

fourteen ● *n.* **1** one more than thirteen. **2** a symbol for this (14, xiv, XIV). **3** a size etc. denoted by fourteen. **4** a set of fourteen persons or things. ● *adj.* that amount to fourteen. □ **fourteenth** *adj., adv. & n.*

fourth ● *n.* **1** the position in a sequence corresponding to that of the number 4 in the sequence 1–4. **2** something occupying this position. **3** the fourth person etc. in a race or competition. **4** each of four equal parts of a thing; a quarter. **5** the fourth (and often highest) in a sequence of gears. **6 a** an interval or chord spanning four consecutive notes in the diatonic scale, e.g. C to F. **b** a note separated from another by this interval. **7** *Baseball* the fourth inning. ● *adj.* that is the fourth. ● *adv.* in the fourth place; fourthly. □ **fourthly** *adv.*

fourth estate *n.* (also **Fourth Estate**) the press; journalists or the profession of journalism.

fourth-generation *adj.* (of a computer) distinguished by large-scale integrated-circuit technology and very large rapid-access memory and belonging essentially to the post-1970 period.

Fourth World *n.* the poorest nations in the least developed parts of the world, esp. in Africa and Asia.

four-wheel *adj.* **1** having four wheels. **2** acting on all four wheels of a vehicle.

four-wheel drive *n.* a system in a motor vehicle which supplies power to all wheels in order to improve traction, cornering, etc.

four-wheeler *n. slang* **1** = ALL-TERRAIN VEHICLE 2. **2** = FOUR-BY-FOUR 1.

fowl (*pl.* same or **fowls**) ● *n.* **1** any domestic cock or hen of various birds of the order Galliformes, kept for eggs and flesh. **2** the flesh of birds, esp. a domestic cock or hen, as food. **3** (in *comb.* or *collect.*) a bird (*guineafowl*; *wildfowl*). ● *v.intr.* catch or hunt wildfowl. □ **fowler** *n.* **fowling** *n.*

fowl supper *n.* (also **fall supper**) *Cdn* a fundraising dinner at which turkey or other fowl is served, held in the autumn by a church or community group.

fox ● *n.* **1 a** any of various wild flesh-eating mammals of the dog family, esp. of the genus *Vulpes*, with a sharp snout, bushy tail, and usu. red or grey fur. **b** the fur of a fox. **2** a cunning or sly person. **3** *N Amer. slang* an attractive young woman. ● *v.tr.* deceive, baffle, trick. □ **foxlike** *adj.*

foxglove *n.* any tall plant of the genus *Digitalis*, with erect spikes of purple or white flowers like the fingers of a glove.

fox grape *n.* a wild grape, *Vitis labrusca*, of the northeastern US and southern Ontario.

foxhole *n. Military* a hole in the ground used as a shelter against enemy fire.

foxhound *n.* a kind of hound bred and trained to hunt foxes.

fox hunt ● *n.* **1** the hunting of foxes with hounds. **2** a particular group of people engaged in this. ● *v.intr.* engage in a fox hunt. □ **fox hunter** *n.* **fox hunting** *n. & adj.*

fox terrier *n.* a short-haired breed of terrier originally used for unearthing foxes.

foxtrot ● *n.* **1** a ballroom dance characterized by varied combinations of slow and quick steps. **2** the music for this. ● *v.intr.* (**foxtrotted**, **foxtrotting**) perform this dance.

foxy *adj.* (**-ier, -iest**) **1** of or like a fox. **2** sly or cunning. **3** reddish brown. **4** *N Amer. slang* (of a woman) sexually attractive. □ **foxily** *adv.* **foxiness** *n.*

foyer /ˈfɔɪeɪ/ *n.* an entrance hall or other large area in a hotel, theatre, apartment building, etc.

FP *abbr.* freezing point.

fp *abbr.* forte-piano.

fps *abbr.* (also **f.p.s.**) feet per second.

FR *abbr. Cdn* Forest Region.

Fr *symbol* francium.

Fr. *abbr.* (also **Fr**) **1** Father. **2** French.

fr. *abbr.* **1** franc(s). **2** from. **3** fragment.

fracas /ˈfrækɑː, ˈfrækɒ, ˈfreɪkɑː/ *n.* a noisy disturbance or quarrel.

fractal /ˈfræktəl/ ● *n.* a curve or geometrical figure, each part of which has the same statistical character as the whole. ● *adj.* of or relating to a fractal.

fraction *n.* **1** a numerical quantity that is not a whole number (e.g. $\frac{1}{2}$, 0.5). **2** a small, esp. very small, part, piece, or amount. **3** a part or subdivision of a whole (*a fraction of the population*). **4** a portion of a mixture separated by distillation etc.

fractional *adj.* **1** of or relating to or being a fraction. **2** very slight; incomplete. **3** *Chem.* relating to the separation of parts of a mixture by making use of their different physical properties (*fractional distillation*). □ **fractionalization** *n.* **fractionalize** *v.tr.* **fractionally** *adv.* (esp. in sense 2).

fractionate *v.tr.* **1** break up into parts. **2** separate (a mixture) by fractional distillation etc. □ **fractionation** *n.*

fractious /ˈfrækʃəs/ *adj.* **1** irritable, bad-tempered. **2** unruly. □ **fractiously** *adv.* **fractiousness** *n.*

fracture ● *n.* **1 a** breakage or breaking, esp. of a bone or cartilage. **b** the result of breaking; a crack or split. **2** the surface appearance of a freshly broken rock or mineral. ● *v.intr. & tr.* **1** undergo or cause to undergo a fracture. **2** break or cause to break.

fragile *adj.* **1** easily broken; weak. **2** of delicate frame or constitution; not strong. **3** vulnerable, easily destroyed (*fragile ecosystem*). □ **fragility** *n.*

fragment ● *n.* **1** a part broken off; a detached piece. **2** an isolated or incomplete part. **3** the remains of an otherwise lost or destroyed whole, esp. the extant remains or unfinished portion of a book or work of art. **4** a scrap; a leftover piece. ● *v.tr. & intr.* break or separate into fragments.

fragmentary *adj.* **1** consisting of fragments. **2** disconnected. **3** *Geol.* composed of fragments of previously existing rocks.

fragmentation *n.* **1** the process or an instance of breaking into fragments. **2** (*attrib.*) designating a weapon that is designed to break up into small rapidly-moving fragments (*fragmentation grenade*).

fragrance *n.* **1** sweetness of smell. **2** a sweet scent. **3** something scented, esp. a perfume, eau de cologne, etc. □ **fragranced** *adj.*

fragrant *adj.* pleasant smelling. □ **fragrantly** *adv.*

frail *adj.* **1** (of a person) physically weak or delicate. **2** easily damaged or broken. **3** morally weak; unable to resist temptation. **4** transient, insubstantial. □ **frailly** *adv.* **frailness** *n.*

frailty *n.* (*pl.* **-ies**) **1** the condition of being frail. **2** liability to err or yield to temptation. **3** a fault, weakness, or foible.

frame ● *n.* **1** a case or border enclosing a picture, window, etc. **2** the basic rigid supporting structure of anything, e.g. of a building or vehicle. **3** (in *pl.*) a structure of metal, plastic, etc. holding the lenses of a pair of eyeglasses. **4** a human or animal body, esp. with reference to its size or structure (*her frame shook with laughter*). **5** a framed work or structure (*the frame of heaven*). **6 a** an established order, plan, or system (*the frame of society*). **b** construction, constitution, build. **7** a temporary state (esp. in **frame of mind**). **8 a** a single complete image or picture on a cinema film or transmitted in a series of lines by television. **b** one of the separate drawings of a comic strip. **9** *Sport informal* an inning, period, etc. **10** *Bowling* **a** any of the ten divisions of a bowling game. **b** one of the compartments on a scorecard where the score from a single frame is recorded. **11 a** esp. *Brit.* = RACK¹ 4. **b** a round of play in pool etc. **12** a boxlike structure of glass etc. for protecting plants. **13** *N Amer. slang* = FRAME-UP. ● *v.tr.* **1 a** set in or provide with a frame. **b** serve as a frame for. **2** construct by a combination of parts or in accordance with a design or plan. **3** formulate or devise the essentials of (a complex thing, idea, theory, etc.). **4** (foll. by *to, into*) adapt or fit. **5** *informal* concoct a false charge or evidence against; devise a plot with regard to. **6** articulate (words). ● *adj.* (of a building) made of a wooden frame covered with boards, siding, etc. (*frame house*). □ **framer** *n.*

frame of reference *n.* a set of standards or principles governing behaviour, thought, etc.

frame-up *n.* *informal* a conspiracy, esp. to make an innocent person appear guilty.

framework *n.* **1** an essential supporting structure. **2** a basic system.

framing *n.* **1** a framework; a system of frames. **2** the act or process of framing or constructing something.

franc *n.* the chief monetary unit of France, Belgium, Switzerland, and several other countries.

franchise ● *n.* **1** the right to vote in elections. **2 a** authorization granted to an individual or group by a company to sell its goods or services. **b** the store, restaurant, etc., granted such authorization. **3 a** authorization granted to an individual or group by a professional sports league to own and operate a team as a member of the league. **b** the team granted such authorization. **4** a right or privilege granted to a person or corporation. ● *v.tr.* grant a franchise to. □ **franchisee** *n.* **franchisor** *n.* (also **franchiser**).

Franciscan /fræn'sɪskən/ ● *n.* a monk or nun of an order founded in 1209 by St. Francis of Assisi (*c.* 1181–1226). ● *adj.* of St. Francis or his order.

francium /'frænsiəm/ *n.* a radioactive metallic element occurring naturally in uranium and thorium ores.

francization *n.* (also **francisation**) *Cdn* (*Que.*) the establishment or adoption of French as the official or working language of business, education, etc.

francization certificate *n.* *Cdn* (*Que.*) a certificate stating that a business etc. has adopted a program of francization.

francize /'frænsaiz/ *v.tr.* (also **francise**) *Cdn* (*Que.*) cause (a person, business, etc.) to adopt French as an official or working language.

Franco /'fræŋko:/ *adj. & n.* (*pl.* **-os**) *Cdn* francophone.

Franco- *comb. form* **1** French; French and (*Franco-German*). **2** regarding France, the French, or French-speakers (*francophile*).

Franco-Albertan *Cdn* ● *n.* a francophone Albertan. ● *adj.* of or relating to Franco-Albertans.

Franco-Canadian *Cdn* ● *n.* = FRENCH CANADIAN *n.* ● *n.* **1** = FRENCH CANADIAN *adj.* **2** of or relating to Canada and France.

Franco-Columbian *Cdn* ● *n.* a francophone British Columbian. ● *adj.* of or relating to Franco-Columbians.

Franco-Manitoban *Cdn* ● *n.* a francophone Manitoban. ● *adj.* of or relating to Franco-Manitobans.

Franco-Ontarian *Cdn* ● *n.* a francophone Ontarian. ● *adj.* of or relating to Franco-Ontarians.

francophile *n.* a person who admires French or francophone culture. □ **francophilia** *n.*

francophone esp. *Cdn* ● *n.* a French-speaking person. ● *adj.* French-speaking.

Francophonie /frɑ̃kəfo:'ni:, fræŋkə-/ *n.* *Cdn* **1** (also **la Francophonie**, **the Francophonie**) a loosely united group of nations in which French is a first, official, or culturally significant language. **2** (also **francophonie**) francophones within Canada.

franglais /'frɑ̃glei/ *n.* often *derogatory* **1** those elements of the French language that have been recently borrowed from English. **2** broken French as spoken by anglophones.

Frank *n.* a member of the Germanic nation or coalition that conquered Gaul in the 6th c.

frank¹ ● *adj.* **1** candid, outspoken (*a frank opinion*). **2** undisguised, avowed (*frank admiration*). **3** ingenuous, open (*a frank face*). ● *v.tr.* stamp (a letter) with an official mark (esp. other than a normal postage stamp) to record the payment of postage. ● *n.* **1 a** franking signature or mark. **2** a franked cover. □ **frankable** *adj.* **franker** *n.* **frankness** *n.*

frank² *n.* *N Amer.* = FRANKFURTER.

Frankenstein /'fræŋkən,stain/ *n.* a thing that becomes terrifying to its maker. □ **Frankensteinian** *adj.*

frankfurter *n.* a seasoned smoked sausage made of beef and pork.

frankincense *n.* an aromatic gum resin obtained from trees of the genus *Boswellia*, used as incense.

Frankish ● *adj.* of or relating to the Franks or their language. ● *n.* any of the West Germanic dialects spoken by the Franks.

Franklin stove *n.* *N Amer.* a cast iron wood stove of the same general shape as a fireplace, usu. having doors on the front.

frankly *adv.* **1** in a frank manner. **2** (qualifying a whole sentence) to be frank.

frankum /'fræŋkəm/ *n.* *Cdn* (*Nfld*) the hardened resin of a spruce tree, often used as chewing gum.

Fransaskois /frɑ̃sæs'kwɒ/ *n.* *Cdn* a francophone resident of Saskatchewan.

frantic *adj.* **1** wildly excited; frenzied. **2** characterized by great hurry or anxiety; desperate. **3** *informal* extreme; very great. □ **frantically** *adv.*

frappé /'fræpei/ ● *adj.* (esp. of wine) iced, cooled. ● *n.* **1** an iced drink. **2** a soft sherbet.

frat *n. N Amer. informal* a fraternity.

fraternal *adj.* **1** of a brother or brothers. **2** suitable to a brother; brotherly. **3** (of twins) developed from separate ova and not necessarily closely similar. **4** *N Amer.* of or concerning a fraternity or other male society or lodge. □ **fraternalism** *n.* **fraternally** *adv.*

fraternal society *n.* an association, usu. of men, devoted to philanthropic, religious, or social activities.

fraternity *n.* (*pl.* **-ies**) **1** *N Amer.* a male students' society in a university or college. **2** a religious brotherhood. **3** a group or company with common interests, or of the same professional class. **4** being fraternal; brotherliness.

fraternize *v.intr.* (often foll. by *with*) **1** associate; make friends; behave as intimates. **2** (of troops) enter into friendly relations with enemy troops or the inhabitants of an occupied country. □ **fraternization** *n.*

frat house *n. N Amer.* a house where members of a fraternity live or hold meetings or parties etc.

fratricide /'frætrɪˌsaid/ *n.* **1** the killing of one's brother or sister. **2** a person who does this. □ **fratricidal** *adj.*

Frau /frau/ *n.* (*pl.* **Frauen** /'frauən/) (often as a title) a married or widowed German woman.

fraud *n.* **1** the action or an instance of deceiving someone in order to make money or obtain an advantage illegally. **2** a person or thing that is not what it is claimed or expected to be. **3** a dishonest trick or stratagem.

fraudulent *adj.* **1** characterized or achieved by fraud. **2** guilty of fraud; intending to deceive. □ **fraudulence** *n.* **fraudulently** *adv.*

fraught *adj.* **1** (foll. by *with*) filled or attended with (*fraught with danger*). **2** *informal* causing or affected by great anxiety or distress.

Fräulein /'frɔilain/ *n.* (often as a title or form of address) an unmarried (esp. young) German woman.

fray¹ *v.* **1** *tr. & intr.* wear through or become worn, esp. (of fabric, rope, etc.) become unwoven as a result of frequent use or abrasion. **2** *intr.* (of nerves, temper, etc.) become strained; deteriorate.

fray² *n.* **1** fighting. **2** a noisy quarrel or brawl.

frazil /'fræzəl/ *n. N Amer.* (also **frazil ice**) slush consisting of small ice crystals formed in water too turbulent to freeze over.

frazzle *informal* ● *n.* a worn or exhausted state. ● *v.tr.* (usu. as **frazzled** *adj.*) wear out; exhaust, esp. from stress. □ **to a frazzle** completely; absolutely (*worn to a frazzle*).

FRCPC *abbr.* Fellow of the Royal College of Physicians of Canada.

FRCS(C) *abbr.* Fellow of the Royal College of Surgeons (Canada).

freak ● *n.* **1** (also **freak of nature**) a monstrosity; an abnormally developed individual or thing. **2** (often *attrib.*) an abnormal, irregular, or bizarre occurrence (*a freak storm*). **3** *informal* **a** an unconventional person. **b** a person with a specified enthusiasm or interest (*health freak*). **c** a person who undergoes hallucinations; a drug addict. **4** a caprice or vagary. ● *v.* (often foll. by *out*) *informal* **1** *intr. & tr.* become or make very angry, frightened, excited, etc. **2** *intr. & tr.* undergo or cause to undergo hallucinations or a strong emotional experience, esp. from use of narcotics. **3** *intr.* adopt a wildly unconventional lifestyle. □ **freakily** *adv.* **freakiness** *n.* **freaky** *adj.* (**-ier, -iest**).

freaking *adj. N Amer. euphemism* expressing annoyance, or as an intensifier (*going out of his freaking mind*).

freakish *adj.* **1** of or like a freak. **2** bizarre, unconventional. □ **freakishly** *adv.* **freakishness** *n.*

freak-out *n. informal* an act of freaking out; a hallucinatory or strong emotional experience.

freak show *n.* a sideshow at a fair, featuring people or animals with abnormal physical features.

freckle ● *n.* (often in *pl.*) any of a number of light brown spots on the skin, often caused by exposure to the sun. ● *v.* **1** *tr.* (usu. as **freckled** *adj.*) spot with freckles. **2** *intr.* be spotted with freckles. □ **freckly** *adj.*

free ● *adj.* (**freer** /'friːər/; **freest** /'friːəst/) **1** not in bondage to or under the control of another; having personal rights and social and political liberty. **2** (of a nation, or its citizens or institutions) subject neither to foreign domination nor to despotic government; having national and civil liberty (*a free society*). **3 a** unrestricted, unimpeded; not restrained or fixed. **b** at liberty; not confined or imprisoned. **c** released from ties or duties; unimpeded. **d** unrestrained as to action; independent (*set free*). **4** (foll. by *of*, *from*) **a** not subject to; exempt from (*free of tax*). **b** not containing or subject to a specified (usu. undesirable) thing (*free from disease*). **5** (foll. by *to* + infin.) able or permitted to take a specified action (*you are free to choose*). **6** unconstrained (*free gestures*). **7 a** available without charge; costing nothing. **b** not subject to tax, duty, trade restraint, or fees. **8 a** clear of engagements or obligations (*are you free tomorrow?*). **b** not occupied or in use. **c** clear of obstructions. **9** spontaneous, unforced (*free compliments*). **10** open to all comers. **11** lavish, profuse; using or used without restraint (*very free with their money*). **12** frank, unreserved. **13** (of a literary style) not observing the strict laws of form. **14** (of a translation) conveying the broad sense; not literal. **15** forward, familiar, impudent. **16** (of movement) under no force other than that of gravity or inertia (*free flight*). **17** *Physics* **a** not modified by an external force. **b** not bound in an atom or molecule. **18** *Chem.* not combined (*free oxygen*). ● *adv.* **1** in a free manner. **2** without cost or payment. ● *v.tr.* **1** make free; set at liberty. **2** (foll. by *of*, *from*) relieve from (something undesirable). **3** disengage, disentangle. □ **for free** *informal* free of charge, gratis. **free and easy** informal, unceremonious. **free on board** (or **rail**) without charge for delivery to a ship or railway car. **free up** *informal* **1** make available. **2** make less restricted. **it's a free country** *informal* the action proposed is not illegal or forbidden. **make free with 1** take liberties with. **2** use as one's own. □ **freely** *adv.*

-free *comb. form* free of or from (*duty-free; cruelty-free*).

free agent *n.* **1** a person with freedom of action. **2** a professional athlete who is not under contract, and may sell his or her services to any team. □ **free agency** *n.* (in sense 2). **free agentry** *n.* (in sense 2).

free association *n.* **1** *Psych.* a method of investigating a person's unconscious by eliciting spontaneous associations with ideas proposed by the examiner. **2** any process in which one thought, word, image, etc. suggests the next without following a logical or conscious direction. □ **free-associate** *v.intr.*

freebase *slang* ● *n.* cocaine that has been purified by heating with ether, and is taken by inhaling the fumes or smoking the residue. ● *v.* **1** *tr.* purify (cocaine) for smoking or inhaling. **2** *tr. & intr.* smoke or inhale (freebased cocaine). □ **freebaser** *n.*

freebie *informal* ● *n.* a thing provided free of charge. ● *adj.* free; provided without charge (*a freebie trip*).

freeboard *n.* the part of a ship's side between the waterline and the deck.

Free Church *n.* a Church dissenting or seceding from an established church.

freedom *n.* **1** the condition of being free or unrestricted. **2 a** personal or civic liberty. **b** absence of slave status. **3** the power of self-determination; independence of fate or necessity. **4** the state of being free to act. **5** the esp. political right to act, speak, etc. as one pleases without interference (*freedom of speech*; *freedom of religion*). **6** frankness; undue familiarity. **7** (foll. by *from*) the condition of being exempt from or not subject to (a defect, burden, etc.). **8** (foll. by *of*) **a** full or honorary participation in (membership, privileges, etc.). **b** unrestricted use of (facilities etc.). **9** facility or ease in action. **10** boldness of conception.

freedom fighter *n.* a person who takes part in violent resistance to a political system etc.

free enterprise *n.* a system in which private business operates in competition and largely free of governmental control. □ **free enterpriser** *n. N Amer.*

free fall ● *n.* (usu. hyphenated when *attrib.*) **1** movement under the force of gravity only, esp.: **a** the part of a parachute descent before the parachute opens. **b** the movement of a spacecraft in space without thrust from the engines. **2** any state of falling rapidly (*prices were in free fall*). ● *v.intr.* (**free-fall**) move in a free fall.

free-floating *adj.* **1** (of an emotion) having no particular focus or cause (*free-floating anxiety*). **2** (of people) not attached or committed to any particular cause, party, etc. **3** able to move relatively freely.

free-for-all *n.* a fight, competition, or argument in which many people take part, usu. having no rules.

free-form *attrib.adj.* of an irregular shape or structure; not constrained by conventional rules etc.

freehand ● *adj.* (of a drawing or plan etc.) done by hand without special instruments or guides. ● *adv.* in a freehand manner.

free hand *n.* freedom to act at one's own discretion.

free-handed *adj.* generous. □ **free-handedly** *adv.* **free-handedness** *n.*

freehold ● *n.* **1** tenure of land or property in fee simple or fee tail or for life. **2** land or property or an office held by such tenure. ● *adj.* held by or having the status of freehold. □ **freeholder** *n.*

free kick *n. Soccer* a set kick allowed to be taken by one side without interference from the other.

freelance ● *n.* (also **freelancer**) a person, usu. self-employed, offering temporary services, esp. to several businesses etc. for particular assignments (also *attrib.*). ● *v.intr.* act as a freelance. ● *adv.* as a freelance.

free-living *adj.* **1** freely indulging in pleasures, esp. that of eating. **2** *Biol.* living freely and independently; not attached to a substrate.

freeloader *n.* esp. *N Amer. slang* a person who eats or drinks at others' expense; a sponger. □ **freeload** *v.intr.* **freeloading** *n.*

free love *n.* sexual relations according to choice and unrestricted by marriage.

free lunch *n.* **1** a lunch provided free of charge. **2** something provided with no obligation on the part of the receiver. □ **there's no (such thing as a) free lunch** nothing is without cost.

freeman *n.* (*pl.* **-men**) **1** a person who has the freedom of a city, company, etc. **2** a person who is not a slave or serf.

free market *n.* a market in which prices are determined by unrestricted competition.

free marketeer *n.* a supporter or advocate of free market economics.

Freemason *n.* a member of an international frater-

nity for mutual help and fellowship (the *Free and Accepted Masons*), with elaborate secret rituals.

Freemasonry *n.* **1** the system and institutions of the Freemasons. **2** (**freemasonry**) instinctive sympathy or understanding.

freer *comparative of* FREE.

free radical *n.* an uncharged atom or group of atoms with one or more unpaired electrons.

free-range *adj.* **1** (of hens etc.) kept in natural conditions with freedom of movement. **2** (of eggs) produced by such birds.

free ride *n.* something obtained at no cost or with no effort. □ **free rider** *n.*

free safety *n. Football* a secondary defensive player who has no assigned position at the snap of the ball but may roam the field behind the line of scrimmage.

freesia /ˈfriːʒə, ˈfriːzɪə/ *n.* an bulbous plant native to Africa, having fragrant coloured flowers.

free skate *n. Figure Skating* (in full **free skating program**) a part of a figure skating competition consisting of a program skated to music chosen by the skater, with the number and type of jumps and other elements chosen freely by the skater.

free speech *n.* the right to express opinions freely.

free spirit *n.* an independent or uninhibited person. □ **free-spirited** *adj.*

freest *superlative of* FREE.

free-standing *adj.* **1** not supported by another structure. **2** autonomous (*a free-standing clinic*).

freestone *n.* a peach or other fruit having a stone which is loose when the fruit is ripe.

freestyle ● *adj.* (of a race or contest) in which all styles are allowed, esp.: **1** *Swimming* in which any stroke may be used. **2** *Wrestling* with few restrictions on the holds permitted. ● *n.* **1** freestyle swimming or wrestling. **2** the front crawl. □ **freestyler** *n.*

free-swimming *adj.* (of an aquatic organism) capable of swimming around freely; not sessile or attached to any object.

freethinker *n.* a person who rejects dogma or authority, esp. in religious belief. □ **freethinking** *n. & adj.*

free throw *n. Sport* **1** an unimpeded throw awarded to a player following a foul etc. **2** *Basketball* such a throw allowing a shot at the basket, taken from behind a marked line.

free trade *n.* international trade free from protectionist tariffs, quotas, export subsidies, and other government intervention.

free trader *n.* **1** an advocate of free trade. **2** *Cdn hist.* a fur trader who was not affiliated with any of the large fur-trading companies.

free verse *n.* irregular or unrhymed verse in which the traditional rules of prosody are disregarded.

free vote *n.* a parliamentary vote in which MPs are not constrained to vote along party lines.

freeware *n.* software available without charge.

freeway *n.* **1** = EXPRESSWAY. **2** a toll-free highway.

free weight *n.* a barbell, dumbbell or other weight not attached to a machine, used for exercise.

freewheel ● *n.* **1** the driving wheel of a bicycle. **2** a device in a vehicle's transmission that automatically disengages the drive shaft whenever it begins to move more quickly than the engine. ● *v.intr.* (usu. **free-wheel**) **1** coast on a bicycle or in a vehicle. **2** move or act without constraint or effort. □ **freewheeler** *n.*

freewheeling *adj.* **1** moving freely. **2** (of a person) unconcerned or unconstrained by rules, responsibilities, or conventions. **3** (of actions, speech, etc.) irresponsible.

free will ● *n.* **1** the power of acting without the constraint of necessity or fate. **2** the ability to act at one's own discretion (*I did it of my own free will*). ● *adj.* (usu. **free-will**) (of a donation etc.) voluntary.

free world *n.* the non-Communist countries.

freeze ● *v.* (*past* **froze**; *past part.* **frozen**) **1** *tr. & intr.* **a** turn or be turned into ice or another solid by cold. **b** (often foll. by *over*, *up*) make or become rigid or solid as a result of the cold. **2** *intr.* be or feel very cold. **3** *tr. & intr.* cover or become covered with ice. **4** *intr.* (foll. by *to*, *together*) adhere or be fastened by frost (*the curtains froze to the window*). **5** *tr. & intr.* be or become obstructed or closed by the formation of ice (*the pipes froze*). **6** *tr.* preserve (food) by refrigeration below freezing point. **7** *tr. & intr.* **a** make or become motionless or powerless through fear, surprise, etc., or when ordered to do so. **b** react or cause to react with sudden aloofness or detachment. **8** *tr.* stiffen or harden, injure or kill, by chilling (*frozen to death*). **9** *tr. informal* make (part of the body) insensitive to pain, esp. by injection of a local anaesthetic. **10** *tr.* make (credits, assets, etc.) temporarily or permanently unrealizable. **11** *tr.* fix or stabilize (prices, wages, etc.) at a certain level. **12** *tr.* prohibit the manufacture, sale, use, or development of (a nuclear weapon, etc). **13** *tr.* arrest (an action) at a certain stage of development. **14** *tr.* = FREEZE-FRAME *v.* **15** *intr. Computing* (of a computer screen) cease to respond to input from the keyboard or mouse. **16** *intr. Curling* draw a rock up against a stationary rock without causing the second rock to move. **17** *tr. Sport* keep possession of (the ball, puck, etc.) for an extended period of time, esp. without attempting to score. ● *n.* **1** a state of frost; a period or the coming of frost or very cold weather. **2** the fixing or stabilization of prices, wages, etc. **3** = FREEZE-FRAME *n.* **4** a decision by one or more nations to stop or limit the manufacture or development of (esp. nuclear) weapons. □ **freeze out** *N Amer. informal* exclude from business, society, etc. by competition or boycott etc. **freeze up** obstruct or be obstructed by the formation of ice.

freeze-dry *v.tr.* (**-dries**, **-dried**) preserve (esp. food) by freezing it and then drying it by the sublimation of ice in a vacuum.

freeze-frame ● *n.* the facility of stopping a film or videotape in order to view a motionless image. ● *v.tr.* use freeze-frame on (an image, recording, etc.).

freezer *n.* a refrigerated cabinet or room for preserving food at very low temperatures.

freezer bag *n.* a bag of heavy plastic used for freezing foods etc.

freeze-up *n.* esp. *Cdn* the freezing up of a river, lake, etc., esp. in the fall.

freezing *adj.* **1** (of temperatures) at or near the freezing point. **2** *informal* (also **freezing cold**) very cold.

freezing point *n.* **1** the temperature at which a liquid freezes. **2** the freezing point of water, 0°C (32°F) (*temperatures will drop below the freezing point*).

freezing rain *n.* rain composed of drops which freeze on hitting the ground or other solid objects.

freight ● *n.* **1** goods transported by water, air, or land. **2** the transportation of such goods. **3** a charge for transportation of goods. **4** a freight train. **5** the hire of a ship or aircraft for transporting goods. **6** a load or burden. ● *v.tr.* **1** transport (goods) as freight. **2** load with freight. **3** hire or let out (a ship) to carry goods and passengers. **4** burden (*freighted with sentiment*).

freight canoe *n.* (also **freighter canoe**) *Cdn hist.* a large canoe used for transporting freight.

freight car *n.* a railway car for carrying freight.

freighter *n.* **1** a ship or aircraft designed to carry freight. **2** a person who loads or charters and loads a ship. **3** a person whose business is to receive and forward freight.

freight ton *n.* see TON.

freight train *n.* a train transporting freight.

French ● *adj.* **1** of or relating to France, a country in W Europe, or its people or language. **2** of or relating to French Canada or French Canadians. **3** having the characteristics attributed to the French people. ● *n.* **1** the Romance language of France, also used in Canada, Belgium, Switzerland, and elsewhere. **2** (**the French**) (treated as *pl.*) **a** the people of France. **b** the people of French Canada. ● *v.tr.* cut (green beans, etc.) into long thin strips before cooking. □ **pardon** (or **excuse**) **my French** *informal* excuse my use of coarse language. □ **Frenchness** *n.*

French bread *n.* white, yeast-raised bread, usu. in a long loaf with a crisp crust.

French Canadian ● *n.* a Canadian whose principal language is French. ● *adj.* (**French-Canadian**) of or relating to French-speaking Canadians.

French door *n.* a long glass door, often one of a pair, and usu. opening onto a patio or balcony.

French dressing *n.* **1** *N Amer.* a creamy, sweet salad dressing, usu. orange in colour. **2** a salad dressing of vinegar and oil, usu. seasoned.

French fact *n. Cdn* (prec. by *the*) francophone culture as a distinct component of Canadian society.

French French *Cdn* ● *n.* the French language as spoken in France, esp. as opposed to that spoken in Quebec. ● *adj.* (**French-French**) of or relating to the French people or language of France, esp. as opposed to those of Quebec.

french fry esp. *N Amer.* ● *n.* (*pl.* **-ies**) a deep-fried strip of potato. ● *v.tr.* (usu. **french-fry**) (**-fried**, **-frying**) fry (food) in deep fat. □ **french-fried** *adj.*

French horn *n.* a valved, brass wind instrument with a long, coiled tube and a wide bell.

Frenchie *var. of* FRENCHY *n.*

Frenchify *v.tr.* (**-ies**, **-ied**) (usu. as **Frenchified** *adj.*) make French in form, character, or manners.

French immersion *n. Cdn* a school program in which anglophone students are taught entirely in French.

French kiss *n.* a kiss with one partner's tongue in the other's mouth. □ **French kiss** *v.tr. & intr.*

Frenchman *n.* (*pl.* **-men**) **1** a native or national of France. **2** a francophone.

French regime *n.* the period of French rule in Canadian history, until 1763.

French safe *n.* esp. *Cdn slang* a condom.

French toast *n.* bread dipped in egg and milk and fried.

French window *n.* = FRENCH DOOR.

Frenchwoman *n.* (*pl.* **-women**) **1** a female native or national of France. **2** a francophone woman.

Frenchy usu. *derogatory* ● *n.* (*pl.* **-ies**) a francophone. ● *adj. informal* French (*a Frenchy restaurant*).

frenetic /frə'nɛtɪk/ *adj.* frantic, frenzied. □ **frenetically** *adv.*

frenzied *adj.* **1** enthusiastic; very excited. **2** frantic; uncontrollably agitated. □ **frenziedly** *adv.*

frenzy ● *n.* (*pl.* **-ies**) **1** mental derangement; wild excitement or agitation. **2** delirious fury. **3** frantic or agitated activity. ● *v.tr.* (**-ies**, **-ied**) drive to frenzy; infuriate.

Freon /'fri:ɒn/ *n. proprietary* any of a group of hydrocarbons containing fluorine, chlorine, and sometimes bromine, used in aerosols, refrigerants, etc.

frequency *n.* (*pl.* **-ies**) **1** commonness of occurrence. **2 a** the state of being frequent; frequent occurrence. **b** the process of being repeated at short intervals. **3 a** the rate of recurrence of a vibration, oscillation, cycle, etc.; the number of repetitions in a given time, esp. per second. Abbr.: **f. b** the number of cycles per second of a carrier wave used for radio transmission. **c** a waveband; a channel. **4** *Statistics* the ratio of the number of actual to possible occurrences of an event.

frequency band *n.* *Electronics* = BAND¹ 4a.

frequency distribution *n.* *Statistics* a measurement of the frequency of occurrence of the values of a variable.

frequency modulation *n.* **1** variation of the frequency of a radio or other wave as a means of carrying information such as an audio signal. **2** the system using such modulation. Abbr.: **FM.**

frequency response *n.* the dependence on signal frequency of the output–input ratio of an amplifier etc.

frequent ● *adj.* /ˈfriːkwənt/ **1** occurring often or in close succession. **2** habitual, constant (*a frequent caller*). **3** found near together; numerous. ● *v.tr.* /ˈfriːkwənt, friˈkwent/ attend or go to habitually. □ **frequently** *adv.*

frequent flyer *n.* **1** a person who travels by air frequently. **2** (*attrib.*) designating programs of rewards offered by airlines to their passengers, or the points accumulated for the rewards.

fresco ● *n.* (*pl.* **-oes**) **1** a painting done in watercolour on a wall or ceiling while the plaster is still wet. **2** this method of painting. ● *v.tr.* (**-oed, -oing**) paint in fresco. □ **frescoed** *adj.*

fresh ● *adj.* **1 a** newly made or obtained (*fresh sandwiches*). **b** (of snow) newly fallen. **2 a** other, different; not previously known or used (*start a fresh page*; *fresh ideas*). **b** additional (*fresh supplies*). **3** (foll. by *from*) lately arrived from (a specified place or situation). **4** not stale or musty or faded (*fresh eggs*; *fresh memories*). **5 a** (of food) not preserved by drying, salting, canning, freezing, etc. **b** (of fruit) not cooked. **6** not salty (*fresh water*). **7 a** pure, untainted, refreshing, invigorating (*fresh air*). **b** bright and pure in colour (*a fresh complexion*). **8** (of the wind) brisk. **9** *informal* **a** cheeky, presumptuous. **b** amorously impudent. **10** young and inexperienced. ● *adv.* newly, recently (esp. in *comb.*: *fresh-baked*). ● *n.* the fresh part of the day, year, etc. (*in the fresh of the morning*). □ **fresh out of 1** recently out of (*fresh out of school*). **2** *N Amer.* having just run out of (*fresh out of bread*). □ **freshly** *adv.* **freshness** *n.*

freshen *v.* **1** *tr.* & *intr.* make or become fresh or fresher. **2** *intr.* *N Amer.* (esp. of a cow) begin to yield new milk after giving birth. **3** *tr.* add fresh wine, spirits, etc., to (a drink which has been standing for some time); top up. □ **freshen up 1** wash, change one's clothes, etc. **2** revive, refresh, renew. □ **freshener** *n.*

freshet /ˈfreʃət/ *n.* **1** a rush of fresh water flowing into the sea. **2** the flood of a river from heavy rain or melted snow.

fresh-faced *adj.* having a clear and young-looking complexion.

Freshie *n.* *Cdn proprietary* a fruit-flavoured powder mixed with water and sugar to make a drink.

freshman ● *n.* (*pl.* **-men**) **1** a first-year student at university or college. **2** *N Amer.* a first-year student in high school or junior high school. ● *adj.* **1** of or relating to a freshman. **2** (of a course, etc.) requisite

or suitable for first-year students (*freshman biology*). **3** inexperienced; doing something for the first time (*a freshman MP*). **4** first (*her freshman year with the force*). **5** (of a level of school sports competition) for younger, less experienced players.

freshwater *adj.* of or found in fresh water, not the sea.

fret¹ ● *v.* (**fretted, fretting**) **1** *intr.* **a** feel or express anxiety, worry, unhappiness, etc. **b** (of a baby) express unhappiness, discomfort, etc., esp. by intermittent whimpering. **2** *tr.* cause anxiety, distress, or irritation to. **3** *tr.* **a** destroy gradually by corrosion, erosion, disease, etc. **b** wear or consume by gnawing or rubbing. **4** *tr.* form (a hole, channel, passage, etc.) by corrosion, erosion, etc. **5** *intr.* (of a stream, the sea, etc.) move in agitation or flow or rise in little waves. ● *n.* irritation, vexation, or agitation of mind (*in a fret*).

fret² ● *n.* **1** an ornamental pattern made of continuous combinations of straight lines joined usu. at right angles. **2** = FRETWORK. ● *v.tr.* (**fretted, fretting**) **1** embellish or decorate with a fret. **2** adorn (esp. a ceiling) with carved or embossed work. □ **fretted** *adj.*

fret³ ● *n.* each of a sequence of bars or ridges on the fingerboard of some stringed musical instruments (esp. the guitar) for fixing the positions of the fingers to produce the desired notes. ● *v.tr.* finger a fretted instrument. □ **fretless** *adj.* **fretted** *adj.*

fretboard *n.* a fretted fingerboard on a guitar etc.

fretful *adj.* anxious, distressed, or irritated. □ **fretfully** *adv.* **fretfulness** *n.*

fretwork *n.* **1** ornamental work in wood, esp. of intersecting straight lines. **2 a** the cutting of wood to form ornamental designs. **b** wood so cut.

Freudian /ˈfrɔɪdiən/ ● *adj.* **1** of or relating to Sigmund Freud (1856–1939), his theories, or his methods of psychoanalysis, esp. with reference to the importance of sexuality in human behaviour. **2** (of a person's speech or behaviour) possibly revealing subconscious feelings. ● *n.* a follower of Freud or his methods. □ **Freudianism** *n.*

Freudian slip *n.* an unintentional, esp. spoken error that seems to reveal subconscious feelings.

Fri. *abbr.* Friday.

friable /ˈfraɪəbl/ *adj.* able to be easily crumbled or reduced to powder. □ **friability** *n.*

friar /ˈfraɪr/ *n.* *Christianity* a member of any of certain religious orders of men, esp. the Augustinians, Carmelites, Dominicans, and Franciscans.

fricassee /ˈfrɪkəˌseɪ, -ˈsiː/ ● *n.* a dish of white meat such as chicken, veal, or rabbit, cut up, stewed in stock, and served in a thick white sauce. ● *v.tr.* (**fricassees, fricasseed**) make a fricassee of.

fricot /frɪˈkoː/ *n.* *Cdn* (*Maritimes*) a hearty Acadian stew containing potatoes and meat, fish, or seafood.

friction *n.* **1** the action of one surface or object rubbing against another. **2** the resistance an object or surface encounters in moving over another. **3** a clash of wills, temperaments, or opinions; mutual animosity arising from disagreement. **4** (*attrib.*) of devices that work or transmit motion by frictional contact (*friction clutch*). □ **frictional** *adj.* **frictionless** *adj.*

Friday ● *n.* the sixth day of the week, following Thursday. ● *adv.* **1** on Friday. **2** (**Fridays**) each Friday.

fridge *n.* *informal* = REFRIGERATOR.

fried ● *adj.* **1** cooked by frying. **2** *N Amer.* *informal* thoroughly worn out, exhausted, etc. **3** *slang* intoxicated. ● *v.* *past and past part. of* FRY¹.

friend *n.* **1** a person with whom one enjoys mutual affection and regard (usu. exclusive of sexual or family bonds). **2** a sympathizer (*a friend of order*). **3 a** a person who is an ally, on the same side, or not an enemy (*friend or foe?*). **b** (usu. in *pl.*) a patron or supporter of a cause etc. (*Friends of the Library*). **4** *euphemism* a romantic or sexual partner. **5 a** a person already mentioned or under discussion (*my friend at the next table then left the room*). **b** an acquaintance, associate, or person known casually. **c** used as a polite or ironic form of address. **6** (**Friend**) a member of the Society of Friends. □ **be friends** (**with**) be on good or intimate terms (with). **friends in high places** highly placed people able or ready to use their influence on one's behalf. **make friends** (**with**) get on good or intimate terms (with). **my honourable friend** *Cdn & Brit.* used in the House of Commons to refer to another member of one's own party. **my learned friend** used by a lawyer in court to refer to another lawyer. □ **friendless** *adj.*

friendly *adj.* (**-ier, -iest**) **1** acting as or like a friend. **2 a** (often foll. by *with*) on amicable terms. **b** not hostile or in opposition. **c** not seriously competitive (*a friendly rivalry*). **3** characteristic of friends, showing or prompted by kindness. **4** favourably disposed, inclined to approve or help. **5 a** (of a thing) serviceable, convenient, opportune. **b** = USER-FRIENDLY. **6** (esp. in *comb.*) not harming; helping (*ozone-friendly*). □ **friendliness** *n.*

friendly fire *n.* *Military* gunfire coming from one's own side, esp. as the cause of accidental injury or death to one's own forces.

friendship *n.* **1 a** the feeling or relationship that friends have. **b** an instance of this (*our friendship is a joy to me*). **2** a friendly disposition felt or shown.

friendship centre *n.* *Cdn* an establishment in a predominantly non-Aboriginal community which provides counselling, social services, etc. to Aboriginal people.

Friesian /ˈfriːʒən, -ziən/ *var. of* FRISIAN.

frieze /friːz/ *n.* **1 a** any broad, horizontal band of sculpted, painted, or other decoration, esp. along a wall near the ceiling. **b** a horizontal paper strip bearing pictures, decorations, etc. for mounting on a wall. **2** (in classical architecture) the part of an entablature between the architrave and the cornice. **3** a horizontal band of sculpture filling this.

frig *coarse slang* • *v.tr. & intr.* (**frigged, frigging**) **1** = FUCK *v.* **2** masturbate. **3** *intr.* (foll. by *about, around*) mess about, fool around. • *n.* = FUCK *n.* 1a, 2.

frigate /ˈfrɪɡət/ *n.* **1** *Cdn & Brit.* a naval escort vessel between a corvette and a destroyer in size. **2** *US* a similar ship between a destroyer and a cruiser in size.

frigging *adj. & adv. coarse slang* = FUCKING.

fright *n.* **1** a sudden or extreme fear. **b** an instance of this (*gave me a fright*). **2** a person or thing looking grotesque or ridiculous. □ **take fright** become frightened.

frighten *v.* **1** *tr.* fill with fright. **2** *tr.* (foll. by *away, off, out of, into*) drive or force by fright (*frightened them into submission*). **3** *intr.* become frightened (*doesn't frighten easily*). □ **frightening** *adj.* **frighteningly** *adv.*

frightful *adj.* **1 a** dreadful, shocking. **b** ugly, hideous. **2** *informal* extremely bad (*a frightful idea*). **3** *informal* very great, extreme. □ **frightfully** *adv.* **frightfulness** *n.*

frigid *adj.* **1** extremely cold. **2** (of a woman) **a** unable to achieve orgasm or experience sexual excitement during intercourse. **b** not showing any sexual desire or responsiveness. **3 a** lacking friendliness or enthusiasm; forced, formal. **b** dull, flat, apathetic, or insipid. **c** (of a thing) chilling, depressing. □ **frigidity** *n.* **frigidly** *adv.*

frill • *n.* **1 a** an ornamental edging of material, having

one side gathered or pleated and the other left loose so as to have a fluted or wavy appearance. **b** a natural fringe of hair, feathers, etc. resembling this on an animal, esp. a bird. **2** an optional or additional extra that is not necessary or essential, but serves for embellishment, decoration, etc. • *v.tr.* **1** decorate with a frill. **2** form into a frill. □ **frilled** *adj.*

frilly • *adj.* (**-ier, -iest**) **1** having a frill or frills. **2** resembling a frill. • *n.* (*pl.* **-ies**) (in *pl.*) *informal* women's underwear. □ **frilliness** *n.*

fringe • *n.* **1 a** an ornamental bordering of threads left loose or formed into tassels or twists. **b** such a bordering made separately. **c** any border or edging. **2** a natural border of hair etc. in an animal or plant. **3** (often *attrib.*) **a** the outer edge or margin of an area etc. (*in the northern fringes of Saskatchewan*). **b** an unofficial, unconventional, and often extreme approach, opinion, etc. (*fringe theatre*). **4** a thing, part, or area of secondary or minor importance. **5** = FRINGE FESTIVAL. • *v.tr.* **1** make into or provide, decorate, or encircle with a fringe. **2** serve as a fringe to. □ **fringed** *adj.* **fringeless** *adj.* **fringy** *adj.*

fringe benefit *n.* an extra benefit given to an employee in addition to salary or wages, e.g. health insurance, a company car, etc.

fringe festival *n.* an arts festival featuring non-mainstream, alternative music, theatre, poetry, etc.

fringetree *n.* a shrub of eastern N America, *Chionanthus virginicus*, with white flowers and plumed seeds.

frippery *n.* (*pl.* **-ies**) **1** unnecessary items of ornament or decoration, e.g. in clothing. **2** empty display or ostentation in speech, writing, etc.

Frisbee *n.* *proprietary* a concave plastic disc for skimming through the air as an outdoor game.

frisée /friːˈzeɪ/ *n.* = ENDIVE 2.

Frisian /ˈfriːʒən, ˈfrɪziən/ • *adj.* of Friesland, a province of the Netherlands, the Frisians, or the Frisian language. • *n.* **1** a native or inhabitant of Friesland. **2** the W Germanic language of Friesland.

frisk • *v.* **1** *tr.* search (a person) by feeling quickly over the body in search of a concealed weapon etc. **2** *intr.* leap, skip, or frolic playfully. • *n.* **1** the act of frisking a person. **2** a playful leap or skip.

frisky *adj.* (**-ier, -iest**) **1** lively, playful. **2** *informal* amorous, sexually excited. □ **friskily** *adv.* **friskiness** *n.*

frisson /ˈfriːsɒn, -sɔ̃/ *n.* an emotional thrill, esp. a shiver of excitement.

frites /friːt/ *n.pl.* french fries, esp. thinly sliced ones.

fritillary /frɪˈtɪləri, ˈfrɪtɪl,eri/ *n.* (*pl.* **-ies**) **1** any plant of the genus *Fritillaria*, having pendent bell-like flowers. **2** any of various butterflies having red-brown wings checkered with black.

frittata /frɪˈtætə/ *n.* a type of omelette in which chopped vegetables, meat, etc. are incorporated into the beaten eggs before they are fried.

fritter[1] *v.tr.* (usu. foll. by *away*) waste (money, time, energy, etc.) triflingly, indiscriminately, etc.

fritter[2] *n.* a piece of fruit, meat, etc., coated in batter and deep-fried (*apple fritter*).

fritz *n.* □ **on the fritz** *N Amer. slang* broken, defective.

frivolous *adj.* **1 a** (of activities) silly or wasteful. **b** (of a claim, charge, etc.) having no reasonable grounds. **2** foolish, lighthearted, not sensible or serious. □ **frivolity** *n.* (*pl.* **-ies**). **frivolously** *adv.*

frizz • *v.* **1** *tr.* form (hair) into tight curls. **2** *intr.* (of hair etc.) curl tightly, esp. so as to be difficult to style. • *n.* frizzy hair. □ **frizzy** *adj.* (**-ier, -iest**).

frizzle[1] *v.intr. & tr.* **1** fry, toast, or grill, with a sputtering noise. **2** (often foll. by *up*) burn or shrivel.

frizzle[2] ● *v.* **1** *tr.* form (hair) into tight curls. **2** *intr.* (of hair etc.) curl tightly. ● *n.* frizzled hair.

frock ● *n.* **1** *Brit.* a woman's or girl's dress. **2** a monk's or priest's long gown with loose sleeves. **3** priestly office. ● *v.tr.* invest with priestly office.

frock coat *n.* a usu. double-breasted coat with skirts extending almost to the knees and not cut away, but of the same length in front as behind.

frog[1] *n.* **1** any of various small amphibians of the order Anura, having a tailless smooth-skinned body with legs developed for jumping, esp. (as distinct from toads) any of those which have a smooth skin and leap rather than walk. **2** (**Frog**) *slang offensive* a French or francophone person. □ **frog in the** (or **one's**) **throat** *informal* hoarseness.

frog[2] *n.* an ornamental coat fastener consisting of a spindle-shaped button and a loop through which it is passed. □ **frogged** *adj.* **frogging** *n.*

froggy ● *adj.* **1** of or like a frog or frogs. **2** abounding in frogs. **3** (also **Froggie**) *slang offensive* French or francophone. ● *n.* (**Froggy**) (*pl.* **-ies**) *slang offensive* a French or French-Canadian person.

frog kick *n.* *Swimming* a type of kick in which the legs are pulled towards the body, then thrust outward, before being brought together again quickly.

frogman *n.* (*pl.* **-men**) a scuba diver engaged in military or police operations.

frogmarch ● *v.tr.* **1** hustle (a person) forward pinning the arms from behind. **2** carry (a person) in a frogmarch. ● *n.* the action or an act of four people carrying a person face downwards with each holding a limb.

frolic ● *v.intr.* (**frolicked, frolicking**) play about cheerfully, gambol. ● *n.* **1** a lively and enjoyable activity. **2** fun, gaiety, or merriment.

from *prep.* expressing separation or origin, followed by: **1** a person, place, time, etc. that is the starting point (*rain comes from the clouds*). **2** a place, object, etc. whose distance or remoteness is reckoned or stated (*ten miles from Tuktoyaktuk; I am far from admitting it*). **3** **a** a source (*dig gravel from a pit; a man from Saskatoon; quotations from Leacock*). **b** a giver or sender (*presents from their parents*). **4** **a** a thing or person avoided, escaped, lost, etc. (*released him from prison; cannot refrain from laughing*). **b** a person or thing deprived (*took his gun from him*). **5** a reason, cause, or motive (*suffering from mumps; did it from jealousy*). **6** a thing or person distinguished or unlike (*know good from bad*). **7** a lower limit (*saw from 10 to 20 boats; tickets from $5*). **8** a state changed for another (*raised the penalty from a fine to imprisonment*). **9** an adverb or preposition of time or place (*from long ago; from abroad*). **10** the position of a person who observes or considers (*saw it from the roof; from his point of view*). **11** a model (*painted it from nature*). □ **from day to day** (or **hour to hour** etc.) daily (or hourly etc.); as the days (or hours etc.) pass. **from now on** henceforward, from now and in the future. **from time to time** occasionally or intermittently. **from year to year** each year; as the years pass.

frond *n.* **1** *Bot.* **a** a leaflike organ formed by the union of stem and foliage in certain flowerless plants, esp. ferns and palms. **b** any large compound leaf, e.g. of the palm. **2** *Zool.* a leaflike structure.

front ● *n.* **1** **a** the side or part of a thing normally nearer or towards the spectator. **b** the side or part of a thing facing forward. **c** a position or place situated directly before or ahead of a thing, observer, etc. (*the front of the mouth*). **2** any face of a building, esp. that of the main entrance. **3** *Military* **a** the foremost line or part of an army, battalion, etc. **b** the line of battle. **c** the foremost part of an occupied territory, area of operations, etc., or the ground next to an enemy. **d** (usu. prec. by *the*) the foremost part of a position or a scene of actual fighting (*go to the front*). **4** **a** a sector of activity regarded as resembling a military front. **b** a political group organized to pursue a particular objective or set of objectives. **5** bearing, demeanour, or degree of composure or confidence while under threat or in danger (*show a bold front*). **6** **a** the most forward or conspicuous position (*come to the front*). **b** a leading position in a race or contest. **7** **a** an outward appearance or show, esp. used as a cover for another trait, motive, etc. **b** a pretext, premise, etc. (*the arguments are false on several fronts*). **8** a person or organization serving as a cover for subversive or illegal activities (also *attrib.: front man*). **9** (prec. by *the*) frontage or the land facing a road or alongside a body of water. **10** *Meteorol.* the forward edge of an advancing mass of cold or warm air. **11** **a** the part of a garment, esp. of a dress or shirt, which covers the upper part of the front of the body. **b** a dickie or false shirt front. ● *attrib.adj.* **1** of or pertaining to the front. **2** situated in front. ● *v.* **1** *intr.* (foll. by *on, to, towards, upon*) have the front facing or directed in a specific direction. **2** *intr.* (foll. by *for*) *slang* act as a front or cover for. **3** *tr.* furnish with a specific front, material, etc. (*fronted with stone*). **4** *tr.* lead or be the most prominent member of (a band, organization, etc.). **5** *tr.* **a** stand opposite to, have the front towards. **b** (of a building) have its front on the side of (a street etc.). **6** *tr.* act as presenter, promoter, or host of (a television program etc.). □ **in front 1** in the lead or in an advanced position. **2** in a position exactly ahead, facing the spectator. **in front of 1** ahead of. **2** in the presence of. **out front** esp. *N Amer.* in front of a building etc. □ **fronted** (in *comb.*) *adj.* **frontward** *adj. & adv.* **frontwards** *adv.*

frontage *n.* **1** **a** the front of a building or lot. **b** the lineal extent of this. **2** **a** land abutting on a street or on water. **b** the land between the front of a building and the road. **3** the way a thing faces.

frontal *adj.* **1** **a** of, at, or on the front (*a frontal attack*). **b** of the front as seen by an onlooker (*a frontal view*). **2** of the forehead or front of the skull. □ **frontally** *adv.*

frontal lobe *n.* each of the paired lobes of the brain lying immediately behind the forehead, including areas concerned with behaviour, learning, and voluntary movement.

front bench *n.* *Cdn*, *Brit.*, *Austral.*, & *NZ* the foremost seats in Parliament, occupied by the leading members of the government and opposition. □ **front-bencher** *n.*

front burner *n.* **1** a position receiving much attention or high priority (*has been brought to the front burner*). **2** a heating element at the front of a stove.

frontcourt *n.* **1** the part of the court closest to the front wall in games such as squash, racquetball, etc. **2** *Basketball* **a** the offensive half of a court for a given team. **b** the centre and two forwards who play offensively in that half of the court.

Front de Libération du Québec /frɔ̃ də li:beiræ'sjɔ̃ du: kei'bek/ *n.* (in Canada) a Quebec separatist terrorist organization esp. active in the 1960s and early 1970s. Abbr.: **FLQ**.

front desk *n.* the registration and reception desk in a hotel etc.

front door *n.* **1** the chief entrance of a house. **2** a

front end *n.* **1** the forward part of a motor vehicle, train, etc. **2** (**front-end**) (often *attrib.*) that part of a computer system that a user deals with directly, esp. a device providing input or access to a central computer or other parts of a network. **3** (**front-end**) (*attrib.*) designating money paid or charged at the beginning of a transaction (*front-end commission*).

front-end loader *n.* **1** a machine with a scoop or bucket on an articulated arm at the front for digging and loading dirt etc. **2** a hydraulic bucket or scoop that fits onto the front of a tractor.

frontier /frʌnˈtiːr, frɒn-, ˈfrʌn-, ˈfrɒn-/ ● *n.* **1 a** the border between two countries. **b** the district on each side of this. **2** the limits of attainment or knowledge in a subject. **3** *N Amer.* the part of a country held to form the furthest limit of its settled or inhabited regions. ● *adj.* **1** of, belonging to, or situated on the frontier. **2** characteristic of life on a frontier, esp. being remote from the comforts of civilization.

frontiersman *n.* (*pl.* **-men**) a man living on a frontier, or on or beyond the borders of civilization.

frontispiece /ˈfrʌntɪsˌpiːs/ *n.* an illustration facing the title page of a book or of one of its divisions.

front line *n.* **1 a** *Military* the line of fighting closest to the enemy. **b** a role or position of immediate involvement with crises, social problems, etc. (*working on the front lines against AIDS*). **2** the most important, advanced, or responsible position (*on the front line of interactive television*). **3** the players in a jazz band other than the rhythm section.

front-loading *adj.* (of a washing machine etc.) being loaded through a door in the front of the machine rather than through the top. □ **front-loader** *n.*

front nine *n.* *Golf* the initial nine holes of an 18-hole course.

front office *n.* a main executive or administrative office of a business, organization, etc.

front page *n.* (also *attrib.*) the first page of a newspaper, esp. as containing important or remarkable news. □ **front-pager** *n.*

front-row seat *n.* **1** a seat in the front row of a theatre etc. **2** a central and prominent position, esp. as an observer or participant.

front-runner *n.* **1** the candidate, contestant, etc. most likely to succeed. **2** an athlete or horse running best when in the lead. □ **front-running** *adj.*

front-wheel drive *n.* a drive system in a car etc. in which power operates through the front wheels.

front yard *n.* *N Amer.* a piece of ground, usu. with a lawn, in front of a house.

frosh *n.* (*pl.* same) *N Amer. slang* = FRESHMAN *n.*

frost ● *n.* **1 a** dew or water vapour frozen into tiny white crystals that cover the ground etc. when the temperature falls below the freezing point. **b** a consistent temperature below freezing point causing frost to form. **2** an influence that chills or depresses, esp. coolness of behaviour or temperament. **3** (of colours of lipstick, eyeshadow, etc.) a silvery, iridescent shade. ● *v.* **1** *intr.* (usu. foll. by *over*, *up*) become covered with frost. **2** *tr.* **a** cover with or as if with frost, powder, etc. **b** freeze and usu. kill or injure (a plant etc.) with frost. **3** *tr.* give an opaque, roughened, or finely granulated surface to (glass, metal) (*frosted glass*). **4** *tr.* *N Amer.* **a** cover or decorate (a cake etc.) with icing. **b** coat with sugar. **5** *tr.* *N Amer.* annoy or anger. **6** *tr.* chemically treat selected strands of hair to produce highlights etc. □ **frosted** *adj.* **frostless** *adj.*

frostbite ● *n.* injury to body tissues caused by

intense cold, in extreme cases resulting in gangrene. ● *v.tr.* (usu. as **frostbitten** *adj.*) affect with frostbite.

frost-free *adj.* **1** (of a region, period, etc.) experiencing no frost. **2** able to defrost automatically.

frost heave *n.* **1** the uplift of soil or other surface deposits, esp. on a road, due to expansion of groundwater on freezing. **2** an uneven area caused by this.

frosting *n.* **1** *N Amer.* icing for a cake etc. **2** a rough surface on glass etc. **3** *N Amer.* a process of treating hair to produce highlights chemically.

frost line *n.* **1** the maximum ground depth below which frost does not penetrate. **2** the lower limit of permafrost.

frosty *adj.* (**-ier**, **-iest**) **1** very cold, esp. cold with frost. **2** covered with or as with hoarfrost. **3** unfriendly in manner, or lacking in warmth of feeling. **4** like frost in appearance. □ **frostily** *adv.* **frostiness** *n.*

froth ● *n.* **1 a** a collection of small bubbles in liquid, caused by shaking, fermenting, etc. **b** impure matter on liquid. **2 a** idle talk or ideas. **b** anything unsubstantial or of little worth. **3** foaming saliva, esp. as in rabies etc. ● *v.* **1** *intr.* **a** emit froth (*frothing at the mouth*). **b** (of liquid) gather froth or run foaming over etc. **2** *tr.* cause (beer etc.) to foam. □ **frothily** *adv.* **frothiness** *n.* **frothing** *adj.* & *n.* **frothy** *adj.* (**-ier**, **-iest**).

frou-frou /ˈfruːfruː/ *n.* **1** frills, frippery. **2** a trivial or insubstantial thing, person, etc.

frown ● *v.* **1** *intr.* **a** contract the eyebrows and wrinkle the forehead, esp. in anger, worry, or deep thought. **b** make a glum expression, esp. with the corners of the mouth turned down. **2** *intr.* (foll. by *at*, *on*, *upon*) express disapproval. **3** *intr.* (of a thing) present a gloomy aspect. **4** *tr.* express (defiance etc.) with a frown. ● *n.* **1** an act of frowning. **2** a look expressing severity, disapproval, or deep thought. □ **frowning** *adj.* **frowningly** *adv.*

frowzy /ˈfrauzi/ *adj.* (also **frowsy**) (**-ier**, **-iest**) **1** musty, ill-smelling, close. **2** slatternly, unkempt, dingy. □ **frowziness** *n.*

froze *past of* FREEZE.

frozen ● *v.* *past part.* of FREEZE. ● *adj.* **1 a** exposed or subject to extreme cold. **b** solidified by exposure to cold. **2** (of food) preserved by refrigeration to below freezing point. **3** emotionally frigid, unfriendly, or unresponsive. **4 a** (of a mechanism etc.) fixed, immobile, e.g. with rust, cold, etc. **b** (of a joint etc.) stiffened or immobile from an injury etc. **5** (of a credit or asset) impossible to liquidate or realize at maturity or some other given time.

frozen yogourt *n.* a dessert of yogourt frozen like ice cream.

fructose /ˈfrʊktoːs, -oːz, ˈfrʌk-/ *n.* a simple sugar found in honey and fruits.

frugal *adj.* **1** (often foll. by *of*) sparing or economical; thrifty. **2** (of things, esp. food) plain, simple, or provided in small quantity and with avoidance of excess. □ **frugality** *n.* **frugally** *adv.*

fruit ● *n.* **1 a** the usu. sweet and fleshy edible product of a plant or tree, containing seed. **b** (in *sing.*) these in quantity (*eats fruit*). **2** the seed-bearing structure with its covering of a plant or tree, as a means of reproduction, e.g. an acorn, pea pod, cherry, etc. **3** (usu. in *pl.*) any plant product used as food, e.g. vegetables, grains, etc. (*fruits of the earth*). **4** (usu. in *pl.*) a product, outcome, or anything concrete or abstract, produced by an activity, process, etc. (*fruits of his labours*). **5** esp. *N Amer. slang derogatory* a male homosexual. ● *v.intr.* & *tr.* bear or cause to bear fruit. □ **fruited** *adj.* (also in *comb.*). **fruiting** *adj.*

fruit bat *n.* any large bat of the suborder Megachiroptera, feeding on fruit.

fruitcake *n.* **1** a cake containing a high proportion of mixed dried fruit and often nuts. **2** *slang* an eccentric or mad person.

fruit cocktail *n.* = FRUIT SALAD.

fruit fly *n.* **1** any of various dipterous flies of the families Tephritidae, whose larvae infest cultivated fruit. **2** any of various dipterous flies of the family Drosophilidae, which feed on rotting or fermenting fruit, much used in genetic research.

fruitful *adj.* **1 a** (of a tree etc.) producing much fruit. **b** (of soil etc.) fertile, inducing fertility in plants etc. **2 a** producing good results; beneficial, successful, rewarding. **b** abundantly productive of ideas or some other immaterial thing. **3** producing offspring, esp. prolifically. □ **fruitfully** *adv.* **fruitfulness** *n.*

fruition /fruːˈɪʃən/ *n.* **1 a** the bearing of fruit. **b** the production of results. **2** the realization or successful outcome of aims, hopes, plans, etc.

fruitless *adj.* **1** useless, unsuccessful. **2** not bearing fruit. □ **fruitlessly** *adv.* **fruitlessness** *n.*

fruit salad *n.* various fruits cut up and served in syrup, juice, etc.

fruit sugar *n.* fructose.

fruity *adj.* (**-ier, -iest**) **1 a** of, relating to, or like fruit, esp. in taste or smell. **b** (of wine) tasting of the grape. **2** (of a voice etc.) of a full rich quality. **3** *slang derogatory* homosexual. □ **fruitiness** *n.*

frump *n.* a dowdy, unattractive woman. □ **frumpily** *adv.* **frumpiness** *n.* **frumpy** *adj.* (**-ier, -iest**)

frustrate *v.tr.* **1** upset or discourage (a person). **2** make (efforts) ineffective (*parliament frustrated his reforms*). **3** prevent (a person) from achieving a purpose. **4** disappoint (a hope). □ **frustrater** *n.* **frustrating** *adj.* **frustratingly** *adv.* **frustration** *n.*

frustrated *adj.* **1** discontented because unable to achieve one's desire. **2** sexually unfulfilled.

fry¹ ● *v.* (**fries, fried**) **1** *tr. & intr.* cook or be cooked in hot fat. **2** *tr. & intr. informal* overload, burn out, etc. (electronic components etc.). **3** *tr. & intr. slang* electrocute or be electrocuted. **4** *tr. & intr. informal* **a** burn or overheat, esp. with effects analogous to those of frying food. **b** (of the sun) scorch (a person etc.). **5** *tr. N Amer. slang* **a** destroy (*drugs fry the brain*). **b** upset or annoy intensely. ● *n.* (*pl.* **fries**) **1** (in *pl.*) *N Amer.* = FRENCH FRY. **2** a dish of fried food, esp. meat. **3** *N Amer.* a party at which fried food is eaten. □ **fry up** heat or reheat (food) in a frying pan.

fry² *n.pl.* **1** young or newly hatched fish. **2** the young of other creatures produced in quantity, e.g. bees or frogs.

fryer *n.* **1** a pot for frying food, esp. in deep fat. **2** a person who fries. **3** *N Amer.* a chicken suitable for frying.

frying pan *n.* (*N Amer.* also **fry pan**) a flat, shallow pan with a long handle, used for frying food. □ **out of the frying pan into the fire** from a bad situation to a worse one.

f-stop *n.* an f-number setting on a camera.

Ft. *abbr.* **1** Fort. **2** (**ft.**) foot, feet.

FTA *abbr.* Free Trade Agreement.

FTP *Computing* ● *abbr.* file transfer protocol. ● *v.tr.* (**FTP's, FTP'd, FTPing**) implement this protocol on (a data item etc.).

fuchsia /ˈfjuːʃə/ *n.* **1** any shrub of the genus *Fuchsia*, with drooping red or purple or white flowers. **2** a bright purple-pink shade of red.

fuck *coarse slang* ● *v.* **1** *tr. & intr.* have sexual intercourse (with). **2** *tr.* (usu. as an exclamation) curse, confound. **3** a *tr.* (often foll. by *over*) deal with (a person) unfairly, unjustly, etc. **b** ruin, spoil, exhaust, or wear out (a thing). **4** *intr.* (foll. by *about, around*) **a** mess about, fool around, or involve oneself in. **b** be sexually promiscuous. ● *interj.* expressing anger or annoyance. ● *n.* **1 a** an act of sexual intercourse. **b** a partner in sexual intercourse. **2** the slightest amount (*don't give a fuck*). **3** a person who is stupid, annoying, hapless, etc. **4** (usu. prec. by *the*) an intensifier (*What the fuck are you doing?*). ¶Although widely used in many sections of society, *fuck* is still generally considered to be one of the most offensive words in the English language. □ **fuck off** go to hell, drop dead, etc. **fuck that** (or **this**) **noise** *N Amer.* expressing total dismissiveness of a suggestion, comment etc. **fuck up 1** blunder, fail, make a serious error. **2** ruin, spoil, mess up. **3** disturb emotionally. □ **fucker** *n.* (often as a term of abuse).

fuck all *n.* *coarse slang* absolutely nothing.

fucking *adj. & adv.* *coarse slang* used as an intensive to express annoyance etc.

fuck-up *n.* *coarse slang* **1** a mess or bungled matter. **2** a person who is a chronic loser or failure.

fucus /ˈfjuːkəs/ *n.* (*pl.* **fuci** /ˈfjuːsaɪ/) any seaweed of the genus *Fucus*, with flat leathery fronds.

fuddle ● *v.* **1** *tr.* confuse or stupefy, esp. with alcoholic liquor. **2** *intr.* tipple. ● *n.* **1** confusion. **2** intoxication.

fuddle duddle *interj.* *Cdn euphemism* go to hell; drop dead.

fuddy-duddy *slang* ● *n.* (*pl.* **-ies**) an old-fashioned or quaintly fussy person. ● *adj.* old-fashioned; quaintly fussy.

fudge ● *n.* **1** a soft crumbly or chewy kind of candy made with milk, sugar, butter, etc. **2** (*attrib.*) esp. *N Amer.* designating rich chocolate cakes, cookies, sauces, etc. **3** nonsense. **4** a piece of dishonesty or faking. ● *v.* **1** *tr.* put together in a makeshift or dishonest way; fake (*fudged the budget figures*). **2** *tr.* deal with vaguely or inadequately, usu. deliberately, so as to mislead or avoid making a definite choice. **3** *intr.* practise such methods (*fudged on the issue of pay raises*). ● *interj.* expressing disbelief or annoyance.

fuel ● *n.* **1** material burned or used as a source of heat or power. **2** food as a source of energy. **3** material used as a source of nuclear energy. **4** anything that sustains or inflames emotion or passion. ● *v.* (**fuelled, fuelling**) **1** *tr.* supply with fuel. **2** *tr.* sustain or inflame (an argument, feeling, etc.). **3** *tr.* give impetus to. **4** *intr.* take in or get fuel.

fuel cell *n.* a cell producing an electric current direct from a chemical reaction.

fuel efficiency *n.* the efficient use of fuel in an engine or other system. □ **fuel-efficient** *adj.*

fuel injection *n.* the direct introduction of fuel under pressure into the combustion chamber of an internal combustion engine. □ **fuel-injected** *adj.*

fuel oil *n.* oil used as fuel in an engine or furnace.

fuel rod *n.* a rod-shaped can of nuclear fuel, esp. one used in a nuclear reactor.

fuelwood *n.* wood burned to provide heat etc.

fugitive ● *n.* a person who flees, esp. from justice, an enemy, danger, or a master. ● *adj.* **1** fleeing; that runs or has run away. **2** fleeting; of short duration. **3** (of literature) of passing interest, ephemeral. **4** (of an impression, colour, etc.) quickly fading. **5** flitting, shifting.

fugue /fjuːg/ *n.* **1** a contrapuntal composition in which a short melody or phrase is introduced by one part and successively taken up by others and developed by interweaving the parts. **2** *Psych.* (in full **fugue state**) loss of awareness of one's identity, often coupled with flight from one's usual environment.

führer /ˈfjʊrər/ *n.* a leader, esp. a tyrannical one.

fulcrum /ˈfʊlkrəm, ˈfʌl-/ *n.* (*pl.* **-s** or **fulcra** /-rə/) **1** the point against which a lever is placed to get a purchase or on which it turns or is supported. **2** the means by which influence etc. is brought to bear.

fulfill *v.tr.* (also **fulfil**) (**fulfilled**, **fulfilling**) **1** carry out (a prophecy or promise). **2** satisfy (a desire or prayer). **3 a** execute, obey (a command or law). **b** perform, carry out (a task). **4** comply with (conditions). **5** answer (a purpose). **6** bring to an end, finish, complete (a period or piece of work). □ **fulfill oneself** develop one's gifts and character to the full. □ **fulfiller** *n.* **fulfillment** *n.* (also **fulfilment**).

fulfilled *adj.* completely happy; satisfied.

fulfilling *adj.* deeply satisfying.

full¹ ● *adj.* **1** holding all its limits will allow (*the bucket is full*). **2** having eaten to one's limits or satisfaction. **3** abundant, copious, satisfying (*led a full life*; *full details*). **4** having or holding an abundance of (*full of interest*; *full of mistakes*). **5 a** engrossed in thinking about (*full of his work*). **b** unable to refrain from talking about (*full of the news*). **6** reaching the specified or usual or utmost limit (*full membership*; *waited a full hour*). **7 a** (of tone or colour) deep and rich; intense. **b** (of light) intense. **c** (of motion etc.) vigorous (*at full gallop*). **d** (of sound) strong, resonant. **e** (of wine etc.) rich in quality or tone. **8** plump, rounded (*a full figure*). **9** (of clothes) amply cut; made of much material arranged in folds or gathers. **10** (of the heart etc.) overcharged with emotion. **11** having all the qualifications or privileges of a designation; of the highest rank (*full professor*). ● *adv.* **1** very (*you know full well*). **2** quite, fully (*full ripe*). **3** exactly (*hit him full on the nose*). ● *n.* **1** height, acme (*season is past the full*). **2** the state or time of full moon. **3** the whole (*cannot tell you the full of it*). ● *v.intr. & tr.* be or become or make (esp. clothes) full. □ **full of oneself** selfish, conceited. **full nine yards** *see* WHOLE. **full speed** (or **steam**) **ahead!** an order to proceed at maximum speed or to pursue a course of action energetically. **full up** completely full. **in full 1** without abridgement. **2** to or for the full amount (*paid in full*). **in full swing** at the height of activity. **in full view** entirely visible. **to the full** to the utmost extent.

full² *v.tr.* cleanse and thicken (cloth). □ **fuller** *n.*

full age *n. Cdn & Brit.* adult status (esp. with reference to legal rights and duties).

fullback *n.* **1** *Football* a running back who lines up behind the rest of his team at the scrimmage. **2** *Soccer etc.* a defensive player, or a position near the goal.

full blood *n.* **1** pure descent; unmixed ancestry. **2** (**full-blood**) a person or animal of unmixed ancestry.

full-blooded *adj.* **1** vigorous, hearty, sensual. **2** not hybrid. **3** of unmixed ancestry. □ **full-bloodedly** *adv.*

full-blown *adj.* **1** fully developed, complete (*full-blown AIDS*). **2** (of flowers) very open.

full-bodied *adj.* rich in quality, tone, flavour, etc.

full bore esp. *N Amer. informal* ● *adv.* at maximum power, speed, etc. (*ran full bore down the street*). ● *adj.* with maximum power, activity, etc.

full brother *n.* a brother born of the same parents.

full colour *n.* the full range of colours (often *attrib.*: *full-colour brochure*).

full-court press *n.* **1** *Basketball* an aggressive defence tactic in which the team without the ball harasses

the opposing team the whole length of the court. **2** *N Amer.* an attack; an offensive campaign.

full deck *n. N Amer.* a complete set of playing cards. □ **not playing with a full deck** *slang* not of normal intelligence or sanity.

full dress ● *n.* clothes worn on ceremonial or formal occasions. ● *adj.* (**full-dress**) thorough, complete (*a full-dress investigation*).

full employment *n.* **1** the condition in which there is no idle capital or labour of any kind that is in demand. **2** the condition in which virtually all who are able and willing to work are employed.

full-face *adv. & adj.* with all the face visible to the observer (*a full-face portrait*).

full-featured *adj.* (of electronic equipment etc.) having many features; technologically up-to-date.

full-figure *adj.* **1** (of a portrait etc.) representing the entire body. **2** (also **full-figured**) **a** plump, stout. **b** large, oversize (*ladies' full-figure blouses*).

full-flavoured *adj.* (of food, wine, etc.) strong and distinct in taste.

full-fledged *adj.* **1** of full rank or status (*a full-fledged political party*). **2** fully developed; mature.

full-grown *adj.* having reached maturity.

full house *n.* **1** a maximum or large attendance at a theatre, stadium, etc. **2** *Cards* a poker hand with three of a kind and a pair.

full-length *adj.* **1** of normal, standard, or maximum length; not shortened or abbreviated. **2** (of a mirror, portrait, etc.) showing the whole height of the human figure.

full marks *n.pl. Cdn & Brit.* **1** the maximum award in an examination, competition, etc. **2** full credit (*I give her full marks for thoughtfulness*).

full moon *n.* **1** the moon in its fullest phase, with its whole disc illuminated. **2** the time when this occurs.

full motion video *n.* digital video data that is transmitted or stored (on videodisc etc.) for real-time reproduction esp. on a computer.

fullness *n.* **1** the state of being full. **2** (of sound, colour, etc.) richness, volume, body. **3** all that is contained (in the world etc.). □ **the fullness of time** the appropriate or destined time.

full out ● *adv.* at full power, speed, etc. ● *adj.* (**full-out**) complete (*full-out drunkenness*).

full page *n.* an entire page of a newspaper etc. (also *attrib.*: *full-page spread*).

full-scale *adj.* **1** not reduced in size; having the same size as the original. **2** utilizing all available resources; all-out (*a full-scale investigation*).

full-service *adj.* **1** designating a gas station, restaurant, etc. where service is provided entirely by staff (*compare* SELF-SERVE 1). **2** providing a wide range of products or services (*a full-service gym*).

full sister *n.* a sister born of the same parents.

full-size ● *adj.* (also **full-sized**) **1** of the standard size of its kind (*a full-size washing machine*). **2** *N Amer.* (of a car) of the largest size, usu. having a wheelbase over 105 inches and a 4 litre engine. ● *n. N Amer.* a full-size car.

full term *n.* the completion of a normal pregnancy.

full throttle *n.* maximum speed, strength, etc.

full-time ● *adj.* occupying or using the whole of the available working time (*a full-time job*). ● *adv.* on a full-time basis (*works full-time*). ● *n.* (**full time**) the total normal duration of work etc.

full-timer *n.* a person who works a full-time job.

fully *adv.* **1** completely, entirely. **2** no less or fewer than (*fully 60*).

fully-fledged *var. of* FULL-FLEDGED.

fulmar /ˈfʊlmər/ *n.* an medium-sized seabird with a stout body, robust bill, and rounded tail.

fulminate /ˈfʌlmɪˌneɪt, ˈfʊl-/ *v.intr.* **1** (often foll. by *against*) express censure loudly and forcefully. **2** explode violently; flash like lightning (*fulminating mercury*). □ **fulmination** *n.* **fulminatory** *adj.*

fulness *var. of* FULLNESS.

fulsome *adj.* **1** (of praise etc.) excessively complimentary or flattering. **2** abundant. ¶Since *fulsome* may have negative connotations to some people and neutral connotations to others, it is advisable to make clear which connotations are intended. □ **fulsomely** *adv.*

fumble ● *v.* **1** *intr.* use the hands awkwardly, grope about (*fumbled for change*). **2** *tr.* handle or deal with clumsily or nervously. **3** *tr. & intr.* Football etc. fail to keep hold of a ball after having touched it or transported it. **4** *tr.* make one's way clumsily (*fumbled his way across the yard*). ● *n.* an act of fumbling. □ **fumblingly** *adv.*

fume ● *n.* (usu. in *pl.*) exuded gas or smoke or vapour, esp. when harmful or unpleasant. ● *v.* **1 a** *intr.* emit fumes. **b** *tr.* give off as fumes. **2** *intr.* (often foll. by *at*) be affected by (esp. suppressed) anger (*was fuming at their inefficiency*). □ **fumeless** *adj.* **fumy** *adj.*

fumigate *v.tr. & intr.* disinfect (a contaminated or infested thing) with the fumes of certain chemicals. □ **fumigant** *n.* **fumigation** *n.* **fumigator** *n.*

fun ● *n.* **1** amusement, esp. lively or playful. **2** a source of this. **3** playfulness; good humour (*she's full of fun*). **4** (in full **fun and games**) lighthearted or amusing activities. ● *adj. informal* amusing, entertaining, enjoyable (*a fun thing to do*). ● *v.intr. informal* have fun; fool, joke. □ **be great** (or **good**) **fun** be very amusing. **for fun** (or **for the fun of it**) not for a serious purpose. **have fun** enjoy oneself. **in fun** as a joke, not seriously. **like fun** *ironic* not at all. **make fun of** (or **poke fun at**) mock; ridicule.

function ● *n.* **1 a** an activity proper to a person or institution. **b** a mode of action or activity by which a thing fulfills its purpose. **c** an official or professional duty; an employment, profession, or calling. **2 a** a public ceremony or occasion. **b** a social gathering, esp. a large, formal, or important one. **3** *Math.* a variable quantity regarded in relation to another or others in terms of which it may be expressed or on which its value depends (*x is a function of y and z*). **4** something dependent on another factor or factors (*university attendance as a function of family income*). **5** *Computing* a part of a program that corresponds to a single value. ● *v.intr.* **1** fulfill a function. **2** operate; be in working order. □ **functionless** *adj.*

functional *adj.* **1** of or serving a function. **2** functioning; able to work (*is this machine functional?*). **3** (esp. of buildings) designed or intended to be practical rather than attractive; utilitarian. **4 a** (esp. of disease) of or affecting only the functions of an organ etc., not structural or organic. **b** (of mental disorder) having no discernible organic cause. **5** *Math.* of a function. □ **functionality** *n.* **functionally** *adv.*

functional illiterate *n.* a person who cannot read or write well enough to complete everyday tasks, such as reading a menu etc. □ **functional illiteracy** *n.* **functionally illiterate** *adj.*

functionalism *n.* **1** the doctrine that the design of an object should be determined solely by its function, rather than by aesthetic considerations. **2** the theory that all aspects of a society serve a function and are necessary for the survival of that society. **3**

belief in or stress on the practical application of a thing. □ **functionalist** *n. & adj.*

functionary *n.* (*pl.* **-ies**) a person who performs official functions or duties; an official.

function key *n.* *Computing* a key which is used to generate instructions.

fund ● *n.* **1** a permanent stock of something ready to be drawn upon (*a fund of knowledge*). **2 a** a reserve of money or investments, esp. one set apart for a purpose. **b** an organization which manages such a reserve (*International Monetary Fund*). **3** (in *pl.*) money resources. ● *v.tr.* **1** provide with money. **2** put into a fund. □ **fundable** *adj.* **funded** *adj.* (usu. in *comb.*). **funder** *n.* **funding** *n.*

fundamental ● *adj.* of, affecting, or serving as a base or foundation; essential. ● *n.* **1** (usu. in *pl.*) a fundamental rule, principle, or article. **2** *Music* a fundamental note or tone. □ **fundamentally** *adv.*

fundamentalism *n.* **1** strict maintenance of traditional Protestant beliefs such as the inerrancy of Scripture and literal acceptance of the creeds as fundamentals of Christianity. **2** strict maintenance of ancient or fundamental doctrines of any religion, esp. Islam. □ **fundamentalist** *n. & adj.*

fundamental note *n.* *Music* the lowest note of a chord in its original (uninverted) form.

fund manager *n.* a person who manages an investment fund at an insurance company, mutual fund company, etc. □ **fund management** *n.*

fundraiser *n.* **1** a person who seeks financial support for a cause, enterprise, etc. **2** a social function held to raise money for a cause, enterprise, etc. □ **fundraising** *n.*

funeral ● *n.* **1 a** a ceremony or service held shortly after a person's death, usu. including the person's burial or cremation. **b** a burial or cremation procession. **2** *informal* one's (usu. unpleasant) concern (*that's your funeral*). ● *attrib.adj.* of or used etc. at a funeral (*funeral oration*).

funeral director *n.* an undertaker.

funeral home *n.* *N Amer.* (also **funeral parlour**, **funeral chapel**) an establishment where the dead are prepared for burial or cremation.

funerary /ˈfjuːnəreri/ *adj.* of or used at a funeral or funerals.

funereal /fjuːˈnɪːrɪəl/ *adj.* **1** of or appropriate to a funeral. **2** gloomy, dismal, dark. □ **funereally** *adv.*

fun fair *n.* a fair consisting of amusements and sideshows.

fungicide /ˈfʌŋɡɪˌsaid, ˈfʌndʒ-/ *n.* a fungus-destroying substance. □ **fungicidal** *adj.*

fungo /ˈfʊŋɡoː/ *n.* *Baseball* (*pl.* **-oes**) **1** a fly ball hit in the air for practice. **2** (in full **fungo bat**) a lightweight practice bat.

fungus /ˈfʌŋɡəs/ *n.* (*pl.* **fungi** /-gai, -dʒai/ or **funguses**) **1** any of a group of unicellular or multicellular spore-producing organisms feeding on organic matter, including moulds, yeast, mushrooms, and toadstools. **2** anything unusual esp. growing suddenly and rapidly. **3** *Med.* a spongy morbid growth. □ **fungal** *adj.* **fungous** *adj.*

funhouse *n.* esp. *N Amer.* (in an amusement park) a equipped with trick mirrors, shifting floors, etc., designed to scare or amuse patrons as they walk through.

funicular /fəˈnɪkjʊlər/ ● *adj.* **1** (of a railway, esp. on a mountainside) operating by cable with ascending and descending cars counterbalanced. **2** of a rope or its tension. ● *n.* a funicular railway.

funk[1] ● *n.* *informal* **1** fear, panic. **2** *N Amer.* a dejected state of mind (*in a funk*). ● *v.* **1** *intr.* flinch, shrink, show cowardice. **2** *tr.* try to evade (an undertaking); shirk. **3** *tr.* be afraid of.

funk² *n.* **1** a style of popular music of US black origin. **2** *N Amer.* a strong, unpleasant smell.

funky *adj.* (**-ier, -iest**) **1** (esp. of jazz or rock music) earthy, bluesy, with a heavy rhythmical beat. **2** *informal* **a** fashionable, trendy. **b** unconventional, striking. **3** *N Amer.* having a strong, unpleasant smell. □ **funkily** *adv.* **funkiness** *n.*

funnel ● *n.* **1** a narrow tube or pipe widening at the top, for pouring liquid, powder, etc., into a small opening. **2** a metal chimney on a steam engine or ship. **3** something resembling a funnel in shape or use. ● *v.* (**funnelled, funnelling**) **1** *tr.* & *intr.* guide or move through or as through a funnel. **2** *tr.* direct, channel (*funnel money to local charities*). □ **funnel-like** *adj.*

funnel cloud *n.* a cloud produced in a low-pressure vortex in the centre of a spiral storm, e.g. a tornado or waterspout.

funny ● *adj.* (**-ier, -iest**) **1** amusing, comical. **2** strange, perplexing, hard to account for. **3** *informal* slightly unwell, nauseous. **4** eccentric, odd (*a funny old man*). **5** underhand, tricky, deceitful. ● *n.* (*pl.* **-ies**) (usu. in *pl.*) *informal* **1** *N Amer.* a comic strip in a newspaper. **2** a joke. □ **funnily** *adv.* **funniness** *n.*

funny bone *n.* **1** the part of the elbow over which the ulnar nerve passes, which, when struck, causes tingling in the arm and hand. **2** a sense of humour.

funny business *n.* **1** *slang* misbehaviour or deception. **2** comic behaviour, comedy.

funny farm *n.* *slang* a psychiatric hospital.

funny money *n.* *informal* **1** inflated or counterfeit currency. **2** *Cdn hist.* twenty-five-dollar certificates issued to Albertans in 1937 by the Social Credit government of William Aberhart.

fun run *n.* *informal* an uncompetitive run, esp. for sponsored runners in support of a charity.

fur *n.* **1 a** the fine, soft, thick hair of certain animals. **b** the skin of such an animal with the fur on it; a pelt. **2 a** the coat of certain animals as material for making, trimming, or lining clothes. **b** a trimming or lining made of the dressed coat of such animals, or of material imitating this. **c** a garment made of or trimmed or lined with fur. **3** (*collect.*) furred animals. **4** a coating formed on the tongue in sickness. □ **the fur is flying** *informal* there is trouble or a disturbance.

furan /ˈfjʊərən, -ˈræn/ *n.* a colourless liquid compound with a planar five-membered ring in its molecule.

furball *n.* *N Amer.* **1** an accumulation of fur ingested by a cat etc. during self-grooming and then regurgitated. **2** *jocular* a small furry animal, esp. a pet.

fur-bearer *n.* a furred animal, esp. one whose fur is of value in the marketplace. □ **fur-bearing** *adj.*

furbish *v.tr.* (often foll. by *up*) **1** remove rust from, polish, burnish. **2** give a new look to, renovate, revive (something antiquated). □ **furbisher** *n.*

fur brigade *n.* *Cdn hist.* a convoy of Red River carts, York boats, canoes, etc. which transported furs etc. to and from isolated trading posts.

furious *adj.* **1** extremely angry. **2** raging, violent, intense. **3** rapid, requiring intense energy (*a furious schedule*). □ **furiously** *adv.* **furiousness** *n.*

furl *v.* **1** *tr.* roll up and secure (a sail, umbrella, flag, etc.). **2** *intr.* become furled.

furlong *n.* an eighth of a mile (201.168 metres).

furlough /ˈfɜːloʊ/ *n.* leave of absence, esp. granted to a soldier or missionary.

furnace *n.* **1** an appliance fired by gas or oil in which air or water is heated to be circulated throughout a building to heat it. **2** an enclosed structure for intense heating by fire, esp. of metals or water. **3** a very hot place.

furnish *v.tr.* **1** provide (a house, room, etc.) with all necessary contents, esp. movable furniture. **2** (foll. by *with*) cause to have possession or use of. **3** provide.

furnished *adj.* (of a house, apartment, etc.) rented with furniture.

furnishings *n.pl.* the furniture, carpets, draperies, etc. in a house, room, etc.

furniture *n.* **1** the movable equipment of a house, room, etc., e.g. tables, chairs, and beds. **2** accessories, e.g. the handles and lock of a door. □ **part of the furniture** *informal* a person or thing taken for granted.

furniture beetle *n.* a beetle, *Anobium punctatum*.

furor /ˈfjʊərɔr, ˈfjɔr-, -ər/ *n.* **1** an uproar; a disturbance or fuss. **2** a wave of enthusiastic admiration, a craze. **3** anger, rage.

furred *adj.* **1** (of a garment) lined or trimmed with fur. **2** (of an animal) with fur. **3** (of a person) clothed in fur. **4** coated with a fur-like substance.

furrier /ˈfɜːrɪər/ *n.* **1** a person who makes, cleans, and repairs fur garments. **2** a person who buys and sells furs. **3** *Cdn* (*Nfld*) a person engaged in hunting or trapping fur-bearing animals.

furrow ● *n.* **1** a narrow trench made in the ground by a plow. **2** a rut, groove, or deep wrinkle. ● *v.* **1** *tr.* plow. **2** *tr.* **a** make furrows, grooves, etc. in. **b** mark with wrinkles. **3** *intr.* (esp. of the brow) become furrowed.

furry *adj.* (**-ier, -iest**) **1** of or like fur. **2** covered with or wearing fur. □ **furriness** *n.*

fur seal *n.* any of several eared seals constituting the genera *Arctocephalus* and *Callorhinus*, with thick fur on the underside.

further ● *adv.* **1 a** to or at a more advanced point in space or time (*unsafe to proceed further*). **b** at a greater distance (*nothing was further from his thoughts*). **2** to a greater extent, more (*will inquire further*). **3** in addition; furthermore (*I may add further*). ● *adj.* **1** more distant or advanced (*on the further side*). **2** more, additional, going beyond what exists or has been dealt with (*threats of further punishment*). ● *v.tr.* promote, favour, help on. ¶The forms *farther* and *farthest* are used esp. with reference to physical distance, although *further* and *furthest* are preferred by many even in this sense. □ **further to** *formal* following on from (esp. an earlier letter etc.). **till further notice** (or **orders**) to continue until explicitly changed. □ **furthermost** *adj.*

furthermore *adv.* in addition, besides (esp. introducing a fresh consideration in an argument).

furthest ● *adj.* **1** most distant in space, direction, or time; most remote. **2** longest; most extended in space. ● *adv.* **1** to or at the greatest distance in space or time; most remote. **2** to the highest degree or extent; most (*she is the furthest advanced of all my students*). ¶See Usage Note at FURTHER.

furtive *adj.* **1** done by stealth, clandestine, meant to escape notice. **2** sly, stealthy. **3** stolen, taken secretly. □ **furtively** *adv.* **furtiveness** *n.*

fur trade *n.* esp. *hist.* the business of trapping, transporting, and selling furs, esp. as carried on between European traders and Aboriginal peoples in N America in the 17th–19th c. □ **fur trader** *n.* **fur-trading** *adj.*

fury *n.* (*pl.* **-ies**) **1 a** wild and passionate anger, rage. **b** a fit of rage (*in a blind fury*). **2** violence of a storm, disease, etc. **3** (**Fury**) (usu. in *pl.*) *Gk Myth* each of three goddesses sent from Tartarus to avenge crime, esp. against kinship. **4** an avenging spirit. **5** an angry or malignant woman. ☐ **like fury** *informal* with great force or effect.

fuse¹ ● *v.* **1** *tr. & intr.* melt with intense heat; liquefy. **2** *tr. & intr.* blend or amalgamate into one whole by or as by melting. **3** *tr.* provide (a circuit, plug, etc.) with a fuse. **4** *intr.* (of anatomical structures, groups of atoms, etc.) coalesce, join. ● *n.* a device or component for protecting an electric circuit, containing a strip of wire of easily melted metal and placed in the circuit so as to break it by melting when an excessive current passes through. ☐ **blow a fuse 1** cause a fuse to melt by passing excessive current through it. **2** lose one's temper.

fuse² ● *n.* **1** a device for igniting a bomb or explosive charge, consisting of a tube or cord etc. filled or saturated with combustible matter. **2** a component in a shell, mine, etc., designed to detonate an explosive charge on impact, after an interval, or when subjected to a magnetic or vibratory stimulation. ● *v.tr.* fit a fuse to. ☐ **have a short fuse** anger easily.

fuse box *n.* a box housing the fuses for circuits in a building.

fuselage /ˈfjuːzə,lɒʒ, ˈfjuːs-, -lɒʒ, -lɪdʒ/ *n.* the body of an airplane, to which the wings and tail are fitted.

fusible /ˈfjuːzəbəl/ *adj.* that can be easily fused or melted. ☐ **fusibility** *n.*

fusil /ˈfjuːzəl, -sɪl/ *n. hist.* a light musket.

fusilier /,fjuːzəˈliːr/ *n.* **1** a member of any of several regiments formerly armed with fusils. **2** *hist.* a soldier armed with a fusil.

fusillade /,fjuːzəˈleɪd, -,lɒd, -sə-/ ● *n.* **1** a continuous discharge of firearms. **2** a sustained outburst of criticism etc. ● *v.tr.* **1** assault (a place) by a fusillade. **2** shoot down (persons) with a fusillade.

fusilli /fuˈzɪli, fjuː-, ˈfjuː-/ *n.pl.* pasta in the form of short spirals.

fusion *n.* **1** the act or an instance of fusing or melting. **2** a fused mass. **3** the blending of different things into one. **4** a coalition. **5** = NUCLEAR FUSION. **6** a kind of music in which elements of more than one popular style are combined, esp. jazz and rock.

fusion bomb *n.* a bomb deriving its energy from nuclear fusion, esp. a hydrogen bomb.

fuss ● *n.* **1** nervous excitement or activity, esp. of an unnecessary kind. **2** a display of excitement, worry, or enthusiasm, esp. over something unimportant. **3** a sustained protest or dispute. ● *v.* **1** *intr.* **a** make a fuss. **b** busy oneself restlessly with trivial things. **c** (often foll. by *about*) move fussily. **d** (of a baby) express discomfort or unhappiness by whimpering etc. **2** *tr.* agitate, worry. ☐ **make a fuss** complain vigorously. **make a fuss over** treat (a person or animal) with great or excessive attention. ☐ **fusser** *n.*

fuss-budget *n. N Amer. informal* (also **fusspot**) a person given to fussing.

fussy *adj.* (**-ier, -iest**) **1** inclined to fuss. **2** full of unnecessary detail or decoration. **3** difficult to please. ☐ **be not fussy about 1** be indifferent about. **2** not like particularly. ☐ **fussily** *adv.* **fussiness** *n.*

fustian /ˈfʌstiən, -tʃən/ ● *n.* **1** thick twilled cotton cloth with a short nap, usu. dyed in dark colours. **2** turgid speech or writing, bombast. ● *adj.* **1** made of fustian. **2** bombastic. **3** worthless.

fusty *adj.* (**-ier, -iest**) **1** stale-smelling, musty. **2** stuffy. **3** old-fashioned. ☐ **fustily** *adv.* **fustiness** *n.*

futile /ˈfjuːtaɪl, -təl/ *adj.* useless, ineffectual. ☐ **futilely** *adv.* **futility** /-ˈtɪlɪti/ *n.*

futon /ˈfuːtɒn/ *n.* **1** a Japanese quilted mattress rolled out on the floor for use as a bed. **2** a type of low wooden sofa bed having such a mattress.

future ● *adj.* **1 a** going or expected to happen or be or become (*his future career*). **b** that will be something specified (*my future wife*). **c** that will be after death (*a future life*). **2 a** of time to come (*future years*). **b** *Grammar* (of a tense or participle) describing an event yet to happen. ● *n.* **1** time to come (*past, present, and future*). **2** what will happen in the future (*the future is uncertain*). **3** the future condition of a person, country, etc. **4** a prospect of success etc. (*there's no future in it*). **5** *Grammar* the future tense. **6** (in *pl.*) *Stock Exch.* **a** goods and stocks sold for future delivery. **b** contracts for these. ☐ **for the future** = IN FUTURE. **in future** from now onward. ☐ **futureless** *adj.*

future perfect *n. Grammar* a tense giving the sense *will have done.*

future shock *n.* a state of distress or disorientation due to rapid social or technological change.

futurism *n.* (also **Futurism**) an early 20th-c. movement in art, literature, music, etc., concerned with celebrating and incorporating into art the energy and dynamism of modern technology.

futurist *n.* (often *attrib.*) **1** (also **Futurist**) an adherent of futurism. **2** a person who is concerned with or studies the future.

futuristic *adj.* **1** suitable for the future; ultra-modern (*futuristic design*). **2** (also **Futuristic**) of futurism. **3** relating to the future. ☐ **futuristically** *adv.*

futurology /,fjuːtʃəˈrɒlədʒi/ *n.* systematic forecasting of the future esp. from present trends in society. ☐ **futurological** *adj.* **futurologist** *n.*

fuze *var. of* FUSE².

fuzz ● *n.* **1** a mass of soft light particles; fluff. **2** fluffy or frizzled hair. **3** *slang* **a** the police. **b** a police officer. **4** an indistinct sound, image, etc. ● *v.tr. & intr.* make or become fluffy or blurred.

fuzzy *adj.* (**-ier, -iest**) **1 a** like fuzz. **b** frayed, fluffy. **c** frizzy. **2 a** blurred, indistinct, esp. in shape or outline. **b** imprecise, vague (*fuzzy thinking*). **c** (of a guitar sound etc.) buzzing, not crisp or distinct. ☐ **fuzzily** *adv.* **fuzziness** *n.*

fwd *abbr.* forward.

f.w.d. *abbr.* **1** four-wheel drive. **2** front-wheel drive.

FX *abbr.* = SPECIAL EFFECTS.

FYI *abbr.* for your information.

Gg

G¹ *n.* (also **g**) (*pl.* **Gs** or **G's**) **1** the seventh letter of the alphabet. **2** *Music* the fifth note in the diatonic scale of C major.

G² *abbr.* (also **G.**) **1** *N Amer. informal* = GRAND *n.* 2. **2** good. **3** Gulf. **4** (in Manitoba) = GENERAL *adj.* 11.

G³ *symbol* **1** gauss. **2** giga-. **3** conductance. **4** guanine.

g¹ *abbr.* (also **g.**) **1** gelding. **2** gas. **3** gauge.

g² *symbol* **1** gram(s). **2 a** gravity. **b** acceleration due to gravity.

GA *abbr.* Georgia (US) (in postal use).

Ga *symbol* gallium.

Ga. *abbr.* Georgia (US).

GAA *abbr.* = GOALS-AGAINST AVERAGE.

gab *informal* ● *n.* talk, chatter. ● *v.intr.* (**gabbed**, **gabbing**) talk, chatter. □ **gift of the gab** the facility of speaking eloquently or profusely. □ **gabby** *adj.* (**-ier, -iest**).

gabardine /'gæbər,di:n, -'di:n/ *n.* (also **gaberdine**) **1** a smooth durable twill-woven cloth esp. of worsted or cotton. **2** a garment made of this, esp. a raincoat.

gabble ● *v.* **1 a** *intr.* speak incoherently or inarticulately. **b** *tr.* utter rapidly and unintelligibly. **2** *intr.* (of geese, chickens, etc.) gaggle, cackle, etc. ● *n.* **1** voluble confused unintelligible talk. **2** the inarticulate noises made by some animals. □ **gabbler** *n.*

gabfest *n.* esp. *N Amer. informal* **1** a gathering in which there is much talking or chattering. **2** a prolonged conversation, esp. with chattering.

gabion /'geibiən/ *n.* an esp. cylindrical metal basket for filling with earth or stones, used in engineering or (formerly) in fortification.

gable *n.* **1 a** the triangular upper part of a wall enclosed by the two sloping planes of a ridged roof. **b** (in full **gable end**) a gable-topped wall. **2** a gable-shaped canopy over a window or door. □ **gabled** *adj.*

gad¹ *v.intr.* (**gadded**, **gadding**) (foll. by *about*, *around*) go about idly or in search of pleasure.

gad² *interj.* (also **Gad**) an expression of surprise or emphatic assertion.

gadabout *n.* an idle pleasure-seeker.

gadfly *n.* (*pl.* **-flies**) **1** a cattle-biting fly, esp. a horsefly. **2** a person who repeatedly criticizes or harasses others, esp. those in authority.

gadget *n.* an ingenious mechanical or electronic device or tool, esp. a non-essential one designed for a specific purpose. □ **gadgety** *adj.*

gadgetry *n.* gadgets collectively.

gadolinium /,gædə'liniəm/ *n.* a soft silvery metallic element occurring naturally.

Gael /geil/ *n.* a Gaelic Celt.

Gaelic /'geilik/ ● *n.* any of the Celtic languages spoken in Ireland and Scotland. ● *adj.* of or relating to the Celts of Ireland and Scotland, or their languages.

gaff ● *n.* **1 a** a stick with an iron hook for landing large fish, seals, etc. **b** a barbed fishing spear. **2** a spar to which the head of a fore-and-aft sail is bent. **3** *N Amer.* rough treatment; criticism. ● *v.tr.* seize (a fish etc.) with a gaff.

gaffe /gæf/ *n.* a blunder; an indiscreet act or remark.

gaffer *n.* **1** the chief electrician in a film or television production unit. **2** an old man; an elderly rustic. **3** *Cdn* (*Nfld*) a boy or youth at work with adults.

gag ● *n.* **1** a piece of cloth etc. thrust into or held over the mouth to prevent speaking or crying out. **2** a thing or circumstance restricting free speech. **3** *Parl.* a closure of a debate in a legislative assembly. **4** a joke or comic scene in a play, film, etc., or as part of a comedian's act. **5** an actor's interpolation in a dramatic dialogue. **6 a** a joke or hoax. **b** a humorous action or situation. **7** a device for keeping the jaws separated during a surgical procedure. ● *v.* (**gagged**, **gagging**) **1** *tr.* apply a gag to. **2** *tr.* silence; deprive of free speech. **3 a** *intr.* choke or retch. **b** *tr.* cause to do this. **4** *intr.* *Theatre* make gags.

gaga /'gɒgɒ/ *adj. slang* **1** senile. **2** slightly crazy. **3** (often foll. by *about*, *over*) exceedingly enthusiastic or infatuated (*went gaga over him*).

gage¹ *n.* **1** a pledge; a thing deposited as security. **2 a** a challenge to fight. **b** a symbol of this, esp. a glove thrown down.

gage² esp. *US var.* of GAUGE.

gaggle ● *n.* **1** a flock of geese. **2** *informal* a disorderly, noisy group. ● *v.intr.* (of geese) cackle.

gag order *n.* *N Amer. informal* **1** a court order banning the publication of information disclosed at a trial etc. **2** (also **gag rule**) any order, law, etc. banning the disclosure of information.

gaiety /'geiəti/ *n.* **1** the state of being lighthearted or merry; mirth. **2** merrymaking, amusement. **3** a bright appearance.

gaily *adv.* **1** in a gay or lighthearted manner. **2** with a bright or colourful appearance.

gain ● *v.* **1** *tr.* obtain or secure (usu. something desired or favourable) (*gain recognition*). **2** *tr.* acquire (a sum) as profits or as a result of changed conditions; earn. **3** *tr.* obtain as an increment or addition (*gain momentum*). **4** *tr.* win (a victory). **5** *intr.* (foll. by *in*) make a specified advance or improvement (*gained in stature*). **6 a** *intr.* (of a clock etc.) have the fault of becoming fast. **b** *tr.* be or become fast by (a specified amount of time). **7** *intr.* (often foll. by *on*, *upon*) come closer to a person or thing pursued. **8** *tr.* bring over to one's interest or views. **9** *tr.* reach or arrive at (a desired place). ● *n.* **1** something gained, achieved, etc. **2** an increase of possessions etc.; a profit, advance, or improvement. **3** the acquisition of wealth. **4** (in *pl.*) sums of money acquired. **5** an increase in amount, weight, etc. □ **gain time** improve one's chances by causing or exploiting a delay. □ **gainer** *n.*

gainful *adj.* **1** (of employment) paid. **2** lucrative, remunerative. □ **gainfully** *adv.* **gainfulness** *n.*

gainsay /gein'sei, 'geinsei/ *v.tr.* (*past* and *past part.* **gainsaid** /-'sed/) deny, contradict. □ **gainsayer** *n.*

gait *n.* **1** a manner of walking. **2** the manner of forward motion of esp. a horse, e.g. walk, gallop.

gaiter *n.* a covering of cloth, leather, etc. for the ankle, or ankle and lower leg, and often extending to the instep, worn over the shoe.

gal *n.* esp. *N Amer. slang* a girl or woman.

gal. *abbr.* gallon(s).

gala /'gɑːlə, 'geɪlə/ n. (often attrib.) a festive or special occasion (a gala performance).

galactic adj. of or relating to a galaxy or galaxies, esp. the Milky Way.

galaxy n. (pl. **-ies**) **1** any of many independent systems of stars, gas, dust, etc., held together by gravitational attraction. **2** (**Galaxy**) = MILKY WAY. **3** (foll. by of) a brilliant company or gathering.

gale n. **1 a** a very strong wind. **b** Meteorol. a wind of force 8 on the Beaufort scale, or 34–40 knots. **2** Naut. a storm. **3** an outburst, esp. of laughter.

galena /gə'liːnə/ n. lead sulphide, the principal ore of lead.

Galician¹ /gə'lɪʃən/ hist. ● n. **1** a Slavic immigrant to W Canada, esp. a Ukrainian. **2** the language of Galicians. ● adj. of or pertaining to Galicians.

Galician² ● n. **1** a person from Galicia, a medieval Castilian kingdom, later a Spanish province. **2** the language of Galicia, closely related to Portuguese. ● adj. of or pertaining to Galicia or its inhabitants.

gall¹ n. **1** impudence; audacity. **2** asperity, rancour. **3** anything bitter (gall and wormwood). **4** the bile of animals. **5** the gallbladder, esp. of an animal.

gall² ● n. **1** a sore on the skin made by chafing. **2** a mental soreness or vexation. **b** a cause of this. ● v.tr. **1** vex, annoy, humiliate. **2** rub sore; injure by rubbing. □ **galling** adj. **gallingly** adv.

gall³ n. **1** a growth produced by insects or fungus etc. on plants and trees, esp. on oak. **2** (attrib.) of insects producing galls (gall wasp).

gall. abbr. gallon(s).

gallant ● adj. /'gælənt/ **1** brave, noble. **2** /'gælənt, gə'lænt/ markedly attentive or polite, esp. to women. **3** (of a ship, horse, etc.) grand, fine, stately. ● n. /'gælənt, gə'lænt/ a ladies' man; a lover or paramour. ● v. /gə'lænt/ **1** tr. flirt with. **2** tr. escort; act as a cavalier to (a lady). **3** intr. **a** play the gallant. **b** (foll. by with) flirt. □ **gallantly** /'gæləntli/ adv.

gallantry n. (pl. **-ies**) **1** bravery; dashing courage. **2** courtliness. **3** a polite act or speech.

gallbladder n. the vessel storing bile after its secretion by the liver and before release into the intestine.

galleon /'gælɪən/ n. hist. a square-rigged ship with three or more decks and masts, having a high forecastle and poop, used chiefly by Spain from the 15th to the 18th c., originally as a warship.

galleria /galə'riːə/ n. a collection of stores under one often high glass roof.

gallery n. (pl. **-ies**) **1** a room or building for showing works of art. **2** a balcony, esp. a platform projecting from the inner wall of a church, hall, etc., providing extra room for spectators etc. or reserved for musicians, the press, etc. **3 a** the highest balcony in a theatre, usu. with the cheapest seats. **b** its occupants. **4 a** a covered space for walking in, partly open at the side; a portico or colonnade. **b** a long narrow passage in the thickness of a wall or supported on corbels, open towards the interior of the building. **5** N Amer. (esp. Que., Nfld, and Gulf States) a veranda, esp. one surrounding a building on all sides. **6** a long narrow room, passage, or corridor. **7** Military & Mining a horizontal underground passage. **8** a collection or assembly, esp. on display. □ **play to the gallery** seek approval by appealing to popular taste. □ **galleried** adj.

galley n. (pl. **-eys**) **1** hist. **a** a low flat single-decked vessel using sails and oars, and usu. rowed by slaves or criminals. **b** an ancient Greek or Roman warship with one or more banks of oars. **c** a large open rowboat, e.g. that used by the captain of a man-of-war. **2** the kitchen in a ship, aircraft, camper, etc. **3**

(in full **galley proof**) a proof in the form of long single-column strips, not in sheets or pages.

Gallic /'gælɪk/ adj. **1** French or typically French. **2** of the Gauls. □ **Gallicize** v.tr. & intr.

Gallicism /'gælɪˌsɪzəm/ n. a French word or usage, esp. one adopted in another language.

gallium /'gælɪəm/ n. a soft bluish-white metallic element which melts just above room temperature, used in high-temperature thermometers etc.

gallivant /'gælɪˌvænt/ v.intr. **1** (often foll. by around) idly search for pleasure; gad about. **2** flirt.

gallon n. **1 a** (in full **imperial gallon**) (in Britain and other Commonwealth countries and formerly in Canada) a measure of capacity equal to eight pints and equivalent to 4.55 litres, used esp. for liquids. **b** (in full **US gallon**) (in the US) a measure of capacity equivalent to 3.79 litres, used for liquids. **2** (usu. in pl.) informal a large amount.

gallop ● n. **1** the fastest pace of a horse or other quadruped, with all the feet off the ground together in each stride. **2** a ride at this pace. ● v. (**galloped**, **galloping**) **1 a** intr. (of a horse etc. or its rider) go at the pace of a gallop. **b** tr. make (a horse etc.) gallop. **2** intr. **a** run with leaping strides, as in a gallop. **b** move or progress rapidly (galloping inflation). □ **at a gallop** at the pace of a gallop.

galloway /'gæləˌweɪ/ n. a breed of hornless black beef cattle.

gallows n.pl. (usu. treated as sing.) **1** a structure, usu. of two uprights and a crosspiece, for the hanging of criminals. **2** (prec. by the) execution by hanging.

gallows humour n. grim and ironic humour.

gallstone n. a small hard mass forming in the gallbladder or bile ducts from bile pigments, cholesterol, and calcium salts.

Gallup poll n. an assessment of public opinion by questioning a representative sample.

galoot n. N Amer. informal a person, esp. a strange or clumsy one.

galore adv. in abundance (flowers galore).

galosh n. (usu. in pl.) a waterproof overshoe, usu. of rubber.

galumph v.intr. informal **1** move noisily or clumsily. **2** go prancing in triumph.

galvanic /gæl'vænɪk/ adj. **1** of or producing an electric current by chemical action. **2 a** sudden and remarkable; convulsive (a galvanic response). **b** stimulating; full of energy; electrifying (a galvanic speech). □ **galvanically** adv.

galvanize /'gælvəˌnaɪz/ v.tr. **1** (often foll. by into) rouse forcefully, esp. by shock or excitement (was galvanized into action). **2** stimulate by or as if by electricity. **3** coat (metal, esp. iron or steel) with zinc (usu. without the use of electricity) as a protection against rust. □ **galvanization** n. **galvanizer** n.

gam n. informal (usu in pl.) a leg, esp. a woman's attractive leg.

Gamay /gæ'meɪ/ n. **1** a variety of black wine grape native to the Beaujolais district of France. **2** a fruity red wine made from this grape.

gambit n. **1** a chess opening in which a player sacrifices a piece or pawn to secure an advantage. **2** an opening move in a discussion etc. **3** a trick or device, esp. to secure an advantage.

gamble ● v. **1** intr. play games of chance for money, esp. for high stakes. **2** tr. **a** bet (a sum of money) in gambling. **b** (often foll. by away) lose (assets) by gambling. **3** intr. take great risks in the hope of substantial gain. **4** intr. (foll. by on) act in the hope or expectation of (*gambled on fine weather*). ● *n.* **1** a risky undertaking or attempt, esp. in the hope of substantial gain. **2** an act of gambling. □ **gambler** *n.*

gambol /'gæmbəl/ ● *v.intr.* (**gambolled**, **gambolling**) frolic playfully. ● *n.* a playful frolic.

gambrel /'gæmbrəl/ *n.* (in full **gambrel roof**) *N Amer.* a two-sided roof with two planes on each side, the lower one steeper.

game¹ ● *n.* **1 a** an amusement, diversion, pastime, etc. **b** a form of contest played according to rules and decided by skill, strength, or luck. **2** a single portion of play forming a scoring unit in some contests, e.g. tennis. **3** (in *pl.*) a meeting for athletic etc. contests (*Olympic Games*). **4** a winning score in a game; the state of the score in a game (*the game is two all*). **5** the apparatus necessary to play a game, esp. a board or computer game. **6** one's level of achievement in, or style of playing a game (*improving their game*). **7 a** a piece of fun; a jest (*was only playing a game with you*). **b** (in *pl.*) dodges, tricks (*none of your games!*). **8** a scheme or undertaking etc. regarded as a game (*so that's your game*). **9 a** a policy or plan of action. **b** = GAME PLAN. **10 a** wild animals or birds hunted for sport or food. **b** the flesh of these. **11** a hunted animal; a quarry or object of pursuit or attack. ● *adj.* **1** spirited; eager and willing. **2** (foll. by *for*, or *to* + infin.) having the spirit or energy; eagerly prepared. ● *v.* **1** *intr.* play at games of chance for money; gamble. **2** *tr.* & *intr.* = WAR GAME. □ **the game is up** the scheme is revealed or foiled. **give the game away** reveal something one would rather keep hidden, esp. inadvertently. **game over** esp. *Cdn slang* all is lost; there is no more hope. **make game** (or **a game**) **of** mock, taunt. **off** (or **on**) **one's game** playing badly (or well). **play the game** behave fairly or according to the rules. □ **gamely** *adv.* **gameness** *n.*

game² *adj.* (of a leg, arm, etc.) lame, crippled.

game bird *n.* **1** a bird shot for sport or food. **2** a bird of the order *Galliformes*, which includes grouse etc.

game farm *n.* an esp. public farm where wild animals are kept.

game fish *n.* (*pl.* same or **game fishes**) a kind of fish caught for sport.

gamekeeper *n.* a person employed to breed and protect game.

gamelan /'gæmə,læn/ *n.* **1** an Indonesian orchestra with a wide range of metal percussion instruments. **2** a kind of xylophone used in this.

game misconduct *n.* *Hockey* a penalty banishing a player for the rest of the current game.

game of chance *n.* a game decided by luck, not skill.

game plan *n.* esp. *N Amer.* **1** a winning strategy worked out in advance for a particular match. **2** a plan of campaign, esp. in politics.

game point *n.* (in tennis etc.) a point which, if won, would win the game.

gamer *n.* **1** *N Amer. informal* an athlete known for consistently making a strong effort. **2** a person who plays a game or games.

game show *n.* a television program in which people compete in a game or quiz, usu. for prizes.

gamesmanship *n.* the art or practice of defeating an opponent by psychological or other questionable (but not strictly illegal) means.

games room *n.* (also **game room**) a room, esp. in a hotel, student residence, etc., equipped for playing games, e.g. table tennis, billiards, darts, etc.

gamete /'gæmi:t, gə'mi:t/ *n.* *Biol.* a mature haploid reproductive cell (male or female) which unites with

another of the opposite sex in sexual reproduction to form a zygote.

game warden *n.* an official locally supervising game, hunting and fishing, etc.

game-winner *n.* the goal, run, etc. that puts one team ahead of the other by the end of the game.

gamey *adj.* = GAMY.

gamine /'gæmi:n, gæ'mi:n/ ● *n.* **1** a girl with mischievous or boyish charm. **2** a girl street urchin. ● *adj.* of or like a gamine (*a short, gamine haircut*).

gaming table *n.* a table used for gambling.

gamma /'gæmə/ *n.* **1** the third letter of the Greek alphabet (Γ, γ). **2** (*attrib.*) designating the third member of a series or set. **3** *Astronomy* the third brightest star in a constellation. **4** (*attrib.*) designating high-energy electromagnetic radiation of wavelengths shorter than those of X-rays (*gamma rays*).

gamma globulin *n.* a mixture of blood plasma proteins, mainly immunoglobulins, of relatively low electrophoretic mobility, often given to boost immunity.

gamut /'gæmət/ *n.* the whole series or range or scope of anything (*the whole gamut of crime*). □ **run the gamut** experience or include the complete range.

gamy *adj.* (**gamier**, **gamiest**) **1** having the strong flavour or scent of game kept until it is high. **2** *N Amer.* scandalous, sensational. **3** = GAME¹ *adj.* □ **gamily** *adv.* **gaminess** *n.*

gander *n.* **1** a male goose. **2** *informal* a look, a glance.

gang *n.* **1 a** an organized group of criminals. **b** *informal* a group of people who regularly associate together. **c** an organized territorial group of esp. urban youth demanding loyalty from members, engaging in various criminal activities, and often violently rivalling other groups. **2** a set of workers, slaves, or prisoners. □ **gang up** *informal* **1** (foll. by *on*) combine against. **2** (often foll. by *with*) act in concert.

gangbang *slang* ● *v. tr.* & *intr.* **1** (of several men) have sexual intercourse successively with the same person, esp. violently. **2** (of a gang) attack members of a rival gang. ● *n.* an instance of gangbanging. □ **gangbanger** *n.*

gangbuster *N Amer. informal* ● *n.* a person who takes part in the aggressive breakup of criminal gangs. ● *adj.* (often as **gangbusters**) outstandingly successful. □ **go gangbusters** be vigorously successful. **like gangbusters** energetically, vigorously; successfully.

gangland *n.* (often *attrib.*) the world of gangs and gangsters (*a gangland killing*).

gangle *v.intr.* move ungracefully.

gangling *adj.* (of a person) loosely built; lanky.

ganglion /'gæŋglian/ *n.* (*pl.* **ganglia** /-liə/ or **-s**) **1 a** an enlargement or knot on a nerve etc. containing an assemblage of nerve cells. **b** a mass of grey matter in the central nervous system forming a nerve nucleus. **2** a cyst, esp. on a tendon sheath.

gangly *adj.* (**-ier**, **-iest**) = GANGLING.

gangplank *n.* a plank usu. with cleats nailed on it for boarding or disembarking from a ship etc.

gang rape *n.* the successive rape of a person by a group of people. □ **gang-rape** *v.tr.*

gangrene /'gæŋgri:n, gæŋ'gri:n/ ● *n.* **1** *Med.* death and decomposition of a part of the body tissue, usu. resulting from obstructed circulation or bacterial infection. **2** moral corruption. ● *v.tr.* & *intr.* affect or become affected with gangrene.

gangsta *n.* **1** *slang* = GANGSTER. **2** (in full **gangsta rap**) a style of rap music, chiefly from the Los Angeles area, the lyrics of which centre on the violence of gang culture, racism, police brutality, etc.

gangster n. a member of a gang of violent criminals. □ **gangsterish** adj. **gangsterism** n.

gangway ● n. **1 a** an opening in the bulwarks by which a ship is entered or left. **b** a bridge laid from ship to shore or to another ship. **c** a passage on a ship, esp. a platform connecting the quarterdeck and forecastle. **2** a temporary arrangement of planks for crossing muddy or difficult ground on a construction site etc. ● interj. make way!

ganja /ˈgændʒə, ˈgɒn-/ n. a potent form of marijuana for smoking.

gannet /ˈgænət/ n. any seabird of the genus Sula, esp. the northern gannet, Sula bassana, catching fish by plunge-diving, and nesting in large colonies on ledges of coastal islands.

gantlet /ˈgæntlət/ N Amer. var. of GAUNTLET².

gantry n. (pl. **-ies**) **1** a bridgelike overhead structure whose span supports railway or road signals etc. **2** a structure supporting a rocket prior to launching.

gaol /dʒeɪl/ n. esp. Brit. var. of JAIL. □ **gaoler** n.

gap n. **1** an unfilled space or interval; a blank; a break in continuity. **2** a breach in a hedge, fence, or wall. **3** a wide (usu. undesirable) divergence in views, sympathies, development, etc. (generation gap). **4** a gorge or pass. □ **fill** (or **close** etc.) **the gap** make up a deficiency. □ **gapped** adj. **gappy** adj.

gape ● v.intr. **1 a** open one's mouth wide, esp. in amazement or wonder. **b** be or become wide open. **2** (foll. by at) gaze curiously or wondrously. **3** split; break apart. **4** yawn. ● n. **1** an open-mouthed stare. **2** a yawn. **3 a** the expanse of an open mouth or beak. **b** the part of a beak that opens. **4** a rent or opening. □ **gaper** n. **gapingly** adv.

gap-toothed adj. having gaps between the teeth.

garage /gəˈrɒʒ, -ˈrɒdʒ, -ˈrædʒ, -ˈræʒ/ n. **1** a building or shed for the storage of a motor vehicle or vehicles. **2 a** an establishment that sells gasoline, repairs motor vehicles, etc. **b** the area at such an establishment where vehicles are serviced. **3** (attrib.) denoting raw, unpolished, usu. energetic guitar-based rock music, esp. as played by amateurs in suburban garages or basements (garage rock).

garage sale n. N Amer. a sale of used household goods, clothes, books, etc. held in the garage or on the lawn of a private house.

garb ● n. **1** clothing, esp. of a distinctive kind. **2** the way a person is dressed. ● v.tr. **1** (usu. in passive or refl.) put (esp. distinctive) clothes on (a person). **2** attire.

garbage n. **1 a** refuse. **b** household waste. **2** anything worthless. **3** nonsense. **4** Computing incorrect or useless data (garbage in, garbage out). □ **garbagey** adj.

garbage bag n. N Amer. a large, often black or dark green plastic bag for holding garbage.

garbage can n. (also **garbage bin, garbage pail**) N Amer. a container for household refuse.

garbage disposal n. (also **garbage disposer**) N Amer. a system installed in a kitchen sink, with blades in the drain to mulch refuse.

garbageman n. N Amer. a person employed to remove garbage, esp. from the curbside, and transport it to a dump.

garbanzo /gɑrˈbɒnzoʊ/ n. = CHICKPEA.

garble ● v.tr. **1** unintentionally distort or confuse (facts, messages, etc.). **2 a** mutilate in order to misrepresent. **b** make (usu. unfair or malicious) selections from (facts, statements, etc.). ● n. garbled speech or sounds.

garburator /ˈgɑrbəˌreɪtər/ n. Cdn a garbage disposal.

garçon /gɑrˈsɔ̃/ n. (pl. **garçons** pronunc. same) a waiter in a French restaurant, hotel, etc.

garden ● n. **1 a** esp. N Amer. a piece of ground adjoining a private house, used for growing flowers, vegetables, etc. **b** a backyard or front yard adjoining a private house, usu. including a lawn and vegetable or flower garden. **2** (often in pl.) ornamental grounds laid out for public enjoyment (botanical gardens). **3** (attrib.) **a** (of plants) cultivated, not wild. **b** for use in a garden (garden tools). **4** an especially fertile region (the Garden of the Gulf). **5** N Amer. (often in pl.) a large hall or sports arena (Maple Leaf Gardens). ● v.intr. cultivate or work in a garden. □ **gardened** adj. **gardening** n.

garden centre n. a store where plants and garden equipment etc. are sold.

gardener n. a person who gardens or is employed to tend a garden.

gardenia /gɑrˈdiːniə/ n. any tree or shrub of the genus Gardenia, with large white or yellow flowers.

garden party n. a social event held on a lawn or in a garden.

garden path n. a path through a garden. □ **lead a person down** (or **up**) **the garden path** mislead a person into error, folly, etc.

garden salad n. N Amer. a salad made with common garden vegetables, e.g. lettuce, tomatoes, cucumbers.

garden-variety attrib.adj. N Amer. commonplace.

gargantuan /gɑrˈgæntʃuən/ adj. enormous, gigantic.

gargle ● v. **1 a** intr. wash one's mouth and throat, esp. for medicinal purposes, with a liquid kept in motion by a stream of air which is breathed out. **b** tr. take (a liquid) in this way. **2** intr. make a sound as when doing this. **3** tr. say with a gargle. ● n. **1** a liquid for gargling. **2** the sound of gargling.

gargoyle n. **1** a grotesque carved human or animal face or figure projecting from the gutter of (esp. a Gothic) building usu. as a spout to carry water clear of a wall. **2** any grotesque figure of a human or animal. □ **gargoylish** adj.

garish /ˈgeərɪʃ, ˈgæ-/ adj. **1** overly bright; showy. **2** overdecorated. □ **garishly** adv. **garishness** n.

garland ● n. **1** a wreath of flowers, leaves, etc., worn on the head or around the neck, or hung as a decoration. **2** a prize or distinction. ● v.tr. **1** adorn with garlands. **2** crown with a garland.

garlic n. **1** any of various plants, esp. Allium sativum. **2** the strong-smelling pungent-tasting bulb of this plant, divided into cloves, used as a flavouring in cooking. □ **garlicky** adj.

garlic bread n. bread, usu. served hot, spread with butter flavoured with garlic.

garment n. **1** an article of clothing. **2** the outward and visible covering of anything.

garner ● v.tr. **1** collect. **2** earn, get (garnered 40 per cent of the vote). **3** store, deposit. ● n. literary a storehouse or granary.

garnet ● n. **1** a vitreous silicate mineral, esp. a transparent, deep red kind used as a gem. **2** a deep red colour. ● adj. of this colour.

garnish ● v.tr. **1** decorate or embellish (esp. food). **2** Law **a** serve notice on (a person) for the purpose of legally seizing money belonging to a debtor or defendant. **b** summon (a person) as a party to litigation started between others. ● n. a decoration or embellishment, esp. to food.

garnishee Law ● n. a third party required to surrender money belonging to a debtor or defendant in compliance with a court order obtained by the creditor or plaintiff. ● *v.tr.* (**garnishees**, **garnisheed**) recover a debt from (a person, his or her wages) by garnishee order.

garnishee order *n.* (also **garnishee proceedings**) a legal order requiring a garnishee to surrender money that he or she holds on behalf of or owes to a debtor.

garret /ˈgerət, ˈgær-/ *n.* **1** a top-floor or attic room, esp. a dismal one. **2** an attic.

garrison ● *n.* **1** the troops stationed in a fortress, town, etc., to defend it. **2** the building occupied by them. ● *v.tr.* **1** provide (a place) with or occupy as a garrison. **2** place on garrison duty.

garrotte /gəˈrɒt/ (also **garotte**) ● *n.* **1** a wire or cord, esp. one with handles attached at each end, used for strangling a person. **2** a method of execution by strangulation in which an iron or wire collar is tightened around the neck. **3** the apparatus used for this. ● *v.tr.* **1** strangle or throttle by means of a wire, cord, etc. **2** execute by means of a garrotte.

garrulous /ˈgerʊləs, ˈgær-/ *adj.* **1** talkative, esp. on trivial matters. **2** loquacious, wordy. □ **garrulity** /gəˈruːlɪti/ *n.* **garrulously** *adv.* **garrulousness** *n.*

garter ● *n.* **1** **a** a band worn to keep a sock or stocking up. **b** a similar band for keeping a shirt sleeve up. **2** *N Amer.* a suspender for a sock or stocking, attached to a garter belt. ● *v.tr.* fasten (a stocking) or encircle (a leg) with a garter.

garter belt *n. N Amer.* an undergarment with suspenders for holding up socks or stockings.

garter snake *n.* any of several harmless, largely semi-aquatic snakes of the genus *Thamnophis*, often with more or less distinct lengthwise stripes on the back, widespread in N America.

gas ● *n.* (*pl.* **gases**) **1** any airlike substance which moves freely to fill any space available, irrespective of its quantity, esp. one that does not become liquid or solid at ordinary temperatures. **2** (often *attrib.*) such a substance (esp. found naturally or extracted from coal) used as a domestic or industrial fuel, e.g. natural gas, propane (*gas stove*). **3** *N Amer.* **a** gasoline. **b** the accelerator of an automotive vehicle. **4** nitrous oxide or another gas used as an anaesthetic (esp. in dentistry). **5** a gas or vapour used as a poisonous agent to disable an enemy in warfare. **6** *informal* pointless idle talk; boasting. **7** *slang* an enjoyable, attractive, or amusing thing or person (*the party was a gas*). **8** *N Amer.* intestinal gas. ● *v.* (**gases**, **gassed**, **gassing**) **1** *tr.* expose to gas, esp. to kill or make unconscious. **2** *tr.* (usu. foll. by *up*) *N Amer. informal* fill (the tank of a motor vehicle) with gasoline. **3** *intr.* give off gas. **4** *intr. informal* talk idly or boastfully. □ **run out of gas** (or **steam**) lose one's impetus or energy.

gasbag *n.* **1** a container of gas, esp. for holding the gas for a balloon or airship. **2** *slang* an idle talker.

gas bar *n. Cdn* a gas station, esp. one without a garage, consisting of a kiosk and pumps only.

gas chamber *n.* an airtight chamber that can be filled with poisonous gas to kill people or animals.

gaseous /ˈgæsɪəs, ˈgæʃəs/ *adj.* **1** of or like gas. **2** *informal* vague, not definite (*a gaseous speech*).

gas-fired *adj.* using natural gas as the fuel.

gas guzzler *n. N Amer.* an esp. large, heavy car which consumes much gas. □ **gas-guzzling** *adj.*

gash ● *n.* **1** a long and deep slash or wound. **2** a cleft such as might be made by a slashing cut. **3** the act of making such a slash or cut. ● *v.tr.* make a gash in.

gasify *v.tr. & intr.* (**-ies**, **-ied**) convert or be converted into gas. □ **gasification** *n.*

gas jet *n.* a jet of burning gas.

gasket *n.* a sheet or ring of rubber etc., shaped to seal the junction of metal surfaces. □ **blow a gasket** *slang* lose one's temper.

gaslight *n.* **1** a jet of burning gas, usu. heating a mantle, to provide light. **2** light emanating from this. □ **gaslit** *adj.*

gas mask *n.* a respirator used as a defence against noxious gas.

gasohol /ˈgæsəhɒl/ *n.* a mixture of gasoline and ethyl alcohol used as fuel.

gasoline *n. N Amer.* a volatile inflammable liquid obtained from petroleum and used as fuel in motor vehicles etc.

gasoline station *n. N Amer.* = GAS STATION.

gasp ● *v.* **1** *intr.* catch one's breath with an open mouth as in exhaustion or astonishment. **2** *intr.* (foll. by *for*) strain to obtain by gasping (*gasped for air*). **3** *tr.* (often foll. by *out*) utter with gasps. ● *n.* a convulsive catching of breath. □ **gaspingly** *adv.*

gas pedal *n.* the accelerator pedal on a car etc.

gasper *n.* a person who gasps.

gaspereau /ˈgæspərəʊ/ *n.* (*pl.* **-eaux**) *Cdn* = ALEWIFE 1.

Gaspesian /gæsˈpeɪʒən/ *Cdn* ● *n.* a native or resident of the Gaspé Peninsula. ● *adj.* of or pertaining to the Gaspé Peninsula.

gas pump *n. N Amer.* a pump with a hose and nozzle for transferring gasoline from a gas station's reservoir to a motor vehicle etc.

gassed *adj.* **1** in senses of GAS *v.* **2** *informal* drunk.

gas station *n. N Amer.* an establishment selling gasoline etc. for refuelling motor vehicles, often including a garage.

gassy *adj.* (**-ier, -iest**) **1 a** of or like gas. **b** full of gas. **2** *informal* (of talk etc.) pointless, verbose.

gastric *adj.* of the stomach.

gastric acid *n.* **1** acid secreted by the stomach as a component of gastric juice. **2** gastric juice considered with respect to its acidic properties.

gastric juice *n.* a thin clear virtually colourless acid fluid secreted by the stomach glands and active in promoting digestion.

gastritis /gæˈstraɪtɪs/ *n.* inflammation of the lining of the stomach.

gastro- /ˈgæstrəʊ/ *comb. form* (also **gastr-** before a vowel) stomach.

gastroenteritis *n. Med.* inflammation of the stomach and intestines.

gastroenterology /ˌgæstrəʊentəˈrɒlədʒi/ *n.* the branch of medicine which deals with disorders of the stomach and intestines. □ **gastroenterological** *adj.* **gastroenterologist** *n.*

gastrointestinal *adj.* of or relating to the stomach and the intestines.

gastronomy /gæˈstrɒnəmi/ *n.* **1** the practice, study, or art of eating and drinking well. **2** = CUISINE. □ **gastronomic** *adj.* **gastronomical** *adj.*

gastropod /ˈgæstrəˌpɒd/ *n.* any mollusc of the class Gastropoda that moves along by means of a large muscular foot, e.g. a snail, slug, etc.

gas turbine *n.* a turbine driven by a flow of gas or by gas from combustion.

gate¹ ● *n.* **1** a barrier, usu. hinged, used to close an opening made for entrance and exit through a wall, fence, etc. **2 a** such an opening, esp. in the wall of a city, enclosure, or large building. **b** a monument resembling a gate or gateway, esp. adorning the entrance to a park etc. **3** a means of entrance or exit. **4** a numbered place of access to aircraft at an airport or trains at a train station. **5** a device for holding the frame of a motion-picture film momentarily in position behind the lens of a camera or projector. **6 a** an electrical signal that causes or controls the passage of other signals. **b** an electrical circuit with an output which depends on the combination of several inputs. **7** a device regulating the passage of water in a lock etc. **8 a** the number of people entering by payment at the gates of a sporting event etc. **b** (in full **gate money**) the proceeds taken for admission. **9** N Amer. slang dismissal. **10** = STARTING GATE. **11** a barrier at a level crossing or at a toll booth. **12** Skiing an arrangement of two flexible poles implanted in the snow of a slalom course between which a skier must pass. ● v.tr. **1** Electricity subject (a signal) to the action of a gate. **2** Cdn retain (an inmate, esp. a dangerous offender) in prison for the full length of a sentence, by arresting the inmate as soon as he or she is released under mandatory supervision. □ **get** (or **be given**) **the gate** N Amer. slang be dismissed.

gate[2] n. **1** (prec. or prefixed by a name) a street (Westgate). **2** Cdn (PEI) a lane or driveway.

-gate comb. form forming nouns denoting an actual or alleged scandal (and usu. an attempted cover-up).

gatecrasher n. an uninvited guest at a party etc. □ **gatecrash** v.tr. & intr.

gated adj. **1** (of a road, fence, etc.) having a gate or gates to control the movement of traffic or animals. **2** (of a subdivision etc.) enclosed by walls etc. with access controlled by security guards.

gatehouse n. a house standing by a gateway, esp. to a large house or park.

gatekeeper n. **1** an attendant at a gate, controlling entrance and exit. **2** a thing or person that controls access to or availability of information etc.

gatepost n. a post on which a gate is hung or against which it shuts. □ **between you and me and the gatepost** informal in strict confidence.

gateway n. **1** an entrance with or opening for a gate. **2** a frame or structure built over a gate. **3** a means of access or entry (gateway to the Prairies). **4** Computing a device or software used to connect two networks.

gather ● v. **1** tr. & intr. bring or come together; assemble, accumulate. **2** tr. (usu. foll. by up) **a** bring together from scattered places or sources. **b** take up together from the ground, a surface, etc. **c** draw together or into a smaller compass (gathered her scarf around her). **d** take (a person) into one's embrace (gathered him into her arms). **3** tr. acquire by gradually collecting. **4** tr. **a** pick a quantity of (flowers etc.). **b** collect (grain etc.) as a harvest. **5** tr. (often foll. by that + clause) infer or understand. **6** tr. be subjected to or affected by the accumulation or increase of (gathering dust; gather speed). **7** tr. (often foll. by up) summon up (one's thoughts, energy, etc.) for a purpose. **8** tr. **a** draw (material) together in folds or wrinkles. **b** pucker or draw together (part of a dress) by running a thread through. ● n. **1** an act or instance of gathering. **2** (in pl.) a part of a garment that is gathered or drawn in. □ **gatherer** n.

gathering ● n. **1** an assembly or meeting. **2** a purulent swelling. **3** a group of leaves taken together in bookbinding. **4** the gathers formed by drawing up a fabric. ● adj. increasing in intensity etc.

gator n. (also **'gator**) esp. N Amer. informal an alligator.

GATT abbr. General Agreement on Tariffs and Trade.

gauche / ɡoʊʃ/ adj. **1** lacking ease or grace; socially awkward. **2** tactless.

gaucho / ˈɡaʊtʃoʊ/ n. (pl. **-os**) **1** a cowboy from the S American pampas. **2** N Amer. (in pl.) (in full **gaucho pants**) wide, calf-length pants.

gaudy adj. (**-ier**, **-iest**) tastelessly or extravagantly bright or showy. □ **gaudily** adv. **gaudiness** n.

gauge ● n. **1** a standard measure to which certain things must conform, esp.: **a** the measure of the inner diameter of an esp. shotgun barrel, representing the number of lead balls of that diameter required to make one pound. **b** the fineness of a textile. **c** the thickness of sheet metal, wire, or other usu. thin materials or objects. **2** any of various instruments for measuring or determining this, or for measuring length, thickness, or other dimensions or properties. **3** the distance between a pair of rails or the wheels on one axle. **4** the capacity, extent, or scope of something. **5** a means of estimating; a criterion or test. **6** a graduated instrument measuring the force or quantity of rainfall, pressure, fuel, wind, etc. ● v.tr. **1** measure exactly (esp. objects of standard size). **2** determine the capacity of. **3** estimate or form a judgment of (a person, temperament, situation, etc.). **4** make uniform; bring to a standard size or shape.

Gaul / ɡɔl/ n. a native or inhabitant of ancient Gaul, a region of Europe corresponding to France, Belgium, the S Netherlands, SW Germany, and N Italy.

gaunch / ɡɔntʃ/ n. Cdn (esp. BC & Alta.) slang underwear.

gaunt adj. **1** lean, haggard. **2** grim or desolate in appearance. □ **gauntly** adv. **gauntness** n.

gauntlet[1] n. **1** a sturdy glove long enough to cover the wrist and part of the forearm. **2** hist. an armoured glove. **3** the part of a glove covering the wrist. □ **take** (or **pick**) **up the gauntlet** see TAKE. **throw down the gauntlet** see THROW. □ **gauntleted** adj.

gauntlet[2] n. **1** a former esp. military punishment in which the offender was required to pass between two rows of people and receive blows from them. **2** the rows of people inflicting this punishment. **3** an ordeal or series of ordeals (the gauntlet of entrance exams). □ **run the gauntlet 1** be subjected to harsh criticism. **2** pass between the two rows of a gauntlet as a punishment.

gauss / ɡaʊs/ n. (pl. same or **gausses**) a unit of magnetic induction, equal to one ten-thousandth of a tesla. Abbr.: **G**.

gauze n. **1** a thin transparent fabric of silk, cotton, etc. **2** Med. thin loosely woven material used for dressings etc. **3** a fine mesh of wire etc. **4** a slight haze.

gauzy adj. (**-ier**, **-iest**) **1** like gauze; thin and translucent. **2** flimsy, delicate. □ **gauzily** adv. **gauziness** n.

gave past of GIVE.

gavel / ˈɡævəl/ ● n. a small hammer used by an auctioneer, or for calling a meeting to order. ● v. (**gavelled**, **gavelling**) **1** intr. use a gavel. **2** tr. call to order or end (a meeting) or dismiss (a speaker) by use of a gavel.

Gawd interj. slang God (see GOD 4).

gawk ● v.intr. informal stare stupidly. ● n. an awkward or bashful person. □ **gawker** n.

gawky adj. (**-ier**, **-iest**) awkward or ungainly. □ **gawkily** adv. **gawkiness** n.

gawp v.intr. informal stare stupidly or obtrusively; gape. □ **gawper** n.

gay ● adj. **1 a** homosexual. **b** of or pertaining to homosexuals (a gay bar). ¶The use of gay to mean 'homosexual' is favoured by homosexuals, and is now well established and in widespread general use. In many instances it is restricted in application to male homosexuals and contrasted with lesbian when discussing homosexuals as a group. **2 a** lighthearted and carefree; mirthful. **b** characterized by cheerfulness or pleasure (a gay life). **c** brightly coloured;

showy, brilliant (*a gay scarf*). ● *n.* a homosexual, esp. male. ☐ **gayness** *n.*

gay bashing *n.* esp. *N Amer. informal* **1** unprovoked verbal and esp. physical attacking of a homosexual or homosexuals. **2** an instance of this. ☐ **gay-bash** *v.intr. & tr.* **gay-basher** *n.*

gaze ● *v.intr.* (foll. by *at*, *into*, *on*, *upon*, etc.) look fixedly. ● *n.* a fixed or intent look. ☐ **gazer** *n.*

gazebo / ɡə'ziːbəː/ *n.* (*pl.* **-os** or **-oes**) a small structure in a garden, park etc., usu. open or with screens on all sides to give a wide view.

gazelle *n.* any of various small antelopes of Asia or Africa, esp. of the genus *Gazella.*

gazette ● *n.* **1** a newspaper (used esp. in names). **2** (in Canada, the UK, and other Commonwealth countries) an official journal with a list of government appointments, bankruptcies, and other public notices. ● *v.tr.* (in Canada, the UK, and other Commonwealth countries) announce in an official gazette.

gazetteer / ˌɡæzə'tiːr/ *n.* a geographical index or dictionary.

gazillion *n. N Amer. informal* **1** an exaggeratedly large number (*gazillions of dictionaries*). **2** (in *pl.*) an exaggeratedly large amount of money (*made gazillions*).

gazpacho / ɡə'spætʃoː/ *n.* (*pl.* **-os**) a Spanish soup made from tomatoes, peppers, cucumbers, garlic, etc., and served cold.

GB *abbr.* Great Britain.

Gbyte *abbr.* gigabyte.

Gd *symbol* gadolinium.

GDP *abbr.* GROSS DOMESTIC PRODUCT.

GDR *abbr. hist.* German Democratic Republic.

Ge *symbol* germanium.

gear ● *n.* **1** (often in *pl.*) **a** a set of toothed wheels that work together to receive and transmit force and motion. **b** a mechanism using gears to transmit and control motion, esp. to the road wheels of a vehicle. **2** a particular state of adjustment of engaged gears (*second gear*). **3** a state of speed or activity (*the campaign moved into top gear*). **4** a mechanism of wheels, levers, etc., usu. for a special purpose (*winding gear*). **5** (in full **landing gear**) the undercarriage of an aircraft. **6** equipment or tackle for a special purpose (*fishing gear*). **7** *informal* clothing, equipment, and accessories, esp. for a specified purpose or of a specified type (*police in riot gear*). **8** an indeterminate quantity of belongings and objects, esp. if perceived as burdensome (*clear all of your old gear out of the attic*). ● *v.* **1** *tr.* (usu. in *passive*; foll. by *to*, *toward*) adjust or adapt to suit a specified purpose, need, or recipient. **2** *tr.* (often foll. by *up*) equip with gears. **3** (usu. foll. by *up*) **a** *tr.* make ready or prepared. **b** *intr.* prepare, get ready. **4** *tr.* put (machinery) in gear. **5** *intr.* be in or come into gear. ☐ **be geared** (or **all geared**) **up** *informal* be ready or enthusiastic. **gear down** engage a lower gear in a vehicle. **gear up 1** (of groups of people, cities, corporate bodies, etc.) prepare or equip, esp. over a period of time in anticipation of some intense activity. **2** speed up or intensify (*gear up production*). **3** engage a higher gear in a vehicle. **gear oneself up** provide oneself with progressively more supplies, courage, etc. in order to face a daunting prospect. **give a person the gears** *Cdn* pester, hassle. **in gear 1** with a gear engaged. **2** operating properly or efficiently. **in high gear** *N Amer.* operating at maximum efficiency. **out of gear 1** with no gear engaged. **2** out of order. **shift** (or **change** etc.) **gears** change one's pace, direction, strategy, etc., esp. in progress.

gearbox *n.* **1** the casing that encloses a set of gears. **2** a set of gears with its casing, esp. in a motor vehicle; transmission.

gearing *n.* a set or arrangement of gears in a machine.

gear ratio *n.* (in a gearbox etc.) the ratio between the rates at which the last and the first gears rotate.

gearshift *n.* a lever used to engage or change gear, esp. in a motor vehicle.

gearwheel *n.* a toothed wheel in a set of gears.

gecko *n.* (*pl.* **-os** or **-oes**) any of various house lizards found in warm climates, with adhesive feet for climbing vertical surfaces.

gee *interj. N Amer. informal* a mild expression of surprise, discovery, dismay, etc.

geek *n.* esp. *N Amer. informal* **1** an uninteresting, ineffectual, socially inept person; a nerd. **2** a person thoroughly devoted to one usu. technical interest, study, etc., often at the expense of social interaction (*computer geek*). ☐ **geeky** *adj.*

geese *pl.* of GOOSE.

gee whiz esp. *N Amer. informal* ● *interj.* = GEE. ● *attrib.adj.* (usu. as **gee-whiz**) characterized by (often naive) astonishment or wonder, usu. at new technologies (*gee-whiz journalism*).

geez *interj. N Amer.* expressing annoyance, frustration, etc.

geezer *n. slang* a person, esp. an old man.

gefilte fish / ɡə'fɪltə/ *n.* a ball etc. of chopped fish mixed with matzo meal, egg, and seasoning, and simmered in fish stock, usu. served cold.

Geiger counter / 'ɡaɪɡər/ *n.* a device which counts ionizing particles to measure radioactivity.

geisha / 'ɡeɪʃə/ *n.* (*pl.* same or **-s**) **1** a Japanese hostess trained in entertaining men with dance and song. **2** a Japanese prostitute.

gel ● *n.* **1** a semi-solid colloidal suspension or jelly, of a solid dispersed in a liquid. **2** a jellylike substance used for setting hair. ● *v.* (**gelled**, **gelling**) **1** *intr.* = JELL. **2** *tr.* apply gel to (hair etc.).

gelatin / 'dʒelətɪn/ *n.* (also **gelatine**) **1** a virtually colourless tasteless transparent water-soluble protein derived from collagen and obtained by prolonged boiling of animal skin, tendons, ligaments, etc., used in food preparation, photography, glue, etc. **2** any similar colloidal substance. ☐ **gelatinize** *v.tr. & intr.* **gelatinization** *n.*

gelatinous / dʒə'lætɪnəs/ *adj.* **1** of or like gelatin. **2** of a jellylike consistency. ☐ **gelatinously** *adv.*

gelato / dʒe'lætoː, -'loːto/ *n.* (*pl.* **gelati** / -tiː/) an Italian sherbet-like ice cream made with milk or cream and relatively low in butterfat.

gelcoat *n.* a polyester resin coating applied to a mould on which fibreglass cloth is subsequently laid, setting to a hard surface over the fibreglass.

geld *v.tr.* **1** deprive (a male animal) of the ability to reproduce; excise the testicles of; castrate. **2** deprive of some essential part; weaken.

gelding *n.* a gelded animal, esp. a male horse.

gelignite / 'dʒelɪɡˌnəit/ *n.* a high explosive made from a gel of nitroglycerine and nitrocellulose in a base of wood pulp and sodium or potassium nitrate, much used in rock blasting.

gem ● *n.* **1** a precious stone, esp. when cut and polished. **2** an object, person, event, etc. of great beauty, or excellence. ● *v.tr.* (**gemmed**, **gemming**) adorn with or as with gems. ☐ **gemlike** *adj.*

Gemara / ɡə'mɑrə/ *n. Judaism* the later of the two parts of the Talmud, consisting of a rabbinical commentary on the first part (the Mishnah).

Gemeinschaft /gə'main‚ʃɒft/ n. a form of social integration based on personal ties; community.

Gemini /'dʒemɪ‚nai, -‚ni:/ n. (pl. **-is**) **1** a constellation between Taurus and Cancer, traditionally regarded as contained in the figures of twins. **2 a** the third sign of the zodiac. **b** a person born when the sun is in this sign, usu. between May 21 and June 20. **3** Cdn any of several awards presented by the Academy of Canadian Cinema and Television for excellence in Canadian English-language television. **b** any of the statuettes symbolizing such an award. □ **Geminian** /‚dʒemɪ'ni:ən, -'naiən/ n. & adj.

gemology n. the study of gems. □ **gemologist** n.

gemstone n. a precious stone used as a gem.

Gen. abbr. General.

gendarme /'ʒɒndɑrm/ n. a soldier employed in specific public police duties, esp. in some French-speaking countries.

gender n. **1 a** the grammatical classification of nouns and related words, roughly corresponding to the two sexes and sexlessness. **b** each of the classes of nouns (see MASCULINE, FEMININE, NEUTER). **2** (of nouns and related words) the property of belonging to such a class. **3 a** a person's sex; either of the sexes. **b** one's characteristics or traits determined socially as a result of one's sex. □ **genderless** adj.

gender-bender n. a person who or thing which adopts or portrays non-traditional gender roles. □ **gender-bending** n. (often attrib.)

gendered adj. of, relating to, or determined by one's sex as expressed by social or cultural distinctions.

gender gap n. the discrepancy in opportunities, status, attitudes, etc. between men and women.

gender-neutral adj. **1** denoting a word which cannot be taken to refer to one sex only, e.g. firefighter as opposed to fireman. **2** (of language etc.) using gender-neutral words whenever appropriate.

gender role n. one's behaviour, lifestyle, etc. regarded in light of one's sex.

gender-specific adj. characteristic of, pertaining to, or referring to one sex only.

gene n. a unit of heredity composed of DNA or RNA and forming part of a chromosome etc., that determines a particular characteristic of an individual.

genealogy /‚dʒi:ni'ɒlədʒi, -æl-/ n. (pl. **-ies**) **1 a** a line of descent traced from an ancestor. **b** an exposition of this. **2** the study and investigation of lines of descent. **3** a plant's or animal's line of development from earlier forms. □ **genealogical** adj. **genealogically** adv. **genealogist** n.

gene mapping n. the determination of a gene's location on a chromosome. □ **gene map** n.

gene pool n. the whole stock of different genes in an interbreeding population.

genera pl. of GENUS.

general ● adj. **1 a** completely or almost universal. **b** including or affecting all or nearly all parts or cases of things. **2** prevalent, widespread, usual. **3** not partial, particular, local, or sectional. **4** not limited in application; relating to whole classes or all cases. **5** including points common to the individuals of a class and neglecting the differences (a general term). **6** not restricted or specialized (general knowledge). **7 a** roughly corresponding or adequate. **b** sufficient for practical purposes. **8** not detailed (a general idea). **9** vague, indefinite (spoke only in general terms). **10** chief or principal (general manager; Secretary-General). **11** (in Alta., BC, Man., & Sask.) designating a film deemed suitable for all audiences. Abbr.: **G. 12** Med. of the entire body (general anaesthetic). **● n. 1** (also **General**;

abbr.: **Gen** Cdn or **Gen.**) **a** (in the Canadian Army or Air Force) an officer of the highest rank. **b** a similar officer in other military forces. **c** a lieutenant general, major general, or brigadier general. **2** a commander of an army. **3** a tactician or strategist of specified merit (a great general). **4** the head of a religious order, e.g. of the Jesuits. □ **as a general rule** in most cases. **in general 1** as a normal rule; usually. **2** for the most part.

general admission n. **1** (often attrib.) admission to unreserved seating at a concert, sports event, etc. (general-admission tickets). **2** the section of a theatre etc. with unreserved seats (sat in general admission). **3** the admission fee to an event etc. charged to those who are not eligible for a discounted rate.

general anaesthetic n. an anaesthetic that affects the whole body, usu. with loss of consciousness.

General Assembly n. **1** the main deliberative body of the UN, with a delegate from each member country. **2** (in Presbyterian churches) an annual national meeting of representative clergy and elders, constituting the highest court of the church.

general contractor n. a person or company that organizes and coordinates construction work performed by employees or subcontractors.

General Council n. (in the United Church of Canada) a national convention of representative clergy and elders, now held every two years, constituting the highest court of the church.

general delivery n. N Amer. the delivery of mail to a post office where addressees can pick it up.

general election n. the election of representatives to a legislature from all constituencies of a country, province, etc.

generalist n. a person competent or knowledgeable in several different fields or activities (opp. SPECIALIST).

generality n. (pl. **-ies**) **1** a statement or principle etc. having general validity or force. **2** applicability to a whole class of instances. **3** vagueness; lack of detail. **4** the state of being general. **5** (foll. by of) the main body or majority.

generalize v. **1** intr. **a** speak in general or indefinite terms. **b** form general principles or notions. **2** tr. reduce to a general statement, principle, or notion. **3** tr. **a** give a general character to. **b** call by a general name. **4** tr. infer (a law or conclusion) by induction. **5** tr. Math. & Philos. express in a general form; extend the application of. **6** tr. bring into general use. **7** intr. (of a disease) spread to other parts of the body. □ **generalizability** n. **generalizable** adj. **generalization** n.

generally adv. **1** usually; in most cases. **2** in a general sense; without regard to particulars or exceptions. **3** for the most part; extensively (generally known). **4** in most respects (are generally well-behaved).

general meeting n. a meeting open to all the members of an association, shareholders of a corporation, etc.

general practitioner n. a doctor working in the community and treating cases of all kinds in the first instance, as distinct from a consultant or specialist. Abbr.: **GP.** □ **general practice** n.

general public n. the people of a community collectively, esp. those not enjoying special privileges.

general-purpose adj. having a range of potential uses or functions; not specialized in design.

general relativity n. see RELATIVITY 2b.

general secretary n. a chief administrator of an organization.

general staff *n.* the staff assisting a military commander in planning and administration.

general store *n.* esp. *N Amer.* a store selling a wide variety of goods for everyday needs.

general strike *n.* a strike of workers in all or most occupations.

General Synod *n.* the highest governing body in some national Anglican churches, including the Anglican Church of Canada.

generate *v.tr.* **1** bring into existence; produce, evolve. **2** produce (electricity).

generation *n.* **1** all the people born at a particular time, regarded collectively (*my generation*). **2** a single step in descent or pedigree (a *second-generation Canadian*). **3** a stage in (esp. technological) development (*fourth-generation computers*). **4** members of a specific group or category who became prominent at the same time (*the new generation of rock guitarists*). **5** the individuals born at about the same time, with a specified common characteristic, attitude, etc. (*the me generation*). **6** the average time in which children are ready to take the place of their parents (usu. reckoned at about 30 years). **7** production by natural or artificial process, esp. the production of electricity or heat. **8 a** procreation; the propagation of species. **b** the act of begetting or being begotten. □ **generational** *adj.*

generation gap *n.* differences of outlook or opinion between those of different generations.

Generation X *n.* the generation born after that of the baby boomers (roughly from the early 1960s to mid-1970s). □ **Generation Xer** *n.*

generative *adj.* **1** of or concerning procreation. **2** able to produce, productive.

generator *n.* **1** a machine for converting mechanical into electrical energy; a dynamo. **2** an apparatus for producing gas, steam, etc. **3** a person or thing that generates something.

generic ● *adj.* **1** characteristic of or relating to an entire class; general, not specific or special. **2** *Biol.* characteristic of or belonging to a genus. **3** designating a word that can apply or refer to both men and women. **4** (of goods, esp. a drug) having no brand name. ● *n.* a generic product, esp. a drug. □ **generically** *adv.*

generous *adj.* **1** (of a person or an institution) giving willingly more of something, esp. money, than is strictly necessary or expected. **2** (of help) given abundantly and willingly. **3** consisting of or representing a large amount of money, esp. when considered excessive or undeserved. **4** (of a person or an action) manifesting an inclination to recognize the positive aspects of someone or something, often disinterestedly. **5** (of something offered) favouring the recipient's interests rather than the giver's (*we offered them generous terms*). **6** liberal, broad, leaning towards the positive (a *generous estimate*). **7 a** ample, abundant, copious (a *generous portion*). **b** (of wine) rich and full. **8** (of rooms etc.) large, spacious; (of clothing) ample. □ **generosity** *n.* **generously** *adv.*

genesis /ˈdʒɛnəsɪs/ *n.* (*pl.* **geneses** /-siːz/) the origin, or mode of formation, of a thing.

gene-splicing *n.* the process of removing a chosen gene or sequence of genes from one organism and causing it to be integrated into the genetic material of another, usu. a bacterium, in order that it may produce the protein for which the gene codes.

gene therapy *n.* the introduction of normal genes into cells in place of missing or defective ones in order to correct genetic disorders.

genetic *adj.* (also **genetical**) **1** of genetics or genes. **2** of, in, or concerning origin. □ **genetically** *adv.*

genetic code *n.* *Biochem.* the means by which genetic information is stored as sequences of nucleotide bases in the chromosomal DNA.

genetic engineering *n.* the deliberate modification of the characters of an organism by the manipulation of the genetic material. □ **genetically engineered** *adj.*

genetic fingerprinting *n.* (also **genetic profiling**) the analysis of characteristic patterns in DNA as a means of identifying individuals. □ **genetic fingerprint** *n.*

geneticist /dʒəˈnɛtɪsɪst/ *n.* a specialist in genetics.

genetic map *n.* a representation of a chromosome including the positions of its genes. □ **genetic mapping** *n.*

genetic marker *n.* an allele used to identify a chromosome or to locate other genes on a genetic map.

genetics *n.pl.* (treated as *sing.*) **1** the study of heredity and the variation of inherited characteristics. **2** (treated as *sing.* or *pl.*) the genetic properties or features of an organism, characteristic, etc. (*the genetics of disease resistance*).

Geneva Convention *n.* an international agreement first made at Geneva in 1864 and later revised, governing the status and treatment of captured and wounded personnel in wartime.

genial /ˈdʒiːnɪəl/ *adj.* **1** jovial, sociable, kindly. **2** (of the climate) mild and warm. **3** cheering, enlivening. □ **geniality** *n.* **genially** *adv.*

genie /ˈdʒiːni/ *n.* **1** (*pl.* **genies** or **genii** /ˈdʒiːni,aɪ/) **a** = JINNI. **b** a spirit of Arabian folklore, esp. one contained within a bottle, lamp, etc., and capable of granting wishes. **2** (**Genie**) *Cdn* **a** any of several awards presented by the Academy of Canadian Cinema and Television for excellence in filmmaking. **b** any of the statuettes symbolizing such an award.

genii *pl.* of GENIUS.

genital ● *adj.* of or relating to the reproductive organs. ● *n.* (in *pl.*) the external reproductive organs.

genital herpes *n.* a disease characterized by genital blisters, caused by a herpes simplex virus.

genitalia /ˌdʒɛnɪˈteɪlɪə/ *n.pl.* the genitals.

genitive /ˈdʒɛnɪtɪv/ *Grammar* ● *n.* the case of nouns and pronouns (and words in grammatical agreement with them) corresponding to *of*, *from*, and other prepositions and indicating possession or close association. ● *adj.* of or in the genitive.

genius *n.* (*pl.* **geniuses** or **genii** /ˈdʒiːni,aɪ/) **1** (*pl.* **geniuses**) **a** an exceptional intellectual or creative power or other natural ability or tendency. **b** a person having this. **c** this ability as manifest in a work of art etc. (*the genius of her painting*). **2** the tutelary spirit of a person, place, institution, etc. **3** a person or spirit regarded as powerfully influencing a person for good or evil. **4** the prevalent feeling or associations etc. of a nation, age, etc.

genlock /ˈdʒɛnlɒk/ *n.* **1** a device for maintaining synchronization between two different video signals, or between a video signal and a computer or audio signal, esp. enabling video images and computer graphics to be mixed. **2** this technique or process.

genoa /ˈdʒɛnoʊə/ *n.* (in full **genoa jib**) a large jib or foresail used esp. on racing yachts.

genocide /ˈdʒɛnəˌsaɪd/ *n.* the mass extermination of human beings, esp. of a particular race or nation. □ **genocidal** *adj.*

genome /ˈdʒiːnoʊm/ *n.* **1** the haploid set of chromosomes of an organism. **2** the genetic material of an organism. □ **genomic** /-ˈnɒmɪk/ adj.

genotype /ˈdʒiːnoːˌtəip, ˈdʒen-/ n. Biol. the genetic constitution of an individual (compare PHENOTYPE). □ **genotypic** /-ˈtɪpɪk/ adj.

genre /ˈʒɑːrə, ˈʒɒnrə/ ● n. **1** a kind or style, esp. of art or literature, e.g. novel, satire, science fiction. **2** (in full **genre painting**) the painting of scenes from ordinary life. ● attrib.adj. denoting a film etc. following the conventions of a recognizable genre.

gent n. informal (often jocular) a gentleman.

genteel adj. **1** affectedly or ostentatiously refined, stylish, or polite. **2** often ironic of or appropriate to the upper classes. □ **genteelly** adv.

gentian /ˈdʒenʃən, -ʃiən/ n. any plant of the genus Gentiana or Gentianella, found esp. in mountainous regions, and usu. having violet or vivid blue trumpet-shaped flowers.

Gentile ● adj. not Jewish. ● n. a person who is not Jewish.

gentility n. **1** refined manners and habits, esp. as associated with wealthy and well-bred people. **2** affected or pretentious refinement or politeness. **3** people of noble birth.

gentle ● adj. (**gentler**, **gentlest**) **1** not rough; mild or kind. **2 a** moderate; not severe or drastic (a gentle rebuke; a gentle breeze). **b** gradual (gentle slope). **c** not harsh (gentle shampoo). **3** (of birth, pursuits, etc.) of or fit for people of elevated social position. **4** (of an animal) docile. ● v.tr. make gentle or docile. □ **gentleness** n. **gently** adv.

gentleman n. (pl. **-men**) **1** a man (in polite or formal use). **2** a chivalrous or well-bred man. **3** a man of good social position or of wealth and leisure. **4** a man of gentle birth attached to a royal household (gentleman in waiting). **5** (in pl. as a form of address) a male audience or the male part of an audience.

gentleman farmer n. (pl. **gentlemen farmers**) a person who farms for pleasure, not to earn a living.

gentlemanly adj. like a gentleman in looks or behaviour; befitting a gentleman.

gentleman's agreement n. (also **gentlemen's agreement**) one which is binding in honour but not legally enforceable.

Gentleman Usher of the Black Rod n. see BLACK ROD.

gentrify /ˈdʒentrɪfai/ v.tr. (**-ies**, **-ied**) convert (a working-class or inner-city neighbourhood etc.) into an area of middle-class residence. □ **gentrification** n. **gentrifier** n.

gentry /ˈdʒentri/ n.pl. **1** people of high social standing. **2** (in the UK) the class of people next below the nobility in position and birth.

genuflect /ˈdʒenjuˌflekt/ v.intr. **1** bend the knee to the ground, esp. in worship or as a sign of respect. **2** (foll. by to, at) display servile obedience or deference to. □ **genuflection** n. **genuflector** n.

genuine /ˈdʒenjuɪn, -ain/ adj. **1** really coming from its stated, advertised, or reputed source. **2** properly so called; not sham. **3** (of an opinion etc.) sincere. **4** (of a person) free from affectation or hypocrisy. □ **genuinely** adv. **genuineness** n.

genuine article n. (prec. by the) a person or thing that is exactly as described or promoted.

genus /ˈdʒiːnəs, ˈdʒenəs/ n. (pl. **genera** /ˈdʒenərə/) **1** Biol. a taxonomic grouping of organisms having common characteristics distinct from those of other genera, usu. containing several or many species and being one of a series constituting a taxonomic family. **2** a kind or class having common characteristics.

Gen X n. slang = GENERATION X. □ **Gen-Xer** n.

geo- comb. form **1** earth (geology). **2** geography (geopolitics).

geocentric adj. **1** having or representing the earth as the centre; not heliocentric. **2** considered as viewed from the centre of the earth.

geochemistry n. the chemistry of the earth and its rocks, minerals, etc. □ **geochemical** adj. **geochemist** n.

geode /ˈdʒiːoːd/ n. **1** a small cavity lined esp. with crystals. **2** a rock containing such a cavity.

geodesic /ˌdʒiːoːˈdiːsɪk, -ˈdesɪk/ ● adj. **1** of or relating to geodesy. **2** of, involving, or consisting of a geodesic line. ● n. (also **geodesic line**) the shortest possible line between two points on a surface.

geodesic dome n. a dome constructed of short struts along geodesic lines, forming a light open framework of triangles or polygons.

geodesy /dʒiːˈɒdɪsi/ n. the branch of mathematics dealing with the figures and areas of the earth or large portions of it.

geoduck /ˈguːiːdvk/ n. a giant mud-burrowing bivalve mollusc, Panopea generosa, occurring on the west coast of N America, where it is collected for food.

geographic information system n. a computer system which allows the user to analyze, display and manipulate spatial data (e.g. data from remote sensing). Abbr.: **GIS**.

geography n. **1** the study of the earth's physical features, resources, and climate, and the physical aspects of its population. **2** the main physical features of an area. **3** the arrangement of features or layout of a region or thing. □ **geographer** n. **geographical** adj. (also **geographic**). **geographically** adv.

geological survey n. **1** a detailed investigation of the geological features and resources of a region. **2** (**Geological Survey**) an official body responsible for conducting such surveys.

geological time n. **1** the time which has elapsed since the earth's formation (up to the beginning of the historical period). **2** time measured with reference to geological events.

geology n. **1** the science of the earth, including the composition, structure, and origin of its rocks. **2** this science applied to any other planet or celestial body. **3** the geological features of a district. □ **geological** adj. (also **geologic**). **geologically** adv. **geologist** n.

geometer /dʒiːˈɒmɪtər/ n. **1** a person skilled in geometry. **2** any moth, esp. of the family Geometridae, having twig-like larvae which move by alternately hunching and stretching the body.

geometric ● adj. (also **geometrical**) **1** of, according to, or like geometry. **2** (of a design, architectural feature, etc.) characterized by or decorated with regular lines and shapes. ● n. a print, pattern, fabric, etc. with a geometric design. □ **geometrically** adv.

geometric mean n. the central number in a geometric progression, also calculable as the nth root of a product of n numbers (as 9 from 3 and 27).

geometric progression n. a progression of numbers with a constant ratio between each number and the one before (as 1, 3, 9, 27).

geometry n. (pl. **-ies**) **1 a** the branch of mathematics concerned with the properties and relations of points, lines, surfaces, and solids. **b** a particular system describing these properties etc. (Euclidean geometry). **2** the relative arrangement of objects or parts. □ **geometrician** n.

geomorphology n. the study of the physical

features of the surface of the earth and their relation to its geological structures. □ **geomorphic** adj. **geomorphological** adj. **geomorphologist** n.

geophysics n. the science concerned with all aspects of the physical properties and processes of the earth and planetary bodies, including seismology, gravity, magnetism, etc. □ **geophysical** adj. **geophysicist** n.

geopolitics n. **1 1** the politics of a country as determined by its geographical features. **2** the study of this. □ **geopolitical** adj. **geopolitically** adv. **geopolitician** n.

Georgian¹ /'dʒɔːrdʒən/ adj. **1 a** of or characteristic of the time of Kings George I–IV of England (1714–1830). **b** of or like the style of architecture of this period, typified in domestic architecture by red-brick houses with regularly spaced sash windows, white paint, and pedimented doorways. **2** of or characteristic of the time of Kings George V and VI of England (1910–52), esp. of the literature of 1910–20.

Georgian² ● adj. of or relating to the US state of Georgia. ● n. a native or resident of Georgia.

Georgian³ ● adj. of or relating to Georgia, a country in SE Europe. ● n. **1** a native of Georgia; a person of Georgian descent. **2** the language of Georgia.

geoscience n. earth sciences, e.g. geology, geophysics. □ **geoscientist** n.

geostationary adj. (of an artificial satellite of the earth) moving in such an orbit as to remain above the same point on the earth's surface.

geosynchronous /ˌdʒiːoʊˈsɪŋkrənəs/ adj. (of an artificial satellite of the earth) moving in an orbit equal to the earth's period of rotation.

geotechnical adj. of or pertaining to practical applications of geological science in building, etc.

geothermal adj. relating to, originating from, or produced by the internal heat of the earth.

Ger. abbr. German.

geranium n. **1** any herb or shrub of the genus *Geranium* bearing fruit shaped like the bill of a crane, e.g. cranesbill. **2** (in general use) a cultivated pelargonium. **3** the colour of the scarlet geranium.

gerbil n. a mouselike desert rodent of the subfamily Gerbillinae, with long hind legs, esp. *Meriones unguiculatus* of Mongolia, commonly kept as a pet.

geriatric ● adj. **1** of or relating to old age or old people. **2** informal old, outdated. ● n. **1** an old person, esp. one receiving special care. **2** offensive a person or thing considered old or outdated.

geriatrics n.pl. (usu. treated as sing.) a branch of medicine or social science dealing with the health and care of old people. □ **geriatrician** n.

germ n. **1** a micro-organism, esp. one which causes disease. **2 a** a portion of an organism capable of developing into a new one; the rudiment of an animal or plant. **b** an embryo of a seed (*wheat germ*). **3** an original idea etc. from which something may develop; an elementary principle. □ **germy** adj.

German ● n. **1** a native or national of Germany, a country in central Europe. **2** a person of German descent. **3** the language of Germany, also used in Austria and Switzerland. ● adj. of or relating to Germany or its people or language.

german adj. **1** having both parents the same (*brother german*). **2** having both grandparents the same on one side (*cousin german*).

germane /dʒɜːrˈmeɪn/ adj. (usu. foll. by to) relevant (to a subject under consideration). □ **germanely** adv.

Germanic /dʒɜːrˈmænɪk/ ● adj. **1** of the languages or language group called Germanic. **2** of the Scandina-vians, Anglo-Saxons, or Germans. **3** having characteristics considered typically German. ● n. **1** the branch of Indo-European languages including English, German, Dutch, and the Scandinavian languages. **2** the (unrecorded) early language from which other Germanic languages developed.

germanium /dʒɜːrˈmeɪniəm/ n. a lustrous brittle semi-metallic element occurring naturally in sulphide ores and used in semiconductors.

German measles n. a contagious disease, rubella, that resembles a mild form of measles but can cause fetal malformations if caught early in pregnancy.

German shepherd n. (also **German shepherd dog**) a large, strong, black and tan dog with a shaggy tail, used as a guard dog and in police work.

germ cell n. **1** a cell containing half the number of chromosomes of a somatic cell and able to unite with one from the opposite sex to form a new individual; a gamete. **2** any embryonic cell with the potential of developing into a gamete.

germicide /'dʒɜːrmɪˌsaɪd/ n. a substance destroying germs, esp. those causing disease. □ **germicidal** adj.

germinate v. **1 a** intr. sprout, bud, or put forth shoots. **b** tr. cause to sprout or shoot. **2 a** tr. cause (ideas etc.) to originate or develop. **b** intr. come into existence. □ **germination** n. **germinator** n.

germplasm n. germ cells collectively; their genetic material.

germ warfare n. the systematic spreading of micro-organisms to cause disease in an enemy population.

Geronimo interj. expressing exultation.

gerontocracy /ˌdʒerɒnˈtɒkrəsi/ n. **1** government by old people. **2** a state or society so governed. □ **gerontocrat** /dʒeˈrɒntəˌkræt/ n. **gerontocratic** adj.

gerontology /ˌdʒerənˈtɒlədʒi/ n. the scientific study of old age, the process of aging, and the special problems of old people. □ **gerontological** adj. **gerontologist** n.

gerrymander ● v.tr. **1** manipulate the boundaries of (a constituency etc.) so as to give undue influence to some party or class. **2** manipulate (a situation etc.) to gain advantage. ● n. this practice.

gerund /'dʒerənd/ n. Grammar a noun formed from a verb, in English ending in -ing, and designating an action or state, e.g. *smoking is bad for you*.

gesso /'dʒesoʊ/ n. (pl. **-oes**) plaster of Paris or gypsum as used in painting as a ground or in sculpture.

gestalt /gəˈʃtɒlt/ n. Psych. an organized whole that is perceived as more than the sum of its parts.

Gestapo /gəˈstɑːpoʊ/ n. **1** the German secret police under Nazi rule. **2** (also **gestapo**) derogatory an organization compared to this.

gestate /'dʒesteɪt/ v.tr. & intr. **1** carry (a fetus) in gestation. **2** develop (an idea etc.).

gestation n. **1 a** the process of carrying or being carried in the womb between conception and birth. **b** this period. **2** the private development of a plan, idea, etc. □ **gestational** adj.

gesticulate /dʒeˈstɪkjʊˌleɪt/ v. **1** intr. use esp. lively gestures instead of or in addition to speech. **2** tr. express with gestures. □ **gesticulation** n.

gesture ● n. **1** a movement of a limb or the body as an expression of thought or feeling. **2** the use of such movements esp. to convey feeling or as a rhetorical device. **3** an action to evoke a response or convey intention, usu. friendly (*goodwill gesture*). ● v.tr. & intr. gesticulate. □ **gestural** adj. **gesturally** adv.

gesundheit /gəˈzʊntaɪt, -haɪt/ interj. expressing a wish of good health, esp. to a person who has sneezed.

get v. (**getting**; past **got**; past part. **got** or **gotten**) **1** tr. come into the possession of; receive or earn (*got $200 a week*; *got first prize*). **2** tr. fetch, obtain, procure, purchase (*get my book for me*; *got a new car*). **3** tr. go to reach or catch (a bus, train, etc.). **4** tr. prepare (a meal etc.). **5** intr. & tr. reach or cause to reach a certain state or condition; become or cause to become (*get rich*; *got them ready*). **6** tr. obtain as a result of calculation. **7** tr. contract (a disease etc.). **8** tr. establish or be in communication with via telephone or radio; receive (a radio signal, television channel, etc.). **9** tr. experience or suffer; have inflicted on one; receive as one's lot or penalty (*got four years in prison*). **10 a** tr. succeed in bringing, placing, etc. (*flattery will get you nowhere*). **b** intr. & tr. succeed or cause to succeed in coming or going (*got absolutely nowhere*). **11** tr. (prec. by *have*) **a** possess (*have not got a penny*). **b** (foll. by *to* + infin.) be bound or obliged (*have got to see you*). **12** tr. (foll. by *to* + infin.) induce; prevail upon (*got them to help me*). **13** tr. informal understand (a person or an argument) (*don't get me wrong*). **14** tr. informal inflict punishment or retribution on, esp. in retaliation (*I'll get you for that*). **15** tr. informal **a** annoy. **b** move; affect emotionally. **c** attract, obsess. **d** amuse. **16** tr. (foll. by *to* + infin.) develop an inclination as specified (*am getting to like it*). **17** intr. (foll. by verbal noun) begin (*get going*). **18** tr. (esp. in past or perfect) catch in an argument; corner, puzzle. **19** tr. establish (an idea etc.) in one's mind. **20** intr. slang be off; go away. **21** tr. answer (a telephone, doorbell, etc.). □ **be getting on for** be approaching (a specified time, age, etc.). **get across 1** manage to communicate (an idea etc.). **2** (of an idea etc.) be communicated successfully. **get ahead** be or become successful. **get along** (or **on**) **1** (foll. by *together*, *with*) live harmoniously. **2** (as imper.) nonsense! **get around 1** (also **get about**) **a** travel extensively or fast; go from place to place. **b** manage to walk, move about, etc. (esp. after illness). **c** (of news) be circulated, esp. orally. **2 a** evade (a law etc.). **b** successfully coax or cajole (a person) esp. to secure a favour. **get around to** deal with (a task etc.) in due course. **get at 1** reach; get hold of. **2** informal imply (*what are you getting at?*). **3** informal nag, criticize, bully. **get away 1** escape. **2** (foll. by *with*) escape blame or punishment for. **get back 1** move back or away. **2** return, arrive home. **3** recover (something lost). **4** (usu. foll. by *to*) contact later (*I'll get back to you*). **get back at** informal retaliate against. **get by** informal **1** just manage, even with difficulty. **2** be acceptable. **get down 1** alight, descend (from a vehicle, ladder, etc.). **2** record in writing. **3** manage to swallow. **4** lower oneself closer to the floor or ground. **5** N Amer. slang be uninhibited or unrestrained, esp. in dancing or socializing. **get a person down** depress or deject a person. **get down to** begin working on or discussing. **get even** (often foll. by *with*) **1** achieve revenge; get in retaliation. **2** equalize the score. **get his** (or **hers** etc.) slang **1** be killed. **2** suffer retribution. **get hold of 1** grasp (physically). **2** grasp (intellectually); understand. **3** make contact with (a person). **4** acquire. **get in 1** enter; gain entrance. **2** arrive. **3** be elected. **get into** become interested or involved in. **get it** slang be punished or in trouble. **get it into one's head** (foll. by *that* + clause) firmly believe or maintain; realize. **get nowhere** fail despite one's efforts. **get off 1** informal be acquitted; escape with little or no punishment. **2** start. **3** alight; alight from (a bus etc.). **4** slang reach orgasm. **get (a crop** etc.) **off** harvest. **get a person off** informal cause a person to be acquitted. **get off on** slang be

excited or aroused by; enjoy greatly. **get on 1** make progress; manage. **2** enter (a bus etc.). **3** = GET ALONG 1. **4** (usu. as **getting on**) informal grow old. **get on to** informal **1** make contact with. **2** understand; become aware of. **get out 1** leave or escape. **2** manage to go outdoors. **3** alight from a vehicle. **4** transpire; become known. **5** succeed in uttering, publishing, etc. **6** (as interj.) (also **get out of here!**, **get out of town!**) expressing disbelief. **get a person out** help a person to leave or escape. **get out of 1** avoid or escape (a duty etc.). **2** abandon (a habit) gradually. **get a thing out of** manage to obtain it from (a person) esp. with difficulty. **get over 1** recover from (an illness, upset, etc.). **2** overcome (a difficulty). **3** manage to communicate (an idea etc.). **4** overcome one's disbelief about. **get a thing over** (or **over with**) complete (a tedious task) promptly. **get one's own back** informal have one's revenge. **get somewhere** make progress; be initially successful. **get through 1** pass or assist in passing (an examination, an ordeal, etc.). **2** finish or use up (esp. resources). **3** make contact by telephone. **4** (foll. by *to*) succeed in making (a person) listen or understand. **get a thing through** cause it to overcome obstacles, difficulties, etc. **get to 1** reach. **2** annoy. **3** = GET DOWN TO. **get together 1** gather, assemble. **2** put (something) in order so as to perform effectively (*get your act together*). **get up 1** rise or cause to rise from sitting etc., or from bed after sleeping or an illness. **2** ascend or mount, e.g. on a bicycle. **3** (of fire, wind, or the sea) begin to be strong or agitated. **4** prepare or organize. **5** enhance or refine one's knowledge of (a subject). **6** work up (a feeling, e.g. anger). **7** produce or stimulate (*get up speed*). **8** (often refl.) dress or arrange elaborately; make presentable. **9** (foll. by *to*) informal indulge or be involved in (*getting up to mischief*). **get it up** slang achieve an erection. **have got it bad** (or **badly**) slang be obsessed or affected emotionally. □ **getter** n.

get-at-able adj. informal accessible.

getaway n. **1** (often attrib.) an escape, esp. after committing a crime. **2 a** a place far from work or home, visited for relaxation, e.g. a cottage, resort, etc. **b** a relaxing holiday, esp. far from one's work or home.

get-go n. esp. N Amer. informal the very beginning (of a project etc.) (*knew from the get-go that it was futile*).

get-out n. □ **as all get-out** see ALL.

get-rich-quick attrib.adj. designed to make a lot of money fast (*a get-rich-quick scheme*).

get-together n. informal a social gathering.

getup n. informal a style or arrangement of dress etc., esp. an elaborate one.

get-up-and-go n. informal energy, enthusiasm.

GeV abbr. gigaelectron volt (10^9 electron volts).

gewgaw n. a gaudy ornament or trinket.

Gewürztraminer /gə'vʊrtstrə,miːnər/ n. **1** a variety of grape grown esp. in the Rhine valley, Alsace, and Austria. **2** the full-bodied and mildly spicy white wine made from this grape.

geyser n. /'gaizər/ an intermittently gushing hot spring that throws up a tall column of water.

GFI abbr. (also **GFCI**) N Amer. ground-fault (circuit) interrupter; a circuit breaker integrated into an outlet, esp. for use in bathrooms or outdoors.

GG abbr. **1** Governor General. **2** Cdn = GOVERNOR GENERAL'S AWARD.

Ghanaian /gə'neiən/ ● adj. of or relating to Ghana, a country in W Africa. ● n. a native or national of Ghana; a person of Ghanaian descent.

ghastly /'gɑːstli/ ● adj. (**-ier**, **-iest**) **1** horrible, frightful. **2** *informal* objectionable, very unpleasant. **3** deathlike, pallid. ● *adv.* in a ghastly or sickly way (*ghastly pale*). □ **ghastliness** *n.*

ghee /giː/ *n.* clarified butter as used in Indian cuisine, esp. from the milk of a buffalo or cow.

gherkin /ˈgɜːkɪn/ *n.* **1** a small variety of cucumber, or a young green cucumber, used for pickling. **2 a** a trailing plant, *Cucumis sativus*, with cucumber-like fruits used for pickling. **b** this fruit.

ghetto *n.* (*pl.* **-os** or **-oes**) **1** a part of a city, esp. a slum area, occupied by a minority group or groups. **2** *hist.* an area of a city in which Jews were required to live. **3** a situation in which a group is segregated because of discrimination or its own preference.

ghetto blaster *n. informal* a large powerful portable radio and cassette/CD player.

ghettoize *v.tr.* restrict to a certain category by prejudice.

ghost ● *n.* **1** the supposed apparition of a dead person or animal; a disembodied spirit. **2** a shadow or mere semblance (*not a ghost of a chance*). **3** a secondary or duplicated image produced by defective television reception or by a telescope. ● *v.* **1 a** *intr.* (often foll. by *for*) act as ghost writer. **b** *tr.* act as ghost writer of (a work). **2** *intr.* move like a ghost. □ **give up the ghost** *informal* die. □ **ghostlike** *adj.*

ghosting *n.* **1** *in senses of* GHOST *v.* **2** the appearance of a 'ghost' (*see* GHOST *n.* 3) in a television picture.

ghostly *adj.* (**-ier, -iest**) like a ghost; spectral.

ghost town *n.* a deserted town with few or no remaining inhabitants.

ghost writer *n.* a person who writes on behalf of the credited author of a work. □ **ghost write** *v.tr. & intr.*

ghoul *n.* **1** an evil spirit or phantom. **2** a person morbidly interested in death, disaster, etc. **3** a spirit in Arabic folklore preying on corpses. □ **ghoulish** *adj.* **ghoulishly** *adv.* **ghoulishness** *n.*

GHQ *abbr.* general headquarters.

GHz *abbr.* gigahertz.

GI[1] ● *n.* a private soldier in the US Army. ● *adj.* of or for US servicemen.

GI[2] *abbr.* gastrointestinal.

giant ● *n.* **1** an imaginary or mythical being of human form but superhuman size. **2** (in Greek mythology) one of such beings who fought against the gods. **3** an abnormally tall or large person, animal, plant, or thing. **4** a person, company, etc. of exceptional ability, prominence, importance, etc. **5 a** a star of relatively great size and luminosity. **b** any of the enormous gaseous planets Jupiter, Saturn, Uranus, and Neptune. ● *attrib.adj.* **1** of extraordinary size or force, gigantic. **2** of exceptional importance, ability, or prominence (*a giant leap in science*). **3** (of a plant or animal) of a very large kind. □ **giantism** *n.* **giant-like** *adj.*

giant slalom *n. Skiing* a downhill event with a longer course and wider turns than standard slalom.

giardia /giˈɑːdɪə/ *n.* a flagellate protozoan, *Giardia lamblia*.

giardiasis /dʒiɑːˈdaɪəsɪs/ *n. Med.* infection of the intestines with giardia, often from drinking untreated lake water, causing diarrhea etc.

gibber /ˈdʒɪbər/ ● *v.* **1** *intr.* speak fast and inarticulately; chatter incoherently. **2** *tr.* utter in a gibber. ● *n.* such speech or sound. □ **gibbering** *n.* (usu. in *pl.*).

gibberish *n.* unintelligible or meaningless speech or writing; nonsense.

gibbon *n.* any small ape of the genus *Hylobates*, native to SE Asia, having a slender body and long arms.

gibe *var. of* JIBE[1].

giblets /ˈdʒɪblɪts/ *n.pl.* the liver, gizzard, heart, neck, etc., of a fowl, usu. removed and kept separate when the bird is prepared for cooking.

GIC *abbr. Cdn* = GUARANTEED INVESTMENT CERTIFICATE.

giddy ● *adj.* (**-ier, -iest**) **1** having a sensation of whirling and a tendency to fall, stagger, or spin around; dizzy. **2 a** overexcited as a result of success, pleasurable emotion, etc.; mentally intoxicated. **b** excitable, frivolous. **3** tending to make one giddy. ● *v.tr.* (**-ies, -ied**) (usu. as **giddying** *adj.*) make giddy. □ **giddily** *adv.* **giddiness** *n.*

GIFT /gɪft/ *n.* gamete intrafallopian transfer, a technique for assisting conception by introducing mixed ova and sperm into a Fallopian tube.

gift ● *n.* **1 a** a thing given freely; a present. **b** (*attrib.*) denoting a usu. decorated container or wrapping for gifts, given along with the presents (*gift bag*). **2** a natural ability or talent. **3** the power to give (*in his gift*). **4** the act or an instance of giving. ● *v.tr.* **1** endow with gifts. **2 a** (foll. by *with*) give to as a gift. **b** bestow as a gift. □ **look a gift horse in the mouth** find fault with what has been given.

gift certificate *n. N Amer.* a certificate or voucher presented as a gift and exchangeable for a specified value of goods, usu. at a specific store.

gifted *adj.* **1** exceptionally talented or intelligent. **2** *N Amer.* designating classes etc. for children of above average intelligence or talent. □ **giftedness** *n.*

gift of tongues *n. see* TONGUE.

gift shop *n.* a small store, often within a museum, hospital, etc., selling articles suitable as gifts.

giftware *n.* goods sold as being suitable as gifts.

gift-wrap ● *v.tr.* (**-wrapped, -wrapping**) wrap attractively as a gift. ● *n.* (**gift wrap**) decorative paper etc. for wrapping gifts.

gig[1] *informal* ● *n.* **1** an engagement of an entertainer, esp. of musicians to play jazz, rock, or dance music, usu. for a single appearance. **2** a performance of this kind. **3** a job or employment, esp. likely to be temporary. ● *v.intr.* (**gigged, gigging**) perform in gigs or a gig.

gig[2] *n.* **1** a light two-wheeled one-horse carriage. **2** a light ship's boat for rowing or sailing.

gig[3] *n.* a gigabyte.

giga- /ˈgɪgə, ˈdʒɪgə, ˈgaɪgə/ *comb. form* **1** denoting a factor of 10^9 (i.e. one billion) (*gigawatt*). **2** *Computing* (in the binary system) denoting a factor of 2^{30} (i.e. 1 073 741 824) (*gigabyte*).

gigabyte /ˈgɪgəbaɪt, ˈdʒɪ-, ˈgaɪ-/ *n. Computing* 1 073 741 824 (i.e. 2^{30}) bytes as a measure of data capacity, or loosely 1 000 000 000.

gigantic *adj.* **1** very large; enormous. **2** like or suited to a giant. □ **gigantically** *adv.*

gigantism /ˈdʒaɪgæn,tɪzəm, dʒaɪˈgæntɪzəm/ *n.* **1** abnormal largeness. **2** *Med.* excessive growth due to hormonal imbalance.

giggle ● *v.intr.* laugh in half-suppressed, high-pitched spasms, esp. in a silly manner or out of nervousness. ● *n.* **1** such a laugh. **2** (**the giggles**) a fit of giggling. **3** *informal* an amusing person or thing; a joke. □ **giggler** *n.* **giggly** *adj.* (**-ier, -iest**). **giggliness** *n.*

GIGO /ˈgaɪgoʊ/ *abbr. Computing* garbage in, garbage out.

gigolo /ˈdʒɪgə,loʊ, ˈʒɪg-/ *n.* (*pl.* **-os**) **1** a young man paid by an older woman to be her escort or lover. **2** a professional male dancing partner or escort.

Gila monster /ˈhiːlə/ *n.* a large carnivorous venomous lizard of Mexico and the southwestern US,

Heloderma suspectum, black with orange or pink markings.

gild[1] *v.tr.* (*past part.* **gilded** or as adj. in sense 1 **gilt**) **1** cover thinly with gold or a substance resembling gold. **2** tinge with a golden colour or light. **3** give a specious or false brilliance to. □ **gild the lily** try to improve what is already beautiful or excellent.

gild[2] *var. of* GUILD.

gilding *n.* **1** the act or art of applying gilt. **2** material used in applying gilt.

gill[1] ● *n.* (usu. in *pl.*) **1** the respiratory organ in fishes and other aquatic animals. **2** the vertical radial plates on the underside of mushrooms and other fungi. **3** the flesh below a person's jaws and ears (*green at the gills*). ● *v.tr.* **1** gut or clean (a fish). **2** catch in a gill net. □ **to the gills** completely, thoroughly, fully (*fed to the gills*). □ **gilled** *adj.* (also in *comb.*).

gill[2] /dʒɪl/ *n.* a unit of liquid measure, equal to a quarter of a pint (142 ml in imperial measure, 118 ml in US measure).

gill net *n.* a net suspended vertically to entangle fish by the gills. □ **gill netting** *n.*

gillnetter *n.* **1** a person who fishes using gill nets. **2** a ship or boat designed for fishing with gill nets.

gilt[1] ● *adj.* **1** covered thinly with gold or a goldlike substance. **2** gold-coloured. ● *n.* gold or a goldlike substance applied in a thin layer to a surface.

gilt[2] *n.* a young unbred sow.

gilt-edged *adj.* **1** (of a page, book, etc.) having a gilded edge. **2** of the highest quality; first-rate. **3** (of securities, stocks, etc.) having a high degree of reliability as an investment.

gimbal /'dʒɪmbəl, 'gɪmbəl/ *n.* (often in *pl.*) a contrivance for keeping objects, esp. instruments such as a compass and chronometer, horizontal aboard a ship or aircraft, etc.

gimcrack /'dʒɪmkræk/ ● *adj.* showy but flimsy and worthless. ● *n.* a knick-knack. □ **gimcrackery** *n.*

gimlet /'gɪmlət/ *n.* **1** a small screw-tipped tool for boring. **2** a cocktail usu. of gin or vodka and lime juice.

gimme *informal* ● *contraction* give me. ● *interj.* give it to me. ● *n. N Amer.* **1** esp. *Sport* a task, e.g. kicking a short field goal, regarded as too easy to bungle; a sure thing. **2** *Golf* (in informal games) a short easy putt one is not required to attempt. ● *adj. N Amer.* designating an item given away, esp. for promotional purposes (*gimme cap*).

gimmick *n. informal* a trick or device, often underhanded, esp. for attracting attention, publicity, or trade. □ **gimmickry** *n.* **gimmicky** *adj.*

gimp[1] /gɪmp/ *n.* a twist of silk etc. with cord or wire running through it, used esp. as a trimming on clothing.

gimp[2] ● *n.* **1** a lame person or leg. **2** a stupid or contemptible person. ● *v.intr.* limp, hobble. □ **gimpy** *adj.*

gin[1] *n.* **1** a hard liquor distilled from grain or malt and flavoured esp. with juniper berries. **2** = GIN RUMMY.

gin[2] ● *n.* **1** a snare or trap. **2** a machine for separating cotton from its seeds. ● *v.tr.* (**ginned**, **ginning**) **1** treat (cotton) in a gin. **2** trap.

ginger ● *n.* **1 a** a hot spicy root usu. powdered for use in cooking, or preserved in syrup, or candied. **b** the plant, *Zingiber officinale*, of SE Asia, having this root. **2** a light reddish-yellow colour. **3** spirit, mettle. **4** *N Amer.* ginger ale. ● *adj.* of a ginger colour. ● *v.tr.* **1** flavour with ginger. **2** (foll. by *up*) rouse or enliven. □ **gingery** *adj.*

ginger ale *n.* a carbonated clear amber drink flavoured with ginger extract.

ginger beer *n.* **1** an effervescent, cloudy soft drink strongly flavoured with ginger. **2** an effervescent mildly alcoholic cloudy drink, made by fermenting a mixture of ginger and syrup.

gingerbread *n.* **1** a cake or cookie made with molasses and flavoured with ginger. **2** (often *attrib.*) elaborate carving or other trim on buildings, usu. along the eaves or on porches etc. **3** gaudy or tawdry decoration or ornament.

ginger group *n. Cdn & Brit.* a group within a party or movement that presses for stronger or more radical policy or action.

gingerly ● *adv.* carefully, cautiously. ● *adj.* showing great care or caution. □ **gingerliness** *n.*

gingersnap *n.* a brittle, ginger-flavoured cookie.

gingham *n.* a plain-woven cotton cloth of dyed yarn, esp. striped or checked.

gingiva /'dʒɪndʒɪvə, dʒɪn'dʒaɪvə/ *n.* (*pl.* **gingivae** /-,viː/) the gum. □ **gingival** /-'dʒaɪvəl/ *adj.*

gingivitis /,dʒɪndʒɪ'vaɪtɪs/ *n.* inflammation of the gums.

ginkgo /'gɪŋkgo/ *n.* (also **gingko** /'gɪŋko:/) (*pl.* **-os** or **-oes**) an originally Chinese and Japanese tree, *Ginkgo biloba*, with fan-shaped leaves and yellow flowers.

gin mill *n. N Amer.* a bar, esp. a disreputable one.

ginormous /dʒaɪ'nɔːrməs/ *adj. Cdn & Brit. slang* very large; enormous.

gin rummy *n. Cards* a form of rummy in which a player holding cards totalling ten or less may terminate play.

ginseng /'dʒɪnseŋ/ *n.* **1** any of several medicinal plants of the genus *Panax*, found in E Asia and N America. **2** the root of this.

gippy tummy /'dʒɪpi/ *n.* esp. *Cdn & Brit. informal* an upset stomach, esp. accompanied by diarrhea and affecting visitors to hot countries.

gipsy *var. of* GYPSY.

giraffe *n.* a ruminant mammal, *Giraffa camelopardalis* of Africa, the tallest animal, with a very long neck.

gird *v.* (*past* and *past part.* **girded**) *literary* **1** *tr.* encircle, attach, or secure with a belt or band. **2** *tr.* secure (clothes) on the body with a girdle or belt. **3** *tr.* enclose or encircle. **4** *tr.* **a** (foll. by *with*) equip with a sword in a belt. **b** fasten (a sword) with a belt. **5** *intr.* (foll. by *for*) prepare for action, a conflict, etc. **6** *tr.* place (cord etc.) around. □ **gird** (**up**) **one's loins** prepare for action.

girder *n.* a large iron or steel beam or compound structure for bearing loads, esp. in bridge-building.

girdle ● *n.* **1** a woman's corset extending from waist to thigh. **2** a belt or cord worn around the waist. **3** a thing that surrounds like a girdle. **4** the bony support for a limb (*pelvic girdle*). **5** the part of a cut gem dividing the crown from the base and embraced by the setting. **6** a ring around a tree made by the removal of bark. ● *v.tr.* **1** surround with or as with a girdle. **2 a** remove a ring of bark from (a branch or tree) to kill it. **b** remove a ring of bark from (a branch) to make the tree more fruitful.

girl *n.* **1** a female child or youth. **2** *informal* a young (esp. unmarried) woman. **3** *informal* a daughter. **4** *informal* a girlfriend or sweetheart. **5** often *offensive* a female servant. **6** often *offensive* a grown woman. **7** a woman belonging to a specified group (*a country girl*). **8** (**the girls**) *informal* a group of women mixing socially. **9** (usu. as a form of address) a female animal (*Steady, girl!*). □ **girlhood** *n.*

girlfriend *n.* **1** a regular female companion or lover. **2** a female friend.

Girl Guide *n. Cdn, Brit., Austral., & NZ* a member of a girls' organization promoting outdoor activity, leadership, and community service.

girlie (also **girly**) *informal* ● *adj.* **1** (of a magazine etc.) depicting nude young women in erotic poses. **2** girlish. ● *n.* (*pl.* **-ies**) *offensive* a young woman.

girlish *adj.* of or like a young girl. □ **girlishly** *adv.* **girlishness** *n.*

girth *n.* **1 a** the distance around a thing. **b** size, esp. of an overweight person. **2** a band around the body of a horse to secure the saddle etc.

GIS *abbr.* **1** *Cdn* GUARANTEED INCOME SUPPLEMENT. **2** GEOGRAPHIC INFORMATION SYSTEM.

gist *n.* the essence of a matter (*the gist of my theory*).

git *interj.* esp. *N Amer. informal* get going; get along.

gitch /gɪtʃ/ *n. Cdn slang* underwear.

Gitksan /ˈgɪtksən/ *n.* **1** an Aboriginal group living along the Skeena River in north central BC. **2** the Tsimshian language of this group.

give ● *v.* (*past* **gave**; *past part.* **given**) **1** *tr. & intr.* (often foll. by *to*) transfer the possession of freely; hand over as a present. **2** *tr.* **a** transfer the ownership of with or without actual delivery (*gave him $200 in her will*). **b** transfer, esp. temporarily or for safekeeping; hand over; provide with (*gave him the dog to hold*). **c** administer (medicine). **d** deliver (a message) (*give her my best wishes*). **3** *tr.* (usu. foll. by *for*) make over in exchange or payment; pay; sell (*gave him $100 for the bicycle*). **4** *tr.* **a** confer (a benefit, honour, etc.). **b** bestow (one's affections, confidence, etc.). **c** award; administer (one's approval etc.); tell, offer (esp. something unpleasant) (*gave him a talking-to*). **d** pledge (*gave her word*). **5** *tr.* **a** effect or perform (an action etc.) (*gave him a kiss*). **b** utter (*gave a shriek*). **6** *tr.* assign; grant (*was given the contract*). **7** *tr.* (in *passive*; foll. by *to*) be inclined to or fond of (*is given to speculation*). **8** *tr.* yield as a product or result (*the field gives fodder for twenty cows*). **9** *intr.* **a** yield to pressure; become relaxed; lose firmness (*this elastic doesn't give properly*). **b** collapse (*the roof gave under the pressure*). **c** *slang* concede defeat; surrender (*I give!*). **10** *intr.* (usu. foll. by *of*) grant; bestow (*gave freely of his time*). **11** *tr.* **a** commit, consign, or entrust (*give her into your care*). **b** sanction the marriage of (a daughter etc.). **12** *tr.* devote; dedicate (*gave his life to table tennis*). **13** *intr. informal* tell what one knows (*What happened? Come on, give!*). **14** *tr.* present; offer; show; hold out (*gave her his arm*). **15** *tr. Theatre* read, recite, perform, act, etc. **16** *tr.* impart; be a source of (*gave him my sore throat; gave its name to the battle*). **17** *tr.* allow (esp. a fixed amount of time) (*can give you five minutes*). **18** *tr.* (usu. foll. by *for*) value (something) (*gives nothing for their opinions*). **19** *tr.* concede (*I give you the victory*). **20** *tr.* deliver (a judgment etc.) authoritatively (*gave his verdict*). **21** *tr.* introduce (a person, cause, etc.) (*I give you our President*). **22** *tr.* provide (a party, meal, etc.) as host (*gave a banquet*). ● *n.* **1** capacity to yield or bend under pressure; elasticity. **2** ability to adapt or comply (*no give in his attitudes*). □ **give and take** exchange (concessions, words, or blows). **give as good as one gets** retort inwardly in words or blows. **give away 1** transfer as a gift. **2** hand over (a bride) ceremonially to a bridegroom. **3** betray or expose to ridicule or detection. **4** esp. *Sport* give inadvertently to the opposition (*gave away a penalty*). **give back** return (something) to its previous owner or in exchange. **give forth** emit; publish; report. **give the game** (or **show**) **away** reveal a secret or intention. **give a person** (or **the devil**) **his or her due** acknowledge, esp. grudgingly, a person's rights, abilities, etc. **give in 1** cease fighting or arguing; yield. **2** hand in (a document etc.) to an official etc. **give in marriage** sanction the marriage of (one's daughter etc.). **give it to a person** *informal* scold or punish. **give me** I prefer or admire (*give me Lake Huron*). **give off** emit (vapour etc.). **give oneself airs** act pretentiously or snobbishly. **give oneself up** surrender to one's pursuers. **give oneself up to 1** abandon oneself to an emotion, esp. despair. **2** addict oneself to. **give on to** (or **into**) (of a window, corridor, etc.) overlook or lead into. **give or take** *informal* add or subtract (a specified amount or number) in estimating. **give out 1** announce; emit; distribute. **2** cease or break down from exhaustion etc. **3** run short. **give over 1** *informal* cease from doing; abandon (a habit etc.); desist (*give over sniffing*). **2** hand over. **3** devote. **give rise to** cause, induce, suggest. **give a person to understand** inform authoritatively. **give up 1** resign; surrender. **2** part with. **3** deliver (a wanted person etc.). **4** pronounce incurable or insoluble; renounce hope of. **5** renounce or cease (an activity). **give a person what for** *informal* punish or scold severely. **give one's word** (or **word of honour**) promise solemnly. **what gives?** *informal* what is the news?; what's happening?; what's the problem? **would give the world** (or **one's right arm**) **for** covet or wish for desperately. □ **giver** *n.*

give-and-take *n.* an exchange of words, concessions, etc.; a compromise.

giveaway *n. informal* **1** an inadvertent betrayal or revelation. **2** an act of giving away. **3** (often *attrib.*) **a** something given away free. **b** something sold at a low price. **4** *Sport* the inadvertent turning over of the puck, ball, etc. to an opponent.

giveback *n. N Amer.* a union's agreement to reduce wages in exchange for benefits.

given ● *adj.* **1** as previously stated or assumed; granted (*given that he is a liar, we cannot trust him*). **2** *Law* (of a document) signed and dated (*given this day the 30th June*). ● *n.* a known fact or situation.

given name *n. N Amer.* a name given to a child at or shortly after birth, distinguished from the surname.

gizmo *n.* (*pl.* **-os**) *informal* a gadget.

gizzard *n.* **1** the second part of a bird's stomach, for grinding food usu. with grit. **2** a muscular stomach of some fish, insects, molluscs, etc. **3** *informal* **a** the stomach, entrails. **b** the throat. □ **stick in one's gizzard** *informal* be distasteful.

glacé /ˈglæsei, glæˈsei/ *adj.* **1** (of fruit, esp. cherries) preserved in sugar, usu. resulting in a glossy surface. **2** (of cloth, leather, etc.) smooth; polished.

glacial *adj.* **1** of ice; icy. **2** of or pertaining to glaciers. **3** *Geomorph.* characterized or produced by the presence or agency of glaciers. **4** (of movement or progress) resembling that of a glacier; extremely slow. □ **glacially** *adv.*

glacial lake *n.* a lake formed by glaciers, esp. a prehistoric lake formed by retreating ice sheets.

glacial period *n.* (also **glacial epoch**) a period when ice sheets were very extensive; an ice age.

glaciated /ˈgleisi,eitəd/ *adj.* **1** marked or polished by the action of ice. **2** covered or having been covered by glaciers or ice sheets. □ **glaciation** *n.*

glacier /ˈgleiʃər, -ʃiər, -siər/ *n.* a slowly-moving mass or river of ice formed by the accumulation and compaction of snow on mountains or in cold climates.

glad[1] *adj.* (**gladder**, **gladdest**) **1** (*predic.*) **a** pleased; delighted. **b** relieved (*glad about the way it turned out*). **c** (usu. foll. by *of*) grateful (*glad of a chance to talk about it*).

d willing and eager (*shall be glad to come*). **2** (*attrib.*) **a** (of news, events, etc.) giving joy (*glad tidings*). **b** expressing joy (*a glad expression*). □ **give a person the glad eye** *informal* cast an amorous glance at a person. □ **gladly** *adv.* **gladness** *n.*

glad² *n. informal* a gladiolus.

gladden *v.tr.* make glad.

glade *n.* an open space in a wood or forest.

glad hand ● *n.* a warm, often superficial, greeting or welcome. ● *v.tr.* (**glad-hand**) (esp. of a politician, celebrity, etc.) greet or welcome warmly, often superficially. □ **glad-hander** *n.*

gladiator *n.* **1** *hist.* a man trained to fight with a sword etc. at ancient Roman shows. **2** a person defending or opposing a cause. □ **gladiatorial** *adj.*

gladiolus /ˌglædiˈoːləs/ *n.* (*pl.* **gladioli** /-laɪ/ or **gladioluses**) (also *informal* **gladiola**) any plant of the genus *Gladiolus* with sword-shaped leaves and usu. brightly coloured flower spikes.

glam *informal* ● *adj.* **1** glamorous. **2** (usu. *attrib.*) designating a kind of pop music characterized by the extravagant dress, makeup, etc. of its performers, originally popular in the early 1970s (*glam rock*). ● *n.* glamour. □ **glammy** *adj.*

glamorize *v.tr.* (also **glamourize**) make glamorous or attractive. □ **glamorization** *n.*

glamour *n.* (also **glamor**) **1** physical attractiveness, esp. when achieved by makeup, elegant clothing, etc. **2** an attractive or exciting quality, esp. one which is inaccessible to the average person. □ **glamorless** *adj.* **glamorous** *adj.* **glamorously** *adv.*

glamour girl *n.* (also **glamour boy**) an attractive young woman (or man), esp. a model etc.

glance ● *v.* **1** *intr.* (often foll. by *down*, *up*, etc.) cast a momentary look. **2** *intr.* (often foll. by *off*) (esp. of a bullet, ball, etc.) bounce (off an object) obliquely. **b** *tr.* (esp. of a weapon etc.) strike (an object) obliquely. **3** *intr.* pass quickly over a subject or subjects (*glances over a number of difficult topics*). **4** *intr.* (of a bright object or light) flash, dart, or gleam; reflect (*the sun glanced off the knife*). ● *n.* **1** (usu. foll. by *at*, *into*, *over*, etc.) a brief look (*took a glance at the paper*). **2** a flash or gleam (*a glance of sunlight*). □ **at a glance 1** immediately upon looking. **2** presented in a manageable format; condensed (*carpentry at a glance*). **at first glance** on the first impression; initially. **glance at 1** give a brief look at. **2** make a passing and usu. sarcastic allusion to. **glance over** (or **through**) read cursorily. □ **glancingly** *adv.*

gland *n.* **1 a** an organ in an animal body secreting substances for use in the body or for ejection. **b** a structure resembling this, such as a lymph gland. **2** *Bot.* a secreting cell or group of cells on the surface of a plant structure.

glandular /ˈglændjʊlər/ *adj.* of or relating to a gland or glands.

glandular fever *n.* an infectious viral disease characterized by swelling of the lymph glands and prolonged lassitude; infectious mononucleosis.

glans /glænz/ *n.* (*pl.* **glandes** /ˈglændiːz/) the rounded part forming the head of the penis or clitoris.

glare¹ ● *v.* **1** *intr.* (usu. foll. by *at*, *upon*) look fiercely or fixedly. **2** *intr.* shine or reflect light dazzlingly or disagreeably. **3** *tr.* express (hate, defiance, etc.) by a look. ● *n.* **1 a** strong fierce (often reflected) light, esp. sunshine. **b** oppressive public attention (*the glare of fame*). **2** a fierce or fixed look (*a glare of defiance*). □ **glareless** *adj.* **glary** *adj.*

glare² *adj.* *N Amer.* (esp. of ice) smooth and glassy.

glaring *adj.* **1** obvious, conspicuous (*a glaring error*). **2**

shining or reflecting light oppressively or harshly. **3** staring fiercely. □ **glaringly** *adv.*

glasnost /ˈglæznɒst, ˈglæs-/ *n. hist.* (in the former USSR) the policy or practice of more open government and wider dissemination of information.

glass ● *n.* **1 a** (often *attrib.*) a hard, brittle, usu. transparent, translucent, or shiny substance, made by fusing sand with soda and lime and sometimes other ingredients. **b** = PLEXIGLAS. **2** (often *collect.*) an object or objects made from, or partly from, glass, esp.: **a** a drinking vessel. **b** a mirror. **c** a window. **d** a greenhouse (*rows of lettuce under glass*). **e** a magnifying lens. **3** (in *pl.*) **a** eyeglasses. **b** binoculars; opera glasses. **4** the amount of liquid contained in a glass. ● *v.tr.* (usu. as **glassed** *adj.*) fit with glass; glaze. □ **glassful** *n.* (*pl.* **-fuls**). **glasslike** *adj.*

glass-blowing *n.* the blowing of semi-molten glass to make glassware. □ **glass-blower** *n.*

glass ceiling *n.* an unacknowledged barrier to personal advancement.

glass eye *n.* a false eye made from glass.

glasshouse *n.* *Cdn & Brit.* a greenhouse.

glass-making *n.* the manufacture of glass. □ **glass-maker** *n.*

glassware *n.* articles made from glass, esp. drinking glasses, tableware, etc.

glassy ● *adj.* (**-ier**, **-iest**) **1** of or resembling glass, esp. in smoothness. **2** (of the eye, expression, etc.) abstracted; dull; fixed (*fixed her with a glassy stare*). ● *n.* (also **glassie**) (*pl.* **-ies**) *Cdn & Austral.* a glass marble. □ **glassily** *adv.* **glassiness** *n.*

glatt kosher /glæt/ *adj.* strictly kosher.

glaucoma /glɒˈkoːmə/ *n.* a condition of the eye with increased pressure within the eyeball, causing gradual loss of sight.

glaucous /ˈglɔːkəs/ *adj.* **1** of a dull greyish green or blue. **2** covered with a powdery bloom as of grapes.

glaze ● *n.* **1** a vitreous substance, usu. a special glass, used to glaze pottery. **2 a** a smooth shiny coating of sugar etc., on food. **b** a semi-liquid icing, often with a glossy sheen. **3** a thin topcoat of transparent paint used to modify the tone of the underlying colour. **4** a smooth surface formed by glazing. **5** *N Amer.* a thin coating of ice. ● *v.* **1** *tr.* **a** fit (a window, picture, etc.) with glass. **b** provide (a building) with glass windows. **2** *tr.* **a** cover (pottery, food, etc.) with a glaze. **b** fix (paint) on pottery with a glaze. **3** *intr.* (often foll. by *over*) (of the eyes) become fixed or glassy. **4** *tr.* give a glassy surface to, e.g. by rubbing. **5** *tr.* coat with a thin layer of ice. □ **glazy** *adj.*

glazier /ˈgleɪziər, -ʒər/ *n.* a person whose trade is glazing windows etc.

glazing *n.* **1** the act or an instance of glazing. **2** windows (*see also* DOUBLE GLAZING). **3** material used to produce a glaze.

gleam ● *n.* **1** a reflected, brief, or faint light (*a gleam of sunlight*). **2** a faint, sudden, intermittent, or temporary show or expression (*a gleam of hope; a gleam in her eye*). ● *v.intr.* **1** emit gleams. **2** shine with a reflected, intermittent, or faint brightness. **3** (of a quality) be indicated (*fear gleamed in his eyes*). □ **gleamingly** *adv.* **gleamy** *adj.*

glean *v.* **1** *tr.* collect or scrape together (news, facts, gossip, etc.) in small quantities. **2 a** *tr. & intr.* gather (ears of grain etc.) after the harvest. **b** *tr.* strip (a field etc.) after a harvest. □ **gleaner** *n.*

gleanings *n.pl.* things gleaned, esp. facts.

glee *n.* mirth; delight, esp. triumphant. □ **gleeful** *adj.* **gleefully** *adv.* **gleefulness** *n.*

glee club *n.* esp. *N Amer.* a choir, esp. at a school.

glen *n.* a narrow valley.

glib *adj.* (**glibber, glibbest**) **1** (of a speaker, speech, etc.) fluent and voluble but insincere and shallow. **2** *Cdn* (esp. *PEI*) (usu. *attrib.*) slippery, smooth (*glib ice*). □ **glibly** *adv.* **glibness** *n.*

glide ● *v.* **1** *intr.* (of a bird, boat, skater, stream, snake, etc.) move with a smooth continuous motion. **2 a** *intr.* (of an aircraft, esp. a glider) fly without engine power. **b** (of a pilot) fly a glider. **3** *intr.* of time etc.: **a** pass gently and imperceptibly. **b** (often foll. by *into*) pass and change gradually and imperceptibly (*night glided into day*). **4** *intr.* move quietly or stealthily. **5** *tr.* cause to glide (*breezes glided the ship on its course*). ● *n.* **1 a** the act of gliding. **b** an instance of this. **2 a** gliding dance or dance step. **3** a flight in a glider. **4** a device affixed to the bottom of chair or table legs so that they can be slid across a floor more easily.

glider *n.* **1 a** an aircraft that flies without an engine. **b** a glider pilot. **2** a person or thing that glides.

glimmer ● *v.intr.* shine faintly or intermittently. ● *n.* **1** a feeble or wavering light. **2** (usu. foll. by *of*) a faint gleam (of hope etc.). **3** a glimpse.

glimmering ● *n.* **1** = GLIMMER *n.* **2** an act of glimmering. ● *adj.* that glimmers. □ **glimmeringly** *adv.*

glimpse ● *n.* (often foll. by *of*) **1** a momentary or partial view (*caught a glimpse of her*). **2** a faint and transient appearance (*glimpses of the truth*). ● *v.* **1** *tr.* see faintly or partly (*glimpsed his face in the crowd*). **2** *intr.* (often foll. by *at*) cast a passing glance.

glint ● *v.intr. & tr.* flash or cause to flash; glitter; sparkle; reflect. ● *n.* a brief flash of light; a sparkle.

glissando /glɪ'sændo:, -'sɒndo/ *n.* (*pl.* **glissandi** /-di/ or **-os**) *Music* a continuous rapid slide of adjacent notes upwards or downwards.

glisten ● *v.intr.* shine, esp. like a wet object, snow, etc.; glitter. ● *n.* a glitter. □ **glisteningly** *adv.*

glitch *n.* a sudden irregularity or malfunction (of equipment, a plan, etc.).

glitter ● *v.intr.* **1** shine, esp. with a bright reflected light; sparkle. **2** (usu. foll. by *with*) **a** be showy or splendid (*glittered with diamonds*). **b** be ostentatious or flashily brilliant (*glittering rhetoric*). ● *n.* **1 a** gleam; a sparkle. **2** showiness; splendour. **3** tiny pieces of sparkling material. **4** *Cdn* (*Nfld*) **a** (often *attrib.*) freezing rain (*glitter storm*). **b** the coating of ice deposited by this. □ **glitteringly** *adv.* **glittery** *adj.*

glitterati /ˌglɪtə'ræti, -'rɒti/ *n.pl.* informal jocular fashionable, wealthy literary or show-business people.

glitz *n.* informal extravagant but superficial display.

glitzy *adj.* (**-ier, -iest**) informal extravagant, ostentatious; tawdry, gaudy. □ **glitzily** *adv.*

gloat ● *v.intr.* (often foll. by *on, upon, over*) consider or contemplate with malice, triumph, etc. ● *n.* **1** the act of gloating. **2** a look or expression of triumphant satisfaction. □ **gloater** *n.* **gloatingly** *adv.*

glob *n.* a lump of semi-liquid substance, e.g. mud.

global *adj.* **1** worldwide (*global marketplace*). **2 a** relating to or embracing a group of items etc.; total. **b** *Computing* operating or applying through the whole of a file, program, etc. □ **globally** *adv.*

globalize *v.tr. & intr.* make or become global. □ **globalization** *n.*

Global Positioning System *n.* a system of satellites and portable receivers able to pinpoint each receiver's location anywhere on the earth's surface, used in navigating and in surveying. Abbr.: **GPS**.

global village *n.* the world seen as one interdependent community linked by telecommunications.

global warming *n.* the increase in temperature of the earth's atmosphere supposedly caused by the greenhouse effect.

globe ● *n.* **1 a** (prec. by *the*) the planet earth. **b** a planet, star, or sun. **c** any spherical body; a ball. **2** a spherical representation of the earth or of the constellations with a map on the surface. **3** a golden sphere as an emblem of sovereignty; an orb. **4** any spherical glass vessel, esp. a fishbowl, a lamp, etc. ● *v.tr. & intr.* make or become globular. □ **globose** *adj.*

globe artichoke *n.* the partly edible head of the artichoke plant.

globe-trotting ● *n.* frequent and extensive travelling. ● *attrib.adj.* engaging in this (*a globe-trotting executive*). □ **globetrotter** *n.*

globin /'glo:bin/ *n.* any of various polypeptides forming the protein component of hemoglobin and related compound proteins.

globular /'glɒbjolər/ *adj.* **1** spherical. **2** composed of globules. □ **globularity** /-'leriti, -'læriti/ *n.*

globule /'glɒbju:l/ *n.* a small globe or round particle; a drop.

globulin /'glɒbjolɪn/ *n.* any of a group of simple proteins soluble only in salt solutions and esp. forming a large fraction of blood serum protein.

glockenspiel /'glɒkən,spi:l, -ˌʃpi:l/ *n.* a musical instrument consisting of a series of bells or metal bars or tubes suspended or mounted in a frame and struck by hammers.

glom /glɒm/ *v.* (**glommed, glomming**) *N Amer. slang* **1** *tr. & intr.* steal. **2** *intr.* (usu. foll. by *on to, into*) **a** grab, clutch. **b** latch on to, get hooked on (an idea etc.).

gloom ● *n.* **1** darkness; obscurity. **2** melancholy; despondency. ● *v.* **1** *intr.* be gloomy or melancholy; frown. **2** *intr.* (of the sky etc.) be dull or threatening; lower. **3** *intr.* appear darkly or obscurely. **4** *tr.* cover with gloom; make dark or dismal.

gloom and doom *n.* = DOOM AND GLOOM.

gloomy *adj.* (**-ier, -iest**) **1** dark; unlighted. **2** depressed; sullen. **3** dismal; depressing. □ **gloomily** *adv.* **gloominess** *n.*

gloop *n.* informal semi-liquid or sticky material.

glop *N Amer. slang* ● *n.* a liquid or sticky mess. ● *v.* (**glopped, glopping**) **1** *tr.* scoop, drop, or toss (a semi-liquid substance). **2** *intr.* (of a semi-liquid substance) drop, collect, ooze, or splat. □ **gloppy** *adj.*

Gloria *n.* **1** any of various Christian prayers or hymns beginning with the word *Gloria.* **2** a musical setting of this.

glorify *v.tr.* (**-ies, -ied**) **1** exalt to heavenly glory; make glorious. **2** transform into something more splendid. **3** extol; praise. **4** (usu. as **glorified** *adj.*) cause to seem or make out to be more splendid than in reality (*just a glorified office boy*). □ **glorification** *n.* **glorifier** *n.*

glorious *adj.* **1** possessing glory; illustrious. **2** conferring glory; honourable (*a glorious sacrifice*). **3** informal splendid; magnificent; delightful (*a glorious day*). **4** ironic intense; unmitigated (*a glorious muddle*). □ **gloriously** *adv.* **gloriousness** *n.*

glory ● *n.* (*pl.* **-ies**) **1** high renown or fame; honour. **2** praise and thanksgiving (*Glory to the Lord*). **3** resplendent majesty or magnificence (*the glory of Versailles*). **4** a thing that brings renown or praise; a distinction. **5** the bliss and splendour of heaven. **6** informal a state of exaltation, prosperity, happiness, etc. (*is in his glory playing with his trains*). ● *v.intr.* (often foll. by *in*, or *to* + infin.) pride oneself; exult (*glory in their skill*). □ **go to glory** *slang* die; be destroyed.

Glory Be ● *n.* a Christian prayer of praise to the Trinity beginning with the words 'Glory be to the

Father'. ● *interj.* (**glory be**) **1** a devout exclamation. **2** *informal* an exclamation of surprise or delight.

glory days *n.pl.* (also **glory years** etc.) the period of one's highest achievement, greatest fame, etc.

gloss¹ ● *n.* **1 a** surface shine or lustre. **b** an instance of this; a smooth finish. **2 a** deceptively attractive appearance. **b** an instance of this. **3** (in full **gloss paint**) paint formulated to give a hard glossy finish. **4** a cosmetic applied to add lustre to skin (*lip gloss*). ● *v.tr.* make glossy. □ **gloss over 1** seek to conceal beneath a false appearance. **2** conceal or evade by mentioning briefly or misleadingly.

gloss² ● *n.* **1 a** an explanatory word or phrase inserted between the lines or in the margin of a text. **b** a comment, explanation, interpretation, or paraphrase. **2 a** a glossary. **b** an interlinear translation or annotation. ● *v.* **1** *tr.* **a** add a gloss or glosses to (a text, word, etc.). **b** read a different sense into; explain away. **2** *intr.* write or introduce glosses.

glossary *n.* (*pl.* **-ies**) **1** (also **gloss**) an alphabetical list of terms or words found in or relating to a specific subject or text, with explanations; a brief dictionary. **2** a collection of glosses.

glossy ● *adj.* (**-ier, -iest**) **1** having a shine; smooth. **2** (of paper etc.) smooth and shiny. **3** (of a magazine etc.) printed on such paper. **4** having a deceptively smooth and attractive appearance. ● *n.* (*pl.* **-ies**) *informal* **1** a glossy magazine. **2** a photograph with a glossy surface. □ **glossily** *adv.* **glossiness** *n.*

glottis /'glɒtɪs/ *n.* the space at the upper end of the windpipe and between the vocal cords, affecting voice modulation through expansion or contraction.

glove ● *n.* **1** a covering for the hand, of wool, leather, cotton, etc., worn esp. for protection against cold or dirt, and usu. having separate fingers. **2** a padded protective glove, esp.: **a** used for catching, as by a goaltender or a baseball player. **b** a hockey player's glove. **c** a boxing glove. ● *v.tr.* **1** (usu. as **gloved** *adj.*) cover or provide with a glove or gloves. **2** *N Amer.* catch (a ball, puck, etc.) in a glove. □ **drop the** (or **one's**) **gloves 1** *N Amer.* (in hockey) remove one's gloves to indicate willingness to fight. **2** *Cdn* engage in or indicate willingness to engage in a debate, confrontation, etc. (*halfway through the interview, he dropped the gloves*). **fit like a glove** fit exactly. **take off the gloves** *Cdn* ready oneself or indicate readiness for a confrontation. **with the gloves off** mercilessly; unfairly.

glovebox *n.* **1** = GLOVE COMPARTMENT. **2** a closed chamber with sealed-in gloves for handling infants, radioactive material, etc.

glove compartment *n.* a recess for small articles in the dashboard of a motor vehicle.

glow ● *v.intr.* **1 a** throw out light and heat. **b** shine with a steady light like something heated in this way. **2** (of the cheeks) redden, esp. from cold or exercise. **3** (often foll. by *with*) **a** (of the body) be heated, esp. from exertion; sweat. **b** express or experience strong emotion, esp. joy (*glowed with pride*). **4** show a warm colour (*the painting glows with warmth*). ● *n.* **1** a glowing state. **2** a bright warm colour, esp. the red of cheeks. **3** ardour; passion. **4** a feeling induced by good health, exercise, etc.; well-being.

glower /'glaʊər/ ● *v.intr.* stare or scowl angrily. ● *n.* a glowering look. □ **gloweringly** *adv.*

glowing *adj.* expressing pride or praise (*a glowing report*). □ **glowingly** *adv.*

glow-worm *n.* any beetle of the genus *Lampyris* whose wingless female has a glowing abdomen.

glucagon /'gluːkəgɒn/ *n.* a polypeptide hormone

formed in the pancreas, which aids the breakdown of glycogen to glucose.

glucose *n.* **1** a simple sugar containing six carbon atoms, which is an important energy source in living organisms and obtainable from some carbohydrates by hydrolysis. **2** a syrup containing glucose sugars from the incomplete hydrolysis of starch.

glue ● *n.* an adhesive substance used for sticking objects or materials together. ● *v.tr.* (**glues, glued, gluing** or **glueing**) **1** fasten or join with glue. **2** keep or put very close. **3** set fixedly (*eyes glued to the TV*). □ **glue-like** *adj.* **gluey** *adj.* (**gluier, gluiest**)

glue gun *n.* an electric tool like a handgun, for melting and applying glue stored as hard sticks.

glue sniffing *n.* the inhalation of intoxicating fumes from the solvents in adhesives etc. □ **glue sniffer** *n.*

glug ● *v.* (**glugged, glugging**) **1** *intr.* make a hollow, usu. repetitive gurgling sound, as of liquid being poured from a bottle. **2** *tr.* pour or drink (a liquid) with such a sound. ● *n.* such a sound.

glum *adj.* (**glummer, glummest**) looking or feeling dejected; sullen, morose. □ **glumly** *adv.* **glumness** *n.*

glut ● *n.* **1** *Econ.* supply exceeding demand; a surfeit (*a glut in the market*). **2** an excessive quantity (*the information glut*). ● *v.tr.* (**glutted, glutting**) **1** *Econ.* overstock (a market) with goods. **2** fill to excess; choke up. **3** feed (a person, one's stomach, etc.) or indulge (an appetite, a desire, etc.) to the full; satiate.

glutamate /'gluːtə,meit/ *n.* any salt or ester of glutamic acid, esp. a sodium salt used to enhance the flavour of food.

glutamic acid /gluː'tæmɪk/ *n.* a naturally occurring amino acid, a constituent of many proteins.

glutch /glʌtʃ/ *Cdn* (*Nfld*) ● *v.tr. & intr.* gulp, swallow. ● *n.* a gulp or swallow.

glute *n.* *slang* (usu. in *pl.*) a gluteus muscle.

gluten *n.* a mixture of proteins present in cereal grains, responsible for the elastic cohesion of dough.

gluteus /'gluːtiəs/ *n.* (*pl.* **glutei** /-ti,ai/) any of the three muscles in each buttock. □ **gluteal** *adj.*

gluteus maximus /'mæksɪməs/ *n.* (*pl.* **glutei maximi** /'mæksimai/) **1** the largest and outermost muscle of each buttock. **2** *slang* the buttocks.

glutinous /'gluːtɪnəs/ *adj.* sticky; like glue.

glutton *n.* **1** an excessively greedy eater. **2** (often foll. by *for*) *informal* a person insatiably eager (*a glutton for work*). □ **a glutton for punishment** a person eager to take on hard or unpleasant tasks. □ **gluttonous** *adj.* **gluttonously** *adv.*

gluttony *n.* habitual greed or excess in eating.

glyceride /'glɪsə,raid/ *n.* any fatty-acid ester of glycerol.

glycerine /'glɪsə,rɪn/ *n.* (esp. *US* **glycerin**) = GLYCEROL.

glycerol /'glɪsə,rɒl/ *n.* a colourless sweet viscous liquid, a by-product in the manufacture of soap, used as an emollient and laxative, in explosives, etc.

glycogen /'glaɪkədʒən/ *n.* a polysaccharide serving as a store of carbohydrates, esp. in animal tissues, and yielding glucose on hydrolysis.

glycol *n.* any alcohol containing two hydroxyl groups in each molecule, esp. ethylene glycol.

glycolysis /glaɪ'kɒlɪsɪs/ *n.* the breakdown of glucose by enzymes in most living organisms to release energy.

glycoprotein /,glaɪko'proːtiːn/ *n.* any of a group of compounds consisting of a protein combined with a carbohydrate.

glycoside /ˈglʌɪkə,saɪd/ n. any compound yielding sugar and other products on hydrolysis.

glyph /glɪf/ n. **1** a sculptured character or symbol. **2** a symbol or pictorial representation, as in computing or on a sign. □ **glyphic** adj.

GM abbr. general manager.

gm abbr. gram(s).

GMT abbr. GREENWICH MEAN TIME.

gnarled /nɑːld/ adj. (of a tree, hands, etc.) knobbly, twisted, rugged.

gnarly adj. **1** = GNARLED. **2** N Amer. slang excitingly rough or dangerous.

gnash v. **1** tr. grind (the teeth), esp. in anger or exasperation. **2** intr. (of the teeth) grind.

gnat n. any small two-winged biting fly, e.g. a midge.

gnaw v. **1** a tr. (usu. foll. by away, off, in two, etc.) bite persistently; wear away by biting. **b** intr. (often foll. by at, into) bite, nibble. **2** a intr. (often foll. by at, into) (of a destructive agent, pain, fear, etc.) corrode; waste away; consume; torture. **b** tr. corrode, consume, torture, etc. with pain, fear, etc. (was gnawed by doubt).

gnawing adj. persistent; worrying. □ **gnawingly** adv.

gneiss /nʌɪs/ n. a usu. coarse-grained metamorphic rock foliated by mineral layers, principally of feldspar, quartz, and mica. □ **gneissic** adj.

gnocchi /ˈnjɒki/ n.pl. an Italian dish of small dumplings usu. made from potato, flour, etc.

gnome¹ n. **1** a a dwarfish legendary creature supposed to guard the earth's treasures underground; a goblin. **b** a figure of a gnome, esp. as a garden ornament. **2** (esp. in pl.) informal a person with sinister influence, esp. financial (gnomes of Zurich). □ **gnomish** adj.

gnome² /noːm, ˈnoːmi/ n. a maxim; an aphorism.

gnomic adj. **1** of, consisting of, or using gnomes or aphorisms (see GNOME²). **2** Grammar (of a tense) used without the implication of time to express a general truth, e.g. men were deceivers ever.

gnomon /ˈnoːmɒn/ n. the rod or pin etc. on a sundial that shows the time by the position of its shadow. □ **gnomonic** adj.

gnosis /ˈnoːsɪs/ n. esoteric spiritual knowledge.

gnostic /ˈnɒstɪk/ ● adj. **1** relating to knowledge, esp. esoteric mystical knowledge. **2** (**Gnostic**) of or concerning Gnosticism or the Gnostics; occult; mystic. ● n. (**Gnostic**) (usu. in pl.) an adherent of Gnosticism.

Gnosticism /ˈnɒstɪˌsɪzəm/ n. a heretical movement prominent in the Christian Church in the 2nd c., emphasizing the power of gnosis to redeem the spiritual element in humankind.

GNP abbr. gross national product.

gnu /nuː, njuː/ n. any antelope of the genus Connochaetes, native to S Africa, with a large erect head and brown stripes on the neck and shoulders.

GNWT abbr. Cdn Government of the Northwest Territories.

go ● v. (3rd sing. present **goes**; past **went**; past part. **gone**) **1** intr. **a** start moving or be moving from one place or point in time to another; travel, proceed. **b** proceed in order to (went to find him; go and buy some bread). **c** informal expressing annoyance (they've gone and broken it). **2** intr. make a special trip for; participate in; proceed to do (went shopping; often goes running). **3** intr. lie or extend in a certain direction (the road goes to Antigonish). **4** intr. leave; depart (they had to go). **5** intr. move, act, work, etc. (the clock doesn't go). **6** intr. **a** make a specified movement (go like this with your foot). **b** make a sound (often of a specified kind) (the gun went bang; the doorbell went). **c** informal say (so he goes to me

'Why not?'). **d** (of an animal) make (its characteristic cry) (the cow went 'moo'). **7** intr. be in a specified state (go hungry). **8** intr. **a** pass into a specified condition (gone bad; went to sleep). **b** informal die. **c** proceed or escape in a specified condition (the crime went unnoticed). **9** intr. (of time or distance) pass, elapse; be traversed (ten days to go; the last mile went quickly). **10** intr. **a** (of a document, verse, song, etc.) have a specified content or wording; run (the tune goes like this). **b** be current or accepted (so the story goes). **c** be suitable; fit; match (the shoes don't go with the hat). **d** be regularly kept or put (the forks go here). **e** find room; fit (this won't go into the cupboard). **11** intr. **a** turn out, proceed (things went well; Montreal went Liberal). **b** be successful (make the party go). **c** progress (we've still a long way to go). **12** intr. **a** be sold (went for $50). **b** (of money) be spent ($200 went on a new jacket). **13** intr. **a** be relinquished, dismissed, or abolished (the car will have to go). **b** fail, decline; give way, collapse (his sight is going). **14** intr. be acceptable or permitted; be accepted without question (anything goes; what Susan says goes). **15** intr. (often foll. by by, with, on, upon) be guided by; judge or act on or in harmony with (a good rule to go by). **16** intr. attend or visit or travel to regularly (goes to church; this train goes to Edmonton). **17** intr. (foll. by pres. part.) informal proceed (often foolishly) to do (don't go making him angry). **18** intr. act or proceed to a certain point (will go so far and no further). **19** intr. (of a number) be capable of being contained in another (6 goes twice into 12). **20** intr. (usu. foll. by to) be allotted or awarded (the job went to his rival). **21** intr. (foll. by to, towards) amount to; contribute to (this will go towards your holiday). **22** intr. (in imper.) begin motion (a starter's order in a race) (ready, set, go!). **23** intr. (usu. foll. by to) refer or appeal (go to him for help). **24** intr. (often foll. by on) take up a specified profession (went on the stage; went to sea). **25** intr. (usu. foll. by by, under) be known or called (goes by the name of Droopy). **26** tr. (in imper.) informal proceed to (go jump in the lake). **27** intr. (foll. by for) apply to; have relevance for (that goes for me too). **28** intr. urinate or defecate (went on the carpet). ● n. (pl. **goes**) **1** the act or an instance of going. **2** mettle; spirit; dash; animation (she has a lot of go in her). **3** vigorous activity (it's all go). **4** informal a success (made a go of it). **5** informal a turn; an attempt (I'll have a go; it's my go). **6** N Amer. a project, undertaking, etc. which has been given the go-ahead (the new subway line is a go). **7** an experience (had a rough go of it). ● adj. informal functioning properly (all systems are go). □ **as** (or **so**) **far as it goes** an expression of caution against taking a statement too positively (the work is good as far as it goes). **as (a person or thing) goes** as the average is (a good actor as actors go). **from the word go** informal from the very beginning. **give it a go** informal make an effort to succeed. **go about 1** busy oneself with; set to work at. **2** be socially active. **3** = GO AROUND 2. **go against 1** be contrary to (goes against my principles). **2** have an unfavourable result for (decision went against them). **go ahead** proceed without hesitation. **go along with** agree to; take the same view as. **go around 1** (foll. by with) be regularly in the company of. **2** (foll. by pres. part.) make a habit of doing (goes around telling lies). **go at** take in hand energetically; attack. **go away** depart, esp. from home for a holiday etc. **go back 1** return (to). **2 a** extend backwards in space or time (goes back to the 18th century). **b** (also **go way back**) (of two or more people or things) have known one another for a very long time (Marty and I go way back). **3** (of the hour, a clock, etc.) be set to an earlier standard time (the clocks go back in the autumn). **go**

back on fail to keep (one's word, promise, etc.). **go by 1** pass. **2** be dependent on; be guided by. **go down 1 a** (of an amount) become less. **b** subside (*the flood went down*). **c** decrease in price; lose value. **2 a** (of a ship) sink. **b** (of an aircraft) crash. **c** (of the sun) set. **3** (usu. foll. by *to*) be continued to a specified point. **4** deteriorate; fail; (of a computer network etc.) cease to function. **5 a** be recorded in writing. **b** be remembered (*this will go down as their greatest triumph*). **6** be swallowed. **7** (often foll. by *with*) find acceptance. **8** (often foll. by *before*) fall (before a conqueror). **9** *N Amer. slang* happen. **go down on** *slang* perform fellatio or cunnilingus on. **go far** be very successful. **go for 1** go to fetch. **2** be accounted as or achieve (*went for nothing*). **3** prefer; choose (*that's the one I go for*). **4** *informal* strive to attain (*go for it!*). **5** *informal* attack (*the dog went for him*). **go forward 1** proceed, progress. **2** (of the hour, a clock, etc.) be set to a later time, esp. daylight time. **go halves** (or **shares**) (often foll. by *with*) share equally. **go in 1** enter a room, house, etc. **2** (of the sun etc.) become obscured by cloud. **go in for** take as one's object, style, pursuit, principle, etc. **going!, gone!** an auctioneer's announcement that bidding is closing or closed. **go into 1** enter (a profession, Parliament, etc.). **2** take part in; be a part of. **3** investigate. **4** allow oneself to pass into (hysterics etc.). **5** dress oneself in (mourning etc.). **6** elaborate on (*went into the family's history*). **go a long way 1** (often foll. by *towards*) have a great effect. **2** (of food, money, etc.) last a long time, buy much. **3** = GO FAR. **go off 1** explode. **2** leave the stage. **3** gradually cease to be felt. **4** (esp. of foodstuffs) deteriorate; decompose. **5** go to sleep; become unconscious. **6** begin. **7** (of an alarm) begin to sound. **8** *informal* lose one's taste or enthusiasm for (*I've gone off sweet things*). **go off well** (or **badly** etc.) (of an enterprise etc.) be received or accomplished well (or badly etc.). **go on 1** continue, persevere (*decided to go on with it; went on trying; unable to go on*). **2** *informal* a talk at great length. **b** (foll. by *at*) admonish (*went on and on at him*). **3** proceed (*went on to become a star*). **4** happen (*what's going on?*). **5** conduct oneself (*shameful, the way they went on*). **6** *Theatre* appear on stage. **7** (of a garment) be large enough for its wearer. **8** take one's turn to do something. **9** *informal* use as evidence (*police don't have anything to go on*). **go on!** *informal* an expression of encouragement or disbelief. **go out 1** leave a room, house, etc. **2 a** be broadcast. **b** be distributed. **3** be extinguished. **4** (often foll. by *with*) be dating. **5** leave one's home for recreation, esp. to visit a restaurant, friends, etc. **6** (of a government) leave office. **7** cease to be fashionable. **8** *informal* lose consciousness. **9** (of workers) strike. **10** (usu. foll. by *to*) (of the heart etc.) expand with sympathy etc. towards (*my heart goes out to them*). **11** *Golf* play the first nine holes in a round. **12** *Cards* be the first to dispose of one's hand. **13** (of a tide) turn to low tide. **14** *Cdn* (of winter ice on a lake, river, etc.) break up in the spring. **go over 1** inspect the details of; rehearse; retouch. **2** (often foll. by *to*) change one's allegiance or religion. **3** (of a play, joke, etc.) be successful (*went over well in Vancouver*). **go round 1** spin, revolve. **2** be long enough to encompass. **3** (of food etc.) suffice for everybody. **4** (usu. foll. by *to*) visit informally. **5** = GO AROUND. **go through 1** be dealt with or completed. **2** discuss in detail; scrutinize in sequence. **3** perform (a ceremony, a recitation, etc.). **4** undergo. **5** *informal* use up; spend (money etc.). **6** make holes in. **7** (of a book) be successively published (in so many editions). **go through with** not leave unfinished; complete. **go to**

hell (or **blazes** etc.) *slang* an exclamation of dismissal, contempt, etc. **go together 1** match; fit. **2** be dating. **go to it!** *informal* begin work! **go to show** (or **prove**) serve to demonstrate (or prove). **go under** sink; fail; succumb. **go up 1** increase in price. **2** be consumed (in flames etc.); explode. **3** (of a building) be under construction. **go well** (or **ill** etc.) (often foll. by *with*) turn out well, (or ill etc.). **go with 1** be harmonious with; match. **2** agree to; take the same view as. **3 a** be a pair with. **b** be dating. **4** follow the drift of. **go without** manage without; forgo. **have a go at 1** attempt, try. **2** esp. *Brit.* attack, criticize. **on the go** *informal* **1** in constant motion. **2** constantly working. **3** in progress; happening. **to go 1** still to be dealt with. **2** *N Amer.* (of food) to be consumed off the premises. **who goes there?** a sentry's challenge.

goad ● *n.* **1** an implement, such as a pointed or electrified rod, used for herding cattle etc. **2** anything that torments, incites, or stimulates. ● *v.tr.* **1** urge on with a goad. **2** (usu. foll. by *on, into*) irritate; stimulate (*goaded him into retaliating*).

go-ahead ● *n.* permission to proceed. ● *adj.* **1** enterprising (*a go-ahead business*). **2** *N Amer. Sport* designating a goal, run, etc. which puts the scoring team ahead.

goal *n.* **1** the object of an ambition or effort; a destination; an aim (*Fredericton was our goal*). **2 a** (in hockey etc.) a pair of posts with a crossbar between which the puck or ball has to be sent to score. **b** a cage or basket used similarly in other sports. **c** a successful attempt to score (*it's a goal!*). **d** a point won (*scored 3 goals*). **3 a** point marking the end of a race. **4** the position of goalkeeper. □ **in goal** in the position of goalkeeper. □ **goalless** *adj.*

goalie *n.* = GOALKEEPER.

goalie pads *n.pl. Hockey* (also **goal pads**) a pair of very thick rectangular pads worn on the legs by a goaltender.

goalkeeper *n.* a player stationed to protect the goal in various sports. □ **goalkeeping** *n.*

goal line *n. Sport* a line across which a ball or puck must cross for points to be scored, esp.: **1** (in hockey) a red line between each pair of goalposts. **2** (in soccer) a line between each pair of goalposts, also extending beyond the posts to form the end boundary of the field of play. **3** (in football) the line separating each end zone from the rest of the field.

goalmouth *n.* (in hockey, soccer, etc.) the space between or directly in front of the goalposts.

goalpost *n.* either of the two upright posts of a goal.

goals-against average *n. Hockey* the average number of goals scored per game against a specified goaltender. Abbr.: **GAA**.

goal scorer *n.* **1** a player who scores a goal. **2** a player good at scoring goals. □ **goal-scoring** *adj. & n.*

goaltender *n. N Amer.* (esp. in hockey) a goalkeeper.

goaltending *n.* **1** *N Amer.* (esp. in hockey) the action of defending a goal. **2** (in basketball) the illegal blocking or deflecting of an attempted basket while the ball is descending or on the rim.

goat *n.* **1 a** a hardy lively frisky short-haired domesticated mammal, *Capra aegagrus*, having horns and (in the male) a beard, and kept for its milk and meat. **b** = MOUNTAIN GOAT. **2** any other mammal of the genus *Capra*, e.g. the ibex. **3** *informal* a foolish person. **4** a lecherous man. □ **get a person's goat** *informal* irritate a person. □ **goatish** *adj.* **goatlike** *adj.* **goaty** *adj.*

goat-antelope *n.* any antelope-like member of the goat family, including the Rocky Mountain goat.

goat cheese *n.* cheese made from goat's milk.

goatee /go:'ti:/ n. a small beard on the point of the chin, like that of a goat. □ **goateed** adj.

goatherd n. a person who tends goats.

goatskin n. **1** the skin of a goat. **2** a garment or bottle made out of goatskin.

goatsucker n. any nocturnal bird of the family Caprimulgidae, including whippoorwills.

gob slang ● n. **1** a clot or lump of esp. slimy or soft matter. **2** slang **a** Cdn spittle. **b** a globule of spittle. **3** (in pl.; foll. by of) N Amer. lots of. ● v.intr. (**gobbed, gobbing**) Cdn & Brit. spit.

gobble¹ v. **1** tr. & intr. eat hurriedly and noisily; devour. **2** tr. (often foll. by up) **a** seize avidly, grab, snatch. **b** consume, use up. □ **gobbler** n.

gobble² ● v.intr. **1** (of a male turkey) make a characteristic swallowing sound in the throat. **2** make such a sound when speaking, esp. when excited, angry, etc. ● n. such a sound.

gobbledegook n. (also **gobbledygook**) informal unintelligible jargon.

gobbler n. informal a turkeycock.

go-between n. an intermediary; a negotiator.

goblet n. a drinking vessel with a foot and a stem, usu. of glass.

goblin n. a mischievous ugly dwarf-like creature of folklore.

goby /'go:bi/ n. (pl. **-ies**) any small marine fish of the family Gabiidae, having ventral fins joined to form a sucker or disc.

go-cart n. **1** = GO-KART. **2** an unpowered esp. homemade riding cart, either sent down a slope or pushed.

god n. **1 a** (in many religions) a superhuman being or spirit worshipped as having power over nature, human fortunes, etc.; a deity. **b** an image, idol, animal, or other object worshipped as divine or symbolizing a god. **2** (**God**) (in monotheistic religions) the creator and ruler of the universe. **3 a** an adored, admired, or influential person. **b** something worshipped like a god (makes a god of success). **4** (**God!**) an exclamation of surprise, anger, etc. □ **by God!** an exclamation of surprise etc. **God bless** an expression of good wishes on parting. **God damn (you, him**, etc.) may (you etc.) be damned. **God grant** (foll. by that + clause) may it happen. **God help (you, him**, etc.) an expression of concern for or sympathy with a person. **God knows 1** it is beyond all knowledge (God knows what will become of him). **2** I call God to witness that (God knows we tried hard enough). **God willing** if Providence allows. **in God's name** an appeal for help. **my** (or **oh**) **God!** an exclamation of surprise, anger, etc. **play God** attempt to control people or events, esp. in matters traditionally outside the realm of human influence. **with God** dead and in Heaven. □ **godhood** n.

godawful adj. slang very unpleasant, inferior, etc.

godchild n. (pl. **-children**) a person in relation to a godparent.

goddammit interj. (also **goddamnit**) informal expressing annoyance, anger, etc.

goddamn adj. (also **goddam** or **goddamned**) slang accursed, damnable.

goddaughter n. a female godchild.

goddess n. **1** a female deity. **2** a woman who is adored, esp. for her beauty.

godfather n. **1** a male godparent. **2** a person directing an illegal organization, esp. the Mafia. **3** the most experienced or influential member of an organization etc., treated with deference and respect.

God-fearing adj. **1** having a deep respect for God and leading a virtuous life. **2** earnestly religious.

godforsaken adj. (also **God-forsaken**) **1** (of a place) dismal; lacking in comfort. **2** remote; isolated.

God-given adj. received as from God; possessed from birth or by divine authority.

godhead n. (also **Godhead**) **1 a** the state of being God or a god. **b** divine nature. **2** a deity. **3** (**the Godhead**) God.

godless adj. **1** impious; wicked. **2** without a god. **3** not recognizing God. □ **godlessness** n.

godlike adj. **1** resembling God or a god in some quality, esp. in omnipotence. **2** befitting or appropriate to God or a god.

godly adj. religious, pious, devout. □ **godliness** n.

godmother n. a female godparent.

godparent n. a person who presents a child at baptism and responds on the child's behalf.

God's country n. N Amer. a natural paradise.

godsend n. an unexpected but welcome event, thing, or person.

God's gift n. often ironic a person or thing that is of supreme benefit to someone or something specified (thinks he's God's gift to women).

godson n. a male godchild.

Godspeed n. (as an expression of good wishes to a person starting a journey etc.) good fortune.

God's truth n. the absolute truth.

godwit n. any wading bird of the genus Limosa, with long legs and a long straight or slightly upcurved bill.

goer n. **1** (often in comb.) a person who attends, esp. regularly (churchgoer; concert-goer). **2** a person or thing that goes (a slow goer).

goes 3rd sing. present of GO¹.

gofer /'go:fər/ n. esp. N Amer. informal a person who runs errands, esp. in an office.

go-getter n. informal an aggressively enterprising person, esp. in business. □ **go-getting** adj.

goggle ● n. **1** (in pl.) **a** eyeglasses for protecting the eyes from glare, dust, water, etc. **b** informal eyeglasses. **2** an expression with wide-open or protuberant eyes. ● v.intr. **1** (often foll. by at) stare with wide, round eyes, esp. in surprise or wonder. **2** (of the eyes) be rolled about; protrude. ● adj. (usu. attrib.) (of the eyes) protuberant or rolling. □ **goggly** adj.

goggle-eyed adj. having staring or protuberant eyes.

go-go adj. **1 a** (of a dancer) performing at a nightclub or disco, esp. in scanty clothing. **b** (of a nightclub etc.) featuring go-go dancers. **2** informal unrestrained; energetic. **3** informal (of investment) speculative.

going ● n. **1 a** the act or process of going. **b** an instance of this; a departure. **2 a** the condition of the ground for walking, riding, etc. **b** progress affected by this (found the going very laborious). **c** progress affected by all circumstances (it'll be tough going for the party this election). ● adj. **1** in or into action (set the clock going). **2** existing, available; to be had (one of the best going). **3** current, prevalent (the going rate). □ **get going** start steadily talking, working, etc. (can't stop them when they get going). **going for one** informal acting in one's favour (he's got a lot going for him). **going on fifteen** etc. esp. N Amer. approaching one's fifteenth etc. birthday. **going on for** approaching (a time, an age, etc.) (must be going on for 64 years). **going to** intending or intended to; about to; likely to (it's going to sink!). **to be going on with** to start with; for the time being. **while the going is good** while conditions are favourable.

going away *n.* a departure, as to another city, job, etc. (often, with hyphen, *attrib.*: *going-away party*).

going concern *n.* a thriving business.

going-over *n.* (*pl.* **goings-over**) *informal* **1** an inspection or overhaul. **2** a thrashing. **3** *N Amer.* a scolding.

goings-on *n.pl.* unusual, surprising, or morally undesirable happenings or events.

goitre /ˈɡɔɪtər/ *n.* (esp. *US* **goiter**) *Med.* a swelling of the neck caused by enlargement of the thyroid. □ **goitrous** *adj.*

go-kart *n.* a miniature race car with a skeleton body.

gold ● *n.* **1** a yellow metallic element occurring naturally in quartz veins and gravel, and precious as a monetary medium, in jewellery, etc. **2** the colour of gold. **3 a** coins or articles made of gold. **b** money in large sums, wealth. **4** something precious, beautiful, or brilliant (*all that glitters is not gold*). **5** = GOLD MEDAL. ● *adj.* **1** made wholly or chiefly of gold. **2** coloured like gold. **3** (of an album, CD, etc.) having sold a specified high number of copies.

gold brick *n. slang* a thing with only a surface appearance of value; a sham or fraud.

gold card *n.* a credit card issued only to people with a high credit rating and giving benefits not available to holders of the standard card.

gold dust *n.* gold in fine particles as often found naturally.

golden *adj.* **1 a** made or consisting of gold. **b** yielding gold. **2** coloured or shining like gold (*golden hair*). **3** precious; valuable; excellent (*a golden opportunity*). **4** (esp. in nicknames for places) wealthy (*Golden Horseshoe*). □ **goldenly** *adv.* **goldenness** *n.*

golden age *n.* **1** a supposed past age when people were happy and innocent. **2** the period of greatest esp. artistic achievement (*the golden age of comics*). **3** (*usu. attrib.*) old age, esp. after retirement.

golden ager *n. N Amer.* an old person, esp. a retired person over 65.

golden boy *n. informal* a popular or successful man.

Golden Delicious *n.* see DELICIOUS *n.*

golden eagle *n.* a large eagle, *Aquila chrysaetos*, with yellow-tipped head feathers.

goldeneye *n.* a diving duck of the genus *Bucephala*, esp. the common goldeneye *B. clangula*, with a large dark head and bright yellow eyes.

golden girl *n. informal* a popular or successful woman.

golden handshake *n. informal* a payment given as compensation for dismissal or compulsory retirement.

golden jubilee *n.* **1** the fiftieth anniversary of a sovereign's accession. **2** any other fiftieth anniversary.

golden oldie *n. informal* **1** an old hit record etc. that is still well known and popular. **2** any person or thing still popular or successful after a long period.

golden parachute *n. informal* financial compensation guaranteed to company executives dismissed as a result of a merger or takeover.

golden retriever *n.* a retriever with a thick coat ranging in colour from pale yellow to golden-orange, and feathering on the neck, legs, and tail.

goldenrod *n.* any plant of the genus *Solidago* with a rod-like stem and a spike of small yellow flowers.

golden rule *n.* a basic principle of action, esp. 'do unto others as you would have them do unto you'.

golden wedding *n.* a fiftieth wedding anniversary.

goldeye *n.* a silvery freshwater fish, *Hiodon alosoides*, with a golden iris, of central N America, much

favoured as a delicacy in Manitoba, esp. when smoked, when it becomes a reddish-gold colour.

goldfield *n.* a district in which gold is found.

goldfinch *n.* any of various bright-coloured songbirds of the genus *Carduelis* with predominantly yellow plumage, esp. the N American *C. tristis*.

goldfish *n.* a small reddish-golden Chinese carp kept for ornament or as a pet, *Carassius auratus*.

goldfish bowl *n.* **1** a globular glass container for goldfish. **2** a situation lacking privacy.

gold foil *n.* gold beaten into a thin sheet.

Gold Glove *n. N Amer. Baseball* an award presented annually in both major leagues to the best defensive player at each position. □ **Gold Glover** *n.*

gold leaf *n.* gold beaten into a very thin sheet (often, with hyphen, *attrib.*: *gold-leaf decor*).

gold medal *n.* a medal of gold, usu. awarded as first prize (often, with hyphen, *attrib.*: *gold-medal performance*). □ **gold medallist** *n.*

gold mine *n.* **1** a place where gold is mined. **2** *informal* a source of wealth. □ **gold miner** *n.* **gold mining** *n.*

gold plate ● *n.* **1** vessels made of gold. **2** material plated with gold. ● *v.tr.* (**gold-plate**) plate with gold.

gold-plated *adj.* **1** plated with gold. **2** wealthy or opulent, esp. excessively so.

gold rush *n.* a rush to a newly discovered goldfield.

gold seeker *n.* a person who searches for gold. □ **gold seeking** *n.*

goldsmith *n.* a person who makes gold articles.

gold standard *n.* a system in which the value of a currency is defined in terms of gold, for which the currency may be exchanged.

gold thread *n.* a thread of silk etc. with gold wire wound around it.

golf ● *n.* a game played on a park-like course, in which a small hard ball is driven with clubs into a series of 18 or 9 holes with the fewest possible strokes (also *attrib.*: *golf ball*). ● *v.intr.* play golf. □ **golfer** *n.*

golf bag *n.* a bag used for carrying golf clubs etc.

golf cart *n.* **1** a trolley used for carrying clubs in golf. **2** a motorized cart for golfers and equipment.

golf club *n.* **1** a long thin club with a metal or wooden head used in golf. **2 a** an association for playing golf. **b** the premises used by a golf club.

golf course *n.* (also **golf links**) the course on which golf is played.

golly *interj.* expressing mild surprise.

gonad /ˈɡoʊnæd/ *n.* an animal organ producing gametes, e.g. the testis or ovary. □ **gonadal** /ɡoʊˈneɪdəl/ *adj.*

gonadotropin /ˌɡoʊnədoʊˈtroʊpɪn, ɡoʊˌnædə-/ *n.* (also **gonadotrophin** /-ˈtroʊfɪn/) *Biochem.* any of various hormones stimulating the activity of the gonads.

gondola /ˈɡɒndələ/ *n.* **1** a light flat-bottomed boat used on Venetian canals, with a central cabin and a high point at each end, worked by one oar at the stern. **2** an enclosed compartment suspended from an airship or balloon. **3** an enclosed cabin suspended from a cable, as in a ski lift. **4** (also **gondola car**) *N Amer.* a railway car with an open top.

gondolier /ˌɡɒndəˈlɪər/ *n.* the oarsman on a gondola.

gone ● *v. past part.* of GO¹. ● *adj.* **1 a** lost; hopeless. **b** dead. **2** used up, consumed. **3** *informal* pregnant for a specified time (*three months gone*). **4** *slang* completely enthralled or entranced, esp. by rhythmic music, drugs, etc. □ **gone on** *slang* infatuated with.

goner /ˈɡɒnər/ *n. slang* a person or thing that is doomed, ended, irrevocably lost, etc.; a person beyond hope or help.

gong ● *n.* **1** a metal disc with a turned rim, giving a resonant note when struck. **2** a saucer-shaped bell. **3** the resonant sound of a struck gong. ● *v.intr.* make a reverberating sound like that of a gong.

gonna *contraction informal* going to (*we're gonna win!*). ¶*Gonna* should generally be avoided in writing.

gonococcus /ˌgɒnəˈkɒkəs/ *n.* (*pl.* **gonococci** /-kaɪ, -ksaɪ, -kɪ, -ksiː/) a bacterium causing gonorrhea.

gonorrhea /ˌgɒnəˈriːə/ *n.* (also esp. *Brit.* **gonorrhoea**) a venereal disease with inflammatory discharge from the urethra or vagina. □ **gonorrheal** *adj.*

gonzo /ˈgɒnzəʊ/ *adj.* esp. *N Amer.* **1** *informal* bizarre; crazy. **2** of or associated with journalistic writing of an exaggerated, subjective, and fictionalized style.

goo *n. informal* **1** a sticky or slimy substance. **2** sickly sentiment.

goober *n.* (in full **goober pea**) *N Amer.* a peanut or peanut plant.

good ● *adj.* (**better, best**) **1** having the right or desired qualities; satisfactory. **2 a** (of a person) efficient, competent (*good at French*; *a good driver*). **b** (of a thing) reliable, efficient (*good brakes*). **c** (of health etc.) strong (*good eyesight*). **3 a** kind, benevolent (*good of you to come*). **b** virtuous (*a good deed*). **c** charitable (*good works*). **d** well-behaved (*a good child*). **4** enjoyable, agreeable (*a good party*; *good news*). **5** thorough, considerable (*a good wash*). **6 a** not less than (*waited a good hour*). **b** considerable in number, quality, etc. (*a good many people*). **7** healthy, beneficial (*milk is good for you*). **8 a** valid, sound (*a good reason*). **b** financially sound (*her credit is good*). **c** (usu. foll. by *for*) *N Amer.* (of a ticket) valid. **9** in exclamations of surprise (*good heavens!*). **10** right, proper, expedient (*thought it good to try*). **11** fresh, eatable, untainted (*is the meat still good?*). **12** (sometimes patronizing) commendable, worthy (*good old Mom*). **13** well shaped, attractive (*has a good body*). **14** in courteous greetings and farewells (*good afternoon*). ● *n.* **1** (only in *sing.*) that which is good (*did it for your own good*; *what good will it do?*). **2** (only in *sing.*) a desirable end or object; a thing worth attaining (*sacrificing the present for a future good*). **3** (in *pl.*) a movable property or merchandise. **b** (prec. by *the*) *informal* what one has undertaken to supply (esp. *deliver the goods*). **c** (prec. by *the*) *slang* the real thing; the genuine article. **4** (as *pl.*; prec. by *the*) virtuous people. ● *adv. N Amer. informal disputed* well (*sings pretty good*). □ **as good as** practically (*he as good as told me*). **as good as gold** extremely well-behaved. **be so good as** (or **be good enough**) **to** (often in a request) be kind and do (a favour) (*be so good as to open the window*). **be (a certain amount) to the good** have as net profit or advantage. **do good** show kindness, act philanthropically. **do a person good** be beneficial to. **for good** (**and all**) finally, permanently. **good and** *informal* used as an intensifier before an adj. or adv. (*raining good and hard*). **good for 1** beneficial to; having a good effect on. **2** able to perform; inclined for (*good for a ten-mile walk*). **3** able to be trusted to pay (*is good for $100*). **good for you!** (or **him!, her!,** etc.) exclamation of approval towards a person. **good God!** (or **good Lord!**) an exclamation of surprise, anger, etc. **good on you!** (or **him!** etc.) = GOOD FOR YOU! **have** (or **get**) **the goods on a person** *slang* have (or acquire) advantageous information about a person. **have a good time** enjoy oneself. **in good faith** with honest or sincere intentions. **in good time 1** with no risk of being late. **2** (also **all in good time**) in due course but without haste. **make good 1** make up for, compensate for, pay (an expense). **2** fulfill (a promise); effect (a purpose or an intended action). **3** demonstrate the truth of (a statement); substantiate (a charge). **4** gain and hold (a position). **5** replace or restore (a thing lost or damaged). **6** accomplish what one intended. **no good** useless (*it is no good arguing*; *my idea was no good*). **to the good** having as profit or benefit. **up to no good** making mischief. □ **goodish** *adj.*

good afternoon ● *interj.* expressing greeting or farewell in the afternoon. ● *n.* an instance of saying this.

Good Book *n.* (prec. by *the*) the Bible.

goodbye ● *interj.* expressing good wishes on parting, ending a telephone conversation, etc., or said with reference to a thing got rid of or irrevocably lost. ● *n.* (*pl.* **goodbyes**) a parting; a farewell.

good cholesterol *n.* high-density lipoprotein.

good cop/bad cop *adj. N Amer. informal* designating a procedure or routine used in interrogating, negotiating, or in public relations, in which one of two partners assumes a harsh, uncompromising attitude and the other a more lenient or mild one.

good day ● *interj.* expressing greeting or farewell during the day. ● *n.* an instance of saying 'good day'.

good egg *n.* a reliable or pleasant person.

good evening ● *interj.* expressing greeting or farewell in the evening. ● *n.* an instance of sayin this.

good faith *n.* honesty or sincerity of intention.

good form *n.* what complies with current social conventions. □ **in good form** in a state of good health or training.

good-for-nothing ● *adj.* worthless. ● *n.* a worthless person.

Good Friday *n.* the Friday before Easter Sunday, commemorating the Crucifixion of Christ.

good guy *n.* esp. *N Amer. informal* a hero; a person viewed favourably in a conflict.

good-hearted *adj.* kindly, well-meaning.

good humour *n.* a genial mood.

good-humoured *adj.* genial, cheerful, amiable. □ **good-humouredly** *adv.*

goodie *var. of* GOODY[1] *n.*

goodie bag *n.* a bag of treats, goodies, or promotional items, given as a gift or prize.

good job *n.* a fortunate state of affairs (*it's a good job you came early*).

good life *n.* (prec. by *the*) esp. *N Amer.* a life of luxury, pleasure, and material comfort.

good-looking *adj.* handsome; attractive.

good luck ● *n.* **1** good fortune. **2** an omen of this. ● *interj.* an exclamation of well-wishing.

goodly *adj.* (**-ier, -iest**) **1** good-looking, handsome. **2** of imposing size etc. □ **goodliness** *n.*

good money *n.* **1** genuine money. **2** *informal* money that might usefully have been spent elsewhere. **3** *informal* high wages.

good morning ● *interj.* expressing greeting in the morning. ● *n.* an instance of saying 'good morning'.

good nature *n.* a friendly disposition.

good-natured *adj.* kind, patient; easygoing. □ **good-naturedly** *adv.*

goodness ● *n.* **1** virtue; excellence, esp. moral. **2** kindness, generosity (*had the goodness to wait*). **3** what is good or beneficial in a thing. ● *interj.* (as a substitution for 'God') expressing surprise, anger, etc. (*goodness knows*; *for goodness' sake!*).

good night ● *interj.* **1** expressing good wishes on parting in the evening or at bedtime. **2** expressing surprise. ● *n.* an instance of saying 'good night'.

good offices *n.pl.* influence, esp. as used to others' benefit; connections.

good riddance *interj.* expressing welcome relief from an unwanted person or thing.

goods and services tax *n. Cdn & NZ* a value-added tax levied on a broad range of consumer goods and services. Abbr.: **GST**.

good-tempered *adj.* having a good temper; not easily annoyed. □ **good-temperedly** *adv.*

good-time *attrib.adj.* recklessly pursuing pleasure.

good times *n.pl.* a period of prosperity.

goodwill *n.* **1** kindly feeling. **2** the established reputation of a business etc. as enhancing its value. **3** cheerful consent or acquiescence; readiness, zeal.

good word *n.* (often in phr. **put in a good word for**) words in recommendation or defence of a person.

good works *n.pl.* charitable acts.

goody ● *n.* (*pl.* **-ies**) **1** (usu. in *pl.*) something good or attractive, esp. to eat, often given as a treat or reward. **2** = GOODY-GOODY *n.* **3** *informal* a good or favoured person, esp. a hero in a story, film, etc. ● *interj.* expressing childish delight.

goody-goody *informal* ● *n.* (*pl.* **goody-goodies**) a smug or obtrusively virtuous person. ● *adj.* obtrusively or smugly virtuous.

goody two-shoes *n.* = GOODY-GOODY.

gooey *adj.* (**gooier, gooiest**) *slang* **1** viscous, sticky. **2** sickly, sentimental. □ **gooeyness** *n.*

goof *informal* ● *n.* **1** a foolish or stupid person. **2** a mistake, a blunder. ● *v.* **1** *tr.* (foll. by *up*) bungle, mess up. **2** *intr.* (often foll. by *up*) blunder, make a mistake. **3** *intr.* (often foll. by *off*) idle. **4** *intr.* (often foll. by *around, about*) fool around, mess about.

goofball esp. *N Amer. informal* ● *n.* **1** a blundering or eccentric person. **2** a pill containing a narcotic drug, esp. a barbiturate. ● *adj.* eccentric or silly.

goof-up *n. informal* a mistake, a blunder.

goofy *adj.* (**-ier, -iest**) silly, ridiculous, odd. □ **goofily** *adv.* **goofiness** *n.*

googlie-eyed /ˈguːgli/ *adj.* (also **googly-eyed**) = GOGGLE-EYED.

goo-goo *adj. N Amer.* **1** designating the behaviour etc. of a baby; infantile (*goo-goo sounds*). **2** indicating excessive or foolish infatuation (*making goo-goo eyes*).

gook *n. N Amer. slang* **1** *offensive* a foreigner, esp. a person of E Asian descent. **2** a slimy or sticky substance.

goon *n. slang* **1** esp. *N Amer.* a person employed to terrorize esp. political or industrial opponents; a thug. **2** *N Amer. informal* a hockey player who intimidates opponents by rough play and fighting. **3** a stupid person; a dolt. □ **goonery** *n.* **goony** *adj.*

goon hockey *n. informal* an excessively rough or violent style of hockey playing.

goop *n.* esp. *N Amer.* = GLOOP. □ **goopy** *adj.* (**-ier, -iest**). **goopiness** *n.*

goose ● *n.* (*pl.* **geese**) **1 a** any of various large water birds of the family Anatidae, with short legs, webbed feet, and a broad bill. **b** the female of this (opp. GANDER). **c** the flesh of a goose as food. **2** *informal* a silly person. ● *v.tr.* **1** *slang* poke (a person) in the buttocks. **2** esp. *US informal* (often foll. by *up*) energize, strengthen, invigorate, or increase. □ **what's good** (or **sauce**) **for the goose is good** (or **sauce**) **for the gander** what is appropriate in one case is appropriate in others.

gooseberry /ˈguːsˌbɛri, -bəri, ˈguːz-/ *n.* (*pl.* **-ies**) **1** a round edible yellowish-green berry with a thin usu. translucent skin enclosing seeds in a juicy flesh. **2** any of various thorny shrubs, esp. *Ribes grossularia*, bearing this fruit.

goosebumps *n.pl.* (also **goose pimples, gooseflesh**) *n.*) *N Amer.* the small pimple-like bumps appearing on the skin because of cold, fright, etc.

goose egg *n. N Amer. informal* **1** a zero score in a game or examination. **2** a lump appearing after hitting one's head etc. or being hit.

goosefoot *n.* (*pl.* **-foots**) any plant of the genus *Chenopodium*, with leaves shaped like the foot of a goose.

gooseneck *n. N Amer.* (often *attrib.*) a long thin flexible metal tube resembling the neck of a goose.

goose step ● *n.* a marching step in which the knees are kept locked and the legs are lifted high, usu. associated with militaristic regimes. ● *v.intr.* (**goosestep**) march in this way.

gopher *n.* **1** a buff-coloured ground squirrel of the prairies of western N America; a Richardson's ground squirrel. **2** (in full **pocket gopher**) any burrowing rodent of the family Geomyidae, native to North and Central America, having external cheek pouches and sharp front teeth. **3** *Computing* a computer program designed to help users reach and search other sites on the Internet. **4** *N Amer.* = GOFER.

Gordian knot /ˈɡɔːdɪən/ *n.* **1** an intricate knot. **2** a difficult problem or task. □ **cut the Gordian knot** solve a problem by force or by evasion.

Gordon setter *n.* a black and tan breed of setter, used as a gun dog.

gore[1] ● *n.* **1** blood shed and clotted. **2** *informal* bloodshed, carnage. ● *v.tr.* pierce with a horn, tusk, etc.

gore[2] *n.* **1** a wedge-shaped piece in a garment. **2** esp. *N Amer.* a small strip or tract of land lying between larger divisions such as townships etc.

Gore-Tex *n. proprietary* a breathable laminated waterproof fabric.

gorge ● *n.* **1** a narrow opening between hills or a rocky ravine, often with a stream running through it. **2** an act of gorging; a feast. **3** the contents of the stomach; what has been swallowed. **4** a mass of ice etc. blocking a narrow passage. ● *v.* **1** *intr.* (usu. foll. by *on*) feed greedily. **2** *tr.* **a** (often *refl.*) satiate, glut. **b** swallow, devour greedily. **c** (often foll. by *with*) fill to excess; glut. □ **one's gorge rises** one is sickened.

gorgeous *adj.* **1** strikingly beautiful. **2** very pleasant, splendid (*gorgeous weather*). **3** richly coloured, sumptuous, magnificent. □ **gorgeously** *adv.* **gorgeousness** *n.*

Gorgonzola /ˌɡɔːɡənˈzoʊlə/ *n.* a type of rich cheese with bluish-green veins.

gorilla *n.* **1** the largest anthropoid ape, *Gorilla gorilla*, native to Central Africa, having a large head, short neck, and prominent mouth. **2** *informal* a heavily built man of aggressive demeanour.

go-round *n.* esp. *N Amer.* **1** each of several recurring turns, opportunities, or chances (*we'll do better on the next go-round*). **2** a fight; a beating; an argument.

gorp *n. N Amer.* = TRAIL MIX.

gorse /ɡɔːs/ *n.* any spiny yellow-flowered shrub of the genus *Ulex*, esp. growing on European wastelands.

gory *adj.* (**-ier, -iest**) **1** involving or depicting bloodshed; bloodthirsty (*a gory film*). **2** covered in gore. **3** resembling gore (*a gory red*). □ **gory details** *jocular* explicit details. □ **gorily** *adv.* **goriness** *n.*

gosh *interj.* expressing mild surprise.

goshawk /ˈɡɒshɔːk/ *n.* a large short-winged hawk, *Accipiter gentilis*.

gosling *n.* a young goose.

go-slow *n.* (usu. *attrib.*) an instance of proceeding slowly, esp. intentionally out of caution.

gospel n. **1** the teaching or revelation of Christ. **2** (**Gospel**) **a** the record of Christ's life and teaching in the first four books of the New Testament. **b** each of these books. **c** a portion from one of them read at a service. **3** (also **gospel truth**) a thing regarded as absolutely true (*take my word as gospel*). **4** a principle one acts on or advocates. **5** (in full **gospel music**) a fervent, spirited style of evangelical religious music, esp. as originally sung by US Blacks.

gospeller n. a person who preaches or promotes the Gospel or a gospel.

gossamer /ˈɡɒsəmər/ ● n. **1** a filmy substance of small spiders' webs. **2** delicate filmy material. **3** a thread of gossamer. ● adj. **1** light and flimsy. **2** frivolous.

gossip ● n. **1 a** easy talk or writing esp. about persons or social incidents. **b** idle talk; groundless rumour. **c** (usu. *attrib.*) denoting a tabloid or section of a newspaper etc. devoted to news or rumours about celebrities (*gossip columnist*). **2** a person who indulges in gossip. ● v.intr. (**gossiped**, **gossiping**) talk or write gossip. □ **gossiper** n. **gossipy** adj.

got past and past part. of GET.

gotch n. (also **gotchies** n.pl.) Cdn slang underpants.

gotcha informal ● interj. esp. N Amer. expressing satisfaction at having exploited another's gullibility or weakness, uncovered another's faults, etc. ● n. **1** (often *attrib.*) an instance of catching someone out, esp. by surprise. **2** a sudden unforeseen difficulty.

Goth /ɡɒθ/ n. **1** a member of a Germanic tribe that invaded the Roman Empire in the 3rd–5th c. **2** an uncivilized or ignorant person. **3** (**goth**) **a** a style of rock music derived from punk, often with apocalyptic or mystical lyrics. **b** a member of a subculture favouring black clothing, white and black makeup, metal jewellery, and goth music.

Gothic ● adj. **1** of the Goths or their language. **2** in the style of architecture prevalent in W Europe in the 12th–16th c., characterized by pointed arches, flying buttresses, and ribbed vaults. **3** (of a novel etc.) in a style popular in the 18th–19th c., with supernatural or horrifying events. **4** barbarous, uncouth. ● n. **1** the Gothic language. **2** Gothic architecture. □ **Gothicism** n.

Gothic revival n. the reintroduction of a Gothic style of architecture toward the middle of the 19th c.

go-to guy n. (also **go-to person** etc.) N Amer. slang (esp. in sports) the person on a team most often relied on to accomplish a task.

gotta informal have got to (*we gotta go*).

gotten N Amer. past part. of GET.

gouache /ɡuːˈɒʃ, gwɒʃ/ n. **1** a method of painting in opaque pigments ground in water and thickened with a gluelike substance. **2** these pigments. **3** a picture painted in this way.

Gouda /ˈɡuːdə/ n. a flat round usu. Dutch cheese with a yellow rind.

gouge ● n. **1** a chisel with a concave blade, used in carpentry, sculpture, and surgery. **2** a groove or mark made by gouging. **3** an act of gouging. ● v. **1** tr. cut with or as with a gouge. **2** tr. **a** (foll. by *out*) force out (esp. an eye with the thumb) with or as with a gouge. **b** force out the eye of (a person). **3** tr. & intr. N Amer. informal take an unjustly large sum of money from (someone); swindle. □ **gouger** n.

goulash /ˈɡuːlæʃ/ n. a Hungarian soup or stew of meat and vegetables, usu. seasoned with paprika.

gourd /ɡʊrd/ n. **1 a** any of various fleshy usu. large fruits with a hard skin, often used as containers, ornaments, etc. **b** any of various climbing or trailing plants of the family Cucurbitaceae bearing this fruit. **2** the hollow hard skin of the gourd fruit, dried and used as a drinking vessel, water container, etc. □ **out of one's gourd** N Amer. slang crazy.

gourmand /ɡʊrˈmɒnd/ n. **1** a glutton. **2** a gourmet.

gourmet /ɡʊrˈmeɪ, ˈɡʊr-, ˈɡɔr-/ ● n. a connoisseur of good food, having a discerning palate. ● attrib.adj. **1** (of food) of very high quality, suitable to refined tastes. **2** of or suitable for a gourmet.

gout n. **1** a disease with inflammation of the smaller joints, esp. the toe, as a result of excess uric acid salts in the blood. **2 a** a drop, esp. of blood. **b** a splash or spot. □ **goutiness** n. **gouty** adj.

Gov. abbr. **1** Governor. **2** Government.

govern v. **1 a** tr. rule or control (a state, subject, etc.) with authority; conduct the policy and affairs of (an organization etc.). **b** intr. be in government. **2 a** tr. control or influence (a person, a function, the course of events, etc.). **b** intr. be the predominating influence. **3** tr. be a standard or principle for; constitute a law for; serve to decide (a case). **4** tr. check or control (esp. passions). **5** tr. be in military command of (a fort, town). □ **governable** adj. **governability** n.

governance n. **1** the act or manner of governing. **2** the office or function of governing. **3** sway, control.

governess n. a woman employed to teach children in a private household.

governing body n. **1** the board of directors of a university or other institution. **2** an organization that establishes and enforces rules for a sport etc.

government n. **1** the act or manner of governing. **2** the system by which a state or community is governed. **3 a** a body of persons governing a state or community. **b** (usu. **Government**) a particular administration in office. **4** the state as an agent. **5** (*attrib.*) denoting something produced, issued, or funded by a government or state. □ **governmental** adj. **governmentally** adv.

Government House n. the official residence of the representative of the Crown, e.g. a Lieutenant-Governor.

Government Leader n. (in Canada) the leader of any of the Territorial governments.

government securities n.pl. bonds etc. issued by the government.

government wharf n. Cdn a wharf built by the government.

governor n. **1** a person who governs; a ruler. **2 a** (also **governor-in-chief**) an official governing a province, town, etc. **b** a representative of the Crown in a colony. **3** the executive head of each state or territory of the US. **4** an officer commanding a fortress or garrison. **5** the head or a member of a governing body of an institution. **6** Cdn hist. **a** the officer in charge of a fort or factory of the Hudson's Bay Company. **b** (in full **governor-in-chief**) the Hudson's Bay Company's chief officer in Canada. □ **governorship** n.

Governor General n. (pl. **Governors General**) the representative of the Crown in a Commonwealth country that regards the Queen as head of state.

Governor General's Award n. (in full **Governor General's Literary Award**) Cdn an award presented annually by the Governor General in each of several categories of Canadian literature.

Governor-in-Council n. (also **Governor-General-in-Council**) the Governor General acting formally as an instrument for legalizing decisions of the cabinet.

Gov. Gen. abbr. Governor General.

Govt. *abbr.* (also **govt.**, **gov't.**) government.

gown ● *n.* **1** a loose flowing garment, esp. a long dress. **2** the official robe of a judge, cleric, member of a university, etc. **3** a protective garment worn in a hospital etc. by a staff member during surgery or by a patient. ● *v.tr.* (usu. as **gowned** *adj.*) attire in a gown.

goy /gɔɪ/ *n.* (*pl.* **goyim** /'gɔɪɪm/ or **goys**) *slang* a non-Jew. □ **goyish** *adj.* (also **goyishe** /'gɔɪʃə/).

GP *abbr.* **1** general practitioner. **2** Grand Prix.

GPA *abbr. N Amer.* GRADE POINT AVERAGE.

GPS *abbr.* GLOBAL POSITIONING SYSTEM.

gr *abbr.* (also **gr.**) **1** gram(s). **2** grains. **3** gross. **4** grey.

grab ● *v.* (**grabbed**, **grabbing**) **1** *tr.* **a** seize suddenly, roughly, or firmly. **b** capture, arrest. **2** *tr.* take greedily or unfairly. **3** *tr. slang* attract the attention of, impress. **4** *intr.* (foll. by *at*) make a sudden snatch at. **5** *tr.* purchase, obtain, or consume (esp. food) hastily (*grabbed a pizza*). **6** *intr.* (of the brakes of a motor vehicle) act harshly or jerkily. ● *n.* **1** a sudden clutch or attempt to seize. **2** a mechanical device for clutching. **3** the practice of grabbing; rapacious proceedings esp. in politics and commerce. □ **up for grabs** *slang* easily obtainable. □ **grabber** *n.*

grab bag *n.* esp. *N Amer.* **1** a bag concealing various prizes, treats, etc., from which one draws blindly. **2** an assortment of small items in a sealed bag which one buys or is given without knowing what the contents are. **3** a miscellaneous assortment.

grab bar *n.* esp. *N Amer.* a bar or rail fixed to a wall as an aid in entering or leaving a bathtub etc.

grabby *adj.* (**-ier**, **-iest**) *informal* tending to grab; greedy, grasping.

grab rail *n.* (also **grab handle** etc.) a handle or rail etc. by grabbing which one may maintain one's balance, steady oneself, etc.

grace ● *n.* **1** attractiveness, esp. in elegance of proportion or manner or movement; gracefulness. **2** courteous good will (*had the grace to apologize*). **3** an attractive feature; an accomplishment (*social graces*). **4 a** (in Christian belief) the unmerited favour of God; a divine saving and strengthening influence. **b** the state of receiving this. **c** a divinely given talent. **5** goodwill, favour (*fall from grace*). **6** delay granted as a favour (*a five-day grace period*). **7** a short thanksgiving before or after a meal. **8** (**Grace**) (in Greek mythology) each of three beautiful sister goddesses, bestowers of beauty and charm. **9** (**Grace**) (prec. by *His*, *Her*, *Your*) forms of description or address for a duke, duchess, or archbishop. ● *v.tr.* (often foll. by *with*) confer honour or dignity on (*graced us with his presence*). □ **days of grace** the time allowed by law for payment of a sum due. **in a person's good** (or **bad**) **graces** regarded by a person with favour (or disfavour). **with good** (or **bad**) **grace** as if willingly (or reluctantly).

graceful *adj.* having or showing grace or elegance. □ **gracefully** *adv.* **gracefulness** *n.*

graceless *adj.* lacking grace or elegance or charm. □ **gracelessly** *adv.* **gracelessness** *n.*

grace note *n.* an extra note as an embellishment not essential to the harmony or melody.

gracious ● *adj.* **1** kindly, courteous. **2** (of God) merciful, benign. **3** condescendingly indulgent and beneficent. **4** characterized by elegance and usu. wealth (*gracious living*). ● *interj.* expressing surprise. □ **graciously** *adv.* **graciousness** *n.*

grackle *n.* any of various New World birds, e.g. of the genus *Quiscalus*, the males of which are shiny black with a blue-green sheen. Also called BLACKBIRD.

grad *n. informal* **1** = GRADUATE *n.* 1. **2** *Cdn* a graduation

ceremony; commencement. **3** *Cdn* a dinner followed by a dance to celebrate graduation; a prom.

gradate *v.* **1** *intr. & tr.* pass or cause to pass by gradations from one shade to another. **2** *tr.* arrange in steps or grades of size etc.

gradation *n.* (usu. in *pl.*) **1** a stage of transition or advance. **2 a** a certain degree in rank, intensity, merit, divergence, etc. **b** an arrangement in such degrees. **3** (of paint etc.) the gradual passing from one shade, tone, etc., to another. □ **gradational** *adj.*

grade ● *n.* **1 a** a certain degree in rank, merit, proficiency, quality, etc. **b** a class of persons or things of the same grade. **2** a step or stage in a process. **3** a mark indicating the quality of a student's work. **4 a** *N Amer.* a class in school, concerned with a particular year's work and usu. numbered from one upwards. **b** (in *comb.*) *Cdn* a pupil of a specified grade in a school (*the grade threes are visiting the museum on Thursday*). **5 a** a gradient or slope. **b** the rate of ascent or descent. **c** *N Amer.* the level at which the ground meets the foundation of a building. ● *v.* **1** *tr.* arrange in or allocate to grades; sort. **2** *intr.* (foll. by *up, down, off, into*, etc.) pass gradually between grades, or into a grade. **3** *tr.* give a grade to (a student or academic work). **4** *intr.* be of good or specified quality; reach a required or expected standard. **5** *tr.* blend so as to affect the grade of colour with tints passing into each other. **6** *tr.* reduce (a road etc.) to easy gradients or to a level. □ **at grade** *N Amer.* on the same level. **make the grade** *informal* reach the desired standard.

grade point *n. N Amer.* (esp. in post-secondary education) a numerical value assigned to a grade received in a course, multiplied by the number of credits awarded for the course.

grade point average *n. N Amer.* an indication of an (esp. post-secondary) student's academic achievement, being the total number of grade points received divided by the number of credits awarded.

grader *n.* **1** a person or thing that grades. **2** (in *comb.*) *N Amer.* a pupil of a specified grade in a school. **3** = ROAD GRADER.

grade school *n. N Amer.* elementary school.

gradient *n.* **1 a** a stretch of road, railway, etc., that slopes from the horizontal. **b** the amount of such a slope. **2** the rate of rise or fall of temperature, pressure, etc., in passing from one region to another.

gradual ● *adj.* **1** taking place or progressing slowly or by degrees. **2** not rapid or steep or abrupt. ● *n. Christianity* **1** an antiphon sung or recited between the Epistle and Gospel in the Mass. **2** a book of music for the sung parts of the Mass. □ **gradually** *adv.*

gradualism *n.* **1** a policy of gradual reform rather than sudden change or revolution. **2** the theory of gradual evolutionary change. □ **gradualist** *n.*

graduate ● *n.* **1 a** a person who has been awarded an academic degree. **b** (*attrib.*) designating or involved in education undertaken beyond the first or bachelor's degree (*graduate student*). **2** *N Amer.* a person who has completed a course of study. ● *v.* **1** *intr.* **a** receive an academic degree or (*N Amer.*) a high school diploma. **b** (foll. by *from*) be a graduate of a specified university. **c** (foll. by *from*) complete a course of study at a specified place or level. **d** (foll. by *in*) be a graduate in a specified subject. **2** *tr. N Amer.* confer a degree, diploma, etc. upon. **3** *intr.* **a** (foll. by *to*) move up to (a higher grade of activity etc.). **b** (foll. by *as, in*) gain specified qualifications. **4** *tr.* mark out in degrees or parts. **5** *tr.* apportion (e.g. tax) according to a scale. **6** *intr.* (foll. by *into, away*) pass by degrees.

graduated *adj.* **1** arranged in grades or gradations;

advancing or proceeding by degrees. **2** marked with lines to indicate degrees, grades, or quantities.

graduated licensing *n.* a gradual process of awarding driving privileges to new drivers, in which novices are allowed to drive only under certain conditions for a specified period and must pass a road test before privileges are increased.

graduate school *n.* N Amer. **1** a department of a university for advanced work by graduates. **2** study undertaken at a university by graduates.

graduation *n.* **1** the act or an instance of graduating or being graduated. **2** a ceremony at which degrees are conferred. **3** each or all of the marks on a vessel or instrument indicating degrees of quantity etc.

Graeco-Roman *var. of* GRECO-ROMAN.

graffiti /grə'fiːtiː/ ● *n.pl.* (often treated as *sing.*) (*sing.* **graffito** /-toː/) inscriptions or drawings scribbled, scratched, or sprayed on a surface. ● *v.tr.* (**graffitied**) **1** cover (a surface) with graffiti. **2** write as graffiti (*graffitied initials*). □ **graffitist** *n.*

graft[1] ● *n.* **1** *Bot.* **a** a shoot or scion inserted into a slit of stock, from which it receives sap. **b** the place where a graft is inserted. **c** an instance or the process of inserting a shoot or scion. **2 a** a piece of living tissue, organ, etc., transplanted surgically. **b** an instance or the process of doing this. ● *v.* **1** *tr.* **a** (often foll. by *into, on*, etc.) insert (a scion) as a graft. **b** insert a graft on (a stock). **2** *intr.* insert a graft. **3** *tr.* transplant (living tissue). **4** *tr.* (foll. by *in, on*) insert or fix (a thing) permanently to another. □ **grafter** *n.*

graft[2] *informal* ● *n.* **1** practices, esp. bribery, used to secure illicit gains in politics or business. **2** such gains. ● *v.intr.* seek or make such gains. □ **grafter** *n.*

graham /'greɪəm, græm/ *adj.* esp. N Amer. designating unbolted whole wheat flour, or crackers etc. made from this.

Grail *n.* (also **grail**) **1** (in medieval legend) the cup or platter used by Christ at the Last Supper, and in which Joseph of Arimathea received Christ's blood at the Cross. **2** any object of a quest.

grain ● *n.* **1 a** wheat or any other cereal plant used as food. **b** their fruit. **c** any particular species of cereal plant. **2** a fruit or seed of a cereal. **3 a** a small hard particle of salt, sand, etc. **b** a discrete particle or crystal, usu. small, in a rock or metal. **4** the smallest unit of weight in the troy and avoirdupois systems (approx. 0.0648 grams), equivalent to $\frac{1}{5760}$ of a pound troy and $\frac{1}{7000}$ of a pound avoirdupois. **5** the smallest possible quantity (*not a grain of truth in it*). **6 a** roughness of surface. **b** *Photog.* each of the tiny light-sensitive particles in a photograph or negative. **7** the texture of skin, wood, stone, etc.; the arrangement and size of constituent particles. **8 a** a pattern of lines of fibre in meat, wood, fabric, or paper. **b** lamination or planes of cleavage in stone, coal, etc. **9** nature, temper, tendency. ● *v.* **1** *tr.* paint in imitation of the grain of wood or marble. **2** *tr.* give a granular surface to. **3** *tr. & intr.* form into grains. □ **against the grain** contrary to one's natural inclination or feeling. □ **grained** *adj.* (also in *comb.*)

grain alcohol *n.* ethanol fermented from grain.

grain elevator *n.* N Amer. = ELEVATOR 2.

grainy *adj.* (**-ier, -iest**) **1** granular. **2** resembling the grain of wood. **3** *Photog.* having a granular appearance. □ **graininess** *n.*

gram *n.* a metric unit of mass equal to one-thousandth of a kilogram.

-gram *comb. form* forming nouns denoting a thing written or recorded or expressed (often in a certain

way) (*epigram; monogram; telegram; kiss-o-gram*). □ **-grammatic** /grə'mætɪk/ *comb. form.*

grama /'græmə/ *n.* (also **grama grass**) any of various chiefly N American pasture and ornamental grasses of the genus *Bouteloua*.

gramma *n.* N Amer. informal = GRANDMA.

grammar *n.* **1 a** the branch of language study which deals with the means of showing the relationship between words in use, traditionally including morphology and syntax, and often phonology. **b** a body of forms and usages in a specified language (*French grammar*). **2** a person's manner of using grammatical forms; speech or writing judged as good or bad according to its conformity to rules of grammar. **3** a book on grammar.

grammarian /grə'meriən/ *n.* an expert in grammar.

grammatical *adj.* **1** of or relating to grammar. **2** conforming to the rules of grammar. □ **grammaticality** *n.* **grammatically** *adv.*

Grammy *n.* (*pl.* **Grammys**) *proprietary* (in the US) any of several annual awards given by the American National Academy of Recording Arts and Sciences for outstanding achievements in the record industry.

gramophone /'græməˌfoːn/ *n.* dated a record player. □ **gramophonic** *adj.*

grampa *n.* (also **gramps**) N Amer. informal = GRANDPA.

gran *n.* informal grandmother.

granary /'greɪnəri, 'græn-/ *n.* (*pl.* **-ies**) **1** a storehouse for threshed grain. **2** a region producing, and esp. exporting, much grain.

grand ● *adj.* **1 a** splendid, magnificent, imposing, dignified. **b** solemn or lofty in conception, execution, or expression. **c** showy, ostentatious. **2** main; of chief importance (*grand staircase*). **3** (also **Grand**) of the highest rank; surpassing all others (*grand champion*). **4** *informal* excellent, enjoyable (*had a grand time; in grand condition*). **5** belonging to high society (*a grand affair*). **6** (in *comb.*) in names of family relationships, denoting the second degree of ascent or descent (*grand-aunt*). **7** great (*Grand Hotel*). **8** comprehensive, final (*grand total*). **9** *Law* serious, important (*grand larceny*) (compare PETTY). ● *n.* **1** = GRAND PIANO. **2** (*pl.* same) (usu. in *pl.*) esp. N Amer. slang a thousand dollars or pounds. □ **grandly** *adv.* **grandness** *n.*

grand chief *n.* the chief of a grand council or national or regional Aboriginal organization.

grandchild *n.* (*pl.* **-children**) a child of one's son or daughter.

grand council *n.* a council of chiefs representing several different First Nations.

granddad *n.* (also **grandad**) *informal* **1** grandfather. **2** an elderly man.

granddaddy *n.* (also **grandaddy**) esp. N Amer. informal **1** = GRANDDAD. **2** the greatest or most notable example or instance of something (*the granddaddy of all winter storms*).

granddaughter *n.* a female grandchild.

grande dame /grãd 'dɒm/ *n.* (*pl.* **grandes dames** *pronunc.* same) **1** a dignified woman of high rank or eminence. **2** a venerable institution, esp. an old and impressive hotel, theatre, etc.

grandee /græn'diː/ *n.* a person of high rank or eminence.

grandeur /'grændər, -djər, -dʒər/ *n.* **1** majesty, splendour; dignity of appearance or bearing. **2** nobility of character.

grandfather ● *n.* **1** a male grandparent. **2** (*attrib.*) Cdn & Brit. designating a long-sleeved collarless esp. flannel shirt with a short buttoned placket at the neck. ●

v.tr. esp. *N Amer.* exempt a pre-existing class of people or things from the requirements of a new regulation. □ **grandfatherly** *adj.*

grandfather clause *n.* *N Amer.* a legal provision exempting certain pre-existing classes of people or things from the requirements of a new regulation.

grandfather clock *n.* a clock in a tall wooden case, driven by weights and a pendulum.

grand finale *n.* **1** the usu. elaborate final scene of a theatrical performance, often involving the whole cast. **2** an elaborate or impressive conclusion to anything (*the grand finale was a chocolate torte*).

grandiflora /ˌgrændɪˈflɔːrə/ *adj.* bearing large flowers.

grandiloquent /ˌgrænˈdɪləkwənt/ *adj.* **1** pompous or inflated in language. **2** given to boastful talk. □ **grandiloquence** *n.* **grandiloquently** *adv.*

grandiose /ˈgrændɪˈoːs, ˈgræn-/ *adj.* **1** producing or meant to produce an imposing effect. **2** planned on an ambitious or magnificent scale. **3** (of speech etc.) characterized by esp. affected grandeur; pompous, arrogant. □ **grandiosity** /-ˈɒsɪtɪ/ *n.*

grandkid *n.* *N Amer. informal* = GRANDCHILD.

grandma *n. informal* grandmother.

grand mal /grɑ̃ ˈmæl/ *n.* a serious form of epilepsy with loss of consciousness (*compare* PETIT MAL).

grandmaster *n.* **1** a chess player of the highest class. **2** (**Grand Master**) the head of a military order of knighthood, of Freemasons, etc.

grandmother *n.* a female grandparent. □ **teach one's grandmother to suck eggs** presume to advise a more experienced person. □ **grandmotherly** *adj.*

grand old man *n.* a venerated person esp. in a specified field or position.

grand opening *n.* *N Amer.* the usu. festive first opening of a new store etc. to the public.

grandpa *n. informal* grandfather.

grandparent *n.* a parent of one's father or mother.

grand piano *n.* a large full-toned piano standing on three legs, with the body, strings, and soundboard arranged horizontally and in line with the keys.

Grand Prix /grɑ̃ ˈpriː/ *n.* (*pl.* **Grands Prix** *pronunc.* same) any of several important international sporting events, esp. in auto racing.

grand prize *n.* the most valuable prize in a raffle etc. for which many prizes are given.

grand slam *n.* **1** *Bridge* the winning of 13 tricks. **2 a** the winning of all of the most important championships or matches in a sport, esp. tennis. **b** (*attrib.*) designating each of these championships. **3** *Baseball* a home run hit when all three bases are occupied by a runner, thus scoring four runs.

grandson *n.* a male grandchild.

grandstand ● *n.* the main stand, usu. roofed, for spectators at a racetrack etc. ● *v.intr.* seek to impress others, esp. by acting showily or ostentatiously. □ **grandstander** *n.*

granite /ˈgrænɪt/ *n.* **1** a granular crystalline igneous rock of quartz, mica, feldspar, etc., used for building. **2** a hard, determined or resolute thing, quality, etc. **3** *Curling* curling rocks. □ **granitic** /grəˈnɪtɪk/ *adj.*

granny *n.* (also **grannie**) (*pl.* **-ies**) *informal* grandmother.

granny flat *n.* part of a house made into self-contained accommodation, as for an elderly relative.

granny glasses *n.pl.* round wire-rimmed eyeglasses.

granny knot *n.* a reef knot crossed the wrong way and therefore insecure.

Granny Smith *n.* an originally Australian variety of bright green apple.

granola *N Amer.* ● *n.* a mixture of rolled oats, nuts, raisins, brown sugar, etc. eaten as a breakfast cereal or pressed into bars. ● *adj. jocular* designating persons with liberal esp. environmental politics, and typified as leading an unconventional or hippy life including the eating of health foods.

grant ● *v.tr.* **1 a** consent to fulfill (a request, wish, etc.) (*granted all they asked*). **b** allow (a person) to have (a thing) (*granted me my freedom*). **c** (as **granted**) *informal* apology accepted; pardon given. **2** give (rights, property, etc.) formally; transfer legally. **3** (often foll. by *that* + clause) admit as true; concede, esp. as a basis for argument. ● *n.* **1** the process of granting or a thing granted. **2 a** a sum of money given by the state for any of various purposes, e.g. to finance education. **b** a tract of land given by the state to private interests. **3** *Law* **a** a legal conveyance by written instrument. **b** formal conferral. □ **take for granted 1** assume something to be true or valid. **2** cease to appreciate through familiarity. □ **grantee** *n.* **grantor** *n.* (both esp. in sense 2 of *v.*).

grant-in-aid *n.* (*pl.* **grants-in-aid**) a grant by a central government to a local government or an institution.

granular *adj.* **1** of or like grains or granules. **2** having a granulated surface or structure. □ **granularity** *n.*

granulate *v.* **1** *tr. & intr.* form into grains (*granulated sugar*). **2** *tr.* roughen the surface of. **3** *intr.* (of a wound etc.) form small prominences as the beginning of healing or joining. □ **granulator** *n.*

granulation *n.* **1** the action or process of forming into granules or grains. **2** the formation of multiple small prominences on the surface of injured tissue, as part of the growth of new connective tissue.

granule /ˈgrænjuːl/ *n.* a small grain.

granuloma /ˌgrænjʊˈloːmə/ *n.* a mass of granulation tissue produced in any of various disease states, usu. in response to infection, inflammation, or the presence of a foreign substance.

grape *n.* **1** a berry (usu. purple, black, or green) growing in clusters on a vine, eaten fresh or dried and used in making wine. **2** (prec. by *the*) *informal* wine. □ **grapey** *adj.* (also **grapy**).

grapefruit *n.* (*pl.* same) **1** a large round yellow citrus fruit with an acid juicy pulp. **2** the tree, *Citrus paradisi*, bearing this fruit.

grape hyacinth *n.* any plant of the genus *Muscari*, with clusters of usu. blue flowers.

grapevine *n.* **1** any of various vines of the genus *Vitis*, esp. *Vitis vinifera*. **2** *informal* the means of transmission of unofficial information or rumour (*heard it through the grapevine*).

graph ● *n.* **1** a diagram showing the relation between variable quantities, usu. of two variables, each measured along one of a pair of axes at right angles. **2** *Math.* a collection of points whose coordinates satisfy a given relation. ● *v.tr.* plot on a graph.

graphic ● *adj.* **1** of or relating to the visual or descriptive arts, esp. writing and drawing. **2** vividly descriptive; conveying all (esp. unwelcome or unpleasant) details. **3** = GRAPHICAL. ● *n.* a visual image (*compare* GRAPHICS). □ **graphically** *adv.*

graphical *adj.* **1** of or in the form of graphs. **2** graphic. □ **graphically** *adv.*

graphical user interface *n.* (also **graphical interface**) software which provides a computer user with icons or other simple graphic representations of a program's available commands or options, which can be manipulated directly, e.g. with a mouse.

graphic arts *n.pl.* the visual and technical arts involving design, writing, drawing, printing, etc. □ **graphic artist** *n.*

graphics *n.pl.* (usu. treated as *sing.*) **1** the products of the graphic arts, esp. commercial design or illustration. **2** the use of diagrams in calculation and design. **3** (in full **computer graphics**) *Computing* **a** the use of computers linked to monitors to generate and manipulate visual images. **b** visual images produced by computer processing.

graphics card *n.* (also **graphics board**) a circuit board which when connected to a computer increases the computer's ability to produce, display, or manipulate graphics.

graphite /ˈɡræfaɪt/ *n.* a crystalline form of carbon used as a solid lubricant, in pencils, and as a moderator in nuclear reactors etc. □ **graphitic** /-ˈfɪtɪk/ *adj.*

graph paper *n.* paper with intersecting lines forming small squares of equal size, used for graphs.

grapnel /ˈɡræpnəl/ *n.* **1** a device with iron claws, attached to a rope and used for dragging or grasping. **2** a small anchor with several flukes.

grappa *n.* a brandy distilled from the fermented residue of grapes after pressing in winemaking.

grapple ● *v.* **1** *intr.* (often foll. by *with*) fight at close quarters or in close combat. **2** *intr.* (foll. by *with*) try to manage or overcome a difficult problem etc. **3** *tr.* **a** grip with the hands; come to close quarters with. **b** seize with or as with a grapnel; grasp. ● *n.* **1 a** a hold or grip in or as in wrestling. **b** a contest at close quarters. **2** a grapnel. □ **grappler** *n.*

grapple yarder *n.* (also **grapple skidder**) a powerful tractor-like vehicle with a large set of claws, used to haul logs to a landing.

grappling hook (also **grappling iron**) = GRAPNEL 1.

grasp ● *v.* **1** *tr.* **a** clutch at; seize greedily. **b** hold firmly; grip. **2** *intr.* (foll. by *at*) try to seize; accept avidly. **3** *tr.* understand or realize (a fact or meaning). ● *n.* **1** a firm hold; a grip. **2** (foll. by *of*) **a** mastery or control (*a grasp of the situation*). **b** a mental hold or understanding (*a grasp of the facts*). □ **within one's grasp** capable of being grasped, achieved, or comprehended by one. □ **graspable** *adj.*

grasping *adj.* avaricious, greedy. □ **graspingly** *adv.*

grass ● *n.* **1 a** vegetation belonging to a group of small plants with green blades that are eaten by cattle, horses, sheep, etc. **b** any species of this. **c** any plant of the family Gramineae (or Poaceae), which includes cereals, reeds, and bamboos. **2** pasture land. **3** lawn (*keep off the grass*). **4** *slang* marijuana. ● *v.tr.* cover with turf. □ **not let the grass grow under one's feet** be quick to act or to seize an opportunity. **out to grass 1** out to graze. **2** in retirement. □ **grassless** *adj.* **grasslike** *adj.*

grass dance *n.* a competitive N American Aboriginal men's dance, originating on the Plains, noted for its fluid movements and sliding steps.

grasshopper *n.* **1** a plant-eating insect of the order Orthoptera, with legs adapted for jumping and a flat-sided head with large compound eyes. **2** a cocktail usu. consisting of cream, crème de cacao, and crème de menthe in equal portions.

grassland *n.* a large open area covered with grass, e.g. a prairie.

grassroots *n.pl.* **1** a fundamental level or source. **2** (often *attrib.*) ordinary people, esp. as voters; the rank and file of an organization, esp. a political party (*a grassroots movement*).

grass snake *n.* *N Amer.* the common greensnake, *Opheodrys vernalis.*

grassy *adj.* (**-ier, -iest**) **1** covered with or abounding in grass. **2** resembling grass. □ **grassiness** *n.*

grate¹ *v.* **1** *tr.* reduce to small shreds by rubbing on a serrated surface. **2** *intr.* (often foll. by *against, on*) rub with a harsh scraping sound. **3** *tr.* utter in a harsh tone. **4** *intr.* (often foll. by *on*) **a** sound harshly or discordantly. **b** have an irritating effect. **5** *tr.* grind (one's teeth). **6** *intr.* (of a hinge etc.) creak.

grate² *n.* **1** = GRATING². **2** a frame of metal bars for holding the fuel in the recess of a fireplace etc. **3** the recess of a fireplace or furnace.

grateful *adj.* **1** thankful; feeling or showing gratitude (*am grateful to you for helping*). **2** pleasant, acceptable. □ **gratefully** *adv.* **gratefulness** *n.*

grater *n.* a device for grating cheese or other food.

gratify *v.tr.* (**-fies, -fied**) **1 a** please, delight. **b** assent to the wish of; satisfy. **2** indulge in or yield to (a feeling or desire). □ **gratification** *n.* **gratifier** *n.* **gratifying** *adj.* **gratifyingly** *adv.*

gratin /ˈɡrætæ̃/ *n.* *Cooking* **1** a crisp brown crust usu. of bread crumbs or melted cheese. **2** a dish cooked with this (compare AU GRATIN).

gratiné /ˈɡrætɪˈneɪ/ (also *fem.* **gratinée**) ● *adj.* = AU GRATIN. ● *n.* = GRATIN.

grating¹ *adj.* **1** sounding harsh (*a grating laugh*). **2** having an irritating effect. □ **gratingly** *adv.*

grating² *n.* a framework of parallel or crossed metal bars.

gratis /ˈɡrætɪs, ˈɡreɪ-/ *adv. & adj.* free; without charge.

gratitude *n.* the feeling of being grateful or the desire to express one's thanks.

gratuitous *adj.* **1** uncalled for; unwarranted (*gratuitous depictions of violence*). **2** given or done free of charge. □ **gratuitously** *adv.* **gratuitousness** *n.*

gratuity *n.* (*pl.* **-ies**) money given in recognition of services; a tip.

grave¹ *n.* **1 a** a hole or trench dug in the ground to receive a dead body. **b** the place where someone is buried, often marked by a mound or stone. **2** (prec. by *the*) death, esp. as indicating mortal finality. **3** something compared to or regarded as a grave. □ **turn** (or **roll**) **over in one's grave** (of a dead person) react with imagined disgust or repugnance at the actions of those still living.

grave² /ɡreɪv/ ● *adj.* **1 a** serious, weighty, important (*a grave matter*). **b** dignified, solemn, sombre (*a grave look*). **2** extremely serious or threatening (*grave danger*). ● *n.* /ɡrɑːv/ a mark (`) placed over a vowel in some languages to denote pronunciation, length, etc. □ **gravely** *adv.* **graveness** *n.*

grave³ *v.tr.* (*past part.* **graven** or **graved**) (foll. by *in, on*) fix indelibly (on one's memory).

gravedigger *n.* a person who digs graves.

gravel ● *n.* **1 a** a mixture of coarse sand and small water-worn or pounded stones, used for paths and roads and as an aggregate. **b** *Geol.* a stratum of this. **2** *Med.* aggregations of crystals formed in the urinary tract. ● *v.tr.* (**gravelled, gravelling**) **1** lay or strew with gravel. **2** perplex, puzzle.

gravelly *adj.* **1** of or like gravel. **2** having or containing gravel. **3** (of a voice) deep and rough-sounding.

graven *past part.* of GRAVE³.

graveside *n.* the ground at the edge of a grave.

gravesite *n.* *N Amer.* the location of a grave.

gravestone *n.* = TOMBSTONE.

graveyard *n.* **1** a cemetery, esp. one located near a church. **2** *informal* = GRAVEYARD SHIFT. **3** a place in which obsolete or derelict objects are stored (*an appliance graveyard*).

graveyard shift *n. esp. N Amer.* **1** a work shift beginning around midnight and lasting until morning. **2** the workers on duty during this period.

gravid /ˈɡrævɪd/ *adj. literary or Zool.* pregnant.

gravitas /ˈɡrævɪ,tæs, -,tɒs/ *n.* seriousness.

gravitate *v.* **1** *intr.* (foll. by *to*, *toward*) move or be attracted to some source of influence. **2** *tr. & intr.* **a** move or tend by force of gravity toward. **b** sink by or as if by gravity.

gravitation *n.* **1** a force of attraction between any particle of matter in the universe and any other. **2** the effect of this, esp. the falling of bodies to the earth. **3** a natural tendency or movement toward a person etc. □ **gravitational** *adj.* **gravitationally** *adv.*

gravitational field *n.* the region of space surrounding a body in which another body experiences a force of attraction.

gravity *n.* **1 a** the force that attracts a body toward the centre of the earth or toward any other physical body having mass. **b** the degree of intensity of this measured by acceleration. **c** gravitational force. **d** (usu. *attrib.*) operating or functioning by the effect of gravity (*gravity bin*). **2** the property of having weight. **3 a** importance, seriousness; the quality of being grave. **b** solemnity, sobriety; serious demeanour.

gravity feed *n.* the supply of material by its fall under gravity. □ **gravity-fed** *adj.*

gravlax /ˈɡrævlæks/ *n.* a Scandinavian dish of dry-cured salmon marinated in salt, sugar, dill, etc.

Gravol *n. Cdn proprietary =* DIMENHYDRINATE.

gravy *n.* (*pl.* **-ies**) **1 a** the juices and fat from cooked meat. **b** a dressing or sauce for food, made from these or from other materials, e.g. stock. **2** *slang* **a** money easily acquired. **b** an unexpected bonus.

gravy browning *n.* = BROWNING.

gravy train *n. slang* a source of easy financial benefit.

gray *var. of* GREY.

grayling *n.* any silver-grey freshwater fish of the genus *Thymallus*, with a long high dorsal fin.

graze¹ *v.* **1** *intr.* (of cattle, sheep, etc.) eat growing grass. **2** *tr.* **a** feed (cattle etc.) on growing grass. **b** feed on (grass). **3** *intr. informal* **a** eat snacks or small meals throughout the day. **b** casually sample something, esp. food on a store shelf. **c** flick rapidly between television channels. □ **grazer** *n.*

graze² *v.* **1** *tr.* rub or scrape (a part of the body, esp. the skin) so as to break the surface without causing bleeding. **2 a** *tr.* touch lightly in passing. **b** *intr.* (foll. by *against*, *along*, etc.) move with a light passing contact. ● *n.* a superficial wound; a scrape.

grazing *n.* **1** *in senses of* GRAZE¹, GRAZE². **2** grassland suitable for pasturage.

GRE *abbr.* Graduate Record Examination.

grease ● *n.* **1** oily or fatty matter esp. in a semi-solid state and as a lubricant in engines etc. **2** the melted fat of a dead animal. **3** oily matter in unprocessed wool. ● *v.tr.* **1** smear or lubricate with grease. **2** smear (a cookie sheet, baking pan, etc.) with butter, margarine, shortening, etc. before using. □ **grease the palm of** *informal* bribe. **like greased lightning** *informal* very fast. □ **greaseless** *adj.*

grease gun *n.* a device for forcing grease into the parts of a machine.

grease monkey *n. slang* a mechanic.

greasepaint *n.* a waxy composition used as makeup for theatrical performers.

greaseproof *adj.* (esp. of paper) impervious to the penetration of grease.

greaser *n.* **1** a person or thing that greases an engine etc., esp. on a ship. **2** *slang* a tough youth, esp. male, with the greased hair characteristic of members of motorcycle gangs of the 1950s.

grease trail *n. Cdn* any of the forest paths connecting the Pacific coast with the interior, used for centuries as trade routes.

greasewood *n.* any of various resinous shrubs of the goosefoot family, esp. *Sarcobatus vermiculatus*, which grow in dry valleys in western N America.

greasy *adj.* (**-ier**, **-iest**) **1 a** of or like grease. **b** smeared or covered with grease. **c** containing or having too much grease. **2 a** slippery. **b** (of a person or manner) unpleasantly unctuous, smarmy. □ **greasily** *adv.* **greasiness** *n.*

greasy pole *n. informal* **1** a pole smeared with grease and difficult to climb. **2** a difficult path to success.

greasy spoon *n. esp. N Amer. informal* a cheap diner serving greasy food.

great ● *adj.* **1 a** of a size, amount, extent, or intensity considerably above the normal or average; big. **b** also with implied surprise, admiration, contempt, etc., esp. in exclamations (*great stuff!*). **c** reinforcing other words denoting size, quantity, etc. (*a great big hole; a great many*). **2** important, pre-eminent (*the great thing is not to get caught*). **3** grand, imposing (*the great hall*). **4 a** (esp. of a public or historic figure) distinguished; prominent. **b** (**the Great**) as a title denoting the most important of the name (*Alexander the Great*). **5 a** (of a person) remarkable in ability, character, achievement, etc. (*a great thinker*). **b** (of a thing) outstanding of its kind (*the Great Lakes*). **6** (foll. by *at*, *on*) competent, skilled. **7** fully deserving the name of; doing a thing habitually or extensively (*a great believer in tolerance*). **8** (also **greater**) the larger of the name, species, etc. (*great horned owl*). **9** (**Greater**) (of a city etc.) including adjacent urban areas (*Greater Toronto*). **10** *informal* very enjoyable or satisfactory; attractive, fine (*had a great time; it would be great if we won*). **11** (*in comb.*) (in names of family relationships) denoting one degree further removed upwards or downwards (*great-uncle*). ● *n.* a great or outstanding person or thing. ● *adv. informal* excellently, well, successfully. ● *interj.* **1** used to express admiration, approval, appreciation, etc. (*Great! Thanks for coming!*). **2** *ironic* used to express dismay, disappointment, etc. (*Great! The tire's flat again!*). □ **great and small** all classes or types. (**the**) **great and** (**the**) **good** often *ironic* distinguished and worthy people. **to a great extent** largely. □ **greatness** *n.*

great blue heron *n.* a mainly greyish-blue heron, *Ardea herodias*, widespread throughout N America.

great circle *n.* a circle on the surface of a sphere whose plane passes through the sphere's centre.

greatcoat *n.* a long heavy overcoat.

Great Dane *n.* a breed of very large, powerful, short-haired dog.

great deal *n. see* DEAL *n.* 1.

Great Depression *n.* = DEPRESSION 2b.

Great Divide *n.* (prec. by *the*) **1** the boundary between life and death. **2** (usu. **great divide**) *jocular* or *literary* the boundary between two contrasting conditions, cultures, etc.

great grey owl *n.* a very large grey hornless owl, *Strix nebulosa*, of northern coniferous forests of N America and Eurasia, having a large facial disc, yellow eyes, and long tail.

great horned owl n. a large powerful N American owl, *Bubo virginianus*, with prominent ear tufts.

greatly adv. by a considerable amount; much (*greatly admired; greatly superior*).

Great Mother n. = MOTHER GODDESS.

great outdoors n. (prec. by *the*) the open air.

great room n. N Amer. a spacious multi-purpose open concept living area in a house.

Great Seal n. the seal used for the authentication of state documents of the highest importance.

great toe n. = BIG TOE.

great unwashed n. informal (prec. by *the*) the rabble.

Great War n. (prec. by *the*) the First World War.

great white hope n. = WHITE HOPE.

Great White North n. Cdn jocular (prec. by *the*) Canada.

great white shark n. a large and dangerous greyish shark, *Carcharadon carcharias*, found in the temperate and tropical regions of all oceans.

grebe /griːb/ n. any diving bird of the family Podicipedidae, with a long neck, lobed toes, and almost no tail.

Grecian /ˈɡriːʃən/ adj. (of architecture or beauty) following Greek models or ideals.

Greco-Roman /ˌɡriːkoːˈroːmən, ˌɡrek-/ adj. **1** of or relating to the Greeks and Romans. **2** Wrestling denoting a style attacking only the upper body.

greed n. an excessive desire, esp. for wealth or food.

greedy adj. (**-ier, -iest**) **1** wanting wealth to excess. **2** having or showing an excessive appetite for food or drink. **3** (foll. by *for*, or *to* + infin.) very keen or eager; needing intensely (*greedy for affection*). □ **greedily** adv. **greediness** n.

Greek ● n. **1 a** a native or national of modern Greece; a person of Greek descent. **b** a native or citizen of any of the ancient states of Greece; a member of the Greek people. **2** the Indo-European language of Greece. ● adj. of Greece or its people or language; Hellenic. □ **Greek to me** informal incomprehensible to me. □ **Greekness** n.

Greek Orthodox Church n. (also **Greek Church**) the national Church of Greece.

Greek salad n. a salad of lettuce, tomatoes, cucumbers, olives, feta, and olive oil vinaigrette.

green ● adj. **1** of the colour between blue and yellow in the spectrum; coloured like grass, emeralds, etc. **2 a** covered with leaves or grass. **b** mild and without snow (*a green Christmas*). **3** (of fruit etc. or wood) unripe or unseasoned. **4 a** not dried, smoked, or tanned. **b** Cdn (Nfld) (of cod) split and salted, but not dried. **5** inexperienced, naive, gullible. **6 a** (of the complexion) pale, sickly-hued. **b** jealous, envious. **7** young, flourishing. **8** not withered or worn out (*a green old age*). **9** vegetable (*green salad*). **10 a** (also **Green**) concerned with or supporting protection of the environment as a political principle. **b** (of a consumer product) not harmful to the environment in its manufacture or use. ● n. **1** a green colour or pigment. **2** green clothes or material (*dressed in green*). **3 a** a piece of public or common grassy land (*village green*). **b** a grassy area used for a special purpose (*putting green*). **c** Golf a putting green. **4** (in pl.) green vegetables. **5** vigour, youth, virility (*in the green*). **6 a** green light. **7** a green ball, piece, etc., in a game or sport. **8** (also **Green**) a member or supporter of an environmentalist group or party. **9** slang money. **10** green foliage or growing plants. ● v.tr. & intr. make or become green. □ **green up** (of vegetation or a landscape etc.) become green, as in the spring. □ **greenish** adj. **greenly** adv. **greenness** n.

green ash n. a variety of the ash *Fraxinus pennsylvanica*, common in the Prairie provinces.

greenback n. **1 a** a US legal tender note. **b** the US dollar. **2** any of various green-backed animals.

green bean n. **1** any bean plant, esp. the French bean *Phaseolus vulgaris*, grown for its edible young pods rather than for its seeds. **2** this pod.

greenbelt n. an area of open land around a city, the development of which is restricted.

Green Beret n. informal an American or British commando.

green card n. US a permit allowing a foreign national to live and work permanently in the US.

greenchain n. Forestry an endless conveyor taking trimmed lumber from the saws to a sorting area.

greenery n. green foliage or growing plants.

green-eyed adj. **1** having green eyes. **2** jealous.

green fee n. a charge for playing one round of golf.

greengrocer n. a retailer of fruit and vegetables.

greenhorn n. an inexperienced or foolish person.

greenhouse n. a transparent glass or plastic building for rearing or hastening the growth of plants.

greenhouse effect n. the heating of the earth's surface and lower atmosphere attributed to an increase in carbon dioxide and other gases, which are more transparent to incoming solar radiation than to reflected radiation from the earth.

greenhouse gas n. any of various gases that contribute to the greenhouse effect.

greenie n. informal a person concerned about environmental issues.

greening n. **1** the process or result of making something green, or becoming green. **2** the planting of trees etc. in urban or desert areas. **3** the process of becoming or making aware of or sensitive to ecological issues. **4** a variety of apple that is green when ripe.

greenkeeper n. = GREENSKEEPER.

Greenlander n. a native or inhabitant of Greenland, a large island lying to the northeast of N America.

green light n. **1** a signal to proceed on a road, railway, etc. **2** informal permission to go ahead with a project. □ **green-light** v.tr.

greenmail n. the practice of buying enough shares in a company to threaten a takeover, thereby forcing the owners to buy them back at a higher price in order to retain control. □ **greenmailer** n.

green manure n. growing plants plowed into the soil as fertilizer.

green onion n. N Amer. an onion taken from the ground before the bulb has formed, with slender green hollow leaves.

Green Paper n. Cdn & Brit. a preliminary report of Government proposals, for discussion.

green pepper n. the unripe fruit of *Capsicum annuum*.

green revolution n. **1** an increase in crop production, esp. in developing countries, achieved by using artificial fertilizers, pesticides, and high-yield crop varieties. **2** a rise of environmental concern in industrialized countries.

green room n. a room in a theatre, studio, etc. in which performers may relax when they are not on stage, on the air, etc.

greens fee n. N Amer. var. of GREEN FEE.

greenskeeper n. esp. N Amer. the keeper of a golf course.

greensward /ˈɡriːnswɔrd/ n. **1** grassy turf. **2** an expanse of this.

green tea n. tea made from steam-dried, not fermented, leaves.

green thumb n. informal esp. N Amer. a talent for gardening. □ **green-thumbed** adj.

greenway n. esp. N Amer. an undeveloped strip of land in an urban area, usu. including a trail and following a natural feature such as a river or ridge.

Greenwich Mean Time /ˈgrenɪtʃ/ n. the local time on the 0° meridian, used as an international basis of time reckoning. Abbr.: **GMT**.

green-winged teal n. see TEAL n. 1.

greeny adj. greenish (greeny yellow).

greet v.tr. **1** welcome or address politely on meeting or arrival. **2** receive or acknowledge in a specified way (was greeted with derision). **3** (of a sight, sound, etc.) become apparent to or noticed by. □ **greeter** n.

greeting n. **1** the act or an instance of welcoming or addressing politely. **2** words, gestures, etc., used to greet a person. **3** (often in pl.) an expression of goodwill.

greeting card n. a decorative card sent to convey greetings.

gregarious /grɪˈgeərəs/ adj. **1** fond of company. **2** living in flocks or communities. **3** growing in clusters. □ **gregariously** adv. **gregariousness** n.

Gregorian calendar /grəˈgɔːriən/ n. the general calendar in use today, introduced in 1582 as a correction of the Julian calendar, with 365 days in standard years and 366 days in all years exactly divisible by 4 except century years, which must be exactly divisible by 400 to have 366 days.

Gregorian chant n. plainsong Christian ritual music.

gremlin n. informal **1** an imaginary mischievous sprite regarded as responsible for mechanical faults. **2** any similar cause of trouble.

Grenache /grəˈnæʃ/ n. a black wine grape.

grenade n. **1** a small bomb thrown by hand (**hand grenade**) or launched mechanically. **2** a similar missile containing chemicals which disperse on impact, used for extinguishing fires etc.

grenadier /ˌgrenəˈdiːr/ n. hist. **1** a soldier armed with grenades. **2** a soldier selected for height and strength to be part of an elite unit.

grenadine[1] /ˈgrenəˌdiːn/ n. a sweet red syrup flavoured with pomegranates.

grenadine[2] n. a dress fabric of loosely woven silk etc.

grew past of GROW.

grey ● adj. **1** of a colour intermediate between black and white, as of ashes or lead. **2 a** (of the weather etc.) dull, dismal; heavily overcast. **b** bleak, depressing; (of a person) depressed. **3 a** (of hair) turning white with age etc. **b** (of a person) having grey hair. **4** nondescript, unidentifiable. ● n. **1 a** a grey colour or pigment. **b** grey clothes or material (dressed in grey). **2** a cold sunless light. **3** a grey or white horse. ● v. **1** tr. & intr. make or become grey. **2** intr. informal become older; age. □ **greyish** adj. **greyness** n.

grey area n. an ill-defined situation etc., not readily categorized or conforming to an existing set of rules.

greybeard n. often derogatory an old man.

Grey Cup n. Cdn **1** the trophy presented each year to the team winning the Canadian Football League championship (often attrib.: Grey Cup game). **2** the game deciding this championship.

greyhound n. a breed of tall slender dog having keen sight and capable of high speed, used in racing.

grey jay n. a common N American jay, Perisoreus canadensis, having grey, black, and white plumage,

notorious for its boldness in scavenging from backwoods camps and picnic grounds.

grey market n. the unofficial but not illegal buying and selling of goods, esp. that bypassing standard channels of distribution. □ **grey marketer** n.

grey matter n. **1** the darker tissues of the brain and spinal cord consisting of nerve cell bodies and branching dendrites. **2** informal intelligence.

grey mullet n. any mullet of the family Mugilidae, usu. found near coasts and having a thick body and blunt head, often used as food.

Grey Nun n. a member of any of five Roman Catholic women's communities, each with a history traceable to the Sisters of Charity of the Hôpital Général, in Montreal.

grey partridge n. see PARTRIDGE 1.

grey power n. informal political or other pressure applied or held by senior citizens.

grey-scale Computing ● attrib.adj. designating the production of black and white images by the assigning of one of several shades of grey to each pixel (compare DITHERING 2). ● n. a grey-scale image.

grey seal n. a large seal, Halichoerus grypus, of the N Atlantic and Baltic.

grey squirrel n. a common grey or black squirrel of eastern N America, Sciurus carolinensis.

greystone n. Cdn **1** grey stones used in building walls, houses, etc. **2** a house etc. made of greystone.

grey water n. mildly contaminated household waste water from sinks, washing machines, etc.

grey whale n. a large mottled grey baleen whale of N Pacific waters, Eschrichtius robustus.

grey wolf n. = WOLF n. 1.

grid n. **1 a** a framework of spaced parallel bars. **b** a network of lines, esp. of two series of regularly spaced lines crossing one another at right angles. **c** a set of points arranged so that lines passing through them would form a grid. **2** a system of numbered squares printed on a map and forming the basis of map references. **3 a** a network of water mains, gas lines, etc. **b** = POWER GRID. **4** a pattern of lines marking the starting places on a motor racing track. **5** an arrangement of town or city streets in a rectangular pattern. □ **gridded** adj.

griddle ● n. a flat pan with little or no rim, used esp. for frying. ● v.tr. cook on a griddle.

gridiron n. **1** a cooking utensil of metal bars for broiling or grilling. **2** N Amer. **a** a football field (with parallel lines marking out the area of play). **b** informal the game of football (the gridiron season). **3** Theatre an open framework over a stage supporting the mechanism for drop scenes etc. **4** = GRID 5.

gridlock n. **1** a traffic jam affecting a whole network of intersecting streets. **2** = DEADLOCK n. 1. □ **gridlocked** adj.

grid road n. Cdn **1** a road following the surveyed divisions of a township, municipality, etc. **2** (Sask.) a road forming part of a provincial grid system constructed in the 1950s, with north-south roads one mile apart, and east-west roads two miles apart.

grief n. **1** deep or intense sorrow or mourning. **2** the cause of this. **3** informal trouble; annoyance. □ **come to grief** meet with disaster; fail. **good grief!** an exclamation of surprise, alarm, etc.

grievance n. **1** a real or fancied cause for complaint. **2** an official allegation that something is unjust, inequitable, or illegal (the union has filed a grievance).

grieve v. **1** intr. suffer grief, esp. at another's death. **2**

tr. cause grief or great distress to. **3** *tr.* file a grievance against (a person or thing). □ **griever** *n.*

grievous *adj.* **1** (of pain etc.) severe. **2** causing grief or suffering. **3** injurious. **4** flagrant, heinous. □ **grievously** *adv.* **grievousness** *n.*

griffin *n.* a mythical creature with an eagle's head and wings and a lion's body.

griffon /'grɪfən/ *n.* **1** a small terrier-like breed of dog with coarse or smooth hair. **2** (in full **griffon vulture**) a large vulture, *Gyps fulvus*.

grift *n. & v. esp. US slang* = GRAFT². □ **grifter** *n.*

grill ● *n.* **1 a** a cooking apparatus consisting of a series of metal bars over a heat source. **b** this series of metal bars, on which food is directly placed for cooking. **2 a** dish of food cooked on a grill. **3** (in full **grill room**) a restaurant serving grilled food. ● *v.* **1** *tr. & intr.* cook or be cooked on a grill or griddle. **2** *tr. & intr.* subject or be subjected to extreme heat, esp. from the sun. **3** *tr.* subject to severe questioning or interrogation. □ **griller** *n.* **grilling** *n.* (in sense 3 of *v.*).

grille /grɪl/ *n.* (also **grill**) **1** a grating or latticed screen, used as a partition or to allow discreet vision. **2** a metal grid protecting the radiator of a vehicle.

grilled cheese *n.* (in full **grilled cheese sandwich**) *N Amer.* a cheese sandwich that has been fried on both sides.

grilse /grɪls/ *n.* (*pl.* same) a young salmon that has returned to fresh water for the first time.

grim *adj.* (**grimmer**, **grimmest**) **1** having a stern or forbidding appearance. **2** harsh, severe. **3** joyless, sinister (*a grim truth*). **4** unpleasant, unattractive. **5** ominous, dreadful. □ **like grim death** with great determination. □ **grimly** *adv.* **grimness** *n.*

grimace /'grɪməs/ ● *n.* a distortion of the face made in disgust etc. or to amuse. ● *v.intr.* make a grimace.

grime ● *n.* dirt or soot, esp. ingrained in a surface. ● *v.tr.* blacken with grime; befoul.

Grim Reaper *n.* a personification of death, esp. as a skeletal or faceless hooded figure with a scythe.

grimy *adj.* (**-ier**, **-iest**) covered with grime; dirty. □ **grimily** *adv.* **griminess** *n.*

grin ● *v.* (**grinned**, **grinning**) **1** *intr.* **a** smile broadly, showing the teeth. **b** make a forced, unrestrained, or stupid smile. **2** *tr.* express by grinning (*grinned his satisfaction*). **3** *intr.* draw back the lips and reveal the teeth, esp. in pain. ● *n.* the act or action of grinning. □ **grin and bear it** take pain or misfortune stoically. □ **grinner** *n.* **grinningly** *adv.*

grinch *n.* a person that seeks to deprive others of joy.

grind ● *v.* (*past* and *past part.* **ground**) **1 a** *tr.* reduce to small particles or powder by crushing, esp. by passing through a mill. **b** *intr.* (of a mill, machine, etc.) move with a crushing action. **2 a** *tr.* reduce, sharpen, or smooth by friction. **b** *tr.* rub or rub together gratingly (*grind one's teeth*). **3** *tr.* (often foll. by *down*) oppress; harass with exactions (*grinding poverty*). **4** *intr.* **a** (often foll. by *away*) work or study hard. **b** (foll. by *out*) produce with effort (*grinding out verses*). **c** (foll. by *on*) (of a sound) continue gratingly or monotonously. **5** *tr.* turn the handle of a barrel organ etc. **6** *intr. slang* rotate the hips or pelvis in a suggestive manner, esp. in a dance. ● *n.* **1** the act or an instance of grinding. **2** *informal* hard dull work; a laborious task (*the daily grind*). **3** the fineness of something that has been ground (*a very coarse grind*). **4** *slang* the action of rotating the hips or pelvis in a dance etc. □ **grind to a halt** stop laboriously. □ **grindingly** *adv.*

grinder *n.* **1** a person or thing that grinds (often in *comb.*: *coffee grinder*). **2** *N Amer. slang* an athlete known

more for consistently working hard than for remarkable skill. **3** a molar tooth.

grindstone *n.* a revolving disc used for grinding, sharpening, and polishing. □ **keep one's nose to the grindstone** work hard and continuously.

gringo /'grɪŋgo/ *n.* (*pl.* **-os**) often *derogatory* a foreigner, esp. a N American, in a Latin American country.

grip ● *v.* (**gripped**, **gripping**) **1 a** *tr.* grasp tightly; take a firm hold of. **b** *intr.* take a firm hold, esp. by friction. **2** *tr.* (of a feeling or emotion) deeply affect (a person) (*was gripped by fear*). **3** *tr.* compel the attention or interest of. ● *n.* **1 a** a firm hold; a tight grasp or clasp. **b** a manner of grasping or holding. **2** the power of holding attention. **3 a** mental or intellectual understanding or mastery. **b** effective control of a situation or one's behaviour etc. (*lose one's grip*). **4 a** a part of a machine that grips or holds something. **b** a part or attachment by which a tool, implement, weapon, etc., is held in the hand. **5 a** a member of a camera crew responsible for moving and setting up equipment. **b** a stagehand. **6** a travelling bag. □ **come to grips with** approach purposefully; begin to deal with. **get a grip** gain or regain composure or control. **in the grip of** dominated or affected by (esp. an adverse circumstance or unpleasant sensation). □ **gripper** *n.* **grippingly** *adv.* **grippy** *adj.* (**-ier**, **-iest**)

gripe ● *v.* **1** *intr. informal* complain, esp. peevishly. **2** *tr.* affect with gastric or intestinal pain. ● *n.* **1** *informal* **a** a complaint. **b** the act of griping. **2** (usu. in *pl.*) gastric or intestinal pain; colic. **3** a grip or clutch. □ **griper** *n.* **gripingly** *adv.*

grisly /'grɪzli/ *adj.* (**-ier**, **-iest**) causing horror, disgust, or fear. □ **grisliness** *n.*

grist *n.* **1 a** grain to be ground. **b** grain that has been ground. **2** malt crushed for brewing. **3** (also **grist for the** (or **one's**) **mill**) a subject to be used, discussed, processed, etc., esp. for profit or advantage.

gristle *n.* tough cartilaginous tissue, esp. as occurring in meat. □ **gristly** *adj.*

gristmill *n.* a mill for grinding grain.

grit ● *n.* **1** small particles of stone or sand. **2** coarse sandstone. **3** the texture or coarseness of sandpaper, stone, etc. **4** (**Grit**) *Cdn* **a** a supporter or member of the Liberal Party. **b** *hist.* = CLEAR GRIT. **5** *informal* pluck, endurance; strength of character. ● *v.* (**gritted**, **gritting**) **1** *tr.* clench (the teeth). **2** *intr.* make or move with a grating sound. □ **grittily** *adv.* **grittiness** *n.* **gritty** *adj.* (**-ier**, **-iest**).

grits *n.pl.* **1** (treated as *sing.* or *pl.*) esp. *US* **a** coarsely ground grain, esp. corn. **b** = HOMINY. **2** oats that have been husked but not ground.

grizzled *adj.* having, or streaked with, grey hair.

grizzly ● *adj.* (**-ier**, **-iest**) grizzled. ● *n.* (*pl.* **-ies**) (in full **grizzly bear**) a large variety of brown bear, *Ursus arctos*, found in N America and N Russia.

groan ● *v.* **1** *intr.* make a deep sound expressing pain, grief, disapproval, or pleasure. **b** *tr.* utter with groans. **2** *intr.* complain inarticulately. **3** *intr.* (usu. foll. by *under*, *beneath*, *with*) be loaded or oppressed. ● *n.* the sound made in groaning. □ **groan inwardly** be distressed. □ **groaningly** *adv.*

groaner *n.* **1** a person who groans or complains. **2** a bad joke or pun.

groats *n.pl.* hulled or crushed grain, esp. oats.

grocer /'groːsər, -ʃər/ *n.* a person who owns or operates a grocery store.

grocery /'groːsəri, -ʃəri, -ʃri/ *n.* (*pl.* **-ies**) **1** (in *pl.*) food and other general household supplies. **2** (in full **grocery store**) a store where groceries are sold.

grocery cart *n. N Amer.* = SHOPPING CART 1.

grog *n.* **1** a drink of spirits (originally rum) and water. **2** *informal* any alcoholic drink.

groggy *adj.* (**-ier, -iest**) dazed or unsteady, as from a hangover, blows, lack of sleep, etc. □ **groggily** *adv.* **grogginess** *n.*

groin[1] ● *n.* **1** the part of the body where the thighs meet the abdomen. **2 a** the lower abdomen. **b** the esp. male genitals. **3** *Archit.* **a** an edge formed by intersecting vaults. **b** an arch supporting a vault. ● *v.tr. Archit.* build with groins.

groin[2] esp. *US var. of* GROYNE.

grommet /'grɒmət/ *n.* a metal, plastic, or rubber eyelet, esp. placed in a hole to protect or insulate a rope or cable etc. passed through it.

groom ● *n.* **1** = BRIDEGROOM. **2** a person employed to take care of horses. ● *v.tr.* **1 a** tend to, esp. brush the coat of (a horse, dog, etc). **b** (of an animal) clean the fur of (another) (also *refl.*). **2 a** give a neat or tidy appearance to (a person etc.). **b** carefully attend to (a lawn). **c** keep (cross-country ski trails etc.) open. **3** prepare or train (a person) for a particular purpose or activity. □ **groomer** *n.*

groomsman *n.* (*pl.* **-men**) = BEST MAN.

groove ● *n.* **1 a** a channel or hollow, esp. one made to guide motion or receive a corresponding ridge. **b** a spiral track cut in a phonograph record. **2** an established routine or habit. **3** *slang* an established rhythmic pattern (*got a groove going*). ● *v.* **1** *tr.* make a groove or grooves in. **2** *intr. slang* **a** play music (esp. jazz or dance music) rhythmically. **b** dance or move rhythmically to music. **c** enjoy oneself. □ **in the groove** *slang* **1** doing or performing well. **2** fashionable.

groovy *adj.* (**-ier, -iest**) **1** *slang* (*dated* or *jocular*) fashionable and exciting; enjoyable, excellent. **2** of or like a groove. □ **groovily** *adv.* **grooviness** *n.*

grope ● *v.* **1** *intr.* (usu. foll. by *for*) feel about or search blindly or uncertainly with the hands. **2** *intr.* (foll. by *for, after*) search mentally (*groping for the answer*). **3** *tr.* feel (one's way) towards something. **4** *tr. slang* fondle clumsily for sexual pleasure. ● *n.* the process or an instance of groping. □ **groper** *n.*

grosbeak /'gro:sbi:k/ *n.* any of various finch-like birds with heavy bills and usu. colourful plumage.

gross ● *adj.* **1** bloated; repulsively fat. **2** (of a person, manners, or morals) coarse, unrefined, or indecent. **3** *slang* repulsive, disgusting. **4** flagrant; conspicuously wrong (*gross negligence*). **5** total; not net (*gross income*). **6 a** luxuriant, rank. **b** thick, solid, dense. **7** (of the senses etc.) dull; lacking sensitivity. ● *v.tr.* produce or earn as gross profit or income. ● *n.* (*pl.* same) **1** gross income, receipts, etc. **2** an amount equal to twelve dozen. □ **gross out** *N Amer. slang* disgust, esp. by repulsive or obscene behaviour. **gross up** increase (a net amount) to its value before deductions. □ **grossly** *adv.* **grossness** *n.*

gross domestic product *n.* the annual total value of goods produced and services provided in a country excluding transactions with other countries.

gross national product *n.* the annual total value of goods produced and services provided in a country.

gross-out *n.* esp. *N Amer. slang* (often *attrib.*) something that is repulsive or disgusting (*a gross-out horror flick*).

gross ton *n. see* TON 5a.

Gros Ventre /'gro: vɒnt/ *n.* (*pl.* same or **Gros Ventres**) **1** a member of an Aboriginal people living in Montana and (formerly) in S Saskatchewan. **2** the Algonquian language of these people.

grotesque /gro:'tesk/ ● *adj.* **1** comically or repulsively distorted; monstrous, unnatural. **2** incongru-

ous, ludicrous, absurd. ● *n.* **1** a decorative form interweaving human and animal features. **2** a comically distorted figure or design. □ **grotesquely** *adv.* **grotesquerie** /-'teskɜri/ *n.* (also **grotesquery**).

grotto *n.* (*pl.* **-oes** or **-os**) **1** a small picturesque cave. **2** an artificial ornamental cave, e.g. in a park.

grotty *adj.* (**-ier, -iest**) *slang* unpleasant, dirty, shabby, unattractive. □ **grottiness** *n.*

grouch *informal* ● *n.* **1** a discontented person. **2** a fit of grumbling or bad temper. **3** a cause of discontent. ● *v.intr.* grumble.

grouchy *adj.* (**-ier, -iest**) *informal* discontented, grumpy. □ **grouchily** *adv.* **grouchiness** *n.*

ground[1] ● *n.* **1 a** the surface of the earth, esp. as contrasted with the air around it. **b** a part of this specified in some way (*low ground*). **2** soil, earth (*stony ground*). **3 a** a position, area, or distance on the earth's surface. **b** the extent of activity etc. achieved or of a subject dealt with (*the book covers a lot of ground*). **4** (often in *pl.*) a foundation, motive, or reason (*excused on the grounds of poor health*). **5** an area of a special kind or designated for special use (often in *comb.*: *fishing grounds*). **6** (in *pl.*) an area of usu. enclosed land attached to a building. **7** an area or basis for consideration, agreement, etc. (*common ground*). **8 a** (in painting) the prepared surface giving the predominant colour or tone. **b** (in embroidery, ceramics, etc.) the undecorated surface. **9** (in *pl.*) solid particles, esp. of coffee, forming a residue. **10** esp. *N Amer. Electricity* a connection between an electrical circuit and the earth, conducting electricity harmlessly to the ground in case of a fault. **11** the bottom of the sea or a large body of water (*the ship touched ground*). **12** (*attrib.*) **a** (of animals) living on or in the ground. **b** (of fish) living at the bottom of water. **c** (of plants) dwarfish or trailing. **d** relating to or concerned with the ground (*ground staff*). **e** *Military* designating units etc. operating on land, as opposed to naval or air units (*ground support*). ● *v.* **1** *tr.* **a** refuse authority for (a pilot or an aircraft) to fly. **b** *informal* temporarily restrict the esp. social activities of (esp. a child or teenager), usu. as a punishment. **2 a** *tr.* run (a ship) aground. **b** *intr.* (of a ship) run aground. **3** *tr.* (foll. by *in*) instruct thoroughly (in a subject). **4** *tr.* (often as **grounded** *adj.*) (foll. by *on*) base (a principle, conclusion, etc.) on. **5** *tr.* (often as **grounded** *adj.*) esp. *N Amer.* connect (an electrical circuit) to the ground, directly or indirectly, so that the electricity is conducted harmlessly to the earth in case of a fault. **6** *intr.* alight on the ground. **7** *intr. Baseball* hit the ball along the ground, esp. for an easy out (*grounded to second*). □ **break ground 1** begin the excavation for a new construction project. **2** (also **break new ground**) introduce or discover a new method, system, etc. **cut the ground from under a person's feet** anticipate and pre-empt a person's arguments, plans, etc. **fall to the ground** (of a plan etc.) fail. **from the ground up** completely, thoroughly. **2** from the most basic stage to the most complex (*redesigned from the ground up*). **gain** (or **make**) **ground 1** advance steadily; make progress. **2** (foll. by *on*) get closer to (a person or thing pursued). **get off the ground** *informal* make a successful start. **ground out** *Baseball* hit the ball along the ground to an infielder and be put out at first base. **hold** (or **stand**) **one's ground** not retreat or give way. **lose ground 1** retreat, decline. **2** lose the advantage or one's position in an argument, contest, etc. **on the ground** at the point of production or operation; in practical conditions. **on one's own ground** on one's own territory or subject; on one's own terms. **thin on the ground** not numerous. **work** (or **run** etc.) **oneself into the ground** informal work etc. to the point of exhaustion.

ground² past and past part. of GRIND.

groundbreaking ● adj. **1** innovative, pioneering. **2** of or relating to a groundbreaking. ● n. the act or ceremony of breaking ground for a new construction project.

ground cover n. **1** a plant covering the surface of the earth, esp. a low-growing spreading plant that inhibits the growth of weeds. **2** such plants collectively.

ground crew n. the people at an airfield whose job is to repair and refuel aircraft.

grounder n. (also **ground ball**) (esp. in baseball) a ball that is hit or passed along the ground.

ground-fault interrupter n. see GFI.

groundfish n. any fish living on or near the bottom of the sea, including halibut, sole, cod, etc.

ground floor n. the floor of a building at ground level. □ **get in on the ground floor** become part of an enterprise in its early stages.

ground glass n. glass made opaque by grinding.

ground hemlock n. a N American yew, *Taxus canadensis*, growing as a straggling shrub.

groundhog n. N Amer. a woodchuck.

Groundhog Day n. N Amer. Feb. 2, when the groundhog is said to come out of hibernation; according to folklore, if it sees its shadow on that day, six more weeks of winter may be expected.

grounding n. basic instruction in a subject.

groundless adj. without motive or foundation. □ **groundlessly** adv. **groundlessness** n.

ground level n. **1** the level of the ground. **2** the ground floor.

groundout n. Baseball a play in which the batter hits a ball along the ground to an infielder and is put out at first base.

ground plan n. **1** the plan of a building at ground level. **2** the general outline of a scheme.

ground rule n. a basic principle.

groundsheet n. a waterproof sheet spread on the ground to protect against moisture, esp. in a tent.

groundskeeper n. N Amer. a person who maintains a playing field or court etc.

groundspeed n. an aircraft's speed relative to the ground (compare AIRSPEED).

ground squirrel n. **1** a squirrel-like rodent, e.g. a chipmunk, gopher, etc. **2** any squirrel of the genus *Spermophilus* living in burrows.

groundstroke n. Tennis a stroke played after the ball has bounced.

groundswell n. **1** a large or extensive swell of the sea caused by a distant or past storm or an earthquake. **2** an increasingly forceful presence (esp. of public opinion).

groundwater n. water held in soil or rock, esp. that below the water table.

groundwood n. (attrib.) designating low-grade newsprint, pulp, etc. that has not been treated or coated.

groundwork n. **1** preliminary or basic work. **2** a foundation or basis.

ground zero n. **1** the point on the ground or on the surface of the water directly under or above an exploding (usu. nuclear) bomb. **2** N Amer. informal the very beginning or starting point.

group ● n. **1** a number of persons or things located close together, or considered or classed together. **2** (attrib.) concerning or done by a group (a *group photograph*). **3** a number of people working together

or sharing beliefs, e.g. part of a political party. **4** a number of commercial companies under common ownership. **5** a small band, esp. one that plays popular music. **6** a division of an air force. **7** Math. a set of elements, together with an associative binary operation, which contains an inverse for each element and an identity element. **8** Chem. **a** a set of ions or radicals giving a characteristic qualitative reaction. **b** a set of elements occupying a column in the periodic table and having broadly similar properties. **c** a combination of atoms having a recognizable identity in a number of compounds. ● v. **1** tr. & intr. form or be formed into a group. **2** tr. (often foll. by with) place in a group or groups. **3** tr. form (colours, figures, etc.) into a well-arranged and harmonious whole. **4** tr. classify.

grouper n. any marine fish of the family Serranidae, with a heavy body, big head, and wide mouth.

group home n. a home where several unrelated people live together under supervision or care.

groupie n. slang **1** an ardent follower of touring pop groups, esp. a young woman seeking sexual relations with them. **2** a fan, enthusiast, or follower.

grouping n. **1** a process or system of allocation to groups. **2** a formation or arrangement in groups.

group insurance n. esp. N Amer. a life, health, or accident insurance policy covering a group of people at a reduced rate under a single contract.

group therapy n. therapy in which patients with a similar condition are brought together to assist one another psychologically.

groupthink n. esp. N Amer. the practice of thinking or making decisions as a group, often resulting in poor quality decision-making.

groupware n. software designed to facilitate collective working by a number of different users.

group work n. work done by a group of people working in close association.

grouse¹ n. (pl. same) **1** any of various game birds of the family Tetraonidae, with a plump body and feathered legs. **2** the flesh of a grouse used as food.

grouse² informal ● v.intr. grumble or complain pettily. ● n. a complaint.

grout ● n. a thin mortar for filling gaps in tiling etc. ● v.tr. provide or fill with grout. □ **grouter** n.

grove n. **1** a small wood or group of trees, esp. one with little or no undergrowth. **2** an orchard planted for the cultivation of citrus fruit, olives, etc.

grovel / ˈgrɒvəl / v.intr. (**grovelled**, **grovelling**) behave obsequiously in seeking favour or forgiveness. □ **groveller** n. **grovelling** adj. **grovellingly** adv.

grow v. (past **grew**; past part. **grown**) **1** intr. increase in size, degree, or in any way regarded as measurable, e.g. authority or reputation (*grew in stature*). **2** intr. **a** develop or exist as a living plant or natural product. **b** develop in a specific way or direction (*growing sideways*). **c** germinate, sprout; spring up. **3** intr. be produced; come naturally into existence; arise. **4** intr. **a** become gradually (*grow rich*). **b** come by degrees (*grew to like it*). **5** intr. (foll. by into) **a** become, having grown or developed (*will grow into a fine athlete*). **b** become large enough for or suited to (*will grow into the coat*; *grew into her new job*). **6** intr. (foll. by on) become gradually more favoured by. **7** tr. **a** produce (plants, fruit, etc.) by cultivation. **b** bring forth. **c** allow (a beard etc.) to develop or increase in length. **8** tr. (in passive; foll. by over, up) be covered with a growth. **9** tr. cause (the economy, a corporation, etc.) to grow or increase in size, value, etc. (a *plan designed to grow the company's market share*). □ **grow out of 1** become too large to wear (a garment). **2** become too mature to retain (a childish habit etc.). **3** be the result or development of. **grow together** coalesce. **grow up 1 a** advance to maturity. **b** (esp. in *imper.*) begin to behave sensibly. **2** (of a custom) arise, become common.

grower *n.* **1** (often in *comb.*) a person growing produce (*fruit grower*). **2** a plant that grows in a specified way (*a fast grower*).

growing pains *n.pl.* **1** early difficulties in the development of an enterprise etc. **2** neuralgic pain in children's legs due to fatigue etc.

growl ● *v.* **1** *intr.* **a** (often foll. by *at*) (esp. of a dog) make a low guttural sound, usu. of anger. **b** murmur angrily. **2** *intr.* rumble. **3** *tr.* (often foll. by *out*) utter with a growl. ● *n.* **1** a growling sound, esp. made by a dog. **2** an angry murmur; a complaint. **3** a rumble. □ **growlingly** *adv.* **growly** *adj.* **(-ier, -iest)**.

growler *n.* **1** a person or thing that growls. **2** a small iceberg.

grown ● *v. past part.* of GROW. ● *adj.* adult.

grown-up ● *adj.* **1** adult. **2** suitable for or characteristic of an adult. ● *n.* an adult person.

growth *n.* **1** the act or process of growing. **2** an increase in size or value. **3** something that has grown or is growing. **4** *Med.* an abnormal formation, esp. a tumour. **5** the cultivation of produce.

growth factor *n.* any substance required by an organism in minute amounts to maintain growth.

growth hormone *n.* a substance which stimulates the growth of a plant or animal.

growth industry *n.* an industry that is developing rapidly.

growth ring *n.* a concentric layer of wood, shell, etc., developed during an annual or other regular period of growth.

groyne *n.* a timber framework or low broad wall built out from a shore to check erosion of a beach.

grub ● *n.* **1** the larva of an insect, esp. of a beetle. **2** *informal* food. ● *v.* **(grubbed, grubbing) 1** *tr. & intr.* dig superficially. **2** *tr.* **a** clear (the ground) of roots and stumps. **b** clear away (roots etc.). **3** *tr.* (foll. by *up, out*) **a** get by digging (*grubbing up weeds*). **b** extract (information etc.) by searching in books etc. **4** *intr.* search in an undignified, or grovelling manner; rummage. **5** *intr.* (foll. by *on, along, away*) toil, plod.

grubber *n.* **1** (usu. in *comb.*) *derogatory* a person devoted to amassing something (*vote-grubber*) (*compare* MONEY-GRUBBER). **2** an implement for digging up weeds etc. **3** a person who or animal which grubs.

grub box *n.* *Cdn* a box or other container for carrying and storing food on an expedition etc.

grubby *adj.* **(-ier, -iest) 1** dirty, grimy. **2** of or infested with grubs. □ **grubbily** *adv.* **grubbiness** *n.*

grubstake *N Amer. informal* ● *n.* material or provisions supplied to an enterprise in return for a share in the resulting profits (originally in prospecting). ● *v.tr.* provide with a grubstake. □ **grubstaker** *n.*

grudge ● *n.* a persistent feeling of ill will or resentment, esp. one due to an insult or injury (*bears a grudge against me*). ● *v.tr.* **1** be resentfully reluctant to give, grant, or allow (a thing). **2** be reluctant to do (a thing) (*grudged paying so much*).

grudge match *n.* esp. *N Amer.* a contest or competition involving antipathy between competitors.

grudging *adj.* reluctant; not willing. □ **grudgingly** *adv.* **grudgingness** *n.*

gruel *n.* a liquid food of oatmeal etc. boiled in milk or water.

gruelling (also **grueling**) ● *adj.* extremely demanding, severe, or tiring. ● *n.* a harsh or exhausting experience. □ **gruellingly** *adv.*

gruesome *adj.* horrible, grisly, disgusting. □ **gruesomely** *adv.* **gruesomeness** *n.*

gruff *adj.* **1 a** (of a voice) low and harsh. **b** (of a person) having a gruff voice. **2** surly, terse, rough-mannered. □ **gruffly** *adv.* **gruffness** *n.*

grumble ● *v.* **1** *intr.* **a** (often foll. by *at, about, over*) complain peevishly. **b** be discontented. **2** *intr.* **a** murmur. **b** rumble. **3** *tr.* (often foll. by *out*) utter complainingly. ● *n.* **1** a complaint. **2 a** a murmur. **b** a rumble. □ **grumbler** *n.* **grumbling** *adj. & n.* **grumblingly** *adv.* **grumbly** *adj.*

grump *informal* ● *n.* **1** a grumpy person. **2** (in *pl.*) a fit of sulks. ● *v.* **1** *intr.* be grumpy. **2** *tr.* utter grumpily.

grumpy *adj.* **(-ier, -iest)** morosely irritable; surly. □ **grumpily** *adv.* **grumpiness** *n.*

Grundy *n.* (*pl.* **-ies**) (in full **Mrs. Grundy**) a person embodying narrow-minded propriety and prudery.

grunge *n.* **1** esp. *N Amer.* grime, dirt. **2** an aggressive style of rock music characterized by a raucous guitar sound and lazy delivery (also *attrib.*: *grunge band*). **3** a style of dress associated with this music, characterized by loose-fitting, often second-hand clothes. □ **grunginess** *n.* **grungy** *adj.* **(-ier, -iest)**.

grunt ● *n.* **1** a low guttural sound made by a pig. **2** a sound resembling this. **3** *slang* a low-ranking labourer (also *attrib.*: *grunt work*). **4** *N Amer. slang* an infantry soldier. **5** any of numerous tropical marine fishes of the family Haemulidae, which produce a grunting sound by grinding together the pharyngeal teeth. **6** *N Amer.* a dessert of berries (esp. blueberries) baked with a doughy topping. ● *v.* **1** *intr.* (of a pig) make a grunt or grunts. **2** *intr.* (of a person) make a low inarticulate sound resembling this, esp. to express fatigue etc. **3** *tr.* utter with a grunt.

grunter *n.* **1** a person or animal that grunts, esp. a pig. **2** a grunting fish, esp. = GRUNT *n.* 5.

Gruyère /'ɡruːjɛr/ *n.* a firm pale yellow cheese made from cow's milk.

gryphon *var. of* GRIFFIN.

GSC *abbr.* Geological Survey of Canada.

G-spot *n.* a highly sensitive and erogenous area of the anterior wall of the vagina.

GST *abbr. Cdn & NZ* GOODS AND SERVICES TAX.

G-string *n.* **1** a narrow strip of cloth etc. covering only the genitals and attached to a string around the waist, as worn esp. by strippers. **2** (usu. **G string**) *Music* a string sounding the note G.

G-suit *n.* a garment with inflatable pressurized pouches, worn by pilots and astronauts to enable them to withstand high acceleration.

GT *n.* a fast high-performance luxury touring sedan.

Gt. *abbr.* Great.

GTA *abbr.* Greater Toronto Area.

GTi /dʒiːtiːˈaɪ/ *adj.* designating a high-performance car with a fuel-injected engine.

guacamole /ˌɡwɒkəˈmoʊli/ *n.* a dip or spread made from mashed avocados mixed with chopped onion, tomatoes, chili peppers, and seasoning.

guanine /'ɡwɒniːn/ *n.* a purine found in all living organisms as a component base of DNA and RNA.

guano /'ɡwɒnoʊ/ (*pl.* **-os**) ● *n.* **1** the excrement of seabirds, esp. that found in the islands off Peru and used as manure. **2** artificial manure, esp. made from fish. ● *v.tr.* **(-oes, -oed)** fertilize with guano.

guar /ɡwɑr/ *n.* a drought-resistant leguminous plant, *Cyamopsis tetragonoloba*, grown esp. in the Indian subcontinent as a vegetable and fodder crop and as a source of guar gum.

guarantee ● *n.* **1 a** a formal promise or assurance,

esp. that an obligation will be fulfilled or that something is of a specified quality and durability. **b** a document giving such an undertaking. **2** = GUARANTY. **3** a person making a guaranty or giving a security. **4** a thing that makes something certain to happen or be the case (*there's no guarantee that she will come*). ● *v.tr.* (**guarantees**, **guaranteed**) **1 a** give or serve as a guarantee for; answer for the due fulfillment of (a contract etc.) or the genuineness of (an article). **b** assure the permanence etc. of. **c** provide with a guarantee. **2** (foll. by *that* + clause, or *to* + infin.) give a promise or assurance. **3 a** (foll. by *to*) secure the possession of (a thing) for a person. **b** make (a person) secure against a risk or in possession of a thing.

Guaranteed Income Supplement *n. Cdn* a federally-supported supplement to the monthly pension payments of those with little income other than that derived from Old Age Security. Abbr.: **GIS**.

guaranteed investment certificate *n. Cdn* a certificate guaranteeing a fixed interest rate on a sum of money deposited for a fixed term, usu. between one and seven years, which may not be withdrawn before term. Abbr.: **GIC**.

guarantor /ˈgerən,tɔr, ˈgerəntɜr, ˈgær-/ *n.* a person who gives a guarantee or guaranty.

guaranty /ˈgerənti, ˈgær-/ *n.* (*pl.* **-ies**) **1** a written or other undertaking to answer for the payment of a debt or for the performance of an obligation by another person liable in the first instance. **2** a thing serving as security for a guaranty.

guard ● *v.* **1** *tr.* (often foll. by *from*, *against*) watch over and defend or protect from harm. **2** *tr.* keep watch by (a door etc.) so as to control entry or exit. **3** *tr.* supervise (prisoners etc.) and prevent from escaping. **4** *tr.* provide (machinery) with a protective device. **5** *tr.* keep (thoughts or speech) in check. **6** *tr.* provide with safeguards. **7** *intr.* (foll. by *against*) take precautions. **8** *tr.* (in various games) protect (a piece, card, etc.) with set moves. ● *n.* **1** a state of vigilance or watchfulness. **2** a person who keeps watch at a prison etc., or who protects. **3** a body of soldiers etc. serving to protect a place or person. **4** a part of an army detached for some purpose (*advance guard*). **5** (in *pl.*) (usu. **Guards**) any of various bodies of troops nominally employed to guard a ruler. **6 a** a thing that protects or defends. **b** a piece of protective equipment designed to prevent injury to a usu. specified part of the body (*mouth guard*). **7** (often in *comb.*) a device fitted to a machine, weapon, etc., to prevent injury or accident to the user. **8** a protective or defensive player, esp.: **a** (in football) the player on either side of the centre on the offensive line. **b** (in basketball) either of the two players positioned in the backcourt. **9** (in curling) a rock positioned in front of the house to protect those behind it. □ **be on** (or **keep** or **stand**) **guard** (of a sentry etc.) keep watch. **lower one's guard** (also **let one's guard down**) reduce vigilance against attack. **off** (or **off one's**) **guard** unprepared for some surprise or difficulty. **on** (or **on one's**) **guard** prepared for all contingencies; vigilant. **raise one's guard** become vigilant against attack.

guard dog *n.* = WATCHDOG 1.

guarded *adj.* **1** (of a remark etc.) cautious, avoiding commitment. **2** defended, protected; kept under guard. □ **guardedly** *adv.* **guardedness** *n.*

guardian *n.* **1** a defender, protector, or keeper. **2** a person having legal custody of another person and his or her property when that person is incapable of managing his or her own affairs. □ **guardianship** *n.*

guardian angel *n.* a spirit conceived as watching over a specific person or place.

guardrail *n.* a rail fitted as a support or to prevent an accident, e.g. along the edge of a highway or balcony.

guardsman *n.* (*pl.* **-men**) a soldier belonging to a body of guards.

guar gum *n.* a fine powder obtained by grinding the endosperm of seeds of guar, used in the food, paper, and other industries.

Guatemalan /ˌgwɒtəˈmɒlən/ ● *n.* a native or inhabitant of Guatemala, a country in Central America. ● *adj.* of or relating to Guatemala.

guava /ˈgwɒvə/ *n.* **1** a small tropical American tree, *Psidium guajava*, bearing an edible pale yellow fruit with pink juicy flesh. **2** this fruit.

gubernatorial /ˌgu:bɜrnəˈtɔriəl/ *adj.* esp. *US* of or relating to a governor.

guck *n.* esp. *N Amer.* slang a sticky or slimy substance.

Guernsey /ˈgɜrnzi/ *n.* (*pl.* **-eys**) a light brown and white dairy cow of a breed originally from Guernsey in the Channel Islands.

guerrilla *n.* (also **guerilla**) **1** a person taking part in an irregular war waged by small bands operating independently, often against a stronger, more organized force, with surprise attacks etc. (also *attrib.*: *guerrilla warfare*). **2** *informal* an activist using controversial or sensational means to support a cause.

guess ● *v.* **1** *tr. & intr.* estimate without calculation or measurement, or on the basis of inadequate data. **2** *tr.* form a hypothesis or opinion about; conjecture; think likely (*I guess it to be around noon*). **3** *tr.* estimate correctly by guessing (*you have to guess the weight*). **4** *intr.* (foll. by *at*) make a conjecture about. **5** *tr. informal* suppose (*I guess you're right*). ● *n.* **1** an estimate or conjecture reached by guessing. **2** an act or instance of guessing. □ **anybody's** (or **anyone's**) **guess** something difficult to determine. **I guess** *informal* I suppose. **keep a person guessing** *informal* withhold information. □ **guessable** *adj.* **guesser** *n.*

guessing game *n. informal* a situation in which desired information is withheld.

guesstimate *informal* ● *n.* /ˈgestɪmət/ an estimate based more on guesswork than calculation. ● *v.tr. & intr.* /ˈgestɪmeɪt/ form a guesstimate of.

guesswork *n.* the process of or results obtained by guessing.

guest ● *n.* **1** a person (usu. invited) visiting another's house or invited to have a meal etc. at the expense of the inviter. **2** a person lodging at a hotel, boarding house, etc. **3 a** a visiting performer invited to take part with a regular body of performers (also *attrib.*: *guest artist*). **b** a person who takes part by invitation in a radio or television program (often *attrib.*: *guest star*). **4** a person attending a social gathering at the request of or accompanying someone invited specifically. **5** (*attrib.*) **a** a serving or set aside for guests (*guest room*). **b** acting as a guest (*guest speaker*). ● *v.intr.* be a guest on a radio or television show or in a theatrical performance etc. □ **be my guest** *informal* make what use you wish of the available facilities.

guest book *n.* a book in which visitors or guests write their names or record comments.

guest house *n.* a private house offering paid accommodation.

guestimate *var. of* GUESSTIMATE.

guest of honour *n.* the most important guest.

guest ranch *n. N Amer.* a ranch where guests pay to lodge and participate in daily activities.

guff *n. slang* **1** nonsense; foolish talk. **2** insolent talk. □ **no guff** *Cdn* **1** a declaration of truthfulness. **2** an expression of mock surprise at a statement.

guffaw ● n. a coarse or boisterous laugh. ● v. **1** intr. utter a guffaw. **2** tr. say with a guffaw.

GUI /'guːiː/ n. Computing a graphical user interface.

guidance n. **1** advice or information aimed at resolving a problem, difficulty, etc. **2** the process of guiding or being guided. **3** the control of a missile or spacecraft in its course.

guidance counsellor n. N Amer. a person, esp. at a school, who counsels others regarding career decisions etc. □ **guidance counselling** n.

guide ● n. **1** a person who leads or shows the way, or directs the movements of a person or group. **2 a** a person who conducts travellers on tours etc. **b** a professional mountain climber in charge of a group. **c** someone hired to lead a hunting or fishing expedition. **3** an adviser. **4** a directing principle or standard (let your conscience be your guide). **5** a book with essential information on a subject, esp. = GUIDEBOOK 1. **6** a thing marking a position or guiding the eye. **7** a soldier, vehicle, or ship whose position determines the movements of others. **8** Mech. **a** a bar, rod, etc., directing the motion of something. **b** a gauge etc. controlling a tool. **9** (**Guide**) Cdn, Brit., Austral., & NZ = GIRL GUIDE. ● v.tr. **1 a** act as guide to; lead or direct. **b** arrange the course of (events). **2** be the principle, motive, or ground of (an action, judgment, etc.). **3** direct the affairs of (a nation etc.). □ **guidable** adj. **guider** n.

guidebook n. **1** a book of information about a place for visitors, tourists, etc. **2** a manual or handbook.

guided missile n. a missile directed to its target by remote control or by equipment within itself.

guide dog n. a dog trained to guide a blind person.

guideline n. (often in pl.) a principle or criterion guiding or directing action.

Guiding n. the Girl Guide movement. **1** an association of people for mutual aid or the pursuit of a common goal. **2** a medieval association of craftsmen or merchants.

guile n. clever and esp. deceitful behaviour. □ **guileful** adj. **guileless** adj. **guilelessly** adv.

guillemot /'gɪlə,mɒt/ n. any of several diving seabirds of northern latitudes constituting the genera Uria and Cepphus, of the auk family, with black (or brown) and white plumage and pointed bills.

guillotine /'gɪlə,tiːn, 'giːə-/ ● n. **1** hist. a machine with a heavy knife blade sliding vertically in grooves, used for beheading. **2** a device for cutting paper, metal, etc. **3** Parl. a method of preventing delay in the discussion of a legislative bill by fixing times at which various parts of it must be voted on. ● v.tr. **1** use a guillotine on. **2** Parl. end discussion of (a bill) by applying a guillotine.

guilt n. **1** the fact of having committed a specified or implied offence. **2 a** culpability. **b** the feeling of this. □ **guilt by association** guilt ascribed to a person not because of any evidence but because of his or her association with an offender.

guilt complex n. a mental obsession with the idea of having done wrong.

guiltless adj. **1** (often foll. by of an offence) innocent; not blameworthy. **2** (foll. by of) not having knowledge or possession of. □ **guiltlessly** adv. **guiltlessness** n.

guilt trip ● n. **1** an intense feeling of guilt, esp. induced by others pointing out offences. **2** an attempt to make another feel guilty by pointing out (supposed) offences. ● v.tr. (**guilt-trip**) (**-tripped**, **-tripping**) attempt to induce a feeling of guilt in (someone), esp. by pointing out (supposed) offences.

guilty adj. (**-ier**, **-iest**) **1** culpable of or responsible for a wrong. **2** conscious of or affected by guilt (a guilty

conscience). **3** concerning guilt (a guilty secret). **4 a** (often foll. by of) having committed a (specified) offence. **b** Law adjudged to have committed a specified offence. □ **guiltily** adv. **guiltiness** n.

guinea fowl n. any originally African fowl of the family Numididae, esp. Numida meleagris, with slate-coloured white-spotted plumage, raised for food.

guinea pig n. **1** a domesticated S American rodent, Cavia porcellus, kept as a pet or for research. **2** a person or thing used as a subject for experiment.

guise n. **1** an assumed appearance; a pretense (under the guise of friendship). **2** external appearance.

guitar n. a usu. six-stringed musical instrument with a fretted fingerboard. □ **guitarist** n.

gulag /'guːlæg/ n. **1** (also **Gulag**) hist. **a** the system of forced-labour camps in the Soviet Union, esp. in the period 1930–55. **b** a camp or prison within this system. **2** any extremely oppressive environment.

gulch /gʌltʃ/ n. N Amer. **1** a ravine, esp. one in which a stream flows. **2** a steep, narrow ravine or cove cutting inland from a shoreline cliff.

gulf n. **1** a stretch of sea consisting of a deep inlet with a narrow mouth. **2** (**the Gulf**) **a** the Gulf of Mexico. **b** the Persian Gulf. **c** the Gulf of St. Lawrence. **3** a deep hollow; a chasm or abyss. **4** a wide difference of feelings, opinion, etc.

Gulf War syndrome n. a disorder of the nervous system alleged to have been contracted by soldiers serving in the Gulf War of 1991.

gull[1] n. any of various long-winged web-footed birds of the family Laridae, usu. having white and black or grey plumage and a bright bill.

gull[2] v.tr. (usu. in passive; foll. by into) dupe, fool.

gullet n. **1** the food passage extending from the mouth to the stomach; the esophagus. **2** the throat.

gullible adj. easily persuaded or deceived; credulous. □ **gullibility** n. **gullibly** adv.

gull-wing adj. **1** (of a car door) hinged along the top and opening outwards and upwards. **2** (of a car) having gull-wing doors.

gully ● n. (pl. **-ies**) (also **gulley** pl. **-eys**) **1** a small ravine, esp. formed by water flowing after heavy rain. **2** a deep artificial channel; a gutter or drain. ● v.tr. (**-ies**, **-ied**) **1** form (channels) by water action. **2** make gullies in.

gulp ● v. **1** tr. (often foll. by down) swallow hastily, or with effort. **2** intr. swallow gaspingly or with difficulty. **3** tr. (foll. by down, back) stifle, suppress (esp. tears). ● n. **1** an act of gulping. **2** an effort to swallow. **3** a large mouthful of a drink. □ **gulper** n. **gulpy** adj.

gum[1] ● n. **1 a** a viscous secretion of some trees and shrubs that hardens on drying but is soluble in water (compare RESIN 1). **b** an adhesive substance made from this. **2** N Amer. **a** = CHEWING GUM. **b** = BUBBLE GUM. **3** = GUM ARABIC. **4** = GUM TREE. ● v. (**gummed**, **gumming**) **1** tr. smear or cover with gum. **2** tr. (usu. foll. by down, together, etc.) fasten with gum. **3** tr. make (a birchbark canoe) watertight by sealing its seams with melted pine gum. **4** intr. exude gum. □ **gum up 1** (of a mechanism etc.) become clogged or obstructed with stickiness. **2** informal interfere with the smooth running of (gum up the works).

gum[2] ● n. (usu. in pl.) the firm flesh around the roots of the teeth. ● v.tr. (of someone without teeth) chew with the gums as though with teeth.

gum[3] n. informal (in oaths) God (by gum!).

gum arabic n. a gum exuded by some acacias, esp. Acacia senegal, used as glue and as an emulsifier.

gumbo n. (pl. **-os**) N Amer. **1 a** okra. **b** a spicy chicken or seafood soup thickened with okra, rice, etc. **2** a heavy clayey soil that is sticky and non-porous when wet; thick clinging mud.

gumboot *n.* a rubber boot usu. reaching the knee.

gumdrop *n.* a soft coloured candy made with gelatin or gum arabic.

gum line *n.* the point where the tooth protrudes from the gum.

gummi /ˈgʌmi/ *n.* a rubbery, coloured and flavoured candy, often in the shape of animals, insects, etc. (also *attrib.*: *gummi spiders*).

gummy¹ *adj.* (**-ier, -iest**) **1** viscous, sticky. **2** abounding in or exuding gum. □ **gumminess** *n.*

gummy² *adj.* (**-ier, -iest**) toothless. □ **gummily** *adv.*

gumption /ˈgʌmpʃən/ *n. informal* **1 a** initiative; enterprising spirit. **b** courage. **2** common sense.

gum resin *n.* a vegetable secretion of resin mixed with gum.

gumshoe ● *n.* **1** a galosh. **2** *N Amer. informal* a detective. ● *v.intr. N Amer. informal* (**-shoed, -shoeing**) **1** move or act stealthily **2** act as a detective.

gum tree *n.* a tree exuding gum, esp. a eucalyptus. □ **up a gum tree** *informal* in great difficulties.

gun ● *n.* **1** a kind of weapon (of any size from a hand-held pistol to a mounted piece of artillery), consisting of a metal tube from which bullets or other missiles are propelled with great force, esp. by a contained explosion. **2** any device imitative of this. **3** a device for discharging something under pressure (often in *comb.*: *grease gun*). **4** *N Amer.* a gunman. **5** the firing of a gun. **6** *N Amer. Sport informal* (esp. in hockey) a prolific scorer. ● *v.* (**gunned, gunning**) **1** *tr.* **a** (often foll. by *down*) shoot (a person) with a gun. **b** shoot at with a gun. **2** *tr. informal* accelerate (an engine or vehicle). **3** *intr.* go hunting with a gun. **4** *intr.* (foll. by *for*) **a** seek out determinedly to attack or rebuke. **b** go determinedly or energetically after. □ **go great guns** *informal* proceed forcefully or vigorously or successfully. **jump the gun** *informal* start before a signal is given, or before an agreed time. **stick to one's guns** *informal* maintain one's position under attack. **under the gun** *informal* under pressure (*we're under the gun to get this done*). □ **gunless** *adj.* **gunned** *adj.*

gunboat *n.* a small vessel of shallow draft and having relatively heavy guns.

gunboat diplomacy *n.* political negotiation supported by the use or threat of military force.

gun carriage *n.* a wheeled support for a gun.

gun control *n. N Amer.* the legislated regulation or restriction of private firearm ownership.

gun dog *n.* a dog bred or trained to assist hunters, e.g. by pointing, retrieving, flushing, etc.

gunfight *n.* a fight with firearms. □ **gunfighter** *n.*

gunfire *n.* **1** the firing of a gun or guns, esp. repeatedly. **2** the noise from this.

gunge *informal* ● *n.* = GUNK *n.* ● *v.tr.* (usu. foll. by *up*) clog or obstruct with gunge. □ **gungy** *adj.* (**-ier, -iest**).

gung-ho *adj.* **1** enthusiastic, eager. **2** uninhibited; quick to take action.

gunk *esp. N Amer. slang* ● *n.* sticky or viscous matter, esp. when messy. ● *v.tr.* (often foll. by *up*) soil or clog with gunk. □ **gunky** *adj.* (**-ier, -iest**).

gunlock *n.* a mechanism by which the charge of a gun is exploded.

gunman *n.* (*pl.* **-men**) a person armed with a gun, esp. in committing a crime.

gunmetal (in full **gunmetal grey, gunmetal blue**) ● *n.* **1** a dull bluish-grey colour. **2** an alloy of copper and tin or zinc, formerly used for guns. ● *adj.* dull bluish grey.

gunnel *var. of* GUNWALE.

gunner *n.* **1 a** (also **Gunner**) a private in the artillery. Abbr.: **Gnr. b** any member of the artillery. **2** a person who operates a gun, esp. on an aircraft or ship. **3** a person who hunts game with a gun.

gunnery *n.* **1** the design and operation of esp. large guns. **2** the firing of guns.

gunny *n.* (*pl.* **-ies**) *N Amer.* **1** coarse sacking, usu. of jute; burlap. **2** (in full **gunny sack**) a sack made of this.

gunplay *n.* the use of guns.

gunpoint *n.* the point of a gun. □ **at gunpoint** threatened with a gun or an ultimatum etc.

gunpowder *n.* an explosive powder made of potassium nitrate, sulphur, and charcoal, used for fuses, fireworks, and blasting.

gunroom *n.* a room in a house for storing guns.

gunrunner *n.* a person engaged in the illegal sale or importing of firearms etc. □ **gun-running** *n.*

gunship *n.* a heavily-armed helicopter etc.

gunshot *n.* **1** a shot fired from a gun. **2** the sound of this. **3** the range of a gun (*within gunshot*).

gun-shy *adj.* **1** (esp. of a hunting dog) afraid of a gun or the sound that it makes. **2** hesitant or nervous, esp. because of a previous unpleasant experience.

gunsight *n.* a sight on a gun (see SIGHT *n.* 7).

gunslinger *n. esp. US slang* a gunfighter. □ **gunslinging** *n. & adj.*

gunsmith *n.* a person who makes, sells, and repairs firearms. □ **gunsmithing** *n.*

gunstock *n.* the esp. wooden mounting for the barrel and firing mechanism of a rifle etc.

gunwale /ˈgʌnəl/ *n.* the upper edge of the side of a boat or ship.

guppy *n.* (*pl.* **-ies**) a small freshwater fish, *Poecilia reticulata*, of the W Indies and S America, frequently kept in aquariums, and giving birth to live young.

gurdwara /gɜrdˈwʊrə/ *n.* a Sikh temple.

gurdy *n.* (*pl.* **-ies**) *Cdn* a winch on a fishing boat used to haul in a line, net, etc.

gurgle ● *v.* **1** *intr.* make a bubbling sound as of water from a bottle or flowing over stones. **2** *intr.* (of liquid) flow with such a sound. **3** *tr.* utter with such a sound. ● *n.* a gurgling sound. □ **gurgly** *adj.*

Gurkha /ˈgɜrkə/ *n.* **1** a member of the principal Hindu race in Nepal. **2** a Nepalese soldier serving in the British army.

gurney /ˈgɜrni/ *n. N Amer.* a wheeled stretcher used to transport patients in a hospital etc.

gurry *n. N Amer.* fish entrails or offal as refuse from cleaning fish.

guru /ˈguːruː, ˈgoru/ *n.* **1** a Hindu spiritual teacher or head of a religious sect. **2** often *derogatory* **a** an influential teacher. **b** a revered mentor.

gush ● *v.* **1** *tr. & intr.* emit or flow in a sudden and copious stream. **2** *intr.* speak or behave with effusiveness or sentimental affectation. ● *n.* **1** a sudden or copious stream. **2** an effusive or sentimental outburst or manner. □ **gushing** *adj.*

gusher *n.* **1** an oil well from which oil flows without being pumped. **2** an effusive person.

gushy *adj.* (**-ier, -iest**) excessively effusive or sentimental. □ **gushily** *adv.* **gushiness** *n.*

gusset *n.* **1** a piece of material let into a garment etc. to strengthen or enlarge a part. **2** a bracket strengthening an angle of a structure.

gussy *v.tr.* (**-ies, -ied**) (esp. in *passive*; foll. by *up*) esp. *N Amer. informal* dress up, esp. for a special occasion.

gust ● *n.* **1** a sudden strong rush of wind. **2** a burst of rain, fire, smoke, or sound. **3** a passionate or emotional outburst. ● *v.intr.* blow in gusts.

gustatory /ˈgʌstəˌtɔri/ *adj.* concerned with tasting or the sense of taste. □ **gustatorial** *adv.*

gusto *n.* zest; enthusiasm or vigour.

gusty *adj.* (**-ier, -iest**) **1** characterized by or blowing in strong winds. **2** marked by sudden bursts of feeling or action. **3** characterized by gusto. □ **gustily** *adv.* **gustiness** *n.*

gut ● *n.* **1 a** the lower alimentary canal or a part of this; the intestine. **b** *informal* the abdomen or belly (*punched in the gut*). **2** (in *pl.*) the bowel or entrails, esp. of animals. **3** (in *pl.*) *informal* personal courage and determination; vigorous application and perseverance. **4** (in *pl.*) *informal* the belly as the source of appetite. **5** (in *pl.*) **a** the contents of anything, esp. representing substantiality. **b** the essence of a thing, e.g. of an issue or problem. **6 a** material for violin or racquet strings or surgical use made from the intestines of animals. **b** material for fishing lines made from the silk glands of silkworms. **7 a** a sound or strait. **b** a defile or narrow passage. **8** (*attrib.*) **a** instinctive (*a gut reaction*). **b** fundamental (*a gut issue*). ● *v.tr.* (**gutted, gutting**) **1** (often in *passive*) remove or destroy (esp. by fire) the internal fittings of (a house etc.). **2** take out the guts of (a fish). **3** remove the essential components of. **4** extract the essence of (a book etc.). □ **hate a person's guts** *informal* dislike a person intensely. **have someone's guts for garters** *Cdn & Brit.* be extremely angry at someone. **sweat** (or **work** etc.) **one's guts out** *informal* work etc. extremely hard or energetically.

gutbucket *adj.* designating a very spirited, robust, or raw style of music, esp. jazz.

gutless *adj.* *informal* lacking courage or determination. □ **gutlessly** *adv.* **gutlessness** *n.*

gut-level *attrib.adj.* instinctive; heartfelt.

gutsy *adj.* (**-ier, -iest**) *informal* courageous; tough. □ **gutsily** *adv.* **gutsiness** *n.*

gutta percha /ˌɡʌtəˈpɜrtʃə/ *n.* a tough plastic substance obtained from the latex of various trees.

gutted *adj.* *in senses of* GUT *v.*

gutter ● *n.* **1 a** a channel at the side of a street to carry away runoff. **b** esp. *US & Brit.* = EAVESTROUGH. **2** (*prec. by the*) **a** a poor or degraded background or environment (*worked their way out of the gutter*). **b** a sordid or vulgar situation (*get your mind out of the gutter*). **3** an open conduit or channel along which liquid etc. flows out. **4** a groove. **5** a track made by the flow of water. **6** the channel running along each side of a bowling lane. **7** the space between open pages of a book, magazine, etc. ● *v.* **1** *intr.* flow in streams. **2** *tr.* furrow, channel. **3** *intr.* **a** (of a candle) melt away as the wax forms channels down the side. **b** (of a candle flame) flicker before being extinguished, esp. as the last wax melts away.

gutter press *n.* sensational journalism concerned esp. with the private lives of public figures.

guttersnipe *n.* **1** a street urchin. **2** an ill-mannered street person or vagrant.

guttural /ˈɡʌtərəl/ *adj.* **1** (of a sound) produced at the back of the throat. **2** (of speech) characterized by guttural sounds. □ **gutturally** *adv.*

gutty *adj.* = GUTSY.

guy¹ ● *n.* **1** *informal* a man; a fellow. **2** (in *pl.*) *N Amer. informal* people of either sex. ● *v.tr.* ridicule.

guy² ● *n.* a rope or chain to secure a tent or steady a load etc. ● *v.tr.* secure with a guy or guys.

Guyanese /ˌɡaɪəˈniːz/ ● *n.* a native or inhabitant of Guyana in S America. ● *adj.* of or relating to Guyana.

guzzle *v.tr. & intr.* eat, drink, or consume excessively or greedily. □ **guzzler** *n.*

Gwich'in /ˈɡwɪtʃɪn/ ● *n.* **1** a member of an Aboriginal people living in Alaska, the Yukon, and the NWT. **2** the Athapaskan language of the Gwich'in. ● *adj.* of or relating to this people.

gybe /dʒaɪb/ ● *v.* **1** *intr.* (of a fore-and-aft sail or boom) swing across in running before the wind. **2** *tr.* cause (a sail) to do this. **3** *intr.* (of a ship or its crew) change course so that this happens. ● *n.* a change of course causing gybing.

gym *n.* *informal* **1** a gymnasium. **2** physical education. **3** gymnastics.

gymnasium *n.* (*pl.* **-s**) a room or building equipped for gymnastics, indoor sports, physical training, etc.

gymnast *n.* an expert in gymnastics.

gymnastic *adj.* of or involving gymnastics. □ **gymnastically** *adv.*

gymnastics *n.pl.* (also treated as *sing.*) **1** exercises developing or dis playing physical agility and co-ordination, usu. in competition. **2** other forms of physical or mental agility (*verbal gymnastics*).

gymnosperm /ˈdʒɪmnoʊˌspɜrm/ *n.* any of various plants having seeds unprotected by an ovary, including conifers, cycads, and ginkgos.

gym shoe *n.* = RUNNING SHOE.

gynecology /ˌɡaɪnəˈkɒlədʒi/ *n.* (also **gynaecology**) the science of the physiological functions and diseases of women and girls, esp. those affecting the reproductive system. □ **gynecologic** *adj.* **gynecological** *adj.* **gynecologically** *adv.* **gynecologist** *n.*

gyp *slang* ● *v.tr.* (**gypped, gypping**) cheat, swindle. ● *n.* an act of cheating; a swindle.

gyppo /ˈdʒɪpoʊ/ *n.* (also **gypo**) (usu. *attrib.*) *N Amer.* a minor or small-time logging operator or contractor.

gyppy tummy *var. of* GIPPY TUMMY.

gyproc /ˈdʒɪprɒk/ *n.* (also **gyprock**) = DRYWALL *n.*

gypsum /ˈdʒɪpsəm/ *n.* a hydrated form of calcium sulphate occurring naturally and used in the building industry and to make plaster of Paris.

gypsumboard *n.* *N Amer.* = DRYWALL.

gypsy *n.* (*pl.* **-ies**) **1** (also **Gypsy**) a member of a nomadic people of Europe and N America, of Hindu origin, speaking a language (Romany) related to Hindi. **2** a person resembling or living like a Gypsy.

gypsy moth *n.* a kind of moth, *Lymantria dispar*, of which the larvae are very destructive to foliage.

gyrate ● *v.intr.* **1** revolve around a fixed point or axis; go in a circle or spiral. **2** move one's hips rhythmically in a circular pattern, esp. in a sexually suggestive way. ● *adj.* *Bot.* arranged in rings or convolutions. □ **gyration** *n.* **gyrator** *n.*

gyre /ˈdʒaɪr/ esp. *literary* ● *v.intr.* whirl, gyrate. ● *n.* **1** a whirling, a vortex; a gyration. **2** a circulatory ocean current.

gyrfalcon /ˈdʒɜrˌfɒlkən/ *n.* a large falcon, *Falco rusticolus*, of the northern hemisphere.

gyro¹ /ˈdʒaɪroʊ/ *n.* (*pl.* **-os**) *informal* **1** = GYROSCOPE. **2** = GYROCOMPASS.

gyro² /ˈjiːroʊ/ *n.* (*pl.* **-os**) *N Amer.* a sandwich of pita bread filled with slices of spiced meat cooked on a spit, tomatoes, onions, etc.

gyrocompass /ˈdʒaɪroʊˌkʌmpəs/ *n.* a non-magnetic compass giving true north and bearings from it by means of a gyroscope.

gyroscope /ˈdʒaɪrəˌskoʊp/ *n.* a wheel or disc mounted so as to spin rapidly about an axis whose orientation is not fixed but is unperturbed by tilting of the mount, esp. used in stabilizers, gyrocompasses, navigation systems, etc. □ **gyroscopic** *adj.*

Hh

H¹ *n.* (also **h**) (*pl.* **Hs** or **H's**) **1** the eighth letter of the alphabet. **2** anything having the form of an H (esp. in *comb.*: *H-girder*).

H² *abbr.* (also **H.**) **1** hardness. **2** (of a pencil lead) hard. **3** *slang* heroin.

H³ *symbol* hydrogen.

h¹ *abbr.* (also **h.**) **1** height. **2** hot. **3** hour(s). **4** husband. **5** *Baseball* hit. **6** hundred.

h² *symbol* hecto-.

Ha *symbol* hahnium.

ha¹ *interj.* expressing surprise, suspicion, triumph, etc.

ha² *abbr.* hectare(s).

habanero /ˌhæbəˈnero/ *n.* a small, green, fiery hot chili pepper.

habeas corpus /ˌheibiəs ˈkɔrpəs/ *n.* **1** a writ requiring a person to be brought before a judge or into court, esp. to investigate the lawfulness of his or her detention. **2** the right to such a writ as protection against unlawful detention.

haberdasher /ˈhæbərˌdæʃər/ *n.* *N Amer.* a dealer in men's clothing and accessories.

haberdashery *n.* (*pl.* **-ies**) **1** the goods and wares sold by a haberdasher. **2** the shop or establishment of a haberdasher, esp. as a department in a store.

habit *n.* **1** (often foll. by *of* + verbal noun) a customary practice or way of acting (*has a habit of ignoring me*). **2** a practice that a person does often and almost without thinking, esp. one that is hard to give up. **3** a person's mental or moral constitution, disposition, qualities, or character. **4** *Psych.* an automatic reaction to a specific situation, acquired by learning or repetition. **5** *informal* **a** a craving for or dependency on an addictive drug or drugs. **b** the practice of taking such a drug or drugs. **6 a** the dress of a particular religious order. **b** (in full **riding habit**) an outfit designed to be worn by a rider on horseback. **7** physical appearance or constitution. **8** *Biol.* & *Mineralogy* the characteristic mode of growth and general external form of a plant or mineral. □ **make a habit of** do regularly.

habitable *adj.* fit or suitable for habitation; that can be inhabited. □ **habitability** *n.*

habitant /ˌæbiˈtɑ̃/ *n.* *hist.* (in Canada) a French settler in rural Quebec, esp. a farmer.

habitat *n.* **1 a** the natural environment characteristically occupied by an organism. **b** an area distinguished by the set of organisms which occupy it. **c** such areas collectively. **2** a dwelling place.

habitation *n.* **1** the action of dwelling in or inhabiting. **2** a house or home.

habit-forming *adj.* causing addiction.

habitual *adj.* **1** done constantly or as a habit. **2** regular, continual, usual. **3** given to a specified habit (*a habitual smoker*). □ **habitually** *adv.*

habituate /həˈbɪtʃʊˌeit/ *v.tr.* (often foll. by *to*) make used to something; accustom. □ **habituation** *n.*

habitué /həˈbɪtʃʊˌei/ *n.* a habitual visitor to a place.

háček /ˈhætʃek/ *n.* a diacritic mark (ˇ) placed over letters to modify the sound in some Slavic and Baltic languages.

hacienda /ˌhæsiˈendə/ *n.* (in Spanish-speaking countries) **1** an estate or plantation, esp. one used for farming or ranching. **2** the house on such an estate.

hack¹ ● *v.* **1** *tr.* cut or chop with heavy blows, esp. in a rough or random fashion. **2** *intr.* (often foll. by *at*) deliver cutting blows. **3** *tr.* cut (a trail, one's way, etc.) through thick foliage etc. **4** *tr.* (of an editor etc.) shorten (a piece of writing, film footage, etc.), esp. detrimentally. **5** *informal* **a** *intr.* (usu. foll. by *into*) use a computer to gain unauthorized access to data in a system. **b** *tr.* gain unauthorized access to (data in a computer etc.). **6** *tr.* *slang* cope with, manage, tolerate, or accept. **7** *intr.* cough repeatedly with a short, dry cough. ● *n.* **1** an act of hacking or chopping, esp. a hacking blow. **2** a gash or wound, esp. from a kick. **3** an implement used in agriculture, mining, etc. for breaking or chopping up, esp. a two-pronged tool resembling a mattock. **4** a short, dry, hard cough. **5** *Curling* a rubber, metal, or wooden insert in the ice, used as a starting block to steady the foot when delivering a stone. **6** *informal* an attempt to break into a computer system. □ **hack around** *informal* **1** idly pass the time or wander aimlessly. **2** pass the time by computer hacking.

hack² ● *n.* **1 a** a writer of mediocre literary or journalistic work. **b** *informal usu. derogatory* a journalist. **2** a person hired to do dull routine work. **3** *N Amer.* **a** a taxi. **b** a taxi driver. **4 a** a horse for ordinary riding. **b** a horse that may be hired. **c** = JADE 3. ● *attrib.adj.* **1** typical of a hack; commonplace (*hack work*). **2** used as a hack. ● *v.* **1** *intr.* write like or work as a hack. **2 a** *intr.* ride on horseback on a road at an ordinary pace. **b** *tr.* ride (a horse) in this way.

hackberry *n.* (*pl.* **-ies**) *N Amer.* **1** any tree of the genus *Celtis*, native to N America, bearing purple edible berries. **2** the berry of this tree.

hacker *n.* **1** a person or thing that hacks or cuts roughly. **2** *informal* **a** a computer user who attempts to gain unauthorized access to computer systems. **b** a computer user who is expert in programming. **3** *N Amer.* a person who engages in esp. a sporting activity in an unskilful fashion. □ **hackery** *n.*

hacking *adj.* (of a cough) short, dry, and persistent.

hackle *n.* **1** a long feather or series of feathers on the neck or saddle of certain birds, e.g. the domestic rooster. **2** (in *pl.*) the erectile hairs along the back of a dog, which rise when it is angry or alarmed. **3** *Fishing* an artificial fly dressed wholly or chiefly with a hackle. □ **make a person's hackles rise** or **raise some** (or **a person's**) **hackles** annoy a person.

hackney *n.* (*pl.* **-eys**) **1 a** a light harness horse with a compact body and a characteristic high-stepping trot. **b** a horse of average size and quality for ordinary riding. **2** (*attrib.*) designating any of various vehicles kept for hire (*hackney carriage*).

hackneyed *adj.* (of a phrase etc.) made commonplace or trite by overuse.

hacksaw *n.* a saw with a narrow blade set in a frame, for cutting metal.

had *past* and *past part.* of HAVE.

haddock /ˈhædək/ n. (pl. same) a marine fish, *Melanogrammus aeglefinus*, of the N Atlantic.

hadj var. of HAJJ.

hadji var. of HAJJI.

hadn't contraction had not.

hadrosaur /ˈhadrəsɔːr/ n. a large herbivorous usu. bipedal dinosaur of the family Hadrosauridae, of the late Cretaceous period, with jaws flattened like the bill of a duck.

haem esp. Brit. var. of HEME.

haemato- etc. esp. Brit. var. of HEMATO- etc.

haemo- etc. esp. Brit. var. of HEMO- etc.

hafnium /ˈhæfniəm/ n. a silvery lustrous metallic element occurring naturally with zirconium, used in tungsten alloys for filaments and electrodes.

haft ● n. the handle of a dagger or knife etc. ● v.tr. provide with a haft.

hag n. 1 an ugly old woman. 2 a witch.

Haggadah /həˈɡædə, hæɡæˈdæ/ n. (pl. **-dahs, -doth**) 1 the non-legal element of the Talmud, consisting esp. of illustrative legends or parables (compare HALACHA). 2 a book containing the text recited at the Seder, on the first two nights of Passover.

haggard /ˈhæɡəd/ adj. looking exhausted and distraught, esp. from fatigue, worry, privation, etc. □ **haggardly** adv. **haggardness** n.

haggis /ˈhæɡɪs/ n. a Scottish dish consisting of a sheep's or calf's offal mixed with suet, oatmeal, etc., and boiled in a bag made from the animal's stomach or in an artificial bag.

haggle ● v.intr. (often foll. by about, over) dispute or wrangle over a price, deal, etc. ● n. a dispute, esp. about a price etc. □ **haggler** n. **haggling** n.

Hagiographa /ˌhæɡiˈɒɡrəfə/ n. the last of the three canonical divisions of the Hebrew Scriptures, additional to the Law and the Prophets.

hagiographer /ˌhæɡiˈɒɡrəfər/ n. 1 a writer of the lives of saints. 2 a writer of any of the Hagiographa.

hagiography n. (pl. **-ies**) 1 the writing of the lives of saints. 2 an idealized biography of any person. □ **hagiographic** adj. **hagiographical** adj.

hah var. of HA¹.

ha ha interj. representing laughter.

hahnium /ˈhɒniəm/ n. an artificially produced radioactive element.

Haida /ˈhaɪdə/ ● n. 1 (pl. same or **Haidas**) a member of an Aboriginal people living on the west coast of Canada. 2 the language of this people. ● adj. of or relating to this people or their language or culture.

haiku /ˈhaɪkuː/ n. (pl. same) 1 a type of very short Japanese poem, having three parts, usu. 17 syllables, and often about a subject in nature. 2 an imitation of this in another language.

hail¹ ● n. 1 pellets of frozen rain falling in showers from cumulonimbus clouds. 2 (foll. by of) a barrage or onslaught (of bullets, curses, questions, etc.). ● v. 1 intr. (prec. by it as subject) hail falls (it is hailing; if it hails). 2 tr. pour down (blows, words, etc.).

hail² ● v. 1 tr. (often foll. by as) acclaim, commend, or endorse vigorously (hailed as a success). 2 tr. signal to or attract the attention of (hailed a taxi). 3 intr. (foll. by from) (of a person) have one's home or origins in (a place) (hails from Windsor). 4 tr. greet enthusiastically. ● interj. expressing greeting. ● n. a greeting or act of hailing. □ **hailer** n.

Hail Mary n. 1 the prayer to the Virgin Mary beginning with the words used by Gabriel in Luke 1:28 and incorporating Elizabeth's words from Luke 1:42. 2

N Amer. Football a long pass made in the final seconds of a half or game as a desperate effort to score.

hailstone n. a pellet of hail.

hailstorm n. a period of heavy hail.

hair n. 1 a any of the fine threadlike strands growing from the skin of mammals, esp. from the human head. b these collectively (has red hair). 2 anything resembling a hair. 3 a fine, elongated plant structure, esp. an outgrowth from the epidermis of a plant, e.g. a root hair. 4 a very small degree, quantity, or extent. □ **get in a person's hair** informal persistently irritate or annoy a person. **hair of the dog (that bit you)** an alcoholic drink taken to cure a hangover. **let one's hair down** informal abandon restraint, behave freely or wildly. **make one's hair stand on end** alarm or horrify one. **not turn a hair** remain apparently unmoved or unaffected. □ **haired** adj. (also in comb.). **hairless** adj. **hairlike** adj.

hairball n. a ball of hair which collects in the stomach of a cat etc. as a result of the animal licking its coat.

hairbrush n. a brush for arranging the hair.

hair colour n. a dye, tint, etc. used on the hair. □ **hair colouring** n. **hair colourist** n.

haircut n. 1 an act of cutting the hair. 2 the style in which the hair is cut. □ **haircutter** n. **haircutting** n.

hairdo n. (pl. **-dos**) the particular way in which esp. a woman's hair is styled.

hairdresser n. 1 a person who cuts and styles hair, esp. professionally. 2 the business or establishment of a hairdresser. □ **hairdressing** n.

hair dryer n. an electrical device for drying the hair by blowing warm air over it.

hairline n. 1 the natural line on a person's head or forehead at which the hair stops growing. 2 (also attrib.) a very thin line or crack. (hairline fracture).

hairnet n. a fine, light net worn on the head to keep the hair in place.

hairpiece n. a piece of false hair augmenting a person's natural hair or covering a bald spot.

hairpin n. 1 a U-shaped pin for fastening the hair. 2 (usu. attrib.) (of a bend in a road etc.) curving sharply.

hair-raising adj. extremely alarming; terrifying.

hair shirt n. 1 a shirt of cloth woven from hair, worn by penitents and ascetics. 2 (**hair-shirt**) (attrib.) austere, harsh, self-sacrificing.

hairsplitting adj. & n. making excessively fine distinctions; quibbling. □ **hairsplitter** n.

hairspray n. a fixative solution sprayed onto the hair to keep it in place.

hairstyle n. a particular way of arranging or dressing the hair. □ **hairstyling** n. **hairstylist** n.

hair-trigger n. 1 a trigger of a firearm set for release at the slightest pressure. 2 (usu. attrib.) (of a reaction, mood, etc.) quickly and easily provoked.

hairy adj. (**-ier, -iest**) 1 made of or covered with hair. 2 having the feel or appearance of hair. 3 slang difficult, frightening, or problematic. □ **hairiness** n.

hairy woodpecker n. a large black and white N American woodpecker, *Picoides villosus*.

Haisla /ˈhaɪslə/ ● n. (pl. same or **Haislas**) 1 a member of a major language group of northern Wakashan, of which the Kitamaat in BC are the only survivors. 2 the language of the Haisla. ● adj. of or relating to this people or their culture or language.

Haitian /ˈheɪʃən/ ● n. 1 a native or inhabitant of Haiti, a country in the Caribbean. 2 (also **Haitian Creole**) the French-based Creole language spoken in Haiti. ● adj. of the Haitians or their language.

hajj /hædʒ/ n. the pilgrimage to Mecca undertaken in the twelfth month of the Muslim year, constituting one of the religious duties of Islam.

hajji /'hædʒi/ n. (pl. **-is**) a Muslim who has been to Mecca as a pilgrim: also (**Hajji**) used as a title.

hake n. **1** any of various blue-grey and silver fishes related to the cod, of shallow temperate seas, of the genus *Merluccius* or the family Merlucciidae. **2** either of two reddish-brown food fishes related to the cod, *Urophycis chuss* and *U. tenuis*, of the NW Atlantic.

Halacha /hɔ'lɒxə/ n. (also **Halakah**) Jewish law and jurisprudence, based on the Talmud, esp. the Mishna, and subsequent rabbinical rulings (compare HAGGADAH 1). □ **Halachic** adj.

halal /hæ'læl/ ● v.tr. (**halalled**, **halalling**) kill (an animal) as prescribed by Muslim law. ● n. (often attrib.) meat prepared in this way.

Halcion /'hælsi:ɒn/ n. N Amer. proprietary a tranquilizer of the benzodiazepine group.

halcyon /'hælsiən/ ● adj. **1** calm, peaceful (*halcyon days*). **2** (of a period) happy, prosperous. ● n. any kingfisher of the genus *Halcyon*, native to Europe, Africa, and Australasia, with brightly coloured plumage.

hale[1] adj. (esp. of an old person) strong and healthy (esp. in **hale and hearty**). □ **haleness** n.

hale[2] v.tr. drag or draw forcibly.

half ● n. (pl. **halves**) **1** either of two equal or corresponding parts, groups, etc. into which a thing is or might be divided. **2** either of two equal periods of play in sports, usu. separated by an interval or intermission. **3** esp. *Soccer & Rugby informal* = HALFBACK. **4** informal half a pint, esp. of beer etc. ● adj. **1** of an amount or quantity equal to a half, or loosely, to a part thought of as roughly a half (*spent half the time reading*; *half a pint*; *half-price*). **2** forming a half (*a half share*). **3** partial, incomplete, imperfect, or falling short of a full or perfect amount, degree, type, etc. (*half measures*). ● adv. **1** (often in comb.) partly, nearly, or to the extent of half (*only half cooked*; *half-laughing*). **2** to a certain extent, somewhat, esp. in idiomatic phrases (*half-dead*; *am half inclined to agree*). **3** (in reckoning time) by the amount of half (an hour etc.) (*half past two*). □ **by half** (prec. by too + adj.) excessively (*too clever by half*). **by halves** imperfectly or incompletely (*never does things by halves*). **go halves** (or **half and half**) share equally in something with another person. **half a chance** informal the slightest opportunity (esp. *given half a chance*). **the half of it** informal the rest or more important part of something (usu. after neg.: *you don't know the half of it*). **half past** (of time) thirty minutes past the hour. **not half 1** not nearly (*not half long enough*). **2** informal not at all (*not half bad*).

half a dozen var. of HALF-DOZEN.

half-and-half ● adv. in equal parts. ● adj. that is half one thing and half another. ● n. **1** something that is half one thing and half another. **2** N Amer. a mixture of milk and cream having 10% milk fat, used esp. in coffee.

half-assed slang ● adj. incompetent, inadequate. ● adv. in an inadequate, inept fashion.

halfback n. **1** Football a back lined up beside the fullback. **2** Soccer a player positioned behind the forwards and in front of the fullbacks. **3** Rugby a forward playing primarily in an offensive capacity.

half-baked adj. **1** incompletely considered or planned. **2** stupid or foolish.

half-blood n. **1** a person having one parent in common with another. **2** this relationship. **3** = HALF-BREED.

half board n. provision of bed, breakfast, and one main meal at a hotel etc.

half-bottle n. **1** a bottle that is half the standard size. **2** its contents or the amount that will fill it.

half-breed n. offensive a person of mixed race.

half-brother n. a male related to one or more other persons, male or female, by having one biological parent in common.

half-circle n. a semicircle.

half-cock n. the position of the hammer of a gun when pulled halfway back.

half-cocked adj. **1** incompletely prepared or realized. **2** (of a gun) at half-cock.

half court n. **1** the section of a court in basketball, tennis, etc. which is the domain of one team, player, etc. **2** (**half-court**) (attrib.) esp. Basketball designating an offensive or defensive game plan devised to be used within one half of the court.

half-cut adj. Cdn & Brit. slang fairly drunk.

half day n. **1** half a working day, esp. taken as a holiday. **2** a period equal either to twelve hours or one half of a work day (also attrib.: *a half-day strike*).

half-dead adj. **1** in a state in which death seems as likely as recovery. **2** in a state of extreme exhaustion or weakness.

half dollar n. **1** (in Canada, the US, etc.) a coin worth fifty cents. **2** the amount represented by this.

half-dozen n. six or about six.

half-drunk adj. **1** partially intoxicated. **2** (of a drink etc.) partially consumed.

half-hardy adj. (of a plant) able to grow in the open air at all times except in severe frost.

half-hear v.tr. (past. and past part. **-heard**) hear (a thing) incompletely.

half-hearted adj. lacking in courage, enthusiasm, or determination. □ **half-heartedly** adv.

half hitch n. a noose or knot formed by passing the end of a rope around its standing part and then through the loop.

half-hour n. **1** (also **half an hour**) a period of 30 minutes. **2** a point of time 30 minutes after any hour o'clock. □ **half-hourly** adj. & adv.

half-life n. **1** the time taken for half of a sample of a particular radioactive isotope to decay into other materials. **2** the time taken for half of a dose of a drug etc. to disappear in the body after administration. **3** an unsatisfactory way of life.

half-light n. a dim, imperfect light, esp. that at dusk or dawn.

half-litre n. (also esp. US **half-liter**) a unit of capacity half as large as a litre.

half-mast n. **1** the position of a flag halfway down the mast, as a mark of respect for a person who has died. **2** informal the position of a garment halfway to that normal (*trousers at half-mast*).

half moon n. **1** the moon when only half its illuminated surface is visible from earth. **2** the time when this occurs. **3** a semicircular object.

half-naked adj. nearly naked; partially unclothed.

half nelson n. Wrestling see NELSON.

half note n. esp. N Amer. Music a note having the time value of two quarter notes or half a whole note and represented by a hollow ring with a stem.

half-pint n. **1** an amount of liquid equal to half a pint. **2** slang a short person.

half-pipe n. a snow tunnel or U-shaped cut in the snow, similar to the stunt ramps used by skateboarders, but used by snowboarders.

half rest *n.* *N Amer. Music* a rest having the time value of a half note.

half section *n.* *N Amer.* (*West*) a half of a square mile of esp. agricultural land, 320 acres (approx. 130 hectares).

half shell *n.* half of the shell of an oyster etc., esp. as used for serving food (*oysters on the half shell*).

half-sister *n.* a female related to one or more other persons, male or female, by having one biological parent in common.

half-slip *n.* an article of lingerie resembling a skirt, worn underneath dresses and skirts.

half-starved *adj.* poorly fed; suffering from malnourishment; having insufficient food.

half-step *n.* **1** *Music* a semitone. **2** a small or partial step in a specific direction.

half-timbered *adj.* (also **half timber**) *Archit.* having walls with a timber frame and a brick or plaster filling. □ **half-timbering** *n.*

halftime *n.* **1** the time at which half of a game is completed. **2** a short interval occurring at this time.

half-ton *n.* *N Amer.* a pickup truck with a carrying capacity of approximately half a ton.

halftone *n.* **1 a** an image, produced by photographic or electronic means, in which an effect of continuous tone is simulated by dots of various sizes or lines of various thicknesses. **b** the process which produces such an image. **2** *N Amer. Music* a semitone. **3** an intermediate tone between the extreme lights and extreme shades.

half-track *n.* **1** a propulsion system for land vehicles with wheels at the front and an endless driven belt at the back. **2** a vehicle equipped with this.

half-truth *n.* **1** a statement that conveys only part of the truth, esp. deliberately.

halfway ● *adv.* **1** at or to a point equidistant between two others (*halfway to Regina*). **2** to some extent, more or less (*is halfway decent*). ● *adj.* midway or equidistant between two points (*reached a halfway point*).

halfway house *n.* **1** a residence where ex-prisoners, mental patients, etc. live and receive treatment to help prepare them for their return to society. **2** the halfway point in a progression.

halfwit *n.* *informal* an extremely foolish or stupid person. □ **halfwitted** *adj.* **halfwittedly** *adv.*

halibut /'hælɪbət/ *n.* (*pl.* same) any of several very large flatfishes fished intensively for food, esp. (also **Atlantic halibut**), *Hippoglossus hippoglossus*, (also **Pacific halibut**) *Hippoglossus stenolepis*, and (also **Greenland halibut**) *Reinhardtius hippoglossoides*.

halide /'hælaɪd, 'heɪl-/ *n.* *Chem.* a binary compound of a halogen with another group or element.

Haligonian /hælɪ'goːnɪən/ ● *n.* a native or resident of Halifax, Nova Scotia. ● *adj.* of or pertaining to Halifax or Haligonians.

Halkomelem /ˌhɒlkə'meɪləm/ ● *n.* (*pl.* same) **1 a** member of an Aboriginal people living in southwestern BC. **2** the Salishan language of the Halkomelem. ● *adj.* of or relating to this people or their culture or language.

hall *n.* **1 a** *N Amer.* a corridor or passage in a building. **b** a space or passage into which the front entrance of a house etc. opens. **2** a large room or building for meetings, meals, concerts, etc. **3** a building containing lecture rooms etc. that is part of a university. **4** (in a college etc.) a common dining room, esp. for members of the institution. **5** the building of a union, fraternity, guild, etc.

hallal *var. of* HALAL.

hallelujah *var. of* ALLELUIA.

hallmark ● *n.* **1** a mark used by British assay offices for indicating the standard of gold, silver, and platinum. **2** any distinctive feature esp. of excellence. ● *v.tr.* **1** stamp with a hallmark. **2** designate as excellent.

Hall of Fame *n.* **1** esp. *N Amer.* a building with memorials of people who have excelled in a specific activity, esp. in a particular sport. **2** (usu. **hall of fame**) a group of people famous in a particular sphere. □ **Hall of Famer** *n.*

halloo /hə'luː/ (also **hallo**) ● *interj.* **1** (in fox hunting) a cry inciting dogs to the chase. **2** calling attention. **3** expressing surprise. ● *n.* the cry 'halloo'. ● *v.* (**halloos, hallooed**) **1** *intr.* cry 'halloo', esp. to dogs. **2** *intr.* shout to attract attention. **3** *tr.* urge on (dogs etc.) with shouts.

hallow *v.tr.* **1** make holy, consecrate. **2** honour as holy. □ **hallowed** *adj.*

Halloween *n.* (also **Hallowe'en**) the eve of All Saints' Day, 31 October.

Halloween apples *interj.* *Cdn* (*Prairies*) uttered by children going door to door on Halloween to collect candies etc.

hallucinate *v.* **1** *intr.* experience hallucinations. **2** *tr.* produce illusions in the mind of (a person). □ **hallucinant** *adj.* & *n.* **hallucinator** *n.*

hallucination *n.* the apparent perception of an object not actually present. □ **hallucinatory** *adj.*

hallucinogen /hə'luːsənədʒən/ *n.* a drug causing hallucinations. □ **hallucinogenic** *adj.*

hallway *n.* an entrance hall or corridor.

halo /'heɪloː/ ● *n.* (*pl.* **-os** or **-oes**) **1** a disc or circle of light shown surrounding the head of a sacred person. **2** the glory associated with an idealized person etc. **3** a circle of white or coloured light around a luminous body, esp. the sun or moon. **4** a circle or ring. ● *v.tr.* (**-oes, -oed**) surround with a halo.

halo effect *n.* the tendency of a favourable (or unfavourable) impression created by an individual in one area to influence one's judgment of him or her in another area.

halogen /'hælədʒən, 'heɪ-/ *n.* *Chem.* **1** any of the group of non-metallic elements (fluorine, chlorine, bromine, iodine, and astatine) which form halides (e.g. sodium chloride) by simple union with a metal. **2** (*attrib.*) (of lamps and radiant heat sources) using a filament surrounded by a halogen, usu. iodine vapour. □ **halogenic** *adj.*

halt[1] ● *n.* **1** a usu. temporary stop; an interruption of progress (*come to a halt*). **2** a temporary stoppage on a march or journey. ● *v.intr.* & *tr.* stop; come or bring to a halt. □ **call a halt** (**to**) decide to stop.

halt[2] *v.intr.* **1** (esp. as **halting** *adj.*) lack smooth progress. **2** hesitate. **3** walk hesitatingly. □ **halting** *adj.* **haltingly** *adv.*

halter ● *n.* **1** a rope or strap with a noose for horses or cattle. **2** (also **halter top**) a style of woman's top fastened behind the neck and across the back, leaving the arms, shoulders, upper back, and often the midriff bare. **3 a** a rope with a noose for hanging a person. **b** death by hanging. ● *v.tr.* **1** put a halter on (a horse etc.). **2** hang (a person) with a halter.

halve *v.tr.* **1** divide into two halves or parts. **2** reduce by half. **3** share equally (with another person etc.). **4** *Golf* use the same number of strokes as one's opponent in (a hole or match).

halves *pl. of* HALF.

halyard /'hæljərd/ *n.* *Naut.* a rope or tackle for raising or lowering a sail or yard etc.

ham ● *n.* **1 a** the upper part of a pig's leg salted and dried or smoked for food. **b** the meat from this. **2** the back of the thigh; the thigh and buttock. **3** *slang* (often *attrib.*) an inexpert or unsubtle actor or piece of acting. **4** *informal* the operator of an amateur radio station (also *attrib.*: *ham radio*). ● *v.intr. & tr.* (**hammed**, **hamming**) *slang* overact; act or treat emotionally or sentimentally. □ **ham it up** overact.

hamadryas /ˌhæməˈdraɪəs/ *n.* (also **hamadryas baboon**) a large Arabian baboon, *Papio hamadryas*, with a silvery-grey cape of hair over the shoulders.

hamatsa /həˈmætsə/ *n.* **1** a dance among the Kwagiulth in which the main dancer is inspired by the spirit of a man-eating monster hungering for human flesh. **2** a dancer embodying the monster.

hamburger *n.* (also *N Amer.* **hamburg**) **1** a patty of ground beef, seasonings, etc. **2** this fried or grilled and eaten in a soft bread roll. **3** *N Amer.* ground beef.

hamburger disease *n. N Amer.* a disease, characterized by diarrhea and kidney failure, caused by toxins produced by *Escherichia coli* bacteria.

ham-handed *adj.* (also **ham-fisted**) *informal* clumsy, heavy-handed. □ **ham-handedly** *adv.* **ham-handedness** *n.*

Hamiltonian /ˌhæmɪlˈtoʊniən/ ● *n.* a native or inhabitant of Hamilton, Ontario. ● *adj.* of or relating to Hamilton.

Hamite /ˈhæmaɪt/ *n.* a member of a group of N African peoples, including the ancient Egyptians and Berbers.

Hamitic /həˈmɪtɪk/ ● *n.* a group of African languages including ancient Egyptian and Berber. ● *adj.* **1** of or relating to this group of languages. **2** of or relating to the Hamites.

Hamito-Semitic *n. & adj.* = AFRO-ASIATIC.

hamlet *n.* a small village, esp. one that is unincorporated.

hammer ● *n.* **1 a** a tool with a heavy metal head at right angles to the handle, used for breaking, driving nails, etc. **b** a machine with a metal block serving the same purpose. **c** a similar contrivance, as for exploding the charge in a gun, striking the strings of a piano, etc. **2** an auctioneer's mallet, indicating by a rap that an article is sold. **3 a** a metal ball of about 7 kg, attached to a wire for throwing in an athletic contest. **b** the sport of throwing the hammer. **4** *Curling* the last rock of an end. ● *v.* **1 a** *tr. & intr.* hit or beat with or as with a hammer. **b** *intr.* strike loudly; knock violently (esp. on a door). **2** *tr.* **a** drive in (nails) with a hammer. **b** fasten or secure by hammering (*hammered the lid down*). **3** *tr.* (often foll. by *in*) inculcate (ideas, knowledge, etc.) forcefully or repeatedly. **4** *tr. informal* utterly defeat; inflict heavy damage on. **5** *intr.* (foll. by *at*, *away at*) work hard or persistently at. □ **under the hammer** to be sold at an auction. **hammer out 1** make flat or smooth by hammering. **2** work out the details of (a plan, agreement, etc.) laboriously. **3** play (a tune, esp. on the piano) loudly or clumsily. □ **hammering** *n.*

hammer and sickle *n.* the symbols of the industrial worker and the peasant used as the emblem of the former USSR and of communism.

hammer and tongs *adv. informal* with great vigour and commotion.

hammered *adj.* **1** (of metal etc.) shaped or formed with a hammer. **2** *N Amer. informal* drunk.

hammerhead *n.* any of a number of sharks of the genus *Sphyrna*, with a flattened, laterally elongated head bearing the eyes and nostrils at the extremities.

hammerlock *n.* **1** a hold in which an opponent's arm is twisted and bent behind the back. **2** a strong hold.

hammock[1] /ˈhæmək/ *n.* a bed of canvas or rope network, suspended by cords at the ends.

hammock[2] *var. of* HUMMOCK 2.

hammy *adj.* (**-ier**, **-iest**) **1** of or like ham. **2** *informal* (of an actor or acting) over-theatrical.

hamper[1] *n.* **1** a large basket usu. with a hinged lid and containing food (*picnic hamper*). **2** a package of food or other essentials for a needy person (*distributing Christmas hampers*). **3** *N Amer.* a usu. covered basket or other receptacle for dirty laundry.

hamper[2] *v.tr.* **1** prevent the free movement or activity of. **2** impede, hinder.

hamster *n.* any of various rodents of the subfamily Cricetinae, esp. *Cricetus cricetus*, having a short tail and large cheek pouches for storing food, kept as a pet or laboratory animal.

hamstring ● *n.* **1** each of five tendons at the back of the knee in humans. **2** the great tendon at the back of the hock in quadrupeds. ● *v.tr.* (*past* and *past part.* **hamstrung**) **1** cripple by cutting the hamstrings of (a person or animal). **2** prevent the activity or efficiency of (a person or enterprise).

Han /hɒn/ ● *n.* **1** a member of a small Aboriginal group living along the Yukon River. **2** the Athapaskan language of this people. ● *adj.* of or relating to this people or their culture or language.

hand ● *n.* **1 a** the end part of the human arm beyond the wrist, including the fingers and thumb. **b** in other primates, the end part of a forelimb, also used as a foot. **2 a** (often in *pl.*) control, management, custody, disposal (*in good hands*). **b** agency or influence (*suffered at their hands*). **c** a share in an action; active support. **3** help or assistance (*Katie gave me a hand*). **4** a thing compared with a hand or its functions, esp. the pointer of a clock or watch. **5** the right or left side or direction relative to a person or thing. **6 a** a skill, esp. in something practical (*a hand for making pastry*). **b** a person skilful in some respect. **7** a person who does or makes something, esp. distinctively (*a picture by the same hand*). **8** an individual's writing or the style of this; a signature (*in one's own hand*). **9** a person etc. as the source of information etc. (*at first hand*). **10** a pledge of marriage. **11** a person as a source of manual labour esp. in a factory, on a farm, or on board ship. **12 a** the playing cards dealt to a player. **b** the player holding these. **c** a round of play. **13** *informal* applause (*got a big hand*). **14** the unit of measure of a horse's height, equal to 4 inches (10.16 cm). **15** (*attrib.*) **a** operated or held in the hand (*hand drill*; *hand baggage*). **b** done by hand and not by machine (*hand-knitted*). ● *v.tr.* **1** (foll. by *in*, *to*, *over*, etc.) deliver; transfer by hand or otherwise. **2** convey verbally (*handed me a lot of abuse*). **3** *informal* give away too readily (*handed them the advantage*). □ **all hands 1** the entire crew of a ship. **2** the entire workforce. **at hand 1** close by. **2** about to happen. **by hand 1** by a person and not a machine. **2** delivered privately, rather than by the post office. **from hand to mouth** satisfying only one's immediate needs (also *attrib.*: *a hand-to-mouth existence*). **get** (or **have** or **keep**) **one's hand in** become (or be or remain) practised in something. **give** (or **lend**) **a hand** assist in an action or enterprise. **hand and foot** completely (*waited on them hand and foot*). **hand down 1** a pass the ownership or use of to another. **b** transmit (a custom etc.) from one generation to the next. **2 a** transmit (a decision) from a higher court etc. **b** *N Amer.* express (an opinion or verdict). **hand in glove** in collusion or association.

hand in hand 1 holding hands. **2** in close association. **hand it to** *informal* acknowledge the merit of. **hand off 1** *Football* hand (the ball) to another player, rather than throwing it. **2** give or hand (a thing) to another person. **hand on** pass (a thing) to the next in a series or succession. **hand out 1** serve, distribute. **2** award, allocate (*the judge handed out stiff sentences*). **hand over** surrender possession of. **hand over fist** *informal* with rapid progress. **hand round** distribute. **hands down** (esp. of winning) with no difficulty. **hands off 1** a warning not to touch or interfere with something. **2** *Computing etc.* not requiring manual use of controls. **hands on 1** *Computing* of or requiring personal operation at a keyboard. **2** involving or offering active participation rather than theory. **hands up!** an instruction to raise one's hands in surrender or to signify assent or participation. **hand-to-hand** (of fighting) at close quarters. **have** (or **take**) **a hand in** share or take part in. **have one's hand in the till** steal from one's employer. **have one's hands full** be fully occupied. **have one's hands tied** *informal* be unable to act. **in hand 1** receiving attention. **2** in reserve; at one's disposal. **3** under one's control. **lay** (or **put**) **one's hands on** *see* LAY¹. **off one's hands** no longer one's responsibility. **on hand 1** available. **2** present, in attendance. **on one's hands** resting on one as a responsibility. **on** (**one's**) **hands and knees** crawling. **on the one** (or **the other**) **hand** from one (or another) point of view. **out of hand 1** out of control. **2** peremptorily (*refused out of hand*). **put** (or **set**) **one's hand to** start work on; engage in. **to hand 1** within easy reach. **2** (of a letter) received. **turn one's hand to** undertake (as a new activity).

hand axe *n.* a prehistoric stone implement, normally oval or pear-shaped and worked on both sides, used for chopping, cutting, and scraping.

handbag *n.* a woman's purse.

handball *n.* **1 a** a game in which a ball is hit with the hand in a walled court. **b** the small, hard ball used in this game. **2** *Soccer* intentional touching of the ball with the hand or arm by a player other than the goalkeeper in the goal area, constituting a foul.

hand barrow *n. Cdn (Nfld)* = BARROW¹ 2.

handbasket *n.* esp. *N Amer.* a small basket. □ **go to hell in a handbasket** degenerate, esp. rapidly.

handbill *n.* a printed notice distributed by hand.

handbook *n.* a short manual or guidebook.

handbrake *n.* a brake operated by hand.

handcart *n.* a small cart pushed or drawn by hand. □ **go to hell in a handcart** = GO TO HELL IN A HANDBASKET (*see* HANDBASKET).

hand-carve *v.tr.* carve (a thing) by hand. □ **hand-carved** *adj.*

handcraft ● *n.* = HANDICRAFT. ● *v.tr.* make by handicraft. □ **handcrafted** *adj.*

hand cream *n.* a cream for softening and moisturizing the skin of the hands.

handcuff ● *n.* (in *pl.*) a pair of lockable linked metal rings for securing a person's wrists. ● *v.tr.* **1** put handcuffs on. **2** prevent (a person) from acting freely or effectively.

-handed *adj.* (in *comb.*) **1** for or involving a specified number of hands (in various senses) (*two-handed*). **2** using chiefly the hand specified (*left-handed*). □ **-handedly** *adv.* **-handedness** *n.* (both in sense 2).

handful *n.* (*pl.* **-fuls**) **1** a quantity that fills the hand. **2** a small number or amount. **3** *informal* a troublesome person or task.

hand game *n.* a usu. gambling game involving

sleight of hand, esp. requiring players to guess in which hand an object is concealed.

hand grenade *n. see* GRENADE 1.

handgrip *n.* **1** a grasp with the hand. **2** a handle designed for easy holding.

handgun *n.* a small firearm fired with one hand.

hand-held ● *adj.* designed to be held in the hand. ● *n.* a small hand-held computer.

handhold *n.* something for the hands to grip on (in climbing, sailing, etc.).

handicap ● *n.* **1 a** a disadvantage imposed on a superior competitor in order to make the chances more equal. **b** a race or contest in which this is imposed. **2** the number of strokes by which a golfer normally exceeds par for the course. **3** a thing that makes progress or success difficult. **4** a physical or mental disability. ● *v.tr.* (**handicapped**, **handicapping**) **1** impose a handicap on. **2** place (a person) at a disadvantage. □ **handicapper** *n.*

handicapped *adj.* suffering from a physical or mental disability.

handicraft *n.* **1** an art, skill, or trade that requires both manual and artistic ability. **2** work produced by such a skill or art. **3** manual skill or dexterity.

handily *adv.* **1** in a handy manner. **2** *N Amer.* easily (*won the contest handily*). **3** conveniently.

handiwork *n.* work done or a thing made by hand, or by a particular person.

handkerchief /ˈhæŋkərtʃɪf, -ˌtʃiːf/ *n.* (*pl.* **-s** or **-chieves** /-ˌtʃiːvz/) a square of cotton, linen, silk, etc., usu. carried in the pocket for wiping one's nose, etc.

handle ● *n.* **1** the part by which a thing is held, carried, or controlled. **2** a fact that may be taken advantage of (*gave a handle to his critics*). **3** *informal* a personal name or title. **4** the feel of goods, esp. textiles, when handled. ● *v.* **1** *tr.* touch, feel, operate, or move with the hands. **2** *tr.* manage or deal with; treat in a particular or correct way (*unable to handle the situation*). **3** *tr.* deal in (goods). **4** *tr.* discuss or write about (a subject). **5** *intr.* (of a vehicle, machine, tool, etc.) react or behave in a specified way in response to use, operation, or direction. **6** *refl.* behave, esp. under pressure. □ **get a handle on** *informal* understand the basis of or reason for a situation, circumstance, etc. □ **handleability** *n.* **handleable** *adj.* **handled** *adj.* (also in *comb.*).

handlebar *n.* (often in *pl.*) the steering bar of a bicycle etc., with a handgrip at each end.

handlebar moustache *n.* a thick moustache with ends curving upwards.

handler *n.* **1** a person or thing that handles something. **2** a person who handles or deals in certain commodities. **3** a person who trains and looks after an animal (esp. a police dog). **4** a person who looks after or represents a public figure, esp. a politician.

handline *n.* a fishing line worked or drawn by hand. □ **handliner** *n.* **handlining** *n.*

handling *n.* **1** the act or an instance of handling. **2** treatment or manner of dealing with something. **3** the process of packing, transporting, and delivering goods etc. (also *attrib.*: *handling charges*). **4** the way in which a vehicle handles.

handlogger *n. N Amer.* a person who logs by hand, using tools such as an axe or saw rather than a feller-buncher etc. □ **handlogging** *n.*

handmade *adj.* made by hand and not by machine, esp. as designating superior quality.

handmaid *n.* (also **handmaiden**) *archaic* a female servant or helper.

hand-me-down *n.* an article of clothing etc. passed on from another person.

hand-off *n.* the act or an instance of handing off.

handout *n.* **1** something given free to a needy person. **2** a statement given to the press etc. **3** a fact sheet, graph, summary of a speech, etc. distributed to a class or audience. **4** anything given away free, e.g. a sample of a product. **5** a payment made by esp. a government to a person, agency, etc. perceived as providing nothing in return.

handover *n.* the act or an instance of handing over.

hand-pick *v.tr.* **1** pick (fruit etc.) by hand. **2** choose carefully or personally. □ **hand-picked** *adj.*

handprint ● *n.* the print or mark of a hand. ● *v.tr.* (usu. **hand-print**) (usu. as **hand-printed** *adj.*) print (something) by hand.

handrail *n.* a narrow rail for holding as a support on stairs etc.

handsaw *n.* a saw worked by one hand.

handset *n.* a telephone mouthpiece and earpiece forming one unit.

hands-free *adj.* (of a telephone etc.) designed to be operated without the use of the hands.

handshake *n.* the shaking of a person's hand with one's own as a greeting etc.

hand signal *n.* a manual indication by a cyclist or driver of his or her intention to stop, turn, etc.

hands-off *adj.* **1** (of a policy, attitude, etc.) characterized by the lack of intervention (*a hands-off approach to the problem*). **2** (of flying, driving, etc.) without the use of the hands (*hands-off piloting*).

handsome /ˈhænsəm/ *adj.* (**handsomer**, **handsomest**) **1** (of a person) good-looking. **2** (of a building etc.) imposing, attractive. **3 a** generous, liberal (*a handsome present*). **b** (of a price, fortune, etc., as assets gained) considerable. □ **handsomeness** *n.*

handsomely *adv.* **1** generously, liberally. **2** finely, beautifully.

hands-on *adj.* characterized by active participation or involvement (*hands-on computer experience*).

handspring *n.* a somersault in which one lands first on the hands and then on the feet.

handstand *n.* the act or an instance of balancing on one's hands with the feet in the air or against a wall.

hand tool *n.* a tool operated by hand, without electricity.

handwashing *n.* **1** washing of the hands. **2** washing by hand. **3** the act of renouncing responsibility.

handwoven *adj.* (of cloth) woven by hand, as opposed to by a machine.

hand-wringing ● *n.* exaggerated lamentation or anguish. ● *adj.* characterized by hand-wringing.

handwriting *n.* **1** writing with a pen, pencil, etc. **2** a person's particular style of writing. □ **the handwriting is on the wall** *N Amer.* there are clear signs of approaching failure or disaster. □ **handwritten** *adj.*

handy *adj.* (**-ier, -iest**) **1** convenient to handle or use; useful. **2** ready to hand; placed or occurring conveniently. **3** clever with the hands.

handyman *n.* (*pl.* **-men**) a person able or employed to do domestic repairs and minor renovations.

handyman's special *n. N Amer.* something, esp. a house, that is for sale at a reduced price because of the many repairs or renovations needed.

hang ● *v.* (*past* and *past part.* **hung** except in sense 7) **1** *tr.* **a** secure or cause to be supported from above, esp. with the lower part free. **b** (foll. by *up, on, on to,* etc.) attach loosely by suspending from the top. **2** *tr.* set up

(a door, gate, etc.) on its hinges so that it moves freely. **3** *tr.* place (a picture) on a wall or in an exhibition. **4** *tr.* attach (wallpaper) in vertical strips to a wall. **5** *tr.* (foll. by *on*) *informal* attach the blame for (a thing) to (a person) (*you can't hang that on me*). **6** *tr.* (foll. by *with*) decorate by hanging pictures or decorations etc. **7** *tr. & intr.* (*past* and *past part.* **hanged**) **a** suspend or be suspended by the neck with a noosed rope until dead, esp. as a form of capital punishment. **b** as a mild oath (*hang the expense*). **8** *tr.* let droop (*hung her head*). **9** *tr.* suspend (meat or game) from a hook and leave it until dry or tender or high. **10** *intr.* be or remain hung (in various senses). **11** *intr.* remain static in the air. **12** *intr.* (often foll. by *over*) be present or imminent, esp. oppressively or threateningly (*a hush hung over the room*). **13** *intr.* (foll. by *on*) **a** be contingent or dependent on (*everything hangs on the discussions*). **b** listen closely to (*hangs on their every word*). **14** *tr.* prevent (a jury) from reaching a verdict. **15** *intr.* (of a computer or computer system) cease to respond to input from the keyboard or mouse. **16** *intr. N Amer. slang* (usu. foll. by *with*) associate with (a person). ● *n.* **1** the way a thing hangs or falls. **2** a downward droop or bend. □ **get the hang of** *informal* understand the technique or meaning of. **hang a left** (or **right**) *N Amer. informal* make a left (or right) turn. **hang around 1 a** loiter. **b** linger near (a person or place). **c** wait. **2** (often foll. by *with*) associate with (a person etc.). **hang back 1** show reluctance to act or move. **2** remain behind. **hang fire** be slow in taking action or in progressing. **hang heavily** (or **heavy**) (of time) pass slowly. **hang in** esp. *N Amer. informal* **1** persist, persevere. **2** linger. **hang loose** *informal* be casual or unconcerned. **hang on** *informal* **1** continue or persevere, esp. with difficulty. **2** (often foll. by *to*) continue to hold or grasp. **3** (foll. by *to*) retain; fail to give back. **4 a** wait for a short time. **b** (in telephoning) continue to listen during a pause in the conversation. **hang one's hat** *N Amer.* be resident. **hang out 1** hang from a window, clothes-line, etc. **2** protrude or cause to protrude downwards. **3** (foll. by *of*) lean out of (a window etc.). **4** *slang* reside or be often present. **5** = HANG AROUND 2. **hang a person out to dry** abandon a person to a usu. unpleasant fate. **hang ten** *slang* (of a surfer) ride (a surfboard) with all ten toes curled over the board's front edge. **hang together 1** make sense. **2** remain associated. **hang tough** *N Amer. informal* be or remain inflexible. **hang up 1** hang from a hook, peg, hanger, etc. **2** (often foll. by *on*) end a telephone conversation, esp. abruptly. **3** cause delay or difficulty to. **4** (usu. in passive, foll. by *on*) *slang* be a psychological or emotional obsession or problem to (*is really hung up on her father*). **5** = HANG *v.* 15. **hang up one's skates** *Cdn* give up; quit or retire (*the premier will hang up his skates next spring*). **let it all hang out** *slang* be uninhibited or relaxed. **might as well be hanged for a sheep as a lamb** if the penalty for a more serious crime, offence, act of foolishness, etc. is no greater than for a less serious one, then one might as well continue in one's criminal, foolish, etc. behaviour. **not care** (or **give**) **a hang** *informal* not care at all.

hangar /ˈhæŋər/ *n.* a building with extensive floor area, for housing aircraft etc. □ **hangarage** *n.*

hangashore /ˈhæŋəʃər/ *n. Cdn* (*Nfld & Maritimes*) **1** a weak or sickly person. **2** an idle or lazy person.

hangdog *adj.* having a dejected or guilty appearance.

hanger *n.* **1** a person or thing that hangs. **2** a shaped piece of wood or plastic etc. from which clothes may be hung.

hanger-on *n.* (*pl.* **hangers-on**) a follower or dependant, esp. an unwelcome one.

hang-glider *n.* **1** a frame with a fabric airfoil stretched over it, from which the operator is suspended and controls flight by body movement. **2** a person who practises hang-gliding. □ **hang-glide** *v.intr.* **hang-gliding** *n.*

hanging ● *n.* **1** the act or practice of executing a person by hanging. **2** a tapestry hung on a wall etc. ● *adj.* **1** that hangs or is hung; suspended. **2** (of a crime) punishable by hanging (*a hanging offence*). **3** (of a judge, jury, etc.) inclined towards giving a death sentence (*a hanging judge*).

hangman *n.* (*pl.* **-men**) **1** an executioner who hangs condemned persons. **2** a word game for two players, in which the tally of failed guesses is kept by drawing a representation of a body on a gallows.

hangnail *n.* **1** a piece of torn skin at the root of a fingernail. **2** the soreness resulting from this.

hangout *n. informal* a place one frequently visits, esp. to relax or socialize etc.

hangover *n.* **1** a severe headache and other after-effects caused by drinking an excess of alcohol. **2** a survival from the past.

Hang Seng index /hæŋ 'sɛŋ/ *n.* a figure indicating the relative price of representative shares on the Hong Kong Stock Exchange.

hang-up *n. slang* an emotional problem or inhibition.

hank *n.* **1** a usu. thick clump of hair. **2** a coil or skein of wool or thread etc. **3** any of several measures of length of cloth or yarn, e.g. 840 yds. (767 m) for cotton yarn.

hanker *v.intr.* (foll. by *for*, *after*, or *to* + infin.) long for; crave. □ **hankerer** *n.* **hankering** *n.*

hanky *n.* (also **hankie**) (*pl.* **-ies**) *informal* a handkerchief.

hanky-panky *n. slang* **1** naughtiness, esp. sexual misbehaviour. **2** dishonest dealing; trickery.

Hansard /'hænsɑrd/ *n.* the official verbatim record of debates in parliaments in Canada, the UK, and many other parliaments throughout the Commonwealth.

hantavirus *n.* any of various viruses of the family Bunyaviridae, spread esp. by rodents and causing acute respiratory disease, kidney failure, etc.

Hanukkah /'hʊnəkə/ *n.* the eight-day Jewish festival of lights, usu. in December, commemorating the purification of the Temple in 165 BC.

hap *archaic* ● *n.* **1** chance, luck. **2** a chance occurrence. ● *v.intr.* (**happed, happing**) **1** come about by chance. **2** (foll. by *to* + infin.) happen to.

haphazard ● *adj.* random. ● *adv.* at random. □ **haphazardly** *adv.* **haphazardness** *n.*

hapless *adj.* unlucky. □ **haplessly** *adv.* **haplessness** *n.*

haploid *Biol.* ● *adj.* (of an organism or cell) with a single set of chromosomes. ● *n.* a haploid organism or cell.

happen *v.intr.* **1** occur (by chance or otherwise). **2** (foll. by *to* + infin.) have the (good or bad) fortune to (*I happened to meet her*). **3** (foll. by *to*) be the (esp. unwelcome) fate or experience of (*what happened to you?*). **4** (foll. by *on*) encounter or discover by chance. **5** esp. *N Amer.* (foll. by *along*, *by*, etc.) come or turn up in a place casually or as if by chance. □ **as it happens** in fact; in reality (*as it happens, it turned out well*).

happening ● *n.* **1** an event or occurrence. **2** an improvised or spontaneous artistic performance. ● *adj. slang* exciting, fashionable, trendy.

happenstance *n.* esp. *N Amer.* a thing that happens by chance.

happy *adj.* (**-ier, -iest**) **1** feeling or showing pleasure or contentment. **2 a** fortunate; characterized by happiness. **b** (of words, behaviour, etc.) apt, pleasing. **3** *informal* slightly drunk. **4** (in comb.) *informal* inclined to use excessively or at random (*trigger-happy*). □ **happily** *adv.* **happiness** *n.*

happy camper *n. N Amer. informal* a happy or contented person.

happy-go-lucky *adj.* cheerfully casual.

happy hour *n.* a period of the day when drinks are sold at reduced prices in bars, hotels, etc.

happy hunting ground *n.* a place where success or enjoyment is obtained.

happy medium *n.* a compromise; the avoidance of extremes.

hara-kiri /ˌhærəˈkɪri/ *n.* **1** ritual suicide by disembowelment with a sword, formerly practised by Samurai to avoid dishonour. **2** a self-destructive action or course (*political hara-kiri*).

harangue /həˈræŋ/ ● *n.* **1** a lengthy and earnest speech. **2** a passionate verbal attack or reprimand. ● *v.tr. & intr.* lecture or make a harangue (to). □ **haranguer** *n.*

harass /həˈræs, ˈherəs, ˈhærəs/ *v.tr.* **1** trouble and annoy continually or repeatedly. **2** make repeated attacks on (an enemy or opponent). ¶The pronunciation with the stress on the second syllable is the most common pronunciation, but is considered incorrect by some people. □ **harasser** *n.* **harassing** *n. & adj.* **harassingly** *adv.* **harassment** *n.*

harbinger /'hɑrbɪndʒər/ *n.* **1** a person or thing that announces or signals the approach of another. **2** a forerunner.

harbour (also **harbor**) ● *n.* **1** a place of shelter for ships. **2** a shelter; a place of refuge or protection. ● *v.* **1** *tr.* give shelter to (esp. a criminal or wanted person). **2** *tr.* keep in one's mind, esp. resentfully (*harbour a grudge*). **3** *intr.* come to anchor in a harbour.

harbourage *n.* (also **harborage**) a shelter or place of shelter, esp. for ships.

harbourfront *N Amer.* ● *n.* (usu. **harbour front**) land adjacent to a harbour. ● *adj.* situated or occurring beside a harbour.

harbour seal *n. N Amer.* a small seal, *Phoca vitulina*, of coastal marine waters and estuaries.

hard ● *adj.* **1** (of a substance, material, etc.) firm and solid; not easily cut. **2 a** difficult to understand or explain (*a hard problem*). **b** difficult to accomplish (*a hard decision*). **c** (foll. by *to* + infin.) not easy to (*hard to believe*). **3** difficult to bear; entailing suffering (*hard luck*). **4** (of a person) unfeeling; severely critical. **5** (of a season or the weather) severe, harsh (*a hard winter*; *a hard frost*). **6** harsh or unpleasant to the senses (*a hard voice*). **7 a** strenuous, enthusiastic, intense (*a hard worker*; *a hard fight*). **b** severe, uncompromising (*a hard bargain*; *hard words*). **c** (of a turn) sharp, extreme (*make a hard left at the corner*). **d** *Politics* extreme; most radical (*the hard right*). **8 a** (of liquor) strongly alcoholic; designating spirits rather than wine or beer. **b** *N Amer.* (of a beverage) containing alcohol; fermented (*hard cider*). **9** (of drugs) potent and addictive. **10** (of pornography) highly explicit. **11** (of water) containing mineral salts that make lathering difficult. **12** *slang* (of the penis) erect. **13** (of a person) disreputable. **14** established; not disputable; reliable (*hard facts*; *hard data*). **15** (of a shape, boundary, etc.) clearly defined, unambiguous. **16** (of wheat) containing a hard kernel rich in gluten, used to make bread flour (compare SOFT adj. 19). **17** (of money) **a** in coins as opposed to paper currency. **b** in currency as opposed to cheques etc. **18** Phonetics (of a consonant) guttural (as c in cat, g in go). ● adv. **1** strenuously, intensely, copiously (is raining hard; hard-working). **2** with difficulty or effort (hard-earned). **3** so as to be hard or firm (frozen hard). **4** in close proximity (following hard on their heels). **5** with great force or genuine sorrow (she took his death very hard). □ **be hard on 1** be difficult for. **2** be severe in one's treatment or criticism of. **3** be unpleasant to (the senses). **be hard put** (usu. foll. by to + infin.) find it difficult. **hard at it** informal busily working or occupied. **hard by** near; close by. **a hard case 1** informal an intractable person. **2** a case of hardship. **a hard** (or **tough**) **nut to crack** informal **1** a difficult problem. **2** a person or thing not easily understood or influenced. **hard on** (or **upon**) close to in pursuit etc. □ **hardish** adj. **hardness** n.

hard and fast adj. (of a rule or a distinction made) definite, unalterable, strict.

hard-ass n. slang a tough, demanding, inflexible person. □ **hard-assed** adj.

hardback adj. & n. = HARDCOVER.

hardball N Amer. ● n. **1** = BASEBALL. **2** slang uncompromising methods or dealings, esp. in politics. ● adj. tough; uncompromising (hardball tactics).

hardboard n. stiff board made of compressed and treated wood pulp.

hard-boiled adj. **1** (also **hard-cooked**) (of an egg) cooked in water in the shell until the white and the yolk are solid. **2** (of a person) tough, shrewd.

hard bread n. Cdn (Nfld) a thick, oval biscuit baked without salt and dried in a kiln.

hard candy n. N Amer. a candy made of corn syrup and boiled sugar, usu. coloured and flavoured.

hard copy n. printed material produced by computer, usu. on paper. □ **hard-copy** adj.

hard core ● n. **1** an irreducible nucleus. **2** informal a the most active or committed members of a society etc. **b** a conservative or reactionary minority. **3** (usu. **hardcore**) a type of punk rock music characterized by a fast tempo and more emphasis on rhythm than melody. ● adj. (usu. **hard-core**) **1** forming a nucleus or centre. **2** blatant, uncompromising. **3** (of pornography) explicit, obscene.

hardcover adj. & n. esp. N Amer. ● adj. (of a book) bound in stiff covers. ● n. a hardcover book.

hard disk n. Computing a large-capacity rigid usu. magnetic storage disk.

hard done by adj. Cdn & Brit. harshly or unfairly treated.

hard-earned adj. that has taken a great deal of effort to earn or acquire.

harden v. **1** tr. & intr. make or become hard or harder. **2** intr. & tr. become, or make (one's attitude etc.), uncompromising or less sympathetic. **3** intr. (of prices etc.) cease to fall or fluctuate. □ **harden off** inure (a plant) to cold by gradual increase of its exposure. □ **hardener** n.

hardening n. **1** the process or an instance of becoming hard. **2** (in full **hardening of the arteries**) = ARTERIOSCLEROSIS.

hard feelings n.pl. feelings of resentment.

hard hat n. **1** protective headgear worn on construction sites etc. **2** informal a construction worker. **3** informal a conservative member of the working class.

hard-headed adj. **1** practical, realistic; not sentimental. **2** esp. N Amer. stubborn. □ **hard-headedly** adv. **hard-headedness** n.

hard-hearted adj. unfeeling, unsympathetic. □ **hard-heartedly** adv. **hard-heartedness** n.

hard hit adj. badly affected.

hard-hitting adj. forceful, tough; not sparing the feelings (a hard-hitting report).

hard labour n. heavy manual work as a punishment, esp. in a prison.

hard line ● n. unyielding adherence to a firm policy. ● attrib.adj. (**hardline**) unyielding, firm. □ **hardliner** n.

hard luck n. worse fortune than one deserves.

hardly adv. **1** scarcely; only just (we hardly knew them). **2** only with difficulty (could hardly speak). **3** probably not or almost certainly not (she will hardly come now). ¶Hardly should not be used with negative constructions. □ **hardly any** almost no; almost none. **hardly ever** very rarely.

hard maple n. = SUGAR MAPLE.

hard news n. news that is of immediate interest to a broad audience, usu. dealing with serious issues such as politics, wars, disasters, etc. (compare SOFT NEWS).

hard-nosed adj. informal realistic, uncompromising.

hard nut n. slang a tough, aggressive person.

hard of hearing adj. somewhat deaf.

hard-on n. coarse slang an erection of the penis.

hardpack n. N Amer. snow with a very dense, tightly packed surface.

hard palate n. the front part of the palate.

hardpan n. Geol. a hardened layer of clay occurring in or below the soil profile.

hard-pressed adj. **1** closely pursued. **2** burdened or oppressed (with work, etc.). **3** in (esp. financial) difficulty (hard-pressed taxpayers). **4** (usu. **hard pressed**) (foll. by to + infin.) unable or barely able.

hard return n. a carriage return inserted by the operator of a word processor, e.g. at the end of a paragraph (compare SOFT RETURN).

hard rock n. rock music characterized by a heavy beat, distorted amplified guitar, and loud vocals.

hardrock mining n. mining underground in large formations of esp. igneous or metamorphic rock, e.g. the Canadian Shield. □ **hardrock miner** n.

hardscrabble adj. N Amer. providing or yielding a meagre output and requiring much effort (earned a hardscrabble living).

hard sell n. aggressive salesmanship or advertising.

hard-shell adj. (also **hard-shelled**) **1** having a hard shell. **2** esp. N Amer. rigid, orthodox, uncompromising.

hardship n. **1** severe suffering or privation. **2** the circumstance causing this.

hard stuff n. slang hard drugs or strong liquor.

hardtack n. = SHIP'S BISCUIT.

hardtop n. **1** N Amer. **a** a road paved with a hard surface, esp. tar and gravel. **b** the material used for such a road. **2** a car with a rigid (sometimes detachable) roof.

hard up adj. **1** short of money. **2** (foll. by for) at a loss for; lacking.

hardware n. **1** tools, building materials, and household articles. **2** heavy machinery or armaments. **3** the mechanical and electronic components of a computer etc. (compare SOFTWARE 1).

hard-wearing adj. able to stand much wear.

hard-wired adj. **1** involving or achieved by permanently connected circuits designed to perform a specific function. **2** furnished or equipped with a natural ability to do something, as if programmed. **3** (of an ability) innate and difficult to modify (fear is hardwired into our brains).

hardwood ● *n.* **1** the wood from a deciduous broadleaf tree, as distinguished from that of conifers. **2** a tree producing such wood. ● *adj.* **1** made of hardwood. **2** containing hardwoods (*hardwood forest*).

hard-working *adj.* diligent.

hardy *adj.* (**-ier, -iest**) **1** robust; capable of enduring difficult conditions. **2** (of a plant) able to withstand winter in the open air. □ **hardily** *adv.* **hardiness** *n.*

hardy annual *n.* an annual plant that may be sown in the open.

hardy har har *var. of* HAR HAR.

Hare *n.* **1** a member of a Dene Aboriginal group living along the north Mackenzie River. **2** the Athapaskan language of this people.

hare *n.* any of various mammals of the family Leporidae, esp. of the genus *Lepus*, like a large rabbit, with tawny fur, long ears, short tail, and hind legs longer than forelegs. □ **hare off** depart, esp. rapidly or impulsively. **run with the hare and hunt with the hounds** try to remain on good terms with both sides.

harebell *n.* a plant, *Campanula rotundifolia*, with slender stems and pale-blue bell-shaped flowers.

hare-brained *adj.* (also **hair-brained**) rash, wild.

Hare Krishna /ˌhɑri ˈkrɪʃnə, ˌheri/ *n.* **1** a sect devoted to the worship of the Hindu deity Krishna. **2** (*pl.* **Hare Krishnas**) a member of this sect.

harelip *n.* often *offensive* = CLEFT LIP. □ **harelipped** *adj.*

harem *n.* **1** (*hist.* or in conservative Muslim communities) **a** the women of a Muslim household, esp. the wives and concubines, living in a separate part of the house. **b** separate women's quarters designed for privacy and seclusion in a Muslim household. **2** a group of female animals sharing a mate.

har har *interj.* expressing (esp. mirthless or disparaging) laughter.

haricot /ˈheriˌko/ *n.* **1** (in full **haricot bean**) a variety of French bean with small white seeds. **2** the dried seed of this used as a vegetable.

hark *v.intr.* (usu. in *imper.*) listen attentively. □ **hark back** mention again or remember an earlier subject, event, etc.

harken *var. of* HEARKEN.

harlequin /ˈhɑrləkwɪn/ ● *n.* (in full **harlequin duck**) a duck of northern coasts and rivers, *Histrionicus histrionicus*, the breeding males having deep greyblue plumage with chestnut and white markings. ● *adj.* **1** gaily coloured. **2** (esp. of an animal) in varied colours; variegated.

harlot /ˈhɑrlət/ *n.* a prostitute or promiscuous woman. □ **harlotry** *n.*

harm ● *n.* **1** hurt, damage. **2** moral evil; wrong. ● *v.tr.* cause harm to. □ **do more harm than good** make matters worse (despite good intentions). **out of harm's way** in safety.

harmful *adj.* causing or likely to cause harm. □ **harmfully** *adv.* **harmfulness** *n.*

harmless *adj.* **1** not able or likely to cause harm. **2** inoffensive. □ **harmlessly** *adv.* **harmlessness** *n.*

harmonic ● *adj.* **1** of or characterized by harmony; harmonious. **2** *Music* **a** of or relating to harmony. **b** (of a tone) produced by vibration of a string etc. in an exact fraction of its length. ● *n.* **1** *Music* an overtone accompanying at a fixed interval (and forming a note with) a fundamental. **2** *Physics* a component frequency of wave motion. □ **harmonically** *adv.*

harmonica *n.* a small rectangular wind instrument with a row of metal reeds along its length, held against the lips and moved from side to side to produce different notes by blowing or sucking.

harmonious *adj.* **1** sweet-sounding, tuneful. **2** forming a pleasing or consistent whole; concordant. **3** free from disagreement or dissent. □ **harmoniously** *adv.* **harmoniousness** *n.*

harmonium *n.* a keyboard instrument in which the notes are produced by air driven through metal reeds by bellows operated by the feet.

harmonize *v.* **1** *tr.* add notes to (a melody) to produce harmony. **2** *tr. & intr.* (often foll. by *with*) bring into or be in harmony. **3** *intr.* sing or play in harmony. **4** *intr.* make or form a pleasing or consistent whole. **5** *tr.* coordinate or make consistent. □ **harmonization** *n.* **harmonizer** *n.*

harmonized sales tax *n.* *Cdn* a value-added tax on goods and services combining the GST and the provincial sales tax in Nova Scotia, New Brunswick, and Newfoundland and Labrador. Abbr.: **HST**.

harmony *n.* (*pl.* **-ies**) **1 a** a combination of simultaneously sounded musical notes to produce chords and chord progressions, esp. as having a pleasing effect. **b** the study of this. **c** the parts of a harmonized piece of music other than the melody. **2 a** an apt or aesthetic arrangement of parts. **b** the pleasing effect of this. **3** agreement, concord. □ **in harmony 1** (of singing etc.) producing chords; not discordant. **2** (often foll. by *with*) in agreement.

harness ● *n.* **1** the equipment of straps and fittings by which a horse or other draft animal is fastened to a cart etc. and controlled. **2** a similar arrangement for fastening a thing to a person's body, for restraining a young child, etc. ● *v.tr.* **1 a** put a harness on (esp. a horse). **b** (foll. by *to*) attach by a harness. **2** make use of (natural resources), esp. to produce energy. ● *adj.* of or relating to harness racing (*harness driver*). □ **in harness** in the routine of daily work.

harness racing *n.* *N Amer.* a form of racing in which a horse pulls a two-wheeled vehicle and its driver with a trotting or pacing gait. □ **harness race** *n.*

harp ● *n.* **1** a large upright musical instrument consisting of a frame housing a graduated series of vertical strings, played by plucking with the fingers. **2** (in full **mouth harp**) *informal* a harmonica. ● *v.intr.* **1** (foll. by *on*, *on about*) talk repeatedly and tediously about. **2** play on a harp. □ **harpist** *n.*

harpoon ● *n.* a barbed spearlike missile with a rope attached, for hunting seals, whales etc. ● *v.tr.* spear with or as with a harpoon. □ **harpooner** *n.*

harp seal *n.* a seal, *Phoca groenlandica*, with a harp-shaped dark mark on its back, of the NW Atlantic and the Barents and White Seas.

harpsichord /ˈhɑrpsɪˌkɔrd/ *n.* a keyboard instrument with horizontal strings which are plucked mechanically. □ **harpsichordist** *n.*

harpy *n.* (*pl.* **-ies**) **1** (in Greek and Roman mythology) a monster with a woman's head and body and bird's wings and claws. **2** a nagging unpleasant woman. **3** a greedy, cruel or grasping person.

harridan /ˈherɪdən/ *n.* a bad-tempered woman.

harrier *n.* **1** a hound used for hunting hares. **2** any bird of prey of the genus *Circus*, with long wings for swooping over the ground. **3** a cross-country runner.

Harris tweed *n.* *proprietary* a kind of tweed woven by hand in the Outer Hebrides, esp. on the island of Lewis with Harris.

harrow ● *n.* a heavy frame with iron teeth dragged over plowed land to break up clods, remove weeds, cover seed, etc. ● *v.tr.* **1** draw a harrow over (land). **2** (usu. as **harrowing** *adj.*) distress greatly. □ **harrower** *n.* **harrowingly** *adv.*

harrumph (also **harumph**) ● *v.* **1** *intr.* clear the throat or make a similar sound, esp. ostentatiously. **2** *tr.* say gutturally, esp. expressing disapproval. ● *interj.* expressing disapproval. ● *n.* a guttural sound made by clearing the throat, expressing disapproval.

harry *v.tr.* (**-ies, -ied**) **1** ravage or despoil. **2** harass; annoy with repeated requests, questions, etc.

harsh *adj.* **1** unpleasantly rough, sharp, or irritating, esp. to the senses. **2** severe, cruel. **3** physically disagreeable; bleak, stark (*harsh terrain*). □ **harshly** *adv.* **harshness** *n.*

hart *n.* the mature male of the European red deer.

harum-scarum /ˌherəmˈskerəm/ *informal* ● *adj.* wild and reckless. ● *n.* such a person. ● *adv.* in a wild and reckless manner.

harvest ● *n.* **1 a** the process of gathering in crops etc. **b** the season when this takes place. **2** the season's yield or crop. **3** the product or result of any action. ● *v.tr.* **1** gather (crops, timber, etc.) as a harvest; reap. **2** kill or remove (wild animals) for food, sport, or population control (*harvest lobsters*). **3** remove (cells, tissues, organs) from a person or animal for experimental or other purposes. **4** experience (consequences). □ **harvestable** *adj.* **harvester** *n.*

harvest excursion *n. Cdn hist.* a low-priced train trip for workers going to the West to harvest crops.

harvest festival *n.* a thanksgiving festival for the harvest.

harvest gold *n. N Amer.* a rich yellow-gold shade, offered as a colour choice for kitchen appliances.

harvest moon *n.* the full moon nearest to the autumnal equinox.

harvest table *n. N Amer.* a large rectangular wooden dining table.

has *3rd sing. present of* HAVE.

has-been *n. informal* a person or thing that has lost a former importance or usefulness.

hash¹ ● *n.* **1** a dish of cooked meat cut into small pieces and recooked, usu. with vegetables. **2 a** a mixture; a jumble. **b** a mess. **3** re-used or recycled material. ● *v.tr.* (often foll. by *up*) **1** cut (meat etc.) into small pieces; make into a hash. **2** *informal* discuss exhaustively. □ **make a hash of** *informal* make a mess of; bungle. **settle a person's hash** *informal* deal with and subdue a person.

hash² *n. informal* hashish.

hash browns *n.pl.* esp. *N Amer.* chopped boiled potatoes, often with onions, fried until brown.

hashish /ˈhæʃiːʃ, ˈhæ-/ *n.* a resinous product of the top leaves and tender parts of hemp, smoked or chewed for its narcotic effects.

hash mark *n.* **1** the symbol #. **2** *Football* either of two marks on each five-yard line, defining a central zone within which all plays must start. **3** *Hockey* one of four short lines on the edges of each faceoff circle.

Hasid /ˈhæsɪd, hæˈsiːd/ *n.* (*pl.* **Hasidim**) (also **Hassid**) a member of any of several mystical Jewish sects, esp. one founded in the 18th c. □ **Hasidic** *adj.* **Hasidism** /ˈhæsɪˌdɪzəm, -ˈsɪdɪzəm/ *n.*

hasn't *contraction* has not.

hasp ● *n.* a hinged metal clasp that fits over a staple and can be secured by a padlock. ● *v.tr.* fasten with a hasp.

hassle *informal* ● *n.* **1** a prolonged trouble or inconvenience. **2** an argument or involved struggle. ● *v.* **1** *tr.* harass, annoy; cause trouble to. **2** *intr.* argue, quarrel.

hassock /ˈhæsək/ *n.* **1** a thick firm cushion used to rest the feet on or, esp. in church, to kneel on. **2** = OTTOMAN 1a. **3** a tuft of matted grass etc.

hast /hæst/ *archaic 2nd sing. present of* HAVE.

haste *n.* **1** quickness or speed of motion or action, esp. as prompted by urgency or pressure. **2** quickness of action without due consideration; rashness. □ **in haste** quickly, hurriedly. **make haste** hurry.

hasten /ˈheɪsən/ *v.* **1** *intr.* (often foll. by *to* + infin.) make haste; hurry. **2** *tr.* cause to occur or be ready or be done sooner.

hasty *adj.* (**-ier, -iest**) **1** hurried; acting quickly or hurriedly. **2** said, made, or done too quickly or too soon; rash. **3** quick-tempered. □ **hastily** *adv.* **hastiness** *n.*

hasty note *n. Cdn* (also **hasti-note**) (usu. in *pl.*) a small folded card or sheet of paper with a decoration on the front and the rest left blank for writing short letters etc.

hat ● *n.* **1** a covering for the head, often with a brim and worn out of doors. **2** *informal* a person's occupation or capacity, esp. one of several (*wearing his managerial hat*). ● *v.tr.* (**hatted, hatting**) cover or provide with a hat. □ **hat in hand** in a supplicatory manner; obsequiously. **hats off** (as *interj.*; foll. by *to*) expressing admiration or appreciation. **keep it under one's hat** *informal* keep it secret. **out of a hat** by random selection. **pass the hat** collect contributions of money. **take off one's hat to** *informal* acknowledge admiration for. **throw (or toss) one's hat in the ring** take up a challenge. □ **hatful** *n.* (*pl.* **-fuls**). **hatless** *adj.* **hatted** *adj.* (also in *comb.*).

hatband *n.* a band of ribbon etc. around a hat above the brim.

hatch¹ *n.* **1 a** an opening in a door, floor, or ceiling of a building. **b** an opening in a wall between two rooms, esp. a kitchen and a dining area, through which dishes etc. are passed. **2** an opening or door in an aircraft, spacecraft, etc. **3** *Naut.* **a** an opening in a ship's deck for lowering cargo into the hold. **b** (often in *pl.*) a trap door or cover for this (*batten the hatches*). **4** the rear hinged door of a hatchback. □ **down the hatch** *slang* (as a drinking toast) drink up, cheers!

hatch² ● *v.* **1** *intr.* **a** (of a young bird or fish etc.) emerge from the egg. **b** (of an egg) produce a young animal. **2** *tr.* incubate (an egg). **3** *tr.* devise (a plot etc.). ● *n.* **1** the act or an instance of hatching. **2** a brood hatched. □ **hatchability** *n.* **hatcher** *n.*

hatch³ *v.tr.* mark (a surface, e.g. a map or drawing) with close parallel lines.

hatchback *n.* **1** a car with a sloping back hinged at the top to form a door. **2** = HATCH¹ 4.

hatchery *n.* (*pl.* **-ies**) a place for hatching eggs.

hatchet *n.* **1** a light short-handled axe. **2** *N Amer.* a tomahawk.

hatchet job *n. informal* a fierce verbal attack on a person, esp. in print.

hatchetman *n.* (*pl.* **-men**) *informal* **1** a hired killer. **2** a harsh or vindictive critic. **3** a person employed to carry out unpleasant tasks, e.g. reducing staff etc.

hatching *n.* close parallel lines forming shading esp. on a map or an architectural drawing.

hatchling *n.* a bird or fish that has just hatched.

hatchway *n.* = HATCH¹ 3a.

hate ● *v.tr.* **1** feel hatred or intense dislike towards. **2** *informal* **a** dislike. **b** (foll. by verbal noun or *to* + infin.) be reluctant (to do something) (*I hate to disturb you*). ● *n.* **1** hatred; intense dislike. **2** *informal* a hated person or thing. **3** (*attrib.*) motivated by sexual, racial, or other forms of intolerance (*hate literature*). □ **hate someone's guts** *informal* dislike (someone) intensely. □ **hater** *n.*

hateful *adj.* **1** arousing hatred; odious. **2** full of hatred (*a hateful diatribe*). □ **hatefulness** *n.*

hate mail *n.* letters sent (usu. anonymously) in which the sender expresses hostility towards the recipient.

hate-monger *n.* a person who promotes hatred and intolerance against an identifiable group. □ **hate-mongering** *n.*

hath /hæθ/ *archaic 3rd sing. present of* HAVE.

hatha yoga /ˈhæθə/ *n.* a system of physical exercises and breathing control used in yoga.

hatpin *n.* a long pin, often decorative, for securing a hat to the head.

hatred *n.* intense dislike or ill will.

hatter *n.* a maker or seller of hats. □ **mad as a hatter** wildly eccentric.

hat trick *n.* **1** the scoring of three goals, points etc. by one person during a game. **2** three successes.

Haudenausanee /hɒdənəˈsɒni/ *n. & adj.* = IROQUOIS.

haughty *adj.* (**-ier, -iest**) arrogantly self-admiring and disdainful. □ **haughtily** *adv.* **haughtiness** *n.*

haul ● *v.tr.* **1** pull or drag forcibly. **2** transport by truck, cart, etc. **3 a** draw (a net) through water to catch fish. **b** lift (fish) in a net or on a line to the surface. **4** (usu. foll. by *into, up*) *informal* bring for reprimand or trial. ● *n.* **1** the act or an instance of hauling. **2 a** an amount gained or acquired. **b** the quantity of fish caught in one draft of the net. **3** a distance to be traversed (*a short haul*). □ **haul ass** *N Amer.* move fast; hurry, leave. **haul off** *N Amer. informal* **1** withdraw a little in preparation (*he hauled off and hit me*). **2** leave, depart. **haul out 1** take or drag out. **2** (of seals and walruses) come out of the water to rest on the rocky slopes of the shore.

haulage *n.* **1** the commercial transport of goods. **2** a charge for this.

haulback *n. Forestry* a lighter line for drawing a cable back to its original position after it has been used to move a log away.

hauler *n.* **1** a person or thing that hauls. **2** a person or firm engaged in the transport of goods.

hauling *n. Forestry* the process of transporting logs from the cutting area to the mill or shipping point.

haulout *n.* **1** the action of hauling a boat out of water. **2** a place along the shore where marine mammals haul out.

haunch *n.* **1** (often in *pl.*) the fleshy part of the buttock with the thigh. **2** the leg and loin of a deer etc. as food.

haunt ● *v.tr.* **1** (of a ghost) visit (a place) regularly, usu. giving signs of its presence. **2** (of a person or animal) frequent or be persistently in (a place). **3** (of a memory etc.) return repeatedly to the mind of, esp. in a distressing manner. **4** (of an action) cause difficulty or problems to (a person, organization, etc.), usu. long after the fact (*that letter will come back to haunt you*). ● *n.* **1** (often in *pl.*) a place frequented by a person. **2** a place frequented by animals, esp. for food and drink. □ **haunter** *n.*

haunted *adj.* **1** frequented by a ghost (*a haunted house*). **2** troubled, world-weary (*a haunted face*).

haunting ● *adj.* (of a memory, melody, etc.) poignant, wistful, evocative. ● *n.* a visitation by a ghost. □ **hauntingly** *adv.*

Hausa /ˈhausə, -zə/ *n.* (*pl.* same or **-s**) **1 a** a people of West Africa and the Sudan. **b** a member of this people. **2** the Hamitic language of this people, widely used in West Africa. ● *adj.* of this people or language.

haute /oːt, hoːt/ *adj.* upper-class, elegant, prestigious.

haute couture *n.* high fashion; the leading fashion houses or their products.

haute cuisine *n.* cooking of a high standard, esp. of the French traditional school.

hauteur /oːˈtɜr/ *n.* haughtiness of manner.

Havana /həˈvænə/ *n.* (in full **Havana cigar**) a cigar made at Havana or elsewhere in Cuba.

havarti /həˈvɑrti/ *n.* a mild, semi-soft Danish cheese with small irregular holes.

have ● *v.* (*3rd sing. present* **has**; *past* and *past part.* **had**) ● *v.tr.* **1** hold in possession as one's property or at one's disposal; be provided with (*has a car*; *had no time to read*). **2** hold in a certain relationship (*has a sister*; *had no equals*). **3** contain as a part or quality (*has green eyes*). **4 a** undergo, experience, enjoy, suffer (*had a good time*; *has a headache*). **b** be subjected to a specified state (*had my car stolen*; *the book has a page missing*). **c** cause, instruct, or invite (a person or thing) to be in a particular state or take a particular action (*had us worried*; *had them over for dinner*). **5 a** engage in (an activity) (*had an argument*; *had sex*). **b** hold (a meeting, party, etc.). **6** eat or drink (*had a beer*). **7** (usu. in *neg.*) accept or tolerate; permit to (*will not have you say such things*). **8 a** let (a feeling etc.) be present (*have no doubt*; *has a lot of sympathy for me*). **b** show or feel (mercy, pity, etc.) towards another person. **c** (foll. by *to* + infin.) show by action that one is influenced by (a feeling, quality, etc.) (*have the goodness to leave now*). **9 a** give birth to (offspring). **b** conceive (an idea etc.). **10** receive, obtain (*not a ticket to be had*). **11** be burdened with or committed to (*has a job to do*). **12 a** have obtained (a qualification) (*has a Ph.D.*). **b** know (a language) (*has no Latin*). **13** *slang* **a** get the better of (*I had him there*). **b** (usu. in *passive*) cheat, deceive (*you were had*). **14** have sexual intercourse with. ● *v.aux.* (with *past part.* or *ellipt.*, to form the perfect, pluperfect, and future perfect tenses, and the conditional mood) (*have worked*; *had I known, I would have gone*). ● *n.* (usu. in *pl.*) *informal* a person who has wealth or resources. □ **had better** would find it prudent to. **have got to** *informal* = HAVE TO. **have had it** *informal* **1** have missed one's chance. **2** be no longer useful or appropriate (*these old boots have had it*). **3** have been killed, defeated, etc. **4** be tired or fed up with (*I've had it with your excuses!*). **have it 1** (foll. by *that* + clause) express the view that. **2** win a decision in a vote etc. **3** *informal* have found the answer etc. **have it coming** can expect unpleasant consequences to follow. **have it in for** *informal* be hostile or ill-disposed towards. **have it out** (often foll. by *with*) *informal* attempt to settle a dispute by discussion or argument. **have on 1** be wearing (clothes). **2** be committed to (an engagement). **3** *informal* tease, play a trick on. **have out** get (a tooth etc.) extracted (*had her tonsils out*). **have something (or nothing) on a person 1** know something (or nothing) discreditable or incriminating about a person. **2** have an (or no) advantage or superiority over a person. **have to** (usu. /hæf/) be obliged to, must. **have up** *informal* bring (a person) before a court of justice etc.

haven *n.* **1** a harbour or port. **2** a place of refuge.

have-not *n.* (usu. in *pl.*) *informal* a person etc. lacking wealth or resources.

have-not province *n. Cdn* a province whose per capita tax revenue falls below a certain average level and which is therefore entitled to receive equalization payments from the federal government.

haven't *contraction* have not.

have province *n. Cdn* a province whose per capita tax revenue exceeds a certain average level and which does not therefore receive equalization payments from the federal government.

havoc ● *n.* widespread destruction; great confusion or disorder. ● *v.tr.* (**havocked, havocking**) devastate. □ **play havoc with** *informal* cause great confusion or difficulty to. **wreak havoc** devastate, cause damage.

haw¹ *n.* the hawthorn or its fruit.

haw² *n.* the nictitating membrane of a horse, dog, etc., esp. when inflamed.

haw³ ● *interj.* expressing hesitation. ● *v.intr. see* HUM¹.

Hawaiian /hə'waiən/ ● *n.* **1 a** a native of Hawaii, a group of 20 islands in the N Pacific. **b** a person of Hawaiian descent. **2** the Malayo-Polynesian language of Hawaii. ● *adj.* **1** of or relating to Hawaii or its people or language. **2** *N Amer.* (of pizza) garnished with ham and pineapple.

Hawaiian guitar *n.* a steel-stringed instrument, usu. held horizontally, in which a characteristic glissando effect is produced by sliding a metal bar along the strings as they are plucked.

Hawaiian shirt *n.* a brightly coloured and gaily patterned shirt.

haw haw *interj.* used to represent the sound of a loud or boisterous laugh.

hawk¹ ● *n.* **1** any of various diurnal birds of prey of the family Accipitridae, having a characteristic curved beak, rounded short wings, and a long tail. **2** *Politics* a person who advocates an aggressive or warlike policy, esp. in foreign affairs. **3** a rapacious person. ● *v.* **1** *intr.* hunt game with a hawk. **2** *intr. & tr.* attack, as a hawk does. **3** *intr.* (of a bird) hunt on the wing for food. □ **watch like a hawk** watch intently and unceasingly. □ **hawkish** *adj.* **hawkishly** *adv.* **hawkishness** *n.* **hawk-like** *adj.*

hawk² *v.tr.* **1** carry about or offer (goods) for sale. **2** (often foll. by *about*) relate (gossip etc.) freely.

hawk³ *v.* **1** *intr.* clear the throat noisily. **2** *tr.* (foll. by *up*) bring (phlegm etc.) up from the throat.

hawker *n.* a person who travels about selling goods.

hawk moth *n.* any darting and hovering moth of the family Sphingidae, having narrow forewings and a stout body.

hawk owl *n.* a somewhat long-tailed, partly diurnal owl, *Surnia ulula*, of northern coniferous woodlands.

hawkweed *n.* any composite plant of the genus *Hieracium*, with yellow or orange flowers.

hawse /hɔz/ *n.* **1** the part of a ship's bows in which hawse holes or hawse pipes are placed. **2** the space between the head of an anchored vessel and the anchors. **3** the arrangement of cables when a ship is moored with port and starboard forward anchors.

hawse hole *n.* a hole in the side of a ship through which a cable or anchor rope passes.

hawse pipe *n.* a metal pipe lining a hawse hole.

hawser /'hɔzər/ *n.* *Naut.* a thick rope or cable for mooring or towing a ship.

hawthorn *n.* any thorny shrub or tree of the genus *Crataegus*, esp. the cultivated *C. monogyna*, with white, red, or pink blossoms and small dark red fruit.

hay ● *n.* grass, clover, alfalfa, etc., cut and dried for animal fodder. ● *v.* **1** *intr.* make hay. **2** *tr.* make (grass etc.) into hay. □ **hit the hay** *informal* go to bed. **make hay of** throw into confusion. **make hay (while the sun shines)** seize opportunities for profit or enjoyment. **make hay out of** turn to one's advantage. □ **haying** *n.*

hay fever *n.* an allergic reaction to the airborne pollen of grasses or other plants, manifested in summer and causing sneezing, nasal congestion, conjunctival irritation, and in some cases asthmatic symptoms.

hayfield *n.* a field where hay is being or is to be made.

haylage /'heilidʒ/ *n.* silage made from grass etc. which has been partially dried.

hayloft *n.* = LOFT *n.* 2.

haymaker *n.* **1** a person who tosses and spreads hay to dry after mowing. **2** an apparatus for shaking and drying hay. **3** *slang* a forceful blow or punch. □ **haymaking** *n.*

haymow /'heimau, -mo:/ *n.* **1** hay stored in a stack or barn. **2** the part of a barn for the storage of hay.

hay privilege *n.* *Cdn* (*Man.*) *hist.* **1** the right of Red River settlers to cut hay on the uncultivated land lying behind each river lot. **2** the land to which this right pertained.

hayride *n.* esp. *N Amer.* a pleasure ride in an open wagon etc. filled with hay or straw.

hayseed *n.* **1** grass seed obtained from hay. **2** *N Amer. informal* a rustic or yokel.

haystack *n.* a packed pile of hay with a pointed or ridged top.

hay wagon *n.* *N Amer.* a wagon for carrying bales of hay etc.

haywire ● *n.* wire for binding bales of hay, straw, etc. ● *adj. informal* **1** badly disorganized, out of control. **2** (of a person) badly disturbed; erratic. □ **go haywire** go wrong; become confused or crazy.

hazard ● *n.* **1** a danger or risk. **2** a source of this. **3** chance. **4** *Golf* an obstruction in playing a shot, e.g. a bunker, water, etc. **5** (in *pl.*) (also **hazard lights**) flashing lights on a vehicle warning that the vehicle is stationary or slowing or reversing unexpectedly. ● *v.tr.* **1** venture on; suggest tentatively (*hazard a guess*). **2** run the risk of. **3** expose to danger; risk.

hazardous *adj.* **1** risky, dangerous. **2** dependent on chance. □ **hazardously** *adv.* **hazardousness** *n.*

haze¹ ● *n.* **1** obscuration of the atmosphere near the earth by fine particles of water, smoke, or dust. **2** mental obscurity or confusion. ● *v.tr. & intr.* make or become hazy.

haze² *v.tr.* **1** *Naut.* harass with overwork. **2** esp. *N Amer.* subject (new students etc.) to abuse and ridicule.

hazel ● *n.* **1** any shrub or small tree of the genus *Corylus*, bearing round brown edible nuts. **2** wood from the hazel. **3** a golden-brown or greenish-brown colour (esp. of the eyes). ● *adj.* (esp. of the eyes) of a golden-brown or greenish-brown colour.

hazelnut *n.* the fruit of the hazel.

hazy *adj.* (**-ier, -iest**) **1** misty. **2** vague, indistinct. **3** confused, uncertain. □ **hazily** *adv.* **haziness** *n.*

HB *abbr.* hard black (pencil lead).

Hb *symbol* hemoglobin.

HBC *abbr. Cdn* Hudson's Bay Company.

H-bomb *n.* = HYDROGEN BOMB.

HC *abbr.* House of Commons.

HCF *abbr.* highest common factor.

HCFC *abbr.* hydrochlorofluorocarbon (similar to CFC but thought to be less harmful to the ozone layer).

hCG *abbr.* HUMAN CHORIONIC GONADOTROPIN.

HDL *abbr.* HIGH-DENSITY LIPOPROTEIN.

HDTV *abbr.* high-definition television.

HE *abbr.* **1** His or Her Excellency. **2** His Eminence. **3** high explosive.

He *symbol* helium.

he ● *pron.* (*obj.* **him**; *poss.* **his**; *pl.* **they**) **1** the male previously named or in question. **2** a person etc. of unspecified sex, esp. referring to one already named or identified (*if anyone comes he will have to wait*).

¶Many people perceive this usage as sexist, and prefer to use *they*; however, this alternative is condemned by others. ● *n.* **1** a male. **2** (in *comb.*) male (*he-goat*).

head ● *n.* **1** the upper part of the human body, or the foremost or upper part of an animal's body, containing the brain, mouth, and sense organs. **2 a** the head regarded as the seat of intellect or repository of information. **b** intelligence; imagination (*use your head*). **c** mental aptitude or tolerance (usu. foll. by *for*: *a good head for business*). **3** *informal* a headache, esp. resulting from a blow or from intoxication. **4** a thing like a head in form or position, esp.: **a** the part of a tool, weapon, golf club, etc. used to strike with. **b** the flattened top of a nail. **c** the ornamented top of a pillar. **d** a mass of leaves or flowers at the top of a stem. **e** the flat end of a drum. **f** the foam on top of a glass of beer etc. **g** the upper horizontal part of a window frame, door frame, etc. **h** = SHOWER HEAD. **5** life when regarded as vulnerable (*it cost him his head*). **6 a** a person in charge; a director or leader. **b** a position of leadership or command. **7** the front or forward part of something, e.g. a procession. **8** the upper end of something, e.g. a table or bed. **9** the top or highest part of something, e.g. a page, stairs, etc. **10** a person or individual regarded as a numerical unit (*$10 per head*). **11** (*pl.* same) **a** an individual animal as a unit. **b** (as *pl.*) a number of cattle or game as specified (*20 head*). **12 a** the side of a coin bearing the image of a head. **b** (usu. in *pl.*) this side as a choice when tossing a coin. **13 a** the source of a river, stream etc. **b** the end of a lake, bay, etc. at which a river enters it. **c** *Cdn* (*Nfld*) the innermost area of a bay, harbour, etc. **14** the height or length of a head as a measure (*his horse won by a head*). **15** the component of a machine that is in contact with or very close to what is being processed or worked on, esp.: **a** the component on a tape recorder that touches the moving tape in play and converts the signals. **b** = PRINTHEAD. **16 a** a confined body of water or steam in an engine etc. **b** the pressure exerted by this. **17** a promontory (esp. in place names). **18** *Naut.* **a** the bows of a ship or boat. **b** (often in *pl.*) a latrine on a ship or boat. **c** *Cdn* (*Nfld*) the seaward end of a wharf. **19** a main topic or category for consideration or discussion. **20** *Journalism* = HEADLINE *n.* **21** a culmination, climax, or crisis. **22** the fully developed top of a boil etc. ● *attrib.adj.* chief or principal (*head office*). ● *v.* **1** *tr.* be at the head or front of. **2** *tr.* (often foll. by *up*) be in charge of. **3** *tr.* **a** provide with a head or heading. **b** (of an inscription, title, etc.) be at the top of, serve as a heading for. **4 a** *intr.* (often foll. by *for*) face or move in a specified direction or towards a specified result (*is heading for trouble*). **b** *tr.* direct in a specified direction. **5** *tr. Soccer* strike (the ball) with the head. **6 a** *tr.* (often foll. by *down*) cut the head off (a plant etc.). **b** *intr.* (of a plant etc.) form a head. □ **above** (**or over**) **one's head** beyond one's ability to understand. **bang one's head against a wall** *informal* be frustrated in an attempt to do something. **come to a head 1** (of a boil etc.) suppurate. **2** reach a crisis or climax. **enter** (**or come into**) **one's head** *informal* occur to one. **from head to toe** (**or foot**) all over a person's body. **get it into one's head** (foll. by *that* + clause or *to* + infin.) form a definite idea or plan, esp. mistakenly or impetuously. **give a person his** (**or her**) **head** allow a person to act freely. **give head** *coarse slang* perform oral sex. **go to one's head 1** (of liquor) make one dizzy or slightly drunk. **2** (of success) make one conceited. **have one's head** (**screwed**) **on**

straight be sensible. **head and shoulders** *informal* by a considerable amount. **head back** return home etc. **head in the sand** refusal to acknowledge an obvious danger or difficulty. **head off 1** get ahead of so as to intercept and turn aside. **2** forestall. **head over heels 1** turning over completely in forward motion as in a somersault etc. **2** topsy-turvy. **3** utterly, completely. **heads will roll** *informal* people will be disgraced or dismissed. **head to head** in direct competition or conflict. **hold up one's head** be confident or unashamed. **in one's head 1** in one's thoughts or imagination. **2** by mental process without use of physical aids. **keep one's head** remain calm. **keep one's head above water** *informal* **1** keep out of debt. **2** avoid succumbing to difficulties. **keep one's head down** *informal* remain inconspicuous in difficult or dangerous times. **lose one's head** lose self-control; panic. **make head(s) or tail(s) of** (usu. with *neg.* or *interrog.*) understand at all. **off one's head** *slang* crazy. **off the top of one's head** *informal* impromptu; without careful thought or investigation. **one's head off** noisily or excessively (*laughed his head off*). **on one's** (or **one's own**) **head** as one's sole responsibility. **out of one's head 1** *slang* crazy or delirious. **2** from one's imagination or memory. **over one's head 1** beyond one's ability to understand. **2** without one's knowledge or involvement, esp. when one has a right to this. **3** with disregard for one's own (stronger) claim (*was promoted over their heads*). **put heads together** consult together. **put into a person's head** suggest to a person. **turn a person's head** make a person conceited. **turn heads** cause people to notice. □ **headed** *adj.* (also in *comb.*). **headless** *adj.*

headache *n.* **1** a continuous pain in the head. **2** *informal* **a** a worrying problem. **b** a troublesome person. □ **headachy** *adj.*

headband *n.* a band worn around the head as decoration or to keep the hair off the face.

headbanger *n.* *slang* a fan of heavy metal music.

headbanging *n.* (often *attrib.*) vigorous head-shaking in time to heavy metal music.

headboard *n.* an upright panel forming or placed behind the head of a bed etc.

head-butt ● *n.* a forceful thrust with the top of the head into the chin or body of another person. ● *v.tr.* attack (another person) with a head-butt.

head case *n.* *informal* a crazy or unstable person.

headcheese *n.* *N Amer.* a jellied preparation of the chopped meat from a boiled pig's head.

head cold *n.* *N Amer.* a cold characterized esp. by sneezing and a stuffy or runny nose.

head count *n.* **1** a counting of individual people or animals. **2** a total number of people, esp. the number of people employed in a particular organization.

headdress *n.* an ornamental covering or band for the head.

headend /ˈhedˌend/ *n.* a control centre in a cable television system, at which the various signals are introduced into the cable network.

header *n.* **1** *Soccer* a shot or pass made with the head. **2** *informal* a headlong fall or dive. **3** a line or block of text appearing at the top of each page of a document etc. (compare FOOTER 2). **4** a brick or stone laid at right angles to the face of a wall (compare STRETCHER 2). **5** a beam crossing and supporting the ends of joists, studs, or rafters.

headfirst ● *adv.* **1** with the head foremost. **2** precipitately. ● *adj.* with the head foremost.

head game *n.* *N Amer. informal* **1** (often in *pl.*) psychological manipulation. **2** a mental exercise to improve memory etc.

headgear *n.* **1 a** something worn on the head, as a hat, cap, or headdress. **b** a protective covering for the head, as a helmet. **2** machinery etc. at the top of a mine shaft. **3** the parts of a harness around a horse's head. **4** orthodontic equipment worn on the head and attached to braces on the teeth.

headhunter *n.* **1** a person who collects the heads of dead enemies as trophies. **2** an agency or agent specializing in the recruitment of skilled personnel. □ **headhunt** *v.tr. & intr.* **headhunting** *n.*

heading *n.* **1 a** a title at the head of a page or section of a book etc. **b** a division or section of a subject of discourse etc. **2** the extension of the top of a curtain above the tape that carries the hooks or the pocket for a wire. **3** the course of an aircraft, ship, etc.

headlamp *n.* **1** = HEADLIGHT. **2** a small lamp attached to a hat or worn strapped to the forehead.

headland *n.* a promontory.

head lettuce *n.* lettuce having tightly clustered, usu. pale leaves forming a round compact head.

headlight *n.* **1** a strong light at the front of a motor vehicle or railway engine. **2** the beam from this. **3** (usu. in *pl.*) *N Amer. slang* a woman's breast.

headline ● *n.* **1** a heading at the top of an article or page, esp. in a newspaper. **2** (in *pl.*) the most important items of news in a newspaper or news broadcast. ● *v.* **1** *tr.* give a headline to. **2** *intr. & tr.* appear as the chief performer (at). □ **hit** (or **make**) **the headlines** *informal* be given prominent attention as news.

headliner *n.* a headlining performer; a star.

headlock *n.* a hold with an arm around the opponent's head.

headlong *adv. & adj.* **1** with the head foremost. **2** in a rush.

headman ● *n.* (*pl.* **-men**) the chief man of a village, tribe etc. ● *v.tr.* (**head-man**) *Hockey* pass (the puck) up ice to a teammate.

headmaster *n.* the principal in charge of a school.

headmistress *n.* a woman principal in charge of a school.

head of hair *n.* the hair on a person's head.

head of state *n.* (*pl.* **heads of state**) the title of the head of a state, usu. the leader of the ruling party or a monarch.

head-on *adj. & adv.* **1** with the front foremost (a *head-on crash*; *hit us head-on*). **2** in direct confrontation.

headphone *n.* (usu. in *pl.*) a pair of earphones for listening to audio equipment etc.

headpiece *n.* **1** any covering for the head, esp. a decorative one worn by a bride. **2** a helmet.

headpond *n.* *Cdn* (*Maritimes*) a pond created behind a dam.

headquarter *v.* esp. *N Amer.* **1** *tr.* (usu. in *passive*) provide with headquarters (at a specific location). **2** *intr.* set up headquarters.

headquarters *n.* (as *sing.* or *pl.*) **1** the administrative centre of an organization. **2** the premises occupied by a military commander and the commander's staff.

headrest *n.* a support for the head attached to a dentist's chair, the seat of a motor vehicle, etc.

headroom *n.* **1** the space above a driver's or passenger's head in a vehicle, between a person's head and a doorway, ceiling, etc. **2** the space or clearance between the top of a vehicle and the underside of a bridge etc. which it passes under.

head scarf *n.* a scarf worn around the head and tied under the chin.

head-scratching *n.* puzzlement.

headset *n.* a set of headphones, often with a microphone attached, used esp. in telephone and radio communication.

headship *n.* the position of chief or leader.

head shop *n.* *slang* a store selling drug paraphernalia.

headspace *n.* **1** space left in the top of a jar, bottle, etc. to allow room for expansion of contents. **2** mindset, attitude.

headstand *n.* an act or instance of balancing on one's head.

head start *n.* an advantage granted or gained at an early stage.

headstone *n.* a (usu. inscribed) stone set up at the head of a grave.

headstrong *adj.* self-willed and obstinate. □ **headstrongly** *adv.* **headstrongness** *n.*

heads-up *N Amer. informal* ● *n.* a warning (*gave them a heads-up*). ● *adj.* alert, perceptive (a *heads-up baseball player*). ● *interj.* (**heads up**) look out!

head table *n.* *N Amer.* a table at a wedding, conference, etc. where the guests of honour sit.

head tax *n.* a tax levied esp. on new immigrants to a country.

head-to-head ● *attrib.adj.* involving two parties confronting each other. ● *adv.* confronting another party.

head waiter *n.* a waiter who supervises other waiters, busboys, etc.

headwater *n.* (in *sing.* or *pl.*) streams flowing from the sources of a river.

headway *n.* **1** progress. **2** the rate of progress of a ship. **3** = HEADROOM.

headwind *n.* a wind blowing from directly in front.

headword *n.* a word forming a heading, e.g. of an entry in a dictionary.

heady *adj.* (**-ier**, **-iest**) **1** (of liquor) potent, intoxicating. **2** light-headed, giddy. **3** affecting the senses strongly (a *heady aroma*). **4** exhilarating; very exciting (the *heady days of youth*). **5** (of a person, thing, or action) impetuous, foolhardy. □ **headily** *adv.* **headiness** *n.*

heal *v.* **1** *intr.* (often foll. by *up*) (of a wound or injury) become healthy again. **2** *tr.* cause (a wound, disease, or person) to heal or be cured. **3** *tr.* repair, correct (an undesirable condition, esp. a breach of relations); put right (differences etc.). **4** *tr.* alleviate (sorrow etc.). **5** *intr.* (of a person) recover from mental trauma. □ **healer** *n.* **healing** *n. & adj.*

health *n.* **1** the state of being well in body or mind. **2** a person's mental or physical condition (often *attrib.*: *health insurance*). **3** soundness, esp. financial or moral. **4** a toast drunk in someone's honour.

health card *n.* *Cdn* a card identifying a person as eligible to receive medical treatment paid for by a public insurance plan.

health care *n.* the maintenance and improvement of health, esp. as administered by organized medical services and facilities.

health centre *n.* the headquarters of a group of local medical services.

health certificate *n.* a certificate attesting fitness or good health.

health club *n.* an establishment providing facilities for exercise, massage, etc.

health food *n.* natural food eaten for its health-giving qualities (often *attrib.*: *health food store*).

healthful *adj.* conducive to good health; beneficial. □ **healthfully** *adv.* **healthfulness** *n.*

health plan n. a medical insurance plan, either one provided by a government or one offered as an employment benefit.

healthy adj. (**-ier, -iest**) **1** having, showing, or promoting good health. **2** beneficial, helpful (a healthy respect for experience). **3** ample, considerable (a healthy portion). **4** (of a business etc.) sound, functioning well. □ **healthily** adv. **healthiness** n.

heap ● n. **1 a** a collection of things lying haphazardly one on another. **b** a mass of something in an untidy pile (she collapsed in a heap on the floor). **2** (esp. in pl.) informal a large number or amount (there's heaps of time). **3** slang an old or dilapidated thing, esp. a motor vehicle or building. ● v. **1** tr. & intr. (foll. by up, together, etc.) collect or be collected in a heap. **2** tr. (foll. by with) load copiously or to excess. **3** tr. (foll. by on, upon) accord or offer copiously to (heaped insults on them).

heaping adj. N Amer. (of a spoonful etc.) with the contents piled above the brim.

hear v. (past and past part. **heard**) **1** tr. & intr. perceive (sound etc.) with the ear. **2** tr. **a** listen to (heard them on the radio). **b** listen to (a recital, religious service, etc.) as a member of an audience or congregation. **3** tr. listen judicially to and judge (a case, plaintiff, etc.). **4** intr. (foll. by about, of, or that + clause) be told or informed. **5** intr. (foll. by from) be contacted by, esp. by letter or telephone. **6** tr. be ready to obey (an order) (you're not going out – do you hear me?). **7** tr. grant (a prayer). □ **be unable to hear oneself think** be unable to think clearly because of the noise. **have heard of** be aware of; know of the existence of. **hear a pin drop** hear the slightest noise. **hear! hear!** interj. expressing agreement (esp. with something said in a speech). **hear a person out** listen to all that a person says. **hear tell** (usu. foll. by of, or that + clause) be informed. **will not hear of** will not allow or agree to. □ **hearable** adj. **hearer** n.

hearing n. **1** the faculty of perceiving sounds. **2** the range within which sounds may be heard; earshot (within hearing). **3** the action or an act of listening. **4** an opportunity to state one's case (give them a fair hearing). **5** the listening to evidence and pleadings in a law court or other officially constituted body.

hearing aid n. a small device to amplify sound, worn by a partially deaf person in or behind the ear.

hearing ear dog n. (also **hearing dog**) a dog trained to guide a deaf person.

hearken /'hɑːkən/ v.intr. (often foll. by to) archaic or literary listen. □ **hearken back** mention again or remember an earlier subject, event, etc.

hearsay n. rumour, gossip.

hearse n. a vehicle for conveying the coffin at a funeral.

heart n. **1** a hollow muscular organ maintaining the circulation of blood by rhythmic contraction and dilation. **2** the region of the heart; the breast. **3 a** the heart regarded as the centre of emotion (esp. love). **b** a person's capacity for feeling emotion (has no heart). **4 a** courage or enthusiasm (lose heart). **b** one's mood or feeling (change of heart). **5 a** the central or innermost part of something. **b** the vital part or essence (the heart of the matter). **6** the close compact head of a cabbage, lettuce, etc. **7 a** a heart-shaped thing. **b** a conventional representation of a heart with two equal curves meeting at a point at the bottom and a cusp at the top. **8 a** a playing card of a suit denoted by a red figure of a heart. **b** (in pl.) this suit. **c** (in pl.) a card game in which players avoid taking tricks containing a card of this suit. **9** a beloved person (dear heart). □ **after one's own heart** sharing one's

tastes. **at heart 1** in one's innermost feelings. **2** basically, essentially. **break a person's heart** overwhelm a person with sorrow, esp. by ending a romantic relationship. **by heart** in or from memory. **close** (or **near**) **to one's heart 1** dear to one. **2** affecting one deeply. **from the heart** (or **the bottom of one's heart**) sincerely, profoundly. **give** (or **lose**) **one's heart** (often foll. by to) fall in love (with). **have a heart** be merciful. **have the heart** (usu. with neg.; foll. by to + infin.) be insensitive or hardhearted enough (didn't have the heart to ask him). **have** (or **put**) **one's heart in** be keenly involved in or committed to (an enterprise etc.). **have one's heart in one's mouth** be greatly alarmed or apprehensive. **have one's heart in the right place** be sincere or well-intentioned. **heart and soul** (with) all one's energies and affections. **heart of gold** a generous nature. **heart of stone** a stern or cruel nature. **hearts and minds** emotional and intellectual support. **heart to heart** candidly, intimately. **in one's heart of hearts** in one's innermost feelings. **sing** (or **play** etc.) **one's heart out** sing or play etc. to the fullest extent of one's ability. **take to heart** be much affected. **wear one's heart on one's sleeve** make one's feelings apparent. **with all one's heart** sincerely; with all goodwill. **with one's whole heart** with enthusiasm; without doubts or reservations. □ **-hearted** adj.

heartache n. mental anguish or grief.

heart attack n. a sudden occurrence of coronary thrombosis usu. resulting in the death of part of a heart muscle.

heartbeat n. **1** a pulsation of the heart. **2** the central or most important part (the heartbeat of the nation). □ **in a heartbeat** without hesitation or delay.

heartbreak n. overwhelming sorrow or distress. □ **heartbreaker** n. **heartbreaking** adj. **heartbreakingly** adv. **heartbroken** adj.

heartburn n. a burning sensation in the chest resulting from indigestion.

hearten v.tr. & intr. make or become more cheerful. □ **heartening** adj. **hearteningly** adv.

heart failure n. a severe failure of the heart to function properly, esp. as a cause of death.

heartfelt adj. sincere; deeply felt.

hearth /hɑːθ/ n. **1 a** the floor of a fireplace. **b** the area in front of a fireplace. **2** this symbolizing the home. **3** the bottom of a blast furnace where molten metal collects. □ **hearth and home** the home and its comforts.

heartily adv. **1** in a hearty manner; with goodwill, appetite, or courage. **2** to a great degree (esp. with reference to personal feelings) (am heartily sick of it).

heartland n. the central or most important part of an area.

heartless adj. unfeeling, pitiless. □ **heartlessly** adv. **heartlessness** n.

heart-lung machine n. a machine that temporarily takes over the functions of the heart and lungs, esp. in surgery.

heart murmur n. = MURMUR 3.

heart rate n. the pulse, calculated by counting the number of beats of the heart per unit of time.

heart-rending adj. causing great sorrow or distress. □ **heart-rendingly** adv.

heart-searching n. the thorough examination of one's own feelings and motives.

heartsick adj. despondent. □ **heartsickness** n.

heart-stopping adj. very suspenseful or thrilling. □ **heart-stopper** n.

heartstrings *n.pl.* one's deepest feelings or emotions.

heartthrob *n.* **1** *informal* an extremely attractive (usu. male) person, esp. an actor or other celebrity. **2** beating of the heart.

heart-to-heart ● *adj.* (of a conversation etc.) candid, intimate. ● *n.* a candid or personal conversation.

heartwarming *adj.* emotionally rewarding or uplifting. □ **heartwarmingly** *adv.*

heartwood *n.* the dense inner part of a tree trunk yielding the hardest timber.

heartworm *n.* **1** a parasitic nematode worm which infests the hearts of dogs. **2** the disease due to infestation by heartworm.

hearty ● *adj.* (**-ier, -iest**) **1** strong, vigorous (*hale and hearty*). **2** spirited. **3** (of a meal or appetite) large. **4** warm, friendly (*a hearty welcome*). **5** heartfelt, genuine, sincere. ● *n.* (*pl.* **-ies**) (usu. in *pl.*) (as a form of address) fellows, esp. fellow sailors. □ **heartiness** *n.*

heat ● *n.* **1 a** the condition of being hot. **b** the sensation or perception of this. **c** high temperature of the body. **2** *Physics* **a** a form of energy arising from the random motion of the molecules of bodies, which may be transferred by conduction, convection, or radiation. **b** the amount of this needed to cause a specific process, or given off in a process. **3** hot weather (*succumbed to the heat*). **4 a** warmth of feeling. **b** anger or excitement (*the heat of the argument*). **5** (foll. by *of*) the most intense part or period of an activity (*in the heat of the battle*). **6** a (usu. preliminary or trial) round in a race or contest. **7** the receptive period of the sexual cycle, esp. in female mammals. **8** redness of the skin with a sensation of heat (*prickly heat*). **9** pungency of flavour. **10** *slang* intensive pursuit, e.g. by the police. **11** *N Amer. slang* adverse criticism; blame. ● *v.* (often foll. by *up*) **1** *tr. & intr.* make or become hot or warm. **2** *tr.* inflame; excite or intensify. □ **in the heat of the moment** during or resulting from intense activity, without pause for thought. **in heat** (of mammals, esp. females) sexually receptive. **turn the heat on** *informal* concentrate an attack or criticism on (a person). □ **heatless** *adj.*

heated *adj.* **1** (of a person, discussions, etc.) angry; inflamed with passion or excitement. **2** made hot. □ **heatedly** *adv.*

heater *n.* **1** a device for warming the air in a room, car, etc. **2** a container with an element etc. for heating the contents (*water heater*). **3** *N Amer. slang* a gun. **4** *Baseball slang* = FASTBALL 1.

heat exchanger *n.* a device for the transfer of heat from one medium to another.

heath *n.* **1** an area of flattish uncultivated land with low shrubs. **2** a plant growing on a heath, esp. of the genus *Erica* or *Calluna* (e.g. heather).

heathen /ˈhiːðən/ ● *n.* **1** *derogatory* a person who does not belong to a widely held religion (esp. who is not Christian, Jewish, or Muslim) as regarded by those that do. **2** an unenlightened person; a person regarded as lacking culture or moral principles. **3** (**the heathen**) heathen people collectively. **4** *Bible* a Gentile. ● *adj.* **1** of or relating to heathens; pagan. **2** having no religion. □ **heathenism** *n.*

heather *n.* **1** an evergreen shrub, *Calluna vulgaris*, with purple bell-shaped flowers. **2** any of various shrubs, e.g. of the genus *Erica* or *Phyllodoce*, growing esp. on moors or in mountainous regions.

heathland *n.* an extensive area of heath.

heating *n.* **1** the imparting or generation of heat. **2** equipment or devices used to provide heat, esp. to a building.

heating pad *n.* a fabric-covered pad containing an electric heating element, placed on the body to relieve aches and pains.

heat lamp *n.* a lamp used for its heat as well as its light.

heatproof *adj.* (also **heat-resistant**) able to resist great heat.

heat pump *n.* a device for the transfer of heat from a colder area to a hotter area by using mechanical energy.

heat rash *n.* = PRICKLY HEAT.

heat-seeking *adj.* (of a missile etc.) able to detect infrared radiation to guide it to its target.

heat sink *n.* a device or substance for absorbing excessive or unwanted heat.

heatstroke *n.* a feverish condition caused by excessive exposure to high temperature.

heat treatment *n.* the use of heat to modify the properties of a metal etc. □ **heat-treat** *v.tr.*

heat wave *n.* a prolonged period of abnormally hot weather.

heave ● *v.* (*past* and *past part.* **heaved** or esp. *Naut.* **hove**) **1** *tr.* lift or haul (a heavy thing) with great effort. **2** *tr.* utter with effort or resignation (*heaved a sigh*). **3** *tr.* throw. **4** *intr.* rise and fall rhythmically or spasmodically. **5** *tr. Naut.* haul by rope. **6** *intr.* retch or vomit. **7** *intr.* rise up above the general surface; expand, shift (*the floor heaved during the winter*). ● *n.* **1 a** an instance of heaving. **b** an uneven area of road etc. caused by heaving due to frost. **2** *Geol.* a sideways displacement in a fault. **3** (in *pl.*; prec. by *the*) *slang* a bout of retching or vomiting. □ **heave in sight** (or **into view**) come into view. **heave to** esp. *Naut.* bring or be brought to a standstill. □ **heaver** *n.*

heave-ho ● *n.* (usu. prec. by *the* or *the old*) *slang* rejection or dismissal (*the bank gave him the heave-ho*). ● *interj.* a sailors' cry, esp. on raising the anchor.

heaven *n.* **1** (also **Heaven**) a place regarded in some religions as the abode of God and the angels, and of the good after death, often characterized as above the sky. **2** a place or state of supreme bliss. **3** *informal* something delightful. **4** God, Providence (often in *sing.* or *pl.* as an exclamation or mild oath: *for heaven's sake*). **5** (**the heavens**) the sky as the abode of the sun, moon, and stars. □ **in seventh heaven** in a state of ecstasy. **move heaven and earth** (foll. by *to* + *infin.*) make extraordinary efforts. □ **heavenward** *adj. & adv.* **heavenwards** *adv.*

heavenly *adj.* **1** of heaven; divine. **2** of the heavens or sky. **3** *informal* very pleasing; wonderful.

heavenly body *n.* a natural object in outer space, e.g. the sun, a star, a planet, etc.

heavenly hash *n.* *N Amer.* a flavour of ice cream combining chocolate ice cream, marshmallow, chocolate chunks, and chocolate-coated almonds.

heavenly host *n.* see HOST[1] 3.

heaven-sent *adj.* providential; wonderfully opportune.

heavier-than-air *adj.* (of an aircraft) weighing more than the air it displaces.

heavy ● *adj.* (**-ier, -iest**) **1 a** of great weight; difficult to lift. **b** (of a person) fat, overweight. **2 a** of great density. **b** *Physics* having a greater than the usual mass (esp. of isotopes and compounds containing them). **3** abundant, considerable (*a heavy crop*). **4** severe, intense, extensive, excessive (*heavy fighting*). **5** doing something to excess (*a heavy drinker*). **6 a** striking or falling with force (*heavy blows; heavy rain*). **b** (of a body of water) having large powerful waves. **7** (of rock music etc.) highly amplified with a strong beat.

8 (of machinery, artillery, etc.) very large of its kind; large in calibre etc. **9** causing a strong impact (*heavy drugs*). **10** needing much physical effort (*heavy work*). **11** (foll. by *with*) laden. **12** carrying heavy weapons (*the heavy brigade*). **13 a** (of a speech, writing, etc.) serious or sombre in tone or attitude; dull, tedious. **b** (of temperament) dignified, stern. **c** (of an issue etc.) grave; important, weighty. **14 a** (of food) hard to digest. **b** (of a literary work etc.) hard to read or understand. **15** (of bread etc.) too dense from not having risen. **16** (of ground) difficult to traverse or work. **17 a** oppressive; hard to endure (*heavy demands*). **b** (of the atmosphere, weather, etc.) overcast; oppressive, sultry. **18 a** coarse, ungraceful (*heavy features*). **b** unwieldy. **19** sad, dejected (*a heavy heart*). **20** loud and deep in sound (*a heavy thud*). **21** *slang* **a** dangerous, threatening (*a heavy scene*). **b** excellent, cool. **c** important, profound. **22** strong, sturdy (*heavy canvas*). ● *n.* (*pl.* **-ies**) **1** *informal* a large violent person; a thug. **2** a villainous or tragic role or actor in a play etc. (usu. in *pl.*). **3** anything large or heavy of its kind, e.g. a piece of artillery. ● *adv.* heavily (esp. in *comb.*: *heavy-laden*). □ **heavy on** using a lot of (*heavy on gas*). □ **heavily** *adv.* **heaviness** *n.*

heavy cream *n. N Amer.* = WHIPPING CREAM.

heavy-duty *adj.* **1** intended to withstand hard use. **2** *N Amer. informal* significant in size, amount, etc.

heavy going *n.* slow or difficult to progress with (*found the book heavy going*).

heavy-handed *adj.* **1** clumsy. **2** overbearing, oppressive. □ **heavy-handedly** *adv.* **heavy-handedness** *n.*

heavy hitter *n. N Amer. informal* an important or powerful person.

heavy hydrogen *n.* = DEUTERIUM.

heavy industry *n.* industry producing metal, machinery, etc.

heavy metal *n.* **1** (often *attrib.*) a type of highly amplified, loud, vigorous rock music with a strong, usu. fast beat and often theatrical performance. **2** metal of high density. **3** heavy guns.

heavy oil *n.* **1** any oil of a high specific gravity. **2** such an oil obtained from coal tar by distillation.

heavy-set *adj.* (of a person) stocky, burly.

heavy water *n.* a form of water consisting of deuterium oxide, used as a moderator in nuclear reactors.

heavyweight *n.* **1 a** a weight in certain sports, in the amateur boxing scale over 81 kg but differing for professional boxers and wrestlers (also *attrib.*: *heavyweight championship*). **b** a sportsman of this weight. **2** a person, animal, or thing of above average weight (also *attrib.*: *heavyweight cotton*). **3** *informal* a person of influence or importance.

Hebrew /ˈhiːbruː/ ● *n.* **1** a member of a Semitic people originally centred in ancient Palestine and traditionally descended from Abraham, Isaac, and Jacob. **2 a** the language of this people. **b** a modern form of this used esp. in Israel. ● *adj.* **1** of or in Hebrew. **2** of the Hebrews or the Jews. □ **Hebraic** *adj.*

Hebrew Bible *n.* the sacred writings of Judaism, called by Christians the Old Testament, consisting of the Torah (the Law or Pentateuch), the Prophets, and the Hagiographa or Writings.

heck *informal* ● *interj.* a mild exclamation of surprise or dismay. ● *adv.* as an intensifier (*a heck of a job*). □ **what the heck** expressing indifference, dismissal of a difficulty, etc.

heckle ● *v.tr.* interrupt and harass (a public speaker). ● *n.* an act of heckling. □ **heckler** *n.*

heckuva /ˈhekəvə/ *adj. & adv. informal* = HELLUVA.

hectare /ˈhekteɪ, -tɑr/ *n.* a metric unit of land measure, equal to 100 ares (2.471 acres or 10,000 square metres). Abbr.: **ha**.

hectic *adj.* busy and confused; characterized by feverish excitement or haste. □ **hectically** *adv.*

hecto- /ˈhektoʊ/ *comb. form* a hundred, esp. of a unit in the metric system. Abbr.: **h**.

hectogram /ˈhektəˌgræm/ *n.* a metric unit of mass, equal to one hundred grams.

hectolitre /ˈhektəˌliːtər/ *n.* (also esp. *US* **hectoliter**) a metric unit of capacity, equal to one hundred litres.

hectometre /ˈhektəˌmiːtər/ *n.* (also esp. *US* **hectometer**) a metric unit of length, equal to one hundred metres.

hector ● *v.* **1** *tr.* bully, intimidate. **2** *intr.* brag, bluster, domineer. ● *n.* a bully. □ **hectoring** *adj.*

he'd *contraction* **1** he had. **2** he would.

heder *var. of* CHEDER.

hedge ● *n.* **1** a fence or boundary formed by closely growing bushes or shrubs. **2** a protection against possible loss or diminution. **3** an equivocal or evasive statement. ● *v.* **1** *tr.* surround or bound with or as with a hedge. **2** *tr.* (foll. by *in*) enclose. **3 a** *tr.* reduce one's risk of loss on (a bet or speculation) by compensating transactions on the other side. **b** *intr.* avoid a definite decision or commitment. **4** *intr.* make or trim hedges. □ **hedge one's bets** protect oneself against loss or error by supporting more than one side in a contest, an argument, etc. □ **hedger** *n.*

hedgehog *n.* **1** any small nocturnal insect-eating mammal of the Old World genus *Erinaceus*, esp. *E. europaeus*, having a piglike snout and a coat of spines, and rolling itself up into a ball for defence. **2** a porcupine or other animal covered with spines.

hedgerow *n.* a row of bushes etc. forming a hedge.

hedge trimmer *n.* an electric device for trimming hedges.

hedonic /hiːˈdɒnɪk, he-/ *adj.* **1** of or characterized by pleasure. **2** *Psych.* of pleasant or unpleasant sensations.

hedonism /ˈhiːdəˌnɪzəm, hed-/ *n.* **1** belief in pleasure as the highest good. **2** behaviour based on this; the pursuit of pleasure. □ **hedonist** *n.* **hedonistic** *adj.*

heebie-jeebies *n.pl.* (prec. by *the*) *slang* a state of nervous depression or anxiety.

heed ● *v.tr.* take notice of. ● *n.* careful attention.

heedful *adj.* (often foll. by *of*) mindful, attentive; careful, cautious. □ **heedfully** *adv.* **heedfulness** *n.*

heedless *adj.* (often foll. by *of*) inattentive, regardless; careless (*went out, heedless of the rain*). □ **heedlessly** *adv.* **heedlessness** *n.*

hee-haw ● *n.* the bray of a donkey. ● *v.intr.* emit a braying sound.

hee hee *interj.* representing laughter, esp. in amusement, derision, triumph, etc.

heel[1] ● *n.* **1** the back part of the foot below the ankle. **2** the corresponding part in vertebrate animals. **3 a** the part of a sock etc. covering the heel. **b** the part of a shoe or boot supporting the heel. **c** (in *pl.*) high-heeled shoes. **4** a thing like a heel in form or position, e.g. the part of the palm next to the wrist, or the part of a hockey stick near where the blade joins the shaft. **5** *informal* a person regarded with contempt or disapproval. **6** (as *interj.*) a command to a dog to walk close to a person's heels. ● *v.* **1** *tr.* fit or renew a heel on (a shoe or boot). **2** *intr.* touch the ground with the heel as in dancing. **3** *intr.* (of a dog) follow obediently at a person's heels. □ **at** (or **on**) **the heels of** following closely after (a person or event). **cool one's heels** be kept waiting. **take to one's heels** run away. **to heel 1** (of a dog) close behind. **2** (of a person etc.) under control. **turn on one's heel** turn sharply round. □ **heelless** adj.

heel² ● v. **1** intr. (of a ship etc.) lean over owing to the pressure of wind or an uneven load (compare LIST²). **2** tr. cause (a ship etc.) to do this. ● n. the act or amount of heeling.

heft ● v.tr. lift (something heavy), esp. to judge its weight. ● n. N Amer. informal weight, heaviness.

hefty adj. (**-ier, -iest**) **1** (of a person) big and strong. **2** (of a thing) large, heavy, powerful. **3** substantial, considerable (a hefty fee increase). □ **heftily** adv.

hegemonic /ˌhedʒə'mɒnɪk, ˌhegə-/ adj. ruling, supreme.

hegemony /hə'dʒeməni, -'gem-, 'hedʒə,mo:ni/ n. (pl. **-ies**) leadership esp. by one state of a confederacy.

hegira /'hedʒɪrə, hɪ'gi:rə/ n. **1** (**Hegira**) **a** Muhammad's departure from Mecca to Medina in AD 622. **b** the Muslim era reckoned from this date. **2** a general exodus or departure.

heh heh interj. expressing chuckling.

heifer n. a female domestic bovine animal that has not borne a calf, or has borne only one calf.

height n. **1** the measurement from base to top or (of a standing person) from head to foot. **2** the elevation above ground or a recognized level (usu. sea level). **3** any considerable elevation. **4** (often in pl.) **a** a high place or area. **b** rising ground. **c** the state of being high above the ground (afraid of heights). **5** the top of something. **6 a** the most intense part or period of anything (the battle was at its height). **b** an extreme instance or example (the height of fashion).

heighten v.tr. & intr. make or become higher or more intense. □ **heightened** adj.

height of land n. esp. Cdn a watershed.

Heiltsuk /'hailtsʊk/ ● n. **1** a member of an Aboriginal group living on the coast of BC. **2** the Wakashan language of this people. ● adj. of or relating to the Heiltsuk or their culture or language.

Heimlich manoeuvre /'haimlɪk/ n. a first aid procedure to dislodge a foreign object from the windpipe of a choking person by administering a sudden upward thrust of the fist to the victim's upper abdomen.

heinous /'heinəs, 'hi:nəs/ adj. (of a crime or criminal) utterly odious or wicked. □ **heinously** adv.

Heinz 57 /hainz/ n. slang a mongrel, esp. a dog.

heir /er/ n. **1** a person entitled to property or rank as the legal successor of its former owner (often foll. by to: heir to the throne). **2** a person deriving or morally entitled to some thing, quality, etc., from a predecessor.

heir apparent n. (pl. **heirs apparent**) **1** an heir whose claim cannot be set aside by the birth of another heir. **2** a person considered likely to succeed another, e.g. as head of political party or corporation. ¶This sense derives from a misunderstanding of the original meaning of heir apparent, but is well established.

heiress /'erəs/ n. **1** a woman entitled to property or rank as the legal successor of its former owner (often foll. by to: heiress to a huge fortune). **2** a woman deriving or morally entitled to some thing, quality, etc., from a predecessor.

heirloom ● n. **1** a piece of personal property that has been in a family for several generations. **2** a piece of property received as part of an inheritance. ● adj. **1** of or designating seeds that have been passed down

from one generation to another. **2** of or designating fruits or vegetables grown with these seeds.

heir presumptive n. (pl. **heirs presumptive**) an heir whose claim may be set aside by the birth of another heir.

heist N Amer. slang ● n. a robbery. ● v.tr. rob.

hejira var. of HEGIRA.

held past and past part. of HOLD¹.

helianthus /ˌhi:li'ænθəs/ n. any plant of the genus Helianthus, including the sunflower.

helical /'helɪkəl/ adj. having the form of a helix.

helices pl. of HELIX.

helichrysum /ˌheli'kraizəm/ n. any composite plant of the genus Helichrysum, with flowers retaining their appearance when dried.

helicopter ● n. a type of aircraft without wings, obtaining lift and propulsion from horizontally revolving overhead blades or rotors, and capable of moving vertically and horizontally. ● v.tr. & intr. transport or fly by helicopter.

heli-logging n. N Amer. the removal of felled timber by helicopter. □ **heli-log** v.tr. **heli-logger** n.

heliocentric /ˌhi:liə'sentrɪk/ adj. **1** having, representing, or regarding the sun as centre. **2** considered as viewed from the sun's centre.

helium n. a colourless, light, inert, gaseous element occurring in deposits of natural gas, used in airships and as a refrigerant.

helix /'hi:lɪks/ n. (pl. **helices** /'hi:lɪ,si:z, 'hel-/) **1** an object of coiled form, either a spiral curve around an axis like a corkscrew or a coiled curve in one plane. **2** Math. a three-dimensional curve on a conical or cylindrical surface which becomes a straight line when the surface is unrolled into a plane.

hell ● n. **1 a** the abode of the dead; in Christian, Jewish, and Islamic belief, the place of punishment or torment where the souls of the damned are confined after death. **b** the kingdom, power, inhabitants, or forces of hell collectively. **2 a** a place or state of suffering, misery, or wickedness. **b** extreme chaos, turmoil, etc. (all hell broke loose). ● interj. informal used as an exclamation of surprise, annoyance, etc. □ **as hell** as an intensifier (sure as hell). **beat** (or **scare,** etc.) **the hell out of** informal beat, scare, etc. severely. **be hell on** slang be unpleasant or harmful to, tough on, etc. (**come**) **hell or high water** (despite) any obstacles or problems. **for the hell of it** informal for fun; on impulse. **from hell** indicating the worst possible example, instance, etc. (the date from hell). **get** (or **catch**) **hell** informal be severely scolded or punished. **give** (**a person**) **hell** informal **1** scold or punish (a person). **2** make things extremely difficult, challenging, or unpleasant for (a person, another team, etc.). **go to hell** be damned, get lost, go away. **the hell** (usu. prec. by what, where, who, etc.) expressing anger, disbelief, etc. or merely emphatic (who the hell are you?). **hell** (or **hell-bent**) **for leather** at full speed. **hell of a** (or **helluva**) exceedingly bad, good, remarkable, etc. (one hell of an athlete). **hell on wheels** a wild or terrible person or thing, esp. one of great speed or ferocity. **hell's bells** expressing anger or annoyance. **hell's half acre** a great distance. **hell to pay** great trouble, discord, pandemonium, etc., esp. as a result of previous action. **in hell** as an intensifier (what in hell have you done?). **like hell** informal **1** recklessly, desperately, exceedingly. **2** ironic not at all, on the contrary. **not a hope in hell** informal no chance at all. **play hell** (or **merry hell**) **with** informal **1** be upsetting or disruptive to. **2** damage. **raise hell** cause trouble, create chaos. **till** (or **until**

or **when**) **hell freezes over** never; to (or at) some date in the impossibly distant future. **to hell** as an intensifier (*shot to hell*). **to hell and gone 1** a great distance. **2** endlessly, forever. **to hell with 1** expressing exasperated dismissal of (a person, thing, etc.). **2** endlessly, forever. **what the hell** *informal* expressing dismissal of a difficulty etc., i.e. it is of no importance. ☐ **hell-like** *adj.*

he'll *contraction* he will; he shall.

hellacious /heˈleɪʃəs/ *adj. N Amer. slang* **1** hellish, extremely awful. **2** tremendous, spectacularly awesome. ☐ **hellaciously** *adv.*

hell-bent *adj.* (foll. by *on*) recklessly determined.

hellebore /ˈhelɪˌbɔr/ *n.* **1** any evergreen plant of the genus *Helleborus*, having large white, green, or purplish flowers, e.g. the Christmas rose. **2** a plant, *Veratrum album*.

Hellene /ˈheliːn/ *n.* **1** a native or citizen of modern Greece. **2** an ancient Greek. ☐ **Hellenic** /heˈlenɪk, -ˈliːnɪk/ *adj.*

Hellenism /ˈhelə,nɪzəm/ *n.* **1** Greek character or culture (esp. of ancient Greece). **2** the study or imitation of Greek culture. ☐ **Hellenize** *v.tr. & intr.* **Hellenization** *n.*

Hellenistic *adj.* of or relating to the period of Greek history, language, and culture 323–31 BC, during which Greek culture spread through the Mediterranean and into the Near East and Asia.

hellfire *n.* **1** the fire or fires of hell. **2 a** the punishments and torments of hell. **b** (*attrib.*) (esp. of preaching) emphasizing the damnation of unsaved souls and the eternal punishments of hell.

hellhole *n.* an extremely oppressive or unbearable place.

hellion /ˈheliən/ *n. N Amer. informal* **1** a rowdy, troublemaking, disreputable person. **2** a rowdy, mischievous, or difficult child.

hellish *adj.* **1** like hell. **2** *informal* extremely difficult or unpleasant. ☐ **hellishly** *adv.* **hellishness** *n.*

hello ● *interj.* **1 a** an expression of informal greeting, or of surprise. **b** used to begin a telephone conversation. **2** used to call attention. **3** *N Amer.* used to reproach ignorance or inattention. ● *n.* (*pl.* **-os**) an instance of saying 'hello'.

hellraiser *n.* a person who causes trouble or creates chaos, esp. habitually. ☐ **hellraising** *adj. & n.*

Hell's Angel *n.* a member of a gang of motorcyclists notorious for violent behaviour and disturbances of the civil order.

helluva *adj. & adv. informal* = HELL OF A (see HELL).

helm ● *n.* **1** a tiller or wheel by which a ship's rudder is controlled. **2** the amount by which this is turned (*more helm needed*). **3** a position of leadership or government. ● *v.tr.* **1** steer or guide with a helm. **2** lead; control. ☐ **at the helm** in control.

helmet *n.* **1** any of various protective head coverings worn by soldiers, miners, athletes, motorcyclists, etc. **2** a device fitting over the head and including a screen on which virtual reality images are displayed. ☐ **helmeted** *adj.* **helmetless** *adj.*

helmsman *n.* (*pl.* **-men**) a person who steers a ship.

help ● *v.* **1** *tr.* aid, assist, or provide (a person etc.) with what is needed or sought (*helped me with my work*; *helped me (to) pay my debts*). **2** *tr.* (foll. by *up*, *down*, *on with*, etc.) assist or give support to (a person) in moving etc. as specified (*helped her into the chair*). **3 a** *tr. & intr.* benefit, do good to, or be of use or service to (a person) (*does that help?*). **b** *tr.* assist in achieving, promote, further, or make (an action, process, etc.) more effective. **4** *tr.* contribute to alleviating (a pain, difficulty, misfortune, etc.). **5** *tr.* prevent, remedy, or cause to be otherwise (*it can't be helped*). **6** (usu. with *neg.*) **a** *tr.* refrain from (*could not help laughing*). **b** *tr.* be unavoidable (*can't help it*). **c** *refl.* make an effort on one's own behalf, extricate oneself from a difficulty (*couldn't help himself*). ● *n.* **1** aid, assistance, or the act of helping or being helped (*we need your help*). **2** a source or means of assistance, esp. a person or thing that helps. **3** an employee or domestic servant, or several collectively. **4** a remedy or escape (*there is no help for it*). ☐ **can't** (or **cannot**) **help but** be obliged to or unable to do other (*can't help but share his worry*). **help oneself** (often foll. by *to*) **1** serve oneself (with food). **2** take without seeking help or permission. **help a person out** give a person help, esp. in difficulty. **not if I can help it** that I can prevent it. **so help me** (or **help me God**) (as an invocation or oath) as I keep my word, as I speak the truth, etc. ☐ **helper** *n.*

helpdesk *n.* a service which assists customers or users who have problems with esp. computer equipment or software.

helpful *adj.* (of a person or thing) giving or productive of help; useful. ☐ **helpfully** *adv.* **helpfulness** *n.*

helping *n.* **1** a portion of food esp. at a meal. **2** a portion of something offered (*generous helpings of propaganda*).

helping hand *n.* an act of assistance.

helping profession *n.* one of the professions whose function is to provide help to people, e.g. medicine, social work, teaching, ministry, etc.

helpless *adj.* **1** unable to function independently or act without help. **2** lacking help or protection; defenceless. **3** unhelpful. ☐ **helplessly** *adv.* **helplessness** *n.*

helpline *n.* a telephone service providing help and advice, either for personal problems or for an item one has bought.

helpmate *n.* a helpful companion or partner, usu. a husband or wife.

help-wanted index *n. Cdn* a rough, seasonally adjusted measure of the job market calculated from help-wanted advertisements in newspapers.

helter-skelter ● *adv. & adj.* in disorderly haste, random order, or confusion. ● *n.* disorder or confusion.

hem[1] ● *n.* **1** the border of a piece of cloth, esp. a cut edge turned under and sewn down. **2** HEMLINE. ● *v.tr.* (**hemmed**, **hemming**) turn under and sew in the edge of (a piece of cloth etc.). ☐ **hem in** confine; restrict the movement of.

hem[2] ● *interj.* calling attention or expressing hesitation by a slight cough or clearing of the throat. ● *n.* an utterance of this. ● *v.intr.* (**hemmed**, **hemming**) hesitate in speech. ☐ **hem and haw** hesitate in speaking, esp. through indecision, disagreement, etc.

he-man *n.* (*pl.* **-men**) *informal* often *ironic* a particularly strong, masterful, or virile man.

hematite /ˈhiːmə,taɪt/ *n.* ferric oxide occurring as a dark red mineral which is an important ore of iron.

hemato- /ˈhiːmətoʊ/ *comb. form* = HEMO-.

hematology /ˌhiːməˈtɒlədʒi/ *n.* the branch of medicine that deals with the blood, esp. in disorders. ☐ **hematologic** *adj.* **hematological** *adj.* **hematologist** *n.*

hematoma /ˌhiːməˈtoʊmə/ *n. Med.* a solid swelling of clotted blood within the tissues.

heme /hiːm/ *n.* a non-protein compound containing iron, responsible for the red colour of hemoglobin.

hemi- /ˈhemi/ *comb. form* half.

hemisphere /ˈhemɪsfɪr/ *n.* **1** a half of the earth, esp. as divided by the equator (into **northern** and

southern hemisphere) or by an imaginary line passing through the poles (into **eastern** and **western hemisphere**). **2** *Anat.* (in full **cerebral hemisphere**) each of the halves of the cerebrum. **3** half of a sphere. □ **hemispheric** /-'sferɪk/ *adj.* **hemispherical** *adj.*

hemline *n.* the line or level of the lower edge of a skirt, dress, or coat.

hemlock *n.* **1 a** a poisonous umbelliferous plant, *Conium maculatum*, with fernlike leaves and small white flowers. **b** a poisonous potion obtained from this. **2** (in full **hemlock fir** or **hemlock spruce**) **a** any coniferous tree of the genus *Tsuga*, having foliage that smells like hemlock when crushed. **b** the timber or pitch of these trees.

hemo- /'hiːmoː/ *comb. form* blood.

hemodialysis *n.* = DIALYSIS 2.

hemoglobin /ˌhiːmə'gloːbɪn/ *n.* a red, oxygen-carrying substance containing iron, present in the red blood cells of vertebrates.

hemolysis /hiː'mɒlɪsɪs/ *n.* the loss of hemoglobin from red blood cells. □ **hemolytic** /-mə'lɪtɪk/ *adj.*

hemophilia /ˌhiːmə'fiːlɪə/ *n.* a usu. hereditary disorder with a tendency to bleed severely from even a slight injury, through the failure of the blood to clot normally. □ **hemophilic** *adj.*

hemophiliac /ˌhiːmə'fiːliˌæk/ *n.* a person with hemophilia.

hemorrhage /'hemərɪdʒ/ • *n.* **1** an escape of blood from a ruptured blood vessel, esp. when profuse. **2** a damaging or uncontrolled outflow of something, esp. of people or assets from a country, organization, etc. • *v.* **1** *intr.* undergo a hemorrhage; bleed heavily. **2** *intr.* be extensively lost or dissipated. **3** *tr.* expend (money etc.) in large amounts; lose or dissipate, esp. wastefully. □ **hemorrhagic** /hemə'rædʒɪk/ *adj.*

hemorrhoid /'hemərɔɪd/ *n.* (usu. in *pl.*) swollen veins at or near the anus; piles.

hemostasis /ˌhiːmoː'steɪsɪs/ *n.* the stopping of the flow of blood. □ **hemostatic** /ˌhiːmoː'stætɪk, ˌhe-/ *adj.*

hemp *n.* **1** (in full **Indian hemp**) a herbaceous plant, *Cannabis sativa*, native to Asia. **2** its fibre extracted from the stem and used to make rope and stout fabrics. **3** any of several narcotic drugs made from the hemp plant (compare CANNABIS, MARIJUANA). **4** any of several other plants yielding fibre, e.g. manila hemp.

hen *n.* **1 a** a female bird, esp. of a domestic fowl. **b** (in *pl.*) domestic fowls of either sex. **2** a female lobster or crab or salmon. □ **rare as hen's teeth** very rare.

hence *adv.* **1** from this time (*two years hence*). **2 a** for this reason; as a result of inference (*hence we seem to be wrong*). **b** from this source, fact, or circumstance.

henceforth *adv.* (also **henceforward**) from this time onward.

henchman *n.* (pl. **-men**) usu. *derogatory* **1** a trusted supporter or faithful follower who always obeys the orders of his or her leader. **2** an often unscrupulous, self-serving, and ambitious subordinate or lackey.

henge /hendʒ/ *n.* any large circular monument, usu. of later neolithic date, comprising a bank and internal ditch which may enclose massive stone or wooden structures.

henhouse *n.* a building in which poultry roost.

henna /'henə/ • *n.* **1** a tropical shrub, *Lawsonia inermis*, having small pink, red, or white flowers. **2** the reddish dye from its shoots and leaves esp. used to colour hair. • *v.tr.* dye with henna. □ **hennaed** *adj.*

henpeck *v.tr.* (of a woman) constantly harass, nag, or domineer over (a man). □ **henpecked** *adj.*

henry *n.* (pl. **-ies** or **-s**) the SI unit of inductance.

hep¹ *var. of* HIP³.

hep² *n.* *informal* hepatitis.

heparin /'hepərɪn/ *n.* a sulphur-containing polysaccharide with anticoagulant properties, present in the blood and various bodily organs and tissues.

hepatic /hɪ'pætɪk/ *adj.* **1** of or relating to the liver. **2** dark brownish red; liver-coloured.

hepatica /hɪ'pætɪkə/ *n.* any plant of the genus *Hepatica*, with reddish-brown lobed leaves resembling the liver.

hepatitis /ˌhepə'taɪtɪs/ *n.* inflammation of the liver.

hepatitis A *n.* a form of viral hepatitis transmitted in food, causing fever and jaundice.

hepatitis B *n.* a severe form of viral hepatitis transmitted in infected blood and other body fluids, causing fever, debility, and jaundice.

hepatitis C *n.* a very serious form of hepatitis, transmitted through untreated blood and blood products and often resulting in chronic disease.

hepcat *n.* *slang* **1** a jazz musician. **2** a hip person.

Hepplewhite /'hepəlˌwaɪt/ *n.* a late 18th-c. style of furniture, originally as made by the English cabinetmaker George Hepplewhite (d.1786), characterized by lightness, delicacy, and graceful curves.

heptagon /'heptəgɒn/ *n.* a plane figure with seven sides and angles. □ **heptagonal** /-'tægənəl/ *adj.*

heptahedron /ˌheptə'hiːdrən/ *n.* (pl. **-hedrons** or **-hedra** /-drə/) a solid figure with seven faces. □ **heptahedral** *adj.*

her • *pron.* **1** *objective case of* SHE (*I like her*). **2** *informal* she (*it's her all right*; *am older than her*). ¶The use of *her* instead of *she* after the verb 'to be' (as in sense 2) is considered by some to be incorrect but is normal in ordinary usage. *Him, me, them,* and *us* are used similarly, e.g. *It's them on the phone again*; *It's us who will have to pay for it.* See also Usage Note at THAN. • *possess.adj.* (*attrib.*) **1** of or belonging to her or herself (*her house*). **2** (**Her**) (in titles) that she is (*Her Majesty*).

herald • *n.* **1** an official messenger bringing news. **2** a forerunner (*spring is the herald of summer*). • *v.tr.* **1** proclaim the approach of; usher in (*her arrival heralds a new era*). **2** acclaim; praise (*heralded as the year's biggest success*).

heraldic /he'rældɪk/ *adj.* of or concerning heraldry. □ **heraldically** *adv.*

heraldry *n.* **1** the science or art of a herald, esp. that of blazoning armorial bearings and deciding the rights of people to bear arms. **2** heraldic pomp, or the ceremony characteristic of a herald. **3 a** the heraldic charge or device which is pictured on a coat of arms. **b** heraldic devices collectively.

herb /hɜrb, ɜrb/ *n.* **1** any non-woody seed-bearing plant which dies down to the ground after flowering. **2** any plant with leaves, seeds, or flowers used for flavouring, food, medicine, scent, etc. □ **herblike** *adj.*

herbaceous /hɜr'beɪʃəs/ *adj.* **1** of or like herbs (*see* HERB 1). **2 a** (of a plant) not woody or not having a woody stem. **b** resembling a leaf in colour or texture.

herbaceous perennial *n.* a plant whose growth dies down annually but whose roots etc. survive.

herbage *n.* **1** herbs collectively. **2** the succulent part of herbs, esp. as pasture.

herbal • *adj.* pertaining to or containing herbs, esp. in therapeutic and culinary use. • *n.* a book with descriptions and accounts of the properties of these.

herbalist *n.* **1 a** a person who practises or advocates the use of herbs to treat disease. **b** a dealer in medicinal herbs. **2** a person skilled in herbs, esp. an early botanical writer. ☐ **herbalism** n.

herbal tea n. (also **herb tea**) an infusion of dried herbs, usu. non-caffeinated.

herbarium /hɑrˈberiəm, ɜrb-/ n. (pl. **herbaria** /-riə/) **1** a systematically arranged collection of dried plants. **2** a book, room, or building for these.

herbed adj. flavoured with herbs.

herbicide /ˈhɜrbɪˌsaɪd, ˈɜrb-/ n. a substance toxic to plants and used to destroy unwanted vegetation. ☐ **herbicidal** adj.

herbivore /ˈhɜrbɪˌvɔr, ˈɜrb-/ n. an animal that feeds on plants. ☐ **herbivorous** /-ˈbɪvɡrəs/ adj.

herby adj. (**-ier, -iest**) **1** abounding in herbs. **2** of the nature of a culinary or medicinal herb.

Herculean /ˌhɜrkjəˈliːən, ˌhɜrˈkjuːliən/ adj. **1** having or requiring great strength or effort. **2** of, like, or pertaining to Hercules.

herd ● n. **1** a large number of animals, esp. cattle, feeding, travelling, or kept together. **2** derogatory **a** a large number of people; a mob. **b** (prec. by the) the majority viewed as mindless followers (prefers not to follow the herd). ● v. **1** intr. & tr. go, drive, or cause to go together in or as in a herd (herded together for warmth). **2** tr. tend (sheep, cattle, etc.). **3** tr. drive (an animal or person) in a particular direction. ☐ **ride herd on** N Amer. keep watch on or control over, esp. by close supervision. ☐ **herder** n. **herding** n.

herdsman n. (pl. **-men**) the owner or keeper of herds (of domestic animals).

here ● adv. **1** in or at or to this place or position (put it here; lives here; comes here every day). **2** indicating a person's presence or a thing offered (here is your coat; my son here will show you). **3** at this point in the argument, situation, etc. (here I have a question). ● n. this place (get out of here; fill it up to here). ● interj. **1** calling attention (here, where are you going with that?). **2** indicating one's presence in a roll call. ☐ **here and now 1** at this very moment; immediately. **2** (prec. by the) the present reality. **here and there** in various places. **here goes!** informal an expression indicating the start of a bold act. **here's to** I drink to the health, success, etc. of. **here we are** informal **1** said as acknowledgement of a given state (here we are, broke again). **2** said on arrival at one's destination. **here we go again** informal the same, usu. undesirable, events are recurring. **here you are 1** said on handing something to somebody. **2** said in acknowledgement of an individual's presence, condition, or achievement (and here you are, a doctor). **neither here nor there** of no importance or relevance.

hereabouts adv. about or near this place.

hereafter ● adv. **1 a** from now on; in the future. **b** formal HEREINAFTER. **2** in the world to come (after death). ● n. **1** the future. **2** life after death.

hereby adv. by this means; as a result of this.

hereditary adj. **1** (of a characteristic, disease, etc.) able to be passed down from one generation to another. **2 a** descending by inheritance. **b** holding a position by inheritance. **3** the same as or resembling what one's parents had (a hereditary hatred). **4** of or relating to inheritance.

hereditary chief n. a chief of an Indian band through hereditary right, as opposed to election.

heredity n. **1 a** the passing on of physical or mental characteristics genetically from one generation to another. **b** these characteristics in a particular individual. **2** the genetic constitution of an individual.

Hereford /ˈhɜrfɜrd, ˈherəfɜrd/ n. a breed of red and white beef cattle.

herein /hiːˈrɪn/ adv. formal **1** in this document, book, etc. **2** in this matter, particular, case, etc.

hereinafter adv. esp. Law formal **1** from this point on. **2** in a later part of this document etc.

heresy /ˈherəsi/ n. (pl. **-ies**) **1 a** belief or practice contrary to the orthodox doctrine of a given religion. **b** an instance of this. **2 a** opinion contrary to what is normally accepted or maintained in any subject, field, etc. **b** an instance of this.

heretic n. **1** the holder of an unorthodox opinion in a subject, field, etc. **2** esp. hist. a person believing in or practising religious heresy. ☐ **heretical** /hɪˈretɪkəl/ adj. **heretically** adv.

hereto adv. formal with regard to this point or to this matter, subject, etc.

heretofore adv. formal formerly, before this time.

herewith /hiːˈwɪð, -ˈwɪθ/ adv. **1** with this (esp. of an enclosure in a letter etc.). **2** hereby.

heritable /ˈherɪtəbəl/ adj. Biol. (of a characteristic) transmissible from parent to offspring. ☐ **heritability** n. **heritably** adv.

heritage n. **1 a** things such as works of art, cultural achievements and folklore that have been passed on from earlier generations. **b** a nation's buildings, monuments, countryside, etc., esp. when regarded as worthy of preservation. **c** (attrib.) esp. Cdn designating a building, site, river, etc. significant for its historic, architectural, or environmental value and which is protected from alteration, development, etc. by the government. **2** that which is or may be inherited. **3** inherited circumstances, benefits, etc. (a heritage of violence). **4** Bible **a** the ancient Israelites. **b** the Church.

Heritage Day n. Cdn **1** the third Monday in February, marked unofficially as a celebration of Canada's history and heritage. **2** (in the Yukon) the fourth Friday in February, observed as a holiday in the public service and some other workplaces. **3** a day designated by a particular region, ethnic group, etc. as a time to celebrate a shared history and culture.

heritage fund n. esp. Cdn (often **Heritage Fund**) a fund established by a province, region, city, etc. from supplementary revenue either as a hedge against difficult economic times or as a resource for future social and cultural development.

heritage language n. Cdn a language, other than English or French, which is a person's mother tongue or that of his or her ethnocultural group.

herky-jerky adj. N Amer. slang (of a movement) spasmodic or occurring at an irregular rate.

hermaphrodite /hɜrˈmæfrəˌdaɪt/ ● n. **1 a** Zool. an animal normally having both male and female sexual organs, e.g. many snails. **b** Bot. a plant having stamens and pistils in the same flower. **2** a human being in whom both male and female sex organs are present, or in which the sex organs contain both ovarian and testicular tissue. **3** a person or thing combining opposite qualities or characteristics. ● adj. **1** combining the characteristics of or consisting of both sexes. **2** combining opposite qualities or characteristics. ☐ **hermaphroditic** /-ˈdɪtɪk/ adj. **hermaphroditical** adj. **hermaphroditism** n.

hermeneutic /ˌhɜrmɪˈnuːtɪk, -ˈnjuː-/ adj. of or concerning interpretation or theories of interpretation, esp. of Scripture or literary texts. ☐ **hermeneutical** adj. **hermeneutically** adv.

hermeneutics n.pl. (also treated as sing.) Bible the branch of knowledge that deals with interpretation and the theories of interpretation, esp. of Scripture or literary texts.

hermetic /hɜrˈmetɪk/ *adj.* (also **hermetical**) **1** completely airtight. **2** protected from outside influences, agencies. **3 a** esoteric. **b** of alchemy or other occult sciences (*hermetic art*). □ **hermetically** *adv.* **hermeticism** /ˈhɜr,metɪsɪzəm/ *n.* (also **hermetism** /ˈhɜrmɪ,tɪzəm/).

hermit *n.* **1** a person who, from religious motives, has retired into the solitary life, esp. an early Christian recluse. **2** any person living in solitude or shunning human society. **3** *N Amer.* a soft spicy cookie, usu. containing raisins and nuts. □ **hermitic** *adj.*

hermitage *n.* **1** a hermit's dwelling. **2** a solitary or secluded dwelling.

hermit crab *n.* any crab of the family Paguridae that lives in a cast-off mollusc shell for protection.

hernia /ˈhɜrniə/ *n.* (*pl.* **-s** or **herniae** /-ni,iː/) a rupture or abnormal displacement and protrusion of part of an organ through the wall of the cavity containing it, esp. of the abdomen. □ **herniated** *adj.* **herniation** *n.*

herniated disc *n.* a disc between vertebrae that has become displaced, causing pain because of pressure on the nerves of the spine.

hero *n.* (*pl.* **-oes**) **1** a person distinguished by courage, noble deeds, outstanding achievements, etc. **2** the chief, esp. male, character in a poem, play, story, etc. **3** *Gk Hist.* a man of superhuman strength, courage, or qualities, favoured by the gods; a demigod. □ **hero's welcome** a rapturous welcome, like that given to a successful warrior.

heroic ● *adj.* **1 a** (of an act or a quality) bold, daring, or characteristic of or fit for a hero. **b** (of an effort etc.) great or courageous, but also desperate. **c** (of a person) like a hero. **2 a** (of language) grand, high-flown, dramatic. **b** (of a work of art) extravagant or unusually large, esp. between life-size and colossal. **3** (of poetry etc.) dealing with heroes and their deeds, esp. those of ancient Greece. ● *n.* (in *pl.*) heroic behaviour, esp. if unduly, extravagantly, or recklessly bold. □ **heroically** *adv.*

heroin *n.* a highly addictive white crystalline analgesic drug derived from morphine, often used as a narcotic.

heroine *n.* **1** a woman noted or admired for nobility, courage, outstanding achievements, etc. **2** the chief female character in a poem, play, story, etc.

heroism *n.* heroic conduct or qualities.

heron *n.* any of various large wading birds of the family Ardeidae, esp. *Ardea herodias*, with long legs and a long S-shaped neck.

hero-worship ● *n.* **1** idealization of an admired person. **2** *Gk Hist.* worship of the ancient heroes. ● *v.tr.* (**-worshipped**, **-worshipping**) idolize or be excessively devoted to (a person). □ **hero-worshipper** *n.*

herpes /ˈhɜrpiːz/ *n.* any of several infectious diseases caused by a herpesvirus and characterized by outbreaks of blisters etc. □ **herpetic** /-ˈpetɪk/ *adj.*

herpes simplex *n.* a viral infection producing usu. localized inflammation, as blisters, cold sores, conjunctivitis, oral and vaginal inflammation, etc.

herpesvirus *n.* any of a group of related viruses that includes those causing shingles and chicken pox, esp. *Herpesvirus hominis*, the cause of herpes simplex.

herpes zoster /ˈzɒstər/ *n.* = SHINGLES.

Herr /her/ *n.* (*pl.* **Herren** /ˈherən/) **1** the title of a German man; Mr. **2** a German man.

herring *n.* any of various chiefly marine fishes of the family Clupeidae, which form shoals in coastal waters at spawning time, including several impor-

tant food fishes, esp. *Clupea harengus* of the N Atlantic or *C. pallasi* of the N Pacific.

herringbone ● *n.* **1** any zigzag pattern or arrangement resembling the pattern of a herring's bones, as of stones, bricks, tiles, etc. **2** a stitch with a similar zigzag pattern. **3** this pattern, or cloth woven in it. **4** *Skiing* a method of ascending a slope with the skis pointing outwards. **5** (*attrib.*) **a** (of cloth) having a zigzag weave. **b** (of brickwork etc.) having a zigzag pattern. **c** resembling the bones of a herring. ● *v.* **1** *tr.* **a** mark with a herringbone pattern. **b** work with a herringbone stitch. **2** *intr. Skiing* ascend a slope using the herringbone technique.

herring choker *n.* *Cdn* esp. (*Maritimes*) *informal* a Maritimer, esp. a New Brunswicker.

herring gull *n.* a large, widely distributed gull, *Larus argentatus*, with dark wing tips, scavenging from fishing boats, garbage dumps, canneries, etc.

herring scull *n.* (also **herring school**) *Cdn* (*Nfld*) a school of herring appearing in inshore waters.

hers *possess.pron.* the one or ones belonging to or associated with her (*it is hers; hers are over there*). □ **of hers** of or belonging to her (*a friend of hers*).

herself *pron.* **1 a** *emphatic form of* SHE or HER (*she herself will do it*). **b** *refl. form of* HER (*she has hurt herself*). **2** in her normal state of body or mind (*does not feel quite herself today*). □ **be herself** act in her normal unconstrained manner.

hertz /hɜrts/ *n.* (*pl.* same) the SI unit of frequency, equal to one cycle per second. Abbr.: **Hz**.

he's *contraction* **1** he is. **2** he has.

he/she *pron.* a written representation of 'he or she' used to indicate both sexes.

hesitant *adj.* tending to be slow in speaking or acting because of uncertainty or unwillingness. □ **hesitance** *n.* **hesitancy** *n.* **hesitantly** *adv.*

hesitate *v.intr.* **1** (often foll. by *about, over*) show or feel indecision or uncertainty; pause in doubt (*hesitated over her choice*). **2** (often foll. by *to* + infin.) be deterred by scruples; be reluctant (*I hesitate to inform against him*). **3** stammer, falter, or pause momentarily in speech. □ **hesitatingly** *adv.* **hesitation** *n.*

Hesquiaht /ˈheskwiɒt/ ● *n.* **1** a member of a Nuu-chah-nulth Aboriginal group living on the west coast of Vancouver Island. **2** the Wakashan language of the Hesquiaht. ● *adj.* of or relating to this people.

Hessian /ˈheʃən/ ● *n.* a native of Hesse in western Germany. ● *adj.* of or concerning Hesse.

het *n.* & *adj.* *slang* = HETEROSEXUAL.

hetero /ˈhetəro/ *informal* ● *n.* (*pl.* **-os**) a heterosexual. ● *adj.* heterosexual.

hetero- *comb. form* other, different.

heterocyclic *adj.* *Chem.* (of a compound) with a bonded ring of atoms of more than one kind.

heterodox /ˈhetərɒ,dɒks/ *adj.* (of a person, opinion, etc.) not orthodox. □ **heterodoxy** *n.*

heterogeneous /,hetəroˈdʒiːniəs/ *adj.* **1** diverse in character. **2** varied in content. **3** *Math.* incommensurable through being of different kinds or degrees. □ **heterogeneity** /-dʒɪˈneiiti/ *n.* **heterogeneously** *adv.*

heteropteran /,hetəˈrɒptərən/ *n.* any insect of the suborder Heteroptera with non-uniform forewings having a thickened base and membranous tip (*compare* HOMOPTERAN). □ **heteropterous** *adj.*

heterosexism *n.* discrimination or prejudice by heterosexuals against or towards homosexuals. □ **heterosexist** *adj.* & *n.*

heterosexual ● *adj.* **1** feeling or involving sexual

attraction to persons of the opposite sex. **2** concerning heterosexual relations or people. **3** relating to the opposite sex. ● *n.* a heterosexual person. □ **heterosexuality** *n.* **heterosexually** *adv.*

het up *adj. informal* excited, overwrought.

heuristic /hjʊˈrɪstɪk/ ● *adj.* **1** allowing or assisting to discover. **2** *Computing* proceeding to a solution by trial and error. ● *n.* **1** the science of heuristic procedure. **2** a heuristic process or method. **3** (in *pl.*, usu. treated as *sing.*) *Computing* the study and use of heuristic techniques in data processing.

hew *v.* (*past part.* **hewn** or **hewed**) **1** *tr.* **a** (often foll. by *down, away, off*) chop or cut (a thing) with an axe, a sword, etc. **b** cut (a block of wood etc.) into shape. **2** *intr.* (often foll. by *at, among*, etc.) strike cutting blows. **3** *intr.* *N Amer.* (usu. foll. by *to*) conform. □ **hew one's way** make a way for oneself by hewing.

hewer *n.* **1** a person who hews. **2** a person who cuts coal from a seam. □ **hewers of wood and drawers of water** menial drudges; labourers.

hex¹ ● *v.* **1** *intr.* practise witchcraft. **2** *tr.* bewitch. ● *n.* **1** a magic spell. **2** a witch.

hex² *adj.* hexagonal (*hex nut*).

hexa- *comb. form* (also **hex-** esp. before a vowel) six.

hexagon /ˈheksəgən/ *n.* a plane figure with six sides and angles. □ **hexagonal** /-ˈsægənəl/ *adj.* **hexagonally** *adv.*

hexagram *n.* **1** a figure formed by two intersecting equilateral triangles. **2** a figure of six lines.

hexahedron /ˌheksəˈhiːdrən/ *n.* (*pl.* **-s** or **-hedra** /-drə/) a solid figure with six faces. □ **hexahedral** *adj.*

hexane /ˈheksein/ *n.* a liquid hydrocarbon of the alkane series.

hexavalent /ˌheksəˈveilənt/ *adj.* having a valence of six.

hexose /ˈheksoːs, -soːz/ *n.* a monosaccharide with six carbon atoms in each molecule, e.g. glucose.

hey *interj.* calling attention or expressing joy, surprise, inquiry, enthusiasm, etc. □ **what the hey** *N Amer.* = WHAT THE HELL (see HELL).

heyday *n.* the flush or full bloom of youth, vigour, prosperity, etc.

hey presto! *interj.* *Cdn & Brit.* a phrase announcing the successful completion of a magical trick or other surprising achievement.

HF *abbr.* HIGH FREQUENCY.

Hf *symbol* hafnium.

HG *abbr.* Her or His Grace.

Hg *symbol* the element mercury.

hg *abbr.* hectogram(s).

HGH *abbr.* HUMAN GROWTH HORMONE.

HH *abbr.* **1** Her or His Highness. **2** His Holiness. **3** double-hard (pencil lead).

HI *abbr.* **1** Hawaii (in postal use). **2** the Hawaiian Islands.

hi *interj.* as a greeting or calling attention.

hiatus /haiˈeitəs/ *n.* (*pl.* **hiatuses**) a break or gap, esp. in a series, account, or chain of proof.

hiatus hernia *n.* the protrusion of an organ, esp. the stomach, through the esophageal opening in the diaphragm.

Hib *n.* a bacterium, *Haemophilus influenzae* type B, causing infant meningitis (often *attrib.*: *Hib vaccine*).

Hibachi /hɪˈbætʃi, hɪˈbɒtʃi/ *n.* (*pl.* **-is**) *proprietary* a small, portable charcoal brazier with a grill.

hibernate *v.intr.* **1** (of some animals) spend the winter in a dormant state. **2** remain inactive. **3** (of human beings) escape or withdraw from a harsh winter. □ **hibernation** *n.* **hibernator** *n.*

Hibernian /haiˈbɜːniən/ ● *adj.* of or concerning Ireland. ● *n.* a native of Ireland.

hibiscus /hɪˈbɪskəs, hai-/ *n.* any plant of the genus *Hibiscus*, cultivated for its large bright flowers.

hic *interj.* expressing the sound of a hiccup, esp. a drunken hiccup.

hiccup ● *n.* **1 a** an involuntary spasm of the diaphragm and respiratory organs, with sudden closure of the glottis and characteristic coughlike sound. **b** (in *pl.*) an attack of such spasms. **2** a temporary or minor stoppage or difficulty. ● *v.* (**hiccuped, hiccuping**) **1** *intr.* make a hiccup or series of hiccups. **2** *tr.* utter with a hiccup. □ **hiccupy** *adj.*

hick *informal derogatory* ● *n.* a country dweller; a provincial. ● *adj.* rural or unsophisticated.

hickey *n.* (*pl.* **-eys**) *N Amer. informal* **1** a red mark on the skin, caused by biting or sucking during sexual play. **2** a gadget (compare DOOHICKEY).

hickory *n.* (*pl.* **-ies**) **1** any N American tree of the genus *Carya*, yielding tough heavy wood, and bearing sometimes edible nuts (see PECAN). **2 a** the wood of these trees. **b** a stick made of this.

hicksville *n.* *N Amer. derogatory* a non-urban area.

hidden *past part.* of HIDE¹. □ **hiddenness** *n.*

hidden agenda *n.* a secret or ulterior motive behind an action, statement, etc.

hidden tax *n.* a tax paid by a manufacturer, distributor, or retailer, that is included in the price charged to the consumer.

hide¹ *v.* (*past* **hid**; *past part.* **hidden** or *archaic* **hid**) **1** *tr.* put or keep out of sight (*hid it under the cushion*). **2** *intr.* conceal oneself. **3** *tr.* (usu. foll. by *from*) keep (a fact) secret. **4** *tr.* conceal (a thing) from sight intentionally or not (*trees hid the house*). □ **hide one's light under a bushel** conceal one's merits. **hide out** (or **up**) remain in concealment. □ **hider** *n.*

hide² ● *n.* **1** the skin of an animal, esp. when tanned or dressed. **2** *informal* the human skin (*saved her own hide*). ● *v.tr.* *informal* flog. □ **neither hide nor hair** not the slightest trace. □ **hided** *adj.* (also in *comb.*).

Hide-A-Bed *n.* *N Amer. proprietary* a couch that folds out into a bed.

hide-and-seek *n.* **1** (also **hide-and-go-seek**) a children's game in which one or more players seek a person who is hiding. **2** a process of attempting to find an evasive person or thing.

hideaway ● *n.* a hiding place or place of retreat. ● *adj.* hidden or concealed, esp. when not in use (*hideaway bed*).

hidebound *adj.* **1 a** narrow-minded; bigoted. **b** conservative; constricted by tradition. **2** (of cattle) with the skin clinging close as a result of bad feeding.

hideous *adj.* **1** frightful, repulsive, or revolting, to the senses or the mind. **2** *informal* unpleasant. □ **hideously** *adv.* **hideousness** *n.*

hideout *n.* *informal* a hiding place.

hidey-hole *n.* (also **hidy-hole**) *informal* a hiding place.

hiding¹ *n.* **1** the act or an instance of hiding. **2** the state of remaining hidden (*go into hiding*).

hiding² *n.* *informal* a thrashing.

hie /hai/ *v.intr. & refl.* (**hies, hied, hieing** or **hying**) *archaic* or *literary* go quickly.

hierarchy /ˈhaiɜrˌɑrki/ *n.* (*pl.* **-ies**) **1 a** a system in which grades or classes of status or authority are ranked one above the other (*ranks third in the hierarchy*). **b** the hierarchical system (of government, management, etc.). **2 a** a priestly government. **b** a priesthood organized in grades. **c** (foll. by *of*) a range in order of importance (*hierarchy of values*). **3 a** each of the three divisions of angels. **b** the angels. ☐ **hierarchic** *adj.* **hierarchical** *adj.* **hierarchize** *v.tr.*

hieratic /ˌhaɪəˈrætɪk/ *adj.* **1** of or concerning priests. **2** of the ancient Egyptian writing of abridged hieroglyphics used by priests (*compare* DEMOTIC *n.* 2). **3** of or concerning Egyptian or Greek traditional styles of art.

hieroglyph /ˈhaɪərəglɪf/ *n.* **1 a** a picture of an object representing a word, syllable, or sound, as used in ancient Egyptian and other writing. **b** a writing consisting of characters of this kind. **2** a secret or enigmatic symbol.

hieroglyphic ● *adj.* **1** of or written in hieroglyphs. **2** symbolical. ● *n.* (in *pl.*) **1** hieroglyphs. **2** handwriting that is difficult to read.

hi-fi *informal* ● *adj.* of or relating to high fidelity. ● *n.* (*pl.* **hi-fis**) a set of equipment for high-fidelity sound reproduction.

higgledy-piggledy ● *adv. & adj.* in confusion or disorder. ● *n.* a state of disordered confusion.

high ● *adj.* **1 a** of great vertical extent (*a high building*). **b** (*predic.*; often in *comb.*) of a specified height (*one inch high*; *waist-high*). **2 a** far above ground or sea level etc. (*a high altitude*). **b** inland, esp. when raised (*High Sierra*). **3** extending above the normal or average level (*high boots*). **4** of exalted, esp. spiritual, quality (*high principles*). **5 a** of exalted social station (*in high society*). **b** (usu. foll. by *up*) placed near the top of a hierarchy (*is high up in the government*). **6 a** great; intense; extreme; powerful (*high praise*; *high temperature*). **b** greater than normal (*high prices*). **7** *Christianity* tending towards or involving an elaborate or formal style of worship (*high Anglican*). **8** (of physical action, esp. athletics) performed at, to, or from a considerable height (*high diving*). **9** *informal* **a** (often foll. by *on*) intoxicated by alcohol or esp. drugs. **b** exhilarated; ecstatic. **10** (of a sound or note) of high frequency; at the top end of the scale or of a singer's register etc. **11** (of a period, an age, a time, etc.) at its peak (*high noon*; *High Renaissance*). **12 a** (of meat) beginning to go bad; off. **b** (of game) well-aged and slightly decomposed. **13** *Geog.* (of latitude) near the North or South Pole. **14** (of a gear) having an output speed relatively close to that of the input speed. **15** (foll. by *in*) having an elevated proportion of (*high in fibre*). ● *n.* **1** a high, or the highest, level or figure. **2** an area of high barometric pressure. **3** *informal* **a** a euphoric drug-induced state. **b** a state of excitement. **4** top gear in a motor vehicle. **5** the setting of a cooking element, microwave oven, etc. giving the most heat or power. **6** the highest temperature reached during a specified period (*highs of 37°*). **7** *N Amer. informal* (esp. in names) high school. ● *adv.* **1** far up; aloft. **2** in or to a high degree. **3** at a high price. **4** (of a sound) at or to a high pitch (*sang high*). ☐ **ace** (or **King** or **Queen** etc.) **high** (in card games) having the ace etc. as the highest-ranking card. **from on high** from heaven or a high place. **high on the agenda** (or **list**) considered a priority for discussion or action. **high opinion of** a favourable opinion of. **high, wide, and handsome** *informal* in a carefree or stylish manner. **on high** in or to heaven or a high place. **on one's high horse** *informal* behaving superciliously or arrogantly. **play high 1** play for high stakes. **2** play a card of high value. **run high 1** (of the sea) have a strong current with high tide. **2** (of feelings) be strong. **to high heaven** to a high degree (*stank to high heaven*).

high achiever *n.* a person who excels at something,

esp. one who excels at many different activities, e.g. academics, sports, work, etc. ☐ **high-achieving** *adj.*

high altar *n.* the chief altar of a church.

high and dry *adv.* (usu. in phr. **leave high and dry**) **1** stranded without resources. **2** (of a ship) out of the water, esp. stranded.

high and low *adv.* everywhere.

high and mighty *adj. informal* arrogant.

High Arctic *n.* the part of the Canadian Arctic that lies within the Arctic Circle.

highball *N Amer.* ● *n.* **1** a drink of liquor diluted with a soft drink etc., served with ice in a tall glass. **2** a railway signal to proceed. ● *v. informal* **1** *intr.* move at full speed. **2** *tr.* drive (a train, car, etc.) at full speed.

highball glass *n. N Amer.* a tall straight glass.

high beam *n. N Amer.* (usu. in *pl.*) a bright headlight beam, used for long-range illumination.

highboy *n. N Amer.* a tall chest of drawers on legs.

highbrow *informal* ● *adj.* intellectual; cultural. ● *n.* an intellectual or cultured person.

highbush *n.* **1** (in full **highbush blueberry**) a shrub of the genus *Vaccinium* of eastern N America, with sweet, juicy, dark blue fruit. **2** (in full **highbush cranberry**) a shrub, *Viburnum triloba*, with lobed leaves and red, juicy berries, found across Canada and the northern US.

high card *n.* a card that outranks others, esp. an ace or a face card.

high chair *n.* an infant's chair with long legs and a tray, for use at meals.

High Church ● *n.* a tradition within the Anglican Church emphasizing ritual, priestly authority, sacraments, and historical continuity with Catholic Christianity. ● *adj.* of or relating to this tradition.

high-class *adj.* of high quality.

high command *n.* **1** the leaders of a military force and associated staff. **2** the chief headquarters of a military force.

High Commission 1 an embassy from one Commonwealth country to another. **2** an international commission, such as one under the auspices of the UN. ☐ **High Commissioner** *n.*

high-concept *n.* (*attrib.*) designating films etc. based on an uncomplicated and easily promoted theme.

High Court *n.* a supreme court of justice for civil cases.

high-cut *adj.* (of shorts, underpants, bodysuits, etc.) having the leg holes cut high up on the side.

high-definition *adj.* designating or providing a relatively clear or distinct image (*high-definition TV*).

high-density lipoprotein *n.* the form of lipoprotein involved in the transport of cholesterol and associated with decreased risk of arteriosclerosis and heart attack.

high-end *adj.* of or associated with the most expensive section of the market (*a high-end stereo*).

higher court *n.* a court that can overrule the decision of another.

higher education *n.* post-secondary education at university, college, etc.

higher-up *n.* (*pl.* **higher-ups**) *informal* a person of higher rank; a superior.

highest bidder *n.* **1** the person who makes the highest bid for an item sold at auction. **2** a person, corporation, etc. that pays a higher price for something than any other contender.

highest common factor *n.* the highest number that can be divided exactly into each of two or more numbers.

high explosive n. an extremely explosive substance used in shells, bombs, etc.

highfalutin adj. (also **highfaluting**) informal absurdly pretentious.

high fashion n. = HAUTE COUTURE.

high fidelity n. the reproduction of sound with little distortion, giving a result very similar to the original (also attrib.: high-fidelity sound).

high-five N Amer. slang ● n. a gesture of celebration or greeting in which two people slap each other's palms with their arms outstretched over their heads. ● v. 1 tr. greet with a high-five. 2 intr. make a high-five. □ **high-fiving** n.

high-flown adj. (of language etc.) extravagant, bombastic.

high flyer n. 1 an ambitious person. 2 a person or thing with great potential for achievement.

high-flying adj. 1 (of a person) ambitious. 2 (of stocks, securities, etc.) having great value or perceived value. 3 flying high in the air.

high frequency n. a frequency, esp. in radio, of 3 to 30 megahertz. Abbr.: **HF**. □ **high-frequency** adj.

high gear n. 1 a gear such that the driven end of a transmission revolves faster than the driving end. 2 a state of intensified activity (moved into high gear).

High German n. standard written and spoken German.

high-grade ● adj. 1 of high quality. 2 (of ore) rich in metal value and commercially profitable. ● v.tr. & intr. 1 steal (high-grade ore) from a mine. 2 N Amer. cut down (the best trees) from a forest. □ **high-grading** n.

high ground n. 1 ground that is naturally elevated and therefore strategically advantageous. 2 the position of esp. moral superiority in a debate etc.

high-handed adj. disregarding others' feelings; overbearing. □ **high-handedly** adv. **high-handedness** n.

high hat ● n. 1 a top hat. 2 = HI-HAT. 3 a snobbish or overbearing person. ● adj. (**high-hat**) supercilious; snobbish. ● v.tr. (**high-hat**) (**-hatted**, **-hatting**) N Amer. treat superciliously.

high heels n.pl. women's shoes with high heels. □ **high-heeled** adj.

High Holidays n.pl. the Jewish festivals of Rosh Hashanah and Yom Kippur.

high-impact adj. 1 (of plastics, etc.) able to withstand great impact without breaking. 2 designating esp. aerobic exercises that place a great deal of potentially harmful stress on the body. 3 having a great effect or lasting impression (a high-impact movie).

highjinks var. of HIJINKS.

high jump n. an athletic event consisting of jumping as high as possible over a bar of adjustable height. □ **high jumper** n. **high jumping** n.

high kick n. 1 a kick high in the air, esp. in dancing. 2 a traditional Inuit game in which participants attempt to kick an object suspended above them and land on the foot used to kick with. □ **high-kicking** attrib.adj.

highland ● n. (usu. in pl.) 1 an area of high land. 2 (**the Highlands**) a the mountainous part of Scotland. b any similar area of hilly plateau (Cape Breton Highlands). ● adj. of or in a highland or the Highlands. □ **highlander** n. (also **Highlander**).

Highland cattle n. a breed of shaggy-haired cattle with long, curved, widely-spaced horns.

Highland fling n. see FLING n. 3.

Highland games n.pl. a Scottish sports meeting and cultural festival, typically consisting of athletic events as well as other activities such as dancing etc.

high lead /liːd/ n. Cdn Forestry the cable or line used to haul logs when using a system of spar trees etc. for yarding (also attrib.: high-lead operation).

high-level adj. 1 (of negotiations etc.) conducted by high-ranking people. 2 Computing (of a programming language) that is not machine-dependent and is usu. at a level of abstraction close to natural language.

high life n. 1 (also **high living**) a luxurious existence. 2 (usu. **highlife**) a West African style of dance music characterized by traditional drumming and syncopated melodies.

highlight ● n. 1 (in a painting etc.) a light area, or one seeming to reflect light. 2 a moment or detail of vivid interest; an outstanding feature. 3 (usu. in pl.) a bright tint in the hair produced by bleaching. ● v.tr. 1 bring into prominence; draw attention to. 2 mark with a highlighter. 3 create highlights in (the hair).

highlighter n. a marker pen which overlays colour on a printed word etc., leaving it emphasized.

highly adv. 1 in a high degree (highly amusing). 2 favourably (think highly of her).

high maintenance adj. requiring much or frequent maintenance, attention, etc.

high marks n.pl. N Amer. 1 the maximum award in an examination, competition, etc. 2 full credit (I give them high marks for resourcefulness).

High Mass n. a Mass in which the prayers are sung rather than spoken.

high-minded adj. having high moral principles. □ **high-mindedly** adv. **high-mindedness** n.

high muckamuck n. N Amer. = MUCKY-MUCK.

highness n. 1 the state of being high. 2 (**Highness**) a title used in addressing and referring to a prince or princess (Her Highness; Your Royal Highness).

high-octane adj. 1 (of fuel used in internal combustion engines) having good anti-knock properties. 2 high-powered; potent (a high-octane dessert).

high-pitched adj. 1 (of a sound) high. 2 (of a roof) steep. 3 (of style etc.) lofty.

high places n.pl. the upper ranks of an organization etc. (has friends in high places).

high point n. the maximum or best state reached.

high-powered adj. (also **high-power**) 1 having great power or energy. 2 important or influential.

high pressure ● n. 1 a high degree of activity or exertion. 2 a condition of the atmosphere with the pressure above 101.3 kilopascals. ● adj. (usu. **high-pressure**) 1 having or involving a pressure that is above the ordinary (high-pressure propane). 2 (of a job, etc.) demanding; having a high level of stress. 3 (of a sales technique, etc.) forceful, persistent.

high-pressure system n. Meteorol. a large expanse of air at high atmospheric pressure.

high priest n. 1 a chief priest in some non-Christian religions. 2 a chief exponent of a political or cultural movement, esp. one who promotes the cause with dogmatism and fervour. □ **high priesthood** n.

high priestess n. 1 a chief priestess in some non-Christian religions. 2 a chief exponent of a political or cultural movement, esp. one who promotes the cause with dogmatism and fervour.

high profile n. exposure to attention or publicity. □ **high-profile** adj.

high-quality adj. of high quality.

high-ranking adj. of high rank, senior.

high relief n. see RELIEF 6a.

high rigger n. the logger responsible for climbing, topping, and rigging the spar tree.

high-rise ● attrib.adj. (of a building) having many storeys. ● n. such a building.

high-risk attrib.adj. involving or exposed to danger.

high road n. (usu. foll. by to) a direct route (on the high road to success).

high roller n. N Amer. slang a person who gambles large sums or spends freely.

high school n. N Amer., Scot., Austral., & NZ a secondary school. □ **high-school** adj.

high sea n. (also **high seas**) open seas not within any country's jurisdiction.

high season n. the period during which the most people travel, book accommodation, etc.

high-security attrib.adj. **1** (of a prison, lock, etc.) extremely secure. **2** (of a prisoner) kept in a high-security prison.

high sign n. N Amer. informal a surreptitious gesture indicating that all is well or that the coast is clear.

high-speed attrib.adj. **1** operating at great speed. **2** (of steel) suitable for tools, cutting so rapidly as to become red-hot.

high-spirited adj. vivacious; cheerful. □ **high-spiritedly** adv. **high-spiritedness** n.

high spirits n.pl. vivacity; energy; cheerfulness.

high spot n. informal an important place or feature.

high-stakes adj. **1** designating a gambling game where the stakes are high. **2** (of an activity) highly risky; dangerous.

high steel n. N Amer. steel used as the framework for high-rise buildings, esp. steel girders high above the ground (also attrib.: high steel workers).

high-step v.intr. walk or move lifting one's feet high off the ground. □ **high-stepping** adj.

high-sticking n. (in ice and field hockey) an illegal raising of the blade of the stick above shoulder level. □ **high stick** n. **high-stick** v.tr.

high-strung adj. very sensitive or nervous.

hightail v.tr. N Amer. informal □ **hightail it** hurry.

high-tech ● adj. **1** (of interior design etc.) imitating styles more usual in industry etc., esp. using steel, glass, or plastic in a functional way. **2** employing, requiring, or involved in high technology. ● n. (**high tech**) = HIGH TECHNOLOGY.

high technology n. advanced technological development, esp. in electronics.

high-tensile adj. having great tensile strength.

high tension n. & adj. = HIGH VOLTAGE.

high tide n. **1** the tide at its fullest. **2** the time of this.

high time n. a time that is late or overdue (it is high time they arrived).

high-toned adj. stylish; dignified; superior.

high-top N Amer. ● adj. designating shoes, esp. athletic shoes, whose uppers come above the ankle bone. ● n. (in pl.) high-top shoes.

high treason n. see TREASON 1.

high voltage ● n. electrical potential large enough to cause injury or damage if diverted. ● adj. (also **high-voltage**) **1** involving high voltage. **2** displaying a great deal of energy (a high-voltage performance).

high water n. = HIGH TIDE.

high-water mark n. **1** the level reached at high water. **2** the maximum recorded value or highest point of excellence.

highway n. **1 a** a main road, esp. one between towns or cities. **b** a public road. **c** a much-travelled route leading directly to a place (the Mackenzie River: history's highway to the Arctic Ocean). **2** a direct course of action (on the highway to success).

highwayman n. (pl. **-men**) hist. a man, usu. mounted and armed with a gun, who robbed travellers on public roads.

highway robbery n. informal a price or charge that is unreasonably or exorbitantly high.

high wire n. a high tightrope.

hi-hat n. a pair of cymbals mounted one above the other on an upright rod, with a sprung pedal at the base to move the upper cymbal down onto the other.

hijab /hɪˈʒʊb, -ˈdʒʊb/ n. a veil worn by some Muslim women to cover the hair, forehead, etc.

hijack ● v.tr. **1** seize control of (an aircraft in flight etc.), esp. to force it to a different destination. **2** seize (goods) in transit. **3** take over (an organization etc.) by force or subterfuge in order to redirect it. ● n. an instance of hijacking. □ **hijacker** n.

hijinks /ˈhaɪdʒɪŋks/ n.pl. boisterous joking or merrymaking.

hijra /ˈhɪdʒrə/ var. of HEGIRA.

hike ● n. **1** a long walk, esp. in the country, taken for pleasure or exercise. **2** an increase (of prices etc.). ● v. **1** intr. go for a long walk, esp. across country. **2** (usu. foll. by up) **a** tr. hitch up (clothing etc.); hoist. **b** intr. work upwards out of place, become hitched up. **3** tr. increase (prices etc.). □ **take a hike** esp. N Amer. go away (told him to take a hike). □ **hiker** n.

hiking boot n. a moderately low-cut leather boot with a heavy tread, worn esp. when hiking.

hila pl. of HILUM.

hilarious adj. **1** exceedingly funny. **2** boisterously merry. □ **hilariously** adv. **hilarity** n.

hill ● n. **1** a naturally raised area of land, not as high as a mountain. **2** (often in comb.) a heap; a mound (anthill). **3** a sloping piece of road. **4** (**the Hill**) (in Canada) = PARLIAMENT HILL. **5 a** a heap formed around a plant by banking up soil. **b** a cluster of plants in such a hill or on level ground. ● v.tr. **1** form into a hill. **2** (usu. foll. by up) bank up (plants) with soil. □ **old as the hills** very ancient. **over the hill** informal **1** past the prime of life; declining. **2** past the crisis.

hillbilly esp. US ● n. (pl. **-ies**) **1** informal, often derogatory a person from a remote or mountainous area, esp. in the Appalachians. **2** country music of or like that of the southern US. ● adj. of, like, or relating to hillbillies.

hillock n. a small hill or mound. □ **hillocky** adj.

hillside ● n. the sloping side of a hill. ● adj. located on the side of a hill.

hilltop n. the summit of a hill.

hilly adj. (**-ier, -iest**) having many hills. □ **hilliness** n.

hilt ● n. **1** the handle of a sword, dagger, etc. **2** the handle of a tool. ● v.tr. provide with a hilt. □ **to the hilt** completely.

hilum /ˈhaɪləm/ n. (pl. **hila** /-lə/) **1** Bot. the point of attachment of a seed to its seed vessel. **2** Anat. a notch or indentation where a vessel enters an organ.

him pron. **1** objective case of HE (I saw him). **2** informal he (it's him; is taller than him).

himself pron. **1 a** emphatic form of HE or HIM (he himself will do it). **b** refl. form of HIM (he has hurt himself). **2** in his normal state of body or mind (does not feel quite himself today). □ **be himself** act in his normal unconstrained manner.

hind[1] adj. (esp. of parts of the body) situated behind or at the back, posterior (hind leg).

hind[2] n. a female deer (usu. a red deer or sika), esp. in and after the third year.

hinder[1] /'hɪndər/ *v.tr. & intr.* impede, delay, prevent, or obstruct.

hinder[2] /'haɪndər/ *adj.* rear, hind (*the hinder part*).

Hindi /'hɪndi/ ● *n.* **1** a group of spoken dialects of N India. **2** a literary form of Hindustani with a Sanskrit-based vocabulary, an official language of India. ● *adj.* of or concerning Hindi.

hindmost *adj.* furthest behind; most remote.

hindquarters *n.pl.* the hind legs and adjoining parts of a quadruped.

hindrance *n.* **1 a** the act or an instance of hindering. **b** the state of being hindered. **2** a person or thing that hinders; an obstacle.

hindsight *n.* wisdom after the event (*realized with hindsight that they were wrong*).

Hindu /'hɪndu/ ● *n.* (*pl.* **Hindus**) a follower of Hinduism. ● *adj.* of or concerning Hindus or Hinduism.

Hinduism *n.* the main religious and social system of India, including a belief in reincarnation, the worship of several gods, and an ordained caste system as the basis of society.

Hindustani /ˌhɪndʊ'stæni/ ● *n. hist.* the Delhi dialect of Hindi, widely used throughout India as a lingua franca. ¶*Hindustani* was the usual term in the 18th and 19th c. for the native language of NW India. The usual modern term is *Hindi*, although *Hindustani* is still sometimes used to refer to the lingua franca. ● *adj.* of or relating to Hindustan (the part of India N of the Deccan plateau) or its people, or Hindustani.

hindwing *n.* either of the posterior wings of an insect.

hinge ● *n.* **1 a** a movable, usu. metal, joint or mechanism on which a lid, door, gate, etc. turns or swings as it opens and closes. **b** *Biol.* a natural joint performing a similar function, e.g. that of a bivalve shell. **2** a central point or principle on which everything depends. ● *v.* **1** *intr.* (foll. by *on*) **a** depend (on a principle, an event, etc.) (*everything hinges on his acceptance*). **b** (of a door etc.) hang and turn (on a post etc.). **2** *tr.* attach with or as if with a hinge. □ **hinged** *adj.*

hint ● *n.* **1** a slight or indirect indication or suggestion. **2** a small piece of practical information; a tip. **3** a very small trace, a slight indication (*a hint of perfume*). ● *v.tr.* suggest slightly or indirectly (*hinted that they were wrong*). □ **hint at** give a hint of or refer indirectly to. **take a** (or **the**) **hint** understand what is meant or stated indirectly and act accordingly.

hinterland *n.* **1** a remote or fringe area; backcountry. **2** the often deserted or uncharted areas beyond a coastal district or a river's banks. **3** an area served by a port or other centre.

hip[1] *n.* **1** a projection of the pelvis and upper thigh bone on each side of the body in human beings and quadrupeds. **2** (often in *pl.*) the part on each side of the human body between the top of the legs and the waist. **3** *Archit.* the sharp edge of a roof from ridge to eaves where two sides meet. □ **hipless** *adj.*

hip[2] *n.* the fruit of a rose, esp. a wild kind.

hip[3] *slang* ● *adj.* (**hipper, hippest**) **1** following the latest fashion in esp. music, clothes, etc.; stylish. **2** (often foll. by *to*) understanding, aware. ● *v.tr.* (**hipped, hipping**) (often foll. by *to*) make (a person) hip; inform, tell. □ **hiply** *adv.* **hipness** *n.*

hip[4] *interj.* introducing a united cheer (*hip, hip, hooray*).

hip bone *n.* a bone forming the hip, esp. the ilium.

hip boot *n.* a tall boot reaching to the hip, usu. made of rubber, worn by firefighters, fly fishermen, etc.

hip check *Hockey* ● *n.* a type of bodycheck in which a player suddenly thrusts his or her hips to the side to obstruct or hit an opponent attempting to skate past. ● *v.tr.* (**hip-check**) hit or obstruct in this way.

hip dysplasia *n.* an abnormal development of the hip joint in some mid- to large-sized dogs.

hip flask *n.* a small metal bottle for liquor etc., carried in a hip pocket.

hip hop *n.* **1** a style of popular music of US black origin, featuring frequently politically inspired raps delivered above spare, electronic backing. **2** the subculture associated with this, including graffiti art, breakdancing, etc. □ **hip-hopper** *n.*

hip joint *n.* the articulation of the head of the thigh bone with the ilium.

hip-length *adj.* (of a garment) reaching down to the hips.

hipped roof *var. of* HIP ROOF.

hippie *n.* (*pl.* **-ies**) *informal* **1** (esp. in the 1960s) a young person who rejected traditional societal values, advocated free love, peace, etc., and adopted an unconventional appearance, typically with long hair, jeans, beads, etc. **2** a person resembling a hippie in dress, beliefs, etc. □ **hippiedom** *n.*

hippo *n.* (*pl.* **-os**) *informal* a hippopotamus.

hippocampus /ˌhɪpə'kæmpəs/ *n.* (*pl.* **hippocampi** /-pi/) **1** a sea horse. **2** *Anat.* the elongated ridges on the floor of each lateral ventricle of the brain, thought to be the centre of emotion and the autonomic nervous system. □ **hippocampal** *adj.*

hip pocket *n.* a pocket just behind the hip on pants etc. □ **in one's hip pocket** *N Amer. informal* completely under control.

hippopotamus /ˌhɪpə'pɒtəməs/ *n.* (*pl.* **-muses** or **-mi** /-ˌmaɪ/) **1** a large thick-skinned four-legged mammal, *Hippopotamus amphibius*, native to Africa, inhabiting rivers, lakes, etc. **2** (in full **pygmy hippopotamus**) a smaller related mammal, *Choeropsis liberiensis*, native to Africa, inhabiting forests and swamps.

hippy[1] *var. of* HIPPIE.

hippy[2] *adj.* having large hips.

hip roof *n.* a roof with both the sides and the ends inclined.

hipster *n. slang* a hip person. □ **hipsterism** *n.*

hip waders *n.pl.* waders that come up to the hips.

hire ● *v.tr.* **1** esp. *N Amer.* employ (a person) for wages or a fee. **2** (often foll. by *from*) procure the temporary use of (a thing) for an agreed payment. ● *n.* **1** an act or instance of hiring or being hired. **2** payment for this. **3** *N Amer.* a recently hired employee. □ **for** (or **on**) **hire** ready to be hired. **hire on** *N Amer.* take a job or obtain employment, esp. at a specific task, company, etc. **hire out 1** grant the temporary use of (a thing) for an agreed payment. **2** *refl.* make oneself available for employment. □ **hireable** *adj.* (also **hirable**). **hirer** *n.*

hired girl *n.* (also **hired man**) *N Amer.* a domestic servant, esp. on a farm.

hired gun *n.* esp. *N Amer. informal* **1 a** an expert brought in to resolve complex esp. legal or financial problems, disputes, etc. **b** a person, e.g. a lobbyist, able to attain power or influence for others quickly and efficiently. **2 a** a bodyguard or other person hired to protect or fight for another. **b** a person contracted to kill another, e.g. a hitman or gunfighter.

hired hand *n.* *N Amer.* a person employed to do usu. manual work on a farm, ranch, etc.

hireling *n.* usu. *derogatory* a person who works primarily for monetary gain, esp. without other motives such as job satisfaction etc.

hirsute /ˈhɜrsuːt, ˈhɜrsuːt, -sjuːt/ *adj.* **1** hairy, shaggy. **2** covered with long soft or moderately stiff hairs.

his *possess.adj.* **1** (*attrib.*) of or belonging to him or himself (*his own business*). **2** the one or ones belonging to or associated with him (*it is his; his are over there*). **3** (**His**) (*attrib.*) (in titles) that he is (*His Majesty*). □ **his and hers** *jocular* (of matching items) for husband and wife, or men and women. **of his** of or belonging to him (*a friend of his*).

Hispanic /hɪˈspænɪk /● *adj.* **1** of or relating to Spain or to Spanish-speaking countries. **2** of or relating to Hispanics. ● *n.* a Spanish-speaking person living in the US or Canada, esp. one of Latin American descent.

hiss ● *v.* **1** *intr.* **a** make a sharp sibilant sound (*the goose hissed angrily*). **b** make this sound to show disapproval or derision (*the audience booed and hissed*). **2** *tr.* express disapproval of (a person etc.) by hisses. **3** *tr.* whisper (a threat etc.) urgently or angrily ('*Get back!' he hissed*). ● *n.* **1** a sharp sibilant sound as of the letter *s*. **2** *Electronics* audible interference. □ **hiss off** hiss (actors etc.) so that they leave the stage. □ **hissy** *adj.*

hissy fit *n. N Amer. informal* a temper tantrum.

histamine /ˈhɪstəmɪn, ˈhɪstəˌmiːn/ *n.* an amine causing contraction of smooth muscle and dilation of capillaries, released by most cells in response to injury and in allergic and inflammatory reactions.

histology /hɪˈstɒlədʒi/ *n.* **1** the study of the microscopic structure of tissues. **2** the microscopic structure of tissues. □ **histologic** *adj.* **histological** *adj.* **histologically** *adj.* **histologist** *n.*

histopathology /ˌhɪstoːpəˈθɒlədʒi/ *n.* **1** changes in tissues caused by disease. **2** the study of these. □ **histopathologic** *adj.* **histopathological** *adj.* **histopathologist** *n.*

historian *n.* **1** a writer of history, esp. a critical analyst, rather than a compiler. **2** a person learned in history, esp. one professionally engaged in teaching and researching history (*Canadian historian*).

historic *adj.* **1** famous or important in history or potentially so (*a historic moment*). **2** *archaic* or *disputed* = HISTORICAL.

historical *adj.* **1** of or concerning history (*historical evidence*). **2** belonging to history, not to prehistory or legend. **3** (of the study of a subject) based on an analysis of its development over a period. **4** belonging to the past, not the present. **5** (of a novel, a film, etc.) dealing or professing to deal with historical events. **6** in connection with history, from the historian's point of view (*of purely historical interest*). □ **historically** *adv.*

historicism *n.* **1 a** the theory that social and cultural phenomena are determined by history. **b** the belief that historical events are governed by laws. **2** the tendency to regard historical development as the most basic aspect of human existence. **3** an excessive regard for past styles etc. □ **historicist** *n.*

historicity /ˌhɪstəˈrɪsɪti/ *n.* the historical genuineness of an event etc.

historicize *v.tr.* make or represent as historical. □ **historicization** *n.* **historicized** *adj.* **historicizing** *n. & adj.*

historiographer /hɪˌstɔːriˈɒɡrəfər, -stɒri-/ *n.* **1** an expert in or student of historiography. **2** a writer of history, esp. an official historian.

historiography *n.* **1** the writing of history. **2** the study of history-writing. **3** written history. □ **historiographic** *adj.* **historiographical** *adj.*

history *n.* (*pl.* **-ies**) **1** a continuous, usu. chronological, record of important or public events. **2 a** the study of past events, esp. human affairs. **b** the total accumulation of past events, esp. relating to human affairs or to the accumulation of developments connected with a particular nation, person, thing, etc. (*the history of Canada; has a history of illness*). **3** an eventful past (*this house has a history*). **4 a** a systematic or critical account of or research into a past event, development, movement, etc. (*the history of radio*). **b** a similar record or account of natural phenomena. **5** a historical play. □ **be history** *informal* be no longer existing, relevant, or important (*one mistake and I'll be history*). **go down in history** be remembered or recorded in history. **make history 1** do or take part in something important enough to be recorded in the world's or one's country's history. **2** do something unusual or important, esp. something never before done in an art, science, profession, sport, etc. **the rest is history** a concluding statement suggesting that the events succeeding those already related are so familiar as to need no repetition.

histrionic /ˌhɪstriˈɒnɪk /● *adj.* **1** (of behaviour) theatrical; dramatically exaggerated. **2** of or concerning actors or acting. ● *n.* **1** (in *pl.*) insincere and dramatic behaviour designed to impress. **2** theatricals; theatrical art. □ **histrionically** *adv.*

hit ● *v.* (**hitting**; *past* and *past part.* **hit**) **1** *tr.* **a** strike with a blow or a flying object. **b** (of a moving object) strike against, crash into, or collide with (*the plane hit the ground*). **c** reach (a target, a person, etc.) with a directed flying object (*hit the window with the ball*). **2** *tr.* affect the feelings, conscience, etc. of a person, esp. deeply or painfully (*the loss hit him hard*). **3** *intr.* (often foll. by *at, against, upon*) direct a blow. **4** *tr.* (often foll. by *against, on*) knock (a part of the body) (*hit his head on the door frame*). **5** *tr.* light upon; get at (a thing aimed at) (*hit the truth at last*) (see HIT ON 1). **6** *tr. informal* **a** encounter (*hit a snag*). **b** arrive at (*hit an all-time low*). **c** indulge in, esp. liquor etc. (*hit the bottle*). **7** *tr.* esp. *N Amer. slang* kill, attack, or rob. **8** *tr.* **a** occur forcefully to (*the seriousness of the situation hit him later*). **b** come suddenly to mind; occur to (a person) (*then it suddenly hit me*). **9** *tr. Sport* **a** propel (a ball etc.) with a bat, club, etc. to score runs or points. **b** score (runs or points) in this way. **c** *Baseball* make (a base hit). **10** *tr. & intr.* give (a person) a playing card, alcoholic drink, etc. **11** *tr.* esp. *N Amer.* (also foll. by *up*) request, ask, or beg (a person), esp. for money. **12** *tr.* represent or imitate exactly (*hit the exact colour*). ● *n.* **1 a** a blow; a stroke. **b** a collision. **2** a shot etc. that hits its target. **3** *informal* **a** a popular success, esp. in entertainment. **b** a successful pop record. **4** a stroke of sarcasm, wit, etc. **5** esp. *N Amer. slang* **a** a violent crime, esp. a contract killing. **b** a dose of something, esp. an illegal drug. **6** *Baseball* = BASE HIT. **7** a successful attempt, esp. an instance of identifying an item of data which matches the requirements of a search etc. □ **hit back** retaliate. **hit below the belt 1** esp. *Boxing* hit an opponent below the waist, esp. in the genitals. **2** treat or behave unfairly. **hit the books** *N Amer.* study, esp. intensely or diligently. **hit the bottle** (or **booze** etc.) *informal* drink too much habitually or over a period of time. **hit the bricks** *N Amer. slang* go on strike. **hit the deck** *informal* fall to the floor, ground, etc. **hit the ground running** esp. *N Amer. informal* **1** begin a task, endeavour, etc. with the basic preparation already completed. **2** proceed with enthusiasm and dynamism. **hit home 1** become fully and often painfully clear. **2** (of remarks etc.) have the intended, often painful, effect. **hit it** *Music* begin playing. **hit it off** (often foll. by *with, together*) *informal* get on well or have a good and harmonious relationship (with a person). **hit the nail on the head** guess correctly or express the truth precisely. **hit on 1** (also **hit upon**) find (what is sought), esp. by chance. **2** *slang* make sexual overtures toward (a person). **hit out** deal vigorous physical or verbal blows (*hit out at her enemies*). **hit the road** (also *N Amer.* **trail**) *slang* depart. **hit the sack** (also **hit the hay**) *informal* go to bed. **make** (or **be**) **a hit** (usu. foll. by *with*) be successful or popular. □ **hitless** *adj.* **hittable** *adj.* **hitter** *n.*

hit-and-miss *adj.* (also **hit-or-miss**) aimed or done carelessly, at random, or haphazardly.

hit and roll *Curling* ● *n.* a play in which a rock strikes and glances off a stationary rock, sliding into a better position and usu. knocking the other rock into a less advantageous position. ● *v.intr.* make such a play.

hit and run ● *n.* **1 a** a motor vehicle accident in which the driver who caused the accident flees the scene. **b** a military etc. attack using swift actions followed by immediate withdrawals. **2** *Baseball* the departure of a runner from his or her base as soon as the pitcher begins to throw to the batter. ● *adj.* (**hit-and-run**) relating to or (of a person) committing a hit and run (*hit-and-run fatalities*).

hit and stay (also **hit and stick**) *Curling* ● *n.* a play in which a rock strikes an opponent's rock directly, knocking it into a less advantageous position and, at the same time, assumes the position of the previously stationary rock. ● *v.intr.* make such a play.

hitch ● *v.* **1 a** *tr.* fasten with a loop, hook, etc. **b** *intr.* (often foll. by *in*, *on to*, etc.) become fastened in this way (*the rod hitched in to the bracket*). **2 a** *tr.* move (a thing) with a jerk; shift slightly. **b** *intr.* move jerkily or unsteadily (*the snowmobile began to hitch*). **3** *informal* **a** *intr.* = HITCHHIKE. **b** *tr.* obtain (a lift) by hitchhiking. **4** *intr.* catch, snag, or become caught on something. ● *n.* **1** an impediment; a temporary obstacle (*the unit ran without a hitch*). **2 a** an abrupt pull or push; a jerk. **b** *Baseball* a flaw in batting style in which the batter brings the bat forward and then draws it back slightly before swinging. **3** any of various kinds of noose or knot used to fasten one thing temporarily to another. **4** a contrivance for fastening one thing to another (*trailer hitch*). **5** *informal* a free ride in a vehicle. □ **get hitched** *informal* marry. **hitch up 1** lift (esp. clothing) with a jerk. **2** meet, join, or become associated with. **hitch one's wagon to a star** associate oneself with a person more prominent than oneself; make use of powers or opportunities greater than one's own. □ **hitcher** *n.*

hitchhike *v.intr.* travel by seeking free lifts in passing vehicles. □ **hitchhiker** *n.* **hitchhiking** *n.*

hi-tech *adj.* = HIGH-TECH *adj.*.

hither *adv.* to or towards this place.

hither and thither *adv.* (also **hither and yon**) here and there, in various directions, to and fro.

hitherto *adv.* until this time, up to now.

Hitler *n.* a tyrannical, dictatorial person, esp. a ruler.

hit list *n.* *slang* **1** a list of prospective victims esp. of assassination. **2** a list of people, programs, etc. against whom some action is being planned.

hitmaker *n.* *informal* an entertainer, esp. a musician, who consistently produces a number of best-selling records etc.

hit man *n.* *slang* a hired assassin.

hit-or-miss *adj.* = HIT-AND-MISS.

hit parade *n.* *informal* **1** a list of the current best-selling records of popular music. **2** any listing of popular people, things, etc. in a specified field.

Hittite /ˈhɪtaɪt/ ● *n.* **1** a member of an ancient, non-Semitic people of Asia Minor and Syria. **2** the Indo-European language of the Hittites, written in cunei-

form and deciphered in the early 20th c. ● *adj.* of or relating to the Hittites or their language.

HIV *abbr.* human immunodeficiency virus, a retrovirus which causes AIDS.

hive ● *n.* **1 a** a beehive. **b** the bees in a hive. **2** a busy, swarming place. **3** a swarming multitude. **4** a thing shaped like a hive in being domed. ● *v.* **1** *tr.* **a** place (bees) in a hive. **b** house (people etc.) snugly. **2** *intr.* **a** (of bees) enter a hive. **b** live or work together like bees. **3** *tr.* gather, hoard, store up, as bees with honey. □ **hive off 1** separate from a larger group. **2 a** form into or assign (work) to a subsidiary department or company. **b** denationalize or privatize (an industry etc.).

hives *n.pl.* any of various skin conditions characterized by itchy red weals caused by allergic reaction, emotional stress, etc.

hiya /ˈhaɪjə/ *interj.* *informal* a word used in greeting.

HK *abbr.* **1** Hong Kong. **2** *N Amer.* housekeeping (*HK cottages*).

hl *abbr.* hectolitre(s).

hm *abbr.* hectometre(s).

h'm *interj. & n.* (also **hmm**) = HEM², HUM².

HMCS *abbr.* Her (or His) Majesty's Canadian Ship (as a designation for a Canadian naval vessel).

HMS *abbr.* Her (or His) Majesty's Ship (as a designation for a British naval vessel).

Ho *symbol* holmium.

ho¹ *interj.* **1** (also in *comb.*) an expression of admiration or (often repeated as **ho! ho!**), derision, surprise, or triumph. **2** a call for attention. **3** (in *comb.*) an addition to the name of a destination etc. (*westward ho*).

ho² *n.* (*pl.* **hos**) esp. *N Amer. slang* **1** a prostitute. **2** *derogatory* a woman.

hoar *literary* ● *adj.* **1** grey-haired with age. **2** greyish-white. **3** (of a thing) grey with age. ● *n.* **1** (also **hoarfrost**) frozen water vapour deposited in clear still weather on vegetation etc. **2** hoariness.

hoard ● *n.* **1** a stock or store (esp. of money) put away. **2** an amassed store of facts etc. **3** *Archaeology* an ancient store of treasure etc. ● *v.* **1** *tr. & intr.* (often foll. by *up*) amass (money etc.) and put away; store. **2** *intr.* accumulate more than one's current requirements of food etc. in a time of scarcity. □ **hoarder** *n.*

hoarding *n.* a temporary board fence erected around a construction site etc.

hoarse *adj.* **1** (of the voice) rough and deep; husky; croaking. **2** having such a voice, due to illness, shouting, etc. □ **hoarsely** *adv.* **hoarseness** *n.*

hoary *adj.* (**-ier, -iest**) **1 a** (of hair) grey or white with age. **b** (of a person) having such hair; aged, venerable. **2** old and trite (*a hoary joke*). **3** *Bot. & Zool.* covered with short white hairs. □ **hoarily** *adv.* **hoariness** *n.*

hoax ● *n.* a humorous or malicious deception. ● *v.tr.* deceive (a person) with a hoax. □ **hoaxer** *n.*

hob¹ *n.* a flat metal shelf at the side of a fireplace, having its surface level with the top of the grate, used esp. for heating a pan etc.

hob² *n.* a hobgoblin. □ **play** (or **raise**) **hob** *N Amer.* cause mischief or act disruptively.

hobble ● *v.* **1** *intr.* **a** walk lamely; limp. **b** proceed haltingly in action or speech (*hobbled lamely to his conclusion*). **2** *tr.* **a** tie together the legs of (a horse etc.) to prevent it from straying etc. **b** tie or fasten (a horse's etc. legs). **3** *tr.* **a** cause (a person etc.) to limp. **b** hinder, interfere with, foil, or perplex (a person, plan, etc.). ● *n.* **1** an uneven or infirm gait. **2** a rope, clog, etc. used for hobbling a horse etc.

hobby *n.* (*pl.* **-ies**) a favourite leisure-time activity or occupation. □ **hobbyist** *n.*

hobby farm *n. N Amer. & Austral.* a small farm operated for pleasure rather than profit. □ **hobby farmer** *n.*

hobby horse *n.* **1** a child's toy consisting of a long stick with a figure of a horse's head on one end. **2** a preoccupation; a favourite topic of conversation. **3** a rocking horse.

hobgoblin *n.* **1** a mischievous imp or sprite. **2** something to be feared superstitiously; a bugbear.

hobnail *n.* **1** a heavy-headed nail used for boot soles. **2** a pattern in glass etc. consisting of closely spaced studs or bosses, often in the shape of diamonds. □ **hobnailed** *adj.*

hobnob *v.intr.* (**hobnobbed, hobnobbing**) (usu. foll. by *with*) mix socially or informally. □ **hobnobber** *n.*

hobo *n.* (*pl.* **-oes** or **-os**) *esp. N Amer.* **1** a tramp or vagrant. **2** an unskilled worker who moves from place to place.

hock¹ *n.* **1** the joint of a quadruped's hind leg between the knee and the fetlock. **2** a knuckle of pork; the lower joint of a ham.

hock² *v.tr. esp. N Amer. informal* pawn. □ **in hock 1** in debt. **2** in pawn.

hockey *n.* (often *attrib.*) *N Amer.* **1** a game played on ice between two teams of six players each, in which players try to shoot a puck into the opposing team's net with sticks. **2** any of a number of variations of this, such as street hockey. *See also* FIELD HOCKEY.

hockey bag *n.* a large esp. nylon bag for carrying hockey equipment, usu. with pockets for skates.

hockey cushion *n. Cdn* a skating rink with hockey boards, esp. an outdoor rink of natural ice.

hockey glove *n.* a padded glove worn by hockey players for protection against slashing etc.

hockey jacket *n. Cdn* an outer jacket, usu. of nylon with a quilted lining, with a hockey team's crest on the chest and the owner's name, position, number, etc. embroidered on the arm.

hockey mom *n.* (also **hockey mother**) *N Amer.* a mother deeply committed to a child's hockey practice, career, etc., who spends much time, effort, and money to ensure the child receives the best training, advantages, etc.

hockey pants *n.pl.* knee-length, high-waisted padded pants worn by hockey players to protect their thighs, hips, and kidneys.

hockey puck *n.* **1** = PUCK 1. **2** an object the size or shape of a hockey puck.

hockey socks *n.pl.* long woollen leggings extending from thigh to ankle, held by a garterbelt and with stirrups for the feet, worn by hockey players.

hockey stick *n.* a stick with a flat, slightly curved blade at the lower end, used to control, pass, and shoot the puck in hockey.

hockey tape *n.* an adhesive tape used esp. on the blade of a hockey stick to strengthen it or on the handle to improve the grip.

hocus-pocus *n.* **1 a** a deception; trickery. **b** magic, dazzle. **2 a** a typical verbal formula used in conjuring. **b** esoteric or in-group jargon.

hod *n.* a V-shaped open trough on a pole used for carrying bricks, mortar, etc.

hodgepodge *n. esp. N Amer.* a mixture of heterogeneous things, a jumble.

Hodgkin's disease /ˈhɒdʒkɪnz/ *n.* a malignant but often curable disease of the lymphatic system usu. characterized by enlargement of the lymph nodes, liver, and spleen.

hoe ● *n.* a long-handled tool with a thin metal blade, used for weeding etc. ● *v.* (**hoes, hoed, hoeing**) **1** *tr.*

weed (crops); loosen (earth); dig up or cut down with a hoe. **2** *intr.* use a hoe. □ **hoer** *n.*

hoedown *n. N Amer.* **1** a lively party with square dancing, country music, etc. **2** the music played at such a party.

hog ● *n.* **1 a** a domesticated pig, esp. a castrated male reared for slaughter. **b** any of several other pigs of the family Suidae, e.g. a warthog. **2** *informal* **a** a greedy person. **b** a person who hoards selfishly or monopolizes something (*a puck hog*). **3** *N Amer. slang* a large, heavy motorcycle. ● *v.* (**hogged, hogging**) **1** *tr. informal* take greedily; hoard selfishly; monopolize. **2** *tr. & intr.* raise (the back), or rise in an arch in the centre. □ **go (the) whole hog** *informal* do something completely or thoroughly. **live high on** (or **off**) **the hog** *N Amer. informal* live luxuriously.

hogback *n.* (also **hog's back**) a ridge of land sloping steeply on each side.

hog line *n. Curling* either of two lines drawn across each end of a rink at one-sixth of the rink's length from the tee, over which a rock must cross to count.

hognose snake *n.* any of several harmless snakes constituting the N American genus *Heterodon*, which have an upturned snout.

hogshead /ˈhɒgzhed/ *n.* **1** a large cask. **2** a liquid or dry measure, varying according to the commodity, but usu. about 220 to 245 litres.

hog-tie *v.tr.* (**-tying**) *N Amer.* **1** secure by fastening the hands and feet or all four feet together. **2** restrain, impede.

hogwash *n.* **1** *informal* nonsense, rubbish. **2** kitchen swill etc. for pigs.

hog-wild *adj. N Amer. informal* exceedingly excited or enthusiastic.

ho ho *interj.* **1** representing deep jolly laughter. **2** expressing surprise, triumph, or derision.

ho-hum ● *adj.* dull, routine, boring. ● *interj.* expressing boredom.

hoick /hɔɪk/ *v. informal* (often foll. by *out*) lift or pull, esp. with a jerk.

hoi polloi /ˌhɔɪ pəˈlɔɪ/ *n.* (often prec. by *the*) the masses; the common people. ¶Some object vehemently to the use with *the*, since *hoi* = 'the', but this construction is well established in English and it is neither necessary nor idiomatic to omit *the*.

hoisin sauce /ˈhɔɪzɪn/ *n.* a sweet, spicy, dark red sauce made from soybeans, vinegar, sugar, garlic, and spices, widely used in southern Chinese cooking.

hoist ● *v.tr.* **1** raise or haul up. **2** raise by means of ropes and pulleys etc. ● *n.* **1** an apparatus for hoisting. **2** an act of hoisting, a lift. **3 a** the perpendicular height of a flag or sail (*compare* FLY¹ *n.* 7a). **b** the part of a flag nearest the staff (*compare* FLY¹ *n.* 7b). **c** a group of flags raised as a signal.

hoity-toity /ˌhɔɪtiˈtɔɪti/ ● *adj.* haughty, snobbish, pretentious. ● *interj.* expressing surprised protest at presumption etc.

hokey *adj.* (**hokier, hokiest**) *N Amer. slang* sentimental, artificial. □ **hokeyness** *n.*

hokum /ˈhoːkəm/ *n.* esp. *N Amer. slang* **1** sentimental, popular, sensational, or unreal situations, dialogue, etc., in a film or play etc. **2** nonsense; rubbish.

Holarctic /hoˈlɑrktɪk/ ● *adj.* of, relating to, or found throughout the Nearctic and Palearctic regions considered together as a single zoogeographical region. ● *n.* the Holarctic region.

hold¹ ● *v.* (*past and past part.* **held**) **1** *tr.* **a** keep fast; grasp (esp. in the hands or arms). **b** (also *refl.*) keep or sustain (a thing, oneself, one's head, etc.) in a particular position (*hold it to the light*). **c** grasp so as to control (*hold the reins*). **2** *tr.* (of a vessel etc.) contain or be capable of containing (*the hall holds 900*). **3** *tr.* possess, gain, or have, esp.: **a** be the owner or tenant of (land, property, stocks, etc.). **b** gain or have gained as an honour, achievement, or qualification (a degree, record, etc.) (*holds the long jump record*). **c** have the position of (a job or office). **d** have (a specified playing card) in one's hand. **e** keep possession of (a place, a person's thoughts, etc.) esp. against attack (*held the fort*). **4** *intr.* remain unbroken; not give way (*the roof held*). **5** *tr.* observe; celebrate, conduct (a meeting, festival, conversation, etc.). **6** *tr.* **a** keep (a person etc.) in a specified condition, place, etc. (*held her prisoner*). **b** detain, esp. in custody (*hold him until I arrive*). **7** *tr.* **a** engross (a person or a person's attention) (*the book held him for hours*). **b** dominate (*held the stage*). **8** *tr.* (foll. by *to*) make (a person etc.) adhere to (terms, a promise, etc.). **9** *intr.* (of weather) remain free of rain, snow etc.; continue sunny and clear. **10** *tr.* (often foll. by *to* + infin., or *that* + clause) think; believe (*held it to be self-evident*). **11** *tr.* regard with a specified feeling (*held him in contempt*). **12** *tr.* **a** cease; restrain (*hold your fire*). **b** *N Amer. informal* withhold; not use (*hold the onions!*). **13** *tr.* keep or reserve (*will you hold our seats please?*). **14** *tr.* be able to drink (liquor) without obvious effect. **15** *tr.* (usu. foll. by *that* + clause) (of a judge, a court, etc.) decide; state as an authoritative opinion; lay down as a point of law. **16** *tr. Music* sustain (a note). **17** *intr.* remain connected by telephone without speaking to someone. **18** *tr.* (of a computer, answering machine, etc.) retain or temporarily store information, data, messages, etc. ● *n.* **1** a grasp (*get hold of him*). **2** (often in *comb.*) a thing to hold by (*handhold*). **3** (foll. by *on, over*) a controlling influence over (*has a strange hold over them*). **4** a manner of holding in wrestling etc. **5** a facility offered by some telephone systems whereby an incoming connection is held open until a specified recipient can take the call. **6** a pause, delay, or postponement. **7** a request ordering or reserving (a book, video, etc.). □ **get** (**a**) **hold of 1** acquire, obtain, etc. **2** contact or communicate with, esp. by telephone. **hold** (**a thing**) **against** (**a person**) resent or regard (a thing) as discreditable to (a person). **hold back 1** impede the progress of; restrain. **2** keep (a thing) to or for oneself. **3** (often foll. by *from*) hesitate; refrain. **hold by** (or **to**) adhere to (a choice, purpose, etc.). **hold court** preside over one's admirers etc., like a sovereign. **hold dear** regard with affection. **hold down 1** repress. **2** *informal* be competent enough to keep (one's job etc.). **3** secure, restrain, or limit. **hold everything!** cease action or movement. **hold the fort 1** act as a temporary substitute. **2** cope in an emergency. **hold forth 1** offer (an inducement etc.). **2** usu. *derogatory* speak at length or tediously. **hold a person's hand** give a person guidance or moral support. **hold hands** grasp one another by the hand as a sign of affection or for support or guidance. **hold one's head high** behave proudly and confidently. **hold one's horses** *informal* stop; slow down. **hold in** keep in check, confine. **hold it!** stop; cease and desist. **hold the line 1** not yield. **2** maintain a telephone connection. **hold one's nose** compress the nostrils to avoid a bad smell. **hold off 1** delay; not begin. **2** keep one's distance. **hold on 1** keep one's grasp on something. **2** wait a moment. **3** (when telephoning) not hang up. **hold out 1** stretch forth (a hand etc.). **2** offer (an inducement etc.). **3** maintain resistance. **4** persist or last. **hold out for** continue to demand. **hold out on** *informal* refuse something to (a person). **hold over 1**

postpone, keep for future consideration. **2** retain for an additional period (*the movie was held over for another week*). **hold something over** threaten (a person) constantly with something. **hold together 1** cohere. **2** cause to cohere. **3** retain one's composure, esp. in difficult circumstances. **hold one's tongue** *informal* be silent. **hold to ransom 1** keep (a person) prisoner until a ransom is paid. **2** demand concessions from by threats of damaging action. **hold true** (or **good**) be valid; apply. **hold up 1 a** support; sustain. **b** maintain (the head etc.) erect. **2** exhibit; display. **3** arrest the progress of; obstruct. **4** stop and rob by violence or threats. **hold water** (of reasoning) be sound; bear examination. **hold with** (usu. with *neg.*) *informal* approve of (*don't hold with motorbikes*). **left holding the bag** *N Amer.* left with unwelcome responsibility. **on hold 1** (when telephoning) holding the line. **2** reserved (*the book is on hold*). **3** (esp. in *phr.* **put on hold**) temporarily inactive or receiving little attention. **take hold** (of a custom or habit) become established. **there is no holding him** (or **her** etc.) he (or she etc.) is restive, high-spirited, determined, etc. **with no holds barred** with no restrictions, all methods being permitted.

hold² *n.* a cavity in the lower part of a ship or aircraft in which the cargo is stowed.

holder *n.* **1** (often in *comb.*) a device or implement for holding something. **2 a** the possessor of a title, record, etc. **b** the occupant of an office etc. **c** a person who holds a bank account, company share, etc.

holding *n.* **1 a** land held by lease. **b** the tenure of land. **2** (usu. in *pl.*) stocks, property, etc. held. **3** *Sport* the action of illegally restraining or obstructing one's opponent. **4** the collection of books, journals, etc. in a library.

holding company *n.* a company created to hold the shares of other companies, which it then controls.

holding pattern *n.* **1** the (usu. circular) flight path maintained by an aircraft awaiting permission to land. **2** a state or period of no progress or change.

holding tank *n.* a tank for short-term storage of a substance.

holdout *n.* **1** an act of holding out against some trend, or of staying out of some activity. **2** a person who does this.

hold-over *n.* **1** *N Amer.* a person or thing left over from the past; a relic. **2** a person who remains in office, on a team, etc. beyond the regular term etc.

holdup *n.* **1** a stoppage or delay by traffic, inclement weather, etc. **2** a robbery, esp. by the use of threats or violence.

hole ● *n.* **1 a** an empty space in a solid body. **b** an aperture in or through something. **2** an animal's burrow. **3** a cavity or receptacle into which the ball must be propelled in various sports or games, e.g. golf. **4** *informal* a small, mean, or dingy abode. **5** a dungeon or prison cell, esp. a cell used for solitary confinement. **6** *informal* an awkward or embarrassing situation. **7** a deep place in a river, stream, etc. (*swimming hole*). **8** *Golf* **a** a point scored by a player who gets the ball from tee to hole with the fewest strokes. **b** the terrain or distance from tee to hole. **9** an opening or vacancy (*the hiring filled a hole in our department*). ● *v.* **1** *tr.* make a hole or holes in. **2** *tr.* put into a hole. **3** *tr. & intr.* (often foll. by *out*) send (a golf ball) into a hole. □ **dig a hole for oneself** create a difficult situation for oneself, from which escape is difficult. **hole up** *N Amer. informal* **1** hide oneself. **2** take shelter (for the night, the winter, etc.). **in the hole**

N Amer. informal in debt. **make a hole in** use a large amount of. ☐ **holey** *adj.*

hole card *n.* **1** (in stud poker) a card which has been dealt face down. **2** *informal* something held in reserve until it can be used to one's advantage.

hole-in-one *n.* (*pl.* **holes-in-one**) *Golf* a shot that enters the hole from the tee.

hole in the wall *n.* a small dingy place (esp. of business).

holiday ● *n.* **1 a** a day on which most work, school, and business ceases, esp. in honour of a person or event. **b** a religious festival. **2** esp. *Cdn, Brit., Austral. & NZ* (often in *pl.*) a period of rest from work, school, etc., usu. for a certain number of weeks per year. **3** (in *pl.*) (also **holiday season**) the festive period surrounding Christmas, Hanukkah, and New Year's. **4** (*attrib.*) (of clothes etc.) festive. ● *vintr.* spend a holiday. ☐ **take a holiday** have a break from work.

holiday weekend *n.* a long weekend on which the Friday or Monday is a holiday.

holier-than-thou *adj. informal* self-righteous.

holiness *n.* **1** sanctity; the state of being holy. **2** (**Holiness**) a title used when referring to or addressing the Pope.

holism /ˈhoːlɪzəm/ *n.* **1** *Philos.* the theory that certain wholes are to be regarded as greater than the sum of their parts (*compare* REDUCTIONISM 2). **2** *Med.* the treating of the whole person including mental and social factors than just the symptoms of a disease. ☐ **holist** *n.* **holistic** *adj.* **holistically** *adv.*

hollandaise sauce /ˈhɒlənˌdeɪz/ *n.* a creamy sauce of melted butter, egg yolks, lemon juice, etc.

holler esp. *N Amer. informal* ● *v.* **1** *intr.* make a loud cry or noise. **2** *tr.* express with a loud cry or shout. ● *n.* a loud cry, noise, or shout.

hollow ● *adj.* **1 a** having a hole or cavity inside; not solid throughout. **b** having a depression; sunken (*hollow cheeks*). **2** (of a sound) echoing, as though made in or on a hollow container. **3** empty; hungry. **4** without significance; meaningless (*a hollow triumph*). **5** insincere; cynical; false (*a hollow laugh*; *hollow promises*). ● *n.* **1** a hollow place; a hole. **2** a valley; a basin. **3** (also **hollow of the hand**) the enclosed space formed by the palm of the hand with the fingers curled inwards. ● *vtr.* (often foll. by *out*) make hollow; excavate. ● *adv. informal* completely (*beaten hollow*). ☐ **hollowly** *adv.* **hollowness** *n.*

hollow-point ● *adj.* (of ammunition) made with a hollow point, so as to shatter on impact. ● *n.* a hollow-point bullet.

holly *n.* (*pl.* **-ies**) **1** any of various shrubs or small trees of the genus *Ilex*, esp. the evergreen *Ilex aquifolium*, with prickly usu. dark green leaves, small white flowers, and red berries. **2** its branches and foliage used as decorations at Christmas.

hollyhock *n.* a tall plant, *Alcea rosea*, with large showy flowers of various colours.

Hollywood *n.* the American motion picture industry or its products, with its principal centre at Hollywood, California.

holm /hoːm/ *n.* (in full **holm oak**) an evergreen oak, *Quercus ilex*, with holly-like young leaves.

holmium /ˈhoːlmiəm/ *n.* a soft silvery metallic element occurring naturally in apatite.

holocaust /ˈhɒləˌkɔːst/ *n.* **1** a case of large-scale destruction, esp. by fire or nuclear war. **2** (**the Holocaust**) the mass murder esp. of Jews under the Nazi regime 1941–5. **3** a sacrifice consumed by fire.

Holocene /ˈhɒləˌsiːn/ ● *adj.* of or relating to the second epoch of the Quaternary period, lasting from about 10,000 years ago to the present, coinciding with the development of human agricultural settlement and civilization. ● *n.* this geological period or system.

hologram /ˈhɒləˌgræm/ *n.* **1** a three-dimensional image formed by the interference of light beams from a coherent light source. **2** a photograph of the interference pattern, which when suitably illuminated produces a three-dimensional image.

holograph /ˈhɒləˌgræf/ ● *adj.* wholly written by hand by the person named as the author. ● *n.* a holograph document.

holography /həˈlɒɡrəfi/ *n. Physics* the study or production of holograms. ☐ **holographic** *adj.* **holographically** *adv.*

holothurian /ˌhɒləˈθjʊəriən/ ● *n.* any echinoderm of the class Holothurioidea, with a wormlike body, e.g. a sea cucumber. ● *adj.* of this class.

Holstein /ˈhoːlstiːn, -staɪn/ *n. N Amer.* (in full **Holstein-Friesian**) a large black and white breed of dairy cattle, noted for high milk production.

holster *n.* a leather case for a pistol or revolver, worn on a belt or under an arm or fixed to a saddle.

holubtsi /ˈhɒlʌpˌtʃi/ *n.pl. Cdn* esp. (*West*) cabbage rolls.

holy (**-ier, -iest**) ● *adj.* **1** morally and spiritually excellent or perfect, and to be revered. **2** belonging to, devoted to, or empowered by, God. **3** consecrated, sacred. **4** used in exclamations (*holy cow!*; *holy Moses!*; *holy smokes!*). ● *interj.* expressing amazement etc.

Holy Ark *n.* a chest or cabinet containing the Torah scrolls in a synagogue.

Holy Bible *n.* = BIBLE 1a.

Holy City *n.* **1** a city held sacred by the adherents of a religion, esp. Jerusalem. **2** Heaven.

Holy Communion *n. see* COMMUNION 3a.

holy day *n.* a religious festival.

Holy Family *n.* **1** the young Jesus with his mother and St. Joseph. **2** (also **Feast of the Holy Family**) *Catholicism* a feast day falling on the first Sunday after Christmas, commemorating the life together of the Holy Family and emphasizing religious family life.

Holy Father *n.* the Pope.

Holy Ghost *n. see* HOLY SPIRIT.

Holy Grail *n.* = GRAIL 1.

Holy Innocents *n.pl.* **1** the children massacred by King Herod in his attempt to kill the child Jesus. **2** (also **Feast of the Holy Innocents**) a feast day commemorating this, celebrated in some Western Christian churches on Dec. 28 and in Eastern churches on Dec. 29.

holy jumpin' *interj. Cdn slang* expressing surprise, disbelief, etc.

holy moly /ˈmoːli/ *interj.* (also **holy moley**) expressing great surprise, admiration, etc.

holy of holies *n.* **1** the inner chamber of the sanctuary in the Jewish temple, separated by a veil from the outer chamber. **2** an innermost shrine. **3** a thing regarded as most sacred.

holy orders *n.pl.* the status of a member of the clergy, esp. the grades of bishop, priest, and deacon.

holy roller *n. slang derogatory* **1** a member of a Pentecostal or other charismatic group characterized by religious excitement. **2** a highly vocal devout person.

Holy Sacrament *n. see* SACRAMENT 3.

Holy Saturday *n.* Saturday in Holy Week.

Holy Scripture *n.* the Bible.

Holy See *n.* the papacy or the papal court.

Holy Spirit (in Christian theology) the third person of the Trinity.

holy terror *n. see* TERROR 2b.

Holy Thursday *n.* the Thursday before Easter.

Holy Trinity *n. see* TRINITY 1.

holy war *n.* a war waged for a religious cause.

holy water *n.* water dedicated to holy uses, or blessed by a priest.

Holy Week *n.* the week before Easter.

homage /ˈhɒmɪdʒ, ˈɒm-/ *n.* **1** acknowledgement of superiority; dutiful reverence (*pay homage to*; *do homage to*). **2** *hist.* formal public acknowledgement of feudal allegiance. **3** an act of homage.

hombre /ˈɒmbreɪ, ˈhɒm-/ *n. N Amer. slang* a man.

homburg /ˈhɒmbɜːrg/ *n.* a man's felt hat with a narrow curled brim and a lengthwise dent in the crown.

home ● *n.* **1 a** the place where one lives; the fixed residence of a family or household. **b** a house or dwelling place. **c** the residence of a person's parents. **d** a building etc. providing a locale for a company's activities. **2** the members of a family collectively; one's family background (*comes from a good home*). **3** the native land of a person or of a person's ancestors. **4** an institution for persons needing care, rest, or refuge (*nursing home*). **5** the place where a thing originates or is native or most common. **6 a** *Baseball* = HOME PLATE. **b** the finishing point in a race. **c** (in games) the place where one is free from attack. **d** (in some sports) the goal. **e** *Lacrosse* a player in an attacking position near the opponents' goal. **7** *Sport* a home game or win. ● *attrib.adj.* **1 a** of or connected with one's home. **b** carried on, done, or made at home (*home movies*). **c** proceeding from home. **2** carried on or produced in one's own country (*the home market*). **3** *Sport* played on one's own ground etc. (*home game*; *home win*). **4** in the neighbourhood of home. **5** main; principal. ● *adv.* **1 a** to one's home or country (*go home*). **b** arrived at home (*is he home yet?*). **c** *N Amer.* at home (*stay home*). **2 a** to the point aimed at (*the thrust went home*). **b** as far as possible (*drove the nail home*). ● *v.* **1** *intr.* (esp. of a trained pigeon) return home (*compare* HOMING 1). **2** *intr.* (often foll. by *on*, *in on*) (of a vessel, missile, etc.) be guided towards a destination or target by a landmark, radio beam, etc. **3** *tr.* send or guide homewards. **4** *tr.* provide with a home. □ **at home 1** in one's own house or native land. **2** at ease as if in one's own home (*make yourself at home*). **3** (usu. foll. by *in*, *on*, *with*) familiar or well informed. **4** available to callers. **come home to** become fully realized by. **heading home** *Curling* in or during the final end of a game. **home free** *N Amer.* assured of success or safety (*if we make it to the border we're home free*). **home, James!** *jocular* drive home quickly! **near home** affecting one closely. □ **homelike** *adj.*

home and school *n.* (in full **home and school association**) esp. *Cdn* a local organization of parents and teachers to promote better communication and improve educational facilities.

home away from home *n.* a place other than one's home where one feels at home; a place providing homelike amenities.

home-baked *adj.* (of food) baked at home or at the restaurant etc. where it is served. □ **home baking** *n.*

home base *n.* **1** headquarters (*our home base is in Brampton*). **2** *Baseball* = HOME PLATE.

home-based *adj.* operating out of a private home.

homebody *n.* (*pl.* **-ies**) a person who likes to stay at home.

homeboy *n.* esp. *US slang* **1** a person from one's own town or neighbourhood. **2** a close friend, esp. a member of one's gang.

homebrew *n.* **1** beer or other alcoholic drink brewed

at home. **2** *Cdn* a person, esp. a sports competitor, who is a native of the country or locality where the competition is held. □ **home-brewed** *adv.*

home builder *n.* **1** a person who builds houses. **2** a person who builds something in their home.

homebuilt *adj.* built in an individual's home.

homebuyer *n.* a person who buys a house etc.

home care *n.* care, esp. medical care, given or received at home (also *attrib.*: *home care nurse*).

home child *n. Cdn* (usu. in *pl.*) one of a number of orphaned or destitute children sent from Britain to Canada from the mid-19th to the early 20th c. to serve as farm or domestic help.

homecoming *n.* **1** arrival at home. **2** *N Amer.* a reunion, esp. of former students of a university, college, or high school.

home ec *n. N Amer.* home economics.

home economics *n.pl.* (often treated as *sing.*) the study of household management, usu. including cooking, nutrition, sewing, child-raising, budgeting, etc. □ **home economist** *n.*

home entertainment *n.* entertainment provided in the home by electronic equipment such as TVs, VCRs, stereos, etc. (also *attrib.*: *home entertainment centre*).

home fires *n.pl.* the fire etc. used to warm a family home. □ **keep the home fires burning** maintain a family home, esp. while one of its members is away for a prolonged period.

home fry *n. N Amer.* (*pl.* **-ies**) (usu. in *pl.*) a slice of usu. boiled potato that has been fried in a frying pan, as opposed to being deep-fried.

homegirl *n.* esp. *US slang* **1** a girl from one's own town or neighbourhood. **2** a close friend, esp. a member of one's gang.

home ground *n.* a subject or area with which one is familiar.

homegrown *adj.* **1** raised or cultivated on one's own land. **2** native to or produced in one's own country, locality, etc.

home ice *n.* the rink where a hockey team or curling rink normally plays its home games.

home invasion *n. N Amer.* a robbery usu. perpetrated by a group while the occupants are present.

homeland *n.* **1** one's native land. **2** *hist.* a partially self-governing area in South Africa set aside for a particular indigenous African people or peoples under the former policy of separate development; the homelands were abolished in 1994. **3** any similar semi-autonomous area.

homeless *adj.* lacking a home. □ **homelessness** *n.*

homely *adj.* (**-ier**, **-iest**) **1** *N Amer.* (esp. of people or their features) unattractive. **2 a** simple, plain. **b** unpretentious. **c** primitive. **3** comfortable in the manner of a home, cozy. □ **homeliness** *n.*

homemade *adj.* made at home.

homemaker *n. N Amer.* **1** one who runs a household for their family, esp. as a primary occupation. **2** one who cooks meals, cleans house, etc. for an elderly, sick, or disabled person. □ **homemaking** *adj. & n.*

home movie *n.* (also **home video**) a film (or video) made at home or of one's own activities.

home office *n.* **1** *N Amer.* an office in a private home. **2** the head office of a corporation.

homeopath /ˈhoːmiːoʊˌpæθ/ *n.* a person who practises homeopathy.

homeopathy /ˌhoːmiˈɒpəθi/ *n.* the treatment of disease by minute doses of drugs that in a healthy person would produce symptoms of the disease. ☐

homeopathic *adj.* **homeopathically** *adv.*

home opener *n. N Amer.* a sports team's first home game of a new season.

homeostasis /hɔːmiːˈsteɪsɪs/ *n.* (*pl.* **-stases** /-siːz/) the tendency towards a relatively stable equilibrium between interdependent elements, esp. as maintained by physiological processes.

homeowner *n.* a person who owns his or her own home. ☐ **home ownership** *n.*

home page *n. Computing* a computer screen that serves as an introduction to a network site, from which a number of options may be selected.

home plate *n. Baseball* a base beside which the batter stands and which a runner must reach to score a run.

home port *n.* the port from which a ship originates.

homer *Baseball* ● *n.* a home run. ● *v.intr.* hit a homer.

Homeric /hɔːˈmɛrɪk, hə'm-/ *adj.* **1** of, or in the style of, the Greek epic poet Homer (*c.* 700 BC) or the epic poems ascribed to him. **2** of Bronze Age Greece as described in these. **3** epic, large-scale (*Homeric conflict*).

homeroom *n. N Amer.* **1** a classroom in which a group of students assembles daily with the same teacher for announcements, opening exercises, etc. before dispersing to other classes. **2** the period during which students assemble in this. **3** the group of students who assemble for a given homeroom.

home rule *n.* (also **Home Rule**) a movement for the government of a colony, dependent country, etc. by its own citizens, esp. the movement advocating devolved government for Ireland, 1870–1914.

home run *n. Baseball* a hit that allows the batter to make a complete circuit of the bases.

home-schooling *n. N Amer.* the practice of teaching one's own children in one's own home. ☐ **home-school** *v.tr.* **home-schooler** *n.*

home shopping *n.* shopping carried out from home using catalogues, satellite TV channels, etc.

home show *n.* a fair or exposition at which home construction and renovation products are displayed.

homesick *adj.* depressed by longing for one's home during absence from it. ☐ **homesickness** *n.*

homesite *n.* esp. *N Amer., Austral. & NZ* a lot or piece of land suitable for building a house on.

homespun ● *adj.* **1 a** (of cloth) made of yarn spun at home. **b** (of yarn) spun at home. **2** plain, simple, unsophisticated, homely. ● *n.* **1** homespun cloth. **2** anything plain or homely.

homestand *n.* a series of games played at a team's own venue.

homestead ● *n.* **1** *N Amer.* an area of public land (usu. a quarter section) granted to a settler in exchange for a small fee, and on certain conditions, usu. that the settler establish a dwelling and cultivate a certain area of land within a specified time. **2** a house, esp. a farmhouse, and outbuildings. ● *v. N Amer.* **1** *tr.* settle on (land) as a homestead. **2** *intr.* settle on a homestead. ☐ **homesteader** *n.*

home stretch *n.* **1** the straight section of a racetrack leading to the finish line. **2** the final stage or phase of anything.

homestyle *adj. N Amer.* (esp. of food) of a kind made or done at home.

home theatre *n.* a home audio-video system designed to simulate as closely as possible the viewing conditions in a movie theatre.

hometown *n.* the town of one's birth or early life or present fixed residence.

home truth *n.* basic but unwelcome information concerning oneself.

home turf *n.* one's own territory.

homeward ● *adv.* (also **homewards**) towards home. ● *adj.* going or leading towards home.

homeward bound ● *adv.* preparing to go, or on the way, home. ● *adj.* (**homeward-bound**) preparing to go, or on the way, home.

homework *n.* **1** work to be done at home, esp. by a school pupil. **2** preparatory work or study.

homeworker *n.* a person who works from home, esp. doing low-paid piecework.

homey *adj.* (**homier, homiest**) suggesting home; cozy. ☐ **homeyness** *n.* (also **hominess**).

homicide /ˈhɒmɪˌsaɪd/ *n.* **1** the killing of a human being by another. **2** a person who kills a human being. ☐ **homicidal** *adj.*

homiletic /ˌhɒmɪˈlɛtɪk/ ● *adj.* (also **homiletical**) of homilies. ● *n.* (usu. in *pl.*) the art of preaching.

homily /ˈhɒmɪli/ *n.* (*pl.* **-ies**) **1** a sermon. **2** a tedious moralizing discourse.

homing *attrib.adj.* **1** (of a pigeon) trained to fly home, bred for long-distance racing, carrying messages, etc. **2** (of a device) for guiding (something) to a target etc. **3** that goes home.

homing instinct *n.* the instinct of certain animals to return to the territory from which they have been moved.

hominid /ˈhɒmɪnɪd/ ● *n.* a primate of the family Hominidae, which includes human beings (*Homo sapiens*), and several fossil forms. ● *adj.* of this family.

hominoid /ˈhɒmɪˌnɔɪd/ ● *adj.* **1** like a human. **2** hominid or pongid. ● *n.* an animal resembling a human.

hominy /ˈhɒmɪni/ *n.* esp. *US* coarsely ground kernels of corn esp. boiled with water or milk.

homme du nord /ɒm duː 'nɔr/ *n.* (*pl.* **hommes du nord**) *Cdn hist.* a voyageur who spent winters in the interior.

hommos *var.* of HUMMUS.

Homo /ˈhoːmoː/ *n.* **1** any primate of the genus *Homo*, including modern humans and various extinct species. **2** (with Latin or mock-Latin adjectives in imitation of zoological nomenclature) in names intended to personify some aspects of human life or behaviour (*Homo economicus*).

homo[1] *n.* (*pl.* **-os**) *informal offensive* a homosexual.

homo[2] *n. Cdn* homogenized milk typically having a butterfat content of 3.25 per cent.

homoerotic /ˌhɒmoːɪˈrɒtɪk/ *adj.* **1** homosexual. **2** arousing sexual desire in a person of the same sex. ☐ **homoeroticism** *n.* (also **homoerotism**).

homogeneous /ˌhɒməˈdʒiːniəs, ˌhoːmə-/ *adj.* (also *disputed* **homogenous** /həˈmɒdʒənəs/) **1** of the same kind. **2** consisting of parts all of the same kind; uniform. **3** *Math.* containing terms all of the same degree. ¶The variant is considered incorrect by many people and is best avoided. ☐ **homogeneity** /-dʒɪˈneɪəti/ *n.* **homogeneously** *adv.*

homogenize *v.* **1** *tr. & intr.* make or become homogeneous. **2** *tr.* treat (milk) so that the fat droplets are emulsified and the cream does not separate. ☐ **homogenization** *n.* **homogenizer** *n.*

homogenized *adj.* **1** homogeneous. **2** (of milk) having the fat droplets emulsified, esp. (in Canada) designating homogenized milk with a butterfat content of 3.25 per cent.

homograph /ˈhɒməˌɡrɑːf/ *n.* a word spelled like another but of different meaning or origin (e.g. POLE[1], POLE[2]).

homologous /həˈmɒləgəs/ *adj.* **1 a** having the same relation, relative position, etc. **b** corresponding. **2** *Biol.* (of organs etc.) similar in position and structure but not necessarily in function. **3** *Biol.* (of chromosomes) pairing at meiosis and having the same structural features and pattern of genes.

homologue /ˈhɒmə،lɒg/ *n.* (also **homolog**) a homologous thing.

homology /həˈmɒlədʒi/ *n.* a homologous state or relation; correspondence. □ **homological** *adj.*

homonym /ˈhɒmənɪm/ *n.* a word of the same spelling or sound as another but of different meaning; a homograph or homophone.

homophobia /،hoːməˈfoːbiə/ *n.* a hatred or fear of homosexuals or homosexuality. □ **homophobe** *n.* **homophobic** *adj.*

homophone /ˈhɒmə،foːn/ *n.* **1** a word having the same sound as another but of different meaning or origin (e.g. *pair*, *pear*). **2** a symbol denoting the same sound as another.

homopteran /həˈmɒptərən/ *n.* any insect of the suborder Homoptera, with wings of uniform texture (compare HETEROPTERAN). □ **homopterous** *adj.*

Homo sapiens /ˈseɪpiɛnz/ *n.* modern humans regarded as a species.

homosexual /،hoːmoːˈsɛkʃʊəl/ ● *adj.* **1** feeling or involving sexual attraction to persons of the same sex. **2** concerning homosexual relations or people. **3** relating to the same sex. ● *n.* a homosexual person. □ **homosexuality** *n.* **homosexually** *adv.*

homunculus /həˈmʌŋkjʊləs/ *n.* (*pl.* **homunculi** /-،laɪ/) a small person.

homy *var. of* HOMEY.

Hon. *abbr.* **1** Honourable. **2** Honorary.

hon /hʌn/ *n. informal* = HONEY 5.

honcho /ˈhɒntʃo/ *N Amer. slang* ● *n.* (*pl.* **-os**) a leader or manager, the person in charge. ● *v.tr.* (**-oes, -oed**) be in charge of, oversee.

hone ● *v.tr.* **1** sharpen on a whetstone. **2** make more effective or focused (*honing her skills as a performer*). ● *n.* **1** a whetstone, esp. for straight razors. **2** any of various stones used as material for this.

honest ● *adj.* **1** fair and just in character or behaviour, not cheating or stealing. **2** free of deceit and untruthfulness, sincere. **3** fairly earned (*an honest living*). **4** (of an act or feeling) showing fairness. **5** (of a thing) unadulterated, unsophisticated. ● *adv. informal* genuinely, really (*I didn't take it, honest!*). □ **do one's honest best** do the best that one can. **make an honest woman of** *informal* marry (esp. a pregnant woman).

honestly ● *adv.* **1** in an honest way. **2** really (*I don't honestly know*). ● *interj.* expressing exasperation, dismay, etc. (*Honestly! You're always complaining!*).

honest-to-God (also **honest-to-goodness**) *informal* ● *adj.* genuine, real. ● *adv.* genuinely, really.

honesty *n.* **1** the quality of being honest. **2** truthfulness. **3** a plant of the genus *Lunaria* with purple or white flowers.

honey *n.* (*pl.* **-eys**) **1** a sweet sticky yellowish fluid made by bees and other insects from nectar collected from flowers. **2** the colour of this. **3 a** sweetness. **b** a sweet thing. **4** a person or thing excellent of its kind (*a honey of a movie*). **5** esp. *N Amer.* (usu. as a form of address) darling, sweetheart. **6** (*attrib.*) designating something that is used to hold or carry sewage, manure, etc. (*honey bucket*). □ **honey-like** *adj.*

honey bag *n. Cdn* (*North*) *informal* a plastic bag used as a receptacle for human waste.

honeybee *n.* the common hive bee, *Apis mellifera*.

honeybun *n.* (also **honeybunch**) (esp. as a form of address) darling.

honeycomb ● *n.* **1** a structure of hexagonal cells of wax, made by bees to store honey and eggs. **2 a** a pattern arranged hexagonally. **b** fabric made with a pattern of raised hexagons etc. **3** tripe from the second stomach of a ruminant. ● *v.tr.* **1** fill with cavities or tunnels, undermine. **2** mark with a honeycomb pattern. □ **honeycombed** *adj.*

honeydew *n.* **1** a sweet sticky substance found on leaves and stems, excreted by aphids. **2** a variety of melon with smooth pale skin and sweet green flesh.

honeyed *adj.* (also **honied**) **1** of or containing honey. **2** sweet, pleasant. **3** flattering.

honey locust *n.* a spiny N American leguminous tree, *Gleditsia triacanthos*, with pinnate leaves.

honeymoon ● *n.* **1** a holiday spent together by a newly married couple. **2** an initial period of enthusiasm or goodwill. ● *v.intr.* (usu. foll. by *in*, *at*) spend a honeymoon. □ **honeymooner** *n.*

honey mushroom *n.* (also **honey fungus**) a parasitic fungus, *Armillaria mellea*, with honey-coloured edible toadstools.

honeysuckle *n.* any shrub of the genus *Lonicera* with fragrant yellow, orange, white or pink flowers.

honey wagon *n. informal* **1** a vehicle which carries away human waste. **2** *N Amer.* a manure spreader.

honk ● *n.* **1** the cry of a goose. **2** the harsh sound of a car horn. **3** a sound similar to either of these, e.g. of a person blowing their nose. ● *v.* **1** *intr.* emit or give a honk. **2** *tr.* cause to do this.

honker *n.* **1** *N Amer. informal* a goose, esp. a wild goose. **2** a person or thing that honks.

honking *adj.* (also **honkin'**) *N Amer. slang* very large.

honky *n.* (*pl.* **-ies**) *N Amer. slang* offensive a white person.

honky-tonk *n. informal* **1** ragtime piano music. **2** a cheap or disreputable nightclub, dance hall, etc.

honorand /ˈɒnə،rænd/ *n.* a person to be honoured, esp. with an honorary degree.

honorarium /،ɒnəˈreriəm/ *n.* (*pl.* **-s** or **honoraria** /-riə/) a fee, esp. a voluntary payment for professional services rendered without the normal fee.

honorary *adj.* (also **honourary**) **1 a** conferred as an honour, without the usual requirements, functions, etc. (*honorary degree*). **b** holding such a title or position (*honorary colonel*). **2** (of an office or its holder) unpaid (*honorary treasurer*). **3** (of an obligation) depending on honour, not legally enforceable.

honorific /،ɒnəˈrɪfɪk/ ● *adj.* **1** conferring honour. **2** (esp. of oriental forms of speech) implying respect. ● *n.* an honorific form of words. □ **honorifically** *adv.*

honoris causa /ɒ،nɔrɪs ˈkauzə/ *adv.* (esp. of a degree awarded without examination) as a mark of esteem.

honour (also **honor**) ● *n.* **1** high respect; glory; credit, reputation, good name. **2** adherence to what is right or to a conventional standard of conduct. **3** nobleness of mind, magnanimity (*honour among thieves*). **4** a thing conferred as a distinction, esp. an official award for bravery or achievement. **5** (foll. by *of* + verbal noun, or *to* + infin.) privilege, special right (*had the honour of being invited*). **6 a** exalted position. **b** (**Honour**) (prec. by *your*, *his*, *her*, etc.) a title of respect given to a lower court judge etc. **7** (foll. by *to*) a person or thing that brings honour (*she is an honour to her profession*). **8** (in *pl.*) **a** special distinction for proficiency in an examination. **b** a course of degree studies more specialized than for a general degree. ● *v.tr.* **1** respect highly. **2** confer honour on. **3** accept or pay (a bill or cheque) when due. **4** acknowledge. □ **do the**

honours perform the duties of a host to guests etc. **in honour of** as a celebration of. **on** (or **upon**) **my honour** an expression of sincerity.

honourable *adj.* (also **honorable**) **1 a** worthy of honour. **b** bringing honour to its possessor. **c** showing honour, not base. **d** consistent with honour. **e** *informal* (of the intentions of a man courting a woman) directed towards marriage. **2** (**Honourable**) a title indicating eminence or distinction, given esp. to an MP, an upper court judge, a Lieutenant-Governor, etc. □ **honourableness** *n.* **honourably** *adv.*

honourable mention *n.* a citation given to a contestant, entry, etc. which has considerable merit but has not been awarded a prize.

honouree *n.* (also **honoree**) a person who is honoured, esp. by receiving an award or special presentation.

honour roll *n. N Amer.* **1** a list of students who have achieved grades above a certain average during a term or school year. **2** a list of the local citizens etc. who died or served in the armed forces.

honours student *n. N Amer.* **1** (also **honour student**) a student who has high grades. **2** a student in an honours program at university.

honour system *n.* a system of conduct which relies on the honour of those concerned to adhere to certain standards of behaviour, unenforced by supervision etc.

hoo *interj.* expressing surprise or apprehension, or requesting attention (*hoo boy!*).

hooch *n. N Amer. informal* alcoholic liquor, esp. inferior or illicit whisky.

hood[1] ● *n.* **1 a** a covering for the head and neck, whether part of a coat etc. or separate. **b** a separate hoodlike garment worn over a university gown or a surplice to indicate the wearer's degree. **2** *N Amer.* a hinged cover over the engine of a motor vehicle. **3** a canopy to protect users of machinery or incorporating a fan to remove fumes, cooking odours, etc. **4** the hoodlike structure or marking on the head or neck of a cobra, seal, etc. ● *v.tr.* cover with a hood. □ **hoodless** *adj.* **hoodlike** *adj.*

hood[2] *n.* esp. *N Amer. slang* a gangster or gunman.

'hood *n.* esp. *US slang* a neighbourhood, esp. one in the inner city.

-hood *suffix* forming nouns: **1** of condition or state (*childhood; falsehood*). **2** indicating a collection or group (*sisterhood*).

hooded *adj.* **1** having a hood; covered with or as with a hood. **2** wearing a hood. **3** (of eyes) having large, partly closed eyelids.

hooded seal *n.* a seal, *Cystophora cristata*, of the Arctic and N Atlantic Oceans, grey with black blotches, the male of which has inflatable nasal sacs used in display.

hooded sweatshirt *n.* a sweatshirt with a hood, often with a front pouch.

hoodie *n. informal* a hooded sweatshirt.

hoodlum /ˈhʊdləm,ˈhuːd-/ *n.* **1** a street hooligan, a young thug. **2** a gangster.

hoodoo /ˈhuːduː/ *n. N Amer.* a fantastic rock pinnacle or column of rock formed by erosion etc.

hoodwink *v.tr.* deceive, delude.

hooey *n. & interj. slang* nonsense, humbug.

hoof /hʊf, huːf/ ● *n.* (pl. **-s** or **hooves** /huːvz, hʊvz/) **1** the horny part of the foot of a horse, antelope, or other ungulate. **2** *jocular* the human foot. ● *v.tr. slang* kick or shove. □ **hoof it** *slang* **1** go on foot. **2** dance. **on**

the hoof 1 (of cattle) not yet slaughtered. **2** (of an action etc.) extempore. □ **hoofed** *adj.* (also in *comb.*).

hoofer *n. informal* a professional dancer, esp. a tap or jazz dancer.

hoofprint *n.* the impression in the ground made by an animal's hoof.

hoo-ha (also **hoo-hah, hoo-haw**) *slang* ● *n.* a commotion, a row; uproar, trouble. ● *interj.* expressing feigned surprise or excitement.

hook ● *n.* **1 a** a piece of metal or other material bent back at an angle or with a round bend, for catching hold or for hanging things on. **b** (in full **fish hook**) a bent piece of wire, usu. barbed and baited, for catching fish. **2** a curved cutting instrument (*pruning hook*). **3 a** a sharp bend, e.g. in a river. **b** a projecting point of land (*Hook of Holland*). **c** a sand spit with a curved end. **4** *Hockey* an instance of hooking. **5** *Golf, Baseball, etc.* **a** a ball or bowl's deviation from a straight line. **b** the action or an act of hooking a ball. **c** = HOOK SHOT. **6** *Boxing* a short swinging blow with the elbow bent and rigid. **7** esp. *N Amer.* **a** something that captures attention or entices (*a marketing hook*). **b** an item or theme around which a news story, radio segment, etc. can be developed. **8** a trap, a snare. **9 a** a curved stroke in handwriting, esp. as made in learning to write. **b** *Music* an added stroke transverse to the stem in the symbol for an eighth note etc. **10** (in *pl.*) *slang* hands or fingers. ● *v.* **1** *tr.* a grasp with a hook. **b** secure with a hook or hooks. **2** (often foll. by *on, up*) **a** *tr.* attach with or as with a hook. **b** *intr.* become attached with a hook. **3** *tr.* catch with or as with a hook (*hooked a fish; hooked a husband*). **4** (foll. by *up*) **a** *tr.* connect or set up (stereo components, a VCR, etc.). **b** *tr.* attach (a house, vehicle, etc.) to a central source of electricity, water, etc. **c** *intr. informal* meet or become involved with (*got hooked up with a guy from Amsterdam*). **5** *tr. slang* steal. **6** *intr.* work as a prostitute. **7** *tr. Hockey* illegally hinder the advancement of the person with the puck by jabbing at his or her body from the side or rear with the blade of one's stick. **8** *tr. & intr. Golf* strike (the ball) so that it deviates towards the striker. **9** *tr. Rugby* secure (the ball) and pass it backward with the foot in the scrum. **10** *tr. Boxing* strike (one's opponent) with the elbow bent and rigid. **11** *tr.* make (a rug) using a hook to pull yarn, rag, etc. through canvas, burlap, etc. □ **by hook or by crook** by one means or another; by fair means or foul. **get one's hooks on** (or **into**) get hold of. **hook, line, and sinker** entirely. **off the hook 1** *informal* no longer in difficulty or trouble. **2** (of a telephone receiver) not on its rest, and so preventing incoming calls. **on the hook** *informal* responsible for (*on the hook for a loan*). □ **hookless** *adj.* **hooklike** *adj.*

hookah /ˈhʊkə/ *n.* an oriental tobacco pipe with a long tube passing through water for cooling the smoke as it is drawn through.

hook and eye *n.* **1** a small metal hook and loop as a fastener on a garment. **2** a similar device consisting of a hook and screw eye used to fasten esp. a door.

hooked *adj.* **1** hook-shaped (*hooked nose*). **2** furnished with a hook or hooks. **3** *in senses of* HOOK *v.* **4** (of a rug or mat) made by pulling woollen yarn through canvas with a hook. **5** *informal* (often foll. by *on*) addicted to or captivated by.

hooker *n.* **1** esp. *N Amer. slang* a prostitute. **2** a person or thing that hooks. **3** *N Amer.* = HOOKTENDER. **4** *Rugby* the player in the middle of the front row of the scrum who tries to hook the ball.

hooking *n. Hockey* an illegal check in which a player

attempts to hinder or pull down an opponent by tugging with the blade of the stick, usu. from behind.

hook shot *n. Basketball* a one-handed shot in which the player lobs the ball over the head with a sweeping movement of the arm.

hooktender *n. N Amer.* a person in charge of the chokermen on a logging crew.

hookup *n.* **1** a connection, esp. an interconnection of broadcasting equipment for special transmissions. **2** a link to a source of electricity, water, etc. in a campground etc. **3** an act or instance of hooking up (also *attrib.: hookup fee*).

hookworm *n.* **1** any of various nematode worms, with hooklike mouthparts for attachment and feeding, infesting humans and animals. **2** a disease caused by one of these, often resulting in severe anemia.

hooky[1] *n. N Amer.* □ **play hooky** *slang* play truant.

hooky[2] *adj.* **1** (of a song) catchy. **2** shaped like a hook.

hooligan *n.* a noisy and violent person. □ **hooliganism** *n.*

hoop ● *n.* **1** a circular band of metal, wood, etc., esp. for binding the staves of casks etc. or for forming part of a framework. **2 a** a ring of wood, plastic, or metal rolled along as a toy or used in various exercises, esp. by children. **b** a large ring usu. with paper stretched over it for circus performers to jump through. **3** *Basketball* **a** the round metal frame of the basket. **b** (also **hoops**) the game of basketball. **4** a circle of flexible material for expanding a woman's skirt etc. **5 a** a circular earring. **b** the circular band of a finger ring. **6** an arch of iron etc. through which the balls are hit in croquet. ● *v.tr.* **1** bind with a hoop or hoops. **2** encircle with or as with a hoop. □ **be put** (or **go**) **through the hoop** (or **hoops**) undergo an ordeal.

hoop dance *n.* a dance among certain N American Aboriginal peoples in which the dancer suspends many, often multicoloured hoops with the arms, legs, and body, to create patterns. □ **hoop dancer** *n.*

hoopla *n. informal* **1** extravagant publicity; hype. **2** commotion; excitement; lively activity.

hoopoe /'hu:pu:/ *n.* a salmon-pink Eurasian bird, *Upupa epops*, with black and white wings and tail.

hoopster *n. N Amer. slang* a basketball player.

hooray *interj.* = HURRAH.

hoosegow /'hu:sgaʊ/ *n. N Amer. slang* a prison.

hoot ● *n.* **1** an owl's cry. **2** the sound made by a train whistle etc. **3** a shout expressing scorn or disapproval; an inarticulate shout. **4** *informal* **a** a shout of laughter. **b** a cause of laughter or merriment. **5** (also **two hoots**) *slang* anything at all (*don't give a hoot*). ● *v.* **1** *intr.* **a** (of an owl) utter its cry. **b** (of a train whistle etc.) make a hoot. **c** (often foll. by *at*) make loud sounds, esp. of scorn or disapproval or merriment (*hooted with laughter*). **2** *tr.* **a** assail with scornful shouts. **b** (often foll. by *out, away*) drive away by hooting.

hootch *var. of* HOOCH.

hooter *n.* **1** *slang* a nose. **2** a person or animal that hoots. **3** (usu. in *pl.*) *N Amer. slang* a woman's breast.

hooves *pl. of* HOOF.

hop[1] ● *v.* (**hopped, hopping**) **1** *intr.* (of a bird, frog, etc.) spring with two or all feet at once. **2** *intr.* (of a person) **a** jump on one foot. **b** make small jumps up and down on both feet. **3** *tr.* move or go quickly (*hopped out of his chair*). **4** *tr.* cross (a ditch etc.) by hopping. **5** *intr. informal* **a** make a quick trip. **b** make a quick change of position or location (*bar-hop*). **6** *tr. informal* jump into or board (a vehicle, plane, etc.). **7** *tr.* (usu. as **hopping** *n.*) (esp. of aircraft) pass quickly

from one (place of a specified type) to another. ● *n.* **1** a hopping movement. **2** *informal* an informal gathering for dancing. **3** a short trip, esp. in an aircraft; a stage of a flight or journey. **4** *N Amer.* a bounce of a ball etc. □ **hop in** (or **out**) *informal* get into (or out of) a car etc.

hop[2] *n.* **1** a climbing plant, *Humulus lupulus*, cultivated for the cones borne by the female. **2** (in *pl.*) **a** the ripe cones of this, used to give a bitter flavour to beer. **b** *informal* beer.

hope ● *n.* **1** (in *sing.* or *pl.*; often foll. by *of, that*) expectation and desire combined, e.g. for a certain thing to occur. **2 a** a person, thing, or circumstance that gives cause for hope. **b** grounds for hope, promise. **3** what is hoped for. ● *v.* **1** *intr.* (often foll. by *for*) feel hope. **2** *tr.* expect and desire (*I hope you can leave early*). **3** *tr.* feel fairly confident; trust. □ **hope against hope** continue to hope for something even though it is very unlikely. **not a hope** (**in hell**) *informal* no chance at all. □ **hoper** *n.*

hope chest *n. N Amer.* a chest containing linen, clothing, china, etc. stored by a woman in preparation for her marriage.

hopeful ● *adj.* **1** feeling hope. **2** causing or inspiring hope. **3** likely to succeed, promising. ● *n.* **1** a person likely to succeed. **2** *ironic* a person likely to be disappointed. □ **hopefulness** *n.*

hopefully *adv.* **1** in a hopeful manner. **2** (qualifying a whole sentence) *disputed* it is to be hoped (*hopefully, the car will be ready by then*). ¶The use of *hopefully* in sense 2 is extremely common, but it is still considered incorrect by some people. However, there are no grounds for condemning this use.

hopeless *adj.* **1** having or feeling no hope; despairing. **2** admitting no hope; irremedial (*a hopeless case*). **3** inadequate, incompetent (*am hopeless at tennis*). **4** without hope of success; futile. □ **hopelessly** *adv.* **hopelessness** *n.*

hop hornbeam *n.* a deciduous tree of eastern N America, *Ostrya virginiana*, with very hard wood.

Hopi /'hoʊpi/ ● *n.* (*pl.* same or **-s**) **1** a member of a N American Aboriginal people living chiefly in NE Arizona. **2** the Uto-Aztecan language of this people. ● *adj.* of or pertaining to the Hopi.

hopped up *adj. N Amer. slang* **1** intoxicated; stimulated with or as with a drug. **2** excited, enthusiastic. **3** (of a motor vehicle) having had its engine altered to give improved performance; souped-up.

hopper *n.* **1** a person who hops. **2** a grasshopper or other hopping insect. **3 a** a container tapering downward through which grain passes into a mill. **b** a similar contrivance in various machines. **4** (in full **hopper car**) a railway car able to discharge grain etc. through openings in its floor. **5** *Baseball slang* a ball which having been struck rebounds from the ground.

hopping *adj.* **1** in senses of HOP[1]. **2** esp. *N Amer. informal* very active, lively (*a hopping party*).

hopping mad *adj. informal* very angry.

hopscotch ● *n.* a children's game of hopping on one foot into and over squares or oblongs marked on the ground in order to retrieve a stone etc. thrown into one of these compartments. ● *v.intr. N Amer.* **1** play hopscotch. **2** jump, as if playing hopscotch. **3** travel from place to place.

hop, skip, and a jump *n.* (also **hop, skip, and jump**) a short distance.

horde *n.* **1 a** usu. *derogatory* a large group, a gang. **b** a moving swarm or pack (of insects, wolves, etc.). **2 a** troop of Tartar or other nomads.

horehound /'hɔːhaʊnd/ *n.* **1** a herbaceous plant, *Mar-*

rubium vulgare, with a white cottony covering on its stem and leaves. **2** its bitter aromatic juice used against coughs etc.

horizon *n.* **1** the line at which the earth and sky appear to meet. **2** range or limit of mental perception, experience, interest, etc. **3** a geological stratum or set of strata, or layer of soil, with particular characteristics. □ **on the horizon** (of an event) just imminent or becoming apparent.

horizontal ● *adj.* **1 a** parallel to the plane of the horizon, at right angles to the vertical. **b** (of machinery etc.) having its parts working in a horizontal direction. **2 a** combining firms engaged in the same stage of production (*horizontal integration*). **b** of or concerned with the same work, status, etc. (*a horizontal move*). **3** of or at the horizon. ● *n.* a horizontal line, plane, etc. □ **horizontality** *n.* **horizontally** *adv.*

hork *slang* ● *v.tr. & intr.* spit. ● *n.* the act of spitting.

hormone *n.* **1** a regulatory substance produced in an organism and transported in tissue fluids such as blood or sap to stimulate cells or tissues into action. **2** a synthetic substance with a similar effect. **3** (in *pl.*) *informal* the hormones regulating the sex drive. □ **hormonal** *adj.* **hormonally** *adv.*

hormone replacement therapy *n.* treatment with estrogens to alleviate menopausal symptoms.

horn *n.* **1 a** a hard permanent outgrowth, often curved and pointed, found singly, in pairs, or one in front of another, on the head of cattle and other esp. hoofed mammals. **b** the structure of a horn, consisting of a core of bone encased in keratinized skin. **2** each of two deciduous branched appendages on the head of (esp. male) deer. **3** a hornlike projection on the head of other animals, e.g. a snail's tentacle etc. **4** the substance of which horns are composed. **5** anything resembling or compared to a horn in shape. **6 a** = FRENCH HORN. **b** a wind instrument played by lip vibration, originally made of horn, now usu. of brass. **c** a horn player. **7** an instrument sounding a warning or other signal (*car horn*; *foghorn*). **8** a receptacle or instrument made of horn, e.g. a drinking vessel. **9** a horn-shaped projection, e.g. on a saddle. **10** *N Amer. informal* a telephone. **11** the extremity of the moon or other crescent. **12** an arm or branch of a river, bay, etc. **13** a representation of an animal's horn as appearing on the head of a supernatural (*esp. evil*) being. □ **horn in** *slang* **1** (usu. foll. by *on*) intrude. **2** interfere. **horn of plenty** a cornucopia. **on the horns of a dilemma** faced with a decision involving equally unfavourable alternatives. **pull** (or **draw**) **in one's horns** become less assertive or ambitious; draw back. □ **hornless** *adj.* **hornlike** *adj.*

hornbeam *n.* any tree of the genus *Carpinus*, with a smooth bark and a hard tough wood.

hornbill *n.* any bird of the family Bucerotidae, with a hornlike excrescence on its large curved bill.

hornblende *n.* a dark brown, black, or green mineral occurring in many igneous and metamorphic rocks, and composed of calcium, magnesium, and iron silicates.

horned *adj.* **1** having a horn or horns. **2** crescent-shaped (*horned moon*).

horned lark *n.* a brown and white lark, *Eremophila alpestris*, which has two black tufts on the head, and is of worldwide distribution.

horned owl *n.* = GREAT HORNED OWL.

hornet *n.* any of various large social wasps of the family Vespidae, with a severe sting.

hornet's nest *n.* a state of trouble, outrage, opposition, etc. (*stir up a hornet's nest*).

hornpipe *n.* **1** a lively dance, usu. for one person, originally to the accompaniment of a wind instrument, and esp. associated with the merrymaking of sailors. **2** the music for this.

horn-rimmed *adj.* (esp. of eyeglasses) having rims made of horn or a substance resembling it. □ **horn-rims** *n.pl.*

hornworm *n.* *N Amer.* any of several hawk moth larvae having a hornlike spike on the tail, esp. the vegetable pests of the genus *Manduca*.

horny *adj.* (**-ier**, **-iest**) **1** of or like horn. **2** hard like horn, callous (*horny-handed*). **3** wearing or having a horn or horns. **4** *slang* **a** sexually excited. **b** lecherous. □ **horniness** *n.*

horoscope *n.* *Astrology* **1** a forecast of a person's future based on a diagram showing the relative positions of the stars and planets at a particular time, e.g. the time of that person's birth. **2** such a diagram.

horrendous *adj.* horrifying; awful. □ **horrendously** *adv.*

horrible *adj.* **1** causing or likely to cause horror; hideous, shocking. **2** unpleasant, excessive (*horrible weather*). □ **horribleness** *n.* **horribly** *adv.*

horrid *adj.* **1** horrible, revolting. **2** unpleasant (*horrid children*). □ **horridly** *adv.* **horridness** *n.*

horrific *adj.* horrifying. □ **horrifically** *adv.*

horrify *v.tr.* (**-ies**, **-ied**) arouse horror in; shock, scandalize. □ **horrifying** *adj.* **horrifyingly** *adv.*

horror *n.* **1** an intense feeling of loathing and fear. **2 a** (often foll. by *of*) intense dislike. **b** (often foll. by *at*) *informal* intense dismay. **3 a** a person or thing causing horror (*the horrors of war*). **b** *informal* a bad or mischievous person etc. **c** *informal* something considered ugly or tacky (*this chesterfield is a horror!*). **4** (in *pl.*; prec. by *the*) *informal* a fit of horror, depression, or nervousness, esp. as in delirium tremens. **5** a genre of literature, film, etc. designed to excite pleasurable feelings of horror by depiction of the supernatural, violence, etc. (often attrib.: *horror movie*).

horrors *interj.* an exclamation of (esp. mock) dismay.

horror-stricken *adj.* (also **horror-struck**) horrified, shocked.

hors d'oeuvre /ɔr'dɜrv/ *n.* (pl. same or **hors d'oeuvres** *pronunc.* same or /dɜrvz/) a small item of food served as an appetizer or at a reception etc.

horse ● *n.* **1 a** a solid-hoofed plant-eating quadruped, *Equus caballus*, with flowing mane and tail, used for riding and to carry and pull loads. **b** an adult male horse; a stallion or gelding. **c** any other four-legged mammal of the genus *Equus*. **d** (collect.; as *sing.*) cavalry. **2 a** a frame or structure on which something is mounted or supported. **b** = SAWHORSE. **c** = CLOTHES HORSE 1. **3** *slang* heroin. **4** *informal* a unit of horsepower. ● *v.* **1** *intr. informal* (foll. by *around*) fool around. **2** *tr.* provide (a person or vehicle) with a horse or horses. **3** *intr.* mount or go on horseback. □ **change horses in midstream** change one's ideas, plans, etc. in the middle of a project or process. **from the horse's mouth** (of information etc.) from the person directly concerned or another authoritative source. **horse of a different** (or **another**) **colour** a thing significantly different. □ **horseless** *adj.* **horselike** *adj.*

horse-and-buggy *attrib.adj.* *N Amer.* old-fashioned, bygone.

horseback ● *n.* the back of a horse, esp. as sat on in riding. ● *adv.* on horseback. □ **on horseback** mounted on a horse.

horse bun *n.* *Cdn slang* a piece of horse manure.

horse chestnut *n.* **1** any large ornamental tree of the genus *Aesculus*, with upright conical clusters of white or pink or red flowers. **2** the dark brown fruit of this.

horse-drawn *adj.* (of a vehicle) pulled by a horse or horses.

horsefly *n.* (*pl.* **-flies**) any of various flies of the family Tabanidae (esp. of the genus *Tabanus*), the females of which inflict a painful bite to suck blood from their victims.

horsehair *n.* hair from the mane or tail of a horse, used for padding etc. (often *attrib.*: *horsehair sofa*).

horsehide *n.* **1** the hide of a horse. **2** leather made from the hide of a horse. **3** *informal* a baseball.

horseman *n.* (*pl.* **-men**) **1** a rider on horseback. **2** a skilled rider. **3** *Cdn slang* a member of the RCMP.

horsemanship *n.* the art of riding on horseback; skill in doing this.

horse opera *n. slang* a western film.

horseplay *n.* boisterous play.

horseplayer *n.* one who gambles on horse races.

horsepower *n.* (*pl.* same) **1** an imperial unit of power equal to 550 foot-pounds per second (about 750 watts). Abbr.: **hp. 2** the power of an engine etc. measured in terms of this.

horse race *n.* **1** a race between horses with riders. **2** any close competition, e.g. an election etc. □ **horse racing** *n.*

horseradish *n.* **1** a cruciferous plant, *Armoracia rusticana*, with long lobed leaves. **2** the pungent root of this scraped or grated as a condiment, often made into a sauce.

horse sense *n. informal* plain common sense.

horseshit *n. coarse slang* **1** excrement from a horse. **2** (often as *interj.*) nonsensical, foolish, or deceptive talk or writing.

horseshoe *n.* **1** an iron shoe for a horse shaped like the outline of the hard part of the hoof. **2** a representation of this as a good luck charm. **3** an object shaped like C or U (e.g. a magnet). **4** (in *pl.*) esp. *N Amer.* a game in which horseshoes are tossed at a stake.

horseshoe crab *n.* a large marine arthropod, *Limulus polyphemus*, with a horseshoe-shaped shell and a long tail spine.

horsetail *n.* **1** the tail of a horse. **2** any plant of the genus *Equisetum*, with a hollow jointed stem and scale-like leaves.

horse-trading *n.* **1** *N Amer.* dealing in horses. **2** shrewd bargaining. □ **horse-trade** *v.intr.* **horse trader** *n.*

horsewhip ● *n.* a whip for driving horses. ● *v.tr.* (**-whipped, -whipping**) beat with a horsewhip.

horsewoman *n.* (*pl.* **-women**) **1** a woman who rides on horseback. **2** a skilled woman rider.

horsey *adj.* (also **horsy**) (**horsier, horsiest**) **1** of, pertaining to, or resembling a horse or horses. **2** concerned with or devoted to horses or horse racing (*the horsey set*). □ **horsily** *adv.* **horsiness** *n.*

horst /hɔrst/ *n. Geol.* a raised elongated block of land bounded by faults on both sides.

horticulture /ˈhɔrtɪˌkʌltʃər/ *n.* the art or science of garden cultivation. □ **horticultural** *adj.* **horticulturally** *adv.* **horticulturist** *n.* (also **horticulturalist**).

hosanna *n. & interj.* a shout of adoration.

hose ● *n.* **1** a flexible tube conveying water for watering plants, putting out fires, etc. **2 a** (as *pl.*) stockings and socks. **b** *hist.* breeches. ● *v.tr.* **1** (often foll. by *down*) water or spray or drench with a hose. **2** provide with hose. **3** *slang* deceive, swindle.

hoser *n. Cdn slang* **1** an idiot; a goof. **2** an uncultivated

person, esp. an unintelligent, inarticulate, beer-drinking lout.

hosiery /ˈhoːzəri, ˈhoːʒəri/ *n.* stockings and socks.

hospice /ˈhɒspɪs/ *n.* a home for people who are ill (esp. terminally).

hospitable *adj.* **1** giving or disposed to give welcome and entertainment to strangers or guests. **2** disposed to welcome something readily; receptive. □ **hospitably** *adv.*

hospital *n.* **1** an institution providing medical and surgical treatment and nursing care for ill or injured people. **2** an establishment for the treatment of sick or injured animals. **3** an establishment that repairs something specified (*doll hospital*).

hospitality *n.* the friendly and generous reception and entertainment of guests or strangers.

hospitality suite *n.* (also **hospitality room**) a suite or room in a hotel etc. set aside for the entertainment of guests.

hospitalize *v.tr.* send or admit (a patient) to hospital. □ **hospitalization** *n.*

Host *n.* the bread consecrated in the Eucharist.

host[1] *n.* **1** (usu. foll. by *of*) a large number of people or things. **2** *archaic* an army. **3** (in full **heavenly host**, **host of heaven**) *Bible* **a** the sun, moon, and stars. **b** the angels.

host[2] ● *n.* **1** a person who receives or entertains another as a guest. **2** an emcee or interviewer, esp. on a television or radio program. **3** *Biol.* an animal or plant having a parasite. **4** an animal or person that has received a transplanted organ etc. ● *v.tr.* act as host to (a person) or at (an event).

hosta /ˈhɒstə/ *n.* any perennial garden plant of the genus *Hosta* with green or variegated leaves and loose clusters of tubular mauve or white flowers.

hostage *n.* **1** a person seized or held as security for the fulfillment of a condition. **2** the state of being held as a hostage.

host computer *n.* a computer attached to a network, which controls or executes certain functions for other linked computers.

hostel *n.* **1** a place providing temporary accommodation for the homeless etc. **2** = YOUTH HOSTEL. **3** *Brit. & Cdn* a house of residence or lodging for students, nurses, etc.

hostelling *n.* the practice of staying in youth hostels, esp. while travelling. □ **hosteller** *n.*

hostelry *n.* (*pl.* **-ies**) *archaic* or *literary* an inn.

hostess *n.* **1** a woman who receives or entertains a guest. **2 a** a woman employed to welcome and seat customers of a restaurant etc. **b** a woman employed to greet and entertain esp. male customers of a nightclub etc. **3** a woman employed as an emcee or interviewer, esp. on a television or radio program. **4** a woman employed to tend to passengers on an aircraft, train, etc. (*air hostess*).

hostile /ˈhɒstaɪl, ˈhɒstəl/ *adj.* **1** of an enemy. **2 a** (often foll. by *to*) aggressively opposed; showing strong rejection. **b** showing strong dislike. **3** (of a takeover bid) liable to be opposed by the management of the target company. □ **hostilely** *adv.*

hostility *n.* (*pl.* **-ies**) **1** being hostile, enmity. **2** a state of warfare. **3** (in *pl.*) acts of warfare. **4** opposition (in thought etc.). **5** a hostile act.

hot ● *adj.* (**hotter, hottest**) **1 a** having a relatively or noticeably high temperature. **b** (of food or drink) prepared by heating and served without cooling. **2** producing the sensation of heat (*hot flash*). **3** (of pepper, spices, etc.) pungent. **4** (of a person) feeling heat. **5 a** ardent, passionate, excited. **b** (often foll. by *for, on*) eager, keen (*in hot pursuit*). **c** angry or upset. **d** lustful. **e** exciting. **f** performing exceptionally well. **6** (of news etc.) fresh, recent. **7** *Hunting* (of the scent) fresh and strong, indicating that the quarry has passed recently. **8 a** (of a player) very skilful. **b** (of a competitor in a race or other sporting event) strongly favoured to win. **c** (of a hit, return, etc., in ball games) difficult for an opponent to deal with. **9** (of music, esp. jazz) strongly rhythmical and emotional. **10** *slang* **a** (of goods) stolen, esp. easily identifiable and hence difficult to dispose of. **b** (of a person) wanted by the police. **11** *slang* radioactive. **12** *informal* (of information) unusually reliable (*hot tip*). **13** (of a colour, shade, etc.) suggestive of heat; intense, bright. **14** *informal* currently popular or in demand (*spring's hottest fashions*). **15** *slang* good-looking; sexy. **16** (of a participant in a children's seeking or guessing game) very close to finding or guessing what is sought. **17** *informal* (of a motor vehicle or aircraft) fast or powerful, esp. in relation to its size. **18** at a high voltage; live (*a hot wire*). **19** as an intensifier (*hot damn!*). **20** (of an oven temperature) above 400° F. ● *v.tr. & intr.* (**hotted, hotting**) (usu. foll. by *up*) *informal* **1** make or become hot. **2** make or become active, lively, exciting, or dangerous. ● *adv.* **1** hotly; in a hot manner. **2** with or to great heat. □ **blow** (or **run**) **hot and cold** *informal* vacillate; be alternately enthusiastic and indifferent. **have the hots for** *slang* be sexually attracted to. **hot and bothered** in a state of exasperated agitation. **hot and heavy** *N Amer.* intense. **hot off the press** very recently published. **hot on the heels of** in close pursuit of. **hot under the collar** feeling anger, resentment, or embarrassment. **make it** (or **things**) **hot for a person** persecute a person. **not so hot** *informal* only mediocre. □ **hotness** *n.* **hottish** *adj.*

hot air *n. informal* empty, boastful, or excited talk.

hot-air balloon *n.* a balloon (see BALLOON *n.* 2) consisting of a bag in which air is heated by burners located below it, causing it to rise. □ **hot-air ballooning** *n.*

hot and sour soup *n.* an Oriental soup having a spicy and slightly acidic broth.

hotbed *n.* **1** a bed of earth heated by fermenting manure, for raising or forcing plants. **2** (foll. by *of*) an environment promoting the growth of something, esp. something unwelcome (*hotbed of vice*).

hot-blooded *adj.* ardent, passionate.

hot button *n.* esp. *N Amer. informal* **1** (often *attrib.*) an emotionally or politically sensitive topic or issue. **2** a commercially attractive feature of a new product.

hotcake *n. US* a pancake. □ **sell like hotcakes** sell rapidly and in great numbers.

hot chocolate *n.* a drink made from cocoa, sugar, and hot water or milk.

hot cross bun *n.* a sweet bun, usu. containing raisins and dried fruit peel, marked with a cross, traditionally eaten on Good Friday.

hot dog ● *n.* **1 a** a hot sausage, usu. a wiener, sandwiched in a soft roll. **b** a wiener. **2** *N Amer. slang* a person who performs stunts, esp. when skiing or surfing. ● *interj. N Amer. slang* expressing approval. ● *v.intr.* (**hot-dog**) (**hot-dogged, hot-dogging**) *N Amer. slang* perform stunts. □ **hot-dogger** *n.*

hotel *n.* **1** an establishment providing accommodation and meals. **2** *Austral., NZ, & Cdn* a tavern.

Hotel-Dieu /ˈhoːteldjɜ/ *n.* a name given to a hospital in French-speaking areas or to one established by a French-speaking order of nuns.

hotelier /hoˈteliɜr/ *n.* a person who owns or manages a hotel.

hot flash *n.* esp. *N Amer.* a sudden feeling of heat during menopause.

hotfoot ● *adv.* in eager haste. ● *v.tr.* hurry eagerly (*hotfoot it*). ● *n.* a prank in which a lighted match is inserted between the soles and uppers of a person's shoe.

hothead *n.* an impetuous, fiery, quick-tempered person. □ **hotheaded** *adj.* **hotheadedly** *adv.* **hotheadedness** *n.*

hothouse ● *n.* **1** a heated building, usu. largely of glass, for rearing plants out of season or in a climate colder than is natural for them (often *attrib.*: *hothouse flowers*). **2** an environment that encourages the rapid growth or development of something. ● *adj.* characteristic of something reared in a hothouse; sheltered, sensitive.

hot key *Computing* ● *n.* a key or combination of keys that has been programmed to cause an immediate change in the operating environment, such as the execution of a program. ● *v.intr.* use such a key or keys.

hotline *n.* **1** a direct exclusive communication link between heads of government etc., esp. for emergencies. **2** a telephone link that is specially arranged and used for a particular purpose (*a hotline for reporting stolen cards*). **3** *Cdn* a radio phone-in show.

hotliner *n. Cdn* **1** an on-air personality who runs a radio phone-in show. **2** a person who calls a radio phone-in show.

hotlink *n. & v.* = HYPERLINK.

hotly *adv.* **1** eagerly (*hotly anticipated*). **2** passionately (*hotly debated*). **3** angrily.

hot pants *n.pl.* very brief, tight shorts for women.

hot pepper *n.* any of various very spicy fruits of plants of the genus *Capsicum*.

hot pink ● *n.* a bright, deep pink colour. ● *adj.* of this colour.

hot plate *n.* an electrical appliance with a flat metal surface, used for cooking or keeping food hot.

hot potato *n. informal* a controversial or awkward matter or situation.

hot rod ● *n.* a motor vehicle modified to have extra power and speed. ● *v.* (**hot-rod**) (**-rodded, -rodding**) **1** *tr.* soup up (a vehicle, amplifier, etc.). **2** *intr.* drive a hot rod. □ **hot rodder** *n.*

hot sauce *n.* a very spicy sauce, usu. made with chilies, used as a condiment.

hot seat *n. slang* **1** a position of difficult responsibility. **2** the electric chair.

hotshot *informal* ● *n.* **1** an important or exceptionally able person. **2** a skilful player of football, basketball, etc., esp. one who is showy. ● *adj.* (*attrib.*) **1** important, able, expert, suddenly prominent (*a hotshot lawyer*). **2** displaying skills in a flamboyant manner (*a hotshot ballplayer*).

hot spot *n.* **1** a small region that is relatively hot. **2** a lively or dangerous place.

hot spring *n.* (usu. in *pl.*) a spring of naturally hot water.

hot stuff *n. informal* **1** an important, impressive, or popular person or thing. **2** a sexually attractive person.

hot-tempered *adj.* impulsively angry.

Hottentot /ˈhɒtən,tɒt/ *often offensive* ● *n.* = NAMA *n.* 1, 2. ● *adj.* = NAMA *adj.* ¶*Nama* is now preferred.

hot tub *n.* a large tub filled with hot aerated water and used by one or several people for recreation or physical therapy. □ **hot tubber** *n.* **hot tubbing** *n.*

hot water *n. informal* difficulty, trouble, or disgrace (*get into hot water*).

hot water bottle *n.* a container, usu. made of rubber, filled with hot water, esp. to warm a bed.

hot-wire ● *v.tr.* esp. *N Amer. slang* start the engine of (a car etc.) by bypassing the ignition system. ● *adj.* operated by the expansion of heated wire.

Houdini /huːˈdiːniː/ *n.* **1** an ingenious escape. **2** a person skilled at escaping.

hound ● *n.* **1 a** a dog used for hunting, esp. one able to track by scent. **b** *informal* any dog. **2** *informal* a despicable man. **3** (usu. in *comb.*) a person keen in pursuit of something (*newshound*). ● *v.tr.* **1** harass or pursue relentlessly. **2** urge on or nag (a person). **3** chase or pursue with a hound. □ **hounder** *n.*

houndstooth *n.* a check pattern with notched corners suggestive of a canine tooth.

hour *n.* **1** a twenty-fourth part of a day and night, 60 minutes. **2** a definite time of day, a specific point in time (*a late hour*). **3** (in *pl.*) with preceding numerals in form 08:00, 20:30, etc.) this number of hours and minutes past midnight on the 24-hour clock (*will assemble at 20:00 hours*). **4 a** a period set aside for some purpose (*lunch hour*). **b** (in *pl.*) a fixed period of time for work, use of a building, etc. (*office hours*). **c** (in *pl.*) one's habitual time of getting up or esp. going to bed (*keeps late hours*). **5** a short indefinite period of time (*an idle hour*). **6** the present time (*question of the hour*). **7 a** a time for action etc. (*the hour has come*). **b** the moment of one's death (*your hour has come*). **8** the distance travelled in one hour (*we are an hour from Fredericton*). **9** *Catholicism* **a** prayers to be said at one of seven fixed times of day (*book of hours*). **b** any of these times. **10** (prec. by *the*) the point of time at which each of the twelve or twenty-four hours measured by a timepiece ends and the next begins (*buses leave on the hour; at quarter past the hour*). **11** *Astronomy & Geog.* 15° of longitude. □ **after hours** after the normally permitted business hours. **at all hours** at any hour of the day, no matter how early or late. **till** (or **until**) **all hours** till very late. **the wee** (**small**) **hours** the hours after midnight, usu. 1 to 4 o'clock.

hourglass *n.* **1** a reversible device with two connected glass bulbs containing sand that takes an hour to pass from the upper to the lower bulb. **2** (*attrib.*) shaped like an hourglass, i.e. narrow in the middle and curving strongly outward above and below (*hourglass figure*).

hour hand *n.* the short hand on a clock or watch which indicates the hours.

hour-long ● *adj.* lasting for one hour. ● *adv.* for one hour.

hourly ● *adj.* **1** done or occurring every hour. **2** frequent, continual. **3** a reckoned hour by hour (*hourly wage*). **b** (of a worker etc.) hired or paid by the hour. ● *adv.* **1** every hour. **2** frequently, continually.

house ● *n.* /haʊs/ (*pl.* /ˈhaʊzɪz, ˈhaʊzɪz/) **1 a** a building for human habitation. **b** a family, household, or occupants of a house collectively (*the head of the house*). **c** (*attrib.*) (of an animal) kept in, frequenting, or infesting houses (*house cat; housefly*). **2** a building for a special purpose (*opera house*). **3** (in *comb.*) a building for keeping animals etc. or for the storage or protection of something (*henhouse*). **4 a** a religious community. **b** the buildings occupied by it. **5** a family, esp. a royal family (*House of Windsor*). **6 a** a firm or institution, esp. a printing or publishing firm, or a couture establishment. **b** its place of business. **c** (*attrib.*) of or pertaining to a specific commercial house or business establishment (*house rules*). **7 a** a legisla-

tive or deliberative assembly. **b** the building where it meets. **8** (**the House**) **a** (in Canada) the House of Commons. **b** (in the US) the House of Representatives. **9 a** an audience in a theatre etc. **b** a theatre. **10** *Astrology* **a** a twelfth part of the heavens. **b** any of the signs of the zodiac considered as the seat of the greatest influence of a particular planet. **11** (*attrib.*) (of wine etc.) selected by the management of a restaurant, hotel, etc. to be offered at a special price. **12** *Curling* the space within the outermost circle drawn around either tee. **13** = HOUSE MUSIC. **14 a** a casino or other establishment for gambling. **b** the management of such an establishment against which bets are placed. **15** the natural habitation of an animal, e.g. a den, burrow, nest, or the shell of a snail or tortoise, etc. **16** *Cdn hist.* a trading post, esp. inland, for the fur trade. ● *v.tr.* /haʊz/ **1** provide (a person, population, etc.) with a house or houses or other accommodation. **2** store (goods etc.). **3** enclose or encase (a part or fitting). **4** fix (a piece of wood etc.) in a socket, joint, mortise, etc. □ **bring the house down** make the audience laugh or applaud loudly. **clean house** *N Amer.* **1** do housework. **2** wipe out corruption, inefficiency, etc. **a house divided** a home, organization, party, etc. with dissension in its ranks. **keep house** provide for, maintain, or manage a household. **like a house on fire 1** vigorously, fast. **2** successfully, excellently. **on the house** at the management's expense; free. **play house** (esp. of children) play by pretending to be a family in its home. **put** (or **get, set,** etc.) **one's house in order** organize one's own affairs efficiently, esp. before telling others how to organize their affairs. **set up house** begin to live in a separate dwelling. □ **houseful** *n.* (*pl.* -**fuls**). **houseless** *adj.*

house and home *n.* (as an emphatic) home (*eating us out of house and home*).

house arrest *n.* detention in one's own house etc.

house band *n.* a band that regularly performs at a certain club.

houseboat *n.* a boat equipped for living in, usu. on inland waters. □ **houseboating** *n.*

housebound *adj.* unable to leave one's house through illness etc.

house brand *n. N Amer.* a food item or household product that bears the name of the store which sells it and usu. costs less than its brand name equivalent.

housebreak *v.tr. N Amer.* train (a pet) not to urinate and defecate inside the house. □ **housebroken** *adj.*

housebreaker *n.* a person who breaks into a house or building with the intent to steal. □ **housebreaking** *n.*

house call *n.* a visit made to a patient in his or her own home by a doctor etc.

housecleaning *n.* **1** the cleaning of the interior of a house or apartment. **2** *N Amer.* the revamping of a company, department, etc. by eliminating personnel, reorganizing systems, etc. □ **houseclean** *v.tr. & intr.*

housecoat *n.* a dressing gown.

housedress *n. N Amer.* a plain dress usu. of light cotton, for wearing around the house while doing housework, etc.

house finch *n.* a red-breasted N American finch, *Carpodacus mexicanus*.

housefly *n.* any fly of the family Muscidae, esp. *Musca domestica*, breeding in decaying organic matter and often entering houses.

house guest *n.* a guest staying for some days in a private house.

household *n.* **1** the occupants of a house regarded as a unit. **2** a house and its affairs. **3** (*attrib.*) of or for use in a house (*household appliances*).

household effects *n.pl.* the movable contents of a house, e.g. furniture, appliances, etc.

householder *n.* **1** a person who owns or rents a house. **2** the head of a household.

household name *n.* (also **household word**) **1** a familiar name or saying. **2** a familiar person or thing.

house hunting *n.* the process of seeking a house to live in. □ **house hunter** *n.*

househusband *n.* a husband who works full-time in the home, taking care of the children, managing the household, etc., while his wife goes out to work.

housekeeper *n.* **1** a person employed to manage a household. **2** a person employed to manage the cleaning staff in a hotel, hospital, etc.

housekeeping *n.* **1 a** the maintenance of a household, including esp. the domestic chores of cleaning etc. **b** operations of maintenance, record-keeping, etc. in an organization. **c** the cleaning staff in a hotel etc. **2** *N Amer.* (usu. *attrib.*) (of rental cottages, etc.) having a stove, refrigerator, and other basic facilities. **3** *Computing* the general maintenance operations enhancing, but not directly affecting, a computer system's performance, e.g. elimination of obsolete files etc. **4** money allowed or set aside for the management of household affairs etc.

house leader *n.* **1** (also **House Leader**) (in Canada) a Member of Parliament chosen by his or her party to coordinate the party's strategy in the House of Commons, schedule speakers during question period, etc. **2** (in the US) a politician holding a position of prominence in the House of Representatives.

house league *n. Cdn* a sports league in which the players on all teams are members of the same school, organization, etc.

housemaid *n.* a female servant in a house, esp. one who cleans rooms etc.

housemate *n.* a fellow occupant of a house, apartment, etc.

house music *n.* a form of popular dance music characterized by the extensive use of drum machines and sampling, and having a fast beat and heavy synthesized bass lines.

House of Assembly *n.* **1** *Cdn* (in Newfoundland and Nova Scotia) the provincial legislature. **2** *Cdn hist.* the legislature in a province of British North America, usu. the lower, elected house. **3** the legislature in certain Commonwealth nations.

house of cards *n.* **1** an insecure scheme etc. **2** a tower-like structure built by balancing playing cards against and on top of each other.

House of Commons *n.* (in Canada and the UK) **1** the lower house of Parliament, composed of elected members. **2** the building in which this meets.

house of God *n.* (also **house of worship**) a place of worship, e.g. a church, chapel, temple, etc.

House of Lords *n.* (in the UK) the chamber of Parliament composed of peers and bishops.

House of Representatives *n.* the lower house of the US Congress and other legislatures.

house party *n.* esp. *N Amer.* a social gathering in a private home, usu. with music, food, dancing, etc.

houseplant *n.* a plant that is suitable for growing indoors.

houseroom *n.* space or accommodation in one's house. □ **not give houseroom to** not have in any circumstances.

house-sit *v.intr.* live in and look after a house while its owner is away. □ **house-sitter** *n.* **house-sitting** *n.*

Houses of Parliament *n.pl.* (in Canada and the UK) the legislative body, composed of a lower elected chamber and an upper appointed chamber.

house sparrow *n.* a common brown and grey sparrow, *Passer domesticus*, which nests in the eaves and roofs of houses.

house style *n.* a particular printer's or publisher's etc. preferred way of presenting text, including rules for spelling, punctuation, etc.

house-to-house *adj. & adv.* calling at each house in turn (*house-to-house inquiries*; *travelled house-to-house*).

house trailer *n. N Amer.* **1** a trailer, such as that used in camping, that can be pulled by a car or truck and is equipped with beds, sinks, etc. **2** = MOBILE HOME.

house-train *v.tr.* esp. *Brit.* = HOUSEBREAK. □ **house-trained** *adj.*

housewares *n.pl. N Amer.* utilitarian household items, esp. kitchen utensils.

housewarming *n.* a party celebrating a move to a new home.

housewife *n.* (*pl.* **-wives**) a woman (usu. married) managing a household, esp. as her primary occupation. □ **housewifely** *adj.*

housework *n.* regular work done in housekeeping, esp. cleaning, laundry, etc.

housing *n.* **1 a** houses, apartments, etc. collectively. **b** the provision of these. **2** shelter, lodging, accommodation. **3** a rigid casing, esp. for moving or sensitive parts of a machine.

housing development *n.* **1** = DEVELOPMENT 5. **2** the planning and building of a large group of homes.

housing project *n. N Amer.* a government-subsidized housing development with relatively low rents.

HOV *abbr. N Amer.* high-occupancy vehicle (*HOV lane*).

hove *past of* HEAVE.

hovel /ˈhʌvəl, ˈhɒv-/ *n.* a small miserable dwelling.

hover /ˈhʌvər / ● *v.intr.* **1 a** (of a bird, insect, etc.) hang suspended in the air, esp. with a fluttering or wavering movement, by rapidly beating the wings. **b** (of a helicopter etc.) maintain a stationary position in the air. **2** (often foll. by *about*, *around*) wait close at hand, linger. **3** be in an indeterminate or irresolute state, waver (*the dollar hovered around 65 cents American*). ● *n.* an act or state of hovering. □ **hoverer** *n.*

hovercraft *n.* (*pl.* same) a vehicle that travels over land or water supported on a cushion of air produced by jet engines.

how¹ ● *interrog. adv.* **1** by what means, in what way or manner (*tell me how you do it*). **2 a** by what name (*how does one address the prime minister?*). **b** *informal* to what effect, with what meaning (*how did he mean that?*). **3** in what condition, esp. of health (*how is the patient?*). **4 a** to what extent (*how far is it?*; *how we laughed!*). **b** to what extent good or well, what ... like (*how was the movie?*). ● *rel. adv.* in whatever way, as (*do it how you can*). ● *conj. informal* that (*told us how he'd been in Scotland*). ● *n.* the way a thing is done (*the how and why of it*). □ **and how!** *slang* very much so (chiefly used ironically or intensively). **how about 1** would you like (*how about a drink?*). **2** what is to be done about. **3** what is the news about. **how many** what number. **how much 1** what amount (*how much do I owe you?*). **2** what price (*how much is it?*). **how so?** how can you show that that is so? **how's that?** what is your opinion or explanation of that? **how's that for ...?** isn't that a remarkable instance of? (*how's that for irony?*).

how² *interj.* a greeting attributed to N American Indians.

how do you do (also informal **how-de-do**) (pl. **-dos**) ●
interj. (also N Amer. informal **howdy**) a greeting on first
being introduced. ● n. **1** an inquiry of 'how do you
do?'. **2** (**how-do-you-do**) an awkward or
embarrassing situation (what a fine how-do-you-do).

Howe Street /haʊ/ n. Cdn **1** a street in Vancouver
where the offices of many financial institutions are
located. **2** the moneyed interests of Vancouver, esp. as
opposed to other regions of Canada.

however adv. **1** nevertheless; yet. **2 a** in whatever way
(do it however you want). **b** to whatever extent, no
matter how (must go however inconvenient). **3** informal (as
an emphatic) in what way, by what means (however did
that happen?).

howitzer /ˈhaʊɪtsər/ n. a short, relatively light gun for
high-angle firing of shells at low velocities.

howl ● n. **1** a long loud doleful cry uttered by a dog,
wolf, etc. **2** a prolonged wailing noise, e.g. as made by
a strong wind. **3** a loud cry of pain, rage, anguish, etc.
4 a yell of derision or merriment. **5** informal a cause of
laughter or merriment. ● v. **1** intr. **a** (of a dog, wolf,
etc.) emit a long, loud, doleful cry. **b** (of a person)
utter a long, loud cry of pain, derision, laughter, etc.
2 intr. (esp. of a child) weep loudly. **3** tr. utter (words)
with a howl. **4** intr. (of an inanimate object, esp. the
wind etc.) make a prolonged wailing noise. □ **howl
down 1** prevent (a speaker) from being heard by
howls of derision. **2** N Amer. move very quickly with or
as with a howling noise.

howler n. **1** (in full **howler monkey**) any of several S
American monkeys constituting the genus Alouatta,
which make loud howling noises. **2** informal a glaring
and usu. amusing mistake, esp. in the use of words. **3**
a person or animal that howls.

howling adj. **1** that howls. **2** slang extreme (a howling
shame).

how-to ● adj. instructive (how-to book). ● n. the instructions for doing something (the how-tos of plumbing).

hoy interj. used to call attention, drive animals, or Naut.
hail or call aloft.

hoya n. any climbing shrub of the genus Hoya, with
pink, white, or yellow waxy flowers.

h.p. abbr. (also **HP**) **1** horsepower. **2** high pressure.

HQ abbr. headquarters.

HR abbr. Baseball home run.

hr. abbr. (pl. **hrs.**) hour.

HRH abbr. Her or His Royal Highness.

HRT abbr. = HORMONE REPLACEMENT THERAPY.

HST abbr. Cdn HARMONIZED SALES TAX.

HT abbr. Physics high tension.

HTLV abbr. human T-cell lymphotrophic virus, a small
family of retroviruses causing diseases of the
immune system, such as certain leukemias.

HTML abbr. HYPERTEXT MARKUP LANGUAGE.

http abbr. Computing hypertext transfer protocol, a protocol that supports the retrieval of data on the Internet, esp. of hypertext on the World Wide Web.

hub n. **1** the central part of a wheel, rotating on or
with the axle, and from which the spokes radiate. **2** a
central point of interest, importance, activity, etc. **3** a
large regional airport serving as a transfer point
between flights. □ **hubless** adj.

hub and spoke adj. of or designating an air transportation system in which local flights take
passengers to a large regional airport, where they are
put on other flights to their final destinations.

Hubbard squash /ˈhʌbərd/ n. a variety of winter
squash, usu. oval with pointed ends, with green skin.

hubbub n. **1** a confused din, esp. from a crowd of
people. **2** a disturbance or uproar.

hubby n. (pl. **-ies**) informal a husband.

hubcap n. a cover for the hub of a vehicle's wheel.

hubris /ˈhjuːbrɪs/ n. **1** arrogant pride or presumption.
2 (in Greek tragedy) excessive pride towards or defiance of the gods, leading to nemesis.

huck v.tr. Cdn (West) informal throw (hucked a rock at it).

huckleberry n. (pl. **-ies**) **1** any of various low-growing N American shrubs, esp. of the genus Gaylussacia.
2 the blue or black soft fruit of this plant.

huckster ● n. **1** a mercenary person ready to make a
profit out of anything. **2** N Amer. a person who uses
aggressive methods to sell things, esp. one working
in advertising. **3** a peddler or hawker. ● v. **1** promote or sell (an often questionable product) aggressively. **2** intr. bargain, haggle. □ **hucksterism** n.

huddle ● v. **1** tr. & intr. (often foll. by up) crowd together;
nestle closely. **2** intr. & refl. (often foll. by up) coil one's
body into a small space. **3** intr. confer, discuss. ● n. **1** (in
team sports, esp. football) a brief gathering of players
during a game to receive instructions on the next
play. **2** informal a close or secret conference (go into a
huddle). **3** a confused or crowded mass of people or
things.

Hudson's Bay blanket n. Cdn (also **Hudson's Bay
point blanket**) a durable woollen blanket woven in a
variety of patterns, including cream with wide
stripes of green, red, yellow, and indigo.

Hudson's Bay blanket coat n. (also **Hudson's
Bay coat**) a warm, heavy, woollen winter coat or
parka, made of Hudson's Bay blanket cloth.

hue n. **1 a** a colour or tint. **b** a variety or shade of
colour caused by the admixture of another. **2** the
attribute of a colour by virtue of which it is discernible as red, green, etc. □ **-hued** adj.

hue and cry n. a loud clamour or outcry.

huevos rancheros /ˌweɪvoːs rænˈtʃeroːs/ n.pl. eggs,
fried or poached with onions and peppers, topped
with salsa, guacamole, etc., and often served on a
tortilla.

huff ● v. **1** intr. give out loud puffs of air, steam, etc. **2**
intr. & tr. take or cause to take offence. **3** intr. bluster
loudly or threateningly. **4** tr. N Amer. slang inhale (gasoline fumes etc.) in a quick gasp of air to get high. ● n. a
fit of petty annoyance. □ **in a huff** annoyed and
offended. □ **huffish** adj.

huffy adj. (**-ier**, **-iest**) **1** apt to take offence. **2**
offended. □ **huffily** adv. **huffiness** n.

hug ● v.tr. (**hugged**, **hugging**) **1** squeeze tightly in
one's arms, esp. with affection. **2 a** keep close to (the
shore, curb, etc.). **b** fit tightly around. **3** cherish or
cling to (beliefs, prejudices etc.). ● n. a strong esp.
affectionate clasp with the arms. □ **huggable** adj.
hugger n. (also in comb.).

huge /hjuːdʒ, juːdʒ/ adj. **1** extremely large; enormous.
2 (of immaterial things) very great (a huge success).

hugely adv. **1** enormously (hugely successful). **2** very
much (enjoyed it hugely).

Huguenot /ˈhjuːɡənɒt, -ˌnoː/ n. hist. a French Protestant in the 16th or 17th c., esp. one persecuted for his
or her beliefs or involved in civil war.

huh interj. **1** expressing disgust, surprise, inquiry, etc.
2 inviting assent (busy, huh?).

hula n. (also **hula-hula**) a Hawaiian dance with flowing arm movements symbolizing or imitating natural phenomena, historical events, etc.

Hula Hoop n. proprietary a large, usu. plastic hoop for

spinning around the body by hula-like movements of the waist and hips.

hula skirt *n.* a long grass skirt as worn by a hula dancer.

hulk ● *n.* **1** the body of a dismantled ship. **2** an unwieldy vessel. **3** *informal* a large unwieldy person or thing. **4** the shell of something abandoned or destroyed (*the empty hulk of the burned out mill*). ● *v.intr.* **1** move or behave in a clumsy or idle way. **2** be bulky or massive; rise like a hulk.

hulking *adj. informal* bulky; large and clumsy.

hull¹ ● *n.* the body or frame of a ship, airship, etc. ● *v.tr.* pierce the hull of (a ship) with gunshot etc.

hull² ● *n.* **1** the outer covering of a fruit, esp. the pod of peas and beans, the husk of grain, or the green calyx of a strawberry. **2** a covering. ● *v.tr.* remove the hulls from (fruit etc.).

hullabaloo /ˌhʌləbəˈluː/ *n.* (*pl.* **-s**) an uproar or clamour.

hum¹ ● *v.* (**hummed, humming**) **1** *intr.* make a low steady continuous sound like that of a bee. **2** *tr. & intr.* sing (a wordless tune) with closed lips. **3** *intr.* utter a slight inarticulate sound. **4** *intr. informal* be in an active state (*really made things hum*). **5** *intr.* Brit. & Cdn informal smell unpleasantly. ● *n.* **1** a humming sound. **2** an unwanted low-frequency noise in an amplifier etc., caused by variation of electric current. □ **hum and haw** hesitate, esp. in speaking. □ **hummable** *adj.* **hummer** *n.*

hum² *interj.* expressing hesitation or dissent.

human /ˈhjuːmən, ˈjuː-/ ● *adj.* **1** of, belonging to, or characteristic of people or humankind. **2** consisting of human beings. **3** of or characteristic of humankind as opposed to God, animals, or machines, esp. susceptible to the weaknesses of humankind (*is only human*). **4** showing (esp. the better) qualities of humankind, e.g. kindness, compassion, etc. (*proved to be very human*). ● *n.* a human being, esp. as distinguished from an animal. □ **humanness** *n.*

human being *n.* any man, woman, or child of the species *Homo sapiens*.

human capital *n.* the training, skills, etc. of an individual or group of individuals collectively, as a resource contributing to economic growth.

human chorionic gonadotropin *n.* gonadotropin secreted by the placenta that stimulates the production of estrogen and progestin. Abbr.: **hCG**.

humane /hjuːˈmeɪn, juː-/ *adj.* **1** benevolent, compassionate. **2** inflicting the minimum of pain (*humane trap*). □ **humanely** *adv.* **humaneness** *n.*

human ecology *n. see* ECOLOGY 2.

humane society *n.* an organization concerned with the protection and humane treatment of animals, which usu. operates shelters for stray, sick, or abused animals.

human geography *n.* the branch of geography dealing with how human activity affects or is influenced by the earth's surface.

human growth hormone *n.* a hormone secreted by the pituitary gland which stimulates the growth of bone and body tissue and affects the metabolism of proteins, carbohydrates, and lipids. Abbr.: **HGH**.

human immunodeficiency virus *n.* = HIV.

human interest *n.* (often *attrib.*) (in a newspaper etc.) reference to personal experience and emotions etc.

humanism *n.* **1** an outlook or system of thought concerned with human rather than divine or supernatural matters. **2** a belief or outlook emphasizing common human needs, seeking solely rational ways of solving human problems, and being concerned

with humanity as responsible and progressive intellectual beings. **3** (often **Humanism**) literary culture, esp. that of the Renaissance humanists.

humanist *n.* **1** an adherent of humanism. **2** a humanitarian. **3** *hist.* a student (esp. in the 14th–16th c.) of Roman and Greek literature and antiquities. □ **humanistic** *adj.* **humanistically** *adv.*

humanitarian /hjuːˌmænɪˈteəriən, juː-/ ● *n.* **1** a person who seeks to promote human welfare. **2** a person who advocates or practises humane action; a philanthropist. ● *adj.* **1** concerned with improving the lives of humanity and reducing suffering, esp. by social reform, aid, etc. **2** relating to or holding the views of humanitarians. □ **humanitarianism** *n.*

humanity /hjuːˈmænɪti, juː-/ *n.* (*pl.* **-ies**) **1 a** the human race. **b** human beings collectively. **c** the fact, quality, or condition of being human. **2** humaneness, kindness, benevolence. **3** (in *pl.*) **a** learning concerned with human culture, esp. the study of literature, art, philosophy, etc. **b** the study of Latin and Greek literature and philosophy.

humanize *v.tr.* **1** make human; give a human character to. **2** make humane; soften, refine, civilize. □ **humanization** *n.*

humankind *n.* human beings collectively.

humanly *adv.* **1** by human means (*it is humanly possible*). **2** in a human manner. **3** from a human point of view. **4** with human kindness or feelings.

human nature *n.* the general characteristics and feelings shared by humankind.

humanoid /ˈhjuːmənɔɪd, ˈjuː-/ ● *adj.* having human form or character. ● *n.* a humanoid animal or thing.

human race *n.* the division of living creatures to which people belong; humankind.

human relations *n.pl.* the study of relations with or between people or individuals usu. to enhance performance, esp. in a work environment.

human resources *n.pl.* **1** people, esp. personnel or workers, as a significant asset of a business, organization, etc. **2** the department in a business, organization, etc. which deals with the hiring, training, management, etc. of employees.

human rights *n.pl.* basic rights held to belong to every living person, e.g. the right to freedom etc.

humble ● *adj.* **1 a** (of a person) not proud; having or showing a low or modest estimate of one's own importance. **b** offered with or affected by such an estimate (*if you want my humble opinion*). **2** of low social or political rank (*humble origins*). **3** (of a thing) of modest pretensions, dimensions, etc. ● *v.tr.* **1** make humble; bring low; abase. **2** lower the rank or status of. □ **eat humble pie** make a humble apology; accept humiliation. □ **humbleness** *n.* **humbly** *adv.*

humbug ● *n.* **1** deceptive or false talk or behaviour. **2** an imposter. **3** Brit. & Cdn a hard candy usu. flavoured with peppermint. **4** nonsense, rubbish. ● *v.* (**humbugged, humbugging**) **1** *intr.* be or behave like an imposter. **2** *tr.* deceive, hoax.

humdinger *n. slang* an excellent or remarkable person or thing.

humdrum ● *adj.* **1** commonplace, dull. **2** monotonous. ● *n.* **1** commonplaceness, dullness. **2** a monotonous routine etc.

humerus /ˈhjuːmərəs/ *n.* (*pl.* **humeri** /-ˌraɪ/) **1** the bone of the upper arm in humans. **2** the corresponding bone in other vertebrates.

humid *adj.* (of the air or climate) warm and damp.

humidex /ˈhjuːmɪdeks/ *n. Cdn* a scale indicating the personal discomfort level resulting from combined heat and humidity.

humidifier *n.* a device for keeping the atmosphere moist in a room etc.

humidify *v.tr.* (**-ies, -ied**) make (air etc.) humid or damp. □ **humidification** *n.*

humidity *n.* (*pl.* **-ies**) **1 a** = RELATIVE HUMIDITY. **b** the degree of moisture esp. in the atmosphere. **2** the state or quality of being humid. **3** moisture or dampness.

humiliate *v.tr.* make humble; injure the dignity or self-respect of. □ **humiliating** *adj.* **humiliatingly** *adv.* **humiliation** *n.* **humiliator** *n.*

humility *n.* **1** humbleness, meekness. **2** a humble condition.

hummingbird *n.* any of numerous very small birds of the New World family Trochilidae having usu. long, thin bills and iridescent plumage, which feed from flowers while hovering and make a characteristic humming sound when in flight.

hummock *n.* **1** a hillock or knoll. **2** *N Amer.* a piece of forested ground rising above a marsh. **3** a hump or ridge in an ice field. □ **hummocky** *adj.*

hummus /ˈhʌməs/ *n.* a thick sauce or spread made from ground chickpeas and sesame oil flavoured with lemon and garlic.

humongous *adj. slang* huge, enormous.

humorist *n.* a person who is known for his or her humorous writing or talking.

humorous *adj.* **1** showing humour or a sense of humour (*a humorous person*). **2** comic, funny. □ **humorously** *adv.* **humorousness** *n.*

humour /ˈhjuːmər, ˈjuːmər/ (also **humor**) ● *n.* **1 a** the condition of being amusing or comic. **b** the expression of humour in literature, speech, etc. **2** (in full **sense of humour**) the ability to perceive or express humour or take a joke. **3** a mood or state of mind (*bad humour*). **4** an inclination or whim. **5** (in full **cardinal humour**) *hist.* each of the four chief fluids of the body, thought to determine a person's physical and mental qualities. ● *v.tr.* **1** gratify or indulge (a person or taste etc.). **2** adapt oneself to; make concessions to. □ **out of humour** displeased. □ **-humoured** *adj.* **-humouredly** *adv.* **humourless** *adj.* **humourlessly** *adv.* **humourlessness** *n.*

hump ● *n.* **1** a rounded protuberance on the back of a camel etc., or as an abnormality on a person's back. **2 a** a rounded, raised mound of earth etc. **b** *N Amer.* a mountain or mountain range. **3** a critical point in an undertaking, ordeal, etc. **4** *Cdn* (*BC*) = PINK SALMON. **5** *coarse slang* an act or instance of sexual intercourse. ● *v.* **1** *tr. informal* lift or carry (heavy objects etc.) with difficulty. **2 a** *tr.* make humped or hump-shaped. **b** *intr.* rise in a hump-like shape. **3** *tr.* annoy, depress. **4** *tr.* & *intr. coarse slang* have sexual intercourse (with). **5** *refl.* & *intr. slang* hurry, move, or act, esp. with effort. □ **over the hump** over the worst; well begun. □ **humped** *adj.* **humpless** *adj.*

humpback *n.* **1** (in full **humpback whale**) a large black baleen whale with white markings on the flippers, *Megaptera novaeangliae*, with a dorsal fin forming a hump. **2** (in full **humpback salmon**) = PINK SALMON. **3** = HUNCHBACK. □ **humpbacked** *adj.*

humph ● *interj.* an inarticulate sound expressing doubt or dissatisfaction. ● *v.intr.* utter 'humph'. ● *n.* an utterance of 'humph'.

humpy *adj.* (**-ier, -iest**) **1** having a hump or humps. **2** humplike.

humungous *var. of* HUMONGOUS.

humus /ˈhjuːməs/ *n.* the organic constituent of soil, usu. formed by the decomposition of plants and leaves by soil bacteria.

Hun /hʌn/ *n.* **1** a member of a warlike Asiatic nomadic people who invaded and ravaged Europe in the 4th–5th c. **2** *dated informal offensive* a German (esp. in military contexts). **3** an uncivilized devastator; a vandal.

hunch ● *v.* **1** *tr.* (usu. in *passive*) bend or arch into a hump. **2** *tr.* thrust out or up to form a hump. **3** *intr.* (often foll. by *up*) esp. *N Amer.* sit with the body hunched. ● *n.* **1** an intuitive feeling or conjecture. **2** a hump. **3** a thick piece.

hunchback *n.* **1** a person having a deformed, hunched, or protruding back. **2** such a back. □ **hunchbacked** *adj.*

hundred ● *n.* (*pl.* **-s** or (in sense 1) **hundred**) (in *sing.*, prec. by *a* or *one*) **1** the number equal to ten times ten. **2** a symbol for this (100, c, C). **3** a set of a hundred things, people, etc. **4** (in *sing.* or *pl.*) *informal* a large number. **5** a hundred-dollar bill, hundred-pound note, etc. **6** (in *pl.*) the years of a specified century (*the seventeen hundreds*). **7** (in *pl.*) the numbers from 100 to 109 (or 199) inclusive, esp. as denoting years of a decade or century or units of a scale of temperature. **8** (in *pl.*) the digit third from the right of a whole number in decimal notation, representing a multiple of one hundred less than a thousand (*numbered in the hundreds*). ● *adj.* **1** that amount to or approximate a hundred. **2** used to express whole hours in the 24-hour system (*thirteen hundred hours*). □ **a** (or **one**) **hundred per cent 1** entire(ly), complete(ly). **2** (usu. with *neg.*) fully recovered. □ **hundredfold** *adj.* & *adv.* **hundredth** *adj.* & *n.*

hundredweight *n.* (*pl.* same or **-weights**) **1** (in full **metric hundredweight**) a unit of weight equal to 50 kg. **2** *US* a unit of weight equal to 100 lb. (about 45.4 kg). Abbr.: **cwt**.

hung ● *v.* past and past part. of HANG. ● *adj.* **1** *N Amer.* (of a jury) unable to agree on a verdict. **2** (of an elected body) in which no political party has a clear majority. **3** *slang* (of a male) having large sexual organs.

Hungarian /hʌŋˈɡeriən/ ● *n.* **1 a** a native or national of Hungary, a country in central Europe. **b** a person of Hungarian descent. **2** the Finno-Ugric language of Hungary. ● *adj.* of or relating to Hungary or its people.

hunger ● *n.* **1 a** a feeling of pain, weakness, or discomfort, or (in extremes) an exhausted condition, caused by lack of food. **b** lack of food; famine (*alleviate world hunger*). **2** (often foll. by *for, after*) a strong desire. ● *v.intr.* **1** (often foll. by *for, after*) have a craving or strong desire. **2** feel hunger.

hunger strike *n.* the refusal of food as a form of protest, esp. by prisoners. □ **hunger striker** *n.*

hungover *adj. informal* suffering from a hangover.

hungry *adj.* (**-ier, -iest**) **1** feeling or showing hunger; needing food. **2** (also in *comb.*) eager, greedy, craving, esp. for money, power, etc. **3** (of a period, place, etc.) marked by famine or a scarcity of food. **4** (of soil) poor, barren. □ **hungrily** *adv.* **hungriness** *n.*

hunk *n.* **1 a** a large piece cut off (*a hunk of bread*). **b** a thick or clumsy piece. **2** *informal* a sexually attractive, well built and ruggedly handsome man.

hunker *v.intr.* (often foll. by *down*) esp. *N Amer.* & *Scot.* **1** squat or crouch with the haunches nearly touching the heels, esp. for shelter or concealment. **2** hide or take shelter (*hunkered down for the winter*). □ **hunker down** apply oneself, knuckle down.

hunky[1] *adj.* (**-ier, -iest**) **1** shaped like a hunk. **2** (of a man) well built and sexually attractive.

hunky[2] *n.* (also **hunkie**) (*pl.* **-ies**) *N Amer. slang offensive* a person of Slavic, esp. Ukrainian, or Hungarian origin or descent.

hunky-dory *adj. informal* excellent.

hunt ● v. **1** tr. & intr. **a** pursue and kill (wild animals or game) for sport or food. **b** (of an animal) chase (its prey). **2** intr. (foll. by *after*, *for*) seek, search (*hunting for a job*). **3** tr. pursue with hostility. **4** tr. scour (a district) in pursuit of game. ● n. **1** an act of looking for something; a search. **2** an act of hunting wild animals (*the seal hunt*). □ **hunt down** pursue and capture. **hunt out** find by searching; track down.

hunted adj. (of a look etc.) expressing alarm or terror as of one being hunted.

hunter n. **1 a** a person or animal that hunts. **b** a horse used in hunting. **2** a person who seeks something.

hunter-gatherer n. a member of a people whose mode of subsistence is based on hunting animals and gathering plants etc.

hunter green ● n. a dark, slightly yellowish green. ● adj. of this colour.

hunting n. the practice of pursuing and killing wild animals (also attrib.: *hunting camp*).

hunting dog n. = GUN DOG.

hunting ground n. **1** a place suitable for hunting. **2** a source of information or object of exploitation likely to be fruitful.

hunting knife n. a large, sharp knife used for cutting up, skinning, and sometimes killing game.

Huntington's chorea /'hʌntɪŋtənz/ n. (also **Huntington's disease**) chorea accompanied by a progressive dementia.

huntsman n. (pl. **-men**) **1** a hunter. **2** a hunt official in charge of hounds.

hurdle ● n. **1** Athletics **a** each of a series of light frames to be cleared by athletes in a race. **b** (in pl.) a hurdle race. **2** an obstacle or difficulty. ● v. **1** Athletics a intr. run in a hurdle race. **b** tr. clear (a hurdle). **2** tr. overcome (a difficulty). □ **hurdler** n.

hurdy-gurdy n. (pl. **-ies**) **1** a musical instrument with a droning sound, played by turning a handle, esp. one with a rosined wheel turned by the right hand to sound the drone strings, and keys played by the left hand. **2** informal a barrel organ.

hurl ● v. **1** tr. throw with great force. **2** tr. utter (abuse etc.) vehemently. **3** intr. N Amer. slang vomit. **4** tr. & intr. Baseball slang pitch. ● n. **1** a forceful throw. **2** the act of hurling.

hurler n. **1** a person or thing that hurls. **2** Baseball a pitcher.

hurley n. **1** (also **hurling**) an Irish game somewhat resembling field hockey, played with broad sticks. **2** a stick used in this.

hurly-burly n. boisterous activity; commotion.

Huron /'hjʊrˌən, -ɒn/ ● n. **1** a member of an Aboriginal group formerly living around Lake Simcoe, with present-day populations living north of Quebec City and in Oklahoma. **2** the Iroquoian language of this people. ● adj. of or relating to the Huron.

hurrah (also **hurray**) ● interj. & n. an exclamation of joy or approval. ● v.intr. cry or shout 'hurrah' or 'hurray'.

hurricane n. **1** a tropical cyclone with winds greater than 65 knots (75 mph) accompanied by heavy rain, esp. one originating in the western North Atlantic. **2** Meteorol. a wind of 65 knots (75 mph) or more, force 12 on the Beaufort scale. **3** a violent commotion.

hurried adj. **1** hasty; done rapidly owing to lack of time (*had a hurried supper*). **2** pressed for time (*hurried waiters*). □ **hurriedly** adv. **hurriedness** n.

hurry ● n. (pl. **-ies**) **1 a** great haste. **b** (with neg. or interrog.) a need for haste (*there's no hurry*; *what's the hurry?*). **2** (often foll. by *for*, or to + infin.) eagerness to

get a thing done quickly. ● v. (**-ies**, **-ied**) **1** move or act with great or undue haste. **2** tr. (often foll. by *away*, *along*) cause to move or proceed in this way. □ **hurry up** (or **along**) make or cause to make haste. **in a hurry 1** hurrying, rushed. **in a rushed manner. 2** informal easily or readily (*you won't beat that in a hurry*).

hurt ● v. (past and past part. **hurt**) **1** tr. & intr. cause pain or injury to. **2** tr. cause mental pain or distress to (a person, feelings, etc.). **3** intr. suffer physical pain or mental anguish (*my arm hurts*; *she's really hurting*). **4** intr. N Amer. (foll. by *for*) have a pressing need for. **5** intr. informal experience harm or misfortune (*sales have been hurting*). **6** tr. influence adversely (*the recession has hurt ticket sales*). ● n. **1** bodily or material injury. **2** harm, wrong. ● adj. **1** physically injured (*a hurt knee*). **2** emotionally wounded (*hurt pride*). **3** (of a facial expression, etc.) suggesting that one has been emotionally injured or offended (*a hurt look*).

hurtful adj. causing (esp. mental) hurt. □ **hurtfully** adv. **hurtfulness** n.

hurting adj. **1** suffering, esp. mentally. **2** (of music, esp. country and western songs) lamenting one's misfortunes. **3** (/'hɜrtɪn/) N Amer. slang pitiful, contemptible.

hurtle v.intr. & tr. move or hurl rapidly or with a clattering sound.

husband ● n. a married man esp. in relation to his wife. ● v.tr. manage thriftily; use (resources) economically. □ **husbander** n. **husbandly** adj.

husbandry n. **1** the cultivation of plants and animals; farming. **2** the application of science to farming, esp. to raising livestock. **3** careful or thrifty management of resources etc.

hush ● v.tr. & intr. make or become silent or quiet. ● interj. calling for silence. ● n. an expectant stillness or silence. □ **hush up** N Amer. **1** be quiet. **2** suppress public mention of (an affair).

hush-hush adj. informal (esp. of an official plan or enterprise etc.) highly secret or confidential.

hush money n. money paid to prevent the disclosure of a discreditable matter.

hush puppy n. (pl. **-ies**) US (South) a deep-fried ball of cornmeal batter.

husk ● n. **1** the dry outer covering of some fruits or seeds, esp. of a nut or grain. **2** N Amer. the coarse leaves enclosing an ear of corn. **3** the worthless outside part of a thing. ● v.tr. remove a husk or husks from.

husky¹ adj. (**-ier**, **-iest**) **1** (of a person or voice) sounding rough as if dry in the throat, often because of emotion; hoarse. **2** of or full of husks. **3** dry as a husk. **4** big and strong. □ **huskily** adv. **huskiness** n.

husky² n. (pl. **-ies**) a breed of dog used in the Arctic for pulling sleds.

hussar /hʊ'zɑr/ n. a soldier of a light cavalry regiment.

hussy /'hʌsi/ n. (pl. **-ies**) derogatory a wanton or impudent girl or woman.

hustings n. the political campaigning leading up to an election, e.g. canvassing and making speeches.

hustle ● v. **1** tr. push or move (someone) in a specified direction in a hurried, esp. rough and aggressive way (*was hustled into a waiting car*). **2** intr. move quickly. **3 a** intr. work hard (*if you want it, you'll have to hustle for it*). **b** tr. obtain by hard work and persistence. **4** tr. & intr. N Amer. sell or obtain (illegal or stolen goods) using aggressive tactics (*they survive by hustling on the streets*). **5** tr. & intr. N Amer. market or sell aggressively. **6 a** intr. slang engage in prostitution. **b** tr. (esp. of a prostitute) solicit (a sexual partner). ● n. **1** (also **hustle and bustle**) busy movement or activity, esp. of many people. **2** the quality or an instance of working hard or aggressively. **3** an act or instance of hustling. **4** *informal* a fraud or swindle. **5** a fast, vigorous dance popular esp. during the 1970s, set to a strong beat and incorporating Latin American, swing, and rock elements. □ **hustle one's buns** (or **butt**) *N Amer. slang* get a move on; move or act quickly.

hustler *n. slang* **1** an active, enterprising, or unscrupulous individual. **2** a prostitute.

hut *n.* a small simple or crude house or shelter.

hutch *n.* **1** a box or cage, usu. with a wire mesh front, for keeping small animals, esp. rabbits. **2** *N Amer.* **a** a usu. open shelving unit placed on top of a sideboard, desk, etc. **b** a piece of furniture incorporating this. **3** *derogatory* a small house.

Hutterite /'hʌtərəit/ ● *n.* a member of an Anabaptist sect living esp. in rural communal settlements and holding all property in common. ● *adj.* of or relating to the Hutterites or their beliefs.

Hutu /'huːtuː/ ● *n.* (*pl.* same or **Hutus**) a member of a Bantu-speaking people forming the majority population in Rwanda and Burundi. ● *adj.* of or relating to the Hutu people.

HVAC *abbr.* heating, ventilating, and air conditioning.

hwy. *abbr. N Amer.* highway.

hyacinth /'haiəsɪnθ/ *n.* **1** any bulbous plant of the genus *Hyacinthus* with racemes of usu. purplish-blue, pink, or white bell-shaped fragrant flowers. **2** any of various plants of the lily family resembling this. **3** = GRAPE HYACINTH. **4** the purplish-blue colour of the hyacinth flower.

hyaluronic acid /ˌhaiəljʊ'rɒnɪk/ *n. Biochem.* a viscous fluid carbohydrate found in synovial fluid etc.

hybrid ● *n.* **1** *Biol.* the offspring of two plants or animals of different species or varieties. **2** *offensive* a person of mixed racial or cultural origin. **3** a thing composed of mixed or incongruous elements. **4** *Linguistics* a word with parts taken from different languages. ● *adj.* **1** bred as a hybrid from different species or varieties. **2** formed from mixed, esp. incongruous elements. □ **hybridist** *n.* **hybridity** *n.*

hybridize *v.* **1** *tr.* subject (a species etc.) to crossbreeding. **2** *intr.* **a** produce hybrids. **b** (of an animal or plant) interbreed. □ **hybridization** *n.*

hybrid offence *n. Cdn* a crime which may be treated as either a summary conviction offence or an indictable offence, at the discretion of the Crown.

hybrid tea *n.* any rose of a group of hybrids now much grown, evolved from crosses between various hybrids, including the tea rose.

hydra /'haidrə/ *n.* **1** a freshwater polyp of the genus *Hydra* with tubular body and tentacles around the mouth. **2** something which is hard to destroy.

hydrangea /hai'dreindʒə, -dʒiə/ *n.* any shrub of the genus *Hydrangea* with large white, pink, or blue flowers.

hydrant *n.* = FIRE HYDRANT.

hydrate /'haidreit/ ● *n. Chem.* a compound of water combined with another compound or with an element. ● *v.tr.* **1** combine chemically with water. **2** cause to absorb water. □ **hydrated** *adj.* **hydration** *n.*

hydraulic /hai'drɒlɪk/ *adj.* **1** (of water, oil, etc.) conveyed through pipes or channels usu. by pressure. **2** (of a mechanism etc.) operated by liquid moving in this manner (*hydraulic lift*). **3** of or concerned with hydraulics (*hydraulic engineer*). **4** hardening under water (*hydraulic cement*). □ **hydraulically** *adv.*

hydraulic brake *n.* **1** a brake that uses a piston or rotor in a liquid-filled chamber to produce the slow-

ing down. **2** a brake on a vehicle that is activated hydraulically but operates through friction.

hydraulics *n.pl.* **1** (usu. treated as *sing.*) the science of the conveyance of liquids through pipes etc. esp. as motive power. **2** hydraulically operated devices.

hydride /'haidraid/ *n. Chem.* a binary compound of hydrogen with an element, esp. with a metal.

hydro ● *n.* (*pl.* **-os**) **1** *Cdn* electricity. **2** hydroelectricity. **3** a hydroelectric power plant. **4** (**Hydro**) *Cdn* an electric utility. ● *adj.* **1** *Cdn* of or relating to electricity (*hydro bill*). **2** of or relating to hydroelectricity (*hydro dam*).

hydrocarbon *n. Chem.* a compound of hydrogen and carbon.

hydrocephalus /ˌhaidrə'sefələs/ *n.* an accumulation of fluid in the brain, esp. in young children, which makes the head enlarge and can cause mental handicap. □ **hydrocephalic** /-sɪ'fælɪk/ *adj.* & *n.*

hydrochloric acid *n.* a solution of the colourless gas hydrogen chloride in water.

hydrochloride *n.* a compound of an organic base with hydrochloric acid.

hydro corridor *n. Cdn* a right-of-way for a hydro line.

hydrocortisone *n. Biochem.* a steroid hormone produced by the adrenal cortex, used medicinally to treat inflammation and rheumatism.

hydrocyanic acid /ˌhaidrəsai'ænɪk/ *n.* a highly poisonous volatile liquid with a characteristic odour of bitter almonds.

hydrodynamics *n.* the science of forces acting on or exerted by fluids. □ **hydrodynamic** *adj.*

hydroelectric *adj.* **1** generating electricity by utilization of water power. **2** (of electricity) generated in this way. □ **hydroelectricity** *n.*

hydrofoil *n.* **1** a boat equipped with a device consisting of planes for lifting its hull out of the water to increase its speed. **2** this device.

hydrogen /'haidrədʒən/ *n.* a colourless gaseous element, without or taste or odour, the lightest of the elements and occurring in water and all organic compounds.

hydrogenate /hai'drɒdʒɪ,neit, 'haidrədʒə,neit/ *v.tr.* **1** charge with or cause to combine with hydrogen. **2** (often as **hydrogenated** *adj.*) add hydrogen to (an edible oil) to convert it into a saturated fat, usu. solid at room temperature. □ **hydrogenation** *n.*

hydrogen bomb *n.* an immensely powerful bomb utilizing the explosive fusion of hydrogen nuclei.

hydrogen peroxide *n.* **1** a colourless viscous unstable liquid with strong oxidizing properties. **2** an aqueous solution of this used esp. as a disinfectant or bleach.

hydrogen sulphide *n.* a poisonous gas with a disagreeable smell, formed by rotting animal matter.

hydrogeology *n.* the branch of geology dealing with underground and surface water. □ **hydrogeological** *adj.* **hydrogeologist** *n.*

hydrography /hai'drɒgrəfi/ *n.* the science of surveying and charting seas, lakes, rivers, etc. □ **hydrographer** *n.* **hydrographic** *adj.* **hydrographical** *adj.* **hydrographically** *adv.*

hydro line *n. Cdn* an elevated or buried wire for the transmission of electricity.

hydrology /hai'drɒlədʒi/ *n.* the science of the properties of the earth's water, esp. of its movement in relation to land. □ **hydrologic** *adj.* **hydrological** *adj.* **hydrologically** *adv.* **hydrologist** *n.*

hydrolysis /hai'drɒlɪsɪs/ *n.* the chemical reaction of a substance with water, usu. resulting in decomposition. □ **hydrolytic** /ˌhaɪdrəˈlɪtɪk/ adj.

hydrolyze /ˈhaɪdrəˌlaɪz/ v.tr. & intr. (also **hydrolyse**) subject to or undergo the chemical action of water.

hydrolyzed vegetable protein n. (also **hydrolyzed plant protein**) a flavour-enhancing food additive made from plant protein that has been broken down into amino acids.

hydrophobia /ˌhaɪdrəˈfoːbɪə/ n. **1** a morbid aversion to water, esp. as a symptom of rabies in humans. **2** rabies, esp. in humans.

hydrophobic adj. **1** of or suffering from hydrophobia. **2 a** lacking an affinity for water. **b** not readily wettable.

hydrophone n. an instrument for the detection of sound waves in water.

hydroplane ● n. **1** a light fast motorboat designed to skim over the surface of water. **2** a finlike attachment which enables a submarine to rise and fall in water. ● v.intr. **1** (of a vehicle) glide uncontrollably on the wet surface of a road. **2** (of a boat) skim over the surface of water with its hull lifted.

hydro pole n. Cdn an esp. wooden vertical pole supporting a hydro line.

hydroponics /ˌhaɪdrəˈpɒnɪks/ n. the process of growing plants in sand, gravel, or liquid, without soil and with added nutrients. □ **hydroponic** adj. **hydroponically** adv.

hydro power n. hydroelectricity.

hydrostatic adj. of the equilibrium of liquids and the pressure exerted by liquid at rest.

hydro station n. Cdn **1** a hydroelectric generating station. **2** a station reducing the high voltage of electric power transmission to that suitable for supply to customers; a substation.

hydrotherapy n. the use of water in the treatment of disorders, usu. exercises in swimming pools for arthritic or partially paralyzed patients. □ **hydrotherapist** n.

hydro tower n. Cdn a tall metal structure erected as a support for high-voltage electrical lines.

hydrous /ˈhaɪdrəs/ adj. containing water.

hydroxide /haɪˈdrɒksaɪd/ n. a metallic compound containing oxygen and hydrogen either in the form of the hydroxide ion (OH-) or the hydroxyl group.

hydroxyl /haɪˈdrɒksɪl/ n. Chem. the monovalent group containing hydrogen and oxygen, as -OH.

hydrozoan /ˌhaɪdrəˈzoːən/ ● n. any aquatic coelenterate of the class Hydrozoa of mainly marine polyp or medusoid forms, including hydra and Portuguese man-of-war. ● adj. of or relating to this class.

hyena n. any of several carnivorous scavenging animals somewhat resembling a dog, but with the hind limbs shorter than the forelimbs, belonging to the genera Hyaena and Crocuta (family Hyaenidae).

hygiene n. **1** the branch of knowledge that deals with the maintenance of health, esp. the conditions and practices conducive to it. **2** conditions or practices conducive to maintaining health. **3** cleanliness.

hygienic /haɪˈdʒenɪk, -ˈdʒiːnɪk/ adj. conducive to health; clean and sanitary. □ **hygienically** adv.

hygienics /haɪˈdʒiːnɪks/ n.pl. (usu. treated as sing.) = HYGIENE 1.

hygienist /haɪˈdʒenɪst, -ˈdʒiːnɪst/ n. a specialist in the promotion and practice of cleanliness for the preservation of health.

hygroscopic /ˌhaɪɡrəˈskɒpɪk/ adj. (of a substance) tending to absorb moisture from the air.

hying pres. part. of HIE.

hymen /ˈhaɪmen/ n. a membrane which partially closes the opening of the vagina and is usu. broken at the first occurrence of sexual intercourse.

hymenopteran /ˌhaɪməˈnɒptərən/ n. any insect of the order Hymenoptera having four transparent wings, including bees. □ **hymenopterous** adj.

hymn ● n. **1** a song of praise, esp. to God in Christian worship, usu. a metrical composition sung in a religious service. **2** a song of praise in honour of a god or other exalted being or thing. ● v. **1** tr. praise or celebrate in hymns. **2** intr. sing hymns. □ **hymnic** adj.

hymnal /ˈhɪmnəl/ n. a book of hymns.

hype[1] slang ● n. **1** extravagant or intensive publicity promotion. **2** a dubious or questionable statement, method, etc., used to promote a product or service. **3** cheating; a trick. ● v.tr. **1** promote (a product) with extravagant publicity. **2** cheat, trick.

hype[2] n. slang **1** a drug addict. **2** a hypodermic needle or injection. □ **hyped up** stimulated by or as if by a hypodermic injection.

hyper adj. slang hyperactive, high-strung.

hyperactive adj. (of a person, esp. a child) abnormally active. □ **hyperactively** adv. **hyperactivity** n.

hyperbaric /ˌhaɪpərˈbærɪk/ adj. (of a gas) at a pressure greater than normal.

hyperbaric chamber n. = DECOMPRESSION CHAMBER.

hyperbola /haɪˈpɜrbələ/ n. (pl. **-s** or **-lae** /-ˌliː/) Geom. the curve produced when a cone is cut by a plane that makes a larger angle with the base than the side of the cone does.

hyperbole /haɪˈpɜrbəliː/ n. **1** an exaggerated statement not meant to be taken literally. **2** extravagant exaggeration.

hyperbolic /ˌhaɪpərˈbɒlɪk/ adj. **1** of or relating to a hyperbola. **2** of the nature of or using hyperbole; exaggerated. □ **hyperbolical** adj. **hyperbolically** adv.

hyperextend v.tr. bend (a limb, digit, etc.) so that it makes an abnormally great angle. □ **hyperextension** n.

hyperglycemia /ˌhaɪpərɡlaɪˈsiːmiə/ n. (also **hyperglycaemia**) an excess of glucose in the bloodstream, often associated with diabetes mellitus. □ **hyperglycemic** adj.

hypericum /haɪˈperɪkəm/ n. any shrub of the genus Hypericum with five-petalled yellow flowers.

hyperinflation n. Econ. inflation at a very high rate.

hyperkinetic adj. **1** characterized by excessive or spasmodic movement. **2** hyperactive.

hyperlink ● n. a software link in a hypertext system connecting cross-referenced items. ● v.tr. connect by means of a hyperlink.

hypermedia n. = MULTIMEDIA n.

hyperplasia /ˌhaɪpərˈpleɪziə/ n. the enlargement of an organ etc.

hyperreal /ˌhaɪpərˈriːl/ adj. (esp. of an artificial environment or an artistic creation) created or represented with such meticulous attention to detail as to appear more real than reality. □ **hyperrealism** n. **hyperrealist** adj. **hyperrealistic** adj. **hyperreality** n.

hypersensitive adj. **1** abnormally or excessively sensitive. **2** (of an individual) having an adverse bodily reaction to a particular substance in doses that do not affect most individuals. □ **hypersensitivity** n.

hypersonic adj. relating to speeds of more than five times the speed of sound (Mach 5).

hyperspace n. space of more than three dimensions, esp. (in science fiction) a notional space-time continuum in which motion and communication at speeds greater than that of light are supposedly possible. ☐ **hyperspatial** *adj.*

hypertension *n.* **1** abnormally high blood pressure. **2** a state of great emotional tension. ☐ **hypertensive** *adj. & n.*

hypertext *n. Computing* a software system allowing extensive cross-referencing between related sections of text and associated graphic material. ☐ **hypertextual** *adj.* **hypertextually** *adv.*

Hypertext Markup Language *n.* the system of tagging used in hypertext to indicate how any downloaded text should be formatted.

hyperthermia /ˌhaɪpərˈθɜrmɪə/ *n. Med.* the condition of having a body temperature greatly above normal.

hyperthyroidism /ˌhaɪpərˈθaɪrɔɪˌdɪzəm/ *n. Med.* overactivity of the thyroid gland, resulting in rapid heartbeat and an increased rate of metabolism. ☐ **hyperthyroid** *n. & adj.*

hypertrophy /haɪˈpɜrtrəfi/ *n.* **1** the enlargement of an organ etc. from the increase in size of its cells. **2** excessive growth or development. ☐ **hypertrophic** /ˌhaɪpərˈtrɒfɪk/ *adj.* **hypertrophied** *adj.*

hyperventilation /ˌhaɪpərˌventɪˈleɪʃən/ *n.* breathing at an abnormally rapid rate, resulting in an increased loss of carbon dioxide, and often accompanied by dizziness. ☐ **hyperventilate** *v.intr.*

hypha /ˈhaɪfə/ *n.* (pl. **hyphae** /-fiː/) a filament in the mycelium of a fungus. ☐ **hyphal** *adj.*

hyphen ● *n.* the sign (-) used to join words semantically or syntactically (as in *pick-me-up*, *rock-forming*), to indicate the division of a word at the end of a line, or to indicate a missing or implied element (as in *man- and womankind*). ● *v.tr.* = HYPHENATE *v.*

hyphenate ● *v.tr.* **1** write (a compound word) with a hyphen. **2** join (words) with a hyphen. ● *n. N Amer.* a person who works in more than one (related) occupation, e.g. both directing a film and acting in it. ☐ **hyphenation** *n.*

hyphenated *adj.* **1** (of a word) spelled with a hyphen. **2** (of a person) having dual nationality or mixed background or ancestry, e.g. *Scottish-Canadian*.

hypnosis *n.* **1** a state like sleep in which the subject acts only on external suggestion. **2** artificially produced sleep.

hypnotherapy /ˌhɪpnoʊˈθerəpi/ *n.* psychotherapy involving hypnotism. ☐ **hypnotherapist** *n.*

hypnotic ● *adj.* **1** of or producing hypnotism. **2** (of a drug) soporific. **3** (of a person's gaze, musical rhythms, etc.) producing a trance-like state or fascination. ● *n.* **1** a thing, esp. a drug, that produces sleep. **2** a person under or open to the influence of hypnotism. ☐ **hypnotically** *adv.*

hypnotism *n.* the study or practice of hypnosis. ☐ **hypnotist** *n.*

hypnotize *v.tr.* **1** produce hypnosis in. **2** fascinate; capture the mind of (a person).

hypo *n.* (pl. **-os**) *informal* = HYPODERMIC *n.*

hypoallergenic *adj.* having little tendency, or a reduced tendency, to cause an allergic reaction.

hypochlorite /ˌhaɪpoʊˈklɔːraɪt/ *n.* a salt of hypochlorous acid.

hypochlorous acid /ˌhaɪpoʊˈklɔːrəs/ *n.* an unstable acid existing only in dilute solution and used in bleaching and water treatment.

hypochondria /ˌhaɪpəˈkɒndrɪə/ *n.* abnormal and unnecessary anxiety about one's health.

hypochondriac /ˌhaɪpəˈkɒndriˌæk/ ● *n.* a person suffering from hypochondria. ● *adj.* (also **hypochondriacal** /-ˈdraɪəkəl/) of or affected by hypochondria.

hypocrisy *n.* (pl. **-ies**) **1** the assumption or postulation of moral standards, principles, etc. to which one's own behaviour does not conform; pretense. **2** an instance of this.

hypocrite *n.* a person given to hypocrisy. ☐ **hypocritical** *adj.* **hypocritically** *adv.*

hypodermic /ˌhaɪpəˈdɜrmɪk/ ● *adj. Med.* **1** of or relating to the area beneath the skin. **2 a** (of a drug etc. or its application) injected beneath the skin. **b** (of a needle, syringe, etc.) used to do this. ● *n.* a hypodermic injection or syringe. ☐ **hypodermically** *adv.*

hypoglycemia /ˌhaɪpoʊglaɪˈsiːmiə/ *n.* (also **hypoglycaemia**) a deficiency of glucose in the bloodstream. ☐ **hypoglycemic** *adj.*

hypotension /ˌhaɪpəˈtenʃən/ *n.* abnormally low blood pressure. ☐ **hypotensive** *adj.*

hypotenuse /haɪˈpɒtəˌnuːs, -ˌnjuːz, -ˌnuːz/ *n.* the side opposite the right angle of a right-angled triangle.

hypothalamus /ˌhaɪpəˈθæləməs/ *n.* (pl. **-mi** /-ˌmaɪ/) the region of the brain which controls body temperature, thirst, hunger, etc. ☐ **hypothalamic** *adj.*

hypothermia /ˌhaɪpoʊˈθɜrmiə/ *n. Med.* the condition of having an abnormally low body temperature. ☐ **hypothermic** *adj.*

hypothesis /haɪˈpɒθɪsɪs/ *n.* (pl. **hypotheses** /-ˌsiːz/) **1** a proposition made as a basis for reasoning, without the assumption of its truth. **2** a supposition made as a starting point for further investigation from known facts. **3** a groundless assumption.

hypothesize /haɪˈpɒθɪˌsaɪz/ *v.* **1** *intr.* frame a hypothesis. **2** *tr.* assume as a hypothesis.

hypothetical /ˌhaɪpəˈθetɪkəl/ ● *adj.* **1** of or based on or serving as a hypothesis. **2** supposed but not necessarily real or true. ● *n.* a hypothetical proposition, phrase, statement, etc. ☐ **hypothetically** *adv.*

hypothyroidism /ˌhaɪpoʊˈθaɪrɔɪˌdɪzəm/ *n. Med.* subnormal activity of the thyroid gland, resulting in cretinism in children, and mental and physical slowing in adults. ☐ **hypothyroid** *n. & adj.*

hypoxia /haɪˈpɒksiə/ *n. Med.* a deficiency of oxygen reaching the tissues. ☐ **hypoxic** *adj.*

hyrax /ˈhaɪræks/ *n.* a mammal of the order Hyracoidea, comprising small animals of Africa and the Middle East, having feet with nails like hoofs.

hyssop /ˈhɪsəp/ *n.* **1** any small bushy aromatic herb of the genus *Hyssopus*, esp. *H. officinalis*, formerly used medicinally. **2** *Bible* **a** a plant whose twigs were used for sprinkling in Jewish rites. **b** a bunch of this used in purification. **3** (in full **giant hyssop**) any of various tall labiate plants of the genus *Agastache*.

hysterectomy /ˌhɪstəˈrektəmi/ *n.* (pl. **-ies**) the surgical removal of the uterus.

hysteria /hɪˈstɪərɪə, -ˈstiːriə/ *n.* **1** an emotional state, caused by grief or fear etc., accompanied by uncontrollable laughter, weeping, etc. **2** a functional disturbance of the nervous system, of psychoneurotic origin. **3** an excited and exaggerated reaction to an event (*public hysteria about AIDS*).

hysteric ● *n.* **1** (in *pl.*) **a** a fit of hysteria. **b** *informal* overwhelming mirth or laughter (*we were in hysterics*). **2** a hysterical person. ● *adj.* = HYSTERICAL.

hysterical *adj.* **1** of or affected with hysteria. **2** morbidly or uncontrolledly emotional. **3** *informal* extremely funny or amusing. ☐ **hysterically** *adv.*

Hz *abbr.* hertz.

Ii

I¹ *n.* (also **i**) (*pl.* **Is** or **I's**) **1** the ninth letter of the alphabet. **2** (as a Roman numeral) 1.

I² ● *pron.* (*obj.* **me**; *possess.* **my, mine**; *pl.* **we**) used by a speaker or writer to refer to himself or herself. ● *n.* (**the I**) *Metaphysics* the ego; the subject or object of self-consciousness.

I³ *symbol* **1** the element iodine. **2** electric current.

I⁴ *abbr.* (also **I.**) **1** Island(s). **2** Isle(s). **3** (in the US) (used in designating highways) interstate (*I-95*). **4** institute.

IA *abbr.* Iowa (in postal use).

Ia. *abbr.* Iowa.

IAEA *abbr.* International Atomic Energy Agency.

iamb /'aɪæmb/ *n.* a foot consisting of a short (or unstressed) followed by a long (or stressed) syllable.

iambic /aɪ'æmbɪk/ *Prosody* ● *adj.* of or using iambs. ● *n.* (usu. in *pl.*) iambic verse. □ **iambically** *adv.*

iambus /aɪ'æmbəs/ *n.* (*pl.* **-buses** or **-bi** /-baɪ/) = IAMB.

IATA /aɪ'ætə, i:-/ *abbr.* International Air Transport Association.

iatrogenic /aɪ,ætrə'dʒɛnɪk/ *adj.* (of a disease etc.) caused by medical examination or treatment.

ib. *var. of* IBID.

IBC *abbr.* Inuit Broadcasting Corporation.

IBD *abbr.* INFLAMMATORY BOWEL DISEASE.

I-beam *n.* a girder with a cross-section like an I.

Iberian /aɪ'bi:riən/ ● *adj.* of ancient Iberia, the peninsula now comprising Spain and Portugal; of Spain and Portugal. ● *n.* **1** a native of ancient Iberia. **2** any of the languages of ancient Iberia.

ibex /'aɪbeks/ *n.* (*pl.* **ibexes**) a wild goat-antelope, *Capra ibex*, esp. of mountainous areas of Europe, N Africa, and Asia, with a chin beard and thick curved ridged horns.

ibid. *abbr.* in the same book or passage etc.

ibis /'aɪbɪs/ *n.* (*pl.* **ibises**) any wading bird of the family Threskiornithidae with a curved bill, long neck, and long legs, and nesting in colonies.

Ibo /'i:bo:/ ● *n.* (*pl.* same or **-os**) **1** a member of a people of SE Nigeria. **2** the Kwa language of this people. ● *adj.* of or relating to this people.

IBRD *abbr.* International Bank for Reconstruction and Development (*see* WORLD BANK).

ibuprofen /aɪbju:'prəʊfən/ *n.* an analgesic and anti-inflammatory drug used esp. as a stronger alternative to ASA.

IC *abbr.* integrated circuit.

i/c *abbr.* in charge.

ICAO *abbr.* International Civil Aviation Organization.

ICBM *abbr.* INTERCONTINENTAL BALLISTIC MISSILE.

ice ● *n.* **1 a** frozen water, a brittle transparent crystalline solid. **b** a sheet of this on the surface of water (*fell through the ice*). **c** a sheet of ice used as a playing surface for hockey, curling, broomball, etc. **2** a frozen mixture of fruit juice or flavoured water and sugar. **3** *slang* diamonds. **4** *slang* a crystalline form of the drug methamphetamine, inhaled or smoked (illegally) as a stimulant. ● *v.* **1** *tr.* mix with or cool in ice (*iced drinks*). **2** *tr.* & *intr.* (often foll. by *over, up*) **a** cover or become covered with ice. **b** freeze. **3** *tr.* spread or cover (a cake etc.) with icing. **4** *tr.* *Hockey* shoot (the puck) from one's own half of the rink to the far end of the other half. **5** *tr.* *Cdn* select (a team or individual) to play in a hockey game. **6** *tr.* *N Amer. slang* murder (a person). **7** *tr.* *N Amer. informal* clinch (a victory, deal, etc.). □ **on ice 1** (of an entertainment etc.) performed by skaters. **2** *informal* held in reserve; awaiting further attention. **on thin ice** in a risky situation.

ice age *n.* a period when ice sheets were particularly extensive, esp. in the Pleistocene epoch.

ice axe *n.* a tool used by mountain climbers and ice climbers for cutting footholds.

Ice Beer *n.* *proprietary* beer brewed at temperatures below freezing.

iceberg *n.* **1** a large floating mass of ice detached from a glacier or ice sheet and carried out to sea. **2** an unemotional or cold-blooded person. □ **the tip of the iceberg** a small perceptible part of something (esp. a difficulty) the greater part of which is hidden.

iceberg lettuce *n.* any of various crisp lettuces with pale, compact leaves.

ice-blue ● *n.* a clear, piercing blue, like that seen in a block of ice. ● *adj.* of this colour.

iceboat *n.* **1** a lightly built boat with runners and a sail for travelling at speed over ice, esp. as a sport. **2** *N Amer.* a fishing vessel with facilities for the refrigeration of fish. □ **iceboat** *v.intr.* **iceboater** *n.* **iceboating** *n.*

icebound *adj.* **1** (of a ship) confined by ice. **2** (of a harbour, coast, etc.) obstructed or sealed off by ice.

icebox *n.* **1** an insulated chest, cabinet, etc. for storing food, cooled by means of a block of ice. **2** esp. *US* a refrigerator.

icebreaker *n.* **1** a ship specially built or adapted for breaking a channel through ice. **2** something that serves to relieve inhibitions, start a conversation, etc. □ **ice breaking** *n.* & *adj.*

ice bridge *n.* *Cdn* a formation of ice across a river solid enough to support traffic.

ice cap *n.* a permanent covering of ice e.g. in polar regions. □ **ice-capped** *adj.*

ice climbing *n.* the action or activity of climbing glaciers etc., esp. as a recreational sport. □ **ice climber** *n.*

ice-cold *adj.* as cold as ice.

ice cream *n.* a frozen dessert made of cream or milk, sugar, flavourings or fruit, etc.

ice cream cone *n.* **1** a crisp, thin, usu. conical wafer for holding ice cream. **2** such a cone containing ice cream.

ice cube *n.* a small block of ice made in a refrigerator.

ice dancing *n.* (also **ice dance**) a form of esp. competitive figure skating based on ballroom dancing and performed by couples. □ **ice dancer** *n.*

iced tea *n.* a cold drink of sweetened tea, often flavoured with lemon etc.

icefall *n.* a steep part of a glacier like a frozen waterfall.

icefield *n.* **1** an expanse of ice, esp. in polar regions. **2** a large flat area of floating ice.

ice fishing n. N Amer. the act or an instance of fishing through holes cut in the ice on the surface of a lake etc. □ **ice-fish** v.intr. **ice fisherman** n.

ice-fishing hut n. Cdn = FISH HUT.

ice floe n. = FLOE.

ice fog n. fog made up of minute ice crystals suspended in the air.

ice-free adj. (of a harbour, river, etc.) free from ice.

ice hockey n. = HOCKEY 1.

ice hole n. Cdn a hole cut through the ice on the surface of a lake etc., used for ice fishing.

ice house n. a building often partly or wholly underground for storing ice.

ice hut n. Cdn = FISH HUT.

ice jam n. N Amer. an obstruction in a river etc. caused by broken ice.

Icelander n. **1** a native or national of Iceland, an island in the N Atlantic. **2** a person of Icelandic descent.

Icelandic ● adj. of or relating to Iceland. ● n. the language of Iceland, a Scandinavian language which is the purest descendant of Old Norse.

icemaker n. **1** an appliance for making ice cubes etc. **2** the person who maintains the ice at a rink.

ice margin n. **1** the edge of a glacier. **2** the edge of an ice floe.

ice milk n. N Amer. a sweet frozen food similar to ice cream but containing less butterfat.

ice-out n. N Amer. the time of year at which a body of water becomes free of ice.

ice pack n. **1** = PACK ICE. **2** a waterproof package containing ice or another frozen substance, used to cool an injured or inflamed part of the body or to keep food cold.

ice pad n. Cdn = RINK 1.

ice palace n. **1** Cdn informal a hockey arena. **2** N Amer. a large building made or carved from ice.

ice pan n. a slab of floating ice.

ice pick n. a pointed implement for breaking up pieces of ice.

ice plant n. **1** a plant, *Mesembryanthemum crystallinum*, with leaves covered with crystals or vesicles looking like ice specks. **2** Cdn a machine or factory for making ice, e.g. at a skating rink.

ice rink n. = RINK 1.

ice road n. Cdn a winter road built across frozen lakes, rivers, muskeg, etc.

icescape n. a landscape covered with ice.

ice sculpture n. **1** the art of carving forms in blocks of ice. **2** a sculpture carved in ice.

ice sheet n. a permanent layer of ice covering an extensive tract of land.

ice shelf n. a floating sheet of ice permanently attached to a land mass.

ice skate ● n. = SKATE[1] n. 1. ● v.intr. (**ice-skate**) skate on ice. □ **ice-skater** n. **ice-skating** n.

ice storm n. esp. N Amer. a storm of freezing rain, that leaves a deposit of ice.

ice tea var. of ICED TEA.

ice time n. esp. Hockey **1** time spent by a hockey etc. player engaged in play (*got a lot of ice time in the playoffs*). **2** the time during which a team, league, etc. may use an ice rink (*could only get ice time at midnight*).

ice water n. water from, or cooled by, ice.

Icewine n. **1** esp. Cdn proprietary a very sweet wine made from ripe grapes left to freeze on the vine before being picked, and still frozen when they go into the press. **2** (**icewine**) a similar wine made in California from artificially frozen grapes.

iceworm n. **1** a small worm of the division Oligochaeta, *Mesenchytraeus solifugus*, found in N American glaciers and icefields. **2** a mythical worm said to inhabit the Northern ice.

ichthyology /ˌɪkθiˈɒlədʒi/ n. the study of fishes. □ **ichthyological** adj. **ichthyologist** n.

ichthyosaur /ˈɪkθiəˌsɔr/ n. (also **ichthyosaurus**) any extinct marine reptile of the order Ichthyosauria, with long head, tapering body, four flippers, and usu. a large tail.

icicle n. **1** a hanging tapering piece of ice, formed by the freezing of dripping water. **2** a long thin strip of foil or silver-coloured Mylar plastic used as a Christmas tree decoration.

icicle lights n.pl. a string of tiny usu. uncoloured Christmas lights hung esp. from eavestroughs to resemble icicles.

icing n. **1** a sweet mixture of sugar with butter or egg whites and flavouring etc., used as a coating or filling for cakes etc. **2** the formation of ice on a ship or aircraft. **3** Hockey **a** the act of icing the puck (see ICE v. 4). **b** the penalty for this. □ **icing on the cake** an attractive though inessential addition or enhancement.

icing sugar n. Cdn, Brit., Austral., & NZ finely powdered sugar, usu. combined with a small amount of cornstarch, for making icing for cakes etc.

ICJ abbr. INTERNATIONAL COURT OF JUSTICE.

ick esp. N Amer. informal ● interj. an expression of distaste or revulsion. ● n. something sticky, congealed, or disgusting.

icky adj. (**-ier, -iest**) informal **1** sweet, sticky, sickly. **2** (as a general term of disapproval) nasty, repulsive. □ **ickiness** n.

icon n. **1** a devotional painting or carving, usu. on wood, of Christ or another holy figure, esp. in the Eastern Church. **2** an image or statue. **3** Computing a symbol or small graphic representation on a computer screen of a program, option, or window, esp. one of several for selection. **4** an object of particular admiration, esp. as a representative symbol of something (*a cultural icon of the 1960s*).

iconic adj. **1** of or having the nature of an image or portrait. **2** of or pertaining to a computer icon. **3** constituting a cultural icon. **4** (of a statue) following a conventional type.

iconoclasm /aɪˈkɒnəˌklæzəm/ n. **1** the breaking of images. **2** the assailing of cherished beliefs or conventions.

iconoclast n. **1** a person who attacks cherished beliefs or conventions. **2** a person who destroys images used in religious worship, esp. hist. during the 8th–9th c. in the Churches of the East, or as a Puritan of the 16th–17th c. □ **iconoclastic** adj.

iconography /ˌaɪkəˈnɒɡrəfi/ n. (pl. **-ies**) **1 a** the visual images and symbols typical of an art form, an artistic movement, an artist, a culture, etc. **b** the interpretation of the significance of these. **2** the illustration of a subject by drawings or figures. **3** the study of portraits, esp. of an individual. □ **iconographer** n. **iconographic** adj. **iconographical** adj. **iconographically** adv.

iconostasis /ˌaɪkəˈnɒstəsɪs, aɪˌkɒnəˈstæsɪs/ n. (pl. **-stases** /-ˌsiːz/) (in the Eastern Church) a screen bearing icons and separating the sanctuary from the nave.

icosahedron /ˌaɪkəsəˈhiːdrən/ n. (pl. **-hedrons** or **-hedra** /-drə/) a solid figure with twenty faces. □ **icosahedral** adj.

ICU abbr. intensive care unit.

icy *adj.* (**-ier, -iest**) **1** very cold. **2** covered with or abounding in ice. **3** (of a tone or manner) unfriendly, hostile (*an icy stare*). **4** like ice (*icy blue eyes*). □ **icily** *adv.* **iciness** *n.*

ID *abbr.* **1** identification, identity (*ID card*). **2** Idaho (in postal use).

I.D. *abbr. Cdn* (*Alta.*) IMPROVEMENT DISTRICT.

Id *var. of* EID.

I'd *contraction* **1** I had. **2** I would.

id /ɪd/ *n. Psych.* the inherited instinctive impulses of the individual as part of the unconscious.

id. *abbr.* = IDEM.

IDA *abbr.* International Development Association.

Ida Red *n.* (also **Idared**) *N Amer.* a large, tart, red apple with greenish-yellow patches.

idea *n.* **1** a conception or plan formed by mental effort. **2 a** a mental impression or notion; a concept. **b** a vague belief or fancy (*had an idea you were married*). **3** an intention, purpose, or essential feature (*the idea is to make money*). **4** an archetype or pattern as distinguished from its realization in individual cases. □ **get** (or **have**) **ideas** *informal* be ambitious, rebellious, etc. **give a person ideas** give a person expectations or hopes that may not be realized. **have no idea** *informal* **1** not know at all. **2** be completely incompetent. **not one's idea of** *informal* not what one regards as (*not my idea of a pleasant evening*). **put ideas into a person's head** suggest ambitions etc. he or she would not otherwise have had. **that's an idea** *informal* that proposal etc. is worth considering. **that's the idea!** that's the correct way to proceed etc. **the (very) idea!** *informal* an exclamation of disapproval or disagreement. **what's the big idea?** expressing disapproval of effrontery, stupidity, etc.

ideal ● *adj.* **1 a** answering to one's highest conception. **b** perfect or supremely excellent. **2 a** existing only as an idea. **b** visionary. **3** embodying an idea. **4** relating to or consisting of ideas; dependent on the mind. ● *n.* **1** a perfect type, or a conception of this. **2** an actual thing as a standard for imitation. **3** (usu. in *pl.*) an esp. moral standard of perfection. □ **ideally** *adv.*

idealism *n.* **1** the practice of forming or following after ideals, esp. unrealistically (*compare* REALISM). **2** the representation of things in ideal or idealized form. **3** imaginative treatment. **4** *Philos.* any of various systems of thought in which the objects of knowledge are held to be in some way dependent on the activity of mind (*compare* REALISM). □ **idealist** *n.* **idealistic** *adj.* **idealistically** *adv.*

idealize *v.tr. & intr.* consider or represent (a person or thing) as perfect or ideal. □ **idealization** *n.*

idem /ˈɪdem/ ● *adv.* in the same author, work, etc. ● *n.* the same work or author etc.

identical *adj.* **1** (often foll. by *with*) (of different things) exactly the same in every detail. **2** (of one thing viewed at different times) one and the same. **3** (of twins) developed from a single fertilized ovum, therefore of the same sex and usu. very similar in appearance. □ **identically** *adv.*

identification *n.* **1** the act or an instance of identifying. **2** a means of identifying a person. **3** (*attrib.*) serving to identify (esp. the bearer) (*identification card*).

identifier *n.* **1** a person or thing that identifies. **2** *Computing* a sequence of characters used to identify or refer to a set of data.

identify *v.* (**-ies, -ied**) **1** *tr.* establish the identity of; recognize. **2** *tr.* establish or select by consideration or analysis of the circumstances (*identify the best method*).

3 *tr.* (foll. by *with*; also *refl.*) associate (a person or oneself) inseparably or very closely (with a party, policy, etc.). **4** *tr.* (often foll. by *with*) treat (a thing) as identical. **5** *intr.* (foll. by *with*) **a** regard oneself as sharing characteristics of (another person). **b** associate oneself. □ **identify oneself** state or show who one is. □ **identifiable** *adj.* **identifiably** *adv.*

Identikit /aɪˈdentɪkɪt/ *n.* (often *attrib.*) proprietary a reconstructed picture of a person (esp. one sought by the police) assembled from transparent strips showing typical facial features according to witnesses' descriptions.

identity *n.* (*pl.* **-ies**) **1 a** the quality or condition of being a specified person or thing. **b** individuality, personality (*lost her identity*). **2** identification or the result of it (*mistaken identity; identity card*). **3** the state of being the same in substance, nature, qualities, etc.; absolute sameness (*no identity of interests between them*). **4** *Algebra* **a** the equality of two expressions for all values of the quantities expressed by letters. **b** an equation expressing this, e.g. $(x + 1)^2 = x^2 + 2x + 1$. **5** *Math.* **a** (in full **identity element**) an element in a set, left unchanged by any operation to it. **b** a transformation that leaves an object unchanged.

identity crisis *n.* a period of emotional disturbance in which a person has difficulty in determining his or her identity and role in relation to society.

ideologue /ˈaɪdiə‚lɒg, ˈɪd-, -ˈdiː-/ *n.* **1** an adherent of an ideology. **2** a theorist; a visionary.

ideology /‚aɪdiˈɒlədʒi, ‚ɪd-/ *n.* (*pl.* **-ies**) a system of ideas or way of thinking, usu. relating to politics or society, or to the conduct of a class or group, and regarded as justifying actions, esp. one that is held implicitly or adopted as a whole and maintained regardless of the course of events. □ **ideological** *adj.* **ideologically** *adv.* **ideologist** *n.*

ides /aɪdz/ *n.pl.* the eighth day after the nones in the ancient Roman calendar (the 15th day of March, May, July, October, the 13th of other months).

idiocy /ˈɪdiəsi/ *n.* (*pl.* **-ies**) **1** utter foolishness; idiotic behaviour or an idiotic action. **2** extreme mental imbecility.

idiom *n.* **1** a group of words established by usage and having a meaning not deducible from those of the individual words, e.g. *down in the dumps*. **2** a form of expression peculiar to a language, person, or group of people. **3 a** the language of a people or country. **b** the specific character of this. **4** a characteristic mode of expression in music, art, etc.

idiomatic *adj.* **1** relating to or conforming to idiom. **2** characteristic of a particular language.

idiopathy /‚ɪdiˈɒpəθi/ *n. Med.* any disease or condition of unknown cause or that arises spontaneously. □ **idiopathic** /‚ɪdiəˈpæθɪk/ *adj.*

idiosyncrasy /‚ɪdiəˈsɪŋkrəsi/ *n.* (*pl.* **-ies**) **1** a person's particular way of thinking, behaving, etc. that is clearly different from that of others. **2** anything highly individualized or eccentric. **3** a mode of expression peculiar to an author. **4** *Med.* a physical constitution peculiar to a person. □ **idiosyncratic** /-ˈkrætɪk/ *adj.* **idiosyncratically** *adv.*

idiot *n.* **1** a stupid person; an utter fool. **2** (in a former system of classification of mental retardation) a person deficient in mind and permanently incapable of rational conduct. □ **idiotic** *adj.* **idiotically** *adv.*

idiot box *n. informal* **1** television. **2** a television set.

idiot-proof *adj.* = FOOLPROOF.

idiot savant /ˈɪdiət səˈvɑ̃/ *n.* (*pl.* **idiot savants** or **idiots savants** *pronunc.* same) a person considered mentally retarded but who displays brilliance in a specific area esp. related to memory skills.

idiot string *n.* (also **idiot strings**) *Cdn* a string attached to each of two mittens or gloves and strung through the sleeves and across the inside back of a child's coat, to prevent the mittens etc. from being lost.

idle ● adj. (**idler, idlest**) **1 a** (of a person) not working, doing nothing. **b** lazy, indolent, having a dislike for work or activity. **2** (of a thing) inactive, not in use, not moving or in operation. **3** (of time etc.) unoccupied. **4 a** (of a thought, speculation, etc.) groundless, meaningless (*idle curiosity*). **b** (of an action, word, etc.) vain, trifling, ineffective, or worthless. **5** useless. **6** (of money) out of circulation; not earning interest, investment income, etc. **● v. 1 a** *intr.* (of an engine) run slowly without doing any work. **b** *tr.* cause (an engine) to idle. **2 a** *intr.* be idle, pass the time in idleness. **b** *tr.* cause to be idle (*the closure idled 750 workers*). **3** *tr.* (foll. by *away*) pass (time etc.) in idleness. **● n. 1** an act of idling. **2** idling or idling speed of an engine. **3** an idle person. □ **idleness** *n.* **idly** *adv.*

idler *n.* **1** a person who idles or is idle. **2** a habitually lazy person.

idol *n.* **1** an image of a deity etc. used as an object of worship. **2** *Bible* a false god. **3** a person or thing that is the object of excessive or supreme adulation.

idolater /aɪˈdɒlətər/ *n.* **1** a worshipper of idols. **2** (often foll. by *of*) a devoted admirer. □ **idolatress** *n.* **idolatrous** *adj.*

idolatry *n.* (*pl.* **-ies**) **1** the worship of idols. **2** excessive devotion to or veneration for a person or thing.

idolize *v.* **1** *tr.* venerate or love extremely or excessively. **2** *tr.* make an idol of. **3** *intr.* practise idolatry. □ **idolization** *n.* **idolizer** *n.*

idyll /ˈɪdɪl/ *n.* (also **idyl**) **1** a short description in verse or prose of a picturesque scene or incident, esp. in rustic life. **2** an episode suitable for such treatment, usu. a love story. **3** a blissful period or scene.

idyllic *adj.* **1** blissfully peaceful and happy. **2** of or like an idyll. □ **idyllically** *adv.*

i.e. *abbr.* that is to say.

if ● conj. 1 introducing a conditional clause: **a** on the condition or supposition that; in the event that (*if you are tired we will rest*). **b** (with past tense) implying that the condition is not fulfilled (*if I were you*). **2** even though (*I'll finish it, if it takes me all day*). **3** whenever (*if I am not sure I ask*). **4** whether (*see if you can find it*). **5 a** expressing wish or surprise (*if I could just try!*; *if it isn't my old hat!*). **b** expressing a request (*if you wouldn't mind coming?*). **6** with implied reservation; = and perhaps not (*very rarely if at all*). **7** (with reduction of the protasis to its significant word) if there is or it is etc. (*took little if any*). **8** despite being (*a useful if cumbersome device*). **● n. 1** a condition or supposition (*too many ifs about it*). **2** an uncertainty (*if he wins — and it's a big if — he'll be the first Canadian to do so*). □ **if and only if** introducing a condition which is necessary as well as sufficient. **if and when** used to express uncertainty about a possible event in the future (*if and when we ever meet again*). **if anything** if any degree, perhaps even (*if anything, it's too large*). **if not 1** otherwise. **2** used after a *yes/no* question to give a promise, warning, etc. (*Are you ready? If not, I'm going without you*). **3** perhaps even (*cost thousands if not millions of dollars*). **4** although not; but not (*it was a good if not very imaginative performance*). **if only 1** even if for no other reason than (*I'll come if only to see her*). **2** (often *ellipt.*) an expression of regret (*if only I could swim!*). **3** an expression of a wish with reference to present or future

time. **ifs, ands, or buts** (usu. in *neg.*) reservations, arguments against. **if so** if that is the case. **only if** only on the condition that.

iffy *adj.* (**-ier, -iest**) *informal* **1** uncertain, doubtful. **2** of questionable quality.

IFR *abbr. Aviation* = INSTRUMENT FLIGHT RULES.

Ig *abbr.* immunoglobulin.

Igbo *var. of* IBO.

igloo *n.* (also **iglu**) **1** a dome-shaped Inuit dwelling built of snow. **2** any other dome-shaped Inuit dwelling.

Iglulik /ɪgˈluːlɪk/ *n.* (also **Igloolik**) **1** a member of an Inuit people inhabiting the eastern Arctic, esp. living on Baffin Island and the Melville Peninsula. **2** the language of the Iglulik.

igneous /ˈɪgnɪəs/ *adj.* **1** *Geol.* (esp. of rocks) produced by volcanic or magmatic action. **2** of fire; fiery.

ignite *v.* **1** *tr.* set fire to; cause to burn. **2** *intr.* catch fire. **3** *tr. Chem.* heat to the point of combustion or chemical change. **4** *tr.* provoke or excite (feelings etc.). □ **ignitability** *n.* **ignitable** *adj.*

igniter *n.* a person who or device which ignites something, esp. a device to set fire to an explosive or combustible.

ignition *n.* **1 a** the action of igniting the fuel in the cylinder of an internal combustion engine. **b** the mechanism for starting this process. **2** the act or an instance of igniting or being ignited.

ignition key *n.* a key to operate the ignition of a motor vehicle.

ignoble /ɪgˈnoʊbəl/ *adj.* (**ignobler, ignoblest**) **1** dishonourable, mean, base. **2** of low birth, position, or reputation. □ **ignobility** *n.* **ignobly** *adv.*

ignominious /ˌɪgnəˈmɪnɪəs/ *adj.* **1** causing or deserving ignominy. **2** humiliating (*an ignominious defeat*). □ **ignominiously** *adv.* **ignominiousness** *n.*

ignominy /ɪgˈnɒməni, ˈɪgnəmɪni/ *n.* (*pl.* **-ies**) dishonour, disgrace.

ignoramus /ˌɪgnəˈreɪməs, -ˈræməs/ *n.* (*pl.* **ignoramuses**) an extremely ignorant person.

ignorance *n.* (often foll. by *of*) lack of knowledge (about a thing).

ignorant *adj.* **1 a** lacking knowledge or experience. **b** (foll. by *of, in*) uninformed (about a fact or subject). **2** *informal* ill-mannered, uncouth. □ **ignorantly** *adv.*

ignore *v.tr.* refuse to take notice of or accept; intentionally disregard. □ **ignorable** *adj.*

iguana /ɪgˈwɒnə/ *n.* any of various large lizards of the family Iguanidae native to America, the W Indies, and the Pacific islands, having a dorsal crest and throat appendages.

IHS *abbr.* Jesus.

IJC *abbr.* INTERNATIONAL JOINT COMMISSION.

ikon *var. of* ICON 1, 2.

IL *abbr.* **1** Illinois (in postal use). **2** = INTERLEUKIN.

ileitis /ˌɪliˈaɪtɪs/ *n. Med.* **1** inflammation of the ileum. **2** = CROHN'S DISEASE.

ileostomy /ˌɪliˈɒstəmi/ *n.* (*pl.* **-ies**) **1** a surgical operation in which a damaged part is removed from the ileum and the cut end directed to an artificial opening in the abdominal wall. **2** the opening created.

ileum /ˈɪliəm/ *n.* (*pl.* **ilea** /ˈɪliə/) *Anat.* the third and last portion of the small intestine. □ **ileal** *adj.*

ilium /ˈɪliəm/ *n.* (*pl.* **ilia** /ˈɪliə/) **1** the bone forming the upper part of each half of the human pelvis. **2** the corresponding bone in animals.

ilk *n. informal* usu. *derogatory* a family, class, or set.

Ill. *abbr.* Illinois.

I'll *contraction* I will; I shall.

ill ● *adj.* **1** (usu. *predic.*; often foll. by *with*) out of health; sick (*is ill*; *was taken ill with pneumonia*). **2** (of health) unsound, disordered. **3** (of an omen, condition, etc.) unlucky, unfavourable, disastrous (*ill fortune*). **4** harmful, disagreeable, objectionable (*ill effects*). **5** hostile, unkind (*ill feeling*). **6** immoral, wicked (*house of ill repute*). **7** faulty, unskilful, inferior, or inefficient. **8** (of manners or conduct) improper, impolite, or rude. ● *adv.* **1** badly, wrongly, unskilfully, or inefficiently (*ill-matched*). **2 a** imperfectly (*ill-provided*). **b** scarcely (*can ill afford to do it*). **3** unfavourably or unhappily (*it would have gone ill with them*). ● *n.* **1** injury, harm. **2** evil; the opposite of good. **3** something unfriendly, unfavourable, or injurious. ☐ **ill at ease** embarrassed, uneasy. **speak ill of** say something unfavourable about.

ill. *abbr.* **1** illustrated. **2** illustration. **3** illustrator.

ill-advised *adj.* **1** acting foolishly or imprudently. **2** (of a plan etc.) not well formed or considered. ☐ **ill-advisedly** *adv.*

ill-assorted *adj.* not well matched.

ill-bred *adj.* badly brought up, badly behaved, rude. ☐ **ill breeding** *n.*

ill-conceived *adj.* badly planned or conceived.

ill-considered *adj.* = ILL-ADVISED 2.

ill-defined *adj.* not accurately analyzed or described (*an ill-defined role*).

ill-disposed *adj.* **1** (often foll. by *toward*) not friendly or pleasant; unfavourably disposed. **2** disposed to evil; malevolent.

ill effect *n.* (usu. in *pl.*) a harmful or unpleasant consequence, result, effect, etc.

illegal ● *adj.* **1** not legal. **2** contrary to law. **3** *Sport* against or prohibited by the rules or regulations. ● *n.* an illegal immigrant. ☐ **illegality** *n.* (*pl.* **-ies**). **illegally** *adv.*

illegible *adj.* difficult or impossible to read; not legible. ☐ **illegibility** *n.* **illegibly** *adv.*

illegitimate ● *adj.* **1** (of a child) born of parents not married to each other. **2 a** not authorized by law or custom; unlawful. **b** not in accordance with a rule; abnormal. **3** improper. **4** wrongly inferred. ● *n.* a person whose position is illegitimate, esp. by birth. ☐ **illegitimacy** *n.* **illegitimately** *adv.*

ill-equipped *adj.* (often foll. by *to* + infin.) not adequately equipped, qualified, or prepared.

ill-fated *adj.* unlucky, doomed; bringing or having bad fortune (*an ill-fated voyage*).

ill-favoured *adj.* (also **ill-favored**) unattractive, displeasing, objectionable.

ill feeling *n.* bad feeling; animosity.

ill-fitting *adj.* fitting badly (*an ill-fitting suit*).

ill-founded *adj.* (of an idea etc.) groundless.

ill-gotten *adj.* gained by dishonest or unlawful means.

ill health *n.* poor physical or mental condition.

illiberal *adj.* **1** intolerant, narrow-minded. **2** not generous; stingy. ☐ **illiberality** *n.* (*pl.* **-ies**). **illiberally** *adv.*

illicit *adj.* **1** unlawful, forbidden (*illicit dealings*). **2** secret, furtive (*an illicit affair*). ☐ **illicitly** *adv.* **illicitness** *n.*

ill-informed *adj.* inadequately or wrongly informed.

illiquid *adj.* (of assets) not easily converted into cash. ☐ **illiquidity** *n.*

illiterate ● *adj.* **1** unable to read or write. **2 a** having or showing little or no education. **b** ignorant in a particular field (*culturally illiterate*). ● *n.* an illiterate person. ☐ **illiteracy** *n.* **illiterately** *adv.*

ill-mannered *adj.* having bad manners; rude.

ill-matched *adj.* badly matched; unsuited.

ill-natured *adj.* churlish, unkind. ☐ **ill-naturedly** *adv.*

illness *n.* **1** a disease, ailment, or malady. **2** the state of being ill.

illogical *adj.* devoid of or contrary to logic. ☐ **illogic** *n.* **illogicality** *n.* (*pl.* **-ies**). **illogically** *adv.*

ill-prepared *adj.* badly or inadequately prepared.

ill-suited *adj.* **1** not suited to doing something; unsuitable. **2** inappropriate.

ill temper *n.* irritability, sullenness. ☐ **ill-tempered** *adj.*

ill-timed *adj.* done or occurring at an inappropriate or unsuitable time.

ill-treat *v.tr.* treat badly or cruelly; abuse. ☐ **ill-treatment** *n.*

illuminate *v.tr.* **1** light up; make bright. **2** help to explain (a subject etc.). **3** decorate (an initial letter etc.) with elaborate designs in gold, silver, or brilliant colours. **4** enlighten spiritually or intellectually. **5** decorate (buildings etc.) with lights as a sign of festivity. **6** make splendid or illustrious. ☐ **illuminating** *adj.* **illuminatingly** *adv.* **illuminator** *n.*

illuminati /ɪˌluːmɪˈnɑːti, -ˈnɒti/ *n.pl.* persons claiming to possess special knowledge or enlightenment.

illumination *n.* **1** the act or an instance of shedding light on something or lighting something up. **2** spiritual or intellectual enlightenment. **3 a** the decoration of a medieval manuscript with elaborate tracery or designs in gold, silver, bright colours, etc. **b** a design or illustration used in such decoration. **c** a page so decorated.

illumine /ɪˈluːmɪn/ *v.tr. literary* **1** light up; make bright. **2** enlighten spiritually.

illus. *abbr.* **1** illustration. **2** illustrated.

ill-use ● *v.tr.* treat unkindly or badly. ● *n.* (also **ill-usage**) ill-treatment. ☐ **ill-used** *adj.*

illusion *n.* **1** deception, delusion. **2** a misapprehension of the true state of affairs. **3** *Psych.* **a** the faulty perception of an external object. **b** an instance of this. **4** a figment of the imagination. **5** = OPTICAL ILLUSION. **6** a thin and transparent kind of tulle. ☐ **be under no illusions** have no esp. positive expectations. **be under the illusion** (foll. by *that* + clause) believe mistakenly.

illusionist *n.* a person who produces illusions, esp. a conjuror. ☐ **illusionism** *n.* **illusionistic** *adj.*

illusory /ɪˈluːsəri, -zəri/ *adj.* (also **illusive** /ɪˈluːsɪv/) **1** deceptive (esp. as regards value or content). **2** having the character of an illusion. ☐ **illusorily** *adv.* **illusoriness** *n.*

illustrate *v.tr.* **1 a** provide (a book etc.) with pictures. **b** elucidate (a description etc.) by drawings or pictures. **2** serve as an example of. **3** explain or make clear, esp. by examples. ☐ **illustrator** *n.*

illustration *n.* **1** a drawing or picture illustrating a book, magazine article, etc. **2** an example serving to elucidate. **3** the act or an instance of illustrating.

illustrative *adj.* (often foll. by *of*) serving as an explanation or example. ☐ **illustratively** *adv.*

illustrious *adj.* distinguished, renowned. ☐ **illustriously** *adv.* **illustriousness** *n.*

ill will *n.* bad feeling; animosity.

ill wind *n.* an unfavourable circumstance.

Illyrian /ɪˈlɪriən/ ● *adj.* **1** of or relating to ancient Illyria, on the east coast of the Adriatic Sea. **2** of the language group represented by modern Albanian. ● *n.* **1 a** a native of Illyria, esp. a member of an Indo-

European people inhabiting ancient Illyria. **b** a person of Illyrian descent. **2 a** the ancient language of Illyria. **b** the language group represented by modern Albanian.

ILO *abbr.* International Labour Organization.

I'm *contraction* I am.

image ● *n.* **1** a representation of a person or thing in sculpture, painting, photography, etc. **2** the character or reputation of a person, organization, product, etc. as generally perceived by the public, esp. a cultivated favourable reputation. **3** an optical appearance or counterpart produced by light or other radiation from an object reflected in a mirror, refracted through a lens, etc. **4** semblance, likeness (*God created man in His own image*). **5** a person or thing that closely resembles another (*is the image of his father*). **6 a** a typical example. **b** a symbol or emblem. **7 a** a simile, metaphor, or figure of speech. **b** a spoken or written description, esp. a vivid or graphic one. **8** an idea or mental representation. ● *v.tr.* **1 a** make an image of; portray. **b** imagine or form a mental picture of. **2** reflect, mirror. **3** describe or depict vividly. **4** obtain a representation of by radar, x-rays, etc. **5** symbolize or typify. □ **imager** *n.*

image-maker *n.* **1** a person employed to create a public image for a politician, product, etc. **2** a carver, sculptor, etc. of images. □ **image-making** *n.*

image processing *n.* (also **image manipulation**) the analysis and manipulation of a usu. digitized image, esp. to improve its quality. □ **image processor** *n.*

imagery *n.* (*pl.* **-ies**) **1** figurative illustration, esp. as used by an author for particular effects. **2** pictures, photographs (*satellite imagery*). **3** mental images collectively. **4** statuary, carving.

imaginable *adj.* that can be conceived or imagined (*the greatest difficulty imaginable*). □ **imaginably** *adv.*

imaginary *adj.* existing only in the imagination.

imagination *n.* **1 a** a mental faculty forming images or concepts of external objects not present to the senses. **b** the action or process of imagining or forming such images. **2** the ability of the mind to be creative or resourceful.

imaginative *adj.* **1** having or showing imagination. **2** given to using the imagination. **3** of or pertaining to the imagination or its use. □ **imaginatively** *adv.* **imaginativeness** *n.*

imagine *v.tr.* **1 a** form a mental image or concept of. **b** picture to oneself (something non-existent or not present to the senses). **2** (often foll. by *to* + infin.) think or conceive (*imagined them to be red*). **3** guess (*cannot imagine what they are doing*). **4** (often foll. by *that* + clause) suppose, be of the opinion. **5** (in *imper.*) as an exclamation of surprise (*just imagine!*). □ **imaginer** *n.*

imaging *n.* **1** *Med.* the creation of images of internal organs etc. through tomography etc., used as a diagnostic tool. **2** *Psych.* the practice of formulating and using mental pictures to control pain etc.

imaginings *n.pl.* things imagined; fancies, fantasies.

imagism /'ɪmə,dʒɪzəm/ *n.* a movement in early 20th-c. poetry which, in revolt against Romanticism, sought clarity of expression through the use of precise images and free verse. □ **imagist** *n.* & *adj.* **imagistic** *adj.* **imagistically** *adv.*

imam /ɪ'mæm, -mɒm/ *n.* **1** a leader of prayers in a mosque. **2** a title of various Muslim leaders, esp. of one succeeding Muhammad as leader of Shiite Islam.

IMAX /'aɪmæks/ *n.* *proprietary* a technique of widescreen cinematography in which 70mm film is shot and projected in such a way as to produce a celluloid image approximately ten times larger than that normally obtained from standard 35 mm film.

imbalance *n.* **1** lack of balance. **2** a lack of proportion or relation between corresponding things.

imbecile /'ɪmbəsəl, -sɪl, -saɪl/ ● *n.* **1** *informal* a stupid person. **2** *Psych.* a person of abnormally weak intellect, esp. an adult with a mental age of about five. ● *adj.* mentally weak; stupid, idiotic. □ **imbecilely** *adv.* **imbecilic** /-'sɪlɪk/ *adj.* **imbecility** /-'sɪlɪti/ *n.* (*pl.* **-ies**).

imbed *var. of* EMBED.

imbibe /ɪm'baɪb/ *v.* **1** *tr.* & *intr.* drink (esp. alcoholic liquor). **2** *tr.* **a** absorb or assimilate (ideas etc.). **b** absorb (moisture, heat, etc.). □ **imbiber** *n.*

imbroglio /ɪm'brəʊlɪəʊ/ *n.* (*pl.* **-os**) **1 a** a complicated, confused, or embarrassing situation, esp. a political or interpersonal one. **b** a confused misunderstanding. **2** esp. *literary* a confused heap.

imbue /ɪm'bjuː/ *v.tr.* (**imbues, imbued, imbuing**) (often foll. by *with*) **1** inspire or permeate (with feelings, opinions, or qualities). **2** saturate, soak through. **3** dye, tinge.

IMF *abbr.* International Monetary Fund, an organization established in 1945 to promote international trade and monetary co-operation and the stabilization of exchange rates.

imitate *v.tr.* **1** follow the example of; copy the action(s) of. **2** mimic. **3** make a copy of; reproduce. **4** be, become, or make oneself like, intentionally or unintentionally. □ **imitable** *adj.* **imitator** *n.*

imitation ● *n.* **1** the act or an instance of imitating or being imitated (*does a good imitation of Elvis*). **2** a copy. **3** a counterfeit; something made to look like something else. ● *adj.* made in imitation of a real or genuine article or substance (*imitation leather*).

imitative *adj.* **1** (often foll. by *of*) imitating; following a model or example. **2** counterfeit. □ **imitatively** *adv.* **imitativeness** *n.*

immaculate *adj.* **1** pure, spotless; perfectly clean and tidy. **2** perfectly or extremely well executed (*an immaculate performance*). **3** free from moral stain or fault; innocent. □ **immaculately** *adv.*

Immaculate Conception *n.* *Catholicism* **1** the doctrine that God preserved the Virgin Mary from the taint of original sin from the moment she was conceived. **2** Dec. 8, the feast of the Immaculate Conception.

immanent /'ɪmənənt/ *adj.* **1** (often foll. by *in*) naturally present, inherent. **2** (of the supreme being) permanently pervading the universe (*opp.* TRANSCENDENT 3). **3** *Philos.* (of an action) performed entirely within the mind of the subject, and producing no external effect. □ **immanence** *n.*

immaterial *adj.* **1** of no essential consequence; unimportant, irrelevant. **2** not material; incorporeal, without physical form or substance. □ **immateriality** *n.* **immaterially** *adv.*

immaterialism *n.* the doctrine that all things exist only as ideas or perceptions of a mind, that matter has no objective existence. □ **immaterialist** *n.*

immature *adj.* **1 a** (of cells, animals, etc.) not mature or fully developed. **b** (of plants, fruit, etc.) unripe. **2** lacking emotional or intellectual development. □ **immaturely** *adv.* **immaturity** *n.*

immeasurable *adj.* not measurable; immense. □ **immeasurably** *adv.*

immediate *adj.* **1** occurring or done at once or without delay (*an immediate reply*). **2 a** nearest in time or space (*the immediate future*). **b** (of family) designating those of closest relation, usu. parents, children, spouses, and siblings. **3** most pressing or urgent; of current concern (*our immediate concern*). **4** (of a thing or action in relation to another) having direct effect; not separated by an intervening medium or agency (*the immediate cause*). ☐ **immediacy** *n.* (*pl.* **-ies**).

immediately *adv.* **1** instantly, without pause or delay (*answered the phone immediately*). **2** without intermediary; in direct connection or relation (*who is immediately responsible?*). **3** with no object, distance, time, etc. intervening (*immediately in front of you*).

immemorial *adj.* **1** ancient beyond memory or record. **2** very old or long established.

immense *adj.* **1** immeasurably large or great; huge. **2** very great; considerable (*made an immense difference*). **3** *informal* very good, splendid. ☐ **immensity** *n.* (*pl.* **-ies**).

immensely *adv.* **1** very much (*enjoyed myself immensely*). **2** to an immense degree.

immerse *v.tr.* **1 a** (often foll. by *in*) dip, plunge, or submerge in a liquid. **b** cause (a person) to be completely under water. **2** (often *refl.* or in *passive*; often foll. by *in*) absorb or involve deeply in a particular activity or condition.

immersion *n.* **1** esp. *N Amer.* **a** (often *attrib.*) a method of teaching a foreign language by the exclusive use of that language, usu. at a special school, in a special class, etc. **b** a class, course, or system of study based on the immersion method. **2 a** the act or an instance of immersing. **b** the process of being immersed. **3** baptism by immersing the whole person in water. **4** mental absorption in an activity etc.

immigrant ● *n.* **1** a person who immigrates. **2 a** an animal or plant that has migrated into a given area, esp. one now living there. **b** an animal (esp. a bird) that regularly or occasionally migrates into a given area. ● *adj.* of, pertaining to, or concerning immigrants or immigration.

immigrate *v.intr.* **1** come as a permanent resident to a country other than one's native land. **2** (of an animal or plant) migrate to a different geographical region, esp. when this leads to continuous occupation of the area by the species.

immigration *n.* **1 a** the process of coming to live in another country permanently. **b** an instance of this. **2** (often *attrib.*) the process of authorizing or monitoring immigration (*immigration officer*). **3** (**Immigration**) the government ministry in charge of regulating immigration. **4** a control point at an airport, border, etc. where the documentation of people wanting to enter a country is checked.

immigration building *n.* (also **immigration hall**, **immigration shed**) *Cdn hist.* a building used to shelter immigrants until they found their own homes.

imminent *adj.* (of an event, esp. danger) impending; about to happen. ☐ **imminence** *n.* **imminently** *adv.*

immobile *adj.* **1** not moving. **2** not able to move or be moved. ☐ **immobility** *n.*

immobilize *v.tr.* **1** make or keep immobile. **2** restrict the free movement of. **3** make (esp. a vehicle or troops) incapable of being moved. **4** keep (a limb or patient) restricted in movement for healing purposes. ☐ **immobilization** *n.* **immobilizer** *n.*

immoderate *adj.* excessive; lacking moderation. ☐ **immoderately** *adv.*

immodest *adj.* **1** lacking modesty. **2** lacking due decency (*immodest dress*). ☐ **immodestly** *adv.* **immodesty** *n.*

immolate /'ɪmə,leɪt/ *v.tr.* **1** kill or offer as a sacrifice. **2** *literary* sacrifice (a valued thing). ☐ **immolation** *n.*

immoral *adj.* **1** not conforming to accepted standards of morality (compare AMORAL). **2** morally wrong, esp. in

sexual matters. **3** depraved, dissolute. ☐ **immorality** *n.* (*pl.* **-ies**). **immorally** *adv.*

immortal ● *adj.* **1 a** living forever; not mortal. **b** divine. **2** incorruptible. **3** likely or worthy to be famous for all time. ● *n.* **1 a** an immortal being. **b** (in *pl.*) the gods of antiquity. **2** a person (esp. an author) of enduring fame. ☐ **immortality** *n.* **immortalize** *v.tr.* **immortalization** *n.* **immortally** *adv.*

immovable (also **immoveable**) ● *adj.* **1** unable to be moved. **2** steadfast, unyielding. **3** emotionless, impassive. **4** fixed, not subject to change (*immovable law*). **5** motionless, stationary. **6** *Law* (of property) permanent, not liable to be removed, e.g. land, houses, etc. ● *n.* (in *pl.*) *Law* immovable property. ☐ **immovability** *n.* **immovably** *adv.*

immune *adj.* **1 a** (often foll. by *against, from, to*) *Biol.* resistant to a particular infection, toxin, etc., owing to the presence of specific antibodies or sensitized white blood cells. **b** of, pertaining to, or producing immunity (*immune mechanism*). **2** (foll. by *from, to*) free or exempt from or not subject to (some undesirable factor or circumstance) (*immune from prosecution*).

immune response *n.* the reaction of the body to the introduction into it of an antigen.

immune system *n.* those structures and functions of an organism responsible for maintaining immunity.

immunity *n.* (*pl.* **-ies**) **1** *Biol.* the ability of an organism to resist a specific infection, toxin, etc. **2** freedom or exemption from an obligation, penalty, or unfavourable circumstance. **3** the ability to be unaffected by something (*immunity to virulent ideas*).

immunize /'ɪmjʊ,naɪz/ *v.tr.* make immune, esp. to infection, usu. by inoculation. ☐ **immunization** *n.* **immunizer** *n.*

immunodeficiency /,ɪmjʊ,noʊdə'fɪʃənsi, ɪ,mjuːnoʊ-/ *n.* (*pl.* **-ies**) a reduction in a person's normal immune defences. ☐ **immunodeficient** *adj.*

immunoglobulin /,ɪmjʊnoʊ'ɡlɒbjʊlɪn, ɪ,mjuːnoʊ-/ *n.* *Biochem.* any of a group of structurally related proteins which function as antibodies. Abbr.: **Ig**.

immunology /,ɪmjʊ'nɒlədʒi/ *n.* (*pl.* **-ies**) the scientific study of resistance to infection in humans and animals. ☐ **immunologic** *adj.* **immunological** *adj.* **immunologically** *adv.* **immunologist** *n.*

immunotherapy /,ɪmjʊnoʊ'θerəpi, ɪ,mjuːnoʊ-/ *n.* (*pl.* **-ies**) the prevention or treatment of disease with substances that stimulate the immune response.

immutable /ɪ'mjuːtəbəl/ *adj.* **1** unchangeable. **2** not subject to variation in different cases. ☐ **immutability** *n.* **immutably** *adv.*

imp *n.* **1** a mischievous child. **2** a small mischievous devil or sprite.

impact ● *n.* **1** (often foll. by *on, against*) the action of one body coming forcibly into contact with another. **2** an effect or influence, esp. when strong. ● *v.tr.* **1** *intr.* (often foll. by *on, against*, etc.) come forcibly into contact with a usu. larger body or surface. **2 a** *intr.* (often foll. by *on*) have an impact. **b** *tr.* have an impact on (*how are the cuts to welfare impacting low-income families?*) ¶Although some people object to these uses of *impact*, they are well established in both spoken and written English and are perfectly acceptable. **3** (often foll. by *in, into*) press closely or fix firmly.

impact crater *n.* a crater or hollow supposedly produced by the impact of a meteorite.

impacted *adj.* **1 a** (of a tooth) wedged between another tooth and the jaw. **b** (of a fractured bone) with the parts crushed together. **c** (of feces) lodged in the intestine. **2 a** (of an area) overcrowded, esp. so as to put severe pressures on public services, etc. **b** pressed closely in, firmly fixed.

impact statement *n.* a formal written account of how a person, place, etc. has been or will be affected by a specific incident, process, etc.

impair *v.tr.* damage or weaken. □ **impairment** *n.*

impaired *adj.* **1** *Cdn* (of driving or the driver of a car, boat, snowmobile, etc.) adversely affected by alcohol or narcotics, specifically for legal purposes, having a blood alcohol level greater than .08. **2** (usu. in *comb.*) disabled, handicapped (*hearing impaired*). **3** that has been impaired.

impala /ɪmˈpælə/ *n.* (*pl.* same) a medium-sized reddish-brown grazing antelope, *Aepyceros melampus*, of southern and eastern African savannah.

impale *v.tr.* (foll. by *on, upon, with*) transfix or pierce with a sharp instrument. □ **impalement** *n.*

impart *v.tr.* (often foll. by *to*) **1** communicate (news etc.). **2** give a share of (a thing).

impartial *adj.* treating all sides in a dispute etc. equally; unprejudiced, fair. □ **impartiality** *n.* **impartially** *adv.*

impassable *adj.* that cannot be traversed. □ **impassability** *n.* **impassably** *adv.*

impasse /ˈɪmpæs/ *n.* a position from which progress is impossible; deadlock.

impassion *v.tr.* fill with passion; arouse emotionally.

impassioned *adj.* ardent (*an impassioned plea*).

impassive *adj.* **1** deficient in or incapable of feeling emotion. **2** undisturbed by passion; serene. □ **impassively** *adv.* **impassivity** *n.*

impasto /ɪmˈpæstoʊ/ *n.* *Art* **1 a** the process of laying on paint thickly. **b** the paint so applied. **2** this technique of painting.

impatiens /ɪmˈpeɪʃəns, -ənz/ *n.* any plant of the genus *Impatiens*.

impatient *adj.* **1 a** (often foll. by *at, with*) lacking patience or tolerance. **b** (of an action) showing a lack of patience. **2** (often foll. by *for*, or *to* + infin.) restlessly eager. □ **impatience** *n.* **impatiently** *adv.*

impeach *v.tr.* **1** esp. *US* charge (the holder of a public office) with misconduct. **2** call in question, disparage (a person's integrity etc.). □ **impeachment** *n.*

impeccable *adj.* **1** (of behaviour, performance, etc.) faultless, exemplary. **2** (of clothing, accommodations, etc.) flawlessly clean and tidy. **3** not liable to sin. □ **impeccability** *n.* **impeccably** *adv.*

impecunious /ˌɪmpɪˈkjuːniəs/ *adj.* having little or no money.

impedance /ɪmˈpiːdəns/ *n.* **1** *Electricity* the total effective resistance of an electric circuit etc. to alternating current, arising from ohmic resistance and reactance. **2** an analogous mechanical property.

impede *v.tr.* retard by obstructing; hinder.

impediment /ɪmˈpedɪmənt/ *n.* **1** a hindrance or obstruction. **2** a defect in speech, e.g. a lisp or stammer. **3** *Law* an obstruction, usu. closeness of blood or affinity, to the making of a marriage contract.

impel *v.tr.* (**impelled, impelling**) **1** drive, force, or urge into action. **2** drive forward; propel.

impeller *n.* **1** a person who or thing which impels. **2** the rotating part of a machine designed to move a fluid by rotation, as a centrifugal pump or compressor.

impend *v.intr.* **1** be about to happen. **2** (often foll. by *over*) (of a danger) be threatening. □ **impending** *adj.*

impenetrable *adj.* **1 a** that cannot be penetrated, pierced or entered. **b** that cannot be seen through. **2** inscrutable, unfathomable; impossible to understand. **3** inaccessible to ideas, influences, etc. □ **impenetrability** *n.* **impenetrably** *adv.*

imperative ● *adj.* **1** urgent. **2** obligatory. **3** commanding, peremptory (*an imperative tone of voice*). **4** *Grammar* (of a mood) expressing a command (e.g. *wait!*). ● *n.* **1** *Grammar* **a** the imperative mood. **b** a word, form, etc. in the imperative mood. **2** a command. **3** an essential or urgent thing (*a moral imperative*). □ **imperatively** *adv.* **imperativeness** *n.*

imperceptible *adj.* **1** that cannot be perceived. **2** very slight, gradual, or subtle. □ **imperceptibility** *n.* **imperceptibly** *adv.*

imperceptive *adj.* not perceptive or perceiving; lacking perception. □ **imperceptively** *adv.* **imperceptiveness** *n.*

imperfect ● *adj.* **1** not fully formed or done; faulty, incomplete. **2** (of a tense) denoting a (usu. past) action in progress but not completed at the time in question (e.g. *they were singing*). ● *n.* **1** the imperfect tense. **2** a word, form, etc. in the imperfect. □ **imperfectly** *adv.*

imperfection *n.* **1** incompleteness. **2 a** faultiness. **b** a fault or blemish.

imperial *adj.* **1** of or characteristic of an empire or comparable sovereign state. **2 a** of or characteristic of an emperor or empress. **b** supreme in authority. **c** majestic, august. **3** (of weights and measures) used or formerly used in the UK and other Commonwealth jurisdictions (*imperial gallon*). **4** designating any of various products or commodities of a certain (esp. great) size or quality. □ **imperially** *adv.*

imperial gallon *n.* = GALLON 1a.

imperialism *n.* **1** an imperial rule or system. **2** usu. *derogatory* a policy of acquiring dependent territories or extending a country's influence over less developed countries through trade, diplomacy, etc. **3** the domination or attempted domination of another country's economic, political, or cultural institutions, without actually seizing governmental control. **4** advocacy or support for imperial interests.

imperialist ● *n.* usu. *derogatory* an advocate or agent of imperial rule or of imperialism. ● *adj.* of or relating to imperialism or imperialists. □ **imperialistic** *adj.* **imperialistically** *adv.*

Imperial Order Daughters of the Empire *n.* a Canadian women's organization founded in 1900, focusing on community affairs.

imperil *v.tr.* (**imperilled, imperilling**) bring or put into danger.

imperious /ɪmˈpiːriəs/ *adj.* **1** overbearing, domineering, expecting obedience. **2** urgent, imperative. □ **imperiously** *adv.* **imperiousness** *n.*

impermanent *adj.* not permanent; transient. □ **impermanence** *n.* **impermanently** *adv.*

impermeable *adj.* **1** that cannot be penetrated. **2** *Physics* that does not permit the passage of fluids. □ **impermeability** *n.*

impermissible *adj.* not allowable. □ **impermissibility** *n.*

impersonal *adj.* **1** not influenced by, showing or involving human emotions (*a vast impersonal organization*). **2** having no personal reference; objective (*an impersonal assessment*). **3** having no personality; not existing as a person (*an impersonal deity*). **4 a** (of a verb) used only with a formal subject (usu. *it*) and expressing an action not attributable to a definite subject (e.g. *it is snowing*). **b** (of a pronoun) = INDEFINITE 3. □ **impersonality** *n.* **impersonally** *adv.*

impersonate *v.tr.* **1** pretend to be (another person) in order to deceive others (*impersonated a police officer*). **2**

mimic the speech, behaviour, etc. of (another person) in order to entertain others. □ **impersonation** n. **impersonator** n.

impertinent adj. **1** rude or insolent; lacking proper respect. **2** out of place; absurd. **3** esp. Law irrelevant, intrusive. □ **impertinence** n. **impertinently** adv.

imperturbable adj. not excitable; calm. □ **imperturbability** n. **imperturbably** adv.

impervious adj. (usu. foll. by to) **1** not responsive (to an argument, outside influence, etc.). **2** not allowing water, gas, etc. to pass through. **3** able to withstand wear and tear; resistant. □ **imperviousness** n.

impetigo /ˌɪmpəˈtaɪgoː/ n. a contagious bacterial skin infection forming pustules and yellow crusty sores.

impetuous /ɪmˈpɛtʃʊəs/ adj. **1** acting or done rashly or with sudden energy. **2** moving forcefully or rapidly. □ **impetuosity** /-ˈɒsɪti/ n. **impetuously** adv. **impetuousness** n.

impetus /ˈɪmpɪtəs/ n. **1** the force or energy with which a body moves. **2** a driving force or impulse.

impiety n. (pl. **-ies**) **1** a lack of piety or reverence. **2** an act etc. showing this.

impinge /ɪmˈpɪndʒ/ v.tr. (usu. foll. by on, upon) **1** make an impact; have an effect. **2** encroach. **3** strike, come into forcible contact; collide. □ **impingement** n. **impinger** n.

impious adj. **1** not pious; lacking reverence for God or a god. **2** wicked, profane. □ **impiously** adv. **impiousness** n.

impish adj. mischievous. □ **impishness** n.

implacable adj. that cannot be appeased; inexorable. □ **implacability** n. **implacably** adv.

implant ● v.tr. **1** (often foll. by in) insert or fix. **2** (often foll. by in) instill (a principle, idea, etc.) in a person's mind. **3** plant, set in the ground. **4** Med. **a** insert (tissue, a substance, or an artificial object) in a living body. **b** (of a fertilized ovum) become attached to the wall of the uterus. ● n. **1** a thing implanted. **2** a thing implanted or grafted into the body, e.g. a piece of tissue, hair, or a capsule containing material for radium therapy. □ **implantation** n.

implausible adj. not plausible. □ **implausibility** n. **implausibly** adv.

implement ● n. **1** a tool, instrument, or utensil. **2** a piece of farm machinery, e.g. a plow, combine, etc. (also attrib.: implement shed). **3** (in pl.) equipment; articles of furniture, dress, etc. **4** an agent, channel (an implement for change). ● v.tr. **1** put (a decision, plan, etc.) into effect. **2** fulfill (an undertaking). □ **implementable** adj. **implementation** n. **implementer** n.

implicate /ˈɪmplɪˌkeɪt/ v.tr. **1** (often foll. by in) show (a person or thing) to be concerned or involved (in a charge, crime, etc.). **2** (in passive; often foll. by in) be affected or involved. **3** lead to as a consequence or inference.

implication n. **1** what is involved in or implied by something else. **2** the act of implicating or implying. □ **by implication** by what is implied or suggested rather than by formal expression.

implicit adj. **1** implied though not plainly expressed. **2** (often foll. by in) virtually contained. **3** absolute, unquestioning, unreserved (implicit obedience). □ **implicitly** adv. **implicitness** n.

implode v. **1** intr. & tr. burst or cause to burst inwards. **2** intr. collapse or disintegrate internally (factors which caused the Soviet Union to implode). □ **implosion** n.

implore v. **1** tr. (often foll. by to + infin.) entreat (a person). **2** tr. beg earnestly for (help, forgiveness, etc.). **3** intr. utter entreaties; supplicate. □ **imploringly** adv.

imply v.tr. (**-ies, -ied**) **1** (often foll. by that + clause) strongly suggest the truth or existence of (a thing not expressly asserted). ¶See INFER. **2** involve as a necessary consequence. **3** insinuate, hint (what are you implying?). **4** (of a word etc.) signify. □ **implied** adj. **impliedly** adv.

impolite adj. ill-mannered, uncivil, rude. □ **impolitely** adv. **impoliteness** n.

impolitic adj. **1** inexpedient, unwise. **2** not politic.

imponderable ● adj. that cannot be estimated or assessed in any definite way. ● n. (often in pl.) something difficult or impossible to assess. □ **imponderability** n. **imponderably** adv.

import ● v.tr. **1** bring in (esp. foreign goods or services) to a country. **2** bring or introduce from an external source or from one use etc. to another (theories imported from the business world.) **3** (often foll. by that + clause) imply, indicate, signify. **4** Computing bring (files etc.) from one application program into another. ● n. **1** the process of importing. **2 a** an imported article or service. **b** (in pl.) an amount imported. **3** what is implied; meaning. **4** importance. **5** Cdn Sport **a** a player who is enlisted from elsewhere to play for a team representing a city, school, etc. **b** any player who is not from the area his or her team represents. **c** Football a professional player who learned to play football outside of Canada (usu. in the US) before the age of seventeen, or who started to learn football after the age of seventeen outside Canada. **6** esp. Cdn a person recently arrived in one country from another. □ **importation** n. **imported** adj. **importer** n. (all in sense 1 of v.).

importance n. **1** the state of being important. **2** weight, significance. **3** personal consequence; dignity (a woman of great importance).

important adj. **1** of great effect or consequence; significant. **2** (of a person) having high rank or status, or great authority. **3** pretentious, pompous. **4** of great concern to; highly prized (my family is very important to me). **5** what is a more, or most, significant point or matter (they are willing and, more important, able). ¶Some commentators have objected to the use of more importantly rather than more important in sentences such as this, but more importantly is overwhelmingly more common and totally unobjectionable. □ **importantly** adv.

importunate /ɪmˈpɔrtʃənət/ adj. **1** making persistent or pressing requests, demands for attention, etc. **2** (of affairs) urgent. □ **importunately** adv.

importune /ˌɪmpɔrˈtuːn, -ˈtjuːn/ v.tr. solicit (a person) pressingly; beg or demand insistently. □ **importunity** n.

impose v. **1** tr. (often foll. by on, upon) require (a tax, duty, charge, or obligation) to be paid or undertaken (by a person etc.). **2** tr. enforce compliance with (imposed his will). **3** intr. & refl. (foll. by on, upon) demand the attention or commitment of (a person); take advantage of. **4** tr. (often foll. by on, upon) palm (a thing) off on (a person). **5** intr. (foll. by on, upon) exert influence by an impressive character or appearance.

imposing adj. impressive, formidable, esp. in appearance. □ **imposingly** adv. **imposingness** n.

imposition n. **1** the act or an instance of imposing; the process of being imposed. **2** an unfair or resented demand or burden. **3** Christianity **a** the laying on of hands in blessing, ordination, etc. **b** the placing of ashes upon a person's forehead on Ash Wednesday.

impossibility n. (pl. **-ies**) **1** the fact or condition of being impossible. **2** an impossible thing or circumstance.

impossible *adj.* **1** not possible; that cannot occur, exist, or be done (*it is impossible to alter them*). **2** (loosely) extremely difficult, inconvenient, or implausible. **3** *informal* (of a person or thing) outrageous, intolerable. □ **impossibly** *adv.*

imposter *n.* (also **impostor**) a person who assumes a false character or pretends to be someone else.

imposture /ɪm'pɒstʃər/ *n.* fraudulent deception.

impotent /'ɪmpətənt/ *adj.* **1 a** powerless; lacking all strength. **b** helpless. **c** ineffective. **2** (of a male) unable, esp. for a prolonged period, to achieve an erection or orgasm. **3** *informal* unable to procreate; sterile. □ **impotence** *n.* **impotently** *adv.*

impound *v.tr.* **1** confiscate; take legal possession of. **2** shut up (animals) in a pound. **3** shut up (a person or thing) as in a pound. □ **impoundable** *adj.* **impounder** *n.* **impoundment** *n.*

impoverish *v.tr.* (often as **impoverished** *adj.*) **1** make poor. **2** exhaust the natural fertility of. **3** weaken or reduce the quality of; deprive of some quality; affect adversely (*a culturally impoverished society*). □ **impoverishment** *n.*

impracticable *adj.* **1** impossible in practice. **2** (of a road etc.) impassable. □ **impracticability** *n.* **impracticably** *adv.*

impractical *adj.* **1** not practical. **2** esp. *N Amer.* not practicable. □ **impracticality** *n.* **impractically** *adv.*

imprecation /ˌɪmprə'keɪʃən/ *n.* **1** a spoken curse. **2** the act of uttering an imprecation. □ **imprecatory** /'ɪmprɪˌkeɪtəri/ *adj.*

imprecise *adj.* not precise. □ **imprecisely** *adv.* **impreciseness** *n.* **imprecision** *n.*

impregnable[1] *adj.* **1** (of a fortress etc.) that cannot be taken by force. **2** resistant to attack or criticism. **3** unable to be broken down or overcome (*impregnable shyness*). □ **impregnability** *n.* **impregnably** *adv.*

impregnable[2] *adj.* that can be impregnated.

impregnate *v.tr.* **1 a** make (a female) pregnant. **b** *Biol.* fertilize (a female reproductive cell or ovum). **2** (often foll. by *with*) fill or saturate. **3** (often foll. by *with*) imbue, fill (with feelings, moral qualities, etc.). □ **impregnation** *n.*

impresario /ˌɪmprə'sɑːriːəʊ, -'seriːəʊ/ *n.* (*pl.* **-os**) an organizer of public entertainments, esp. a manager or promoter of performing arts companies or productions.

impress ● *v.* **1** (often foll. by *with*) **a** *tr.* affect or influence deeply. **b** *tr. & intr.* evoke a favourable opinion or reaction from (a person) (*was most impressed with your efforts*). **2** *tr.* (often foll. by *on, upon*) emphasize (an idea etc.) (*must impress on you the need to be prompt*). **3** *tr.* (often foll. by *on*) **a** imprint or stamp. **b** apply (a mark etc.) with pressure. **4** *tr.* make a mark or design on (a thing) with a stamp, seal, etc. ● *n.* **1** the act or an instance of impressing. **2** a mark made by a seal, stamp, etc. **3** a characteristic mark or quality. **4** = IMPRESSION 1. □ **impressible** *adj.*

impression *n.* **1 a** an effect produced (esp. on the mind, conscience, or feelings). **b** a striking or positive effect (*made an impression on the talent scout*). **2** a notion or belief (esp. a vague or mistaken one) (*my impression is they are afraid*). **3** an imitation of a person or sound, esp. done to entertain. **4 a** the impressing of a mark. **b** a mark impressed. **5** a reprint without editorial corrections. **6 a** the number of copies of a book, newspaper, etc., issued at one time. **b** the printing of these. **7** a print taken from a wood engraving. **8** *Dentistry* a mould (from which a positive cast is usu. made) of the teeth or mouth made by pressing them into a soft substance.

impressionable *adj.* easily influenced; susceptible to impressions. □ **impressionability** *n.* **impressionably** *adv.*

Impressionism *n.* (also **impressionism**) **1** an artistic style or movement originating in France in the late 19th c., characterized by a concern with depicting the visual impression of the moment, esp. in terms of the shifting effect of light and colour. **2** a style of music or writing that seeks to describe a feeling or experience rather than achieve accurate depiction or systematic structure.

impressionist ● *n.* **1** an entertainer who impersonates famous people etc. **2** (**Impressionist**) an adherent or practitioner of Impressionism. ● *adj.* (**Impressionist**) of or relating to Impressionism or Impressionists.

impressionistic *adj.* **1** (**Impressionistic**) in the style of Impressionism. **2** subjective, unsystematic; based on impressions. □ **impressionistically** *adv.*

impressive *adj.* **1** impressing the mind or senses, esp. so as to cause approval or admiration. **2** (of language, a scene, etc.) tending to excite deep feeling. □ **impressively** *adv.* **impressiveness** *n.*

imprimatur /ˌɪmprɪ'mætər, -'meɪtər, -tʊr/ *n.* **1** *Catholicism* an official licence to print (an ecclesiastical book etc.). **2** official approval.

imprint ● *v.tr.* **1** (often foll. by *on*) impress or establish firmly, esp. on the mind. **2 a** (often foll. by *on*) make a stamp or impression of (a figure etc.) on a thing. **b** make an impression on (a thing) with a stamp etc. **3** (usu. in *passive*; often foll. by *on* or *to*) *Biol.* cause (a young animal etc.) to recognize another as a parent or object of habitual trust. ● *n.* **1** a mark produced by pressure on a surface; an impression or stamp. **2 a** lasting impression or sign of some emotion, experience, action, etc.; an influence, an effect. **3 a** the printer's or publisher's name and other details printed in a book, usu. on the title page or at the foot of a single sheet. **b** a line of specific titles issued by a publishing company.

imprison *v.tr.* **1** put into prison. **2** confine; shut up. □ **imprisonment** *n.*

improbable *adj.* **1** not likely to be true or to happen. **2** difficult to believe. □ **improbability** *n.* **improbably** *adv.*

impromptu /ɪm'prɒmptuː, -tjuː/ ● *adj. & adv.* without preparation; on the spur of the moment. ● *n.* **1** an improvised performance or speech. **2** a short piece of usu. solo instrumental music, often song-like.

improper *adj.* **1 a** unseemly; indecent. **b** not in accordance with accepted rules of behaviour. **2** wrong or incorrect (*improper use of a tool*). **3** dishonest, irregular (*improper business practices*). □ **improperly** *adv.*

impropriety *n.* (*pl.* **-ies**) **1** lack of propriety; indecency. **2** an instance of improper conduct, language etc. **3** incorrectness, inaccuracy. **4** unfitness, inappropriateness.

improv *n.* (often *attrib.*) *informal* **1** improvisation, esp. as a theatrical technique. **2** an instance of this.

improve *v.* **1 a** *tr. & intr.* make or become better. **b** *intr.* (foll. by *on, upon*) produce something better than. **2** *tr.* make (land) more productive or valuable by cultivation, clearing, etc. □ **improvable** *adj.* **improvability** *n.* **improved** *adj.* **improver** *n.*

improvement *n.* **1** the act or an instance of improving or being improved. **2** something that improves, esp. an addition or alteration that adds to value (*home improvements*). **3** something that has been improved.

Improvement District *n.* *Cdn* (Alta., Ont., & BC) a

sparsely populated region which does not have a municipal government and is therefore administered by provincial officials. Abbr.: **I.D.**

improvident /ɪmˈprɒvɪdənt/ adj. **1** lacking foresight or care for the future. **2** not frugal; wasteful. **3** heedless, incautious. □ **improvidence** n.

improvise /ˈɪmprəˌvaɪz/ v.tr. & intr. **1 a** compose or perform (music, dialogue, etc.) on the spur of the moment, not working from a text or score, etc. **b** say or do (something) without preparation (I didn't know the answer, so I had to improvise). **2** provide or construct (a thing) from whatever is available, without preparation. □ **improvisation** n. **improvisational** adj. **improvisatory** /-ˈprɒvəzə,tɔri/ adj. **improviser** n.

imprudent adj. rash, indiscreet. □ **imprudence** n. **imprudently** adv.

impudent adj. **1** insolently disrespectful; impertinent. **2** shamelessly presumptuous. □ **impudence** n. **impudently** adv.

impugn /ɪmˈpjuːn/ v.tr. challenge or call in question (a statement, action, someone's character, etc.).

impulse n. **1** the act or an instance of impelling; a push. **2** impetus (gave an impulse to industrial expansion). **3** incitement or stimulus to action arising from a state of mind or feeling (a selfish impulse). **4** a sudden desire or tendency to act without reflection (did it on impulse). **5** Physics **a** an indefinitely large force acting for a very short time but producing a finite change of momentum (e.g. the blow of a hammer). **b** the change of momentum produced by this or any force. **6** a stimulating force in a nerve or electric circuit that causes a reaction.

impulse buying n. the unpremeditated buying of goods as a result of a whim or impulse. □ **impulse buy** n. & v.intr. **impulse buyer** n.

impulsive adj. **1** (of a person or conduct etc.) apt to be affected or determined by sudden impulse. **2** tending to impel. **3** Physics acting as an impulse. □ **impulsively** adv. **impulsiveness** n. **impulsivity** n.

impunity /ɪmˈpjuːnɪti/ n. exemption from punishment or from the injurious consequences of an action. □ **with impunity** without having to suffer the normal injurious consequences (of an action).

impure adj. **1** mixed with foreign matter; adulterated (impure metals). **2 a** dirty or contaminated. **b** ceremonially unclean. **3** unchaste; not morally pure (impure thoughts). **4** (of a colour) mixed with another colour. □ **impurely** adv.

impurity n. (pl. **-ies**) **1** the quality or condition of being impure. **2 a** an impure thing or constituent. **b** a trace element added to a semiconductor.

impute /ɪmˈpjuːt/ v.tr. (foll. by to) **1** regard (esp. something undesirable) as being done or caused or possessed by. **2** (in Christian theology) ascribe (righteousness, guilt, etc.) to (a person) by virtue of a similar quality in another. **3** Econ. attribute or assign (value) to a product or process by inference from the value of the products or processes to which it contributes. □ **imputable** adj. **imputation** n.

IN abbr. Indiana (in postal use).

In symbol indium.

in ● prep. **1** expressing inclusion or position within limits of space, time, circumstance, etc. (in Canada; in the rain). **2** during the time of (in the night; in 1999). **3** within the time of (will be back in two hours). **4 a** with respect to (good in parts). **b** as a kind of (the latest thing in luxury). **5** as a proportionate part of (one in three failed). **6** with the form or arrangement of (packed in tens). **7** as a member of (in the army). **8** concerned with (is in politics). **9** as or regarding the content of (there is something in what you say). **10** within the ability of (does he have it in him?). **11** having the condition of; affected by (in bad health; in danger). **12** having as a purpose (in search of; in reply to). **13** by means of or using as material (drawn in pencil). **14 a** using as the language of expression (written in French). **b** (of music) having as its key (symphony in C). **15** wearing as dress (in blue; in a suit). **16** with the identity of (found a friend in Mary). **17** (of an animal) pregnant with (in calf). **18** into (with a verb of motion or change: put it in the box; cut it in two). **19** introducing an indirect object after a verb (believe in). **20** forming adverbial phrases (in any case; in reality). **21** in the process of; in the act of (in climbing the wall he fell). ● adv. expressing position within limits, or motion to such a position: **1** into a room, house, etc. (come in). **2** at home, in one's office, etc. (is not in). **3** so as to be enclosed or confined (locked in). **4** in a publication (is the ad in?). **5** in or to the inward side (rub it in). **6 a** in fashion, season, or office (long skirts are in). **b** elected (the Liberal got in). **7** exerting favourable action or influence (their luck was in). **8** Sport **a** (of a shot, serve, etc.) within the boundary of the playing area. **b** (of a player or side) having the turn to play. **c** (of a hockey puck, soccer ball, etc.) between and behind the goalposts. **d** (of a baseball infielder or outfielder) playing closer to home plate than usual. **9** (of transport) at the platform etc. (the train is in). **10** (of a season, harvest, order, etc.) having arrived or been received. **11** denoting effective action (join in). **12** (of the tide) at the highest point. **13** (in comb.) informal denoting prolonged or concerted action, esp. by large numbers (sit-in). ● adj. **1** internal; living in; inside (in-patient). **2** fashionable, esoteric (the in thing to do). **3** confined to or shared by a group of people (in-joke). ● n. (foll. by with) informal an introduction to, or influence with, a person of power or authority. □ **in at** present at; contributing to (in at the kill). **in for 1** about to undergo (esp. something unpleasant). **2** competing in or for. **3** involved in; committed to. **in on** sharing in; privy to (a secret etc.). **ins and outs** (often foll. by of) all the details (of a procedure etc.). **in that** because; in so far as. **in with** on good terms with.

in. abbr. inch(es).

in- prefix **1** adjectives, meaning 'not' (inedible; insane). **2** nouns, meaning 'without, lacking' (inaction).

in absentia /ˌɪn æbˈsenʃə, -ʃiə, -tiə/ adv. in (his, her, or their) absence.

inactivate v.tr. make inactive or inoperative. □ **inactivation** n.

inactive adj. **1** not active or inclined to act. **2** passive. **3** sedentary, indolent (an inactive lifestyle). **4** not participating fully in a club, team, etc. (an inactive member). □ **inactively** adv. **inactivity** n.

inadequate adj. (often foll. by to) **1** not adequate; insufficient. **2** (of a person) incompetent; unable to

inability n.	**inaccessible** adj.	**inaccuracy** n. (pl. **-ies**).	**inaccurately** adv.
inaccessibility n.	**inaccessibly** adv.	**inaccurate** adj.	**inaction** n.

deal with a situation. □ **inadequacy** n. (pl. **-ies**). **inadequately** adv.

inadvertent adj. **1** (of an action) unintentional. **2 a** not properly attentive. **b** negligent. □ **inadvertence** n. **inadvertently** adv.

inane /ɪˈneɪn/ adj. **1** silly, senseless (inane remarks). **2** literary empty, void. □ **inanely** adv. **inanity** /-ˈænɪti/ n. (pl. **-ies**).

inanimate adj. **1** not animate; not endowed with (esp. animal) life. **2** lifeless; showing no sign of life. **3** spiritless, dull; lacking energy and vitality.

inapt adj. **1** not apt or suitable. **2** unskilful, awkward. ¶See INEPT. □ **inaptitude** n. **inaptly** adv.

inarticulate adj. **1** unable to speak distinctly or express oneself clearly or fluently. **2** (of speech, a sound, etc.) **a** not articulate; indistinctly pronounced. **b** having no distinct meaning; unintelligible (inarticulate gibberish). **3** not clearly or well expressed (an inarticulate speech). **4** unable to speak (inarticulate with anger). **5** not expressed; unspoken. **6** Zool. & Bot. not jointed or hinged. □ **inarticulately** adv. **inarticulateness** n.

inartistic adj. **1** not following the principles of art. **2 a** lacking skill or talent in art. **b** not appreciating art. □ **inartistically** adv.

inasmuch adv. (foll. by as) **1** since, because, seeing or considering that. **2** in so far as, to the extent that.

inaugural /ɪˈnɒɡjʊrəl, -ɡɜr-/ ● adj. **1** of or forming part of an inauguration or inauguration ceremony. **2** (of a lecture, series, etc.) first in a series or course. ● n. an inaugural speech, ceremony, etc.

inaugurate /ɪˈnɒɡjʊˌreɪt, -ɡɜr-/ v.tr. **1** admit (a person) formally to office. **2** open or dedicate (a building etc.) to public use by a ceremony. **3 a** begin, introduce, initiate (the moon landing inaugurated a new era in space exploration). **b** enter into (an undertaking, course of action, etc.) formally or ceremoniously. □ **inauguration** n.

inauspicious adj. **1** unpropitious. **2** unlucky. □ **inauspiciously** adv. **inauspiciousness** n.

in-basket n. N Amer. a tray on an office desk etc. for incoming documents, letters, etc.

in-between informal ● attrib.adj. intermediate. ● n. a person or thing that fills, occupies, or takes up an intermediate space, position, or attitude.

inboard ● adj. & adv. (situated) within or towards the centre of a boat, aircraft, vehicle, etc. ● n. esp. N Amer. **1** a boat equipped with a motor mounted within the hull. **2** a motor so mounted.

inborn adj. **1** (of a quality etc.) innate, existing from birth. **2** (of a disorder etc.) congenital and hereditary.

inbound ● adj. coming in, headed inward, or homeward bound. ● v.tr. Basketball throw (the ball) in bounds from the sidelines.

inbounds attrib.adj. Basketball (of a pass) thrown in bounds from the sidelines.

inbred adj. **1** inborn, innate, inherent. **2** characterized or produced by inbreeding.

inbreeding n. breeding from closely related animals or persons. □ **inbreed** v.tr. & intr. (past and past part. **inbred**).

Inc. abbr. **1** N Amer. Incorporated. **2** (**inc.**) including, included.

Inca /ˈɪŋkə/ n. a member of a S American Aboriginal people who established an empire in the central Andes before the Spanish conquest in the early 16th c. □ **Incan** adj.

incalculable adj. **1** too great for calculation. **2** that cannot be estimated or reckoned beforehand. **3** (of a person, character, etc.) uncertain, unpredictable. □ **incalculability** n. **incalculably** adv.

incandescent adj. **1** (of an electric or other light) produced by a glowing white-hot filament. **2** glowing with heat. **3** becoming warm or intense in feeling etc. □ **incandescence** n. **incandescently** adv.

incantation n. **1 a** a magical formula chanted or spoken. **b** the use of this. **2** a spell or charm. □ **incant** v.tr. & intr. **incantatory** adj.

incapable adj. **1** (often foll. by of) **a** incompetent, not capable. **b** lacking the required quality or characteristic (favourable or adverse) for a specified purpose, action, etc. (incapable of hurting anyone). **2** not, esp. legally, capable of rational conduct or of managing one's own affairs. □ **incapability** n. **incapably** adv.

incapacitate v.tr. **1** render incapable or unfit. **2** disqualify, esp. legally. □ **incapacitation** n.

incapacity n. (pl. **-ies**) **1** inability; lack of the necessary power or resources. **2** legal disqualification. **3** an instance of incapacity.

incarcerate /ɪnˈkɑrsəˌreɪt/ v.tr. imprison or confine. □ **incarceration** n. **incarcerator** n.

incarnate ● adj. /ɪnˈkɑrnət/ **1** (of a person, spirit, quality, etc.) embodied in flesh, esp. in human form (is the devil incarnate). **2** represented in a recognizable or typical form (folly incarnate). ● v.tr. /ɪnˈkɑrneɪt/ **1** embody in flesh or esp. a human form. **2** put (an idea etc.) into concrete form. **3** (of a person etc.) be the living embodiment or type of (a quality etc.).

incarnation n. **1 a** the form, appearance, or mode of presentation assumed by a person or thing at a particular time (the party's present incarnation). **b** the period of time spent in such an incarnation. **2 a** the embodiment of a deity etc. in esp. human flesh. **b** (**the Incarnation**) (in Christian theology) the embodiment of God the Son in human flesh as Jesus Christ. **3** (often foll. by of) a living type or embodiment (of a quality etc.) (she's the incarnation of femininity).

incendiary /ɪnˈsendiəri/ ● adj. **1** (of a substance or device, esp. a bomb) designed to cause fires. **2** of or relating to the malicious setting on fire of property. **3** tending to stir up strife. **4** informal powerful, impressive (an incendiary guitar solo). ● n. (pl. **-ies**) **1** an incendiary bomb or device. **2 a** an arsonist. **b** a person who stirs up strife; an agitator.

---

inadmissibility n.
inadmissible adj.
inadmissibly adv.
inadvisability n.
inadvisable adj.
inalienability n.
inalienable adj.
inalienably adv.

inapparent adj.
inapparently adv.
inapplicability n.
inapplicable adj.
inapplicably adv.
inappreciation n.
inappreciative adj.
inappropriate adj.

inappropriately adv.
inappropriateness n.
inattention n.
inattentive adj.
inattentively adv.
inattentiveness n.
inaudibility n.
inaudible adj.

inaudibly adv.
inauthentic adj.
inauthenticity n.
incaution n.
incautious adj.
incautiously adv.

incense¹ /'ɪnsens/ • n. **1** a gum or spice producing a sweet smell when burned. **2** the smoke or perfume of this, used esp. in religious ceremonies. • v.tr. **1 a** treat or perfume (a person or thing) with incense. **b** suffuse with fragrance. **2** burn incense to (a deity etc.).

incense² /ɪn'sens/ v.tr. (often foll. by at, with, against) enrage; make angry.

incentive /ɪn'sentɪv/ • n. **1** (often foll. by to) a motive or incitement, esp. to action. **2** a payment or concession to stimulate greater output by workers. • adj. serving to motivate or incite. □ **incentivize** v.tr.

inception /ɪn'sepʃən/ n. a beginning.

incessant /ɪn'sesənt/ adj. unceasing, continual, repeated. □ **incessancy** n. **incessantly** adv.

incest /'ɪnsest/ n. sexual intercourse between parent and child or grandchild, or siblings or half-siblings.

incestuous adj. **1** involving incest. **2** unwholesomely close; interconnected (the incestuous literary world). □ **incestuously** adv. **incestuousness** n.

inch • n. **1** a unit of linear measure equal to one-twelfth of a foot (2.54 cm). **2 a** (as a unit of rainfall) a quantity that would cover a horizontal surface to a depth of 1 inch. **b** (of atmospheric or other pressure) an amount of pressure that balances the weight of a column of mercury 1 inch high. **3** (as a unit of scale on a map) so many inches representing 1 mile on the ground. **4** a small amount (usu. with neg.: would not budge an inch). • v.tr. & intr. move gradually in a specified way (inched forward). □ **by inches 1** only just (missed me by inches). **2** gradually (dying by inches). **every inch 1** (often foll. by a, the) entirely (looked every inch a lady). **2** (usu. foll by of) the whole distance or area (combed every inch of the garden). **give a person an inch and he** (or **she**) **will take a mile** a person once conceded to will demand much. **inch by inch** gradually; bit by bit. **within an inch of** almost to the point of. **within an inch of one's life 1** extremely severely. **2** almost to death.

inchoate /ɪn'kəʊət, -eit, 'ɪn-/ adj. **1** incipient, just begun. **2** undeveloped, rudimentary, unformed.

inchworm n. the caterpillar of the geometer moth.

incidence n. **1** (often foll. by of) the fact, manner, or rate of occurrence or action of a phenomenon among a group of people (high incidence of suicide). **2** the range, scope, or extent of a thing or a thing's influence. **3** Physics the way in which esp. a ray of light strikes a surface. **4** the act or an instance of falling upon, affecting, or coming into contact with a thing.

incident • n. **1 a** an event or occurrence. **b** a minor or detached event attracting general attention or noteworthy in some way. **2 a** a hostile clash, esp. of troops of countries at war (a border incident). **b** an accident, public disturbance, or other trouble (the night passed without incident). **3** a distinct piece of action in a play or a poem. **4** Law a privilege, burden, etc., attaching to an obligation or right. • adj. **1 a** (often foll. by to) apt to happen. **b** (foll. by to) naturally connected with or forming an expected part of something. **2** (often foll. by on, upon) (of light etc.) falling upon or striking against a surface.

incidental • adj. **1** (often foll. by to) having a minor role in relation to a more important thing, event, etc. **b** not essential. **2** (foll. by to) liable to happen. **3** (foll. by on, upon) following as a subordinate event. **4** (of an expense or charge) incurred apart from the main sum disbursed. • n. (usu. in pl.) a minor detail, expense, event, etc.

incidentally adv. **1** by the way; as a further thought or unconnected remark. **2** in an incidental way.

incinerate /ɪn'sɪnə,reit/ v.tr. destroy completely by burning; reduce to ashes. □ **incineration** n.

incinerator n. a furnace or apparatus for burning esp. waste to ashes.

incipient /ɪn'sɪpiənt/ adj. **1** beginning. **2** in an initial or early stage. □ **incipiently** adv.

incise /ɪn'saɪz/ v.tr. **1** cut into or make a cut in. **2** engrave (letters, an inscription, etc.). □ **incised** adj.

incision /ɪn'sɪʒən/ n. **1 a** a cut; a division produced by cutting. **b** the esp. initial cut through the surface of the body made during surgery. **2** the act of cutting into a thing.

incisive /ɪn'saɪsɪv/ adj. **1** mentally sharp; acute. **2** clear and effective. **3** (of a comment etc.) cutting, penetrating. □ **incisively** adv. **incisiveness** n.

incisor /ɪn'saɪzər/ n. a sharp cutting tooth, esp. in humans, any of the eight at the front of the mouth.

incite /ɪn'saɪt/ v.tr. (often foll. by to) urge or stir up. □ **incitement** n.

incivility n. (pl. **-ies**) **1** rudeness, discourtesy. **2** a rude or discourteous act.

incl. abbr. **1** including. **2** inclusive.

inclement adj. (of the weather or climate) severe, esp. cold, rainy, or stormy. □ **inclemency** n. (pl. **-ies**).

inclination n. **1** (often foll. by to) a disposition, tendency, or propensity. **2** (often foll. by for) a liking or affection. **3 a** a leaning, slope, or slant. **b** the amount of the deviation (of a surface etc.) from the normal horizontal or vertical position. **4** the act or action of bending towards something, esp. a bending of the body or head in a bow. **5** Math. the difference of direction of two lines or planes, esp. as measured by the angle between them. **6** the dip of a magnetic needle. •

incline • v. **1** tr. (usu. in passive; often foll. by to, for, or to + infin.) **a** make (a person, feelings, etc.) willing or favourably disposed (am inclined to think so). **b** give a specified tendency to (a thing) (the door is inclined to bang). **2** intr. **a** be disposed (I incline to think so). **b** (often foll. by to, towards) tend. **3** intr. & tr. lean or turn away from a given direction (the land inclines towards the shore). **4** tr. bend (the head, body, or oneself) forward, downward, or toward a thing. • n. **1** a slope, esp. on a road or railway. **2** an inclined plane or surface. □ **incline one's ear** (often foll. by to) listen favourably.

inclined adj. **1** sloping, slanted. **2** having a natural ability in a specified subject (musically inclined).

inclined plane n. a sloping plane, esp. as a means of reducing the force needed to raise a load.

include v.tr. **1** involve, comprise, or reckon in as part of a whole. **2** treat or regard as part of the whole.

including prep. if one takes into account, inclusive of.

inclusion n. **1** the act of including someone or something. **2 a** the fact or condition of being included. **b** an instance of this. **3** a thing which is included.

inclusive adj. **1** (often foll. by of) including, comprising. **2** with the inclusion of the extreme limits stated (pages 7 to 26 inclusive). **3** including all the normal services etc. (a hotel offering inclusive terms). **4 a** not excluding any section of society. **b** (of language) deliberately non-sexist, esp. avoiding the use of masculine pronouns to cover men and women. □ **inclusively** adv. **inclusiveness** n. **inclusivity** n.

incognito /,ɪnkɒg'niːtəʊ/ • adj. & adv. with one's name or identity kept secret (travelling incognito). • n. (pl. **-os**) **1** a person who is incognito. **2** the pretended identity or anonymous character of such a person.

incoherent adj. **1** (of a person) unable to speak intelligibly. **2** (of speech, thought, etc.) disjointed, lacking logic or consistency. ☐ **incoherence** n. **incoherency** n. (pl. **-ies**). **incoherently** adv.

income /'ɪnkʌm, 'ɪŋkəm/ n. the money or other assets received, esp. periodically or in a year, from one's business, work, investments, etc.

income group n. a section of the population determined by income.

incomer /'ɪn,kʌmər/ n. a person who comes in.

income tax n. a tax levied on income.

incoming ● adj. **1 a** coming in (incoming calls). **b** starting, beginning (incoming students). **2** succeeding another person or persons (the incoming tenant). **3** (of profit) accruing. ● n. the act of arriving or entering.

incommensurable ● adj. **1** (often foll. by with) having no common standard of measurement; not comparable in respect of magnitude or value. **2** (foll. by with) not worthy of being compared with; utterly disproportionate to. **3** Math. **a** (often foll. by with) (of a magnitude or magnitudes) having no common factor, integral or fractional. **b** irrational. ● n. (usu. in pl.) an incommensurable quantity. ☐ **incommensurability** n. **incommensurably** adv.

incommensurate adj. **1** (often foll. by with, to) out of proportion; inadequate. **2** = INCOMMENSURABLE adj. 1.

incommunicable adj. **1** that cannot be communicated or shared. **2** that cannot be uttered or told. **3** that does not communicate; uncommunicative. ☐ **incommunicability** n.

incommunicado /ˌɪnkəˌmjuːˈnɪˈkædoː/ adj. & adv. **1** without or deprived of the means of communication with others. **2** in solitary confinement (the prisoner was held incommunicado).

incomparable adj. **1** without an equal; matchless. **2** (often foll. by with, to) not to be compared. ☐ **incomparability** n. **incomparably** adv.

incompatible adj. **1** opposed in character; discordant. **2** (often foll. by with) not consistent or in logical agreement. **3** (of persons) unable to live, work, etc., together in harmony. **4** (of drugs) not suitable for taking at the same time. **5** (of equipment etc.) not capable of being used in combination with some other item. ☐ **incompatibility** n.

incompetent ● adj. **1 a** not qualified or able to perform a particular task or function (an incompetent builder). **b** (of a witness, evidence, etc.) not legally qualified or qualifying. **2** showing a lack of skill (an incompetent performance). **3** Med. (esp. of a valve or sphincter) not able to perform its function. ● n. an incompetent person. ☐ **incompetence** n. **incompetency** n. (pl. **-ies**). **incompetently** adv.

incomplete adj. **1** not complete, finished, or fully formed. **2** imperfect, lacking something. **3** Football (of a forward pass) not completed. ☐ **incompletely** adv. **incompleteness** n. **incompletion** n.

inconceivable adj. **1** unthinkable, unimaginable. **2** unbelievable. ☐ **inconceivability** n. **inconceivably** adv.

inconclusive adj. (of an argument, evidence, or action) not leading to a definite conclusion or result. ☐ **inconclusively** adv. **inconclusiveness** n.

incongruous adj. **1** not appropriate; out of place. **2** (often foll. by with) discordant, inconsistent; disagreeing in character or qualities. **3** having disparate or inharmonious parts or elements. ☐ **incongruity** n. (pl. **-ies**). **incongruously** adv.

inconnu /'ɪnkənuː/ n. (pl. same) a predatory freshwater salmonid game fish Stenodus leucichthys, of the Eurasian and N American Arctic.

inconsequent adj. **1** irrelevant. **2** lacking logical sequence. **3** (of ideas or subjects) disconnected; haphazard. ☐ **inconsequence** n.

inconsequential adj. **1** trivial, unimportant, of no consequence. **2** = INCONSEQUENT. ☐ **inconsequentiality** n. (pl. **-ies**). **inconsequentially** adv.

inconsiderable adj. **1** of small size, value, etc. **2** not worth considering.

inconsiderate adj. **1** lacking or showing a lack of consideration or regard for the feelings of others. **2** (of a person or action) thoughtless, rash. ☐ **inconsiderately** adv. **inconsiderateness** n.

inconsistent adj. **1** acting at variance with one's own principles or former conduct. **2** (often foll. by with) not in keeping; discordant, at variance. **3** (of a single thing) incompatible or discordant; having self-contradictory parts. ☐ **inconsistency** n. (pl. **-ies**). **inconsistently** adv.

inconspicuous adj. **1** not conspicuous; not easily noticed. **2** Bot. (of flowers) small, pale, or green. ☐ **inconspicuously** adv.

inconstant adj. **1** (of a person) fickle, changeable. **2** frequently changing; variable, irregular. ☐ **inconstancy** n. (pl. **-ies**). **inconstantly** adv.

incontinent adj. **1** unable to control movements of the bowels or bladder or both. **2** lacking self-restraint, esp. in regard to sexual desire; promiscuous. **3** unrestrained, unchecked (incontinent bombing). ☐ **incontinence** n.

incontrovertible /ˌɪnkɒntrəˈvɜrtɪbəl/ adj. indisputable, indubitable. ☐ **incontrovertibility** n. **incontrovertibly** adv.

inconvenience ● n. **1** lack of suitability to personal requirements or ease. **2** a cause or instance of this. ● v.tr. cause inconvenience to.

inconvenient adj. causing trouble, difficulty, or discomfort; not convenient. ☐ **inconveniently** adv.

incorporate v. /ɪn'kɔrpəˌreɪt/ **1** tr. (often foll. by in, with) unite; form into one body or whole. **2** intr. become incorporated. **3** tr. combine (ingredients) into one substance. **4** tr. admit as a member of a company etc. **5** tr. combine or form into an organization, esp. constitute as a legal corporation. ☐ **incorporation** n. **incorporator** n.

incorporated adj. forming a legal corporation.

incorporeal adj. **1** without a body or material form. **2** of or characteristic of immaterial beings.

incorrect adj. **1** not in accordance with fact; wrong. **2** not in accordance with accepted standards (incorrect behaviour). ☐ **incorrectly** adv. **incorrectness** n.

incorrigible /ɪn'kɒrɪdʒɪbəl/ ● adj. **1** (of a person or habit) incurably bad or depraved. **2** not readily improved. ● n. an incorrigible person. ☐ **incorrigibility** n. **incorrigibly** adv.

---

incombustibility n.	**incomprehensibly** adv.
incombustible adj.	**incomprehension** n.
incomprehensibility n.	**incompressible** adj.
incomprehensible adj.	**inconsolability** n.

inconsolable adj.	**incontestably** adv.
inconsolably adv.	**inconvenient** adj.
incontestability n.	**inconveniently** adv.
incontestable adj.	**incoordination** n.

incorruptible /ˌɪnkəˈrʌptɪbəl/ adj. **1** unable to be corrupted, esp. unable to be bribed. **2** not susceptible to decay; everlasting. □ **incorruptibility** n. **incorruptibly** adv.

increase ● v. **1** tr. & intr. make or become greater in size, amount, etc., or more numerous. **2** intr. advance (in quality, attainment, etc.). **3** tr. intensify (a quality). ● n. **1** the act or process of becoming greater or more numerous; growth, enlargement. **2** (of people, animals, or plants) growth in numbers; multiplication. **3** the amount or extent of an increase. □ **on the increase** increasing, esp. in frequency. □ **increasingly** adv.

incredible adj. **1** that cannot be believed. **2** informal amazing, extraordinary (we had an incredible time in Scotland). □ **incredibility** n. **incredibly** adv.

incredulous adj. **1** unwilling to believe, skeptical. **2** showing disbelief (an incredulous look). □ **incredulity** n. **incredulously** adv.

increment /ˈɪnkrəmənt/ n. **1 a** the action or process of increasing or becoming greater, esp. gradually. **b** an increase or addition, esp. one of a series on a fixed scale. **c** the amount of this. **2** Math. a small amount by which a variable quantity increases. □ **incremental** adj. **incrementalism** n. **incrementally** adv.

incriminate /ɪnˈkrɪmɪˌneɪt/ v.tr. **1** (esp. as **incriminating** adj.) tend to prove the guilt of (incriminating evidence). **2** involve in an accusation. **3** charge with a crime. □ **incrimination** n. **incriminatory** adj.

incubate /ˈɪŋkjʊbeɪt/ v. **1** tr. sit on or artificially heat (eggs) in order to bring forth young birds etc. **2** tr. maintain (cells, micro-organisms, etc.) in a controlled environment suitable for growth and development. **3** intr. **a** sit on eggs; brood. **b** undergo incubation. **4** tr. & intr. develop or grow slowly (incubate a plan).

incubation n. **1** the act of incubating. **2 a** (in full **incubation period**) the period between exposure to an infection and the appearance of the first symptoms. **b** the processes occurring during this.

incubator n. **1** an apparatus used to provide a suitable temperature and environment for a premature baby or one of low birth weight. **2** an apparatus used to hatch eggs or grow micro-organisms under artificially controlled conditions. **3** a place, organization, etc. providing a supportive and nurturing environment for the growth of an idea, business, etc.

incubus /ˈɪŋkjʊbəs/ n. (pl. **-buses** or **-bi** /-ˌbaɪ/) **1** a male demon believed to have sexual intercourse with sleeping women. **2** a nightmare. **3** a person or thing that oppresses or troubles like a nightmare.

inculcate /ˈɪnkʌlˌkeɪt/ v.tr. (often foll. by in) urge or impress (a fact, habit, idea, etc.) persistently (inculcate in young people a respect for the law). □ **inculcation** n.

incumbency n. (pl. **-ies**) the position, tenure, or sphere of an incumbent.

incumbent ● adj. **1** currently holding office (the incumbent prime minister). **2** (foll. by on, upon) resting or falling upon a person as a duty or obligation (it is incumbent on you to warn them). **3** esp. literary (often foll. by on) lying, pressing. ● n. the holder of an office or post.

incur v.tr. (**incurred**, **incurring**) suffer, experience, or become subject to (something unpleasant) as a result of one's own behaviour etc. (incurred huge debts).

incurable adj. **1** unable to be cured. **2** inveterate; not likely to change (an incurable romantic). □ **incurability** n. **incurably** adv.

incursion /ɪnˈkɜrʒən/ n. **1** an invasion or attack, esp. when sudden or brief. **2** an interruption or disturbance.

Ind. abbr. **1** Independent. **2 a** India. **b** Indian. **3** Indiana.

indebted adj. (usu. foll. by to) **1** owing gratitude or obligation. **2** owing money. □ **indebtedness** n.

indecent adj. **1** offending against recognized standards of decency. **2** unbecoming; highly unsuitable (with indecent haste). □ **indecency** n. (pl. **-ies**). **indecently** adv.

indecent exposure n. the intentional act of publicly and indecently exposing one's body, esp. the genitals.

indecisive adj. **1** not decisive or conclusive (an indecisive battle). **2** (of a person) undecided, hesitating. **3** characteristically unable to make decisions. □ **indecisively** adv. **indecisiveness** n.

indecorous adj. **1** improper. **2** in bad taste.

indecorum n. **1** lack of decorum. **2** improper behaviour.

indeed ● adv. **1** in truth; really (they are, indeed, a remarkable family). **2** expressing emphasis or intensification (indeed it is). **3** admittedly (there are indeed exceptions). **4** in point of fact (if indeed such a thing is possible). **5** expressing an approving or ironic echo (who is this Mr. Smith? — who is he indeed?). ● interj. expressing irony, contempt, incredulity, etc.

indefatigable /ˌɪndɪˈfætɪɡəbəl/ adj. (of a person, quality, etc.) that cannot be tired out. □ **indefatigability** n. **indefatigably** adv.

indefensible adj. that cannot be defended, justified, or maintained in argument. □ **indefensibility** n. **indefensibly** adv.

indefinite adj. **1** not clearly defined or stated; vague. **2** of undetermined extent, amount or number; unlimited. **3** Grammar not determining the person, thing, time, etc., referred to. □ **indefiniteness** n.

indefinite article n. Grammar a word (a and an in English) preceding a noun and implying lack of specificity (as in bought me a book; government is an art).

indefinitely adv. **1** for an unlimited time (was postponed indefinitely). **2** in an indefinite manner; vaguely.

indefinite pronoun n. a pronoun indicating a person, amount, etc., without being definite or particular, e.g. any, some, anyone.

indelible /ɪnˈdeləbəl/ adj. **1** that cannot be rubbed out or (in abstract senses) removed; permanent. **2** (of ink etc.) that makes indelible marks. □ **indelibly** adv.

indelicate adj. **1** coarse, unrefined. **2** tactless. **3** tending to indecency. □ **indelicacy** n. (pl. **-ies**). **indelicately** adv.

indemnify /ɪnˈdemnəˌfaɪ/ v.tr. (**-ies**, **-ied**) **1** (often foll. by from, against) protect or secure (a person) against harm, loss, etc. **2** (often foll. by for) secure (a person) against legal responsibility for actions. **3** (often foll. by for) compensate (a person) for a loss, expenses, etc.

indemnity /ɪnˈdemnɪti/ n. (pl. **-ies**) **1 a** compensation for loss incurred. **b** a sum paid for this, esp. a sum exacted by a victor in war etc. as one condition of peace. **2** security against loss. **3** legal exemption from penalties etc. incurred. **4** Cdn the salary paid to a Member of Parliament or of a Legislative Assembly.

---

incuriosity n.
incurious adj.

indecipherable adj.
indecision n.

indefinable adj.

indefinably adv.

indent¹ ● *v.tr.* **1** start (a line of print or writing) further from the margin than other lines, e.g. to mark a new paragraph. **2** make toothlike notches in. **3** form deep recesses in (a coastline etc.). ● *n.* **1** an indentation in printing or writing; an indented line. **2** an incision in the edge of a thing.

indent² ● *v.tr.* **1** make a dent in the surface of (a thing). **2** impress (a mark etc.). ● *n.* a dent or depression in a surface.

indentation *n.* **1** the act or an instance of indenting; the process of being indented. **2** a cut or notch. **3** a zigzag. **4** a deep recess in a coastline etc.

indenture ● *n.* **1** (usu. in *pl.*) **a** a sealed agreement or contract. **b** a contract binding a person to service. **2** a formal list, certificate, voucher, etc. ● *v.tr.* bind (a person) by indentures, esp. as an apprentice or servant. □ **indentured** *adj.*

indépendantiste /æˈdeipãdãˈtiːst/ *Cdn* ● *n.* a person who supports the idea of Quebec independence; a sovereignist. ● *adj.* of or relating to the sovereignist movement in Quebec.

independence *n.* **1** (often foll. by *of*, *from*) the state of being independent. **2** the fact or process of becoming independent.

Independence Day *n.* a day celebrating the anniversary of national independence, esp. (*US*) July 4.

independent ● *adj.* **1 a** (often foll. by *of*) not depending on authority or control. **b** (of a state) self-governing. **2 a** not depending on another person for one's opinion or livelihood. **b** (of income or resources) making it unnecessary to earn one's living (*a woman of independent means*). **3** unwilling to be under an obligation to others. **4** *Politics* not belonging to or supported by a party. **5** not depending on something else for its validity, efficiency, value, etc. (*independent proof*). **6** impartial; originating or conducted outside a given institution, group, etc. (*an independent inquiry*). **7** (of broadcasting, a school, etc.) not supported by public funds. **8 a** (of a film, recording, etc.) produced without the support of a major studio, record label, etc. **b** (of a store, business, business person, etc.) not part of a chain or larger corporate structure (*an independent bookstore; an independent contractor*). **9** *Grammar* (of a clause) able to stand alone as a complete sentence. ● *n.* **1** a person who or thing which is independent, esp. a retailer whose store is not part of a chain. **2** a person who is politically independent. □ **independently** *adv.*

independent variable *n.* *Math.* a variable whose variation does not depend on that of another.

in-depth *attrib.adj.* thorough; done in depth.

indescribable *adj.* **1** too unusual or extreme to be described. **2** vague, indefinite. □ **indescribability** *n.* **indescribably** *adv.*

indeterminate *adj.* **1** not fixed in extent, character, etc. **2** left doubtful; vague. **3** *Math.* (of a quantity) not limited to a fixed value by the value of another quantity. **4** (of a judicial sentence) such that the convicted person's conduct determines the date of release. □ **indeterminacy** *n.* **indeterminately** *adv.*

index ● *n.* (*pl.* **indexes** or esp. in technical use **indices** /ˈɪndɪˌsiːz/) **1** an alphabetical list of names, subjects, etc., with references, usu. at the end of a book. **2** = CARD INDEX. **3** a scale relating the level of prices, wages, etc. at a particular time to those at a date taken as a base (*consumer price index*). **4** *Math.* **a** the exponent of a number. **b** the power to which it is raised. **5 a** a pointer, esp. on an instrument, showing a quantity, a position on a scale, etc. **b** (usu. foll. by *of*) a sign, token, or indication of something. **6** *Physics* a number expressing a physical property etc. in terms of a standard (*refractive index*). **7** *Computing* a set of items each of which specifies one of the records of a file and contains information about its address. ● *v.tr.* **1** provide (a book etc.) with an index. **2** enter in an index. **3** relate (wages etc.) to the value of a price index. **4** serve as an index to; indicate. □ **indexer** *n.*

indexation *n.* the adjustment in rates of payment etc. to reflect variations in the cost-of-living index or other economic indicator.

index card *n.* a small rectangular card made of heavy paper, used in writing or recording notes etc.

index finger *n.* the forefinger.

India ink *n.* esp. *N Amer.* **1** a black pigment made originally in China and Japan. **2** a dark ink made from this, used esp. in drawing and technical graphics.

Indian ● *n.* **1 a** a native or national of India. **b** a person of Indian descent. **2 a** a member of the Aboriginal peoples of N and S America, or their descendants. **b** any of the languages of the Aboriginal peoples of N and S America. **c** *Cdn* a status Indian. ¶Although the use of *Indian* in sense 2 has declined because it is thought to reflect Columbus's mistaken idea that he had landed in India in 1492, it is common in the usage of many Aboriginal people and embedded in legislation that is still in effect. It is also the only clear way to distinguish among the three general categories of Aboriginal people (Indians, Inuit, and Metis). ● *adj.* **1** of or relating to India, or to the subcontinent comprising India, Pakistan, and Bangladesh. **2** of or relating to the Aboriginal peoples of N and S America.

Indian agent *n.* *Cdn hist.* a person appointed by the Department of Indian Affairs to supervise government programs on a reserve or in a specific region.

Indian corn *n.* maize.

Indian elephant *n.* the elephant, *Elephas maximus*, of India, which is smaller than the African elephant.

Indian hemp *n.* = HEMP 1.

Indian ice cream *n.* *Cdn* (*BC*) a dessert or drink made from whipped soapberries, sugar, and water.

Indian paintbrush *n.* *N Amer.* any of various plants of the genus *Castilleja*, chiefly of western N America, with flowers hidden by brightly coloured bracts.

Indian summer *n.* **1** a period of unusually dry warm weather sometimes occurring in late autumn. **2** a late period (of life, of an epoch etc.) characterized by comparative calm.

Indian title *n.* *Cdn* the claim by Indians to rights of ownership of land by virtue of its being occupied by Indians before the arrival of Europeans.

India rubber *n.* = RUBBER¹ 1.

Indic /ˈɪndɪk/ ● *adj.* of or relating to a group of Indo-European languages comprising Sanskrit and the modern Indian languages which are its descendants. ● *n.* this language group.

indicate *v.tr.* (often foll. by *that* + clause) **1** point out; make known; show. **2** be a sign or symptom of; express the presence of. **3** (often in *passive*) suggest; call for; require or show to be necessary (*stronger measures are indicated*). **4** admit to or state briefly (*indicated his disapproval*). **5** (of a gauge etc.) give as a reading.

indication n. **1 a** the act or an instance of indicating. **b** something that suggests or indicates; a sign or symptom. **2** something indicated or suggested. **3** a reading given by a gauge or instrument.

indicative /ɪnˈdɪkətɪv/ ● adj. **1** (foll. by of) suggestive; serving as an indication. **2** Grammar (of a mood) denoting simple statement of a fact. ● n. Grammar **1** the indicative mood. **2** a verb in this mood.

indicator n. **1** a person or thing that indicates, esp. performance, change, etc. (economic indicators). **2 a** a device indicating the condition of a machine etc. **b** a pointer, light, etc., which draws attention or gives warning. **3** a recording instrument attached to an apparatus, e.g. a dial indicating the movement of an elevator. **4** a substance which changes to a characteristic colour in the presence of a particular concentration of an ion, so indicating e.g. acidity. **5** Biol. a species or group which acts as a sign of particular environmental conditions (also attrib.: indicator species).

indices pl. of INDEX.

indict /ɪnˈdaɪt/ v.tr. **1** charge (a person) with a crime, esp. formally by legal process. **2** bring accusations against (a person or thing). □ **indicter** n.

indictable adj. **1** (of an offence) rendering the person who commits it liable to be charged with a crime. **2** (of a person) so liable.

indictable offence n. Cdn & Brit. a serious criminal offence, such as murder, which is triable by way of indictment (compare SUMMARY CONVICTION OFFENCE).

indictment n. **1** the act of indicting or the state of being indicted. **2 a** a formal accusation. **b** a legal process in which this is made. **c** a document containing a charge. **3** something that serves to condemn (the book is an indictment of the government).

indie informal ● n. **1** an independent record or film company. **2 a** a musician or band whose music is recorded by an independent company. **b** a film produced by an independent company. ● adj. **1** (of a pop group, record label, film, etc.) independent, not belonging to one of the major record companies or film studios. **2** characteristic of the deliberately unpolished or uncommercialized style of indie bands.

indifference n. **1** lack of interest or attention. **2** unimportance (a matter of indifference).

indifferent adj. **1** (foll. by to) having no partiality for or against; having no interest in or sympathy for. **2** neither good nor bad; average, mediocre. **3 a** not especially good. **b** fairly bad. **4** (often prec. by very) decidedly inferior. □ **indifferently** adv.

indigene /ˈɪndɪdʒiːn/ n. a native or aboriginal inhabitant of a region etc.

indigenize /ɪnˈdɪdʒənaɪz/ v.tr. make indigenous; subject to native influence. □ **indigenization** n.

indigenous /ɪnˈdɪdʒənəs/ adj. **1 a** (esp. of flora or fauna) originating naturally in a region. **b** (of people) born in a region. **c** (of a musical style, sport, etc.) characteristic of or originating in a region. **2** (foll. by to) belonging naturally to a place. **3** of, pertaining to, or concerned with the aboriginal inhabitants of a region. □ **indigenously** adv. **indigenousness** n.

indigent /ˈɪndɪdʒənt/ ● adj. needy, poor. ● n. an indigent person. □ **indigence** n.

indigestible /ˌɪndɪˈdʒestəbəl/ adj. **1** difficult or impossible to digest. **2** too complex or awkward to read or comprehend easily. □ **indigestibility** n.

indigestion /ˌɪndɪˈdʒestʃən/ n. **1** difficulty in digesting food. **2** pain or discomfort caused by this.

indignant /ɪnˈdɪɡnənt/ adj. feeling or showing scornful anger. □ **indignantly** adv.

indignation /ˌɪndɪɡˈneɪʃən/ n. scornful anger at supposed unjust or unfair conduct or treatment.

indignity /ɪnˈdɪɡnɪti/ n. (pl. **-ies**) **1** unworthy treatment. **2** a slight or insult. **3** the humiliating quality of something (the indignity of my position).

indigo /ˈɪndɪˌɡoː/ ● n. (pl. **-os**) **1 a** a natural blue dye obtained from the indigo plant. **b** a synthetic form of this dye. **2** any plant of the genus Indigofera. **3** (in full **indigo blue**) a colour between blue and violet in the spectrum. ● adj. of this colour.

indigo bunting n. a N American bunting, Passerina cyanea, the male of which has bright blue plumage.

indirect adj. **1 a** allusive; not going straight to the point (an indirect answer). **b** not acting or exercised with direct force; roundabout. **2** (of a route etc.) not straight; circuitous. **3** not directly sought or aimed at (indirect result). **4** (of lighting) from a concealed source and diffusely reflected. □ **indirection** n. **indirectly** adv. **indirectness** n.

indirect object n. Grammar a person or thing affected by a verbal action but not primarily acted on, e.g. him in give him the book.

indirect question n. Grammar a question in reported speech, e.g. they asked who I was.

indirect speech n. (esp. N Amer. also **indirect discourse**) = REPORTED SPEECH.

indirect tax n. a tax that is paid to the government by the taxpayer through an intermediary rather than directly, e.g. sales tax.

indiscernible adj. that cannot be discerned or distinguished from another. □ **indiscernibility** n.

indiscreet adj. **1** not discreet; revealing secrets. **2** injudicious, unwary. □ **indiscreetly** adv.

indiscrete adj. not divided into distinct parts.

indiscretion n. **1** lack of discretion; indiscreet conduct. **2** an indiscreet action, remark, etc.

indiscriminate /ˌɪndɪˈskrɪmɪnət/ adj. **1** (of an action etc.) not distinguished by discernment or discrimination; haphazard, not selective. **2** (of a person) acting without careful judgment; not exercising discrimination. □ **indiscriminately** adv.

indispensable ● adj. **1** (often foll. by to, for) that cannot be dispensed with; necessary. **2** (of a law, duty, etc.) that is not to be set aside. ● n. an indispensable person or thing. □ **indispensably** adv.

indispose v.tr. **1** (often foll. by for, or to + infin.) make unfit or unable. **2** (often foll. by toward, from, or to + infin.) make averse.

indisposed adj. **1** slightly unwell. **2** averse or unwilling.

indisposition n. **1** ill health, a slight or temporary ailment. **2** disinclination.

indisputable adj. **1** that cannot be disputed. **2** unquestionable. □ **indisputability** n. **indisputably** adv.

indissoluble /ˌɪndɪˈsɒljʊbəl/ adj. **1** that cannot be dissolved or decomposed. **2** lasting, stable (an indissoluble bond). □ **indissolubly** adv.

indistinct adj. **1** not distinct. **2** confused, obscure. □ **indistinctly** adv. **indistinctness** n.

indistinguishable adj. (often foll. by from) not distinguishable. □ **indistinguishability** n. **indistinguishably** adv.

indium /ˈɪndɪəm/ n. a soft silvery-white metallic element occurring naturally in zinc blende etc., used for electroplating and in semiconductors.

individual ● *adj.* **1** single, separate. **2** particular, special; not general. **3** having a distinct character. **4** characteristic of a particular person. **5** designed for use by one person (*individual portions*). ● *n.* **1** a single human being as distinct from a family or group. **2** a person (*a most unpleasant individual*). **3** a person who does not conform to the majority. **4** a single member of a class or group.

individualism *n.* **1** the habit or principle of being independent and self-reliant. **2** a social theory favouring the free action of individuals. **3** self-centred feeling or conduct; egoism. **4** = INDIVIDUALITY 1. □ **individualist** *n.* **individualistic** *adj.* **individualistically** *adv.*

individuality *n.* (*pl.* **-ies**) **1** the sum of the attributes which distinguish one person or thing from others of the same kind; strongly marked individual character. **2** the fact or condition of separate existence.

individualize *v.tr.* **1** give an individual character to. **2** specify. **3** (esp. as **individualized** *adj.*) personalize or tailor to suit the individual (*individualized training course*). □ **individualization** *n.*

individually *adv.* **1** personally; in an individual capacity. **2** in a distinctive manner. **3** one by one; not collectively.

individuate /ˌɪndɪˈvɪdʒʊˌeɪt/ *v.tr.* individualize; form into an individual or distinct entity. □ **individuation** *n.*

indivisible *adj.* **1** not divisible. **2** not distributable among a number. □ **indivisibility** *n.* **indivisibly** *adv.*

Indo-Aryan /ˌɪndoˈerɪən/ ● *n.* **1** a member of any of the Indo-European peoples of India. **2** the Indic group of languages. ● *adj.* of the Indo-Aryans or Indo-Aryan.

Indo-Canadian ● *n.* a Canadian born in the Indian subcontinent, esp. India, or one of Indian descent. ● *adj.* of or relating to Indo-Canadians.

indoctrinate *v.tr.* **1** teach (a person or group) systematically or for a long period to accept (esp. partisan or tendentious) ideas uncritically. **2** teach, instruct. □ **indoctrination** *n.* **indoctrinator** *n.*

Indo-European ● *adj.* **1** of the family of languages spoken over the greater part of Europe and Asia as far as N India. **2** of the hypothetical parent language of this family. ● *n.* **1** the Indo-European family of languages. **2** the hypothetical parent language of all languages belonging to this family. **3** (usu. in *pl.*) a speaker of an Indo-European language.

Indo-Iranian ● *adj.* of or relating to the subfamily of Indo-European languages spoken esp. in northern India and Iran. ● *n.* this subfamily.

indole /ˈɪndoːl/ *n.* an organic compound with a characteristic odour formed on the reduction of indigo.

indolent /ˈɪndələnt/ *adj.* **1** lazy; wishing to avoid activity or exertion. **2** *Med.* causing no pain (*an indolent tumour*). □ **indolence** *n.* **indolently** *adv.*

indomitable /ɪnˈdɒmɪtəbəl/ *adj.* **1** that cannot be subdued; unyielding. **2** stubbornly persistent. □ **indomitability** *n.* **indomitably** *adv.*

Indonesian /ˌɪndəˈniːʒən/ ● *n.* **1 a** a native or national of Indonesia in SE Asia. **b** a person of Indonesian descent. **2** a member of the chief pre-Malay population of the E Indies. **3 a** the western branch of the Austronesian language family. **b** = BAHASA. ● *adj.* of or relating to Indonesia or its people or language.

indoor *adj.* situated, carried on, or used within a building or under cover.

indoor-outdoor *adj.* N *Amer.* designating a sturdy carpet that can be used both inside and outside of a house etc.

indoors *adv.* into or within a building.

indubitable /ɪnˈdjuːbɪtəbəl, -ˈdjuː-/ *adj.* that cannot be doubted. □ **indubitably** *adv.*

induce /ɪnˈdjuːs, -ˈdjuːs/ *v.* **1** *tr.* (often foll. by *to* + infin.) prevail on; persuade. **2** *tr.* bring about; give rise to. **3** *tr.* & *intr. Med.* bring on (labour) artificially, esp. by use of drugs. **4** *tr.* produce (a current) by induction. **5** *tr. Physics* cause (radioactivity) by bombardment. **6** *tr.* infer; derive as a deduction. □ **inducer** *n.* **inducible** *adj.*

inducement *n.* **1** (often foll. by *to*) an attraction that leads one on. **2** a thing that induces (*a financial inducement*).

induct *v.tr.* (often foll. by *to, into*) **1 a** introduce formally into an office, position, etc. **b** introduce (a member of the clergy) formally into possession of a benefice. **2** introduce, initiate (*inducted into a secret brotherhood*). **3** admit as a new member (*inducted him into the band*). □ **inductee** *n.*

inductance *n. Electricity* **1** the property of an electric circuit that causes an electromotive force to be generated by a change in the current flowing. **2** INDUCTOR 1.

induction *n.* **1** the act or an instance of inducting or inducing. **2** *Med.* the process of bringing on (esp. labour) by artificial means. **3** *Logic* **a** the inference of a general law from particular instances (*compare* DEDUCTION 2a). **b** *Math.* a means of proving a theorem by showing that if it is true of any particular case it is true of the next case in a series, and then showing that it is indeed true in one particular case. **c** (foll. by *of*) the production of (facts) to prove a general statement. **4** *Electricity* **a** the production of an electric or magnetic state by the proximity (without contact) of an electrified or magnetized body. **b** the production of an electric current in a conductor by a change of magnetic field. **5** the drawing of a fuel mixture into the cylinders of an internal combustion engine.

induction coil *n.* a coil for generating intermittent high voltage from a direct current.

inductive *adj.* **1** (of reasoning etc.) of or based on induction. **2** of electric or magnetic induction. □ **inductively** *adv.* **inductiveness** *n.*

inductor *n.* **1** *Electricity* a component (in a circuit) which possesses inductance. **2** a person who inducts or initiates.

indulge *v.* **1** *intr.* (often foll. by *in*) allow oneself to enjoy the pleasure of something. **2** *tr.* yield freely to (a desire etc.). **3** *tr.* gratify the wishes of; favour (*indulged them with money*). **4** *refl.* give free rein to one's inclination or liking. **5** *intr. informal* take alcoholic liquor.

indulgence *n.* **1 a** the act of indulging. **b** the state of being indulgent. **c** lenient or liberal treatment. **2** something indulged in. **3** *Catholicism* the remission of punishment in purgatory, still due for sins even after sacramental absolution. **4** a privilege granted.

indulgent *adj.* **1** ready or too ready to overlook faults etc. **2** indulging or tending to indulge. □ **indulgently** *adv.*

industrial ● *adj.* **1 a** of or relating to industry or industries. **b** employed in industry (*industrial workers*). **2** designed or suitable for industrial use (*industrial alcohol*). **3** characterized by highly developed industries (*the industrial nations*). **4** of or relating to a form of popular dance music characterized by a heavy mechanical beat and a dissonant sound. ● *n.* **1** (in *pl.*) shares in industrial companies. **2** a promotional film profiling an industry, company, etc. □ **industrially** *adv.*

industrial arts *n.pl.* N *Amer.* woodworking, metalwork, etc., esp. as taught in schools etc.

industrial design *n.* the act or art of designing objects for manufacture. ☐ **industrial designer** *n.*

industrialism *n.* a social or economic system in which manufacturing industries are prevalent.

industrialist *n.* a person engaged in the management of an industrial enterprise.

industrialize *v.* **1** *tr.* introduce industries to (a country or region etc.). **2** *intr.* become industrialized. ☐ **industrialization** *n.*

industrial mall *n.* N Amer. a strip mall or plaza housing a number of individual industrial enterprises, usu. located in a suburban area.

industrial relations *n.pl.* **1** the relations between management and workers in industries. **2** the study or management of such relations.

Industrial Revolution *n.* the dramatic transformation of society resulting from the bulk of the working population turning from agriculture to industry, esp. in Britain in the second half of the 18th c. and the first half of the 19th c.

industrial-strength *adj.* (often *attrib.*) esp. N Amer. often *jocular* strong, powerful (*industrial-strength coffee*).

industrious *adj.* diligent, hard-working. ☐ **industriously** *adv.* **industriousness** *n.*

industry *n.* (*pl.* **-ies**) **1 a** a branch of trade or manufacture. **b** trade and manufacture collectively. **c** any commercial undertaking that provides services (*hospitality industry*). **2** concerted or copious activity (*a hive of industry*). **3 a** diligence. **b** *informal* the diligent study of a particular topic (*the Shakespeare industry*).

Indy *n.* **1** (in full **Indy 500**) the annual Indianapolis 500-mile motor race. **2** (usu. *attrib.*) any of a series of similar competitive circuit races.

Indycar *n.* **1** a rear-engine, turbocharged race car designed to compete in Indy racing. **2** (*attrib.*) = INDY 2 (*Indycar champion*).

inebriate ● *v.tr.* /ɪˈniːbrɪˌeɪt/ **1** make drunk; intoxicate. **2** excite. ● *adj.* /ɪˈniːbrɪət/ drunken. ● *n.* /ɪˈniːbrɪət/ a drunken person, esp. a habitual drunkard. ☐ **inebriated** *adj.* **inebriation** *n.*

inedible *adj.* not edible, esp. not suitable for eating (*compare* UNEATABLE). ☐ **inedibility** *n.*

ineffable /ɪnˈɛfəbəl/ *adj.* **1** unutterable; too great for description in words; indefinable. **2** that must not be uttered. ☐ **ineffability** *n.* **ineffably** *adv.*

ineffective *adj.* **1** not producing any effect or the desired effect. **2** (of a person) inefficient; not achieving results. ☐ **ineffectively** *adv.* **ineffectiveness** *n.*

ineffectual *adj.* **1 a** without effect. **b** not producing the desired or expected effect. **2** (of a person) lacking the ability to achieve results (*an ineffectual leader*). ☐ **ineffectuality** *n.* **ineffectually** *adv.*

inefficient *adj.* **1** (of a machine, process, etc.) wasting time or resources (*an inefficient heating system*). **2** (of a person or organization) failing to make the best use of the available time and resources. ☐ **inefficiency** *n.* **inefficiently** *adv.*

inelastic *adj.* **1** not elastic. **2** unadaptable, inflexible, unyielding. **3** *Econ.* (of demand or supply) unresponsive to, or varying less than in proportion to, changes in price. ☐ **inelastically** *adv.* **inelasticity** *n.*

inelegant *adj.* **1** not elegant. **2 a** unrefined. **b** (of a style) unpolished. ☐ **inelegance** *n.* **inelegantly** *adv.*

ineluctable *adj.* unable to be resisted or avoided; inescapable (*ineluctable fate*). ☐ **ineluctability** *n.* **ineluctably** *adv.*

inept /ɪnˈɛpt, ɪˈnɛpt/ *adj.* **1 a** unskilful, incompetent. **b** absurd, silly. **2** out of place; inappropriate. ¶ *Inapt* is more common in this sense. The difference is illustrated by *Her after-dinner speech was both inept and inapt*, i.e. both clumsy and inappropriate. ☐ **ineptitude** *n.* **ineptly** *adv.* **ineptness** *n.*

inequality *n.* (*pl.* **-ies**) **1 a** lack of equality between persons or things; disparity in size, number, quality, etc. **b** an instance of this. **2 a** a difference of rank or circumstance; social or economic disparity (*inequality between rich and poor*). **b** unfairness, inequity. **3** the state of being variable. **4** unevenness, irregularity. **5** *Math.* a formula affirming that two expressions are not equal.

inequity *n.* (*pl.* **-ies**) **1** unfairness, bias. **2** an instance of this.

ineradicable /ˌɪnɪˈrædɪkəbəl/ *adj.* unable to be eradicated or rooted out. ☐ **ineradicably** *adv.*

inert *adj.* **1** without inherent power of action, motion, or resistance. **2** without active chemical or other properties. **3** inactive, slow. **4** lacking vigour or interest. ☐ **inertly** *adv.* **inertness** *n.*

inert gas *n.* = NOBLE GAS.

inertia /ɪˈnɜːrʃə/ *n.* **1** *Physics* a property of matter by which it continues in its existing state of rest or uniform motion in a straight line, unless that state is changed by an external force. **2 a** inertness; lack of vigour or will to move. **b** a tendency to remain unchanged. ☐ **inertial** *adj.*

inestimable *adj.* too great, intense, precious, etc., to be estimated. ☐ **inestimably** *adv.*

inevitable /ɪnˈɛvɪtəbəl/ ● *adj.* **1 a** unavoidable; sure to happen. **b** that is bound to occur or appear. **2** *informal* that is tiresomely familiar. ● *n.* **1** (prec. by *the*) that which is inevitable. **2** an inevitable fact, event, truth, etc. ☐ **inevitability** *n.* **inevitably** *adv.*

inexhaustible *adj.* **1** that cannot be used up (*an inexhaustible resource*). **2** tireless (*an inexhaustible canoeist*). ☐ **inexhaustibility** *n.*

inexorable /ɪnˈɛksərəbəl/ *adj.* **1** relentless. **2** (of a person or attribute) that cannot be persuaded by request or entreaty. ☐ **inexorability** *n.* **inexorably** *adv.*

in extremis /ˌɪn ɛkˈstriːmɪs, -triːmɪs, -tremɪs/ *adj.* **1** at the point of death. **2** in great difficulties.

inextricable /ɪnˈɛkstrɪkəbəl, ˌɪnɪkˈstrɪk-/ *adj.* **1** (of a circumstance) that cannot be escaped from. **2** (of a knot, problem, etc.) that cannot be unravelled or solved. **3** intricately confused. ☐ **inextricably** *adv.*

INF *abbr.* intermediate-range nuclear force(s).

---

ineligibility *n.*
ineligible *adj.*
ineligibly *adv.*
inequitable *adj.*
inequitably *adv.*
inescapability *n.*
inescapable *adj.*

inescapably *adv.*
inessential *adj. & n.*
inexact *adj.*
inexactly *adv.*
inexactness *n.*
inexcusable *adj.*
inexcusably *adv.*

inexpediency *n.*
inexpedient *adj.*
inexpensive *adj.*
inexpensively *adv.*
inexpensiveness *n.*
inexperience *n.*
inexperienced *adj.*

inexpert *adj.*
inexpertly *adv.*
inexplicability *n.*
inexplicable *adj.*
inexplicably *adv.*
inexpressible *adj.*
inexpressibly *adv.*

infallible / ɪnˈfælɪbəl/ *adj.* **1** incapable of error. **2** (of a method, test, proof, etc.) unfailing; sure to succeed. **3** *Catholicism* (of the Pope) unable to err in pronouncing dogma as doctrinally defined. □ **infallibility** *n.* **infallibly** *adv.*

infamous / ˈɪnfəməs/ *adj.* **1** well-known for being bad, wicked, etc.; notorious. **2** abominable. □ **infamously** *adv.* **infamy** *n.* (*pl.* **-ies**).

infancy *n.* (*pl.* **-ies**) **1** early childhood; babyhood. **2** an early state in the development of an idea, undertaking, etc. **3** *Law* the state of being a minor.

infant *n.* **1** a child during the earliest period of its life. **2** (*attrib.*) **a** of or relating to infants or infancy. **b** made or intended for young children (*infant car seat*). **3** (esp. *attrib.*) a person or thing in an early stage of its development. **4** *Law* a minor; a person under 18.

infanticide / ɪnˈfæntɪˌsaɪd/ *n.* **1** the killing of an infant soon after birth. **2** the practice of killing newborn infants. **3** a person who kills an infant. □ **infanticidal** *adj.*

infantile / ˈɪnfənˌtaɪl/ *adj.* **1 a** like or characteristic of a child. **b** childish, immature (*infantile humour*). **2** in its infancy.

infantilism / ɪnˈfæntɪˌlɪzəm/ *n.* **1** childish behaviour. **2** *Psych.* the persistence of infantile characteristics or behaviour in adult life; abnormal physical, sexual, or psychological immaturity.

infantilize / ɪnˈfæntɪlaɪz/ *v.tr.* **1** prolong or inculcate a state of infancy or infantile behaviour in. **2** treat (a person) as infantile.

infant mortality *n.* death before the age of one.

infantry *n.* (*pl.* **-ies**) a body of soldiers who march and fight on foot; foot soldiers collectively.

infantryman *n.* (*pl.* **-men**) a soldier of an infantry regiment.

infarct / ˈɪnfɑrkt/ *n. Med.* a small localized area of dead tissue caused by an inadequate blood supply. □ **infarcted** *adj.* **infarction** *n.*

infatuate / ɪnˈfætʃuːˌeɪt, -tjuː-/ *v.tr.* **1** inspire with intense usu. transitory fondness or admiration. **2** affect with extreme folly. □ **infatuation** *n.*

infatuated *adj.* (often foll. by *with*) affected by an intense fondness or admiration.

infect / ɪnˈfekt/ *v.tr.* **1** contaminate (air, water, etc.) with harmful organisms or noxious matter. **2 a** affect (a person) with disease etc.; introduce a disease-causing micro-organism into. **b** affect (a computer system) with a virus. **3** instill bad feeling or opinion into (a person).

infection *n.* **1 a** the process of infecting or state of being infected. **b** an instance of this; an infectious disease. **c** the presence of a virus in, or its entry into, a computer system. **2** communication of disease, esp. by the agency of air or water etc.

infectious *adj.* **1** infecting with disease. **2** (of a disease) liable to be transmitted by air, water, etc. **3** (of emotions etc.) apt to spread; quickly affecting others. □ **infectiously** *adv.* **infectiousness** *n.*

infectious hepatitis *n.* = HEPATITIS A.

infective *adj.* capable of infecting with disease. □ **infectiveness** *n.* **infectivity** *n.*

infer *v.tr.* (**inferred, inferring**) (often foll. by *that* + clause) **1** deduce or conclude from facts and reasoning. **2** *disputed* imply, suggest. ¶The use of *infer*

in sense 2 is considered incorrect by many people since it is the reverse of the primary sense of the verb. It should be avoided by using *imply* or *suggest*.

inference / ˈɪnfərəns/ *n.* **1** the act or an instance of inferring. **2** *Logic* **a** the forming of a conclusion from premises. **b** a thing inferred. □ **inferential** /-ˈrenʃəl/ *adj.* **inferentially** *adv.*

inferior ● *adj.* **1** of lower rank, quality, etc. **2** lower; in a lower position. **3** poor in quality. **4** (of a planet) having an orbit within the earth's. **5** *Bot.* situated below an ovary or calyx. **6** (of figures or letters) written or printed below the line, e.g. the 2 in CO_2. ● *n.* **1** a person inferior to another, esp. in rank. **2** an inferior letter or figure. □ **inferiorly** *adv.*

inferiority *n.* the state of being inferior.

inferiority complex *n.* an unrealistic feeling of general inadequacy caused by actual or supposed inferiority in one sphere, sometimes marked by aggressive behaviour in compensation.

infernal *adj.* **1 a** of hell or the underworld. **b** hellish, fiendish. **2** *informal* detestable, tiresome. □ **infernally** *adv.*

inferno *n.* (*pl.* **-os**) **1** a raging fire. **2** a scene of horror or distress. **3** hell.

infest *v.tr.* (of harmful persons or things, esp. vermin or disease) overrun (a place) in large numbers. □ **infestation** *n.*

infidel / ˈɪnfɪdəl/ ● *n.* **1** usu. *derogatory* a person who does not believe in religion or in a particular religion; an unbeliever. **2** *hist.* an adherent of a religion other than one's own, esp.: **a** (from a Christian point of view) a Muslim. **b** (from a Muslim point of view) a Christian. **c** (from a Jewish point of view) a Gentile. ● *adj.* **1** that is an infidel. **2** of unbelievers.

infidelity *n.* (*pl.* **-ies**) **1 a** disloyalty, or esp. unfaithfulness to a sexual partner. **b** an instance of this. **2** lack of faith; disbelief in religious matters or a particular religion, esp. Christianity.

infield *n.* **1** *Baseball* **a** the area bounded by the baselines. **b** the fielders positioned along the baseline from first base to third base. **c** a team's defensive ability in the infield. **2** *N Amer.* the area enclosed by a racetrack.

infielder *n. Baseball* any of the fielders, i.e. the first baseman, second baseman, third baseman, and shortstop, stationed in the infield.

infighting *n.* **1** hidden conflict or competitiveness within an organization. **2** boxing at closer quarters than arm's length. □ **infighter** *n.*

infill ● *n.* (also **infilling**) **1** material used to fill a hole, gap, etc. **2** the placing of buildings to occupy the space between existing ones. **3 a** the building of a house on a lot cleared by demolishing an existing, usu. smaller house. **b** a house built where the previous one has been demolished. ● *v.tr.* fill in (a cavity etc.).

infiltrate *v.* **1 a** *tr. & intr.* gain entrance or access to surreptitiously and by degrees (as spies etc.). **b** *tr.* cause to do this. **2** *tr. & intr.* permeate by filtration. **3** *tr. & intr.* (often foll. by *into, through*) introduce (fluid) by filtration. □ **infiltration** *n.* **infiltrator** *n.*

---

infeasibility *n.*   **infeasible** *adj.*   **infertile** *adj.*   **infertility** *n.*

infinite ● *adj.* **1** boundless, endless. **2** very great. **3** (usu. with *pl.*) innumerable; very many (*infinite resources*). **4** *Math.* **a** greater than any assignable quantity or countable number. **b** (of a series) that may be continued indefinitely. ● *n.* **1** (**the Infinite**) God. **2** (**the infinite**) infinite space. □ **infinitely** *adv.*

infinitesimal /ˌɪnfɪnɪˈtesɪml/ ● *adj.* infinitely or very small. ● *n.* an infinitesimal amount. □ **infinitesimally** *adv.*

infinitesimal calculus *n.* the differential and integral calculi regarded as one subject.

infinitive ● *n.* a form of a verb expressing the verbal notion without reference to a particular subject, tense, etc. (e.g. *see* in *we came to see*, or *let her see*). ● *adj.* having this form.

infinity *n.* (*pl.* **-ies**) **1** the state of being infinite. **2** an infinite number or extent. **3** infinite distance. **4** *Math.* infinite quantity. Symbol: ∞.

infirm *adj.* **1** physically weak, esp. through age. **2** (of a person, mind, judgment, etc.) weak, irresolute. □ **infirmity** *n.* (*pl.* **-ies**).

infirmary *n.* (*pl.* **-ies**) **1** a place for those who are ill in a boarding school, prison, etc. **2** a hospital.

inflame *v.* **1** *tr. & intr.* provoke or become provoked to strong feeling, esp. anger. **2** *tr. Med.* cause inflammation or fever in (a body etc.). **3** *tr.* aggravate.

inflamed *adj.* **1** (of a part of the body) red, painful, and often swollen, esp. as a reaction to injury or infection. **2** full of anger or violent feelings.

inflammable ● *adj.* **1** easily set on fire; flammable. **2** easily excited. ¶See FLAMMABLE. ● *n.* (usu. in *pl.*) an inflammable substance. □ **inflammability** *n.*

inflammation *n.* **1** the act or an instance of inflaming. **2** *Med.* a localized physical condition with heat, swelling, redness, and usu. pain, esp. as a reaction to injury or infection.

inflammatory *adj.* **1** (esp. of speeches, leaflets, etc.) tending to cause anger etc. **2** of or tending to inflammation of the body.

inflammatory bowel disease *n.* either of two diseases, Crohn's disease and ulcerative colitis, which cause an inflammation of the bowel.

inflatable ● *adj.* that can be inflated. ● *n.* an inflatable plastic or rubber object, esp. an inflatable boat.

inflate *v.* **1** *tr.* distend (a balloon etc.) with air. **2** *tr.* (usu. foll. by *with*; usu. in *passive*) puff up (a person with pride etc.). **3 a** *tr. & intr.* bring about inflation (of the currency). **b** *tr.* raise (prices) artificially. **4** *tr.* exaggerate or embellish. **5** *intr.* become inflated. □ **inflator** *n.* (also **inflater**).

inflated *adj.* **1** swollen or distended. **2** (esp. of language, sentiments, etc.) bombastic. **3** (of prices, costs, etc.) unreasonably increased in amount, level, etc. **4** puffed up (with pride etc.). **5** *Bot. & Zool.* having a bulging form and hollow interior, as if filled with air.

inflation *n.* **1** *Econ.* **a** a general increase in prices and fall in the purchasing value of money. **b** an increase in available currency regarded as causing this. **2 a** the act or condition of inflating or being inflated. **b** an instance of this. □ **inflationary** *adj.*

inflation-adjusted *adj. N Amer.* (of income, a return, etc.) adjusted to take inflation into account.

inflect *v.* **1** *tr.* change the pitch of (the voice, a musical note, etc.). **2** *Grammar* **a** *tr.* change the form of (a word) to express tense, gender, number, mood, etc. **b** *intr.* (of a word, language, etc.) undergo such change. **3** *tr.* bend inwards; curve. **4** *tr.* (usu. as **inflected** *adj.*, in *comb.*) influence or modify, esp. by the addition of characteristics of another culture, musical style, etc. (*jazz-inflected style of singing*). □ **inflective** *adj.*

inflection *n.* **1 a** the act or condition of inflecting or being inflected. **b** an instance of this. **2** *Grammar* **a** the process or practice of inflecting words. **b** an inflected form of a word. **c** a suffix etc. used to inflect, e.g. *-ed*. **3** a modulation of the voice. □ **inflectional** *adj.* **inflectionless** *adj.*

inflexible *adj.* **1** that cannot be changed or adapted to particular circumstances (*an inflexible system*). **2** (of a person) unwilling to change or adapt. **3** unbendable. □ **inflexibility** *n.* **inflexibly** *adv.*

inflict *v.tr.* (usu. foll. by *on*, *upon*) **1** cause (injury, defeat, damage, punishment etc.). **2** (also *refl.*) often *jocular* impose (something objectionable or unwelcome) on.

infliction *n.* **1** the act or an instance of inflicting. **2** something inflicted.

inflight *attrib.adj.* occurring or provided during an aircraft flight.

inflorescence /ˌɪnfləˈresəns/ *n.* **1** *Bot.* **a** the complete flower head of a plant including stems, stalks, bracts, and flowers. **b** the arrangement of this. **2** the process of flowering.

inflow *n.* **1** a flowing in. **2** something, e.g. a liquid, money, etc., that flows in. □ **inflowing** *n. & adj.*

influence ● *n.* **1 a** (usu. foll. by *on*, *upon*) the effect a person or thing has on another. **b** (usu. foll. by *over*, *with*) moral ascendancy or power. **c** a thing or person exercising such power (*is a good influence on them*). **2** the ability to obtain favourable treatment by means of acquaintance, wealth, status, etc. **3** *Astrology* an ethereal fluid supposedly flowing from the stars and affecting character and destiny. ● *v.tr.* **1** exert influence on; have an effect on. **2** persuade or induce (a person) to do or think something. □ **under the influence** *informal* affected by alcoholic drink. □ **influencer** *n.*

influence peddler *n. N Amer.* a person who uses his or her position or political influence in exchange for money or favours. □ **influence-peddling** *n.*

influential /ˌɪnfluˈenʃəl/ ● *adj.* having great influence or power. ● *n.* an influential person. □ **influentially** *adv.*

influenza /ˌɪnfluˈenzə/ *n.* a highly contagious virus infection causing fever, severe aching, weakness, and coughing.

influx *n.* **1** a continual entry of people (esp. visitors or immigrants) into a place, esp. in large numbers. **2** (usu. foll. by *into*) a flowing in of a substance, esp. in large quantities. **3** the point at which a stream or river flows into another body of water.

info *n. & comb. form informal* information.

Infobahn /ˈɪnfoːˌbɒn/ *n. informal* = INFORMATION SUPERHIGHWAY.

info centre *n. Cdn* a booth or office etc. providing information to the public on a particular subject or region.

infold ● *v.tr. & intr.* fold inwards. ● *n.* a convolution; a fold. □ **infolding** *n.*

infomercial /ˌɪnfoːˈmɜrʃəl/ *n.* esp. *N Amer.* a television commercial made to look like a regular program, so as to disguise the fact that it is a paid advertisement.

inform *v.* **1** *tr.* (usu. foll. by *of*, *about*, or *that*, *how* + clause) tell (*informed them of their rights*). **2** *intr.* (usu. foll. by *against*, *on*) make an accusation. **3** *tr.* (usu. foll. by *with*) *literary* inspire or imbue (a person, heart, or thing) with a feeling, principle, quality, etc. **4** *tr.* impart its quality to; permeate. **5** *intr.* give or supply information or knowledge (*the book's task is to inform*).

informal *adj.* **1** without ceremony or formality (*just an informal chat*). **2** (of clothing, etc.) everyday; casual.

3 (of language, writing, etc.) relaxed or conversational in style; not formal. □ **informality** n. (pl. **-ies**). **informally** adv.

informant n. **1** a person who gives information. **2** a person who informs against another, esp. in criminal matters; an informer. **3** a person from whom a linguist, anthropologist, etc., obtains information about language, dialect, or culture.

informatics /ˌɪnfərˈmætɪks/ n.pl. (usu. treated as sing.) information science.

information n. **1 a** something told; knowledge. **b** (usu. foll. by on, about) items of knowledge; news (the latest information on the crisis). **2** a booth, office or agency providing information, esp. on a specific subject or location (ask at information). **3** Law (usu. foll. by against) a charge or complaint lodged with a court or magistrate. **4 a** the act of informing or telling. **b** an instance of this. **5** data as processed or stored etc. by a computer system. □ **informational** adj.

information age n. the current historical period, characterized by the capacity to store, retrieve, and transmit large volumes of information using computer technology.

information science n. the study of the processes for storing and retrieving information.

information superhighway n. (also **information highway**) a means of rapid transfer of information in different digital forms (e.g. video, sound, and graphics) via an extensive electronic network.

information technology n. the study or use of systems (esp. computers, telecommunications, etc.) for storing, retrieving, and sending information.

informative adj. giving information; instructive. □ **informatively** adv. **informativeness** n.

informed adj. **1** with knowledge of the facts (badly informed). **2** educated; knowledgeable (informed readers).

informed consent n. a patient's agreement to a certain course of treatment etc. given after being advised of the relevant medical facts, risks, etc.

informer n. **1** a person who informs against another. **2** a person who informs or advises.

infotainment /ˌɪnfoʊˈteɪnmənt/ n. broadcast material intended both to entertain and to inform.

infra- comb. form below.

infraction /ɪnˈfrækʃən/ n. esp. Law a violation or infringement. □ **infract** v.tr. **infractor** n.

infrared /ˌɪnfrəˈred/ ● adj. **1** having a wavelength just greater than the red end of the visible light spectrum but less than that of radio waves. **2** of or using such radiation. ● n. the infrared part of the spectrum.

infrastructure /ˈɪnfrəˌstrʌktʃər/ n. **1 a** the basic structural foundations of a society or enterprise; a substructure or foundation. **b** roads, bridges, sewers, etc., regarded as a country's economic foundation. **2** permanent installations as a basis for military etc. operations. □ **infrastructural** adj.

infrequent adj. not frequent. □ **infrequency** n. **infrequently** adv.

infringe v. **1** tr. **a** act contrary to; violate (a law, an oath, etc.). **b** act in defiance of (another's rights etc.). **2** intr. (usu. foll. by on, upon) affect something so as to limit or restrict it (they are infringing on our privacy). □ **infringement** n. **infringer** n.

infuriate /ɪnˈfjʊriˌeit/ v.tr. fill with fury; enrage. □ **infuriating** adj. **infuriatingly** adv.

infuse /ɪnˈfjuːz/ v. **1** tr. (usu. foll. by with) imbue; pervade (anger infused with resentment). **2** tr. steep (herbs, tea, etc.) in liquid to extract the content. **3** tr. (usu. foll. by into) instill (grace, spirit, life, etc.). **4** intr. undergo infusion (let it infuse for five minutes).

infusion n. **1** a liquid obtained by infusing. **2** the introduction of someone or something new that will have a positive influence (an infusion of cash). **3** Med. a slow injection of a substance into a vein or tissue. **4 a** the act of infusing. **b** an instance of this.

ingenious /ɪnˈdʒiːniəs/ adj. **1** clever at inventing, constructing, organizing, etc.; skilful; resourceful. **2** (of a machine, theory, etc.) cleverly contrived. ¶See INGENUOUS. □ **ingeniously** adv. **ingeniousness** n.

ingenue /ˈæʒəˈnjuː, -nuː/ n. **1** an innocent or unsophisticated young woman. **2 a** such a part in a play. **b** the actress who plays this part.

ingenuity /ˌɪndʒɪˈnjuːɪti/ n. skill in devising or contriving; ingeniousness.

ingenuous /ɪnˈdʒenjʊəs/ adj. **1** innocent; artless. **2** open; frank. ¶Ingenuous, meaning 'open, frank, innocent', should not be confused with ingenious, which means 'clever at inventing, resourceful'. □ **ingenuously** adv. **ingenuousness** n.

ingest v.tr. take in (food etc.); eat. □ **ingestion** n.

inglorious adj. **1** shameful; ignominious. **2** not famous. □ **ingloriously** adv. **ingloriousness** n.

ingoing adj. going in; entering.

ingot /ˈɪŋɡət/ n. a usu. oblong piece of cast metal, esp. of gold, silver, or steel.

ingrain ● adj. **1** inherent; ingrained. **2** (of textiles) dyed in the fibre, before being woven. ● v.tr. implant (a habit, belief, or attitude) ineradicably in a person.

ingrained adj. **1** deeply rooted; inveterate. **2** thorough. **3** (of dirt etc.) deeply embedded.

ingrate ● n. an ungrateful person. ● adj. ungrateful.

ingratiate /ɪnˈɡreɪʃiˌeit/ v.refl. (usu. foll. by with) bring oneself into favour. □ **ingratiating** adj. **ingratiatingly** adv.

ingredient n. **1** any of the foods that are combined to make a particular dish. **2** any of the things or qualities of which something is made (the ingredients of a good mystery story).

ingress n. Astronomy the start of an eclipse or transit.

in-ground attrib.adj. N Amer. (of a swimming pool etc.) sunk into the earth.

in-group n. a small exclusive group of people with a common interest.

ingrowing adj. growing inwards, esp. (of a toenail) growing into the flesh.

ingrown adj. (of a toenail etc.) grown into the flesh.

inguinal /ˈɪŋɡwɪnəl/ adj. of the groin.

inhabit v.tr. (**inhabited, inhabiting**) (of a person or animal) dwell in; occupy (a region, town, house, etc.). □ **inhabitability** n. **inhabitable** adj. **inhabitant** n. **inhabitation** n.

inhabited adj. having inhabitants; lived-in (an inhabited planet).

inhalant /ɪnˈheilənt/ ● n. **1** a medicinal preparation for inhaling. **2** a substance inhaled by drug abusers. ● adj. of or relating to inhalation or inhalants.

---

infusibility n.   **infusible** adj.   **ingratitude** n.

inhale v. **1** tr. & intr. breathe in. **2** tr. & intr. take (esp. tobacco smoke) into the lungs. **3** tr. N Amer. informal devour (food etc.) rapidly (inhaled the meal). □ **inhalation** n.

inhaler n. a portable device for administering a medicinal or anaesthetic gas or vapour, esp. to relieve nasal or bronchial congestion, e.g. in asthmatics.

inhere v.intr. (often foll. by in) **1** exist essentially or permanently in. **2** (of rights etc.) be vested in (a person etc.).

inherent /ɪnˈherənt, ɪnˈhiːr-/ adj. (often foll. by in) **1** existing in something, esp. as a permanent or characteristic attribute. **2** vested in (a person etc.) as a right or privilege. □ **inherence** n. **inherently** adv.

inherit v. (**inherited, inheriting**) **1** tr. & intr. receive (property, rank, title, etc.) by legal descent or succession. **2** intr. succeed as an heir. **3** tr. receive or have from a predecessor or predecessors in office etc. (inherited a lot of problems). **4** tr. come into possession of (clothing, etc.) from someone else (inherits all her clothes from her sisters). **5** tr. derive (a characteristic, disorder, etc.) genetically from one's ancestors.

inheritable adj. **1** capable of being inherited. **2** capable of inheriting. □ **inheritability** n.

inheritance n. **1** something that is inherited. **2 a** the act of inheriting. **b** an instance of this.

inheritance tax n. a tax levied on property etc. acquired by inheritance.

inheritor n. an heir; a person who inherits.

inhibit v.tr. (**inhibited, inhibiting**) **1** hinder, restrain, or prevent (an action or progress). **2** prevent (a person) from acting freely. □ **inhibitive** adj. **inhibitor** n. **inhibitory** adj.

inhibited adj. subject to inhibition; unable to express feelings or impulses.

inhibition n. **1** Psych. a restraint on the direct expression of an instinct. **2** a feeling of nervousness or embarrassment which prevents one from relaxing or behaving naturally. **3 a** the act of inhibiting. **b** the process of being inhibited.

inhospitable adj. **1** not hospitable. **2** (of a region, coast, etc.) not affording shelter etc. □ **inhospitableness** n. **inhospitably** adv.

in-house ● adj. done or existing within an institution, company, etc. (an in-house project). ● adv. internally, without outside assistance.

inhuman adj. **1** (of a person, conduct, etc.) brutal; unfeeling; barbarous. **2** not of a human type. **3** not suitable for humans. □ **inhumanly** adv.

inhumane adj. not humane. □ **inhumanely** adv.

inhumanity n. (pl. **-ies**) **1** brutality; barbarousness; callousness. **2** an inhumane act.

inimical /ɪˈnɪmɪkəl/ adj. (usu. foll. by to) **1** hostile. **2** harmful. □ **inimically** adv.

inimitable adj. impossible to imitate. □ **inimitability** n. **inimitably** adv.

iniquity /ɪˈnɪkwɪti/ n. (pl. **-ies**) **1** wickedness. **2** a gross injustice. □ **iniquitous** adj.

initial ● adj. of, existing at, or occurring at the beginning; first (initial stage). ● n. **1** (usu. in pl.) the first letters of two or more names of a person, or of words forming any name or phrase. **2** (in full **initial letter**, **initial consonant**) a letter or consonant at the beginning of a word. ● v.tr. (**initialled, initialling**) mark or sign with one's initials. □ **initially** adv.

initialism n. a group of initial letters used as an abbreviation for a name or expression, each letter being pronounced separately, e.g. CBC.

initialize v.tr. **1** Computing **a** set to the value or put in the condition appropriate to the start of an operation. **b** format (a disk). **2** designate by or use an initial or initials instead of the full name. □ **initialization** n.

initiate ● v.tr. /ɪˈnɪʃiˌeit/ **1** begin, introduce; set going; originate. **2 a** (usu. foll. by into) admit (a person) into a society, an office, a secret, etc., esp. with a ritual. **b** (usu. foll. by in, into) instruct (a person) in science, art, etc. ● n. /ɪˈnɪʃiət/ a person who has been newly initiated; a beginner, a novice. ● adj. /ɪˈnɪʃiət/ (of a person) newly initiated (an initiate member). □ **initiation** n. **initiator** n.

initiative /ɪˈnɪʃətɪv, ɪˈnɪʃiətɪv/ ● n. **1** the ability to initiate things; enterprise, self-motivation (he lacks initiative). **2 a** the action of initiating something or of taking the first step or the lead. **b** a proposal made by one group, nation, etc. to another, with a view to improving relations between them (a peace initiative). **3** the power or right to begin something. ● adj. beginning; originating. □ **have the initiative** esp. Military be able to control the enemy's movements. **on one's own initiative** without being prompted by others. **take the initiative** (usu. foll. by in + verbal noun) be the first to take action.

inject v.tr. **1 a** (usu. foll. by into) drive or force (a fluid, medicine, etc.) under pressure into a passage, cavity, or solid material. **b** (usu. foll. by with) introduce by injection. **c** administer medicine etc. to (a person) by injection. **2** introduce suddenly, with force, or by way of interruption; interject (injected a note of realism). **3** introduce (a new quality, element, etc.) into something (inject some fresh ideas; inject $200,000). □ **injectable** adj. & n. **injector** n.

injection n. **1 a** the act of injecting. **b** an instance of this. **2** a liquid or solution (to be) injected. **3** = FUEL INJECTION.

injection moulding n. the shaping of rubber or plastic articles by injecting heated material into a mould. □ **injection-moulded** adj.

in-joke n. a joke which can be appreciated by only a limited group of people because of shared experiences etc.

injudicious adj. showing lack of judgment or discretion. □ **injudiciously** adv. **injudiciousness** n.

injunction n. **1** an authoritative warning or order. **2** Law a judicial order restraining a person or a corporation from an act or compelling redress to an injured party. □ **injunctive** adj.

injure v.tr. **1** do esp. physical harm or damage to; hurt. **2** harm or impair (injured her reputation). **3** do injustice or wrong to. □ **injurer** n.

injured adj. **1** harmed or hurt (the injured passengers). **2** offended; wronged (in an injured tone).

injurious /ɪnˈdʒɔːriəs/ adj. **1** hurtful. **2** (of language) insulting; libellous. **3** wrongful. □ **injuriously** adv.

injury n. (pl. **-ies**) **1 a** physical harm or damage. **b** an instance of this (suffered head injuries). **2** esp. Law **a** wrongful action or treatment, esp. the violation of another's rights. **b** an instance of this. **3** damage to one's feelings, reputation, etc.

injustice n. **1** a lack of fairness or justice. **2** an unjust act. □ **do a person an injustice** judge a person unfairly.

---

inharmonious adj.

ink ● *n.* **1** a coloured fluid used for writing, drawing, printing, etc. **2** *Zool.* a black liquid ejected by a cuttlefish, octopus, etc. to confuse a predator. **3** *informal* press coverage; publicity. ● *v.tr.* **1** (usu. foll. by *in*, *over*, etc.) **a** mark with ink. **b** go over or trace around with ink. **2** cover (type etc.) with ink before printing. **3** apply ink to. **4** *esp. N Amer. informal* sign, put one's signature to (a contract etc.). □ **ink out** obliterate with ink.

Inkatha /ɪnˈkætə/ *n.* (in full **Inkatha Freedom Party**) a mainly Zulu political party and organization in South Africa, founded in 1928 as a cultural and social movement and revived in 1975.

ink blot test *n.* a Rorschach test.

ink cap *n.* any fungus of the genus *Coprinus*.

ink-jet printer *n. Computing* a printer that creates characters and graphics by firing a stream of minute ink drops at a surface from one or more banks of tiny nozzles. □ **ink-jet printing** *n.*

inkling *n.* (often foll. by *of*) a slight knowledge or suspicion; a hint.

ink pad *n.* = STAMP PAD.

inky *adj.* (**-ier, -iest**) of, as black as, or stained with ink. □ **inkiness** *n.*

inlaid ● *v.tr. past and past part. of* INLAY. ● *adj.* (of a piece of furniture etc.) ornamented by inlaying.

inland ● *adj.* **1** pertaining to or situated in the interior of a country. **2** inhabiting the interior of a country (*inland Algonquians*). **3** *esp. Cdn & Brit.* carried on within the limits of a country; domestic (*inland trade*). ● *n.* **1** the parts of a country remote from the coast or borders; the interior. **2** *Cdn hist.* (attrib.) denoting persons, places, or things involved with the inland fur trade (*an inland post*). ● *adv.* **1** in or towards the interior of a country. **2** conducted or occurring away from the coast or borders (*inland fishing*). □ **inlander** *n.*

inland navigation *n.* transportation by rivers and canals.

Inland Tlingit *n.* **1** a member of an Aboriginal group living in northern BC and the southern Yukon Territory. **2** the Tlingit language of this people.

in-law ● *n.* (usu. in *pl.*) a relative by marriage. ● *comb. form* denoting a relation by marriage (*father-in-law*).

in-law suite *n.* (also **in-law apartment**) *N Amer.* an extension added or a room, suite, etc. renovated to form a small apartment within an existing house.

inlay ● *v.tr.* (*past and past part.* **inlaid**) **1** (usu. foll. by *in*) embed (a thing in another) so that the surfaces are even. **2** (usu. foll. by *with*) ornament (a thing) by inserting another material in its surface in a decorative design. ● *n.* **1** inlaid work. **2** a piece of material inlaid or prepared for inlaying. **3** a filling shaped to fit a tooth cavity.

inlet *n.* **1** a small arm of the ocean, a lake, or a river. **2** a valve, device, etc. that controls incoming air, water, etc. **3** a way of entry.

in-line *adj.* **1 a** having parts arranged in a line. **b** (of an internal combustion engine) having usu. vertical cylinders arranged in one or more rows. **2** involving, employing, or forming part of a continuous, usu. linear, sequence of operations or machines, as in an assembly line. **3** *Computing* designating data processing which does not require input data to be sorted into batches.

in-line skate *n.* a skate resembling an ice skate, but having a line of usu. four rubber wheels instead of a blade, for use on paved surfaces etc. □ **in-line skater** *n.* **in-line skating** *n.*

Inmarsat *n.* an international organization that operates a system of satellites providing telecommunication services, as well as distress and safety communication services, to the world's shipping, aviation, and offshore industries.

inmate *n.* (often foll. by *of*) a person confined in a prison, hospital, etc.

in memoriam /ɪn məˈmɔːriəm/ ● *prep.* in memory of (a dead person). ● *n.* a written article or notice etc. in memory of a dead person; an obituary.

inmost *adj.* **1** most inward. **2** most intimate; deepest.

inn *n.* **1** a small hotel, esp. in the country. **2** a tavern.

innards /ˈɪnərdz/ *n.pl. informal* **1** entrails. **2** the inner workings (of an engine etc.).

innate /ɪˈneɪt, ˈɪ-/ *adj.* **1** inborn; natural (*an innate sense of style*). **2** *Philos.* originating in the mind. □ **innately** *adv.* **innateness** *n.*

inner ● *adj.* (usu. *attrib.*) **1 a** further in; inside; interior (*the inner compartment*). **b** further inshore, nearer the land (*inner islands*). **2** (of thoughts, feelings, etc.) deeper, more secret. **3** designating the mind or soul; mental; spiritual. ● *n.* the inner part of something. □ **innermost** *adj.*

inner cabinet *n.* a small group of powerful decision-makers within a ministerial cabinet.

inner child *n.* **1** a person's supposed original or authentic self, esp. regarded as damaged or concealed by negative childhood experiences. **2** that part of an individual's personality which manifests itself in or enjoys childish activities.

inner circle *n.* an exclusive group of close friends or associates within a larger group.

inner city *n.* the central area of a city, esp. if dilapidated, or characterized by overcrowding, poverty, etc. (also *attrib.*: *inner-city housing*).

inner ear *n.* the semicircular canals and cochlea, which form the organs of balance and hearing and are embedded in the temporal bone.

inner tube *n.* an inflatable rubber tube inside a tire.

innervate /ˈɪnər veɪt, ɪˈnɜːr-/ *v.tr.* supply (an organ etc.) with nerves or nervous stimulation. □ **innervation** *n.*

inning *n. N Amer.* each of the divisions of a baseball game during which both sides have a turn at bat.

innkeeper *n.* a person who manages or owns an inn.

innocent ● *adj.* **1** free from moral wrong; sinless. **2** (usu. foll. by *of*) not guilty (of a crime etc.). **3** free from responsibility for an event yet suffering its consequences (*innocent bystanders*). **4** simple; guileless; naive. **5** not intending to hurt or offend (*an innocent question*). **6** (foll. by *of*) *informal* without, lacking (*innocent of hypocrisy*). ● *n.* **1** an innocent person, esp. a young child. **2** a person involved by chance in a situation, esp. a victim of crime or war. **3** (in *pl.*) the young children killed by Herod after the birth of Jesus. □ **innocence** *n.* **innocently** *adv.*

innocuous /ɪˈnɒkjuəs/ *adj.* **1** harmless. **2** inoffensive. □ **innocuously** *adv.* **innocuousness** *n.*

innominate bone /ɪˈnɒmɪnət/ *n.* the bone formed from the fusion of the ilium, ischium, and pubis.

innovate /ˈɪnə veɪt/ *v.* **1** *intr.* bring in new methods, ideas, etc. **2** *intr.* (often foll. by *in*) make changes. **3** *tr.* introduce (a product) for the first time, esp. to the market. □ **innovation** *n.* **innovative** *adj.* **innovatively** *adv.* **innovativeness** *n.* **innovator** *n.*

inn-to-inn *adj. Cdn* designating a network of trails for cross-country skiing, snowmobiling, etc. on which inns are strategically located as rest stops.

Innu /ˈɪnu/ ● *n.* **1** a member of an Aboriginal people living in Labrador and northern Quebec (*see also*

MONTAGNAIS, NASKAPI). **2** the Cree language of this people. ● *adj.* of or relating to this people.

innuendo /ˌɪnjʊˈendo:/ *n.* (*pl.* **-oes** or **-os**) **1** an allusive or oblique remark or hint, usu. disparaging. **2** a remark with a double meaning, usu. suggestive.

innumerable *adj.* too many to be counted. □ **innumerability** *n.* **innumerably** *adv.*

inoculate /ɪˈnɒkjʊˌleɪt/ *v.tr.* **1 a** treat (a person or animal) with a vaccine containing a dead or modified disease-causing agent, usu. by injection, to promote immunity against the disease. **b** introduce (an infective agent) into an organism. **c** introduce (cells or organisms) into a culture medium. **2** indoctrinate (a person) with ideas or opinions. □ **inoculation** *n.* **inoculative** / -lətɪv/ *adj.* **inoculator** *n.*

inoculum /ɪˈnɒkjʊləm/ *n.* (*pl.* **inocula** /-lə/) (also **inoculant**) any substance used for inoculation.

inoffensive *adj.* **1** not objectionable or offensive; not causing offence. **2** innocuous, harmless; doing or causing no harm. □ **inoffensively** *adv.* **inoffensiveness** *n.*

inoperable *adj.* **1** *Surgery* that cannot be operated on successfully (*inoperable cancer*). **2** that cannot be operated; inoperative. **3** impractical, unworkable. □ **inoperability** *n.*

inoperative *adj.* **1** not working or taking effect. **2** *Law* without practical force, invalid.

inordinate /ɪnˈɔrdɪnət/ *adj.* **1** beyond proper or normal limits; excessive (*inordinate delays*). **2** intemperate. **3** disorderly. □ **inordinately** *adv.*

inorganic ● *adj.* **1** without organized physical structure or systematic arrangement. **2** not arising or growing naturally from an organization or structure; artificial, extraneous. ● *n.* an inorganic chemical. □ **inorganically** *adv.*

inorganic chemistry *n.* the branch of chemistry that deals with the properties and reactions of inorganic compounds.

in-patient *n.* a patient who stays in hospital for a period of days while receiving treatment.

input ● *n.* **1 a** what is put in or taken in, or operated on by any process or system. **b** the total resources including raw materials, manpower, etc. necessary to production, which are deducted from output in calculating profits. **2** *Electronics* **a** a place where, or a device through which, energy, information, etc., enters a system. **b** energy supplied to a device or system; an electrical signal. **3** the information fed into a computer. **4** the action or process of putting in or feeding in. **5** a contribution of information etc. ● *v.tr.* (**inputting**; *past* and *past part.* **input** or **inputted**) (often foll. by *into*) **1** put in. **2** *Computing* supply (data, programs, etc., to a computer, program, etc.).

input device *n.* a piece of equipment by which data, programs, or signals are transferred from a memory store to a computer.

input/output *attrib.adj.* (also **input-output**) *Computing* etc. of, relating to, or for input and output. Abbr.: **I/O**.

inquest *n.* **1** *Law* **a** an inquiry by a coroner's court into the cause of a sudden, unexplained, or suspicious death. **b** a coroner's jury. **2** *informal* a discussion analyzing the outcome of a game etc.

inquire *v.* **1 a** *intr.* (often foll. by *of*) seek information; ask a question (of a person). **b** *tr.* ask for information as to (*inquired my name*; *inquired whether we were coming*). **2** *intr.* seek information formally; make a

formal investigation. **3** *intr.* (foll. by *after, for*) ask about a person, a person's health, etc. **4** *intr.* (foll. by *for*) ask about the availability of. □ **inquirer** *n.* **inquiring** *adj.* **inquiringly** *adv.*

inquiry /ɪnˈkwaɪri/ *n.* (*pl.* **-ies**) **1** the act or an instance of asking or seeking information. **2** a question, a query. **3** (also /ˈɪnkwəri/) a formal or judicial investigation into a matter of public concern, esp. one conducted by a tribunal and granted jurisdictive powers.

inquisition *n.* **1** usu. *derogatory* **a** an intensive search or investigation. **b** a relentless, sustained, or unwelcome questioning of a person. **2** a judicial or official inquiry. **3** (**the Inquisition**) *Catholicism hist.* **a** an ecclesiastical court established *c.* 1232 for the detection of heretics, at a time when certain heretical groups were regarded as enemies of society. **b** (in full **Spanish Inquisition**) a similar but separate body, established by the Spanish crown in 1478 and directed originally against converts from Judaism and Islam. □ **inquisitional** *adj.*

inquisitive *adj.* **1** seeking knowledge; inquiring. **2** unduly curious; prying. □ **inquisitively** *adv.* **inquisitiveness** *n.*

inquisitor *n.* **1** an official investigator, esp. one who proceeds ruthlessly, unrelentingly, etc. **2** *hist.* an officer of the Inquisition.

inquisitorial *adj.* **1** of or like an inquisitor. **2** offensively prying.

INRI *abbr.* Jesus of Nazareth, King of the Jews.

inroad *n.* **1** (usu. in *pl.*) **a** a usu. foll. by *on, into*) an encroachment; a using up of resources etc. (*makes inroads on my time*). **b** (usu. foll by *in, into*) progress; an advance (*making inroads into a difficult market*). **2** a hostile attack; a raid.

inrush *n.* a rushing in; an influx. □ **inrushing** *adj. & n.*

ins. *abbr.* **1** inches. **2** insurance.

insane *adj.* **1 a** mentally deranged; not of sound mind. **b** characteristic of an insane person (*an insane laugh*). **2** (of an action) extremely foolish; irrational. □ **insanely** *adv.* **insanity** *n.* (*pl.* **-ies**).

insatiable /ɪnˈseɪʃəbəl/ *adj.* **1** unable to be satisfied. **2** (usu. foll. by *of*) extremely greedy. □ **insatiability** *n.* **insatiably** *adv.*

inscribe *v.tr.* **1 a** (usu. foll. by *in, on*) write or carve (words etc.) on stone, metal, paper, a book, etc. **b** (usu. foll. by *with*) mark (a sheet, tablet, etc.) with characters. **2** (usu. foll. by *to*) write an informal dedication (to a person) in or on (a book etc.). **3** enter the name of (a person) on an official document or list; enrol. **4** *Math.* draw (a figure) within another so that some or all of their boundaries touch but do not intersect (*compare* CIRCUMSCRIBE). □ **inscriber** *n.*

inscription *n.* **1** words inscribed, esp. on a monument, coin, stone, or in a book etc. **2 a** the act of inscribing, esp. the informal dedication of a book etc. **b** an instance of this.

inscrutable /ɪnˈskruːtəbəl/ *adj.* wholly mysterious, impenetrable. □ **inscrutability** *n.* **inscrutably** *adv.*

inseam *n. N Amer.* the inner seam on the leg of a pair of pants, extending from crotch to cuff.

insect *n.* **1 a** any arthropod of the class Insecta, having a head, thorax, abdomen, two antennae, three pairs of thoracic legs, and usu. one or two pairs of thoracic wings. **b** (loosely) any other small invertebrate animal esp. with several pairs of legs. **2** an insignificant or contemptible person or creature. □ **insectile** /ɪnˈsektaɪl/ *adj.*

inopportune *adj.* **inopportunely** *adv.*

insecticide /ɪn'sektə,saɪd/ n. a substance used for killing insects. □ **insecticidal** adj.

insectivore /ɪn'sektɪ,vɔr/ n. **1** any animal that feeds on insects, esp. a mammal of the order Insectivora, including shrews, hedgehogs, and moles. **2** any plant which captures and absorbs insects. □ **insectivorous** /-'tɪvərəs/ adj.

insecure adj. **1** (of a person or state of mind) uncertain; lacking confidence. **2 a** unsafe, not firm or fixed. **b** (of ice, ground, etc.) not providing good support, liable to give way. □ **insecurely** adv. **insecurity** n. (pl. **-ies**).

inseminate /ɪn'semə,neɪt/ v.tr. introduce semen into (a female) by natural or artificial means. □ **insemination** n.

insensibility n. (pl. **-ies**) **1** unconsciousness. **2** a lack of mental feeling or emotion; hardness. **3** (often foll. by to) indifference.

insensible adj. **1 a** without one's mental faculties; unconscious. **b** (of the extremities etc.) numb; without feeling. **2** (usu. foll. by of, to) unaware; indifferent (insensible to her needs). **3** without emotion; callous. **4** too small or gradual to be perceived. □ **insensibly** adv.

insensitive adj. (often foll. by to) **1** showing or feeling no sympathetic or emotional response; indifferent, callous. **2** not sensitive to physical stimuli. **3** (of a substance, device, etc.) not susceptible or responsive to some physical influence, e.g. light etc. □ **insensitively** adv. **insensitivity** n. (pl. **-ies**).

inseparable /ɪn'sepriabal, -'sepərəbəl/ adj. unable or unwilling to be separated (inseparable friends). □ **inseparability** n. **inseparably** adv.

insert ● v.tr. **1** (usu. foll. by in, into, between, etc.) place, fit, or thrust (a thing) into another (insert the key in the lock). **2** (usu. foll. by in, into) introduce (a letter, word, etc.) into a piece of text etc. (inserted a new paragraph). ● n. something inserted, e.g. an additional section in a magazine, a piece of cloth in a garment, a shot in a film, etc. □ **insertable** adj.

insertion n. **1** the act or an instance of inserting. **2** an amendment etc. inserted in writing or printing. **3** each appearance of an advertisement in a newspaper etc.

in-service ● attrib.adj. (of training) intended for those actively engaged in the profession or activity concerned. ● n. an in-service training session.

inset ● n. **1** (often attrib.) something set in or inserted (an inset photo). **2 a** a small map, photograph, etc., inserted within the border of a larger one. **b** an extra page or pages inserted in a folded sheet or in a book; an insert. **3** a piece set into a garment as decoration etc. ● v.tr. (**insetting**; past and past part. **inset**) **1** set or put in as an inset; insert. **2** decorate with an inset.

inshallah /ɪn'ʃælə/ interj. if Allah wills it.

inshore ● adj. **1** situated at sea close to the shore. **2** of or pertaining to fishing conducted from small boats in coastal waters. ● adv. **1** at sea but close to the shore. **2** towards the shore.

inside ● n. **1 a** the inner side or surface of a thing. **b** the inner part; the interior. **2 a** the side of a path or sidewalk furthest away from the road. **b** the part of a track or curving road nearest to the inner or shorter side of the curve. **3** (usu. in pl.) informal **a** the stomach and bowels (something wrong with my insides). **b** the operative part of a machine etc. **4** informal a position affording inside information (knows someone on the inside). ● adj. **1** situated on or in, or derived from, the inside. **2** (of information etc.) available only to those on the inside. **3** Baseball **a** (of a pitched ball) missing the plate on the batter's side. **b** (of the strike zone) nearest the batter. ● adv. **1 a** on, in, or to the inside. **b** indoors. **2** slang in prison. **3** Cdn (North) within the Yukon or Northwest Territories. ● prep. **1** on the inner side of; within (inside the house). **2** in less than (inside an hour). □ **inside of** informal in less than (a week etc.)

inside information n. information not accessible to outsiders.

inside job n. informal a crime committed by or involving the help of a person living or working on the premises burgled etc.

inside out ● adv. with the inner surface turned outwards. ● attrib.adj. (**inside-out**) in this condition. □ **know a thing inside out** know a thing thoroughly. **turn inside out 1** turn the inner surface outwards. **2** informal cause confusion or a mess in.

insider n. **1** a person who is within a society, organization, etc. **2** a person privy to a secret, esp. when using it to gain advantage.

insider trading n. Stock Exch. the illegal use of confidential information as a basis for share trading.

inside track n. **1** a position of advantage. **2** the track of a racecourse etc. which is shorter, because of the curve.

insidious /ɪn'sɪdiəs/ adj. **1** proceeding or progressing inconspicuously but harmfully (an insidious disease). **2** treacherous; crafty. □ **insidiously** adv. **insidiousness** n.

insight n. **1 a** the capacity of understanding hidden truths etc., esp. of character or situations. **b** an instance of this. **2** a sudden perception of the solution to a problem. □ **insightful** adj. **insightfully** adv.

insignia /ɪn'sɪɡniə/ n. (treated as sing. or pl.; usu. foll. by of) **1** badges or other symbols of rank or authority. **2** distinguishing marks or tokens indicative of something specific.

insignificant adj. **1** unimportant; trifling. **2** (of a person) undistinguished. **3** meaningless. □ **insignificance** n. **insignificantly** adv.

insincere adj. not sincere; not candid. □ **insincerely** adv. **insincerity** n. (pl. **-ies**).

insinuate /ɪn'sɪnjʊ,eɪt/ v.tr. **1** (often foll. by that + clause) convey indirectly or obliquely; hint (insinuated that she was lying). **2** (often refl.; usu. foll. by into) **a** introduce (oneself, a person, etc.) into favour, office, etc., by subtle manipulation. **b** introduce (a thing, oneself, etc.) subtly or deviously into a place. □ **insinuating** adj. **insinuatingly** adv. **insinuation** n.

insipid adj. **1** lacking vigour or interest; dull, boring. **2** lacking flavour. □ **insipidity** n. **insipidly** adv.

insist v.tr. & intr. (usu. foll. by that + clause) maintain or demand positively and assertively (insisted that he was innocent). □ **insist on** insistently maintain or make a persistent demand for (something) (I insist on being present). □ **insistingly** adv.

insistent adj. **1** insisting; demanding positively or continually. **2** regular and repeated; demanding attention (the insistent rattle of the window). □ **insistence** n. **insistency** n. **insistently** adv.

in situ /ɪn 'sɪtju:, sɪtu:, 'si:-/ adv. in its original or proper place.

insofar adv. (usu. foll. by as) to the extent that.

insole n. **1** a removable sole worn in a boot or shoe for comfort, warmth, etc. **2** the fixed inner sole of a boot or shoe.

insolent /'ɪnsələnt/ adj. rude, disrespectful; offensively contemptuous or arrogant. □ **insolence** n. **insolently** adv.

insoluble adj. **1** (of a difficulty, problem, etc.) incapable of being solved. **2** incapable of being dissolved in a liquid. □ **insolubility** n. **insolubly** adv.

insolvent ● adj. **1** unable to pay one's debts. **2** relating to insolvency. ● n. a debtor. □ **insolvency** n. (pl. **-ies**).

insomnia /ɪnˈsɒmnɪə/ n. habitual sleeplessness; inability to sleep. □ **insomniac** n. & adj.

insouciant /ɪnˈsuːsɪənt/ adj. carefree; unconcerned. □ **insouciance** n. **insouciantly** adv.

Insp. abbr. Inspector.

inspect v.tr. **1** look closely at or into, esp. to assess quality or check for shortcomings. **2** examine (a document etc.) officially. □ **inspection** n.

inspector n. **1** a person who inspects. **2** an official employed to supervise a service, system, machine, etc., and make reports (building inspector). **3** Cdn **a** (in some municipal police forces) an officer ranking above staff sergeant. **b** (in the SQ and Quebec municipal police forces) an officer ranking above captain. **c** (in the OPP) an officer ranking above sergeant major. **d** (in the Royal Newfoundland Constabulary) an officer ranking above lieutenant. **e** (in the RCMP) an officer ranking above corps sergeant major. □ **inspectorate** n.

inspector general n. a chief inspector.

inspiration n. **1 a** a supposed force or influence on poets, artists, musicians, etc., stimulating creativity, ideas, etc. **b** a person, principle, faith, etc. as a source of esp. artistic creativity or moral fervour. **c** a similar divine influence supposed to have led to the writing of Scripture etc. **2** a sudden brilliant, creative, or timely idea etc. **3** a drawing in of breath; inhalation. □ **inspirational** adj. **inspirationally** adv.

inspire v. **1** tr. (often foll. by to) stimulate or arouse (a person) to esp. creative activity or moral fervour (inspired her to write; inspired by God). **2** tr. **a** (usu. foll. by with) animate (a person) with a feeling. **b** (usu. foll. by into) instill (a feeling) into a person etc. **c** (usu. foll. by in) create (a feeling) in a person. **3** tr. prompt; give rise to (the poem was inspired by the autumn). □ **inspirer** n. **inspiring** adj. **inspiringly** adv.

inspired adj. **1** (of a work of art etc.) as if prompted by or emanating from a supernatural source; characterized by inspiration (an inspired speech). **2** (of a guess) intuitive but accurate.

Inst. abbr. **1** institute. **2** institution.

instability n. (pl. **-ies**) **1 a** a lack of stability. **b** an instance of instability. **2** Psych. a tendency to unpredictable behaviour or erratic changes of mood. **3** a meteorological tendency towards precipitation, high winds, etc.

install v.tr. (also **instal**) (**installed**, **installing**) **1** place (equipment, machinery, etc.) in position ready for use. **2** take (software), e.g. from a floppy disk, CD-ROM, etc., and place it in its permanent location from where it will be executed. **3** place (a person) in an office or rank with ceremony. **4** establish (oneself, a person, etc.) in a place, condition, etc. (installed herself at the head of the table). □ **installer** n.

installation n. **1 a** the act or an instance of installing. **b** the process or an instance of being installed. **2** a piece of apparatus, a machine, etc. installed. **3 a** a large work of art, esp. a sculpture or mixed media piece, specially created or constructed for display in a gallery, museum, or other site. **b** an exhibition of such works. **4** a subsidiary military or industrial establishment.

installment n. (also **installment**) **1** a sum of money due as one of several usu. equal payments for something, spread over an agreed period of time. **2** any of

several parts, esp. of a television or radio series or a magazine story, broadcast or published in sequence at intervals.

instalment plan n. a method of buying something by paying for it in instalments.

instance ● n. **1** an example or illustration of (another instance of his lack of determination). **2** a particular case (that's not true in this instance). **3** Law a legal suit. ● v.tr. cite (a fact, case, etc.) as an instance. □ **at the instance of** at the request or suggestion of. **for instance** as an example. **in the first** (or **second** etc.) **instance** in the first (or second etc.) place; at the first (or second etc.) stage of a proceeding.

instant ● adj. **1 a** occurring immediately (instant results). **b** designed to produce quick or immediate results (instant camera). **2 a** (of food etc.) processed to allow quick preparation. **b** prepared hastily and with little effort (I have no instant solution). **3** urgent; pressing. **4** of the present moment. ● n. **1** a precise moment of time, esp. the present (come here this instant). **2** a short space of time (was there in an instant). **3** an instant food or beverage, esp. instant coffee.

instantaneous /ˌɪnstənˈteɪnɪəs/ adj. **1** occurring or done in an instant or instantly. **2** Physics existing at a particular instant. □ **instantaneously** adv.

instant coffee n. **1** dried coffee granules. **2** the beverage made by adding boiling water to these.

instantiate /ɪnˈstænʃɪˌeɪt/ v.tr. represent by an instance. □ **instantiation** n.

instantly adv. immediately; at once.

instant replay n. esp. N Amer. **1** the recording and immediate rebroadcasting of part of a televised sports event, often in slow motion. **2** the part recorded and rebroadcast. **3** any immediate recollection, re-enactment, or review of an event, conversation, etc.

instate v.tr. (often foll. by in) install; establish.

instead adv. **1** (foll. by of) as a substitute or alternative to; in place of (stayed instead of going). **2** as an alternative (took me instead) (compare STEAD).

instep n. **1** the inner arch of the foot between the toes and the ankle. **2** the part of a shoe etc. fitting over or under this.

instigate /ˈɪnstɪˌgeɪt/ v.tr. **1** bring about by incitement or persuasion; provoke. **2** (usu. foll. by to) urge on, incite (a person etc.) to esp. a foolhardy or drastic act. □ **instigation** n. **instigator** n.

instill v.tr. (also **instil**) (**instilled**, **instilling**) (often foll. by into) **1** introduce (a feeling, idea, etc.) into a person's mind etc. gradually. **2** put (a liquid) into something in drops. □ **instillation** n.

instinct n. **1 a** an innate, usu. fixed, pattern of behaviour in most animals in response to certain stimuli. **b** a similar propensity in human beings to act without conscious intention. **2** (usu. foll. by for) unconscious skill; intuition. □ **instinctual** adj. **instinctually** adv.

instinctive adj. **1** relating to or prompted by instinct. **2** apparently unconscious or automatic (an instinctive reaction). □ **instinctively** adv.

institute /ˈɪnstɪˌtjuːt, ˌ-tjuːt/ ● n. **1 a** a society or organization for the promotion of science, education, etc. **b** a building used by an institute. **c** Law (usu. in pl.) a digest of the elements of a legal subject (Institutes of Justinian). **3** a principle of instruction. **4** N Amer. a brief course of instruction for teachers etc. **5** a unit within a university, college, etc. devoted to advanced teaching and research in a specialized field. **6** Cdn a collegiate institute. ● v.tr. **1** establish; found. **2 a** initiate (an inquiry etc.). **b** begin (proceedings) in a court. **3**

(usu. foll. by *to*, *into*) place (a person, esp. a cleric) officially in a new post with a formal ceremony.

institution *n.* **1** the act or an instance of instituting. **2 a** a society or organization founded esp. for charitable, religious, educational, or social purposes. **b** a business or governmental establishment providing a service to the public, e.g. a bank, prison, etc. (*financial institution*). **c** a building used by an institution. **3** a residential centre for the care of psychiatric or disabled patients etc. **4** an established law, practice, or custom (*the institution of marriage*). **5** *informal* (of a person, custom, etc.) a familiar object. **6 a** the establishment of a sacrament by Christ, esp. the Eucharist. **b** a passage, e.g. *this is my body*, of the prayer used in consecrating the Eucharist.

institutional *adj.* **1** of or like an institution. **2** typical of institutions, esp. in being regimented or unimaginative. **3** (of religion) expressed or organized through institutions (churches etc.). □ **institutionalism** *n.* **institutionally** *adv.*

institutional investor *n.* a large institution, e.g. an insurance company, bank, etc. that invests substantial amounts of money in the stock exchange.

institutionalize *v.tr.* **1** (esp. as **institutionalized**) establish in practice or custom (*institutionalized racism*). **2** place or keep (a person) in an institution. **3** convert into an institution; make institutional. □ **institutionalization** *n.*

institutionalized *adj.* (of a prisoner, long-term patient, etc.) made apathetic and dependent after a long period in an institution.

in-store ● *adj.* available or occurring inside a store (*an in-store promotion*). ● *adv.* inside a store.

instruct *v.tr.* **1** (often foll. by *in*) teach (a person) a subject etc. (*instructed her in French*). **2** (usu. foll. by *to* + infin.) direct; command (*instructed him to fill in the hole*). **3** (often foll. by *of*, or *that* etc. + clause) inform (a person) of a fact etc. **4** *N Amer.* (of a judge) advise (a jury), prior to its deliberations, of the legal principles applicable to the case.

instruction *n.* **1** (often in *pl.*) a direction; an order (*read the instructions*). **2** teaching; education (*individualized instruction*). **3** *Law* (in *pl.*) *N Amer.* a judge's directions to a jury, prior to its deliberations, on the legal principles applicable to the case under consideration. **4** the act or an instance of teaching or directing. **5** a direction in a computer program defining and effecting an operation. □ **instructional** *adj.*

instructive *adj.* tending to instruct; conveying a lesson; enlightening (*found the experience instructive*). □ **instructively** *adv.* **instructiveness** *n.*

instructor *n.* **1** a person who instructs; a teacher. **2** *N Amer.* a university teacher ranking below assistant professor. □ **instructorship** *n.*

instrument ● *n.* **1** a tool or implement, esp. for delicate or scientific work. **2** (in full **musical instrument**) a device for producing musical sounds by vibration, wind, percussion, etc. **3 a** a thing used in performing an action; a means (*the meeting was an instrument in her success*). **b** a person made use of (*is merely their instrument*). **4** a measuring device, esp. in a car or aircraft, serving to gauge position, speed, etc. **5** a formal, esp. legal, document. **6** an investment option such as derivatives, stocks, bonds, etc. ● *v.tr.* **1** arrange (music) for instruments. **2** equip with instruments (for measuring, controlling, etc.).

instrumental ● *adj.* **1** (usu. foll. by *to*, *in*, or *in* + verbal noun) serving as an instrument or means (*was instrumental in finding the money*). **2** (of music) performed on instruments, without singing (compare VOCAL *adj.* 3). **3** of, or arising from, an instrument (*instrumental error*). **4** *Grammar* of or in the instrumental. ● *n.* **1** a piece of music performed by instruments, not by the voice. **2** *Grammar* the case of nouns and pronouns (and words in grammatical agreement with them) indicating a means or instrument. □ **instrumentalist** *n.* **instrumentality** *n.* **instrumentally** *adv.*

instrumentation *n.* **1 a** the arrangement or composition of music for a particular group of musical instruments. **b** the instruments used in any one piece of music. **2 a** the design, provision, or use of instruments in industry, science, etc. **b** such instruments collectively.

instrument flight rules *n.pl.* rules for controlling and navigating an aircraft by using instruments only.

instrument panel *n.* a surface, esp. in a car etc., containing the dials etc. of measuring devices.

insubordinate *adj.* refusing to obey instructions or show respect. □ **insubordinately** *adv.* **insubordination** *n.*

insubstantial *adj.* **1** lacking solidity or substance; weak, flimsy. **2** not real; imaginary (*an insubtantial vision*). **3** not large in size or amount (*an insubstantial raise*). □ **insubstantiality** *n.* **insubstantially** *adv.*

insufferable *adj.* **1** intolerable. **2** unbearably arrogant or conceited etc. □ **insufferableness** *n.* **insufferably** *adv.*

insufficiency *n.* (*pl.* **-ies**) **1 a** the condition of being insufficient; inadequacy. **b** an instance of this. **2** *Med.* the inability of an organ to perform its normal function (*renal insufficiency*).

insular /ˈɪnsʊlər, ˈɪnsjʊ-/ *adj.* **1 a** of or like an island. **b** separated or remote, like an island. **c** inhabiting or situated on an island. **2** ignorant of or indifferent to cultures, peoples, etc., outside one's own experience; narrow-minded. □ **insularity** /-ˈlærɪti/ *n.*

insulate /ˈɪnsəˌleɪt, ˈɪnsjə-/ *v.tr.* **1** prevent the passage of electricity, heat, or sound from (a thing, room, etc.) by interposing non-conductors. **2** detach (a person or thing) from its surroundings; isolate. □ **insulative** *adj.*

insulation *n.* **1** the action of insulating or the condition of being insulated against the passage of electricity, heat, or sound. **2** materials used for this, such as foam or fibreglass.

insulator *n.* **1** a thing or substance used for insulation against electricity, heat, or sound. **2** an insulating device to support telephone wires etc. **3** a device preventing contact between electrical conductors.

Insulbrick /ˈɪnsɒlbrɪk/ *n.* *Cdn* simulated-brick asphalt siding used on houses etc.

insulin /ˈɪnsəlɪn, ˈɪnsjə-/ *n.* **1** a polypeptide hormone produced in the pancreas by the islets of Langerhans, which regulates the amount of glucose in the blood. **2** a commercial preparation of this substance, used in the treatment of diabetes.

insult ● *v.tr.* **1** speak to or treat with scornful abuse or indignity. **2** offend the self-respect or modesty of. ● *n.* **1** an insulting remark or action. **2** something so worthless or contemptible as to be offensive (*an insult to his intelligence*). □ **add insult to injury** behave offensively as well as harmfully. □ **insulting** *adj.* **insultingly** *adv.*

insuperable /ɪnˈsuːpərəbəl, ɪnˈsjuː-, -prəbəl/ *adj.* **1** (of a barrier) impossible to surmount. **2** (of a difficulty etc.) impossible to overcome. □ **insuperability** *n.* **insuperably** *adv.*

insurable earnings *n.pl. Cdn* income on which employment insurance premiums are paid.

insurance *n.* **1** the act or an instance of insuring property, life, etc. **2 a** a sum paid for this; a premium. **b** a sum paid out as compensation for theft, damage, loss, etc. **3** the business of providing insurance policies. **4** = INSURANCE POLICY. **5** a measure taken to provide for a possible contingency (*take an umbrella as insurance*). **6** a system of contributions from workers and employers, or one funded entirely by tax revenue, to provide government assistance in sickness, unemployment, etc. (*health insurance*).

insurance agent *n.* a person employed by an insurance company to sell insurance policies.

insurance broker *n.* a self-employed person who buys and sells insurance policies on behalf of clients.

insurance company *n.* a company engaged in the business of insurance.

insurance policy *n.* **1** a contract of insurance. **2** a document detailing such a policy and constituting a contract.

insure *v.* **1** *tr. & intr.* (often foll. by *against*) secure the payment of a sum of money in the event of loss or damage to (property, life, a person, etc.) by regular payments or premiums (*insured the house for $250,000*; *insured against flood damage*). **2** *tr.* (of the owner of a property, an insurance company, etc.) secure the payment of (a sum of money) in this way. **3** *tr.* (usu. foll. by *against*) provide for (a possible contingency) (*insured themselves against the rain by taking umbrellas*). **4** *tr. N Amer.* = ENSURE 1-3. □ **insurable** *adj.* **insurability** *n.*

insured ● *adj.* covered by insurance. ● *n.* (usu. prec. by *the*) a person etc. covered by insurance.

insurer *n.* a person or company offering insurance policies for premiums; an underwriter.

insurgent /ɪnˈsɜrdʒənt/ ● *adj.* rising in active revolt; rebellious. ● *n.* a rebel; a revolutionary. □ **insurgence** *n.* **insurgency** *n.* (*pl.* **-ies**)

insurrection *n.* a rising in open resistance to established authority; a rebellion. □ **insurrectionary** *adj.* **insurrectionist** *n. & adj.*

int. *abbr.* **1** interior. **2** internal. **3** international.

intact *adj.* **1** entire; undamaged. **2** untouched.

intaglio /ɪnˈtælioʊ/ ● *n.* (*pl.* **-os**) **1** a gem with an incised design (*compare* CAMEO 1). **2** an engraved design. **3** a carving, esp. incised, in hard material. **4** a printing process in which the image is engraved or etched into a metal plate or cylinder so that it lies below the non-printing areas. ● *v.tr.* (**-oes, -oed**) **1** engrave (material) with a sunken pattern or design. **2** engrave (such a design).

intake *n.* **1 a** the action of taking in. **b** an instance of this. **2 a** a number (of people etc.) or the amount taken in or received (*this year's intake of students*). **b** such people etc. **3** a place where water is taken into a channel or pipe from a river, or fuel or air enters an engine etc.

intangible ● *adj.* **1** unable to be touched; not solid. **2** unable to be grasped mentally. **3** (of a business asset, e.g. a patent, trademark, or copyright) saleable, but having no value in itself. ● *n.* something that cannot

be precisely measured or assessed. □ **intangibility** *n.* **intangibly** *adv.*

integer /ˈɪntɪdʒər/ *n.* **1** a whole number. **2** a thing complete in itself.

integral ● *adj.* **1 a** of a whole or necessary to the completeness of a whole. **b** forming a whole (*integral design*). **c** whole, complete. **d** included as part of the whole, rather than supplied from outside (*a machine with an integral power source*). **2** *Math.* **a** of or denoted by an integer. **b** involving only integers, esp. as coefficients of a function. ● *n. Math.* **1** a quantity of which a given function is the derivative, i.e. which yields that function when undifferentiated, and which may express the area under the curve of a graph of the function. **2** a function satisfying a given differential equation. □ **integrally** *adv.*

integral calculus *n.* mathematics concerned with finding integrals, their properties and application, etc. (*compare* DIFFERENTIAL CALCULUS).

integrate *v.* **1** *tr.* **a** combine (parts) into a whole. **b** complete (an imperfect thing) by the addition of parts. **2** *tr. & intr.* bring or come into equal participation in or membership of society, a school, etc. **3** *tr.* desegregate, esp. racially (a school etc.). □ **integrative** /ˈɪntəɡrətɪv/ *adj.*

integrated *adj.* **1** combined into a whole; united; undivided. **2** designating or characterized by a personality in which the component elements combine harmoniously. **3** uniting several components previously regarded as separate. **4** (of an institution, group, etc.) not divided by considerations of race, culture, ability, etc.; not segregated.

integrated circuit *n.* a small chip etc. of material replacing several separate components in a conventional electrical circuit.

integrated school *n. Cdn* (*Nfld*) a public school established, maintained, and operated jointly by members of the Anglican, United, and Presbyterian Churches and the Salvation Army.

integrated services digital network *n.* a telecommunications network through which sound, images, and data can be transmitted as digitized signals. *Abbr.:* **ISDN**.

integration *n.* **1** the act or an instance of integrating. **2** the intermixing of persons previously segregated. **3** *Psych.* the combination of the diverse elements of perception etc. in a personality. **4** *Math.* the process or an instance of obtaining the integral of a function. □ **integrationist** *n. & adj.*

integrator *n.* **1** an instrument for indicating or registering the total amount or mean value of some physical quality, as area, temperature, etc. **2** a person or thing that integrates.

integrity *n.* **1** moral uprightness; honesty. **2** wholeness; completeness. **3** soundness; unimpaired or uncorrupted condition.

integument /ɪnˈtɛɡjʊmənt/ *n.* **1** a natural outer covering, as a skin, husk, rind, etc. **2** something with which an object is covered, enclosed, or clothed.

intellect *n.* **1 a** the faculty of reasoning, knowing, and thinking, as distinct from feeling. **b** the understanding or mental powers (of a particular person etc.). **2 a** a clever or knowledgeable person. **b** the intelligentsia regarded collectively.

intellectual ● *adj.* **1** of or relating to the intellect. **2 a** possessing a high level of understanding or intelligence. **b** valuing or interested in matters appealing to the intellect. **3** requiring, appealing to, or engaging the intellect. ● *n.* **1** a person of superior intelligence. **2** a person who is interested in intellectual matters. **3** a person professionally engaged in intellectual activity. □ **intellectuality** *n.* **intellectually** *adv.*

intellectualism *n.* **1** devotion to intellectual pursuits. **2** the exercise, esp. when excessive, of the intellect at the expense of the emotions. **3** *Philos.* the theory that knowledge is wholly or mainly derived from pure reason. □ **intellectualist** *n.*

intellectualize *v.* **1** *tr.* make intellectual; give an intellectual character to. **2** *intr.* exercise the intellect; talk or write intellectually. □ **intellectualization** *n.*

intellectual property *n.* *Law* non-tangible property that is the result of creativity, such as patents, copyrights, etc.

intelligence *n.* **1 a** the intellect; the understanding. **b** (of a person or an animal) quickness of understanding and reasoning; wisdom. **2 a** the collection of information, esp. of military or political value (also *attrib.: intelligence operation*). **b** a group or agency that collects such information (also *attrib.: intelligence agency*). **c** information so collected. **d** information in general; news.

intelligence quotient *n.* a number denoting the ratio of a person's intelligence to the statistical norm, 100 being average. Abbr.: **IQ**.

intelligent *adj.* **1** having the faculty of understanding; possessing or showing intelligence, esp. of a high level (*intelligent life; an intelligent remark*). **2** clever. **3 a** (of a machine) able to vary its behaviour in response to varying situations and requirements and past experience. **b** (esp. of a computer terminal) having its own data-processing capability; incorporating a microprocessor (*opp.* DUMB *adj.* 6). **c** (of a building, office, etc) equipped with sophisticated telecommunications and computer technology. □ **intelligently** *adv.*

intelligent agent *n.* a computer program which can seek or sort information with minimal supervision by the user.

intelligentsia /ˌɪntelɪˈdʒentsɪə/ *n.* **1** the class of intellectuals regarded as possessing culture and political initiative. **2** people doing intellectual work; intellectuals.

intelligible /ɪnˈtelɪdʒəbəl/ *adj.* **1** (often foll. by *to*) able to be understood; comprehensible. **2** *Philos.* able to be understood only by the intellect, not by the senses. □ **intelligibility** *n.* **intelligibly** *adv.*

Intelsat /ˈɪntelˌsæt/ *n.* an international organization of countries operating a system of commercial communication satellites.

intemperate *adj.* **1** immoderate; unbridled; violent (*used intemperate language*). **2 a** given to excessive indulgence in alcohol. **b** excessively indulgent in one's appetites. **c** characterized by overindulgence or profligateness (*an intemperate lifestyle*). □ **intemperance** *n.* **intemperately** *adv.*

intend *v.tr.* **1** have as one's purpose; propose (*we intend to go*). **2** (usu. foll. by *to* + infin.) design or destine (*I intend him to go*). **3** (often foll. by *as*) mean (*intended it as a warning*). **4** (in *passive*; foll. by *for*) **a** be meant for a person to have or use etc. (*they are intended for the children*). **b** be designed for (*intended for a small child's hand*).

intendant *n.* **1** (often **Intendant**) *hist.* a high-ranking administrative official in French, Portuguese, and Spanish provinces and colonies, responsible for economic development, settlement, and the administration of justice. **2** a superintendent or manager of a department of public business etc. □ **intendancy** *n.*

intended ● *adj.* **1** done on purpose; intentional. **2** designed, meant (*the intended audience*). **3** future; prospective (*my intended spouse*). ● *n.* informal one's fiancé or fiancée (*is this your intended?*).

intending *adj.* who intends to be (*an intending visitor*).

intense *adj.* (**intenser, intensest**) **1** (of a quality, feeling etc.) existing in a high degree; extremely strong, esp. so severe as to be difficult to withstand or endure (*intense cold*). **2 a** (of an emotion) deeply or strongly felt. **b** (of a person) extremely earnest and serious (*very intense about her music*). **c** (of an activity) characterized by emotional tension. **d** expressing strong emotion. **3** (of a colour) very strong or deep. **4** (of an action etc.) requiring a great deal of emotional, intellectual, or physical effort concentrated in a short time (*intense thought*). □ **intensely** *adv.*

intensifier *n.* **1** a person or thing that intensifies. **2** a word or prefix used to give force or emphasis.

intensify *v.* (**-ies, -ied**) **1** *tr.* (often in *passive*) **a** (of a person) make (esp. something that causes stress) more intense. **b** increase the quantity or strength of (something). **2** *intr.* (of any activity, esp. a conflict; also of emotions, colours, physical sensations) become much stronger, esp. rapidly. □ **intensification** *n.*

intensity *n.* (*pl.* **-ies**) **1** the quality of being intense. **2** concentration of feeling, emotional depth, earnestness or passion. **3** esp. *Physics* the measurable amount of some quality, e.g. brightness etc.

intensive ● *adj.* **1** characterized by a great deal of concentrated effort, usu. over a short period of time (*intensive study*). **2** of or relating to intensity as opposed to extent; producing intensity. **3** serving to increase production in relation to costs (*intensive farming methods*). **4** (usu. in *comb.*) *Econ.* making much use of (*labour-intensive*). **5** *Grammar* (of an adjective, adverb, etc.) expressing intensity; giving force, as *really* in *my feet are really cold.* ● *n.* *Grammar* an intensifier. □ **intensively** *adv.* **intensiveness** *n.*

intensive care *n.* **1** medical treatment with constant monitoring etc. of a dangerously ill patient (also *attrib.: intensive care unit*). **2** a part of a hospital devoted to this.

intent ● *n.* (usu. without article) **1** intention; a purpose. **2** *Law* a person's state of mind that directs him or her to perform an action (*with intent to defraud*). ● *adj.* **1** (usu. foll. by *on*) **a** resolved; bent; determined (*was intent on succeeding*). **b** attentively occupied (*intent on her books*). **2** (esp. of a look) earnest; eager; meaningful. □ **to** (or **for**) **all intents and purposes** practically; virtually. □ **intently** *adv.* **intentness** *n.*

intention *n.* **1** a thing intended; an aim or purpose (*have no intention of staying*). **2** the action or fact of intending (*done without intention*). **3** informal (usu. in *pl.*) a person's, esp. a man's, designs in respect to marriage (*are his intentions honourable?*). □ **intentioned** *adj.* (usu. in *comb.*).

intentional *adj.* **1** done with an aim or purpose; deliberate. **2** of or pertaining to intention; existing only in intention. **3** *Philos.* of or pertaining to the operation of the mind; existing in or for the mind. □ **intentionality** *n.* **intentionally** *adv.*

intentional walk *n.* *Baseball* a tactical play in which a pitcher deliberately walks a batter.

inter /ɪnˈtɜr/ v.tr. (**interred, interring**) deposit (a corpse etc.) in the earth, a tomb, etc.; bury.

inter- /ˈɪntər/ comb. form **1** between, among (*intercontinental*). **2** mutually, reciprocally (*interbreed*).

Interac n. Cdn proprietary a system of payment by means of a debit card, in which funds are transferred electronically from the cardholder's bank account to the account of a merchant etc.

interact v.intr. **1** act reciprocally; act on each other. **2** (of people) work together or communicate.

interaction n. **1** reciprocal action or influence. **2** Physics the action of atomic and subatomic particles on each other. □ **interactional** adj.

interactive adj. **1** reciprocally active; acting upon or influencing each other. **2** (of a computer, television, or other electronic device) allowing a two-way flow of information between it and a user, responding to the user's input. □ **interactively** adv. **interactivity** n.

inter alia /ˌɪntər ˈeɪlɪə, ˈælɪə/ adv. among other things.

interbank adj. agreed, arranged, or operating between banks (*interbank loan*).

interbreed v.tr. & intr. (past and past part. **-bred**) breed or cause to breed with members of a different stock, race, or species to produce a hybrid.

intercalary /ɪnˈtɜrkələri, -ˈkæləri/ adj. **1** (of a day or a month) inserted in the calendar to harmonize it with the solar year, e.g. Feb. 29 in leap years. **2** (of a year) having such an addition.

intercalate /ɪnˈtɜrkəˌleɪt/ v.tr. **1** insert (an intercalary day etc.). **2** interpose (anything out of the ordinary course). □ **intercalation** n.

intercede v.intr. **1** (usu. foll. by with) interpose or intervene on behalf of another; plead (*they interceded with the authorities for her release*). **2** mediate between two people, groups, etc. □ **interceder** n.

intercellular adj. located or occurring between cells.

intercept ● v.tr. **1** seize, catch, or stop (a person, message, vehicle, ball, puck, etc.) going from one place to another. **2** check or stop (motion etc.). **3** overtake and destroy (an aircraft, missile, etc.). **4** Math. mark off (a space) between two points etc. ● n. **1** Math. the part of a line between two points of intersection with usu. the coordinate axes or other lines. **2** a message, signal, etc. intended for someone else and obtained by covert means, esp. in espionage or warfare. □ **interception** n. **interceptive** adj.

interceptor n. **1** an aircraft used to intercept enemy aircraft. **2** a person or thing that intercepts.

intercession n. **1** the act of interceding, esp. by prayer. **2** an instance of this, esp. a prayer on behalf of another. □ **intercessional** adj. **intercessor** n. **intercessory** adj.

interchange ● v.tr. **1** (of two people) exchange (things) with each other. **2** put each of (two things) in the other's place; alternate. ● n. **1** (often foll. by of) a reciprocal exchange between two people etc. **2** alternation (*the interchange of woods and fields*). **3** an intersection of two or more highways designed on several levels to allow vehicles to go from one road to another without crossing a flow of traffic. □ **interchangeable** adj. **interchangeability** n. **interchangeably** adv.

inter-church adj. concerning or composed of several Christian denominations (*an inter-church coalition*).

intercity adj. existing or travelling between cities.

intercollegiate adj. existing or conducted between colleges or universities.

intercolonial adj. existing or conducted between colonies.

intercom n. **1** a system of intercommunication by radio or telephone between or within offices, aircraft, etc. **2** an instrument used in this.

intercommunicate v.intr. **1** communicate reciprocally. **2** (of rooms etc.) have free passage into each other; have a connecting door. □ **intercommunication** n.

interconnect v.tr. & intr. connect with each other. □ **interconnected** adj. **interconnectedness** n. **interconnecting** adj. **interconnection** n. **interconnectivity** n.

intercontinental adj. connecting or travelling between continents.

intercontinental ballistic missile n. a ballistic missile able to be sent from one continent to another.

interconvert v.tr. & intr. convert into each other. □ **interconversion** n. **interconvertible** adj.

intercooler n. an apparatus for cooling gas between successive compressions, esp. in a car or truck engine. □ **intercool** v.tr.

intercostal /ˌɪntərˈkɒstəl/ ● adj. between the ribs (of the body or a ship). ● n. (in pl.) intercostal muscles, nerves, arteries, etc.

intercourse n. **1** communication or dealings between individuals etc. **2** = SEXUAL INTERCOURSE.

intercultural adj. taking place between cultures; belonging to or derived from different cultures. □ **interculturalism** n.

intercut (**-cutting**; past and past part. **-cut**) Film ● v. **1** tr. alternate (scenes or shots) with contrasting scenes or shots to make one composite scene. **2** intr. switch from one shot or scene to another. ● n. a sequence or scene in a film, video, etc. formed by intercutting.

inter-denominational adj. concerning more than one (religious) denomination.

interdepartmental adj. concerning more than one department. □ **interdepartmentally** adv.

interdependent adj. dependent on each other. □ **interdepend** v.intr. **interdependence** n.

interdict ● n. **1** an authoritative prohibition. **2** Catholicism a sentence barring a person, or esp. a place, from ecclesiastical functions and privileges. ● v.tr. **1** prohibit (an action). **2** forbid the use of. **3** (usu. foll. by from + verbal noun) restrain (a person). **4 a** Military impede (an enemy force), esp. by bombing lines of communication or supply. **b** intercept (a prohibited commodity); prevent (its movement). □ **interdiction** n. **interdictory** adj.

interdisciplinary adj. of or between more than one branch of learning. □ **interdisciplinarity** n.

interest ● n. **1 a** concern; curiosity (*have no interest in fishing*). **b** a quality exciting curiosity or holding the attention (*this magazine lacks interest*). **c** the power of an issue, action, etc. to hold the attention; noteworthiness, importance (*findings of no particular interest*). **2** a subject, hobby, etc., in which one is concerned. **3** advantage or profit, esp. when financial (*it is in your interest to go*). **4 a** money paid for the use of money lent, or for not requiring the repayment of a debt. **b** = INTEREST RATE. **5** (usu. foll. by in) **a** a financial stake (in an undertaking etc.). **b** a legal concern, title, or right (in property). **6 a** a party or group having a common interest (*the brewing interest*). **b** a principle in which a party or group is concerned. **7** self-interest. ● v.tr. **1** excite the curiosity or attention of. **2** (usu. foll. by in) cause (a person) to take a personal interest or share (*can I interest you in a drink?*). □ **declare an** (or **one's**) **interest** make known one's financial etc. interests in an undertaking before it is discussed. **in the best interests of** to the greatest advantage or benefit of.

in the interest (or **interests**) **of** as something that is advantageous to. **lose interest** become bored or boring. **with interest 1** with interest charged or paid. **2** with increased force etc. (*returned the blow with interest*).

interested *adj.* **1** showing or having curiosity or concern (*an interested audience*). **2** having a private interest; not impartial or disinterested (*an interested party*). □ **interestedly** *adv.* **interestedness** *n.*

interest group *n.* a group of people sharing a common identifying interest, concern, or purpose.

interesting *adj.* causing curiosity; holding the attention. □ **interestingly** *adv.* **interestingness** *n.*

interest rate *n.* a charge made for borrowing a sum of money, expressed as a percentage of the total sum loaned, for a stated period of time.

inter-ethnic *adj.* occurring or existing between ethnic groups.

interface ● *n.* **1** esp. *Physics* a surface forming a common boundary between two regions. **2** a point where interaction occurs between two systems, processes, subjects, etc. (*the interface between psychology and education*). **3** *Computing* **a** an apparatus for connecting two pieces of equipment or systems so that they can be operated jointly or communicate with each other. **b** the way in which a program accepts information from or presents information to the user, e.g. the layout of the screen, command structure, etc. ● *v.* **1** *tr.* & *intr.* (often foll. by *with*) connect with (another piece of equipment etc.) by an interface. **2** *intr.* interact with (another person etc.).

interfacing *n.* a stiffish material between two layers of fabric in collars etc. **2** *in senses of* INTERFACE *v.*

interfaith *adj.* of, relating to, or between different religions or members of different religions.

interfere *v.intr.* **1** (usu. foll. by *with*) **a** (of a person) meddle; obstruct a process etc. **b** (of a thing) be a hindrance; get in the way. **2** (usu. foll. by *in*) take part or intervene, esp. without invitation or necessity. **3** *Sport* (foll. by *with*) unlawfully obstruct an opposing player. **4** (foll. by *with*) *Cdn & Brit.* molest or assault sexually. **5** *Physics* (of light or other waves) combine so as to cause interference. □ **interferer** *n.* **interfering** *adj.* **interferingly** *adv.*

interference *n.* **1** (usu. foll. by *with*) **a** the act of interfering. **b** an instance of this. **2 a** the fading or disturbance of received radio signals by the interference of waves from different sources, or esp. by atmospherics or unwanted signals. **b** the distorted reception caused by this. **3** *Physics* the combination of two or more wave motions to form a resultant wave in which the displacement is reinforced or cancelled. **4 a** *Football* the legal blocking of an opposing player to clear a way for the ball carrier. **b** *Sport* the illegal blocking or hindering of an opponent. □ **run interference** *N Amer.* intervene on someone's behalf, esp. to protect them from distraction, annoyance, etc.

interferon /ˌɪntərˈfiːərɒn/ *n.* *Biochem.* any of various proteins released by cells, usu. in response to a virus, and able to inhibit viral replication.

intergalactic *adj.* of or situated between two or more galaxies. □ **intergalactically** *adv.*

intergenerational *adj.* **1** existing or occurring between different generations of people. **2** involving more than one generation.

interglacial ● *adj.* of or relating to a period of milder climate between glacial periods. ● *n.* such a period.

intergovernmental *adj.* concerning between two or more governments. □ **intergovernmentally** *adv.*

inter-group *adj.* existing or occurring between different groups or members of different groups, esp. different social or political groups.

interim ● *n.* the intervening time (*in the interim she died*). ● *adj.* intervening; provisional, temporary.

interim moderator *n.* (in Presbyterian churches) a minister who takes temporary responsibility for a pastoral charge.

interior ● *adj.* **1** inner (*opp.* EXTERIOR). **2** remote from the coast or frontier; inland. **3** internal; domestic (*opp.* FOREIGN). **4** (usu. foll. by *to*) situated further in or within. **5** existing in the mind or soul; inward. **6** drawn, photographed, etc. within a building. **7** coming from inside. ● *n.* **1** the interior part; the inside. **2** the interior part of a country or region. **3 a** the home affairs of a country. **b** a department dealing with these (*Minister of the Interior*). **4 a** the inside of a building, room, etc. **b** a representation of this in art or photography. **5** the inner nature; the soul. □ **interiority** /ɪnˌtiːriˈɒrɪti/ *n.* **interiorize** *v.tr.* **interiorization** *n.* **interiorly** *adv.*

interior angle *n.* the angle between adjacent sides of a rectilinear figure.

interior design *n.* (also **interior decoration**) the decoration or design of the interior of a building etc. □ **interior designer** *n.* (also **interior decorator**).

interject *v.tr.* introduce abruptly, esp. into a conversation; remark parenthetically or as an interruption. □ **interjector** *n.* **interjectory** *adj.*

interjection *n.* an exclamation, esp. as a part of speech (e.g. *hey!*, *dear me!*).

interlace *v.* **1** *tr.* bind intricately together; interweave. **2** *tr.* mingle, intersperse. **3** *intr.* cross each other intricately.

interleave *v.tr.* **1** insert (usu. blank) leaves between the leaves of (a book etc.). **2** insert something at regular intervals between (the parts of).

interleukin /ˌɪntərˈluːkɪn/ *n.* *Biochem.* any of several glycoproteins produced by leukocytes for regulating immune responses. Abbr.: **IL**.

interlibrary *adj.* between libraries (*interlibrary loan*).

interline[1] ● *v.* **1** *tr.* insert words between the lines of (a document etc.). **2** *tr.* insert (words) in this way. **3** *intr.* **a** make use of transportation by more than one route, service, etc. **b** provide interconnections with another route, service, etc. ● *adj.* of or relating to the transfer of passengers or freight from one route or service to another during travel (*interline service*).

interline[2] *v.tr.* put an extra lining between the ordinary lining and the fabric of (a garment) esp. for added stiffness or warmth.

interlinear *adj.* written or printed between the lines.

interlink *v.tr.* & *intr.* link or be linked together. □ **interlinkage** *n.* **interlinked** *adj.*

interlock ● *v.* **1** *intr.* engage with each other by overlapping or by the fitting together of projections and recesses. **2** *tr.* (usu. in *passive*) lock or clasp within each other. **3** *intr.* be intimately connected (*interlocking responsibilities*). ● *adj.* (of a fabric) knitted with closely interlocking stitches. ● *n.* **1** a device or mechanism for connecting or coordinating the function of different components. **2** a knitted fabric with closely interlocking stitches. **3** *N Amer.* = INTERLOCKING BRICK.

interlocking brick *n.* (also **interlocking stone**) a paving material formed into shapes that interlock.

interlocutor /ˌɪntərˈlɒkjʊtər/ *n.* a person who takes part in a dialogue or conversation. □ **interlocution** /-ləˈkjuːʃən/ *n.*

interlocutory /ˌɪntərˈlɒkjʊtəri/ *adj.* **1** of dialogue or conversation. **2** *Law* (of a decree etc.) given provisionally in a legal action.

interloper *n.* an intruder. ☐ **interlope** *v.intr.*

interlude /ˈɪntərˌluːd/ *n.* **1 a** an intervening time, space, or event that contrasts with what goes before or after. **b** a temporary amusement or entertaining episode. **2** a piece of music, esp. an instrumental passage, played between other pieces etc. **3 a** a pause between the acts of a play. **b** something performed or done during this pause.

intermarriage *n.* **1** marriage between people of different races, tribes, religions, etc. **2** marriage between near relations.

intermarry *v.intr.* (**-ies, -ied**) (foll. by *with*) (of people belonging to different races, tribes, religions, etc.) become connected by marriage.

intermediary /ˌɪntərˈmiːdiˌeri/ ● *n.* (*pl.* **-ies**) **1** a person who acts as a link or helps to negotiate between two or more others; a mediator. **2** something acting between persons or things. ● *adj.* serving as a means of mediation or interaction.

intermediate /ˌɪntərˈmiːdiət/ ● *adj.* coming between two things in time, place, character, etc. ● *n.* an intermediate thing. ● *v.intr.* /-diˌeit/ (foll. by *between*) act as intermediary; mediate. ☐ **intermediation** *n.*

interment *n.* burial. ¶See INTERNMENT.

intermezzo /ˌɪntərˈmetsoː/ *n.* (*pl.* **intermezzi** /-tsi/ or **-os**) **1 a** a short connecting instrumental movement in an opera or other musical work. **b** a similar piece performed independently. **c** a short piece for a solo instrument. **2** a short light dramatic or other performance inserted between the acts of a play.

interminable *adj.* **1** endless; having no prospect of an end. **2** tediously long or habitual. ☐ **interminableness** *n.* **interminably** *adv.*

intermingle *v.tr. & intr.* (often foll. by *with*) mix together; mingle.

intermission *n.* **1** a pause or break between parts of a play, film, concert, etc. **2** a pause or cessation. **3** a period of inactivity.

intermittent *adj.* occurring at intervals; not continuous or steady. ☐ **intermittently** *adv.*

intermix *v.tr. & intr.* mix together. ☐ **intermixture** *n.*

intermodal *adj.* involving two or more different modes, esp. modes of transport in conveying goods.

intern ● *n.* esp. *N Amer.* **1** a recent medical graduate, resident and working under supervision in a hospital as part of his or her training. **2** a person in any profession gaining practical experience under supervision. ● *v.* **1** *intr.* esp. *N Amer.* serve as an intern. **2** *tr.* confine; oblige (a prisoner, alien, etc.) to reside within prescribed limits. ☐ **internship** *n.*

internal ● *adj.* **1** of or situated in the inside or invisible part. **2** relating or applied to the inside of the body (*internal injuries*). **3** of or relating to political, economic, etc. activity happening entirely within a country rather than with other countries; domestic (*internal flight*). **4** used or applying within an organization. **5 a** of the inner nature of a thing; intrinsic. **b** of the mind or soul. ● *n.* (in *pl.*) **1** intrinsic qualities. **2** internal parts, organs, etc. ☐ **internally** *adv.*

internal combustion engine *n.* an engine in which motive power is generated by the expansion of exhaust gases from the burning of fuel (e.g. gasoline, diesel, etc.) with air inside the engine.

internalize *v.tr.* **1** *Psych.* make (attitudes, behaviour, etc.) part of one's nature by learning or unconscious assimilation. **2** *Econ.* incorporate (costs) as part of the internal structure, esp. social costs resulting from

the manufacture and use of a product. ☐ **internalization** *n.*

internal medicine *n.* the branch of medicine that deals with the diagnosis and treatment, by nonsurgical means, of diseases of internal organs.

Internal Revenue Service *n.* (in the US) the government department responsible for collecting domestic taxes. Abbr.: **IRS**.

international ● *adj.* **1** existing, involving, or carried on between two or more nations. **2** agreed on or used by all or many nations (*international money order*). **3** of or pertaining to relations between nations (*international law*). **4** available for the use of all nations (*international waters*). ● *n.* (**International**) **1** any of four associations founded (1864–1936) to promote socialist or communist action. **2** a member of any of these. ☐ **internationality** *n.* **internationally** *adv.*

International Court of Justice *n.* an international judicial court of the UN, which meets at The Hague and adjudicates disputes between nations in accordance with international law.

International Date Line *n.* see DATE LINE *n.* 1.

Internationale /ˌɪntərˌnæʃəˈnæl/ *n.* (prec. by *the*) an (originally French) revolutionary song adopted by socialists.

internationalism *n.* **1** the advocacy of a community of interests among nations. **2** the quality or state of being international. **3** (**Internationalism**) the principles of any of the Internationals. ☐ **internationalist** *n. & adj.*

internationalize *v.tr.* **1** make international. **2** bring under the protection or control of two or more nations. ☐ **internationalization** *n.*

International Joint Commission *n.* a commission comprising 3 Canadian and 3 US members dealing with questions concerning water resources along the Canada-US boundary.

international law *n.* a body of rules established by custom or treaty and agreed as binding by nations in their relations with one another.

International Monetary Fund *n.* see IMF.

International Phonetic Alphabet *n.* an internationally recognized set of phonetic symbols used to transcribe the pronunciation of words etc.

International Style *n.* a 20th c. style of architecture characterized by simple geometric forms and the use of unornamented glass, steel, and concrete.

international system of units *n.* a system of physical units based on the metre, kilogram, second, ampere, kelvin, candela, and mole, with prefixes to indicate multiplication or division by a power of ten.

international unit *n.* a standard quantity of a vitamin etc.

internecine /ˌɪntərˈnesiːn, -ain, -niːs-/ *adj.* **1** mutually destructive. **2** of or relating to conflict within a group or organization etc.

internee *n.* a person interned.

Internet *n.* an international computer network linking computers from educational institutions, government agencies, industry, etc.

internetwork *n.* several computer networks connected together to form a single, higher-level network. ☐ **internetworking** *n.*

internist *n.* esp. *N Amer.* a specialist in internal medicine.

internment *n.* **1** the act of interning someone. **2** confinement; the state of being interned. ¶*Internment* should not be confused with either *interment* 'burial' or *internship* 'position of an intern'.

internship n. esp. N Amer. **1** the position of an intern. **2** the period of such a position. ¶See INTERNMENT.

inter-office adj. serving to communicate or occurring between the offices of a corporation etc.

interoperable /ɪntər'ɒpərəbəl/ adj. able to operate in conjunction. □ **interoperability** n.

interpenetrate v. **1** intr. (of two things) penetrate each other. **2** tr. pervade; penetrate thoroughly. □ **interpenetration** n. **interpenetrative** adj.

interpersonal adj. **1** (of relations) occurring between persons, esp. reciprocally. **2** of or relating to relationships between people (interpersonal skills). □ **interpersonally** adv.

interplanetary adj. **1** between planets. **2** relating to travel between planets.

interplant v.tr. plant (a specified crop or plant) together with another crop or plant.

interplay n. the way in which two or more things influence or affect each other.

Interpol /'ɪntər,pɒl/ n. the International Criminal Police Organization, which coordinates investigations with an international dimension made by the police forces of member countries.

interpolate /ɪn'tɜrpə,leit/ v.tr. **1** interject (a remark) in a conversation. **2** insert as something additional or different. **3** estimate (values) from known ones in the same range (compare EXTRAPOLATE 2). **4 a** insert (words) in a book etc., esp. to give false impressions as to its date etc. **b** make such insertions in (a book etc.). □ **interpolation** n. **interpolator** n.

interpose v. **1** tr. (often foll. by between) place or insert (a thing) between others. **2** tr. say (words) as an interruption. **3** tr. exercise or advance (a veto or objection) so as to interfere. **4** intr. (foll. by between) intervene (between parties).

interpret v. (**interpreted, interpreting**) **1** tr. explain the meaning of. **2** tr. perform a piece of music, a dramatic role, etc. **3** tr. & intr. translate orally or in sign language from one language into another. **4** tr. explain or understand (behaviour etc.) in a specified manner. □ **interpretable** adj. **interpretability** n. **interpretation** n. **interpretational** adj. **interpretative** adj. **interpretive** adj. **interpretively** adv.

interpreter n. **1** a person who translates from one language to another either orally or using sign language. **2** a person who interprets. **3** Computing a program that can analyze and execute a program line by line. **4** an employee of a park, museum, etc. who gives tours, answers visitors' questions, etc.

interpretive centre n. a building or complex at a historic site, national park, etc., which contains a variety of displays and exhibits related to the site.

interprovincial adj. situated or carried on between provinces.

interracial adj. existing between or affecting different races. □ **interracially** adv.

interrelate v. **1** tr. relate (two or more things) to each other. **2** intr. (of two or more things) relate to each other. □ **interrelatedness** n. **interrelation** n. **interrelationship** n.

interrogate /ɪn'terə,geit/ v.tr. **1** ask questions of (a person) esp. closely, thoroughly, or formally. **2** examine closely (data, social systems, etc.) so as to find answers. □ **interrogator** n.

interrogation n. **1** the act or an instance of interrogating; the process of being interrogated. **2** a question or inquiry. □ **interrogational** adj.

interrogative /ɪntə'rɒgətɪv/ ● adj. **1 a** of or like a question; used in questions. **b** (of an adjective or pronoun) asking a question (e.g. who?, which?). **2** having the form or force of a question. **3** suggesting inquiry. ● n. an interrogative word (e.g. what?, why?). □ **interrogatively** adv.

interrogatory ● adj. questioning; of or suggesting inquiry (an interrogatory eyebrow). ● n. (pl. **-ies**) a formal set of questions, esp. Law one formally put to an accused person etc.

interrupt ● v. **1 a** tr. act so as to break the continuous progress of (something) temporarily. **b** tr. & intr. stop (someone) speaking, by speaking oneself or causing some other disturbance. **2** tr. obstruct (a person's view etc.). **3** tr. break an even or continuous line, surface, etc. ● n. Computing a signal causing an interruption of a program, e.g. to allow immediate execution of another program. □ **interruptible** adj. **interruption** n. **interruptive** adj.

interrupter n. (also **interruptor**) **1** a person or thing that interrupts. **2** a device for interrupting, esp. an electric circuit.

intersect v. **1** tr. divide (a thing) by passing or lying across it. **2** intr. (of lines, roads, etc.) cross or cut each other. **3** intr. Geom. have one or more points in common.

intersection n. **1 a** esp. N Amer. a place where two or more roads intersect. **b** the place where two things intersect or cross. **2** a point or line common to lines or planes that intersect. **3** Math. & Logic the set which comprises all the elements common to two or more given sets, and no others. **4** the act of intersecting.

intersession n. Cdn a short university term, usu. in May and June, in which the course material usually covered in thirteen weeks is condensed into five or six weeks of intensive study.

interspecific adj. (also **interspecies**) **1** relating to or occurring between one or more species. **2** formed from different species.

intersperse v.tr. **1** (often foll. by between, among) scatter; place here and there. **2** (foll. by with) diversify (a thing or things with others as scattered). □ **interspersion** n.

interstate ● adj. existing or carried on between states, esp. of the US or Australia. ● n. US each of a system of highways between states.

interstellar adj. occurring or situated between stars.

interstice /ɪn'tɜrstɪs/ n. **1** an intervening space. **2** a chink or crevice.

interstitial /ɪntər'stɪʃəl/ adj. of, forming, or occupying interstices. □ **interstitially** adv.

intertextuality n. the relationship between esp. literary texts; the fact of relating or alluding to other texts. □ **intertextual** adj.

intertidal adj. of or relating to the area which is under water at high tide and exposed at low tide.

inter-tribal adj. existing or occurring between different tribes.

intertwine v. **1** tr. (often foll. by with) entwine (together). **2** intr. become entwined.

interval /'ɪntɜrvəl/ n. **1** an intervening time or space. **2** an open space between two things or two parts of the same thing; a gap or opening. **3** the difference in pitch between two sounds. □ **at intervals** here and there; now and then. □ **intervallic** /-'vælɪk/ adj. (also **intervalic**).

intervale /'ɪntɜr,veil/ n. N Amer. (Maritimes, Nfld, & New England) a low, level tract of land, esp. along a river.

interval house n. Cdn = WOMEN'S SHELTER.

intervene v.intr. (often foll. by between, in) **1** occur in time between events. **2** interfere; come between so as to prevent or modify the result or course of events. **3**

be situated between things. **4** come in as an extraneous factor or thing. **5** *Law* interpose in a lawsuit as a third party. □ **intervenor** *n.* (also **intervener**).

intervention *n.* **1** the act or an instance of intervening. **2** interference, esp. by one country in another's affairs. **3** mediation. □ **interventional** *adj.*

interventionism *n.* the principle or practice of intervention. □ **interventionist** *n. & adj.*

intervertebral *adj.* between vertebrae.

interview ● *n.* **1** a meeting at which a job applicant, student, etc. is questioned to determine their suitability. **2 a** a conversation between a reporter etc. and a person of public interest, used as a basis of a broadcast or publication. **b** the published or broadcast result of this. **3** a meeting of persons face to face, esp. for consultation. **4** a session of formal questioning by the police. ● *v.* **1** *tr.* hold an interview with. **2** *tr.* question to discover the opinions or experience of (a person). **3** *intr.* participate in an interview; perform (well etc.) at an interview. □ **interviewee** *n.* **interviewer** *n.*

interwar *attrib.adj.* existing in the period between two wars, esp. the two world wars.

interweave *v.* (*past* **-wove**; *past part.* **-woven**) **1** *tr.* (often foll. by *with*) weave together. **2** *tr.* blend intimately. **3** *intr.* be or become interwoven.

interwoven *adj.* **1** woven together; interlaced. **2** intimately linked.

intestate /ɪn'testeɪt/ ● *adj.* not having made a will before death. ● *n.* a person who has died intestate.

intestinal flora *n.pl.* = FLORA 3.

intestine /ɪn'testaɪn, -ɪn/ *n.* (in *sing.* or *pl.*) **1** the lower part of the alimentary canal from the end of the stomach to the anus. **2** *Zool.* (esp. in invertebrates) the whole alimentary canal. □ **intestinal** (also /ˌɪntɛ'staɪnəl/) *adj.*

intifada /ˌɪntɪ'fɑdə/ *n.* a movement of Palestinian uprising in the Israeli-occupied West Bank and Gaza Strip, beginning in 1987.

intimacy /'ɪntɪməsɪ/ *n.* (*pl.* **-ies**) **1** close familiarity or friendship; closeness. **2** an intimate act, esp. sexual intercourse. **3** a private cozy atmosphere. **4** an intimate remark; an endearment.

intimate[1] /'ɪntɪmət/ ● *adj.* **1** closely acquainted; familiar, close (*an intimate friend*). **2** private and personal (*intimate thoughts*). **3** (usu. foll. by *with*) having sexual relations. **4** (of knowledge) detailed, thorough. **5** (of a relationship between things) close. **6** (of mixing etc.) thorough. **7** essential, intrinsic. **8** (of a place etc.) cozy; suggesting intimacy (*an intimate restaurant*). ● *n.* a very close friend. □ **intimately** *adv.*

intimate[2] /'ɪntɪˌmeɪt/ *v.tr.* **1** (often foll. by *that* + clause) state or make known. **2** imply, hint. □ **intimation** *n.*

intimidate *v.tr.* frighten or overawe, esp. to subdue or influence. □ **intimidating** *adj.* **intimidatingly** *adv.* **intimidation** *n.* **intimidator** *n.*

intinction *n.* *Christianity* the dipping of the Eucharistic bread in the wine.

into *prep.* **1** expressing motion or direction to a point on or within (*walked into a tree*; *ran into the house*). **2** expressing direction of attention or concern (*will look into it*). **3** expressing a change of state (*turned into a dragon*; *separated into groups*). **4** *informal* interested in; knowledgeable about (*is really into ballet*). **5** after the beginning of (*five minutes into the game*). **6** *Math.* expressing the relationship of a divisor to a dividend (*8 into 24 is 3*).

intolerable *adj.* that cannot be endured. □ **intolerably** *adv.*

intolerance *n.* **1** lack of tolerance for difference of

opinion or practice, esp. in political or religious matters. **2** severe sensitivity or allergy to a substance, esp. a food or drug (*lactose intolerance*).

intolerant *adj.* **1** not tolerant, esp. of views, beliefs, or behaviour differing from one's own. **2** (usu. foll. by *of*) not having the capacity to tolerate or endure a specified thing. □ **intolerantly** *adv.*

intonation /ˌɪntə'neɪʃən/ *n.* **1** modulation of the voice; accent. **2** the act of intoning. **3** accuracy of pitch in playing or singing. **4** the opening phrase of a plainsong melody. □ **intonational** *adj.*

intone *v.tr.* **1** recite (prayers etc.) with prolonged sounds, esp. in a monotone. **2** chant (psalms etc.). **3** utter in a solemn or pompous tone.

in toto /ɪn 'toːtoː/ *adv.* completely.

intoxicant ● *n.* an intoxicating substance. ● *adj.* intoxicating.

intoxicate *v.tr.* **1** make drunk. **2** excite or elate beyond self-control. □ **intoxicating** *adj.* **intoxicatingly** *adv.* **intoxication** *n.*

intra- *prefix* forming adjectives usu. from adjectives, meaning 'on the inside, within' (*intramural*).

intracellular *adj.* *Biol.* located or occurring within a cell or cells. □ **intracellularly** *adv.*

intractable *adj.* **1** hard to control or deal with. **2** (of a disease) not easily treated. **3** (of a person or animal) not manageable or docile; stubborn. □ **intractability** *n.* **intractably** *adv.*

intramural /ˌɪntrə'mjʊərəl/ ● *adj.* **1 a** esp. *N Amer.* taking place within a single (esp. educational) institution (*intramural floor hockey league*). **b** forming part of normal university or college studies. **2** situated or done within walls. ● *n.* (in *pl.*) *N Amer.* intramural sports. □ **intramurally** *adv.*

intramuscular *adj.* in or into a muscle or muscles.

intranet *n.* *Computing* a communications network within an organization, employing the same technology as the Internet.

intransigent /ɪn'trænzɪdʒənt, -sɪdʒənt/ ● *adj.* uncompromising, stubborn. ● *n.* an intransigent person. □ **intransigence** *n.* **intransigently** *adv.*

intransitive *adj.* (of a verb or sense of a verb) that does not take or require a direct object (whether expressed or implied), e.g. *look* in *look at the sky* (opp. TRANSITIVE). □ **intransitively** *adv.* **intransitivity** *n.*

intraspecific *adj.* produced, occurring, or existing within a single taxonomic species or between individuals of a single species.

intrauterine *adj.* within the uterus.

intrauterine device *n.* a contraceptive device fitted inside the uterus and physically preventing the implantation of fertilized ova. Abbr.: **IUD.**

intravascular *adj.* situated or occurring within a vessel of an animal or plant, esp. a blood vessel.

intravenous /ˌɪntrə'viːnəs/ ● *adj.* in or into a vein or veins. ● *n.* an intravenous injection or feeding. □ **intravenously** *adv.*

in-tray *n.* = IN-BASKET.

intrepid *adj.* fearless; very brave. □ **intrepidly** *adv.*

intricate *adj.* very complicated; perplexingly detailed. □ **intricacy** *n.* (*pl.* **-ies**). **intricately** *adv.*

intrigue ● *v.* (**intrigues, intrigued, intriguing**) **1** *tr.* provoke (a person's) interest or curiosity (*what you say intrigues me*). **2** *intr.* (foll. by *with*) make and carry out secret plans, often with other people, with the aim of causing someone harm, doing something illegal, etc. ● *n.* **1** the making of secret plans to cause somebody harm, do something illegal, etc. (*a novel of mystery and intrigue*). **2 a** a secret plan to cause someone harm, etc. (*political intrigues*). **b** a secret arrangement (*amorous intrigues*). ☐ **intriguer** n. **intriguing** adj. (esp. in sense 1 of v.). **intriguingly** adv.

intrinsic adj. inherent, essential; belonging naturally (*intrinsic value*). ☐ **intrinsically** adv.

intro informal ● n. (pl. **-os**) an introduction. ● adj. introductory.

intro- comb. form into (*introspection*).

introduce /ˌɪntrəˈduːs, -ˈdjuːs/ v.tr. **1** (foll. by to) make (a person or oneself) known by name to another, esp. formally. **2** announce or present to an audience. **3** bring (a custom, idea, etc.) into use. **4** bring (a piece of legislation) before a legislative assembly. **5** (foll. by to) draw the attention or extend the understanding of (a person) to a subject, activity, etc. **6** insert; place in. **7** bring in; usher in; bring forward. **8** begin; occur just before the start of. **9** bring (a plant, animal, disease, etc.) to a place where it does not normally occur. ☐ **introducer** n.

introduction n. **1** the act or an instance of introducing; the process of being introduced. **2** a formal presentation of one person to another. **3** an explanatory section at the beginning of a book etc. **4** a preliminary section in a piece of music, often thematically different from the main section. **5** an introductory treatise on a subject. **6** a thing introduced. ☐ **introductory** adj.

introit /ˈɪntrɔɪt/ n. **1** a psalm or antiphon sung or said while the priest approaches the altar for the Eucharist. **2** a choral response used at the start of a worship service.

introspection /ˌɪntrəˈspekʃən/ n. the examination or observation of one's own mental and emotional processes etc. ☐ **introspective** adj. **introspectively** adv.

introvert ● n. /ˈɪntrəˌvɜrt/ **1** Psych. a person predominantly concerned with his or her own thoughts and feelings rather than with external things. **2** a shy, inwardly thoughtful person (compare EXTROVERT). ● adj. /ˈɪntrəˌvɜrt/ (also **introverted**) typical or characteristic of an introvert. ● v.tr. /ˌɪntrəˈvɜrt/ Psych. direct (one's thoughts or mind) inwards. ☐ **introversion** n.

intrude v. (foll. by on, upon, into) **1** intr. come uninvited or unwanted; force oneself abruptly on others. **2** tr. thrust or force (something unwelcome) on a person. **3** Geol. **a** tr. thrust or force (esp. molten rock material) into. **b** intr. (of rock material) be forced or thrust into as an intrusion.

intruder n. a person who intrudes, esp. into a building with criminal intent.

intrusion n. **1** the act or an instance of intruding. **2** an unwanted interruption etc. **3** Geol. an influx of molten rock between or through strata etc. but not reaching the surface.

intrusive adj. **1** that intrudes or tends to intrude. **2** characterized by intrusion. ☐ **intrusively** adv. **intrusiveness** n.

intuit /ɪnˈtuːɪt, -tjuː-/ v. **1** tr. know by intuition. **2** intr. receive knowledge by direct perception.

intuition n. **1** the power of understanding situations or people's feelings immediately, without the need for conscious reasoning or study (*use your intuition*). **2** an idea or piece of knowledge gained by this power (*had an intuition you were here*).

intuitive adj. **1** of, characterized by, or possessing intuition. **2** perceived by intuition. **3** capable of being easily understood or grasped by intuition. ☐ **intuitively** adv. **intuitiveness** n.

in-turn n. Curling **1** an inward turn of the elbow and an outward turn of the hand made in delivering a stone, thus giving it a clockwise rotation. **2** a stone delivered with such a motion.

Inuit /ˈɪnjuːɪt, ˈɪnɔɪt/ ● n. (pl. same) **1** any of several Aboriginal peoples inhabiting the Arctic coasts of Canada and Greenland. **2** the language of the Inuit; Inuktitut. ● adj. of or relating to the Inuit.

Inuit Tapirisat of Canada n. a national organization, founded in 1971, representing the Inuit of the NWT, northern Quebec and Labrador.

Inuk /ɪnˈuːk/ n. (pl. **Inuit**) a member of any of the Inuit peoples.

Inukshuk /ˈɪnʊkˌʃʊk/ n. a figure of a human made of stones, originally used to scare caribou into an ambush, and now as a marker to guide travellers.

Inuktitut /ɪnˈʊktɪtʊt/ n. the language of the Inuit.

inundate /ˈɪnənˌdeɪt/ v.tr. (often foll. by with) **1** flood. **2** overwhelm (*inundated with inquiries*). ☐ **inundation** n.

Inupiaq /ɪˈnuːpiæk/ n. an Inuit language spoken in Canada, Alaska, and Greenland.

Inupiat /ɪˈnuːpiæt/ (pl. same) ● n. **1** a member of an Inuit people inhabiting areas of northern Alaska. **2** the Inuit language spoken by the Inupiat. ● adj. of or relating to the Inupiat.

inure /ɪˈnjɔr/ v.tr. (often in passive; foll. by to) accustom (a person) to something esp. unpleasant.

in utero /ɪn ˈjuːtəˌroː/ adv. in the womb; before birth.

Inuvialuit /ˌɪˌnuːviˈæluːɪt/ ● n. an Inuit people of the W Canadian Arctic, speaking Inuvialuktun. ● adj. of or relating to this people.

Inuvialuktun /ɪˈnuːviəˌlʊktuːn/ n. an Inuit language of the western Arctic.

invade v.tr. & intr. **1** enter (a country etc.) under arms, with intent to control or subdue it. **2** enter in large numbers; swarm into (*every summer tourists invade the city*). **3** (of a disease) attack (a body etc.). **4** encroach upon (a person's rights, esp. privacy). ☐ **invader** n.

invalid¹ /ˈɪnvəˌlɪd/ ● n. **1** a person weakened or disabled by illness or injury, esp. chronically or permanently. **2** (attrib.) **a** being an invalid (*caring for her invalid mother*). **b** of or for invalids. ● v.tr. (**invalided**, **invaliding**) **1** esp. Brit. (often foll. by out etc.) remove from active service (one who has become an invalid). **2** (usu. in passive) disable (a person) by illness. ☐ **invalidism** n.

invalid² /ɪnˈvælɪd/ adj. **1** not officially acceptable or usable, esp. having no legal force. **2** not true or logical (*an invalid argument*).

invalidate v.tr. **1** make (esp. an argument etc.) invalid. **2** remove the validity or force of (a treaty, contract, etc.). ☐ **invalidation** n.

invalidity /ˌɪnvəˈlɪdɪti/ n. (pl. **-ies**) **1** lack of validity. **2** the condition of being an invalid; bodily infirmity.

invaluable adj. above valuation; inestimable. ☐ **invaluableness** n. **invaluably** adv.

invariable adj. **1** unchangeable; always the same. **2** Math. constant, fixed. ☐ **invariability** n. **invariably** adv.

invasion n. **1** the act of invading or process of being invaded. **2** an entry of a hostile army into a country or territory. **3** the entry or arrival of a large number of people in a place (*an invasion of tourists*). **4** a harmful incursion of any kind, e.g. of disease, moral evil, etc. **5** the spreading to new sites of pathogenic microorganisms or malignant cells already in the body. **6** intrusion; encroachment upon a person's property, rights, privacy, etc.

invasive adj. **1** (of weeds, cancer cells, etc.) tending to spread. **2** (of medical procedures etc.) involving the introduction of instruments into the body. **3** tending to encroach on the privacy, rights, etc., of others. □ **invasiveness** n.

invective n. **1 a** strongly attacking words. **b** the use of these. **2** abusive rhetoric.

inveigle /ɪn'veɪgəl, -'viːgəl/ v.tr. (foll. by into, or to + infin.) entice; persuade by guile.

invent v.tr. **1** create by thought; devise; originate (a new method, an instrument, etc.). **2** concoct (a false story etc.).

invention n. **1** the process of inventing. **2** a thing invented; a contrivance, esp. one for which a patent is granted. **3** a fictitious statement or story; a fabrication. **4** creativity, inventiveness. **5** a short piece for keyboard, developing a simple idea.

inventive adj. **1** able or inclined to invent; original in devising. **2** showing ingenuity of devising. **3** of or pertaining to invention. □ **inventively** adv. **inventiveness** n.

inventor n. a person who invents things, esp. as an occupation.

inventory • n. (pl. **-ies**) **1 a** a complete list of goods in stock, house contents, etc. **b** the goods listed in this. **c** the action of compiling such a list. **2** any list, catalogue, or detailed account (an inventory of jobs to do). **3** N Amer. the total of a firm's commercial assets. **4** N Amer. a means of taking stock of the quality, characteristics, and growth of various forest areas through aerial mapping and sampling on the ground. • v.tr. (**-ies, -ied**) **1** make an inventory of. **2** enter (goods) in an inventory.

inverse • adj. inverted in position, order, or relation. • n. **1** the state or condition of being inverted. **2** (often foll. by of) a thing that is the opposite or reverse of another. **3** Math. an element which, when combined with a given element in an operation, produces the identity element for that operation. □ **inversely** adv.

inverse proportion n. (also **inverse ratio**) a relation between two quantities such that one increases in proportion as the other decreases.

inversion n. **1 a** the act of turning upside down, inside out, or inward. **b** the state of being so turned. **2** the reversal of a normal order, position, sequence, or relation. **3** the reversal of the order of words, for rhetorical effect. **4 a** the reversal of the normal variation of air temperature with altitude, i.e. an increase of temperature with height instead of the normal decrease. **b** a layer of air having such a reversed gradient. **5 a** the decomposition of an optically active carbohydrate, esp. sucrose, by which the direction of the optical rotatory power is reversed. **b** the reversal of direction of rotation of a plane of polarized light. **6** Psych. homosexuality. **7** the conversion of direct current into alternating current.

invert • v.tr. **1** turn upside down, inside out, or inward. **2** reverse the position, order, sequence, or relation of. **3** subject to inversion. • n. Psych. a homosexual. □ **inverter** n. **invertibility** n. **invertible** adj.

invertebrate /ɪn'vɜːtəbreɪt, -,brət/ • adj. (of an animal) not having a backbone or spinal column. • n. an invertebrate animal.

invert sugar n. a mixture of glucose and fructose obtained by the hydrolysis of sucrose.

invest v. **1** tr. (often foll. by in) **a** apply or use (money), esp. for profit. **b** devote (time, effort etc.) to an enterprise. **2** intr. (foll. by in) **a** put money for profit (into stocks etc.). **b** informal buy (something useful) (invested in a new car). **3** tr. **a** (foll. by with) provide or

credit (a person or thing with qualities, insignia, or rank). **b** (foll. by in) attribute or entrust (qualities or feelings to a person). □ **investable** adj. **investor** n.

investigate v. **1** tr. **a** inquire into; examine; study carefully. **b** make an official inquiry into. **2** intr. make a systematic inquiry or search. □ **investigator** n.

investigation n. **1** the process or an instance of investigating. **2** a formal examination or study.

investigative /ɪn'vestɪ,geɪtɪv, -gətɪv/ adj. **1 a** (of journalism or broadcasting) investigating and seeking to expose malpractice, miscarriage of justice, etc. **b** (of a journalist etc.) engaged in this. **2** characterized by or inclined to investigation.

investiture n. the formal investing of a person with honours or rank.

investment n. **1 a** the act or process of investing money, time, effort, etc. **b** an instance of this. **2** money etc. invested. **3** property etc. in which money is or may be invested.

investment bank n. a financial institution that specializes in financing commercial loans, mergers and acquisitions, foreign trade, etc. □ **investment banker** n. **investment banking** n.

investment company n. a company that invests the funds provided by shareholders in a variety of securities, its profits being made from the income and capital gains provided by these securities.

investment dealer n. Cdn **1** = INVESTMENT COMPANY. **2** a person who is a broker for an investment company.

investment income n. **1** a person's income derived from investments. **2** the income of a business derived from its outside investments rather than from its trading activities.

inveterate /ɪn'vetərət/ adj. **1** (of a person) confirmed in an esp. undesirable habit etc. (an inveterate gambler). **2 a** (of a habit etc.) long established, ingrained. **b** (of an activity, esp. an undesirable one) habitual. □ **inveterately** adv.

invidious /ɪn'vɪdɪəs/ adj. (of an action, conduct, attitude, etc.) likely to excite resentment or indignation against the person responsible, esp. by real or seeming injustice (an invidious position). □ **invidiously** adv. **invidiousness** n.

invigorate v.tr. give vigour or strength to. □ **invigorating** adj. **invigoratingly** adv. **invigoration** n.

invincible adj. **1** unconquerable; that cannot be defeated. **2** insurmountable. □ **invincibility** n. **invincibly** adv.

inviolable /ɪn'vaɪələbəl/ adj. not to be violated, dishonoured, or profaned (inviolable rights). □ **inviolability** n. **inviolably** adv.

inviolate /ɪn'vaɪələt/ adj. **1** not violated or profaned. **2** safe from violation or harm.

invisible adj. **1 a** unable to be seen; that by its nature is not perceivable by the eye. **b** not in sight; hidden, obscured, secret. **2** too small or inconspicuous to be seen or noticed; imperceptible. **3** artfully concealed (invisible mending). □ **invisibility** n. **invisibly** adv.

invisible ink n. ink which becomes invisible when on paper so that writing cannot be seen until the paper is heated or otherwise treated.

invitation n. **1** the process of inviting or fact of being invited, esp. to a social occasion. **2** the spoken or written form in which a person is invited. **3** the action or an act of enticing; attraction, allurement.

invitational esp. N Amer. • adj. (of a tournament, contest etc.) open only to those invited. • n. an invitational contest etc.

invite ● *v.* **1** *tr.* (often foll. by *to*, or *to* + infin.) ask (a person) courteously to come, or to do something (*invited her to lunch*). **2** *tr.* make a formal courteous request for (*invited comments*). **3** *tr.* tend to call forth unintentionally (something unwanted) (*inviting trouble*). **4 a** *tr.* attract. **b** *intr.* be attractive. ● *n.* /ˈɪnvaɪt/ *informal* an invitation. □ **invitee** *n.* **inviter** *n.*

inviting *adj.* **1** attractive. **2** enticing, tempting. □ **invitingly** *adv.*

in vitro /ɪn ˈviːtroː/ *adv. Biol.* (of processes or reactions) performed, obtained, or occurring in a test tube, culture dish, or elsewhere outside a living organism.

in vitro fertilization *n.* a method of fertilizing an ovum in a test tube, culture dish, etc. and then implanting it in a uterus for gestation. Abbr.: **IVF**.

in vivo /ɪn ˈviːvoː/ *adv. Biol.* (of processes) taking place in a living organism.

invocation /ˌɪnvəˈkeɪʃən/ *n.* **1 a** the act or an instance of invoking an authority, a precedent, etc. **b** the act or an instance of calling upon God, a deity, etc. in prayer. **2** an appeal to a supernatural being or beings, e.g. the Muses, for psychological or spiritual inspiration. **3** *Christianity* the words 'In the name of the Father' etc. used at the beginning of a religious service, as the preface to a sermon, etc.

invoice ● *n.* a list of goods shipped or sent, or services rendered, with prices and charges; a bill. ● *v.tr.* **1** make an invoice of (goods and services). **2** send an invoice to (a person).

invoke *v.tr.* **1 a** appeal to (the law, a person's authority, etc.), esp. for support, confirmation, etc. **b** put or call (a law, model, etc.) into operation or effect. **2** call on (a deity etc.) in prayer or as a witness. **3** ask earnestly for (vengeance, help, etc.). **4** summon (a spirit) by charms. **5** *Computing* cause (a procedure etc.) to be carried out.

involuntary *adj.* **1** not done willingly or by choice; unintentional. **2** (of a nerve, muscle, or movement) not under the control of the will. □ **involuntarily** *adv.* **involuntariness** *n.*

involve *v.tr.* **1** (often foll. by *in*) cause (a person or thing) to participate, or share the experience or effect (of a situation, activity, etc.). **2** imply, entail, make necessary. **3** (foll. by *in*) implicate (a person in a charge, crime, etc.). **4** include or affect in its operations.

involved *adj.* **1** (often foll. by *in*) **a** connected or associated with (*involved in biotechnology*). **b** implicated (*involved in drug dealing*). **2** complicated in thought or form (*an involved process*). **3** (often foll. by *with*) engaged in a romantic relationship (*involved with a married man*).

involvement *n.* **1** (often foll. by *in*, *with*) **a** the action or process of involving something or someone. **b** the fact or condition of being involved. **2** a complicated affair, relationship, or concern.

invulnerable *adj.* **1** that cannot be wounded or hurt, physically or mentally. **2** unassailable; not liable to damage or harm, esp. from attack. □ **invulnerability** *n.* **invulnerably** *adv.*

-in-waiting *comb. form* **1** attending another person (*lady-in-waiting*). **2** future (*leader-in-waiting*).

inward ● *adj.* **1** directed toward the inside; going in. **2** situated within; that is the inner or innermost part. **3** mental, spiritual. ● *adv.* (also **inwards**) **1** towards the inside. **2** in the mind or soul.

inwardly *adv.* **1** on the inside. **2 a** in the mind or soul. **b** at heart, in reality, secretly. **3** (of speaking) not aloud; inaudibly.

inwardness *n.* **1** inner nature; essence. **2** the condi-

tion of being inward. **3 a** introspection. **b** spirituality.

in-your-face *adj.* (also **in your face** *predic.*) *slang* aggressively blatant or provocative (*an in-your-face attitude*).

I/O *abbr. Computing* = INPUT/OUTPUT.

IOC *abbr.* International Olympic Committee.

IODE *abbr. Cdn* IMPERIAL ORDER DAUGHTERS OF THE EMPIRE.

iodide /ˈaɪəˌdaɪd/ *n. Chem.* any compound of iodine with another element or group.

iodine /ˈaɪəˌdaɪn, -ˌdiːn/ *n.* **1** a non-metallic element of the halogen group, forming black crystals and a violet vapour, used in medicine and photography, and an essential element for living organisms. **2** a solution of this in alcohol used as a mild antiseptic.

iodize /ˈaɪəˌdaɪz/ *v.tr.* treat or impregnate with iodine. □ **iodization** *n.*

IOF *abbr.* Independent Order of Foresters.

ion /ˈaɪɒn, ˈaɪən/ *n.* an atom, molecule, or group that has lost one or more electrons (= CATION), or gained one or more electrons (= ANION).

ion exchange *n.* the exchange of ions of the same charge between a usu. aqueous solution and a solid, used in water-softening, separation of chemical compounds, etc. □ **ion exchanger** *n.*

Ionic /aɪˈɒnɪk/ ● *adj.* **1** of the order of Greek architecture characterized by a column with scroll shapes on either side of the capital. **2** of the ancient Greek dialect used in Ionia, the central part of the west coast of Asia Minor. ● *n.* the Ionic dialect.

ionic /aɪˈɒnɪk/ *adj.* of, relating to, or using ions.

ionization chamber *n.* an instrument for gauging radiation intensity by measuring the charge on the ions produced by the radiation in a volume of gas.

ionize /ˈaɪəˌnaɪz/ *v.tr. & intr.* convert or be converted into an ion or ions. □ **ionizable** *adj.* **ionization** *n.*

ionizer *n.* any thing which produces ionization, esp. a device used to improve air quality in a room etc.

ionizing radiation *n.* a radiation of sufficient energy to cause ionization in the medium through which it passes.

ionosphere /aɪˈɒnəˌsfiːr/ *n.* an ionized region of the atmosphere above the stratosphere, extending to about 1 000 km above the earth's surface. □ **ionospheric** /-ˈsferɪk/ *adj.*

IOOF *abbr.* Independent Order of Oddfellows.

iota /aɪˈoːtə/ *n.* **1** the ninth letter of the Greek alphabet (Ι, ι). **2** (usu. with *neg.*) the smallest possible amount.

IOU *n.* a signed document acknowledging a debt.

IPA *abbr.* **1** INTERNATIONAL PHONETIC ALPHABET. **2** International Phonetic Association.

IPO *abbr.* initial public offering, the first offering by a private company of stock for public purchase, usu. to raise start-up or expansion capital.

ips *abbr.* (also **i.p.s.**) inches per second.

ipso facto /ˌɪpsoː ˈfæktoː/ *adv.* **1** by that very fact or act. **2** thereby.

IQ *abbr.* = INTELLIGENCE QUOTIENT.

IR *abbr.* infrared.

Ir *symbol* iridium.

IRA *abbr.* = IRISH REPUBLICAN ARMY.

Iranian /ɪˈreɪniən, -ˈrɒniən/ ● *adj.* **1** of or relating to Iranians or Iran, a country in the Middle East. **2** of the Indo-European group of languages including Persian, Pashto, Avestan, and Kurdish. ● *n.* **1 a** a native or national of Iran. **b** a person of Iranian descent. **2** the Iranian languages.

Iraqi /ɪˈræki, -ˈrɒki/ ● *adj.* of or relating to Iraqis or

Iraq, a country on the Persian Gulf. ● n. (pl. **Iraqis**) **1 a** a native or national of Iraq. **b** a person of Iraqi descent. **2** the form of Arabic spoken in Iraq.

irascible /ɪˈræsɪbəl/ adj. **1** irritable, hot-tempered, easily provoked to anger or resentment. **2** (of an emotion, action, etc.) characterized by, arising from, or exhibiting anger. □ **irascibility** n. **irascibly** adv.

irate /aɪˈreɪt/ adj. **1** angry, enraged. **2** (of an action etc.) characterized by, arising from, or exhibiting anger (an irate letter).

IRB abbr. Cdn Immigration and Refugee Board.

IRBM abbr. intermediate-range ballistic missile.

IRC abbr. Computing Internet Relay Chat.

ire n. anger, wrath.

iridescent /ˌɪrɪˈdesənt/ adj. **1** showing rainbow-like luminous or gleaming colours. **2** changing colour with position. □ **iridescence** n. **iridescently** adv.

iridium /ɪˈrɪdɪəm/ n. a hard white metallic element, used esp. in alloys.

iridology /ɪrɪˈdɒlədʒi/ n. (in alternative medicine) diagnosis by examination of the iris of the eye. □ **iridologist** n.

iris n. **1** the flat circular coloured membrane behind the cornea of the eye, with a circular opening (pupil) in the centre. **2** any herbaceous plant of the genus Iris, usu. with tuberous roots, sword-shaped leaves, and showy flowers. **3** (in full **iris diaphragm**) an adjustable diaphragm of thin overlapping plates for regulating the size of a central hole esp. for the admission of light to a lens.

Irish ● adj. of or relating to Ireland, an island of the British Isles, or its people, or the Celtic language of Ireland. ● n. **1** (prec. by the; treated as pl.) the people of Ireland, or their immediate descendants in other countries, esp. those of Celtic origin. **2** the Celtic language of Ireland. **3** informal temper, passion (don't get your Irish up). □ **Irishness** n.

Irish bull n. = BULL³.

Irish coffee n. hot coffee mixed with Irish whiskey and served with whipped cream on top.

Irishman n. (pl. **-men**) a man who is Irish by birth or descent.

Irish moss n. = CARRAGEEN.

Irish Republican Army n. the military arm of Sinn Fein, aiming for union between the Republic of Ireland and Northern Ireland.

Irish setter n. a breed of setter with a long silky dark red coat and a long feathered tail.

Irish terrier n. a rough-haired, light reddish-brown breed of terrier.

Irish whiskey n. a whisky made in Ireland from malted barley and seldom blended.

Irish wolfhound n. a breed of large, rough-coated hound, often grey in colour.

Irishwoman n. (pl. **-women**) a woman who is Irish by birth or descent.

irk v.tr. (often prec. by it as subject) irritate, bore, annoy.

irksome adj. tedious, annoying, tiresome. □ **irksomely** adv. **irksomeness** n.

IRO abbr. International Refugee Organization.

iron ● n. **1** a silver-white metallic element occurring naturally as hematite, magnetite, etc., much used for tools and implements, and an essential element in all living organisms. **2** this as a type of unyieldingness or a symbol of firmness (will of iron). **3** a tool or implement made of iron (branding iron). **4** a household appliance with a flat base which uses dry heat or steam to remove wrinkles from fabric when passed over it. **5** a golf club with an iron or steel sloping head which is angled in order to loft the ball (often in comb. with a number indicating the degree of angle: seven-iron). **6** a preparation of iron as a tonic or dietary supplement, used to treat anemia etc. (iron pills). **7** (usu. in pl.) a fetter (clapped in irons). ● adj. **1 a** consisting or made of iron. **b** resembling iron, esp. in appearance or hardness. **2** very robust, tough, enduring. **3 a** firm, inflexible, stubborn, unyielding (iron determination). **b** cruel, merciless, implacable, severe. ● v. **1 a** tr. smooth (clothes etc.) with an iron. **b** intr. (of a garment, material, etc.) become smooth by being pressed with an iron. **2** tr. shackle with irons. □ **in irons** handcuffed, chained, etc. **iron in the fire** an undertaking, opportunity, or commitment (too many irons in the fire). **iron out** remove or smooth over (difficulties etc.).

Iron Age n. the period following the Bronze Age when iron replaced bronze in the making of implements and weapons.

ironclad adj. **1** strict, rigorous, hard and fast. **2** clad or protected with iron.

Iron Curtain n. the notional barrier to the passage of people and information which existed between the West and the countries of the former Soviet bloc until the decline of Communism.

iron fist n. firmness or ruthlessness.

iron hand n. = IRON FIST. □ **ironhanded** adj.

ironic /aɪˈrɒnɪk/ adj. (also **ironical**) **1** using or displaying irony. **2** in the nature of irony. ¶It is not recommended to use ironic to describe any mildly surprising, unexpected, coincidental, or paradoxical state of affairs. □ **ironically** adv.

ironing n. **1** the pressing and smoothing of clothes etc. with a heated iron. **2** clothes etc. which are to be or have just been ironed.

ironing board n. a long narrow flat surface usu. on legs and of adjustable height, on which clothes etc. are ironed.

ironist /ˈaɪrnɪst/ n. a person who uses irony. □ **ironize** v.intr.

iron man n. **1** a brave or robust man, esp. a powerful athlete. **2** (**Ironman**) a multi-event sporting contest demanding stamina, esp. a consecutive triathlon of swimming, cycling, and running.

iron-on adj. able to be fixed to the surface of a fabric etc. by ironing.

iron ore n. any rock or mineral from which iron is or may be extracted.

ironstone n. **1** any rock containing a substantial proportion of an iron compound. **2** a kind of hard white opaque stoneware.

ironwood n. any of various trees with strong wood, esp. the hornbeam and hop hornbeam of the birch family, growing in eastern N America.

ironwork n. **1** things made of iron. **2** work in iron. □ **ironworker** n.

ironworks n. (as sing. or pl.) a place where iron is smelted or iron goods are made.

irony¹ /ˈaɪroni, ˈaɪrni/ n. (pl. **-ies**) **1 a** the expression of meaning using language that normally expresses the opposite. **b** an instance of this; an ironic utterance or expression. **2** a discrepancy between the expected and actual state of affairs. **3** a literary technique in which the audience can perceive hidden meanings unknown to the characters.

irony² /ˈaɪrni/ adj. of or like iron.

Iroquoian /ˌɪrəˈkwɔɪən/ ● n. **1** a major Aboriginal linguistic group, including Cayuga, Mohawk, Oneida, Onondaga, Seneca, and Tuscarora. **2** a member of the Iroquois. ● *adj.* of or relating to the Iroquois or the Iroquoian linguistic group or one of its members.

Iroquois /ˈɪrəˌkwɒɪ/ ● *n.* (*pl.* same) **1 a** a confederacy of Iroquoian peoples (originally including the Cayuga, Mohawk, Oneida, Onondaga, and Seneca, and later the Tuscarora) living in Ontario, Quebec, and New York. **b** a member of any of the peoples of this confederacy. **2** any of the languages of these peoples. ● *adj.* of or relating to the Iroquois or their languages.

irradiate *v.tr.* **1** subject to any form of radiation. **2** make brighter, light up (*faces irradiated with joy*). **3** throw light on (a subject).

irradiation *n.* **1 a** the action or process of irradiating. **b** an instance of this. **2 a** the use of radiation for diagnostic or therapeutic purposes. **b** the process of exposing food to gamma rays to kill micro-organisms.

irrational *adj.* **1** illogical; unreasonable. **2** not capable of reasoning. **3** *Math.* (of a root etc.) not rational; not commensurate with the natural numbers, e.g. a non-terminating decimal. ☐ **irrationalism** *n.* **irrationalist** *n.* **irrationality** *n.* **irrationalize** *v.tr.* **irrationally** *adv.*

irreconcilable ● *adj.* **1** implacably hostile. **2** (of ideas, actions, etc.) incompatible, unable to be made consistent or brought into harmony (*irreconcilable differences*). ● *n.* **1** an uncompromising opponent of a political measure etc. **2** (*usu.* in *pl.*) any of two or more items, ideas, etc., that cannot be made to agree. ☐ **irreconcilability** *n.* **irreconcilably** *adv.*

irrecoverable *adj.* **1** that cannot be recovered or retrieved. **2** that cannot be remedied or rectified. ☐ **irrecoverably** *adv.*

irredeemable *adj.* **1** that cannot be redeemed or bought back. **2 a** hopeless, absolute. **b** beyond redemption, thoroughly depraved. ☐ **irredeemably** *adv.*

irreducible *adj.* **1 a** that cannot be reduced or made smaller. **b** that cannot be simplified. **2** (often foll. by *to*) that cannot be brought to a desired condition. ☐ **irreducibility** *n.* **irreducibly** *adv.*

irrefutable *adj.* that cannot be refuted or disproved. ☐ **irrefutably** *adv.*

irregular ● *adj.* **1** not regular; unsymmetrical, uneven; varying in form. **2** (of a surface) uneven. **3** contrary to a rule, moral principle, or custom. **4** uneven in duration, order, etc.; not occurring at regular intervals. **5** (of troops) not belonging to the regular or established army. **6** *Grammar* (of a verb, noun, etc.) not inflected according to the usual rules. **7** *N Amer.* (of clothing, cloth, etc.) flawed or damaged, and thus often offered for sale at a reduced price. **8** (of a flower) having unequal petals etc. **9** (of a galaxy) having an irregular shape, esp. lacking any apparent axis of symmetry or central nucleus. **10** not having regular bowel movements or menstrual periods. ● *n.* **1 a** (in *pl.*) irregular troops. **b** a member of an irregular military force. **2** *N Amer.* (*usu.* in *pl.*) an imperfect piece of merchandise, esp. cloth or clothing, often sold at a reduced price. ☐ **irregularity** *n.* (*pl.* **-ies**). **irregularly** *adv.*

irrelevant *adj.* (often foll. by *to*) not relevant; not applicable (to a matter in hand). ☐ **irrelevance** *n.* **irrelevancy** *n.* (*pl.* **-ies**). **irrelevantly** *adv.*

irreligious *adj.* **1** indifferent or hostile to religion. **2** lacking a religion. ☐ **irreligiousness** *n.*

irremediable *adj.* that cannot be remedied. ☐ **irremediably** *adv.*

irreparable *adj.* (of an injury, loss, etc.) that cannot

be rectified or made good. ☐ **irreparability** *n.* **irreparably** *adv.*

irreplaceable *adj.* that cannot be replaced if lost or damaged (*an irreplaceable vase*). ☐ **irreplaceably** *adv.*

irrepressible *adj.* that cannot be repressed or restrained. ☐ **irrepressibility** *n.* **irrepressibly** *adv.*

irreproachable *adj.* faultless, blameless. ☐ **irreproachability** *n.* **irreproachably** *adv.*

irresistible *adj.* **1** too strong or convincing to be resisted. **2** delightful; alluring. ☐ **irresistibility** *n.* **irresistibly** *adv.*

irresolute *adj.* **1** hesitant, undecided. **2** lacking in resoluteness. ☐ **irresolutely** *adv.* **irresolution** *n.*

irrespective *adj.* (foll. by *of*) not taking into account; regardless of. ☐ **irrespectively** *adv.*

irresponsible *adj.* **1** acting or done without due sense of responsibility. **2** not responsible for one's conduct. ☐ **irresponsibility** *n.* **irresponsibly** *adv.*

irretrievable *adj.* that cannot be retrieved or restored. ☐ **irretrievability** *n.* **irretrievably** *adv.*

irreverent *adj.* lacking reverence; disrespectful. ☐ **irreverence** *n.* **irreverently** *adv.*

irreversible *adj.* not reversible or alterable, irrevocable. ☐ **irreversibility** *n.* **irreversibly** *adv.*

irrevocable /ɪˈrevəkəbəl, ɪrəˈvoːk-/ *adj.* **1** unalterable. **2** gone beyond recall. ☐ **irrevocability** *n.* **irrevocably** *adv.*

irrigate *v.tr.* **1** supply (land or a crop) with water, esp. by means of specially constructed channels or pipes. **2** *Med.* supply (a wound etc.) with a constant flow of liquid. ☐ **irrigation** *n.* **irrigator** *n.*

irritable *adj.* **1** easily annoyed or angered. **2** (of an organ etc.) very sensitive to contact. **3** *Biol.* responding actively to physical stimulus. ☐ **irritability** *n.* **irritably** *adv.*

irritable bowel syndrome *n.* a condition involving abdominal pain and diarrhea or constipation, associated with stress, depression, etc.

irritant ● *adj.* causing irritation. ● *n.* an irritant substance. ☐ **irritancy** *n.*

irritate *v.tr.* **1** excite to anger; annoy. **2** stimulate discomfort or pain in (a part of the body). **3** *Biol.* stimulate (an organ) to action. ☐ **irritatedly** *adv.* **irritating** *adj.* **irritatingly** *adv.* **irritation** *n.* **irritative** *adj.*

IRS *abbr.* (in the US) INTERNAL REVENUE SERVICE.

Is. *abbr.* **1** Island(s). **2** Isle(s).

is *3rd sing. present of* BE.

ISBN *abbr.* international standard book number.

ischium /ˈɪskiəm/ *n.* (*pl.* **ischia** /-kiə/) the curved bone forming the base of each half of the pelvis.

ISDN *abbr.* INTEGRATED SERVICES DIGITAL NETWORK.

-ish *suffix* forming adjectives: **1** from nouns, meaning: **a** having the qualities or characteristics of (*boyish*). **b** of the nationality of (*Danish*). **2** from adjectives, meaning 'somewhat' (*thickish*). **3** *informal* denoting an approximate age or time of day (*fortyish*; *six-thirtyish*).

Islam /ˈɪzlæm, -lɒm, -ˈlæm/ *n.* **1** the religion of the Muslims, a monotheistic faith regarded as revealed through Muhammad as the Prophet of Allah. **2** the Muslim world. ☐ **Islamic** /ɪzˈlæmɪk/ *adj.* **Islamism** *n.* **Islamist** *n.* **Islamize** *v.tr.* **Islamization** *n.*

island ● *n.* **1** a piece of land surrounded by water. **2** anything compared to an island, esp. in being isolated or surrounded in some way. **3** a free-standing cupboard unit with a countertop, esp. in a kitchen, allowing access from all sides. **4** = TRAFFIC ISLAND. **5** a clump of woodland surrounded by prairie. **6 a** a detached or isolated thing. **b** *Physiol.* a detached portion of tissue or group of cells (*compare* ISLET). ● *v.tr.* **1** make into an island. **2** isolate.

islander *n.* **1** a native or inhabitant of an island. **2** (**Islander**) (in Canada) a native or resident of Prince Edward Island, Vancouver Island, etc.

island-hop *v.tr.* move from one island to another, esp. as a tourist in an area of small islands. □ **island-hopping** *n.*

isle /aıl/ *n.* an island, esp. a small one.

islet /'aılət/ *n.* **1** a small island. **2** *Anat.* a portion of tissue structurally distinct from surrounding tissues.

islets of Langerhans /'lɒŋɜrhɒnz/ *n.pl.* groups of pancreatic cells secreting insulin and glucagon.

ism *n. informal* usu. *derogatory* any distinctive but unspecified doctrine or practice of a kind with a name ending in *-ism*.

-ism *suffix* forming nouns, esp. denoting: **1** a system, principle, or ideological movement (*Conservatism*; *feminism*). **2** a basis of prejudice or discrimination (*racism*). **3** a peculiarity or characteristic of a nation, individual, etc., esp. in language (*Canadianism*).

Ismaili /ɪz'maıli/ *n.* (*pl.* **Ismailis**) a member of a Shiite Muslim branch that seceded from the main group in the 8th c. over the question of succession to the position of imam.

isn't *contraction* is not.

ISO /'aıso:/ *abbr.* **1** International Organization for Standardization. **2** the numerical exposure index assigned to a photographic film to indicate its sensitivity to light.

iso- /'aıso:/ *comb. form* **1** equal (*isometric*). **2** *Chem.* isomeric, esp. of a hydrocarbon with a branched chain of carbon atoms (*isobutane*).

isobar /'aıso:,bɑr/ *n.* **1** a line on a map connecting positions having the same atmospheric pressure at a given time or on average over a given period. **2** each of two or more isotopes of different elements, with the same atomic weight. □ **isobaric** /-'bærɪk/ *adj.*

isolate ● *v.tr.* **1 a** place apart or alone, cut off from society. **b** place (a patient thought to be contagious or infectious) in quarantine. **2 a** identify and separate for attention (*isolated the problem*). **b** *Chem.* separate (a substance) from a mixture. **3** insulate (electrical apparatus). ● *adj.* = ISOLATED. ● *n.* an isolated person or thing. □ **isolable** /'aısələbəl/ *adj.* **isolator** *n.*

isolated *adj.* **1** lonely; cut off from society or contact; remote (*feeling isolated*; *an isolated farmhouse*). **2** untypical, unique (*an isolated incident*).

isolation *n.* **1** the act or an instance of isolating. **2** the state of being isolated or separated. **3** (*attrib.*) designating a hospital ward etc. for patients with contagious or infectious diseases. □ **in isolation** considered singly and not relatively.

isolationism *n.* the policy of holding aloof from the affairs of other countries or groups esp. in politics. □ **isolationist** *n. & adj.*

isolation pay *n. Cdn* a financial supplement to the salary of an employee who works in an isolated area.

isomer /'aısəmər/ *n.* **1** *Chem.* one of two or more compounds with the same molecular formula but a different arrangement of atoms and different properties. **2** *Physics* one of two or more atomic nuclei that have the same atomic number and the same mass number but different energy states. □ **isomeric** /-'merɪk/ *adj.* **isomerize** /aı'sɒmə,raız/ *v.tr.* **isomerization** *n.*

isometric /,aıso:'metrɪk/ *adj.* **1** of equal measure. **2** *Physiol.* (of muscle action) developing tension while the muscle is prevented from contracting. **3** (of a drawing etc.) with the plane of projection at equal

angles to the three principal axes of the object shown. **4** *Math.* (of a transformation) without change of shape or size. □ **isometrically** *adv.* **isometry** /aı'sɒmɪtri/ *n.* (in sense 4).

isometrics *n.pl.* a system of physical exercises in which muscles are caused to act against each other or against a fixed object.

isomorph /'aıso:,mɔrf/ *n.* an isomorphic substance or organism.

isomorphic *adj.* (also **isomorphous**) **1** exactly corresponding in form and relations. **2** *Mineralogy* having the same form. □ **isomorphism** *n.*

isopropyl alcohol /,aıso'pro:pəl/ *n.* a colourless secondary alcohol used in antifreeze and as a solvent.

isosceles /aı'sɒsɪ,li:z/ *adj.* (of a triangle) having two sides equal.

isostasy /aı'sɒstəsi/ *n. Geol.* the general state of equilibrium thought to exist within the earth's crust. □ **isostatic** /,aıso:'stætɪk/ *adj.* **isostatically** *adv.*

isotherm *n.* **1** a line on a map connecting places having the same temperature at a given time or on average over a given period. **2** a curve for changes in a physical system at a constant temperature. □ **isothermal** *adj.* **isothermally** *adv.*

isotonic /,aıso:'tɒnɪk/ *adj.* **1** designating or relating to a solution having the same osmotic pressure as some particular solution (esp. that in a cell, or a body fluid). **2** of or relating to a solution having the same salt concentration as blood, used esp. by athletes to restore lost salt. **3** *Physiol.* (of muscle action) taking place with normal contraction. □ **isotonically** *adv.*

isotope /'aıso,to:p/ *n. Chem.* each of two or more forms of an element differing from each other in nuclear but not chemical properties. □ **isotopic** /-'tɒpɪk/ *adj.* **isotopically** *adv.* **isotopy** /aı'sɒtəpi/ *n.*

I spy *n.* a children's game in which players try to identify something observed by one of them and identified by its colour or initial letter.

Israeli /ɪz'reıli/ ● *adj.* of or relating to the modern state of Israel. ● *n.* **1** a native or national of Israel. **2** a person of Israeli descent.

Israelite /'ızrıə,laıt, -rə,laıt/ ● *n.* a member of the ancient Hebrew nation or people, esp. an inhabitant of the northern kingdom of the Hebrews (*c.* 930–721 BC). ● *adj.* of or relating to the Israelites.

Issei /'i:seı/ *n. N Amer.* (*pl.* same) a member of the first generation of Japanese immigrants to N America, who immigrated in the late 19th and early 20th c.

ISSN *abbr.* international standard serial number.

issue ● *n.* **1 a** a giving out or circulation of shares, notes, stamps, etc. **b** a quantity of coins, supplies, copies of a newspaper or book etc., circulated or put on sale at one time. **c** an item or amount given out or distributed, esp. by a military force. **d** each of a regular series of a magazine etc. (*the May issue*). **2 a** an outgoing, an outflow. **b** a way out, an outlet, esp. the place of the emergence of a stream etc. **3** a point in question; an important subject of debate or litigation. **4** a result, outcome, or decision. **5** *Law* children, progeny (*died without issue*). ● *v.* (**issues**, **issued**, **issuing**) **1** *intr.* (often foll. by *out*, *forth*) *literary* go or come out. **2** *tr.* **a** send forth; publish; put into circulation. **b** (foll. by *to*, *with*) supply, esp. officially or authoritatively (*issued them with passports*; *issued orders to the staff*). **3** *intr.* **a** (often foll. by *from*) be derived or result. **b** (foll. by *in*) end, result. **4** *intr.* (foll. by *from*) emerge from a condition. □ **at issue 1** under discussion; in dispute. **2** at variance. **make an issue of** make a fuss about; turn into a subject of contention.

take issue (foll. by *with*) disagree. □ **issuance** *n.*

issueless *adj.* **issuer** *n.*

-ist *suffix* forming personal nouns (and in some senses related adjectives) denoting: **1** an adherent of a system etc. in *-ism: see* -ISM **2** (*Marxist*; *fatalist*). **2** a person who subscribes to a prejudice or practises discrimination (*racist*; *sexist*).

isthmus /ˈɪsməs, ˈɪsθ-/ *n.* **1** a narrow piece of land connecting two larger bodies of land. **2** *Anat.* a narrow part connecting two larger parts.

IT *abbr.* information technology.

It. *abbr.* Italian.

it *pron.* (*possess.* **its**; *pl.* **they**) **1** the thing (or occas. the animal or child) previously named or in question (*took a stone and threw it*). **2** the person in question (*Who is it? It is I*; *is it a boy or a girl?*). **3** as the subject of an impersonal verb (*it is raining*; *it is Tuesday*; *it is two kilometres to Whitehorse*). **4** as a substitute for a deferred subject or object (*it is silly to talk like that*; *I take it that you agree*). **5** as a substitute for a vague object (*run for it!*). **6** as the antecedent to a relative word (*it was an owl I heard*). **7** exactly what is needed (*absolutely it*). **8** the extreme limit of achievement. **9** *informal* **a** sexual intercourse. **b** sex appeal. **10** (in children's games) a player who has to perform a required feat, esp. to catch the others. □ **that's it** *informal* that is: **1** what is required. **2** the difficulty. **3** the end, enough. **this is it** *informal* **1** the expected event is at hand. **2** this is the difficulty.

ital. *abbr.* italic (type).

Italian ● *n.* **1 a** a native or national of Italy, a country in S Europe. **b** a person of Italian descent. **2** the Romance language used in Italy and parts of Switzerland. ● *adj.* of or relating to Italy or its people or language.

Italianate /ɪˈtæljəˌneit/ *adj.* of Italian style or appearance.

italic /aiˈtælɪk, ɪ-/ ● *adj.* **1 a** *Typography* of the sloping kind of letters now used esp. for emphasis or distinction and in foreign words. **b** (of handwriting) compact and pointed. **2** (**Italic**) of ancient Italy. ● *n.* **1** a letter in italic type. **2** this type.

italicize /ɪˈtælɪˌsaɪz/ *v.tr.* print in italics. □ **italicization** *n.*

Italo- /ˈɪtələ/ *comb. form* Italian; Italian and.

itch ● *n.* **1** an irritation in the skin. **2** an impatient desire; a hankering. **3** (prec. by *the*) (in general use) scabies. ● *v.intr.* **1** feel an irritation in the skin, causing a desire to scratch it. **2** (usu. foll. by *to* + infin.) (of a person) feel a desire to do something (*am itching to tell you the news*). □ **itching palm** avarice.

itchy *adj.* (**-ier, -iest**) having or causing an itch. □ **have itchy feet** *informal* **1** be restless. **2** have a strong urge to travel. □ **itchiness** *n.*

it'd *contraction* **1** it had. **2** it would.

-ite *suffix* forming nouns meaning 'a person or thing connected with': **1** as natives or residents of a country, city, etc. (*Israelite*; *Vancouverite*). **2** often *derogatory* as followers of a movement etc. (*Trotskyite*).

item *n.* **1 a** any of a number of enumerated or listed things. **b** an entry in an account. **2** an article, esp. one for sale (*household items*). **3** a separate or distinct piece of news, information, etc. **4** *informal* a couple in a romantic or sexual relationship.

itemize *v.tr.* state or list item by item. □ **itemization** *n.* **itemizer** *n.*

iterate /ˈɪtəˌreit/ *v.tr.* repeat; state repeatedly. □ **iteration** *n.*

iterative /ˈɪtərətɪv/ *adj.* characterized by repeating or being repeated. □ **iteratively** *adv.*

itinerant /aiˈtɪnərənt, ɪ-/ ● *adj.* **1** travelling from place to place. **2** (of a judge, minister, etc.) travelling within a circuit. **3** (of a teacher) working at more than one school. ● *n.* a person who travels from place to place, esp. as a minister etc. □ **itinerancy** *n.*

itinerary /aiˈtɪnərəri, ɪ-/ *n.* (*pl.* **-ies**) **1** a detailed route. **2 a** a record of a journey. **b** a listing of the departure and arrival times etc. of aircraft, trains, or other means of transport taken on a journey, usu. accompanying the ticket. **3** a guidebook.

-itis /ˈʌɪtɪs/ *suffix* forming nouns, esp.: **1** names of inflammatory diseases (*bronchitis*). **2** *informal* in extended uses with reference to conditions compared to diseases (*electionitis*).

it'll *contraction* it will; it shall.

ITO *abbr.* International Trade Organization.

its *possess.adj.* of it; of itself (*can see its advantages*). ¶Care should be taken not to confuse *its* with *it's*. *Its*, meaning 'of or belonging to it', does not have an apostrophe. The apostrophe is used only in the short form of *it is* or *it has*, e.g. *It's raining*.

it's *contraction* **1** it is. **2** it has. ¶See ITS.

itself *pron.* emphatic and refl. form of IT. □ **by itself** apart from its surroundings, automatically. **in itself** viewed in its essential qualities (*not in itself bad*).

itsy-bitsy *adj.* (also **itty-bitty**) *informal* usu. *derogatory* tiny, insubstantial, slight.

ITU *abbr.* International Telecommunication Union.

IU *abbr.* INTERNATIONAL UNIT.

IUD *abbr.* INTRAUTERINE DEVICE.

IV *abbr.* intravenous.

I've *contraction* I have.

ivermectin /aivərˈmektɪn/ *n.* a medication used for treating heartworm in dogs.

IVF *abbr.* in vitro fertilization.

ivory (*pl.* **-ies**) ● *n.* **1** a hard creamy-white substance composing the main part of the tusks of an elephant, hippopotamus, walrus, or narwhal. **2** the colour of this. **3** a substance resembling ivory, or made in imitation of it. **4** (usu. in *pl.*) **a** an article made of ivory. **b** *slang* a piano key or a tooth. ● *adj.* of the colour of ivory; creamy white. □ **tickle** (or **tinkle**) **the ivories** *informal* play the piano.

ivory tower *n.* a state or place of seclusion or separation from the ordinary world and the harsh realities of life.

ivy *n.* (*pl.* **-ies**) **1** a climbing evergreen shrub, *Hedera helix*, with usu. dark green shining five-angled leaves. **2** any of various other climbing plants including poison ivy.

Ivy League ● *n.* a group of universities in the eastern US, with a reputation for scholastic and social prestige. ● *adj.* of or relating to the schools of the Ivy League or their students.

IWC *abbr.* International Whaling Commission.

-ize *suffix* forming verbs, meaning: **1** make or become such (*Canadianize*; *realize*). **2** treat in such a way (*monopolize*; *pasteurize*). **3 a** follow a special practice (*economize*). **b** have a specified feeling (*sympathize*). **4** affect with, provide with, or subject to (*oxidize*; *hospitalize*). □ **-ization** *suffix.* **-izer** *suffix.*

Jj

J¹ *n.* (also **j**) (*pl.* **Js** or **J's**) **1** the tenth letter of the alphabet. **2** (as a Roman numeral) = *i* in a final position (*ij*; *vj*).

J² *abbr.* (also **J.**) **1** Judge. **2** Justice. **3** (in cards) jack.

J³ *symbol* joule(s).

jab ● *v.* (**jabbed**, **jabbing**) **1** *tr.* pierce or poke with the end or point of something. **2** *tr.* punch, esp. with a short, sharp blow. **3** *tr.* (foll. by *into*) thrust (a thing) hard or abruptly. **4** *intr.* punch or poke with short, sharp blows (*jabbed at it with a stick*). ● *n.* **1** an abrupt blow with one's fist etc. **2** *N Amer. informal* a satirical or cutting remark or comment.

jabber ● *v.* **1** *intr.* chatter volubly and incoherently. **2** *tr.* utter (words) fast and indistinctly. ● *n.* meaningless jabbering; a gabble. □ **jabberer** *n.*

jacaranda /ˌdʒækəˈrændə/ *n.* **1** any tropical American tree of the genus *Jacaranda*, with trumpet-shaped blue flowers. **2** any tropical American tree of the genus *Dalbergia*, with hard scented wood.

jack ● *n.* **1** a device for lifting heavy objects, esp. the axle of a vehicle off the ground while changing a wheel etc. **2** a playing card with a picture of a soldier, servant, etc. **3** a ship's flag, esp. one flown from the bow and showing nationality. **4** a female connecting device in an electrical circuit (*telephone jack*). **5** a small white ball in lawn bowling, at which the players aim. **6 a** = JACKSTONE. **b** (in *pl.*) a game of jackstones. **7** (**Jack**) typifying the common man (*I'm all right, Jack*). **8** *N Amer. informal* = LUMBERJACK. **9 a** any of various marine perchlike fish of the family Carangidae, including the amberjack. **b** a pike or pickerel. **10** the male of various animals (*jackass*). **11** a species or variety of animal smaller than other similar kinds. **12** (in full **jack boat**) *Cdn* (*Nfld*) *hist.* a small fishing schooner with two masts. ● *v.* **1** *tr.* (usu. foll. by *up*) **a** raise (a car, etc.) with or as with a jack (in sense 1). **b** *informal* increase (prices, volume, etc.) (*jacked up the rent*). **2** *tr. & intr. N Amer.* hunt or fish using a jacklight. □ **every man jack** each and every person. **jack around** *N Amer. slang* deal deceitfully or dishonestly with. **jack into** *slang* access (the Internet, a home page, etc.). **jack off** *coarse slang* masturbate.

jackal *n.* any of various wild doglike mammals of the genus *Canis*, esp. *C. aureus*, found in Africa and S Asia, usu. hunting or scavenging for food in packs.

Jack and Jill *N Amer.* ● *adj.* **1** open to both men and women. **2** designating a party held for a couple soon to be married, to which both men and women are invited. ● *n.* a Jack and Jill party.

jackass *n.* **1** a male donkey or ass. **2** a stupid person.

jackboot *n.* **1** a large boot reaching above the knee worn chiefly by soldiers, e.g. those under the Nazi regime. **2** this as a symbol of fascism or military oppression. □ **jackbooted** *adj.*

jacket ● *n.* **1 a** a sleeved short outer garment. **b** a thing worn esp. round the torso for protection or support (*life jacket*). **2** a casing or covering, e.g. as insulation around a boiler. **3** = DUST JACKET. **4** the skin of a potato, esp. when baked whole. **5** an animal's coat. ● *v.tr.* (**jacketed**, **jacketing**) cover with a jacket. □ **jacketed** *adj.* **jacketless** *adj.*

Jack Frost *n.* frost personified.

jackhammer esp. *N Amer.* ● *n.* a portable pneumatic hammer or drill. ● *v.tr.* drill or break up using a jackhammer.

jack-in-the-box *n.* a toy in the form of a box with a figure inside on a spring that jumps up when the lid is opened.

jack-in-the-pulpit *n.* any of several small woodland plants of the arum family, in N America esp. of the genus *Arisaema*.

jackknife ● *n.* (*pl.* **-knives**) **1** a large pocket knife. **2** a dive in which the body is first bent at the waist and then straightened. ● *v.* (**-knifed**, **-knifing**) **1** *intr.* (of an articulated vehicle) fold against itself in an accidental skidding movement. **2** *intr. & tr.* fold like a jackknife. **3** *intr.* perform a jackknife dive.

jacklight *N Amer.* ● *n.* a light used illegally as a lure when hunting or fishing at night. ● *v.intr.* hunt or fish using a jacklight. □ **jacklighting** *n.*

jack of all trades *n.* a person who can do many different kinds of work.

jack-o'-lantern *n.* a lantern made esp. from a hollowed-out pumpkin carved to resemble a face.

Jack pine *n.* a pine of northern N America, *Pinus banksiana*, with short needles.

jackpot *n.* a large prize or amount of winnings, esp. accumulated in a game or lottery etc. □ **hit the jackpot** *informal* **1** win a large prize. **2** have remarkable luck or success.

jackrabbit *n.* any of various large N American prairie hares of the genus *Lepus* with very long ears and hind legs.

jackstone *n.* **1** a small piece of metal etc. used with others in tossing games. **2** (in *pl.*) **a** a game with a ball and jackstones. **b** the game of jacks.

Jacobean /ˌdʒækəˈbiːən/ ● *adj.* **1** of the reign of James I of England. **2** (of furniture) in the style prevalent then, esp. of the colour of dark oak. ● *n.* a person of the time of James I.

Jacobin /ˈdʒækəbɪn/ *n.* **1** *hist.* a member of a radical democratic club established in Paris in 1789. **2** any extreme radical.

Jacobite /ˈdʒækəbaɪt/ *n.* a supporter of the deposed James II and his descendants in their claim to the British throne after the Revolution of 1688.

Jacob's ladder *n.* **1** a plant, *Polemonium caeruleum*, with corymbs of blue or white flowers, and leaves suggesting a ladder. **2** *Naut.* a rope or chain ladder.

jacquard /ˈdʒækɑːrd/ *n.* **1** an apparatus with perforated cards, fitted to a loom to facilitate the weaving of figured fabrics. **2** (in full **jacquard loom**) a loom fitted with this. **3** a fabric or article made with this, with an intricate variegated pattern.

Jacuzzi /dʒəˈkuːzi/ *n.* (*pl.* **Jacuzzis**) *proprietary* **1** a whirlpool bath. **2** = HOT TUB.

jade ● *n.* **1 a** a hard usu. green stone composed of silicates of calcium and magnesium, or of sodium and aluminum, used for ornaments etc. **b** an ornament etc. made of jade. **2** the green colour of jade. **3**

an inferior or worn-out horse. **4** *derogatory* a disreputable woman. ● *adj.* of the colour jade.

jaded *adj.* tired or worn out; surfeited. □ **jadedly** *adv.* **jadedness** *n.*

jade plant *n.* a succulent plant, *Crassula argentea*, with thick shiny dark green leaves, frequently grown as a houseplant.

jaeger /ˈjeigər/ *n. N Amer.* a seabird of the skua family, esp. one of the smaller kinds, of the genus *Stercorarius*.

jag¹ ● *n.* a sharp projection of rock etc. ● *v.tr.* (**jagged, jagging**) **1** cut or tear unevenly. **2** make indentations in.

jag² *n. esp. N Amer. informal* **1** a drinking bout. **2** a period of indulgence in an activity, emotion, etc.

jagged *adj.* **1** with an unevenly cut or torn edge. **2** deeply indented; with sharp points. **3** having a harsh or irregular quality; not smooth. □ **jaggedly** *adv.* **jaggedness** *n.*

jaguar /ˈdʒægwɑr, -juɑr/ *n.* a large carnivorous feline, *Panthera onca*, of Central and S America, mainly yellowish-brown with dark spots grouped in rosettes.

jail ● *n.* **1** a public prison for the detention of persons committed by process of law. **2** confinement in a jail. ● *v.tr.* put in jail.

jailbird *n.* a prisoner or habitual criminal.

jailbreak *n.* an escape from jail.

jailer *n.* (also **jailor**) **1** a person in charge of a jail or of the prisoners in it. **2** a person who keeps another person forcibly confined.

jailhouse *n. esp. N Amer.* a prison.

Jain /dʒain/ ● *n.* an adherent of a non-Brahmanical Indian religion characterized by its stress on non-violence and strict asceticism as means to liberation. ● *adj.* of or relating to this religion. □ **Jainism** *n.* **Jainist** *n.*

jake *adj. slang* all right; satisfactory.

jalapeno /hæləˈpiːnoː, -ˈpiːnjoː, -ˈpeinoː, -ˈpeinjoː/ *n.* (*pl.* **-os**) (also **jalapeno pepper**) a very hot green chili pepper, used esp. in Mexican-style cooking.

jalopy /dʒəˈlɒpi/ *n.* (*pl.* **-ies**) *informal* a dilapidated old car, truck, etc.

jam ● *v.tr. & intr.* (**jammed, jamming**) **1 a** *tr.* (usu. foll. by *into*) squeeze or wedge into a space. **b** *tr.* (usu. foll. by *in*) bruise or crush by pressure (*jammed my finger in the drawer*). **c** *tr.* become wedged. **2 a** *tr.* cause (machinery etc.) to become wedged or immovable so that it cannot work. **b** *intr.* become jammed in this way. **3** *tr.* push or cram together in a compact mass. **4** *intr.* (foll. by *in, on* to) push or crowd (*they jammed on to the bus*). **5 a** *tr.* block (a passage, road, etc.) by crowding or obstructing. **b** *tr.* (foll. by *in*) obstruct the exit of (*we were jammed in*). **c** *intr.* (of ice, logs, etc.) form an obstruction in a river, stream, etc. **6** *tr.* (usu. foll. by *on*) **a** apply (brakes etc.) forcefully or abruptly. **b** put on (an item of clothing etc.) in a determined or angry manner. **7** *tr.* make (a radio transmission) unintelligible by causing interference. **8** *intr. informal* extemporize with other musicians. ● *n.* **1** a conserve of fruit and sugar boiled to a thick consistency. **2** a squeeze or crush. **3** a crowded mass (*traffic jam*). **4** *informal* an awkward situation or predicament. **5** a stoppage (of a machine etc.) due to jamming. **6** (in full **jam session**) *informal* improvised playing by a group of jazz etc. musicians. □ **jammer** *n.*

Jamaican /dʒəˈmeikən/ ● *adj.* of or relating to Jamaica, an island country in the Caribbean Sea, or the Jamaicans. ● *n.* **1** a native or inhabitant of Jamaica. **2** the variety of English spoken in Jamaica.

Jamaican patty *n.* a half-moon-shaped turnover of yellow pastry with a spicy filling of ground meat.

jamb /dʒæm/ *n.* a side post or surface of a doorway, window, or fireplace.

jambalaya /ˌdʒæmbəˈlaiə/ *n.* **1** a Cajun dish of rice with shrimps, chicken, etc. **2** a mixture; jumble.

jamboree /ˌdʒæmbəˈriː/ *n.* **1** a celebration or merrymaking. **2** a large rally of Scouts.

jambuster *n. Cdn* (*Man. & NW Ont.*) a jelly-filled doughnut.

jammies *n.pl. N Amer. slang* = PYJAMAS 1.

jammy *adj.* (**-ier, -iest**) of or like jam in taste, consistency, etc.

jam-packed *adj. informal* full to capacity.

jam session *n. see* JAM¹ *n.* 6.

Jan. *abbr.* January.

jangle ● *v.* **1** *intr. & tr.* make, or cause (a bell etc.) to make, a harsh metallic sound. **2** *tr.* irritate (the nerves etc.) by discordant sound or speech etc. ● *n.* a harsh metallic sound. □ **jangly** *adj.*

janitor *n.* a caretaker of a school, office building, etc., responsible for its cleaning, heating, etc. □ **janitorial** /ˌdʒænɪˈtɔriəl/ *adj.*

janny *n.* (*pl.* **-ies**) (also **janney**) *Cdn* (*Nfld*) a mummer. □ **jannying** *n.*

January *n.* (*pl.* **-ies**) the first month of the year.

Jap *n. & adj. informal offensive* = JAPANESE.

japan ● *n.* **1** a hard usu. black varnish, esp. of a kind originally from Japan. **2** work in a Japanese style. ● *v.tr.* (**japanned, japanning**) **1** varnish with japan. **2** make black and glossy as with japan.

Japanese ● *n.* (*pl.* same) **1 a** a native or national of Japan, a country in E Asia occupying an archipelago in the Pacific. **b** a person of Japanese descent. **2** the language of Japan. ● *adj.* of or relating to Japan, its people, or its language.

Japanese beetle *n.* a chafer, *Popillia japonica*, which is a plant pest in eastern N America.

Japanese maple *n.* any of several maples native to Japan cultivated for their decorative foliage.

jape ● *n.* a jest or joke. ● *v.intr.* say or do something in jest or mockery; joke. □ **japer** *n.* **japery** *n.*

japonica /dʒəˈpɒnɪkə/ *n.* any flowering shrub of the genus *Chaenomeles*, esp. *C. speciosa*, with round white, green, or yellow edible fruits and bright red flowers.

jar¹ *n.* **1 a** a container of glass, earthenware, plastic, etc., usu. cylindrical. **b** the contents of this. **2** *Brit. & Cdn informal* a glass of beer etc. □ **jarful** *n.* (*pl.* **-fuls**).

jar² ● *v.* (**jarred, jarring**) **1** *intr.* (often foll. by *on*) (of sound, words, manner, etc.) sound discordant or grating (on the nerves etc.). **2 a** *tr.* (foll. by *against, on*) strike or cause to strike with vibration or a grating sound. **b** *intr.* (of a body affected) vibrate gratingly. **3** *tr.* send a shock through (a part of the body) (*the fall jarred his neck*). **4** *intr.* (often foll. by *with*) (of an opinion, fact, etc.) be at variance; be in conflict or in dispute. ● *n.* **1** a jarring sound or sensation. **2** a physical shock or jolt. **3** lack of harmony; disagreement. □ **jarring** *adj.* **jarringly** *adv.*

jargon *n.* **1** words or expressions used by a particular group or profession (*medical jargon*). **2** language marked by affected or convoluted syntax, vocabulary, or meaning. **3** unintelligible or meaningless talk or writing; gibberish. **4** a pidgin (*Chinook Jargon*).

jasmine /ˈdʒæzmɪn/ *n.* (also **jasmin**) any of various ornamental shrubs of the genus *Jasminum* usu. with white or yellow flowers.

jasper *n.* an opaque variety of quartz, usu. red, yellow, or brown in colour.

Jat /dʒæt/ n. a member of an Indic people widely distributed in NW India.

jaundice /'dʒɒndɪs/ ● n. 1 Med. a condition with yellowing of the skin or whites of the eyes, often caused by obstruction of the bile duct or by liver disease. 2 envy, resentment, jealousy. ● v.tr. 1 affect with jaundice. 2 (esp. as **jaundiced** adj.) affect (a person) with envy, resentment, or disillusionment.

jaunt ● n. a short excursion for enjoyment. ● v.intr. take a jaunt.

jaunty adj. (**-ier, -iest**) 1 cheerful and self-confident; carefree. 2 dashing, pert (a jaunty hat). □ **jauntily** adv. **jauntiness** n.

Java /'dʒɑːvə, jʊvə/ n. proprietary a programming language used esp. for creating applications for the Internet and other networks.

java /'dʒævə, jʊvə/ n. N Amer. slang coffee.

Javanese /ˌdʒɑːvəˈniːz/ (also **Javan**) ● n. (pl. same) 1 **a** a native or inhabitant of Java, a large island in the Malay Archipelago. **b** a person of Javanese descent. 2 the Austronesian language of central Java. ● adj. of Java, its people, or its language.

javelin /'dʒævəlɪn, -vlɪn/ n. 1 a light spear thrown in a competitive sport or as a weapon. 2 the athletic event or sport of throwing the javelin.

Javex n. Cdn proprietary chlorine bleach.

jaw ● n. 1 **a** each of the upper and lower bony structures forming the framework of the mouth and containing the teeth. **b** the parts of certain invertebrates used for the ingestion of food. 2 **a** (in pl.) the mouth with its bones and teeth. **b** the narrow mouth of a valley, channel, etc. **c** the gripping parts of a tool or machine. **d** gripping power (jaws of death). 3 informal **a** talkativeness; tedious talk (hold your jaw). **b** a conversation. ● v. informal 1 intr. speak esp. at tedious length; gossip. 2 tr. admonish or lecture. □ **jawed** adj. (also in comb.). **jawless** adj.

jawbone ● n. a bone of the jaw, esp. that of the lower jaw (the mandible), or either half of this. ● v.tr. & intr. seek to restrain (a union or other body in a dispute) by persuasion. □ **jawboning** n.

jawbreaker n. informal 1 a word that is very long or hard to pronounce. 2 a large, round, hard candy. □ **jawbreaking** adj.

jawline n. the outline of the jaw.

Jaws of Life n. a powerful hydraulic tool that can pry apart twisted metal, used esp. to rescue people trapped in wrecked vehicles.

jay n. 1 any of various medium-sized birds of the crow family, often colourful, plumage, e.g. a blue jay. 2 a person who chatters impertinently.

Jaycee n. N Amer., Austral., & NZ a member of a Junior Chamber of Commerce.

jaywalk v.intr. (of a pedestrian) cross a street at a place other than an intersection, crosswalk, etc. or against a red light, esp. with disregard for traffic. □ **jaywalker** n. **jaywalking** n.

jazz ● n. 1 **a** a type of music of African-American origin, characterized by improvisation, syncopated phrasing, and a regular rhythm. **b** (attrib.) designating a style of music containing elements of jazz (jazz-rock). 2 (also **jazz ballet**, **jazz dance**) a style of theatrical dance performed to jazz or popular music, and incorporating elements of popular dance. 3 slang pretentious talk or behaviour, nonsensical stuff. 4 slang energy, excitement. ● v. 1 intr. play or dance to jazz. 2 tr. excite, energize. □ **all that jazz** all that sort of thing. **jazz up** brighten or enliven. □ **jazzer** n.

jazzman n. (pl. **-men**) a male jazz musician.

jazzy adj. (**-ier, -iest**) 1 of or like jazz. 2 slang spirited,

lively, exciting. 3 slang flashy, showy (a jazzy car). □ **jazzily** adv. **jazziness** n.

Jct. abbr. JUNCTION 2.

jealous adj. 1 (often foll. by of) envious or resentful (of a person or a person's advantages etc.). 2 suspicious or resentful of rivalry in love or affection. 3 (often foll. by of) fiercely protective (of rights etc.). 4 (of God) intolerant of disloyalty. □ **jealously** adv.

jealousy n. (pl. **-ies**) 1 a jealous state or feeling. 2 an instance of this.

jean n. 1 a heavy twilled cotton fabric, now usu. denim (usu. attrib.: jean jacket). 2 (usu. in pl.) hard-wearing pants made of this fabric.

Jeep n. proprietary a sturdy, four-wheel drive motor vehicle, suitable for off-road travel.

jeepers interj. (also **jeepers creepers**) N Amer. slang expressing surprise etc.

jeer ● v. 1 intr. (usu. foll. by at) speak or call out in derision or mockery; scoff derisively. 2 tr. scoff at; deride. 3 tr. (usu. foll. by down, from, out, etc.) drive or force away by jeering. ● n. a scoff or taunt. □ **jeeringly** adv.

jeez interj. (also **jeeze**) slang a mild expression of surprise, discovery, etc. (compare GEE).

jeezly adj. (also **jeezely**, **jeesly**) Cdn slang used as an intensifier (you're a jeezly fool!).

jehad var. of JIHAD.

Jehovah /dʒəˈhoʊvə/ n. a form of the Hebrew name of God used in some translations of the Bible.

Jehovah's Witness n. a member of a fundamentalist millenarian Christian sect rejecting the supremacy of the state and religious institutions over personal conscience, faith, etc.

jejunum /dʒɪˈdʒuːnəm/ n. the part of the small intestine between the duodenum and ileum.

Jekyll and Hyde /ˌdʒekəl ənd ˈhaɪd/ n. a person alternately displaying opposing good and evil personalities (also attrib.: a Jekyll-and-Hyde existence).

jell v.intr. informal 1 **a** set as a jelly. **b** (of ideas etc.) take a definite form. 2 (of people) readily co-operate or reach an understanding.

jellied adj. 1 set into a jelly (jellied chicken stock). 2 containing jelly as an ingredient (jellied salad).

Jell-O n. N Amer. proprietary 1 a fruit-flavoured gelatin dessert. 2 the powder used to make this.

jelly ● n. (pl. **-ies**) 1 **a** a type of jam made of fruit juice boiled with sugar and cooled to a semi-solid consistency. **b** a dessert made of juice, fruit-flavoured water, etc., sugar and gelatin, set to a soft semi-solid consistency, often in a mould. **c** a similar preparation derived from meat, bones, etc., and gelatin. 2 any substance of a similar consistency (petroleum jelly). ● v. (**-ies, -ied**) 1 intr. & tr. set or cause to set as a jelly, congeal. 2 tr. set (food) in a jelly. □ **jellylike** adj.

jelly bean n. a bean-shaped candy with a gelatinous centre and a hard sugar coating.

jelly doughnut n. N Amer. a round jam-filled doughnut, usu. coated in icing sugar.

jellyfish n. (pl. usu. same) 1 a marine coelenterate of the class Scyphozoa having an umbrella-shaped jelly-like body and stinging tentacles. 2 informal a feeble person.

jelly roll n. N Amer. a thin, flat, rectangular sponge cake spread with jam or other filling and rolled up to form a cylindrical cake with a spiral cross-section.

je ne sais quoi /ʒə nə sei ˈkwʌ/ n. an indefinable something.

jenny n. (pl. **-ies**) a female donkey or female bird.

jeopardize v.tr. endanger; put into jeopardy.

jeopardy /'dʒepərdi/ n. **1** danger, esp. of severe harm or loss. **2** Law the risk of being convicted and punished for a criminal offence.

jeremiad /ˌdʒerəˈmaiəd, -æd/ n. a doleful complaint or lamentation; a list of woes.

jerk¹ ● n. **1** a sharp sudden pull, twist, twitch, etc. **2** a spasmodic muscular twitch. **3** slang a fool; a stupid or annoying person. **4** (prec. by the) the raising of a barbell to above the head by a rapid extension of the arms, following an initial lift to shoulder level. ● v. **1** intr. move with a jerk. **2** tr. pull, thrust, twist, etc., with a jerk. **3** tr. throw with a suddenly arrested motion. **4** tr. (in weightlifting) raise (a weight) from shoulder level to above the head. □ **jerk around** N Amer. slang deal with unfairly; deceive or mislead. **jerk off** coarse slang (of a male) masturbate. □ **jerker** n.

jerk² ● v.tr. cure (meat) by cutting it in slices and drying it in the sun. ● n. (attrib.) designating an originally Jamaican method of preparing meat by cutting it into strips, seasoning highly with pepper and spices, and barbecuing (jerk chicken).

jerkin n. a sleeveless jacket.

jerkwater adj. N Amer. informal (of a town etc.) small and remote; insignificant.

jerky¹ adj. (-ier, -iest) having sudden abrupt movements; spasmodic. □ **jerkily** adv. **jerkiness** n.

jerky² n. jerked meat.

jerry-built adj. **1** built insubstantially from inferior materials. **2** developed or produced in a slapdash manner. □ **jerry-build** v.tr. **jerry-building** n.

jerry can n. (also **jerrican**) a kind of gasoline or water can.

jersey n. (pl. **-eys**) **1** a soft, fine, usu. stretchy knitted fabric. **2** a knitted usu. woollen pullover or similar garment. **3** a distinguishing sweater or shirt worn by members of a hockey, soccer, etc. team. **4** (**Jersey**) a light brown dairy cow of a breed originally from Jersey in the Channel Islands.

Jerusalem artichoke n. **1** a species of sunflower, Helianthus tuberosus, with edible underground tubers. **2** this tuber used as a vegetable.

jest ● n. **1 a** a joke. **b** fun. **2 a** banter. **b** an object of derision (a standing jest). ● v.intr. **1** joke; make jests. **2** fool about; play or act triflingly. □ **in jest** in fun. □ **jestingly** adv.

jester n. hist. a professional joker or fool at a medieval court etc., traditionally wearing a cap and bells.

Jesu /'dʒiːzuː, 'dʒei-/ Jesus (as an archaic form of address).

Jesuit /'dʒezʊɪt, 'dʒez-, -jʊɪt/ n. a member of the Society of Jesus, a Catholic order founded in 1534.

Jesus¹ the central figure of the Christian religion.

Jesus² /'dʒiːzəs/ interj. (also **Jesus Christ**) taboo slang an exclamation of surprise, dismay, anger, etc.

Jesus freak n. slang a (usu. young) person combining a hippie lifestyle with fervent evangelical Christianity.

Jesus, Mary, and Joseph interj. informal an exclamation of surprise, dismay, etc.

jet¹ ● n. **1** a stream of liquid, gas, or (more rarely) solid particles shot out, esp. from a small opening. **2** a spout or nozzle for emitting water etc. in this way. **3 a** a jet engine (also attrib.: jet fighter). **b** an aircraft powered by one or more jet engines. ● v.tr. & intr. (**jetted, jetting**) **1** spurt out or cause to spurt out in jets. **2** send or travel by jet plane.

jet² ● n. **1 a** a hard black variety of lignite capable of being carved and highly polished. **b** (attrib.) made of this. **2** a deep glossy black. ● adj. of this colour.

jet black ● n. a black colour like jet; a glossy black. ● adj. (**jet-black**) of this colour.

jet boat n. a small boat without a propeller, the engine of which expels a jet of water to provide thrust. □ **jet boater** n. **jet boating** n.

jet engine n. an engine using jet propulsion for forward thrust, esp. of an aircraft.

jet lag n. extreme tiredness and disrupted biological rhythms felt after a long flight in which different time zones are crossed in a relatively short time. □ **jet-lagged** adj.

jetliner n. a commercial airplane equipped with jet engines.

jet-propelled adj. **1** having jet propulsion. **2** (of a person etc.) very fast.

jet propulsion n. propulsion by the backward ejection of a high-speed jet of gas etc.

jetsam /'dʒetsəm/ n. discarded material washed ashore, esp. that thrown overboard to lighten a ship etc. (compare FLOTSAM).

jet set n. informal wealthy people frequently travelling by air, esp. for pleasure (also attrib.: a jet-set lifestyle). □ **jet-setter** n. **jet-setting** adj.

Jet Ski ● n. proprietary a jet-propelled watercraft ridden like a motorbike. ● v.intr. ride on a jet ski. □ **jet skier** n. **jet skiing** n.

jet stream n. **1** a narrow current of very strong winds encircling the globe several miles above the earth. **2** the stream from a jet engine.

jettison /'dʒetɪsən, -zən/ ● v.tr. **1** throw (esp. heavy material) overboard to lighten an aircraft, ship, hot-air balloon, etc. **2** release or drop from a spacecraft in flight. **3** abandon; get rid of (something no longer wanted). ● n. the act of jettisoning.

jetty n. (pl. **-ies**) **1** a landing pier. **2** a pier or breakwater constructed to protect or defend a harbour, coast, etc.

Jew n. a person of Hebrew descent or whose religion is Judaism.

jewel ● n. **1 a** a precious stone; a gem. **b** this as used for its hardness as a bearing in watchmaking. **2** a personal ornament containing a jewel or jewels. **3** something of great beauty or worth. **4** (attrib.) cut or shaped like a jewel (a jewel neckline). **5** (attrib.) having the intense colour of a jewel (jewel tones). ● v.tr. (**jewelled, jewelling**) **1** (esp. as **jewelled** adj.) adorn or set with jewels. **2** (in watchmaking) set with jewels. □ **jewel in the crown** the best in a particular class of assets. □ **jewel-like** adj.

jewel box n. **1** (also **jewellery box**) a small, usu. ornamental box for storing jewellery or other valuables. **2** (also **jewel case**) the hinged plastic case in which a compact disc is packaged.

jeweller n. (also esp. US **jeweler**) a person who makes or sells jewels or jewellery.

jewellery /'dʒuːləri, 'dʒuːəlri, dʒuːlri/ n. (also **jewelry**) ornamental objects for personal adornment, e.g. rings and necklaces, esp. made of precious metal and set with jewels.

Jewish adj. **1** of or relating to Jews. **2** of Judaism. □ **Jewishly** adv. **Jewishness** n.

Jewry n. (pl. **-ies**) the Jewish people, nation, or community; Jews collectively.

Jew's harp n. a small lyre-shaped musical instrument held between the teeth and struck with the finger.

J.H.S. abbr. N Amer. JUNIOR HIGH SCHOOL.

jib ● n. **1** a triangular staysail from the outer end of the jib-boom to the top of the foremast or from the bowsprit to the masthead. **2** the projecting arm of a crane. ● *v.tr. & intr.* (**jibbed, jibbing**) (of a sail etc.) pull or swing round from one side of the ship to the other; gybe.

jib-boom *n.* a spar run out from the end of the bowsprit.

jibe[1] ● *n.* an instance of mocking or taunting. ● *v.* **1** *intr.* (often foll. by *at*) jeer, mock. **2** *tr.* sneer at, taunt, mock.

jibe[2] *var. of* GYBE.

jibe[3] *v.intr. N Amer.* (usu. foll. by *with*) *informal* agree; be in accord.

jiffy *n.* (*pl.* **-ies**) (also **jiff**) *informal* a short time; a moment (*in a jiffy*).

jig ● *n.* **1 a** a lively dance with springs and hops. **b** the music for this, usu. in triple time. **2** a device that holds a piece of work and guides the tools operating on it. **3** a device for catching fish that is jerked up and down through the water. ● *v.* (**jigged, jigging**) **1** *intr.* dance a jig. **2** *tr. & intr.* move quickly and jerkily up and down. **3** *tr.* work on or equip with a jig or jigs. **4** *tr. & intr.* fish (for) or catch with a jig or jigger. ☐ **in jig time** *N Amer. informal* extremely quickly; in a short time. **the jig is up** *N Amer. informal* the scheme is revealed or foiled.

jigger[1] ● *n.* **1 a** a small tackle consisting of a double and single block with a rope. **b** a small sail at the stern. **c** a small fishing boat having this. **2 a** a small glass or metal cup marked for measuring liquor. **b** the quantity of liquor contained in this. **3** *Cdn* **a** a device upon which a gill net is hung underneath ice. **b** a piece of lead shaped like a fish, with two hooks in the mouth, fastened on the end of a heavy fishing line. **4** a person or thing that jigs. ● *v.tr.* (usu. in phr. **I'll be jiggered**) *slang* confound, damn.

jigger[2] *n.* = CHIGOE.

jiggle ● *v.* **1** *tr. & intr.* shake lightly; rock jerkily. **2** *intr.* fidget. ● *n.* a light shake. ☐ **jiggly** *adj.*

Jiggs' dinner *n. Cdn* (*Nfld*) a boiled dinner of corned beef, potatoes, and other vegetables, esp. cabbage.

jigsaw *n.* **1 a** (in full **jigsaw puzzle**) a puzzle consisting of a picture on board or wood etc. cut into irregular interlocking pieces to be reassembled. **b** a mental puzzle resolvable by assembling various pieces of information. **2** (**jig saw**) a machine saw with a fine blade enabling it to cut curved lines in a sheet of wood, metal, etc.

jihad /dʒɪˈhæd/ *n.* **1** a holy war undertaken by Muslims for the propagation or defence of Islam. **2** a campaign or crusade in some cause.

jillion *n. N Amer. informal* a great many, an extremely large quantity. ☐ **jillionth** *adj.*

jilt ● *v.tr.* abruptly reject or abandon (a lover etc.). ● *n.* a person (esp. a woman) who jilts a lover.

Jim Crow *n. US* the practice of segregating or discriminating against blacks (also *attrib.*: *Jim Crow laws*). ☐ **Jim Crowism** *n.*

jim-dandy ● *adj.* excellent; outstanding. ● *n.* an excellent person or thing.

jim-jams *n.pl. slang* a fit of depression or nervousness.

jimmy *N Amer.* ● *n.* (*pl.* **-ies**) a burglar's short crowbar, usu. made in sections. ● *v.tr.* (**-ies, -ied**) force open with a jimmy.

jingle ● *n.* **1 a** a mixed noise as of bells or light metal objects being shaken together. **b** a thing that jingles, esp. a bell. **2 a** a repetition of the same sound in words, esp. as an aid to memory or to attract attention. **b** a short verse of this kind used in advertising etc. ● *v.* **1** *intr. & tr.* make or cause to make a jingling sound. **2** *intr.* proceed or move with such a sound. **3** *intr.*

(of writing) be full of alliterations, rhymes, etc. ☐ **give a person a jingle** *N Amer. informal* telephone a person. ☐ **jingly** *adj.* (**-ier, -iest**).

jingo *n.* (*pl.* **-oes**) a supporter of policy favouring war; a blustering patriot. ☐ **by jingo!** a mild oath. ☐ **jingoism** *n.* **jingoist** *n.* **jingoistic** *adj.*

jink ● *v.intr.* move elusively; dodge. ● *n.* an act of dodging or eluding.

jinni /dʒɪˈniː/ *n.* (also **jinnee, jinn**) (*pl.* **jinn**) (in Muslim mythology) an intelligent being lower than the angels, able to appear in human and animal forms, and having power over people.

jinx *informal* ● *n.* a person or thing that seems to cause bad luck. ● *v.tr.* (often in *passive*) subject (a person) to an unlucky force.

JIT *abbr. Business* just-in-time.

jitter *informal* ● *n.* **1** (**the jitters**) extreme nervousness. **2** *Electronics* **a** slight random or irregular variation, esp. in the shape or timing of a regular pulse. **b** unsteadiness of an image etc. due to this. ● *v.intr.* be or act nervous. ☐ **jitteriness** *n.* **jittery** *adj.*

jitterbug ● *n.* **1** *hist.* a fast dance popular in the 1940s, performed chiefly to swing music. **2** a person fond of dancing this. ● *v.intr.* (**-bugged, -bugging**) dance the jitterbug. ☐ **jitterbugger** *n.*

jiu-jitsu /dʒuːˈdʒɪtsuː/ *n.* a Japanese system of unarmed combat using an opponent's strength and weight to his or her disadvantage, now also practised as physical training.

jive ● *n.* **1** a jerky lively style of dance esp. popular in the 1950s, performed to jazz or rock'n'roll music. **2** music for this dance. **3** a variety of American black English associated esp. with jazz musicians and enthusiasts. **4** *slang* talk, conversation, esp. when misleading or pretentious. ● *v.* **1** *intr.* dance the jive. **2** *intr.* play jive music. **3** *slang* **a** *tr.* mislead, fool (*are you jiving me?*). **b** *intr.* fool around; talk nonsense. **4** *intr. N Amer. informal var. of* JIBE[3]. ☐ **jiver** *n.*

JK *abbr. Cdn* (*Ont.*) JUNIOR KINDERGARTEN.

Jnr. *abbr.* Junior.

job ● *n.* **1** a piece of work, esp. one done for hire or profit. **2** a paid position of employment. **3 a** anything one has to do. **b** responsibility (*it's your job to do the dishes*). **c** a specified operation or other matter, esp. an operation involving plastic surgery (*nose job; paint job*). **4 a** *informal* a difficult task (*had a job to find them*). **b** performance (*did a poor job on the exam*). **5** *slang* an example of its type (*that car's a neat little job*). **6** *Computing* an item of work regarded separately. **7** *slang* a crime, esp. a robbery. **8** a transaction in which private advantage prevails over duty or public interest. **9** *informal* a state of affairs or set of circumstances (*is a bad job*). ● *v.* (**jobbed, jobbing**) **1 a** *intr.* do jobs; do piecework. **b** *tr.* (usu. foll. by *out*) let or deal with for profit; subcontract. **2 a** *intr.* deal in stocks. **b** *tr.* buy and sell (stocks or goods) as a middleman. **3 a** *intr.* turn a position of trust to private advantage. **b** *tr.* deal corruptly with (a matter). **4** *tr. N Amer. slang* swindle. ☐ **do the job** succeed in doing what is required or desired. **get on with the job** proceed with one's work; continue with one's affairs. **on the job** at work; in the course of doing a piece of work. **out of a job** unemployed.

job action *n. N Amer.* an organized protest by employees, such as a work slowdown.

jobber *n.* **1** a wholesaler. **2** a pieceworker. **3** a person who uses a public office or position of trust for private or party advantage.

jobbie *n. slang* = JOB *n.* 5.

jobbing *adj.* working on separate or occasional jobs.

job creation n. the provision of new opportunities for paid employment.

job description n. a written description of the exact responsibilities of a job.

job-hunt v.intr. seek employment. □ **job hunter** n. **job-hunting** n.

jobless adj. unemployed. □ **joblessness** n.

job lot n. a miscellaneous group of articles, esp. bought together.

job satisfaction n. fulfillment gained from doing one's job.

job-sharing n. an arrangement by which a full-time job is done jointly by two or more part-time employees who share the remuneration etc. □ **job-share** n. & v.intr. **job-sharer** n.

Jock n. slang a Scotsman.

jock n. informal **1** N Amer. = JOCKSTRAP. **2** N Amer. an esp. male athlete or sports fan, esp. one not interested in intellectual or artistic pursuits. **3** a disc or video jockey. **4** an enthusiast or devotee of some activity (computer jock). **5** a jockey. □ **jockdom** n. **jockish** adj.

jockey ● n. (pl. **-eys**) **1** a rider in horse races, esp. a professional one. **2** esp. N Amer. informal (usu. in comb.) a person having control, guidance, or direction of something (desk jockey). ● v. (**-eys, -eyed**) **1** intr. (usu. foll. by for) try to gain an advantageous position esp. by skilful manoeuvring or unfair action (jockey for position). **2** tr. ride (a horse) as a jockey. **3** tr. trick, cheat, or outwit (a person).

Jockey Club n. (also **jockey club**) a club or association for the promotion and regulation of horse racing.

Jockey shorts n.pl. N Amer. proprietary men's or boys' close-fitting underpants with elasticized waist and leg openings and a triangular flap at the front.

jock itch n. a fungal infection of the groin area.

jockstrap n. a close-fitting undergarment providing support or protection for the male genitals.

jocular /'dʒɒkjʊlər/ adj. **1** (of speech, action, etc.) of the nature of a joke; said, done, etc. jokingly. **2** (of a person, disposition, etc.) fond of joking; speaking or acting in jest or merriment. □ **jocularity** /-'lærɪti/ n. (pl. **-ies**). **jocularly** adv.

jodhpurs /'dʒɒdpərz/ n.pl. long breeches for riding etc., wide around the hips and thighs but close-fitting from the knee to the ankle.

joe n. slang **1** (also attrib.) a fellow or average man (the average joe). **2** N Amer. coffee.

Joe Blow n. N Amer. informal a hypothetical average man.

joe-boy n. N Amer. informal a person required to perform menial tasks for another.

joe job n. Cdn a menial or monotonous task.

Joe Public n. informal (a member of) the general public.

joey n. (pl. **-eys**) Austral. a young kangaroo.

jog¹ ● v. (**jogged, jogging**) **1** intr. run at a slow pace, esp. as physical exercise. **2** intr. (of a horse) move at a jogtrot. **3** intr. (often foll. by on, along) proceed, go on one's way, get through the time, esp. laboriously (the industry is jogging along at a respectable growth rate). **4** tr. nudge (a person), esp. to arouse attention. **5** tr. shake or bump with a push or jerk. **6** tr. give a gentle reminder to (a person's or one's own memory). ● n. **1 a** a slow walk or trot. **b** a gentle run taken as a form of exercise. **2** a shake, push, or nudge.

jog² N Amer. ● n. **1** a short bend, turn, or change of direction in a road etc., after which the road continues in its original direction. **2** a notch, step, or jag in

an otherwise level surface or straight line. ● v.intr. bend, turn, or suddenly change course or direction.

jogger n. **1** a person who jogs, esp. regularly for exercise. **2** Cdn & Brit. = RUNNING SHOE.

jogging n. running at a gentle, regular pace as a form of exercise (also attrib.: jogging suit).

joggle ● v.tr. & intr. shake or move by or as if by repeated jerks. ● n. **1** a slight shake. **2** the act or action of joggling.

jogtrot ● n. **1** a slow regular trot or pace. **2** a steady, monotonous way of doing something. ● v.intr. go or move at a jogtrot.

john n. N Amer. informal **1** a toilet. **2** a washroom. **3** a prostitute's customer.

johnboat n. N Amer. a small, square-ended, flat-bottomed boat chiefly for use on inland waterways.

John Doe n. N Amer. **1 a** a person whose real name is unknown. **b** Law an anonymous party, usu. the plaintiff, in a legal action. **2** informal = JOE BLOW.

johnnycake n. N Amer. a cornmeal bread usu. baked or fried on a griddle.

Johnny Canuck n. Cdn informal **1** a native, inhabitant, or citizen of Canada. **2** a Canadian soldier, esp. during the world wars. **3** Canada personified.

johnny-come-lately n. (pl. **-latelies**) informal a person who has recently arrived or come to prominence; an upstart.

joie de vivre /ˌʒwɒ də 'viːvrə/ n. a feeling of healthy and exuberant enjoyment of life.

join ● v. **1** tr. (often foll. by to, together) put together; fasten, unite. **2** tr. connect (points) by a line etc. **3** tr. become a member of (an association, society, organization, etc.). **4** tr. take one's place with or in (a company, group, etc.). **5** tr. **a** come into the company of (a person). **b** (foll. by in) take part with (others) in an activity etc. (join me in eating). **c** (foll. by for) share the company of (a person) for a specified occasion (may I join you for lunch?). **6** intr. (often foll. by with, to) come together, be united, esp. in action or purpose. **7** intr. (often foll. by in) take part with others in an activity etc. **8** tr. be or become connected or continuous with (the Liard joins the Mackenzie at Fort Simpson). **9** tr. link or unite (people etc. together) in marriage, friendship, or other alliance. ● n. a point, line, or surface at which two or more things are joined. □ **join battle** begin fighting. **join forces** combine efforts. **join hands 1 a** clasp each other's hands. **b** clasp one's hands together. **2** combine in an action or enterprise. **join up 1** enlist for military service. **2** (often foll. by with) unite, connect. □ **joinable** adj.

joiner n. **1** informal a person who readily joins groups, associations, etc. **2** a device used for making carpentry joints.

joinery n. **1** the construction of wooden furniture etc. **2** carpentry joints collectively.

joint ● n. **1 a** a place at which things or parts are joined together. **b** a point at which, or a contrivance by which, two parts of an artificial structure are joined either rigidly or so as to allow movement. **2 a** a structure in an animal body by which two bones are fitted and held together, usu. so that relative movement is possible. **b** the place of connection of two movable parts in an invertebrate, esp. an arthropod. **3 a** any of the parts into which an animal carcass is divided for food. **b** a part of a plant, animal, etc. connected by a joint to an adjacent part, esp. such a part of a digit or limb. **4** slang **a** often derogatory a place where people go for eating, drinking, entertainment, etc. (strip joint; burger joint). **b** a residence or establishment. **c** N Amer. prison. **5** slang a marijuana cigarette. **6** the part of a stem from which a leaf or branch grows. ● *adj.* **1** (of a single thing) held or done by, or belonging to, two or more persons etc. in conjunction (*a joint venture*). **2** (of a person or persons) sharing with another in some action, state, etc. (*joint author*). **3** of, concerning, or involving both houses of a bicameral parliament. ● *v.tr.* **1** connect or fasten by joints. **2** divide (a body or member) at a joint or into joints. **3** prepare (a board etc.) for being joined to another by planing its edge. □ **joint and several** (of a bond etc.) signed by more than one person, of whom each is liable for the whole sum. **out of joint 1** (of a bone) dislocated. **2** disordered, out of order. □ **jointless** *adj.* **jointly** *adv.*

joint account *n.* a bank account held by more than one person, each of whom has the right to deposit and withdraw funds.

Joint Chiefs of Staff *n.pl.* (in the US) the chief military advisory body to the President.

joint committee *n.* a committee composed of members nominated by two or more distinct bodies.

joint custody *n.* legal custody of a child or children shared by both parents after separation or divorce.

jointed *adj.* **1** provided with, constructed with, or having joints. **2** having joints of a specified kind. **3** *Bot.* **a** having or appearing to have joints. **b** separating readily at the joints.

joint stock *n.* capital held jointly; a common fund.

joint-stock company *n.* a company, usu. unincorporated, that has its members' capital pooled in a common fund.

joint venture *n.* a commercial enterprise undertaken jointly by two or more parties otherwise retaining their separate identities.

joist *n.* each of a series of parallel supporting beams of timber, steel, etc., used in floors, ceilings, etc.

jojoba /ho:ˈhoːbə/ *n.* a plant, *Simmondsia chinensis*, with seeds yielding an extract used in cosmetics etc.

joke ● *n.* **1 a** a thing said or done to excite laughter. **b** a witticism, jest, or short humorous anecdote. **2** a ridiculous thing, person, or circumstance. **3 a** something trifling; a matter that is not serious, true, or worthy of concern (*that theory is a joke*). **b** *N Amer. informal* something very easy (*that exam was a joke*). ● *v.* **1 a** *intr.* make a joke or jokes. **b** *tr.* utter as a joke. **2** *tr.* make the object of a joke; poke fun at; banter. □ **(all) joking aside** speaking seriously. **no joke** *informal* a serious matter. □ **jokey** *adj.* **jokiness** *n.* **jokingly** *adv.*

joker *n.* **1** a person who jokes. **2** a person who is considered foolish or inept and so not treated seriously. **3** a playing card usu. with a figure of a jester, used in some games esp. as a wild card. **4** an unexpected factor or resource.

jollity /ˈdʒɒlɪti/ *n.* (*pl.* **-ies**) **1** the quality or condition of being jolly, cheerful, or festive. **2** merrymaking; festiveness.

jolly[1] ● *adj.* (**-ier, -iest**) **1** cheerful and good-humoured. **2** lively and very pleasant; delightful or enjoyable. ● *v.tr.* (**-ies, -ied**) **1** (usu. foll. by *up, along*) *informal* keep or make (a person) jolly or cheerful by friendly behaviour etc. **2** poke fun at, tease. ● *n.* (*pl.* **-ies**) *N Amer. informal* (usu. in *pl.*) a thrill or cause of excitement or pleasure. □ **jolliness** *n.*

jolly[2] *n.* (*pl.* **-ies**) (in full **jolly boat**) a ship's boat smaller than a cutter, with a bluff bow.

Jolly Jumper *n. Cdn proprietary* an infant swing which suspends a baby in a harness in a standing position just above the floor, allowing the child to jump, exercise its legs, etc.

Jolly Roger *n.* a pirates' black flag, usu. with the skull and crossbones.

jolt ● *v.* **1** *tr.* disturb or shake from the normal position with a jerk. **2** *tr.* give a mental shock to; perturb. **3** *tr.* invigorate suddenly or abruptly. **4** *intr.* **a** move with a jolt. **b** (of a vehicle) move along with jerks, as on a rough road. ● *n.* **1** an abrupt movement or jerk. **2** a surprise or mental shock. **3** a sudden invigorating sensation (*caffeine provides a jolt*).

Jordanian /dʒɔːˈdeɪniən/ ● *adj.* of or relating to the kingdom of Jordan in the Middle East. ● *n.* a native or inhabitant of Jordan.

josh *slang* ● *v.* **1** *tr.* tease or joke with. **2** *intr.* indulge in banter. ● *n.* a good-natured or teasing joke. □ **joshing** *n.*

joss *n.* **1** a Chinese figure of a god. **2** (in full **joss stick**) a stick of fragrant tinder mixed with clay, burned as incense.

jostle ● *v.* **1** *tr.* knock or come into rough collision with. **2** *tr.* (often foll. by *away, from*, etc.) push (a person) roughly or unceremoniously. **3** *intr.* push, shove, or come into collision with, esp. in a crowd. **4** *intr.* (foll. by *for, with*) vie, struggle, or compete forcefully in order to gain something. ● *n.* **1** the act or an instance of jostling. **2** a collision, rough push, or thrust. □ **jostler** *n.*

jot ● *v.tr.* (**jotted, jotting**) (usu. foll. by *down*) write briefly or hastily. ● *n.* (often with *neg.* expressed or implied) a very small amount (*not one jot or tittle*).

jotting *n.* **1** (usu. in *pl.*) a note; something jotted down. **2** the act or an instance of hastily writing something down.

joual /ʒuːˈɒl/ *n.* a variety of Canadian French considered to be uneducated, characterized by non-standard grammar and syntax and, esp. in cities, numerous English borrowings.

joule /dʒuːl/ *n.* the SI unit of work or energy equal to the work done by a force of one newton when its point of application moves one metre in the direction of action of the force. Symbol: **J**.

jounce /dʒaʊns/ ● *v.tr. & intr.* bump, bounce, jolt. ● *n.* a jolt or a jolting pace. □ **jouncing** *n. & adj.*

journal *n.* **1** a daily record of events; a diary. **2 a** a periodical, esp. an academic one dealing with a specialized subject. **b** an esp. daily newspaper. **3** a book in which business transactions are entered, with a statement of the accounts to which each is to be debited and credited. **4** the part of a shaft or axle that rests on bearings. **5** (**the Journals**) a record of daily proceedings in a legislative assembly.

journalese *n.* a hackneyed style of language characteristic of some newspaper writing.

journalism *n.* **1** the work of collecting, writing, and reporting news items in the press or on television etc. **2** the news media collectively. **3** material broadcast etc. by the news media. □ **journalist** *n.* **journalistic** *adj.* **journalistically** *adv.*

journey ● *n.* (*pl.* **-eys**) **1** an act of going from one place to another, esp. at a long distance. **2** the distance travelled in a specified time (*a day's journey*). **3** the travelling of a vehicle along a route at a stated time. **4** one's passage or progress through life. ● *v.intr.* (**-eys, -eyed**) make a journey. □ **journeyer** *n.*

journeyman *n.* (*pl.* **-men**) **1** a person who, having served an apprenticeship, is qualified to work in a craft or trade under the direction of a more qualified person. **2** a reliable but not outstanding worker.

joust /dʒaʊst/ ● *n.* **1** *hist.* a combat between two knights on horseback with lances. **2** a verbal, political, etc. encounter or contest, esp. between two individuals. ● *v.intr.* engage in a joust. □ **jouster** *n.*

Jove /dʒoːv/ *n.* □ **by Jove!** an exclamation of surprise or approval.

jovial /'dʒoːviəl/ *adj.* merry, convivial, hearty and good-humoured. □ **joviality** /-'æliti/ *n.* **jovially** *adv.*

Jovian /'dʒoːviən/ *adj.* of the planet Jupiter.

jowl¹ *n.* **1** the jaw or jawbone. **2** the cheek (*cheek by jowl*). □ **-jowled** *adj.* (in *comb.*).

jowl² *n.* **1** the external loose skin on the throat or neck when prominent. **2** the dewlap of oxen, wattle of a bird, etc. **3 a** *Cdn* (*Nfld*) the meat of the cheek of cod eaten as food. **b** *N Amer.* the meat of the cheek of a pig eaten as food. □ **jowly** *adj.*

joy *n.* **1** (often foll. by *at*, *in*) a vivid emotion of pleasure; extreme gladness. **2** a thing that causes joy. **3** *informal* satisfaction, success (*got no joy*). □ **wish a person joy of** *ironic* be gladly rid of (what that person has to deal with). □ **joyless** *adj.* **joylessly** *adv.*

joy buzzer *n.* *N Amer.* a device concealed in the palm of the hand with which, as a practical joke, one surprises another with a buzzing noise and unpleasant vibrating sensation while shaking hands.

Joycean /'dʒɔisiən/ ● *adj.* of or characteristic of the Irish novelist and short-story writer James Joyce (1882–1941) or his work. ● *n.* a specialist in or admirer of Joyce's works.

joyful *adj.* full of, showing, or causing joy. □ **joyfully** *adv.* **joyfulness** *n.*

joyous *adj.* (of an occasion, circumstance, etc.) characterized by pleasure or joy; joyful. □ **joyously** *adv.* **joyousness** *n.*

joyride *informal* ● *n.* **1** a car ride taken for fun and excitement, usu. without the owner's permission. **2** a pleasurable, often exciting, and usu. brief experience. ● *v.intr.* (*past* **-rode**; *past part.* **-ridden**) go for a joyride. □ **joyrider** *n.* **joyriding** *n.*

joystick *n.* a lever that can be moved in several directions to control the movement of an image on a video or computer screen.

JP *abbr.* JUSTICE OF THE PEACE.

Jr. *abbr.* Junior.

jubilant /'dʒuːbɪlənt/ *adj.* exultant, rejoicing, joyful. □ **jubilance** *n.* **jubilantly** *adv.*

jubilate /'dʒuːbɪˌleit/ *v.intr.* exult; be joyful. □ **jubilation** *n.*

jubilee /dʒuːbɪ'liː, 'dʒuː-/ *n.* **1** an anniversary, esp. the 25th, 50th, or 60th. **2** a time or season of rejoicing. **3 a** *Jewish Hist.* a year of emancipation and restoration, kept every 50 years. **b** a time of restitution, remission, or release. **4** *Catholicism* a period, usu. every 25 years, during which indulgences are granted under certain conditions. **5** exultant joy.

Judaeo- *comb. form var. of* JUDEO-.

Judaic /dʒuː'deiɪk/ *adj.* of the Jews or Judaism.

Judaica *n.pl.* (treated as *sing.*) **1** the literature, customs, ritual objects, artifacts, etc. which are of particular relevance to Jews or Judaism. **2** such items or aspects of Jewish life individually.

Judaism *n.* **1** the religion of the Jews, with a belief in one God and a basis in Mosaic and rabbinical teachings. **2** the cultural practices, social identity, etc. based on this religion.

Judaize *v.* **1** *intr.* follow Jewish customs or rites. **2** *tr.* **a** make Jewish. **b** convert to Judaism. **3** *tr.* imbue with Jewish customs or principles. □ **Judaization** *n.* **Judaized** *adj.* **Judaizer** *n.*

Judas /'dʒuːdəs/ *n.* a person who betrays a friend.

judder /'dʒʌdər/ ● *v.intr.* (esp. of a mechanism) shake or

vibrate noisily or violently. ● *n.* **1** an instance of this. **2** the condition of juddering. □ **juddery** *adj.*

Judeo- /dʒuː'deiːoː/ *comb. form* **1** pertaining to the Jews, Judaism, or things Jewish. **2** Jewish and (*Judeo-Christian*).

judge ● *n.* **1 a** a public officer appointed to hear and try causes in a court of justice. **2** a person appointed to decide a competition, contest, dispute, etc. **3 a** a person who decides anything in question. **b** a person regarded in terms of capacity to decide on the merits of a thing or question (*am no judge of that*). **4** *Jewish Hist.* a leader having temporary authority in Israel in the period between Joshua and the Kings. ● *v.* **1** *tr.* **a** try (a cause) in a court of justice. **b** pronounce sentence on (a person). **2** *tr.* form an opinion about; estimate, appraise. **3** *tr.* act as a judge of (a dispute or contest). **4** *tr.* (often foll. by *to* + infin. or *that* + clause) conclude, consider, or suppose. **5** *intr.* **a** form a judgment. **b** act as judge. □ **judgeship** *n.*

judgment *n.* (also **judgement**) **1** the critical faculty; discernment (*an error of judgment*). **2** good sense. **3** an opinion or estimate (*in my judgment*). **4 a** the sentence of a court of justice. **b** judicial decision or order in court. **5** criticism. **6 a** a divine decree, decision, or sentence. **b** often *jocular* a misfortune viewed as a deserved recompense (*it is a judgment on you for getting up late*). **7** (**Judgment**) = LAST JUDGMENT. □ **against one's better judgment** contrary to what one really feels to be advisable.

judgmental *adj.* (also **judgemental**) **1** of, concerning, or by way of judgment. **2** condemning, critical, esp. in moral matters. □ **judgmentally** *adv.*

judgment call *n.* a decision made on personal observation, by subjective determination, etc., esp. when the facts of a situation are indeterminate.

Judgment Day *n.* the day on which the Last Judgment is believed to take place; doomsday.

judicare /'dʒuːdɪkər/ *n.* *Cdn* a form of legal aid in which lawyers bill the province for services to poor clients rather than receiving a salary.

judicial /dʒuː'dɪʃəl/ *adj.* **1** of, done by, or proper to a court of law. **2** invested with the authority to judge causes (*a judicial assembly*). **3** of or proper to a judge. **4** giving or being disposed to pass judgment on a matter; critical. **5** judicious, impartial, having or showing sound judgment. **6** regarded as a divine judgment. □ **judicially** *adv.*

Judicial Committee *n.* *Cdn* a committee made up of chief judges, either nationally or from a specific province or territory, which considers proposed appointments to the bench etc.

Judicial Committee of the Privy Council *n.* esp. *hist.* the final court for the disposal of appeals made to the King or Queen in Council from colonial countries.

judicial district *n.* *Cdn* (in certain provinces) a territory, county, or district subdivided for purposes of holding district or county courts, with a judge having jurisdiction over each subdivision.

judicial review *n.* *Law* a procedure by which a superior judicial body may pronounce on (in Canada) the conduct of an inferior court, committee, etc. to ensure the conduct was proper.

judiciary /dʒuː'dɪʃɪriː/ ● *n.* (*pl.* **-ies**) the judges of a nation collectively. ● *adj.* = JUDICIAL 1, 2, 3.

judicious /dʒuː'dɪʃəs/ *adj.* **1** sensible, prudent, proceeding from or showing sound judgment esp. in practical matters. **2** (of a person, the faculties, etc.) sound in discernment and judgment. □ **judiciously** *adv.* **judiciousness** *n.*

judo /'dʒuːdoː/ n. a refined form of jiu-jitsu using principles of movement and balance, practised as a sport or form of physical exercise. □ **judoist** n.

jug ● n. **1 a** N Amer. a large, deep vessel, usu. of glass or earthenware, with a narrow neck and usu. a handle. **b** Cdn & Brit. a deep vessel for holding liquids, with a handle and often with a spout or lip shaped for pouring. **2** the contents of a jug. **3** slang prison. **4** (in pl.) N Amer. slang a woman's breasts. ● v.tr. (**jugged**, **jugging**) **1** (in rock or ice climbing etc.) climb a rope like a ladder. **2** slang imprison.

jug band n. a folk or blues band in which jugs are played by blowing across the opening to produce bass notes, usu. accompanied by other makeshift or simple instruments.

juggernaut /'dʒʌɡərˌnɒt/ n. **1** a huge or overwhelming force or object. **2** an institution or notion to which persons blindly sacrifice themselves or others.

juggle ● v. **1 a** intr. (often foll. by with) perform feats of dexterity, esp. by tossing objects in the air and catching them, keeping several in the air at the same time. **b** tr. perform such feats with. **2** tr. continue to deal with (several activities) at once, esp. with ingenuity. **3** intr. & tr. **a** change the arrangement of something adroitly to achieve a more viable or satisfactory result (juggle bookings). **b** manipulate or misrepresent (facts etc.), esp. to deceive or cheat. ● n. an act or instance of juggling.

juggler n. **1** a person who juggles. **2** a trickster or imposter. □ **jugglery** n.

jughead n. a stupid person.

jug milk n. (also **jug milk store**, **jug milk outlet**, etc.) Cdn (Ont.) a convenience store at which milk may be bought in returnable plastic jugs.

Jugoslav var. of YUGOSLAV.

jugular /'dʒʌɡjʊlər/ ● adj. **1 a** of the neck or throat. **b** designating or pertaining to any of several large veins of the neck. **2** (of fish) having ventral fins in front of the pectoral fins, in the throat region. ● n. **1** (in full **jugular vein**) any of several large veins of the neck which carry blood from the face, head, brain, etc. **2** the weakest point in an opponent's argument etc., esp. when subject to fierce attack (a go-for-the-jugular campaign).

juice ● n. **1** the extractable liquid part of a vegetable or fruit, commonly containing its characteristic flavour etc. **2 a** the fluid part of an animal body or substance, esp. a secretion. **b** the fluid naturally contained in or coming from anything. **3 a** the essence or spirit of anything. **b** (in pl.) a person's vitality or creative, expressive, etc. faculties. **c** strength or vigour. **4** informal gasoline or electricity. **5** N Amer. slang **a** influence or money, esp. that obtained by or used in corrupt or criminal activities. **b** money lent at a usurious rate of interest or the interest extorted usuriously. **6** N Amer. slang gossip, rumour, scandal. **7** N Amer. slang alcoholic drink; liquor. ● v.tr. extract the juice from (a fruit etc.). □ **juice up 1** increase the power, potential, or performance of. **2** heighten the enthusiasm, energy, or style of. □ **juiceless** adj.

juice bar n. N Amer. **1** a café-style establishment serving esp. freshly squeezed fruit juices. **2** a nightclub for teenagers, where only non-alcoholic beverages are served.

juice box n. N Amer. a small box comprising layers of foil, plastic, waxed cardboard, etc., with a straw attached, containing an individual serving of juice.

juiced adj. **1** N Amer. slang intoxicated. **2** N Amer. slang (of a baseball, card deck, etc.) being inexplicably and

perhaps illicitly altered and enhanced for superior results. **3** (of fruit etc.) having had its juice extracted.

juicer n. **1** an appliance or device used to extract juice from fruit or vegetables. **2** N Amer. an alcoholic.

juicy adj. (-**ier**, -**iest**) **1** full of juice; succulent. **2** informal **a** substantial or interesting (always gets the juicy roles). **b** racy, scandalous (juicy gossip). **3** informal profitable. □ **juicily** adv. **juiciness** n.

ju-jitsu /dʒuːˈdʒɪtsuː/ (also **ju-jutsu**) var. of JIU-JITSU.

juju /'dʒuːdʒuː/ n. **1** a charm or fetish of some W African peoples. **2** a supernatural power attributed to this. **3** Music a flowing, sonorous, and complex musical style of Yoruba origin, usu. combining numerous interrelating drums, guitars, and call-and-response singing.

jujube /'dʒuːdʒuːb/ n. **1 a** any plant of the genus Zizyphus bearing edible acidic berry-like fruits. **b** this fruit. **2** a small, flavoured, jellylike candy.

juke ● n. **1** US **a** = JUKE JOINT. **b** = JUKEBOX. **2** a feigned move or gesture, esp. intended to confuse or deceive. ● v. **1** tr. & intr. feign or make a sham move to confuse or mislead (one's opponent). **2** intr. move in a zigzag fashion. **3** intr. dance, esp. at a juke joint or to the music of a jukebox.

jukebox n. **1** a machine that automatically plays a selected musical recording when a coin is inserted. **2** a device for holding a number of CD-ROMs in such a way that any of them can be played or assessed.

juke joint n. N Amer. a roadhouse, nightclub, etc., esp. one providing food, drinks, and music for dancing.

Jul. abbr. July.

julep /'dʒuːlep/ n. **1** N Amer. = MINT JULEP. **2 a** a sweet drink, esp. as a vehicle for medicine. **b** a medicated drink as a mild stimulant etc.

Julian /'dʒuːliən/ adj. **1** of or associated with the Roman general and statesman Julius Caesar (100–44 BC). **2** of or pertaining to the calendar reform instituted by him in 46 BC.

Julian calendar n. a calendar introduced by Julius Caesar, in which the year consisted of 365 days, every fourth year having 366 (compare GREGORIAN CALENDAR).

julienne /ˌdʒuːliˈen/ ● n. **1** food, esp. vegetables, cut into short thin strips. **2** a dish of assorted vegetables cut into thin strips. ● adj. **1** (of a vegetable etc.) cut into thin strips. **2** (of a dish or garnish) consisting of or containing such strips. ● v.tr. slice (esp. vegetables) into short, thin strips. □ **julienned** adj.

July n. (pl. **Julys**) the seventh month of the year.

jumble ● n. a confused state or heap; a muddle. ● v. **1** tr. (often foll. by up) **a** mix or mingle (objects etc.) in a confused and disordered way. **b** confuse or mix up (memories etc.) mentally. **2** intr. move about in disorder. □ **jumbled** adj.

jumbo informal ● n. (pl. -**os**) **1** a large animal (esp. an elephant), person, or thing. **2** (in full **jumbo jet**) a large airliner with capacity for several hundred passengers. ¶Usu. applied specifically to the Boeing 747. ● adj. **1** very large of its kind. **2** extra large.

jump ● v. **1** intr. move off the ground or other surface by sudden muscular effort in the legs. **2** intr. (often foll. by up, from, in, out, etc.) move suddenly or hastily in a specified way. **3** intr. give a sudden bodily movement from shock or excitement etc. **4** intr. undergo a rapid change, esp. an advance in status. **5** intr. (often foll. by around, about) change or move rapidly from one idea or subject to another, omitting intermediate stages. **6 a** intr. rise or increase suddenly (prices jumped). **b** tr. cause to do this. **7** tr. **a** pass over (an obstacle, barrier, etc.) by jumping. **b** move or pass over (an intervening thing) to a point beyond. **8** tr. skip, ignore, or pass over (a passage in a book etc.). **9** *tr.* cause (a thing, or an animal, esp. a horse) to jump. **10** *intr.* (foll. by *to, at*) reach a conclusion hastily, esp. without examining the premises. **11** *tr.* (of a train) leave (the rails). **12** *tr.* **a** anticipate and respond prematurely to (permission or a signal to act). **b** ignore and pass (a red traffic light etc.). **13** *tr.* get on or off (a train etc.) quickly, esp. illegally or dangerously. **14** *tr.* pounce on or attack (a person) unexpectedly. **15** *tr.* take summary possession of (a claim allegedly abandoned or forfeit by the former occupant). **16** *tr. slang* have sexual intercourse with. **17** *tr.* start (a car) using jumper cables. **18** *intr.* (often foll. by *in, into*) join in eagerly and enthusiastically. **19** *intr.* parachute from a flying plane. **20** *intr.* **a** (of a nightclub, etc.) be full of excitement, pulsate with activity. **b** (of jazz or similar music) have a strong or exciting rhythm. • *n.* **1** the act or an instance of jumping. **2** *Sport* **a** an act or type of jumping, as an athletic performance. **b** a distance jumped. **c** a place to be jumped from, as in ski jumping etc. **3** an obstacle to be jumped, esp. by a horse. **4** a sudden bodily movement caused by shock or excitement. **5** an abrupt rise in amount, price, value, status, etc. **6 a** a sudden transition from one thing, idea etc. to another, omitting intermediate stages. **b** an interval or gap in argument, technological development, etc. ☐ **get** (or **have**) **the jump on** *informal* get (or have) an advantage over (a person) by prompt action. **jump at** accept eagerly. **jump down a person's throat** *informal* berate, reprimand, or contradict a person fiercely. **jump for joy** be joyfully excited; show one's delight by excited movements. **(go) jump in the lake** *informal* (usu. in *imper.*) go away and stop being a nuisance. **jump on** *informal* attack or criticize severely and without warning. **jump out at 1** grab the attention; be blatantly apparent. **2** suddenly spring out at and surprise (a person). **jump out of one's skin** *informal* be extremely startled. **jump the queue** take unfair precedence over others. **jump rope** *N Amer.* skip with a skipping rope. **jump ship 1** abandon an organization, effort, etc. before one's commitment is up, an undertaking is finished, etc. **2** (of a seaman) desert. **jump to it** *informal* act promptly and energetically. **one jump ahead** one stage further on than a rival etc. ☐ **jumpable** *adj.* **jumping** *n. & adj.*

jump ball *n. Basketball* a ball thrown vertically between two opposing players by the referee to start or resume play.

jump-cut *Film* • *n.* **1** the excision of part of a shot in order to break its continuity of action and time. **2** the abrupt transition from one scene to another which is discontinuous in time. • *v.tr.* join (a scene) to others via a jump-cut.

jumped-up *adj. informal* newly or suddenly risen in status or importance, esp. when presumptuously arrogant.

jumper[1] *n. N Amer.* a collarless, sleeveless dress worn over a blouse or sweater.

jumper[2] *n.* **1** a person or animal that jumps, esp.: **a** a horse trained for show jumping. **b** an athlete in a sport such as ski jumping, high jump, etc. **c** *informal* a person who commits suicide by leaping from a bridge, tall building, etc. **d** *slang* a person who frequently or dramatically changes jobs, religions, etc. **2** *Electricity* **a** a short wire used to make or break a circuit. **b** (usu. in *pl.*) = JUMPER CABLE. **3** *Basketball slang* **a** = JUMPSHOT. **b** = JUMP BALL. **4** *Cdn* = JOLLY JUMPER.

jumper cable *n.* esp. *N Amer.* either of a pair of heavy electric cables ending in alligator clips, used for conveying current from the battery of one motor vehicle to boost (or recharge) another.

jumping jack *n.* **1** *N Amer.* an exercise performed by standing with legs together and arms at one's side, jumping to a position with legs spread and arms fully extended above the head, then returning to the initial stance. **2** a toy figure with movable limbs esp. attached to strings.

jumping-off point *n.* (also **jumping-off place** etc.) **1** the place or point from where a journey, plan, campaign, etc. is begun or launched. **2** *N Amer.* a place regarded as being the furthest limit of civilization or settlement. **3** a place from which a person moves into another esp. remote region beyond.

jump rope *n. N Amer.* **1** a skipping rope. **2** an exercise or child's game done or played with a skipping rope.

jump seat *n. N Amer.* a folding extra seat in a motor vehicle, aircraft, etc.

jumpshot *n. Basketball* a shot at the net made at the apex of a vertical leap.

jump-start • *v.tr.* **1** start (a motor vehicle) with jumper cables. **2** revitalize, energize, or stimulate (a team, effort, etc.). • *n.* the action of jump-starting.

jumpsuit *n.* a one-piece garment for the whole body, of a kind originally worn by paratroopers.

jumpy *adj.* (**-ier, -iest**) **1** nervous; easily startled. **2** making sudden movements, esp. of nervous excitement. ☐ **jumpily** *adv.* **jumpiness** *n.*

Jun. *abbr.* **1** June. **2** (also **jun.**) Junior.

junco /'dʒʌŋko:/ *n.* (*pl.* **-os**) any of several small birds of Central and N America of the genus *Junco.*

junction *n.* **1** a point at which two or more things are joined. **2** a place where two or more railway lines or roads meet, unite, or cross. **3** the act or an instance of joining. **4** *Electronics* a region of transition in a semiconductor between regions where conduction is mainly by electrons and regions where it is mainly by holes. ☐ **junctional** *adj.*

junction box *n.* a rigid box or casing used to enclose and protect junctions of electrical wires, cables, etc.

juncture *n.* **1** a critical convergence of events; a critical point of time (*at this juncture*). **2** a place where things join. **3** an act of joining.

June *n.* the sixth month of the year.

Juneberry *n.* (*pl.* **-ies**) **1** any of several N American shrubs of the genus *Amelanchier,* of the rose family, with showy white flowers. **2** the fruit of this shrub.

June bug *n.* (also **June beetle**) any of various large beetles of the genus *Phyllophaga* esp. N American chafers, appearing in early summer.

Jungian /'jʊŋiən/ • *adj.* of or relating to the Swiss psychologist Carl Jung (1875–1961) or his system of analytical psychology. • *n.* a supporter of Jung or of his system.

jungle *n.* **1 a** land overgrown with undergrowth or tangled vegetation, esp. in the tropics. **b** the luxuriant and often almost impenetrable vegetation covering such land. **2** a wild tangled mass. **3 a** a scene or place of ruthless competition, struggle, or exploitation (*urban jungle*). **b** a place of bewildering complexity or confusion. **4** (in full **jungle music**) a type of fast dance music with an exaggerated bass line, influenced by reggae and soul. **5** *N Amer. slang* an often illicit camp for and established by the homeless, unemployed, etc. ☐ **law of the jungle** a state of ruthless competition. ☐ **jungly** *adj.*

Jungle Gym *n. proprietary* monkey bars for a children's playground, usu. having various bars, tubes, slides, etc.

junior • *adj.* **1 a** (foll. by *to*) inferior in age, standing, or position. **b** of less or least standing; of the lower or lowest position (*junior partner*). **2 a** less advanced in age. **b** intended for children or young people (*junior dictionary*). **3** the younger (esp. appended to a name for distinction from an older person of the same name). **4** smaller than usual. **5** *Sport* of, for, or pertaining to (usu. amateur) athletes under 20 years of age. **6** esp. *US* of the year before the final year at university, high school, etc. • *n.* **1** a person who holds a low rank in a profession, is inferior in length of service, etc. **2** a person who is a specified number of years younger than another (*10 years his junior*). **3** *Sport* **a** a junior athlete. **b** the level of competition for junior athletes (*spent three years playing junior*). **4** esp. *US* a student in the third year of a four-year program at high school, college, or university. **5** *N Amer. informal* a young male child, esp. in relation to his family.

Junior A *n. Hockey* the highest level of amateur competition, for players under 20 years of age.

Junior B *n. Hockey* the second-highest level of amateur competition, for players under 20 years of age.

Junior C *n. Hockey* the third-highest level of amateur competition, for players under 20 years of age.

junior college *n.* **1** *Cdn (Que.) informal* a CEGEP. **2** *US* a college offering the first two years of a university education.

Junior Forest Wardens *n.pl. Cdn (West)* an organization for young people interested in conservation, hunter education, etc.

junior high school *n. N Amer.* (also *informal* **junior high**) a school intermediate between elementary school and high school, usu. from Grade 7 to Grade 9.

junior kindergarten *n. Cdn (Ont.)* a class for young children, usu. ages 3 to 4, which prepares them for kindergarten through games, socialization, etc.

junior management *n.* **1** the lowest level of management in an organization. **2** the managers at this level usu. with supervisory rather than full management responsibility.

junior minister *n. Cdn & Brit.* a cabinet minister with responsibility for certain matters within a larger portfolio, assisting and reporting to the minister in charge.

juniper /ˈdʒuːnɪpər/ *n.* any evergreen shrub or tree of the genus *Juniperus*, esp. *J. communis*, with prickly leaves and dark blue berry-like cones.

junk[1] • *n.* **1** anything regarded as useless or of little value. **2** old or unwanted articles that are discarded or sold cheaply. **3** *slang* a narcotic drug, esp. heroin. **4** *Baseball* a pitch effective because of unpredictable movement rather than speed, e.g. a knuckleball. **5** *Cdn* (esp. *Maritimes & Nfld*) a short log, esp. cut to fit a stove, fireplace, etc. **6** = JUNK FOOD. **7** (in full **junk bond**) a high-yielding high-risk security, esp. one issued to finance a takeover. **8** a lump of fibrous tissue in the sperm whale's head, containing spermaceti. • *v.tr.* discard as junk.

junk[2] *n.* a flat-bottomed sailing vessel used in the China seas, with a prominent stem and lugsails.

Junker /ˈjʊŋkər/ *n. hist.* **1** a member of an exclusive (Prussian) aristocratic party concerned with maintaining the exclusive privileges of their class. **2** a German noble, esp. a younger, narrow-minded, overbearing one.

junker *n. N Amer. informal* **1** an old, dilapidated automotive vehicle, boat, etc. **2** a junk dealer.

junket /ˈdʒʌŋkət/ • *n.* **1 a** esp. *N Amer.* an extensive tour taken esp. for promotional purposes, usu. with the traveller's expenses paid. **b** a pleasure outing, esp. with eating, drinking, etc. **2** a dish of sweetened

and flavoured curds, often served with fruit or cream. • *v.intr.* (**junketed, junketing**) esp. *N Amer.* go on a pleasure excursion. □ **junketeer** *n.* **junketeering** *n.* & *adj.* **junketing** *n.*

junk food *n.* food with low nutritional value.

junk heap *n.* **1** an accumulation of junk. **2** a notional place to which discarded ideas, trends, etc. are consigned.

junkie *n. informal* **1** a drug addict. **2** *informal* an aficionado of some specified activity.

junk mail *n.* unsolicited advertising material etc. sent to large numbers of people by mail.

junk shop *n.* a shop selling cheap second-hand goods or antiques.

junky • *adj.* (**-ier, -iest**) of or like junk. • *n.* (*pl.* **-ies**) *var. of* JUNKIE.

junkyard *n.* a place where junk is collected for storage or resale.

Juno /ˈdʒuːnoʊ/ *n. Cdn* (*pl.* **-os**) **1** any of several awards presented by the Canadian Academy of Recording Arts and Sciences for excellence in Canadian music recording. **2** any of the statuettes symbolizing such an award.

junta /ˈhʊntə, ˈhʌn-, ˈdʒʌn-/ *n.* **1 a** a political or military clique or faction taking power after a revolution or coup. **b** a secretive group; a cabal. **2** a deliberative or administrative council in Spain, Portugal, or Latin America.

Jurassic /dʒʊˈræsɪk/ *Geol.* • *adj.* of or relating to the second period of the Mesozoic era, between 213 and 144 million years ago, between the Triassic and Cretaceous periods, with evidence of many large dinosaurs, the first birds, and mammals. • *n.* the Jurassic period or geological system.

juridical /dʒʊˈrɪdɪkəl/ *n.* **1** of judicial proceedings. **2** relating to the law. □ **juridically** *adv.*

juried *adj.* judged or selected by a jury or panel.

jurisdiction /ˌdʒʊrɪsˈdɪkʃən/ *n.* **1** (often foll. by *over*) the administration of justice. **2 a** legal or other authority. **b** the territory it extends over.

jurisprudence /ˌdʒʊrɪsˈpruːdəns/ *n.* **1** the science or philosophy of law. **2** a system or body of law. **3** a branch of law. **4** legal decisions collectively.

jurist /ˈdʒʊrɪst/ *n.* a person who is knowledgeable in legal matters. □ **juristic** *adj.*

juror /ˈdʒʊrər/ *n.* **1** a member of a jury. **2** a person who takes an oath.

jury /ˈdʒʊri, ˈdʒɜːri/ • *n.* (*pl.* **-ies**) **1** a body of usu. twelve persons sworn to render a verdict on the basis of evidence submitted to them in a court of justice. **2** a body of persons selected to award prizes in a competition. • *v.tr.* select or judge (entries etc.) by or as if by a jury. □ **the jury is** (or **is still**) **out** (often foll. by *on*) a decision has not yet been reached.

jury box *n.* the enclosure for the jury in a law court.

jury-rig *v.tr.* (often as **jury-rigged** *adj.*) assemble (something) hastily, using materials at hand.

just • *adj.* **1** acting or done in accordance with what is morally right or fair. **2** (of treatment etc.) deserved (a *just reward*). **3** (of feelings, opinions, etc.) well-grounded (*just resentment*). **4** right in amount etc.; proper. • *adv.* **1** exactly (*just what I need*). **2** exactly or nearly at this or that moment; a little time ago (*I have just seen them*). **3** *informal* simply, merely (*we were just good friends*). **4** barely; no more than (*I just managed it*). **5** *informal* positively (*it is just splendid*). **6** quite (not just yet). **7** *informal* as an intensifier (*just you wait!*). **8** in questions, seeking precise information (*just how did you manage?*). □ **just about** *informal* almost exactly; almost completely. **just as well** convenient; fortunate (*it is just as well that I checked*). **just in case** as a precaution. **just now 1** at this moment. **2** a little time ago. **just so 1** exactly arranged (*likes everything just so*). **2** it is exactly as you say. □ **justly** *adv.* **justness** *n.*

justice *n.* **1** just conduct; fairness. **2** the law and its administration (*the criminal justice system*). **3** judgment by legal process (*was brought to justice*). **4 a** a judge, esp. of a court of appeal. **b** (**Justice**) (usu. prec. by (*Cdn & Brit.*) *Mr.*, (*Cdn*) *Madame*, or (*Brit.*) *Mrs.*) a title given to an appeal court judge. □ **do justice to** treat fairly or appropriately; show due appreciation of. **do oneself justice** perform in a manner worthy of one's abilities. **in justice to** out of fairness to. **with** (**some**) **justice** reasonably. □ **justiceship** *n.* (in sense 4).

Justice of the Peace *n.* a local public official appointed to hear minor cases, take oaths, etc.

Justice of the Peace Court *n. Cdn* (in the NWT) a court presided over by a Justice of the Peace, with jurisdiction to hear all summary conviction matters, offences against municipal bylaws, etc.

justifiable *adj.* that can be justified or defended. □ **justifiability** *n.* **justifiably** *adv.*

justifiable homicide *n.* killing regarded as lawful and without criminal guilt, esp. the execution of a death sentence.

justify *v.tr.* (**-ies, -ied**) **1** show the justice or rightness of (a person, act, etc.). **2** demonstrate the correctness of (an assertion etc.). **3** provide adequate grounds for (conduct, a claim, etc.). **4** (esp. in *passive*) (of circumstances) be a good reason or excuse for (*an increase in prices can't be justified*). **5** (as **justified** *adj.*) just, right (*am justified in assuming*). **6** (of God) free (a person) from the consequences of sin. **7** adjust (a line of type) to fill a space evenly. □ **justification** *n.* **justificatory** /ˈdʒʌstɪfɪˌkeɪtəri/ *adj.* **justifier** *n.*

just-in-time *n.* (often *attrib.*) **1** a manufacturing system in which production is operated in very small batches. **2** a factory system in which materials are delivered immediately before they are required in order to minimize storage costs.

jut ● *v.intr.* (**jutted, jutting**) (often foll. by *out, into*) protrude, project. ● *n.* a protruding point.

Jute *n.* a member of a Germanic tribe that settled in Britain in the 5th–6th c.

jute *n.* **1** a rough fibre made from the bark of a jute plant, used for making twine and rope, and woven into sacking, mats, etc. **2** an Asian plant of the genus *Corchorus* yielding this fibre.

juvenile ● *adj.* **1 a** young, youthful. **b** of or for young persons. **2** suited to or characteristic of youth. **3** often *derogatory* immature (*behaving in a very juvenile way*). **4** *Cdn* (of a sports team, league, player, etc.) involving teenagers, esp. between the ages of 15 and 19. **5** of or relating to a juvenile bird, animal, etc. (*juvenile feathers*). ● *n.* **1** a young person. **2** a book intended for young people. **3** a young bird, animal, etc., esp.: **a** a bird in its first full plumage, but not yet having adult plumage. **b** a two-year-old racehorse. **4** an actor playing the part of a youthful person. □ **juvenilely** *adv.* **juvenility** *n.*

juvenile court *n.* = YOUTH COURT.

juvenile delinquency *n.* offences committed by a person or persons below the age of legal responsibility. □ **juvenile deliquent** *n.*

juvenile diabetes *n.* (also **juvenile-onset diabetes**) a type of diabetes mellitus in which insulin is not produced by the body in sufficient quantities and must therefore be injected.

juxtapose /ˌdʒʌkstəˈpoːz/ *v.tr.* **1** place (things) side by side. **2** (foll. by *to, with*) place (a thing) beside another. **3** set (something) in close association with another, esp. to highlight a contrast. □ **juxtaposition** *n.* **juxtapositional** *adj.*

Kk

K¹ n. (also **k**) (pl. **Ks** or **K's**) the eleventh letter of the alphabet.

K² abbr. (also **K.**) **1** kelvin(s). **2** King, King's. **3** Köchel (catalogue of Mozart's works). **4** (also **k**) (prec. by a numeral) **a** Computing a unit of 1,024 (i.e. 2^{10}) bytes or bits, or loosely 1,000. **b** 1,000. **5** informal one thousand dollars. **6** N Amer. kindergarten. **7** kilometre. **8** (in pl.) kilometres per hour.

K³ symbol **1** potassium. **2** Baseball strikeout.

K⁴ n. N Amer. a strikeout.

k¹ abbr. knot(s).

k² symbol **1** kilo-. **2** Math. a constant.

K-9 abbr. designating police canine units.

Kabbalah /kə'bɒlə, 'kæbələ/ n. (also **Kabbala**, **Cabbala**) **1** a Jewish mystical tradition. **2** (**kabbalah**) var. of CABBALA 1. □ **Kabbalism** n. **Kabbalist** n. **Kabbalistic** adj.

Kabinett /ˌkæbɪ'net/ n. a wine of exceptional quality, esp. one made in Germany from grapes that can ferment without added sugar.

kabloona /kə'blu:nə/ n. (pl. same or **-s** or **kabloonat**) a person who is not Inuit, esp. a white person.

kabob /kə'bɒb/ var. of KEBAB.

kaboodle esp. N Amer. var. of CABOODLE.

kaboom n. a sudden loud sound, as of an explosion.

kabuki /kə'bu:ki/ n. a form of popular traditional Japanese drama with highly stylized song, acted by males only.

ka-ching /kə'tʃɪŋ/ interj. imitating the sound made by a cash register.

Kaddish /'kædɪʃ/ n. **1** a Jewish mourner's prayer. **2** a formula of praise used in the synagogue service.

kaffeeklatsch /'kæfei,klætʃ/ n. = COFFEE KLATCH.

Kaffir /'kæfər/ n. **1 a** hist. a member of the Xhosa-speaking peoples of South Africa. **b** the language of these peoples. **2** South Africa offensive any black African.

Kafir /'kæfər/ n. a native of the Hindu Kush mountains of NE Afghanistan.

Kafkaesque /ˌkæfkə'esk/ adj. (of a situation etc.) impenetrably oppressive, nightmarish, in a manner characteristic of the fictional world of the Czech novelist Franz Kafka (1883–1924).

kaftan var. of CAFTAN.

kafuffle Cdn var. of KERFUFFLE.

kahuna n. see BIG KAHUNA.

Kaigani /kai'gæni/ n. a member of a division of the Haida, who left the Queen Charlotte Islands in the early 18th c. and settled on the southern shores of Prince of Wales Island.

kaiser n. **1** hist. an emperor, esp. the German Emperor, the Emperor of Austria, or the head of the Holy Roman Empire. **2** N Amer. (in full **kaiser roll**) a large crusty bread roll with the dough forming a pinwheel pattern.

kalamata /kælə'mætə/ n. a medium-sized, firm, flavourful, Greek variety of purplish-black olive.

Kalashnikov /kə'læʃnɪkɒf/ n. (also attrib.) a type of rifle or submachine gun made in Russia.

kale /keil/ n. a variety of cabbage which forms no compact head.

kaleidoscope /kə'laidə,skoʊp/ n. **1** a tube containing mirrors and pieces of coloured glass or paper, whose reflections produce changing patterns when the tube is rotated. **2** a constantly and quickly changing pattern. □ **kaleidoscopic** adj.

Kama Sutra /ˌkɑːmə 'suːtrə/ n. an ancient Sanskrit treatise on the art of erotic love.

kamik /'kʌmɪk, 'kæm-/ n. a traditional Inuit boot made from seal or caribou skin.

kamikaze /ˌkæmɪ'kɑːzi/ ● n. hist. (during WW II) **1** a Japanese aircraft loaded with explosives and deliberately crashed on its target. **2** the pilot of such an aircraft. ● adj. **1** of or relating to a kamikaze. **2** reckless, dangerous, potentially self-destructive.

Kamloops trout n. Cdn a bright silvery rainbow trout found in lakes.

Kampuchean /ˌkæmpʊ'tʃiən/ n. & adj. = CAMBODIAN.

kana /'kɒnə/ n. **1** Japanese syllabic writing. **2** a character or syllabary in this.

kangaroo n. (pl. **-s**) **1** a plant-eating marsupial of the genus Macropus, native to Australia and New Guinea, with a long tail and strongly developed hind quarters enabling it to travel by jumping. **2** Cdn (attrib.) designating a hooded garment, usu. of fleece material, with a front pouch (kangaroo jacket).

kangaroo court n. **1** an illegal court formed by a group of prisoners, strikers, etc. to settle disputes among themselves. **2** any trial, court, public hearing, or disciplinary proceeding operating unfairly and rendering an unjust verdict. **3** a mock trial, usu. for comic effect and often to raise funds for a charity, where participants are tried for trivial offences and given comic punishments.

kangaroo rat n. any burrowing rodent of the genus Dipodomys, having elongated hind feet.

kanji /'kændʒi/ n. Japanese writing using Chinese characters.

Kansan ● adj. of or relating to the US state of Kansas. ● n. a native or inhabitant of Kansas.

kaolin /'keiəlin/ n. a fine soft white clay produced by the decomposition of other clays or feldspar, used esp. for making porcelain and in medicines.

Kaposi's sarcoma /kə'pɒ:si:z/ n. a form of cancer involving multiple tumours of the lymph nodes or skin, occurring esp. in people with depressed immune systems, e.g. as a result of AIDS. Abbr.: **KS**.

kapow n. N Amer. informal a sudden sharp sound, like a gunshot or explosion.

kappa /'kæpə/ n. the tenth letter of the Greek alphabet (K, κ).

kaput predic.adj. slang broken, ruined; done for.

karabiner var. of CARABINER.

karakul /'kærə,kʊl/ n. **1** a variety of Asian sheep with a dark curled fleece when young. **2** fur made from or resembling this.

karaoke /ˌkeri'oʊki/ n. a form of entertainment in which people sing popular songs as soloists against a pre-recorded backing (often attrib.: karaoke bar).

karat /'kerət/ n. a measure of purity of gold, pure gold being 24 karats. Abbr.: **kt**.

karate /kə'rɒti/ n. a Japanese system of unarmed combat using the hands and feet as weapons.

karate chop ● n. a forceful, usu. downward motion with the side of the hand. ● v.tr. (**karate-chop**) (**-chopped, -chopping**) strike with a karate chop.

karma /'kɑrmə/ n. **1 a** Buddhism & Hinduism the sum of a person's actions in previous states of existence, viewed as deciding his or her fate in future existences. **b** Jainism subtle physical matter which binds the soul as a result of bad actions. **2** destiny. **3** the positive or negative feelings or energy felt to be produced by a person or thing. □ **karmic** adj.

karst /kɑrst/ n. a limestone region with underground drainage and many cavities and passages caused by the dissolution of the rock. □ **karstic** adj.

kart n. = GO-KART.

kasha /'kɑʃə/ n. a soft food made of boiled or baked grain, esp. buckwheat.

Kashmir goat n. a goat of a Himalayan breed yielding fine soft wool (used to make cashmere).

Kashmiri /kaʃ'mi:ri/ ● adj. of or relating to Kashmir, on the northern border between India and Pakistan, or its people or language. ● n. **1** a native or inhabitant of Kashmir. **2** the Indic language of Kashmir.

Kashruth /'kæʃruː:θ/ n. (also **Kashrut** /'kæʃruː:t/) Judaism **1** the body of religious laws relating to the suitability of food, ritual objects, etc. **2** the condition of being fit for ritual use.

Kaska /'kæskə/ ● n. **1** a member of a Dene Aboriginal group living in northwestern BC. **2** the Athapaskan language of this people. ● adj. of or relating to this people or their culture or language.

kata /'kɒtɒ/ n. a system of basic exercises or postures used to teach and improve the execution of techniques in judo and other martial arts.

katydid /'keitidɪd/ n. any of various N American green grasshoppers of the family Tettigoniidae.

kayak ● n. **1** an Inuit one-man enclosed canoe consisting of a light wooden frame covered with sealskins. **2** a small covered canoe modelled on this, used for touring or sport. ● v. (**kayaked, kayaking**) **1** intr. travel by kayak. **2** tr. paddle a kayak on or along (a river, the ocean, etc.). □ **kayaker** n. **kayaking** n.

kayo informal ● v.tr. (**-oes, -oed**) knock out; stun by a blow. ● n. (pl. **-os**) a knockout.

Kazakh /kə'zʊk/ (also **Kazak**) ● n. **1** (pl. **-s**) a member of a Turkic people of central Asia, esp. of Kazakhstan. **2** the language of this people. ● adj. of or relating to the Kazakhs or their language.

kazillion n. N Amer. = GAZILLION.

kazoo n. a toy or jazz musical instrument consisting of a tube with a membrane at each end or over a hole in the side, which produces a buzzing noise when hummed into.

KB abbr. **1** kilobyte(s). **2** KING'S BENCH.

Kb abbr. kilobit(s).

kb abbr. kilobar(s).

KBps abbr. kilobytes per second.

Kbps abbr. kilobits per second.

kbyte abbr. kilobyte(s).

KC abbr. **1** KING'S COUNSEL. **2** Kennel Club.

kcal abbr. kilocalorie(s).

kebab /kə'bʊb, -bæb/ n. a dish of pieces of marinated meat and vegetables cooked and served on a skewer.

keel ● n. **1** the lengthwise timber or steel structure along the base of a ship, airship, or some aircraft, on which the framework of the whole is built up. **2** a ridge along the breastbone of many birds. ● v.tr. & intr. turn keel upwards. □ **keel over 1** fall down; faint. **2**

fall over sideways. **3** die. **4** capsize. **on an even keel 1** (of a ship or aircraft) not listing. **2** (of a plan or person) untroubled. □ **keelless** adj.

keelhaul v.tr. **1** drag (a person) through the water under the keel of a ship as a punishment. **2** scold or rebuke severely.

keen[1] adj. **1** (of a person, desire, or interest) eager, ardent (a keen curler). **2** (foll. by on) much attracted by; fond of or enthusiastic about. **3 a** (of the senses) sharp; highly sensitive. **b** (of feelings) intense, strong, deep. **4** intellectually acute. **5 a** having a sharp edge or point. **b** (of an edge etc.) sharp. **6** (of a sound, light, etc.) penetrating, vivid, strong. **7** (of a wind, frost, etc.) piercingly cold. **8** (of a pain etc.) acute, bitter. **9** informal excellent. □ **keenly** adv. **keenness** n.

keen[2] ● n. an Irish funeral song accompanied with wailing. ● v. **1** intr. make a high-pitched sound like wailing. **2** intr. utter the keen. **3** tr. bewail (a person) in this way. **4** tr. utter in a wailing tone.

keener n. Cdn informal a person, esp. a student, who is extremely eager, zealous, or enthusiastic.

keep ● v. (past and past part. **kept** /kept/) **1** tr. have continuous charge of; retain possession of. **2** tr. (foll. by for) retain or reserve for a future occasion or time. **3** tr. & intr. retain or remain in a specified condition, position, course, etc. (keep them happy). **4** tr. put or store in a regular place. **5** tr. (foll. by from) cause to avoid or abstain from something (will keep you from going too fast). **6** tr. detain; cause to be late (what kept you?). **7** tr. **a** observe or pay due regard to (a law, custom, etc.). **b** honour or fulfill (a commitment, undertaking, etc.) (keep one's word). **c** respect the commitment implied by (a secret etc.). **d** act fittingly on the occasion of (keep the Sabbath). **8** tr. own and look after (animals) for amusement or profit (keeps bees). **9** tr. **a** provide for the sustenance of (a person, family, etc.). **b** (foll. by in) maintain (a person) with a supply of. **10** tr. carry on; manage (a shop, business, etc.). **11** tr. **a** maintain (accounts, a diary, etc.) by making the requisite entries. **b** maintain (a house) in proper order. **12** tr. have (a commodity) regularly on sale (we don't keep that book in stock). **13** tr. guard or protect (a person or place, a goal in hockey, etc.). **14** tr. preserve in being; continue to have (keep order). **15** intr. continue or do repeatedly or habitually (why do you keep saying that?). **16** tr. continue to follow (a way or course). **17** intr. **a** (esp. of perishable commodities) remain in good condition. **b** (of news or information etc.) admit of being withheld for a time. **18** tr. remain in (one's bed, room, house, etc.). **19** tr. retain (one's seat, ground, etc.) against opposition or difficulty. **20** tr. maintain (a person) in return for sexual favours. ● n. **1** food, clothes, and other things needed for living (earn your keep). **2** charge or control (is in your keep). □ **for keeps** informal permanently, indefinitely. **how are you keeping?** how are you? **keep at** persist or cause to persist with. **keep away** (often foll. by from) **1** avoid being near. **2** prevent from being near. **keep back 1** remain or keep at a distance. **2** retard the progress of. **3** conceal; decline to disclose. **4** retain, withhold (kept back $50). **keep one's balance** remain stable; avoid falling. **keep down 1** hold in subjection. **2** keep low in amount. **3** lie low; stay hidden. **4** manage not to vomit (food eaten). **keep one's feet** manage not to fall. **keep in 1** confine or restrain (one's feelings etc.). **2** remain or confine indoors. **keep off 1** stay or cause to stay away from. **2** ward off; avert. **3** abstain from. **4** avoid (a subject). **keep on 1** continue to do something; do continually. **2** continue to use or employ. **3** (foll. by at) pester or harass. **keep out 1** keep or remain outside. **2** exclude. **keep one's temper** control one's anger. **keep to 1** adhere to (a course, schedule, etc.). **2** observe (a promise). **3** confine oneself to. **keep to oneself 1** avoid contact with others. **2** refuse to disclose or share. **keep together** remain or keep in harmony. **keep under** hold in subjection. **keep up 1** maintain (progress etc.). **2** prevent (prices, one's spirits, etc.) from sinking. **3** keep in repair, in an efficient or proper state, etc. **4** carry on (a correspondence etc.). **5** prevent (a person) from going to bed, esp. when late. **6** (often foll. by *with*) manage not to fall behind. **keep up with the Joneses** strive to compete socially with one's neighbours.

keeper *n.* **1** a person who keeps or looks after something or someone (also in *comb.*: *zookeeper*). **2** a device for keeping something in place, esp. a loop securing the end of a buckled strap. **3** a fruit or other product that keeps in a specified way. **4** *Football* an offensive play in which the quarterback runs with the ball. **5** *informal* something that one wishes to keep. **6** *N Amer.* a fish that is large enough that it need not be released if caught. **7 a** a plain stud or ring worn to preserve a hole in a pierced earlobe. **b** a ring worn to guard against the loss of a more valuable one.

keeping *n.* **1** custody, charge (*into your keeping*). **2** agreement, harmony (*in keeping*).

keepsake *n.* a thing kept for the sake of or in remembrance of the giver.

keester *N Amer. var. of* KEISTER.

kef /kef/ *n.* **1** a drowsy state induced by marijuana etc. **2** the enjoyment of idleness. **3** a substance smoked to produce kef.

keg *n.* a small barrel.

keg beer *n.* beer supplied from a sealed metal container.

keister *n. N Amer. slang* the buttocks.

kelly green *N Amer.* ● *n.* a bright yellowish-green colour. ● *adj.* of this colour.

kelp *n.* **1** any of several large broad-bladed brown seaweeds esp. of the genus *Laminaria*, suitable for use as fertilizer. **2** the calcined ashes of seaweed used for the salts of sodium, potassium, and iodine which they contain.

Kelt *var. of* CELT.

kelt /kelt/ *n.* a salmon or sea trout after spawning.

kelvin *n.* the SI unit of thermodynamic temperature, equal in magnitude to the degree celsius. Abbr.: **K**.

Kelvin scale *n.* a scale of temperature with absolute zero as zero.

kendo /'kendo:/ *n.* a Japanese form of fencing with two-handed bamboo swords.

kennel ● *n.* **1** a small shelter for a dog. **2** (in *pl.*) a breeding or boarding establishment for dogs. ● *v.* (**kennelled, kennelling**) **1** *tr.* put into or keep in a kennel. **2** *intr.* live in or go to a kennel.

kennel club *n.* an organization which establishes dog breeds, records pedigrees, issues the rules for dog shows and trials, etc.

keno /ki:no/ *n.* a game of chance resembling bingo, based on the drawing of numbers and covering of corresponding numbers on cards.

kente /'kentei/ *n.* (in full **kente cloth**) a brightly coloured banded woven fabric of Ghanaian origin.

Kentuckian ● *n.* a native or inhabitant of the US state of Kentucky. ● *adj.* of or relating to Kentucky.

Kentucky bluegrass *n.* the grass *Poa pratensis*, used for fodder and in lawns.

Kentucky Derby *n.* an annual horse race for three-year-olds held at Louisville, Kentucky.

Kenyan /'kenjən, 'ki:n-/ ● *adj.* of or relating to Kenya in E Africa. ● *n.* a native or inhabitant of Kenya.

kept *past and past part. of* KEEP.

keratin /'kerətɪn/ *n.* a fibrous protein which occurs in hair, feathers, hooves, claws, horns, etc.

keratinize *v.tr. & intr.* cover or become covered with a deposit of keratin. □ **keratinization** *n.*

kerchief /'kɜrtʃɪf, -tʃiːf/ *n.* a cloth used to cover the head. □ **kerchiefed** *adj.*

kerf /kɜrf/ ● *n.* a slit made by cutting, esp. with a saw. ● *v.tr.* make a kerf in (a piece of wood etc.).

kerfuffle *n. Cdn, Brit., & Austral. informal* a fuss or commotion.

kermode /'kɜr'mo:di/ *n.* (also **kermode bear**) a subspecies of the black bear, *U. americanus kermodei*, with either black or white fur, found in the coastal mainland and some islands of BC.

kern *Printing* ● *n.* the part of a metal type projecting beyond its body or shank. ● *v.tr.* **1** provide (type) with kerns; make (letters) overlap. **2** adjust the spacing between (characters). □ **kerned** *adj.*

kernel *n.* **1** a central, softer, usu. edible part within a hard shell of a nut, fruit stone, seed, etc. **2** the whole seed of a cereal. **3** the nucleus or essential part of anything. **4** *Computing* the lowest layer into which a large operating system is subdivided, responsible for allocating hardware resources to processes etc.

kerosene *n. esp. N Amer.* a petroleum distillate widely used as a fuel and solvent.

kestrel /'kestrəl/ *n.* any of several falcons distinguished by the habit of hunting by sustained hovering.

keta /ki:tə/ *n.* = CHUM[3].

kétaine /kei'ten/ *adj. Cdn (Que.)* in poor taste; tacky.

ketamine /'ki:təmi:n/ *n.* an anaesthetic and pain-killing drug, also used (illicitly) as a hallucinogen.

ketch *n.* a two-masted fore-and-aft rigged sailing boat with a mizzen-mast located forward of the rudder and smaller than its foremast.

ketchup *n.* a thick sauce made from tomatoes, vinegar, sugar, etc., used as a condiment.

ketone /'ki:to:n/ *n.* any of a class of organic compounds in which two hydrocarbon groups are linked by a carbonyl group, e.g. acetone.

kettle *n.* **1** a vessel with a spout and handle, for boiling water in. **2** a large usu. open pot for cooking foods, boiling liquids, etc. **3** = KETTLE HOLE. □ **a different kettle of fish** a different matter altogether. **a pretty** (or **fine**) **kettle of fish** an awkward state of affairs. □ **kettleful** *n.* (*pl.* **-fuls**).

kettledrum *n.* a large drum shaped like a bowl with a membrane adjustable for tension (and so pitch) stretched across. □ **kettledrummer** *n.*

kettle hole *n.* a depression in the ground resulting from the melting of an ice block trapped in glacial deposits.

keV *abbr.* kilo-electron volt.

Kevlar /'kevlɑr/ *n. proprietary* a synthetic fibre of high tensile strength used esp. as a reinforcing agent in the manufacture of rubber products, e.g. tires.

kewpie doll /'kju:pi/ *n.* (also **kewpie**) a small chubby doll with a curl or topknot.

key[1] ● *n.* (*pl.* **keys**) **1** an instrument, usu. of metal, for moving the bolt of a lock forwards or backwards to lock or unlock. **2** a similar implement for operating a switch in the form of a lock. **3** an instrument for grasping screws, pegs, nuts, etc., e.g. one for winding a clock etc. **4** a lever depressed by the finger in playing the organ, flute, etc. **5** (often in *pl.*) each of several buttons for operating a typewriter, computer terminal, etc. **6** what gives or precludes the opportunity for or access to something. **7** a place that by its position gives control of a sea, territory, etc. **8 a** a solution or explanation. **b** a word or system for solving a cipher or code. **c** an explanatory list of symbols used in a map, table, etc. **d** a book of solutions to mathematical problems etc. **9** *Music* a system of notes definitely related to each other, based on a particular note, and predominating in a piece of music (*a study in the key of C major*). **10** a tone or style of thought or expression. **11** a piece of wood or metal inserted between others to secure them. **12** the samara of a maple etc. **13** a mechanical device for making or breaking an electric circuit, e.g. in telecommunications. **14** (in basketball) the area beneath each basket, extending from the end line to a circle surrounding the free throw line. ● *adj.* essential (*the key element*; *productivity is key*). ● *v.tr.* (**keys, keyed**) **1** (foll. by *in*, *on*, etc.) fasten with a pin, wedge, bolt, etc. **2** (often foll. by *in*) enter (data) by means of a keyboard. **3** (foll. by *to*) align or link (one thing to another). □ **key** (**in**) **on** focus on; zero in on. **key up** (often foll. by *to*, or *to* + infin.) make (a person) nervous or tense; excite. □ **keyer** *n.* **keyless** *adj.*

key² *n.* a low-lying island or reef, esp. off the coast of Florida or in the W Indies.

keyboard ● *n.* **1** a set of keys on a typewriter, computer, piano, etc. **2** an electronic musical instrument with keys arranged as on a piano. ● *v.* **1** *tr.* enter (data) by means of a keyboard. **2** *intr.* work at a keyboard. □ **keyboarder** *n.* (in sense 1 of *n.*). **keyboardist** *n.* (in sense 2 of *n.*).

key chain *n.* a short, often decorated chain for carrying keys.

keyhole *n.* **1** a hole by which a key is put into a lock. **2** a means to very private or intimate information. **3** something shaped like a keyhole, with a circle above a vertical oblong, often flared at the bottom.

key lime *n.* a small yellowish tart lime.

key money *n.* a payment demanded from a tenant for the provision of a key to the premises.

Keynesian /ˈkeinziən/ ● *adj.* of or relating to the theories of the English economist J. M. Keynes (1883–1946), esp. regarding state control of the economy through money and taxation. ● *n.* an adherent of these theories. □ **Keynesianism** *n.*

keynote *n.* **1** a prevailing tone or idea (*the keynote of the whole occasion*). **2** (*attrib.*) intended to set the prevailing tone at a meeting or conference (*keynote address*). **3** *Music* the note on which a key is based.

keypad *n.* a miniature keyboard or set of buttons for operating an electronic device, telephone, etc.

key ring *n.* a ring for keeping keys on.

key signature *n.* any of several combinations of sharps or flats after the clef at the beginning of each staff indicating the key of a piece of music.

keystone *n.* **1** the central principle of a policy, etc., on which all the rest depends. **2** a central stone at the summit of an arch locking the whole together.

keystroke *n.* a single depression of a key on a keyboard.

keyway *n.* a slot for receiving a machined key.

keyword *n.* **1** the key to a cipher etc. **2** a word of great significance. **b** a significant word used in indexing.

kg *abbr.* kilogram(s).

KGB *abbr.* the Soviet secret police (1953–91).

khaki /ˈkæki, ˈkɒki, ˈkɑrki/ ● *adj.* dust-coloured; dull brownish yellow. ● *n.* (*pl.* **khakis**) **1** khaki fabric of twilled cotton or wool, used esp. in military dress. **2** the dull brownish-yellow colour of this. **3** (in *pl.*) esp. military clothing made from this.

Khalsa /ˈkɒlsə/ *n.* the fraternity of warriors into which Sikh males are initiated at puberty.

khan /kɒn, kæn/ *n.* **1** a title given to rulers and officials in Central Asia etc. **2** *hist.* **a** the supreme ruler of the Turkish, Tartar, and Mongol tribes. **b** the emperor of China in the Middle Ages.

khat /kɒt/ *n.* **1** a shrub, *Catha edulis*, grown in Arabia. **2** the leaves of this, chewed or infused as a stimulant.

Khmer /kmer/ ● *n.* **1** a native of the ancient Khmer kingdom in SE Asia, or of modern Cambodia. **2** the language of this people. ● *adj.* of the Khmers or their language.

Khoikhoi /ˈkɔikɔi/ *n. see* NAMA.

Khoisan /ˈkɔisɒn/ *n.* **1** a collective term for the Nama (Khoikhoi) and the San (Bushmen) of southern Africa. **2** a southern African language family, the smallest in Africa, spoken mainly by the Nama and the San.

kHz *abbr.* kilohertz.

KIA *abbr.* killed in action.

kibble ● *n.* N Amer. ground meal shaped into pellets esp. for pet food. ● *v.tr.* grind or chop (dried grain, beans, etc.) coarsely.

kibbutz /kɪˈbʊts/ *n.* (*pl.* **kibbutzim** /-ˈtsiːm/) a collective esp. farming settlement in Israel.

kibitz /ˈkɪbɪts/ *v.intr.* N Amer. informal **1** chat or joke lightheartedly. **2** offer unwanted advice to card players. **3** give unsolicited advice. □ **kibitzer** *n.*

kibosh /ˈkaɪbɒʃ/ esp. N Amer. slang ● *n.* nonsense. ● *v.tr.* put an end to; dispose of. □ **put the kibosh on** put an end to; finally dispose of.

kick ● *v.* **1** *tr.* strike or propel forcibly with the foot or hoof etc. **2** *intr.* (usu. foll. by *at*, *against*) **a** strike out with the foot. **b** extend the leg and foot forcefully out from the body. **c** express annoyance at or dislike of (treatment, a proposal, etc.); rebel against. **3** *tr.* informal give up (a habit). **4** *tr.* (often foll. by *out* etc.) expel or dismiss forcibly. **5** *refl.* be annoyed with oneself (*I'll kick myself if I'm wrong*). **6** *tr.* (in soccer, football, etc.) score (a goal or fieldgoal) by a kick. ● *n.* **1 a** a blow with the foot or hoof etc. **b** the delivery of such a blow. **c** an instance of extending the leg and foot forcefully out from the body. **2** *informal* **a** a sharp stimulant effect, esp. of alcohol (*a cocktail with a kick*). **b** (often in *pl.*) a pleasurable thrill (*did it for kicks*). **3** strength, resilience (*have no kick left*). **4** *informal* a specified temporary interest or enthusiasm. **5** the recoil of a gun when discharged. □ **kick around** (or **about**) *informal* **1 a** drift idly from place to place. **b** be unused or unwanted. **2 a** treat roughly or scornfully. **b** discuss (an idea) unsystematically. **kick** (**some**) **ass** (or **butt**) N Amer. slang act forcefully or in a domineering manner; dominate. **kick at the can** (or **cat**) Cdn informal an opportunity to achieve something. **kick back 1** recoil. **2** relax. **kick the bucket** slang die. **kick in 1** knock down (a door etc.) by kicking. **2** esp. N Amer. slang contribute (esp. money); pay one's share. **3** become activated, start. **kick in the pants** informal **1** a reprimand or setback seen as an incentive. **2** (also **in the teeth**, **ass**, etc.) a humiliating punishment or setback. **kick off 1 a** (in football or soccer) begin or resume a match. **b** informal begin. **2** remove (shoes etc.) by kicking. **kick up** stir up; cause to move upward. **kick up a fuss** informal create a disturbance; object or register strong disapproval. **kick up one's heels**

esp. *N Amer.* have a lively, enjoyable time. □ **kickable** *adj.*

kick-ass *attrib.adj.* (also **kick-butt**) *N Amer. slang* **1** forceful, aggressive. **2** impressive, powerful.

kickback *n. informal* **1** the force of a recoil. **2** payment for collaboration, esp. collaboration for illicit profit.

kick-boxing *n.* a form of boxing characterized by the use of blows with the feet as well as with gloved fists. □ **kick-boxer** *n.*

kicker *n.* **1** a person or thing that kicks, esp. a football player. **2** *N Amer.* a surprising fact, circumstance, etc. which comes as a conclusion, often as a disappointment. **3** a small, electrically powered outboard motor.

kicking *adj. slang* lively, exciting; excellent.

kickoff *n.* **1** (in football or soccer) the start or resumption of a match. **2** the kick marking this. **3** an event marking the beginning of a campaign etc.

kickplate *n.* a protective covering for the lowest portion of a door.

kickstand *n.* a rod attached to a bicycle or motorcycle and kicked into a vertical position to support the vehicle when stationary.

kick-start ● *n.* **1** (also **kick-starter**) a device to start the engine of a motorcycle etc. by the downward thrust of a pedal. **2** an act of starting a motorcycle etc. in this way. **3** an impetus given to get a thing started or restarted. ● *v.tr.* **1** start (a motorcycle etc.) in this way. **2** start or restart (a process etc.) by providing some initial impetus.

kick the can *n. N Amer.* a children's game involving chasing and capturing, in which a can must be kicked to set free those captured.

kicky *adj.* (**-ier**, **-iest**) *N Amer. informal* exciting, amusing, pleasurable.

kid[1] ● *n.* **1** a young goat. **2** the leather made from its skin. **3** *informal* **a** a child or young person. **b** (*attrib.*) designating something pertaining to or characteristic of children. **4** (as a form of address) any person (*here's lookin' at you, kid!*). ● *v.intr.* (**kidded**, **kidding**) (of a goat) give birth. □ **kids'** (or **kid** or **kid's**) **stuff** *informal* something very simple. **new kid on the block** *N Amer.* a person, company, etc., newly arrived within a group.

kid[2] *v.* (**kidded**, **kidding**) *informal* **1** *tr.* (also *refl.*) deceive, trick (*don't kid yourself*). **2** *tr. & intr.* tease, joke with (*only kidding*). □ **no kidding** (also **I kid you not**) *informal* that is the truth. □ **kidder** *n.* **kiddingly** *adv.*

kid brother *n.* (also **kid sister**) *informal* a younger brother or sister.

kiddie *n.* (also **kiddy**) (*pl.* **-ies**) *informal* = KID[1] *n.* 3.

kiddo *n.* (*pl.* **-os**) *informal* (esp. as a form of address) = KID[1] *n.* 3, 4.

kid glove *n.* **1** a glove made from kid leather. **2** (*attrib.*) dainty or delicate. □ **handle with kid gloves** handle in a gentle or delicate manner.

kidnap (**kidnapped**, **kidnapping**) ● *v.tr.* carry off (a person etc.) by illegal force or deception, esp. to obtain a ransom. ● *n.* (usu. *attrib.*) an instance of kidnapping. □ **kidnapper** *n.* **kidnapping** *n.*

kidney *n.* (*pl.* **-eys**) **1** either of a pair of organs in the abdominal cavity of mammals, birds, and reptiles, which remove nitrogenous wastes from the blood and excrete urine. **2** the kidney of a pig etc. as food. **3** temperament, nature, kind (*of the right kidney*).

kidney bean *n.* an edible esp. dark red kidney-shaped bean.

kidney dish *n.* a kidney-shaped dish, esp. one used in surgery.

kidney-shaped *adj.* shaped like a kidney, with one side concave and the other convex.

kidskin *n.* = KID[1] *n.* 2.

kielbasa /kiːlˈbɒsə/ *n.* a type of highly seasoned sausage of E European origin, usu. containing garlic.

kif /kɪf/ *var. of* KEF.

kike *n.* esp. *N Amer. slang offensive* a Jew.

Kikuyu /kɪˈkuːjuː/ ● *n.* (*pl.* same or **-s**) **1** a member of a Bantu-speaking people constituting the largest ethno-linguistic group in Kenya. **2** the language of this people. ● *adj.* of or relating to this people.

kilim /kɪˈliːm, ˈkiːlɪm/ ● *n.* a pileless woven rug etc., made in Turkey, Kurdistan, and neighbouring areas. ● *attrib.adj.* designating such a rug etc.

kill ● *v.* **1** *tr. & intr.* deprive of life or vitality; put to death; cause the death of. **2** *tr.* destroy; put an end to (feelings etc.). **3** *refl.* (often foll. by pres. part.) *informal* **a** overexert oneself. **b** laugh heartily. **4** *tr. informal* overwhelm (a person) with amusement, disbelief, etc. (*the things he says really kill me*). **5** *tr.* switch off (a spotlight, engine, etc.). **6** *tr. Computing* **a** delete (a line, paragraph, etc.) from a computer file. **b** cause (a process) to stop running. **7** *tr. informal* cause pain or discomfort to (*my feet are killing me*). **8** *tr.* pass (time, or a specified amount of it) usu. while waiting for a specific event. **9** *tr.* defeat (a bill in a legislative assembly). **10** *tr. informal* consume the entire contents of (a bottle of wine etc.). **11** *tr. Hockey* **a** (often foll. by off) (of a team) endure (a penalty) without being scored on. **b** (of a player) play during (a penalty) while the team is short-handed. **12** *tr.* **a** *Tennis etc.* hit (the ball) so skilfully that it cannot be returned. **b** stop (the ball) dead. **13** *tr.* neutralize or render ineffective (taste, sound, etc.). **14** *tr.* cancel publication or broadcast of (a news story etc.). ● *n.* **1** an act of killing (esp. an animal). **2** an animal or animals killed, esp. by a hunter. **3** *informal* the destruction or disablement of an enemy aircraft etc. □ **dressed to kill** dressed showily, alluringly, or impressively. **in at the kill** present at or benefiting from the successful conclusion of an enterprise. **kill off 1** get rid of or destroy completely (esp. a number of persons or things). **2** (of an author) bring about the death of (a fictional character). **kill two birds with one stone** achieve two aims at once. **kill with kindness** spoil (a person) with overindulgence.

killdeer *n.* a large N American plover, *Charadrius vociferus*, with a plaintive song.

killer *n.* **1 a** a person, animal, or thing that kills. **b** a murderer. **2** *informal* **a** an impressive, formidable, or excellent thing. **b** a decisive blow.

killer bee *n. informal* a very aggressive hybrid bee.

killer whale *n.* a predatory toothed whale, *Orcinus orca*, with black and white markings and a high narrow dorsal fin.

killifish /ˈkɪlɪfɪʃ/ *n.* **1** any of several small, often brightly coloured fish found esp. in sheltered rivers and estuaries of eastern N America. **2** a brightly-coloured tropical aquarium fish.

killing ● *n.* **1** *in senses of* KILL *v.* **2** a great (esp. financial) success (*make a killing*). ● *adj.* **1** that kills (*a killing frost*). **2** *informal* overwhelmingly funny. **3** *informal* exhausting; very strenuous.

killing field *n.* (usu. in *pl.*) (also **killing ground**) an area where mass killing is carried out.

killjoy *n.* a person who throws gloom over or prevents other people's enjoyment.

kiln *n.* a furnace or oven for burning, baking, or drying, esp. for firing pottery, drying lumber, etc.

kilo /ˈkiːlo/ *n.* (*pl.* **-os**) **1** a kilogram. **2** a kilometre.

kilo- /ˈkɪloː/ *comb. form* denoting a factor of 1,000 (esp. in metric units). Abbr.: **k**, or **K** in *Computing*.

kilobit /ˈkɪləbɪt/ *n. Computing* a unit of memory size equal to 1,024 (i.e. 2^{10}) bits.

kilobyte /ˈkɪləbəit/ *n. Computing* 1,024 (i.e. 2^{10}) bytes as a measure of memory size. Abbr.: **KB** or **kbyte**.

kilocalorie /ˈkɪlə,kælərɪ/ *n.* = CALORIE 1.

kilogram /ˈkɪləgræm/ *n.* the SI unit of mass, equivalent to the international standard kept at Sèvres near Paris (approx. 2.205 lb.). Abbr.: **kg**.

kilohertz /ˈkɪlə,hɜrts/ *n.* a measure of frequency equivalent to 1,000 cycles per second. Abbr.: **kHz**.

kilojoule /ˈkɪlə,dʒuːl/ *n.* 1,000 joules, esp. as a measure of the energy value of foods. Abbr.: **kJ**.

kilolitre /ˈkɪlə,liːtər/ *n.* (also **-liter**) 1,000 litres (equivalent to 220 imperial gallons). Abbr.: **kl**.

kilometre /kɪˈlɒmɪtər, ˈkɪlə,miːtər/ *n.* (also **kilometer**) a metric unit of measurement equal to 1,000 metres (approx. 0.62 miles). Abbr.: **km**. □ **kilometric** /ˌkɪləˈmetrɪk/ *adj.*

kilopascal /ˈkɪlo:,pæskəl, ˌkɪlo:ˈpæsˈkæl/ *n.* a metric unit of pressure equal to 1,000 pascals. Abbr.: **kPa**.

kiloton /ˈkɪlə,tʌn/ *n.* a unit of explosive power equivalent to 1,000 tons of TNT. Abbr.: **kt**.

kilowatt /ˈkɪlə,wɒt/ *n.* 1,000 watts. Abbr.: **kW**.

kilowatt hour *n.* a measure of electrical energy equivalent to a power consumption of 1,000 watts for one hour. Abbr.: **kWh**.

kilt ● *n.* a wraparound knee-length pleated tartan skirt, worn by women and girls and as part of traditional Highland male dress. ● *v.tr.* tuck up (skirts) around the body.

kilted *adj.* **1** provided with or wearing a kilt. **2** gathered in vertical pleats.

kilter *n.* good working order (*out of kilter; off-kilter*).

kimberlite /ˈkɪmbərləit/ *n.* a rare igneous blue-tinged rock sometimes containing diamonds, found in northern Canada, South Africa, and Siberia.

kimono /kɪˈmoːnoː, -nə/ *n.* (*pl.* **-os**) **1** a long loose Japanese robe worn with a sash. **2** a wraparound dressing gown modelled on this.

kin ● *n.* **1** one's relatives or family. **2** a group of similar or related things. ● *predic.adj.* (of a person) related. □ **kinless** *adj.*

kinaesthesia *var. of* KINESTHESIA.

kinase /ˈkaineiz, ˈkɪneiz, -eis/ *n. Biochem* any of various enzymes that catalyze the transfer of a phosphate group from ATP to another molecule.

kind¹ *n.* **1 a** a race or species (*human kind*). **b** a natural group of animals, plants, etc. (*the wolf kind*). **2** type (*what kind of job are you looking for?*). ¶In sense 2, *these* (or *those*) *kind* is often encountered when followed by a plural, as in *I don't like these kind of things*, but *this kind* and *these kinds* are usually preferred. **3** each of the elements of the Eucharist (*communion in both kinds*). **4** the manner or fashion natural to a person etc. (*act after their kind*). **5** character, quality (*differ in degree but not in kind*). □ **all kinds of** very many, esp. of different varieties. **in kind 1** in the same form, likewise (*was insulted and replied in kind*). **2** (of payment) in goods or labour as opposed to money (*received their wages in kind*). **kind of** *informal* to some extent. **a** (or **some**) **kind of** used to imply looseness, vagueness, exaggeration, etc., in the term used (*a kind of Jane Austen of our times; some kind of doctor*). **nothing of the kind 1** not at all like the thing in question. **2** (expressing denial) not at all. **of a kind 1** similar in some important respect (*they're two of a kind*). **2** *derogatory* scarcely deserving the name (*a choir of a kind*). **something of the kind** something like the thing in question.

kind² *adj.* **1** of a friendly, generous, or gentle nature. **2** (usu. foll. by *to*) showing friendliness, affection, or consideration. **3** showing kindness (*kind words*).

kinda *adv. informal* = KIND OF (*see* KIND¹).

kindergarten *n.* a class or school for young children, usu. five-year-olds, in preparation for grade one. Abbr.: **K**. □ **kindergartner** *n.*

kind-hearted *adj.* of a kind disposition. □ **kind-heartedly** *adv.* **kind-heartedness** *n.*

kindle *v.* **1** *tr.* light or set on fire, esp. gradually. **2** *intr.* catch fire, burst into flame. **3** *tr.* arouse or inspire (*kindle enthusiasm*). **4** *intr.* become animated, glow with passion etc. (*her imagination kindled*). **5** *tr. & intr.* make or become bright (*kindle the embers to a glow*). □ **kindler** *n.*

kindling *n.* small sticks etc. for lighting fires.

kindly ● *adv.* **1** in a kind manner. **2** often *ironic* used in a polite request or demand (*kindly leave me alone*). ● *adj.* (**-ier, -iest**) **1** kind, kind-hearted. **2** (of climate etc.) pleasant, genial. **3** □ **look kindly upon** regard sympathetically. **take a thing kindly** like or be pleased by it. **take kindly to** be pleased by or endeared to. **thank kindly** thank very much. □ **kindliness** *n.*

kindness *n.* **1** the state or quality of being kind. **2** a kind act.

kindred /ˈkɪndrəd/ ● *n.* **1** one's relatives, referred to collectively. **2** a relationship by blood. **3** a resemblance or affinity in character. ● *adj.* **1** related by blood or marriage. **2** allied or similar in character.

kindred spirit *n.* a person whose character and outlook have much in common with one's own.

kinematics /ˌkɪnəˈmætɪks, ˌkai-/ *n.pl.* (usu. treated as *sing.*) the branch of mechanics concerned with the motion of objects without reference to the forces which cause the motion. □ **kinematic** *adj.*

kinesiology /kɪ,niːsiˈɒlədʒi, -zi-/ *n.* the study of the mechanics of esp. human body movements.

kinesis /kɪˈniːsɪs, kai-/ *n.* **1** movement, motion. **2** *Biol.* undirected movement of an organism in response to a stimulus (*compare* TAXIS 2).

kinesthesia /ˌkɪnəsˈθiːziə, -ʒə/ *n.* a sense of awareness of the position and movement of the voluntary muscles of the body. □ **kinesthetic** /-ˈθetɪk/ *adj.*

kinetic /kɪˈnetɪk, kai-/ *adj.* of or due to motion. □ **kinetically** *adv.*

kinetic energy *n.* energy which a body possesses by virtue of being in motion.

kinetics *n.pl.* (usu. treated as *sing.*) **1** = DYNAMICS 1a. **2** the branch of physical chemistry or biochemistry concerned with measuring and studying the rates of chemical or biochemical reactions.

kinetic theory *n.* a theory which explains the physical properties of matter in terms of the motions of its constituent particles.

Kinette /kɪˈnet/ *n. Cdn* a member of a women's organization associated with the Kinsmen.

kinfolk *n.pl.* people to whom one is related by blood.

king ● *n.* **1** (as a title usu. **King**) a male sovereign, esp. the hereditary ruler of an independent state. **2** a person or thing pre-eminent in a specified field or class (*railway king*). **3** a large (or the largest) kind of plant, animal, etc. (*king penguin*). **4** *Chess* **a** a piece on each side which can move only one square in any direction, and which the opposing side has to checkmate to win. **b** (**king's**) designating pieces that start on the king's side of the board. **5** a piece in checkers with extra capacity of moving, made by crowning an ordinary piece that has reached the far end of the board. **6** a playing card bearing a representation of a king and usu. ranking next below an ace. **7** (**the King**) (in Canada and the UK) the anthem 'God Save the King'. ● *v.tr.* make (a person) king. ● *adj.* denoting a king-size bed, mattress, sheets, etc. (*see* KING-SIZE 2). □ **kinglike** *adj.* **kingly** *adj.* **kingliness** *n.*

kingbird *n.* any of several N American tyrant fly-catchers of the genus *Tyrannus*.

king cobra *n.* a large and venomous hooded Indian snake, *Ophiophagus hannah*.

king crab *n.* **1** = HORSESHOE CRAB. **2** any of various very large crabs of the family Lithodidae, which resemble the spider crabs and are found in cold waters of the N Pacific.

kingdom *n.* **1** an organized community headed by a king or queen. **2** the territory subject to a king or queen. **3** *Christianity* **a** the spiritual reign attributed to God. **b** the sphere of this (*kingdom of heaven*). **4** a domain belonging to a person, animal, etc. **5** a province of nature (*the vegetable kingdom*). **6** a specified mental or emotional province (*kingdom of the heart*). **7** *Biol.* the highest category in taxonomic classification.

kingdom come *n. informal* the next world. □ **till kingdom come** forever; for an indefinitely long period.

king eider *n.* an Arctic eider distinguished by the orange bill and frontal shield of the male.

kingfish *n.* any of various large fish, esp. the opah or croaker.

kingfisher *n.* any bird of the family Alcedinidae, often stocky with crested heads, which dive for fish in rivers etc., esp. the N American belted kingfisher.

King James Version *n.* (also **King James Bible**) a 1611 English translation of the Bible made under James I and still widely used. Abbr.: **KJV**.

kinglet *n.* **1** any of several tiny N American birds of the genus *Regulus*, e.g. the golden-crowned kinglet and the ruby-crowned kinglet. **2** a petty king.

kingmaker *n.* a person who makes kings, leaders, etc., through the exercise of political influence.

king of beasts *n.* the lion.

King of the Castle *n. Cdn & Brit.* a children's game consisting of trying to displace a rival from an elevated position.

kingpin *n.* **1** an essential person or thing, esp. in a complex system. **2 a** a main or large bolt in a central position. **b** a vertical bolt used as a pivot.

king salmon *n.* = CHINOOK 2.

King's Bench *n. see* QUEEN'S BENCH.

King's Counsel *n.* = QUEEN'S COUNSEL.

King's English *n.* = QUEEN'S ENGLISH.

kingship *n.* the office or the fact of ruling as a king.

king-size *adj.* (also **king-sized**) **1** larger than normal. **2** designating the largest standard size of mattress, usu. 193 by 203 cm (76 by 80 in.), or the sheets etc. designed for such a mattress.

kink ● *n.* **1 a** a short twist or bend in wire or tubing etc. such as may cause an obstruction. **b** a tight wave in human or animal hair. **2** a flaw or glitch in a mechanism, plan, etc. **3** a crick or stiffness in the neck or back. **4** an esp. mental twist or quirk. **5** kinky sex. ● *v.intr. & tr.* form or cause to form a kink.

kinky *adj.* (**-ier, -iest**) *informal* **1 a** given to or involving bizarre or unusual sexual behaviour. **b** (of clothing etc.) bizarre in a sexually provocative way. **2** strange, eccentric. **3** having kinks or twists. □ **kinkiness** *n.*

kinnikinnick /ˌkɪnɪkɪˈnɪk/ *n.* **1** a mixture formerly used by some Aboriginal peoples of N America as a tobacco substitute or extender, usu. consisting of dried bearberry or sumac leaves and the inner bark of dogwood or willow. **2** any of the various plants used for this, esp. bearberry.

kinsfolk *var. of* KINFOLK.

kinship *n.* **1** blood relationship. **2** the sharing of characteristics or origins.

kinsman *n.* (*pl.* **-men**) **1** a blood relative or *disputed* a relative by marriage. **2** a member of one's own tribe or people. **3** (**Kinsman**) *Cdn* a member of a fraternal organization for esp. businessmen and professionals, founded in 1920. □ **kinswoman** *n.* (*pl.* **-women**).

kiosk /ˈkiːɒsk/ *n.* a light open-fronted booth or cubicle from which refreshments, newspapers, tickets, etc. are sold or information for tourists is provided.

kipper ● *n.* **1** a fish, esp. herring that has been cured by splitting, salting, and drying in the open air or smoke. **2** a male salmon in the spawning season. ● *v.tr.* cure (a herring etc.) by splitting open, salting, and drying in the open air or smoke.

kirk *n.* **1** esp. *Scot.* a church. **2** (**the Kirk** or **the Kirk of Scotland**) the Church of Scotland (Presbyterian).

kirk session (in Presbyterian churches) = SESSION 6.

kirpan /kərˈpæn, -ˈpɒn/ *n.* the dagger or sword worn by Sikhs as a religious symbol.

kirsch /kɪərʃ/ *n.* a brandy distilled from the fermented juice of cherries.

kismet /ˈkɪzmet, ˈkɪs-/ *n.* destiny, fate.

kiss ● *v.* **1** *tr.* touch with the lips, esp. as a sign of love, greeting, or reverence. **2** *tr.* express (greeting or farewell) in this way. **3** *intr.* (of two persons) touch each other's lips in this way. **4** *tr.* touch very lightly or briefly. ● *n.* **1** a touch with the lips in kissing. **2** a very light or brief touch. **3** a bite-sized baked meringue or esp. chocolate candy. □ **kiss and tell** recount one's romantic encounters or sexual exploits. **kiss ass** (or **kiss a person's ass**) *coarse slang* act obsequiously (towards a person). **kiss away** remove (tears etc.) by kissing. **kiss goodbye to** *informal* accept the loss of. **kiss the ground** prostrate oneself as a token of homage. **kiss off** esp. *N Amer. slang* dismiss, get rid of, esp. roughly or abruptly. **kiss up to** *N Amer.* act obsequiously toward in order to obtain something. □ **kissable** *adj.*

kiss-and-cry *n.* (usu. *attrib.*) the area beside the ice in which figure skaters and their coaches etc. await the posting of the judges' marks at a competition.

kiss-and-tell *adj.* revealing confidential material.

kiss-ass *n.* esp. *N Amer. coarse slang* an obsequious, boot-licking toady; a sycophant.

kisser *n.* **1** a person who kisses. **2** *slang* the mouth; the face.

kissing cousin *n.* **1** a relative or friend with whom one is on close enough terms to greet with a kiss. **2** something related or similar.

kiss of death *n.* an act or situation (often apparently friendly) which causes ruin.

kiss-off *n. slang* an abrupt or rude dismissal.

kiss of life *n.* **1** mouth-to-mouth resuscitation. **2** an act or thing which revitalizes.

kiss of peace *n. Christianity* a ceremonial kiss or other greeting, esp. during the Eucharist, as a sign of unity.

kissy *adj. informal* pertaining to or given to kissing (*not the kissy type*).

kit[1] *n.* **1** a set of articles, equipment, documents, or clothing needed for a specific purpose (*first aid kit*; *press kit*). **2** a container for such a set. **3** the clothing, gear, etc. needed for any activity (*battle kit*). **4** a set of all the parts needed to assemble an item, e.g. a piece of furniture, a model, etc. **5** = DRUM KIT.

kit² *n.* **1** a kitten. **2** a young fox, beaver, etc.

kit bag *n.* a large, often cylindrical bag or sack used for carrying the equipment of a soldier, traveller, etc.

kitchen *n.* **1 a** a room or area where food is prepared and cooked. **b** kitchen appliances, fixtures, etc., esp. as sold together. **2** (*attrib.*) of or belonging to the kitchen (*kitchen table*). **3** the staff working in the kitchen of a restaurant etc. □ **everything but the kitchen sink** everything imaginable.

kitchen cabinet *n.* a group of unofficial advisers thought to be unduly influential.

kitchenette *n.* a small kitchen or part of a room, boat, etc. fitted as a kitchen.

kitchen garden *n.* a garden where vegetables and sometimes fruit or herbs are grown for personal use.

kitchen midden *n.* a prehistoric refuse-heap which marks an ancient settlement.

kitchen party *n.* Cdn (*Maritimes*) an informal entertainment held in a person's home, at which participants play music, sing, dance, etc.

kitchen racket *n.* Cdn (*Nfld & Cape Breton*) = KITCHEN PARTY.

kitchen-sink *adj.* (in art forms) depicting extreme realism, esp. drab or sordid (*kitchen-sink drama*).

kitchenware *n.* the utensils used in the kitchen.

kite ● *n.* **1** a toy consisting of a light frame with thin material stretched over it, flown in the wind at the end of a long string. **2** any of various medium-sized birds of prey with long wings and usu. a forked tail and soaring flight. **3** *slang* a fraudulent cheque, bill, or receipt. **4** *slang* a letter or note, esp. one that is illicit or surreptitious. ● *v.* **1** *intr.* soar like a kite. **2** *tr. & intr.* N Amer. originate or pass (fraudulent cheques, bills, or receipts). **3** *tr. & intr.* raise (money) by dishonest means (*kite a loan*). □ **go fly a kite** *informal* get lost; go away. **high as a kite** *informal* **1** intoxicated by alcohol or drugs. **2** excited; happy. □ **kiting** *n.*

kith /kɪθ/ *n.* friends, acquaintances, or neighbours. □ **kith and kin** friends and relations.

kitsch /kɪtʃ/ *n.* garish, tasteless, or sentimental art. □ **kitschy** *adj.* (**-ier, -iest**). **kitschiness** *n.*

Kitselas /ˈkɪtsələs/ *n.* **1** a member of an Aboriginal people living along the Skeena River in northwestern BC. **2** the Tsimshian language of this people.

kitten ● *n.* **1** a young cat. **2** the young of certain other animals, as the fox, ferret, etc. ● *v.intr. & tr.* (of a cat etc.) give birth or give birth to. □ **have kittens** *informal* be extremely upset, anxious, or nervous.

kittenish *adj.* **1** like a young cat; playful and lively. **2** flirtatious. □ **kittenishly** *adv.* **kittenishness** *n.*

kittiwake /ˈkɪti,weik/ *n.* either of two small gulls, *Rissa tridactyla* and *R. brevirostris*, nesting on sea cliffs.

kitty¹ *n.* (*pl.* **-ies**) **1** a fund of money for communal use. **2** a pool of money in some card games made up of contributions from each player and used as winnings or for refreshments etc. **3** the jack in bowls.

kitty² *n.* (*pl.* **-ies**) a pet name or a child's name for a kitten or cat.

kitty-corner N Amer. ● *adj.* placed or situated diagonally. ● *adv.* diagonally.

Kitty Litter *n.* proprietary = CAT LITTER.

Kiwanis /kɪˈwɒnɪs/ *n.* N Amer. a society of business and professional people founded in 1915 for the maintenance of commercial ethics and as a social and charitable organization. □ **Kiwanian** *n.*

kiwi *n.* (*pl.* **kiwis**) **1** a flightless New Zealand bird of the genus *Apteryx* with hairlike feathers and a long

bill. **2 a** a climbing plant, *Actinidia chinensis*, bearing fruits with a thin hairy skin, green flesh, and black seeds. **b** (also **kiwi fruit**) this fruit. **3** (**Kiwi**) *informal* a New Zealander.

kJ *abbr.* kilojoule(s).

KJV *abbr.* KING JAMES VERSION.

KKK *abbr.* KU KLUX KLAN.

kl *abbr.* kilolitre(s).

Klan *n.* (usu. prec. by *the*) KU KLUX KLAN.

Klansman *n.* (*pl.* **-men**) a member of the Ku Klux Klan.

Klanswoman *n.* (*pl.* **-women**) a female member of the Ku Klux Klan.

klaxon /ˈklæksən/ *n.* a horn, originally on a motor vehicle.

Kleenex *n.* (*pl.* same or **Kleenexes**) proprietary an absorbent disposable paper tissue, used esp. as a handkerchief.

kleptomania /ˌklepto:ˈmeiniə/ *n.* a recurrent urge to steal, usu. without regard for need or profit. □ **kleptomaniac** *n. & adj.*

klezmer /ˈklezmər/ *n.* **1** a member of a group of musicians playing traditional eastern European Jewish music. **2** (in full **klezmer music**) this type of music.

klick *n.* N Amer. slang a kilometre.

klister /ˈklɪstər/ *n.* Skiing a soft wax for applying to the running surface of skis to facilitate movement, used esp. when the temperature is above freezing.

Klondike *n.* a source of valuable material.

Klondiker *n.* hist. a prospector who took part in the Klondike gold rush of 1897–8.

klutz /klʌts/ *n.* esp. N Amer. informal **1** a clumsy, awkward person. **2** a fool. □ **klutzy** *adj.*

km *abbr.* kilometre(s).

km/h *abbr.* kilometres per hour

kn. *abbr.* Naut. knot(s).

knack *n.* **1** an acquired or intuitive faculty of doing a thing adroitly. **2** a trick or habit of action or speech etc. (*has a knack of offending people*).

knapsack *n.* a bag of canvas, nylon, or other weatherproof material, carried strapped on the back.

knave *n.* **1** a rogue, a scoundrel. **2** = JACK¹ *n.* 2. □ **knavery** *n.* (*pl.* **-ies**). **knavish** *adj.*

knead *v.tr.* **1 a** work (dough, clay, etc.) into a smooth mass by pressing and folding. **b** make (bread, pottery, etc.) in this way. **2** blend or weld together (*kneaded them into a unified group*). **3** massage or pummel (muscles etc.) as if kneading. □ **kneader** *n.*

knee ● *n.* **1 a** (often *attrib.*) the joint between the thigh and the lower leg in humans. **b** the corresponding joint in other animals. **c** the area around this. **d** the upper surface of the thigh of a sitting person; the lap (*held her on his knee*). **2** the part of a garment covering the knee. **3** anything resembling a knee in shape or position, esp. a piece of wood or iron bent at an angle, a sharp turn in a graph, etc. ● *v.tr.* (**knees, kneed, kneeing**) touch or strike with the knee. □ **bend the knee 1** kneel in submission, worship, or supplication. **2** submit. **bring to its** (or **his** or **her**) **knees** reduce (a thing or person) to a state of weakness or submission. **learn (something) at one's mother's knee** at an early age. **on bended knee** (also **on one's bended knees**) kneeling, esp. in supplication, submission, or worship. **on one's knees 1** kneeling. **2** seriously weakened, just short of total collapse.

kneeboard ● *n.* a short surfboard ridden in a kneel-

ing position. ● *v.intr.* ride a kneeboard. □
kneeboarder *n.* **kneeboarding** *n.*

kneecap ● *n.* **1** the convex bone in front of the knee;
the patella. **2** a protective covering for the knee. ● *v.tr.*
(**-capped, -capping**) shoot (a person) in the knee or
leg as a punishment, esp. for betraying a terrorist
group. □ **kneecapper** *n.* **kneecapping** *n.*

knee-deep *adj.* **1** (usu. foll. by *in*) **a** immersed up to
the knees. **b** deeply involved. **c** having more than one
needs or wants of a specified thing. **2** (of water, snow,
mud, etc.) so deep as to reach the knees.

knee-high ● *adj.* **1** reaching as high as the knees. **2**
(of a person) very small or very young. ● *n.* (usu. in *pl.*)
N Amer. a sock reaching just below the knee. □
knee-high to a grasshopper very small or very
young.

knee-jerk ● *n.* a sudden involuntary kick caused by a
blow on the tendon just below the knee. ● *attrib.adj.*
predictable, stereotyped (*a knee-jerk reaction*).

knee joint *n.* **1** = KNEE *n.* 1a, b. **2** a joint made of two
pieces hinged together.

kneel *v.intr.* (*past* and *past part.* **knelt** or esp. *N Amer.*
kneeled) fall or rest on the knees or a knee.

knee-length *adj.* reaching the knees.

kneeler *n.* **1** a low padded bench or cushion used for
kneeling, esp. in church. **2** a person who kneels.

knee pad *n.* a pad of foam, plastic, etc. worn to
protect the knee, esp. in sports activities.

knee sock *n.* (usu. in *pl.*) = KNEE-HIGH *n.*.

knell ● *n.* **1** the sound of a bell, esp. when rung
solemnly for a death or funeral. **2** an announcement,
event, etc., regarded as a solemn warning of disaster.
● *v. intr.* **1 1** (of a bell) ring solemnly, esp. for a death or
funeral. **2** make a doleful or ominous sound. □ **ring
the knell of** announce or herald the end of.

knelt *past and past part. of* KNEEL.

Knesset /ˈknɛsɪt/ *n.* the parliament of modern Israel,
established in 1949.

knew *past of* KNOW.

knickerbocker *n.* **1** (in *pl.*) loose-fitting breeches
gathered at the knee or calf. **2** (**Knickerbocker**) **a** a
New Yorker. **b** a descendant of the original Dutch
settlers in New York.

knickers *n.pl. N Amer.* **1** knickerbockers. **2** a boy's
short trousers. □ **get one's knickers** (or **shirt**) **in a
knot** (or **twist**) become agitated or upset.

knick-knack *n.* **1** a useless and usu. worthless ornament; a trinket. **2** a small, dainty article of furniture,
dress, etc. □ **knick-knackery** *n.*

knife ● *n.* (*pl.* **knives**) **1 a** a metal blade used as a
cutting tool with usu. one long sharp edge fixed
rigidly in a handle or hinged. **b** a similar tool used as
a weapon. **2** a cutting blade forming part of a
machine. ● *v.* **1** *tr.* cut or stab with or as with a knife. **2**
tr. slang bring about the defeat of (a person) by underhand means. **3** *intr.* (usu. foll. by *through*) cut or move
through like a knife. □ **go under the knife** *informal*
have surgery. **like a (hot) knife through butter**
easily; without meeting any resistance or difficulty.
that one could cut with a knife *informal* (of an
accent, atmosphere, etc.) very obvious, oppressive,
etc. □ **knifelike** *adj.* **knifer** *n.*

knife-edge *n.* **1** the edge of a knife. **2** a position of
extreme danger or uncertainty. **3** a steel wedge on
which a pendulum etc. oscillates. **4** = ARÊTE.

knifepoint *n.* the pointed end of a knife, esp. as
directed at a person as a threat. □ **at knifepoint**
under threat of being stabbed.

knifing *n.* an instance of stabbing with a knife.

knight ● *n.* **1** a man awarded a non-hereditary title
(*Sir*) by a sovereign in recognition of merit or service.
2 *hist.* **a** a man, usu. noble, raised esp. by a sovereign
to honourable military rank after service as a page
and squire. **b** a military follower or attendant, esp. of
a lady as her champion in a war or tournament. **3** a
man devoted to the service of a woman, cause, etc. **4**
Chess a piece usu. shaped like a horse's head. ● *v.tr.*
confer a knighthood on. □ **knighthood** *n.* **knightly**
adj. **knightliness** *n.*

knight errant *n.* **1** *hist.* a medieval knight wandering
in search of chivalrous adventures. **2** a man of a
chivalrous or quixotic nature.

knight in shining armour *n.* a chivalrous rescuer
or helper, esp. of a woman.

Knight of Columbus *n.* a member of an esp. N
American society of Catholic men founded in 1882.

knish /knɪʃ/ *n.* a dumpling of flaky dough filled with
cheese etc. and baked or fried.

knit ● *v.* (**knitting**; *past* and *past part.* **knitted** or (esp.
in senses 2–4) **knit**) **1** *tr. & intr.* **a** make (a garment,
blanket, etc.) by interlocking loops of yarn with knitting needles or by machine **b** make (a plain stitch) in
knitting (*knit one, purl one*). **2 a** *tr.* contract (the forehead) in vertical wrinkles. **b** *intr.* (of the forehead)
contract; frown. **3** *tr. & intr.* (often foll. by *together*) make
or become close or compact esp. by common interests
etc. (*a close-knit group*). **4** *intr.* (often foll. by *together*) (of
parts of a broken bone) become joined; heal. ● *n.*
knitted material or a knitted garment (also *attrib.*: *a
knit sleeper*). □ **knit up 1 a** make or repair by knitting.
b *Cdn* (*Nfld & PEI*) knot twine into meshes to make a
fishnet or the heads on a lobster trap. **2** conclude,
finish, or end. □ **knitter** *n.*

knitting *n.* **1** a garment etc. in the process of being
knitted. **2 a** the act of knitting. **b** an instance of this.

knitting needle *n.* a thin pointed rod of steel, wood,
plastic, etc., used esp. in pairs for knitting.

knitwear *n.* knitted garments.

knives *pl. of* KNIFE.

knob ● *n.* **1 a** a rounded protuberance, esp. at the end
or on the surface of a thing. **b** a handle of a door,
drawer, etc., shaped like a knob. **c** a knob-shaped
attachment for pulling, turning, etc. (*press the knob
under the desk*). **2 a** a small, usu. round, piece (of
butter, coal, etc.). **b** *Cdn* (*Nfld*) a hard candy. **3** esp.
N Amer. a prominent round hill. **4** *coarse slang* the penis.
● *v.tr.* (**knobbed, knobbing**) provide with knobs. □
knobby *adj.* **knob-like** *adj.*

knobbly *adj.* having many small knobs.

knock ● *v.* **1 a** *tr.* strike (a hard surface) with an
audible sharp blow. **b** *intr.* strike, esp. a door to gain
admittance. **2** *tr.* make (a hole, dent, etc.) by knocking.
3 *tr.* drive (a thing, a person, etc.) by striking (*knocked
the ball into the hole*; *knocked her hand away*). **4** *tr. informal*
criticize. **5** *intr.* come into collision with something (*he
knocked into the desk*). **6** *tr.* cause (a person) to be in a
certain state or position by striking (*knocked me
senseless*). **7** *intr.* (of a motor or other engine) make a
thumping or rattling noise, esp. due to faulty
combustion. ● *n.* **1** an act of knocking. **2** a sharp rap,
esp. at a door. **3** an audible sharp blow. **4** the sound of
knocking in an engine, esp. in a motor engine. **5 a** a
misfortune, a setback. **b** adverse criticism. □ **knock
around** (or **about**) **1** strike repeatedly; treat roughly.
2 lead a wandering adventurous life; wander
aimlessly. **3** be present without design or volition
(*there's a cup knocking about somewhere*). **4** discuss
casually. **knock against** collide with. **knock back**
1 *informal* eat or drink, esp. quickly. **2** *Brit. & Cdn informal*

disconcert. **3** reverse the progress of. **knock down 1** strike (esp. a person) to the ground with a blow. **2** demolish. **3** (usu. foll. by *to*) (at an auction) dispose of (an article) to a bidder by a knock with a hammer (*knocked the Picasso down to him for a million*). **4** *informal* lower the price of (an article). **5** take (machinery etc.) apart for transportation. **knock one's head against** come into collision with (unfavourable facts or conditions). **knock into the middle of next week** *informal* send (a person) flying, esp. with a blow. **knock it off!** stop it! **knock off 1** strike off with a blow. **2** *informal* finish work. **3** *informal* rapidly produce (a work of art, verses, etc.). **4** (often foll. by *from*) deduct (a sum) from a price, bill, etc. **5** *slang* **a** steal or burglarize. **b** copy, plagiarize. **6** *slang* kill. **7** *N Amer. slang* defeat (*knocked off the top team in the league*). **8** remove or reduce by (*knocked a second off the previous world record*). **knock on the head** stun or kill (a person) by a blow on the head. **knock (on) wood** *N Amer.* = TOUCH WOOD (see TOUCH). **knock out 1** make (a person) unconscious by a blow on the head. **2** knock down (a boxer) for a count of 10, thereby winning the contest. **3 a** defeat, esp. in a knockout competition. **b** get rid of; destroy (*a computer program to knock out viruses*). **4** *informal* astonish, esp. by unexpected excellence, generosity, etc. **5** (*refl.*) *informal* exhaust (*knocked themselves out swimming*). **6** *informal* make or write (a plan etc.) hastily. **knock over 1** cause to fall, spill, or overturn. **2** *slang* rob, burglarize. **knock one's socks off** astound, amaze. **knock together** put together or assemble hastily or roughly. **knock up 1** esp. *N Amer. slang* make pregnant. **2 a** become exhausted or ill. **b** exhaust or make ill. **take a knock** be hard hit financially or emotionally.

knock-down ● *attrib.adj.* **1** (of a blow, misfortune, argument, etc.) overwhelming. **2** *informal* (of a price) very low. **3** (of a price at auction) reserve. **4** (of furniture etc.) easily dismantled and reassembled. **5** (of an insecticide) rapidly immobilizing. ● *n.* an act or instance of knocking down.

knock-down, drag-out *adj.* esp. *N Amer.* (also **knock-down, drag-'em-out**) (of a brawl, argument, etc.) violent, vicious.

knocker *n.* **1** a metal or wooden instrument hinged to a door for knocking to call attention. **2** a person or thing that knocks. **3** (in *pl.*) *coarse slang* a woman's breasts. **4** *informal* a person who continually finds fault.

knock knees *n.pl.* an abnormal condition with the legs curved inwards at the knee. □ **knock-kneed** *adj.*

knock-knock joke *n.* a joke beginning with the line 'knock knock' and usu. ending with a pun.

knock-off *n.* (often *attrib.*) *informal* a copy or imitation made esp. for commercial gain.

knockout *n.* **1** the act of making unconscious by a blow. **2** *Boxing etc.* a blow that knocks an opponent out. **3** a competition in which the loser in each round is eliminated (also *attrib.*: *a knockout round*). **4** *informal* an outstanding or irresistible person or thing.

knoll /noːl/ *n.* a small hill or mound.

knot ● *n.* **1 a** an intertwining of a rope, string, tress of hair, etc., with another, itself, or something else to join or fasten together. **b** a set method of tying a knot (*a reef knot*). **c** a ribbon etc. tied as an ornament and worn on a dress etc. **d** a tangle in hair, knitting, etc. **2 a** a unit of a ship's or aircraft's speed equivalent to one nautical mile per hour (see NAUTICAL MILE). **b** a division marked by knots on a line or rope attached to a ship's log, used as a measure of speed. **c** *informal* a

nautical mile. **3** (usu. foll. by *of*) a group or cluster. **4** something forming or maintaining a union; a bond or tie, esp. of wedlock. **5** a hard lump of tissue in an animal or human body. **6 a** a knob or protuberance in a stem, branch, or root. **b** a hard mass formed in a tree trunk at the intersection with a branch. **c** a round cross-grained piece in timber where a branch has been cut through. **d** a node on the stem of a plant. **7** a difficulty; a problem. **8** a central point in a problem or the plot of a story etc. **9** a sensation of contortion felt in the stomach or throat, caused by stress or nervousness. ● *v.* (**knotted, knotting**) **1** *tr.* **a** tie (a string etc.) in a knot. **b** secure (something) with a knot. **2 a** *tr.* entangle. **b** *intr.* become entangled. **3** *tr.* form lumps, knobs, or knots on or in; make knotty. **4** *tr. N Amer. slang* tie (a score, game, etc.). □ **tie in knots** *informal* baffle or confuse completely. **tie the knot** *informal* get married. □ **knotless** *adj.* **knotter** *n.*

knothead *n. N Amer. informal* a stupid person or animal. □ **knotheaded** *adj.*

knothole *n.* **1** a hole in a piece of timber where a knot has fallen out. **2** a hollow formed in a tree trunk by the decay of a branch.

knotty *adj.* (**-ier, -iest**) **1** full of knots. **2** hard to explain; puzzling. □ **knottily** *adv.* **knottiness** *n.*

know ● *v.* (*past* **knew**; *past part.* **known**) **1 a** *tr.* have in the mind; have learned; be able to recall (*knows a lot about cars; knows what to do*). **b** *tr. & intr.* be aware of (a fact) (*she knows I am waiting*). **c** *tr.* have a good command of (a subject or language) (*knew German; knows her times tables*). **2** *tr.* be acquainted or friendly with (a person or thing). **3** *tr.* **a** recognize; identify (*I knew him at once*). **b** be aware of (a person or thing) as being or doing what is specified (*knew them to be thugs*). **c** (foll. by *from*) be able to distinguish (one from another) (*did not know him from Adam*). **4** *tr.* be subject to (*her joy knew no bounds*). **5** *tr.* have personal experience of (fear etc.). **6** *intr.* have understanding or knowledge. ● *n.* (in phr. **in the know**) *informal* well informed; having special knowledge. □ **before one knows it** with baffling speed. **be not to know 1** have no way of learning (*wasn't to know they'd arrive late*). **2** be not to be told (*she's not to know about the party*). **don't I know it!** *informal* an expression of rueful assent. **don't you know** *informal* or *jocular* an expression used for emphasis (*such a bore, don't you know*). **for all I know** so far as my knowledge extends. **have been known to** have occasionally in the past (*they have been known to turn up late*). **I knew it!** I was sure that this would happen. **I know what** I have a new idea, suggestion, etc. **know about** have information about. **know best** be or claim to be better informed etc. than others. **know better than** (foll. by *that*, or *to* + infin.) be wise, well informed, or well-mannered enough to avoid (specified behaviour etc.). **know by name** have heard the name of. **2** be able to give the name of. **know by sight** recognize the appearance (only) of. **know how** know the way to do something. **know of** be aware of; have heard of (*not that I know of*). **know one's own mind** be decisive, not vacillate. **know the ropes** (or **one's stuff**) be fully knowledgeable or experienced. **know a thing or two** be experienced or shrewd. **know what's what** have adequate knowledge of the world, life, etc. **know who's who** be aware of who or what each person is. **not know from** *N Amer.* not know anything about. **not know that ...** *informal* be fairly sure that ... not (*I don't know that I want to go*). **not know the meaning of the word** behave as if one does not know such an idea exists. **not know what hit one** be suddenly injured, killed, disconcerted, etc. **not want to know** refuse to take any notice of. **what do you know** (or **know about that**)? *informal* an expression of surprise. **you know** *informal* **1** an expression implying something generally known or known to the hearer (*you know, the restaurant on the corner*). **2** an expression used as a gap-filler in conversation. **you know something** (or **what**)? I am going to tell you something. **you never know** nothing in the future is certain. ☐ **knowable** *adj.* **knower** *n.*

know-how *n.* **1** practical knowledge; technique; expertise. **2** natural skill or invention.

knowing ● *n.* the state of being aware or informed of any thing. ● *adj.* **1** usu. *derogatory* cunning; sly. **2** showing knowledge or awareness; shrewd. ☐ **there is no knowing** no one can tell. ☐ **knowingness** *n.*

knowingly *adv.* **1** intentionally (*had never knowingly hurt him*). **2** in a knowing manner (*smiled knowingly*).

know-it-all *n. esp. N Amer. informal* (often *attrib.*) a person who seems or pretends to know everything.

knowledge *n.* **1 a** (usu. foll. by *of*) awareness or familiarity gained by experience (of a person, fact, or thing). **b** a person's range of information. **2 a** (usu. foll. by *of*) a theoretical or practical understanding of a subject, language, etc. (*has a good knowledge of Greek*). **b** the sum of what is known (*every branch of knowledge*). ☐ **come to one's knowledge** become known to one. **to** (**the best of**) **my knowledge 1** so far as I know. **2** as I know for certain.

knowledgeable *adj.* (also **knowledgable**) well-informed; intelligent. ☐ **knowledgeability** *n.* **knowledgeably** *adv.*

knowledge base *n.* **1** the underlying set of facts, assumptions, and inference rules which a computer system has available to solve a problem. **2** a store of information available to draw upon.

knowledge-based *adj.* **1** (of an industry etc.) producing information rather than manufactured goods, natural resources, etc. **2** (of a computer system) incorporating a set of facts, assumptions, or inference rules derived from human knowledge.

known ● *v. past part. of* KNOW. ● *adj.* **1** publicly acknowledged (*a known thief; a known fact*). **2** *Math.* (of a quantity etc.) having a value that can be stated.

know-nothing *n.* an ignorant person.

knuckle ● *n.* **1** the bone at a finger joint, esp. that adjoining the hand. **2 a** a projection of the carpal or tarsal joint of a quadruped. **b** a joint of meat consisting of this with the adjoining parts, esp. of bacon or pork. **3** something shaped, angled, or protruding like a knuckle. ● *v.tr.* strike, press, or rub with the knuckles. ☐ **knuckle down 1** apply oneself seriously (to a task etc.). **2** (also **knuckle under**) give in; submit. ☐ **-knuckled** *adj.* (in *comb.*). **knuckly** *adj.*

knuckleball *n. Baseball* a slow erratically-moving pitch made by gripping the ball with the knuckles or fingernails and throwing it with little spin. ☐ **knuckleballer** *n.*

knucklebone *n.* **1** bone forming a knuckle. **2** the bone of a sheep or other animal corresponding to or resembling a knuckle. **3** a knuckle of meat.

knuckle-duster *n.* a metal guard worn over the knuckles in fighting to increase the effect of blows.

knucklehead *n. informal* a stupid or dull-witted person. ☐ **knuckleheaded** *adj.*

knuckler *n. N Amer. slang* a knuckleball.

knurl /nɜrl/ ● *n.* a small projecting knob, ridge, etc. ● *v.tr.* make knurls on the edge of (a coin etc.). ☐ **knurled** *adj.*

KO /ˈkeɪoʊ/ ● *n.* a knockout in boxing etc. ● *v.tr.* (**KO's,**

KO'd KO'ing) **1** knock out (an opponent) in boxing etc. **2** *informal* destroy, defeat. ● *abbr.* knockout.

koala /koˈɑːlə/ *n.* (in full **koala bear**) an Australian bearlike marsupial, *Phascolarctos cinereus*, having thick grey fur and feeding on eucalyptus leaves.

koan /ˈkoʊæn/ *n.* a paradoxical anecdote or riddle without a solution, used in Zen Buddhism to demonstrate the inadequacy of logical reasoning and provoke enlightenment.

Köchel number /ˈkɜːʃəl/ *n.* a number given to each of Mozart's compositions in the complete catalogue of his works compiled by L. von Köchel (d. 1877) and his successors.

Kodiak *n.* (in full **Kodiak bear**) a large variety of grizzly found in Alaska.

kohl /koʊl/ *n.* a black powder, usu. antimony sulphide or lead sulphide, used as eye makeup esp. in Eastern countries.

kohlrabi /koʊlˈrɑːbi/ *n.* (*pl.* **-ies**) a variety of cabbage with an edible turnip-like swollen stem.

koi *n.* (also **koi carp**) (*pl.* same) a carp of a large ornamental variety bred in Japan.

kokanee /koʊˈkæni/ *n.* (*pl.* same) a non-migratory sockeye salmon found in lakes in western N America.

kola *var. of* COLA 1.

kolbassa /koʊbɒˈsɒ, ˈkuːbɒ̩sɒ, koʊˈbæsə/ *n.* a type of highly seasoned sausage, usu. containing garlic.

komatik /ˈkɒmətɪk/ *n.* an Inuit sled consisting of two parallel wooden runners connected by wooden slats, usu. pulled by a dog team.

Komodo dragon /kəˈmoʊdoʊ/ *n.* (also **Komodo monitor**) a large monitor lizard, *Varanus komodoensis*, native to the E Indies.

kook /kuːk/ *n. slang* a strange or eccentric person.

kookaburra /ˈkʊkəˌbʌrə/ *n.* any Australian kingfisher of the genus *Dacelo*, esp. *D. novaeguineae*, which makes a strange laughing cry.

kooky *adj.* (**-ier, -iest**) *slang* strange, eccentric. ☐ **kookily** *adv.* **kookiness** *n.*

Kool-Aid *n. N Amer. proprietary* **1** a fruit-flavoured powder mixed with water and sugar to make a drink. **2** such a drink.

Kootenay (also **Kootenai**) *var. of* KUTENAI.

kora /ˈkɔːrə/ *n.* a stringed W African instrument resembling a harp.

Koran /kɔːˈræn, kə-/ *n.* the Islamic sacred book, believed to be the word of God as dictated to Muhammad and written down in Arabic. ☐ **Koranic** /-ˈrænɪk/ *adj.*

Korean /kəˈriːən/ ● *n.* **1** a native or national of N or S Korea in SE Asia. **2** the language of Korea. ● *adj.* of or relating to Korea or its people or language.

kosher /ˈkoʊʃər/ ● *adj.* **1** (of food or premises in which food is sold, cooked, or eaten) fulfilling the requirements of Jewish law. **2** *informal* correct; genuine; legitimate. ● *n.* **1** kosher food. **2** the Jewish law regarding food (*keep kosher*). ● *v.tr.* prepare (food) according to the Jewish law.

Kosovar /ˈkɒsəˌvɑr/ ● *n.* an esp. Albanian-speaking native or inhabitant of Kosovo, in S Yugoslavia. ● *adj.* of or relating to Kosovo or its inhabitants.

koto /ˈkoʊtoʊ/ *n.* (*pl.* **-os**) a Japanese musical instrument with 13 long esp. silk strings.

kowtow /ˈkaʊtaʊ/ ● *n. hist.* the Chinese custom of kneeling and touching the ground with the forehead in worship or submission. ● *v.intr.* **1** (usu. foll. by *to*) act obsequiously. **2** *hist.* perform the kowtow.

kPa *abbr.* kilopascal(s).

k.p.h. *abbr.* kilometres per hour.

Kr *symbol* krypton.

kraft *n.* (in full **kraft paper**) a kind of strong smooth brown wrapping paper.

Kraut /kraʊt/ *n. slang offensive* a German.

kremlin /'kremlɪn/ *n.* **1** a citadel within a Russian town. **2** (**the Kremlin**) **a** the citadel in Moscow, the capital of Russia. **b** the Russian or (formerly) USSR government housed within it.

krill *n.* **1** a small shrimp-like planktonic crustacean of the order Euphausiacea, important as food for fish, and for some whales and seals. **2** these collectively.

krona /'kroːnə/ *n.* **1** (*pl.* **kronor** /'kroːnɔr/) the chief monetary unit of Sweden. **2** (*pl.* **kronur** /'kroːnʊr/) the chief monetary unit of Iceland.

krone /'kroːnə/ *n.* (*pl.* **kroner** /'kroːnɔr/) the chief monetary unit of Denmark and of Norway.

krypton /'krɪptɒn/ *n.* an inert gaseous element, forming a small portion of the earth's atmosphere and used in fluorescent lamps etc.

KS *abbr.* **1** Kansas (in official postal use). **2** KAPOSI'S SARCOMA.

Kt. *abbr.* Knight.

kt. *abbr.* **1** knot. **2** karat. **3** kiloton.

Ktunaxa Kinbasket /ktuː'nɒxɒ 'kɪn,bæsket/ *n.* **1** a member of an Aboriginal people living in southeastern BC and northeastern Washington. **2** the language of this people. ● *adj.* of or relating to this people.

Ku *symbol* kurchatovium.

kubasa /kuːbɒ'sɒ, 'kuːbəsɒ/ *n. Cdn* a garlic sausage of Ukrainian origin.

kuchen /'kuːxən/ *n.* a cake topped with sliced fruit and sprinkled with sugar before baking.

kudlik /'kuːdlɪk/ *n.* an Inuit soapstone seal oil lamp, providing both light and heat.

kudos /'kuːdɒːz, -doːs, -dɒs/ *n. informal* **1** *N Amer.* (often treated as *pl.*) expressions of praise. **2** glory; renown. ¶The plural use of *kudos* has been criticized, but it is well established in N American English.

kudzu /'kʌdzuː/ *n.* (in full **kudzu vine**) a quick-growing climbing plant with reddish-purple flowers.

kugel /'kuːgəl/ *n.* a baked sweet or savoury dish of potatoes or noodles mixed with eggs, cottage cheese, etc. and served as a separate course or as a side dish.

Ku Klux Klan *n.* a secret society of white people in the United States, originally formed in the southern states after the Civil War and revived in 1915 to harass and intimidate Blacks and other ethnic or religious minorities through violence, terrorism, and murder. ☐ **Ku Klux Klansman** *n.* (*pl.* **-men**).

kumquat /'kʌmkwɒt/ *n.* **1** an orange-like fruit with a sweet rind and acid pulp, used in preserves. **2** any shrub or tree of the genus *Fortunella* yielding this.

Kuna /'kuːnə/ (*pl.* same or **-as**) ● *n.* **1** a member of an Indian people of the isthmus of Panama. **2** the language of this people. ● *adj.* of or pertaining to the Kuna or their language.

kundalini /'kuːndəliːni/ *n.* **1** (in yoga) the latent, female energy believed to lie coiled at the base of the spine. **2** (in full **kundalini yoga**) a type of meditation which aims to direct and release this energy.

Kung /kuŋ/ ● *n.* (*pl.* same) **1** a member of a San (Bushman) people of the Kalahari Desert in southern Africa, maintaining to some extent a nomadic way of life dependent on hunting and gathering. **2** the Khoisan language of the Kung. ● *adj.* of or relating to the Kung or their language.

kung fu /kʌŋ 'fuː/ *n.* the Chinese form of unarmed combat similar to karate.

kurchatovium /,kɜrtʃə'toːviəm/ *n.* = RUTHERFORDIUM.

Kurd /kɜrd/ *n.* a member of a mainly pastoral Muslim people living chiefly in eastern Turkey, northern Iraq, western Iran, and eastern Syria.

Kurdish ● *adj.* of or relating to the Kurds or their language. ● *n.* the Iranian language of the Kurds.

Kutchin /kuː'tʃɪn/ *n.* = GWICH'IN.

Kutenai /'kuːtən,ei/ *n. & adj.* = KTUNAXA KINBASKET.

Kuwaiti /kʊ'weiti/ ● *n.* **1** (*pl.* **-s**) a native or inhabitant of Kuwait, a country on the NW coast of the Persian Gulf. **2** the dialect of Arabic spoken in Kuwait. ● *adj.* of or relating to Kuwait or the Kuwaitis.

kvetch /kvetʃ/ *esp. N Amer. slang* ● *v.tr.* complain and whine, esp. continually. ● *n.* (also **kvetcher**) a person who complains a great deal. ☐ **kvetching** *n.*

kW *abbr.* kilowatt(s).

Kwa /kwɑ/ ● *n.* **1** the group of related languages, spoken from Ivory Coast to Nigeria, which includes Ibo and Yoruba. **2** (*pl.* same) a member of a Kwa-speaking people. ● *adj.* of or relating to this group of languages.

Kwagiulth /kwʊ'giːuːlθ/ ● *n.* (*pl.* same) **1** a member of an Aboriginal people living in parts of coastal BC and northern Vancouver Island. **2** the Kwa-kwa-la language of this people. ● *adj.* of or relating to this people.

Kwakiutl /,kwɒki:'uːtəl/ *n. & adj.* (*pl.* same) = KWAGIULTH.

Kwakwaka'wakw /kwʊ'kwʊki,wʊk/ ● *n.* (*pl.* same) a member of an Aboriginal people living in south-western BC. ● *adj.* of or relating to this people.

Kwa-kwa-la /kwʊ'kwʊlə/ *n.* the Wakashan language of the Kwakwaka'wakw and Kwagiulth.

Kwanza /'kwɒnzɒ/ *n.* (also **Kwanzaa**) *N Amer.* a festival observed from 26 Dec. to 1 Jan. in celebration of black cultural heritage.

kwashiorkor /,kwɒʃi'ɔrkɔr/ *n.* a form of malnutrition caused by a severe dietary protein deficiency, esp. in young children in the tropics.

kWh *abbr.* kilowatt hour(s).

KWIC /kwɪk/ *n. Computing etc.* keyword in context.

KY *abbr.* Kentucky (in official postal use).

Ky. *abbr.* Kentucky.

Kyrie /'kiːri,ei/ *n.* (in full **Kyrie eleison** /ei'leii,sɒn, e'lei-, i'lei-, -,zɒn/) **1** a short repeated invocation (in Greek or translated) beginning with the words 'Lord, have mercy' used in many Christian liturgies, esp. at the beginning of the Eucharist or as a response in a litany. **2** a musical setting of the Kyrie.

LI

L¹ *n.* (also **l**) (*pl.* **Ls** or **L's**) **1** the twelfth letter of the alphabet. **2** (as a Roman numeral) 50. **3** a thing shaped like an L, esp. a joint connecting two pipes.
L² *abbr.* (also **L.**) **1** Lake. **2** (esp. on clothing etc.) large. **3** Liberal. **4** (in academic degrees) Licentiate. **5** Lire. **6** litre.
l *abbr.* (also **l.**) **1** left. **2** line. **3** litre(s). **4** length. **5** (esp. *pl.* **ll.**) (of poetry) line. **6** liquid.
£ *abbr.* (preceding a numeral) pounds (of money).
LA *abbr.* **1** Los Angeles. **2** Louisiana (in postal use).
La *symbol* lanthanum.
La. *abbr.* Louisiana.
la /lɪ/ *n. Music* **1** (in tonic sol-fa) the sixth note of a major scale. **2** the note A in the fixed-do system.
Lab *n.* esp. *N Amer.* a Labrador retriever.
Lab. *abbr.* Labrador.
lab *n. informal* a laboratory.
lab coat *n.* a coat of a light, usu. white fabric, worn over clothing to protect it, esp. in a laboratory etc.
label ● *n.* **1** a usu. small piece of paper, card, cloth, metal, etc. attached to or beside an object, item of food, etc., giving its name, information about it, instructions for use, etc. **2** esp. *derogatory* a short classifying phrase or name applied to a person, a work of art, etc. **3 a** a small fabric label sewn into a garment bearing the maker's name. **b** the logo, title, or trademark of esp. a fashion or recording company. **c** the clothing or recordings produced under such a trademark. **d** the identifying material affixed to or imprinted upon a CD, cassette, etc. describing its contents etc. **e** a recording company or part of one producing CDs, cassettes, etc. under a distinctive name. **4** a paper sticker used for addressing envelopes, magazines etc. for mailing. **5** a word placed before, after, or in the course of a dictionary definition etc. to specify its subject, register, nationality, etc. **6** *Biol.* & *Chem.* a radioactive isotope, fluorescent dye, etc. used to label another substance. **7** *Computing* **a** an arbitrary name for a statement in a program which facilitates reference to it elsewhere in the program. **b** a set of data recorded on a reel of magnetic tape describing its contents and serving for identification by a computer. ● *v.tr.* (**labelled**, **labelling**) **1** attach a label to, mark with a label. **2** (usu. foll. by *as*) assign to a category, describe or designate as with a label (*labelled them as irresponsible*). **3** make (a substance, molecule, etc.) experimentally recognizable but essentially unaltered in behaviour, so that its path may be followed or its distribution ascertained. □ **labeller** *n.*
labial /ˈleɪbɪəl/ *adj.* **1 a** of the lips. **b** *Zool.* pertaining to, of the nature of, associated with, or situated on a lip or labium. **2** *Dentistry* designating the surface of a tooth adjacent to the lips.
labiate /ˈleɪbɪət/ ● *n.* any plant of the family Labiatae, including mint and rosemary, having square stems and a corolla or calyx divided into two parts suggesting lips. ● *adj.* **1** *Bot.* of or relating to the Labiatae. **2** *Bot.* & *Zool.* like a lip, lips, or labium.
labium /ˈleɪbɪəm/ *n.* (*pl.* **labia** /-bɪə/) **1** (usu. in *pl.*) *Anat.*

each of the two pairs of skin folds that enclose the vulva. **2** the lower lip in the mouthparts of an insect or crustacean. **3** a lip, esp. the lower one of a labiate plant's corolla.
labor etc. *var.* of LABOUR etc.
laboratory /ˈlæbrə.tɔrɪ, ləˈbɔrə-, ləˈbɒrətrɪ/ *n.* (*pl.* **-ies**) **1** a room or building fitted out for scientific experiments, research, teaching, or the manufacture of drugs and chemicals. **2** a class in which students engage in learning activities such as language drill, mapping, conducting experiments, etc.
laboratory animal *n.* any animal, such as a rat, monkey, mouse, etc. commonly used for experiments in a laboratory.
laboratory technician *n.* a person trained to perform practical tasks in a laboratory, e.g. conducting tests, compiling data, etc.
laborious /ləˈbɔrɪəs/ *adj.* **1** needing hard work or toil (*a laborious task*). **2** (esp. of literary style) showing signs of toil; not fluent. □ **laboriously** *adv.* **laboriousness** *n.*
labour (also **labor**) ● *n.* **1 a** physical or mental work; exertion; toil. **b** such work considered as supplying the needs of a community. **2** workers, esp. manual, considered as a class or political force. **3** the process of childbirth, esp. the period from the start of uterine contractions to delivery. **4** a particular task, esp. of a difficult nature. **5** (**Labour**) = LABOUR PARTY. ● *v.* **1** *intr.* **a** work hard or exert oneself physically or mentally. **b** do esp. manual work to earn one's living. **2** *intr.* (usu. foll. by *for*, or *to* + infin.) strive for a purpose (*laboured to fulfill his promise*). **3** *tr.* treat at or insist upon at excessive length; elaborate needlessly (*I will not labour the point*). **4** *intr.* (often foll. by *under*) suffer under (a disadvantage or delusion) (*laboured under universal disapproval*). **5** *intr.* proceed with trouble or difficulty (*laboured slowly up the hill*). **6** *intr.* (of an engine) work noisily and with difficulty, esp. when under load. **7** *intr.* (of a woman) be in labour, give birth. □ **labour in vain** make a fruitless effort. **labour of love** a task done for pleasure, not reward. □ **labouringly** *adv.*
labour board *n.* (in full **Labour Relations Board**) a tribunal, either provincial or federal, empowered to mediate and resolve labour disputes.
labour camp *n.* **1** a prison camp enforcing a regime of hard labour. **2** a camp providing shelter for migratory workers, esp. farm labourers.
labour coach *n. N Amer.* a person who provides emotional and physical help to a woman in labour, e.g. by helping with breathing exercises, etc.
Labour Day *n.* (*US* **Labor Day**) a holiday in celebration of working people, observed in Canada and the US on the first Monday in September and elsewhere on 1 May.
laboured *adj.* **1** not natural or spontaneous; showing signs of too much effort. **2** (esp. of breathing) slow and difficult.
labourer *n.* (also **laborer**) **1** a person doing unskilled, usu. manual, work for wages. **2** a person who labours.
labour force *n.* **1** the number of people in the

population employed or seeking work. **2** the body of workers employed, esp. at a plant, company, etc.

labour-intensive *adj.* (of a process or industry) having labour as the largest factor or cost.

labour law *n.* **1** the area of law pertaining to and governing the relationship between employers and employees, management and unions, etc. **2** a law affecting or controlling working conditions etc.

labour market *n.* the supply of labour considered with reference to the demand on it.

labour movement *n.* **1** the effort by organized labour to improve conditions for workers. **2** the organizations and individuals involved in this.

Labour Party *n.* **1** a British political party formed to represent the interests of ordinary working people. **2** any similar political party in other countries.

labour relations *n.* (often treated as *sing.*) the relations between management and employees.

labour-saving *adj.* (of an appliance etc.) designed to reduce or eliminate the work needed to do something.

labour union *n.* N Amer. an organized association of workers formed to protect and further their rights and interests and bargain collectively with employers.

Labrador *n.* (in full **Labrador dog**, **Labrador retriever**) a breed of retriever with a black or golden coat often used as a gun dog or as a guide for a blind person.

Labradorian ● *n.* a native or inhabitant of Labrador, a coastal region of E Canada, which forms the mainland part of the province of Newfoundland and Labrador. ● *adj.* of or relating to Labrador or Labradorians.

Labrador Inuit *n.* **1** the Inuit people living in N Labrador. **2** the language of this people.

labradorite *n.* a kind of plagioclase feldspar, often showing iridescence from internal reflective planes.

Labrador tea *n.* **1** a shrub of the genus *Ledum* of the heath family, which has leathery evergreen leaves. **2** an infusion made from these leaves.

lab technician *n.* (also N Amer. informal **lab tech**) = LABORATORY TECHNICIAN.

laburnum /ləˈbɜːnəm/ *n.* any small tree of the genus *Laburnum* with racemes of golden flowers yielding poisonous seeds.

labyrinth /ˈlæbərɪnθ/ *n.* **1** a complicated irregular network of passages or paths etc. **2 a** an intricate or tangled arrangement, esp. of streets or buildings. **b** a complex or confusing situation. **3** Anat. the complex arrangement of canals and chambers of the inner ear which constitute the organs of hearing and balance. **4** any of various devices containing or consisting of winding passages, esp. a series of chambers designed to absorb unwanted vibrations in a loudspeaker. □ **labyrinthine** /-ˈrɪnθaɪn/ *adj.*

lac /læk/ *n.* a resinous substance secreted as a protective covering by the lac insect, and used to make varnish and shellac.

lace ● *n.* **1** a fine open fabric, esp. of cotton or silk, made by weaving thread in patterns and used esp. as a trim or to make tablecloths. **2** a cord or leather strip passed through eyelets or hooks on opposite sides of a shoe, skate, garment, etc., pulled tight and fastened. **3** braid used for trimming esp. dress uniforms. ● *attrib.adj.* made of lace. ● *v.* **1** *tr.* (usu. foll. by up) **a** fasten or tighten (a shoe, garment, etc.) with a lace or laces usu. passed alternately through two rows of eyelet holes or around two rows of hooks, studs, etc. **b** fasten (a person) into a garment etc. by

means of a lace or laces. **2** *tr.* **a** (usu. foll. by with) add an ingredient to (a drink etc.) to enhance or adulterate flavour, strength, effect, etc. **b** intermingle (ribaldry laced with philosophy). **3** *tr.* (usu. foll. by with) **a** streak (a sky etc.) with colour. **b** interlace or embroider (fabric) with thread etc. **4** *tr.* & *intr.* informal thrash, beat, or abuse, physically or verbally. **5** *tr.* (often foll. by through) pass (a shoelace etc.) through. **6** *tr.* pass (film, tape, etc.) between the guides and other parts of a projector, tape recorder, etc. so it runs from one spool to the other.

lace curtain ● *n.* a window curtain made of lace which lets in light but makes seeing into the room difficult. ● *adj.* (also **lace-curtain**) **1** having social pretensions. **2** genteel.

laced *adj.* **1 a** (of shoes etc.) made to be fastened or tightened with a lace or laces. **b** (of a shoe etc.) so fastened. **2 a** (of a drink etc.) mixed with a small measure of some other substance such as liquor etc. **b** marked with streaks of colour. **3** ornamented or trimmed with lace or laces.

lacerate /ˈlæsəˌreɪt/ *v.tr.* **1** tear or cut (esp. flesh or tissue). **2** distress or cause pain to (the feelings etc.). □ **lacerated** *adj.* **laceration** *n.*

lace-up ● *n.* a shoe, boot, etc. fastened with a lace. ● *attrib.adj.* (of a shoe etc.) fastened by a lace or laces.

lacewing *n.* any of various predatory insects with delicate lacelike wings.

lacing *n.* **1** the act or an instance of lacing something. **2** something that laces or fastens, esp. a laced fastening on a shoe etc. **3** ornamental lace trimming or braiding. **4** informal a beating.

lac insect *n.* an Asian scale insect, *Laccifer lacca*, living in trees.

lack ● *n.* (usu. foll. by of) an absence, want, or deficiency. ● *v.tr.* be without or deficient in (lacks courage). □ **for lack of** owing to the absence of. **lack for** lack (never lacks for odd jobs).

lackadaisical /ˌlækəˈdeɪzɪkəl/ *adj.* unenthusiastic, lacking vigour. □ **lackadaisically** *adv.*

lackey *n.* (pl. **-eys**) **1** derogatory **a** a servile political follower. **b** an obsequious parasitical person. **2 a** a usu. liveried footman or manservant. **b** a servant.

lacking *predic.adj.* **1** (of a thing) not available, missing (money was lacking). **2** inadequate or deficient (is lacking in determination).

lacklustre *adj.* (also esp. US **lackluster**) **1** lacking in vitality, force, or conviction. **2** (of the eye, hair, etc.) dull.

laconic /ləˈkɒnɪk/ *adj.* **1** (of a style of speech or writing) brief; concise; terse. **2** (of a person) laconic in speech etc. □ **laconically** *adv.*

lacquer /ˈlækər/ ● *n.* **1** a sometimes coloured varnish made of shellac dissolved in alcohol, or of synthetic substances, that dries to form a hard protective coating. **2** any of the various resinous wood varnishes capable of taking a hard polish, esp. the sap of the lacquer tree. ● *v.tr.* coat with lacquer. □ **lacquered** *adj.*

lacquer tree *n.* an E Asian tree, *Rhus verniciflua*, the sap of which is used as a varnish for wood.

lacrosse /ləˈkrɒs/ *n.* a game, originally played by N American Indians, in which a ball is thrown, carried and caught with a lacrosse stick.

lacrosse stick *n.* the stick used in lacrosse, having a curved L-shaped or triangular frame at one end with a piece of shallow netting in the angle.

lactase /ˈlækteɪz, -teɪs/ *n.* Biochem. any of a group of enzymes which catalyze the hydrolysis of lactose.

lactate[1] /læk'teit/ v.intr. (of mammals) secrete milk. □ **lactating** adj.

lactate[2] /'lækteit/ n. any salt or ester of lactic acid.

lactation n. **1** the secretion of milk by the mammary glands. **2 a** the period of milk secretion normally following childbirth. **b** the suckling of young.

lactic adj. Chem. of or obtained from milk.

lactic acid n. a clear odourless syrupy carboxylic acid formed in sour milk, and produced in the muscle tissues during strenuous exercise.

lactobacillus /,læktəbə'sıləs/ n. (pl. **-bacilli** /-lai/) Biol. any rod-shaped bacterium of the genus Lactobacillus, producing lactic acid from the fermentation of carbohydrates.

lactose /'læktəʊs, -təʊz/ n. a sugar that occurs in milk, and is less sweet than sucrose.

lacuna /lə'kjuːnə/ n. (pl. **lacunae** /-niː/ or **lacunas**) **1** a hiatus, blank, or gap. **2 a** a missing portion or empty page, esp. in an ancient manuscript, book, etc. **b** something missing or left out, esp. by oversight, incompetence, etc. **3** Anat. a space, cavity, or depression within or between the tissues of an organism, esp. in bone.

lacy adj. (**-ier, -iest**) of, trimmed with, or resembling lace. □ **lacily** adv. **laciness** n.

lad n. **1 a** a boy or youth. **b** a young son. **2** (esp. in pl.) informal a man; a fellow, esp. a workmate, drinking companion, etc. (he's one of the lads).

ladder n. **1 a** a fixed or portable device usu. made of wood, metal, or rope, consisting of a series of bars, rungs, or steps fixed between two supports and used as a means of climbing up or down. **b** anything resembling a ladder in appearance or function (fish ladder). **2 a** a hierarchical structure perceived as resembling a ladder. **b** such a structure as a means of advancement, promotion, etc.

ladderback n. an upright chair with a back formed of horizontal pieces of wood, resembling a ladder.

laddie n. informal a young boy or lad.

lade v. (past part. **laden**) **1** tr. **a** put cargo on board (a ship). **b** ship (goods) as cargo. **2** intr. take on cargo.

laden adj. **1** (in comb.) having a high proportion of the specified quality, substance, etc. (debt-laden; sugar-laden). **2** (usu. foll. by with) heavily loaded, abundantly filled. **3** (of the conscience, spirit, etc.) painfully burdened with guilt etc.

la-di-da /,lɒ:di:'dɑ:/ adj. informal (also **la-de-da, lah-di-dah**) affectedly genteel or refined.

ladies pl. of LADY.

Ladies' Aid n. (in full **Ladies' Aid Society**) N Amer. an organization of women who support a church's work by fundraising, arranging social activities, etc.

ladies' man n. (also **lady's man**) a man fond of and very successful with women.

ladies' night n. **1** a designated night at a bar, club, etc. on which admission for women is free or at a reduced price. **2** a function at a men's club etc. to which women are invited.

ladies' room n. a women's washroom.

lading n. **1** a cargo. **2** the act or process of lading.

ladle n. **1** a long-handled spoon with a cup-shaped bowl for serving or transferring liquids. **2** a vessel for transporting molten metal in a foundry. ● v.tr. (often foll. by out) transfer (liquid) from one receptacle to another. □ **ladle out** distribute, esp. lavishly. □ **ladleful** n. (pl. **-fuls**).

lady n. (pl. **-ies**) **1 a** a woman regarded as being of superior social status or as having the refined manners associated with this (compare GENTLEMAN). **b**

(**Lady**) a title used by peeresses, female relatives of peers, the wives and widows of knights, etc. **2 a** any woman (ask that lady over there). **b** often offensive as a form of address (hey, lady, move your car). **3** informal **a** a wife or consort. **b** a man's girlfriend or mistress. **4** the female head of a household (lady of the house). **5** (in pl. as a form of address) a female audience or the female part of an audience. **6** hist. a woman who is the object of chivalrous devotion, esp. one loved and courted by a knight. **7** an honorific title, used preceding the names of goddesses, allegorical figures, personifications, etc. (Lady Philosophy). □ **the Ladies** (or **Ladies'**) a women's public washroom.

ladybug n. N Amer. (also esp. Brit. **ladybird**) a coleopterous insect of the family Coccinellidae, with wing covers usu. of a reddish colour with black spots.

ladyfinger n. N Amer. a finger-shaped sponge cake.

lady friend n. a regular female companion or lover.

lady-in-waiting n. a lady attending a queen etc.

ladylike adj. with the modesty, comportment, etc., thought characteristic of a well brought-up lady.

Lady Luck n. informal a female personification of luck.

lady of the house n. the female head of a household.

lady of the night n. a prostitute.

ladyship n. □ **her** (or **your** or **their**) **ladyship** (or **ladyships**) **1** a respectful form of reference or address to a Lady or Ladies. **2** ironic a form of reference or address to a woman thought to be giving herself airs.

lady's mantle n. any plant of the genus Alchemilla with yellowish-green clustered flowers.

lady's slipper n. any orchid of the genus Cypripedium, with a slipper-shaped lip on its flowers.

laevorotatory var. of LEVOROTATORY.

lag ● v.intr. (**lagged, lagging**) (often foll. by behind) fall behind; not keep pace. ● n. **1 a** = LAG TIME. **b** a delay. **2** Physics **a** retardation in a current or movement. **b** the amount of this. □ **lagger** n.

lager /'lɒgɜr/ n. **1** a kind of beer, effervescent and light in colour and body. **2** a serving of this.

laggard /'lægɜrd/ ● n. a dawdler; a person who lags behind. ● adj. dawdling; slow; lagging behind.

lagoon n. **1** a bay separated from the sea, a large lake, etc. by a low sandbank or similar barrier. **2** the enclosed water of an atoll or inside a barrier reef. **3** an artificial pool for the treatment of effluent or to accommodate an overspill from surface drains during heavy rain. □ **lagoonal** adj.

lag time n. a period of time separating two events, esp. an action and its effect.

lah var. of LA.

laid past and past part. of LAY[1].

laid-back adj. informal relaxed, unbothered, easygoing.

laid up predic.adj. **1** (of a person) confined to bed or the house, esp. because of illness or injury. **2** (of a ship, vehicle, etc.) taken out of service. **3 a** (of goods, provisions, etc.) saved, stored up, or put away for safety. **b** informal (of a person etc.) hidden.

lain past part. of LIE[1].

lair /ler/ n. **1** a wild animal's den or resting place. **2** a person's hiding place, retreat, or secret base. □

laissez-faire /,lesei'fer/ n. (also **laisser-faire**) **1** the theory or practice of governmental abstention from interference in the workings of the market etc. **2** non-interference or non-involvement in, or indifference to, the affairs of others generally.

laity /'leɪɪti/ n. (usu. prec. by the; usu. treated as pl.) **1** lay people, as distinct from the clergy. **2** non-professionals.

lake[1] n. **1** a large body of water surrounded by land. **2** an expanse or surplus of liquid.

lake[2] n. **1** a reddish colouring originally made from lac. **2** a complex formed by the action of dye and mordants applied to fabric to fix colour. **3** any insoluble product of a soluble dye and mordant.

lake boat n. Cdn a boat or ship designed for sailing on the Great Lakes.

lake effect n. the influence of a lake on weather patterns, esp. increasing snowfall on its leeward side and moderating the temperature of surrounding areas (also attrib.: lake effect snow).

lakefront n. N Amer. the shore of a lake (also attrib.: lakefront cottages).

lakehead n. Cdn the area along a lakeshore farthest from the lake's outlet.

lakeland n. an area with many lakes.

laker n. informal **1** N Amer. = LAKE TROUT. **2** a ship designed for sailing on lakes, esp. the Great Lakes.

lakeshore n. N Amer. the shore of a lake.

lakeside attrib.adj. beside a lake.

lake trout n. the salmonid Salvelinus namaycush, of N American lakes, an important sport fish.

lakeview attrib.adj. N Amer. overlooking a lake.

la-la land n. N Amer. informal **1** a fanciful state or dream world. **2** (**La-La Land**) **a** California, esp. the world of movies and television based there. **b** Cdn British Columbia.

lalapalooza var. of LOLLAPALOOZA.

lallygag /'læli,gæg/ v.intr. (**-gagged**, **-gagging**) N Amer. slang **1** loiter. **2** cuddle amorously.

lam[1] v. (**lammed**, **lamming**) slang **1** tr. thrash; hit. **2** intr. (foll. by into) hit hard with a stick etc.

lam[2] n. □ **on the lam** N Amer. slang in flight, esp. from the police.

lama /'lɒmə/ n. a Tibetan or Mongolian Buddhist monk.

Lamaism /'lɒmə,ɪzəm/ n. the system of doctrine and observances inculcated and maintained by lamas.

Lamaze /lə'mɒz/ n. (attrib.) N Amer. designating a method of childbirth emphasizing the use of psychological and physical preparation and breathing routines to control pain.

lamb ● n. **1** a young sheep. **2** the flesh of a lamb as food. **3** a mild or gentle person, esp. a young child. **4** = LAMB OF GOD. ● v. **1 a** tr. (in passive) (of a lamb) be born. **b** intr. (of a ewe) give birth to lambs. **2** tr. tend (lambing ewes). □ **like a lamb** meekly, obediently.

lambada /ləm'bɒdə/ n. a fast erotic Brazilian dance which couples perform with their stomachs touching.

lambaste /læm'beist/ v.tr. **1** thrash; beat. **2** criticize severely.

lambda /'læmdə/ n. **1** the eleventh letter of the Greek alphabet (Λ, λ). **2** (as λ) the symbol for wavelength.

lambent /'læmbənt/ adj. **1** (of a flame or a light) playing on a surface with a soft radiance but without burning. **2** (of the eyes, sky, etc.) softly radiant. **3** (of wit etc.) lightly brilliant. □ **lambency** n.

Lamb of God n. **1** a name for Christ. **2** = AGNUS DEI 2.

lambskin prepared skin from a lamb, with the wool on or as leather.

lamb's lettuce n. a plant, Valerianella locusta, used in salad.

lamb's quarters n. a herbaceous European plant of the goosefoot family, naturalized in N America.

lambswool n. soft fine wool from a young sheep used in knitted garments etc.

lame ● adj. **1 a** disabled, esp. in the foot or leg, so as to walk awkwardly or with difficulty. **b** limping; unable to walk normally. **2** (of an argument, story, excuse, etc.) unconvincing; unsatisfactory; weak. **3** N Amer. pathetic or contemptible, esp. because unfashionable. ● v.tr. **1** make lame; disable. **2** harm permanently. □ **lamely** adv. **lameness** n.

lamé /læ'mei, 'læmei/ ● n. a fabric with gold or silver threads interwoven. ● adj. (of fabric, a dress, etc.) having such threads.

lamebrain n. N Amer. informal a stupid person. □ **lame-brained** adj.

lame duck n. (often, with hyphen, attrib.) **1** a disabled or powerless person or thing. **2** (in the US) the President in the final period of office, after the election of a successor. **3** any person or thing soon to be replaced.

lament ● n. **1** a passionate expression of grief. **2** a song or poem of mourning or sorrow. ● v. **1** tr. & intr. express or feel grief (for or about). **2** tr. regret (lamented the lack of information). **3** tr. utter with a lament. □ **lament for** (or **over**) mourn or regret.

lamentable /lə'mentəbəl, 'læməntəbəl/ adj. (of an event, fate, condition, character, etc.) deplorable; regrettable. □ **lamentably** adv.

lamentation /,læmən'teiʃən/ n. **1** the act or an instance of lamenting. **2** a lament.

lamented adj. a conventional expression referring to a recently dead person (your late lamented father).

lamina /'læmɪnə/ n. (pl. **laminae** /-,ni:/) a thin plate or scale, e.g. of bone, stratified rock, etc.

laminate ● v. /'læmɪ,neit/ **1** tr. beat or roll (metal) into thin plates. **2** tr. overlay with a thin plastic layer, metal plates, etc. **3** tr. manufacture by placing layer on layer. **4** tr. & intr. split or be split into layers or leaves. ● n. /'læmɪnət/ a laminated structure or material, esp. of layers fixed together to form rigid or flexible material. ● adj. /'læmɪnət/ in the form of lamina or laminae. □ **lamination** n. **laminator** n.

lamp n. **1** a device for producing a steady light, esp.: **a** an electric bulb, and usu. its holder and shade or cover (bedside lamp). **b** an oil lamp. **c** a usu. glass holder for a candle. **d** a gas jet and mantle. **2** a source of spiritual or intellectual inspiration. **3** literary the sun, the moon, or a star. **4** a device producing ultraviolet, infrared, or other radiation, for tanning skin, keeping food warm, etc. □ **lampless** adj.

lampblack n. a black pigment made from soot.

lamplight n. light given by a lamp or lamps. □ **lamplit** adj.

lampoon ● n. a satirical attack. ● v.tr. satirize.

lamppost n. (also **lamp standard**) a tall post supporting a street light.

lamprey /'læmpri/ n. (pl. **-eys**) any eel-like aquatic vertebrate of the family Petromyzonidae, without scales, paired fins, or jaws, but having a sucker mouth with horny teeth and a rough tongue.

lampshade n. a cover for a lamp, used to soften or direct its light.

LAN /læn/ n. Computing local area network.

lance ● n. **1 a** a long weapon with a wooden shaft and a pointed steel head, used by a horseman in charging. **b** a similar weapon used for spearing a fish, killing a harpooned whale, etc. **2** = LANCER. ● v. **1** tr. Surgery prick or cut open with a lancet. **2** tr. pierce with or as with a lance. **3** intr. (of a ray of light etc.) pierce through a narrow opening. □ **lance the boil**

relieve simmering tension or an unpleasant situation, esp. by taking drastic or painful measures.

lancer *n. hist.* a soldier of a cavalry regiment armed with lances.

lancet /ˈlænsət/ *n.* **1** a small broad double-edged surgical knife with a sharp point. **2** (in full **lancet arch, lancet window**) a narrow arch or window with a pointed head. □ **lanceted** *adj.*

land ● *n.* **1 a** the solid part of the earth's surface, as opposed to large bodies of water or air. **b** (*attrib.*) designating armies rather than navies or air forces (*land forces*). **2 a** an expanse of country; ground; soil. **b** such land in relation to its use, quality, etc., or (often prec. *by the*) as a basis for agriculture. **3** a country, nation, or state (*our home and native land*). **4 a** landed property. **b** (in *pl.*) estates. **5** a figurative domain or sphere (*TV land*). ● *v.* **1 a** *tr. & intr.* set or go ashore. **b** *intr.* (often foll. by *at*) disembark (*landed at the harbour*). **2** *tr.* bring (an aircraft, its passengers, etc.) to the ground or the surface of water. **3** *intr.* (of an aircraft, bird, parachutist, etc.) alight on the ground or water. **4** *tr.* bring (a fish) to land, esp. with a hook or net. **5** *tr. & intr.* (also *refl.*; often foll. by *up*) *informal* bring to, reach, or find oneself in a certain situation, place, or state (*landed her in trouble*). **6** *tr. informal* deal (a person etc. a blow etc.) (*landed him one in the eye*). **7** *tr.* set down (a person, cargo, etc.) from a vehicle, ship, etc. **8** *tr. informal* win or obtain (a prize, job, etc.) esp. against strong competition. □ **how the land lies** what the state of affairs is. **in the land of the living** *jocular* still alive. **land of Nod** sleep. **land on one's feet** emerge unharmed from a difficult situation. □ **landless** *adj.*

land agent *n. Cdn hist.* an agent who helped settlers find homesteads, esp. on the Prairies. □ **land agency** *n.*

landau /ˈlændau/ *n.* **1** a four-wheeled horse-drawn carriage, with folding front and rear hoods enabling it to travel open, half-open, or closed. **2** a car with a folding leather hood over the rear seats.

land bank *n.* **1** a bank issuing banknotes on the securities of landed property. **2** land held in trust, esp. for future development.

land base *n. esp. Cdn* a territory under the control of a specified group, e.g. a logging company or Aboriginal group.

land bridge *n.* a neck of land joining two large land masses.

land claim *n. esp. Cdn* a legal claim by an Aboriginal group concerning the use of an area of land.

landed *adj.* **1** *Cdn* denoting official recognition of immigration to Canada (*landed immigrant*; *landed status*). **2** owning land (*landed gentry*). **3** consisting of, including, or relating to land (*landed property*).

lander *n.* a spacecraft designed to land on the surface of a planet or moon.

landfall *n.* the first sight of or approach to land after a journey by sea or by air over open water.

landfast *attrib.adj. N Amer.* (of ice covering a frozen body of water) firmly attached to the shore.

landfill *n.* **1** the disposal of refuse by burying it under layers of earth. **2** refuse disposed of in this way. **3** an area filled in by this process. ● *v.* **1** *tr. & intr.* dispose of (refuse) in this way. **2** *tr.* fill (a piece of land) with refuse in this way.

Land Forces Command *n. Cdn* the official name for the Canadian army.

landform *n.* a natural feature of the earth's surface.

land grant *n. N Amer.* **1** the donation of land by a government to an individual, institution, etc. **2** the

land so granted. **3** the agreement, treaty, etc. authorizing the grant.

landholder *n.* the owner or the tenant of land.

landholding *n.* **1** a piece of land owned or rented. **2** the owning or renting of land.

landing *n.* **1 a** the act or process of coming to land or the ground, floor etc. **b** an instance of this. **c** a place in a harbour for disembarking, loading, unloading, etc. **2** a level place between two flights of stairs, or at the top or bottom of a flight. **3** *Cdn Forestry* an area where logs are piled before transportation.

landing craft *n.* any of several types of craft esp. designed for putting troops and equipment ashore.

landing gear *n.* the undercarriage of an aircraft.

landing light *n.* **1** a light on a runway to guide an aircraft in a night landing. **2** a powerful light attached to an aircraft to illuminate the landing path ahead.

landing pad *n.* a small area designed for helicopters to land on and take off from.

landing stage *n.* a platform, often floating, on which goods and passengers are disembarked.

landing strip *n.* an airstrip.

landlady *n.* (*pl.* **-ies**) **1** a woman who rents land, a building, part of a building, etc., to a tenant. **2** a woman who keeps a boarding or rooming house.

landlocked *adj.* **1** almost or entirely enclosed by land. **2** (of fish, esp. salmon) living in fresh water cut off from the sea.

landlord *n.* **1** a person who rents land, a building, part of a building, etc., to a tenant. **2** a person who keeps a boarding or rooming house.

landlubber *n.* a person unfamiliar with the sea or sailing.

landmark *n.* **1 a** a conspicuous object in a district etc. **b** an object marking the boundary of an estate, country, etc. **c** an important building, monument, etc. **2** an event etc. marking a stage or turning point in history etc. (also *attrib.*: *a landmark decision*).

land mass *n.* a large area of land.

land mine *n.* an explosive mine laid in or on the ground.

land office *n. N Amer.* an office recording dealings in public land.

landowner *n.* an owner of land. □ **landownership** *n.* **landowning** *adj. & n.*

land registry office *n. Cdn* (in the Atlantic provinces, Quebec, and parts of Ontario and Manitoba) a government office where documents concerning property are kept but where the government does not guarantee their validity (compare LAND TITLES OFFICE).

landscape ● *n.* **1** natural or imaginary scenery, as seen in a broad view. **2** (often *attrib.*) a picture representing this; the genre of landscape painting. **3** (of a page, book, etc., or the manner in which it is set or printed) having or in a rectangular shape with the width greater than the height (compare PORTRAIT). **4** the general characteristics of an activity, field, sphere, etc. (*the political landscape*). ● *v.tr. & intr.* alter (a piece of land) by landscape gardening. □ **landscaper** *n.* **landscaping** *n.* **landscapist** *n.*

landscape architecture *n.* the art or practice of planning and designing the environment, esp. with reference to built areas. □ **landscape architect** *n.*

landscape gardening *n.* the art or practice of laying out ornamental grounds or grounds imitating natural scenery. □ **landscape gardener** *n.*

landslide *n.* **1 a** the sliding down of a mass of land from a mountain, cliff, etc. **b** the mass of land which has so fallen. **2** an overwhelming majority for one side in an election.

land titles office *n. Cdn & Austral.* a government agency which keeps track of ownership of property by maintaining documents pertaining to the property once it has determined their validity (*compare* LAND REGISTRY OFFICE).

landward ● *adj.* facing the land, as opposed to the sea. ● *adv.* (also **landwards**) towards the land.

landwash *n. Cdn* (*Nfld*) the area along a shore between the high-water mark and the sea.

lane *n.* **1** a narrow road, street, or path. **2** a division of a road for a stream of traffic (*four-lane highway*; *bicycle lane*). **3** a strip of track or water for a runner, rower, or swimmer, usu. marked out and separated from parallel ones by lines or ropes. **4** a path or course prescribed for or regularly followed by a ship, aircraft, etc. (*ocean lane*). **5** the long alley down which a bowling ball is thrown. **6** a gangway between crowds of people, objects, etc. **7** *Basketball* **a** = KEY *n.* 17. **b** any open area on the court through which a player can move towards the hoop (*drive the lane*).

laneway *n.* **1** = LANE 1. **2** *Cdn* a narrow urban street, esp. behind houses or stores; a back alley.

langoustine /ˌlãgu:ˈsti:n, ˈlɒŋgu,sti:n/ *n.* = NORWAY LOBSTER.

language *n.* **1** the method of human communication, either spoken or written, consisting of the use of words in an agreed way. **2** the language of a particular community or country etc. **3** any method of expression (*body language*). **4 a** the faculty of speech. **b** a style or the faculty of expression; the use of words, etc. (*his language was poetic*). **c** (also **bad language**) coarse, crude, or abusive speech (*didn't like his language*). **5** a system of symbols and rules for writing computer programs or algorithms. **6** a professional or specialized vocabulary. **7** literary style. □ **speak the same language** have a similar outlook, manner of expression, etc.

language arts *n.pl.* those subjects (as reading, writing, spelling, etc.) taught in schools to develop oral and written communication skills.

language police *n. derogatory* **1** *Cdn* (*Que.*) the officials of the Commission de Protection de la Langue Française responsible for ensuring that Quebec's language laws are enforced. **2** a group, often self-appointed, which criticizes what it considers to be unacceptable language.

languid /ˈlæŋgwɪd/ *adj.* **1** moving slowly and involving little physical effort or emotion. **2** (of ideas etc.) lacking force; uninteresting. **3** faint; weak. □ **languidly** *adv.*

languish /ˈlæŋgwɪʃ/ *v.intr.* **1** be or grow feeble; lose or lack vitality. **2** live under conditions which lower the vitality or depress the spirits (*languished in graduate school*). **3** (foll. by *for*) pine or long for. **4** suffer neglect.

languor /ˈlæŋgər/ *n.* **1** the state or feeling, often pleasant, of being lazy and lacking energy. **2** faintness; fatigue. **3** a soft or tender mood or effect. **4** an oppressive stillness (of the air etc.). □ **languorous** *adj.* **languorously** *adv.*

lank *adj.* **1** (of hair, grass, etc.) long, limp, and straight. **2** thin and tall. □ **lankly** *adv.* **lankness** *n.*

lanky *adj.* (**-ier**, **-iest**) (of limbs, a person, etc.) ungracefully thin and long or tall. □ **lankily** *adv.* **lankiness** *n.*

lanolin /ˈlænəlɪn/ *n.* a fat found naturally on sheep's wool and used purified for cosmetics etc.

lantern *n.* **1 a** a portable lamp with a transparent or translucent case, e.g. of glass or paper, protecting a flame. **b** a similar electric etc. lamp. **c** its case. **2 a** a raised structure on a dome, room, etc., glazed to admit light. **b** a similar structure for ventilation etc. **3** the light chamber of a lighthouse.

lanthanide /ˈlænθə,naɪd/ *n.* an element of the lanthanide series, 15 metallic elements in the periodic table having similar chemical properties.

lanthanum /ˈlænθənəm/ *n.* a silvery metallic element used in the manufacture of alloys and catalysts.

Laotian /ˈlaʊʃən, lɑˈoːʃən/ ● *n.* **1 a** a native or national of Laos in SE Asia. **b** a person of Laotian descent. **2** the language of Laos. ● *adj.* of or relating to Laos or its people or language.

lap¹ *n.* **1 a** the front of the body from the waist to the knees of a sitting person (*sat on her lap*; *caught it in his lap*). **b** the clothing, esp. a skirt, covering the lap. **c** the front of a skirt held up to catch or contain something. **2** care, charge, etc. (*thrown into the laps of the teachers*). **3** a condition or position of extreme comfort, ease, etc. (*in the lap of luxury*).

lap² ● *n.* **1 a** one circuit of a racetrack etc. **b** a swim from one end of a pool to the other and back again; two lengths. **c** a swim from one end of a pool to the other; a length. **d** a section of a journey etc. **2 a** an amount of overlapping. **b** an overlapping or projecting part. ● *v.* (**lapped**, **lapping**) **1** *tr.* lead or overtake (a competitor in a race) by one or more laps. **2** *tr.* (often foll. by *about, round*) coil, fold, or wrap (a garment etc.) around esp. a person. **3** *tr.* (usu. foll. by *in*) enfold or swathe (a person) in wraps etc. **4** *tr.* surround (a person) with an influence etc. **5** *intr.* (usu. foll. by *over*) project; overlap. **6** *tr.* cause to overlap.

lap³ ● *v.* (**lapped**, **lapping**) **1 a** *tr. & intr.* (usu. of an animal) drink (liquid) with the tongue. **b** *tr.* (usu. foll. by *up, down*) consume (liquid) greedily. **c** *tr.* (usu. foll. by *up*) consume (gossip, praise, etc.) greedily. **2 a** *tr.* (of water) move or beat upon (a shore) with a rippling sound as of lapping. **b** *intr.* (of waves etc.) move in ripples; make a lapping sound. ● *n.* **1 a** the process or an act of lapping. **b** the amount of liquid taken up. **2** the sound of wavelets on a beach.

laparoscope /ˈlæpərə,skoːp/ *n.* a fibre optic instrument inserted through the abdominal wall to give a view of the organs in the abdomen. □ **laparoscopic** *adj.* **laparoscopy** *n.* (*pl.* **-ies**).

laparotomy /ˌlæpəˈrɒtəmi/ *n.* (*pl.* **-ies**) a surgical incision into the abdominal cavity for exploration or diagnosis.

lap belt *n.* a seat belt worn across the lap.

lapdog *n.* a small pet dog.

lapel /ləˈpel/ *n.* the part of the front of a coat, jacket, etc., which is folded over towards either shoulder.

lapidary /ˈlæpɪ,deri/ ● *adj.* **1** concerned with stone or stones. **2** engraved upon stone. **3** (of writing style) dignified and concise, suitable for inscriptions. ● *n.* (*pl.* **-ies**) a cutter, polisher, or engraver of gems.

lapis lazuli /ˌlæpɪs ˈlæzʊlaɪ, -li, -jʊ-/ (also **lapis**) ● *n.* **1 a** blue mineral containing sodium aluminum silicate and sulphur, used as a gemstone. **2** a bright blue pigment formerly made from this. **3** its colour. ● *adj.* of this mineral, pigment, or colour.

lap joint *n.* the joining of rails, shafts, etc., by halving the thickness of each at the joint and fitting them together.

Lapp ● *n.* **1** a member of the indigenous population of the extreme north of Scandinavia. **2** the language of this people. ● *adj.* of or relating to the Lapps or their language. ¶The Lapps' own name for themselves, *Sami*, is now often preferred with reference to the people.

lapped *adj.* (usu. foll. by *in*) protectively encircled; enfolded caressingly.

lap pool *n. N Amer.* a narrow pool suitable for swimming laps.

lap robe *n. N Amer.* a thick blanket draped over the lap and legs for warmth.

lapse ● *n.* **1** a slight error; a slip of memory etc. **2** a weak or careless decline into an inferior state. **3** (foll. by *of*) an interval or passage of time (*after a lapse of three years*). **4** *Law* the termination of a right or privilege through disuse or failure to follow appropriate procedures. ● *v.intr.* **1** fail to maintain a position or standard. **2** (foll. by *into*) fall back into an inferior or previous state. **3** (of a right or privilege etc.) become invalid because it is not used or claimed or renewed.

lapsed *adj.* designating a person who has abandoned a formerly adhered-to religion, philosophy, etc.

laptop *n.* (often *attrib.*) a portable microcomputer.

lapwing *n.* a plover, *Vanellus vanellus*, with black and white plumage, crested head, and a shrill cry.

larceny /ˈlɑrsəni/ *n.* (*pl.* **-ies**) the theft of personal property. □ **larcenist** *n.* **larcenous** *adj.*

larch *n.* **1** a deciduous coniferous tree of the genus *Larix*, with soft needles and producing tough timber. **2** (also **larchwood**) its wood.

lard ● *n.* the internal fat of the abdomen of pigs, esp. when rendered and clarified for use in cooking. ● *v.tr.* **1** insert strips of fat or bacon in (meat etc.) before cooking. **2** (foll. by *with*) embellish or enrich (esp. talk or writing) with foreign material, esp. to excess.

larder *n.* **1** a room or cupboard for storing food. **2** a store of food.

large ● *adj.* **1** of considerable or relatively great size or extent. **2** of the larger kind (*the large intestine*). **3** of wide range; comprehensive. **4** pursuing an activity on a large scale (*large manufacturer*). ● *n.* **1** a garment of a size suited for people moderately larger than average. **2** a large serving of a beverage or food that is sold in more than one size. □ **at large 1** at liberty; not confined. **2** as a body or whole (*popular with the people at large*). **3** (of a narration etc.) at full length and with all details. **4** without a specific target (*scatters insults at large*). **in large measure** (or **part**) to a significant extent. □ **largeness** *n.* **largish** *adj.*

large calorie *n. see* CALORIE 1.

large cap *n.* a company with a relatively large market capitalization (usu. *attrib.*: *large-cap stocks*).

large intestine *n.* the cecum, colon, and rectum collectively.

largely *adv.* to a great extent; principally.

largemouth *n.* (*pl.* same or **largemouths**) (in full **largemouth bass**) a N American freshwater bass, *Micropterus salmoides* of the sunfish family, an important sport fish.

large-print *adj.* designating a book etc. printed in large type.

large-scale *adj.* made or occurring on a large scale or in large amounts.

largesse /lɑrˈdʒes, -ˈʒes/ *n.* (also **largess**) **1** money or gifts freely given, esp. on an occasion of rejoicing, by a person in high position. **2** the bestowal of such gifts. **3** generosity, beneficence.

largetooth aspen *n.* a poplar of eastern N America, *Populus gradidentata*, similar to trembling aspen, with leaves with large teeth.

largo /ˈlɑrgoː/ *Music* ● *adv. & adj.* in a slow tempo and dignified in style. ● *n.* (*pl.* **-os**) a largo passage etc.

lariat /ˈleriət, ˈlæriət/ *n.* **1** a lasso. **2** a tethering rope, esp. used by cowboys.

lark[1] *n.* **1** any small singing bird of the family Alaudidae with brown plumage and an elongated hind claw, esp. the Eurasian skylark or the horned lark. **2** any of various birds resembling but not related to the true larks, e.g. the meadowlark.

lark[2] *informal* ● *n.* a carefree frolic or spree; an amusing incident; a practical joke. ● *v.intr.* (usu. foll. by *about*) play tricks; frolic. □ **larky** *adj.*

larkspur *n.* **1** a plant of the genus *Consolida*, with spurred flowers. **2** a delphinium.

larva /ˈlɑrvə/ *n.* (*pl.* **larvae** /-viː/) **1** the stage of development of an insect between egg and pupa, e.g. a caterpillar. **2** an immature form of other animals that undergo some metamorphosis, e.g. a tadpole. □ **larval** *adj.*

laryngitis /ˌlerɪnˈdʒəitəs/ *n.* inflammation of the larynx.

larynx /ˈlerɪŋks/ *n.* (*pl.* **larynges** /ləˈrɪndʒiːz/) the hollow muscular organ forming an air passage to the lungs and holding the vocal cords in humans and other mammals.

lasagna /ləˈzɒnjə/ *n.* (also **lasagne**) **1** pasta in the form of wide ribbons. **2** a baked dish made from layers of lasagna, usu. filled with tomato sauce, cheese, and ground meat.

lascivious /ləˈsɪvias/ *adj.* **1** lustful. **2** inciting to or evoking lust. □ **lasciviously** *adv.* **lasciviousness** *n.*

lase /leiz/ *v.intr.* **1** function as or in a laser. **2** (of a substance) undergo the physical processes employed in a laser.

laser ● *n.* a device that generates an intense beam of coherent monochromatic light (or other electro-magnetic radiation) by stimulated emission from excited atoms or molecules. ● *v.* **1** *tr.* remove or treat (cells, tissue, etc.) with a laser. **2** *tr.* inscribe or engrave (words, a design, etc.) onto a surface using a laser. **3** *intr.* travel with great speed and precision (*the ball lasered toward his head*).

laser disc *n.* a disc on which signals and data are recorded digitally as a series of pits and bumps under a protective coating, and which is read optically by a laser beam reflected from the surface.

laser printer *n.* a high-speed computer printer in which a laser is used to form a pattern of dots on a photosensitive drum corresponding to the pattern of print required on the page.

lash ● *v.* **1** *tr. & intr.* make a sudden whip-like movement (*lashed his tail*). **2** *tr.* beat with a whip, rope, etc. **3** *intr.* pour or rush with great force. **4** *intr.* (foll. by *at*, *against*) strike violently. **5** *tr.* castigate in words. **6** *tr.* urge on as with a lash. **7** *tr.* (foll. by *down*, *together*, etc.) fasten with a cord, rope, etc. **8** *tr.* (of rain, wind, etc.) beat forcefully upon. ● *n.* **1 a** a sharp blow made by a whip, rope, etc. **b** (prec. by *the*) punishment by beating with a whip etc. **c** something that goads or hurts like a blow from a whip (*the lash of her tongue*). **d** a powerful impact (*the lash of the storm*). **2** the flexible end of a whip. **3** (usu. in *pl.*) an eyelash. □ **lash out** (often foll. by *at*) speak or hit out angrily.

lashing *n.* **1 a** a beating. **b** a scolding; reprimand. **2** cord used for lashing.

LASIK /ˈleizɪk/ *n.* laser in situ keratomileusis, a form of eye surgery which uses a laser to carve the interior of the cornea, e.g. to correct myopia (*compare* PRK).

lass *n. Scot. & Northern England* or *literary* a girl or young woman.

lassie *n. informal* = LASS.

lassitude /ˈlæsɪˌtuːd, -ˌtjuːd/ n. **1** languor, weariness. **2** disinclination to exert or interest oneself.

lasso /ləˈsuː, ˈlæsoː/ ● n. (pl. **-os** or **-oes**) a rope with a noose at one end, used esp. in N America for catching cattle etc. ● v.tr. (**-oes, -oed**) catch with or as with a lasso.

last¹ ● adj. **1** after all others; coming at or belonging to the end. **2 a** most recent; next before a specified time (last Christmas; last week). **b** preceding; previous in a sequence (got on at the last station). **3** only remaining; final (our last chance). **4** (prec. by the) least likely or suitable (the last person I'd want). **5** the lowest in rank (the last place). **6** individual, single. ● adv. **1** after all others (esp. in comb.: last-mentioned). **2** on the last occasion before the present (when did you last see her?). **3** (esp. in enumerating) lastly. ● n. **1** a person or thing that is last, last-mentioned, most recent, etc. **2** (prec. by the) the last mention or sight etc. (shall never hear the last of it). **3** the last performance of certain acts (breathed his last). **4** (prec. by the) **a** the end or last moment. **b** death. □ **at last** (or **long last**) in the end; after much delay. **last but not least** last in order of mention or occurrence but not of importance. **to** (or **till**) **the last** till the end; esp. till death.

last² v.intr. **1** remain unexhausted or adequate or alive for a specified or considerable time; suffice (enough food to last us a week). **2** continue for a specified time. □ **last out** remain adequate or in existence for the whole of a period previously stated or implied.

last³ n. a shoemaker's model for shaping or repairing a shoe or boot.

last call n. N Amer. the final opportunity to order alcoholic drinks from a bar before it must legally stop serving alcohol for the evening.

last-ditch adj. (of an effort etc.) made at the last minute in an attempt to avert disaster.

last gasp ● n. **1** the final attempt to draw breath before dying. **2** the final hours, days etc. of an event, season, etc. (the last gasp of winter). ● adj. (**last-gasp**) last-minute (last-gasp negotiations).

last hurrah n. **1** any final performance, effort, or success. **2** the final act in a politician's career.

lasting adj. **1** continuing, permanent. **2** durable. □ **lastingly** adv. **lastingness** n.

Last Judgment n. (in some beliefs) the judgment of humankind expected to take place at the end of the world, when each person is rewarded or punished according to his or her merits.

lastly adv. finally; in the last place.

last minute ● n. (also **last moment**) the time just before an important event. ● adj. (**last-minute**) done at the last minute (last-minute shopping).

last name n. surname.

last post n. Brit. & Cdn **1** the last of several bugle calls giving notice of the hour of retiring at night. **2** this call blown at military funerals etc.

last rites n. sacred rites for a person about to die.

Last Supper n. the supper eaten by Christ and his disciples on the eve of the Crucifixion, as recorded in the New Testament.

last word n. (prec. by the) **1** a final or definitive statement (always has the last word). **2** (often foll. by in) the latest fashion.

lat n. (usu. in pl.) slang = LATISSIMUS DORSI.

lat. abbr. latitude.

latch ● n. **1** a bar with a catch and lever used as a fastening for a gate etc. **2** a spring lock preventing a door from being opened from the outside without a key after being shut. ● v.tr. & intr. fasten or be fastened with a latch. □ **latch on** (often foll. by to) informal **1**

attach oneself (to). **2** N Amer. obtain, get. **3** associate oneself strongly with. **4** become very interested in.

latchkey n. (pl. **-eys**) a key of an outer door.

latchkey child n. (also informal **latchkey kid**) a child who is alone at home after school until a parent returns from work.

late ● adj. **1 a** after the due or usual time; occurring or done after the proper time (late for dinner; a late delivery). **b** informal (of a woman) whose menstrual period has failed to occur at the expected time. **2 a** far on in the day or night or in a specified time or period (the late 1500s). **b** belonging to an advanced stage in the development of a person or thing, the history of a science, language, etc. **3** flowering or ripening toward the end of the season (late strawberries). **4** (prec. by the or my, his, etc.) no longer alive or having the specified status (my late husband; the late president). **5** (esp. in superlative) of recent date (the late storms; the latest songs). ● adv. **1** after the due or usual time (arrived late; married late). **2** far on in time (this happened later on). **3** at or till a late hour. **4** at a late stage of development. **5** formerly but not now (late of Halifax). **6** (in comparative) subsequently (later in the book; three months later). □ **at the latest** as the latest time envisaged (will have done it by six at the latest). **late in the day** (or **game**) informal at a late stage in the proceedings, esp. too late to be useful. **of late** lately, recently. **the latest** the most recent news, fashion, etc. □ **lateness** n.

late bloomer n. N Amer. **1** a flower that blooms toward the end of the season. **2** a person who develops a skill, interest, etc. later in life. □ **late-blooming** adj.

latecomer n. **1** a person who arrives late. **2** a recent arrival; a newcomer.

lateen /ləˈtiːn/ adj. (of a ship) rigged with a lateen sail.

lateen sail n. a triangular sail on a long yard at an angle of 45° to the mast.

late Loyalist n. Cdn hist. an American settler who came to Canada between 1790 and 1800.

lately adv. not long ago; recently; in recent times.

late-model adj. (of a car, electronic component, etc.) of a recent make.

latent /ˈleɪtənt/ adj. **1** concealed, dormant. **2** existing but not developed or manifest. □ **latency** n. **latently** adv.

latent image n. Photog. an image not yet made visible by developing.

lateral ● adj. **1** of, at, toward, or from the side or sides. **2** of or pertaining to a new job which is neither a promotion nor a demotion (a lateral move). ● n. **1 a** side part etc., esp. a lateral shoot or branch. **2** (in full **lateral pass**) Football a sideways pass. ● v. (**lateralled, lateralling**) Football **1** intr. make a side-ways pass. **2** tr. throw (the ball) in a lateral pass. □ **laterally** adv.

lateral thinking n. a method of solving problems indirectly or by apparently illogical methods.

latex /ˈleɪteks/ n. (pl. **latexes** or **latices** /-təˌsiːz/) **1** a milky fluid of mixed composition found in various plants and trees, esp. the rubber tree, and used for commercial purposes. **2** a synthetic product resembling this, used in paints etc. **3** (in full **latex paint**) paint having latex as its binding medium.

lath /læθ/ n. (pl. **laths** /læθs, læðz/) **1** a thin flat strip of wood, esp. each of a series forming a framework or support for plaster etc. **2** (esp. in phr. **lath and plaster**) laths collectively as a building material, esp. as a foundation for supporting plaster.

lathe /leɪð/ n. a machine for shaping wood, metal,

etc., by means of a rotating drive which turns the piece being worked on against cutting tools.

lather ● *n.* **1** a froth produced by agitating soap etc. and water. **2** frothy sweat, esp. of a horse. **3** a state of agitation. ● *v.* **1** *intr.* (of soap etc.) form a lather. **2** *tr.* cover with lather. **3** *intr.* (of a horse etc.) develop or become covered with lather. **4** *tr. informal* thrash. □ **lathery** *adj.*

Latin /'lætɪn/ ● *n.* **1** the Italic language of ancient Rome and its empire, originating in Latium. **2** *Rom. Hist.* an inhabitant of ancient Latium in Central Italy. **3** a native or inhabitant of any of the various countries in Europe (France, Italy, Spain, etc.) and Latin America whose language is developed from Latin. ● *adj.* **1** of or in Latin. **2 a** of the countries or peoples using languages developed from Latin. **b** Latin-American. **3** of or relating to ancient Latium or its inhabitants. **4** of the Roman Catholic Church. **5** of or relating to the Latin alphabet.

Latina /læ'ti:nə/ ● *n.* a female Latin American inhabitant of N America. ● *adj.* of or relating to Latinas.

Latin America *n.* the parts of the Americas where Spanish or Portuguese is the main language. □ **Latin American** *adj. & n.*

Latino /lə'ti:nɔ:/ ● *n.* (*pl.* **-os**) a Latin American inhabitant of N America. ● *adj.* of or relating to Latinos.

Latin rite *n.* a religious ceremony using Latin, esp. in the Roman Catholic Church.

latissimus dorsi /lə'tɪsəməs dɔ:rsai, dɔrsi/ *n.* (*pl.* **latissimi dorsi** /lə'tɪsəmai/) either of a pair of large, roughly triangular muscles covering the lower part of the back, from the sacral, lumbar, and lower thoracic vertebrae to the armpits.

latitude *n.* **1 a** the angular distance on its meridian of any place on the earth's surface from the equator, expressed in degrees and minutes north or south of the equator. **b** (usu. in *pl.*) regions or climes, esp. with reference to temperature (*warm latitudes*). **2** freedom from narrowness; liberality of interpretation. **3** tolerated variety of action or opinion (*was allowed much latitude*). □ **latitudinal** *adj.* **latitudinally** *adv.*

latke /'lætkə/ *n.* (in Jewish cooking) a pancake made with grated potato.

latrine *n.* a communal lavatory, esp. in a camp etc.

latte /'lætei/ *n.* espresso coffee with hot milk.

latter ● *n.* (prec. by *the*) the second-mentioned or *disputed* last-mentioned person or thing (*opp.* FORMER[1] *n.*). ¶The use of *latter* to mean 'last-mentioned of three or more' is considered incorrect by some people. ● *adj.* **1** nearer to the end (*the latter part of the year*). **2** recent. **3** belonging to the end of a period, of the world, etc.

latter-day *attrib.adj.* modern, contemporary.

Latter-day Saint *n.* a member of the Mormon Church (officially called the Church of Jesus Christ of Latter-day Saints).

latterly *adv.* **1** in the latter part of life or of a period. **2** recently.

lattice /'lætɪs/ *n.* **1 a** a structure of crossed laths or bars with spaces between, used as a screen, fence, etc. **b** = LATTICEWORK. **2** something with an open interlaced structure like that of a lattice. **3** a regular periodic arrangement of atoms, ions, or molecules in a crystalline solid. □ **latticed** *adj.*

lattice window *n.* a window with small panes set in diagonally crossing strips of lead.

latticework *n.* laths arranged in lattice formation.

Latvian /'lætvɪən/ ● *n.* **1 a** a native or inhabitant of Latvia, a country on the eastern shore of the Baltic Sea. **b** a person of Latvian descent. **2** the language of Latvia. ● *adj.* of or relating to Latvia or its people.

laud /lɔd/ ● *v.tr.* praise or extol. ● *n.* (in *pl.*) the office of the first canonical hour of prayer, originally said at daybreak.

laudable *adj.* commendable, praiseworthy. ¶*Laudable* 'praiseworthy' is sometimes confused with *laudatory* 'expressing praise'. □ **laudably** *adv.*

laudanum /'lɔdənəm/ *n.* a solution containing morphine and prepared from opium, formerly used as a narcotic painkiller.

laudatory /'lɔdətɔri/ *adj.* expressing praise. ¶See LAUDABLE.

laugh ● *v.* **1** *intr.* **a** make the spontaneous sounds and movements usual in expressing lively amusement, scorn, derision, etc. **b** have the emotion expressed by laughing (*laughed inwardly at his foolishness*). **2** *tr.* express by laughing. **3** *intr.* (foll. by *at*) ridicule, make fun of (*laughed at us for going*). **4** *intr.* (in phr. **be laughing**) *informal* be in a fortunate or successful position. **5** *intr.* esp. *literary* make sounds reminiscent of laughing (*the wind laughed in the trees*). ● *n.* **1** the sound or act or manner of laughing. **2** *informal* a comical, entertaining or ridiculous person or thing (*the party was a laugh*). □ **for laughs** for amusement or enjoyment. **have the last laugh** be the ultimate winner. **laugh all the way to the bank** be in an enviable financial position. **a laugh a minute** very funny or amusing. **laugh in a person's face** show open scorn for a person. **laugh off** get rid of (embarrassment or humiliation) by joking. **laugh out of the other side of one's face** (or **mouth**) change from enjoyment or amusement to displeasure, shame, apprehension, etc. **laugh out of court** deprive of a hearing by ridicule. **laugh over** discuss with laughter or amusement. **laugh up one's sleeve** be secretly or inwardly amused.

laughable *adj.* ludicrous; highly amusing. □ **laughably** *adv.*

laugher *n.* **1** a person who laughs. **2** *N Amer. Sport slang* an easily won game; a walkover.

laughing ● *n.* laughter. ● *adj. in senses of* LAUGH *v.* □ **no laughing matter** something serious. □ **laughingly** *adv.*

laughing gas *n.* nitrous oxide as an anaesthetic, formerly used without oxygen and causing an exhilarating effect when inhaled.

laughingstock *n.* a person or thing open to general ridicule.

laugh-line *n.* **1** (usu. in *pl.*) a wrinkle around the eye or mouth formed over the years by smiling or laughing. **2** a line in a play, movie, etc. designed to make the audience laugh.

laughter *n.* the act or sound of laughing.

laugh track *n.* *N Amer.* pre-recorded laughter added to a radio or television show to simulate or encourage audience response.

launch[1] ● *v.* **1 a** *tr.* set (a vessel) afloat. **b** *tr.* set afloat (a newly built vessel) for the first time, often with ceremonies. **c** *intr.* (often foll. by *out*) (of a vessel) put out to sea etc. **2** *tr.* hurl or send forth (a weapon, rocket, etc.). **3** *tr.* start or set in motion (an enterprise, a person on a course of action, etc.). **4** *tr.* formally introduce (a new product) with publicity etc. **5** *intr.* **a** (foll. by *out*, *into*) make a start, esp. on an ambitious enterprise. **b** (foll. by *into*) begin suddenly (a tirade, speech, song, etc.). ● *n.* the act or an instance of launching.

launch[2] *n.* a large motorboat, used esp. for pleasure.

launcher n. a structure or device to hold a rocket, missile, etc. during launching.

launching pad n. (also **launch pad**) **1** a platform with a supporting structure, from which rockets are launched. **2** a starting point for a career etc.

launder v. **1 a** tr. & intr. wash and dry (clothes, bed or table linen, etc.). **b** intr. (of a fabric, garment, etc.) bear laundering without damage to the texture, colour, etc. **2** tr. informal transfer (funds) to conceal a dubious or illegal origin. **3** tr. treat or process (something) to make it appear acceptable. □ **launderer** n.

launderette /lɒn'drɛt/ n. (also **laundrette**) a laundromat.

laundromat n. an establishment with coin-operated washing machines and dryers for public use.

laundry n. (pl. **-ies**) **1** clothes etc. for laundering or newly laundered. **2 a** a room or building for washing clothes etc. **b** a business washing clothes etc. commercially. **3** the action of laundering clothes etc.

laundry list n. esp. N Amer. a long list of assorted items (a laundry list of complaints).

laureate /'lɔːrɪət/ ● n. **1** a person who is honoured for outstanding creative or intellectual achievement (Nobel laureate). **2** = POET LAUREATE. ● adj. wreathed with laurel as a mark of honour.

laurel /'lɒrəl/ ● n. **1** = BAY² 1. **2 a** (in sing. or pl.) the foliage of the bay tree used as an emblem of victory or distinction in poetry, usu. formed into a wreath or crown. **b** (in pl.) honour or distinction. **3** any plant with dark green glossy leaves like a bay tree. ● v.tr. (**laurelled**, **laurelling**) **1** wreathe with laurel. **2** confer honourable distinction upon. □ **look to one's laurels** beware of losing one's pre-eminence. **rest on one's laurels** be satisfied with what one has done and not seek further success.

Laurentian /lə'rɛnʃən/ adj. **1** designating or pertaining to a geological region in eastern Canada of Precambrian age or the period in which it was formed, esp. designating a group of granites found northwest of the St. Lawrence River. **2** of or pertaining to the Laurentian Mountains.

lav /læv/ n. informal a lavatory.

lava n. **1** the molten matter which flows from a volcano. **2** the solid substance which it forms on cooling. □ **lavalike** adj.

lava flow n. a mass of flowing or solidifed lava.

lava lamp n. a lamp designed as an upright tube containing coloured liquid which swirls and separates like lava when the lamp is plugged in.

lavatory /'lævətɔːrɪ/ n. (pl. **-ies**) **1** = TOILET 1. **2** a room or compartment containing one or more toilets.

lavender ● n. **1 a** any small evergreen shrub of the genus Lavandula, with narrow leaves and blue, purple, or pink aromatic flowers. **b** its flowers and stalks dried and used to scent clothes etc. **2** (in full **oil of lavender** or **lavender oil**) the oil obtained by distillation of the blossoms of cultivated lavender, used in medicine and perfume. **3** a pale blue colour with a trace of mauve. ● adj. **1** of the colour or fragrance of lavender flowers. **2 a** refined, sentimental, genteel. **b** informal of or relating to homosexuality.

lavish ● adj. **1** giving or producing in large quantities; profuse. **2** generous, unstinting. **3** excessive, overabundant. **4** great in extent, rich in quality, and usu. expensive (a lavish new production). ● v.tr. (often foll. by on) bestow or spend (money, effort, praise, etc.) abundantly. □ **lavishly** adv. **lavishness** n.

law n. **1 a** a rule enacted or customary in a community and recognized as enjoining or prohibiting certain actions and enforced by the imposition of penalties. **b** a body of such rules (forbidden under Canadian law). **2** the controlling influence of laws; a state of respect for laws (law and order). **3** laws collectively as a social system or subject of study. **4** (with defining word) any of the specific branches or applications of law (commercial law; law of contract). **5** binding force or effect (Jo's word is law). **6** (prec. by the) **a** the legal profession. **b** informal the police. **7** the statute and common law (opp. EQUITY 2). **8** jurisprudence. **9 a** litigation. **b** the law courts as providing this (go to law). **10** a rule of action or procedure, e.g. in a game, social context, form of art, etc. **11** a regularity in natural occurrences, esp. as formulated or propounded in particular instances (the law of gravity). **12 a** the body of divine commandments as expressed in the Bible or other sources. **b** (**Law of Moses**) the precepts of the Pentateuch. **c** (**the Law**) the Pentateuch as distinguished from the other parts of the Hebrew Bible (the Prophets and the Writings) (compare TORAH). □ **be a law unto oneself** do what one feels is right; disregard custom. **go to law** take legal action; make use of the law courts. **in** (or **at**) **law** according to the laws. **lay down the law** be dogmatic or authoritarian. **take the law into one's own hands** redress a grievance by one's own means, esp. by force.

law-abiding adj. obedient to the laws.

lawbreaker n. a person who breaks the law. □ **law-breaking** n. & adj.

law clerk n. **1** = CLERK 4b. **2** = ARTICLED CLERK.

law court n. a court of law.

lawful adj. conforming with, permitted by, or recognized by law; not illegal or (of a child) illegitimate. □ **lawfully** adv. **lawfulness** n.

lawgiver n. a person who lays down laws.

lawless adj. **1** having no laws or enforcement of them. **2** disregarding laws. **3** unbridled, uncontrolled. □ **lawlessly** adv. **lawlessness** n.

lawmaker n. a legislator. □ **law-making** adj. & n.

lawman n. (pl. **-men**) esp. US a law-enforcement officer, esp. a sheriff or police officer.

lawn¹ n. a piece of grass kept mown and smooth.

lawn² n. a fine linen or cotton fabric used for clothes.

lawn bowling n. N Amer. any of several bowling games played on grass or dirt surfaces in which players attempt to roll a ball as close as possible to a smaller ball. □ **lawn bowler** n.

lawn chair n. a usu. folding chair for use outdoors.

lawn mower n. a machine for cutting grass.

lawn tennis n. the usual form of tennis, played with a soft ball on outdoor grass or a hard court.

law of the jungle n. a state of ruthless competition.

lawrencium /lɒ'rɛnsɪəm/ n. an artificially made radioactive metallic element.

law reports n.pl. a publication of accounts of judicial proceedings and judgments.

law school n. an institution of higher education, usu. part of a university, at which lawyers are trained.

Law Society n. Cdn & Brit. a professional body representing lawyers.

lawsuit n. the process of bringing a dispute, claim, etc. before a law court for settlement.

lawyer ● n. a member of the legal profession. ● v.intr. follow the profession of lawyer; act as a lawyer. □ **lawyerly** adj.

lax adj. not strict or severe enough. □ **laxity** n. **laxly** adv. **laxness** n.

laxative /'læksətɪv/ ● adj. tending to facilitate evacuation of the bowels. ● n. a laxative medicine.

lay¹ ● *v.* (*past* and *past part.* **laid**) **1** *tr.* place on a surface, esp. horizontally in a position of rest (*laid the book on the table*). **2** *tr.* **a** put or bring into a certain or the required position or state (*lay a carpet*). **b** deposit (a corpse) in a grave; bury. **3** *intr. disputed* lie. ¶Although this sense is very common, esp. in spoken English, it is considered erroneous. Its use arises probably as a result of confusion with *lay* as the past of *lie*, as in *The dog lay on the floor* which is correct. *The dog is laying on the floor* is not considered standard by many people, and in this sentence *laying* should be *lying*. **4** *tr.* make by laying (*lay the foundations*). **5** *tr.* & *intr.* (of a female bird) produce (an egg). **6** *tr.* **a** cause to subside or lie flat. **b** deal with to remove (a ghost, fear, etc.). **7** *tr.* place or present for consideration (a case, proposal, etc.). **8** *tr.* set down as a basis or starting point. **9** *tr.* (usu. foll. by *on*) attribute or impute (blame etc.). **10** *tr.* prepare or make ready (a plan or a trap). **11** *tr.* prepare (a table) for a meal. **12** *tr.* place or arrange the material for (a fire). **13** *tr.* put down as a wager; stake. **14** *tr.* (foll. by *with*) coat or strew (a surface). **15** *tr. slang offensive* have sexual intercourse with. ● *n.* **1** the way, position, or direction in which something lies. **2** *slang offensive* **a** a partner in sexual intercourse. **b** an act of sexual intercourse. □ **lay about one 1** hit out on all sides. **2** criticize indiscriminately. **lay aside 1** put to one side. **2** cease to practise or consider. **3** save (money etc.) for future needs. **lay back** cause to slope back from the vertical. **lay bare** expose, reveal. **lay a charge** make an accusation. **lay claim to** claim as one's own. **lay down 1** put on the ground or other surface. **2** relinquish; give up (an office). **3** formulate or insist on (a rule or principle). **4** pay or wager (money). **5** begin to construct (a ship or railway). **6** store (wine) in a cellar. **7** set down on paper. **8** sacrifice (one's life). **9** record (esp. popular music). **lay hands on 1** seize or attack. **2** place one's hands on or over, esp. in confirmation, ordination, or spiritual healing. **3** (also **lay one's hands on**) obtain, acquire, locate. **lay hold of** seize or grasp. **lay in** provide oneself with a stock of. **lay into** *informal* attack violently with words or blows. **lay it on** (**thick** or **with a shovel**) *informal* flatter or exaggerate grossly. **lay low 1** overthrow, kill, or humble. **2** incapacitate by illness. **3** *disputed* lie low. **lay off 1** discharge (workers) temporarily or permanently because of a shortage of work; make redundant. **2** *informal* (often in *imper.*) stop bothering (a person). **3** *informal* stop working (*laid off around 4:00*). **4** abstain from or stop using (something) (*lay off beer*). **lay on 1** provide (a facility, amenity, etc.). **2** impose (a penalty, obligation, etc.). **3** inflict (blows, damage, etc.). **4** spread on (paint etc.). **lay open 1** break the skin of. **2** (foll. by *to*) expose (to criticism etc.). **lay out 1** spread out. **2** expose to view. **3** prepare (a corpse) for burial. **4** *informal* knock unconscious. **5** dispose (grounds etc.) according to a plan. **6** expend (money). **7** reveal or explain in detail (*she laid out the rules for us*). **lay up 1** store, save. **2** put (a ship etc.) out of service. **3** (usu. in *passive*) confine to bed through illness, injury, etc.; be taken ill (*was laid up with a cold*).

lay² *adj.* **1 a** non-clerical. **b** designating a person who has taken the vows of a religious order but is not ordained and is employed in ancillary or manual work (*lay sister*). **2 a** not professionally qualified, esp. in law or medicine. **b** of or done by such persons.

lay³ *n.* **1** a short lyric or narrative poem meant to be sung. **2** a song.

lay⁴ *past of* LIE¹.

layabout *n.* a habitual loafer or idler.

layaway *n. N Amer.* a system of purchasing an article by making usu. monthly payments until the entire cost has been paid, at which point the article is released to the customer.

layer ● *n.* **1** a thickness of matter, esp. one of several, laid over a surface or forming a horizontal division (*wore layers of clothing*; *ozone layer*). **2** a person or thing that lays. **3** a hen that lays eggs, esp. with reference to its productivity (*a good layer*). ● *v.* **1** *tr.* **a** arrange (something) in layers. **b** cut (hair) in layers. **2** *intr.* form layers. □ **layered** *adj.* **layering** *n.*

layer cake *n.* esp. *N Amer.* a cake of two or more layers with icing, filling, etc. between.

layette /leɪˈet/ *n.* a set of clothing, toilet articles, and bedclothes for a newborn child.

laying on of hands *n.* **1** a rite in which a person being ordained, confirmed, etc. is touched by a cleric. **2** the act of placing the hands, esp. by a faith healer etc., on a person seeking healing, faith, etc.

layman *n.* (*pl.* **-men**) **1** any non-ordained member of a church. **2** a person without professional or specialized knowledge in a subject.

layoff *n.* **1** a temporary or permanent dismissal of workers. **2** a period when this is in force. **3** a rest or respite (*came back from a six-month layoff to win the race*).

layout *n.* **1** the disposing or arrangement of a site, ground, etc. **2** the way in which plans, printed matter, etc., are arranged or set out. **3** something arranged or set out in a particular way. **4** the makeup of a book, newspaper, etc.

layover *n.* a period of rest or waiting before a further stage in a journey etc.; a stopover.

layperson *n.* (*pl.* **lay people** or **-s**) a layman or laywoman.

lay reader *n.* (in the Anglican Church) a layperson licensed to conduct some religious services.

layup *n.* **1** *Basketball* a shot made close to the basket, in which the shooter often lays the ball against the backboard so it will rebound into the basket. **2** plies or layers assembled for the manufacture of plywood or other laminated material.

laywoman *n.* (*pl.* **-women**) **1** any non-ordained female member of a church. **2** a woman without professional or specialized knowledge in a subject.

laze *v.* **1** *intr.* spend time lazily or idly. **2** *tr.* (often foll. by *away*) pass (time) in this way.

lazy *adj.* (**-ier**, **-iest**) **1** disinclined to work, doing little work. **2** of or inducing idleness. **3** (of a river etc.) slow-moving. □ **lazily** *adv.* **laziness** *n.*

lazybones *n.* (*pl.* same) *informal* a lazy person.

lazy eye *n.* an amblyopic eye in which underuse has contributed to its poor vision.

Lazy Susan *n.* (also **lazy Susan**) **1** a revolving stand on a table to hold condiments etc. **2** *N Amer.* an esp. kitchen cupboard or shelf designed to revolve in order to provide easy access to its contents.

lb. *abbr.* a pound or pounds (weight).

LBO *abbr.* LEVERAGED BUYOUT.

LC *abbr.* **1** LIBRARY OF CONGRESS CLASSIFICATION. **2** *Cdn* LIQUOR COMMISSION.

l.c. *abbr.* **1** in the passage etc. cited. **2** lower case.

LCBO *abbr. Cdn* (*Ont.*) Liquor Control Board of Ontario.

LCD *abbr.* **1** LIQUID CRYSTAL DISPLAY. **2** lowest common denominator.

LCdr *abbr. Cdn* LIEUTENANT COMMANDER.

LCM *abbr.* lowest (or least) common multiple.

LCol *abbr. Cdn* LIEUTENANT COLONEL.

LD *abbr.* learning disability.

Ld. *abbr.* Lord.

LDC *abbr.* less developed country.

LDL *abbr.* LOW-DENSITY LIPOPROTEIN.

LDS *abbr.* Latter-day Saints.

lea /liː/ *n.* *literary* a piece of meadow or arable land.

leach *v.* **1** *tr.* make (a liquid) percolate through some material. **2** *tr.* subject (bark, ore, or soil) to the action of percolating fluid. **3** *tr. & intr.* (foll. by *away, out*) remove (soluble matter) or be removed in this way. **4** *tr.* slowly deprive of. □ **leachable** *adj.* **leachability** *n.*

leachate /ˈliːtʃeɪt/ *n.* a quantity of liquid that has percolated through a solid and leached out some of the constituents.

lead¹ /liːd/ ● *v.* (*past* and *past part.* **led**) **1** *tr.* cause to go with one, esp. by guiding or showing the way or by going in front and taking a person's hand or an animal's halter etc. **2** *tr.* **a** direct the actions or opinions of. **b** (often foll. by *to*, or *to* + infin.) guide by persuasion or example or argument (*what led you to that conclusion?*). **c** (of a lawyer) put a question to (a witness) in such a way as to suggest the answer desired. **3** *tr. & intr.* provide access to; bring to a certain position or destination (*this door leads into a small room; the road leads to Moncton*). **4** *tr.* pass or go through (a life etc. of a specified kind) (*led a miserable existence*). **5 a** *tr.* have the first place in (*led the parade; leads the world in sugar production*). **b** *intr.* go first; be ahead in a race or game. **c** *intr.* be pre-eminent in some field. **d** *intr.* guide one's partner through the steps of a dance. **6** *tr.* be in charge of (*leads a team of researchers*). **7** *tr.* **a** direct by example. **b** set (a fashion). **c** be the principal player of (a group of musicians). **8** *tr. & intr. Cards* begin a round of play by playing (a card) or a card of (a particular suit). **9** *intr.* (foll. by *to*) have as an end or outcome; result in (*what does all this lead to?*). **10 a** *intr.* (foll. by *with*) (of a newspaper, newscast, etc.) use a particular item as the main story (*led with the Stock Market crash*). **b** *tr.* (of a story) be the main feature of (a newspaper or part of it or a newscast) (*the election will lead the front page*). **11** *tr.* (foll. by *through*) make (a liquid, strip of material, etc.) pass through a pulley, channel, etc. ● *n.* **1** guidance given by going in front; example (*follow her lead*). **2 a** a leading place; the leadership (*is in the lead; take the lead*). **b** the amount by which a competitor is ahead of the others (*a lead of ten points*). **3** a clue, esp. an early indication of the resolution of a problem (*is the first real lead in the case*). **4** = LEASH *n.* **5** a conductor (usu. a wire) conveying electric current from a source to an appliance. **6 a** the chief part in a play etc. **b** the person playing this. **c** the chief performer or instrument of a specified type (also *attrib.*: *lead guitar*). **7** (in full **lead story**) the item of news given the greatest prominence in a newspaper, magazine, or newscast. **8** the member of a curling rink who delivers the first two rocks for their rink in each end. **9 a** the act or right of playing first in a game or round of cards. **b** the card led. **10 a** an artificial watercourse, esp. one leading to a mill. **b** a channel of water in an icefield. **11** *Cdn* (*Nfld*) a stretch of low, open land passing through an area covered with lakes, trees, or hills. □ **lead by the nose** cajole (a person) into compliance. **lead off 1** begin; make a start. **2** *Baseball* be the first batter for a team in (an inning or game). **lead on 1** entice into going further than was intended. **2** mislead or deceive.

lead² /led/ ● *n.* **1** a heavy bluish-grey soft ductile metallic element occurring naturally in galena and other minerals. **2 a** graphite. **b** a thin length of this for use in a pencil. **3** a lump of lead used in sounding water. **4** (in *pl.*) lead frames holding the glass of a lattice or stained glass window. **5** (*attrib.*) made of lead.

6 bullets collectively. ● *v.tr.* **1** cover, weight, or frame (a roof or windowpanes) with lead. **2** add a lead compound to (gasoline etc.). □ **get the lead out** *N Amer. slang* hurry up; move or work more quickly. **go over like a lead balloon** *N Amer. slang* (of an idea etc.) fail to generate enthusiasm or interest.

lead crystal *n.* leaded crystal.

lead dog *n.* *N Amer.* the primary dog in a team, responsible for leading the rest of the team in response to the driver's commands.

leaded *adj.* **1** (of gasoline) containing tetraethyl lead as an additive. **2** (of glass or crystal) containing a high proportion of lead oxide, making it more refractive. **3** (of a window) containing panes of glass set in lead strips.

leaden *adj.* **1** of or like lead. **2** heavy, slow, burdensome (*leaden limbs*). **3** inert, depressing (*leaden rule*). **4** lead-coloured (*leaden skies*). □ **leadenly** *adv.*

leader *n.* **1 a** a person or thing that leads. **b** a person followed by others. **2 a** the principal player in a music group. **b** a conductor, esp. of a small musical group. **3** a short strip of non-functioning material at each end of a reel of film or recording tape for connection to the spool. **4** a shoot of a plant at the apex of a stem or of the main branch. **5** the horse or dog placed at the front of a team. **6** a length of line or wire connecting the end of a fishing line to a hook or fly. □ **leaderless** *adj.* **leadership** *n.*

leaderboard *n.* a scoreboard, esp. at a golf course, showing the names etc. of the leading competitors.

leadership convention *n.* *Cdn* a convention held by a political party to elect a new leader.

lead foot /led/ *n.* *N Amer. informal* the practice of driving too quickly, esp. habitually (*has a lead foot*).

lead-footed *adj.* *N Amer.* **1** slow or sluggish (*a lead-footed skater*). **2** tending to drive too quickly.

lead-free *adj.* (of gasoline) without added tetraethyl lead.

lead head /led/ *n.* (in full **lead head jig**) a simple fishing lure consisting of a single hook extending horizontally from a blob of lead.

lead-in *n.* **1** an introduction, opening, etc. **2** a wire leading in from outside, esp. from an antenna to a receiver or transmitter.

leading ● *adj.* **1** chief; most important (*a leading cause of death*). **2** first in position (*the leading runner*). **3** best-selling; most popular. **4** most likely to succeed, win, etc. ● *n.* guidance, leadership.

leading edge *n.* **1** the foremost edge of an airfoil, esp. a wing or propeller blade. **2** the forefront of development, esp. in technology (also *attrib.*: *leading-edge company*).

leading lady *n.* the actress or film star who plays the principal female part in a play or film.

leading light *n.* a prominent and influential person.

leading man *n.* the actor or film star who plays the principal male part in a play or film.

leading question *n.* **1** *Law* a question that prompts the answer wanted. **2** a craftily worded question intended to lead the questioned person to say something incriminating.

leading seaman *n.* **1** (also **Leading Seaman**) a member of the Canadian Navy of the rank above able seaman and below master seaman. Abbr.: **LS**. **2** a person of similar rank in other navies.

leadoff ● *n.* an action beginning a process. ● *adj.* **1** *Baseball* of or relating to the player who bats first in the batting order or an inning. **2** of or relating to something that serves as a beginning or introduction.

lead pencil /led/ n. a pencil of graphite enclosed in wood.

lead poisoning n. acute or chronic poisoning by absorption of lead into the body.

lead shot /led/ n. = SHOT¹ 3b.

lead tetraethyl n. = TETRAETHYL LEAD.

lead time /liːd/ n. the time between the initiation and completion of a process.

leaf ● n. (pl. **leaves**) **1 a** each of several flattened usu. green structures of a plant, usu. on the side of a stem or branch and the main organ of photosynthesis. **b** other similar plant structures, e.g. bracts, sepals, and petals. **2 a** foliage regarded collectively. **b** the state of having leaves out (a tree in leaf). **3** a single thickness of paper, esp. in a book with each side forming a page. **4** a very thin sheet of metal, esp. gold or silver. **5 a** the hinged part or flap of a door, shutter, table, etc. **b** an extra section inserted to extend a table. ● v.intr. put forth leaves. □ **leaf through** turn over the pages of (a book etc.). **take a leaf out of a person's book** imitate a person. **turn over a new leaf** improve one's conduct or performance. □ **leafed** adj. (also in comb.). **leafless** adj. **leaflike** adj.

leaf blower n. a device for blowing leaves off a lawn or into piles etc., used as an alternative to raking.

leafcutter n. **1** (in full **leafcutter ant, leaf-cutting ant**) an ant which cuts pieces from leaves to cultivate fungus. **2** (in full **leafcutter bee**) a solitary bee which lines its nest with leaf fragments.

leaf-green ● n. the colour of green leaves. ● adj. of this colour.

leaflet ● n. **1** a printed sheet of paper, usu. folded and free of charge, containing information. **2** a young leaf. **3** any division of a compound leaf. ● v.tr. (**leafleted, leafleting** or **leafletted, leafletting**) distribute leaflets to.

leaf lettuce n. lettuce with loose leaves.

leaf miner n. any of various larvae burrowing in leaves.

leaf mould n. soil consisting chiefly of decayed leaves.

leaf spot n. any of numerous fungal and bacterial plant diseases which cause leaves to develop discoloured spots.

leaf spring n. a spring consisting of a number of strips of metal curved slightly upwards and clamped together one above the other.

leaf stalk n. a petiole.

leafy adj. (**-ier, -iest**) **1 a** having many leaves. **b** (of a place) rich in foliage; verdant. **2** producing broad-bladed leaves, as distinct from other types of foliage (green leafy vegetables). **3** resembling a leaf.

league¹ ● n. **1 a** collection of people, countries, etc., combining for a particular purpose, esp. mutual protection or co-operation. **2** an agreement to combine in this way. **3** a group of sports teams of a similar level organized to compete among themselves. **4** a class or category (I'm not in your league). ● v.intr. (**leagues, leagued, leaguing**) (often foll. by together) join in a league. □ **in league** allied, conspiring.

league² n. archaic a variable measure of distance, usu. about three miles (4.8 km).

league-leading adj. **1** (of a team or player) occupying first place in any classification of all teams or players in a league. **2** designating a statistic which surpasses that of every other player or team in a league (a league-leading 43 goals).

League of Nations n. an association of countries established in 1919 to promote international co-operation and achieve international peace and security; it was replaced after World War II by the UN.

leaguer n. esp. N Amer. a member of a league (esp. in comb.: minor-leaguer).

leak ● n. **1 a** a hole in a pipe, container, etc. caused by wear or damage, through which matter, esp. liquid or gas, passes accidentally in or out. **b** the matter passing in or out through this. **c** the act or an instance of leaking. **2 a** a similar escape of electrical charge. **b** the charge that escapes. **3** the intentional disclosure of secret information. ● v. **1 a** intr. (of liquid, gas, etc.) pass in or out through a leak. **b** tr. lose or admit (liquid, gas, etc.) through a leak. **2** tr. intentionally disclose (secret information). **3** intr. (often foll. by out) (of a secret, secret information) become known. □ **have** (or **take**) **a leak** slang urinate. □ **leaker** n.

leakage n. **1** the action or result of leaking. **2** what leaks in or out. **3** an intentional disclosure of secret information.

leak-proof adj. designed so as to prevent leakage.

leaky adj. (**-ier, -iest**) having a leak or leaks. □ **leakiness** n.

lean¹ ● v. (past and past part. **leaned** or (esp. Brit.) **leant**) **1** intr. & tr. be or place in a sloping position; incline from the perpendicular. **2** intr. & tr. rest or cause to rest for support against etc. **3** intr. (foll. by on, upon) rely on; derive support from. **4** intr. (foll. by to, toward) be inclined or partial to; have a tendency toward. ● n. a deviation from the perpendicular (has a lean to the right). □ **lean on** informal put pressure on (a person) to act in a certain way.

lean² ● adj. **1** (of a person or animal) thin; having no superfluous fat. **2** (of meat) containing little fat. **3** meagre; of poor quality (lean crop). **4** (of a business, sector of the economy, etc.) rendered more efficient or competitive through the reduction of unnecessary costs or expenditure. **5** (of a period of time) not prosperous; marked by austerity and restraint. **6** (of a vaporized fuel mixture) having a high proportion of air (compare RICH 7). ● n. the lean part of meat. □ **leanly** adv. **leanness** n.

lean-burn adj. of or relating to an internal combustion engine designed to run on a lean mixture to reduce pollution.

leaning n. a tendency or partiality.

lean-to n. (pl. **-tos**) **1** N Amer. a usu. temporary shelter consisting of an inclined roof supported at one side by trees or posts and covered with canvas, branches, etc. **2** a roof that has a single slope and is supported at its upper end by a wall or building etc. **3** a room or building with such a roof.

leap ● v. (past and past part. **leaped** or **leapt**) **1** intr. jump or spring forcefully. **2** tr. jump across. **3** intr. (of prices etc.) increase dramatically. **4** intr. move quickly or suddenly; rush (leaped into the car). **5** intr. spring or arise quickly, as if by a leap (the idea just leapt into my mind). **6** intr. (foll. by up) spring suddenly to one's feet; rise with a bound from a sitting or reclining position. **7** intr. (often foll. by at) accept something eagerly (leaped at the chance to go to Yellowknife). ● n. **1** a forceful jump. **2** a large, sudden increase (a leap in prices). **3** an abrupt or sudden transition. **4** the distance covered by a leap or jump. **5** a thing to be leaped over or from. □ **by leaps and bounds** with startlingly rapid progress. **leap in the dark** a daring step or enterprise whose consequences are unpredictable. **leap to the eye** be immediately apparent. □ **leaper** n.

leapfrog ● n. a game in which players in turn vault

with parted legs over another who is bending down. ● v. (**-frogged, -frogging**) **1** intr. (foll. by over) perform such a vault. **2** tr. vault over in this way. **3** tr. & intr. (of two or more people, vehicles, etc.) overtake alternately. **4** tr. & intr. (of a person, corporation, etc.) overtake or surpass a competitor or competitors.

leap of faith n. the act or an instance of accepting or believing something that cannot be proven.

leap year n. a year, occurring once in four, with 366 days (including Feb. 29 as an intercalary day).

learn v. (past and past part. **learned** or **learnt** /lɜrnt/) **1** tr. gain knowledge of or skill in by study, experience, or being taught. **2** tr. (foll. by to + infin.) acquire or develop a particular ability (learn to swim). **3** tr. commit to memory (will try to learn your names). **4** intr. (foll. by of) be informed about. **5** tr. (foll. by that, how, etc. + clause) become aware of by information or from observation. **6** intr. receive instruction; acquire knowledge or skill. **7** tr. slang or archaic teach. ¶Usually regarded as an uneducated use, and unacceptable in spoken and written English except jocularly or in fixed informal phrases, e.g. that'll learn you! □ **learnable** adj. **learnability** n.

learned /'lɜrnəd/ adj. **1** (of a person) having much knowledge acquired by study. **2** showing or requiring learning (a learned work). **3** studied or pursued by learned persons. **4** concerned with the interests of learned persons; scholarly (a learned journal). **5** (/lɜrnd/) acquired by learning or experience; not innate (learned behaviour). **6** Cdn & Brit. as a courteous description of a lawyer in certain formal contexts (my learned friend). □ **learnedly** adv. **learnedness** n.

learner n. **1** a person who is learning a subject, language, or skill. **2** a person who is learning to drive a motor vehicle and has not yet passed a driving test.

learning n. **1** knowledge acquired by study. **2** the act or process of learning (also attrib.: learning experience).

learning curve n. **1** the rate of progress in learning or gaining experience. **2** a graph of this.

learning disability n. a difficulty in learning caused by a physical or psychological dysfunction. □ **learning disabled** adj.

lease ● n. **1** an agreement by which the owner of a property, a vehicle, etc. allows another to use it for a specified time in return for payment. **2** the period of time for which such an agreement is made. ● v.tr. grant or take on lease. □ **a new lease on life** a substantially improved prospect of living, or of use after repair. □ **leasable** adj. **leaser** n.

leasehold ● n. **1** the holding of property by lease. **2** property held by lease. ● adj. held by lease. □ **leaseholder** n.

leash ● n. a strip of rope etc. for leading or controlling a dog. ● v.tr. **1** put a leash on. **2** restrain. □ **keep a person on a long** (or **short**) **leash** give a person considerable (or little) freedom of action. **straining at the leash** eager to begin.

least ● adj. **1** smallest, slightest, most insignificant. **2** (prec. by the; esp. with neg.) any at all (it does not make the least difference). **3** (of a species or variety) very small. ● n. the least amount. ● adv. in the least degree. □ **at least 1** at all events; anyway; even if there is doubt about a more extended statement. **2** (also **at the least**) not less than. **in the least** (usu. with neg.) in the smallest degree; at all (not in the least offended). **to say the least** (or **the least of it**) used to imply the moderation of a statement (that is doubtful to say the least).

least bittern n. a small bittern, Ixobrychus exilis, found from southern Canada to S America.

least common denominator n. = LOWEST COMMON DENOMINATOR.

leastways adv. (also **leastwise**) informal at least, rather.

leather ● n. **1** material made from the skin of an animal by tanning or a similar process. **2** a thing made wholly or partly of leather. **3 a** (usu. in pl.) leather clothes, esp. for wearing on a motorcycle. **b** leather clothing, esp. as intended to express extreme masculinity, aggression, or sado-masochistic tendencies, or to arouse sexual desire. **4** a thong. **5** dried puréed fruit cut into sheets (fruit leather). ● adj. **1** made of or resembling leather. **2** of or relating to leather clothing or persons wearing it (leather bar). ● v.tr. **1** cover with leather. **2** polish or wipe with a leather. **3** beat, thrash.

leatherback n. a large marine turtle, Dermochelys coriacea, having a thick leathery carapace.

leather-bound adj. (esp. of a book) bound in leather.

leatherette n. imitation leather.

leatherleaf n. an ericaceous shrub, Chamaedaphne calyculata, found across Canada, with leathery leaves and small white flowers.

leathery adj. **1** like leather. **2** (esp. of meat etc.) tough. □ **leatheriness** n.

leave[1] v. (past and past part. **left**) **1 a** tr. go away from. **b** intr. (often foll. by for) depart (we leave tomorrow; has just left for St. John's). **2** tr. cause to or let remain; depart without taking (has left his gloves; left a bad impression). **3** tr. & intr. cease to reside at or attend or belong to or work for (has left the school; am leaving for another job). **4** tr. abandon, forsake, desert. **5** tr. have remaining after one's death (leaves a husband and two children). **6** tr. bequeath. **7** tr. allow (a person or thing) to do something without interference or assistance (leave the future to take care of itself). **8** tr. (foll. by to) commit or refer to another person (leave that to me). **9** tr. a abstain from consuming or dealing with. **b** (in passive; often foll. by over) remain over. **10** tr. a deposit or entrust (a thing) to be attended to, collected, delivered, etc., in one's absence (left a message). **b** depute (a person) to perform a function in one's absence. **11** tr. allow to remain or cause to be in a specified state or position (left the door open; the performance left them unmoved). **12** to have a particular amount remaining after subtraction (six from seven leaves one). □ **be left with 1** retain (a feeling etc.). **2** be burdened with (a responsibility etc.). **have left** have remaining (has no friends left). **leave alone 1** refrain from disturbing, not interfere with. **2** not have dealings with. **3** = LET ALONE (see LET[1]). **leave be** informal refrain from disturbing, not interfere with. **leave behind 1** go away without. **2** leave as a consequence or a visible sign of passage. **3** pass. **leave a person cold** (or **cool**) not impress or excite a person. **leave go** informal relax one's hold. **leave hold of** cease holding. **leave it at that** informal abstain from comment or further action. **leave much** (or **a lot** etc.) **to be desired** be highly unsatisfactory. **leave off 1** come to or make an end. **2** discontinue (leave off work). **3** omit from (was left off the list). **4** cease to wear. **leave out** omit, not include. **leave a person to himself** (or **herself**) **1** not attempt to control a person. **2** leave a person solitary. **left at the post** beaten from the start of a race. **leave for dead** abandon as being beyond rescue. □ **leaver** n.

leave[2] n. **1** permission. **2 a** (in full **leave of absence**) permission to be absent from duty, work, etc. **b** the period for which this lasts. □ **on leave** legitimately absent from duty, work, etc. **take one's**

leave bid farewell. **take one's leave of** bid farewell to. **take leave to** venture or presume to.

leaved *adj.* **1** having leaves. **2** (in *comb.*) having a leaf or leaves of a specified kind or number (*broad-leaved*).

leaven /'levən/ ● *n.* **1** *archaic* a substance added to dough to make it ferment and rise, esp. yeast. **2 a** a pervasive transforming influence. **b** (foll. by *of*) a small amount of a specified quality. ● *v.tr.* **1** ferment (dough) with leaven. **2 a** permeate and transform. **b** (foll. by *with*) modify with a tempering element.

leavening *n.* **1** a substance, e.g. yeast or baking powder, that causes dough or batter to rise. **2** the act or an instance of causing fermentation by using leaven. **3** = LEAVEN *n.* 2.

leaves *pl.* of LEAF.

leave-taking *n.* the act of taking one's leave.

leavings *n.pl.* things left over, esp. as worthless.

Lebanese /ˌlebə'niːz/ ● *adj.* of or relating to Lebanon, a country in the Middle East, or its inhabitants. ● *n.* a native or inhabitant of Lebanon.

lech /letʃ/ *informal* ● *v.intr.* feel lecherous; behave lustfully. ● *n.* **1** a strong, esp. sexual, desire. **2** a lecher.

lecher *n.* a lecherous man.

lecherous *adj.* lustful; having excessive sexual desire. □ **lecherously** *adv.* **lecherousness** *n.*

lechery *n.* unrestrained indulgence of sexual desire.

lecithin /'lesɪθɪn/ *n.* **1** any of a group of phospholipids found naturally in animals, egg yolk, and some plants. **2** a preparation of this used as an emulsifier.

lectern /'lektərn/ *n.* **1** a stand for holding a book in a church, esp. for a Bible from which readings are made. **2** a similar stand for a lecturer etc.

lectionary /'lekʃənəri/ *n.* (*pl.* **-ies**) **1** a list of portions of Scripture for reading at a religious service. **2** a book containing such portions of Scripture.

lector /'lektər/ *n.* *Catholicism* a person designated to read aloud certain readings, prayers, etc. at Mass.

lecture ● *n.* **1** a discourse giving information about a subject to a class or other audience. **2** a long serious speech esp. as a scolding or reprimand. ● *v.* **1** *intr.* (often foll. by *on*) deliver a lecture or lectures. **2** *tr.* talk seriously or reprovingly to (a person). **3** *tr.* instruct or entertain (a class or other audience) by a lecture.

lecturer *n.* **1** a person who lectures, esp. as a teacher in post-secondary education. **2** *N Amer.* a university professor ranking below assistant professor.

lectureship *n.* a position as a lecturer.

LED *abbr.* light-emitting diode, a semiconductor diode which glows when a voltage is applied.

led *past and past part.* of LEAD[1].

lederhosen /'leɪdər,hoːzən/ *n.pl.* leather shorts with braces worn by men in Bavarian traditional dress.

ledge *n.* **1** a narrow horizontal surface projecting from a wall etc. **2** a shelf-like projection on the side of a rock or mountain. **3** a ridge of rocks, esp. below water. □ **ledged** *adj.* **ledgy** *adj.*

ledger *n.* a book or computer document in which a business, bank, etc. records its financial accounts.

lee *n.* **1** shelter given by a neighbouring object (*under the lee of*). **2** (in full **lee side**) the side away from the wind (opp. WEATHER SIDE).

leech *n.* **1** any freshwater or terrestrial annelid worm of the class Hirudinea with suckers at both ends, esp. *Hirudo medicinalis*, a bloodsucking parasite of vertebrates formerly much used medically. **2** a person who extorts profit from or sponges on others. □ **like a leech** persistently or clingingly present.

leek *n.* a plant, *Allium porrum*, with flat overlapping leaves forming an elongated cylindrical bulb, used as food and as a Welsh national emblem.

leer ● *v.intr.* look slyly or lasciviously or maliciously. ● *n.* a leering look. □ **leeringly** *adv.*

leery *adj.* (**-ier, -iest**) *slang* (usu. foll. by *of*) wary. □ **leeriness** *n.*

lees /liːz/ *n.pl.* **1** the sediment of wine etc. (*drink to the lees*). **2** dregs, refuse.

leeward /'liːwərd, *Naut.* 'luːərd/ ● *adj. & adv.* on or toward the side sheltered from the wind (opp. WINDWARD). ● *n.* the leeward region, side, or direction (*to leeward*).

leeway *n.* **1 a** allowable deviation or freedom of action. **b** additional or extra time, materials, etc. **2** the sideways drift of a ship to leeward of the desired course.

left[1] ● *adj.* **1 a** on or toward the side of the human body which corresponds to the position of west if one regards oneself as facing north. **b** on or toward the part of an object which is analogous to a person's left side or (with opposite sense) which is nearer to an observer's left hand (opp. RIGHT 5). **2** (also **Left**) *Politics* of the Left. ● *adv.* on or to the left side. ● *n.* **1** the left side or area (*on my left*). **2 a** the road etc. on the left (*take the next left*). **b** a left turn. **3** *Boxing* **a** the left hand. **b** a blow with this. **4** (often **Left**) *Politics* a group or section favouring socialism; socialists collectively. **5** = STAGE LEFT. □ **have two left feet** *informal* be clumsy. **left and right** (also **left, right, and centre**) = RIGHT AND LEFT (see RIGHT). □ **leftish** *adj.*

left[2] *past and past part.* of LEAVE[1].

left bank *n.* the bank of a river on the left facing downstream.

left brain *n.* the left cerebral hemisphere, controlling the right side of the body and, in humans, language skills and numerical calculations.

left-centre *n.* (in full **left-centre field**) *Baseball* the part of the outfield between centre field and left field.

left field *n.* **1** *Baseball* **a** the part of the outfield to the left of the batter as he or she faces the pitcher. **b** the position of the fielder who covers this area (*playing left field*). **2** *N Amer. informal* a position, state, experience, etc., that is removed from the mainstream or ordinary (*the proposal came from left field*). □ **out in left field** *N Amer. slang* completely wrong or mistaken. □ **left fielder** *n.*

left-hand *adj.* **1** on or toward the left side of a person or thing. **2** to the left (*a left-hand turn*). **3** done with the left hand. **4 a** (of rope) twisted counter-clockwise. **b** (of a screw) = LEFT-HANDED 4b.

left-handed ● *adj.* **1 a** using the left hand by preference as more serviceable than the right. **b** using a tool etc. by preference on one's left side (*left-handed batter*). **2** (of a tool etc.) designed for use by left-handed people. **3** (of a blow) struck with the left hand. **4 a** turning to the left; toward the left. **b** (of a screw) advanced by turning counter-clockwise. **5** awkward, clumsy. **6 a** (of a compliment) ambiguous. **b** of doubtful sincerity or validity. ● *adv.* with the left hand or to the left side (*writes left-handed*). □ **left-handedly** *adv.* **left-handedness** *n.*

left-hander *n.* **1** a left-handed person. **2** a left-handed blow.

leftie *var.* of LEFTY.

leftism *n.* *Politics* the principles or policy of the left. □ **leftist** *n. & adj.*

left-leaning *adj.* (of a person, group, etc.) favouring or tending toward the political left.

leftmost *adj.* furthest to the left.

left-of-centre adj. (of political parties, voters, etc.) having somewhat leftist views, policies, etc.

leftover ● n. (usu. in pl.) an item (esp. of food) remaining after the rest has been used. ● adj. remaining over.

leftward ● adv. (also **leftwards**) toward the left. ● adj. going toward or facing the left.

left wing ● n. **1** the radical or socialist section of a political party. **2** Hockey **a** the forward position to the left of centre (facing the opponent's goal). **b** the player at this position. **3** the left side of an army. ● adj. (usu. **left-wing**) socialist or radical. □ **left-winger** n.

lefty ● n. (pl. **-ies**) informal **1** a left-handed person. **2** Politics a left-winger. ● adj. (of a person) **1** left-handed. **2** leftist. ● adv. esp. Baseball with the left hand or to the left side (batting lefty).

leg n. **1 a** each of the limbs on which a person or animal walks and stands. **b** the part of this from the hip to the ankle. **2** a leg of an animal or bird as food. **3** a part of a garment covering a leg or part of a leg. **4** a support of a chair, table, bed, etc. **5 a** a section of a journey. **b** a section of a relay race. **c** a stage in a competition. **d** one of two or more games constituting a round. **6** one branch of a forked object (the leg of a compass). **7** one of the sides of a triangle other than the base or hypotenuse. **8** N Amer. a device for lifting grain in a grain elevator, consisting of a series of buckets attached to a vertical conveyor belt. □ **as fast as one's legs can** (or **would**) **carry one** as fast as one is able to. **find one's legs 1** gain momentum. **2** acquire or regain mastery of a skill. **give a person a leg up** help a person to mount a horse etc. or get over an obstacle or difficulty. **have no legs** informal (of a golf ball etc.) have not enough momentum to reach the desired point. **leg it** informal walk or run hard. **not have a leg to stand on** be unable to support one's argument by facts or sound reasons. **on one's last legs** near death or the end of one's usefulness etc.

legacy n. (pl. **-ies**) **1** a gift left in a will. **2** something handed down by a predecessor (legacy of corruption).

legal adj. **1** of or based on law; concerned with law; falling within the province of law. **2** appointed or required by law. **3** permitted by law, lawful. **4** Sport permitted by the rules. **5** N Amer. **a** designating a size of paper 22 by 35.5 cm (8¹⁄₂ by 14 inches). **b** designating office supplies, e.g. file folders etc., designed to be used with this size of paper. **6** recognized by law, as distinct from equity. □ **legally** adv.

legal aid n. payment from public funds allowed, in cases of need, to help pay for legal advice.

legal clinic n. N Amer. a clinic offering legal advice and assistance, paid for by legal aid.

legal eagle n. (also **legal beagle**) informal a lawyer, esp. one who is keen or astute.

legalese /ˌliːɡəˈliːz/ n. informal the technical language of legal documents.

legal fiction n. an assertion accepted as true (though probably fictitious) to achieve a useful purpose, esp. in legal matters.

legal holiday n. N Amer. = STATUTORY HOLIDAY.

legalism n. excessive adherence to law or formula. □ **legalist** n. **legalistic** adj. **legalistically** adv.

legality /lɪˈɡælti, liː-/ n. (pl. **-ies**) **1** lawfulness. **2** legalism. **3** (in pl.) obligations imposed by law.

legalize v.tr. **1** make lawful. **2** bring into harmony with the law. □ **legalization** n.

legal tender n. currency that cannot legally be refused in payment of a debt.

legate /ˈlɛɡət/ n. a member of the clergy representing the Pope. □ **legateship** n.

legation /lɪˈɡeɪʃən/ n. **1** a body of deputies. **2 a** the office and staff of a diplomatic minister (esp. when not having ambassadorial rank). **b** the official residence of a diplomatic minister. **3** a legateship. **4** the sending of a legate or deputy.

legato /ləˈɡɒtoʊ/ Music ● adv. & adj. in a smooth flowing manner, without breaks between notes. ● n. (pl. **-os**) **1** a legato passage. **2** legato playing.

leg curl n. an exercise for strengthening the leg muscles in which the heels, with or without added weights, are drawn up to the buttocks.

legend n. **1 a** a traditional story sometimes popularly regarded as historical but unauthenticated; a myth. **b** such stories collectively. **c** a popular but unfounded belief. **d** informal a subject of such beliefs (became a legend in her own lifetime). **2 a** an inscription, esp. on a coin or medal. **b** a caption. **c** a key to the symbols used on a map etc.

legendary adj. **1** of or connected with legends. **2** described in a legend. **3** remarkable enough to be a subject of legend. **4** based on a legend. □ **legendarily** adv.

legerdemain /ˌlɛdʒɜrdəˈmeɪn/ n. **1** sleight of hand; conjuring or juggling. **2** trickery, sophistry.

legged /ˈlɛɡd/ adj. having legs, esp. of a specified kind or number (long-legged).

legging n. (usu. in pl.) **1** close-fitting stretch trousers for women or children. **2** an outer garment for keeping the legs warm.

leggy ● adj. (**-ier, -iest**) **1 a** long-legged. **b** (of a woman) having attractively long legs. **2** long-stemmed. ● n. Cdn (Nfld) (pl. **-ies**) a small cod that has been cleaned, salted, and dried but not split, usu. intended for home consumption. □ **legginess** n.

leghold trap n. (also **leghold**) a type of trap which catches and holds an animal by one of its legs.

leghorn n. **1** (**Leghorn**) **a** a bird of a small hardy breed of domestic fowl. **b** this breed. **2 a** fine braided straw. **b** a hat of this.

legible adj. (of handwriting, print, etc.) clear enough to read; readable. □ **legibility** n. **legibly** adv.

legion ● n. **1** a vast host, multitude, or number. **2** (**Legion**) any of various national associations of exservicemen and ex-servicewomen (Royal Canadian Legion). **3** N Amer. = LEGION HALL. **4** Rom. Hist. a division of 3,000–6,000 soldiers, including a complement of cavalry. **5** a large military force. ● predic.adj. great in number (her good works have been legion).

legionary ● adj. of a legion or legions. ● n. (pl. **-ies**) a soldier of a legion.

legionella /ˌliːdʒəˈnɛlə/ n. the bacterium Legionella pneumophila, which causes legionnaires' disease.

legion hall n. N Amer. a building serving as the headquarters for a local Legion branch, usu. incorporating facilities for entertainment, e.g. an auditorium, banquet hall, bar, etc.

legionnaire n. **1** a member of a foreign legion. **2** a member of a Legion.

legionnaires' disease n. a form of bacterial pneumonia spread esp. by water droplets through air conditioning systems etc.

legislate v. **1** intr. make laws. **2** tr. create or control by means of legislation (legislating pay equity).

legislation n. **1** the process of making laws. **2** a law or series of laws.

legislative adj. of or empowered to make legislation. □ **legislatively** adv.

legislative assembly n. **1** the legislative body of a

nation, province, etc. **2** (in Canada) an elected provincial or (*hist.*) colonial legislature.

legislative building *n. Cdn* the building in which a provincial legislature meets.

legislative council *n. Cdn hist.* **1** the upper house of a provincial legislature, consisting of members appointed by the government. **2** (in colonial governments) a body of advisers appointed by the governor, serving either as a unicameral legislature or as the upper house of a bicameral legislature.

legislator *n.* **1** a member of a legislative body. **2** a lawgiver.

legislature *n.* **1** the legislative body of a nation, province, etc. **2** *Cdn* = LEGISLATIVE BUILDING.

legit *adj. informal* legitimate.

legitimate ● *adj.* /lɪˈdʒɪtɪmət/ **1 a** (of a child) born of parents lawfully married to each other, entitled in law to full filial rights. **b** (of a parent, birth, descent, etc.) with, of, through, etc., a legitimate child. **2 a** sanctioned or authorized by law or principle; lawful. **b** conforming to a recognized standard. **3** sanctioned by the laws of reasoning; logical. **4** (of a monarch, sovereignty, etc.) justified or validated by the strict principle of hereditary right. **5** designating or pertaining to art considered to have aesthetic merit or serious intent, esp.: **a** conventional theatre or drama as distinct from musical comedy, farce, etc. **b** classical music as distinct from jazz or other popular music. **●** *v.tr.* /lɪˈdʒɪtɪˌmeɪt/ **1** make legitimate by decree, enactment, or proof. **2** authorize or justify by word or example; serve as a justification for. □ **legitimacy** *n.* **legitimately** *adv.* **legitimating** *adj.* **legitimation** *n.*

legitimize *v.tr.* **1** make legitimate. **2** serve as a justification for. □ **legitimization** *n.* **legitimizing** *n. & adj.*

legless *adj.* having no legs.

legman *n.* (pl. **-men**) a person employed to go about gathering news or running errands etc.

Lego /ˈlɛɡoʊ/ *n. proprietary* a construction toy consisting of interlocking plastic building blocks.

legroom *n.* the space available for the legs of a seated person in a car, theatre, etc.

legume /ˈlɛɡjuːm/ *n.* **1** any seed, pod, or other edible part of a leguminous plant used as food. **2** a leguminous plant. **3** the seed pod of a leguminous plant.

leguminous *adj.* of or like the family Leguminosae, including peas and beans, having seeds in pods and usu. root nodules able to fix nitrogen.

leg warmer *n.* either of a pair of tubular, usu. knitted garments covering the leg from ankle to thigh, but often worn gathered below the knee to the ankle.

legwork *n.* work which involves a lot of walking, travelling, or physical activity to collect information, deliver messages, etc.

lei /ˈleiː, leɪ/ *n.* a garland of flowers, feathers, shells, etc. often given as a symbol of affection.

Leicester /ˈlɛstər/ *n.* a kind of mild firm cheese, usu. orange-coloured and originally made in Leicestershire, England.

leishmaniasis /ˌliːʃməˈnaɪəsɪs/ *n.* any of several diseases caused by parasitic protozoans of the genus *Leishmania* transmitted by the bite of sandflies.

leisure /ˈliːʒər, ˈlɛ-/ *n.* **1** free time; time at one's own disposal. **2** enjoyment of free time. **3** (usu. foll. by *for*, or to + infin.) opportunity afforded by free time. □ **at leisure 1** not occupied. **2** in an unhurried manner. **at one's leisure** when one has time.

leisure centre *n.* (also **leisure complex**) *Cdn & Brit.* a large building with sports facilities, bars, etc.

leisured *adj.* **1** having ample leisure (*the leisured classes*). **2** leisurely.

leisurely ● *adj.* **1** relaxed, having leisure, able to proceed without haste. **2** (of an action or agent) performed or operating at leisure or without haste; unhurried. **●** *adv.* without haste or hurry. □ **leisureliness** *n.*

leisure wear *n.* informal clothes, esp. track suits and other sportswear.

leitmotif /ˈlaɪtmoʊˌtiːf/ *n.* (also **leitmotiv**) **1** a recurrent theme associated throughout a musical, literary, etc. composition with a particular person, idea, or situation. **2** any recurring theme, symbol, etc.

Lekwiltok /ˈlɛkwɪltɒk/ *n.* **1** a member of large group of the Kwakwaka'wakw living between Knight and Bute Inlets, on the west coast of BC. **2** the Kwa-kwa-la language of the Lekwiltok.

lemma *n.* **1** an assumed or demonstrated proposition used in an argument or proof. **2 a** a word or phrase defined in a dictionary, glossed in a glossary, entered in a word list, etc. **b** the form of a word or phrase chosen to represent all inflectional and spelling variants in a dictionary entry etc.

lemme /ˈlɛmi/ *informal* let me.

lemming *n.* **1** any of several short-tailed esp. Arctic rodents of the genus *Lemmus* and related genera of the family Muridae, noted for their fluctuating populations and periodic mass migrations. **2** a person who unthinkingly joins a mass movement, esp. a headlong rush to destruction. □ **lemming-like** *adj.*

lemon ● *n.* **1 a** a pale-yellow thick-skinned oval citrus fruit with acidic juice. **b** a tree of the species *Citrus limon* which produces this fruit. **2** = LEMON YELLOW. **3** *informal* **a** a thing which is bad, unsatisfactory, or disappointing, esp. a substandard or defective car. **b** a loser, simpleton, or person who is easily deluded or taken advantage of. **●** *adj.* of or resembling the colour, flavour, or fragrance of a lemon. □ **lemony** *adj.*

lemonade *n.* a drink made of lemon juice and water, usu. sweetened with sugar.

lemon balm *n.* a bushy plant, *Melissa officinalis*, with leaves smelling and tasting of lemon.

lemon grass *n.* any fragrant tropical grass of the genus *Cymbopogon*, yielding an oil smelling of lemon.

lemon meringue *n.* (in full **lemon meringue pie**) an open pie with a lemon filling and meringue topping.

lemon-scented *adj.* having a smell suggestive of lemons.

lemon sole *n.* **1** a flatfish, *Microstomus kitt*, of the flounder family, an important food fish. **2** the flesh of any of various other flounders as food.

lemon yellow ● *n.* a pale yellow colour. **●** *adj.* (hyphenated when *attrib.*) of this colour.

lemur /ˈliːmər/ *n.* any arboreal primate of the family Lemuridae native to Madagascar, with a pointed snout and long tail.

lend *v.tr.* (*past* and *past part.* **lent**) **1** (usu. foll. by *to*) grant (to a person) the use of (a thing) on the understanding that it or its equivalent shall be returned. **2** allow the use of (money) at interest. **3** bestow or contribute (something temporary) (*lend assistance*; *lends a certain charm*). □ **lend an ear** (or **one's ears**) listen. **lend itself to** (of a thing) allow, be suitable for. **lend oneself to** accommodate oneself to (a policy or purpose). **lend one's name to** allow one's self, name, or reputation to be associated with some cause etc. □ **lender** *n.* **lending** *n. & adj.*

lending library *n.* a library from which books may be borrowed with or without direct payment.

length /leŋkθ, leŋθ/ n. **1 a** the linear extent of a thing from end to end. **b** the greater of two or the greatest of three dimensions of a body or figure. **c** the quality or fact of being long. **2 a** extent from beginning to end, esp. of a period of time, etc. (*the length of a speech*). **b** a period or duration of time, esp. a long period (*a stay of some length*). **3** the distance a thing extends. **4 a** the length of a swimming pool as a measure of the distance swum. **b** the length of a horse, boat, etc., as a measure of the lead in a race. **c** the length of a car, usu. as a measure of separation from the vehicle in front. **5** a long stretch, piece, or extent of land, hair, tubing, etc. **6** a degree of thoroughness in action (*went to great lengths; prepared to go to any length*). **7** a piece of material of a certain or distinct length (*a length of cloth*). **8** the quantity, esp. long quantity, of a vowel or syllable. **9** the extent of a garment, curtains, etc. in a vertical direction when worn or hung (*a floor-length veil*). **10** the full extent of one's body. □ **at length 1** (also **at full** or **great** etc. **length**) in detail, without curtailment. **2** after a long time, at last. **length and breadth** all places or directions.

lengthen v.tr. & intr. make or become longer. □ **lengthener** n. **lengthening** n. & adj.

lengthwise ● adv. in a direction parallel with a thing's length. ● adj. lying or moving lengthwise.

lengthy adj. (**-ier, -iest**) **1** (of a period of time) long, extended, of unusual length. **2** (of speech, writing, style, a speaker, etc.) tedious, excessively detailed. □ **lengthily** adv. **lengthiness** n.

lenient /ˈliːnɪənt/ adj. **1** merciful, tolerant, not disposed to severity. **2** (of punishment etc.) mild. □ **lenience** n. **leniency** n. **leniently** adv.

Leninism /ˈlenɪnˌɪzəm/ n. Marxism as interpreted and applied by Vladimir Ilyich Lenin (1870–1924), the first premier of the Soviet Union. □ **Leninist** n. & adj.

lens ● n. **1** a piece of a transparent substance with one or usu. both sides curved for concentrating or dispersing light rays esp. in optical instruments. **2** (also **compound lens**) such a lens or combination of lenses used in photography. **3** Anat. = CRYSTALLINE LENS. **4** Physics a device for focusing or otherwise modifying the direction of movement of light, sound, electrons, etc. **5 a** a piece of glass or plastic enclosed in a frame for wearing in front of the eyes to correct the vision. **b** = CONTACT LENS. **6** a biconvex body of any material, as rock, ice, water, etc. **7** a viewpoint, perspective (*see life through a new lens*). ● v. **1** tr. film (a movie etc.). **2** intr. (of a movie etc.) be filmed. □ **lensed** adj. **lensing** n. **lensless** adj.

lens cap n. (also **lens cover**) a protective cover that fits over the end of a camera lens tube.

Lent n. Christianity the period from Ash Wednesday to Holy Saturday, of which the 40 weekdays are devoted to fasting and penitence.

lent past and past part. of LEND.

Lenten adj. of, in, or appropriate to Lent.

lentil /ˈlentil/ n. **1** a leguminous plant, *Lens culinaris*, yielding edible biconvex seeds. **2** this seed, esp. used as food with the husk removed.

lento /ˈlento:/ Music ● adj. slow. ● adv. slowly.

leopard /ˈlepərd/ n. **1** any large African or Asian flesh-eating cat, *Panthera pardus*, with either a black-spotted yellowish-fawn or all black coat. **2** (*attrib.*) spotted like a leopard (*leopard moth*).

leopard frog n. **1** a N American frog, *Rana pipiens*, that is green with black pale-ringed blotches. **2** any of various similar N American frogs.

leopard skin n. **1** the skin of a leopard. **2** (also **leopard print**) fabric printed in imitation of a leopard skin, with tawny colours and brown blotches.

leotard /ˈliːəˌtard/ n. **1** a close-fitting one-piece garment worn by dancers, gymnasts, etc. **2** N Amer. (usu. in pl.) heavy tights.

leper /ˈlepər/ n. **1** a person suffering from leprosy. ¶Now usu. avoided in medical usage. **2** a person who is shunned, esp. on moral grounds; an outcast.

leprechaun /ˈleprəˌkɒn/ n. a small, usu. mischievous being of human form in Irish folklore.

leprosy /ˈleprəsi/ n. **1** a contagious bacterial disease that affects the skin, mucous membranes, and nerves, causing disfigurement. **2** corruption or contagion, esp. social, moral, etc.

lesbian /ˈlezbiən/ ● n. a woman who is sexually attracted to other women. ● adj. of or pertaining to lesbians. □ **lesbianism** n.

lesion /ˈliːʒən/ n. **1** Med. a pathological change in the functioning or structure of an organ, organism, etc. **2** injury, harm, damage; a wound or blemish.

less ● adj. **1** smaller in extent, degree, number, etc. (*of less importance*). **2** of smaller quantity, not so much (opp. MORE) (*find less difficulty; eat less meat*). **3** disputed fewer (*eat less cookies*). ¶The use with countable nouns is considered incorrect in formal English. Strictly, *less* should be used only with uncountable nouns as the comparative of *little*, e.g. *I have little time; she has even less*, but *I have few books; she has even fewer*. **4** of lower rank, status, etc. (*no less a person than; St. James the Less*). ● adv. to a smaller extent, in a lower degree. ● pron. a smaller amount, quantity, or number (*cannot take less; is little less than disgraceful*). ● prep. minus (*made $1,000 less GST*). □ **in less than no time** informal very quickly or soon. **less and less** to an extent that is becoming continuously smaller. **less of** to a smaller extent. **much** (or **still**) **less** with even greater force of denial (*do not suspect him of negligence, much less of dishonesty*). **no less** (as an intensifier) what's more.

-less suffix forming adjectives and adverbs: **1** from nouns, meaning 'not having, without, free from' (*doubtless*). **2** from verbs, meaning 'not affected by or doing the action of the verb' (*fathomless; tireless*). □ **-lessly** suffix. **-lessness** suffix.

lessee /leˈsiː/ n. a person to whom a lease is granted or who holds a property by lease, esp. a tenant.

lessen v.tr. & intr. make or become less, diminish.

lesser adj. (usu. attrib.) **1 a** not so great or much as the other or the rest (*the lesser evil*). **b** (attrib.) smaller, inferior, or of lower status or worth. **2** designating the smaller of two similar or related plants, animals, anatomical parts, or places.

lesser-known adj. known less well than others of the same kind.

lesson n. **1 a** a continuous portion of teaching given to a student or class at one time. **b** the time assigned to this. **c** any of the portions into which a course of instruction is divided. **2** (in pl.; foll. by *in*) systematic instruction (*gives lessons in dancing; took lessons in French*). **3** a thing learned or to be learned by a student, esp. a section of a book etc. to be studied. **4 a** an occurrence, example, rebuke, or punishment, that serves or should serve to warn or encourage (*let that be a lesson to you*). **b** a thing inculcated by experience or study. **5** a passage from the Bible read aloud during a church service. □ **learn one's lesson** be wiser as a result of an unpleasant, painful, etc. experience. **teach a person a lesson** punish a person, esp. as a deterrent.

lessor /leˈsɔr/ n. a person who lets a property by lease.

lest *conj.* **1** in order that not, for fear that (*lest we forget*). **2** that (*afraid lest we should be late*). ¶The verb in the clause introduced by *lest* is usually in the subjunctive; less frequently, it is preceded by *should*.

let[1] *v.* (**letting**; *past* and *past part.* **let**) **1** *tr.* **a** allow to, not prevent or forbid (*we let them go*). **b** cause to (*let me know*; *let it be known*). **2** *tr.* (foll. by *into*) **a** allow to enter. **b** make acquainted with (a secret etc.). **3** *tr.* allow or cause (liquid or air) to escape (*let blood*). **4** *tr.* award (a contract for work). **5** *aux.* supplying the first and third persons of the imperative in exhortations (*let's eat!*), commands (*let it be done at once*), assumptions (*let AB be equal to CD*), and permission or challenge (*let him do his worst*). □ **let alone 1** not to mention, far less or more (*hasn't got a television, let alone a VCR*). **2** = LET BE. **let be** not interfere with, attend to, or do. **let down 1** lower. **2** fail to support or satisfy, disappoint. **3** lengthen (a garment). **4** loosen, untie, or allow to hang freely. **let down gently** avoid disappointing or humiliating abruptly. **let fly 1** (often foll. by *at*) attack physically or verbally. **2** (often foll. by *with*) throw, hurl, or hit vigorously. **let go 1** release, set at liberty. **2 a** (often foll. by *of*) relax or relinquish one's hold. **b** lose hold of. **3 a** cease to think or talk about; dismiss from one's thoughts. **b** cease to attend to or control; take no further action concerning. **c** dismiss (an employee). **let oneself go 1** give way to enthusiasm, impulse, etc. **2** cease to take trouble, neglect one's appearance or habits. **let in 1** allow to enter. **2** (usu. foll. by *for*) involve (a person, often oneself) in loss or difficulty. **3** (foll. by *on*) allow (a person) to share privileges, information, etc. **4** inlay (a thing) in another. **let oneself in** enter someone else's residence etc. by means of a key. **let it drop** (usu. in *imper.*) let the matter end there, not continue with the matter. **let know** inform (a person). **let loose 1** release or unleash. **2** loosen. **3** (also foll. by *with*) emit abruptly (a scream, tirade, etc.). **4** (often foll. by *on*) allow (a person) free access to (*once they're trained, we'll let them loose on the new computers*). **let off 1 a** fire (a gun). **b** explode (a bomb or firework). **2** allow or cause (steam, liquid, etc.) to escape. **3** allow to alight from a vehicle etc. **4 a** not punish or compel. **b** (foll. by *with*) punish lightly. **c** excuse, free (*was let off work early*). **let on** *informal* **1** reveal a secret. **2** pretend (*let on that he had succeeded*). **let out 1** allow to go out, esp. through a doorway. **2** release from restraint. **3** (often foll. by *that* + clause) reveal (a secret etc.). **4** make (a garment) looser esp. by adjustment at a seam. **5** *N Amer.* (of a class, meeting, etc.) finish, come to an end. **let (a person) have it 1** direct a blow or shot at a person. **2** assail with blows or words. **let through** allow to pass. **let up** *informal* **1** become less intense or severe. **2** relax one's efforts. **to let** esp. *Brit.* available for rent.

let[2] *n.* (in tennis, squash, etc.) an obstruction of a ball or a player in certain ways, requiring the ball to be served again.

letdown *n.* a disappointment, drawback, or disadvantage.

lethal /ˈliːθəl/ *adj.* **1** causing or sufficient to cause death. **2** harmful, injurious, destructive. □ **lethality** /lɪˈθælɪti/ *n.* **lethally** *adv.*

lethal dose *n.* the amount of a toxic compound or drug that causes death in humans or animals.

lethal injection *n.* an injection of various deadly chemicals used for capital punishment.

lethargy /ˈleθərdʒi/ *n.* **1** lack of energy or vitality; a torpid, inert, or apathetic state. **2** *Med.* a pathological state of sleepiness or deep unresponsiveness and inactivity. □ **lethargic** /lɪˈθɑrdʒɪk/ *adj.* **lethargically** *adv.*

let's *contraction* let us (*let's go now*).

letter ● *n.* **1 a** a character representing one or more of the simple or compound sounds used in speech; any of the alphabetic symbols. **b** (in *pl.*) *informal* the initials of a degree etc. after the holder's name. **2 a** a written, typed, or printed communication, usu. sent by mail or messenger. **b** (in *pl.*) an addressed legal or formal document for any of various purposes. **3** the precise terms or strict verbal interpretation of a statement or document (*opp.* SPIRIT *n.* 6) (*the letter of the law*). **4** (in *pl.*) **a** literature in general. **b** acquaintance with books, erudition (*a man of letters*). **c** authorship (*the profession of letters*). **5 a** types collectively. **b** a font of type. **6** *N Amer.* (*attrib.*) **a** designating a size of paper 22 by 28 cm ($8\frac{1}{2}$ by 11 inches). **b** designating office supplies, e.g. files etc., designed to hold this size paper. ● *v.tr.* **1** write, paint, inscribe, etc. letters on. **2** write, paint, inscribe, etc. (a word or words) on. □ **to the letter 1** with adherence to every detail. **2** in accordance with a strict literal interpretation.

letter bomb *n.* a terrorist explosive device disguised as a letter and sent through the mail.

letter box *n.* **1** esp. *Brit.* a public mailbox into which letters are deposited for delivery by the postal service. **2** esp. *Brit.* **a** a private mailbox to which letters etc. are delivered. **b** = MAIL SLOT. **3** (**letterbox**) (usu. *attrib.*) designating an adaptation of a motion picture for showing on television, maintaining the aspect ratio of a movie screen and thus producing an image with black borders above and below. ● *v.tr.* (**letterbox**) adapt a film for television broadcast in this format. □ **letterboxed** *adj.* **letterboxing** *n.*

letter carrier *n. N. Amer.* a person who delivers mail for the postal service.

lettered *adj.* **1** printed, marked, inscribed, etc. with or as with letters. **2** well read or educated; literate, learned.

letter grade *n. N Amer.* a grade given for schoolwork expressed as a letter (A, B, C, etc.).

letterhead *n.* **1** a printed heading on stationery, containing the address etc. of an organization or individual. **2** stationery with this.

lettering *n.* **1** the process of writing, inscribing, etc. letters. **2** letters written, painted, inscribed, etc. on something.

letter of intent *n.* a document containing a declaration of the intentions of the writer.

letter opener *n.* a knife with a long, narrow, blunt blade for slitting open envelopes etc.

letter-perfect *adj.* **1 a** literally correct, verbally exact. **b** flawless. **2** knowing one's part perfectly.

letter-quality *adj.* **1** (esp. of a printer attached to a computer) producing print of a quality suitable for a business letter. **2** (of text) printed to this quality.

letters patent *n.pl.* an open document issued by a sovereign or government in order to record a contract, authorize or command an action, or confer a right, privilege, title, etc.

lettuce *n.* **1** a composite plant, *Lactuca sativa*, with crisp edible leaves used in salads. **2** any of various plants resembling this.

let-up *n. informal* **1** a reduction in intensity or severity. **2** a relaxation of effort.

leukemia /luːˈkiːmiə/ *n.* (also esp. *Brit.* **leukaemia**) any of a group of malignant diseases in which the bone marrow and other blood-forming organs produce increased numbers of leukocytes.

leukocyte /ˈluːkəˌsəɪt/ *n.* (also **leucocyte**) **1** a white

blood cell. **2** any blood cell that contains a nucleus. □
leukocytic /-'sɪtɪk/ *adj.*

levee¹ /'levi/ *n.* **1** *Cdn* a New Year's Day reception held
by the Governor General, a Lieutenant-Governor, a
mayor, etc. **2** *N Amer.* an assembly of visitors or guests,
esp. at a formal reception.

levee² /'levi, lɪ'vi:/ *n.* *N Amer.* **1 a** an embankment
against river floods. **b** any of a series of continuous
embankments surrounding irrigated fields. **2** a natural embankment built up by a river. **3** a landing
place, a pier, or a quay.

level ● *n.* **1 a** a horizontal line or plane. **b** a horizontal position or the condition of being horizontal. **2 a**
a position marked by a horizontal line (*eye level*). **b** a
position on a real or imaginary scale with respect to
amount, intensity, extent, etc. (*danger level*). **c** a relative height, amount, or value (*sugar level in the blood*).
3 a standard or plane in social, moral, or intellectual
matters. **4** a plane of rank or authority, esp. in a
hierarchy (*discussions at Cabinet level*). **5 a** an instrument giving a line parallel to the plane of the horizon
for testing whether things are horizontal. **b** *Surveying*
an instrument for giving a horizontal line of sight. **c**
a real or imaginary horizontal line in relation to
which elevation is measured. **6 a** a more or less level
or flat surface. **b** a floor or storey in a building. **c** a
stratum in the earth. **7** a flat tract of land; a stretch of
land without hills. **8 a** a facet or layer of significance
or meaning, esp. in a literary or artistic work. **b** the
aspect or aspects of a subject, situation, etc. being
considered at a particular time. ● *adj.* **1** having a flat
and even surface; not bumpy. **2 a** horizontal; perpendicular to the plumb line. **b** lying, moving, or
directed in an approximately horizontal plane. **3**
(often foll. by *with*) **a** (of two or more things) situated
in the same horizontal plane. **b** having equality with
something else. **c** (of a spoonful etc.) with the contents even with the brim; not rounded or heaped. **4 a**
(of a person, judgment, etc.) well-balanced, sensible,
not agitated or confused. **b** of even, uniform, or
equable quality, tone, style, etc. ● *v.* (**levelled**,
levelling) **1** *tr.* make (a surface) level, even, or uniform, esp. by removing or reducing irregularities. **2** *tr.*
a raze or demolish. **b** beat or knock (a person) down.
3 *tr. & intr.* aim (a missile or gun). **4** *tr. & intr.* (foll. by *at,
against*) direct (an accusation, criticism, or satire). **5** *tr.*
standardize, reduce or remove (distinctions) to produce evenness or equality. **6** *intr.* (usu. foll. by *with*)
informal be frank or honest. **7** *tr.* place (two or more
things, people, etc.) on the same level. **8** *tr. & intr.*
Surveying **a** ascertain differences in the height of
(land). **b** determine the height of a point or points
relative to a given horizontal plane. **9** *tr. & intr.* (foll. by
off, out) **a** bring (an aircraft) into horizontal flight. **b**
(of an aircraft) assume or resume horizontal flight. □
do one's level best *informal* do one's utmost; make
all possible efforts. **find its level** (or **its own level**)
1 (of a liquid) reach the same height in containers
etc. which communicate with each other. **2** reach a
stable level, value, position, etc. with respect to something else (*the dollar found its level against the yen*). **find
one's level** reach the right social, intellectual, etc.
place in relation to others. **level down** bring down
to a standard. **level off 1** make or become level or
smooth. **2** cease or cause to cease ascending or descending, increasing or decreasing. **level out** make or
become level, remove differences, irregularities, etc.
from. **level up** bring up to a standard. **on the level**
informal **1** honest(ly), truthful(ly). **2** on a given plane,
horizontal, etc. **on a level with 1** equal with. **2** in

the same horizontal plane as. □ **levelly** *adv.*
levelness *n.*

level crossing *n.* *Cdn & Brit.* a place at which a road
and a railway cross each other at the same level.

level-headed *adj.* mentally balanced, cool, sensible.
□ **level-headedly** *adv.* **level-headedness** *n.*

leveller *n.* **1 a** a person who advocates the abolition
of social distinctions. **b** a thing which brings all
people to a common level (*death the great leveller*). **2**
(**Leveller**) *hist.* an extreme radical dissenter in 17th-c.
England, professing egalitarian principles. **3** a person or thing that levels.

level playing field *n.* a state of equitable conditions
for trading or competing.

lever /'li:vər, levər/ ● *n.* **1** a projecting handle moved
to operate a mechanism. **2** a bar resting on a pivot,
used to help lift or dislodge a heavy or firmly fixed
object. **3** *Mech.* a simple machine consisting of a rigid
bar pivoted about a fulcrum (fixed point) which can
be acted upon by a force (effort) in order to move a
load. **4** a means of exerting moral pressure. ● *v.* **1** *tr.*
use a lever. **2** *tr.* (often foll. by *away, out, up,* etc.) lift,
move, or act on with or as with a lever.

leverage /'levərɪdʒ, 'li:vər-/ ● **1** the action of a lever; a
way of applying a lever. **2** the power of a lever. **3**
advantage for accomplishing a purpose; increased
power or influence of action. **4** *N Amer. Business* **a** the
earning potential created by the ratio of capital to
shares. **b** the use of borrowed capital to enhance this.
5 *N Amer. Business* **a** the ratio of a company's loan
capital (debt) to the value of its common shares
(equity). **b** the effect of this on share prices. ● *v.* **1** *tr. &
intr.* speculate or cause to speculate financially on
borrowed capital expecting profits made to be
greater than interest payable. **2** *tr.* bring into a specified, usu. advantageous, position by or as by applying
a lever.

leveraged buyout *n.* esp. *N Amer.* the buyout of a
company by its management using outside capital.

leviathan /lə'vaɪəθən/ *n.* **1** *Bible* a sea monster. **2** an
imaginary or real aquatic animal of enormous size. **3**
anything monstrously large. **4** an autocratic monarch or nation.

levitate /'levɪ,teɪt/ *v.* **1** *intr.* rise and float in the air
(esp. with reference to spiritualism). **2** *tr.* cause to do
this. **3** *tr.* cause (something heavier than the surrounding medium) to rise or remain suspended without visible means, e.g. using magnetic forces. □
levitation *n.* **levitator** *n.*

levity /'levɪti/ *n.* **1** a tendency to make light of serious
matters. **2** lack of constancy or resolution. **3** undignified behaviour, impropriety.

levorotatory /,li:vo:'rotətəri/ *adj.* *Chem.* having the
property of rotating the plane of a polarized light ray
to the left.

levy ● *v.* (**-ies, -ied**) **1 a** *tr.* raise (contributions, taxes)
or impose (a rate, toll, fee, etc.) as a levy. **b** *tr. & intr.* raise
(a sum of money) by legal execution or process (*the
debt was levied on the debtor's goods*). **c** *tr.* seize (goods) in
this way. **2** *tr.* enlist or enrol (troops etc.). **3** *tr.* (usu. foll.
by *upon, against*) wage, proceed to make (war). ● *n.* (*pl.*
-ies) **1 a** the collecting of a contribution, tax, etc., or
of property to satisfy a legal judgment. **b** a contribution, tax, etc., levied. **2 a** the act or an instance of
enrolling troops etc. **b** (in *pl.*) troops enrolled. **c** a
body of troops enrolled.

lewd *adj.* **1** lustful, lecherous, wanton. **2** indecent,
obscene. □ **lewdly** *adv.* **lewdness** *n.*

lexical *adj.* **1** of the words of a language. **2** of or as of
a lexicon. □ **lexically** *adv.*

lexical item *n.* (also **lexical unit**) a word or string of words (e.g. an idiomatic phrase, a compound word, etc.) having a distinct meaning.

lexicography /ˌleksɪˈkɒɡrəfi/ *n.* the compiling, writing, or editing of dictionaries. ▢ **lexicographer** *n.* **lexicographic** *adj.* **lexicographical** *adj.* **lexicographically** *adv.*

lexicon /ˈleksɪkɒn/ *n.* **1** a dictionary, esp. of Greek, Hebrew, or Arabic. **2 a** the vocabulary of a person, language, branch of knowledge, etc. **b** a book listing this vocabulary.

LF *abbr.* low frequency.

LGen *abbr. Cdn* LIEUTENANT GENERAL.

LH *abbr.* LUTEINIZING HORMONE.

l.h. *abbr.* left hand.

Lhasa /ˈlæsə/ *n.* (in full **Lhasa Apso** /æpso:/ *pl.* **-os**) a breed of small long-coated dog, often gold or grey and white.

Li *symbol* lithium.

liability /ˌlaɪəˈbɪlɪti/ *n.* (*pl.* **-ies**) **1** the state of being liable. **2** a person or thing that causes one problems or puts something at risk. **3** what a person or company is liable for, esp. (in *pl.*) debts or pecuniary obligations.

liability insurance *n.* insurance that covers compensation payments and court costs for which a policyholder is legally liable because of claims for injury to other people or damage to their property resulting from the policyholder's negligence.

liable /ˈlaɪəbəl/ *predic.adj.* **1** legally bound. **2** (foll. by *to*) subject to (a tax or penalty). **3** (foll. by *to* + infin.) under an obligation. **4** (foll. by *to*) exposed or open to (something undesirable). **5** *disputed* apt, likely (*these sorts of people are liable to suffer from depression*). ¶Although there is a long tradition of objection to this use of *liable*, it is well established. **6** (foll. by *for*) answerable.

liaise /liˈeɪz/ *v.intr.* (foll. by *with, between*) establish co-operation, act as a link.

liaison /liˈeizɒn, ˌliːeiˈzɒn/ *n.* **1 a** communication or co-operation, esp. between groups within an organization. **b** a person or association coordinating the co-operation of different groups. **2** an illicit sexual relationship.

liaison officer *n.* **1** an officer acting as a link between allied forces or units of the same force. **2** a person whose job is to promote communication between different groups within an organization or between organizations and the public etc.

liana /liˈænə/ *n.* (also **liane** /-ˈæn/) any of several climbing and twining plants of tropical forests.

liar /ˈlaɪər/ *n.* a person who tells a lie or lies, esp. habitually.

Lib. *abbr.* Liberal.

lib *n. informal* **1** liberation (*women's lib*). **2** a liberal. **3** (**Lib**) a Liberal.

libation /laɪˈbeiʃən/ *n.* **1 a** the pouring out of a drink offering to a god. **b** such an offering. **2** *jocular* a drink.

libber *n. informal* **1** an advocate of women's liberation. **2** an advocate of the liberation of a specified group (*animal libbers*).

libel /ˈlaibəl/ ● *n.* **1** *Law* **a** a published false statement damaging to a person's reputation (*compare* SLANDER 3). **b** the act or crime of publishing this. **2 a** a false and defamatory written statement. **b** (foll. by *on*) a thing that brings discredit by misrepresentation etc. (*the book is a libel on human nature*). ● *v.tr.* (**libelled, libelling**) **1** defame by libellous statements. **2** accuse falsely and maliciously. **3** *Law* publish a libel against. ▢ **libeller** *n.* **libellous** *adj.* **libellously** *adv.*

liberal ● *adj.* **1 a** given freely. **b** ample, abundant. **2** (often foll. by *with*) giving freely, generous, not sparing. **3** open-minded, not prejudiced. **4** not strict or rigorous; (of interpretation) not literal. **5** for general broadening of the mind, not professional or technical (*liberal education*). **6 a** favouring a relaxing of social traditions and a significant role for the state in matters of economics and social justice. **b** favouring individual liberty and limited government involvement in economic affairs. **7** (**Liberal**) of or characteristic of Liberals or a Liberal Party. **8** *Theol.* regarding many traditional beliefs as dispensable, invalidated by modern thought, or liable to change (*liberal Protestant*). ● *n.* **1** a person of liberal views. **2** (**Liberal**) a supporter or member of a Liberal Party. ▢ **liberally** *adv.* **liberalness** *n.*

liberal arts *n.pl. N Amer.* the humanities, esp. as studied at university, leading to a broad general education.

Liberal-Conservative Party *n. Cdn hist.* the dominant political party of the Province of Canada, formed in the mid-19th c. as a coalition of moderate Reformers and Tories.

liberalism *n.* **1** a political and social philosophy emphasizing the freedom of the individual, democratic government characterized by progress and reform, and the protection of civil liberties. **2** the quality of being liberal; open-mindedness. **3** (**Liberalism**) the principles and practices of a Liberal party.

liberality *n.* **1** generosity. **2** respect for political, moral, or religious views which one does not share.

liberalize *v.tr. & intr.* make or become more liberal or less strict. ▢ **liberalization** *n.* **liberalizer** *n.*

Liberal Party *n.* (in Canada) one of the two historically most important political parties, generally advocating a centrist position.

liberate *v.tr.* **1** (often foll. by *from*) set at liberty, set free. **2** free (a country etc.) from an oppressor or an enemy occupation. **3** (often as **liberated** *adj.*) free (a person or group) from rigid social conventions or stigmas. **4** *slang jocular* steal. **5** *Chem.* release (esp. a gas) from a state of combination. ▢ **liberator** *n.* **liberatory** /ˈlɪbrəˌtɔri/ *adj.*

liberation *n.* **1** the act or an instance of liberating; the state of being liberated. **2** the freeing of a person or group from restrictive social conventions. ▢ **liberationist** *n. & adj.*

liberation theology *n. Christianity* a theory which interprets liberation from social, political, and economic oppression as an anticipation of ultimate salvation.

Liberian /laiˈbiːriən/ ● *adj.* of or relating to Liberia, a country on the Atlantic coast of W Africa, or its people. ● *n.* a native or inhabitant of Liberia.

libertarian /ˌlɪbərˈteriən/ ● *n.* an advocate of liberty, esp. of an almost absolute freedom of expression and action. ● *adj.* believing in free will. ▢ **libertarianism** *n.*

libertine /ˈlɪbərˌtiːn, -ˌtain/ ● *n.* **1** a man who behaves without moral principles or a sense of responsibility, esp. in sexual matters. **2** a free thinker on religion. **3** a person who follows his or her own inclinations in spite of social conventions. ● *adj.* **1** licentious, dissolute. **2** freethinking. **3** following one's own inclinations. ▢ **libertinism** *n.*

liberty *n.* (*pl.* **-ies**) **1 a** freedom from captivity, imprisonment, slavery, or despotic control. **b** a personification of this. **2 a** the right or power to do as one pleases. **b** (foll. by *to* + infin.) right, power, opportunity, permission. **c** *Philos.* freedom from control by fate or necessity. **3** (usu. in *pl.*) a right, privilege, or immunity, enjoyed by prescription or grant. **4** setting aside of rules or convention, esp. concerning intimacy (*permitted no liberties*). □ **at liberty 1** free, not imprisoned (*set at liberty*). **2** (foll. by *to* + infin.) entitled, permitted. **3** available, disengaged. **take liberties 1** (often foll. by *with*) behave in an unduly familiar manner. **2** (foll. by *with*) deal freely or superficially with rules or facts. **take the liberty** (foll. by *to* + infin., or *of* + verbal noun) presume, venture.

libidinous /lɪˈbɪdɪnəs/ *adj.* lustful. □ **libidinously** *adv.* **libidinousness** *n.*

libido /lɪˈbiːdoʊ/ *n.* (*pl.* **-os**) **1** the sexual drive or instinct. **2** *Psych.* psychic drive or energy inherent in instinctive mental desires and drives. □ **libidinal** /lɪˈbɪdɪnəl/ *adj.* **libidinally** *adv.*

Libra /ˈliːbrə/ *n.* **1** a constellation near Virgo, traditionally regarded as contained in the figure of scales. **2 a** the seventh sign of the zodiac. **b** a person born when the sun is in this sign, usu. between Sept. 23 and Oct. 22. □ **Libran** *n. & adj.*

librarian *n.* **1** a person professionally trained in library science. **2** a person in charge of, or an assistant in, a library. □ **librarianship** *n.*

library *n.* (*pl.* **-ies**) **1 a** a collection of books, periodicals, recordings, electronic reference materials, etc. for use by the public or by members of a group. **b** a person's collection of books. **2** a room or building containing a collection of books (for reading or reference rather than for sale). **3 a** a similar collection of films, records, computer routines, etc. **b** the place where these are kept. **4** a series of books issued by a publisher in similar bindings etc., usu. as a set. **5** a public institution charged with the care of a collection of books, films, etc.

library card *n.* a card entitling the bearer to borrow books from a library.

Library of Congress Classification *n. N Amer.* a classification system for library holdings based on that of the Library of Congress in Washington and used in most N American academic libraries.

library science *n.* the study of the collection, organization, use, and dissemination of information resources within libraries and other information institutions.

libretto /lɪˈbretoʊ/ *n.* (*pl.* **-os** or **libretti** /-tiː/) the text of an opera or other long musical vocal work. □ **librettist** *n.*

Librium /ˈlɪbriəm/ *n. proprietary* a benzodiazepine drug used as a tranquilizer.

Libyan /ˈlɪbiən, ˈlɪbjən/ ● *adj.* **1** of or relating to modern Libya, a country in N Africa. **2** of ancient N Africa west of Egypt. **3** of or relating to the Berber group of languages. ● *n.* **1 a** a native or national of modern Libya. **b** a person of Libyan descent. **2** an ancient language of the Berber group.

Lic. *abbr.* licensed.

lice *pl. of* LOUSE 1.

licence *n.* (also *US* **license**) **1** a permit from an authority to own or use something (esp. a dog, gun, or vehicle), do something (esp. construct a building, drive a motor vehicle, or marry), or carry on a trade (esp. in liquor). **2 a** liberty of action, esp. when excessive; disregard of law or propriety, abuse of freedom. **b** licentiousness. **3** a writer's or artist's irregularity in grammar, metre, perspective, etc., or deviation from fact, esp. for effect (*poetic licence*).

licence number *n. N Amer.* a unique sequence of numbers or letters identifying a motor vehicle.

licence plate *n. N Amer.* a plate fixed prominently to all licensed motor vehicles, bearing the licence number.

license *v.tr.* (also **licence**) **1** grant a licence to (a person). **2** authorize the use of (premises) for a certain purpose, esp. the sale and consumption of alcoholic liquor. **3** authorize the publication of (a book etc.) or the performance of (a play). **4** authorize the use of a logo or proprietary name on (merchandise). □ **licensor** *n.* (also **licenser**).

licensed *adj.* (also **licenced**) **1** having a specified or appropriate licence (*licensed mechanic*). **2** (of a restaurant etc.) having a licence to sell alcoholic drinks. **3** (of a consumer product) bearing a logo, trademark, etc. which the manufacturer was licensed to use. **4** (of a Baptist preacher) authorized by the Church to preach but not ordained.

licensed practical nurse *n.* a person who has a licence to perform basic nursing tasks under the direction of a physician or registered nurse.

licensee *n.* the holder of a licence.

licentiate /laɪˈsenʃiət, -ʃət/ *n.* a holder of a certificate of competence to practise a certain profession.

licentious /laɪˈsenʃəs/ *adj.* sexually promiscuous or unrestrained. □ **licentiously** *adv.* **licentiousness** *n.*

lichee *var. of* LYCHEE.

lichen /ˈlaɪkən/ *n.* **1** any plant organism of the group Lichenes, composed of a fungus and an alga in symbiotic association, usu. of green, grey, or yellow tint and growing on and colouring rocks, tree trunks, roofs, walls, etc. **2** any of several types of skin disease in which small round hard lesions occur close together. □ **lichened** *adj.* (in sense 1).

licit /ˈlɪsɪt/ *adj.* not forbidden; lawful. □ **licitly** *adv.*

lick ● *v.* **1** *tr.* pass the tongue over, esp. to taste, eat, moisten, or (of animals) clean. **2** *tr.* bring into a specified condition or position by licking (*licked it all up*; *licked it clean*). **3 a** *tr.* (of a flame, waves, etc.) touch; play lightly over. **b** *intr.* move gently or caressingly. **4** *tr. informal* **a** defeat, excel. **b** surpass the comprehension of (*has got me licked*). **5** *tr. informal* thrash. **6** *tr. N Amer.* solve (a problem); overcome (a difficulty). ● *n.* **1** an act of licking with the tongue. **2** = SALT LICK. **3** *informal* a fast pace (*at a lick*). **4** *informal* **a** a small amount (foll. by *of*: *doesn't make a lick of sense*). **b** a hastily-done activity, esp. a wash. **5** a smart blow with a stick etc. **6** *slang Music* a short ornamental solo passage. □ **a lick and a promise** *informal* a hasty performance of a task, esp. of housecleaning etc. **lick a person's boots** (or **shoes**) toady; be servile. **lick one's lips** (or **chops**) **1** look forward with relish. **2** show one's satisfaction. **lick one's wounds** try to recover one's strength or confidence after defeat or disappointment. □ **licker** *n.* (also in *comb.*).

lickety-split *informal* ● *adv.* at full speed; headlong. ● *attrib.adj.* quick.

licking *n. informal* **1** a thrashing. **2** a defeat.

licorice /ˈlɪkərɪʃ, ˈlɪkrɪʃ, -rɪs/ *n.* **1** the leguminous plant *Glycyrrhiza glabra*. **2** a black substance extracted from its root, used as a sweet and in medicine. **3** candy flavoured with this, usu. in long black rubbery strips. **4** a rubbery candy similar to this, in any of several flavours and colours.

licorice root *n. N Amer.* **1** a leguminous plant, *Glycyrrhiza lepidota* of western and central N America. **2** a leguminous plant, *Hedysarum alpinum*.

lid *n.* **1** a hinged or removable cover, esp. for the top of a container. **2** = EYELID. **3** *informal* a restraint, check, or brake (*keep a lid on the information*). **4** *slang* a hat or helmet. ☐ **blow the lid off** *informal* expose (a scandal etc.). **put a lid on it** *informal* stop talking. ☐ **lidded** *adj.* (also in *comb.*). **lidless** *adj.*

lie¹ ● *v.intr.* (**lying**; *past* **lay**; *past part.* **lain**) **1** be in or assume a horizontal position on a supporting surface; be at rest on something. **2** (of a thing) rest flat on a surface (*snow lay on the ground*). **3** (of abstract things) remain undisturbed or undiscussed etc. (*let matters lie*). **4 a** be kept or remain or be in a specified, esp. concealed, state or place (*lie hidden*; *malice lay behind those words*; *they lay dying*). **b** (of abstract things) exist, reside; be in a certain position or relation (foll. by *in*, *with*, etc.; *my sympathies lie with the family*). **5 a** be situated or stationed (*the village lay to the east*). **b** (of a road, route, etc.) lead (*the road lies over mountains*). **c** be spread out to view (*the desert lay before us*). **6** (of the dead) be buried in a grave. **7** (foll. by *with*) *archaic* have sexual intercourse. ● *n.* the way or direction or position in which a thing lies. ☐ **as far as in me lies** to the best of my power. **let lie** not raise (a controversial matter etc.) for discussion etc. **lie ahead** be going to happen; be in store. **lie around** (or **about**) be left carelessly out of place. **lie back** recline so as to rest. **lie down** assume a lying position; have a short rest. **lie heavy** cause discomfort or anxiety. **lie in state** (of a deceased great personage) be laid in a public place of honour before burial. **lie low 1** keep quiet or unseen. **2** be discreet about one's intentions. **lie off** *Naut.* stand some distance from shore or from another ship. **lie over** be deferred. **lie with** (often foll. by *to* + infin.) be the responsibility of (a person) (*it lies with you to answer*). **take lying down** (usu. with *neg.*) accept (defeat, rebuke, etc.) without resistance or protest etc.

lie² ● *n.* **1** an intentionally false statement. **2** imposture; false belief (*live a lie*). ● *v.intr. & tr.* (**lies, lied, lying**) **1** *intr.* tell a lie or lies. **b** (of a thing) be deceptive (*the camera cannot lie*). **2** *tr.* (usu. *refl.*; foll. by *into*, *out of*) get (oneself) into or out of a situation by lying. ☐ **give the lie to** serve to show the falsity of (a supposition etc.). **lie through one's teeth** lie brazenly.

lied /liːd, liːt/ *n.* (*pl.* **lieder** /ˈliːdər/) a type of German song, esp. of the Romantic period, usu. for solo voice with piano accompaniment.

lie detector *n.* an instrument for determining whether a person is telling the truth by testing for physiological changes considered to be symptomatic of lying.

lie-down *n.* a short rest.

liege /liːdʒ, liːʒ/ usu. *hist.* ● *adj.* entitled to receive or bound to give feudal service or allegiance. ● *n.* **1** (in full **liege lord**) a feudal superior or sovereign. **2** (usu. in *pl.*) a vassal or subject.

lien /liːn, ˈliːən/ *n. Law* a right over another's property to protect a debt charged on that property.

lieu /luː, ljuː/ *n. Cdn* designating time taken off work in compensation for overtime worked (also *attrib.*: *lieu time*). ☐ **in lieu 1** instead. **2** (foll. by *of*) in the place of.

Lieut. *abbr.* Lieutenant.

lieutenant /lefˈtenənt, luː-/ *n.* **1** a deputy or substitute acting for a superior (*the prime minister's Quebec lieutenant*). **2** (also **Lieutenant**) **a** (in the Canadian Army and Air Force and the British Army) an officer next in rank below captain. **b** (in the Canadian Navy and other navies) an officer next in rank below lieutenant commander, equivalent to a captain in the other commands. **3** (in Quebec and the US) a police officer next in rank below captain. **4** (in the Royal

Newfoundland Constabulary) an officer of a rank between staff sergeant and inspector. ¶The pronunciation /lefˈtenənt/ is used in the Canadian Forces. Many Canadians object to /luːˈtenənt/ as being American, but outside of the Armed Forces, it is probably somewhat more common among Canadians than /lefˈtenənt/, except for the word *Lieutenant-Governor*, where usage is more equally divided. ☐ **lieutenancy** *n.* (*pl.* **-ies**).

lieutenant colonel *n.* (also **Lieutenant Colonel**) an officer ranking next below colonel and above major.

lieutenant commander *n.* (also **Lieutenant Commander**) a naval officer ranking below a commander and above a lieutenant.

lieutenant general *n.* (also **Lieutenant General**) (in the Canadian or US Army or Air Force and other armies) an officer ranking above a major general.

lieutenant-governor *n.* (*pl.* **lieutenant-governors**) **1** (**Lieutenant-Governor**) *Cdn* the representative of the Crown in a province. Abbr.: **Lt.-Gov. 2** the acting or deputy governor of a state, province, etc., under a governor or Governor General.

LIF /lɪf/ *abbr. Cdn* LIFE INCOME FUND.

life *n.* (*pl.* **lives**) **1** the condition which distinguishes active animals and plants from inorganic matter, including the capacity for growth, functional activity, and continual change preceding death. **2 a** living things and their activity (*insect life*; *is there life on Mars?*). **b** human presence or activity (*no sign of life*). **c** the human condition; existence (*such is life*). **3 a** the period during which life lasts, or the period from birth to the present time or from the present time to death (*have done it all my life*). **b** the duration of a thing's existence or of its ability to function; validity, efficacy, etc. (*the battery has a life of two years*). **4 a** a person's state of existence as a living individual (*took many lives*). **b** a living person (*many lives were lost*). **c** life seen as a right to which the unborn are entitled (*pro-life*). **5 a** an individual's occupation, actions, or fortunes; the manner of one's existence (*that would make life easy*). **b** a particular aspect of this (*how's your love life?*). **c** one's romantic life (*is there someone in your life?*). **6** the active part of existence; the business and pleasures of the world (*travel is the best way to see life*). **7** earthly or supposed future existence (*this life and the next*). **8 a** energy, liveliness, animation (*put some life into it!*). **b** an animating influence (*was the life of the party*). **9** the living, esp. nude, form or model (*life drawing classes*). **10** a biography. **11** *informal* a sentence of imprisonment for life (*serving life*). **12** a chance; a fresh start. ☐ **come to life 1** emerge from unconsciousness or inactivity; begin operating. **2** (of an inanimate object) assume an imaginary animation. **for dear** (or **one's**) **life** as if or in order to escape death; as a matter of extreme urgency (*hang on for dear life*; *run for your life*). **for life** for the rest of one's life. **for the life of** (foll. by pers. pron.) even if (one's) life depended on it (*cannot for the life of me remember*). **get a life** begin to live a meaningful or useful life. **give one's life 1** (foll. by *for*) die; sacrifice oneself. **2** (foll. by *to*) dedicate oneself. **large as life** *informal* in person, esp. prominently (*stood there large as life*). **larger than life 1** exaggerated. **2** (of a person) having an exuberant personality. **life and limb** life and personal health and safety (*she would risk life and limb to save him*). **lose one's life** be killed. **not on your life** *informal* most certainly not. **save a person's life 1** prevent a person's death. **2** save a person from serious difficulty. **take one's life in one's hands** take a crucial personal risk. **to the life** true to the original.

life-and-death adj. **1** determining life or death (a life-and-death struggle). **2** vitally important.

life assurance n. esp. Brit. = LIFE INSURANCE.

lifebelt n. a belt of buoyant or inflatable material for keeping a person afloat in water.

lifeblood n. **1** the blood, as being necessary to life. **2** the vital factor or influence.

lifeboat n. a small rescue or safety boat for use during emergencies.

lifebuoy n. a buoyant support (usu. a ring) for keeping a person afloat in water, esp. in an emergency.

life cycle n. **1** the series of developmental stages through which an organism passes, from one state to the same state in the next generation. **2** the series of developmental stages of any thing, from beginning to end.

life expectancy n. the average period that a person at a specified age etc. may expect to live.

life force n. the vital force which gives energy, inspiration, etc. to a living being.

life form n. an organism.

life-giving adj. that sustains life or uplifts and revitalizes.

lifeguard n. an expert swimmer employed to rescue swimmers from drowning.

life history n. the story of the development of a person or thing, from beginning to end.

life income fund n. Cdn a tax-sheltered fund providing annual income to its holder, not falling below an established minimum percentage of the fund, but also not exceeding a maximum payment.

life insurance n. insurance for a sum to be paid to named beneficiaries on the death of the insured person.

life jacket n. a buoyant jacket for keeping a person afloat in water, esp. in an emergency.

lifeless adj. **1** lacking life; no longer living; dead. **2** unconscious. **3** lacking movement or vitality. □ **lifelessly** adv. **lifelessness** n.

lifelike adj. closely resembling the person or thing represented.

lifeline n. **1 a** a rope etc. used for life-saving, e.g. that attached to a lifebuoy. **b** a diver's signalling line. **2 a** a sole means of communication or transport. **b** a vital source of aid or sustenance. **3** a fold in the palm of the hand, regarded as significant in palmistry. **4** an emergency telephone counselling service.

lifelong adj. lasting a lifetime.

life member n. a person who has lifelong membership of a society etc.

life-or-death adj. = LIFE-AND-DEATH.

life partner n. a person engaged in a permanent sexual and romantic relationship with another.

life preserver n. a life jacket etc.

lifer n. slang **1** a person serving a life sentence. **2** a person seemingly destined to remain in the same job, position, etc. for life.

life raft n. an inflatable or timber etc. raft for use in an emergency instead of a boat.

lifesaver n. **1** a buoyant ring for keeping a person afloat in an emergency. **2** informal a thing that saves one from serious difficulty. □ **life-saving** n. & adj.

life sciences n.pl. biology and related subjects.

life sentence n. **1** a sentence of imprisonment for life. **2** (in Canada) a jail sentence of 25 years. **3** an

illness or commitment etc. perceived as a continuing threat to one's freedom.

life-sized adj. (also **life-size**) of the same size as the person or thing represented.

life skills n.pl. the basic skills needed to function normally in society.

lifespan n. the length of time for which a person or creature lives, or for which a thing exists or is functional.

life story n. the story of a person's life, esp. told at tedious length.

lifestyle n. **1** the particular way of life of a person or group; a way or style of living. **2** (attrib.) of or relating to a particular way of living, esp. designating advertising, products, etc. designed to appeal to a consumer by association with a particular, desirable lifestyle.

life-support ● attrib.adj. (of equipment or a system of machines) allowing vital functions, such as breathing, to continue in an adverse environment or during severe disability. ● n. a life-support system.

life's work n. (also **life work**) the work of a lifetime; a task, project, etc. pursued throughout one's life.

life-threatening adj. (of an illness etc.) that endangers life.

lifetime n. **1** the duration of a person's life. **2** the duration of a thing or its usefulness. **3** informal an exceptionally long time. □ **of a lifetime** such as does not occur more than once in a person's life.

lifeway n. esp. Anthropology a way of life or lifestyle, esp. of a specific group or community.

lift ● v. **1** tr. raise or remove to a higher position. **2** intr. go up; be raised; yield to an upward force (the window will not lift). **3** tr. give an upward direction to (the eyes or face). **4** tr. **a** elevate to a higher plane of thought or feeling (lifted their spirits). **b** make less heavy or dull; add interest to (something esp. artistic). **c** enhance, improve (lifted their game in the third period). **5** intr. (of a cloud, fog, rain, etc.) rise, disperse. **6** tr. remove (a barrier or restriction). **7** tr. transport supplies, troops, etc. by air. **8** tr. informal **a** steal. **b** plagiarize (a passage of writing etc.). **9** tr. dig up (esp. potatoes etc.). **10** intr. (of a floor) swell upwards, bulge. **11** tr. hold or have on high (the church lifts its spire). **12** tr. hit (a baseball, puck, etc.) into the air (lifted one over second base). **13** tr. (usu. in passive) perform cosmetic surgery on (esp. the face or breasts) to reduce sagging. ● n. **1** the act of lifting or process of being lifted. **2** a free ride in another person's vehicle (gave them a lift). **3 a** an apparatus for carrying persons up or down a mountain etc. (see SKI LIFT). **b** a device for lifting things. **4 a** transport by air (see AIRLIFT n.). **b** a quantity of goods transported by air. **5** the upward pressure which air exerts on an airfoil to counteract the force of gravity. **6** a supporting or elevating influence; a feeling of elation (that really gave me a lift). **7** a layer of leather in the heel of a boot or shoe, esp. to correct shortening of a leg or increase height. **8** a rise in the level of the ground. **9** a movement in which a dancer or figure skater lifts another in the air. **10** cosmetic surgery to reduce sagging. **11** an exercise consisting of lifting a limb or other part of the body repeatedly to develop strength. □ **lift down** pick up and bring to a lower position. **lift a finger** (or **hand** etc.) (in neg.) make the slightest effort (didn't lift a finger to help). **lift off 1** (of a spacecraft or rocket) rise from the launching pad. **2** (of an aircraft) rise from the runway during takeoff. **lift his leg** (of a male dog) urinate. **lift up one's head** hold one's head high with pride. **lift up one's voice** sing out. □ **lifter** n.

liftoff n. **1** the vertical takeoff of a spacecraft etc. **2** an aircraft's rising from the runway during takeoff.

lift ticket n. N Amer. a ticket or tag entitling the bearer to use a ski lift.

ligament /'lɪgəmənt/ n. Anat. **1** a short band of tough flexible fibrous connective tissue linking bones together. **2** any membranous fold keeping an organ in position. □ **ligamentous** /-'mentəs/ adj.

ligate /lɪ'geɪt/ v.tr. Surgery tie up (a bleeding artery etc.). □ **ligation** n.

ligature /'lɪgətʃər/ ● n. **1** a tie or bandage, esp. in surgery for a bleeding artery etc. **2** Music a slur; a tie. **3** Printing two or more letters joined, e.g. æ. **4** a bond; a thing that unites. **5** the act of tying or binding. ● v.tr. bind or connect with a ligature.

light¹ ● n. **1** the natural agent (electromagnetic radiation of wavelength between about 390 and 740 nm) that stimulates sight and makes things visible. **2** the medium or condition of the space in which this is present. **3** an appearance of brightness (saw a distant light). **4 a** a source of light, e.g. the sun, a lamp, fire, etc. **b** an illuminated, usu. coloured electrical device used as a signal. **5** (often in pl.) a traffic light (ran a red light; stop at the lights). **6 a** the amount or quality of illumination in a place (bad light). **b** one's fair or usual share of this (you are standing in my light). **7 a** a flame or spark serving to ignite (struck a light). **b** a device producing this (have you got a light?). **8** the aspect in which a thing is regarded or considered (in a new light). **9 a** mental illumination; elucidation, enlightenment. **b** hope, happiness; a happy outcome. **c** spiritual illumination by divine truth. **10** vivacity, enthusiasm, or inspiration visible in a person's face, esp. in the eyes. **11** (in pl.) a person's mental powers or ability (according to one's lights). **12** an eminent person (a leading light). **13 a** the bright part of a thing; a highlight. **b** the bright parts of a picture etc. esp. suggesting illumination (light and shade). **14 a** a window or opening in a wall to let light in. **b** the perpendicular division of a mullioned window. **c** a pane of glass, esp. in a door. ● v. (past **lit**; past part. **lit** or (attrib.) **lighted**) **1** tr. & intr. set burning or begin to burn; ignite. **2** tr. provide with light or lighting. **3** tr. show (a person) the way or surroundings with a light. ● adj. **1** well provided with light; not dark. **2** (of a colour) pale (light blue). ● comb. form forming compounds designating the distance travelled by light in a specified time (light-year). □ **bring** (or **come**) **to light** reveal or be revealed. **in a good** (or **bad**) **light** giving a favourable (or unfavourable) impression. **in** (**the**) **light of** considering; in view of; drawing information from. **light at the end of the tunnel** a long-awaited sign that a period of hardship or adversity is coming to an end. **light of one's life** usu. jocular a much-loved person. **light up 1** informal begin to smoke a cigarette etc. **2** switch on lights or lighting; illuminate a scene. **3** (of a light or a panel etc. covered with lights) become illuminated. **4** (of the face or eyes) brighten with animation. **out like a light** deeply asleep or unconscious. **throw** (or **shed**) **light on** help to explain. □ **lightish** adj. **lightless** adj. **lightness** n.

light² ● adj. **1** of little weight; not heavy; easy to lift. **2 a** relatively low in weight, amount, density, intensity, etc. (light traffic; a light breeze). **b** deficient in weight (light coin). **c** (of an isotope etc.) having not more than the usual mass. **3 a** carrying or suitable for small loads (light aircraft). **b** (of a ship) unladen. **c** carrying only light arms, armaments, etc. (light infantry). **d** (of a locomotive) with no train attached. **4 a** (of food, a meal, etc.) small in amount; easy to digest (a light

lunch). **b** (of a foodstuff) low in fat, cholesterol, or sugar, etc. **c** (of a foodstuff) lower in calories, fat, etc. than a comparable product. **d** (of drink) not heavy on the stomach or not strongly alcoholic. **5 a** (of entertainment, music, etc.) intended for amusement, rather than edification; not profound. **b** frivolous, thoughtless, trivial (a light remark). **6** (of sleep or a sleeper) easily disturbed. **7** easily borne or done (light housekeeping). **8** nimble; quick-moving (a light step). **9** (of a building etc.) graceful, elegant, delicate. **10** (of type) not heavy or bold. **11 a** free from sorrow; cheerful (a light heart). **b** giddy (light in the head). **12** (of soil) not dense; porous. **13** (of a dessert) fluffy and well-aerated. ● adv. **1** in a light manner (sleep light). **2** with a minimum load or minimum luggage (travel light). ● v.intr. (past and past part. **lit** or **lighted**) (foll. by on, upon) come upon or find by chance. □ **light into** informal attack. **light out** informal depart. **make light of** treat as unimportant. **make light work of** do a thing quickly and easily. □ **lightish** adj. **lightness** n.

light box n. any apparatus with a translucent surface lit from behind, used to view slides, film, etc.

light breeze n. **1** a light wind, force 2 on the Beaufort scale (7–12 km/h, or 4–7 mph). **2** any light wind.

light bulb n. a glass bulb containing an inert gas and a metal filament, providing light when an electric current is passed through.

light cream n. **1** Cdn a table cream having 7% fat. **2** esp. US a table cream generally with 18% fat.

light-emitting diode n. = LED.

lighten¹ v. **1 a** tr. & intr. make or become lighter in weight. **b** tr. reduce the weight or load of. **2** tr. bring relief to (the heart, mind, etc.). **3** tr. mitigate (a penalty). □ **lighten up** informal become less earnest or intense; relax. □ **lightener** n.

lighten² v. **1 a** tr. shed light on. **b** tr. & intr. make or grow bright. **c** make less dark. **2** intr. **a** shine brightly; flash. **b** emit lightning (it is lightening). □ **lightener** n.

lighter n. **1** a device for lighting cigarettes, barbecues, etc. **2** a boat, usu. flat-bottomed, for transferring goods from a ship to a wharf or another ship.

lighter fluid n. a petrochemical fuel, esp. naphtha, used to work a cigarette lighter.

lighter-than-air attrib.adj. (of an aircraft) weighing less than the air it displaces, e.g. a blimp.

lightfast adj. (of a dye, pigment, etc.) resistant to alteration on exposure to light. □ **lightfastness** n.

light-fingered adj. given to stealing.

light flyweight n. **1** a weight in amateur boxing up to 48 kg. **2** an amateur boxer of this weight.

light-footed adj. nimble. □ **light-footedly** adv.

light-handed adj. having a light, delicate, or deft touch.

light-headed adj. giddy, faint. □ **light-headedly** adv. **light-headedness** n.

lighthearted adj. **1** cheerful. **2** (unduly) casual, thoughtless. □ **lightheartedly** adv. **lightheartedness** n.

light heavyweight n. **1** the weight in some sports between middleweight and heavyweight, in the amateur boxing scale 75-81 kg. **2** an athlete of this weight.

lighthouse n. a tower or other structure containing a beacon light to warn or guide ships.

light industry n. the manufacture of small or light articles, esp. consumer goods.

lighting n. **1** equipment on a street, in a room, etc. for producing light. **2** the arrangement or effect of lights.

lightkeeper n. a person in charge of a lighthouse.

lightly *adv. in senses of* LIGHT² *adj.* □ **get off lightly** escape with little or no punishment. **take lightly** not be serious about (a thing).

light middleweight *n.* **1** a weight in amateur boxing of 67-71 kg. **2** a boxer of this weight.

lightning ● *n.* a flash of bright light produced by an electric discharge between clouds or between clouds and the ground. ● *attrib.adj.* very quick (*lightning speed*).

lightning rod *n.* **1** a metal rod or wire fixed to an exposed part of a building or to a mast to divert lightning into the earth or sea. **2** a person or thing that attracts criticism.

light of day *n.* **1** daylight, sunlight. **2** general notice; public attention.

light opera *n.* = OPERETTA.

light pen *n.* **1** a penlike photosensitive device held to the screen of a computer terminal for passing information on to it. **2** a light-emitting device used for reading bar codes.

light pollution *n.* excessive brightening of the night sky by street lights etc., esp. as obscuring the stars etc.

lightproof *adj.* (of a container, barrier, etc.) not permitting the passage of light.

lights *n.pl.* the lungs of sheep, pigs, steers, etc., used as a food esp. for pets. □ **punch a person's lights out** beat a person soundly.

light show *n.* a display of changing coloured lights for entertainment.

lights out *n.* the time all lights are to be shut off in a dormitory etc.

light station *n.* = LIGHTHOUSE.

light touch *n.* delicate or tactful treatment.

lightweight ● *adj.* **1** (of a person, garment, etc.) of below average weight. **2** of little importance or influence. ● *n.* **1** a lightweight person, animal, or thing. **2 a** a weight in certain sports intermediate between featherweight and welterweight, in the amateur boxing scale 57–60 kg but differing for professionals and wrestlers. **b** an athlete of this weight. **3** a person of little influence or significance.

light-year *n.* **1** the distance light travels in one mean solar year, approximately 9.46×10^{12} km (5.88×10^{12} miles). **2** (in *pl.*) a long distance or great amount.

lignin /'lɪgnɪn/ *n.* a complex organic polymer deposited in the cell walls of many plants making them rigid and woody.

lignite /'lɪgnaɪt/ *n.* a soft brown coal showing traces of plant structure, intermediate between bituminous coal and peat.

likable *var. of* LIKEABLE.

like¹ ● *adj.* (often governing a noun as if a transitive participle such as *resembling*) (**more like**, **most like**) having some or all of the qualities of another or each other or an original; alike (*in like manner; is very like her brother*). ● *prep.* **1** resembling in some way, such as; in the same class as (*good writers like Dickens*). ¶When *like* means 'such as', some people prefer *such as* to be used in formal contexts when more than one example is mentioned, e.g. *good writers such as Dickens, Shakespeare, and Hardy.* **2** (usu. in pairs correlatively) as one is so will the other be (*like mother, like daughter*). **3** characteristic of (*it is not like them to be late*). **4** in a suitable state or mood for (doing or having something) (*felt like working; felt like a cup of tea*). **5** in the manner of; to the same degree as (*acted like an idiot*). ● *adv.* **1** *slang* so to speak (*like, I'm no Shakespeare*). **2** *informal* likely, probably (*as like as not*). ● *conj. informal disputed* **1** as (*cannot do it like you do*). **2** as if (*ate like they were starving*). ¶The use of *like* as a conjunction, e.g. *He did it like he'd never done it before*, is very common, esp.

in spoken English. However, there is a long tradition of opposition to this usage, and it is therefore best avoided in formal contexts by using instead *as* or *as if*. ● *n.* **1** a counterpart; an equal; a similar person or thing (*shall not see its like again*). **2** (prec. by *the*) a thing or things of the same kind (*never did the like again*). □ **and the like** and similar things; et cetera (*music, painting, and the like*). **be nothing like** be in no way similar or comparable or adequate. **like** (or **as like**) **as not** *informal* probably. **like so** *informal* like this; in this manner. **the likes of** *informal* a person such as. **more like it** *informal* nearer what is required. **of like** (or **of a like**) **mind** = LIKE-MINDED. **what is he** (or **she** or **it** etc.) **like?** what sort of characteristics does he (or she, or it, etc.) have?

like² ● *v.* **1** *tr.* **a** find agreeable or enjoyable or satisfactory (*like reading; like to dance*). **b** be fond of (a person). **2** *tr.* **a** choose to have; prefer (*like my coffee black; do not like such things discussed*). **b** wish for or be inclined to (*would like a cup of tea; would like to come*). **3** *tr.* (usu. in *interrog.*; prec. by *how*) feel about; regard (*how would you like it if it happened to you?*). **4** *intr.* feel inclined; choose (*we could go out if you like*). ● *n.* (in *pl.*) the things one likes or prefers. □ **like it or not** *informal* whether it is acceptable or not.

-like *comb. form* forming adjectives from nouns, meaning 'similar to, characteristic of' (*doglike; shell-like; tortoise-like*).

likeable *adj.* pleasant; easy to like. □ **likeability** *n.* **likeableness** *n.* **likeably** *adv.*

likelihood *n.* probability; the quality or fact of being likely. □ **in all likelihood** very probably.

likely ● *adj.* **1** probable; such as well might happen or be true (*it is not likely that they will come; the most likely place is Saskatoon*). **2** (foll. by *to* + infin.) to be reasonably expected (*he is not likely to come now*). **3** promising; apparently suitable (*this is a likely spot*). ● *adv.* probably (*is very likely true*). ¶Although some people consider it incorrect, use of the adverb *likely* without a qualifying adverb such as *more*, *most*, or *very* is common among educated speakers. □ **as likely as not** probably. **not likely** *informal* certainly not. □ **likeliness** *n.*

like-minded *adj.* having the same tastes, opinions, etc. □ **like-mindedly** *adv.* **like-mindedness** *n.*

liken *v.tr.* (foll. by *to*) represent as similar; point out the resemblance of (a person or thing to another).

likeness *n.* **1** (foll. by *between*, *to*) resemblance. **2** (foll. by *of*) a semblance or guise (*in the likeness of a ghost*). **3** a portrait or representation (*is a good likeness*).

likewise *adv.* **1** moreover, too. **2** similarly (*do likewise*).

liking *n.* **1** what one likes; one's taste (*is it to your liking?*). **2** (foll. by *for*) regard or fondness; taste or fancy (*had a liking for toffee*).

li'l /lɪl/ *adj. informal jocular* little.

lilac /'laɪlək, -lɒk, -læk/ ● *n.* **1** any shrub or small tree of the genus *Syringa*, esp. *S. vulgaris* with fragrant purple, pink, or white blossoms. **2** a pale pinkish-violet colour. **3** the scent of lilac. ● *adj.* of this colour.

Lilliputian /,lɪlɪ'pjuːʃən/ ● *n.* a diminutive person or thing. ● *adj.* **1** tiny, diminutive. **2** of petty mind or character.

Lillooet /'lɪloːet/ *n.* **1** a member of an Aboriginal people living in southwestern BC, northeast of Vancouver. **2** the Salishan language of this people.

lilt ● *n.* **1** a light springing rhythm or gait. **2** a characteristic rising and falling cadence or inflection (of a voice, accent, music, etc.). ● *v.intr.* (esp. as **lilting** *adj.*) move or speak etc. with a lilt (*a lilting melody*).

lily *n.* (*pl.* **-ies**) **1** any bulbous plant of the genus *Lilium* with large trumpet-shaped often spotted flowers on a tall slender stem, e.g. the tiger lily. **2** any of several other plants of the lily family with similar flowers, e.g. the day lily. **3** the water lily. □ **lily-like** *adj.*

lily-livered *adj.* cowardly.

lily of the valley *n.* (*pl.* **lilies of the valley**) any plant of the genus *Convallaria*, with oval leaves and racemes of white bell-shaped fragrant flowers.

lily pad *n.* a floating leaf of a water lily.

lily-white *adj.* **1** as white as a lily. **2** faultless. **3** in favour of, committed to, or pertaining to a policy excluding non-whites.

lima bean /ˈlaimə/ *n.* **1** a tropical American bean plant, *Phaseolus limensis*, having large flat white edible seeds. **2** the seed of this plant.

limb ● *n.* **1** a projecting part of a person's or animal's body such as an arm, leg, or wing. **2** a large branch of a tree. **3** a projecting part of a thing, e.g. the branch of a cross. **4** a section, element, or component part of something. ● *v.tr.* remove branches from (a tree). □ **out on a limb** alone; without supporters. **tear limb from limb** violently dismember. □ **limbed** *adj.* (also in *comb.*). **limbless** *adj.*

limber ● *adj.* **1** lithe, agile, nimble. **2** flexible. ● *v.* (usu. foll. by *up*) **1** *tr.* make (oneself or a part of the body etc.) supple. **2** *intr.* warm up in preparation for athletic etc. activity. □ **limberness** *n.*

limbic /ˈlɪmbɪk/ *adj.* of or relating to a part of the brain concerned with basic emotions and instinctive actions.

limbo¹ *n.* (*pl.* **-os**) **1** (in some Christian beliefs) the supposed abode of the souls of unbaptized infants, and of the just who died before Christ. **2** an intermediate state or condition of awaiting a decision etc. **3** prison, confinement. **4** a state of neglect or oblivion.

limbo² *n.* (*pl.* **-os**) a W Indian dance in which the dancer bends backwards to pass under a horizontal bar which is progressively lowered to a position just above the ground.

Limburger /ˈlɪm,bɜrgər/ *n.* a soft white cheese with a characteristic strong smell.

lime¹ ● *n.* **1** (in full **quicklime**) a white caustic alkaline substance obtained by heating limestone and used for making mortar or as a fertilizer or bleach etc. **2** a white substance (calcium hydroxide) made by adding water to quicklime, used esp. in cement. **3** calcium or calcium salts, esp. calcium carbonate in soil etc. ● *v.tr.* treat (wood, skins, land, etc.) with lime. □ **limy** *adj.* (**-ier, -iest**).

lime² ● *n.* **1 a** a rounded citrus fruit like a lemon but greener, smaller, and more acid. **b** (in full **lime tree**) the tree, *Citrus aurantifolia*, bearing this. **2** (in full **lime juice**) the juice of limes, used in drinks and cooking. **3** (also **lime green**) a bright pale green colour. ● *adj.* (**lime-green**) of this colour.

lime³ *n.* **1** (in full **lime tree**) any ornamental tree of the genus *Tilia*, esp. *T. europaea* with heart-shaped leaves and fragrant yellow blossoms. **2** its wood.

limelight *n.* **1** an intense white light used formerly in theatres. **2** (prec. by *the*) the full glare of publicity; the focus of attention.

limerick /ˈlɪmərɪk/ *n.* a humorous or comic form of five-line poem with a rhyme scheme *aabba*.

limestone *n.* a sedimentary rock composed mainly of calcium carbonate, used as building material and in the making of cement.

Limey *N Amer. slang offensive* ● *n.* (*pl.* **-eys**) a British person or ship. ● *adj.* British.

liminal /ˈlɪmɪnəl/ *adj.* **1 a** of or relating to a transitional or initial stage. **b** marginal, insignificant. **2** occupying a position on, or on both sides of, a boundary or threshold. □ **liminality** *n.*

limit ● *n.* **1** a point, line, or level beyond which something does not or may not extend or pass. **2** (often in *pl.*) the boundary of an area. **3** *Cdn Forestry* an area of forested land in which an individual or company has the right to fell and remove timber. **4** the greatest or smallest amount permissible or possible (*lower limit*). ● *v.tr.* (**limited, limiting**) **1** set or serve as a limit to. **2** (foll. by *to*) restrict. □ **be the limit** *informal* be intolerable or extremely irritating. **go (to) the limit** behave in an extreme way. **2** allow sexual intercourse. **off limits** out of bounds; forbidden. **within limits** to a moderate extent. **without limit** with no restriction. □ **limitable** *adj.* **limiting** *adj.*

limitation *n.* **1** the act or an instance of limiting; the process of being limited. **2** (often in *pl.*) a condition of limited ability (*know one's limitations*). **3** (often in *pl.*) a limiting rule or circumstance (*has its limitations*). **4** a legally specified period beyond which an action cannot be brought, or a property right is not to continue.

limited *adj.* **1** confined within limits. **2** not great in scope or talents (*has limited experience*). **3 a** few, scanty, restricted (*a limited budget*). **b** restricted to a few examples (*limited printing*). **4** (**Limited**) *Cdn & Brit.* (after a company name) being a limited company. **5** (of a monarchy, government, etc.) exercised under limitations of power prescribed by a constitution. **6** *N Amer.* (of a train, bus, etc.) making few stops; express.

limited company *n.* (also **limited liability company**) *Cdn & Brit.* a company whose owners are legally responsible only to a limited amount for its debts.

limited edition *n.* an edition of a book, or reproduction of an object, limited to some specific number of copies.

limited liability *n. Cdn & Brit.* the status of being legally responsible only to a limited amount for debts of a trading company.

limited partnership *n.* a partnership in which the liability of some partners is legally limited to the extent of their investment. □ **limited partner** *n.*

limiter *n.* **1** a person or thing that limits something. **2** *Electronics* a device whose output is restricted to a certain range of values irrespective of the size of the input.

limitless *adj.* **1** extending or going on indefinitely (*a limitless expanse*). **2** unlimited (*limitless generosity*). □ **limitlessly** *adv.* **limitlessness** *n.*

limn /lɪm/ *v.tr.* **1** paint or draw (a picture or portrait); portray (a subject). **2** portray or represent (esp. a person) in words. □ **limner** /ˈlɪmnər/ *n.*

limo *n.* (*pl.* **-os**) *informal* a limousine.

Limousin /liːmuːˈzæ̃/ *n.* a breed of red beef cattle.

limousine /ˌlɪməˈziːn, ˈlɪmə,ziːn/ *n.* **1** a large luxurious automobile, often with a partition behind the driver. **2** *N Amer.* a large sedan or minibus for carrying people over a fixed route to and from an airport etc.

limp¹ ● *v.intr.* **1** walk lamely. **2** (of a damaged ship, aircraft, etc.) proceed with difficulty. **3** (of a business, an event, etc.) progress slowly or weakly (*the company limped along for years*). ● *n.* a lame walk.

limp² *adj.* **1** not stiff or firm; easily bent. **2** without energy or will. □ **limply** *adv.* **limpness** *n.*

limpet /ˈlɪmpət/ *n.* **1** any of various marine gastropod molluscs, esp. the common limpet *Patella vulgata*, with a shallow conical shell and a broad muscular foot that sticks tightly to rocks. **2** a clinging person.

limpid /ˈlɪmpɪd/ *adj.* **1** (of water, eyes, etc.) clear, transparent. **2** (of writing) clear and easily comprehended. **3** calm, tranquil. □ **limpidity** n. **limpidly** adv. **limpidness** n.

LINC /lɪŋk/ abbr. Cdn Language Instruction for Newcomers to Canada.

linchpin /'lɪntʃpɪn/ n. **1** a pin passed through the end of an axle to keep a wheel in position. **2** a person or thing vital to an enterprise, organization, etc.

lindane /'lɪndeɪn/ n. Chem. a toxic colourless isomer of benzene hexachloride used as an insecticide.

linden /'lɪndən/ n. a basswood tree.

lindy (in full **lindy hop**) ● n. a dance originating as a form of the jitterbug among blacks in Harlem, New York. ● v.intr. dance the lindy.

line¹ ● n. **1** a continuous mark or band made on a surface (drew a line). **2** use of lines in art, esp. engraving etc. (boldness of line). **3** a thing resembling such a mark, e.g. a furrow or wrinkle. **4** Music **a** each of (usu. five) horizontal marks forming a staff in musical notation. **b** a sequence of notes or tones forming an instrumental or vocal melody. **5 a** a straight or curved continuous extent of length without breadth. **b** the track of a moving point. **6 a** a contour or outline, esp. as a feature of design (the ship's lines). **b** a facial feature (the cruel line of his mouth). **7 a** (on a map or graph) a curve connecting all points having a specified common property. **b** (**the Line**) the Equator. **8 a** a real or notional limit or boundary (town line). **b** a border, esp. the border between Canada and the US. **c** a mark limiting or dividing the area of play, the starting or finishing point in a race, etc. **d** the boundary between a credit and a debit in an account. **9 a** a row of persons or things. **b** a direction as indicated by them (line of march). **c** N Amer. a row or sequence of people, vehicles, etc. awaiting their turn to be attended to or to proceed. **10 a** a row of printed or written words. **b** a portion of verse written in one line. **11** (in pl.) **a** a piece of poetry. **b** the words of an actor's part. **c** a specified amount of text etc. to be written out as a school punishment. **12** a short letter or note (drop me a line). **13 a** a length of cord, rope, wire, etc., usu. serving a specified purpose, esp. a fishing line or clothesline. **b** a pipe, conduit, etc. through which a substance is conveyed (fuel line). **14 a** a wire or cable for a telephone or telegraph. **b** a connection by means of this (am trying to get a line). **c** an individual telephone number or extension (she's on the other line; a toll-free line). **d** a wire or cable serving as a conductor of electric current (hydro lines). **15 a** a single track of a railway. **b** one branch or route of a railway system, or the whole system under one management. **c** a bus route. **16 a** a regular succession of buses, ships, aircraft, etc., plying between certain places. **b** a company conducting this (shipping line). **17** a connected series of persons following one another in time (esp. several generations of a family); stock, succession (a long line of craftsmen; next in line to the throne). **18 a** a course or manner of procedure, conduct, thought, etc. (along these lines; don't take that line with me). **b** policy (the party line). **c** conformity (bring them into line). **19** a direction, course, or channel (lines of communication). **20** a department of activity; a branch of business (not in my line). **21** a class of commercial goods (a new line in hats). **22** informal **a** a false or exaggerated account or story (gave me a line about missing the bus). **b** a piece of information (I've got a line on a job). **c** an utterance, esp. when rehearsed (my opening line). **23** a sequence of events in a story etc. (plot line). **24 a** a connected series of military fieldworks, defences, etc. (behind enemy lines). **b** an arrangement of soldiers or ships side by side; a line of battle. **c** the fighting forces of an army or navy (excluding auxiliary forces). **25** each of the very narrow horizontal sections forming a television picture. **26** a narrow range of the spectrum that is noticeably brighter or darker than the adjacent parts. **27** the level of the base of most letters in printing and writing. **28** (as a measure) one twelfth of an inch. **29** an assembly line. **30** a dose of cocaine laid out in a line for snorting. **31** Football **a** = LINE OF SCRIMMAGE. **b** either of the two front rows of opposing players facing each other on the line of scrimmage. **32** Hockey & Lacrosse a shift of players, esp. the three forwards. **33** Cdn (esp. Ont) = CONCESSION 4b. **34** a series of traps for catching game. ● v. **1** tr. mark with lines. **2** tr. cover with lines (a face lined with pain). **3** tr. & intr. position or stand at intervals along (crowds lined the route). **4** tr. delineate, sketch. **5** tr. & intr. Baseball hit (a ball) straight and low above the ground; play (a shot) as a line drive. **6** tr. & intr. N Amer. guide or control (a boat or canoe) from the bank or shore of a stretch of inland water by means of a rope or ropes. □ **all along the line** at every point. **bring into line** make conform. **come into line** conform. **end of the line 1** the point at which further effort is unproductive or one can go no further. **2** the terminus of a rail, subway, or bus route. **get a line on** informal learn something about. **in line 1** arranged or standing in a line. **2** under control. **in line for** likely to receive. **in the line of** in the course of (esp. duty). **in** (or **out of**) **line with** in (or not in) accordance with. **keep in line** control (kept me in line). **lay** (or **put**) **it on the line 1** speak frankly. **2** pay money. **line up 1** arrange or be arranged in a line or lines. **2** have ready; organize (had a job lined up). **on the line 1** at risk (put my reputation on the line). **2** speaking on the telephone. **3** immediately; at the time of the transaction (pay cash on the line). **out of line 1** not in alignment; discordant. **2** failing to conform to a rule or convention; behaving inappropriately.

line² v.tr. **1 a** cover the inside surface of (a garment, box, etc.) with a layer of usu. different material. **b** serve as a lining for. **2** cover as if with a lining (shelves lined with books). **3** fill, esp. plentifully. □ **line one's pocket** make money, usu. by corrupt means.

lineage /'lɪniɪdʒ/ n. lineal descent; ancestry.

lineal /'lɪniəl/ adj. **1** in the direct line of descent or ancestry. **2** linear; of or in lines. □ **lineally** adv.

linear /'lɪniɜr/ adj. **1 a** of or in lines; in lines rather than masses (linear development). **b** of length (linear extent). **2** long and narrow and of uniform breadth. **3** involving one dimension only. **4** progressing in a single series of steps or stages; sequential (linear thinking). □ **linearity** /-'erɪti/ n. **linearize** /'lɪniəraɪz/ v.tr. **linearly** adv.

Linear B n. a form of Bronze Age writing found in Crete and parts of Greece and recording a form of Mycenaean Greek: an earlier undeciphered form (**Linear A**) also exists.

linear equation n. an equation between two variables that, plotted on a graph, gives a straight line.

linear measure n. a measure of length (metres, miles, etc.).

linebacker n. Football a player or position just behind the defensive line.

line dancing n. a type of country-and-western dancing in which dancers line up in a row without partners and follow a choreographed pattern of steps to music. □ **line dance** n. & v.intr. **line dancer** n.

line drawing *n.* a drawing in which images are produced from variations of lines.

line drive *n. Baseball* a ball hit straight and low above the ground.

lineman *n.* (*pl.* **-men**) **1 a** a person who repairs and maintains telephone or electrical etc. lines. **b** a person who tests the safety of railway lines. **2** *Football* a centre, guard, tackle, or end.

linemate *n. Hockey* a player who plays on the same line as another.

linen /'lɪnɪn/ ● *n.* **1 a** cloth woven from flax. **b** a particular kind of such cloth. **2** (*collect.*) articles made or originally made of linen, cotton, etc., as sheets, cloths, shirts, undergarments, etc. ● *adj.* made of linen or flax (*linen cloth*). ☐ **wash** (or **air**) **one's dirty linen in public** be indiscreet about one's domestic quarrels etc.

linen closet *n.* (also **linen cupboard**) a closet for bed and table linen, towels, etc.

line of credit *n.* an amount of credit extended to a borrower.

line of defence *n.* a strategy or argument for protecting one's position, opinion, etc.

line of fire *n.* **1** the expected path of gunfire, a missile, etc. **2** the intended direction of criticism, controversy, etc.

line of scrimmage *n. Football* the imaginary line separating two teams at the beginning of a scrimmage.

line of sight *n.* a straight line along which an observer has unobstructed vision or along which radio waves etc. may be transmitted directly.

line of vision *n.* the straight line along which an observer looks.

line printer *n.* a machine that prints output from a computer a line at a time rather than character by character.

liner¹ *n.* **1** a ship or aircraft etc. carrying passengers on a regular line. **2** = EYELINER. **3** = LINE DRIVE.

liner² *n.* **1** a lining in an appliance, device, or container, esp. a removable one. **2** a lining of a garment, esp. one made of a synthetic fibre.

linerboard *n.* a paperboard used as a facing on fibreboard.

liner notes *n.pl.* explanatory text about a record, cassette, etc., appearing on the cover or included inside the package.

linesman *n.* (*pl.* **-men**) **1** *Hockey* an on-ice official whose tasks include making offside and icing calls, breaking up fights, etc. **2** (in games played on a field or court) an umpire's or referee's assistant who decides whether a ball falls within the playing area or not. **3** *Football* an official who marks the distances won or lost on each play.

lineup *n.* **1** a line of people formed for a particular reason, e.g. to buy tickets etc. **2** the personnel or configuration of persons on a team, in a musical group, etc. **3** (in police work) a line of persons from whom a suspect is to be identified. **4** a schedule of television programs, events, etc. **5** a line of items or services offered by a company.

ling *n.* **1** any of several long slender predatory fishes of the cod family of the genus *Molva*, esp. *M. molva*, an important food fish found chiefly in the E Atlantic. **2** a burbot.

ling cod *n.* a large food fish, *Ophiodon elongatus*, found in the N Pacific.

linger *v.intr.* **1 a** be slow or reluctant to depart. **b** stay about. **c** (foll. by *over*, *on*, etc.) dally (*lingered over dinner*). **2** (foll. by *on*) (of an action or condition) be protracted; drag on (*the memory lingers on*). **3** (foll. by *on*) (of a dying person or custom) be slow in dying; drag on feebly. ☐ **lingerer** *n.* **lingeringly** *adv.*

lingerie /lɔ̃ʒə'reɪ, lā-, -ri:/ *n.* women's underwear and nightclothes.

lingo *n.* (*pl.* **-os** or **-oes**) *informal* **1** the vocabulary of a special subject or group of people. **2** a foreign language.

lingonberry /'lɪŋɡənberi/ *n.* (*pl.* **-ies**) **1** the cowberry, *Vaccinium vitis-idaea*, of northern regions, esp. typically in Scandinavia, where the berries are used in cooking. **2** an Arctic variety of this occurring in the former USSR and N America.

lingua franca /ˌlɪŋɡwə 'fræŋkə/ *n.* (*pl.* **lingua francas**) **1** a language adopted as a common language between speakers whose native languages are different. **2** a system of communication providing mutual understanding.

lingual /'lɪŋɡwəl/ *adj.* **1** of or formed by the tongue. **2** of speech or languages. ☐ **lingually** *adv.*

linguine /lɪŋ'ɡwiːni/ *n.pl.* (also **linguini**) pasta in the form of narrow ribbons.

linguist /'lɪŋɡwɪst/ *n.* a person skilled in languages or linguistics.

linguistic *adj.* of or relating to language or the study of languages. ☐ **linguistically** *adv.*

linguistics *n.* the scientific study of language and its structure.

liniment /'lɪnəmənt/ *n.* a medicated lotion, usu. made with oil, for rubbing onto the body to relieve pain.

lining *n.* **1** a layer of material used to line a surface etc. **2** an inside layer or surface etc. (*stomach lining*). **3** the technique of guiding or controlling a canoe or boat from the bank or shore of a stretch of inland water by means of a rope or ropes.

link ● *n.* **1** one loop or ring of a chain etc. **2 a** a connecting part, esp. a thing or person that unites or provides continuity; one in a series. **b** a state or means of connection. **c** an instruction or code that serves as a connection between two parts of a computer program, or between consecutive elements of a computerized list. **3** a means of contact by radio, telephone, television, or computer between two points. **4** a means of travel or transport between two places (*a link to the mainland*). **5** = CUFFLINK. **6** a measure equal to one-hundredth of a surveying chain (20.12 cm or 7.92 inches). **7** (usu. in *pl.*) any of the divisions of a chain of sausages. ● *v.* **1** *tr.* (foll. by *together*, *to*, *with*) connect or join (two things or one to another). **2** *tr.* (foll by. *to*, *with*) connect causally, associate in speech, thought, etc. (*many diseases have been linked to smoking*) **3** *tr.* clasp or intertwine (hands or arms). **4** *intr.* (foll. by *on*, *to*, *in to*) be joined; attach oneself to (a system, company, etc.). ☐ **link up** (foll. by *with*) connect or combine. ☐ **linker** *n.*

linkage *n.* **1** the action of linking; a link or system of links. **2** the linking of different issues in political negotiations. **3** an assembly of interconnected rods for transmitting or controlling the motion of a mechanism.

links *n.pl.* (treated as *sing.* or *pl.*) a golf course, esp. one having undulating ground, coarse grass, etc.

link-up *n.* an act or result of linking up.

linoleic acid /lɪnoː'liːɪk, -/ *n.* a polyunsaturated fatty acid occurring as a glyceride in linseed and other oils and essential in the human diet.

linolenic acid /lɪnoː'lenɪk, -'liːnɪk/ *n.* a polyunsaturated fatty acid (with one more double bond than linoleic acid) occurring as a glyceride in linseed and other oils and essential in the human diet.

linoleum /lɪˈnoːlɪəm/ n. a material consisting of a canvas backing thickly coated with a preparation of linseed oil and powdered cork etc., used esp. as a floor covering. □ **linoleumed** adj.

linseed n. the seed of flax.

linseed oil n. oil extracted from linseed and used in paint and varnish.

lint n. **1** tiny threads or fibres of fabric; fluff. **2** a soft material used esp. for dressing wounds, originally made by ravelling or scraping linen cloth. **3** an accumulation of dirt, dead skin cells, etc. in the navel. □ **linty** adj.

lintel n. a horizontal supporting piece of timber, stone, etc., across the top of a door or window.

Linux /ˈlɪnəks, ˈlaɪnəks, ˈliːnəks/ n. Computing a freely available Unix-like operating system.

liny adj. (**-ier, -iest**) marked with lines; wrinkled.

lion n. **1** a large flesh-eating cat, *Panthera leo*, of Africa and S Asia, with a tawny coat and, in the male, a flowing shaggy mane. **2** a brave or celebrated person. **3** (**Lion**) a member of a Lions Club. □ **lion-like** adj.

lioness n. **1** a female lion. **2** (**Lioness**) a member of a Lioness Club.

Lioness Club n. a women's service club, affiliated with the Lions Club.

lionize v.tr. treat as a celebrity. □ **lionization** n.

Lions Club n. any of numerous associated clubs devoted to social and international service, the first of which was founded in Chicago in 1917.

lion's share n. the largest or best part.

lip ● n. **1 a** either of the two fleshy parts forming the edges of the mouth. **b** a thing resembling these. **c** = LABIUM. **2 a** the edge of a cup, vessel, etc., esp. the part shaped for pouring from. **b** the edge of an opening or cavity, e.g. of a canyon, the crater of a volcano, etc. **3** informal impudent talk (*that's enough of your lip!*). ● v.tr. (**lipped, lipping**) **1 a** touch with the lips; apply the lips to. **b** touch lightly. **2** informal insult, abuse; be impudent to (someone). □ **bite one's lip** repress an emotion; stifle laughter, a retort, etc. **curl one's lip** express scorn. **pass a person's lips** be eaten, drunk, spoken, etc. **smack one's lips** open and close the lips noisily in relish or anticipation, esp. of food. □ **lipless** adj. **liplike** adj. **lipped** adj.

lip balm n. a greasy or waxy preparation, usu. in stick form, to prevent or relieve chapped lips.

lip gloss n. a glossy cosmetic applied to the lips.

lipid /ˈlɪpɪd/ n. any of a group of organic compounds that are insoluble in water but soluble in organic solvents, including fatty acids, oils, waxes, etc.

Lipizzaner var. of LIPPIZANER.

lipliner n. a cosmetic applied as a line around the lips, to accentuate them and keep lipstick from bleeding.

lipoprotein /ˌlɪpoʊˈproʊtiːn, ˌlaɪ-/ n. Biochem. any of a group of soluble proteins that combine with and transport fat or other lipids in the blood plasma.

liposome /ˈlɪpoʊˌsoʊm, ˈlaɪ-, -pə-/ n. Biochem. a minute artificial spherical sac usu. of a phospholipid membrane enclosing an aqueous core, esp. used to carry drugs to specific tissues.

liposuction /ˈlɪpoʊˌsʌkʃən, ˈlaɪ-/ n. a technique in cosmetic surgery for removing excess fat from under the skin by suction.

Lippizaner /ˌlɪpɪtˈsænər/ n. (also **Lippizan**) a breed of white horse used esp. in displays of dressage.

lippy adj. (**-ier, -iest**) informal **1** insolent, impertinent. **2** having large lips.

lip-read v. intr. (past and past part. **-read** /-red/) (esp. of a deaf person) understand (speech) entirely from observing a speaker's lip movements. □ **lip-reader** n. **lip-reading** n.

lip service n. an insincere expression of support etc.

lip-smacking adj. **1** (of food etc.) delicious. **2** tantalizing; tempting.

lipstick n. a small stick of cosmetic for colouring the lips, usu. a shade of red or pink. □ **lipsticked** adj.

lipstick lesbian n. informal a lesbian of glamorous or manifestly feminine appearance.

lip-synch (also **lip-sync**) ● n. (in film acting etc.) the movement of a performer's lips in sychronization with a pre-recorded soundtrack. ● v.tr. & intr. perform (esp. a song) on film using this technique. □ **lip-syncher** n. **lip-synching** n.

liquefy /ˈlɪkwəˌfaɪ/ v.tr. & intr. (**-ies, -ied**) make or become liquid. □ **liquefaction** /-ˈfækʃən/ n. **liquefiable** adj. **liquefier** n.

liqueur /lɪˈkjɜr, -kjʊr/ n. any of several strong sweet alcoholic spirits, variously flavoured, usu. drunk after a meal.

liquid ● adj. **1** (of a material substance) having a consistency like that of water or oil, flowing freely but of constant volume. **2** (of light, fire, the eyes, etc.) like water in appearance; clear, bright, translucent (*a liquid lustre*). **3** (of a gas, e.g. oxygen) reduced to a liquid state by intense cold or high pressure. **4 a** (of sounds) clear and pure; harmonious, fluent. **b** (of movement) unconstrained. **5 a** (of assets) easily converted into cash. **b** having ready cash or liquid assets (*prompting investors to stay liquid*). **6** not fixed; fluid (*liquid opinions*). ● n. **1** a liquid substance. **2** (usu. in pl.) liquid food. □ **liquidly** adv. **liquidity** adj.

liquidate v. **1 a** tr. wind up the affairs of (a company or firm) by ascertaining liabilities and apportioning assets. **b** intr. (of a company) be liquidated, go into liquidation. **2** tr. clear or pay off (a debt). **3** tr. put an end to or get rid of (esp. by violent means); kill.

liquidation n. **1 a** the process of liquidating a company etc. **b** the state or condition of being wound up. **2** the action or process of abolishing or eliminating something or someone, esp. the doing away with or killing of unwanted people. □ **go into liquidation** (of a company etc.) be wound up and have its assets apportioned.

liquidator n. **1** a person called in to wind up the affairs of a company etc. **2** a person who implements a policy of liquidation.

liquid crystal n. a substance that flows like a liquid but has some degree of ordering in the arrangement of its molecules.

liquid crystal display n. a form of visual display in electronic devices, esp. of segmented numbers or letters, in which liquid crystals are made visible by temporarily modifying their capacity to reflect light.

liquidity /lɪˈkwɪdɪti/ n. (pl. **-ies**) **1** the state of being liquid. **2** availability of liquid assets.

liquid measure n. a unit for expressing the volume of liquids.

liquify var. of LIQUEFY.

liquor /ˈlɪkər/ ● n. **1** an alcoholic drink, esp. produced by distillation. **2** a liquid of a particular kind used or produced in a chemical or industrial process etc. **3** other liquid, esp. that produced in cooking. **4** Pharm. a solution of a specified drug in water. ● v.tr. **1** slang (usu. foll. by up; usu. in passive) cause to drink alcoholic liquor. **2** steep (malt etc.) in water.

liquor commission n. Cdn **1** (in the territories and certain provinces) a regulatory body controlling the sale and distribution of alcoholic beverages. **2** a liquor store operated by this body. Abbr.: **LC**.

liquor control board n. (also **liquor board**) Cdn (in certain provinces) a regulatory body controlling the sale and distribution of alcoholic beverages.

liquorice var. of LICORICE.

liquor licence n. a permanent licence allowing the sale and serving of liquor for consumption in a restaurant, bar, etc.

liquor permit n. a temporary, special-occasion permit allowing the sale or consumption of liquor in a place not generally open to the public.

LIRA /'li:rə/ abbr. Cdn LOCKED-IN RETIREMENT ACCOUNT.

lira /'li:rə/ n. (pl. **lire** /'li:re, 'li:ri/) **1** the chief monetary unit of Italy, used also in San Marino and the Vatican City. **2** the chief monetary unit of Turkey.

LISP /lɪsp/ abbr. Computing a high-level programming language devised for list processing.

lisp ● n. **1 a** a speech defect in which s is pronounced like th in thick and z is pronounced like th in this. **b** the action or act of lisping; a lisping pronunciation. **2** a sound resembling a lisp, e.g. the rippling of waters, rustling of leaves, etc. ● v. intr. & tr. speak or utter with a lisp. □ **lisper** n. **lisping** adj. & n.

list¹ ● n. **1** a number of connected items, names, etc., written or printed together usu. consecutively to form a record or aid to memory (shopping list). **2 a** a catalogue of the titles of books published, or to be published, by a particular publisher. **b** the books in such a catalogue collectively (Oxford has a very strong fall list). **3** Computing a formalized representation of the concept of a list, used for the storage of data or in list processing. **4** (in pl.) **a** a palisades enclosing an area for a tournament. **b** the scene of a contest. **5** LIST PRICE. ● v. **1** tr. make a list of. **2** tr. **a** enter in a list. **b** include as if in a list or catalogue; report, mention. **3** tr. N Amer. **a** place (a property) in the hands of a real estate agent for sale or rent. **b** add to the list or properties advertised by a real estate agent. **4** tr. enter (a name and address) in a telephone directory. **5** tr. Computing display or print out (the contents of a file etc.). **6** tr. (usu. in passive) approve (securities etc.) for dealings on a stock exchange. **7** intr. (usu. foll. by at, for) be specified in a price list (the fishing reel lists at $4.95). □ **enter the lists** issue or accept a challenge. □ **lister** n.

list² ● v. intr. **1** (of a ship etc.) lean over to one side, esp. owing to a leak or shifting cargo (compare HEEL²). **2** (of a building etc.) lean over, tilt. ● n. the process or an instance of listing.

listed adj. **1** included in a list, directory, or catalogue. **2** (of securities etc.) approved for dealings on a stock exchange.

listen ● v. intr. **1 a** make an effort to hear something. **b** pay attention to (a person speaking or an utterance). **2** (foll. by to) **a** give attention with the ear (listened to my story). **b** pay heed, respond, or yield to advice, a request, etc. (listen to your mother). **3** (also **listen out**) (often foll. by for) be eager or make a careful effort to catch the sound of. ● n. an act or instance of listening. □ **listen in 1** listen secretly to or tap a private communication by telephone etc. **2** listen to a broadcast radio program etc. **3** listen to the conversation of others, often covertly and usu. without contributing. **listen up** esp. N Amer. informal pay attention.

listenable adj. easy or pleasant to listen to. □ **listenability** n.

listener n. **1** a person who listens. **2** a person receiving broadcast radio programs.

listening n. **1** in senses of LISTEN. **2** (with qualifying adj.) broadcast, recorded, or other matter for listening to, esp. with reference to its quality or kind (easy listening).

listening post n. **1 a** a point near an enemy's lines for detecting movements by sound. **b** a station for intercepting electronic communications. **2** a place for the gathering of information from reports etc.

listeria /lɪ'stɪːrɪə/ n. any motile rod-like bacterium of the genus Listeria, esp. L. monocytogenes infecting humans and animals eating contaminated food.

listeriosis /lɪ,stiːrɪ'oːsɪs/ n. infection with, or a disease caused by, listerias.

listing¹ n. **1** a list or catalogue (see LIST¹ 1). **2 a** the drawing up of a list. **b** an entry in a catalogue, telephone directory, or other list. **3** N Amer. **a** the placing of a property on the list of a real estate agent. **b** a real estate agent's register of properties available for sale. **c** a property so listed. **4** Computing a printed or displayed copy of a program or the contents of a file.

listing² adj. (of a ship etc.) inclining to one side.

listless adj. lacking energy or enthusiasm; disinclined for exertion. □ **listlessly** adv. **listlessness** n.

list price n. the price shown for an article in a printed list issued by the maker, or by the general body of makers of the particular class of goods.

list processing n. Computing the manipulation and use of chained lists and of data in them.

listserv /'lɪstsɜːrv/ n. Computing an e-mail system which automatically sends messages to all subscribers on specific mailing lists, in special interest groups, etc.

lit¹ past and past part. of LIGHT¹, LIGHT².

lit² n. informal literature.

lit. abbr. **1** literary. **2** literature.

litany /'lɪtəni/ n. (pl. **-ies**) **1** a series of petitions for use in church services or processions, usu. recited by the clergy and responded to in a recurring formula by the people. **2 a** a continuous repetition or long enumeration; a repeated formula. **b** a tedious recital (a litany of woes).

litchi var. of LYCHEE.

lit crit n. literary criticism.

lite ● adj. **1** (also proprietary **Lite**) applied to low-fat or low-sugar versions of manufactured food or drink products, esp. to low-calorie beer. **2** N Amer. informal lacking in substance; facile, over-simplified. ● n. **1** (also proprietary **Lite**) a light beer with relatively few calories. **2** a light, esp. a courtesy light in a motor vehicle. **3** a pane of glass, esp. in a door.

liter esp. US var. of LITRE.

literacy n. **1** the ability to read and write. **2** competence in some field of knowledge, technology, etc. (computer literacy).

literal adj. **1** taking words in their usual or primary sense without metaphor or allegory (literal interpretation). **2 a** (of a translation, version, transcript, etc.) following the letter, text, or exact or original words. **b** (of a representation in art or literature) exactly copied, true to life, realistic. **3** (in full **literal-minded**) (of a person) apt to take what is spoken or written at face value, missing irony, humorous exaggeration, etc.; matter of fact. **4 a** without metaphor, exaggeration, or inaccuracy (the literal truth). **b** so called without exaggeration (a literal extermination). **5** informal disputed (as an intensifier) so called with some exaggeration or using metaphor (a literal avalanche of mail). ¶The use of literal and literally simply as intensifiers is better avoided in writing or formal speech. **6** of, in, or expressed by a letter or the letters of the alphabet. ☐ **literalize** v.tr. **literally** adv. **literalness** n.

literalism n. **1** insistence on a literal interpretation; adherence to the letter. **2** literal representation in art or literature. ☐ **literalist** n. **literalistic** adj.

literary adj. **1** of, constituting, or occupied with books or literature or written composition, esp. of the kind valued for quality of form. **2** well informed about literature. **3** (of a word or idiom) used chiefly in literary works or other formal writing. **4** (of painting, sculpture, etc.) depicting or representing a story. ☐ **literarily** adv. **literariness** n.

literary criticism n. the art or practice of estimating the qualities and character of literary works. ☐ **literary critic** n. **literary-critical** adj.

literary device n. = DEVICE 4.

literary history n. **1** a history of the major literary traditions, movements, works, and authors of a country, region, etc. **2** the history of the treatment of, and references to, a specified subject in literature, e.g. a legend, historical person, event, etc.

literate ● adj. **1** able to read and write. **2 a** well-read, cultured. **b** educated. **3** competent or well-versed in a specified area (computer literate). **4** (of a text etc.) lucid, articulate, polished. ● n. a literate person.

literati /ˌlɪtəˈrɒti/ n.pl. educated and intelligent people who produce or are well-versed in literature.

literature n. **1** written works, esp. those whose value lies in beauty of language or in emotional effect. **2** literary work or production as a whole. **3** the body of writings produced in a particular country or period. **4** printed matter, leaflets, etc. **5** the material in print on a particular subject.

lithe /laɪð/ adj. **1** moving or bending easily and gracefully; supple. **2** gracefully slim and muscled. ☐ **lithely** adv. **litheness** n.

lithium /ˈlɪθɪəm/ n. a soft silver-white metallic element, the lightest metal, used in alloys and in batteries.

litho /ˈlaɪθəʊ/ informal ● n. **1** = LITHOGRAPHY. **2** = LITHOGRAPH. ● v.tr. (**-oes**, **-oed**) produce by lithography.

lithograph /ˈlɪθəˌɡræf/ ● n. a lithographic print. ● v.tr. print by lithography.

lithography /lɪˈθɒɡrəfi/ n. (pl. **-ies**) a process of obtaining prints from a stone or metal surface so treated that what is to be printed can be inked but the remaining area rejects ink. ☐ **lithographer** n. **lithographic** adj. **lithographically** adv.

lithosphere /ˈlɪθəˌsfɪːr/ n. the rigid outer portion of the earth including the crust and the outermost mantle. ☐ **lithospheric** /-ˈsferɪr/ adj.

Lithuanian /ˌlɪθuːˈeɪnɪən, ˌlɪθjuː-/ ● n. **1 a** a native or inhabitant of Lithuania, a country on the shore of the Baltic Sea. **b** a person of Lithuanian descent. **2** the language of Lithuania. ● adj. of or relating to Lithuania or its people or language.

litigant /ˈlɪtɪɡənt/ ● n. a party to a lawsuit. ● adj. engaged in a lawsuit.

litigate /ˈlɪtɪˌɡeɪt/ v. **1** intr. take a claim or dispute to a law court; be a party to a lawsuit. **2** tr. contest (a point) in a lawsuit.

litigation n. **1** the action or process of carrying on a lawsuit. **2** an instance of legal proceedings.

litigator n. esp. N Amer. a person who litigates, esp. a trial lawyer.

litigious /lɪˈtɪdʒəs/ adj. **1** fond of or given to litigation or carrying on lawsuits, esp. unreasonably so. **2** disputable in a law court; liable to become the subject of a lawsuit. **3** of or pertaining to lawsuits. ☐ **litigiously** adv. **litigiousness** n.

litmus /ˈlɪtməs/ n. a dye obtained from lichens that is red under acid conditions and blue under alkaline conditions.

litmus paper n. a paper stained with litmus to be used as a test for acids or alkalis.

litmus test n. **1** informal a circumstance, phenomenon, question, etc., one's reaction to which serves to establish decisively the true character of an individual etc. **2** a test for acids or alkalis using litmus paper.

litre /ˈliːtər/ n. (also esp. US **liter**) a metric unit of capacity, formerly defined as the volume of one kilogram of water under standard conditions, now equal to 1 cubic decimetre (about 35 oz.).

Litt.D. abbr. Doctor of Letters.

litter ● n. **1 a** garbage discarded in an open or public place. **b** odds and ends lying about. **c** (attrib.) for disposing of litter (litter bin). **2** a state of untidiness, disorderly accumulation of papers etc. **3** a group of young mammalian animals comprising all those born at one birth. **4** decomposing but still recognizable vegetable debris from plants etc. forming a distinct layer above the soil, esp. in a forest. **5** esp. hist. a vehicle containing a couch shut in by curtains and carried on men's shoulders or by beasts of burden. **6** a stretcher or portable bed for transporting the sick and wounded. **7 a** straw, rushes, etc., as bedding, esp. for animals. **b** straw and dung in a farmyard. **8** = CAT LITTER. ● v. **1 a** tr. make (a place) untidy with litter. **b** intr. leave paper, garbage, etc. lying about, esp. in a public place. **2** tr. **a** scatter (paper etc.) untidily and leave lying about. **b** (of things) lie about untidily on (old car parts littered the premises). **3** tr. (of an animal) give birth to (whelps etc.). **4** tr. (often foll. by down) **a** provide (a horse etc.) with litter as bedding. **b** spread litter or straw on (a floor) or in (a stable). ☐ **litterer** n.

littérateur /ˌlɪtərəˈtɜːr/ n. a literary person.

litter box n. a tray for cat litter.

litterbug n. a person who carelessly leaves litter in a public place.

little ● adj. (**littler**, **littlest**; **less** or **lesser**; **least**) **1 a** (of a material object, immaterial thing, area of space, etc.) small in size, amount, degree, etc.; not large, great, or big. **b** often used to convey affectionate or emotional overtones, or condescension, not implied by small (a silly little fool). **2 a** (of a person) short in stature. **b** of short distance or duration (wait a little while). **3** (prec. by a) of something though small amount of (a little cream). **4** trivial; relatively unimportant (exaggerates every little difficulty). **5** not much; inconsiderable (gained little advantage from it). **6** operating on a small scale (the little store owner). **7** as a distinctive epithet: **a** of a smaller or the smallest size of the things or the class specified (little finger). **b** that is the smaller or smallest of the name, type, or kind (little auk). **c** (of a town, district, etc.) less large or important, later established, or suggestive of another or others of that name (Little Italy). **8** young or younger (a little boy; my little sister). **9** (of a collective unity) having few members, small in number (a little group of students). **10** as of a child, evoking tenderness, condescension, amusement, etc. (we know their little ways). **11** mean, paltry, contemptible (you little sneak). ● n. **1** not much; only a small amount (got very little out of it). **2** (usu. prec. by a) **a** a certain but no great amount (knows a little of everything). **b** a short time or distance (after a little). ● adv. (**less**, **least**) **1 a** to a small extent only (little-known authors; is little more than speculation). **b** infrequently, rarely. **2** (prec. by a) somewhat (is a little deaf). **3** not at all; hardly (they little thought). ☐ **a little 1** to a little or slight extent. **2** for or at a short time or distance. **little by little** by degrees; gradually. **little or nothing** hardly anything. **no little** considerable, a good deal of (*took no little trouble over it*). **not a little 1** much; a great deal. **2** extremely (*not a little concerned*). **quite a little** a lot, much, considerably.

little auk n. a small Arctic auk, *Alle alle*.

little-bitty adj. N Amer. informal very small; tiny.

little black book n. a record or list of information, esp. of names and addresses of sexual partners.

little boys' room n. jocular a men's washroom.

little finger n. the smallest finger, at the outer end of the hand.

little girls' room n. jocular a women's washroom.

little guy n. N Amer. (prec. by the) the common person, esp. weak or unimportant in contrast to the wealthy and powerful.

little ice age n. any period of comparatively cold climate occurring outside the major glacial periods, esp. (**Little Ice Age**) such a period which reached its peak in the 17th c.

little known adj. (hyphenated when attrib.) not widely known; obscure.

Little League n. N Amer. a baseball league for children between the ages 8 and 12.

little man n. esp. jocular **1** the average 'man in the street'. **2** a person working or producing on a small scale. **3** (as a form of address) a boy.

littleneck n. (in full **littleneck clam**) a small variety of quahog.

little ones n.pl. young children or animals.

little people n.pl. **1** fairies, elves, leprechauns, etc. **2** the poor, ordinary people. **3** children.

little red schoolhouse n. N Amer. **1** a one-room schoolhouse, esp. one of red brick, of a design that was typical throughout N America, esp. in rural areas, from the 19th to the mid-20th c. **2** (prec. by the) this as a symbol of old-fashioned educational practice, with all grades taught in the same room, emphasis on basics, rote learning, etc.

little theatre n. a small playhouse, esp. one used for experimental drama or for community, non-commercial productions.

little toe n. the outermost and smallest toe.

little woman n. informal offensive (prec. by the) one's wife.

littoral /ˈlɪtərəl/ • adj. **1** of or on the shore of the sea, a lake, etc. **2** = INTERTIDAL. • n. a region lying along a shore.

liturgical /lɪˈtɜːdʒɪkəl/ adj. of or related to liturgies or public religious worship. □ **liturgically** adv.

liturgy /ˈlɪtɜːdʒi/ n. (pl. **-ies**) **1 a** a public worship, esp. in accordance with a prescribed form. **b** a collection of set forms for the conducting of divine services. **2** the Communion office of the Orthodox Church.

livable adj. **1** (of a house, room, climate, etc.) fit to live in. **2** (of a life) bearable; worth living. **3** (of a person) companionable; easy to live with. □ **livability** n. **livableness** n.

live¹ /lɪv/ v. **1** intr. be alive; have animal or vegetable life. **2** intr. (foll. by on) subsist or feed (*lives on fruit*). **3** intr. (foll. by on, off) depend on for a livelihood or subsistence (*lives on income from investments*). **4** intr. (foll. by on, by) sustain one's position or repute (*live on their reputation*). **5** tr. **a** spend, pass, experience (*lived a happy life*). **b** express in one's life (*lives her faith*). **6** intr. conduct oneself in a specified way, esp. with reference to moral behaviour, personal aims or principles, etc. (*lived in a state of anxiety*). **7** intr. arrange one's

habits, expenditure, feeding, etc. (*live modestly*). **8** intr. **a** make or have one's abode (*lived in Brandon*). **b** informal (of an inanimate object) have as its usual storage place (*where does the kettle live?*). **9** intr. (foll. by in) spend much non-working time, the daytime, etc. (*the room didn't seem to be lived in*). **10** intr. **a** (of a person etc.) continue in life, have one's life prolonged. **b** (of a thing, experience, etc.) continue in actuality (*the horrors of war live on*). **c** (of a thing, experience, etc.) continue in memory, escape obliteration or oblivion (*ideals live on*). **11** intr. enjoy life intensely or to the full (*you haven't lived till you've seen it*). □ **live and breathe** be utterly absorbed or consumed by (an interest). **live and learn** expressing surprise at some new or unexpected information. **live and let live** be tolerant towards others of different opinions, lifestyles, etc. **live dangerously** take risks habitually. **live down** (usu. with neg.) cause (past guilt, embarrassment, etc.) to be forgotten by different conduct over a period of time (*you'll never live that down!*). **live for** regard as the aim or purpose of one's life (*she lives for her work*). **live in** (of a domestic employee, student, etc.) reside on the premises of one's work, school, etc. **live in hope** remain hopeful. **live in the past** behave as though circumstances, values, etc. have not changed from what they were previously. **live it up** informal pursue pleasure, live extravagantly. **live off the land** subsist on the produce of the land. **live one's own life** follow one's own plans or principles; live independently. **live out 1** spend the rest of (one's life) (*will I live out my days as a lexicographer?*). **2** experience or execute in reality (one's fantasies, ideas, etc.). **3** (of a domestic employee etc.) reside away from one's place of work. **live through** survive; remain alive at the end of. **live to** survive and reach (*lived to a great age*). **live together** (esp. of an unmarried couple) share a home and have a sexual relationship. **live up to 1** honour or fulfill; put into practice (principles etc.). **2** reach and maintain an expected standard, either good or bad. **live well 1** thrive, survive. **2** have plenty; be in comfortable circumstances. **3** live a virtuous, satisfying life. **live with 1** share a home with. **2** share a home and have a sexual relationship with. **3** tolerate; endure. **live with oneself** retain one's self-respect. **long live ...!** an exclamation of support, loyalty, or endorsement (to a person etc. specified). **where one lives** N Amer. at, to, or in the right, vital, or most vulnerable spot (*hits me where I live*).

live² /laɪv/ • adj. **1 a** (attrib.) that is alive; living. **b** actual, genuine (*real live musicians*). **2 a** (of a broadcast) heard or seen at the time of its performance, not from a recording. **b** (of a recording, film, etc.) made of a live performance. **c** taking place concurrently (*live telephone bidding*). **3 a** (of a person etc.) lively, alert, energetic; full of life. **b** (of a question, issue, etc.) of current interest, not obsolete or exhausted. **4** Sport **a** (of a ball in baseball, football, etc.) in play. **b** (of a tennis ball etc.) having ample bounce or rebound. **5** expending or still able to expend energy in various forms, esp.: **a** (of coals) glowing, burning. **b** (of a shell) unexploded and capable of exploding. **c** (of a cartridge) containing a bullet; not a blank. **d** (of a wire etc.) connected to a source of electrical power. **e** (of a microphone) switched on, receptive to sound. **6 a** (of a volcano) not extinct. **b** (of a mineral or rock) still forming part of the earth's mass. **7** (of a room, auditorium, etc.) having a relatively long reverberation time. **8** (of a vaccine) containing living but weakened disease-causing micro-organisms. • adv. in order to make a live broadcast; as a live performance (*going over live now to the House of Commons*). □ **go live** *Computing* (of a system) become operational. □ **liveness** *n.*

liveable *var. of* LIVABLE.

live-aboard ● *n.* **1** a yacht etc. equipped with basic facilities for daily, and often year-round, living. **2** a person who lives on a yacht etc. ● *adj.* (of a yacht etc.) equipped with the necessary facilities for daily living.

live action *n.* (often *attrib.*) *Film* action involving real people or animals, as opposed to animation etc.

live bait *n.* a living worm, small fish, etc. used as bait.

live birth *n.* a birth in which the child is born alive.

lived-in *adj.* **1** (of a room etc.) showing signs of habitation. **2** *informal* (of a face) marked by experience.

live-in ● *attrib.adj.* **1** (of a sexual partner) cohabiting. **2** (of a domestic employee etc.) residing on the premises of one's work. ● *n.* a live-in employee, lover, etc.

livelihood /ˈlaivli,hʊd/ *n.* a way of earning a living; an occupation.

livelong /ˈlɪvlɒŋ/ *adj.* in its entire length or apparently so (*the livelong day*).

lively /ˈlaivli/ *adj.* (**-ier, -iest**) **1** full of life; vigorous, energetic. **2** brisk (*a lively pace*; *a lively tune*). **3** vivid, stimulating (*a lively discussion*; *a lively imagination*). **4** (of a person, group, etc.) vivacious, jolly, sociable. **5** *jocular* exciting, dangerous, difficult (*the press is making things lively for them*). **6** (of a colour) bright and vivid. **7 a** (of an image, picture, etc.) lifelike, realistic, animated (*a lively description*). **b** (of feelings, impressions, memories, etc.) strong, intense, striking. **8** (of a narrative) full of action and incident. **9** (of food) tasty, esp. spicy. □ **step** (or **look**) **lively** move (more) quickly or energetically. □ **livelily** *adv.* **liveliness** *n.*

liven *v.tr. & intr.* (usu. foll. by *up*) *informal* **1** make or become more lively. **2** cheer; brighten.

live-out *adj.* (of a domestic employee etc.) residing away from one's place of work.

liver¹ *n.* **1 a** a large, lobed, glandular organ in the abdomen of vertebrates, functioning in many metabolic processes including the regulation of toxic materials in the blood, secreting bile, etc. **b** a similar organ in other animals. **2** the flesh of an animal's liver as food. **3** a dark reddish brown.

liver² *n.* a person who lives in a specified way (*a clean liver*).

liver spots *n.pl.* brown spots or patches of melanin on the skin, characteristic of any of several medical conditions. □ **liverspotted** *adj.*

liverwurst /ˈlɪvərwɜrst/ *n.* (also **liver sausage**) *N Amer.* a cooked sausage having a high proportion of esp. pork liver.

livery /ˈlɪvəri/ *n.* (pl. **-ies**) **1** a distinctive uniform worn by servants in a particular household etc. **2** a distinctive guise, marking, or outward appearance (*birds in their winter livery*). **3** an emblem, device, or distinctive colour scheme on a vehicle, product, etc. indicating its owner or manufacturer. **4** *N Amer.* a place where horses can be hired. □ **liveried** *adj.* (esp. in senses 1, 3).

livery stable *n.* (also **livery barn**) a stable where horses are kept for their owners in return for payment, or from which horses may be rented.

lives *pl. of* LIFE.

livestock /ˈlaivstɒk/ *n.* (usu. treated as *pl.*) animals kept esp. on a farm for use or profit, e.g. cattle etc.

live trap ● *n.* a box-like trap for catching esp. wild animals alive and without hurting them. ● *v.tr.* (**live-trap**) catch (an animal) in such a trap for relocation, ear tagging, etc.

livewell *n.* a tub-like container of water in a fishing boat, often aerated and sunk flush with the deck, in which caught fish are kept alive and fresh.

live wire *n.* **1** an energetic and forceful person. **2** a wire conveying an electric current.

liveyer *Cdn* (*Nfld*) *var. of* LIVYER.

livid /ˈlɪvɪd/ *adj.* **1** *informal* furiously angry. **2** *disputed* of an intense reddish colour. ¶This sense is contrary to the word's original meaning and is therefore often regarded as incorrect. It is, however, widely used. **3 a** of a bluish leaden colour. **b** discoloured as by a bruise. □ **lividity** *n.* **lividly** *adv.*

living ● *n.* **1 a** a means of keeping alive or living in a certain style (*made my living as a journalist*). **b** a way of earning this (*what does she do for a living?*). **2** the action of leading one's life in a particular moral, physical, etc. manner. **3** (prec. by *the*; treated as *pl.*) those who are alive. ● *adj.* **1 a** that lives or has life; not dead or extinct. **b** contemporary; now existent (*the greatest living poet*). **2** (of a likeness or image of a person) exact. **3** (of a language) still in vernacular use. **4** (of water) perennially flowing. **5** (of rock etc.) = LIVE² 6b. **6** *informal* complete, entire (*scared the living daylights out of him*). □ **within living memory** within the memory of people still living.

living area *n.* an area in a room or house for general use during the day.

living colour *n.* vivid or true-to-life colour.

living fossil *n.* a plant or animal that has survived relatively unchanged since the extinction of others of its group, known only as fossils.

living legend *n.* a person widely celebrated, while still alive, as very famous (or notorious) in a particular field.

living museum *n.* (also **living history museum**) **1** a historic site, or a recreation of one, at which historical interpreters dress in period costume, perform period-specific tasks and trades, etc. **2** a site in which flora etc. no longer usu. found elsewhere is preserved in its natural state.

living room *n.* a room in a private home for general use during the daytime.

living space *n.* **1** an area in a room or house for general use during the day. **2** space for accommodation.

living standard *n.* the level of consumption in terms of food, clothing, services, etc. estimated for a person, group, or nation.

living wage *n.* the lowest wage on which a person can afford a reasonable standard of living without undue hardship.

living will *n.* a written declaration, morally though in many jurisdictions not legally binding, by a person setting out the circumstances in which artificial means of maintaining his or her life should be withdrawn.

livre /ˈliːvrə/ *n.* an old French monetary unit, worth one pound of silver.

livyer /ˈlɪvjər/ *n. Cdn* (*Nfld*) a resident or permanent settler in Newfoundland or Labrador.

lizard *n.* **1** any reptile of the suborder Lacertilia, having usu. a long body and tail, four legs, movable eyelids, and a rough or scaly hide. **2** leather made from lizard skin.

ll. *abbr.* lines (in references).

'll *v.* **1** (usu. after pronouns) shall, will (*I'll*; *that'll*). **2** *informal* (usu. after verbs) till (*wait'll they see me!*).

llama /'læmə/ *n.* **1** a S American ruminant, *Lama glama*, kept as a beast of burden and for its soft woolly fleece. **2** the wool from this animal, or cloth made from it.

LL.B. *abbr.* Bachelor of Laws.

LLBO *abbr. Cdn* Liquor Licence Board of Ontario.

LL.D. *abbr.* Doctor of Laws.

LL.M. *abbr.* Master of Laws.

LNG *abbr.* liquefied natural gas.

lo[1] *interj. archaic* or *jocular* calling attention to an amazing sight. □ **lo and behold** a formula introducing a surprising or unexpected fact.

lo[2] *adj.* low, used esp. in advertising etc. *(lo-cal).*

load ● *n.* **1 a** a thing that is being carried or to be carried, esp. if heavy. **b** (often in *comb.*) an amount usu. or actually carried, esp. by a specified vehicle *(busload; truckload).* **2 a** the quantity of a particular substance which it is customary to load at one time. **b** a unit of measure or weight based on this. **3 a** a burden of care, grief, affliction, etc. **b** an amount of work, teaching, responsibility, etc. to be done or borne by a person. **4** *informal* **a** (in *pl.*; often foll. by *of*) plenty; a lot. **b** a quantity of *(a load of nonsense).* **5 a** the amount of electric power that a generating system is delivering or required to deliver at any moment. **b** the amount of power supplied by a generating system at any given time. **c** an impedance or circuit that receives or develops the output of a transistor or other device. **6** the weight or force borne by the supporting part of a structure. **7** a material object or force which acts or is conceived as a weight, clog, etc. **8** the resistance of machinery to motive power. **9** a quantity of items washed or to be washed in a washing machine or dishwasher at one time. **10** the charge of a firearm. **11** a commission charged on the purchase of mutual funds. ● *v.* **1** *tr.* **a** put a load on or aboard (a person, vehicle, ship, etc.). **b** place (a load or cargo) aboard a ship, on a vehicle, etc. **2** *intr.* (often foll. by *up*) **a** (of a ship, vehicle, or person) take a load aboard, pick up a load. **b** (of a vehicle) fill with passengers. **3** *tr.* (often foll. by *with*) **a** add weight to; be a weight or burden upon *(a stomach loaded with food).* **b** oppress with affliction, responsibility, etc. **4** *tr.* strain the bearing capacity of *(a table loaded with food).* **5** *tr.* (also **load up**) (foll. by *with*) **a** supply overwhelmingly *(loaded us with work).* **b** assail overwhelmingly *(loaded us with abuse).* **6** *tr. & intr.* put a charge of ammunition into (a firearm). **7** *tr.* **a** insert a photographic film or plate in (a camera). **b** insert (a film) into a camera. **8** *tr.* transfer (a program or data) into memory, or into the central processing unit from a more remote part of memory. **9** *tr. Electricity* provide with a load consisting of any kind of impedance. **10** *tr.* add an extra charge to (an insurance premium) in the case of a poorer risk. **11** *tr.* give a bias to (dice, a roulette wheel, etc.) with weights. **12** *tr.* place items for washing in (a washing machine or dishwasher). □ **a load off one's mind** (or **back** etc.) a source of anxiety removed. **get a load of** *slang* listen attentively to; notice. **load the bases** *Baseball* place baserunners on all three bases. **take a load off (one's feet)** *informal* sit or lie down; take the body's weight off the feet. □ **loadable** *adj.*

load-bearing *adj.* (of a wall, beam, etc.) supporting much of the weight of a structure.

loaded *adj.* **1** bearing or carrying a load. **2** *slang* **a** wealthy. **b** drunk. **c** *N Amer.* drugged. **3** (of dice etc.) weighted or given a bias. **4** (of a question or statement) charged with some hidden or improper implication. **5** *N. Amer. informal* (of a car etc.) equipped with optional extras. □ **loaded for bear** *slang* fully

prepared, esp. for a fight, challenge, or confrontation.

loader *n.* **1 a** a machine or device for loading things. **b** = FRONT-END LOADER. **2** *Computing* a program which controls the loading of other programs. **3** (in *comb.*) a gun, machine, vessel, etc. that is loaded in a specified way. □ **-loading** *adj.* (in *comb.*) (in sense 3).

loading *n.* **1 a** the act of one who loads. **b** the load or cargo of a vehicle, vessel, etc. **2** *Electricity* the maximum current or power taken by an appliance. **3** an increase in an insurance premium due to a factor increasing the risk involved (*see* LOAD *v.* 10). **4** *Archit. & Engin.* the loads collectively that act on a structure or part of one. **5** *Psych.* the extent to which a factor or variable contributes to or is correlated with some resultant quality or overall situation, usu. represented by a number arrived at by statistical analysis of test results. **6 a** the use of some added material for the purpose of adulteration or falsification. **b** the substance added. **7** *informal* massive consumption of a particular substance etc. to enhance one's performance *(carbo-loading).*

loading dock *n. N Amer.* a raised platform, e.g. at a warehouse etc., from which trucks or railway cars are loaded or unloaded.

load line *n.* a marking on a ship's side showing the limit of legal submersion under various conditions.

loaf[1] *n.* (*pl.* **loaves**) **1** a portion of baked bread, usu. of a standard size or shape. **2** a quantity of other food formed into a particular, usu. oblong shape (*meat loaf*). **3** (in full **loaf cake**) a plain cake, usu. including fruit or nuts, baked in an oblong shape. □ **half a loaf is better than none** (or **no bread**) **1** having to accept less than one expects or feels entitled to is better than having nothing at all. **2** it is better to compromise in one's demands than to risk losing all.

loaf[2] *v.* **1** *intr.* (often foll. by *about, around*) spend time idly; hang about. **2** *tr.* (foll. by *away*) waste (time) idly *(loafed away the morning).* **3** *intr.* saunter.

loafer *n.* **1** an idle person. **2** (**Loafer**) *proprietary* a leather shoe shaped like a moccasin with a flat heel.

loafing *n.* (*attrib.*) designating a barn or part of one or an outdoor area in which cattle etc. are allowed to roam freely, rather than being tied, penned, or at pasture *(loafing barn).*

loam *n.* **1** a fertile soil of clay and sand containing decayed vegetable matter. **2** a paste of clay and water with sand, chopped straw, etc., used in making bricks, plastering, etc. □ **loamy** *adj.* **loaminess** *n.*

loan ● *n.* **1** something lent, esp. a sum of money to be returned, normally with interest. **2** the act of lending or state of being lent. **3** a word, custom, etc., adopted by one people from another. ● *v.tr.* lend (esp. money). □ **on loan** acquired or given as a loan.

loaner *n.* **1** a car, computer, etc. lent to a customer while the customer's is kept for repair or service (also *attrib.: loaner car*). **2** a lender.

loan shark *n. informal* a person who lends money at exorbitant rates of interest. □ **loansharking** *n.*

loan word *n.* a word adopted, usu. with little modification, from a foreign language.

loath /loʊθ/ *predic.adj.* disinclined, reluctant, unwilling *(was loath to admit it).*

loathe /loʊð/ *v.tr.* regard with disgust; detest. □ **loather** *n.* **loathing** *n.*

loathsome /'loʊðsəm, 'loʊθ-/ *adj.* arousing hatred or disgust; offensive, repulsive. □ **loathsomely** *adv.* **loathsomeness** *n.*

loaves *pl.* of LOAF[1].

LOB *abbr. Baseball* left on base.

lob ● *v.tr.* (**lobbed, lobbing**) **1** hit or throw (a ball etc.) slowly or in a high arc. **2** fire (a rocket or other missile) in a high arc. **3** send (an opponent) a lobbed ball. **4** direct (questions, insults, accusations, etc.) at a person. ● *n.* **1 a** a ball struck in a high arc. **b** a stroke producing this result. **2** *Cdn* (also **lob ball**) a question that is easy to answer, esp. one that is made intentionally so in order to make the respondent look competent, articulate, etc.

lobate /ˈloːbeit/ *adj.* *Biol.* having a lobe or lobes; lobed.

lobby ● *n.* (*pl.* **-ies**) **1** a usu. large area inside the main entrance of a public building leading to other rooms, or to the auditorium in a theatre etc. **2 a** a body of persons seeking to influence legislators on behalf of a particular interest (*the anti-abortion lobby*). **b** an organized attempt by members of the public to influence legislators. **3** (also **division lobby**) each of two areas on either side of the Commons chamber in which MPs may relax or discuss party strategy and in which they assemble before a vote. ● *v.* (**-ies, -ied**) **1** *tr.* solicit the support of (an influential person). **2 a** *tr.* (of members of the public) seek to influence (the members of a legislature). **b** *intr.* attempt to persuade a politician to support or oppose changes in the law (*fishermen lobbying for higher quotas*). □ **lobbying** *n.* & *adj.* **lobbyist** *n.*

lobe *n.* **1** a roundish and flattish projecting or pendulous part, often each of two or more such parts divided by a fissure (*lobes of the brain*). **2** = EARLOBE. □ **lobed** *adj.*

lobelia /ləˈbiːliə/ *n.* any plant of the genus *Lobelia*, with blue, scarlet, white, or purple flowers having a deeply cleft corolla.

Lobo /ˈloːboː/ *n.* *N Amer.* a large, yellow-green eating apple with red streaks.

lobotomize /ləˈbɒtəmaiz/ *v.tr.* **1** perform a lobotomy on. **2** (usu. as **lobotomized** *adj.*) make (a person) apathetic or zombie-like.

lobotomy /ləˈbɒtəmi/ *n.* (*pl.* **-ies**) *Surgery* **1** surgical incision into a lobe, esp. the prefrontal lobe of the brain, formerly used to treat intractable psychiatric disorders. **2** an instance of this.

lobster (*pl.* **-s** or same) ● *n.* **1** any large marine crustacean of the family Nephropidae, with stalked eyes and two pincer-like claws as the first pair of ten limbs. **2** its flesh as food. ● *v.intr.* catch lobsters. □ **lobstering** *n.*

lobster boat *n.* a boat used in lobster fishing, with a well in which to keep the lobsters alive.

lobsterman *n.* (*pl.* **-men**) *N Amer.* a person who traps lobsters for a living.

lobster pot *n.* a device for trapping lobsters, esp. one made of wooden slats.

lobster pound *n.* a place where lobsters trapped during the season are kept alive until they are sold and shipped.

lobster roll *n.* *N Amer.* (*Maritimes & New England*) a long bread roll stuffed with lobster salad, usu. including celery, sweet peppers, sour cream, basil, etc.

lobster supper *n.* *Cdn* (*Maritimes*) a meal, usu. served in a community hall, featuring boiled lobster, salads, bread rolls, clam chowder, and cake or pie.

lobster thermidor /ˈθɜːrmɪdɔːr/ *n.* a mixture of lobster meat, mushrooms, cream, egg yolks, and sherry, cooked in a lobster shell.

local ● *adj.* **1** belonging to, existing in, or pertaining to a particular locality as opposed to the country as a whole. **2** limited, peculiar to, or only encountered in a particular place or places. **3 a** of or belonging to the neighbourhood (*the local doctor*). **b** (of a train, bus, etc.) serving a particular district or stopping at all or most stations or stops on the line or route. **4** of or affecting a part and not the whole, esp. of the body (*local pain*; *a local anaesthetic*). **5** (of a telephone call) to a nearby place and not subject to long-distance charges. ● *n.* **1** an inhabitant of a particular place regarded with reference to that place. **2** a local train, bus, etc. **3** *N Amer.* a local branch of a trade union. **4** a local anaesthetic. □ **locally** *adv.* **localness** *n.*

local area network *n.* a computer network in which computers in close proximity are able to communicate with each other and share resources.

local bus *n.* **1** a bus service operating over short distances. **2** a computer connection from a microprocessor to an adjacent peripheral device such as a video system, allowing rapid transmission of data.

local colour *n.* **1** the detailed representation of the characteristic features of a place or period in order to convey a sense of actuality. **2** such features themselves in real life; picturesque qualities.

locale /loːˈkæl/ *n.* a scene or locality, esp. with reference to an event etc. taking place there.

local government *n.* **1** a system of administration of a city, municipality, etc. by the elected representatives of those who live there. **2** a governing body, e.g. a council, in such a system.

localism *n.* **1** preference for what is local. **2** a local idiom, custom, etc. **3 a** attachment to a locality, esp. to the place where one lives. **b** a limitation of ideas, sympathies, and interests resulting from such attachment.

locality *n.* (*pl.* **-ies**) **1** an area or district considered as the site occupied by certain people or things or as the scene of certain activities; a neighbourhood. **2** the site or scene of something, esp. in relation to its surroundings. **3** the situation or position of an object, esp. the geographical place or situation of a plant, mineral, etc.

localize *v.* **1 a** *tr.* restrict or assign to a particular place. **b** *Med.* *intr.* (foll. by *in*) (of a disease or causative agent of disease) be confined to (a specified area of the body). **2** *tr.* invest with the characteristics of a particular place. **3** *tr.* attach to districts; decentralize. □ **localizable** *adj.* **localization** *n.* **localized** *adj.* **localizer** *n.*

local municipality *n.* *Cdn* (*Ont. & Que.*) = URBAN MUNICIPALITY.

local paper *n.* a newspaper distributed only in a certain area and usu. featuring local news.

local talent *n.* the singers, artists, etc. from a given city, region, etc.

local time *n.* **1** the time as reckoned in a particular place. **2** time measured from the sun's transit over the meridian of a place.

locate *v.* **1** *tr.* discover the exact place or position of (*locate the enemy's camp*). **2** *tr.* establish in a place or in its proper place. **3** *tr.* state the locality of. **4** *tr.* (in *passive*) be situated. **5** *intr.* (often foll. by *in*) *N Amer.* take up residence or business (in a place). □ **locator** *n.*

location *n.* **1** a particular place; the place or position in which a person or thing is. **2** the act of locating or process of being located. **3** an actual place or natural setting featured in a film or broadcast, as distinct from a simulation in a studio (*filmed on location*). **4** *Computing* = ADDRESS 1c, 1d. □ **locational** *adj.*

location ticket *n.* *Cdn hist.* a certificate entitling a settler to take possession of a piece of land as a homestead, but not conveying legal title.

loc. cit. *abbr.* in the passage already cited.

loch /lɒk, lɒx/ *n. Scot.* **1** a lake. **2** an arm of the sea, esp. when narrow or partially landlocked.

loci¹ *pl. of* LOCUS.

loci² /ˈloːkiː/ *n.* (also **locie**) *Cdn informal* an engine used in logging or mining.

lock¹ ● *n.* **1** a device for fastening a door, lid, etc., which can only be opened by means of a key, combination, code, etc. **2** a confined section of a canal or river where the level can be changed for raising and lowering boats between adjacent sections by the use of gates and sluices. **3 a** the turning of the front wheels of a vehicle to change its direction of motion. **b** the maximum extent of this. **4** an interlocked or jammed state. **5** *Wrestling* a hold that keeps an opponent's limb fixed. **6** an appliance to keep a wheel from revolving or slewing. **7** a mechanism for exploding the charge of a gun. **8** = AIRLOCK 2. **9** *N Amer. informal* a sure thing; a person or thing that is certain to succeed (*she is a lock to win the election*). ● *v.* **1 a** *tr.* fasten with a lock. **b** *intr.* (of a door, window, box, etc.) have the means of being locked. **2** *tr.* (foll. by *up*, *in*, *into*) enclose (a person or thing) by locking or as if by locking. **3** *tr.* (often foll. by *up*, *away*) store or allocate inaccessibly (*capital locked up in land*). **4** *tr. & intr.* make or become rigidly fixed or immovable. **5** *intr. & tr.* become or cause to become jammed or caught. **6** *tr.* (often in *passive*; foll. by *in*) entangle in an embrace or struggle. **7** *intr.* interlace or intertwine (*the protesters locked arms*). **8** *intr.* go through a lock on a canal etc. □ **lock down** *N Amer.* subject (a prisoner or prisoners) to a lockdown. **have a lock on** *N Amer. informal* have an unbreakable hold on or total control over (*she has a lock on her seat in the legislature*). **lock horns** come into conflict; engage in an argument. **be locked into** be irrevocably committed to (*am locked into going to this stupid party*). **lock in 1** (usu. in *passive*) convert (a mortgage) from a floating to a fixed rate of interest. **2** (of an investor) be unable to sell or convert (investments). **3** fix (a pension, investment, etc.) so that it cannot be transferred or sold. **lock on to** locate or cause to locate by radar, a heat-seeking device, etc., and then track. **lock oneself out** accidentally prevent oneself from entering a place, esp. by losing the key or locking it inside (*locked myself out of my car*). **lock out 1** keep (a person) out by locking the door. **2** (of an employer) submit (employees) to a lockout. **lock up 1** shut and secure (esp. a building) by locking (*I'll lock up*). **2** imprison (*locked up for life*). **3** commit to a psychiatric institution. **4** (of a computer or computer screen) cease to respond to input from the keyboard or mouse. **5** (esp. of a turning object) cease to move; seize (*slammed on the brakes and her wheels locked up*). **6** store; hold in reserve (*Canada's forests lock up huge amounts of carbon*). **7** *N Amer.* have complete control of; be assured of success in (*her party has locked up Ontario*). **under lock and key** securely locked up. □ **lockable** *adj.* **lockless** *adj.*

lock² *n.* **1 a** a portion of hair that coils or hangs together. **b** (in *pl.*) the hair of the head. **2** a tuft of wool or cotton. □ **-locked** *adj.* (in *comb.*).

lockdown *n. N Amer.* the confining of prisoners to their cells, esp. to gain control during a riot etc.

locked-in retirement account *n. Cdn* a retirement savings account created with money transferred out of a registered pension plan and from which funds can only be transferred to a life income fund, a locked-in retirement income fund, or a life annuity. Abbr.: **LIRA**.

locked-in retirement income fund *n. Cdn* a tax-sheltered savings plan which provides retirement income. Abbr.: **LRIF**.

locker *n.* **1** a small lockable cupboard or compartment, esp. one of several in a school, bus station, locker room, etc. **2** *Naut.* a chest or compartment for clothes, stores, ammunition, etc. **3** a person or thing that locks.

locker room ● *n.* a change room at a swimming pool, fitness club, etc., with lockers for storing one's clothes etc. ● *adj.* (usu. **locker-room**) (of language etc.) characteristic of or suited for a men's locker room; coarse, ribald (*locker-room humour*).

locket *n.* a small ornamental case holding a portrait, lock of hair, etc., and usu. hung from the neck.

lockjaw *n.* a variety of tetanus with sustained contractions of the jaw muscles causing the mouth to remain tightly closed.

lockout *n.* the exclusion of employees by their employer from their place of work until certain terms are agreed to.

locksmith *n.* a person who makes, repairs, and replaces locks. □ **locksmithing** *n.*

lockstep ● *n.* marching with each person as close as possible to the one in front. ● *adj.* (usu. **lock-step**) rigid; inflexible. □ **in lockstep** exactly parallel; in exact synchronism.

lock, stock, and barrel ● *n.* the whole of a thing. ● *adv.* completely.

lock-up *n.* **1** *informal* = JAIL *n.* 1. **2** *Cdn* a type of press conference where members of the media are allowed to examine a government budget in a locked room before it is brought down in the legislature, but are not allowed to leave the room or file any reports until the budget is officially brought down. **3 a** the locking up of premises for the night. **b** the time of doing this. **4 a** the unrealizable state of invested capital. **b** an amount of capital locked up.

loco¹ *n.* (*pl.* **-os**) *informal* a locomotive engine.

loco² ● *adj. slang* crazy. ● *n.* (*pl.* **-os**) (in full **locoweed**) a poisonous leguminous plant of N America causing brain disease in cattle eating it.

locomotion *n.* motion or the power of motion from one place to another.

locomotive ● *n.* an engine, powered by diesel fuel or electricity, used for pulling trains. ● *adj.* **1** of or relating to or effecting locomotion (*locomotive power*). **2** having the power of or given to locomotion; not stationary.

locomotor *adj.* of or relating to locomotion.

locus /ˈloːkəs/ *n.* (*pl.* **loci** /-saɪ/) **1** a position or point, esp. in a text, treatise, etc. **2** *Math.* a curve etc. formed by all the points satisfying a particular equation of the relation between coordinates, or by a point, line, or surface moving according to mathematically defined conditions. **3** *Biol.* the position of a gene, mutation, etc. on a chromosome. **4** the centre or source of something (*the locus of power has shifted*).

locust /ˈloːkəst/ *n.* **1** any of various grasshoppers of the family Acrididae, migrating in swarms and destroying vegetation. **2** *N Amer.* a cicada. **3** (in full **locust bean**) a carob. **4** (in full **locust tree**) **a** a carob tree, *Robinia pseudoacacia*, native to N America, bearing fragrant white flowers and black pods, grown for ornament. **c** any of various other trees of the legume family.

locution /ləˈkjuːʃən/ *n.* **1** a word or phrase, esp. considered in regard to style or idiom. **2** style of speech. □ **locutionary** *adj.*

lode *n.* **1** a vein of metal ore. **2** a rich source or plentiful supply (*your book is a lode of wisdom*).

lodestone *n.* **1** magnetite. **2 a** a piece of this used as a magnet. **b** a thing that attracts.

lodge ● *n.* **1** a hotel or inn, esp. in a resort area. **2** *N Amer.* the main building in a resort or summer camp, usu. containing a dining area etc. **3** *Cdn* (esp. in proper names) an old people's home. **4** a house occupied in the hunting or fishing season. **5** a N American Indian's tent or wigwam. **6** a small house at the gates of a park or in the grounds of a large house, occupied by a gatekeeper, gardener, etc. **7 a** the meeting place of a branch of a society such as the Freemasons. **b** the members of such a local branch. **8** a beaver's or otter's lair. ● *v.* **1** *tr.* deposit in court or with an official a formal statement of (complaint or information). **2** *tr.* deposit (money etc.) for security. **3** *tr.* bring forward (an objection etc.). **4** *tr.* (foll. by *in*, *with*) place (power etc.) in a person or group. **5** *tr. & intr.* make or become fixed or caught without further movement (*the bullet lodged in his brain*). **6** *tr.* **a** provide with sleeping quarters. **b** receive as a guest or inhabitant. **c** establish as a resident in a house or room or rooms. **7** *intr.* reside or live, esp. as a guest paying for accommodation. **8** *tr.* serve as a habitation for; contain. **9** *tr.* (in *passive*; foll. by *in*) be contained in.

lodgepole *n.* *N Amer.* **1** a pole used to support a teepee or wigwam. **2** (in full **lodgepole pine**) a pine native to mountainous regions of northwestern N America, *Pinus contorta* var. *latifolia*.

lodger *n.* a person receiving accommodation in another's house for payment.

lodging *n.* **1** temporary accommodation (*a lodging for the night*). **2** (in *pl.*) a room or rooms rented for lodging in on a relatively long-term basis. **3** a dwelling place.

lods et ventes /loːz eɪ vãt/ *n. Cdn* (*Que.*) *hist.* a seigneurial right to one-twelfth of the purchase price of an estate changing hands by sale or transfer.

loess /ˈloːes/ *n.* a deposit of fine light-coloured wind-blown dust found esp. in the basins of large rivers and very fertile when irrigated.

loft ● *n.* **1** a room or space directly under the roof of a house, used as storage or living space. **2** a space under the roof of a barn or stable etc., used esp. for storing hay and straw. **3** a gallery or upper level in a church or hall (*choir loft*). **4** *N Amer.* **a** an upper room or floor of a large building, factory, etc., sometimes converted into apartments, studios, etc. **b** = LOFT APARTMENT. **5** *N Amer.* the resilience of a fabric, esp. wool. **6** *N Amer.* the thickness of insulating matter in something, e.g. a sleeping bag or down-filled coat. **7** *Golf* **a** a backward slope on the head of a club. **b** a lofting stroke. ● *v.tr.* **1** a send (a ball etc.) high up. **b** clear (an obstacle) in this way. **2** (esp. as **lofted** *adj.*) give a loft to (a golf club).

loft apartment *n.* *N Amer.* an apartment built into a former warehouse or office building, esp. one having high ceilings and an open concept design.

lofty *adj.* (**-ier, -iest**) **1** (of things) of imposing height, towering (*lofty heights*). **2** consciously haughty, aloof, or dignified (*lofty contempt*). **3** exalted or noble; sublime (*lofty ideals*). □ **loftily** *adv.* **loftiness** *n.*

log¹ ● *n.* **1 a** a part of the trunk of a tree or of a large branch that has fallen or been cut down. **b** something long and cylindrical (*shape the dough into a log*). **2 a** *hist.* a float attached to a line wound on a reel for gauging the speed of a ship. **b** any other apparatus for the same purpose. **3** a record of events occurring during and affecting the voyage of a ship or aircraft. **4** = LOGBOOK. **5** any systematic record of things done, experienced, etc. ● *v.* (**logged, logging**) **1** *tr.* clear (a region) of trees. **2** *tr.* cut (a tree) into logs. **3** *intr.* fell timber and cut the wood into logs. **4** *tr.* **a** enter (the distance made or other details) in a ship's logbook. **b** enter details about (a person or event) in a logbook. **c** (of a ship) achieve (a certain distance). **5** *tr.* **a** enter (information) in a regular record. **b** attain (a cumulative total of time etc. recorded in this way) (*logged 50 hours*). □ **log off** (or **out**) go through the procedures to conclude use of a computer system. **log on** (or **in**) go through the procedures to begin use of a computer system.

log² *n.* a logarithm (esp. prefixed to a number or algebraic symbol whose logarithm is to be indicated).

logan /ˈlogən/ *n. Cdn* (*Nfld*) a leather boot with a rubber foot, reaching to below the knee, worn in winter or when working in the bush.

loganberry *n.* (*pl.* **-ies**) **1** a hybrid, *Rubus loganobaccus*, between a blackberry and a raspberry, with dark red acid fruits. **2** the fruit of this plant.

logarithm /ˈlɒgə,rɪðəm/ *n.* a figure representing the power to which a fixed number or base must be raised to produce a given number (*the logarithm of 1,000 to base 10 is 3*), used to simplify calculations as the addition and subtraction of logarithms is equivalent to multiplication and division. □ **logarithmic** *adj.* **logarithmically** *adv.*

log barge *n.* *Cdn* (*BC*) a large barge used to transport logs from the log dump to the mill.

logbook *n.* **1** a book containing a detailed record of things done or experienced. **2** a book in which particulars of aircraft flights etc. are recorded.

log boom *n.* *N Amer.* = BOOM² 2.

log bronc *n.* *Cdn* (*BC*) a tugboat used to direct a log boom or to gather logs together in the booming grounds.

log cabin *n.* **1** (also **log house**) a house or cabin with walls made of logs. **2** (*attrib.*) designating a quilt pattern in which square blocks are made up of a small square centre section surrounded by rectangular strips of increasing length.

log chute *n.* *Cdn* a chute constructed to allow logs being driven down a river to bypass a waterfall etc.

log drive *n.* *Cdn* the transporting of logs from the bush to the mills by floating them down rivers etc. □ **log driver** *n.*

log dump *n.* *N Amer.* = DUMP *n.* 6.

loge /loːʒ/ *n.* **1** a seating area in a theatre, usu. elevated above the orchestra level and on the side. **2** a private box or enclosure in a theatre.

logged-over *attrib.adj.* (also **logged-off, logged-out**) *N Amer.* (of a tract of forest) that has been logged.

logger *n.* *N Amer.* a person who fells trees and prepares timber for milling.

loggerhead *n.* **1** an iron instrument with a ball at the end heated for melting pitch etc. **2** any of various large-headed animals, esp. a turtle (*Caretta caretta*) or shrike (*Lanius ludovicianus*). □ **at loggerheads** (often foll. by *with*) disagreeing or disputing.

loggia /ˈloːdʒə, ˈlɒ-/ *n.* **1** an open-sided gallery or arcade. **2** an open-sided extension of a house.

logging *n.* the work of cutting and preparing forest timber.

logging chain *n.* *Cdn* a heavy-duty steel chain of the type used esp. in logging.

logging division *n.* *Cdn* a tract of forest being logged by loggers resident in a single logging camp.

logging road *n.* *N Amer.* an unimproved road into a forest area, used for logging purposes.

logic *n.* **1 a** the science of reasoning, proof, thinking, or inference. **b** a particular scheme of or treatise on this. **2 a** a chain of reasoning (*I don't follow your logic*). **b** the correct or incorrect use of reasoning (*your logic is flawed*). **c** ability in reasoning (*argues with great learning and logic*). **d** arguments (*is not governed by logic*). **3 a** the inexorable force or compulsion of a thing (*the logic of events*). **b** the necessary consequence of (an argument, decision, etc.). **4 a** a system or set of principles underlying the arrangements of elements in a computer or electronic device so as to perform a specified task. **b** logical operations collectively. □ **logician** /ləˈdʒɪʃən/ n.

-logic *comb. form* (also **-logical**) forming adjectives corresponding esp. to nouns in *-logy* (*geologic*).

logical *adj.* **1** of logic or formal argument. **2** not contravening the laws of thought, correctly reasoned. **3** deducible or defensible on the ground of consistency; reasonably to be believed or done. **4** capable of correct reasoning. □ **logically** *adv.*

logical positivism *n.* (also **logical empiricism**) a form of positivism regarding all valid philosophical problems as solvable by logical analysis. □ **logical positivist** *n.*

logic bomb *n. Computing* a set of instructions secretly incorporated into a program so that if a particular logical condition is satisfied they will be carried out, usu. with harmful effects.

log-in *n. Computing* **1** the action of logging in (also *attrib.*: *log-in screen*). **2** a code, password, etc. used in logging in.

-logist /lədʒɪst/ *comb. form* forming nouns denoting a person skilled or involved in a branch of study etc. with a name in *-logy* (*archaeologist*).

logistics /ləˈdʒɪstɪks/ *n.pl.* **1** the organization of moving, lodging, and supplying troops and equipment. **2** the detailed organization and implementation of a plan or operation. □ **logistic** *adj.* **logistical** *adj.* **logistically** *adv.*

log-jam *n.* **1** a crowded mass of logs in a river. **2** a deadlock. **3** *Sport* a situation in which several contestants are tied at the same place in the standings.

logo *n.* (*pl.* **-os**) a symbol designed for and used by a company or organization as its special sign, e.g. in advertising and packaging.

log-on *n.* = LOG-IN.

Logos /ˈlɒgɒs/ *n.* (in Christian theology) the Word of God, or Second Person of the Trinity.

log-rolling *n. N Amer.* **1** *informal* the practice of exchanging favours, esp. (in politics) of exchanging votes to mutual benefit. **2** the action of causing a floating log to rotate by treading, esp. as a competitive sport. □ **log-roll** *v.intr. & tr.* **log-roller** *n.*

log scaler *n. Cdn* a person who measures cut logs and calculates the amount of lumber that they contain.

logwood *n.* **1** a Caribbean tree, *Haematoxylon campechianum*. **2** the wood of this, producing a substance used in dyeing.

logy /ˈloːgi/ *adj.* (**-ier, -iest**) *N Amer.* dull and heavy in motion or thought.

-logy /lədʒi/ *comb. form* forming nouns denoting: **1** (usu. as **-ology**) a subject of study or interest (*zoology*). **2** a characteristic of speech or language (*tautology*). **3** discourse (*trilogy*).

loin *n.* **1** (in *pl.*) the part of the body on both sides of the spine between the floating ribs and the hip bones. **2** (in *pl.*) *literary* the source of reproductive power (*fruit of his loins*). **3** a cut of meat that includes the loin vertebrae.

loincloth *n.* a cloth worn around the loins, esp. as a sole garment.

loiter *v.intr.* **1** hang about; linger idly. **2** linger indolently on the way when on an errand, journey, etc. □ **loiterer** *n.*

loll /lɒl/ *v.intr.* **1** (often foll. by *about, around*) stand, sit, or recline in a lazy attitude. **2** hang loosely.

lollapalooza /lɒləpəˈluːzə/ *n. N Amer. slang* an excellent or attractive person or thing.

lollipop /ˈlɒli,pɒp/ *n.* a large flat or round candy on a small stick, held in the hand and sucked.

lolly /ˈlɒli/ *n. Cdn* (*Nfld & Maritimes*) = FRAZIL.

lollygag *var. of* LALLYGAG.

Lombard /ˈlɒmbɑrd/ ● *n.* **1** a native of Lombardy in N Italy. **2** a member of a Germanic people who conquered Italy in the 6th c. **3** the dialect of Lombardy. ● *adj.* of or relating to the Lombards or Lombardy. □ **Lombardic** *adj.*

Lombardy poplar /ˈlɒmbərdi/ *n.* a variety of poplar, *Populus nigra* var. *italica*, with an especially tall slender form.

Londoner *n.* a native or inhabitant of London, England, or London, Ontario.

lone *attrib.adj.* **1** (of a person) solitary; without a companion or supporter. **2** single, only. **3** (of a place) unfrequented, uninhabited, lonely (*the lone prairie*). **4** unmarried, single (*lone parent*).

lonely *adj.* (**-ier, -iest**) **1** solitary, isolated, without companions. **2** (of a place) unfrequented. **3** sad because without friends or company. **4** imparting a sense of loneliness; dreary. □ **loneliness** *n.*

lonely heart *n.* (usu. in *pl.*) a lonely person, esp. one seeking companionship by advertising in a newspaper etc. (usu. *attrib.*: *a lonely hearts column*).

loner *n.* a person who prefers not to associate with others.

lonesome *adj.* **1** solitary, lonely. **2** feeling lonely or forlorn. **3** causing such a feeling. □ **by** (or **on**) **one's lonesome** all alone. □ **lonesomely** *adv.* **lonesomeness** *n.*

lone wolf *n.* a person who prefers to act alone.

long¹ ● *adj.* (**longer; longest**) **1** measuring much from end to end in space or time; not soon traversed or finished (*a long line; a long time ago*). **2** (following a measurement) in length or duration (*4 metres long; two months long*). **3** relatively great in extent or duration (*a long meeting*). **4 a** consisting of a large number of items (*a long list*). **b** seemingly more than the stated amount; tedious, lengthy (*ten long miles; a long day*). **5** of elongated shape. **6 a** lasting or reaching far back or forward in time (*a long friendship*). **b** (of a person's memory) retaining things for a long time. **7** far-reaching; acting at a distance; involving a great interval or difference. **8** *Phonetics & Prosody* (of a vowel or syllable: **a** having the greater of the two recognized durations. **b** stressed. **c** (of a vowel in English) having the pronunciation shown in the name of the letter (as in *pile* and *cute* which have a long *i* and *u*, as distinct from *pill* and *cut*) (*compare* SHORT *adj.* 6). **9** (of odds or a chance) reflecting or representing a low level of probability. **10** *Stock Exch.* **a** (of stocks, bonds, etc.) bought in large quantities in advance, with the expectation of a rise in price. **b** (of a broker etc.) buying etc. on this basis. **11** (of a bill of exchange) maturing at a distant date. **12** (of a mixed drink) containing a relatively large proportion of mixer to liquor. **13** *informal* (of a person) tall. **14** (foll. by *on*) *informal* well supplied with. **15** (of a thrown or hit ball) travelling a long distance. ● *n.* **1** a long interval or period (*shall not be away for long; it will not take long*). **2** *Phonetics* **a** a long syllable or vowel. **b** a mark indicating that a vowel is long. ● *adv.* (**longer; longest**) **1** by or for a long time (*long before*; *long live the king!*). **2** (following nouns of duration) throughout a specified time (*all day long*). **3** (in *comparative*; with *neg.*) after an implied point of time (*shall not wait any longer*). **4** esp. *Sport* at or to a great distance (*kick the ball long*). □ **as** (or **so**) **long as 1** during the whole time that. **2** provided that; only if. **before long** fairly soon. **be long** (often foll. by *pres. part.* or *in* + verbal noun) take a long time; be slow (*was long in coming*; *I won't be long*). **in the long run 1** over a long period. **2** eventually; finally. **long ago** in the distant past. **the long and the short of it 1** all that can or need be said. **2** the eventual outcome. **long in the tooth** rather old (originally of horses). **long time no see** *informal* (used as a greeting) it is a long time since we last met. □ **longish** *adj.*

long[2] *v.intr.* (foll. by *for* or *to* + infin.) have a strong wish or desire for.

long. *abbr.* longitude.

long- *comb. form* forming adverbs meaning 'for or lasting for a long time' (*long-expected*; *long-lasting*).

long-ago *adj.* that is in the distant past.

long-awaited *adj.* that has been awaited for a long time.

longboat *n.* a sailing ship's largest boat.

longbow *n.* a bow drawn by hand and shooting a long feathered arrow.

long-chain *adj.* (of a molecule) containing a chain of many carbon atoms.

long-dead *adj.* that has been dead for a long time.

long-distance ● *adj.* **1** (of a telephone call) made between places that are sufficiently far apart as to require extra payment. **2** of, relating to, or providing such service (*a long-distance company*). **3** covering relatively great distances (*long-distance race*; *long-distance trucker*). ● *adv.* (also **long distance**) between distant places (*phone long-distance*). ● *n.* (usu. **long distance**) **1** long-distance telephone service (*we pay a lot for long distance*). **2** a long-distance telephone call.

long division *n.* division of numbers with details of the calculations written down.

long-drawn-out *adj.* (also **long-drawn**) prolonged, esp. unduly.

longe *var. of* LUNGE[2].

longer /ˈlɒŋgər/ *n.* (usu. in *pl.*) *Cdn* (*Nfld & Maritimes*) a long pole, esp. from the trunk of a conifer, used for building fences, fishing stages, roofs, floors, etc.

longevity /lɒnˈdʒevɪti/ *n.* **1** long life. **2** duration of life (*studying longevity*). **3** duration or length of service, employment, tenure, etc.

long face *n.* a dismal or disappointed expression. □ **long-faced** *adj.*

long gone *adj.* (usu. *predic.*; hyph. when *attrib.*) that has been gone for a long time (*she was long gone by the time he got there*).

longhair *n.* **1** an intellectual. **2** a person interested in the arts, esp. a classical musician. **3** a long-haired cat.

longhand *n.* ordinary handwriting (as opposed to shorthand or typing or printing).

long haul *n.* **1** the transport of goods or passengers over a long distance (also *attrib.*: *long-haul flights*). **2** a prolonged effort or task. □ **over the long haul** over a long period; in the long run.

longhorn *n.* **1** one of a breed of cattle with long horns. **2** any of numerous usu. elongate beetles of the family Cerambycidae, having very long, slender, backwardly flexed antennae, and found worldwide esp. in woodland.

longhouse *n.* a dwelling shared by several nuclear families, esp. among the Iroquois and the Aboriginal peoples of the northwest coast of N America.

longing ● *n.* a feeling of intense desire. ● *adj.* having or showing this feeling. □ **longingly** *adv.*

longitude /ˈlɒŋgɪˌtuːd, ˈlɒndʒ-, -ˌtjuːd/ *n.* **1** *Geog.* the angular distance east or west from a standard meridian such as Greenwich to the meridian of any place. Symbol: λ. **2** *Astronomy* the angular distance of a celestial body north or south of the ecliptic measured along a great circle through the body and the poles of the ecliptic.

longitudinal *adj.* **1** of or in length. **2** running lengthwise. **3** of longitude. **4** (of research, a study, etc.) involving information about an individual or group at different times throughout a long period. □ **longitudinally** *adv.*

longitudinal wave *n.* a wave vibrating in the direction of propagation.

long john *n.* **1** (in *pl.*) *informal* close-fitting cotton or wool knit underpants with full-length legs. **2** *N Amer.* a long, cream-filled doughnut, usu. iced.

long jump *n.* an athletic contest of jumping as far as possible along the ground in one leap. □ **long-jumper** *n.*

long-lasting *adj.* that lasts, or has lasted, for a long time.

long-legged *adj.* **1** having long legs. **2** *informal* speedy.

long-life *adj.* **1** (of perishable foods etc.) treated to preserve freshness. **2** (esp. of batteries etc.) manufactured in such a way as to last for a long time.

longline *n.* a deep-sea fishing line with a large number of baited hooks. □ **longlining** *n.*

longliner *n.* a fishing boat using longlines.

long-lived *adj.* having a long life; durable.

long-lost *attrib.adj.* that has been lost or not seen for a long time.

long lot *n.* *Cdn* = RIVER LOT.

long neck *n.* *N Amer. slang* **1** a beer bottle with a long neck. **2** a beer in such a bottle.

long-playing *adj.* (of a microgroove record) designed to be played at $33\frac{1}{3}$ revolutions per minute.

long-range *adj.* **1** (of a missile, aircraft, etc.) having a long range. **2** of or relating to a period of time far into the future.

long-run *adj.* occurring or running over a long period of time (*long-run costs*).

long-running *adj.* continuing for a long time.

longshore *adj.* **1** existing on or frequenting the shore. **2** directed along the shore.

longshoreman *n.* (*pl.* **-men**) *N Amer.* a person employed to load and unload ships.

long shot *n.* **1** a competitor or team etc. that is unlikely to succeed. **2** an undertaking or venture that has great potential but little chance of success. **3** a wild guess. **4** a bet at long odds. **5** *Film* a shot including objects at a distance. □ **by a long shot** by any means (*it isn't over by a long shot*).

long-sleeved *adj.* with sleeves reaching to the wrist.

longspur *n.* a N American bunting of the genus *Calcarius*.

long-standing *adj.* that has long existed; not recent (*a long-standing agreement*).

long-suffering *adj.* bearing provocation patiently.

long suit *n.* **1** many cards of one suit in a hand (esp. more than 3 or 4 in a hand of 13). **2** a thing at which one excels (*car repair is not my long suit*).

long-term *adj.* **1** of or for a long period of time (*long-term plans*). **2** (of an investment, loan, etc.) maturing or coming down after a long period of time.

long-time *adj.* that has been such for a long time.

long ton *n.* see TON 2.

long view *n.* (prec. by *the*) a broad and forward-looking assessment of circumstances etc. □ **take the long view** consider what is likely to happen, be relevant, etc. over the long term.

long wave *n.* a radio wave of frequency less than 300 kHz.

longways *adv.* (also **longwise**) = LENGTHWISE.

long weekend *n.* a three-day weekend consisting of Saturday, Sunday, and a statutory holiday on the Friday or Monday.

long-winded *adj.* **1** (of speech or writing) tediously lengthy. **2** (of a person) verbose; given to long discourses. □ **long-windedly** *adv.* **long-windedness** *n.*

loo *n.* esp. *Brit.* informal a toilet or washroom.

loofah /ˈluːfə/ *n.* (also **loofa**) **1** a climbing gourdlike plant, *Luffa cylindrica*, native to Asia, producing edible marrow-like fruits. **2** the dried fibrous vascular system of this fruit used as a sponge.

look ● *v.* **1 a** *intr.* (often foll. by *at*) use one's sight; turn one's eyes in some direction. **b** *tr.* turn one's eyes on; contemplate or examine (*looked me in the eyes*). **2** *intr.* **a** make a visual or mental search. **b** (foll. by *at*) consider, examine (*must look at the facts*). **3** *intr.* (foll. by *for*) **a** search for. **b** hope or be on the watch for. **c** expect. **4** *intr.* inquire (*when one looks deeper*). **5** *intr.* **a** have a specified appearance (*look foolish*). **b** seem; appear (*it looks to me as if you ought to go*). **6** *intr.* (foll. by *to*) **a** consider; take care of; be careful about (*look to the future*). **b** rely on (a person or thing) (*you can look to me for support*). **c** expect; count on; aim at. **7** *intr.* (foll. by *into*) investigate or examine. **8** *tr.* (foll. by *what, where,* etc. + clause) ascertain or observe by sight (*look where we are*). **9** *intr.* (of a thing) face or be turned, or have or afford an outlook, in a specified direction. **10** *tr.* express, threaten, or show (an emotion etc.) by one's looks. **11** *intr.* (foll. by *that* + clause) take care; make sure. **12** *intr.* (foll. by *to* + infin.) expect (*am looking to finish this today*). **13** *intr.* informal (foll. by *at*) be faced with an estimated expense, deficit, etc. (*you're looking at $40 to get to the airport*). ● *n.* **1** an act of looking; the directing of the eyes to look at a thing or person; a glance. **2** (in *sing.* or *pl.*) the appearance of a face; a person's expression or personal aspect. **3** the (esp. characteristic) appearance of a thing (*the place has a European look*). **4** style, fashion (*this year's look*). **5** (in *comb.*) designating imitation fabrics etc. that have the appearance of a natural substance (*a linen-look suit*). ● *interj.* (also **look here!**) calling attention, expressing a protest, etc. □ **look after 1** attend to; take care of. **2** follow with the eye. **3** seek for. **look one's age** appear to be as old as one really is. **look alive** (or **lively**) informal be brisk and alert. **look around 1** look in every or another direction. **2** examine the objects of interest in a place. **3** examine the possibilities etc. with a view to deciding on a course of action. **look as if** suggest by appearance the belief that (*it looks as if she's gone*). **look back 1** (foll. by *on, upon, to*) turn one's thoughts to (something past). **2** (usu. with *neg.*) cease to progress (*since then we have never looked back*). **look before you leap** avoid precipitate action. **look down on** (or **upon** or **look down one's nose at**) regard with contempt or a feeling of superiority. **look forward to** await (an expected event) eagerly or with specified feelings. **look in** make a short visit or call. **look a person in the eye** (or **eyes** or **face**) look directly and unashamedly at him or her. **look like 1** have the appearance of. **2** indicate the presence of (*it looks like mice*). **3** threaten or promise (*it looks like rain*). **look on 1** (often foll. by *as*) regard (*looks on you as a friend*). **2** be a spectator; avoid participation. **look oneself** appear in good health (esp. after illness etc.). **look out 1** direct one's sight or put one's head out of a window etc. **2** (often foll. by *for*) be vigilant or prepared. **3** (foll. by *on, over,* etc.) have or afford a specified outlook. **4** search for and produce (*shall look one out for you*). **look over 1** inspect or survey (*looked over the house*). **2** examine (a document etc.) esp. cursorily. **look sharp** act promptly; make haste. **look through 1** examine the contents of, esp. cursorily. **2** penetrate (a pretense or pretender) with insight. **3** ignore by pretending not to see (*I waved, but you just looked through me*). **look up 1** search for (esp. information in a book). **2** informal go to visit (a person) (*had intended to look them up*). **3** raise one's eyes (*Mary Jane looked up when I went in*). **4** improve, esp. in price, prosperity, or well-being (*things are looking up all over*). **look a person up and down** scrutinize a person keenly or contemptuously. **look up to** respect or venerate. **not like the look of** find alarming or suspicious. □ **-looking** *adj.* (in *comb.*).

look-alike ● *n.* a person or thing closely resembling another (*an Elvis look-alike*). ● *adj.* closely similar, esp. in appearance; identical.

looker *n.* **1** a person having a specified appearance (*a good-looker*). **2** informal an attractive person, esp. a woman. **3** a person who looks.

look-in *n.* informal an informal call or visit.

looking glass *n.* archaic a mirror.

lookism *n.* prejudice or discrimination on the basis of looks or appearance. □ **lookist** *adj.* & *n.*

lookit *interj.* N Amer. informal **1** demanding attention or protesting. **2** look at (someone or something).

lookout *n.* **1** a watch or looking out (*on the lookout for bargains*). **2 a** a post of observation. **b** a person or party or boat stationed to keep watch. **3** a view over a landscape. **4** a prospect of luck (*it's a bad lookout for them*). **5** informal a person's own concern.

look-see *n.* informal a survey or inspection.

looky *v.intr.* N Amer. informal (in *imper.*; usu. as **looky here**) demanding attention.

loom[1] *n.* an apparatus in which yarn or thread is woven into fabric by the crossing of vertical and horizontal threads.

loom[2] *v.intr.* (often foll. by *up*) **1** come into sight dimly, esp. as a vague and often magnified or threatening shape. **2** (of an event or prospect) be ominously close. **3** (often foll. by *over*) be ominously above (*the castle loomed over us*). □ **loom large** figure significantly.

loon *n.* **1** N Amer. any aquatic diving bird of the family Gaviidae, with a long slender body and a sharp bill, esp. the common loon, *Gavia immer*, with a haunting yodel-like call, red eyes, bands of alternating black and white on the collar, and a checkered black and white back. **2** informal a crazy person. **3** Cdn = LOONIE.

loonie *n.* (also **loony**) (*pl.* **-ies**) Cdn **1** the Canadian one-dollar coin. **2** informal the Canadian dollar.

loony slang ● *n.* (*pl.* **-ies**) a mad or silly person; a lunatic. ● *adj.* (**-ier, -iest**) crazy, silly. □ **looniness** *n.*

loony bin *n.* slang a mental home or hospital.

loony-tune *adj.* & *n.* (also **looney tune**) informal ● *adj.* (also **-tunes**) crazy; bizarre. ● *n.* a crazy or silly person.

loop ● *n.* **1 a** the esp. oval or circular figure produced by a curve or string etc. that crosses itself. **b** anything forming this figure. **2** a similarly shaped attachment or ornament formed of cord or thread etc. and fastened at the crossing. **3** a ring or curved piece of material as a handle etc. **4** a contraceptive coil. **5 a** (in full **loop line**) a railway or telephone line etc. that diverges from a main line and joins it again. **b** a trail etc. that returns to its starting point. **c** a short circular stretch of track or roadway where a bus, streetcar, etc. turns at the end of its run. **6** a manoeuvre in which an airplane describes a vertical loop. **7** *Figure Skating* **a** a compulsory figure describing a curve that crosses itself, made on a single edge. **b** a jump from the back outside edge of one foot, landing on the back outside edge of the same foot, with rotation in the air. **8** *Electricity* a complete circuit for a current. **9** an endless strip of tape or film allowing continuous repetition. **10** *Computing* a programmed sequence of instructions that is repeated until or while a particular condition is satisfied. **11** *N Amer.* the circle of influential people or those keeping up to date (*has been out of the loop for a while now*). **12** any continuously-repeated process or routine. ● *v.* **1** *tr.* form (thread etc.) into a loop or loops. **2** *tr.* enclose with or as with a loop. **3** *tr.* (often foll. by *up*, *back*, *together*) fasten or join with a loop or loops. **4** *intr.* **a** form a loop. **b** move in looplike patterns. **5** *intr.* loop the loop (see LOOP-THE-LOOP). □ **throw** (or **knock**) **one for a loop** *N Amer.* surprise, astonish; catch off-guard.

looped *adj.* **1** coiled or wreathed in loops. **2** consisting of a loop (*looped hiking trails*). **3** *N Amer. slang* drunk.

looper *n.* **1** a caterpillar of the geometer moth which progresses by arching itself into loops; inchworm. **2** a device for making loops.

loophole ● *n.* **1** a means of evading a rule etc. without infringing the letter of it. **2** a narrow vertical slit in a wall for shooting or looking through or to admit light or air. ● *v.tr.* make loopholes in (a wall etc.).

loop-the-loop ● *n.* the feat of circling in an aircraft in a vertical loop. ● *v.intr.* (**loop the loop**) perform this feat.

loopy *adj.* (**-ier**, **-iest**) **1** *slang* crazy. **2** having many loops.

loose ● *adj.* **1 a** not or no longer held by bonds or restraint. **b** (of an animal) not confined or tethered etc. **2** detached or detachable from its place (*has come loose*). **3** not held together or contained or fixed. **4** not specially fastened or packaged (*loose papers*; *had her hair loose*). **5** hanging partly free (*a loose end*). **6** slack, relaxed; not tense or tight. **7** (of a person's joints) easily moved. **8** not compact or dense (*loose soil*). **9** (of language, concepts, etc.) inexact; conveying only the general sense. **10** (preceding an agent noun) doing the expressed action in a loose or careless manner (*a loose thinker*). **11** morally lax; dissolute (*loose living*). **12 a** (of talk) indiscrete. **b** (of the tongue) likely to speak indiscreetly. **13** (of the bowels) lax; afflicted with diarrhea. **14** *Sport* **a** (of a ball, puck, etc.) in play but not in any player's possession. **b** (of play etc.) with the players not close together. **15** (of a partnership, coalition, etc.) allowing for substantial independence among its members. ● *adv.* **1** (in *comb.*) loosely (*loose-fitting*). **2** without constraint (*the dog runs loose*). **3** without attachment (*pried her fingers loose*). ● *v.tr.* **1** release; set free; free from constraint. **2** untie or undo (something that constrains). **3** detach from moorings. **4** relax (*loosed my hold on it*). **5** discharge (a gun or arrow etc.). □ **on the loose 1** escaped from captivity. **2** having a free enjoyable time. **stay loose** remain relaxed. □ **loosely** *adv.* **looseness** *n.*

loose cannon *n.* a reckless person or thing causing unintentional or misdirected damage.

loose change *n.* a relatively insignificant amount of money for casual use, as coins kept in a pocket.

loose end *n.* an unfinished detail. □ **at loose ends** (of a person) with nothing to do; unsettled, without a place or purpose.

loose-leaf ● *adj.* **1** (of a notebook, manual, etc.) with each leaf separate and removable. **2** pertaining to or for use with a loose-leaf binder etc. (*loose-leaf paper*). ● *n.* loose-leaf paper.

loosen *v.* **1** *tr. & intr.* make or become less tight or compact or firm. **2** *tr.* make (a regime etc.) less severe. **3** *tr.* release (the bowels) from constipation. **4** *tr.* relieve (a cough) from dryness. □ **loosen a person's tongue** make a person talk freely. **loosen up 1** limber up (see LIMBER *v.*). **2** lighten up (see LIGHTEN¹). □ **loosener** *n.*

loosestrife *n.* **1** any plant of the genus *Lysimachia*, e.g. the European garden loosestrife, *L. vulgaris*, naturalized in N America. **2** any plant of the genus *Lythrum*, esp. the purple loosestrife, *L. salicaria*, with racemes of star-shaped purple flowers.

loosey-goosey *adj. N Amer. informal* laid back; very relaxed.

loot ● *n.* **1** goods taken from an enemy; spoil. **2** booty; illicit gains made by an official. **3** *slang* money. **4** *informal* a collection or mass of recently-obtained goodies (*Halloween loot*). ● *v.tr.* **1** rob (premises) or steal (goods) left unprotected, esp. after riots or other violent events. **2** plunder or sack (a city, building, etc.). **3** carry off as booty. □ **looter** *n.* **looting** *n.*

loot bag *n. N Amer.* a bag containing candy, trinkets, etc., given to each child at a birthday party etc.

lop¹ ● *v.* (**lopped**, **lopping**) **1** *tr.* **a** (often foll. by *off*, *away*) cut or remove (a part or parts) from a whole, esp. branches from a tree. **b** remove branches from (a tree). **2** *tr.* (often foll. by *off*, *away*) remove (items) as superfluous. **3** *intr.* (foll. by *at*) make lopping strokes on (a tree etc.). ● *n.* parts lopped off, esp. branches and twigs of trees. □ **lopper** *n.*

lop² *v.* (**lopped**, **lopping**) **1** *intr. & tr.* hang limply. **2** *intr.* move with short bounds. □ **loppy** *adj.*

lop³ *n.* **1** a state of the sea in which the waves are short and choppy. **2** the sea or its surface when in this condition. □ **loppy** *adj.*

lope ● *v.intr.* **1** run with a long bounding stride. **2** move with long, easy strides. ● *n.* a long bounding stride.

loppet /ˈlɒpət/ *n.* a long-distance cross-country ski race in which all competitors start together.

lopsided *adj.* **1** with one side lower or smaller than the other; unevenly balanced. **2** *Sport* (of a score, victory, etc.) with one side greatly outscoring the other. □ **lopsidedly** *adv.* **lopsidedness** *n.*

loquacious /loˈkweɪʃəs/ *adj.* talkative. □ **loquaciously** *adv.* **loquacity** /-ˈkwæsɪti/ *n.*

loran /ˈlɔːræn/ *n.* a system of long-distance navigation in which position is determined from the intervals between signal pulses received from widely spaced radio transmitters.

lord ● *n.* **1 a** a master or ruler. **b** a powerful person in a specified field or group (*drug lord*). **2** *hist.* a feudal superior, esp. of a manor. **3** (**Lord**) (often prec. by *the*) **a** a name for God. **b** a name for Christ. **4** (in the UK) a peer of the realm or a person entitled to the title *Lord*, esp. a marquess, earl, viscount, or baron. **5** (**Lord**) (in the UK) **a** prefixed to the designation of a marquess, earl, viscount, or baron. **b** prefixed to the first name of the younger son of a duke or marquess. **c** (**the Lords**) = HOUSE OF LORDS. ● *interj.* (**Lord**) expressing surprise, dismay, etc. □ **lord it over 1** domineer. **2** adopt an attitude of superiority over. **Lord knows** God knows (see GOD). **lord over** (usu. in *passive*) rule over. □ **lordless** *adj.* **lordlike** *adj.*

lord and lady n. (pl. **lords and ladies**) esp. Cdn (usu. in pl.) the harlequin duck.

lordly adj. (**-ier, -iest**) **1** haughty, imperious. **2** suitable for a lord. ☐ **lordliness** n.

Lord's Day n. Sunday.

lordship n. (foll. by of, over) dominion, rule, or ownership. ☐ **his** (or **your**) **Lordship** (or **lordship**) (pl. **their** (or **your**) **Lordships** or **lordships**) **1** Brit. a respectful form of reference or address to a Lord or a bishop. **2** Cdn & Brit. a respectful form of reference or address to a judge. **3** ironic a form of reference or address to a man thought to give himself airs.

Lord's Prayer n. the prayer taught by Christ to his disciples, beginning with the words 'Our Father'.

Lord's Supper n. the Eucharist.

Lordy interj. = LORD interj.

lore /lɔr/ n. a body of traditions and knowledge on a subject or held by a particular group (herbal lore).

lorikeet /ˈlɒrɪˌkiːt, ˈlɒri-/ n. any of various small brightly coloured parrots of the subfamily Loriinae.

lose v. (past and past part. **lost**) **1** tr. be deprived of or cease to have, esp. by negligence or misadventure. **2** tr. **a** be deprived of (a person, esp. a close relative or patient) by death. **b** suffer the death of (a baby) in childbirth or through miscarriage. **3** tr. become unable to find; fail to keep in sight or follow or mentally grasp (lose one's way). **4** tr. let or have pass from one's control or reach (lose one's chance; lose one's bearings). **5** tr. & intr. be defeated in (a game, race, lawsuit, battle, etc.). **6** tr. evade; get rid of (lost our pursuers). **7** tr. fail to apprehend by sight or hearing; not catch (words etc.). **8** tr. forfeit (a stake, deposit, right to a thing, etc.). **9** tr. spend (time, efforts, etc.) to no purpose (lost no time in raising the alarm). **10 a** intr. suffer loss or detriment; incur a disadvantage. **b** intr. be worse off, esp. financially. **c** tr. experience a deficit of expenditure over income (lost money on her house). **11** tr. cause (a person) the loss of (will lose you your job). **12** (of a timepiece) **a** intr. become slow. **b** tr. become slow by (a specified amount of time). **13** tr. (in passive) disappear, perish; be dead (was lost in the war; is a lost art). **14** tr. informal get rid of; discard. **15** tr. undergo a reduction of; shed (weight). **16** tr. vomit (lost my lunch). ☐ **lose one's balance** fail to remain stable; fall. **lose one's cool** informal lose one's composure. **lose face** be humiliated; lose one's credibility. **lose heart** be discouraged. **lose it 1** lose one's composure suddenly and completely. **2** lose one's mind, sense of reality, sanity, etc. **3** cease to excel or be proficient in a specified field. **lose one's nerve** become timid or irresolute. **lose out** informal **1** (often foll. by on) be unsuccessful; not get a fair chance or advantage (in). **2** (foll. by to) be beaten in competition or replaced by. **lose one's temper** become angry. **lose time** allow time to pass with something unachieved etc. **lose the** (or **one's**) **way** become lost; fail to reach one's destination. ☐ **losing** n. & adj.

lose-lose attrib.adj. informal designating a condition, settlement, etc. which is damaging or disadvantageous to everyone involved (a lose-lose situation).

loser n. **1** a person or thing that loses or has lost (esp. a contest or game). **2** informal **a** a person who regularly fails. **b** a socially awkward person; a misfit.

losing battle n. a contest or effort in which failure seems inevitable.

loss n. **1 a** the act or an instance of losing; the state of being lost. **b** the fact of being deprived of a person by death, estrangement, etc. **2** a person, thing, or amount lost. **3** the detriment or disadvantage resulting from losing (that is no great loss). ☐ **at a loss** (sold etc.) for less than was paid for it. **be at a loss** be puzzled or uncertain. **be at a loss for words** not know what to say.

loss leader n. an item sold at a loss to attract customers.

lost ● v. past and past part. of LOSE. ● adj. **1** unable to find one's way; not knowing where one is. **2** confused or in difficulties. **3** that cannot be found or recovered. **4** damned, fallen (lost souls). ☐ **be lost for words** be so surprised, confused, etc. that one cannot think what to say. **be lost in** be engrossed in. **be lost on** be wasted on, or not noticed or appreciated by. **be lost to** be no longer affected by or accessible to (is lost to the world). **be lost without** have great difficulty if deprived of (am lost without my address book). **get lost** (usu. in imper.) slang go away.

lost and found n. a place where misplaced items are collected for retrieval by their owners.

lost cause n. **1** an enterprise etc. with no chance of success. **2** a person one can no longer hope to influence.

lost generation n. the generation reaching maturity c. 1915–25, a high proportion of whose men were killed in WW I, characterized by disillusionment.

lost soul n. **1** a soul that is damned. **2** a person who is unable to cope with everyday life; a bewildered or pitiful person.

lot ● n. **1** informal (prec. by a or in pl.) **a** a large number or amount (a lot of people; lots of chocolate). **b** informal much (a lot warmer; is lots better). **2 a** each of a set of objects used in making a chance selection. **b** this method of deciding (chosen by lot). **3** a share, or the responsibility resulting from it. **4** a person's destiny, fortune, or condition. **5** esp. N Amer. **a** a portion of land assigned to a particular owner; each of the portions into which a tract of land is divided when offered for sale. **b** land near a film studio where outside filming may be done. **c** a plot of land used for parking vehicles. **d** the area at a car dealership where cars for sale are kept. **6** an article or set of articles for sale at an auction etc. **7** a number or quantity of associated persons or things. ● v.tr. (**lotted, lotting**) divide into lots. ☐ **cast** (or **draw**) **lots** decide by means of lots. **throw in one's lot with** decide to share the fortunes of. **the** (or **the whole**) **lot** the whole number or quantity. **a whole lot** informal very much (is a whole lot better).

Lothario /ləˈθɑːrioʊ, -ˈθɛrioʊ/ n. (pl. **-os**) a man known for many sexual conquests.

lotion n. a medicinal or cosmetic liquid preparation applied externally.

lotsa adv. informal lots of.

lotta n. informal a lot of.

lottery n. (pl. **-ies**) **1 a** a means of raising money, usu. on a large scale and government-operated, by selling numbered tickets and giving prizes to the holders of numbers drawn at random. **b** any game of chance involving the sale of tickets. **c** a process of selection which relies on random drawing. **2** an enterprise, process, etc., whose outcome is governed by chance (life is a lottery).

lotto n. **1** N Amer. (also esp. Que. **loto**) a lottery. **2** a game of chance like bingo, but with numbers drawn by the players instead of being called.

lotus /ˈloʊtəs/ n. **1** (in Greek mythology) a legendary plant inducing luxurious languor when eaten. **2 a** any water lily of the genus Nelumbo, esp. N. nucifera of India, with large pink flowers. **b** this flower used symbolically in Hinduism and Buddhism. **3** an Egyptian water lily, *Nymphaea lotus*, with white flowers. **4** any plant of the genus *Lotus*.

lotus land *n.* **1** a place of indolent enjoyment. **2** (**Lotus Land**) *Cdn jocular* southern British Columbia.

lotus position *n.* a cross-legged position of meditation with the feet resting on the thighs.

louche /luːʃ/ *adj.* disreputable, shifty.

loud ● *adj.* **1 a** strongly audible, esp. noisily or oppressively so. **b** able or liable to produce loud sounds (*a loud engine*). **c** clamorous, insistent (*loud complaints*). **2** (of colours, design, etc.) gaudy, obtrusive. **3** (of behaviour) aggressive and noisy. ● *adv.* in a loud manner. □ **loud and clear 1** loudly and clearly (*speak loud and clear*). **2** without misunderstanding (*got the hint loud and clear*). **out loud 1** aloud. **2** loudly (*laughed out loud*). □ **louden** *v.tr. & intr.* **loudly** *adv.* **loudness** *n.*

loud-hailer *n.* a bullhorn.

loudmouth *n. informal* a noisily self-assertive or vociferous person. □ **loud-mouthed** *adj.*

loudspeaker *n.* an apparatus that converts electrical impulses into sound, esp. music and voice.

Lou Gehrig's disease /ˌluː ˈgɛrɪɡz/ *n.* = AMYOTROPHIC LATERAL SCLEROSIS.

lounge ● *v.intr.* **1** recline comfortably and casually; loll. **2** (often foll. by *around, about*) stand or move about idly. ● *n.* **1** a place where people may sit and relax, esp.: **a** a public room or bar, e.g. in a hotel. **b** a place in an airport etc. with seats for waiting passengers. **c** a room where staff, students, etc. may congregate informally. **2** (*attrib.*) designating live easy listening musical entertainment characteristic of lounges (*lounge singer*). **3** a sitting room in a house.

lounge chair *n. N Amer.* any chair for lounging or reclining in.

lounge lizard *n. informal* **1** an esp. smarmy or unctuous idler who frequents lounges. **2** an idler in fashionable society. **3** a singer or other performer of esp. pop songs in lounges.

lounger *n.* **1** a person who lounges. **2** a piece of furniture for relaxing on. **3** a casual garment for wearing when relaxing.

lour /laʊr/ *var. of* LOWER³.

louse /laʊs/ ● *n.* **1** (*pl.* **lice**) **a** a parasitic insect, *Pediculus humanus*, infesting the human hair and skin and transmitting various diseases. **b** any insect of the order Anoplura or Mallophaga parasitic on mammals, birds, fish, or plants. **2** (*pl.* **louses**) *slang* a contemptible or unpleasant person. ● *v.tr.* (also /laʊz/) remove lice from. □ **louse up** *slang* mess up.

lousy /ˈlaʊzi/ *adj.* (**-ier, -iest**) **1** infested with lice. **2** *informal* very bad; disgusting (also as a term of general disparagement). **3** *informal* (often foll. by *with*) well supplied, teeming. □ **lousily** *adv.* **lousiness** *n.*

lout *n.* a rough, crude, or ill-mannered person (usu. a man). □ **loutish** *adj.* **loutishly** *adv.* **loutishness** *n.*

louvre /ˈluːvər/ *n.* (also **louver**) **1** each of a set of overlapping slats, esp. in a door, designed to admit air and some light. **2** a domed structure on a roof with side openings for ventilation etc. □ **louvred** *adj.*

lovable *adj.* inspiring or deserving love or affection. □ **lovability** *n.* **lovableness** *n.* **lovably** *adv.*

lovage /ˈlʌvɪdʒ/ *n.* **1** a S European herb, *Levisticum officinale*, used for flavouring etc. **2** a white-flowered umbelliferous plant, *Ligusticum scoticum*.

love ● *n.* **1** an intense feeling of deep affection or fondness for a person or thing; great liking. **2** sexual passion. **3** sexual relations. **4** a beloved one; a sweetheart (often as a form of address). **5** *informal* a person of whom one is fond. **6** affectionate greetings (*give him*

my love). **7** (in some sports) no score; nil. **8** a formula for ending an affectionate letter etc. ● *v.* **1** *tr. & intr.* feel love or deep fondness (for). **2** *tr.* delight in; admire; greatly cherish. **3** *tr.* like very much (*loves books*). **4** *tr.* (foll. by verbal noun, or *to* + infin.) be inclined, esp. as a habit; greatly enjoy; find pleasure in (*loves to find fault*). □ **fall in love** (often foll. by *with*) develop a great (esp. sexual) love (for). **for love** for pleasure not profit. **for the love of** for the sake of. **in love** (often foll. by *with*) deeply enamoured (of). **make love 1** (often foll. by *to, with*) have sexual intercourse (with). **2** (often foll. by *to*) *archaic* pay amorous attention (to). **no love lost between** mutual dislike between (two people etc.). **not for love or money** *informal* not in any circumstances. **out of love** no longer in love. □ **loveworthy** *adj.*

loveable *var. of* LOVABLE.

love affair *n.* **1** an esp. extramarital romantic or sexual relationship between two people in love. **2** an intense enthusiasm or liking for something.

lovebird *n.* **1** any of various African parrots, esp. *Agapornis personata*. **2** (in *pl.*) *informal* lovers.

loved one *n.* a person whom one loves deeply.

lovefest *n.* **1** a gathering involving or celebrating free love. **2** = LOVE-IN 2.

love handles *n.pl.* esp. *N Amer. slang* excess fat at the waist.

love-hate relationship *n.* **1** an intensely emotional relationship in which one or each party has ambivalent feelings of love and hate for the other. **2** a situation in which feelings of liking and disliking are combined (*our love-hate relationship with raccoons*).

love-in *n.* (*pl.* **-ins**) *informal* **1** a gathering (esp. of hippies) expressing or advocating love and peace. **2** *jocular* a gathering of like-minded people.

love interest *n.* a person or character in a film etc. in whom another has a romantic or sexual interest.

loveless *adj.* without love; unloving or unloved or both. □ **lovelessly** *adv.* **lovelessness** *n.*

love letter *n.* a letter expressing feelings of sexual love.

love life *n.* a person's life with regard to relationships with lovers.

lovelorn *adj.* pining from or pertaining to unrequited love.

lovely ● *adj.* (**-ier, -iest**) **1** exquisitely beautiful. **2** pleasing, delightful. ● *n.* (*pl.* **-ies**) *informal* a pretty woman. □ **lovelily** *adv.* **loveliness** *n.*

lovemaking *n.* amorous sexual activity, esp. sexual intercourse.

love nest *n.* a place of intimate lovemaking.

lover *n.* **1** a person in love with another. **2** a person with whom another is having sexual relations. **3** (in *pl.*) a couple in love or having sexual relations. **4** a person who likes or enjoys something specified (*a music lover; a lover of words*).

loveseat *n.* a small sofa for two.

lovesick *adj.* languishing with romantic love.

love slave *n.* a person kept willingly or unwillingly in thrall to another to provide sexual favours.

lovestruck *adj.* completely smitten by love.

love triangle *n.* a situation in which one person is romantically involved with two others.

lovey *informal* ● *n.* (*pl.* **-eys**) esp. *Brit.* love, sweetheart (esp. as a form of address). ● *adj.* (also **lovey-dovey**) fondly affectionate, esp. unduly sentimental.

loving ● *adj.* feeling or showing love. ● *n.* affection; active love. □ **lovingly** *adv.* **lovingness** *n.*

loving-kindness *n.* tenderness and consideration.

low¹ ● *adj.* **1** of less than average height; not high or tall or reaching far up (*a low fence*). **2 a** situated close to ground or sea level etc.; not elevated in position (*low altitude*). **b** (of the sun) near the horizon. **c** (of latitude) near the equator. **3** of or in humble rank or position (*of low birth*). **4** of small or less than normal amount or extent or intensity (*low price; low in calories*). **5** small or reduced in quantity (*supplies are low*). **6** coming below the normal level (*a dress with a low neck*). **7 a** dejected; lacking vigour (*feeling low; in low spirits*). **b** poorly nourished; indicative of poor nutrition. **8 a** (of a sound, voice, etc.) not high-pitched. **b** (of a sound) not loud. **9** not exalted or sublime; commonplace. **10** unfavourable (*a low opinion*). **11** vulgar; coarse (*low humour*). **12** contemptible; underhanded. **13** (of an oven etc.) warm but not hot (*cook over low heat*). ● *n.* **1** a low or the lowest level, number, or thing (*the dollar has reached a new low*). **2** an area of low barometric pressure; a depression. **3** the lowest temperature reached during a specified period (*overnight low of minus 36°*). **4** the lowest setting of a cooking element, microwave oven, etc. ● *adv.* **1** in or to a low position or state. **2** in a low tone (*speak low*). **3** at or to a low pitch (*I can't sing so low*). **4** at or to a moral position considered contemptible (*how low can you stoop?*). ☐ **lowness** *n.*

low² ● *n.* a sound made by cattle; a moo. ● *v.tr. & intr.* utter (with) this sound.

Low Arctic *n.* the part of the Canadian Arctic south of the Arctic Circle.

lowball ● *attrib.adj.* **1** designating a deceptively or unrealistically low price or estimate. **2** inexpensive. ● *v.* **1** *tr. & intr.* deceptively offer (someone) an unrealistically low price or estimate. **2** *tr.* deceptively make (an offer, estimate, etc.) lower than is realistic.

low beam *n.* *N Amer.* (usu. in *pl.*) a headlight beam used for short-range illumination.

low blow *n.* **1** a cruel or unfair criticism or attack. **2** a punch below the belt in boxing.

low-born *adj.* of humble birth.

lowboy *n.* *N Amer.* a low chest or table with drawers and short legs.

lowbrow ● *adj.* not highly intellectual or cultured. ● *n.* a lowbrow person. ☐ **lowbrowed** *adj.*

low-budget *adj.* produced or operated with a limited amount of money (*a low-budget film*).

lowbush *n.* **1** (in full **lowbush blueberry**) a low shrub of northeastern N America, *Vaccinium angustifolium*, with sweet edible blue berries. **2** (in full **lowbush cranberry**) a shrub of northern N America, *Viburnum edule*, with lobed leaves and red, edible fruit.

low-cal /ˈloː kæl/ *adj.* (in full **low-calorie**) (of food, a diet, etc.) low in calories.

Low Church *n.* a tradition within Anglicanism stressing evangelicalism and giving little emphasis to ritual, priestly authority, and the sacraments.

low-cut *adj.* **1** (of a dress etc.) having a low neckline. **2** (of a running shoe etc.) not covering the ankle.

low-density lipoprotein *n.* the form of lipoprotein in which cholesterol is transported in the blood.

lowdown ● *n.* *informal* (usu. foll. by *on*) the relevant information (about). ● *adj.* dishonourable, contemptible.

low-E *adj.* (in full **low-emissivity**) *N Amer.* designating a window which has been coated to prevent the escape or entry of heat, yet which permits the passage of visible light.

low-end *adj.* designating or pertaining to relatively cheap models of consumer products, services, etc. (*bought low-end equipment*).

lower¹ /ˈloːər/ ● *adj.* (*comparative of* LOW¹) **1** less high in position or status. **2** situated below another part (*lower lip; lower atmosphere*). **3 a** situated on less high land (*the lower town*). **b** situated to the south (*Lower California*). **c** situated along or pertaining to the downstream part of a river, esp. the part closest to the mouth (*the Lower St. Lawrence*). **4** (of an animal or plant) showing relatively primitive characteristics, e.g. a platypus or a fungus. **5** (often **Lower**) *Geol. & Archaeology* designating an older, and hence usu. deeper, part of a stratigraphic division, archaeological deposit, etc., or the period in which it was formed or deposited. ● *adv.* in or to a lower position, status, etc. ☐ **lowermost** *adj.*

lower² /ˈloːər/ *v.* **1** *tr.* let or haul down. **2** *tr. & intr.* make or become lower. **3** *tr.* reduce the height or pitch or elevation of (*lower your voice*). **4** *tr.* degrade. **5** *tr. & intr.* diminish. ☐ **lower the boom on** *N Amer. slang* **1** inflict a physical defeat on (a person). **2** treat (a person) severely. **3** put a stop to (an activity).

lower³ /laur, ˈloːər/ ● *v.intr.* **1** frown; look sullen. **2** (of the sky etc.) look dark and threatening. ● *n.* **1** a scowl. **2** a gloomy look (of the sky etc.).

Lower Canadian *Cdn hist.* ● *n.* a native or inhabitant of the former British colony of Lower Canada (1791–1841), now Labrador and southern Quebec. ● *adj.* of or relating to the colony of Lower Canada.

lower case ● *adj.* designating the smaller characters most often used in printing and writing, often differing in shape as well as size from the capital forms. ● *n.* lower case letters.

lower class ● *n.* working-class people and their families. ● *adj.* (**lower-class**) of the lower class.

lower court *n.* a court of law that is not a court of appeal.

lower deck *n.* the deck of a ship situated immediately over the hold.

lower house *n.* the usu. larger and more representative body of a bicameral legislature, esp. (in Canada) the House of Commons.

lower middle class ● *n.* the class of society between the lower and middle classes. ● *adj.* (**lower-middle-class**) of the lower middle class.

lower world *n.* (also **lower regions** *n.pl.*) the realm of the dead; hell.

lowest common denominator *n.* **1** the lowest common multiple of the denominators of several fractions. **2** the least desirable common feature of members of a group.

lowest common multiple *n.* the lowest quantity that is a multiple of two or more given quantities.

low frequency *n.* (in radio) 30–300 kilohertz.

low gear *n.* a gear such that the driven end of a transmission revolves slower than the driving end.

Low German *n.* the group of dialects of Germany spoken in the lowland areas of the north, most closely related to Dutch and Frisian.

low-grade *adj.* of low quality or strength.

low-impact *adj.* **1** designating esp. aerobic exercises designed to put little or no potentially harmful stress on the body. **2** (of camping etc.) affecting or altering the natural environment as little as possible.

low-income *attrib.adj.* of or relating to the income group comprising those earning relatively low wages.

low-intensity *attrib.adj.* (of warfare, conflicts, etc.) relatively restrained, localized, or small-scale.

low-key *adj.* (also **low-keyed**) lacking intensity or prominence; restrained.

lowland ● *n.* **1** (usu. in *pl.*) low-lying country. **2** (**Lowland**) (usu. in *pl.*) the region of Scotland lying south and east of the Highlands. ● *adj.* of or in lowland or the Scottish Lowlands. □ **lowlander** *n.* (also **Lowlander**).

low latitudes *n.pl.* regions near the equator.

low-level *adj.* **1** designating an activity conducted on or at a low level (*low-level negotiations; low-level flight*). **2** *Computing* (of a programming language) close in form to machine language.

low-life *n.* (*pl.* **-lifes**) (also **low-lifer**) **1** a degenerate person or a member of the underworld. **2** such people collectively.

lowlight *n.* **1** a monotonous or dull period; a feature of little prominence (*the lowlights of the evening*). **2** (usu. in *pl.*) a dark tint in the hair produced by dyeing.

lowly *adj.* (**-ier, -iest**) **1** humble in feeling, behaviour, or status. **2** modest, unpretentious. □ **lowliness** *n.*

low-lying *adj.* (of land) at low altitude (above sea level etc.).

low maintenance *adj.* requiring little or infrequent maintenance, attention, etc. (*a low maintenance machine*).

low-minded *adj.* vulgar or ignoble in mind or character. □ **low-mindedness** *n.*

lowpass *adj.* designating a filter that attenuates only those components with a frequency greater than some cut-off frequency.

low-pitched *adj.* **1** (of a sound) low. **2** (of a roof) having only a slight slope.

low post *n. Basketball* the area below the opponent's basket (often, with hyphen, *attrib.*: *low-post scorer*).

low-pressure ● *adj.* **1** characterized by or exerting below-average pressure. **2** (of a job, situation, etc.) not demanding or stressful. ● *n.* (**low pressure**) an atmospheric condition with pressure below 101.3 kilopascals.

low-pressure system *n. Meteorol.* a large expanse of air at low atmospheric pressure.

low profile *n.* an attitude or manner characterized by the avoidance of attention or publicity (often, with hyphen, *attrib.*: *a low-profile position*).

low relief *n. see* RELIEF 6a.

low-rent *adj.* **1** (in full **low-rental**) designating housing or a neighbourhood for tenants with relatively low incomes. **2** *informal* inferior; second-rate.

low-rider *n.* (often *attrib.*) *US* **1** a car customized with hydraulics, enabling the chassis to be lowered very close to the ground. **2** the usu. young owner or driver of such a car. □ **low-riding** *n.*

low-rise ● *adj.* (of a building) having few storeys. ● *n.* a low-rise building.

low-risk *adj.* that does not constitute a troubling risk.

low season *n.* the period during which the fewest people travel, book accommodation, etc.

low-slung *adj.* **1** suspended; sagging. **2 a** with a low and wide profile (*low-slung houses*). **b** close to the ground (*low-slung furniture*).

low spirits *n.pl.* dejection, depression. □ **low-spirited** *adj.* **low-spiritedness** *n.*

low-tech *n.tr.* (in full **low-technology**) (usu. *attrib.*) relatively unsophisticated tools, machines, procedures, etc. (*a low-tech kitchen*).

low tide *n.* (also **low water**) the time or level of the tide at its ebb.

low-water mark *n.* **1** the level reached at low water. **2** a minimum recorded level or value etc.

lox[1] *n.* liquid oxygen.

lox[2] *n. N Amer.* smoked salmon.

loyal *adj.* **1** (often foll. by *to*) true or faithful (to duty, a friend, cause, etc.). **2** steadfast in allegiance; devoted to the sovereign or government of one's country. □ **loyally** *adv.*

loyalist *n.* **1** a person who remains loyal to the existing sovereign, government, etc., esp. in the face of rebellion or usurpation. **2** (**Loyalist**) **a** any of the colonists of the American revolutionary period who supported the British cause, many of whom afterwards migrated to Canada. **b** *Cdn* a descendant of such a person. **3** a person loyal to a specific person, cause, etc. □ **loyalism** *n.*

loyal Opposition *n.* = OFFICIAL OPPOSITION.

loyalty *n.* (*pl.* **-ies**) **1** the state of being loyal. **2** (often in *pl.*) a feeling or application of loyalty.

lozenge /ˈlɒzɪndʒ/ *n.* **1** a rhombus or diamond figure. **2** a small candy or medicinal tablet, originally lozenge-shaped, for dissolving in the mouth. **3** a lozenge-shaped pane in a window. **4** the lozenge-shaped facet of a cut gem.

LP *n.* a long-playing record.

LPG *abbr.* liquefied petroleum gas.

LPN *abbr.* LICENSED PRACTICAL NURSE.

Lr *symbol* lawrencium.

LRB *abbr.* Labour Relations Board.

LRC *abbr.* (of trains) light, rapid, comfortable.

LRIF /ˈelrɪf/ *abbr. Cdn* LOCKED-IN RETIREMENT INCOME FUND.

LRT *abbr.* light rail (or rapid) transit.

LS *abbr. Cdn* LEADING SEAMAN.

LSAT /ˈelsæt/ *abbr.* Law School Admission Test.

LSD *abbr.* LYSERGIC ACID DIETHYLAMIDE.

LSI *abbr. Computing* large-scale integration; the technology integrating thousands of circuits on one chip.

Lt *abbr.* **1** (also **Lt.**) LIEUTENANT. **2** (**Lt.**) light.

Lt. Cdr. *abbr.* LIEUTENANT COMMANDER. ¶The Canadian Forces use the abbreviation *LCdr.*

Lt. Col. *abbr.* LIEUTENANT COLONEL. ¶The Canadian Forces use the abbreviation *LCol.*

Ltd. *abbr.* Limited.

Lt. Gen. *abbr.* LIEUTENANT GENERAL. ¶The Canadian Forces use the abbreviation *LGen.*

Lt.-Gov. *abbr.* Lieutenant-Governor.

Lu *symbol* lutetium.

luau /ˈluːaʊ/ *n.* a Hawaiian party or feast usu. accompanied by some form of entertainment.

Lubavitcher /ˈluːbəˌvɪtʃər, luːˈbɒ-/ ● *n.* a member of a group of Hasidic Jews founded in the 18th c., stressing piety and missionary work. ● *adj.* (also **Lubavitch**) of or pertaining to Lubavitchers.

lubber *n.* **1** a big clumsy fellow; a lout. **2** = LANDLUBBER. □ **lubberly** *adj. & adv.*

lube *esp. N Amer. & Austral. informal* ● *n.* **1** = LUBRICANT. **2** an application of lubricant (esp. to a motor vehicle). ● *v.tr.* = LUBRICATE.

Lubicon /ˈluːbɪkɒn/ *n.* (also **Lubicon Cree**, **Lubicon Lake Cree**) **1** an Aboriginal group living near Peace River, Alberta. **2** the Algonquian language of the Lubicon.

lubricant ● *n.* a substance used to reduce friction. ● *adj.* lubricating.

lubricate *v.tr.* **1** reduce friction in (machinery etc.) by applying oil or grease etc. **2** make slippery or smooth; make smooth the motion or action of (something) by applying a fluid or unguent. **3** (usu. as **lubricated** *adj.*) *informal* drunk. □ **lubrication** *n.* **lubricator** *n.*

lubricious /lu:'brɪʃəs/ adj. (also **lubricous** /'lu:brɪkəs/) **1** lewd, prurient. **2** slippery, smooth, oily. ☐ **lubricity** n.

lucent /'lu:sənt/ adj. literary **1** shining, luminous. **2** translucent. ☐ **lucency** n.

lucerne /lu:'sɜːn/ n. (also **lucern**) = ALFALFA.

lucid /'lu:sɪd/ adj. **1 a** expressing or expressed clearly; easy to understand. **b** (of a dream) vivid; clear. **2** of or denoting intervals of sanity between periods of insanity or dementia. ☐ **lucidity** n. **lucidly** adv.

Lucifer /'lu:sɪfər/ n. Satan.

Lucite /'lu:saɪt/ n. proprietary a solid transparent plastic resin.

luck ● n. **1** chance regarded as the bringer of good or bad fortune. **2** circumstances of life (beneficial or not) brought by this. **3** good fortune; success due to chance (in luck; out of luck). ● v.intr. esp. N Amer. informal **1** (foll. by into) acquire by good fortune. **2** (foll. by out, in) achieve success or advantage by good luck. **3** (foll. by out) fail or be disadvantaged by bad luck. ☐ **as luck would have it** by chance; because of luck. **for luck** to bring good fortune. **no such luck** informal unfortunately not. **try one's luck** make a venture. **with luck** if all goes well. **worse luck** informal unfortunately.

luckily adv. **1** (qualifying a whole sentence or clause) fortunately (luckily there was enough food). **2** in a lucky or fortunate manner.

luckless adj. having no luck; unfortunate.

lucky adj. (**-ier**, **-iest**) **1** having or resulting from good luck, esp. as distinct from skill or design or merit. **2** bringing good luck (a lucky charm). **3** fortunate, appropriate (a lucky guess). ☐ **get lucky** informal have sex, esp. with a date. **thank one's lucky stars** be extremely grateful to fate. ☐ **luckiness** n.

lucrative /'lu:krətɪv/ adj. profitable, yielding financial gain. ☐ **lucratively** adv. **lucrativeness** n.

lucre /'lu:kər/ n. derogatory financial profit or gain.

Luddite /'lʌdaɪt/ ● n. **1** hist. a member of any of the bands of English artisans who rioted against mechanization and destroyed machinery (1811–16). **2** a person opposed to increased industrialization or new technology. ● adj. of the Luddites or their beliefs. ☐ **Luddism** n.

'lude n. (also **lude**) N Amer. slang a Quaalude.

ludic /'lu:dɪk/ adj. spontaneously playful.

ludicrous /'lu:dɪkrəs/ adj. absurd or ridiculous; laughable. ☐ **ludicrously** adv.

luff /lʌf/ ● n. the edge of the fore-and-aft sail next to the mast or stay. ● v. **1** tr. & intr. steer (a ship) nearer the wind. **2** tr. turn (the helm) so as to achieve this. **3** tr. raise or lower (the jib of a crane or derrick). **4** intr. (of a sail) flap from being set too close to the wind.

Luftwaffe /'lʊft,vɒfə/ n. hist. the German air force up to the end of World War II.

lug[1] ● v. (**lugged**, **lugging**) **1** tr. **a** drag or tug (a heavy object) with effort or violence. **b** (usu. foll. by around, about) carry (something heavy) around with one. **2** tr. (usu. foll. by in, into) introduce (a subject etc.) irrelevantly. **3** intr. (usu. foll. by at) pull hard. ● n. **1** a hard or rough pull. **2** a projection on an object by which it may be carried, fixed in place, etc. **3** a ridge on the sole of a shoe or boot, or on a tire, designed to provide traction. **4** slang an awkward or stupid person, esp. a man. **5** either of two flaps of a hat, for covering the ears.

lug[2] n. = LUGWORM.

luge /lu:ʒ/ ● n. **1** a light sled with runners for one or two people, ridden in a sitting or supine position. **2**

the sport in which these are raced. ● v.intr. ride on a luge. ☐ **luger** n.

Luger /'lu:gər/ n. proprietary a type of German automatic pistol.

luggage n. suitcases, bags, etc. to hold a traveller's belongings.

lugsail /'lʌgseɪl, -səl/ n. a quadrilateral sail which is bent on and hoisted from a yard.

lugubrious /lu:'gu:brɪəs, lə-/ adj. doleful, mournful, dismal. ☐ **lugubriously** adv. **lugubriousness** n.

lugworm n. any polychaete worm of the genus *Arenicola*, living in muddy sand and often used as bait by fishermen.

lukewarm adj. **1** moderately warm; tepid. **2** unenthusiastic, indifferent. ☐ **lukewarmly** adv. **lukewarmness** n.

lull ● v. **1** tr. soothe or send to sleep gently. **2** tr. (usu. foll. by into) deceive (a person) into confidence (lulled into a false sense of security). **3** tr. allay (suspicions etc.) usu. by deception. **4** intr. (of noise, a storm, etc.) abate or fall quiet. ● n. a temporary quiet period in a storm or in any activity. ☐ **lulling** adj. **lullingly** adv.

lullaby ● n. (pl. **-ies**) **1** a soothing song to send a child to sleep. **2** the music for this. ● v.tr. (**-ies**, **-ied**) sing to sleep.

lulu n. slang a remarkable, incredible, or memorable person or thing, esp. for its unpleasantness.

lumbar /'lʌmbər, -bɑːr/ adj. Anat. relating to the loin, esp. the lower back area.

lumber[1] v.intr. move in a slow clumsy noisy way. ☐ **lumbering** adj. **lumberingly** adv.

lumber[2] ● n. **1** N Amer. partly or fully prepared timber. **2** slang a hockey stick. ● v. **1** N Amer. **a** intr. perform the labour or carry on the business of cutting and preparing timber. **b** tr. (often foll. by over) go over (ground) cutting down timber. **2** tr. (usu. in passive; usu. foll. by with) burden or leave (a person etc.) with something unwanted or unpleasant (I always get lumbered with the chores). ☐ **lay on the lumber** slang check heavily with a hockey stick.

lumber baron n. N Amer. a leading or wealthy timber merchant.

lumber camp n. N Amer. a camp in which loggers live.

lumbering n. esp. N Amer. **1** the lumber or timber trade. **2** the work of cutting and preparing forest timber.

lumberjack n. N Amer. esp. hist. = LOGGER.

lumberjack jacket n. N Amer. (also **lumberjacket**) a jacket, usu. of warm, red and black checked material, originally worn by loggers.

lumberjack shirt n. esp. N Amer. a long-sleeved shirt of brushed cotton or flannel, usu. in red and black check.

lumberman n. (pl. **-men**) N Amer. **1** a lumber company owner or manager. **2** = LOGGER.

lumber mill n. N Amer. a factory where logs and lumber are dressed.

lumber road n. N Amer. = LOGGING ROAD.

lumberyard n. N Amer. **1** a place where lumber is stored and sold. **2** a business operating such a place.

luminance /'lu:mɪnəns/ n. Physics **1** the state or quality of reflecting light. **2** the intensity of light emitted from a surface per unit area in a given direction.

luminary /'lu:mɪneri/ n. (pl. **-ies**) **1** a prominent member of a group or gathering (business luminaries). **2** a person as a source of intellectual light or moral inspiration. **3** a lamp or artificial light.

luminescence /,lu:mɪ'nesəns/ n. **1** the emission of

light by a substance other than as a result of incandescence. **2** the light emitted by a luminescent object or surface. □ **luminescent** *adj.*

luminous /'lu:mɪnəs/ *adj.* **1** full of or shedding light; radiant, bright. **2** phosphorescent, visible in darkness (*luminous paint*). **3** shedding intellectual, moral, or spiritual light. **4** of visible radiation (*luminous intensity*). □ **luminosity** /-'nɒsɪti/ *n.* **luminously** *adv.*

lummox /'lʌməks/ *n.* esp. *N Amer. informal* a clumsy or stupid person.

lump[1] ● *n.* **1 a** a compact shapeless or unshapely mass (*a lump of dirt*). **b** a cube of sugar for putting in tea or coffee. **2** *slang* a quantity or heap. **3** a tumour, swelling, or bruise. **4** a heavy, dull, or ungainly person. **5** (in *pl.*) *slang* hard knocks, attacks, defeats (*take one's lumps*). ● *v.* **1** *tr.* (usu. foll. by *together, with, in with, under*, etc.) mass together or group indiscriminately. **2** *tr. & intr.* make or become lumpy. **3** *intr.* (usu. foll. by *along*) proceed heavily or awkwardly. □ **lump in the throat** a feeling of pressure there, caused by emotion.

lump[2] *v.tr. informal* endure or suffer (a situation); tolerate reluctantly. □ **like it or lump it** put up with something whether one likes it or not.

lumpectomy /lʌm'pɛktəmi/ *n.* (*pl.* **-ies**) the surgical removal of a usu. cancerous lump from the breast.

lumpen /'lʌmpən/ *derogatory* ● *adj.* ignorantly contented, boorish, stupid; uninterested in revolutionary advancement. ● *n.* the class of those who are lumpen.

lumper *n.* **1** *N Amer.* a person employed in loading and unloading cargo; a longshoreman. **2** a person (esp. a taxonomist) who attaches importance to similarities rather than differences in classification or analysis and so favours inclusive categories (*compare* SPLITTER 2).

lumpish *adj.* **1** heavy and clumsy. **2** stupid, lethargic. **3** shaped like a lump; lumpy. □ **lumpishly** *adv.* **lumpishness** *n.*

lump sum *n.* **1** a sum covering a number of items. **2** money paid down at once (*opp.* INSTALMENT 3).

lumpy *adj.* (**-ier, -iest**) **1** full of or covered with lumps. **2** (of water) cut up by the wind into small waves. **3** (of a person, style, etc.) heavy and clumsy. □ **lumpily** *adv.* **lumpiness** *n.*

lun /lʌn/ *n. Cdn (Nfld)* a lee; a sheltered spot.

lunacy /'lu:nəsi/ *n.* (*pl.* **-ies**) **1** insanity (originally of the intermittent kind attributed to changes of the moon); the state of being a lunatic. **2** great folly or eccentricity; a foolish act.

luna moth /'lu:nə/ *n.* a N American moth, *Actias luna*, with crescent-shaped spots on its pale green wings.

lunar /'lu:nər/ *adj.* **1** of, relating to, resembling, or determined by the moon. **2** concerned with travel to the moon and related research. **3** crescent-shaped. **4** of or containing silver.

lunar eclipse *n.* an eclipse of the moon.

lunar month *n.* the period of the moon's revolution, esp. the interval between new moons of about $29\frac{1}{2}$ days.

lunar orbit *n.* **1** the orbit of the moon around the earth. **2** an orbit around the moon.

lunar year *n.* a period of 12 lunar months.

lunatic /'lu:nətɪk/ ● *n.* **1** an insane person. **2** someone foolish or eccentric. ● *adj.* mad, foolish.

lunatic fringe *n.* a fanatical, eccentric, or visionary minority of any group, society, etc.

lunch ● *n.* **1** the meal eaten in the middle of the day. **2** a light meal eaten at any time. ● *v.intr.* eat one's lunch. □ **do lunch** *informal* have lunch with a person,

esp. a business associate. **out to lunch** *slang* out of touch with reality; unaware; crazy. □ **luncher** *n.*

lunch box *n.* a plastic or metal container with a handle, for carrying a packed meal to school or work.

lunch break *n.* = LUNCH HOUR.

lunch bucket ● *n.* = LUNCH BOX. ● *adj. N Amer.* (**lunch-bucket**) = LUNCH PAIL *adj.*

lunch counter *n. N Amer.* **1** a counter in a department store etc., where light lunches and snacks are served. **2** = LUNCHEONETTE.

luncheon /'lʌntʃən/ *n.* a lunch, esp. a formal one.

luncheonette *n. N Amer.* a small restaurant or snack bar serving light lunches.

luncheon meat *n.* a usu. tinned block of ground meat, usu. sliced and eaten cold in sandwiches etc.

lunch hour *n.* a break from work, usu. around the middle of the day, when lunch is eaten.

lunch kit *n.* = LUNCH BOX.

lunch pail *N Amer.* ● *n.* = LUNCH BOX. ● *adj.* (**lunch-pail**) working-class; blue-collar (*lunch-pail town*).

lunchroom *n.* **1** *N Amer.* a room in a school, office, etc. where lunch is served or where people may eat lunches brought from home. **2** = LUNCHEONETTE.

lunchtime *n.* the time around the middle of the day when lunch is usually eaten (often *attrib.*: *lunchtime drinking*).

lung *n.* either of the pair of respiratory organs which bring air into contact with the blood in humans and many other vertebrates. □ **-lunged** *adj.* (in *comb.*). **lungful** *n.* (*pl.* **-fuls**). **lungless** *adj.*

lunge[1] /lʌndʒ/ ● *n.* **1** a sudden movement forward. **2** a thrust with a sword etc., esp. the basic attacking move in fencing. **3** a movement forward by bending the front leg at the knee while keeping the back leg straight. ● *v.intr.* **1** make a lunge. **2** *Fencing* make a thrust with a foil or rapier.

lunge[2] ● *n.* (in full **lunge line**) a long rope on which a horse is held and made to move in a circle around its trainer. ● *v.tr.* (**lungeing**) exercise (a horse) with or in a lunge.

lunge[3] *n.* = MUSKELLUNGE.

lungfish *n.* any freshwater fish of the order Dipnoi, having gills and a modified swim bladder used as lungs.

lunker /'lʌŋkər/ *n. N Amer. slang* an animal, esp. a fish, which is an exceptionally large example of its species; a whopper.

lunkhead *n.* (also **lunk**) esp. *N Amer. slang* a slow-witted, unintelligent person. □ **lunkheaded** *adj.*

lupine[1] /'lu:pɪn/ *n.* (also **lupin**) any plant of the genus *Lupinus*, with long tapering spikes of blue, purple, pink, white, or yellow flowers.

lupine[2] /'lu:paɪn/ *adj.* of or like a wolf or wolves.

lupus /'lu:pəs/ *n.* any of various ulcerous or erosive skin diseases, esp. lupus erythematosus.

lupus erythematosus /ˌɛrəθiːməˈtoːsəs/ *n.* an inflammatory disease of the skin giving rise to scaly red patches, esp. on the face, and sometimes also involving internal organs.

lurch[1] /lɜːtʃ/ ● *n.* a sudden unsteady movement or leaning; a stagger. ● *v.intr.* **1** (of a person etc.) stagger, move unsteadily. **2** (of a ship etc.) move suddenly to one side.

lurch[2] *n.* □ **leave in the lurch** desert (a friend etc.) in difficulties.

lure /lʊr, lɜr/ ● *v.tr.* **1** (usu. foll. by *away, into*) entice (a person, an animal, etc.) usu. with some form of bait. **2** attract back again or recall (a person, animal, etc.) with the promise of a reward. ● *n.* **1** a thing used to entice. **2** (usu. foll. by *of*) the attractive or compelling qualities (of a pursuit etc.). **3** live or esp. artificial bait used to entice fish or animals; a decoy.

lurid /'lʊrɪd, lɜr-/ *adj.* **1** sensational, horrifying, or terrible (*lurid details*). **2** showy, gaudy (*paperbacks with lurid covers*). **3** vivid or glowing in colour (*lurid orange*). **4** of an unnatural glare (*lurid nocturnal brilliance*). **5** ghastly, wan (*lurid complexion*). □ **luridly** *adv.* **luridness** *n.*

lurk *v.intr.* **1** linger furtively or unobtrusively. **2 a** lie in ambush. **b** (usu. foll. by *in*, *under*, *about*, etc.) hide, esp. for sinister purposes. **3** exist latently or semi-consciously (*a lurking suspicion*). **4** *Computing* read messages on an on-line bulletin board without contributing messages oneself. □ **lurker** *n.*

luscious *adj.* **1 a** richly sweet in taste or smell. **b** *informal* delicious. **2** (of literary style, music, etc.) over-rich in sound, imagery, or voluptuous suggestion. **3** voluptuously attractive. □ **lusciously** *adv.* **lusciousness** *n.*

lush¹ *adj.* **1 a** (of vegetation, esp. grass) luxuriant, abundant. **b** characterized by luxuriance of vegetation (*a lush forest*). **2** luxurious. **3** (of colour, sound, etc.) rich, voluptuous. □ **lushly** *adv.* **lushness** *n.*

lush² *slang* ● *n.* **1** an alcoholic, a drunkard. **2** alcohol, liquor. ● *v.tr. & intr. N Amer.* drink (alcohol).

lust ● *n.* **1** strong sexual desire. **2 a** (usu. foll. by *for*, *of*) a passionate desire for (*a lust for power*). **b** (usu. foll. by *of*) a passionate enjoyment of (*the lust of battle*). **3** (usu. in *pl.*) a sensuous appetite regarded as sinful (*the lusts of the flesh*). ● *v.intr.* (usu. foll. by *after*, *for*) have a strong or excessive (esp. sexual) desire. □ **lustful** *adj.* **lustfully** *adv.* **lustfulness** *n.*

lustre /'lʌstər/ (esp. *US* **luster**) ● *n.* **1** gloss, brilliance, or sheen. **2** a shiny or reflective surface. **3** a thin metallic coating giving an iridescent glaze to ceramics. **4** a radiance or attractiveness; splendour, glory, distinction (of achievements etc.) (*add lustre to*; *shed lustre on*). **5 a** a prismatic glass pendant on a chandelier etc. **b** a cut-glass chandelier or candelabra. **6** any fabric or yarn with a sheen or gloss. ● *v.tr.* put lustre on (pottery, a cloth, etc.). □ **lustreless** *adj.* (esp. *US* **lusterless**). **lustrous** *adj.* **lustrously** *adv.* **lustrousness** *n.*

lusty *adj.* (**-ier**, **-iest**) **1** healthy and strong. **2** vigorous or lively. **3** lustful; full of sexual desire. **4** (of a meal etc.) hearty, abundant. □ **lustily** *adv.* **lustiness** *n.*

lute *n.* a guitar-like instrument with a long neck and a pear-shaped body, much used in the 14th–17th c.

lutein /'lu:tiɪn/ *n. Chem.* a pigment of a deep yellow colour found in egg yolk etc.

luteinizing hormone /'lu:tənaɪzɪŋ/ *n. Biochem.* a hormone secreted by the anterior pituitary gland that in females stimulates ovulation and in males stimulates the synthesis of androgen. Abbr.: **LH**.

lutetium /lu:'ti:ʃiəm/ *n.* a silvery metallic element.

Lutheran /'lu:θərən/ ● *n.* **1** a member of the Church which accepts the Augsburg Confession of 1530, with justification by faith alone as a cardinal doctrine. **2** a follower of the German reformer Martin Luther (1483–1546). ● *adj.* **1** of or relating to Lutherans or the Lutheran church. **2** of or characterized by the theology of Luther. □ **Lutheranism** *n.*

Lutz /lʌts/ *n.* (also **lutz**) *Figure Skating* a jump in which the skater takes off from the back outside edge of one skate, using the toe of the free foot to assist the takeoff, and lands, after at least one complete rotation in the air, on the back outside edge of the other skate.

lux /lʌks/ *n.* (*pl.* same) *Physics* the SI unit of illumination.

luxe /lʌks, lʊks/ ● *n.* luxury (*compare* DELUXE). ● *adj.* deluxe, sumptuous.

luxuriant /lʌɡ'ʒʊriənt, lʌk'ʃʊr-/ *adj.* **1** (of vegetation, hair, etc.) lush, profuse in growth. **2** prolific, exuberant (*luxuriant imagination*). **3** (of literary or artistic style) florid, richly ornate. □ **luxuriance** *n.* **luxuriantly** *adv.* ¶*Luxuriant*, meaning 'growing profusely, exuberant' is sometimes confused with *luxurious*, the adjective relating to luxury.

luxuriate *v.intr.* **1** (foll. by *in*) take self-indulgent delight in, enjoy in a luxurious manner. **2** take one's ease, relax in comfort. **3** (of a plant etc.) grow profusely.

luxurious *adj.* **1** characterized by luxury; sumptuous, rich (*a luxurious estate*). **2** extremely comfortable. **3** self-indulgent, voluptuous. □ **luxuriously** *adv.* **luxuriousness** *n.* ¶See Usage Note at LUXURIANT.

luxury /'lʌkʃəri, 'lʌɡʒəri/ *n.* (*pl.* **-ies**) **1** choice or costly surroundings, possessions, food, etc.; luxuriousness (*a life of luxury*). **2** (often in *pl.*) something desirable for comfort or enjoyment, but not indispensable. **3** a means of indulging one's tastes and desires (*the luxury of only having to work when one wants to*). **4** (*attrib.*) providing great comfort, expensive (*luxury holiday*).

Lw *symbol* lawrencium.

lx *abbr.* lux.

-ly¹ *suffix* forming adjectives esp. from nouns, meaning: **1** having the qualities of (*princely*). **2** recurring at intervals of (*daily*; *hourly*).

-ly² *suffix* forming adverbs from adjectives, denoting esp. manner or degree (*boldly*; *happily*; *deservedly*).

lychee /'li:tʃi/ *n.* **1** a sweet fleshy fruit with a thin spiny skin. **2** the tree, *Nephelium litchi*, originally from China, bearing this.

Lycra /'laɪkrə/ *n. proprietary* an elastic polyurethane fibre or fabric used esp. for close-fitting sports clothing and foundation garments.

lye /laɪ/ *n.* **1** any strong alkaline solution, esp. of potassium hydroxide used for washing or cleansing. **2** water that has been made alkaline by percolation through vegetable ashes.

lying¹ *pres. part. of* LIE¹.

lying² ● *v. pres. part. of* LIE². ● *adj.* deceitful, false. □ **lyingly** *adv.*

Lyme disease /laɪm/ *n.* a form of arthritis which mainly affects the large joints and is caused by spirochete bacteria transmitted by ticks.

lymph /lɪmf/ *n. Physiol.* a colourless fluid containing white blood cells, drained from the tissues and conveyed through the body in the lymphatic system. □ **lymphoid** *adj.*

lymphatic /lɪm'fætɪk/ ● *adj.* **1** of or secreting or conveying lymph. **2** (of a person) pale, flabby, or sluggish. ● *n.* a veinlike vessel conveying lymph.

lymphatic system *n.* a network of vessels conveying lymph.

lymph node *n.* (also **lymph gland**) a small mass of tissue in the lymphatic system where lymph is purified and lymphocytes are formed.

lymphocyte /'lɪmfə,saɪt/ *n.* a form of leukocyte occurring in the blood, in lymph, etc. □ **lymphocytic** /-'sɪtɪk/ *adj.*

lymphoma /lɪm'fəʊmə/ *n.* (*pl.* **-s** or **lymphomata** /-mətə/) any malignant tumour of the lymph nodes, excluding leukemia.

lynch /lɪntʃ/ *v.tr.* (of a body of people) put (a person) to death, esp. by hanging, for an alleged offence without a legal trial. □ **lyncher** n. **lynching** n.

lynch mob n. **1** a mob intent on lynching someone. **2** any unruly, angry crowd of people.

lynchpin var. of LINCHPIN.

lynx /lɪŋks/ n. (pl. same) **1** any of various small to medium-sized members of the cat family typically having a short tail, tufted ears, and mottled or spotted fur, esp. *Lynx canadensis* of northern N America or the smaller *Lynx lynx*, which inhabits forests in NW Europe and northern Asia. **2** its fur.

lyre /laɪr/ n. an ancient stringed instrument like a small U-shaped harp, played usu. with a plectrum and accompanying the voice.

lyric /ˈlɪrɪk / ● adj. **1** (of poetry) expressing the writer's emotions, usu. briefly and in stanzas or recognized forms. **2** (of a poet) writing in this manner. **3** of or for the lyre. **4** meant to be sung, fit to be expressed in song, song-like (*lyric opera*). **5** (of a singing voice) using a light register (*a lyric soprano*). ● n. **1** a lyric poem or verse. **2** (in pl.) lyric verses. **3** (usu. in pl.) the words of a song.

lyrical adj. **1** = LYRIC 1, 2, 5. **2** resembling, couched in, or using language appropriate to, lyric poetry. **3** informal highly enthusiastic (*wax lyrical about*). □ **lyrically** adv.

lyricism /ˈlɪrɪˌsɪzəm/ n. **1** the character or quality of being lyric or lyrical. **2** a lyrical expression. **3** high-flown sentiments.

lyricist n. a person who writes the words to a song.

lyse /laɪz, laɪs/ v.tr. & intr. bring about or undergo lysis.

lysergic acid /laɪˈsɜrdʒɪk/ n. a crystalline acid extracted from ergot or prepared synthetically.

lysergic acid diethylamide /daɪˌeθəˈlæmaɪd, daɪˈeθələˌmaɪd/ n. a powerful hallucinogenic drug.

lysis /ˈlaɪsɪs/ n. (pl. **lyses** /-siːz/) the disintegration of a cell.

-lysis /lɪsɪs/ comb. form forming nouns denoting disintegration or decomposition (*electrolysis*).

Lysol /ˈlaɪsɒl/ n. proprietary a mixture of cresols and soft soap, used as a disinfectant.

Mm

M¹ *n.* (also **m**) (*pl.* **Ms** or **M's**) **1** the thirteenth letter of the alphabet. **2** (as a Roman numeral) 1,000.

M² *abbr.* (also **M.**) **1** Monsieur. **2** (in sizes) medium. **3** *Chem.* molar. **4** Middle. **5** Monday.

M³ *symbol* mega-.

m¹ *abbr.* (also **m.**) **1 a** masculine. **b** male. **2** married. **3** mile(s). **4** million(s). **5** minute(s). **6** month.

m² *symbol* **1** metre(s). **2** milli-. **3** *Physics* mass.

m³ *possess.adj.* = MY (*m'dear*).

'm¹ *abbr.* *informal* am (*I'm sorry*).

'm² *n.* *informal* madam (*yes'm*).

M-16 *n.* (*pl.* **M-16s**) a lightweight, automatic or semi-automatic magazine-fed rifle.

MA *abbr.* Massachusetts (in postal use).

M.A. *abbr.* Master of Arts.

ma /mɒ/ *n.* *informal* mother.

ma'am /mæm, mɔm/ *n.* madam.

ma-and-pa *adj.* *N Amer.* = MOM-AND-POP.

Ma Bell *n.* *informal* the Bell Telephone Company.

Mac *n.* *N Amer.* *informal* **1** a form of address to a male stranger. **2** a McIntosh apple.

macabre /mə'kʊbrə, -'kæbrə, -'kɒb/ *adj.* **1** grim, gruesome. **2** dealing with death.

macadam /mə'kædəm/ *n.* **1** material for road building with successive layers of compacted broken stone. **2** = TARMACADAM. □ **macadamize** *v.tr.*

macadamia /,mækə'deimiə/ *n.* any evergreen tree of the genus *Macadamia*, esp. *M. ternifolia*, bearing edible nutlike seeds.

macaque /mə'kæk/ *n.* any monkey of the genus *Macaca*, including the rhesus monkey, having prominent cheek pouches and usu. a long tail.

macaroni *n.* a tubular variety of pasta, usu. cut into short pieces.

macaroni and cheese *n.* a savoury dish consisting of macaroni baked or served with a cheese sauce.

macaroon *n.* a small light cookie made with egg whites, sugar, and ground almonds or coconut.

macaw /mə'kɔ/ *n.* any long-tailed brightly coloured parrot of the genus *Ara* or *Anodorhynchus*, native to S and Central America.

Mace ● *n.* *proprietary* an irritant chemical preparation used in aerosol form as a disabling weapon. ● *v.tr.* (also **mace**) spray (a person) with Mace.

mace¹ *n.* **1** a staff of office, esp. the symbol of the Speaker's authority in the House of Commons. **2** *hist.* a heavy club usu. having a metal head and spikes. **3** (in full **mace-bearer**) an official who carries a mace on ceremonial occasions.

mace² *n.* the dried outer covering of the nutmeg, used as a spice.

Macedonian ● *n.* **1 a** a native of ancient Macedonia in SE Europe. **b** a native or inhabitant of the modern republic of Macedonia in the Balkans. **c** a native or inhabitant of the region of Macedonia in modern Greece. **2 a** the Slavic language of modern Macedonia. **b** the language of ancient Macedonia. ● *adj.* of or pertaining to Macedonians.

macerate /'mæsə,reit/ *v.tr. & intr.* make or become soft by soaking. □ **maceration** *n.* **macerator** *n.*

Mach /mɒk, mæk/ *n.* (in full **Mach number**) the ratio of the speed of a body to the speed of sound in the surrounding medium. ¶Often as *Mach 1, 2*, etc., (the speed of sound, twice the speed of sound, etc.).

mâche /mɒʃ/ *n.* = LAMB'S LETTUCE.

machete /mə'ʃeti, mə'tʃeti/ *n.* a broad heavy knife, originally used in Central America and the W Indies as an implement and weapon.

Machiavellian /,mækiə'veliən/ ● *adj.* **1** elaborately cunning; scheming, unscrupulous. **2** of, pertaining to, or characteristic of the Italian statesman and political philosopher Niccolò di Bernardo dei Machiavelli (1469–1527) or his principles, esp. that the acquisition and effective use of power may necessitate unethical methods that are not in themselves desirable. ● *n.* **1** a person preferring expediency to morality. **2** a person who adopts the principles recommended by Machiavelli in his treatise on statecraft. □ **machiavellianism** *n.*

machination *n.* (usu. in *pl.*) a cunning plot or scheme.

machine ● *n.* **1** an apparatus using or applying mechanical power, having several parts, each with a definite function which together perform certain kinds of work. **2** a particular kind of machine, e.g. a vehicle, piece of electrical or electronic apparatus, etc. **3** an instrument that transmits a force or directs its application. **4 a** the controlling system of a political party, a similar organization, etc. (*the Big Blue Machine*). **b** a well-organized group acting with often ruthless efficiency. **5** a person who acts mechanically and with apparent lack of emotion. **6** (esp. in *comb.*) a coin-operated dispenser (*pop machine*). ● *v.tr.* **1** cut, make, form, or operate on by means of a machine. **2** engrave, shape, print, or sew (a thing) by means of a machine. □ **machining** *n. & adj.*

machine code *n.* (also **machine language**) a language that a particular computer can handle or act on directly, without further translation (*compare* SOURCE CODE).

machine gun ● *n.* **1** a mounted or portable gun which is mechanically loaded and fired, giving continuous fire while the trigger is pressed. **2** (**machine-gun**) (*attrib.*) like a machine gun, esp. in rapidly and usu. noisily repeated action. ● *v.tr.* (**machine-gun**) (**-gunned, -gunning**) shoot at with a machine gun. □ **machine-gunner** *n.*

machine-readable *adj.* (of data) in a form that a computer can process.

machinery *n.* (*pl.* **-ies**) **1** machines collectively or in general. **2** the moving parts or mechanism of a machine. **3** (foll. by *of*) an organized system (*the machinery of government*). **4** (foll. by *for*) the means or procedures devised or available (*the machinery for decision-making*).

machine shed *n.* *Cdn* (*West*) a small, auxiliary structure or outbuilding in which machines, equipment, implements, etc. are kept.

machine shop *n.* a workshop for making or repairing machines or parts of machines.

machine tool *n.* a mechanically operated tool for working on metal, wood, or plastics.

machine washable *adj.* (of clothes etc.) able to be washed in a washing machine without damage. □ **machine wash** *v.tr.*

machinist *n.* **1** a person who operates a machine, esp. a machine tool. **2** a person who makes, invents, or controls machines or machinery; an engineer.

machismo /məˈtʃɪzmoː, -ˈkɪzmo/ *n.* **1** exaggerated or aggressive pride in being male. **2** a show of such assertive manliness or masculinity.

Mach number *n. see* MACH.

macho /ˈmɒtʃoː, ˈmætʃo/ ● *adj.* aggressively or ostentatiously masculine. ● *n.* = MACHISMO.

mack *var. of* MAC.

mackerel *n.* (*pl.* same or **-s**) any of various swift-swimming pelagic fishes of the family Scombridae, of which several are commercially important as food fishes, esp. *Scomber scombrus*, of the N Atlantic and Mediterranean, which approaches the shore in shoals in summer for spawning.

mackinaw /ˈmækɪnd/ *n. N Amer.* **1 a** a heavy, napped and felted woollen cloth, now usu. with a plaid design. **b** (in full **mackinaw coat** or **mackinaw jacket**) a thick, double-breasted jacket, usu. short and often belted, made of this cloth. **2** (**Mackinaw**; in full **Mackinaw trout**) = LAKE TROUT.

mackintosh *n.* (also **macintosh**) **1** esp. *Brit.* a waterproof coat etc. **2** cloth waterproofed with rubber.

macramé /ˈmækrəmei/ *n.* **1** the art of knotting cord or string in patterns to make decorative articles. **2** articles made in this way.

macro ● *n. Computing* a series of abbreviated instructions expanded automatically when required. ● *adj.* **1** large-scale. **2** overall, comprehensive.

macro- *comb. form* **1** long, large, large-scale. **2** comprehensive. **3** *Med.* abnormally enlarged or elongated.

macrobiotic /ˌmækroʊbaɪˈɒtɪk/ ● *adj.* **1** relating to or following a dietary system intended to prolong life, usu. comprised of pure vegetable foods, brown rice, etc. **2** tending to prolong life; relating to the prolongation of life. ● *n.* (in *pl.*; treated as *sing.*) the use or theory of such a dietary system.

macrocosm /ˈmækroʊˌkɒzəm/ *n.* **1** the universe; the whole of all nature. **2** a complex structure or whole, esp. one considered to be epitomized by some constituent portion or microcosm. □ **macrocosmic** /-ˈkɒzmɪk/ *adj.* **macrocosmically** *adv.*

macroeconomics *n.* the study of large-scale or general economic factors, e.g. national productivity. □ **macroeconomic** *adj.* **macroeconomist** *n.*

macromolecule *n.* a molecule containing a very large number of atoms and having a very high molecular weight. □ **macromolecular** *adj.*

macronutrient *n.* a chemical required in relatively large amounts for the growth and development of living organisms.

macrophage /ˈmækroʊˌfeɪdʒ/ *n.* a large phagocytic white blood cell usu. occurring at points of infection.

macroscopic *adj.* **1** visible to the naked eye. **2** general, comprehensive; regarded in terms of large units. □ **macroscopically** *adv.*

macula /ˈmækjʊlə/ *n.* (*pl.* **maculae** /-ˌliː/) **1** a dark spot, esp. a permanent one, in the skin, e.g. a freckle. **2** (in full **macula lutea** /ˈluːtɪə/) an oval yellowish area near the centre of the retina, where visual acuity is most pronounced. □ **macular** *adj.*

MAD /mæd/ *n.* = MUTUAL ASSURED DESTRUCTION.

mad *adj.* (**madder, maddest**) **1** insane; having a disordered mind. **2** (of a person, conduct, or an idea) wildly foolish. **3** (often foll. by *about, on*) carried away by enthusiasm or desire (*mad about hockey; is powermad*). **4** *informal* **a** beside oneself with anger; furious. **b** annoyed, exasperated. **5** (of an animal) **a** suffering from rabies. **b** abnormally furious. **6 a** frantic, wild, desperate (*a mad dash*). **b** wildly lighthearted. **7** (of a storm, wind, etc.) wild, violent. □ **like mad** *informal* with great energy, intensity, or enthusiasm.

madam /ˈmædəm/ *n.* **1** a polite or respectful form of address or mode of reference to a woman. **2** a woman who keeps a brothel.

Madame /məˈdæm, ˈmædəm/ *n.* **1** (*pl.* **Mesdames** /meɪˈdæm/) a title or form of address used of or to a French-speaking woman, corresponding to Mrs. or madam. **2** (**madame**) = MADAM 1.

madcap ● *adj.* **1** (of a person) reckless, wildly impulsive. **2** (of an endeavour etc.) undertaken without forethought. ● *n.* a wildly impulsive person.

mad cow disease *n. informal* = BSE 1.

madden *v.* **1** *tr.* & *intr.* make or become mad. **2** *tr.* irritate intensely. □ **maddening** *adj.* **maddeningly** *adv.*

madder *n.* **1** a herbaceous plant, *Rubia tinctorum*, with yellowish flowers. **2** a reddish-purple dye obtained from the root of the madder, or its synthetic substitute.

madding *adj.* □ **far from the madding crowd** (of a place) secluded, removed from public notice.

made ● *v. past and past part. of* MAKE. ● *adj.* (usu. in *comb.*) **1** (of a person or thing) built or formed artificially or in a specified manner (*well-made*). **2** successful (*a self-made man*). □ **be made for** be ideally suited to. **be made of** consist of. **have it made** *informal* be sure of success.

made beaver *n. Cdn hist.* (*pl.* same or **made beavers**) **1** a unit of exchange formerly used among fur traders, equivalent to the value of the prepared skin of one adult beaver in prime condition. **2** a coin or token equivalent to this.

made-for-TV *adj.* (also **made-for-television**) **1** (of a film etc.) specially made for first showing on television, not in theatres. **2** (of a set, event, sound bite, etc.) ideally suited to televison.

Madeira /məˈdiːrə/ *n.* a fortified white wine from the island of Madeira, off the NW coast of Africa.

madeleine /ˈmædəˌlen/ *n.* a small, shell-shaped sponge cake.

Madelinot /mædəliˈno/ *n. Cdn* a resident or native of the Magdalen Islands.

made man *n.* a man who has attained success or whose success in life is assured.

Mademoiselle /ˌmædmwəˈzel/ *n.* (*pl.* **Mesdemoiselles**) /ˌmeɪdm-/ **1** a title or form of address used of or to an unmarried French-speaking woman, corresponding to Miss or madam. **2** (**mademoiselle**) a young Frenchwoman.

made-to-measure *adj.* **1** (of clothing, draperies, etc.) made to a specific customer's measurements, specifications, etc. **2** conceived, designed, or particularly suited for a specific situation etc.

made up *adj.* (hyphenated when *attrib.*) **1** invented, not true. **2** (of a person) wearing makeup. **3** (of a meal etc.) already prepared.

madhouse *n.* **1** esp. *hist.* a home or hospital for the mentally ill. **2** *informal* a scene of extreme confusion or uproar.

Madison Avenue *n.* **1** a street in New York where many American advertising agencies have their offices. **2 a** the American advertising industry. **b** the attitudes and methods characteristic of this industry. **c** American advertising agents collectively.

madly adv. **1** in a mad, insane, or foolish manner. **2 a** passionately, fervently. **b** extremely, very.

madman n. (pl. **-men**) an insane, wildly foolish, or furious man.

madness n. the quality or state of being mad.

Madonna n. Christianity **1** (prec. by the) a name for the Virgin Mary. **2** (usu. **madonna**) a picture or statue of the Madonna.

madras /mə'dræs/ n. **1** a strong cotton fabric with brightly coloured or white stripes, checks, etc. **2** (**Madras**; in full **Madras curry**) a hot spiced curry dish usu. made with chicken or beef.

madrigal /'mædrɪgəl/ n. **1** a usu. 16th or 17th-c. part-song for several voices, usu. arranged in elaborate counterpoint and without instrumental accompaniment. **2** a short love poem.

madroño /mə'dro:njo:/ n. (pl. **-os**) (also **madroña**, **madrone** /-njə/) an evergreen tree, Arbutus menziesii, of western N America, with white flowers, red berries, and glossy leaves.

mad scientist n. a wildly eccentric or dangerously insane scientist, esp. as a stock figure in melodramatic horror stories.

madwoman n. (pl. **-women**) an insane, wildly foolish, or furious woman.

M.A.Ed. abbr. Master of Arts in Education.

maelstrom /'meilstrəm/ n. **1** a great whirlpool. **2** a state of turbulence or confusion.

maestoso /mai'sto:zo:/ Music ● adj. & adv. to be performed majestically. ● n. (pl. **-os**) a piece of music to be performed in this way.

maestro /'maistro:/ n. (pl. **-os** or **maestri** /-stri/) (often as a form of address) **1** a distinguished musician, esp. a conductor or performer. **2** a great performer in any sphere, esp. artistic.

Mafia /'mɒfiə, 'mæ-/ n. **1** an organized secret society of criminals, originating in Sicily but now operating internationally, esp. in the US. **2** (**mafia**) any closely united group regarded as exerting a secret and often sinister influence.

Mafioso /ˌmæfi'o:so:, ˌmɒ-/ n. (pl. **-si** /-si/) **1** a member of the Mafia. **2** (**mafioso**) a member of a group regarded as exerting a hidden sinister influence.

mag n. **1** informal **a** a magazine (periodical). **b** a magazine (in a rifle etc.). **2** informal **a** a magnesium. **b** magneto. **c** magnetic. **3** magnitude.

magazine n. **1** a periodical publication containing articles, stories, etc. by various writers, usu. with photographs, illustrations, etc. **2** a chamber for holding a supply of cartridges to be fed automatically to the breech of a repeating rifle, machine gun, etc. **3** a similar device feeding a camera, slide projector, etc. **4 a** a building for the storage of arms, ammunition, and provisions for use in war. **b** a store for large quantities of explosives. **5** a regular television or radio broadcast format comprising a variety of entertainment or news items.

Magen David /mɒ'gɪn dɒ'vɪd/ n. = STAR OF DAVID.

magenta /mə'dʒentə/ ● n. **1** a brilliant mauvish-crimson shade. **2** an aniline dye of this colour. ● adj. of or coloured with magenta.

maggot n. any soft-bodied limbless larva, esp. of a housefly, blowfly, or other dipterous fly, typically found in decaying organic matter. □ **maggoty** adj.

magi pl. of MAGUS.

magic ● n. **1 a** the supposed art of influencing events by the occult control of nature or spirits. **b**

witchcraft. **2** the art of producing by sleight of hand, optical illusion, etc. apparently inexplicable phenomena. **3** an inexplicable or remarkable influence producing surprising results. **4** an enchanting quality or phenomenon. **5** informal exceptional skill or talent. ● adj. **1 a** of, pertaining to, working, or produced by magic. **b** (of a material object) used or usable in magic rites; having supernatural powers (magic wand). **2** producing surprising results, like those attributed to magic. **3** informal wonderful, exciting, fantastic. ● v.tr. (**magicked**, **magicking**) change or create by magic, or apparently so. □ **like magic 1** very rapidly. **2** without any apparent explanation.

magical adj. **1** of or relating to magic. **2 a** resembling magic in action or effect. **b** produced as if by magic. **3** wonderful, enchanting. □ **magically** adv.

magic bullet n. informal = SILVER BULLET.

magic carpet n. a mythical carpet able to transport a person on it to any desired place.

magician n. **1** a person skilled in or practising magic or sorcery. **2** a conjuror. **3** a person with exceptional skill.

Magic Marker n. proprietary a felt-tipped indelible marker pen.

magic mushroom n. a hallucinogenic mushroom, esp. one producing psilocybin.

magic realism n. (also **magical realism**) a literary or artistic genre in which realism and narrative are combined with surreal, fantastic, dreamlike, or mythological elements. □ **magical realist** n. & adj.

magic word n. a word or phrase the utterance of which effects magic or creates a desired effect.

magisterial /ˌmædʒɪ'stiːriəl/ adj. **1** imperious, dictatorial. **2 a** (of a person) invested with authority. **b** of, pertaining to, or befitting a master, teacher, or someone qualified to speak with authority. **3** of or conducted by a magistrate. **4** (of a work, opinion, etc.) highly authoritative. □ **magisterially** adv.

magisterium /ˌmædʒɪ'stiːriəm/ n. Catholicism the teaching function and authority of the Church.

magistracy /'mædʒɪstrəsi/ n. (pl. **-ies**) **1** the office or authority of a magistrate. **2** magistrates collectively.

magistrate /'mædʒɪstreit, -ˌstrət/ n. **1** an official conducting a court for minor cases and preliminary hearings. **2** a civil officer administering the law.

Magistrate's Court n. Cdn = PROVINCIAL COURT.

maglev /'mæglev/ n. (usu. attrib.) magnetic levitation, a system in which magnetic repulsion supports a train above the rail or rails on which it runs, allowing it to glide along in a magnetic field.

magma /'mægmə/ n. (pl. **magmata** /-mətə/ or **-s**) **1** a hot fluid or semi-liquid material beneath the crust of the earth or other planet, which erupts as lava and from which igneous rock is formed by cooling. **2** a crude pasty mixture of mineral or organic matter. □ **magmatic** /-'mætik/ adj. **magmatically** adv.

Magna Carta n. (also **Magna Charta**) **1** a charter of liberty and political rights obtained from King John of England in 1215. **2** any similar document.

magna cum laude /ˌmægnə ku:m 'laudei, -'laudə/ adv. & adj. N Amer. (of a degree, diploma, etc.) with or of great distinction; of a higher standard than average, though not the highest (compare SUMMA CUM LAUDE).

magnanimous /mæg'næniməs/ adj. nobly generous; not petty in feelings or conduct. □ **magnanimity** /ˌmægnə'nimiti/ n. **magnanimously** adv.

magnate /'mægneit, -nət/ n. a wealthy and influential person, esp. in business (shipping magnate).

magnesia /mæg'ni:ʒə, -ʃə, -zjə/ n. **1** magnesium oxide, a white refractory solid used in ceramics etc. **2**

(in general use) hydrated magnesium carbonate, a white powder used as an antacid and laxative.

magnesium /mæg'niːziəm/ n. a naturally-occurring silvery metallic element, used for making light alloys and an essential element in living organisms.

magnesium flare n. an intense white light produced by burning magnesium wire.

magnet n. **1** a piece of iron, steel, alloy, ore, etc., usu. in the form of a bar or horseshoe, having properties of attracting or repelling iron. **2** a person or thing that attracts. **3** = LODESTONE.

magnetic adj. **1 a** having the properties of a magnet. **b** pertaining to a magnet or magnetism. **c** producing, produced by, or acting by magnetism. **2** capable of being attracted by or acquiring the properties of a magnet. **3** very attractive or alluring (a *magnetic personality*). **4** (of a bearing, direction, etc.) measured relative to magnetic north. □ **magnetically** adv.

magnetic compass n. = COMPASS 1.

magnetic disk n. see DISK 1a.

magnetic equator n. an irregular line, passing around the earth near the geographical equator, on which the earth's magnetic field is horizontal so that a magnetic needle has no dip.

magnetic field n. a region of variable force around magnets or current-carrying conductors.

magnetic flux n. a measure of the quantity of magnetism, taking account of the strength and extent of a magnetic field.

magnetic moment n. the measured total intensity of magnetization of a magnet or current-carrying coil, irrespective of the volume or weight of the magnet or coil itself.

magnetic needle n. a piece of magnetized steel used as an indicator of direction, esp. on the dial of a compass or in magnetic and electrical apparatus in telegraphy etc.

magnetic north n. the north magnetic pole, usu. the point indicated by a compass needle.

magnetic pole n. **1** each of the points of the earth's surface, near to but not corresponding to the geographical poles, where the lines of force of the earth's magnetic fields are vertical. **2** a point at which magnetic force is concentrated, esp. either of two such opposite points or regions of a magnet.

magnetic resonance imaging n. a form of medical imaging using the nuclear magnetic resonance of protons in the body. Abbr.: **MRI**.

magnetic stripe n. (also **magnetic strip**) a strip of magnetized material on the back of a credit card, etc. containing electronically coded information.

magnetic tape n. a tape coated with magnetic material for recording sound or pictures or for the storage of information.

magnetism n. **1 a** the characteristic properties of magnetic phenomena, esp. attraction. **b** the property of matter producing these phenomena. **2** the branch of knowledge that deals with magnetic phenomena. **3** an attractive power or influence, esp. personal charm.

magnetite n. magnetic iron oxide, an important ore of iron.

magnetize v.tr. **1** give magnetic properties to; make into a magnet. **2** attract as or like a magnet. □ **magnetizable** adj. **magnetization** n.

magneto /mæg'niːtoː/ n. (pl. **-os**) an electric generator using permanent magnets and producing high voltage, esp. for the ignition of an engine.

magnetometer /ˌmægnə'tɒmɪtər/ n. an instrument

measuring magnetic forces, esp. the earth's magnetism. □ **magnetometric** /mægniːˌtoː'metrɪk/ adj. **magnetometry** n.

magnetosphere /mæg'niːtəˌsfiːr/ n. the not necessarily spherical region surrounding a planet, star, etc. in which its magnetic field is effective and prevails over other magnetic fields. □ **magnetospheric** /-'sfiːrɪk/ adj.

magnet school n. a public school specializing in a particular field or subject area to attract students from various neighbourhoods, regions, etc.

Magnificat /mæg'nɪfɪˌkæt/ n. **1** the hymn of the Virgin Mary (Luke 1:46–55) used as a canticle. **2** a musical setting of this.

magnification n. **1 a** the act or an instance of magnifying by or as by a lens. **b** the process of being so magnified. **2** the amount or degree of magnification. **3** a magnified reproduction.

magnificent adj. splendid; remarkable; impressive. □ **magnificence** n. **magnificently** adv.

magnify v.tr. (**-ies**, **-ied**) **1** make (a thing) appear larger than it is, as with a lens. **2** exaggerate. **3** intensify. **4** archaic extol, glorify, esp. render honour to (God). □ **magnifier** n.

magnifying glass n. a convex lens used to increase the apparent size of an object viewed through it.

magnitude n. **1** great size or extent. **2** importance. **3 a** each of a set of classes into which stars are arranged according to their brilliance, stars of the first magnitude being the most brilliant, those of the sixth barely visible to the naked eye. **b** the relative brightness of a star according to this scale. **4** the intrinsic size of an earthquake or underground explosion, as distinct from local intensity. □ **of the first magnitude** very important.

magnolia /mæg'noːliə/ n. **1** any tree or shrub of the genus *Magnolia*, cultivated for its dark green foliage and large waxlike flowers in spring. **2** a pale, creamy pink colour.

magnum n. (pl. **-s**) **1 a** a wine bottle of about twice the standard size. **b** the quantity of liquor held by such a bottle. **2** (**Magnum**) proprietary **a** a cartridge or shell that is especially powerful or large. **b** (often attrib.) a cartridge or gun adapted so as to be more powerful than its calibre suggests.

magnum opus /ˌmægnəm 'oːpəs/ n. **1** a great and usu. large work of art, literature, etc. **2** the most important work of an artist, writer, etc.

magpie /'mægpaɪ/ n. **1** a European and N American bird of the crow family, *Pica pica*, with a long pointed tail, black and white plumage, and a noisy chattering call, proverbial for its habit of taking and hoarding bright objects. **2** an idle chatterer. **3** a person who collects things indiscriminately.

M.Agr. abbr. Master of Agriculture.

maguey /'mægweɪ/ n. an agave plant, esp. one yielding pulque.

magus /'meɪɡəs/ n. (pl. **magi** /'meɪdʒaɪ/) **1** a member of a priestly caste of ancient Persia. **2** a sorcerer. **3** Christianity (**the** (**three**) **Magi**) the 'wise men' from the East who brought gifts to the infant Christ.

mag wheel n. a lightweight, steel wheel for a motor vehicle, often with an intricate pattern of holes and spokes.

Magyar /'mægjɑr/ ● n. **1** a member of a Ural-Altaic people now predominant in Hungary. **2** the language of this people; Hungarian. ● adj. **1** of or relating to this people or language. **2** designating a style of blouse, bodice, etc. in which the sleeves are cut in one piece with the main part of the garment.

Mahabharata /məˈhɒ,bɑrətə/ n. an ancient Hindu epic relating a feud between two great families.

maharaja /,mɒhəˈrɑdʒə/ n. (also **maharajah**) hist. a title of some Indian princes of high rank.

maharishi /,mɒhəˈriːʃi/ n. **1** a great Hindu sage or spiritual leader. **2** a popular leader of spiritual thought.

mahatma /məˈhætmə/ n. **1** (in India etc.) a person regarded with reverence, love, and respect. **2 a** each of a class of persons in India and Tibet supposed by some to have preternatural powers. **b** a sage.

Mahayana /,mɒhəˈjɑnə/ n. a school of Buddhism with syncretistic features, practised in China, Japan, and Tibet.

Mahdi /ˈmɒdi/ n. (pl. **Mahdis**) **1** a spiritual and temporal messiah expected by Muslims. **2** a leader claiming to be this Messiah. □ **Mahdist** n.

mahi mahi /ˈmɒhi:,mɒhi/ n. N Amer. the common dolphin, eaten as food.

mah-jong /mɒˈdʒɒŋ/ n. (also **mah-jongg**) a Chinese game for four resembling rummy and played with 136 or 144 pieces called tiles.

mahogany /məˈhɒɡəni/ ● n. (pl. **-ies**) **1** a rich, reddish-brown wood used for furniture. **2** any tropical tree of the genus Swietenia, esp. S. mahagoni, yielding this wood. **3** a deep rich reddish-brown. ● adj. of a rich reddish-brown colour.

maid n. **1** a female domestic servant. **2** literary a girl or young woman.

maiden n. **1 a** literary a girl; a young unmarried woman. **b** (attrib.) unmarried (maiden aunt). **2** (attrib.) (of a female animal) unmated. **3** (often attrib.) **a** a horse that has never won a race. **b** a race open only to such horses. **4** (attrib.) being or involving the first attempt or occurrence (maiden voyage). **5** (attrib.) **a** (of soil etc.) that has never been disturbed; unworked. **b** (of a plant or tree) grown from seed as opposed to a stock; not pruned or transplanted. □ **maidenly** adj.

maidenhair n. (in full **maidenhair fern**) a fern of the genus Adiantum, esp. A. capillus-veneris, with fine hairlike stalks and delicate fronds.

maidenhead n. **1** virginity. **2** the hymen.

maiden name n. a wife's surname before marriage.

maid of honour n. **1** esp. N Amer. an unmarried woman who acts as a bride's principal bridesmaid (compare MATRON OF HONOUR). **2** an unmarried lady attending a queen or princess.

mail¹ ● n. **1 a** letters, parcels, etc. conveyed by the postal system. **b** the postal system. **c** one complete delivery or collection of mail. **d** one delivery of letters to one place, esp. to a business on one occasion. **2 a** = ELECTRONIC MAIL. **b** = VOICE MAIL. **3** a vehicle carrying mail. **4** (pl.) (prec. by the) N Amer. the postal service, esp. serving remote areas such as the North etc. ● v.tr. esp. N Amer. **1** send (a letter etc.) through the postal service. **2 a** send e-mail to (a person). **b** send by e-mail.

mail² ● n. **1** armour made of interlaced rings or chains, or overlapping plates, joined together flexibly. **2** the protective shell etc. of an animal. ● v.tr. clothe with or as if with mail. □ **mailed** adj.

mailbag n. **1** a large sack or bag for carrying mail. **2** the correspondence, comments, etc. received by a radio station, television program, etc.

mail bomb ● n. **1** an explosive device disguised as a letter or package and sent through the mail. **2** a huge, useless file sent by electronic mail to take up a large amount of the recipient computer's memory, disk space, etc. ● v.tr. send a mail bomb.

mailbox n. N Amer. **1 a** a public receptacle into which letters are dropped for delivery by the postal service.

b a private receptacle to which letters are delivered. **2** the file etc. in which electronic or voice mail is received and stored.

mailer n. **1** an advertising pamphlet, brochure, or catalogue sent out in the mail. **2** a container such as a cardboard tube etc. for the conveyance of items, esp. papers, by mail. **3** a person who or thing which dispatches messages etc. by mail, electronic mail, etc.

mail-in ● adj. **1** (of an item, such as a rebate coupon etc.) that is or can be sent through the mail. **2** (of a ballot, survey, etc.) conducted through the mail. ● n. an item as a coupon etc. sent out or returned by mail.

mailing n. **1 a** the action or process of sending something by mail. **b** a letter or parcel sent by mail. **2** a batch of mail or a number of items mailed at one time, esp. as part of a publicity campaign, survey, etc.

mailing address n. N Amer. the address to which one has one's mail sent, esp. if different from one's street address.

mailing list n. a list of people to whom advertising matter, information, etc. is to be mailed regularly.

mailman n. (pl. **-men**) N Amer. a postman.

mail merge n. Computing **1** a program that draws on a file of names and addresses and a text file to produce multiple copies of a letter, each addressed to a different recipient. **2** the facility for doing this.

mail order ● n. **1** an order for goods sent by mail. **2 a** a system of buying and selling goods by mail. **b** (hyphenated when attrib.) a company etc. offering mail-order goods (mail-order catalogue). ● v.tr. (**mail-order**) buy through mail-order catalogues etc.

mailroom n. a room in a company etc. where mail is collected, sorted, or otherwise dealt with.

mail slot n. N Amer. a slit in the door of a house, apartment, etc. through which letters are delivered.

maim v.tr. **1** cripple, disable, mutilate. **2** harm, impair, render powerless or essentially incomplete (emotionally maimed by neglect).

main ● adj. **1** chief in size, importance, extent, etc.; principal (the main part; the main point). **2** (of strength etc.) exerted to the full; sheer (by main force). ● n. **1 a** principal channel, duct, etc., for water, sewage, etc. (water main). **2** esp. Brit. (usu. in pl.; prec. by the) **a** the central distribution network for electricity, gas, water, etc. **b** a domestic electricity supply as distinct from batteries. **3** literary **a** the ocean or oceans (the Spanish main). **b** the mainland. **4** (**the Main**) Cdn informal Saint-Laurent Boulevard in Montreal. □ **in the main** for the most part. **with might and main** with all one's strength.

main chance n. something which is of principal importance. □ **an eye for** (or **to**) **the main chance** consideration for one's own interests.

main clause n. Grammar a clause that alone forms a complete sentence (compare SUBORDINATE CLAUSE).

main course n. (also **main dish**) **1** the chief course of a meal. **2** any of a number of substantial dishes in a large menu.

main deck n. the principal deck of a ship, usu. the uppermost enclosed one running the whole length.

main drag n. N Amer. informal = MAIN STREET.

main floor n. esp. N Amer. = GROUND FLOOR.

mainframe n. **1** (often attrib.) a large or general-purpose computer, esp. one supporting numerous peripherals etc. **2** the central processing unit and primary memory of a computer.

mainland n. **1** a large continuous extent of land, including the greater part of a country or territory and excluding neighbouring islands, peninsulas, etc. **2** (**Mainland**) Cdn (Nfld) **a** the provinces of Canada other than Newfoundland. **b** (to those on the coastal islands) the coast of Labrador. ☐ **mainlander** n.

mainline ● adj. (of an institution etc.) established, normative, and usu. moderate in opinions, attitudes, etc. (*mainline churches*). ● n. **1** (usu. **main line**) a principal railway line. **2** N Amer. Forestry the primary, heavy cable used to haul logs from the forest to the landing. **3** slang a principal vein, esp. as a site for a drug injection. ● v. slang **1** intr. take drugs intravenously. **2** tr. inject (drugs) intravenously.

mainly adv. for the most part; chiefly.

main man n. **1** a principal figure on a team, in a political campaign, etc. **2** the principal performer in a band. **3** slang a close and usu. trusted friend or companion.

mainmast n. the principal mast of a ship.

main memory n. Computing random access memory.

mainsail /'meinseil, -səl/ n. **1** (in a square-rigged vessel) the lowest sail on the mainmast. **2** (in a fore-and-aft rigged vessel) a sail set on the after part of the mainmast.

mainsheet n. Naut. the rope which controls the boom of the mainsail when set.

mainspring n. **1** a chief motive, reason, or incentive. **2** the principal spring of a mechanical clock, etc.

main squeeze n. N Amer. slang a lover.

mainstage n. the stage of the principal theatre operated by a theatrical company, usu. the one on which major works are performed.

mainstay n. a chief support or principal element (a *mainstay of the repertoire*).

mainstream ● adj. **1** belonging to or characteristic of an established field of activity. **2** of or pertaining to the mainstream. ● n. **1** the prevailing trend in opinion, fashion, etc. **2** the stream of education or a class at school etc. for students without special needs. **3** a type of jazz based on the swing style of the 1930s and consisting esp. of solo improvisation on chord sequences. **4** the principal current of a river. ● v.tr. & intr. **1** a place (a child with a disability) in a school or class for those without special needs for all or part of the school day. **b** educate in such an integrated environment. **2** incorporate into the mainstream. ☐ **mainstreamer** n. **mainstreaming** n.

main street n. the principal street of a town or city.

mainstreeting n. Cdn political campaigning in main streets to win support. ☐ **mainstreet** v.intr.

maintain v.tr. **1** cause to continue; keep up, preserve (a state of affairs, an activity, etc.) (*maintained friendly relations*). **2** (often foll. by in) support (life, a condition, etc.) by work, nourishment, expenditure, etc. (*maintained him in comfort*). **3** (often foll. by that + clause) support or uphold, esp. in speech or argument (*maintained that she was the best*). **4** preserve or provide for the preservation of (a building, machine, road, etc.) in good repair. **5** give aid to (a cause, party, etc.). **6** pay for the upkeep, repair, or equipping of (a garrison etc.). ☐ **maintainability** n. **maintainable** adj. **maintainer** n.

maintenance n. **1 a** the action or process of maintaining or being maintained. **b** the state or fact of being maintained. **2 a** the provision of the means to support life, esp. by work etc. **b** a husband's or wife's provision for a spouse after separation or divorce. **3** (attrib.) (of a drug, dosage, treatment, etc.) sufficient to sustain an esp. beneficial effect on the body.

maintenance man n. a man employed for caretaking and janitorial duties.

maiolica /mə'jɒlɪkə/ var. of MAJOLICA.

maison de la culture /me'zɔ̃ də læ kʊltʊr/ n. Cdn

(Que.) a cultural centre, usu. containing a library, theatre, and exhibition space for visual arts.

mai tai /'maitai/ n. a cocktail of rum, curaçao, and fruit juices.

maître d' /ˌmeitrə 'di:, ˌmeitər, ˌmetrə/ = MAÎTRE D'HOTEL.

maître d'hotel /ˌmeitrə do:'tel, ˌmet-/ n. **1** the manager etc. of a hotel. **2** a head waiter.

maize n. esp. Brit. = CORN[1] 1.

Maj abbr. (also **Maj.**) MAJOR n. 1.

majestic /mə'dʒestɪk/ adj. showing majesty; stately and dignified; grand, imposing. ☐ **majestically** adv.

majesty n. (pl. **-ies**) **1** impressive dignity or beauty. **2** a royal power. **b** (**Majesty**) (prec. by your, her, his, their, etc.) a title used to refer to or address a sovereign or a sovereign's wife or widow.

Maj. Gen. abbr. MAJOR GENERAL.

majolica /mə'dʒɒlɪkə, mə'jɒl-/ n. a type of earthenware with coloured decoration on a white glaze.

major ● adj. **1** important, large, serious, significant (a *major road; the major consideration is their health*). **2** (of an operation) serious or life-threatening. **3** Music **a** (of a scale) having intervals of a semitone between the third and fourth, and seventh and eighth degrees. **b** (of an interval) greater by a semitone than a minor interval (*major third*). **c** (of a key) based on a major scale, tending to produce a bright or joyful effect (D *major*). **4** of full age. **5** Logic **a** (of a term) occurring in the predicate or conclusion of a syllogism. **b** (of a premise) containing a major term. ● n. **1** Military **a** (in the Canadian or US Army and Air Force and other armies) an officer of a rank next below lieutenant colonel and above captain. **b** an officer in charge of a section of band instruments (*pipe major*). **2** a person of full age. **3** Music a major key etc. **4** N Amer., Austral. & NZ **a** the principal subject or course of a student at university or college. **b** a student specializing in a specified subject (a *philosophy major*). **5** N Amer. (in pl.) the major leagues. **6** Hockey = MAJOR PENALTY. **7** designating levels of amateur hockey for competitors between the ages of 18 and 21, or for younger players if their skills are adequate to compete with older players. ● v.intr. (foll. by in) N Amer., Austral., & NZ study or qualify in a subject (*majored in history*).

majorette n. = DRUM MAJORETTE.

major general n. (in the Canadian or US Army and Air Force and other armies) an officer of a rank next below a lieutenant general and above brigadier general or brigadier. Abbr.: **MGen** Cdn or **Maj. Gen.**

majoritarian /məˌdʒɒrɪ'teriən, -dʒɒrɪ-/ ● adj. **1** governed by or believing in majority rule. **2** of, relating to, or constituting a majority. ● n. a person who supports majority rule. ☐ **majoritarianism** n.

majority n. (pl. **-ies**) **1** (usu. foll. by of) the greater number or part. ¶Some feel that *majority* in this sense should be used only with countable nouns, e.g. a *majority of people*, and not with mass nouns, e.g. a *majority of the work*, although use with mass nouns is both widespread and standard. To avoid wordiness and possible criticism, *most* may be used in such cases, e.g. *most of the work*. When *majority* is followed by a plural noun, a plural verb is used, e.g. The *majority of her books are best-sellers*. **2** Politics **a** the number by which the votes cast for one party, candidate, etc. exceed those of the next in rank (*won by a majority of 151*) (compare PLURALITY 3). **b** a party etc. receiving the greater number of votes. **3** full legal age (*attained her majority*). ☐ **in the majority** belonging to or constituting a majority party etc.

majority government n. Cdn, Brit., Austral., & NZ a

government that has more than half of the total number of parliamentary seats.

majority leader *n.* (in the US) the floor leader of the party having the majority in a legislature.

majority rule *n.* the principle that the greater number should exercise greater power.

major junior *n. Cdn* the highest level of amateur hockey competition.

major league *N Amer.* ● *n.* **1** either of the two principal professional baseball leagues in N America, the American League and the National League. **2** a similar league in other sports. **3** a category in any field considered to be the most demanding, most professional, or of the highest calibre. ● *adj.* (usu. **major-league**) **1** of or relating to a major league (*set a major-league record*). **2** of the highest order. □ **major-leaguer** *n.*

majorly *adv. N Amer. slang* to a great extent.

major penalty *n. Hockey* a five minute penalty, given esp. for fighting.

major planet *n. see* PLANET 1.

major prophet *n.* each of the prophets (Isaiah, Jeremiah, and Ezekiel) for whom the longer prophetic books of the Bible are named and whose prophecies they record.

majuscule /ˈmædʒəˌskjuːl/ ● *n.* **1** a large letter, whether capital or uncial. **2** large lettering. ● *adj.* of, written in, or concerning majuscules.

make ● *v.* (*past* and *past part.* **made**) **1** *tr.* construct; create; form from parts or other substances (*made it out of cardboard*). **2** *tr.* (foll. by *to* + infin.) cause or compel (a person etc.) to do something (*make her repeat it*). **3** *tr.* **a** cause to exist; create; bring about (*made a noise*). **b** cause to become or seem (*made him angry*). **c** appoint; designate (*made her a senator*). **4** *tr.* compose; prepare; draw up (*made her will; made a film*). **5** *tr.* constitute; amount to (*2 and 2 make 4*). **6** *tr.* **a** undertake or agree to (an aim or purpose) (*made a promise; make an effort*). **b** execute or perform (a bodily movement, a speech, etc.) (*made a face*). **7** *tr.* gain, acquire, procure (money, a profit, etc.). **8** *tr.* prepare (a drink, dish, etc.) for consumption. **9** *tr.* **a** arrange bedclothes tidily on (a bed) ready for use. **b** arrange and light materials for (a fire). **10** *intr.* **a** proceed (*made towards the river*). **b** (foll. by *to* + infin.) begin an action (*she made to go*). **11** *tr. informal* **a** arrive at (a place) or in time for (a train etc.) (*made the town before dark; made the six o'clock train*). **b** manage to attend; manage to attend on (a certain day) or at (a certain time) (*can make any day except Friday*). **c** achieve a place in (*made the six o'clock news*). **d** esp. *N Amer.* achieve the rank of (*made colonel in three years*). **12** *tr.* establish or enact (a distinction, rule, law, etc.). **13** *tr.* consider to be; estimate as (*what do you make the time?*). **14** *tr.* secure the success or advancement of (*it made my day*). **15** *tr.* accomplish (a distance, speed, score, etc.) (*made 120 km/h on the highway*). **16** *tr.* **a** become by development or training (*made a great leader*). **b** serve as (*makes a useful seat*). **17** *tr.* (usu. foll. by *out*) represent as; cause to appear as (*makes him out a liar*). **18** *tr.* form in the mind; feel (*I make no judgment*). **19** *tr.* (foll. by *it* + compl.) **a** determine, establish, or choose (*let's make it Tuesday*). **b** bring to (a chosen value etc.) (*decided to make it a dozen*). **20** *tr. slang* have sexual relations with. **21** *intr.* (of the tide) begin to flow or ebb. **22** *tr. Cdn* (esp. *Nfld*) preserve (fish) by drying and salting. ● *n.* **1** (esp. of a product) a type, origin, brand, etc. of manufacture. **2** a kind of mental, moral, or physical structure or composition. □ **make as if** (or **though**) (foll. by *to* + infin. or conditional) act as if the speci-

fied circumstances applied (*made as if she had not noticed*). **make away** (or **off**) depart hastily. **make away with 1** get rid of; kill. **2** squander. **make a day** (or **night** etc.) **of it** devote a whole day (or night etc.) to an activity. **make do 1** manage with the limited or inadequate means available. **2** (foll. by *with*) manage with (something) as an inferior substitute. **make for 1** tend to result in (happiness etc.). **2** proceed towards (a place). **3** assault; attack. **4** confirm (an opinion). **make it** *informal* **1** succeed in reaching, esp. in time. **2** be successful. **3** (usu. foll. by *with*) *slang* have sexual intercourse (with). **make it up 1** be reconciled, esp. after a quarrel. **2** fill in a deficit. **make it up to** remedy negligence, an injury, etc. to (a person). **make like** *informal* pretend to be; imitate. **make much** (or **little**) **of 1** derive much (or little) advantage from. **2** give much (or little) attention, importance, etc., to. **make of 1** construct from. **2** conclude to be the meaning or character of (*can you make anything of it?*). **make off** = MAKE AWAY. **make off with** carry away; steal. **make or break** cause the success or ruin of. **make out 1 a** distinguish by sight or hearing. **b** decipher (handwriting etc.). **2** understand (*can't make him out*). **3** assert; pretend (*made out she liked it*). **4** *informal* make progress; fare (*how did you make out?*). **5** (usu. foll. by *to*, *in favour of*) draw up; write out (*made out a cheque to her*). **6** *N Amer. informal* indulge in sexual activity usu. stopping short of intercourse. **7** prove or try to prove (*how do you make that out?*). **make over 1** transfer the possession of (a thing) to a person. **2** refashion (a garment etc.). **3** change (a person, an institution) to fit a new image. **make up 1** serve or act to overcome (a deficiency). **2** complete (an amount, a party, etc.). **3** compensate. **4** be reconciled. **5** put together; compound; prepare. **6** sew (parts of a garment etc.) together. **7** get (a sum of money, a company, etc.) together. **8** concoct (a story). **9** (of parts) compose (a whole). **10 a** apply cosmetics. **b** apply cosmetics to. **11** settle (a dispute). **12** prepare (a bed) for use with fresh sheets etc. **13** compile (a list, an account, a document, etc.). **make up to** curry favour with; court. **on the make** *informal* **1** intent on gain. **2** looking for sexual partners.

make-believe ● *n.* pretense. ● *adj.* pretended.

make-do *adj.* makeshift.

make-over *n.* a complete transformation or remodelling.

maker *n.* **1** (often in *comb.*) a person or thing that makes. **2** a manufacturer. **3** (**our**, **the**, etc. **Maker**) God. **4** a person who executes a legal document, esp. a promissory note. □ **meet one's maker** *informal* die.

makeshift ● *adj.* temporary (*a makeshift arrangement*). ● *n.* a temporary substitute or device.

makeup *n.* **1** cosmetics for the face etc., either generally or to create a performer's appearance or disguise. **2** the appearance of the face etc. when cosmetics have been applied (*his makeup was not convincing*). **3** a person's character, temperament, etc. **4** the composition or constitution (of a thing). **5** *N Amer.* a supplementary test or assignment given to a student who missed or failed the original one (also *attrib.*: *makeup exam*).

make-work *n.* **1** esp. *N Amer.* work or activity of little or no value, devised mainly to keep someone busy (also *attrib.*: *a make-work project*). **2** esp. *Cdn* (*attrib.*) designating an esp. government-sponsored project, program, grant, etc. intended to create jobs.

making *n.* **1** in senses of MAKE *v.* **2** (in *pl.*) **a** earnings; profit. **b** (usu. foll. by *of*) essential qualities or ingredients (*has the makings of a general*; *we have the* *makings of a meal*). **c** *N Amer. & Austral. informal* paper and tobacco for rolling a cigarette. □ **be the making of** ensure the success or favourable development of. **in the making** in the course of being made or formed.

mako /ˈmækəː/ *n.* (*pl.* **-os**) a large blue shark of the genus *Isurus* (family Lamnidae), of tropical and temperate oceans worldwide.

malacca /məˈlækə/ *n.* (in full **malacca cane**) a cane from the stem of the palm tree *Calamus scipionum* having a rich brown colour, used for walking sticks etc.

malachite /ˈmæləˌkaɪt/ *n.* a bright green mineral of hydrous copper carbonate, taking a high polish and used ornamentally.

maladaptive *adj.* (of an individual, species, etc.) failing to adjust adequately to the environment, and undergoing emotional, behavioural, physical, or mental repercussions. □ **maladapted** *adj.*

maladjusted *adj.* **1** not correctly adjusted. **2** (of a person) unable to adapt to or cope with the demands of a social environment. □ **maladjustment** *n.*

maladroit /ˌmæləˈdrɔɪt/ *adj.* clumsy; bungling. □ **maladroitly** *adv.* **maladroitness** *n.*

malady /ˈmælədi/ *n.* (*pl.* **-ies**) **1** an ailment; a disease. **2** a morbid or depraved condition; something requiring a remedy.

Malagasy /ˌmæləˈgæsi/ ● *adj.* of or relating to Madagascar, an island country off the E coast of Africa. ● *n.* **1** the language of Madagascar. **2** a native or inhabitant of Madagascar.

malaise /məˈleɪz/ *n.* **1** a non-specific bodily discomfort not associated with the development of a disease. **2** a feeling of uneasiness.

malamute /ˈmæləˌmjuːt/ *n.* a dog of a breed developed in Alaska, with a thick grey or black and white coat, pointed ears, and a plumed tail curling over the back.

malapropism /ˈmæləprɒpˌɪzəm/ *n.* (also **malaprop**) the use of a word in mistake for one sounding similar, to comic effect, e.g. *consummated* for *consommé*.

malaria /məˈleriə/ *n.* an intermittent and remittent fever caused by a protozoan parasite of the genus *Plasmodium*, introduced by the bite of a mosquito. □ **malarial** *adj.*

malarkey /məˈlɑrki/ *n. informal* humbug; nonsense.

malathion /ˌmæləˈθaɪɒn/ *n.* an insecticide containing phosphorus, with low toxicity to other animals.

Malay /məˈleɪ/ ● *n.* **1 a** a member of a people inhabiting Malaysia and Indonesia in SE Asia. **b** a person of Malay descent. **2** the language of this people, the official language of Malaysia. ● *adj.* of or relating to this people or language.

Malayan /məˈleɪən/ ● *n.* = MALAY *n.* 1. ● *adj.* of or relating to Malays or Malaya (now part of Malaysia).

Malayo-Polynesian /məˈleɪjoː-/ ● *adj.* of or relating to the Malays and the Polynesians, or to Malayo-Polynesian. ● *n.* = AUSTRONESIAN *n.*.

Malaysian /məˈleɪʒən/ ● *n.* **1** a native or inhabitant of Malaysia in SE Asia. **2** a person of Malaysian descent. ● *adj.* of or relating to Malaysia or its people.

malcontent ● *n.* a discontented person; a rebel. ● *adj.* discontented or rebellious.

male ● *adj.* **1** of the sex that can beget offspring by fertilization or insemination. **2** of men or male animals, plants, etc.; masculine (*playing a male role; male choir*). **3** (of plants or their parts) containing only fertilizing organs. **4** (of parts of machinery etc.) designed to enter or fill the corresponding female part (*a male plug*). ● *n.* a male person, animal, or plant. □ **maleness** *n.*

male bonding *n.* the formation of friendship and loyalty between males, esp. between a particular pair of male associates.

male chauvinist *n.* (also **male chauvinist pig**) *informal derogatory* a man who is prejudiced against women or regards women as inferior. □ **male chauvinism** *n.*

Malecite /ˈmæləˌsəit/ *var. of* MALISEET.

malefactor /ˈmæləˌfæktər/ *n.* a criminal; an evildoer. □ **malefaction** /-ˈfækʃən/ *n.*

male menopause *n.* a crisis of potency, confidence, etc., supposed to afflict men in middle life.

malemute *var. of* MALAMUTE.

malevolent /məˈlevələnt/ *adj.* wishing evil to others. □ **malevolence** *n.* **malevolently** *adv.*

malfeasance /mælˈfiːzəns/ *n. Law* evildoing; illegal action.

malformation *n.* faulty formation. □ **malformed** *adj.*

malfunction ● *n.* a failure to function in a normal or satisfactory manner. ● *v.intr.* fail to function normally or satisfactorily.

malic acid /ˈmælɪk/ *n.* an organic acid found in apples and other fruits.

malice *n.* **1** the intention to do evil or to injure another person. **2** *Law* wrongful intention, esp. as increasing the guilt of certain offences.

malice aforethought *n. Law* the intention to commit a crime, esp. murder.

malicious /məˈlɪʃəs/ *adj.* characterized by malice; intending or intended to do harm. □ **maliciously** *adv.* **maliciousness** *n.*

malign /məˈlaɪn/ ● *adj.* **1** (of a thing) injurious. **2** malevolent. ● *v.tr.* speak ill of; slander. □ **malignity** /məˈlɪgnɪti/ *n.* (*pl.* **-ies**).

malignant /məˈlɪgnənt/ *adj.* **1 a** (of a disease) very virulent or infectious (*malignant cholera*). **b** (of a tumour) tending to invade normal tissue and recur after removal; cancerous. **2** harmful; feeling or showing intense ill will. □ **malignancy** *n.* (*pl.* **-ies**). **malignantly** *adv.*

malinger /məˈlɪŋgər/ *v.intr.* exaggerate or feign illness in order to escape duty, work, etc. □ **malingerer** *n.*

Maliseet /ˈmæləˌsiːt/ (*pl.* same) ● *n.* **1** a member of an Aboriginal people now occupying northwestern New Brunswick and eastern Quebec. **2** the Algonquian language of this people. ● *adj.* of or relating to this people or their language or culture.

mall *n.* **1** a retail complex containing several stores, restaurants, etc., in a single building or adjacent buildings. **2** a sheltered walk or promenade.

mallard /ˈmælərd, -ɑrd/ *n.* (*pl.* same or **-s**) a common wild duck or drake, *Anas platyrhynchos*, of the northern hemisphere, the male of which has a green head, narrow white collar, chestnut breast, and a blue patch on the wings.

mall crawl *n. N Amer. slang* the act of visiting a large number of stores in a shopping mall.

malleable /ˈmæliəbəl/ *adj.* **1** (of metal etc.) able to be hammered or pressed permanently out of shape without breaking or cracking. **2** (of a person) adaptable; pliable, flexible. □ **malleability** *n.*

mallet /ˈmælət/ *n.* **1** a type of hammer, usu. made of wood and having a relatively large head, used for driving chisels, beating metal, etc. **2** a light hammer used for playing the vibraphone etc. **3** a long-handled wooden hammer for striking a croquet or polo ball.

mallow *n.* **1** any plant of the genus *Malva*, esp. *M. sylvestris*, naturalized in N America with pink or purple flowers. **2** any of several other plants of the family Malvaceae, including marsh mallow.

mall rat *n. N Amer. informal* a person, esp. a teenager, who frequents malls to socialize etc.

malmsey /'mɒmzi/ *n.* a strong sweet wine originally from Greece, now chiefly from Madeira.

malnourished *adj.* suffering from malnutrition.

malnutrition *n.* (also **malnourishment**) a dietary condition resulting from the absence of some foods or essential elements necessary for health.

malocclusion *n.* imperfect positioning of the teeth when the jaws are closed.

malodorous *adj.* foul smelling.

malolactic /mælo:'læktɪk/ *adj.* designating bacterial fermentation which converts malic acid (in wine) to lactic acid.

Malpeque oyster /'mɒlpek/ *n. Cdn* a large edible oyster raised in Malpeque Bay in PEI.

malpractice *n.* **1** improper or negligent professional treatment, esp. medical. **2 a** criminal wrongdoing; misconduct. **b** an instance of this.

malt ● *n.* **1** barley or other grain that is steeped, germinated, and dried, esp. for brewing or distilling and vinegar making. **2 a** = MALT WHISKY. **b** = MALT LIQUOR. **3** *N Amer.* = MALTED MILK. **●** *v.* **1** *tr.* convert (grain) into malt. **2** *intr.* (of seeds) become malt when germination is checked by drought.

malted ● *adj.* **1** converted into malt. **2** mixed with malt or a malt extract. **●** *n. N Amer.* = MALTED MILK.

malted milk *n.* **1** a powder made from dried milk and malted cereals. **2** a drink made of this and milk, usu. with ice cream and flavouring.

Maltese /mɒl'ti:z/ **●** *n.* **1** (*pl.* same) **a** a native or national of Malta, an island country in the central Mediterranean. **b** a person of Maltese descent. **2** the Semitic language of Malta, heavily influenced by Italian. **●** *adj.* of or relating to Malta or its people.

Maltese cross *n.* a cross with arms of equal length broadening from the centre, often indented at the ends.

Malthusian /mæl'θu:ziən/ **●** *adj.* of or relating to T. R. Malthus, English clergyman and economist (1766–1834) or his theories, esp. that the increase of populations is checked only by the limits of their means of subsistence. **●** *n.* a follower of Malthus. **□ Malthusianism** *n.*

malt liquor *n.* alcoholic liquor made from malt by fermentation as opposed to distillation, e.g. beer etc.

maltose /'mɒltoz/ *n. Chem.* a sugar produced by the hydrolysis of starch under the action of the enzymes in malt, saliva, etc.

maltreat *v.tr.* ill-treat. **□ maltreatment** *n.*

malt whisky *n.* whisky made from malted barley.

malty *adj.* (**-ier, -iest**) of, containing, or resembling malt. **□ maltiness** *n.*

mama *n. informal* (esp. as a child's term) mother.

mama's boy *n. N Amer. informal* a boy or man who is excessively influenced by or devoted to his mother.

mambo ● *n.* (*pl.* **-os**) **1** a Latin American dance like the rumba. **2** the music for this. **●** *v.intr.* (**-oes, -oed**) perform the mambo.

mamilla /mə'mɪlə/ *n.* (*pl.* **-illae** /-li:/) **1** the nipple of a woman's breast. **2** a nipple-shaped organ etc.

mamma¹ *informal var. of* MAMA.

mamma² /'mæmə/ *n.* (*pl.* **mammae** /-mi:/) **1** a milk-secreting organ of female mammals. **2** a corresponding non-secretory structure in male mammals.

mammal *n.* any warm-blooded animal of the vertebrate class Mammalia, members of which are charac-

terized by the possession of mammary glands in the female and a four-chambered heart. **□ mammalian** /mæ'meiliən/ *adj. & n.*

mammary /'mæməri/ *adj.* of the human female breasts or milk-secreting organs of other mammals.

mammary gland *n.* the milk-producing gland of female mammals.

mammilla *var. of* MAMILLA.

mammogram /'mæməgram/ *n.* an image obtained by mammography.

mammography /mæ'mɒgrəfi/ *n.* an X-ray technique of diagnosing and locating abnormalities (esp. tumours) of the breasts.

Mammon /'mæmən/ *n.* wealth regarded as an idol or as an evil influence. **□ Mammonism** *n.*

mammoth ● *n.* any large extinct elephant of the genus *Mammuthus*, with a hairy coat and curved tusks. **●** *adj.* huge.

mammy *n.* (*pl.* **-ies**) *dated* a child's word for mother.

Man. *abbr.* Manitoba.

man ● *n.* (*pl.* **men**) **1** an adult human male, esp. as distinct from a woman or boy. **2 a** a human being; a person (*no man is perfect*). **b** the human race (*man is mortal*). ¶The generic use of *man* to mean 'a human being' or 'the human race' is regarded by many as sexist. **3** a person showing characteristics associated with males (*she's more of a man than he is*). **4 a** a worker; an employee (*spoke to the men*). **b** a manservant or valet. **5 a** (usu. in *pl.*) soldiers, sailors, etc., esp. non-officers. **b** an individual, usu. male, person (*fought to the last man*). **c** (usu. prec. by *the*, or *possess.adj.*) a person regarded as suitable or appropriate in some way; a person fulfilling requirements (*not the man for the job*). **6 a** a husband (*man and wife*). **b** *informal* a boyfriend or lover. **7 a** a human being of a specified historical period or character (*Renaissance man*). **b** a type of prehistoric man named after the place where the remains were found (*Peking man*). **8** any one of a set of pieces used in playing chess, checkers, etc. **9** (as second element in *comb.*) a man of a specified nationality, profession, skill, etc. (*Dutchman; clergyman; horseman*). **10 a** an expression of impatience etc. used in addressing a male (*nonsense, man!*). **b** *informal* a general mode of address (*blew my mind, man!*). **11** (prec. by *a*) a person; one (*what can a man do?*). **12 a** a person pursued; an opponent etc. (*the Mounties always get their man*). **●** *v.tr.* (**manned, manning**) **1** supply (a ship, fort, factory, etc.) with a person or people for work or defence etc. **2** work or service or defend (a specified piece of equipment, a fortification, etc.) (*man the pumps*). **3** *Naut.* place men at (a part of a ship). **4** fill (a post or office). **●** *interj.* esp. *N Amer. informal* expressing surprise, admiration, etc. **□ as one man** in unison; in agreement. **be a man** be courageous; not show fear. **be one's own man 1** be free to act; be independent. **2** be in full possession of one's faculties etc. **man to man** with candour; honestly. **my** (or **my good**) **man** a patronizing mode of address to a man. **separate** (or **sort out**) **the men from the boys** *informal* find those who are truly virile, competent, etc. **to a man** all without exception. **□ manless** *adj.*

mana /'mɒnə/ *n.* an impersonal supernatural power which can be associated with people or objects and which can be transmitted or inherited.

man about town *n.* a sophisticated man who frequently goes to fashionable clubs, parties etc.

manacle /'mænəkəl/ **●** *n.* (usu. in *pl.*) **1** a fetter or shackle for the hand; a handcuff. **2** a restraint. **●** *v.tr.* fetter with manacles.

manage *v.* **1** *tr.* organize; regulate; be in charge of (a business, household, team, a person's career, etc.). **2** *tr.* succeed in achieving; contrive (*managed a smile*; *managed to ruin the day*). **3** *intr.* **a** (often foll. by *with*) succeed in one's aim, esp. against heavy odds (*managed with one assistant*). **b** meet one's needs with limited resources etc. (*just about manages on her pension*). **4** *tr.* gain influence with or maintain control over (a person etc.) (*cannot manage their teenage son*). **5** *tr.* & *intr.* (often prec. by *can*, *be able to*) **a** cope with; make use of (*couldn't manage another bite*; *can you manage by yourself?*). **b** be free to attend on (a certain day) or at (a certain time) (*can you manage Thursday?*). **6** *tr.* handle or wield (a tool, weapon, etc.).

manageable *adj.* able to be easily managed, controlled, or accomplished etc. □ **manageability** *n.* **manageableness** *n.* **manageably** *adv.*

management *n.* **1** the process or an instance of managing or being managed. **2 a** the professional administration of business concerns, public undertakings, etc. **b** the people engaged in this. **c** (prec. by *the*) a governing body; a board of directors or the people in charge of running a business, regarded collectively. **3** (usu. foll. by *of*) *Med.* the technique of treating a disease etc.

management buyout *n.* the purchase of at least a controlling share in a company by its directors.

manager *n.* **1** a person controlling or administering a business or part of one. **2** a person controlling the affairs, training, etc. of a person or team in sports, entertainment, etc. **3** a person regarded in terms of skill in household or financial or other management (*a good manager*). □ **managerial** /ˌmænɪˈdʒɪːrɪəl/ *adj.* **managerially** *adv.*

managing *adj.* (in *comb.*) having executive control or authority (*managing director*).

mañana /mænˈjɒnə/ ● *adv.* in the indefinite future (esp. to indicate procrastination). ● *n.* an indefinite future time.

manatee /ˌmænəˈtiː/ ● *n.* any large aquatic plant-eating mammal of the genus *Trichechus*, with paddle-like forelimbs, no hind limbs, and a powerful tail.

Manchu /mænˈtʃuː/ ● *n.* (*pl.* **Manchus**) **1** a member of a people in China, descended from a Tartar people, who formed the last imperial dynasty (1644-1912). **2** the language of the Manchus, now spoken in parts of NE China. ● *adj.* of or relating to the Manchu people or their language.

mandala /ˈmændələ/ *n.* **1** a symbolic circular figure representing the universe in Hinduism and Buddhism. **2** *Psych.* such a symbol in a dream, representing the dreamer's search for completeness and self-unity.

mandarin *n.* **1** (**Mandarin**) the most widely spoken form of Chinese and the official language of China. **2** *hist.* a Chinese official in any of nine grades of the pre-Communist civil service. **3 a** a bureaucrat. **b** a powerful member of the establishment. **4** (in full **mandarin orange**) **a** a small flattish deep-coloured orange with a loose skin. **b** the tree, *Citrus reticulata*, yielding this.

mandate ● *n.* **1** an order given to a person, organization, etc. to carry out a certain task. **2 a** support for a policy or course of action, regarded by a victorious party, candidate, etc., as derived from the wishes of the people in an election. **b** *Cdn* the period during which a government is in power. **3** a commission to act for another. **4** *Law* a commission by which a party is entrusted to perform a service, often gratuitously and with indemnity against loss by that party. ● *v.tr.* **1**

require, esp. by law; make mandatory. **2** instruct (a delegate) to act or vote in a certain way.

mandatory /ˈmændəˌtɔri/ *adj.* **1** compulsory. **2** of or conveying a command. □ **mandatorily** *adv.*

mandatory supervision *n.* *Cdn Law* supervision by a parole officer of a convict serving the last part of a sentence in the community after being released from prison, usu. because of good behaviour in the first two-thirds of the sentence.

man-day *n.* a day of work etc. by one person, as a unit of measure.

mandible /ˈmændɪbəl/ *n.* **1** the jaw, esp. the lower jaw in mammals and fishes. **2** the upper or lower part of a bird's beak. **3** either half of the crushing organ in an arthropod's mouthparts. □ **mandibular** /-ˈdɪbjʊlər/ *adj.*

mandolin /ˌmændəˈlɪn, ˈmæn-, -dɒ-/ *n.* **1** a musical instrument resembling a lute, having paired metal strings plucked with a plectrum. **2** (also **mandoline**) a kitchen utensil fitted with cutting blades and used for slicing vegetables. □ **mandolinist** *n.* (in sense 1).

mandrake *n.* a poisonous plant, *Mandragora officinarum*, with white or purple flowers and large yellow fruit, having emetic and narcotic properties and possessing a root once thought to resemble the human form and to shriek when plucked.

mandrel /ˈmændrəl/ *n.* **1** a shaft inserted into a workpiece to secure it to a lathe (*compare* CHUCK² 2). **2** a cylindrical rod round which metal or other material is forged or shaped.

mandrill /ˈmændrɪl/ *n.* a large W African baboon, *Papio sphinx*, the adult of which has a bright red and blue face and blue buttocks.

mane *n.* **1** long hair growing in a line on the neck of a horse, lion, etc. **2** a person's long, thick hair. □ **maned** *adj.* (also in *comb.*).

man-eater *n.* **1** an animal, esp. a shark or tiger, that eats or has a propensity for eating human flesh. **2** *informal* a woman who has many men as lovers and is perceived as using them for her own advantage.

maneuver *var. of* MANOEUVRE.

man Friday *n.* a male helper or follower; a right-hand man.

manful *adj.* brave; resolute. □ **manfully** *adv.*

manganese /ˈmæŋgəˌniːz/ *n.* **1** a grey brittle metallic element used with steel to make alloys. **2** (in full **manganese oxide**) the black mineral oxide of this used in the manufacture of glass.

mange /meɪndʒ/ *n.* a skin disease in hairy and woolly animals, caused by an arachnid parasite and occasionally communicated to humans.

manger *n.* a long open box or trough in a barn etc. for livestock to eat from.

manger scene *n.* *N Amer.* = NATIVITY SCENE.

mangia-cake *n.* *Cdn derogatory* or *jocular* (among Italian-Canadians) a non-Italian white person, esp. of British stock, with characteristically N American traits or customs.

mangle¹ *v.tr.* **1** crush, bend, break, or mutilate (something), esp. so that it is difficult to ascertain its original form. **2** spoil (a quotation, text, etc.) by misquoting, mispronouncing, etc. **3** cut roughly so as to disfigure. □ **mangler** *n.*

mangle² ● *n.* **1** esp. *Brit. hist.* a machine having two or more cylinders usu. turned by a handle, between which wet clothes etc. are squeezed and pressed. **2** *US* a large machine for ironing usu. damp sheets etc. using heated rollers. ● *v.tr.* press in a mangle.

mango *n.* (*pl.* **-oes** or **-os**) **1** a fleshy yellowish-red fruit, eaten ripe or used green for pickles etc. **2** the Indian evergreen tree, *Mangifera indica*, bearing this.

mangrove /'mæŋgrəʊv/ *n.* **1** any tropical tree or shrub of the genus *Rhizophora*, growing in shore mud with many tangled roots above ground. **2** any of various other trees or shrubs resembling this.

mangy /'meɪndʒi/ *adj.* (**-ier, -iest**) **1** (esp. of a domestic animal) having mange. **2** squalid; shabby. □ **mangily** *adv.* **manginess** *n.*

manhandle *v.tr.* **1** move (heavy objects) by human effort. **2** *informal* handle (a person) roughly.

manhattan *n.* a cocktail made of vermouth, whisky, etc.

Manhattan clam chowder *n. N Amer.* a soup of clams, tomatoes, onion, and potatoes.

Manhattanite *n.* a native or inhabitant of Manhattan, a borough of New York City occupying an island at the mouth of the Hudson River.

Manhattan Project *n.* the code name for the American project set up in 1942 to develop an atom bomb.

manhole *n.* a covered opening allowing access to a sewer, tunnel, boiler, etc.

manhood *n.* **1** the state of being a man rather than a child or woman. **2 a** manliness; courage. **b** a man's sexual potency. **c** *informal euphemism* the penis. **3** men collectively. **4** the state of being human.

man-hour *n.* an hour regarded in terms of the amount of work that could be done by one person within this period.

manhunt *n.* an organized search for a person, esp. a criminal.

mania *n.* **1** *Psych.* mental illness marked by periods of great excitement and violence. **2** (often foll. by *for*) an extreme or abnormal desire or enthusiasm (*has a mania for jogging*).

-mania *comb. form* **1** *Psych.* denoting a special type of mental abnormality or obsession (*megalomania*; *nymphomania*). **2** denoting extreme enthusiasm or admiration (*Trudeaumania*).

maniac ● *n.* **1** a person exhibiting extreme symptoms of wild behaviour etc.; an insane person. **2** an obsessive enthusiast. ● *adj.* of or behaving like a maniac. □ **-maniac** *comb. form.* **maniacal** *adj.* **maniacally** *adv.*

manic /'mænɪk/ *adj.* **1** of or affected by mania. **2** frenzied, elated, or abnormally energetic as if affected by a manic disorder. □ **manically** *adv.*

manic-depressive *Psych.* ● *adj.* affected by or relating to a mental disorder with alternating periods of elation and depression. ● *n.* a person having such a disorder. □ **manic depression** *n.*

Manichaean /manɪ'kiːən/ (also **Manichean**) ● *n.* **1** an adherent of a religious system of the 3rd–5th c., representing Satan in a state of everlasting conflict with God. **2** *Theol. & Philos.* a dualist (see DUALISM 2, 3a). ● *adj.* of or relating to Manichaeans. □ **Manichaeism** /-'kiːɪzəm/ *n.* (also **Manicheism**).

manicotti /manɪ'kɒti/ *n.* large tubular pasta, usu. served stuffed with ricotta cheese and covered with tomato sauce.

manicure ● *n.* **1** a usu. professional cosmetic treatment of the hands and fingernails. **2** = MANICURIST. ● *v.tr.* **1** apply a manicure to (the hands or a person). **2** trim or cut neatly (*manicured the lawn*). □ **manicured** *adj.*

manicurist *n.* a person who manicures hands and fingernails professionally.

manifest /'manɪfɛst/ ● *adj.* clear or obvious to the eye or mind (*her distress was manifest*). ● *n.* a list of the cargo or passengers carried by a ship, truck, aircraft, etc. ● *v.* **1** *tr.* display or show (a quality, feeling, etc.) by one's acts etc. **2** *tr.* show plainly to the eye or mind. **3** *tr.* be evidence of; prove. **4** *intr. & refl.* (of a thing) reveal itself. **5** *intr.* (of a ghost) appear. **6** *tr.* record (names, cargo, etc.) in a manifest. □ **manifestation** *n.* **manifestly** *adv.*

manifest destiny *n.* the esp. 19th c. belief that the US was intended by God to expand to the Pacific coast, and eventually to cover all of N America.

manifesto /manɪ'fɛstəʊ/ *n.* (pl. **-os** or **-oes**) a public declaration of principles, intentions, purposes, etc.

manifold /'manɪfəʊld/ ● *adj. literary* **1** many and various (*manifold vexations*). **2** having various forms, parts, applications, etc. **3** performing several functions at once. ● *n.* **1** a thing with many different forms, parts, applications, etc. **2** *Mech.* a pipe or chamber branching into several openings.

manikin /'manɪkɪn/ *n.* **1** a little person; a dwarf. **2** a dummy or jointed figure of a human body used by artists for arranging drapery on etc. **3** an anatomical model of the body.

manila /mə'nɪlə/ *n.* (also **manilla**) **1** (in full **manila hemp**) the strong fibre of a Philippine tree, *Musa textilis*, used for rope etc. **2** a strong brown paper made from manila hemp or other material and used for wrapping paper, envelopes, etc.

man in the moon *n.* the semblance of a face seen on the surface of a full moon.

man in the street *n.* an ordinary average person, as distinct from an expert.

manioc /'manɪɒk/ *n.* = CASSAVA.

manipulate /mə'nɪpjʊleɪt/ *v.tr.* **1** handle, treat, or use, esp. skilfully (a tool, question, material, etc.). **2** manage (a person, situation, etc.) to one's own advantage, esp. unfairly or unscrupulously. **3** manually examine and treat (a part of the body). **4** *Computing* alter, edit, or move (text, data, etc.). □ **manipulable** /-ləbəl/ *adj.* **manipulation** *n.* **manipulator** *n.*

manipulative /mə'nɪpjʊlətɪv/ *adj.* **1** characterized by unscrupulous exploitation of a situation, person, etc. for one's own ends. **2** of, concerning, or causing manipulation. □ **manipulatively** *adv.* **manipulativeness** *n.*

Manitoba maple *n.* a fast-growing N American maple, *Acer negundo*, with pinnate leaves, found east of the Rockies.

Manitoban ● *adj.* of or relating to Manitoba. ● *n.* a resident or native of Manitoba.

manitou /'manɪtuː/ *n.* (esp. among the Cree and Ojibwa) **1** a good or evil spirit as an object of reverence. **2** something regarded as having supernatural power.

mankind *n.* **1** the human species. ¶Some people consider use of this sense sexist and prefer to use *humankind* or *the human race*. **2** male people, as distinct from female.

manlike *adj.* **1** having the qualities of a man. **2** (of an animal, shape, etc.) resembling a human being.

manly *adj.* (**-ier, -iest**) **1** having qualities regarded as admirable in a man, such as courage, frankness, etc. **2** (of things, qualities, etc.) befitting a man. □ **manliness** *n.*

man-made *adj.* made by humans; synthetic.

manna *n.* **1** *Bible* the substance miraculously supplied as food to the Israelites in the wilderness. **2** (also **manna from heaven**) an unexpected benefit. **3** spiritual nourishment, esp. the Eucharist.

Mann Cup *n.* a trophy awarded annually to the

Canadian senior amateur lacrosse champions, first presented in 1910.

manned *adj.* (of an aircraft, spacecraft, etc.) having a human crew.

mannequin /ˈmænəkɪn/ *n.* **1** a three-dimensional model of a human body, used when making clothes or esp. for displaying them in stores. **2** a model employed by a couturier etc. to show clothes to customers.

manner *n.* **1** a way a thing is done or happens (*always dresses in that manner*). **2** (in *pl.*) **a** the social habits and customs, esp. of a particular group (*18th-century aristocratic manners*). **b** polite or well-bred behaviour (*has no manners*). **3** a person's outward bearing, way of speaking, etc. (*has an imperious manner*). **4 a** a style in literature, art, etc. (*in the manner of Leacock*). **b** = MANNERISM 2. **5** a kind or sort (*what manner of man is he?*). □ **all manner of** many different kinds of. **in manner of speaking** in some sense; to some extent; so to speak. **to the manner born 1** *informal* naturally at ease in a specified job, situation, etc. **2** destined by birth to follow a custom or way of life.

mannered *adj.* **1** (in *comb.*) behaving in a specified way (*ill-mannered*). **2** (of a style, artist, writer, etc.) showing idiosyncratic mannerisms. **3** (of a person) eccentrically affected in behaviour.

mannerism *n.* **1** a habitual gesture or way of speaking etc.; an idiosyncrasy. **2** excessive addiction to a distinctive style in art or literature. **3** (usu. **Mannerism**) a style of Italian art preceding the Baroque, characterized by unusual and often bizarre effects of scale, lighting, and perspective, and the use of bright colours. □ **mannerist** *n.* **manneristic** *adj.*

mannerly *adj.* well-mannered; polite.

mannikin *var. of* MANIKIN.

manning depot *n.* *Cdn hist.* (during World War II) a training depot for recruits to the RCAF.

mannish *adj.* **1** usu. *derogatory* (of a woman) masculine in appearance or manner. **2** characteristic of a man. □ **mannishly** *adv.* **mannishness** *n.*

mano-a-mano /ˌmæno: ə ˈmæno:/ *adv. & adj.* hand to hand; one on one.

manoeuvre /məˈnuːvər/ (also **maneuver**, **manoeuver**) ● *n.* **1** a planned and controlled movement or series of moves. **2** (in *pl.*) a large-scale exercise of troops, warships, etc. **3 a** an often deceptive planned or controlled action designed to gain an objective. **b** a skilful plan. ● *v.* **1** *intr. & tr.* perform or cause to perform a manoeuvre (*manoeuvred the car into the space*). **2** *intr. & tr.* perform or cause (troops etc.) to perform military manoeuvres. **3 a** *tr.* (usu. foll. by *into*, *out*, *away*) force, drive, or manipulate (a person, thing, etc.) by scheming or adroitness. **b** *intr.* use artifice. □ **manoeuvrability** /-vrəˈbɪlɪti/ *n.* **manoeuvrable** *adj.* **manoeuvrer** *n.*

man of God *n.* **1** a clergyman. **2** a male saint.

man of letters *n.* a scholar or author.

man of the cloth *n.* a clergyman.

man of the house *n.* the male head of a household.

man-of-war *n.* an armed ship.

man on the street *var. of* MAN IN THE STREET.

manor *n.* **1** (also **manor house**) a large house with lands. **2** *Brit.* **a** a unit of land consisting of a lord's estate and lands rented to tenants etc. **b** *hist.* a feudal lordship over lands. □ **manorial** /məˈnɔːriəl/ *adj.*

manpower *n.* **1** the power generated by a person working, as opposed to by a machine etc. **2** people available for work, service, etc. **3** *Cdn* (often **Manpower**) a government department offering job refer-

ral services for the unemployed (also *attrib.*: *manpower centre*). ¶No longer in official use.

manqué /ˈmɒŋkei/ *adj.* (placed after noun) that might have been but is not (*a comic actor manqué*).

mansard /ˈmænsɑrd/ *n.* a roof which has four sloping sides, each of which becomes steeper halfway down.

manse /mæns/ *n.* the house, owned by a congregation, of an esp. Presbyterian or United Church minister. □ **son** (or **daughter**) **of the manse** a child of an esp. Presbyterian minister.

manservant *n.* (*pl.* **-s**) a male servant.

mansion *n.* a large house.

man-sized *adj.* (also **man-size**) **1** of the size of a man. **2** big enough for a man (*a man-sized sandwich*). **3** *informal* very large (*a man-sized project*).

manslaughter *n.* **1** the killing of a human being. **2** *Law* the unlawful killing of a human being without malice aforethought.

manta *n.* any large ray of the family Mobulidae, esp. *Manta birostris*, having wing-like pectoral fins and a whip-like tail.

man-tailored *adj.* *N Amer.* (of a style of women's clothing) tailored after the conventional fashion of a man's garment (*a man-tailored jacket*).

mantel /ˈmæntəl/ *n.* (also **mantelpiece**) **1** a structure of wood, marble, etc. above and around a fireplace. **2** (also **mantelshelf**) a shelf above a fireplace.

mantid *n.* = MANTIS.

mantis *n.* (*pl.* same or **mantises**) any insect of the family Mantidae, feeding on other insects etc.

mantle ● *n.* **1** a loose sleeveless cloak. **2** a covering (*a mantle of snow*). **3** a spiritual influence or authority. **4** a fragile lacelike tube fixed around a gas jet to give an incandescent light. **5** an outer fold of skin enclosing a mollusc's viscera. **6** the plumage of the back and folded wings of a bird, esp. if distinct in colour. **7** the region between the crust and the core of the earth. ● *v.* **1** *tr.* clothe in or as if in a mantle; cover, conceal, envelop. **2** *intr.* **a** (of the blood) suffuse the cheeks. **b** (of the face) glow with a blush. **3** *intr.* (of a liquid) become covered with a coating or scum.

mantra /ˈmæntrə/ *n.* **1** *Hinduism & Buddhism* a word or sound repeated to aid concentration in meditation. **2** a Vedic hymn. **3** a frequently repeated word, phrase, etc.; a slogan.

mantrap *n.* a trap for catching trespassers etc.

manual ● *adj.* **1** of or relating to the hand or hands. **2** done or performed with the hands. **3** involving physical rather than mental effort (*manual labour*). **4** worked by hand, not by automatic equipment or with electronic assistance etc. (*manual transmission*). **5** not involving computers or electronic transmission of data etc. ● *n.* **1 a** a book of instructions, esp. for operating a machine or learning a subject; a handbook (*a computer manual*). **b** any small book. **2** an organ keyboard played with the hands, not the feet. □ **manually** *adv.*

manufacture ● *n.* **1 a** the making of articles esp. in a factory etc. **b** a branch of an industry (*woollen manufacture*). **2** a manufactured item or product. ● *v.tr.* **1** make (articles), esp. on an industrial scale. **2** invent or fabricate (evidence, a story, etc.). **3** esp. *derogatory* make or produce (literature, art, etc.) in a mechanical way. □ **manufacturability** *n.* **manufacturable** *adj.* **manufacturer** *n.*

manumit /ˌmænjoˈmɪt/ *v.tr.* (**-mitted**, **-mitting**) *hist.* set (a slave) free. □ **manumission** /-ˈmɪʃən/ *n.*

manure ● *n.* **1** animal dung used for fertilizing land.

2 any compost or artificial fertilizer. *See also* GREEN MANURE. ● *v.tr.* apply manure to (land etc.).

manuscript ● *n.* **1** a book, document, etc. written by hand. **2** an author's text submitted for publication. **3** handwritten form (*produced in manuscript*). ● *adj.* written by hand.

Manx /mæŋks/ ● *adj.* of or relating to the Isle of Man, a British Crown possession in the Irish Sea. ● *n.* **1** the now extinct Celtic language spoken in the Isle of Man. **2** (prec. by *the*; treated as *pl.*) the Manx people.

many /'meni/ ● *adj.* (**more** /mɔr/; **most** /moːst/) great in number; numerous. ● *n.* (as *pl.*) a large number (*many like skiing*). □ **have one too many** become drunk. **as many** the same number of (*six mistakes in as many lines*). **as many again** the same number additionally (*sixty here and as many again there*). **be too** (or **one too**) **many for** outwit, baffle. **a good** (or **great**) **many** a large number. **many's the time** often (*many's the time we saw it*). **many a time** many times.

many-sided *adj.* having many sides, aspects, interests, capabilities, etc. □ **many-sidedness** *n.*

manzanilla /ˌmænzə'nɪlə/ *n.* **1** a pale very dry Spanish sherry. **2** a variety of olive, distinguished by small thin-skinned fruit.

Maoism /'mauɪzəm/ *n.* the Communist doctrines of the Chinese statesman Mao Zedong (1893–1976) as formerly practised in China, having as a central idea permanent revolution and stressing the importance of the peasantry, of small-scale industry, and of agricultural collectivization. □ **Maoist** *n.* & *adj.*

Maori /'mauri/ ● *n.* (*pl.* same or **Maoris**) **1** a member of the Polynesian aboriginal people of New Zealand. **2** the language of the Maori. ● *adj.* of or concerning the Maori or their language.

MAP *abbr. N Amer.* MODIFIED AMERICAN PLAN.

map ● *n.* **1 a** a usu. flat representation of the earth's surface, or part of it, showing physical features, cities, etc. (*compare* GLOBE 2). **b** a diagrammatic representation of a route etc. (*drew a map of the journey*). **2** a two-dimensional representation of the stars, the heavens, etc., or of the surface of a planet, the moon, etc. **3** a diagram showing the arrangement or components of a thing, esp. of the sequence of genes on a chromosome or of bases in a DNA or RNA molecule. **4** *Math.* a correspondence by which each element of a given set has associated with it one or more elements of a second set. ● *v.tr.* (**mapped**, **mapping**) **1** represent (a country etc.) on a map. **2** *Math.* associate each element of (a set) with one element of another set. □ **all over the map** *N Amer.* disorganized; lacking a central focus (*the presentation was all over the map*). **map out** arrange in detail; plan (a course of conduct etc.). **put on the map** *informal* establish as prominent or important. **wipe off the map** *informal* obliterate. □ **mappable** *adj.* **mapper** *n.*

maple *n.* **1** any tree or shrub of the genus *Acer*, with usu. lobed leaves, frequently grown for shade, ornament, wood, or its sugar. **2** the wood of the maple. **3** (also *attrib.*) the flavour of maple syrup or maple sugar.

maple bush *n. Cdn* = SUGAR BUSH.

maple butter *n. Cdn* **1** a spread made by heating maple syrup, then rapidly cooling it while stirring until it has a creamy consistency. **2** butter blended with maple syrup or maple sugar.

maple leaf *n.* **1** the leaf of the maple, used as an emblem of Canada. **2** (**Maple Leaf**) the Canadian flag. **3** (**Maple Leaf**; *pl.* **Maple Leafs**) a one ounce gold coin, bearing the image of a maple leaf, produced by the Royal Canadian Mint.

maple sugar *n.* a sugar produced by evaporating the sap of the sugar maple etc.

maple syrup *n.* a syrup produced from the sap of the sugar maple etc.

map-maker *n.* a cartographer. □ **map-making** *n.*

map-reading *n.* the inspection and interpretation of a map. □ **map-reader** *n.*

map reference *n.* a set of numbers and letters specifying a location as represented on a map.

maquette /mə'ket/ *n.* **1** a sculptor's or architect's small preliminary model. **2** a preliminary sketch.

maquiladora /ˌmækiːlæ'dɔrə/ *n.* a Mexican factory taking advantage of cheap labour, run by a foreign company and exporting its products to the country of that company.

Mar. *abbr.* March.

mar *v.tr.* (**marred**, **marring**) **1** ruin. **2** impair the perfection of; spoil; disfigure.

marabou /'mærə,buː/ *n.* (also **marabout**) **1** a large W African stork, *Leptoptilos crumeniferus*. **2** *N Amer.* a lead head jig used in freshwater fishing, with a marabou feather or something resembling it attached to simulate the appearance of a small fish. **3** a tuft of down from the wing or tail of the marabou used as a trimming for hats etc.

maraca /mə'rɒkə, -ræk/ *n.* a hollow gourd or gourd-shaped container filled with beans, pebbles, etc. and usu. shaken in pairs as a percussion instrument.

maraschino /ˌmærə'ʃiːnoː, -'skiːnoː, ˌmerə-/ *n.* (*pl.* **-os**) a strong sweet liqueur made from a small black cherry.

maraschino cherry *n.* a cherry preserved in maraschino or maraschino-flavoured syrup.

marasmus /mə'ræzməs/ *n.* severe loss of weight in a person, esp. an undernourished child. □ **marasmic** *adj.*

marathon *n.* **1** a long-distance running race, usu. of 26 miles 385 yards (42.195 km). **2** a long-lasting or difficult task, operation, etc. (often *attrib.: a marathon shopping expedition*). □ **marathoner** *n.*

maraud /mə'rɒd/ *v.* **1** *intr.* go about in search of things to steal, people to attack, etc. **2** *tr.* plunder (a place). □ **marauder** *n.*

marble ● *n.* **1** limestone in a metamorphic crystalline (or granular) state, capable of taking a polish, used in sculpture and architecture. **2** (often *attrib.*) **a** anything made of marble (*a marble clock*). **b** anything resembling marble in hardness, coldness, durability, etc. (*her features were marble*). **3 a** a small ball of marble, glass, clay, etc., used as a toy. **b** (in *pl.*; treated as *sing.*) a game using these. **4** (in *pl.*) *slang* one's mental faculties (*he's lost his marbles*). **5** (*attrib.*) (esp. of a food) made with two or more colours swirled together (*marble cheese*). **6** a marble sculpture. ● *v.tr.* stain or colour (paper, the edges of a book, soap, etc.) to look like variegated marble. □ **marbly** *adj.*

marbled *adj.* **1** (of meat) streaked with alternating layers of lean and fat. **2** stained or coloured to look like variegated marble.

marbled murrelet *n.* a murrelet, *Brachyramphus marmoratus* of the N Pacific, with mottled brown and white underparts.

marbling *n.* **1** colouring or marking like marble. **2** streaks of fat in lean meat.

marc *n.* **1** the residue of pressed grapes etc. **2** a brandy made from this.

March *n.* the third month of the year.

march¹ ● *v.* **1** *intr.* (usu. foll. by *away*, *off*, *out*, etc.) walk in a military manner with a regular measured tread.

2 *tr.* (often foll. by *away*, *on*, *off*, etc.) cause to march or walk (*marched the cadets back to camp*; *marched him out of the room*). **3** *intr.* **a** walk or proceed steadily, esp. across country. **b** (of events etc.) continue unrelentingly (*time marches on*). **4** *intr.* take part in a protest march. ● *n.* **1 a** the act or an instance of marching. **b** the uniform step of troops etc. (*a slow march*). **2 a** long difficult walk. **3** a procession as a protest or demonstration. **4** (usu. foll. by *of*) progress or continuity (*the march of events*). **5 a** a piece of music composed to accompany a march. **b** a composition of similar character and form. □ **march on 1** advance towards (a military objective). **2** proceed. **on the march 1** marching. **2** in steady progress.

march² ● *n. hist.* **1** (usu. in *pl.*) a boundary, a frontier (esp. between England and Scotland or Wales). **2** a tract of often disputed land between two countries. ● *v.intr.* (foll. by *upon*, *with*) (of a country, an estate, etc.) have a common frontier with, border on.

March break *n. Cdn* a school holiday, usu. about a week long, in March.

marcher *n.* a person who marches or takes part in a march.

March hare *n.* a hare in the breeding season, characterized by excessive leaping, strange behaviour, etc. (*mad as a March hare*).

marching band *n.* a usu. brass band which performs while marching in parades etc.

marching orders *n.pl.* **1** a dismissal (*gave him his marching orders*). **2** instructions or directions given authoritatively. **3** *Military* the direction for troops to depart for war etc.

marchioness /ˌmɑːʃəˈnes, ˈmɑː-/ *n.* **1** the wife or widow of a marquess. **2** a woman holding the rank of marquess in her own right (*compare* MARQUISE 1b).

march past *n.* the marching of troops past a saluting point at a review.

marconi /mɑːˈkoʊni/ *n. Cdn* (*Nfld*) *informal* a radio, esp. one used for two-way communications (also *attrib.*: *marconi station*).

Mardi Gras /ˈmɑːdi ˌɡrɒ/ *n.* **1** the last Tuesday before Lent, celebrated in some areas (esp. New Orleans) as a day of great revelry. **2** the period of festivities culminating in this.

mare¹ *n.* the female of any equine animal, esp. the horse.

mare² /ˈmɒreɪ, -ri/ *n.* (*pl.* **maria** /ˈmɒriə/ or **mares**) **1** any of a number of large dark flat areas on the surface of the moon, once thought to be seas. **2** a similar area on Mars.

margarine *n.* a butter substitute made from vegetable oils or animal fats with milk etc.

margarita /mɑːɡəˈriːtə/ *n.* a cocktail made with tequila, lime juice, and orange liqueur, typically served in a glass with a salt-coated rim.

margin ● *n.* **1 a** the edge or border of a surface. **b** (in *pl.*) the ignored or unimportant sections of a group etc. **2 a** the blank border on each side of the print on a page etc. **b** a line ruled esp. on exercise paper, marking off a margin. **3** an amount (of time, money, etc.) by which a thing exceeds, falls short, etc. (*won by a narrow margin*; *a margin of profit*). **4** the lower limit of possibility, success, etc. **5** a sum deposited with a stockbroker to cover the risk of loss on a transaction on account. ● *v.tr.* (**margined, margining**) provide with a margin or marginal notes.

marginal *adj.* **1 a** of or written in a margin. **b** having marginal notes. **2 a** of or at the edge; not central. **b** not significant or decisive (*the work is of merely marginal interest*). **3** *Cdn*, *Brit.*, *Austral.*, & *NZ* (of a parliamen-

tary seat or constituency) having a small majority at risk in an election. **4** close to the limit, esp. of profitability. **5** (of the sea) adjacent to the shore of a country. **6** (of land) that cannot produce enough to be profitable except when prices of farm products are high. **7** barely adequate; unprovided for (*living a marginal existence*). **8** (of a person) not fitting into the mainstream. **9** (of a rate of taxation) imposed on the portion of income exceeding the limit of a tax bracket, rather than on the total income. □ **marginality** *n.* **marginally** *adv.*

marginal cost *n.* the cost added by making one extra item of a product.

marginalia /ˌmɑːdʒɪˈneɪliə/ *n.pl.* marginal notes.

marginalize *v.tr.* make or treat as insignificant. □ **marginalization** *n.*

margin call *n.* a demand by a broker that an investor deposit further cash or securities to guarantee the margin on an investment.

margin of error *n.* a usu. small difference allowed for miscalculation, change of circumstances, etc.

marguerite /ˌmɑːɡəˈriːt/ *n.* a daisy, esp. the ox-eye daisy, *Chrysanthemum leucanthemum*.

maria *pl. of* MARE².

mariachi /meriˈætʃi, -ˈɒtʃi/ *n.* **1** an itinerant Mexican folk band. **2** a member of such a band.

Marian /ˈmeriən/ *adj.* of or relating to the Virgin Mary (*Marian devotion*).

marigold *n.* any plant of the genus *Calendula* or *Tagetes*, with golden or bright yellow flowers.

marijuana /ˌmerɪˈwɒnə/ *n.* **1** the dried leaves, flowering tops, and stems of the hemp, used as an intoxicating drug usu. smoked in cigarettes; cannabis. **2** the plant yielding these (*compare* HEMP).

marimba /məˈrɪmbə/ *n.* a kind of deep-toned xylophone, originating in Africa and consisting of wooden keys on a frame with a tuned resonator beneath each key.

marina /məˈriːnə/ *n.* a specially designed harbour with moorings for pleasure boats etc.

marinade ● *n.* **1** a mixture of wine, vinegar, oil, spices, etc., in which meat, fish, etc., is soaked before cooking, esp. to tenderize or add flavour. **2** meat, fish, etc., soaked in such a mixture. ● *v.tr.* = MARINATE.

marinara /ˌmerəˈnerə, mɑːrəˈnɑːrə/ *adj.* designating a sauce made from tomatoes, onions, herbs, etc., usu. served with pasta.

marinate *v.tr.* soak (meat, fish, etc.) in a marinade. □ **marination** *n.*

marine ● *adj.* **1 a** of, found in, or produced by the sea. **b** of, found in, or produced by any esp. large body of water. **2 a** of or relating to shipping or naval matters (*marine insurance*). **b** for use at sea. ● *n.* **1 a** country's shipping, fleet, or navy (*mercantile marine*; *merchant marine*). **2 a** a member of a body of troops trained to serve on land or sea. **b** (**Marine**) (in the US) a member of the Marine Corps, a branch of the armed forces trained to attack land targets from the sea.

marine park *n.* **1** an area of an ocean or other body of water set aside as an ecological preserve. **2** a theme park featuring marine wildlife.

mariner /ˈmærɪnər/ *n.* a sailor.

marionette /ˌmeriəˈnet/ *n.* a puppet worked from above by strings.

mariposa lily /ˌmerəˈpoʊsə/ *n.* any of various lilies of western N America of the genus *Calochortus*, with showy flowers of three petals.

marital *adj.* of marriage or the relations between husband and wife. □ **maritally** *adv.*

marital status *n.* a person's situation as regards being single, married, divorced, separated, or in a common-law relationship.

maritime *adj.* **1** connected with the sea or seafaring (*maritime insurance*). **2** living or found near the sea. **3** (**Maritime**) *Cdn* of or relating to the Maritime provinces.

Maritime Command *n. Cdn* the official name for the Canadian navy.

Maritimer *n. Cdn* a native or resident of the Maritime provinces.

Maritimes *n.pl.* (also **Maritime provinces**) New Brunswick, Nova Scotia, and Prince Edward Island.

marjoram /'mɑrdʒərəm/ *n.* **1** either of two aromatic herbaceous plants, (in full **wild marjoram**), *Origanum vulgare*, or (in full **sweet marjoram**), *Origanum marjorana*. **2** the fresh or dried leaves of sweet marjoram used as a flavouring in cooking.

mark¹ • *n.* **1** a trace, sign, stain, scar, etc., on a surface, face, page, etc. **2** (esp. in *comb.*) **a** a written or printed symbol (*question mark*). **b** a numerical or alphabetical award denoting a degree of excellence, conduct, proficiency, etc. (*got good marks for effort; how are your marks?*). **3** (usu. foll. by *of*) a sign or indication of quality, character, feeling, etc. (*took off his hat as a mark of respect*). **4 a** a sign, seal, etc., used for distinction or identification. **b** a cross etc. made in place of a signature by an illiterate person. **5 a** a target, object, goal, etc. (*missed the mark*). **b** a standard for attainment (*his work falls below the mark*). **c** a level considered important or critical (*sales have reached the million mark*). **d** a point in time (*scored at the three-minute mark*). **e** a record (*broke her own world mark*). **6** a line etc. indicating a position; a marker. **7** (usu. **Mark**) (followed by a numeral) a particular design, model, etc., of a car, aircraft, etc. (*this is the Mark 2 model*). **8** a runner's starting point in a race. **•** *v.tr.* **1 a** make a mark on (a thing or person), esp. by writing, cutting, scraping, etc. **b** put a distinguishing or identifying mark, initials, name, etc., on (clothes etc.). **c** (of an animal) leave a scent mark on. **2 a** allot marks to; correct (a student's work etc.). **b** record (the points gained in games etc.). **3** attach a price to (goods etc.) (*marked the doll at $5*). **4** (often foll. by *by*) show or manifest (displeasure etc.) (*marked his anger by leaving early*). **5** notice or observe (*she marked his agitation*). **6 a** characterize or be a feature of (*the day was marked by storms*). **b** acknowledge, recognize, celebrate (*marked the occasion with a toast*). **c** constitute (a significant event) (*this year marks our hundredth anniversary*). **7** name or indicate (a place on a map, the length of a syllable, etc.) by a sign or mark. **8** characterize (a person or a thing) as (*marked them as weak*). **9** keep close to so as to prevent the free movement of (an opponent in sport); cover. **10** (of a graduated instrument) show, register (so many degrees etc.). □ **hit** (or **miss**) **the mark** succeed (or fail) in an attempt to do something. **leave** (or **make**) **one's mark on** have a long-lasting (often harmful) effect on. **make one's mark** attain distinction. **mark down 1** mark (goods etc.) at a lower price. **2** make a written note of. **3** choose (a person) as one's victim. **4** reduce the examination marks of. **mark off** (often foll. by *from*) separate (one thing from another) by a boundary etc. (*marked off the subjects for discussion*). **mark out 1** plan (a course of action etc.). **2** destine (*marked out for success*). **3** trace out boundaries, a course, etc. **mark time 1** *Military* march on the spot, without moving forward. **2** act routinely; go through the motions. **3** await an opportunity to advance. **mark up 1** mark

(goods etc.) at a higher price. **2** mark or correct (text etc.) for typesetting or alteration. **off the mark 1** having made a start. **2** (also **wide of the mark**) not accurate. **quick** (or **slow**) **off the mark** fast (or slow) in responding to a situation or understanding something. **on the mark 1** accurate. **2** ready to start. **on your mark** (or **marks**) (as an instruction) get ready to start (esp. a race). **up to the mark** reaching the usual or normal standard, esp. of health.

mark² *n.* **1** = DEUTSCHMARK. **2** *hist.* a denomination of weight for gold and silver.

markdown *n.* a reduction in price.

marked /mɑrkt/ *adj.* **1** having a visible mark. **2** clearly noticeable; evident (*a marked difference*). **3** (of playing cards) having distinctive marks on their backs to assist cheating. **4** designating a person whose conduct is watched with suspicion or hostility (*marked man*). □ **markedly** /-kədli/ *adv.*

marker *n.* **1** a stone, post, etc., used to mark a position etc. **2** a person or thing that marks. **3** a felt-tipped pen with a broad tip. **4** a person who records a score, esp. in billiards. **5** a flare etc. used to direct a pilot to a target. **6** a bookmark. **7** = GENETIC MARKER. **8** any distinguishing characteristic or mark. **9** a person who marks school assignments or examination papers. **10** *N Amer. slang* a promissory note.

market • *n.* **1** the gathering of people for the purchase and sale of provisions, livestock, etc., esp. with a number of different vendors. **2** an open space or covered building used for this. **3 a** (often foll. by *for*) a demand for a commodity or service (*a ready market*). **b** a place or group providing such a demand (*Canada is a small market*). **4** conditions as regards, or opportunity for, buying or selling. **5** the rate of purchase and sale, market value (*the market fell*). **6** (prec. by *the*) the trade in a specified commodity (*the market in soft drinks*). **7** = STOCK MARKET. **•** *v.* (**marketed**, **marketing**) **1** *tr.* sell. **2** *tr.* **a** offer for sale. **b** promote an item for sale. **3** *intr.* buy or sell goods in a market. □ **be in the market for** wish to buy. **be on** (or **come into**) **the market** be offered for sale. **put on the market** offer for sale.

marketable *adj.* **1** able or fit to be sold. **2** (of an attribute, skill, etc.) in demand. □ **marketability** *n.*

market-driven *adj.* determined solely by consumer demand (*a market-driven program*).

market economy *n.* an economy subject to and determined by free competition.

marketeer *n.* **1** a person involved in or promoting a usu. specified market (*black marketeer*). **2** = MARKETER. □ **marketeering** *n.*

marketer *n.* a person trained in the marketing of products etc.

market garden *n.* esp. *Brit.* & *Cdn* a place where vegetables and fruit are grown for the market etc. □ **market gardener** *n.* **market gardening** *n.*

marketing *n.* **1** the action or business of promoting and selling products, including market research and advertising. **2** in senses of MARKET *v.*

marketing board *n. Cdn* & *Brit.* an association of agricultural producers controlling the marketing of a specific commodity, often setting prices and imposing production quotas.

market leader *n.* **1** the company that sells the largest quantity of a particular product. **2** a product which sells more than all its competitors.

marketplace *n.* **1** an open space where a market is held in a town. **2** the world of commerce or trade. **3** any place or environment where ideas etc. are exchanged or evaluated.

market price *n.* the current price which a commodity or service fetches in the market.

market research *n.* the study of consumers' needs and preferences. □ **market researcher** *n.*

market share *n.* a single company's or product's proportion of the total sales of a commodity or service.

market value *n.* the value of a product or service as determined by consumer demand (opp. BOOK VALUE).

marking *n.* (usu. in *pl.*) **1** an identification mark, esp. a symbol on an aircraft. **2** the colouring of an animal's fur, feathers, etc. **3** the action of MARK¹ *v.*

marksman *n.* (*pl.* **-men**) a person skilled in shooting, esp. with a pistol or rifle. □ **marksmanship** *n.*

markup *n.* **1** the amount added to the cost price of goods to cover overhead charges, profit, etc. **2** an act or instance of increasing the price of goods. **3** the corrections made in marking up text. **4** a system of tagging used to identify the structure of a text held electronically.

marl ● *n.* soil consisting of clay and lime, with fertilizing properties. ● *v.tr.* apply marl to (the ground). □ **marly** *adj.*

marlin *n.* any of several large marine game fishes and food fishes of the swordfish family (genera *Makaira* and *Tetrapterus*) with the upper jaw elongated to form a pointed snout.

marmalade /ˈmɑrməˌleɪd/ ● *n.* **1** a preserve of citrus fruit, usu. bitter oranges, made like jam. **2** a preserve made of other fruits or vegetables, esp. onions. ● *attrib.adj.* (esp. of a cat) orange tabby; ginger.

marmoset /ˈmɑrməˌzet/ *n.* any of several small tropical American monkeys of the family Callitricidae, having a long bushy tail.

marmot /ˈmɑrmət/ *n.* any burrowing rodent of the genus *Marmota*, with a heavy-set body and short bushy tail.

maroon¹ *adj.* brownish crimson.

maroon² *v.tr.* **1** leave (a person) isolated in a desolate place (esp. an island). **2** (of a person or a natural phenomenon) cause (a person) to be unable to leave a place.

marque /mɑrk/ *n.* a make or brand, esp. of motor vehicle.

marquee /mɑrˈki:/ *n.* **1** esp. *N Amer.* a canopy over the entrance to a large building. **2 a** a usu. brightly-lit sign over the entrance to a theatre etc., listing the names of featured performers. **b** (*attrib.*) *N Amer.* popular enough to be listed on a marquee; famous (*a marquee player*; *marquee status*). **3** a large tent used for social or commercial functions.

marquess /ˈmɑrkwɪs/ *n.* a British nobleman ranking between a duke and an earl (compare MARQUIS).

marquetry /ˈmɑrkɪtri/ *n.* (also **marqueterie**) inlaid work in wood, ivory, etc., esp. as used for the decoration of furniture.

marquis /ˈmɑrˈki:/ *n.* a European nobleman ranking between a duke and a count (compare MARQUESS).

marquise /mɑrˈki:z/ *n.* **1 a** the wife or widow of a marquis. **b** a woman holding the rank of marquis in her own right (compare MARCHIONESS). **2** a pointed oval shape cut of diamond, usu. with 58 facets. **3** a chilled chocolate mousse-like dessert.

Marquis wheat /ˈmɑrkwɪs/ *n.* a variety of wheat which ripens in a relatively short growing season, allowing wheat to be grown further north in Canada.

marram /ˈmerəm, ˈmæ-/ *n.* a coarse shore grass, *Ammophila brevigulata* or *A. arenaria*, that binds sand with its tough rhizomes.

marriage /ˈmerɪdʒ, ˈmæ-/ *n.* **1** the legal or religious union of a man and a woman in order to live together and often to have children. **2** an act or ceremony establishing this union. **3** one particular union of this kind (*by a previous marriage*). **4** a close association or intimate union (*the marriage of true minds*). **5** a combination of different elements. □ **by marriage** as a result of a marriage (*related by marriage*). **in marriage** as husband or wife (*take in marriage*).

marriageable *adj.* **1** (of a person) fit for marriage, esp. of an appropriate age. **2** (of age) fit for marriage. □ **marriageability** *n.*

marriage commissioner *n. Cdn* (in some provinces) an official who conducts civil marriages.

marriage of convenience *n.* a marriage concluded to achieve some practical purpose, esp. financial or political.

married ● *adj.* **1** united in marriage. **2** of or relating to marriage (*married name*; *married life*). **3** bound by strong, almost irrevocable ties (*married to her job*). ● *n.* (usu. in *pl.*) a married person (*young marrieds*).

married quarters *n.pl.* housing provided to married personnel and their families by the armed forces, usu. for a low rent.

marrow *n.* **1** = BONE MARROW. **2** the essential part. **3** (in full **vegetable marrow**) **a** a large usu. white-fleshed gourd used as food. **b** the plant, *Cucurbita pepo*, yielding this.

marrow bone *n.* a bone containing edible marrow.

marry *v.* (**-ies, -ied**) **1** *tr.* **a** take as one's wife or husband in marriage. **b** (of a person authorized to perform marriages) join (persons) in marriage. **c** (of a parent or guardian) give (a son, daughter, etc.) in marriage. **2** *intr.* **a** enter into marriage. **b** (foll. by *into*) become a member of (a family, a social group) by marriage. **3** *tr.* **a** unite intimately. **b** correlate (things) as a pair. **4** *tr. & intr.* combine or be combined successfully with something else. □ **marry money** marry a rich person. **marry off** find a wife or husband for.

Marsala /mɑrˈsælə, -ˈsɒlə/ *n.* a dark sweet fortified dessert wine.

marsh *n.* **1** low land flooded in wet weather and usu. watery at all times. **2** (*attrib.*) of or inhabiting marshes. □ **marshy** *adj.* (**-ier, -iest**). **marshiness** *n.*

marshal ● *n.* **1 a** (in titles of ranks) a high-ranking officer in the armed forces of some countries. **b** an officer of the highest rank in the armies of some countries. **c** a high-ranking officer of state. **2** a person arranging ceremonies, controlling procedure at parades, races, etc. **3** *US* **a** a federal or municipal law officer. **b** the head of a fire department. ● *v.* (**marshalled, marshalling**) **1** *tr.* **a** arrange or draw up (armed forces) in order for fighting, exercise, or review. **b** arrange (people) in a body or procession or for a race etc. **c** dispose, arrange, or set (things, material or immaterial) in methodical order, esp. in preparation for something (*marshalling my thoughts*). **2** *tr.* conduct (a person) ceremoniously. **3** *intr.* take up positions in due arrangement.

Marshall Plan *n.* a US plan to supply financial assistance to certain western European countries after the Second World War to further their recovery.

marsh hawk *n. N Amer.* = NORTHERN HARRIER.

marshland *n.* land consisting of marshes.

marshmallow *n.* **1** a very soft, fluffy, usu. white candy made of sugar, egg white, gelatin, etc. **2** an excessively tender-hearted or unassertive person.

marsh mallow *n.* a shrubby herbaceous plant, *Althaea officinalis*, the roots of which were formerly used to make marshmallow.

marsh marigold n. a golden-flowered herbaceous plant of the buttercup family, *Caltha palustris*, growing in moist meadows etc.

marsupial /mɑr'su:piəl/ ● n. any mammal of the order Marsupialia, characterized by being born incompletely developed and usu. carried and suckled in a pouch on the mother's belly. ● adj. **1** of or belonging to this order. **2** of or like a pouch (*marsupial muscle*).

mart n. N Amer. (usu. in proper names) a store (*Drug Mart*).

marten n. **1** any weasel-like carnivore of the genus *Martes* found in forests of Eurasia and N America, esp. the pine marten. **2** the pelt or fur of the marten.

martial adj. **1** of or appropriate to warfare or the military. **2** warlike, brave; fond of fighting.

martial art n. any of various fighting techniques or sports including judo and karate.

martial law n. military government, involving the suspension of ordinary law.

Martian ● adj. of the planet Mars. ● n. a hypothetical inhabitant of Mars.

martin n. any of several birds belonging to the swallow family Hirundinidae, e.g. the purple martin.

martini /mɑr'ti:ni/ n. a cocktail made of dry vermouth and usu. gin.

Martin Luther King Day n. (in some US states) a holiday on the third Monday in January, commemorating the civil rights activist Martin Luther King (1929–68).

martyr /'mɑrtər/ ● n. **1 a** a person who is put to death for refusing to renounce a faith or belief. **b** a person who suffers for adhering to a principle, cause, etc. **c** a person who suffers or pretends to suffer in order to obtain sympathy or pity. **2** (foll. by *to*) a constant sufferer from (an ailment etc.). ● v.tr. **1** put to death as a martyr. **2** torment.

martyrdom n. **1** the sufferings or death of a martyr. **2** torment.

marvel ● n. **1** a wonderful thing. **2** (foll. by *of*) a wonderful example of (a quality). ● v.intr. (**marvelled**, **marvelling**) **1** (foll. by *at*, or *that* + clause) feel or express surprise or wonder. **2** (foll. by *how*, *why*, etc. + clause) wonder. □ **marveller** n.

marvellous adj. (also esp. US **marvelous**) **1** astonishing. **2** excellent. **3** extremely improbable. □ **marvellously** adv. **marvellousness** n.

Marxism n. the political and economic theories based on the writings of Karl Marx (1818–83), predicting the overthrow of capitalism, the taking over of the means of production by the proletariat, and the eventual attainment of a classless society, in accordance with scientific laws determined by dialectical materialism. □ **Marxist** n. & adj.

Marxism-Leninism n. Marxism as developed by Lenin and as implemented in the Soviet Union and subsequently in China. □ **Marxist-Leninist** n. & adj.

Mary Jane n. esp. N Amer. **1** a flat, low-cut shoe for girls, with a single strap across the top. **2** slang marijuana.

marzipan /'mɑrzɪˌpæn, -'pæn/ ● n. a paste of ground almonds, sugar, etc., moulded into decorative shapes or used to coat large cakes. ● v.tr. (**marzipanned**, **marzipanning**) cover with or as with marzipan.

mas /mæs/ n. (originally in Trinidad) a masquerade, esp. one held as part of an annual carnival parade.

masa /'mæsə/ n. a type of dough made from cornmeal and used to make tortillas etc.

Masai /'mæsai/ ● n. (pl. same or **Masais**) **1 a** a pastoral people living in Kenya and Tanzania. **b** a member of this people. **2** the Nilotic language of the Masai. ● adj. of or relating to the Masai.

masala /mə'sælə/ n. **1** any of various spice mixtures ground into a paste or powder for use in Indian cooking. **2** a dish flavoured with this.

M.A.Sc. abbr. Master of Applied Science.

masc. abbr. = MASCULINE.

mascara n. a cosmetic applied to the eyelashes to make them darker and thicker. □ **mascaraed** adj.

mascarpone /mæskɑr'poːni/ n. a soft mild Italian cream cheese.

mascot n. **1** a person, animal, or thing that is supposed to bring good luck to or represent a team, school, etc. **2** N Amer. a costumed figure representing a sports team, usu. leading cheers among the spectators watching games.

masculine ● adj. **1** of or characteristic of men. **2** manly, vigorous. **3** (of a woman) having qualities considered appropriate to a man. **4** Grammar of or denoting the gender proper to certain words or grammatical forms, including those referring to males. ● n. Grammar the masculine gender; a masculine word. □ **masculinity** n. **masculinize** v.tr.

masculinist ● n. an advocate of the rights of men. ● adj. of or relating to the advocacy of the rights of men.

maser /'meizər/ n. a device using the stimulated emission of radiation by excited atoms to amplify or generate coherent monochromatic electromagnetic radiation in the microwave range (compare LASER).

mash ● n. **1** a soft mixture. **2** a mixture of boiled grain, bran, etc., given warm to horses etc. **3** a mixture of malt grains and hot water used esp. to form wort for brewing. **4** a soft pulp made by crushing, mixing with water, etc. ● v.tr. **1** reduce (potatoes etc.) to a uniform mass by crushing. **2** crush or pound to a pulp. **3** mix (malt) with hot water to form wort. □ **masher** n.

mask ● n. **1** a covering for all or part of the face: **a** worn as a disguise, as part of a costume, or to amuse or terrify. **b** made of wire, gauze, paper, etc., and worn for protection, e.g. by an athlete, or by a medical practitioner to prevent infection of a patient. **c** worn to conceal the face at balls etc. and usu. made of velvet or silk. **2** a respirator used to filter inhaled air or to supply gas for inhalation. **3** a likeness of a person's face, esp. one made by taking a mould from the face (*death mask*). **4** a disguise or pretense (*mask of respectability*). **5** a hollow model of a human head worn by ancient Greek and Roman actors. **6** the face or head of an animal, esp. a fox. **7** = FACE MASK 2. ● v.tr. **1** cover (the face etc.) with a mask. **2** disguise or conceal (a taste, one's feelings, etc.). **3** protect from a process. **4** Military **a** conceal (a battery etc.) from the enemy's view. **b** hinder (an army etc.) from action by observing with adequate force. **c** hinder (a friendly force) by standing in its line of fire. □ **masker** n.

masked adj. **1** wearing a mask; disguised or hidden by or as by a mask. **2** (of an animal etc.) having facial markings or features suggesting a mask.

masked ball n. a ball at which masks are worn.

masking tape n. usu. cream coloured adhesive tape used in painting to cover areas on which paint is not wanted, and in various household tasks.

masochism /'mæsəˌkɪzəm/ n. **1** the condition or state of deriving (esp. sexual) gratification from one's own pain or humiliation. **2** the enjoyment of what appears to be painful or tiresome. □ **masochist** n. **masochistic** adj. **masochistically** adv.

mason n. **1** a person who builds with stone or brick. **2** (**Mason**) a Freemason.

Masonic /mə'sɒnɪk/ adj. of or relating to Freemasons.

Masonite n. esp. N Amer. proprietary fibreboard made from wood fibre pulped under steam at high pressure.

masonry n. **1 a** the work of a mason. **b** stonework or brickwork. **2** (**Masonry**) Freemasonry.

masque /mɑːsk/ n. **1** a dramatic and musical entertainment esp. of the 16th and 17th c., originally of pantomime, later with metrical dialogue. **2** a dramatic composition for this.

masquerade /ˌmæskə'reɪd/ ● n. **1** a false show or pretense. **2** a masked ball. ● v.intr. (often foll. by as) have or assume a false appearance. □ **masquerader** n.

Mass. abbr. Massachusetts.

Mass n. (also **mass**) **1** the Eucharist, esp. in the Catholic Church. **2** a celebration of this. **3** the liturgy used in the Mass. **4** a musical setting of parts of this.

mass ● n. **1** a coherent body of matter of indefinite shape. **2** a dense aggregation of objects (a mass of fibres). **3** (in sing. or pl.; foll. by of) a large number or amount. **4** (usu. foll. by of) an unbroken expanse (of colour etc.). **5** (foll. by of) covered or abounding in (was a mass of cuts and bruises). **6** a main portion (of a painting etc.) as perceived by the eye. **7** (prec. by the) **a** the majority. **b** (in pl.) the ordinary people. **8** Physics the quantity of matter a body contains. **9** (attrib.) relating to, done by, or affecting large numbers of people or things; large-scale (mass murder). ● v.tr. & intr. (usu. as **massed** adj.) **1** assemble into a mass or as one body (massed bands). **2** Military (with reference to troops) concentrate or be concentrated. □ **in the mass** in the aggregate; collectively. □ **massless** adj.

massacre /'mæsəkər/ ● n. **1** a general slaughter (of persons, occasionally of animals). **2** informal an utter defeat or destruction. ● v.tr. **1** murder (esp. a large number of people) cruelly or violently. **2** informal defeat heavily; destroy.

Massacre of the Innocents n. New Testament the killing of all male infants in Bethlehem on Herod's orders.

massage /mə'sɒʒ, -dʒ/ ● n. **1** the rubbing, kneading, etc., of muscles and joints of the body esp. with the hands, for relaxation, to stimulate circulation, increase suppleness, etc. **2** an instance of this. ● v.tr. **1** apply massage to. **2** (usu. foll. by into, onto) apply (a lotion etc.) by rubbing. **3** manipulate (statistics etc.) to give an acceptable result. **4** flatter (a person's ego etc.). □ **massager** n.

massage parlour n. an establishment at which massages and often sexual services are provided.

massage therapy n. the therapeutic use of massage. □ **massage therapist** n.

massasauga /ˌmæsə'sɒgə/ n. (also **massasauga rattlesnake**) a small spotted venomous N American rattlesnake, Sistrurus catenatus.

masseur /mə'sɜːr/ n. a person who provides massage professionally.

masseuse /mə'suːs, -'sɜːz/ n. a woman who provides massage professionally.

massif /mæ'siːf, 'mæsɪf/ n. a large mountain mass; a compact group of mountain heights.

massive adj. **1** large and heavy or solid. **2** (of the features, head, etc.) relatively large in scale; of solid build. **3** exceptionally large, substantial, or far-reaching. **4** (of a mineral) not visibly crystalline. **5** (of architectural or artistic style) presenting great, solid masses. □ **massively** adv. **massiveness** n.

massively parallel adj. of or relating to a computer which consists of many individual processing units, and which is thus able to carry out simultaneous calculations on a substantial scale.

mass market ● n. the market for mass-produced goods. ● adj. (**mass-market**) designed for or appealing to a large segment of the population. ● v.tr. (**mass-market**) market (a product) on a mass scale. □ **mass-marketed** adj. **mass marketing** n.

mass media n. = MEDIA 2.

mass meeting n. a meeting of a large body of people, esp. of all or most of the members of a workforce, community, etc.

mass murder n. the killing of several people, esp. at once by one person. □ **mass murderer** n.

mass noun n. a noun that is not countable and cannot be used with the indefinite article or in the plural.

mass number n. the total number of protons and neutrons in an atomic nucleus.

mass-produce v.tr. manufacture by mass production. □ **mass-produced** adj.

mass production n. the production of large quantities of a standardized article, esp. by a standardized mechanical process.

mass society n. a society in which the population is largely homogeneous and is strongly influenced by the mass media.

mass transit n. N Amer. public transportation, esp. in urban areas.

mast[1] ● n. **1** a long upright post of timber, iron, etc., set up on a ship's keel, esp. to support sails. **2** a post or latticework upright for supporting a radio or television antenna. **3** a flagpole (half-mast). ● v.tr. furnish (a ship) with masts. □ **before the mast** serving as an ordinary seaman. □ **masted** adj. (also in comb.). **master** n. (also in comb.).

mast[2] n. the fruit of the beech, oak, chestnut, and other forest trees, esp. as food for pigs.

mast cell n. a cell in connective tissue which releases histamine etc. during inflammatory and allergic reactions.

mastectomy /mæ'tektəmi/ n. (pl. **-ies**) the surgical removal of all or part of a breast.

master ● n. **1 a** a person having control of persons or things. **b** an employer, esp. of domestic servants. **c** a male head of a household (master of the house). **d** the owner of a pet, horse, etc. **e** the owner of a slave. **f** Naut. the captain of a merchant ship. **g** Cdn (Nfld) the person in charge of a fishing crew. **2 a** the head of a college, school, etc. **b** the head or presiding officer of a society, institution, lodge, etc. **3** a person who has or gets the upper hand (we shall see which of us is master). **4 a** a person skilled in a particular trade and able to teach others (often attrib.: master carpenter). **b** a person highly accomplished in a particular skill, activity, etc. (a master of manipulation). **5 a** (in full **master's degree**) a graduate degree, usu. awarded after at least one full year of study beyond the undergraduate level. **b** a holder of such a university degree, originally giving authority to teach in the university (Master of Arts). **6 a** a revered teacher in philosophy etc. **b** (**the Master**) Christianity Christ. **7 a** an artist of great skill, esp. one regarded as a model of excellence. **b** a work of painting or sculpture by such an artist. **8 a** Chess etc. a player of proved ability at international level. **b** Sport (in pl.) (usu. attrib.) a class for competitors over the usual age for the highest level of competition (Masters tournament). **9** the original copy of a sound recording, film, data file, etc. from which

a series of copies can be made. **10 (Master)** a title prefixed to the name of a boy not old enough to be called *Mr.* **11** (in Ontario) a judicial officer with jurisdiction over interlocutory matters. **12** *Mech.* a machine, device, or component directly controlling another (compare SLAVE 5). ● *adj.* **1** main, principal (*master bedroom*). **2 a** (of a material or immaterial thing) main, principal; controlling, supreme (*master plan*). **b** designating a device or component which directly controls the action of others (*master switch*). **3** designating the copy of a tape, disc, file, etc. which is the authoritative source for copies. **4** commanding, superior, great, leading (*a master spirit*). ● *v.tr.* **1** overcome, defeat, get the better of in a contest or struggle. **2** break, tame, reduce to subjection, or compel to obey. **3** acquire complete knowledge of (a subject), facility in using (an instrument etc.), or skill at (performing a task). **4** rule as a master. **5 a** record the master disc or tape for (a sound recording). **b** make a recording of (a performance) from which a master can be created. □ **be master of 1** know how to control. **2** have at one's disposal. **be one's own master** be independent or free to do as one wishes.
master bedroom *n.* the largest bedroom in a dwelling, usu., in a family dwelling, the one intended for the parents.
master class *n.* **1** an advanced class given by a person of distinguished skill, esp. in music. **2** the most powerful or influential class in a society.
master corporal *n.* (also **Master Corporal**) *Cdn* (in the Canadian Army and Air Force) a non-commissioned officer of a rank above corporal.
masterful *adj.* **1** imperious, domineering. **2** characterized by the skill that constitutes a master; masterly. ¶*Masterful* is normally used of a person, whereas *masterly* is used of achievements, abilities, etc. □ **masterfully** *adv.* **masterfulness** *n.*
master key *n.* a key that opens several locks, each of which also has its own key that will not open any of the rest.
masterly *adj.* worthy of a master; very skilful (*a masterly piece of work*). □ **masterliness** *n.*
master mason *n.* **1** a skilled mason, or one in business on his or her own account. **2 (Master Mason)** a fully qualified Freemason, who has passed the third degree.
mastermind ● *n.* **1** the person directing an intricate operation. **2** a person with an outstanding intellect. ● *v.tr.* plan and direct (a scheme or enterprise).
master of ceremonies *n.* **1** a person introducing speakers at a banquet, entertainers in a variety show, etc. **2** a person in charge of ceremonies at a state or public occasion. Abbr.: **MC.**
masterpiece *n.* **1** an outstanding piece of artistry or workmanship. **2** a person's best work.
master seaman *n.* (also **Master Seaman**) *Cdn* (in the Canadian Navy) a non-commissioned officer of a rank above leading seaman and equivalent to a master corporal in the other commands.
master stroke *n.* an outstandingly skilful act of policy etc.
master switch *n.* a switch controlling the supply of electricity etc. to an entire system.
master warrant officer *n.* (also **Master Warrant Officer**) *Cdn* (in the Canadian Army and Air Force) a non-commissioned officer of a rank above warrant officer and below chief warrant officer.
masterwork *n.* = MASTERPIECE.
mastery *n.* **1** (often foll. by *of*) comprehensive knowledge or use of a subject or instrument. **2** masterly

skill. **3** dominion, sway. **4** (prec. by *the*) superiority or ascendancy in competition or strife.
masthead *n.* **1 a** the title of a newspaper etc. at the head of the front or editorial page. **b** *N Amer.* a box in a newspaper or magazine listing the names of owners and staff etc. **2** the highest part of a ship's mast, esp. that of a lower mast as a place of observation or punishment.
mastic /ˈmæstɪk/ *n.* **1** a gum or resin exuded from the bark of the mastic tree, used in making varnish. **2** (in full **mastic tree**) the evergreen tree, *Pistacia lentiscus*, yielding this. **3** a waterproof, putty-like filler and sealant used in building.
masticate /ˈmæstɪˌkeɪt/ *v.tr.* grind or chew (food) with one's teeth. □ **mastication** *n.* **masticatory** *adj.*
mastiff /ˈmæstɪf/ *n.* a dog of a large strong breed with drooping ears and pendulous lips.
mastitis /mæˈstaɪtɪs/ *n.* an inflammation of the mammary gland (the breast or udder).
mastodon /ˈmæstəˌdɒn/ *n.* a large extinct mammal of the genus *Mammut*, resembling the elephant but having nipple-shaped tubercles on the crowns of its molar teeth.
mastoid /ˈmæstɔɪd/ ● *adj.* **1** shaped like a woman's breast. **2** of or pertaining to the mastoid process or bone. ● *n.* (in full **mastoid process**) a conical prominence on the temporal bone behind the ear, to which muscles are attached.
masturbate /ˈmæstərˌbeɪt/ *v.intr. & tr.* arouse oneself or cause (another person) to be aroused by manual stimulation of the genitals. □ **masturbation** *n.* **masturbator** *n.* **masturbatory** *adj.*
M.A.T. *abbr.* Master of Arts in Teaching.
mat[1] ● *n.* **1** a small piece of carpeting or other heavy material, used as a covering on a floor. **2** a usu. thin piece of cork, rubber, plastic, etc., to protect a surface from the heat or moisture of an object placed on it. **3** a piece of padded, resilient material for landing on in gymnastics, wrestling, etc. **4** a piece of coarse fabric of braided rushes, straw, etc. **5** a thick tangled mass of hair, vegetation, etc., esp. forming a layer. ● *v.* (**matted, matting**) **1** *intr.* become matted. **2** *tr.* cover or furnish with mats. □ **go to the mat** vigorously engage in an argument or contention, esp. on behalf of a particular person or cause.
mat[2] ● *n.* **1** a sheet of cardboard forming a margin around a picture inside a frame. **2** a sheet of cardboard on which a picture etc. is mounted. ● *v.tr.* (**matted, matting**) **1** mount (a print etc.) on a cardboard backing. **2** provide (a print etc.) with a border.
mat[3] *n.* = MATRIX 2.
matador /ˈmætəˌdɔr/ *n.* a bullfighter whose task is to kill the bull.
match[1] ● *n.* **1** a person, thing, action, etc. equal to another in some quality (*this river is a match for the most skilled anglers*). **2** a person or thing exactly or corresponding to another (*this vase is an exact match for the one that was broken*). **3** a person or thing that associates or combines well with another (*ginger and peaches are a wonderful match*). **4** a contest or game of skill etc. in which persons or teams compete against each other. **5 a** a marriage. **b** a close association of two people (*as partners they are a perfect match*). **6** a person viewed in regard to his or her eligibility for marriage, esp. as to rank or fortune (*an excellent match*). **7** *Computing* a record, string, etc. that matches the requirements of a search or is identical with a given record etc. **8** an incident in which the participants vie to outdo each other (*slanging match*). ● *v.* **1 a** *tr.* combine well with, esp. in colour (*the curtains match*

the wallpaper). **b** *intr.* (often foll. by *with*) correspond; harmonize (*his socks do not match*). **2** *tr.* (foll. by *against, with*) place (a person, aptitudes, etc.) in competition with (another) (*match your skill against the experts*). **3** *tr.* find material etc. that matches (another) (*can you match this paint?*). **4** *tr.* find a person or thing suitable for another (*matching workers with positions*). **5** *tr.* be equal to (*the players are well matched*). **6** *tr.* find or provide something equal to (*can you match that story?*). **7** *tr. Electronics* produce or have an adjustment of (circuits) such that maximum power is transmitted between them. □ **match up** (often foll. by *with*) pair up; fit to form a coherent whole or relation. **match up to** be as good as or equal to. **meet one's match** meet someone who has as much skill, determination, etc. as oneself, and perhaps more. **to match** corresponding in some essential respect with what has been mentioned (*yellow dress with gloves to match*).

match² *n.* **1** a short thin piece of wood, paper, etc., tipped with a composition that can be ignited by friction. **2** a piece of wick, cord, etc., designed to burn at a uniform rate, for firing a cannon, igniting a trail of gunpowder, etc. □ **put a match to** set fire to.

matchbook *n. N Amer.* a small folder, usu. with a striking surface on the back, containing paper matches.

matchbox *n.* **1** a small box for holding matches. **2** (often *attrib.*) something very small, esp. a very small house or apartment.

matching *adj.* **1** that matches (*shoes and matching gloves*). **2** (of financial grants) of an amount based on the amount raised from other sources (*matching grant*).

matchless *adj.* without an equal, incomparable. □ **matchlessly** *adv.*

matchmaker *n.* **1 a** a person who schemes to bring couples together. **b** a person who arranges marriages. **2** a person who arranges matches between employers and prospective employees, corporate deal makers, etc. □ **matchmake** *v.intr.* **matchmaking** *n. & adj.*

match penalty *n. Hockey* = GAME MISCONDUCT.

match point *n. Tennis etc.* **1** the state of a game when one side needs only one more point to win the match. **2** this point.

matchstick ● *n.* the stem of a match. ● *adj.* **1** very thin, skeletal. **2** made of or as though of matchsticks.

matchup *n.* **1** the action of pairing or setting in opposition. **2** (esp. in sports or politics) a two suited or equal persons, teams, or things. **b** a pair so matched. **c** a contest between such a pair.

mate¹ ● *n.* **1** (in *comb.*) a fellow member or joint occupant of (*roommate*). **2** a partner in marriage or a lover. **3** either of a pair of mated animals. **4** either of a pair of things (*I have the left shoe, but I can't find its mate*). **5** *Naut.* **a** an officer on a merchant ship subordinate to the master, the rank being divided into *first, second, third,* etc. *mate* according to seniority. **b** an assistant to an officer on board ship (*boatswain's mate*). **6** an assistant to a skilled worker (*plumber's mate*). ● *v.* (often foll. by *with*) **1 a** *tr.* bring (animals or birds) together for breeding. **b** *intr.* (of animals or birds) come together for breeding. **2 a** *tr.* join (persons) in marriage. **b** *intr.* (of persons) be joined in marriage. **c** *intr.* copulate. **3** *intr. Mech.* (of a part) fit well, make a good or proper fit.

mate² *n. & v.tr. Chess* = CHECKMATE.

matelot /ˈmætlo:/ *n. Cdn & Brit. slang* a sailor.

material ● *n.* **1** the matter from which a thing is made. **2** cloth, fabric. **3** (in *pl.*) things needed for an activity (*building materials*; *writing materials*). **4** a per-

son or thing suitable for a specific role or purpose (*officer material*). **5** (in *sing.* or *pl.*) information, ideas, evidence, etc. to be used in creating an artistic or literary work, drawing a conclusion, etc. (*materials for a biography*). **6** (in *sing.* or *pl.*, often foll. by *of*) the elements or constituent parts of a substance. ● *adj.* **1** formed or consisting of matter; corporeal. **2 a** concerned with bodily comfort etc. (*material well-being*). **b** relating to the physical, not intellectual or spiritual, aspect of things. **3** (of conduct, points of view, etc.) not elevated or spiritual. **4 a** (often foll. by *to*) pertinent, essential, relevant (*at the material time*). **b** serious, important, of consequence. **5** *Law* (of evidence, a fact, etc.) significant, influential, esp. to the extent of determining a cause, affecting a judgment, etc. (*material witness*). □ **materiality** /-iˈælɪti/ *n.*

material culture *n.* the physical objects (tools, articles of domestic and religious use, dwelling places, etc.) which give evidence of the type of culture developed by a social group.

materialism *n.* **1 a** a tendency to prefer material possessions and physical comfort to spiritual values. **b** a way of life based on material interests. **2** *Philos.* **a** the doctrine that nothing exists but matter and its movements and modifications. **b** the doctrine that consciousness and will are wholly due to material agencies. **3** *Art* a tendency to lay stress on the material aspect of objects represented. □ **materialist** *n. & adj.* **materialistic** *adj.* **materialistically** *adv.*

materialize *v.* **1** *intr.* become actual fact. **2** *intr.* appear, arrive, or be present when expected. **3 a** *tr.* cause (a spirit) to appear in bodily form. **b** *intr.* (of a spirit) appear in this way. **4** *tr.* represent or express in material form. **5** *tr.* make materialistic. □ **materialization** *n.*

materially *adv.* **1** substantially, considerably. **2** with respect to matter.

matériel /məˌtiːriˈel/ *n.* available means or resources, esp. materials and equipment used in warfare (opp. PERSONNEL 1).

maternal *adj.* **1** of or like a mother. **2** motherly, having the instincts of motherhood. **3 a** related through the mother (*maternal uncle*). **b** inherited from the mother (*maternal chromosome*). **4** of or pertaining to the mother in pregnancy and childbirth. □ **maternalistic** *adj.* **maternally** *adv.*

maternity *n.* **1** (*attrib.*) **a** for women during and just after childbirth (*maternity ward*; *maternity leave*). **b** designed for a pregnant woman (*maternity dress*). **2** a maternity ward or hospital. **3 a** motherhood. **b** motherliness.

matey *adj.* (**matier, matiest**) (often foll. by *with*) sociable; familiar and friendly. □ **mateyness** *n.* (also **matiness**).

math *n. N Amer. informal* mathematics.

mathematical *adj.* **1** of or relating to mathematics. **2 a** (of a concept, object, etc.) as understood or defined in mathematics. **b** (of a proof etc.) rigorously precise. □ **mathematically** *adv.*

mathematics *n.* **1** the abstract, deductive science of number, quantity, space, and arrangement studied in its own right (**pure mathematics**), or as applied to other disciplines such as physics, engineering, etc. (**applied mathematics**). **2** (as *pl.*) the use of mathematics in calculation etc. □ **mathematician** /-məˈtɪʃən/ *n.*

matinee /ˌmætɪˈnei/ *n.* an afternoon performance at a theatre, concert hall, etc.

matinee idol *n.* esp. *dated* a handsome actor.

mating ● *n.* an act or instance of matching, marrying, or pairing (of animals etc.) for breeding purposes. ● *adj.* of or pertaining to the act of mating (*mating season*).

matins /ˈmætɪnz/ *n.* (as *sing* or *pl.*) **1** *Anglicanism* a service of morning prayer. **2** *Catholicism* the office of one of the canonical hours of prayer, properly a night office, but also recited with lauds at daybreak or on the previous evening.

matriarch /ˈmeɪtriˌɑrk/ *n.* **1 a** a woman who is the head of a family or tribe. **b** a woman who dominates an organization. **2** an elderly woman who is highly respected. □ **matriarchal** *adj.*

matriarchy *n.* (*pl.* **-ies**) **1** a form of social organization in which the mother is the head of the family and descent is reckoned through the female line. **2 a** a society etc. governed by a woman or women. **b** government by a woman or women.

matriculate /məˈtrɪkjʊˌleɪt/ *v.* **1** *intr.* be enrolled at a college or university. **2** *tr.* admit (a student) to membership of a college or university.

matriculation *n.* the act or an instance of matriculating, esp. formal admission into a university, college, etc.

matrilineal /ˌmætrɪˈlɪniəl/ *adj.* of or based on kinship with the mother or the female line. □ **matrilineage** *n.* **matrilineally** *adv.*

matrimonial cake *n. Cdn* (*Prairies*) = DATE SQUARE.

matrimony /ˈmætrɪˌmoʊni/ *n.* (*pl.* **-ies**) **1** the rite or institution of marriage. **2 a** the state of being married. **b** the relation between married persons. □ **matrimonial** *adj.* **matrimonially** *adv.*

matrix /ˈmeɪtrɪks/ *n.* (*pl.* **matrices** /-ˌsiːz/ or **matrixes**) **1** an environment or substance in which a thing is developed. **2 a** a mould in which a thing is cast or shaped, such as printing type, an engraved die to strike coins, etc. **b** a positive or negative copy of an original disc recording used in making other copies. **3 a** the rock material in which a gem, fossil, etc. is embedded. **b** any relatively fine or homogeneous substance in which coarser or larger particles are embedded. **4** *Math.* a rectangular array of symbols, elements, etc. in rows and columns that is treated as a single element. **5** *Computing* a gridlike array of interconnected circuit elements. **6** an organizational structure in which two or more lines of command, responsibility, or communication run through the same individual.

matron /ˈmeɪtrən/ *n.* **1** a middle-aged or elderly married woman, esp. a dignified, staid, or portly one of high social standing. **2** esp. *N Amer.* a female prison officer.

matronly *adj.* like or characteristic of a matron, esp. as regards staidness or portliness.

matron of honour *n.* a married woman attending the bride at a wedding.

matryoshka /mæˈtrɪʃkə/ *n.* (often *attrib.*) = RUSSIAN DOLL.

Matsqui /ˈmætskwiː/ *n.* (*pl.* same) a member of a Salishan Aboriginal people, a subdivision of the Halkomelem, living in the Lower Fraser valley of BC.

matte¹ /mæt/ (also esp. *Brit.* **matt**) ● *adj.* **1** (of a colour, surface, etc.) dull, without lustre. **2** (of lipstick, face powder, paint, etc.) having a flat, not shiny or glossy, finish. ● *n.* paint formulated to give a dull flat finish (*compare* GLOSS¹ 3, SEMIGLOSS).

matte² /mæt/ *n.* an impure product of the smelting of sulphide ores, esp. those of copper or nickel.

matte³ /mæt/ *n. Film* a mask to obscure part of an image and allow another image to be superimposed, giving a combined effect.

matted *adj.* **1** (esp. of plants, hair, etc.) tangled and interlaced. **2** covered with a dense growth. **3** (of a picture) provided with a mat.

matter ● *n.* **1 a** physical substance in general, as distinct from mind and spirit. **b** that which has mass and occupies space. **2** a constituent substance, esp. of a particular kind (*colouring matter*). **3** (prec. by *the*; often foll. by *with*) the thing that is amiss (*there's something the matter with him*). **4** fact or thought as material for expression. **5** the content of a book, speech, etc., as distinct from its stylistic manner or form. **6** a thing or things collectively of a specified kind or relating to a specified thing (*printed matter*). **7** a an affair or situation being considered, esp. in a specified way (*a serious matter*). **b** (in *pl.*) events, circumstances, etc. generally which are objects of consideration or practical concern. **8 a** any substance in or discharged from the body (*fecal matter*). **b** pus. **9** (foll. by *of, for*) a ground, reason, or what is or may be a good reason for (complaint, regret, etc.). **10** *Law* **a** a thing which is to be tried or proved. **b** statements or allegations which come under the consideration of a court. ● *v. intr.* (often foll. by *to*) be of importance; have significance (*it does not matter to me*). □ **as a matter of course** be a regular habit or usual procedure. **be another** (or **a different**) **matter** be completely different. **for that matter 1** as far as that is concerned. **2** and indeed also. **in the matter of** as regards. **make matters worse** make an already difficult sitation more difficult. **a matter of 1** approximately (*a matter of hours*). **2** a thing that relates to, depends on, or is determined by (*it's simply a matter of experience*). **a matter of life and death** a matter of vital importance. **it's all** (or **only**) **a matter of time** (**before…**) this consequence is inevitable though it may not happen immediately. **no matter 1** (foll. by *when, how*, etc.) regardless of (*will do it no matter what the consequences*). **2** it is of no importance. **take matters into one's own hands** act decisively and independently. **what is the matter with** surely there is no objection to. **what matter?** that need not worry us.

matter of fact ● *n.* **1** what belongs to the sphere of fact as distinct from opinion etc. **2** *Law* the part of a judicial inquiry concerned with the truth of alleged facts. ● *adj.* (**matter-of-fact**) **1** unimaginative, prosaic. **2** unemotional. **3** pertaining to, having regard to, or depending on actual fact as distinct from what is speculative or fanciful. □ **as a matter of fact** actually, in reality (esp. to correct a falsehood or misunderstanding). □ **matter-of-factly** *adv.* **matter-of-factness** *n.*

matter of form *n.* **1** a point of correct procedure. **2** a mere routine.

matter of law *n.* the part of a judicial inquiry concerned with the interpretation of the law and correctness of procedure.

matting *n.* **1** fabric of hemp, bast, grass, etc., for mats (*coconut matting*). **2** in senses of MAT¹,² *v.*

mattins *var.* of MATINS.

mattock /ˈmætək/ *n.* an agricultural tool shaped like a pickaxe, with an adze and a chisel edge as the ends of the head.

mattress *n.* a large fabric case stuffed with soft, firm, or springy material, or a similar case filled with air or water, used on or as a bed.

maturation /ˌmætʃʊˈreɪʃən/ *n.* **1 a** the act or instance of maturing. **b** the state of being matured. **2** *Med.* **a** the formation of purulent matter. **b** the causing of this.

mature ● *adj.* (**maturer, maturest**) **1 a** with fully developed powers of body and mind; adult. **b** sensible, wise. **c** middle aged or elderly. **2 a** complete in natural development or growth. **b** (of wine, cheese, etc.) ready for consumption. **c** (of fruit) ripe. **3** (of thought, intentions, etc.) duly careful and adequate. **4** fully developed or established; at a point after which further development, expansion, or improvement is unlikely or impossible (*mature technology*). **5** (of a bond etc.) due for payment. **6 a** (in Alberta) a film classification which requires that viewers under 14 years of age be accompanied by an adult. **b** (in BC) a film classification which advises of content which may be inappropriate for young viewers, without indicating an age restriction. ● *v.* **1 a** *tr. & intr.* bring to or reach a mature state; develop fully. **b** *tr. & intr.* ripen. **c** *intr.* come to maturity. **2** *tr.* perfect (a plan etc.). **3** *intr.* (of a bond etc.) become due for payment. □ **maturely** *adv.* **maturity** *n.*

mature student *n.* a person, usu. an adult, who undertakes a course of study at a later age than normal.

matzo /ˈmɒtsoː/ *n.* (also **matzoh, matzah** /ˈmɒtsə/) (*pl.* **-os, -ohs, -ahs** or **matzoth** /-oːt/) **1** a flat, crisp, unleavened bread for the Passover. **2** a slab of this.

matzo ball *n.* a small dumpling made of seasoned matzo meal bound together with egg and chicken fat, typically served in chicken soup.

maudlin /ˈmɔːdlɪn/ *adj.* **1** foolishly sentimental or self-pitying. **2** tearful and effusive from drunkenness.

maul ● *v.tr.* **1** (of an animal) tear and mutilate (a person, prey etc.). **2 a** beat and bruise (a person). **b** handle roughly or carelessly; damage by rough handling. **3** subject to damaging criticism; injure by criticizing. ● *n.* **1** a special heavy hammer, commonly of wood, esp. for driving piles. **2** a wooden club. □ **mauler** *n.* **mauling** *n.*

maunder *v.intr.* **1** talk in a dreamy or rambling manner. **2** move or act listlessly or idly.

Maundy Thursday *n.* the Thursday before Easter.

Mauser /ˈmauzər/ *n.* proprietary a type of firearm, originally a repeating rifle, now also a pistol.

mausoleum /ˌmɔːzəˈliːəm, ˌmɒsə-/ *n.* **1** a large and grand tomb. **2** a very large and sombre building.

mauve pale purple.

mauzy /ˈmɒzi/ *adj.* (also **mausy**) *Cdn* (*Nfld*) (of weather) foggy, damp, or misty, esp. producing condensation on objects.

maven /ˈmeivən/ *n.* *N Amer.* *informal* an expert or connoisseur.

maverick *n.* **1** an unorthodox or independent-minded person (also *attrib.*: *maverick politicians*). **2** *N Amer.* a calf etc. not branded with its owner's mark.

maw *n.* **1 a** the stomach of an animal. **b** the jaws or throat of a voracious animal or (*jocular*) person. **2** a thing perceived as a consuming mouth or entrance (*the voracious maw of the publicity machine*).

mawkish *adj.* **1** sentimental in a feeble or sickly way. **2** having a faint sickly flavour. □ **mawkishly** *adv.* **mawkishness** *n.*

max *N Amer.* *slang* ● *n.* (a) maximum. ● *adj.* maximal. ● *adv.* maximally; at most. ● *v.* **1** *intr.* (foll. by *out*) achieve or attain a maximum in something (*prices max out at fifty thousand*). **2** *tr.* (foll. by *out*) *informal* spend to the limit of (a credit card). □ **to the max 1** completely. **2** to the furthest possible extreme.

max. *abbr.* maximum.

maxi *n.* (*pl.* **maxis**) *informal* **1** a maxi-coat, -skirt, etc. **2** = MAXI-PAD.

maxi- *comb. form* very large or long (*maxi-coat*).

maxilla /mækˈsɪlə/ *n.* (*pl.* **maxillae** /-liː/) **1** the jaw or jawbone, esp. the upper jaw in most vertebrates. **2** the mouthpart of many arthropods used in chewing. □ **maxillary** *adj.*

maxim *n.* a general truth or rule of conduct expressed in a sentence.

maximal *adj.* **1** being or relating to a maximum. **2** the greatest possible in size, duration, etc. □ **maximally** *adv.*

maximalist *n.* a person who rejects compromise and expects a full response to demands.

maximize *v.tr.* increase or enhance to the utmost. □ **maximization** *n.* **maximizer** *n.*

maximum ● *n.* (*pl.* **-s** or **maxima**) the highest possible or attainable amount or magnitude. ● *adj.* of or pertaining to a maximum; that is a maximum.

maximum-security *adj.* (of a correctional institution) intended for offenders who require the greatest degree of physical security and so usu. having high walls, double fences, security posts with armed guards, electronic monitoring systems, etc.

maxi-pad *n.* a sanitary pad designed to absorb heavy menstrual flow.

maxwell *n.* a unit of magnetic flux in the cgs system, equal to that induced through one square centimetre by a perpendicular magnetic field of one gauss.

May *n.* **1** the fifth month of the year. **2** (**may**) the hawthorn or its blossom.

may *v.aux.* (*3rd sing. present* **may**; *past* **might**) **1** (often foll. by *well* for emphasis) expressing possibility (*it may be true; you may well lose your way*). **2** expressing permission (*may I come in?*). ¶Both *can* and *may* are used to express permission; in more formal contexts *may* is usual since *can* also denotes capability (*can I move?* = am I physically able to move?; *may I move?* = am I allowed to move?). **3** expressing a wish (*may he live to regret it*). **4** expressing uncertainty or irony in questions (*who may you be?; who are you, may I ask?*). **5** in purpose clauses and after *wish, fear,* etc. (*take such measures as may avert disaster; hope she may succeed*). □ **be that as it may** (or **that is as may be**) despite the fact that it may be so (*be that as it may, I still want to go*). **may as well** = MIGHT AS WELL (see MIGHT¹).

Maya /ˈmaɪə/ ● *n.* **1** (*pl.* same or **Mayas**) a member of an ancient Indian people of Central America. **2** the language of this people. ● *adj.* of or relating to this people or language. □ **Mayan** *adj. & n.*

maya /ˈmaɪə/ *n.* **1** *Hindu Philos.* illusion, magic, the supernatural power wielded by gods and demons. **2** *Hinduism & Buddhism* the power by which the universe becomes manifest, the illusion or appearance of the phenomenal world.

maybe ● *adv.* perhaps, possibly. ● *n.* an uncertain response, a possibility; what may be.

May Day *n.* May 1 esp. as a festival with dancing, or as an international holiday in honour of workers.

mayday *n.* an international radio distress signal used esp. by ships and aircraft.

May-December *adj.* (of a romance, marriage, etc.) involving two people of widely disparate ages, usu. a young woman and a much older man.

mayest archaic *var.* of MAYST.

mayflower *n.* any of various flowers that bloom in May, esp. the trailing arbutus, *Epigaea repens*.

mayfly *n.* (*pl.* **-flies**) **1** any insect of the order Ephemeroptera, living briefly in spring in the adult stage. **2** an imitation mayfly used by anglers.

mayhem *n.* violent or damaging action.

mayn't contraction may not.

mayo *n.* esp. *N Amer. informal* mayonnaise.

mayonnaise *n.* a thick creamy dressing made of egg yolks, oil, vinegar, etc.

mayor *n.* the head of a municipal corporation, esp. of a city or town. □ **mayoral** *adj.*

mayoralty *n.* (pl. **-ies**) **1** the office of mayor. **2** a mayor's period of office.

maypole *n.* a tall pole painted and decked with flowers and ribbons, for dancing around on May Day.

mayst *archaic 2nd sing. present of* MAY.

maze *n.* **1 a** a network of paths and passages arranged in bewildering complexity, usu. with a correct path concealed by blind alleys etc. **b** such a pattern, represented on paper by a pattern of lines, designed as a puzzle. **2** any complex system, arrangement, process, etc. that bewilders, confuses, or perplexes. □ **mazed** *adj.* **mazy** *adj.* (**-ier, -iest**).

mazel tov /'mɒzəltɒv, -tɒf, -toːv/ *interj.* good luck, congratulations.

mazurka /məˈzɜːrkə/ *n.* **1** a usu. lively Polish dance in triple time, usu. with a slide and hop. **2** a piece of music for this dance or composed in its rhythm, usu. with accentuation of the second or third beat.

MB *abbr.* **1** (also **Mb**) *Computing* megabyte. **2** Manitoba (in postal use). **3** *Cdn* MEDAL OF BRAVERY. **4** Mennonite Brethren.

M.B.A. ● *abbr.* Master of Business Administration. ● *n.* a person who holds this degree.

Mbps *abbr.* megabytes per second.

Mbyte *abbr.* megabyte.

MC ● *n.* a master of ceremonies. ● *v.tr.* (**MCs, MCd, MCing**) act as master of ceremonies for.

Mc *abbr.* megacycle(s).

McCarthyism *n.* **1** *hist.* (esp. in the US) the policy of hunting out suspected Communists and removing them from government departments or other positions, esp. as pursued by the Republican politician Joseph McCarthy (1908–57). **2** any use of unfair or unsubstantiated accusations to hound, harass, or investigate. □ **McCarthyite** *adj. & n.*

McCoy *n. informal* □ **the** (or **the real**) **McCoy** the real thing; the genuine article.

mCi *abbr.* millicurie(s).

McIntosh *n. N Amer.* a medium-sized, deep red cooking and eating apple with green blotches.

McJob *n. informal* a low paying, low status, and usu. unstimulating job with few benefits and little chance for advancement, esp. in a service industry.

MCP *abbr. informal* male chauvinist pig.

MCpl *abbr. Cdn* MASTER CORPORAL.

M.C.S. *abbr.* Master of Computer Science.

Mc/s *abbr.* megacycles per second.

MD *abbr.* **1** Doctor of Medicine. **2** Maryland (in postal use). **3** *Cdn* (*Prairies & North*) MUNICIPAL DISTRICT. **4** Mini Disc.

Md *symbol* mendelevium.

Md. *abbr.* Maryland.

MDA *abbr.* methylenedioxyamphetamine, a synthetic hallucinogenic drug.

MDF *abbr.* medium density fibreboard.

M.Div. *abbr.* Master of Divinity.

MDMA *abbr.* methylenedioxymethamphetamine, an amphetamine-based drug that causes euphoric and hallucinatory effects (see ECSTASY 3).

MDT *abbr.* MOUNTAIN DAYLIGHT TIME.

ME *abbr.* **1** Maine (in postal use). **2** myalgic encephalomyelitis, an obscure disease with symptoms like those of influenza and prolonged periods of tiredness and depression.

Me. *abbr.* Maine.

me¹ ● *pron.* **1** objective case of I² (*he saw me*). **2** *N Amer. informal* myself, to or for myself (*I got me a gun*). **3** *informal* used in exclamations (*dear me!*). ● *adj.* of or displaying an excessive preoccupation with personal fulfillment and gratification (*the me generation*). ● *n.* one's personality, the ego (*the real me*). ¶ See HER.

me² *var. of* MI.

mea culpa /meiə ˈkʊlpə, -ˈkʌlpə/ ● *n.* an acknowledgement of one's fault or error. ● *interj.* expressing such an acknowledgement.

mead *n.* an alcoholic drink of fermented honey and water.

meadow *n.* **1** a piece of grassland, esp. one used for hay or for grazing animals. **2** a piece of low well-watered ground, esp. near a river. □ **meadowy** *adj.*

meadowland *n.* land used for the cultivation of grass, esp. for hay.

meadowlark *n.* any of several N American songbirds of the genus *Sturnella* related to the blackbirds but speckled brown with yellow underparts, esp. the eastern meadowlark, *S. magna*, or western meadowlark, *S. neglecta*, which has a characteristic bubbling song.

meagre /ˈmiːgər/ *adj.* (also **meager**) **1** lacking in amount or quality (*a meagre salary*). **2** (of literary composition, ideas, etc.) lacking fullness, unsatisfying. **3** (of a person or animal) lean, thin. □ **meagrely** *adv.* **meagreness** *n.*

meal¹ *n.* **1** an occasion when food is eaten. **2** the food eaten on one occasion. □ **make a meal of** consume as a meal.

meal² *n.* **1** the edible part of any grain or pulse (usu. other than wheat) ground to powder. **2** any powdery substance made by grinding.

Meals on Wheels *n.pl.* (usu. treated as *sing.*) a service by which meals are delivered to old people, invalids, etc.

meal ticket *n.* **1** a ticket entitling one to a meal, esp. at a specified place with reduced cost. **2** *informal* a person or thing that is a source of food or income.

mealtime *n.* any of the usual times of eating.

mealworm *n.* the larva of any of several beetles of the genus *Tenebrio*, infesting cereal products, and often raised as food for pet fish or reptiles.

mealy *adj.* (**-ier, -iest**) **1 a** of or like meal; soft and powdery. **b** containing meal. **c** covered with or as with meal, flour, or any fine dust or powder. **2** (of a complexion) pale. □ **mealiness** *n.*

mealy bug *n.* any insect of the genus *Pseudococcus*, infesting vines etc., whose body is covered with white powder, a pest of citrus trees and greenhouses.

mealy-mouthed *adj.* not willing to speak directly.

mean¹ *v.tr.* (*past and past part.* **meant**) **1 a** (often foll. by *to* + infin.) have as one's purpose or intention; have in mind (*I didn't mean to break it*). **b** (foll. by *by*) have as a motive in explanation (*what do you mean by that?*). **2** (often in *passive*) design or destine for a purpose (*is meant to be a gift*). **3** intend to convey or indicate or refer to (a particular thing or notion) (*I mean London in Ontario*). **4** entail, involve (*it means catching the early flight*). **5** (often foll. by *that* + clause) portend, signify (*this means trouble; your refusal means that we must look elsewhere*). **6** (of a word) have as its explanation in the same language or as its equivalent in another language. **7** (foll. by *to*) be of some specified importance to (a person), esp. as a source of benefit or object of affection etc. (*that means a lot to me*). □ **mean it** not be joking or exaggerating. **mean to say** really admit (usu. in *interrog.*: *do you mean to say you have lost it?*). **mean well** (often foll. by *by*) have good intentions.

mean² *adj.* **1** uncooperative, unkind or unfair. **2** stingy; not generous. **3 a** malicious, ill-tempered. **b** *N Amer.* vicious or aggressive in behaviour. **4 a** low in the social hierarchy; humble (*mean origins*). **b** (of housing etc.) shabby; characterized by poverty. **5** (of a person's capacity, understanding, etc.) inferior, poor. **6** *informal* **a** (of a person) skilful, formidable (*is a mean fighter*). **b** (of a thing) excellent, impressive (*a mean batch of chili*). □ **no mean** a very good (*that is no mean achievement*). □ **meanly** *adv.* **meanness** *n.*

mean³ ● *n.* **1** a condition, quality, virtue, or course of action equally removed from two opposite (usu. unsatisfactory) extremes. **2** *Math.* **a** the term or one of the terms midway between the first and last terms of an arithmetical or geometrical etc. progression. **b** the quotient of the sum of several quantities and their number; the average. ● *adj.* **1** (of a quantity) equally far from two extremes. **2** calculated as a mean.

meander /miˈændər/ ● *v.intr.* **1** wander at random. **2** (of a stream) wind about. ● *n.* **1** (often in *pl.*) a curve in a winding river. **2** a crooked or winding path etc. **3** a circuitous journey. □ **meandering** *adj. & n.*

meanie *n.* (*pl.* **-ies**) *informal* a mean, stingy, or ill-tempered person.

meaning ● *n.* **1** what is meant by a word, action, idea, etc. **2** significance. **3** importance. ● *adj.* expressive, significant (*a meaning glance*). □ **meaningly** *adv.*

meaningful *adj.* **1** full of meaning; significant. **2** able to be interpreted. **3** intended to communicate something not directly expressed (*a meaningful look*). □ **meaningfully** *adv.* **meaningfulness** *n.*

meaningless *adj.* having no meaning or significance. □ **meaninglessly** *adv.* **meaninglessness** *n.*

means *n.pl.* **1** (often treated as *sing.*) an action, object, system, etc. by which a result is brought about; a method or methods (*an effective means of communication*). **2 a** money resources (*live beyond one's means*). **b** wealth (*a man of means*). □ **by all means** certainly. **by any means** in any way (*not by any means rich*). **by means of** by the agency or instrumentality of (a thing or action). **by no means** (or **not by any manner of means**) not at all; certainly not.

means of production *n.* (in Marxist doctrine) the raw materials and means of labour (machines, implements, etc.) used in the production process.

mean-spirited *adj.* petty; spiteful; selfish. □ **mean-spiritedly** *adv.* **mean-spiritedness** *n.*

means test ● *n.* an official inquiry to establish need before financial assistance from public funds is given. ● *v.tr.* (**means-test**) **1** assess (a grant etc.) by a means test. **2** subject (a person) to a means test.

mean streets *n.pl.* **1** streets where the poor or socially deprived live or work. **2** streets noted for violence and crime.

meant *past and past part.* of MEAN¹.

meantime ● *n.* the intervening period (*in the meantime*). ● *adv.* = MEANWHILE.

meanwhile ● *adv.* **1** in the intervening period of time. **2** at the same time. ● *n.* the intervening period (*in the meanwhile*).

meany *var.* of MEANIE.

measles *n.pl.* (also treated as *sing.*) **1** an acute infectious viral disease marked by red spots on the skin. **2** the spots of measles.

measly *adj.* (**-ier, -iest**) *informal* ridiculously small in

size, amount, or value. **2** *informal* inferior, contemptible, worthless. **3** of or affected with measles.

measurable *adj.* **1** that can be measured. **2** noticeable; definite (*a measurable improvement*). □ **measurability** *n.* **measurably** *adv.*

measure ● *n.* **1** a size or quantity found by measuring. **2** a system of measuring (*linear measure*). **3** a rod or tape etc. for measuring. **4** a vessel of standard capacity for transferring or determining fixed quantities of liquids etc. (*a pint measure*). **5 a** the degree, extent, or amount of a thing. **b** (foll. by *of*) some degree of (*gained a measure of acceptance*). **6** a unit of capacity, e.g. a bushel (*20 measures of wheat*). **7** a factor by which a person or thing is reckoned or evaluated (*their success is a measure of their determination*). **8** suitable action to achieve some end (*a stop-gap measure*; *drastic measures*). **9** a legislative enactment. **10** a quantity contained in another an exact number of times. **11** a prescribed extent or quantity. **12** *N Amer.* a bar of music. ● *v.* **1 a** *tr.* ascertain the extent or quantity of (a thing) by comparison with a fixed unit or with an object of known size. **b** *intr.* take measurements; use a measuring instrument. **2** *intr.* be of a specified size (*it measures six centimetres*). **3** *tr.* ascertain the size and proportion of (a person) for clothes. **4** *tr.* estimate (a quality, person's character, etc.) by some standard or rule. **5** *tr.* (often foll. by *off*) mark (a line etc. of a given length). **6** *tr.* (foll. by *out*) deal or distribute (a thing) in measured quantities. **7** *tr.* (foll. by *with*, *against*) bring (oneself or one's strength etc.) into competition with. □ **beyond measure** very greatly. **for good measure** as something beyond the minimum; as a finishing touch. **have** (or **get**) **the measure of** have an accurate opinion of the abilities or character of. **in a** (or **some**) **measure** partly. **measure up 1 a** determine the size etc. of by measurement. **b** take comprehensive measurements. **2** (often foll. by *to*) have the necessary qualifications (for).

measured *adj.* **1** ascertained by measurement. **2** rhythmical; regular in movement (*a measured pace*). **3** (of language) carefully considered; restrained. □ **measuredly** *adv.*

measureless *adj.* not measurable; infinite. □ **measurelessly** *adv.*

measurement *n.* **1** the act or an instance of measuring. **2** a size, quantity, or extent determined by measuring. **3** (in *pl.*) **a** detailed dimensions. **b** the measured circumference or length of the parts of a person's body used in fitting clothes, esp. the chest, waist, and hips. **4** a system of measuring or of measures (*metric measurement*).

measuring cup *n.* a cup used for measuring, esp. one marked with gradations, or in a standard size.

measuring tape *n.* a tape marked to measure length.

meat *n.* **1** the flesh of animals (esp. mammals) as food. **2 a** (foll. by *of*) the essence or chief part of. **b** significant content; substance. **3** the edible part of fruits, nuts, eggs, shellfish, etc. **4 a** *informal* human flesh. **b** *coarse slang* the penis. □ **meatless** *adj.*

meat and potatoes esp. *N Amer.* ● *n.* basics; ordinary but fundamental things. ● *adj.* (**meat-and-potatoes**) basic, fundamental, down-to-earth.

meatball *n.* **1** minced meat compressed into a small round ball. **2** *N Amer.* a stupid, clumsy, or ineffectual person.

meathead *n.* a stupid person.

meathook *n.* **1** a hook on which to hang meat carcasses etc. **2** *slang* an arm or hand.

meat loaf n. esp. N Amer. a dish of ground meat mixed with onion, bread crumbs, etc., baked in a loaf pan.

meat market n. **1** a butcher's shop. **2** slang a place, esp. a bar, club, etc. where people seek to meet others for sexual encounters.

meat-packing n. the business of processing and packing meat and distributing it to retailers. □ **meat packer** n.

meaty adj. (**-ier, -iest**) **1** full of meat; fleshy. **2** of or like meat. **3** full of substance. □ **meatily** adv. **meatiness** n.

mecca /ˈmekə/ n. (also **Mecca**) **1** a place which attracts people of a particular group (tourist mecca). **2** the birthplace of a policy, pursuit, etc.

Meccano /məˈkænɒ/ n. proprietary a construction set of reusable metal components, for making model machines, vehicles, etc.

mechanic n. a skilled worker who makes or uses or repairs machinery, esp. engines.

mechanical ● adj. **1** of or relating to machines or mechanisms. **2** working or produced by machinery. **3** (of a person or action) like a machine; automatic; lacking originality. **4 a** (of an agency, principle, etc.) belonging to mechanics. **b** (of a theory etc.) explaining phenomena by the assumption of mechanical action. **5** of or relating to mechanics as a science. ● n. (in pl.) the working parts of a machine, esp. of an automobile. □ **mechanically** adv.

mechanical engineering n. the branch of engineering that deals with the design, construction, and maintenance of machines. □ **mechanical engineer** n.

mechanical excavator n. a machine for removing soil from the ground by means of a crane to which a scoop is attached.

mechanics n.pl. **1** (treated as sing.) the branch of applied mathematics dealing with motion and tendencies to motion. **2** (treated as sing.) the science of machinery. **3** (usu. treated as pl.) **a** the construction, workings, or routine operation of a thing (mechanics of a lawn mower). **b** the practicalities or details of a thing (mechanics of laundering money).

mechanism n. **1** the structure or adaptation of parts of a machine. **2** a system of mutually adapted parts working together in or as in a machine. **3** the mode of operation of a process. **4** a means (no mechanism for complaints). **5** Philos. the doctrine that all natural phenomena, including life, allow mechanical explanation by physics and chemistry. **6** an unconscious, structured set of mental processes underlying a person's behaviour or responses (defence mechanism).

mechanist n. **1** a person skilled in constructing machinery. **2** Philos. a person who holds the doctrine of mechanism. □ **mechanistic** adj. **mechanistically** adv.

mechanize v.tr. **1** make mechanical; give a mechanical character to. **2** introduce machines or machinery in or into (a factory, process, etc.). **3** Military equip with tanks, armoured cars, etc. □ **mechanization** n. **mechanizer** n.

mechoui /ˈmeiʃwi/ n. Cdn (Que.) **1** a meal of meat, esp. lamb or mutton, roasted on a spit over a fire. **2** a party, usu. outdoors and for large numbers of people, at which meat, usu. a whole animal, is cooked in this way and served.

M.Ed. abbr. Master of Education.

Med n. informal the Mediterranean Sea.

med esp. N Amer. informal ● adj. medical (med school). ● n. (usu. in pl.) medication (take your meds!).

med. abbr. medium.

medal ● n. **1** a piece of metal, usu. in the form of a disc, struck or cast with an inscription or device to commemorate an event etc., or awarded as a distinction to a soldier, scholar, athlete, etc., for services rendered, for proficiency, etc. **2** a similar object marked with a religious image, inscription, etc. **3** (attrib.) designating the part of a competition that will determine the medal winners or a sport eligible for medals (curling is now a medal sport). ● v. (**medalled, medalling**) **1** tr. (usu. in passive) decorate or honour with a medal. **2** intr. (esp. of an athlete) receive a medal. □ **medalled** adj.

medallion /məˈdæljən/ n. **1** a large medal. **2** a thing shaped like this, e.g. a decorative panel or tablet, portrait, etc. **3** a small, flat, round or oval cut of meat or fish.

medallist n. (also esp. US **medalist**) **1** a recipient of a (specified) medal (gold medallist). **2** an engraver or designer of medals.

Medal of Bravery n. Canada's third highest decoration for bravery. Abbr.: **MB**.

meddle v.intr. (often foll. by with, in) interfere in or busy oneself unduly with others' concerns. □ **meddler** n.

meddlesome adj. fond of meddling; interfering.

Mede n. hist. a member of an Indo-European people which established an empire in Media in Persia (modern Iran) in the 7th c. BC. □ **Median** adj.

medevac /ˈmedəvæk/ ● n. the transportation of sick or wounded patients by air to hospital, esp. from a remote location, a battlefield, etc. ● v.tr. (**medevaced, medevacing**; also **medevacked, medevacking**) transport by medevac.

media n.pl. **1** pl. of MEDIUM. **2** (usu. prec. by the; treated as pl. or sing.) the main means of mass communication (esp. newspapers and broadcasting) regarded collectively (often attrib.: media coverage). ¶Although considerable opposition has been expressed to the use of media as a mass noun with a singular verb, e.g. the media is on our side, this usage is fairly well established.

mediaeval esp. Brit. var. of MEDIEVAL.

media event n. an event primarily intended to attract publicity.

medial /ˈmiːdɪəl/ adj. **1 a** situated in the middle. **b** (of a letter etc.) occurring in the middle of a word or between words. **2** of average size. □ **medially** adv.

median /ˈmiːdɪən/ ● adj. **1** situated in the middle. **2** Statistics designating or pertaining to the midpoint of a frequency distribution, such that the variable has an equal probability of falling above or below it. **3** Anat., Bot., & Zool. of, pertaining to, or designating the plane which divides a body, organ, or limb into roughly symmetrical halves. ● n. **1** Math. the middle value of a series of values arranged in order of size. **2** (also **median strip**) N Amer. a paved or landscaped strip of ground, or a physical barrier such as a raised curb, dividing a street or highway. **3** Math. a straight line drawn from any vertex of a triangle to the middle of the opposite side.

mediate ● v. /ˈmiːdɪˌeit/ **1** intr. (often foll. by between) intervene (between parties in a dispute) to produce agreement or reconciliation. **2** tr. be the medium for bringing about (a result) or for conveying (a gift etc.). **3** tr. form a connecting link between. ● adj. /ˈmiːdɪət/ **1** connected not directly but through some other person or thing. **2** involving an intermediate agency. □ **mediator** /ˈmiːdɪˌeitər/ n. **mediatory** /ˈmiːdɪətɔri/ adj.

mediation /ˌmiːdɪˈeiʃən/ n. Law the process or action

of mediating between parties in a dispute to produce agreement or reconciliation.

medic n. informal a doctor or medical student.

Medicaid n. US a federal and state system of health insurance for those requiring financial assistance.

medical ● adj. **1** of or relating to the science or practice of medicine in general. **2** of or relating to conditions requiring medical and not surgical treatment (medical ward). **3** of or relating to the condition of one's health (medical leave). ● n. informal a medical examination. □ **medically** adv.

medical certificate n. a certificate of fitness or unfitness to work etc., usu. issued by a doctor.

medical doctor n. a physician.

medical examination n. an examination to determine the state of a person's physical health or fitness.

medical examiner n. **1** N Amer. a medically qualified public officer who investigates unusual or suspicious deaths, performs post-mortems, and initiates inquests. **2** a doctor who performs medical examinations.

medical history n. **1** the medically significant events and phenomena in a person's life. **2** a record of these.

medicalize v.tr. involve medicine in; view in medical terms, esp. unwarrantedly (medicalize menopause). □ **medicalization** n.

medical officer n. a doctor appointed by a company or public authority to attend to matters relating to health.

medical officer of health n. Cdn & Brit. a person in charge of a public health department, responsible for enforcing public health regulations. Abbr.: **MOH**.

medical practitioner n. a physician or surgeon.

medicare n. **1** (in Canada) a national health care program financed by taxation and administered by the provinces and territories. **2** (**Medicare**) (in the US) a federal system of health insurance for persons over 65 years of age.

medicate v.tr. **1** treat medically; administer medication to. **2** add a medicinal substance to (medicated shampoo). □ **medicative** adj.

medication n. **1** a substance used for medical treatment. **2** treatment using drugs.

medicinal /mə'dısənəl/ ● adj. **1** (of a substance) having healing properties. **2** (of a taste, smell, etc.) resembling that of medicine. ● n. a medicinal substance. □ **medicinally** adv.

medicine n. **1** the science or practice of the diagnosis, treatment, and prevention of disease, esp. as distinct from surgical methods. **2** any drug or preparation used for the treatment or prevention of disease, esp. one taken by mouth. **3** a spell, charm, or fetish which is thought to cure afflictions. **4** (attrib.) (in Aboriginal societies) used to designate the healing power that may reside in physical objects or in the knowledge and techniques of healing rites. □ **a taste** (or **dose**) **of one's own medicine** treatment such as one is accustomed to giving others. **take one's medicine** submit to something disagreeable.

medicine ball n. a large heavy stuffed usu. leather ball thrown and caught for exercise.

medicine bundle n. a collection of objects, often wrapped in hide, which have sacred and personal power for the owner, used by Plains Aboriginal peoples as a religious object.

medicine cabinet n. (also **medicine chest**) a small cupboard containing medicines, items for first aid, etc.

Medicine Line n. Cdn (West) esp. hist. the Canada-US border, esp. from Ontario westward.

medicine man n. a person believed to have magical powers of healing, esp. among some N American Aboriginal peoples.

medicine wheel n. a wheel-shaped arrangement of stones at which acts of ritual and meditation were or are performed by certain Aboriginal peoples, located at various places throughout N America.

medico /'medɪˌko:/ n. (pl. **-os**) informal a doctor or medical student.

medieval /mɪd'i:vəl, med-, ˌmedi-/ adj. **1** of, or in the style of, the Middle Ages. **2** informal old-fashioned, archaic. □ **medievalism** n. **medievalist** n.

medina /mə'di:nə/ n. the old Arab or non-European quarter of a N African town.

mediocre /ˌmi:di'o:kər/ adj. **1** of middling quality, neither good nor bad. **2** second-rate.

mediocrity /ˌmi:di'ɒkrɪti/ n. (pl. **-ies**) **1** the state of being mediocre. **2** a mediocre person or thing.

meditate v. **1** intr. **a** exercise the mind in (esp. religious) contemplation. **b** (usu. foll. by on, upon) focus on a subject in this manner. **2** tr. plan mentally; design. □ **meditation** n. **meditational** adj. **meditator** n.

meditative /'medɪtətɪv, -ˌteitɪv/ adj. **1** inclined to meditate. **2** indicative of meditation. □ **meditatively** adv.

Mediterranean /ˌmedɪtə'reiniən/ ● n. **1** (prec. by the) **a** the Mediterranean Sea. **b** the countries bordering on the Mediterranean Sea. **2** a native of a country bordering on the Mediterranean Sea. ● adj. **1** of or characteristic of the Mediterranean, countries bordering it, or their inhabitants (Mediterranean cooking). **2** (of climate) characterized by hot dry summers and warm wet winters.

medium ● n. (pl. **media** or **-s**) **1** the middle quality, degree, etc. between extremes (find a happy medium). **2** the means by which something is communicated (the medium of television). **3** the intervening substance through which impressions are conveyed to the senses etc. (light passing from one medium into another). **4** Biol. the physical environment or conditions of growth, storage, or transport of a living organism. **5** an agency or means of doing something (the medium through which money is raised). **6** the material or form used by an artist, composer, etc. **7** the liquid, e.g. oil or gel, with which pigments are mixed for use in painting. **8** (pl. **mediums**) a person claiming to be in contact with the spirits of the dead and to communicate between the dead and the living. **9 a** a garment size designed to fit the average figure. **b** an article of clothing in this size. ● adj. **1** between two qualities, degrees, etc. **2** average; moderate (of medium height). □ **mediumistic** adj. **mediumship** n. (both in sense 8).

medium dry adj. (of sherry, wine, etc.) having a flavour intermediate between dry and sweet.

medium of exchange n. something that serves as an instrument of commercial transactions, e.g. coin.

medium-range adj. (of an aircraft, missile, etc.) able to travel a medium distance.

medium-security adj. (of a correctional institution) having perimeter security, ranging from fences to armed posts.

medium-sized adj. of average size.

medivac var. of MEDEVAC.

medley n. (pl. **-eys**) **1** a varied mixture; a miscellany. **2** a collection of musical items from one work or various sources arranged as a continuous whole. **3** a dish of assorted vegetables. **4** (in full **medley relay**) a relay race between teams in which each team member runs a different distance, swims a different stroke, etc.

medulla /mɪˈdʌlə/ *n.* **1** *Anat.* the inner region of certain organs or tissues usu. when it is distinguishable from the outer region or cortex, as in hair or a kidney. **2** (in full **medulla oblongata** /ˌɒblɒŋˈɡætə/) the continuation of the spinal cord within the skull, forming the lowest part of the brain stem. **3** *Bot.* the soft internal tissue of plants.

medusa /mɪˈdjuːsə, -ˈdjuː-/ *n.* (*pl.* **medusae** /-siː/ or **medusas**) **1** a jellyfish. **2** a free-swimming form of any coelenterate, having tentacles round the edge of a usu. umbrella-shaped jellylike body, e.g. a jellyfish.

meek *adj.* **1** humble and submissive; suffering injury etc. tamely. **2** piously gentle in nature. □ **meekly** *adv.* **meekness** *n.*

meet[1] ● *v.* (*past* and *past part.* **met**) **1 a** *tr.* encounter (a person or persons) by accident or design; come face to face with. **b** *intr.* (of two or more people) come into each other's company by accident or design. **c** *tr.* come to the notice of; confront (*an amazing sight met their eyes*). **2** *tr.* go to a place to be present at the arrival of (a person, train, etc.). **3 a** *tr.* (of a moving object, line, feature of landscape, etc.) come together or into contact with (*where the road meets the bridge*). **b** *intr.* come together or into contact (*where the lake and the sky meet; their eyes met*). **c** *tr.* & *intr.* (of an artistic style, a culture, etc.) influence or be influenced by another (*where jazz meets hip hop*). **4 a** *tr.* make the acquaintance of (*delighted to meet you*). **b** *intr.* (of two or more people) make each other's acquaintance. **5** *intr.* & *tr.* come together or come into contact with for the purposes of conference, business, worship, etc. (*the committee meets every week*). **6** *tr.* **a** (of a person or group) deal with or answer (a demand, objection, etc.) (*met the original proposal with hostility*). **b** satisfy or conform with (proposals, deadlines, a person, etc.) (*agreed to meet the new terms; did my best to meet them on that point; it's a challenge we can meet*). **7** *tr.* pay (a bill etc.); provide the funds required by (a cheque etc.) (*meet the cost of the move*). **8** *tr.* & *intr.* experience, encounter, or receive (success, disaster, a difficulty, etc.) (*met with many problems*). **9** *tr.* oppose in battle, contest, or confrontation. **10** *intr.* (of clothes, curtains, etc.) join or fasten correctly. ● *n.* the assembly of competitors for various sporting activities (*track meet*). □ **meet the eye** (or **the ear**) be visible (or audible). **meet a person's eye** check if another person is watching and look into his or her eyes in return. **meet a person halfway** make a compromise; respond in a friendly way to the advances of another person. **meet up** (often foll. by *with*) *informal* meet or make contact, esp. by chance. **meet with 1** see sense 8 of *v.* **2** receive (a reaction) (*met with the committee's approval*). **3** esp. *N Amer.* = sense 1a of *v.* **more (to it) than meets the eye** hidden qualities or complications.

meet[2] *adj. archaic* suitable, fit, proper.

meeting *n.* **1** in senses of MEET[1]. **2** an assembly of people, esp. the members of a society, committee, etc., for discussion or entertainment. **3** an assembly (esp. of Quakers) for worship. **4** the persons assembled (*address the meeting*).

meeting house *n.* **1** a place of worship for Quakers. **2** *hist.* a Protestant place of worship.

meeting place *n.* a place where people often meet.

meg /meg/ *n. slang* megabyte(s).

mega /ˈmeɡə/ *slang* ● *adj.* of enormous size, importance, etc. ● *adv.* extremely (*mega famous*).

mega- /ˈmeɡə/ *comb. form* **1** large. **2** denoting a factor of one million (10^6) in the metric system of measurement. **3** to a great degree, extent, etc.

megabit *n.* 1,048,576 (i.e. 2^{20}) bits as a measure of data capacity, or loosely 1,000,000 bits.

megabuck *n. informal* **1** a million dollars (also *attrib.*: *megabuck salary*). **2** (in *pl.*) a huge sum of money.

megabyte *n.* 1,048,576 (i.e. 2^{20}) bytes as a measure of data capacity, or loosely 1,000,000 bytes.

mega-city *n.* (*pl.* **-ies**) a very large city, esp. one with a population of over 10 million.

megadeal *n.* a business transaction involving large amounts of money, property, etc.

megadose *n.* a very large dose, esp. of a vitamin etc.

megafauna *n.* the large animals, esp. the large vertebrates, of a given area, habitat, or epoch.

megaflop *n.* **1** a unit of computing speed equal to one million floating-point operations per second. **2** *slang* a complete failure.

megahertz *n.* (*pl.* same) one million hertz, esp. as a measure of frequency of radio transmissions.

megahit *n.* a highly successful enterprise, product, etc.

megalithic /ˌmeɡəˈlɪθɪk/ *adj. Archaeology* made of or marked by the use of large stones.

megalomania /ˌmeɡələˈmeɪnɪə/ *n.* **1** a mental disorder producing delusions of grandeur. **2** a passion for grandiose schemes. **3** lust for power. □ **megalomaniac** *adj.* & *n.* **megalomaniacal** /-məˈnaɪəkəl/ *adj.*

megalopolis /ˌmeɡəˈlɒpəlɪs/ *n.* **1** a very large city. **2** an urban region consisting of a city and its environs.

mega-mall *n.* an extremely large shopping mall, usu. including elaborate entertainment facilities.

megaphone ● *n.* a large funnel-shaped device for amplifying the sound of the voice. ● *v.intr.* speak through or as through a megaphone.

megaproject *n.* a very large-scale, costly construction or engineering project, e.g. the building of a dam, the development of a transportation infrastructure, etc.

megastar *n.* a very famous person, esp. in the world of entertainment. □ **megastardom** *n.*

megastore *n.* a large store, selling many different types of goods, usu. situated on the outskirts of a town or city.

megaton *n.* **1** a unit of explosive power equal to one million tons of TNT. **2** *informal* a very large or heavy amount (*sold megatons of albums*). □ **megatonnage** *n.*

megavolt *n.* one million volts, esp. as a unit of electromotive force.

megawatt *n.* one million watts, esp. as a measure of electrical power as generated by power stations.

Meiji /ˈmeɪdʒɪ/ ● *n.* the period of the rule of the Japanese emperor Meiji Tenno (1852–1912, emperor 1867–1912), which saw the country's emergence as a major world power. ● *adj.* pertaining to or characteristic of this period.

meiosis /maɪˈəʊsɪs/ *n.* (*pl.* **meioses** /-siːz/) *Biol.* a type of cell division that results in daughter cells with half the chromosome number of the parent cell (*compare* MITOSIS). □ **meiotic** /-ˈɒtɪk/ *adj.*

-meister *comb. form* often *jocular* a person skilled in or famous for something specified by the initial element (*schlockmeister*).

melamine /ˈmeləˌmiːn/ *n.* **1** a white crystalline compound that can be copolymerized with formaldehyde to give thermosetting resins. **2** (in full **melamine resin**) a plastic made from melamine and used esp.

for laminated coatings and for moulded items, e.g. dishes, utensils, etc.

melancholia /melən'koːliə/ n. **1** a mental illness marked by depression and ill-founded fears. **2** = MELANCHOLY n. **1**. □ **melancholic** adj. & n. **melancholically** adv.

melancholy /'melənkɒli/ ● n. (pl. **-ies**) **1 a** a pensive sadness. **b** a tendency to this. **2** hist. one of the four humours; black bile (see HUMOUR n. 5). ● adj. **1** (of a person) sad, gloomy. **2** (of a thing) saddening, depressing. **3** (of words, a tune, etc.) expressing sadness.

Melanesian /ˌmeləˈniːʒən, -ziən/ ● n. **1** a member of the dominant Negroid people of Melanesia, a region of the W Pacific south of Micronesia and west of Polynesia. **2** any of the Austronesian languages of this people. ● adj. of or relating to this people or their language.

mélange /meiˈlɑ̃ʒ/ ● n. a mixture, a medley. ● adj. (of a fabric) made of a blend of fibres (*mélange flannel*).

melanin /'melənɪn/ n. a dark brown to black pigment occurring in the hair, skin, and iris of the eye, that is responsible for tanning of the skin when exposed to sunlight.

melanoma /ˌmeləˈnoːmə/ n. a usu. malignant tumour of melanin-forming cells, usu. in the skin.

melatonin /meləˈtoːnɪn/ n. Biochem. an indole derivative formed in the pineal gland of various mammals, which inhibits melanin formation and is thought to be concerned with regulating the reproductive cycle.

Melba n. Cdn an early, sweet, yellow cooking and eating apple with pink and red stripes.

Melba toast n. very thin crisp toast.

meld¹ ● v.tr. & intr. (in rummy etc.) lay down or declare (one's cards) in order to score points. ● n. a completed set or run of cards in any of these games.

meld² ● v.tr. & intr. merge, blend, combine. ● n. a thing formed by merging or blending.

melee /'meilei, 'melei, me'lei/ n. **1** a confused fight, skirmish, or scuffle. **2** a muddle.

melisma /məˈlɪzmə/ n. (pl. **melismata** /-mətə/ or **-s**) Music the prolongation of one syllable of text over a number of notes. □ **melismatic** /-ˈmætɪk/ adj.

mellifluous /məˈlɪfluːəs/ adj. (of a voice, words, etc.) pleasing, musical, flowing. □ **mellifluent** adj.

mellow ● adj. **1** (of sound, colour, light) soft and rich, free from harshness. **2** (of character) softened or matured by age or experience. **3** good-humoured, relaxed, genial. **4** informal partly intoxicated, esp. pleasantly. **5** (of fruit) soft, sweet, and juicy with ripeness. **6** (of wine, cheese, etc.) well-matured, smooth. **7** (of earth) rich, loamy. ● v.tr. & intr. **1** make or become mellow. **2** N Amer. informal (often foll. by out) relax, become less intense. □ **mellowly** adv. **mellowness** n.

Melmac n. proprietary melamine.

melodic /məˈlɒdɪk/ adj. **1** of or relating to melody. **2** having or producing melody. □ **melodically** adv.

melodious /məˈloːdiəs/ adj. **1** of, producing, or having melody. **2** sweet-sounding. □ **melodiously** adv. **melodiousness** n.

melodrama n. **1** a sensational dramatic piece with crude appeals to the emotions and usu. a happy ending. **2** the genre of drama of this type. **3** language, behaviour, or an occurrence suggestive of this. □ **melodramatic** adj. **melodramatically** adv. **melodramatist** n. **melodramatize** v.tr.

melodramatics n.pl. melodramatic behaviour, action, or writing.

melody n. (pl. **-ies**) **1** an arrangement of single notes in a musically expressive succession. **2** the principal part in harmonized music. **3** a musical arrangement of words; a song. **4** sweet music, either vocal or instrumental (*the haunting melody of the meadowlark*).

melon n. **1** the sweet fruit of various gourds. **2** the gourd producing this. **3 a** a mass of waxy material in the head of some toothed whales, thought to focus acoustic signals. **b** the dome this forms on the forehead. **4** a yellowish pink colour. **5** slang (in pl.) a woman's (esp. large) breasts. □ **melony** adj.

melt ● v. **1** intr. become liquefied by heat. **2** tr. change to a liquid condition by heat (see also MOLTEN). **3** intr. & tr. soften, disintegrate, or liquefy, esp. by the action of moisture; dissolve. **4** intr. **a** (of a person, feelings, the heart, etc.) be softened as a result of pity, love, etc. **b** dissolve into tears. **5** tr. soften (a person, feelings, the heart, etc.) (*a look to melt a heart of stone*). **6** intr. (usu. foll. by into) change or merge imperceptibly into another form or state (*night melted into dawn*). **7** intr. (often foll. by away) (of a person) leave or disappear unobtrusively (*melted into the background*). **8** intr. informal (of a person) perspire excessively, suffer extreme heat. ● n. **1** the process or an instance of melting. **2** N Amer. **a** a period of melting, esp. of the snow in spring. **b** = MELTWATER. **3** N Amer. a sandwich, hamburger, or other dish having melted cheese on top (*tuna melt*). **4** metal etc. in a melted condition. **5** an amount of a substance melted at any one time. □ **melt away** disappear or make disappear by or as if by liquefaction. **melt down 1** melt (esp. metal articles) in order to reuse the raw material. **2** become liquid and lose structure. **3** (of a part of a nuclear reactor) lose structural integrity, creating a potential for the catastrophic release of radiation (compare MELTDOWN 1). **melt in the mouth** (of food) be delicious and esp. very light. □ **melter** n.

meltdown n. **1** the melting of (and consequent damage to) a structure, esp. the overheated core of a nuclear reactor. **2 a** any uncontrolled and usu. disastrous transformation with far-reaching repercussions. **b** a collapse or reversal of fortune, esp. a sudden rapid drop in the value of assets, shares, etc.

melting adj. **1** that melts or is melting. **2** (of a person, a mood, etc.) yielding to emotion, esp. feeling or showing pity, love, etc. **3** (of sound) soft and liquid (*melting chords*). □ **meltingly** adv.

melting point n. the temperature at which any given solid will melt.

melting pot n. **1** a place where races, ethnic groups, etc. are integrated and mixed together. **2** an imaginary pool where theories, ideas, etc. are mixed together. **3** a pot in which metals etc. are melted and mixed.

melt-in-the-mouth adj. (also **melt-in-your-mouth**) (of food) delicious and of a very fine texture.

melton n. (also **melton cloth**) cloth with a close-cut nap, used for jackets, overcoats, etc.

meltwater n. water formed by the melting of snow and ice, esp. from a glacier.

member n. **1** a person or thing belonging to an organization, team, etc. **2** (**Member**) a person formally elected to take part in the proceedings of certain organizations (*Member of Parliament*). **3** (also attrib.) a part or branch of a political, social, etc. body (*a member of NATO; member agencies*). **4** a constituent part of a complex structure. **5** a part of a sentence, equation, group of figures, mathematical set, etc. **6 a** any part or organ of the body, esp. a limb. **b** slang the penis. **c** Biol. any part of a plant or animal viewed with regard to its form and position. **7** used in the title awarded to a person admitted to (usu. the lowest grade of) certain honours (*Member of the Order of Canada*). □ **memberless** *adj.*

membership *n.* **1** the state or condition of being a member. **2** the number of members in a particular body. **3** the body of members collectively.

membrane *n.* **1** any pliable sheetlike structure acting as a boundary, lining, or partition in an organism. **2** a thin pliable sheet or skin of various kinds. □ **membranous** /'membrənəs/ *adj.*

meme /mi:m/ *n. Biol.* an element of a culture or system of behaviour that is passed from one individual to another by non-genetic means, esp. imitation.

memento /mə'mento:/ *n.* (*pl.* **-oes** or **-os**) an object kept as a reminder or souvenir of a person or event.

memo *n.* (*pl.* **-os**) a memorandum.

memoir /'memwɑr/ *n.* **1** (in *pl.*) an autobiography or a written account of one's memory of certain events or people. **2** a historical account or biography written from personal knowledge or special sources. **3** an essay on a learned subject specially studied by the writer. □ **memoirist** *n.*

memorabilia /,memərə'bi:liə, -bi:ljə/ *n.pl.* souvenirs of memorable events, people, periods, etc.

memorable /'memərəbəl/ *adj.* **1** worth remembering, not to be forgotten. **2** easily remembered. □ **memorability** *n.* **memorably** *adv.*

memorandum /,memə'rændəm/ *n.* (*pl.* **memoranda** /-də/ or **memorandums**) **1 a** a written note or communication esp. in business between people working for the same organization. **b** an informal diplomatic message, esp. summarizing the state of a question etc. **2** a note or record made for future use. **3** *Law* a document summarizing or embodying the terms of a contract or other legal details.

memorandum of understanding *n.* a formal document embodying the firm commitment of two or more parties to an undertaking, and setting out its general principles, but falling short of constituting a detailed contract or agreement. Abbr.: **MOU.**

memorial ● *n.* an object, institution, or custom established in memory of a person or event (*the Terry Fox Memorial*). ● *adj.* intending to commemorate a person or thing (*memorial service*).

Memorial Cup *n.* a trophy awarded annually to the Canadian major junior amateur hockey champions.

Memorial Day *n.* **1** *Cdn* (*Nfld*) a statutory holiday, 1 July, commemorating losses to the Newfoundland Regiment at the battle of the Somme. **2** *US* a day on which those who died on active service are remembered, usu. the last Monday in May.

memorialize *v.tr.* **1** commemorate. **2** address a memorial to (a person etc.). □ **memorialization** *n.*

memorial service *n.* a service of commemoration of the dead, usu. without the body or bodies being present.

memorize *v.* **1** *tr.* commit to memory, learn by heart. **2** *intr.* learn things by heart. □ **memorization** *n.* **memorizing** *n.*

memory *n.* (*pl.* **-ies**) **1 a** the faculty by which things are recalled to or kept in the mind. **b** an individual's capacity to remember things (*my memory is poor*). **2** one's store of things remembered (*buried deep in my memory*). **3** a recollection or remembrance (*the memory of better times*). **4 a** the capacity of a computer or other electronic machinery to store data or program instructions in such a way that they may be retrieved when required. **b** a device in which data or program instructions may be stored and from which they may

be retrieved when required. **c** = MEMORY BOARD. **5** the remembrance of a person or thing (*his mother's memory haunted him*). **6 a** the reputation of a dead person (*Dad's memory lives on*). **b** in formulaic phrases used of a dead sovereign etc. (*of blessed memory*). **7** the length of time over which the memory or memories of any given person or group extends. **8** the act of remembering (*a deed worthy of memory*). **9 a** the capacity of a substance etc. for manifesting effects of its previous state, behaviour, or treatment. **b** the capacity of a substance etc. for returning to a previous state when the cause of the transition from that state is removed. **c** such effects or such a state. □ **commit to memory** learn (a thing) so as to be able to recall it at will. **down memory lane** through a succession of sentimental memories deliberately pursued. **from memory** without reading from or referring to books etc. **in memory of** to keep alive the remembrance of.

memory bank *n.* **1** the memory device of a computer etc. **2** *informal* the store of memories of an individual or group.

memory board *n.* a detachable storage device, containing additional memory capacity, which can be installed in a computer.

memory card *n.* a memory chip housed in a rectangular plastic case which plugs into a computer enabling data storage and retrieval.

memory chip *n. Computing* a semiconductor chip made as a memory, e.g. a ROM or a RAM, containing many separately addressable locations.

men *pl. of* MAN.

menace ● *n.* **1** a dangerous thing or person. **2** *jocular* a pest, a nuisance. **3** a threat. ● *v.tr. & intr.* threaten, esp. in a malignant or hostile manner. □ **menacing** *adj.* **menacingly** *adv.*

ménage /mei'næʒ, -nɒʒ/ *n.* **1** a domestic establishment, a household. **2** the members of a household.

ménage à trois /mei,nɒʒ æ 'trwɒ/ *n.* a sexual relationship involving three people, esp. in one household.

menagerie /mə'næʒəri, -'nædʒ-, -'nɒʒ-/ *n.* **1 a** a collection of wild animals in captivity for exhibition etc. **b** the place where these are housed. **2** a heterogeneous collection of animals. **3** a collection of strange or outlandish people etc.

menarche /me'nɑrki/ *n.* the onset of first menstruation.

mend ● *v.* **1** *tr.* restore to a sound condition; repair (a broken article, a damaged road, torn clothes, etc.). **2** *intr.* regain health; heal. **3** *tr.* improve or put right (a fault, something wrong, etc.) (*mend matters*). ● *n.* a darn or repair in material etc. (*a mend in my shirt*). □ **mend (one's) fences** make peace with a person; reconcile differences. **mend one's manners** improve one's behaviour. **mend one's ways** reform, improve one's habits. **mend or end** improve or abolish. **on the mend** improving in health or condition. □ **mender** *n.*

mendacious /men'deiʃəs/ *adj.* untruthful; false. □ **mendaciously** *adv.* **mendacity** /-'dæsɪti/ *n.* (*pl.* **-ies**).

mendelevium /,mendə'li:viəm/ *n.* an artificially made radioactive metallic element.

mendicant /'mendɪkənt/ ● *adj.* **1** begging. **2** designating or belonging to any of the religious orders, e.g. the Franciscans, Dominicans, etc., whose members support themselves by work and charitable contributions. ● *n.* **1** a beggar. **2** a mendicant friar.

mending *n.* **1** the action of a person who mends. **2** things, esp. clothes, to be mended.

menfolk *n.pl. informal* **1** men in general. **2** the men of one's family.

M.Eng. *abbr.* Master of Engineering.

menhaden /men'heidən/ *n.* any large herring-like fish of the genus *Brevoortia*, of the E coast of N America, yielding valuable oil and used for fertilizer.

menial /'mi:niəl / ● *adj.* (esp. of unskilled work) of the nature of drudgery; servile, degrading. ● *n.* **1** a domestic servant. **2** a servile person. □ **menially** *adv.*

Ménière's disease /mein'jers/ *n.* a disease of the labyrinth of the ear associated with tinnitus, progressive deafness, and intermittent vertigo.

meninges /mɪ'rɪndʒi:z/ *n.pl.* (*sing.* **meninx** /'mi:nɪŋks/) (usu. in *pl.*) the three membranes that line the skull and vertebral canal and enclose the brain and spinal cord. □ **meningeal** /mɪ'rɪndʒiəl/ *adj.*

meningitis /,menɪn'dʒaɪtɪs/ *n.* an inflammation of the meninges of the brain or spinal cord due to infection by viruses or bacteria.

meningococcus /me,nɪŋgə'kɒkəs, -,nɪndʒə-/ *n.* (*pl.* **-cocci** /-'kɒkai, -'kɒksi:/) a bacterium, *Neisseria meningitidis*, involved in some forms of meningitis and cerebrospinal infection. □ **meningococcal** *adj.*

meniscus /mə'nɪskəs/ *n.* (*pl.* **menisci** /-sai/) **1** the curved upper surface of a liquid in a tube etc., caused by surface tension etc. **2** a lens that is convex on one side and concave on the other, esp. one thickest in the middle, with a crescent-shaped section. **3** a thin fibrous cartilage between the surfaces of some joints, e.g. the knee. **4** a crescent-shaped figure. □ **meniscoid** *adj.*

Mennonite /'menə,nəit/ ● *n.* a member of a Protestant denomination originating in 16th-c. Friesland, emphasizing adult baptism and rejecting military service and the holding of public office. ● *adj.* of or pertaining to Mennonites. □ **Mennonitism** *n.*

menopause /'menə,pɒz/ *n.* **1** the final cessation of menstruation. **2** the period in a woman's life, usu. between 45 and 50, when this occurs (*see also* MALE MENOPAUSE). □ **menopausal** *adj.*

menorah /mə'nɔrə/ *n. Judaism* **1** a candelabrum with usu. seven branches, used at home and in the synagogue on Sabbaths and holidays. **2** a candelabrum used during Hanukkah, having eight branches and a holder for the candle used to light the others. **3** a representation of either as a symbol of Judaism.

mensch *n.* an admirable or honourable person.

menservants *pl. of* MANSERVANT.

menses /'mensi:z/ *n.pl.* **1** blood and mucosal tissue etc. discharged from the uterus at menstruation. **2** the time of menstruation.

Menshevik /'menʃə,vɪk/ *n.* a member of a minority faction of the Russian Socialist Party; they were defeated by the Bolsheviks in the power struggle following the overthrow of the czar in 1917.

men's room *n.* (also **men's**) esp. *N Amer.* a public washroom for men.

menstrual /'menstrəl, -struəl/ *adj.* of or relating to the menses or menstruation.

menstrual cycle *n.* the process of ovulation and menstruation in sexually mature women and female primates.

menstruation /men'streiʃən/ *n.* the process of discharging blood and mucosal tissue etc. from the uterus through the vagina that occurs in sexually mature, non-pregnant women, normally at intervals of about one lunar month, until menopause. □ **menstruate** *v.intr.* **menstruating** *adj.*

menswear *n.* clothes for men.

-ment *suffix* **1** forming nouns expressing the means, product, or result of the action of a verb (*abridgement*). **2** forming nouns from adjectives (*merriment*).

mental *adj.* **1** of or pertaining to the mind. **2** carried on or performed by, or taking place in, the mind. **3** *informal derogatory* insane, crazy (*this is driving me mental*). **4** designating a medical establishment for the care and treatment of the mentally ill (*mental institution*). □ **mentally** *adv.*

mental age *n.* the degree of a person's mental development expressed as an age at which the same degree is attained by an average person.

mental block *n.* a sudden and temporary inability to continue a thought process or mental link, esp. due to subconscious emotional factors.

mental case *n. informal derogatory* a person suffering from some kind of mental impairment, esp. one under or requiring medical care for mental illness.

mental cruelty *n. Law* conduct which inflicts suffering on the mind of another person, rendering continued relations impossible, esp. as grounds for divorce.

mental handicap *n.* **1** the condition of being of such low intelligence, or having the intellectual capacities so underdeveloped, esp. through illness or injury, as to inhibit normal social functioning. **2** an instance of this.

mental health *n.* the condition of a person or a group in respect to the functioning of the mind etc.

mental health day *n. N Amer.* a day taken off school or work as a sick day, spent in relaxation or enjoyable activities, on the pretext that this is necessary for one's mental health.

mental illness *n.* **1** disordered functioning of the mind. **2** an instance of this.

mentalism *n. Philos.* the theory that physical and psychological phenomena are ultimately only explicable in terms of a creative and interpretative mind. □ **mentalist** *n.* **mentalistic** *adj.*

mentality /men'tælɪti/ *n.* (*pl.* **-ies**) **1** mental character or disposition. **2** outlook; what is in or of the mind. **3** kind or degree of intelligence.

mentally handicapped *adj.* (of a person) having a mental handicap.

mentally ill *adj.* (of a person) having a mental illness.

mentally incompetent *adj.* (of a person) mentally ill or mentally handicapped to an extent that care, supervision, and control are required.

mentally retarded *adj.* (of a person) suffering from mental retardation.

mental note *n.* a fixing of something in one's mind, to be remembered subsequently.

mental patient *n.* a sufferer from mental illness, esp. while in a hospital or under active treatment.

mental retardation *n.* a developmental disorder in which a person has impaired learning ability and a lower than normal IQ.

menthol /'menθɒl/ *n.* a mint-tasting organic alcohol found in oil of peppermint etc., used as a flavouring and to relieve local pain.

mentholated /'menθə,leitəd/ *adj.* treated with or containing menthol.

mention ● *v.tr.* **1** refer to or remark on incidentally. **2** specify by name or otherwise. **3** reveal or disclose (*do not mention this to anyone*). **4** (in dispatches) award (a person) a minor honour for meritorious, usu. gallant, military service. ● *n.* **1** an incidental reference, esp. by name, to a person or thing. **2** (in dispatches) a military honour awarded for outstanding conduct. □ **don't mention it** said in polite dismissal of an apology or thanks. **make mention** (or **no mention**) **of** refer (or not refer) to. **not to mention** introducing a fact or thing of secondary or (as a rhetorical device) of primary importance. ☐ **mentionable** *adj. & n.*

mentor /ˈmɛntɔr/ ● *n.* an experienced and trusted adviser or guide. ● *v.tr.* act as a mentor to (a person). ☐ **mentoring** *n. & adj.* **mentorship** *n.*

menu *n.* **1 a** a list of dishes to be served at a meal, available in a restaurant, etc. **b** a card, folder, etc. on which such a list is written or printed. **c** the food served or available. **2** a list of available commands, options, etc., displayed on a television or computer screen, for selection by the operator.

menu bar *n.* a graphically represented bar in which the primary menus and menu options for a software program are displayed and from which these can be accessed.

menu-driven *adj.* (of a program or computer) used by making selections from menus.

meow ● *n.* one of the characteristic sounds made by a domestic cat. ● *v.intr.* make this sound.

meperidine /meˈperɪdiːn/ *n.* esp. *N Amer.* a narcotic analgesic used for moderate to severe pain.

Mephistopheles /ˌmefɪˈstɒfɪˌliːz/ *n.* a fiendish person. ☐ **Mephistophelian** /-ˈfiːliən/ *adj.*

mercantile /ˈmɜrkənˌtaɪl/ ● *adj.* **1** of or pertaining to trade, traders, or trading. **2** concerned with the exchange of merchandise; commercial. **3** mercenary, having payment or gain as the motive. ● *n. N Amer.* (*West*) a local general store.

mercantilism /ˈmɜrkəntɪˌlɪzəm/ *n. hist.* the economic theory that trade generates wealth and is stimulated by the accumulation of bullion, which a government should encourage by promoting exports and restricting imports. ☐ **mercantilist** *n.* **mercantilistic** *adj.*

Mercator projection /mɜrˈkeɪtər/ *n.* (also **Mercator's projection**) a cylindrical map projection in which all parallels of latitude have the same length and meridians are represented by equidistant straight lines at right angles to the equator and any course that follows a constant compass bearing is represented by a straight line.

mercenary /ˈmɜrsəˌneri/ ● *adj.* primarily concerned with money or other material reward (*mercenary motives*). ● *n.* (*pl.* **-ies**) **1** a professional soldier serving a foreign power for money. **2** a hireling; a person whose services are available for money.

merchandise ● *n.* /ˈmɜrtʃənˌdaɪs, -daɪz/ the commodities of commerce, goods to be bought and sold. ● *v.tr.* /ˈmɜrtʃənˌdaɪz/ (also **-ize**) **1** put on the market, promote the sale of (goods etc.). **2** advertise, publicize (an idea or person). ☐ **merchandiser** *n.* **merchandising** *n. & adj.*

merchant ● *n.* **1** a person whose occupation is the purchase and sale of goods for profit. **2** a wholesale trader, esp. with foreign countries. **3** esp. *N Amer. & Scot.* a retail trader, a store keeper. **4** *informal usu. derogatory* a person showing a partiality for a specified activity or practice (*speed merchant*). **5** *Cdn* (*Nfld*) an entrepreneur involved in the fish trade, usu. purchasing and exporting salt cod, financing fishing operations, etc. ● *adj.* **1 a** connected with or relating to trade or commerce. **b** connected with merchandise. **2** (of a ship, fleet, etc.) serving for or involved in the transport of merchandise.

merchantable *adj.* marketable.

merchant bank *n.* esp. *Brit.* a bank dealing primarily in long-term commercial loans and financing. ☐ **merchant banker** *n.* **merchant banking** *n.*

merchant marine *n. N Amer.* a fleet or number of ships used in trade; a nation's commercial shipping. ☐ **merchant mariner** *n.*

merchant navy *n.* = MERCHANT MARINE.

merchant ship *n.* a ship conveying merchandise.

merciful *adj.* having, showing, or feeling mercy. ☐ **mercifulness** *n.*

mercifully *adv.* **1** in a merciful manner. **2** (qualifying a whole sentence) fortunately.

merciless *adj.* **1** pitiless, unrelenting. **2** showing no mercy. ☐ **mercilessly** *adv.* **mercilessness** *n.*

Mercosur /ˈmɛrkəsʊr/ *n.* the *Mercado del Sur*, a common market agreement permitting the movement of goods and services between Argentina, Brazil, Paraguay, and Uruguay.

mercurial /mɜrˈkjʊriəl/ ● *adj.* **1** (of a person) lively, quick to react and often changing. **2** of or containing mercury. **3** (**Mercurial**) of or pertaining to the planet Mercury. ● *n.* a drug containing mercury. ☐ **mercurially** *adv.*

mercury *n.* **1** a toxic silvery-white heavy liquid metallic element used in barometers, thermometers, and amalgams. **2 a** the column of mercury in a thermometer or barometer. **b** the temperature or barometric pressure indicated by this, esp. as rising or falling. **3** any plant of the genus *Mercurialis*. ☐ **mercuric** *adj.*

mercury vapour *n.* (often *attrib.*) a vapour of mercury atoms or ions above liquid mercury or at low pressure.

mercury vapour lamp *n.* (also **mercury vapour light**) a lamp in which bluish light is produced by an electric discharge through mercury vapour.

mercy ● *n.* (*pl.* **-ies**) **1** compassion or forbearance shown to a powerless person, esp. an offender or one with no claim to kindness. **2** the disposition to forgive or show compassion; mercifulness. **3** an act of mercy. **4** (*attrib.*) administered or performed out of mercy or pity for a suffering person (*mercy killing*). **5** something to be thankful for (*small mercies*). ● *interj.* expressing surprise or fear. ☐ **at the mercy of 1** wholly in the power of. **2** liable to danger or harm from. **have mercy on** (or **upon**) show mercy to.

mercy killing *n.* = EUTHANASIA.

mere[1] *attrib.adj.* (**merest**) **1** having no greater extent, range, value, power, or importance than the designation implies (*a mere child*). **2** insignificant, ordinary. ☐ **merely** *adv.*

mere[2] *n.* esp. *literary* a lake or pond.

mere mortal *n.* a person with no outstanding skills or characteristics; an average person.

merengue /məˈrɛŋgeɪ/ *n.* **1** a dance of Dominican and Haitian origin, with alternating long and stiff-legged steps. **2** a piece of music for this dance, usu. in duple and triple time.

meretricious /ˌmerəˈtrɪʃəs/ *adj.* **1** (of decorations, literary style, etc.) showily attractive but valueless. **2** of or befitting a prostitute. ☐ **meretriciously** *adv.* **meretriciousness** *n.*

merganser /mɜrˈgænsər/ *n.* any of various diving fish-eating northern ducks of the genus *Mergus*, with a long narrow serrated hooked bill, esp. the common merganser, *M. merganser*, and the red-breasted merganser, *M. serrator*.

merge ● *v.* **1** *tr. & intr.* (often foll. by *with*) **a** combine or be combined. **b** join or blend gradually. **2** *intr. & tr.* (foll. by *in*) lose or cause to lose character and identity by absorption in (something else). **3** *tr. Computing* combine (multiple files, sets of data, etc.) to produce only one file, set, etc., usu. in an ordered sequence. **4** *intr.* **a** (of lanes of traffic etc.) be gradually integrated into fewer lanes. **b** (of a vehicle) join a lane of traffic. ● *n.* **1** an act or instance of merging, esp. a merger. **2 a** *Computing* (often *attrib.*) a function that enables file or data merging (*merge facility*). **b** = MAIL MERGE. **3** an instance or the site of a traffic merge. □ **merged** *adj.* **merging** *n. & adj.*

merger *n.* **1** the combining of two commercial companies etc. into one. **2** a merging, esp. of one estate in another.

meridian /məˈrɪdɪən/ *n.* **1 a** a great circle passing through the celestial poles and zenith of a given place on the earth's surface. **b** the circle of the earth which lies on the same plane. **2 a** half the circle of the earth which extends from pole to pole through a place, corresponding to a line of longitude. **b** a line on a map, globe, etc. representing one of these. **3** any of the pathways in the body along which energy is said to flow, esp. each of twelve associated with specific organs for acupuncture etc. **4 a** any great circle of a sphere that passes through the poles. **b** any line on a surface of revolution that is in a plane with its axis.

meringue /məˈræŋ/ *n.* **1** a mixture of stiffly beaten egg white and sugar. **2** this used as a topping for pies or cakes, browned on top but still soft inside. **3** a round of this mixture, baked until crisp, usu. decorated or filled with whipped cream etc.

merino /məˈriːnoː/ *n.* (*pl.* **-os**) **1** (in full **merino sheep**) a variety of sheep with long fine wool. **2** a soft woollen or wool-and-cotton material like cashmere, originally of merino wool. **3** a fine woollen yarn.

meristem /ˈmerɪˌstem/ *n.* a plant tissue consisting of actively dividing cells forming new tissue.

merit ● *n.* **1** the quality of being entitled to reward or gratitude. **2** excellence, worth. **3** (usu. in *pl.*) **a** a thing that entitles one to reward or gratitude. **b** claim or title to commendation or esteem. **4** esp. *Law* intrinsic rights and wrongs or excellences and defects (*the merits of a case*). **5** *Theol.* **a** good deeds viewed as entitling a person to a future reward from God. **b** *Buddhism* the quality of actions in one of a person's states of existence which helps determine a better succeeding state. ● *v.tr.* (**merited**, **meriting**) deserve or be worthy of (reward, punishment, consideration, etc.). □ **on its merits** with regard only to its intrinsic worth.

meritocracy /ˌmerɪˈtɒkrəsi/ *n.* (*pl.* **-ies**) **1** government or the holding of power by persons selected competitively according to merit. **2** a group of persons selected in this way. **3** a society governed by meritocracy. □ **meritocratic** *adj.*

meritorious /ˌmerɪˈtɔːrɪəs/ *adj.* **1** (of a person or act) having merit; deserving reward, praise, or gratitude. **2** deserving commendation for thoroughness etc.

merle /mɜːrl/ ● *n.* a dog, esp. a collie, having a light coloured coat with dark markings, esp. blue-grey fur speckled or streaked with black. ● *adj.* (of a dog) having such a colour pattern.

merlin *n.* a small European or N American falcon, *Falco columbarius*, that hunts small birds.

Merlot /mɜːrˈloː, mer-/ *n.* **1** a variety of black grape used in winemaking. **2** the vine on which this grape grows. **3** a red wine made from Merlot grapes.

mermaid *n.* an imaginary half-human sea creature, with the head and trunk of a woman and tail of a fish.

merman *n.* (*pl.* **-men**) an imaginary half-human sea

creature, with the head and trunk of a man and the tail of a fish.

merriment *n.* **1** exuberant enjoyment; being merry. **2** mirth, fun.

merry *adj.* (**-ier, -iest**) **1** joyous. **2** full of laughter or gaiety. □ **make merry** be festive; enjoy oneself. □ **merrily** *adv.* **merriness** *n.*

merry-go-round *n.* **1** a revolving platform with wooden horses, cars, etc. for people to ride on at a fair etc.; a carousel. **2** a cycle of bustling activities.

merrymaking *n.* festivity, fun. □ **merrymaker** *n.*

merry widow *n.* a waist-length, usu. lace-trimmed corselette, with attached stocking garters.

M.E.S. *abbr.* Master of Environmental Studies.

mesa /ˈmeɪsə/ *n. N Amer.* an isolated flat-topped hill with steep sides, found in landscapes with horizontal strata.

mescal /ˈmeskæl/ *n.* **1 a** any of several plants of the genus *Agave* found in Mexico and the southwestern US, used as sources of fermented liquor, food, or fibre, esp. the American aloe, *Agave americana*. **b** a strong liquor distilled from this (compare TEQUILA). **2 a** a peyote cactus. **b** a preparation of this used as a hallucinogenic drug (compare MESCALINE, PEYOTE).

mescal button *n.* the disc-shaped dried top from the peyote cactus, eaten or chewed for its hallucinogenic effects.

mescaline /ˈmeskəˌliːn/ *n.* (also **mescalin** /-lɪn/) a hallucinogenic alkaloid present in mescal buttons.

mesclun /ˈmesklən/ *n.* a kind of green salad made from a selection of lettuces, typically with other edible leaves and flowers.

Mesdames *pl. of* MADAME.

Mesdemoiselles *pl. of* MADEMOISELLE.

mesentery /ˈmesənˌteri/ *n.* (*pl.* **-ies**) a double layer of peritoneum attaching the stomach, small intestine, pancreas, spleen, and other abdominal organs to the posterior wall of the abdomen. □ **mesenteric** *adj.*

mesh ● *n.* **1** an interlaced fabric or structure; netting. **2 a** each of the open spaces or interstices between the strands of a net or sieve etc. **b** (in *pl.*) the strands between the interstices of a net etc. **3** a network. **4 a** the coarseness or spacing of the strands of a grid, net, or screen. **b** (with preceding numeral) a measure of this (representing the number of openings per unit length), or of the size of particles which will just pass through such a grid etc. **5 a** *Math.* a set of discrete ordered points, which can be chosen arbitrarily, at which a numerical function or mathematical model is evaluated. **b** (in computer graphics and computer-aided design) a set of finite elements used to represent a geometric object for modelling or analysis. **6** (in *pl.*) *Physiol.* an interlaced structure. ● *v.* **1 a** *intr.* (often foll. by *with*, *together*) fit in, be harmonious, combine. **b** *tr.* bring together, harmonize, reconcile. **2** *intr.* (often foll. by *with*) (of the teeth of a wheel) be engaged (with another piece of machinery). **3** *tr.* entangle, catch in or as in a net. □ **in mesh** (of the teeth of wheels) engaged. □ **meshed** *adj.* **meshing** *n. & adj.*

meshuga /məˈʃʌgə/ *adj.* (also **meshugga**, **meshuggah**) *slang* mad, crazy; stupid.

mesmerism /ˈmezməˌrɪzm/ *n.* **1** the process or practice of inducing a hypnotic state by the influence of an operator over the will and nervous system of the patient. **2** the state so induced. □ **mesmeric** /mezˈmerɪk/ *adj.* **mesmerically** *adv.* **mesmerist** *n.*

mesmerize /ˈmezməˌraɪz/ *v.tr.* **1** fascinate, hold spellbound. **2** *Psych.* hypnotize; exercise mesmerism on. □ **mesmerization** *n.* **mesmerizer** *n.*

meso- /ˈmesoː, ˈmez-/ *comb. form* middle, intermediate.

Meso-American ● *adj.* of or relating to Meso-America, the central region of America from central Mexico to Nicaragua, esp. as a region of ancient civilizations and Aboriginal cultures. ● *n.* a member of a Meso-American people.

mesolithic /ˌmezoːˈlɪθɪk/ (also **Mesolithic**) ● *adj.* of or concerning the part of the Stone Age between the paleolithic and neolithic periods. ● *n.* this period.

meson /ˈmezɒn, ˈmiːzɒn/ *n.* any of a class of elementary particles believed to participate in the forces that hold nucleons together in the atomic nucleus.

Mesopotamian /ˌmesəpəˈteɪmiən/ ● *adj.* of or relating to Mesopotamia, an ancient region of SW Asia in present-day Iraq, between the Tigris and Euphrates rivers. ● *n.* a native or inhabitant of Mesopotamia.

mesosphere *n.* the region of the atmosphere extending from the top of the stratosphere to an altitude of about 50 miles. ☐ **mesospheric** *adj.*

mesothelioma /ˌmesoːθiːliːˈoːməˌ/ *n.* a tumour of the lungs, or of the lining of the pleural or abdominal cavities, associated esp. with exposure to asbestos.

Mesozoic /ˌmesoːˈzoːɪk, ˌmez-/ ● *adj.* of or relating to the geological era between the Paleozoic and Cenozoic, comprising the Triassic, Jurassic, and Cretaceous periods, lasting from about 248 to 65 million years BP. ● *n.* this geological era.

mesquite /ˈmeskiːt/ *n.* **1** any N American leguminous tree of the genus *Prosopis*, esp. *P. juliflora*. **2** the wood of this used for grilling food.

mess ● *n.* **1 a** a dirty, untidy state of affairs (*the room is a mess*; *made such a mess*). **b** a bungled state of affairs. **2** a state of confusion, embarrassment, or trouble (*my life's a mess*). **3** something causing a mess, e.g. spilled liquid etc. **4 a** a person whose life or affairs are confused. **b** a dirty or unkempt person. **5** excrement, esp. of a domestic animal or child. **6 a** a company of persons who take meals together, esp. in the armed forces. **b** a place where such meals or recreation take place communally. **c** a meal taken there. **7** esp. *US* **a** a prepared dish (of a specified kind of food). **b** a quantity of food sufficient to make a dish. **8** *N Amer. informal* a large quantity of something (*a whole mess of preconceptions*). ● *v.* **1** *intr. informal* (foll. by *with*) interfere or get involved with. **2** *intr.* take one's meals, esp. as the member of a mess. **3** *intr. & tr. informal* (esp. of an animal or infant) defecate or soil by defecating. ☐ **make a mess of** bungle (an undertaking). **mess around** (or **about**) **1** act desultorily; putter. **2** *informal* make things awkward for; cause arbitrary inconvenience to (a person). **3** esp. *N Amer. informal* **a** engage in sexual activity. **b** engage in adulterous sexual activity. **mess up 1** make a mess of; dirty. **2** muddle; make a mess of a situation. **3** make unhappy, confused, or dysfunctional (*messed-up kids*). **4** ruin or damage.

message ● *n.* **1** a usu. brief oral or written communication. **2** an inspired or significant communication from a prophet, writer, or preacher. **3** the central import of something, an implicit esp. polemical meaning in an artistic work etc. ● *v.tr.* **1** send a message to (a person) (*message me tomorrow*). **2** transmit (a plan etc.) by e-mail etc. (*messaged the examples*). ☐ **get the message** *informal* understand what is meant. **send a message** make a significant statement, esp. implicitly or by one's actions. ☐ **messaging** *n.*

message board *n.* *N Amer.* **1** = BULLETIN BOARD 1. **2** a computerized bulletin board on the Internet for the posting of electronic messages. **3** an electronic board in an arena, train station, etc., which displays instructions to fans, information to travellers, etc.

Messeigneurs *pl. of* MONSEIGNEUR.

messenger *n.* **1** a person who carries a message. **2** a person employed to carry messages. **3** *Biol.* a molecule or substance that carries (esp. genetic) information.

messenger RNA *n.* the form of RNA in which genetic information transcribed from DNA as a sequence of bases is transferred to a ribosome.

mess hall *n.* a military dining area.

Messiah /məˈsaɪə/ *n.* **1 a** the promised deliverer of the Jews, as prophesied in the Hebrew Bible. **b** (usu. prec. by *the*) (in Christian theology) Jesus Christ regarded as fulfilling this prophecy, and as saviour of humankind. **2** (usu. **messiah**) a liberator or would-be liberator of an oppressed people, country, etc.

messianic /ˌmesiˈænɪk/ *adj.* (also **Messianic**) **1** of, pertaining to, or characteristic of the Messiah or a messiah. **2** inspired by hope or belief in the Messiah or a messiah. ☐ **messianism** /məˈsaɪəˌnɪzəm/ *n.*

Messieurs *pl. of* MONSIEUR.

Messrs. /ˈmesərz/ *pl. of* MR.

mess-up *n.* a mess, a muddle; a confused situation.

messy *adj.* (**-ier**, **-iest**) **1** untidy or dirty. **2** causing or accompanied by a mess. **3** difficult to deal with; full of awkward complications (*a messy divorce*). ☐ **messily** *adv.* **messiness** *n.*

mestiza /meˈstiːzə/ *n.* (*pl.* **-as**) a woman who is a mestizo.

mestizo /meˈstiːzoː/ *n.* (*pl.* **-os**) a person of mixed ancestry, esp. (in Latin and South America), the offspring of a European and an American Indian.

met¹ *past and past part. of* MEET¹.

met² *adj. informal* **1** meteorological. **2** metropolitan.

metabolism /məˈtæbəˌlɪzəm/ *n.* all the chemical processes that occur within a living organism, resulting in energy production (**destructive metabolism**) and growth (**constructive metabolism**). ☐ **metabolic** /ˌmetəˈbɒlɪk/ *adj.* **metabolically** *adv.*

metabolite /məˈtæbəˌlaɪt/ *n.* a substance formed in or necessary for metabolism.

metabolize /məˈtæbəˌlaɪz/ *v.tr. & intr.* process or be processed by metabolism.

metacarpus /ˌmetəˈkɑːpəs/ *n.* (*pl.* **metacarpi** /-paɪ/) **1** the set of five bones of the hand that connects the wrist to the fingers. **2** this part of the hand.

metafiction *n.* a work of fiction in which the author self-consciously alludes to the artificiality or literariness of a work by parodying or departing from novelistic conventions and traditional narrative techniques. ☐ **metafictional** *adj.*

metal ● *n.* **1 a** any of a class of substances (including many chemical elements) which are in general lustrous, malleable, fusible, ductile solids and good conductors of heat and electricity, e.g. gold, iron, brass, steel. **b** a material of this kind. **2** material used for making glass, in a molten state. **3** = HEAVY METAL 1. ● *adj.* made of metal. ● *v.tr.* (**metalled, metalling**) provide or fit with metal.

metalanguage *n.* a language used for the description or analysis of another language.

metal detector *n.* an electronic device giving a signal when it locates metal.

metal fatigue *n.* fatigue (*see* FATIGUE *n.* 2) in metal.

metalhead *n.* *slang* a fan of heavy metal music.

metallic ● *adj.* **1** of, consisting of, or characteristic of metal or metals. **2** sounding sharp and ringing, like struck metal. **3** having the sheen or lustre of metals. ● *n.* (usu. in *pl.*) **1** an article or substance made of or containing metal, esp. a fabric. **2** a paint or colour having the sheen or lustre of metal. □ **metallically** *adv.*

metallurgy /ˈmetəˌlɜrdʒi, məˈtælərdʒi/ *n.* the science concerned with the production, purification, and properties of metals and their application. □ **metallurgic** /ˌmetəˈlɜrdʒɪk/ *adj.* **metallurgical** *adj.* **metallurgically** *adv.* **metallurgist** *n.*

metalwork *n.* **1** the art of working in metal. **2** metal objects collectively. □ **metal worker** *n.* **metalworking** *n. & attrib.adj.*

metamorphic /ˌmetəˈmɔrfik/ *adj.* **1** of or marked by metamorphosis. **2** (of rock) that has undergone transformation by natural agencies such as heat and pressure. □ **metamorphism** *n.*

metamorphose /ˌmetəˈmɔrfoːz/ *v.* **1** *tr.* change in form. **2** *tr.* (foll. *by to, into*) **a** turn (into a new form). **b** change the nature of. **3** *intr.* undergo metamorphosis.

metamorphosis /ˌmetəˈmɔrfəsɪs, ˌmetəmɔrˈfoːsɪs/ *n.* (*pl.* **metamorphoses** /-ˌsiːz/) **1** a change of form (by natural or supernatural means). **2** a changed form. **3** a change of character, conditions, etc. **4** the transformation between an immature form and an adult form, e.g. from a pupa to an insect.

metaphor /ˈmetəfɔr/ *n.* **1 a** the application of a name or descriptive term or phrase to an object or action to which it is imaginatively but not literally applicable, e.g. *a glaring error*. **b** an instance of this. **2** (often foll. by *of* or *for*) a symbol of a usu. abstract thing. □ **metaphoric** /-ˈfɔrik/ *adj.* **metaphorical** *adj.* **metaphorically** *adv.*

metaphysical /ˌmetəˈfizikəl/ ● *adj.* **1** of or relating to metaphysics. **2** based on abstract general reasoning. **3** excessively subtle or theoretical. **4** incorporeal; supernatural. **5** (of certain 17th-c. English poets or their poetry) exhibiting subtlety of thought and complex imagery. ● *n.* (**the Metaphysicals**) the metaphysical poets. □ **metaphysically** *adv.*

metaphysics *n.pl.* (usu. treated as *sing.*) **1** the branch of philosophy that deals with the first principles of things, including such concepts as being, knowing, substance, essence, cause, identity, time, and space. **2** the philosophy of mind. **3** *informal* abstract or subtle talk; mere theory. □ **metaphysician** *n.*

metapsychology /ˌmetəsaiˈkɒlədʒi/ *n.* the study of the nature and functions of the mind beyond what can be studied experimentally.

metastasis /məˈtæstəsɪs/ *n.* (*pl.* **metastases** /-ˌsiːz/) **1** the transfer of a disease, etc. from one part of the body to another; esp. the development of secondary tumours at a distance from a primary site of cancer. **2** a secondary tumour. □ **metastasize** *v.intr.* **metastatic** /ˌmetəˈstætik/ *adj.*

metatarsus /ˌmetəˈtɑrsəs/ *n.* (*pl.* **metatarsi** /-saɪ/) **1** the part of the human foot between the ankle and the toes. **2** the set of bones in this. **3** the corresponding bones in other vertebrates. □ **metatarsal** *adj.*

mete *v.tr.* (usu. foll. by *out*) apportion or allot (a punishment or reward).

meteor *n.* a small body of matter from outer space that becomes incandescent as a result of friction with the earth's atmosphere and is visible as a streak of light.

meteoric *adj.* **1** of meteors or meteorites. **2** rapid like a meteor; dazzling, transient (*meteoric rise to fame*). **3** of or relating to the atmosphere.

meteorite *n.* a rock or metal fragment formed from a meteor of sufficient size to reach the earth's sur-

face without burning up completely in the atmosphere. □ **meteoritic** *adj.*

meteoroid *n.* any small body moving in the solar system that becomes visible as it passes through the earth's atmosphere as a meteor.

meteorology *n.* **1** the study of the processes and phenomena of the atmosphere, esp. in forecasting the weather. **2** the atmospheric character of a region. □ **meteorological** *adj.* **meteorologist** *n.*

meteor shower *n.* a group of meteors appearing to come from one point in the sky, esp. around a particular date each year.

meter¹ ● *n.* **1** a thing that measures, esp. an instrument for recording a quantity of gas, electricity, etc. supplied, present, or needed, or a device in a taxi measuring the time and distance travelled and the fare payable. **2** = PARKING METER. ● *v.* **1** *tr. & intr.* measure by means of a meter. **2** *tr.* deliver in measured amounts (*to meter one's sentences*). **3** *tr.* provide with a meter or meters.

meter² *var. of* METRE¹, METRE².

meth *n. slang* methamphetamine.

methadone *n.* a potent narcotic analgesic drug used to relieve severe pain, and as a substitute for morphine or heroin.

methamphetamine /ˌmeθæmˈfetəmiːn, -mɪn/ *n.* an amphetamine derivative with quicker and longer action, used as a stimulant.

methane /ˈmeθein/ *n. Chem.* a colourless odourless inflammable gaseous hydrocarbon, the main constituent of natural gas.

methanol /ˈmeθənɒl/ *n. Chem.* a colourless volatile inflammable liquid, used as a solvent.

methaqualone /meˈθækwəloːn/ *n.* a hypnotic and sedative drug derived from quinazoline.

methinks *v.intr.* (*past* **methought**) *archaic or jocular* it seems to me.

methionine /meˈθaiəˌniːn/ *n.* an amino acid which is an important constituent of proteins.

method *n.* **1** a mode of procedure; a defined or systematic way of doing a thing. **2** orderliness; regular habits. **3** the orderly arrangement of ideas etc. □ **method in one's madness** sense in what appears to be foolish or strange behaviour.

méthode champenoise /ˈmeitɒd ʃɑ̃pənˈwɒz/ *n.* **1** the method of introducing a sparkle into wine by allowing the last stage of fermentation to take place in the bottle. **2** a sparkling wine made in this way.

methodical /məˈθɒdikəl/ *adj.* characterized by method or order. □ **methodically** *adv.*

Methodist /ˈmeθədɪst/ ● *n.* **1** a member of any of various branches of a Protestant denomination originating in the 18th-c. evangelistic movement of Charles (1707–88) and John (1703–91) Wesley and George Whitefield (1714–70). **2** (**methodist**) a person who follows or advocates a particular method or system of procedure. ● *adj.* of or relating to Methodists or Methodism. □ **Methodism** *n.*

methodology /ˌmeθəˈdɒlədʒi/ *n.* (*pl.* **-ies**) **1** a body of methods used in a particular branch of activity. **2** the branch of knowledge that deals with method and its application in a particular field. □ **methodological** *adj.* **methodologically** *adv.* **methodologist** *n.*

methotrexate /ˌmeθoːˈtrekseit/ *n. Pharm.* a cytotoxic orange-brown powder which is a folic acid antagonist used to treat certain cancers.

methought *past of* METHINKS.

Methuselah /məˈθuːzələ, -ˈθjuːzələ/ *n.* **1** a very old person or thing. **2** (**methuselah**) a wine bottle of about eight times the standard size.

methyl /'meθəl/ *n.* the monovalent hydrocarbon radical —CH₃, found in many organic compounds.

methyl alcohol *n.* = METHANOL.

methylate /'meθə,leit/ *v.tr.* **1** mix or impregnate with methanol. **2** introduce a methyl group into (a molecule or compound). ☐ **methylation** *n.*

methylated spirits *n.* (also **methylated spirit**) alcohol impregnated with methanol to make it unfit for drinking and exempt from duty.

methylene /'meθə,li:n/ *n. Chem.* the highly reactive divalent group of atoms CH₂.

meticulous /mə'tıkjʊləs/ *adj.* **1** giving great or excessive attention to details. **2** very careful and precise. ☐ **meticulously** *adv.* **meticulousness** *n.*

métier /mei'tjei, 'mei-/ *n.* **1** one's trade, profession, or department of activity. **2** one's forte.

Metis /mei'ti:/ *n.* (*pl.* same) (esp. in Canada) a person of mixed Aboriginal and European descent.

metonym /'metənım/ *n.* a word used in metonymy.

metonymy /mı'tɒnəmi/ *n.* the substitution of the name of an attribute or adjunct for that of the thing meant, e.g. *Crown* for *monarch*. ☐ **metonymic** /metə'nımık/ *adj.* **metonymical** *adj.* **metonymically** *adv.*

me-too *adj.* **1** (of a person or course of action) adopting or acquiescing in the views, policies, etc. of someone else, often those of one's political or other opponents. **2** (of a product) designed to emulate or rival another which has already been commercially successful. **3** (of policies, techniques, or companies) emulating a rival in this way.

metre¹ *n.* (also **meter**) a metric unit and the base SI unit of linear measure, equal to about 39.4 inches.

metre² *n.* (also **meter**) **1 a** any form of poetic rhythm, determined by the number and length of feet in a line. **b** a metrical group or measure. **2** the basic pulse and rhythm of a piece of music.

metre-kilogram-second *adj.* denoting a system of measure using the metre, kilogram, and second as the basic units of length, mass, and time. Abbr.: **mks**.

metric ● *adj.* **1** of or pertaining to the metre or metric system. **2** of or relating to measurement; metrical. ● *n.* **1** = METRIC SYSTEM. **2** a system or standard of measurement. **3** a mathematical function based on distances, or on quantities treated as analogous to distances for the purpose of analysis.

metrical *adj.* **1** of, relating to, or composed in metre (*metrical psalms*). **2** of or involving measurement (*metrical geometry*). ☐ **metrically** *adv.*

metric hundredweight *n.* see HUNDREDWEIGHT 1.

metric system *n.* the decimal measuring system with the metre, litre, and gram (or kilogram) as units of length, volume, and mass.

metric ton *n.* (also **metric tonne**) 1,000 kilograms (2205 lb.).

Metro *n.* **1** an informal name for (Metropolitan) Toronto. **2** an informal name for the urban area of Halifax-Dartmouth.

metro¹ *n.* (*pl.* **-os**) a subway system in some cities, e.g. Montreal and Paris.

metro² *adj. N Amer.* metropolitan (*metro council*).

metronome /'metrə,noːm/ *n. Music* an instrument marking time at a selected rate by giving a regular tick. ☐ **metronomic** /-'nɒmık/ *adj.*

metropolis /mə'trɒpəlıs/ *n.* **1** a large, busy city, esp. the main city of a country or region. **2** a city or town

which is a local centre of activity. **3** a metropolitan bishop's see.

metropolitan /,metrə'pɒlıtən/ ● *adj.* **1** of or relating to a metropolis. **2** encompassing a city and its suburbs (*metropolitan Toronto*). **3** belonging to, forming or forming part of, a mother country as distinct from its colonies etc. (*metropolitan France*). **4** of an ecclesiastical metropolis. ● *n.* **1** (in full **metropolitan bishop**) a bishop having authority over the bishops of a province, in the Western Church equivalent to archbishop, in the Orthodox Church ranking above archbishop and below patriarch. **2** an inhabitant of a metropolis. ☐ **metropolitanism** *n.*

mettle *n.* **1** the quality of a person's disposition or temperament (*a chance to show your mettle*). **2** spirit, courage. **3** the natural vigour of an animal, esp. a horse. ☐ **on one's mettle** incited to do one's best.

MeV *abbr.* mega-electron volt(s).

mew ● *v.intr.* (of a cat, gull, etc.) utter its characteristic cry. ● *n.* this sound, esp. of a cat.

mewl *v.intr.* cry feebly; whimper.

Mexican ● *n.* **1 a** a native or national of Mexico, a country in N America south of the US. **b** a person of Mexican descent. **2** an indigenous language of Mexico, esp. Nahuatl. ● *adj.* **1** of or relating to Mexico or its people or indigenous languages. **2** of Mexican descent.

Mexican standoff *n.* a situation in which there is no clear winner; an impasse.

mezuzah /mə'zu:zə/ *n.* (*pl.* **-s** or **mezuzoth** /-zo:θ/) a parchment inscribed with religious texts and attached in a case to the doorpost of a Jewish house as a sign of faith.

mezzanine /'mezəni:n, mezə'ni:n/ *n.* (also *attrib.*) **1** a low storey between two others (usu. between the ground floor and the second floor). **2** *N Amer.* the lowest balcony or foremost part of a single balcony in a theatre.

mezzo /'metso:/ *Music* ● *adv.* half, moderately. ● *n.* (in full **mezzo-soprano**) (*pl.* **-os**) **1 a** a female voice between soprano and contralto. **b** a singer with this voice. **2** a part written for mezzo-soprano.

mezzo-forte *adj. & adv.* fairly loud. Abbr.: **mf**.

mezzo-piano *adj. & adv.* fairly soft. Abbr.: **mp**.

MF *abbr.* milk fat.

M.F. *abbr.* Master of Forestry.

mf *abbr.* mezzo-forte.

M.F.A. *abbr.* Master of Fine Arts.

mfg. *abbr.* manufacturing.

MFN *abbr.* MOST FAVOURED NATION.

mfr. *abbr.* manufacturer's.

Mg *symbol* magnesium.

mg *abbr.* milligram(s).

MGen *abbr. Cdn* MAJOR GENERAL.

Mgr. *abbr.* **1** Manager. **2** Monseigneur. **3** Monsignor.

MHA *abbr.* (in Newfoundland and Australia) Member of the House of Assembly.

M.H.A. *abbr.* Master of Health Administration.

MHR *abbr.* (in the US and Australia) Member of the House of Representatives.

M.H.Sc. *abbr.* Master of Health Sciences.

MHz *abbr.* megahertz.

MI *abbr.* **1** Michigan (in postal use). **2** Military Intelligence.

mi *n.* (also **me**) *Music* **1** (in tonic sol-fa) the third note of a major scale. **2** the note E in the fixed-do system.

mi. *abbr.* mile(s).

MIA *abbr.* missing in action.

miasma /mi:'æzmə, mai-/ *n.* (*pl.* **miasmas** or

miasmata /-mətə/ **1** an infectious or noxious vapour, esp. from rotting organic matter, which pollutes the atmosphere. **2** a polluting, oppressive or foreboding atmosphere or influence.

mic /maɪk/ *n.* microphone.

mica /'maɪkə/ *n.* any of a group of silicate minerals with a layered structure, esp. muscovite.

mice pl. of MOUSE.

Mich. *abbr.* Michigan.

Michaelmas daisy /'mɪkəlməs/ *n.* an autumn-flowering aster.

Michigander /ˌmɪʃɪ'gændər/ *n.* a native or inhabitant of the US state of Michigan.

mick *n.* (also **Mick**) *slang offensive* **1** an Irishman. **2** a Roman Catholic.

mickey *n.* (pl. **-eys**) **1** *Cdn* a half bottle of liquor, usu. 375 ml. **2** = MICKEY FINN.

Mickey Finn *n.* (also **mickey, Mickey**) *slang* **1** a strong alcoholic drink, esp. adulterated with a narcotic or laxative. **2** the adulterant itself.

Mickey Mouse *adj. informal* **1** of inferior quality. **2** ridiculous, trivial. **3** (of a university course etc.) requiring little work or intellectual ability.

Micmac *var. of* MI'KMAQ.

micro *informal* ● *n.* (pl. **-os**) **1** = MICROCOMPUTER. **2** = MICROPROCESSOR. **3** = MICROWAVE. ● *adj.* **1** microscopic; very small. **2** small-scale.

micro- *comb. form* **1** small (*microchip*). **2** denoting a factor of one millionth (10⁻⁶) (*microgram*). Symbol: μ. **3** *Med.* involving arrested development or underdevelopment of a part (*microencephaly*). **4** (in names of instruments, techniques, and disciplines) dealing with small effects or small quantities. **5** involving the use of a microscope. **6** containing or pertaining to something in minute form, quantity, or degree (*microvascular*). **7** pertaining to or obtained by micrography (*microtext*).

microbe /'maɪkroːb/ *n.* a minute living being; a micro-organism (esp. a bacterium causing disease or fermentation). □ **microbial** *adj.* **microbic** *adj.*

microbiology *n.* the scientific study of micro-organisms, e.g. bacteria, viruses, and fungi. □ **microbiological** *adj.* **microbiologist** *n.*

microbrewery *n.* esp. *N Amer.* a brewery which produces beer on a small scale, and which usu. specializes in high-quality brands made with natural ingredients. □ **microbrew** *n.* & *v.tr.* **microbrewer** *n.*

microcassette *n.* a small audio cassette for use in a tape recorder, answering machine, etc.

microcephaly /ˌmaɪkroː'sefəli/ *n.* an abnormal smallness of the head in relation to the rest of the body. □ **microcephalic** /-sə'fælɪk/ *adj. & n.*

microchip ● *n.* a tiny wafer of semiconducting material used to make an integrated circuit. ● *v.tr.* implant a microchip under the skin of (a pet) for identification purposes.

microcircuit *n.* a minute electric circuit, esp. an integrated circuit. □ **microcircuitry** *n.*

microclimate *n.* the climate of a small local area or enclosed space, esp. as differing from the surroundings. □ **microclimatic** *adj.*

microcode *n.* **1** microinstruction. **2** microprogram.

microcomputer *n.* a small computer that contains a microprocessor as its central processing unit.

microcosm /'maɪkrəˌkɒzəm/ *n.* **1** (often foll. by *of*) a miniature representation. **2** humankind viewed as the epitome of the universe. **3** any community or complex unity viewed in this way. □ **microcosmic** *adj.* **microcosmically** *adv.*

microdot *n.* **1** a microphotograph of a document etc. reduced to the size of a dot. **2** a tiny capsule or tablet of LSD.

microeconomics *n.* the branch of economics that deals with small-scale economic factors such as individual commodities, producers, consumers, etc. (*compare* MACROECONOMICS). □ **microeconomic** *adj.*

microelectronics *n.* the design, manufacture, and use of microchips and microcircuits. □ **microelectronic** *adj.*

microenvironment *n. Biol. & Bot.* the immediate small-scale environment of a thing, esp. as a distinct part of a larger environment.

microfibre *n.* a lightweight, water-resistant polyester used esp. for outerwear, swimsuits, etc.

microfiche /'maɪkroːˌfiːʃ/ *n.* (pl. same or **-es**) a flat rectangular piece of film bearing microphotographs of the pages of a printed text or document.

microfilm ● *n.* a length of film bearing microphotographs of documents etc. ● *v.tr.* photograph (a document etc.) on microfilm.

microform *n.* microphotographic reproduction on film or paper of a manuscript etc.

microgram *n.* one-millionth of a gram.

micrograph *n.* a photograph taken by means of a microscope.

microgravity *n.* very weak gravity, as in an orbiting spacecraft.

microgroove *n.* a very narrow groove on a long-playing record.

microinstruction *n.* a machine-code instruction that effects a basic operation in a computer system.

micromanage *v.tr.* supervise or control with excessive attention to small details. □ **micromanagement** *n.* **micromanager** *n.*

micrometer /maɪ'krɒmɪtər/ *n.* a gauge for accurately measuring small distances, thicknesses, etc.

micrometre /'maɪkroːˌmiːtər/ *n.* one-millionth of a metre.

micro-mini ● *adj.* **1** (of a skirt etc.) very short. **2** (of a car, computer, etc.) very small. ● *n.* an object that is very short in length or very small in size.

micron /'maɪkrɒn/ *n.* one-millionth of a metre. Symbol: μ.

Micronesian /ˌmaɪkroː'niːʒən, -ziən/ ● *adj.* of or relating to Micronesia, a region of the W Pacific to the north of Melanesia, or its people or their languages. ● *n.* **1** a native of Micronesia. **2** the group of Austronesian languages spoken in Micronesia.

micronutrient *n.* a chemical element or substance required in trace amounts for the growth and development of living organisms.

micro-organism *n.* any of various microscopic organisms, esp. a bacterium or virus.

microphone *n.* an instrument for converting sound waves into electrical energy variations which may be reconverted into sound after transmission by wire or radio or after recording. □ **microphonic** *adj.*

microphotograph *n.* **1** a photograph reduced to a very small size. **2** a photograph of a microscopic object on a magnifed scale. □ **microphotography** *n.*

microprocessor *n.* an integrated circuit that contains all the functions of a central processing unit of a computer.

microprogram *n.* a microinstruction program that controls the functions of a central processing unit of a computer.

microproof *adj.* (of a dish, container, etc.) able to be used in a microwave oven.

microscope n. an instrument magnifying small objects by means of a lens or lenses so as to reveal details invisible to the naked eye. □ **under the microscope** examined in great detail.

microscopic /ˌmaɪkrə'skɒpɪk/ adj. **1** so small as to be visible only with a microscope. **2** extremely small. **3** regarded in terms of small units; concerned with minute detail. **4** of the microscope. □ **microscopical** adj. **microscopically** adv.

microscopy /maɪ'krɒskəpi/ n. the use of the microscope. □ **microscopist** n.

microsecond n. one-millionth of a second.

microstructure n. (in a metal or other material) the arrangement of crystals etc. which can be made visible and examined with a microscope. □ **microstructural** adj.

microsurgery n. intricate surgery performed using microscopes, enabling the tissue to be operated on with miniaturized precision instruments. □ **microsurgeon** n. **microsurgical** adj.

microswitch n. a switch that can be operated rapidly by a small movement.

microtubule /ˌmaɪkrəʊ'tuːbjuːl/ n. a minute protein filament occurring in cytoplasm and involved in forming the spindles during cell division etc.

microwave ● n. **1** an electromagnetic wave with a wavelength in the range 0.001–0.3m. **2** (in full **microwave oven**) an oven that uses microwaves to cook or heat food. ● v.tr. cook in a microwave oven. □ **microwaveable** adj. (also **microwavable**).

mid[1] attrib.adj. **1** (usu. in comb.) that is the middle of (mid-air). **2** that is in the middle; medium, half.

mid[2] prep. literary = AMID.

mid-air n. (also attrib.) some part or section of the air above ground level or above another surface (suspended in mid-air; mid-air collision).

Midas touch /'maɪdəs/ n. the ability to turn one's activities to esp. financial advantage.

midbrain n. the part of the brain developing from the middle of the primitive or embryonic brain.

midday n. the middle of the day; noon.

midden /'mɪdən/ n. **1** a refuse heap near a dwelling. **2** = KITCHEN MIDDEN.

middle ● attrib.adj. **1** at an equal distance from the extremities of a thing. **2** (of a member of a group) so placed as to have the same number of members on each side. **3** intermediate in rank, quality, order, etc. **4** average (of middle height). **5** (of a language) of the period between the old and modern forms. ● n. **1** (often foll. by of) the middle point or position or part. **2** a person's waist. **3** a position between two rivals, subject to attack from both (caught in the middle). □ **in the middle of** (often foll. by verbal noun) in the process of; during. **up the middle** Baseball (of a ground ball or line drive) (hit) down the centre of the field, past the pitcher and second baseman.

middle age n. the period between youth and old age, about 40 to 60. □ **middle-aged** adj.

Middle Ages n.pl. the period of European history generally considered as beginning either with the fall of the Roman Empire in the West (5th c.) or with the end of the Dark Ages (c. 1000), and ending either with the start of the Renaissance in Italy (14th c.) or with the fall of Constantinople (1453).

Middle America n. **1** the middle class in the US, esp. seen as having conventional attitudes, tastes, etc. **2** Mexico and Central America.

middlebrow informal ● adj. claiming to be or regarded as only moderately intellectual. ● n. a middlebrow person.

middle C n. the C near the middle of the piano keyboard, the note between the treble and bass staffs, at about 260 Hz.

middle class ● n. the class of society between the upper class and the lower class, including professional and business workers and their families. ● adj. (**middle-class**) of the middle class.

middle distance n. **1** (in a painted or actual landscape) the part between the foreground and the background. **2** Athletics a race distance of esp. 400, 800, or 1500 metres (also attrib.: middle-distance runner).

middle ear n. the cavity of the central part of the ear behind the drum.

Middle East n. a term applied to an extensive area of SW Asia and N Africa, stretching from the Mediterranean to Pakistan, including the Arabian peninsula, and having a predominantly Muslim population. □ **Middle Eastern** adj.

Middle English n. the English language c.1150–1500.

middle finger n. the finger between the index finger and the ring finger.

middle ground n. **1** the thought, area, or path, tending to moderation and compromise. **2** the people regarded as holding moderate views.

middle-income attrib.adj. of or relating to the group of people earning average salaries.

middleman n. (pl. **-men**) **1** any of the traders who handle a commodity between its producer and the retailer or consumer. **2** an intermediary.

middle management n. **1** the level in an organization between senior and junior management. **2** the managers at this level.

middle name n. **1** a person's name placed after the first name and before the surname. **2** a characteristic quality of a person etc. (punctuality is my middle name).

middle-of-the-road adj. **1** (of a person etc.) moderate; avoiding extremes. **2** (of music) intended to appeal to a wide audience. □ **middle-of-the-roader** n. **middle-of-the-roadism** n.

middle power n. a nation with average political or military influence on world affairs.

middle school n. N Amer. = JUNIOR HIGH SCHOOL.

middle-sized adj. of medium size.

middleweight n. **1** a weight in certain sports intermediate between welterweight and light heavyweight, in the amateur boxing scale 71·5 kg but differing for professionals and wrestlers. **2** an athlete of this weight.

Middle West n. = MIDWEST.

middling /'mɪdlɪŋ/ adj. **1** moderately good (fair to middling). **2** informal (of a person's health) fairly good. **3** second-rate. ● adv. fairly or moderately (middling good). □ **middlingly** adv.

middy n. (pl. **-ies**) **1** informal a midshipman. **2** (in full **middy blouse**) a woman's or child's loose blouse with a sailor collar.

Mideast n. N Amer. = MIDDLE EAST.

Midewiwin /mɪ'deɪwɪwɪn/ n. (also **Midewin** /mɪ'deɪwɪn/) a shamanic society among the Ojibwa and Algonquin, devoted to the understanding of herbal remedies and spiritual knowledge.

midfield n. **1** (in football, soccer, etc.) the central part of the playing field, away from the goals or end zones. **2** (in soccer) the players positioned in the midfield. □ **midfielder** n.

midge n. **1** informal **a** a gnatlike insect. **b** a small person. **2 a** any small dipterous non-biting insect of the family Chironomidae, accumulating in swarms.

b any similar insect of the family Ceratopogonidae with piercing mouthparts for sucking blood or eating smaller insects.

midget *n.* **1** an extremely small person or thing. **2** (*attrib.*) very small. **3** *Cdn* **a** a level of amateur sport, usu. involving players aged 16 to 17. **b** a player in this age group.

MIDI /'mɪdi/ *n.* a standard system for transferring data between electronic musical instruments, synthesizers, computers, etc., allowing them to be used simultaneously (also *attrib.*: *MIDI keyboard*).

midi *n.* (*pl.* **midis**) a garment of medium length, usu. reaching to mid-calf.

midland ● *n.* **1** (**the Midlands**) the inland counties of central England. **2** the middle part of a country. ● *adj.* of or in the midland or Midlands.

mid-life *n.* middle age (often *attrib.*: *mid-life planning*).

mid-life crisis *n.* an emotional crisis of self-confidence that can occur in early middle age.

midline ● *n.* a median line, or plane of bilateral symmetry. ● *adj.* (**mid-line**) designating or pertaining to consumer products or services that are of a general quality, neither expensive nor cheap; mid-range.

midnight *n.* **1** 12 o'clock at night. **2** the middle of the night.

midnight blue very dark blue.

midnight Mass *n.* esp. *Catholicism* a Mass beginning at midnight on Christmas Eve.

midnight sun *n.* the sun visible at midnight during the summer in polar regions.

midpoint *n.* the middle point.

mid-range ● *adj.* (esp. of a consumer product etc.) mid-priced; of average cost, capability, etc. ● *n.* the middle part of the range of audible frequencies (also *attrib.*: *mid-range speakers*).

Midrash /'mɪdræʃ/ *n.* (*pl.* **Midrashim** /-'ʃɪm/) an ancient commentary on part of the Hebrew scriptures. □ **Midrashic** /mɪd'ræʃɪk/ *adj.*

midriff *n.* **1 a** the region of the front of the body between the chest and the waist. **b** the diaphragm. **2** a garment or part of a garment covering the abdomen. **3** a garment exposing the midriff.

midsection *n.* **1** the middle part of something. **2** the middle part of the human torso; midriff.

midship *n.* the middle part of a ship or boat.

midshipman *n.* (*pl.* **-men**) (in the Royal Navy and *hist.* in the Royal Canadian Navy) a naval officer ranking below sub-lieutenant.

midships *adv.* = AMIDSHIPS.

midshore *attrib.adj. Cdn* designating the fishery an intermediate distance from shore, between the inshore and the offshore fisheries.

mid-size ● *adj.* (also **mid-sized**) **1** *N Amer.* (of a car) of a size between compact and full-size, usu. having a wheelbase of 100 to 105 inches and a four- or six-cylinder engine from 2 to 3.5 litres in size. **2** of intermediate size. ● *n. N Amer.* a mid-size car.

midsole *n.* a shock-absorbing layer in the sole of a running shoe etc.

midst □ **in the midst of** among; in the middle of. **in our** (or **your** or **their**) **midst** among us (or you or them).

midstream ● *n.* the middle of a stream, river, etc. ● *adv.* (also **in midstream**) in the middle of an action etc. (*abandoned the project midstream*).

midsummer *n.* the period of or near the summer solstice, about June 21.

Midsummer Day *n.* (also **Midsummer's Day**) June 24.

mid-term ● *adj.* occurring in the middle of a term. ● *n. N Amer.* a mid-term exam.

midtown *n. N Amer.* an area of a city at a moderate distance from the downtown area.

midway ● *adv.* in or toward the middle of the distance or interval between two points. ● *n. N Amer.* a fair or an area with amusements, sideshows, rides, etc.

mid-week ● *n.* the middle of the week ● *adj.* occurring at mid-week. ● *adv.* at mid-week.

Midwest *n.* (in the US) the region of northern states from Ohio west to the Missouri valley. □ **Midwestern** *adj.* **Midwesterner** *n.*

midwife *n.* (*pl.* **-wives**) **1** a person (usu. a woman) trained to assist women in childbirth. **2** a person or thing that brings about change. □ **midwifery** /mɪd'wɪfəri/ *n.*

mid-winter *n.* **1** the middle of the winter (also *attrib.*: *mid-winter blues*). **2** the period of or near the winter solstice, about Dec. 22.

mien /miːn/ *n.* a person's look or bearing, as showing character or mood.

miffed *adj. informal* put out of humour; offended.

might[1] *v.aux.* (*3rd. sing.* **might**) *past of* MAY, used esp.: **1** in reported speech, expressing possibility (*said he might come*) or permission (*asked if I might leave*) (*compare* MAY 1, 2). **2** expressing a possibility based on a condition not fulfilled (*if you'd looked you might have found it*). **3** expressing complaint that an obligation or expectation is not or has not been fulfilled (*they might have asked*). **4** expressing a request (*you might give them a call*). **5** *informal* **a** = MAY 1 (*it might be true*). **b** (in tentative questions) = MAY 2 (*might I have the pleasure of this dance?*). **c** = MAY 4 (*who might you be?*). □ **might as well** expressing that it is probably at least as desirable to do a thing as not to do it (*might as well go to lunch; won't win but might as well try*).

might[2] *n.* **1** great bodily or mental strength. **2** power to enforce one's will (usu. in contrast with *right*). □ **with all one's might** to the utmost of one's power.

might-have-been *n. informal* **1** a past possibility that no longer applies. **2** a person or thing that could have been more eminent.

mightn't *contraction* might not.

mighty ● *adj.* (**-ier, -iest**) **1** powerful or strong, in body, mind, or influence. **2** massive, bulky. **3** *informal* great, considerable. ● *adv. informal* very (*a mighty difficult task*). □ **mightily** *adv.* **mightiness** *n.*

migraine /'maɪɡreɪn/ *n.* a recurrent throbbing headache that usually affects one side of the head, often accompanied by nausea and disturbance of vision.

migrant /'maɪɡrənt/ ● *adj.* that migrates. ● *n.* a migrant person or animal, esp. a bird.

migrate *v.intr.* **1** (of people) move from one place of residence to another, esp. in a different country. **2** (of an animal, esp. a bird or fish) change its area of habitation with the seasons. **3** (of a cell, atom, molecule, etc.) move in a non-random manner from one position or region to another or in a particular direction. □ **migration** *n.* **migrational** *adj.* **migrator** *n.* **migratory** /'maɪɡrətəri/ *adj.*

Mike *n.* □ **for the love of Mike** *slang* an exclamation of entreaty or dismay.

mike *informal* ● *n.* **1** a microphone. **2** a microwave oven. ● *v.tr.* (**miked, miking**) put a microphone near, in, or on (a person, place, etc.) in order to transmit, amplify, or record sounds.

Mi'kmaq /'mɪkmæk, 'miːmɒ, 'mɪɡmɒ/ ● *n.* **1** a member of an Aboriginal people living in Nova Scotia, New Brunswick, PEI, and the Gaspé Peninsula. **2** the

Algonquian language of this people. ● *adj.* of or relating to this people.

mikveh /ˈmɪkvə/ *n.* (also **mikvah, mikva**) a bath in which certain Jewish ritual purifications are performed.

mil¹ *n.* one thousandth of an inch (0.0254 mm), as a unit of measure for the diameter of wire, thickness of a film, etc.

mil² *n.* (*pl.* same) (usu. in *pl.*) esp. *N Amer. informal* a million dollars (or pounds).

Milanese /ˌmɪləˈniːz/ ● *adj.* of or relating to Milan in NW Italy. ● *n.* (*pl.* same) a native or inhabitant of Milan.

mild *adj.* **1** (esp. of a person) gentle and conciliatory. **2** moderate; not severe or harsh. **3** (of the weather, esp. in winter) moderately warm. **4** (of food, tobacco, etc.) not sharp or strong in taste etc. **5** (of medicine, soap, etc.) operating gently; not harsh. **6** tame, feeble; lacking energy or vivacity. □ **mildness** *n.*

mildew /ˈmɪldjuː, -djuː/ ● *n.* **1** a destructive growth of minute fungi on plants. **2** a similar growth on paper, leather, etc. exposed to damp. ● *v.tr. & intr.* taint or be tainted with mildew. □ **mildewed** *adj.*

mildly *adv.* in a mild fashion; to a limited extent. □ **to put it mildly** as an understatement (implying the reality is more extreme).

mild-mannered *adj.* = MILD *adj.* 1.

mild steel *n.* steel containing a small percentage of carbon, strong and tough but not readily tempered.

mile *n.* **1** (also **statute mile**) a unit of linear measure equal to 1,760 yards (approx. 1.609 kilometres). **2** (in *pl.*) *informal* a great distance or amount (*miles better*). **3** a race extending over a mile. □ **miles away** *informal* lost in thought; preoccupied. (**talk** etc.) **a mile a minute** (talk etc.) very quickly. **go the extra mile** extend or exert oneself for another's benefit, esp. beyond what is strictly necessary.

mileage *n.* **1 a** the distance travelled. **b** the distance a vehicle is capable of travelling per unit of fuel. **2** expenses per distance travelled. **3** *informal* use, benefit, advantage (*got good mileage out of that story*).

miler *n.* *informal* a person or horse qualified or trained specially to run a mile.

milestone *n.* (also *N Amer. & Austral.* **milepost**) **1** a stone (or post) set up beside a road to mark a distance in miles. **2** a significant event or stage in a life, history, project, etc.

milieu /miːlˈjuː, miːlˈjɜː/ *n.* (*pl.* **milieux** or **milieus** /-ljɜːz/) one's environment or social surroundings.

militant /ˈmɪlɪtənt/ ● *adj.* **1** combative; aggressively active esp. in support of a (usu. political) cause. **2** engaged in warfare. ● *n.* a militant person, esp. a political activist. □ **militancy** *n.* **militantly** *adv.*

militarism /ˈmɪlɪtəˌrɪzəm/ *n.* **1** the policy of maintaining a strong military capability. **2** the attachment of undue importance to military values and military strength. **3** the spirit or tendencies of a professional soldier. □ **militaristic** *adj.* **militaristically** *adv.*

militarist ● *n.* **1** a person dominated by militaristic ideas. **2** a student of military science. ● *adj.* militaristic.

militarize /ˈmɪlɪtəˌraɪz/ *v.tr.* **1** equip with military resources. **2** make military or warlike. **3** imbue with militarism. □ **militarization** *n.*

military ● *adj.* of, relating to, or characteristic of soldiers or armed forces. ● *n.* (as *sing.* or *pl.*; prec. by *the*) members of the armed forces, as distinct from civilians and the police. □ **militarily** *adv.*

military honours *n.* marks of respect paid by troops at the burial of a soldier, to royalty, etc.

military-industrial complex *n.* esp. *N Amer.* a nation's military and the industries supplying it, esp. as a single powerful influence on public policy.

military police *n.* (treated as *pl.*) a corps responsible for police and disciplinary duties in the armed forces. □ **military policeman** *n.*

militate *v.intr.* (usu. foll. by *against*) (of facts or evidence) have force or effect (*what you say militates against our opinion*). ¶See MITIGATE.

militia /mɪˈlɪʃə/ *n.* **1** a military force raised from the civilian population and supplementing a regular army in an emergency. **2** any usu. small military force not sanctioned by a nation or government.

militiaman *n.* (*pl.* **-men**) a member of a militia.

milk ● *n.* **1** an opaque white fluid secreted by female mammals for the nourishment of their young. **2** the milk of cows, goats, or sheep as food. **3** the milklike juice of plants, e.g. in the coconut. **4** a milklike preparation of herbs, drugs, etc. ● *v.* **1** *tr.* draw milk from (a cow, ewe, goat, etc.). **2** *tr.* **a** exploit (a person or thing) esp. financially. **b** get all possible advantage from (a situation or thing). **3** *tr.* extract sap, venom, etc. from. **4** *intr.* (of a cow etc.) yield milk. □ **cry over spilt milk** lament an irremediable loss or error.

milk and honey *n.* abundance, comfort, prosperity.

milk chocolate *n.* chocolate made with milk.

milker *n.* **1** an animal, esp. a cow, yielding milk or kept for milking. **2** a person who, or a machine which, milks.

milk fat *n.* = BUTTERFAT. Abbr.: **MF**.

milk house *n.* a room or building on a dairy farm where milk is cooled and stored.

milkmaid *n.* a girl or woman who milks cows or works in a dairy.

milkman *n.* (*pl.* **-men**) a person who sells or delivers milk.

milk of human kindness *n.* kindness regarded as natural to humanity.

milk of magnesia *n.* a white suspension of magnesium hydroxide usu. in water as an antacid or laxative.

milk powder *n.* milk dehydrated by evaporation.

milk pudding *n.* a dessert made of flavoured milk thickened with cornstarch.

milk run *n.* **1** the regular route followed by a person delivering milk. **2** a routine trip or train route with many regular stops. **3** a routine or easy task, expedition, etc.

milkshake *n.* a frothy drink, usu. cold, of milk, flavouring, and usu. ice cream, mixed in a blender.

milk snake *n.* a harmless, usu. brightly coloured N American snake, *Lampropeltis triangulum*.

milk store *n. Cdn* = CONVENIENCE STORE.

milk sugar *n.* lactose.

milk tooth *n.* a temporary tooth in young mammals; a baby tooth.

milkweed *n.* **1** any of various N American plants of the genus *Asclepias*, which have milky juice and seeds plumed with long silky hairs. **2** any of various other plants with milky juice.

milk-white *adj.* (usu. *attrib.*) white like milk.

milky *adj.* (**-ier, -iest**) **1** of, like, or mixed with milk. **2** (of a gem, liquid, etc.) cloudy. □ **milkiness** *n.*

Milky Way *n.* **1** (in full **Milky Way Galaxy**) the galaxy of which the solar system is part. **2** this viewed as a faintly luminous band of light encircling the heavens, formed of countless indistinguishable stars.

mill¹ ● *n.* **1 a** a building fitted with a mechanical apparatus for grinding grain. **b** such an apparatus. **2**

an apparatus for grinding any solid substance to powder or pulp (*pepper mill*). **3 a** a building fitted with machinery for manufacturing processes etc. (*paper mill*). **b** such machinery. **4 a** any group etc. generating something specified (*rumour mill*). **b** any institution etc. operating impersonally or inhumanely and concerned solely with output (*puppy mill*). ● *v.* **1** *tr.* **a** grind (grain), produce (flour), or hull (seeds) in a mill. **b** extract (a mineral) from rock by crushing the rock in a mill. **2** *tr.* produce regular ribbed markings on the edge of (a coin). **3** *tr.* cut or shape (metal) with a rotating tool. **4** *intr.* (often foll. by *about*, *around*) (of people or animals) move in an aimless manner, esp. in a confused mass. □ **go** (or **put** or **run**) **through the mill** undergo (or cause to undergo) intensive work or a difficult ordeal.

mill² *n. N Amer.* one thousandth of a dollar, esp. in calculating tax rates.

mille feuille /miːl ˈfɔj/ *n.* **1** a dessert comprised of thin layers of puff pastry and a filling of cream, custard, etc. **2** a similar savoury dish of layers of pastry alternating with filling.

millenarian /mɪlɪˈnɛriən/ ● *adj.* **1** of or related to the millennium. **2** believing in the imminence of the millennium or a millennium. ● *n.* a person who believes in the imminence of the millennium or a millennium. □ **millenarianism** *n.*

millennium /mɪˈlɛniəm/ *n.* (*pl.* **-s** or **millennia** /-niə/) **1 a** a period of 1,000 years. **b** any millennium reckoned from the supposed date of the birth of Christ (*the third millennium*). **2** *Christianity* the period of 1,000 years during which (according to one interpretation of Revelation 20:1–5) Christ will reign in person on earth. **3** a period of good government, great happiness, and prosperity. □ **millennial** *adj.*

millennium bug *n.* computer problems arising from the inability of certain software and firmware to deal correctly with dates of 1 January 2000 or later.

miller *n.* **1** the proprietor or tenant of a grain mill. **2** a person who works or owns a mill.

millet *n.* **1** any of various cereal plants, esp. *Panicum miliaceum*, bearing a large crop of small nutritious seeds. **2** the seed of this.

mill hand *n.* a worker in a mill or factory.

milli- /ˈmɪlɪ/ *comb. form* a thousand, esp. denoting a factor of one thousandth. Abbr.: **m.**

milliampere *n.* (also **milliamp**) one thousandth of an ampere, a measure for small electrical currents.

millibar *n.* one thousandth of a bar, the cgs unit of atmospheric pressure equivalent to 100 pascals.

milligram *n.* one thousandth of a gram.

millilitre *n.* (also esp. *US* **milliliter**) one thousandth of a litre.

millimetre *n.* (also esp. *US* **millimeter**) one thousandth of a metre (0.039 in.).

milliner /ˈmɪlɪnər/ *n.* a person who makes or sells women's hats. □ **millinery** *n.*

milling frolic *n. Cdn* (*NS*) **1** *hist.* a gathering at which participants pound new wool to raise the nap, usu. with singing etc. **2** a cultural event at which songs traditionally sung at these are performed.

million ● *n.* (*pl.* same or (in sense 2) **-s**) (in *sing.* prec. by *a* or *one*) **1** a thousand thousand. **2** (often in *pl.*) *informal* a very large number (*millions of years*; *thanks a million*). **3** (prec. by *the*) the bulk of the population. **4** a million dollars, pounds, etc. ● *adj.* that amount to a million. □ **look** (or **feel** etc.) (**like**) **a million bucks** (or **dollars** etc.) look (or feel) extremely good. □ **millionfold** *adj. & adv.* **millionth** *adj. & n.*

millionaire *n.* **1** a person whose assets are worth at least one million dollars, pounds, etc. **2** a person of great wealth.

millipede *n.* any arthropod of the class Diplopoda, having a long segmented body with two pairs of legs on each segment.

millisecond *n.* one thousandth of a second.

millivolt *n.* one thousandth of a volt. Abbr.: **mV**.

millpond *n.* a pool of water retained by a dam for the operation of a mill. □ **like a millpond** (of a stretch of water) very calm.

millrace *n.* a current of water that drives a mill wheel.

millstone *n.* **1** each of two circular stones used for grinding grain. **2** a heavy burden or responsibility.

mill wheel *n.* a wheel used to drive a water mill.

millwork *n.* **1** work done in a mill. **2** wood products manufactured in a mill, e.g. trim or mouldings.

mill worker *n.* a worker in a factory or mill.

millwright *n.* **1** one who maintains or repairs mill machinery. **2** one who designs or builds mills.

milo /ˈmaɪloː/ *n.* a drought-resistant variety of sorghum grown esp. in the central US.

milquetoast /ˈmɪlktoːst/ *n.* a timid person.

milt *n.* **1 a** a sperm-filled reproductive gland of a male fish. **b** the semen of a male fish. **2** the spleen in mammals. **3** an analogous organ in other vertebrates.

mime ● *n.* **1** the theatrical technique of suggesting action, character, etc. by gesture and expression without using words. **2** a theatrical performance using this technique. **3** (also **mime artist**) a practitioner of mime. ● *v.tr. & intr.* **1** convey (an idea or emotion) by gesture without words. **2** (often foll. by *to*) (of singers etc.) mouth (the words of a song etc.) along with a soundtrack.

mimesis /mɪˈmiːsɪs, maɪ-/ *n.* **1** *Biol.* = MIMICRY 3. **2** the representation of the real world in art, poetry, etc.

mimetic /mɪˈmɛtɪk/ *adj.* **1** relating to or habitually practising mimesis or mimicry. **2** *Biol.* of or exhibiting mimicry. □ **mimetically** *adv.*

mimic ● *v.tr.* (**mimicked**, **mimicking**) **1** imitate (a person, gesture, manner of speech, etc.) esp. to entertain or ridicule. **2** copy minutely or servilely. **3** (of a thing) resemble closely. ● *n.* a person skilled in imitation. ● *adj.* having an aptitude for mimicry; imitating; imitative, esp. for amusement. □ **mimicker** *n.*

mimicry *n.* (*pl.* **-ies**) **1** the act or art of mimicking. **2** a thing that mimics another. **3** *Biol.* a close external resemblance of an animal (or part of one) to another animal or to a plant or inanimate object; a similar resemblance in a plant.

mimosa /mɪˈmoːzə, -sə/ *n.* **1** any leguminous shrub of the genus *Mimosa*, esp. *M. pudica*, having globular flowers and sensitive leaves which droop when touched. **2** any of various acacia plants with showy yellow flowers. **3** a drink of champagne and orange juice.

mimulus /ˈmɪmjʊləs/ *n.* any flowering plant of the genus *Mimulus*, including the N American plants musk and the monkey flower.

Min *n.* any of the Chinese languages or dialects spoken in the Fukien province in SE China and in parts of Taiwan.

Min. *abbr.* **1** Minister. **2** Ministry.

min *abbr.* **1** minute(s). **2** (**min.**) minimum.

Minamata disease /mɪnəˈmɒtə/ *n.* chronic poisoning by alkyl mercury compounds, characterized by impairment of brain functions such as speech, sight, and muscular coordination.

minaret /ˌmɪnəˈret, ˈmɪnəˌret/ n. a slender turret connected with a mosque and having a balcony from which the muezzin calls at hours of prayer.

mince ● v. 1 tr. a cut up into very small pieces. b grind (meat). 2 tr. (usu. with neg.) restrain (one's words etc.) within the bounds of politeness. 3 intr. speak or walk with an affected delicacy. ● n. esp. Brit. minced meat. □ **mincer** n. **mincing** adj. (in sense 3 of v.). **mincingly** adv.

mincemeat n. a mixture of currants, raisins, sugar, apples, candied peel, spices, and often suet. □ **make mincemeat of** utterly defeat (a person, argument, etc.).

mince pie n. a pie containing mincemeat.

mind ● n. 1 a the seat of consciousness, awareness, thought, volition, and feeling. b attention, concentration (my mind keeps wandering). 2 the intellect; intellectual powers. 3 remembrance, memory (it went out of my mind). 4 one's opinion (we're of the same mind). 5 a way of thinking or feeling (the Victorian mind). 6 the focus of one's thoughts or desires (put one's mind to it). 7 the state of normal mental functioning (lose one's mind). 8 a person as embodying mental faculties (a great mind). ● v. 1 (usu. with neg. or interrog.) a tr. object to (I don't mind your being late). b intr. object, be annoyed (do you think they'd mind?). 2 tr. remember; take care to (mind you come on time). 3 tr. have charge of temporarily (mind the house while I'm away). 4 tr. apply oneself to, concern oneself with (business, affairs, etc.) (I try to mind my own business). 5 tr. a be careful about (mind the step; mind you don't drop it). b pay attention to; concern oneself with (don't mind the expense). 6 tr. N Amer. & Irish be obedient to (mind what your mother says). 7 tr. N Amer. & Scot. recall, recollect. □ **bear** (or **keep**) **in mind** retain an awareness of; remember. **be of one mind** be in agreement; share an opinion. **be of two minds** be undecided. **change one's mind** adopt a different opinion or plan. **come into a person's mind** be remembered. **come** (or **spring**) **to mind** (of a thought, idea, etc.) suggest itself. **don't mind me 1** often ironic do as you please. 2 do not let yourself be disturbed by me. **do you mind!** ironic an expression of annoyance. **give a person a piece of one's mind** scold or reproach a person. **give one's mind to** concentrate on or direct all one's attention to. **have a good** (or **half a**) **mind to** (often as a threat, usu. unfulfilled) feel tempted to (I've a good mind to report you). **have (it) in mind** intend. **have in mind** be considering as suitable (who do you have in mind for the job?). **have a mind of one's own** be capable of independent opinion or action. **have on one's mind** be troubled by the thought of. **I don't mind if I do** used when accepting something offered. **make up one's mind** decide, resolve. **mind over matter** the power of the mind asserted over the physical universe. **mind one's Ps & Qs** be careful in one's behaviour. **mind the store** have charge of affairs temporarily. **mind you** an expression used to qualify a previous statement (I found it — mind you, it wasn't easy). **never mind 1** an expression used to comfort or console. 2 (also **never you mind**) an expression used to evade a question. 3 not to mention; let alone. **open** (or **close**) **one's mind to** be receptive (or unreceptive) to (changes, new ideas, etc.). **out of one's mind 1** insane. 2 to a great extent (I was bored out of my mind). **not pay a person any mind** N Amer. not pay any attention to a person. **put a person in mind of** remind a person of. **put** (or **set**) **a person's mind at rest** (or **ease**) reassure a person. **put a person or thing out of one's mind**

deliberately forget. **read a person's mind** discern a person's thoughts. **spring to mind** = COME TO MIND. **take a person's mind off** help a person not to think or worry about. **to my mind** in my opinion.

mind-altering adj. (of a drug) hallucinogenic.

mind-bending adj. informal (esp. of a psychedelic drug) influencing or altering one's state of mind.

mind-blowing adj. slang 1 overwhelming, bewildering. 2 (esp. of drugs etc.) inducing hallucinations. □ **mind-blowingly** adv.

mind-boggling adj. informal overwhelming, startling. □ **mind-bogglingly** adv.

mind candy n. N Amer. slang enjoyable but intellectually undemanding entertainment.

minded adj. 1 (in comb.) a inclined to think in some specified way (mathematically minded; fair-minded). b having a specified kind of mind (high-minded). c interested in or enthusiastic about a specified thing (car-minded). 2 (usu. foll. by to + infin.) disposed or inclined (to an action). □ **mindedly** adv. **mindedness** n.

minder n. a person whose job it is to attend to a person or thing (often in comb.: netminder).

mindfuck esp. N Amer. coarse slang ● v.tr. manipulate or disturb (someone) psychologically. ● n. an instance of this. □ **mindfucker** n.

mindful adj. (often foll. by of) taking heed or care; being conscious. □ **mindfully** adv. **mindfulness** n.

mind game n. 1 (usu. in pl.) informal an instance of psychological manipulation. 2 a game designed to test or exercise the intellect.

mindless adj. 1 lacking intelligence; stupid. 2 not requiring thought or skill (totally mindless work). 3 (of an action, condition, thing, etc.) characterized by a lack of thought. 4 (usu. foll. by of) heedless of (advice etc.). □ **mindlessly** adv. **mindlessness** n.

mind-numbing adj. (esp. of tedium) that numbs the mind. □ **mind-numbingly** adv.

mind reader n. a person capable of discerning the thoughts of another. □ **mind reading** n.

mindscape n. reality as imagined in one's mind, and often as portrayed in art.

mindset n. a frame of mind, a mental attitude.

mind's eye n. informal the mind as viewer of memories or things imagined. □ **in one's mind's eye** in one's imagination or mental view.

mine[1] possess.pron. 1 the one or ones belonging to or associated with me (it is mine; mine are over there). 2 (attrib. before a vowel) archaic = MY (mine eyes have seen). □ **of mine** of or belonging to me (a friend of mine).

mine[2] ● n. 1 an excavation in the earth for extracting metal, coal, salt, etc. 2 an abundant source (of information etc.). 3 a receptacle filled with explosive and placed in the ground or in the water for destroying enemy personnel, ships, etc. 4 a subterranean gallery in which explosive is placed to blow up fortifications. ● v.tr. 1 a obtain (metal, coal, etc.) from a mine. 2 tr. & intr. (often foll. by for) dig in (the earth etc.) for ore etc. 3 tr. a dig or burrow in (usu. the earth). b make (a hole, passage, etc.) underground. 4 tr. lay explosive mines under or in. 5 tr. = UNDERMINE. □ **minable** adj.

minefield n. 1 an area planted with explosive mines. 2 a subject or situation presenting unseen hazards.

miner n. 1 a person who works in a mine. 2 any burrowing insect or grub.

mineral ● n. 1 a substance that occurs naturally in the earth and is not formed from animal or vegetable matter. 2 a substance obtained by mining. 3 any of the elements, e.g. calcium, iron, etc., that are essential for good nutrition. ● adj. **1** of or containing a mineral or minerals. **2** obtained by mining.

mineralize v. **1** tr. & intr. change wholly or partly into a mineral. **2** tr. impregnate (water etc.) with a mineral substance. **3** tr. change (a metal) into an ore. □ **mineralization** n.

mineralogy /ˌmɪnəˈrɒlədʒi, -ælədʒi/ n. the scientific study of minerals. □ **mineralogical** adj. **mineralogically** adv. **mineralogist** n.

mineral oil n. a colourless odourless oily liquid obtained from petroleum and used as a lubricant, laxative, etc.

mineral rights n.pl. ownership rights to the minerals located on or below a property.

mineral spirits n.pl. N Amer. a volatile liquid distilled from petroleum and used esp. as a paint thinner.

mineral water n. water found in nature with some dissolved salts present.

mine shaft n. a shaft giving access to a mine.

minestrone /ˌmɪnɪˈstroːni/ n. a soup containing vegetables and pasta, beans, or rice.

minesweeper n. a ship for clearing away floating and submarine mines.

mineworker n. = MINER 1.

Ming n. **1** the Chinese dynasty founded in 1368 after the collapse of Mongol authority in China, and ruling until succeeded by the Manchus in 1644. **2** Chinese porcelain made during this dynasty.

mingle v. (often foll. by with) **1** tr. & intr. mix, blend. **2** intr. socialize, esp. at a party etc. □ **mingle with** go about among. □ **mingler** n.

mingy /ˈmɪndʒi/ adj. (-ier, -iest) informal **1** mean, stingy. **2** small. □ **mingily** adv.

mini n. (pl. **minis**) informal **a** a miniskirt. **b** a garment, e.g. a dress, with a miniskirt. **2** a minicomputer.

mini- comb. form miniature; very small or minor of its kind (minibus; mini-budget).

miniature /ˈmɪnɪtʃər, ˈmɪniətʃər/ ● adj. **1** much smaller than normal. **2** represented on a small scale. ● n. **1** any object reduced in size. **2** a small-scale minutely finished portrait. **3** this branch of painting (portrait in miniature). **4** a picture or decorated letters in an illuminated manuscript. □ **in miniature** on a small scale. □ **miniaturist** n. (in senses 2 and 3 of n.).

miniature golf n. a game patterned on golf, but played on a small obstacle course.

miniaturize v.tr. produce in a smaller version; make small. □ **miniaturization** n.

mini-bar n. a small fridge containing mainly alcoholic drinks and snacks placed in a hotel room for the use of guests, the contents being charged to the bill if used.

mini-blind n. N Amer. a type of venetian blind with narrow slats.

mini-budget n. an interim budget, usu. limited in scope, brought down by a government.

minibus n. a small bus for about twelve passengers.

mini-cam n. a hand-held video camera.

mini-camp n. N Amer. Sport a short training camp, held esp. in addition to the regular training camp, to which players are invited to try out for a team or prepare for the coming season.

minicomputer n. a computer of medium power, more than a microcomputer but less than a mainframe.

Mini Disc n. proprietary a small recordable version of a compact disc.

minigolf n. = MINIATURE GOLF.

minim n. Music = HALF NOTE.

minima pl. of MINIMUM.

minimal adj. **1** as small as possible; minimum. **2** a Art etc. characterized by the use of simple or primary forms or structures etc., often geometric or massive (huge minimal forms in a few colours). **b** Music characterized by the repetition of short phrases which change very gradually as the music proceeds. □ **minimally** adv. (in sense 1).

minimalist ● adj. **1** (esp. of an aesthetic style) constituting or characterized by the minimum required; not elaborate. **2** advocating moderate policies. **3** of or relating to minimal art or music. ● n. **1** (also attrib.) a person advocating minor or moderate reform in politics (opp. MAXIMALIST). **2** a person who advocates or practises minimal art or music. □ **minimalism** n. **minimalistic** adj.

mini-mall n. N Amer. a mall containing a relatively small number of stores etc. and with access to each store from the outdoors rather than from an interior hallway.

mini-mart n. N Amer. = CONVENIENCE STORE.

mini-mill n. a small steel plant, esp. one that produces steel by melting down scrap.

minimize v.tr. **1** reduce to, or estimate at, the smallest possible amount or degree. **2** estimate or represent at less than the true value or importance. □ **minimization** n. **minimizer** n.

minimum (pl. **-s** or **minima**) ● n. **1** the least possible or attainable amount (reduced to a minimum). **2** the lowest amount of a varying quality, e.g. temperature, pressure, etc., attained or recorded within a particular period. ● adj. that is a minimum.

minimum-security adj. (of a correctional institution) having no extraordinary security measures such as perimeter fences, barred windows, etc.

minimum wage n. the lowest wage permitted by law or special agreement.

mining n. the process or industry of removing metals, coal, etc. from a mine.

mining recorder n. Cdn a government official who registers mining claims.

minion /ˈmɪnjən/ n. derogatory a servile follower or attendant.

minipill n. a contraceptive pill containing a progestin only (not estrogen).

mini-putt n. Cdn = MINIATURE GOLF.

miniseries n. a film shown on television in several segments broadcast within a few days of each other.

miniskirt n. a very short skirt. □ **miniskirted** adj.

minister ● n. **1** Parl. (in Canada, the UK, and other Commonwealth countries) a head of a government department. **2** (in full **minister of religion**) a member of the clergy, esp. in some Protestant denominations. **3** a diplomatic agent, usu. ranking below an ambassador. ● v.intr. **1** (usu. foll. by to) render aid or service (to a person, cause, etc.). **2** serve as or perform the functions of a minister of religion (ministered there for 17 years).

ministerial /ˌmɪnɪˈstiːriəl/ adj. **1** of a government minister. **2** of a minister of religion or a minister's office. **3** instrumental or subsidiary in achieving a purpose (ministerial in bringing about a settlement).

ministering angel n. a kind-hearted person, esp. a woman, who nurses or comforts others.

minister of state n. (in Canada) a federal government minister having responsibility for a certain policy area but without direct control over a department established by statute with a dedicated budget. ¶This position was superseded in 1993 by the creation of that of SECRETARY OF STATE.

Minister of the Crown n. (in Canada, the UK, and other Commonwealth countries) a member of the Cabinet.

Minister's Permit n. Cdn a permit issued by a visa or immigration officer that allows a person not otherwise eligible to immigrate to Canada to enter or remain in Canada for a period of up to three years.

minister without portfolio n. a government minister who has Cabinet status, but is not in charge of a specific department or ministry. ¶This position no longer exists in Canada.

ministration /ˌmɪnɪˈstreɪʃən/ n. **1** (usu. in pl.) aid or service (the kind ministrations of her neighbours). **2** ministering, esp. in religious matters. **3** (usu. foll. by of) the supplying (of help, justice, etc.).

ministry n. (pl. **-ies**) **1 a** a government department headed by a minister. **b** the building or buildings which it occupies. **2 a** (prec. by the) the vocation or profession of a religious minister (called to the ministry). **b** the office of a religious minister, priest, etc. **c** the period of tenure of this. **d** a form of Christian service effected by a layperson. **3** (prec. by the) the body of ministers of a government or of a religion. **4** a period of government under one prime minister. **5** ministering, ministration.

minivan n. a small passenger van, usu. having side windows and removable rear seats.

mink n. **1** either of two small semi-aquatic ermine-like animals of the genus *Mustela*, *M. vison* of N America and *M. intreola* of Europe. **2** the thick brown fur of these. **3** a coat made of this.

minke /ˈmɪŋkə/ n. a small baleen whale, *Balaenoptera acutorostrata*, with a pointed snout.

Minn. abbr. Minnesota.

Minnesotan ● n. a native or inhabitant of the US state of Minnesota. ● adj. of or relating to Minnesota.

minnow n. any of various small freshwater fish, esp. of the carp family.

Minoan /mɪˈnoʊ:ən/ ● adj. of or relating to the Bronze Age civilization centred on Crete (c.3000–1100 BC). ● n. **1** an inhabitant of Minoan Crete or the Minoan world. **2** the language or scripts associated with the Minoans.

minor ● adj. **1** lesser or comparatively small in size or importance (minor poet; minor operation). **2** Music **a** (of a scale) having intervals of a semitone between the second and third, fifth and sixth, and seventh and eighth degrees. **b** (of an interval) less by a semitone than a major interval. **c** (of a key) based on a minor scale, tending to produce a melancholy effect. **3** Cdn designating organized amateur team sport for children (minor hockey). ● n. **1** a person under the legal age limit or majority (no unaccompanied minors). **2** Music a minor key etc. **3** N Amer., Austral., & NZ a student's subsidiary subject or course (compare MAJOR 4). **4** Hockey = MINOR PENALTY. **5** (in pl.) N Amer. the minor leagues. ● v.intr. (foll. by in) N Amer., Austral., & NZ (of a student) undertake study in (a subject) as a subsidiary to a main subject. □ **in a minor key** (of novels, events, people's lives, etc.) understated, subdued, often with a melancholy tinge.

minority n. (pl. **-ies**) **1** (often foll. by of) a smaller number or part, esp. within a political party or structure. **2** the state of having less than half the votes or of being supported by less than half of the body of opinion (in the minority). **3 a** (also **minority group**) a relatively small group of people differing from others in the society of which they are a part in race, religion, language, political persuasion, etc. **b** a member of such a group. **4** (attrib.) relating to or done by the minority (minority interests). **5 a** the state of being under full legal age. **b** the period of this.

minority government n. Cdn, Brit., Austral., & NZ a government that has fewer seats in parliament than the total number held by all other parties.

minority leader n. (in the US) the floor leader of the party having a minority in a legislature.

minor league N Amer. ● n. **1** (esp. in hockey and baseball) a league of professional clubs other than the major leagues. **2** Cdn an amateur league for children and youth, esp. in hockey, football, etc. ● adj. (usu. **minor-league**) **1** of or relating to a minor league (set a minor-league record). **2** of inferior quality; small-time. □ **minor-leaguer** n.

minor penalty n. Hockey a two minute penalty given for lesser infractions.

minor planet n. see PLANET 2.

minor prophet n. Bible any of the Hebrew prophets from Hosea to Malachi.

Minotaur /ˈmɪnə.tɔr, ˈmaɪn-/ n. (in Greek mythology) a man with a bull's head, kept in a Cretan labyrinth and fed with human flesh.

minoxidil /mɪˈnɒksɪˌdɪl/ n. a pyrimidine derivative used to treat hypertension, which can also promote hair growth when applied topically.

minstrel /ˈmɪnstrəl/ n. **1** a medieval singer or musician, esp. singing or reciting poetry. **2** hist. a person who entertained patrons with singing, buffoonery, etc.

mint¹ ● n. **1** any aromatic plant of the genus *Mentha*. **2** a mint-flavoured candy. **3** the flavour or scent of mint. ● adj. having the flavour of mint (mint icing). □ **minty** adj. (**-ier**, **-iest**).

mint² ● n. **1** a place where money is coined under governmental control. **2** a vast sum of money (making a mint). **3** a source of invention etc. (a mint of ideas). ● adj. in perfect condition; as new (the bike was in mint condition). ● v.tr. **1** make (coin) by stamping metal. **2** invent, coin (a word, phrase, etc.).

minted¹ adj. flavoured with mint.

minted² adj. recently created (newly minted MBAs).

mint green ● n. a pale pastel green. ● adj. of this colour.

mint julep n. N Amer. a sweet iced alcoholic drink of bourbon flavoured with mint.

Minto Cup n. Cdn a trophy awarded annually to the Canadian junior amateur lacrosse champions.

minuend /ˈmɪnjʊˌend/ n. Math. a quantity or number from which another is to be subtracted.

minuet /ˌmɪnjʊˈet/ n. **1** a slow stately dance for two in triple time, popular esp. in the 17th and 18th c. **2** the music for this, or music in the same rhythm and style, often as a movement in a suite, sonata, or symphony.

minus ● prep. **1** with the subtraction of (7 minus 4 equals 3). Symbol: –. **2** (of temperature) below zero (minus 2°). **3** lacking; deprived of (Stephen returned minus the dog). ● adj. **1** Math. negative. **2** Electronics having a negative charge. **3** (after a grade etc.) of a standard slightly lower than the one stated (got a B minus). ● n. **1** = MINUS SIGN. **2** Math. a negative quantity. **3** a disadvantage.

minuscule /ˈmɪnə.skjuːl/ ● adj. **1** extremely small or unimportant. **2** lower case. ● n. **1** a lower case letter. **2** a kind of cursive script developed in the 7th c.

minus sign n. the symbol –, indicating subtraction or a negative value.

minute¹ ● n. **1** the sixtieth part of an hour. **2** a distance covered in one minute (ten minutes from the *subway*). **3 a** a moment; an instant; a point of time (*Shannon will be home any minute*). **b** a short time (*I'll be there in a minute*; *do you have a minute?*). **c** (prec. by *the*) *informal* the present time (*what are you doing at the minute?*). **d** (foll. by clause) as soon as (*call me the minute you get back*). **4** the sixtieth part of an angular degree. **5** (in *pl.*) a brief summary of the proceedings at a meeting. **6** a note or memorandum authorizing or recommending a course of action. ● *v.tr.* record (proceedings) in the minutes. □ **in a minute 1** very soon (*I'll get up in a minute*). **2** very readily (*she'd marry him in a minute*). **just** (or **wait**) **a minute 1** a request to wait for a short time. **2** as a prelude to a query or objection. **not for a minute** not at all (*I never thought for a minute that you would refuse*).

minute² /maɪˈnjuːt, -nuːt/ *adj.* (**minutest**) **1** very small. **2** trifling, petty. **3** (of an inquiry, inquirer, etc.) accurate, detailed, precise. □ **minutely** *adv.* **minuteness** *n.*

minute hand *n.* the hand on an analog watch or clock which indicates minutes.

Minuteman /ˈmɪnɪtˌmæn/ *n.* (*pl.* **-men**) *US* **1** a type of three-stage intercontinental ballistic missile. **2** *hist.* an American militiaman of the revolutionary period.

minute steak *n.* a thin slice of steak to be cooked quickly, esp. one that has been tenderized.

minutia /mɪˈnuːʃɪə, -juː-, -ʃə, mai-/ *n.* (*pl.* **-iae** /-ʃai, -ʃiə, -ʃə/) (usu. in *pl.*) a precise, trivial, or minor detail.

minx *n.* a mischievous or pert girl. □ **minxish** *adj.*

minyan /ˈmɪnjən, mɪnˈjɒn/ *n.* the quorum of ten males over thirteen years of age required for traditional Jewish public worship.

Miocene /ˈmaɪəˌsiːn/ *Geol.* ● *adj.* of or relating to the fourth epoch of the Tertiary period, between the Oligocene and the Pliocene, lasting from about 24.6 to 5.1 million years ago. ● *n.* this geological epoch.

miosis /maɪˈoːsɪs/ *n.* (also **myosis**) excessive constriction of the pupil of the eye. □ **miotic** /maɪˈɒtɪk/ *adj.*

MIPS /mɪps/ *n.* a unit of computing speed equivalent to a million instructions per second.

miracle *n.* **1** an extraordinary event attributed to some supernatural agency. **2 a** any remarkable occurrence. **b** a remarkable development in some specified area (*an economic miracle*). **3** (usu. foll. by *of*) a remarkable or outstanding specimen (*the plan was a miracle of ingenuity*).

miraculous *adj.* **1** of the nature of a miracle; supernatural. **2** remarkable, surprising. **3** having the power to work miracles. □ **miraculously** *adv.* **miraculousness** *n.*

mirage /mɪˈrɒʒ/ *n.* **1** an optical illusion caused by atmospheric conditions, esp. the appearance of a sheet of water in a desert or on a hot road from the reflection of light. **2** an illusory thing.

Miranda /mɪˈrændə/ *adj.* *US* *Law* designating or pertaining to the duty of the police to inform a person taken into custody of his or her right to legal counsel and the right to remain silent under questioning (*Miranda rights*).

mire ● *n.* **1** a stretch of swampy or boggy ground. **2** wet or soft mud; muck. **3** a difficult situation from which it is difficult to extricate oneself. ● *v.* **1** *tr. & intr.* plunge or sink in a mire. **2** *tr.* (usu. in *passive*) involve in difficulties. □ **miry** *adj.*

mirin /miːˈrɪn/ *n.* a sweet, golden coloured Japanese rice wine, used esp. in cooking.

mirror ● *n.* **1** a polished surface, usu. of amalgam-coated glass or metal, which reflects an image. **2** anything regarded as giving an accurate reflection or

description of something else. ● *v.tr.* reflect as in a mirror.

mirror ball *n.* a large ball covered with small pieces of mirror glass, suspended esp. above dance floors to reflect light in revolving patterns.

mirrored *adj.* **1** fitted with a mirror or mirrors (*a mirrored wall*). **2** having a reflective surface (*mirrored sunglasses*).

mirror image *n.* **1** an identical image, but with the structure reversed, as in a mirror. **2** a phenomenon or occurrence which is identical to another. □ **mirror-image** *adj.*

mirth *n.* merriment, laughter. □ **mirthful** *adj.* **mirthfully** *adv.* **mirthfulness** *n.* **mirthless** *adj.* **mirthlessly** *adv.*

MIS *abbr.* *Computing* management information systems.

mis- *prefix* added to verbs and verbal derivatives: meaning 'amiss', 'badly', 'wrongly', 'unfavourably' (*mislead*; *misshapen*).

misadventure *n.* **1** a misfortune. **2** bad luck. **3** *Law* an accident without concomitant crime or negligence (*death by misadventure*).

misalign *v.tr.* give the wrong alignment to. □ **misaligned** *adj.* **misalignment** *n.*

misanthrope /ˈmɪsənˌθroːp, mɪz-/ *n.* (also **misanthropist** /mɪˈsænθrəpɪst, -ˈzæn-/) **1** a person who hates humans. **2** a person who avoids human society. □ **misanthropic** /-ˈθrɒpɪk/ *adj.* **misanthropy** /mɪˈzænθrəpi/ *n.*

misapply *v.tr.* (**-ies**, **-ied**) apply (a theory, a term, funds, etc.) wrongly. □ **misapplication** *n.*

misapprehend *v.tr.* misunderstand (words, a person). □ **misapprehension** *n.*

misappropriate /ˌmɪsəˈproʊpriˌeɪt/ *v.tr.* apply (usu. another's money) to one's own use or to a wrong use. □ **misappropriation** *n.*

misbegotten *adj.* **1** illegitimate, bastard. **2** contemptible, disreputable.

misbehave *v.intr. & refl.* (of a person, machine, etc.) behave badly. □ **misbehaviour** *n.*

misc. *abbr.* miscellaneous.

miscalculate *v.tr. & intr.* calculate (amounts, results, etc.) wrongly. □ **miscalculation** *n.*

miscarriage *n.* **1** the expulsion of a fetus from the womb before it can survive independently, esp. before the 28th week of pregnancy. **2** the failure of a plan etc. to reach completion.

miscarriage of justice *n.* any failure of the judicial system to attain the ends of justice.

miscarry *v.* (**-ies**, **-ied**) **1 a** *intr.* (of a woman or female animal) have a miscarriage. **b** *tr.* suffer the miscarriage of (a fetus). **2** *tr.* (of a business, plan, etc.) fail, be unsuccessful.

miscast *v.tr.* (*past* and *past part.* **-cast**) assign an unsuitable role to (a performer).

miscegenation /mɪsˈedʒɪˌneɪʃən, ˌmɪsɪdʒɪˈneɪʃən/ *n.* **1** the interbreeding of races, esp. of whites and non-whites. **2** marriage between people of different races.

miscellaneous /ˌmɪsəˈleɪnɪəs/ *adj.* **1** of mixed composition or character. **2** (foll. by *pl. noun*) of various kinds.

miscellany /ˈmɪsəˌleɪni, -ˈseləni/ *n.* (*pl.* **-ies**) **1** a mixture, a medley. **2** a book containing a collection of stories etc., or various literary compositions.

mischief *n.* **1** conduct which is troublesome, but not malicious, esp. in children. **2** pranks, scrapes (*keep out of mischief*). **3** playful malice, archness (*eyes full of mischief*). **4** harm or injury caused by a person or thing. **5** a person or thing responsible for harm or annoyance (*that loose connection is the mischief*). □ **do a person a mischief** wound or kill a person. **get up to** (or **make**) **mischief** create discord.

mischief-maker *n.* a person who encourages discord, esp. by gossip etc. □ **mischief-making** *n.*

mischievous /'mistʃivəs, disputed mis'tʃi:viəs, -'tʃi:vəs/ *adj.* **1** (of a person) disposed to mischief. **2** (of conduct etc.) teasing; playfully malicious. **3** (of a thing) having harmful effects. ¶Although the pronunciation /mis'tʃi:viəs/ is very common, it is not considered standard by many people. Likewise, the spelling *mischevious* is not standard.

miscible /'misibəl/ *adj.* (often foll. by *with*) capable of being mixed. □ **miscibility** *n.*

misconceive *v.* **1** *intr.* (often foll. by *of*) have a wrong idea or conception. **2** *tr.* misunderstand (a word, person, etc.).

misconceived *adj.* badly planned, organized, etc.

misconception *n.* a misunderstanding; a wrong idea.

misconduct ● *n.* **1** improper or unprofessional behaviour. **2** bad management. **3** *Hockey* a penalty, usu. lasting for five minutes or more, called against a player for fighting or arguing with the referee etc. (*game misconduct*). ● *v. tr.* mismanage.

misconstrue *v.tr.* (**-construes, -construed, -construing**) **1** interpret (a word, action, etc.) wrongly. **2** mistake the meaning of (a person). □ **misconstruction** *n.*

miscount ● *v.tr. & intr.* count wrongly. ● *n.* a wrong count.

miscreant /'miskriənt/ ● *n.* an immoral or criminal person. ● *adj.* depraved, villainous.

miscue ● *n.* **1** an error or blunder. **2** (in pool etc.) the failure to strike the ball properly with the cue. ● *v.intr.* (**-cues, -cued, -cueing** or **-cuing**) make a miscue.

misdeal ● *v.tr. & intr.* (*past* and *past part.* **-dealt**) make a mistake in dealing (cards). ● *n.* **1** a mistake in dealing cards. **2** a misdealt hand.

misdeed *n.* an evil deed, a wrongdoing; a crime.

misdemeanour /,misdə'mi:nər/ *n.* (also **misdemeanor**) **1** a minor wrongdoing. **2** *Law* a minor criminal offence, esp. (in the US) one less serious than a felony. ¶Not used in Canadian law.

misdiagnose *v.tr.* diagnose incorrectly. □ **misdiagnosis** *n.*

misdial *v.tr. & intr.* (**-dialed, -dialing**) dial (a telephone number etc.) incorrectly.

misdirect *v.tr.* **1** direct (a person, letter, blow, etc.) wrongly. **2** (of a judge) instruct (the jury) wrongly. □ **misdirection** *n.*

misdirected *adj.* **1** sent in the wrong direction (*a misdirected pass*). **2** used or applied wrongly or inappropriately (*misdirected energies*). **3** undeserved by its target or victim (*misdirected anger*).

mise en scène /,mi:z ã 'sen/ *n.* **1** *Theatre* **a** the scenery and properties of a play. **b** the way in which these are arranged. **2** *Film* the disposition of all the visual elements in a frame. **3** the setting or surroundings of an event.

miser *n.* **1** a person who hoards wealth and lives miserably. **2** an avaricious person.

miserable *adj.* **1** wretchedly unhappy or uncomfortable (*felt miserable*). **2** contemptible, mean. **3** causing wretchedness or discomfort (*miserable weather*). **4** *informal* (of a person) gloomy, morose. □ **miserableness** *n.* **miserably** *adv.*

miserly *adj.* like a miser, stingy. □ **miserliness** *n.*

misery *n.* (*pl.* **-ies**) **1** great discomfort of mind or body. **2** a thing causing this. □ **put out of its** etc. **misery 1** release (a person, animal, etc.) from suffering or suspense. **2** kill (an animal in pain).

misfire ● *v.intr.* **1** (of a gun, motor engine, etc.) fail to go off or start or function regularly. **2** (of an action etc.) fail to have the intended effect. ● *n.* a failure of function or intention.

misfit *n.* **1** a person unsuited to a particular kind of environment, occupation, etc. **2** something that does not fit or suit well.

misfortune *n.* **1** bad luck. **2** an instance of this.

misgiving *n.* (usu. in *pl.*) a feeling of mistrust or apprehension.

misguide *v.tr.* mislead, misdirect. □ **misguidance** *n.*

misguided *adj.* mistaken in thought or action (*a misguided attempt to rescue the hostages*). □ **misguidedly** *adv.* **misguidedness** *n.*

mishandle *v.tr.* **1** deal with incorrectly or ineffectively. **2** handle (a person or thing) roughly or rudely; ill-treat.

mishap *n.* an unlucky accident.

mishear *v.tr.* (*past* and *past part.* **-heard**) hear incorrectly or imperfectly.

mis-hit ● *v.tr.* (**-hitting**; *past* and *past part.* **-hit**) hit (a ball etc.) faultily. ● *n.* a faulty or bad hit.

mishmash *n.* a confused mixture.

Mishnah /'mɪʃnə/ *n.* an authoritative collection of exegetical material embodying the oral tradition of Jewish law, which forms the first part of the Talmud.

misidentify *v.tr.* (**-ies, -ied**) identify erroneously. □ **misidentification** *n.*

misinform *v.tr.* give wrong information to, mislead. □ **misinformation** *n.*

misinformed *adj.* **1** (of a person) incorrectly informed; having an incorrect or imperfect knowledge of or acquaintance with the facts. **2** (of an argument etc.) based on incorrect information.

misinterpret *v.tr.* (**-interpreted, -interpreting**) interpret wrongly; draw a wrong inference from. □ **misinterpretation** *n.* **misinterpreter** *n.*

misjudge *v.tr. & intr.* **1** judge wrongly. **2** have a wrong opinion of. □ **misjudgment** *n.* (also **misjudgement**)

mislabel *v.tr.* (**-labelled, -labelling**) **1** attach an incorrect label to. **2** describe or designate wrongly.

mislay *v.tr.* (*past* and *past part.* **-laid**) **1** unintentionally put (a thing) where it cannot readily be found. **2** lose.

mislead *v.tr.* (*past* and *past part.* **-led**) cause (a person) to have a wrong idea or im-pression about something. □ **misleader** *n.*

misleading *adj.* giving the wrong idea or impression. □ **misleadingly** *adv.* **misleadingness** *n.*

mismanage *v.tr.* manage badly or dishonestly. □ **mismanagement** *n.*

mismatch ● *v.tr.* match unsuitably or incorrectly. ● *n.* a bad match.

misname *v.tr.* call by a wrong or inappropriate name.

misnomer /mis'no:mər/ *n.* **1** a name or term used wrongly. **2** the wrong use of a name or term.

miso /'mi:so:/ *n.* a paste made from fermented soybeans and barley or rice malt, used in Japanese cooking.

misogyny /mi'sɒdʒini/ *n.* the hatred of women. □ **misogynist** *n.* **misogynistic** *adj.* **misogynous** *adj.*

misperception *n.* a wrong or incorrect perception.

misplace *v.tr.* (usu. as **misplaced** *adj.*) **1** put in the wrong place. **2** bestow (affections, confidence, etc.) on an inappropriate object.

misplaced modifier *n.* a word, phrase, or clause

which is intended to modify a noun or pronoun but is placed in an ambiguous grammatical relationship to it, e.g. *as a single woman, he found her very interesting*.

misplay ● *v.tr.* play (a ball, card, etc.) in a wrong or ineffective manner. ● *n.* an instance of this.

misprint ● *n.* a mistake in printing. ● *v.tr.* print wrongly.

mispronounce *v.tr.* pronounce (a word etc.) wrongly. □ **mispronunciation** *n.*

misquote *v.tr.* quote wrongly.

misread *v.tr.* (*past* and *past part.* **-read** /-'red/) read or interpret (text, a situation, etc.) wrongly. □ **misreading** *n.*

misrepresent *v.tr.* represent wrongly; give a false or misleading account of. □ **misrepresentation** *n.*

misrule ● *n.* **1** bad government. **2** disorder. ● *v.tr.* govern badly.

Miss. *abbr.* Mississippi.

miss¹ ● *v.* **1** *tr. & intr.* fail to hit, reach, find, capture, etc. (an object or goal). **2** *tr.* fail to catch (a bus, train, etc.). **3** *tr.* fail to experience, see, or attend (an occurrence or event). **4** *tr.* fail to meet (a person), keep (an appointment), etc. **5** *tr.* fail to take advantage of (an opportunity etc.) (*I missed my chance*). **6** *tr.* fail to hear, observe, or understand (*I'm sorry, I missed what you said*). **7** *tr.* **a** regret the loss or absence of (a person or thing) (*did you miss me while I was away?*). **b** notice the loss or absence of (an object) (*bound to miss the key if it isn't there*). **8** *tr.* avoid (*go early to miss the traffic*). **9** (often foll. by *out*) **a** *tr.* omit, leave out (*you missed my name*). **b** *tr. & intr.* fail to get or experience (*missed out on the fun*). **10** *intr.* (of an engine etc.) fail, misfire. **11** *tr.* fail to take (medication, food, etc.), either intentionally or unintentionally. **12** *intr.* fail (*you can't miss if you serve chicken*). ● *n.* a failure to hit, reach, attain, connect, etc. □ **be missing** not have (see also MISSING *adj.*). **give** (**a thing**) **a miss** avoid, leave alone (*gave the party a miss*). **miss a beat** (usu. with *neg.*) hesitate in making a transition from one activity to another or in conversation (*she carried on without missing a beat*). **miss the boat 1** lose an opportunity. **2** fail to understand the point. **a miss is as good as a mile** the fact of failure, escape, or success is not affected by the narrowness of the margin. **not miss much** be alert. **not miss a trick** never fail to seize an opportunity, advantage, etc. □ **missable** *adj.*

miss² *n.* **1** (**Miss**) **a** a title for an unmarried woman or girl without a higher, honorific, or professional title. **b** the title of a married woman retaining her maiden name for professional purposes. **2 a** the title of a young woman representing a country, group, etc., esp. in a beauty contest (*Miss Canada*). **b** *ironic* or *jocular* a mock title of a young woman supposedly personifying a particular state, condition, etc. (*little Miss Innocent*). **3 a** a girl or unmarried woman. **b** usu. *derogatory* or *jocular* a girl, esp. a schoolgirl, with implications of silliness etc. **4** used as a term of address to a waitress, female schoolteacher, sales clerk, etc. **5** *N Amer.* (in *pl.*) = MISSY 1.

missal /'misəl/ *n. Catholicism* **1** a book containing the texts used in the service of the Mass throughout the year. **2** a book of prayers, esp. an illuminated one.

misshape *v.tr.* give a bad, ugly, or wrong shape or form to; distort.

misshapen *adj.* ill-shaped, deformed, distorted. □ **misshapenly** *adv.* **misshapenness** *n.*

missile /'misəl, 'misail/ *n.* **1** a destructive, self-propelling projectile, esp. a nuclear weapon, that is directed automatically or by remote control. **2** an object or

weapon suitable for throwing at a target or discharging from a machine.

missing *adj.* **1** not in its place; lost. **2** not present, absent. **3** (of a person) not yet traced or confirmed as alive but not known to be dead.

missing link *n.* **1** a thing lacking to complete a series. **2** a hypothetical intermediate animal assumed to be an evolutionary link between humans and apes.

mission ● *n.* **1 a** a particular task or goal assigned to a person or group. **b** a journey with a purpose. **c** a person's duty, vocation, or work, esp. that enthusiastically accepted or assumed (*mission in life*). **2 a** a military or scientific operation or expedition for a particular purpose. **b** the dispatch of an aircraft or spacecraft on an operational flight. **3 a** a body of persons sent, esp. to a foreign country, to conduct negotiations, establish political or commercial relations, etc. **b** *US* a permanent diplomatic establishment, embassy, or legation. **4 a** members of a religious organization sent to propagate their faith abroad. **b** a field of missionary activity. **c** a missionary post or organization. **d** a place of worship attached to a mission. **e** a body of people established to do missionary, evangelical, or humanitarian work in their own country, esp. among the poor or disadvantaged. **f** (in *pl.*) organized missionary activities (*world missions*). **5** a particular, usu. intensive, course or period of preaching, services, etc., undertaken to stimulate interest in the work of a parish, a community, the faith, etc. **6** (often **Mission**) *N Amer.* (*attrib.*) (of furniture) of a plain, solid style modelled originally on the furniture of Spanish missions in N America. ● *v.tr.* (usu. in *passive*) send on a mission; give (a person) a mission to perform.

missionary ● *adj.* **1** of, concerned with, or characteristic of, religious missions. **2** characteristic of a person engaged in a religious mission (*missionary zeal*). ● *n.* (*pl.* **-ies**) a person doing missionary work.

mission boat *n. Cdn* (*BC*) *hist.* a vessel carrying spiritual and medical services to isolated villages on coastal inlets, inland rivers, etc.

mission control *n.* a group or organization responsible for directing a spacecraft and its crew.

mission statement *n.* a declaration made by a company etc. of its general principles of operation.

missis *var. of* MISSUS.

Mississauga /ˌmɪsɪ'sɒgə/ *n.* (*pl.* same or **-s**) **1** a member of an Ojibwa Aboriginal people living in S Ontario. **2** the Algonquian language of this people.

Mississippian /mɪsɪ'sɪpiən/ ● *n.* **1** a native or resident of the US state of Mississippi. **2** *Geol.* **a** the Mississipian period. **b** the system of rocks dating from this time. ● *adj.* **1** of or pertaining to the state of Mississippi or its inhabitants. **2** designating or pertaining to the period of the Paleozoic era in N America following the Devonian and preceding the Pennsylvanian, from about 360 to 320 million years BP. **3** designating a culture which flourished in the Mississippi basin from about AD 800 until the arrival of the Europeans, based on intensive agriculture, esp. of corn, and characterized by large towns in river valleys.

missive /'mɪsɪv/ *n.* **1** an esp. official letter. **2** *jocular* a letter, esp. a long and serious one.

Missourian /mɪ'zɔriən/ ● *n.* a native or inhabitant of the US state of Missouri. ● *adj.* of or relating to Missouri.

misspell *v.tr.* (*past* and *past part.* **-spelled** or **-spelt**) spell wrongly. □ **misspelled** *adj.* **misspelling** *n.*

misspend v.tr. (past and past part. **-spent**) spend amiss or wastefully.

misspent adj. wastefully or irresponsibly spent, passed, etc. (misspent money; misspent youth).

misstate v.tr. state wrongly or inaccurately. □ **misstatement** n.

misstep n. an inappropriate or clumsy action.

missus n. **1** a form of address to a woman. **2** slang or jocular a wife. □ **the missus** the wife of the person speaking, addressed, or referred to.

missy n. (pl. **-ies**) **1** N Amer. (also **misses'**) a standard size of clothing designed for well-proportioned and well-developed women, usu. around 5 feet 6 inches. **2** an affectionate or derogatory form of address to a young girl.

mist ● n. **1 a** a diffuse cloud of water droplets on or near the ground that limits visibility, but to a lesser degree than fog. **b** any condensed vapour settling in fine droplets on a surface and obscuring glass etc. **2** dimness or blurring of the sight caused by tears etc. **3 a** a diffuse cloud of small particles resembling mist. **b** a haze or haziness produced by distance, time, etc. (lost in the mists of time). ● v. **1** tr. & intr. (usu. foll. by up, over) cover or become covered with mist or as with mist. **2** tr. spray (a plant, one's hair, etc.) with vaporized moisture.

mistake ● n. **1 a** a misconception about the meaning of something; an incorrect idea or opinion. **b** a thing incorrectly done or thought. **2** an error of judgment. ● v.tr. (past **mistook**; past part. **mistaken**) **1** misunderstand the meaning or intention of (a person, a statement, etc.). **2** (foll. by for) wrongly take or identify (mistook me for you). **3** choose wrongly (mistake one's vocation). □ **and** (or **make**) **no mistake** informal undoubtedly; have no doubt about. **by mistake** accidentally; in error. **there is no mistaking** one is sure to recognize (a person or thing).

mistaken adj. **1** wrong in opinion or judgment. **2** based on or resulting from an error, misapprehension, etc. (mistaken identity). □ **mistakenly** adv.

Mistassini Cree /ˌmɪstəˈsiːni/ n. a member of a Cree people living on the shores of Lac Mistassini in north central Quebec.

mister¹ n. **1** = MR. **2** slang or jocular a form of address to an adult male stranger.

mister² n. device for producing or dispensing mist, esp. for misting plants, hair, etc.

mistime v.tr. say or do at the wrong time. □ **mistiming** n.

mistletoe n. **1** a parasitic plant, Viscum album, growing on apple and other trees and bearing white glutinous berries in winter. **2** a similar plant, Phoradendron flavescens, native to N America.

mistranslate v.tr. translate incorrectly. □ **mistranslation** n.

mistreat v.tr. treat wrongly, badly, or abusively. □ **mistreatment** n.

mistress n. **1** a woman (other than his wife) with whom a married man has a (usu. prolonged) sexual relationship. **2** (often foll. by of) a woman with power to control, use, or dispose of something at will (mistress of the situation). **3** a female head of a household. **4 a** a woman in authority over others. **b** the female owner of a pet. **5** literary a woman loved and courted by a man.

mistrial n. **1** a trial rendered invalid through some error in the proceedings. **2** US a trial in which the jury cannot agree on a verdict.

mistrust ● v.tr. **1** be suspicious of; doubt the truth, validity, or genuineness of. **2** feel no confidence in (a person, oneself, one's powers, etc.). ● n. **1** suspicion. **2** lack of confidence.

mistrustful adj. **1** (foll. by of) distrustful, suspicious. **2** lacking confidence or trust. □ **mistrustfully** adv.

misty adj. (**-ier**, **-iest**) **1 a** clouded, obscured, or accompanied by mist. **b** consisting of or covered with mist or fine particles resembling mist. **2** indistinct or dim in outline. **3** obscure, vague. □ **mistily** adv. **mistiness** n.

misty-eyed adj. **1** emotional; sentimental, maudlin. **2** having eyes blurred by tears.

mistype v.tr. type wrongly.

misunderstand v.tr. (past and past part. **-understood**) fail to understand correctly.

misunderstanding n. **1** a failure to understand correctly. **2** a slight disagreement or quarrel.

misunderstood adj. **1** (of word, actions, etc.) misinterpreted. **2** (of a person) unappreciated, not valued sympathetically.

misuse ● v.tr. **1** use wrongly or improperly; apply to the wrong purpose. **2** subject to ill-treatment; maltreat. ● n. **1 a** wrong or improper use or application of power, a word, etc. **b** the non-therapeutic use of a drug. **2** an instance of misuse. □ **misuser** n.

mite¹ n. **1** any small arachnid of the order Acarina, having four pairs of legs when adult. **2** N Amer. **a** an initiation level of sports competition for young children, usu. between the ages of 5 and 8. **b** a player at this level.

mite² ● adv. (usu. prec. by a) informal somewhat (is a mite shy). ● n. **1** a small object or person, esp. a child. **2** a modest contribution; the best one can do (offered my mite of comfort). **3** any small monetary unit.

miter esp. US var. of MITRE.

mitigate /ˈmɪtɪˌgeɪt/ v.tr. make milder or less intense or severe; moderate or give relief from (how can we mitigate the suffering?). ¶Care should be taken not to confuse mitigate 'make less intense or severe' with militate 'have force or effect' as is often done in the phrase mitigate against, which attracts criticism. □ **mitigation** n.

mitigating circumstances n. Law extenuating circumstances which, while not excusing a crime etc., permit greater leniency in sentencing or imposing penalties.

mitochondrion /ˌmaɪtəˈkɒndrɪən/ n. (pl. **-dria** /-drɪə/) Biol. an organelle found in most eukaryotic cells, containing enzymes for respiration and energy production. □ **mitochondrial** adj.

mitosis /mɪˈtoʊsɪs, maɪ-/ n. a type of cell division that results in two daughter cells each having the same number and kind of chromosomes as the parent nucleus (compare MEIOSIS).

mitre /ˈmaɪtər/ (also esp. US **miter**) ● n. **1** a tall, deeply-cleft headdress worn by bishops and abbots, forming in outline the shape of a pointed arch. **2 a** (in full **mitre joint**) the joint of two pieces of wood or other material at an angle of 90°, such that the line of junction bisects this angle. **b** either of the shaped ends or edges which form such a joint. **c** a 45° angle such as these ends or edges have. **3** a diagonal join of two pieces of fabric that meet at a corner, made by folding. ● v. **1 a** tr. & intr. join with a mitre or mitre joint. **b** tr. make a mitre joint in. **c** tr. cut or shape to a mitre. **2** tr. bestow or confer a mitre on (a bishop or abbot). □ **mitred** adj.

mitre box n. a block or frame of wood with slits for guiding a saw when cutting mitre joints.

mitt n. **1** a covering for the hand with two sections, one for the thumb and the other for all four fingers.

2 *Baseball* a protective glove worn by the catcher or first baseman for catching the ball. **3** *N Amer.* a padded cloth mitten worn as protection from heat etc. (*oven mitt*). **4** *slang* a hand or fist. **5** *slang* (in *pl.*) boxing gloves.

mitten *n.* **1** = MITT 1. **2** a glove leaving the tips of the fingers and thumb exposed. □ **mittened** *adj.*

mitzvah /ˈmɪtsvɑ/ *n.* (*pl.* **mitzvoth** /-vɒt/) *Judaism* **1** a a precept or commandment. **b** a religious obligation. **2** a good deed or considerate act.

-miut /ˈmiːʊt/ *suffix* meaning 'the people of' designating subgroups of the Inuit (*Sadlermiut*).

mix ● *v.* **1** *tr.* **a** combine or put together (two or more substances or things) so that the constituents of each are diffused among those of the other(s). **b** combine or blend (different principles, qualities, etc.). **2** *tr.* prepare (a cocktail etc.) by combining various ingredients. **3** *tr.* combine an activity etc. with another simultaneously (*mix business and pleasure*). **4** *intr.* **a** join, be mixed, or combine, esp. readily (*oil and water will not mix*). **b** be compatible. **c** be sociable, esp. at a party. **5** *intr.* **a** (foll. by *with*) (of a person) be harmonious or sociable with; have regular dealings with. **b** (foll. by *in*) participate in. **6** *tr.* drink different kinds of (alcoholic liquor) in close succession. **7** *Film* **a** *tr.* blend (two pictures or sounds) temporarily by fading one out as the other is faded in. **b** *tr.* combine (two or more sound signals) into one, with or without modulation, in a mixer. **c** *intr.* (foll. by *from*, *to*) pass from one picture or sound to another by fading one out as the other is faded in. **8** *tr.* produce (a recording) by combining a number of separate recordings or soundtracks. **9** *tr.* (foll. by *down*) convert (a multi-track sound recording or multiple signal) to one consisting of fewer tracks or a single signal. **10** *tr. & intr.* crossbreed (animals etc.). ● *n.* **1** the result of mixing or combining, esp. disparate elements; a mixture. **2 a** a number of ingredients mixed together (*trail mix*). **b** the proportion or combination of different components that make up a product, plan, policy, or other integrated whole. **3** a group of persons or things of different types (*a mix of housing types*). **4** a commercially prepared mixture of ingredients for making a cake etc., or for a process such as making concrete. **5 a** the action or process of combining or merging film pictures or soundtracks. **b** a transition between two pictures or sounds in which one fades out as the other fades in; a dissolve. **6** *Music* **a** a version of a recording in which the component tracks are mixed in a different way. **b** a recording made by mixing other recordings. **7** the soft drink, fruit juice, etc. with which an alcoholic drink is diluted. **8** a crossbred animal (*a Labrador-collie mix*). □ **be** (or **get**) **mixed up in** be or become involved in (esp. something undesirable). **be** (or **get**) **mixed up with** be or become associated with (esp. someone dishonest). **mix in 1** combine, blend. **2** (of a person) blend sociably or harmoniously with a group. **mix and match** select from a range of alternative combinations. **mix it up** *informal* **1** fight, argue; cause trouble. **2** interact vigorously, boisterously, or roughly. **mix up 1** mix thoroughly. **2** confuse; mistake the identity of. □ **mixable** *adj.*

mix-and-match ● *adj.* **1** suitable for or selected by mixing and matching. **2** complementary, coordinating; assorted. ● *n.* **1** an instance of mixing and matching. **2** a combination of complementary or coordinating items.

mixed *adj.* **1 a** consisting of diverse qualities or elements. **b** formed by mingling, blending, or combining different substances, individuals, etc. **2** containing persons from various backgrounds etc. **3** for or involving persons of both sexes (*mixed curling*). **4** (of wooded land) consisting of several species of trees. **5 a** (of reactions, reviews, results, etc.) having both negative and positive aspects. **b** (of a message, a signal, etc.) ambiguous, unclear.

mixed bag *n.* a diverse assortment of things or persons.

mixed blessing *n.* a thing having advantages and disadvantages.

mixed-blood ● *adj.* (of a person) having parents or ancestors from two or more races. ● *n.* (**mixed blood**) a person having parents or ancestors from two or more races.

mixed breed *n.* a crossbreed.

mixed doubles *n.pl. Tennis* a doubles game with a man and a woman as partners on each side.

mixed drink *n.* an alcoholic beverage consisting of several ingredients, usu. liquor with fruit juice or a soft drink etc.

mixed economy *n.* an economic system combining private and government enterprise.

mixed farming *n.* farming of both crops and livestock. □ **mixed farm** *n.* **mixed-farm** *attrib.adj.*

mixed feelings *n.pl.* (also **mixed emotions**) a mixture of pleasure and dismay about something.

mixed grass *n.* (hyphenated when *attrib.*) grass combining a variety of species, esp. blue grama and wheat grass (*mixed-grass prairie*).

mixed marriage *n.* a marriage between persons of different races or religions.

mixed media ● *n.* the use of a variety of mediums in a work of art, public performance, show, etc. ● *attrib.adj.* (also **mixed-media**) = MULTIMEDIA *adj.*

mixed metaphor *n.* a combination of inconsistent metaphors, e.g. *this tower of strength will forge ahead*.

mixed race *adj.* = MIXED-BLOOD *adj.*

mixed-up *adj. informal* **1** mentally or emotionally confused. **2** socially ill-adjusted.

mixed-use *adj.* (of a building, development, etc.) designed to accommodate diverse functions, usu. including residential units, work places, public areas, etc.

mixer *n.* **1 a** a kitchen appliance for mixing or beating foods, usu. one with two rotating beaters. **b** a machine or device for mixing or processing other materials. **2 a** a person who manages socially in a specified way (*a good mixer*). **b** *N Amer.* a social gathering to enable people to get to know one another. **3** = MIX *n.* 7. **4 a** a device for merging input signals to produce a combined output in the form of sound or pictures. **b** a person who operates this.

Mixmaster *n.* **1** *proprietary* a type of electric food mixer. **2** a person or thing constantly on the move.

mixture *n.* **1** the result of mixing; something mixed; a combination. **2** *Chem.* the product of the mechanical mixing of substances without chemical change, as opposed to a chemical compound. **3** a medicinal or other preparation consisting of two or more ingredients mixed together, esp. a liquid medicine as opposed to pills, powders, etc. (*cough mixture*). **4 a** gas, vaporized gasoline, or oil mixed with air, forming an explosive charge in an internal combustion engine. **b** a combination of gasoline with a small proportion of oil, used as a fuel and lubricant in some two-stroke engines. **5** the process of mixing or being mixed.

mix-up *n.* a confusion, misunderstanding, or mistake.

mizzen *n.* (also **mizen**) *Naut.* (in full **mizzen-sail**) the lowest fore-and-aft sail of a fully rigged ship's mizzen-mast.

mizzen-mast *n.* the mast next aft of the mainmast on a sailing ship.

Mk. *abbr.* **1** the German mark. **2** (also **Mk**) mark (*the Mk III version*).

mks *abbr.* metre-kilogram-second.

ml *abbr.* **1** (also **mL**) millilitre(s). **2** mile(s).

MLA *abbr.* **1** *Cdn & Ind.* Member of the Legislative Assembly. **2** Modern Language Association (of America). **3** (**M.L.A.**) Master of Landscape Architecture.

MLD *abbr.* minimum lethal dose.

M.L.I.S. *abbr.* Master of Library and Information Studies.

M.Litt. *abbr.* Master of Letters.

Mlle *abbr.* (*pl.* **Mlles**) Mademoiselle.

MLS *abbr.* **1** = MULTIPLE LISTING SERVICE. **2** (**M.L.S.**) Master of Library Sciences. **3** *Aviation* microwave landing system.

MM *abbr.* **1** Messieurs. **2** *Cdn & Brit.* Military Medal.

mm *abbr.* millimetre(s).

M.Math. *abbr.* Master of Mathematics.

Mme *abbr.* (*pl.* **Mmes**) Madame.

m.m.f. *abbr.* magnetomotive force.

MMM *abbr.* *Cdn* Member of the Order of Military Merit.

mmm *interj.* expressing hesitation or inarticulate interrogation, assent, reflection, or satisfaction.

MMR *abbr.* measles, mumps, and rubella (vaccine).

MMT *abbr.* methylcyclopentadienyl manganese tricarbonyl, an octane-boosting gasoline additive.

M.Mus. *abbr.* Master of Music

MN *abbr.* **1** Minnesota (in postal use). **2** (**M.N.**) Master of Nursing.

Mn *symbol* the element manganese.

MNA *abbr.* *Cdn* (in Quebec) Member of the National Assembly.

mnemonic /nɪˈmɒnɪk/ ● *adj.* **1** of or designed to aid the memory. **2** of or pertaining to mnemonics. **3** (of a formula, code, etc.) easy to remember or understand. ● *n.* a mnemonic device, formula, or code. □ **mnemonically** *adv.*

mnemonics *n.pl.* (usu. treated as *sing.*) **1** the art of improving memory, esp. by artificial aids. **2** a system of precepts and rules intended to aid the memory.

MO *abbr.* **1** Missouri (in official postal use). **2** = MODUS OPERANDI. **3** Medical Officer. **4** money order.

Mo *symbol* molybdenum.

Mo. *abbr.* Missouri.

mo. *abbr.* *N Amer.* month.

moa /ˈmoʊə/ *n.* (*pl.* **moas**) any extinct flightless New Zealand bird of the family Dinornithidae, resembling the ostrich.

moan ● *n.* **1** a long, low mournful sound expressing physical or mental suffering etc. **2** a low plaintive sound made by wind etc. **3** a complaint or grievance. ● *v.* **1** *intr.* make a moan. **2** *intr. informal* complain or grumble. **3** *tr.* utter with moans. □ **moaner** *n.*

moat ● *n.* a deep defensive ditch around a castle, town, etc., usu. filled with water. ● *v.tr.* surround with or as with a moat.

mob ● *n.* **1 a** a disorderly crowd; a rabble. **b** an assembly of people; a crowd or group. **2** (prec. by *the*) usu. *derogatory* the ordinary people; the populace. **3** (**the Mob**) *informal* the Mafia or a similar criminal organization. ● *v.* (**mobbed, mobbing**) **1** *tr.* **a** crowd round in order to attack or admire. **b** (of a mob) attack. **c** *N Amer.* crowd into (a building). **2** *intr.* assemble in a mob.

mobile /ˈmoʊbail/ ● *adj.* (also /ˈmoʊbəl/) **1 a** movable; not fixed; free or able to move or flow easily. **b** (of troops, police patrols, etc.) that may be easily and rapidly moved from place to place. **2 a** (of a person) able to move into different social levels or change environments, fields of employment, etc. **b** (of a society) not rigidly stratified, able to accommodate social or professional movement. **3** (of the face etc.) readily changing its expression. **4** (of a service, library, etc.) accommodated in a vehicle so as to serve various places. ● *n.* a decorative structure, usu. consisting of pieces of metal, plastic, etc., hung so as to turn freely. □ **mobility** /məˈbɪlɪti/ *n.*

Mobile Command *n.* *Cdn* the division of the Armed Forces encompassing all combat-ready land forces, including land reserves.

mobile home *n.* a large, transportable structure equipped with living accommodations, permanently parked, and used as a residence.

mobile phone *n.* (also **mobile telephone**) = CELLULAR TELEPHONE.

mobilize *v.* **1 a** *tr.* organize or make ready for service or action (originally troops in time of war). **b** *intr.* be organized or made ready for action. **2** *tr.* render movable or capable of movement; bring into circulation. □ **mobilization** *n.* **mobilizer** *n.*

Möbius strip /ˈmɜːbiəs, moː-/ *n.* (also **Möbius loop**) **1** *Math.* a surface with only one side and one edge, formed by twisting a long, narrow, rectangular strip through 180° and joining the ends. **2** a stylized version of this used as a symbol for recycling etc.

mob rule *n.* rule imposed and enforced by a mob.

mobster *n.* *slang* a gangster.

moccasin *n.* **1 a** a type of soft leather slipper or shoe with combined sole and heel, as originally worn by some N American Aboriginal peoples. **2** a hard-soled shoe with a low heel resembling this. **3** *N Amer.* a venomous N American snake of the genus *Agkistrodon*, esp. (also **water moccasin**) the semi-aquatic *A. piscivorus* of the southern US. □ **moccasined** *adj.*

moccasin flower *n.* = LADY'S SLIPPER.

moccasin telegraph *n.* esp. *Cdn* (esp. *North*) *informal* **1** a means of transmitting rumours or unofficial information by word of mouth; the grapevine. **2** information so relayed.

mocha /ˈmoʊkə/ *n.* **1** a coffee of fine quality. **2** a flavouring made from this, often with chocolate added, used in cakes etc. **3** a dark brown colour as that of mocha coffee.

mochaccino /ˌmoʊkəˈtʃiːnoʊ/ *n.* a cappuccino flavoured with chocolate syrup.

mock ● *v.* **1 a** *tr.* ridicule; scoff at. **b** *intr.* (foll. by *at*) act or speak with scorn or contempt for; use ridicule. **2** *tr.* mimic contemptuously. **3** *tr.* jeer or defy contemptuously. ● *attrib.adj.* **1** sham, imitation (esp. without intention to deceive). **2** pretended, fake (*a mock battle*; *mock chicken*). □ **mockable** *adj.* **mocker** *n.* **mocking** *adj.* **mockingly** *adv.*

mockery *n.* (*pl.* **-ies**) **1** a derision, ridicule. **b** a subject or occasion of this. **2** (often foll. by *of*) a counterfeit or absurdly inadequate representation. **3 a** a ludicrously futile action. **b** something insultingly unfitting. □ **make a mockery of something** make something appear foolish or worthless.

mock-heroic ● *adj.* (of a literary style) burlesquing a heroic style. ● *n.* such a style.

mockingbird *n.* a bird that mimics the notes of

other birds, esp. the American songbird *Mimus polyglottos*.

mock orange *n.* any of various white-flowered, heavy-scented shrubs, esp. *Philadelphus coronarius*.

mocktail *n. N Amer.* a drink consisting of the same mixes etc. as the various cocktail recipes and usu. served in the same glasses, but without the spirits.

mock turtle soup *n.* soup made from a calf's head etc. to resemble turtle soup.

mock-up *n.* an experimental model or replica of a proposed structure, page layout, etc.

mod[1] *adj.* modern, esp. in style of dress.

mod[2] *n.* (in Scotland, Cape Breton, etc.) an event at which Gaelic music, poetry, and dancing are performed, often with a competitive element.

modal /'mo:dəl/ ● *adj.* **1** of or relating to mode or form as opposed to substance. **2** *Grammar* **a** of or denoting the mood of a verb. **b** (of an auxiliary verb, e.g. *would*) used to express the mood of another verb. **3** *Statistics* **a** of, pertaining to, or of the nature of a mode. **b** (of a value etc.) occurring most frequently in a sample or population. **4** *Music* denoting a style of music using a particular mode. **5** *Logic* **a** (of a proposition) in which the predicate is affirmed of the subject with some qualification, or which involves the affirmation of possibility, impossibility, necessity, or contingency. **b** (of an argument) containing a modal proposition as a premise. ● *n.* **1** *Grammar* a modal verb. **2** *Logic* a modal proposition. □ **modally** *adv.*

modality /mo'dælıti/ *n. (pl.* **-ies**) **1 a** the state of being modal. **b** a modal quality or circumstance. **2** (in *sing.* or *pl.*) a prescribed method or technique of procedure, treatment, behaviour, etc.

mode *n.* **1** a way or manner in which a thing is done; a method of procedure. **2** a prevailing fashion, custom, or style, esp. of a particular place or period. **3 a** any of a number of distinct ways in which a machine, computer system, etc. operates (*print mode*). **b** *informal* or *jocular* a specified way in which a person functions, behaves, etc., esp. by conscious choice (*as soon as this is over I'm switching into holiday mode*). **4** *Statistics* the value or range of values that occurs most frequently in a given set of data etc. **5** *Music* **a** each of the scale systems that result when the white notes of the piano are played consecutively over an octave. **b** each of the two main modern scale systems, the major and minor (*minor mode*). **6** *Logic* the character of a modal proposition. **b** = MOOD[2] 2. **7** *Physics* any of the distinct kinds or patterns of vibration that an oscillating system can sustain. **8** *N Amer. Grammar* = MOOD[2] 1.

model ● *n.* **1** (often *attrib.*) a representation in three dimensions of an existing person or thing or of a proposed structure, esp. in smaller scale (*model airplane; architect's model*). **2** a simplified description of a system, process, etc. put forward as a basis for theoretical or empirical understanding; a conceptual or mental representation of a thing. **3** a figure in clay, wax, etc. to be reproduced in another, usu. more durable material. **4 a** a car etc. of a particular design or produced in a specified year. **b** each of a series of varying designs of the same type of structure, commodity, or object. **5** an exemplary person or thing (*a model of self-discipline*). **6** (often foll. by *for*) a person or thing used, or for use, as an example to copy or imitate (*the Canadian model of federalism*). **7 a** a person employed to pose for an artist, photographer, etc. **b** a person employed to display clothes etc. by wearing them. **8** an actual person, place, etc. on which a fictional character, location, etc. is based. ● *adj.* **1** serving as an example; exemplary, ideally perfect. **2**

designating a small-scale model of the object or kind of object specified. ● *v.* (**modelled, modelling**) **1 a** *intr.* act or pose as an esp. fashion or photographic model. **b** *tr.* (of a person acting as a model) display (a garment). **2** *tr.* **a** fashion or shape (a figure) in clay, wax, etc. **b** (foll. by *after, on*, etc.) form, frame, or give shape to (a document, argument, other immaterial object, etc.), esp. in imitation of another. **3** *tr.* devise a (usu. mathematical) model or simplified description of (a phenomenon, system, etc.). **4** *tr. Art* (in drawing, painting, etc.) form with or assume the appearance of natural relief; cause to appear three-dimensional. □ **modeller** *n.* **modelling** *n. & adj.*

model home *n. N Amer.* a finished house, sometimes furnished and decorated, in a subdivision under construction, used to give potential buyers an idea of what other houses of its type would look like.

modem *n.* a combined device for modulation and demodulation, e.g. between a computer and a telephone line, used for converting digital electrical signals to analog or audio ones and vice versa.

moderate ● *adj.* /'mɒdərət/ **1** avoiding extremes in conduct, opinions, or expression. **2** of medium quantity, quality, size, or extent. **3** (of a process, condition, or agency) intermediate in strength or degree; not intense, violent, or severe. **4** (of a wind) of medium strength. **5** (of prices, charges, etc.) reasonable, fairly low. **6** (of an oven temperature for baking) between 350° and 375° F. ● *n.* /'mɒdərət/ a person who holds moderate views, esp. in politics, religion, etc. ● *v.* /'mɒdə,reit/ **1** *tr. & intr.* make or become less violent, intense, rigorous, etc. **2** *tr.* preside over (a deliberative body) or at (a debate etc.). **3** *tr. Physics* retard (neutrons), esp. with a moderator. □ **moderately** /-rətli/ *adv.* **moderatism** /'mɒdərə,tızəm/ *n.*

moderation /,mɒdə'reiʃən/ *n.* **1** the process or an instance of moderating. **2** the quality of being moderate, esp. in conduct, opinion, etc. **3** *Physics* the action or process of slowing down neutrons by the use of a moderator. □ **in moderation** in a moderate manner or degree.

moderato /,mɒdə'rɒto:/ *Music* ● *adj. & adv.* performed at a moderate pace. ● *n. (pl.* **-os**) a piece of music to be performed in this way.

moderator *n.* **1** *N Amer.* a chairperson of a discussion on television or radio. **2** a person chosen to preside over a meeting or assembly and conduct its business. **3** (in the United Church) a person elected by the General Council to serve as the head of the church. **4** (in the Presbyterian Church) **a** a person elected by the General Assembly to moderate the Assembly. **b** a person appointed or elected by a synod or presbytery to preside over meetings, officiate at services, etc. **5** *Physics* a substance used in a nuclear reactor to retard neutrons and control the rate of fission. **6** an arbitrator or mediator.

modern ● *adj.* **1** of the present and recent times. **2** in current fashion; not antiquated. **3** (of a person) up-to-date in lifestyle, outlook, opinions, etc. **4** designating the form of a language currently used, or the form representing the most recent significant stage of development (*modern Hebrew*). **5** designating or pertaining to art, architecture, etc. of the 20th c. marked by a departure from traditional styles and values. **6** *Zool., Geol., etc.* belonging to a comparatively recent period in the history of the earth. ● *n.* **1** (usu. in *pl.*) a person living in or belonging to modern times. **2** a person with modern tastes or opinions. **3** = MODERN DANCE. □ **modernity** *n.* **modernly** *adv.* **modernness** *n.*

modern conveniences *n.pl.* gadgets, amenities, labour-saving devices, etc. typical of a well-equipped modern home.

modern dance *n.* a style of theatrical dance developed in the 20th c., not constrained by the rules and techniques of classical ballet.

modern-day *adj.* of the present; contemporary.

modern dress *n.* costuming for a theatrical production which reflects current styles rather than those in fashion at the time the play etc. was written or depicts.

modern English *n.* English from about 1500 onward.

modern history *n.* history from the end of the Middle Ages, or after the fall of the Western Roman Empire, to the present day.

modernism *n.* **1 (Modernism)** the methods, style, or attitudes of modern artists, writers, architects, composers, etc., esp. a style of art etc. rejecting classical and traditional methods of expression. **2** a movement towards modifying traditional religious beliefs and doctrines in accordance with modern ideas. **3 a** modern character or quality of thought, expression, etc. **b** a modern term or expression. □ **modernist** *n.*

modernistic *adj.*

modernize *v.* **1** *tr.* make modern; adapt to modern needs, habits, standards, or styles. **2** *intr.* adopt modern ways, views, styles, etc. □ **modernization** *n.*

modernizer *n.*

modern jazz *n.* jazz as developed in the 1940s and 1950s, esp. bebop.

modern language *n.* a language that is spoken or written currently, esp. a European language.

modern Latin *n.* Latin since 1500, used esp. in scientific classification.

modern pentathlon *n.* an athletic competition in which participants engage in five different events usu. in a single day or over two days, including fencing, shooting, swimming, riding, and cross-country running.

modest *adj.* **1 a** having or expressing a humble or moderate estimate of one's own merits or achievements. **b** (of an action, attribute, etc.) proceeding from or indicating such a quality. **2** diffident, bashful, not bold or forward. **3 a** decorous in manner and conduct, avoiding impropriety or indecency. **b** reserved in sexual matters. **4** moderate or restrained in amount, extent, severity, etc.; not excessive or exaggerated (*a modest sum*). **5** (of a thing) unpretentious in appearance etc.; unostentatious. □ **modestly** *adv.*

modesty *n.* the quality of being modest.

modicum /'mɒdɪkəm/ *n.* (foll. by *of*) a small quantity.

modification *n.* **1** the act or an instance of modifying or being modified. **2** a change made. **3** *Biol.* **a** the development of non-heritable changes in an organism. **b** the non-heritable changes produced in an organism in response to a particular environment.

modified American plan *n.* *N Amer.* (in hotels etc.) a method of charging a fixed rate that covers bed and breakfast, plus one other meal. Abbr.: **MAP**.

modifier *n.* **1** a person or thing that modifies or alters something. **2** a word, esp. an adjective or noun used attributively, that qualifies the sense of another word, e.g. *good* and *family* in *a good family house*.

modify *v.tr.* (**-ies, -ied**) **1** make partial or minor changes in; alter without radical transformation. **2** make less severe or extreme; tone down (*modify one's demands*). **3** *Grammar* limit, qualify, or expand the

sense of (a word, phrase, etc.). **4** *Chem.* change or replace all the substituent radicals of a polymer, thereby changing its physical properties such as solubility etc. (*modified starch*). □ **modifiable** *adj.*

modish /'moʊdɪʃ/ *adj.* fashionable. □ **modishly** *adv.*

modishness *n.*

modular /'mɒdjʊlər, -ʒʊlər/ *adj.* **1** of or pertaining to modules. **2 a** employing or involving a module or modules as the basis of design, measurement, or construction. **b** part of a system so designed or constructed. **3 a** (of an educational course) designed as a series of units or discrete sections. **b** (of a facility, service, etc.) provided in a number of discrete stages. □ **modularity** /-'lærɪti/ *n.* **modularization** *n.*

modulate /'mɒdjʊˌleɪt, 'mɒdʒəˌleɪt/ *v.* **1** *tr.* **a** regulate or adjust. **b** moderate, temper. **2** *tr.* adjust or vary the tone or pitch of (the speaking voice etc.). **3** *tr.* alter the amplitude or frequency of (a wave) by a wave of a lower frequency to convey a signal. **4** *intr. & tr. Music* (often foll. by *from, to*) change or cause to change from one key to another. □ **modulation** *n.* **modulator** *n.*

module /'mɒdjuːl/ *n.* **1** a standardized part or independent unit used in construction or assembly, esp. of furniture, a building, or an electronic system. **2** an independent self-contained unit of a spacecraft (*lunar module*). **3** a distinct unit or period of training or education which can be combined with others to make up a course. **4** *Computing* any of a number of distinct but interrelated units from which a program may be built up or into which a complex activity may be analyzed. **5 a** a standard or unit of measurement. **b** a length chosen as a basis for the dimension of parts of a building, items of furniture, etc. so that all lengths are integral multiples of it.

modus operandi /ˌmoʊdəs ˌɒpəˈrændi/ *n.* (*pl.* **modi operandi** /ˌmoʊdiː/) **1** the particular way in which a person performs a task or action. **2** the way a thing operates.

modus vivendi /ˌmoʊdəs vɪˈvendi/ *n.* (*pl.* **modi vivendi** /ˌmoʊdiː/) **1** a way of living or coping. **2 a** an arrangement whereby those in dispute can carry on pending a settlement. **b** an arrangement between people who agree to differ.

mogul¹ /'moʊɡəl/ *n.* **1** *informal* an important or influential person. **2 (Mogul)** *hist.* **a** = MUGHAL. **b** (often **the Great Mogul**) any of the emperors of Delhi in the 16th–19th c.

mogul² *n.* **1** a mound of hard snow on a ski slope. **2** (in *pl.*) a freestyle skiing event in which skiers negotiate the moguls on a run with as much speed and élan as possible.

MOH *abbr.* MEDICAL OFFICER OF HEALTH.

mohair ● *n.* **1** the hair of the angora goat. **2** a yarn or fabric from this, either pure or mixed with wool or cotton. ● *adj.* made or consisting of mohair.

Mohammedan /moʊˈhæmədæn/ *n. & adj.* = MUSLIM. ¶A term not used or favoured by Muslims, and often regarded as *offensive*.

Mohawk *n.* **1 a** a member of an Iroquois people, one of the five of the original Iroquois federation, now inhabiting parts of southern Ontario and northern New York. **b** the Iroquoian language of this people. **2** *Figure Skating* a step from either edge of the skate to the same edge on the other foot in the opposite direction (*compare* CHOCTAW 2). **3 (mohawk)** (also **mohawk haircut**) esp. *N Amer.* a haircut, supposedly resembling that worn by the Mohawk, in which the head is shaved except for a brushlike strip of hair over the top of the head to the back of the neck.

Mohegan /moʊˈhiːɡən/ ● *n.* **1** a member of an Algonquian people formerly inhabiting part of Connecticut. **2** the language of this people. ● *adj.* designating or pertaining to this people or their language.

mohel /mɒ'hel, 'mo:həl/ *n. Judaism* a person trained to perform ritual circumcisions.

moi /mwɒ/ *interj. jocular* as a tongue-in-cheek rejoinder to being accused of something of which one knows one is guilty; what, me? (*pretentious? moi?*).

moiety /'mɔɪəti/ *n.* (*pl.* **-ies**) **1** *Law* or *literary* a half, either of two equal parts. **2** *Law* or *literary* each of the two parts into which a thing is divided. **3** *Anthropology* either of two primary social divisions of a tribe.

moil ● *v.intr.* **1** toil, work hard, drudge (*toil and moil*). **2** swirl, mill about; move around in agitation or confusion. ● *n.* **1** turmoil, confusion, trouble. **2** drudgery.

moiré /mɔr'ei, mwɔr-/ ● *n.* **1** a fabric, often silk, having a pattern of glossy wavy bars. **2** a variegated or clouded appearance like that of this fabric, esp. as an ornamental finish applied to metal. **3** (in full **moiré pattern**) light and dark fringes observed when a pattern of lines, dots, etc. is visually superimposed on another similar or identical pattern slightly out of alignment with the first. ● *adj.* having a moiré pattern.

moist *adj.* **1** slightly wet; damp. **2 a** (of the season, climate, etc.) rainy; having some or considerable rainfall. **b** (of the eyes) wet with tears, ready to shed tears. □ **moistly** *adv.* **moistness** *n.*

moisten *v.tr. & intr.* make or become moist; wet superficially or moderately.

moisture *n.* water or other liquid diffused in a small quantity as vapour, or within a solid, or condensed on a surface.

moisturize *v.tr.* make less dry (esp. the skin by use of a cosmetic). □ **moisturizer** *n.* **moisturizing** *adj.*

mojo *n.* (*pl.* **-os**) esp. *US* **1** magic, voodoo. **2** a charm or amulet.

mol /mo:l/ *abbr.* = MOLE⁴.

mol. *abbr.* **1** molecular. **2** molecule.

molar¹ ● *adj.* **1** (of a tooth) serving to grind, esp. designating any of the back teeth of mammals. **2** of or pertaining to a molar tooth. ● *n.* a molar tooth.

molar² *adj.* **1** of or relating to mass. **2** acting on or by means of large masses or units.

molar³ *adj. Chem.* **1** of a mass of substance usu. per mole (*molar latent heat*). **2** (of a solution) containing one mole, or a specified number of moles, of solute per litre of solvent. □ **molarity** /mə'læriti/ *n.*

molasses /mə'læsɪs, -sɪz/ *n.* **1** a thick, dark, uncrystallized syrup drained from raw sugar during refining. **2** *N Amer.* a lighter, sweeter version of this substance combined with invert sugar and corn syrup for use as a table syrup, in baking, etc.

mold *var. of* MOULD¹, MOULD², MOULD³.

molder *var. of* MOULDER.

molding *var. of* MOULDING.

moldy *var. of* MOULDY.

mole¹ *n.* **1** any small burrowing insect-eating mammal of the family Talpidae, with dark velvety fur and very small eyes. **2** *informal* **a** a spy established deep within an organization and usu. dormant for a long period while attaining a position of trust. **b** a betrayer of confidential information. **3** a remotely operated or automatic machine capable of tunnelling through rock.

mole² *n.* a small often slightly raised dark blemish on the skin caused by a high concentration of melanin.

mole³ *n.* **1** a massive structure serving as a pier, breakwater, or causeway. **2** an artificial harbour.

mole⁴ *n. Chem.* the SI unit of amount of substance equal to the quantity containing as many elementary units as there are atoms in 0.012 kg of carbon-12.

mole⁵ /'mo:lei/ *n.* a highly spiced Mexican sauce made chiefly from chili peppers and chocolate, served with meat.

molecular /mə'lekjolər/ *adj.* of, relating to, or consisting of molecules. □ **molecularly** *adv.*

molecular biology *n.* the study of the structure and function of large molecules associated with living organisms. □ **molecular biologist** *n.*

molecular weight *n.* the ratio of the average mass of one molecule of an element or compound to one twelfth of the mass of an atom of carbon-12.

molecule /'mɒlə,kju:l/ *n.* **1** the smallest fundamental unit (usu. a group of atoms) of a chemical compound that can take part in a chemical reaction. **2** (in general use) a small particle.

molehill *n.* a small mound thrown up by a mole in burrowing. □ **make a mountain out of a molehill** exaggerate the importance of a minor difficulty.

mole rat *n.* any of various rat-like rodents with reduced eyes which live underground, esp. of the African family Bathyergidae, often living communally.

moleskin *n.* **1** the skin of a mole used as fur. **2 a** kind of cotton fustian with its surface shaved before dyeing. **b** (in *pl.*) clothes, esp. trousers, made of this. **3** an adhesive-backed felt put on parts of the feet to reduce abrasion from shoes.

molest *v.tr.* **1** attack or interfere with (a person), esp. sexually. **2** annoy or pester (a person) in a hostile or injurious way. □ **molestation** /,mɒlə'steiʃən/ *n.* **molester** *n.*

moll *n. slang* a gangster's female companion.

mollify /'mɒlə,fai/ *v.tr.* (**-ies**, **-ied**) **1** appease, pacify. **2** reduce the severity of; soften. □ **mollification** *n.* **mollifier** *n.*

mollusc /'mɒləsk/ *n.* (also esp. *US* **mollusk**) any invertebrate of the phylum Mollusca, with a soft body and usu. a hard shell, including limpets, snails, oysters, mussels, etc. □ **molluscan** /mə'lʌskən/ *adj.*

molly *n.* (also **mollie**) a small American freshwater fish of the genus *Poecilia*, bearing live young, esp. *P. sphenops*, bred in many colours for aquariums.

Molotov cocktail /'mɒlə,tɒf/ *n.* a homemade incendiary device, usu. consisting of a bottle filled with inflammable liquid, usu. with a rag stuffed in the neck that is ignited just before throwing.

Molson muscle *n. Cdn slang* a beer belly.

molt esp. *US var. of* MOULT.

molten /'mo:ltən/ *adj.* melted, esp. made liquid by heat.

molto /'mɒlto:/ *adv. Music* very (*allegro molto*).

moly /'mo:li/ *n.* (*pl.* **-ies**) **1** a plant, *Allium moly*, with small yellow flowers. **2** a mythical herb with white flowers and black roots, endowed with magic properties.

molybdenum /mə'lɪbdənəm/ *n.* a silver-white brittle metallic element occurring naturally and used in steel to give strength and resistance to corrosion.

mom /mʌm, mɒm/ *n. N Amer. informal* mother.

mom-and-pop *attrib.adj. N Amer.* designating a store, restaurant, etc. run by a married couple or other members of a family.

moment *n.* **1** a very brief portion of time; an instant. **2** a short period of time (*wait a moment*) (*see also*

MINUTE[1] 3a). **3 a** an exact or particular point of time (*I came the moment you called*). **b** a brief period of time marked by a particular quality or experience (*a revolutionary moment*). **4** importance (*of no great moment*). **5** *Physics & Mech.* etc. **a** the turning effect produced by a force acting at a distance on an object. **b** this effect expressed as the product of the force and the distance from its line of action to a point. □ **at the moment** at this time; now. **have one's moments** be impressive, happy, etc., on occasions. **in a moment 1** very soon. **2** instantly. **man** (or **woman** etc.) **of the moment** the one of importance at the time in question. **not for a** (or **one**) **moment** never; not at all. **this moment** immediately; at once (*come here this moment*).

momentarily *adv.* **1** for a moment; fleetingly. **2 a** *N Amer.* at any moment; very soon. **b** instantly.

momentary *adj.* **1** lasting only a moment. **2** short-lived; transitory.

moment of truth *n.* a time of crisis or test.

momentous /mo:'mentəs/ *adj.* having great importance. □ **momentously** *adv.* **momentousness** *n.*

momentum /mo:'mentəm/ *n.* (*pl.* **momenta** /-tə/) **1** *Physics* the quantity of motion of a moving body, measured as a product of its mass and velocity. **2** the impetus gained by movement. **3** strength or continuity derived from an initial effort.

momma /'mɒmə, 'mʌmə/ *n.* esp. *N Amer. var.* of MAMMA[1].

mommy /'mʌmi, 'mɒmi/ *n.* (*pl.* **-ies**) *N Amer. informal* mother.

mommy track *n.* esp. *N Amer. informal* a career path for women who sacrifice some promotions and pay raises in order to devote more time to raising their children. □ **mommy tracker** *n.* **mommy tracking** *n.*

Mon. *abbr.* Monday.

Mona Lisa /'mo:nə li:sə/ *adj.* (of a smile etc.) enigmatic.

monarch *n.* **1** a sovereign with the title of king, queen, emperor, empress, or the equivalent. **2** a powerful or pre-eminent person. **3** (in full **monarch butterfly**) a large migrating orange and black butterfly, *Danaus plexippus*, found mainly in the Americas. **4** (in full **monarch flycatcher**) a flycatcher of the Old World family Monarchidae. □ **monarchic** /mə'nɑrkɪk/ *adj.* **monarchical** *adj.*

monarchism *n.* the advocacy of or the principles of monarchy. □ **monarchist** *n. & adj.*

monarchy *n.* (*pl.* **-ies**) **1** a form of government with a monarch at the head. **2** a state with this.

monastery /'mɒnə,steri/ *n.* (*pl.* **-ies**) **1** the residence of a religious community, esp. of monks living in seclusion. **2** the community itself.

monastic /mə'næstɪk/ ● *adj.* **1** of or relating to monasteries or the religious communities living in them. **2** resembling these or their way of life; solitary and celibate. ● *n.* a monk or other follower of a monastic rule. □ **monastically** *adv.* **monasticism** /-,sɪzəm/ *n.*

Monday ● *n.* the second day of the week, following Sunday. ● *adv.* **1** on Monday. **2** (**Mondays**) on Mondays; each Monday.

Monday-morning quarterback *n. N Amer. informal* a person who, having the advantage of hindsight, criticizes the actions of another.

mondo /'mɒndo/ *slang* ● *adj.* big, large, considerable (*mondo waves*). ● *adv.* very, extremely (*mondo cool*).

monetarism /'mɒnətə,rɪzəm/ *n.* the theory or practice of controlling the supply of money as the chief method of stabilizing the economy. □ **monetarist** *n. & adj.*

monetary /'mɒnəteri/ *adj.* **1** of or pertaining to coinage or currency. **2** of or pertaining to money. □ **monetarily** *adv.*

monetary policy *n.* the means by which a government tries to affect macroeconomic conditions by increasing or decreasing the supply of money.

monetary unit *n.* a standard unit of currency in a country, related to monetary units of other countries by a foreign exchange rate.

money *n.* **1 a** a current medium of exchange in the form of coins and banknotes. **b** a particular form of this (*paper money*). **2** (*pl.* **-ies** or **-eys**) (in *pl.*) sums of money. **3 a** wealth; property etc. viewed as convertible into money. **b** wealth as giving power or influence (*money talks*). **c** a rich person or family (*married into money*). **4 a** money as a resource (*time is money*). **b** profit, remuneration (*in it for the money*). **c** a salary, wage (*makes good money*). **5** money earmarked for a particular purchase or purpose (*grocery money*). □ **for my money** in my opinion or judgment; for my preference (*is too aggressive for my money*). **in the money** *informal* having or winning a lot of money. **made of money** *informal* very rich. **put one's money where one's mouth is** produce, bet, or pay out money to support one's statements or opinions. **put money into** invest in. (**right**) **on the money 1** on target; carried out with skill and precision. **2** correct in a prediction, observation, etc.

money-back guarantee *n.* a guarantee by a manufacturer, retailer, etc. to refund the full purchase price of a product or service which the purchaser finds to be defective or unsatisfactory.

moneybags *n.pl.* (treated as *sing.*) usu. *derogatory* a wealthy person.

moneybelt *n.* a belt with a compartment for carrying money, passports, etc., worn underneath clothing esp. by tourists.

money bill *n.* a government bill to impose, change, or regulate taxation, supply government monetary requirements, etc.

money-changer *n.* a person whose business it is to change money, esp. at an official rate. □ **money-changing** *n. & adj.*

moneyed *adj.* **1** having much money; wealthy. **2** consisting of money (*moneyed assistance*).

money-grubber *n. informal* a person greedily intent on amassing money. □ **money-grubbing** *adj. & n.*

money laundering *n.* the practice or system of transferring funds to conceal a dubious or illegal origin (also *attrib.*: *money-laundering operation*). □ **money launderer** *n.*

moneylender *n.* a person who lends money, esp. as a business, at interest. □ **moneylending** *n. & adj.*

money-loser *n.* an unprofitable business venture etc. □ **money-losing** *adj.*

money-maker *n.* **1** a person who earns much money. **2** a thing, idea, etc. that produces much money. □ **money-making** *n. & adj.*

money man *n. informal* a financier or financial expert.

money manager *n.* a person who manages mutual funds and other investments at a mutual fund company etc. □ **money management** *n.*

money market *n.* the market in short-term debt instruments issued by governments, corporations, etc. such as treasury bills, short-term bonds etc.

money market fund *n.* a mutual fund that invests

in the money market, usu. highly liquid, very secure, and offering higher interest than bank accounts.

money order *n.* an order for payment of a specified sum, issued by a bank or post office.

money pit *n. informal* **1** a project, program, etc. that eats up large amounts of money and is often perceived as wasteful and unnecessary. **2** = PIT¹ *n.* 6.

money supply *n.* the total amount of money in circulation or in being in a country.

money's worth *n.* (prec. by *your, my, one's*) good value for one's money.

monger /'mʌŋgər, 'mʌŋgər/ *n.* (usu. in *comb.*) **1** a dealer or trader (*fishmonger*). **2** usu. *derogatory* a person who promotes or deals in something specified (*warmonger*). □ **-mongering** *comb. form.*

Mongol /'mɒŋgəl/ ● *adj.* **1** of or relating to the Asian people now inhabiting Mongolia or their language. **2** resembling this people, esp. in appearance. **3** (**mongol**) *offensive* suffering from Down's syndrome. ● *n.* **1 a** a Mongolian. **b** the Mongolian language. **2** (**mongol**) *offensive* a person suffering from Down's syndrome.

Mongolian /mɒŋ'goːliən/ ● *n.* **1** a native or inhabitant of Mongolia, a country in E Asia bordered by Russia and China. **2** the language of Mongolia, usu. considered a member of the Altaic family. ● *adj.* of or relating to Mongolia or its people or language.

mongolism /'mɒŋgə,lɪzəm/ *n. offensive* = DOWN'S SYNDROME.

Mongoloid /'mɒŋgə,lɔɪd/ ● *adj.* **1** of or relating to the division of humankind including the indigenous peoples of E Asia, SE Asia, and the Arctic region of N America, characteristically having dark eyes, straight hair, pale ivory to dark skin, and little facial or body hair. **2** (**mongoloid**) *offensive* affected with Down's syndrome. ● *n.* **1** a person of Mongoloid physical type. **2** *offensive* a person affected with Down's syndrome.

mongoose /'mɒŋguːs/ *n.* (*pl.* **mongooses**) any of various short-legged carnivorous mammals of the family Viverridae, native to southern Asia and Africa, and noted for the ability to kill venomous snakes.

mongrel /'mʌŋgrəl/ ● *n.* **1** a dog of no definable type or breed. **2** any other animal or plant resulting from the crossing of different breeds or types. **3** *offensive* a person of mixed race. ● *adj.* of mixed origin, nature, or character. □ **mongrelize** *v.tr.* **mongrelization** *n.*

'mongst *literary var. of* AMONGST (see AMONG).

monied *var. of* MONEYED.

monies *see* MONEY 2.

moniker /'mɒnɪkər/ *n.* (also **monicker**) *slang* a name.

monism /'mɒnɪzəm, 'moːn-/ *n.* **1** any theory denying the duality of matter and mind. **2** *Philos. & Theol.* the doctrine that only one ultimate principle or being exists (*compare* PLURALISM 3). □ **monist** *n.* **monistic** *adj.*

monitor ● *n.* **1** any of various persons or devices for checking or warning about a situation, operation, etc. (*fetal monitor*). **2** a school pupil with disciplinary or other special duties. **3 a** a television receiver used in a studio to select or verify the picture being broadcast. **b** a loudspeaker used in a studio for listening to what is being recorded. **c** any large or powerful speaker, esp. one used on stage by a band. **4** *Computing* **a** a component displaying data as characters on a screen. **b** a computer program which monitors the running of other programs or the operation of a system. **5** a detector of radioactive contamination. **6** any tropical lizard of the genus *Varanus*, supposed to give warning of the approach of crocodiles. ● *v.tr.* **1** watch and check something over a period of time. **2** maintain regular surveillance over. **3** regulate the

strength of (a recorded or transmitted signal). □ **monitoring** *n. & adj.*

monk *n.* a member of a religious community of men living under certain vows esp. of poverty, chastity, and obedience. □ **monkish** *adj.*

monkey ● *n.* (*pl.* **-eys**) **1** any of various mainly long-tailed agile tree-dwelling primates of the families *Cebidae, Callithricidae,* and *Cercopithecidae.* **2** a mischievous person, esp. a child (*young monkey*). ● *v.intr.* (**-eys, -eyed**) **1** (often foll. by *with*) tamper or play mischievous tricks. **2** (foll. by *around, about*) fool around. □ **have a monkey on one's back** *slang* be a drug addict. **make a monkey of** humiliate by making appear ridiculous.

monkey bars *n.pl. N Amer.* a playground structure of joined bars for children to climb on.

monkey business *n. informal* **1** mischief. **2** suspicious or dishonest activities or behaviour.

monkey flower *n.* a mimulus, esp. *Mimulus guttatus,* with bright yellow flowers.

monkey in the middle *n. N Amer.* **1** a children's game in which two people throw a ball over the head of a third person standing in the middle, who tries to catch it. **2** a person who is placed in an awkward situation between two others.

monkey suit *n. informal* **1** a tuxedo. **2** any uniform.

monkey trail *n. Cdn (West)* a narrow trail, in a park, field, along a riverbank, etc. created by the passage of walkers, cyclists, etc.

monkey wrench ● *n.* a wrench with an adjustable jaw. ● *v.tr.* (**monkeywrench**) sabotage, esp. as a means of environmentalist protest. □ **throw a monkey wrench into (the works etc.)** *N Amer.* cause confusion or disruption. □ **monkeywrencher** *n.* **monkeywrenching** *n.*

monkfish *n.* **1** an anglerfish, esp. *Lophius americanus.* **2** a large bottom-dwelling shark, *Squatina squatina,* with a flattened body and large pectoral fins.

monkshood *n.* an aconite, esp. the cultivated *Aconitum napellus,* with hood-shaped blue or purple flowers.

mono *informal* ● *adj.* monophonic. ● *n.* **1** (*pl.* **-os**) a monophonic record, reproduction, etc. **2** *N Amer.* = MONONUCLEOSIS. **3** *N Amer.* = MONOFILAMENT 2.

mono- *comb. form* (usu. **mon-** before a vowel) **1** one, alone, single. **2** *Chem.* (forming names of compounds) containing one atom or group of a specified kind.

monobloc /'mɒnəblɒk/ *adj.* made as, contained in, or involving a single casting (*a monobloc chair*).

monochromatic /,mɒnəkrə'mætɪk/ *adj.* **1** (of light or other radiation) of a single wavelength or frequency. **2** containing only one colour. **3** (of a musical performance etc.) lacking any distinguishing or inspiring characteristics. □ **monochromatically** *adv.*

monochrome ● *n.* **1** a photograph or picture done in one colour or different tones of this, or in black and white. **2** *Photog. etc.* black and white. ● *adj.* having or using only one colour or in black and white only.

monocle /'mɒnəkəl/ *n.* a single eyeglass, kept in position by the muscles around the eye. □ **monocled** *adj.*

monoclonal /,mɒnə'kloːnəl/ *adj.* forming a single clone; derived from a single individual or cell.

monoclonal antibodies *n.pl.* antibodies produced artificially by a single clone of cells or cell line and consisting of identical antibody molecules.

monocoque /'mɒnə,kɒk/ *n.* (also *attrib.*) an aircraft or vehicle structure in which the chassis is integral with the body.

monocular /mə'nɒkjʊlər/ ● adj. of or pertaining to one eye only. ● n. a field glass or microscope for use with one eye.

monoculture /'mɒnə,kʌltʃər/ n. **1 a** the cultivation of a single crop to the exclusion of others. **b** an area in which such a practice prevails. **2** a society which is ethnically or culturally homogeneous. ☐ **monocultural** adj.

monocyte /'mɒnə,saɪt/ n. a large leukocyte with a simple nucleus, developing into a macrophage.

monofilament n. **1** a single strand of synthetic fibre. **2** a type of fishing line using this.

monogamy /mə'nɒɡəmi/ n. **1 a** the practice or state of being married to one person at a time. **b** the practice or state of having only one sexual partner at a time. **2** Zool. the habit of having only one mate at a time. ☐ **monogamous** adj.

monogram n. two or more letters, esp. a person's initials, combined in one design and marked on items of clothing etc. ☐ **monogrammed** adj.

monograph ● n. a separate treatise on a single subject or an aspect of it. ● v.tr. write a monograph on. ☐ **monographic** adj.

monohull n. a boat with a single hull.

monolingual /,mɒnə'lɪŋɡwəl, -lɪŋɡju:əl/ ● adj. **1** knowing or using only one language. **2** written in a single language. ● n. a person who knows only one language. ☐ **monolingualism** n.

monolith /'mɒnəlɪθ/ n. **1** a single block of stone, esp. shaped into a pillar or monument. **2 a** a person or thing like a monolith in being massive, immovable, or solidly uniform. **b** a large impersonal political or corporate body. **3** a large block of concrete, brickwork, etc., sunk in water, e.g. in the building of a dock. ☐ **monolithic** adj. **monolithically** adv.

monologue /'mɒnə,lɒɡ/ n. **1 a** a long speech in a play, film, etc. spoken by one actor, esp. when alone. **b** a dramatic composition, esp. in verse, told or performed by one person. **2** a long speech by one person in a conversation etc. **3** a stand-up comedy routine, esp. one performed at the beginning of a talk show by the host. ☐ **monologic** /-'lɒdʒɪk/ adj. **monological** adj. **monologist** /'mɒnə,lɒɡɪst, mə'nɒlədʒɪst/ n. (also **monologuist** /-ɡɪst/).

monomania /,mɒnə'meɪniə/ n. obsession of the mind by one idea or interest. ☐ **monomaniac** n. **monomaniacal** /-mə'naɪəkəl/ adj.

monomer /'mɒnəmər/ n. **1** a unit in a dimer, trimer, or polymer. **2** a molecule or compound that can be polymerized (compare DIMER). ☐ **monomeric** /-'merɪk/ adj.

monomial /mə'no:miəl/ Math. ● adj. (of an algebraic expression) consisting of one term. ● n. a monomial expression.

mononucleosis /,mɒno:,nju:kli'o:sɪs, -,nju:k-/ n. an abnormally high proportion of monocytes in the blood, esp. = GLANDULAR FEVER.

monophonic /,mɒnə'fɒnɪk/ adj. **1** (of sound reproduction) using only one channel of transmission (compare STEREOPHONIC). **2** Music having a simple melodic line predominating over other parts. ☐ **monophonically** adv.

monoplane n. an airplane with one set of wings (compare BIPLANE).

monopole n. **1** Physics a single electric charge or magnetic pole, esp. a hypothetical isolated magnetic pole. **2** a radio antenna, pylon, etc. consisting of a single pole or rod.

monopolist /mə'nɒpəlɪst/ n. a person who has or advocates a monopoly. ☐ **monopolistic** adj.

monopolize /mə'nɒpə,laɪz/ v.tr. **1** obtain exclusive possession or control of (a trade or commodity etc.). **2** dominate or prevent others from sharing in (a conversation, person's attention, etc.). ☐ **monopolization** n. **monopolizer** n.

monopoly /mə'nɒpəli/ n. (pl. **-ies**) **1 a** the exclusive possession or control of the trade in a commodity or service. **b** this conferred as a privilege by the state. **2 a** a commodity or service that is subject to a monopoly. **b** a company etc. that possesses a monopoly. **3** (foll. by of, on) exclusive possession, control, or exercise. **4** (**Monopoly**) proprietary a board game in which players use imitation money to engage in simulated property and financial dealings.

Monopoly money n. **1** imitation money used in the game of Monopoly. **2** money that has no real existence or value.

monorail n. a railway in which the track consists of a single rail, usu. elevated with the train units suspended from it.

monosaccharide /,mɒnə'sækə,raɪd/ n. a sugar that cannot be hydrolyzed to give a simpler sugar, e.g. glucose.

monosodium glutamate /,mɒnə'so:diəm 'ɡlu:tə,meɪt/ n. a sodium salt of glutamic acid used in foods as a flavour enhancer (compare GLUTAMATE).

monosyllable n. a word of one syllable. ☐ **in monosyllables** in simple direct words. ☐ **monosyllabic** adj.

monotheism /'mɒnə,θiːɪzəm/ n. the doctrine or belief that there is only one God. ☐ **monotheist** n. **monotheistic** adj.

monotone ● n. **1** a sound or utterance continuing or repeated on one note without change of pitch. **2** sameness of style in writing, expression, etc. ● adj. **1** without change of pitch or tone. **2** containing only one tone of one colour.

monotonic /,mɒnə'tɒnɪk/ adj. **1** uttered in a monotone. **2** Math. (of a function or quantity) varying in such a way that it either never decreases or never increases. ☐ **monotonically** adv.

monotonous /mə'nɒtənəs/ adj. **1** lacking in variety; tedious through sameness. **2** (of a sound or utterance) without variation in tone or pitch. ☐ **monotonously** adv.

monotony /mə'nɒtəni/ n. **1** lack of interesting variety; dull or tedious routine. **2** sameness of tone or pitch; lack of variety in cadence or inflection.

monotreme /'mɒnə,triːm/ n. any mammal of the order Monotremata, native to Australia and New Guinea, including the duckbill and echidna, laying large yolky eggs through a common opening for urine, feces, etc.

monounsaturated adj. (of a compound, esp. a fat or oil molecule) containing one double bond.

monovalent /mɒnə'veɪlənt/ adj. Chem. having a valence of one.

monoxide n. Chem. an oxide containing one oxygen atom.

Monseigneur /,m̃ɔsen'jɜr/ n. (pl. **Messeigneurs** /,mesen'jɜr/) a title given to an eminent French person, esp. a prince, cardinal, archbishop, or bishop.

Monsieur /mə'sjø/ n. (pl. **Messieurs** /me'sjø/) the title or form of address used of or to a French-speaking man, corresponding to Mr. or sir.

Monsignor /mɒn'siːnjər, mɒn-/ n. (pl. **Monsignori** /-'njɔri/) **1** a title in the Roman Catholic Church bestowed by the Pope on priests, either in conjunction with an office or as an honorary title for distinguished service. **2** a person holding this title.

monsoon /mɒn'suːn/ n. **1** a wind in S Asia, esp. in the Indian Ocean, blowing from the southwest in summer (**wet monsoon**) and the northeast in winter (**dry monsoon**). **2** a rainy season accompanying a wet monsoon. **3** any other wind with periodic alternations. □ **monsoonal** adj.

mons pubis /mɒnz 'pjuːbɪs/ n. a rounded mass of fatty tissue lying over the joint of the pubic bones, esp. = MONS VENERIS.

monster n. **1** an imaginary creature, usu. large and frightening, often compounded of incongruous elements. **2** an inhumanly cruel or wicked person. **3** a misshapen or ugly person, animal, or plant. **4** a large animal or thing. **5** (attrib.) **a** huge; extremely large of its kind (monster home). **b** very successful (had a monster season).

monstrance /'mɒnstrəns/ n. Catholicism a receptacle, usu. of gold or silver, with an open or transparent compartment in which the consecrated Host is exposed for veneration.

monstrosity /mɒn'strɒsɪti/ n. (pl. **-ies**) **1** a huge, hideous, or outrageous thing, esp. an unsightly building. **2** the condition or fact of being monstrous. **3** = MONSTER 3.

monstrous adj. **1** of or like a monster in appearance, fearsomeness, etc. **2** huge. **3 a** outrageously wrong or absurd. **b** atrocious; horrible (a monstrous crime). □ **monstrously** adv. **monstrousness** n.

mons Veneris /mɒnz 'venərɪs/ n. a rounded mass of fatty tissue on a woman's lower abdomen above the vulva.

Mont. abbr. Montana.

montage /mɒn'tɒʒ/ ● n. **1** Film **a** a combination of images in quick succession to compress background information or provide atmosphere. **b** a system of editing in which the narrative is modified or interrupted to include images that are not necessarily related to the dramatic development. **2 a** the technique of producing a new composite whole from fragments of pictures, words, music, etc. **b** a composition produced in this way. ● v.tr. make or integrate into a montage.

Montagnais /'mɒntən‚jei/ ● n. **1** a member of an Innu people living in the barrens between Hudson Bay and the Labrador coast. **2** the Cree language of this people. ● adj. of or relating to this people or their culture or language.

Montagnais-Naskapi n. = INNU n.

Montanan ● n. a native or inhabitant of the US state of Montana. ● adj. of or relating to Montana.

montane /'mɒntein/ adj. **1** of or inhabiting mountainous country. **2** designating or pertaining to the belt of upland vegetation below the timberline.

monte /'mɒnti/ n. **1** a Spanish game of chance, played with 40 cards. **2** (in full **three-card monte**) a game of Mexican origin played with three cards, similar to three-card trick.

Monterey Jack /‚mɒntə'rei/ n. a mild, white cheddar cheese.

Montessori /‚mɒntə'sɔːri/ n. (usu. attrib.) the system of education (esp. of young children) propounded by the Italian physician and educator Maria Montessori (1870–1952) that seeks to develop natural interests and activities rather than use formal teaching methods.

Montezuma's revenge /‚mɒntə'zuːməz/ n. diarrhea suffered by travellers, esp. visitors to Mexico.

month n. **1 a** (in full **calendar month**) each of usu. twelve periods into which a year is divided. **b** a period of time between the same dates in successive calendar months. **2** a period of 30 days or of four weeks. **3** = LUNAR MONTH. **4** the period of a woman's menstrual cycle. □ **month of Sundays** a very long period.

monthly ● adj. done, produced, or occurring once a month. ● adv. once a month; from month to month. ● n. (pl. **-ies**) **1** a monthly periodical. **2** (in pl.) informal a menstrual period.

Montrachet /mɔːrræ'ʃei/ n. **1** a white burgundy made from Chardonnay grapes from a single vineyard in the Côte de Beaune district of the Côte d'Or. **2** a kind of goat cheese produced in this area.

Montreal bagel n. Cdn a type of bagel, originally made in Montreal, which is lighter, thinner, and sweeter than other kinds of bagel.

Montreal canoe n. Cdn = CANOT DU MAÎTRE.

Montrealer n. a native or inhabitant of Montreal.

Montreal smoked meat n. Cdn = SMOKED MEAT 2.

monty n. Brit. □ **the full monty** everything necessary or appropriate; to the utmost (insisted on nothing less than the full monty; promised to go the full monty in fighting crime).

monument n. **1** anything enduring that serves to commemorate or make celebrated, esp. a structure or building. **2** a stone or other structure placed over a grave or in a church etc. in memory of the dead. **3** an ancient building or site etc. that has survived or been preserved. **4** (foll. by of, to) a typical or outstanding example (a monument of indiscretion). **5** a lasting reminder. **6** a written record.

monumental adj. **1 a** extremely great; stupendous (a monumental achievement). **b** (of a literary work etc.) impressive and of lasting importance. **2** of or serving as a monument. **3** informal (as an intensifier) very great; calamitous (a monumental blunder). □ **monumentality** n. **monumentally** adv.

moo ● v.intr. (**moos, mooed**) make the characteristic vocal sound of cattle. ● n. (pl. **moos**) this sound.

mooch informal ● v. **1** tr. **a** (often foll. by off) beg, scrounge. **b** esp. N Amer. steal. **2** intr. loiter or saunter desultorily. **3** tr. & intr. N Amer. fish with light tackle allowed to drift. ● n. a person who mooches. □ **moocher** n.

mood[1] n. **1** a state of mind or feeling. **2** a fit of melancholy or bad temper. **3** (attrib.) inducing a particular mood (mood music). **4** the atmosphere or pervading tone of a place, event, composition, etc. □ **in the** (or **no**) **mood** (foll. by for, or to + infin.) inclined (or disinclined) (was in no mood to go dancing).

mood[2] n. **1** Grammar **a** a form or set of forms of a verb serving to indicate whether it is to express fact, command, wish, etc. (subjunctive mood). **b** the distinction of meaning expressed by different moods. **2** Logic any of the classes into which each of the figures of a valid categorical syllogism is subdivided.

mood swing n. an abrupt and unaccountable change of mood.

moody adj. (**-ier, -iest**) given to changes of mood; gloomy, sullen. □ **moodily** adv. **moodiness** n.

Moog /moːg, muːg/ n. (in full **Moog synthesizer**) proprietary an electronic instrument with a keyboard, for producing a wide variety of musical sounds (see SYNTHESIZER).

moolah n. (also **moola**) slang money.

moon ● n. **1 a** the natural satellite of the earth, orbiting it monthly, illuminated by the sun and reflecting some light to the earth. **b** this regarded in terms of its waxing and waning in a particular month (new moon). **c** moonlight (there is no moon tonight). **2** a satellite of any planet. **3** (prec. by the) something desirable but unattainable (promised them *the moon*). **4** a month. ● *v.* **1** *intr.* (often foll. by *about*, *around*, etc.) move or look listlessly. **2** *tr.* (foll. by *away*) spend (time) in a listless manner. **3** *intr.* (foll. by *over*) act aimlessly or inattentively from infatuation for (a person). **4** *slang* **a** *tr.* expose one's buttocks to (another person) (*mooned the crowd*). **b** *intr.* expose one's buttocks. □ **many moons ago** a long time ago. **over the moon** extremely happy or delighted. □ **moonless** *adj.*

moonbeam *n.* a ray of moonlight.

moon boot *n.* a thickly-padded boot designed for low temperatures.

moon-faced *adj.* having a round face. □ **moon face** *n.*

moonfish *n.* any of various pale or silver-coloured marine fishes with round, usu. thin bodies.

Moonie *n.* *slang* a member of the Unification Church.

moonlight ● *n.* **1** the light of the moon. **2** (*attrib.*) lighted by the moon. ● *v.intr.* (**-lighted**) *informal* have a second job, esp. at night, in addition to one's regular day job. □ **moonlighter** *n.*

moonlit *adj.* lighted by the moon.

moonquake *n.* a tremor of the moon's surface.

moonrise *n.* **1** the rising of the moon. **2** the time of this.

moonscape *n.* **1** the surface or landscape of the moon. **2** an area resembling this; a wasteland.

moonseed *n.* a vine of moist places east of the Rockies, *Menispermum canadense*, with fruit like wild grapes.

moonset *n.* **1** the setting of the moon. **2** the time of this.

moonshine *n.* **1** *slang* illicitly distilled alcoholic liquor. **2** foolish or unrealistic talk or ideas.

moonshiner *n.* *N Amer.* *slang* an illicit distiller of alcoholic liquor.

moon shot *n.* the launching of a spacecraft to the moon.

moonstone *n.* any of various milky, opalescent varieties of albite and other minerals, used in jewellery.

moonstruck *adj.* **1** romantically captivated. **2** mentally deranged.

moonwalk *n.* **1** a walk by an astronaut on the surface of the moon. **2** a dance step in which a person moves backwards while making the motions of walking forwards. □ **moonwalk** *v.intr.*

moony *adj.* (**-ier**, **-iest**) **1** listless; stupidly dreamy. **2** of or like the moon.

Moor /mʊər, mɔːr/ *n.* a member of a Muslim people of mixed Berber and Arab descent inhabiting NW Africa, who conquered the Iberian peninsula in the 8th c. and retained control of portions of Spain until the 15th c. □ **Moorish** *adj.*

moor¹ /mʊər, mɔːr/ *n.* a tract of open, uncultivated, usu. poorly drained upland.

moor² *v.* **1** *tr.* make fast (a boat, buoy, etc.) by attaching a cable etc. to a fixed object. **2** *intr.* (of a boat) be moored. □ **moorage** *n.*

moorhen *n.* a small aquatic bird, *Gallinula chloropus*, with long legs and a short red-yellow bill.

mooring *n.* **1 a** a fixed object to which a boat, buoy, etc., is moored. **b** (often in *pl.*) a place where a boat etc. is moored. **2** (in *pl.*) a set of permanent anchors and chains laid down for ships to be moored to. **3** (in *pl.*) a source of stability or security (*spiritual moorings*).

moorland *n.* esp. *Brit.* an extensive area of moor.

moose *n.* (*pl.* same) esp. *N Amer.* **1** the largest living deer, *Alces alces*, found in northern parts of Europe, Asia, and N America, and having a growth of skin

hanging from the neck and (in males) very large antlers. **2** (also **moose meat**) the flesh of the moose as food.

moosehair *n.* stiff, pale hair from the shoulders, back, rump, and chest of a moose, dyed and used by some Aboriginal peoples to form decorative patterns on garments.

moosehide *n.* esp. *N Amer.* the skin of a moose, esp. when tanned (also *attrib.*: *moosehide leggings*).

moose milk *n.* *Cdn* **1** a drink including alcoholic liquor (usu. rum), milk, and often eggs etc. **2** home-distilled liquor. **3** any alcoholic drink.

moose pasture *n.* *Cdn slang* **1** a piece of land promoted as having mining potential but in fact unproductive. **2** worthless land, useful only for grazing moose.

moo shu pork *n.* a Chinese dish consisting of shredded pork, mushrooms, bean sprouts, etc. stir-fried together and wrapped in a thin pancake.

moot ● *adj.* **1** debatable, undecided. **2** having little or no practical significance. **3** *N Amer. Law* (of a case etc.) hypothetical. ● *v.tr.* raise (a question) for discussion. ● *n. Law* a discussion of a hypothetical case as an academic exercise.

moot point *n.* **1** a statement or question that is not or is no longer of any practical purpose. **2** a statement or question that is undecided or debatable.

mop ● *n.* **1** a tool for cleaning floors etc., consisting of a bunch of thick strings or soft material fastened to a long handle. **2** a similarly-shaped large or small implement for various purposes. **3** anything resembling a mop, esp. a thick mass of hair. **4** an act of mopping or being mopped (*gave it a mop*). ● *v.tr.* (**mopped**, **mopping**) **1** wipe or clean with or as with a mop. **2 a** wipe tears or sweat etc. from (one's face or brow etc.). **b** wipe away (tears etc.). □ **mop up 1** wipe up with or as with a mop. **2** *informal* absorb (profits etc.). **3** dispatch; make an end of.

mope ● *v.intr.* **1** be gloomily depressed or listless; behave sulkily. **2** wander about listlessly. ● *n.* **1** a person who mopes. **2** (**the mopes**) low spirits. □ **moper** *n.* **mopey** *adj.* (also **mopy**) (**mopier**, **mopiest**). **mopily** *adv.* **mopiness** *n.*

moped *n.* a small motorcycle equipped with both a low-powered engine and pedals.

moppet *n.* *informal* (esp. as a term of endearment) a baby or small child.

MOR *abbr.* MIDDLE-OF-THE-ROAD.

moraine /məˈreɪn/ *n.* a ridge or mound of rock debris etc. carried and deposited by a glacier. □ **morainal** *adj.* **morainic** *adj.*

moral ● *adj.* **1 a** concerned with goodness or badness of human character or behaviour, or with the distinction between right and wrong. **b** concerned with accepted rules and standards of human behaviour. **2 a** conforming to accepted standards of general conduct. **b** capable of moral action (*humans are moral creatures*). **3** (of rights or duties etc.) founded on moral law. **4 a** concerned with morals or ethics (*moral philosophy*). **b** (of a literary work etc.) dealing with moral conduct. **5** concerned with or leading to a psychological state associated with confidence in a right action (*moral support; moral victory*). ● *n.* **1 a** a moral lesson (esp. at the end) of a fable, story, event, etc. **b** a moral maxim or principle. **2** (in *pl.*) moral behaviour, e.g. in sexual conduct. □ **morally** *adv.*

morale *n.* the amount of confidence, enthusiasm, etc. that a person or group has at a particular time.

moralism *n.* **1** a natural system of morality. **2** religion regarded as moral practice.

moralist *n.* **1** a person who practises or teaches morality. **2** a person who follows a natural system of ethics.

moralistic *adj.* **1** pertaining to or characteristic of a moralist. **2** fond of moralizing. **3** having or showing definite but narrow beliefs and judgments about what is right and wrong. □ **moralistically** *adv.*

morality *n.* (*pl.* **-ies**) **1** the degree of conformity of an idea, practice, etc., to moral principles. **2** right moral conduct. **3** a lesson in morals. **4** a particular system of morals (*commercial morality*).

morality squad *n. Cdn* a police unit dealing with infractions of legislation concerning prostitution, pornography, drugs, gambling, etc.

moralize *v.* **1** *intr.* (often foll. by *on*) indulge in moral reflection or talk. **2** *tr.* interpret morally; explain the moral meaning of. **3** *tr.* make moral or more moral. □ **moralization** *n.* **moralizer** *n.* **moralizingly** *adv.*

Moral Majority *n.* (in the US) a right-wing conservative political movement composed mainly of Protestant fundamentalists.

moral philosophy *n.* the branch of philosophy concerned with ethics.

moral pressure *n.* persuasion by appealing to a person's moral sense.

moral sense *n.* the ability to distinguish right and wrong.

morass /məˈræs/ *n.* **1** a disordered situation, esp. one impeding progress. **2** a bog or marsh.

moratorium /ˌmɒrəˈtɔːriəm/ *n.* (*pl.* **-s** or **moratoria** /-riə/) **1** (often foll. by *on*) a temporary prohibition or suspension (of an activity). **2 a** a legal authorization to debtors to postpone payment. **b** the period of this postponement.

Moravian /məˈreɪviən/ ● *n.* **1** a native of Moravia, a region of the Czech Republic. **2** a member of a Protestant denomination founded in Saxony by emigrants from Moravia, accepting the Bible as the only source of faith. ● *adj.* **1** of, relating to, or characteristic of Moravia or its people. **2** of or relating to the Moravian Church.

moray *n.* any tropical eel-like fish of the family Muraenidae.

morbid *adj.* **1** (of the mind, ideas, etc.) having or showing an unusual interest in sad or unpleasant things, esp. death. **2** gruesome, grisly. **3** *Med.* of the nature of or indicative of disease. □ **morbidity** *n.* **morbidly** *adv.*

mordant ● *adj.* **1** (of sarcasm etc.) caustic, biting. **2** pungent, smarting. **3** corrosive or cleansing. **4** (of a substance) serving to fix colouring matter or gold leaf on another substance. ● *n.* a mordant substance. □ **mordantly** *adv.*

more ● *adj.* **1** existing in a greater or additional quantity, amount, or degree (*more problems than last time*; *bring some more water*). **2** greater in degree (*more's the pity*; *the more fool you*). ● *n.* a greater quantity, number, or amount (*more than three people*; *more to it than meets the eye*). ● *adv.* **1** in a greater degree (*do it more carefully*). **2** to a greater extent (*people like to walk more these days*). **3** forming the comparative of adjectives and adverbs, esp. those of more than one syllable (*more absurd*; *more easily*). **4** again (*once more*). **5** moreover. □ **more and more** in an increasing degree. **more of** to a greater extent (*more of a poet than a musician*). **more or less** **1** in a greater or less degree. **2** approximately; as an estimate. **more so** of the same kind to a greater degree.

morel /məˈrel/ *n.* an edible fungus, *Morchella esculenta*, with a honeycombed cap.

moreover *adv.* (introducing or accompanying a new statement) further, besides.

mores /ˈmɔːreɪz, -riːz/ *n.pl.* customs or conventions regarded as essential to or characteristic of a community.

morgue *n.* **1** a mortuary. **2** (esp. in a newspaper office or television studio) a room or file of miscellaneous cuttings, photographs, videotape, etc. for future use.

moribund /ˈmɒrɪˌbʌnd/ *adj.* **1** at the point of death. **2** lacking vitality.

Mormon ● *n.* a member of the Church of Jesus Christ of Latter-day Saints, a millenarian religion founded in 1830 by Joseph Smith (1805–44), having as its central scripture (apart from the Bible) the Book of Mormon. ● *adj.* of or relating to the Mormons or their beliefs. □ **Mormonism** *n.*

morn *n. literary* morning.

mornay /ˈmɔːrneɪ/ *n.* a cheese-flavoured white sauce.

morning ● *n.* **1** the early part of the day, esp. from sunrise to noon (*this morning*; *morning coffee*). **2** sunrise, daybreak. **3** a time compared with the morning, esp. the early part of one's life etc. ● *interj.* = GOOD MORNING *interj.* □ **in the morning** during or in the course of the morning.

morning after *n.* (also **morning after the night before**) *informal* a morning when one feels the effects of previous overindulgences, esp. with alcohol.

morning-after pill *n.* a contraceptive pill effective when taken some hours after intercourse.

morning coat *n.* a coat with tails, and with the front cut away below the waist.

morning glory *n.* (*pl.* **-ies**) any of various twining plants of the genus *Ipomoea* or related genera of the bindweed family, with trumpet-shaped flowers which fade in the afternoon.

morning paper *n.* a newspaper published early in the morning.

morning person *n. N Amer.* a person who likes to get up early in the morning.

morning sickness *n.* nausea experienced during early pregnancy, often in the morning.

morning star *n.* a planet, usu. Venus, seen in the east before sunrise.

Moroccan /məˈrɒkən/ ● *n.* **1** a native or national of Morocco in N Africa. **2** a person of Moroccan descent. ● *adj.* of or relating to Morocco.

morocco /məˈrɒkoː/ *n.* (*pl.* **-os**) **1** a fine flexible leather made from goatskins tanned with sumac, used esp. in bookbinding and shoemaking. **2** an imitation of this in grained calf etc.

moron *n.* **1** *informal* a very stupid or foolish person. **2** an adult with a mental age of about 8–12. □ **moronic** /məˈrɒnɪk/ *adj.* **moronically** *adv.*

morose /məˈroːs/ *adj.* sullen and ill-tempered. □ **morosely** *adv.* **moroseness** *n.*

morph[1] *n.* a variant form of an animal or plant.

morph[2] *v.* **1** *tr.* alter or transform (an image) by computer. **2** *intr. slang* be transformed.

morpheme /ˈmɔːrfiːm/ *n. Linguistics* **1** a morphological element considered with respect to its functional relations in a linguistic system. **2** a meaningful morphological unit of a language that cannot be further divided (e.g. *in*, *come*, *-ing*, forming *incoming*). □ **morphemic** *adj.*

morphine /ˈmɔːrfiːn/ *n.* an analgesic and narcotic drug obtained from opium and used medicinally to relieve pain.

morphing *n.* a technique that changes a film image into a numerical code, enabling it to be manipulated by a computer so that the effect can be created of transforming an image smoothly into another.

morphogenesis /ˌmɔrfə'dʒenɪsɪs/ n. Biol. the development of form in organisms. □ **morphogenetic** /-dʒɪ'netɪk/ adj.

morphology /mɔr'fɒlədʒi/ n. **1** Biol. the study of the forms of organisms. **2** Linguistics **a** the study of the forms of words. **b** the system of forms in a language. **3** the shape, form, or external arrangement of something, esp. as an object of study. □ **morphologic** adj. **morphological** adj. **morphologically** adv. **morphologist** n.

morrow n. (usu. prec. by the) literary the following day.

Morse n. (in full **Morse code**) an alphabet or code in which letters are represented by combinations of long and short light or sound signals.

morsel n. a small amount or piece of something, esp. food.

mortadella /ˌmɔrtə'delə/ n. a large spiced sausage usu. made of pork and pork fat and eaten cold.

mortal ● adj. **1** subject to death. **2** causing death; fatal. **3** (of a battle) fought to the death. **4** associated with death (mortal agony). **5** (of an enemy) implacable. **6** (of pain, fear, an affront, etc.) intense, very serious. **7** informal a very great (in a mortal hurry). **8** long and tedious (for two mortal hours). **8** informal conceivable, imaginable (of no mortal use). ● n. **1** a mortal being, esp. a human. **2** jocular a person described in some specified way (a thirsty mortal). □ **mortally** adv.

mortality n. (pl. **-ies**) **1** the state of being subject to death. **2** loss of life on a large scale. **3 a** the number of deaths in a given period etc. **b** (in full **mortality rate**) = DEATH RATE.

mortal sin n. a grave sin that is regarded as depriving the soul of divine grace.

mortar ● n. **1** a mixture of lime with cement, sand, and water, used in building to bond bricks or stones. **2** a short large-bore cannon for firing shells at high angles (also attrib.: mortar fire). **3** a contrivance for firing a lifeline or firework. **4** a vessel made of hard material, in which ingredients are pounded with a pestle. ● v.tr. **1** plaster or join with mortar. **2** attack or bombard with mortar shells.

mortarboard n. **1** an academic cap with a stiff flat square top. **2** a flat board with a handle on the undersurface, for holding mortar in bricklaying etc.

mortgage ● n. **1 a** an agreement by which money is lent by a bank, trust company, etc. for buying a house or other property, the property itself being the security. **b** a deed effecting this (burned our mortgage). **2 a** a debt secured by a mortgage. **b** a loan resulting in such a debt. **3** see CHATTEL MORTGAGE. ● v.tr. **1** give a bank, trust company, etc. the legal right to take possession of (a house or some other property) as a security for money lent. **2** pledge; place under an obligation (have mortgaged our future to foreign investment). □ **mortgageable** adj.

mortgagee n. the creditor in a mortgage, e.g. a bank, trust company, etc.

mortgage rate n. the rate of interest charged by a mortgagee.

mortgagor n. (also **mortgager**) the debtor in a mortgage.

mortician /mɔr'tɪʃən/ n. N Amer. an undertaker.

mortify v. (**-ies**, **-ied**) **1** tr. **a** cause (a person) to feel shamed or humiliated. **b** wound (a person's feelings). **2** tr. bring (the body, the flesh, the passions, etc.) into subjection by self-denial or discipline. **3** intr. (of flesh) be affected by gangrene or necrosis. □ **mortification** n. **mortifying** adj. **mortifyingly** adv.

mortise /'mɔrtɪs/ (also **mortice**) ● n. a hole in a piece of wood etc. designed to receive the end of another part, esp. a tenon. ● v.tr. **1** join securely, esp. by mortise and tenon. **2** cut a mortise in. □ **mortiser** n.

mortuary /'mɔrtʃuˌeri/ ● n. (pl. **-ies**) a room or building in which dead bodies may be kept until burial or cremation. ● adj. of or concerning death or burial.

Mosaic /moː'zeɪɪk/ adj. of or associated with Moses.

mosaic ● n. **1 a** a picture or pattern produced by an arrangement of small variously coloured pieces of glass or stone etc. **b** the process of producing such a work. **2** something that resembles a mosaic, esp. in its diversity of composition (the Canadian cultural mosaic). **3** an arrangement of photosensitive elements in a television camera. **4** (in full **mosaic disease**) a virus disease causing mottled leaves in plants, esp. tobacco, corn, and sugar cane. **5** (attrib.) **a** of or like a mosaic. **b** diversified. ● v.tr. (**mosaicked**, **mosaicking**) **1** adorn with mosaics. **2** combine into or as into a mosaic.

Mosaic Law n. the laws attributed to Moses and listed in the Pentateuch.

mosasaur /ˌmoːsə'sɔr/ n. (also **mosasaurus** /ˌmoːsə'sɔrəs/) any large extinct marine reptile of the genus Mosasaurus, with a long slender body and flipper-like limbs.

moselle /moː'zel/ n. a light medium-dry white wine produced in the valley of the Mosel River in Germany.

mosey v.intr. (**-eys**, **-eyed**) informal walk in a leisurely or aimless manner.

mosh v.intr. dance in a violent manner, involving jumping up and down and deliberately hitting other dancers, esp. at a rock concert. □ **mosher** n. **moshing** n.

mosh pit n. the area in front of the stage at a rock concert, where moshing usually takes place.

Moslem /'mɒzləm/ var. of MUSLIM.

mosque /mɒsk/ n. a Muslim place of worship.

mosquito n. (pl. **-oes** or **-os**) **1** any of various slender biting insects, esp. of the genus Culex, Anopheles, or Aedes, the female of which punctures the skin of humans and other animals with a long proboscis to suck their blood and transmits diseases such as malaria and encephalitis. **2** Cdn **a** an initiation level of sports competition for young children. **b** a player at this level.

mosquito coil n. a slowly-burning spiral made with a dried paste of pyrethrum powder, which produces a smoke that inhibits mosquitos from biting.

mosquito net n. (also **mosquito netting**) a net to keep off mosquitoes. □ **mosquito-netted** adj.

moss ● n. **1** any small plant of the class Musci, growing in dense clusters on the surface of the ground, in bogs, on trees, stones, etc. **2** a mass or growth of moss. **3** see IRISH MOSS. ● v.tr. cover with moss. □ **mosslike** adj. **mossy** adj.

Mossad /mɒ'sæd, 'mɒs-/ n. the principal intelligence service of Israel.

mossback n. N Amer. **1** informal an old-fashioned or extremely conservative person. **2** a large and old fish. □ **mossbacked** adj.

moss green n. a yellowish-green colour resembling that of moss.

moss-grown adj. overgrown with moss.

most ● adj. **1** existing in the greatest quantity or degree (the most noise). **2** the majority of; nearly all of (most people). ● n. **1** the greatest quantity or number (the most I can do). **2** (**the most**) slang the best of all. **3** the majority (most of them). ● adv. **1** in the highest degree (this is most interesting). **2** forming the superlative of adjectives and adverbs, esp. those of more than one syllable (*most certain*; *most easily*). **3** *N Amer. informal* almost. □ **at most** no more or better than. **at the most 1** as the greatest amount. **2** not more than. **for the most part 1** as regards the greater part. **2** usually. **make the most of 1** employ to the best advantage. **2** represent at its best or worst.

Most Favoured Nation *n.* a country which is afforded beneficial trade terms with another, e.g. lower import tariffs than others.

Most High *n.* (prec. by *the*) God.

mostly *adv.* **1** as regards the greater part. **2** usually.

Most Reverend *n.* the official title of certain high-ranking clergy, e.g. archbishops and bishops.

mot /mo:/ *n.* (*pl.* **mots** *pronunc.* same) a witty saying.

mote *n.* a speck of dust.

motel *n.* a hotel designed for motorists, usu. having direct access from each room to the parking lot.

motet /mo:'tet/ *n.* a short sacred choral composition.

moth *n.* **1** any of the large group of insects (including clothes moths) which together with butterflies constitute the order Lepidoptera and are distinguished from butterflies by nocturnal activity, hairlike or slender antennae, thicker bodies, the usu. folded position of the wings when at rest, and duller colouring. **2** any small insect of the family Tineidae breeding in cloth etc., on which its larva feeds.

mothball ● *n.* a ball of naphthalene etc. placed in stored clothes to keep away moths. ● *v.tr.* **1** place in mothballs. **2** a take out of use or active service. **b** put in storage for an indefinite time. □ **in mothballs** stored unused for a considerable time.

moth-eaten *adj.* **1** damaged or destroyed by moths. **2** antiquated, time-worn.

mother ● *n.* **1 a** a woman in relation to a child or children to whom she has given birth. **b** a woman who serves as a mother, e.g. a stepmother, adoptive mother, or foster mother. **2** any female animal in relation to its offspring. **3** a quality or condition etc. that gives rise to another (*necessity is the mother of invention*). **4** (in full **Mother Superior**) the head of a female religious community. **5** (*attrib.*) a designating an institution etc. regarded as having maternal authority (*Mother Church*; *mother earth*). **b** designating the main ship, spacecraft, etc., in a convoy or mission (*the mother craft*). **6** esp. *N Amer.* **a** *slang* a person or thing that is very large, powerful, etc. **b** *coarse slang* = MOTHERFUCKER. **7** (in full **mother of vinegar**) a ropy mucilaginous substance produced on the surface of liquids during fermentation, and used to ferment other liquids, as in changing wine to vinegar. ● *adj.* **1** that is a mother (*a mother bird*). **2** characteristic of a mother (*mother love*). **3** inherited or learned from, or as if from, one's mother; native (*mother tongue*). ● *v.tr.* **1** give birth to; be the mother of. **2** protect as a mother. **3** give rise to; be the source of. □ **every mother's son** *informal* every man; everyone. **the mother of all ...** the largest ... of all. □ **motherless** *adj.* **motherlike** *adj. & adv.*

motherboard *n.* a printed circuit board containing the principal components of a microcomputer etc.

Mother Carey's chicken *n.* = STORM PETREL.

Mother Corp. *n.* (also **Mother Corporation**) *Cdn informal* the CBC.

mother country *n.* **1** the country which colonized or settled a particular place. **2** one's native country.

mother figure *n.* an older woman who is regarded as a source of nurture, support, etc.

motherfucker *n.* esp. *N Amer. coarse slang* an obnox-

ious or very unpleasant person or thing. □ **motherfucking** *adj.*

mother goddess *n.* a mother-figure deity, goddess of the entire complex of birth and growth, commonly a central figure of early nature cults where maintenance of fertility was of prime religious importance.

Mother Goose *n.* the fictitious author of a collection of nursery rhymes first published in England in the late 18th c.

mother hen *n.* **1** a person who sees to the needs of others, esp. in a fussy or annoying way. **2** a hen with a brood of chicks.

motherhood *n.* **1** the state or condition of being a mother. **2** the qualities or attributes characteristic of a mother. **3** *N Amer.* (*attrib.*) having an inherent goodness or justness that is obvious or cannot be disputed (*a motherhood issue*).

mother house *n.* a convent or monastery having authority over other houses of the same order.

Mother Hubbard *n.* **1** *Cdn* (in full **Mother Hubbard parka**) a type of woman's parka, worn esp. in the Western Arctic, consisting of an inner duffle shell covered in a bright print fabric, edged with fur at the hood and cuffs and having a deep ruffle around the bottom. **2** a woman's long unfitted dress.

mother-in-law *n.* (*pl.* **mothers-in-law**) the mother of one's husband or wife.

mother-in-law suite *n.* *N Amer.* = IN-LAW SUITE.

motherland *n.* **1** one's native country. **2** the land in which one's ancestors lived.

motherlode *n.* **1** *Mining* the main vein of a system. **2** a rich or important source of something.

motherly *adj.* **1** like or characteristic of a mother in affection, care, etc. **2** of or relating to a mother. □ **motherliness** *n.*

mother-of-pearl *n.* a smooth iridescent substance forming the inner layer of the shell of some molluscs.

mother's allowance *n.* *Cdn hist.* = FAMILY ALLOWANCE.

Mother's Day *n.* *N Amer.* the second Sunday in May, set aside as a day to honour mothers.

mother ship *n.* **1** a ship escorting or having charge of a number of other, smaller, vessels. **2** an aircraft or spacecraft from which another aircraft or spacecraft is launched or controlled.

Mother Superior *n.* see MOTHER[1] *n.* 4.

mother-to-be *n.* a woman who is expecting a baby.

mother tongue *n.* **1** one's native language. **2** a language from which others have evolved.

mothproof ● *adj.* (of clothes) treated so as to repel moths. ● *v.tr.* treat (clothes) in this way.

mothy *adj.* (**-ier**, **-iest**) infested with moths.

motif /mo:'ti:f/ *n.* **1** a distinctive feature or dominant idea in artistic or literary composition. **2** *Music* = FIGURE *n.* 12. **3** a decorative design or pattern. **4** an ornament of lace etc. sewn separately on a garment.

motile /'mo:tail/ *adj. Zool. & Bot.* capable of motion. □ **motility** /-'tɪlɪti/ *n.*

motion ● *n.* **1** the act or process of moving or of changing position. **2** a particular manner of moving the body in walking etc. **3** a change of posture. **4** a gesture. **5** a formal proposal put to a committee, legislature, etc. **6** *Law* an application for a rule or order of court. ● *v.* (often foll. by *to* + infin.) **1** *tr.* direct (a person) by a sign or gesture. **2** *intr.* (often foll. by *to* a person) make a gesture directing (*motioned to me to leave*). □ **go through the motions 1** make a pretense; do something perfunctorily or superficially. **2** simulate an action by gestures. **in motion** moving;

not at rest. **put** (or **set**) **in motion** set going or working. □ **motionless** *adj.* **motionlessly** *adv.*

motion detector *n.* (also **motion sensor**) a security device, usu. emitting an infrared beam which triggers an alarm when interrupted by any movement through it.

motion picture *n.* a continuous picture of events obtained by projecting a sequence of photographs taken at very short intervals (also *attrib.: the motion picture industry*).

motion sickness *n.* nausea induced by motion, esp. by travelling in a vehicle.

motivate *v.tr.* **1** supply a motive to; be the motive of. **2** cause (a person) to act in a particular way. **3** stimulate the interest of (a person in an activity). □ **motivation** *n.* **motivational** *adj.* **motivator** *n.*

motive ● *n.* **1** a factor or circumstance that induces a person to act in a particular way. **2** a motif in art, literature, or music. ● *adj.* **1** tending to initiate movement. **2** concerned with movement. **3** motivating. □ **motiveless** *adj.*

motive power *n.* a moving or impelling power, esp. a source of energy used to drive machinery.

mot juste /mo: 'ʒu:st/ *n.* (*pl.* ***mots justes*** *pronunc.* same) the most appropriate expression.

motley ● *adj.* (**motlier, motliest**) **1** of varied character (*a motley crew*). **2** diversified in colour. ● *n.* **1** an incongruous mixture. **2** *hist.* the parti-coloured costume of a jester.

motocross /'mo:to:,krɒs/ *n.* cross-country racing on motorcycles. □ **motocrosser** *n.*

motor ● *n.* **1** a thing that imparts motion. **2** a machine (esp. one using electricity or internal combustion) supplying motive power for a vehicle etc. or for some other device with moving parts. ● *adj.* **1** giving, imparting, or producing motion. **2** driven by a motor. **3** of or for motor vehicles. **4** of or for motorists (*motor hotel*). **5** relating to muscular movement or the nerves activating it (*motor skills*). ● *v.* **1** *intr.* travel by or in a motor vehicle. **2** *intr.* move under motor power in a boat.

motorbike *n. informal* **1** = MOTORCYCLE. **2** = DIRT BIKE.

motorboat ● *n.* a motor-driven boat. ● *v.intr.* travel in or by motorboat.

motorcade *n.* a procession of motor vehicles.

motorcoach *n.* a bus that is comfortably equipped for long journeys.

motorcycle *n.* a two-wheeled motor-driven road vehicle without pedal propulsion. □ **motorcycling** *n.* **motorcyclist** *n.*

motorhome *n.* esp. *N Amer.* a large motor vehicle equipped as a self-contained home for camping or long trips.

motorist *n.* the driver of a car.

motorize *v.tr.* **1** provide with a motor. **2** equip (troops etc.) with motor transport. □ **motorization** *n.*

motormouth *n. N Amer. slang* a person who talks incessantly and trivially. □ **motor-mouthed** *adj.*

motor nerve *n.* a nerve carrying impulses from the brain or spinal cord to a muscle.

motorsailer *n.* a boat equipped with both sails and an engine.

motor scooter *n.* see SCOOTER.

motorsport *n.* (also **motor racing**) the racing of motorized vehicles, esp. cars, as a sport.

motor vehicle *n.* a road vehicle powered by an internal combustion engine.

motor yacht *n.* a motor-driven yacht.

Motown *n.* music with rhythm and blues and soul elements, associated with Detroit.

mottle ● *v.tr.* (esp. as **mottled** *adj.*) mark with spots or smears of colour. ● *n.* **1** an irregular arrangement of spots or patches of colour. **2** any of these spots or patches. □ **mottling** *n.*

motto *n.* (*pl.* **-oes, -os**) **1** a short sentence or phrase chosen and used as a guide or rule of behaviour or as an expression of the aims or ideals of a family, a country, an institution, etc. **2** a phrase or sentence accompanying a coat of arms or crest.

MOU *abbr.* MEMORANDUM OF UNDERSTANDING.

mould[1] ● *n.* **1** a hollow container into which molten metal etc. is poured or soft material is pressed to harden into a required shape. **2** a metal, earthenware, or plastic vessel used to give shape to puddings, jellies, etc. **3** something formed in a mould. **4** *Archit.* a moulding or group of mouldings. **5** a frame or template for producing mouldings. **6** a usual or expected type of something (*Martha doesn't fit into the traditional mould of an academic*). ● *v.* **1** *tr.* make (an object) in a required shape or from certain ingredients (*was moulded out of clay*). **2** *tr.* give a shape to. **3** *tr.* influence the formation or development of (*consultation helps to mould policies*). **4** *tr.* (esp. of clothing) fit closely to (*the gloves moulded his hands*). **5** *intr.* (foll. by *to*) conform to the shape of (*the shoe moulds to my foot*). □ **break the mould 1** (also **break out of the mould**) change people's expectations of something, esp. in a dramatic or challenging way. **2** make impossible the repetition of a certain type of creation (*they broke the mould when Alex was born*). □ **mouldable** *adj.* **moulder** *n.*

mould[2] *n.* a woolly, furry, or staining growth of minute fungi, as that which forms on food, textiles, etc., esp. in moist conditions.

mould[3] *n.* **1** loose earth. **2** the upper soil of cultivated land, esp. when rich in organic matter.

mouldboard *n.* the curved board or blade in a plow that turns over the furrow.

moulded *adj.* **1** formed, shaped. **2** made from a mould.

moulder *v.intr.* **1** decay to dust. **2** (foll. by *away*) rot or crumble. **3** deteriorate.

moulding *n.* **1 a** an ornamentally shaped outline as an architectural feature, esp. in a cornice. **b** a strip of material in wood or stone etc. for use as moulding. **2** similar material in wood or plastic etc. used for other decorative purposes, e.g. in picture framing.

mouldy *adj.* (**-ier, -iest**) **1** covered with mould; smelling of mould. **2** old and decaying. **3** old-fashioned. □ **mouldiness** *n.*

moult ● *v.* **1** *intr.* shed feathers, hair, a shell, etc., in the process of renewing plumage, a coat, etc. **2** *tr.* (of an animal) shed (feathers, hair, etc.). ● *n.* the act or an instance of moulting (*is in moult once a year*).

mound ● *n.* **1** a raised mass of earth, stones, or other compacted material. **2** a heap or pile. **3** a hillock. **4** *Baseball* a slight elevation on which the pitcher stands. ● *v.tr.* **1** heap up in a mound or mounds. **2** enclose with mounds. □ **take the mound** *Baseball* (of a pitcher) start or enter a game.

mound builder *n.* a member of a prehistoric N American Aboriginal people whose culture was characterized by the erection of mounds for burial and other purposes.

mount[1] ● *v.* **1** *tr.* ascend or climb (a hill, stairs, etc.). **2** *tr.* **a** get up on (an animal, esp. a horse) to ride it. **b** set (a person) on horseback. **c** provide (a person) with a horse. **3** *tr.* go up or climb on to (a raised surface). **4** *intr.*

a move upwards. **b** (often foll. by *up*) increase, accumulate. **c** (of a feeling) become stronger or more intense (*excitement was mounting*). **5** *tr.* (esp. of a male animal) get on to (a female) to copulate. **6** *tr.* (often foll. by *on*) place (an object) on an elevated support. **7** *tr.* **a** set in or attach to a backing, setting, or other support. **b** attach (a picture etc.) to a mount or frame. **c** fix (an object for viewing) on a microscope slide. **8** *tr.* **a** arrange (a play, exhibition, etc.) or present for public view or display. **b** conduct or take action to initiate (a program, campaign, etc.). **9** *tr.* prepare (specimens) for preservation. **10** *tr.* **a** bring into readiness for operation. **b** put (a gun, missile, etc.) into position for use. **c** (usu. in *passive*; foll. by *with*) fit (a military vehicle etc.) with a weapon. ● *n.* **1** a backing or setting on which a photograph, gem, etc. is set for display. **2** a support for a gun, camera, etc. **3** a glass microscope slide for securing a specimen etc. to be viewed. **4** a small piece of gummed transparent paper used for fixing stamps in an album etc. **5 a** a horse available for riding. **b** an opportunity to ride a horse, esp. as a jockey. □ **mount guard** (often foll. by *over*) perform the duty of guarding; take up sentry duty. □ **mountable** *adj.* **mounter** *n.*

mount² *n.* mountain, hill (*Mount Everest*).

mountain *n.* **1** a large natural elevation of the earth's surface rising abruptly from the surrounding level; a large or high and steep hill. **2** a large heap or pile; a huge quantity (*a mountain of work*). □ **move mountains 1** achieve spectacular results. **2** make every possible effort. □ **mountainy** *adj.*

mountain ash *n.* any of various small trees of the genus *Sorbus*, with pinnate leaves and scarlet berries.

mountain avens *n.* a alpine plant of the genus *Dryas*, bearing white or yellow flowers; one species, *D. octopetala*, is the floral emblem of the NWT.

mountain bike *n.* a bicycle with a light sturdy frame, broad deep-treaded tires, and multiple gears, originally designed for riding on mountainous terrain. □ **mountain biker** *n.* **mountain biking** *n.*

mountain chain *n.* a connected series of mountains.

mountain climber *n.* a person who climbs mountains, esp. as a sport. □ **mountain climbing** *n.*

mountaineer ● *n.* **1** a person skilled in mountain climbing. **2** a person living in an area of high mountains. ● *v.intr.* climb mountains as a sport. □ **mountaineering** *n.*

mountain goat *n.* **1** (in full **Rocky Mountain goat**) a white snow-antelope, *Oreamnos americanus*, of mountains in western N America. **2** a goat which lives on mountains, proverbial for agility.

mountain lion *n.* a cougar.

mountain man *n.* **1** a person who inhabits or frequents mountains or mountainous country. **2** (in N America) an early European pioneer, esp. living in the wilderness.

mountain maple *n.* a shrub or small tree, *Acer spicatum*, with three-lobed leaves, found from Newfoundland to Saskatchewan.

mountainous *adj.* **1** (of a region) having many mountains. **2** huge.

mountain range *n.* a line of mountains connected by high ground.

mountain sheep *n.* a sheep native to mountain regions, esp. a bighorn sheep or a Dall sheep.

mountainside *n.* the side of a mountain; slope.

Mountain Time *n.* the time in a zone including Alberta, the US states in or near the Rocky Mountains, and Mexico. **Mountain Standard Time** is

seven hours behind GMT; **Mountain Daylight Time** is six hours behind GMT.

mountaintop *n.* the top of a mountain.

mounted ● *adj.* **1** *in senses of* MOUNT¹ *v.* **2** serving on horseback (*mounted police*). ● *n. Cdn* a mounted police force (*officers of the mounted*).

Mountie *n. informal* a member of the RCMP.

Mountie hat *n. Cdn* the characteristic tan hat of the RCMP, with a broad flat encircling brim.

mounting *n.* **1** = MOUNT¹ *n.* 1, 2. **2** *in senses of* MOUNT¹ *v.*

mourn *v.* **1** *tr. & intr.* feel or show sorrow or regret for (a dead person, a lost thing, a past event, etc.). **2** *intr.* show conventional signs of grief after a person's death.

mourner *n.* a person who mourns, esp. at a funeral.

mournful *adj.* **1** doleful, sad, sorrowing. **2** expressing or suggestive of mourning. □ **mournfully** *adv.* **mournfulness** *n.*

mourning *n.* **1** the expression of deep sorrow, esp. for a loss, death, etc. **2** the wearing of solemn clothing as a convention to indicate sorrow after a death. **3** the clothes worn in mourning. □ **in mourning** assuming the signs of mourning, esp. in dress.

mourning cloak *n. N Amer.* a butterfly, *Nymphalis antiopa*, with deep purple yellow-bordered wings.

mourning dove *n.* a small slender N American dove, *Zenaida macroura*, with a long pointed tail and a plaintive call.

mourvèdre /muːrˈvedrə/ *n.* **1** a variety of vine of the species *Vitis vinifera*, yielding black grapes used in winemaking. **2** the grape of this variety, noted for its intense fruity flavour and often used in blends. **3** the red wine made from this grape.

mouse ● *n.* (*pl.* **mice**) **1 a** any of various small rodents of the family Muridae, esp. of the genus *Mus*, usu. having a pointed snout and relatively large ears and eyes. **b** any of several similar rodents such as a small shrew or vole. **2** a timid or feeble person. **3** *Computing* a small hand-held device moved over a flat surface to produce a corresponding movement of a cursor or arrow on a computer screen, usu. having fingertip controls for selecting a function or entering a command. ● *v.intr.* **1** (esp. of a cat, owl, etc.) hunt for or catch mice. **2** (foll. by *around*, *about*) search industriously; prowl about as if searching. □ **mouselike** *adj.* & *adv.* **mouser** *n.*

mouse pad *n.* a flat pad across which a computer mouse is moved.

mousetrap ● *n.* **1** a trap with bait for catching and usu. killing mice. **2** (often *attrib.*) cheese of poor quality. ● *v.tr. N Amer.* entice (a person) to destruction or defeat.

mousey *var. of* MOUSY.

moussaka /moˈsɒkə/ *n.* a Greek and eastern Mediterranean baked dish of ground meat, eggplant, etc. with white sauce.

mousse /muːs/ ● *n.* **1 a** a dessert of whipped cream, eggs, etc., usu. flavoured with fruit or chocolate. **b** a meat or fish purée made with whipped cream etc. **2** a foamy preparation applied to the hair enabling it to be styled more easily. ● *v.tr.* apply mousse to (hair). □ **moussed** *adj.*

moustache /ˈmʌstæʃ, məˈstæʃ/ *n.* **1** the hair on the upper lip, esp. as left to grow by men. **2** a similar growth around the mouth of some animals. □ **moustached** *adj.*

moustachio *var. of* MUSTACHIO.

mousy *adj.* (**-ier, -iest**) **1** of or like a mouse. **2** (of a person) shy or timid; ineffectual. **3** (esp. of hair) nondescript light brown. **4** dark grey with a yellow tinge.

mouth ● *n.* (*pl.* **mouths**) **1 a** an external opening in the head, through which most animals admit food and emit communicative sounds. **b** (in humans and some animals) the cavity behind it containing the means of biting and chewing and the vocal organs. **2 a** the opening of a container such as a bag or sack. **b** the opening of a cave, volcano, etc. **c** the muzzle of a gun. **3 a** the place where a river enters a sea or lake. **b** the expanse of water connecting a bay or harbour with a lake or the sea. **4** *informal* **a** talkativeness. **b** impudent talk; cheek. **c** boastful talk. **5** an individual regarded as needing sustenance (*an extra mouth to feed*). ● *v.* **1** *tr.* & *intr.* utter or speak solemnly or with affectations; rant, declaim (*mouthing platitudes*). **2** *tr.* say (words) with movement of the mouth but no sound. **3** *tr.* utter very distinctly. **4** *intr.* **a** move the lips silently. **b** grimace. **5** *tr.* take (food) in the mouth. **6** *tr.* touch with the mouth. □ **have a big mouth** talk indiscreetly. **keep one's mouth shut** *informal* refrain from saying something inappropriate. **mouth off 1** (often foll. by *at*) talk insolently or disrespectfully. **2** talk loudly; express one's opinions forcefully. **put words into a person's mouth** inaccurately represent a person as having said something. **take the words out of a person's mouth** say what another was about to say. **watch one's mouth** be careful not to say something offensive. □ **mouthed** *adj.* (also in *comb.*).

mouth feel *n.* the sensation produced in the mouth by the texture of food etc., regardless of the taste.

mouthful *n.* (*pl.* **-fuls**) **1** a quantity, esp. of food, that fills or is in the mouth. **2** a small quantity. **3** a long or complicated word or phrase. □ **say a mouthful** *N Amer.* say something important.

mouthguard *n.* a piece of esp. sports equipment protecting the mouth, teeth, etc.

mouth organ *n.* (also **mouth harp**) = HARMONICA.

mouthpart *n.* any of the (usu. paired) organs surrounding the mouth of an insect or other arthropod and adapted for feeding.

mouthpiece *n.* **1 a** the part of a musical instrument placed between or against the lips. **b** the part of a telephone for speaking into. **c** the part of a tobacco pipe placed between the lips. **2** any apparatus or part of one that fits into the mouth, e.g. of scuba equipment, a bridle, etc. **3 a** a person, organization, etc. that speaks for another or others. **b** *informal* a lawyer.

mouth-to-mouth *n.* a method of resuscitation in which a person breathes into a subject's lungs through the mouth (also *attrib.*: *mouth-to-mouth resuscitation*).

mouthwash *n.* a liquid antiseptic etc. for rinsing the mouth or gargling.

mouth-watering *adj.* **1** (of food etc.) having a delicious smell or appearance; appetizing. **2** tempting, alluring.

mouthy *adj.* (**-ier**, **-iest**) **1** ranting, railing, bombastic. **2** *informal* impudent, cheeky.

movable (also **moveable**) ● *adj.* **1** that can be moved. **2** *Law* (of property) of the nature of a chattel, as distinct from land or buildings. **3** (of a religious feast or festival) variable in date from year to year. ● *n.* **1** an article of furniture that may be removed from a house, as distinct from a fixture. **2** (in *pl.*) personal property. □ **movability** *n.*

movable-do *attrib.adj.* applied to a system of sight-singing in which do is the keynote of any major scale (*compare* FIXED-DO).

move ● *v.* **1** *intr.* & *tr.* **a** shift one's position or posture, or cause to do this. **b** change (*Russia is moving towards a market economy*; *moved the meeting to Friday*). **2** *tr.* & *intr.* **a** put or keep in motion; rouse, stir. **b** maintain a fairly quick pace or tempo. **3** *intr.* (often foll. by *about*, *around*, etc.) go or pass from place to place. **4** *intr.* take action, esp. promptly (*moved to reduce unemployment*). **5** *intr.* **a** (often foll. by *ahead*) make progress (*the project is moving fast*). **b** (foll. by *on*) advance, progress (*moved on to the quarter-finals*). **6** *intr.* change (one's place of residence or work). **7 a** *intr.* make a move in a board game. **b** *tr.* change the position of (a piece) in a board game. **8** *intr.* (foll. by *in*) live or be socially active in (a specified place or group etc.) (*moves in the best circles*). **9** *tr.* affect (a person) with (usu. tender or sympathetic) emotion. **10** *tr.* (foll. by *to*) provoke (a person to laughter etc.). **11** *tr.* (foll. by *to*, or *to* + infin.) prompt or incline (a person to a feeling or action). **12** *tr.* & *intr.* (cause to) change in attitude or opinion (*nothing can move me on this issue*). **13 a** *tr.* cause (the bowels) to be emptied. **b** *intr.* (of the bowels) be emptied. **14** *tr.* (often foll. by *that* + clause) propose in a meeting, deliberative assembly, etc. **15** *intr.* (foll. by *for*) make a formal request or application. **16 a** *intr.* (of merchandise) be sold. **b** *tr.* sell. ● *n.* **1** the act or an instance of moving. **2** a change of house, business premises, etc. **3** a step taken to secure some action or effect; an initiative. **4 a** the changing of the position of a piece in a board game. **b** a player's turn to do this. **5** *Sport* a manoeuvre employed by a single player esp. to avoid or deceive an opponent. □ **get a move on** *informal* **1** hurry up. **2** make a start. **get moving** *informal* begin, leave, etc. quickly (*it's late - we'd better get moving*). **get something moving** *informal* cause something to make vigorous progress. **make a move** take action. **move along** (or **on**) change to a new position, esp. to avoid crowding, getting in the way, etc. **move away** go to live in another area. **move house** esp. *Cdn* & *Brit.* transfer one's furniture, goods, etc. from one residence to another. **move in 1** take possession of a new house etc. **2** get into a position of influence, interference, etc. **3** (often foll. by *on*) get into a position of readiness or proximity (for an offensive action etc.). **move in with** start to share accommodation with (an existing resident). **move off** (esp. of a vehicle) start a journey. **move on** move to another place, topic, job, etc. **move out 1** leave one's home; change one's place of residence. **2** leave a position, job, etc. **move over** adjust one's position to make room for another. **move up 1** improve one's position or condition, esp. in a career. **2** *Baseball* (of a baserunner) move to the next base. **on the move 1** progressing. **2** moving around. **put the move** (or **moves**) **on** make sexual advances towards.

movement *n.* **1 a** the act or an instance of moving or being moved. **b** an act of changing position, esp. as a planned and controlled act by armed forces (*troop movements*). **2** (usu. in *pl.*) a person's activities and whereabouts, esp. at a particular time. **3 a** a body of persons with a common object (*the peace movement*). **b** a campaign undertaken by such a body. **4** a direction of thought or opinion; a social trend. **5** a change in amount. **6 a** the moving parts of a mechanism (esp. a clock or watch). **b** a particular group of these. **7** *Music* **a** a principal division of a longer musical work, self-sufficient in terms of key, tempo, structure, etc. **b** rhythmical character in music; tempo. **8** the progressive development of a poem, story, etc. **9** (of the bowels) the action of discharging feces. **10 a** an activity in a market for some commodity. **b** a rise or fall in price. **11** *Baseball* the deviation of a pitched ball from a straight trajectory.

mover *n.* **1** a person or thing that moves. **2** *N Amer.* a person or company that transports furniture etc. for clients changing residence or business location. **3** a person who makes a motion in a formal meeting etc. **4** (esp. in **movers and shakers**) a person who incites or instigates to action; an enterprising person.

movie *n.* esp. *N Amer. informal* **1** a motion-picture film. **2** a movie theatre. **3** (in *pl.*) the motion-picture industry. **4** (also *pl.*) a showing of a motion-picture film (*were at a movie; went to the movies*).

moviegoer *n.* esp. *N Amer.* a person who attends movies. □ **movie-going** *n.*

movieland *n. informal* the motion-picture industry.

moviemaker *n.* esp. *N Amer.* a filmmaker. □ **moviemaking** *n.*

movie theatre *n.* (also **movie house**) esp. *N Amer.* a theatre where motion-picture films are shown.

moving *adj.* **1** that moves or causes to move. **2** affecting with emotion. □ **movingly** *adv.* (in sense 2).

moving picture *n.* = MOTION PICTURE.

moving sidewalk *n.* a structure like a conveyor belt for pedestrians.

moving target *n.* **1** a target that is in motion when aimed at. **2** a person, thing, or phenomenon that changes character so frequently as to be difficult to assess, deal with, etc.

mow[1] *v.tr.* (*past part.* **mowed** or **mown**) **1** cut down (grass, hay, etc.) with a machine or scythe. **2** cut down the grass etc. of (a lawn) or the produce of (a field) by mowing. □ **mow down** kill or destroy randomly or in great numbers. □ **mower** *n.*

mow[2] /mau/ *n.* **1** a pile or heap of hay, grain, etc. **2** a place in a barn where hay or straw is stored.

moxa /'mɒksə/ *n.* a downy substance from the dried leaves of *Artemisia moxa* etc., burned on the skin in oriental medicine as a counterirritant.

moxie *n.* *N Amer. slang* force of character, energy, ingenuity.

Mozambican /ˌmoːzæm'biːkən/ ● *n.* **1** a native or inhabitant of Mozambique, a country on the east coast of southern Africa. **2** a person of Mozambican descent. ● *adj.* of or relating to Mozambique.

mozzarella /ˌmɒtsə'relə, ˌmʌt-/ *n.* a white Italian cheese originally made of buffalo milk.

MP *abbr.* **1** Member of Parliament. **2 a** military police. **b** military policeman.

mp *abbr.* mezzo-piano.

m.p. *abbr.* melting point.

M.P.A. *abbr.* Master of Public Administration.

MPD *abbr.* multiple personality disorder.

M.P.E. *abbr.* Master of Physical Education.

mpg *abbr.* miles per gallon.

mph *abbr.* miles per hour.

M.Phil. *abbr.* Master of Philosophy.

M.P.M. *abbr.* Master of Public Management.

MPP *abbr. Cdn* (*Ont.*) Member of Provincial Parliament.

MPV *abbr.* multi-purpose vehicle, a minivan.

Mr. *n.* (*pl.* **Messrs.**) **1** a title prefixed to the name of a man not having a higher, honorific, or professional title. **2** a title prefixed to a designation of office etc. (*Mr. Speaker*). **3** a title prefixed to a characteristic of a certain man (*Mr. Nice Guy*).

MRC *abbr. Cdn* (in Quebec) *Municipalité Régionale de Comté.*

M.R.E. *abbr.* Master of Religious Education.

MRI *abbr.* MAGNETIC RESONANCE IMAGING.

mRNA *abbr. Biol.* messenger RNA.

Mr. Right *n. jocular* the man who would make the ideal husband for a particular woman.

Mrs. *n.* (*pl.* same or **Mesdames**) a title prefixed to the name of a married woman not having a higher, honorific, or professional title.

MS *abbr.* **1** manuscript. **2** Mississippi (in postal use). **3** MULTIPLE SCLEROSIS. **4** *Cdn* MASTER SEAMAN.

M.S. *abbr.* **1** Master of Science. **2** Master of Surgery.

Ms. *n.* a title prefixed to the name of a woman regardless of her marital status.

ms *abbr.* millisecond(s).

M.Sc. *abbr.* Master of Science.

M.Sc.F. *abbr.* Master of Science in Forestry.

MS-DOS /ˌemes'dɒs/ *n. proprietary* an operating system for personal computers.

MSG *abbr.* MONOSODIUM GLUTAMATE.

Msgr. *abbr.* **1** Monseigneur. **2** Monsignor.

MSRP *abbr.* manufacturer's suggested retail price.

MSS *abbr.* manuscripts.

MST *abbr.* Mountain Standard Time.

M.S.W. *abbr.* Master of Social Work.

MT *abbr.* **1** Montana (in postal use). **2** MOUNTAIN TIME.

Mt. *abbr.* **1** Mount (*Mt. Logan*). **2** Mountain.

MTB *abbr.* **1** motor torpedo boat. **2** mountain bike.

M.Th. *abbr.* Master of Theology.

Mtl. *abbr.* Montreal.

M.T.S. *abbr.* Master of Theological Studies.

mu /mjuː/ *n.* **1** the twelfth Greek letter (M, μ). **2** (μ, as a symbol) = MICRO- 2.

MUC *abbr.* Montreal Urban Community.

much ● *adj.* **1** existing or occurring in a great quantity (*much trouble; not much rain; too much noise*). **2** (prec. by *as*, *how*, *that*, etc.) with relative rather than distinctive sense (*I don't know how much money you want*). ● *n.* **1** a great quantity (*much of that is true*). **2** (prec. by *as*, *how*, *that*, etc.) with relative rather than distinctive sense (*we do not need that much*). **3** (usu. in *neg.*) a noteworthy or outstanding example (*not much of a party*). ● *adv.* **1 a** in a great degree (*much to my surprise; is much the same*). **b** (qualifying a verb or past participle) greatly (*they much regret the mistake; much annoyed*). **c** qualifying a comparative or superlative adjective (*much better*). **2** for a large part of one's time (*is much away from home*). ● *interj. informal* expressing strong disagreement. □ **as much** the extent or quantity just specified; the idea just mentioned (*I thought as much; as much as that?*). **a bit much** *informal* somewhat excessive or immoderate. **much as** even though (*cannot come, much as I would like to*). **too much** *informal* an intolerable situation etc. (*that really is too much*). **too much for 1** more than a match for. **2** beyond what is endurable by. □ **muchly** *adv. jocular.*

mucho /'muːtʃo/ *jocular* much.

mucilage /'mjuːsɪlɪdʒ/ *n.* **1** a solution of gum or glue in water, used as an adhesive. **2** a viscous or gelatinous solution obtained from plant roots, seeds, etc., used in medicines and adhesives. **3** any viscous or gummy solution or secretion, e.g. mucus. □ **mucilaginous** /-'lædʒɪnəs/ *adj.*

muck ● *n.* **1** mud. **2** very dark and highly organic soil. **3** *informal* dirt or filth; anything disgusting. **4** farmyard manure. **5** *informal* an untidy state; a mess. **6** waste material removed during mining or civil engineering operations. ● *v.* **1** *tr.* (usu. foll. by *up*) *informal* ruin, spoil, mess up. **2** *tr.* make dirty. **3** *tr.* manure with muck. **4** *intr.* (in hockey) play tenaciously and physically, esp. along the boards in an attempt to gain control of the puck. □ **muck about** (or **around**) *informal* **1** putter or fool about. **2** (foll. by *with*) fool or interfere with. **muck out** clean (a barn etc.) of manure.

mucker n. slang **1** a person or machine that removes mining waste. **2** N Amer. a person, esp. a hockey player, known more for tenacity and hard work than for remarkable talent.

muckrake v.intr. search out and reveal scandal, esp. among famous people. □ **muckraker** n. **muckraking** n.

mucky adj. (**-ier, -iest**) **1** covered with muck. **2** dirty. □ **muckiness** n.

mucky-muck n. (also **muckamuck, muckety-muck**) N Amer. slang a person of great self-importance.

mucosa /mju:ˈkoːsə/ n. (pl. **mucosae** /-si:/) a mucous membrane. □ **mucosal** adj.

mucous /ˈmjuːkəs/ adj. of, resembling, secreting, or covered with mucus.

mucous membrane n. a mucus-secreting epithelial tissue lining many body cavities and tubular organs.

mucus /ˈmjuːkəs/ n. **1** a slimy substance, usu. not miscible with water, secreted by a mucous membrane or gland. **2** a gummy substance found in plants.

mud n. **1** wet soft earthy matter. **2** hard ground from the drying of an area of this. □ **as clear as mud** informal not at all clear. **drag through the mud** denigrate publicly. **fling** (or **sling** or **throw**) **mud** speak disparagingly or slanderously. **here's mud in your eye!** informal a toast made when drinking. **one's name is mud** one is unpopular or in disgrace.

mudbank n. a bank of mud, esp. on the bed of a river or the bottom of the sea.

mud bath n. **1** a bath in the mud of mineral springs, esp. to relieve rheumatism etc. **2** a muddy scene or occasion.

mud brick n. a brick made from baked mud (also attrib.: mud-brick huts).

mudcat n. **1** Cdn = BULLHEAD 1. **2** N Amer. a large N American catfish, Pylodictis olivaris, with a long slender body and a flat head.

muddle ● v. **1** tr. (often foll. by up) bring into disorder. **2** tr. bewilder, confuse. **3** tr. mismanage (an affair). **4** intr. (often foll. by with) busy oneself in a confused and ineffective way. ● n. **1** a state of disorder. **2** mental confusion. □ **make a muddle of 1** bring into disorder. **2** bungle. **muddle along** (or **on**) progress in a haphazard way. **muddle through** succeed by perseverance rather than skill or efficiency. □ **muddler** n. **muddlingly** adv.

muddle-headed adj. stupid, confused.

muddler n. N Amer. a type of fly used in trout fishing.

muddy ● adj. (**-ier, -iest**) **1** like mud. **2** covered in or full of mud. **3** (of liquid) turbid. **4** mentally confused. **5** obscure. **6** (of light) dull. **7** (of colour) impure. ● v.tr. (**-ies, -ied**) make muddy. □ **muddy the waters** confuse matters. □ **muddily** adv. **muddiness** n.

mud flap n. a flap hanging behind the wheel of a vehicle, to catch mud and stones etc. thrown up from the road.

mud flat n. a stretch of muddy land left uncovered at low tide.

mudguard n. a curved strip or cover over a wheel of a bicycle, motorcycle, etc. to reduce the amount of mud etc. thrown up from the road.

mudhole n. **1** a water hole dried so as to become mud. **2** a muddy hole in a road.

mud pie n. **1** mud made into a pie shape by a child. **2** N Amer. a rich chocolate ice cream pie.

mud puppy n. N Amer. a large nocturnal salamander, Necturus maculosus, of central N America.

mud room n. N Amer. a small room, often a vestibule, in a house, in which wet or muddy footwear and outer clothes are removed.

mudslide n. an avalanche of mud etc.

mudslinging n. informal abuse, slander, or malevolent criticism. □ **mudslinger** n.

mud trout n. Cdn (Nfld) the eastern brook trout, Salvelinus fontinalis.

mud wrestling n. an activity in which usu. female contestants wrestle in a mud-filled ring for the amusement of spectators. □ **mud-wrestle** v.tr. & intr. **mud wrestler** n.

Muenster /ˈmɒnstər/ n. a fairly strong soft-ripened cheese, having a washed rind cured in a solution of brine or seasoned wine or beer.

muesli /ˈmjuːzli/ n. a breakfast food of crushed cereals (usu. oats), dried fruits, nuts, etc., eaten with milk.

muezzin /muːˈezɪn/ n. a Muslim crier who proclaims the hours of prayer usu. from a minaret.

muff[1] n. **1** a fur or other covering, usu. in the form of a tube with an opening at each end for the hands to be inserted for warmth. **2** = EARMUFF.

muff[2] ● v.tr. **1** bungle; deal clumsily with. **2** fail to catch or receive (a ball etc.). **3** blunder in (a theatrical part etc.). ● n. a failure, esp. to catch a ball.

muffin n. N Amer. a quick bread made of flour, milk, eggs, and fat, often also with oats or bran, etc., leavened with baking powder or baking soda, and baked in a small cup-shaped pan.

muffin tin n. N Amer. a baking pan having a series of small round wells, for cooking muffins.

muffle v.tr. **1** (often foll. by up) wrap or cover for warmth. **2** cover or wrap up (a source of sound) to reduce its loudness. **3** (usu. as **muffled** adj.) stifle (an utterance, e.g. a curse). **4** prevent from speaking.

muffler n. **1** N Amer. a device attached to a motor vehicle's exhaust system to reduce noise. **2** a scarf worn for warmth. **3** any of various devices used to deaden sound in musical instruments.

mufti[1] /ˈmʌfti/ n. a Muslim legal expert empowered to give rulings on religious matters.

mufti[2] /ˈmʌfti/ n. plain clothes worn by a person who also wears (esp. military) uniform (in mufti).

mug ● n. **1 a** a drinking vessel, usu. cylindrical and with a handle and used without a saucer. **b** its contents. **2** slang the face or mouth of a person. ● v. (**mugged, mugging**) **1** tr. rob (a person) with violence esp. in a public place. **2** intr. slang make faces, esp. before an audience, camera, etc. □ **a mug's game** informal a foolish or unprofitable activity. □ **mugger** n. (in sense 1 of v.). **mugful** n. (pl. **-fuls**). **mugging** n. (in sense 1 of v.).

muggy adj. (**-ier, -iest**) (of the weather etc.) oppressively damp and warm; humid. □ **mugginess** n.

Mughal /ˈmuːɡʊl/ n. **1** a Mongolian. **2** (attrib.) denoting the Muslim dynasty in India in the 16th–19th c. (compare MOGUL[1] 2b).

mug shot n. slang a photograph of a face, esp. for official purposes.

mug-up n. Cdn (esp. Nfld) a break for a hot drink (esp. tea) and snacks, esp. while on a hike, journey, etc.

mujahedeen /ˌmuːdʒəhəˈdiːn/ n.pl. (also **mujahideen, mujahidin**) guerrilla fighters in Islamic countries, esp. supporting Muslim fundamentalism.

mukluk /ˈmʌklʌk/ n. N Amer. **1** a winter boot with a

heavy rubber sole and a high fabric upper, usu. with laces. **2** a traditional Inuit boot, usu. made from seal or caribou skin.

mulatto /məˈlætoː, -ˈlɒtoː, mjuː-/ n. (pl. **-oes** or **-os**) a person of mixed white and black parentage.

mulberry ● n. (pl. **-ies**) **1** (also **mulberry tree** or **mulberry bush**) any deciduous tree of the genus *Morus*, esp. *M. alba* (**white mulberry**), grown originally for feeding silkworms, and *M. rubra* of eastern N America (**red mulberry**), with juicy edible fruit. **2** the dark red or white berry of such a tree. **3** a dark red or purple colour. ● adj. of this colour.

mulch ● n. a mixture usu. of vegetable matter spread around or over a plant to enrich or insulate the soil or suppress weeds. ● v.tr. treat with mulch.

mule[1] n. **1** the offspring (usu. sterile) of a male donkey and a female horse, or (in general use) of a female donkey and a male horse, used as a beast of burden. **2** a stupid or obstinate person. **3** (often attrib.) a hybrid and usu. sterile plant or animal (*mule canary*). **4** esp. N Amer. slang a person acting as a courier for illicit drugs. **5** (in full **spinning mule**) a kind of spinning machine producing yarn on spindles.

mule[2] n. a light shoe or slipper without a back.

mule deer n. a long-eared black-tailed deer of prairies and mountains of western N America, *Odocoileus hemionus*.

muley n. (also **mulie**) N Amer. informal = MULE DEER.

mulish adj. **1** like a mule. **2** stubborn. □ **mulishly** adv. **mulishness** n.

mull[1] v.tr. & intr. (often foll. by over) ponder or consider.

mull[2] v.tr. (esp. as **mulled** adj.) warm (wine or beer) with added sugar, spices, etc.

mullah /ˈmʌlə, ˈmʊlə/ n. a Muslim learned in Islamic theology and sacred law.

mullein /ˈmʌlən/ n. any herbaceous plant of the genus *Verbascum*, with woolly leaves and yellow flowers.

mullet /ˈmʌlət/ n. any fish of the family Mullidae (**red mullet**) or Mugilidae (**grey mullet**), usu. with a thick body and a large blunt-nosed head, commonly used as food.

mulligan /ˈmʌlɪgən/ n. (in full **mulligan stew**) N Amer. a stew made from odds and ends of food.

mulligatawny /ˌmʌlɪgəˈtɒni/ n. a highly seasoned soup originally from India.

mullion /ˈmʌljən/ n. a vertical bar dividing the lights in a window (compare TRANSOM 1). □ **mullioned** adj.

multi- comb. form many; more than one.

multi-billion attrib.adj. costing or involving several billion dollars, pounds, etc.

multicellular adj. Biol. having or involving many cells. □ **multicellularity** n.

multi-channel adj. employing or possessing many communication or television channels.

multicoloured adj. (also **multicolour**) of many colours.

multiculti adj. (also Cdn **multicult**) informal = MULTICULTURAL.

multicultural adj. **1** designating or pertaining to a society consisting of many culturally distinct groups. **2 a** (of a person etc.) advocating or receptive to the establishment of a multicultural society. **b** (of a group etc.) consisting of individuals from various, culturally distinct groups. □ **multiculturalism** n. **multiculturalist** n. & adj. **multiculturally** adv.

multi-dimensional adj. of or involving more than three dimensions.

multidirectional adj. of, involving, or operating in several directions.

multidisciplinary adj. combining or involving many separate disciplines or fields of endeavour.

multi-ethnic adj. composed of or involving several ethnic groups.

multi-faceted adj. having several facets, aspects, etc.

multi-family adj. (esp. of housing) designed for or occupied by more than one family.

multifarious /ˌmʌltɪˈfɛriəs/ adj. **1** (foll. by pl. noun) many and various. **2** having great variety or diversity. □ **multifariously** adv. **multifariousness** n.

multi-function adj. (also **multi-functional**) having or fulfilling several functions.

multi-generational adj. **1** (of a family or group) including more than two generations. **2** lasting over several generations (*multi-generational poverty*).

multigrade n. (usu. attrib.) **1** an engine oil, paper, etc. meeting the requirements of several standard grades. **2** N Amer. (of a class etc.) having students from more than one academic year studying together.

multi-grain adj. (of baked goods, cereals, etc.) incorporating many grains.

multihull n. a boat having more than one hull.

multi-lane adj. (of a road) having many lanes, usu. more than two in each direction.

multilateral adj. **1 a** (of an agreement, treaty, conference, etc.) in which three or more parties participate. **b** performed by more than one party (*multilateral disarmament*). **2** having many sides. □ **multilateralism** n. **multilateralist** n. & adj. **multilaterally** adv.

multi-layered adj. (also **multi-layer**) composed of, occurring in, or having many layers.

multi-level adj. **1** having, involving, or operating on many levels. **2** designating a method of direct selling in which buyers at each level of a hierarchy secure the participation of further buyers at a level below them. □ **multi-levelled** adj.

multilingual /ˌmʌltiˈlɪŋgwəl, -ˈlɪŋjuəl/ adj. **1** in or using several languages. **2** (of a person) speaking several languages fluently. □ **multilingualism** n.

multimedia ● attrib.adj. (of art, education, etc.) using more than one medium of expression, communication, etc. ● n. an extension of hypertext allowing the provision of audio and video material cross-referenced to a computer text (also attrib.: *multimedia applications*).

multi-million attrib.adj. costing or involving several million dollars, pounds, etc.

multi-millionaire n. a person with a fortune of several million dollars, pounds, etc.

multinational ● adj. **1** (of a business organization) operating in several countries. **2** relating to or including several nationalities or ethnic groups. ● n. a multinational company.

multi-pack n. a composite package containing several units of a product, sold at a lower price than the equivalent number of units sold separately.

multi-party attrib.adj. **1 a** comprising members of several esp. political parties (*multi-party talks*). **b** sponsored by or involving more than one person, interest group, etc. (*multi-party lawsuit*). **2** designating or pertaining to an electoral system in which the interests of the electorate are represented by three or more political parties. □ **multi-partyism** n.

multiple ● adj. **1** having many parts, elements, or individual components. **2** (foll. by pl. noun) many and various. **3** *Med.* (of a disease or symptom) affecting several parts, organs, etc. ● *n.* **1** a number that may be divided by another a certain number of times without a remainder (*56 is a multiple of 7*). **2** *Business* a number expressing the current market price of a company share divided by the earnings per share of the company. **3** an inexpensive work of art able to be mass-produced by industrial methods. □ **multiply** *adv.*

multiple-choice *adj.* **1** (of a question in an examination) accompanied by several possible answers from which the correct one is to be chosen. **2** (of a test, questionnaire, etc.) consisting of such questions.

multiple listing service *n.* *N Amer.* a co-operative real estate market system in which the seller signs an agreement with one vendor and broker allowing other brokers to sell the property for part of the agreed upon commission.

multiple personality *n.* (in full **multiple personality disorder**) a dissociative condition in which an individual's personality is apparently split into two or more distinct sub-personalities, each of which may become dominant at different times.

multiple sclerosis *n.* a chronic, progressive disease of the nervous system, in which sclerosis occurs in patches in the brain and spinal cord, resulting in tremor, paralysis, speech and sight defects, etc.

multiplex ● *adj.* **1** manifold; of many elements; having many related features. **2** involving simultaneous transmission of several messages along a single channel of communication. **3** of or relating to a single-site complex of two or more cinemas. ● *n.* **1** a multiplex cinema. **2** a multiplex system or signal. ● *v.tr.* incorporate into a multiplex signal or system. □ **multiplexer** *n.* (also **multiplexor**). **multiplexing** *n.* & *adj.*

multiplication *n.* **1** the arithmetical process of multiplying. **2** the act or an instance of multiplying. **3** the reproduction of people or animals, or the propagation of plants. □ **multiplicative** *adj.*

multiplication sign *n.* the sign (×) to indicate that one quantity is to be multiplied by another, as in 2×3.

multiplication table *n.* a list of multiples of a particular number, usu. from 1 to 12.

multiplicity /ˌmʌltɪˈplɪsɪtɪ/ *n.* (*pl.* **-ies**) **1** manifold variety. **2** (foll. by *of*) a great number.

multiplier *n.* **1 a** a thing which or person who multiplies or causes something to increase. **b** a quantity by which a given number is multiplied. **2** *Econ.* a factor by which an increment of income exceeds the resulting increment of saving or investment. **3** *Electricity* an instrument for increasing by repetition the intensity of a current, force, etc.

multiply /ˈmʌltɪˌplaɪ/ *v.* (**-ies, -ied**) **1** *tr.* & *intr.* obtain from (a number) another that is a specified number of times its value (*multiply 6 by 4 and you get 24*). **2** *intr.* a increase in number by accumulation or repetition. **b** increase in number by reproduction or procreation. **3** *tr.* produce a large number of (instances etc.). **4** *tr.* **a** breed (animals). **b** propagate (plants).

multi-point *adj.* having or serving several points.

multipolar *adj.* **1** having or pertaining to many poles. **2** consisting of or divided into more than two esp. political alliances, parties, etc. □ **multipolarity** *n.*

multiprocessing *n.* *Computing* processing by a number of processors sharing a common memory and common peripherals.

multiprocessor *n.* a computer capable of performing multiprocessing.

multiprogramming *n.* *Computing* the execution of two or more independent programs concurrently.

multi-purpose *adj.* having many purposes.

multiracial *adj.* relating to or made up of many human races. □ **multiracialism** *n.*

multi-sensory *adj.* pertaining to or affecting more than one of the five senses.

multi-stage *attrib.adj.* consisting of, occurring in, or involving many stages.

multi-storey *attrib.adj.* (of a building) having many esp. similarly designed storeys.

multi-tasking ● *n.* the execution of a number of tasks at the same time. ● *adj.* capable of multi-tasking. □ **multi-task** *v.tr.* & *intr.*

multi-threading *n.* a programming technique whereby several processes can use the same applications software concurrently without interference. □ **multi-threaded** *adj.*

multi-track ● *attrib.adj.* **1** relating to or made by the mixing of separately recorded soundtracks. **2** (of a school) having students divided into several groups on overlapping schedules esp. to ease overcrowding. ● *n.* a multi-track recording. ● *v.tr.* & *intr.* **1** record using multi-track recording. **2** divide a student body into several groups on overlapping schedules to ease overcrowding etc. □ **multi-tracked** *adj.* **multi-tracking** *n.*

multitude *n.* **1** (often foll. by *of*) a great number. **2** a large gathering of people; a crowd. **3** (**the multitude**) the common people. **4** the state of being numerous.

multitudinous /ˌmʌltɪˈtuːdɪnəs, -ˈtjuːdɪnəs/ *adj.* **1** very numerous. **2** consisting of many individuals or elements.

multi-use *adj.* serving many uses.

multi-user *attrib.adj.* **1** having many users. **2** (of a computer system) able to be used by more than one person and accessed from more than one terminal concurrently.

multivalent /ˌmʌltɪˈveɪlənt/ *adj.* **1** having or susceptible of many applications, interpretations, meanings, or values. **2** *Chem.* **a** having a valence of more than two. **b** having a variable valence. □ **multivalence** *n.*

multivariate /ˌmʌltɪˈveərɪət/ *adj.* *Statistics* involving or having two or more variable quantities.

multivitamin ● *n.* a nutritional supplement, esp. a pill, incorporating several vitamins. ● *adj.* designating a nutritional supplement of this sort.

multi-year *adj.* lasting or covering many years.

multi-year ice *n.* polar ice that is more than two years old.

mum[1] *n.* *Cdn* & *Brit.* informal mother.

mum[2] *adj.* informal silent (*keep mum*). □ **mum's the word** say nothing.

mum[3] *v.intr.* (**mummed, mumming**) play as a mummer.

mum[4] *n.* informal = CHRYSANTHEMUM.

mumble ● *v.* **1** *intr.* & *tr.* speak or utter indistinctly. **2** *tr.* bite or chew with or as with toothless gums. ● *n.* an indistinct utterance. □ **mumbler** *n.* **mumbling** *n.* & *adj.* **mumblingly** *adv.*

mumbo-jumbo *n.* (*pl.* **-jumbos**) **1** meaningless or ignorant ritual. **2** obscure language or action intended to mystify or confuse. **3** an object of superstitious veneration.

mummer ● *n.* **1** an actor in a traditional masked mime. **2** *jocular* or *derogatory* an actor in the theatre. **3** (in Newfoundland) (also *attrib.*) a person participating in Christmas mumming. ● *v.intr.* (in Newfoundland) participate in mumming activities.

mummichog /'mʌmiːtʃʊg/ *n.* a black and silver killifish, *Fundulus heteroclitus*, common in marshy coastal waters of N America.

mummify *v.tr.* (**-ies, -ied**) **1** embalm and preserve (a body) in the form of a mummy (see MUMMY²). **2** shrivel or dry up (tissues etc.). □ **mummification** *n.* **mummified** *adj.*

mumming *n.* (also **mummering**) **1** a performance, esp. of a folk play, by disguised actors, often accompanied by an outdoor procession or visits to private houses. **2** (in Newfoundland) the visiting of private houses by disguised merrymakers during the twelve days of Christmas.

mummy¹ *n.* (*pl.* **-ies**) *Cdn & Brit. informal* mother.

mummy² *n.* (*pl.* **-ies**) **1** a body of a human being or animal embalmed for burial, esp. in ancient Egypt. **2** a dried-up body.

mumps *n.pl.* (treated as *sing.*) an acute contagious and infectious viral disease, esp. of children, characterized by fever and swelling of the parotid glands.

munch *v.tr. & intr.* eat steadily and usu. audibly with a marked action of the jaws, esp. with great enjoyment. □ **muncher** *n.* **munchy** *adj.*

Munchausen's syndrome /'mʌntʃhauzənz/ *n.* a mental illness in which a person repeatedly feigns severe illness so as to obtain hospital treatment.

Munchausen's syndrome by proxy *n.* (also **Munchausen by proxy**) a mental condition in which a person seeks attention by inducing illness in another person, esp. a child.

munchies *n.pl. informal* **1** snacks; food suitable for snacks. **2** (prec. by *the*) hunger, esp. desire for snack food.

munchkin *n. N Amer. informal* **1** a small or dwarf-like person, animal, etc. **2** a child.

mundane /mʌn'dein/ *adj.* **1** dull, routine; of or pertaining to everyday life. **2** of this world; worldly. □ **mundanely** *adv.* **mundanity** /-'dæniti/ *n.* (*pl.* **-ies**).

mung *n.* the seed of either of two widely cultivated, originally Asian leguminous plants, (in full **mung bean**) the green gram, *Vigna radiata*, or the black gram, *V. mungo*.

municipal /mju:'nɪsɪpəl, ˌmju:nɪ'sɪpəl/ *adj.* of, concerning, or operated by a municipality. □ **municipalize** *v.tr.* **municipalization** *n.* **municipally** *adv.*

municipal court *n. N Amer.* a lower court with limited jurisdiction, usu. extending to bylaw infractions, certain civil matters, etc.

municipal district *n. Cdn* (*Prairies & North*) a large, lightly populated rural area administered by a regional municipal government. Abbr.: **MD.**

municipalité régionale de comté /mu:ni:si:pæli:'tei reiʒi'næl də kɔ̃'tei/ *n. Cdn* (*Que.*) = REGIONAL COUNTY MUNICIPALITY.

municipality /mju:ˌnɪsɪ'pælɪti/ *n.* (*pl.* **-ies**) **1** a city, town, or district having local government. **2** the governing body of this area.

munificent /mju:'nɪfɪsənt/ *adj.* (of a giver or a gift) splendidly generous, bountiful. □ **munificence** *n.* **munificently** *adv.*

munition /mju:'nɪʃən/ ● *n.* (usu. in *pl.*) military weapons, ammunition, equipment, and stores. ● *v.tr.* supply with munitions.

Munsee /'mʌnsi:/ ● *n.* **1** a member of either of two groups of Aboriginal people living esp. in New Jersey and New York, but with a small population near St.

Thomas, Ont. **2** either of the Algonquian languages of these peoples. ● *adj.* of or relating to this people.

muon /'mju:ɒn/ *n. Physics* an unstable elementary particle like an electron, but with a much greater mass. □ **muonic** *adj.*

M.U.P. *abbr.* Master of Urban Planning.

mural ● *n.* a painting executed directly on a wall. ● *adj.* **1** of or like a wall. **2** placed or painted on a wall. □ **muralist** *n.*

MURB *abbr. Cdn* multiple unit residential building.

murder ● *n.* **1 a** the unlawful premeditated killing of a human being by another (compare MANSLAUGHTER). **b** an instance of this. **2** *informal* an unpleasant, troublesome, or dangerous state of affairs (*it was murder here*). **3** something very damaging (*chlorine is murder on hair*). ● *v.tr.* **1** kill (a human being) unlawfully, esp. wickedly or inhumanly. **2** *Law* kill (a human being) with malice and a premeditated motive. **3** *informal* **a** put an end to or destroy. **b** spoil by bad execution, performance, mispronunciation, etc. (*murdered the soliloquy*). **4** *slang* conclusively defeat (an opponent etc.), esp. at a game or sport. □ **scream** (or **shout, yell,** etc.) **bloody** (or **blue**) **murder** *slang* shout loudly. **get away with murder** *informal* do whatever one wishes and escape punishment. **murder will out** murder cannot remain undetected. □ **murderer** *n.* **murderess** *n.*

murderball *n. Cdn* a game in which players in opposing teams attempt to hit their opponents with a large, inflated ball.

murder mystery *n.* a novel, play, etc. about a murder in which the murderer's identity is concealed until the denouement.

murderous *adj.* **1** (of a person, weapon, action, etc.) capable of, intending, or involving murder or great harm. **2** *informal* extremely arduous or unpleasant. □ **murderously** *adv.* **murderousness** *n.*

murex /'mju:rəks/ *n.* (*pl.* **murexes** or **murices** /-rɪ,si:z/) any of various spiny-shelled predatory gastropod molluscs of the genus *Murex* and related genera, of tropical and temperate seas.

muriatic acid /mjuri'ætɪk/ *n.* = HYDROCHLORIC ACID.

murk *n.* **1** darkness, gloom; poor visibility. **2 a** air obscured by fog, dense vapour, etc. **b** confusion, obscurity, vagueness, or incomprehensibility.

murky *adj.* (**-ier, -iest**) **1** dark, gloomy. **2** (of darkness) thick, dense. **3** suspiciously obscure (*a murky past*). **4** indistinct, confused, not easily understood. □ **murkiness** *n.*

murmur ● *n.* **1** a softly spoken or nearly inarticulate utterance. **2** a subdued expression of discontent. **3** *Med.* a recurring sound heard in the auscultation of the heart and usu. indicating abnormality. **4** a subdued continuous sound, as made by waves, a brook, etc. ● *v.* **1** *tr.* utter (words) in a low voice. **2** *intr.* make a subdued continuous sound. **3** *intr.* (usu. foll. by *at, against*) complain in low tones, grumble. □ **murmurer** *n.* **murmuring** *adj. & n.* **murmurous** *adj.*

Murphy's Law *n. jocular* any of various maxims about the apparent perversity of things, esp. the principle that if anything can go wrong, it will.

murre /mɜr/ *n.* esp. *N Amer.* an auk or guillemot.

murrelet /'mɜrlət/ *n.* any of several small auks of the N Pacific, of the genera *Brachyramphus* and *Synthliboramphus.*

muscadine /'mʌskədɪn, -,dain/ *n.* a variety of grape with a musk flavour, used chiefly in winemaking.

muscat /'mʌskæt/ *n.* **1** a sweet fortified white wine made from muscadines. **2** a muscadine.

muscle ● *n.* **1** a fibrous tissue with the ability to contract, producing movement in or maintaining the position of an animal body. **2** the part of an animal body that is composed of muscles. **3 a** physical power or strength. **b** force, influence (*more marketing muscle*). **4** *slang* a person employed to threaten or use violence. **5** (*attrib.*) *N Amer.* designating an exceptionally powerful vehicle (*muscle boat*). ● *v.* **1** *informal* **a** *tr. N Amer.* move by the exercise of physical power. **b** *intr.* make one's way by the exercise of physical power (*muscled through the crowds*). **c** *tr.* Baseball (of a batter) propel (the ball) forcefully with the part of the bat nearest the hands, relying more on muscle strength than on swing momentum. **2** *tr. slang* coerce by violence, intimidation, etc., esp. by economic or political pressure. □ **not move a muscle** be completely motionless. **muscle in** (**on**) *informal* involve oneself in something when one has no right to do so, for one's own advantage. □ **muscled** *adj.* (usu. in *comb.*). **muscleless** *adj.* **muscly** *adj.*

muscle-bound *adj.* **1** with muscles stiff and inelastic through excessive exercise or training. **2** *informal* usu. *derogatory* (of a person) very, esp. excessively muscular.

muscle car *n.* esp. *N Amer. informal* a powerful car, esp. a hot rod.

muscle fibre *n.* each of the elongated contractile cells of which muscular tissue is composed.

muscle-flexing *n.* an assertion of strength or power.

muscleman *n.* (*pl.* **-men**) **1** a man with highly developed muscles. **2** a person who employs or threatens violence on behalf of another, esp. a professional criminal.

muscle shirt *n. N Amer.* a man's tight-fitting, sleeveless T-shirt, usu. with a low scoop neck in front and back.

Muscovite /ˈmʌskə,vəit/ ● *n.* a native or citizen of Moscow. ● *adj.* of or relating to Moscow, the capital of Russia.

muscovite *n.* a silver-grey form of mica with a sheetlike crystalline structure that is used in the manufacture of electrical equipment etc.

Muscovy duck /ˈmʌskəvi/ *n.* a tropical American duck, *Cairina moschata*, having a small crest and red markings on its head.

muscular *adj.* **1** having well-developed muscles. **2** of or affecting the muscles. **3** robust, vigorous. □ **muscularity** *n.* **muscularly** *adv.*

muscular dystrophy *n.* a hereditary progressive weakening and wasting of the muscles.

musculature /ˈmʌskjʊlətʃər/ *n.* **1** the muscular system of a body or organ. **2** a person's or animal's muscles collectively, esp. if well-developed.

musculoskeletal /,mʌskjulo:ˈskelətəl/ *adj.* of or relating to the musculature and skeleton together.

Mus.D. *abbr.* (also **Mus. Doc.**) Doctor of Music.

muse¹ *n.* **1** (**Muse**) *Gk & Rom. Myth* any of the goddesses who presided over the arts and sciences (traditionally nine in number). **2** (usu. *prec.* by *the*) **a** a poet's inspiring goddess. **b** a poet's genius. **3** a source of inspiration for creativity.

muse² *v.* **1** *intr.* **a** (usu. *foll.* by *on, upon*) ponder, reflect. **b** (usu. *foll.* by *on*) gaze meditatively (on a scene etc.). **2** *tr.* say or murmur meditatively.

museology /mju:ziˈɒlədʒi/ *n.* the science or practice of organizing and managing museums. □ **museological** *adj.* **museologist** *n.*

museum *n.* a building used for storing, preserving, and exhibiting objects considered to be of lasting historical, scientific, or cultural interest.

museum piece *n.* **1** a specimen of art etc. fit for a museum. **2** *derogatory* an old-fashioned or quaint person or object.

mush¹ ● *n.* **1** a soft pulpy or formless mass. **2** feeble sentimentality. **3** *US* porridge, esp. cornmeal boiled in water until it thickens. ● *v.tr.* reduce to mush; mash.

mush² *N Amer.* ● *v.intr.* **1 a** travel through snow with a dogsled. **b** (of dogs) pull a sled. **2** (in *imper.*) used as a command to dogs pulling a sled to urge them forward. ● *n.* a journey across snow with a dogsled. □ **musher** *n.* **mushing** *n.*

mushroom ● *n.* **1** the usu. edible spore-producing body of various fungi, esp. *Agaricus campestris*, with a stem and domed cap, proverbial for its rapid growth. **2** the pinkish-brown colour of this. **3** any item resembling a mushroom in shape. **4** (usu. *attrib.*) something that appears or develops suddenly or is ephemeral; an upstart. ● *v.intr.* **1** appear or develop rapidly. **2** expand and flatten like a mushroom cap. **3** gather mushrooms. □ **mushrooming** *adj. & n.* **mushroomy** *adj.*

mushroom cloud *n.* a cloud of smoke, vapour, etc. suggesting the shape of a mushroom, esp. from a nuclear explosion.

mushy *adj.* (**-ier, -iest**) **1** like mush, soft and pulpy. **2** feebly sentimental. □ **mushiness** *n.*

music *n.* **1** the art of combining vocal or instrumental sounds (or both) to produce beauty of form, harmony, and expression of emotion. **2** the sounds so produced. **3** musical compositions collectively. **4** the written or printed score of a musical composition. **5** certain pleasant sounds, e.g. birdsong, the sound of a stream, etc. □ **face the music** *informal* put up with or stand up to unpleasant consequences, esp. criticism. **music to one's ears** something very pleasant to hear.

musical ● *adj.* **1** of or relating to music. **2** (of sounds, a voice, etc.) melodious, harmonious. **3** fond of or skilled in music (*the musical one of the family*). **4** set to or accompanied by music. ● *n.* a musical comedy or music theatre. □ **musicalize** *v.tr.* **musically** *adv.*

musical chairs *n.pl.* **1** a party game in which the players compete in successive rounds for a decreasing number of chairs, sitting down on a chair whenever the music stops. **2** a series of esp. minor changes, manoeuvres, etc. after the manner of the game.

musical comedy *n.* a light drama on stage or film, consisting of dialogue, songs, and dancing.

musical instrument *n.* *see* INSTRUMENT *n.* 2.

musicality /mju:ziˈkælɪti/ *n.* **1** the quality or character of being musical. **2** (of a dancer, choreographer, etc.) the ability to suit or fit dance steps to music particularly pleasingly.

musical ride *n. Cdn* an exhibition in which riders on horseback (usu. members of a mounted police force) perform choreographed manoeuvres to music.

music box *n.* **1** a mechanical instrument playing a tune by causing a toothed cylinder to strike a comb-like metal plate within a box. **2** a figurine, toy, or other decorative item incorporating a music box.

music director *n.* (also **musical director**) the person responsible for the musical aspects of a performance, production, arts organization, etc., usu. the conductor of an orchestra, band, etc.

music hall *n.* **1** a public hall or theatre used for musical performances. **2** variety entertainment, popular *c.* 1850–1914, consisting of singing, dancing, and novelty acts; vaudeville.

musician *n.* a person who performs esp. instrumental music, esp. professionally. □ **musicianly** *adj.* **musicianship** *n.*

musicology *n.* the branch of knowledge that deals with music as a subject of study rather than as a skill or performing art; esp. academic research in music. □ **musicological** *adj.* **musicologist** *n.*

music stand *n.* a rest or frame on which sheet music or a score is supported.

music theatre *n.* in late 20th-c. music, the combination of elements from music and drama in new forms distinct from traditional opera, esp. as designed for small groups of performers.

music video *n.* a dramatization of a song or piece of music on videotape, esp. for broadcast on television.

musing *n.* **1** an act or instance of being absorbed in thought. **2** (often in *pl.*) an expression of one's thoughts or opinions. □ **musingly** *adv.*

musk *n.* **1 a** a strong-smelling reddish-brown substance produced by a gland in the male musk deer and used as an ingredient in perfumes. **b** any of various similar odorous substances secreted by other animals, esp. for scent-marking. **2 a** a substance designed to imitate musk, esp. for use in perfumes. **b** an aromatic odour resembling that of musk, esp. worn as a fragrance. **3** the plant, *Mimulus moschatus*, with pale-green oval leaves and yellow flowers. □ **musky** *adj.* (**-ier, -iest**). **muskiness** *n.*

musk deer *n.* any small Asian deer of the genus *Moschus*, having no antlers and in the male having long protruding canine teeth.

muskeg *n.* **1** a swamp or bog in northern N America, consisting of a mixture of water and partly dead vegetation, often covered by a layer of sphagnum or other mosses. **2** terrain characterized by these.

muskellunge /ˈmʌskəˌlʌndʒ/ *n.* a large N American pike, *Esox masquinongy*, esp. of the Great Lakes.

musket *n. hist.* an infantryman's usu. smoothbore light gun, fired from shoulder level.

musketeer *n. hist.* **1** a soldier armed with a musket. **2** a member of either of two bodies forming part of the household troops of the French king in the 17th and 18th c.

muskie *n. N Amer.* = MUSKELLUNGE.

muskmelon *n.* the common yellow or green melon, *Cucumis melo*, usu. with a raised network of markings on the skin.

Muskogean /ˌmʌskəˈgiːən, mʌˈskoːgiən/ ● *n.* a language family of southeastern N America, including Creek, Seminole, Choctaw, and Chickasaw. ● *adj.* of or pertaining to this language family.

Muskogee /mʌˈskoːgiː/ ● *n.* **1** a member of a N American Aboriginal people forming part of the Creek Confederacy. **2** the Muskogean language of this people. ● *adj.* of or relating to this people.

Muskoka chair /məˈskoːkə/ *n. Cdn* a slatted wooden lawn chair with a fan-shaped back and broad arms.

muskox *n.* (*pl.* same or **muskoxen**) **1** a large goat-antelope, *Ovibos moschatus*, of the tundra, esp. in Canada and Greenland, with a thick shaggy coat and small curved horns, the male of which emits a strong odour during rutting. **2** the flesh of this used as food.

muskrat *n.* **1** a large semi-aquatic rodent, *Ondatra zibethicus*, native to N America, having a musky smell. **2** the fur of this.

Muslim /ˈmʌzlɪm, -ləm/ ● *n.* a follower of the Islamic religion. ● *adj.* of or relating to Muslims or their religion.

muslin /ˈmʌzlɪn/ *n.* a cotton or cotton blend fabric of a plain weave.

muss *N Amer. informal* ● *v.tr.* (often foll. by *up*) mess, make untidy (*don't muss my hair*). ● *n.* a mess; a state of confusion or untidiness. □ **mussy** *adj.*

mussel *n.* **1** any bivalve mollusc of the genus *Mytilus*, living in sea water and often used for food. **2** any similar freshwater mollusc of the genus *Margaritifer* or *Anodonta*, forming pearls.

mussel mud *n. Cdn* (*Maritimes*) thick sea mud, rich in lime from the remains of mussels etc., as fertilizer.

must[1] ● *v.aux.* (*3rd sing.* present **must**; *past* **had to** or in indirect speech **must**) (foll. by infin., or *absol.*) **1 a** be obliged or required to (*you must go to school*; *must we leave now?*). **b** be necessary that (*it must be done now*). **2** used in ironic questions (*must you slam the door?*). **3** be certain to (*we must win in the end*; *you must be her sister*). **4** should, ought to (*we must see what can be done*; *it must be said that*). **5** expressing insistence (*I must ask you to leave*). **6** (foll. by *not* + infin.) **a** not be permitted to, be forbidden to (*you must not smoke*). **b** ought not; need not (*you mustn't think he's angry*). **c** expressing insistence that something should not be done (*they must not be told*). ● *n. informal* (also *attrib.*) a thing that cannot or should not be overlooked or missed (*if you go to Halifax the Citadel is a must*; *a must-read*). □ **I must say** often *ironic* I cannot refrain from saying (*a fine way to behave, I must say*).

must[2] *n.* grape juice before or during fermentation.

must[3] *n.* mustiness, mould.

must[4] ● *adj.* (of a male elephant or camel) in a state of dangerous frenzy, associated with the rutting season. ● *n.* this state.

mustache *var. of* MOUSTACHE.

mustachio /məˈstæʃioː/ *n.* (*pl.* **-os**) (often in *pl.*) a moustache, esp. a large one. □ **mustachioed** *adj.*

mustang *n.* a small wild horse of the American plains.

mustard ● *n.* **1 a** any of various plants of the genus *Brassica* with slender pods and yellow flowers, esp. *B. nigra*. **b** any of various plants of the genus *Sinapis*, esp. *S. alba*, eaten at the seedling stage. **c** any of various other plants, esp. of the mustard family (*Cruciferae, Brassicaceae*), resembling these in appearance, pungency, etc. **2** a paste made from the crushed seeds of these and used as a spicy condiment. **3** (also **mustard yellow**) the brownish-yellow colour of this condiment. ● *adj.* of a brownish-yellow colour. □ **mustardy** *adj.*

mustard gas *n.* a colourless oily liquid, whose vapour is a powerful irritant, used in chemical warfare.

mustard plaster *n.* a poultice made with mustard.

muster ● *v.* **1** *tr. & intr.* collect, gather together. **2** *tr.* collect or assemble (originally soldiers) for inspection, to check numbers, etc. **3** *tr.* (often foll. by *up*) summon up (courage, strength, etc. ● *n.* **1 a** the assembly of persons for inspection. **b** an act of mustering soldiers, sailors, etc. **2** an assembly, a collection. □ **pass muster** come up to the required standard.

musth *var. of* MUST[4].

must-have ● *n.* an item regarded as indispensable. ● *adj.* indispensable.

mustn't *contraction* must not.

must-see ● *n.* a site, event, film, etc. that must be seen. ● *adj.* that must be seen.

musty *adj.* (**-ier, -iest**) **1** mouldy; having a smell or taste indicative or suggestive of mouldiness or decay. **2** stale-smelling or fusty. **3** having lost newness, interest, or liveliness. □ **mustiness** *n.*

mutable /ˈmjuːtəbəl/ *adj. literary* **1** liable or subject to change or alteration. **2** fickle. **3** *Biol.* able or liable to undergo esp. frequent mutation. □ **mutability** *n.*

mutagen /ˈmjuːtədʒən, -dʒen/ *n.* an agent causing or promoting mutation, e.g. radiation. □ **mutagenesis** /-ˈdʒenəsɪs/ *n.* **mutagenic** /-ˈdʒenɪk/ *adj.* **mutagenicity** /-dʒəˈnɪsɪtɪ/ *n.*

mutant ● *adj.* **1** resulting from mutation. **2** having the characteristics or attributes of a mutant. ● *n.* **1** an individual, gene, etc. which has arisen by or undergone mutation. **2** (esp. in science fiction) an individual with freak or grossly abnormal anatomy, abilities, etc.

mutate *v.intr. & tr.* undergo or cause to undergo mutation. □ **mutated** *adj.*

mutation *n.* **1** the process or an instance of change or alteration. **2 a** a genetic change which, when transmitted to offspring, gives rise to heritable variations. **b** the process by which such changes arise. **3** a distinct form produced by genetic change; a mutant. □ **mutational** *adj.*

mute ● *adj.* **1** silent, refraining from, or temporarily bereft of speech. **2** (of a person) lacking the faculty of speech. **3** (of an animal) naturally lacking the power of articulate speech. **4 a** not expressed in speech (*mute protest*). **b** characterized by an absence of sound; quiet, still (*the mute forest*). **5** (of a letter) not pronounced. ● *n.* **1** a person who cannot or will not speak (*a deaf mute*). **2** *Music* a clip placed over the bridge of a violin etc. to dampen the resonance without affecting the vibration of the strings. **b** a pad or cone inserted into the bell of a wind instrument to soften the sound. **3** = MUTE BUTTON 2. ● *v.tr.* **1 a** deaden, muffle, or soften the sound of (a thing, esp. a musical instrument). **b** suppress the volume of (a loudspeaker) or the output of (an amplifier or other circuit component). **2** tone down, make less intense. □ **mutely** *adv.* **muteness** *n.*

mute button *n.* **1** a device on a telephone etc. to temporarily prevent the caller from hearing what is being said at the receiver's end. **2** a device on a television etc. that temporarily suppresses all sound.

muted *adj.* **1** (of colours etc.) subdued (*a muted green*). **2** (of a musical instrument) having a muffled tone or employing a mute. **3 a** silent, quiet, muffled. **b** understated.

mute swan *n.* the common white swan, *Cygnus olor*, native to Eurasia.

mutilate *v.tr.* **1** injure or damage (a person or animal or a part of the body) very severely, e.g. by removal of a limb or organ. **2** render (a book etc.) imperfect by excision or some act of destruction. □ **mutilation** *n.* **mutilator** *n.*

mutinous *adj.* (of a person or their conduct) rebellious, tending to mutiny. □ **mutinously** *adv.*

mutiny ● *n.* (*pl.* **-ies**) an open revolt against constituted authority, esp. by soldiers or sailors against their officers. ● *v.intr.* (**-ies, -ied**) (often foll. by *against*) revolt; engage in mutiny.

Mutsu /ˈmʌtsuː/ *n.* = CRISPIN.

mutt *n.* **1** *derogatory* or *jocular* a dog, esp. a mongrel. **2** *slang* an ignorant, stupid, or blundering person.

Mutt and Jeff *n.* a seemingly ill-matched pair of people.

mutter ● *v.* **1** *tr. & intr.* speak in a barely audible manner. **2** *intr.* murmur or grumble about. **3** *tr.* say or express (complaints etc.), esp. in secret. **4** *intr.* make a low rumbling sound. ● *n.* **1** low, indistinct muttered words or sounds. **2** an act of muttering. □ **mutterer** *n.* **muttering** *n.* & *adj.* **mutteringly** *adv.*

mutton *n.* the flesh of sheep used for food. □ **mutton**

dressed as lamb *informal* a usu. middle-aged or elderly woman dressed or made up to appear younger.

mutton chop *n.* **1** (usu. in *pl.*) (in full **mutton chop whisker**) a side whisker, narrow at the top and broad and rounded at the bottom. **2** a piece of mutton, usu. the rib and half vertebra to which it is attached.

mutual *adj.* **1** (of feelings, actions, etc.) experienced or done by each of two or more parties with reference to the other or others; reciprocal (*mutual affection*). **2** held in common or shared between two or more persons (*mutual friend; a mutual interest*). **3** (of people) having the same specified relationship to each other (*mutual well-wishers*). □ **mutuality** /ˌmjuːtʃuˈælɪtɪ/ *n.* **mutually** *adv.*

mutual admiration society *n.* two or more people who think very highly of one another, even to the extent of overestimating one another's merits.

mutual assured destruction *n.* a US military scenario in which nuclear war is deterred by each side knowing that the other is capable of inflicting unacceptable damage if attacked. Abbr.: **MAD**.

mutual fund *n.* *N Amer.* a fund in which contributions from many persons combined are invested in various securities and in which dividends are paid in proportion to the contributors' holdings.

mutual insurance *n.* insurance in which some or all of the profits are divided among the policyholders.

mutuel /ˈmjuːtʃuəl/ *n.* *N Amer.* = PARIMUTUEL.

muumuu /ˈmuːmuː/ *n.* a woman's usu. brightly coloured and patterned loose-fitting dress.

Muzak /ˈmjuːzæk/ *n.* **1** *proprietary* a system for transmitting background music for playing in public places. **2** (**muzak**) **a** a recorded light background music. **b** bland, undemanding music.

muzzle ● *n.* **1** the projecting part of an animal's face, including the nose and mouth. **2** a guard, usu. made of straps or wire, fitted over an animal's nose and mouth to stop it biting or feeding. **3** the open end of a firearm. ● *v.tr.* **1** put a muzzle on (an animal etc.). **2** impose silence upon. □ **muzzler** *n.*

muzzleloader *n.* a gun that is loaded through the muzzle. □ **muzzle-loading** *adj.* & *n.*

muzzy *adj.* (**-ier, -iest**) **1 a** mentally hazy; dull, spiritless. **b** dazed or fuddled from drinking alcohol. **2** blurred, indistinct. □ **muzzily** *adv.*

MV *abbr.* **1** motor vessel. **2** megavolt(s).

mV *abbr.* millivolt(s).

MVA *abbr.* *Cdn* market value assessment (of property values for tax purposes).

MVP *abbr.* *N Amer.* *Sport* most valuable player.

MW *abbr.* megawatt(s).

mW *abbr.* milliwatt(s).

MWO *abbr.* *Cdn* MASTER WARRANT OFFICER.

Mx. *abbr.* maxwell(s).

my ● *possess.adj.* (*attrib.*) **1** of or belonging to me or myself (*my house; my own business*). **2** as a form of address in affectionate, sympathetic, respectful, jocular, or patronizing contexts (*my dear boy*). **3** in various expressions of surprise (*my God!*). ● *interj.* expressing surprise, admiration, etc. (*my, she's beautiful!*)

myalgia /maiˈældʒə, -dʒiə/ *n.* a pain in a muscle or group of muscles. □ **myalgic** *adj.*

myasthenia gravis /ˌmaiəsˈθiːniə ˈɡrævɪs/ *n.* a rare chronic autoimmune disease marked by muscular weakness without atrophy.

mycelium /maiˈsiːliəm/ *n.* (*pl.* **mycelia** /-liə/) the vegetative part of a fungus, consisting of microscopic threadlike hyphae. □ **mycelial** adj.

Mycenaean /ˌmaɪsəˈniːən/ ● adj. of or relating to the late Bronze Age civilization in Greece depicted in the Homeric poems and represented by finds at Mycenae and elsewhere. ● n. an inhabitant of Mycenae or the Mycenaean world.

mycobacterium /ˌmaɪkoʊˌbækˈtiːriəm/ n. (pl. **-bacteria**) any of various aerobic, filament-forming bacteria of the genus *Mycobacterium* or the family Mycobacteriaceae, including the causative agents of tuberculosis and leprosy. □ **mycobacterial** adj.

mycology /maɪˈkɒlədʒi/ n. **1** the study of fungi. **2** the fungi of a particular region. □ **mycological** adj. **mycologically** adv. **mycologist** n.

mycoplasma /ˌmaɪkoʊˈplæzmə/ n. (pl. **-s** or **mycoplasmata** /-mətə/) any of a group of mainly parasitic micro-organisms smaller than bacteria and without a cell wall.

mycorrhiza /ˌmaɪkəˈraɪzə/ n. (pl. **mycorrhizae** /-ziː/ or **-s**) a symbiotic association of a fungus and the roots of a plant. □ **mycorrhizal** adj.

mycosis /maɪˈkoʊsɪs/ n. (pl. **-coses** /-ˈkoʊsiːz/) any disease caused by a fungus, e.g. ringworm.

mycotoxin /ˌmaɪkəˈtɒksɪn/ n. any toxic substance produced by a fungus.

myelin /ˈmaɪəlɪn/ n. a white substance which forms a sheath around certain nerve fibres. □ **myelination** n. **myelinated** adj.

myeloma /ˌmaɪəˈloʊmə/ n. (pl. **-s** or **myelomata** /-mətə/) a malignant tumour of the bone marrow.

Mylar /ˈmaɪlɑr/ n. proprietary a polyester film used to make audio tapes, insulation, etc.

myna /ˈmaɪnə/ n. (also **mynah**) any of various SE Asian starlings, esp. *Gracula religiosa* able to mimic the human voice.

myocardium /ˌmaɪoʊˈkɑrdiəm/ n. (pl. **myocardia** /-diə/) the muscular tissue of the heart. □ **myocardial** adj. **myocarditis** /-ˈdaɪtɪs/ n.

myopia /maɪˈoʊpiə/ n. **1** short-sightedness. **2** lack of imagination or intellectual insight. □ **myopic** /-ˈɒpɪk/ adj. **myopically** adv.

myosis var. of MIOSIS.

myriad /ˈmɪriəd/ ● n. an indefinitely great number. ● adj. **1** of an indefinitely great number. **2** having countless phases or aspects.

myrrh /mɜr/ n. **1** a gum resin from several trees of the genus *Commiphora* used, esp. in the Near East, in perfumery, medicine, incense, etc. **2** Cdn (Nfld) fir or spruce resin, often used as a component of home remedies.

myrtle /ˈmɜrtəl/ n. **1** an evergreen shrub of the genus *Myrtus* with aromatic foliage and white flowers, esp. *M. communis*, bearing purple-black ovoid berries. **2** N Amer. the periwinkle, *Vinca minor*.

myself pron. **1** emphatic form of I² or ME¹ (*I saw it myself; I like to do it myself*). **2** refl. form of ME¹ (*able to dress myself; as bad as myself*). **3** in my normal state of body and mind (*I'm not myself today*). □ **I myself** I for my part (*I myself am doubtful*).

mysterious adj. **1** full of or wrapped in mystery. **2** puzzling; enigmatic. □ **mysteriously** adv. **mysteriousness** n.

mystery n. (pl. **-ies**) **1** a secret, hidden, or inexplicable matter (*the reason remains a mystery*). **2** secrecy or obscurity (*wrapped in mystery*). **3** (attrib.) secret, undisclosed (*mystery guest*). **4** the practice of making a secret of (esp. unimportant) things (*engaged in mystery and intrigue*). **5** a fictional work dealing with a puzzling event, esp. a crime (also attrib.: *a well-known mys-*

tery writer*). **6 a** a religious truth divinely revealed, esp. one beyond human reason. **b** Catholicism a decade of the rosary. **7** (in pl.) the secret religious rites of the ancient Greeks, Romans, etc. □ **make a mystery of** treat as an impressive secret.

mystic /ˈmɪstɪk/ ● n. a person who seeks by contemplation and self-surrender to obtain unity or identity with or absorption into the Deity or the ultimate reality, or who believes in the spiritual apprehension of truths that are beyond the understanding. ● adj. **1** mysterious and awe-inspiring. **2** spiritually allegorical or symbolic. **3** occult, esoteric. **4** of hidden meaning. □ **mysticism** /-ˌsɪzəm/ n.

mystical adj. **1** of mystics or mysticism. **2** mystic. □ **mystically** adv.

mystify /ˈmɪstɪˌfaɪ/ v.tr. (**-ies**, **-ied**) **1** bewilder, confuse. **2** wrap up in mystery. □ **mystification** n. **mystifying** adj. **mystifyingly** adv.

mystique /mɪˈstiːk/ n. an atmosphere of mystery and importance evoking admiration, surrounding some activity or person; charisma.

myth n. **1** a traditional narrative usu. involving supernatural or imaginary persons and embodying popular ideas on natural or social phenomena etc. **2** such narratives collectively. **3** a widely held but false notion. **4** a fictitious person, thing, or idea. **5** an idealized version of the past, esp. as embodying significant cultural realities. **6** an allegory (the Platonic myth). □ **mythic** adj. **mythical** adj. **mythically** adv.

mythmaker n. a creator of myths or folklore. □ **mythmaking** n.

mythology n. (pl. **-ies**) **1** a body of myths (Greek mythology). **2** the study of myths. **3** myths collectively. **4** a body of traditions or stories, usu. somewhat idealized, concerning a particular person, institution, event, etc. □ **mythologic** adj. **mythological** adj. **mythologically** adv. **mythologist** n. **mythologization** n. **mythologize** v.tr. & intr. **mythologizer** n.

mythopoeia /ˌmɪθoʊˈpiːə/ n. the making of myths. □ **mythopoeic** adj. (also **mythopoetic** /-poʊˈetɪk/).

mythos /ˈmɪθɒs, ˈmaɪθɒs/ n. (pl. **mythoi** /-θɔɪ/) literary a myth; a body of myths. **2** a narrative theme or pattern.

Nn

N¹ *n.* (also **n**) (*pl.* **Ns** or **N's**) **1** the fourteenth letter of the alphabet. **2** *Printing* en.

N² *abbr.* (also **N.**) **1 a** North. **b** Northern. **2** New. **3** nuclear.

N³ *symbol Chem.* **1** nitrogen. **2** newton(s).

n¹ *abbr.* (also **n.**) **1** name. **2** neuter. **3** noon. **4** note. **5** noun.

n² *symbol* **1** *Math.* an indefinite number. **2** nano-. □ **to the nth** (or **nth degree**) **1** *Math.* to any required power. **2** to any extent; to the utmost.

'n *conj.* (also **'n'**) *informal* and.

NA *abbr.* **1** North America. **2** North American.

Na *symbol* sodium.

n/a *abbr.* **1** not applicable. **2** not available.

NAACP *abbr.* (in the US) National Association for the Advancement of Colored People.

naan *var. of* NAN².

nab *v.tr.* (**nabbed, nabbing**) *informal* **1** arrest; catch in wrongdoing. **2** capture, catch.

nabob /'neibɒb/ *n. informal* a very rich or influential person.

NAC *abbr.* (in Canada) National Action Committee (on the Status of Women).

nacho /'nɒtʃo:, 'nætʃo:/ *n.* (*pl.* **-os**) (usu. in *pl.*) a tortilla chip topped with cheese, salsa, etc. and broiled.

nacre /'neikɜr/ *n.* = MOTHER-OF-PEARL.

NAD *abbr. Biochem.* nicotinamide adenine dinucleotide, a coenzyme important in many biological oxidation reactions.

nada /'nɒdə/ *n. informal* nothing (*has said nada*).

nadir /'neidi:r, -dɜr, 'næd-/ *n.* **1** the part of the celestial sphere directly below an observer (*opp.* ZENITH). **2** the lowest point in one's fortunes; a time of deep despair.

naevus *var. of* NEVUS.

NAFTA /'næftə/ *abbr.* North American Free Trade Agreement.

nag¹ ● *v.* (**nagged, nagging**) **1 a** *tr.* annoy or irritate (a person) with persistent fault-finding or continuous urging. **b** *intr.* (often foll. by *at*) find fault, complain, or urge, esp. persistently. **2** *intr.* (of a pain) ache dully but persistently. **3 a** *tr.* worry or preoccupy (a person, the mind, etc.) (*his mistake nagged him*). **b** *intr.* (often foll. by *at*) worry or gnaw. ● *n.* a persistently nagging person. □ **nagger** *n.*

nag² *n.* **1** an old or broken-down horse. **2** *informal* a horse, esp. a racehorse. **3** a small riding horse or pony.

naga /'nɒgə/ *n. Hinduism* a member of a race of semi-divine creatures, half-snake half-human.

nagging ● *n.* the action of persistent fault-finding or urging. ● *adj.* **1** worrying or preoccupying (a *nagging feeling*). **2** aching dully and persistently (a *nagging headache*). □ **naggingly** *adv.*

nah *adv. informal* no.

Nahuatl /'nɒːwɒtəl, 'nɑ-/ ● *n.* **1** a member of a group of Aboriginal peoples of S Mexico and Central America, including the Aztecs. **2** the language of these peoples. ● *adj.* of or concerning the Nahuatl peoples or language.

naïf /nɒˈiːf/ ● *adj.* = NAIVE *adj.* ● *n.* a naive person.

nail ● *n.* **1** a small usu. sharpened metal spike with a broadened flat head, driven in esp. with a hammer to join things together. **2 a** a horny covering on the upper surface of the tip of the human finger or toe. **b** a claw or talon. ● *v.tr.* **1** fasten with a nail or nails (*nail it to the wall; nailed them together*). **2** fix or hold (one's eyes, attention, etc.) on something. **3** hit, strike, or punch (a person, ball, etc.). **4 a** secure, catch, or get hold of (a person or thing). **b** arrest (a person). **5** *Baseball* put (a runner) out (*nailed him at first*). **6** complete or perform (something) well or perfectly (*nailed a triple somersault*). □ **hard as nails 1** callous; unfeeling. **2** in good physical condition. **nail one's colours to the mast** persist; refuse to give in. **nail down 1** bind (a person) to a promise etc. **2** define precisely. **3** fasten (a thing) with nails. **nail in the coffin** something to make imminent a person's death or the end or failure of something. **nail up 1** close (a door etc.) with nails. **2** fix (a thing) at a height with nails. □ **nailed** *adj.* (also in *comb.*). **nailless** *adj.*

nail-biter *n.* **1** something that causes anxiety or tension (*the game was a real nail-biter*). **2** a person who habitually bites his or her fingernails.

nail-biting ● *adj.* **1** causing severe anxiety or tension. **2** (of a person) having a tendency to bite his or her fingernails, esp. habitually. ● *n.* the act or an instance of biting one's fingernails.

nail brush *n.* a small brush for cleaning the nails.

nail enamel *n. N Amer.* = NAIL POLISH.

nail file *n.* a roughened metal or emery strip used for smoothing the nails.

nail gun *n.* a tool that uses electric power or an explosive charge to drive nails into wood.

nailhead *n.* the flat head of a nail.

nail polish *n.* a varnish applied to the nails to colour them or make them shiny.

naive /naiˈiːv/ *adj.* **1** artless; innocent; unaffected. **2** foolishly credulous. **3** (of art etc.) produced in a sophisticated society but deliberately rejecting conventional expertise. □ **naively** *adv.* **naiveness** *n.*

naïveté /nai,iːvəˈtei, naiˈiːvəti/ *n.* (also **naivety** /naiˈiːvəti/) **1** the state or quality of being naive. **2** a naive action.

naked *adj.* **1** unclothed; nude. **2** plain; undisguised; exposed (*the naked truth*). **3 a** (of a flame etc.) unprotected from the wind etc. **b** (of a light bulb) unshaded. **4** defenceless. **5 a** (of landscape) barren; treeless. **b** (of rock) exposed; without soil etc. **6** (of a sword etc.) unsheathed. **7** without leaves, hairs, scales, shell, etc. **8** (of a room, wall, etc.) without decoration, furnishings, etc.; empty, plain. □ **nakedly** *adv.* **nakedness** *n.*

naked eye *n.* unassisted vision, e.g. without a telescope, microscope, etc.

Nam /næm, nɒm/ an informal name for Vietnam.

Nama /'nɒmə/ ● *n.* (*pl.* same or **Namas**) **1** a member of a people of South Africa and Namibia. **2** the language of this people. ● *adj.* of or relating to this people or their language.

namby-pamby ● *adj.* **1** lacking vigour or drive;

weak. **2** insipidly pretty or sentimental. ● *n.* (*pl.* **-ies**) a namby-pamby person.

name ● *n.* **1 a** the word by which an individual person, animal, place, or thing is known, spoken of, etc. (*mentioned you by name; her name is Sandra*). **b** all who go under one name; a family, clan, or people in terms of its name (*brought dishonour to his name*). **2 a** a usu. abusive term used of a person etc. (*called me names*). **b** a word denoting an object or esp. a class of objects, ideas, etc. (*what is the name of that kind of vase?; that sort of behaviour has no name*). **3** a famous person (*big names*). **4** a reputation, esp. a good one (*has a name for honesty; their name is guarantee enough*). **5** something existing only nominally (*opp.* FACT, REALITY). ● *v.tr.* **1** give a usu. specified name to (*what will we name her?*). **2** call (a person or thing) by the right name (*named the child in the photograph*). **3** mention; specify; cite (*named a time for the meeting*). **4** nominate, appoint, etc. (*was named the new director*). **5** specify as something desired (*named it as her dearest wish*). **6** *Cdn & Brit. Parl.* (of the Speaker) mention (a member of a legislative assembly) as disobedient to the chair, thus banning her or him from the House. ● *adj.* **1** famous; widely-known (*a name band*). **2** designating the person that gives his or her name to a firm, theatrical production, etc. (*one of the name partners*). □ **by name 1** called (*Erin by name*). **2** using the name or names of someone (*knows all her students by name*). **by the name of** called (*a young girl by the name of Joelene*). **enter one's name** apply to enter an educational institution, competition, course, etc. **give a bad name** cause disrepute to (*this kind of behaviour gives students a bad name*). **give one's name to something** invent or originate something which then becomes known by one's own name. **have one's name on a thing** be destined or particularly suited to receive that thing (*a bullet out there with my name on it*). (**have**) **to one's name** (possess) as one's own. **in all but name** virtually. **in name** (or **in name only**) as a mere formality; hardly at all (*was the manager in name only*). **in the name of 1** calling to witness; invoking (*in God's name, what are you doing?*). **2** by the authority of (*stop in the name of the law*). **3** for the sake of (*they did it all in the name of friendship*). **in one's own name** independently; without authority. **make a name for oneself** (also **make one's name**) become famous. **name after** (also *N Amer.* **name for**) call (a person) by the name of (a specified person) (*named him after his grandfather*). **name the day** arrange a date for one's wedding. **name names** mention specific names, esp. in accusation. **name of the game** *informal* the purpose or essence of an action etc. **put a name to a person or a thing** know or remember what a person or thing is called (*I know that tune but I can't put a name to it*). **put one's name down for 1** apply for. **2** promise to subscribe (a sum). **under the name** using as a pseudonym. **what's in a name?** names are arbitrary labels. **you name it** *informal* no matter what; whatever you like. □ **nameable** *adj.* **namer** *n.*

name brand *n.* (also *attrib.*) = BRAND NAME.

name-calling *n.* abusive language.

name-dropping *n.* the practice of casually mentioning the names of famous people one knows or pretends to know in order to impress others. □ **name-drop** *v.intr.* (**-dropped**, **-dropping**). **name-dropper** *n.*

nameless *adj.* **1** having no name or inscription. **2** inexpressible; indefinable (*a nameless sensation*). **3** unnamed; anonymous, esp. deliberately (*our inform-ant, who shall be nameless*). **4** too loathsome or horrific to be named (*nameless vices*). **5** obscure; inglorious. □

namelessly *adv.* **namelessness** *n.*

namely *adv.* that is to say; in other words.

nameplate *n.* **1** a plate or panel bearing the name of an occupant of a room etc. **2 a** a plate attached to a car, computer, etc. bearing the name of the manufacturer or model. **b** a line of products produced under a single name.

namesake *n.* a person or thing having the same name as another (*was her aunt's namesake*).

name tag *n.* **1** a label, sticker, etc. bearing a person's name and often other relevant information and worn as identification. **2** a label sewn inside a garment etc. and bearing the name of the owner.

Namibian /nəˈmɪbiən/ ● *n.* a native or inhabitant of Namibia, a country in southern Africa. ● *adj.* of or relating to Namibia or the Namibians.

nam pla /ˈnæm plæ/ *n.* a pungent, salty fish sauce used in Thai cooking.

nan¹ *n. Brit. & Cdn* (*Nfld*) *informal* grandmother.

nan² *n.* (in Indian cooking) a type of flat, oval, leavened bread cooked esp. in a clay oven.

nana *n. informal* grandmother.

Nanaimo bar /nəˈnaɪmoː/ *n. Cdn* a dessert consisting of a crust of chocolate and cookie crumbs, usu. also including coconut and nuts, covered with a usu. vanilla buttercream filling and a chocolate glaze, served cut into squares.

nancy (also **nance**) *slang offensive* ● *n.* (*pl.* **-ies**) (in full **nancy boy**) an effeminate man, esp. a homosexual. ● *adj.* effeminate.

nanny ● *n.* (*pl.* **-ies**) **1 a** a person employed, esp. on a full-time basis, to care for a child, usu. in the child's home. **b** an unduly protective person, institution, etc. **2** = NAN¹. **3** (in full **nanny goat**) a female goat. ● *v.tr.* (**-ies**, **-ied**) be unduly protective towards.

nanny suite *n.* a self-contained apartment within a house, as for a live-in nanny.

nano- /ˈnænoː, ˈneɪno/ *comb. form* **1** denoting a factor of 10^{-9} (*nanosecond*). **2** very small; minute.

nanometre *n.* (also **nanometer**) one billionth of a metre. *Abbr.:* **nm**.

nanosecond *n.* **1** one billionth of a second. **2** an extremely short interval.

nanotechnology *n.* the branch of technology that deals with dimensions and tolerances of less than 100 nanometres, esp. the manipulation of individual atoms and molecules. □ **nanotechnological** *adj.*

nap¹ ● *v.intr.* (**napped**, **napping**) sleep lightly or briefly. ● *n.* a short sleep or doze, esp. by day. □ **catch a person napping 1** find a person asleep or off guard. **2** detect in negligence or error.

nap² ● *n.* **1** the raised pile on textiles, esp. velvet. **2** a soft downy surface. ● *v.tr.* (**napped**, **napping**) raise a nap on (cloth). □ **napless** *adj.* **napped** *adj.*

nap³ *v.tr.* (**napped**, **napping**) (usu. *in passive*) cover (food) with a sauce (*clams napped with a white sauce*).

napa¹ /ˈnæpə/ *n.* a soft leather made by a special process from the skin of sheep or goats.

napa² /ˈnæpə/ *n.* a plant, *Brassica rapa pekinensis*, with a long, dense head of whitish, broad leaves used in salads and Oriental cooking.

napalm /ˈneɪpɑm/ ● *n.* **1** a thickening agent produced from naphthenic acid, other fatty acids, and aluminum. **2** a jellied gasoline made from this, used in incendiary bombs. ● *v.tr.* attack with napalm bombs.

nape *n.* the back of the neck.

napery /'neɪpəri/ n. N Amer. & Scot. household linen, esp. table linen.

naphtha /'næpθə, 'næf-/ n. a colourless, flammable petroleum distillate used as a fuel and solvent.

naphthalene /'næfθə,li:n/ n. a white crystalline aromatic substance produced by the distillation of coal tar and used in mothballs and the manufacture of dyes etc.

naphthene /'næfθi:n/ n. any of a group of cycloalkanes. □ **naphthenic** /næf'θi:nɪk/ adj.

napkin n. (in full **table napkin**) a square piece of linen, paper, etc. used for wiping the lips, fingers, etc. at meals; a serviette.

napkin ring n. a ring used to hold a rolled table napkin when not in use.

napoleon /nə'poːliən/ n. **1** N Amer. = MILLE FEUILLE 1. **2** hist. a gold twenty-franc piece minted in the reign of Napoleon I (1769–1821), emperor of France.

Napoleonic /nə,poːli'ɒnɪk/ adj. of, relating to, or characteristic of Napoleon I (1769–1821), emperor of France, or his time.

nappa var. of NAPA[1], NAPA[2].

nappy n. (pl. **-ies**) N Amer. a small, shallow, glass or ceramic bowl for serving fruit, ice cream, etc.

naproxen /nə'prɒksen/ n. an anti-inflammatory analgesic substance given orally as a painkiller and in the treatment of some forms of arthritis.

narc n. esp. N Amer. slang a police narcotics officer.

narcissism /'nɑrsɪ,sɪzəm/ n. Psych. excessive or erotic interest in oneself, one's physical features, etc. □ **narcissist** n. **narcissistic** adj.

narcissus /nɑr'sɪsəs/ n. (pl. **narcissi** /-saɪ/ or **narcissuses**) any bulbous plant of the genus Narcissus, esp. N. poeticus bearing a heavily scented single flower with an undivided corona edged with crimson and yellow.

narcolepsy /'nɑrkə,lepsi/ n. a disease with fits of sleepiness and drowsiness. □ **narcoleptic** adj. & n.

narcosis /nɑr'koːsɪs/ n. a state of drowsiness or unconsciousness induced by a narcotic drug.

narcotic ● adj. **1** (of a substance) inducing drowsiness, sleep, stupor, or insensibility. **2** (of a drug) affecting the mind. **3** of or involving narcosis. **4** soporific. ● n. a narcotic substance, drug, or influence.

nark var. of NARC.

narrate /'nereit, nə'reit/ v. **1** tr. give a continuous story or account of. **2** tr. provide a spoken commentary or accompaniment for (a film etc.). **3** intr. recount or relate a story, events, experiences, etc. □ **narration** /nə'reɪʃən/ n.

narrative ● n. **1** a spoken or written account of connected events in order of happening. **2** the practice or art of narration. ● adj. in the form of, or concerned with, narration (narrative verse). □ **narratively** adv.

narratology /nerə'tɒlədʒi/ n. the branch of knowledge that deals with the structure and function of narrative. □ **narratological** adj. **narratologist** n.

narrator /'ner,eitər, nə'reit-/ n. **1** a character in a play, film, etc., who relates part of the plot to the audience. **2** a person who speaks a commentary in a film, broadcast, etc. **3** a character who recounts the events in a plot, esp. that of a novel or narrative poem. **4** the imagined voice recounting a story in a novel, etc., as distinct from the author (the omniscient narrator). □ **narratorial** adj.

narrow ● adj. (**narrower, narrowest**) **1 a** of small width in proportion to length; lacking breadth. **b** confined or confining; constricted (within narrow bounds). **2** of limited scope; restricted (in the narrowest sense). **3** with little margin (a narrow escape). **4** searching; precise; exact (a narrow examination). **5** = NARROW-MINDED. **6** of small size. ● n. **1** (usu. in pl.) the narrow part of a strait, river, sound, etc. **2** a narrow pass or street. ● v. **1** intr. become narrow; diminish; contract; lessen. **2** tr. make narrow; constrict; restrict. □ **narrow down** reduce the number of possibilities or choices, esp. by eliminating those that are less appropriate or desirable. □ **narrowly** adv. **narrowness** n.

narrowcast esp. N Amer. ● v.intr. & tr. (past and past part. **narrowcast** or **narrowcasted**) transmit (a television program etc.), esp. by cable, to an audience targeted by interests or location. ● n. **1** transmitting in this way. **2** a transmission or program of this kind. □ **narrowcaster** n. **narrowcasting** n.

narrow gauge ● n. a railway track that has a smaller gauge than the standard one. ● adj. (usu. **narrow-gauge**) of or relating to a railway with a narrow gauge.

narrow-minded adj. rigid or restricted in one's views; intolerant, prejudiced. □ **narrow-mindedly** adv. **narrow-mindedness** n.

narrow squeak n. **1** a narrow escape. **2** a success barely attained.

narthex /'nɑrθeks/ n. a lobby inside the main entrance to a church building.

narwhal /'nɑrwəl/ n. a white Arctic whale, Monodon monoceros, the male of which has a long straight spirally fluted tusk developed from one of its teeth.

nary adj. informal or jocular not a; no (nary a one).

NASA /'næsə, 'næsə/ abbr. (in the US) National Aeronautics and Space Administration.

nasal ● adj. **1** of, for, or relating to the nose. **2** Phonetics (of a letter or a sound) pronounced with the breath passing through the nose, e.g. m, n, ng, or French en, un, etc. **3** (of the voice or speech) having an intonation caused by breathing through the nose. ● n. Phonetics a nasal letter or sound. □ **nasally** adv.

NASCAR abbr. National Association for Stock Car Auto Racing.

nascent /'neisənt, 'næs-/ adj. **1** just beginning to be; not yet mature (nascent talents). **2** in the act of being born. **3** Chem. just being formed and therefore unusually reactive (nascent hydrogen).

NASDAQ /'næsdæk, 'næz-/ n. (in the US) National Association of Securities Dealers Automated Quotations, a system for quoting prices on over-the-counter securities.

Naskapi /nə'skæpi/ ● n. **1** a member of an Innu people living along the north shores of the Gulf of St. Lawrence and the St. Lawrence River. **2** the Cree language of this people. ● adj. of or relating to this people.

Nass-Gitksan /,næsgɪt'ksæn/ n. an Aboriginal language spoken by the Nisga'a and Gitksan.

nasturtium /nə'stɜrʃəm/ n. **1** a trailing plant, Tropaeolum majus, with rounded edible leaves and bright orange, yellow, or red flowers. **2** any plant of the genus Nasturtium, including watercress.

nasty ● adj. (**-ier, -iest**) **1 a** highly unpleasant (a nasty experience). **b** annoying; objectionable (has a nasty habit of breaking). **2** difficult to negotiate; dangerous, serious (a nasty question; a nasty illness). **3** (of a person or animal) ill-natured, ill-tempered, spiteful; violent, offensive (nasty to her mother). **4** (of the weather) unpleasant because of cold, wind, precipitation, etc. **5 a** disgustingly dirty, filthy. **b** unpalatable; disagreeable (*nasty smell*). **6** obscene. ● *n.* (*pl.* **-ies**) *informal* a nasty person, animal, thing, etc. □ **a nasty bit** (or **piece**) **of work** *informal* an unpleasant or contemptible person. □ **nastily** *adv.* **nastiness** *n.*

Nat. *abbr.* **1** National. **2** Natural.

natal /'neitəl/ *adj.* **1** of or pertaining to one's birth. **2** (of a place) native; connected with one from birth.

natch *adv. informal* = NATURALLY.

nation *n.* **1 a** a community of people of mainly common descent, history, language, etc., forming a state or inhabiting a territory. **b** the state or territory itself. **2** *N Amer.* a group of Aboriginal people with common ancestry who are socially, culturally, and linguistically united. □ **nationhood** *n.*

national ● *adj.* **1** of or pertaining to a nation or the nation, esp. as a whole. **2** peculiar to or characteristic of a particular nation. **3** owned, controlled, or financially supported by the state (*a national library*). ● *n.* **1** a citizen of a specified country, usu. entitled to hold that country's passport (*French nationals*). **2** (in *pl.*) a national tournament or competition. □ **nationally** *adv.*

national anthem *n.* a song adopted by a nation, expressive of its identity etc. and intended to inspire patriotism.

National Assembly *n.* **1** *Cdn* the provincial legislature of Quebec. **2** an elected house of legislature in various countries.

national bank *n.* **1** *US* a bank chartered under the federal government and required to be a member of the Federal Reserve System. **2** a bank owned and operated by the state.

national debt *n.* the money owed by a central government, including both internal and overseas debts.

national forest *n.* (in the US) a tract of forestland under federal supervision, set aside for conservation and recreation.

National Guard *n.* (in the US) a militia recruited on a state-by-state basis but serving as the primary reserve force of the US army, and available for federal use in emergencies.

National Historic Site *n.* (in Canada) a place designated by the federal government as historically significant, identified by an associated building, archaeological remains, or commemorative statue, cairn or plaque.

national holiday *n.* (also **national day**) a holiday commemorating the creation or celebrating the existence of a nation.

national income *n.* the total annual money value of the goods and services produced by a country.

nationalism *n.* **1 a** patriotic feeling, principles, etc. **b** an extreme form of this. **2** a policy of national independence. □ **nationalist** *n. & adj.* **nationalistic** *adj.* **nationalistically** *adv.*

nationality *n.* (*pl.* **-ies**) **1 a** the status of belonging to a particular nation (*what is your nationality?*). **b** a nation. **2** the condition of being national; distinctive national qualities. **3** an ethnic group forming a part of one or more political nations. **4** existence as a nation; nationhood. **5** patriotic sentiment.

nationalize *v.tr.* **1** take over (an industry, transportation service, land, etc.) from private ownership on behalf of the state. **2 a** make national. **b** make into a nation. □ **nationalization** *n.*

national park *n.* an area of natural beauty or ecological or historical significance, protected by the nation for the use of the general public.

National Policy *n.* *Cdn hist.* a policy of tariff protection for Canadian manufacturers brought into effect in 1879 by Sir John A. Macdonald and espoused by subsequent Conservative prime ministers.

national service *n.* service in the armed forces under conscription for a specified period.

National Socialism *n. hist.* the doctrines of nationalism, racial purity, etc., adopted by the Nazis. □ **National Socialist** *n. & adj.*

Nation of Islam *n.* a black Islamic organization founded *c.*1930 in Detroit.

nation-state *n.* a sovereign state of which most of the citizens or subjects are united also by factors such as language, common descent, etc.

nationwide *adj. & adv.* extending over the whole nation.

native ● *n.* **1 a** (usu. foll. by *of*) a person born in a specified place (*a native of Kamloops*). **b** a local inhabitant. **2** a member of an indigenous people of a country, region, etc., as distinguished from settlers, immigrants, etc. or their descendants. **3** (usu. foll. by *of*) an indigenous animal or plant. ● *adj.* **1** (usu. foll. by *to*) belonging to a person or thing by nature; inherent; innate (*native intelligence*). **2** of one's birth or birthplace (*our home and native land*). **3** belonging to one by right of birth (*native language*). **4** (usu. foll. by *to*) belonging to a specified place (*the anteater is native to South America*). **5** (also **Native**) **a** (of a person) indigenous; descended from the original inhabitants of a region or country. **b** of, pertaining to, or characteristic of the indigenous people of a place (*native customs*). **6** unadorned; simple; artless. **7** *Computing* designed for or built into a given system. □ **go native** (of a settler, traveller, etc.) adopt the way of life of the indigenous inhabitants of a place. □ **natively** *adv.* **nativeness** *n.*

Native American *n.* an American Indian, esp. of the US. ¶The term *Native American* is now often preferred to *American Indian*. However, when used to include the Indian peoples of Canada as well as of the US, it can cause offence. Ambiguity can be avoided by using *American Indian* or *Canadian Indian* as appropriate. See also Usage Note at INDIAN.

native-born *adj.* belonging to a particular place or country by birth.

Native Canadian *n.* an Aboriginal Canadian; a Canadian Indian, Inuit, or Metis.

native friendship centre *n.* *Cdn* = FRIENDSHIP CENTRE.

native son *n.* *N Amer.* a male native of a particular city, province or state, etc.

native speaker *n.* a person who has spoken a specified language from early childhood.

nativism *n.* **1** the attitude, practice, or policy of protecting the interests of native-born or existing inhabitants against those of immigrants. **2** *Anthropology* a return to or emphasis on a way of life or customs under threat from outside influences. **3** *Philos.* the doctrine of innate ideas. □ **nativist** *adj. & n.*

nativity /nə'tɪvɪti/ *n.* (*pl.* **-ies**) **1** (esp. **the Nativity**) **a** the birth of Christ. **b** the festival of Christ's birth; Christmas. **2** a picture of the Nativity. **3** birth. **4 a** the birth of the Virgin Mary or St. John the Baptist. **b** the festival of the nativity of the Virgin (Sept. 8) or St. John (June 24).

nativity scene *n.* a usu. three-dimensional depiction of Christ's birth in a stable, with Mary and Joseph, farm animals, visiting shepherds, etc.

NATO /'neito:/ *abbr.* North Atlantic Treaty Organization.

natter *informal* ● *v.intr.* **1** chatter idly. **2** grumble; talk fretfully. ● *n.* **1** aimless chatter. **2** grumbling talk.

natty *adj.* (**-ier, -iest**) *informal* **1 a** smartly or neatly dressed, dapper. **b** spruce; trim; smart (*a natty suit*). **2** deft. □ **nattily** *adv.* **nattiness** *n.*

natural ● *adj.* **1 a** existing in or caused by nature; not artificial (*natural landscape*). **b** uncultivated; wild (*existing in its natural state*). **2** in the course of nature; not exceptional or miraculous (*died of natural causes*). **3** (of human nature etc.) not surprising; to be expected (*natural for her to be upset*). **4 a** (of a person or a person's behaviour) unaffected, easy, spontaneous. **b** (foll. by *to*) spontaneous, easy (*friendliness is natural to him*). **5 a** (of qualities etc.) inherent; innate (*a natural talent*). **b** (of a person) having such qualities (*a natural comedian*). **6** not disguised or altered (as by makeup, hair dye etc.). **7** lifelike; as if in nature (*the portrait looked very natural*). **8** likely by its or their nature to be such (*natural enemies*). **9** having a physical existence as opposed to what is spiritual, intellectual, etc. (*the natural world*). **10** having genetically the specified familial relationship; actually begotten, not adopted (*her natural son*). **11** based on the innate moral sense; instinctive (*natural justice*). **12** *Music* **a** (of a note) not sharpened or flattened (*B natural*). **b** (of a scale) not containing any sharps or flats. **c** (of a key) having no sharps or flats. **13** (of cotton, silk, etc.) having a colour characteristic of the unbleached and undyed state; off-white, creamy beige. **14** not refined or treated (*natural wood*). **15** containing no additives, preservatives, or other artificial ingredients (*natural foods*). ● *n.* **1** (usu. foll. by *for*) *informal* a person or thing naturally suitable, adept, expert, etc. (*a natural for the championship*). **2** *Music* **a** a sign (♮) denoting a return to natural pitch after a sharp or a flat. **b** a natural note. **c** a white key on a piano. **3** a pale fawn colour. □ **naturalness** *n.*

natural-born *adj.* (usu. *attrib.*) having a character or position by birth.

natural childbirth *n.* childbirth with minimal medical or technological intervention.

natural death *n.* death by age or disease, not by accident, violence, etc.

natural gas *n.* an inflammable mainly methane gas found in the earth's crust, not manufactured.

natural history *n.* **1** the study of animals or plants, esp. as set forth for popular use. **2** an aggregate of the facts concerning the flora and fauna etc. of a particular place or class (*a natural history of Vancouver Island*). □ **natural historian** *n.*

naturalism *n.* **1** the theory or practice in art and literature of representing nature, character, etc. realistically and in great detail. **2 a** *Philos.* a theory of the world that excludes the supernatural or spiritual. **b** any moral or religious system based on this theory. **3** action based on natural instincts. **4** indifference to conventions.

naturalist ● *n.* **1** an expert or student of natural history. **2** a person who believes in or practises naturalism. ● *adj.* = NATURALISTIC.

naturalistic *adj.* **1** imitating nature closely; lifelike. **2** of or according to naturalism. **3** of natural history.

naturalize *v.* **1** *tr.* admit (a person of foreign birth) to the citizenship of a country. **2** *tr.* introduce (an animal, plant, etc.) into another region so that it flourishes in the wild. **3** *tr.* adopt (a foreign word, custom, etc.). **4** *intr.* become naturalized. **5** *tr.* *Philos.* exclude from the miraculous. **6** *tr.* free from conventions; make natural. **7** *tr.* cause to appear natural. □ **naturalization** *n.*

natural language *n.* a language used natively by people, as opposed to an artificial language or code.

natural law *n.* **1** *Philos.* unchanging moral principles common to all people by virtue of their nature as human beings. **2 a** an observable law relating to natural phenomena. **b** these collectively (*where they saw chance, we see natural law*).

natural life *n.* the duration of one's life on earth.

natural logarithm *n.* a logarithm to the base *e* (2.71828.....). Abbr.: **log**$_e$.

naturally *adv.* **1** in a natural manner (*spoke very naturally*). **2** as a natural result. **3** (qualifying a whole sentence) as might be expected; of course. **4** by nature; instinctively (*a naturally talented actor*). **5** without artificial help, special treatment, etc. (*her hair curls naturally*).

natural numbers *n.* the integers 1, 2, 3, etc., sometimes with the addition of 0.

natural philosophy *n.* *hist.* natural science, esp. physical science. □ **natural philosopher** *n.*

natural resources *n.* materials or conditions occurring in nature and capable of economic exploitation.

natural science *n.* **1** the sciences used in the study of the physical world, e.g. physics, chemistry, geology, biology, botany. **2** any one of these sciences.

natural selection *n.* the Darwinian theory of the survival and propagation of organisms best adapted to their environment.

nature *n.* **1** a thing's or person's innate or essential qualities or character (*not in their nature to be cruel; is the nature of iron to rust*). **2** (often **Nature**) **a** the physical power causing all the phenomena of the material world (*Nature is the best physician*). **b** these phenomena, including plants, animals, landscape, etc. **3** a kind, sort, or class (*things of this nature*). **4** = HUMAN NATURE. **5** a specified element of human character (*our animal nature*). **6 a** an uncultivated or wild area, condition, community, etc. **b** the countryside, esp. when picturesque. **7** inherent impulses determining character or action. **8** heredity as an influence on or determinant of personality (*opp.* NURTURE *n.* 3). **9** a living thing's vital functions or needs (*such a diet will not support nature*). □ **against nature** unnatural; immoral. **back to nature** returning to a preindustrial or natural state. **by nature** innately. **from nature** *Art* using natural objects as models. **in nature 1** actually existing. **2** anywhere; at all. **3** in the natural world. **in** (or **of**) **the nature of** characteristically resembling or belonging to the class of (*the answer was in the nature of an excuse*). **in the nature of things** inevitably. **in a state of nature** in an uncivilized or uncultivated state. **one's better nature** the good side of one's character; one's capacity for tolerance, generosity, etc.

-natured *adj.* (in *comb.*) having a specified disposition (*good-natured*).

nature reserve *n.* a tract of land managed so as to preserve its flora, fauna, physical features, etc.

nature spirit *n.* a spirit supposed to reside in some natural element or object.

nature trail *n.* a signposted path through the countryside designed to draw attention to natural phenomena.

nature walk *n.* (also **nature hike**) *N Amer.* a walk through woods, marshland, etc. to observe plants, animals, physical phenomena, etc.

naturism *n.* **1** nudism. **2** naturalism in religion or philosophy. **3** the worship of natural objects. □ **naturist** *n.* & *adj.*

naturopathy /ˌnætʃəˈrɒpəθi, ˌneɪ-/ *n.* **1** the treatment of disease etc. without drugs, usu. involving diet, exercise, massage, etc. **2** this regimen used preventively. □ **naturopath** /ˈnætʃərəˌpæθ, ˈneɪ-/ n. **naturopathic** adj.

Naugahyde /ˈnɒgəhaɪd/ n. proprietary a material used in upholstery, consisting of a fabric base coated with a layer of rubber or vinyl resin and finished with a leather-like grain.

naught archaic or literary ● n. nothing, nought. ● adj. (usu. predic.) worthless; useless. □ **come to naught** be ruined or baffled. **set at naught** disregard; despise.

naughty adj. (**-ier, -iest**) **1** (esp. of children) disobedient; badly behaved. **2** informal jocular connected with sex in a rude or funny way (a naughty postcard). □ **naughtily** adv. **naughtiness** n.

nausea /ˈnɔːzɪə/ n. **1** a feeling of sickness with an inclination to vomit. **2** loathing; revulsion.

nauseate /ˈnɔːzɪˌeɪt/ v.tr. **1** affect with nausea; cause to feel sick (was nauseated by the smell). **2** disgust; appall. □ **nauseated** adj. **nauseating** adj. **nauseatingly** adv.

nauseous /ˈnɔːʃəs, ˈnɔːzɪəs/ adj. **1** affected with nausea, sick (felt nauseous all day). ¶Objections to the use of nauseous in this sense on the grounds that nauseated should be used instead are ill-founded. This is in fact by far the most common sense of nauseous. **2** causing nausea, offensive to the taste or smell. **3** disgusting; loathsome.

nautical adj. of or concerning sailors or ships; naval; maritime. □ **nautically** adv.

nautical mile n. a unit of approx. 1 852 metres (2,025 yards).

nautilus /ˈnɔːtɪləs/ n. (pl. **nautiluses** or **nautili** /-ˌlaɪ/) any cephalopod of the genus Nautilus with a light brittle spiral shell.

NAV abbr. net asset value.

nav. abbr. **1** navigation. **2** naval.

nav n. informal **1** (usu. attrib.) navigation (nav lights). **2** navigator.

Navajo /ˈnævəhoʊ/ (also **Navaho**) ● n. (pl. same or **-os**) **1** a member of an Athapaskan people of Arizona, Utah, and New Mexico. **2** the Athapaskan language of this people. ● adj. of this people.

naval adj. **1** of, in, for, etc. the navy or a navy. **2** of or concerning ships or boats (a naval battle).

naval base n. a seaport from which naval operations can be carried out.

nave n. the central longitudinal part of a church, usu. from the main entrance to the chancel and excluding the side aisles.

navel n. **1** a rounded depression in the centre of the belly caused by the detachment of the umbilical cord; the umbilicus. **2** a central point.

navel-gazing n. usu. profitless meditation; complacent introversion; self-absorption.

navel orange n. a large seedless orange with a navel-like formation at the top.

navigable /ˈnævɪgəbəl/ adj. (of a river, the sea, etc.) affording a passage for ships. □ **navigability** n.

navigate /ˈnævɪgeɪt/ v. **1 a** tr. manage or direct the course of (a ship, aircraft, etc.). **b** intr. find one's way; steer the correct course. **2** tr. **a** sail on or across (a sea, river, etc.). **b** travel or fly through (the air). **3** intr. (of a passenger in a vehicle) assist the driver by map-reading etc. **4** tr. informal steer (oneself, a course, etc.) through a crowd etc.

navigation n. **1** the act or process of navigating. **2** any of several methods of determining or planning a

ship's or aircraft's position and course by geometry, astronomy, radio signals, etc. □ **navigational** adj.

navigation light n. a light on a ship or aircraft, indicating its position and direction.

navigator n. **1** a person skilled or engaged in navigation. **2** an explorer by sea.

navvy n. (pl. **-ies**) Brit. & Cdn informal a labourer excavating or constructing roads, canals, railways, etc.

navy ● n. (pl. **-ies**) **1 a** the whole body of a nation's ships of war, including crews, maintenance systems, and related material such as aircraft etc. **b** the officers and other ranks of a navy. **2** (in full **navy blue**) a dark blue colour as used in naval uniform. ● adj. (in full **navy blue**) dark blue.

navy bean n. = HARICOT.

naw adv. slang = NO interj.

nay ● adv. **1** or rather; and even; and more than that (impressive, nay, magnificent). **2** Parl. or archaic = NO interj. 1. ● n. **1** the word 'nay'. **2** a negative vote.

naysayer n. N Amer. **1** a person who expresses negative, cynical, or gloomy views. **2** a person who does this habitually. □ **naysaying** n.

Nazarene /ˈnæzəˌriːn/ ● n. **1** (prec. by the) Christ. **2** a native or inhabitant of Nazareth, a town in N Israel. **3 a** a member of an early Jewish-Christian sect living in Syria. **b** a member of a Protestant denomination called the Church of the Nazarene. ● adj. of or concerning Nazareth, the Nazarenes, etc.

Nazi /ˈnɒtsi, ˈnætsi/ ● n. (pl. **Nazis**) **1** hist. a member of the German National Socialist party, led by Adolf Hitler. **2** derogatory a person holding extreme racist or authoritarian views or behaving brutally. **3** a person belonging to any organization similar to the Nazis. ● adj. of or concerning the Nazis, Nazism, etc. □ **Nazidom** n. **Nazification** n. **Nazify** v.tr. (**-ies, -ied**) **Naziism** /-iːˌɪzəm/ n. **Nazism** /ˈnætsɪzəm/ n.

NB abbr. **1** New Brunswick. **2** nota bene.

Nb symbol niobium.

NBA abbr. National Basketball Association.

NBC abbr. (of armaments or warfare) nuclear, biological, and chemical.

NC abbr. North Carolina (also in postal use).

NCAA abbr. (in the US) National Collegiate Athletic Association.

NCC n. (in Canada) National Capital Commission.

NCM abbr. Cdn non-commissioned member.

NCO abbr. non-commissioned officer.

ND abbr. North Dakota (also in postal use).

Nd symbol neodymium.

n.d. abbr. no date.

N.Dak. abbr. North Dakota.

NDE abbr. near-death experience.

NDP abbr. Cdn NEW DEMOCRATIC PARTY. □ **NDPer** n.

NDT abbr. Newfoundland Daylight Time.

NE abbr. **1** northeast. **2** northeastern. **3** Nebraska (in postal use).

Ne symbol the element neon.

né /neɪ/ adj. born (indicating a man's previous name) (Lord Beaconsfield, né Benjamin Disraeli).

Neanderthal /niˈændərˌθɒl, -ˌtɒl/ ● adj. **1** of or belonging to the type of human widely distributed in paleolithic Europe, with a retreating forehead and massive brow ridges. **2** (also **neanderthal**) jocular or derogatory **a** primitive, uncivilized, uncouth. **b** reactionary; extremely conservative. ● n. **1** a Neanderthal hominid. **2** (also **neanderthal**) jocular or derogatory **a** a primitive, uncivilized, or uncouth person. **b** a reactionary or extremely conservative person.

neap n. (in full **neap tide**) a tide just after the first and third quarters of the moon when there is least difference between high and low water.

Neapolitan /niəˈpɒlɪtən/ ● *n.* a native or citizen of Naples, Italy. ● *adj.* of or relating to Naples.

Neapolitan ice cream *n.* ice cream made in layers of chocolate, vanilla, and strawberry.

near ● *adv.* **1** (often foll. by *to*) to or at a short distance in space or time; close by (*the time drew near; dropped near to them*). **2** closely (*as near as one can guess*). **3** *informal* almost, nearly (*damn near died*). ● *prep.* (comparative & superlative also used) **1** to or at a short distance (in space, time, condition, or resemblance) from (*stood near the back; occurs nearer the end*). **2** (in *comb.*) **a** that is almost (*near-hysterical*). **b** intended as a substitute for; resembling (*near-beer*). ● *adj.* **1** close at hand; close to, in place or time (*the end is near; in the near future*). **2 a** closely related (*a near relation*). **b** intimate (*a near friend*). **3** (of a part of a vehicle, animal, or road) left-hand (as seen from the driver's or rider's point of view) (*near side front wheel* (opp. OFF *adj.* 2). **4** close; narrow (*a near escape; a near guess*). **5** similar (to) (*is nearer the original*). **6** niggardly, mean. ● *v.* **1** *tr.* approach; draw near to (*neared the harbour*). **2** *intr.* draw near (*could distinguish them as they neared*). □ **come near** (foll. by verbal noun, or *to* + verbal noun) be on the point of, almost succeed in (*came near to falling*). **near at hand 1** within easy reach. **2** in the immediate future. **nearest and dearest** one's closest friends and relatives collectively. □ **nearness** *n.*

near bank *n.* (in Canada) a financial institution, e.g. a credit union or caisse populaire, that provides banking services but does not have the status or privileges of a chartered bank.

nearby ● *adj.* situated in a near position (*a nearby hotel*). ● *adv.* (also **near by**) close; not far away.

Nearctic /niːˈɑːrktɪk, -ˈɑːrtɪk/ ● *adj.* of or relating to the Arctic and the temperate parts of N America as a zoogeographical region. ● *n.* the Nearctic region.

near-death experience *n.* an out-of-body experience taking place on the brink of death, recounted by a person on recovery.

Near East *n.* (prec. by *the*) **1** = MIDDLE EAST. **2** *hist.* the Balkans. □ **Near Eastern** *adj.*

nearly *adv.* **1** almost (*we are nearly there*). **2** closely (*they are nearly related*). **3** with a close degree of approximation. □ **not nearly** nothing like; far from (*not nearly enough*).

near miss *n.* **1** a bomb etc. falling close to the target. **2** a narrowly avoided collision. **3** an attempt that is almost but not quite successful.

Near North *n. Cdn* the southern edge of the Subarctic, extending across Canada in a band just north of the heavily settled areas of the Fraser Valley, the Prairies, S Ontario, and the St. Lawrence Valley.

nearsighted *adj.* esp. *N Amer.* **1** unable to distinguish objects clearly at a distance; myopic. **2** = SHORT-SIGHTED 2. □ **nearsightedly** *adv.* **nearsightedness** *n.*

near-term *adj.* occurring in or pertaining to the near future.

near thing *n.* a narrow escape.

neat ● *adj.* **1 a** (of a room etc.) tidy; clean; in an orderly condition. **b** (of a person) liking to keep things in order; fastidious (*a neat worker*). **2** elegantly simple in form etc.; well-proportioned. **3** (of language, style, etc.) brief, clear, and pointed; epigrammatic. **4 a** cleverly executed (*a neat piece of work*). **b** deft; dexterous. **5** (of esp. alcoholic liquor) undiluted. **6** *N Amer. slang* (as a general term of approval) good, pleasing, excellent. ● *adv. informal*

neatly. ● *n.* (in *pl.*) a small pattern or design of dots, geometrics, etc. found esp. on ties, socks, etc. □ **neatly** *adv.* **neatness** *n.*

neaten *v.tr.* make neat.

'neath *prep.* (also **neath**) *literary* beneath.

neat-o *adj. N Amer. slang* = NEAT[1] *adj.* 6.

NEB *abbr.* (in Canada) National Energy Board.

Neb. *abbr.* (also **Nebr.**) Nebraska.

Nebbiolo /nebiˈoːloː/ ● *n.* **1** a black wine grape grown in Piedmont in northern Italy. **2** red wine made from this. ● *adj.* of or pertaining to this grape or wine.

nebbish /ˈnebɪʃ/ *informal* ● *n.* an ineffectual or timid person. ● *adj.* ineffectual; timid. □ **nebbishy** *adj.*

Nebraskan ● *n.* a native or inhabitant of the US state of Nebraska. ● *adj.* of or relating to Nebraska.

nebula /ˈnebjʊlə/ *n.* (*pl.* **nebulae** /-ˌliː, -ˌlaɪ/ or **-s**) **1 a** cloud of gas and dust in space, sometimes glowing and sometimes appearing as a dark silhouette against other glowing matter. **2** a clouded spot on the cornea causing defective vision. □ **nebular** *adj.*

nebulous /ˈnebjʊləs/ *adj.* **1** hazy, indistinct, vague (*nebulous ideas*). **2** *Astronomy* of or like a nebula or nebulae. □ **nebulosity** /-ˈlɒsɪti/ *n.* **nebulously** *adv.*

necessarily *adv.* **1** as a necessary result; inevitably. **2** by force of necessity (*we don't necessarily have to leave*).

necessary ● *adj.* **1** requiring to be done, achieved, etc.; requisite, essential (*it is necessary to work*; *lacks the necessary documents*). **2** determined, existing, or happening by natural laws, predestination, etc., not by free will; inevitable (*a necessary evil*). ● *n.* (*pl.* **-ies**) (usu. in *pl.*) any of the basic requirements of life, such as food, warmth, etc. □ **the necessary** an action, item, etc., needed for a purpose (*they will do the necessary*).

necessitate *v.tr.* make necessary (esp. as a result) (*will necessitate some sacrifice*).

necessity *n.* (*pl.* **-ies**) **1 a** (often in *pl.*) an indispensable thing (*central heating is a necessity*; *the necessities of life*). **b** (usu. foll. by *of*) indispensability (*the necessity of a warm overcoat*). **2** a state of affairs or circumstances enforcing a certain course (*there was a necessity to hurry*). **3** imperative need (*necessity is the mother of invention*). **4** want; poverty; hardship (*stole because of necessity*). **5** constraint or compulsion regarded as a natural law governing all human action. □ **of necessity** unavoidably.

neck ● *n.* **1 a** the part of the body connecting the head to the shoulders. **b** the part of a shirt, dress, etc. around or close to the neck. **c** = NECKLINE. **2 a** something resembling a neck, such as the narrow part of a cavity or vessel, a passage, channel, pass, isthmus, etc. **b** the narrow part of a bottle, vase, etc. near the mouth. **3** the part of a violin, guitar, etc. bearing the fingerboard. **4** the length of a horse's head and neck as a measure of its lead in a race. ● *v.* **1** *intr. informal* kiss and caress amorously. **2 a** *tr.* form a narrowed part in. **b** *intr.* form a narrowed part. □ **get it in the neck** *informal* **1** receive a severe reprimand or punishment. **2** suffer a fatal or severe blow. **neck and neck** very close in a race, competition, etc. **up to one's neck** (often foll. by *in*) *informal* very deeply involved; very busy. □ **necked** *adj.* (also in *comb.*). **necker** *n.* (in sense 1 of *v.*). **neckless** *adj.*

neckband *n.* a strip of material around the neck of a garment.

neckerchief /ˈnekərtʃɪf, -tʃiːf/ *n.* a square of cloth worn around the neck.

necklace *n.* **1** a chain or string of beads, precious stones, links, etc., worn as an ornament around the

neck. 2 a series of towns, buildings, objects, etc., spread over an area.

neckline *n.* the edge or shape of the opening of a garment at the neck (*a square neckline*).

neck of the woods *n. informal* a community or locality.

necktie *n.* esp. *N Amer.* = TIE *n.* 2.

necromancy /'nekrə,mænsi/ *n.* **1** the prediction of the future by the supposed communication with the dead. **2** witchcraft. □ **necromancer** *n.* **necromantic** *adj.*

necrophilia /nekrə'filiə/ *n.* a morbid and esp. erotic attraction to corpses. □ **necrophiliac** *n.* **necrophilic** *adj.*

necropolis /nə'krɒpəlɪs/ *n.* **1** an ancient cemetery or burial place. **2** a cemetery, esp. a large one in or near a city.

necropsy /'nekrɒpsi/ *n.* (*pl.* **-ies**) = AUTOPSY 1.

necrosis /nə'krəʊsɪs/ *n.* the death or decay of part or all of an organ or tissue due to disease, injury, or deficiency of nutrients, esp. as one of the symptoms of gangrene or pulmonary tuberculosis. □ **necrotic** /-'krɒtɪk/ *adj.* **necrotize** /'nekrətaɪz/ *v.intr.*

nectar *n.* **1** a sugary substance produced by plants to attract pollinating insects and made into honey by bees. **2 a** (in Greek and Roman mythology) the drink of the gods. **b** a drink compared to this. **3** a drink of usu. undiluted fruit juice or a blend of fruit juices.

nectarine *n.* **1** a variety of peach with a thin brightly-coloured smooth skin and firm flesh. **2** the tree bearing this.

née /neɪ/ *adj.* (also **nee**) (used in adding a married woman's maiden name after her surname) born (*Mrs. Patricia Barber, née Clarke*).

need ● *v.* **1** *tr.* stand in want of; require (*needs a new coat*; *this needs revising*). **2** *tr.* **a** (foll. by *to* + infin.) (esp. in positive and declarative contexts) be under a necessity or obligation (*it needs to be done carefully*). **b** (3rd sing. present **need**) (without *to*) (esp. in neg. or interrog. contexts) be under the necessity or obligation (*he need not come*). **3** *intr. N Amer. informal* must get (*I need in there, now!*). ● *n.* **1 a** a want or requirement (*my needs are few*). **b** a thing wanted (*my greatest need is a car*). **2** circumstances requiring some course of action; necessity (*there is no need to worry*). **3 a** a condition of lacking or requiring some necessary thing, either physically or psychologically. **b** destitution; poverty. **4** a crisis, time of difficulty, distress, or trouble; an emergency (*failed them in their need*). □ **at need** in time of need. **have need of** require; want. **have no need to** not be obliged to (*I have no need to prove my manhood*). **if need be** if necessary. **in need** requiring help. **in need of** requiring. **need not have** did not need to (but did).

needful ● *adj.* **1** requisite; necessary; indispensable. **2** having a need or needs. ● *n.* **1** (prec. by *the*) what is necessary. **2** *informal* money or action needed for a purpose.

needle ● *n.* **1 a** a very thin small piece of smooth steel etc. pointed at one end and with a slit (eye) for thread, used in sewing. **b** a larger plastic, wooden, etc. slender stick without an eye, used in knitting. **2 a** a slender, usu. pointed, indicator on a dial or other measuring instrument, esp. a speedometer. **b** = MAGNETIC NEEDLE. **3** any of several small thin pointed instruments, esp.: **a** a surgical instrument for stitching. **b** the end of a hypodermic syringe. **c** a thin metal rod used in acupuncture. **d** = STYLUS 3. **e** an etching tool. **4 a** a hypodermic syringe. **b** an injection of a drug, vaccine, etc. through the needle of such a syringe. **5 a** a pointed peak or mass of rock. **b** a long narrow pointed crystal or spicule. **6** any of the sharp, stiff, slender leaves characteristic of a coniferous tree. ● *v.tr.* **1** *informal* **a** incite or irritate; provoke. **b** tease, harass. **2** sew, pierce, or operate on with a needle. □ **needle in a haystack** something almost impossible to find because it is concealed by so many other things etc. □ **needled** *adj.* (also in *comb.*). **needler** *n.* **needling** *n.*

needle-nose *attrib.adj.* (of pliers) having long, thin, pincers suitable for gripping in very narrow spaces.

needlepoint ● *n.* embroidery worked over canvas etc., esp. petit point. ● *v.tr. & intr.* work or create through needlepoint.

needless *adj.* unnecessary, uncalled for, not needed or wanted. □ **needless to say** of course; it goes without saying. □ **needlessly** *adv.* **needlessness** *n.*

needle stick *n.* (often *attrib.*) an act or instance of being, usu. accidentally, stuck by a hypodermic needle, esp. if possibly contaminated by HIV etc. (*needle-stick injury*).

needlework *n.* **1** the action of producing something with a needle, esp. by embroidery, tapestry, etc. **2** a piece of work so produced (also *attrib.*: *needlework cushion*). □ **needleworker** *n.*

needn't *contraction* need not.

needs *adv.* (usu. prec. or foll. by *must*) of necessity (*must needs decide*).

need-to-know *adj.* designating the principle or practice of telling people only what is necessary for them to carry out a task effectively.

needy *adj.* (**-ier**, **-iest**) **1** (of a person) **a** poor; destitute. **b** lacking some essential emotional or psychological quality, experience, etc. **2** (of circumstances) characterized by poverty or need. □ **neediness** *n.*

neem /niːm/ *n.* a tree, *Azadirachta indica* (mahogany family), whose leaves and bark are used medicinally in the Indian subcontinent.

ne'er /neə/ *adv.* **1** *literary* = NEVER. **2** *Cdn* (*Nfld*) not one, not a; no.

ne'er-do-well ● *n.* a good-for-nothing person. ● *adj.* good-for-nothing.

nefarious /nə'feəriəs/ *adj.* wicked; iniquitous. □ **nefariousness** *n.*

neg *n. informal* a photographic negative.

neg. *abbr.* negative.

negate *v.tr.* **1** nullify, make ineffective, invalidate. **2** imply, involve, or assert the non-existence of; deny. **3** *Grammar* make (a clause, sentence, etc.) negative in meaning.

negation *n.* **1** (often foll. by *of*) **a** the act of refusing, or of contradicting or denying a statement or allegation. **b** an instance of this; a contradiction, denial, or refusal. **c** a negative statement or doctrine. **2** the absence or opposite of something actual or positive (*death is the negation of life*). **3** *Grammar* **a** the grammatical process by which the truth of a clause or sentence is denied, involving the use of a negative word, e.g. *not*, *no*, *never*. **b** an instance of this. **4** a negative or unreal thing; a nonentity.

negative ● *adj.* **1** expressing or implying denial, prohibition, or refusal (*a negative vote*; *a negative answer*). **2 a** (of a person, attitude, etc.) unhelpful, critical, or destructive; pessimistic, defeatist. **b** not having or showing an interested attitude, aiming to improve something, etc.; uncooperative. **3** (of an effect) harmful (*eliminate the negative side effects of the drug*). **4 a** (of the results of a test or an experiment) indicating that a substance or condition is not present (*the biopsy was negative*). **b** (in *comb.*) (of a person, blood, etc.) not having a specified condition, substance, etc. (*HIV-negative*). **5** marked by the absence rather than the presence of qualities. **6** of the opposite nature to a thing regarded as positive (*debt is negative capital*). **7** *Grammar* (of a word, clause, etc.) expressing negation. **8** *Algebra* (of a quantity) less than zero, to be subtracted from others or from zero (*opp.* POSITIVE *adj.* 9). **9** *Electricity* **a** of the kind of charge carried by electrons (*opp.* POSITIVE *adj.* 10a). **b** containing or producing such a charge. **10** *Photog.* (of a visual image, esp. a photograph) showing the lights, shades, and colour values reversed from those of the original. ● *n.* **1** a negative statement or reply. **2** *Photog.* **a** an image with black and white reversed or colours replaced by complementary ones, from which positive pictures are obtained. **b** a developed film or plate bearing such an image. **3** *Grammar* = NEGATOR 2. **4** (prec. by *the*) the side or aspect of a question which is opposed to the affirmative or positive. **5 a** a negative quality or characteristic. **b** an absence of something. **6** a negative result on a medical test, experiment, etc. ● *interj.* esp. *N Amer.* no. ● *v.tr.* **1** refuse to accept or countenance; veto; reject. **2** disprove (an inference or hypothesis). **3** contradict (a statement). **4** neutralize (an effect). □ **in the negative** in rejection of a proposal or suggestion, with negative effect; no (*the answer was in the negative*). □ **negatively** *adv.* **negativeness** *n.* **negativity** *n.*

negative equity *n.* the indebtedness arising when the market value of a property falls below the outstanding amount of a mortgage secured on it.

negative feedback *n.* **1** the return of part of an output signal to the input, tending to decrease the amplification etc. **2** esp. *Biol.* the diminution or counteraction of an effect by its own influence on the process giving rise to it. **3** a negative response to a questionnaire, an experiment, etc.

negativism *n.* **1 a** the tendency to be negative in attitude, action, or position. **b** extreme skepticism, criticism, etc. **2** denial of accepted beliefs. □ **negativist** *n.* **negativistic** *adj.*

negator /nəˈgeitər/ *n.* **1** a person who denies something. **2** *Grammar* a word or particle expressing negation, e.g. *not, don't.*

neglect ● *v.tr.* **1** fail to care for or to do; be remiss about (*neglected their duty; neglected his children*). **2** (foll. by *to* + infin.) fail; overlook or forget the need to (*neglected to inform them*). **3** not pay due attention to; disregard (*this area of research has been largely neglected*). ● *n.* **1** lack of caring; negligence (*the house suffered from neglect*). **2 a** the act or fact of neglecting. **b** the state or condition of being neglected (*the house fell into neglect*). **3** (usu. foll. by *of*) disregard. □ **neglected** *adj.* **neglectful** *adj.*

negligee /ˈneglɪˌʒei/ *n.* a woman's light dressing gown, usu. made of delicate, semi-transparent fabric and trimmed with lace etc.

negligence /ˈneglɪdʒəns/ *n.* **1 a** a lack of reasonable or proper care and attention; carelessness. **b** an act or instance of carelessness or inattention. **2** *Law* **a** = CONTRIBUTORY NEGLIGENCE. **b** = CRIMINAL NEGLIGENCE. □ **negligent** *adj.* **negligently** *adv.*

negligible /ˈneglɪdʒɪbəl/ *adj.* not worth considering or noticing; insignificant. □ **negligibility** *n.*

negotiable /nəˈgoʊʃəbəl/ *adj.* **1 a** able to be decided or arranged by negotiation or mutual agreement. **b** subject to modification of meaning or interpretation. **2** (of a bill, draft, cheque, etc.) transferable or assignable in the course of business from

one person to another simply by delivery. **3** (of an obstacle) that may be crossed or got over, around, or through. □ **negotiability** *n.*

negotiable instrument *n.* a freely negotiable legal document such as a cheque, promissory note, etc. that is payable to the bearer.

negotiate /nəˈgoʊʃiˌeit/ *v.* **1** *intr.* (usu. foll. by *with*) confer with others in order to reach a compromise or agreement. **2** *tr.* arrange or settle (a matter) or bring about (a result) by negotiating (*negotiated a settlement; negotiate a loan*). **3** *tr.* find a way over, through, etc. (an obstacle, difficulty, etc.). **4** *tr.* **a** transfer or assign (a cheque etc.) to another. **b** convert (a cheque etc.) into cash or banknotes. **c** get or give value for (a cheque etc.) in money. □ **negotiated** *adj.* **negotiating** *n.* **negotiation** /-ʃɪˈeiʃən, -sɪˈeiʃən/ *n.* **negotiator** *n.*

negotiating table *n.* a place or meeting etc. at which disputes, esp. labour disputes, armed conflicts, constitutional matters, etc., are negotiated.

Negro /ˈniːgroʊ/ ¶Now usu. considered *offensive.* ● *n.* (*pl.* **-oes**) a member of the black or dark-skinned group of human populations that exist or originated in Africa south of the Sahara, now distributed around the world. ● *adj.* of or concerning this people.

Negroid /ˈniːgroid/ ● *adj.* **1** denoting, concerning, or belonging to one of the group of human populations having dark skin, tightly curled hair, and a broad flattish nose, indigenous to sub-Saharan Africa and parts of Melanesia. **2** (of features etc.) characteristic of these peoples. ● *n.* a member of one of these peoples.

Negro spiritual *n.* = SPIRITUAL *n.*

Nehru jacket /ˈneiru:/ *n.* a long, narrow jacket with a high stand-up collar.

neigh ● *n.* **1** the high whinnying sound of a horse. **2** any similar sound, e.g. a laugh. ● *v.* **1** *intr.* make such a sound. **2** *tr.* utter with such a sound.

neighbour (also **neighbor**) ● *n.* **1** a person, institution, etc., resident or established next door to or near or nearest another. **2 a** a person or thing near or next to another (*my neighbour at dinner*). **b** a country etc. adjacent to or near another (*Canada and the US are neighbours*). **c** (in *pl.*) a resident of such a country etc. (*our neighbours to the South*). **3** a person regarded as a fellow human being, esp. as entitled to kindness, compassion, consideration, etc. **4** (*attrib.*) a neighbouring (*a neighbour nation*). **b** living in the vicinity or next door (*neighbour kids*). ● *v.* **1** *tr.* border on; adjoin. **2** *intr.* (often foll. by *on, upon*) border; adjoin. □ **neighbouring** *adj.*

neighbourhood *n.* (also **neighborhood**) **1 a** a district, esp. considered in reference to the character or circumstances of its inhabitants. **b** a small, relatively self-contained section of a larger urban area. **2** the people of a district; one's neighbours. **3** (often foll. by *of*) the nearby or surrounding area, the vicinity. **4** (*attrib.*) belonging to or serving a particular neighbourhood (*neighbourhood eatery*). □ **in the neighbourhood of** roughly; about (*paid in the neighbourhood of $100*).

neighbourhood watch *n.* systematic local vigilance by householders to discourage crime.

neighbourly *adj.* (also **neighborly**) characteristic of a good neighbour. □ **neighbourliness** *n.*

neither /ˈnaiðər, ˈni:ð-/ ● *adj. & pron.* (foll. by sing. verb) **1** not the one nor the other (of two things); not either (*neither of the accusations is true; neither wish was granted; neither went to the fair*). **2** *Cdn* (*Nfld*) no, none, not any. ● *adv.* **1** (foll. by *nor*; introducing the first of two or more things in the negative) not either; not on the one hand (would neither come in nor go out; neither the teachers nor the parents nor the children). **2** not either; also not (if you do not, neither shall I). ● conj. nor yet; nor (I do not know, neither can I guess). ¶As a pronoun, neither is singular: Neither of us likes tennis. However, in informal English, it is often treated as a plural: Neither of them are good players. When two subjects are linked by neither...nor, either a singular or a plural verb is permissible: Neither the television nor the radio works properly; Neither the television nor the radio work properly; some people feel, however, that singular subjects require a singular verb.

nelly n. (pl. **-ies**) a silly or effeminate person. □ **not on your nelly** Cdn & Brit. slang certainly not.

nelson n. a wrestling hold in which one arm is passed under the opponent's arm from behind and the hand is applied to the neck (**half nelson**), or both arms and hands are applied (**full nelson**).

nematode /'nemə,toːd/ n. any parasitic or free-living worm of the phylum Nematoda, with a slender unsegmented cylindrical shape.

nemesis /'neməsɪs/ n. (pl. **nemeses** /-,siːz/) **1** esp. N Amer. a long-standing or persistent rival, enemy, or tormentor. **2** retributive justice. **3 a** a downfall caused by this. **b** an agent of such a downfall.

neo- /'niːoː/ comb. form **1** new, modern. **2** a new or revived form of.

neo-classical adj. (also **neo-classic**) **1** of or relating to a revival or development of a classical style or treatment in art, literature, music, etc. **2** Econ. of, pertaining to, or characteristic of a body of theory primarily concerned with supply and demand rather than with the source and distribution of wealth. □ **neoclassicism** n. **neoclassicist** n.

neo-colonialism n. the use of economic, political, or other pressures to control or influence other countries, esp. former dependencies. □ **neo-colonialist** n. & adj.

neo-con adj. & n. = NEO-CONSERVATIVE.

neo-conservative ● adj. of or pertaining to a form of political conservatism advocating a moderate type of democratic capitalism. ● n. an advocate or supporter of neo-conservative principles or beliefs. □ **neo-conservatism** n.

neocortex n. (pl. **-tices** /-tɪsəs/) the most recently evolved part of the cerebral cortex, involved in sight and hearing in advanced reptiles and in mammals.

neodymium /,niːoˈdɪmiəm/ n. a silver-grey naturally-occurring metallic element used in colouring glass etc.

neo-fascist ● adj. of or relating to a political belief, movement, etc. based on, inspired by, or emulating fascism, Nazism, etc. ● n. **1** an adherent or advocate of a fascist belief or movement. **2** a person belonging to an organization based on the Italian Fascist movement of the early 20th c. □ **neo-fascism** n.

neo-Gothic adj. of or relating to a revival of the medieval Gothic style in art or architecture.

neo-liberal ● adj. of or designating a modern political belief or movement that modifies certain doctrines of classical liberalism, esp. attitudes toward trade unions, big business, and military spending. ● n. an adherent or advocate of such a belief or movement. □ **neo-liberalism** n.

neolithic /,niːoˈlɪθɪk/ (also **Neolithic**) ● adj. of or relating to the later Stone Age, when ground or polished stone weapons and implements prevailed. ● n. the neolithic period.

neologism /niːˈɒlədʒ,ɪzəm/ n. **1** a new word or

expression. **2** the coining or use of new words. □ **neologist** n. **neologistic** adj. **neologize** v.intr.

neomycin /,niːoˈmaɪsɪn/ n. an antibiotic, related to streptomycin, used to treat a wide variety of bacterial infections.

neon ● n. **1** (often attrib.) an inert gaseous element occurring in traces in the atmosphere and giving an orange glow when electricity is passed through it in a sealed low-pressure tube, used in lights and illuminated advertisements (neon sign). **2** a neon lamp or tube; neon lighting. ● adj. **1** of, pertaining to, or involving neon. **2 a** resembling a neon light in colour or brilliance. **b** harshly bright, gaudy, or glowing.

neonate /'niːə,neɪt/ n. **1** a newborn child, esp. an infant less than four weeks old. **2** a newly born animal, bird, etc. □ **neonatal** /-'neɪtəl/ adj.

neonatology /,niːənəˈtɒlodʒi/ n. the branch of medicine that deals with the disorders and problems of newly born infants. □ **neonatologist** n.

neo-Nazi ● n. (pl. **neo-Nazis**) a person belonging to an organization based on or deriving from the German National Socialist Party, or holding extreme racist views. ● adj. of or relating to neo-Nazis or neo-Nazism. □ **neo-Nazism** n.

neophyte /'niːə,faɪt/ n. **1** a beginner; a novice (also attrib.: neophyte sailor). **2** a new convert, esp. to a religious faith. **3** Catholicism **a** a novice of a religious order. **b** a newly ordained priest.

neoplasm /'niːə,plæzəm/ n. a new and abnormal growth of tissue in some part of the body, esp. a tumour. □ **neoplastic** adj.

Neoplatonism n. a philosophical and religious system based on Platonic ideas, which emphasizes the distinction between a supposed eternal world and the changing physical world, and combines this with a mystic possibility of union with the supreme being from which all reality is supposed to derive. □ **Neoplatonic** adj. **Neoplatonist** n.

neoprene /'niːoː,priːn/ n. any of various strong synthetic rubbers which are resistant to oil, heat, and weathering.

neo-realism n. the doctrine of realism in philosophy, art, literature, etc. revived at the beginning of the 20th c. to refute certain tenets of idealism. □ **neo-realist** n.

neo-traditionalism adj. a revival of traditional styles, customs, etc., esp. in architecture etc.

neotropical adj. of or relating to tropical and S America as a biogeographical region.

Nepalese /,nepəˈliːz/ adj. & n. (pl. same) = NEPALI.

Nepali /nəˈpɒli/ ● n. (pl. same or **Nepalis**) **1 a** a native or national of Nepal, a mountainous landlocked country in S Asia. **b** a person of Nepali descent. **2** the language of Nepal. ● adj. of or relating to Nepal or its language or people.

nephew n. a son of one's brother or sister, or of one's brother-in-law or sister-in-law.

nephritis /nɪˈfraɪtɪs/ n. inflammation of the kidneys.

nephron /'nefrɒn/ n. each of the functional units in the kidney, through which filtrate passes before emerging as urine.

ne plus ultra /,neɪ plʊs 'ʊltrɑ/ n. **1** the culmination, acme, or perfection. **2** the furthest attainable point.

nepotism /'nepə,tɪzəm/ n. favouritism shown to relatives in bestowing employment or conferring privileges. □ **nepotist** n. **nepotistic** adj.

neptunium /nep'tjuːniəm/ n. a radioactive metallic element produced from uranium.

nerd *n. esp. N Amer. slang* a foolish, feeble, or uninteresting person, esp. one ridiculed as studious, puny, or unfashionable. □ **nerdiness** *n.* **nerdish** *adj.* **nerdy** *adj.*

nerve ● *n.* **1 a** a fibre or bundle of fibres that transmits impulses of sensation or motion between the brain or spinal cord and other parts of the body. **b** the material constituting these. **2 a** coolness in danger; bravery; assurance. **b** *informal* impudence, audacity (*they've got nerve*). **3** (in *pl.*) **a** the bodily state in regard to physical sensitivity and the interaction between the brain and other parts. **b** a state of heightened nervousness or sensitivity; a condition of mental or physical stress (*need to calm my nerves*). **4** a rib of a leaf. ● *v.tr.* (usu. *refl.*) brace (oneself) to face danger, suffering, etc. □ **get on a person's nerves** irritate or annoy a person. **have nerves of steel** (of a person etc.) be not easily upset or frightened. **hit** (or **touch**) **a nerve** remark on or draw attention to a sensitive subject or point. □ **nerved** *adj.* (also in *comb.*).

nerve cell *n.* an elongated branched cell transmitting impulses in nerve tissue.

nerve centre *n.* **1** a group of closely connected nerve cells associated in performing some function. **2** the centre of control of an organization etc.

nerve ending *n.* the branched or specialized end of a nerve fibre.

nerve gas *n.* a poisonous gas or vapour that disrupts the functioning of the nervous system, esp. for use in warfare.

nerve impulse *n.* a signal transmitted along a nerve fibre, consisting of a wave of electrical depolarization.

nerveless *adj.* **1** inert, lacking vigour or spirit. **2** confident; not nervous. **3** *Anat. & Zool.* without nerves. □ **nervelessly** *adv.* **nervelessness** *n.*

nerve-racking *adj.* (also **nerve-wracking**) stressful, frightening; straining the nerves.

nervous *adj.* **1 a** worried, anxious. **b** timid, reluctant, afraid. **c** resulting from or reflecting these feelings (*nervous smile*). **2 a** excitable; high-strung; easily agitated. **b** resulting from this temperament, from a disorder of the nervous system, etc. (*a nervous headache*). **3** pertaining to or affecting the nerves (*a nervous disorder*). □ **nervously** *adv.* **nervousness** *n.*

nervous breakdown *n.* a period of incapacitating mental and emotional disturbance, severe depression, etc.

nervous system *n.* the body's network of specialized cells which transmit nerve impulses between parts of the body.

nervous wreck *n. informal* a person suffering from mental stress, emotional exhaustion, etc.

nervy *adj.* (**-ier, -iest**) *N Amer.* impudent, audacious. □ **nervily** *adv.* **nerviness** *n.*

-ness *suffix* forming nouns from adjectives, and occasionally other words, expressing: **1** state or condition, or an instance of this (*happiness; a kindness*). **2** something in a certain state (*wilderness*).

nest ● *n.* **1** a structure or place where a bird lays eggs and shelters its young. **2** an animal's or insect's breeding ground or lair. **3** a snug or secluded retreat, shelter, home, etc. **4** (often foll. by *of*) a place fostering something undesirable (*a nest of vice*). **5** a number of birds, insects, etc. occupying the same nest or habitation; a brood or swarm. **6** a group or set of similar objects, often of different sizes and fitting together for storage (*a nest of tables*). **7** a group of machine guns, snipers, etc. **8** a set of nested procedures, sub-

routines, syntactic units, etc. ● *v.* **1** *intr.* use or build a nest. **2** *intr.* take or collect wild birds' nests or eggs. **3 a** *intr.* (of objects) fit together or one inside another. **b** *tr.* place or fit (a thing) inside another, similar one, esp. in a hierarchical arrangement. □ **nestable** *adj.* **nested** *adj.* **nester** *n.*

nest egg *n.* a sum of money saved for the future.

nesting box *n.* (also **nest box**) a box provided for a bird to make its nest in.

nestle *v.* **1** *tr. & intr.* (often in *passive*; often foll. by *in*, *against*, *among*) place or lie in a partly hidden, snug, or sheltered position. **2** *intr.* (often foll. by *down*, *in*, etc.) settle down in a snug or comfortable manner. **3** *tr.* (foll. by *in*, *into*, etc.) rest or settle (a head, shoulder, etc.) in a snug or affectionate manner. **4** *intr.* draw or press close to a person or thing, esp. in an affectionate manner.

nestling /'neslɪŋ, 'nest-/ *n.* a bird that is too young to leave its nest.

Net *n. informal* (also **net**) (usu. prec. by *the*) the Internet.

net¹ ● *n.* **1** an open-meshed fabric of cord, rope, fibre, etc. **2** a piece of net used esp. to restrain, contain, or to catch fish or other animals. **3 a** a structure backed by a net, forming the goal in hockey, lacrosse, etc. **b** a structure from which a net is suspended dividing the court in tennis etc. **4** a system or procedure for catching or entrapping a person or persons. **5 a** a network of spies. **b** a broadcasting network. **c** a network of interconnected computers. **6** a number of lines, veins, fibres, etc. arranged like or resembling the threads of a net. **7** = SAFETY NET 2. ● *v.tr.* (**netted, netting**) **1 a** cover, confine, or catch with a net. **b** procure as with a net. **2** *Sport* hit or shoot etc. (a puck or ball) into a net. **3** cover or confine with or as with a net or nets. **4** fish (a river etc.) with nets; set or use nets in. **5** make (a purse, hammock, etc.) by knotting etc. threads together to form a net. **6** mark with a netlike pattern. □ **netlike** *adj.* **netted** *adj.* (also in *comb.*). **netter** *n.*

net² ● *adj.* **1** (esp. of money) remaining after all necessary deductions, or free from deductions (*net income*). **2** (of a price) to be paid in full; not reducible. **3** (of a weight) excluding that of the packaging or container etc. **4** (of an effect, result, etc.) ultimate. **5** after all factors have been calculated (*a net importer of oil*). ● *n.* a net sum, income, result, etc. ● *v.tr.* (**netted, netting**) gain or yield (a sum) as net profit.

netball *n.* a team game, esp. for women, similar to basketball, in which players cannot run or walk with the ball but must throw or hand it to each other.

nether *adj. esp. literary* or *jocular* = LOWER¹ *adj.* 1, 2. □ **nethermost** *adj.*

Netherlander /'neðərl,ændər/ *n.* **1** a native or national of the Netherlands, a country in W Europe, on the North Sea. **2** a person of Dutch descent. □ **Netherlandish** *adj.*

nether regions *n.pl.* **1** *jocular* the parts of the human body below the waist, esp. the buttocks and genitals. **2** hell; the abode of the dead. **3** a place or situation viewed as an unpleasant exile.

netherworld *n.* **1** the infernal regions; hell. **2** the world of the criminal underground. **3** a state of neglect or oblivion; limbo.

netiquette /'netɪ,kət/ *n. informal* the informal code of conduct governing effective and polite use of the Internet.

netminder *n.* a goaltender. □ **netminding** *n.*

net profit *n.* the effective profit; the actual gain after working expenses have been paid.

Net surfer *n.* (also **net surfer**) a person who uses the

Internet, esp. habitually. □ **Net surf** *v.intr.* **Net surfing** *n. & adj.*

netting *n.* **1** netted fabric. **2** a piece of this. **3** the action of fishing with a net or nets. **4 a** the action or process of making a net, nets, or a network. **b** enclose an area etc. with nets, wire, etc.

nettle ● *n.* **1** any plant of the genus *Urtica*, esp. *U. dioica*, with leaves covered with stinging hairs. **2** any of various plants resembling this. ● *v.tr.* **1** irritate, provoke, annoy. **2** sting with nettles.

net ton *n. see* TON *n.* 5b.

network ● *n.* **1** a group of interconnected or inter-communicating things, points, or people. **2** an arrangement of intersecting horizontal and vertical lines, like the structure of a net. **3** a complex system of railways, roads, telephone lines, etc. **4** a group of people who exchange information, contacts, and experience for professional or social purposes. **5** a chain of interconnected computers, machines, or operations. **6** a system of connected electrical conductors. **7 a** a group of broadcasting stations connected for a simultaneous broadcast of a program. **b** a nationwide broadcasting company or broadcasting companies collectively. ● *v.* **1** *intr.* communicate or foster relationships with a network of people, esp. for personal advantage. **2** *tr. & intr.* **a** link (machines, esp. computers) together to allow the sharing of data and efficient utilization of resources. **b** incorporate (a computer, data, etc.) into a computer network. □ **networked** *adj.* **networking** *n.*

network computer *n.* a low-cost personal computer without local disk storage, designed to be connected to the Internet, a local area network, etc., from which it would access applications and data.

networker *n.* **1** *Computing* a member of an organization or computer network who operates from home or from an external office. **2** a member of a professional or social network.

net worth *n.* the monetary value of a person's or organization's holdings when liabilities have been deducted from the value of assets.

neural /ˈnjʊərəl, ˈnɜrəl/ *adj.* of or relating to a nerve or the central nervous system. □ **neurally** *adv.*

neuralgia /njʊˈrældʒə, nəˈræl-/ *n.* an intense intermittent pain along the course of a nerve, esp. in the head or face. □ **neuralgic** *adj.*

neural network *n.* (also **neural net**) **1** a system of interconnections which resembles or is based on the arrangement of neurons in the brain and nervous system. **2** a configuration of computers designed to simulate this.

neural tube *n.* a hollow structure from which the brain and spinal cord develop.

neural tube defect *n.* any of a range of congenital abnormalities, including spina bifida, resulting from incomplete fusion of the neural tube.

neurasthenia /ˌnjʊərəsˈθiːniə, ˌnɜrəs-/ *n.* an ill-defined medical condition characterized by lassitude, fatigue, headache, and irritability, associated chiefly with emotional disturbance. □ **neurasthenic** /-ˈθenɪk/ *adj. & n.*

neuritis /njʊˈraɪtɪs, nəˈraɪt-/ *n.* inflammation of a nerve or nerves, usu. with pain and loss of function. □ **neuritic** /-ˈrɪtɪk/ *adj.*

neuro- /ˈnjʊərəʊ:, ˈnɜrəʊ:-/ *comb. form* a nerve or nerves.

neuroanatomy *n.* the anatomy of the nervous system. □ **neuroanatomical** *adj.* **neuroanatomist** *n.*

neurobiology *n.* the biology of the nervous system. □ **neurobiological** *adj.* **neurobiologist** *n.*

neurochemical ● *adj.* of or pertaining to the chemistry of the nervous system. ● *n.* a drug, chemical, or other substance that acts on the nervous system. □ **neurochemist** *n.* **neurochemistry** *n.*

neurology /njʊˈrɒlədʒi, nəˈrɒ-/ *n.* the branch of biology or esp. medicine that deals with the anatomy, functions, and organic disorders of nerves and the nervous system. □ **neurologic** *adj.* **neurological** *adj.* **neurologically** *adv.* **neurologist** *n.*

neuroma /njʊˈrəʊmə, nəˈrəʊ-/ *n.* (*pl.* **-s** or **neuromata** /-mətə/) a tumour on a nerve or in nerve tissue.

neuromuscular *adj.* pertaining to, consisting of, or resembling both nerves and muscle tissue.

neuron /ˈnjʊərɒn, ˈnɜrɒn/ *n.* a specialized cell transmitting nerve impulses; a nerve cell. □ **neuronal** /-ˈrəʊnəl/ *adj.*

neuropathology *n.* the branch of pathology that deals with diseases and disorders of the nervous system. □ **neuropathological** *adj.* **neuropathologist** *n.*

neuropathy /njʊˈrɒpəθi, nəˈrɒ-/ *n.* a disease or dysfunction of one or more peripheral nerves, typically causing numbness or weakness.

neurophysiology *n.* the physiology of the nervous system. □ **neurophysiological** *adj.* **neurophysiologist** *n.*

neuropsychology *n.* the study of the relationship between the nervous system (esp. the brain) and behaviour. □ **neuropsychological** *adj.* **neuropsychologist** *n.*

neuroscience *n.* any or all of the sciences dealing with the structure and function of the nervous system and brain. □ **neuroscientist** *n.*

neurosis /njʊˈrəʊsɪs, nəˈrəʊ-/ *n.* (*pl.* **neuroses** /-siːz/) **1** a mild mental illness, not attributable to organic cause, characterized by symptoms of stress such as anxiety, depression, obsessive behaviour, hypochondria, etc., without loss of contact with reality. **2** any more or less specific anxiety or malaise experienced by an individual, group, nation, etc.

neurosurgery *n.* surgery performed on the nervous system, esp. the brain and spinal cord. □ **neurosurgeon** *n.* **neurosurgical** *adj.*

neurotic /njʊˈrɒtɪk, nəˈrɒ-/ ● *adj.* **1** caused by or relating to neurosis. **2** (of a person) suffering from neurosis. **3** *informal* abnormally sensitive or obsessive. ● *n.* a neurotic person. □ **neurotically** *adv.* **neuroticism** /-ˌsɪzəm/ *n.*

neurotoxin *n.* any poison which acts on the nervous system. □ **neurotoxic** *adj.* **neurotoxicity** *n.*

neurotransmitter *n.* a chemical substance released from a nerve fibre that effects the transfer of an impulse to another nerve or muscle. □ **neurotransmission** *n.*

neuter ● *adj.* **1** (of a noun etc.) neither masculine nor feminine. **2** (of a plant) having neither pistils nor stamen. **3** (of an insect) having no functional sexual organs, sterile. **4** having no sexual characteristics, being neither male nor female; asexual. ● *n.* **1** *Grammar* **a** the neuter gender. **b** a neuter word. **2 a** a non-fertile insect, esp. a worker bee or ant. **b** a castrated animal. **3** an asexual or genderless person. ● *v.tr.* **1** castrate or spay (an animal). **2** deprive of potency, vigour, or force. □ **neutered** *adj.* **neutering** *n.*

Neutral *n.* a member of an Iroquoian people formerly living on the shores of Lake Erie.

neutral ● *adj.* **1** not helping or supporting either of two opposing sides, esp. countries at war or in dispute; impartial. **2** belonging to a neutral party, nation, etc. (*neutral ships*). **3** indistinct, vague, indeterminate. **4** occupying a middle position with regard to two extremes. **5** (of colours, esp. white, beige, or grey) not strong or intense; harmonizing well with most other colours. **6** *Chem.* neither acid nor alkaline. **7** having neither a positive nor a negative electrical charge. **8** *Biol.* having either no sexual characteristics or no functional sexual organs; asexual, neuter. **9** *Physics* designating or situated at a point, on a line or plane, etc. where opposing forces are in equilibrium. **10** (in *comb.*) having neither a positive nor a negative effect (*revenue-neutral*). **11** (in *comb.*) specifying neither male nor female characteristics (*gender-neutral*). ● *n.* **1 a** a neutral country or person. **b** a citizen of a neutral country. **2** a position of the driving and driven parts in a gear mechanism in which no power is transmitted. **3** a state in which no progress is made (*this government seems to be stuck in neutral on this issue*). **4** a neutral colour. □ **neutrality** *n.* **neutrally** *adv.*

neutral corner *n.* **1** either of the two corners of a boxing ring not allocated to a boxer as a base between rounds etc. **2** any similar position removed from a scene of battle, confrontation, argument, etc.

neutralism *n.* a policy of political neutrality. □ **neutralist** *n.*

neutralize *v.tr.* **1** counterbalance; render ineffective by an opposite force or effect. **2 a** make (an acidic or alkaline solution etc.) chemically neutral. **b** eliminate a charge difference in; make electrically neutral. **3** exempt or exclude (a place) from the sphere of hostilities. **4** *euphemism* kill or make (a person) harmless or ineffective. □ **neutralization** *n.* **neutralizer** *n.*

neutral zone *n.* **1** *Hockey* the central area of a rink, extending from blue line to blue line. **2** an esp. demilitarized area acting as a buffer between two belligerents.

neutral-zone trap *n.* *Hockey* a conservative, defensive strategy in which a team positions all its skaters in the neutral zone to challenge their opponents' rush, rather than send players into the opponents' end to forecheck.

neutrino /nuːˈtriːnoː, njuː-/ *n.* (*pl.* **-os**) any of a group of stable elementary particles with zero electric charge and probably zero mass, which travel at the speed of light.

neutron /ˈnuːtrɒn, ˈnjuː-/ *n.* an elementary particle of about the same mass as a proton but without an electric charge, present in all atomic nuclei except those of ordinary hydrogen.

neutron bomb *n.* a kind of atomic bomb producing large numbers of neutrons but little blast, so causing great damage to life but little destruction to property.

neutron star *n.* a very small, dense star composed mainly of closely packed neutrons.

Nev. *abbr.* Nevada.

Nevadan ● *n.* a native or inhabitant of the US state of Nevada. ● *adj.* of or relating to Nevada.

névé /ˈneɪveɪ/ *n.* an expanse of crystalline or granular snow on the upper part of a glacier, not yet compressed into ice.

never *adv.* **1 a** at no time; on no occasion; not ever. **b** *informal* as an emphatic negative (*I never heard you come in*). **2** not at all, in no way (*never fear*). **3** *informal* (expressing surprise or incredulity) surely not (*you never left the key in the lock!*). □ **never ever** (also **never, ever**) never at all, absolutely never. **well I never!** expressing great surprise.

never-ending *adj.* never coming to an end, endless.

nevermore *adv.* at no future time; never again.

never-never land *n.* an imaginary, utopian or illusory place.

nevertheless *adv.* in spite of that; notwithstanding; all the same.

nevus /ˈniːvəs/ *n.* (*pl.* **nevi** /-vaɪ/) **1** a birthmark in the form of a raised red patch on the skin. **2** = MOLE².

new ● *adj.* **1 a** of recent origin or arrival. **b** made, invented, discovered, acquired, or experienced recently or now for the first time (*a new star; new ideas*). **2** in original condition; not worn or used. **3 a** renewed or reformed (*a new life*). **b** reinvigorated (*felt like a new person*). **4** different from a recent previous one (*has a new job*). **5** in addition to others already existing (*a new supermarket*). **6** (often foll. by *to*) unfamiliar or strange (*the idea was new to me*). **7** (often foll. by *at*) (of a person) inexperienced, unaccustomed (to doing something) (*am new at this*). **8** (usu. prec. by *the*) often *derogatory* **a** later, modern. **b** newfangled. **c** given to new or modern ideas (*the new woman*). **d** recently affected by social change (*the new rich*). **9** (often prec. by *the*) advanced in method or theory (*the new formula*). **10** (in place names) discovered or founded later than and named after (*New Brunswick*). **11** (of vegetables, esp. potatoes) recently harvested and usu. small, with a thin light skin. ● *adv.* (usu. in *comb.*) newly, recently (*new-found*). □ **a new one** (often foll. by *on*) *informal* an account or idea not previously encountered (by a person). □ **newish** *adj.* **newness** *n.*

New Age *n.* a broad movement characterized by alternative approaches to traditional Western culture, with interest in spiritual matters, mysticism, holistic ideas, environmentalism, etc. (often *attrib.*: *New Age philosophy*). □ **New Ager** *n.* **New Agey** *adj.*

newbie *n.* *slang* a novice on the Internet.

newborn ● *adj.* **1** (of a child etc.) recently born. **2** spiritually reborn; regenerated. ● *n.* a newborn child.

New Brunswicker *n.* a native or inhabitant of New Brunswick.

new Canadian *n.* a person who has recently immigrated to Canada.

newcomer *n.* **1** a person who has recently arrived. **2** a beginner in some activity.

new country *n.* a style of country music blending traditional country and western elements with elements of rock music, including elaborate production values, and a more urban focus.

New Criticism *n.* an approach to the analysis of literary texts which concentrates on the organization of the text itself, with particular emphasis on irony, ambiguity, etc., rather than on its historical or biographical context. □ **New Critic** *n.* **New Critical** *adj.*

new deal *n.* **1** new arrangements or conditions, esp. when better than the earlier ones. **2** (**New Deal**) the economic measures introduced by US President Franklin D. Roosevelt in 1933 to counteract the effects of the Great Depression. □ **New Dealer** *n.*

New Democrat *n.* **1** *Cdn* a member or supporter of the New Democratic Party. **2** *US* a member of the Democratic party, esp. in the 1990s, espousing policies differing from traditional Democratic ones.

New Democratic *adj.* *Cdn* of, belonging to or constituted by the New Democratic Party.

New Democratic Party *n.* (in Canada) a left-of-centre political party, more successful provincially than federally, formed from the Co-operative Commonwealth Federation in 1961. Abbr.: **NDP**.

newel /ˈnuːəl, ˈnjuː-/ *n.* **1** the supporting central post of winding stairs. **2** (in full **newel post**) a post at the head or foot of a staircase supporting a handrail.

newfangled *adj. derogatory* different from what one is used to; objectionably new.

Newfie (also **Newf**) *informal* ● *n.* **1** a Newfoundlander. **2** Newfoundland. **3** a Newfoundland dog. ● *adj.* (esp. *attrib.*) of or relating to Newfoundland or Newfoundlanders.

Newfie joke *n.* *Cdn* a joke in which the humour is derived from the purported lack of sophistication or intelligence of Newfoundlanders.

new-found *adj.* newly discovered.

Newfoundland /ˌnuːfənˈlænd, ˈnuːfəndlənd, ˈnuːfəndlænd, njuːˈfaundlənd/ *n.* (in full **Newfoundland dog**) a very large breed of dog with a thick coarse coat and webbed feet, noted for its intelligence, strength, and swimming ability.

Newfoundlander *n.* a native or inhabitant of Newfoundland.

Newfoundland Time *n.* the time in a zone including the island of Newfoundland. **Newfoundland Standard Time** is three and a half hours behind GMT; **Newfoundland Daylight Time** is two and a half hours behind GMT.

new-generation *attrib.adj.* designating the latest model, type, etc. of a thing (*new-generation audio*).

new guard *n.* the new or progressive members of a group (compare OLD GUARD).

New International Version *n.* a version of the Bible completed in the 1970s and used esp. by conservative Protestant churches.

new jack *adj.* of or relating to new jack swing, or the clothes, culture, etc. associated with it.

new jack swing *n.* a form of dance music combining elements from among rhythm and blues, soul, hip-hop, and rap music.

New Jerseyan ● *n.* a native or inhabitant of the US state of New Jersey. ● *adj.* of or relating to New Jersey.

New Jerusalem *n.* **1** *Christianity* the abode of the saints in heaven. **2** *informal* an ideal place or situation.

New Journalism *n.* a style of journalism characterized by the use of subjective and fictional elements so as to elicit an emotional response from the reader. □ **New Journalist** *n.*

New Left *n.* a movement initiated in the 1960s by young left-wing radicals opposed to the philosophy of the old liberal society. □ **New Leftist** *n.*

new look ● *n.* **1** a new or revised appearance or presentation, esp. of something familiar. **2** (often **New Look**) a style of women's clothing introduced after World War II, featuring long full skirts and a generous use of material. ● *attrib.adj.* (**new-look**) having a new image; restyled.

newly *adv.* **1** recently. **2** afresh, anew (*newly painted*). **3** in a new or different manner (*newly arranged*).

newlywed *n.* a recently married person.

new man *n.* (usu. prec. by *the*) a man who rejects the traditional male role in favour of more caring or sensitive attitudes.

New Mexican ● *n.* a native or inhabitant of the US state of New Mexico. ● *adj.* of or relating to New Mexico.

new money *n.* *informal* **1** recently acquired money or wealth. **2** the recently wealthy.

new moon *n.* **1 a** the moon when first seen as a crescent after conjunction with the sun. **b** the time of its appearance. **2** *Astronomy* the time at which the moon is in conjunction with the sun.

New Revised Standard Version *n.* a 1990 revision of the Revised Standard Version of the Bible.

New Right *n.* a political movement characterized by rejection of all forms of socialism and an emphasis on traditional conservative values.

news *n.pl.* (usu. treated as *sing.*) **1** information about important or interesting recent events, esp. when published or broadcast. **2** (prec. by *the*) a broadcast report of news. **3** newly received or noteworthy information. **4** (foll. by *to*) *informal* information not previously known (to a person) (*that's news to me*). **5** a person or thing much in the news.

news agency *n.* an organization that collects and distributes news items.

newsboy *n.* esp. *hist.* a boy who sells or delivers newspapers.

news bulletin *n.* a short broadcast or published news item or collection of news items.

newscast *n.* a radio or television broadcast of news reports.

newscaster *n.* a person who reads news broadcasts.

news conference *n.* a press conference.

news flash *n.* a single item of important news broadcast separately and often interrupting other programs.

newsgroup *n.* *Computing* (on the Internet or other network) a forum for the discussion of, and exchange of information about, a particular subject.

newshound *n.* *informal* a newspaper reporter, esp. an aggressive one.

newsletter *n.* a usu. informal printed report issued periodically by a society, business, organization, etc.

newsmagazine *n.* *N Amer.* **1** a publication reporting and commenting on current events, usu. issued weekly on glossy paper, typically with many photographs. **2** a television news program consisting of in-depth reports on selected current events.

newsmaker *n.* a person or thing at the centre of newsworthy events. □ **newsmaking** *n.*

newsman *n.* (*pl.* **-men**) a reporter, newscaster, or journalist.

newspaper *n.* **1** a printed publication (usu. daily or weekly) containing news, advertisements, correspondence, etc. **2** the sheets of paper forming this (*wrapped in newspaper*).

newspapering *n.* the business etc. of producing newspapers.

newspaperman *n.* (*pl.* **-men**) a journalist. □ **newspaperwoman** (*pl.* **-women**) *n.*

Newspeak *n.* ambiguous euphemistic language used esp. in political propaganda.

newsprint *n.* a type of low-quality paper on which newspapers are printed.

news reader *n.* = NEWSCASTER.

newsreel *n.* *hist.* a short motion picture of recent events.

news release *n.* = PRESS RELEASE.

newsroom *n.* a room in a newspaper or broadcasting office where news is processed.

news service *n.* = NEWS AGENCY.

newsstand *n.* a stall for the sale of newspapers.

New Style *n.* dating reckoned by the Gregorian Calendar (compare OLD STYLE).

new-style *attrib.adj.* having a new style (*new-style contracts*).

newsweekly *n.* (*pl.* **-ies**) *N Amer.* a weekly newspaper or newsmagazine.

news wire *n.* a service transmitting the latest news stories, e.g. via teleprinter, satellite, or the Internet.

newswoman *n.* (*pl.* **-men**) a female reporter, newscaster, or journalist.

newsworthy *adj.* of sufficient interest to the public to warrant mention in the news; topical. □ **newsworthiness** *n.*

newsy *adj.* (**-ier, -iest**) **1** (of a newspaper etc.) full of esp. gossipy news. **2** (of a news item) light, gossipy.

newt *n.* any of various small rough-skinned amphibians, esp. of the genus *Notophthalmus* or *Taricha*, having a well-developed tail.

New Testament *n.* the second part of the Christian Bible concerned with the life and teachings of Christ and his earliest followers.

newton *n. Physics* the SI unit of force that, acting on a mass of one kilogram, increases its velocity by one metre per second every second along the direction that it acts. Abbr.: **N**.

Newtown /'nuːtən, 'njuː-/ *n.* a medium-sized greenish-yellow eating and cooking apple.

new wave *n.* (also *attrib.*) **1** a recent trend in a given field (*the new wave in fitness; a new wave diet*). **2** (often prec. by *the*) a movement in French cinema of the late 1950s and early 1960s, characterized by frequent use of jump-cuts, on-location shooting, hand-held cameras, etc. **3** a style of pop music of the late 1970s and early 1980s, influenced by punk but characterized by a greater use of synthesizers and a more mainstream sound.

New World *n.* North and South America regarded collectively in relation to Europe.

new world order *n.* often *ironic* a state of co-operation, peace, and justice among all nations.

new year *n.* the calendar year just begun or about to begin.

New Year's *n.* **1** (in full **New Year's Eve**) the evening of Dec. 31. **2** (in full **New Year's Day**) the first day of the year, Jan. 1.

New Yorker ● *n.* **1** a native or inhabitant of the US state of New York. **2** a native or inhabitant of New York City. ● *adj.* of or relating to New York State or New York City.

New York steak *n.* (also **New York strip**) *N Amer.* a steak cut from the outer side of a T-bone.

New Zealander *n.* a native or inhabitant of New Zealand, an island country east of Australia.

next /nekst/ ● *adj.* **1** (often foll. by *to*) being or positioned or living nearest (*the chair next to the fire*). **2 a** the nearest in order of time; the first or soonest encountered or considered (*next Friday; ask the next person*). **b** following the nearest in order of time; the second to be encountered or considered (*not this Monday, but next Monday*). ● *adv.* **1** (often foll. by *to*) in the nearest place or degree (*put it next to mine; came next to last*). **2** on the first or soonest occasion (*when we next meet*). **3** subsequently, afterwards (*next beat in the eggs*). **4** (with superlatives) following in the specified order (*the next oldest building is the church*). **5** expressing surprise (*whatever next!*). ● *n.* the next person or thing. ● *prep. informal* next to. □ **as good** (or **well** or **much** etc.) **as the next person** as good, well, etc. as the average person (*I can take a joke as well as the next guy*). **next to 1** adjacent to. **2** almost (*next to nothing left*). **3** following in order after (*next to skiing her favourite sport was skating*).

next door *adv. & adj.* (as adj. often hyphenated) in or to the next house, room, etc. □ **next door to 1** in the next house etc. to. **2** nearly, almost, near to.

next-generation *attrib.adj.* designating an imminent technology, style, model, etc.

next of kin *n.* the closest living relative or relatives.

next-to-last *adj.* penultimate.

next world *n.* a supposed life after death.

nexus /'neksəs/ *n.* (*pl.* **nexuses**) **1** a connected group, series, or network. **2** a bond; a connection.

NF *abbr.* Newfoundland (in postal use).

NFB *abbr.* National Film Board of Canada.

NFC *abbr.* (in the US) National Football Conference.

NFL *abbr.* (in the US) National Football League.

Nfld. *abbr.* Newfoundland.

NGO *abbr.* non-governmental organization.

Nguni / əŋ'guːni/ ● *n.* **1** (*pl.* same) a member of a group of Bantu-speaking peoples living mainly in southern Africa. **2** the group of closely related Bantu languages spoken by these peoples. ● *adj.* of or relating to these peoples or this group of languages.

NGV *abbr.* natural gas vehicle.

NH *abbr.* New Hampshire (also in postal use).

NHL *abbr.* National Hockey League. □ **NHLer** *n.*

NI *abbr.* Northern Ireland.

Ni *symbol* the element nickel.

niacin /'naɪəsɪn/ *n.* a vitamin of the B complex, found in milk, liver, and yeast, a deficiency of which causes pellagra.

Niagara *n.* (also **niagara**; usu. foll. by *of*) an outpouring, a deluge (*a Niagara of fan mail*).

nib ● *n.* **1** the point of a pen, which touches the writing surface. **2** (in *pl.*) shelled and crushed coffee or cocoa beans. **3** the point of a tool etc. ● *v.tr.* (**nibbed, nibbing**) provide with a nib.

nibble ● *v.* **1** *tr. & intr.* **a** take small bites at. **b** eat in small amounts. **c** bite at gently or cautiously or playfully. **2** *intr.* (often foll. by *at*) show cautious interest in. ● *n.* **1** an instance of nibbling. **2 a** a very small amount of food. **b** (also **nibbly** *pl.* **-ies**) (usu. in *pl.*) a small food item. **3** *Computing* half a byte, i.e. 4 bits. **4** a tentative display of interest. □ **nibble away** (**at**) consume or wear away slowly or gradually. □ **nibbler** *n.*

niblet *n.* a small piece of food, e.g. a kernel of corn.

nibs *n.* □ **his nibs** *jocular informal* a mock title used with reference to an important or self-important person.

NIC /ˌenaɪˈsiː, nɪk/ *abbr.* newly industrialized (or industrializing) country.

nicad /'naɪkæd/ *n.* (often *attrib.*) a battery, often rechargeable, with a nickel anode and a cadmium cathode.

Nicaraguan /ˌnɪkəˈrɒgwən, -ˈræg-/ ● *adj.* of or relating to Nicaragua, the largest country in Central America. ● *n.* a native or inhabitant of Nicaragua.

nice *adj.* **1** pleasant, agreeable, satisfactory. **2** (of a person) kind, good-natured. **3** *ironic* bad or awkward (*a nice mess*). **4 a** fine or subtle (*a nice distinction*). **b** requiring careful thought or attention (*a nice problem*). **5** fastidious; delicately sensitive. **6** punctilious, scrupulous (*were not too nice about their methods*). **7** (foll. by an adj., often with *and*) satisfactory or adequate in terms of the quality described (*nice and warm*). □ **make nice** (also **make nice-nice**) *N Amer. informal* be pleasant when one would rather not. **nice one** *informal* expressing approval or commendation. □ **nicely** *adv.* **niceness** *n.*

nice-guy *attrib.adj.* *N Amer.* characteristic of a nice, agreeable person (*a nice-guy image*).

Nicene Creed /'naɪsiːn, 'nəɪ-, -'siːn/ *n.* (also **Nicaean Creed** /-'siːən/) a formal statement of Christian belief based on that adopted at the first Council of Nicaea in 325.

nicety /'naɪsəti/ *n.* (*pl.* **-ies**) **1** a subtle distinction or detail. **2** precision, accuracy. **3** intricate or subtle quality (*a point of great nicety*). **4** (in *pl.*) **a** minutiae; fine details. **b** refinements, trimmings.

niche /niːʃ, nɪtʃ/ *n.* **1** a shallow recess, esp. in a wall to contain a statue etc. **2** a comfortable or suitable position in life or employment. **3** a specialized but profitable corner of the market (also *attrib.*: *niche marketing*). **4** *Ecology* a position or role taken by a kind of organism within its community. □ **niched** *adj.*

nick ● *n.* **1** a small cut or notch. **2** a scratch or light wound. ● *v.tr.* make a nick or nicks in. □ **in the nick of time** only just in time; just at the right moment. **nick (someone) for** *informal* defraud someone of (a sum).

nickel ● *n.* **1** a malleable ductile silver-white metallic element, occurring naturally in various minerals and used in special steels, in magnetic alloys, and as a catalyst. **2** *N Amer.* **a** a five-cent coin. **b** five cents. ● *v.tr.* (**nickelled, nickelling**) coat with nickel.

nickel and dime ● *v.tr.* (**nickel-and-dimed** or **nickelled and dimed**, **nickel-and-diming** or **nickelling and diming**) put a financial strain on (someone) by charging small amounts for many minor services etc. ● (**nickel-and-dime**) *attrib.adj.* petty, insignificant.

nickelodeon /nɪkəˈloːdiən/ *n.* *N Amer.* *hist.* **1** *informal* a jukebox. **2** a movie theatre with an admission fee of one nickel.

nicker *v.intr.* neigh.

nickname ● *n.* **1** a familiar or humorous name given to a person or thing instead of or as well as the real name. **2** a familiar or abbreviated form of a first name. ● *v.tr.* give a nickname to; call (a person or thing) by a nickname.

niçoise /niːˈswɒz/ *adj.* designating food (esp. a salad) garnished with tomatoes, capers, anchovies, etc.

nicotiana /ˌnɪkoːtiˈænə, -ʃiˈænə/ *n.* the tobacco plant.

nicotinamide /nɪkəˈtiːnəmaid, -ˈtɪnə-/ *n.* the amide of niacin, having a similar role in the diet, and important as a constituent of NAD.

nicotine /ˈnɪkəˌtiːn, ˌnɪkəˈtiːn/ *n.* a poisonous alkaloid present in tobacco. □ **nicotinic** *adj.*

nicotine patch *n.* a patch applied to the skin of those addicted to nicotine, releasing a measured amount of the drug into the bloodstream in order to break the addiction.

nictitating membrane /ˈnɪktɪˌteɪtɪŋ/ *n.* a clear membrane forming a third eyelid in amphibians, birds, and some other animals, that can be drawn across the eye to give protection without loss of vision.

niece *n.* a daughter of one's brother or sister, or of one's brother-in-law or sister-in-law.

Nielsen ratings /ˈniːlsən/ *n.pl.* (also **Nielsens**) popularity ratings for television programs provided by A. C. Nielsen Co. and calculated from figures obtained from a sample survey of receiving sets fitted with a device to record listening or viewing patterns.

nifty *adj.* (**-ier, -iest**) *informal* **1** cleverly designed, executed, etc. **2** clever, adroit. **3** smart, stylish. □ **niftily** *adv.* **niftiness** *n.*

Nigerian /naiˈdʒiːriən/ ● *n.* a native or inhabitant of Nigeria, a country on the coast of W Africa. ● *adj.* of or relating to Nigeria or the Nigerians.

niger seed /ˈnaidʒər/ *n.* the seeds of *Guizotia abyssinica*, an African composite plant, used as bird seed and for their oil.

niggardly /ˈnɪɡərdli/ ● *adj.* **1** stingy, parsimonious. **2** meagre, scanty. ● *adv.* in a stingy or meagre manner. ¶Some people have claimed that *niggardly* is derived

from *nigger*, and as such is racist, but the two words are totally unrelated. □ **niggardliness** *n.*

nigger *n.* *offensive* **1** a black person. **2** a dark-skinned person. □ **a nigger in the woodpile** a hidden cause of trouble or inconvenience.

niggle ● *v.* **1** *intr.* be over-attentive to details. **2** *intr.* find fault in a petty way. **3** *tr.* *informal* irritate; nag pettily. ● *n.* a trifling complaint or criticism; a worry or annoyance.

niggling *adj.* **1** troublesome or irritating in a petty way. **2** trifling or petty. □ **nigglingly** *adv.*

nigh *often jocular* ● *adj.* (esp. of a momentous event) near; approaching. ● *adv.* almost (*nigh impossible*). □ **nigh on** almost.

night ● *n.* **1** the period of darkness between one day and the next; the time from sunset to sunrise. **2** nightfall (*get there before night*). **3** the darkness of night (*as black as night*). **4** a night or evening appointed for some activity, or spent or regarded in a certain way (*parent-teacher night*; *a great night out*). ● *interj.* *informal* = GOOD NIGHT *interj.* 1. □ **night and day** all the time; unceasingly. □ **nightless** *adj.*

nightcap *n.* **1** *hist.* a cap worn in bed. **2** a hot or alcoholic drink taken at bedtime. **3** *Baseball* the second game of a doubleheader when played in the evening.

nightclothes *n.* clothes for wearing in bed.

nightclub *n.* a club that is open at night for drinking, eating, dancing, entertainment, etc.

nightclubbing *n.* the frequenting of nightclubs. □ **nightclubber** *n.*

night crawler *n.* *N Amer.* an earthworm.

nightfall *n.* the onset of night; the end of daylight.

nightgown *n.* (also **nightdress**) a woman's or girl's loose garment worn in bed.

nighthawk *n.* **1** a nocturnal insectivorous N American bird of the genus *Chordeiles*. **2** a person who is active at night.

nightie *n.* *informal* a nightgown.

nightingale *n.* any small reddish-brown bird of the genus *Luscinia*, esp. *L. megarhynchos*, of which the male sings melodiously, esp. at night.

nightlife *n.* activity or entertainment occurring at night in a city, as in nightclubs etc.

night light *n.* **1** a dim light kept on in a room or hallway at night. **2** any light at night, e.g. a street light.

night-long *attrib.adj.* throughout the night.

nightly ● *adj.* **1** happening, done, or existing in the night. **2** recurring every night. ● *adv.* every night.

nightmare *n.* **1** a frightening or unpleasant dream. **2** a terrifying or very unpleasant experience or situation. **3** a haunting or obsessive fear. □ **nightmarish** *adj.* **nightmarishly** *adv.*

night night *interj.* = GOOD NIGHT *interj.* 1.

night owl *n.* a person active at night.

night person *n.* a person who functions best (esp. late) at night.

night school *n.* an institution providing evening classes for those working by day.

nightshade *n.* **1** any of various poisonous plants, esp. of the genus *Solanum*, including *S. nigrum* (**black nightshade**) with black berries, and *S. dulcamara* (**woody nightshade**) with red berries. **2** (in full **deadly nightshade**) = BELLADONNA.

night shift *n.* a shift of workers employed during the night.

nightshirt *n.* a long shirt worn in bed.

night side *n.* **1** the side of a planet or satellite that is facing away from the sun and is therefore in darkness. **2** the dark or bad aspect of a person or thing.

nightspot *n.* a nightclub.

nightstick *n. N Amer.* a police officer's truncheon.

night table *n.* (also **nightstand**) *N Amer.* a small low bedside table, often with drawers.

nighttime *n.* the time between evening and morning; the time of night or darkness.

night vision *n.* **1** the faculty of seeing during the night or in the dark. **2** (**night-vision**) (*attrib.*) designating equipment enabling one to see in the dark (*night-vision goggles*).

night watchman *n.* a person whose job is to keep watch by night.

nightwear *n.* clothing suitable for wearing in bed.

nighty-night /ˈnɔɪtiˌnɔɪt/ *interj.* = GOOD NIGHT *interj.* 1.

nihilism /ˈnaɪɪlɪzəm, ˈnaɪhɪlɪzəm, ˈniː-/ *n.* **1** the rejection of all moral and religious principles. **2** an extreme form of skepticism maintaining that nothing has a real existence. ☐ **nihilist** *n.* **nihilistic** *adj.*

nihil obstat /ˌnaɪhɪl ˈɒbstæt, ˌniː-/ *n.* **1** *Catholicism* a certificate that a book is not open to objection on doctrinal or moral grounds. **2** an authorization or official approval.

-nik /nɪk/ *suffix* forming nouns denoting a person associated with a specified thing or quality (*beatnik*).

Nikkei /ˈniːkeɪ/ *n.* (in full **Nikkei index, Nikkei average**) a figure indicating the relative price of representative shares on the Tokyo Stock Exchange.

nil *n.* nothing; no number or amount (often as a score in games).

Nilotic /naɪˈlɒtɪk/ *adj.* **1** of or relating to the Nile or the Nile region of Africa. **2** of or relating to a group of E African Negroid peoples, or the languages spoken by them.

nimble *adj.* (**nimbler, nimblest**) **1** quick and light in movement or action; agile. **2** (of the mind) quick to comprehend; clever; versatile. ☐ **nimbleness** *n.* **nimbly** *adv.*

nimbostratus /ˌnɪmboʊˈstreɪtəs/ *n.* cloud forming a low diffuse dark grey layer, often with falling rain or snow.

nimbus /ˈnɪmbəs/ *n.* (*pl.* **nimbuses** or **nimbi** /-baɪ/) **1 a** a bright cloud or halo investing a deity or person or thing. **b** the halo of a saint etc. **2** a rain cloud.

NIMBY /ˈnɪmbi/ *n.* (*pl.* **NIMBYs**) (often *attrib.*) a person who objects to unwanted groups or developments appearing in his or her neighbourhood.

nimrod *n.* **1** *N Amer. slang* an inept person. **2** (also **Nimrod**) a skilled hunter.

nincompoop *n.* a simpleton; a fool. ☐ **nincompoopery** *n.*

nine ● *n.* **1** one more than eight. **2** a symbol for this (9, ix, IX). **3 a** a size etc. denoted by nine. **b** a shoe, garment, etc., of such a size. **4** a set or team of nine individuals. **5** nine o'clock. **6** a playing card with nine pips. ● *adj.* that amount to nine. ☐ **dressed to the nines** dressed very elaborately or elegantly. **have nine lives** appear to recover repeatedly from disastrous circumstances. **nine days' wonder** a person or thing that is briefly famous. **nine-tenths** nearly all (*possession is nine-tenths of the law*). **nine times out of ten** nearly always.

ninefold *adj. & adv.* **1** nine times as much or as many. **2** consisting of nine parts.

900 number *n. N Amer.* a telephone number, with the digits '900' in place of an area code, used to access information or entertainment provided for a fee charged by the minute.

ninepin *n.* **1** (in *pl.*; usu. treated as *sing.*) a game in which nine pins are set up at the end of an alley and bowled at in an attempt to knock them down. **2** a pin used in this game. ☐ **go down** (or **drop** or **fall**) **like ninepins** topple or succumb in large numbers.

niner *n. Cdn* (esp. *Ont.*) *slang* a student in grade nine, the first year of high school.

nineteen ● *n.* **1** one more than eighteen, nine more than ten. **2** the symbol for this (19, xix, XIX). **3** a size etc. denoted by nineteen. ● *adj.* that amount to nineteen. ☐ **nineteenth** *adj., adv. & n.*

nineteenth hole *n. Golf slang* the bar at a golf club.

nine-to-five *attrib.adj.* of or involving standard office hours (typically 9 a.m. to 5 p.m.). ☐ **nine-to-fiver** *n.*

ninety ● *n.* (*pl.* **-ies**) **1** the product of nine and ten. **2** a symbol for this (90, xc, XC). **3** (in *pl.*) the numbers from 90 to 99, esp. the years of a century or of a person's life. ● *adj.* that amount to ninety. ☐ **ninety-first, -second**, etc. the ordinal numbers between ninetieth and a hundredth. **ninety-one, -two**, etc. the cardinal numbers between ninety and a hundred. ☐ **ninetieth** *adj., adv. & n.*

ninja /ˈnɪndʒə/ *n.* **1** a person skilled in an originally Japanese martial art characterized by stealthy movement and camouflage. **2** *informal* any fanciful warrior using acrobatics and various bladed weapons.

ninny *n.* (*pl.* **-ies**) a foolish or simple-minded person.

ninth ● *n.* **1** the position in a sequence corresponding to the number 9 in the sequence 1–9. **2** something occupying this position. **3** each of nine equal parts of a thing. **4** *Music* **a** an interval or chord spanning nine consecutive notes in the diatonic scale, e.g. C to D an octave higher. **b** a note separated from another by this interval. **5** *Baseball* the ninth inning. ● *adj.* that is the ninth. ● *adv.* in the ninth place; ninthly. ☐ **ninthly** *adv.*

niobium /naɪˈoʊbiəm/ *n.* a rare grey-blue metallic element used in alloys for superconductors.

Nip *n. slang offensive* a Japanese person.

nip[1] ● *v.* (**nipped, nipping**) **1** *tr.* pinch, squeeze, or bite sharply. **2** *tr.* (often foll. by *off*) remove by pinching etc. **3** *tr.* (of the cold, frost, etc.) cause pain or harm to. **4** *intr.* (foll. by *in, out*, etc.) *informal* go quickly. **5** *tr. N Amer. informal* (of an athlete, team, etc.) overtake or defeat (an opponent) by a narrow margin. **6** *tr.* make (the waist of a garment) very narrow in comparison to the shoulders, bust, and hips. ● *n.* **1 a** a pinch, a sharp squeeze. **b** a bite. **2 a** a biting cold. **b** a check to vegetation caused by this. **3** *Cdn* (*Man. & NW Ont.*) a hamburger. ☐ **nip at someone's heels** (or **heels**) pursue someone very closely. **nip in the bud** suppress or destroy (esp. an idea) at an early stage. ☐ **nipping** *adj.*

nip[2] ● *n.* a small quantity of an alcoholic beverage. ● *v.tr.* (**nipped, nipping**) drink (alcohol).

nip and tuck ● *n.* (*pl.* **nips and tucks**) *informal* **1** a cosmetic surgical operation. **2** a minor renovation or improvement. ● *adj. N Amer.* (of a competition) not decided until the last possible moment.

nipper *n.* **1** a person or thing that nips. **2** *Cdn* (*Maritimes & Nfld*) a glove worn while handling lines to protect the hands from friction. **3** *Cdn* (*Nfld*) a large mosquito. **4** the claw of a crab, lobster, etc. **5** (in *pl.*) any tool for gripping or cutting, e.g. forceps or pincers.

nipple *n.* **1 a** a small projection in which the mammary ducts of female mammals terminate and from which milk is secreted for the young. **b** an analogous structure in the male. **2** a rubber device shaped like this on a baby's or animal's feeding bottle. **3** a device like a nipple in function, e.g. the tip of a grease gun. **4** a nipple-like protuberance. **5** *N Amer.* a short section of pipe with a screw thread at each end for coupling. □ **nippleless** *adj.*

Nipponese ● *n.* (*pl.* same) a Japanese person. ● *adj.* Japanese.

nippy *adj.* (**-ier, -iest**) *informal* **1** chilly, cold. **2** (of food, esp. cheese) piquant, sharp. **3** quick, nimble, active. □ **nippily** *adv.*

nirvana /nɜr'vɒnə, -'vænə/ *n.* **1** (in Buddhism) perfect bliss and release from karma, attained by the extinction of individuality. **2** *informal* a state of perfection. □ **nirvanic** *adj.*

Nisei /niː'seɪ/ *N Amer.* (*pl.* same) ● *n.* a Canadian or American whose parents were immigrants from Japan. ● *adj.* of or relating to the Nisei.

Nisga'a /'nɪsgə/ (also **Nishga** /'nɪʃgə/) ● *n.* **1** a member of a Tsimshian Aboriginal people living in the Skeena River valley in northwestern BC. **2** the language of this people, a dialect of Nass-Gitksan. ● *adj.* of or relating to this people or their language.

Nishnawbe-Aski /nɪʃ'nɒbeɪ'æski/ *n.* an Aboriginal political organization representing bands within the area of NW Ontario covered by Treaty number 9.

nit *n.* the egg or young form of a louse or other parasitic insect, esp. of human head lice or body lice. □ **pick nits** search for and criticize small, esp. insignificant faults or errors; nitpick.

nite *n. N Amer. informal* night.

Nitinat /'nɪtənæt/ ● *n.* **1** a member of an Aboriginal people, part of the Nuu-chah-nulth, living on southern Vancouver Island. **2** the Wakashan language of this people. ● *adj.* of or relating to this people.

nitpicking *n. & adj. informal* searching for and criticizing small, esp. insignificant faults or errors. □ **nitpick** *v.intr.* **nitpicker** *n.* **nitpicky** *adj.*

nitrate /'naɪtreɪt/ ● *n.* **1** any salt or ester of nitric acid. **2** potassium or sodium nitrate when used as a fertilizer. ● *v.tr. Chem.* treat, combine, or impregnate with nitric acid. □ **nitration** /-'treɪʃən/ *n.*

nitre /'naɪtər/ *n.* (also esp. *US* **niter**) saltpetre.

nitric /'naɪtrɪk/ *adj.* of or containing nitrogen.

nitric acid *n.* a colourless corrosive poisonous liquid.

nitric oxide *n.* a colourless toxic gas, involved in physiological processes in minute quantities, and forming nitrogen dioxide in air.

nitride /'naɪtraɪd/ *n.* a binary compound of nitrogen with a more electropositive element.

nitrite /'naɪtraɪt/ *n.* any salt or ester of nitrous acid.

nitro /'naɪtroʊ/ *n. informal* nitroglycerine.

nitro- /'naɪtroʊ/ *comb. form* **1** of or containing nitric acid, nitre, or nitrogen. **2** made with or by use of any of these. **3** of or containing the monovalent -NO₂ group.

nitrocellulose *n.* a highly flammable material made by treating cellulose with concentrated nitric acid, used in the manufacture of explosives and celluloid.

nitrogen /'naɪtrədʒən/ *n.* a colourless odourless unreactive gaseous element that forms four-fifths of the earth's atmosphere and is an essential constituent of proteins, nucleic acids, and other biological molecules. □ **nitrogenous** /-'trɒdʒɪnəs/ *adj.*

nitrogen cycle *n.* the interconversion of nitrogen and its compounds in nature.

nitrogen dioxide *n.* a reddish brown poisonous gas.

nitrogen fixation *n.* a chemical process in which atmospheric nitrogen is assimilated into organic compounds in living organisms and hence into the nitrogen cycle. □ **nitrogen-fixing** *adj.*

nitroglycerine /ˌnaɪtroʊ'glɪsərɪn/ *n.* (also **nitroglycerin**) an explosive yellow liquid made by reacting glycerol with a mixture of concentrated sulphuric and nitric acids, used as an explosive and medically as a vasodilator.

nitrous /'naɪtrəs/ *adj.* of, like, or impregnated with nitrogen, esp. in the trivalent state.

nitrous acid *n.* a weak acid existing only in solution and in the gas phase.

nitrous oxide *n.* a colourless gas used as an anaesthetic and as an aerosol propellant.

nitty-gritty *n. slang* the realities or practical details of a matter.

nitwit *n. informal* a stupid person.

NIV *abbr.* NEW INTERNATIONAL VERSION.

nix *slang* ● *n.* **1** nothing. **2** a denial or refusal. ● *v.tr.* **1** cancel. **2** reject. ● *adv.* no.

NJ *abbr.* New Jersey (also in postal use).

NL *abbr. Baseball* National League.

Nlaka'pamux /ˌənθlɒ'kʊpəm/ ● *n.* **1** a member of an Aboriginal people living near the Thompson River in the Fraser River Valley of BC. **2** the Salishan language of this people. ● *adj.* of or relating to this people.

NLCS *abbr. Baseball* National League Championship Series.

NM *abbr.* New Mexico (in postal use).

nm *abbr.* **1** nanometre. **2** nautical mile.

NMR *abbr.* nuclear magnetic resonance.

NNE *abbr.* north-northeast.

NNW *abbr.* north-northwest.

No¹ *symbol* nobelium.

No² *n.* traditional Japanese drama with dance and song, evolved from Shinto rites.

No. *abbr.* **1** number. **2** *US* North.

no ● *adj.* **1** not any (*there is no excuse*; *no two of them are alike*). **2** not a, quite other than (*is no fool*; *caused no slight inconvenience*). **3** hardly any (*did it in no time*). **4** used elliptically as a slogan, notice, etc., to forbid, reject, or deplore the thing specified (*no parking*; *no surrender*). ● *interj.* equivalent to a negative sentence: the answer to your question is negative, your request or command will not be complied with, the statement made or course of action intended or conclusion arrived at is not correct or satisfactory, the negative statement made is correct. ● *adv.* (foll. by *comparative*) by no amount; not at all (*no better than before*). ● *n.* (*pl.* **noes**) **1** an utterance of the word *no*. **2** a denial or refusal. **3** a negative vote. □ **no man** no person, nobody. **no sweat** *informal* no bother, no trouble. **no two ways about it** (or **that**) *informal* there is no question; undoubtedly. **no way** *informal* **1** it is impossible. **2** I will not agree etc. **3** you're kidding. **... or no ...** regardless of the ... (*rain or no rain, I shall go out*). **there is no ...ing** it is impossible to ... (*there was no mistaking what they meant*).

no-account ● *adj.* unimportant, worthless. ● *n.* an unimportant or worthless person or thing.

Noah's ark *n.* **1** the ship in which Noah, his family, and the animals were saved from the Biblical flood. **2** an imitation of this as a child's toy.

nob *n. slang* the head.

no-bake *attrib.adj.* designating a recipe or food item (esp. a dessert) requiring no baking (*no-bake treat*).

Nobelist /noː'bɛlɪst/ *n. N Amer.* a Nobel Prize winner.

nobelium /noː'biːliəm/ *n.* an artificially produced radioactive metallic element.

Nobel Prize /'noːbel/ *n.* (also **Nobel**) any of six international prizes awarded annually for physics, chemistry, physiology or medicine, literature, economics, and the promotion of peace.

nobility *n.* (*pl.* **-ies**) **1** nobleness of character, mind, birth, or rank. **2** (prec. by *a, the*) an aristocracy.

noble ● *adj.* (**nobler, noblest**) **1** belonging by rank, title, or birth to the aristocracy. **2** of excellent character; having lofty ideals; free from pettiness and meanness. **3** of imposing appearance, splendid, magnificent, stately. **4** (of a metal or element) unreactive; inert. **5** excellent, admirable. **●** *n.* a nobleman or noblewoman. □ **nobleness** *n.* **nobly** *adv.*

noble gas *n.* any gaseous element of a group that almost never combine with other elements.

nobleman *n.* (*pl.* **-men**) a man of noble rank or birth.

noble savage *n.* an idealized concept, prevalent esp. in Romantic literature, of an innately good humanity uncorrupted by exposure to civilization.

noblesse oblige /noː'bles ɒ'bliːʒ/ *n.* the moral obligation incumbent upon rich or noble people to act generously and honourably.

noblewoman *n.* (*pl.* **-women**) a woman of noble rank or birth.

nobody ● *pron.* no person. **●** *n.* (*pl.* **-ies**) a person of no importance, authority, or position.

no-brainer *n.* esp. *N Amer. informal* something that requires a minimum of thought or mental effort.

nock ● *n.* **1** a notch at either end of a bow for holding the string. **2 a** a notch at the butt-end of an arrow for receiving the bowstring. **b** a notched piece of metal or plastic etc. serving this purpose. **●** *v.tr.* set (an arrow) on the string.

no-confidence motion *n.* a non-confidence motion.

nocturnal *adj.* **1** of or relating to the night. **2** done at night. **3** active at night. □ **nocturnally** *adv.*

nocturne /'nɒktɜːn/ *n.* **1** *Music* a short composition of a romantic nature, usu. for piano. **2** a picture of a night scene.

nod ● *v.* (**nodded, nodding**) **1** *intr.* incline one's head slightly and briefly in greeting, assent, or command. **2** *intr.* let one's head fall forward in drowsiness; be drowsy. **3** *tr.* incline (one's head). **4** *tr.* signify (assent etc.) by a nod. **5** *intr.* (of flowers, plumes, etc.) bend downwards and sway, or move up and down. **6** *intr.* make a mistake due to a momentary lack of alertness or attention. **●** *n.* **1** a nodding of the head. **2** an indication of approval, acceptance, or merit. **3** a passing or superficial reference, allusion, or acknowledgement (*a nod to the 1960s*). □ **get the nod** *N Amer.* be chosen or approved. **nod off** *informal* fall asleep. □ **noddingly** *adv.*

nodal /'noːdəl/ *adj.* of or pertaining to a node or nodes.

nodding acquaintance *n.* (usu. foll. by *with*) a very slight acquaintance with a person or subject.

noddy *n.* (*pl.* **-ies**) **1** a simpleton. **2** any of various tropical seabirds of the genus *Anous*, resembling terns. **3** *Cdn* (*Nfld*) the Atlantic fulmar, *Fulmaris glacialis glacialis*. **4** *Cdn* (*Nfld*) *derogatory* = BAYMAN 1.

node *n.* **1** *Bot.* **a** the part of a plant stem from which one or more leaves emerge. **b** a knob on a root or branch. **2** *Anat.* a natural swelling or bulge in an organ or part of the body. **3** *Astronomy* either of two points at which a planet's orbit intersects the plane of the ecliptic or the celestial equator. **4** *Math.* **a** a point at which a curve intersects itself. **b** a vertex in a graph. **5** a point in a computer network where information is

received and distributed among various communication lines.

nodule /'nɒdjuːl/ *n.* **1** a small rounded lump of anything. **2** a small swelling or aggregation of cells, e.g. a small tumour, node, or ganglion, or a swelling on a root of a legume containing bacteria. □ **nodular** *adj.*

Noel /noː'el/ *n.* (also **Noël**) Christmas.

noes *pl. of* NO *n.*

no-fault *attrib.adj.* esp. *N Amer.* **1** (of automobile insurance) valid regardless of the allocation of blame for an accident etc. **2** not assigning responsibility to either party (*a no-fault divorce*).

no-fly zone *n.* an area where esp. military aircraft are forbidden to fly.

no-frills *adj.* **1** providing only the strict minimum necessary (*no-frills flights*). **2** lacking ornament or embellishment.

nog *n.* = EGGNOG.

noggin *n.* **1** *informal* the head. **2** a small mug. **3** a small measure, usu. $^1/_4$ pint, of hard liquor.

no go ● *n.* **1** a project, proposal, etc. that cannot proceed. **2** an athlete who cannot play, esp. because of injury. **●** *adj.* impossible. **●** *interj.* indicating impossibility, inadvisability, etc.

no-go area *n.* (also **no-go zone**) an area forbidden to unauthorized people.

no-good *informal* **●** *attrib.adj.* useless. **●** *n.* a useless person or thing.

Noh *var. of* NO[2].

no-hitter *n.* *Baseball* a game in which a team's pitchers yield no hits. □ **no-hit** *adj.*

no-hoper *n.* *slang* a useless person; a person who has no chance of succeeding.

nohow *adv.* *N Amer.* in no way; by no means. ¶Not used in standard English.

noise ● *n.* **1** a sound, esp. a loud or unpleasant or undesired one. **2** a series of loud sounds, esp. shouts; a confused sound of voices and movements. **3 a** irregular fluctuations accompanying a transmitted signal but not relevant to it. **b** *Computing* a signal that interrupts a program, usu. causing an error. **4** (in *pl.*) remarks expressing a specified feeling, which may or may not be genuine (*made sympathetic noises*). **●** *v.tr.* (usu. in *passive*) make public; spread abroad (a person's fame or a fact). □ **make noises** (usu. foll. by *about*) speak indirectly about one's attitude or intentions (*management is making noises about layoffs*).

noises off sounds made off stage to be heard by the audience of a play.

noiseless *adj.* **1** silent. **2** making no avoidable noise. □ **noiselessly** *adv.* **noiselessness** *n.*

noisemaker *n.* a device for making a loud noise at a party, celebration, etc.

noise pollution *n.* harmful or annoying noise in public places.

noisette /nwɒ'zet/ *n.* a small round piece of meat etc.

noisy *adj.* (**-ier, -iest**) **1** full of or attended with noise. **2** making or given to making much noise. **3** clamorous, turbulent. □ **noisily** *adv.* **noisiness** *n.*

no-load *adj.* *N Amer.* (of a mutual fund share) sold without a commission being charged to the buyer.

nom. *abbr.* nominal.

nomad ● *n.* **1** a member of a people roaming from place to place for food or fresh pasture. **2** a wanderer. **●** *adj.* **1** living as a nomad. **2** wandering. □ **nomadic** *adj.* **nomadically** *adv.* **nomadism** *n.*

no man's land *n.* **1** *Military* the space between two opposing armies. **2** an area not assigned to any owner. **3** an area not clearly belonging to any one subject etc.

nom de / ˌnɒm də, ˈnɔ də / n. jocular an assumed name in a specified field or activity (her nom de Net was Piggy).

nom de guerre / ˈger, nɔ - / n. (pl. **noms de guerre** pronunc. same) an assumed name under which a person fights, plays, writes, etc.

nom de plume / ˈpluːm, nɔ - / n. (pl. **noms de plume** pronunc. same) an assumed name under which a person writes.

nomenclature   / ˈnoːmənˌkleitʃər,   ˈnɒm-, noːˈmenklətʃər / n. a set or system of names, esp. as used in a particular science etc. □ **nomenclatural** adj.

nomenklatura / ˌnoːmənklæˈtʊrə / n. (in the former Soviet Union) a select list or group of people from whom upper-level government positions were filled.

nominal adj. **1** existing in name only; not real or actual (nominal ruler). **2** (of a sum of money, rent, etc.) virtually nothing; much below the actual value of a thing. **3** of or in names (nominal and essential distinctions). **4** consisting of or giving the names (nominal list of officers). **5** of or as or like a noun. □ **nominally** adv.

nominal value n. the face value (of a coin, shares, etc.).

nominate v.tr. **1 a** propose (a candidate) for election. **b** propose (a person or thing) formally for an honour, office, or task (was nominated for six Genies). **2** appoint to an office (a board of six nominated and six elected members). **3** name or appoint (a date or place). **4** mention by name. **5** call by the name of, designate. □ **nominator** n.

nomination n. **1** the act or an instance of nominating; the state of being nominated. **2** the right of nominating for an appointment.

nomination day n. Cdn a day on which nominations for esp. municipal offices are closed.

nominative / ˈnɒmɪnətɪv / ● n. Grammar the case of nouns, pronouns, and adjectives, expressing the subject of a verb. ● adj. **1** Grammar of or in this case. **2** / -neitɪv / of, or appointed by, nomination (as distinct from election).

nominee n. **1 a** a person who is nominated for an office. **b** a person, creative work, etc. nominated for an award. **2** Commerce a person (not necessarily the owner) in whose name a stock etc. is registered.

no more ● n. nothing further (have no more to say). ● adj. not any more (no more wine?). ● adv. **1** no longer. **2** never again. **3** to no greater extent (could no more do it than fly in the air). **4** just as little, neither (you did not come, and no more did she).

non n. something or someone that is not a thing previously specified (Which section would you prefer, smoking or non?).

non- prefix giving the negative sense of words with which it is combined, esp.: **1** not doing or having or involved with (non-productive; nonpayment). **2 a** not of the kind or class described (non-member). **b** forming

terms used adjectivally (non-union). **3** a lack of. **4** (with adverbs) not in the way described (non-aggressively). **5** forming adjectives from verbs, meaning 'that does not' or 'that is not meant to (or to be)' (non-skid). **6** used to form a neutral negative sense when a form in in- or un- has a special sense or (usu. unfavourable) connotation (non-controversial; non-effective; non-human). ¶The number of words that can be formed with this prefix is unlimited; consequently only a selection, considered the most current or noteworthy, can be given here.

nonagon / ˈnɒnəgɒn / n. a plane figure with nine sides and angles.

non-aligned adj. (of a country etc.) not aligned with another (esp. major) power. □ **non-alignment** n.

no-name ● adj. (attrib.) **1** designating a person or thing that is not well known or famous (a movie starring no-name actors). **2** not having a well-known brand name (no-name computers). ● n. a no-name person or thing (a team of no-names).

non-A, non-B hepatitis n. = HEPATITIS C.

non-appearance n. failure to appear or be present.

nonce / nɒns / n. (attrib.) designating a word or phrase etc. coined for one specific occasion (nonce formation). □ **for the nonce** for the time being; for the present occasion.

nonchalant / ˌnɒnʃəˈlɒnt, ˈnɒnʃəˌlɒnt, -lənt / adj. calm and casual, unmoved, unexcited, indifferent. □ **nonchalance** n. **nonchalantly** adv.

non-com n. informal a non-commissioned officer.

non-combatant n. **1** a member of a military force who is not engaged in combat, e.g. a doctor, chaplain, etc. **2** a person not fighting in a war, esp. a civilian.

non-commissioned adj. Military (of an officer) not holding a commission.

non-communist (also **non-Communist** with reference to a particular party) ● adj. not advocating or practising communism. ● n. a non-communist person.

non-conductor n. a substance that does not conduct heat or electricity.

non-confidence n. Cdn a lack of majority support for a government, policy, etc. expressed by a legislature (also attrib.: a non-confidence motion).

nonconformist ● n. **1** a person who does not conform to a prevailing principle. **2** (usu. **Nonconformist**) (in the UK) a Protestant belonging to a denomination other than the established church. ● adj. of or relating to a nonconformist or to Nonconformism. □ **nonconformism** n. **Nonconformism** n.

nonconformity n. **1 a** nonconformists or (**Nonconformity**) Nonconformists as a body. **b** the principles or practice of nonconformists or (**Nonconformity**) of Nonconformists. **2** (usu. foll. by to) failure to conform to a rule etc. **3** lack of correspondence between things.

non-contributory adj. **1** not contributing. **2** (esp. of a pension plan) not supported by contributions made by the beneficiary.

<table>
<tr><td>

non-Aboriginal adj.
non-aggression n.
non-aggressive adj.
non-aggressively adv.
non-alcoholic adj. & n.

</td><td>

non-allergenic adj.
non-believer n.
non-binding adj.
non-biodegradability n.
non-biodegradable adj.

</td><td>

non-Canadian adj. & n.
non-Catholic adj. & n.
non-Christian adj. & n.
non-commercial adj.
noncommittal adj.

</td><td>

noncommittally adv.
non-competitive adj.
non-compliance n.
non-compliant adj.

</td></tr>
</table>

non-controversial *adj.* not controversial. ¶Neutral in sense: see NON- 6, UNCONTROVERSIAL.

non-custodial *adj.* **1** (of a parent) not having custody of a child or children, e.g. after a divorce. **2** (of a criminal sentence) served outside of a traditional correctional institution.

non-dairy *adj.* containing no milk products (*a nondairy creamer*).

nondescript ● *adj.* **1** lacking distinctive characteristics; uninteresting, dull. **2** not easily classified, neither one thing nor another. ● *n.* a nondescript person or thing.

none[1] ● *pron.* **1** (foll. by *of*) **a** not any of (*none of them*; *none of your impudence!*). **b** not any one of (*none of them has come*). ¶The verb following *none* in this sense can be singular or plural according to the sense. **2 a** no persons (*none but fools have ever believed it*). **b** no person (*none can tell*). ● *adj.* (usu. with a preceding noun implied) **1** no; not any (*you have money and I have none*). **2** not to be counted in a specified class (*if a linguist is wanted, I am none*). ● *adv.* (foll. by *the* + comparative, or *so, too*) by no amount; not at all (*none the wiser*; *none too fond of it*). □ **none other** (usu. foll. by *than*) no other person.

none[2] /noːn/ *n.* (also in *pl.*) **1** the office of the fifth of the canonical hours of prayer, originally said at the ninth hour (3 p.m.). **2** this hour.

nonentity *n.* (*pl.* **-ies**) **1** a person or thing of no importance. **2 a** non-existence. **b** a non-existent thing, a figment.

nones /noːnz/ *n.pl.* in the ancient Roman calendar, the ninth day before the ides by inclusive reckoning, i.e. the 7th day of March, May, July, October, the 5th of other months.

non-essential ● *adj.* not essential. ¶Neutral in sense: see NON- 6, INESSENTIAL. ● *n.* a non-essential thing.

nonesuch *var. of* NONSUCH.

nonetheless *adv.* (also **none the less**) nevertheless.

non-event *n.* an unimportant or anticlimactic occurrence.

non-fat *adj.* (of a food) containing little or no fat.

non-ferrous *adj.* (of a metal) other than iron or steel.

non-fiction *n.* literary work other than fiction, including biography and reference books. □ **non-fictional** *adj.*

non-flammable *adj.* not flammable. ¶See FLAMMABLE.

non-functional *adj.* **1** not having a function. **2** not functioning; out of order.

non-governmental *adj.* not belonging to or associated with a government.

non-human ● *adj.* (of a being) not human. ● *n.* a non-human being. ¶Neutral in sense: see NON- 6, INHUMAN, UNHUMAN.

non-import *n. Cdn Football* a player who is a Canadian or who has played with a Canadian team for five years or more.

non-intervention *n.* the principle or practice of not becoming involved in others' affairs, esp. by one country in regard to another. □ **non-interventionist** *adj. & n.*

non-invasive *adj.* **1** (of a medical procedure) not requiring incision into the body or the removal of tissue. **2** (of an infection etc.) not tending to spread.

non-issue *n.* something that is of little or no importance (*the debate was a non-issue*).

non-Jew *n.* a person who is not Jewish. □ **non-Jewish** *adj.*

nonlogical *adj.* not involving logic. ¶Neutral in sense: see NON- 6, ILLOGICAL. □ **nonlogically** *adv.*

non-military *adj.* not military; not involving armed forces; civilian.

non-moral *adj.* not concerned with morality. ¶Neutral in sense: see NON- 6, AMORAL, IMMORAL. □ **non-morally** *adv.*

non-natural *adj.* not involving natural means or processes. ¶Neutral in sense: see NON- 6, UNNATURAL.

non-nuclear *adj.* **1** not involving nuclei or nuclear energy. **2** not having nuclear weapons.

no-no *n. informal* something that is not possible or acceptable.

no-nonsense *adj.* serious, sensible; without flippancy.

non-operational *adj.* **1** that does not operate. **2** out of order.

non-organic *adj.* not organic. ¶Neutral in sense: see NON- 6, INORGANIC.

nonpareil /ˈnɒnpərəl, ˌnɒnpəˈreil/ ● *adj.* unrivalled or unique. ● *n.* such a person or thing.

non-penetrative *adj.* (of sexual activity) in which penetration does not take place.

non-performing *adj.* (of an investment, loan, etc.) producing no income.

non-person *n.* a person regarded as non-existent or insignificant (*compare* UNPERSON).

nonplussed /nɒnˈplʌst/ *adj.* **1** perplexed. **2** *N Amer.* unfazed.

non-prescription *adj.* (of medication) available without a prescription.

non-productive *adj.* not productive. ¶Neutral in sense: see NON- 6, UNPRODUCTIVE. □ **non-productively** *adv.*

non-professional ● *adj.* not professional (esp. in status). ¶Neutral in sense: see NON- 6, UNPROFESSIONAL. ● *n.* a non-professional person.

non-profit *adj.* (of an organization, institution, event, etc.) not involving or making a profit.

non-proliferation *n.* the prevention of an increase in something, esp. possession of nuclear weapons (also *attrib.*: *nuclear non-proliferation treaty*).

---

non-denominational *adj.*	**non-judgmental** *adj.*	**non-negotiable** *adj.*	**non-porous** *adj.*
non-destructive *adj.*	**non-linear** *adj.*	**non-partisan** *adj.*	**non-racial** *adj.*
non-European *adj. & n.*	**non-magnetic** *adj.*	**nonpayment** *n.*	**non-reactive** *adj.*
non-existence *n.*	**non-member** *n.*	**non-physical** *adj.*	**non-refundable** *adj.*
non-existent *adj.*	**non-membership** *n.*	**non-physically** *adv.*	**non-renewable** *adj.*
non-infectious *adj.*	**non-metal** *adj.*	**non-poisonous** *adj.*	
non-interference *n.*	**non-metallic** *adj.*	**non-political** *adj.*	

non-resident ● *adj.* (of a person) not residing in a particular place. ● *n.* a non-resident person. □ **non-residence** *n.* **non-residential** *adj.*

non-scientific *adj.* not involving science or scientific methods. ¶Neutral in sense: *see* NON- 6, UNSCIENTIFIC. □ **non-scientist** *n.*

nonsense *n.* **1** spoken or written words that have no meaning, or make no sense. **2** foolish talk, ideas, etc. **3** unacceptable behaviour (*she tolerates a lot of nonsense from her staff*). **4** (often *attrib.*) a form of literature meant to amuse by absurdity (*nonsense verse*). □ **nonsensical** *adj.* **nonsensicality** *n.* (*pl.* **-ies**). **nonsensically** *adv.*

non sequitur /nɒn ˈsekwɪtər/ *n.* **1** a conclusion that does not logically follow from the premises. **2** a remark, response, etc. not logically following from what has gone before.

non-skid *adj.* **1** that does not skid. **2** that inhibits skidding.

non-slip *adj.* **1** that does not slip. **2** that inhibits slipping.

non-smoker *n.* a person who does not smoke. □ **non-smoking** *adj.* & *n.*

non-specialist *n.* a person who is not a specialist (in a particular subject).

non-standard *adj.* **1** not standard. **2** (of language) containing features which are widely used but generally considered incorrect.

non-starter *n.* **1** a person or animal that does not start in a race. **2** *informal* a person or thing that is unlikely to succeed or be effective.

non-status *adj.* (in Canada) designating a person of Indian ancestry who is not registered as an Indian under the Indian Act.

non-steroidal *adj.* of or relating to a drug etc. that is not a steroid but which has similar effects.

non-stick *adj.* **1** that does not stick. **2** that does not allow things to stick to it.

non-stop ● *adj.* **1** (of a train, flight, journey, etc.) without any stops (*a non-stop flight to Victoria*). **2** without any breaks or pauses (*a non-stop meeting*). ● *adv.* without stopping or pausing (*cried non-stop for three hours*). ● *n.* a non-stop train, flight, etc.

nonsuch *n.* a person or thing that is unrivalled, a paragon.

non-tariff barrier *n.* something, such as a system of grants to domestic manufacturers, that has the effect of limiting imports without the use of tariffs.

non-technical *adj.* **1** not technical. **2** without technical knowledge.

non-treaty *adj.* designating status or non-status Indian people who have not signed a treaty with the Canadian government.

non-union *adj.* **1** not belonging to a trade union. **2** not done or produced by members of a trade union. □ **non-unionized** *adj.*

non-use *n.* failure to use. □ **non-user** *n.*

non-violence *n.* the avoidance of violence, esp. as a principle. □ **non-violent** *adj.* **non-violently** *adv.*

non-voting *adj.* not having or using a vote. □ **non-voter** *n.*

noodle[1] *n.* a thin, flat strip of pasta used in soups etc.

noodle[2] *n. informal* **1** a foolish person. **2** the head (*use your noodle!*).

noodle[3] *v.intr.* (**noodled, noodling**) **1** improvise or play esp. jazz music in a casual or desultory manner. **2** do or say something in an unproductive or undirected way (*I wish he'd stop noodling around*).

nook *n.* **1** a corner or recess; a secluded place. **2** a small or inaccessible place (*every nook and cranny*).

nookie *n.* (also **nooky**) *slang* sexual activity.

noon *n.* twelve o'clock in the day, midday.

noonday *n.* midday (also *attrib.*: *noonday meal*).

no one *n.* (also **no-one**) no person; nobody.

noon hour *n.* the time around midday when students, workers, etc. are given a lunch break.

noontime *n.* midday (also *attrib.*: *noontime concert*).

noose ● *n.* **1** a loop with a running knot, tightening as the rope or wire is pulled, esp. in a snare, lasso, or hangman's halter. **2** a snare or bond. ● *v.tr.* **1** catch with or enclose in a noose, ensnare. **2 a** make a noose on (a cord). **b** (often foll. by *round*) arrange (a cord) in a noose. □ **put one's head in a noose** bring about one's own downfall.

Nootka /ˈnuːtkə/ = NUU-CHAH-NULTH. □ **Nootkan** *adj.*

nope *interj. informal* = NO *interj.* 1.

no place *adv. N Amer.* nowhere.

nor *conj.* **1** and not; and not either (*I said I had not seen it, nor had I; can neither read nor write*). **2** and no more; neither (*'I cannot go' — 'Nor can I'*).

nor' *n., adj.,* & *adv.* (esp. in compounds) = NORTH (*nor'wester*).

NORAD *abbr.* North American Aerospace Defence Command.

noradrenalin /ˌnɔrəˈdrenəlɪn/ *n.* (also **noradrenaline**) a hormone released by the adrenal medulla and by sympathetic nerve endings as a neurotransmitter.

Nor-Am *adj.* esp. *Skiing* North American.

Nordic ● *adj.* **1** of or relating to a physical type of northern Germanic peoples characterized by tall stature and fair colouring. **2** of or relating to Scandinavia or Finland. **3** of or relating to cross-country skiing or ski jumping (*compare* ALPINE *adj.* 3). ● *n.* a Nordic person, esp. a native of Scandinavia or Finland.

nordicity /nɔrˈdɪsɪti/ *n. Cdn* a measure of the degree of northernness of a high-latitude place, calculated by assigning values to ten criteria, including latitude, summer heat, and annual cold.

nor'easter *n. N Amer.* = NORTHEASTER.

norepinephrine /ˌnɔrepəˈnefrɪn/ *n.* = NORADRENALIN.

Norfolk Island pine /ˈnɔrfək/ *n.* (also **Norfolk pine**) a large pyramidal coniferous tree, *Araucaria heterophylla*, with tiered branches and small needles, grown as a pot-bound houseplant.

---

nonresistance *n.*
nonresistant *adj.*
non-returnable *adj.*
non-sectarian *adj.*
non-sexist *adj.*

non-sexual *adj.*
non-sexually *adv.*
non-specific *adj.*
non-surgical *adj.*
non-toxic *adj.*

non-traditional *adj.*
non-transferable *adj.*
non-uniform *adj.*
non-verbal *adj.*
non-verbally *adv.*

non-volatile *adj.*
non-white *adj.* & *n.*

nori /ˈnɔri/ n. edible seaweed of the genus *Porphyra*, eaten either fresh or dried in sheets.

norm n. **1** a standard or pattern or type. **2** a standard quantity to be produced or amount of work to be done. **3** customary behaviour, appearance, etc. (*social norms*). **4** the average or general level (*temperature well below the seasonal norm*).

normal ● adj. **1** constituting or conforming to a standard; regular, usual, typical. **2 a** physically or mentally sound; healthy. **b** about average in intelligence, emotional development, ability, etc. ● n. **1 a** the normal value of a temperature etc. **b** the usual state, level, etc. (*things have returned to normal*). **2** a person or thing that is normal. □ **normalcy** n. esp. N Amer. **normality** n.

normalize v. **1** tr. make normal or regular. **2** tr. make (relations) normal or standard between countries etc. **3** intr. become normal. **4** tr. cause to conform to a standard. □ **normalization** n. **normalizer** n.

normally adv. **1** in a normal manner. **2** usually.

normal school n. esp. N Amer. hist. a school or college for training teachers.

Norman ● n. **1** a native or inhabitant of Normandy. **2** a descendant of the people of mixed Scandinavian and Frankish origin established there in the 10th c., who conquered England in 1066. **3** Norman French. **4** Archit. the style of Romanesque architecture found in Britain under the Normans. **5** any of the English kings from William I (c. 1027–87) to Stephen (c. 1097–1154). ● adj. **1** of or relating to the Normans or Normandy. **2** of or relating to the Norman style of architecture.

Norman French n. French as spoken by the Normans or (after 1066) in English law courts.

normative /ˈnɔrmətɪv/ adj. of or establishing a norm. □ **normatively** adv. **normativity** n.

Norse ● n. **1 a** the Norwegian language. **b** the Scandinavian language group. **2** (prec. by the; treated as pl.) **a** the Norwegians. **b** the Vikings. ● adj. **1** of or relating to Norway or the Norse language. **2** of or relating to ancient Scandinavia or its inhabitants. □ **Norseman** n. (pl. **-men**)

north ● n. **1 a** the point of the horizon 90° counterclockwise from east. **b** the compass point corresponding to this. **c** the direction in which this lies. **2** (usu. **the North**) **a** the Arctic. **b** (in Canada) (from Labrador to the west) the northern part of a province. **c** the part of the world or a country or a town lying to the north, esp. = NORTH COUNTRY 1 or NORTHERN STATES. **d** the industrialized nations. ● adj. **1** towards, at, near, or facing north. **2** coming from the north (*north wind*). ● adv. **1** towards, at, or near the north. **2** (foll. by *of*) further north than. **3** informal (foll. by *of*) more than (*paid him north of $40,000*). □ **north by east** (or **west**) between north and north-northeast (or north-northwest). **up north** to or in the north.

North American ● adj. of or relating to North America. ● n. a native or inhabitant of North America, esp. a citizen of the US or Canada.

North American Free Trade Agreement n. an agreement which came into effect in January 1994 between Canada, the US, and Mexico to remove barriers to trade between the three countries over a ten-year period. Abbr.: **NAFTA**.

North Americanism n. **1** a word or expression originating in Canada and the US. **2** a word or expression used only in Canada and the US.

North Atlantic Treaty Organization n. an association of European and N American states, formed in 1949 for the defence of Europe and the N Atlantic against the perceived threat of Soviet aggression.

northbound adj. travelling or leading northwards.

north canoe n. Cdn = CANOT DU NORD.

North Carolinian ● adj. of or relating to the US state of North Carolina. ● n. a resident or native of North Carolina.

North Country n. (also **north country**) **1** the northern part of England (north of the Humber). **2** the northern part of any country.

North Dakotan /dəˈkoʊtən/ ● adj. of or relating to the US state of North Dakota. ● n. a resident or native of North Dakota.

northeast ● n. **1** the point of the horizon midway between north and east. **2** the compass point corresponding to this. **3** the direction in which this lies. **4** (**Northeast**) the part of a country, city, etc. lying to the northeast. ● adj. of, towards, or coming from the northeast. ● adv. towards, at, or near the northeast. □ **northeastern** adj.

northeaster n. a northeast wind.

northeasterly ● adj. & adv. = NORTHEAST. ● n. (pl. **-ies**) a northeast wind.

northeastward adj. & adv. (also **northeastwards**) towards the northeast.

northerly ● adj. & adv. **1** in a northern position or direction. **2** (of wind) blowing from the north. ● n. (pl. **-ies**) (usu. in pl.) a wind blowing from the north.

northern ● adj. **1** of or in the north; inhabiting the north. **2** lying or directed towards the north. **3** (of a wind) blowing from the north. ● n. N Amer. = NORTHERN PIKE. □ **northernmost** adj. **northernness** n.

northerner n. a native or inhabitant of the north.

northern fulmar n. a fulmar, *Fulmarus glacialis*, breeding in immense colonies along the N Atlantic and Arctic coasts.

Northern Games n. Cdn a festival of arts and crafts, dancing, and games held in a different Arctic community every year.

northern gannet n. see GANNET.

northern harrier n. a common harrier, *Circus cyaneus*, having a partial facial disk reminiscent of an owl's, and a conspicuous white rump patch.

northern hemisphere the half of the earth north of the equator.

northern lights n.pl. a northern occurrence of aurora (see AURORA 1).

northern oriole n. a N American oriole, *Icterus galbula*, with black and orange or yellowish-orange plumage.

northern pike n. a large species of pike, *Esox lucius*, found in northern waters and valued as a game fish.

northern pintail n. see PINTAIL.

northern sea lion n. = STELLER'S SEA LION.

Northern Spy n. (pl. **Spys** or **Spies**) N Amer. a large bright red cooking apple streaked with green.

Northern States n.pl. the states in the north of the US, esp. those lying roughly north of the Mason-Dixon Line and the Ohio river forming the Union side in the Civil War.

North Germanic ● n. the northern group of Germanic languages, comprising the Scandinavian languages. ● adj. of or relating to North Germanic.

North Korean ● adj. of or relating to North Korea, a country in the Far East, occupying the northern part of the peninsula of Korea. ● n. a native or inhabitant of North Korea.

northland n. (also **northlands**) the northern lands; the northern part of a country.

Northman n. (pl. **-men**) **1** a Viking. **2** Cdn hist. = HOMME DU NORD.

north-northeast ● n. the point or direction midway between north and northeast. ● adj. & adv. in, from, or towards this direction.

north-northwest ● n. the point or direction midway between north and northwest. ● adj. & adv. in, from, or towards this direction. Abbr.: **NNW**.

north of 60 n. Cdn informal the areas of Canada north of 60 degrees latitude.

North Pole n. see POLE² 1.

north-south attrib.adj. of or relating to countries of the north and south (north-south divide).

North Star n. Polaris.

northward ● adv. (also **northwards**) towards the north. ● adj. **1** situated or directed towards the north. **2** moving or facing towards the north. ● n. a northward direction or region.

northwest ● n. **1** the point of the horizon midway between north and west. **2** the compass point corresponding to this. **3** the direction in which this lies. **4** (**Northwest**) the part of a country, city, etc. lying to the northwest. ● adj. of, towards, or coming from the northwest. ● adv. towards, at, or near the northwest. □ **northwestern** adj.

northwester n. **1** a northwest wind. **2** (**Northwester**) Cdn hist. **a** a wintering partner or employee of the North West Company. **b** (in pl.) the North West Company collectively.

northwesterly ● adj. & adv. = NORTHWEST. ● n. (pl. **-ies**) a northwest wind.

North West Mounted Police n. Cdn hist. a federal police force established in 1873, renamed the Royal North West Mounted Police in 1904 and the Royal Canadian Mounted Police in 1920. Abbr.: **NWMP**.

Northwest Rebellion n. Cdn an armed uprising of Metis, Indians, and white settlers in Saskatchewan in 1885, led by Louis Riel (1844–85), who proclaimed a provisional government for Western Canada with the capital at Batoche.

northwestward adj. & adv. (also **northwestwards**) towards the northwest.

north woods n.pl. N Amer. the vast regions of forest in northern Canada and parts of the northern US.

Norway lobster n. a small European lobster, Nephrops norvegicus.

Norway maple n. a European maple tree with leaves similar to the sugar maple, Acer platanoides, with many cultivated varieties, frequently planted in eastern N America.

Norway spruce n. a large Eurasian spruce, Picea abies, with many cultivated varieties planted both as a forest tree and as an ornamental.

Norwegian /nɔr'wiːdʒən/ ● n. **1 a** a native or national of Norway, a country in N Europe. **b** a person of Norwegian descent. **2** the language of Norway. ● adj. of or relating to Norway or its people or language.

nor'wester n. **1** = NORTHWESTER 1. **2** an oilskin hat. **3** (**Nor'Wester**) Cdn hist. = NORTHWESTER 2.

Nos. abbr. (also **nos.**) numbers.

nose ● n. **1** an organ above the mouth on the face or head of a human or animal, containing nostrils and used for smelling and breathing. **2 a** the sense of smell (dogs have a good nose). **b** the ability to detect a particular thing (a nose for scandal). **3** the odour or perfume of wine, tea, tobacco, hay, etc. **4** the open end or nozzle of a tube, pipe, etc. **5** the front end or projecting part of a thing, e.g. of a car or aircraft. **6** Cdn the northeast portion of the Grand Banks of Newfoundland, lying outside Canada's 320-km (200-mile) fishing zone. ● v. **1** tr. (often foll. by out) **a** perceive the smell of, discover by smell. **b** detect. **2** tr. **a** thrust or rub one's nose against or into, esp. in order to smell. **b** smell or sniff (wine etc.). **3** intr. (usu. foll. by about, around, through, etc.) pry or search. **4 a** intr. (often foll. by out) move forward slowly and cautiously. **b** tr. make (one's or its way) forward slowly and cautiously. □ **as plain as the nose on your face** easily seen. **by a nose** by a very narrow margin (won the race by a nose). **count noses** count those present, one's supporters, etc.; decide a question by mere numbers. **cut off one's nose to spite one's face** disadvantage oneself in the course of trying to disadvantage another. **have one's nose in** (a book etc.) informal read intently. **keep one's nose clean** slang stay out of trouble, behave properly. **nose out** defeat by a narrow margin. **on the nose** N Amer. slang precisely. **poke** (or **stick**) **one's nose into** informal pry or intrude into (esp. a person's affairs). **put a person's nose out of joint** informal upset or annoy a person. **see no further than one's nose** be shortsighted, esp. in foreseeing the consequences of one's actions etc. **turn up one's nose** (usu. foll. by at) informal show disdain. **under a person's nose** informal right before a person (esp. of defiant or unnoticed actions). **with one's nose in the air** haughtily. □ **nosed** adj. (also in comb.)

noseband n. the lower band of a bridle, passing over the horse's nose.

nosebleed ● n. an instance of bleeding from the nose. ● adj. N Amer. **1** (of seats in an arena, theatre, etc.) situated in a high level. **2** (of a price etc.) very high.

nose candy n. N Amer. slang cocaine.

nose cone n. the cone-shaped nose of a rocket etc.

nose-dive ● n. **1** a steep downward plunge by an aircraft. **2** a sudden plunge, drop, or decline (his career took a nose-dive). ● v.intr. (**-dived, -diving**) make a nose-dive.

no-see-um n. N Amer. a small bloodsucking insect, esp. a midge of the family Ceratopogonidae.

nosegay n. a small bunch of flowers; a posy.

nose job n. informal = RHINOPLASTY.

nose-piece n. **1** the part of eyeglass frames that goes over the bridge of the nose. **2** = NOSEBAND. **3** the part of a helmet etc. protecting the nose. **4** the part of a microscope to which the objective lenses are attached.

nose ring n. a ring fixed in the nose of an animal (esp. a bull) for leading it, or of a person for ornament.

nose tackle n. Football **1** the defensive player who lines up in the centre of the linemen in formation. **2** this field position.

nose-thumbing ● n. behaviour meant to show one's contempt (for a person, establishment, etc.) ● adj. derisory; contemptuous.

nose wheel n. a landing wheel under the nose of an aircraft.

nosh slang ● v.tr. & intr. **1** eat or drink. **2** N Amer. eat between meals; snack. ● n. **1** food or drink. **2** N Amer. a snack. □ **nosher** n.

no-show n. a person who is expected at an event, has a ticket reserved for a trip, etc. but does not appear for it.

nostalgia /nɒ'stældʒə, -dʒiə, nə-/ n. **1** (often foll. by for) sentimental yearning for a period of the past; regretful or wistful memory of an earlier time. **2** a thing or things which evoke a former era. **3** severe homesickness. ☐ **nostalgic** *adj.* **nostalgically** *adv.* **nostalgist** *n.*

nostril *n.* either of two external openings of the nasal cavity in vertebrates that admit air to the lungs and smells to the olfactory nerves.

nostrum /ˈnɒstrəm/ *n.* **1** a quack remedy, esp. one prepared by the person recommending it. **2** a pet scheme, esp. for political or social reform.

nosy *adj.* (also **nosey**) (**-ier, -iest**) *informal* inquisitive, prying. ☐ **nosily** *adv.* **nosiness** *n.*

Nosy Parker *n. informal* a nosy person.

not *adv.* expressing negation, esp.: **1** (also **n't** joined to a preceding verb) following an auxiliary verb or *be* or (in a question) the subject of such a verb (*I cannot say*; *she isn't there*; *am I not right?*). **2** used elliptically for a negative sentence or verb or phrase (*I hope not*; *Certainly not!*). **3** used to express the negative of other words (*not a single one was left*; *he is not my cousin, but my nephew*). **4** *informal* following and emphatically negating an affirmative statement (*great party ... not!*). ☐ **not at all** (in polite reply to thanks) there is no need for thanks. **not least** with considerable importance, notably. **not quite 1** almost (*am not quite there*). **2** noticeably not (*not quite proper*). **not in the slightest** not at all. **not a thing** nothing at all. **not that** (foll. by clause) it is not to be inferred that (*if he said so — not that he ever did — he lied*).

nota bene /ˌnəʊtə ˈbeneɪ/ *v.tr.* (as *imper.*) observe what follows, take notice.

notability *n.* (*pl.* **-ies**) **1** the state of being notable (*historical notability*). **2** a prominent person.

notable ● *adj.* worthy of note; striking, remarkable, eminent. ● *n.* **1** an eminent person. **2** a noteworthy fact or thing. ☐ **notably** *adv.*

notarize /ˈnəʊtəˌraɪz/ *v.tr. N Amer.* certify (a document) as a notary.

notary /ˈnəʊtəri/ *n.* (*pl.* **-ies**) **1** (in full **notary public**, *pl.* **notaries public**) a person authorized to perform certain legal formalities, esp. to draw up or certify contracts, deeds, etc. **2** *Cdn* (*Que.*) a member of the legal profession not authorized to plead in court but qualified to draft deeds, contracts, and other legal documents, e.g. wills, real estate transactions, etc. ☐ **notarial** /nəʊˈtɛrɪəl/ *adj.*

notate *v.tr.* write in notation. ☐ **notated** *adj.* **notator** *n.*

notation *n.* **1 a** the representation of numbers, quantities, pitch and duration etc. of musical notes, dance movements, chess moves, etc. by symbols. **b** any set of such symbols. **2** esp. *N Amer.* **a** a note or annotation. **b** a record. ☐ **notational** *adj.*

notch ● *n.* **1** a V-shaped indentation on an edge or surface. **2** one of a series of holes for the tongue of a buckle on a belt, shoe, etc. **3** each of a series of indentations marking graduated points on a regulating dial etc. **4** a nick made on a stick etc. in order to keep count. **5** *informal* a step or degree (*move up a notch*). **6** *N Amer.* a deep gorge. ● *v.tr.* **1** make notches in. **2** (often foll. by *up*) record or score with or as with notches. **3** secure or insert by notches. ☐ **notched** *adj.* **notchy** *adj.* (**-ier, -iest**).

note ● *n.* **1** a brief record of facts, topics, thoughts, etc., as an aid to memory, for use in writing, public speaking, etc. (often in *pl.*: *spoke without notes*). **2** an observation, usu. unwritten, of experiences etc. (*compare notes*). **3** a short or informal letter. **4** a formal diplomatic or parliamentary communication. **5** a short annotation or additional explanation in a book etc.; a footnote. **6 a** = BANKNOTE (*a five-pound note*). **b** a written promise or notice of payment of various

kinds. **7 a** notice, attention (*worthy of note*). **b** distinction, eminence (*a person of note*). **8 a** a written sign representing the pitch and duration of a musical sound. **b** a single tone of definite pitch made by a musical instrument, the human voice, etc. **c** a key of a piano etc. **9 a** a bird's song or call. **b** a single tone in this. **10** a quality or tone of speaking, expressing mood or attitude etc.; a hint or suggestion (*ended on a note of optimism*). **11** a characteristic; a distinguishing feature. ● *v.tr.* **1** observe, notice; give or draw attention to. **2** (often foll. by *down*) record as a thing to be remembered or observed. **3** (in *passive*; often foll. by *for*) be famous or well known (for a quality, activity, etc.). ☐ **hit** (or **strike**) **the right** (or **a false**) **note** speak or act in an appropriate (or inappropriate) manner. **of note** important, distinguished (*a person of note*). **take note** (often foll. by *of*) observe; pay attention (to). ☐ **noted** *adj.* (in sense 3 of *v.*). **noteless** *adj.*

notebook *n.* **1** a small book for making or taking notes. **2** (in full **notebook computer**) a portable computer smaller than a laptop.

notepad *n.* **1** a pad of paper for writing notes on. **2** a small hand-held computer taking input from an electronic stylus rather than a keyboard.

notepaper *n.* paper for writing letters.

noteworthy *adj.* worthy of attention; remarkable. ☐ **noteworthiness** *n.*

not-for-profit *adj.* = NON-PROFIT.

nothing ● *n.* **1** not anything (*have nothing to do*). **2** no thing (often foll. by complement: *I see nothing that I want*). **3 a** a person or thing of no importance or concern; a trivial event or remark (*was nothing to me*; *murmured sweet nothings in her ear*). **b** (*attrib.*) *informal* of no value; indeterminate (*a nothing sort of day*). **4** no part, share, etc., of some thing (*the singer had nothing of his former power*). **5** non-existence; what does not exist. **6** (in calculations) no amount; nought (*a third of nothing is nothing*). ● *adv.* **1** not at all, in no way (*is nothing like enough*). **2** *informal* not at all (*Is he ill? — Ill nothing, he's dead.*). ☐ **be nothing to 1** not concern. **2** not compare with. **3** have no claim on a person's affections. **be** (or **have**) **nothing to do with 1** have no connection with. **2** not be involved or associated with. **for nothing 1** at no cost; without payment. **2** with no reward or result; to no purpose (*did all that work for nothing*). **have nothing on 1** be naked. **2** have no engagements. **have nothing on a person 1** have much less of a certain quality or ability than something else (*today's pop music has nothing on the old musicals*). **2** (of the police etc.) have no information that could show a person to be guilty of something. **make nothing of 1** do without hesitation. **2** treat as a trifle. **3** be unable to understand, use, or deal with. **no nothing** *informal* (concluding a list of negatives) nothing at all. **nothing doing** *informal* **1 a** there is no prospect of success or agreement. **b** I refuse. **2** nothing is happening. **nothing** (or **nothing else**) **for it** (often foll. by *but to* + infin.) no alternative (*nothing for it but to pay up*). **nothing less than** at least (*nothing less than a disaster*). **nothing** (or **not much**) **to it 1** untrue or unimportant. **2** simple to do. **think nothing of it** do not apologize or feel bound to show gratitude.

nothingness *n.* **1** non-existence; the non-existent. **2** worthlessness, triviality, insignificance.

notice ● *n.* **1** attention, observation (*it escaped my notice*). **2** a displayed sheet etc. bearing an announcement or other information. **3 a** an intimation or warning, esp. a formal one to allow preparations to be made (*give notice*; *at a moment's notice*). **b** (often foll. by *to* + infin.) a formal announcement or declaration of intention to end an agreement or leave employment at a specified time (*hand in one's notice*). **4 a** a short published review or comment about a new play, book, etc. **b** a small advertisement or announcement in a newspaper or magazine (*death notices*). ● *v.tr.* **1** (often foll. by *that*, *how*, etc. + clause) perceive, observe; take notice of. **2** remark upon; speak of. **3** treat (a person) with some degree of attention, favour, or politeness; recognize or acknowledge (a person). □ **at short** (or **a moment's**) **notice** with little warning. **put on notice** alert or warn (a person). **take notice** (or **no notice**) show signs (or no signs) of interest. **take notice of 1** observe; pay attention to. **2** act upon.

noticeable *adj.* **1** easily seen or noticed; perceptible. **2** worthy or deserving notice. □ **noticeably** *adv.*

notice board *n.* a board for displaying notices.

notify *v.tr.* (**-ies, -ied**) (often foll. by *of*, or *that* + clause) inform or give notice to (a person). □ **notification** *n.*

notion *n.* **1 a** a concept or idea; a conception (*an absurd notion*). **b** an opinion (*has the notion that people are honest*). **c** a vague view or understanding. **2** an inclination, impulse, or intention (*has no notion of conforming*). **3** (in *pl.*) esp. *N Amer.* small articles related to sewing, such as thread, ribbons, buttons, etc.

notional *adj.* **1 a** existing only in the mind; imaginary. **b** (of knowledge etc.) speculative; not based on experiment etc. **2** *Grammar* of or pertaining to semantic content as opposed to grammatical structure or behaviour. □ **notionally** *adv.*

notorious /noː'tɔriəs, nə-/ *adj.* well known, esp. unfavourably (*a notorious criminal*; *notorious for its climate*). □ **notoriety** /-tə'raiəti/ *n.* **notoriously** *adv.*

notwithstanding /ˌnɒtwɪθ'stændɪŋ, -wɪð-/ *prep.* in spite of; without prevention by (*notwithstanding your objections*). ● *adv.* nevertheless; all the same. ● *conj.* (usu. foll. by *that* + clause) although.

notwithstanding clause *n.* *Cdn* Section 33 of the Canadian Charter of Rights and Freedoms, which allows Parliament and the provincial legislatures to override Charter clauses covering fundamental freedoms and legal and equality rights.

nougat /'nuːgət/ *n.* a candy made from sugar or honey, nuts, and egg white.

nought *n.* *literary* or *archaic* (in certain phrases) nothing (compare NAUGHT).

noun *n.* *Grammar* a word (other than a pronoun) or group of words used to name or identify any of a class of persons, places, or things (**common noun**), or a particular one of these (**proper noun**).

nourish *v.tr.* **1 a** sustain with food. **b** enrich; promote the development of (the soil etc.). **c** provide with intellectual or emotional sustenance or enrichment. **2** foster or cherish (a feeling etc.). □ **nourisher** *n.*

nourishing *adj.* (esp. of food) containing much nourishment; sustaining. □ **nourishingly** *adv.*

nourishment *n.* **1** something that nourishes; sustenance, food. **2** the action, process, or fact of nourishing someone or something.

nouveau /'nuːvoː, nuː'voː/ *adj.* **1** derogatory or jocular (of a person) having recently become the thing specified (*nouveau gentry*). **2** modern; up-to-date (*nouveau chic*).

nouveau riche /ˌnuːvoː 'riːʃ/ ● *n.* (*pl.* **nouveaux riches** pronunc. same) a person who has recently acquired (usu. ostentatious) wealth. ● *adj.* of, pertaining to, or characteristic of a nouveau riche.

nouveau roman /'nuːvoː roː'mã/ *n.* a style of avant-garde French novel that came to prominence in the 1950s, rejecting the plot, characters, and omniscient narrator central to the traditional novel.

nouvelle /nuː'vel/ *adj.* of, pertaining to, or characteristic of nouvelle cuisine.

nouvelle cuisine /kwɪ'ziːn/ *n.* a modern style of (esp. French) cooking that avoids traditional rich sauces and emphasizes the freshness of the ingredients and attractive presentation.

Nov. *abbr.* November.

nova *n.* (*pl.* **novae** /'noːviː/ or **-s**) a star showing a sudden increase of brightness and then subsiding.

Nova Scotian ● *n.* a native or inhabitant of Nova Scotia. ● *adj.* of or relating to Nova Scotia.

Nova Scotia duck tolling retriever *n.* a breed of smallish dog trained to attract ducks along a shoreline and then retrieve them.

novel¹ *n.* **1** a fictitious prose story of considerable length and complexity, esp. one representing character and action with some degree of realism. **2** (prec. by *the*) this type of literature.

novel² *adj.* of a new kind or nature; strange; previously unknown.

novelette *n.* a short novel.

novelist *n.* a writer of novels. □ **novelistic** *adj.*

novelize *v.tr.* make into a novel. □ **novelization** *n.*

novella /nə'velə/ *n.* (*pl.* **novellas**) a short novel or narrative story.

novelty ● *n.* (*pl.* **-ies**) **1 a** newness; new character. **b** originality. **2** a new or unusual thing or occurrence. **3** a small toy or decoration etc. of novel design. **4** (*attrib.*) having novelty; appealing through newness; faddish (*novelty song*).

November *n.* the eleventh month of the year.

novena /noː'viːnə/ *n.* *Catholicism* a devotion consisting of special prayers or services on nine successive days.

novice *n.* **1** a beginner; an inexperienced person (also *attrib.*: *novice programmer*). **2** a probationary member of a religious order, before the taking of vows. **3** a horse, dog, etc. that has not won a major prize in a competition. **4** *Cdn* **a** a level of children's sports, usu. involving children aged 8 to 9. **b** a player in this age group.

novitiate /noː'vɪʃiət, -ieit/ *n.* **1** the period of being a novice. **2** a religious novice. **3** novices' quarters.

Novocaine /'noːvəˌkein/ *n.* *proprietary* a local anaesthetic derived from benzoic acid.

no vote *n.* a vote in opposition to a proposal etc.

now ● *adv.* **1** at the present or mentioned time. **2** immediately (*I must go now*). **3** by this or that time (*it was now clear*). **4** under the present circumstances (*I cannot now agree*). **5** on this further occasion (*what do you want now?*). **6** in the immediate past (*just now*). **7** in these times; nowadays. **8** (esp. in a narrative or discourse) then, next (*now to consider the next point*). **9** (without reference to time, giving various tones to a sentence) surely, I insist, I wonder, etc. (*now what do you mean by that?*; *oh come now!*). ● *conj.* (often foll. by *that* + clause) as a consequence of the fact (*now that I am older*). ● *n.* this time; the present (*should be there by now*). ● *adj.* *informal* modern, fashionable. □ **as of now** from or at this time. **for now** until a later time (*goodbye for now*). **now and again** (or **then**) from time to time; intermittently. **now now** used to reprimand or pacify a person. **now or never** an expression of urgency. □ **nowness** *n.*

nowadays *adv.* at the present time or age; in these times.

Nowel *n.* (also **Nowell**) *archaic var.* of NOEL.

nowhere ● *adv.* in, at, or to no place; not anywhere. ●

n. **1** no place. **2** a remote, dull, or nondescript place. ● *adj. slang* **1** remote, insignificant. **2** unsatisfactory, dull (*a nowhere job*). □ **come out of** (or **from**) **nowhere** be suddenly evident or successful. **get nowhere** make or cause to make no progress. **in the middle of nowhere** *informal* remote from urban life. **nowhere near** not nearly.

no win *attrib.adj.* of or designating a situation in which success is impossible.

noxious /'nɒkʃəs/ *adj.* **1** harmful, injurious (*noxious fumes*). **2** morally harmful; unwholesome.

noxious weed *n.* a plant considered harmful to animals or the environment.

nozzle *n.* **1** a spout on a hose etc. through which a stream of air or liquid issues. **2** a duct in a jet or rocket engine in which the speed of the ejected fuel is increased.

NP *abbr.* **1** Notary Public. **2** NURSE PRACTITIONER.

Np *symbol* neptunium.

NPT *abbr.* Non-Proliferation Treaty.

NRA *abbr.* (in the US) National Rifle Association.

NRC *abbr.* National Research Council of Canada.

NRSV *abbr.* NEW REVISED STANDARD VERSION.

NS *abbr.* Nova Scotia.

ns *abbr.* nanosecond.

NSAID /'ensed/ *abbr.* non-steroidal anti-inflammatory drug.

NSERC /'ensɜrk/ *abbr.* Natural Sciences and Engineering Research Council of Canada.

NSF *abbr.* not sufficient funds.

NST *abbr.* Newfoundland Standard Time.

NSW *abbr.* New South Wales.

NT *abbr.* **1** New Testament. **2** NEWFOUNDLAND TIME. **3** Northwest Territories (in official postal use).

n't *adv.* (in *comb.*) = NOT 1 (usu. with *is, are, have, must,* and the auxiliary verbs *can, do, should, would, might, ought*) (*isn't; mustn't*).

nth /enθ/ *see* N².

NTSC *abbr.* National Television Standards Committee.

nu /nju/ *n.* the thirteenth letter of the Greek alphabet (*N, ν*).

nuance /'nu:ɒns, 'nju:-/ ● *n.* a subtle difference in or shade of meaning, feeling, colour, etc. ● *v.tr.* give a nuance or nuances to. □ **nuanced** *adj.*

nub *n.* **1** the point or gist (of a matter or story). **2** a small lump or chunk. **3** a stub; a protuberance. **4** a knot or irregularity in fabric. □ **nubby** *adj.*

nubbin *n. N Amer.* a small lump or stub.

nubile /'nu:bail, 'nju:-/ *adj.* (of a woman) sexually attractive. □ **nubility** *n.*

nuclear /'nu:kliɜr, 'nju:-/ *adj.* **1** of, relating to, or constituting a nucleus. **2** using, producing, or resulting from nuclear energy (*nuclear reactor*). **3** of, involving, or possessing nuclear weapons.

nuclear bomb *n.* a bomb using the release of energy by nuclear fission or fusion or both.

nuclear disarmament *n.* the gradual or total reduction by a state of its nuclear weapons.

nuclear energy *n.* = ATOMIC ENERGY.

nuclear family *n.* a couple and their children, regarded as a basic social unit.

nuclear fission *n.* a nuclear reaction in which a heavy nucleus splits spontaneously or on impact with another particle, with the release of energy.

nuclear force *n.* a strong attractive force between nucleons in the atomic nucleus that holds the nucleus together.

nuclear-free *adj.* (of a country or region) free from nuclear weapons, power, etc.

nuclear fuel *n.* a substance that will sustain a fission chain reaction so that it can be used as a source of nuclear energy.

nuclear fusion *n.* a nuclear reaction in which atomic nuclei of low atomic number fuse to form a heavier nucleus with the release of energy.

nuclear magnetic resonance *n.* the absorption of electromagnetic radiation by a nucleus having a magnetic moment when in an external magnetic field, used mainly as an analytical technique and in body imaging for diagnosis. Abbr.: **NMR**.

nuclear physics *n.* the physics of atomic nuclei and their interactions, esp. in the generation of nuclear energy. □ **nuclear physicist** *n.*

nuclear power *n.* **1** electric or motive power generated by a nuclear reactor. **2** a country that has nuclear weapons. □ **nuclear-powered** *adj.*

nuclear reactor *n. see* REACTOR 2.

nuclear warfare *n.* warfare in which nuclear weapons are used.

nuclear waste *n.* radioactive waste material e.g. from the use or reprocessing of nuclear fuel.

nuclear weapon *n.* a missile, bomb, etc., using the release of energy by nuclear fission or fusion or both.

nuclear winter *n.* a period of abnormal cold and darkness predicted to follow a nuclear war.

nucleate ● *adj.* /'nu:kliɜt, 'nju:-/ having a nucleus. ● *v.intr. & tr.* /'nu:klieit, 'nju:-/ form or form into a nucleus. □ **nucleation** *n.*

nucleic acid /nu:'kli:ɪk, -'kleiɪk, nju:-/ *n.* either of two complex organic substances (DNA and RNA), whose molecules consists of many nucleotides linked in a long chain, and present in all living cells.

nucleon /'nu:kliɒn, 'nju:-/ *n.* a proton or neutron.

nucleoside /'nu:kliə,said, 'nju:-/ *n. Biochem.* an organic compound consisting of a purine or pyrimidine base linked to a sugar, e.g. adenosine.

nucleotide /'nu:kliə,taid, 'nju:-/ *n. Biochem.* an organic compound consisting of a nucleoside linked to a phosphate group.

nucleus /'nu:kliəs, 'nju:-/ *n.* (*pl.* **nuclei** /-li,ai/) **1 a** the central part or thing around which others are collected. **b** the kernel of an aggregate or mass. **2** an initial part meant to receive additions. **3** *Astronomy* the solid part of a comet's head. **4** *Physics* the positively charged central core of an atom that contains most of its mass. **5** *Biol.* a large dense organelle of eukaryotic cells, containing the genetic material. **6** a discrete mass of grey matter in the central nervous system. **7** *Chem.* a ring structure or other arrangement of atoms which is characteristic of a group of compounds.

nuclide /'nu:klaid, 'nju:-/ *n. Physics* a distinct kind of atom or nucleus characterized by a specific number of protons and neutrons.

nude ● *adj.* **1 a** (of a person, body part, etc.) naked, unclothed, bare. **b** (of performance etc.) involving a naked or scantily clad person or persons. **c** (of a thing) lacking natural coverage, foliage, etc. **2** (of hosiery etc.) flesh-coloured and very sheer. **3** (of beaches etc.) used by nudists. ● *n.* **1** a painting, sculpture, etc. of a nude human figure. **2** a nude person. **3** (prec. by *the*) an unclothed state (*sleeps in the nude*).

nudge ● *v.* **1** *tr.* prod gently esp. with the elbow to attract attention. **2** *tr.* push gently or gradually. **3** *tr.* coax or give a gentle reminder or encouragement to (a person). **4** *intr.* move slightly or slowly, esp. by gradual pushing (*we nudged through the bushes*). ● *n.* **1 a** the act or an instance of nudging. **b** a gentle push. **2** a gentle reminder. □ **nudge, nudge, wink, wink**

used to imply a sexual innuendo in the preceding phrase or clause.

nudie *n. informal* **1** (usu. *attrib.*) a film, photograph, etc. feauturing nudity (*nudie magazine*). **2** a nude person.

nudist *n.* a person who advocates or practises going unclothed. □ **nudism** *n.*

nudity *n.* nakedness.

nuff *n. slang* enough (*nuff said*).

nugget *n.* **1 a** a lump of gold, platinum, etc., as found in the earth. **b** a lump of anything compared to this. **2** a small, valuable, and esp. abstract thing concealed in a larger mass (*a nugget of information*). **3** N Amer. a small piece of chicken etc. covered with batter and deep-fried.

nuisance *n.* **1** a person, thing, or circumstance causing trouble, annoyance, or inconvenience. **2** anything harmful or offensive to the community or a member of it and for which a legal remedy exists.

nuisance grounds *n.pl. Cdn (West) informal* a garbage dump.

nuke *informal* ● *n.* **1** a nuclear weapon. **2** a nuclear power station. ● *v.tr.* **1** bomb or destroy with nuclear weapons. **2** *informal* cook (food) in a microwave. **3** *slang* destroy.

null ● *adj.* **1** (esp. **null and void**) invalid; having no legal or binding force. **2 a** associated with, producing, or having the value zero. **b** designating or pertaining to a point or region in which no effect or force occurs or in which effects or forces cancel each other out. **3** (of a class or set) **a** empty; having no elements (*null list*). **b** all the elements of which are zeros (*null matrix*). **4** without distinctive character or expression. ● *n.* **1 a** *Computing* (in full **null character**) a character denoting nothing, usu. represented by a zero. **b** a dummy letter in a cipher. **2** a zero; nothing. ● *v.tr.* annul, cancel, make void.

nullify *v.tr.* (**-ies, -ied**) **1** make legally null and void; annul, invalidate. **2** make of no value or use; cancel out, neutralize. □ **nullification** *n.* **nullifier** *n.*

nullity /ˈnʌlɪti/ *n.* (*pl.* **-ies**) **1** *Law* **a** the fact of being null and void; invalidity, esp. of marriage. **b** an act, document, etc., that is null. **c** a fact or circumstance causing nullity. **2 a** nothingness; the condition of being non-existent. **b** a mere nonentity; a nonentity.

numb ● *adj.* **1** (often foll. by *with*) deprived of feeling or the power of motion (*numb with cold*). **2** unable to experience emotion (*I felt numb after his death*). ● *v.tr.* **1** make numb. **2** stupefy, paralyze. □ **numbing** *adj.* (also in *comb.*). **numbingly** *adv.* **numbly** *adv.* **numbness** *n.*

number ● *n.* **1 a** an arithmetical value representing a particular quantity and used in counting and making calculations. **b** a word, symbol, or figure representing this. **c** an arithmetical value showing position in a series esp. for identification, reference, etc. (*registration number*). **d** = TELEPHONE NUMBER. **2** (often foll. by *of*) the total count or aggregate (*the number of accidents has decreased*). **3 a** (in *pl.*) arithmetic (*not good at numbers*). **b** numerical reckoning (*the laws of number*). **4 a** (in *sing.* or *pl.*) a quantity or amount; a total; a count (*a large number of people*; *only in small numbers*). **b** (**a number of**) several (of), some (of). ¶ In this sense, *a number of* is normally used with a plural verb, e.g. *a number of problems remain*. **c** (in *pl.*) numerical preponderance (*safety in numbers*). **5 a** a person or thing having a place in a series, esp. a single issue of a magazine, an item in a program, etc. **b** a song, dance, etc. **6** company, collection, group (*among our number*). **7** *Grammar* **a** the classification of words by their singular or plural forms. **b** a particular such form. **8** *informal* a person or thing regarded familiarly or affec-

tionately (usu. qualified in some way: *an attractive little number*). **9** *informal* a garment. ● *v.tr.* **1** count or class among people or things of a specified category (*I number you among my friends*). **2** assign a number or numbers to. **3** have, equal, or amount to (a specified number). **4 a** count or ascertain the number of. **b** include or comprise in a specified number. □ **any number of 1** *informal* a large unspecified number of. **2** any particular whole quantity of. **by (the) numbers** following simple instructions (as if) identified by numbers. **one's days are numbered** one does not have long to live, prosper, etc. **do a number on (a person)** *N Amer. slang* **1** disparage, speak, or write of with contempt. **2** deceive. **have a person's number** *informal* understand a person's real motives, character, etc. **have a person's number on it** (of a bomb, bullet, etc.) be destined to hit a specified person. **one's number is up** *informal* one is finished or doomed to die. **without number** innumerable. □ **numbered** *adj.* **numbering** *adj. & n.*

number cruncher *n. slang* **1** *Computing & Math.* a machine capable of complex calculations etc. **2** a person, esp. an accountant or statistician, whose primary concern is with numbers, statistics, etc. □ **number crunching** *n.* (usu. hyphenated when *attrib.*).

numbered company *n. Cdn* a corporation the name of which is simply its registration number followed by the province in which it is registered.

numbered treaty *n.* any of a number of land cession treaties signed from 1871 to 1921 between the Canadian government and Aboriginal nations throughout the north and west of Canada.

numberless *adj.* **1** innumerable, countless. **2** without a number or numbers.

number one *informal* ● *n.* **1** oneself, one's own person and interests (*always takes care of number one*). **2** the best; the finest quality (*we're number one!*). **3** *euphemism* an act of urination. ● *adj.* **1** leading; most important (*number one priority*). **2** best; finest quality.

numbers game *n.* **1** *N Amer.* (also **numbers, numbers racket**) a lottery based on the occurrence of unpredictable numbers in the results of races etc. **2** a comparison, contest, etc. regarded merely in terms of numerical statistics.

number theory *n.* the branch of mathematics that deals with the properties and relationships of numbers, esp. the positive integers.

number two *n.* **1** (often *attrib.*) something second-rate. **2** a second-in-command. **3** *euphemism* an act of defecation.

numbskull *n.* a stupid or foolish person.

numerable /ˈnuːmərəbəl, ˈnjuː-/ *adj.* that can be counted.

numeral ● *n.* a word, figure, or group of figures denoting a number. ● *adj.* expressing or denoting a number or numbers.

numerate /ˈnuːmərət, ˈnjuː-/ *adj.* acquainted with the basic principles of mathematics, esp. arithmetic. □ **numeracy** *n.*

numeration *n.* **1 a** a method or process of numbering or computing. **b** calculation. **2** the expression in words of a number written in figures.

numerator *n.* **1** the number above the line in a vulgar fraction showing how many of the parts indicated by the denominator are taken (e.g. 2 in $^2/_3$). **2** a person or device that numbers.

numerical *adj.* (also **numeric**) **1** of, pertaining to, or characteristic of a number or numbers (*numerical superiority*). **2** (of a figure, symbol, etc.) expressing a number. □ **numerically** *adv.*

numerology /ˌnuːˈmɜrɒlədʒi, ˌnjuː-/ n. (pl. **-ies**) the study of the supposed occult or esoteric significance of numbers. ☐ **numerological** adj. **numerologist** n.

numero uno /ˌnuːmɜroːˈuːno/ n. informal = NUMBER ONE n. 1, 2.

numerous adj. **1** (with pl.) great in number. **2** consisting of many (a numerous family). ☐ **numerously** adv.

numinous /ˈnuːmɪnəs, ˈnjuː-/ adj. **1 a** spiritual. **b** indicating the presence of a divinity. **2 a** awe-inspiring, uplifting. **b** aesthetically appealing.

numismatic /ˌnuːmɪzˈmætɪk, ˌnjuː-/ adj. of or relating to coins or medals.

numismatics n.pl. (usu. treated as sing.) the study of coins or medals, esp. from an archaeological or historic standpoint. ☐ **numismatist** n.

nummy adj. N Amer. informal delicious.

numskull var. of NUMBSKULL.

nun n. a member of a Christian community of women living under vows of poverty, chastity, and obedience, according to the rule of a particular order. ☐ **nunlike** adj. **nunnish** adj.

nunatak /ˈnʌnəˌtæk/ n. an isolated peak of rock projecting above a surface of inland ice or snow.

Nunavummiut /ˌnʌnəˈvɒmiːət/ n.pl. the people inhabiting the territory of Nunavut.

Nunc Dimittis /ˌnʌŋk dɪˈmɪtɪs/ n. Christianity Luke 2:29-32 used as a canticle.

nuncio /ˈnʌnsioː, nʊn-/ n. (pl. **-os**) Catholicism a papal ambassador to a foreign court or government.

nunnery n. (pl. **-ies**) hist. a convent.

nunny-bag n. Cdn (Nfld) a knapsack of sealskin, burlap, or canvas, used to carry supplies when hunting, sealing, etc.

nuoc mam /nwɒkˈmæm/ n. a spicy Vietnamese fish sauce.

nuptial /ˈnʌpʃəl/ ● adj. **1** of or relating to marriage or weddings. **2** Zool. of or pertaining to mating or the breeding season, esp. designating characteristic breeding coloration or behaviour. ● n. (usu. in pl.) a wedding.

nurse ● n. **1** a person professionally trained to care for the sick or infirm, assist in surgery, treat minor medical problems, and give medical advice. **2** (formerly) a person employed or trained to take charge of young children. **3** archaic = WET NURSE. ● v. **1 a** intr. work as a nurse. **b** tr. care for (a person) during sickness or infirmity. **c** tr. give medical attention to (an illness or injury). **2 a** tr. & intr. (of a woman) breast-feed (a baby). **b** intr. feed or be fed at the breast or teat; suckle. **3** tr. harbour or nurture (a grievance, hatred, etc.). **4** tr. **a** foster; promote the development of. **b** tend or cultivate (a plant) carefully. **5** tr. consume (a drink) slowly. **6** tr. hold or treat carefully or caressingly (stood nursing the teapot).

nurse practitioner n. a specially trained registered nurse who is qualified to diagnose and treat common diseases, minor injuries, etc.

nursery n. (pl. **-ies**) **1 a** a room or place equipped for young children. **b** = DAYCARE 3. **2 a** a place where plants, trees, etc., are reared for sale or transplantation. **b** a place which breeds or supports animals, esp. a pond etc. where young fry are reared. **3** any sphere or place in or by which qualities or types of people are fostered or bred.

nursery rhyme n. a simple traditional song or story in rhyme for children.

nursery school n. a school for children below the age for compulsory education, usu. between the ages of three and five.

nurse's aide n. a person who assists registered nurses in hospital or home care by performing basic tasks such as making beds, serving meals, etc.

nursing n. **1 a** the practice or profession of providing health care as a nurse. **b** the duties of a nurse. **2** (attrib.) concerned with or suitable for nursing the sick or infirm etc. **3** the action of breast-feeding.

nursing assistant n. a person who is trained to provide nursing care for patients who are not acutely ill, and to assist nurses in the care of the acutely ill.

nursing home n. an institution providing long-term health care, esp. for the elderly.

nursing mother n. a mother who is breast-feeding her baby.

nursing station n. **1** Cdn a clinic or small hospital in a remote community, staffed by nurses and visited regularly by a doctor. **2** the central desk on a hospital floor or ward where nurses complete paperwork, store medications, etc.

nurture ● n. **1** the process of bringing up or training (esp. children). **2** that which nurtures; food, nourishment. **3** the social environment as an influence on or determinant of personality (opp. NATURE 8). ● v.tr. **1** foster the development of; encourage. **2** bring up to maturity. **3** feed, nourish. ☐ **nurturer** n.

nut ● n. **1 a** a fruit consisting of a hard or tough shell around an edible kernel. **b** this kernel. **2** a small usu. square or hexagonal flat piece of metal or other material with a threaded hole through it for screwing on the end of a bolt to secure it. **3** slang **a** an obsessive enthusiast or devotee (a health-food nut). **b** a crazy or eccentric person. **4** (in pl.) coarse slang the testicles. **5** slang a person's head. ● v.intr. (**nutted**, **nutting**) seek or gather nuts (go nutting). ☐ **off one's nut** slang crazy. **a tough** (or **hard**) **nut to crack** a problem resisting easy solution. ☐ **nutlike** adj.

nutbar n. N Amer. informal an eccentric or crazy person. **2** (also **nut bar**) a bar made from chopped nuts and other vegetarian ingredients.

nut brown ● n. a dark brown colour. ● adj. (hyphenated when attrib.) of this colour.

nutcase n. slang a crazy, eccentric, or foolish person.

nutcracker n. a device for cracking the shell of a nut to reach the edible kernel.

nuthatch /ˈnʌthætʃ/ n. any small bird of the family Sittidae, climbing up and down tree trunks and feeding on nuts, insects, etc.

nuthouse n. slang a mental home or hospital.

nutmeg n. **1** an evergreen E Indian tree, Myristica fragrans, yielding a hard aromatic spheroidal seed. **2** the seed of this grated or ground and used as a spice.

nutrient ● n. any substance that provides essential nourishment for the maintenance of life. ● adj. serving as or providing nourishment.

nutriment /ˈnuːtrɪmənt, ˈnjuː-/ n. a nourishing substance.

nutrition n. **1** the process by which humans or animals utilize food for the proper functioning of the organism. **2** the scientific study of this and of dietary requirements. ☐ **nutritional** adj. **nutritionally** adv.

nutritionist n. a person who studies or is an expert on the processes of esp. human nourishment.

nutritious adj. rich in nutrients.

nutritive adj. **1** of, pertaining to, or concerned in nutrition. **2** serving as nutritious food.

nuts informal ● adj. crazy, mad, eccentric. ● interj. an expression of contempt or derision (nuts to you). ☐ **be nuts about** be enthusiastic about or very fond of.

nuts and bolts ● n.pl. the practical details. ● adj.

(usu. **nuts-and-bolts**) pertaining to the practical details.

nutsedge *n.* any of various plants of the sedge family, esp. *Cyperus esculenta*, cultivated in the southwestern US for its edible tuber.

nutshell *n.* the hard exterior covering of a nut. □ **in a nutshell** in a few words; concisely stated.

nutso *N Amer. informal* ● *n.* (*pl.* **-os**) a crazy or eccentric person. ● *adj.* crazy, eccentric.

nutsy *adj.* (**-ier, -iest**) *N Amer. informal* = NUTSO *adj.*

nut tree *n.* any tree bearing nuts, esp. a hazel.

nutty *adj.* (**-ier, -iest**) **1 a** tasting like nuts. **b** having a rich mellow flavour. **2** *informal* crazy, eccentric. **3** enthusiastic (*nutty about boats*). **4** full of or having many nuts. □ **nutty as a fruitcake** *informal* crazy, extremely eccentric. □ **nuttily** *adv.* **nuttiness** *n.*

Nuu-chah-nulth /nuːˈtʃɒnuːl/ ● *n.* **1** a member of a major linguistic group of the Wakashan living on the west coast of Vancouver Island. **2** the Wakashan language of this people. ● *adj.* of or relating to this people.

Nuxalk /nuːˈxɒlk/ ● *n.* **1** a member of a Salishan Aboriginal people of the central BC coast. **2** the Salishan language of this people. ● *adj.* of or relating to this people.

nuzzle *v.* **1** *tr.* touch or rub gently with the nose. **2** *intr.* (foll. by *against, up to*) press the nose or mouth gently. **3** *tr. & intr.* (foll. by *up to, against, into*) move so as to touch; snuggle.

NV *abbr.* Nevada (in postal use).

NW *abbr.* **1** northwest. **2** northwestern.

NWC *abbr. Cdn hist.* North West Company.

NWMP *abbr. Cdn hist.* = NORTH WEST MOUNTED POLICE.

NWO *abbr.* Northwestern Ontario.

NWT *abbr.* (also **N.W.T.**) **1** Northwest Territories. **2** *Cdn hist.* North-West Territories.

NY *abbr.* New York (also in postal use).

NYC *abbr.* New York City.

nylon *n.* **1** any of various synthetic polyamide fibres having a protein-like structure, with tough, lightweight, elastic properties, used for textiles, cord, etc. **2** a nylon fabric. **3** (in *pl.*) pantyhose or stockings made of nylon. □ **nyloned** *adj.* (in sense 3).

nymph ● *n.* **1** any of various mythological semi-divine spirits regarded as maidens and associated with aspects of nature, esp. rivers and woods. **2** esp. *literary* a beautiful young woman. **3 a** an immature form of some insects. **b** a young dragonfly or damselfly. **4** a fishing fly made to resemble the aquatic larva of a mayfly. ● *v.intr.* fish using a nymph.

nymphet /nɪmˈfet, ˈnɪmfət/ *n. informal* a sexually attractive girl or young woman.

nympho *n.* (*pl.* **-os**) *informal* a nymphomaniac.

nymphomania /ˌnɪmfəˈmeɪniə/ *n.* excessive or uncontrollable sexual desire in women. □ **nymphomaniac** *n. & adj.*

NYSE *abbr.* New York Stock Exchange.

NZ *abbr.* New Zealand.

Oo

O¹ *n.* (also **o**) (*pl.* **Os** or **O's**) **1** the fifteenth letter of the alphabet. **2** (**0**) = OH². **3** a human blood type of the ABO system. **4** a round thing, as a circle, spot, etc.

O² *abbr.* (also **O.**) Old.

O³ *symbol* the element oxygen.

O⁴ *interj.* **1** *var. of* OH¹. **2** prefixed to a name in the vocative (*O Canada*).

o' *prep.* of, on (*o'clock*; *will-o'-the-wisp*).

OAC *abbr.* **1** (also **o.a.c.**) on approved credit. **2** *Cdn* (*Ont.*) Ontario Academic Credit, a senior level high school course, taken in preparation for university.

oaf *n.* (*pl.* **oafs**) **1** an awkward lout. **2** a stupid person. □ **oafish** *adj.* **oafishness** *n.*

oak *n.* **1** any tree or shrub of the genus *Quercus* usu. having lobed leaves and bearing acorns. **2** the durable wood of this tree, used esp. for furniture and in building. **3** (*attrib.*) made of oak (*oak table*). □ **oaken** *adj.*

oakum /'oːkəm/ *n.* a loose fibre obtained by picking old rope to pieces, used esp. in caulking.

oaky *adj.* (of wine etc.) having the coconut-like aroma or flavour of oak, acquired from the wood of the barrel in which it is aged. □ **oakiness** *n.*

OAP *abbr. Cdn* Old Age Pension.

oar *n.* **1** a pole with a wide, flat blade at one end used for rowing or steering a boat by leverage against the water. **2** a rower. □ **rest on one's oars** relax one's efforts. □ **oared** *adj.* (also in *comb.*).

oarlock *n. N Amer.* a device on a boat's gunwale serving as a fulcrum for an oar and keeping it in place.

oarsman *n.* (*pl.* **-men**) a rower.

oarswoman *n.* (*pl.* **-women**) a female rower.

OAS *abbr.* **1** *Cdn* OLD AGE SECURITY. **2** Organization of American States.

oasis /oː'eɪsɪs/ *n.* (*pl.* **oases** /-siːz/) **1** a fertile spot in a desert, where water is found. **2** an area or period of calm in the midst of turbulence.

oat *n.* **1 a** a cereal plant, *Avena sativa*, cultivated in cool climates. **b** (in *pl.*) the grain yielded by this, used as food. **2** any other cereal of the genus *Avena*, esp. the wild oat, *A. fatua*. □ **feel one's oats** *informal* **1** be lively or frisky. **2** *N Amer.* revel in one's own power. **sow one's oats** (or **wild oats**) indulge in youthful excess or promiscuity. □ **oaten** *adj.* **oaty** *adj.*

oatcake *n.* a thin, unleavened, biscuit made of oatmeal, common in Scotland and northern England.

oath *n.* (*pl.* **oaths** /oːðs, oːðz/) **1** a solemn promise (often naming God) regarding a future action or behaviour. **2** a sworn promise to tell the truth, esp. in a law court. **3** a curse. □ **under** (or **on**) **oath** having sworn a solemn oath.

oatmeal ● *n.* **1 a** rolled oats (also *attrib.*: *oatmeal cookies*). **b** meal made from ground oats. **2** *N Amer.* porridge made from oats. **3** a greyish-fawn colour flecked with brown. ● *adj.* of this colour.

OB *abbr. N Amer.* **1** obstetric. **2** obstetrics. **3** obstetrician.

O/B *abbr.* (also **o/b**) outboard.

obbligato /ˌɒblɪ'ɡɒtoː/ *n.* (*pl.* **-os**) *Music* an accompaniment, usu. special and unusual in effect, forming an integral part of a composition.

obdurate /'ɒbdjʊrət, -dʊr-/ *adj.* **1** stubborn, unyielding. **2** hardened against esp. moral persuasion or influence. □ **obduracy** *n.* **obdurately** *adv.*

obeah /'oːbɪə/ *n.* a kind of sorcery or witchcraft practised esp. in the W Indies.

obedience *n.* **1** the act of obeying. **2** submission to another's rule or authority. **3** compliance with a law or command. **4** (*attrib.*) designating courses, trials, etc. pertaining to the training of dogs. □ **in obedience to** actuated by or in accordance with.

obedient *adj.* obeying or ready to obey. □ **obediently** *adv.*

obeisance /oː'beɪsəns, -biː-/ *n.* **1** homage, submission, deference (*pay obeisance*). **2** a bow, curtsy, or other respectful or submissive gesture.

obelisk /'ɒbəlɪsk/ *n.* **1** a tapering four-sided stone pillar set up as a monument or landmark. **2** = OBELUS.

obelus /'ɒbələs/ *n.* (*pl.* **obeli** /-laɪ, -liː/) a symbol (†) used as a reference mark in printed matter or to indicate that a person is deceased.

obese *adj.* very fat; corpulent. □ **obesity** *n.*

obey *v.* **1** *tr.* **a** carry out the command of (*you will obey me*). **b** carry out (a command) (*obey orders*). **2** *intr.* do what one is told to do. **3** *tr.* be actuated by, respond to (a force or impulse). □ **obeyer** *n.*

obfuscate /'ɒbfʌˌskeɪt/ *v.tr.* **1** obscure or confuse (a mind, topic, etc.). **2** stupefy, bewilder. □ **obfuscation** *n.* **obfuscatory** *adj.*

OB/GYN *abbr.* (also **ob-gyn**) *N Amer.* **1** obstetrics and gynecology. **2** obstetrician-gynecologist.

obi /'oːbiː/ *n.* (*pl.* **-s**) a sash worn with a kimono.

obit /'oːbɪt/ *n. informal* an obituary.

obiter dictum /ˌɒbɪtər 'dɪktəm/ *n.* (*pl.* ***obiter dicta*** /-tə/) **1** a judge's expression of opinion uttered in court or giving judgment, but not essential to the decision and therefore without binding authority. **2** an incidental remark.

obituary /oː'bɪtʃʊˌeri, ə'bɪt-/ *n.* (*pl.* **-ies**) **1** a notice of a death, esp. in a newspaper, usu. comprising a brief biographical sketch of the deceased. **2** (*attrib.*) of, relating to, or serving as an obituary.

object ● *n.* **1** a material thing that can be seen or touched. **2** (foll. by *of*) a person or thing to which action or feeling is directed (*the object of attention*). **3** a thing sought or aimed at; a purpose. **4** *Grammar* a noun or its equivalent governed by an active transitive verb or by a preposition. **5** *Philos.* **a** a thing external to the thinking mind or subject. **b** a thing or being of which a person thinks or has cognition. **6** *derogatory* a person or thing of esp. a pathetic or ridiculous appearance. **7** *Computing* a package of information, containing both data and a description of its manipulation, that can perform specific tasks. ● *v.* **1** *intr.* **a** (often foll. by *to*, *against*) express or feel opposition, disapproval, or reluctance; protest (*I object to being treated like this*). **b** have an objection (*I object!*). **2** *tr.* (foll. by *that* + clause) state as an objection (*objected that they were kept waiting*). □ **no object** not forming an important or restricting factor (*money is no object*). **object of the exercise** the main point of an activity. □ **objector** *n.*

objectify *v.tr.* (**-ies, -ied**) **1** make into or present as an object of perception. **2** embody, make objective, or express in an external or concrete form. **3** reduce to the status of an object. □ **objectification** *n.*

objection *n.* **1** an expression or feeling of opposition, disapproval, or protest. **2** the act of objecting. **3** an adverse reason or statement.

objectionable *adj.* **1** offensive, disapproved of. **2** open to objection. □ **objectionably** *adv.*

objective ● *adj.* **1** (of a person, an opinion, etc.) not influenced by personal bias (compare SUBJECTIVE 1). **2 a** (of writing, art, etc.) concerned with outward things or events; dealing with or stressing what is external to the mind. **b** external to or independent of the mind. **3** *Grammar* (of a case or word) constructed as or appropriate to the object of a transitive verb or preposition (compare ACCUSATIVE). **4** (of symptoms) observed by another and not only felt by the patient. ● *n.* **1** something sought or aimed at; a target, goal, or aim. **2** *Grammar* **a** the objective case. **b** a word etc. in this case. □ **objectively** *adv.* **objectivity** *n.*

objectivism *n.* **1** the tendency to lay stress on what is external to or independent of the mind. **2** *Philos.* the belief that certain things, esp. moral truths, exist apart from human knowledge or perception of them. □ **objectivist** *n.* **objectivistic** *adj.*

object lesson *n.* a practical example or illustration of some principle.

object-oriented *adj.* denoting a component-based form of computer programming in which objects communicate with other objects to order a program.

objet /ɒb'ʒei/ *n.* an object displayed as an ornament.

objet d'art /,ɒbʒei 'dɑr/ *n.* (*pl.* **objets d'art** *pronunc.* same) a small decorative or artistic object.

Oblate /'ɒbleit, ɔ:-/ ● *n.* a member of the Oblates of Mary Immaculate. ● *adj.* of or pertaining to the Oblates of Mary Immaculate.

oblate /'ɒbleit/ *n.* a person dedicated to a monastic or religious life or work.

Oblates of Mary Immaculate *n.pl.* a Roman Catholic missionary order of priests and brothers founded in France in 1816 and very active in Canada from 1841, esp. in the west and north. Abbr.: **OMI**.

oblation /oʊ'bleiʃən/ *n.* **1** a thing offered to a divine being. **2** *Christianity* the presentation of bread and wine to God in the Eucharist.

obligate *v.tr.* (usu. in *passive*; foll. by *to* + infin.) bind (a person) legally or morally.

obligation *n.* **1** a duty, what one is morally or legally required to do. **2** the constraining power of a law, precept, duty, contract, etc. **3** a binding agreement, esp. one enforceable under legal penalty. **4 a** a service, benefit, or kindness done or received (*repay an obligation*). **b** indebtedness for this (*be under an obligation*). □ **day of obligation** *Catholicism* a day on which all are required to attend Mass.

obligato *var.* of OBBLIGATO.

obligatory /ə'bligətɔri/ *adj.* **1** required by rule, law, or custom. **2** legally or morally binding. **3** creating or constituting an obligation.

oblige *v.* **1** *tr.* (foll. by *to* + infin.) constrain, compel. **2** *tr.* be binding on. **3 a** *tr.* make indebted by conferring a favour. **b** *tr.* (foll. by *with*, or *by* + verbal noun) gratify (*oblige me by leaving*). **c** *tr. & intr.* perform a service for (*will you oblige?*). **4** *tr.* (in *passive*; foll. by *to*) be indebted (*am obliged to you for your help*). **5** *intr. informal* (foll. by *with*) make a contribution of a specified kind (*Beth obliged with a song*). □ **much obliged** an expression of thanks. □ **obliger** *n.*

obliging *adj.* courteous, accommodating. □ **obligingly** *adv.* **obligingness** *n.*

oblique /ə'bliːk, ɔ:-/ ● *adj.* **1 a** slanting. **b** diverging from a straight line or course. **2** not going straight to the point; indirect. **3** *Math.* **a** (of a line, plane figure, or surface) inclined at other than a right angle. **b** (of an angle) acute or obtuse. **c** (of a cone, cylinder, etc.) with an axis not perpendicular to the plane of its base. **4** *Anat.* neither parallel nor perpendicular to the long axis of a body or limb. **5** (of a leaf) with unequal sides. **6** *Grammar* denoting any case other than the nominative or vocative. ● *n.* **1** an oblique stroke (/). **2** an oblique muscle. □ **obliquely** *adv.* **obliqueness** *n.* **obliquity** /ə'blikwiti/ *n.*

obliterate /ə'blitə,reit/ *v.tr.* **1** blot out; efface, erase, destroy. **2** leave no clear traces of. □ **obliteration** *n.*

oblivion *n.* **1** a state in which one is no longer aware of what is happening (*drink oneself into oblivion*). **2** the state of being forgotten (*rescued from oblivion*).

oblivious /ə'bliviəs/ *adj.* **1** (foll. by *to*, *of*) unaware or unconscious of. **2** (often foll. by *of*) forgetful, unmindful. □ **obliviously** *adv.* **obliviousness** *n.*

oblong ● *adj.* **1** deviating from a square form by having one long axis, esp. rectangular with adjacent sides unequal. **2** greater in breadth than in height. ● *n.* an oblong figure or object.

obloquy /'ɒblǝkwi/ *n.* (*pl.* **-quies**) **1** the state of being generally ill spoken of. **2** abuse, detraction.

obnoxious /ɒb'nɒkʃəs, əb-/ *adj.* annoying, irritating, offensive. □ **obnoxiously** *adv.* **obnoxiousness** *n.*

OBO *abbr.* N Amer. or best offer.

oboe *n.* **1** a woodwind double-reed treble instrument with a plaintive tone. **2** its player. □ **oboist** *n.*

obscene *adj.* **1** offensively or repulsively indecent, esp. by offending accepted sexual morality. **2** *informal* highly offensive or repugnant (*an obscene accumulation of wealth*). □ **obscenely** *adv.*

obscenity *n.* (*pl.* **-ies**) **1** an obscene word, action, etc. **2** the state or quality of being obscene.

obscurantism /ɒb'skjʊrən,tizəm, əb-,ɒbskjʊ'ræntizəm/ *n.* opposition to knowledge and enlightenment. □ **obscurant** /əb'skjʊrənt/ *n. & adj.* **obscurantist** *n. & adj.*

obscure ● *adj.* **1** not clearly expressed or easily understood. **2** unexplained, doubtful. **3** dark, dim. **4** indistinct; not clear. **5** hidden; remote from observation. **6 a** unnoticed. **b** undistinguished, hardly known. **7** (of a colour) dingy, dull, indefinite. ● *v.tr.* **1** prevent from being seen, heard, detected, understood, etc. **2** dim the glory of; outshine. **3** conceal. □ **obscuration** *n.* **obscurely** *adv.*

obscurity *n.* (*pl.* **-ies**) **1** the state of not being well known. **2** an obscure thing, esp. one that is difficult to understand. **3** darkness; poor light.

obsequious /ɒb'siːkwiəs/ *adj.* servilely obedient or attentive. □ **obsequiously** *adv.* **obsequiousness** *n.*

observance *n.* **1** the act or process of keeping or performing a law, duty, custom, ritual, etc. **2** an act of a religious or ceremonial character; a customary rite. **3** the rule of a religious order.

observant *adj.* **1** acute or diligent in taking notice. **2** attentive in esp. religious observances (*an observant few*). □ **observantly** *adv.*

observation *n.* **1 a** an act or instance of noticing; the condition of being noticed. **b** an observed truth or fact; a thing learned by observing. **2** perception; the faculty of taking notice. **3** a comment on something heard or noticed etc. **4 a** the scientific study or investigation of a phenomenon etc. **b** a measurement etc. obtained from this. **c** the noting of the symptoms of a patient, the behaviour of a suspect, etc. **5** the taking of the sun's or another celestial body's altitude to find a latitude or longitude. **6** *Military* the watching of a fortress or hostile position. □ **under observation** being watched or monitored. □ **observational** *adj.* **observationally** *adv.*

observation deck *n.* a platform or area designed for viewing e.g. animals at a wildlife sanctuary etc.

observatory *n.* (*pl.* **-ies**) a room or building equipped for the observation of natural, esp. astronomical or meteorological, phenomena.

observe *v.tr.* **1** (often foll. by *that, how* + clause) perceive, note; take notice of. **2** watch carefully. **3 a** follow or adhere to (a law, command, method, principle, etc.). **b** keep or adhere to (an appointed time). **c** maintain (silence). **d** duly perform (a rite). **e** celebrate (an anniversary). **4** examine and note (phenomena) without the aid of experiment. **5** (often foll. by *that* + clause) say, esp. by way of comment. □ **observable** *adj.* **observably** *adv.*

observer *n.* **1** a person who observes. **2** a person who attends a conference etc. to note the proceedings but does not participate.

obsess *v.* **1** *tr.* (often in *passive*) preoccupy, haunt; fill the mind of (a person) continually. **2** *intr.* *N Amer.* (foll. by *about, on, over*) be continually preoccupied with. □ **obsessed** *adj.* (also in *comb.*). **obsessive** *adj. & n.* **obsessively** *adv.* **obsessiveness** *n.*

obsession *n.* **1** the act of obsessing or the state of being obsessed. **2** a persistent idea or thought dominating a person's mind. **3** a condition in which such ideas are present. □ **obsessional** *adj.* **obsessionality** *n.* **obsessionally** *adv.*

obsessive-compulsive *adj.* of or designating a disorder in which a person has an obsessive compulsion to perform meaningless acts repeatedly.

obsidian / ɒbˈsɪdiən, əb-/ *n.* a dark glassy volcanic rock formed from hardened lava.

obsolescent / ˌɒbsəˈlesənt/ *adj.* becoming obsolete; going out of use or date. □ **obsolescence** *n.*

obsolete *adj.* **1** disused, discarded, antiquated, outmoded, out of date. **2** *Biol.* less developed than formerly or than in a cognate species; rudimentary. □ **obsoletely** *adv.* **obsoleteness** *n.*

obstacle *n.* a person or thing that obstructs progress.

obstacle course *n.* (also **obstacle race**) **1** a course or race in which various obstacles have to be negotiated. **2** an endeavour in which there are many problems to overcome.

obstetric *adj.* (also **obstetrical**) of or relating to childbirth and associated processes. □ **obstetrically** *adv.*

obstetrician / ˌɒbstəˈtrɪʃən/ *n.* a physician specializing in obstetrics.

obstetrics *n.* the branch of medicine and surgery concerned with pregnancy and childbirth.

obstinate *adj.* **1** stubborn, intractable. **2** firmly adhering to one's chosen course of action or opinion despite dissuasion. **3** not readily responding to treatment etc. □ **obstinacy** *n.* **obstinately** *adv.*

obstreperous / ɒbˈstrepərəs, əb-/ *adj.* **1** unruly; resisting control. **2** noisy, vociferous. □ **obstreperously** *adv.* **obstreperousness** *n.*

obstruct *v.tr.* **1** block up; make hard or impossible to pass along or through. **2** prevent or retard the progress of; impede. **3** block (a view). □ **obstructor** *n.*

obstruction *n.* **1** the act or an instance of blocking; the state of being blocked. **2** the act of making or the state of becoming more or less impassable. **3** an obstacle or blockage. **4** the retarding of progress by deliberate delays. **5** *Sport* the act of unlawfully obstructing another player. **6** *Med.* a blockage in a bodily passage, esp. in an intestine. □ **obstructionism** *n.* **obstructionist** *n.* (both in sense 4).

obstruction of justice *n.* interference with the course of justice by influencing jurors, intimidating witnesses, being influenced by bribes or threats as a juror or witness, etc.

obstructive *adj.* causing or intended to cause an obstruction. □ **obstructiveness** *n.*

obtain *v.* **1** *tr.* acquire, secure; have granted to one. **2** *intr.* be prevalent or established or in vogue; apply, hold good. □ **obtainable** *adj.* **obtainability** *n.*

obtrude / ɒbˈtruːd, əb-/ *v.* **1** *intr.* be or become obtrusive. **2** *tr.* (often foll. by *on, upon*) thrust forward (oneself, one's opinion, etc.) importunately.

obtrusive *adj.* unpleasantly or unduly noticeable. □ **obtrusively** *adv.* **obtrusiveness** *n.*

obtuse / ɒbˈtuːs, əb-, -tjuːs/ *adj.* **1 a** dull-witted; slow to understand. **b** difficult to understand; obscure. **2** of blunt form; not sharp. **3** (of an angle) more than 90° and less than 180°. **4** (of pain or the senses) dull; not acute. □ **obtusely** *adv.* **obtuseness** *n.*

obverse ● *n.* **1 a** the side of a coin or medal etc. bearing the head or principal design. **b** this design (*compare* REVERSE 7). **2** the front or proper or top side of a thing. **3** the counterpart of a fact or truth. ● *adj.* that is an obverse. □ **obversely** *adv.*

obviate / ˈɒbvi.eɪt/ *v.tr.* get around or do away with (a need, inconvenience, etc.). □ **obviation** *n.*

obvious *adj.* **1** easily seen or recognized or understood; palpable, indubitable. **2** not subtle; revealing sentiments, intentions, etc. clearly. □ **obviously** *adv.* **obviousness** *n.*

OC *abbr.* Officer of the Order of Canada.

ocarina / ˌɒkəˈriːnə/ *n.* a small egg-shaped wind instrument with finger holes.

occasion ● *n.* **1 a** a special or noteworthy event or happening. **b** the time or occurrence of this (*on the occasion of their marriage*). **2** (often foll. by *for*, or *to* + infin.) a reason, ground, or justification (*there is no occasion to be angry*). **3** a juncture suitable for doing something; an opportunity. **4** an immediate but subordinate or incidental cause (*the assassination was the occasion of the war*). ● *v.tr.* **1** be the occasion or cause of; bring about esp. incidentally. **2** (foll. by *to* + infin.) cause (a person or thing to do something). □ **on occasion** now and then; when the need arises. **rise to the occasion** produce the necessary will, energy, ability, etc., in unusually demanding circumstances. **take the** (or **this** etc.) **occasion** (foll. by *to* + infin.) make use of the opportunity.

occasional *adj.* **1** happening, done, consumed, etc. infrequently; not regular. **2** made or meant for, or associated with, a special occasion. **3** acting on a special occasion. **4** constituting or serving as the occasion or incidental cause of something. **5** (of furniture etc.) used from time to time and for various purposes. □ **occasionally** *adv.*

Occident / ˈɒksɪdənt/ *n.* *literary* **1** (prec. by *the*) the West. **2** western Europe. **3** Europe, the Americas, or both, as distinct from the Orient. **4** European in contrast to Oriental civilization.

occidental ● *adj.* **1** of the Occident, as distinct from oriental. **2** western. **3** of western Europe. **4** relating to European or Western (in contrast to oriental) civilization. ● *n.* (**Occidental**) a native or inhabitant of the Occident.

occiput /'ɒksɪˌpʌt/ n. the back of the head. □ **occipital** adj.

occlude /ə'kluːd/ v.tr. **1** stop up or close (pores, an orifice, a passage, etc.). **2** Chem. absorb and retain (gases or impurities).

occlusion n. **1** the act or process of occluding. **2** Meteorol. a phenomenon in which the cold front of a depression overtakes the warm front, causing upward displacement of warm air between them. **3** Dentistry the position of the teeth when the jaws are closed. **4** the blockage or closing of a hollow organ etc. (coronary occlusion). □ **occlusive** adj.

occult ● adj. **1** involving the supernatural; mystical. **2** kept secret; esoteric. **3** mysterious; beyond the range of ordinary knowledge. **4** Med. not obvious on inspection. ● n. (prec. by the) supernatural phenomena. ● v.tr. (of a celestial body) conceal (an apparently smaller body) by passing or being in front of it. □ **occultation** n. **occultism** n. **occultist** n.

occupancy n. (pl. **-ies**) **1** the act, condition, or fact of occupying something or of being occupied. **2** N Amer. the number of people occupying or meant to be occupying a room, vehicle, etc. (high-occupancy vehicle).

occupant n. **1** a person who occupies, resides in, or is in a place etc. **2** a person holding property, esp. land, in actual possession. **3** a person who establishes a title by taking possession of something previously without an established owner.

occupation n. **1** what occupies one; a means of passing one's time. **2** a person's temporary or regular employment. **3** the act of occupying or state of being occupied. **4 a** the act of taking or holding possession of (a country, district, etc.) by military force. **b** the state or time of this. **5** tenure, occupancy.

occupational adj. **1** of or in the nature of an occupation or occupations. **2** (of a disease, etc.) rendered more likely by one's occupation.

occupational hazard n. **1** a risk or danger connected with a particular job. **2** an unpleasant but not necessarily dangerous consequence of one's job, hobby, etc.

occupational therapy n. mental or physical activity designed to assist recovery from disease or injury. □ **occupational therapist** n.

occupy v.tr. (**-ies, -ied**) **1** reside in; be the tenant of. **2** take up or fill (space or time or a place). **3** hold (a position or office). **4** take military possession of (a country, region, town, strategic position). **5** place oneself in (a building etc.) forcibly or without authority. **6** (usu. in passive; often foll. by in, with) keep busy or engaged. □ **occupier** n.

occur v.intr. (**occurred, occurring**) **1** come into being as an event or process at or during some time; happen. **2** exist or be encountered in some place or conditions (fossils occur throughout this area). **3** (foll. by to; usu. foll. by that + clause) come into the mind of, esp. as an unexpected or casual thought.

occurrence n. **1** the act or an instance of occurring. **2** an incident or event. **3** the rate or measure of occurring; incidence.

OCdt abbr. Cdn OFFICER CADET.

ocean n. **1 a** a large expanse of sea, esp. each of the main areas called the Atlantic, Pacific, Indian, Arctic, and Antarctic Oceans. **b** (usu. prec. by the) these collectively; the sea. **2** (often in pl.) a very large expanse or quantity of anything (oceans of time). □ **oceanward** adv. & adj.

oceanfront ● attrib.adj. on the shore of an ocean. ● n. a property or land on the shore of an ocean.

ocean-going adj. (of a ship) able to cross oceans.

Oceania /ˌoːʃi' æniə, ˌoːsi-/ n. the islands of the Pacific and adjacent seas, sometimes including Australasia and the Malay Archipelago. □ **Oceanian** adj. & n.

oceanic /ˌoːʃi'ænɪk, ˌoːsi-/ adj. **1** of, like, or near the ocean. **2** (of a climate) governed by the ocean. **3** of the part of the ocean beyond the edge of the continental shelf. **4** immense, vast. **5** (**Oceanic**) of Oceania.

oceanography /ˌoːʃə'nɒgrəfi/ n. the study of the oceans. □ **oceanographer** n. **oceanographic** adj.

ocean perch n. **1** the flesh of various species of redfish marketed as food. **2** any of various fish of the scorpion fish family.

oceanside attrib.adj. near, by, on, or along the shore of an ocean (oceanside resort).

ocellus /ɒ'seləs/ n. (pl. **ocelli** /-laɪ/) **1** each of the simple, as opposed to compound, eyes of insects etc. **2** a spot of colour surrounded by a ring of a different colour on the wing of a butterfly etc.

ocelot /'ɒsəˌlɒt, 'oː-/ n. **1** a medium-sized cat, Felis pardalis, native to S and Central America, having a deep yellow or orange coat with black striped and spotted markings. **2** its fur.

ochre /'oːkər/ (US also **ocher**) ● n. **1** a mineral of clay and ferric oxide, used as a pigment varying from light yellow to brown or red. **2** a pale brownish yellow. ● adj. of the colour of ochre.

o'clock adv. **1** of the clock (used to specify the hour) (6 o'clock). **2** used after a numeral to indicate direction or bearing with reference to an imaginary clock face, twelve o'clock being directly above or in front of the observer or at the top of a circular target etc.

OCR abbr. optical character recognition.

Oct. abbr. October.

octa- comb. form (also **oct-** before a vowel) eight.

octagon /'ɒktəgɒn/ n. **1** a plane figure with eight sides and angles. **2** an object or building with this cross-section. □ **octagonal** /-'tægənəl/ adj.

octahedron /ˌɒktə'hiːdrən/ n. (pl. **-s** or **-dra** /-drə/) **1** a solid figure contained by eight plane faces. **2** a crystal etc. in the form of an octahedron. □ **octahedral** adj.

octane n. a colourless inflammable hydrocarbon of the alkane series.

octane number n. (also **octane rating**) a figure indicating the anti-knock properties of a fuel.

octave /'ɒktɪv/ n. **1** Music **a** a series of eight notes occupying the interval between (and including) two notes, one having twice or half the frequency of vibration of the other. **b** this interval. **c** each of the two notes at the extremes of this interval. **d** these two notes sounding together. **2** a group or stanza of eight lines; an octet. **3 a** the seventh day after a church festival. **b** a period of eight days including a festival and its octave. **4** a group of eight.

octavo /ɒk'tɒvoː, ɒk'teɪvoː/ n. (pl. **-os**) **1** a size of book or page given by folding a standard sheet three times to form a quire of eight leaves. **2** a book or sheet of this size. Abbr.: **8vo**.

octet /ɒk'tet/ n. **1** Music **a** a composition for eight voices etc. **b** the performers of such a piece. **2** a group of eight. **3** the first eight lines of a sonnet.

octo- comb. form (also **oct-** before a vowel) eight.

October n. the tenth month of the year.

October Crisis n. Cdn the kidnapping of the British diplomat James Cross and the Quebec labour and immigration minister Pierre Laporte by cells of the Front de Libération du Québec in October of 1970.

octogenarian /ˌɒktədʒə'neriən/ ● n. a person from

80 to 89 years old. ● *adj.* **1** of this age. **2** of octogenarians.

octopus *n.* (*pl.* **octopuses** or **octopi** /'ɒktəpai/) any mollusc of the genus *Octopus* having eight suckered arms, a soft saclike body, and strong beaklike jaws.

ocular /'ɒkjʊlər/ ● *adj.* of or connected with the eyes or sight; visual. ● *n.* the eyepiece of an optical instrument. □ **ocularly** *adv.*

OD *esp. N Amer. slang* ● *n.* an overdose, esp. of a narcotic drug. ● *v.intr.* (**ODs**, **OD'd**, **ODing**) take an overdose.

O.D. *abbr.* Doctor of Optometry.

Odawa /oːˈdɒwə/ ● *n.* **1** a member of an Aboriginal people formerly living along the Ottawa River, and now living esp. on Manitoulin Island. **2** the Ojibwa dialect of this people. ● *adj.* of or relating to this people or their language.

odd *adj.* **1** strange, queer, eccentric. **2** casual, occasional, unconnected (*odd jobs*). **3** not normally noticed or considered; unpredictable (*picks up odd bargains*). **4** additional; beside the reckoning (*earned the odd dollar*). **5 a** (of numbers such as 3 and 5) not integrally divisible by two. **b** (of things or persons numbered consecutively) bearing such a number (*no parking on odd dates*). **6** left over when the rest have been distributed or divided into pairs (*odd socks*). **7** detached from a set or series (*a few odd volumes*). **8** (appended to a number, sum, etc.) somewhat more than (*forty odd; forty-odd people*). **9** by which a round number, given sum, etc., is exceeded (*we have 102—what'll we do with the odd 2?*). □ **oddly** *adv.* **oddness** *n.*

oddball *informal* ● *n.* an odd or eccentric person. ● *adj.* strange, bizarre.

Oddfellow *n.* a member of a fraternal society similar to the Freemasons.

oddity *n.* (*pl.* **-ies**) **1** a strange person, thing, or occurrence. **2** a peculiar trait. **3** oddness.

odd jobs *n.pl.* small, esp. domestic, jobs of various types, usu. done for others.

odd man out *n.* (also **odd one out**) **1** a person or thing differing from all the others in a group in some respect. **2** a method of selecting one of three or more persons e.g. by tossing a coin.

odd-man rush *n. Hockey* a situation in which the players leading an offensive rush outnumber the skaters defending against it.

oddments *n.pl.* miscellaneous articles.

odds *n.pl.* **1** the ratio between the amounts staked by the parties to a bet, based on the expected probability either way. **2 a** the chances or balance of probability in favour of or against some result (*the odds are against it*). **b** this probability expressed as a ratio (*the odds against winning are 50 to 1*). **3** the balance of advantage (*the odds are in your favour*). **4** an equalizing allowance to a weaker competitor; a handicap. **5** a difference giving an advantage (*it makes no odds*). □ **at odds** (often foll. by *with*) in conflict or at variance. **by all odds** certainly. **take odds** accept a bet.

odds and ends *n.pl.* miscellaneous articles.

odds-on *attrib.adj.* designating the outcome or chance most favoured by the odds (*odds-on favourite*).

ode *n.* **1** a lyric poem, usu. rhymed and in the form of an address, in varied or irregular metre. **2** *hist.* a poem meant to be sung. **3** an artistic creation praising something (*this film is an ode to fly fishing*).

odious /'oːdiəs/ *adj.* hateful, repulsive. □ **odiously** *adv.* **odiousness** *n.*

odium /'oːdiəm/ *n.* **1** a general or widespread dislike or reprobation incurred by a person or associated with an action. **2** hatred.

odometer /oːˈdɒmətər/ *n.* an instrument for measuring the distance travelled by a vehicle.

odorous *adj.* having a scent or odour.

odour *n.* (also **odor**) **1** a distinctive, usu. unpleasant smell. **2** a lasting esp. unpleasant quality or trace of something (*an odour of intolerance*). **3** regard, repute (*in bad odour*). □ **odourless** *adj.* (in sense 1).

odyssey *n.* (*pl.* **-eys**) a series of wanderings; a long adventurous journey.

OE *abbr.* Old English.

OECD *abbr.* Organization for Economic Co-operation and Development.

oedema /ɪˈdiːmə/ *Brit. var. of* EDEMA.

Oedipus complex /'iːdɪpəs/ *n. Psych.* (according to Freud etc.) the complex of emotions aroused in a young (esp. male) child by a subconscious sexual desire for the parent of the opposite sex and wish to exclude the parent of the same sex. □ **Oedipal** *adj.*

OEM *abbr.* original equipment manufacturer.

oenology /iːˈnɒlədʒi/ *n.* the study of wines. □ **oenological** *adj.* **oenologist** *n.*

o'er /'oːr/ *adv. & prep. literary* = OVER.

oesophagus *esp. Brit. var. of* ESOPHAGUS.

oestrogen *Brit. var. of* ESTROGEN.

oestrus *Brit. var. of* ESTRUS.

oeuvre /'ɜːvrə/ *n.* (*pl.* **oeuvres** *pronunc.* same) **1** the works of an author, painter, composer, etc., esp. regarded collectively. **2** a work of art, music, etc.

OF *abbr.* Baseball outfielder.

of *prep.* connecting a noun (often a verbal noun) or pronoun with a preceding noun, adjective, adverb, or verb, expressing a wide range of relations broadly describable as follows: **1** origin, cause, or authorship (*paintings of Thomson; people of Rome; died of malnutrition*). **2** the material or substance constituting or identifying a thing (*a house of logs; built of brick*). **3** belonging, connection, or possession (*articles of clothing; the head of the business*). **4** identity or close relation (*the city of Halifax; a pound of apples; a fool of a man*). **5** removal, separation, or privation (*north of the city; got rid of them*). **6** reference, direction, or respect (*beware of dog; suspected of lying; short of money*). **7** objective relation (*love of music*). **8** partition, classification, or inclusion (*no more of that; part of the story; a friend of mine*). **9** description, quality, or condition (*a person of tact; a girl of ten; on the point of leaving*). **10** *N Amer.* time in relation to the following hour (*a quarter of three*). □ **be of** possess intrinsically; give rise to (*is of great interest*). □ **of all** designating the (nominally) least likely or expected example (*you of all people!*). **of all the nerve** (or **cheek** etc.) an exclamation of indignation at a person's impudence etc. **of an evening** (or **morning** etc.) *informal* **1** on most evenings (or mornings etc.). **2** at some time in the evenings (or mornings etc.). **of it** *informal* concerning what is being discussed (*had a hard time of it*).

off ● *adv.* **1 a** away; at or to a distance in time or space (*drove off; is three miles off; summer is not far off*). **b** distant or remote in fact, nature, likelihood, etc. **2** out of position; not on or touching or attached (*has come off; take your coat off*). **3** so as to be rid of (*sleep it off*). **4** so as to break continuity or continuance; stopped, cancelled (*turn off the radio; take a day off; the wedding is off*). **5** starting a journey, race, etc. (*she's off to Hong Kong*). **6** to the end; entirely; so as to be clear (*finish off; pay off*). **7** situated as regards money, supplies, etc. (*is not very well off*). **8** offstage (*noises off*). **9** taken from the price (*all shirts are 10 per cent off*). **10** into operation; activated (*the alarm went off at 6:30*). **11** (of crops) harvested (*get the wheat off*). ● *prep.* **1 a** from;

away or down or up from (*fell off the chair*; *took $10 off the price*; *jumped off the edge*). **b** not on (*was already off the ice*). **2 a** (temporarily) relieved of or abstaining from (*off duty*; *am off my diet*). **b** not attracted by for the time being (*off their food*; *off drinking*). **c** not achieving or doing one's best in (*off one's game*). **3** using as a source or means of support (*live off the land*). **4** leading from; not far from (*a laneway off King Street*). **5** at a short distance to sea from (*sank off Cape Horn*). **6** *informal* from (a specified source) (*bought it off my neighbour*). ● *adj.* **1** far, further (*the off side of the wall*). **2** (of a part of a vehicle, animal, or road) right (*the off front wheel*) (*opp.* NEAR *adj.* 3). **3** (*predic.*) *informal* **a** strange, eccentric (*she's a little off*). **b** *Brit.* & *Cdn* unwell (*am feeling a bit off*). **c** (of food etc.) unfit for consumption; no longer fresh. **4** not up to the usual standard (*his game was off*). **5** not on; no longer in operation or effect (*the radio is off*; *our agreement is off*). **6** decreased in price, quantity etc. (*tourism is off this summer*). ● *v.tr. N Amer. slang* kill, murder. ● *n. N Amer.* (in *comb.*) a competition (*cook-off*). □ **off and on** intermittently. **off of** *slang disputed* = OFF *prep.* 1a (*picked it up off of the floor*). ¶This use of *off of* is non-standard and should be avoided in writing.

off-air *adj.* & *adv.* **1** of or relating to the reception of broadcast programs. **2** associated with a radio or TV program but not broadcast (*off-air comments*).

offal /ˈɒfəl/ *n.* **1** the less valuable edible parts of a carcass, esp. the entrails and internal organs. **2** refuse or waste stuff.

offbeat ● *adj.* **1** eccentric, unconventional. **2** *Music* not coinciding with the beat. ● *n. Music* any of the normally unaccented beats in a bar.

off-Broadway ● *n.* (often *attrib.*) New York City theatres, theatrical productions, or theatre life outside the area of Broadway, characteristically being more experimental and less commercial. ● *adv.* occurring outside New York City's main theatre district.

off-camera *adj.* & *adv.* out of the range of a film or television camera.

off-campus *adj.* & *adv.* away from a university or college campus.

off-centre ● *adj.* **1** slightly away from the centre; not quite coinciding with a central position. **2** unconventional, eccentric (*off-centre ideas*). ● *adv.* positioned away from the centre.

off chance *n.* (prec. by *the*) the slight possibility.

off-colour *adj.* esp. *N Amer.* slightly indecent or obscene (*an off-colour joke*).

offcut *n.* a remnant of wood etc. after cutting.

off-day *n.* **1** a day when one is not at one's best. **2** *N Amer.* a day off from work, sports training, etc.

off-duty *adj.* **1** not engaged in one's regular work (*an off-duty police officer*). **2** pertaining to or during the time when one is not at work (*off-duty activities*).

offence *n.* (also **offense**) **1** an illegal act; a breach of the law. **2** resentment of a perceived insult etc. (*no offence was meant*). **3** the act of attacking or taking the offensive. **4** an offensive person or thing. **5** esp. *N Amer. Sport* **a** the role of scoring points, goals, etc. for one's team (*he plays offence*). **b** the plays, moves, or tactics for achieving this. **c** the players on a team who perform this role. □ **give offence** cause hurt feelings. **take offence** suffer hurt feelings.

offend *v.* **1** *tr.* cause offence to or resentment in; wound the feelings of. **2** *tr.* displease or anger. **3** *intr.* commit an illegal act. **4** *intr.* (often foll. by *against*) do wrong; transgress. □ **offender** *n.* **offending** *adj.*

offensive ● *adj.* **1** giving or meant or likely to give offence; insulting (*offensive language*). **2** disgusting,

foul-smelling, nauseous, repulsive. **3 a** aggressive, attacking. **b** (of a weapon) meant for use in attack. **4** esp. *N Amer. Sport* of or relating to a team in possession of the ball, puck, etc. (*offensive line*). ● *n.* **1** (usu. prec. by *the*) an aggressive action or attitude (*take the offensive*). **2** an attack, an offensive campaign or stroke. **3** aggressive or forceful action in pursuit of a cause (*a peace offensive*). □ **offensively** *adv.* **offensiveness** *n.*

offer ● *v.* **1** *tr.* present for acceptance or refusal or consideration. **2** *intr.* (foll. by *to* + infin.) express readiness or show intention (*offered to take the children*). **3** *tr.* provide; give an opportunity for. **4** *tr.* make available for sale. **b** propose as payment; bid (*offered $30 for the table*). **5** *tr.* (of a thing) present to one's attention or consideration (*each day offers new opportunities*). **6** *tr.* present (a sacrifice, prayer, etc.) to a deity. **7** *intr.* present itself; occur (*as opportunity offers*). **8** *tr.* give an opportunity for (battle) to an enemy. **9** *tr.* attempt, or try to show (violence, resistance, etc.). **10** *tr.* say tentatively or helpfully (*'It's a nice day,' she offered*). ● *n.* **1** an expression of readiness to do or give if desired, or to buy or sell (for a certain amount). **2** an amount offered. **3** a proposal (esp. of marriage). **4** a bid. **5** *Law* a proposal made by one party that will establish a binding contract if accepted unconditionally by the party to whom it is made.

offering *n.* **1** a contribution, esp. of money, to a church. **2** a thing offered as a religious sacrifice or token of devotion. **3** anything contributed or offered.

offertory /ˈɒfətɔri, ˈɒfrə-/ *n.* (*pl.* **-ies**) **1** *Christianity* **a** the offering of the bread and wine at the Eucharist. **b** a hymn accompanying this. **2 a** the collection of money at a religious service. **b** music played or sung while this is collected. **c** the money collected.

off-field *adj. Sport* situated or taking place away from a playing field.

off-gas ● *n.* a gas which is given off, esp. one emitted as the by-product of a chemical process. ● *v.intr.* emit a chemical, esp. a harmful one, in the form of a gas. □ **off-gassing** *n.*

offhand ● *adj.* curt or casual in manner. ● *adv.* **1** in an offhand manner. **2** without preparation or premeditation. □ **offhanded** *adj.* **offhandedly** *adv.* **offhandedness** *n.*

off-hour ● *n.* an hour when one is not working. ● *adj.* of or taking place during an off-hour.

off-ice *adj.* & *adv. Hockey etc.* not occurring or positioned on the ice (*off-ice training*; *off-ice official*).

office *n.* **1 a** a room or building used as a place of business, esp. for clerical or administrative work. **b** the employees who work in such a place of business (*called the office together*). **2** a room or department or building for a particular kind of business (*post office*). **3** the local centre of a large business (*our London office*). **4** *N Amer.* **a** a suite of rooms in which a doctor, dentist, etc. treats patients. **b** the staff of this. **5** a position with duties attached to it; a place of authority or trust or service, esp. of a public nature. **6** tenure of an official position, esp. that of a government minister or of the party forming the government (*hold office*; *out of office for 13 years*). **7** (**Office**) a government agency, or a subdivision of such an agency (*Land Titles Office*). **8** a duty attaching to one's position; a task or function. **9** (usu. in *pl.*) a piece of kindness or attention; a service (*through the good offices of*). **10** *Christianity* **a** an authorized form of worship (*Office for the Dead*). **b** (in full **divine office**) the daily service recited by those in Catholic orders (*say the office*). **11** a ceremonial duty.

office block *n.* a large building designed to contain business offices.

office-holder *n.* an esp. elected official.

office hours *n.* the hours during which business is normally conducted.

officer ● *n.* **1** a person holding a position of authority or trust, esp. one with a commission in the armed services, in the mercantile marine, or on a passenger ship. **2** a policeman or policewoman. **3** a holder of a post in a society or organization, e.g. the president or secretary. **4** a holder of a public, civil, or ecclesiastical office; an appointed or elected functionary (usu. with a qualifying word: *probation officer; returning officer*). **5** a person who acts in an official capacity in a company. **6** a bailiff (*the sheriff's officer*). **7** (**Officer**) a member of the grade below Companion in the Order of Canada. ● *v.tr.* **1** provide with officers. **2** act as the commander of.

officer cadet *n.* *Cdn & Brit.* a person training to be an officer in the armed forces. Abbr.: **OCdt**.

office tower *n.* a tall building housing offices.

office worker *n.* an employee in a business office.

official ● *adj.* **1** of or relating to an office (see OFFICE *n.* 5, 6) or its tenure or duties. **2** (often *derogatory*) characteristic of officials and bureaucracy. **3** emanating from or attributable to a person in office. **4** holding office; employed in a public capacity. **5** formal; ceremonial (*an official reception*). ● *n.* a person holding office or engaged in official duties. □ **officialdom** *n.* **officially** *adv.*

official language *n.* the language or languages under which government services etc. must be provided to citizens upon their request.

official opposition *n.* *Cdn & Brit.* (in a legislature) the opposition party which has the most seats and is thereby granted certain parliamentary privileges.

official receiver *n.* see RECEIVER 3.

official secrets *n.pl.* *Cdn & Brit.* confidential information involving national security.

officiate /əˈfɪʃɪˌeɪt/ *v.* **1** *intr.* act in an official capacity, esp. on a particular occasion. **2** *intr.* perform a religious service etc. **3** *tr. & intr.* act as a referee etc. at (a competition or game). □ **officiation** *n.* **officiator** *n.*

officious /əˈfɪʃəs/ *adj.* **1** asserting one's authority aggressively; domineering. **2** intrusive or excessively enthusiastic in offering help etc.; meddlesome. □ **officiously** *adv.* **officiousness** *n.*

offing *n.* the more distant part of the sea in view. □ **in the offing** not far away; likely to happen soon.

off-island ● *adj.* situated or occurring away from an island, esp. (in Canada) PEI. ● *adv.* away from an island, esp. (in Canada) PEI (*travelled off-island*).

off-key *adj.* **1** out of tune. **2** not suitable or appropriate; incongruous.

off-line ● *adj.* **1** *Computing* (of a computer terminal or process) not directly controlled by or connected to a central processing unit. **2** designating or relating to the initial stage of video editing, in which the material is viewed and the desired selections are made. ● *adv.* with a delay between the production of data and its processing; while not directly controlled by or connected to a central processing unit.

off-load *v.tr.* **1** get rid of (esp. something unpleasant) by giving it to someone else. **2** unload (cargo etc.).

off-peak ● *adj.* used or for use at times other than those of greatest demand. ● *adv.* at times other than those of greatest demand.

off-piste *attrib.adj. & adv.* *Skiing* away from prepared ski runs.

off-price *adj.* *N Amer.* involving merchandise sold at a lower price than that recommended by the manufacturer.

off-putting *adj.* **1** disconcerting; disturbing. **2** repellent; unpleasant. □ **off-puttingly** *adv.*

off-ramp *n.* *N Amer.* a sloping one-way road leading off a highway.

off-reserve *Cdn* ● *adj.* located on or inhabiting land which is not part of a designated reserve for Aboriginal people (*off-reserve housing*). ● *adv.* not on a reserve.

off-road ● *attrib.adj.* (of a vehicle etc.) designed for rough terrain or for cross-country driving. ● *adv.* away from the road, on rough terrain.

off-roading *n.* the activity of driving over rough terrain, esp. as a sport. □ **off-roader** *n.*

off-sale *Cdn* (*BC*, *Alta.*, *& North*) ● *n.* **1** the sale of liquor for consumption elsewhere than at the place of sale. **2** (usu. in *pl.*) an alcoholic drink sold for consumption elsewhere. ● *adj.* designating a place where liquor is sold in this manner (*an off-sale outlet*).

off-screen ● *adj.* **1** not appearing on a movie, television, or computer screen. **2** (*attrib.*) in private life or in real life as opposed to a film or television role. ● *adv.* **1** outside the view presented by a movie, television or computer screen. **2** in private life or in real life as opposed to a film or television role.

off-season *n.* **1** *Sport* the period following the conclusion of the regular season and playoffs, during which no competition takes place. **2** a time when business etc. is slack (often *attrib.*: *off-season prices*).

offset ● *n.* **1** a side shoot from a plant serving for propagation. **2** an offshoot or scion. **3** a consideration or amount diminishing or neutralizing the effect of a contrary one. **4** (often *attrib.*) a method of printing in which ink is transferred from a plate or stone to a uniform rubber surface and from there to paper etc. (*offset litho*). ● *v.tr.* (**-setting**; *past* and *past part.* **-set**) **1** counterbalance, compensate. **2** place out of line. **3** print by the offset process.

offshoot *n.* **1** a side shoot or branch. **2** a thing which originated as a branch of something else.

offshore ● *adj.* **1 a** situated at sea some distance from the shore. **b** of or pertaining to fishing conducted from large vessels on the grounds and banks at some distance from the shore. **2** (of the wind) blowing seawards. **3 a** (of goods, funds, etc.) made or registered abroad. **b** living abroad (*offshore investors*). ● *adv.* **1** at some distance from the shore. **2** in a direction away from the shore. **3** abroad.

offside ● *adj.* **1** *Hockey, Soccer, etc.* **a** (of a player) in an illegal position ahead of the ball or puck. **b** of or relating to such a position (*offside pass*). **2** not in agreement with. ● *adv.* in an offside position (*caught offside*). ● *n.* (/ˈɒfsaɪd/) the infraction of being offside.

off-site *adj. & adv.* away from a site; removed from the premises (*off-site storage*).

off-speed *adj.* *Baseball* (of a pitch or ball) delivered at less than full speed.

offspring *n.* (*pl.* same) **1** a person's child or children or descendant(s). **2** an animal's young or descendant(s). **3** something derived or descended from another (*ringette is an offspring of hockey*).

offstage *attrib.adj. & adv.* **1** not on the stage and so not visible or audible to the audience. **2** in private or real life as opposed to a theatre etc. role.

off-the-rack *adj.* *N Amer.* (esp. of clothes) ready-made.

off-the-shelf ● *attrib.adj.* (of goods) supplied ready-made; available from existing stock. ● *adv.* (**off the shelf**) ready-made; from existing stock.

off-the-shoulder *attrib.adj.* (of a dress etc.) leaving the shoulders bare.

off-the-wall *adj. slang* crazy, absurd, outlandish.

off-track *adj.* **1** situated or taking place away from a racetrack (*off-track betting*). **2** (of skiing, hiking, etc.) not performed on a groomed trail. **3** situated or taking place away from a railway track. **4** (**off track**) away from the subject, goal, etc.

off-white ● *n.* a white colour with a grey or yellowish tinge. ● *adj.* of this colour.

off-world *esp. US* ● *n.* (esp. in science fiction) any place away from earth, or from that world which serves as the location of a given narrative. ● *adj.* involving, located in, inhabiting, or coming from a place outside the native world. ● *adv.* away from the native world. □ **off-worlder** *n.*

oft *adv.* (in *comb.*) often (*oft-recurring*; *oft-quoted*).

often *adv.* (**oftener**, **oftenest**) **1 a** frequently; many times. **b** at short intervals. **2** in many instances. □ **as often as not** in roughly half the instances. **more often than not** in more than (roughly) half the instances.

oftentimes *adv.* often.

ogle /ˈoːɡəl/ ● *v.* **1** *tr.* eye amorously, lecherously, or covetously. **2** *intr.* look amorously. **3** *tr.* stare at; keep an eye on. ● *n.* an amorous or lecherous look. □ **ogler** *n.*

ogre /ˈoːɡər/ *n.* **1** a man-eating giant in folklore etc. **2** a cruel, irascible, or ugly person. □ **ogreish** *adj.*

OH *abbr.* Ohio (in official postal use).

oh ● *interj.* (also **O**) expressing surprise, pain, entreaty, etc. (*oh, what a mess*; *oh for a holiday*). ● *n.* (also **O**) zero (*the big four-oh*; *the Jays are five and oh*). □ **oh boy** expressing surprise, excitement, etc. **oh well** expressing resignation.

OHC *abbr.* overhead camshaft.

Ohioan /oˈhaioːən/ ● *n.* a native or inhabitant of the US state of Ohio. ● *adj.* of or relating to Ohio.

OHIP /ˈoːhɪp/ *abbr. Cdn* Ontario Health Insurance Plan.

ohm /oːm/ *n. Electricity* the SI unit of resistance, transmitting a current of one ampere when subjected to a potential difference of one volt. Symbol: Ω. □ **ohmic** *adj.*

oho /oˈhoː/ *interj.* expressing surprise or exultation.

-oholic *var. of* -AHOLIC.

OHOSP /ˈoːhɒsp/ *abbr. Cdn* Ontario Home Ownership Savings Plan.

oi *var. of* OY.

-oid /ɔid/ *suffix* forming adjectives and nouns, denoting form or resemblance (*asteroid*; *rhomboid*; *thyroid*). □ **-oidal** *suffix.* **-oidally** *suffix.*

oil ● *n.* **1** any of various thick, viscous, usu. inflammable liquids insoluble in water but soluble in organic solvents, obtained from animal, plant, or mineral sources. **2** petroleum. **3** (in *comb.*) using oil as fuel (*oil furnace*). **4** = COOKING OIL. **5 a** (usu. in *pl.*) = OIL PAINT. **b** a picture painted in oil paints. **6** any of various thick liquids used on the hair, skin, etc. (*suntan oil*). **7** (in *pl.*) shares in an oil company. ● *v.tr.* **1** apply oil to; moisten, smear, cover, or lubricate with oil. **2** impregnate or treat with oil (*oiled silk*). □ **oil the wheels** help make things go smoothly.

oil and water *n.* two elements or factors which do not agree or blend together.

oil-based *adj.* (esp. of paint etc.) having oil as the main ingredient.

oil can *n.* a can containing oil, esp. one with a long nozzle for oiling machinery.

oilcloth *n.* **1** a fabric waterproofed with oil. **2** a canvas coated with linseed or other oil and used to cover a table or floor.

oil drum *n.* a metal drum used for transporting oil.

oiler *n.* **1** an oil can for oiling machinery. **2** an oil tanker. **3** a person who oils machinery. **4** *N Amer.* **a** an oil well. **b** (in *pl.*) oilskins.

oil field *n.* an area of land or seabed underlain by strata which contain oil, usu. in amounts that justify commercial exploitation.

oil-fired *adj.* using oil as fuel.

oil lamp *n.* a lamp using oil as fuel.

oilman *n.* (*pl.* **-men**) an owner or employee of an oil company.

oil paint *n.* a mix of ground colour pigment and oil.

oil painting *n.* **1** the art of painting in oils. **2** a picture painted in oils. □ **oil painter** *n.*

oil palm *n.* either of two trees, *Elaeis guineensis* of W Africa, or *E. oleifera* of the US, yielding palm oil.

oil pan *n.* (in an internal combustion engine) the bottom part of the crankcase, in which the oil used to lubricate the engine collects.

oil paper *n.* a paper made transparent or waterproof by soaking in oil.

oil patch *n.* esp. *N Amer. slang* **1** a petroleum-rich region in a country etc. **2** the petroleum industry.

oil rig *n.* a structure with equipment for drilling an oil well. □ **oil rigger** *n.*

oil sand *n.* (usu. in *pl.*) a deposit of loose sand or partly consolidated sandstone containing bitumen.

oilseed *n.* any of various seeds from cultivated crops yielding oil, e.g. rape, peanut, or cotton.

oil shale *n.* a fine-grained rock from which oil can be extracted.

oilskin *n.* **1** cloth waterproofed with oil. **2** (often in *pl.*) a garment made of this.

oil slick *n.* a patch of floating oil, esp. on the sea.

oilstone *n.* a fine-grained flat stone used with oil for sharpening flat tools, e.g. chisels, planes, etc.

oil tanker *n.* a ship designed to carry oil in bulk.

oil well *n.* a well from which petroleum is drawn.

oily *adj.* (**-ier**, **-iest**) **1** of, like, or containing much oil. **2** covered or soaked with oil. **3** (of a manner etc.) fawning, insinuating, unctuous. □ **oiliness** *n.*

oink ● *v.intr.* **1** (of a pig) make its characteristic grunt. **2** (of a person) grunt like a pig. ● *n.* the grunt of a pig or a sound resembling this.

ointment *n.* a smooth greasy healing or cosmetic preparation for the skin.

OJ *n. N Amer. informal* (also **O.J.**) orange juice.

Ojibwa /oˈdʒɪbweɪ/ (also **Ojibway**, **Ojibwe**) ● *n.* (*pl.* same or **-s**) **1** a member of an Algonquian people living esp. around Lake Superior. **2** the Algonquian language of this people. ● *adj.* of the Ojibwa.

Oji-Cree /ˈɒdʒɪkriː/ *n.* a mixture of the Cree and Ojibwa spoken in NW Ontario and Manitoba.

OK¹ (also **okay**) *informal* ● *adj.* all right; satisfactory. ● *adv.* well, satisfactorily (*that worked out OK*). ● *n.* (*pl.* **OKs** or **okays**) approval, sanction. ● *interj.* all right, yes. ● *v.tr.* (**OK's** or **okays**, **OK'd** or **okayed**, **OK'ing** or **okaying**) give an OK to; approve, sanction.

OK² *abbr.* Oklahoma (in official postal use).

Oka /ˈoːkə/ *n. Cdn* a variety of semi-soft cured cheese originally made by Trappist monks.

Okanagan /ˌoːkəˈnɒɡən/ *n.* **1** a member of an Aboriginal people living in southern BC. **2** the Salishan language of this people.

okey-doke *adj., interj., & adv.* (also **okey-dokey**) = OK¹.

Okie *n. informal* **1** a native or inhabitant of the US state of Oklahoma. **2** a migrant agricultural worker, esp.

one from Oklahoma who was forced to leave a farm during the Great Depression.

Okla. *abbr.* Oklahoma.

Oklahoman /ˌoːkləˈhoːmən/ ● *n.* a native or inhabitant of the US state of Oklahoma. ● *adj.* of Oklahoma.

okra /ˈoːkrə/ *n.* **1** an African plant, *Abelmoschus esculentus*, with long seed pods. **2** the seed pods eaten as a vegetable and used to thicken soups etc.

Oktoberfest *n.* **1** an annual beer festival celebrated in Munich, Germany in late September and early October. **2** a similar autumn festival held elsewhere.

old *adj.* (**older**, **oldest**) (*compare* ELDER¹, ELDEST). **1 a** advanced in age; far on in the natural period of existence. **b** not young or near its beginning. **2 a** of a particular age (*is four years old; a four-year-old boy*). **b** (in comb., as a noun) a person or animal of the age specified (*our four-year-old*). **3** made long ago. **4** long in use. **5 a** dilapidated or shabby from the passage of time. **b** familiar through repetition (*an old joke*). **6** having the characteristics (experience, wisdom, etc.) of age (*the child is old beyond her years*). **7** practised, inveterate (*an old offender*). **8** belonging only or chiefly to the past; lingering on; former (*old times*). **9** dating from far back; long established or known (*old friends*). **10** (of language) as used in former or earliest times. **11** *informal* as a term of affection or casual reference (*good old Charlie*). **12** the former or first of two or more similar things (*wants his old job back*). **13** used as an intensifier (*a grand old time*). **14** Cdn (of cheddar) aged 10-24 months. □ **of old** formerly; long ago. □ **oldish** *adj.* **oldness** *n.*

old age *n.* the later part of normal life.

old-age home *n.* = OLD PEOPLE'S HOME.

old-age pension *n.* a pension paid by the state to citizens above a certain age. □ **old-age pensioner** *n.*

old age security *n.* Cdn a system of government-funded pensions for those over 65. Abbr.: **OAS**.

old bat *n.* *derogatory* an older woman, esp. one regarded as unattractive and unpleasant.

Old Believer *n.* a member of a Russian Orthodox group which refused to accept the liturgical reforms of the patriarch Nikon (1605-81).

old boy *n.* **1** esp. Brit. a former male pupil of a school. **2** *informal* **a** an elderly man. **b** an affectionate form of address to a boy or man.

old boys' network *n.* *informal* (also **old boy network**) an informal network through which men from the same social background, profession, school, etc. help each other in business, politics, etc.

old country *n.* (*prec. by the*) the native country of an immigrant, settler, etc.

old dear *n.* *informal* an elderly woman.

olden *adj.* *archaic or literary* of old; of a former age (esp. *in the olden days*).

Old English *n.* the English language up to c.1150.

Old English sheepdog *n.* a breed of large sheepdog with a shaggy blue-grey and white coat.

olde worlde /ˈoːldi ˈwɜːldi/ *adj.* *jocular* old and quaint, often in a mock old style.

old-fashioned *adj.* **1** in or according to the style, fashion, or tastes of an earlier period; antiquated. **2** believing in old ways, customs, etc.; conservative.

old folks' home *n.* *informal* = OLD PEOPLE'S HOME.

Old French *n.* the French language up to c.1400.

old girl *n.* **1** esp. Brit. a former female pupil of a school. **2** *informal* **a** an elderly woman. **b** an affectionate term of address to a girl or woman.

old-growth *adj.* (of a tree etc.) mature, never felled.

old guard *n.* the original or past or conservative members of a group.

old hand *n.* a person with much experience.

old hat *adj.* *informal* tediously familiar or out of date.

Old High German *n.* High German up to c.1200.

old home week *n.* N Amer. *informal* **1** a festival during which former residents of a town return home. **2** any similar event or reunion.

Old Icelandic *n.* Icelandic up to the 16th c., a form of Old Norse.

oldie *n.* *informal* **1** a thing that is old or familiar, esp. an old song or film. **2** an elderly person.

old lady *n.* *informal* or *offensive* one's mother, wife, or girlfriend.

old-line *adj.* N Amer. **1** conservative; traditional. **2** long-established; venerable.

old man *informal* **1** one's father, husband, or boyfriend. **2** an affectionate form of address to a boy or man.

old man's beard *n.* any of various plants with plumed seeds, esp. fringetree, *Chionanthus virginica*, and species of clematis.

Old Master *n.* **1** a great artist of former times, esp. of the 13th-17th c. in Europe. **2** a painting by such a painter.

old money *n.* **1** wealth accumulated in a family over several generations. **2** people endowed with this.

old moon *n.* the moon in its last quarter, before the new moon.

Old Norse *n.* the North Germanic language of Norway and its colonies until the 14th c., from which the Scandinavian languages are derived.

Old Order *adj.* of or relating to various sects of the Mennonite church in N America, which strictly observe the oldest forms of worship and preserve the most conservative codes of behaviour, dress, etc.

old people's home *n.* an institution providing accommodation and nursing care for the elderly, esp. for those too infirm to live alone.

Old Saxon *n.* = SAXON *n.* 1b.

old school *n.* **1** traditional attitudes. **2** people having such attitudes.

oldsquaw *n.* N Amer. a duck, *Clangula hyemalis*, the male of which has a very long tail.

oldster *n.* an old person.

Old Style ● *n.* dating reckoned by the Julian calendar (*compare* NEW STYLE). ● *attrib.adj.* (**old-style**) of an old style, outmoded (*old-style communists*).

Old Testament *n.* the first part of the Christian Bible containing the scriptures of the Hebrews.

old-time *attrib.adj.* belonging to or typical of former times (*old-time rock'n'roll*). □ **old-timey** *adj.*

old-timer *n.* **1** a person who has lived in a place or been associated with an organization, job, etc. for a long time. **2** an elderly person. **3** N Amer. Sport **a** a retired professional player, esp. one who participates in sports charity events (*NHL old-timers*). **b** a member of a team of middle-aged or elderly amateur players.

Old West *n.* the western US and Canada before the influx of settlers and establishment of government.

old wives' tale *n.* a foolish or unscientific tradition or belief.

old woman *n.* *informal* or *offensive* **1** one's wife, mother, or girlfriend. **2** a fussy or timid man.

Old World *n.* Europe, Asia, and Africa, regarded collectively as the part of the world known before the European discovery of the Americas.

old-world *adj.* belonging to or associated with old times.

oleander /ˌoːliˈændər/ n. an evergreen poisonous shrub, *Nerium oleander*, native to the Mediterranean and bearing clusters of white, pink, or red flowers.

oleaster /ˌoːliˈæstər/ n. any of various sometimes thorny trees of the genus *Elaeagnus*, esp. *E. angustifolia* bearing olive-shaped yellowish fruits.

oleoresin /ˌoːlioːˈrezɪn/ n. a natural or artificial mixture of essential oils and a resin, e.g. balsam.

Olestra /ʊˈlestrə/ n. *proprietary* a synthetic sucrose polyester used as a calorie-free substitute for fat in various foods.

olfactory /oːlˈfæktəri, ɒl-/ adj. of or relating to the sense of smell (*olfactory nerves*).

oligarch /ˈɒlɪˌɡɑːrk/ n. a member of an oligarchy.

oligarchy n. (pl. **-ies**) **1** government by a small group of people. **2** a state governed in this way. **3** the members of such a government. □ **oligarchic** adj. **oligarchical** adj. **oligarchically** adv.

Oligocene /ˈɒlɪɡəˌsiːn/ ● adj. of or relating to the third epoch of the Tertiary period, between the Eocene and the Miocene, lasting from about 38 to 24.6 million years ago. ● n. this geological epoch.

oligopoly /ˌɒlɪˈɡɒpəli/ n. (pl. **-ies**) a state of limited competition between a small number of producers or sellers. □ **oligopolistic** adj.

olive ● n. **1** any evergreen tree of the genus *Olea*, having dark green lance-shaped leathery leaves with silvery undersides. **2** the small oval fruit of this, having a hard stone and bitter flesh, green when unripe and bluish black when ripe. **3** (in full **olive green**) the greyish-green colour of an unripe olive. **4** the wood of the olive tree. ● adj. **1** (in full **olive green**) coloured like an unripe olive. **2** (of the complexion) yellowish brown, sallow.

olive branch n. **1** the branch of an olive tree as a symbol of peace. **2** a gesture of reconciliation.

olive drab ● n. the dull olive green colour used in certain army uniforms. ● adj. of this colour.

olive oil n. a faintly scented oil extracted from olives, used esp. in cooking.

-ology /ˈɒlədʒi/ comb. form see -LOGY.

Olympiad /əˈlɪmpiˌæd/ n. **1 a** a period of four years between Olympic Games, used by the ancient Greeks in dating events. **b** a four-yearly celebration of the ancient Olympic Games. **2** a celebration of the modern Olympic Games. **3** a regular international contest in chess, bridge, etc.

Olympian /əˈlɪmpiən/ ● adj. **1 a** of or associated with Mount Olympus in Greece, traditionally the home of the Greek gods. **b** celestial, godlike. **2** (of manners etc.) condescending, superior (*Olympian detachment*). **3 a** of or relating to ancient Olympia in southern Greece. **b** = OLYMPIC. ● n. **1** any of the pantheon of twelve gods regarded as living on Olympus. **2** a competitor in the Olympic Games.

Olympic ● adj. **1** of or pertaining to the modern Olympic Games. **2** of ancient Olympia or the ancient Olympic Games. ● n. (**the Olympics**) the Olympic Games.

Olympic Games n. **1** a modern international sports competition, traditionally held every four years since 1896 in different venues. **2** hist. an ancient Greek festival held at Olympia every four years, with athletic, literary, and musical competitions.

Olympic-sized adj. (also **Olympic-size**) of the dimensions prescribed for modern Olympic competitions (*an Olympic-sized pool*).

om /oːm/ n. *Hinduism & Buddhism* a mystic syllable used as a mantra at the beginning and end of prayers.

oma /oːmə/ n. (among people of German descent) grandmother.

Omaha /ˈoːməhɒ/ ● n. (pl. same or **-s**) **1** a member of an Aboriginal people of NE Nebraska. **2** the Siouan language of this people. ● adj. of or pertaining to the Omaha or their language.

ombudsman /ˈɒmbʌdzmən, -bʊdz-, -ˈbʌdz-/ n. (pl. **-men**) (also **ombudsperson** pl. **-s**) **1** an official appointed by a government to investigate individuals' complaints against public authorities etc. **2** N Amer. an official within an institution who investigates complaints from employees, students, etc.

omega /oːˈmeiɡə, -meɡə/ n. **1** the last (24th) letter of the Greek alphabet (Ω, ω). **2** the last of a series.

omega-3 fatty acid n. a long-chain polyunsaturated fatty acid found esp. in fish oil, believed to help reduce blood cholesterol levels.

omelette /ˈɒmlət, -əlɪt/ n. (also **omelet**) a dish of beaten eggs cooked in a frying pan and served plain or filled with cheese, meat, vegetables, etc.

omen ● n. **1** an occurrence or object regarded as portending good or evil. **2** prophetic significance (*of good omen*). ● v.tr. (usu. in *passive*) portend; foreshow. □ **omened** adj. (also in comb.).

omentum /oːˈmentəm/ n. (pl. **-ta** /-tə/) a fold of peritoneum connecting the stomach with other organs.

omertà /oːˈmertə/ n. a code of silence, esp. as practised by the Mafia.

OMI abbr. OBLATES OF MARY IMMACULATE.

omicron /ˈɒmɪkrɒn, ˈoː-/ n. the fifteenth letter of the Greek alphabet (O, o).

ominous /ˈɒmənəs/ adj. threateningly inauspicious; indicating disaster or difficulty. □ **ominously** adv. **ominousness** n.

omission n. **1** the act or an instance of omitting or being omitted. **2** something that has been omitted.

omit v.tr. (**omitted, omitting**) **1** leave out; not insert or include. **2** (foll. by verbal noun or to + infin.) fail or neglect (*omitted to say*).

OMM abbr. Cdn Officer of the Order of Military Merit.

omni- comb. form **1** all; of all things. **2** in all ways or places.

omnibus /ˈɒmnɪbʌs/ ● n. (pl. **-es**) **1** hist. = BUS n. 1. **2** a volume containing several novels etc. previously published separately. ● adj. **1** serving several purposes at once. **2** comprising several items.

omnidirectional adj. of equal sensitivity or power in all directions (*omnidirectional microphone*).

OMNIMAX n. *proprietary* (often attrib.) a technique of wide-screen cinematography in which 70mm film is projected through a fish-eye lens onto a hemispherical screen.

omnipotent /ɒmˈnɪpətənt/ adj. **1** having great or absolute power. **2** having great influence. □ **omnipotence** n. **omnipotently** adv.

omnipresent /ˌɒmnɪˈprezənt/ adj. **1** present everywhere at the same time. **2** widely or constantly encountered. □ **omnipresence** n.

omniscient /ɒmˈnɪsiənt, -ʃənt/ adj. having infinite or very extensive knowledge. □ **omniscience** n. **omnisciently** adv.

omnivorous /ɒmˈnɪvərəs/ adj. **1** feeding on many kinds of food, esp. on both plants and flesh. **2** making use of everything available. □ **omnivore** /ˈɒmnɪˌvɔːr/ n. **omnivorously** adv. **omnivorousness** n.

ON abbr. Ontario (in official postal use).

on ● prep. **1** (so as to be) supported by or attached to or covering or enclosing (*sat on a chair*; *stuck on the wall*; *leaned on his elbow*). **2** carried with; about the person of (*do you have a pen on you?*). **3** (of time) exactly at; during; contemporaneously with (*on March 28; on the hour; on schedule*). **4** immediately after or before (*I saw them on my return*). **5** as a result of (*on further examination I found this*). **6** (so as to be) having membership etc. of or residence at or in (*she is on the board of directors*; *lives on Cape Breton Island*). **7** supported financially by (*lives on $200 a week; lives on her wits*). **8** close to; just by (*a cabin on the lake; lives on the main road*). **9** in the direction of; against. **10** so as to threaten; touching or striking (*pulled a knife on me; a punch on the nose*). **11** having as an axis or pivot (*turned on his heels*). **12** having as a basis or motive (*works on a ratchet; arrested on suspicion*). **13** having as a standard, confirmation, or guarantee (*did it on purpose; I promise on my word*). **14** concerning or about (*writes on folklore*). **15** using or engaged with (*is on the pill; here on business*). **16** so as to affect (*walked out on me*). **17** at the expense of (*the drinks are on me; the joke is on him*). **18** added to (*five cents on a litre of gas*). **19** in a specified manner or style (often foll. by *the* + adj. or noun: *on the run*). ● *adv.* **1** (so as to be) covering or in contact with something, esp. of clothes (*put your boots on*). **2** in the appropriate direction; towards something (*look on*). **3** further forward; in an advanced position or state (*time is getting on; it happened later on*). **4** with continued movement or action (*went plodding on; keeps on complaining*). **5** in operation or activity (*the light is on; the chase was on*). **6** due to take place as planned (*is the party still on?*). **7** *informal* (of a person) willing to participate or approve, or make a bet. **8** being shown or performed (*a good movie on tonight*). **9 a** (of a performer) on stage; performing. **b** (of a radio or television host etc.) on the air (*we're on in 5 minutes*). **10** (of an employee) on duty. **11** forward (*head on*). □ **be on about** refer to or discuss esp. tediously or persistently (*what are they on about?*). **be on at** *informal* nag or grumble at. **be on to 1** realize the significance or intentions of. **2** get in touch with (esp. by telephone). **on and off** intermittently; now and then. **on and on** continually; at tedious length. **on side** *see* ONSIDE. **on time** punctual, punctually. **on to** to a position or state on or in contact with (*compare* ONTO).

on-again, off-again *adj.* operating or occurring at irregular and often unpredictable intervals.

on-air *adj.* on the air; broadcasting.

on-base percentage *n. Baseball* a statistic indicating the number of times a player reaches base in relation to his or her at-bats.

on-board *attrib.adj.* provided or situated on board a vehicle, ship, etc. (*on-board computer*) (*compare* ON BOARD (*see* BOARD)).

on-camera *adj. & adv.* within the range of a film or television camera (*an on-camera interview*).

once ● *adv.* **1** on one occasion or for one time only. **2** at some point or period in the past. **3** ever or at all (*if you once forget it*). **4** by one degree (*a cousin once removed*). ● *conj.* as soon as (*once they have gone we can relax*). ● *n.* one time or occasion (*just the once*). □ **all at once 1** without warning; suddenly. **2** all together. **at once 1** immediately. **2** simultaneously. **for once** on this (or that) occasion, even if at no other. **once again** (or **more**) another time. **once and for all** (or **once for all**) (done) in a final or conclusive manner, esp. so as to end hesitation or uncertainty. **once and future** that has been in the past and will be again. **once** (or **every once**) **in a while** occasionally. **once or twice** a few times. **once upon a time 1** at some vague time in the past. **2** formerly.

once-in-a-lifetime *adj.* (of an experience, opportu-

nity, etc.) so extraordinary that it is not likely to be repeated in one's lifetime.

once-over *n. informal* a rapid preliminary inspection or piece of work.

oncology /ɒŋ'kɒlədʒi/ *n.* the branch of medicine dealing with the diagnosis and treatment of cancerous tumours. □ **oncologist** *n.*

oncoming ● *adj.* approaching from the front. ● *n.* an approach or onset.

on-deck circle *n. Baseball* a circular area outside the team's dugout where the next batter warms up etc.

one ● *adj.* **1** single and integral in number. **2** a single person or thing of the kind expressed or implied (*one of the best; a nasty one*). **3 a** particular but undefined, esp. as contrasted with another (*that is one view*). **b** *informal* (as an emphatic) a noteworthy example of (*that is one difficult question*). **4** only such (*the one person who can do it*). **5** forming a unity (*one and undivided*). **6** identical; the same (*of one opinion*). **7** a certain (*issued a warrant for one Donald Smith*). ● *n.* **1 a** the lowest cardinal number. **b** a symbol for this (1, i, I). **c** a thing numbered with it. **2** unity; a unit (*came in ones and twos*). **3** a single thing or person or example (often referring to a noun previously expressed or implied: *the big dog and the small one*). **4** *informal* an alcoholic drink (*have one on me*). **5** a story or joke (*the one about the frog*). **6** one o'clock. ● *pron.* **1** a person of a specified kind (*loved ones; like one possessed*). **2** any person, as representing people in general (*one is bound to lose in the end*). ¶The use of the pronoun *one* in this sense is usually regarded as a formal usage. □ **at one** in agreement. **for one** being one, even if the only one (*I for one do not believe it*). **for one thing** as a single consideration, ignoring others. **one and all** everyone. **one and only 1** unique. **2** superb, unequalled. **one by one** singly, successively. **one day 1** on an unspecified day. **2** at some unspecified future date. **one or two** *see* OR. **one thing and another** *informal* various events, items, matters, tasks, etc.

one-and-a-half *n. Cdn (Que.)* an apartment having one room plus a bathroom.

one another *pron.* each the other or others (esp. as a formula of reciprocity) (*love one another*).

one-armed bandit *n. informal* a slot machine worked by a long handle at the side.

one-dimensional *adj.* **1** having or pertaining to a single dimension. **2** lacking depth or scope; superficial. □ **one-dimensionality** *n.*

one-handed ● *adj.* **1** having only one hand, or only one hand capable of use. **2** used, worked, or performed with one hand. ● *adv.* using only one hand.

one-horse *adj.* **1** using a single horse. **2** *informal* small, unimportant; obscure (*a one-horse town*).

Oneida /oː'naɪdə/ ● *n.* **1** a member of an Iroquois people formerly living in New York State, and now living near London, Ont. **2** the Iroquoian language of this people. ● *adj.* of or relating to this people.

one-liner *n. informal* a short witty remark; a joke consisting of only one sentence.

one-man *adj.* **1** involving, done, or operated by only one man. **2** committed or attached to one man only.

one-man band *n.* **1** an entertainer who plays a number of musical instruments at the same time. **2** a person who does everything personally or operates without assistance.

oneness *n.* **1** the fact or state of being one; singleness. **2** uniqueness. **3** agreement; unity of opinion. **4** identity, sameness.

one-night stand *n.* **1** *informal* a sexual liaison lasting only one night. **2** a single performance of a play etc. in a place.

one-off *informal* ● *attrib.adj.* made or happening only once; not repeated. ● *n.* a thing that is made or happens only once.

one-on-one ● *adj.* involving direct communication, competition, confrontation, etc. between two people; person-to-person. ● *adv.* in direct communication, confrontation, etc. (*spoke one-on-one*). ● *n.* a one-on-one meeting, encounter, confrontation, etc.

one per cent *n.* (also **1 per cent, 1%**) *N Amer.* partly skimmed milk containing one per cent milk fat.

one-piece ● *adj.* **1** (of a bathing suit, snowsuit, etc.) made as a single garment. **2** made or consisting of a single piece. ● *n.* a thing that is made or consists of one piece.

one-room schoolhouse *n.* (also **one-room school**) *N Amer. esp. hist.* a school in which all grades are taught by one teacher in a single classroom.

onerous /'ɒnərəs, 'ɔːn-/ *adj.* **1** burdensome; causing or requiring trouble. **2** *Law* involving heavy obligations. □ **onerously** *adv.*

oneself *pron.* the reflexive and emphatic form of *one* (*hurt oneself*; *one has to do it oneself*).

one-shot *adj.* **1** achieved or done with a single attempt, stroke, etc. **2** occurring, produced, used, etc. only once (*a one-shot deal*).

one-sided *adj.* **1** favouring one side in a dispute; unfair, partial. **2** having or occurring on one side only. **3** larger or more developed on one side. □ **one-sidedly** *adv.* **one-sidedness** *n.*

one-size-fits-all *adj.* **1** (of clothing) available in one size only. **2** *informal* suitable for or used in all circumstances (*a one-size-fits-all solution*).

one-step *adj.* done or made etc. in a single step (*one-step installation process*).

one-stop *attrib.adj.* (of a store etc.) capable of supplying all a customer's needs within a particular range of goods or services (*a one-stop building supply centre*).

one-time ● *adj.* **1** former (*the one-time champ*). **2** done or occurring etc. only once (*a one-time payment*). ● *v.tr.* *Hockey* shoot (a moving puck) without stopping it first.

one-timer *n.* *Hockey* a shot that has been one-timed.

one-to-one *adj.* **1** with each member of a group corresponding to a member of another group. **2** = ONE-ON-ONE *adj.*

one-track mind *n.* a mind preoccupied with one subject.

one-two *informal* ● *n.* *Boxing* the delivery of two punches in quick succession. ● *adj.* (of two teams, competitors, etc.) holding first and second place.

one-up *informal* ● *adj.* having a particular advantage. ● *v.tr.* (**one-upped, one-upping**) do better than (someone) (*always trying to one-up me*).

one-upmanship *n.* *informal* the art or practice of maintaining an advantage in a competitive relationship.

one-way *adj.* **1** allowing movement or travel in one direction only. **2** characterized by or entailing no reciprocal feeling, communication, responsibility, etc. (*a one-way relationship*). **3** (of a window etc.) permitting vision from one side only.

one-way street *n.* **1** a street on which vehicular travel is allowed in only one direction. **2** a situation, relationship, etc., in which there is no reciprocity or possibility of returning to a previous state.

one-woman *adj.* **1** involving, done, or operated by

only one woman (*a one-woman show*). **2** committed or attached to one woman only.

ongoing *adj.* **1** continuing to exist or be operative etc. **2** that is or are in progress (*ongoing discussions*).

on-ice *adj. & adv. Hockey & Curling* occurring or positioned on the ice (*on-ice violence*).

onion *n.* **1** a plant, *Allium cepa*, having a short stem and bearing greenish-white flowers. **2** the swollen bulb of this, used as a vegetable. □ **oniony** *adj.*

onion dome *n.* a bulbous dome, esp. on an Eastern Orthodox church etc. □ **onion-domed** *adj.*

onion ring *n.* a ring of onion coated in batter and deep-fried.

onion skin *n.* **1** the outer skin of an onion. **2** thin smooth translucent paper.

on-line ● *adj.* (of equipment or a process) directly controlled by or connected to a central processing unit. ● *adv.* while thus controlled or connected.

onlooker *n.* a non-participating observer; a spectator. □ **onlooking** *adj.*

only ● *adv.* **1** solely, merely, exclusively (*I only want to sit down*; *needed six only*; *is only a child*). **2** no longer ago than (*saw them only yesterday*). **3** not until (*arrives only on Tuesday*). **4** with no better result than (*hurried home only to find her gone*). ¶In informal English *only* is usually placed between the subject and verb regardless of what it refers to (e.g. *I only want to talk to you*); in more formal English it is often placed more exactly, esp. to avoid ambiguity (e.g. *I want to talk only to you*). ● *attrib.adj.* **1** existing alone of its or their kind (*their only son*). **2** best or alone worth knowing (*the only place to eat*). ● *conj. informal* **1** except that; but for the fact that (*I would go, only I feel ill*). **2** but then (as an extra consideration) (*he always makes promises, only he never keeps them*). □ **only too** extremely (*only too willing*).

on-off *adj.* **1** (of a switch) having two positions, 'on' and 'off'. **2** = ON AND OFF (see ON).

onomatopoeia /ˌɒnəˌmætə'piːə/ *n.* **1** the formation of a word from a sound associated with what is named (e.g. *sizzle*). **2** the use of such words. □ **onomatopoeic** *adj.*

Onondaga /ˌɒnɒn'dɒɡə/ ● *n.* **1** a member of an Iroquois people now living esp. on the Six Nations reserve near Brantford, Ont. **2** the Iroquoian language of this people. ● *adj.* of this people.

on-ramp *n.* *N Amer.* a sloping one-way road leading onto a highway.

on-reserve *Cdn* ● *adj.* located on or inhabiting land which is part of a designated reserve for Aboriginal people. ● *adv.* on a reserve (*works on-reserve*).

onrush *n.* an onward rush. □ **onrushing** *adj.*

onscreen ● *adj.* appearing on a movie, television, or computer screen. ● *adv.* **1** on or by means of a screen. **2** within the view presented by a movie scene.

onset *n.* **1** the beginning of some esp. unpleasant operation, situation, condition, etc. **2** an attack.

on-set *attrib.adj.* taking place or occurring on the set of a play or film.

onshore ● *adj.* **1** on the shore. **2** (of the wind) blowing from the sea towards the land. ● *adv.* on or towards the land.

onside /'ɒnsaɪd, ɒn'saɪd/ *adj. & adv.* **1** *Sport* (of a player) in a legal position; not offside. **2** (also **on side**) in or into a position of agreement with (another person).

on-site *attrib.adj.* taking place or available on a site or premises.

onslaught /'ɒnslɔt/ *n.* a fierce attack.

onstage *adj. & adv.* on the stage; before an audience.

Ont. *abbr.* Ontario.

Ontarian ● *n.* a native or inhabitant of Ontario. ● *adj.* of or relating to Ontario.

Ontario Court *n.* *Cdn* (in Ontario) a provincial court with two divisions, the **General Division**, which has jurisdiction over all indictable offences and most civil cases, and the **Provincial Division**, which has jurisdiction over cases involving family law and also acts as a youth court and small claims court.

on-the-job *adj.* done or occurring while one is at work.

onto *prep.* to a position or state on or in contact with (*compare* ON TO: see ON).

ontogenesis /ˌɒntəˈdʒenɪsɪs/ *n.* the origin and development of an individual (*compare* PHYLOGENY). □ **ontogenetic** /-dʒɪˈnetɪk/ *adj.* **ontogenetically** *adv.*

ontogeny /ɒnˈtɒdʒəni/ *n.* = ONTOGENESIS. □ **ontogenic** *adj.*

ontology /ɒnˈtɒlədʒi/ *n.* the branch of metaphysics dealing with the nature of being. □ **ontological** *adj.* **ontologically** *adv.*

onus /ˈoːnəs/ *n.* (*pl.* **onuses**) a burden, duty, or responsibility.

onward ● *adv.* (also **onwards**) **1** further on. **2** towards the front. **3** with advancing motion. **4** into the future (*from 1998 onward*). ● *adj.* directed onward.

onyx /ˈɒnɪks/ *n.* a semi-precious variety of agate with different colours in layers.

oodles /ˈuːdəlz/ *n.pl.* *informal* a very great amount.

ooh ● *interj.* expressing surprise, delight, pain, etc. ● *n.* an exclamation of 'ooh'. ● *v.intr.* (**oohed, oohing**) (in *phr.* **ooh and aah**) express delight, a favourable reaction, etc.

Ookpik /ˈuːkpɪk/ *n.* *Cdn proprietary* a doll resembling an owl, originally handcrafted of sealskin by Inuit artisans, now mass-produced and sold as a souvenir.

oolichan *var. of* EULACHON.

oomiak *var. of* UMIAK.

oompah *n.* (also **oompahpah**) a representation of the repetitive rhythmical playing of lower brass instruments, esp. in German and E European dance music.

oomph / umf/ *n.* *slang* **1** energy, liveliness. **2** attractiveness, esp. sexual appeal.

oops *interj.* *informal* expressing surprise or apology, esp. on making an obvious mistake.

oopsy daisy *var. of* UPSY-DAISY.

ooze[1] ● *v.* **1** *intr.* (of fluid) pass slowly through the pores of a body. **2** *intr.* trickle or leak slowly out. **3** *intr.* (of a substance) exude moisture. **4** *tr.* exude or exhibit (a feeling, an ambience) liberally (*oozes history*). ● *n.* a sluggish flow or exudation. □ **oozy** *adj.*

ooze[2] *n.* **1** a deposit of wet mud or slime, esp. at the bottom of a river, lake, or estuary. **2** a bog or marsh; soft muddy ground. □ **oozy** *adj.*

OP *abbr.* **1** *Catholicism* Order of Preachers (used after the name of a member of the Dominican order). **2** *Military* observation post. **3** out of print.

Op. *abbr.* *Music* opus.

op *n.* *informal* operation (in surgical and military senses).

o.p. *abbr.* overproof.

opa /ˈoːpə/ *n.* (among people of German descent) grandfather; grandpa.

opacity /əˈpæsɪti/ *n.* **1** the state of being opaque. **2** the degree to which a substance is opaque. **3** obscurity of meaning. **4** obtuseness of understanding.

opah /ˈoːpə/ *n.* a large rare deep-sea fish, *Lampris guttatus*, usu. having a silver-blue back with white spots and crimson fins.

opal /ˈoːpəl/ *n.* a quartzlike form of hydrated silica, usu. white or colourless and sometimes showing changing colours, often used as a gemstone.

opalescent /ˌoːpəˈlesənt/ *adj.* showing changing colours like opal. □ **opalesce** *v.intr.* **opalescence** *n.*

opaque /oːˈpeik/ ● *adj.* (**opaquer, opaquest**) **1** not transmitting light. **2** impenetrable to sight. **3** obscure; not lucid. **4** obtuse, dull-witted. ● *n.* **1** an opaque thing or substance. **2** a substance for producing opaque areas on negatives. □ **opaquely** *adv.*

op. cit. *abbr.* in the work already quoted.

OPEC /ˈoːpek/ *abbr.* Organization of Petroleum Exporting Countries.

op-ed *n.* a newspaper page usu. located opposite the editorial page and containing signed opinion pieces, letters to the editor, etc. (also *attrib.*: *op-ed article*).

open ● *adj.* **1** not closed or locked or blocked up; allowing entrance or passage or access. **2 a** (of a room, field, or other area) having its door or gate in a position allowing access, or part of its confining boundary removed. **b** (of a container) not fastened or sealed. **3 a** unconfined, unobstructed (*the open road*). **b** unenclosed or unprotected on at least one side (*an open fire*). **4** uncovered, bare, exposed (*open drain; open wound*). **5** *Sport* (of a goal or player etc.) unguarded. **6** undisguised, public, manifest; not exclusive or limited (*an open disregard for the law*). **7** expanded, unfolded, or spread out. **8** (of land etc.) having few trees, buildings, etc. **9** (of a fabric) not close; with gaps or intervals. **10 a** (of a person) frank and communicative. **b** (of the mind) accessible to new ideas; unprejudiced or undecided. **11 a** (of an exhibition, store, etc.) accessible to visitors or customers; ready for business. **b** (of a meeting) admitting all, not restricted to members etc. **12 a** (of a race, competition, scholarship, etc.) unrestricted as to who may compete. **b** (of a champion, scholar, etc.) having won such a contest. **13** *Cdn* (of a mortgage etc.) that may be paid off in full without penalty before the expiry of the stated term. **14** (of government) conducted in an informative manner receptive to inquiry, criticism, etc., from the public. **15** (foll. by *to*) a willing to receive (*is open to offers*). **b** (of a choice, offer, or opportunity) still available. **c** likely to suffer from or be affected by (*open to abuse*). **16** relating to that part of a body of water which is not surrounded by headlands etc. (*lost on the open lake*). **17 a** (of the mouth) with lips apart, esp. in surprise or incomprehension. **b** (of the ears or eyes) eagerly attentive. **18** (of a compound word) written as separate words, e.g. *garbage truck*. **19** *Music* **a** (of a string) allowed to vibrate along its whole length. **b** (of a pipe) unstopped at each end. **c** (of a note) sounded from an open string or pipe. **20** (of an electrical circuit) having a break in the conducting path. **21** (of the bowels) not constipated. **22** (of a return ticket) not restricted as to day of travel. **23** (of a boat) without a deck. **24** (of a river or harbour) free of ice. **25** (of the weather or winter) mild. **26** (of a sandwich etc.) = OPEN-FACED 2. ● *v.* **1** *tr. & intr.* make or become open or more open. **2 a** *tr.* change from a closed or fastened position so as to allow access (*opened the box*). **b** *intr.* (of a door, lid, etc.) have its position changed to allow access (*the door opened slowly*). **3** *tr.* remove the sealing or fastening element of (a container) to get access to the contents (*opened the envelope*). **4** *intr.* (foll. by *into, on to*, etc.) (of a door, room, etc.) afford access as specified (*opened onto a large garden*). **5 a** *tr.* start or establish (a business, activity, etc.). **b** *intr.* start, begin (*the session opens tomorrow; the story opens with a murder*). **c** *tr.* (of a counsel in a law court) make a preliminary statement in (a case) before calling witnesses. **6 a** *tr.* spread out or unfold (a map, newspaper, etc.). **b** *tr. & intr.* refer to the contents of (a book). **7** *intr.* (often foll. by *with*) (of a person) begin speaking, writing, etc. (*he opened with a joke*). **8** *intr.* (of a prospect) come into view; be revealed. **9** *tr.* reveal or communicate (one's feelings, intentions, etc.). **10** *tr.* make (one's mind, heart, etc.) more sympathetic or enlightened. **11** *tr.* ceremonially declare (a building etc.) to be completed and in use. **12** *intr. Cards* play the first card, or make the first bid, in a hand; lead. **13** *tr.* cause (the bowels) to empty. • *n.* **1** (prec. by *the*) **a** open space or country or air. **b** public notice or view; general attention (*brought the affair into the open*). **2** an open championship, competition, or scholarship. □ **be open with** speak frankly to. **open fire** start shooting. **open out 1** unfold; spread out. **2** develop, expand. **3** accelerate. **open up 1** unlock (premises). **2** make accessible. **3** reveal; bring to notice. **4** accelerate esp. a motor vehicle. **5** begin shooting or sounding. **6** talk or speak openly. □ **openable** *adj.* **openness** *n.*

open air • *n.* (usu. prec. by *the*) a free or unenclosed space outdoors. • *attrib.adj.* (**open-air**) **1** out of doors. **2** having no cover or shelter (*an open-air vehicle*).

open-and-shut *adj.* (of an argument, case, etc.) straightforward and conclusive.

open bar *n.* N Amer. a bar, e.g. at a reception, where the drinks are paid for by the host or through an admission fee rather than purchased directly by the guests (*compare* CASH BAR).

open book • *n.* a person or thing that is easily understood. • *adj.* (usu. **open-book**) (of an exam etc.) written with the use of one's textbook, notes, etc.

open concept *adj.* Cdn (of a house, office, etc.) having few or no internal walls or partitions.

open custody *n.* Cdn custody in a correctional facility that has relatively little supervision or security, e.g. a group home (also *attrib.*: *open-custody institution*).

open door *n.* **1** a policy or practice of allowing trade with all nations on an equal basis. **2** free or unrestricted admittance, esp. for immigration etc. (also *attrib.*: *open door policies*).

open-ended *adj.* **1** having no predetermined limit or boundary. **2** (of a question etc.) not limiting the respondent in the range of his or her answer. □ **open-endedness** *n.*

opener *n.* **1** a person or thing that opens (something). **2** a device for opening cans, bottles, etc. **3** the first item in a program, series, season, etc. □ **for openers** *informal* to start with.

open-faced *adj.* **1** having a frank or ingenuous expression. **2** (also **open-face**) (of a sandwich etc.) without an upper layer of bread etc.

open flame *n.* a source of combustion, esp. when exposed to combustible gases (*store away from open flame*).

open-handed *adj.* generous. □ **open-handedly** *adv.* **open-handedness** *n.*

open-heart *adj.* of or relating to surgery in which the heart has been temporarily bypassed and opened.

open house *n.* **1** N Amer. a reception or party during which guests are invited to drop in to a person's home. **2** a time during which an institution, such as a school, is open to visitors. **3** N Amer., Austral., & NZ a time during which a house for sale may be viewed by prospective buyers without an appointment. □ **keep open house** provide general hospitality.

open ice *n.* Hockey ice that is free of opposing players and away from the boards (also *attrib.*: *open-ice play*).

opening • *n.* **1** an aperture or gap, esp. one allowing access. **2** a favourable situation or opportunity. **3** an available position or opportunity in a business etc. A a beginning. **5** the process of becoming open or making something open. **6** a ceremony to celebrate a new building, facility, etc. **7** esp. N Amer. the first performance of a theatrical production etc. (also *attrib.*: *opening night*). **8** N Amer. a tract of land that is thinly wooded in comparison to the surrounding forest. **9** Cdn a period of fixed length determined by the government during which herring fishing may be undertaken. **10** a counsel's preliminary statement of a case in a law court. • *adj.* initial, first.

opening line *n.* **1** the first line of a book, movie, etc. **2** a phrase or sentence initiating a conversation, esp. with someone to whom one is sexually attracted.

open letter *n.* a letter, esp. of protest, addressed to an individual and published in a newspaper etc.

open-line *adj.* designating a radio or television program in which the public can participate by phone.

open-liner *n.* Cdn the host of an open-line program.

openly *adv.* **1** frankly, honestly. **2** publicly; without concealment.

open market *n.* an unrestricted market with free competition of buyers and sellers.

open-minded *adj.* unprejudiced; accessible to new ideas. □ **open-mindedly** *adv.* **open-mindedness** *n.*

open-mouthed *adj.* with the mouth open, esp. in surprise.

open-necked *adj.* (of a shirt) worn with the top button unfastened.

open-plan *adj.* (usu. *attrib.*) = OPEN CONCEPT.

open question *n.* a matter on which differences of opinion are legitimate.

open season *n.* **1** the season when restrictions on hunting are lifted. **2** (often foll. by *on*) a time of no restraint, esp. of criticism (*open season on unions*).

open secret *n.* a supposed secret that is known to many people.

open shop *n.* **1** a business etc. where employees do not have to be members of a labour union (*opp.* CLOSED SHOP). **2** this system.

open skies *n.* a system allowing unrestricted access to the airspace over a country.

open society *n.* a society with wide dissemination of information and freedom of belief.

open stock *n.* N Amer. merchandise, e.g. dishes, which may be purchased as individual pieces rather than as a set.

open system *n.* (often in *pl.*) a computer system in which the components conform to non-proprietary standards rather than to the standards of a specific supplier of hardware or software, thus allowing greater compatibility.

open-toed *adj.* (of shoes) leaving a toe or toes exposed.

open university *n.* (often **Open University**) a university that teaches mainly by broadcasting and correspondence, and is open to those without formal academic qualifications.

openwork *n.* a pattern with intervening spaces in metal, leather, lace, etc.

opera[1] *n.* **1 a** a dramatic work in one or more acts, set to music for singers and instrumentalists. **b** this as a genre. **c** the score for an opera. **d** a performance of an opera. **2** a building for the performance of opera. **3** a company performing opera.

opera[2] *pl.* of OPUS.

operable /ˈɒpərəbəl/ *adj.* **1** that can be operated. **2**

suitable for treatment by surgical operation. □ **operability** n.

opera glasses n.pl. small binoculars for use in a theatre.

opera house n. **1** a theatre for the performance of opera, also often used for ballet performances. **2** N Amer. a theatre, esp. in a small town.

operate v. **1** tr. manage, work, control; put or keep in a functional state. **2** intr. be in action; function. **3** intr. produce an effect; exercise influence (the tax operates to our disadvantage). **4** intr. (often foll. by on) **a** perform a surgical operation. **b** conduct a military or naval action. **c** be active in business etc., esp. dealing in stocks and shares. **5** intr. (foll. by on) influence or affect (feelings etc.). **6** tr. bring about; accomplish.

operatic /ˌɒpəˈrætɪk/ adj. **1** of or relating to opera. **2** resembling or characteristic of opera. □ **operatically** adv.

operatics n.pl. the production and performance of operas.

operating profit n. gross profit before deduction of expenses.

operating room n. (also **operating theatre**) a room for surgical operations.

operating system n. the basic software that enables the running of a computer program.

operating table n. a table on which surgical operations are performed.

operation n. **1 a** the action or process or method of working or operating. **b** the state of being active or functioning. **c** the scope or range of effectiveness of a thing's activity. **2** an active process; a discharge of a function (the operation of breathing). **3** a piece of work, esp. one in a series (often in pl.: begin operations). **4** an act of surgery performed on a patient. **5 a** a strategic movement of troops, ships, etc. for military action. **b** preceding a code name for such a movement (Operation Overlord). **6** a financial transaction. **7** a business (owned a dairy operation near Goderich). **8** Math. the subjection of a number or quantity or function to a process affecting its value or form, e.g. multiplication, differentiation.

operational adj. **1 a** of or used for operations. **b** engaged or involved in operations. **2** able or ready to function. □ **operationally** adv.

operations room n. a room etc. from which military or police operations are directed.

operative /ˈɒprətɪv, ˈɒpərətɪv/ ● adj. **1** in operation; having effect. **2** having the principal relevance ('may is the operative word). **3** of or by surgery. **4** Law expressing an intent to perform a transaction. ● n. **1** a worker, esp. a skilled one. **2** esp. N Amer. a secret service agent; a spy.

operator n. **1** a person operating a machine etc., esp. one who operates a telephone switchboard. **2** a person operating or engaging in business. **3** a person acting in a specified way (a smooth operator). **4** Math. a symbol or function denoting an operation (e.g. ×, +).

operetta /ˌɒpəˈretə/ n. a theatrical production, usu. of a comic nature, combining songs with spoken dialogue.

ophthalmia /ɒfˈθælmɪə, ɒp-/ n. an inflammation of the eye, esp. conjunctivitis.

ophthalmic /ɒfˈθælmɪk, ɒp-/ adj. of or relating to the eye and its diseases.

ophthalmology /ˌɒfθəlˈmɒlədʒi, ɒp-/ n. the scientific study of the eye. □ **ophthalmological** adj. **ophthalmologist** n.

opiate ● n. /ˈoːpɪət/ **1** a drug containing or derived from opium, usu. to ease pain or induce sleep. **2** a

thing which soothes or stupefies. ● adj. /ˈoːpɪət/ **1** containing opium. **2** narcotic, soporific.

opine /oˈpaɪn/ v. **1** tr. (often foll. by that + clause) hold or express as an opinion. **2** intr. express an opinion.

opinion n. **1** a belief or assessment based on grounds short of proof. **2** a view held as probable. **3** (often foll. by on) what one thinks about a particular topic or question (my opinion on capital punishment). **4 a** a formal statement of professional advice (get a second opinion). **b** Law a formal statement of reasons for a judgment given. **5** an estimation (had a low opinion of it). □ **be of the opinion that** believe or maintain that. **in one's opinion** according to one's view or belief. **a matter of opinion** a disputable point.

opinionated adj. conceitedly assertive or dogmatic in one's opinions.

opinion poll n. = GALLUP POLL.

opium /ˈoːpɪəm/ n. **1** a heavy-scented addictive drug prepared from the juice of the opium poppy, used in medicine as an analgesic and narcotic; it is the source of both morphine and heroin. **2** anything regarded as soothing or stupefying.

opium den n. a place where opium may be purchased and used.

opium poppy n. a poppy, Papaver somniferum, with white, red, pink, or purple flowers.

opossum /əˈpɒsəm/ n. **1** any mainly tree-living marsupial of the family Didelphidae, having a prehensile tail and hind feet with an opposable thumb, esp. (in full **Virginia opossum**) the common N American species, Didelphis virginiana, which is the size of a cat. **2** an opossum, Chironectes minimus, suited to an aquatic habitat and having webbed hind feet.

OPP abbr. (in Canada) Ontario Provincial Police.

opp. abbr. opposite.

opponent ● n. a person who opposes or belongs to an opposing side. ● adj. opposing, contrary, opposed.

opportune adj. **1** (of a time) well-chosen or especially favourable or appropriate. **2** (of an action or event) done or occurring at a favourable or useful time. □ **opportunely** adv. **opportuneness** n.

opportunism n. **1** the adaptation of policy or judgment to circumstances or opportunity, esp. regardless of principle. **2** the seizing of opportunities when they occur. □ **opportunist** n.

opportunistic adj. **1** of or relating to opportunism. **2** Ecology (of a species) able to spread quickly in a previously unexploited habitat. **3** Med. **a** (of a microorganism) rarely causing disease except in unusual circumstances, e.g. in patients with depressed immune systems. **b** (of an infection) caused by such a micro-organism. □ **opportunistically** adv.

opportunity n. (pl. **-ies**) **1** a good chance; a favourable occasion. **2** a chance or opening offered by circumstances. **3** good fortune. □ **opportunity knocks** an opportunity occurs.

opposable adj. **1** able to be opposed. **2** (of the thumb in primates) capable of facing and touching the other digits on the same hand.

oppose v. **1** tr. & intr. resist; set oneself against; argue against. **2** tr. & intr. be hostile (to). **3** tr. take part in a game, sport, etc., against (another competitor or team). **4** tr. (foll. by to) place in opposition or contrast. □ **as opposed to** in contrast with. □ **opposing** adj.

opposite ● adj. **1** (often foll. by to) having a position on the other or further side. **2** (often foll. by to, from) **a** of a contrary kind; diametrically different. **b** being the other of a contrasted pair. **3** (of angles) between opposite sides of the intersection of two lines. **4** (of leaves etc.) placed at the same height on the opposite sides of the stem, or placed straight in front of another organ. ● *n.* an opposite thing or person or term. ● *adv.* **1** in an opposite position (*the tree stands opposite*). **2** (of a leading theatrical etc. part) in a complementary role to (another performer). ● *prep.* in a position opposite to. □ **oppositely** *adv.*

opposite field *n. Baseball* the part of the diamond on the opposite side of the plate from the batter, e.g. right field for right-handed hitters (also *attrib.*: *opposite-field home run*).

opposite number *n.* a person holding an equivalent position in another group or organization.

opposite sex *n.* women in relation to men or vice versa.

opposition *n.* **1** resistance, antagonism. **2** the state of being hostile or in conflict or disagreement. **3** contrast or antithesis. **4** a group or party of opponents or competitors. **5** *Cdn., Brit., Austral.* & *NZ* **a** (**the Opposition**) the principal parliamentary party opposed to that in office (*see also* OFFICIAL OPPOSITION). **b** (often **Opposition**) all the members of a parliament who are not of the governing party (often *attrib.*: *opposition parties*). **6** the act of opposing or placing opposite. **7 a** diametrically opposite position. **b** *Astrology* & *Astronomy* the position of two heavenly bodies when their longitude differs by 180°, as seen from the earth. □ **oppositional** *adj.* **oppositionality** *n.* **oppositionist** *n.*

oppress *v.tr.* **1** keep in subservience by coercion. **2** govern or treat harshly or with cruel injustice. **3** weigh down (with cares or unhappiness). □ **oppressed** *adj.* **oppressor** *n.*

oppression *n.* **1** the act or an instance of oppressing; the state of being oppressed. **2** prolonged harsh or cruel treatment or control. **3** mental distress.

oppressive *adj.* **1** oppressing; harsh or cruel. **2** difficult to endure. **3** (of weather) close and sultry. □ **oppressively** *adv.* **oppressiveness** *n.*

opprobrium /əˈprəʊbrɪəm/ *n.* **1** disgrace or bad reputation attaching to some act or conduct. **2** a cause of this.

ops room *n.* = OPERATIONS ROOM.

opt *v.intr.* (usu. foll. by *for* or *to* + infin.) exercise an option; make a choice. □ **opt out** (often foll. by *of*) **1** choose not to participate. **2** (in Canada) (of a doctor, health clinic, etc.) operate with private rather than government funding. **opt in** choose to participate.

opted-out *attrib.adj.* designating a person or thing that has opted out (*an opted-out clinic*).

optic ● *adj.* of or relating to the eye, vision, or light (*optic nerve*). ● *n.* a lens etc. in an optical instrument.

optical *adj.* **1** of sight; visual. **2 a** of or concerning sight or light in relation to each other. **b** belonging to optics. **3** (esp. of a lens) constructed to assist sight or on the principles of optics. □ **optically** *adv.*

optical character recognition *n.* the identification of printed characters using photoelectric devices. Abbr.: **OCR**.

optical disk *n. see* DISK *n.* 1b.

optical fibre *n.* thin glass fibre through which signals can be transmitted as modulated light.

optical illusion *n.* **1** a thing having an appearance so resembling something else as to deceive the eye. **2** an instance of mental misapprehension caused by this.

optical microscope *n.* a microscope using the direct perception of light (*compare* ELECTRON MICROSCOPE). □ **optical microscopy** *n.*

optical scanning *n.* = OPTICAL CHARACTER RECOGNITION. □ **optical scanner** *n.*

optician /ɒpˈtɪʃən/ *n.* a maker or seller of optical instruments, esp. eyeglasses and contact lenses.

optic nerve *n.* each of the second pair of cranial nerves, transmitting impulses to the brain from the retina at the back of the eye.

optics *n.pl.* **1** (treated as *sing.*) the scientific study of sight and the behaviour of light, or of other radiation or particles (*electron optics*). **2** the optical components of an instrument or apparatus.

optimal /ˈɒptɪməl/ *adj.* best or most favourable, esp. under a particular set of circumstances. □ **optimality** /-ˈmælɪti/ *n.* **optimally** *adv.*

optimism *n.* **1** a tendency to take a favourable view of circumstances or prospects; confidence. **2** *Philos.* **a** the doctrine that this world is the best of all possible worlds. **b** the theory that good must ultimately prevail over evil in the universe (opp. PESSIMISM 2).

optimist *n.* **1** a person inclined to or professing optimism. **2** (**Optimist**) a member of an international social and charitable association founded in 1911, dedicated esp. to helping children and youth. □ **optimistic** *adj.* **optimistically** *adv.*

optimize *v.* **1** *tr.* **a** make the best or most effective use of (a situation, an opportunity, etc.). **b** make optimal; improve to the utmost. **2** *tr.* make (a computer program) as efficient as possible. **3** *intr.* be an optimist. □ **optimization** *n.* **optimizer** *n.*

optimum ● *n.* (*pl.* **optima** or **optimums**) **1 a** the most favourable conditions (for growth, reproduction, etc.). **b** the best or most favourable situation. **2** the best possible compromise between opposing tendencies. ● *adj.* = OPTIMAL.

option ● *n.* **1 a** the act or an instance of choosing; a choice. **b** a thing that is or may be chosen; an alternative. **2** the liberty of choosing; freedom of choice. **3 a** the right, obtained by payment, to buy, sell, etc. specified stocks etc. at a specified price within a set time. **b** the provision in a contract allowing one to extend the terms of the contract for a specified time (also *attrib.*: *option year*). **4** (in full **option play**) *Football* a play in which a player, esp. the quarterback, has the option of throwing the ball or running with it. ● *v.tr. N Amer.* buy or sell under option; have an option on. □ **have no option but to** must. **keep** (or **leave**) **one's options open** not commit oneself. □ **optional** *adj.* **optionally** *adv.*

optometry /ɒpˈtɒmətri/ *n.* the science or profession of measuring eyesight, detecting eye disease, and prescribing corrective lenses (but not drugs or medicines). □ **optometrist** *n.*

opt-out *n.* (*attrib.*) designating a provision in a contract etc. allowing one to opt out (*opt-out clause*).

opulent /ˈɒpjʊlənt/ *adj.* **1** ostentatiously rich; wealthy. **2** luxurious (*opulent surroundings*). **3** abundant; profuse. □ **opulence** *n.* **opulently** *adv.*

opus /ˈəʊpəs/ *n.* (*pl.* **opuses** or **opera** /ˈɒprə/) **1** *Music* **a** a separate musical composition or set of compositions of any kind. **b** used before a number given to a composer's work, usu. indicating the order of publication. Abbr.: **Op. 2** any artistic or creative work (*compare* MAGNUM OPUS).

OR *abbr.* **1** (**O.R.**) *N Amer.* operating room. **2** Oregon (in official postal use). **3** other ranks.

or *conj.* **1 a** introducing the second of two alternatives (*white or black*). **b** introducing all but the first, or only the last, of any number of alternatives (*white or grey or black*; *white, grey, or black*). **2** (often prec. by *either*) introducing the only remaining possibility or choice given (*either come in or go out*). **3** (prec. by *whether*) introducing the second part of an indirect question or conditional clause (*ask him whether he was there or not*). **4** introducing a synonym or explanation of a preceding word etc. (*suffered from vertigo or giddiness*). **5** introducing a significant afterthought (*he must know - or is he bluffing?*). **6** = OR ELSE (*run or you'll be late*). □ **one or two** (or **two or three** etc.) *informal* a few. **or else 1** otherwise (*watch out, or else you'll get hit*). **2** *informal* expressing a warning or threat (*hand over the money or else*). **or rather** introducing a rephrasing or qualification of a preceding statement etc. (*he was there, or rather I heard he was*). **or so** (after a quantity or a number) or thereabouts (*send ten or so*).

-or *suffix* forming nouns denoting a person or thing performing the action of a verb (*actor*).

oracle *n.* **1 a** a place at which advice or prophecy was sought from the gods in classical antiquity. **b** the usu. ambiguous or obscure response given at an oracle. **c** a prophet or prophetess at an oracle. **2 a** a person or thing regarded as an infallible guide to future action etc. **b** a saying etc. regarded as infallible guidance. **3** divine inspiration or revelation.

oracular /ə'rækjʊlər/ *adj.* **1** of or concerning an oracle or oracles. **2** (esp. of advice etc.) mysterious or ambiguous. **3** prophetic. □ **oracularly** *adv.*

oral ● *adj.* **1 a** by word of mouth; spoken; not written. **b** designating a society or culture which has not reached the stage of literacy. **2** done or taken by the mouth (*oral contraceptive*). **3** of the mouth. **4** *Psych.* of or concerning a supposed stage of infant emotional and sexual development, in which the mouth is of central interest. ● *n.* (usu. in *pl.*) *informal* a spoken test etc. □ **orality** *n.* **orally** *adv.*

oralism *n.* the principle that profoundly deaf people should learn to communicate by speech and lip-reading, not by sign language. □ **oralist** *adj. & n.*

oral sex *n.* sexual activity in which the genitals of one partner are stimulated by the mouth of the other.

-orama /əræmə/ *comb. form* = -RAMA.

orang /o:'ræŋ/ *n.* = ORANGUTAN.

Orange *adj.* **1** of or relating to Orangemen. **2** of or relating to the House of Orange. □ **Orangeism** *n.*

orange ● *n.* **1 a** a round citrus fruit with a bright reddish-yellow rind. **b** any of various trees or shrubs of the genus *Citrus*, bearing fragrant white flowers and yielding this fruit. **2** a fruit or plant resembling this. **3 a** the reddish yellow colour of an orange. **b** orange pigment. ● *adj.* **1** orange coloured; reddish yellow. **2** orange flavoured. □ **orangey** *adj.* (also **orangy**).

Orangeman *n.* (*pl.* **-men**) a member of the Orange Order.

Orange Order *n.* (also **Orange Lodge**) a fraternal society formed in 1795 to support Protestantism in Ireland, established in Canada in the 19th c., where its anti-Catholic and conservative attitudes had a considerable political and social influence.

orange peel *n.* **1** the skin of an orange. **2** (**orange-peel**) (*attrib.*) designating a rough surface like this.

orange pekoe *n.* a black tea made from very small leaves.

orange roughy *n.* an orange-coloured fish, *Hoplostethus atlanticus*, much prized for food.

orangewood *n.* the wood of the orange tree.

orangutan /o:,ræŋu:'tæn/ *n.* a large red long-haired tree-living ape, *Pongo pygmaeus*, native to Borneo and Sumatra, with long arms and hooked hands and feet.

oration *n.* **1** a formal speech, discourse, etc., esp. when ceremonial. **2** *Grammar* a way of speaking; language.

orator /'ɔrətər, 'ɒ-/ *n.* **1** a person making a speech. **2** an eloquent public speaker.

oratorio /,ɔrə'tɔ:rɪo:, ,ɒ-/ *n.* (*pl.* **-os**) a semi-dramatic work for orchestra and voices esp. on a sacred theme, performed without costume, scenery, or action.

oratory /'ɔrə,tɔri, 'ɒ-/ *n.* (*pl.* **-ies**) **1** the art or practice of formal speaking, esp. in public. **2** exaggerated, eloquent, or highly coloured language. **3** a small chapel, esp. for private worship. **4** (**Oratory**) *Catholicism* **a** (in full **Institute of the Oratory of St. Philip Neri**) a religious society of priests living in community without vows. **b** a church, branch, or house of this society. □ **oratorical** /-'tɔrɪkəl/ *adj.*

orb ● *n.* **1** a globe surmounted by a cross esp. carried by a sovereign at a coronation. **2** a sphere; a globe. **3** *literary* a heavenly body, esp. the sun or moon. **4** *literary* an eyeball; an eye. ● *v.* **1** *tr.* enclose in (an orb); encircle. **2** *intr.* form or gather into an orb.

orbit ● *n.* **1 a** the regularly repeated elliptical course of a satellite around a star or a planet. **b** (prec. by *in, into, out of*, etc.) the state of motion in an orbit. **c** one complete passage around an orbited body. **2** the path of an electron around an atomic nucleus. **3** a range or sphere of action or influence. **4 a** the eye socket. **b** the area around the eye of a bird or insect. ● *v.* (**orbited, orbiting**) **1** *tr. & intr.* (of a satellite) go around in orbit. **2** *intr.* fly in a circle. **3** *tr.* put into orbit. □ **into orbit** into a state of heightened performance etc. (*sales went into orbit*). □ **orbital** *adj.*

orbital sander *n.* a sander having a circular motion.

orbiter *n.* a spacecraft designed to remain in orbit.

orca *n.* the killer whale.

orchard *n.* a piece of enclosed land with fruit trees. □ **orchardist** *n.*

orchestra *n.* **1** a usu. large group of instrumentalists, esp. combining strings, woodwinds, brass, and percussion. **2 a** (in full **orchestra pit**) the part of a theatre, opera house, etc., where the orchestra plays, usu. in front of the stage and on a lower level. **b** *N Amer.* the seats on the ground floor in a theatre. □ **orchestral** *adj.* **orchestrally** *adv.*

orchestrate *v.tr.* **1** arrange, score, or compose (music) for orchestral performance. **2** arrange or direct (elements of a situation) for maximum effect. □ **orchestration** *n.* **orchestrator** *n.*

orchid /'ɔrkɪd/ *n.* **1** any epiphytic or terrestrial plant of the family Orchidaceae, bearing colourful flowers in fantastic shapes, usu. having one petal larger than the others. **2** a flower of any of these plants.

orchis /'ɔrkɪs/ *n.* **1** an orchid with a tuberous root and an erect fleshy stem having a spike of usu. purple or red flowers. **2** any of various wild orchids.

ordain *v.tr.* **1** bestow the office of minister, priest, or deacon on (a person). **2** (in the Presbyterian Church) bestow the office of elder on (a person). **3 a** (often foll. by *that* + clause) decree. **b** (of God, fate, etc.) destine; appoint (*has ordained us to die*).

ordeal *n.* a painful or trying experience.

order ● *n.* **1 a** the condition in which every part, unit, etc. is in its right place; tidiness. **b** a usu. specified sequence, succession, etc. (*alphabetical order*). **2** (in *sing.* or *pl.*) an authoritative command, instruction, etc. **3** a state of peaceful harmony under a constituted authority (*law and order*). **4** rank, class, kind, sort (*an engine of a higher order*). **5** a kind; a sort (*talents of a high order*). **6 a** a direction to a manufacturer, seller, waiter, etc. to supply something. **b** the quantity of goods etc. supplied. **7** the constitution or nature of the world, society, etc. (*the order of things*). **8** *Biol.* a taxonomic rank below a class and above a family. **9** a body or society of persons living by common consent under the same religious, moral, or social regulations and discipline (*the Franciscan order*). **10 a** any of the grades of the Christian ministry. **b** (in *pl.*) the status of a member of the clergy. **11 a** any of the five classical styles of architecture based on the proportions of columns, amount of decoration, etc. **b** any style or mode of architecture subject to uniform established proportions. **12** (esp. **Order**) **a** a company of distinguished people to which appointments are made as an honour or reward (*Order of Canada*). **b** the insignia worn by members of an order. **13** *Math.* **a** a degree of complexity of a differential equation (*equation of the first order*). **b** the order of the highest derivative in the equation. **14** *Christianity* the stated form of divine service (*the order of confirmation*). **15** the principles of procedure, decorum, etc., accepted by a meeting, legislative assembly, etc. or enforced by its president. **16** a Masonic or similar fraternity. **17** *Christianity* any of the nine ranks of angelic beings. ● *v.* **1** *tr.* (usu. foll. by *to* + infin., or *that* + clause) command; bid; prescribe (*ordered him to go*). **2** *tr.* command or direct (a person) to a specified destination (*was ordered to Singapore*). **3** *tr. & intr.* direct a manufacturer, waiter, seller, etc. to supply (*ordered a new suit*). **4** *tr.* put in order; regulate (*ordered her affairs*). **5** *tr.* (of God, fate, etc.) ordain. **6** *tr. N Amer.* command (a thing) done or (a person) dealt with (*ordered him expelled*). □ **by order** according to the proper authority. **in bad** (or **good** etc.) **order** not working (or working properly etc.). **in order 1** one after another according to some principle. **2** ready or fit for use. **3** according to the rules (of procedure at a meeting etc.). **in order that** with the intention; so that. **in order to** with the purpose of doing; with a view to. **keep order** enforce orderly behaviour. **made to order 1** made according to individual requirements, measurements, etc. (*opp.* READY-MADE 1). **2** exactly what is wanted. **of** (or **in** or **on**) **the order of 1** approximately. **2** having the order of magnitude specified by (*of the order of one in a million*). **on order** (of goods etc.) ordered but not yet received. **order about 1** dominate; command officiously. **2** send hither and thither. **Order! Order!** a call for silence or calm, esp. by the Speaker of a legislative assembly. **order out** (or **in**) *N Amer.* order food to be delivered to one's home etc. **out of order 1** not working properly. **2** not in the correct sequence. **3** not according to the rules (of a meeting, organization, etc.). **4** *informal* **a** not behaving in an acceptable fashion. **b** (of behaviour) not acceptable. **take orders 1** accept commissions. **2** accept and carry out commands. **3** (also **take holy orders**) be ordained.

order book *n.* **1** a listing or record of orders for a product etc. **2** the level of incoming orders.

order form *n.* a printed form on which customers enter details concerning their orders.

Order-in-Council *n.* (*pl.* **Orders-**) *Cdn & Brit.* an administrative order determined by the cabinet and formally issued by the sovereign or the sovereign's representative, usu. to deal with routine matters or to establish detailed regulations concerning acts passed by Parliament.

orderly ● *adj.* **1** methodically arranged; regular. **2** obedient to discipline; well-behaved; not unruly. **3** *Military* **a** of or concerned with orders. **b** charged with the conveyance or execution of orders. ● *n.* (*pl.* **-ies**) **1** an attendant in a hospital responsible for the non-medical care of patients and the maintenance of

order and cleanliness. **2** a soldier who carries orders for an officer etc. □ **orderliness** *n.*

order of business *n.* *N Amer.* a subject or task requiring attention, esp. one in a series.

Order of Canada *n.* an order of merit established in 1967 to honour Canadians for exemplary achievement, awarded in three ranks.

order of magnitude *n.* a class in a system of classification determined by size, usu. by powers of 10.

Order of Military Merit *n.* an order of merit established in 1972 to honour members of the Canadian Forces in recognition of special achievement, awarded in three grades.

order of the day *n.* **1** the prevailing state of affairs. **2** a principal topic of action or a procedure decided upon. **3** business set down for treatment; a program. **4** what is called for by necessity, fashion, etc.

Order Paper *n.* esp. *Parl.* an agenda, esp. a daily list of topics etc. to be discussed or voted on in a legislature. □ **die on the Order Paper** *Cdn* (of a bill) fail to be voted on before the end of a legislative session.

ordinal ● *n.* **1** (in full **ordinal number**) a number defining a thing's position in a series, e.g. 'first', 'second', 'third', etc. (*compare* CARDINAL NUMBER). **2** *Christianity* a service book, esp. one with the forms of service used at ordinations. ● *adj.* **1 a** of or relating to an ordinal number. **b** defining a thing's position in a series etc. **2** *Biol.* of or concerning an order.

ordinance /'ɔrdɪnəns/ *n.* **1** an authoritative order; a decree. **2** an enactment by a local authority. **3** a religious rite.

ordinary ● *adj.* **1** regular, normal, customary, usual (*ordinary circumstances*). **2** boring; commonplace (*an ordinary house*). ● *n.* (*pl.* **-ies**) **1** (**the Ordinary**) a person who has immediate jurisdiction in ecclesiastical cases, as the archbishop in a province, or the bishop in a diocese. **2** usu. (**Ordinary**) *Catholicism* those parts of a service, esp. the Mass, which do not vary from day to day. □ **out of the ordinary** unusual. □ **ordinarily** *adv.* **ordinariness** *n.*

ordinary seaman *n.* a sailor of the lowest rank, that below able seaman. Abbr.: **OS.**

ordinate *n.* *Math.* **1** a straight line from any point drawn parallel to one coordinate axis and meeting the other, usually a coordinate measured parallel to the vertical. **2** the distance of a point from the horizontal axis measured parallel to the vertical axis.

ordination *n.* **1 a** the act of ordaining or conferring holy orders on a priest, minister, etc. **b** the admission of a priest etc. to church ministry. **2** the arrangement of things etc. in ranks; classification. **3** the act of decreeing or ordaining.

ordnance /'ɔrdnəns/ *n.* **1** mounted guns; cannon. **2** a branch of government service or the military dealing esp. with military stores and materials.

Ordovician /ˌɔrdə'vɪʃən/ *Geol.* ● *adj.* of or relating to the second period of the Paleozoic era, lasting from about 505 to 438 million years ago, between the Cambrian and Silurian periods. ● *n.* this geological period or system.

ordure /'ɔrdjʊr/ *n.* **1** excrement; dung. **2** obscenity; filth; foul language.

Ore. *abbr.* (also **Oreg.**) Oregon.

ore *n.* a naturally occurring solid material from which metal or other valuable minerals may be extracted.

ore body *n.* a large mass of mineral-bearing rock etc.

oregano /ɔ'regəno:/ *n.* **1** the dried leaves of wild marjoram used as a culinary herb (*compare* MARJORAM). **2** the plant, *Origanum vulgare*, bearing these.

Oregonian /ˌɔrəˈgoːniən/ ● *n.* a native or inhabitant of the US state of Oregon. ● *adj.* of Oregon.

Oreo /ˈɔriːo/ *n.* esp. *US slang derogatory* a black person who is considered, esp. by other blacks, to have adopted values of the white establishment.

org *n.* organization.

organ *n.* **1 a** a usu. large musical instrument having pipes supplied with air from bellows, played using a keyboard or by an automatic mechanism. **b** a smaller instrument without pipes, producing similar sounds electronically. **c** = HARMONIUM. **d** = BARREL ORGAN. **2 a** a usu. self-contained part of an organism having a special vital function (*digestive organs*). **b** esp. *jocular* the penis. **3** a medium of communication, esp. a newspaper, sectarian periodical, etc. **4** a means of action or operation.

organdy /ˈɔrgəndi/ *n.* (*pl.* **-ies**) a fine translucent cotton muslin, usu. stiffened.

organelle /ˌɔrgəˈnel/ *n.* *Biol.* any of various organized or specialized structures which form part of a cell.

organ grinder *n.* the player of a barrel organ.

organic ● *adj.* **1** of or relating to plants or animals. **2 a** *Physiol.* of or relating to a bodily organ or organs. **b** *Med.* (of a disease) affecting the structure of an organ. **3** (of a plant or animal) having organs or an organized physical structure. **4** produced or involving production without the use of chemical fertilizers, pesticides, etc. (*organic farming*). **5** (of a compound etc.) containing carbon (opp. INORGANIC). **6 a** structural, inherent. **b** constitutional, fundamental. **7** organized, systematic, coordinated (*an organic whole*). **8** characterized by or designating continuous or natural development (*the company expanded through organic growth rather than acquisitions*). ● *n.* (esp. in *pl.*) an organic substance, esp. a fertilizer, pesticide, etc. □ **organically** *adv.*

organic chemistry *n.* the chemistry of carbon compounds.

organicism /ɔrˈgænɪˌsɪzəm/ *n.* **1** the doctrine that everything in nature has an organic basis or is part of an organic whole. **2** the use or advocacy of literary or artistic forms in which the parts are connected or coordinated in the whole. **3** the use or advocacy of organic farming methods. □ **organicist** *n. & adj.*

organism *n.* **1** a living individual consisting of a single cell or of a group of interdependent parts sharing the life processes; an individual plant or animal. **2** a whole with interdependent parts compared to a living being.

organist *n.* the player of an organ.

organization *n.* **1** the act or an instance of organizing; the state of being organized. **2** an organized body, esp. a business, government department, charity, etc. **3** systematic arrangement; tidiness. □ **organizational** *adj.* **organizationally** *adv.*

organize *v.* **1** *tr.* **a** give an orderly structure to, systematize. **b** bring the affairs of (another person or oneself) into order; make arrangements for (a person). **2** *tr.* **a** arrange for or initiate (a scheme etc.). **b** provide; take responsibility for (*organized some sandwiches*). **3 a** *tr.* enrol (new members) in a trade union, political party, etc. **b** *tr.* form (a trade union etc.). **c** *intr.* form a trade union etc. **4** *tr.* **a** form (different elements) into an organic whole. **b** form (an organic whole). **5** *tr.* (esp. as **organized** *adj.*) make organic; make into a living being or tissue.

organized crime *n.* esp. *N Amer.* widespread criminal activity organized under powerful leadership.

organizer *n.* **1** a person who organizes an event, the creation of a trade union, a political party, etc. **2** a

thing used for organizing objects, such as a handbag or folder with many compartments. **3** = PERSONAL ORGANIZER.

organ loft *n.* a gallery in a church etc. for an organ.

organ pipe *n.* *Music* any of the pipes on an organ.

organ stop *n.* **1** a set of pipes of a similar tone in an organ. **2** the handle of the mechanism that brings it into action.

organza /ɔrˈgænzə/ *n.* a thin stiff transparent silk or synthetic dress fabric.

orgasm /ˈɔrgæzəm/ ● *n.* **1 a** the culmination or climax of sexual excitement, arousing an intensely pleasurable sensation in both sexes, and accompanied in the male by ejaculation of semen. **b** an instance of this. **2** violent excitement. ● *v.intr.* experience a sexual orgasm. □ **orgasmic** /-ˈgæzmɪk/ *adj.*

orgy /ˈɔrdʒi/ *n.* (*pl.* **-ies**) **1** a wild festivity esp. with much drinking and indiscriminate sexual activity. **2** excessive indulgence in an activity.

orient ● *n.* **1** (**the Orient**) **a** the Far East. **b** (formerly) the Middle East. **2 a** the special lustre of a high-quality pearl. **b** a pearl having this lustre. **3** (**the Orient**) *literary* the east. ● *adj.* (of a pearl or other precious stone, originally from the East) of superior value and brilliancy; lustrous, sparkling. ● *v.tr.* **1 a** (also *refl.*) establish one's position in relation to one's surroundings, the points of the compass, etc. (*tried to orient themselves by the stars*). **b** bring (oneself, different elements, etc.) into a clearly understood position or relationship, esp. to known facts or principles. **c** place, align, or determine exactly the position of (a structure etc.), esp. with the aid of a compass; find the bearings of. **2** direct (a person) toward a particular interest, action, career, etc. **3** direct or aim (something) at (*programs oriented toward immigrants*).

oriental ● *adj.* **1** (often **Oriental**) of, relating to, or characteristic of E Asia, or Asiatic countries generally. **2** (often **Oriental**) of or characteristic of Eastern civilizations etc. generally. **3** (often **Oriental**) designating a person of E Asian origin. **4** (of a pearl etc.) orient. ● *n.* (esp. **Oriental**) *offensive* a person of East Asian origin. □ **orientalize** *v.intr. & tr.* **orientalizing** *adj. & n.*

orientalism *n.* **1** (often **Orientalism**) **a** the representation or concept of the Orient, esp. the Middle East, in Western academic writing, art, or literature. **b** this representation perceived as romanticized, idealized, or stereotyped, esp. as embodying a colonialistic attitude. **2** the study or knowledge of Oriental languages, literatures, etc. □ **orientalist** *n.*

oriental poppy *n.* a perennial garden poppy, *P. orientale*, with showy usu. scarlet flowers, native to SW Asia.

oriental rug *n.* (also **oriental carpet**) a rug or carpet hand-knotted in or as in the Orient.

orientate *v.tr. & intr.* = ORIENT *v.*

orientation *n.* **1 a** a person's esp. political or psychological attitude or adjustment in relation to circumstances, ideas, etc. **b** = SEXUAL ORIENTATION. **2** an introduction to a subject or situation; a briefing. **3** the position of a building, object, etc. relative to specific defined data, the points of the compass, etc. **4 a** the act or an instance of orienting. **b** the state of being oriented. **5** the faculty by which birds etc. find their way home from a distance. □ **orientational** *adj.*

orientation program *n.* esp. *N Amer.* (also **orientation course** etc.) a course giving information to newcomers to a university, organization, etc.

oriented *adj.* **1** (with preceding n. or adv.) having a specified emphasis, bias, or interest (*job-oriented*). **2** having a particular orientation.

orienteering *n.* a competitive sport in which participants have to find their way on foot, skis, etc. across rough country with the aid of map and compass. □ **orienteer** *n. & v.intr.*

orifice /'ɒrɪfɪs, 'ɒr-/ *n.* a usu. small opening, esp. the mouth of a bodily organ or other cavity.

origami /ˌɒrɪ'gɑːmi, ˌɒr-/ *n.* the Japanese art of folding paper into decorative shapes and figures.

origin *n.* **1 a** a beginning, cause, or ultimate source of something. **b** that from which a thing is derived; a source or starting point (*a word of Latin origin*). **2** (often in *pl.*) a person's social background, family, etc. (*middle-class origins*). **3 a** a place at which a muscle is firmly attached. **b** a place where a nerve or blood vessel begins or branches from a main nerve or blood vessel. **4** *Math.* **a** a fixed point from which measurement or motion begins. **b** the point of intersection of axes in Cartesian coordinates.

original ● *adj.* **1** existing from the beginning or earliest stages. **2** novel; inventive; creative (*has an original mind*). **3 a** that is the origin or source of something. **b** (of a picture, text, etc.) from which another is copied, translated, etc. (*in the original Greek; an original Rembrandt*). **c** not derivative or imitative, esp. made, composed, etc. by a person himself or herself (*an original poem*). ● *n.* **1 a** an original model, pattern, picture, etc. from which another is copied or translated. **b** a person represented in a picture or upon whom a literary character is based. **2** an unusual or eccentric person. **3 a** a garment specially designed for a fashion collection. **b** a copy of such a garment made to order. □ **originally** *adv.*

originality *n.* (*pl.* **-ies**) **1** the quality or fact of being original, esp. the power of creating or thinking creatively. **2** newness or freshness, esp. of literary or artistic style. **3** an original act, thing, trait, etc.

original sin *n. Christianity* the innate tendency to evil or depravity of all humans, held to be inherited from Adam as a consequence of the Fall.

originate *v.* **1** *intr.* (usu. foll. by *from, in, with*) begin, arise, be derived, take its origin. **2** *tr.* cause to begin; initiate. **3** *intr. N Amer.* (of an aircraft, bus, etc.) begin a scheduled trip at a particular place. □ **origination** *n.* **originator** *n.*

o-ring *n.* a gasket in the form of a ring with a circular cross-section.

oriole /'ɔːriəl, -ɒl/ *n.* **1** any New World bird of the genus *Icterus*, esp. the northern oriole. **2** any Old World bird of the genus *Oriolus*, many of which have brightly coloured plumage.

ormolu /'ɔːməluː/ *n.* (often *attrib.*) gilded bronze; a gold-coloured alloy of copper, zinc, and tin used to decorate furniture, make ornaments, etc.

ornament ● *n.* **1 a** a thing used or serving to adorn, esp. a small trinket, vase, figure, etc. (*a mantelpiece crowded with ornaments; her only ornament was a brooch*). **b** a person who adds honour or distinction to his or her sphere, time, etc. (*an ornament to her profession*). **c** a quality or circumstance that confers beauty, grace, or honour. **2** decoration added to embellish esp. a building. **3** (in *pl.*) *Music* embellishments and decorations made to a melody. ● *v.tr.* adorn, beautify, provide with ornaments. □ **ornamentation** *n.*

ornamental ● *adj.* serving as an ornament; decorative. ● *n.* a thing considered to be ornamental rather than essential, esp. a cultivated plant. □ **ornamentalism** *n.* **ornamentally** *adv.*

ornate /ɔː'neɪt/ *adj.* **1** elaborately adorned; highly

decorated. **2** (of literary style etc.) convoluted; flowery. □ **ornately** *adv.* **ornateness** *n.*

ornery /'ɔːnəri/ *adj. N Amer. informal* **1** grumpily stubborn. **2** crotchety, cantankerous. □ **orneriness** *n.*

ornithology /ˌɔːnɪ'θɒlədʒi/ *n.* the branch of zoology that deals with the study of birds. □ **ornithological** *adj.* **ornithologist** *n.*

orphan ● *n.* (often *attrib.*) **1 a** a child or young animal deprived by death of one or usu. both parents. **b** a child bereft of parental care, esp. through abandonment or neglect. **2** a person, country, policy, etc. bereft of previous protection, advantages, etc. **3** *Printing* the first line of a paragraph at the foot of a page or column (*compare* WIDOW *n.* 3). ● *v.tr.* **1** bereave (a child etc.) of its parents or a parent. **2** abandon or deprive of previously provided assistance, support, etc. □ **orphaned** *adj.*

orphanage *n.* a usu. residential institution for the care and education of orphans.

ortho- *comb. form* **1** straight, rectangular, upright. **2** normal, proper, correct.

orthodontics /ˌɔːθə'dɒntɪks/ *n.pl.* (treated as *sing.*) (also **orthodontia** /-'tiə/) the branch of dentistry that deals with treatment of irregular alignment of the teeth and jaws. □ **orthodontic** *adj.* **orthodontist** *n.*

orthodox *adj.* **1 a** holding correct or currently accepted opinions, esp. on religious doctrine, morals, etc. **b** conventional, not independent-minded. **2 a** (of opinion, doctrine, etc.) right, correct, in accordance with what is generally accepted or authoritatively established. **b** (of standards of morality etc.) approved, in accordance with what is regarded as proper or usual. **3** (usu. **Orthodox**) (of Judaism or Jews) adhering strictly to the rabbinical interpretation of Jewish law and its traditional observances. **4** (**Orthodox**) of or relating to the Orthodox Church. **Orthodox Church** *n.* the family of Eastern Churches, having the Patriarch of Constantinople as its head, and including the national Churches of Russia, Romania, Greece, etc.

orthodoxy *n.* (*pl.* **-ies**) **1 a** the quality or character of being orthodox. **b** belief in or agreement with what is, or is currently held to be, right, esp. in religious matters. **c** the body of orthodox doctrine. **2** an authorized or generally accepted theory, doctrine, etc. **3** (also **Orthodoxy**) **a** the Orthodox practice of Judaism. **b** the body of Orthodox Jews. **4 a** the Orthodox Church or Churches. **b** the body of Orthodox Christians.

orthogonal /ɔː'θɒɡənəl/ *adj.* of, involving, or at right angles; rectangular. □ **orthogonality** /-'nælɪti/ *n.*

orthography /ɔː'θɒɡrəfi/ *n.* (*pl.* **-ies**) **1** correct or conventional spelling. **b** spelling with reference to its correctness (*dreadful orthography*). **c** the branch of grammar which deals with letters and their combinations to represent sounds and words; the subject of spelling. **2 a** perspective projection used in maps and elevations in which the projection lines are parallel. **b** a map etc. so projected. □ **orthographic** *adj.* **orthographical** *adj.*

orthopaedic /ˌɔːθə'piːdɪk/ *adj.* (also **orthopedic**) **1** pertaining to or concerned with orthopaedics. **2 a** (of a bed etc.) designed to relieve back problems, usu. having a very firm mattress or board. **b** (of footwear etc.) designed to ease or correct deformities of the feet.

orthopaedics *n.pl.* (treated as *sing.*) (also **orthopedics**) the branch of medicine dealing with the correction of deformities of bones or muscles or the treatment of impairments of the skeletal system. □ **orthopaedist** n.

orthotic /ɔːˈθɒtɪk/ n. (usu. in pl.) **1** a moulded insert for a shoe etc. designed to improve posture and gait. **2** an artificial external device, as a brace or splint, serving to prevent or assist relative movement in the limbs. □ **orthotist** /ˈɔːθɒtɪst/ n.

Orwellian /ɔːˈwelɪən/ adj. of or characteristic of the writings of George Orwell (1903–50), esp. with reference to the totalitarian development of the state as depicted in *Nineteen Eighty-four* and *Animal Farm*.

oryx /ˈɒrɪks/ n. any large straight-horned antelope of the genus *Oryx*, native to Africa and Arabia.

orzo n. a variety of pasta shaped like grains of rice or barley.

OS abbr. **1** Computing operating system. **2** old style. **3** ORDINARY SEAMAN. **4** outsize. **5** out of stock.

Os symbol osmium.

Osage orange /oːˈseɪdʒ, ˈoː-/ n. **1** a hardy thorny tree, *Maclura pomifera*, of the US, bearing inedible wrinkled orange-like fruit. **2** the durable orange-coloured timber from this.

OSAP /ˈoːsæp/ abbr. Cdn (Ont.) Ontario Student Assistance Program, a program administering financial aid to post-secondary students.

OSC abbr. Cdn (Ont.) Ontario Securities Commission.

Oscar n. any of the statuettes awarded by the US Academy of Motion Picture Arts and Sciences for excellence in film acting, directing, etc.

oscillate /ˈɒsɪleɪt/ v. **1** intr. & tr. **a** swing to and fro like a pendulum. **b** move to and fro between points. **2** intr. vacillate; vary between extremes of opinion, action, etc. **3** intr. Physics move with periodic regularity. **4** intr. Electricity (of a current) undergo high-frequency alternations. **5** intr. (of a radio receiver) radiate electromagnetic waves owing to faulty operation. **6** intr. Math. (of a series or function) increase and decrease alternately as successive items are taken or as the variable tends to infinity. □ **oscillating** adj. **oscillation** n. **oscillator** n. **oscillatory** /ˈɒsɪlətəri, ˈɒsɪˌleɪtəri/ adj.

oscilloscope /əˈsɪləˌskoːp/ n. a device for viewing oscillations by a display on the screen of a cathode ray tube. □ **oscilloscopic** adj.

osier /ˈoːzɪər/ n. **1** any of various willows, esp. *Salix viminalis*, with long flexible shoots used in basketwork. **2** a shoot of a willow.

osmium /ˈɒzmɪəm/ n. a hard bluish-white element, the heaviest known metal, occurring naturally in association with platinum and used in certain alloys.

osmosis /ɒzˈmoːsɪs, ɒs-/ n. **1** Biochem. the passage of a solvent through a semi-permeable partition into a more concentrated solution, so as to make the concentration on the two sides more nearly equal. **2** gradual, usu. unconscious assimilation or absorption of ideas, knowledge, etc. □ **osmotic** /-ˈmɒtɪk/ adj. **osmotically** adv.

osprey /ˈɒspreɪ, -prɪ/ n. (pl. **-eys**) a large bird of prey, *Pandion haliaetus*, with a brown back and white markings, feeding on fish, which it catches in its claws after making a spectacular dive from the air.

Ossie var. of AUSSIE.

ossify /ˈɒsɪfaɪ/ v.tr. & intr. (**-ies, -ied**) **1** turn into bone or bony tissue; harden. **2 a** make or become emotionally callous. **b** make or become rigid, fixed, or unprogressive in attitude. □ **ossification** n.

osso bucco /ˌɒsoː ˈbʊkoː/ n. (also **osso buco**) an Italian dish of veal shanks containing marrow bone stewed in wine with vegetables.

ostensible /ɒˈstensɪbəl/ adj. **1** apparent, but not necessarily real (*his brother's ostensible detachment*). **2** declared, professed, esp. while concealing the actual or genuine (*her ostensible function was that of interpreter*). □ **ostensibly** adv.

ostentation /ˌɒstenˈteɪʃən/ n. **1** a pretentious and vulgar display esp. of wealth and luxury. **2** the attempt or intention to attract notice; showing off. □ **ostentatious** adj. **ostentatiously** adv.

osteo- /ˈɒstɪoː/ comb. form bone.

osteoarthritis n. a degenerative disease of joint cartilage causing pain and stiffness esp. in those middle aged and older.

osteology /ˌɒstiˈɒlədʒi/ n. the study of the structure and function of the skeleton. □ **osteological** adj. **osteologically** adv. **osteologist** n.

osteopathy /ˌɒstiˈɒpəθi/ n. a system of healing based on the theory that some disorders can be alleviated by treatment of the skeleton and musculature using manipulation and massage. □ **osteopath** /ˈɒstiəˌpæθ/ n. **osteopathic** adj.

osteoporosis /ˌɒstioːpəˈroːsɪs/ n. a condition of fragile, porous bones caused by loss of the protein and mineral content of bone tissue, esp. as a result of hormonal changes, or deficiency of calcium or vitamin D. □ **osteoporotic** /-ˈrɒtɪk/ adj. & n.

ostinato /ˌɒstiˈnæːtoː/ n. (pl. **-os** or **-i**) (often attrib.) Music a persistent phrase or rhythm repeated through all or part of a piece.

ostracize /ˈɒstrəˌsaɪz/ v.tr. exclude (a person) from a society, favour, privileges, etc. by common consent; refuse to associate with. □ **ostracism** n.

ostrich n. **1** a large African swift-running flightless bird, *Struthio camelus*, with long legs and two toes on each foot. **2** a person who refuses to accept facts. □ **ostrichlike** adj.

Oswego tea /ɒsˈwiːgoː/ n. a N American bergamot, *Monarda didyma*, grown for its showy heads of scarlet flowers.

OT abbr. **1 a** overtime. **b** Football offensive tackle. **2 a** occupational therapy. **b** occupational therapist. **3** Old Testament.

OTC abbr. = OVER-THE-COUNTER.

other ● adj. **1** not the same as one or some already mentioned or implied; separate in identity or distinct in kind (*other people; use other means*). **2 a** further; additional (*a few other examples*). **b** alternative of two (*open your other eye*) (*compare* EVERY OTHER (*see* EVERY)). **3** (prec. by *the*) that remains after all except the one or ones in question have been considered, eliminated, etc. (*must be in the other pocket; the other three men left*). **4** (foll. by *than*) **a** apart from; excepting (*any person other than you*). **b** different in kind or quality (*might be other than what she seemed*). ● n. or pron. **1** an additional, different, or extra person, thing, example, etc. (*one or other of us will be there; some others have come*). **2** (in pl.; prec. by *the*) the ones remaining, the different ones (*where are the others?*). **3** (usu. **Other** or in quotation marks, prec. by *the*) *Philos.* & *Sociol.* that which is distinct from, different from, or opposite to something or oneself (*fear of the 'other'*). ● adv. (usu. foll. by *than*) disputed otherwise (*cannot react other than angrily*). □ **of all others** out of the many possible or likely (*on this night of all others*). **the other day** (or **night** or **week**) a few days etc. ago (*heard from him the other day*). **other things being equal** if conditions are or were alike in all but the point in question. **someone** (or **something** or **somehow** etc.) **or other** some unspecified person, thing, manner, etc.

other half n. **1** jocular one's wife or husband. **2** informal (prec. by *the*) a group of people having different, esp. markedly superior or inferior, social, cultural, or economic standing (*how the other half lives*). **3** the rest, the remainder, or esp. the second of two equal parts.

otherness *n.* **1** the state or fact of being other or different. **2** a thing or existence separate from or other than the thing mentioned and the thinking subject.

other place *n.* (prec. by *the*) *jocular* **1** hell (as opposed to heaven). **2** *Cdn* the Senate as regarded by the House of Commons and vice versa.

other ranks *n.pl. Cdn, Brit., Austral.,* & *NZ* noncommissioned officers and ordinary soldiers etc.

otherwise ● *adv.* **1** else; or else; in the circumstances other than those considered etc. (*bring your umbrella, otherwise you will get wet*). **2** in other respects (*he is untidy, but otherwise very suitable*). **3** (often foll. by *than*) in another way, differently (*could not have acted otherwise*). **4** as an alternative (*otherwise known as Josh*). ● *adj.* (*predic.*) different, other (*the matter is quite otherwise*). □ **and** (or **or**) **otherwise** the negation or opposite (of a specified thing) (*experiences pleasant and otherwise*).

other woman *n.* a married man's mistress.

other world *n.* **1** = NEXT WORLD. **2** (also **otherworld**) **a** an alternate reality or state of consciousness. **b** (esp. in science fiction etc.) a fantastic or extraterrestrial planet or culture.

otherworldly *adj.* **1** concerned with spiritual matters, life after death, etc. **2** of or pertaining to an imaginary, ideal, or fantastic world. **3** unworldly; impractical. □ **otherworldliness** *n.*

Ottawa /ˈɒtəwɒ, -wə/ *n. & adj.* = ODAWA.

Ottawan ● *n.* a native or inhabitant of Ottawa. ● *adj.* of or relating to Ottawa.

otter *n.* **1 a** any of several semi-aquatic fish-eating mammals of the family Mustelidae, esp. of the genus *Lutra,* having strong claws and webbed feet and noted for its agile swimming. **b** its fur or pelt. **2** = SEA OTTER.

otter board *n.* a device, usu. consisting of two boards or metal plates attached to the ends of a trawl net, for keeping the mouth of the net open.

otter trawl *n.* a cone-shaped net, the mouth held open with an otter board, that is dragged along the ocean floor to catch groundfish, e.g. cod.

Ottoman /ˈɒtəmən/ ● *adj. hist.* **1** of or concerning the dynasty of Osman or Othman I (late 13th c.), the branch of the Turks to which he belonged, or the empire ruled by his descendants. **2** Turkish. ● *n.* an Ottoman person; a Turk.

ottoman /ˈɒtəmən/ *n.* **1** an upholstered seat, usu. square and without a back or arms, sometimes a box with a padded top. **2** a footstool of similar design.

ouananiche /ˈwɒnənɪʃ/ *n. Cdn* a landlocked lake variety of Atlantic salmon, found in Newfoundland and Labrador, Quebec, and Ontario.

ouch *interj.* expressing pain or annoyance.

ought[1] *v.aux.* (usu. foll. by *to* + infin.) **1** expressing duty or rightness (*we ought to love our neighbours*). **2** expressing shortcoming (*it ought to have been done*). **3** expressing advisability or prudence (*you ought to go for your own good*). **4** expressing esp. strong probability (*he ought to be there by now*).

ought[2] *n. informal* a figure denoting nothing; nought.

oughtn't *contraction* ought not.

Ouija /ˈwiːdʒiː, -dʒə/ *n.* (in full **Ouija board**) *proprietary* a board having letters or signs at its rim to which a planchette points under supposedly spiritualistic influence in answer to questions from attenders at a seance etc.

ounce *n.* **1 a** a unit of weight of one-sixteenth of a pound avoirdupois (approx. 28 grams). Abbr.: **oz. b** a unit of one-twelfth of a pound troy or apothecaries' measure, equal to 480 grains (approx. 31 grams). **2** = FLUID OUNCE. **3** a small quantity.

ouncer *n.* (in *comb.*) a thing that weighs or consists of a specified number of ounces (*a forty-ouncer of rye*).

our *possess.adj.* (*attrib.*) **1** of or belonging to us or ourselves (*our house; our own business*). **2** of or belonging to all people (*our children's future*). **3** (esp. as **Our**) of Us the king or queen, emperor or empress, etc. (*given under Our seal*). **4** of us, the editorial staff of a newspaper etc. (*a foolish adventure in our view*).

Our Father *n. Christianity* **1** the Lord's Prayer. **2** God.

Our Lady *n. Christianity* **1** the Virgin Mary. **2** an image or representation of the Virgin Mary.

Our Lord *n.* **1** *Christianity* Jesus Christ. **2** God.

ours *possess.pron.* the one or ones belonging to or associated with us (*it is ours; ours are over there*). □ **of ours** of or belonging to us (*a friend of ours*).

ourself *pron.* **1** *archaic* a word formerly used instead of *myself* by a sovereign, newspaper editorial staff, etc. (compare OUR 3, 4). **2** *disputed*= OURSELVES. ¶The use of *ourself* rather than *ourselves* in contexts such as *We see ourself as the biggest club in Canada* is considered incorrect by some people.

ourselves *pron.* **1 a** *emphatic form of* WE or US (*we ourselves did it; made it ourselves*). **b** *refl. form of* US (*are pleased with ourselves*). **2** in our normal state of body or mind (*not quite ourselves today*). □ **be ourselves** act in our normal unconstrained manner.

oust /ʌʊst/ *v.tr.* **1** remove (a person) from a job or position of power, esp. by forcing oneself in. **2** (usu. foll. by *of*) *Law* put (a person) out of possession; deprive. □ **ousted** *adj.*

ouster *n.* **1** a removal (of a person), esp. from a position of power, as a result of physical action, judicial process, or political upheaval. **2** esp. *N Amer.* dismissal, expulsion.

out ● *adv.* **1 a** away from or not in or at a place etc. (*keep her out; get out of here*). **b** *Cdn* (North) in or to the more southern or heavily populated part of the country. **2** (forming part of phrasal verbs) **a** indicating dispersal away from a centre etc. (*hire out*). **b** indicating a progression to a conclusion or resolution (*fight it out*). **c** indicating coming or bringing into the open for public attention etc. (*stand out*). **d** indicating a need for attentiveness (*watch out*). **3** a not in one's house, office, etc. (*out for a walk*). **b** occupied elsewhere, esp. socially (*out with friends*). **c** no longer detained in prison. **4 a** completely; thoroughly (*tired out*). **b** in its entirety (*typed it out*). **5** (of a fire, candle, etc.) not burning. **6** in error (*was 3 per cent out in my calculations*). **7** *informal* unconscious (*she was out for five minutes*). **8 a** (of a tooth) extracted. **b** (of a joint, bone, etc.) dislocated (*put his shoulder out*). **9** (of a party, politician, etc.) not in office. **10** (of a jury) considering its verdict in secrecy. **11** (of workers) on strike. **12 a** (of a secret) revealed. **b** *informal* (of a person) having declared to others that one is homosexual (*I've only been out for two years*). **13** (of a flower) blooming, open. **14** (of a book etc.) **a** published; on the market (*their new CD is just out*). **b** not in the library; currently on loan to someone else. **15** (of a star) visible after dark. **16** unfashionable (*wide ties are out*). **17 a** *Baseball* (of a batter) having failed to get on base. **b** *Baseball* (of a runner) having failed to advance from one base to another. **c** (of a shot, serve, etc.) outside the boundary of the playing area. **18** not worth considering; rejected (*that idea is out*). **19** *informal* (prec. by *superlative*) known to exist (*the best game out*). **20** (of a stain, mark, etc.) not visible, removed (*painted out the sign*). **21** (of time) not spent working (*took five minutes out*). **22** having lost in a transaction (*am out $50 on the deal*). **23** (of the tide) at the lowest point. **24** *Boxing* unable to rise from the floor (*out for the count*). **25 a** at an end; over (*before the week is out*). **b** (in a radio conversation etc.) indicating that a transmission has come to an end (*over and out*). ● *prep.* out of (*looked out the window*). ● *n.* **1** *informal* a way of escape; an excuse. **2** *Baseball* the action or an act of putting a player out. ● *adj. informal* (of a person) openly homosexual (*an out lesbian*). ● *interj.* a peremptory dismissal, reproach, etc. ● *v.* **1** *tr.* **a** put out. **b** *informal* eject forcibly. **2** *intr.* come or go out; emerge (*murder will out*). **3** *tr. informal* **a** reveal the homosexuality of (esp. a prominent person). **b** reveal a previously unknown fact about (a person). **4** *tr. Boxing* knock out. □ **on the outs** *N Amer.* at variance or enmity. **out and about** (of a person, esp. after an illness) engaging in normal activity. **out and away** by far. **out for** having one's interest or effort directed to; intent on. **out of 1** from within (*came out of the house*). **2** not within (*out of the province*). **3** from among (*nine out of ten*). **4** beyond the range of (*is out of reach*). **5** without or so as to be without (*was swindled out of her money; out of breath*). **6** from (*get the money out of your parents*). **7** owing to; because of (*asked out of curiosity*). **8** by the use of (material) (*what did you make it out of?*). **9** at a specified distance from (a town, port, etc.) (*seven miles out of Moncton*). **10** beyond (*something out of the ordinary*). **11** as depicted in (a fictional work) (*a scene straight out of Dickens*). **out of it** *N Amer. informal* **1** dazed, dopey. **2** out of touch; not up to date. **out to** keenly striving to do. **out with** an exhortation to expel or dismiss (an unwanted person). **out with it** say what you are thinking.

out- *prefix* added to verbs and nouns, meaning: **1** so as to surpass or exceed (*outnumber*). **2** external, separate (*outline*). **3** out of; away from; outward (*outgrowth*).

outa *var. of* OUTTA.

outage *n.* **1** an interruption in supply, esp. of electricity. **2** a period of time during which this happens.

out-and-out ● *adj.* in every respect; complete (*an out-and-out crook*). ● *adv.* completely; totally.

outback *n.* esp. *Austral.* the remote and usu. uninhabited inland districts. □ **outbacker** *n.*

out basket *n. N Amer.* a tray or basket, esp. on a person's desk, for outgoing documents etc.

outbid *v.tr.* (**-bidding**; *past* and *past part.* **-bid**) bid higher than (another person) at an auction etc.

outboard ● *adj.* **1** (of a motor) portable and attachable to the outside of the stern of a boat. **2** (of a boat) having an outboard motor. **3** located on, near, or towards the outside of an aircraft, ship, etc. ● *adv.* on, towards, or near the outside of a ship, aircraft, etc. ● *n.* **1** an outboard engine. **2** a boat with an outboard engine.

outbound *adj.* outward bound.

outbreak *n.* a usu. sudden eruption of emotion, war, disease, rebellion, etc.

outbuilding *n.* a detached building, e.g. a shed, barn, garage, etc., that is separate from but within the grounds of a main building.

outburst *n.* **1** an explosion of anger etc., expressed in words. **2** a sudden eruption or explosion of activity etc.

outcast ● *n.* **1** a person cast out from or rejected by his or her home, country, society, etc. **2** a tramp or vagabond. ● *adj.* rejected; homeless; friendless.

outclass *v.tr.* **1** belong to a higher class than. **2** defeat easily. **3** (usu. in *passive*) be superior to.

outcome *n.* a result; a visible effect.

outcrop ● *n.* (also **outcropping**) **1 a** the emergence of a stratum, vein, or rock, at the surface. **b** a stratum etc. emerging. **2** a noticeable manifestation or occurrence. ● *v.intr.* (**-cropped**, **-cropping**) appear as an outcrop; crop out.

outcry *n.* (*pl.* **-ies**) **1** a vehement or prolonged public protest. **2** an uproar. **3** an act or instance of crying out.

outdated *adj.* out of date; obsolete.

outdistance *v.tr.* **1** leave (a competitor) behind completely. **2** be vastly superior to.

outdo *v.tr.* (3rd *sing. present* **-does**; *past* **-did**; *past part.* **-done**) exceed or surpass in doing or performance.

outdoor *adj.* **1** done, existing, or used out of doors. **2** fond of the open air (*an outdoor type*).

outdoors ● *adv.* in or into the open air; out of doors. ● *adj.* = OUTDOOR *adj.* 2. ● *n.* the world outside buildings; the open air.

outdoorsman *n.* (*pl.* **-men**) a person who enjoys or frequently participates in outdoor activities.

outdoorswoman *n.* (*pl.* **-women**) a woman who enjoys or frequently participates in outdoor activities.

outdoorsy *adj.* **1** associated with or characteristic of the outdoors. **2** (of a person) fond of an outdoor life or outdoor activities.

outer *adj.* **1** outside; external (*pierced the outer layer*). **2** farther from the centre or inside; relatively far out. **3** objective or physical, not subjective.

outer garment *n.* an article of clothing worn over other clothes or outdoors.

outermost *adj.* furthest from the inside; the most far out.

outer space *n.* = SPACE *n.* 3a.

outerwear *n.* clothing, such as a coat, that is worn over other clothing to provide warmth or protection while outdoors.

outfall *n.* the outlet of a river, drain, sewer, etc.

outfield *n.* **1** the part of a baseball field that lies outside of the baseline. **2** the positions in this space, i.e. right, left, and centre field. **3** the players who occupy these positions. □ **outfielder** *n.*

outfit ● *n.* **1** a set of clothes worn or esp. designed to be worn together. **2** a complete set of equipment etc. for a specific purpose. **3** a business or company engaged in a particular type of work (*a construction outfit*). **4** a military unit. **5** a group of musicians (*a jazz outfit*). ● *v.tr.* (also *refl.*) (**-fitted**, **-fitting**) provide with an outfit, e.g. of clothes or equipment.

outfitter *n. N Amer.* **1** a supplier of equipment for outdoor activities such as hiking trips etc. **2** a person who acts as guide on wilderness trips etc.

outflank *v.tr.* **1 a** extend one's flank beyond that of (an enemy). **b** outmanoeuvre (an enemy) in this way. **2** get the better of (an opponent).

outflow *n.* **1** an outward flow. **2** the amount that flows out.

outfox *v.tr. informal* outwit.

outgas *v.* (**-gases**, **-gassed**, **-gassing**) **1** *intr.* release or give off a gas or vapour. **2** *tr.* **a** release or give off (a substance) as a gas or vapour. **b** drive off a gas or vapour from.

outgo *n.* (*pl.* **-goes**) expenditure of money, effort, etc.

outgoing ● *adj.* **1** friendly; sociable; extrovert. **2** retiring from office. **3** going out or away. ● *n.* **1** (in *pl.*) expenditure. **2** the act or an instance of going out.

outgroup *n.* a group perceived as outsiders by members of an in-group.

outgrow *v.tr.* (*past* **-grew**; *past part.* **-grown**) **1** grow too big for (one's clothes). **2** leave behind (a childish habit, taste, ailment, etc.) as one matures. **3** grow faster or taller than (a person, plant, etc.).

outgrowth *n.* **1** something that grows out. **2** an offshoot; a natural product. **3** the process of growing out.

outgun *v.tr.* (**-gunned**, **-gunning**) **1** surpass in military or other power or strength. **2** shoot better than.

outharbour *n. Cdn* (*Nfld*) = OUTPORT 1.

outhouse *n.* **1** *N Amer.* an outdoor toilet that is enclosed but separate from the main building. **2** an outbuilding.

outing *n.* **1** a short holiday away from home, esp. of one day or part of a day; a pleasure trip, an excursion. **2** any brief journey from home. **3** a public appearance in a game, race, etc. **4** *informal* the practice or policy of revealing the homosexuality of a prominent person.

outlander *n.* a foreigner, alien, or stranger.

outlandish *adj.* bizarre, strange, unfamiliar. □ **outlandishly** *adv.* **outlandishness** *n.*

outlast *v.tr.* last longer than or beyond; survive (*outlasted its usefulness*).

outlaw ● *n.* **1** a fugitive from the law. **2** a person who does not conform to traditional or established practices. ● *v.tr.* **1** make illegal; prohibit. **2** declare (a person) an outlaw. □ **outlawry** *n.*

outlay *n.* **1** an amount of money spent; an expenditure. **2** an act or instance of spending money.

outlet *n.* **1** a means of exit or escape. **2** *N Amer.* a socket in a wall etc. for connecting an electrical appliance to a wiring system. **3** (usu. foll. by *for*) a means of expression (of a talent, emotion, etc.) (*an outlet for tension*). **4 a** a place that sells merchandise made by a particular company or of a particular type. **b** = FACTORY OUTLET. **5 a** a stream, river, or channel flowing out of and draining a larger body of water, e.g. a lake. **b** the mouth of a river.

outlet box *n.* **1** an electrical outlet. **2** a small metal box inserted in a wall etc., for containing an electrical outlet.

outline ● *n.* **1** a rough statement of the main facts or points to be presented in a piece of writing, etc. **2** a sketch containing only contour lines. **3** (in *sing.* or *pl.*) **a** lines enclosing or indicating an object (*the outline of a shape under the blankets*). **b** a contour. **c** an external boundary. **4** (in *pl.*) the main features or general principles (*the outlines of a plan*). ● *v.tr.* **1** describe the main features of; summarize. **2** draw in outline. **3** draw a line around (*outlined in red*). □ **in outline** sketched or represented as an outline.

outlive *v.tr.* **1** live longer than (another person). **2** live beyond (a specified date or time). **3** live through (an experience).

outlook *n.* **1** the prospect for the future (*the outlook is bleak*). **2** one's mental attitude or point of view (*narrow in their outlook*). **3** a view on which one looks out (*a pleasant outlook over the valley*).

outlying *adj.* situated far from a centre; remote.

outmanoeuvre *v.tr.* (also **outmaneuver**) **1** use skill and cunning to secure an advantage over (a person). **2** outdo in manoeuvring.

out-migration *n.* the action of migrating from one place to another, esp. in the same country.

outmoded *adj.* **1** no longer in fashion. **2** obsolete.

outnumber *v.tr.* exceed in number.

out-of-body experience *n.* a sensation of being outside one's body, esp. of floating and being able to observe oneself from a distance.

out-of-court *attrib.adj.* (esp. of a settlement) made or done outside or without the intervention of a court.

out of date *adj.* (hyphenated when *attrib.*) old-fashioned, obsolete.

out-of-pocket *adj.* (of costs etc.) paid out in cash.

out of print *adj.* (of a book) no longer available from the publisher.

out-of-province *adj. Cdn* in, from, or pertaining to another province (*out-of-province health insurance*).

out-of-sight *adj.* **1** not visible. **2** *informal* excellent.

out-of-the-way *adj.* **1** remote; far from a main road or centre of population. **2** unusual; extraordinary.

out-of-town *attrib.adj.* **1** originating from outside of a particular place (*had some out-of-town visitors*). **2** occurring in another place (*an out-of-town hockey tournament*). □ **out-of-towner** *n.*

out-of-work *adj.* unemployed.

outpace *v.tr.* **1** go faster than. **2** outdo in a contest.

outpatient *n.* a person receiving treatment at a hospital without being hospitalized.

outperform *v.tr.* **1** perform better than. **2** surpass in a specified field or activity. □ **outperformance** *n.*

outplacement *n.* the act or process of finding new employment for esp. executive workers who have been dismissed or made redundant (also *attrib.*).

outplay *v.tr.* surpass in playing; play better than.

outpoll *v.tr.* receive more votes than (an opponent) in an election, opinion poll, etc. (*outpolled her closest competitor three to one*).

outport *n.* **1** *Cdn* **a** (*Nfld*) any port other than St. John's, esp. an isolated fishing village. **b** (*Maritimes*) a coastal fishing village. **2** a subsidiary port.

outporter *n. Cdn* (*Nfld*) an inhabitant or native of an outport.

outpost *n.* **1** a detachment set at a distance from the main body of an army, esp. to prevent surprise. **2** a distant branch or settlement.

outpost camp *n. Cdn* a remote hunting or fishing camp.

outpouring *n.* **1** a large amount of something produced in a short time (*a remarkable outpouring of new ideas*). **2** (usu. in *pl.*) an expression of very strong feelings (*outpourings of public grief*). **3** something that pours out (*an outpouring of water from the lake*).

output ● *n.* **1** the product of a process, esp. of manufacture, or of mental or artistic work. **2** the quantity or amount of this. **3** the printout, results, etc. supplied by a computer. **4** the power etc. delivered by an apparatus. **5** a place where energy, information, etc. leaves a system. ● *v.tr.* (**-putting**; *past* and *past part.* **-put** or **-putted**) **1** put or send out. **2** (of a computer) supply (results etc.).

outrage ● *n.* **1** an extreme or shocking violation of others' rights, sentiments, etc. **2** a gross offence or indignity. **3** fierce anger or resentment (*a feeling of outrage*). ● *v.tr.* **1** subject to outrage. **2** injure, insult, etc. flagrantly. **3** shock and anger. □ **outraged** *adj.*

outrageous /ʌut'reidʒəs/ *adj.* **1** deeply shocking and unacceptable. **2** grossly cruel. **3** immoral, offensive. **4** highly unusual or unconventional. □ **outrageously** *adv.* **outrageousness** *n.*

outran *past of* OUTRUN.

outrank *v.tr.* **1** be superior in rank to. **2** take priority over.

outré /ˈuːtrei/ *adj.* outside the bounds of what is usual or proper.

outreach ● *v.tr.* **1** reach further than. **2** surpass. ● *n.* **1** the activity of an organization in contacting, educating, and providing services, advice, etc. to people in the community, esp. outside its usual centres. **2** the extent or length of reaching out.

outrider *n.* **1** a mounted attendant riding ahead of, or with, a carriage etc. **2** a motorcyclist acting as a guard in a similar manner. □ **outriding** *n.*

outrigger *n.* **1** a beam, spar, or framework, rigged out and projecting from or over a ship's side for various purposes. **2** a similar projecting beam etc. in a building. **3** a log etc. fixed parallel to a canoe to stabilize it. **4** a chassis extension supporting the body of a motor vehicle.

outright ● *adv.* **1** altogether, entirely (*proved outright*). **2** not gradually, nor by degrees, nor by instalments (*bought it outright*). **3** without reservation, openly (*denied the charge outright*). ● *adj.* **1** downright, direct, complete (*outright anger*). **2** undisputed, clear (*the outright winner*). □ **outrightness** *n.*

outro / ˈʌutro: / *n.* (*pl.* **-os**) *informal* a concluding section, esp. of a broadcast program or a piece of music.

outrun *v.tr.* (**-running**; *past* **-ran**; *past part.* **-run**) **1** a run faster or farther than. **b** escape from. **2** go beyond (a specified point or limit).

outscore *v.tr.* score more than (an opponent) in a game etc.

outsell *v.tr.* (*past* and *past part.* **-sold**) **1** sell more than. **2** be sold in greater quantities than.

outset *n.* the start, beginning. □ **at** (or **from**) **the outset** from the beginning.

outshine *v.tr.* (*past* and *past part.* **-shone**) **1** shine brighter than. **2** surpass in ability, excellence, etc.

outshoot *v.tr.* (*past* and *past part.* **-shot**) **1** shoot better or further than (another person). **2** esp. *N Amer.* (in hockey, etc.) make more shots on (an opposing team) than the opposing team is able to make.

outside ● *n.* **1** the external side or surface; the outer parts. **2** the external appearance; the outward aspect of a building etc. **3** (of a path) the side away from the wall or next to the road. **4** (also *attrib.*) all that is without; the world as distinct from the thinking subject (*viewed from the outside the problem is simple*). **5** a position on the outer side (*the gate opens from the outside*). **6** *informal* the highest computation (*a mile at the outside*). **7** *Cdn* (*North*) the rest of the world, esp. a more heavily populated or urban area. ● *adj.* **1** of or on or nearer the outside; outer. **2** not of or belonging to some circle or institution (*outside help*). **3** (of a chance etc.) remote; very unlikely. **4** (of an estimate etc.) the greatest or highest possible (*the outside price*). **5** (of a player in football etc.) positioned nearest to the edge of the field. **6** *Baseball* **a** (of a pitched ball) missing the plate on the side opposite the batter. **b** (of the strike zone) furthest away from the batter. **7** *Cdn* (*North*) of or relating to the rest of the world, esp. to a more heavily populated or urban area. ● *adv.* **1** on or to the outside. **2** in or to the open air. **3** not within or enclosed or included. **4** *Cdn* (*North*) in or to the rest of the world, esp. a more heavily populated or urban area. **5** *slang* not in prison. ● *prep.* **1** not in; to or at the exterior of (*outside the post office*). **2** external to, not included in, beyond the limits of (*outside the law*). ¶The use of *outside of* as a preposition, e.g. *There is nothing like it outside of Newfoundland*, is considered incorrect by some, but is acceptable in both written and spoken English. □ **at the outside** (of an estimate etc.) at the most. **get outside of** *slang* eat or drink. **outside and in** outside and inside. **outside**

in = INSIDE OUT. **outside of** esp. *N Amer. informal* apart from.

outside interest *n.* a hobby; an interest not connected with one's work or normal way of life.

outsider *n.* **1 a** a non-member of some circle, party, profession, etc. **b** an uninitiated person, a layman. **2** a competitor, applicant, etc. thought to have little chance of success.

outsize ● *adj.* **1** unusually large. **2** (of garments etc.) of an exceptionally large size. ● *n.* an exceptionally large person or thing, esp. a garment. □ **outsized** *adj.*

outskirts *n.pl.* the outer border or fringe of a town, district, subject, etc.

outsmart *v.tr.* outwit, be cleverer than.

outsold *past and past part. of* OUTSELL.

outsole *n.* the outer sole of a boot or shoe, esp. a sports shoe.

outsource *v.tr.* esp. *N Amer. Commerce* **1** obtain (goods etc.) by contract from an outside source. **2** contract (work) out. □ **outsourcing** *n.*

outspend *v.tr.* (*past* and *past part.* **-spent**) spend more than (one's resources or another person).

outspoken *adj.* given to or involving plain speaking; frank in stating one's opinions. □ **outspokenly** *adv.* **outspokenness** *n.*

outspread ● *adj.* spread out; fully extended or expanded. ● *v.tr. & intr.* (*past* and *past part.* **-spread**) spread out; expand.

outstanding *adj.* **1 a** conspicuous, eminent, esp. because of excellence. **b** (usu. foll. by *at*, *in*) remarkable in (a specified field). **2** (esp. of a debt) not yet settled. □ **outstandingly** *adv.*

outstay *v.tr.* **1** stay beyond the limit of (one's welcome, invitation, etc.). **2** stay or endure longer than (another person etc.).

outstep *v.tr.* (**-stepped**, **-stepping**) step outside or beyond.

outstretch *v.tr.* **1** (usu. as **outstretched** *adj.*) reach out or stretch out (esp. one's hands or arms). **2** reach or stretch further than.

outstrip *v.tr.* (**-stripped**, **-stripping**) **1** pass in running etc. **2** surpass in competition or relative progress or ability. **3** be or become faster than (*demand is outstripping supply*).

outta *prep.* esp. *N Amer. informal* out of.

outtake *n.* a length of film etc. rejected in editing.

out-think *v.tr.* (*past* and *past part.* **-thought**) outwit; outdo in thinking.

out-thrust ● *adj.* extended; projected (*ran forward with out-thrust arms*). ● *v.tr.* (*past* and *past part.* **-thrust**) thrust out. ● *n.* **1** the act or an instance of thrusting forcibly outward. **2** the act or an instance of becoming prominent or noticeable.

out to lunch *adj. informal* out of touch with reality; unaware; crazy.

out tray *n.* = OUT BASKET.

out-turn *n. Curling* **1** an inward turn of the elbow and an outward turn of the hand made in delivering a stone, giving it a clockwise rotation. **2** a stone delivered with such a motion.

outvote *v.tr.* defeat by a majority of votes.

outward ● *adj.* **1** situated on or directed towards the outside. **2** going out (*on the outward voyage*). **3** bodily, external, apparent, superficial (*in all outward respects*). ● *adv.* (also **outwards**) in an outward direction; towards the outside. ● *n.* the outward appearance of something; the exterior. □ **outwardly** *adv.*

outward bound *adj.* **1** (of a ship, passenger, etc.) going away from home. **2** (**Outward Bound**) a movement to provide adventure training, naval training, and other outdoor activities for young people.

outwash *n.* the material carried from a glacier by meltwater and deposited beyond the moraine.

outwear ● *v.tr.* (*past* **-wore**; *past part.* **-worn**) **1** exhaust; wear out; wear away. **2** live or last beyond the duration of. ● *n.* outer clothing.

outweigh *v.tr.* exceed in weight, importance, etc.

outwent *past of* OUTGO.

outwit *v.tr.* (**-witted, -witting**) be too clever or crafty for; deceive by greater ingenuity.

outwork ● *v.tr.* work harder or faster than. ● *n.* an advanced or detached part of a fortification.

outworn ● *v. past part. of* OUTWEAR. ● *adj.* **1** obsolete; out-of-date. **2** worn out.

ouzo /'uːzoː/ *n.* (*pl.* **-os**) a Greek aniseed-flavoured spirit.

ova *pl. of* OVUM.

oval ● *adj.* **1** egg-shaped, ellipsoidal. **2** having the outline of an egg, elliptical. ● *n.* **1** an egg-shaped or elliptical closed curve. **2** any object with an oval outline. **3** an oval speed skating rink, racetrack, etc.

Oval Office *n.* **1** the office of the US President in the White House. **2** this seen as representing the executive power of the US presidency.

ovary /'oːvəri/ *n.* (*pl.* **-ies**) **1** each of the female reproductive organs in which ova are produced. **2** the hollow base of the carpel of a flower, containing one or more ovules. □ **ovarian** /ə'veriən/ *adj.* **ovariectomy** /-rɪ'ektəmɪ/ *n.* (*pl.* **-ies**) (in sense 1).

ovation /oː'veiʃən/ *n.* an enthusiastic reception, esp. spontaneous and sustained applause. □ **ovational** *adj.*

oven *n.* **1** an enclosed compartment, e.g. as part of a stove, used for baking, roasting, heating, etc. **2** a small furnace or kiln used in chemistry etc.

oven mitt *N Amer.* an insulated mitten (usu. one of a pair) for handling hot pans etc.

ovenproof *adj.* suitable for use in an oven.

oven-ready *adj.* (of food) prepared before sale so as to be ready for immediate cooking in the oven.

ovenware *n.* dishes that can be used for cooking food in the oven.

over ● *adv.* expressing movement or position or state above or beyond something stated or implied: **1** outward and downward from a brink or from any erect position (*knocked the lamp over*). **2** so as to cover or touch a whole surface (*paint it over*). **3** so as to produce a fold, or reverse a position; with the effect of being upside down. **4 a** across a street or other space (*came over from Europe*). **b** for a visit etc. (*invited them over last night*). **5** with transference or change from one hand or part to another (*went over to the Tories*; *handed them over*). **6** with motion above something; so as to pass across something (*fly over*; *boil over*). **7** from beginning to end with repetition or detailed concentration (*think it over*; *did it six times over*). **8** in excess; more than is right or required (*had one left over*). **9** for or until a later time (*held over*). **10** at an end; settled (*the crisis is over*; *all is over between us*). ● *prep.* **1** above, in, or to a position higher than; upon. **2** out and down from; down from the edge of (*fell over the cliff*). **3** so as to cover (*a hat over her eyes*). **4** above and across; so as to clear (*a bridge over the river*). **5** concerning; as a result of (*had an argument over money*). **6** while engaged or occupied with (*fell asleep over the newspaper*). **7 a** superior to (*a victory over the enemy*; *it was Calgary over Toronto 6–5*). **b** in charge of (*ruled over three kingdoms*). **c** in preference to (*I'd choose you over her any day*). **8** divided by. **9 a** throughout; covering the extent of

(*travelled over most of the prairies*; *a blush spread over his face*). **b** so as to deal with completely (*went over the plans*). **10 a** for the duration of (*stay over Saturday night*). **b** at any point during the course of (*I'll do it over the weekend*). **11** beyond; more than (*over $50*; *travelled over 60 miles*; *are you over 18?*). **12** transmitted by (*heard it over the radio*). **13** in comparison with (*gained 20 per cent over last year*). **14** having recovered from (*am now over my cold*). ● *adj.* **1** upper, outer. **2** superior. **3** extra. ● *interj.* (in full **over to you**) (in radio conversations etc.) said to indicate that it is the other person's turn to speak. □ **not over** not very; not at all (*not over friendly*). **over again** once again. **over against** in an opposite situation to; adjacent to, in contrast with. **over all** taken as a whole. **over and above** in addition to; not to mention (*$100 over and above the asking price*). **over and over** so that the same thing or the same point comes up again and again (*said it over and over*). **over with** (also **over and done with**) (esp. of an unpleasant or disagreeable task, experience, etc.) finished, completed (*let's get it over with*). **start** (or **begin** etc.) **over** *N Amer.* begin again.

over- *prefix* added to verbs, nouns, adjectives, and adverbs, meaning: **1** excessively; to an unwanted degree (*overheat*). **2** upper, outer, extra (*overcoat*; *overtime*). **3** 'over' in various senses (*overhang*; *overshadow*). **4** completely, utterly (*overjoyed*).

overabundant *adj.* in excessive quantity. □ **overabundance** *n.* **overabundantly** *adv.*

overachieve *v.* **1** *intr.* do more than might be expected (esp. scholastically). **2** *tr.* achieve more than (an expected goal or objective etc.). □ **overachievement** *n.* **overachiever** *n.*

overact *v.tr. & intr.* act in an exaggerated manner.

overactive *adj.* excessively active. □ **overactivity** *n.*

overage /'oːvəridʒ/ *n.* a surplus or excess, esp. an amount greater than estimated.

over-age *adj.* over a certain age limit; too old.

overall ● *adj.* **1** total, inclusive of all (*overall cost*). **2** taking everything into account, general (*overall improvement*). **3** from end to end (*overall length*). ● *adv.* **1** in all parts; taken as a whole (*overall, the performance was excellent*). **2** when everything is included (*finished second in their division and eighth overall*). ● *n.* (in *pl.*) = BIB OVERALLS. □ **overalled** *adj.*

overarching *adj.* **1** all-embracing; comprehensive. **2** forming an arch over.

overarm *adj. & adv.* **1** = OVERHAND 1. **2** *Swimming* with one or both arms lifted out of the water during a stroke.

overate *past of* OVEREAT.

overawe *v.tr.* cause (a person) to feel a great deal of fear, respect, etc.

overbalance ● *v.* **1** *tr.* cause (a person or thing) to lose its balance and fall. **2** *intr.* fall over, capsize. **3** *tr.* outweigh. ● *n.* **1** an excess. **2** the amount of this.

overbear *v.tr.* (*past* **-bore**; *past part.* **-borne**) **1** bear down; upset by weight, force, or emotional pressure. **2** put down or repress by power or authority. **3** surpass in importance etc.; outweigh.

overbearing *adj.* **1** domineering, masterful. **2** overpowering. □ **overbearingly** *adv.*

overbite *n.* the overlapping of the lower teeth by the upper.

overblown *adj.* **1** excessively inflated or pretentious. **2** (of a flower etc.) past its prime.

overboard *adv.* from on a ship into the water (*fall overboard*). □ **go overboard 1** be highly enthusiastic. **2** behave immoderately; go too far. **throw overboard** abandon, discard.

overbook *v.tr. & intr.* accept too many bookings or reservations for (an aircraft, hotel, etc.).

overbuild *v.tr.* (*past* and *past part.* **-built**) **1** build over or upon. **2** place too many buildings on (land etc.). □ **overbuilding** *n.*

overburden ● *v.tr.* burden (a person, thing, etc.) to excess. ● *n.* **1** rock etc. that must be removed prior to mining the mineral deposit beneath it. **2** an excessive burden.

overcapacity *n.* the resources to produce more goods, handle more business, etc. than is needed at a particular time.

overcapitalize *v.tr.* fix or estimate the capital of (a company etc.) too high.

overcast ● *adj.* **1** (of the sky, weather, etc.) covered with cloud; dull and gloomy. **2** (in sewing) edged with stitching to prevent fraying. ● *v.tr.* (*past* and *past part.* **-cast**) **1** cover (the sky etc.) with clouds or darkness. **2** stitch over (a raw edge etc.) to prevent fraying. ● *n.* a covering, esp. of clouds.

overcautious *adj.* excessively cautious. □ **overcautiously** *adv.* **overcautiousness** *n.*

overcharge ● *v.* **1** *tr. & intr.* charge too high a price to (a person) or for (a thing). **2** *tr.* put too much charge into (a battery, gun, etc.). **3** *tr.* put exaggerated or excessive detail into (a description, picture, etc.). ● *n.* an excessive charge (of explosive, money, etc.).

overcoat *n.* **1** a heavy coat, esp. one worn over indoor clothes for warmth outdoors in cold weather. **2** a protective coat of paint etc.

overcome ● *v.* (*past* **-came**; *past part.* **-come**) **1** *tr.* prevail over, master. **2** *intr.* be victorious. ● *adj.* (usu. foll. by *with*, *by*) **1** exhausted, made helpless. **2** affected by (emotion etc.).

overcompensate *v.* **1** *tr.* (usu. foll. by *for*) compensate excessively for (something). **2** *intr. Psych.* strive for power etc. in an exaggerated way, esp. to make allowance or amends for a real or fancied grievance, defect, handicap, etc. □ **overcompensation** *n.*

overconfident ● *adj.* excessively confident. □ **overconfidence** *n.* **overconfidently** *adv.*

overcook *v.tr.* cook too much or for too long. □ **overcooked** *adj.*

overcrowd *v.tr.* fill (a space, object, etc.) beyond what is usual or comfortable. □ **overcrowded** *adj.* **overcrowding** *n.*

overcutting *n.* the act or an instance of cutting too many trees in an area of forest at one time. □ **overcut** *v.tr.*

overdetermine *v.tr.* **1** determine, account for, or cause in more than one way, or with more conditions than are necessary. **2** (in *passive*) have more determining factors than the minimum necessary, have more than one cause. **3** *Psych.* give expression to more than one need or desire. □ **overdetermination** *n.*

overdevelop *v.tr.* (**-developed**, **-developing**) **1** develop too much. **2** *Photog.* treat with developer for too long. □ **overdevelopment** *n.*

overdo *v.tr.* (*3rd sing. present* **-does**; *past* **-did**; *past part.* **-done**) carry to excess, go too far, exaggerate (*overdid the sarcasm*). □ **overdo it** (or **things**) exhaust oneself.

overdone *adj.* **1** overcooked. **2** excessive, exaggerated.

overdose ● *n.* an excessive dose (of a drug, sensation, etc.). ● *v.* **1** *intr.* (often foll. by *on*) take an overdose of a drug. **2** *tr.* give an excessive dose of (a drug etc.) or to (a person). □ **overdosage** *n.*

overdraft *n.* **1** a deficit in a bank account caused by drawing more money than is credited to it. **2** the amount of this.

overdramatize *v.tr. & intr.* express or react to in an excessively dramatic way. □ **overdramatic** *adj.*

overdraw *v.* (*past* **-drew**; *past part.* **-drawn**) **1** *tr.* draw a sum of money in excess of the amount credited to (one's bank account). **2** *intr.* overdraw one's account. **3** *tr.* exaggerate in describing or depicting.

overdrawn *adj.* **1** (of a bank account) having an overdraft. **2** (of a person) having overdrawn one's bank account.

overdress ● *v.* **1** *tr.* dress (a person, esp. a child) too warmly. **2** *tr.* dress with too much display or formality. **3** *intr.* overdress oneself. ● *n.* a dress worn over another dress or a blouse etc. □ **overdressed** *adj.*

overdrive *n.* **1 a** a mechanism in a motor vehicle providing a gear ratio higher than that of the usual gear. **b** an additional speed-increasing gear. **2** (usu. prec. by *in*, *into*) a state of high or excessive activity.

overdub ● *v.tr. & intr.* (**-dubbed**, **-dubbing**) impose (additional sounds) on an existing recording. ● *n.* the act or an instance of overdubbing.

overdue *adj.* **1** past the time when due or ready. **2** not yet paid, arrived, etc., though after the expected time. **3** (of a library book etc.) retained longer than the period allowed. **4 a** (of a baby) not yet born, though past the due date. **b** (of a woman) having passed her due date without having given birth.

overeager *adj.* excessively eager. □ **overeagerly** *adv.* **overeagerness** *n.*

over easy *adj.* *N Amer.* (of a fried egg) flipped when almost cooked and fried lightly on the other side, so that the yolk remains slightly liquid.

overeat *v.intr.* (*past* **-ate**; *past part.* **-eaten**) eat too much. □ **overeater** *n.* **overeating** *n.*

over-elaborate *adj.* excessively elaborate. □ **over-elaborately** *adv.*

over-emotional *adj.* excessively emotional. □ **over-emotionally** *adv.*

overemphasis *n.* excessive emphasis. □ **overemphasize** *v.tr. & intr.*

overenthusiasm *n.* excessive enthusiasm. □ **overenthusiastic** *adj.* **overenthusiastically** *adv.*

overestimate ● *v.tr. & intr.* form too high an estimate of (a person, ability, cost, etc.). ● *n.* too high an estimate. □ **overestimation** *n.*

overexcite *v.tr.* excite excessively. □ **overexcited** *adj.* **overexcitement** *n.*

overexert *v.tr. & refl.* exert too much. □ **overexertion** *n.*

overexpose *v.tr. & intr.* **1** expose too much, esp. to the public eye. **2** *Photog.* expose (film) for too long a time. □ **overexposure** *n.*

overextend *v.tr.* **1** extend (a thing) too far. **2** *refl.* take on (oneself) an excessive burden of work etc. □ **overextended** *adj.*

overfamiliar *adj.* excessively familiar. □ **overfamiliarity** *n.*

overfeed *v.tr.* (*past* and *past part.* **-fed**) feed excessively.

overfill *v.tr. & intr.* fill to excess or to overflowing.

overfish *v.tr.* deplete (a body of water) by too much fishing. □ **overfishing** *n.*

overflight *n.* an instance of overflying.

overflow ● *v.* **1** *tr.* **a** flow over (the brim, limits, etc.). **b** flow over the brim or limits of. **c** cause to overflow; fill (a container) so full that the contents spill out. **2** *intr.* **a** (of a receptacle etc.) be so full that the contents overflow it. **b** (of contents) overflow a container. **3** *tr.* (of a crowd etc.) extend beyond the limits of (a room etc.). **4** *tr.* flood (a surface or area). **5** *intr.* (foll. by *with*) be full of. **6** *intr.* (of kindness, a harvest, etc.) be very abundant. ● *n.* (also *attrib.*) **1** what overflows or is superfluous (*an overflow crowd*). **2** an instance of overflowing. **3** (esp. in a bathtub or sink) an outlet for excess water etc. **4** an excess (*an overflow of ideas*). **5** *Computing* the generation of a number having more digits than the assigned location. □ **to overflowing** so as to be more than full; so as to overflow.

overfly *v.tr.* (**-flies**; *past* **-flew**; *past part.* **-flown**) fly over or beyond (a place or territory).

overfull *adj.* filled excessively or to overflowing.

overgraze *v.tr.* allow (grassland) to be so heavily grazed, or (of livestock) feed on (grassland) so heavily, that the vegetation is damaged and ground becomes liable to erosion. □ **overgrazed** *adj.* **overgrazing** *n.*

overgrow *v.tr.* (*past* **-grew**; *past part.* **-grown**) **1** grow over, overspread, esp. so as to choke. **2** grow too big for (one's strength etc.).

overgrown *adj.* **1** abnormally large (*he's like an overgrown child*). **2** wild; grown over with vegetation.

overgrowth *n.* **1** growth that is excessive or too rapid; an instance of this. **2** a growth over or on something.

overhand *adj. & adv.* **1** (in tennis, baseball, etc.) thrown or played with the hand above the shoulder. **2** *Swimming* = OVERARM 2. **3 a** with the palm of the hand downward or inward. **b** with the hand above the object held.

overhang *v.* (*past and past part.* **-hung**) *tr. & intr.* project or hang over. ● *n.* **1** the overhanging part of a structure etc. **2** the amount by which this projects. **3** an excess or buildup of any factor in an economy or market which has, or is likely to have, an undesirable effect upon it. □ **overhanging** *adj.*

overharvesting *n.* the act or an instance of killing too many trees, animals, fish, etc., by logging, hunting, fishing, etc. □ **overharvest** *v.tr. & n.*

overhaul ● *v.tr.* **1** take to pieces in order to examine. **2** examine the condition of (and improve or repair as necessary). ● *n.* a thorough examination, with adjustments or repairs as necessary.

overhead ● *adv.* above one's head. ● *adj.* **1** placed overhead. **2** (of a driving mechanism etc.) above the object driven. **3** (of expenses) arising from general running costs, as distinct from particular business transactions. ● *n.* **1** (also in *pl.*) overhead expenses. **2** (in full **overhead projector**) a device that projects an enlarged image of a transparency onto a screen or wall. **3** a transparency for use on an overhead projector.

overhear *v.tr. & intr.* (*past and past part.* **-heard**) hear as an eavesdropper or as an unobserved or unintentional listener.

overheat *v.tr. & intr.* **1** make or become too hot; heat to excess. **2** suffer, or cause to suffer, from marked inflation as a result of placing excessive pressure on resources at a time of expanding demand. □ **overheating** *n.*

overheated *adj.* **1** excessively hot. **2** excessively passionate about a matter (*an overheated editorial*). **3** (of an economy etc.) suffering from marked inflation.

overhype *v.tr.* promote with excessive hype. □ **overhyped** *adj.*

overindulge *v.tr. & intr.* indulge to excess. □ **overindulgence** *n.* **overindulgent** *adj.*

overjoyed *adj.* (often foll. by *at*, *to hear*, etc.) filled with great joy.

overkill *n.* **1** an excess of what is necessary or appropriate. **2** the amount by which destruction or the capacity for destruction exceeds what is necessary for victory or annihilation.

overland *adj. & adv.* by land.

Overlander *n. Cdn hist.* one of a group of people who journeyed overland from Ontario to the Cariboo goldfields in BC in 1862.

overlap ● *v.* (**-lapped**, **-lapping**) **1** *tr.* (of part of an object) partly cover (another object). **2** *tr.* cover and extend beyond. **3** *intr.* (of two things) partly coincide; not be completely separate (*where psychology and philosophy overlap*). ● *n.* **1** an instance of overlapping. **2** the amount of this. □ **overlapping** *n. & adj.*

overlay ● *v.tr.* (*past* and *past part.* **-laid**) **1** lay over. **2** (foll. by *with*) cover the surface of (a thing) with (a coating etc.). **3** overlie. ● *n.* **1** a thing laid over another. **2** (in printing etc.) a transparent sheet to be superimposed on another sheet. **3** *Computing* **a** the process of transferring a block of data etc. to replace what is already stored. **b** a section so transferred. **4** a coverlet, small tablecloth, etc.

overlie *v.tr.* (**-lying**; *past* **-lay**; *past part.* **-lain**) lie on top of.

overload ● *v.tr.* (esp. in *passive*) **1** put too great a load on or into something. **2** (often foll. by *with*) give (a person or thing) too much of something. **3** put too great a demand on a computer, electrical system, etc., causing it to fail. ● *n.* an excessive quantity; a demand etc. which surpasses capability or capacity.

overlong *adj. & adv.* too or excessively long.

overlook ● *v.tr.* **1 a** miss or fail to see or notice (a thing). **b** see (a mistake, wrongdoing, etc.) but decide officially to ignore it (*have overlooked your lateness*). **c** consider (a person or thing) not good or important enough and so ignore them or it (*was repeatedly overlooked for promotion*). **2** have a view from above, be higher than. **3** supervise, oversee. ● *n. N Amer.* a place giving a view of the scene below. □ **overlooker** *n.*

overlord *n.* **1** a lord superior to other lords or rulers. **2** a person in a position of superiority or supreme power.

overly *adv.* excessively; too.

overmatch *v.tr.* esp. *N Amer.* **1** be more than a match for; defeat by superior strength etc. **2** match (a person) against a superior opponent.

overmuch ● *adv.* to too great an extent; excessively. ● *adj.* excessive.

overnight ● *adv.* **1** for the duration of a night (*stay overnight*). **2** during the course of a night. **3** suddenly, immediately (*the situation changed overnight*). ● *adj.* **1** done, happening, operating, etc. overnight (*an overnight stop*). **2** staying for one night (*an overnight guest*). **3** for use overnight (*an overnight bag*). **4** lasting or valid for one night. **5** (of a delivery etc.) occurring before opening time the next business day. **6** sudden, instant (*an overnight success*). ● *v.* **1** *tr.* send (a package etc.) by overnight delivery. **2** *intr.* stay for the night at or in (*overnighted at Kingston*).

overnight bag *n.* a piece of luggage large enough to hold clothing and toiletries etc. for an overnight trip.

overnighter *n.* **1** *N Amer.* an overnight trip, stay, etc. **2** a person who stays at a place overnight. **3** an overnight bag.

over-optimistic *adj.* excessively or unjustifiably optimistic. □ **over-optimism** *n.*

overpackaging *n.* excessive packaging of a product, e.g. consisting of several layers of wrapping. □ **overpackaged** *adj.*

overpass *n.* a road or railway line that passes over another by means of a bridge.

overpay *v.tr.* (*past* and *past part.* **-paid**) **1** recompense (a person etc.) too highly. **2** pay more than (an amount owing). □ **overpayment** *n.*

overplay v.tr. **1** play (a part) to excess. **2** give undue importance to; overemphasize. □ **overplay one's hand 1** be unduly optimistic about one's capabilities. **2** spoil a good case by exaggerating its value.

overpopulated adj. having too large a population.□ **overpopulation** n.

overpower v.tr. **1** reduce to submission, subdue. **2** make (a thing) ineffective or imperceptible by greater intensity. **3** (of heat, emotion, etc.) be too intense for, overwhelm. □ **overpowering** adj. **overpoweringly** adv.

over-prescribe v.tr. & intr. prescribe an excessive amount of (a drug) or too many (drugs). □ **over-prescription** n.

overprice v.tr. price (a thing) too highly. □ **overpriced** adj.

overprint ● v.tr. **1** print further matter on (a surface already printed, esp. a postage stamp). **2** print (further matter) in this way. ● n. **1** the words etc. overprinted. **2** an overprinted postage stamp.

overproduce v.tr. & intr. **1** produce more of (a commodity) than is wanted. **2** produce to an excessive degree. □ **overproduction** n.

overproof adj. containing more alcohol than proof spirit does.

overprotective adj. excessively protective, esp. of a person in one's charge. □ **overprotected** adj.

overqualified adj. too highly qualified (esp. for a particular job etc.).

overran past of OVERRUN.

overrate v.tr. rate or esteem too highly. □ **overrated** adj.

overreach v.tr. **1** exceed (the limits of a person's authority etc.). **2** (usu. refl.) **a** strain oneself by reaching too far. **b** defeat one's object by attempting what is beyond one's abilities. **3** circumvent, outwit; get the better of by cunning or artifice. □ **overreacher** n. **overreaching** n. & adj.

overreact v.intr. respond more forcibly etc. than is justified. □ **overreaction** n.

overrefine v.tr. & intr. **1** refine too much. **2** make too subtle distinctions in (an argument etc.). □ **overrefinement** n.

overreliance n. excessive reliance.

overrepresent v.tr. (usu. in passive) cause to be present in numbers higher than would be expected statistically.

override ● v.tr. (past **-rode**; past part. **-ridden**) **1** have or claim precedence or superiority over. **2** intervene and make ineffective. **3** interrupt the action of (an automatic device) esp. to take manual control. ● n. **1** the action or process of suspending an automatic function. **2** a device for this.

overriding adj. foremost; taking precedence (accuracy is our overriding concern).

overripe adj. (esp. of fruit etc.) past its best; excessively ripe. □ **overripeness** n.

overrule v.tr. **1** set aside (a decision, argument, proposal, etc.) by exercising a superior authority. **2** annul a decision by or reject a proposal of (a person) in this way.

overrun ● v.tr. (**-running**; past **-ran**; past part. **-run**) **1** (esp. of something undesirable) swarm or spread over. **2** conquer or ravage (territory) by force. **3** (of time, expenditure, production, etc.) exceed (a fixed limit). **4** Printing carry over (a word etc.) to the next line or page. **5** Mech. rotate faster than. ● n. **1** an instance of overrunning. **2** the amount of this. **3** the movement of a vehicle at a speed greater than is imparted by the engine.

oversampling n. a process used in CD players by which each component of the signal is repeated electronically so as to increase the apparent sampling frequency, making it easier to remove spurious signals introduced by the original sampling process.

overseas ● adv. abroad (was sent overseas). ● adj. (also **oversea**) **1** foreign; across or beyond the sea. **2** of or connected with movement or transport over the sea (overseas postage rates).

oversee v.tr. (**-sees**; past **-saw**; past part. **-seen**) officially supervise (workers, work, etc.).

overseer n. a person who supervises others, esp. workers.

oversell v.tr. & intr. (past and past part. **-sold**) **1** sell more of (a commodity etc.) than one can deliver. **2** exaggerate the merits of.

oversexed adj. having unusually strong sexual desires.

overshadow v.tr. **1** appear much more prominent or important than. **2** cast into the shade; shelter from the sun. **3** (usu. in passive) make an occasion less happy than it should be (victory was overshadowed by the terrible loss of life).

overshirt n. a shirt worn over another shirt or without being tucked in.

overshoe n. a shoe worn over another as protection from wet, cold, etc.

overshoot ● v.tr. & intr. (past and past part. **-shot**) **1** pass or send beyond (a target or limit). **2** (of an aircraft) fly beyond or taxi too far along (the runway) when landing or taking off. ● n. **1** the act of overshooting. **2** the amount of this. □ **overshoot the mark** go beyond what is intended or proper.

oversight n. **1** a failure to notice something. **2** an inadvertent mistake. **3** supervision.

oversimplify v.tr. & intr. (**-ies**, **-ied**) distort (a problem etc.) by stating it in too simple terms. □ **oversimplification** n. **oversimplified** adj.

oversized adj. (also **oversize**) of more than the usual size.

overskate v. (of a hockey player) **1** tr. skate faster than or past (the puck). **2** intr. overskate the puck.

oversleep v.intr. (past and past part. **-slept**) sleep too long.

oversold past and past part. of OVERSELL.

overspend v. (past and past part. **-spent**) **1** intr. & refl. spend too much. **2** tr. spend more than (a specified amount). □ **overspender** n. **overspending** n.

overspill n. **1** what is spilled over or overflows. **2** the surplus population leaving a country or city to live elsewhere.

overspread ● v.tr. (past and past part. **-spread**) **1** become spread or diffused over. **2** cover or occupy the surface of. ● adj. (usu. foll. by with) covered (hills overspread with trees).

overstate v.tr. **1** state (esp. a case or argument) too strongly. **2** exaggerate. □ **overstatement** n.

overstay v.tr. stay longer than (one's welcome, a time limit, etc.).

oversteer ● v.intr. (of a motor vehicle) have a tendency to turn more sharply than was intended. ● n. this tendency.

overstep v.tr. (**-stepped**, **-stepping**) **1** pass beyond (a boundary or mark). **2** violate (certain standards of behaviour etc.). □ **overstep the mark** (or **bounds**) violate conventions of behaviour.

overstimulate v.tr. stimulate or excite excessively. □ **overstimulation** n.

overstock ● *v.tr.* stock excessively. ● *n.* esp. *N Amer.* a supply in excess of demand or requirement.

overstorey *n.* (also **overstory** *pl.* **-ies**) the uppermost canopy level of a forest ecosystem, formed by the taller trees.

overstress ● *v.tr.* stress too much. ● *n.* an excessive degree of stress.

overstretch ● *v.tr.* **1** stretch too much. **2** (esp. as **overstretched** *adj.*) make excessive demands on (resources, a person, etc.). ● *n.* the fact or an instance of overstretching.

overstuff *v.tr.* stuff more than is necessary.

overstuffed *adj.* (of furniture) made soft and comfortable by thick upholstery.

oversubscribe *v.tr.* (usu. as **oversubscribed** *adj.*) subscribe for more than the amount available of (a commodity offered for sale etc.) (*the offer was oversubscribed*).

oversupply ● *v.tr.* (**-ies**, **-ied**) supply with too much. ● *n.* an excessive supply.

overt /ɔːˈvɜːt, ˈɔːvɜːt/ *adj.* unconcealed; done openly. □ **overtly** *adv.* **overtness** *n.*

overtake *v.tr.* (*past* **-took**; *past part.* **-taken**) **1** catch up with and pass in the same direction. **2** (of a storm, misfortune, etc.) come suddenly or unexpectedly upon. **3** become level with and exceed (a compared value etc.).

overtax *v.tr.* **1** make excessive demands on (a person's strength etc.). **2** tax too heavily.

over-the-counter *attrib.adj.* **1** obtainable from a store, esp. (of drugs) without a prescription. *See also* OVER THE COUNTER (*see* COUNTER¹). **2 a** (of stocks and other securities) not listed on or traded in an organized stock exchange. **b** (of a market) trading in such securities. Abbr.: **OTC**.

over-the-top *adj. informal* (esp. of behaviour, dress, etc.) outrageous, excessive.

overthrow ● *v.tr.* (*past* **-threw**; *past part.* **-thrown**) **1** remove forcibly from power. **2** put an end to (an institution etc.). **3** conquer, overcome. **4** knock down, upset. **5 a** throw (a ball) too far. **b** throw a ball past or over (a person, base, spot, etc.). ● *n.* **1** a defeat or downfall. **2** the act or an instance of overthrowing.

overtime ● *n.* **1** the time during which a person works at a job in addition to the regular hours. **2** payment for this. **3** *N Amer. Sport* a further period of play at the end of a game when the score is tied. ● *adj.* **1** pertaining to overtime (*overtime pay*). **2** happening in overtime (*an overtime goal*). ● *adv.* in addition to regular hours.

overtired *adj.* excessively tired.

overtone *n.* **1** a subtle or elusive quality or implication (*sinister overtones*). **2** *Music* any of the tones above the lowest in a harmonic series.

overtook *past of* OVERTAKE.

overtop ● *v.tr.* (**-topped**, **-topping**) **1** be or become higher than. **2** surpass. ● *prep.* above. ● *adv.* over the top of.

overture *n.* /ˈɔːvɜːr,tʃər/ *n.* **1** an orchestral piece opening an opera, ballet, etc. **2** a one-movement composition in this style. **3** (usu. in *pl.*) an approach or proposal made to a person with the aim of starting a discussion, establishing a relationship, etc. **4** something that serves as an introduction.

overturn ● *v.* **1** *tr.* cause to fall down or over; upset. **2** *tr.* overthrow; destroy. **3** *tr.* reverse; invalidate (*overturned the verdict*). **4** *intr.* turn over; capsize. ● *n.* a subversion, an act of upsetting.

overuse ● *v.tr.* use too much or too frequently. ● *n.* excessive use.

overvalue *v.tr.* (**-values**, **-valued**, **-valuing**) value too highly; have too high an opinion of.

overview *n.* a general survey.

overwater ● *v.tr. & intr.* water (a plant etc.) too much. ● *attrib.adj.* situated above the water.

overweening *adj.* **1** arrogant, presumptuous, conceited. **2** (of an opinion, emotion, etc.) excessive, exaggerated.

overweight ● *adj.* **1** in excess of a weight considered normal or desirable. **2** beyond an allowed or suitable weight. ● *n.* excessive or extra weight; preponderance. ● *v.tr.* (usu. foll. by *with*) load unduly.

overwhelm *v.tr.* **1** overpower with emotion. **2** (usu. foll. by *with*) overpower with an excess of work, responsibility, etc. **3** bring to sudden ruin or destruction; crush. **4** bury or drown beneath a huge mass, submerge utterly.

overwhelming *adj.* **1** very great or very strong; overpowering (*your affection is overwhelming*). **2** complete; total, or nearly so (*an overwhelming success; the overwhelming majority*). □ **overwhelmingly** *adv.*

overwind *v.tr.* (*past* and *past part.* **-wound**) wind (a mechanism, esp. a watch) beyond the proper stopping point.

overwinter *v.* **1** *intr.* (usu. foll. by *at, in, on,* etc.) spend the winter. **2** *intr.* (of insects, fungi, etc.) live through the winter. **3** *tr.* keep (animals, plants, etc.) alive through the winter.

overwork ● *v.* **1** *intr.* work too hard. **2** *tr.* cause (another person) to work too hard. **3** *tr.* weary or exhaust with too much work. **4** *tr.* make excessive use of. ● *n.* excessive work. □ **overworked** *adj.*

overwrite *v.* (*past* **-wrote**; *past part.* **-written**) **1** *tr.* write on top of (other writing). **2** *tr. Computing* destroy (data) in (a file etc.) by entering new data. **3** *intr.* (esp. as **overwritten** *adj.*) write too elaborately or too ornately. **4** *intr. & refl.* write too much; exhaust oneself by writing. **5** *tr.* write too much about.

overwrought /ˌoʊvɜːrˈrɔːt/ *adj.* **1** overexcited, nervous, distraught. **2** overdone; too elaborate.

overzealous *adj.* too zealous in one's attitude, behaviour, etc.; excessively enthusiastic.

ovoid /ˈoʊvɔɪd/ ● *adj.* **1** (of a solid or a surface) egg-shaped. **2** oval, with one end more pointed than the other. ● *n.* an ovoid body or surface.

ovulate /ˈɒvjʊˌleɪt/ *v.intr.* produce ova or ovules, or discharge them from the ovary. □ **ovulation** *n.*

ovule /ˈoʊvjuːl/ *n.* the part of the ovary of seed plants that contains the germ cell; an unfertilized seed.

ovum /ˈoʊvəm/ *n.* (*pl.* **ova** /ˈoʊvə/) **1** a mature reproductive cell of female animals, produced by the ovary. **2** the egg cell of plants.

ow *interj.* expressing sudden pain.

owe *v.* **1 a** *tr.* be under obligation (to a person etc.) to pay or repay (money etc.). **b** *intr.* (usu. foll. by *for*) be in debt (*still owe for my car*). **2** *tr.* (often foll. by *to*) render (honour, gratitude, etc.) to a person (*owe grateful thanks to my father*). **3** *tr.* (usu. foll. by *to*) be indebted to a person or thing for (*we owe the discovery of insulin to Banting and Best*). □ **owe it to oneself** (often foll. by *to* + infin.) need (to do) something in order to avoid unfairness to oneself.

owing *predic.adj.* **1** owed; yet to be paid (*the balance owing*). **2** (foll. by *to*) **a** caused by; attributable to (*the cancellation was owing to lack of public interest*). **b** (foll. by *to*) because of (*delayed owing to bad weather*).

owl *n.* **1** any nocturnal bird of prey of the order

Strigiformes, with large eyes and a hooked beak. **2** *informal* a person compared to an owl, esp. in looking solemn or wise. □ **owlish** *adj.* **owl-like** *adj.*

owlet *n.* a small or young owl.

owly *adj.* (esp. of a person) owlish.

own ● *adj.* (prec. by possessive) **1 a** belonging to oneself or itself; not another's (*with my own eyes*). **b** individual, peculiar, particular (*a charm all of its own*). **2** used to emphasize identity rather than possession (*cooks his own meals*). ● *pron.* **1** private property (*is it your own?*). **2** kindred (*among my own*). ● *v.* **1** *tr.* have as property; possess. **2 a** *tr.* confess; admit as valid, true, etc. (*owns he did not know*). **b** *intr.* (foll. by *to*) confess to (*owned to a prejudice*). **3** *tr.* acknowledge paternity, authorship, or possession of. □ **come into one's own 1** receive one's due. **2** achieve recognition. **get one's own back** (often foll. by *on*) *informal* get revenge. **hold one's own** maintain one's position; not be defeated or lose strength. **of one's own** belonging to oneself alone. **on one's own 1** alone. **2** independently, without help. **own up** (often foll. by *to*) confess frankly. □ **-owned** *adj.* (in *comb.*).

owner *n.* a person who owns something. □ **ownerless** *adj.* **ownership** *n.*

ox *n.* (*pl.* **oxen**) **1** any bovine animal, esp. a large usu. horned domesticated ruminant used for draft, for supplying milk, and for eating as meat. **2** a castrated male of a domesticated species of cattle, *Bos taurus*. **3** a foolish, clumsy person.

oxbow *n.* **1** a U-shaped collar of an ox yoke. **2 a** a loop formed by a horseshoe bend in a river. **b** (also **oxbow lake**) a lake formed when the river cuts across the narrow end of the loop.

Oxbridge *n.* **1** (also *attrib.*) Oxford and Cambridge universities regarded together, esp. in contrast to newer institutions. **2** (often *attrib.*) the characteristics of these universities or of their students (*an Oxbridge accent*).

ox cart *n.* a cart pulled by an ox or oxen.

oxen *pl.* of OX.

ox-eye *n.* a plant with a flower like the eye of an ox.

ox-eye daisy *n.* a daisy, *Chrysanthemum leucanthemum*, having flowers with white petals and a yellow centre.

oxford *n.* (in full **oxford shoe**) a low, sturdy shoe laced over the instep.

oxidant /'ɒksɪdənt/ *n.* an oxidizing agent.

oxidase /'ɒksɪˌdeɪs, -ˌdeɪz/ *n.* any of a class of enzymes that react with molecular oxygen to form water or hydrogen peroxide.

oxidation /ɒksɪ'deɪʃən/ *n.* the process or result of oxidizing or being oxidized.

oxidation state *n.* **1** a number indicating the number of electrons actually or notionally lost or gained by an atom of an element when chemically combined. **2** the state represented by a value of this.

oxide /'ɒksaɪd/ *n.* a binary compound of oxygen.

oxidize /'ɒksɪdaɪz/ *v.tr. & intr.* **1** combine or cause to combine with oxygen. **2** cover (metal) or (of metal) become covered with a coating of oxide etc.; make or become rusty or tarnished. **3** *Chem.* undergo or cause to undergo a loss of electrons (*opp.* REDUCE 12b). □ **oxidization** *n.* **oxidized** *adj.* **oxidizer** *n.*

oxidizing agent *n.* a substance that brings about oxidation by being reduced and gaining electrons.

oxtail *n.* the tail of an ox, esp. as an ingredient in soup.

oxyacetylene /ˌɒksɪə'setɪˌliːn/ *adj.* of or using a mixture of oxygen and acetylene, esp. in cutting or welding metals (*oxyacetylene torch*).

oxygen *n.* a colourless tasteless odourless gaseous element, occurring naturally in air, water, and most minerals and organic substances, and essential to plant and animal life.

oxygenate /'ɒksɪdʒəˌneɪt, ɒk'sɪ-/ *v.tr.* **1** supply, treat, or mix with oxygen; oxidize. **2** charge (blood) with oxygen by respiration. □ **oxygenation** *n.*

oxygenator *n.* **1** an apparatus for oxygenating the blood. **2** an aquatic plant which enriches the surrounding water with oxygen.

oxygen mask *n.* a mask placed over the nose and mouth through which oxygen or oxygen-enriched air is supplied to relieve breathing difficulties.

oxygen tent *n.* a tent-like enclosure containing oxygen-enriched air, placed over a patient to aid breathing.

oxymoron /ˌɒksɪ'mɔːrɒn/ *n.* a figure of speech in which apparently contradictory terms appear in conjunction, e.g. *faith unfaithful kept him falsely true*. □ **oxymoronic** /ˌɒksɪː'mɒrɒnɪk/ *adj.*

oxytocin /ˌɒksɪ'toːsɪn/ *n.* **1** a hormone released by the pituitary gland that causes increased contraction of the uterus during labour and stimulates the ejection of milk into the ducts of the breasts. **2** a synthetic form of this used to induce labour etc.

oy *interj.* calling attention or expressing alarm, dismay, exasperation, etc.

oyster ● *n.* **1** any of various bivalve molluscs of the family Ostreidae or Aviculidae. **2** something regarded as containing all that one desires (*the world is my oyster*). ● *v.intr.* fish for or gather oysters. □ **oystering** *n.*

oyster bar *n.* **1** a bar or counter in a restaurant where patrons gather to eat oysters and drink. **2** a restaurant having an oyster bar.

oyster bed *n.* a part of the sea floor where oysters breed or are bred.

oystercatcher *n.* any usu. coastal wading bird of the genus *Haematopus*, with a strong orange-coloured bill, feeding on shellfish.

oyster mushroom *n.* an edible fungus, *Pleurotus ostreatus*, which grows on trees.

oyster sauce *n.* a dark brown sauce made from soy sauce and oyster extract, used in Asian cooking.

oy vey /ɔɪ veɪ/ *interj.* an exclamation of dismay etc.

Oz¹ *slang* ● *n.* **1** Australia. **2** an Australian. ● *adj.* Australian.

Oz² *n.* any place thought to resemble Oz, a city and land in a children's fantasy by L. Frank Baum (1856–1919), esp. any fantastic, ideal, or imaginary domain.

oz. *abbr.* ounce(s).

ozone /'oːzoːn/ *n.* **1** a colourless unstable toxic gas with a pungent odour and powerful oxidizing properties, formed from normal oxygen by electrical discharges or ultraviolet light. **2** = OZONE LAYER.

ozone depletion *n.* a reduction of ozone concentration in the stratosphere, believed to be due to atmospheric pollution. □ **ozone depleter** *n.*

ozone-friendly *adj.* (of manufactured articles) containing chemicals that are not destructive to the ozone layer.

ozone hole *n.* a region of marked thinning of the ozone layer, esp. above each pole.

ozone layer *n.* a layer of ozone in the stratosphere that absorbs most of the sun's ultraviolet radiation.

Ozzie *var.* of AUSSIE.

Pp

P¹ *n.* (also **p**) (*pl.* **Ps** or **P's**) the sixteenth letter of the alphabet.

P² *abbr.* (also **P.**) **1 a** (on road signs) parking. **b** (on an automatic transmission display) park. **2** (also Ⓟ) proprietary. **3** (of a grade) pass. **4** *Baseball* pitcher. **5** president.

P³ *symbol* **1** phosphorus. **2** *Physics* **a** a poise (unit). **b** proton.

p *abbr.* (also **p.**) **1** (*pl.* **pp**) page. **2** pico-. **3** piano (softly).

PA¹ *abbr.* **1** Pennsylvania (in official postal use). **2** production assistant. **3** *Cdn* (*Sask. & Man.*) PARENTAL ACCOMPANIMENT.

PA² /ˈpiːˈeɪ/ *n.* a public address system.

Pa *symbol* protactinium.

pa *n. informal* father.

p.a. *abbr.* per annum.

paan /pæn/ *n.* the leaf of the betel palm wrapped around a preparation of betel nuts and lime and chewed.

PABA /ˈpæbə/ *abbr.* para-aminobenzoic acid.

Pablum *n.* **1** *proprietary* a soft cereal for infants. **2** (**pablum**) bland or insipid intellectual fare, entertainment, etc.; pap.

pabulum /ˈpæbjələm/ *n.* **1** food, esp. for the mind (*mental pabulum*). **2** = PABLUM 2.

PAC *abbr.* pre-authorized chequing.

pace ● *n.* **1 a** a single step in walking or running. **b** the distance covered in this. **c** the distance between two successive stationary positions of the same foot in walking. **2** speed in walking or running. **3** speed or tempo in theatrical or musical performance. **4 a** the rate at which something progresses (*learn at your own pace*). **b** the speed at which life is led (*the pace of city life*). **5 a** a manner of walking or running. **b** any of various gaits, esp. of a trained horse etc. ● *v.* **1** *intr.* **a** walk (esp. repeatedly or methodically) with a slow or regular pace (*pacing up and down*). **b** (of a horse) = AMBLE *v.* 2. **2** *tr.* traverse by pacing. **3** *tr.* set the pace for (a rider, runner, etc.). **4** *tr.* (often foll. by *off*) measure (a distance) by pacing. **5** *refl.* distribute one's energy, efforts, etc. equally over the time allotted for a task, so as not to exhaust oneself too soon. □ **change of pace** a change from what one is used to. **keep pace** (often foll. by *with*) advance at an equal rate (as). **off the pace 1** slower than the leading horse in a race. **2** behind the leader in any race or contest. **put a person through his** (or **her**) **paces** test a person's qualities in action etc. **set the pace** determine the speed, esp. by leading. □ **-paced** *adj.*

pace /ˈpɑːtʃeɪ, ˈpeɪsiː/ *prep.* despite the opinion of; with due deference to (*I was not — pace Mr. Smith — defending prostitution*). ¶*Pace* does not mean 'according to (someone)' or 'notwithstanding (something)'.

pacemaker *n.* **1** a device which supplies electrical signals to the heart, stimulating it to beat at an appropriate rate. **2** the part of the heart which determines the rate at which it contracts and where the contractions begin. **3** a competitor who sets the pace for another in racing etc. **4** = PACESETTER 1.

pacer *n.* **1** a horse bred to take part in harness racing. **2** a person who paces or sets the pace.

pacesetter *n.* **1** a person, etc. that serves as a model for others. **2** = PACEMAKER 3. □ **pace-setting** *adj. & n.*

pacha *var. of* PASHA 1.

pachinko /pəˈtʃɪŋkoː/ *n.* a Japanese form of pinball.

pachyderm /ˈpækɪˌdɜrm/ *n.* any thick-skinned mammal, esp. an elephant or rhinoceros.

pacific *adj.* **1** characterized by or tending to peace. **2** (**Pacific**) of or adjoining the Pacific Ocean.

pacification /ˌpæsəfɪˈkeɪʃən/ *n.* the act of pacifying or the process of being pacified.

Pacific dogwood *n.* an ornamental dogwood tree, *Cornus nuttallii*, of the west coast of N America, with white floral bracts and red fruits; it is the floral emblem of BC.

Pacific loon *n.* a loon, *Gavia pacifica*, which breeds in the Arctic and winters on the coast of BC, similar in appearance to the common loon but smaller.

Pacific Rim *n.* (usu. prec. by *the*) the countries and regions bordering the Pacific Ocean, esp. regarded collectively as a group with shared political, economic, and environmental interests.

Pacific salmon *n.* any of the five species constituting the genus *Oncorhynchus*, of the N Pacific: the pink, chum, coho, sockeye, and chinook.

Pacific sardine *n.* a sardine, *Sardinops sagax caeruleus*, of the Pacific coast of N America.

Pacific Scandal *n. Cdn hist.* a scandal surrounding financial contributions to Sir John A. Macdonald's 1872 election campaign by businessmen who were subsequently given the charter to build the CPR.

Pacific Time *n.* the time in a zone including BC and the Pacific states of the US. **Pacific Standard Time** is eight hours behind GMT; **Pacific Daylight Time** is seven hours behind GMT.

Pacific yew *n.* a small yew tree of the west coast of N America, *Taxus brevifolia*.

pacifier *n.* **1** a person or thing that pacifies. **2** *N Amer.* a baby's soother.

pacifism /ˈpæsəˌfɪzəm/ *n.* the belief that all disputes should be settled by peaceful means rather than war. □ **pacifist** *n. & adj.* **pacifistic** *adj.*

pacify /ˈpæsəˌfaɪ/ *v.tr.* (**-ies, -ied**) **1** appease (a person, anger, etc.). **2** bring (a country etc.) to a state of peace.

pacing *n.* **1** in senses of PACE *v.* **2** = PACE *n.* 3. **3** the tempos and overall rhythm, taken as a whole, selected by a conductor for a performance of a work.

pack¹ ● *n.* **1 a** a collection of things wrapped up or tied together for carrying. **b** = BACKPACK *n.* **2 a** a set of items packaged for use or disposal together. **b** a package, esp. of cigarettes. **3** usu. *derogatory* **a** a lot or set (of similar things or persons) (*a pack of lies*). **b** a group of journalists regarded as a predatory mob which hounds those in the news (also *attrib.*: *pack journalism*). **4** a set of playing cards. **5** a group of wild animals or hounds, esp. wolves, hunting together. **6** *Cdn & Brit.* an organized group of Cubs, Brownies, etc. **7 a** *Sport* the main body of competitors following the leader or leaders, esp. in a race. **b** any group of competitors. **8 a** a medicinal or cosmetic substance applied to the skin. **b** a hot or cold pad of absorbent material for treating a wound etc. **9** (also **ice pack**) an area of pack ice. **10** *Med.* **a** the wrapping of a body or part of a body in a wet sheet etc. **b** a sheet etc. used for this. ● *v.* **1** (often foll. by *up*) **a** *tr.* fill (a suitcase, bag, box, etc.) with clothes or other items for transport or storage. **b** *tr.* put (things) together in a bag, suitcase, box, etc. esp. for travelling or moving. **c** *intr.* pack clothes etc. for travelling or moving. **2** *intr. & tr.* come or put closely together; crowd or cram (*packed a lot into a few hours*). **3** *tr.* (in *passive*; often foll. by *with*) be filled (with); contain extensively (*the restaurant was packed*; *packed with information*). **4** *tr.* fill (a hall, theatre, etc.) with an audience etc. **5** *tr.* cover (a thing) with something pressed tightly around (*pack a wound*). **6** *intr.* be suitable for packing (*these skirts pack well*). **7** *tr. informal* **a** carry (a gun etc.). **b** be capable of delivering (a punch, impression, etc.) with skill or force. **8** *N Amer.* **a** *tr.* carry (goods, equipment, etc.), esp. on the back. **b** *intr.* = BACKPACK *v.* **9** *tr. Computing* compress (stored data) in a way that permits subsequent recovery. **10** *tr.* place (food items) in a bag or box for later consumption, e.g. at work or school or while travelling. **11** *tr.* store (food items) in a preservative substance (*peaches packed in sugar syrup*). **12** *tr.* form a hard thick mass (*the wind had packed the snow against the door*). ● *adj.* (of an animal) used for carrying a load (*pack dog*). □ **pack in** *informal* stop, give up (*packed in his job*). **pack it in** (or **up**) *informal* end or stop it. **pack off** *informal* send (a person) away, esp. abruptly or promptly. **pack one's bags** prepare to leave. **send packing** *informal* dismiss (a person) summarily. □ **packable** *adj.*

pack² *v.tr.* select (a jury etc.) or fill (a meeting) so as to secure a decision in one's favour.

package ● *n.* **1 a** an object or objects wrapped in paper or packed in a box; a parcel. **b** a box etc. in which things are packed. **2** (also **package deal**) a set of things offered or agreed to as a whole. **3** a portfolio, folder, etc., containing publicity materials (*information package*). **4** a group of related objects viewed or organized as a unit. **5** *Computing* a piece of software suitable for various applications. **6** (in full **package tour**, **package holiday**) a tour, vacation, etc. with all arrangements made at an inclusive price. □ **packager** *n.*

packaging *n.* **1** a wrapping or container for goods. **2** the action or process of packing goods. **3** the creation of an image for promotional purposes; the style and context in which a particular product, person, or idea is marketed.

pack animal *n.* an animal for carrying packs.

packed *adj.* **1** full to capacity (*a packed auditorium*). **2** filled with something packed in. **3 a** (*predic.*) (of a person) having finished packing for a trip. **b** (of a suitcase etc.) that has been packed. **4** having a specified quality in abundance (*an action-packed movie*). **5** compressed into a hardened mass (*packed snow*). **6** (of a food) packed in a specified substance for preservation (*oil-packed tuna*).

packer *n.* **1** a person or thing that packs, esp. a dealer who prepares and packs food for transportation and sale. **2** *N Amer.* **a** a pack animal. **b** a person who transports goods by means of pack animals. **c** a person who carries goods on his or her back.

packet *n.* **1** a small package. **2** *Computing* a unit of data transmitted over a network. **3** = PACKAGE *n.* 3.

packet switching *n.* a method of data transmission in which parts of a message are sent indepen-

dently by the optimum route for each part and then reassembled. □ **packet-switched** *adj.*

pack horse *n.* a horse for carrying loads.

pack ice *n.* an area of large crowded pieces of floating ice in the sea.

packing *n.* **1** the process of packing. **2** material used to fill up space around or in something, esp. to protect a fragile article in transit. **3** material used to seal a joint or lubricate an axle.

packing house *n.* a factory where meat, produce, etc. is processed and packaged for shipping and sale.

packing plant *n.* a factory where meat or fish is processed and packaged for shipping and sale.

packing snow *n.* wet snow that holds together when compressed, good for making snowballs etc.

pack rat *n.* **1** a N American woodrat of the genus *Neotoma cinerea*, which accumulates hoards of litter in its den. **2** *N Amer.* a person who hoards things.

packsack *n.* *N Amer.* a knapsack.

packsaddle *n.* a saddle adapted for supporting packs.

pack train *n.* *N Amer.* a train of pack animals with their loads.

pact *n.* an agreement or treaty between two or more people, groups, or countries.

pad¹ ● *n.* **1 a** a piece of material used to reduce friction or jarring, fill out hollows, hold or absorb liquid, etc. **b** = SANITARY PAD. **2** a number of sheets of paper fastened together at one edge. **3** = STAMP PAD. **4** the fleshy underpart of an animal's foot or of a human finger. **5** a guard for the leg, elbow, etc. in sports. **6 a** a flat surface for helicopter takeoff or rocket-launching. **b** a broad, flat expanse of concrete etc. used as a floor or foundation. **7** *informal* an apartment. **8** the floating leaf of a water lily. **9** = CUSHION *n.* 3. **10** = TOUCHPAD. ● *v.tr.* (**padded, padding**) **1** provide with a pad or padding; stuff. **2** lengthen or fill out (a book etc.) with unnecessary material. **3** inflate or falsify figures in an expense account, budget, etc.

pad² ● *v.intr.* (**padded, padding**) **1** (often foll. by *around*, *over*, etc.) walk with a soft dull steady step. **2** travel on foot. ● *n.* the sound of soft steady steps.

PA day *abbr. Cdn* = PROFESSIONAL DEVELOPMENT DAY.

padding *n.* **1** soft material used to pad or stuff with. **2** superfluous matter added to lengthen a book etc. **3** inflated or fraudulent entries in a budget etc.

paddle ● *n.* **1** a short broad-bladed oar used without a oarlock. **2** a paddle-shaped instrument or part of a machine, esp. one used for beating or mixing food. **3 a** *Sport* a short-handled bat used esp. in table tennis. **b** a numbered bat shaped like this, used to signal bids in an auction. **4** *Zool.* a fin or flipper. **5** each of the boards fitted around the circumference of a paddlewheel or mill wheel. **6** the action of paddling; a period spent paddling. **7** a plastic-covered electrode used in cardiac stimulation. ● *v.* **1** *intr. & tr.* move or propel over water by means of paddles. **2** *intr. & tr.* row gently. **3** *tr.* transport (a person) by paddling (*we paddled her to the island*). **4** *tr.* esp. *N Amer. informal* spank. **5** *tr.* stir or mix with or as with a paddle. **6** *intr.* dog-paddle. **7** *intr. Brit. & Cdn* walk, esp. barefoot, in shallow water. **8** *intr.* dabble the feet or hands in shallow water. □ **paddle one's own canoe** *N Amer.* manage one's own affairs. □ **paddler** *n.* **paddling** *n.*

paddleboat *n.* **1** a boat propelled by a paddlewheel. **2** = PEDAL BOAT. □ **paddle boating** *n.*

paddlewheel *n.* a wheel with blades fitted around its circumference, which propels a boat when revolved by pushing backwards against the water.

paddlewheeler *n.* *N Amer.* a steamer propelled by paddlewheels.

paddock /'pædək/ ● *n.* **1** a small field, esp. for keeping horses in. **2** an enclosure adjoining a racetrack where horses or cars are gathered before a race. ● *v.tr.* keep or enclose in a paddock.

Paddy *n.* (*pl.* **-ies**) *informal* often *offensive* an Irishman.

paddy *n.* (*pl.* **-ies**) **1** (in full **paddy field**) a field where rice is grown. **2** rice before threshing or in the husk.

paddy wagon *n.* *N Amer.*, *Austral.*, & *NZ slang* a police van for transporting prisoners or people who have been arrested.

padlock ● *n.* a detachable lock hanging by a pivoted hook on the object fastened. ● *v.tr.* secure with a padlock.

Padlock Law *n.* *Cdn hist.* a 1937 Quebec statute allowing the Attorney General to close any premises suspected of being used to propagate communism.

padre /'pɑdrei, 'pæd-/ *n.* **1** a Christian clergyman, esp. a Roman Catholic priest. **2** a chaplain in any of the armed services.

pad Thai *n.* a spicy Thai dish of rice noodles and shrimp, chicken, vegetables, etc.

paean /'piːən/ *n.* **1** a song of praise or triumph. **2** a written or spoken attribution of praise.

paediatrics esp. *Brit.* var. of PEDIATRICS.

paedophile esp. *Brit.* var. of PEDOPHILE.

paella /pai'eiə, pæ-, -elə/ *n.* a Spanish dish of rice, saffron, chicken, seafood, etc.

pagan /'peigən/ ● *n.* **1** a person holding religious beliefs other than those of any of the main religions of the world. **2** a person considered to be hedonistic or irreligious. ● *adj.* **1 a** of or associated with pagans. **b** irreligious. **2** identifying divinity or spirituality in nature. □ **paganism** *n.*

page¹ ● *n.* **1 a** a leaf of a book etc. **b** each side of this. **c** what is written or printed on this. **2** *Computing* **a** a section of stored data, esp. that can be displayed on a screen at one time. **b** a hypertext document containing text and/or images which can be accessed by users of a network, esp. the Internet. **3 a** an episode that might fill a page in written history etc. **b** a memorable event. ● *v.* **1** *tr.* paginate. **2** *intr.* **a** (foll. by *through*) leaf through (a book etc.). **b** (foll. by *through*, *up*, *down*) *Computing* display (text etc.) one page at a time.

page² ● *n.* **1 a** an attendant of a person of rank, a bride, etc., esp. a boy. **b** *N Amer.* a person employed in a legislative assembly to deliver members' messages. **2** a boy or man, usu. in livery, employed to run errands, attend to a door, etc. **3** *hist.* a boy in training for knighthood and attached to a knight's service. ● *v.tr.* **1** summon by making an announcement or by sending a messenger. **2** summon by means of a pager. □ **paging** *n.*

pageant /'pædʒənt/ *n.* **1 a** a brilliant spectacle or parade. **b** a procession or play depicting historical events (*Christmas pageant*). **c** a contest or show (*beauty pageant*). **2** a tableau etc. on a fixed stage or moving vehicle. **3** something resembling a pageant in its grandeur, sweep, etc. (*the pageant of history*).

pageantry *n.* **1 a** elaborate show or display. **b** empty or specious show or display. **2** an instance of this.

pageboy *n.* **1** a woman's hairstyle with the hair reaching to the shoulder and rolled under at the ends. **2** a youth employed as a page.

page break *n.* **1** the point in a piece of continuous text where a page ends and its successor begins. **2** *Computing* a character which, inserted into a text, causes a computer to display or print a new page.

pager *n.* a radio device with a beeper, activated from a central point to alert the person wearing it.

page-turner *n.* **1** a book so exciting or engrossing that one is compelled to read it quickly. **2** a person who turns the pages of a musical score for a pianist etc. □ **page-turning** *adj.*

page wire *n.* smooth wiring in a grid pattern, used as fencing material to enclose fields etc. (often *attrib.*: *page-wire fence*).

paginate /'pædʒə,neit/ *v.tr.* assign numbers to the pages of a book etc. □ **pagination** *n.*

pagoda /pə'goːdə/ *n.* **1** a Hindu or Buddhist temple or sacred building, esp. a many-tiered tower, in India and the Far East. **2** an ornamental imitation of this.

PAH *abbr.* polycyclic aromatic hydrocarbon.

pah *interj.* expressing disgust or contempt.

paid ● *v.* past and past part. of PAY¹. ● *adj.* recompensed or reimbursed (*paid vacation*).

pail *n.* **1** a bucket. **2** an amount contained in this.

pain ● *n.* **1 a** an unpleasant bodily sensation such as is produced by illness or injury; the condition of hurting. **b** a particular kind or instance of this (often in *pl.*: *stomach pains*; *labour pains*). **2** mental suffering or distress. **3** (in *pl.*) careful effort; trouble taken (*take pains*). **4** (also **pain in the neck**) *informal* a nuisance. ● *v.tr.* cause pain to. □ **be at** (or **take**) **pains** (usu. foll. by *to* + infin.) take great care in doing something. **in pain** suffering pain. **no pain, no gain** one cannot make progress (esp. in physical activity) without experiencing some pain. **on** (or **under**) **pain of** with (death etc.) as the penalty.

pained *adj.* expressing pain (*a pained expression*).

painful *adj.* **1** causing bodily or mental pain or distress. **2** (esp. of part of the body) suffering pain. **3** causing trouble or difficulty; laborious (*a painful climb*). **4** very bad (*painful jokes*). □ **painfully** *adv.*

painkiller *n.* a medicine or drug for alleviating pain. □ **painkilling** *adj.*

painless *adj.* **1** not causing or suffering pain. **2** effortless; easy. □ **painlessly** *adv.*

painstaking *adj.* careful, industrious, thorough. □ **painstakingly** *adv.*

paint ● *n.* **1 a** a colouring matter, esp. in liquid form, for imparting colour to a surface. **b** this as a dried film or coating (*the paint peeled off*). **2** *jocular* or *archaic* makeup, esp. rouge or nail polish. **3** *Basketball* = KEY¹ 14. ● *v.* **1** *tr.* cover the surface of (a wall, object, etc.) with paint esp. of a specified colour (*paint the door green*). **2** *tr.* depict (an object, scene, etc.) with paint; produce (a picture) by painting. **3** *tr.* describe vividly as if by painting. **4** *tr.* **a** apply makeup to (the face, skin, etc.). **b** apply nail polish to (fingernails or toenails). **5** *tr.* apply (a liquid) to a surface with a brush etc. **6** *intr.* practise the art of painting. **7** *tr.* cause (text, images, etc.) to be displayed or represented on a computer screen. □ **paint a picture** describe in vivid detail. **paint into a corner** force (a person, oneself) into a situation from which it is not easy to escape. **paint over** (or **out**) efface with paint. **paint the town red** *informal* enjoy oneself flamboyantly. □ **paintable** *adj.*

paintball *n.* a game in which participants simulate military combat using air guns to shoot capsules of paint at each other. □ **paintballer** *n.*

paintbox *n.* a box holding dry paints for painting pictures.

paintbrush *n.* **1** a brush for applying paint. **2** any of various plant species of the chiefly western N American genus *Castilleja*, with showy, brightly coloured bracts. **3** = HAWKWEED.

paint-by-number *adj.* **1** denoting a painting set or book in which the pictures are divided into sections with numbers indicating the colour to be used. **2** unoriginal; lacking individuality.

paint chip *n.* **1** *N Amer.* a card showing a colour or a range of related colours available in a type of paint. **2** a small area on a painted surface where the paint has been chipped away.

painted *adj.* **1** that has been painted. **2** (of a plant or animal) brightly coloured; variegated.

painted lady *n.* any of several orange-red butterflies, esp. *Vanessa cardui* or *V. virginiensis*, with black and white spots.

painted turtle *n.* a small freshwater turtle of N America, *Chrysema picta*, that is black or olive with red and yellow markings on the head and shell.

painter[1] *n.* **1** an artist who paints pictures. **2** a professional who paints houses etc.

painter[2] *n.* a rope attached to the bow of a boat for tying it to a quay etc.

painterly *adj.* **1** like, characteristic of, or pertaining to a painter or paintings; artistic. **2** (of a painting or style of painting) characterized by qualities of colour, stroke, and texture rather than of contour or line. □ **painterliness** *n.*

painting *n.* **1** the process or art of using paint. **2** a painted picture.

paint stripper *n.* a heating device or a solvent for removing paint.

paint thinner *n.* a volatile liquid, e.g. turpentine, mineral spirits, etc., used to dilute paint, clean paintbrushes, etc.

paintwork *n.* **1** a painted surface or area in a building, on a car, etc. **2** the work of painting.

pair ● *n.* **1** a set of two persons or things used together or regarded as a unit (*a pair of gloves*). **2** an article, e.g. scissors, pants, etc., consisting of two joined or corresponding parts not used separately. **3 a** a dating or married couple. **b** a mated couple of animals. **4** two horses harnessed side by side. **5** the second member of a pair in relation to the first (*cannot find its pair*). **6** two playing cards of the same denomination. **7** (in *pl.*) **a** = PAIRS SKATING. **b** a sporting event, e.g. synchronized swimming or rowing, performed by teams of two. ● *v.tr. & intr.* **1** (often foll. by *off*) arrange or be arranged in couples. **2** match or be matched together (*pair a wool vest with a silk shirt*). **3 a** join or be joined in marriage, close friendship, etc. **b** (of animals) mate. □ **in pairs** in twos.

paired *adj.* occurring in pairs or as a pair.

pairing *n.* an arrangement or match resulting from organizing or forming into pairs.

pairs skating *n.* a type of figure skating in which a couple perform together a choreographed routine of jumps, lifts, throws, etc. to music. □ **pairs skater** *n.*

paisa /ˈpaɪzə/ *n.* (*pl.* **paise** /-zeɪ or -zə/) a coin and monetary unit of India, Pakistan, and Nepal, equal to one-hundredth of a rupee.

paisley /ˈpeɪzli/ *n.* (often *attrib.*) **1** a distinctive detailed pattern of curved feather-shaped figures. **2** a soft woollen fabric having this pattern. **3** a garment, esp. a shawl, made from this fabric.

pajamas *N Amer. var. of* PYJAMAS.

pak *n.* (esp. in *comb.*) = PACK[1] *n.* 2a (*econo-pak*).

Paki /ˈpæki/ *n.* (*pl.* **Pakis**) *slang offensive* a Pakistani, esp. an immigrant.

Pakistani /ˌpækəˈstæni, ˌpæk-/ ● *n.* (*pl.* **-is**) a person of Pakistani nationality or descent. ● *adj.* of or relating to Pakistan.

pakora /pəˈkɔrə/ *n.* a piece of cauliflower, carrot, etc. in seasoned batter and deep-fried.

pal ● *n. informal* **1** a friend. **2** a form of address to an esp. male stranger. ● *v.intr.* (**palled, palling**) (usu. foll. by *around*) associate; form a friendship.

palace *n.* **1** the official residence of a sovereign, president, archbishop, or bishop. **2** a splendid mansion. **3** a spacious building used for exhibitions, concerts, etc. (*cow palace*). **4** an establishment noted for the provision of a specified thing (*movie palace*).

palace coup *n.* the (usu. non-violent) overthrow of a sovereign, government, etc. by senior officials.

palacsinta /ˌpæləˈtʃɪntə/ *n.* (also **palacinke** /-ˈsɪŋkə/) (in Hungarian cuisine) a thin dessert pancake filled esp. with jam, cottage cheese, nuts, or chocolate.

paladin /ˈpælədɪn/ *n.* **1** *hist.* a knight errant. **2** a dedicated advocate or supporter of a cause.

Palaearctic *esp. Brit. var. of* PALEARCTIC.

palaeo- *esp. Brit. var. of* PALEO-.

Palaeocene *esp. Brit. var. of* PALEOCENE.

Palaeozoic *esp. Brit. var. of* PALEOZOIC.

palatable /ˈpælətəbəl/ *adj.* **1** pleasant to taste. **2** (of an idea, suggestion, etc.) acceptable, satisfactory. □ **palatability** *n.* **palatably** *adv.*

palatal /ˈpælətəl/ ● *adj.* **1** of the palate. **2** (of a sound) made by placing the surface of the tongue against the hard palate, e.g. *y* in *yes*. ● *n.* a palatal sound. □ **palatalization** *n.*

palate /ˈpælət/ *n.* **1** a structure closing the upper part of the mouth cavity in vertebrates. **2** the sense of taste. **3** flavour, taste, esp. of wine or beer. **4** a mental taste or inclination; liking.

palatial /pəˈleɪʃəl/ *adj.* (of a building) like a palace, esp. spacious and splendid. □ **palatially** *adv.*

palaver /pəˈlævər/ ● *n.* **1** fuss and bother, esp. prolonged. **2** profuse or idle talk. **3** flattery, cajolery. **4** *informal* a prolonged or tiresome matter. ● *v.* **1** *intr.* talk profusely. **2** *tr.* flatter, wheedle. **3** *intr.* confer.

palazzo /pəˈlætsoː, -ˈlɒtsoː/ ● *n.* (*pl.* **-os**) **1** a large palatial building or mansion. **2** loose, wide-legged pants worn by women. ● *adj.* denoting a loose, wide-legged garment.

pale[1] ● *adj.* **1** (of a person or complexion) of a whitish or ashen appearance. **2 a** (of a colour) not dark or deep. **b** faintly coloured. **3** of faint lustre; dim. **4** feeble; weak (*a pale imitation*). ● *v.* **1** *intr. & tr.* grow or make pale. **2** *intr.* (often foll. by *before, beside*) be feeble in comparison (with). □ **palely** *adv.* **paleness** *n.*

pale[2] *n.* **1** a pointed piece of wood for fencing etc.; a stake. **2** a boundary. **3** an enclosed or delimited area. □ **beyond the pale** outside the bounds of acceptable behaviour. □ **paling** *n.*

Palearctic /ˌpeɪliˈɑrktɪk, ˌpæli-, -ˈɑrtɪk/ *adj.* *Zool.* of the Arctic and temperate parts of the Old World.

paleface *n.* a name supposedly used by the N American Indians for the white man.

paleo- /ˈpeɪlioː, ˈpælioː/ *comb. form* (also esp. *Brit.* **palaeo-**) of ancient (esp. prehistoric) times.

paleoanthropology *n.* the branch of anthropology concerned with fossil hominids. □ **paleoanthropological** *adj.* **paleoanthropologist** *n.*

paleobotany *n.* the study of fossil plants. □ **paleobotanical** *adj.* **paleobotanist** *n.*

Paleocene /ˈpeɪlioˌsiːn/ *Geol.* ● *adj.* of or relating to the earliest epoch of the Tertiary period, between the Cretaceous period and the Eocene epoch, lasting from about 65 to 55 million years BP, characterized by a sudden diversification of mammals. ● *n.* this geological epoch or system.

paleoclimatology *n.* the study of the climate in past epochs. □ **paleoclimatologist** *n.*

paleoecology *n.* the ecology of extinct and prehistoric organisms. □ **paleoecological** *adj.* **paleoecologist** *n.*

paleogeography *n.* the study of the geographical features at periods in the geological past. □ **paleogeographer** *n.*

paleography /ˌpeɪliˈɒɡrəfi/ *n.* the study of writing and documents from the past. □ **paleographer** *n.* **paleographic** *adj.* **paleographical** *adj.* **paleographically** *adv.*

paleolithic /ˌpeɪliːˈlɪθɪk/ ● *adj.* of or relating to the early phase of the Stone Age, lasting for about 2.5 million years until the end of the last ice age. ● *n.* the paleolithic period.

paleomagnetism *n.* the study of the magnetism remaining in rocks. □ **paleomagnetic** *adj.*

paleontology /ˌpeɪliɒnˈtɒlədʒi/ *n.* the branch of science that deals with extinct and fossil animals and plants. □ **paleontological** *adj.* **paleontologist** *n.*

Paleozoic /ˌpeɪliːəˈzoʊɪk/ *Geol.* ● *adj.* of or relating to the geological era between the Precambrian and the Mesozoic, lasting from about 590 to 248 million years ago. ● *n.* this geological era.

Palestinian /ˌpæləˈstɪniən/ ● *adj.* of or relating to Palestine. ● *n.* **1** a native of Palestine in ancient or modern times. **2** an Arab, or a descendant of one, born or living in the area formerly called Palestine.

palette /ˈpælət/ *n.* **1** a thin board or slab or other surface, usu. with a hole for the thumb, on which an artist lays and mixes colours. **2** the range of colours used by an artist. **3** the range or variety of tonal or instrumental colour in a musical piece, composer's work, etc. **4** *Computing* the range of colours or shapes available to a user of a computer graphics card.

Pali /ˈpæliː/ ● *n.* an Indic language used in the canonical books of Buddhists. ● *adj.* of this language.

palimony /ˈpæliˌmoʊni/ *n.* esp. *N Amer. informal* an allowance made by one member of an unmarried couple to the other after separation.

palimpsest /ˈpælɪmpˌsest/ *n.* **1** a piece of writing material or manuscript on which the original has been effaced to make room for other writing. **2** a place, experience, etc., in which something new is superimposed over traces of something earlier.

palindrome /ˈpælɪnˌdroʊm/ *n.* a word or phrase that reads the same backwards as forwards, e.g. *rotator*, or *nurses run*. □ **palindromic** /-ˈdrɒmɪk/ *adj.*

palisade /ˌpælɪˈseɪd/ ● *n.* **1** a fence of pales or iron railings. **2** a strong pointed stake used in a close row for defence. ● *v.tr.* enclose or provide with a palisade.

pall¹ /pɔl/ *n.* **1** a cloth spread over a coffin, hearse, or tomb. **2** a dark or gloomy covering.

pall² /pɔl/ *v.* **1** *intr.* (often foll. by *on*) become uninteresting (to). **2** *tr.* satiate, cloy.

Palladian /pəˈleɪdiən/ *adj.* in the neoclassical style of the Italian architect Andrea Palladio (1508–80). □ **Palladianism** *n.*

palladium /pəˈleɪdiəm/ *n.* a white metallic element occurring naturally and used in chemistry as a catalyst and for making jewellery.

pallbearer *n.* a person helping to carry or officially escorting a coffin at a funeral.

pallet¹ /ˈpælət/ *n.* **1** a straw mattress. **2** a makeshift or small, uncomfortable bed.

pallet² /ˈpælət/ *n.* **1** a portable platform for transport-

ing and storing loads. **2** = PALETTE. **3** a flat wooden blade with a handle, used for shaping clay.

palliate /ˈpæliˌeɪt/ *v.tr.* **1** alleviate (disease or its symptoms) without curing it. **2** excuse, extenuate.

palliative /ˈpæliətɪv/ ● *n.* anything used to alleviate pain, anxiety, etc., esp. without eliminating its source. ● *adj.* serving to palliate or alleviate.

palliative care *n.* medical care provided for the terminally ill, aimed at relieving symptoms.

pallid /ˈpælɪd/ *adj.* **1** pale. **2** feeble or insipid.

pallor /ˈpælər/ *n.* paleness.

pally /ˈpæli/ *adj.* (**-ier, -iest**) *informal* friendly.

palm¹ /pɑm, pɑlm/ *n.* **1** any usu. tropical tree of the family Palmae, with no branches and a mass of large pinnate or fan-shaped leaves at the top. **2 a** the leaf of this tree as a symbol of victory or excellence. **b** a prize for this.

palm² /pɑm, pɑlm/ ● *n.* **1** the inner surface of the hand between the wrist and fingers. **2** the part of a glove that covers this. ● *v.tr.* **1** conceal in the hand. **2** take or pass on stealthily. **3** touch, move, etc. with the palm. □ **in the palm of one's hand** under one's control or influence. **palm off 1** (often foll. by *on*) **a** impose or thrust fraudulently (on a person). **b** cause a person to accept unwillingly or unknowingly (*palmed my old computer off on him*). **2** (often foll. by *with*) cause (a person) to accept unwillingly or unknowingly (*palmed him off with my old computer*). □ **palmed** *adj.*

palmful *n.* (pl. **-fuls**).

palmate /ˈpælmeɪt/ *adj.* (also **palmated**) **1** shaped like an open hand. **2** having lobes etc. like spread fingers.

palmcorder *n.* a small, hand-held camcorder.

Palme d'Or /pɑmˈdɔr/ *n.* an annual award for the best film at the Cannes International Film Festival.

palmetto /pælˈmeto, pɒl-/ *n.* (pl. **-os**) a small palm tree of the genus *Sabal* or *Chamaerops*.

palmistry /ˈpɑmɪstri, ˈpɑlm-/ *n.* supposed divination from lines and other features on the palm of the hand. □ **palmist** *n.*

palm oil *n.* oil from the fruit of any of various palms.

palm reader *n.* a person who practises palmistry.

Palm Sunday *n. Christianity* the Sunday before Easter, celebrating Christ's entry into Jerusalem.

palmtop *n.* a computer small and light enough to be held in one hand.

palmy *adj.* (**-ier, -iest**) **1** of or like or abounding in palms. **2** prosperous (*palmy days*).

palomino /ˌpæləˈmiːno/ *n.* (pl. **-os**) a golden or tan-coloured horse with a light-coloured mane and tail, originally bred in the southwestern US.

palooka /pəˈluːkə/ *n.* esp. *N Amer. slang* an oaf or lout.

palpable /ˈpælpəbəl/ *adj.* **1** that can be touched or felt. **2** readily perceived by the senses or mind; obvious. □ **palpably** *adv.*

palpate /ˈpælpeɪt/ *v.tr.* examine (esp. medically) by touch. □ **palpation** *n.*

palpitate /ˈpælpɪˌteɪt/ *v.intr.* **1** pulsate, throb. **2** tremble, quiver.

palpitation *n.* **1** throbbing, trembling, fluttering. **2** (often in *pl.*) increased beating or fluttering of the heart due to exertion, excitement, or disease.

palsa /ˈpælsə/ *n.* a mound or ridge containing a core of frozen peat or soil, found in the subarctic.

palsy /ˈpɔlzi/ ● *n.* (pl. **-ies**) paralysis, esp. with involuntary tremors. ● *v.tr.* (**-ies, -ied**) affect with palsy. □ **palsied** *adj.*

paltry /ˈpɒltri/ *adj.* (**-ier, -iest**) **1** meagre. **2** worthless, contemptible. □ **paltriness** *n.*

pampas /'pæmpəs/ *n.pl.* (*sing.* **pampa**) large treeless plains in S America.

pamper *v.tr.* (also *refl.*) treat (a person or animal) with abundant or excessive kindness or comfort. □ **pampered** *adj.* **pampering** *n.*

pamphlet ● *n.* **1** a small booklet or leaflet containing information. **2** a short treatise on a controversial, esp. political subject. ● *v.intr.* (**pamphleted, pamphleting**) distribute pamphlets.

pamphleteer ● *n.* a writer or issuer of (esp. political) pamphlets. ● *v.intr.* write or issue pamphlets. □ **pamphleteering** *n.*

pan¹ ● *n.* **1 a** a cooking vessel of metal, earthenware, heat-resistant glass, etc. **b** the contents of this. **2** a panlike vessel in which substances are heated etc. **3** any similar shallow container such as the bowl of a pair of scales. **4** *N Amer.* = ICE PAN. **5** a hollow in the ground. **6** a hard substratum of soil. **7 a** a metal drum in a steel band. **b** steel-band music and the associated culture. ● *v.* (**panned, panning**) **1** *tr. informal* criticize severely. **2 a** *tr.* wash (gold-bearing gravel) in a shallow pan. **b** *intr.* search for gold by panning gravel. **c** *intr.* (foll. by *out*) (of gravel) yield gold. □ **pan out** (of an action etc.) turn out well or in a specified way. □ **panful** *n.* (*pl.* **-fuls**). **panlike** *adj.*

pan² ● *v.* (**panned, panning**) **1** *tr.* swing (a movie camera) horizontally to give a panoramic effect or to follow a moving object. **2** *intr.* (of a movie camera) be moved thus. ● *n.* a panning movement.

pan- *comb. form* **1** all; the whole of. **2** relating to the whole or all the parts or members of (*pan-American*).

panacea /ˌpænə'si:ə/ *n.* a cure for all ills.

panache /pə'næʃ/ *n.* flamboyance of style or manner.

panama hat /'pænə,mɒ/ *n.* (also **panama**) a hat of strawlike material made from the leaves of a palmlike plant.

Panamanian /ˌpænə'meiniən/ ● *adj.* of or relating to the Republic of Panama, in Central America. ● *n.* a person of Panamanian nationality or descent.

pan and scan *n.* a technique for adjusting a wide-screen film to fit the squarer shape of a television screen (also *attrib.*: *pan-and-scan video*).

pan-broil *v.tr.* cook (meat) in a pan with little fat.

pancake ● *n.* **1** any of various thin, flat, usu. round cakes of batter, grated potatoes, etc., fried on both sides, esp. one made of flour, milk, eggs, and leavening, served with butter and maple syrup. **2** (also **pancake makeup**) a thick layer of makeup, esp. foundation. **3** (in full **pancake landing**) an emergency landing in which an aircraft levels out close to the ground and drops vertically with its undercarriage retracted. ● *v.* **1 a** *intr.* make a pancake landing. **b** *tr.* cause (an aircraft) to pancake. **2** *tr. & intr. N Amer. informal* flatten. □ **flat as a pancake** completely flat.

pancake breakfast *n. N Amer.* a breakfast for large numbers of people at which pancakes and usu. sausages or bacon are served, often as a fundraiser.

Pancake Day *n.* Shrove Tuesday.

pancake syrup *n. N Amer.* a maple- or caramel-flavoured syrup for pouring on pancakes.

pancetta /pæn'tʃetə/ *n.* cured belly of pork, usu. in a long casing.

pancreas /'pæŋkriəs/ *n.* a gland near the stomach supplying the duodenum with digestive fluid and secreting insulin into the blood. □ **pancreatic** /-'ætɪk/ *adj.* **pancreatitis** /-'taɪtɪs/ *n.*

panda *n.* **1** (also **giant panda**) a bearlike mammal, *Ailuropoda melanoleuca*, native to China and Tibet, having black and white markings. **2** (also **red panda**) a reddish-brown Himalayan raccoon-like mammal, *Ailurus fulgens*, with a long bushy tail.

pandemic /pæn'demɪk/ ● *adj.* (of a disease) prevalent over a whole country or the world. ● *n.* a pandemic disease.

pandemonium *n.* utter confusion; chaos.

pander ● *n.* **1** a go-between in illicit love affairs. **2** a person who provides another with a means of gratifying lust; a pimp. ● *v.intr.* **1** (foll. by *to*) gratify or indulge a person, a desire or weakness, etc. **2** act as a pimp. □ **panderer** *n.* **pandering** *n.*

P & H *abbr.* postage and handling.

pandit *var. of* PUNDIT 1.

P & L *abbr.* profit and loss.

Pandora's box /pæn'dɔrəz/ *n.* a process that once begun will generate many difficult problems.

pane *n.* a single sheet of glass in a window or door. □ **paned** *adj.*

panegyric /ˌpænɪ'dʒaɪrɪk, -'dʒɪ-/ *n.* a discourse etc. expressing high praise.

panel ● *n.* **1 a** a distinct, usu. rectangular, section of a surface, e.g. of a wall, door, or vehicle. **b** a board on which a number of electrical switches or controls are fixed. **c** = INSTRUMENT PANEL. **2** a strip of material as part of a garment. **3** a group of people invited to decide on or discuss a matter. **4** a list of available jurors. ● *v.tr.* (**panelled, panelling**) **1** fit or provide with panels. **2** cover or decorate with panels.

panelling *n.* (also esp. *US* **paneling**) panels collectively, esp. wooden panels used for a decorative wall covering.

panellist *n.* (also esp. *US* **panelist**) a member of a panel (esp. in broadcasting).

panel truck *n. N Amer.* a robust small truck capable of carrying heavy loads, with an enclosed compartment behind the driver's cab.

panfish *n. N Amer.* any small freshwater fish suitable for frying whole in a pan, esp. one caught by an angler rather than bought. □ **panfishing** *n.*

pan-fry *v.tr.* sauté in a pan. □ **pan-fried** *adj.*

pang *n.* a sudden sharp pain or painful emotion.

Pangnirtung hat /'pæŋnɜrtʌŋ/ *n. Cdn* (*North*) a knitted wool hat in bright colours, with a tassel at the crown and earflaps, traditional in the E Arctic.

panhandle *N Amer.* ● *n.* a narrow strip of territory surrounded on three sides by water or the territory of another country or state. ● *v.tr. & intr. informal* beg for money in the street. □ **panhandler** *n.*

panic ● *n.* **1** sudden uncontrollable fear or alarm leading to unreasoned behaviour, esp. that which may suddenly spread through a crowd. **2** widespread apprehension in relation to financial and commercial matters leading to hasty measures to guard against loss (also *attrib.*: *panic selling*). **3** an agitated busyness as when making hurried preparations for something. ● *v.tr. & intr.* (**panicked, panicking**) affect or be affected with panic. □ **panicky** *adj.*

panic attack *n.* a sudden overwhelming feeling of intense and disabling anxiety.

panic button *n.* a button for summoning help in an emergency. □ **push** (or **press**) **the panic button** react in an unduly alarmed manner.

panic-stricken *adj.* affected with panic.

panjandrum /pæn'dʒændrəm/ *n.* an official etc. claiming to have great importance or authority.

pannier /'pænjɜr/ *n.* **1** a basket, esp. one of a pair carried by a beast of burden. **2** each of a pair of bags or boxes on either side of the rear wheel of a bike.

panoply /'pænəpli/ *n.* (*pl.* **-ies**) an impressive array.

panorama *n.* **1** an unbroken view of a surrounding region. **2** a complete survey or presentation of a subject, sequence of events, etc. **3** a picture or photograph containing a wide view. **4** a continuous passing scene. □ **panoramic** *adj.*

pan pipe *n.* (in *sing.* or *pl.*) a musical instrument made of a series of short pipes graduated in length and fixed together with the mouthpieces in line.

pansy *n.* (*pl.* **-ies**) **1** any garden plant of the genus *Viola*, with richly coloured flowers. **2** *informal derogatory* an effeminate man or homosexual.

pant[1] ● *v.* **1** *intr.* breathe with short quick breaths, as from exertion or excitement. **2** *tr.* utter breathlessly. **3** *intr.* (often foll. by *for*) yearn or crave. ● *n.* a panting breath. □ **pantingly** *adv.*

pant[2] *n. esp. N Amer.* = PANTS (often *attrib.*: *pant leg*).

pantaloons /ˌpæntəˈluːnz/ *n.pl.* **1** *hist.* men's close-fitting breeches fastened below the calf or at the foot. **2** *informal* pants. **3** baggy pants (esp. for women) gathered at the ankles.

pantheism /ˈpænθiˌɪzəm/ *n.* **1** the belief or philosophical theory that God and the universe are identical (implying a denial of the personality and transcendence of God); the identification of God with the forces of nature and with natural substances. **2** worship that admits or tolerates all gods. □ **pantheist** *n.* **pantheistic** *adj.* **pantheistical** *adj.* **pantheistically** *adv.*

pantheon /ˈpænθiɒn/ *n.* **1** a building in which illustrious dead are buried or have memorials. **2** the deities of a people collectively. **3** a temple dedicated to the gods, esp. (**the Pantheon**) the circular one at Rome. **4** a group of famous or respected people.

panther *n.* **1** *N Amer.* a cougar. **2** a leopard, esp. with black fur.

panties *n.pl.* legless underwear for women and girls.

pantomime ● *n.* **1 a** the use of gestures and facial expressions to convey meaning, esp. in drama and dance. **b** a performance of this. **2** an esp. British theatrical entertainment based on a fairy tale, with music, jokes, etc., usu. produced around Christmas. **3** *informal* an absurd or outrageous piece of behaviour. ● *v.tr.* represent by pantomime.

pantry *n.* (*pl.* **-ies**) a small room or cupboard in which food, dishes, cutlery, table linen, etc., are kept.

pants *n.pl. esp. N Amer.* any of various garments reaching from the waist at least as far as the thighs, but usu. to the ankles, divided into two parts to cover each leg separately. □ **scare** (or **beat** etc.) **the pants off** *informal* scare, beat, etc., thoroughly. **with one's pants down** *informal* in an embarrassingly unprepared state.

pantsuit *n. esp. N Amer.* a women's suit of pants and a matching jacket.

panty *n.* (often *attrib.*) = PANTIES.

pantyhose *n.pl. N Amer.* very thin or sheer nylon tights for women.

panzer /ˈpænzər/ *n.* a German armoured unit or tank (*panzer division*).

panzerotto /pænzəˈrɒtoː/ *n.* (*pl.* **-ti**) *Cdn* a baked pizza-like turnover, consisting of dough folded into a sealed pocket, filled with tomato sauce, cheese, etc.

pap *n.* **1 a** soft or semi-liquid food for infants or invalids. **b** a mash or pulp. **2** unchallenging or trivial reading matter, ideas, entertainment, etc.; nonsense.

papa *n. archaic* father (esp. as a child's word).

papacy /ˈpeɪpəsi/ *n.* (*pl.* **-ies**) **1** a pope's office or tenure. **2** the papal system.

papal *adj.* of a pope or the papacy. □ **papally** *adv.*

paparazzo /ˌpæpəˈrætso:/ *n.* (*pl.* **paparazzi** /-tsi/) (usu. in *pl.*) a freelance photographer who pursues celebrities to get photographs of them.

papaw /pəˈpɒ/ *var. of* PAWPAW.

papaya /pəˈpaɪjə/ *n.* **1** an elongated melon-shaped fruit with edible orange flesh and small black seeds. **2** a tropical tree, *Carica papaya*, bearing this.

paper ● *n.* **1 a** a material manufactured in thin sheets from the pulp of wood or other fibrous substances, used for writing or drawing or printing on, or as wrapping material etc. **b** a piece of this. **2** (*attrib.*) made of or using paper. **3** = NEWSPAPER. **4 a** a document printed on paper. **b** (in *pl.*) personal documents, esp. verifying identity or credentials. **5** *Commerce* a negotiable documents, e.g. bills of exchange. **b** (*attrib.*) recorded on paper though not existing (*paper profits*). **6** = WALLPAPER. **7** a scholarly essay or dissertation. **8** *Theatre slang* free tickets or the people admitted by them (*the house is full of paper*). **9 a** a set of questions in an exam. **b** the written answers to these. ● *v.tr.* **1** apply paper to, esp. decorate (a wall etc.) with wallpaper. **2** (foll. by *over*) **a** cover (a hole or blemish) with paper. **b** disguise or try to hide (a fault etc.). **3** *Theatre* fill (a theatre) by giving free tickets. □ **on paper 1** in writing. **2** in theory; to judge from written or printed evidence. **push paper** engage in office work. □ **paperer** *n.* **paperless** *adj.* **papery** *adj.*

paperback ● *adj.* (of a book) bound in stiff paper not boards. ● *n.* a paperback book.

paperbark *n.* any of various trees with flaking bark, esp. the paperbark maple, *Acer griseum*.

paper birch *n.* = WHITE BIRCH.

paperboard *n.* a sheet of stiff material made by pasting and pressing together sheets of paper.

paper boy *n.* (also **paper girl**) a boy or girl who delivers or sells newspapers.

paper carrier *n.* a person who delivers newspapers.

paper chase *n.* **1** *informal* any process involving much paperwork. **2** a cross-country run in which runners follow a trail marked by torn-up paper.

paper clip ● *n.* a clip of bent wire or of plastic for holding several sheets of paper together. ● *v.tr.* (**paper-clip**) attach with a paper clip.

paperhanger *n.* a person who applies wallpaper, esp. professionally.

papermaker *n.* a person who makes paper for a living. □ **papermaking** *n. & adj.*

paper money *n.* money in the form of banknotes.

paper-pusher *n.* *informal* a menial clerical or office worker. □ **paper-pushing** *n.*

paper route *n. N Amer.* **1** a job of regularly delivering newspapers. **2** a route taken doing this.

paper-thin *adj. & adv.* very thin

paper tiger *n.* an apparently threatening but ineffectual person or thing.

paper towel *n. N Amer.* an absorbent paper sheet for drying hands, wiping up spills, etc., usu. sold in rolls.

paper trail *n. N Amer.* documentation linking a person or group to an esp. incriminating event or series of events.

paperweight *n.* a small heavy object for keeping loose papers in place.

paperwork *n.* **1** routine clerical or administrative work. **2** paper documents collectively.

paperworker *n.* a person employed in the pulp and paper industry.

papier mâché /ˌpeɪpər mæˈʃeɪ, ˌpæpjeɪ ˈmæʃei/ *n.* paper pulp or strips of paper mixed with glue, used for making moulded figures etc.

papilla /pə'pɪlə/ n. (pl. **papillae** /-liː/) **1** a small nipple-like protuberance in a part or organ of the body. **2** Bot. a small fleshy projection on a plant.

papilloma /ˌpæpɪ'loːmə/ n. (pl. **-mas** or **-mata** /-mətə/) a wartlike usu. benign tumour.

papist /'peɪpɪst/ offensive ● n. a Roman Catholic. ● adj. of or relating to Roman Catholics.

papoose /pə'puːs/ n. a N American Indian child.

pappardelle /ˌpæpar'delei/ n.pl. pasta in the form of broad flat ribbons, usu. served with a meat sauce.

pappy n. (pl. **-ies**) esp. US father.

paprika /'pæprɪkə, pə'priːkə/ n. a spice made from the dried ground fruits of certain (esp. red) varieties of the sweet pepper, Capsicum annuum.

Pap smear n. (also **Pap test**) a procedure for detecting cervical cancer involving the scraping and microscopic examination of cells from the cervix.

Papuan /'pæpjuːən/ ● n. **1** a native or inhabitant of Papua, the SE part of the island of New Guinea in the W Pacific. **2** a group of around 750 languages spoken in New Guinea and neighbouring islands. ● adj. of or relating to Papua or its people or to Papuan.

papyrus /pə'paɪrəs/ n. (pl. **papyri** /-raɪ/) **1** an aquatic plant, Cyperus papyrus, with dark green stems topped with fluffy inflorescences. **2 a** a writing material prepared in ancient Egypt from the pithy stem of this. **b** a document written on this.

par ● n. **1** the average or normal amount, degree, condition, etc. (feel below par). **2** an equal standing (on a par with). **3** Golf the number of strokes a first-class player should normally require for a hole or course. **4** the face value of a stock or bond. **5** the recognized value of one country's currency in terms of another's. ● v.tr. Golf complete (a hole or course) with a score equal to par. □ **par for the course** informal what is normal or expected in any given circumstances.

par. abbr. (also **para.**) paragraph.

para n. informal **1** a paratrooper. **2** a paragraph.

para- comb. form of or using parachutes (parasailing).

parable n. **1** a narrative of imagined events used to illustrate a moral or spiritual lesson. **2** an allegory.

parabola /pə'ræbələ/ n. a symmetrical curve like the path of a projectile under the influence of gravity.

parabolic /ˌperə'bɒlɪk, ˌpæ-/ adj. **1** of or expressed in a parable. **2** of or like a parabola.

parachute ● n. a cloth canopy that fills with air and allows a person etc. attached to it to fall from an airplane at a safe rate, or which is released from the rear of a landing aircraft as a brake. ● v.tr. & intr. **1** drop or land by parachute. **2** appoint or be appointed as an outsider to a position or job. □ **parachutist** n.

parade ● n. **1 a** a public procession, usu. celebrating a special day. **b** a series of people or things appearing in succession (a parade of players to the penalty box). **2** an ostentatious display. **3 a** a formal or ceremonial march or assembling of troops for inspection or display. **b** = PARADE GROUND. ● v. **1** intr. march in or assemble for a parade. **2** tr. & intr. (often foll. by around, through) present or appear publicly in an ostentatious way. **3** tr. & intr. pass by or cause to pass by in procession. □ **on parade 1** on display. **2** taking part in a parade. □ **parader** n.

parade ground n. (also Cdn **parade square**) an outdoor area where soldiers etc. gather for inspection, roll call, etc.

paradigm /'perəˌdaɪm/ n. **1** a typical example or pattern; a model. **2** a mode of viewing the world which underlies the theories and methodology of science etc. in a particular period of history. **3** a list

serving as an example or pattern of the inflections of a noun, verb, etc. □ **paradigmatic** /-dɪg'mætɪk/ adj.

paradigm shift n. a fundamental change (in approach, philosophy, etc.).

paradise n. **1** (in some religions) heaven as the ultimate abode of the just. **2 a** an idyllic place or state. **b** an ideal or perfect place (a walker's paradise). **3** the abode of Adam and Eve in the Biblical account of Creation; the garden of Eden. □ **paradisal** adj.

paradox n. **1 a** a seemingly self-contradictory or absurd statement which, when investigated or explained, may prove to be well-founded or true. **b** a statement that is actually self-contradictory, absurd, or false. **2** a phenomenon that conflicts with preconceived notions of what is reasonable or possible. **3** a situation, person, or thing that combines contradictory qualities or features.

paradoxical adj. **1** of or involving paradox (in sense 1a). **2** (of a person etc.) characterized by paradox. □ **paradoxically** adv.

paraffin n. **1** a translucent, inflammable, waxy or oily substance distilled from petroleum and shale and used esp. in candles, cosmetics, and polishes, and for coating and sealing. **2** Chem. = ALKANE.

paraffin wax n. paraffin in its solid form.

paragliding n. a sport resembling hang-gliding, using a wide, parachute-like canopy attached to the body by a harness, allowing a person to glide after jumping from or being hauled to a height. □ **paraglide** v.intr. **paraglider** n.

paragon n. **1** a person or thing seen as a model of excellence. **2** (foll. by of) a model (of virtue etc.).

paragraph ● n. **1 a** a distinct passage of a text, dealing with one particular point of the subject, the words of one speaker, etc., and beginning on a new, usu. indented line. **b** a distinct, usu. numbered, article or section of a legal document. **2 a** symbol (usu. ¶) used to mark a new paragraph or section of a text, to introduce an editorial comment, or as a reference mark. ● v.tr. arrange (text) in paragraphs.

Paraguayan /ˌpærə'gwaɪən/ ● adj. of or relating to Paraguay, a country in northern S America. ● n. a native or inhabitant of Paraguay.

parakeet n. a small usu. long-tailed parrot.

paralegal esp. N Amer. ● n. a person trained in subsidiary legal matters, but not fully qualified as a lawyer; a legal aide. ● adj. of or relating to auxiliary aspects of the law.

parallax /'perəˌlæks/ n. **1 a** the apparent difference in the position or direction of an object caused when the observer's position is changed. **b** such a difference or change in the position of a celestial object as seen from different points on the earth's surface or opposite points in its orbit. **2** the angular amount of such a difference or change.

parallel ● adj. **1 a** (of lines or planes) side by side with the same distance continuously between them. **b** (foll. by to, with) (of a line or plane) having this relation (to another). **2** (of circumstances etc.) precisely similar, analogous, or corresponding. **3** running through the same period of time, contemporary in duration (parallel universe). **4** Computing **a** involving the concurrent performance of multiple operations (parallel processing). **b** of or involving the simultaneous transmission of data over separate wires (parallel port). **5** (of a text etc.) having two or more translations etc. printed in a format which allows direct comparison, usu. on facing or consecutive pages (a parallel Bible). ● n. **1** a comparison. **2** a person or thing precisely analogous or equal to another in essential particulars. **3** (in full **parallel of latitude**) **a** each of the imaginary parallel circles of constant latitude on the earth's surface. **b** a corresponding line on a map. **4** *Printing* two parallel lines (‖) used as a reference mark. ● *v.tr.* (**paralleled, paralleling**) **1** be parallel to; correspond to. **2** compare. **3** esp. *N Amer.* run parallel with, alongside of, or in the same general direction as. **4** *literary* adduce as a parallel instance. ● *adv.* in a parallel direction or manner (*main streets ran parallel to the shoreline*). ▢ **in parallel 1** (of electric circuits) arranged so as to join at common points at each end. **2** concurrently, simultaneously, contemporaneously.

parallel bars *n.pl.* **1** a gymnastics event in which participants perform feats on a pair of parallel rails on posts. **2** these rails.

parallelism *n.* **1 a** the state, position, or character of being parallel. **b** an instance of this. **c** a parallel case, passage, etc. **2** correspondence, in sense or esp. construction, of successive clauses or passages in writing. **3** *Computing* **a** the execution of operations concurrently by separate parts of a computer, esp. separate microprocessors. **b** the capability of a computer to operate in this way.

parallelogram /ˌperəˈleləˌgræm/ *n.* a four-sided plane rectilinear figure with opposite sides parallel.

parallel parking *n.* the parking of a vehicle parallel to the roadside. ▢ **parallel park** *v.tr. & intr.*

parallel turn *n.* a turn in skiing with the skis kept parallel to each other.

Paralympics *n.pl.* (also **Paralympic Games**) an international athletic competition for the disabled. ▢ **Paralympian** *n.* **Paralympic** *attrib.adj.*

paralysis *n.* (*pl.* **paralyses**) **1** loss of the ability to move a part of the body, usu. as a result of disease or injury to the nervous system. **2** a state of utter powerlessness; inability to act or function.

paralytic *adj.* of, causing, or suffering from paralysis.

paralyze *v.tr.* (also **paralyse**) **1** affect with paralysis. **2** render incapable of action. **3** bring to a standstill.

paramecium /ˌperəˈmiːsiəm/ *n.* any freshwater protozoan of the genus *Paramecium*, of a characteristic slipper-like shape covered with cilia.

paramedic *n.* a paramedical worker, trained in first aid, esp. one who works in ambulances.

paramedical *adj.* (of services etc.) supplementing and supporting medical work.

parameter /pəˈræmətər/ *n.* **1 a** a distinguishing or defining characteristic or feature, esp. one that may be measured or quantified. **b** a constant element or aspect, esp. serving as a limit or boundary. **2** *Math.* a quantity constant in the case considered but varying in different cases. ▢ **parametric** /ˌperəˈmetrɪk/ *adj.*

paramilitary ● *adj.* (of forces etc.) organized similarly to military forces. ● *n.* (*pl.* **-ies**) **1** a paramilitary force or organization. **2** a member of such a force.

paramoecium esp. *Brit. var.* of PARAMECIUM.

paramount *adj.* **1** superior to others in importance, influence, etc. **2** (of a person, nation, etc.) above others in rank or order. ▢ **paramountcy** *n.*

paramour /ˈperəˌmʊr/ *n.* **1** an illicit lover of a married person. **2** any lover; a sweetheart.

paranoia /ˌperəˈnɔiə/ *n.* **1** a mental illness characterized by delusions of persecution, unwarranted jealousy, or exaggerated self-importance. **2** unjustified suspicion and mistrust of others. ▢ **paranoiac** *adj. & n.* **paranoic** /-ˈnoːɪk, -ˈnɔɪɪk/ *adj.* **paranoid** /ˈperəˌnɔid/ *adj. & n.*

paranormal *adj.* of phenomena or powers whose

operation is outside the scope of known laws of nature or normal objective investigation.

parapet /ˈperəpət/ *n.* **1** a low wall at the edge of a roof, balcony, etc., or along the sides of a bridge etc. **2** a bank of earth or stone erected to provide protection from observation and attack, esp. one on top of a wall or rampart, or in front of a trench.

paraphernalia /ˌperəfəˈneiljə/ *n.pl.* (also treated as *sing.*) miscellaneous belongings, items of equipment, accessories, etc.

paraphrase ● *n.* rewording. ● *v.tr. & intr.* express the meaning of in other words. ▢ **paraphrasable** *adj.*

paraplegia /ˌperəˈpliːdʒə/ *n.* paralysis of the legs and part or all of the trunk. ▢ **paraplegic** *adj. & n.*

paraprofessional ● *n.* a person without professional training to whom a particular aspect of a professional task is assigned. ● *adj.* of or designating such a person.

parapsychology *n.* the study of mental phenomena outside the sphere of the ordinary, e.g. hypnosis, telepathy, etc. ▢ **parapsychological** *adj.* **parapsychologist** *n.*

parasailing *n.* a sport in which participants wearing open parachutes glide through the air while being towed by a speedboat. ▢ **parasail** *v.intr. & n.*

parasite *n.* **1** an organism living in or on another and benefiting at the expense of the other. **2** a person who lives off others. ▢ **parasitic** *adj.* **parasitical** *adj.* **parasitically** *adv.* **parasitism** *n.* **parasitize** *v.tr.* **parasitologist** *n.* **parasitology** *n.*

parasol *n.* a light umbrella used to give shade from the sun.

parasympathetic *adj.* relating to one of the major divisions of the autonomic nervous system, whose nerves leave the spinal cord in the cranial or sacral region, and which is associated more with calmness and rest than with alertness (compare SYMPATHETIC 8).

parathyroid ● *n.* a gland next to the thyroid, secreting a hormone that regulates calcium and phosphate levels in the body. ● *adj.* of this gland.

paratroops *n.pl.* troops equipped to be dropped by parachute from aircraft. ▢ **paratrooper** *n.*

paratyphoid ● *n.* a fever like typhoid but less severe and caused by different bacteria. ● *adj.* of this fever.

parboil *v.tr.* partly cook by boiling.

parcel ● *n.* **1** an item or quantity of goods etc. wrapped up in a single package. **2** a piece of land. **3** (esp. in **part and parcel**) an integral part. ● *v.tr.* (**parcelled, parcelling**) **1** (foll. by *up*) wrap as a parcel. **2** (foll. by *out*) divide into portions.

parcel post *n.* *N Amer.* a postal rate for packages weighing over 500g, cheaper than first-class mail.

parch *v.* **1** *tr. & intr.* make or become hot and dry with heat. **2** *tr.* roast (peas, grain, etc.) lightly.

parched *adj.* **1** dried out, esp. by heat. **2** thirsty.

parchment *n.* **1 a** the skin of esp. a sheep or goat, prepared as a writing or painting surface. **b** a manuscript written on this. **2** (also **parchment paper**) high-grade translucent paper made to resemble parchment, used for lampshades, as a writing surface, and in baking. **3** *N Amer.* a diploma.

pardner *n.* *N Amer. jocular* a partner or comrade.

pardon ● *n.* **1 a** the act of excusing or forgiving an offence, error, sin, etc. **b** courteous forbearance or indulgence. **2 a** a remission of the legal consequences of a crime or conviction. **b** a document conveying a legal pardon. **3** *Catholicism hist.* an indulgence. ● *v.tr.* **1** release from the consequences of a legal offence or sin. **2** forgive or excuse (a person, error, or offence). **3** make esp. courteous allowances for, excuse (a person, fact, or action). ● *interj.* (also **pardon me** or **I beg your pardon**) **1** a formula of apology or disagreement. **2** a request to repeat something said. □ **pardonable** *adj.* **pardonably** *adv.*

pare *v.tr.* **1** a cut away the skin or outer covering of (esp. fruit or vegetables). **b** trim by cutting away the surface or edge (*pared his nails*). **c** (often foll. by *off*, *away*) cut off (the surface or edge). **2** (usu. foll. by *down*) gradually reduce in size, extent, or number, esp. so as to arrive at the essentials. □ **parer** *n.*

pared-down *adj.* simplified, reduced esp. to a minimum (*pared-down companies*).

parent ● *n.* **1** a biological father or mother. **2** a person who holds the position or exercises the function of such a parent, e.g. by adopting a child. **3** an ancestor. **4** (also *attrib.*) an animal or plant considered in relation to its offspring. **5** (also *attrib.*) a thing from which another is derived or has its existence. **6** a (also *attrib.*) an initiating organization or enterprise. **b** = PARENT COMPANY. ● *v.* **1** *tr.* **a** be or act as a parent to (a child). **b** beget, produce. **2** *intr.* be a parent; take care of one's children. □ **parental** *adj.* **parenthood** *n.*

parentage *n.* descent from or through parents (*their parentage is unknown*).

Parental Accompaniment *n.* **1** (in Manitoba) a film classification which recommends that viewers under 15 years of age be accompanied by a parent or guardian. **2** (in Saskatchewan) a film classification which requires that viewers under 14 years of age be accompanied by a parent or guardian. Abbr.: **PA**.

Parental Guidance *n.* **1** (in Alberta, Saskatchewan, and Ontario) a film classification which advises of content that should be subject to parental discretion, without specifying an age restriction. **2** (in Manitoba and the Maritimes) a film classification which advises of content most suitable for mature viewers over 12 years of age. Abbr.: **PG**.

parental leave *n.* a paid or unpaid leave from work afforded to either parent to care for a child, esp. a newborn.

parent company *n.* a company of which other companies are subsidiaries.

parenthesis *n.* (*pl.* **parentheses**) **1** a a word, clause, or sentence inserted as an explanation or afterthought into a passage, usu. set off in text by brackets, dashes, or commas. **b** (usu. in *pl.*) either of a pair of round brackets ( ) used for this. **2** an interval.

parenthetical /ˌpɛrənˈθɛtɪkəl/ *adj.* **1** of or by way of a parenthesis. **2** interposed. □ **parenthetically** *adv.*

parenting *n.* the raising of children by parents.

parent-in-law *n.* (*pl.* **parents-in-law**) a father-in-law or mother-in-law.

parent-teacher association *n.* a local organization of parents and teachers for promoting closer relations and improving educational facilities at a school. Abbr.: **PTA**.

pareve /ˈparəvə, ˈparvə/ *adj.* Judaism (of food) being or containing neither meat nor dairy and so kosher for use with either, according to the dietary laws (includes fruit, vegetables, fish, etc.).

par excellence /ˌpar ɛksəˈlãs/ *adj.* being the supreme example of its kind (*the short story par excellence*).

parfait /parˈfeɪ/ *n.* **1** ice cream, sauces, crushed fruit, etc. layered in a tall glass. **2** a frozen dessert made with egg whites, sugar, whipped cream, and flavouring.

parfleche /ˈparflɛʃ/ *n. N Amer.* a hide, esp. of buffalo,

from which the hair has been removed and which has been dried on a frame (*parfleche bag*).

parge (also **parget**) ● *v.tr.* (**parged, parging** or **pargeted, pargeting**) **1** apply parging to (a wall, brickwork, etc.). **2** plaster (a wall etc.) esp. with an ornamental pattern. ● *n.* **1** plaster applied in this way; ornamental plasterwork. **2** roughcast.

parging *n.* **1** a thin layer of mortar, roughcast, etc. covering a wall for protection or to create a smooth surface. **2** the mortar used for parging.

pariah /pəˈraɪə/ *n.* **1** a social outcast. **2** a despised person. **3** (also **pariah state**) a country against which political or diplomatic sanctions are in force.

parietal /pəˈraɪətəl/ *adj.* **1** *Anat.* **a** of the wall of the body or the lining of any of its cavities. **b** of or near the parietal bones. **2** *Bot.* of the wall of a hollow structure, esp. an ovary.

parietal bone *n.* either of a pair of bones forming the central part of the sides and top of the skull.

parimutuel /ˌpariˈmjuːtʃuˌel/ *n.* **1** a form of betting in which those backing the first three places divide the losers' stakes (less the operator's commission). **2** a booth etc. for placing bets under this system.

paring *n.* **1** (often in *pl.*) a thin portion cut or peeled from a surface; a shaving. **2** an act of cutting, shaving, or peeling such a strip.

paring knife *n.* a kitchen knife with a short, firm, pointed blade used for paring fruit, vegetables, etc.

parish *n.* **1** a an area of ecclesiastical jurisdiction having a church and clergy. **b** the people who are members of a parish. **2** *Cdn* **a** (*Que.*) a county subdivision functioning as both a political and an ecclesiastical unit. **b** (*NB*) a county subdivision, the unit of representation at county councils.

parish hall *n.* **1** a large meeting room, usu. part of or connected to a parish church, in which social events, meetings, etc. are held. **2** the building in which this is housed, if separate from the church.

parishioner *n.* **1** a member or attendee of a particular church. **2** an inhabitant of a parish.

parish priest *n.* a priest in charge of a parish.

Parisian /pəˈriːʒən, -ˈriːziən/ ● *adj.* of or typical of the people or city of Paris, France. ● *n.* **1** a native or inhabitant of Paris. **2** the kind of French spoken in Paris.

Parisienne /pærizːˈiːˈɛn/ *n.* a Parisian girl or woman.

parity /ˈpɛrɪti/ *n.* **1** equality or equal status. **2** equality of nature, character, or tendency; parallelism or analogy. **3** a equivalence of pay for jobs or categories of work perceived as being comparable or analogous. **b** the practice or system of setting pay levels according to such perceived comparability. **4** *Math.* & *Computing* **a** the property of an integer by virtue of which it is odd or even. **b** the property of employing odd or even numbers. **5** *Computing* a function whose being odd or even provides a check on a set of binary values. **6** *Physics* (of a quantity) the fact of changing its sign or remaining unaltered under a given transformation of coordinates etc. **7** equivalence of one currency with another.

park ● *n.* **1** a piece of land with lawns, gardens, etc. in a town or city, maintained at public expense for recreational use. **2** a large area of government land kept in its natural state for recreational use, wildlife conservation, etc. **3** a large enclosed area of land, either public or private, used to accommodate wild animals in captivity (*wildlife park*). **4** (usu. in *comb.*) an area developed for a specified purpose or form of recreation (*industrial park*; *water park*; *theme park*). **5** *N Amer.* a stadium etc. for sports events (*ballpark*). **6** an area for motor vehicles etc. to be left in (*trailer park*). **7** the gear position or function in automatic transmission in which the gears are locked, preventing the vehicle's movement. **8** a large enclosed piece of ground, usu. with woodland and pasture, attached to a stately home etc. ● **1** *v.tr. & intr.* leave (a vehicle) temporarily, in a parking lot, by the side of the road, etc. **2** *tr. informal* leave, deposit, or settle (a person or thing) in a convenient place, usu. temporarily. **3** *intr. N Amer. slang* make out in a parked car. □ **park oneself** *informal* sit down. □ **park-like** *adj.*

parka *n.* a warm, hooded coat extending to the thighs or calves.

parkade *n. Cdn* a parking garage.

park-and-ride ● *n.* a system whereby commuters, shoppers, etc. travel by car to parking lots on the outskirts of a city and continue into the city by public transportation. ● *adj.* of or designating this system.

park belt *n. Cdn (West)* = PARKLAND 1b.

Parker House roll *n. N Amer.* an oval bread roll formed by folding a flat disk of dough in half.

parkette *n. Cdn (S Ont.)* a small park in a city.

parking *n.* **1** (also *attrib.*) the act of stopping a vehicle at a place and leaving it for a time (*parking attendant*). **2** an area for leaving vehicles (*underground parking*). **3** *N Amer. slang* the act of making out in a parked car.

parking brake *n.* = EMERGENCY BRAKE.

parking garage *n.* a structure with space for parking vehicles.

parking light *n.* a small light on either side of the front and rear of a vehicle.

parking lot *n. N Amer.* a usu. outdoor area for parking vehicles.

parking meter *n.* a coin-operated meter which receives fees for vehicles parked in the street and indicates the time available.

parking space *n.* (also **parking spot**) a space for parking a single vehicle.

parking stall *n. Cdn (West) & US* a parking space in a parking garage or parking lot.

parking ticket *n.* a notice of a fine etc. imposed for parking illegally.

Parkinson's disease *n.* (also **Parkinsonism**) a progressive disease of the nervous system which produces tremor, muscular rigidity, and slowness and imprecision of movements. □ **parkinsonian** *adj.*

parkland *n.* **1 a** open grassland scattered with clumps of trees etc. **b** *Cdn* the lightly wooded grasslands between the open prairie and the northern forests in Manitoba, Saskatchewan, and Alberta. **c** *Cdn* the grassy region between the Prairies and the foothills of the Rockies. **2** a piece of land set aside by the government for public recreation, wildlife conservation, etc.

parks officer *n. Cdn* = PARK WARDEN.

park warden *n.* (also **park ranger**) an official responsible for patrolling and maintaining in a national, provincial, etc. park, having the powers of a peace officer in matters of park regulations.

parkway *n. N Amer.* a highway or main road with trees, grass, etc. planted alongside.

parlance /ˈpɑrləns/ *n.* a particular way of speaking, esp. as regards choice of words, idiom, etc.

parlay /pɑrˈlei, ˈpɑrlei/ *N Amer.* ● *v.tr.* **1** (foll. by *into*) transform (an advantage etc.) into something greater. **2** use (money won on a bet) as a further stake. **3** increase (capital) by gambling. ● *n.* a bet made by parlaying.

parley /ˈpɑrli/ ● *n.* (*pl.* **-eys**) an informal conference,

under truce, with an enemy, for discussing the mutual arrangement of matters such as terms for armistice, exchange of prisoners, etc. ● *v.intr.* (**-leys**, **-leyed**) (often foll. by *with*) hold a parley.

parliament *n.* **1** (usu. **Parliament**) the highest legislative body in certain countries, including Canada. **2** a legislative body of a province, state, etc. (*provincial parliament*). **3** the members of a parliament. **4** a period during which the members of a parliament are assembled, following a general election and until dissolution. **5** a place where parliament meets. **6** the House of Commons.

parliamentarian ● *n.* **1** a member of a parliament, esp. one well versed in its procedures. **2** *hist.* (**Parliamentarian**) = ROUNDHEAD. ● *adj.* = PARLIAMENTARY.

parliamentary *adj.* **1** of or relating to a parliament. **2** enacted or established by a parliament. **3** according to the constitution of a parliament (*parliamentary democracy*). **4** (of language) admissible in a parliament; polite, civil, courteous.

parliamentary committee *n.* see COMMITTEE 2.

parliamentary government *n.* a government in which a prime minister (or premier) chooses MPs, usu. from his or her own party, to be Ministers of the Crown who will form the Cabinet and be responsible to Parliament for the conduct of the government.

parliamentary secretary *n.* an MP belonging to the party in government, appointed by the prime minister to assist a senior cabinet minister.

parliament building *n.* **1** a building in which a parliament meets. **2** a complex of buildings housing the parliament and offices of its members and staff, esp. (**Parliament Buildings**) (in Canada) those in Ottawa.

Parliament Hill *n. Cdn* **1** the hill in Ottawa on which the Parliament Buildings stand. **2** the federal government of Canada.

parlour *n.* (also **parlor**) **1** a sitting room in a house. **2 a** esp. *N Amer.* a business providing specified goods or services (*beauty parlour*). **b** *Cdn* = BEER PARLOUR. **3** (in full **milking parlour**) a room or building equipped for milking cows. **4** a room in a hotel, club, etc. for the private use of guests. **5** a room in a convent or monastery set aside for conversation. **6** (*attrib.*) *derogatory* denoting a person who professes but does not actively support a specified political cause (*parlour socialist*).

parlour game *n.* a game, e.g. charades, played by a number of people indoors.

Parmesan /ˈpɑrmɪˌzɒn, -zən, -zæn/ *n.* (also **parmigiano** /pɑrmɪˈdʒɛɪnoː/) hard dry cheese used esp. in grated form.

parmigiana /pɑrmɪˈdʒɒnə, -ˌdʒɒnə, -ˌʒɛnə, -dʒɪˈænə/ *adj.* made or served with Parmesan cheese.

parochial /pəˈroːkiəl/ *adj.* **1** of a parish. **2** (of views etc.) merely local, narrow or restricted in scope. □ **parochialism** *n.* **parochially** *adv.*

parochial school *n. N Amer.* a primary or secondary school established and run by a religious body.

parody ● *n.* (*pl.* **-ies**) **1** humorous exaggerated imitation of an author, literary work, etc., esp. for purposes of ridicule. **2** a thing done so badly that it seems to be an intentional mockery of what it should be. **3** a comic or satirical imitation of a person, event, etc. ● *v.tr.* (**-ies**, **-ied**) **1** compose or perform a parody of. **2** imitate in a poor or feeble manner. □ **parodic** /pəˈrɒdɪk/ *adj.* **parodically** *adv.* **parodist** *n.*

parole ● *n.* **1** the release of a prisoner, temporarily for a special purpose or completely, before the expiry of a sentence, on the promise of good behaviour. **2**

the system or practice of granting or accepting such a conditional release. ● *v.tr.* put (a prisoner) on parole.□ **on parole** released esp. from a custodial sentence on the terms of parole. □ **parolee** *n.*

parotid /pəˈrɒtɪd/ ● *adj.* of or situated near the parotid glands. ● *n.* (in full **parotid gland**) a salivary gland in front of the ear.

paroxysm /ˈpærəkˌsɪzəm/ *n.* **1** (often foll. by *of*) a sudden attack or outburst (of rage, laughter, etc.). **2 a** a sudden fit or convulsion. **b** a sudden attack, recurrence, or worsening of disease etc. □ **paroxysmal** /-ˈsɪzməl/ *adj.*

parquet /parˈkei, ˈpar-/ *n.* / (often *attrib.*) a flooring of short strips or blocks of wood arranged in a pattern, usu. sold in square, interlocking tiles.

parr *n.* a young salmon between the stages of fry and smolt, distinguished by dark rounded patches evenly spaced along its sides.

parrot ● *n.* any of various vividly coloured esp. tropical birds of the order Psittaciformes, some of which can mimic the human voice. ● *v.tr.* (**parroted**, **parroting**) repeat the words or actions of another mindlessly or mechanically.

parrotfish *n.* any fish of the genus *Scarus*, with a mouth like a parrot's hooked bill.

parry ● *v.tr.* (**-ies**, **-ied**) **1** ward off (a weapon or attack), esp. with a countermove. **2** deal skilfully with (an awkward question etc.). ● *n.* (*pl.* **-ies**) an act of parrying.

parse /pars, parz/ *v.tr.* **1** analyze (a word) grammatically, stating its inflection, relation to the sentence, etc. **2** resolve (a sentence) into its component parts and describe them grammatically. **3** *Computing* analyze (a string) into syntactic components. □ **parser** *n.*

Parsi /parˈsiː/ *n.* (also **Parsee**) an adherent of Zoroastrianism, esp. a descendant of the Zoroastrian Persians who fled to India in the 7th–8th c. to escape Muslim persecution.

parsimony /ˈparsɪˌmoːni/ *n.* extreme unwillingness to use money or other resources. □ **parsimonious** /-ˈmoːniəs/ *adj.* **parsimoniously** *adv.*

parsley *n.* a biennial herb, *Petroselinum crispum*, with white flowers and flavourful leaves, used for seasoning and garnishing food. □ **parsleyed** *adj.*

parsnip *n.* **1** a biennial umbelliferous plant, *Pastinaca sativa*, with a large pale-yellow tapering root. **2** this root eaten as a vegetable.

parson *n.* **1** any (esp. Protestant) member of the clergy. **2** an Anglican parish priest.

parsonage *n.* a church house provided for a parson.

part ● *n.* **1** some but not all of a thing or number of things. **2** an essential member or constituent of anything (*part of the family; a part of the job*). **3** a component of a machine etc. **4** a portion of the body. **5** a division of a book, serial, etc. **6 a** each of several equal portions of a whole (*the recipe has 3 parts sugar to 2 parts flour*). **b** (prec. by ordinal number) a specified fraction of a whole (*each received a fifth part*). **7 a** a portion allotted; a share. **b** a person's share in an action or enterprise (*will have no part in it*). **c** one's duty (*was not my part to interfere*). **8 a** a character assigned to an actor etc. **b** the words spoken by an actor. **9** *Music* a melody or other constituent of harmony assigned to a particular voice or instrument (often in *comb.*: *four-part harmony*). **10** each of the sides in an agreement or dispute. **11** (often in *pl.*) a region or district (*from parts unknown*). **12** (in *pl.*) abilities (*a man of many parts*). **13** esp. *N Amer.* the dividing line of combed hair. ● *v.* **1** *tr. & intr.* divide or separate into parts (*the crowd parted to let them through*). **2** *intr.* **a** leave

one another's company (*they parted the best of friends*). **b** (foll. by *from*) say goodbye to. **3** *tr.* cause to separate (*they fought hard and had to be parted*). **4** *intr.* (foll. by *with*) give up possession of. **5** *tr.* separate (the hair of the head on either side of a part) with a comb. ● *adv.* to some extent; partly. □ **for one's part** as far as one is concerned. **in part** (or **parts**) to some extent; partly. **look the part** have an appearance suitable for a role, job, or position. **on the part of** proceeding from (*concern on the part of parents*). **part and parcel** (usu. foll. by *of*) an essential part. **play a part 1** be significant or contributory. **2** perform a dramatic role. **take part** (often foll. by *in*) participate (in). **take the part of** support; back up.

partake *v.intr.* (*past* **-took**; *past part.* **-taken**) **1** (foll. by *in*, *of*) participate in (*partook in the festivities*). **2** (foll. by *of*) eat or drink a part or amount (of a thing). **3** (foll. by *of*) have some (of a quality etc.). □ **partaker** *n.*

parter *comb. form.* something having a specified number of parts, esp. a radio or television production in a specified number of episodes (*three-parter*).

parterre /parˈter/ *n.* **1** a level space in a garden occupied by flower beds arranged formally. **2** *N Amer.* the ground floor of a theatre auditorium, esp. the section overhung by balconies.

parthenogenesis /ˌparθənoʊˈdʒenəsɪs/ *n.* *Biol.* reproduction from an ovum without fertilization, esp. as a normal process in invertebrates and lower plants. □ **parthenogenetic** *adj.* **parthenogenetically** *adv.*

partial ● *adj.* **1** not complete; forming only part (*a partial success*). **2** biased, unfair. **3** (foll. by *to*) having a liking for. ● *n.* a denture replacing some but not all of the teeth. □ **partially** *adv.* **partialness** *n.*

partial eclipse *n.* an eclipse in which only part of the sun or moon is covered or darkened.

partiality /ˌparʃiˈælɪti/ *n.* bias, favouritism.

Participaction *n.* *Cdn* **1** a private, non-profit organization which promotes physical fitness through regular exercise. **2** (**participaction**) *informal* physical activity; exercise.

participant ● a person who participates in something. ● *adj.* participating.

participate *v.intr.* (usu. foll. by *in*) share or take part. □ **participation** *n.* **participative** *adj.* **participatory** *adj.*

participatory democracy *n.* involvement of citizens in the political decision-making process.

participle /ˈpartɪˌsɪpəl, parˈtɪsəpəl/ *n.* *Grammar* a word formed from a verb, e.g. *going*, *gone*, *being*, *been*, and used in compound verb forms, e.g. *is going*, *has been*, or as an adjective, e.g. *working woman*, *burnt toast*. □ **participial** /-ˈsɪpiəl/ *adj.*

particle *n.* **1** a very small bit or piece of something (*dirt particles*). **2** *Physics* any of numerous subatomic constituents of the physical world that interact with each other, including electrons, neutrinos, and photons. **3** the least possible amount (*not a particle of sense*). **4** *Grammar* **a** a minor part of speech, esp. a short word that does not change its form. **b** a common prefix or suffix such as *in-*, *-ness*.

particle accelerator *n.* an apparatus for accelerating subatomic particles to high velocities by means of electric or electromagnetic fields.

particle beam *n.* a stream of subatomic particles produced by a particle accelerator, used for studying nuclear structure etc., or as a military weapon.

particleboard *n.* a rigid sheet made from compressed wood chips, splinters, sawdust, and resin.

particle physics *n.* the branch of physics concerned with the properties and interactions of sub-atomic particles. □ **particle physicist** *n.*

parti-coloured *adj.* of several colours.

particular ● *adj.* **1** relating to or considered as one thing or person as distinct from others; individual (*in this particular case*). **2** more than is usual; exceptional (*took particular trouble*). **3** paying close attention to detail; fastidious. **4** detailed (*a full and particular account*). **5** *Logic* (of a proposition) in which something is asserted of some but not all of a class (*opp.* UNIVERSAL *adj.* 2). ● *n.* **1** a detail; an item. **2** (in *pl.*) points of information; a detailed account. □ **in particular** especially, specifically.

particularism *n.* **1** exclusive devotion to one party, sect, etc. **2** the principle of leaving political indepen-dence to each state in an empire or federation. **3** the theological doctrine of individual redemption or election. □ **particularist** *n.* & *adj.* **particularistic** *adj.*

particularity *n.* (*pl.* **-ies**) **1** the quality of being individual or particular. **2** fullness or minuteness of detail in a description. **3** (usu. in *pl.*) **a** a particular point or circumstance; a detail. **b** a special or distinc-tive quality or feature; a peculiarity.

particularize *v.tr.* mention or describe particularly; treat individually or in detail.

particularly *adv.* **1** especially, very. **2** specifically. **3** in a fussy manner.

particulate /parˈtɪkjʊˌlət, -leit/ ● *adj.* in the form of separate particles. ● *n.* matter in this form.

partier *n.* **1** a person who parties. **2** *slang* a person who drinks or uses drugs recreationally.

parting *n.* **1** a leave-taking or departure (often *attrib.*: *parting words*). **2** a division; an act of separating. **3** a point at which things part or are parted.

parting shot *n.* a remark or glance etc. reserved for the moment of departure.

Parti Québécois *n. Cdn* a political party in Quebec, founded in 1968 and dedicated to achieving Quebec sovereignty. Abbr.: **PQ**.

Parti Rouge *n. Cdn hist.* a radical French-Canadian political party founded about 1848 and first led by Louis-Joseph Papineau.

partisan /ˈpɑrtɪˌzæn, -ən, -ˈzæn/ ● *n.* **1** an esp. zealous supporter of a party, person, or cause. **2** a guerrilla. ● *adj.* **1** of partisans. **2** biased towards a particular cause. □ **partisanship** *n.*

partition ● *n.* **1** division into parts, esp. of a country with separate areas of government. **2** a structure dividing a space into two parts, esp. a light interior wall. **3** *Computing* **a** a self-contained part of a program, or a group of programs within a program library. **b** each of a number of blocks into which some opera-ting systems divide memory in order to facilitate storage and retrieval of information. ● *v.tr.* **1** divide into parts. **2** (foll. by *off*) separate (part of a room etc.) with a partition. **3** *Computing* divide (memory) into partitions. □ **partitioned** *adj.*

partly *adv.* to some extent; not completely.

partner ● *n.* **1 a** a person, organization, country, etc. who shares or takes part with another or others in some activity (*Canada's trading partners*). **b** a person who is associated with another or others in the carrying on of a business with shared risks and profits. **2** a colleague or associate. **3** a dancer, figure skater, tennis player, etc. paired with another. **4 a** either member of a married couple or an established unmarried couple. **b** a person with whom one has sexual relations. ● *v.* **1** *tr.* be or act as the partner of. **2** *intr.* (foll. by *with*) associate as partners. □ **partnering** *n.* **partnerless** *adj.*

partnership *n.* **1** the state of being a partner or partners. **2** a joint business. **3** a pair or group of partners.

part of speech *n.* each of the categories to which words are assigned according to their grammatical and semantic functions (e.g. noun, verb).

partook *past of* PARTAKE.

part owner *n.* a person who owns something jointly with another. □ **part ownership** *n.*

partridge *n.* (*pl.* same or **-s**) **1** any game bird of the genus *Perdix*, esp. the grey partridge, *P. perdix* native to Europe and Asia and introduced in N America. **2** any of various similar birds of the family Phasiani-dae, esp. the ruffed grouse or the ptarmigan.

partridgeberry *n.* (*pl.* **-ies**) **1** either of two N Ameri-can plants with edible red berries, *Mitchella repens* or *Gaultheria procumbens*. **2** the fruit of these plants.

part-skim *adj.* made partly with skim milk.

part-time ● *adj.* employed, occurring, or lasting less than full-time (*part-time student*). ● *adv.* on a part-time basis (*he works part-time*). □ **part-timer** *n.*

partway *adv.* **1** part of the way. **2** partly.

party ● *n.* (*pl.* **-ies**) **1** a social gathering, usu. of invited guests (often *attrib.*: *party hats*). **2** a group of people engaged in an activity or travelling together (*search party*). **3** a political group organized to campaign for election (often *attrib.*: *party policy*). **4** a person or people forming one side in an agreement or dispute. **5** (foll. by *to*) *Law* an accessory (to an action). **6** *informal* a person. ● *v.intr.* (**-ies, -ied**) **1** go to parties frequently. **2** revel, carouse (*partied all night*). □ **partying** *n.*

party animal *n. informal* a person who parties.

partyer *var. of* PARTIER.

party-goer *n.* a person who attends a party or parties.

party line *n.* **1** the official policies adopted by a political party. **2** an official position or interpreta-tion of events etc. put forth publicly by members of an organization, institution, etc. **3** a telephone line shared by two or more subscribers.

party politics *n.pl.* political activity carried out through, by, or for political parties.

party-pooper *n.* (also **party-poop**) esp. *N Amer. slang* a person whose manner or behaviour inhibits other people's enjoyment; a killjoy. □ **party-pooping** *n.*

parvenu /ˈpɑrvəˌnju/ ● *n.* **1** a person of obscure origin who has gained wealth or position. **2** an upstart. ● *adj.* **1** of or characteristic of such a person. **2** upstart.

parvovirus /ˈpɑrvoˌvaɪrəs/ *n.* any of a class of small viruses affecting vertebrate animals, esp. one which causes contagious disease in dogs.

pascal *n.* **1** /ˈpæskəl/ the SI unit of pressure, equal to one newton per square metre. **2** (**Pascal**) /pæsˈkæl/ a programming language esp. used in education.

paschal /ˈpæskəl/ *adj.* **1** of or relating to Easter. **2** of or relating to Passover.

pas de deux /pɒ də ˈdə/ *n.* (*pl.* same; /-ˈdə, -ˈdəz/) a dance for two persons, esp. a man and a woman.

pasha /ˈpæʃə/ *n.* **1** *hist.* the title (placed after the name) of a Turkish officer of high rank, e.g. a military commander, the governor of a province, etc. **2** *informal* a wealthy, powerful person.

Pashto /ˈpʌʃtoː/ ● *n.* the Indo-Iranian language of the Pathans, the official language of Afghanistan, also spoken in NW Pakistan. ● *adj.* of this language.

paska /ˈpɒskə, ˈpæskə/ *n. Cdn* a rich, usu. decorated,

egg bread, often containing dried fruits, traditional at Easter among people of Ukrainian origin.

pasque flower *n.* either of two spring flowering anemones, the prairie crocus, *Anemone (Pulsatilla) patens*, of N America or *A. vulgaris* of Europe.

pass¹ ● *v.* (*past part.* **passed**) (*see also* PAST) **1** *intr.* (often foll. by *along, by, down, on*, etc.) proceed, esp. past some point of reference. **2** *tr.* **a** go past; leave (a thing etc.) on one side or behind in proceeding. **b** overtake, esp. in a vehicle. **c** go across (a frontier, mountain range, etc.). **3** *tr. & intr.* transfer or be transferred from one person or place to another (*pass the butter; the title passes to his son*). **4** *tr.* surpass; be too great for (*it passes my comprehension*). **5** *intr.* get through; effect a passage. **6** *intr.* **a** be accepted as adequate (*let the matter pass*). **b** (foll. by *as, for*) be accepted as or taken for. **7** *tr.* move; cause to go (*passed her hand over her face*). **8 a** *tr. & intr.* (of a student) be successful in completing (a test or course). **b** *tr.* be successful in (a course, test, etc.). **c** *tr.* (of a teacher etc.) judge the performance of (a student) to be satisfactory. **9 a** *tr.* (of a bill) be examined and approved by (a parliamentary body or process). **b** *tr.* cause or allow (a bill) to proceed to further legislative processes. **c** *intr.* (of a bill or proposal) be approved. **10** *intr.* **a** occur, elapse (*the remark passed unnoticed; time passes slowly*). **b** happen, occur (*heard what passed between them*). **11 a** *intr.* circulate; be current. **b** *tr.* put into circulation (*was passing forged cheques*). **12** *tr.* spend (a certain time or period) (*passed the afternoon reading*). **13** *tr. & intr.* (in hockey, football, etc.) send (the puck or ball) to a teammate. **14** *intr.* **a** forgo one's turn or chance in a game etc. **b** (often foll. by *on*) decline an offer etc. **15** *intr.* (foll. by *to, into*) change from one form (to another). **16** *intr.* come to an end. **17** *tr.* discharge (urine, feces, a kidney stone, etc.) from the body. **18** *tr.* (foll. by *on, upon*) **a** utter (criticism) about. **b** pronounce (a judicial sentence) on. **19** *intr.* (often foll. by *on, upon*) adjudicate. ● *n.* **1** an act or instance of passing. **2 a** success in an examination, course, etc. **b** *Brit. & Cdn* the status of a university degree without honours. **3** written permission to pass into or out of a place, or to be absent from quarters. **4 a** a ticket or permit giving free entry or access etc. **b** a purchased ticket giving unlimited usage, access, etc. for a certain period (*bus pass*). **5 a** (in hockey, football, etc.) a transference of the puck or ball to a teammate. **b** *Baseball* = WALK *n.* **7**. **6** *Cards* an act of declining or being unable to make a bid or act in one's turn. **7** an act of passing the hands over anything, as in conjuring or hypnotism. **8** a critical position; a state of affairs (*how have things come to such a pass?*). **9** a short sweeping movement or dive made by an aircraft. □ **in passing 1** by the way. **2** in the course of speech, conversation, etc. **make a pass at** *informal* make amorous or sexual advances to. **pass around 1** distribute. **2** send or give to each of a number in turn. **pass away** *euphemism* die. **pass by 1** go past. **2** disregard, omit. **pass one's eye over** read (a document etc.) cursorily. **pass off** (foll. by *as*) misrepresent (a person or thing) as something else. **pass on 1** transmit to the next person in a series. **2** *euphemism* die. **3** proceed on one's way. **pass out 1** become unconscious. **2** distribute. **pass over 1** omit, ignore, or disregard. **2** ignore the claims of (a person) to promotion or advancement. **pass through 1** experience. **2** be in a place temporarily while on the way to somewhere else. **pass up** *informal* refuse or neglect (an opportunity etc.). □ **passer** *n.*

pass² *n.* **1** a narrow passage through mountains. **2** a navigable channel, esp. at the mouth of a river. **3** a

road or route. **4** *Cdn* a migration route followed by animals. □ **head** (or **cut**) **off at the pass** deter (a person) or prevent (a problem) early on.

passable *adj.* **1** barely satisfactory; just adequate. **2** (of a road etc.) that can be passed. □ **passably** *adv.*

passage *n.* **1** the process, action, or means of passing (*the passage of time; a passage through the crowd*). **2 a** a sea route around a large land mass, usu. between two oceans (*Northwest Passage*). **b** a narrow strait between islands etc. **3** the liberty or right to pass through. **4 a** the right of conveyance as a passenger, esp. by sea. **b** a journey, esp. by sea. **5 a** a short extract from a book etc. **b** a section of a piece of music. **6** = PASSAGEWAY. **7** a transition from one state to another. **8** the passing of a bill etc. into law. **9** *Anat.* a duct etc. in the body (*nasal passages*).

passageway *n.* a corridor.

Passamaquoddy /ˌpæsəmə'kwɒdi/ ● *n.* **1** a member of a N American Aboriginal people inhabiting parts of SE Maine and (formerly) SW New Brunswick. **2** the Algonquian language of this people. ● *adj.* of this people or their language.

passbook *n.* a small book issued by a financial institution to an account holder recording sums deposited and withdrawn.

pass card *n.* a plastic card with an encoded magnetic strip, which, when passed through a scanner, acts as a key to open a locked door etc.

passé /pæ'sei/ *adj.* **1** no longer fashionable or topical; out of date. **2** past one's prime.

passed ball *n.* *Baseball* a pitch dropped by the catcher, allowing a runner to advance one or more bases.

passenger *n.* a traveller in or on a public or private conveyance (other than the driver, pilot, crew, etc.).

passenger pigeon *n.* a wild pigeon of N America, noted for migrating in huge flocks and hunted to extinction by 1914.

passerby *n.* (*pl.* **passersby**) a person who goes past, esp. by chance.

passerine /'pæsəˌriːn/ ● *n.* any perching bird of the order Passeriformes, having feet with three toes pointing forward and one pointing backwards, including sparrows and most land birds. ● *adj.* of or relating to this order.

passim /'pæsɪm/ *adv.* (of allusions or references in a published work) to be found at various places throughout the text.

passing ● *adj.* **1** transient, fleeting (*a passing glance*). **2** cursory, incidental (*a passing reference*). ● *n.* the death of a person. □ **passingly** *adv.*

passing lane *n.* **1** a traffic lane in which drivers may pass other vehicles. **2** *Basketball* any open space on the court through which players attempt to pass the ball.

passion *n.* **1** strong barely controllable emotion. **2** intense sexual love or desire. **3** strong enthusiasm (*a passion for football*). **4** a person or thing arousing passion. **5** an outburst of anger (*flew into a passion*). **6** (**the Passion**) a *Christianity* the suffering of Christ during his last days. **b** a narrative of this from the Gospels. □ **passionless** *adj.*

passionate *adj.* **1** dominated by or easily moved to strong feeling, esp. love or anger. **2** showing or caused by passion. □ **passionately** *adv.*

passion flower *n.* any climbing plant of the genus *Passiflora*, with a flower that was supposed to suggest the instruments of the Crucifixion.

passion fruit *n.* the edible fruit of some species of passion flower, esp. *Passiflora edulis*.

Passion play *n.* (also **passion play**) a play depicting the events of Christ's Passion, usu. performed during Lent.

Passion Sunday *n.* the fifth Sunday in Lent.

passive ● *adj.* **1** suffering action; acted upon. **2** offering no opposition; submissive. **3 a** not active; inert. **b** (of a metal) abnormally unreactive owing to a surface coating of oxide. **4** *Grammar* designating the voice in which the subject undergoes the action of the verb, e.g. in *they were killed*. **5** of or designating a system in which energy for heating etc. is obtained by the absorption of existing radiant energy, usu. sunlight. **6** (of radar, a satellite, etc.) not generating its own signal; receiving or reflecting radiation from a transmitter etc. ● *n.* the passive voice or form of a verb. □ **passively** *adv.* **passivity** *n.*

passive smoking *n.* the involuntary inhaling, esp. by a non-smoker, of smoke from others' cigarettes etc. □ **passive smoke** *n.* **passive smoker** *n.*

Passover *n.* the Jewish spring festival commemorating the liberation of the Israelites from slavery in Egypt, held from the 14th to the 21st day of the seventh month of the Jewish year.

passport *n.* **1** a document issued by a government certifying the holder's identity and citizenship, and entitling the holder to travel abroad under its protection. **2** (foll. by *to*) a thing that ensures admission or attainment (*a passport to success*).

pass rush *n.* *Football* the elements of a team's defensive play aimed at thwarting the quarterback's pass attempts. □ **pass rusher** *n.* **pass-rushing** *adj.*

pass-through *N Amer.* ● *n.* an opening in a wall between two rooms, esp. a kitchen and a dining area, through which dishes etc. are passed. ● *adj.* (of costs) chargeable to the customer.

password *n.* **1** a selected word or phrase securing recognition, admission, etc., when used by those to whom it is disclosed. **2** *Computing* a confidential sequence of characters that has to be typed in order to gain access to a particular computer, network, etc.

past ● *adj.* **1** gone by in time and no longer existing (*in past years*; *the time is past*). **2** recently completed or gone by (*the past month*). **3** relating to a former time (*past president*). **4** *Grammar* expressing a past action or state. ● *n.* **1** (prec. by *the*) a past time. **b** what has happened in past time (*cannot undo the past*). **2** a person's past life or career, esp. if discreditable (*a man with a past*). **3** a past tense or form. ● *prep.* **1** beyond in time or place (*is past two o'clock*; *ran past the house*). **2** beyond the range, duration, or compass of (*past belief*). ● *adv.* so as to pass by (*hurried past*). □ **not put it past a person** believe it possible of a person. **past it** *informal* old and useless. □ **pastness** *n.*

pasta / ˈpæstə, ˈpɒstə/ *n.* **1** a type of dough extruded or stamped into various shapes for cooking, e.g. lasagna or spaghetti. **2** a dish made from this.

paste ● *n.* **1** a moist thick mixture, esp. of powder and liquid. **2** an adhesive, esp. for sticking paper and other light materials. **3** a puréed preparation of ground meat, fish, vegetable, etc. (*tomato paste*). **4 a** a hard vitreous composition used in making imitation gems. **b** imitation jewellery made of this. **5** a mixture of clay, water, etc., used in making ceramics. ● *v.tr.* **1** fasten or coat with paste. **2** *Computing* insert or reproduce (already existing text) at a new location in a document, file, etc. **3** *slang* **a** beat or thrash. **b** bomb or bombard heavily. □ **pasting** *n.*

pasteboard *n.* a sheet of stiff material made by pasting together sheets of paper.

pastel ● *n.* **1** a crayon consisting of powdered pigments bound with a gum solution. **2 a** the art or

technique of drawing with pastels. **b** a work of art in pastel. **3** a light and subdued shade of a colour. ● *adj.* of a light and subdued shade. □ **pastellist** *n.*

pastern *n.* **1** the part of a horse's foot between the fetlock and the hoof. **2** a similar part in other animals.

paste-up *n.* a document prepared for copying etc. by pasting various sections of text on a backing.

pasteurize *v.tr.* subject (milk etc.) to the process of partial sterilization by heating. □ **pasteurization** *n.*

pastiche /pæˈstiːʃ/ ● *n.* **1** a medley, esp. a picture or a musical composition, made up from or imitating various sources. **2** a literary or other work of art composed in the style of a well-known writer, artist, etc. ● *v.tr.* copy or imitate the style of (an artist, author, time period, etc.) □ **pasticheur** /pæstiˈʃɜr/ *n.*

pastille /pæˈstiːl, -ˈstɪl/ *n.* a small candy or lozenge.

pastime *n.* a recreational activity or hobby.

past master *n.* **1** a person who is especially adept or expert in an activity, subject, etc. **2** a person who has been a master in a guild, Freemason's lodge, etc.

pastor ● *n.* **1** (also **Pastor**) (often as a title or form of address) a minister or priest in charge of a church or a congregation. **2** a person exercising spiritual guidance. ● *v.tr. & intr.* be pastor of (a church).

pastoral /ˈpæstərəl/ ● *adj.* **1 a** of or associated with shepherds or flocks and herds. **b** of or pertaining to the country; rural. **2** (of a poem, picture, etc.) portraying country life, usu. in a romantic or idealized form. **3** (of land) used for pasture. **4** of or pertaining to a pastor or the spiritual care of a congregation. ● *n.* **1** a pastoral poem, play, etc. **2** (in full **pastoral letter**) a letter from a pastor (esp. a bishop) to the clergy or people. □ **pastoralism** *n.*

pastoralist /ˈpæstərəlɪst/ ● *n.* a farmer of sheep or cattle. ● *adj.* = PASTORAL *adj.* 1a.

pastorate /ˈpæstərət/ *n.* **1** the office or tenure of a pastor. **2** a body of pastors; pastors collectively.

past perfect *n.* = PLUPERFECT.

pastrami /pəˈstrɒmi/ *n.* seasoned smoked beef brisket, usu. cut in thin slices for sandwiches.

pastry *n.* (*pl.* **-ies**) **1** a dough of flour, fat, and water baked and used as a base and covering for pies etc. **2 a** food made wholly or partly of this. **b** a piece or item of this food. **3** a sweet bread or cake.

pastry bag *n.* a cloth funnel through which icing etc. is squeezed to decorate the top of a cake etc.

pastry chef *n.* (also **pastry cook**) a cook who specializes in pastry, esp. for public sale.

pasturage *n.* land for pasture.

pasture ● *n.* **1** (also **pasture land**) an area of land covered with grass etc. suitable for grazing animals, esp. cattle or sheep. **2** herbage for animals. **3** the circumstances of a person's life, work, etc. (*find greener pastures*). ● *v.tr. & intr.* graze in a pasture. □ **out to pasture 1** out to graze. **2** *informal* **a** (of a person) in retirement. **b** (of a thing) out of service.

pasty[1] /ˈpæsti/ *n.* (*pl.* **-ies**) esp. *Brit.* a savoury turnover.

pasty[2] /ˈpeɪsti/ ● *adj.* (**-ier**, **-iest**) **1** unhealthily pale. **2** like paste. ● *n.* (*pl.* **-ies**) (usu. in *pl.*) a decorative covering for the nipple worn by a stripper. □ **pastiness** *n.*

PA system *n.* = PUBLIC ADDRESS SYSTEM.

pat[1] ● *v.* (**patted, patting**) **1** *tr.* **a** tap gently with the hand or a flat surface. **b** tap (a person) gently, esp. as a sign of affection, sympathy, or congratulation. **2** *tr.* flatten or mould by patting. **3** *tr. & intr.* (foll. by *on, upon*) tap or beat lightly on (a surface), esp. making a gentle sound. ● *n.* **1** a light tap, esp. with the hand. **2** the sound made by this, or by light footsteps. **3** a small mass (esp. of butter) formed by patting.

pat² ● *adj.* **1** known thoroughly and ready for any occasion. **2** apposite or opportune, esp. unconvincingly so (*a pat answer*). ● *adv.* **1** in a pat manner. **2** opportunely.□ **have down pat** know or have memorized perfectly. **stand pat** esp. *N Amer.* **1** stick stubbornly to one's opinion or decision. **2** *Poker* retain one's hand as dealt. □ **patly** *adv.* **patness** *n.*

pat. *abbr.* patent.

patch ● *n.* **1** a piece of material used to mend or reinforce clothing etc. **2** a pad or shield worn over an eye or eye socket. **3** a dressing etc. put over a wound. **4** a small area or piece of ground, esp. one that contrasts with a surrounding area (*a patch of ice*; *a vegetable patch*). **5** a small scrap, piece, or remnant (*fog patches*). **6** an adhesive patch worn on the skin, which releases measured amounts of a drug into the bloodstream. **7** *Cdn* (*Nfld*) a herd of seals. **8** *informal* a period of time (*went through a bad patch*). **9 a** a temporary electrical connection. **b** *Computing* a small piece of code inserted to correct or enhance a program. ● *v.* **1** *tr.* **a** (often foll. by *up*) mend with a patch or patches. **b** repair the damage to (*patch a pothole*). **2** *tr.* (often foll. by *together*) construct hastily or in a makeshift way. **3** *tr.* (foll. by *up*) settle (differences etc.) after a quarrel or dispute. **4** *tr. & intr.* (often foll. by *through, into*) connect or be connected by a temporary electrical, radio, etc. connection. **5** *tr. Computing* correct or enhance (a routine, program, etc.) by inserting a patch. □ **patcher** *n.*

patchouli /pə'tʃuːli/ *n.* **1** a strongly scented E Indian plant, *Pogostemon cablin*. **2** the perfume obtained from this.

patchwork ● *n.* **1** needlework in which small pieces of cloth in different designs are sewn together to form a quilt etc. **2** a thing composed of different pieces or elements. ● *attrib.adj.* **1** composed of patchwork pieces. **2 a** resembling patchwork (*patchwork fields*). **b** pieced together with lack of uniformity.

patchy *adj.* (**-ier, -iest**) **1** uneven in quality. **2** having or existing in patches. □ **patchily** *adv.* **patchiness** *n.*

pate *n. jocular* the head, esp. if bald.

pâté /pæ'tei, 'pætei/ *n.* a rich paste of finely ground or puréed and seasoned meat or fish etc., served as an appetizer.

pâté de foie gras *n. see* FOIE GRAS.

patella /pə'telə/ *n.* (*pl.* **patellas** or **patellae** /-liː/) the kneecap. □ **patellar** *adj.* **patellate** /-lət/ *adj.*

patent /'pætənt, 'peit-/ ● *n.* **1** a government licence conferring a right or title, esp. the sole right to make, use, or sell some invention. **2** an invention or process protected by this. **3** *N Amer.* the right or title to an area of public land granted to an individual by the government. ● *adj.* **1** obvious, plain. **2** protected by patent. **3** made and marketed under a patent; proprietary. **4** concerning patents (*patent law*). **5** made of patent leather. ● *v.tr.* **1** obtain a patent for. **2** *N Amer.* grant (an area of public land) by a patent. □ **patentable** *adj.* **patently** *adv.* (in sense 1 of *adj.*).

patentee /ˌpætən'tiː:, ˌpeit-/ *n.* a person, company, etc. that takes out or holds a patent.

patent leather *n.* leather with a glossy varnished surface, used for shoes and accessories (often *attrib.*: *patent-leather pumps*).

paternal *adj.* **1** fatherly. **2** related through the father (*paternal grandmother*). **3** inherited from the male parent (*paternal chromosome*). **4** (of an organization, government, etc.) limiting freedom and responsibility by well-meant regulations. □ **paternally** *adv.*

paternalism *n.* the policy of governing in a paternal

way, or behaving paternally to one's associates or subordinates. □ **paternalist** *adj. & n.* **paternalistic** *adj.* **paternalistically** *adv.*

paternity *n.* **1** fatherhood. **2** one's paternal origin. **3** the source or authorship of a thing.

paternity leave *n.* a leave of absence taken by a father to care for a new baby.

paternity suit *n.* a lawsuit held to determine whether a certain man is the father of a certain child.

path *n.* (*pl.* **-s**) **1 a** a track laid down for walking or made by continual treading. **b** a track laid for a special purpose (*bike path*). **2** the line along which a person or thing moves (*flight path*). **3** a course of action or conduct (*career path*). **4** *Computing* a sequence of movements or operations taken by a system. □ **pathless** *adj.*

Pathan /pə'tæn/ *n.* a member of a Pashto-speaking people inhabiting NW Pakistan and SE Afghanistan.

path-breaking = GROUNDBREAKING *adj.* 1 □ **path-breaker** *n.*

pathetic *adj.* **1** arousing pity or sadness or contempt. **2** *informal* miserably inadequate; useless or worthless (*a pathetic performance*). □ **pathetically** *adv.*

pathetic fallacy *n.* the attribution of human feelings and responses to inanimate things, esp. in art and literature.

pathfinder *n.* **1** a person who explores new territory, investigates a new subject, etc. **2** an aircraft or its pilot sent ahead to locate and mark the target area for bombing. **3** (**Pathfinder**) *Cdn* a member of the branch of the Girl Guides for 12- to 15-year-olds.

pathogen /'pæθədʒən/ *n.* an agent causing disease. □ **pathogenic** *adj.* **pathogenicity** /-'nɪsɪti/ *n.*

pathogenesis /ˌpæθə'dʒenəsɪs/ *n.* the manner of development of a disease.

pathological /ˌpæθə'lɒdʒɪkəl/ *adj.* (also **pathologic**) **1** of pathology. **2** of or caused by a physical or mental disorder (*pathological depression*). **3** *informal* extreme and unreasonable (*pathological fear of spiders*). **b** compulsive (*pathological liar*). □ **pathologically** *adv.*

pathology *n.* (*pl.* **-ies**) **1** the science of bodily diseases. **2** the symptoms of a disease. **3** any abnormal or unhealthy condition. □ **pathologist** *n.*

pathos /'peiθɒs/ *n.* a quality in speech, writing, events, etc. that excites pity or sadness.

pathway *n.* **1** a path or course. **2** *Biochem.* a sequence of reactions undergone in a living organism.

patience *n.* the capacity to accept or endure delay, provocation, or hardship calmly without anger. □ **have no patience with** (or **for**) be unable to tolerate; be irritated by.

patient ● *adj.* having or showing patience. ● *n.* a person receiving medical treatment. □ **patiently** *adv.*

patina /pə'tiːnə, 'pætɪnə/ *n.* (*pl.* **-s**) **1** a film, usu. green, formed on the surface of old bronze. **2** a similar film on other surfaces. **3** a gloss produced by age on woodwork etc. **4** a superficial appearance (*a patina of class*). □ **patinated** /-ˌneitəd/ *adj.* **patination** *n.*

patio *n.* (*pl.* **-os**) a paved usu. roofless area adjoining a house, used for outdoor recreation.

patio door *n.* (often in *pl.*) a set of sliding glass doors.

patisserie /pə'tiːsəri/ *n.* a bakeshop where fancy, esp. French, pastries are made, sold, and usu. served.

Patna rice /'pætnə/ *n.* a variety of rice with long firm grains.

patois /'pætwɒ, 'pæt-/ *n.* (*pl.* same /-wɒz/) a nonstandard local dialect.

patriarch /'peitriˌɑːrk/ *n.* **1** the male head of a family or tribe. **2** (often in *pl.*) *Bible* **a** each of the twelve sons of Jacob, from whom the tribes of Israel were descended. **b** Abraham, Isaac, and Jacob, and their forefathers. **3** *Christianity* **a** the title of a chief bishop or the heads of certain Orthodox Churches. **b** *Catholicism* a bishop ranking next above primates and metropolitans, and immediately below the pope. **4 a** the founder of an order, science, etc. **b** a venerable old man. **c** the oldest member of a group.

patriarchal *adj.* of a patriarch or patriarchy.

patriarchy *n.* (*pl.* **-ies**) **1** a system of society, government, etc., ruled by a man and with descent through the male line. **2** the attitudes, structures, etc. of a society seen as ensuring male dominance.

patriate /'peitri,eit/ *v.tr. Cdn* bring (legislation, esp. a constitution) under the authority of the autonomous country to which it applies, used with reference to laws passed on behalf of that country by its former mother country. □ **patriation** *n.*

patrician /pə'trɪʃən/ ● *n.* **1** *hist.* a member of the ancient Roman nobility (*compare* PLEBEIAN *n.* 1). **2** an aristocrat. **3** *N Amer.* a refined or well-bred person. ● *adj.* **1** noble, aristocratic. **2** *hist.* of the ancient Roman nobility. **3** *N Amer.* refined, well-bred.

patrilineal /,pætrɪ'lɪnɪəl/ *adj.* of or based on kinship with the father or descent through the male line.

patrimony /'pætrɪ,moːni/ *n.* (*pl.* **-ies**) **1** a heritage. **2** property inherited from one's father or ancestor. □ **patrimonial** *adj.*

patriot *n.* a person who is ardently devoted to the well-being or interests of his or her country. □ **patriotic** *adj.* **patriotically** *adv.* **patriotism** *n.*

Patriote /pætri'ɒt/ *n. Cdn hist.* a supporter of Louis-Joseph Papineau (1786–1871) in the Rebellion of Lower Canada in 1837.

patristic /pə'trɪstɪk/ *adj.* of the early Christian theologians or their writings.

patrol ● *n.* **1** the act of going around an area, esp. at regular intervals, in order to protect or supervise it. **2** one or more persons or vehicles sent out on patrol. **3 a** a detachment of troops sent out to reconnoitre. **b** such reconnaissance. **4** a routine operational voyage of a ship or aircraft. **5** a unit of six to eight Scouts or Guides. ● *v.* (**patrolled, patrolling**) **1** *tr.* carry out a patrol of. **2** *intr.* act as a patrol. □ **patroller** *n.*

patrol car *n. N Amer.* a police car used in patrolling roads and streets.

patrolman *n.* (*pl.* **-men**) *N Amer.* a police officer on a patrol.

patron *n.* **1** a person who gives financial or other support to a person, cause, arts organization, work of art, etc. **2** a usu. regular customer of a store etc. **3** = PATRON SAINT. □ **patroness** *n.*

patronage /'peitrənɪdʒ, pæt-/ *n.* **1** the support, promotion, or encouragement given by a patron. **2 a** the control of appointments to office, privileges, etc., esp. in public service. **b** the appointing of friends, supporters, etc. to office etc. **3** a customer's support for a store etc.

patronize /'peitrə,naiz, pæt-/ *v.tr.* **1** treat condescendingly. **2** act as a patron towards (a person, cause, artist, etc.); support; encourage. **3** frequent (a store etc.) as a customer. □ **patronization** *n.* **patronizer** *n.* **patronizing** *adj.* **patronizingly** *adv.*

patron saint *n.* the protecting saint of a person, place, occupation, etc.

patronymic /,pætrə'nɪmɪk/ ● *n.* a name derived from the name of a father or ancestor, e.g. *Johnson, O'Brien, Ivanovich*. ● *adj.* **1** (of a name) so derived. **2** (of an affix) indicating such a derivation.

patsy *n.* (*pl.* **-ies**) esp. *N Amer. slang* a person who is deceived, ridiculed, tricked, etc.

patter¹ ● *v.* **1** *intr.* make a rapid succession of taps, as of rain on a window. **2** *intr.* run with quick short steps. ● *n.* a rapid succession of taps, light steps, etc.

patter² ● *n.* **1** rapid speech used by a comedian or salesman. **2** rapid speech included in an esp. comic song. ● *v.* **1** *tr.* repeat in a rapid mechanical way. **2** *intr.* talk glibly or mechanically.

pattern ● *n.* **1** a repeated decorative design on fabric, paper, etc. **2** an esp. regular or logical form, order, or arrangement. **3** a model or design from which copies, garments, etc. can be made. **4** an example of excellence (*a pattern of elegance*). **5** a wooden or metal figure from which a mould is made for a casting. **6** a sample (of cloth, wallpaper, etc.). **7** a random combination of shapes or colours. ● *v.tr.* **1** (usu. foll. by *after, on*) model (a thing) on a design etc. **2** decorate with a pattern. □ **patterning** *n.* **patternless** *adj.*

patty *n.* (also **pattie**) (*pl.* **-ies**) **1** a quantity of any substance formed into a disc-like shape, esp. ground meat etc. **2 a** a little pie or pastry. **b** = JAMAICAN PATTY.

patty cake *n. N Amer.* a child's game in which partners clap their own and each other's hands to the rhythm of a recited rhyme or song.

paucity /'pɒsɪti/ *n.* smallness of number or quantity.

Pauline /'pɒliːn/ *adj.* of or relating to St. Paul.

paunch *n.* the belly or stomach, esp. when protruding. □ **paunchiness** *n.* **paunchy** *adj.*

pauper *n.* a very poor person. □ **pauperize** *v.tr.* **pauperization** *n.*

pause ● *n.* **1** a temporary stop or break. **2** *Music* a mark (⌒) over a note or rest that is to be held for an unspecified time. **3** (also **pause button**) a control allowing the interruption of the operation of a VCR, CD player, etc. ● *v.intr.* **1** make a pause; wait. **2** (usu. foll. by *upon*) linger over (a word etc.). □ **give pause to** cause (a person) to hesitate.

pave *v.tr.* **1** cover (a street etc.) with asphalt, concrete, stone, etc. **2** cover or strew (a floor etc.) with anything (*paved with flowers*). □ **pave the way for** prepare a situation conducive to (*legislation paving the way for economic growth*).

pavement *n.* **1** a paved area or surface, as a roadway, playground, etc. **2** the asphalt, concrete, or densely packed stones etc. used to pave a surface.

paver *n.* **1** a person or machine that paves roads etc. **2** a stone, brick, etc. used in paving a surface.

pavilion *n.* **1** a summer house or other decorative building in a garden. **2** a usu. large tent at a show, fair, etc. **3** a building at a fair or exhibition housing displays or exhibits esp. on a common theme.

paving *n.* the material used to pave a surface.

paving stone *n.* a large flat usu. rectangular piece of stone etc. for paving.

Pavlovian /pæv'loːviən/ *adj.* **1** of or relating to the Russian physiologist I. P. Pavlov (1849–1936) or his work, esp. on conditioned reflexes. **2** of the nature of a reaction or response made unthinkingly or under the influence of others.

paw ● *n.* **1** a foot of an animal having claws or nails. **2** *informal* a person's hand. ● *v.* **1** *tr. & intr.* strike or scrape (the ground) with a paw, hoof, or foot. **2** *tr. informal* fondle awkwardly or indecently.

pawl *n.* a pivoted, usu. curved, bar or lever whose free end engages with the teeth of a cogwheel or ratchet so that it can only turn or move one way.

pawn¹ *n.* **1** *Chess* a piece of the lowest value. **2** a person used by others for their own purposes.

pawn² ● *v.tr.* **1** deposit an object, esp. with a pawnbroker, as security for money lent. **2** pledge or wager (one's life, honour, word, etc.). ● *n.* an object left as security for money etc. lent. □ **in pawn** (of an object etc.) held as security. **pawn off** pass off (a responsibility, something unwanted).

pawnbroker *n.* a person who lends money at interest on the security of personal property pawned. □ **pawnbroking** *n.*

pawnshop *n.* a shop where pawnbroking is conducted and often where property collected from defaulted loans is sold.

pawpaw *n.* **1** a N American tree, *Asimina triloba*, with purple flowers and edible fruit. **2** = PAPAYA.

pax *n.* **1** (often **Pax**; usu. foll. by Latin or Modern Latin adj.) the peace or political stability due to the dominance of one state or power (*Pax Romana; Pax Americana*). **2** the kiss of peace.

pay ● *v.* (*past* and *past part.* **paid**) **1** *tr. & intr.* give (a person etc.) what is due for services done, goods received, debts incurred, etc. **2** *tr.* **a** give (money) for work done, a debt, a ransom, etc. **b** (of a stock etc.) yield (a specified return). **3** *tr.* **a** give, bestow, or express (attention, respect, a compliment, etc.). **b** make (a visit, call, etc.). **4** *intr.* (of an undertaking, attitude, etc.) be profitable or advantageous. **5** *tr. & intr.* suffer or account for a fault etc. (*you'll pay!; paid the penalty*). **6** *tr.* (usu. foll. by *out, away*) let out (a rope etc.) by slackening it. ● *n.* wages; payment. ● *attrib.adj.* designating a service or object the use of which requires payment (*pay phone*). □ **in the pay of** employed by. **pay back 1** return (money). **2** take revenge on (a person). **3** recompense. **pay dearly 1** obtain at a high cost, great effort, etc. **2** suffer for a wrongdoing etc. **pay down** reduce (debt etc.) by repayment. **pay one's dues** esp. *N Amer.* **1** fulfill one's obligations. **2** undergo hardship to succeed or gain experience. **pay for 1** hand over the price of. **2** bear the cost of. **3** suffer or be punished for (a fault etc.). **pay into** pay (money) into a bank account, savings plan, etc. **pay one's (own) way** cover costs; not be indebted. **pay one's last respects** show respect towards a dead person by attending the funeral home or funeral. **pay off 1** *informal* yield good results; succeed. **2** pay (a debt) in full. **3** dismiss (workers) with a final payment. **pay out** pay (money) from funds under one's control; spend. **pay the piper (and call the tune)** pay the cost of (and so have the right to control) an activity or undertaking. **pay a** (or **the**) **price** suffer a disadvantage or loss in return for a gain. **pay one's respects** make a polite visit. **pay through the nose** *informal* pay much more than a fair price. **pay up** pay the full amount. **put paid to** *informal* **1** eliminate. **2** terminate; negate. **3** deal effectively with (a person). □ **payee** /pei'i:/ *n.* **payer** *n.*

payable ● *adj.* **1** that must be paid; due (*payable in April*). **2** that may be paid. ● *n.* (in *pl.*) debts owed by a business; liabilities.

pay-as-you-go *n.* a system or the practice of paying debts and meeting costs as they arise.

payback *n.* **1** a financial return; a reward. **2** the profit from an investment etc., esp. one equal to the initial outlay. **3** (in full **payback period**) the length of time required for an investment to pay for itself in terms of profits or savings.

paycheque *n.* **1** an esp. regular payment given to an employee. **2** a cheque for this.

payday *n.* **1** a day on which payment, esp. of wages, is collected or expected to be collected. **2** *N Amer. informal*

the winning or gaining of a large sum, as from gambling, a contest, etc.

pay dirt *n.* *N Amer. Mining* ground worth working for ore. □ **hit** (or **strike**) **pay dirt** find or reach a source of profit or reward.

paydown *n.* the lowering of debt by repayment.

pay envelope *n.* *N Amer.* = PAY PACKET.

pay equity *n.* the practice of ensuring that men and women in occupations of equal or comparable value receive equal pay.

payload *n.* **1 a** the part of a transport vehicle's load from which revenue is derived. **b** goods transported. **2 a** the explosive warhead carried by an aircraft or rocket. **b** the instruments etc. carried by a spaceship.

paymaster *n.* **1** an official who pays troops, workers, etc. **2** a person etc. to whom another owes duty or loyalty because of payment given.

payment *n.* **1** the act or an instance of paying. **2** an amount paid. **3** reward, recompense.

payoff *n.* *informal* **1** an act of payment. **2** a deserved benefit, reward, or punishment. **3** a bribe.

payola /pei'o:lə/ *n.* esp. *N Amer.* bribery or a bribe offered for unofficial promotion of a product etc. in the media, esp. paid to radio disc jockeys for the playing of specific recordings.

payout *n.* an instance of money being paid out, esp. compensation or dividends.

pay packet *n.* **1** a packet or envelope containing an employee's wages. **2** an employee's wages.

pay-per-view *n.* (usu. *attrib.*) a television service requiring viewers to pay a fee in order to watch a specific broadcast (*a pay-per-view movie*).

pay phone *n.* a telephone operated by the insertion of coins, a credit card, a phone card, etc.

payroll *n.* **1** a list of employees receiving regular pay. **2** the personnel costs of a company etc.

payroll tax *n.* a tax paid by an employer calculated as a percentage of employees' salaries.

pay stub *n.* (also **pay slip**, **pay statement**) a note given to an employee when paid, detailing the amount of pay and deductions for tax etc.

pay-TV *n.* (also **pay television**) any television service requiring payment from viewers, esp. one in which viewers subscribe to a specific channel.

PB *n.* *N Amer. informal* peanut butter.

Pb *symbol* the element lead.

pb. *abbr.* paperback.

PC *abbr.* **1** PERSONAL COMPUTER. **2** *Cdn* Progressive Conservative. **3** politically correct; political correctness. **4** *Cdn* postal code. **5** *Cdn & Brit.* privy councillor. **6** police constable. **7** protective custody.

pc. *abbr.* (also **pce.**) piece (*3 pc. bath*).

PCB *abbr.* polychlorinated biphenyl, any of several toxic aromatic compounds containing two benzene molecules in which hydrogens have been replaced by chlorine atoms, formed as industrial waste.

PCMCIA *abbr.* Personal Computer Memory Card International Association, denoting a standard specification for memory cards and interfaces in small computers.

PCO *abbr.* *Cdn* PRIVY COUNCIL OFFICE.

PCP *abbr.* **1** = PHENCYCLIDINE. **2** *Med.* pneumocystis carinii pneumonia, a fatal lung infection esp. of immunodeficient patients.

PCR *abbr.* polymerase chain reaction, a means of detecting and reproducing nucleic acid.

pct. *abbr.* *N Amer.* per cent.

PD *abbr.* US Police Department.

Pd *symbol* palladium.

pd. *abbr.* paid.

PD day *n.* *Cdn* PROFESSIONAL DEVELOPMENT DAY.

PDQ *abbr. informal* pretty damn quick.

PDT *abbr.* Pacific Daylight Time.

PE *abbr.* **1** physical education. **2** (in official postal use) Prince Edward Island.

pea /piː/ *n.* **1 a** a hardy climbing plant, *Pisum sativum*, of the legume family, with seeds growing in pods and used for food. **b** its seed. **2** any of several similar leguminous plants or seeds (*sweet pea*; *chickpea*).

pea brain *n. informal* a stupid or dim-witted person. □ **pea-brained** *adj.*

peace /piːs/ *n.* **1 a** quiet (*needs peace to work well*). **b** mental calm (*peace of mind*). **2 a** (often *attrib.*) freedom from or the cessation of war (*peace talks*). **b** (esp. **Peace**) a peace treaty between countries at war (*the Peace of Paris*). **3 a** freedom from civil disorder. **b** freedom from quarrels or dissension between individuals. **4** *Christianity* a ritual liturgical greeting. □ **at peace 1** in a state of friendliness. **2** serene. **3** *euphemism* dead. **hold one's peace** keep silence. **keep the peace** prevent, or refrain from, strife. **make one's peace** (often foll. by *with*) re-establish friendly relations. **make peace** bring about peace; reconcile.

peaceable *adj.* **1** disposed to peace; unwarlike. **2** free from disturbance; peaceful. □ **peaceably** *adv.*

peace bond *n.* *N Amer.* a written undertaking to a court of law to keep the peace, esp. to refrain from damaging property or inflicting personal injury.

Peace Corps *n.* *US* an organization sending young people to work as volunteers in developing countries.

peace dividend *n.* public money which becomes available for other spending on defence is reduced.

peaceful *adj.* **1** characterized by peace; tranquil. **2** not violating or infringing peace (*peaceful coexistence*). **3** pertaining to a state of peace. □ **peacefully** *adv.* **peacefulness** *n.*

peacekeeping *n.* the active maintenance of a truce between nations or communities, esp. by international military forces (also *attrib.*: *peacekeeping mission*). □ **peacekeeper** *n.*

peacemaker *n.* a person, group, or nation who brings about peace. □ **peacemaking** *n. & adj.*

peace officer *n.* a civil officer, e.g. a police officer, appointed to preserve the public peace.

peace pipe *n.* = CALUMET.

peace process *n.* a process of negotiation toward a peace treaty.

peace sign *n.* **1** a sign of peace made by holding up the hand with the palm outwards and the first two fingers forming a V. **2** a symbol consisting of a circle divided into thirds by lines, with the central line extended to cover the whole diameter of the circle.

peacetime *n.* a period without war.

peach[1] ● *n.* **1 a** a round juicy fruit with downy skin. **b** the tree, *Prunus persica*, bearing it. **2** the orange-pink colour of a peach. **3** *informal* an impressive or attractive person or thing. ● *adj.* of an orange-pink colour.

peach[2] *v.intr.* (usu. foll. by *against*, *on*) *informal* turn informer; inform.

peaches and cream *n.* **1** *N Amer.* (usu. with *neg.*) an excellent or desirable situation (*it wasn't all peaches and cream*). **2** (often, with hyphens, *attrib.*) a fair complexion characterized by creamy skin and pink cheeks. **3** a variety of corn with alternating white and yellow kernels.

peach fuzz *n.* *N Amer. informal* the down on the chin of an adolescent boy whose beard has not yet developed.

peach Melba *n.* a dish of ice cream and peaches with raspberry sauce.

peachy *adj.* (**-ier, -iest**) **1** like a peach in colour or flavour. **2** (also **peachy-keen**) *N Amer. informal* attractive, outstanding. □ **peachiness** *n.*

peacock *n.* **1** a male peafowl, having brilliant plumage and a fan-like tail with eyelike markings. **2** an ostentatious strutting person.

peacock blue ● *n.* the lustrous greenish blue of a peacock's neck. ● *adj.* (hyphenated when *attrib.*) of this colour.

peafowl *n.* a pheasant of the genus *Pavo*.

pea green ● *n.* a bright green colour. ● *adj.* (hyphenated when *attrib.*) of this colour.

peahen *n.* a female peafowl.

peak ● *n.* **1** a projecting usu. pointed part, esp.: **a** the pointed top of a mountain. **b** a mountain with a peak. **c** a stiff brim at the front of a cap. **d** *Naut.* the upper outer corner of a sail extended by a gaff. **e** the highest point of a roof. **2 a** the highest point in a curve (*on the peak of the wave*). **b** the time of greatest success (in a career etc.). **c** the highest point on a graph etc. **3** (usu. in *pl.*) a pointed mass of beaten egg white, whipped cream, etc. ● *v.intr.* reach the highest value, quality, etc. ● *attrib.adj.* of or at the highest value, quality, level, etc. (*peak shopping times*).

peaked[1] *adj.* having a peak.

peaked[2] /piːkəd/ *adj.* = PEAKY.

peaky *adj.* (**-ier, -iest**) **1** sickly. **2** white-faced.

peal ● *n.* **1 a** the loud ringing of a bell or bells. **b** a set of bells. **2** a loud repeated sound, esp. of thunder, laughter, etc. ● *v.* **1** *intr.* sound forth in a peal. **2** *tr.* utter sonorously. **3** *tr.* ring (bells) in peals.

peameal bacon *n.* *Cdn* back bacon rolled in a coating of fine cornmeal.

peanut *n.* **1** a leguminous plant, *Arachis hypogaea*, bearing pods that ripen underground and contain seeds used as food and yielding oil. **2** the seed of this plant. **3** (in *pl.*) *informal* a paltry or trivial thing or amount, esp. of money. □ **peanutty** *adj.*

peanut butter *n.* a paste of ground roasted peanuts.

peanut gallery *n.* *N Amer. slang* **1** the uppermost balcony in a theatre, where the cheapest seats are. **2** a group of hecklers or rowdy spectators.

pear *n.* **1** a yellowish or brownish-green fleshy fruit, tapering towards the stalk. **2** any of various trees of the genus *Pyrus* bearing it, esp. *P. communis*.

pearl ● *n.* **1 a** (often *attrib.*) a usu. white or bluish-grey hard mass formed within the shell of a pearl oyster or other bivalve mollusc, highly prized as a gem for its lustre. **b** an imitation of this. **c** (in *pl.*) a necklace of pearls. **d** (usu. *attrib.*) = MOTHER-OF-PEARL. **2** a precious thing; the finest example. **3** anything resembling a pearl. **4** an iridescent off-white colour. ● *adj.* of the colour of pearl. ● *v.intr.* form pearl-like drops. □ **cast pearls before swine** offer a treasure to a person unable to appreciate it.

pearl barley *n.* barley reduced to small round grains by grinding.

pearl onion *n.* a very small onion, usu. pickled.

pearl oyster *n.* any of various marine bivalve molluscs of the genus *Pinctada*, esp. *P. margaritifera*, a major commercial source of pearls.

pearly *adj.* (**-ier, -iest**) **1** resembling a pearl; lustrous. **2** containing pearls or mother-of-pearl. **3** adorned with pearls. □ **pearliness** *n.*

Pearly Gates *n.pl. informal* the gates of Heaven.

pearly whites *n.pl. informal* the teeth.

Peary caribou /'pɪːri/ *n.* a small caribou of the Arctic islands of Canada.

peasant ● *n.* **1** (esp. formerly or in poorer countries) a member of a class of farm labourers or subsistence farmers. **2** *derogatory* an ignorant, stupid, or unsophisticated person. ● *adj.* **1** of or characteristic of peasants. **2** (of a style of dress, art, etc.) inspired by Western folk traditions. □ **peasanty** *adj.*

peasantry *n.* peasants collectively.

peashooter *n.* a toy weapon consisting of a small tube through which peas, rolled paper, or other pellets are propelled by blowing.

pea soup *n.* **1** a thick soup, usu. dull yellow or green, made from dried split peas. **2** (also **pea-souper**) *informal* a thick fog. **3** *Cdn* (also **pea-souper**) *slang offensive* (also, with hyphen, *attrib.*) a French Canadian.

peat *n.* vegetable matter partly decomposed in wet acid conditions to form a brown deposit like soil, used for fuel, in gardening, etc. □ **peaty** *adj.*

peat moss *n.* **1** any of various mosses of the genus *Sphagnum*, which grow in damp conditions and form peat as they decay. **2** such moss when dried, used in gardening as a mulch, soil conditioner, etc.

peavey /'piːvi/ *n.* (also **peavy**) (*pl.* **-eys**, **-ies**) *N Amer.* a logging implement consisting of a long pole ending in a metal spike and hinged hook.

pea vine *n.* **1** any of various leguminous plants esp. of the genus *Lathryus*. **2** the climbing stem and leaves of the pea, esp. when dried as hay.

pebble ● *n.* **1** a small smooth stone worn by the action of water. **2** a dimpled texture, as of leather, the ice surface in curling, etc. **3** an agate or other gem, esp. when found as a pebble in a stream etc. ● *v.tr.* give a dimpled texture to (leather, the ice surface in curling, etc.) □ **pebbled** *adj.* **pebbly** *adj.*

pec *n.* (usu. in *pl.*) *informal* a pectoral muscle.

pecan /pɪ'kæn, 'piːkæn, pɪ'kɒn/ *n.* **1** a pinkish-brown smooth nut with an edible kernel. **2** a hickory, *Carya illinoensis*, of the southern US, producing this.

peccadillo /ˌpekə'dɪloː/ *n.* (*pl.* **-oes** or **-os**) a trifling offence; a minor sin.

peccary /'pekəri/ *n.* (*pl.* **-ies**) any of several dark-furred gregarious pig-like mammals inhabiting forest and forest scrub in Central and S America.

peck¹ ● *v.tr.* **1** strike or bite (something) with a beak or pointed instrument. **2** kiss (esp. a person's cheek) hastily or perfunctorily. **3 a** make (a hole) by pecking. **b** (foll. by *out*, *off*) remove or pluck out by pecking. **4** (also foll. by *away*, *out*) type at a typewriter etc. ● *n.* **1** a stroke or bite with a beak or pointed instrument. **2** a hasty or perfunctory kiss. □ **peck at 1** eat (food) listlessly. **2** strike (a thing) repeatedly with a beak.

peck² *n.* **1 a** (in Britain and other Commonwealth countries) a measure of capacity for dry goods, equal to 2 imperial gallons (9.09 litres). **b** (in the US) a measure of capacity for dry goods, equal to 8 US quarts (8.81 litres). **2** a vessel used to contain this amount. □ **a peck of** a large number or amount of (troubles, dirt, etc.).

pecker *n.* **1** esp. *N Amer. coarse slang* the penis. **2** a bird that pecks (*woodpecker*).

pecking order *n.* **1** a hierarchy based on rank or status. **2** a pattern of behaviour observed among animals in which those of high rank attack those of lower rank without provoking an attack in return.

peckish *adj. informal* moderately hungry.

pecorino /ˌpekə'riːnoː/ *n.* (*pl.* **-os**) an Italian cheese made from ewes' milk.

pectin *n.* any of various soluble gelatinous polysaccharides found in ripe fruits etc. and used as a setting agent in jams and jellies.

pectoral /'pektərəl/ ● *adj.* of, relating to, or worn on the chest. ● *n.* **1** (esp. in *pl.*) a pectoral muscle. **2** a pectoral fin.

peculiar *adj.* **1** strange. **2 a** (usu. foll. by *to*) belonging exclusively (*peculiar to the time*). **b** belonging to the individual (*their own peculiar brand of art*). **3** particular (*a point of peculiar interest*). □ **peculiarly** *adv.*

peculiarity *n.* (*pl.* **-ies**) **1 a** idiosyncrasy; oddity. **b** an instance of this. **2** a distinguishing characteristic or habit. **3** the state of being peculiar.

pecuniary /pə'kjuːniˌeri/ *adj.* **1** of, concerning, or consisting of money (*pecuniary aid*). **2** (of an offence) entailing a fine.

pedagogue /'pedəˌgɒg/ *n.* a teacher.

pedagogy /'pedəˌgɒdʒi/ *n.* (*pl.* **-ies**) the science of teaching. □ **pedagogic** /-'gɒdʒɪk/ *adj.* **pedagogics** *n.* **pedagogical** *adj.* **pedagogically** *adv.*

pedal ● *n.* any of several types of foot-operated levers or controls for mechanisms, esp.: **1** either of a pair of levers for transmitting power to a bicycle or tricycle wheel etc. **2** any of the foot-operated controls in a motor vehicle. **3** a bar on a musical instrument, e.g. a piano, organ, or harp, that is operated by the foot in order to produce or affect sound. ● *v.* (**pedalled**, **pedalling**) **1** *intr.* operate a bicycle, organ, etc. by using the pedals. **2** *tr.* work (a bicycle etc.) with the pedals. □ **pedal to the metal** *N Amer.* **1** full speed, full out. **2** with the gas pedal of a vehicle pressed completely to the floor. □ **pedaller** *n.*

pedal boat *n.* a small recreational pontoon boat usu. with pedal-operated paddlewheels.

pedant /'pedənt/ *n.* **1** a person excessively concerned with trifling details or who insists on strict adherence to formal rules or literal meaning at the expense of a wider view. **2** a person who parades or reveres academic learning or technical knowledge above everything. □ **pedantic** /pɪ'dæntɪk/ *adj.* **pedantically** *adv.* **pedantry** *n.* (*pl.* **-ies**).

peddle *v.* **1** *tr.* sell (goods), esp. in small quantities, as a peddler. **2** *tr.* sell (goods). **3** *tr.* advocate or promote (ideas, a way of life, etc.). **4** *intr.* engage in selling as a peddler. **5** *tr.* sell (drugs) illegally.

peddler *n.* **1** a travelling seller of small items esp. carried in a pack etc. **2 a** a person who sells drugs illegally. **b** (usu. foll. by *of*) a spreader of gossip etc.

pederast /'pedəˌræst/ *n.* a man who engages in sexual relations with boys. □ **pederasty** *n.*

pedestal *n.* **1** a base supporting a column, statue, etc. **2** either of the two supports at either end of the writing surface of a desk, usu. containing drawers. **3** (often *attrib.*) an upright, column-like support for a seat, machine, etc. (*pedestal sink*). □ **put** (or **set**) **on a pedestal** admire disproportionately, idolize.

pedestrian ● *n.* a person on foot rather than in a vehicle. ● *adj.* **1** (esp. of writing) dull. **2** of, relating to, or for walkers or walking (*pedestrian crossing*).

pediatrics /ˌpiːdi'ætrɪks/ *n.pl.* (treated as *sing.*) the branch of medicine dealing with children and their diseases. □ **pediatric** *adj.* **pediatrician** /-ə'trɪʃən/ *n.*

pedicure /'pedɪˌkjʊr/ *n.* **1** remedial or cosmetic treatment of the feet. **2** a session of such treatment. □ **pedicured** *adj.*

pedigree *n.* **1** (often *attrib.*) a recorded line of descent of a person or esp. a purebred animal. **2** *informal* the history of a person, thing, idea, etc., esp. a list of achievements. **3** a genealogical table. □ **pedigreed** *adj.*

pediment /ˈpedɪmənt/ n. **1** the triangular part crowning the front of a building in the classical style. **2** a similar part of a building in other styles, irrespective of shape. **3** a similar feature surmounting a door etc. □ **pedimented** adj.

pedlar var. of PEDLAR.

pedophile /ˈpedə‚faɪl, piːd-/ n. a person who desires children sexually. □ **pedophilia** n. **pedophiliac** adj.

pedway n. esp. N Amer. a walkway designed to separate pedestrians from urban traffic.

pee informal ● v. (**pees, peed**) **1** intr. urinate. **2** tr. pass (urine etc.) from the bladder. **3** refl. urinate into one's clothes. **4** tr. wet (esp. bedclothes, one's clothing) by urinating. ● n. **1** an act of urination. **2** urine. □ **peed off** annoyed.

peek ● v.intr. (usu. foll. by in, out, at) look quickly or furtively. ● n. a quick or furtive look.

peekaboo ● n. the game of hiding one's face and suddenly revealing it, as played with a young child. ● interj. the utterance made when doing this. ● adj. (of a garment) transparent or having a pattern of small holes so as to reveal the body.

peel ● v. **1** tr. **a** strip the skin etc. from. **b** strip (skin, peel, wrapping, etc.) from a fruit etc. **2** intr. **a** (of a tree, an animal's or person's body, a painted surface, etc.) have the outer layer of bark, skin, paint, etc. flake off. **b** (often foll. by off) (of bark, a person's skin, paint, etc.) flake off. **3 a** tr. remove or separate (a label, a banknote, etc.) from the outside or top of something. **b** tr. turn back so as to expose something underneath. **4** intr. separate from a body of people, vehicles, etc. (peeled away from the line of cars). **5 a** tr. (often foll. by off) informal (of a person) take off (a garment). **b** intr. (foll. by down) undress. **6** intr. N Amer. (of a vehicle etc.) move quickly, leave a place, etc. suddenly (peeled out of her driveway). **7** tr. & intr. Curling remove (a rock) from play with a rock that itself also goes out of play. ● n. **1** the outer covering of a fruit, vegetable, shrimp, etc. **2** the chemical removal of superficial layers of skin on the face, usu. to remove scars etc. **3** Curling an instance of peeling a rock (also attrib.: peel game). □ **peel off** veer away and detach oneself from a group of marchers, a formation of aircraft, etc.

peeler n. **1** a utensil for peeling fruit etc. **2** (in full **peeler crab**) a crab when it casts its shell.

peeling n. a strip of the outer skin of a vegetable, fruit, etc. (potato peelings).

peen n. the wedge-shaped or thin or curved end of the head of a hammer (opp. FACE n. 5a).

peep¹ ● v.intr. **1** (usu. foll. by at, in, out, into) look quickly and secretly, esp. through a small opening. **2** (usu. foll. by out) come slowly into view; emerge. ● n. **1** a furtive or peering glance. **2** the first appearance.

peep² ● v.intr. make a shrill feeble sound as of young birds, mice, etc. ● n. **1** such a sound. **2** a slight sound, utterance, or complaint (not a peep out of them). **3** N Amer. any of several sandpipers.

pee-pee n. informal **1** urine. **2** the penis.

peeper¹ n. **1** a person who peeps. **2** informal (usu. in pl.) an eye. **3** N Amer. slang a private investigator.

peeper² n. = SPRING PEEPER.

peephole n. a small hole to be looked through.

peeping Tom n. a person who surreptitiously observes others, esp. women undressing.

peep show n. **1** a show of live nudes or an erotic film viewed from a coin-operated booth. **2** a series of small pictures viewed through a magnifying lens placed in a small opening of a box etc.

peer¹ v.intr. (usu. foll. by into, at, etc.) look keenly or with difficulty (peered into the fog).

peer² n. **1** a person who is equal in ability, standing, rank, or value (a jury of his peers). **2** a noble or person of high rank. □ **without peer** unequalled, unrivalled. □ **peerless** adj.

peerage n. **1** peers as a class; the nobility. **2** the rank of peer or peeress (a life peerage). **3** a book containing a list of peers with their genealogy etc.

peeress n. **1** the wife or widow of a peer. **2** a woman having the rank of a peer by creation or descent.

peer group n. a group of people of the same age, status, interests, etc.

peer pressure n. influence from members of one's peer group.

peer review n. **1** the evaluation by experts of a research project for which a grant is sought, a paper received for publication, etc. **2** a review of commercial, professional, or academic efficiency, competence, etc. by others in the same occupation. □ **peer review** v.tr. **peer-reviewed** adj. **peer reviewer** n.

peeve informal ● n. a cause of annoyance. ● v.tr. (usu. in passive) annoy.

peevish adj. **1** easily annoyed, esp. by unimportant things; bad-tempered. **2** (of a quality, action, etc.) characterized by or exhibiting petty vexation or spite. □ **peevishly** adv. **peevishness** n.

peewee ● n. **1** Cdn **a** a level of amateur sport, usu. involving children aged 12–13 (also attrib.: peewee hockey). **b** a player in this age group. **2** N Amer. a very small or young person or thing. ● adj. very small.

peg ● n. **1** a usu. cylindrical pin or bolt of wood, metal, etc., often tapered at one end, and used for: **a** fastening two things together. **b** hanging garments. **c** anchoring a tent etc. **d** tightening or loosening the strings of a violin etc. **e** keeping score on a cribbage board. **2** Baseball informal a strong throw, esp. to a base. **3** an occasion, pretext, excuse, theme, etc. (used the incident as a peg for the article). **4** a short blunt structure or outgrowth in a plant, animal, etc. ● v.tr. (**pegged, pegging**) **1 a** fix (a thing) with a peg. **b** drive or insert a peg or pegs into. **2** (usu. foll. by as) esp. N Amer. informal identify, categorize, form an opinion of (a person etc.). **3** N Amer. informal **a** throw (a ball). **b** Baseball put out (a runner) with such a throw. **4** informal measure, mark, set (the cost was pegged at $5.5 million). **5 a** fix (prices, wages, etc.) at a certain level or in line with a certain standard. **b** stabilize the price of (stock etc.) by freely buying or selling at a given price. □ **peg out 1** slang die. **2** measure, extend, or mark the boundaries of (land etc.). **3** score the winning point in cribbage. **a round** (or **square**) **peg in a square** (or **round**) **hole** a person in a situation unsuited to his or her capacities, disposition, etc.; a misfit. **take a person down a peg or two** humble a person.

Pegboard n. proprietary a type of perforated board having a regular pattern of small holes for pegs.

pegged adj. **1** in senses of PEG v. **2** (attrib.) N Amer. (of a garment) wide at the top and narrow at the bottom.

peg leg informal ● n. **1** an artificial leg, esp. a wooden leg. **2** offensive a person with an artificial leg. ● adj. **1** (also **peg-legged**) informal having a peg leg. **2** = PEGGED 2.

Peguis /ˈpegwɪs/ n. a member of a Cree- and Ojibwa-speaking Aboriginal group living about 200 km north of Winnipeg.

PEI abbr. Prince Edward Island.

Peigan /piːˈgæn/ ● n. **1** a member of an Aboriginal people, a part of the Blackfoot Confederacy, living in S Alberta and NW Montana. **2** the Algonquian language of this people. ● adj. of this people or language.

pejorative /pɪˈdʒɔrətɪv/ ● *adj.* (of a word, an expression, etc.) expressing contempt and criticism or disapproval. ● *n.* a derogatory word or form. □ **pejoratively** *adv.*

pekan /ˈpekən/ *n.* = FISHER 1.

Peke *n. informal* a Pekingese dog.

Peking duck *n.* a Chinese dish consisting of duck that has been coated with honey, hung to dry, and then roasted, served in shreds with vegetables, sauce, and small pancakes.

Pekingese (also **Pekinese**) ● *n.* (*pl.* same) **1** a lapdog of a short-legged breed with long hair and a snub nose. **2** a citizen of Peking (Beijing). **3** the form of the Chinese language used in Beijing. ● *adj.* of or concerning Beijing or its language or citizens.

pekoe /ˈpiːkoː/ *n.* a high-quality black tea.

pelagic /pɛˈlædʒɪk/ *adj.* of, performed on, or inhabiting the open sea.

pelargonium /ˌpelɑrˈgoːniəm/ *n.* any plant of the genus *Pelargonium*, with red, pink, or white flowers and fragrant leaves.

pelican *n.* any large gregarious waterfowl of the family Pelecanidae with a large bill and a pouch in the throat for storing fish.

pellagra /pəˈlægrə, -ˈleɪgrə, -lɒgrə/ *n.* a disease caused by niacin deficiency, characterized by dermatitis, diarrhea, and mental disturbance.

pellet ● *n.* **1** a small, hard, compressed mass of something. **2 a** a bullet or piece of small shot. **b** an imitation bullet for a toy gun (also *attrib.*: *pellet gun*). **3 a** a small mass of bones, feathers, etc. regurgitated by a bird of prey. **b** a small hard piece of animal excreta. ● *v.tr.* (**pelleted, pelleting**) **1** make into a pellet or pellets. **2** hit with pellets. □ **pelletization** *n.* **pelletize** *v.tr.* **pelletizing** *n. & adj.*

pell-mell ● *adv.* **1** headlong, recklessly. **2** in disorder or confusion. ● *adj.* confused, tumultuous.

pellucid /pəˈluːsɪd, -ˈljuːsɪd/ *adj.* very clear.

pelt[1] *v.* **1** *tr.* (usu. foll. by *with*) **a** hurl many small objects at. **b** strike repeatedly with esp. many small things. **c** assail (a person etc.) with insults, abuse, etc. **2** *intr.* (usu. foll. by *down*) (of rain etc.) fall quickly and torrentially. **3** *intr.* move or run fast or vigorously. □ **(at) full pelt** as fast as possible.

pelt[2] *n.* the dressed or undressed skin of a fur-bearing mammal with hair, wool, etc. still on.

pelvic floor *n.* the muscular base of the abdomen, attached to the pelvis.

pelvic girdle *n.* the bony or cartilaginous structure in vertebrates to which the posterior limbs are attached.

pelvic inflammatory disease *n.* an inflammation of the female reproductive organs, caused by bacterial infection. *Abbr.:* **PID**.

pelvis *n.* (*pl.* **pelvises** or **pelves**) **1 a** a basin-shaped cavity at the lower end of the torso of most vertebrates, formed from the innominate bone with the sacrum and other vertebrae. **b** these bones collectively, constituting the pelvic girdle. **c** the part of the abdomen containing the pelvis. **2** the basin-like cavity of the kidney. □ **pelvic** *adj.*

pemmican *n.* pounded, dried meat (usu. buffalo) mixed to a paste with melted fat, berries, etc. originally made by N American Indians and adapted by fur traders etc.

Pen. *abbr.* Peninsula.

pen[1] ● *n.* **1** an instrument for writing or drawing with ink. **2** (usu. prec. by *the*) the occupation or practice of writing. **3** an instrument resembling a pen in form or function. **4** an electronic pen-like device used with a writing surface to enter commands or data into a computer. ● *v.tr.* (**penned, penning**) **1** write. **2** compose and write. □ **the pen is mightier than the sword** persuasion, legislation, and education can achieve more than the use of armed force. **put pen to paper** begin writing.

pen[2] ● *n.* **1 a** a small enclosure for cows, sheep, poultry, etc. **b** a number of animals in a pen or sufficient to fill a pen. **2** a place of confinement. **3** an enclosure for sheltering submarines. ● *v.tr.* (**penned, penning**) enclose or shut in a pen.

pen[3] *n.* a female swan.

pen[4] *n. N Amer. slang* = PENITENTIARY *n.* 1.

penal /ˈpiːnəl/ *adj.* **1 a** of or concerning punishment or its infliction. **b** (of an act or offence) punishable, esp. by law. **2** extremely severe (*penal taxation*). □ **penally** *adv.*

penal code *n.* a system of laws relating to crime and its punishment.

penalize /ˈpiːnəˌlaiz, pen-/ *v.tr.* **1 a** subject to a penalty for breaking a rule etc. **b** put at a comparative disadvantage; handicap unfairly. **2** make or declare (an action) penal. □ **penalization** *n.*

penalty /ˈpenəlti/ *n.* (*pl.* **-ies**) **1** a punishment, esp. a fine, for a breach of law, contract, etc. **2** a disadvantage, loss, etc., esp. as a result of one's own actions. **3** a disadvantage imposed on a competitor for a breach of the rules etc. □ **under** (or **on**) **penalty of** under the threat of (dismissal etc.).

penalty area *n. Soccer* the ground in front of the goal in which a foul by defenders involves the award of a penalty kick.

penalty box *n. Hockey & Lacrosse* an area of seating reserved for players temporarily withdrawn from play as a penalty.

penalty kick *n. Soccer* a free kick at the goal, given after a foul in the penalty area.

penalty killer *n. Hockey* a player who plays while the team is short-handed due to a penalty. □ **penalty killing** *n.*

penalty shootout *n.* = SHOOTOUT 2.

penalty shot *n. Hockey* **1** a shot by an offensive player on a goal defended only by the goaltender, allowed as a penalty for certain infractions. **2** such a shot used esp. to decide the outcome of a tied game.

penance /ˈpenəns/ *n.* **1** an act of self-punishment as reparation for guilt. **2 a** (in the Catholic and Orthodox Churches) a sacrament including confession of and contrition and absolution for a sin. **b** a punishment or discipline imposed esp. by a priest, or undertaken voluntarily, in expiation of a sin. **3** an unpleasant task or situation, esp. one regarded as a punishment for something.

pen and ink ● *n.* **1** the instruments of writing or drawing. **2** writing. **3** a drawing made using pen and ink. ● *adj.* (**pen-and-ink**) (esp. of a drawing) done in ink.

pen-based *adj.* (of a computer etc.) taking input from an electronic pen rather than a keyboard.

pence /pens/ *n. Brit.* **1** *pl.* of PENNY. **2** *informal* a penny, esp. in British decimal currency.

penchant /ˈpenʃənt, ˈpɑ̃ʃɑ̃/ *n.* an inclination; a strong or habitual liking.

pencil ● *n.* **1 a** an instrument for writing or drawing, usu. consisting of a thin rod of graphite etc. enclosed in a cylinder. **b** a cosmetic or medication in pencil form (*eyebrow pencil*). **2** (*attrib.*) **a** resembling a pencil in shape (*pencil bomb*). **b** for, with, or of a pencil (*pencil sketch*; *pencil stub*). ● *v.tr.* (**pencilled, pencilling**) **1**

write, sketch, etc. with or as if with a pencil. **2** (usu. foll. by *in*) **a** note down or arrange tentatively or provisionally (*have pencilled in the wedding*). **b** fill (an area) with thin or delicate pencil strokes (*pencilled in her eyebrows*). □ **pencilled** *adj.*

pencil case *n.* a small bag, box, etc. for holding pencils, pens, etc.

pencil crayon *n.* Cdn a pencil with a coloured core used for art, colouring, etc.

pencil line *n.* **1** a line drawn with or resembling one drawn with a pencil. **2** (also **pencil-line**) (*attrib.*) (of a moustache) very thin.

pencil-pusher *n.* N Amer. informal derogatory a person, esp. a clerk, whose job involves a lot of boring paperwork. □ **pencil-pushing** *n. & adj.*

pencil-thin *adj.* very thin or narrow.

pendant /'pendənt/ *n.* **1** a hanging jewel etc., esp. one attached to a necklace, bracelet, etc. (also *attrib.*: *pendant earrings*). **2** a light fixture, ornament, etc., hanging from a ceiling.

pendent /'pendənt/ *adj.* **1** hanging. **2** overhanging.

pending ● *adj.* **1** awaiting decision or settlement, undecided (*a settlement was pending*). **2** about to come into existence (*patent pending*). ● *prep.* **1** until (*pending his return*). **2** during (*pending these negotiations*).

pendulous /'pendjʊləs/ *adj.* **1** (of a part of the body) tending to droop heavily. **2** (of flowers, bird's nests, etc.) hanging down, drooping, and esp. swinging.

pendulum /'pendjʊləm/ *n.* **1** a weight suspended so as to swing freely, esp. a rod with a weighted end regulating the movement of a clock's works. **2** popular opinion etc. characterized by oscillation or regular movement from one extreme to another.

penetrate *v.* **1** *tr.* **a** find access into or through, esp. forcibly. **b** (usu. foll. by *with*) imbue (a person or thing) with. **2** *tr.* see into, find out, or discern (a person's mind, the truth, etc.). **3** *tr.* see through (darkness, fog, etc.). **4** *intr.* be understood, fully realized, or absorbed by the mind. **5** *tr.* breach or get through (an opponent's defence). **6** *tr.* enter (a market) to establish a new brand, product, etc. **7** *intr.* (usu. foll. by *into, through, to*) make a way. **8** *tr.* (of a male) put the penis into the vagina or anus of (a sexual partner). □ **penetrability** *n.* **penetrable** *adj.* **penetration** *n.* **penetrative** *adj.* **penetrator** *n.*

penetrating *adj.* **1** that permeates, gets, or forces a way into or through something. **2** having or suggesting sensitivity or insight (*a penetrating remark*). **3 a** (of a voice etc.) easily heard through or above other sounds. **b** (of a smell) sharp, pungent. **4** capable of penetrating an opponent's defence.

penfriend *n.* = PEN PAL.

penguin *n.* any black-and-white flightless seabird of the family Spheniscidae of the southern hemisphere, with wings developed into scaly flippers for swimming underwater.

penicillin *n.* any of various antibiotics produced naturally by moulds of the genus *Penicillium*, or synthetically, and able to prevent the growth of certain disease-causing bacteria.

penile /'pi:naɪl/ *adj.* of or concerning the penis.

peninsula /pə'nɪnsjələ, -sə-/ *n.* a piece of land almost surrounded by water or projecting far into a sea or lake etc. □ **peninsular** *adj.*

penis *n.* (*pl.* **penises** or **penes**) the male genital organ which carries the duct for the emission of sperm, in mammals consisting largely of erectile tissue and serving also for the elimination of urine.

penis envy *n.* the supposed female envy of the male's possession of a penis, postulated by Freud to

account for various behavioural characteristics in women.

penitent /'penɪtənt/ ● *adj.* regretting and wishing to atone for sins etc. ● *n.* **1** a person who repents, a repentant sinner. **2** a person doing penance under the direction of a confessor. □ **penitence** *n.* **penitential** *adj.* **penitentially** *adv.* **penitently** *adv.*

penitentiary /ˌpenɪ'tenʃəri/ ● *n.* (*pl.* **-ies**) **1** Cdn a federal corrections institution for convicted offenders serving a sentence of two years or more. **2** US a state or federal prison, esp. for serious offenders. ● *adj.* **1** intended for or pertaining to the penal and reformatory treatment of criminals. **2** N Amer. (of an offence) making a culprit liable to imprisonment.

penknife *n.* (*pl.* **-knives**) a small folding knife, esp. for carrying in a pocket.

penlight *n.* a small, pen-shaped flashlight.

penmanship *n.* **1** handwriting. **2** the skill or art of handwriting.

Penn. *abbr.* (also **Penna.**) Pennsylvania.

pen name *n.* a literary pseudonym.

pennant *n.* **1 a** a tapering flag, esp. that flown at the masthead of a vessel in commission. **b** N Amer. such a flag identifying a team, club, cause, etc. **2** N Amer. Sport **a** a flag symbolizing a league championship, esp. in professional baseball. **b** such a championship.

pennant race *n.* N Amer. Baseball an esp. close competition among teams for the league pennant.

penne /'peneɪ/ *n.* pasta in the form of short tubes with the ends cut diagonally.

penniless *adj.* having no money. □ **pennilessly** *adv.* **pennilessness** *n.*

Pennsylvania Dutch (also **Pennsylvania German**) ● *n.* **1** a dialect of High German spoken by 17th–18th-c. German and Swiss immigrants to Pennsylvania, still spoken by some of their descendants in Pennsylvania and nearby areas and S Ontario, esp. the Amish. **2** (as *pl.*) these settlers or their descendants. ● *adj.* of, pertaining to, or designating these people or their dialect.

Pennsylvanian ● *n.* **1** a native or inhabitant of the US state of Pennsylvania. **2** (prec. by *the*) esp. N Amer. the upper Carboniferous period or system. ● *adj.* **1** of or relating to Pennsylvania. **2** esp. N Amer. of or relating to the upper Carboniferous period or system.

penny *n.* (*pl.* for separate coins **-ies**, Brit. for a sum of money **pence**) **1** N Amer. a one-cent coin. **2** Brit. a coin and monetary unit equal to one-hundredth of a pound. **3** Brit. hist. a former coin and monetary unit equal to one 240th of a pound. **4** a very little or the least amount of wealth, money, etc. (*worth every penny*). □ **in for a penny, in for a pound** an exhortation to total commitment to an undertaking. **like a bad penny** continually returning when unwanted. **pennies from heaven** unexpected esp. financial benefits. **a penny for your thoughts** a request to a person to confide in the speaker. **a pretty penny** a considerable sum of money.

penny ante N Amer. ● *n.* **1** poker played for small, esp. penny, stakes. **2** a matter, concern, etc. involving an insignificant sum of money. ● *adj.* (**penny-ante**) contemptible, trivial.

penny auction *n.* **1** a fundraising auction where items are sold for very small sums. **2** an auction of goods repossessed or seized as collateral, in which the bidders collude to pay absurdly low prices so that the repossessor sees no financial gain from the sale and the owner can regain the property at little cost.

penny-pinching ● *n.* stinginess, miserliness. ● *adj.* stingy, miserly. □ **penny-pincher** *n.*

pennyroyal n. **1** a creeping mint, *Mentha pulegium*, cultivated for its supposed medicinal properties. **2** N Amer. an aromatic plant, *Hedeoma pulegioides*.

penny stock n. common stock valued at less than a dollar a share, and therefore highly speculative.

pennywhistle n. a tin pipe with six holes.

penny-wise adj. careful, esp. overly careful, in saving small amounts or in small expenditures. □ **penny-wise and pound foolish** thrifty in small expenditures but careless or wasteful in large ones.

pennywort n. any of several round-leafed wild plants, esp.: **1** (**wall pennywort**) *Umbilicus rupestris*, growing in crevices. **2** (**marsh** or **water pennywort**) *Hydrocotyle vulgaris*, growing in marshy places.

pen pal n. esp. N Amer. a person with whom one builds a friendship by exchanging letters, esp. someone in a foreign country whom one has never met.

pen-pusher n. informal derogatory = PENCIL-PUSHER. □ **pen-pushing** n.

pension ● n. **1** a regular payment made by a government to people above a specified age, to the disabled, or to such a person's surviving dependents. **2** a similar payment made by an employer etc. to a retired employee. **3** a regular payment from a fund etc. to which the recipient has contributed (usu. with an employer) as an investment during his or her working life in order to realize a return upon retirement (also attrib.: *pension plan*). ● v.tr. grant a pension to. □ **pension off 1** dismiss with a pension. **2** cease to employ or use.

pension /pãˈsjɔ̃/ n. a European, esp. French, hotel providing full or half board at a fixed rate.

pensionable adj. **1** entitled to a pension. **2** (of a service, job, etc.) entitling an employee to a pension. **3** of, pertaining to, or affecting a person's pension (*pensionable earnings*). □ **pensionability** n.

pensioner n. a recipient of (esp. an old-age) pension.

pensive /ˈpensiv/ adj. **1** deep in thought. **2** sorrowfully thoughtful. □ **pensively** adv.

penstemon /penˈstiːmən, ˈpenstəmən/ n. any N American herbaceous plant of the genus *Penstemon*, with showy flowers and five stamens.

pent adj. (usu. foll. by *up*) closely confined; shut in.

penta- comb. form five.

pentagon n. **1** a plane figure with five sides and angles. **2** (**the Pentagon**) **a** a pentagonal building in Arlington, Virginia, containing the headquarters of the US armed forces. **b** the leaders of the US armed forces. □ **pentagonal** /-ˈtægənəl/ adj.

pentahedron /ˌpentəˈhiːdrən/ n. (pl. **-hedrons** or **-hedra** /-drə/) a solid figure with five faces.

pentameter /penˈtæmətər/ n. a verse of five feet, e.g. English iambic verse of ten syllables.

pentamidine /penˈtæmɪˌdiːn/ n. a drug used to treat protozoal infections, esp. in AIDS patients.

pentane /ˈpentein/ n. Chem. a hydrocarbon of the alkane series.

Pentateuch /ˈpentəˌtuːk, -ˌtjuːk/ n. the first five books of the Bible (Genesis, Exodus, Leviticus, Numbers, and Deuteronomy), called the Torah by Jews, and traditionally ascribed to Moses. □ **Pentateuchal** adj.

pentathlon /penˈtæθlɒn/ n. **1** = MODERN PENTATHLON. **2** any athletic event comprising five different events. □ **pentathlete** /-ˈtæθliːt/ n.

Pentecost n. **1** a Christian festival observed on the seventh Sunday after Easter, commemorating the descent of the Holy Spirit on the disciples. **2 a** the Jewish harvest festival, on the fiftieth day after the second day of Passover. **b** a synagogue ceremony on the anniversary of the giving of the Law on Mount Sinai. **3** (in some Christian denominations) the liturgical season extending from Pentecost to the beginning of Advent.

Pentecostal ● adj. (also **pentecostal**) **1** of or relating to Pentecost. **2** of or designating Christian denominations and individuals who emphasize charismatic forms of worship, e.g. speaking in tongues, healing, etc., and are often fundamentalist in outlook. ● n. a member of a Pentecostal church. □ **Pentecostalism** n. **Pentecostalist** adj. & n.

penthouse n. **1** an apartment or suite on the top floor of a tall building. **2** a structure on the roof of a building to house elevator machinery etc.

pentobarbital n. a narcotic and sedative barbiturate formerly used to relieve insomnia.

Pentothal n. proprietary = THIOPENTAL SODIUM.

pentstemon /penˈstiːmən/ var. of PENSTEMON.

pentyl /ˈpentil/ n. = AMYL.

penultimate /pəˈnʌltɪmət/ ● adj. last but one; second-last. ¶ Often mistakenly used and understood to mean 'absolutely ultimate; unsurpassable'. ● n. **1** the last but one. **2** the last syllable but one.

penumbra /pəˈnʌmbrə/ n. (pl. **penumbrae** /-briː/ or **penumbras**) **1** the partly shaded region around the shadow of an opaque body, esp. that around the total shadow of the moon or earth in an eclipse. **2** a partial shadow. □ **penumbral** adj.

penury /ˈpenjʊri/ n. (pl. **-ies**) **1** destitution. **2** a lack.

peon /ˈpiːɒn/ n. **1** N Amer. a menial or drudge. **2 a** a Spanish American farm worker. **b** a poor or destitute South American. □ **peonage** n.

peony /ˈpiːəni/ n. (pl. **-ies**) any herbaceous plant of the genus *Paeonia*, with large globular red, pink, or white flowers, often double in cultivated varieties.

people ● n. **1** (treated as pl.) **a** human beings, esp. as opposed to animals etc. **b** persons in general. **2** (usu. as pl.) persons composing a community, race, nation, etc. **3** (prec. by *the*; treated as pl.) **a** the mass of people in a country etc. not having special rank or position. **b** these considered as an electorate. **4** (treated as pl.) family (*my people came from Scotland*). ● v.tr. **1** fill with people; populate. **2** (esp. as **peopled** adj.) inhabit; occupy as inhabitants, fictional characters, etc. (*a novel peopled with unlovable characters*).

peoplehood n. the condition, state, or awareness of being a people.

people person n. a person who enjoys or is particularly good at interacting with other people.

people power n. **1** political or other pressure applied by the people, esp. through the public demonstration of popular organization. **2** physical power exerted by people as opposed to machines etc.

people skills n.pl. character traits that allow one to deal effectively with other people.

people-watching n. the action of observing people as they pass by, esp. noting idiosyncrasies, styles, etc. □ **people-watch** v.intr. **people-watcher** n.

pep informal ● n. liveliness; energy and enthusiasm. ● v.tr. (**pepped, pepping**) (usu. foll. by *up*) fill with energy or liveliness.

pepper ● n. **1 a** a hot aromatic condiment from the dried berries of certain plants used whole or ground. **b** any climbing vine of the genus *Piper*, esp. *P. nigrum*, yielding these berries. **2 a** the bell-shaped, smooth-skinned, mildly pungent fruit of certain varieties of the plant *Capsicum annuum*. **b** the plant of the nightshade family bearing this fruit. **3** = CAYENNE. ●

v.tr. **1** sprinkle or treat with or as if with pepper. **2** sprinkle liberally (*peppered with quotations from Shakespeare*). **3** pelt with missiles.

peppercorn *n.* the dried pepper berry as a condiment.

pepper mill *n.* (also **pepper grinder**) a device for grinding pepper by hand.

peppermint *n.* **1 a** a mint plant, Mentha piperita, grown for the strong-flavoured oil obtained from its leaves. **b** the oil from this. **2** a candy flavoured with peppermint. □ **pepperminty** *adj.*

peppermint knob *n.* Cdn (Nfld) a hard, usu. spherical peppermint candy.

pepperoni *n.* a hard, highly-seasoned sausage made with beef and pork.

pepper spray *n.* an aerosol spray of oils derived from cayenne pepper, used to overcome an assailant.

pepper squash *n.* Cdn a variety of winter squash with dark green to orange skin and yellow flesh.

pepper steak *n.* **1** a dish of beefsteak coated in coarsely crushed peppercorns before cooking. **2** steak coated with peppercorns as a basis for this dish. **3** a stew-like dish of steak with bell peppers.

peppery *adj.* **1** of, like, or containing much pepper. **2** hot-tempered. **3** pungent. □ **pepperiness** *n.*

pep pill *n.* informal a pill containing a stimulant drug.

peppy *adj.* (**-ier, -iest**) informal vigorous, energetic.

pep rally *n.* (*pl.* **-ies**) N Amer. a meeting or gathering to inspire enthusiasm, esp. before a sports event.

pepsi *n.* (*pl.* **-sis**) Cdn informal derogatory a French Canadian.

pepsin *n.* an enzyme contained in the gastric juice, which hydrolyzes proteins.

pep talk *n.* a usu. short talk intended to enthuse, encourage, etc.

peptic *adj.* concerning or promoting digestion.

peptic ulcer *n.* an ulcer in the stomach or duodenum.

peptide *n.* any of a group of organic compounds consisting of two or more amino acids bonded in sequence.

Péquiste /pei'ki:st/ *n.* Cdn a supporter or member of the Parti Québécois.

per *prep.* **1** for each. **2** by means of. **3** (in full **as per**) in accordance with (*as per instructions*). □ **as per usual** informal as usual.

perambulate /pə'ræmbjʊ,leit/ *v.* **1** *tr.* walk through, over, or about (streets, the country, etc.). **2** *intr.* walk from place to place. □ **perambulation** *n.*

per annum *adv.* for each year.

percale /pər'keil/ *n.* a closely woven cotton fabric used esp. for bedsheets.

per capita *adv. & adj.* per person.

perceive *v.tr.* **1** notice, esp. through the sight; observe. **2** understand. **3** regard mentally in a specified manner. □ **perceivable** *adj.* **perceiver** *n.*

per cent (also **percent**) ● *adv.* in every hundred. ● *n.* **1** percentage. **2** one part in every hundred (*half a per cent*).

percentage *n.* **1** a rate or proportion per cent. **2** a proportion. **3** informal personal benefit or advantage.

percentile *n.* Statistics one of 99 values of a variable dividing a population into 100 equal groups as regards the value of that variable.

perceptible *adj.* capable of being perceived. □ **perceptibility** *n.* **perceptibly** *adv.*

perception *n.* **1 a** the faculty of perceiving. **b** an instance of this. **2 a** the intuitive recognition of a truth, aesthetic quality, etc. **b** an instance of this (a

sudden perception of the true position). **3** an interpretation or impression based on one's understanding of something. □ **perceptual** *adj.* **perceptually** *adv.*

perceptive *adj.* **1** capable of perceiving. **2** sensitive; discerning; observant (*a perceptive remark*). □ **perceptively** *adv.* **perceptiveness** *n.*

perch¹ ● *n.* **1** a usu. horizontal bar, branch, etc. used by a bird to rest on. **2** a usu. high or precarious place for a person or thing to rest on. ● *v.intr. & tr.* (usu. foll. by on) settle or rest, or cause to settle or rest, on or as if on a perch etc. (*a bird perched on a branch; a town perched on a hill*). □ **knock something off its perch** **1** vanquish, destroy. **2** make less confident or secure.

perch² *n.* (*pl.* same or **-es**) **1** any spiny-finned freshwater fish of the genus Perca, esp. P. flavescens of N America. **2** = WHITE PERCH. **3** = OCEAN PERCH.

Percheron /'pɑrtʃə,rɒn/ *n.* a breed of heavy draft horse combining strength with agility and speed.

perchloroethylene /pər,klɔro:'eθili:n/ *n.* an inert colourless liquid used as a dry-cleaning fluid.

percolate *v.* **1** *intr.* (often foll. by through) **a** (of liquid etc.) filter or ooze gradually (esp. through a porous surface). **b** (of an idea etc.) permeate gradually. **2 a** *tr.* prepare (coffee) by repeatedly passing boiling water through ground beans. **b** *intr.* (of coffee) be or become made by percolating. □ **percolation** *n.*

percolator *n.* a machine for making coffee by circulating boiling water through ground beans.

percuss /pər'kʌs/ *v.tr.* tap (a part of the body) gently as part of a diagnosis.

percussion /pər'kʌʃən/ *n.* **1 a** the playing of music by striking instruments with sticks etc. **b** the section of such instruments in an orchestra. **2** the forcible striking of one esp. solid body against another. □ **percussionist** *n.* **percussive** *adj.* **percussively** *adv.*

percussion cap *n.* = CAP *n.* 5.

per diem /pər 'di:em/ ● *adv. & adj.* for each day. ● *n.* an allowance or payment for each day.

peregrine /'perəgrən/ *n.* (in full **peregrine falcon**) a falcon, Falco peregrinus, much prized for hawking on account of its fast and accurate flight.

peremptory /pə'rempt3ri/ *adj.* **1** (of a statement or command) admitting no denial or refusal. **2** (of a person, a person's manner, etc.) dogmatic; imperious. **3** Law not open to appeal or challenge. □ **peremptorily** *adv.*

perennial /pə'reniəl/ ● *adj.* **1** (of a plant) lasting several years. **2** constantly occurring; recurring (a perennial problem). **3** lasting for a long time (a perennial source of hope). **4** (of a stream) flowing through all seasons of the year. ● *n.* a perennial plant. □ **perennially** *adv.*

perestroika /,pere'strɔikə/ *n.* (in the former Soviet Union) the policy or practice of restructuring or reforming the economic and political system, esp. under Mikhail Gorbachev 1985–91.

perfect ● *adj.* **1** complete. **2** flawless. **3** very satisfactory (a perfect evening). **4** exact; precise (a perfect circle). **5** entire; unqualified (a perfect stranger). **6** Grammar (of a tense) denoting a completed action or event in the past, formed in English with have or has and the past participle, as in they have eaten. **7** Baseball **a** designating a pitcher who has not allowed an opposing batter to reach base safely (has been perfect over four innings). **b** designating a game or inning in which a pitcher is perfect. **8** eminently suitable (sausage is perfect in this dish). ● *v.tr.* **1** make perfect; improve. **2** carry through; complete. ● *n.* Grammar the perfect tense. □ **perfecter** *n.* **perfectibility** *n.* **perfectible** *adj.*

perfection /pər'fekʃən/ n. **1** the act or process of making perfect. **2** the state of being perfect; faultlessness. **3** a perfect person, thing, or example. **4** full development; completion. □ **to perfection** exactly; completely.

perfectionism n. the uncompromising pursuit of perfection. □ **perfectionist** n. & adj. **perfectionistic** adj.

perfectly adv. **1** completely; absolutely (I understand you perfectly). **2** quite, completely (is perfectly capable of doing it). **3** in a perfect way.

perfect pitch n. = ABSOLUTE PITCH.

perfidy /'pərfidi/ n. breach of faith; treachery. □ **perfidious** /-'fidiəs/ adj.

perforate v.tr. **1** make a hole or holes through; pierce. **2** make a row of small holes in (paper etc.) so that a part may be torn off easily. **3** make an opening into; pass into or extend through. □ **perforation** n. **perforated** adj. **perforator** n.

perforce adv. unavoidably; necessarily.

perform v. **1** tr. & intr. carry out, execute, or do (something). **2** tr. & intr. fulfill or carry into effect (a promise etc.). **3** tr. act in an official way; conduct (a ceremony etc.) (performed the marriage). **4** tr. **a** act or stage (a play, role, etc.). **b** play or sing (a piece of music etc.) for an audience. **c** accomplish (a feat, act of skill, etc.), esp. for an audience. **5** intr. **a** give a performance to entertain an audience (is performing in Saint John). **b** be engaged in the performing arts, esp. as a professional. **6** intr. function, esp. in a specified way (the car performs well). **7** intr. (of an investment) yield a return; be profitable. **8** intr. slang have sexual intercourse (esp. satisfactorily). □ **performer** n. **performing** adj.

performance n. **1 a** the act or process of performing or carrying out. **b** the execution or fulfillment (of a duty etc.). **2 a** a staging or production (of a drama, piece of music, etc.). **b** the action of performing a part, a piece of music, etc. **3** a person's achievement (put up a good performance). **4** informal a fuss; a scene; a public exhibition (made such a performance about leaving). **5 a** the capabilities of a machine, esp. a car or aircraft. **b** (attrib.) of high capability (a performance car). **6** the return on an investment, esp. in stocks and shares etc.

performance art n. a kind of visual art in which the activity of the artist forms a central feature. □ **performance artist** n.

performing arts n.pl. the arts, e.g. drama, music, and dance, that require performance for their realization.

perfume /'pərfju:m, -'fju:m/ ● n. **1** a sweet smell. **2** fluid containing the essence of flowers etc. ● v.tr. (usu. as **perfumed** adj.) impart a sweet scent to; impregnate with a sweet smell. □ **perfumy** adj.

perfumer /pər'fju:mər/ n. a maker or seller of perfumes. □ **perfumery** n. (pl. **-ies**).

perfunctory /pər'fʌŋktəri/ adj. **1** done merely for the sake of getting through a duty. **2** unenthusiastic. □ **perfunctorily** adv.

pergola /'pərgələ/ n. an arbour or covered walk, formed of growing plants trained over trellises.

perhaps adv. **1** possibly (perhaps it is lost). **2** introducing a polite request (perhaps you would open the window?).

pericardium /,peri'kardiəm/ n. (pl. **pericardia** /-diə/) the membranous sac enclosing the heart. □ **pericardial** adj.

pericarp n. the part of a fruit formed from the wall of the ripened ovary.

perigee /'peri,dʒi:/ n. the point in the orbit of a celestial body or satellite where it is nearest the earth (opp. APOGEE).

peril n. **1** serious and immediate danger. **2** a thing that causes or may cause damage or loss, esp. as covered by an insurance policy. □ **at one's peril** at one's own risk.

perilous adj. dangerous. □ **perilously** adv. **perilousness** n.

perimeter n. **1 a** the circumference or outline of a closed figure. **b** the length of this. **2** the outer edges of an area, away from the centre of activity, population, interest, etc. **3 a** the outer boundary of an enclosed area. **b** a defended boundary.

perinatal /,peri'neitəl/ adj. of or relating to the time immediately before and after birth.

perineum /,peri'ni:əm/ n. the region of the body between the anus and the scrotum or vulva. □ **perineal** adj.

period ● n. **1** a length or portion of time (sunny with cloudy periods). **2** a distinct portion of history, a person's life, etc. (the pre-Confederation period). **3** a time forming part of a geological era (the Quaternary period). **4 a** an interval between recurrences of an astronomical or other phenomenon. **b** the time taken by a planet to rotate about its axis. **5** a division of an academic day allotted to a particular subject, course, etc. **6** each of the intervals into which the playing time of a sporting event etc. is divided. **7** an occurrence of menstruation. **8** esp. N Amer. **a** a punctuation mark (.) used at the end of a sentence or an abbreviation. **b** used at the end of a sentence etc. to indicate finality, absoluteness, etc. (we want the best, period). ● adj. belonging to or characteristic of some past period (period furniture). □ **of the period** of the era under discussion (the custom of the period).

periodic adj. **1** appearing or occurring at regular intervals. **2** intermittent; appearing or occurring at irregular intervals (periodic outbreaks of meningitis). **3** of or concerning the period of a celestial body (periodic motion). □ **periodically** adv. **periodicity** n.

periodical ● n. a magazine etc. that is published at regular intervals, e.g. monthly or weekly. ● adj. **1** published at regular intervals. **2** of or relating to periodicals (a periodical article). **3** occasional.

periodic function n. Math. a function returning to the same value at regular intervals.

periodic table n. an arrangement of chemical elements in order of increasing atomic number and in which elements of similar chemical properties appear at regular intervals.

periodization n. the division of history into periods.

periodontics /,periə'dɒntiks/ n.pl. (treated as sing.) the branch of dentistry concerned with the gums and other structures surrounding and supporting the teeth. □ **periodontal** adj. **periodontist** n.

period piece n. a work of art, furniture, literature, etc., considered in relation to its associations with or evocativeness of a past period.

peripatetic /,peripə'tetik/ ● adj. **1** (of a teacher) working in more than one school etc. **2** going from place to place. ● n. a peripatetic person, esp. a teacher.

peripheral /pə'rifərəl/ ● adj. **1** of minor importance. **2** of the periphery. **3** near the surface of the body, with special reference to the circulation and nervous system. **4** (of equipment) used with a computer etc. but not an integral part of it. ● n. a peripheral device or piece of equipment, e.g. a keyboard, printer, disk or tape drive, etc. □ **peripherally** adv.

peripheral nervous system *n.* the nervous system outside the brain and spinal cord.

peripheral vision *n.* that which is visible to the eye outside of the main area of focus.

periphery /pə'rɪfəri/ *n.* (*pl.* **-ies**) **1** the boundary of an area or surface. **2** an outer or surrounding region.

periscope *n.* an apparatus with mirrors or prisms in a tube so that the user can view the area above, e.g. the surface of the sea from a submerged submarine.

perish *v.intr.* **1** be destroyed; suffer death or ruin. **2** fade away; disappear. □ **perish the thought** an exclamation of horror against an unwelcome idea.

perishable ● *adj.* liable to perish; subject to decay. ● *n.* (in *pl.*) a thing, esp. a foodstuff, subject to speedy decay. □ **perishability** *n.*

peristalsis /ˌperə'stælsɪs/ *n.* the involuntary muscular wavelike movements by which the contents of the alimentary canal etc. are propelled along. □ **peristaltic** *adj.*

peritoneum /ˌperɪtə'niːəm/ *n.* (*pl.* **-s** or **peritonea** /-'niːə/) the serous membrane lining the cavity of the abdomen. □ **peritoneal** *adj.*

peritonitis /ˌperɪtə'naɪtɪs/ *n.* an inflammatory disease of the peritoneum.

periwinkle[1] /'peri,wɪŋkəl/ ● *n.* **1** any plant of the genus *Vinca*, esp. an evergreen trailing plant with blue or white flowers. **2** a tropical shrub, *Catharanthus roseus*, native to Madagascar. **3** a purple-blue colour like that of the periwinkle flower. ● *adj.* of the colour of a periwinkle.

periwinkle[2] /'peri,wɪŋkəl/ *n.* = WINKLE.

perjure /'pɜːrdʒər/ *v.refl. Law* wilfully tell an untruth when under oath. □ **perjurer** *n.* **perjury** *n.*

perk[1] *v.tr.* (often foll. by *up*) raise (esp. one's ears) briskly. □ **perk up 1** recover confidence, liveliness, etc. **2** restore confidence or courage or liveliness in (esp. another person). **3** smarten up (*perk up an outfit with a scarf*).

perk[2] *n. informal* a perquisite.

perk[3] *informal* ● *v.* **1** *intr.* (of coffee) percolate. **2** *tr.* percolate (coffee). ● *n. Cdn* a coffee percolator.

perky *adj.* (**-ier, -iest**) **1** lively; cheerful. **2** bright, jaunty. **3** self-assertive. □ **perkily** *adv.* **perkiness** *n.*

perlite /'pɜːrlaɪt/ *n.* a glassy type of vermiculite, expandable to a solid form by heating, used for insulation, as a plant growth medium, etc.

perm ● *n.* a permanent wave. ● *v.tr.* give a permanent wave to (a person or person's hair).

permaculture *n.* the development of agricultural ecosystems meant to be self-sustaining and complete. □ **permacultural** *adj.* **permaculturist** *n.*

permafrost *n.* subsoil which remains below the freezing point all year, as in polar regions.

permanent ● *adj.* **1** lasting, or intended to last or function, indefinitely without change (*his permanent address*). **2** persistent, enduring (*a permanent stoop*). **3 a** (of hair dye) producing colour that lasts until the hair grows out. **b** (of ink etc.) indelible. **4** (of an employee or position) not having a specified date of termination; not contractual. ● *n.* a perm. □ **permanence** *n.* (also **permanency**). **permanently** *adv.*

permanent magnet *n.* a magnet retaining its magnetic properties in the absence of an inducing field or current.

permanent press *n.* **1** a process for producing fabrics which retain their crease, press, shape, etc. **2** a fabric treated by this process (also *attrib.*: *permanent-press slacks*).

permanent resident *n.* an immigrant deemed to have settled in a country permanently and entitled to all privileges of citizenship except voting rights; a landed immigrant. □ **permanent residence** *n.*

permanent wave *n.* a long-lasting wave set into the hair by applying chemicals, heat, etc.

permeable /'pɜːrmiəbəl/ *adj.* capable of being permeated. □ **permeability** *n.*

permeate /'pɜːrmi,eɪt/ *v.* **1** *tr.* penetrate throughout; pervade; saturate. **2** *tr.* pass through (a membrane etc.) by osmosis or diffusion. **3** *intr.* (usu. foll. by *through*) diffuse itself. □ **permeation** *n.*

permethrin /pɜːr'miːθrɪn/ *n.* a synthetic compound used as an insecticide, esp. against disease-carrying insects.

Permian /'pɜːrmiən/ ● *adj.* of or relating to the final period of the Paleozoic era, lasting from about 286–248 million years ago, between the Carboniferous and Triassic periods. ● *n.* this geological period.

permissible *adj.* allowable. □ **permissibility** *n.* **permissibly** *adv.*

permission *n.* consent; authorization.

permissive *adj.* **1** tolerant; liberal, esp. in sexual matters (*the permissive society*). **2** giving permission. □ **permissively** *adv.* **permissiveness** *n.*

permit ● *v.* (**permitted, permitting**) **1** *tr.* give permission or consent to. **2 a** *tr.* allow; give an opportunity to (*the new design permits easier storage*). **b** *intr.* give an opportunity (*weather permitting*). **3** *intr.* (foll. by *of*) admit; allow for. ● *n.* **1** a document granting legal permission (*liquor permit*). **2** a document etc. which allows entry into a specified zone.

permit book *n. Cdn* a document issued annually by the Canadian Wheat Board to farmers to record deliveries of and payments for wheat and barley.

permutate /'pɜːrmjuˌteɪt/ *v.tr.* change the order or arrangement of.

permutation *n.* **1 a** an ordered arrangement or grouping of a set of numbers, items, etc. **b** any one of the range of possible groupings (*the permutations of x, y, and z are xyz, xzy, yxz, yzx, zxy, and zyx*). **2** any combination or selection of a specified number of things from a larger group. □ **permutational** *adj.*

pernicious /pɜːr'nɪʃəs/ *adj.* **1** destructive; ruinous; fatal. **2** wicked, evil. □ **perniciously** *adv.*

pernicious anemia *n.* a defective formation of red blood cells through a lack of vitamin B_{12} or folic acid.

pernickety *adj. informal* = PERSNICKETY.

perogy *n.* (*pl.* **-ies**) (also **perogie, perogi**) *N Amer.* a dough dumpling stuffed with potato, cheese, etc., boiled and then optionally fried, and usu. served with onions, sour cream, etc.

peroration /ˌperə'reɪʃən/ *n.* **1** the concluding part of a speech, forcefully summing up what has been said. **2** a long, often rhetorical speech.

peroxide ● *n.* **1 a** = HYDROGEN PEROXIDE. **b** (often *attrib.*) a solution of hydrogen peroxide used to bleach the hair or as an antiseptic. **2** a compound of oxygen with another element containing the greatest possible proportion of oxygen. **3** any salt or ester of hydrogen peroxide. ● *v.tr.* bleach (the hair) with peroxide.

perp *n.* esp. *N Amer.* slang the perpetrator of a crime.

perpendicular ● *adj.* **1 a** at right angles to the plane of the horizon. **b** (usu. foll. by *to*) *Geom.* at right angles (to a given line, plane, or surface). **2** upright, vertical. **3** (of a slope etc.) very steep. **4** *jocular* in a standing position. ● *n.* **1** a perpendicular line. **2** (prec. by *the*) a perpendicular line or direction (*is out of the perpendicular*). □ **perpendicularly** *adv.*

perpetrate v.tr. commit or perform (a crime, blunder, etc.). □ **perpetration** n. **perpetrator** n.

perpetual adj. **1** eternal; lasting indefinitely. **2** uninterrupted. **3** frequent, much repeated (perpetual interruptions). **4** permanent during life. □ **perpetually** adv.

perpetual motion n. the motion of a hypothetical machine which once set in motion would run forever unless subject to an external force or to wear.

perpetuate v.tr. **1** make perpetual; make continue indefinitely. **2** preserve from oblivion. □ **perpetuation** n.

perpetuity /ˌpɜːpəˈtʃuːɪti/ n. (pl. **-ies**) the state or quality of being perpetual. □ **in perpetuity** forever.

perplex v.tr. **1** puzzle, disconcert. **2** complicate or confuse (a matter). □ **perplexed** adj. **perplexing** adj. **perplexingly** adv.

perplexity /pərˈpleksɪti/ n. (pl. **-ies**) **1** the state of being perplexed. **2** a thing which perplexes.

perquisite /ˈpɜːkwəzɪt/ n. **1** an incidental benefit attached to employment etc., e.g. the use of a company car. **2** a customary extra right or privilege. **3** an extra sum of money additional to a main income etc.

per se /pɜː ˈseɪ/ adv. by or in itself; intrinsically.

persecute v.tr. **1** subject (a person etc.) to hostility or ill-treatment, esp. on the grounds of race or political or religious belief. **2** harass; annoy persistently. □ **persecutor** n. **persecutory** adj.

persecution n. the act or an instance of persecuting; the state of being persecuted.

persevere v.intr. continue steadfastly or determinedly; persist. □ **perseverance** n.

Persian ● n. **1 a** a native or inhabitant of ancient or modern Persia (now Iran). **b** a person of Persian descent. **2** the language of ancient Persia or modern Iran. ¶The preferred terms for the language are *Iranian* and *Farsi* respectively. **3** (in full **Persian cat**) a cat of a breed with a broad round head, long silky hair and a thick tail. **4** Cdn (NW Ont.) an oblong doughnut covered with pink or white icing. ● adj. of or relating to Persia or its people or language.

Persian carpet n. (also **Persian rug**) a carpet or rug of a traditional pattern, made by hand in the Middle East from silk or wool.

Persian lamb n. the silky tightly curled fur of a young karakul, used in clothing.

persimmon /pərˈsɪmən/ n. **1** any evergreen tree of the genus *Diospyros* bearing edible orange pulpy fruits. **2** its fruit.

persist v.intr. **1** (often foll. by *in*) continue firmly or obstinately (in an opinion or a course of action) esp. despite obstacles, objections, etc. **2** (of a custom, institution, phenomenon, etc.) survive. **3** be insistent with a statement or question.

persistent adj. **1** continuing in spite of obstacles, attempts at control, etc. **2** enduring. **3** constantly repeated (persistent nagging). **4** (of horns, leaves, etc.) remaining instead of falling off in the normal manner. **5** (of a chemical) remaining within the environment for a long time after its introduction. □ **persistence** n. **persistently** adv.

persnickety adj. N Amer. informal **1** fussy; fastidious. **2** requiring tact or careful handling.

person n. **1** an individual human being. **2** the living body of a human being (hidden about your person). **3** Philos. a self-conscious or rational being. **4** Grammar a category used in the classification of pronouns, verb forms, etc., according to whether they indicate the speaker (**first person**), the addressee (**second person**), or a third party (**third person**). **5** (in comb.)

used to replace *-man* in offices open to either sex (salesperson). **6** (in Christianity) God as Father, Son, or Holy Spirit (three persons in one God). **7** an individual or a group of individuals as a corporation regarded as having rights and duties recognized by law. **8** an individual characterized by a preference or liking for a specified thing (not a party person). **9** (in comb.) used as a unit of measure of work etc. (person-day; person-year). **10** an individual as distinguished from a thing, a type, or an animal, esp. an individual regarded as having human dignity, personality, or responsibility. □ **in one's own person** oneself; as oneself. **in person** physically present.

persona /pərˈsoʊnə/ n. (pl. **personas** or **personae** /-naɪ, -niː/) **1** an aspect of the personality as shown to or perceived by others (opp. ANIMA 1). **2** a character assumed by an author, performer, etc. in his or her writing, work, etc. **3** a character in a fictional work.

personable adj. agreeable. □ **personably** adv.

personage n. **1** a person, esp. of rank or importance. **2** a character in a play etc.

personal ● adj. **1** one's own; individual; private. **2** done or made in person (made a personal appearance). **3** directed to or concerning an individual (a personal letter). **4 a** referring (esp. in a hostile way) to an individual's private life or concerns (personal remarks; no need to be personal). **b** close, intimate (a personal friend). **5** of the body and clothing (personal hygiene). **6** existing as a person, not as an abstraction or thing (a personal God). **7** Grammar of or denoting one of the three persons (personal pronoun). **8** intended for a particular person rather than a group (my personal coach; a personal favour). ● n. esp. N Amer. (also **personal ad**) an advertisement or notice in a personal column, on a computer bulletin board, etc.

personal best n. a person's best achievement in a sporting endeavour.

personal column n. a part of a newspaper in which personal messages, advertisements for companions, etc. are published.

personal computer n. a general-purpose microcomputer designed for use by one person at a time, esp. in the home or office. Abbr.: **PC**. □ **personal computing** n.

personal digital assistant n. a small hand-held computer, often pen-based, used as a personal organizer.

personal flotation device n. a life jacket or other buoyant or inflatable device for keeping a person afloat in water, esp. in an emergency. Abbr.: **PFD**.

personal identification number n. a number serving as a password esp. for a bank machine, automatic debit terminal, etc. Abbr.: **PIN**.

personality n. (pl. **-ies**) **1 a** all the qualities or characteristics which make a person a distinctive individual (an attractive personality). **b** socially attractive qualities (has no personality). **c** the unique characteristics of a place, situation, or thing. **2** a famous person (a TV personality). **3** a person who stands out from others by virtue of his or her character (is a real personality). **4** the condition of being a person.

personality disorder n. any of several psychiatric disorders characterized by a tendency to behave in certain abnormal ways that cause harm to oneself or others.

personality type n. a classification of personality according to a person's preponderant traits.

personalize v.tr. **1** make personal; adapt to individual persons' needs etc. **2** mark or inscribe with a particular person's name, initials, etc. **3** cause (a discussion etc.) to become concerned with personal matters or feelings rather than with general issues. ☐

personalization n.

personal loan n. a loan to a private person by a bank etc. for buying a car, renovating a home, etc.

personally adv. **1** in person (see to it personally). **2** for one's own part (speaking personally). **3** as a person (I don't know him personally, but I've read his books). ☐ **take personally** be offended by.

personal organizer n. **1** a loose-leaf notebook with sections for various kinds of information, such as appointments, addresses, etc. **2** a hand-held microcomputer serving the same purpose.

personal pronoun n. each of the pronouns I, you, he, she, it, we, they, me, him, her, us, them. ¶Reflexive pronouns (myself, ourselves, etc.) and possessive pronouns (my, your, etc.) are sometimes included in the category of personal pronouns.

personal property n. Law all one's property except land and those interests in land that pass to one's heirs (compare REAL adj. 6).

personal space n. **1** the immediate area around a person where encroachment is considered threatening or uncomfortable. **2** space for an individual's use.

personal stereo n. a small portable audio cassette player, often with radio, or compact disc player, used with lightweight headphones.

personal touch n. **1** a characteristic or individual approach to a situation. **2** a personal element added to something otherwise impersonal.

personal trainer n. a fitness expert hired to come to a person's home etc. to plan and supervise workouts.

personal watercraft n. N Amer. a jet-propelled recreational boat for one or two persons, ridden like a motorcycle. Abbr.: **PWC.**

persona non grata /nɒn 'grɑːtə/ n. (pl. **personae non gratae** /'grɑːtaɪ, -tiː/) an unacceptable or unwelcome person.

personhood n. the quality or condition of being an individual person.

personification n. **1** the act of personifying. **2** (foll. by of) a person or thing viewed as a striking example of (a quality etc.) (the personification of ugliness).

personify /pər'sɒnə,faɪ/ v.tr. (**-ies, -ied**) **1** attribute a human nature or characteristics to (an abstraction or thing). **2** symbolize (a quality etc.) by a figure in human form. **3** (usu. as **personified** adj.) embody (a quality) in one's own person (is love personified).

personnel n. **1** a body of employees, persons involved in a public undertaking, armed forces, etc. **2** (in full **personnel department**) the part of an organization concerned with the hiring, training, and welfare of employees.

personnel carrier n. an armoured vehicle for transporting troops etc.

person-to-person ● attrib.adj. **1** involving personal contact between individuals. **2** (of a phone call) booked through the operator to a specified person. ● adv. in person; face to face.

perspective ● n. **1 a** the art of drawing solid objects on a two-dimensional surface so as to give the right impression of relative positions, size, etc. **b** a picture drawn in this way. **2** the apparent relation between visible objects as to position, distance, etc. **3 a** a point of view (a Marxist perspective). **b** a mental view of the relative importance of things (keep the right perspective). ● adj. of or in perspective. ☐ **in** (or **out of**) **perspective 1** drawn or viewed according (or not according) to the rules of perspective. **2** correctly (or

incorrectly) regarded in terms of relative importance. ☐ **perspectival** /-'taɪvəl/ adj.

perspicacious /ˌpɜːspɪ'keɪʃəs/ adj. having or showing discernment; perceptive. ☐ **perspicacity** /-'kæsɪti/ n.

perspiration n. **1** = SWEAT n. 1. **2** sweating.

perspire v. **1** intr. sweat. **2** tr. exude (fluid etc.).

persuade v.tr. & refl. **1** cause (another person or oneself) to believe; convince. **2** induce (another person or oneself) (persuaded us to join them). ☐ **persuadable** adj. **persuader** n.

persuasion n. **1** persuading (yielded to persuasion). **2** persuasiveness (use all your persuasion). **3** a belief or conviction (my private persuasion). **4** a religious or political belief, or the group holding it (of a different persuasion). **5** informal or jocular **a** any group or party (the male persuasion). **b** kind or type.

persuasive adj. able to persuade; convincing. ☐ **persuasively** adv. **persuasiveness** n.

pert adj. **1** impudent, esp. in speech or conduct. **2** (of clothes etc.) neat and jaunty. ☐ **pertly** adv.

pertain v.intr. **1** (foll. by to) relate or have reference to (evidence pertaining to the case). **2** belong to as a part or appendage or accessory.

pertinent adj. (often foll. by to) relevant to the matter in hand. ☐ **pertinence** n. **pertinently** adv.

perturb v.tr. **1** (usu. in passive) disturb mentally. **2** throw into confusion or disorder.

perturbation n. **1** the act or an instance of perturbing; the state of being perturbed. **2** a cause of disturbance or agitation. **3** Physics a slight alteration of a physical system, e.g. of the electrons in an atom, caused by a secondary influence. **4** Astronomy a minor deviation in the course of a celestial body, caused by the attraction of a neighbouring body.

pertussis /pər'tʌsɪs/ n. whooping cough.

Peruvian ● n. **1** a native or national of Peru in S America. **2** a person of Peruvian descent. ● adj. of or relating to Peru.

peruse v.tr. **1** read or study thoroughly or carefully. **2** read in a casual manner. **3** examine (a person's face etc.) carefully. ☐ **perusal** n. **peruser** n.

perv n. slang a sexual pervert. ☐ **pervy** adj.

pervade v.tr. **1** spread throughout. **2** (of influences etc.) become widespread among, in, or through. ☐ **pervasion** n.

pervasive adj. **1** pervading. **2** able to pervade. ☐ **pervasively** adv. **pervasiveness** n.

perverse adj. **1** (of a person or action) deliberately or stubbornly departing from what is reasonable or required. **2** persistent in error. **3** peevish. **4** perverted. **5** (of a verdict etc.) against the weight of evidence or the judge's direction. ☐ **perversely** adv. **perversity** n. (pl. **-ies**)

perversion n. **1** an act of perverting; the state of being perverted. **2** a perverted form of an act or thing. **3** a preference for an abnormal form of sexual activity. **b** such an activity.

pervert ● v.tr. **1** turn (a person or thing) aside from its proper use or nature. **2** misapply or misconstrue (words etc.). **3** lead astray right opinion or conduct; corrupt. ● n. a person showing sexual perversion. ☐ **perverted** adj. **pervertedly** adv.

Pesach /'peɪsɑːx/ n. Judaism Passover.

pesky adj. (**-ier, -iest**) esp. N Amer. informal annoying. ☐ **peskily** adv. **peskiness** n.

peso /'peɪsoː/ n. (pl. **-os**) the basic monetary unit of several Latin American countries and the Philippines.

pessimism n. **1** a tendency to take a gloomy view of circumstances or expect the worst outcome. **2** Philos. a belief that this world is as bad as it could be or that all things tend to evil (opp. OPTIMISM 2). □ **pessimist** n. **pessimistic** adj. **pessimistically** adv.

pest n. **1** a troublesome or annoying person or thing; a nuisance. **2** a destructive animal, esp. an insect which attacks crops, livestock, etc.

pester v.tr. trouble or annoy, esp. with frequent or persistent requests.

pesticide n. a chemical preparation for destroying insects or other organisms harmful to cultivated plants or to animals.

pestilence /'pestɪləns/ n. **1** a fatal epidemic disease, esp. bubonic plague. **2** something evil or destructive.

pestilent adj. **1** destructive to life, deadly. **2** harmful or morally destructive. **3** informal annoying.

pestle /'pesəl/ n. a club-shaped instrument for pounding substances in a mortar.

pesto n. a sauce of crushed basil leaves, pine nuts, garlic, Parmesan cheese, and olive oil, usu. served with pasta.

PET abbr. **1** POSITRON EMISSION TOMOGRAPHY. **2** polyethylene terephthalate, a plastic used in recyclable packaging.

pet¹ ● n. **1** a domestic or tamed animal kept for pleasure or companionship. **2** a darling, a favourite (often as a term of endearment). ● attrib.adj. **1** kept as a pet (pet lamb). **2** of or for pets (pet food). **3** often jocular favourite or particular (pet peeve). **4** expressing fondness or familiarity (pet name). ● v.tr. & intr. (**petted**, **petting**) **1** tr. treat as a pet. **2** tr. stroke (an animal). **3** intr. engage in erotic caressing.

pet² n. a feeling of petty resentment or irritability.

petal n. each of the parts of the corolla of a flower. □ **petalled** adj. (also in comb.).

petard /pɪ'tɑrd/ n. □ **hoist with one's own petard** adversely affect oneself by schemes against others.

peter¹ v.intr. (foll. by out) decrease, diminish, or fade gradually before coming to an end.

peter² n. slang the penis.

Peterborough canoe n. Cdn a type of all-wood canoe originally built at Peterborough, Ontario.

Peterhead n. Cdn a decked launch or large whaleboat with a sail and a small motor, used in the E Arctic.

Peter Pan n. a person who retains youthful features, or who is immature.

Peter Pan collar n. a flat collar with rounded points.

Peter Principle n. jocular the principle that members of a hierarchy are promoted until they reach a level at which they are no longer competent.

petiole /'peti,oːl/ n. **1** Bot. the slender stalk joining a leaf to a stem. **2** Zool. a slender stalk between two structures, as that connecting the abdomen and thorax in wasps, ants, and other insects.

petit bourgeois /,peti 'bʊrʒwʌ, pə'tiː/ ● n. (pl. **petits bourgeois** pronunc. same) a member of the lower middle class. ● adj. pertaining to or characteristic of the lower middle class.

petite ● adj. **1** (of a woman) of small and dainty build. **2** (of a thing) small in size. **3** designating a size in women's clothing for shorter women. ● n. a petite size in women's clothing.

petite bourgeoisie /'peti ,bʊrʒwɒ'ziː/ n. the lower middle class.

petition ● n. **1** a supplication or request. **2** a formal written request, esp. one signed by many people,

appealing to authority in some cause. **3** an application to a court for a writ etc. ● v. **1** tr. make or address a petition to (petition your MP). **2** intr. appeal earnestly or humbly. □ **petitioner** n.

petit mal /,peti 'mæl, ,pəti/ n. (also, with hyphen, attrib.) a mild form of epilepsy with only momentary loss of consciousness (compare GRAND MAL).

petit point /'peti pɔint/ n. embroidery on canvas using small stitches.

pet name n. N Amer. an affectionate nickname.

petrel /'petrəl/ n. any of various seabirds with mainly black (or brown) and white plumage and usu. a hooked bill, usu. flying far from land.

Petri dish /'piːtri/ n. a shallow covered dish used for the culture of bacteria etc.

petrify v. (**-ies**, **-ied**) (usu. as **petrified** adj.) **1** tr. paralyze with fear, astonishment, etc. **2** tr. change (organic matter) into a stony substance. **3** intr. become like stone. **4** tr. deprive (the mind, a doctrine, etc.) of vitality; deaden.

petrochemical ● n. a substance industrially obtained from petroleum or natural gas. ● adj. of or relating to petrochemistry or petrochemicals.

petrochemistry n. **1** the branch of chemistry dealing with petroleum and natural gas. **2** the branch of chemistry dealing with rocks.

petrodollar n. a unit of currency earned by a country etc. from petroleum exports.

petroglyph /'petro:glɪf/ n. a rock carving, esp. a prehistoric one.

petrolatum /,petrə'lɒtəm/ n. N Amer. petroleum jelly.

petroleum n. a dark viscous hydrocarbon oil found in the upper strata of the earth, refined for use as a fuel for heating and in internal combustion engines, for lighting, as a solvent, etc.

petroleum jelly n. a soft, greasy, translucent semisolid mixture of hydrocarbons used as a lubricant, ointment, etc.

petticoat n. **1** an undergarment in the form of a skirt or a skirt and bodice. **2** slang a woman or girl.

petting zoo n. (also **petting farm**) N Amer. a collection of wild or farm animals displayed so that visitors, esp. children, may walk among the animals to pet or feed them etc.

petty adj. (**-ier**, **-iest**) **1** unimportant. **2** small-minded. **3** on a small scale (petty princes). **4** (of a crime) of lesser importance (compare GRAND 9). □ **pettily** adv. **pettiness** n.

petty bourgeois n. = PETIT BOURGEOIS.

petty bourgeoisie n. = PETITE BOURGEOISIE.

petty cash n. a small amount of money kept from or for small payments.

petty officer n. (also **Petty Officer**) **1** Cdn (in the Canadian navy) an officer of either of two ranks: petty officer first class (Abbr.: **PO1**), ranking below chief petty officer second class, or petty officer second class (Abbr.: **PO2**), ranking next below it, equivalent to sergeant in the other commands. **2** a noncommissioned officer in other navies.

petulant /'petjʊlənt, 'petʃu-/ adj. peevishly impatient or irritable. □ **petulance** n. **petulantly** adv.

Petun /pə'tuːn/ ● n. **1** a member of an Aboriginal people formerly living in SW Ontario; defeated by the Iroquois in the mid 17th c., they were absorbed into neighbouring Aboriginal groups. **2** the Iroquoian language of this people. ● adj. of or relating to this people or their culture or language.

petunia n. any plant of the genus Petunia with white, purple, red, etc., funnel-shaped flowers.

pew n. **1** (in a church) a long bench with a back. **2** an enclosed compartment or section in a church, for a family or other group. □ **take a pew** have a seat.

pewter ● n. **1** a grey alloy of tin, antimony and copper (formerly, tin and lead). **2** utensils made of this. **3** a bluish or silvery grey. ● adj. of a bluish or silvery grey colour. □ **pewtery** adj.

peyote /peɪˈoːti/ n. **1** any Mexican cactus of the genus Lophophora, esp. L. williamsii having no spines and button-like tops when dried. **2** a hallucinogenic drug containing mescaline prepared from this, taken sacramentally by some American Indians.

PFD abbr. N Amer. PERSONAL FLOTATION DEVICE.

PG abbr. (of films) classified as suitable for children subject to parental guidance.

pg. abbr. (pl. **pgs.**) page.

PGA abbr. Professional Golfers' Association.

PGP abbr. 'Pretty Good Privacy', a computer program which encrypts and decrypts messages for secure transmission over digital circuits.

pH n. a measure of acidity or alkalinity; a pH of 7 corresponds to a neutral solution, one less than 7 to an acidic solution, and one greater than 7 to an alkaline solution.

phagocyte /ˈfæɡəˌsaɪt/ n. a type of cell capable of engulfing and absorbing foreign matter, esp. a leukocyte ingesting bacteria in the body. □ **phagocytic** /-ˈsɪtɪk/ adj.

phalanx /ˈfælæŋks, ˈfeɪ-/ n. (pl. **-es** or **phalanges** /-ˈlæn,dʒiːz/) **1** a set of people etc. forming a compact mass, or banded for a common purpose. **2** a bone of the finger or toe. **3** a bundle of stamens united by filaments.

phalarope /ˈfæləˌroːp/ n. any small wading or swimming bird of the subfamily Phalaropodinae, with a straight bill and lobed feet.

phallic /ˈfælɪk/ adj. **1** of, relating to, or resembling a phallus. **2** Psych. denoting the stage of male sexual development characterized by preoccupation with the genitals. □ **phallically** adv.

phallocentric /ˌfælɒˈsentrɪk/ adj. **1** centred on a belief in male superiority. **2** centred on the phallus. □ **phallocentrism** /-trɪzəm/ n.

phallus /ˈfæləs/ n. (pl. **phalluses** or **phalli** /-laɪ/) **1** the (esp. erect) penis. **2** an image of this as a symbol of generative power in nature.

phantasm /ˈfæn,tæzəm/ n. **1** an illusion, a phantom. **2** (usu. foll. by of) an illusory likeness. **3** a supposed vision of an absent (living or dead) person. □ **phantasmal** /-ˈtæzməl/ adj.

phantasmagoria /ˌfæn,tæzməˈɡɒriə/ n. a shifting series of real or imaginary figures as seen in a dream or as created as an effect in a film etc. □ **phantasmagoric** adj. **phantasmagorical** adj.

phantom ● n. **1** a ghost; an apparition. **2** a form without substance or reality; a mental illusion. ● adj. merely apparent; illusory.

Pharaoh /ˈfeːroː/ n. **1** the ruler of ancient Egypt. **2** the title of this ruler. □ **Pharaonic** /ˌfeɪreɪˈɒnɪk/ adj.

Pharisee /ˈfærɪsiː/ n. **1** a member of an ancient Jewish sect, distinguished by strict observance of the traditional and written law, and commonly held to have pretensions to superior sanctity. **2** a self-righteous person; a hypocrite. □ **Pharisaic** /ˌfærɪˈseɪɪk/ adj. **Pharisaical** adj. **Pharisaism** /ˈfærɪseɪˌɪzəm/ n.

pharmacare n. Cdn (in some provinces) a system of subsidization of drug costs, esp. by the government.

pharmaceutical /ˌfɑrməˈsuːtɪkəl, -sjuːt-/ ● adj. **1** of or engaged in pharmacy. **2** pertaining to the prepara-

tion, use, or sale of medicinal drugs. ● n. a medicinal drug. □ **pharmaceutically** adv.

pharmacist n. a person qualified to prepare and dispense drugs and to give expert advice on their use.

pharmacology n. the branch of medicine that deals with the uses, effects, and modes of action of drugs. □ **pharmacologic** adj. **pharmacological** adj. **pharmacologically** adv. **pharmacologist** n.

pharmacy n. (pl. **-ies**) **1** the preparation and the dispensing of (medicinal) drugs. **2** a pharmacist's store or dispensary.

pharyngeal /fəˈrɪndʒiəl/ adj. of, pertaining to, or involving the pharynx.

pharynx /ˈferɪŋks/ n. (pl. **pharynges** /-rɪn,dʒiːz/) a cavity, with enclosing muscles and mucous membrane, behind the nose and mouth, and connecting them to the esophagus.

phase ● n. **1** a distinct period or stage in a process of change or development. **2** each of the aspects of the moon or a planet, according to the amount of its illumination. **3** Physics a particular stage or point in the cycle of a periodic phenomenon, esp. an alternating current or a light wave. **4** a difficult or unhappy period, esp. in adolescence. **5** a genetic or seasonal variety of an animal's coloration etc. ● v.tr. **1** carry out (a program etc.) in phases or stages. **2** adjust the phase of; bring into phase, synchronize. □ **in phase** having the same phase at the same time. **out of phase** not in phase. **phase in** (or **out**) bring gradually into (or out of) use. □ **phasic** adj.

phase-in n. the process of bringing something into use or availability gradually (phase-in period).

phase-out n. the gradual removal of something from use or availability.

phaser n. (esp. in science fiction) a usu. hand-held weapon incorporating a laser beam whose 'phase' can supposedly be altered to create different effects (such as stunning, annihilation, etc.) on the target.

phat /fæt/ adj. (**phatter, phattest**) slang excellent.

Ph.D. abbr. Doctor of Philosophy.

pheasant n. any of several long-tailed game birds of the family Phasianidae, originally from Asia.

phencyclidine /fenˈsaɪklɪˌdiːn/ n. a veterinary anaesthetic and a hallucinogenic drug. Abbr.: **PCP**.

phenobarbital /ˌfiːnoːˈbɑrbɪˌtɒl/ n. a narcotic and sedative barbiturate drug used esp. to treat epilepsy.

phenol /ˈfiːnɒl/ n. **1** a white hygroscopic mildly acidic crystalline solid, used diluted as an antiseptic and disinfectant. **2** any hydroxyl derivative of an aromatic hydrocarbon.

phenolic /fəˈnɒlɪk/ ● adj. **1** of the nature of, derived from, or containing a phenol, esp. containing or designating a hydroxyl group bonded directly to a benzene ring. **2 a** designating a large class of usu. thermosetting polymeric materials that have wide industrial applications as plastics or resins and are prepared from phenols by condensation with aldehydes. **b** made of such a material. ● n. **1** a phenolic plastic or resin. **2** any compound containing a hydroxyl group bonded directly to a benzene ring, esp. in plants.

phenolphthalein /ˌfiːnɒlˈθeɪliːn/ n. Chem. a white crystalline solid used in solution as an acid-base indicator and medicinally as a laxative.

phenom /ˈfiːnɒm/ n. N Amer. informal an unusually gifted person, a prodigy.

phenomenal /fəˈnɒmənəl/ adj. **1** extraordinary. **2** of the nature of a phenomenon. **3** perceptible by, or perceptible only to, the senses. □ **phenomenally** adv.

phenomenology /fəˌnɒməˈnɒlədʒi/ n. Philos. **1** the

science of phenomena as distinct from that of being (ontology). **2** a philosophical approach concentrating on the study of consciousness and the objects of direct experience. □ **phenomenological** *adj.* **phenomenologically** *adv.* **phenomenologist** *n.*

phenomenon /fə'nɒmə,nɒn, -nən/ *n.* (*pl.* **phenomena** /-nə/) **1** a fact, circumstance, or occurrence that appears or is perceived, esp. one of which the cause is in question. **2** a renowned, remarkable person or thing. **3** *Philos.* the object of a person's perception (as distinguished from substance, or the thing in itself).

phenothiazine /ˌfiːnoʊ'θaiəziːn/ *n.* **1** a heterocyclic compound used to treat parasitic infestations of animals. **2** any of various derivatives of this, used as tranquilizers, esp. in the treatment of mental illnesses.

phenotype /'fiːnoʊˌtaip/ *n.* *Biol.* a set of observable characteristics of an individual or group as determined by its genotype and environment. □ **phenotypic** /-'tipik/ *adj.* **phenotypically** *adv.*

phenyl /'fenɒl, 'fiː-/ *n.* the monovalent radical formed from benzene by the removal of a hydrogen atom.

phenylalanine /ˌfenəl'ælə,niːn, ˌfiː-/ *n.* *Biochem.* an amino acid widely distributed in plant proteins and essential in the human diet.

phenylketonuria /ˌfenəl,kiːtə'nʊriə, ˌfiː-, -'njʊriə/ *n.* an inherited inability to metabolize phenylalanine, ultimately leading to mental deficiency if untreated. Abbr.: **PKU**.

phenytoin /ˌfeni'toʊɪn/ *n.* an anticonvulsant used to treat epilepsy.

pheromone /'ferəˌmoʊn/ *n.* a chemical substance secreted and released by an animal for detection and response by another usu. of the same species. □ **pheromonal** /-'moʊnəl/ *adj.*

phew *interj.* an expression of relief, discomfort, astonishment, or disgust.

phi /fai/ *n.* the twenty-first letter of the Greek alphabet (Φ, φ).

phial /'faiəl/ *n.* a small glass bottle, esp. for liquid medicine.

phil- *comb. form var. of* PHILO-.

-phil /fil/ *comb. form var. of* -PHILE.

philander /fi'lændər/ *v.intr.* have casual affairs with many women; womanize. □ **philanderer** *n.*

philanthropic /ˌfilən'θrɒpik/ *adj.* **1** loving humanity. **2** benevolent to others, esp. in giving generously to charity. □ **philanthropically** *adv.*

philanthropy /fi'lænθrəpi/ *n.* **1** a love of humankind. **2** the disposition or effort to promote the happiness and well-being of one's fellow people, esp. by gifts of money, work, etc. □ **philanthropist** *n.*

philately /fi'lætəli/ *n.* the collection and study of postage stamps. □ **philatelic** /ˌfilə'telik/ *adj.* **philatelically** *adv.* **philatelist** *n.*

-phile /fail/ *comb. form* forming nouns and adjectives with the sense 'lover of, that loves' something specified, designating either a fondness or affection (*bibliophile*), or an esp. sexual obsession (*pedophile*).

philharmonic /ˌfilhɑr'mɒnik, ˌfilər-/ *adj.* **1** fond of music. **2** used in the names of orchestras, choirs, etc.

Philippine *adj.* of or relating to the Philippines, an archipelago and nation in the South China Sea or their people.

Philistine /'fili,stiːn, -stain/ ● *n.* **1** a member of a people opposing the Israelites in ancient Palestine. **2** (usu. **philistine**) a person who is hostile or indiffer-

ent to culture, the arts, etc., or one whose interests or tastes are commonplace or material. ● *adj.* hostile or indifferent to culture; commonplace, prosaic. □ **philistinism** /-stinizəm/ *n.*

Phillips *n.* (usu. *attrib.*) *proprietary* denoting a screw with a cross-shaped slot, or a corresponding screwdriver.

philo- /'filoʊ/ *comb. form* denoting a liking for what is specified.

philodendron /ˌfilə'dendrən/ *n.* (*pl.* **-s** or **-dra** /-drə/) any tropical American climbing plant of the genus *Philodendron*, with bright foliage, often grown as a houseplant.

philology /fi'lɒlədʒi/ *n.* **1** the branch of language that deals with the structure, historical development, and relationships of a language or languages. **2** the branch of knowledge that deals with the linguistic, historical, interpretative, and critical aspects of literature. □ **philologist** *n.* **philological** *adj.* **philologically** *adv.*

philosophe /'filəˌsɒf/ *n.* a philosopher, esp. any of the humanistic French philosophers of the 18th c.

philosopher *n.* **1** a person engaged or learned in philosophy or a branch of it. **2** a person who shows philosophic calmness in trying circumstances.

philosophical *adj.* (also **philosophic**) **1** of or according to philosophy. **2** skilled in or devoted to philosophy. **3** wise. **4** calm in adversity. □ **philosophically** *adv.*

philosophize *v.* **1** *intr.* reason like a philosopher. **2** *intr.* speculate; theorize. □ **philosophizer** *n.*

philosophy *n.* (*pl.* **-ies**) **1** the use of reason and argument in seeking truth and knowledge of reality, esp. of the causes and nature of things and of the principles governing existence, the material universe, perception of physical phenomena, and human behaviour. **2 a** a particular system or set of beliefs reached by this. **b** a personal rule of life. **3 a** serenity; calmness. **b** conduct governed by a particular philosophy. **4** the branch of knowledge that deals with the principles of a particular field or subject (*philosophy of science*).

phlebitis /flə'baitis/ *n.* inflammation of the walls of a vein.

phlegm /flem/ *n.* **1** the thick viscous substance secreted by the mucous membranes of the respiratory passages, discharged by coughing. **2 a** coolness and calmness of disposition. **b** sluggishness or apathy. □ **phlegmy** *adj.*

phlegmatic /fleg'mætik/ *adj.* **1** stolidly calm. **2** dull, sluggish, apathetic.

phloem /'floʊem/ *n.* the tissue conducting food material in plants (*compare* XYLEM).

phlox /flɒks/ *n.* any cultivated plant of the genus *Phlox*, with scented clusters of esp. white, blue, and red flowers.

-phobe *comb. form* forming nouns and adjectives denoting a person having a fear or dislike of what is specified (*xenophobe*).

phobia *n.* an abnormal fear. □ **phobic** *adj.* & *n.*

-phobia /'foʊbiə/ *comb. form* forming abstract nouns denoting a fear of or aversion to what is specified (*agoraphobia*). □ **-phobic** *comb. form.*

phoebe /'fiːbi/ *n.* any small N American tyrant flycatcher of the genus *Sayornis*.

Phoenician /fə'niːʃən/ ● *n.* **1** a member of a people of ancient Phoenicia in S Syria or of its colonies. **2** the Semitic language of the Phoenicians. ● *adj.* of or relating to Phoenicia, its colonies, or its people.

phoenix /'fiːniks/ *n.* **1** a mythical bird that, after living for centuries in the Arabian desert, burned itself on a funeral pyre and rose from the ashes with renewed youth to live through another cycle. **2** a thing which is renewed after apparent destruction.

phone ● *n.* = TELEPHONE. ● *v.* **1** *tr.* speak to (a person) by telephone. **2** *tr.* send (a message) by telephone. **3** *intr.* make a telephone call. **4** *tr.* dial (a telephone number). **5** *tr.* make a telephone call to (a place) (*phone the store*; *phone England*). □ **phone in** call a radio show etc. on the telephone to participate in a broadcast discussion. **phone up** call (somebody) on the telephone. □ **phoner** *n.*

phone book *n.* a book listing telephone subscribers in a particular area, their telephone numbers, and usu. their addresses.

phone booth *n.* = TELEPHONE BOOTH.

phone card *n.* a prepaid card for use with a public telephone.

phone-in *n.* a broadcast program during which the listeners or viewers phone the studio etc. and participate (also *attrib.*: *phone-in show*).

phoneme /ˈfoːniːm/ *n.* any of the units of sound in a specified language that distinguish one word from another, e.g. *p*, *b*, *d*, *t* as in pad, pat, bad, bat, in English. □ **phonemic** *adj.*

phone phreak *n. see* PHREAK.

phone sex *n.* (also, with hyphen, *attrib.*) an activity in which customers pay to listen to or to participate in sexually explicit phone messages or conversations.

phonetic /fəˈnetɪk/ *adj.* **1** representing vocal sounds. **2 a** designating the difference between any two sounds; e.g. in English the *b* of *bin*, the *p* of *pin*, and the *p* of *spin* are phonetically different. **b** (of a system of spelling etc.) reflecting phonetic differences; having a direct correspondence between symbols and sounds. **3** of or relating to phonetics. □ **phonetically** *adv.*

phonetics *n.pl.* (usu. treated as *sing.*) **1** vocal sounds and their classification. **2** the study of these. □ **phonetician** /ˌfoːnəˈtɪʃən/ *n.*

phonic /ˈfɒnɪk, ˈfoː-/ *adj.* **1** of sound; acoustic; of vocal sounds. **2** of, designating, or pertaining to phonics.

phonics /ˈfɒnɪks/ *n.pl.* (treated as *sing.*) a method of teaching reading by associating letters or groups of letters with particular sounds.

phono /ˈfoːnoː/ ● *n.* = PHONOGRAPH (esp. on a button or as a setting on a stereo system). ● *attrib.adj.* designating a type of plug (and the corresponding socket) used with audio and video equipment, in which one conductor is cylindrical and the other is a central part that extends beyond it.

phono- /ˈfoːnoː/ *comb. form* denoting sound.

phonograph /ˈfoːnəˌɡræf/ *n.* N Amer. a record player.

phonology /fəˈnɒlədʒi/ *n.* **1** the study of sounds in a language. **2** the system of sounds in a specific language. □ **phonological** *adj.* **phonologically** *adv.* **phonologist** *n.*

phony *informal* (also **phoney**) ● *adj.* (**phonier**, **phoniest**) **1** sham; counterfeit; fake. **2** insincere. ● *n.* (*pl.* **-ies** or **-eys**) a phony person or thing. □ **phoniness** *n.*

phony-baloney *adj. & n.* N Amer. *slang* = PHONY.

phooey *interj.* an expression of disgust or contempt.

phosphate *n.* any salt or ester of phosphoric acid.

phospholipid *n.* Biochem. any lipid consisting of a phosphate group and one or more fatty acids, including those forming cell membranes.

phosphor *n.* **1** a synthetic fluorescent or phosphorescent substance esp. used in cathode ray tubes. **2** (in *comb.*) = PHOSPHORUS.

phosphorescence *n.* **1** radiation similar to fluorescence but detectable after excitation ceases. **2** the emission of light without combustion or perceptible heat. □ **phosphoresce** *v.intr.* **phosphorescent** *adj.* **phosphorescently** *adv.*

phosphoric acid *n.* a crystalline solid which has many commercial uses, e.g. in fertilizer and soap manufacture and food processing.

phosphorous *adj.* Chem. containing phosphorus, esp. in its lower valence of three (*phosphorous acid*).

phosphorus *n.* a non-metallic element occurring naturally in various phosphate rocks and existing in allotropic forms, esp. as a poisonous whitish waxy substance burning slowly at ordinary temperatures and so appearing luminous in the dark, and a reddish form used in matches, fertilizers, etc.

photo *n.* (*pl.* **-os**) = PHOTOGRAPH *n.*

photo- *comb. form* denoting: **1** light. **2** photography.

photo-aging *n.* skin damage such as wrinkles, brown spots, changes in texture, etc. caused by the sun's ultraviolet light.

Photo CD *n. proprietary* **1** a compact disc from which still photographs can be displayed on a television screen. **2** the technology for storing and reproducing photographs in this way.

photochemical *adj.* of or relating to the chemical action of light. □ **photochemically** *adv.*

photochemical smog *n.* a condition caused by the action of sunlight on pollutants in the air, resulting in haze and high levels of ozone and nitrogen oxide.

photocopier *n.* an electrical machine for producing immediate photographic copies of text or graphic matter by a process usu. involving the electrical or chemical action of light. □ **photocopiable** *adj.* **photocopied** *adj.* **photocopy** *n. & v.tr. & intr.*

photodegradable *adj.* capable of being decomposed by the action of light, esp. sunlight.

photoelectric *adj.* marked by or using emissions of electrons from substances exposed to light. □ **photoelectricity** *n.*

photoelectric cell *n.* a device which generates an electric current or voltage dependent on the degree of illumination.

photo essay *n.* an essay consisting of text matter and numerous photographs.

photo finish *n.* a close finish of a race or contest, esp. one where the winner is distinguishable only on a photograph.

photofinishing *n.* the commercial development and printing of films. □ **photofinisher** *n.*

photog *n.* N Amer. *informal* photographer.

photogenic /ˌfoːtoːˈdʒenɪk, -ˈdʒiːnɪk/ *adj.* **1** (esp. of a person) having an appearance that looks pleasing in photographs. **2** Biol. producing or emitting light. □ **photogenically** *adv.*

photogrammetry /ˌfoːtoːˈɡræmətri/ *n.* the use of photography for surveying and mapping. □ **photogrammetric** /-ˈmetrɪk/ *adj.* **photogrammetrist** *n.*

photograph ● *n.* a picture formed by means of the chemical action of light or other radiation on sensitive film. ● *v.* **1** *tr.* take a photograph of (a person etc.). **2** *intr.* appear (in a particular way) when in a photograph. □ **photographable** *adj.* **photographer** *n.* **photographic** *adj.* **photographically** *adv.*

photographic memory *n.* a memory allowing the precise recall of images with the accuracy of a photograph.

photography n. **1** the process or art of taking photographs. **2** the business of producing and printing photographs. **3** a collection of photographs.

photo ID n. identification containing a photograph of the bearer.

photojournalism n. the art or practice of relating news through the use of photographs, with or without an accompanying text, esp. in magazines etc. □ **photojournalist** n. **photojournalistic** adj.

photometer /foˈtɒmətər/ n. an instrument for measuring the intensity of light. □ **photometric** /ˌfoːtoˈmetrɪk/ adj. **photometry** /-ˈtɒmɪtri/ n.

photon /ˈfoːtɒn/ n. a quantum of light or other electromagnetic radiation, the energy of which is proportional to the frequency of radiation. □ **photonic** /-ˈtɒnɪk/ adj.

photo opportunity n. (also esp. N Amer. informal **photo op**) an opportunity for media photographers to take pictures of a politician, celebrity, etc.

photoperiod n. the period of daily illumination which an organism receives. □ **photoperiodic** adj.

photo radar n. a computer-operated radar system which takes a photograph of the licence plate of a speeding car, the picture and a ticket being subsequently delivered in the mail to the car's owner.

photo-realism n. detailed and idealized representation in art, esp. of mundane or sordid aspects of life. □ **photo-realist** n. **photo-realistic** adj.

photoreceptor n. any living structure that responds to incident light, esp. a cell in which light is converted to a nervous or other signal.

photosensitive adj. reacting chemically, electrically, etc., to light. □ **photosensitivity** n.

photosynthesis n. the process in which the energy of sunlight is used by organisms, esp. green plants, to synthesize carbohydrates from carbon dioxide and water. □ **photosynthesize** v.tr. & intr. **photosynthetic** adj. **photosynthetically** adv.

photovoltaic adj. relating to the production of electric current at the junction of two substances exposed to light. Abbr.: **PV**.

photovoltaics n. the branch of science and technology dealing with photovoltaic effects and devices.

phr. abbr. phrase.

phrasal adj. Grammar of the nature of or consisting of a phrase. □ **phrasally** adv.

phrasal verb n. an idiomatic phrase consisting of a verb and an adverb, e.g. break down or a verb and a preposition, e.g. see to.

phrase ● n. **1** a small group of words forming a conceptual unit, but not a sentence, esp. such a group without a predicate or finite verb. **2** an idiomatic or short pithy expression. **3** a manner or mode of expression (a nice turn of phrase). **4** Music a group of notes forming a more or less distinct unit within a larger passage or piece. ● v.tr. **1** express in words (phrased the reply badly). **2** (esp. when reading aloud or speaking) divide (sentences etc.) into units so as to convey the meaning of the whole. **3** divide (music) into phrases etc. in performance; play so as to give due expression to phrasing. □ **phrasing** n.

phrase book n. a book for tourists etc. listing useful expressions translated into another language.

phraseology /freizɪˈɒlədʒi/ n. (pl. **-ies**) **1** a choice or arrangement of words. **2** a mode of expression. □ **phraseological** adj.

phreak ● n. (in full **phone freak**) a person who makes fraudulent use of a telephone system by electronic means, esp. for computer hacking etc. ● v.tr. & intr. use an electronic device to obtain (a telephone call) without payment. □ **phreaking** n.

phrenology /frəˈnɒlədʒi/ n. hist. the study of the shape and size of the cranium as a supposed indication of character and mental faculties. □ **phrenological** adj. **phrenologist** n.

phthalic acid /ˈfθælɪk/ n. Chem. one of three isomeric dicarboxylic acids derived from benzene.

phyla pl. of PHYLUM.

phylactery /fɪˈlæktəri/ n. (pl. **-ies**) **1** either of two small leather boxes containing Biblical texts in Hebrew, worn by Jewish men during morning prayer on all days except the Sabbath as a reminder to keep the law. **2** an amulet or charm.

phyllo /ˈfiːlo/ n. **1** a dough that can be stretched into very thin leaves which may then be layered to make pastries, e.g. baklava. **2** pastry made this way.

phylloquinone /ˌfailoˈkwɪnoːn/ n. one of the K vitamins, found in leafy green vegetables, and essential for blood clotting.

phylloxera /fɪlɒkˈsiːrə, fɪˈlɒksərə/ n. any louse of the genus Phylloxera, esp. attacking vines.

phylogeny /faiˈlɒdʒəni/ n. (also **phylogenesis** /ˌfailoˈdʒenəsɪs/) **1** the evolutionary development and diversification of groups of organisms, or particular features of organisms. **2** a history of this (compare ONTOGENESIS). □ **phylogenetic** adj. **phylogenetically** adv.

phylum /ˈfailəm/ n. (pl. **phyla** /-lə/) **1** a taxonomic rank below kingdom comprising a class or classes and subordinate taxa. **2** a group of languages related to each other less closely than those of a family.

phys. ed. n. N Amer. = PHYSICAL EDUCATION.

physiatrist /fəˈzaiətrɪst/ n. a person who uses physical agents such as light, heat, etc. to diagnose or treat deformity, disease, or injury.

physical ● adj. **1 a** of or concerning the body (physical exercise; physical abuse). **b** of or concerning observable aspects or features of the environment. **2** of or pertaining to matter, the world of the senses, or things material as opposed to things mental or spiritual. **3 a** of or in accordance with the laws of nature (a physical impossibility). **b** of or pertaining to physics. **4 a** (of a person or action) inclined to be aggressive or violent, making frequent use of bodily contact, etc. **b** (of an attribute etc.) involving the body rather than the mind (physical charms). ● n. (in full **physical examination**) a medical examination to determine health or physical fitness. □ **get physical 1** become violent or physically aggressive. **2** become sexually involved. **3** exercise, become physically fit or toned. □ **physicality** n. **physically** adv.

physical chemistry n. the application of the techniques and theories of physics to the study of chemical systems, behaviour, etc.

physical education n. instruction in physical exercise and sports, esp. in schools.

physical force n. **1** material or corporal rather than moral means of persuasion etc. **2** the use of armed power to effect or repress political changes.

physical geography n. the branch of geography dealing with natural features and forces.

physically challenged adj. N Amer. euphemism (of a person) having a physical disability.

physical object n. Philos. an object that exists in space and time and that can be perceived.

physical plant n. = PLANT 2c.

physical science n. any branch of the sciences that deals with inanimate matter and energy, e.g. physics, chemistry, geology, astronomy, etc.

physical therapy n. esp. *US* = PHYSIOTHERAPY. ☐ **physical therapist** n.

physical training n. the systematic use of exercises to promote bodily fitness and strength. Abbr.: **PT**.

physician n. a person legally qualified to practise medicine, esp. a specialist in non-surgical medical diagnosis and treatment.

physicist n. an expert in or student of physics.

physicochemical adj. of or relating to physics and chemistry or to physical chemistry.

physics n. the science dealing with the properties and interactions of matter and energy.

physio n. *Cdn & Brit. informal* **1** (pl. **-os**) a physiotherapist. **2** physiotherapy.

physiognomy /ˌfɪziˈɒnəmi/ n. (pl. **-ies**) **1 a** a person's face or expression, esp. viewed as indicative of the mind or character. **b** the art of supposedly judging character from facial characteristics etc. **2** the external features of a landscape, plant community, etc. **3** the ideal, mental, moral, or political aspect of anything as an indication of its character.

physiological adj. (also **physiologic**) of or concerning physiology. ☐ **physiologically** adv.

physiology n. **1** the science that deals with the normal functioning of living organisms and their parts. **2** the physiological features of a thing. ☐ **physiologist** n.

physiotherapy n. esp. *Cdn & Brit.* the treatment of disease, injury, etc., by physical methods including manipulation, massage, exercise, etc., rather than by drugs. ☐ **physiotherapist** n.

physique n. the form, size, and development of a person's body.

phytoplankton /ˌfəitoˈplæŋktən/ n. plankton consisting of microscopic plants.

PI abbr. private investigator.

pi /pai/ n. **1** the sixteenth letter of the Greek alphabet (Π, π). **2** (as π) the symbol of the ratio of the circumference of a circle to its diameter (approx. 3.14159).

pia mater /ˌpaiə ˈmeitər, ˌpiːə/ n. *Anat.* the delicate, fibrous, and highly vascular innermost membrane enveloping the brain and spinal cord (see MENINGES).

pianism /ˈpiːəˌnɪzəm/ n. **1** the art or technique of piano playing. **2** the skill or style of a composer of piano music. ☐ **pianistic** adj. **pianistically** adv.

pianissimo /ˌpiəˈnɪsɪˌmo/ *Music* ● adj. performed very softly. ● adv. very softly.

pianist /ˈpiːənɪst, piˈænɪst, ˈpjænɪst/ n. a person who plays the piano, esp. professionally.

piano¹ /piˈænoː, ˈpjænoː/ n. (pl. **-os**) **1** a large musical instrument played by pressing down keys on a keyboard and causing hammers to strike metal strings, the vibration from which is stopped by dampers when the keys are released. **2** an instrument operated in the same way and producing the same tone by electronic means.

piano² adj. *Music* performed softly. ● adv. softly.

piano bar n. a cocktail lounge having a piano and featuring live entertainment.

piano bench n. a low rectangular bench, often of adjustable height and with a hinged seat serving as a lid for a compartment for music.

pianoforte /ˌpiænoːˈfɔrtei/ n. *formal* a piano.

piano nobile /ˌpjænoː ˈnoːbɪˌlei/ n. **1** the main floor of a large house, containing the principal rooms, when this is the floor above the ground floor. **2** a mezzanine, usu. above the lobby, in a theatre etc.

piano stool n. a low round stool with a seat that may be raised or lowered, usu. by a screw mechanism.

piano wire n. a special kind of strong steel wire used for the strings of pianos.

piazza /piˈætsə, piˈɒtsə/ n. a public square or marketplace esp. in an Italian town.

pic n. (pl. **pix** or **pics**) *informal* **1** a motion picture. **2** a picture, painting, or photograph.

pica /ˈpaikə/ n. **1** a unit of type size equal to 12 points (approximately ¹/₆ inch). **2** a size of letters in typewriting (10 per inch).

picante /piˈkɒntei/ adj. (of food) spicy.

picaresque /ˌpikəˈresk/ adj. **1** (of a style of fiction) dealing with the episodic adventures of rogues etc. **2** drifting, wandering.

picayune /ˌpikəˈjuːn/ adj. **1** contemptible; petty. **2** insignificant.

piccaninny var. of PICKANINNY.

piccolo /ˈpikəˌlo/ n. (pl. **-os**) **1** a small flute sounding an octave higher than the ordinary flute. **2** its player.

pick¹ ● v. **1** tr. & intr. choose carefully from a number of alternatives. **2** tr. detach or pluck (a flower, fruit, etc.) from a stem, tree, etc. **3** tr. **a** probe (the teeth, nose, a pimple, etc.) with the finger, an instrument, etc. to remove unwanted matter. **b** clear (a bone, carcass, etc.) of scraps of meat etc. **c** make (a hole) by piercing or probing with a pointed instrument. **4** tr. & intr. (of a person) eat (food, a meal, etc.) fastidiously, in small mouthfuls, or without interest. **5** tr. & intr. esp. *N Amer.* play (a guitar etc.) by plucking the strings. **6** tr. **a** select (a route or path) carefully over difficult terrain on foot. **b** place (one's steps etc.) carefully. ● n. **1** the act or an instance of picking. **2 a** that which is picked. **b** *N Amer.* a person chosen as a member of a team etc. **c** *informal* the favourite to win a game, race, or competition. **d** the right to select (*had first pick of the prizes*). **3** (usu. foll. by *of*) the best (*the pick of the bunch*). **4** *Basketball* a permissible block. ☐ **pick and choose** select carefully or fastidiously. **pick apart** esp. *N Amer.* **1** find fault, criticize harshly. **2** break up or dismantle. **pick at 1** eat (food) without interest; nibble. **2** = PICK ON 1. **pick a person's brains** extract ideas, information, etc., from a person for one's own use. **pick a fight** (or **quarrel**) start an argument or a fight deliberately. **pick holes in 1** find fault with (an idea etc.). **2** make holes in (material etc.) by plucking, poking, etc. **pick a lock** open a lock with an instrument other than the proper key, esp. with intent to steal. **pick off 1** pluck (leaves etc.) off. **2** shoot (people etc.) one by one without haste. **3** eliminate (opposition etc.) singly. **4** *Baseball* put out (a runner) by throwing the ball to a base. **pick on 1** find fault with; nag at. **2** single out (a person) for criticism, victimization, etc. **pick out 1** take from a larger number, esp. with care and deliberation (*picked him out from the others*). **2** distinguish from surrounding objects or at a distance. **3** play (a tune) by ear on the piano etc. **4** accentuate (decoration etc.) with a contrasting colour. **pick over** select the best from. **pick a person's pockets** steal the contents of a person's pockets. **pick to pieces** = PICK APART. **pick up 1** grasp and raise (from the ground etc.). **2 a** learn or acquire with little effort. **b** catch (an illness). **c** buy (a thing) cheaply or luckily. **d** hear or learn (news etc.). **3 a** fetch (a person, animal, or thing) left in another person's charge. **b** stop for and take along with one, esp. in a vehicle. **4** make the acquaintance of (a person) casually, esp. as a sexual overture. **5** (of one's health, the weather, share prices, etc.) recover, prosper, improve. **6 a** gather (speed); accelerate (a pace). **b** (of the wind) become stronger. **7** (of the police etc.) take into charge; arrest. **8** detect by scrutiny or with a telescope, searchlight, radio, etc. **9 a** (often foll. by *with*) form or renew a friendship. **b** resume, take up anew. **10** (esp. in phr. **pick up the tab**) accept the responsibility of paying (a bill etc.). **11** (*refl.*) raise or recover (oneself etc.) after a fall, setback, etc. **12** (esp. in phrase **pick up your feet**) raise (the feet) clear of the ground so as to walk without stumbling. **13** esp. *N Amer. informal* tidy or clean up (a room etc.). **pick up on** become aware of. **pick up the gauntlet** = TAKE UP THE GAUNTLET (see TAKE). **pick up the pieces** restore to normality or make better (a situation etc.), esp. after a setback. **take one's pick** make a choice. □ **picker** *n.*

pick² *n.* **1** a long-handled tool having a usu. curved iron bar pointed at one or both ends, used for breaking up hard ground, masonry, etc. **2** a plectrum. **3** (usu. in *comb.*) an instrument with a sharp point, used for a specified purpose (*toothpick*; *ice pick*). **4** a comb with long, widely spaced teeth used esp. for curly hair. **5** *Figure Skating* = TOE PICK.

pickaninny *n.* (*pl.* **-ies**) *offensive* a small Black or Australian Aboriginal child.

pickaxe (*US* **pickax**) ● *n.* = PICK² *n.* 1. ● *v.* **1** *tr.* break with a pick. **2** *intr.* work with a pick.

pickerel *n.* (*pl.* same or **pickerels**) **1** *N Amer.* a walleye. **2** *N Amer.* **a** a northern pike. **b** any of various other small pikes of the genus *Esox*. **3** a sauger.

pickerelweed *n.* an aquatic plant of eastern N America, *Pontederia cordata*, with a spike of blue flowers and large arrowhead-shaped leaves.

picket ● *n.* **1 a** a person or group of people outside a place as a protest or to persuade esp. workers not to enter during a strike etc. **b** an occasion on which people act as pickets (*a mass picket of the embassy*). **2 a** pointed stake or peg driven into the ground to form a fence etc. **3** *Military* a small body of troops sent out to watch for the enemy, held in readiness, etc. ● *v.* (**picketed, picketing**) **1 a** *tr.* form a picket outside (a place of work etc.). **b** *intr.* demonstrate as a picket. **2** *tr.* & *intr.* post or station (soldiers) as a picket. **3** *tr.* enclose or fence (a place) with stakes. **4** *tr.* tether (an animal). □ **picketer** *n.*

picket fence *n.* *N Amer.* **1** a fence consisting of vertical pickets nailed to horizontal rails between fence posts. **2** (also **white picket fence**) this as a symbol of middle-class esp. suburban domesticity and contentment (also *attrib.*: *the ideal white-picket-fence life*).

picket line *n.* a boundary established by workers on strike, esp. at the entrance to the place of work, which others are asked not to cross.

pickings *n.pl.* **1** profits or gains that are easily or dishonestly obtained. **2** remaining scraps.

pickle ● *n.* **1 a** *N Amer.* a vegetable, esp. a small cucumber, preserved in brine, vinegar, etc. **b** a condiment of chopped vegetables preserved in brine, vinegar, mustard, etc. **c** the brine, vinegar, etc. in which food is preserved. **2** *informal* a difficult or unpleasant predicament (*in a pickle!*). ● *v.tr.* **1** preserve (food) in brine, vinegar, etc. **2** treat (metal, wood, etc.) with an acid or other chemical for cleaning, bleaching, etc.

pickled *adj.* **1** (of food) preserved in brine or vinegar. **2** *slang* drunk. **3** (of wooden furniture etc.) artificially aged with acid or other chemicals.

pickler *n.* **1** a vegetable grown or suitable for pickling. **2** a person who pickles vegetables etc.

pick-me-up *n.* **1** an esp. alcoholic drink taken as a tonic or restorative when feeling weak, tired, ill, etc. **2** a good experience, good news, etc. that cheers.

pickoff *n.* (often *attrib.*) *Baseball* a play in which a runner is caught off the base and tagged out.

pickpocket ● *n.* a person who steals from the pockets of others. ● *v.tr.* & *intr.* steal from the pockets of (a person). □ **pickpocketing** *n.*

pickup *n.* **1** (in full **pickup truck**) a light truck having a usu. open bed with low sides. **2** a device that produces an electrical signal in response to some other kind of signal or change, esp.: **a** a device on a musical instrument which converts sound vibrations into electrical signals for amplification. **b** the part of a record player carrying the stylus. **c** an analogous part of a compact disc player. **3** *slang* a person met casually, esp. for sexual purposes. **4 a** the act or action of picking up (*free pickup and delivery*). **b** something picked up. **5 a** *N Amer.* the capacity for increasing speed; acceleration. **b** an increase in or recovery of health, prosperity, etc. **6** (*attrib.*) **a** impromptu, done on the spur of the moment or with whatever is at hand (*pickup hockey*). **b** (of a performing group, esp. musicians or dancers) assembled for a particular performance etc. rather than as a permanent ensemble. **7** the tendency to pick up or absorb a substance (*prevents dirt pickup*). **8** *Music* a note or series of notes before a bar line as the beginning of a phrase. **9** *Fishing* a loop of metal for guiding the line back on to the spool as it is reeled in.

pick-up sticks *n.* a game in which players use two small thin sticks to try to remove other sticks from a jumbled pile without disturbing it.

picky *adj.* (**-ier, -iest**) *informal* excessively choosy.

pick-your-own *n.* (usu. *attrib.*) (of commercially grown fruit and vegetables) dug or picked by the customer at the place of production.

picnic ● *n.* **1** an outing including a packed meal eaten outdoors (also *attrib.*: *picnic basket*). **2** any meal eaten outdoors or without tables, chairs, etc. **3** (usu. with *neg.*) *informal* something agreeable or easily accomplished (*work was no picnic*). **4** *N Amer.* = PICNIC SHOULDER. ● *v.intr.* (**picnicked, picnicking**) take part in a picnic. □ **picnicker** *n.*

picnic shelter *n.* a usu. open-sided shelter at a picnic area etc. to protect picnickers from rain.

picnic shoulder *n.* (also **picnic ham**) a cut of meat taken from the shoulder and upper foreleg of a pig, with most of the butt removed, often smoked.

picnic table *n.* a rectangular table with benches attached along each long side.

pico- /ˈpiːkəʊ/ *comb. form* denoting a factor of 10^{-12}.

Pict *n.* a member of an ancient people of N Britain who resisted the Roman invaders and eventually amalgamated with the Scots. □ **Pictish** *adj.*

pictograph *n.* (also **pictogram**) **1 a** a pictorial symbol or sign. **b** an ancient record consisting of pictorial symbols, as in cave paintings etc. **2** a pictorial representation of statistics etc. on a chart, graph, etc. □ **pictographic** *adj.* **pictography** *n.*

pictorial ● *adj.* **1** of or expressed in a picture or pictures. **2** containing or illustrated by a picture or pictures. ● *n.* **1** a periodical, article, etc. having pictures as the main feature. **2** a postage stamp printed with a picture or scene. □ **pictorially** *adv.*

picture ● *n.* **1 a** a painting, drawing, photograph, etc. (also *attrib.*: *picture frame*). **b** a portrait, esp. a photograph, of a person. **c** a beautiful or picturesque person or thing. **2 a** a total esp. mental impression or image. **b** a scene, situation, or state of affairs (*the picture looks bleak*). **c** a written or spoken description. **3** a film. **4** a visible image on a television or radar screen etc. **5** *informal* **a** a person or thing exemplifying something (*he was the picture of innocence*). **b** a person or thing resembling another closely (*the picture of her* aunt). **c** *ironic* or *informal* a comic or striking sight (*her face was a picture*). ● *v.tr.* **1** represent in a picture or pictorial form. **2** (also *refl.*) imagine, esp. visually or vividly (*picture yourself hiking*). □ **get the picture** *informal* grasp or become aware of a particular situation, set of circumstances, etc. **in the picture 1** actively involved. **2** fully informed or noticed. **out of the picture** no longer involved, inactive; irrelevant.

picture book ● *n.* a book containing many illustrations, usu. for children. ● *adj.* **(picture-book)** characteristic of a children's picture book, esp. excessively or sentimentally pretty.

picture-perfect *adj.* **1** ideal, perfectly ordered in every detail. **2** precisely accurate.

picture postcard ● *n.* a postcard with a picture or view on one side. ● *adj.* **(picture-postcard)** (of a view etc.) conventionally attractive.

picturesque *adj.* **1 a** (of landscape, buildings, etc.) beautiful or striking, esp. in a quaint way. **b** (of a route etc.) affording views of this kind. **2** (of language etc.) vivid. **3** *informal* of (a person, appearance, manner, etc.) unique, strange, or unusual; eccentric. □ **picturesquely** *adv.* **picturesqueness** *n.*

picture tube *n.* the cathode ray tube of a TV set.

picture window *n.* a large window, esp. one consisting of one pane of glass without mullions.

PID *abbr.* = PELVIC INFLAMMATORY DISEASE.

piddle ● *v.intr.* **1** *informal* urinate. **2 a** work or act in a petty or trifling way. **b** while or fritter away time etc. ● *n. informal* **1** urination. **2** urine.

piddling *adj.* (also **piddly**) *informal* trivial; trifling.

pidgin /ˈpɪdʒɪn/ *n.* a form of a language altered by non-native speakers, with vocabulary from two or more languages, used for communication between people not having a common language.

pidgin English *n.* a pidgin in which the chief language is English.

pie *n.* **1** any of various dishes with a pastry crust or topping or both, with a filling of fruit, meat, etc. **2** anything resembling a pie in form (*a mud pie*). **3 a** *informal* wealth, market share, etc. considered as something to be shared out (*they each claimed a piece of the pie*). **b** *N Amer. slang* political favour or patronage. □ **easy as pie** *informal* very easy. **pie in the sky** *informal* **1** an extravagant promise unlikely to be fulfilled. **2** an unrealistic prospect of future happiness, esp. after present suffering.

piebald /ˈpaɪbɔld/ ● *adj.* **1** having irregular patches of two colours, esp. black and white. **2** motley; mongrel. ● *n.* a piebald animal, esp. a horse.

piece ● *n.* **1 a** (often foll. by *of*) one of the distinct portions forming part of or broken off from a larger object; a bit; a part (*a piece of string*). **b** a single, usu. small sample, instance, or quantity of a substance or non-material thing (*a piece of paper; a new piece of software*). **c** each of the parts of which a set or category is composed (*a five-piece band; a piece of furniture*). **d** any of the irregular sections of a jigsaw or similar puzzle. **2** a coin of specified value (*50-cent piece*). **3 a** a usu. short literary or musical composition or a picture. **b** an essay or article for a magazine, newspaper, etc. **c** a work of art, esp. a painting, statue, or play. **4** an item, instance, or example (*a piece of news*). **5 a** any of the objects used to make moves in board games. **b** a chessman (strictly, other than a pawn). **6 a** definite quantity in which a thing is sold, e.g. cloth etc. **7** (often foll. by *of*) an enclosed portion (of land etc.). **8** (also **piece of ass, piece of tail**) esp. *N Amer. coarse slang* **a** a woman regarded as an object of sexual gratification. **b** sexual intercourse with a woman. **9**

(foll. by *of*) *N Amer. informal* involvement or a share or esp. financial interest in (a business, project, etc.) (*has a piece of the new production*). **10 a** esp. *N Amer. slang* a small portable firearm, esp. a handgun. **b** a large but still portable gun, cannon, etc. (*artillery pieces*). **11** *N Amer. informal* a short distance, part of the way (*down the road a piece*). ● *v.tr.* **1** (usu. foll. by *together*) **a** join together to form one thing, mend or make by putting pieces together (*pieced together a parliamentary majority*). **b** infer or construct from previously unrelated facts (*finally pieced his story together*). **2** (usu. foll. by *out*) **a** eke out. **b** form (a theory etc.) by combining parts etc. □ **break to pieces** break into fragments. **by the piece** (paid) according to the quantity of work done. **go to pieces 1** break up, lose cohesion. **2** collapse emotionally or mentally; suffer a breakdown. **in one piece 1** (of a thing) unbroken; consisting of a single piece or mass. **2** (of a person etc.) whole, unharmed, without injury or loss. **in pieces** broken, in fragments. **(all) of a piece** (often foll. by *with*) uniform, consistent, in keeping. **piece by piece** with one piece or part after another in succession; gradually. **a piece of the action** *slang* **1** a share in the profits. **2** a share in the excitement. **a piece of one's mind** a sharp rebuke or lecture. **a piece of the puzzle** an item of information that helps to understand a larger problem. **say one's piece** give one's opinion or make a statement. **take to pieces** = PICK APART (see PICK[1]).

pièce de résistance /ˌpjes də reiˈziːstɑ̃s/ *n.* (*pl.* **pièces de résistance** *pronunc.* same) **1** the most important or remarkable item. **2** the most substantial dish at a meal.

piecemeal ● *adv.* piece by piece; gradually; separately. ● *adj.* consisting of pieces; done bit by bit; gradual; unsystematic.

piece of work *n.* **1 a** a thing made by working. **2 a** a task, a difficult thing. **b** *informal* a commotion, a to-do. **3** a person of a specified and usu. unpleasant kind (*he's a nasty piece of work*).

piecework *n.* work paid for by the amount produced. □ **pieceworker** *n.*

pie chart *n.* a circle divided into sectors to represent relative quantities.

pie crust *n.* **1** the crust of a pie, made of pastry or a mixture of crushed cookies and fat. **2** pie pastry.

pied /paɪd/ *adj.* parti-coloured.

piedmont /ˈpiːdmɒnt/ *n.* a gentle slope leading from the foot of mountains to a region of flat land.

Pied Piper *n.* **1** (in German legend) a piper who rid the town of Hamelin (Hameln) of rats by enticing them away with his music. **2** a person enticing followers esp. to their doom.

pie-eyed *adj. slang* drunk.

Piegan *var. of* PEIGAN.

pie plate *n.* (also **pie pan**) a shallow usu. round dish with sloping sides, in which pies are baked.

pier *n.* **1** a structure raised on piles and leading out into the sea, a lake, etc., used as a landing stage and promenade. **2** a long narrow structure projecting from the main body of an airport terminal, along which passengers walk to and from their aircraft. **3 a** a support of an arch or of the span of a bridge. **b** solid masonry between windows etc.

pierce *v.* **1** *tr.* **a** (of a sharp instrument etc.) penetrate the surface of. **b** (often foll. by *with*) prick with a sharp instrument, esp. to make a hole in. **c** make a hole, opening, or tunnel into or through (something), bore through. **d** make (a hole etc.) (*pierced a hole in the belt*). **e** (of cold, grief, etc.) affect keenly or sharply. **f** (of a light, glance, sound, etc.) penetrate keenly or sharply. **2** *tr.* force (a way etc.) through or into (something) (*pierced their way through the undergrowth*). **3** *intr.* (usu. foll. by *through*, *into*) penetrate. □ **piercer** *n.*

pierced *adj.* **1** having a hole or holes. **2** (of a part of the body) having a hole in which a ring etc. is worn (*pierced ears*). **3** (of an earring) designed to be worn in a pierced ear.

piercing *adj.* **1** (of voices, sounds, etc.) very high and loud; shrill. **2 a** (of eyes) very bright and seeming to see through the person they are looking at. **b** (of a look) very direct; searching. **3** (of a feeling, comment, etc.) very perceptive. **4** (of wind, cold, etc.) bitter; penetrating. □ **piercingly** *adv.*

pierogi *var. of* PEROGY.

pie-shaped *adj.* N Amer. shaped like a triangular piece cut out of a round pie, having one curved side.

Pietà /ˌpiːeˈtɒ/ *n.* a picture or sculpture of the Virgin Mary holding the dead body of Christ.

piety /ˈpaɪəti/ *n.* (*pl.* **-ies**) **1** the quality of being pious. **2** a pious act, remark, etc.

piezoelectricity /paɪˌiːzoːˌɪlekˈtrɪsɪti/ *n.* electric polarization in a substance resulting from the application of mechanical stress, esp. in certain crystals. □ **piezoelectric** *adj.*

piffle *informal* ● *n.* nonsense; empty speech. ● *v.intr.* talk or act feebly; trifle. □ **piffling** *adj.*

pig *n.* **1 a** a domesticated even-toed ungulate with a large head, a broad flat snout, and a stout often almost hairless body, raised as a source of meat. **b** N Amer. a piglet. **c** (often in *comb.*) any similar animal (*guinea pig*). **2** the flesh of esp. a young or sucking pig as food (*roast pig*). **3** *informal* **a** a selfish and greedy person. **b** an ill-mannered, insensitive, or vulgar person. **c** a fat person. **4** an oblong mass of metal (esp. iron or lead) from a smelting furnace. **5** *slang derogatory* a police officer. □ **buy a pig in a poke** buy, accept, etc. something without knowing its value or esp. seeing it. **make a pig of oneself** overeat. **pig out** (**pigged**, **pigging**) esp. N Amer. informal eat gluttonously (*pigging out on cookies*). □ **piglike** *adj.*

pigeon *n.* **1** any of several large usu. grey and white birds of the family Columbidae, esp. *Columba livia*, often domesticated and bred and trained to carry messages etc. **2** *informal* a person easily swindled.

pigeon guillemot *n.* a guillemot of the N Pacific, *Cepphus columba*.

pigeonhole ● *n.* **1** each of a set of compartments in a cabinet or on a wall for papers, letters, etc. **2** a small recess for a pigeon to nest in. ● *v.tr.* **1** deposit (a document) in a pigeonhole. **2** put (a matter) aside for future consideration or to forget it. **3** assign (a person or thing) to a preconceived category.

piggish *adj.* **1** of or relating to pigs. **2** having a quality associated with pigs, esp. greedy, dirty, or stubborn. □ **piggishness** *n.*

piggy ● *n.* (also **piggie**) (*pl.* **piggies**) *informal* **1** a little pig. **2** a child's word for a pig. ● *adj.* (**-ier**, **-iest**) **1** like a pig; piggish. **2** (of features etc.) like those of a pig.

piggyback ● *n.* (also **piggyback ride**) a ride on the back and shoulders of another person. ● *v.* **1** *intr.* ride (as if) on a person's back and shoulders. **2** *tr.* **a** give a piggyback ride to. **b** carry or mount on top of another thing. **3** *intr.* (usu. foll. by *on*) use an already established situation as a basis so as to gain an advantage. ● *adv.* **1** on the back and shoulders of another person. **2** on top of a larger object.

piggy bank *n.* a container, esp. in the shape of a pig with a slot in the top, used for saving coins in.

pigheaded *adj.* obstinate.

pig in a blanket *n.* (*pl.* **pigs in a blanket**) a small sausage wrapped in dough and baked.

pig iron *n.* crude iron from a smelting furnace.

pig Latin *n.* a jargon formed from English by transferring the initial consonant or consonant cluster of each word to the end of the word and adding a vocalic syllable (usu. /eɪ/).

piglet *n.* a young pig.

pigment ● *n.* **1** colouring matter used as paint or dye. **2** the natural colouring matter of animal or plant tissue, e.g. chlorophyll, hemoglobin. ● *v.tr.* colour with or as if with pigment.

pigmentation *n.* **1** the natural colouring of plants, animals, etc. **2** the colouring of tissue by the deposition of pigment.

pigmy *var. of* PYGMY.

pig-out *n.* N Amer. slang an instance of eating to excess.

pigskin *n.* **1** the hide of a pig. **2** leather made from this. **3** N Amer. a football.

pigsty *n.* (*pl.* **-ies**) (N Amer. also **pigpen**) **1** a pen or enclosure for a pig or pigs. **2** a filthy room etc.

pigtail *n.* **1** the tail of a pig. **2** a braid of hair hanging from the back of the head, or either of a pair at the sides. □ **pigtailed** *adj.* (in sense 2).

pigweed *n.* **1** any herb of the genus *Amaranthus*, grown for grain or fodder. **2** = GOOSEFOOT.

pika /ˈpaɪkə/ *n.* any small rabbit-like mammal of the genus *Ochotona*, with small ears and no tail, found in the mountains and deserts of western N America.

pike[1] *n.* (*pl.* same) **1** a large voracious freshwater fish, *Esox lucius*, with a long narrow snout and sharp teeth. **2** any other fish of the family Esocidae.

pike[2] *n.* hist. an infantry weapon with a pointed steel or iron head on a long wooden shaft.

pike[3] *n.* **1** a tollgate; a toll. **2** a turnpike road. □ **come down the pike** N Amer. appear on the scene.

pike[4] *n.* a jackknife position in diving or gymnastics.

pike-perch *n.* any of various pike-like perches of the genus *Lucioperca* or *Stizostedion*, e.g. the walleye.

pike pole *n.* Cdn a long pole with a sharp point and hook, used for moving floating logs.

piker *n.* **1** a cheap or stingy person. **2** a cautious or timid person.

pilaf /ˈpiːlæf, pɪˈlæf/ *n.* (also **pilau** /pɪˈlaʊ/) a Middle Eastern or Indian dish of spiced rice or wheat with meat, fish, vegetables, etc.

pilaster /pɪˈlæstər/ *n.* a rectangular column, esp. projecting from a wall.

Pilates /pəˈlɒtiːz/ *n.* a system of exercises using specialized apparatus, designed to improve physical strength, flexibility, and posture, and enhance mental awareness and control of body movement (usu. attrib.: *Pilates method*).

pilchard /ˈpɪltʃərd/ *n.* **1** a small marine fish, *Sardinia pilchardus*, the young of which are often marketed as sardines. **2** a Pacific sardine, esp. as tinned.

pile[1] ● *n.* **1** a heap of things laid or gathered upon one another. **2 a** a large imposing building. **b** a large group of tall buildings. **3** *informal* **a** a large quantity. **b** a large amount of money; a fortune. **4** Cdn (Nfld) a stack of split and salted cod at any stage in the drying and curing process. **5 a** a series of plates of dissimilar metals laid one on another alternately to produce an electric current. **b** = ATOMIC PILE. **6** a funeral pyre. ● *v.* **1** *tr.* **a** (often foll. by *up*, *on*) heap up. **b** (foll. by *with*) load (*piled the bed with coats*). **2** *intr.* (usu. foll. by *in*, *into*, *on*, *out of*, etc.) crowd hurriedly or tightly (*piled into the car*). □ **pile it on** *informal* exaggerate. **pile up 1** accumulate; heap up. **2** *informal* cause (a vehicle etc.) to crash.

pile² ● *n.* a heavy beam driven vertically into the bed of a river, soft ground, etc., to support the foundations of a superstructure. ● *v.tr.* **1** provide with piles. **2** drive (piles) into the ground etc.

pile³ *n.* **1** the soft projecting surface on velvet, plush, etc., or esp. on a carpet; nap. **2** soft hair or down, or the wool of a sheep. □ **pileless** *adj.*

pileated /ˈpiliˌeitəd/ *n.* (of a bird) having a conspicuous cap or crest.

pileated woodpecker *n.* a N American woodpecker, *Dryocopus pileatus*, with a red-topped head.

piledriver *n.* a machine for driving piles into the ground.

piles *n.pl.* hemorrhoids.

pileup *n. informal* **1** a multiple crash of road vehicles. **2** an accumulation (of things, tasks, etc.). **3** a confused mass of people fallen on top of one another.

pilfer *v.tr. & intr.* steal (objects) esp. in small quantities. □ **pilferage** *n.* **pilferer** *n.*

pilgrim *n.* **1** a person who journeys to a sacred place for religious reasons. **2** a wanderer or traveller. **3** (usu. **Pilgrim**) one of a group of 102 people who pioneered British colonization of North America, sailing in the *Mayflower* and founding a settlement at Plymouth, MA, in 1620.

pilgrimage ● *n.* **1** a pilgrim's journey (*go on a pilgrimage*). **2** life viewed as a journey. **3** any journey taken for nostalgic or sentimental reasons. ● *v.intr.* go on a pilgrimage.

Pilgrim Fathers *n.pl.* the Pilgrims.

piling *n.* **1** a group or mass of piles. **2** a structure made of piles.

Pilipino *n.* the national language of the Philippines.

pill¹ *n.* **1 a** a solid medicine formed into a ball or a flat disc for swallowing whole. **b** (usu. prec. by *the*) a contraceptive pill. **2** an unpleasant or painful necessity (*a bitter pill*). **3** *informal* an objectionable annoying person. □ **sugar** (or **sweeten**) **the pill** make an unpleasant necessity acceptable.

pill² *v.intr.* (of esp. knitted fabric) form balls of fluff on the surface (*this sweater is pilling*).

pillage /ˈpilidʒ/ ● *v.tr. & intr.* plunder; sack (a place or a person). ● *n.* the act or an instance of pillaging, esp. in war. □ **pillager** *n.*

pillar *n.* **1** a tall, upright column of stone, wood, metal, etc., used as a support for a building or as an ornament or monument etc. **2 a** a strong supporter or important member of something (*a pillar of society*). **b** a fundamental part or feature of a system, organization, etc. (*dismantled the pillars of the welfare state*). **3** an upright mass of air, water, rock, etc. (*pillar of salt*). □ **pillar of strength** a person regarded as showing or giving great moral support etc. □ **pillared** *adj.*

pillbox *n.* **1** a small shallow cylindrical box for holding pills. **2** a hat of a similar shape. **3** *Military* a small partly underground enclosed concrete fort.

pillion *n.* **1** seating for a passenger behind a motorcyclist. **2** *hist.* **a** a woman's light saddle. **b** a cushion attached to the back of a saddle for a usu. female passenger. □ **ride pillion** travel seated behind a motorcyclist etc.

pillory /ˈpiləri/ ● *n.* (*pl.* **-ies**) *hist.* a wooden framework with holes for the head and hands, enabling the public to assault or ridicule a person so imprisoned. ● *v.tr.* (**-ies**, **-ied**) **1** expose (a person) to ridicule or public contempt. **2** *hist.* put in the pillory.

pillow ● *n.* **1** a usu. oblong support for the head, esp. in bed, with a cloth cover stuffed with feathers, flock, foam rubber, etc. **2** any pillow-shaped block or support. ● *v.tr.* **1** rest (the head etc.) on or as if on a

pillow (*pillowed his head on his arms*). **2** serve as a pillow for (*moss pillowed her head*). □ **pillowy** *adj.*

pillowcase *n.* (also **pillow slip**) a washable fabric cover for a pillow.

pillow fight *n.* a mock fight in which the participants try to hit one another with pillows.

pillow talk *n.* intimate conversation in bed.

pill-popper *n.* **1** a person who takes pills in abundance. **2** a drug addict. □ **pill-popping** *n. & attrib.adj.*

pilot ● *n.* **1** a person who operates the flying controls of an aircraft. **2** a person qualified to take charge of a ship entering or leaving harbour, moving through dangerous waters, etc. **3 a** (usu. *attrib.*) an experimental undertaking or test, esp. in advance of a larger one (*a pilot project*). **b** a test episode of a television series used to assess audience reaction etc. **4** = PILOT LIGHT. **5** a guide; a leader. ● *v.tr.* (**piloted, piloting**) **1** act as a pilot on (a ship) or of (an aircraft). **2** conduct or lead; guide (*piloted the new bill through the Commons*). **3** produce a pilot or test for (an idea, scheme, etc.); try out. □ **pilotless** *adj.*

pilot hole *n.* a small hole drilled into something to receive a nail or screw, or to guide a larger drill bit.

pilothouse *n.* = WHEELHOUSE 1.

pilot light *n.* **1** a small flame that burns continuously, e.g. on a gas stove or oil furnace, and lights a larger flame when the valve controlling the fuel opens. **2** an electric indicator light or control light.

pilot whale *n.* a small whale of the genus *Globicephala*, of temperate or subtropical waters.

Pilsner /ˈpilznər, -snər/ *n.* (also **Pilsener**) a pale lager beer with a strong flavour of hops.

pimento /piˈmentoʊ/ *n.* (also **pimiento** /ˌpimiˈento:, pimˈjento:/) (*pl.* **-os**) **1** = SWEET PEPPER. **2** a small tropical tree, *Pimenta dioica*, native to Jamaica. **3** the unripe dried berries of this, crushed for culinary use. Also called ALLSPICE.

pimp ● *n.* a man who lives off the earnings of a prostitute or a brothel. ● *v.* **1** *intr.* act as a pimp. **2** *tr.* (also *refl.*) cause to act as a prostitute. □ **pimping** *n.*

pimple *n.* a small, hard, inflamed, usu. raised spot on the skin. □ **pimpled** *adj.* **pimply** *adj.*

PIN *n.* a confidential identification number issued by a bank etc. to validate electronic transactions.

pin ● *n.* **1 a** a small thin pointed piece of esp. steel wire with a round or flattened head used (esp. in sewing) for holding things in place, attaching one thing to another, etc. **b** any of several types of pin (*safety pin*; *hairpin*). **c** a small brooch (*diamond pin*). **d** a badge fastened with a pin. **2** a peg or dowel used as a fastener or support. **3** a club-shaped usu. wooden peg used as a target in bowling. **4** a piece of metal on a hand grenade that keeps the grenade from exploding until it is removed. **5** a steel rod used to join the ends of fractured bones while they heal. **6** *Wrestling* a throw which keeps one's opponent on the mat for a specified period of time. **7** *Golf* a stick with a flag placed in a hole to mark its position. **8** *Music* a peg around which one string of a musical instrument is fastened. ● *v.tr.* (**pinned, pinning**) **1 a** (often foll. by *to, up, together*) fasten with a pin or pins (*pinned up the hem*; *pinned the papers together*). **b** transfix with a pin, lance, etc. **2** (usu. foll. by *on*) fix (blame, responsibility, etc.) on a person etc. (*pinned the blame on others*). **3** (often foll. by *against, on,* to, etc.) seize and hold fast. **4** *Wrestling* capture (one's opponent) in a pin. □ **neat as a pin** very tidy. **pin down 1** (often foll. by *to*) bind (a person etc.) to a promise, arrangement, etc. **2** force (a person) to declare his or her intentions. **3** restrict the actions or movement of (an enemy etc.). **4** specify (a thing) precisely (*could not pin down my unease to a particular cause*). **5** hold (a person etc.) down by force. **pin one's hopes** (or **faith** etc.). **on** rely completely on.

pina colada /ˌpiːnə kəˈlɒdə/ n. a drink made from pineapple juice, rum, and coconut.

pinafore n. an apron-like garment, usu. fastened at the back, worn over a dress, esp. by small girls.

pinata /pɪˈnjɒtə, piː-/ n. (also **piñata**) an originally Mexican brightly decorated papier mâché figure filled with small treats and suspended overhead to be broken by a blindfolded person waving a stick.

pinball n. a game in which small metal balls are shot across a board and score points by striking pins with lights etc. (also *attrib.*: *pinball machine*).

pince-nez /ˈpænsneɪ, pæ̃sˈneɪ/ n. (*pl.* same) a pair of eyeglasses held in place only by a clip on the nose.

pincers /ˈpɪnsəz/ n.pl. **1** (also **pair of pincers**) a gripping tool resembling scissors but with blunt usu. concave jaws to hold a nail etc. for extraction. **2** the front claws of lobsters and some other crustaceans.

pinch ● v. **1 a** tr. grip (esp. skin or flesh) tightly, e.g. between finger and thumb, two hard surfaces, etc. (*pinched my finger in the door*; *stop pinching me!*). **b** tr. & intr. (of a shoe, garment, etc.) constrict (the flesh) painfully. **2** tr. *slang* a steal; take without permission. **b** arrest (a person). **3** intr. be niggardly with money, food, etc. **4** tr. (usu. foll. by *out*, *back*, *down*) remove (leaves, buds, etc.) to encourage bushy growth. **5** intr. sail very close to the wind. ● n. **1** the act or an instance of pinching the flesh. **2** an amount that can be taken up with fingers and thumb (*a pinch of salt*). **3** the stress or pain caused by poverty, cold, hunger, etc. **4** *Baseball* (*attrib.*) (of a hit, run, etc.) made by a pinch hitter (*pinch homer*). **5** *slang* **a** an arrest. **b** a theft. □ **feel the pinch** experience the effects of poverty. **in a pinch** in an emergency; if necessary. **pinch oneself** check to make sure that one is awake and not dreaming. **pinch pennies** live frugally.

pinched adj. (of the features) drawn, as with cold, hunger, worry, etc.

pin cherry n. a N American wild cherry, *Prunus pensylvanica*, with very small fruit.

pinch-hitter n. **1** a baseball player who bats instead of another. **2** *N Amer.* a person acting as a substitute for another, esp. in an emergency. □ **pinch hit** n. **pinch-hit** v.intr.

pinch-run v.intr. *Baseball* substitute for another runner, esp. at a critical point in the game. □ **pinch-runner** n.

pincushion n. a small cushion for holding pins.

pine¹ n. **1** any evergreen tree of the genus *Pinus*, native to northern temperate regions, with needle-shaped leaves growing in clusters. **2** the soft timber of this, often used to make furniture. **3** (*attrib.*) made of pine. **4** *Sport informal* the bench (*warming the pine*).

pine² v.intr. **1** (often foll. by *away*) decline or waste away, esp. from grief, disease, etc. **2** (usu. foll. by *for*, *after*, or *to* + infin.) long eagerly; yearn.

pineal gland /ˈpɪnɪəl, ˈpaɪ-/ n. a pea-sized conical mass of tissue in the brain, secreting a hormone-like substance in some mammals.

pineapple n. **1** a tropical plant, *Ananas comosus*, with a spiral of sword-shaped leaves and a thick stem bearing a large fruit developed from many flowers. **2** the fruit of this, consisting of yellow flesh surrounded by a tough segmented skin and topped with a tuft of stiff leaves.

pine cone n. the cone-shaped fruit of the pine tree.

pine grosbeak n. a large finch, *Pinicola enucleator*, of

coniferous forests in N America and Eurasia, the male of which is predominantly dull red.

pine marten n. **1** *N Amer.* the most common marten of N America, *Martes americana*, with predominantly dark brown fur with a splash of orange on the chest. **2** the European marten *Martes martes*, with a dark brown coat and white throat and stomach.

pine nut n. the edible seed of various pine trees.

pinesap n. a N American saprophytic plant with a stem of several nodding flowers.

pine siskin n. a siskin, *Carduelis pinus*, of N American coniferous forests.

pine tar n. a sticky, dark liquid obtained by distilling pinewood, used in making paints, roofing, etc.

pinewood n. **1** the timber of the pine. **2** (also **pine wood**) a forest of pines.

piney adj. of, like, or full of pines.

ping ● n. **1** a single short high ring. **2** *N Amer.* = KNOCK n. 4. ● v.intr. **1** make a ping. **2** *N Amer.* = KNOCK v. 7.

pinger n. a device that transmits pings at short intervals for purposes of detection or measurement.

pingo n. (*pl.* **-os**) a dome-shaped mound found in permafrost areas, consisting of a layer of soil over a large core of ice.

ping-pong n. *proprietary* = TABLE TENNIS.

pinhead n. **1** the head of a pin. **2** a very small thing. **3** *informal* a stupid or foolish person.

pinhole n. a hole made by a pin.

pinion¹ /ˈpɪnjən/ ● n. the outer part of a bird's wing, usu. including the flight feathers. ● v.tr. **1** cut off the pinion of (a wing or bird) to prevent flight. **2 a** bind the arms of (a person). **b** (often foll. by *to*) bind (the arms, a person, etc.) esp. to a thing.

pinion² n. **1** a small cogwheel engaging with a larger one. **2** a cogged spindle engaging with a wheel.

pink¹ ● n. **1** a pale red colour. **2 a** any cultivated plant of the genus *Dianthus*, with sweet-smelling white, pink, crimson, etc. flowers. **b** the flower of this plant. **3** *informal* often derogatory a person with socialist tendencies. **4** = PINK SALMON. **5** (prec. by *the*) the most perfect condition etc. (*the pink of elegance*). ● adj. **1** (often in *comb.*) of a pale red colour of any of various shades (*salmon-pink*). **2** esp. *derogatory* tending to socialism. **3** (of wine) rosé. □ **in the pink** *informal* in very good health. □ **pinkish** adj. **pinkly** adv. **pinkness** n. **pinky** adj.

pink² v.tr. **1** cut a scalloped or zigzag edge on (esp. fabric). **2** pierce slightly with a sword etc. **3** (often foll. by *out*) ornament (leather etc.) with perforations.

pink-collar adj. (usu. *attrib.*) (of a profession etc.) traditionally associated with women.

pink eye n. **1** contagious ophthalmia in humans and some livestock. **2** a contagious fever in horses.

pinking shears n.pl. a dressmaker's serrated shears for cutting a zigzag edge.

pinko n. (*pl.* **-os**) esp. *N Amer. derogatory* a socialist.

pink salmon n. a medium-sized pink-fleshed migratory salmon, *Oncorhynchus gorbuscha*, of the Pacific and more recently Atlantic Oceans, the male of which has a humped back at spawning time.

pink slip esp. *N Amer.* ● n. a notice of dismissal from employment. ● v.tr. (usu. **pink-slip**) dismiss (a person) from employment (*was pink-slipped last week*).

pinky n. (also **pinkie**) (*pl.* **-ies**) esp. *N Amer. & Scot.* the little finger.

pin money n. a very small sum of money, esp. for spending on inessentials.

pinnacle ● n. **1** the culmination or climax (e.g. of success). **2** a natural peak, e.g. of rock etc. **3** a small ornamental turret usu. ending in a pyramid or cone, crowning a buttress, roof, etc. ● *v.tr.* **1** set on or as if on a pinnacle. **2** provide with pinnacles.

pinnate /ˈpɪneɪt/ *adj.* **1** (of a compound leaf) having leaflets arranged on either side of the stem, usu. in pairs opposite each other. **2** having branches, tentacles, etc., on each side of an axis.

PIN number *n.* = PIN.

pin oak *n.* a N American oak, *Quercus palustris*, with dead branches resembling pegs fixed into the trunk.

pinochle /ˈpiː,nʌkəl/ *n. N Amer.* **1** a card game with a double pack of 48 cards (nine to ace only). **2** the combination of queen of spades and jack of diamonds in this game.

piñon /piːˈnjoːn/ *n.* **1** a pine, *Pinus cembra*, bearing edible seeds. **2** the seed of this, a type of pine nut.

Pinot /piːˈnoː/ *n.* **1** any of several varieties of black or white grape used in winemaking. **2** the vine on which these grapes grow. **3** a red or white wine made from these grapes.

pinpoint ● *n.* **1** the point of a pin. **2** something very small or sharp. **3** (*attrib.*) **a** very small. **b** precise, accurate. ● *v.tr.* locate or determine with precision or accuracy (*pinpointed the problem*).

pinprick *n.* **1** a prick caused by a pin. **2** a trifling irritation.

pins and needles *n.pl.* a tingling sensation in a limb recovering from numbness. □ **on pins and needles** in an agitated state of suspense.

pinstripe *n.* **1** a very narrow white stripe in a fabric (*pinstripe suit*). **2** (in *sing.* or *pl.*) a pinstripe suit (*wearing pinstripes*). □ **pinstriped** *adj.*

pint *n.* **1** a measure of capacity for liquids etc., equal to one-eighth of a gallon (0.568 litre in Imperial measure, or 0.473 litre in US measure). **2** a dry measure, equal to a half quart or (in the US) one sixty-fourth of a bushel (0.5506 litre). **3** *Cdn* (*Maritimes*) a mickey of liquor. **4** *esp. Brit. informal* a pint of beer.

pintail *n.* a duck, esp. the northern pintail, *Anas acuta*, with a pointed tail.

pinto *N Amer.* ● *adj.* piebald. ● *n.* (*pl.* **-os**) **1** a piebald horse. **2** (in full **pinto bean**) a variety of kidney bean with mottled seeds.

pint-sized *adj.* (also **pint-size**) *informal* very small.

pintuck *n.* a very narrow ornamental tuck. □ **pintucking** *n.*

pin-up *n.* **1** a photograph of a popular or sexually attractive person, affixed to a wall. **2** a person shown in such a photograph.

pinwheel ● *n.* **1** a hand-held toy consisting of a stick with a small vaned wheel which rotates. **2** a firework which can be fixed at the centre and which rotates rapidly when lit. **3** something shaped like a pinwheel (*pastry pinwheels*). ● *v.tr. & intr.* rotate or cause to rotate like a pinwheel.

pinworm *n.* a small parasitic nematode worm, *Enterobius vermicularis*.

piny *var. of* PINEY.

Pinyin /pɪnˈjɪn/ *n.* a system of romanized spelling for transliterating Chinese.

pinyon *var. of* PIÑON.

pion /ˈpaɪɒn/ *n. Physics* a meson having a mass approximately 270 times that of an electron.

pioneer *n.* **1** an initiator of a new enterprise, an inventor, etc. **2** a settler in a previously unsettled land (also *attrib.: a pioneer settlement*). ● *v.* **1** *tr.* initiate or originate (an enterprise etc.). **2** *intr.* act or prepare the way as a pioneer. □ **pioneering** *adj.*

pious *adj.* **1** devout; religious. **2** hypocritically virtuous; sanctimonious. □ **piously** *adv.*

pip[1] *n.* **1** the seed of an apple, orange, grape, etc. **2** *informal* an excellent thing or person; a fine example.

pip[2] *n.* **1** any of the spots on a playing card, dice, or domino. **2** a diamond-shaped segment of the surface of a pineapple. **3** = BLIP 2.

pipe ● *n.* **1** a tube of metal, plastic, wood, etc. used to convey water, gas, exhaust, etc. **2** a **a** narrow wooden or clay etc. tube with a bowl at one end containing burning tobacco, opium, etc., the smoke from which is drawn into the mouth. **b** the quantity of tobacco etc. held by this (*smoked a pipe*). **3** *Music* **a** a wind instrument consisting of a single tube. **b** any of the tubes by which sound is produced in an organ. **c** (in *pl.*) bagpipes. **4 a** a tubal organ, vessel, etc. in an animal's body. **b** (in *pl.*) *informal* the human circulatory, respiratory, or digestive system. **5** *informal* or *jocular* the voice or vocal cords, esp. in reference to singing. **6** a high note or song, esp. of a bird. **7** a cylindrical vein of ore. **8 a** a boatswain's whistle. **b** the sounding of this. ● *v.* **1** *tr. & intr.* play (a tune etc.) on a pipe or pipes. **2** *tr.* **a** convey (oil, water, gas, etc.) by pipes. **b** provide with pipes. **3** *tr.* (often foll. by *in*) transmit (music, a radio program, etc.) by wire or cable. **4** *tr.* (usu. foll. by *up*, *on*, *to*, etc.) *Naut.* **a** summon (a crew) to a meal, work, etc. **b** signal the arrival of (an officer etc.) on board. **5** *intr.* utter in a shrill voice; whistle. **6** *tr.* arrange (icing, cream, etc.) in decorative lines or twists on a cake etc. **7** *tr.* trim (a dress etc.) with piping. **8** *tr.* lead or bring (a person etc.) by the sound of a pipe. □ **between the pipes** *Hockey* playing goal. **pipe down** *informal* be quiet or less insistent. **pipe up** begin to play, sing, speak, etc. **put that in your pipe and smoke it** *informal* a challenge to another to accept something frank or unwelcome. □ **pipeful** *n.* (*pl.* **-fuls**).

pipe band *n.* a band of bagpipers and drummers.

pipe bomb *n.* a homemade bomb contained in a metal tube.

pipeclay *n.* a fine white clay used for tobacco pipes, whitening leather, etc.

pipe cleaner *n.* a piece of flexible covered wire, used for cleaning a tobacco pipe and for crafts.

pipe dream *n.* an unattainable or fanciful hope.

pipefitter *n.* a worker who installs and repairs pipe systems. □ **pipefitting** *n.*

pipeline ● *n.* **1** a long, usu. underground, pipe for conveying oil, gas, etc. **2** a channel supplying goods, information, etc. **3** *Computing* a linear sequence of specialized modules used for pipelining. ● *v.tr.* **1** convey by a pipeline. **2** *Computing* design or execute using the technique of pipelining. □ **in the pipeline** being planned, worked on, or produced.

pipelining *n.* a form of computer organization in which successive steps of a process are executed in turn by a sequence of modules able to operate concurrently, so that another process can be begun before the previous one is finished.

pipe major *n.* a person responsible for training and leading a pipe band.

pipe organ *n. Music* an organ using pipes instead of or as well as reeds.

piper *n.* **1** a bagpiper. **2** a person who plays a pipe, esp. an itinerant musician.

pipestem ● *n.* the shaft of a tobacco pipe. ● *adj.* slender like a pipestem (*pipestem arms*).

pipe-stone *n.* a hard red clay of the central US, used by Aboriginal peoples to make tobacco pipes.

pipette /paɪˈpɛt, pɪ-/ ● *n.* a slender tube for transferring or measuring small quantities of liquids esp. in chemistry. ● *v.tr.* transfer or measure using a pipette.

pipe wrench *n.* a wrench with one fixed and one movable jaw, designed so as to grip a pipe etc. when turned in one direction only.

piping ● *n.* **1** the act or an instance of piping, esp. whistling or singing. **2** lengths of pipe, or a system of pipes, esp. in domestic use. **3** a thin pipelike fold used to edge hems or frills on clothing, seams on upholstery, etc. **4** ornamental lines of icing, cream, potato, etc. on a cake or other dish. ● *adj.* (of a noise) high; whistling.

piping hot *adj.* & *adv.* very or suitably hot (esp. as required of food, water, etc.).

piping plover *n.* a small buff-coloured N American bird with a whistling call, *Charadrius melodus*.

pipit *n.* any of various birds of the family Motacillidae, esp. of the genus *Anthus*, with brown plumage often heavily streaked with a lighter colour.

pippin *n.* **1** an apple grown from seed. **2** a red and yellow dessert apple.

pipsqueak *n. informal* a contemptibly small, weak, or insignificant person or thing.

piquant /piː'kænt, -'kɒnt, 'piː'kænt/ *adj.* **1** agreeably pungent, sharp, or appetizing. **2** pleasantly exciting and stimulating (*a piquant bit of gossip*). □ **piquancy** *n.*

pique /piːk/ ● *v.tr.* (**piques, piqued, piquing**) **1** wound the pride of, irritate. **2** arouse (curiosity, interest, etc.). ● *n.* ill-feeling; enmity; resentment.

piqué /piː'keɪ/ *n.* a stiff ribbed cotton or other fabric.

piracy *n.* (*pl.* **-ies**) **1** the practice or an act of robbery of ships at sea. **2** a similar practice or act in other forms, esp. hijacking. **3** the infringement of copyright by unauthorized reproduction or use of a book, recording, computer program, etc.

piranha /pɪ'rɒnə, -'rænə/ *n.* any of various freshwater predatory fish of the genera *Pygocentrus*, *Rooseveltiella*, or *Serrasalmus*, native to S America and having sharp cutting teeth.

pirate ● *n.* **1** a person who commits piracy. **2** a person who infringes another's copyright or other business rights. **3** (often *attrib.*) a person, organization, etc., that broadcasts without official authorization (*pirate radio station*). ● *v.tr.* **1** appropriate or reproduce (the work or ideas etc. of another) without permission, for one's own benefit. **2** plunder. □ **pirated** *adj.* **piratical** /-'rætɪkəl/ *adj.*

piri piri /pɪri 'pɪri/ *n.* a sauce made with hot peppers, lemon rind and juice, and other flavourings.

pirogi *var. of* PEROGY.

pirogue /pɪ'roːg/ *n.* a long narrow canoe made from a single tree trunk.

piroshki /pɪ'rɒʃki/ *n.* (*pl.* same or **-s**) a small turnover of pastry filled with meat, fish, rice, etc.

pirouette /ˌpɪru'et/ ● *n.* a rapid turn or spin on the point of the toe or the ball of the foot, made esp. by a dancer. ● *v.intr.* perform a pirouette.

piscatorial /ˌpɪskə'tɔːriəl/ *adj.* **1** of or concerning fish or fishing. **2** *formal* enthusiastic about fishing.

Pisces /'paɪsiːz/ *n.* (*pl.* same) **1** a large constellation between Aries and Aquarius, traditionally regarded as contained in the figure of a pair of fish. **2** a the twelfth sign of the zodiac. **b** a person born when the sun is in this sign, usu. between Feb. 19 and Mar. 20.□ **Piscean** /'paɪsiən/ *n.* & *adj.*

pish *interj.* an expression of contempt or impatience.

piss *coarse slang* ● *v.* **1** *intr.* urinate. **2** *tr.* **a** discharge (blood etc.) when urinating. **b** wet with urine. **3** *refl.* **a**

wet one's clothing with urine. **b** be very frightened, amused, or excited. ● *n.* **1** urine. **2** an act of urinating. **3** an unpalatable drink. □ **piss around** fool or mess around. **piss away** squander; waste (*pissed away his money*). **piss down** rain heavily. **piss in** (or **into** or **against**) **the wind** do something to no effect or against one's own interests. **piss off 1** go away. **2** (often as **pissed off** *adj.*) annoy; anger. **piss on** show utter contempt for, esp. by humiliating.

piss and vinegar *n. coarse slang* energy; aggression.

pissed *adj.* **1** drunk. **2** *N Amer.* annoyed; angry.

pisser *n. coarse slang* **1** a difficult or annoying thing. **2** a urinal or toilet. **3** a person who urinates.

piss-poor *adj. coarse slang* very bad; inferior.

pissy *adj.* (**-ier, -iest**) *coarse slang* **1** disagreeable; foul (*a pissy mood*). **2** inferior; second-rate.

pistachio /pɪ'stæʃiːˈ/ ● *n.* (*pl.* **-os**) **1** an evergreen tree, *Pistacia vera*, bearing small brownish-green flowers and ovoid reddish fruit. **2** (in full **pistachio nut**) the edible pale green seed of this. **3** (in full **pistachio green**) a pale green colour. ● *adj.* (in full **pistachio green**; hyph. when *attrib.*) pale green.

piste /piːst/ *n.* a ski run of compacted snow.

pistil /'pɪstɪl/ *n.* the female organs of a flower, comprising the stigma, style, and ovary.

pistol ● *n.* a small hand-held firearm. ● *v.tr.* (**pistolled, pistolling**) shoot with a pistol.

pistol-grip *n.* a handle shaped like the butt of a pistol.

pistol-whip *v.tr.* (**-whipped, -whipping**) beat with a pistol.

piston *n.* **1** a disc or short cylinder fitting closely within a tube in which it moves up and down against a liquid or gas, used in an internal combustion engine to impart motion, or in a pump to receive motion. **2** a sliding valve in a trumpet etc.

pit¹ ● *n.* **1 a** a usu. large deep hole in the ground. **b** a hole made in digging for industrial purposes (*gravel pit*). **c** a mine, esp. a coal mine. **d** a covered hole as a trap for esp. wild animals. **2 a** an indentation left after smallpox, acne, etc. **b** a hollow in a plant or animal body or on any surface. **3 a** = ORCHESTRA 2a. **b** the people in the pit. **4 a** (**the pit** or **bottomless pit**) hell. **b** (**the pits**) *slang* a wretched or the worst imaginable place, situation, person, etc. **5 a** an area at the side of a track where race cars are serviced and refuelled. **b** a sunken area in a garage floor for access to a car's underside. **6** esp. *N Amer.* the area of a stock market or commodity exchange in which a particular stock or commodity is traded, esp. one in which dealings in certain commodities take place by open outcry (*wheat pit*). **7** an enclosure in which animals are made to fight (*compare* COCKPIT 3). **8** = MOSH PIT. ● *v.* (**pitted, pitting**) **1** *tr.* (usu. foll. by *against*) **a** set (people or things) in opposition or rivalry. **b** match (one's wits, strengths, etc.) against an opponent. **2** *tr.* (usu. as **pitted** *adj.*) make pits, esp. scars, in. **3** *intr.* (of the flesh etc.) retain the impression of a finger etc. when touched. **4** *intr.* (of a race-car driver) make a pit stop.

pit² *N Amer.* ● *n.* the stone of a fruit. ● *v.tr.* (**pitted, pitting**) remove pits from (fruit).

pita /'piːtə/ *n. N Amer.* a flat hollow unleavened bread which can be split and filled with salad etc.

pit-a-pat *var. of* PITTER-PATTER.

pit bull *n.* **1** (in full **pit bull terrier**) a dog of an American variety of bull terrier, noted for its ferocity. **2** (*attrib.*) aggressive; fierce (*pit-bull personality*).

pitch¹ ● *v.* **1** *tr.* erect and fix (a tent, camp, etc.). **2** *tr.* throw; fling. **3** *Baseball* **a** *tr.* throw (the ball) to the batter. **b** *tr.* serve as pitcher of (a game, inning, etc.). **c**

intr. fill the position of pitcher. **d** *tr.* throw the ball to (a batter) in a specific way (*pitch him low and away*). **e** *intr.* throw a pitch. **4** *tr.* fix or plant (a thing) in a definite position. **5 a** *tr.* express in a particular style or at a particular level (*pitched his argument at the most basic level*). **b** *tr. informal* promote (a product, idea, etc.); attempt to win sales or approval for (*pitched his outline to the editor*). **c** *intr.* make a bid or offer for business. **6** *intr.* (often foll. by *against*, *into*, etc.) fall heavily, esp. headlong. **7** *intr.* (of a ship etc.) plunge in a longitudinal direction (*compare* ROLL *v.* 8a). **8** *tr. Music* set at a particular pitch. **9** *intr.* move with a vigorous jogging motion, as in a train, carriage, etc.; lurch. ● *n.* **1** height, degree, intensity, etc. (*the pitch of despair*). **2 a** the steepness of a slope, esp. of a roof, stratum, etc. **b** the degree of such a pitch. **c** a downward inclination or slope, esp. a steep one. **3** *Baseball* the act or manner of pitching the ball to a batter. **4** *Music* **a** the degree of highness or lowness of a tone. **b** a standard scale of this used in performance etc. (*compare* CONCERT PITCH). **5** the pitching motion of a ship etc. **6** *informal* behaviour or speech intended to influence or persuade, esp. for the purpose of sales or advertising. **7** (also **pitch shot**) *Golf* a high approach shot with a short run. **8** *Mech.* the distance between successive corresponding points or lines, e.g. between the teeth of a cogwheel. **9** *Computing* the density of characters on a line, usu. per inch. **10** a measure of the angle of the blades of a screw propeller. □ **pitch in** *informal* **1** assist, co-operate. **2** set to work vigorously. **pitch into** *informal* attack forcibly with blows, words, etc.

pitch² ● *n.* **1** a sticky resinous black or dark brown substance obtained by distilling tar or turpentine, semi-liquid when hot, hard when cold, used for caulking the seams of ships etc. **2** any of various bituminous substances including asphalt. **3** the resin or crude turpentine which exudes from pine and fir trees. ● *v.tr.* cover, coat, or smear with pitch.

pitch-black *adj.* (also **pitch-dark**) very or completely dark.

pitchblende /ˈpɪtʃblend/ *n.* a mineral form of uranium oxide occurring in pitchlike masses and yielding radium.

pitched battle *n.* **1** a vigorous fight, argument etc. **2** *Military* a battle planned beforehand and fought on chosen ground.

pitched roof *n.* a sloping roof.

pitcher¹ *n.* **1** esp. *N Amer.* **a** a vessel, usu. of glass, earthenware or plastic, with a lip and a handle, for holding liquids. **b** the amount of liquid contained in this (*a pitcher of lemonade*). **2** the modified leaf of the pitcher plant. □ **pitcherful** *n.* (*pl.* **-fuls**).

pitcher² *n.* **1** *Baseball* the player who throws the ball to the batter. **2** a person or thing that pitches.

pitcher plant *n.* any of various plants, esp. *Sarracenia purpurea* of eastern N America, with pitcher leaves that can hold liquids and trap insects and a dark red flower with a large flattened pistil.

pitchfork ● *n.* a long-handled fork for pitching hay etc. ● *v.* **1** *tr. & intr.* throw with or as if with a pitchfork. **2** *tr.* (usu. foll. by *into*) thrust (a person) forcibly into a position, office, etc.

pitchman *n.* (*pl.* **-men**) *N Amer.* a person delivering a sales pitch, esp. in a radio or television commercial.

pitchout *n.* **1** *Baseball* a pitch purposely thrown wide of the plate, to make it easier for the catcher to throw out a baserunner who is attempting to steal. **2** *Football* a short lateral pass thrown behind the line of scrimmage.

pitch pine *n.* any of various pine trees, esp. *Pinus rigida* or *P. palustris*, yielding much resin.

pitch pipe *n.* a small pipe blown to set the pitch for singing or tuning.

pitchy *adj.* (**-ier, -iest**) of, like, or dark as pitch.

piteous /ˈpɪtiəs/ *adj.* deserving or causing pity; wretched. □ **piteously** *adv.*

pitfall *n.* **1** an unsuspected snare, danger, or drawback. **2** a covered pit for trapping animals etc.

pith *n.* **1** spongy white tissue lining the rind of an orange, lemon, etc. **2** the essential part; quintessence. **3** *Bot.* the spongy cellular tissue in the stems and branches of dicotyledonous plants. **4** force; energy, esp. of words or speech.

pithead *n.* **1** the top of a mine shaft. **2** the area surrounding this.

pith helmet *n.* a light helmet made from the dried pith of the sola or a similar plant, worn by explorers etc. in the tropics for protection from the sun.

pithy *adj.* (**-ier, -iest**) **1** (of style, speech, etc.) condensed, terse, and forcible. **2** of, like, or containing much pith. □ **pithily** *adv.* **pithiness** *n.*

pitiable *adj.* **1** deserving or causing pity. **2** contemptible.

pitiful *adj.* **1** deserving of or arousing pity. **2** contemptible. □ **pitifully** *adv.* **pitifulness** *n.*

pitiless *adj.* **1** showing no pity; cruel (*a pitiless tyrant*). **2** very harsh or severe; unrelenting (*the pitiless heat of the desert*). □ **pitilessly** *adv.*

pit-lamping *n.* *Cdn* (*BC*) the hunting practice of using strong portable lights to blind an animal temporarily so that it freezes in its tracks, thus allowing the hunter an easy shot.

piton /ˈpiːtɒn/ *n.* a peg or spike driven into a rock or crack to support a climber or a rope.

pit socks *n.pl.* *Cdn* (*Cape Breton*) standard grey work socks, esp. worn by miners.

pit stop *n.* **1** *Motor Racing* a stop at a pit for servicing and refuelling. **2 a** a brief stop during a trip for a rest etc. **b** a place where one makes such a stop.

pittance *n.* **1** a scanty or meagre allowance, remuneration, etc. **2** a small number or amount.

pitter-patter ● *adv.* **1** with a sound like quick light steps. **2** with a rapid beat (*heart went pitter-patter*). ● *n.* such a sound.

pituitary /pɪˈtuːɪteri, -ˈtjuː-/ ● *n.* (*pl.* **-ies**) a small ductless gland at the base of the brain secreting various hormones essential for growth and other bodily functions. ● *adj.* of or relating to this gland.

pit viper *n.* any of various American and Asian snakes of the subfamily Crotalinae, which have sensory pits on the head that can detect the heat of prey.

pity ● *n.* (*pl.* **-ies**) **1** sorrow and compassion aroused by another's condition. **2** something to be regretted; grounds for regret or mild annoyance (*what a pity!*). ● *v.tr.* (**-ies, -ied**) feel (often contemptuous) pity for (*I pity you if you think that*). □ **for pity's sake** an exclamation of urgent supplication, anger, etc. **take** (or **have**) **pity on** feel or act compassionately towards. □ **pitying** *adj.* **pityingly** *adv.*

pivot ● *n.* **1** a short shaft or pin on which something turns or oscillates. **2** a crucial or essential person, point, etc., in a scheme or enterprise. **3** a pivoting movement. **4** *Basketball* **a** a movement in which the ball carrier may take one or more paces in any direction with one foot, while keeping the other foot in place. **b** an offensive position in the frontcourt, usu. played by the centre, in which the player stands facing away from the basket. **c** the player who plays in the pivot position. **5** *Hockey* a centre. • *v.* (**pivoted, pivoting**) **1** *intr.* turn on or as if on a pivot. **2** *intr.* (foll. by *on, upon*) hinge on; depend on. **3** *tr.* provide with or attach by a pivot. □ **pivotal** *adj.*

pix *n.pl. informal* **1** pictures, esp. photographs. **2** movies.

pixel /'pɪksəl/ *n. Electronics* any of the minute areas of uniform illumination of which an image on a television or computer screen is composed.

pixie *n.* (also **pixy**) (*pl.* **-ies**) **1** a small fairy, often portrayed with pointed ears and a pointed hat. **2** a small, mischievous person. □ **pixieish** *adj.*

pizza *n.* a food consisting of a flat round base of dough baked with a topping of tomato sauce and cheese and other garnishes, e.g. meat, vegetables, etc.

pizzazz *n.* (also **pizazz**) *informal* verve, energy, liveliness, sparkle.

pizzeria *n.* a place where pizzas are made or sold.

pizzicato /ˌpɪtsɪ'kɑːtəː, -'kɒtəː/ *Music* • *adv.* plucking the strings of a violin etc. with the finger (*compare* ARCO). • *adj.* (of a note, passage, etc.) performed pizzicato. • *n.* (*pl.* **-os** or **pizzicati** /-ti/) a note, passage, etc. played pizzicato.

PJs *n.pl. esp. N Amer. informal* = PYJAMAS 1.

pk. *abbr.* **1** pack. **2** park. **3** peak.

PK *abbr. N Amer. slang* preacher's (or pastor's) kid.

pkg. *abbr.* package.

PKU *abbr.* PHENYLKETONURIA.

pl. *abbr.* plural.

placable /'plækəbəl/ *adj.* easily placated; mild.

placard /'plækɑrd, -kɑrd/ • *n.* a printed or handwritten poster used esp. as an advertisement, in protest demonstrations, picket lines, etc. • *v.tr.* **1** set up placards on (a wall etc.). **2** advertise by placards. **3** display (a poster etc.) as a placard.

placate /plə'keɪt, 'plæ-, 'pleɪ-/ *v.tr.* make less angry; calm. □ **placatingly** *adv.* **placatory** /plə'keɪtəri/ *adj.*

place • *n.* **1 a** a particular portion of space. **b** a portion of space occupied by a person or thing (*it has changed its place*). **c** a proper or natural position (*take your places*). **d** situation, circumstances (*put yourself in my place*). **2** a city, town, village, etc. (*was born in this place*). **3 a** a residence or dwelling (*has a place in the country*; *come to my place*). **b** a particular building, room or outdoor site (*looking for a place to eat*). **c** (usu. with *neg.*) a suitable, proper, or safe area (*is no place for a child*). **4** a person's rank or status (*a place in history*). **5** role, position or function (*the place of computers in modern society*). **6** a point reached in a book etc. (*lost my place*). **7** a particular spot or area on a surface, e.g. on the body (*a tattoo in an embarrassing place*). **8 a** employment or office (*friends in high places*). **b** the duties or entitlements of office etc. (*is not my place to judge*). **9 a** position as a member of a team, a student in a college, etc. **10 a** any of the first three or sometimes four positions in a race. **b** *N Amer.* the second position, esp. in a horse race. **11** the position of a figure in a series indicated in decimal or similar notation. • *v.* **1** *tr.* put (a thing etc.) in a particular place or state; arrange. **2** *tr.* identify, classify, or remember correctly (*cannot place him*). **3** *tr.* assign to a particular place; locate. **4** *tr.* **a** appoint (a person, esp. a member of the clergy) to a post. **b** find a job, home, etc. for. **c** (usu. foll. by *with*) consign to a person's care etc. (*placed her with her aunt*). **5** *tr.* assign rank, importance, or worth to. **6** *tr.* **a** dispose of (goods) to a customer. **b** make (an order for goods etc.). **7** *tr. esp. N Amer.* order or obtain a connection for (a telephone call), esp. through an operator. **8** *tr.* (often foll. by *in, on*, etc.) have (confidence, trust, etc.). **9** *tr.* invest (money). **10** *intr.* **a** *N Amer.* finish second in a horse race. **b** finish among the first

three or sometimes four in a race. □ **all over the place** *informal* **1** everywhere (*companies are going bankrupt all over the place*). **2** in disorder; chaotic. **give place to 1** make room for. **2** yield precedence to. **3** be succeeded by. **go places** *informal* be successful. **in place 1** in the right position; suitable. **2** *N Amer.* not moving; on the spot (*running in place*). **in place of** in exchange for; instead of. **in places** at some places or in some parts, but not others. **keep a person in his** or **her place** suppress a person's aspirations or pretensions. **out of place 1** in the wrong position. **2** unsuitable. **put oneself in another's place** imagine oneself in another's position. **put a person in his** or **her place** deflate or humiliate a person. **take place** occur. **take one's place** go to one's correct position, be seated, etc. **take the place of** be substituted for; replace. □ **placeless** *adj.*

placement *n.* **placing** *n.*

placebo /plə'siːbəː/ *n.* (*pl.* **-os**) **1 a** a pill, medicine, etc. prescribed for psychological reasons but having no physiological effect. **b** a blank sample used as a control in testing new drugs etc. **2** something that is said or done to calm or humour a person but does not address the cause of his or her anxiety.

place in the sun *n.* a good situation or position.

place kick *n. Football* a kick in which the ball is placed on the ground and held upright. □ **place-kick** *v.intr.* **place-kicker** *n.*

placemat *n.* a small mat of cloth, cork, paper, etc. used to protect and keep clean a table or other surface on which dishes and eating utensils are set.

place name *n.* the name of a city, hill, lake, etc.

placenta /plə'sentə/ *n.* (*pl.* **-s** or **placentae** /-tiː/) **1** a flattened circular organ in the uterus of some pregnant mammals, nourishing and maintaining the fetus through the umbilical cord and expelled after birth. **2** (in flowers) part of the ovary wall carrying the ovules. □ **placental** *adj.*

placer /'plæsər/ *n.* a deposit of sand, gravel, etc., in the bed of a stream etc., containing minerals, e.g. gold, in particles (often *attrib.*: *placer mining*).

place setting *n.* a set of plates, cutlery, etc. for one person at a meal.

placid *adj.* **1** (of a person) not easily aroused or disturbed; peaceful. **2** calm; serene. □ **placidly** *adv.*

placket *n.* **1** an opening or slit in a garment, for fastenings or access to a pocket. **2** the flap of fabric under this.

plagiarize /'pleɪdʒəˌraɪz/ *v.tr. & intr.* **1** take and use (the thoughts, writings, inventions, etc. of another person) as one's own. **2** pass off the thoughts etc. of (another person) as one's own. □ **plagiarism** *n.* **plagiarist** *n.* **plagiaristic** *adj.* **plagiarizer** *n.*

plagioclase /'pleɪdʒiəˌkleɪz/ *n.* a series of feldspar minerals forming glassy crystals.

plague • *n.* **1 a** (prec. by *the*) a contagious bacterial disease characterized by fever and delirium, with the formation of buboes (**bubonic plague**) and sometimes infection of the lungs (**pneumonic plague**). **b** any severe or fatal contagious disease spreading rapidly over a wide area. **2** (foll. by *of*) an unusual infestation of a pest etc. (*a plague of frogs*). **3 a** great trouble. **b** an affliction, esp. as regarded as divine punishment. **4** *informal* a nuisance. • *v.tr.* (**plagues, plagued, plaguing**) **1** afflict, torment (*plagued by war*). **2** *informal* pester or harass continually.

plaice *n.* (*pl.* same) either of two flatfishes having a brown back and a white underside, much used for food, the N Atlantic fish *Hippoglossoides platessoides* or the European *Pleuronectes platessa*.

plaid /plæd/ n. **1** (often attrib.) **a** checkered or tartan, esp. woollen, twilled cloth. **b** a checkered or tartan pattern. **2** a long piece of plaid worn over the shoulder as part of Highland Scottish costume.

plain ● adj. **1** clear; evident (is plain to see). **2 a** readily understood; simple (in plain words). **b** frank; straightforward (the plain truth). **3 a** ordinary; basic (plain common sense). **b** downright; utter (plain stupidity). **4 a** (of cooking, sewing, decoration, etc.) uncomplicated; not elaborate; unembellished; simple. **b** (of food) without added flavours, toppings, etc. (plain popcorn). **c** (of a fabric, item of clothing, etc.) without a decorative pattern. **5** (esp. of a woman or girl) not beautiful or pretty. **6** (of manners, dress, etc.) unsophisticated; homely. ● adv. **1** clearly; unequivocally (to speak plain, I don't approve). **2** simply (plain stupid). ● n. **1** a level tract of esp. treeless and flat grassland; prairie. **2 (the Plains)** the region of western N America originally characterized by such grassland. □ **be plain with** speak bluntly to. □ **plainly** adv. **plainness** n.

plainchant n. = PLAINSONG.

plain clothes ● n.pl. ordinary clothes worn esp. as a disguise by police officers etc. ● attrib.adj. **(plainclothes)** not wearing a uniform.

plain-Jane ● adj. ordinary, simple, unremarkable (a plain-Jane dress). ● n. **(plain Jane)** a plain or unattractive girl or woman.

plains bison n. (also **plains buffalo**) a subspecies of the N American bison, distinguished by a yellow-ochre cape of hair over the shoulders.

Plains Cree n. **1** a member of a Cree people who moved west to the Plains in the 18th c. and now live in Manitoba, S Saskatchewan, and central Alberta. **2** the dialect of Cree spoken by this people.

Plains Indian n. a member of any of a number of Aboriginal peoples inhabiting the Plains of western N America, including the Assiniboine, Blackfoot, Gros Ventres, Peigan, Blood, and Sarcee.

plainsong n. church music, usu. unaccompanied, sung in unison in medieval modes and in free rhythm corresponding to the accentuation of the words (compare GREGORIAN CHANT).

plain-spoken adj. outspoken; blunt.

plaintiff n. Law a person who brings a case against another into court (opp. DEFENDANT).

plaintive adj. expressing sorrow; mournful, sad. □ **plaintively** adv. **plaintiveness** n.

plain-vanilla adj. **1** ordinary, plain, unexciting. **2** (esp. of a computer, program, or other product) having no interesting or unusual feature.

plain weave n. a weave made with the weft alternately over and under the warp.

plait ● n. a length of hair, straw, etc., in three or more interlaced strands; a braid. ● v.tr. **1** form (hair etc.) into a plait. **2** make (a belt etc.) by plaiting.

plan ● n. **1 a** a formulated and esp. detailed method by which a thing is to be done. **b** an intention or proposed proceeding (my plan was to distract them). **c** an arrangement for the regular payment of contributions toward a pension, insurance policy, etc. **d** the fund thus established. **e** a scheme for economic development. **2 a** a drawing or diagram made by projection on a horizontal plane, esp. showing a building or one floor of a building (compare ELEVATION). **b** (often in pl.) a detailed diagram of the parts of a machine etc. esp. with instructions for construction. **3** a large-scale detailed map of part of a town, a group of buildings, etc. **4** a way of arranging things (seating plan). ● v. **(planned, planning) 1** tr. (often foll. by that + clause or to + infin.) arrange (a procedure etc.) beforehand; form a plan. **2** tr. **a** design (a building, urban area, etc.). **b** make a plan of (an existing building, an area, etc.). **3** intr. make plans. □ **go according to plan** proceed as expected or planned. **plan on** informal **1** aim at doing; intend. **2** (also **plan for**) anticipate, expect; work under a specified assumption.

planar /ˈpleɪnər/ adj. Math. of, relating to, or in the form of a plane.

Plan B n. a secondary plan or program of action resorted to when the original plan fails.

planchette /plænˈʃet/ n. a small usu. heart-shaped board on casters with a pencil that is supposedly caused to write spirit messages when a person's fingers rest lightly on it.

plane¹ ● n. **1 a** a flat surface on which a straight line joining any two points on it would wholly lie. **b** an imaginary flat surface through or joining etc. material objects. **2** a level surface. **3** informal = AIRPLANE. **4** a flat surface producing lift by the action of air or water over and under it (usu. in comb.: hydroplane). **5** (often foll. by of) a level of attainment, knowledge, etc. **6** a flat thin object such as a tabletop. ● adj. **1** (of a surface etc.) perfectly level. **2** (of an angle, figure, etc.) lying in a plane. ● v.intr. **1** (often foll. by down) travel or glide in an airplane. **2** (of a speedboat etc.) skim over water. **3** soar.

plane² ● n. **1** a tool consisting of a wooden or metal block with a projecting steel blade, used to smooth a wooden surface by paring shavings from it. **2** a similar tool for smoothing metal. ● v.tr. **1** smooth (wood, metal, etc.) with a plane. **2** (often foll. by away, down) pare (irregularities) with a plane.

plane³ n. any tree of the genus Platanus often growing to great heights, with maple-like leaves and bark which peels in uneven patches.

planeload n. as much as can be carried in an airplane.

planer n. = PLANE² n. 1.

planet n. **1** a celestial body moving in an elliptical orbit around a star, esp. (in full **major planet**) any of the nine large rocky or gaseous bodies orbiting the sun. **2** (in full **minor planet**) an asteroid. **3** (prec. by the) the earth. □ **planetwide** adj.

planetarium n. (pl. **-s** or **-taria**) **1** a domed building in which images of stars, planets, constellations, etc. are projected for public entertainment or education. **2** the device used for such projection.

planetary adj. **1** of or like planets (planetary influence). **2** terrestrial; mundane. **3** global, worldwide. **4** Mech. of or involving a gear in which one wheel travels around the outside or the inside of another wheel with which it meshes.

plane tree n. see PLANE³.

plangent /ˈplændʒənt/ adj. **1** (of a sound) loud and reverberating. **2** (of a sound) plaintive; sad. □ **plangency** n. **plangently** adv.

plank ● n. **1** a long flat piece of timber used esp. in building etc. **2** a single item of a political or other program (compare PLATFORM 6). ● v. **1** tr. provide, cover, or floor, with planks. **2** tr. & intr. (usu. foll. by down) esp. N Amer. informal **a** put (a thing etc.) down roughly or violently. **b** pay (money) on the spot or abruptly (planked down $20). □ **walk the plank** hist. (of a pirate's captive etc.) be made to walk along a plank over the side of a ship to one's death in the sea. □ **planked** adj.

plank house n. a large rectangular timber-framed dwelling covered with planks, used esp. by the Aboriginal peoples of the Pacific coast of N America.

planking n. planks as flooring etc.

plank road n. Cdn a road of planks laid across logs running end to end over rough ground.

plankton n. the chiefly microscopic organisms drifting or floating in the sea or fresh water. □ **planktonic** adj.

planned adj. in accordance with a plan (his planned arrival; planned parenthood).

planned economy n. an economy in which production, prices, incomes, etc. are determined centrally by government.

planner n. 1 = URBAN PLANNER. 2 a person who makes plans. 3 a list, table, organizer, etc., with information helpful in planning.

planning n. 1 in senses of PLAN v. 2 the coordinating of land use and development.

plant ● n. 1 a any living organism of the kingdom Plantae, usu. containing chlorophyll enabling it to live wholly on inorganic substances and lacking specialized sense organs and the power of voluntary movement. b a small organism of this kind, as distinguished from a shrub or tree. 2 a machinery, fixtures, etc., used in industrial processes. b a factory. c (also **physical plant**) the premises, fittings, and equipment of a business or institution. 3 informal a something, esp. incriminating or compromising, positioned or concealed so as to be discovered later. b a person stationed as a spy or source of information. ● v.tr. 1 place (a seed, bulb, or growing thing) in the ground so that it may take root and flourish. 2 (often foll. by in, on, etc.) a put or fix in position. b refl. take up a position (planted myself by the door). 3 deposit (young fish, spawn, oysters, etc.) in a river or lake. 4 station (a person etc.), esp. as a spy or source of information. 5 cause (an idea etc.) to be established, esp. in another person's mind. 6 deliver (a blow, kiss, etc.) with a deliberate aim. 7 informal position or conceal (something incriminating or compromising) for later discovery. 8 settle or establish (a colony, city, etc.). □ **plant out** transfer (a plant) from a pot or frame to the open ground; set out (seedlings) at intervals. □ **plantlike** adj.

plantain¹ /ˈplæntein, ˈplæn-/ n. any plant of the genus Plantago, with a rosette of leaves and seeds used as food for birds and as a mild laxative.

plantain² n. 1 a banana plant, Musa paradisiaca. 2 the starchy fruit of this containing less sugar than a standard banana and chiefly used in cooking.

plantain lily n. = HOSTA.

plantar /ˈplæntər/ adj. relating to the sole of the foot.

plantation n. 1 a large farm, esp. in tropical or subtropical areas, on which cotton, tobacco, sugar, etc. is cultivated, usu. by resident farm workers. 2 an area planted with trees etc., esp. as part of a reforestation program. 3 hist. a colony; colonization.

planter n. 1 a large container for growing plants, usu. outdoors. 2 the owner or manager of a coffee, cotton, tobacco, etc. plantation. 3 a person employed to plant seedlings in reforestation programs. 4 a machine for planting seeds etc. 5 hist. a colonist. 6 a person who cultivates the soil.

planter's punch n. a cocktail consisting of rum and lime or lemon juice with water and sugar.

plant food n. 1 food of vegetable origin consumed by humans or animals. 2 fertilizer for plants.

planting n. 1 in senses of PLANT v. 2 an arrangement of plants in a garden or other setting.

plantlet n. an undeveloped or diminutive plant.

plant louse n. a small insect that infests plants, esp. an aphid.

plaque n. 1 an ornamental usu. metal tablet, esp. affixed to a building in commemoration. 2 a sticky deposit on teeth where bacteria proliferate. 3 Med. a a patch or eruption of skin etc. as a result of damage. b a fibrous lesion in atherosclerosis.

plasma n. (also **plasm**) 1 a the colourless fluid in blood, lymph, or milk, in which corpuscles or fat globules are suspended. b this taken from donated blood for use in transfusions. 2 = PROTOPLASM. 3 a gas of positive ions and free electrons with an approximately equal positive and negative charge. □ **plasmic** adj.

plasma membrane n. a membrane in a cell which regulates the passage of molecules in and out of the cytoplasm.

plasmodium /plæzˈmoːdiəm/ n. (pl. **plasmodia** /-diə/) 1 any parasitic protozoan of the genus Plasmodium, including those causing malaria in humans. 2 a form within the life cycle of various micro-organisms including slime moulds, usu. consisting of a mass of naked protoplasm containing many nuclei.

plaster ● n. 1 a soft pliable mixture esp. of lime or gypsum with sand and water for spreading on walls, ceilings, etc., to form a smooth hard surface when dried. 2 = PLASTER OF PARIS. 3 a protective substance spread on a bandage etc. ● v.tr. 1 cover (a wall etc.) with plaster or a similar substance. 2 (often foll. by with) cover (a surface, etc.) with a lot of something (pictures plastered all over her office). 3 stick or apply (a thing) thickly like plaster (plastered glue all over it). 4 (often foll. by down) make (esp. hair) smooth with water, cream, etc.; fix flat. 5 apply a medical plaster cast to. 6 slang bomb heavily. □ **plasterer** n.

plasterboard n. two boards with a filling of plaster used to form or line the inner walls of houses etc.

plaster cast n. 1 a bandage stiffened with plaster of Paris and applied to a broken limb etc. 2 a statue or mould made of plaster.

plastered adj. slang drunk.

plaster of Paris n. fine white plaster made of gypsum and used for making plaster casts etc.

plasterwork n. work done in plaster, esp. the plaster-covered surface of a wall.

plastic ● n. 1 any of a number of synthetic polymeric substances that can be given any required shape. 2 informal (also **plastic money**) credit cards or other types of plastic card that can be used instead of money. 3 = PLASTIC WRAP. ● adj. 1 a made of plastic. b artificial, insincere. 2 capable of being moulded; pliant; supple. 3 moulding or giving form to clay, wax, etc. 4 Biol. exhibiting an adaptability to environmental changes. □ **plastically** adv. **plasticity** n. **plasticize** v.tr. **plasticizer** n. **plasticky** adj.

plastic explosive n. a putty-like explosive capable of being moulded by hand.

Plasticine n. proprietary a soft plastic material used, esp. by children, for modelling.

plastic surgery n. the process of reconstructing or repairing parts of the body by the transfer of tissue, either in the treatment of injury or for cosmetic reasons. □ **plastic surgeon** n.

plastic wrap n. N Amer. a very thin clinging transparent plastic film, used esp. to cover food.

plate ● n. 1 a a shallow usu. circular and ceramic vessel from which food is eaten or served. b the contents of this (a plate of beans). 2 a similar vessel usu. of metal or wood, used esp. for taking a collection in a church etc. 3 N Amer. a main course of a meal, served on one plate. 4 one person's meal at a banquet etc. (*$100 per plate*). **5** (*collect.*) **a** utensils of silver, gold, or other metal. **b** objects of plated metal. **6 a** a piece of metal with a name or inscription for affixing to a door, container, etc. **b** = LICENCE PLATE. **7** an illustration on special paper in a book. **8** a thin sheet of metal, glass, etc., coated with a sensitive film for photography. **9** a flat thin usu. rigid sheet of metal etc. with an even surface and uniform thickness, often as part of a mechanism or protective armour. **10 a** a smooth piece of metal etc. for engraving. **b** an impression made from this. **11 a** a silver or gold cup as a prize for a horse race etc. **b** a race with this as a prize. **12 a** a thin piece of plastic material to which artificial teeth are attached. **b** *informal* a complete denture. **13** *Geol.* each of several rigid sheets of rock thought to form the earth's outer crust. **14** a stereotype or plastic cast of a page of composed movable types, or a metal or plastic copy of filmset matter, from which sheets are printed. **15** *Baseball* a flat piece of white rubber marking the station of a batter or pitcher. **16** a horizontal timber laid along the top of a wall to support the ends of joists or rafters. ● *v.tr.* **1** apply a thin coat esp. of silver, gold, or tin to (another metal). **2** cover with plates of metal, esp. for protection. **3** make a plate of (type etc.) for printing. □ **on a plate** = ON A PLATTER (see PLATTER). **on one's plate** for one to deal with or consider. □ **plateful** *n.* (*pl.* **-fuls**). **plater** *n.*

plate armour *n.* armour of metal plates.

plateau /plæ'to:/ ● *n.* (*pl.* **-s** or **-teaux** /-to:z/) **1** an area of fairly level high ground. **2** a state of little variation after an increase. ● *v.intr.* (**plateaus**, **plateaued**) reach a level or stable state after an increase.

plate glass *n.* fine-quality glass for windows etc., originally cast in plates.

platelet *n.* a small colourless disc-shaped cell fragment without a nucleus, found in large numbers in blood and involved in clotting.

plate tectonics *n.pl.* (usu. treated as *sing.*) a theory of the earth's surface based on the interaction of rigid lithospheric plates which move slowly on the underlying mantle.

platform *n.* **1** a raised level surface. **2 a** a raised surface from which a speaker addresses an audience. **b** an opportunity to express one's opinions; a forum. **3 a** a raised elongated structure along the side of a track in a railway or subway station. **b** *N Amer.* a slightly raised area of concrete etc. used by passengers for boarding and alighting from a bus at a bus station. **4** the floor area at the entrance to a train. **5 a** a thick sole of a shoe (often *attrib.*: *platform shoes*). **b** (usu. in *pl.*) a platform shoe, boot, etc. **6** the declared policy or policies of a political party etc. **7** a computer system whose hardware and software make it sufficiently different from all other computer systems for it to require unique software versions. **8** a rigid diving board, esp. used in diving competitions. **9** (also **drilling platform**) a structure designed to stand on the bed of the sea (or a lake) to provide a stable base above water level from which several oil or gas wells can be drilled or regulated.

plating *n.* **1** a coating of gold, silver, etc. **2** armour consisting of metal plates.

platinum ● *n.* **1** a ductile malleable silvery-white metallic element occurring naturally in nickel and copper ores, unaffected by simple acids and fusible only at a very high temperature, used in making jewellery and laboratory apparatus. **2** a greyish-white or silvery colour like that of platinum. ● *adj.* **1** (of an

album or other recording) having attained the highest recognition for sales exceeding a specified high figure. **2** platinum-coloured. **3** designating a group of similar metallic elements often associated in ores, comprising platinum, iridium, palladium, osmium, rhodium, and ruthenium.

platinum blond ● *adj.* silvery-blond. ● *n.* a person with silvery-blond hair.

platitude *n.* a trite or commonplace remark, esp. one solemnly delivered. □ **platitudinous** *adj.*

Platonic /plə'tɒnɪk/ *adj.* **1** of or associated with the Greek philosopher Plato (*c.*429–*c.*347 BC). **2** (**platonic**) (of love or friendship) not involving sex. **3** constituting or pertaining to ideal, transcendent or eternal realities. □ **Platonically** *adv.*

Platonism /'pleɪtə,nɪzəm/ *n.* the philosophy of Plato or his followers, esp. his theory of 'ideas' or 'forms', in which abstract entities are contrasted with objects in the material world. □ **Platonist** *n.*

platoon ● *n.* **1** *Military* a subdivision of a company, a tactical unit usu. divided into three sections of ten to twelve soldiers. **2** a group of persons acting together. **3** *N Amer.* a pair or group of players on a team who alternate at the same position. **4** *Football* a group of offensive or defensive players sent on or off the field as a unit. ● *v.tr. & intr. N Amer. Sport* alternate (a player) with or (of a player) interchange with another player at the same position on a team.

platter *n.* **1 a** a large usu. oval dish or plate for presenting or serving food. **b** a serving of food on such a plate, usu. consisting of several different items (*cheese platter*). **2** the rotating metal disc of a record player turntable. **3** *Computing* a rigid disk used to store data magnetically. □ **on a platter** *informal* available with little trouble to the recipient.

platypus /'plætɪpəs/ *n.* (*pl.* **-es**) an Australian egg-laying aquatic mammal, *Ornithorhynchus anatinus*, with a ducklike bill, webbed feet, and grey fur.

plaudit /'plɔːdɪt/ *n.* (usu. in *pl.*) **1** an emphatic expression of approval. **2** a round of applause.

plausible /'plɔːzɪbəl/ *adj.* **1** (of an argument, statement, etc.) seeming reasonable, believable, or probable. **2** (of a person) persuasive. □ **plausibility** *n.* **plausibly** *adv.*

play ● *v.* **1** *intr.* (often foll. by *with*) occupy or amuse oneself pleasantly with some recreation, game, exercise, etc. **2** *intr.* (foll. by *with*) act lightheartedly or flippantly (with feelings etc.). **3 a** *tr.* perform on or be able to perform on (a musical instrument). **b** *tr.* perform (a piece of music etc.). **c** *tr.* cause (a cassette player etc.) to produce or (of a cassette player etc.) produce sounds, video images, etc. **4 a** *intr.* (foll. by *in*) perform a role in (a drama etc.). **b** *tr.* perform (a drama or role) on stage, or in a film or broadcast. **c** *tr.* perform a play or concert or play a game etc. at (a theatre, concert hall, stadium, etc.). **d** *intr.* be performed or shown in a theatre etc. (*what's playing?*). **9** *intr.* (of a theatrical performance, a concept, political action, etc) receive acceptance by an audience, the general public, etc. (*will it play in the suburbs?*). **5** *tr.* act in real life the part of (*play the fool*). **6** *tr.* (foll. by *on*) perform (a trick or joke etc.) on (a person). **7** *tr.* (foll. by *for*) regard (a person) as (something specified) (*played me for a fool*). **8** *intr. informal* participate, co-operate; do what is wanted (*they won't play*). **9** *intr.* gamble. **10** *tr.* gamble on. **11 a** *tr. & intr.* take part in (a game or recreation). **b** *tr.* compete with (another player or team) in a game. **c** *tr.* occupy (a specified position) in a team for a game. **d** *tr.* (foll. by *in, on, at,* etc.) assign (a player) to a position. **12** *tr.* move (a piece) or display (a playing card) in one's turn in a game. **13** *tr.* strike (a ball etc.) or execute (a stroke) in a game. **14** *intr.* move about in a lively or unrestrained manner. **15** *intr.* (often foll. by *on*) **a** touch gently. **b** emit light, water, etc. (*fountains gently playing*). **16** *tr.* allow (a fish) to exhaust itself pulling against a line. **17** *intr.* (often foll. by *at*) **a** engage in a half-hearted way (in an activity). **b** pretend to be. **18 a** *intr.* act or behave (as specified) (*play fair*). **b** *tr.* engage in (an activity) (*play footsie*). ● *n.* **1** recreation, amusement, esp. as the spontaneous activity of children and young animals. **2 a** the playing of a game. **b** the action or manner of this. **c** the status of the ball etc. in a game as being available to be played according to the rules (*out of play*). **d** an action or manoeuvre, esp. in or as in a game (*what a play!*). **3** a dramatic piece for the stage, radio, etc. **4 a** activity or operation (*brought into play*). **b** behaviour, activity (*foul play*). **5 a** freedom of movement. **b** space or scope for this. **6** brisk, light, or fitful movement. **7** gambling. **8** the button on a VCR, compact disc player, etc., which causes it to play when pushed.□**at play** engaged in recreation. **in play** for amusement; not seriously. **make a play for** *informal* make a conspicuous attempt to acquire. **make play with** use ostentatiously. **play along 1** co-operate, comply. **2** pretend to agree or co-operate. **play around 1** behave playfully or irresponsibly. **2** (often foll. by *with*) have casual or extramarital sexual relations. **play back** play (sounds or video images recently recorded), esp. to monitor recording quality etc. **play both ends against the middle** keep one's options open by trying to keep favour with opposing sides. **play by ear 1** perform (music) without having seen a score of it. **2** (also **play it by ear**) proceed instinctively or step by step according to results and circumstances. **play one's cards right** (or **well**) make good use of opportunities; act shrewdly. **play down** minimize the importance of. **play fast and loose** act unreliably; ignore one's obligations. **play favourites** show favouritism. **play for time** seek to gain time by delaying. **play host** act as host to. **play a** (or **one's**) **hunch** make an instinctive choice. **play into a person's hands** act so as unwittingly to give a person an advantage. **play it cool** *informal* **1** affect indifference. **2** be relaxed or unemotional. **play the man** *Sport* focus one's attention on the opposing player, not the puck, stick, ball, etc. **play the market** speculate in stocks etc. **play off** (usu. foll. by *against*) **1** oppose (one person against another), esp. for one's own advantage. **2** play an extra match to decide a draw or tie. **play on 1** continue to play. **2** take advantage of (a person's feelings etc.). **play out 1 a** use up. **b** tire. **2** finish, bring or come to an end or resolution. **3** perform to the end. **play it safe** avoid risks. **play up** emphasize, make the most of. **play up to 1** flatter, esp. to win favour. **2** perform as expected considering (one's capability, reputation, etc.). **play with 1** consider (an idea etc.), but not seriously. **2** touch or fondle idly (*played with her scarf*). **play with fire** take foolish risks. **play with oneself** masturbate. □ **playable** *adj.* **playability** *n.*

playa /'plæjə/ *n.* a flat area of silt or sand at the bottom of a desert basin, dry except after rain.

play-act *v.* **1** *intr.* act in a play. **2** *intr.* behave affectedly or insincerely. **3** *tr.* act (a scene, part, etc.). □ **play-acting** *n.* **play-actor** *n.*

play-action *n. Football* a play in which the quarterback fakes a hand-off and then passes the ball forward.

playback *n.* a playing back of a recording.

playbill *n.* **1** a poster announcing a theatrical performance. **2** a slate of theatrical productions to be performed in a season etc. **3** a theatre program.

playbook *n. N Amer.* **1** *Sport* (esp. *Football*) a book containing descriptions of a team's strategies and plays. **2** a set of strategies employed by a company etc.

playboy *n.* **1** a sexually promiscuous man. **2** an irresponsible, pleasure-seeking, esp. wealthy man.

play-by-play *n. N Amer.* the verbal description of a sports match etc. as it unfolds, esp. as part of a broadcast (also *attrib.*: *play-by-play announcer*).

playdough *n.* a soft, malleable, coloured doughlike substance used esp. by children for modelling.

playdown *n.* (usu. in *pl.*) esp. *Cdn & Scot. Sport* a playoff match in a tournament etc.

player *n.* **1** a person taking part in a sport or game. **2** a person playing a musical instrument. **3** a person who plays a part on the stage; an actor. **4** a machine that plays audio or video recordings. **5** a person or company important in an industry, activity, etc.

player piano *n.* a piano fitted with an apparatus enabling it to play automatically.

playful *adj.* **1** fond of or inclined to play. **2** done in fun; humorous. □ **playfully** *adv.* **playfulness** *n.*

playground *n.* **1** an outdoor area for children to play on. **2** any place of recreation, e.g. a resort.

playgroup *n.* a group of esp. preschool children who play regularly together under supervision.

playhouse *n.* **1** a theatre. **2** a toy house for children to play in.

playing card *n.* each of a set of usu. 52 cards with an identical pattern on one side and different values represented by numbers and symbols on the other, used to play various games.

playing field *n.* **1** a field used for outdoor team games. **2** the sphere of any competition (*ensured a level playing field for the election*).

playlet *n.* a short play or dramatic piece.

playlist ● *n.* a list of pieces to be played, esp. on a radio show. ● *v.tr.* place on a playlist.

playmaker *n.* a player in a team game who leads attacks or brings other players in the same side into a position to score. □ **playmaking** *n. & attrib.adj.*

playmate *n.* **1** a child's companion in play. **2** a lover.

play money *n.* pieces of paper made to look like money, used in some board games etc.

playoff *n. Sport* **1** (usu. in *pl.*, except when *attrib.*) a tournament played to determine a champion among competitors having advanced from preliminary competition. **2** a game or match in such a tournament. **3** a match played to decide a draw or tie.

play on words *n.* a pun.

playpen *n.* a portable enclosure for young children to play in.

playroom *n.* a room set aside for playing in.

playschool *n.* a nursery school.

playset *n.* a set of swings incorporating a slide, monkey bars, etc.

playsuit *n.* a usu. one-piece outfit combining shorts and a top, worn by children and women.

plaything *n.* **1** a toy or other thing to play with. **2** a person or thing treated as a toy.

playtime *n.* time for play or recreation.

playwright *n.* a person who writes plays.

playwriting *n.* the activity of writing plays.

plaza *n.* **1** *N Amer.* a shopping centre or mall. **2** an open square in an urban area.

plea *n.* **1** an earnest appeal or entreaty. **2** *Law* a formal statement by or on behalf of a defendant., esp. in response to a charge. **3** an argument or excuse.

plea bargaining n. N Amer. an arrangement between prosecutor and defendant whereby the defendant pleads guilty to a lesser charge in the expectation of leniency. □ **plea bargain** n. & v.intr.

plead v. (past and past part. **pleaded** or esp. US **pled**) **1** a intr. make an earnest appeal. **b** tr. say pleadingly. **2** intr. Law address a law court as an advocate on behalf of a party. **3** tr. maintain (a cause) esp. in a law court. **4** tr. Law declare to be one's state as regards guilt in or responsibility for a crime (plead guilty). **5** tr. offer as an excuse (pleaded forgetfulness). □ **pleader** n.

pleading ● n. (usu. in pl.) a formal statement of the cause of an action or defence. ● adj. expressing an earnest entreaty. □ **pleadingly** adv.

pleasant adj. **1** pleasing to the mind, feelings, or senses. **2** polite and friendly. □ **pleasantly** adv. **pleasantness** n.

pleasantry n. (pl. **-ies**) a pleasant or amusing remark, esp. made in casual conversation.

please ● v. **1** tr. & intr. be agreeable (to); make (a person) glad; give pleasure (to). **2** tr. (in passive) **a** (foll. by to + infin.) be glad or willing to (am pleased to help). **b** (often foll. by about, at, with) derive pleasure or satisfaction (from). **3** tr. (with it as subject; usu. foll. by to + infin.) be the wish of (it did not please them to attend). **4** intr. think fit; have the will or desire (take as many as you please). ● interj. **1** used as a polite way of making a request or giving an order (please come in). **2** used to add force to a request or statement (Children, please! I'm trying to work!). **3** used when accepting an offer emphatically ('Do you want some help?' 'Please!'). **4** informal used to express scorn ('He said he was too busy to help.' 'Oh please!'). □ **if you please 1** used in making a polite request (come this way, if you please). **2** used to express annoyance when reporting something, esp. something unexpected. **please God** may God let it happen; if it is pleasing to God (please God, things will improve). **please oneself** do as one likes. □ **pleased** adj. **pleasing** adj. **pleasingly** adv.

pleasurable adj. causing pleasure; agreeable. □ **pleasurably** adv.

pleasure ● n. **1** a feeling of satisfaction or joy. **2** enjoyment. **3** a source of pleasure or gratification. **4** formal the will or desire. **5** sensual gratification or enjoyment (a life of pleasure). **6** (attrib.) done or used for pleasure (pleasure boat). ● v. **1** tr. give (esp. sexual) pleasure to. **2** intr. (often foll. by in) take pleasure. □ **take pleasure in** like doing. **with pleasure** gladly.

pleat ● n. a fold or crease, esp. a flattened fold in cloth doubled upon itself. ● v.tr. (usu. as **pleated** adj.) make a pleat or pleats in. □ **pleating** n.

pleb /pleb/ n. informal usu. derogatory = PLEBEIAN.

plebeian /plɪˈbiːən/ ● n. **1** a commoner, esp. in ancient Rome. **2** derogatory a member of the lower classes, esp. an uncultured one. ● adj. **1** of the common people. **2** uncultured; unrefined.

plebiscite /ˈplebɪˌsaɪt/ n. **1** the direct vote of all electors on an important public question, e.g. a change in the constitution. **2** the public expression of a community's opinion, with or without binding force. □ **plebiscitary** /-ˈbɪsɪteri/ adj.

plectrum /ˈplektrəm/ n. (pl. **-s** or **plectra** /-trə/) **1** a thin flat piece of plastic or horn etc. held in the hand and used to pluck a string, esp. of a guitar. **2** the corresponding mechanical part of a harpsichord etc.

pled esp. US past of PLEAD.

pledge ● n. **1** a solemn promise or undertaking. **2** a thing given as security for the fulfillment of a con-

tract, the payment of a debt, etc., and liable to forfeiture in the event of failure. **3** a thing put in pawn. **4 a** the promise of a donation to charity, a fundraising campaign, etc. **b** such a donation. **5** a thing given as a token of love, favour, or something to come. **6** a toast. **7** a solemn undertaking to abstain from alcohol (sign the pledge). **8** the state of being pledged (goods lying in pledge). ● v. **1** tr. **a** deposit as security. **b** pawn. **2** tr. promise solemnly by the pledge of (one's honour, word, etc.). **3** tr. (often refl.) bind by a solemn promise. **4** tr. & intr. promise solemnly (we pledged our support). **5** tr. commit oneself to donate (a sum).

Pleistocene /ˈplaɪstəˌsiːn/ Geol. ● adj. of or relating to the first epoch of the Quaternary period, lasting from about 2,000,000 to 10,000 years BP. ● n. this geological epoch or system.

plenary /ˈplenəri, ˈpliːn-/ ● adj. **1** entire, unqualified, absolute. **2** (of an assembly, presentation, etc.) to be attended by all members or participants. ● n. (pl. **-ies**) a plenary session etc.

plenipotentiary /ˌplenɪpəˈtenʃieri/ ● n. (pl. **-ies**) a person (esp. a diplomat) invested with the full power of independent action. ● adj. **1** having this power. **2** (of power) absolute.

plenitude n. literary **1** fullness. **2** abundance.

plenteous /ˈplentiəs/ adj. literary plentiful. □ **plenteously** adv. **plenteousness** n.

plentiful adj. abundant, copious. □ **plentifully** adv.

plenty ● n. a situation in which there is an ample supply of food, money, etc. ● pron. (often foll. by of) a great or sufficient quantity or number. ● adj. informal existing in an ample quantity. ● adv. **1** informal fully, entirely (is plenty large enough). **2** a lot (plenty more; it costs plenty).

plenum /ˈpliːnəm/ n. **1** a full assembly of people or a committee etc. **2** Physics space filled with matter.

plethora /ˈpleθrə/ n. **1** an abundance. **2** an excess.

pleura[1] /ˈplʊərə/ n. (pl. **pleurae** /-riː/) **1** each of a pair of serous membranes lining the thorax and enveloping the lungs. **2** lateral extensions of the body wall in arthropods. □ **pleural** adj.

pleura[2] pl. of PLEURON.

pleurisy /ˈplʊərɪsi/ n. inflammation of the pleura, marked by pain in the chest or side, fever, etc.

pleuron /ˈplʊərɒn/ n. (pl. **pleura** /-rə/) = PLEURA[1] 2.

Plexiglas n. proprietary a tough light transparent acrylic thermoplastic used instead of glass.

plexus n. (pl. same or **plexuses**) **1** Anat. **a** a network of nerves or blood vessels in an animal body (solar plexus). **b** a structure consisting of a bundle of minute closely interwoven and intercommunicating fibres or tubes. **2** any network or weblike formation.

pliable adj. **1** bending easily; supple. **2** flexible in disposition or character; compliant. □ **pliability** n.

pliant adj. **1** flexible; able to be bent or folded. **2** (of a person etc.) readily influenced.

pliers n.pl. pincers with gripping jaws usu. having parallel serrated surfaces, used for holding small objects, bending wire, etc.

plight[1] n. an esp. unfortunate condition or state.

plight[2] v.tr. **1** pledge or promise solemnly (one's faith, loyalty, etc.). **2** (foll. by to) engage, esp. in marriage.

Plimsoll line /ˈplɪmsəl/ n. (also **Plimsoll mark**) a marking on a ship's side showing the limit of legal submersion under various sea conditions.

plink ● v.intr. **1** emit a short, sharp, metallic, or ringing sound. **2** play a musical instrument in this manner. ● n. the sound or action of plinking. □ **plinky** adj.

plinth n. **1** the lower square slab at the base of

acolumn or pedestal. **2** a base supporting a vase or statue etc. **3** *Archit.* the projecting part of a wall immediately above the ground.

Pliocene /'plaɪə,siːn/ *Geol.* ● *adj.* of or relating to the last epoch of the Tertiary period, lasting from about 5.1 to 2 million years ago. ● *n.* this geological epoch.

PLO *abbr.* Palestine Liberation Organization.

plod ● *v.* (**plodded, plodding**) **1** *intr.* (often foll. by *along, on*, etc.) walk doggedly or laboriously; trudge. **2** *intr.* work slowly and steadily. **3** *tr.* tread or make (one's way) laboriously. ● *n.* the act or a period of plodding. □ **plodder** *n.* **plodding** *adj.* **ploddingly** *adv.*

plonk[1] ● *v.tr.* set down hurriedly, clumsily, or firmly. ● *n.* a heavy thud, as of one hard object hitting another.

plonk[2] *n. informal* cheap or inferior wine.

plop ● *n.* an abrupt, hollow sound as of a smooth object dropping into water without a splash. ● *v.intr. & tr.* (**plopped, plopping**) **1** make a plop. **2** fall or drop with a plop. □ **plop down** (also **plop oneself down**) sit down abruptly.

plot ● *n.* **1 a** a defined and usu. small piece of ground, esp. one used for a special purpose. **b** a grave or area of graves, esp. as belonging to a particular family. **2** a plan or an outline of the main events in a novel, film, etc. **3** a conspiracy or secret plan, esp. for unlawful purposes. ● *v.* (**plotted, plotting**) **1** *tr. & intr.* plan or contrive secretly (a crime, conspiracy, etc.). **2** *tr.* make a ground plan, map, or diagram of (an existing object, a place or thing to be laid out, constructed, etc.); draw to scale. **3** *tr.* **a** mark (a point or course etc.) on a chart or diagram. **b** divide (land) for registration etc. **4** *tr.* **a** mark out or allocate (points) on a graph. **b** make (a curve etc.) by marking out a number of points on a graph. **5** *tr.* devise the plot of (a novel, film, etc.). □ **plotless** *adj.*

plot line *n.* the main features of the plot of a play, novel, film, etc.

plotter *n.* **1** a person who plots something esp. unlawful. **2** an instrument for automatically plotting a graph etc. **3** a device capable of drawing with a pen under the control of a computer.

ploughman *n.* (*pl.* **-men**) (also **plowman**) a person who uses a plough.

ploughshare *n.* (also **plowshare**) the large cutting blade of a plough.

plover /'plʌvər/ *n.* any plump-breasted shorebird of the family Charadriidae, usu. with a pigeon-like bill.

plow (also **plough**) ● *n.* **1** (often **plough**) a farm implement with a cutting blade fixed in a frame drawn by a tractor or by horses, for cutting furrows in the soil and turning it up. **2** an implement resembling this and having a comparable function, esp. for deflecting material against which it moves (*snowplow*). ● *v.* **1** (often **plough**) *tr. & intr.* make furrows in and turn up (the earth) with a plow, esp. before sowing. **2** *tr.* (often **plough**) **a** (foll. by *out, up, down*, etc.) turn or extract (roots, weeds, etc.) with a plow. **b** (foll. by *under*) bury in the soil by plowing. **3** *tr.* **a** remove (snow) from a surface with a plow. **b** clear (a surface) of snow with a plow. **4** *tr.* furrow or scratch (a surface) with or as if with a plow. **5** *tr.* produce (a furrow or line) in this way. **6** *intr.* (foll. by *through*) advance laboriously, esp. through work, a book, etc. **7** (of a ship etc.) **a** *intr.* (often foll. by *through*) cleave the surface of the water. **b** *tr.* cleave (the surface of the water); cut (a course) through the water. **8** *intr.* (foll. by *through, into*) (esp. of a car etc.) travel or be propelled clumsily or violently into or through (an obstacle). **9** *tr.* (foll. by *into*) invest (money, usu. a large amount) in (a project

etc.). □ **plow back** reinvest (profits) in the business producing them. □ **plowed** *adj.*

plowing match *n.* a rural fair featuring plowing competitions, farm machinery demonstrations, new product displays, and entertainment.

ploy *n. informal* a stratagem; a cunning manoeuvre to gain an advantage.

ploye /plɔɪ/ *n. Cdn* an Acadian buckwheat pancake.

pluck ● *v.* **1** *tr.* (often foll. by *out, off*, etc.) remove by picking or pulling out or away. **2** *tr.* **a** pull off (the feathers, hair, fur, etc.) from. **b** shape or thin (the eyebrows) by removing hairs. **3** *tr.* pull at, esp. abruptly or with a jerk. **4** *intr.* (foll. by *at*) tug or snatch at. **5** *tr.* sound (the string of a musical instrument) by doing this with the finger or pick. **6** *tr.* rescue (a person) from a difficult or unpleasant situation. **7** *tr.* remove (a person) from obscurity. ● *n.* **1** courage, spirit, boldness. **2** an act of plucking; a twitch. □ **pluck up** summon up (courage etc.). □ **plucker** *n.*

plucky *adj.* (**-ier, -iest**) brave, spirited. □ **pluckily** *adv.* **pluckiness** *n.*

plug ● *n.* **1** a piece of solid material fitting tightly into a hole, used to fill a gap or cavity, act as a wedge, stop a sink, etc. **2 a** a device of metal pins in an insulated casing fitting into holes in a socket for making an electrical connection. **b** *informal* an electric socket. **3** = SPARK PLUG 1. **4** *informal* a piece of (often free) publicity for an idea, product, etc. **5** a mass of solidified lava filling the neck of a volcano. **6** a cake or stick of tobacco, esp. for chewing. **7** *Fishing* a lure with one or more hooks attached. **8** a small area of scalp with strong hair growth grafted on to a balding area. **9** esp. *N Amer.* a small piece of turf or pre-planted soil used esp. for filling or seeding a lawn. **10** *N Amer. informal* a baby's pacifier. ● *v.tr.* (**plugged, plugging**) **1** (often foll. by *up*) stop, fill, or obstruct (a hole etc.) with or as if with a plug etc. **2** *informal* seek to popularize (an idea, product, etc.) by repeated recommendation; give free publicity to. **3** *slang* shoot or hit (a person etc.). □ **plug away** *informal* (often foll. by *at*) work steadily away (at); persevere doggedly. **plug a gap** remedy a deficiency. **plug in 1 a** connect electrically by inserting a plug in a socket. **b** be able to be connected by a plug. **2** *informal* incorporate, account for (*must plug in the data*). **plug into** become connected with (a source of information, a trend, etc.).

plug and play *n. Computing* a standard of compatibility for peripherals, software, etc. that makes installation simpler by allowing automatic configuration of the system.

plugged *adj.* **1** stopped up, closed, or filled with a plug. **2** esp. *N Amer.* (of a coin) having a portion removed and the space filled with base material.

plugged-in *adj.* **1** connected by means of a plug. **2** *informal* aware of what is happening, in fashion etc.

plugged nickel *n. N Amer.* (also **plug nickel**) a negligible amount (*not worth a plugged nickel*).

plugger *n.* **1** a person who or thing which plugs something. **2** *N Amer. informal* = DIGGER 4.

plug-in ● *adj.* able to be connected by means of a plug. ● *n.* **1** a plug-in device or unit. **2** *Cdn* an electrical outlet in a garage, near a parking space, etc. for plugging in the block heater of a car etc.

plum ● *n.* **1 a** an oval fleshy fruit, usu. purple, reddish, or yellow when ripe, with sweet pulp and a flattish pointed stone. **b** (also **plum tree**) any of various deciduous trees of the genus *Prunus* (rose family), esp. *P. domestica*, which bears this fruit. **2** a deep reddish-purple colour. **3** a highly desirable thing; the pick of a collection, esp. a choice appointment etc. ● *adj.* **1** (also **plum-coloured**) of a reddish-purple colour. **2** choice, valuable, coveted.

plumage /'pluːmɪdʒ/ *n.* a bird's feathers. □ **plumaged** *adj.* (usu. in *comb.*).

plumb¹ ● *n.* a ball of lead or other heavy material, esp. one attached to the end of a line for finding the depth of water or determining the vertical. ● *adv.* **1** exactly (*plumb in the centre*). **2** vertically, perpendicularly, straight down. **3** *N Amer. slang* completely (*plumb crazy*). ● *adj.* **1** vertical, perpendicular. **2** downright, sheer (*plumb nonsense*). ● *v.tr.* **1 a** measure the depth of (water) with a plumb. **b** determine (a depth). **2 a** test (an upright surface) to determine the vertical. **b** make vertical. **3** emotionally reach or experience (*plumb the depths of fear*). **4** get to the bottom of, learn in detail the facts about (a matter). □ **out of** (or **off**) **plumb** not vertical.

plumb² *v.* **1** *tr.* provide (a building or room etc.) with plumbing. **2** *tr.* (often foll. by *in*) fit as part of a plumbing system. **3** *intr.* work as a plumber.

plumb bob *n.* = PLUMB¹.

plumber *n.* a person who fits and repairs the water pipes, water tanks, etc. in a building.

plumber's friend *n.* (also **plumber's helper**) a plunger.

plumber's snake *n.* a long flexible wire for clearing obstacles in pipes, toilets, etc.

plumbing *n.* **1** the system of water pipes etc. in a building. **2** *jocular* **a** the excretory system. **b** the reproductive system. **3** the work of a plumber.

plumb line *n.* a line with a plumb attached.

plume ● *n.* **1** a feather, esp. a large one used for ornament. **2** a trail of vapour etc. issuing from a localized source and spreading out as the trail travels (*a plume of smoke*). **3** an ornament of feathers etc. attached to a headdress etc., usu. symbolizing dignity or rank. **4** a feather-like part or formation. ● *v.* **1** *tr.* decorate or provide with a plume or plumes. **2** *intr.* (of a trail of smoke, vapour, etc.) form a plume. **3** *tr.* (of a bird) preen (itself or its feathers). □ **plumed** *adj.* **plumelike** *adj.*

plummet ● *v.intr.* (**plummeted**, **plummeting**) drop, fall, or plunge rapidly. ● *n.* **1** a plumb or plumb line. **2** a sounding line. **3** a weight attached to a fishing line to keep the float upright.

plummy *adj.* (**-ier**, **-iest**) **1 a** resembling a plum or plums, esp. in taste or colour. **b** consisting of or rich in plums. **2** *informal* (of a voice) deep, thick-sounding, esp. as supposedly characteristic of the British upper classes. **3** *informal* good, desirable.

plump¹ ● *adj.* having a full rounded shape; fleshy; filled out. ● *v.tr. & intr.* (often foll. by *up*, *out*) make or become plump. □ **plumpish** *adj.* **plumpness** *n.* **plumpy** *adj.*

plump² ● *v.* **1** *intr. & tr.* (often foll. by *down*) drop, fall, or set down abruptly, esp. heavily or with a dull thud (*plumped down on the chair*). **2** *intr.* (foll. by *for*) decide, campaign, etc. in favour of (one of two or more possibilities). ● *n.* an abrupt plunge; a heavy fall.

plum pudding *n.* a rich boiled or steamed suet pudding with raisins, currants, spices, etc., traditionally served at Christmas.

plum sauce *n.* a yellowish brown, slightly sweet sauce made from salted plums, vinegar, sugar, and spices, used as a condiment in Chinese cuisine.

plum tomato *n.* a plum-shaped tomato.

plunder ● *v.* **1** *tr. & intr.* rob (a place or person), esp. systematically or as in war. **2** *tr. & intr.* steal or embezzle (goods). **3** *tr.* steal from (another's writings etc.). ● *n.* **1** the violent or dishonest acquisition of property. **2** property acquired by plundering. **3** *informal* profit, gain. □ **plunderer** *n.*

plunge ● *v.* **1** (usu. foll. by *in*, *into*) **a** *tr.* thrust forcefully or abruptly. **b** *intr.* dive; propel oneself forcibly. **c** *intr. & tr.* enter or cause to enter a certain condition or embark on a certain course abruptly or impetuously (*plunged into a lively discussion*; *the room was plunged into darkness*). **2** *tr.* immerse completely. **3** *intr.* **a** move suddenly and dramatically downward. **b** (foll. by *down*, *into*, etc.) move with a rush (*plunged down the stairs*). **c** diminish rapidly. **4** *intr.* (of currency, prices, etc.) drop sharply in value or amount. **5** *intr.* (of a horse) start violently forward. **6** *intr.* (of a ship) pitch. ● *n.* **1** a sudden violent movement or fall. **2** an act of jumping or diving. □ **take the plunge** *informal* **1** take a decisive first step; commit oneself irrevocably to a course of action. **2** get married.

plunge pool *n.* **1** a deep basin excavated at the foot of a waterfall by the falling water. **2** a cold water pool, esp. forming part of the equipment of a sauna.

plunger *n.* **1** a part of a mechanism that works with a plunging or thrusting movement. **2** a rubber cup on a handle for clearing blocked pipes by a plunging and sucking action.

plunk ● *n.* **1** the sound made by the sharply plucked string of a stringed instrument. **2** *N Amer.* the sound of something dropping, esp. heavily. ● *v.* **1** *N Amer.* (often foll. by *down*) *tr. & intr.* drop down heavily or abruptly. **2 a** *tr.* cause (a string) to sound with a plunk; play (a note) with a plunk. **b** *intr.* sound with a plunk. □ **plunk down** spend (money).

pluperfect /pluː'pɜːfɪkt/ ● *adj.* **1** *Grammar* (of a tense) denoting an action completed prior to some past point of time specified or implied, formed in English by *had* and the past participle, as: *he had gone by then*. **2** esp. *N Amer. informal* more than perfect; complete, thorough. ● *n.* the pluperfect tense.

plural ● *adj.* **1** a more than one in number. **b** (of a society etc.) composed of or reflecting different ethnic groups or cultural traditions. **2** *Grammar* (of a word or form) denoting more than one, or (in languages with dual number) more than two. ● *n.* *Grammar* **1** a plural word. **2** the plural number. □ **plurally** *adv.*

pluralism *n.* **1 a** a form of society in which the members of minority groups maintain their independent cultural traditions. **b** the toleration or acceptance of a diversity of opinions, values, theories, etc. **2 a** a political theory or system of power-sharing among a number of political parties. **b** a theory or system of devolution and autonomy for individual bodies rather than monolithic state control. **3** *Philos.* **a** a theory or system that recognizes more than one ultimate principle (*compare* MONISM 2). **b** the theory that the knowable world is made up of a plurality of interacting things. **4** the holding of more than one office, esp. an ecclesiastical office, at a time. □ **pluralist** *n.* **pluralistic** *adj.* **pluralistically** *adv.*

plurality *n.* (*pl.* **-ies**) **1** the state or fact of being plural. **2 a** a large number or quantity; a multitude. **b** the greater number or part; more than half of the whole. **3** *N Amer.* **a** the number of votes cast for a candidate who receives more than any other but does not receive an absolute majority. **b** the number by which this exceeds the number of votes cast for the candidate placing second. **4** = PLURALISM 4.

pluralize *v.* **1** *tr. & intr.* make or become plural. **2** *tr.* express in or form the plural. □ **pluralization** *n.*

plus ● *prep.* **1 a** *Math.* made more by, increased by (3 *plus 4 equals* 7). Symbol: +. **b** with the addition of, inclusive of (*five plus me*). **2** (of temperature) above zero (*plus 2° C*). **3** *informal* with; having gained; newly possessing (*returned plus a new car*). ● *adj.* **1** (after a number) at least; more than indicated (*fifteen plus*). **2 a** (after a grade etc.) rather better than (*B plus*). **b** *informal* of superior quality, excellent in its kind. **3** *Math.* positive. **4** having a positive electrical charge. **5** *N Amer.* (of a women's clothing size) designed for people larger and usu. heavier than most. ● *n.* (*pl.* **-es**) **1** = PLUS SIGN. **2** *Math.* an additional or positive quantity. **3** an advantage; a positive quality (*experience is a plus*). ● *conj. informal disputed* and furthermore (*they arrived late, plus they were hungry*). ¶ The use of *plus* as a conjunction is considered incorrect by some. It is to be avoided in formal writing. □ **on the plus side** as an advantage. **plus or minus 1** give or take, add or subtract. **2** more or less, roughly.

Plus-15 *n. Cdn* (in Calgary) an enclosed overhead walkway between buildings.

plus ça change /plu: sa ʃaʒ/ *interj.* expressing the intrinsic immutability of human nature.

plush ● *n.* a type of cloth with a cut pile surface like, but longer and smoother than, velvet. ● *adj.* **1** made of or resembling plush. **2** stylish, luxurious. □ **plushness** *n.* **plushy** *adj.* (**-ier, -iest**).

plus-minus *n. Hockey* (also **plus/minus**) a statistic indicating a player's effectiveness on offence and defence, adjusted every time an even-strength goal is scored while the player is on the ice.

plus sign *n.* the symbol +, indicating addition or a positive value.

plutocracy /plu:'tɒkrəsi/ *n.* (*pl.* **-ies**) **1 a** government by the wealthy. **b** a nation governed in this way. **2 a** wealthy elite or ruling class.

plutocrat /'plu:tə,kræt/ *n.* **1** *derogatory* a wealthy and influential person. **2** a member of a plutocracy or wealthy elite. □ **plutocratic** *adj.*

plutonium /plu:'to:niəm/ *n.* a dense silvery radioactive metallic element of the actinide series, used in some nuclear reactors and weapons.

ply¹ *n.* (*pl.* **-ies**) **1** a thickness or layer of certain materials, esp. wood, cloth, or tissue paper (*three-ply*). **2** = PLYWOOD *n.* **3** a strand or twist of rope, yarn, or thread. **4** a reinforcing layer of fabric in a tire.

ply² *v.* (**-ies, -ied**) **1** *tr.* work steadily at (one's business or trade). **2 a** *intr.* (often foll. by *between*) (of a vehicle, esp. a ship) travel regularly (to and fro between two points). **b** *tr.* work (a route) in this way. **3** *tr.* (foll. by *with*) **a** supply (a person) continuously (with food, drink, etc.). **b** approach repeatedly (with questions, demands, etc.). **4** *tr.* use or wield vigorously (a tool, weapon, etc.). **5** *intr.* (of a taxi driver etc.) attend regularly for custom (*ply for trade*).

Plymouth Brethren /'plɪməθ/ *n.pl.* a strict Calvinistic religious body formed *c.*1830, having no formal creed and no official order of ministers.

plywood ● *n.* a strong warp-resistant board consisting of two or more layers of wood glued and pressed together with the directions of the grains alternating. ● *adj.* of or made of plywood.

PM *abbr.* **1** Prime Minister. **2** post-mortem.

Pm *symbol* promethium.

p.m. *abbr.* (also **P.M.**) after noon.

PMG *abbr.* Postmaster General.

PMO *abbr. Cdn* PRIME MINISTER'S OFFICE.

PMS *abbr.* premenstrual syndrome.

PNE *abbr. Cdn* Pacific National Exhibition.

pneumatic /nu:'mætɪk, nju:-/ *adj.* **1** of or relating to air, wind, or gases. **2** containing or operated by compressed air. **3** connected with or containing air cavities esp. in the bones of birds or in fish. □ **pneumatically** *adv.*

pneumatic drill *n.* a heavy, mechanical drill driven by compressed air, for breaking up a hard surface.

pneumocystis carinii pneumonia /nu:məu,sɪstɪs kə'raɪniaɪ, nju:-/ *n.* = PCP 2.

pneumonia *n.* a bacterial or other infection causing inflammation of the lungs causing the air sacs to fill with pus and become solid.

pneumonic plague /nju:'mɒnɪk/ *n. see* PLAGUE *n.* 1a.

PNG *abbr.* Papua New Guinea.

PO *abbr.* **1** Post Office. **2** postal order. **3** purchase order. **4** PETTY OFFICER.

Po *symbol* polonium.

poach¹ *v.tr.* cook (a shelled egg, fish, etc.) in simmering water. □ **poacher** *n.*

poach² *v.* **1** *tr. & intr.* catch (game or fish) illegally. **2** *intr.* (often foll. by *on*) trespass or encroach (on another's property, ideas, etc.). **3** *tr.* appropriate illicitly or unfairly (a person, thing, idea, etc.). □ **poacher** *n.*

pock ● *n.* **1 a** small pus-filled spot on the skin, esp. caused by chicken pox etc. **2 a** scar or pit left by a pustule, pimple, etc. **b** a disfiguring mark, hole, or pit. ● *v.tr.* mark with pocks or disfiguring spots. □ **pocked** *adj.* **pocky** *adj.*

pocket ● *n.* **1** a small bag sewn into or on clothing, for carrying small articles. **2 a** a pouchlike compartment in a suitcase, car door, etc. **b** any small bag-like pouch, esp. made of pastry etc. **3** one's financial resources. **4 a** an isolated group or area contrasted with or differing from its surroundings (*a few pockets of resistance*). **b** a wide or deep hollow among hills or mountains; a distinct area of depth within a pond or lake, etc. **5** a cavity in a rock or stratum. **6** a pouch at the corner or on the side of a billiard table or snooker table into which balls are driven. **7 a** = AIR POCKET. **b** a local atmospheric condition. **8** (*attrib.*) **a** of a suitable size and shape for carrying in a pocket. **b** smaller than the usual size. **9 a** *Sport* a position in a race etc. in which a competitor is hemmed in by others and has no chance of winning. **b** *Football* a shielded area formed by blockers, from which the quarterback throws a pass. **c** *Baseball* the deep centre of a baseball mitt or glove. ● *v.tr.* (**pocketed, pocketing**) **1** put into one's pocket. **2** take possession of or appropriate, esp. dishonestly. **3** confine or enclose in a small space. **4** *Sport* hem in (a competitor) during a race so as to remove the chance of winning. **5** conceal or suppress (one's feelings). **6** *Billiards etc.* drive (a ball) into a pocket. □ **dig into one's pockets** spend or provide money. **in pocket 1** having gained in a transaction. **2** (of money) available. **in a person's pocket 1** under a person's control. **2** close to or intimate with a person. **out of pocket** having lost in a transaction. □ **pocketable** *adj.* **pocketful** *n.*

pocketbook *n. N Amer.* **1** one's stock of cash or financial resources. **2** (**pocket book**) a small book.

pocket door *n.* a sliding door which emerges from and disappears into a narrow, door-sized recess contained in the adjacent wall.

pocket gopher *n.* = GOPHER 2.

pocket knife *n.* a knife with a folding blade.

pocket money *n.* **1** money for minor expenses. **2** esp. *Brit.* an allowance of money made to a child.

pocket protector *n.* **1** a plastic insert for a shirt pocket, designed to protect the garment from rips and ink stains caused by pens. **2** this viewed as typical of the attire of a computer nerd.

pocket-sized adj. (also **pocket-size**) **1** small enough to be carried in a pocket. **2** petty, small-scale.

pocket watch n. a watch intended to be carried in the pocket of a waistcoat, jacket, etc.

pockmark n. = POCK n. 2. □ **pockmarked** adj.

PO'd adj. annoyed.

pod¹ ● n. **1** a long seed vessel esp. of a leguminous plant, e.g. a pea. **2 a** a streamlined compartment suspended under an aircraft for an engine, fuel tanks, equipment etc. **b** a detachable compartment in a spacecraft. **3** any protruding, detachable, or more or less enclosed part of a tool, craft, vehicle, etc. **4** the cocoon of a silkworm. ● v. (**podded, podding**) **1** intr. bear, form, or have a pod or pods. **2** tr. remove (peas etc.) from pods. □ **podded** adj.

pod² n. a small group of marine animals, esp. whales.

podiatry /pə'daiətri/ n. esp. N Amer. a medical specialty involving the care of the feet and treatment of foot disorders. □ **podiatrist** n.

podium n. (pl. **-s** or **-dia**) **1** a raised platform or dais at the front of a hall or stage. **2** a platform from which a conductor conducts an orchestra etc. **3** a lectern.

poem n. **1** a metrical composition of words expressing facts, thoughts, feelings, or imaginative description. **2** an esp. non-metrical composition of words having some esp. aesthetic quality or qualities in common with poetry. **3** something, other than a composition of words, with poetic qualities.

poesy /'po:əzi/ n. literary **1** poetry. **2** the art or composition of poetry.

poet n. **1** a writer of poems. **2** a person possessing high powers of imagination or expression etc.

poetess n. often offensive a female poet.

poetic adj. (also **poetical**) **1 a** of, like, or pertaining to poetry or poets. **b** written in verse. **2** elevated or sublime in expression. □ **poetically** adv.

poetic justice n. well-deserved unforeseen retribution or reward.

poetic licence n. a writer's or artist's transgression of established rules of language for effect.

poetics n. **1** the art of writing poetry. **2** the study of poetry and its techniques.

Poet Laureate n. a poet honoured by a state as its most eminent or representative.

poetry n. **1 a** the expression or embodiment of beautiful or elevated thought, imagination, or feeling, in language and a form adapted to stir the imagination and the emotions. **b** composition in verse, metrical language, or some equivalent patterned arrangement of language. **2** poems collectively. **3** a poetic or tenderly pleasing quality. **4** anything compared to poetry.

pogey n. (also **pogy**) Cdn informal **1** unemployment insurance benefits. **2** welfare benefits.

pogo ● n. (pl. **-os**) **1** (in full **pogo stick**) a toy consisting of a spring-loaded stick with rests for the feet, for jumping about on. **2** (**Pogo**) Cdn proprietary (in full **Pogo stick**) a hot dog covered in cornmeal batter, deep-fried or baked, and served on a stick. **3** a dance with movements suggestive of jumping on a toy pogo stick. ● v.intr. **1** (also **pogo-stick**) move or jump on or as on a toy pogo stick. **2** dance the pogo.

pogrom /po:'grom, 'pogrəm, -rom/ n. **1** an organized massacre, originally and especially of Jews in Russia. **2** an organized, officially tolerated attack on any community or group.

poi /pɔi/ n. a Hawaiian dish made from the fermented root of the taro, *Colocasia esculenta*.

poignant /'poinjənt/ adj. **1 a** deeply moving, touching. **b** painfully sharp to the emotions or senses; distressing. **2** arousing sympathy. □ **poignancy** n. (also **poignance**). **poignantly** adv.

poinsettia /poin'setə, -setiə/ n. a shrub, *Euphorbia pulcherrima*, with large esp. scarlet bracts surrounding small yellow flowers.

point ● n. **1** the sharp or tapered end of a tool, weapon, pencil, etc. **2** a tip, apex, extreme end, or sharp projection. **3** Math. that which is conceived as having a position, but no extent, magnitude, or dimension, e.g. the intersection of two lines. **4 a** a specific place or position, esp. as being in a particular direction etc. (*points south*; *point of contact*). **b** (in the Presbyterian and United churches) each of the individual congregations served by a common minister (*Rev. Bisset's two-point charge in southern Ontario*). **5 a** a precise or particular moment at which something happens (*at the point of death*). **b** the critical or decisive moment for action (*when it came to the point, he refused*). **6** a very small mark on a surface; a speck. **7 a** a dot or other punctuation mark, esp. a period. **b** any of various dots or small strokes used in Semitic languages to indicate vowels or distinguish consonants. **8** = DECIMAL POINT. **9** a step, stage, or degree in progress, development, increase, or decrease (*at that point we gave up*). **10** a level of temperature at which a change of state occurs (*freezing point*). **11** a separate or single item, element, detail, or particular (*it is a point of principle*). **12 a** a unit of count in scoring in a game etc. **b** a unit in appraising the qualities of a competitor or of an exhibit in a competitive show. **c** a unit of credit toward an award, benefit, etc. **d** an advantage or success in an argument, discussion, or other less quantifiable contexts (*scored points with the boss*). **13 a** a recognized unit in quoting variations in price or value, as of stocks and shares etc. **b** a percentage point in quoting interest rates. **c** a unit of weight (2 mg) for diamonds. **14 a** (usu. prec. by *the*) a topic or subject for discussion, esp. the essential or most important part of a discourse (*that was the point of the question*). **b** (usu. with *neg.* or *interrog.*; often foll. by *in*) sense, purpose, advantage, or value (*saw no point in staying*). **15** a distinctive or distinguishing feature, quality, or characteristic, esp. as the basis for a judgment (*tact is not his strong point*). **16** a marking woven into a Hudson's Bay blanket to indicate weight. **17 a** each of 32 directions marked at equal distances around the circumference of a compass. **b** the corresponding direction toward the horizon. **18** (usu. in pl.) (in an engine) **a** either of the metal pieces on a spark plug between which the spark jumps. **b** either of the metal surfaces of a contact breaker which touch to complete the circuit in the distributor of a motor vehicle. **19 a** Hockey either of two areas to the left and right of the net, just inside the blue line where it meets the boards (*a shot from the point*). **b** Basketball a frontcourt position, usu. manned by the guard who sets up the team's defence. **20** Lacrosse **a** a player stationed a short distance in front of the goalkeeper and behind the cover-point. **b** this position. **21** a tapering piece of land jutting out into a body of water. **22** Printing a unit of measurement for type bodies (in the UK and N America 0.0138 in.). ● v. **1 a** tr. (usu. foll. by *to*) indicate or direct (a person, a person's attention, etc.). **b** tr. (usu. foll. by *at*) direct, level, or aim (a finger, weapon, etc.). **c** intr. direct attention in a certain direction (*pointed to the house* *across the road).* **d** *intr. Computing* use a device such as a mouse to move the cursor until it reaches a desired item. **2** *intr.* (foll. by *at, toward*) **a** lie, face, or have its point or length directed in a certain direction etc. (*the needle points north*). **b** have a motion or tendency toward, to do, etc. **3** *intr.* (foll. by *to*) suggest, indicate, or be evidence of (*it all points to murder*). **4** *tr.* give point or force to (words or actions). **5** *tr.* fill in or repair the joints of (brickwork) with smoothly finished mortar or cement. **6** *tr.* **a** punctuate. **b** insert points indicating vowels etc. in (written Hebrew etc.). **7** *tr.* sharpen (a pencil, tool, etc.). **8** *tr. & intr.* (of a dog) indicate the presence of (game) by acting as pointer. **9** *tr.* extend (the toes or feet) so as to form a point. □ **at** (or **in**) **all points** in every part or respect. **at the point of** on the verge of; about to do (the action specified). **beside the point** irrelevant or irrelevantly. **case in point** an instance that is relevant or (prec. by *the*) under consideration. **have a point** be correct or effective in one's contention. **make** (or **prove**) **a** (or **one's**) **point** establish a proposition; prove one's contention. **make a point of** (often foll. by verbal noun) **1** insist on; treat or regard as essential. **2** make a special project of (doing). **on** (or **upon**) **the point of** (foll. by verbal noun) about to do (the action specified). **point out** (often foll. by *that* + clause) indicate, show; draw attention to. **point up** emphasize; show as important. **score points off** get the better of in an argument etc. **take a person's point 1** concede that a person has made a valid contention. **2** understand the import or significance of what a person is saying. **to the point** relevant or relevantly. **to the point of** to the stage of; to such a degree as to justify. **up to a (certain) point** to some extent, but by no means completely.

point-and-click *n.* (*attrib.*) designating computer interfaces where the user selects an action by pointing the cursor to an icon on the screen and clicks with a mouse to initiate the action.

point-and-shoot ● *attrib.adj.* designating a camera which does not require any manual adjustments to advance the film or take properly exposed and focused photographs. ● *n.* a point-and-shoot camera.

point-blank ● *adj.* **1 a** (of a shooting distance or range) very close to the target. **b** (of a shot or shooting) aimed or fired from or within such a range. **2** (of a remark, question, etc.) straightforward, blunt, direct. ● *adv.* **1** at very close range. **2** directly, bluntly, straightforwardly.

point blanket *n.* a type of Hudson's Bay blanket with distinctive markings or points, usu. in the form of short black lines, woven in to indicate weight.

point-counterpoint *n.* a situation in which opposing views etc. are heard in alternation.

pointe /point/ *n. Ballet* **1** the tip of the toe or toes, or the toe of a pointe shoe. **2** (in full **pointe work**) dance performed on the tips of the toes.

pointed *adj.* **1** sharpened or tapering to a point. **2** (of a remark etc.) a penetrating, cutting, having particular force. **b** precisely aimed, exactly directed. **3** emphasized; made evident. **4** having a point of a specified kind. □ **pointedly** *adv.* **pointedness** *n.*

pointer *n.* **1** a thing that points, e.g. the index hand of a gauge etc. **2** a rod for pointing to features on a map, chart, etc. **3** *informal* a hint, clue, or indication; a suggestion. **4** *Computing* a numerical representation of the address in memory of a piece of data, esp. as part of a composite data type. **5** a dog of a breed that on scenting game stands rigid looking toward it. **6** *Cdn* a flat-bottomed rowboat, pointed at both ends and

having a shallow draft, used by loggers. **7** a movable image on a computer screen, often in the shape of an arrow, used to activate a window, point to an icon, etc. **8** (usu. prec. by a numeral) a thing having or earning so many points (*a three-pointer*).

pointe shoe *n.* a soft heelless shoe worn by female ballet dancers, with a stiffened toe allowing the dancer to dance on the tip of the toes.

point form *n.* an abbreviated form of writing, not using full sentences or developed paragraphs.

point guard *n. Basketball* a small fast guard with good ball-handling skills who directs the team's offence.

pointillism /ˈpwæntɪˌlɪzəm/ *n. Art* a technique of Impressionist painting in which luminous effects are produced by tiny dots of pure colours, which seem to blend when viewed. □ **pointillist** *n. & adj.*

pointing *n.* **1** *in senses of* POINT *v.* **2 a** cement or mortar filling the joints of brickwork. **b** facing produced by this. **c** the process of producing this.

pointless *adj.* **1** lacking force, purpose, or meaning. **2** without a sharp or tapering point; having a rounded or blunt end. **3** (in games) without a point scored. □ **pointlessly** *adv.* **pointlessness** *n.*

point man *n.* esp. *N Amer.* **1** the soldier at the head of a patrol. **2** a person who leads a new endeavour etc. **3** *Hockey* the player taking a position at the point during a power play.

point of departure *n.* **1** an initial assumption or the starting point of a thought, action, etc. **2** a time or place at which a journey begins.

point of honour *n.* an action or circumstance that affects one's reputation.

point of no return *n.* a point in a journey or enterprise at which it becomes essential or more practical to continue to the end.

point of order *n.* a query in a debate etc. as to whether correct procedure is being followed.

point of reference *n.* = REFERENCE POINT.

point-of-sale *n.* (also **point-of-purchase**) (usu. *attrib.*) designating, pertaining to, for use at, or associated with the place at which goods are retailed.

point of view *n.* **1** a position from which a thing is viewed. **2** a particular way of considering a matter. **3** (in fiction etc.) the narrator's position relative to the story being told (*first-person point of view*).

point source *n.* a source of light, sound, etc. of negligible dimensions.

point spread *n.* esp. *N Amer.* the number of points constituting the margin by which a stronger team is expected to defeat a weaker one, for betting purposes.

point-to-point *adj.* (of a dedicated communication link etc.) joining only two nodes in a network.

pointy *adj.* (**-ier, -iest**) having a noticeably sharp end; pointed.

pointy-headed *adj. N Amer. informal derogatory* supposedly expert or intellectual (*pointy-headed bureaucrat*). □ **pointy head** *n.*

poise ● *n.* **1** composure or self-possession of manner. **2** equilibrium; a stable state. **3** carriage (of the head etc.). ● *v.* (usu. in *passive*) **1** *tr.* balance; hold suspended or supported. **2** *tr.* carry (one's head etc. in a specified way). **3** *intr.* hover in the air etc.

poised *adj.* **1** composed, self-assured. **2** (often foll. by *for,* or *to* + infin.) ready for action.

poison ● *n.* **1 a** a substance that when absorbed by a living organism causes death or injury, esp. quickly. **2** a harmful influence or principle etc. ● *v.tr.* **1** administer poison to. **2** kill or injure or infect (a person or animal) with poison. **3** infect (air, water, etc.) with poison. **4** (esp. as **poisoned** adj.) treat (a weapon) with poison. **5** corrupt or pervert (a person or mind). **6** spoil or destroy (a person's pleasure etc.). **7** render (land etc.) unusable, e.g. by the accumulation of chemicals or toxins etc. □ **what's your poison?** informal what can I get you to drink? □ **poisoner** n. **poisoning** n. **poisonous** adj. **poisonously** adv.

poison gas n. = GAS n. 5.

poison ivy n. a N American climbing plant, Rhus radicans, secreting an irritant oil from its leaves.

poison oak n. either of two N American shrubs, Rhus toxicodendron and R. diversilobia, related to poison ivy and having similar properties.

poison pill n. **1** a pill containing esp. fast-acting poison. **2** any of various ploys used by a company threatened with an unwelcome takeover bid to make itself unattractive to the bidder.

poison sumac n. a small tree or shrub with pinnate leaves, Rhus vernix, of eastern N America, related to poison ivy and having similar properties.

poke[1] ● v. **1** (foll. by in, up, down, etc.) **a** tr. thrust or push with the hand, point of a stick, etc. **b** intr. be thrust forward. **2** intr. (foll. by at etc.) make thrusts with a stick etc. **3** tr. **a** thrust the end of a finger etc. against. **b** informal punch, hit. **4** tr. (foll. by in) produce (a hole etc. in a thing) by poking. **5** tr. thrust forward, esp. obtrusively (poked her head out of the window). **6** tr. stir (a fire) with a poker. **7** intr. (often foll. by along) move or go slowly or in an aimless manner. **8** tr. & intr. (foll. by around, about) pry; search casually. ● n. **1** the act or an instance of poking. **2** a thrust or nudge. □ **poke fun at** ridicule, tease.

poke[2] n. hist. a small miners' bag for nuggets etc.

poke[3] n. = POKEWEED.

poke check n. Hockey a defensive play in which a player holds his or her stick low along the ice and pokes the puck out of the puck carrier's control. □ **poke-check** v.tr. **poke-checking** n.

poker[1] n. a stiff metal rod for stirring an open fire.

poker[2] n. a card game in which bluff is used as players bet on the value of their hands.

poker face n. the impassive countenance appropriate to a poker player. □ **poker-faced** adj.

poker run n. (also **poker derby**) Cdn a competition in which participants race to a series of points (usu. over a large area) collecting one playing card at each, the winner being determined by a combination of time taken and the poker hand collected.

pokeweed n. a tall N American plant, Phytolacca americana, with spikes of cream flowers and purple berries that yield emetics and purgatives.

pokey n. esp. N Amer. slang prison.

poky adj. (**-ier, -iest**) **1** (of a room etc.) small and cramped. **2** N Amer. annoyingly slow. □ **pokiness** n.

pol n. N Amer. informal a politician.

polack n. N Amer. offensive a person of Polish origin.

polar adj. **1 a** of or near a pole of the earth or a celestial body, or of the celestial sphere. **b** (of a species or variety) living in the north polar region. **2** having magnetic polarity. **3 a** (of a molecule) having a positive charge at one end and a negative charge at the other. **b** (of a compound) having electric charges. **4** Math. of or relating to a pole. **5** directly opposite in character or tendency.

polar bear n. a very large white bear, Ursus maritimus, of Arctic regions.

polar bear swim n. (also **polar bear dip**) N Amer. an organized swim in cold or partially ice-covered water, esp. on a holiday such as New Year's Day.

polar cap n. a region of ice or other frozen matter surrounding a pole of a planet.

polar coordinates n. a system by which a point can be located with reference to two angles.

polar desert n. a type of arid region found near the poles, characterized by frost-shattered rock, small flowering plants, and few or no lichens or mosses.

Polar Fleece n. proprietary a thick fleece fabric.

polar ice cap n. = POLAR CAP.

Polaris /pə'lɑrəs, pə-/ n. a type of submarine-launched ballistic missile.

polarity /pə'lerɪti/ n. (pl. **-ies**) **1** the tendency of a lodestone, magnetized bar, etc., to point with its extremities to the magnetic poles of the earth. **2** the condition of having two poles with contrary qualities. **3** the state of having two opposite tendencies, opinions, etc. **4** the electrical condition of a body (positive or negative).

polarize v. **1** tr. restrict the vibrations of (a transverse wave, esp. light) to one direction. **2** tr. give magnetic or electric polarity to (a substance or body). **3** tr. & intr. divide into two groups of opposing opinion etc. □ **polarization** n. **polarizer** n.

Polaroid n. proprietary **1** a type of camera with internal processing that produces a finished print rapidly after each exposure. **2** a photograph taken with this.

Pole n. **1** a native or national of Poland. **2** a person of Polish descent.

pole[1] ● n. **1** a long slender rounded piece of wood, metal, etc., esp. with the end placed in the ground as a support etc. **2** Athletics a long slender flexible rod used by a competitor in pole vaulting. **3** esp. N Amer. = FISHING ROD. ● v. **1** tr. provide with poles. **2** tr. push or propel (a boat etc.) with a pole. **3** intr. use poles, esp. to propel a boat or oneself on skis.

pole[2] n. **1** (in full **north pole, south pole**) **a** each of the two points in the celestial sphere about which the stars appear to revolve. **b** each of the extremities of the axis of rotation of the earth or another body. **c** see MAGNETIC POLE. ¶The spelling is North Pole and South Pole when used as geographical designations. **2** each of the two opposite points on the surface of a magnet at which magnetic forces are strongest. **3** each of two terminals (positive and negative) of an electric cell or battery etc. **4** each of two opposed principles or ideas. **5** Math. each of two points in which the axis of a circle cuts the surface of a sphere. **6** a fixed point to which others are referred. □ **be poles apart** differ greatly, esp. in nature or opinion. □ **poleward** adj. **polewards** adj. & adv.

poleaxe ● n. a battle-axe. ● v.tr. **1** hit or kill with or as if with a poleaxe. **2** (usu. passive) affect (a person) very greatly with surprise, distress, etc.

polecat n. N Amer. a skunk.

polemic /pə'lemɪk/ ● n. **1** a controversial discussion. **2** Politics a verbal or written attack, esp. on a political opponent. **3** (in pl.; also treated as sing.) the art of controversial discussion, esp. in theology. ● adj. (also **polemical**) controversial. □ **polemically** adv. **polemicist** /-sɪst/ n.

polenta /pə'lentə/ n. cornmeal boiled in water and often baked or fried.

pole position n. the most favourable position at the start of a motor race.

pole vault n. the sport of vaulting over a high bar with the aid of a long flexible pole. □ **pole-vault** v.intr. **pole vaulter** n.

police ● n. (treated as pl.) **1** (usu. prec. by the) a civil force responsible for enforcing the law, maintaining public order, etc. **2** the members of a police force (*several hundred police*). **3** a force with similar functions of enforcing regulations (*military police*). **4** a group, often self-appointed, which criticizes or attempts to stop practices that it considers unacceptable (*fashion police*). ● *v.tr.* **1** control (a country or area) by means of police. **2** provide with police. **3** keep order in; control.

police action *n.* **1** the deeds or activity of the police. **2** military intervention without a formal declaration of war.

police constable *n.* = CONSTABLE 1. Abbr.: **PC**.

police dog *n.* a dog used in police work.

police force *n.* the body of police of a city etc.

police informer *n.* a person who gives police information about crimes and offenders.

policeman *n.* (*pl.* **-men**) a member of a police force.

police officer *n.* a policeman or policewoman.

police state *n.* a totalitarian state or country controlled by political police supervising the citizens' activities.

police station *n.* the office of the police in a certain district or community.

police village *n.* *Cdn* (*Ont.*) a small, unincorporated village administered by a group of elected trustees.

policewoman *n.* (*pl.* **-women**) a female member of a police force.

policy¹ *n.* (*pl.* **-ies**) **1** a course or principle of action adopted or proposed by a government, party, individual, etc. **2** prudent conduct; sagacity.

policy² *n.* (*pl.* **-ies**) **1** a contract of insurance. **2** a document containing this.

policyholder *n.* a person or body holding an insurance policy.

policy-maker *n.* a person who helps to determine government etc. policy. □ **policy-making** *n. & adj.*

policy wonk *n.* = WONK 2.

polio *n.* = POLIOMYELITIS.

poliomyelitis /ˌpoːlioˌmaiəˈlaitis/ *n.* an infectious viral disease that affects the central nervous system and which can cause permanent paralysis.

polis /ˈpoːlɪs/ *n.* (*pl.* **poleis**) *hist.* a city state, esp. in ancient Greece.

poli-sci /ˈpɒliˌsai/ *n.* *N Amer.* *informal* political science (also *attrib.*: *poli-sci class*).

Polish ● *adj.* **1** of or relating to Poland. **2** of the Poles or their Slavic language. ● *n.* this language.

polish ● *v.* **1** *tr. & intr.* make or become smooth or glossy by rubbing. **2** *tr.* (esp. as **polished** *adj.*) refine or improve; add finishing touches to. ● *n.* **1** a substance used for polishing. **2** smoothness or glossiness produced by friction. **3** the act or an instance of polishing. **4** refinement or elegance of manner, conduct, etc. □ **polish off 1** finish (esp. food) quickly. **2** get rid of (an enemy, etc.). **polish up** revise or improve (a skill etc.). □ **polisher** *n.*

Polish sausage *n.* = KIELBASA.

politburo /ˈpɒlɪtˌbjʊroː/ *n.* (*pl.* **-os**) the principal policy-making committee of a Communist party.

polite *adj.* (**politer**, **politest**) **1** having good manners; courteous. **2** cultivated, cultured. **3** refined, elegant (*not used in polite society*). □ **politely** *adv.* **politeness** *n.*

politic ● *adj.* **1** (of an action) judicious, expedient. **2** (of a person) prudent, sagacious. **3** political (*body politic*). ● *v.intr.* (**politicked**, **politicking**) engage in politics. □ **politicking** *n.*

political *adj.* **1 a** of or concerning the state or its government, or public affairs generally. **b** of, relating to, or engaged in politics. **c** belonging to or forming part of a civil administration. **2** having an organized form of society or government. **3** taking or belonging to a side in politics. **4** relating to or affecting interests of status or authority rather than matters of principle (*a political decision*). □ **politically** *adv.*

political asylum *n.* protection given by a country to a political refugee from another country.

political correctness *n.* the avoidance of forms of expression or action that exclude, marginalize, or insult certain racial or cultural groups.

political economy *n.* the study of the economic aspects of government. □ **political economist** *n.*

political geography *n.* geography dealing with boundaries and the possessions of countries, etc.

politically correct *adj.* exhibiting political correctness.

politically incorrect *adj.* failing to exhibit political correctness.

political prisoner *n.* a person imprisoned for political beliefs or actions.

political science *n.* the study of the state and systems of government. □ **political scientist** *n.*

political will *n.* support by the public for policies.

politician *n.* **1** a person engaged in or concerned with politics. **2** a person skilled in politics.

politicize *v.* **1** *tr.* **a** give a political character to. **b** make politically aware. **2** *intr.* engage in or talk politics. □ **politicization** *n.*

politico *n.* (*pl.* **-os**) *informal* a politician or political enthusiast.

politics *n.pl.* **1** (treated as *sing.* or *pl.*) **a** the art and science of government. **b** public life and affairs as involving authority and government. **2** (usu. treated as *pl.*) **a** a particular set of ideas, principles, or commitments in politics (*what are their politics?*). **b** activities concerned with the acquisition or exercise of authority or power (*office politics*). **c** an organizational process or principle affecting authority, status, etc. (*the politics of the decision*).

polity /ˈpɒlɪti/ *n.* (*pl.* **-ies**) **1** a form or process of civil government or constitution. **2** an organized society; a state as a political entity.

polka /ˈpoːlkə, ˈpoːkə/ ● *n.* **1** a lively dance of Bohemian origin for couples in duple time. **2** the music for this. ● *v.intr.* (**polkas**, **polkaed** /-kəd/ or **polka'd**, **polkaing** /-kəɪŋ/) dance the polka.

polka dot *n.* a round dot as one of many forming a regular pattern on fabric etc. □ **polka-dot** *adj.* **polka-dotted** *adj.*

poll ● *n.* **1** = GALLUP POLL, OPINION POLL. **2 a** the process of voting at an election. **b** the counting of votes at an election. **c** the result of voting. **d** the number of votes recorded (*a heavy poll*). **e** (usu. in *pl.*) a place where votes are cast. **3 a** a human head. **b** the part of this on which hair grows. **4** a hornless animal, esp. one of a breed of hornless cattle. **5** the part of an animal's (esp. a horse's) head between the ears. ● *v.* **1** *tr.* **a** take the vote or votes of. **b** (in *passive*) have one's vote taken. **c** (of a candidate) receive (so many votes). **d** give (a vote). **2** *tr.* record the opinion of (a person or group) in an opinion poll. **3** *intr.* give one's vote. **4** *tr.* cut off the top of (a tree or plant), esp. make a pollard of. **5** *tr.* (esp. as **polled** *adj.*) cut the horns off (cattle). **6** *tr.* *Computing* check the status of (a computer system) at intervals. □ **go to the polls** have an election.

pollack *var. of* POLLOCK.

pollard /ˈpɒlərd/ ● *n.* **1 a** an animal that has lost its horns **b** an ox, sheep, or goat of a hornless breed. **2** a tree with branches cut off to encourage the growth of new young branches. ● *v.tr.* make (a tree) a pollard.

poll captain *n. Cdn* a person who directs an election campaign for a candidate in a given area.

pollen *n.* the fine dustlike grains discharged from the male part of a flower containing the gamete that fertilizes the female ovule.

pollen count *n.* an index of the amount of pollen in the air, published esp. for those allergic to it.

pollinate *v.tr. & intr.* fertilize (a plant) with pollen. □ **pollination** *n.* **pollinator** *n.*

polling *n.* the registering or casting of votes.

polling booth *n.* a compartment in which a voter stands or sits to mark a ballot paper.

polling day *n.* the day of a local or general election.

polling station *(N Amer.* also **polling place)** a building where voting takes place during an election.

polliwog *var. of* POLLYWOG.

pollock *n.* **1** an important food fish of the cod family, *Pollachius virens*, of the N Atlantic, having a protruding jaw. **2** a similar European fish, *P. pollachius.*

pollster *n.* a person who conducts opinion polls.

poll tax *n.* a tax levied on every adult.

pollute *v.tr.* **1** contaminate or defile (the environment). **2** make foul or filthy. **3** destroy the purity or sanctity of. □ **pollutant** *adj. & n.* **polluter** *n.*

polluted *adj.* **1** made unclean; contaminated. **2** *N Amer. slang* drunk.

pollution *n.* the presence in the environment, or the introduction into it, of substances, features, etc. that have harmful or unpleasant effects.

Pollyanna *n.* a cheerful optimist; an excessively cheerful person. □ **Pollyannaish** *adj.*

pollywog *n. N Amer.* a tadpole.

polo *n.* **1** a game in which players riding on horses try to hit a ball into a goal using long wooden mallets. **2** (in full **polo shirt)** a short-sleeved casual shirt with a collar and a short buttoned placket at the neckline.

polonaise /ˌpɒləˈneiz/ *n.* **1** a dance of Polish origin, consisting chiefly of an intricate march or procession in triple time. **2** the music for this.

polonium /pəˈloːniəm/ *n.* a rare radioactive metallic element, occurring naturally in uranium ores.

poltergeist /ˈpoːltər,ɡaist/ *n.* a noisy mischievous ghost, esp. one manifesting itself by physical damage.

poly *n.* **1** polyester. **2** polyethylene.

polyamide /ˌpɒliˈæmaid/ *n. Chem.* any of a class of condensation polymers produced from the interaction of an amino group of one molecule and a carboxylic acid group of another, and which includes many synthetic fibres such as nylon.

polyanthus /ˌpɒliˈænθəs/ *n.* (*pl.* **-es**) a plant cultivated from hybridized primulas.

polybag ● *n.* a bag made of polyethylene, used esp. for packaging etc. ● *v.tr.* place or package (something) in a polybag.

polycarbonate /ˌpɒliˈkɑrbə,neit/ *n.* any of a class of polymers in which the units are linked through a carbonate group, mainly used in moulding.

polychaete /ˈpɒli,kiːt/ *n.* any aquatic annelid worm of the class Polychaeta, having numerous bristles on the fleshy lobes of each body segment. □ **polychaetan** /-ˈkiːtən/ *adj.* **polychaetous** *adj.*

polychlorinated biphenyl *n. see* PCB.

polychrome ● *adj.* painted or decorated in many colours. ● *n.* **1** a work of art in several colours, esp. a statue. **2** varied colouring. □ **polychromed** *adj.*

polycotton *n.* fabric made from a mixture of cotton and polyester fibre.

polycyclic /ˌpɒliˈsaiklik/ *adj. Chem.* having more than one ring of atoms in the molecule.

polyester *n.* **1** any of a group of condensation polymers used to form synthetic fibres or to make resins. **2** a fabric made from such a polymer.

polyethylene *n.* a tough light thermoplastic polymer of ethylene, used for packaging and insulating.

polygamous /pəˈliɡəməs/ *adj.* **1** having more than one spouse at the same time. **2** having more than one mate. **3** *Bot.* bearing some flowers with stamens only, some with pistils only, some with both, on the same or different plants. □ **polygamy** *n.*

polyglot /ˈpɒli,ɡlɒt/ ● *adj.* **1** of many languages. **2** (of a person) speaking or writing several languages. **3** (of a book, esp. the Bible) with the text translated into several languages. ● *n.* **1** a polyglot person. **2** a polyglot book, esp. a Bible.

polygon /ˈpɒli,ɡɒn/ *n.* a plane figure with usu. four or more sides and angles. □ **polygonal** /pəˈliɡənəl/ *adj.*

polygraph /ˈpɒli,ɡræf/ *n.* **1** a machine designed to detect and record changes in physiological characteristics (e.g. rates of pulse and breathing), used esp. as a lie detector. **2** a test using a polygraph to determine whether a person is telling the truth.

polygyny /pəˈlidʒini/ *n.* **1** polygamy in which a man has more than one wife. **2** (of male animals) the fact or state of having more than one female mate.

polyhedron /ˌpɒliˈhiːdrən, -ˈhedrən/ *n.* (*pl.* **-s** or **-hedra** /-drə/) a solid figure with many (usu. more than six) faces. □ **polyhedral** *adj.*

polymath /ˈpɒli,mæθ/ *n.* a person of much or varied learning; a great scholar. □ **polymathic** *adj.*

polymer /ˈpɒlimər/ *n.* a compound composed of one or more large molecules formed from repeated units of smaller molecules. □ **polymeric** /-ˈmerik/ *adj.* **polymerize** *v.intr. & tr.* **polymerization** *n.*

polymerase /ˈpɒləmə,reiz/ *n. Biochem.* any enzyme which catalyzes the formation of a polymer, esp. of DNA or RNA.

polymerase chain reaction *n. see* PCR.

polymorphism /ˌpɒliˈmɔrfizəm/ *n. Biol.* the existence of various different forms in the successive stages of the development of an organism. □ **polymorphic** *adj.* **polymorphous** *adj.*

Polynesian ● *adj.* of or relating to Polynesia. ● *n.* **1 a** a native of Polynesia. **b** a person of Polynesian descent. **2** the Polynesian languages as a group, including Maori, Hawaiian, and Samoan.

polynomial /ˌpɒliˈnoːmiəl/ *Math.* ● *n.* an expression of more than two algebraic terms, esp. the sum of several terms that contain different powers of the same variable(s). ● *adj.* of or being a polynomial.

polynya /pəˈlinjə/ *n.* a stretch of open water surrounded by ice, esp. in the Arctic seas.

polyp /ˈpɒlip/ *n.* **1** *Zool.* an individual coelenterate. **2** *Med.* a small usu. benign growth protruding from a mucous membrane. □ **polypoid** /ˈpɒli,pɔid/ *adj.*

polypeptide /ˌpɒliˈpeptaid/ *n.* a peptide formed by the combination of about ten or more amino acids.

polyphonic /ˌpɒliˈfɒnik/ *adj. Music* (of vocal music etc.) in two or more relatively independent parts.

polyphony /pəˈlifəni/ *n.* (*pl.* **-ies**) *Music* polyphonic style in musical composition; counterpoint.

polypropylene /ˌpɒliˈproːpi,liːn/ *n. Chem.* any of various polymers of propylene including thermoplastic materials used for films, fibres, or moulding materials.

polyrhythm /ˈpɒliriθəm/ *n. Music* the use of two or more different rhythms simultaneously. □ **polyrhythmic** *adj.*

polysaccharide /ˌpɒliˈsækə,raid/ *n.* any of a group

of carbohydrates, including starch, cellulose, and insulin, whose molecules consist of long chains of monosaccharides.

polysemy /pə'lɪsəmi, ˌpɒli'si:mi, 'pɒl-/ n. Linguistics the existence of many meanings (of a word etc.). □ **polysemic** /-'si:mɪk/ adj. **polysemous** adj.

polystyrene /ˌpɒli'staɪˌri:n/ n. a thermoplastic polymer of styrene, usu. hard or expanded with a gas to produce a lightweight rigid substance, used for insulation and in packaging.

polytechnic /ˌpɒli'teknɪk/ ● n. an institution of higher education offering courses in many (esp. vocational) subjects at degree level or below. ● adj. dealing with or devoted to various vocational or technical subjects.

polytetrafluoroethylene /ˌpɒli,tetrə,flʊəro:'eθɪˌli:n/ n. Chem. a tough translucent polymer resistant to chemicals and used as a non-stick coating on cooking utensils etc. Abbr.: **PTFE**.

polytheism n. the belief in or worship of more than one god. □ **polytheist** n. **polytheistic** adj.

polyunsaturate n. a polyunsaturated fat etc.

polyunsaturated adj. Chem. (of a compound, esp. a fat or oil molecule) containing several double or triple bonds and thus not encouraging the formation of cholesterol in the blood.

polyurethane n. any polymer containing the urethane group, used in adhesives, paints, plastics, rubbers, foams, etc.

polyvinyl acetate n. Chem. a soft plastic polymer used in paints and adhesives. Abbr.: **PVA**.

polyvinyl chloride n. a tough transparent solid polymer of vinyl chloride, easily coloured and used for a wide variety of products including pipes, flooring, etc. Abbr.: **PVC**.

pom n. a Pomeranian dog.

Poma /'po:mə/ n. N Amer. proprietary a type of ski lift with detachable supports for the passengers.

pomegranate /'pɒmə,grænɪt, 'pɒm,grænɪt/ n. **1** an orange-sized fruit with a tough golden-orange outer skin containing many seeds in a red pulp. **2** the tree bearing this, Punica granatum, of N Africa and W Asia.

Pomeranian /ˌpɒmə'reiniən/ n. a breed of small dog with long silky hair, a pointed muzzle, a tail curling over the back, and pricked ears.

pommel /'pʌməl/ ● n. **1** a knob, esp. at the end of a sword hilt. **2** the upward projecting front part of a saddle. ● v.tr. (**pommelled, pommelling**) = PUMMEL.

pommes frites /pɒm'fri:t/ n.pl. thin french fries.

po-mo ● adj. postmodern. ● n. postmodernism.

pomp n. **1** a splendid display; splendour. **2** (often in pl.) vainglory.

pompadour /'pɒmpə,dɔr, -dʊr/ n. **1** a woman's hairstyle with the hair in a high turned-back roll around the face. **2** a man's hairstyle with the hair combed high off the forehead. □ **pompadoured** adj.

pompano /'pɒmpəno:/ n. (pl. **-os**) **1** any of various tropical fishes having a deep, laterally compressed, angular body, many of which are caught for sport. **2** any of various similar fishes, e.g. the Pacific pompano, Peprilus simillimus.

pompom n. (also **pompon**) **1 a** a ball or bobble made of tufts of yarn etc. used for decoration. **b** a bundle of strips of fabric, paper, etc. waved or shaken by cheerleaders or spectators at a sporting event. **2** the round tuft on a soldier's cap etc. **3** (often attrib.) a dahlia or chrysanthemum with small tightly-clustered petals. □ **pompommed** adj.

pompous adj. **1** self-important, affectedly grand or

solemn. **2** (of language) pretentious; unduly grand in style. □ **pomposity** n. (pl. **-ies**). **pompously** adv.

poncho n. (pl. **-os**) **1** a S American cloak made of a blanket-like piece of cloth with a slit in the middle for the head. **2** a garment in this style, esp. a raincoat. □ **ponchoed** adj.

pond ● n. **1** a fairly small body of still water formed naturally or by hollowing etc. **2** (prec. by the) jocular the Atlantic Ocean. ● v.intr. (of water) form a pond.

ponder v. **1** tr. weigh mentally; think over; consider. **2** intr. (usu. foll. by on, over) think; muse.

ponderosa /ˌpɒndə'ro:sə/ n. **1** a pine of western N America, P. ponderosa. **2** the red timber of this tree.

ponderous adj. **1** heavy; unwieldy. **2** laborious. **3** (of style etc.) dull; tedious. □ **ponderously** adv.

pond lily n. a water lily of the genus Nuphar.

pond scum n. **1** a mass of scummy freshwater algae floating in stagnant water. **2** N Amer. derogatory a worthless or contemptible person or thing.

pondweed n. any of various aquatic plants, esp. of the genus Potamogeton.

pongid /'pɒndʒɪd/ ● n. any ape of the family Pongidae, including gorillas, chimpanzees, and orangutans. ● adj. of or relating to this family.

pontiff n. the Pope. □ **pontifical** adj.

pontificate ● v.intr. /pɒn'tɪfɪˌkeɪt/ be pompously dogmatic. ● n. /pɒn'tɪfɪkət/ **1** the office of bishop or pope. **2** the period of this. □ **pontification** n.

pontoon n. **1** a flat-bottomed boat. **2 a** each of several boats, hollow metal cylinders, etc., used to support a temporary bridge. **b** a hollow tube or other float for keeping a boat, float plane, etc., buoyant. □ **pontooned** adj.

pony n. (pl. **-ies**) **1** a horse of any small breed. **2** a small drinking glass. **3** (in pl.) slang **a** racehorses. **b** (prec. by the) horse racing. □ **pony up** N Amer. hand over (money etc.) esp. in settlement of an account.

ponytail n. a person's hair drawn back, tied, and hanging down like a pony's tail. □ **ponytailed** adj.

Ponzi /'pɒnzi/ attrib.adj. N Amer. designating a form of fraud in which belief in the success of a non-existent enterprise is fostered by payment of quick returns to the first investors from money invested by others.

poo esp. Cdn & Brit. ● n. excrement. ● v. **1** intr. defecate. **2** tr. defecate in (one's pants etc.). ● interj. var of POOH.

poobah var. of POOH-BAH.

pooch n. esp. N Amer. slang a dog.

poodle n. a breed of dog with a coat of usu. clipped tight curls.

poof interj. announcing something sudden, esp. a disappearance or appearance.

pooh ● interj. expressing impatience or contempt. ● n. var. of POO.

pooh-bah n. **1** a person with much influence in an organization etc. **2** a pompous self-important person.

pooh-pooh v.tr. express contempt for; ridicule; dismiss (an idea etc.) scornfully.

pooja var. of PUJA.

pool[1] ● n. **1** a small body of still water or other liquid. **2** a receptacle or hole filled with water for swimming, wading, etc. **3** a deep place in a river. ● v. **1** tr. form into a pool. **2** intr. (of blood) become static.

pool[2] ● n. **1** esp. N Amer. any of various games of billiards, esp. eight ball. **2 a** a common supply of persons, commodities, resources, etc. (gene pool). **b** esp. Cdn a grain farmers' co-operative for marketing etc. **c** a group of persons sharing duties, resources, etc. (car pool). **3 a** the collective amount of players' stakes in gambling etc. **b** a bet in which players contribute to a pool, all of which is taken by one winner or divided among a few. **4 a** a joint commercial venture, esp. an arrangement between competing parties to fix prices and share business to eliminate competition. **b** the common funding for this. **5** a group of contestants who compete against each other in a tournament for the right to advance to the next round. ● *v.tr.* **1** put (resources etc.) into a common fund. **2** share (things) in common.

pool hall *n.* a place for playing billiards.

poolroom *n. N Amer.* **1** a place for playing billiards. **2** a betting establishment.

poolside ● *n.* the area adjoining a swimming pool (often *attrib.*: *poolside bar*). ● *adv.* to, toward, or beside a swimming pool (*sat poolside*).

poop[1] *n.* the stern of a ship; the deck that is highest and furthest aft.

poop[2] *v.tr.* (esp. as **pooped** *adj.* or foll. by *out*) *N Amer. informal* exhaust; tire out.

poop[3] *n. & v.* (also **poo-poo**) = POO. □ **poopy** *adj.*

poop[4] *n.* esp. *N Amer. slang* = SCOOP *n.* 4b.

poop[5] *n. informal* a stupid or ineffectual person.

pooper scooper *n.* an implement for clearing up (esp. dog) excrement.

poor *adj.* **1** lacking adequate money or means; characterized by poverty. **2** (often foll. by *in*) deficient in (a possession or quality) (*oxygen-poor*). **3 a** scanty, inadequate (*a poor crop*). **b** less good than is usual or expected (*poor visibility*). **c** paltry; inferior (*poor condition*). **d** not good or skilled at (*a poor judge of character*; *a poor loser*). **4 a** deserving pity or sympathy; unfortunate (*you poor thing*). **b** with reference to a dead person (*my poor father*). **5** spiritless; despicable (*is a poor creature*). **6** often *jocular* humble; insignificant (*in my poor opinion*). □ **poor man's** an inferior or cheaper substitute for.

poor-boy *attrib.adj.* designating coarse knitwear reminiscent of a kind worn by the poor in the 1920s and 1930s (*poor-boy sweater*).

Poor Clare *n.* a member of an order of Franciscan nuns founded by St. Clare of Assisi *c.* 1212.

poorhouse *n. hist.* a house for poor people living on public charity.

poorly ● *adv.* **1** scantily; defectively. **2** with no great success. ● *predic.adj.* unwell.

poor-mouth *N Amer.* ● *n.* a person who claims to be poor, either to receive more money or to avoid giving money. ● *v.* **1** *intr.* plead poverty. **2** *tr.* bad-mouth, speak disparagingly of.

poorness *n.* **1** defectiveness. **2** the lack of some good quality or constituent.

poor relation *n.* an inferior or subordinate member of a family or any other group or one treated as such.

poor white *n. offensive* a white person, esp. in the southern US, lacking money and social status.

POP *abbr.* probability of precipitation.

pop[1] ● *n.* **1** a sudden sharp explosive sound as of a cork when drawn, or of a bursting toy balloon. **2** any carbonated, sweetened, non-alcoholic drink, e.g. cola, ginger ale, etc. **3** a single item or instance of service for which a price is set; a person paying for such an item or service (*charged us $75 a pop*). ● *v.* (**popped**, **popping**) **1** *intr. & tr.* make or cause to make a pop. **2 a** *intr. & tr.* (foll. by *in*, *out*, *up*, *down*, etc.) go, move, come, or put unexpectedly or in a quick or hasty manner (*pop out to the store*; *pop in for a visit*). **b** *tr.* engage, open, release, etc. quickly or suddenly (*pop the hood*). **3 a** *intr. & tr.* burst, making a popping sound. **b** *tr.* heat (popcorn etc.) until it pops. **4** *tr.* **a** take (a pill etc.). **b** *slang* inject (a drug etc.). **5** *intr.* (usu. foll. by *up*)

Baseball hit the ball high but not far, esp. for an easy out. **6** *intr.* (of eyes) protrude. **7** *intr.* (of the ears) discern a faint pop as a result of a change in altitude, pressure, etc. **8** *tr. N Amer. informal* hit, punch. ● *attrib.adj.* sudden, unexpected (*pop quiz*). □ **pop off** *informal* **1** die. **2** quietly slip away (*compare sense 2 of v.*). **pop out** *Baseball* be put out by having one's pop-up caught. **pop the question** *informal* propose marriage. **pop up** appear, esp. unexpectedly.

pop[2] *informal* ● *adj.* **1** in or relating to a popular or modern style. **2** performing or relating to pop music (*pop star*). ● *n.* **1** (in full **pop music**) commercial popular music, esp. that since the 1950s. **2** pop art. **3** (in *pl.*) pieces of light classical music, show tunes, etc. (*a pops concert*)

pop[3] *n.* esp. *US informal* father.

pop[4] *n.* a snack of flavoured frozen water, yogourt, etc. with a stick embedded in it for holding.

pop. *abbr.* population.

pop art *n.* art based on modern popular culture and the mass media, esp. as a critical comment on traditional fine art values.

popcorn *n.* **1** corn which bursts open when heated. **2** these kernels when popped. **3** (*attrib.*) resembling popcorn in appearance (*popcorn shrimp*).

pop culture *n.* commercial culture based on popular taste.

pope *n.* **1** (as title usu. **Pope**) the Bishop of Rome as head of the Roman Catholic Church. **2** the head of the Coptic Church, the patriarch of Alexandria.

pop-eyed *adj. informal* **1** having bulging eyes. **2** wide-eyed (with surprise etc.).

pop fly *n.* = FLY BALL.

popgun *n.* a child's toy gun which shoots a pellet, cork, etc. by the compression of air with a piston.

popinjay / ˈpɒpɪnˌdʒeɪ / *n.* a conceited person.

poplar *n.* any tree of the genus *Populus*, with a usu. rapidly growing trunk and tremulous leaves.

popout ● *n. Baseball* an instance of popping out. ● *attrib.adj.* (**pop-out**) designating a part of a machine etc. that is easily removable (*pop-out panel*).

popover *n. N Amer.* **1** a food made from a thin batter of milk, eggs, and flour, which rises to form a hollow shell when baked. **2** a loose casual garment put on by slipping it over the head.

poppa *n. N Amer. informal* (esp. as a child's word) **1** father. **2** grandfather.

popper *n.* **1** a person or thing that pops. **2** a pan or electric appliance for popping popcorn. **3** *informal* any of a number of inhalant muscle relaxants and vasodilators used as a stimulant. **4** *N Amer. Angling* a plug that makes a popping sound at the surface of the water as it moves.

pop-psych *attrib.adj.* (in full **pop-psychology**) characterized by or relating to usu. superficial psychological concepts as popularly understood.

poppy[1] *n.* (*pl.* **-ies**) **1** any plant of the genus *Papaver*, with showy often red flowers and a milky narcotic sap. **2** *Cdn & Brit.* an artificial red poppy distributed for Remembrance Day.

poppy[2] *adj.* (of music, a group, etc.) having a sound characteristic of pop music.

poppycock *n. slang* nonsense.

Poppy Day *n. Brit. & Cdn* = REMEMBRANCE DAY.

poppy seed *n.* the small black seed of the poppy, used in fillings and toppings for bread, cakes, etc. (also *attrib.*: *poppy-seed cake*).

Popsicle *n.* esp. *N Amer. proprietary* a piece of frozen flavoured and coloured water, juice, etc. on a stick.

Popsicle stick *n. N Amer.* a thin, flat stick with rounded ends on which a Popsicle is frozen, often used in arts and crafts.

popster *n. informal* a pop musician.

populace / 'pɒpjʊləs / *n.* **1** the people living in a given area. **2 a** the common people. **b** *derogatory* the rabble.

popular *adj.* **1** liked or admired by many people or by a specified group. **2 a** of or carried on by the general public (*popular meetings*). **b** prevalent among the general public (*popular discontent*). **3** adapted to the understanding or taste of the people (*popular science*). □ **popularity** *n.* **popularly** *adv.*

popular culture *n.* = POP CULTURE.

popular front *n.* a party etc. representing the populace against an esp. totalitarian government.

popularize *v.tr.* **1** make popular. **2** cause (a person, principle, etc.) to be generally known or liked. **3** present (a technical subject etc.) in a popular or readily understandable form. □ **popularization** *n.* **popularizer** *n.*

popular music *n.* **1** songs, folk tunes, etc., appealing to popular tastes. **2** pop music.

popular vote *n.* the total number of votes cast by voters in an election.

populate *v.tr.* **1** inhabit; form the population of (a town, country, etc.). **2** supply with inhabitants; people (*a densely populated district*).

population *n.* **1 a** the inhabitants of a place, country, etc. referred to collectively. **b** any specified group within this (*the Italian population of Toronto*). **2** the total number of any of these (*a population of eight million; the seal population*). **3** the act or process of supplying with inhabitants. **4** *Statistics* any finite or infinite collection of items under consideration.

population explosion *n.* a sudden large increase of population.

populist ● *n.* **1** a member or adherent of a political party seeking support mainly from the ordinary people. **2** a person who holds, or who is concerned with, the views of the populace. ● *adj.* of or relating to a populist or populists. □ **populism** *n.*

populous *adj.* having many inhabitants.

pop-up ● *attrib.adj.* **1** *Computing* (of a menu etc.) able to be superimposed on the screen and suppressed rapidly. **2** (of a toaster etc.) operating so as to move the object (toast when ready etc.) quickly upwards. **3** (of a book etc.) containing three-dimensional figures etc. that rise up when the page is turned. ● *n.* **1** *Baseball* an instance of popping up. **2** *Computing* a pop-up menu etc.

porcelain *n.* **1** a hard vitrified translucent ceramic. **2** objects made of this.

porch *n.* **1** a covered shelter for the entrance of a building. **2** *N Amer.* a veranda. □ **porched** *adj.*

porcine / 'pɔrsaɪn / *adj.* of or like pigs.

porcini / pɔr't∫ini / *n.* an edible mushroom.

porcupine *n.* **1** any rodent with defensive spines or quills, esp. (in the Americas) the common porcupine *Erethizon dorsatum.* **2** (*attrib.*) denoting any of various animals or other organisms with spines.

pore¹ *n.* a minute opening in a surface, e.g. the skin, through which gases or fluids may pass.

pore² *v.intr.* (foll. by *over*) **1** be absorbed in studying (a book etc.). **2** meditate on (a subject).

porgy / 'pɔrgi / *n.* (*pl.* **-ies**) *N Amer.* any of numerous fishes found esp. in N American Atlantic coastal waters, esp. a fish of the family Sparidae, which includes several food fishes.

pork *n.* **1** the flesh of a pig, used as food. **2** esp. *US slang* an instance of pork-barrel politics.

pork and beans *n. N Amer.* baked beans with some salt pork or bacon.

pork barrel *n.* (hyphenated when *attrib.*) *N Amer. informal* **1** a source of government funds for projects designed to win votes. **2** the funds themselves. □ **pork-barreller** *n.* **pork-barrelling** *n.*

pork belly *n.* (*pl.* **-ies**) a side of pork, esp. as a commodity.

porker *n.* **1** a pig raised for food. **2** a young fattened pig.

pork pie *n.* a pie of ground pork etc. eaten cold.

porky¹ *adj.* (**-ier, -iest**) **1** *informal* fleshy, fat. **2** of or like pork.

porky² *n.* (*pl.* **-ies**) *N Amer. informal* a porcupine.

porn (also **porno**) *informal* ● *n.* pornography. ● *adj.* pornographic.

pornography *n.* **1** the explicit description or exhibition of sexual activity in literature, films, etc., intended to stimulate erotic rather than aesthetic or emotional feelings. **2** literature etc. characterized by this. □ **pornographer** *n.* **pornographic** *adj.*

porous *adj.* **1** full of pores. **2** letting through air, water, etc. **3** (of an argument, structure, etc.) leaky, admitting infiltration. □ **porosity** / pɔr'bsɪti / *n.*

porphyry / 'pɔrfɪri / *n.* (*pl.* **-ies**) **1** a hard rock quarried in ancient Egypt, composed of crystals of white or red feldspar in a red matrix. **2** an igneous rock with large crystals scattered in a matrix of much smaller crystals.

porpoise / 'pɔrpəs / *n.* any of various small toothed whales of the family Phocaenidae, esp. of the genus *Phocaena,* with a low triangular dorsal fin and a blunt rounded snout.

porridge *n.* a dish consisting of oats or another cereal boiled in water or milk. □ **porridgy** *adj.*

port¹ *n.* **1** a harbour. **2** a town or place possessing a harbour where ships load or unload. □ **any port in a storm** any refuge in difficult or troubled circumstances.

port² *n.* (also **port wine**) a strong, sweet, usu. dark red fortified wine of Portugal.

port³ ● *n.* the left-hand side (looking forward) of a ship, boat, or aircraft. ● *v.tr. & intr.* turn (the helm) to port. ● *adj.* situated on or turned toward the left-hand side (looking forward) of a ship or aircraft.

port⁴ ● *n.* **1 a** an opening in the side of a ship for entrance etc. **b** a porthole. **2** an aperture for the passage of steam, water, etc. **3** a socket or aperture in an electronic circuit, esp. in a computer network, where connections can be made with peripheral equipment. ● *v.tr. Computing* transfer (software) from one operating system etc. to another.

portable ● *adj.* **1 a** easily movable or transportable, convenient for carrying (*portable TV*). **b** not fixed; movable (*portable classroom*). **2** (of a right, privilege, etc.) capable of being transferred or adapted in altered circumstances (*portable pension*). **3** (of software etc.) not restricted to one machine or computer system; able to be transferred from one machine or system to another. ● *n.* **1** a portable object, e.g. a radio etc. **2** esp. *N Amer. & Austral.* a small transportable building used as a classroom. □ **portability** *n.*

portage ● *n.* **1** / pɔr'tɒʒ / the carrying of boats or goods between two navigable waters or around an unnavigable section of a river etc. **2** / pɔr'tɒʒ / **a** a place at which this is necessary. **b** the route taken during a portage. **3** / 'pɔrtɪdʒ / the act or instance of carrying or transporting. ● *v.* / pɔr'tɒʒ / **1** *tr. & intr.* convey (a boat or goods) between navigable waters. **2** *tr.* carry a boat or goods at (a portage). **3** *tr.* circumvent (a stretch of unnavigable waters) by means of a portage.

portage trail *n. Cdn* a trail created by people performing a portage.

portal *n.* a doorway or gate etc., esp. a large and elaborate one.

porta-potty *n.* (*pl.* **-potties**) a portable toilet.

portend *v.tr.* **1** foreshadow as an omen. **2** give warning of.

portent /'pɔrtent, -tənt/ *n.* **1** an omen, a sign of something to come. **2** a prodigy; a marvellous thing.

portentous /pɔr'tentəs/ *adj.* **1** like or serving as a portent. **2** pompously solemn. □ **portentously** *adv.* **portentousness** *n.*

porter¹ *n.* **1 a** a person employed to carry luggage etc., esp. a railway, airport, or hotel employee. **b** a hospital employee who moves patients, equipment, trolleys, etc. **2** a dark brown bitter beer brewed from charred or browned malt. **3** *N Amer.* a sleeping car attendant.

porter² *n.* a gatekeeper or doorman.

porterhouse *n.* esp. *N Amer.* (in full **porterhouse steak**) a thick steak cut from between the prime ribs and the sirloin.

portfolio *n.* (*pl.* **-os**) **1** a case for keeping loose sheets of paper, drawings, etc. **2** a range of investments held by a person, company, etc. **3** the office or responsibility of a government minister. **4** samples of an artist's or photographer's work.

porthole *n.* a usu. round window in the side of a ship or an aircraft.

portico /'pɔrtɪko:/ *n.* (*pl.* **-oes** or **-os**) a colonnade; a roof supported by columns at regular intervals usu. attached as a porch to a building.

portion ● *n.* **1** a part or share. **2** the amount of food allotted to one person; a helping. **3** a specified or limited quantity. **4** one's destiny or lot. ● *v.tr.* **1** divide (a thing) into portions. **2** (foll. by *out*) distribute. **3** (foll. by *to*) assign (a thing) to (a person).

Portland cement *n.* a cement manufactured from chalk and clay.

portly *adj.* (**-ier, -iest**) corpulent; stout. □ **portliness** *n.*

portmanteau /pɔrt'mænto:/ *n.* (*pl.* **-teaus** /-to:z/ or **-teaux**) a travelling bag for clothes etc., esp. of leather and opening into two equal parts.

portobello *n.* an edible brown variety of the common mushroom, *Agaricus bisporus*.

port of call *n.* a place where a ship or a person stops on a journey.

port of entry *n.* a port etc. by which people and goods may enter a country.

portrait *n.* **1** a representation of a person or animal, esp. of the face, made by drawing, painting, photography, etc. **2** a description in words of a person. **3** a person etc. resembling or typifying another (*is the portrait of his father*). **4** (in graphic design etc.) a format in which the height of an illustration etc. is greater than the width (*compare* LANDSCAPE 3).

portraitist *n.* a person who takes or paints portraits.

portraiture *n.* **1** the art of painting or taking portraits. **2** graphic description. **3** a portrait.

portray *v.tr.* **1** make a likeness of. **2** describe graphically. **3** represent, esp. dramatically (*immigrants as portrayed in the media*). □ **portrayal** *n.*

Portuguese ● *n.* (*pl.* same) **1 a** a native or national of Portugal. **b** a person of Portuguese descent. **2** the Romance language of Portugal, also used in Brazil etc. ● *adj.* of or relating to Portugal.

Portuguese man-of-war *n.* a dangerous tropical or subtropical marine hydrozoan of the genus *Physalia* with a large crest and a poisonous sting.

POS *abbr.* point-of-sale.

pose¹ ● *v.* **1** *intr.* assume a certain attitude of body, esp. when being photographed or being painted for a portrait. **2** *intr.* (foll. by *as*) set oneself up as or pretend to be (another person etc.) (*posing as a celebrity*). **3** *intr.* behave affectedly in order to impress others. **4** *tr.* put forward or present (a question, threat, etc.). **5** *tr.* place (an artist's model etc.) in a certain attitude or position. ● *n.* **1** an attitude of body or mind, esp. assumed when being photographed etc. **2** an attitude or pretense, esp. one assumed for effect (*his generosity is a mere pose*).

pose² *v.tr.* puzzle (a person) with a question or problem.

poser *n.* **1** a person who poses (*see* POSE¹ *v.* 3). **2** a puzzling question or problem.

poseur /po:'zɜr/ *n.* a person who poses for effect or behaves affectedly.

posh *adj.* stylish; luxurious. □ **poshness** *n.*

posit /'pɒzɪt/ *v.tr.* (**posited, positing**) state or assume as a fact; postulate.

position ● *n.* **1** a place occupied by a person or thing. **2 a** the way in which a thing or its parts are placed or arranged. **b** a disposition of the parts of the body; a posture (*an uncomfortable position*). **3** the proper place (*in position*). **4** the state of being advantageously placed (*jockeying for position*). **5** an attitude or policy concerning a question or issue (*their position on nuclear disarmament*). **6** a person's situation in relation to others (*puts one in an awkward position*). **7** rank or status; high social standing. **8** paid employment. **9** (in team games) a set of functions considered as the responsibility of a particular player (*what position does he play?*). **10** a place where troops etc. are posted for strategical purposes (*the position was stormed*). **11** the configuration of chessmen etc. during a game. **12** a specific disposition of the legs and feet or arms in ballet etc. (*first position*). **13** the extent to which an investor, dealer, or speculator has made a commitment in the market by buying or selling securities, currencies, commodities, etc. (*long position*). ● *v.tr.* **1** place in position. **2** promote (a product or service) esp. within a chosen sector of a market. □ **in a position to** enabled by circumstances, resources, information, etc. to (do, state, etc.). □ **positional** *adj.* **positionally** *adv.* **positioner** *n.*

position paper *n. N Amer.* a written report of policy on a particular issue, prepared by a business etc.

positive ● *adj.* **1** (of a person) convinced, confident, or overconfident in his or her opinion (*positive that I was not there*). **2 a** having a helpful and constructive intention or attitude toward something (*positive criticism*). **b** optimistic, hopeful (*a positive outlook*). **c** affirmative; expressing or showing assent (*a positive answer*). **3** formally or explicitly stated; definite, unquestionable (*positive proof*). **4 a** absolute; not relative. **b** *Grammar* (of an adjective or adverb) expressing a simple quality without comparison. **5** *informal* downright; complete (*it would be a positive miracle*). **6 a** marked by the presence rather than absence of qualities or (*Med.*) symptoms (*a positive reaction to the plan*; *the test was positive*). **b** (of a person, blood, etc.) having a specified condition, substance, etc. (*HIV-positive*). **7** esp. *Philos.* dealing only with matters of fact; practical (*compare* POSITIVISM 1). **8** tending in a direction naturally or arbitrarily taken as that of increase or progress. **9** greater than zero (*opp.* NEGATIVE *adj.* 8). **10 a** *Electricity* designating electric charge, potential, etc. having the same polarity as that electrode of a galvanic cell from which the current is held to flow (and toward which the actual flow of electrons occurs). **b** designating a north-seeking pole of a magnet. **11** (of a photographic image) showing lights and shades or colours true to the original (*compare* NEGATIVE *adj.* 11). ● *n.* a positive adjective, photograph, quantity, result, etc. □ **positively** *adv.* **positiveness** *n.* **positivity** *n.*

positive discrimination *n. Cdn & Brit.* the practice of making distinctions in favour of groups considered to be disadvantaged or underprivileged, esp. in the allocation of resources and opportunities.

positive feedback *n.* **1** a constructive response to a presentation, experiment, questionnaire, etc. **2** *Electronics* the return of part of an output signal to the input, tending to increase the amplification etc.

positive reinforcement *n.* reinforcement achieved by a pleasurable or satisfying stimulus provided after a desired response to increase the probability of its repetition.

positive thinking *n.* the practice or result of concentrating one's mind on the good and constructive aspects of a matter so as to eliminate destructive attitudes and emotions.

positivism *n.* **1 a** the philosophical system of the French philosopher Auguste Comte (1798–1857), recognizing only non-metaphysical facts and observable phenomena, and rejecting metaphysics and theism. **b** a religious system founded on this. **2** = LOGICAL POSITIVISM. □ **positivist** *n. & adj.* **positivistic** *adj.*

positron /'pɒzɪ,trɒn/ *n.* a subatomic particle with a positive charge equal to the charge of an electron.

positron emission tomography *n.* a form of tomography used esp. for brain scans which employs positron-emitting isotopes introduced into the body as a source of radiation.

posse /'pɒsɪ/ *n.* **1** a body of men summoned by a sheriff etc. to find a criminal, maintain order, etc. **2** *slang* an esp. criminal gang. **3** *informal* usu. *derogatory* a band of persons acting or going about together.

possess *v.tr.* **1** hold as property; own. **2** have a faculty, quality, etc. (*they possess a special value for us*). **3 a** (of a demon etc.) occupy; have power over (a person etc.) (*possessed by the devil*). **b** (of an emotion, infatuation, etc.) dominate, be an obsession of (*possessed by fear*). **4** have sexual intercourse with (esp. a woman). □ **be possessed of** own, have. **what possessed you?** an expression of incredulity. □ **possessor** *n.* **possessory** *adj.*

possession *n.* **1** the act or state of possessing or being possessed. **2** the thing possessed. **3** the act or state of actual holding or occupancy. **4** *Law* **a** power or control over a thing, esp. land, which is similar to lawful ownership but which may exist separately from it. **b** *informal* the state of possessing an illegal drug or drugs (*charged with possession*). **5** (in *pl.*) property, wealth, subject territory, etc. **6** *Football, Hockey, etc.* **a** temporary control of the ball or puck by a particular player or team. **b** a period of such control. □ **in possession 1** (of a person) possessing. **2** (of a thing) possessed. **in possession of 1** having in one's possession. **2** maintaining control over (*in possession of one's wits*). **in the possession of** held or owned by. **take possession** (often foll. by *of*) become the owner or possessor (of a thing).

possessive ● *adj.* **1** showing a desire to possess or

retain what one already owns. **2** showing jealous and domineering tendencies toward another person. **3** *Grammar* indicating possession. ● *n.* (in full **possessive case**) the case of nouns and pronouns expressing possession. □ **possessiveness** *n.*

possessive pronoun *n.* each of the pronouns indicating possession (*my, your, their,* etc.) or the corresponding absolute forms (*mine, yours, theirs,* etc.).

possibility *n.* (*pl.* **-ies**) **1** the state or fact of being possible, or an occurrence of this (*outside the range of possibility; saw no possibility of going*). **2 a** a thing that may exist or happen (*there are three possibilities*). **b** a possible candidate, member of a team, etc. **3** (usu. in *pl.*) the capability of being used, improved, etc.; the potential of an object or situation (*it has possibilities*).

possible ● *adj.* **1** capable of existing or happening; that may be managed, achieved, etc. (*came as early as possible*). **2** that is likely to happen etc. (*few thought their victory possible*). **3** acceptable; potential (*a possible way of doing it*). **4** that is perhaps true or a fact (*it's possible that he has left*). **5** that is or perhaps will be (what is denoted by the noun) (*looking for a possible serial killer*). ● *n.* **1** = POSSIBILITY *n.* 2b. **2** (prec. by *the*) whatever is likely, manageable, etc.

possibly *adv.* **1** perhaps. **2** in accordance with possibility (*cannot possibly refuse*).

possum *n. informal* = OPOSSUM. □ **play possum** *informal* pretend to be asleep or unaware.

post¹ ● *n.* **1** a long piece of wood or metal set upright in the ground etc., esp.: **a** to support something, esp. in building. **b** to mark a position, boundary, etc. **c** to carry notices. **2** any of the principal upright supports of a piece of furniture, such as a chair or four-poster bed. **3 a** a pole etc. marking the start or finish of a race. **b** = GOALPOST. ● *v.tr.* **1** (often foll. by *up*) **a** attach (a paper etc.) in a prominent place; stick up (*post no bills*). **b** announce or advertise by placard, in a published text, on a computer bulletin board, etc. **2** achieve (a score in a game, etc.).

post² ● *n.* esp. *Brit.* **1** the official conveyance of parcels, letters, etc. (*send it by post*). **2** a single collection, dispatch, or delivery of these; the letters etc. dispatched. ● *v.* **1** *tr.* esp. *Brit.* put (a letter etc.) in the mail. **2** *tr.* (esp. as **posted** *adj.*) supply a person with information (*keep me posted*). **3** *tr.* **a** enter (an item) in a ledger. **b** (often foll. by *up*) complete (a ledger) in this way. **c** (an entry) from an auxiliary book to a more formal one, or from one account to another. **4** *intr.* (of a rider) rise and fall in the saddle in rhythm with the horse at a trot.

post³ ● *n.* **1** a job; a position of paid employment. **2** a place where a soldier is stationed or which he or she patrols. **3** a place where an official is on duty (*customs post*). **4 a** a position taken up by a body of soldiers. **b** a force occupying a fort. **c** a fort. **5** = TRADING POST. **6** *Basketball* the area in the vicinity of the opponent's basket. ● *v.tr.* **1** place or station (soldiers, an employee, etc.). **2** appoint to a post or command. □ **post up** *Basketball* position oneself in the post.

post⁴ *v.tr.* put up, provide (esp. bail money).

post⁵ *n. informal* POST-PRODUCTION.

post- *prefix* after in time or order.

postage *n.* the amount charged for sending a letter etc. by post, usu. prepaid in the form of a stamp.

postage and handling *n.* a price charged for the mailing, packing, and delivery of a package etc.

postage meter *n. N Amer.* a machine that officially marks letters with an inked stamp in lieu of a postage stamp, and records the cost of postage incurred.

postage stamp *n.* **1** an official stamp affixed to or imprinted on a letter etc. indicating the amount of postage paid. **2** (*attrib.*) very small (*a postage-stamp lawn*).

postal *adj.* of or relating to the post office or mail delivery. □ **postally** *adv.*

postal code *n. Cdn* a series of six alternating letters and numerals used as part of a postal address to expedite the processing of machine-sorted mail.

postal station *n. Cdn* one of a number of branch post offices in a community too large to be serviced by a single post office.

post-and-beam *adj.* (of a method of construction or a building) having a framework of upright and horizontal beams.

postcard *n.* **1** a card with a photograph or picture on one side, for sending a short message by mail without an envelope. **2** (*attrib.*) picturesque.

post-coital *adj.* occurring or existing after sexual intercourse. □ **post-coitally** *adv.*

post-colonial *adj.* occurring or existing after the end of colonial rule. □ **post-colonialism** *n.* **post-colonialist** *adj.* & *n.*

post-concussion syndrome *n.* a lingering condition experienced as a result of a serious head injury, characterized esp. by recurrent headaches, dizziness, difficulty concentrating, sensitivity to light, blurred vision, and nausea.

post-Confederation *adj. Cdn* **1** of or pertaining to the period after 1867 in Canada. **2** relating to or characteristic of the period after a province or territory entered Confederation.

post-consumer *adj.* designating waste thrown away by consumers and used in recycled products.

postdate *v.tr.* **1** affix or assign a date later than the actual one to (a document, cheque, event, etc.). **2** follow in time; belong to a later date.

post-doc *n. informal* a post-doctoral scholar or appointment.

post-doctoral *adj.* of or relating to research undertaken after the completion of doctoral research.

poster ● *n.* **1** a printed or written notice posted or displayed in a public place as an announcement or advertisement. **2** a large printed picture suitable for decorative display on a wall. **3** *Computing* a person who posts a message on a BBS etc. ● *v.* **1** *tr.* affix posters on (a wall, building, etc.). **2** *intr.* place posters throughout a neighbourhood etc.

poster boy *n.* esp. *N Amer.* **1** a male poster child. **2** a male model who appears in a print advertisement.

poster child *n.* esp. *N Amer.* **1** a child who appears on a poster or in an advertisement for a charitable organization. **2** a person who epitomizes or represents a quality, cause, etc.

poster girl *n.* esp. *N Amer.* **1** a female poster child. **2** a female model who appears in a print advertisement.

posterior ● *adj.* **1** situated behind or at the back. **2** later; coming after in series, order, or time. ● *n.* the buttocks. □ **posteriorly** *adv.*

posterity /pɒ'stɛrɪti/ *n.* **1** all succeeding generations. **2** the descendants of a person.

post-feminist ● *adj.* **1** relating to or occurring in the period after the feminist movement of the 1970s. **2** of or relating to ideas, theories, etc. in feminism after the 1970s. ● *n.* a person who holds post-feminist ideas and attitudes. □ **post-feminism** *n.*

postglacial ● *adj.* formed or occurring after a glacial period. ● *n.* a postglacial period or deposit.

post-grad *adj.* & *n. informal* = POST-GRADUATE.

post-graduate ● *adj.* **1** (of a course of study) carried

on after completing a bachelor's degree. **2** of or relating to students following this course of study. ● *n.* a post-graduate student.

posthole *n.* a hole for the insertion of a fence post.

posthumous /'pɒstjəməs, -juːməs, 'pɒstʃəməs/ *adj.* **1** occurring after death. **2** (of a book etc.) published after the author's death. **3** (of a child) born after the death of its father. □ **posthumously** *adv.*

postie *n. Cdn* & *Brit. informal* a postal worker, esp. a letter carrier.

Post-Impressionism *n.* artistic aims and methods developed from, or as a reaction against, Impressionism, intending to express the artist's conception of the objects represented rather than the general observer's view. □ **Post-Impressionist** *n.* & *adj.*

post-industrial *adj.* relating to or characteristic of a society or economy which no longer relies on heavy industry. □ **post-industrialism** *n.*

posting *n.* **1** an appointment to a position. **2** a message posted to a discussion group etc. on the Internet.

Post-it *n.* (also **Post-it Note**) *proprietary* **1** a small pad of paper with an adhesive strip on the bottom of each sheet, designed for easy positioning on and removal from smooth surfaces. **2** a sheet from such a pad.

postlude /'pəʊstljuːd/ *n. Music* a piece of esp. organ music played at the conclusion of a church service.

postman *n.* (*pl.* **-men**) a person who is employed to deliver letters etc.

postmark ● *n.* an official mark stamped on a letter, esp. one giving the place, date, etc. of dispatch or arrival, and serving to cancel the stamp. ● *v.tr.* mark (an envelope etc.) with this.

postmaster *n.* a person in charge of a post office.

postmaster general *n.* the head of the postal service in certain countries.

post-menopausal *adj.* of or occurring after menopause. □ **post-menopause** *n.*

postmistress *n.* a woman in charge of a post office.

postmodernism *n.* a late 20th-c. style and concept in the arts, architecture, and criticism, which represents a departure from modernism and has at its heart a general distrust of grand theories and ideologies. □ **postmodern** *adj.* **postmodernist** *adj.* & *n.* **postmodernity** *n.*

post-mortem ● *n.* **1** an examination made after death, esp. to determine its cause. **2** *informal* a discussion analyzing the course and result of a game, election, etc. ● *adv.* & *adj.* after death.

postnatal *adj.* characteristic of or relating to the period after childbirth. □ **postnatally** *adv.*

post office *n.* **1** the public department or corporation responsible for postal services and (in some countries) telecommunication. **2** a building, counter in a drugstore, etc., where stamps can be bought, letters can be mailed, etc. **3** *N Amer.* a children's game in which imaginary letters are delivered in exchange for kisses.

post office box *n.* a numbered locked box at a post office, in which mail for an individual or company is put and kept until called for.

post-op *informal* ● *adj.* post-operative. ● *adv.* post-operatively.

post-operative *adj.* of the period following a surgical operation. □ **post-operatively** *adv.*

postpaid *adj.* & *adv.* on which postage has been paid.

postpartum *adj.* following childbirth.

postpartum depression *n.* depression suffered by a mother following childbirth.

postpone v.tr. put off to a future time; arrange (an event etc.) to take place at a later time; defer. □
postponable adj. **postponement** n. **postponer** n.

post-production n. work done on a film, broadcast, etc. after filming or recording has taken place.

post-punk adj. of or occurring after the punk music wave in the late 1970s to early 1980s.

postscript n. **1** an additional paragraph or remark, usu. at the end of a letter after the signature and introduced by 'PS'. **2** any additional information, action, etc.

post-season N Amer. Sport • adj. of or occurring after the conclusion of the regular season (post-season play). • n. the playoffs.

post-secondary adj. N Amer. of or relating to education occurring after completion of high school.

post-structuralism n. an extension and critique of structuralism, esp. as used in critical textual analysis, which emphasized plurality and deferral of meaning, rejecting the fixed binary oppositions of structuralism and the validity of authorial authority. □
post-structural adj. **post-structuralist** n. & adj.

post-tax attrib.adj. (of income) after deduction of taxes.

post time n. N Amer. the time at which a horse race starts.

post-traumatic stress disorder n. (also **post-traumatic stress syndrome**) Med. a condition of mental and emotional stress that sometimes follows injury or severe psychological shock, characterized by withdrawal and anxiety, and a tendency to physical illness. Abbr.: **PTSD**, **PTSS**.

postulant /'pɒstjʊlənt, 'pɒstʃʊ-/ n. a candidate, esp. for admission into a religious order.

postulate /'pɒstjʊˌleɪt, 'pɒstʃʊ-/ • v.tr. **1** (often foll. by that + clause) assume as a necessary condition, esp. as a basis for reasoning. **2** claim. • n. (/-lət/) **1** a thing postulated. **2** a fundamental prerequisite or condition. **3** Math. an assumption used as a basis for mathematical reasoning. □ **postulation** n.

posture • n. **1** the relative position of parts, esp. of the body (in a reclining posture). **2** carriage or bearing (good posture and balance). **3** a mental or spiritual attitude or condition. **4** the condition or state (of affairs etc.). • v.intr. assume a mental or physical attitude, esp. for effect. □ **postural** adj.

post-war adj. occurring or existing after a war (esp. the most recent major war).

postwoman n. (pl. **-women**) a woman who is employed to deliver letters etc.

posy n. (pl. **-ies**) a small bunch of flowers.

pot¹ • n. **1 a** a vessel, usu. rounded, of ceramic ware or metal or glass for holding liquids or solids or for cooking in. **b** such a vessel designed to hold a particular substance (coffee pot; teapot). **2 a** = FLOWERPOT 1. **b** = LOBSTER POT. **c** = CHAMBER POT, POTTY² 2. **3** a drinking vessel of pewter etc. **4** the contents of a pot. **5** the total amount of the bet in a game etc. **6** N Amer. informal a fund established by a group of people for a common purpose, esp. for buying food and drinks. **7** informal a large sum (pots of money). **8** = POT-BELLY. • v. (**potted**, **potting**) **1** tr. place (a plant) in a flowerpot. **2** tr. **a** (usu. as **potted** adj.) preserve in a sealed pot (potted shrimps). **b** cook (food) in a pot. **3** tr. Hockey score (a goal). **4** tr. shoot at, hit, or kill (an animal) with a potshot. **5** tr. seize or secure. **6** intr. make pottery. **7** intr. informal take a potshot; shoot at. □ **go to pot** informal deteriorate; be ruined. **not have a pot to piss in** coarse slang be very poor. **the pot calling the kettle black** a case of accusing someone of something of

which one is oneself guilty. **pot of gold** an imaginary reward; an ideal; a jackpot. □ **potful** n. (pl. **-fuls**).

pot² n. slang marijuana.

potable /'pɒtəbəl/ • adj. drinkable. • n. (usu. in pl.) a drinkable substance. □ **potability** n.

potash /'pɒtæʃ/ n. an alkaline potassium compound, usu. potassium carbonate or hydroxide.

potassium n. a soft silver-white metallic element occurring naturally in sea water and various minerals, an essential element for living organisms, forming many compounds used industrially.

potassium chloride n. a white crystalline solid used as a fertilizer and in photographic processing.

potassium cyanide n. a highly toxic solid that can be hydrolyzed to give poisonous hydrogen cyanide gas.

potassium iodide n. a white crystalline solid used as an additive to salt to prevent iodine deficiency.

potato n. (pl. **-oes**) **1** a starchy plant tuber that is cooked and used for food. **2** the plant, Solanum tuberosum, bearing this.

potato blight n. a destructive disease of potatoes caused by a parasitic fungus, Phytophthora infestans.

potato chip n. N Amer. = CHIP n. 2a.

potato pancake n. a pancake made with grated potato.

potato salad n. cold cooked potato chopped and mixed with mayonnaise, onion, etc.

potato skins n.pl. N Amer. wedges of baked potato skin with most of the pulp removed, topped with bacon, cheese, etc. and broiled, served esp. as an appetizer.

pot-au-feu /pɒtɔː'fə/ n. (pl. same) a French soup or stew of usu. beef and vegetables cooked in a large pot.

pot-bellied stove n. (also **pot-belly stove**) N Amer. a small bulbous stove for burning esp. wood.

pot-belly n. (pl. **-ies**) a protruding stomach. □ **pot-bellied** adj.

potboiler n. a mediocre work of literature or art done merely to make the writer or artist money.

pot-bound adj. (of a plant) having roots which fill the flowerpot, leaving no room to expand.

potent adj. **1** powerful; strong. **2** (of a drug, alcoholic drink, poison, etc.) having strong physical or chemical properties. **3** (of a reason) cogent; forceful. **4** (of a male) capable of sexual erection or orgasm. **5** literary mighty. □ **potency** n. **potently** adv.

potentate /'pəʊtənˌteɪt/ n. a person who possesses great power, esp. a monarch or ruler.

potential • adj. capable of coming into being or action; latent. • n. **1** the possibility of something developing or happening (potential for error). **2** qualities that exist and can be developed (she has artistic potential). **3** usable resources. **4** Physics the quantity determining the energy of mass in a gravitational field or of charge in an electric field. □ **potentiality** /-ʃɪ'ælɪti/ n. **potentially** adv.

potential difference n. the difference of electric potential between two points.

potentilla /ˌpəʊtən'tɪlə/ n. cinquefoil.

pothead¹ n. slang a habitual user of marijuana.

pothead² n. (also **pothead whale**) the pilot whale, Globicephala melaena.

pot holder n. esp. N Amer. a piece of quilted or thick fabric for handling hot dishes etc.

pothole n. **1** a hole in a road surface caused by wear or extremes of weather. **2** (also **pothole lake**) N Amer. (West & North) a shallow pond or lake formed by a natural hollow in the ground in which water has collected. **3** a deep hole in the ground or a riverbed. **4** a deep hole or system of caves and underground riverbeds formed by the erosion of rock esp. by the action of water. □ **potholed** adj.

potion n. a liquid medicine, poison, magic charm, etc. (love potion).

potlatch n. (among some Aboriginal peoples of the Pacific coast of N America) a ceremonial giving away or destruction of property to enhance status. □ **potlatching** n.

pot light n. Cdn a light encased in a cylindrical shell, recessed into a ceiling. □ **pot lighting** n.

potluck n. **1** N Amer. (in full **potluck supper**, **potluck dinner**, etc.) a party to which each guest brings a dish to be shared. **2** whatever is available.

pot pie n. a pie of beef, chicken, etc. with vegetables, baked and topped with a crust.

potpourri /po:pʊˈriː/ n. **1** a mixture of dried petals and spices used to perfume a room etc. **2** a musical or literary medley. **3** any miscellaneous grouping.

pot roast ● n. a piece of meat, esp. beef, cooked slowly in a covered dish with a small amount of liquid. ● v.tr. cook (a piece of meat) in this way.

potshot n. **1** a random shot at a person or animal. **2** a shot aimed at an animal etc. within easy reach. **3** a piece of esp. random or opportunistic criticism.

potted adj. **1** planted or grown in a flowerpot, esp. indoors. **2** N Amer. slang intoxicated by alcohol or drugs. **3** abridged; summarized (a potted history).

potter[1] v. esp. Brit. = PUTTER[3].

potter[2] n. a maker of ceramic vessels.

potter's wheel n. a flat revolving disc on which wet clay is shaped by a potter.

pottery n. (pl. **-ies**) **1** vessels etc. made of fired clay. **2** a potter's work. **3** a potter's workshop.

potting shed n. a building in which plants are potted and tools etc. are stored.

potting soil n. nutrient-rich soil used esp. for potted plants.

potty[1] adj. (**-ier**, **-iest**) slang esp. Brit. foolish or crazy.

potty[2] n. (pl. **-ies**) informal **1** a small seat fitting over a toilet seat, used by a young child during toilet training. **2** a child's commode.

pouch ● n. **1** a small bag. **2 a** a pocket-like receptacle in which marsupials carry their young during lactation. **b** any of several pocket-like structures in various other animals, e.g. in the cheeks of rodents. **3** a baggy area of skin underneath the eyes etc. **4** a soldier's leather ammunition bag. **5** a lockable bag for mail or dispatches. **6** Bot. a bag-like cavity, esp. the seed vessel, in a plant. ● v.tr. put or make into a pouch. □ **pouched** adj. **pouchy** adj.

pouf /puːf/ n. a soft projecting mass of material on a dress, headdress, etc. □ **poufed** adj.

poultice /ˈpoʊltɪs/ ● n. a soft medicated and usu. heated mass applied to the body and kept in place with muslin etc., for relieving soreness and inflammation. ● v.tr. apply a poultice to.

poultry n. domestic fowls (chickens, turkeys, ducks, geese, etc.), esp. as a source of food.

pounce ● v.intr. **1** spring or swoop, esp. as in capturing prey. **2** (often foll. by on, upon) **a** make a sudden attack. **b** seize eagerly upon an object, remark, etc. (pounced on what we said). ● n. **1** the act or an instance of pouncing. **2** the claw or talon of a bird of prey.

pound[1] n. **1** a unit of weight equal to 16 oz. avoirdupois (453.6 g), or 12 oz. troy (373.2 g). **2** (in full **pound sterling**) (pl. same or **pounds sterling**) the chief monetary unit of the UK and several other countries. **3** = POUND SIGN 2.

pound[2] v. **1** tr. **a** crush or beat with repeated heavy blows. **b** thump or pummel, esp. with the fists. **c** grind to a powder or pulp. **2** intr. deliver heavy blows or gunfire. **3 a** intr. (foll. by along, down, etc.) make one's way heavily or clumsily. **b** tr. informal walk (the streets etc.); cover on foot, esp. in search of work, business, etc. (pounded the pavement). **4** intr. **a** (of the heart) beat heavily. **b** (of the head) throb painfully. □ **pound into** instill (an attitude, behaviour, etc.) forcefully. **pound out** produce with or as if with heavy blows (pound out a tune). □ **pounder** n.

pound[3] ● n. **1** an enclosure, esp. one maintained by public authorities, where stray or homeless animals are kept. **2** a place where impounded vehicles are kept until redeemed. **3** a place of confinement. **4** Cdn hist. = BUFFALO POUND. **5** N Amer. hist. = BUFFALO JUMP. **6** (in full **pound net**) an enclosure of nets in the water near the shore, consisting of a long straight wall of net leading the fish into a first enclosure, and a second enclosure from which they cannot escape. ● v.tr. enclose (cattle etc.) in a pound.

poundage n. **1** a weight stated in pounds. **2** a person's weight, esp. that which is regarded as excess.

pound cake n. a cake made with equal weights of butter, sugar, flour, and eggs.

pounder n. (usu. in comb.) **1** a thing or person weighing a specified number of pounds (a five-pounder). **2** a gun carrying a shell of a specified number of pounds.

pounding n. a resounding defeat; an onslaught resulting in heavy losses (our team took a pounding).

pound sign n. **1** the sign £, representing a pound sterling. **2** the sign #, esp. on a telephone keypad or computer keyboard.

pour ● v. **1** intr. & tr. (usu. foll. by down, out, over, etc.) flow or cause to flow esp. downwards in a stream or shower. **2** tr. & intr. dispense (a drink, e.g. tea) by pouring. **3** intr. (of rain, or with it as subject) fall heavily. **4** intr. (usu. foll. by in, out, etc.) come or go in profusion or rapid succession (the crowd poured out; letters poured in). **5** tr. bestow or spend (money) lavishly or freely. **6** tr. discharge or send freely (poured forth arrows). **7** tr. (often foll. by out) utter at length or in a rush (poured out their story). **8** tr. (also refl.) informal put or fit a person into a tight-fitting garment, esp. in such a way that every part of it is 'filled out' by the wearer. ● n. **1** the act of pouring. **2** a pouring stream. **3** a heavy fall of rain; a downpour. □ **it never rains but it pours** misfortunes rarely come singly. **pour it on** proceed, work, etc. very quickly, with all one's energy. **pour oil on the waters** (or **on troubled waters**) calm a disagreement or disturbance, esp. with conciliatory words. □ **pourable** adj. **pourer** n.

pout ● v.intr. **1** push the lips forward as an expression of displeasure or sulking. **2** (of the lips) be pushed forward. ● n. **1** such an action or expression. **2** a fit of sulking (in a pout). □ **poutingly** adv. **pouty** adj.

poutine /puːˈtiːn/ n. Cdn **1** a dish of french fries topped with cheese curds and a sauce, usu. gravy. **2** NB **a** a potato dumpling. **b** a pudding or pie.

POV abbr. point of view.

poverty n. **1** the state of being poor; want of the necessities of life. **2** (often foll. by of) scarcity or lack. **3** inferiority, poorness, meanness. **4** Christianity renunciation of the right to individual ownership of property.

poverty line n. the minimum income level needed to secure the necessities of life.

poverty-stricken adj. extremely poor.

POW *abbr.* prisoner of war.

pow *interj.* expressing the sound of a blow or explosion.

powder ● *n.* **1** a substance in the form of fine dry particles. **2** a medicine or cosmetic in this form. **3** = GUNPOWDER. **4** loose, usu. freshly-fallen snow, esp. when considered as a type of terrain for skiing. **●** *v.tr.* **1 a** apply powder to. **b** sprinkle or decorate with or as with powder. **2** (esp. as **powdered** *adj.*) reduce to a fine powder. □ **keep one's powder dry** be cautious and alert. **powder one's nose 1** apply powder to one's nose. **2** *euphemism* go to a washroom. □ **powdery** *adj.*

powder blue ● *n.* pale blue. **●** *adj.* (hyphenated when *attrib.*) of this colour.

powder keg *n.* **1** a barrel of gunpowder. **2** a dangerous or volatile situation.

powderman *n.* (*pl.* **-men**) (also **powder monkey**) *N Amer.* the member of a logging crew responsible for the use of explosives.

powder-puff *n.* **1** a soft pad for applying powder to the skin, esp. the face. **2** a soft or weak person (also *attrib.*: *a powder-puff performance*).

powder room *n.* **1** *N Amer.* a small room containing a toilet and sink, located off a bedroom, hallway, etc. **2** *euphemism* a women's washroom, esp. in a public building.

powdery mildew *n.* **1** a plant disease caused by a parasitic fungus of the family Erysiphaceae and characterized by a white floury covering of spores. **2** the fungus itself.

power ● *n.* **1** the ability to do or act (*has the power to change colour*). **2** a particular faculty of body or mind (*lost the power of speech*). **3 a** government, influence, or authority. **b** political or social ascendancy or control (*the party in power*; *people power*). **4** authorization; delegated authority (*power of attorney*). **5** (often foll. by *over*) personal ascendancy. **6** an influential person, group, or organization (*the press is a power in the land*). **7** a military strength. **b** a nation etc. having international influence, esp. based on military strength (*the leading powers*). **8** vigour, energy. **9** an active property or function (*has a high heating power*). **10** *informal* a large number or amount (*has done me a power of good*). **11** the capacity for exerting mechanical force or doing work (*horsepower*). **12** mechanical or electrical energy as distinct from hand labour. **13 a** a public supply of (esp. electrical) energy. **b** a particular source or form of energy (*hydroelectric power*). **14** a mechanical force applied e.g. by means of a lever. **15** *Physics* the rate of energy output. **16** the product obtained when a number is multiplied by itself a certain number of times (*2 to the power of 3 = 8*). **17** the magnifying capacity of a lens. **18** a deity. **●** *v.* **1** *tr.* supply with mechanical or electrical energy. **2** *tr.* (foll. by *up*, *down*) increase or decrease the power supplied to (a device); switch on or off. **3** *intr. informal* move or travel with great speed or force (*they powered along the highway*). **●** *adj.* **1** of or relating to the generation or distribution of electricity (*power plant*). **2** driven by mechanical or electrical energy (*power steering*). **3** *informal* expressing esp. corporate power; characteristic of or involving authority or influence (*wore a power suit*). **4** *Baseball* of or relating to a player who displays power rather than finesse (*power hitter*; *power pitcher*). **5** designating an activity engaged in with maximum intensity (*a power nap*). □ **in the power of** under the control of. **power behind the throne** a person who asserts authority or influence without having formal

status. **the powers that be** those in authority. □ **powered** *adj.* (also in *comb.*).

power-assisted *adj.* (esp. of steering and brakes in a motor vehicle) employing an inanimate source of power to assist manual operation.

power bar *n.* *N Amer.* an electrical cord containing a number of outlets, an on-off switch, and often a surge suppressor, used esp. for computer equipment.

power base *n.* a source of authority or support.

powerboat *n.* a powerful motorboat.

power-broker *n.* esp. *N Amer.* a person who exerts influence or affects the equilibrium of political power by intrigue. □ **power-broking** *n. & adj.*

power centre *n.* **1** the centre of power in an organization, country, etc. **2** a person, organization, etc. that is at the centre of power. **3** *N Amer.* a shopping centre having large discount stores or superstores as its major tenants.

power failure *n.* (also **power cut**) a temporary withdrawal or failure of an electric power supply.

power forward *n.* **1** *Basketball* **a** a large forward who plays in the low post and usu. has good shot-blocking and rebounding skills. **b** this position. **2** *Hockey* an effective forward known as much for strength and toughness as for skill and scoring ability.

powerful *adj.* **1** having much power or strength. **2** politically or socially influential. **3** having a strong emotional effect (*powerful drama*). □ **powerfully** *adv.* **powerfulness** *n.*

power grab *n. informal* an attempt to seize power.

power grid *n.* a system of electricity distribution over a wide area, consisting of a network of high-voltage power lines between major power stations.

powerhouse *n.* **1** = POWER STATION. **2** a very strong, energetic, or successful person, organization, or thing (also *attrib.*: *a powerhouse performance*).

powerless *adj.* **1** without power or strength. **2** (often foll. by *to* + infin.) wholly unable (*powerless to help*). □ **powerlessly** *adv.* **powerlessness** *n.*

powerlifting *n.* a form of competitive weightlifting emphasizing sheer strength, consisting of three types of lift. □ **powerlifter** *n.*

power line *n.* a conductor supplying electrical power, esp. one supported by poles etc.

power of attorney *n.* the authority to act for another person in legal or financial matters.

power of sale *n.* the authority by which a bank, trust company, etc., may seize and sell a mortgaged property on which the mortgage is in default.

power outage *n.* = POWER FAILURE.

power pack *n.* **1** a unit for supplying power. **2** the equipment for converting an alternating current to a direct current at a different (usu. lower) voltage.

power plant *n.* **1** an apparatus or installation which provides power for an industry, machine, etc. **2** = POWER STATION.

power play *n.* **1** *Hockey* **a** a temporary situation in which a team has a numerical advantage over the opposing team because one or more of the opposing players are serving a penalty. **b** an offensive strategy adopted by a team having such an advantage. **2** *Football* a running play in which a number of offensive players clear a path for the ball carrier. **3** an (often underhanded) attempt to gain or maintain power in personal relationships, politics, etc.

power politics *n.pl.* political action based on power or influence.

power-sharing *n.* a policy agreed between parties or within a coalition to share responsibility for decision-making and political action (also *attrib.*: *a power-sharing agreement*).

power skating *n. Cdn* a skating technique aiming to increase a skater's power, speed, and agility by the most efficient use of the skate blades and of the muscles and alignment of the body.

power station *n.* a facility where electricity is generated for distribution.

power stroke *n.* **1** the stroke of an internal combustion engine, in which the piston is moved downward by the expansion of gases. **2** a powerful action of the arm or leg in canoeing, cycling, etc.

power supply *n.* a device that provides electrical power, esp. independently of the main electrical system or at a different voltage.

power surge *n.* a sudden marked increase in voltage of an electric current.

power takeoff *n.* a device for the transmission of mechanical power from an engine, esp. that of a tractor etc.

power tool *n.* an electrically powered tool.

powertrain *n.* **1** the mechanism that transmits the drive from the engine of a vehicle to its axle. **2** this together with the engine and axle.

power trip *n. slang* something done primarily for the enjoyment of exercising power over other people (*the director is on a real power trip*).

power walking *n.* brisk walking for exercise, often accompanied by vigorous swinging of the arms to increase the aerobic demand. □ **power walker** *n.*

powwow ● *n.* **1** a cultural gathering among some N American Aboriginal peoples, with dancing, music, eating, etc. **2** a conference or meeting for discussion. ● *v.intr.* hold a powwow.

pox *n.* **1** any virus disease producing a rash of pimples that become pus-filled and leave pockmarks on healing. **2** *informal* = SYPHILIS.

pp *abbr.* **1** pianissimo. **2** pages.

ppb *abbr.* parts per billion.

ppm *abbr.* parts per million.

PPS *abbr.* additional postscript.

PPV *abbr.* pay-per-view.

PQ *abbr.* **1** Parti Québécois. **2** Province of Quebec.

PR *abbr.* **1** public relations. **2** proportional representation. **3** Puerto Rico. **4** (**pr.**) pair.

Pr *symbol* praseodymium.

practicable /ˈpræktɪkəbəl/ *adj.* **1** that can be done or used. **2** possible in practice. □ **practicability** *n.* **practicably** *adv.*

practical *adj.* **1** of or concerned with practice or use rather than theory. **2** suited to use or action; designed mainly to fulfill a function (*practical shoes*). **3 a** (of a person) inclined to action rather than speculation. **b** sensible as regards the conduct of everyday affairs, financial matters, etc. **4 a** that is such in effect though not nominally (*for all practical purposes*). **b** virtual (*in practical control*). **5** feasible; concerned with what is actually possible (*practical politics*). □ **practicality** *n.* (*pl.* **-ies**).

practical joke *n.* a trick played on a person which makes them look foolish and is intended to amuse others. □ **practical joker** *n.*

practically *adv.* **1** virtually, almost (*practically nothing*). **2** in a practical way.

practical nurse *n. N Amer. see* LICENSED PRACTICAL NURSE, REGISTERED PRACTICAL NURSE.

practice ● *n.* (also **practise**) **1** the actual doing of something; action as contrasted with ideas (*put a plan into practice*). **2** a way of doing something that is

common, habitual, or expected (*standard practice*). **3** a habit or custom. **4 a** repeated exercise in an activity requiring the development of skill (also *attrib.*: *practice clothes*). **b** a session of this (*time for target practice*). **5** action or execution as opposed to theory. **6** the professional work or business of a doctor, lawyer, etc. (*has a practice in town*). **7** an established method of legal procedure. **8** procedure generally, esp. of a specified kind (*bad practice*). ● *v. var. of* PRACTISE. □ **in practice 1** when actually applied; in reality. **2** skilful because of recent exercise in a particular pursuit. **out of practice** lacking a former skill from lack of recent practice. **put into practice** actually apply (an idea, method, etc.).

practicum *n. N Amer.* a course of practical training through experience working in a particular field.

practise ● *v.* (also **practice**) **1** *tr.* perform habitually; carry out in action (*practise the same method*). **2** *tr. & intr.* do repeatedly as an exercise to improve a skill; exercise oneself in or on (an activity requiring skill). **3** *tr.* pursue or be engaged in (a profession, religion, etc.). ● *n. var. of* PRACTICE. □ **practise what one preaches** do what one tells others to do. □ **practiser** *n.*

practised *adj.* **1** experienced, expert (*with a practised hand*). **2** gained or perfected through practice (*a practised accent*).

practising *adj.* currently active or engaged in (a profession or activity) (*a practising Christian*).

practitioner /prækˈtɪʃənər/ *n.* **1** a person practising a profession, esp. medicine. **2** a person who regularly does a particular activity, esp. one requiring skill.

pragmatic /prægˈmætɪk/ *adj.* **1** dealing with matters with regard to their practical requirements or consequences. **2** treating the facts of history with reference to their practical lessons. **3** concerning pragmatism. □ **pragmatically** *adv.*

pragmatism /ˈprægməˌtɪzəm/ *n.* **1** a pragmatic attitude or procedure. **2** a philosophy that evaluates assertions solely by their practical consequences and bearing on human interests. □ **pragmatist** *n.*

prairie *n.* **1** a large area of usu. treeless and flat grassland, esp. in western Canada. **2** (also **the prairies**) the region of western N America originally characterized by such grassland. **3** (**the Prairies**) = PRAIRIE PROVINCES.

prairie chicken *n.* **1** a medium-sized grouse of the N American prairies, *Tympanuchus cupido*. **2** = SHARP-TAILED GROUSE.

prairie crocus *n. Cdn* a spring-flowering plant of the buttercup family, found from BC to Manitoba and the US, *Anemone (Pulsatilla) nuttalliana*, covered with silky hairs and with purple or white flowers and long plumed seeds; floral emblem of Manitoba.

prairie dog *n.* any N American rodent of the genus *Cynomys*, living in burrows and making a barking sound.

prairie fire *n. N Amer.* an uncontrolled fire that burns off the grasses etc. of the prairie.

prairie lily *n.* a N American lily, *Lilium philadelphicum*, with upright reddish-orange flowers with spotted petals; floral emblem of Saskatchewan.

prairie oyster *n.* **1** a seasoned raw egg, swallowed without breaking the yolk. **2** *N Amer.* the testicle of a calf eaten as a delicacy.

Prairie provinces *n.pl.* Alberta, Saskatchewan, and Manitoba.

prairie schooner *n. N Amer.* a covered wagon used by the 19th-c. pioneers in crossing the prairies.

prairie smoke *n. Cdn* either of two plants with long-plumed seeds, purple or three-flowered avens, *Geum triflorum*, or the prairie crocus.

prairie wool *n. Cdn* the natural grassy plant cover of prairie land.

praise ● *v.tr.* **1** express warm approval or admiration of. **2** glorify (God or a deity) in words. ● *n.* the act or an instance of praising; commendation. □ **praise be!** an exclamation of pious gratitude. **sing the praises of** commend (a person) highly.

praiseworthy *adj.* worthy of praise; commendable.

praline /ˈpreɪliːn, ˈprɒ-/ *n.* **1** a confection made by browning nuts in boiling sugar, often crushed and used as a topping or in ice cream etc. **2** a fudge-like, cookie-shaped candy made of sugar, cream, nuts etc.

prana /ˈprɑːnə/ *n.* **1** (in Hinduism) breath as a life-giving force. **2** the breath; breathing.

prance ● *v.intr.* **1** (of a horse) raise the forelegs and spring from the hind legs. **2** (often foll. by *about*) walk or behave in an elated or arrogant manner. ● *n.* **1** the act of prancing. **2** a prancing movement.

prank *n.* a practical joke; a piece of mischief. □ **prankish** *adj.* **prankster** *n.* **pranksterism** *n.*

praseodymium /ˌpreɪziəˈdɪmiəm/ *n.* a soft silvery metallic element of the lanthanide series, occurring in various minerals and used in catalyst mixtures.

prate ● *v.* **1** *intr.* chatter; talk too much. **2** *intr.* talk foolishly or irrelevantly. **3** *tr.* tell or say in a prating manner. ● *n.* prating; idle talk. □ **prating** *adj.*

pratfall *n. N Amer. informal* **1** a fall on the buttocks. **2** a humiliating failure or blunder.

prattle ● *v.intr. & tr.* chatter or say in a childish way. ● *n.* **1** childish chatter. **2** inconsequential talk. □ **prattler** *n.* **prattling** *adj.*

prawn ● *n.* **1** any of various marine crustaceans, resembling a shrimp but usu. larger. **2** *esp. Brit.* a large shrimp. ● *v.intr.* fish for prawns.

praxis *n.* **1** accepted practice or custom. **2** the practising of an art or skill.

pray *v.* **1** *intr.* say prayers (to God etc.); make devout supplication. **2** *tr.* say or offer (a prayer). **3 a** *tr.* entreat, beseech. **b** *tr. & intr.* ask earnestly (*prayed to be released*). □ **pray tell** (used when adding emphasis to question or request, sometimes ironically) please say (*and what, pray tell, would be the point?*).

prayer¹ *n.* **1 a** a solemn request or thanksgiving to God or an object of worship (*say a prayer*). **b** a formula or form of words used in praying (*the Lord's prayer*). **c** the act of praying (*be at prayer*). **d** a religious service consisting largely of prayers. **2 a** an entreaty to a person. **b** a thing entreated or prayed for. □ **not have a prayer** *N Amer. informal* have no chance (of success etc.).

prayer² *n.* a person who prays.

prayer book *n.* a book containing prayers for use in religious services or private devotions.

prayerful *adj.* **1** (of a person) given to praying; devout. **2** (of speech, actions, etc.) characterized by or expressive of prayer. □ **prayerfully** *adv.*

prayer meeting *n. N Amer.* a gathering of esp. evangelical Christians to offer prayers.

prayer rug *n.* (also **prayer mat**) a small carpet used by Muslims when praying.

prayer shawl *n.* = TALLIS.

praying mantis *n.* a mantis, *Mantis religiosa*, that holds its forelegs in a position suggestive of hands folded in prayer, while waiting to pounce on its prey.

pre- *prefix* before (in time, place, order, degree, etc.).

preach *v.* **1 a** *intr.* deliver a sermon or religious address. **b** *tr.* deliver (a sermon); proclaim or expound (the Gospel etc.). **2** *intr.* give moral advice in an obtrusive way. **3** *tr.* advocate or inculcate (a quality or practice etc.). □ **preach to the converted** commend an opinion to a person or persons already in agreement.

preacher *n.* a person who preaches, esp. a minister of religion. □ **preacherly** *adj.*

preachy *adj.* (**-ier**, **-iest**) *informal* inclined to preach or moralize. □ **preachiness** *n.*

preadolescent ● *adj.* **1** (of a child) having nearly reached adolescence. **2** of or relating to the two or three years preceding adolescence. ● *n.* a preadolescent child. □ **preadolescence** *n.*

preamble /priːˈæmbəl, ˈpriː-/ *n.* **1** a preliminary statement or introduction. **2** the introductory part of a statute or deed etc. **3** a preceding fact or circumstance.

preamplifier *n.* (also **preamp**) an electronic device that amplifies a very weak signal (e.g. from a microphone or pickup) and transmits it to a main amplifier. □ **preamplified** *adj.*

pre-arrange *v.tr.* arrange beforehand. □ **pre-arranged** *adj.* **pre-arrangement** *n.*

pre-board *v.tr. & intr.* admit to, or go on board, an aircraft, train, etc. in advance of others. □ **pre-boarding** *n.*

pre-book *v.tr.* book in advance.

Precambrian /priːˈkæmbriən/ *Geol.* ● *adj.* of or relating to the earliest geological era including the whole of the earth's history from its origin about 4,600 million years ago to the beginning of the Cambrian period. ● *n.* this geological era.

precarious /prɪˈkɛəriəs/ *adj.* **1** uncertain; dependent on chance. **2** insecure, perilous (*precarious health*). □ **precariously** *adv.* **precariousness** *n.*

precast *adj.* (of concrete) cast in its final shape before positioning.

precaution *n.* an action taken in advance to avoid danger, prevent problems, etc. □ **precautionary** *adj.*

precede *v.tr.* **1 a** come or go before in time, order, importance, etc. (*the preceding paragraph*). **b** walk etc. in front of (*preceded by our guide*). **2** (foll. by *by*) cause to be preceded (*must precede this measure by milder ones*).

precedence /ˈprɛsɪdəns/ *n.* **1** priority in time, order, or importance, etc. **2** the right of preceding others on formal occasions. □ **take precedence** (often foll. by *over, of*) have priority (over).

precedent /ˈprɛsɪdənt/ *n.* **1** a previous case or legal decision etc. taken as a guide for subsequent cases or as a justification. **2** a similar event or action that occurred earlier (*there is no precedent for such a study*).

precept /ˈpriːsɛpt/ *n.* **1** a command; a rule of conduct. **2** moral instruction. **3** a writ or warrant.

pre-Christian *adj.* before Christ or Christianity.

precinct *n.* **1** an enclosed or clearly defined area, e.g. around a cathedral, college, etc. **2** a specially designated area in a town, esp. with the exclusion of traffic (*shopping precinct*). **3** (in *pl.*) **a** the surrounding area or environs. **b** the boundaries. **4** *N Amer.* **a** a subdivision of a county, city, etc., for police or electoral purposes. **b** *informal* the police station of such a subdivision. **c** (in *pl.*) a neighbourhood.

precious ● *adj.* **1** of great value or worth. **2** beloved; much prized (*precious memories*). **3** affectedly refined, esp. in language or manner. **4** *informal* often *ironic* **a** considerable (*a precious lot you know about it*). **b** expressing contempt or disdain (*you can keep your precious flowers*). ● *adv. informal* extremely, very (*had precious little left*). □ **preciousness** *n.*

precious metal *n.* any of the metals gold, silver, and platinum.

precious stone *n.* a piece of mineral having great value esp. as used in jewellery.

precip *n.* *N Amer. informal* precipitation.

precipice /ˈprɛsɪpɪs/ *n.* **1** a vertical or steep face of a rock, cliff, mountain, etc. **2** a dangerous situation.

precipitate ● *v.* /prɪˈsɪpɪˌteɪt/ **1** *tr.* hasten the occurrence of; cause to occur prematurely. **2** *tr.* (foll. by *into*) send rapidly into a certain state or condition (*were precipitated into war*). **3** *tr.* throw down headlong. **4** *Chem.* **a** *tr.* cause (a substance) to be deposited in solid form from a solution. **b** *intr.* be deposited as a solid from a solution, or from suspension in a gas; settle as a precipitate. **5** *tr. Physics* **a** cause (dust etc.) to be deposited from the air on a surface. **b** condense (vapour) into drops and so deposit it. ● *adj.* /prɪˈsɪpɪtət/ **1** headlong; violently hurried (*precipitate departure*). **2** hasty, rash, inconsiderate. ● *n.* /prɪˈsɪpɪtət/ **1** *Chem.* a substance precipitated from a solution. **2** *Physics* moisture condensed from vapour by cooling and depositing, e.g. rain or dew. ☐ **precipitately** /-tətli/ *adv.* **precipitator** *n.*

precipitation *n.* **1** rain or snow etc. falling to the ground. **b** a quantity of this. **2** the act of precipitating or the process of being precipitated. **3** rash haste.

precipitous /prɪˈsɪpɪtəs/ *adj.* **1 a** of or like a precipice. **b** dangerously steep. **2** precipitate. ☐ **precipitously** *adv.* **precipitousness** *n.*

précis /ˈpreɪsiː/ ● *n.* (*pl.* same /-siːz/) a summary or abstract, esp. of a text or speech. ● *v.tr.* (**-cises** /-siːz/; **-cised** /-siːd/; **-cising** /-siːɪŋ/) make a précis of.

precise *adj.* **1 a** accurately expressed. **b** definite, exact. **2** scrupulous in being exact, observing rules, etc. **3** identical, exact (*at that precise moment*). **4** (of an instrument) accurate; exact.

precisely *adv.* **1** in a precise manner; exactly. **2** (as a reply) quite so; as you say.

precision *n.* **1** the condition of being precise; accuracy. **2** the degree of refinement in measurement etc. **3** (*attrib.*) marked by or adapted for precision (*precision instruments*).

precision skating *n.* *Cdn* figure skating performed in unison by a team of 12 to 32 skaters. ☐ **precision skater** *n.*

preclinical *adj.* **1** (of a stage in a disease) before symptoms can be identified. **2** relating to the first, chiefly theoretical, stage of a medical education.

preclude *v.tr.* **1** (often foll. by *from*) prevent, exclude (*precluded from taking part*). **2** make impossible; remove (*so as to preclude all doubt*). ☐ **preclusion** *n.* **preclusive** *adj.*

precocious *adj.* **1** often *derogatory* (of a person, esp. a child) prematurely developed in some faculty or characteristic. **2** (of an action etc.) indicating such development. **3** (of a plant) flowering or fruiting early. ☐ **precociously** *adv.* **precocity** *n.*

precognition *n.* (supposed) foreknowledge, esp. of a supernatural kind. ☐ **precognitive** *adj.*

pre-colonial *adj.* of or relating to the period before a region or territory became a colony.

pre-Columbian *adj.* of or pertaining to the period of history in the Americas before the arrival of Columbus in 1492.

preconceive *v.tr.* form (an idea etc.) beforehand.

preconception *n.* **1** a preconceived idea. **2** a prejudice.

precondition ● *n.* a prior condition, that must be fulfilled before other things can be done. ● *v.tr.* bring into a required condition beforehand.

pre-Confederation *adj.* *Cdn* **1** of or pertaining to the period before 1867 in Canada. **2** relating to or characteristic of the period before a province or territory entered Confederation.

pre-contact *adj.* of or relating to an Aboriginal society before contact with Europeans.

precook *v.tr.* cook in advance.

precursor /priːˈkɜrsər/ *n.* **1 a** a forerunner. **b** a person who precedes in office etc. **2** a harbinger. **3** a substance from which another is formed by decay or chemical reaction etc.

precut *v.tr.* (*past* and *past part.* **precut**) cut in advance.

predate *v.tr.* exist or occur at a date earlier than.

predation /prɪˈdeɪʃən/ *n.* **1** (usu. in *pl.*) = DEPREDATION. **2** *Zool.* the natural preying of one animal on others.

predator *n.* **1** an animal naturally preying on others. **2** a predatory corporation, country, individual, etc.

predatory *adj.* **1** (of an animal) preying naturally upon others. **2** (of a corporation, country, individual, etc.) plundering or exploiting others.

predatory pricing *n.* the setting of uneconomically low prices in order to put smaller competitors out of business.

pre-dawn ● *n.* the period of time just before dawn. ● *adj.* relating to or occurring during this time.

predecease *v.tr.* die earlier than (another person).

predecessor *n.* **1** a former holder of an office or position with respect to a later holder (*my immediate predecessor*). **2** a thing to which another has succeeded (*the new plan resembles its predecessor*).

predestination *n.* *Theol.* (as a belief or doctrine) the divine foreordaining of all that will happen, esp. with regard to the salvation of some and not others.

predestine /priːˈdɛstɪn/ *v.tr.* **1** determine beforehand. **2** ordain in advance by divine will or fate.

predetermine *v.tr.* **1** determine or decree beforehand. **2** predestine. ☐ **predetermination** *n.*

predicament /prɪˈdɪkəmənt/ *n.* a difficult, unpleasant, or embarrassing situation.

predicate ● *v.tr.* /ˈprɛdɪˌkeɪt/ **1** assert or affirm as true or existent. **2** (foll. by *on*) found or base (a statement etc.) on. ● *n.* /ˈprɛdɪkət/ **1** *Grammar* what is said about the subject of a sentence etc. (e.g. *went home* in *Earl went home*). **2** *Logic* **a** what is predicated. **b** what is affirmed or denied of the subject by means of the copula (e.g. *mortal* in *all humans are mortal*).

predicative /prɪˈdɪkətɪv/ *adj.* **1** (of an adjective or noun) forming or contained in the predicate, as *old* in *the dog is old* and *house* in *there is a large house* (opp. ATTRIBUTIVE). **2** that predicates. ☐ **predicatively** *adv.*

predict *v.* **1** *tr.* (often foll. by *that* + clause) make a statement about the future; foretell, prophesy. **2** *intr.* make a prediction; foretell the future. ☐ **predictive** *adj.* **predictively** *adv.* **predictor** *n.*

predictable *adj.* **1** that can be predicted or is to be expected. **2** likely to behave in a way that is easy to predict. ☐ **predictability** *n.* **predictably** *adv.*

prediction *n.* **1** the art of predicting or the process of being predicted. **2** a thing predicted; a forecast.

predigest *v.tr.* **1** render (food) easily digestible before being eaten. **2** make (reading matter, etc.) easier to read, understand, appreciate, etc.

predilection /ˌpriːdɪˈlɛkʃən/ *n.* (often foll. by *for*) a preference or special liking.

predispose *v.tr.* **1** influence favourably in advance. **2** (foll. by *to*, or *to* + infin.) render liable or inclined beforehand. ☐ **predisposition** *n.*

prednisone /ˈprɛdnɪˌzoːn/ *n.* a synthetic drug similar

to cortisone, used to relieve rheumatic and allergic conditions and to treat leukemia.

predominant *adj.* **1** prevailing, exerting control. **2** being the main or most numerous or widespread element. □ **predominance** *n.*

predominantly *adv.* mainly; for the most part.

predominate *v.intr.* **1** (foll. by *over*) have or exert control. **2** be superior. **3** be the strongest, main, or most numerous or widespread element (*a garden in which dahlias predominate*).

pre-eclampsia /ˌpriːɪˈklæmpsɪə/ *n.* a condition of pregnancy characterized by high blood pressure and other symptoms associated with eclampsia. □ **pre-eclamptic** *adj. & n.*

preemie *n.* a baby born prematurely.

pre-eminent *adj.* **1** excelling others. **2** outstanding; distinguished in some quality. □ **pre-eminence** *n.* **pre-eminently** *adv.*

pre-empt *v.tr.* **1 a** forestall; act in advance to render (something) unnecessary, ineffective, etc. **b** acquire or appropriate in advance. **2** prevent (an attack) by disabling the enemy. **3** obtain by pre-emption. **4** *N Amer.* take for oneself (esp. public land) so as to have the right of pre-emption. **5** *N Amer.* (of a news bulletin etc.) interrupt and take the place of (a television or radio broadcast). □ **pre-emptor** *n.* **pre-emptory** *adj.*

pre-emption *n.* **1 a** the purchase or appropriation by one person or party before the opportunity is offered to others. **b** the right to purchase (esp. public land) in this way. **2** prior appropriation or acquisition. **3** *Military* the action or strategy of making a pre-emptive attack.

pre-emptive *adj.* **1** serving to pre-empt. **2** (of military action) intended to prevent attack by disabling the enemy (*a pre-emptive strike*). □ **pre-emptively** *adv.*

preen *v.tr. & intr.* **1** (of a bird) tidy (the feathers or itself) with its beak. **2** (also *refl.*) (of a person) smarten or admire (oneself, one's hair, clothes, etc.).

pre-exist *v.intr.* (esp. as **pre-existing** *adj.*) exist at an earlier time or already. □ **pre-existence** *n.* **pre-existent** *adj.*

prefab *informal* ● *adj.* prefabricated. ● *n.* a prefabricated building etc.

prefabricate *v.tr.* **1** manufacture (a building etc. or a component of one) prior to assembly on a site. **2** produce in an artificially standardized way. □ **prefabrication** *n.*

preface ● *n.* **1** an introduction to a book stating its subject, scope, etc. **2** the preliminary part of a speech. ● *v.tr.* **1** introduce or begin (a speech or event) (*prefaced my remarks with a warning*). **2** provide (a book etc.) with a preface. **3** (of an event etc.) lead up to (another). □ **prefatory** *adj.*

prefect *n.* **1** a chief officer, magistrate, governor, etc. **2** the chief administrative officer of certain departments in France. **3** a senior pupil in a school etc. authorized to enforce discipline.

prefecture *n.* **1 a** a district under the government of a prefect. **b** an administrative division of a Japanese or Chinese province. **2 a** a prefect's office or tenure. **b** the official residence of a prefect. □ **prefectural** *adj.*

prefer /prəˈfɜr/ *v.tr.* (**preferred**, **preferring**) **1** choose instead; like better (*would prefer to stay*; *prefers coffee to tea*). **2** submit (information, an accusation, etc.) for consideration. **3** give preference to as a creditor. **4** promote or advance (a person).

preferable /ˈprefrəbəl, ˈprefərəbəl, prəˈfɜrəbəl/ *adj.* **1** to be preferred. **2** more desirable. □ **preferability** *n.* **preferably** *adv.*

preference *n.* **1** the act or an instance of preferring or being preferred. **2** a thing preferred. **3 a** the favouring of one person etc. before others. **b** *Commerce* the favouring of one country by admitting its products at a lower import duty. **4** *Law* a prior right, esp. to the payment of debts. □ **in preference to** as a thing preferred over (another).

preferential *adj.* **1** of or involving preference (*preferential treatment*). **2** giving or receiving a favour. **3** (of a tariff etc.) favouring particular countries. **4** (of voting) in which the voter puts candidates in order of preference. □ **preferentially** *adv.*

preferment *n.* promotion to office.

preferred share *n.* (also **preferred stock**) *N Amer.* a share in a company which yields a fixed rate of interest and takes preference over common stock in entitlement to dividends.

prefigure *v.tr.* **1** represent beforehand by a figure or type. **2** imagine beforehand. □ **prefiguration** *n.*

prefix ● *n.* **1** a verbal element placed at the beginning of a word to adjust or qualify its meaning, e.g. *ex-, non-, re-*. **2** a title placed before a name, e.g. *Mr.* ● *v.tr.* (often foll. by *to*) **1** add as an introduction. **2** join (a word or element) as a prefix.

pre-flight *attrib.adj.* occurring or provided before an aircraft flight.

preform *v.tr.* form or shape beforehand.

prefrontal *adj.* **1** in front of the frontal bone of the skull. **2** in the forepart of the frontal lobe.

pre-game *attrib.adj.* occurring just before a sporting event (*pre-game jitters*; *pre-game show*).

preggers *adj. informal* = PREGNANT 1.

pregnancy *n.* (*pl.* **-ies**) the condition or an instance of being pregnant.

pregnant *adj.* **1** (of a woman or female animal) having a child or young developing in the uterus. **2** full of meaning; significant or suggestive (*a pregnant pause*). **3** (esp. of a person's mind) imaginative, inventive. **4** (foll. by *with*) plentifully provided (*pregnant with danger*). □ **pregnantly** *adv.* (in sense 2).

pre-hearing *n.* a hearing preparatory to a full hearing, trial, etc.

preheat *v.tr.* heat beforehand.

prehensile /prɪˈhensaɪl/ *adj.* (of a tail or limb) capable of grasping.

prehistoric *adj.* **1** of or relating to the period before written records. **2** *informal* utterly out of date. □ **prehistorian** *n.* **prehistorically** *adv.* **prehistory** *n.*

pre-industrial *adj.* of or relating to the time before industrialization.

prejudge *v.tr.* **1** form a premature judgment on (a person, issue, etc.). **2** pass judgment on (a person) before a trial or proper inquiry. □ **prejudgment** *n.*

prejudice ● *n.* **1 a** a preconceived opinion. **b** (foll. by *against*, *in favour of*) bias or partiality. **c** dislike or distrust of a person, group, etc. **2** harm or injury that results or may result from some action or judgment (*to the prejudice of*). ● *v.tr.* **1** impair the validity or force of (a right, claim, statement, etc.). **2** cause (a person) to have a prejudice. □ **without prejudice** (often foll. by *to*) without detriment (to any existing right or claim).

prejudiced *adj.* not impartial; bigoted.

prejudicial *adj.* causing or characterized by prejudice. □ **prejudicially** *adv.*

pre-lapsarian /ˌpriːlæpˈserɪən/ *adj.* before the Fall; innocent.

prelate /ˈprelət/ *n.* a high ecclesiastical dignitary.

pre-law *n.* *N Amer.* (often *attrib.*) a program of studies taken as preparation for law school.

prelim /ˈpriːlɪm, prɪˈlɪm/ *n. informal* **1** (often in *pl.*) a preliminary match, contest, round, etc. **2** a preliminary examination, esp. at a university. **3** a preliminary hearing or trial.

preliminary ● *adj.* introductory, preparatory; initial. ● *n.* (*pl.* **-ies**) (usu. in *pl.*) **1** a preliminary action or arrangement (*dispense with the preliminaries*). **2** a preliminary trial or contest. ● *adv.* (foll. by *to*) preparatory to; in advance. □ **preliminarily** *adv.*

preliterate *adj.* of or relating to a society or culture that has not developed the use of writing.

preload *v.tr.* (esp. as **preloaded** *adj.*) load (esp. software) beforehand.

prelude /ˈpreɪljuːd, -ljuːd, ˈprel-/ ● *n.* (often foll. by *to*) **1** an action, event, or situation serving as an introduction. **2 a** an introductory piece of music, often preceding a fugue or forming the first piece of a suite or beginning an act of an opera. **b** a short piece of music of a similar type, esp. for the piano. **3** the introductory part of a poem etc. ● *v.tr.* **1** serve as a prelude to. **2** introduce with a prelude.

premarital *adj.* existing or (esp. of sexual relations) occurring before marriage.

premature *adj.* **1 a** occurring or done before the usual or proper time; too early (*a premature decision*). **b** too hasty (*must not be premature*). **2** born (esp. three or more weeks) before the end of the full term of gestation. □ **prematurely** *adv.* **prematurity** *n.*

pre-med *n.* (often *attrib.*) **1** a program of studies taken in preparation for medical school. **2** a pre-med student.

premeditate *v.tr.* (esp. as **premeditated** *adj.*) think out or plan (an action) beforehand (*premeditated murder*). □ **premeditation** *n.* **premeditative** *adj.*

premenopausal *adj.* preceding menopause.

premenstrual *adj.* of, occurring, or experienced before menstruation (*premenstrual tension*).

premenstrual syndrome *n.* any of a complex of symptoms (including tension, fluid retention, etc.) experienced by some women in the days immediately before menstruation. Abbr.: **PMS.**

premier /ˈpriːmjiːr, ˈpriːmjər, ˈpriːmiːr, ˈpremjər/ ● *n.* **1** *Cdn* the first minister of a province or territory. **2** a prime minister or head of government in any of several other countries. ● *adj.* first in importance, order, or time. □ **premiership** *n.*

premiere /premˈjer, prəˈmjer, ˈpremjer, ˈpriːmjiːr, -ˈmjiːr/ ● *n.* the first performance or showing of a play, film, etc. ● *v.* **1** *tr.* give a premiere of. **2** *intr.* (of a play, film, etc.) be presented for the first time. ● *adj.* = PREMIER.

premise ● *n.* /ˈpremɪs/ **1** (also **premiss**) *Logic* a previous statement or proposition from which another is inferred or follows as a conclusion. **2** the basic plot or circumstances on which a play, film, etc., is based. **3** (in *pl.*) /ˈpremɪsɪs, -sɪz/ **a** a house, building, etc., with any buildings or property near it belonging to it. **b** *Law* houses, lands, or tenements previously specified in a document etc. ● *v.tr.* /ˈpremɪs/ **1 a** say or write by way of introduction. **b** assume from a premise. **2** (foll. by *on*) base on. □ **on the premises** in the building etc. concerned.

premium ● *n.* **1** an amount to be paid for a contract of insurance. **2 a** a sum added to interest, wages, etc.; a bonus. **b** a sum added to ordinary charges. **3** a reward or prize. ● *attrib.adj.* (of a commodity) of best quality and therefore more expensive. □ **at a premium 1** highly valued; above the usual or nominal price. **2** scarce and in demand. **put a premium**

on 1 provide or act as an incentive to. **2** attach special value to.

premix ● *v.tr.* (esp. as **premixed** *adj.*) mix beforehand. ● *n.* a mixture prepared beforehand of various materials, e.g. animal feed.

premolar ● *adj.* in front of a molar tooth. ● *n.* (in an adult human) each of eight teeth situated in pairs between each of the four canine teeth and each first molar.

premonition /ˌpremɪˈnɪʃən/ *n.* a forewarning; a presentiment. □ **premonitory** /prɪˈmɒnɪˌtɔri/ *adj.*

prenatal *adj.* of or concerning the period before childbirth. □ **prenatally** *adv.*

prenup /priːˈnʌp/ *n.* a prenuptial agreement.

prenuptial /priːˈnʌptʃəl, -ˈnʌpʃʊəl, -ˈnʌpʃəl/ *adj.* **1** existing or occurring before marriage. **2** (of an agreement, contract, etc.) entered into by a couple before marriage, specifying how their assets are to be split in the event of divorce.

preoccupation *n.* **1** the state of being preoccupied. **2** a thing that engrosses the mind.

preoccupied *adj.* otherwise engrossed; mentally distracted.

preoccupy *v.tr.* (**-ies, -ied**) **1** (of a thought etc.) dominate or engross the mind of (a person) to the exclusion of other thoughts. **2** occupy beforehand.

pre-op *adj.* = PREOPERATIVE.

preoperative *adj.* of or related to the period or a condition before an operation.

preordain *v.tr.* (esp. as **preordained** *adj.*) ordain or determine beforehand.

pre-owned *adj.* second-hand, used.

prep *informal* ● *n.* **1** = PREPARATION. **2** *N Amer.* = PREPPY. **3** *N Amer.* a horse race that is a preparation for a more important event. ● *attrib.adj.* **1** = PREPARATORY (*prep time*). **2** relating to a preparatory school (*prep athlete*). ● *v.* (**prepped, prepping**) *N Amer. informal* **1** *tr.* prepare, make ready or suitable. **2** *intr.* prepare oneself for an event.

prepackage *v.tr.* (esp. as **prepackaged** *adj.*) package (goods) on the site of production or before retail.

preparation *n.* **1** the act or an instance of preparing; the process of being prepared. **2** (often in *pl.*) something done to make ready. **3** a specially prepared substance, esp. a food or medicine.

preparative *adj.* preparatory. □ **preparatively** *adv.*

preparatory /ˈprepərəˌtɔri, prəˈperətɔri/ ● *adj.* (often foll. by *to*) serving to prepare; introductory. ● *adv.* (often foll. by *to*) in a preparatory manner (*preparatory to departure*). □ **preparatorily** *adv.*

preparatory school *n. N Amer.* a usu. private school preparing pupils for college or university.

prepare *v.* **1** *tr.* make or get ready for use, consideration, etc. **2** *tr.* make ready or assemble (food, a meal, etc.) for eating. **3 a** *tr.* make (a person or oneself) ready or disposed in some way (*prepares students for university; prepared them for a shock*). **b** *intr.* put oneself or things in readiness, get ready (*prepare to jump*). **4** *tr.* make (a chemical product etc.) by a regular process. □ **be prepared 1** (usu. foll. by *for*) be ready or disposed (*was prepared for a legal battle*). **2** (foll. by *to*) be willing to. □ **preparer** *n.*

preparedness *n.* a state of readiness, e.g. for war.

prepay *v.tr.* (*past* and *past part.* **prepaid**) **1** pay (a charge) in advance. **2** pay for (goods or a service) in advance. □ **prepayable** *adj.* **prepayment** *n.*

preplan *v.tr.* (**-planned, -planning**) plan in advance.

preponderant *adj.* surpassing in influence, power,

number, or importance; predominant. □ **preponderance** n. **preponderantly** adv.

preponderate v.intr. (often foll. by over) **1 a** be greater in influence, quantity, or number. **b** predominate. **2** be of greater importance.

preposition n. Grammar a word governing (and usu. preceding) a noun or pronoun and expressing a relation to another word or element, as in: 'the man on the platform', 'came after dinner', 'what did you do it for?'. □ **prepositional** adj.

prepossessing adj. attractive, appealing.

preposterous adj. utterly absurd; outrageous; contrary to nature, reason, or common sense. □ **preposterously** adv. **preposterousness** n.

preppy N Amer. informal (also **preppie**) ● n. (pl. **-ies**) a person attending an expensive private school or who looks like such a person (with neat and stylish hair, clothing, etc.). ● adj. (**-ier**, **-iest**) **1** of, like, or pertaining to a preppy or preppies. **2** neat and fashionable.

preprint v.tr. (esp. as **preprinted** adj.) print beforehand.

preprocess v.tr. subject to a preliminary processing.

preprocessor n. a computer program that modifies data to conform with the input requirements of another program.

pre-production n. work done on a film, broadcast, etc. before production begins (often attrib.: pre-production discussions).

pre-program v.tr. (**-programmed**, **-programming**) program (a computer etc.) beforehand.

prep school n. = PREPARATORY SCHOOL.

prepubescent ● adj. (also **prepubertal**) **1** occurring prior to puberty. **2** that has not yet reached puberty. ● n. a prepubescent boy or girl.

prepublication ● attrib.adj. produced or occurring before publication. ● n. publication in advance or beforehand.

pre-qualify v.intr. qualify in advance, as for a mortgage, sporting event, etc.

prequel n. a story, film, etc., whose events or concerns precede those of an existing work.

Pre-Raphaelite /pri'ræfiə‚laɪt/ ● n. a member of a group of English 19th-c. artists whose early work was marked by bright colours, strong boundary lines, and meticulous detail; later works typically depict scenes from classical mythology or medieval romance in a dreamy style. ● adj. **1** of or relating to the Pre-Raphaelites. **2** (**pre-Raphaelite**) (esp. of a woman) like a type painted by a Pre-Raphaelite, e.g. with long thick curly auburn hair.

pre-record v.tr. (esp. as **pre-recorded** adj.) record (a message, material for broadcasting, etc.) in advance.

pre-release ● attrib.adj. /‚pri:ri'li:s/ of or pertaining to the period before the release of a prisoner, consumer product, etc. ● n. /'pri:ri‚li:s/ a film, record, software, etc., given restricted availability before being generally released.

prerequisite ● adj. required as a precondition. ● n. a prerequisite thing.

prerogative /prə'rɒgətɪv/ n. **1** a right or privilege exclusive to an individual or class. **2** the right or privilege exercised by a monarch or head of state over all other people, which overrides the law and is in theory subject to no restriction.

Pres. abbr. President.

presage ● n. /'presɪdʒ/ **1** an omen or portent. **2** a presentiment or foreboding. ● v.tr. /'presɪdʒ, prə'seɪdʒ/ **1** portend, foreshadow. **2** give warning of (an event

etc.) by natural means. **3** (of a person) predict or have a presentiment of.

presbyter /'presbɪtər, 'prez-/ n. **1** an elder in the early Christian Church. **2** (in the Presbyterian Church) an elder. **3** (in the Episcopal Church) a minister of the second order; a priest. □ **presbyterial** /-'tɪəriəl/ adj.

Presbyterian ● n. a member of any of various branches of a more or less Calvinistic Protestant denomination with ecclesiastical government by presbyteries. ● adj. of or relating to Presbyterians or Presbyterianism. □ **Presbyterianism** n.

presbytery /'presbɪtri, 'prez-/ n. (pl. **-ies**) **1 a** (in the Presbyterian and United Churches) an ecclesiastical body made up of all of the ministers from a district together with an equal number of elders, ranking next above a Session. **b** a district represented by this. **2** the house of a Catholic priest. **3** the eastern part of a chancel beyond the choir; the sanctuary.

preschool ● adj. of or relating to the time before a child is old enough to go to school. ● n. = NURSERY SCHOOL. □ **preschooler** n.

prescient /'presiənt, pri:-, -ʃi-, 'preʃənt/ adj. having foresight or foreknowledge. □ **prescience** n. **presciently** adv.

pre-screen v.tr. screen beforehand; make a preliminary selection among (candidates etc.).

prescribe v. **1** tr. **a** advise the use of (a medicine etc.), esp. by an authorized prescription. **b** recommend, esp. as a benefit (prescribed a change of scenery). **2** tr. lay down or impose authoritatively. **3** intr. (foll. by to, for) assert a prescriptive right or claim. □ **prescriber** n.

prescript n. an ordinance, law, or command.

prescription n. **1 a** a doctor's (usu. written) instruction for the composition and use of a medicine. **b** a medicine prescribed (also attrib.: prescription drugs). **2 a** the act or an instance of prescribing. **b** a thing considered as bringing about a specified condition (a prescription for anarchy). **3** uninterrupted use or possession from time immemorial or for the period fixed by law as giving a title or right. **4 a** an ancient custom viewed as authoritative. **b** a claim founded on long use.

prescriptive adj. **1** prescribing. **2** Linguistics concerned with or laying down rules of usage. **3** based on prescription (prescriptive right). **4** prescribed by custom. □ **prescriptivism** n. **prescriptivist** n. & adj.

pre-season n. the period before a season (esp. a sports season) begins (often attrib.: pre-season game).

pre-select v.tr. select in advance. □ **pre-selection** n.

presence n. **1** the state or condition of being present. **2** a place where a person is (was admitted to their presence). **3** a person's appearance, bearing, or force of personality, esp. when imposing (stage presence). **4** a person, spirit, etc., that is present (there was a presence in the room). **5** the maintenance by a nation of political interests and influence in another country or region (maintained a presence). □ **in the presence of** in front of; observed by.

presence of mind n. calmness and self-control in sudden difficulty etc.

present[1] ● adj. **1** (usu. predic.) **a** being in the place in question (was present at the trial). **b** occurring or existing (oxygen is present in water). **2 a** now existing, occurring, or being such (the present premier). **b** now being considered or discussed etc. (in the present case). **3** Grammar expressing an action etc. now going on or habitually performed (present tense). ● n. (prec. by the) **1** the time now passing (no time like the present). **2** Grammar the present tense. □ **at present** now. **for the**

present¹ 1 just now. 2 as far as the present is concerned. □ **presentness** n.

present² v. 1 tr. introduce, offer, or exhibit, esp. for public attention or consideration. 2 tr. a (with a thing as object, foll. by to) offer or give as a gift (to a person), esp. formally or ceremonially. b (with a person as object, foll. by with) make available to; cause to have (presented them with a new car; that presents us with a problem). 3 tr. a (of a company, producer, etc.) put (a form of entertainment) before the public. b (of a performer, master of ceremonies, etc.) introduce or put before an audience. 4 tr. introduce (a person) formally (may I present my fiancé?). 5 tr. offer, give (compliments etc.) (may I present my card). 6 tr. a (of a circumstance) reveal (some quality etc.) (this presents some difficulty). b exhibit (an appearance etc.) (presented a rough exterior). 7 tr. (of an idea etc.) offer or suggest itself. 8 tr. deliver (a cheque, bill, etc.) for acceptance or payment. 9 tr. a (usu. foll. by at) aim (a weapon). b hold out (a weapon) in a position for aiming. 10 intr. & refl. Med. (of a patient or illness etc.) come forward for or undergo initial medical examination. 11 intr. Med. (of a part of a fetus) be directed toward the cervix at the time of delivery. 12 tr. (foll. by to) Law bring formally under notice, submit (an offence, complaint, etc.). □ **present arms** hold a rifle etc. vertically in front of the body as a salute. **present oneself** 1 appear. 2 come forward for examination etc. □ **presenter** n.

present³ n. a gift; a thing given or presented. □ **make a present of** give as a gift.

presentable adj. 1 of good appearance; fit to be presented to other people. 2 fit for presentation. □ **presentability** n. **presentably** adv.

presentation /ˌprezənˈteiʃən, ˌpriː-/ n. 1 a the act or an instance of presenting; the process of being presented. b a thing presented. 2 the manner or quality of presenting. 3 a demonstration or display of materials, information, etc.; a lecture. 4 an exhibition or theatrical performance. 5 a formal introduction. 6 the position of the fetus in relation to the cervix at the time of delivery. 7 Cdn (Prairies) a a wedding at which the bride and groom receive gifts of money rather than things. b a gift of money at such a wedding. □ **presentational** adj.

present company n. those who are here now.

present-day attrib.adj. of this time; modern.

presentiment /priˈzentimənt, -ˈsentimənt/ n. a vague expectation; a foreboding (esp. of misfortune).

presently adv. 1 esp. N Amer. & Scot. at the present time; now. 2 soon; after a short time.

presentment /priˈzentmənt/ n. the act or an instance of presenting or being presented, esp. the presentation of a statement on oath by a jury, or of a bill, note, etc., as payment.

preservation n. 1 the act of preserving or process of being preserved. 2 a state of being well or badly preserved (in an excellent state of preservation).

preservationist n. a supporter or advocate of preservation, esp. of historic buildings, natural areas, etc.

preservative ● n. a substance for preserving perishable foodstuffs, wood, etc. ● adj. tending to preserve.

preserve ● v.tr. 1 a keep safe or free from harm, decay, etc. b keep alive (a name, memory, etc.). 2 maintain (a thing) in its existing state. 3 retain (a quality or condition). 4 a treat or refrigerate (food) to prevent decomposition or fermentation. b prepare (fruit) by boiling it with sugar, for long-term storage. 5 keep (a natural area, wildlife, etc.) undisturbed for protection or private use. ● n. (in sing. or pl.) 1 preserved fruit; jam. 2 a place where game or fish etc. is preserved. 3 a sphere or area of activity regarded as a person's own. □ **preserver** n.

pre-set ● v.tr. (-setting; past and past part. -set) set or fix in advance of operation or use. ● n. (preset) a setting or control, esp. on an electronic instrument, configured or adjusted beforehand to facilitate use.

pre-settlement attrib.adj. N Amer. designating the time before the arrival of European settlers.

pre-shrink v.tr. (past and past part. -shrunk) treat (a fabric or garment) so that it shrinks during manufacture and not in use.

preside v.intr. 1 (often foll. by at, over) be in a position of authority, esp. as the chairperson or president of a meeting. 2 exercise control or authority.

presidency n. (pl. -ies) 1 the office of president. 2 the period of this.

president n. 1 the elected head of a republican state. 2 the head of an association, union, council, etc. 3 N Amer. the head of a company, etc. 4 the head of a college or university. 5 a person in charge of a meeting, assembly, etc. □ **presidential** adj.

president-elect n. (pl. **presidents-elect**) a president who has been elected but has not yet taken office.

presoak ● v.tr. soak (esp. food or laundry) prior to cooking, washing, etc. ● n. liquid in which something is presoaked.

press¹ ● v. 1 tr. apply steady force to (a thing in contact). 2 tr. a compress or apply pressure to a thing to flatten, shape, or smooth it, as by ironing. b squeeze (a fruit etc.) to extract its juice. c manufacture (a phonograph record etc.) by moulding under pressure. 3 tr. (foll. by out of, from, etc.) squeeze (juice etc.). 4 tr. embrace or caress by squeezing (pressed my hand). 5 intr. a (foll. by on, against, etc.) exert pressure. b (of an athlete, team, etc.) apply offensive pressure. 6 intr. be urgent; demand immediate action (time was pressing). 7 intr. (foll. by for) make an insistent demand. 8 intr. (foll. by around, etc.) form a crowd. 9 intr. (foll. by on, forward, etc.) hasten insistently. 10 tr. (often foll. by for, or to + infin.) urge or entreat (pressed me to stay). 11 tr. (foll. by on, upon) a put forward or urge (an opinion, claim, or course of action). b insist on the acceptance of (an offer, a gift, etc.). 12 tr. insist on (did not press the point). 13 tr. Weightlifting raise (a specified weight) esp. by first lifting it to shoulder height, and then gradually pushing it upwards above the head. ● n. 1 the act or an instance of pressing (give it a slight press). 2 a a device for compressing, flattening, shaping, extracting juice, etc. (garlic press). b a frame for preserving the shape of a racquet when not in use. c a machine that applies pressure to a workpiece by means of a tool, in order to punch shapes, bend it, etc. 3 = PRINTING PRESS. 4 (prec. by the) a the art or practice of printing. b newspapers, journalists, etc., generally or collectively (pursued by the press). 5 treatment given to or opinions expressed in newspapers etc. about something or someone; publicity (got good press). 6 (**Press**) a a printing house or establishment. b a publishing company (Oxford University Press). 7 a crowding. b a crowd (of people etc.). 8 the pressure of affairs. 9 Weightlifting a raising of a weight up to shoulder height followed by its gradual extension above the head. 10 Basketball any of various forms of close guarding by the defending team. □ **at** (or **in**) **press** (or **the press**) being printed. **be pressed for** have barely enough (time etc.). **go** (or **send**) **to press** go or send to be printed. **press the button** 1 set machinery in motion. 2 informal initiate an action or train of events, esp. nuclear war. **press (the) flesh** esp. *N Amer.* shake hands. □ **presser** *n.*

press² *v.tr.* **1** *hist.* force to serve in the army etc. **2** bring into use as a makeshift (*was pressed into service*).

press agent *n.* a person employed by an organization to deal with press publicity.

pressback *adj. N Amer.* designating a type of antique wooden chair with a design pressed rather than carved into the chair back.

pressboard *n.* a material made of compressed paper laminations, used as a separator or insulator in electrical equipment.

press box *n.* a reporters' enclosure esp. at a sports event.

press clipping *n. N Amer.* an article, photo, etc. cut from a newspaper, magazine, etc.

press conference *n.* a session to which journalists are invited to hear an announcement, ask questions, etc.

press corps *n.* a group of reporters from various publications, networks, etc. who regularly cover the same beat.

pressed glass *n.* glass shaped or given its pattern by being poured under pressure into a mould.

press gallery *n.* a gallery for reporters esp. in a legislative assembly.

press gang ● *n. hist.* a body of men employed to press men into service in the army or navy. ● *v.tr.* (**press-gang**) force into service; coerce.

pressing ● *adj.* calling for immediate attention; urgent (*pressing business*). ● *n.* **1** a thing made by pressing, esp. a phonograph record. **2** a series of these made at one time. **3** the act or an instance of pressing a thing, esp. a phonograph record or olives etc. □ **pressingly** *adv.*

press kit *n.* a portfolio, folder, etc. containing printed matter or other multimedia materials relating to a certain issue, product, etc., prepared by an organization for distribution to the media.

press office *n.* a department, e.g. of a business firm or political party, responsible for dealings with the press. □ **press officer** *n.*

press release *n.* an official statement issued to the media by a government department, business, etc., for information and possible publication.

press run *n.* = PRINT RUN.

press secretary *n.* a person who deals with publicity and public relations for an individual or organization.

press time *n.* the time at which a print run of a newspaper, magazine, etc. begins.

pressure ● *n.* **1 a** the exertion of continuous force on or against a body by another in contact with it. **b** the force exerted. **c** the amount of this (expressed by the force on a unit area) (*atmospheric pressure*). **d** = BLOOD PRESSURE. **2** urgency; the need to meet a deadline etc. (*work under pressure*). **3** affliction or difficulty (*under financial pressure*). **4** constraining influence (*if pressure is brought to bear*). ● *v.tr.* **1** apply (esp. psychological or moral) pressure to. **2** (often foll. by *into*) persuade; coerce (*was pressured into attending*).

pressure cooker *n.* **1** an airtight pot in which food can be cooked quickly under steam pressure. **2** an environment or situation of great pressure or stress. □ **pressure-cook** *v.tr.*

pressure gauge *n.* a gauge showing the pressure of steam, air in a tire, etc.

pressure group *n.* a group that promotes a particular interest or cause by influencing public policy.

pressure point *n.* **1** a small area on the skin esp. sensitive to pressure. **2** a point where an artery can be pressed against a bone to inhibit bleeding. **3** a target for political pressure or influence.

pressure ridge *n.* a ridge caused by pressure, esp. a ridge of ice in the polar sea forced up by lateral pressure.

pressure-treated *adj.* (of wood) impregnated with a preservative fluid to reduce decay and rotting. □ **pressure-treat** *v.tr.*

pressurize *v.tr.* **1** (esp. as **pressurized** *adj.*) maintain normal atmospheric pressure in (an aircraft cabin etc.) at a high altitude. **2** raise to a high pressure. □ **pressurization** *n.*

prestige /pre'sti:3, -'sti:d3/ *n.* **1** respect, reputation, or influence derived from achievements, power, wealth, etc. **2** (*attrib.*) having or conferring prestige. □ **prestigious** /pre'sti:d3əs, -'stɪd3əs/ *adj.*

presto /'presto:/ ● *adv. Music* in quick tempo. ● *n.* (*pl.* **-os**) *Music* a movement to be played in a quick tempo. ● *interj.* (also **presto chango** /tʃeɪnd3o:/) used to announce the successful completion of a magical trick or other surprising, esp. rapid, achievement.

presumably *adv.* as may reasonably be presumed.

presume *v.* **1** *tr.* **a** (often foll. by *that* + clause) suppose to be true; take for granted. **b** assume (a person) to be (*presumed dead*). **2** *tr.* (often foll. by *to* + infin.) **a** take the liberty; be impudent enough (*presumed to question their authority*). **b** dare (*may I presume to ask?*). **3** *intr.* be presumptuous; take liberties. **4** *intr.* (foll. by *on*, *upon*) take advantage of or make unscrupulous use of (a person's good nature etc.). □ **presumedly** *adv.*

presumption *n.* **1** arrogance; presumptuous behaviour. **2 a** the act of presuming a thing to be true. **b** a thing that is or may be presumed to be true. **3** a ground for presuming (*a presumption against their being guilty*). **4** *Law* an inference from known facts.

presumption of innocence *n.* the legal presumption that every person charged with a criminal offence is innocent until proven guilty.

presumptive *adj.* giving grounds for presumption (*presumptive evidence*). □ **presumptively** *adv.*

presumptuous *adj.* unduly or overbearingly confident. □ **presumptuously** *adv.* **presumptuousness** *n.*

presuppose *v.tr.* (often foll. by *that* + clause) **1** assume beforehand. **2** require as a precondition; imply.

presupposition *n.* **1** the act or an instance of presupposing. **2** a thing assumed beforehand as the basis of argument etc.

prêt-à-porter /ˌpretapɔr'tei/ ● *adj.* (of clothes) sold ready-to-wear. ● *n.* ready-to-wear clothes.

pre-tax *adj.* (of income or profits) before the deduction of taxes.

preteen ● *adj.* of or relating to a child just under the age of thirteen. ● *n.* a preteen child.

pretend ● *v.* **1** *tr.* (usu. foll. by *to* + infin., or *that* + clause) claim or assert falsely so as to deceive. **2 a** *tr.* imagine to oneself in play (*pretended it was a ship*). **b** *intr.* make pretense, esp. in imagination or play; make believe (*they're just pretending*). **3** *tr.* profess, esp. falsely or extravagantly (*does not pretend to be a scholar*). **4** *intr.* (foll. by *to*) **a** lay claim to (a right or title etc.). **b** profess to have (a quality etc.). **5** *tr.* (foll. by *to*) aspire or presume; venture (*I cannot pretend to guess*). ● *adj. informal* pretended; in pretense (*pretend money*).

pretended *adj.* **1** falsely claimed to be such; so-called (*a pretended friend*). **2** professed falsely or insincerely.

pretender *n.* **1** a person who claims a throne or title etc. **2** a person who pretends.

pretense /'priːtens, prɪ'tens/ n. (also **pretence**) **1 a** a pretext or excuse (*on the slightest pretense*). **b** a false show of intentions or motives (*the pretense of friendship; false pretenses*). **2** (foll. by *to*) a claim, esp. a false or ambitious one (*has no pretense to any great talent*). **3** pretending, make-believe. **4 a** affectation, display. **b** pretentiousness, ostentation (*stripped of pretense*).

pretension n. **1** (often foll. by *to*) **a** an assertion of a claim. **b** a justifiable claim (*has pretensions to the throne*). **2** (usu. in *pl.*) an unwarranted claim to some quality, merit, etc. (*literary pretensions*). **3** pretentiousness.

pretentious adj. **1** making an excessive claim to great merit, importance, fashionableness, etc. esp. without good cause. **2** ostentatious, showy. ☐ **pretentiously** adv. **pretentiousness** n.

preterm adj. born or occurring prematurely.

preternatural /ˌpriːtər'nætʃərəl, -'nætʃrəl/ adj. outside the ordinary course of nature. ☐ **preternaturally** adv.

pretext n. **1** an ostensible or alleged reason or intention. **2** an excuse offered. ☐ **on** (or **under**) **the pretext** (foll. by *of*, or *that* + clause) professing as one's object or intention.

pre-treat v.tr. treat beforehand. ☐ **pre-treatment** n.

pretrial ● adj. **1** of or pertaining to the period before a trial (*pretrial publicity*). **2** of or pertaining to a preliminary hearing before a trial (*pretrial testimony*). ● n. a preliminary hearing before a trial.

prettify v.tr. (**-ies, -ied**) make (a thing or person) pretty esp. in an affected or superficial way. ☐ **prettification** n. **prettifier** n.

pretty ● adj. (**-ier, -iest**) **1** (of a person, esp. a woman or girl) attractive in a delicate, dainty, or graceful way without stateliness. **2** (of a thing) pleasing to the eye, the ear, or the aesthetic sense (*a pretty dress*). **3** *ironic* considerable, fine (*a pretty penny*). ● adv. *informal* **1** fairly, moderately (*pretty difficult*). **2** very, considerably (*you're pretty strong!*). ● n. (pl. **-ies**) a pretty person (esp. as a form of address to a child). ● v.tr. (**-ies, -ied**) (often foll. by *up*) make pretty or attractive. ☐ **pretty much** (or **nearly** or **well**) *informal* almost; very nearly. **pretty please** an emphatic form of request. **sitting pretty** *informal* in a favourable or advantageous position. ☐ **prettily** adv. **prettiness** n.

pretty boy n. *slang* **1** a foppish or effeminate man. **2 a** gay man.

pretzel ● n. a crisp salted biscuit made in the shape of a knot or a stick. ● v.tr. (**-lled, -lling**) twist, bend, or contort (an object, a part of the body, etc.).

prevail v.intr. **1** (often foll. by *against, over*) be victorious or gain mastery. **2** be the more usual or predominant. **3** exist or occur in general use or experience; be current. **4** (foll. by *on, upon*) persuade.

prevailing adj. **1** most usual or widespread (*prevailing opinion*). **2** (of a wind) that blows in an area most frequently. ☐ **prevailingly** adv.

prevalent /'prevələnt/ adj. **1** generally existing or occurring. **2** predominant. ☐ **prevalence** n. **prevalently** adv.

prevaricate /prɪ'værɪˌkeɪt/ v.intr. **1** speak or act evasively or misleadingly. **2** quibble, equivocate. ☐ **prevarication** n. **prevaricator** n.

prevent v.tr. (often foll. by *from* + verbal noun) stop from happening or doing something; hinder; make impossible (*the weather prevented me from going*). ☐ **preventability** n. **preventable** adj. **preventer** n. **prevention** n.

preventive (also **preventative**) ● adj. serving to prevent, esp. preventing disease, breakdown, etc. (*preventive maintenance*). ● n. a preventive agent, measure, drug, etc. ☐ **preventively** adv.

preview ● n. **1** the act of seeing in advance. **2 a** the showing of a film, exhibition, etc., before the official opening. **b** a film trailer. **3** a foretaste, a preliminary glimpse. ● v.tr. see or show in advance.

previous ● adj. (often foll. by *to*) coming before in time or order (*previous attempts*). ● adv. (foll. by *to*) before (*previous to writing*). ☐ **previously** adv.

pre-war adj. existing or occurring before a war (esp. the most recent major war).

prewash ● n. a preliminary wash, esp. as performed in an automatic washing machine. ● v.tr. give a preliminary wash to, esp. before selling.

pre-wire v.tr. wire beforehand, esp. put in during construction wiring for services such as alarms or communications that are normally installed afterwards.

prey ● n. **1** an animal that is hunted or killed by another for food. **2** (often foll. by *to*) a person or thing that is influenced by or vulnerable to (something undesirable) (*fell prey to morbid fears*). ● v.intr. (foll. by *on, upon*) **1** seek or take as prey. **2** make a victim of. **3** (of a disease, emotion, etc.) exert a harmful influence (*fear preyed on his mind*). ☐ **preyer** n.

prez n. esp. *US slang* a president.

price ● n. **1 a** the amount of money or goods for which a thing is bought or sold. **b** value or worth (*beyond price*). **2** what is or must be given, done, sacrificed, etc., to obtain or achieve something. **3** the amount of money etc. needed to bribe a person (*everyone has a price*). **4** a sum of money offered or given as a reward, esp. for the capture or killing of a person. ● v.tr. **1** fix or find the price of (a thing for sale). **2** estimate the value of. ☐ **at any price** no matter what the cost, sacrifice, etc. (*peace at any price*). **at a price** at a high cost. **beyond** (or **without**) **price** so valuable that no price can be stated. **price on a person's head** a reward for a person's capture or death. **price oneself out of the market** lose to one's competitors by charging more than customers are willing to pay. **put a price on** value in terms of money (*can't put a price on loyalty*). **what price ...?** (often foll. by verbal noun) *informal* **1** what is the chance of ...? (*what price your finishing the course?*). **2** what is the value or use of ...? (*what price success?*). ☐ **priced** adj. (also in comb.).

price controls n.pl. restrictions by a government on the prices of consumer goods, usu. imposed on a short-term basis as a measure to control inflation.

price-fixing n. the maintaining of prices at a certain level by agreement between competing sellers.

price gouging n. N Amer. the practice of charging unjustly high prices for items, services, etc.

price index n. an index showing the variation in the prices of a set of goods etc. since a chosen base period.

priceless adj. **1** beyond price. **2** *informal* very amusing or absurd. ☐ **pricelessly** adv. **pricelessness** n.

price list n. a list of current prices of items on sale.

price support n. government policy of providing support for certain basic, usu. agricultural, products to stop the price falling below an agreed level.

price tag n. **1** the label on an item showing its price. **2** the cost of an enterprise or undertaking.

price war n. a period of fierce competition between two or more firms in the same industry that are seeking to increase their shares of the market by cutting the prices of their products.

pricey adj. (also **pricy**) (**pricier, priciest**) informal expensive. □ **priciness** n.

prick ● v. 1 tr. pierce slightly; make a small hole in. 2 tr. (foll. by off, out) mark (esp. a pattern) with small holes or dots. 3 tr. trouble mentally (my conscience is pricking me). 4 intr. feel a pricking sensation. 5 tr. spur or urge on (a horse etc.). ● n. 1 the act or an instance of pricking. 2 a small hole or mark made by pricking. 3 a pain caused as by pricking. 4 a mental pain (the pricks of conscience). 5 coarse slang a the penis. b derogatory (as a term of contempt) an objectionable man. □ **kick against the pricks** persist in futile resistance. **prick (up) one's ears** 1 (of a dog etc.) make the ears erect when on the alert. 2 (of a person) become suddenly attentive. □ **pricker** n.

prickle ● n. 1 a a small thorn. b Bot. a thornlike process developed from the epidermis of a plant. 2 a prickling sensation. ● v.tr. & intr. affect or be affected with a sensation as of pricking.

prickly adj. (**-ier, -iest**) 1 (esp. in the names of plants and animals) having prickles. 2 a (of a person) ready to take offence; touchy. b (of a topic, argument, etc.) full of contentious or complicated points; thorny. 3 tingling. □ **prickliness** n.

prickly heat n. an itchy rash of small raised red spots caused by inflammation of the sweat glands.

prickly pear n. 1 any cactus of the genus Opuntia, native to arid regions of N and S America, bearing barbed bristles and large pear-shaped prickly fruits. 2 its fruit.

prickly rose n. a wild rose, Rosa acicularis, with deep pink flowers and stems thickly covered with bristles; floral emblem of Alberta.

pride ● n. 1 a a feeling of elation or satisfaction at achievements or qualities or possessions etc. that do one credit. b (prec. by the; foll. by of) an object of this feeling (the pride of the museum's collection). c the foremost or best of a group. 2 a high or overbearing opinion of one's worth or importance. 3 knowledge of one's own worth or character; a sense of dignity and respect for oneself. 4 a group or company (of animals, esp. lions). ● v.refl. (foll. by on, upon) be proud of. □ **one's pride and joy** a thing of which one is very proud. **take pride** (or **a pride**) **in** 1 be proud of. 2 maintain in good condition or appearance. □ **prideful** adj. **pridefully** adv.

pride of place n. the most important or prominent position.

priest n. 1 an ordained minister of the Catholic or Orthodox Church, or of the Anglican Church (above a deacon and below a bishop), authorized to perform certain rites and administer certain sacraments. 2 an official minister of a non-Christian religion. 3 a devotee or minister of a practice or thing. □ **priesthood** n. **priestlike** adj. **priestly** adv.

priestess n. 1 a female priest of a non-Christian religion. 2 a female devotee or minister of a practice or thing (priestess of reason).

prig n. a self-righteously correct or moralistic person. □ **priggery** n. **priggish** adj. **priggishness** n.

prim adj. (**primmer, primmest**) 1 a (of a person or manner) stiffly formal and precise. b (of a thing) ordered, regular, formal (a prim garden). 2 (of a woman or girl) demure. 3 prudish; prissy. □ **primly** adv. **primness** n.

prima ballerina /ˌpriːmə ˌbæləˈriːnə/ n. the chief female dancer in a ballet or ballet company.

primacy /ˈpraɪməsɪ/ n. (pl. **-ies**) 1 the state or position of being first in order, importance, or authority; pre-eminence. 2 the office of a primate.

prima donna /ˌpriːmə ˈdɒnə/ n. 1 the chief female singer in an opera or opera company. 2 a temperamentally self-important person. □ **prima donna-ish** adj.

primaeval var. of PRIMEVAL.

prima facie /ˌpraɪmə ˈfeɪʃɪ/ ● adv. at first sight; from a first impression. ● adj. (of evidence) based on the first impression (can see a prima facie reason for it).

primal adj. 1 primitive, primeval. 2 chief, fundamental.

primal scream n. a scream releasing emotion.

primary ● adj. 1 a of the first importance; chief (our primary concern). b fundamental, basic. 2 earliest, original; first in a series. 3 of the first rank in a series; not derived (the primary meaning of a word). 4 (of education) for young children, esp. below the age of 12. 5 (of a battery or cell) generating electricity by irreversible chemical reaction. 6 Biol. belonging to the first stage of development. 7 (of an industry or source of production) concerned with obtaining or using raw materials. ● n. (pl. **-ies**) 1 a thing that is primary. 2 (in full **primary election**) (in the US) a preliminary election to appoint delegates to a party conference or to select the candidates for a principal (esp. presidential) election. □ **primarily** /ˈpraɪmerɪlɪ, -ˈmerɪlɪ/ adv.

primary colour n. any of the colours red, green, and blue, or (for pigments) red, blue and yellow, from which all other colours can be obtained by mixing.

primary school n. N Amer. a school for young children, esp. one covering the first three or four grades and sometimes kindergarten.

primate /ˈpraɪmeɪt/ n. 1 any animal of the order Primates, the highest order of mammals, including lemurs, apes, monkeys, and humans. 2 (also /ˈpraɪmət/) an archbishop or bishop ranked first among all the bishops of a country, region, etc.

primavera /ˌpriːməˈvɛrə/ adj. N Amer. designating a pasta dish made with lightly sautéed spring vegetables.

prime¹ ● adj. 1 chief, most important (the prime motive). 2 of the best or highest quality or value; first-rate, excellent (prime real estate). 3 primary, fundamental. 4 Math. a (of a number) divisible only by itself and unity, e.g. 2, 3, 11. b (of numbers) having no common factor but unity. ● n. 1 the state of the highest perfection of something (in the prime of life). 2 (prec. by the; foll. by of) the best part. 3 the beginning or first age of anything. 4 a prime number. 5 = PRIME RATE. 6 Christianity the office of the second canonical hour of prayer, originally said at the first hour of the day (i.e. 6 a.m.). 7 Printing a symbol (′) added to a letter etc. as a distinguishing mark, or to a figure as a symbol for minutes or feet.

prime² v.tr. 1 prepare (a thing) for use or action. 2 prepare (a gun) for firing or (an explosive) for detonation. 3 a pour (a liquid) into a pump to prepare it for working. b inject gasoline into (the cylinder or carburetor of an internal combustion engine). 4 prepare (wood etc.) for painting by applying a substance that prevents paint from being absorbed. 5 equip (a person) with information etc. 6 ply (a person) with food or drink in preparation for something. □ **prime the pump** (esp. of a government) encourage the growth of a new or weak business or industry by investing money in it.

prime meridian n. 1 the meridian from which longitude is reckoned, esp. that passing through Greenwich. 2 the corresponding line on a map.

prime minister n. the head of the executive branch

of government in most countries with a parliamentary system. ☐ **prime ministerial** *adj.* **prime ministership** *n.*

Prime Minister's Office *n. Cdn* the political staff of the prime minister, responsible for scheduling engagements, press and public relations, etc.

prime mover *n.* **1** a person who originates or promotes an action, event, etc.; an initiator. **2** an initial natural or mechanical source of motive power.

primer¹ *n.* **1** a substance used to prime wood etc. **2** a cap, cylinder, etc., used to ignite the powder of a cartridge etc. **3** *Biochem.* a molecule that serves as a starting material for a polymerization. **4** a person who primes something.

primer² /'praɪmər, 'prɪmər/ *n.* **1** an elementary textbook for teaching children to read. **2** an introductory book.

prime rate *n.* the rate of interest at which banks lend money to their best-rated customers.

prime rib *n. N Amer.* a roast or steak cut from the seven ribs immediately before the loin.

prime time *n.* the time at which a radio or television audience is expected to be at its highest, usu. between 7 and 11 p.m. (often *attrib.*: *prime-time viewing*).

primeval /praɪ'miːvəl/ *adj.* **1** of or relating to the first age of the world. **2** ancient, primitive.

priming *n.* **1** a mixture used by painters for a preparatory coat. **2 a** gunpowder placed in the pan of a firearm. **b** a train of powder connecting the fuse with the charge in blasting etc.

primitive ● *adj.* **1** early, ancient; at an early stage of civilization (*primitive man*). **2** undeveloped, crude, simple (*primitive methods*). **3** original, primary. **4** antiquated; outmoded. **5** *Geol.* of the earliest period. **6** *Biol.* appearing in the earliest or a very early stage of growth or evolution. **7 a** pertaining to or designating pre-Renaissance western European art. **b** (of art etc.) simple or straightforward in style, eschewing subtlety or conventional technique. ● *n.* **1** a primitive person or thing. **2 a** painter of the period before the Renaissance. **b** a modern imitator of such. **c** an untutored painter with a direct naive style. **d** a picture by such a painter. ☐ **primitively** *adv.* **primitiveness** *n.*

primitivism *n.* **1** primitive behaviour. **2** belief in the superiority of what is primitive. **3** the practice of primitive art. ☐ **primitivist** *n. & adj.*

primo /'priːmoː/ *adj. slang* first-class; first-rate.

primordial /praɪ'mɔːrdɪəl/ *adj.* **1** existing at or from the beginning; primeval. **2** original, fundamental.

primp *v.* **1** *intr.* make oneself well-groomed, esp. in a fussy or affected manner. **2** *tr.* make (the hair, one's clothes, etc.) tidy.

primrose ● *n.* **1** any plant of the genus *Primula*, esp. *P. vulgaris*, bearing pale yellow flowers. **2** (in full **primrose yellow**) a pale yellow colour. ● *adj.* (in full **primrose yellow**) pale yellow.

primula /'prɪmjʊlə/ *n.* any plant of the genus *Primula*, bearing flowers in a wide variety of colours during the spring, including primroses and cowslips.

Primus /'praɪməs/ *n. proprietary* a brand of portable stove burning vaporized oil for cooking etc.

prince *n.* (as a title usu. **Prince**) **1** a male member of a royal family other than a reigning king. **2** a son or grandson of a British monarch. **3** a ruler of a small state, actually or nominally subject to a king or emperor. **4** (as an English rendering of foreign titles) a noble usu. ranking next below a duke. **5 a** (as a courtesy title in some connections) a duke, marquess, or earl. **b** *Catholicism* a title applied to a Cardinal (*Prince of the Church*). **6** (often foll. by *of*) the chief or greatest

(*the prince of novelists*). **7** a powerful or influential man, esp. a magnate in a specified industry etc. (*merchant prince*). **8** *N Amer. informal* an admirable or generous man. ☐ **princelike** *adj.*

prince consort *n.* (a title conferred on) the husband of a reigning female sovereign who is himself a prince.

princeling /'prɪnslɪŋ/ *n.* **1** a young prince. **2** the ruler of a small principality or domain.

princely *adj.* (**-ier, -iest**) **1 a** of or worthy of a prince. **b** held by a prince (*princely state*). **2** sumptuous, generous, splendid. ☐ **princeliness** *n.*

Prince of Peace *n.* Christ.

Prince of Wales *n.* (a title conferred on) the nominal ruler of Wales, from 1301 the heir apparent to the English or British throne.

princess ● *n.* (as a title usu. **Princess**) **1** the wife of a prince. **2** a female member of a royal family other than a reigning queen. **3** a daughter or granddaughter of a British monarch. **4** a pre-eminent woman or thing personified as a woman. **5** *informal* a girl or woman regarded or treated as a princess, esp. one who is pampered, egocentric, demanding, etc. ● *adj.* designating a style of dress, coat, etc. with a close fitted bodice and a flared skirt with a seamless waist.

principal ● *adj.* **1** (usu. *attrib.*) first in rank or importance; chief. **2** main, leading (*a principal cause of my success*). **3** (of money) constituting the original sum invested or lent. ● *n.* **1** a head, ruler, or superior. **2** the head of some schools, colleges, and universities. **3** the leading performer in a concert, play, etc. **4** a capital sum as distinguished from interest or income. **5** a person for whom another acts as agent etc. **6** *Cdn* a lawyer who supervises an articling student. **7** the person actually responsible for a crime. **8** a person for whom another is surety. **9** *Music* the leading player in each section of an orchestra (also *attrib.*: *principal horn*). **10** (in full **principal dancer**) a dancer who is of the highest rank in a ballet company. ☐ **principally** *adv.* **principalship** *n.*

principal clause *n. Grammar* = MAIN CLAUSE.

principality *n.* (*pl.* **-ies**) **1** a state ruled by a prince. **2** the government of a prince.

principal meridian *n. Cdn* **1** a geographical meridian established by an authority as a meridian of reference for land surveying purposes. **2** (**Principal Meridian**) = FIRST MERIDIAN.

principle *n.* **1** a fundamental truth or law as the basis of reasoning or action (*arguing from first principles*; *moral principles*). **2 a** a personal code of conduct (*a person of high principle*). **b** (in *pl.*) such rules of conduct (*has no principles*). **3** a general law in physics etc. **4** a law of nature forming the basis for the construction or working of a machine etc. **5** a fundamental source; a primary element (*held water to be the first principle of all things*). **6** *Chem.* a constituent of a substance, esp. one giving rise to some quality, etc. ☐ **in principle** as regards fundamentals but not necessarily in detail. **on principle** on the basis of a moral attitude (*I refuse on principle*).

principled *adj.* based on or having (esp. praiseworthy) principles of behaviour.

print ● *n.* **1 a** an indentation or mark on a surface left by the pressure of a thing in contact with it. **b** = FINGERPRINT. **c** = FOOTPRINT. **2 a** printed lettering or writing (*large print*). **b** words in printed form. **c** a printed publication, esp. a newspaper. **d** the quantity of a book etc. printed at one time. **e** the state of being printed. **3** a picture or design printed from a block or plate. **4** *Photog.* a picture produced on paper from a negative. **5 a** a pattern printed on fabric. **b** a fabric printed in this way. **c** a piece of clothing made of such a fabric. **6** a positive copy of a finished motion picture, ready for release. ● *v.* **1** *tr.* **a** produce or reproduce (text, a picture, etc.) by mechanically transferring characters or designs to paper, cloth, etc., esp. from inked types, blocks, or plates. **b** (of an author, publisher, or editor) cause (a book or manuscript etc.) to be produced or reproduced in this way. **2** *tr.* express or publish in print. **3** *tr.* **a** (often foll. by *on*, *in*) impress or stamp (a mark or figure on a surface). **b** (often foll. by *with*) impress or stamp (a soft surface, e.g. of butter or wax, with a seal, die, etc.). **4** *intr. & tr.* write (words or letters) without joining, in imitation of typography. **5** *tr.* (often foll. by *off*, *out*) *Photog.* produce (a picture) by the transmission of light through a negative. **6** *tr.* (usu. foll. by *out*) (of a computer etc.) produce output in printed form. **7** *tr.* mark (a textile fabric) with a decorative design in colours. **8** *tr.* (foll. by *on*) impress (an idea, scene, etc. on the mind or memory). ● *adj.* **1** (of an article of clothing) made of a printed fabric (*a print dress*). **2** of or relating to newspapers or magazines (*the print media*). □ **appear in print** have one's work published. **in print 1** (of a book etc.) available from the publisher. **2** in printed form. **out of print** no longer available from the publisher. □ **printable** *adj.*

printed circuit *n.* an electric circuit with thin strips of conductor on a flat insulating sheet.

printer *n.* **1** a person or company that prints books etc. **2** the owner of a printing business. **3** a device that prints, esp. as part of a computer system.

printhead *n.* the component in a printer (*see* PRINTER 3) that assembles and prints the characters on the paper.

printing *n.* **1** the production of printed books etc. **2** a single impression of a book. **3** printed letters or writing imitating them.

printing press *n.* a machine for printing from types or plates etc.

printmaker *n.* **1** a person, esp. a graphic artist, who makes prints (*a noted Inuit printmaker*). **2** a person who makes print. □ **printmaking** *n.*

printout *n.* computer output in printed form.

print run *n.* the number of copies of a book etc. printed at one time.

prior ● *adj.* **1** earlier. **2** (often foll. by *to*) coming before in time, order, or importance. ● *adv.* (foll. by *to*) before (*decided prior to their arrival*). ● *n.* **1** the superior officer of a religious house or order. **2** (in an abbey) the officer next under the abbot. **3** *N Amer. slang* a prior criminal conviction (*has three priors*).

prioress *n.* **1** a female superior of a house of any of various orders of nuns. **2** (in an abbey) the officer next under the abbess.

priority *n.* (*pl.* **-ies**) **1** something that is given prior or special attention or considered more important. **2** precedence in rank etc. **3** the fact or condition of being earlier or antecedent. □ **prioritize** *v.tr.* **prioritization** *n.*

priory *n.* (*pl.* **-ies**) a monastery governed by a prior or a convent governed by a prioress.

prise esp. *Brit.* ● *v.tr.* = PRY[2]. ● *n.* leverage, purchase.

prism *n.* **1** a solid geometric figure whose two ends are similar, equal, and parallel rectilinear figures, and whose sides are parallelograms. **2** a transparent body in this form, usu. triangular with refracting surfaces at an acute angle with each other, which separates white light into a spectrum of colours. **3** *Crystallog.* a form having three or more faces that meet in edges parallel to the vertical axis.

prismatic *adj.* **1** of, like, or using a prism. **2 a** (of colours) distributed by or as if by a transparent prism. **b** (of light) displayed in the form of a spectrum. □ **prismatically** *adv.*

prison *n.* **1** a place in which a person is kept in captivity, esp. a building to which persons are legally committed while awaiting trial or for punishment; a jail. **2** any place of real or perceived confinement.

prison camp *n.* a camp for political prisoners or prisoners of war.

prisoner *n.* **1** a person kept in prison. **2** (in full **prisoner at the bar**) a person in custody on a criminal charge and on trial. **3** a person or thing confined by illness, another's grasp, etc. **4** (in full **prisoner of war**) a person who has been captured in war. □ **take no prisoners** deal very aggressively with a person or thing. **take prisoner** seize and hold as a prisoner.

prisoner of conscience *n.* a person imprisoned by a state for holding political or religious views it does not tolerate.

prissy *adj.* (**-ier**, **-iest**) prim, prudish. □ **prissily** *adv.* **prissiness** *n.*

pristine /'prɪstiːn, -'stiːn/ *adj.* **1** in its original condition (*a pristine copy of the book*). **2** fresh and clean, as if new (*a pristine bedroom*). **3** unspoiled (*pristine wilderness*). ¶Although there is a tradition of objection to senses 2 and 3, they are quite common and acceptable in both spoken and written English.

privacy /'praɪvəsi, 'prɪ-/ *n.* **1 a** the state of being private and undisturbed. **b** a person's right to this. **2** freedom from intrusion or public attention. **3** avoidance of publicity.

Privacy Commissioner *n. Cdn* the official responsible for investigating the collection and storage of personal information on private citizens by federal government departments.

private ● *adj.* **1** belonging to an individual; one's own; personal (*private property*). **2** confidential; not to be disclosed to others (*private talks*). **3** kept or removed from public knowledge or observation. **4 a** not open to the public. **b** for an individual's or group's exclusive use (*private room*). **5** (of a place) affording privacy. **6** (of a person) not holding public office or an official position (*private citizens*). **7** (of a service, business, etc.) provided or owned by an individual or group of individuals rather than the government or a public body. **8** (of education) paid for directly by the student or parent rather than through taxes. **9** (of health care) paid for by an individual or insurance company rather than by the government. ● *n.* **1** (also **Private**) (in the Canadian Army and Air Force and other armies) a person holding the lowest rank. **2** (in *pl.*) *informal* the genitals. □ **in private** privately; in private company or life. □ **privately** *adv.*

private bill *n.* a parliamentary bill affecting an individual or corporation only.

private company *n. Cdn*, *Brit.*, *Austral.*, & *NZ* a company with restricted membership and no issue of shares.

private detective *n.* = PRIVATE INVESTIGATOR.

private enterprise *n.* **1** a business or businesses not under government control. **2** = FREE ENTERPRISE.

privateer *n.* **1** an armed vessel owned and officered by private individuals and authorized for war service. **2 a** a commander of such a vessel. **b** a crew member of such a vessel. □ **privateering** *n.*

private eye *n. informal* a private investigator.

private investigator *n.* a usu. freelance detective carrying out investigations for a private employer.

private label *n.* a make of goods manufactured specially for a retailer and bearing the retailer's name (also *attrib.*: *private label products*).

private law *n.* a law relating to individual persons and private property.

private life *n.* life as a private person, not as an official, public performer, etc.

private member *n. Cdn., Brit., Austral., & NZ* a member of a legislative body not holding a government office.

private member's bill *n. Cdn., Brit., Austral., & NZ* a bill introduced by a private member, not part of government legislation.

private parts *n.pl.* the genitals.

private school *n.* a school established and supported by a private group rather than through taxes etc.

private secretary *n.* a secretary dealing with the personal and confidential concerns of a business person.

private sector *n.* the part of the economy that is free of direct governmental control.

private soldier *n.* an ordinary soldier other than the officers.

privation /praɪˈveɪʃən/ *n.* **1** lack of the comforts or necessities of life (*suffered many privations*). **2** (often foll. by *of*) loss or absence (of a quality).

privatize *v.tr.* make private, esp. assign (a business etc.) to private as distinct from governmental control or ownership. □ **privatization** *n.*

privet /ˈprɪvɪt/ *n.* any evergreen shrub of the genus *Ligustrum*, esp. *L. vulgare* bearing small white flowers and black berries, and used for hedges.

privilege ● *n.* **1** a special right or advantage available only to a particular person or a group of people. **2** the rights and advantages possessed by the rich and powerful (*had led a life of luxury and privilege*). **3** (also **parliamentary privilege**) the freedom of members of a legislative assembly to speak at its meetings without risking legal action. **4** a special benefit or honour, esp. one restricted to a small group (*it is a privilege to meet you*). **5** a monopoly or patent granted to an individual, corporation, etc. ● *v.tr.* **1** invest with a privilege. **2** (foll. by *to* + infin.) allow (a person) as a privilege (to do something). **3** (often foll. by *from*) exempt (a person from a liability etc.). **4** consider or treat as more important; favour.

privileged *adj.* **1** having a privilege or privileges. **2** (usu. *predic.*) honoured. **3 a** legally protected from being made public (*privileged communication*). **b** (of an exchange of information) made between such people and in such circumstances that it is not actionable. **4** (of information) kept within a select group and not divulged to others.

privy /ˈprɪvɪ/ ● *adj.* (foll. by *to*) sharing in the secret of (a person's plans etc.). ● *n.* (*pl.* **-ies**) **1** *N Amer.* an outhouse. **2** *Law* a person having a part or interest in any action, matter, or thing.

Privy Council *n.* (in Canada) a (now chiefly honorary) body of advisers appointed by the Governor General, made up of current and former Cabinet ministers, provincial premiers, etc.

privy councillor *n.* (also **privy counsellor**) a member of a Privy Council.

Privy Council Office *n.* (in Canada) an administrative body which coordinates the activities of the federal Cabinet, provides advice to the prime minister, and implements government objectives.

prix fixe /pri: fiks/ *n.* a fixed price for a restaurant meal chosen from a usu. limited menu. **2** a meal that is served for such a price.

prize¹ ● *n.* **1** something that can be won in a competition or lottery etc. **2** a reward given as a symbol of victory or superiority. **3** something striven for or worth striving for (*missed all the great prizes of life*). **4** a person considered highly (*he's no prize*). **5** (*attrib.*) **a** to which a prize is awarded (*a prize bull*). **b** supremely excellent or outstanding of its kind. ● *v.tr.* value highly (*a prized possession*). □ **keep one's eyes on the prize** remain focused on the ultimate goal. **no prizes for guessing** it is obvious.

prize² ● *n.* **1** a ship or property captured in naval warfare. **2** a find or windfall. ● *v.tr.* make a prize of.

prize³ *US var. of* PRISE.

prizefight *n.* a boxing match fought for prize money. □ **prizefighter** *n.* **prizefighting** *n.*

prize money *n.* money offered as a prize.

prizewinner *n.* a winner of a prize. □ **prizewinning** *adj.*

PRK *abbr.* photorefractive keratectomy, a form of eye surgery which uses a laser to carve away part of the outer surface of the cornea (*compare* LASIK).

pro¹ ● *n.* (*pl.* **-os**) a professional. ● *adj.* professional.

pro² ● *adj.* (of an argument or reason) for; in favour. ● *n.* (*pl.* **-os**) a reason or argument for or in favour. ● *prep. & adv.* in favour of. □ **pros and cons** reasons or considerations for and against a proposition etc.

pro-¹ *prefix* favouring or supporting (*pro-government*).

pro-² *prefix* before in time, place, order, etc.

proactive *adj.* **1** (of a person, policy, etc.) creating or controlling a situation by taking the initiative. **2** of or relating to mental conditioning or a habit etc. which has been learned. □ **proactively** *adv.*

pro-am ● *adj.* (of a sports event etc.) involving professionals and amateurs. ● *n.* a pro-am event.

prob *n. informal* a problem.

probability *n.* (*pl.* **-ies**) **1** the state or condition of being probable. **2** the likelihood of something happening. **3** a probable or most probable event (*the probability is that they will come*). **4** *Math.* the extent to which an event is likely to occur, measured by the ratio of the favourable cases to the whole number of cases possible. □ **in all probability** most probably.

probable ● *adj.* (often foll. by *that* + clause) that may be expected to happen or prove true; likely (*the probable explanation*). ● *n.* a probable candidate, member of a team, etc. □ **probably** *adv.*

probate ● *n.* **1** the official proving of a will. **2** a verified copy of a will with a certificate as handed to the executors. ● *v.tr. N Amer.* establish the validity of (a will).

probate court *n.* = SURROGATE COURT.

probation *n.* **1** *Law* a system of suspending the sentence on an offender subject to a period of good behaviour under supervision. **2** a process or period of testing the character or abilities of a person in a certain role, esp. of a new employee. □ **on probation** undergoing probation. □ **probationary** *adj.*

probationary constable *n.* (in the OPP) the lowest ranking officer.

probationer *n.* **1** a person on probation, e.g. a newly appointed nurse etc. **2** an offender on probation.

probation officer *n.* an official supervising offenders on probation.

probe ● *n.* **1** a penetrating investigation. **2** any small device, esp. an electrode, for measuring, testing, etc. **3** a blunt-ended surgical instrument usu. of metal for exploring a wound etc. **4** an unmanned exploratory spacecraft transmitting information about its environment. ● *v.* **1** *tr.* examine or inquire into closely. **2** *tr.* explore (a wound or part of the body) with a probe. **3** *tr.* penetrate with a sharp instrument. **4** *intr.* pierce or explore with or as with a probe. □ **prober** *n.* **probingly** *adv.*

probity /'prəʊbɪtɪ, 'prɒ-/ *n.* uprightness, honesty.

problem *n.* **1** a doubtful or difficult matter requiring a solution. **2** something hard to understand or accomplish or deal with. **3** (*attrib.*) **a** causing problems; difficult to deal with (*problem child*). **b** (of a play, novel, etc.) in which a social or other problem is treated. **4 a** *Physics & Math.* an inquiry starting from given conditions to investigate or demonstrate a fact, result, or law. **b** *Math.* a proposition in which something has to be constructed (*compare* THEOREM 1). **5** a puzzle or question for solution. □ **no problem** *informal* that is simple or easy. **that's your** (or **his, her,** etc.) **problem** said to disclaim responsibility or involvement.

problematic *adj.* (also **problematical**) **1** attended by difficulty. **2** doubtful or questionable. □ **problematically** *adv.*

problematize *v.tr.* make into or regard as a problem requiring a solution. □ **problematization** *n.*

pro bono /pro: 'bo:no: / *attrib.adj.* *N Amer.* **1** (of legal work) done without charge. **2** doing such work.

proboscis /prəʊ'bɒskɪs, -'bɒsɪs/ *n.* **1** the long flexible trunk or snout of some mammals, e.g. an elephant or tapir. **2** the elongated mouthparts of some insects. **3** the sucking organ in some worms. **4** *jocular* the human nose.

procaryote *var. of* PROKARYOTE.

procedure *n.* **1** a way of proceeding, esp. a mode of conducting business or a legal action. **2** a mode of performing a task. **3** a series of actions conducted in a certain order or manner. **4** a proceeding. **5** *Computing* = SUBROUTINE. □ **procedural** *adj.* **procedurally** *adv.*

proceed *v.intr.* **1** (often foll. by *to*) go forward or on further; make one's way. **2** (often foll. by *with*, or to + infin.) continue; go on with an activity. **3** (of an action) be carried on or continued (*the case will now proceed*). **4** adopt a course of action (*how shall we proceed?*). **5** go on to say. **6** (foll. by *against*) start a lawsuit (against a person). **7** (often foll. by *from*) come forth or originate.

proceeding *n.* **1** an action or piece of conduct (*a high-handed proceeding*). **2** (in *pl.*) (in full **legal proceedings**) an action at law; a lawsuit. **3** (in *pl.*) a published report of discussions or a conference.

proceeds *n.pl.* money produced by a transaction or other undertaking.

process[1] /'prəʊ.ses, 'prɒ-/ ● *n.* (*pl.* **processes** /-sesəz, -sesi:z/) **1** a course of action or proceeding, esp. a series of stages in manufacture or some other operation. **2 a** the progress or course of something (*in process of construction*). **b** the course of becoming, happening, etc. (*regeneration is in process*). **3** a natural or involuntary operation or series of changes (*the process of growing old*). **4** a summons or writ. **5** (*attrib.*) (of food etc.) that has been processed. **6** a natural appendage or outgrowth on an organism. ● *v.tr.* **1** put (a raw material, a food, etc.) through an industrial or manufacturing process in order to change or preserve it etc. **2** deal with (a document, request, etc.) officially. **3** *Computing* operate on (data) by means of a program. **4** mix, chop, etc. (food) using a food processor. **5** = DEVELOP *v.* 7.

process[2] /prə'ses/ *v.intr.* walk in procession.

procession *n.* **1** a number of people or vehicles etc.

moving forward in orderly succession, esp. at a ceremony, demonstration, or festivity. **2** the movement of such a group (*go in procession*).

processional ● *adj.* **1** of processions. **2** used, carried, or sung in processions. ● *n.* *Christianity* a hymn etc. sung during a procession.

processor /'prəʊ.sesər, 'prɒ-/ *n.* **1** a person or company etc. that processes something, esp. food. **2** a machine that processes things. **3** = CENTRAL PROCESSING UNIT. **4** a piece of software that performs operations on data (*word processor*). **5** = FOOD PROCESSOR.

pro-choice *adj.* favouring the right of a woman to choose to have an abortion.

proclaim *v.tr.* **1** (often foll. by *that* + clause) announce or declare publicly or officially. **2** declare (a person) to be (a king, traitor, etc.). **3** reveal as being (*an accent that proclaims you a Scot*). □ **proclaimer** *n.* **proclamation** /ˌprɒklə'meɪʃən/ *n.*

proclivity /prə'klɪvɪtɪ/ *n.* (*pl.* **-ies**) a tendency or inclination.

procrastinate /prəʊ'kræstɪˌneɪt/ *v.intr.* delay or postpone action. □ **procrastination** *n.* **procrastinator** *n.*

procreate /'prəʊkrɪˌeɪt/ *v.tr. & intr.* bring (offspring) into existence by the natural process of reproduction. □ **procreative** *adj.* **procreation** *n.* **procreator** *n.*

proctology /prɒk'tɒlədʒɪ/ *n.* the branch of medicine concerned with the anus and rectum. □ **proctologist** *n.*

proctor *N Amer.* ● *n.* a person who supervises students in an examination etc. ● *v.tr. & intr.* supervise an examination etc.

procure *v.* **1** *tr.* obtain, esp. by care or effort; acquire (*managed to procure a copy*). **2** *tr.* bring about (*procured their dismissal*). **3** *tr. & intr.* obtain (a prostitute) for another person. □ **procurable** *adj.*

procurement *n.* **1** the act or an instance of procuring. **2** the act of buying or purchasing, esp. by a government (also *attrib.*: *federal procurement budget*).

prod ● *v.* (**prodded, prodding**) **1** *tr.* poke with the finger or a pointed object. **2** *tr.* stimulate to action. **3** *intr.* (foll. by *at*) make a prodding motion. ● *n.* **1** a poke or thrust. **2** a stimulus to action. **3** an implement, such as a pointed or electrified rod, used for herding cattle etc. □ **prodder** *n.*

prodigal ● *adj.* **1** recklessly wasteful. **2** (foll. by *of, with, in,* etc.) lavish. **3** having returned after an absence. ● *n.* **1** a prodigal person. **2** a repentant wastrel etc. **3** a person who returns back to a place, family, etc., after an absence. □ **prodigality** /-'gælɪtɪ/ *n.*

prodigious /prə'dɪdʒəs/ *adj.* **1** marvellous; amazing. **2** enormous. **3** abnormal. □ **prodigiously** *adv.*

prodigy /'prɒdɪdʒɪ/ *n.* (*pl.* **-ies**) **1** a person endowed with exceptional qualities or abilities, esp. a precocious child. **2** something that causes wonder or amazement. **3** (foll. by *of*) a wonderful example (of a quality).

produce ● *v.tr.* **1** bring (something) into existence (*produced dinner; produced a masterpiece*). **2** manufacture (goods) from raw materials etc. **3** yield (fruit, a harvest, etc.) (*grain produced in the West*). **4** give birth to (a child). **5** cause or bring about (a reaction, sensation, etc.). **6** bring forward for consideration, inspection, or use (*produced the tickets*). **7 a** bring (a play, performer, book, etc.) before the public. **b** supervise the making of (a film, broadcast, etc.). ● *n.* **1** something that has been produced. **2** agricultural and natural products collectively (*the produce of Canada's* *oceans).* **3** fruits and vegetables (also *attrib.: located in the produce aisle).*

producer *n.* **1** a person, company, country, etc. that produces goods or materials *(milk producers).* **2 a** a person in charge of a film, play, etc., who obtains the money to pay for it and arranges rehearsals, filming, publicity, etc. **b** the director of a theatrical event or broadcast program.

product *n.* **1** a thing that is grown or produced, usu. for sale. **2** a thing or substance produced during a natural, chemical, or manufacturing process *(the products of combustion).* **3** a thing or state that is the result of something *(the product of their labours).* **4** a person who has been greatly influenced by something *(a product of her times).* **5** *Math.* a quantity obtained by multiplying quantities together.

production *n.* **1** the act or an instance of producing; the process of being produced. **2** the process of being manufactured, esp. in large quantities *(go into production).* **3 a** a total yield. **b** the rate at which something is produced. **4 a** the process or administrative management of making a film, play, record, etc. **b** a film, play, record, etc., produced. **5** the sets, costumes, props, lighting, etc. and other physical aspects of a theatrical entertainment. **6** *informal* an exaggeratedly or needlessly complicated situation or event *(always makes such a production out of doing the housework).* **7** *(attrib.)* (of a car etc.) mass-produced; not custom-made *(a production model).*

production line *n.* = ASSEMBLY LINE.

production values *n.pl.* the quality of a film, television, or theatrical production as regards the sets, costumes, props, authenticity of period detail, music, etc. as distinct from the acting, direction, etc.

productive *adj.* **1** of or engaged in the production of goods. **2** producing much. **3** *Econ.* producing commodities of exchangeable value *(productive labour).* **4** (foll. by *of*) producing or giving rise to *(productive of great annoyance).* □ **productively** *adv.*

productivity *n.* **1** the capacity to produce. **2** the quality or state of being productive. **3** the effectiveness of productive effort, esp. in industry. **4** production per unit of effort.

Prof. *abbr.* (also **prof**) Professor.

pro-family *adj.* *N Amer.* **1** promoting or supporting traditional family life. **2** = ANTI-ABORTION.

profane ● *adj.* **1** secular; not sacred. **2 a** irreverent, blasphemous. **b** (of language) blasphemous or obscene. **3** (of a rite etc.) heathen. **4** not initiated into religious rites or any esoteric knowledge. ● *v.tr.* **1** treat (a sacred thing) with irreverence or disregard. **2** violate (what is entitled to respect). □ **profanation** *n.* **profanely** *adv.* **profaner** *n.*

profanity *n.* *(pl.* **-ies**) **1** a profane act. **2 a** profane language; blasphemy. **b** a swear word.

profess *v.tr.* **1** claim openly to have (a quality or feeling). **2** (foll. by *to* + infin.) pretend. **3** declare *(profess ignorance).* **4** affirm one's faith in or allegiance to. **5** receive into a religious order under vows. **6** have as one's profession or business.

professed *adj.* **1** self-acknowledged *(a professed Christian).* **2** alleged, ostensible. **3** claiming to be duly qualified. **4** (of a monk or nun) having taken the vows of an order. □ **professedly** *adv.* (in senses 1, 2).

profession *n.* **1** a vocation or calling, esp. one that involves some branch of advanced learning or science *(the medical profession).* **2** a body of people engaged in a profession. **3** a declaration or avowal. **4** a declaration of belief in a religion. **5 a** the declara-

tion or vows made on entering an order. **b** the ceremony or fact of being professed in a religious order.

professional ● *adj.* **1** of or belonging to or connected with a profession. **2 a** having or showing the skill of a professional, competent. **b** worthy of a professional *(professional conduct).* **3** engaged in a specified activity as one's main paid occupation *(compare* AMATEUR) *(a professional lexicographer).* **4** *derogatory* engaged in a specified activity regarded with disfavour *(a professional agitator).* ● *n.* **1** a person qualified or employed in one of the professions *(health professionals).* **2** a professional player or performer. **3** a highly skilled and experienced person *(Mary Jane is a real professional).* **4** an expert player of a game, esp. golf or tennis, who provides instruction to members of a club etc. □ **professionally** *adv.*

professional development *n.* development in one's profession, e.g. through seminars, courses, etc.

professional development day *n.* esp. *Cdn* a day on which classes are cancelled so that teachers may attend seminars etc. for professional development.

professionalism *n.* **1** the skill or qualities required or expected of members of a profession. **2** great skill and ability.

professionalize *v.* **1** *tr.* make (an occupation, activity, etc.) professional. **2** *intr.* become professional. □ **professionalization** *n.*

professor *n.* **1** *N Amer.* a university teacher. **2** (often as a title) a university teacher of the highest rank. □ **professorial** *adj.* **professoriate** *n.* **professorship** *n.*

proffer ● *v.tr.* offer (a gift, services, a hand, etc.). ● *n.* an offer or proposal.

proficient *adj.* (often foll. by *in, at*) adept, expert. □ **proficiency** *n.* **proficiently** *adv.*

profile ● *n.* **1 a** an outline (esp. of a human face) as seen from one side. **b** a representation of this. **2 a** a short biographical or character sketch. **3** *Statistics* a representation by a graph or chart of information (esp. on certain characteristics) recorded in a quantified form. **4** the extent to which a person, company, organization, etc., attracts public notice or comment *(try to raise our profile).* **5** a vertical cross-section of a structure etc. ● *v.tr.* **1** represent in profile. **2** give a profile to. □ **in profile** as seen from one side. **keep a low profile** remain inconspicuous. □ **profiler** *n.*

profit ● *n.* **1** financial gain; excess of returns over outlay. **2** an advantage or benefit. ● *v.* **(profited, profiting) 1** *tr. & intr.* be beneficial to. **2** *intr.* obtain an advantage or benefit *(profited by the experience).* **3** *intr.* make or earn a profit. □ **at a profit** with financial gain. □ **profitless** *adj.*

profitable *adj.* **1** yielding profit; lucrative. **2** beneficial; useful. □ **profitability** *n.* **profitably** *adv.*

profit and loss *n.* the gain and loss made in a commercial transaction or series of transactions, esp. as shown on a balance sheet (also *attrib.: profit and loss account).*

profit centre *n.* **1** a part of a business organization with its own profits and costs and hence ascertainable profitability. **2** a profitable part of an organization.

profiteer ● *v.intr.* make or seek to make excessive profits, esp. illegally or in black market conditions. ● *n.* a person who profiteers.

profit margin *n.* the difference between the cost of buying or producing something and the price for which it is sold *(increase the profit margin to 20 per cent).*

profit-sharing *n.* the sharing of profits esp. between

employer and employees (also *attrib.*: *profit-sharing plan*).

profit-taking *n.* the sale of shares etc. at a time when profit will accrue.

profligate /'prɒflɪgət/ ● *adj.* **1** shamelessly immoral. **2** recklessly extravagant. ● *n.* a profligate person. □ **profligacy** /-gəsi/ *n.* **profligately** *adv.*

pro forma /pro: 'fɔrmə/ ● *adj.* **1** done or produced as a matter of form. **2** (of an invoice etc.) sent in advance of goods supplied. ● *adv.* as a matter of form.

profound *adj.* (**profounder, profoundest**) **1 a** having or showing great knowledge or insight (*a profound treatise*). **b** demanding deep study or thought (*profound doctrines*). **2** (of a state or quality) deep, intense, unqualified (*profound indifference*). **3** at or extending to a great depth (*profound crevasses*). **4** (of a sigh) deepdrawn. □ **profoundly** *adv.* **profundity** /prə'fʌndɪti/ *n.* (*pl.* **-ies**).

profuse /prə'fju:s/ *adj.* **1** (often foll. by *in, of*) lavish; extravagant (*was profuse in her praise*). **2** (of a thing) exuberantly plentiful; abundant (*profuse bleeding*). □ **profusely** *adv.* **profusion** /prə'fju:ʒən/ *n.*

prog *n.* *Cdn* (*Nfld*) food, e.g. for a meal, the winter, etc. (also *attrib.*: *prog bag*).

progenitor /pro:'dʒenɪtər/ *n.* **1** the ancestor of a person, animal, or plant. **2** a political or intellectual predecessor. **3** something that serves as a model; precursor.

progeny /'prɒdʒəni/ *n.* **1** the offspring of a person or other organism. **2** a descendant or descendants. **3** an outcome or issue.

progesterone /pro:'dʒestə,ro:n/ *n.* a steroid hormone released by the corpus luteum which stimulates the preparation of the uterus for pregnancy.

progestin /pro:'dʒestɪn/ *n.* (also **progestogen** /-ədʒɪn/) **1** any of a group of steroid hormones (including progesterone) that maintain pregnancy and prevent further ovulation during it. **2** a similar hormone produced synthetically.

prognosis /prɒg'no:sɪs/ *n.* (*pl.* **prognoses** /-si:z/) **1** a forecast; a prognostication. **2** a forecast of the course of a disease or other medical condition.

prognostic /prɒg'nɒstɪk/ ● *n.* **1** (often foll. by *of*) an advance indication or omen, esp. of the course of a disease etc. **2** a prediction; a forecast. ● *adj.* acting as or pertaining to an advance indication of a disease. □ **prognostically** *adv.*

prognosticate /prɒg'nɒstɪ,keɪt/ *v.tr.* **1** (often foll. by *that* + clause) foretell; foresee; prophesy. **2** (of a thing) betoken; indicate (future events etc.). □ **prognostication** *n.* **prognosticator** *n.*

program (also **programme**) ● *n.* **1 a** a usu. printed list of a series of events, pieces of music, performers, etc. at a public function, performance, etc. **b** the performance itself (*a program of pieces for violin*). **2** a radio or television broadcast. **3 a** a course of activities or actions undertaken to achieve a certain result (*fitness program*). **b** a plan of future events (*the program is dinner and a movie*). **4 a** a course of study; curriculum (*a graduate of Carleton's journalism program*). **b** a system of extracurricular, usu. athletic activities (*football program*). **5** a plan offering subscribers certain benefits (*frequent flyer program*). **6** a series of coded instructions to control the operation of a computer or other machine. ● *v.tr.* (**programmed, programming**) **1** make a program or definite plan of. **2** provide (a computer etc.) with coded instructions for the automatic performance of a particular task. **3** train to behave in a predetermined way. **4** choose or schedule (films, plays, pieces of music, etc.)

for performance. □ **get with the program** *N Amer. slang* become aware of and attuned to the realities of a situation. □ **programmability** *n.* **programmable** *adj.* **programmatic** *adj.* **programmatically** *adv.*

programmer *n.* **1** a person who writes computer programs. **2** a person responsible for the programming of broadcast programs, films, etc.

programming *n.* **1** the writing of computer programs. **2** the choice, arrangement, or broadcasting of radio or television programs, films, etc. **3** the action of programming; planning for management or administrative purposes.

programming language *n.* a notation for the precise description of computer programs or algorithms.

progress ● *n.* /'prɒgres, 'pro:-/ **1** forward or onward movement towards a destination. **2** advance or development towards completion, betterment, etc.; improvement (*has made little progress this term*). ● *v.* /prə'gres/ **1** *intr.* move or be moved forward or onward; continue (*the argument is progressing*). **2** *intr.* advance or develop towards completion, improvement, etc. (*science progresses*). **3** *tr.* cause (a situation, condition, person etc.) to advance or improve. □ **in progress** in the course of developing; going on.

progression *n.* **1** the act or an instance of progressing. **2** a succession; a series. **3 a** = ARITHMETIC PROGRESSION. **b** = GEOMETRIC PROGRESSION. **4** *Music* passing from one note or chord to another.

progressive ● *adj.* **1** moving forward (*progressive motion*). **2** proceeding step by step; cumulative (*progressive drug use*). **3 a** (of a political party, government, etc.) favouring or implementing rapid progress or social reform. **b** holding liberal views; modern (*this is a progressive company*). **c** (of music) modern, experimental, avant-garde (*progressive jazz*). **4** (of disease, violence, etc.) increasing in severity or extent. **5** (of taxation) at rates increasing with the sum taxed. **6** *Grammar* (of an aspect) expressing an action in progress, e.g. *am writing, was writing*. **7** (of education) informal and without strict discipline, stressing individual needs. ● *n.* an advocate of progressive political policies or social reform. □ **progressively** *adv.* **progressiveness** *n.* **progressivism** *n.* **progressivist** *n.* & *adj.*

Progressive Conservative (in Canada) ● *n.* a member or supporter of the Progressive Conservative Party. ● *adj.* of or relating to the Progressive Conservative Party or its policies.

Progressive Conservative Party *n.* (in Canada) one of the two historically most important political parties, advocating right-of-centre policies.

progressive rock *n.* (also **prog rock**) a style of rock music popular in the 1970s which sought to expand the boundaries of popular music through the use of complex instrumentation and arrangement and non-traditional subject matter.

prohibit *v.tr.* (**prohibited, prohibiting**) (often foll. by *from* + verbal noun) **1** formally forbid, esp. by authority. **2** prevent; make impossible (*his accident prohibits him from playing football*). □ **prohibitory** *adj.*

prohibition *n.* **1** the act or an instance of forbidding; a state of being forbidden. **2** *Law* **a** an edict or order that forbids. **b** *Brit.* & *Cdn* a writ from a superior court forbidding an inferior court from proceeding in a suit deemed to be beyond its cognizance. **3** (usu. **Prohibition**) **a** the prevention by law of the manufacture and sale of alcoholic drink, esp. as in the US 1920–33. **b** the period during which this is in effect. □ **prohibitionism** *n.* **prohibitionist** *n.*

prohibitive *adj.* **1** prohibiting. **2** (of prices, taxes, etc.) so high as to prevent purchase, use, abuse, etc. (*published at a prohibitive price*). □ **prohibitively** *adv.*

project ● *n.* /ˈprɒdʒekt, ˈprɒ-/ **1 a** a plan; a scheme. **2 a** an undertaking that is carefully planned and designed to achieve a particular aim. **b** any planned activity (*a do-it-yourself project*). **3** a usu. long-term exercise or study of a set topic undertaken by a student or group of students to be submitted for assessment. **4** an individual or collaborative enterprise undertaken usu. for industrial or scientific research, or having a social purpose (*Manhattan Project*). **5** *N Amer.* = HOUSING PROJECT. ● *v.* /prəˈdʒekt/ **1** *tr.* plan or contrive (a course of action, scheme, etc.). **2** *intr.* protrude; jut out. **3** *tr.* throw; cast; impel (*projected the stone into the water*). **4** *tr.* extrapolate (results etc.) to a future time; forecast (*the unemployment rate is projected to fall*). **5** *tr.* cause (light, shadow, images, etc.) to fall on a surface, screen, etc. **6 a** *tr.* cause (a sound, esp. the voice) to be heard at a distance. **b** *intr.* use the voice loudly enough to be heard in a large room etc. **7** *tr. & intr.* express or convey (feelings, a particular image, etc.) forcefully or effectively, e.g. to an audience. **8** *tr. Geom.* **a** draw straight lines from a centre or parallel lines through every point of (a given figure) to produce a corresponding figure on a surface or a line by intersecting it. **b** draw (such lines). **c** produce (such a corresponding figure). **9** *Psych.* **a** *tr. & intr.* attribute (an emotion etc.) to an external object or person, esp. unconsciously. **b** *refl.* project (oneself) into another's feelings, the future, etc.

projectile /prəˈdʒektaɪl, -tɪl/ ● *n.* **1** a missile, fired by a rocket. **2** a bullet, shell, etc. fired from a gun. **3** any object thrown as a weapon. ● *adj.* **1** capable of being projected by force, esp. from a gun. **2** projecting or impelling.

projection *n.* **1** the act or an instance of projecting; the process of being projected. **2** a thing that projects or obtrudes. **3 a** the presentation of an image etc. on a surface or screen. **b** the image etc. presented. **4 a** a forecast or estimate based on present trends (*a projection of next year's profits*). **b** this process. **5** the projecting quality of the voice, a sound, etc. **6 a** a mental image or preoccupation viewed as an objective reality. **b** the unconscious transfer of one's own impressions or feelings to external objects or persons. **7** *Math.* the act or an instance of projecting a figure. **8** the representation on a plane surface of any part of the surface of the earth or a celestial sphere (*Mercator projection*). □ **projectionist** *n.* (in sense 3).

projective *adj.* **1** *Geom.* **a** relating to or derived by projection. **b** (of a property of a figure) unchanged by projection. **2** *Psych.* mentally projecting or projected.

projector *n.* **1 a** an apparatus containing a source of light and a system of lenses for projecting slides or film onto a screen. **b** an apparatus for projecting rays of light. **2** a person who forms or promotes a project.

prokaryote /proːˈkærɪɒt, -ɒt, -əʊt/ *n.* a single-celled organism which has neither a distinct nucleus with a membrane nor other specialized organelles, e.g. a bacterium. □ **prokaryotic** /-ˈɒtɪk/ *adj.*

prolapse ● *n.* **1** the forward or downward displacement of a part or organ. **2** the prolapsed part or organ, esp. the uterus. ● *v.intr.* undergo prolapse.

prole *derogatory informal* ● *adj.* proletarian. ● *n.* a proletarian.

proletarian /ˌproːləˈteːrɪən/ ● *adj.* of or concerning the proletariat. ● *n.* a member of the proletariat. □ **proletarianization** *n.* **proletarianize** *v.tr.*

proletariat /ˌproːləˈteːrɪət/ *n.* **1** *Econ.* wage earners collectively, esp. those without capital and dependent on selling their labour. **2** esp. *derogatory* the lowest class of the community, esp. when considered as uncultured.

pro-life *adj.* in favour of preserving life, esp. in opposing abortion. □ **pro-lifer** *n.*

proliferate /prəˈlɪfəreɪt/ *v.* **1** *intr.* **a** reproduce. **b** increase rapidly in numbers. **2** *tr.* produce (cells etc.) rapidly. □ **proliferation** *n.* **proliferative** /-rətɪv/ *adj.*

prolific *adj.* **1** producing many offspring or much output. **2** abundantly productive. **3** (often foll. by *in*) abounding, copious. □ **prolificacy** *n.* **prolifically** *adv.*

prolix /ˈproːlɪks, prəˈlɪks/ *adj.* **1** (of speech, writing, etc.) lengthy; tedious. **2** (of a speaker, writer, etc.) verbose; long-winded. □ **prolixity** /-ˈlɪksɪti/ *n.*

prologue ● *n.* **1 a** a preface or introduction to a literary or musical work, esp. an introductory speech or short poem addressed to the audience by one of the actors in a play (*compare* EPILOGUE 2). **b** the actor speaking the prologue. **2** a short preliminary time trial held before a cycling race to obtain a leader. **3** (usu. foll. by *to*) any act or event serving as an introduction. ● *v.tr.* (**-logues, -logued, -loguing**) introduce with or provide with a prologue.

prolong *v.tr.* **1** extend (an action, condition, etc.) in time or space. **2** lengthen the pronunciation of (a syllable etc.).

prom /prɒm/ *n.* *N Amer. informal* a semiformal or formal dance for high school or university students (often *attrib.*: *prom dress*).

promenade /ˌprɒməˈnæd, -ˈnɒd, -ˈneɪd/ ● *n.* **1** a walk, or sometimes a ride or drive, taken esp. for display, leisure, etc. **2 a** esp. *Brit.* a paved public walk along the seafront at a resort. **b** any paved public walk. **3** *N Amer.* = PROM. **4** (in square dancing) a movement resembling a march made by couples in formation. ● *v.* **1** *intr.* make a promenade. **2** *tr.* lead (a person etc.) about a place esp. for display. **3** *tr.* make a promenade through (a place). □ **promenader** *n.*

promethium /prəˈmiːθɪəm/ *n.* a radioactive metallic element occurring in nuclear waste material.

prominence *n.* **1** the state of being prominent. **2** a prominent thing, esp. a jutting outcrop etc.

prominent ● *adj.* **1** jutting out; projecting. **2** conspicuous. **3** distinguished; important. ● *n.* (in full **prominent moth**) a moth of the family Notodontidae, with tufted forewings and larvae with humped backs. □ **prominently** *adv.*

promiscuous /prəˈmɪskjʊəs/ *adj.* **1 a** having frequent and diverse sexual relationships, esp. transient ones. **b** (of sexual relationships) of this kind. **2** of mixed and indiscriminate composition or kinds; indiscriminate. **3** *informal* carelessly irregular; casual. □ **promiscuity** /-ˈskjuːɪti/ *n.* **promiscuously** *adv.*

promise ● *n.* **1** an assurance that one will or will not undertake a certain action, behaviour, etc. (*a promise of help*; *gave a promise to be generous*). **2** a sign or signs of future achievements, good results, etc. (*shows great promise*). ● *v.* **1** *tr. & intr.* (usu. foll. by *to* + infin., or *that* + clause) make (a person) a promise, esp. to do, give, or procure (a thing). **2** *tr.* afford expectations of (*promises to be a good evening*). **3** *tr.* *informal* assure, confirm (*I promise you, it won't be easy*). □ **promise well** (or **ill** etc.) hold out good (or bad etc.) prospects.

promised land *n.* (prec. by *the*) **1** (**Promised Land**) *Bible* Canaan. **2 a** any place where happiness is expected, esp. heaven. **b** any coveted situation (*a promised land of economic freedom*).

promising *adj.* likely to turn out well; hopeful; full of promise (*a promising start*). □ **promisingly** *adv.*

promissory /ˈprɒmɪsəri/ *adj.* **1** conveying or implying a promise. **2** (often foll. by *of*) full of promise.

promissory note *n. esp. N Amer.* a signed document containing a written promise to pay a stated sum to a specified person or the bearer at a specified date or on demand.

promo *informal* ● *n.* (*pl.* **-os**) **1** an advertising or publicity campaign for a particular product. **2** a trailer for a television program, theatrical production, etc. ● *adj.* of or relating to publicity for a performer, commercial product, etc.; promotional (*a promo video*).

promontory /ˈprɒməntəri/ *n.* (*pl.* **-ies**) **1** a point of high land jutting out into the sea etc.; a headland. **2** *Anat.* a prominence or protuberance in the body.

promote *v.tr.* **1** (often foll. by *to*) advance or raise (a person) to a higher office, rank, etc. (*was promoted to captain*). **2** help forward; encourage; support actively (a cause, process, desired result, etc.) (*promoted women's rights; rest promotes recovery*). **3** publicize and sell (a product). **4** advance (a student) to the next grade. □ **promotion** *n.* **promotional** *adj.*

promoter *n.* **1** a person who promotes. **2** a person who finances, organizes, etc. a sporting event, theatrical production, etc. **3** a person involved in setting up and funding a new company.

prompt ● *adj.* **1** (of a person) acting without delay (*prompt in paying our bills*). **2** made, done, etc. readily or at once (*a prompt reply*). ● *v.tr.* **1** (usu. foll. by *to*, or to + *infin.*) incite; urge (*prompted them to action*). **2 a** supply a forgotten word, sentence, etc., to (an actor, reciter, etc.). **b** assist (a hesitating speaker) with a suggestion. **3** give rise to; inspire (a feeling, action, etc.). ● *n.* **1 a** an act of prompting. **b** a thing said to help the memory of an actor etc. **2** *Computing* an indication or sign on a computer screen to show that the system is waiting for input. **3** the time limit for the payment of an account for goods purchased. □ **prompting** *n.* **promptly** *adv.* **promptness** *n.*

prompter *n.* **1** *Theatre* a person seated out of sight of the audience who prompts the actors. **2** a person or thing that prompts.

promulgate /ˈprɒməlɡeɪt/ *v.tr.* **1** make known to the public; disseminate; promote (a cause etc.). **2** proclaim (a decree, news, etc.). □ **promulgation** *n.*

prone *adj.* **1 a** lying face downwards (*compare* SUPINE *adj.* 1). **b** lying flat; prostrate. **c** having the front part downwards, esp. the palm of the hand. **2** (usu. foll. by *to*, or *to* + *infin.*) disposed or liable, esp. to a bad action, condition, etc. (*is prone to depression*). **3** (usu. in *comb.*) more than usually likely to suffer (*accident-prone*). □ **proneness** *n.*

prong ● *n.* each of two or more projecting pointed parts at the end of a fork etc. ● *v.tr.* pierce or stab with or as with a fork.

pronged *adj.* **1** having a prong or prongs. **2** (in *comb.*) having a specified number of points of attack, perspectives, etc. (*a three-pronged theory*).

pronghorn *n.* (also **pronghorn antelope**) a small, very swift deer-like ruminant, *Antilocapra americana*, inhabiting the plains of western N America.

pronoun *n.* a word used instead of and to indicate a noun already mentioned or known, esp. to avoid repetition, e.g. *we, their, this, ourselves.*

pronounce *v.* **1** *tr. & intr.* utter or speak (words, sounds, etc.), esp. in a certain way. **2** *tr.* utter or deliver (a judgment, sentence, curse, etc.) formally or solemnly. **b** proclaim or announce officially (*I pronounce you man and wife*). **3** *tr.* state or declare, as being one's opinion (*pronounced dessert excellent*). **4** *intr.* pass judg-

ment; give one's opinion (*pronounced for the defendant*). □ **pronounceability** *n.* **pronounceable** *adj.* **pronouncement** *n.*

pronounced *adj.* **1** very noticeable; marked (*a pronounced limp*). **2** (of opinions etc.) strongly felt; definite (*has very pronounced views*). **3** (of a word, sound, etc.) uttered. □ **pronouncedly** *adv.*

pronto *adv. informal* promptly, quickly.

pronunciation /prəˌnʌnsiˈeɪʃən/ *n.* **1** the way in which a word, language, etc. is pronounced, esp. with reference to a standard. **2** the act or an instance of pronouncing. **3** a person's way of pronouncing words etc. **4** a phonetic transcription of a word.

proof ● *n.* **1** facts, evidence, argument, etc. establishing or helping to establish a fact (*proof of their honesty; no proof that he was there*). **2** *Law* the spoken or written evidence in a trial. **3** a demonstration or act of proving. **4** a test or trial (*put them to the proof*). **5** the standard of strength of distilled alcoholic liquors, in which the strongest measure is 100%. **6** *Printing* a trial impression taken from type or film, used for making corrections before final printing. **7** the stages in the resolution of a mathematical or philosophical problem. **8** each of a limited number of impressions from an engraved plate before the ordinary issue is printed and usu. before an inscription or signature is added. **9** a photographic print made for selection etc. **10** any of various preliminary impressions of coins struck as specimens. ● *adj.* **1** impervious to penetration, ill effects, etc. (*proof against the severest weather*). **2** (in *comb.*) able to withstand penetration, damage, or destruction by a specified agent (*soundproof; childproof*). **3** (of a distilled alcholic liquor) of standard strength. ● *v.tr.* **1** make (something) proof, esp. make (fabric) waterproof. **2** make a proof of (a printed work, engraving, etc.). **3** proofread (printer's proofs, copy, etc.). □ **the proof of the pudding is in the eating** (also **the proof is in the pudding**) the true value of something can be judged only from practical experience.

proof line *n. Cdn* (*Ont.*) BASELINE 5.

proof of purchase *n.* (*pl.* **proofs of purchase**) a sales receipt, label, box top, etc. associated with a product, which may be used as evidence that the product has been purchased.

proof positive *n.* absolutely certain proof.

proofread *v.tr.* (*past* and *past part.* **-read**) read (printer's proofs, copy, etc.) and mark any errors. □ **proofreader** *n.* **proofreading** *n.*

proof spirit *n.* a mixture of alcohol and water having proof strength.

prop. *abbr.* **1** proprietor. **2** proposition.

prop¹ ● *n.* **1** a rigid support, esp. one not an integral part of the thing supported. **2** a person who supplies support, assistance, comfort, etc. **3** *Rugby* a forward at either end of the front row of a scrum. ● *v.* (**propped**, **propping**) **1** *tr.* (often foll. by *up*) support with or as if with a prop. **2** *tr.* (often foll. by *against*, etc.) lean (something) against a support.

prop² *n.* a movable object used on a theatre stage etc.

prop³ *n. informal* a propeller.

propaganda *n.* **1 a** an organized program of publicity, selected information, etc., used to propagate a doctrine, practice, etc. **b** usu. *derogatory* the information, doctrines, etc., propagated in this way, esp. regarded as misleading or dishonest. **2** (**Propaganda**) *Catholicism* a committee of cardinals responsible for foreign missions.

propagandist ● *n.* a member or agent of a propaganda organization; a person who spreads

propaganda. ● *adj.* consisting of or spreading propaganda. ☐ **propagandistic** *adj.* **propagandistically** *adv.* **propagandize** *v.intr. & tr.*
propagate *v.* **1 a** *tr.* breed specimens of (a plant, animal, etc.) by natural processes from the parent stock. **b** *refl. & intr.* (of a plant, animal, etc.) reproduce itself. **2** *tr.* disseminate; spread (a statement, belief, etc.). **3** *tr.* hand down (a quality etc.) from one generation to another. **4 a** *tr.* extend the operation of; transmit (a vibration, earthquake, etc.). **b** *intr.* be transmitted; travel. ☐ **propagation** *n.* **propagator** *n.*
propane *n.* a gaseous hydrocarbon of the alkane series used as bottled fuel.
propel *v.tr.* (**propelled, propelling**) **1** drive or push forward. **2** urge on; encourage.
propellant ● *n.* **1** a thing that propels. **2** an inert compressed fluid in which the active contents of an aerosol are dispersed. **3** an explosive that fires bullets etc. from a firearm. **4** a substance used as a reagent in a rocket engine etc. to provide thrust. ● *adj.* = PROPELLENT.
propellent *adj.* propelling; capable of driving or pushing forward.
propeller *n.* **1** a revolving shaft with blades, esp. for propelling a ship or aircraft. **2** a person or thing that propels.
propeller-head *n. slang* a computer geek; a nerd.
propensity /prəˈpensɪti/ *n.* (*pl.* **-ies**) an inclination or tendency (*has a propensity for wandering*).
proper ● *adj.* **1 a** accurate, correct (*the proper amount*). **b** fit, suitable, right (*at the proper time*). **2** decent; respectable, esp. excessively so (*not quite proper*). **3** (*usu. foll. by* *to*) belonging or relating exclusively or distinctively (*with the respect proper to them*). **4** (*usu.* placed after noun) strictly so called; real (*this is the crypt, not the cathedral proper*). **5** *Christianity* (of a psalm, lesson, etc.) appointed for a particular day, occasion, or season. ● *n. Christianity* the part of a service that varies with the season or feast. ☐ **properness** *n.*
properly *adv.* **1** fittingly; suitably (*do it properly*). **2** accurately; correctly (*properly speaking*). **3** rightly (*he very properly refused*). **4** with decency; respectably (*behave properly*).
proper name *n.* (also **proper noun**) *Grammar* a name used for an individual person, place, animal, country, title, etc., and spelled with a capital letter, e.g. Jane, Whitehorse, Everest.
propertied *adj.* having property, esp. land.
property *n.* (*pl.* **-ies**) **1 a** something owned; a possession, either tangible, e.g. a house, land, etc., or intangible, e.g. patents, copyrights, etc. (*intellectual property*). **b** *Law* the right to possession, use, etc. **c** possessions collectively, esp. real estate (*has money in property*). **2** an attribute, quality, or characteristic (*medicinal properties*). **3** = PROP². **4** an artist, performer, athlete, or work regarded as a commercial asset, success, or sensation (*a hot property*). **5** *Logic* a quality common to a whole class but not necessary to distinguish it from others. ☐ **propertyless** *adj.*
property manager *n.* a person whose job is to administer rental properties on behalf of a landlord.
property tax *n.* a tax based on the value of property.
prop forward *n.* = PROP¹ 3.
prophecy /ˈprɒfəsi/ *n.* (*pl.* **-ies**) **1 a** a divinely inspired utterance. **b** a prediction of future events (*a prophecy of massive inflation*). **2** the faculty, function, or practice of prophesying (*the gift of prophecy*).
prophesy /ˈprɒfəˌsaɪ/ *v.* (**-ies, -ied**) **1** *tr.* (*usu. foll. by* *that, who,* etc.) foretell (an event etc.). **2** *intr.* speak as a prophet; foretell future events.
prophet *n.* **1 a** a teacher or interpreter of the sup-

posed will of God. **b** one of the major or minor Hebrew prophets. **2 a** a person who foretells events. **b** a person who advocates and speaks innovatively for a cause (*a prophet of the new order*). **3** (**the Prophet**) **a** Muhammad. **b** Joseph Smith (1805–44), founder of the Mormons, or one of his successors. ☐ **prophetess** *n.*
prophetic *adj.* **1** (often foll. by *of*) containing a prediction. **2** of or concerning a prophet. ☐ **prophetical** *adj.* **prophetically** *adv.*
prophylactic /ˌprɒfəˈlæktɪk/ ● *adj.* **1** tending to prevent disease. **2** protective; precautionary. ● *n.* **1** a preventive medicine or course of action. **2** esp. *N Amer.* a condom. ☐ **prophylactically** *adv.*
propitiate /prəˈpɪʃiˌeɪt/ *v.tr.* appease (an offended person etc.). ☐ **propitiation** *n.* **propitiatory** /-ˈpɪʃiətəri/ *adj.*
propitious /prəˈpɪʃəs/ *adj.* **1** (of an omen etc.) favourable. **2** (often foll. by *for, to*) (of the weather, an occasion, etc.) suitable. **3** well-disposed (*the fates were propitious*). ☐ **propitiously** *adv.* **propitiousness** *n.*
prop-jet *n.* a turboprop.
proponent /prəˈpoːnənt/ *n.* a person advocating a motion, theory, or proposal.
proportion ● *n.* **1 a** a comparative part or share (*a large proportion of the profits*). **b** a comparative ratio (*the proportion of births to deaths*). **2** (usu. in *pl.*) a correct or ideal relationship in size, degree, etc. between one thing and another, or between the parts of a whole. **3** (in *pl.*) dimensions; size (*large proportions*). **4** *Math.* **a** an equality of ratios between two pairs of quantities, e.g. 3:5 and 9:15. **b** a set of such quantities. ● *v.tr.* adjust or regulate in proportion to something, make (a thing) proportional. ☐ **in proportion 1** by the same factor. **2** without exaggerating (importance etc.) (*must get the facts in proportion*). **out of (all) proportion 1** badly proportioned. **2** exaggerated, overemphasized. **3** (often foll. by *to, with*) disproportionate. ☐ **proportioned** *adj.* (also in *comb.*).
proportional *adj.* in due proportion; comparable (*a proportional increase; resentment proportional to his injuries*). ☐ **proportionality** *n.* **proportionally** *adv.*
proportional representation *n.* an electoral system in which all parties gain seats in proportion to the number of votes cast for them. Abbr.: **PR**.
proportionate *adj.* = PROPORTIONAL. ☐ **proportionately** *adv.*
proposal *n.* **1 a** the act or an instance of proposing something. **b** a course of action etc. so proposed (*the proposal was never carried out*). **c** a written document outlining a proposed undertaking. **2** an offer of marriage.
propose *v.* **1** *tr. & intr.* put forward for consideration or as a plan. **2** *tr.* (usu. foll. by *to* + infin., or verbal noun) intend; purpose (*propose to open a restaurant*). **3** *intr.* make an offer of marriage. **4** *tr.* nominate (a person) as a member of a society, for an office, etc. **5** *tr.* offer (a person's health, a person, etc.) as a subject for a toast. ☐ **proposer** *n.*
proposed *adj.* suggested (*the proposed site*).
proposition ● *n.* **1** a plan proposed; a proposal. **2 a** an offer of terms for a business transaction. **b** an enterprise or undertaking esp. with regards to its financial success (*the company is a profitable proposition*). **3** a statement or assertion. **4** *Logic* a statement consisting of subject and predicate that is subject to proof. **5** a problem, opponent, prospect, etc. that is to be dealt with (*a difficult proposition*). **6** *Math.* a formal statement of a theorem or problem, often including the demonstration. **7** *informal* a proposal to have sexual relations, esp. one made bluntly

or offensively. ● v.tr. informal make a proposal (esp. of sexual relations) to. □ **propositional** adj.

propound v.tr. **1** offer for consideration; propose. **2** Cdn & Brit. Law produce (a will etc.) before the proper authority so as to establish its legality. □ **propounder** n.

proprietary adj. **1 a** (of a name) owned and used for a particular product only by a particular company. **b** (of goods) manufactured and sold by a particular firm (proprietary medicines). **2** of or relating to an owner or ownership (proprietary rights). **3** of, holding, or concerning property.

proprietor n. **1** the owner of a business. **2** a holder of property. □ **proprietorial** adj. **proprietorially** adv. **proprietorship** n.

proprietress n. **1** a woman who owns a business. **2** a woman who is the holder of property.

propriety /prə'praiiti/ n. (pl. **-ies**) **1** (often foll. by of) suitability; rightness (doubt the propriety of refusing them). **2** correctness of behaviour or morals. **3** (in pl.) the details or rules of correct conduct.

proprioceptive /ˌprəʊprɪə'septɪv/ adj. relating to stimuli produced and perceived within an organism, esp. relating to the position and movement of the body. □ **proprioception** n. **proprioceptor** n.

propulsion n. **1** the act or an instance of driving or pushing forward. **2** an impelling influence. □ **propulsive** adj.

propyl /'prəʊ.pəl/ n. Chem. either of two isomeric radicals, C₃H₇, derived from propane.

propylene /'prəʊpə,liːn/ n. a gaseous hydrocarbon used in the manufacture of chemicals.

propylene glycol n. either of two isomeric liquid alcohols, esp. one which is used as a solvent, in antifreeze, and in the food and plastics industries.

pro-rate v.tr. esp. N Amer. (usu. in passive) calculate or distribute proportionally (pension pro-rated to years of service). □ **pro-rated** adj. **pro-ration** n.

prorogue /prə'rəʊg/ v. (**-rogues, -rogued, -roguing**) **1** tr. discontinue the meetings of (a parliament etc.) without dissolving it. **2** intr. (of a parliament) be prorogued. □ **prorogation** /-rə'geɪʃən/ n.

prosaic /prə'zeɪɪk, prəʊ-/ adj. **1** like prose, lacking poetic beauty. **2** unromantic; dull; commonplace (took a prosaic view of life). □ **prosaically** adv.

proscenium /prə'siːnɪəm, prəʊ-/ n. (pl. **-s** or **proscenia** /-nɪə/) **1** (also **proscenium arch**) an arch that forms a frame at the front of a stage. **2** the part of the stage in front of the drop or curtain, usu. with the enclosing arch.

prosciutto /prəʊ'ʃuːtəʊ/ n. Italian cured ham, usu. served raw and thinly sliced as an hors d'oeuvre.

proscribe v.tr. **1** reject or denounce (a practice etc.) as dangerous etc. **2** banish, exile (proscribed from the club). **3** put (a person) outside the protection of the law. □ **proscription** n.

prose ● n. **1** the ordinary form of the written or spoken language (Milton's prose works). **2** a passage of prose, esp. for translation into a foreign language. **3 a** dull or commonplace speech, writing, etc. **b** an instance of this. ● v.intr. (usu. foll. by about) talk tediously.

prosecute v. **1** tr. & intr. **a** institute legal proceedings against (a person). **b** institute a prosecution with reference to (a claim, crime, etc.). **2** tr. & intr. (of a lawyer) represent a person or an organization that prosecutes. **3** tr. follow up, pursue (an inquiry, studies, etc.). **4** tr. carry on (a war, pursuit, etc.). □ **prosecutable** adj.

prosecution n. **1 a** the institution and carrying on of a criminal charge in a court. **b** the carrying on of

legal proceedings against a person. **c** the prosecuting party in a court case. **2** the action of carrying out or the process of being occupied with something (the prosecution of war).

prosecutor n. a person who prosecutes, esp. in a criminal court. □ **prosecutorial** adj.

proselyte /'prɒsɪ,laɪt/ n. a person converted, esp. recently, from one opinion, creed, party, etc., to another. □ **proselytism** /-lə,tɪzəm/ n.

proselytize /'prɒsələ,taɪz/ v.tr. & intr. **1** attempt to persuade others to adopt one's own belief, esp. in religion. **2** champion or promote a cause or opinion. □ **proselytization** n. **proselytizer** n.

prose poem n. a piece of imaginative poetic writing in prose.

pro shop n. N Amer. a store run by a golf or tennis club, ski resort etc. and often supervised by a resident professional or coach, where sports equipment may be bought or rented.

prosody /'prɒzədi, 'prɒsədi/ n. **1** the systematic study of versification, covering the principles of metre, rhythm, rhyme, and stanza forms. **2** patterns of stress and intonation in ordinary speech. □ **prosodic** /prə'sɒdɪk/ adj. **prosodically** adv.

prospect ● n. **1 a** the chance or hope that something will happen (there's little prospect of a settlement). **b** (often in pl.) the chances of being successful (her prospects for a new job were good). **c** a vision or idea of the future (she dreaded the prospect of the visit). **2 a** something viewed in terms of its profitability (a good prospect for investment). **b** a candidate or competitor who is likely to be successful. **3** a possible or probable customer, subscriber, etc. **4** an extensive view of landscape. ● v. **1** intr. (usu. foll. by for) explore a region for minerals. **2** tr. **a** explore (a region) for minerals. **b** work (a mine) experimentally. **c** (of a mine) promise (a specified yield). **3** intr. (often foll. by for) search around, look out for something (prospecting for customers). □ **prospecting** n. **prospector** n.

prospective attrib.adj. **1** expected; potential (prospective buyer). **2** concerned with or applying to the future (prospective analysis) (compare RETROSPECTIVE 1). □ **prospectively** adv.

prospectus n. **1** a printed document advertising or describing a commercial enterprise etc., esp. to attract investors. **2** a brochure or pamphlet detailing the courses etc. of an educational institution.

prosper v. **1** intr. succeed; thrive. **2** tr. make successful (Heaven prosper him).

prosperity n. the state of being prosperous.

prosperous adj. **1** successful; rich (a prosperous entrepreneur). **2** flourishing; thriving (a prosperous enterprise). □ **prosperously** adv.

prostaglandin /ˌprɒstə'glændɪn/ n. any of a group of hormone-like substances that cause muscle contraction and which may be used to induce labour.

prostate /'prɒsteɪt/ n. (in full **prostate gland**) gland surrounding the neck of the bladder in male mammals and releasing a fluid forming part of the semen.

prosthesis /prɒs'θiːsɪs/ n. (pl. **-theses** /-,siːz/) an artificial part supplied to remedy a deficiency, e.g. a false breast, leg, tooth, etc. □ **prosthetic** /-'θetɪk/ adj.

prosthetics n.pl. (usu. treated as sing.) the branch of surgery that deals with the replacement of defective or missing parts of the body by artificial substitutes.

prostitute ● n. **1 a** a woman or girl who engages in sexual activity for payment. **b** a man or boy who engages in sexual activity, esp. with men, for payment. **2** a person who misuses his or her talents or skills esp. for money. ● *v.tr. & refl.* **1** use one's abilities etc. wrongly or in a way that is not worthy of them, esp. in order to earn money. **2** make a prostitute of (esp. oneself). □ **prostitution** *n.*

prostrate ● *adj.* /ˈprɒstreɪt/ **1 a** lying face downwards. **b** lying horizontally. **2** overcome, esp. by grief, exhaustion, etc. (*prostrate with self-pity*). **3** *Bot.* growing along the ground. ● *v.tr.* /prɒˈstreɪt, prə-/ **1** lay (a person etc.) flat on the ground. **2** (*refl.*) throw (oneself) down in submission etc. **3** (of fatigue, illness, etc.) overcome; reduce to extreme physical weakness. □ **prostration** /prɒˈstreɪʃən, prə-/ *n.*

prosy *adj.* (**-ier, -iest**) **1** resembling or characteristic of prose. **2** tedious; commonplace (*a prosy lecture*).

protactinium /ˌprɒʊtækˈtɪnɪəm/ *n.* a radioactive metallic element whose chief isotope yields actinium by decay.

protagonist /prɒʊˈtægənɪst/ *n.* **1** the principal character in a work of fiction, film, drama, etc. **2** (often in *pl.*) the most prominent or most important individual in a situation or course of events. **3** a leading or respected supporter of a cause, movement, etc. (*a protagonist of women's rights*).

protasis /ˈprɒtəsɪs/ *n.* (*pl.* **protases** /-ˌsiːz/) the clause expressing the condition in a conditional sentence, e.g. *If you asked my opinion* in *If you asked my opinion, I would agree*.

protean /ˈprɒʊtɪən, -ˈtiːən/ *adj.* **1** variable, taking many forms. **2** (of an artist, writer, etc.) versatile.

protease /ˈprɒʊtɪˌeɪs, -ˌeɪz/ *n.* any enzyme able to hydrolyze proteins and peptides by proteolysis.

protect *v.* **1** *tr.* keep (a person or thing) safe from harm, injury, etc. **2** *tr.* **a** attempt to preserve (a threatened plant or animal species) by legislating against hunting, collecting, etc. **b** restrict by law access to or development of (land) in order to preserve its wildlife or its undisturbed state. **3** *tr. Computing* restrict access (to a file, disk, etc.) to a specified user or users. **4** *tr.* shield (domestic industry) from competition by imposing import duties on foreign goods. **5** *intr.* (usu. foll. by *against*) keep a person, thing, etc. safe from something (*this vaccine protects against several diseases*). □ **protected** *adj.*

protected list *n.* *N Amer.* a list of players whose rights are owned by a professional hockey, baseball, football team, etc. who may not play for another team in the same league.

protection *n.* **1 a** the act or an instance of protecting, or the state of being protected. **b** a means of protecting against something (*bought a gun for protection*). **2** = PROTECTIONISM. **3 a** (in full **protection money**) money extorted by racketeers in exchange for a guarantee against threatened violence. **b** freedom from violence thus obtained. **4** insurance coverage (*health protection*).

protectionism *n.* the theory or practice of protecting domestic industries. □ **protectionist** *n. & adj.*

protective *adj.* **1** protecting; intended to protect (*protective equipment*). **2** having or showing the tendency to protect a person or thing (*a protective mother*). □ **protectively** *adv.* **protectiveness** *n.*

protective colouring *n.* colouring disguising or camouflaging a plant or animal.

protective custody *n.* the detention of a person for his or her own protection.

protector *n.* **1** a person who protects. **2** (often in *comb.*) a thing or device that protects (*surge-protector*). **3** (**Protector**) (in full **Lord Protector of the Commonwealth**) *Brit. hist.* the title of Oliver Cromwell 1653–58 and his son Richard 1658–59.

protectorate *n.* **1 a** a territory that is controlled and protected by a larger state. **b** such a relation of one state to another. **2** *hist.* **a** the office of the protector of a kingdom or country. **b** the period of this, esp. (**Protectorate**) in England 1653–59.

protege /ˈprɒʊtəˌʒeɪ, ˈprɒt-/ *n.* (also **protegé**) a person whose welfare and career are looked after by an influential person, esp. over a long period.

protein *n.* **1** any of a group of organic compounds composed of one or more chains of amino acids and forming an essential part of all living organisms. **2** such substances collectively, esp. as a dietary component.

proteinaceous /ˌprɒʊtiːˈneɪʃəs/ *adj.* of the nature of or consisting of protein.

pro tem *adj. & adv.* for the time being; temporarily.

proteolysis /ˌprɒʊtiːˈɒlɪsɪs/ *n.* the splitting of proteins or peptides by the action of enzymes esp. during the process of digestion. □ **proteolytic** /-əˈlɪtɪk/ *adj.*

Proterozoic /ˌprɒʊtərɒˈzɒʊɪk/ ● *adj.* of or relating to the later part of the Precambrian era, from about 2.5 billion to 550 million years ago. ● *n.* this time.

protest ● *n.* **1** a statement of dissent, disapproval, or complaint; a remonstrance. **2** (often *attrib.*) a usu. public demonstration of objection to government etc. policy (*protest demonstration*). **3** *Law* a written declaration that a bill has been presented and payment or acceptance refused. ● *v.* **1 a** *intr.* (usu. foll. by *against, at, about,* etc.) make a protest against an action, proposal, etc. ¶Although some have disputed 'protest against' as redundant, this structure is long established, esp. in British English, and unobjectionable. **b** *tr. N Amer.* object to (he *protested their decision*). **c** *tr. & intr.* maintain a difference of opinion, stubbornly disagree ('I *am not too tired,' she protested*.). **2** *tr.* (often foll. by *that* + clause) affirm (one's innocence etc.) solemnly, esp. in reply to an accusation etc. **3** *tr. Law* write or obtain a protest in regard to (a bill). □ **under protest** unwillingly. □ **protestingly** *adv.*

Protestant /ˈprɒtəstənt/ (also **protestant**) ● *n.* **1** a member or follower of any of the western Christian Churches that are separate from the Catholic Church in accordance with the principles of the Reformation. **2** (**protestant**) (also /prəˈtestənt/) a protesting person. ● *adj.* **1** of or relating to any of the Protestant Churches or their members etc. **2** (**protestant**) (also /prəˈtestənt/) protesting. □ **Protestantism** *n.*

Protestant Reformation *n.* = REFORMATION 2.

Protestant work ethic *n.* (also **Protestant ethic**) hard work seen as a Christian duty and as morally beneficial, esp. as perceived to be exemplified by Calvinists.

protestation /ˌprɒtəˈsteɪʃən, ˌprɒʊ-/ *n.* **1** a strong affirmation. **2** an objection.

protester *n.* (also **protestor**) a person who participates in a protest.

protest vote *n.* a vote for a party or candidate representing a protest against the actions or policies of another party or candidate.

prothonotary warbler /ˌprɒʊθəˈnɒʊtəri, prəˈθɒnəˌtɜri/ *n.* a N American wood warbler, *Protonotarius citrea*, with a deep yellow head and breast, green back, and blue-grey wings.

proto- *comb. form* **1** first. **2** designating or pertaining to the earliest attested or hypothetically-reconstructed form of a language (*Proto-Algonquian*).

protocol *n.* **1 a** official, esp. diplomatic, formality and etiquette observed on state occasions etc. **b** the rules, formalities, etc. of any procedure, group, etc. **2** the original draft of a diplomatic document, esp. of the terms of a treaty agreed to in conference and signed by the parties. **3** a formal statement of a transaction. **4** Computing a set of rules governing the exchange or transmission of data electronically between devices.

proton /ˈprɒːtɒn/ n. Physics a stable elementary particle with a positive electric charge, equal in magnitude to that of an electron, and occurring in all atomic nuclei.

protoplasm /ˈprɒːtəˌplæzəm/ n. the material comprising the living part of a cell, consisting of a nucleus embedded in membrane-enclosed cytoplasm. □ **protoplasmic** /-ˈplæzmɪk/ adj.

prototype /ˈprɒːtəˌtəɪp/ ● n. **1** an original thing or person of which or whom copies, imitations, improved forms, representations, etc. are made. **2** a trial model or preliminary version of a vehicle, machine, etc. ● v.tr. make a prototype of (a product). □ **prototypic** /-ˈtɪpɪk/ adj.

prototypical adj. **1** constituting the essential type of; ideal (the prototypical skater). **2** of or relating to a prototype (a prototypical model). □ **prototypically** adv.

protozoan /ˌprɒːtəˈzoːən/ ● n. (also **protozoon** /-ˈzoːɒn/) (pl. **-zoa** /-ˈzoːə/ or **-s**) any usu. unicellular and microscopic organism of the subkingdom Protozoa, including amoebae and ciliates. ● adj. of or relating to this phylum. □ **protozoal** adj.

protract v.tr. **1** prolong or lengthen esp. in time or in space. **2** (of a muscle) extend (a limb, etc.). □ **protraction** n.

protracted adj. of excessive length or duration (a protracted debate).

protractor /prəˈtræktər, ˈprɒːtræktər/ n. **1** an instrument for measuring angles, usu. in the form of a semicircle graduated by degrees. **2** a muscle that serves to extend a limb etc.

protrude v. **1** intr. extend beyond or above a surface; project. **2** tr. thrust or cause to thrust forth. □ **protrusion** n.

protuberant /prəˈtuːbərənt, -ˈtjuːb-/ adj. bulging out; prominent (protuberant eyes). □ **protuberance** n.

proud adj. **1** feeling greatly honoured or pleased. **2 a** (often foll. by of) valuing oneself, one's possessions, etc. highly, or esp. too highly; haughty; arrogant (she wasn't too proud to take the money). **b** suitably satisfied with one's achievements (proud of a job well done). **3 a** (of an occasion etc.) justly arousing pride (a proud day for us). **b** (of an action etc.) showing pride (a proud wave). **4** (of a thing) imposing; distinguished (the statue stands tall and proud). □ **do proud** informal **1** be a source of pride to (someone) (her achievements did her family proud). **2** treat (a person) with lavish generosity or honour (they did us proud on our anniversary). □ **proudly** adv.

Prov. abbr. **1** (also **prov.**) Provincial, provincial. **2** (also **prov.**) Province, province.

prove v.tr. (past part. **proven** or **proved**) **1 a** (often foll. by that + clause) demonstrate the truth of by evidence or argument. **b** assert or reveal (something). **c** show (a thing or person) to be (right, wrong, etc.) (the facts will prove me right). **2 a** be found (the tool proved useless for the job). **b** turn out to be, emerge as, become (jealousy will prove his downfall). **3** test the accuracy of (esp. a calculation); subject to a testing process. **4** establish the genuineness and validity of (a will). □ **prove oneself** show one's abilities, courage, etc. □ **provable** adj. **provably** adv.

proven attrib.adj. **1** shown to be such through trial and experience (a proven performer). **2** (also in comb.) demonstrated to be effective (a time-proven technique).

provenance /ˈprɒvənəns/ n. **1** the place of origin or history, esp. of a work of art etc. **2** origin.

Provençal /ˌprɒːvãˈsæl, ˌprɒvɒnˈsæl, ˌprɒvãˈsæl/ ● adj. **1** of or concerning the language, inhabitants, landscape, etc. of Provence in SE France. **2** (also **provençale**) containing olive oil, garlic, and often tomato, and normally flavoured with mixed herbs such as tarragon, rosemary, etc. ● n. **1** a native of Provence. **2** the Romance language of Provence, closely related to French, Italian, and Catalan.

proverb n. a short pithy saying in general use, held to embody a general truth.

proverbial adj. **1** (esp. of a specific characteristic etc.) as well-known as a proverb; notorious (his proverbial honesty). **2** of or referred to in a proverb (the proverbial ill wind). □ **proverbially** adv.

provide v. **1** tr. **a** supply, furnish. **b** offer or present (an answer, example, opportunity, etc.) (darkness provided a chance for escape). **2** tr. (foll. by that) ensure or specify (this agreement provides that profits will be divided equally). □ **provide for 1** supply money and other necessities, e.g. food, for (she provides for her family). **2** make the necessary plans to deal with something that may happen (had not provided for rain). **3** (of a law, etc.) make it possible for something to be done later (freedom of speech is provided for in the constitution).

provided conj. (also **providing**) (often foll. by that) on the condition or understanding (that).

providence /ˈprɒvɪdəns/ n. **1** esp. Christianity the protective care of God or nature. **2** (**Providence**) esp. Christianity God as exercising prescient and beneficient power and direction. **3** timely care or preparation; foresight; thrift.

provident adj. **1** having or showing foresight. **2** thrifty. □ **providently** adv.

providential /ˌprɒvɪˈdenʃəl/ adj. **1** of or by divine foresight or intervention. **2** opportune, lucky. □ **providentially** adv.

provider n. **1** a person or thing that provides. **2** the breadwinner of a family etc.

province n. **1** a principal administrative division of a country etc., esp. (in Canada) one of the ten principal political units which, along with the Territories, constitute Canada. **2** (in pl.) the whole of esp. a European country outside the capital city, often regarded as uncultured, unsophisticated, etc. **3** a sphere of action, concern, or responsibility. **4** a branch of learning etc. (in the province of aesthetics). **5** an area, zone, or region containing a distinct group of animal or plant communities; a division of a biogeographical region. **6** an extensive region all parts of which have a broadly similar geology and topography. **7** (in Catholic and Anglican churches) a district under an archbishop or a metropolitan, usu. consisting of adjacent dioceses. **8** a territorial division of a religious order. **9** Rom. Hist. a territory outside Italy under a Roman governor.

provincehood n. Cdn the quality or status of being a province.

Province House n. the name of the legislative building in Nova Scotia and PEI.

province-wide adj. esp. Cdn extending throughout or pertaining to a whole province.

provincial ● adj. **1** of, pertaining to, or under the jurisdiction of a province or provinces. **2** of or concerning the whole of esp. a European country outside the capital city (French provincial furniture). **3** derogatory having or showing a narrow or limited view of life and current affairs (provincial attitudes). ● n. **1** Cdn (in pl.) a provincial tournament or championship. **2** an inhabitant of esp. a European region outside the capital city. **3** an unsophisticated or uncultured person. **4** *Christianity* the head or chief of a province or of a religious order in a province. □ **provinciality** *n.* **provincially** *adv.*

provincial building *n.* *Cdn* a building housing provincial government offices.

provincial constable *n.* (in the OPP) an officer ranking above probationary constable.

provincial court *n.* *Cdn* a court established by provincial legislation, usu. having both criminal and civil divisions, which conducts hearings by judge alone on offences of a relatively minor nature.

provincialism *n.* **1 a** an attitude or manners reflecting a limited or restricted view of life and current events; narrow-mindedness. **b** an unsophisticated outlook. **2** allegiance to or concern for one's province rather than one's country. □ **provincialist** *n. & adj.*

provincialization *n.* *Cdn* the transfer (of responsibilities, etc.) to the provincial level. □ **provincialize** *v.tr.*

provincial park *n.* *Cdn* an area of land owned and preserved by a provincial government for public benefit and enjoyment and conservation of wildlife.

provincial parliament *n.* *Cdn* a provincial legislative assembly.

provincial police *n.* *Cdn* (esp. *Ont. & Que.*) a police force under provincial authority responsible for jurisdictions without municipal police protection.

provincial right *n.* *Cdn* (usu. in *pl.*) the right of a province or provinces to maintain and exercise authority over specified areas under provincial jurisdiction.

proving ground *n.* any area or situation in which a person or thing is tested or proven.

provision ● *n.* **1 a** the act or an instance of providing (*the provision of services*). **b** something provided (*a provision of bread*). **c** preparation that is made to meet future needs or eventualities (*make provision for one's old age*). **2** (in *pl.*) food, drink, etc., esp. for an expedition. **3 a** a legal or formal statement providing for something. **b** a clause of this. ● *v.tr.* supply (an expedition etc.) with provisions. □ **provisioner** *n.* **provisioning** *n.*

provisional ● *adj.* **1** providing for immediate needs only; temporary. **2** (**Provisional**) designating the unofficial wing of the IRA established in 1970, advocating terrorism. ● *n.* (**Provisional**) a member of the Provisional wing of the IRA. □ **provisionally** *adv.*

proviso /prə'vaizo:/ *n.* (*pl.* **-os**) **1** a stipulation. **2** a clause of stipulation or limitation in a document.

provocateur /prɒ'vɒkə,tɜr, prə-/ *n.* a person who provokes a disturbance; an agitator.

provocation *n.* **1** the act or an instance of provoking; a state of being provoked (*did it under severe provocation*). **2** a cause of annoyance. **3** *Cdn & Brit. Law* an action, insult, etc. deemed likely to provoke physical retaliation or an irrational response.

provocative *adj.* **1** intentionally causing anger, annoyance, controversy, etc. (*a provocative editorial*). **2** tending to arouse sexual desire. **3** intellectually stimulating (*a provocative book*). □ **provocatively** *adv.* **provocativeness** *n.*

provoke *v.tr.* **1** annoy, disturb, or harass (*don't provoke the dog*). **2** cause a person to do something by behaving in a certain way. annoying way (*provoked her into leaving him*). **3** cause a particular reaction in a person etc. (*provoked an angry response*). **4** cause, give rise to (*will provoke fermentation*).

provoking *adj.* **1** exasperating, irritating, annoying.

2 (in *comb.*) prompting (thought, anxiety, laughter, etc.) (*thought-provoking*). □ **provokingly** *adv.*

provolone /,pro:və'lo:nei/ *n.* a type of mellow cow's-milk cheese originally made in S Italy, often smoked after drying and moulded into the shape of a pear.

provost /'prɒvəst/ *n.* *N Amer.* a high administrative officer in a university.

prow *n.* the bow of a ship. □ **prowed** *comb. form.*

prowess /prau'es, 'praues, -əs/ *n.* **1** skill. **2** valour; gallantry.

prowl ● *v.* **1 a** *intr.* move quietly and carefully, esp. when looking or hunting for something. **b** *tr.* move through or in a place in this way (*prowling the streets*). **2** *intr.* walk or wander, e.g. because one is anxious or unable to relax (*prowling about the house*). ● *n.* the act or an instance of prowling. □ **on the prowl** moving about secretively; prowling. □ **prowler** *n.*

proximal /'prɒksıməl/ *adj.* situated towards the centre of the body or point of attachment.

proximate /'prɒksımət/ *adj.* **1** nearest or next before or after (in place, order, time, causation, thought process, etc.). **2** approximate. □ **proximately** *adv.*

proximity /prɒk'sımətı/ *n.* nearness in space, time, etc.

proxy *n.* (*pl.* **-ies**) (also *attrib.*) **1** the authorization given to a substitute or deputy. **2** a person authorized to act as a substitute etc. **3 a** a document giving the power to act as a proxy, esp. in voting. **b** a vote given by this.

Prozac *n. proprietary* **1** the antidepressant drug fluoxetine hydrochloride. **2** a capsule etc. of this.

prude *n.* a person having or affecting an attitude of extreme propriety or modesty, esp. in sexual matters. □ **prudery** *n.* (*pl.* **-ies**). **prudish** *adj.* **prudishness** *n.*

prudent *adj.* **1** careful to provide for the future. **2** discreet or cautious; circumspect. **3** having or exercising good judgment. □ **prudence** *n.* **prudently** *adv.*

prudential /pru:'denʃəl/ *adj.* of, involving, or marked by prudence.

prune¹ *n.* **1** a dried plum. **2** (also **prune plum**) esp. *N Amer.* a variety of plum suitable for drying. □ **pruney** *adj.*

prune² *v.tr.* **1 a** (often foll. by *down*) trim (a tree etc.) by cutting away dead or overgrown branches etc. **b** (usu. foll. by *off, away*) lop (branches etc.) from a tree. **2** reduce (costs etc.) (*try to prune expenses*). **3** reduce the extent of (something) by cutting or removing unnecessary parts etc. (*must prune the list*). □ **pruner** *n.*

pruning hook *n.* a long-handled hooked cutting tool used for pruning.

prurient /'prorıənt/ *adj.* **1** having or showing an excessive interest in sexual matters. **2** encouraging such an excessive interest. □ **prurience** *n.*

Prussian /'prʌʃən/ ● *adj.* of or relating to Prussia, a former German state, or the militaristic tradition associated with it. ● *n.* a native of Prussia.

pry¹ *v.intr.* (**pries, pried**) **1** (usu. foll. by *into*) inquire impertinently (into a person's private affairs etc.). **2** (usu. foll. by *into, about,* etc.) look or peer inquisitively. □ **prying** *adj.* **pryingly** *adv.*

pry² *v.tr.* (**pries, pried**) *N Amer.* **1** (often foll. by *open, up,* etc.) move, open, raise, etc., by leverage (*pry up the lid*; *pried the box open*). **2** remove, obtain, or separate with difficulty (*could not pry the secret out of her*).

pry bar *n.* a metal bar used for prying up nailed boards etc.

PS *abbr.* **1** (also **ps**) postscript. **2** *N Amer.* Public School. **3** power steering.

PSA *abbr.* **1** prostate specific antigen, a blood test used to detect prostate cancer. **2** N Amer. PUBLIC SERVICE ANNOUNCEMENT.

PSAC abbr. Public Service Alliance of Canada.

psalm /sɒm/ n. **1 a** (also **Psalm**) any of the sacred songs contained in the Biblical Book of Psalms. **b** a musical setting for a Psalm. **2** a sacred song or hymn.

pseudo /'suːdoː, 'sjuː-/ ● adj. **1** sham; spurious. **2** insincere. ● n. (pl. **-os**) a pretentious or insincere person.

pseudo- /'suːdoː, 'sjuː-/ comb. form (also **pseud-** before a vowel) **1** supposed or purporting to be but not really so (pseudo-intellectual). **2** resembling or imitating (often in technical applications) (pseudo-language).

pseudoephedrine /ˌsuːdoː'fedrɪn, -'efə,driːn, ˌsjuː-/ n. a dextrorotatory compound commonly used as a nasal decongestant.

pseudonym /'suːdənɪm, 'sjuː-/ n. a fictitious name, esp. one assumed by an author.

pseudo-science n. a pretended or spurious science. ☐ **pseudo-scientific** adj.

pshaw interj. an expression of contempt or impatience.

psi¹ /psaɪ/ n. **1** the twenty-third letter of the Greek alphabet (Ψ, ψ). **2** supposed parapsychological faculties, phenomena, etc. regarded collectively.

psi² abbr. pounds per square inch.

psilocybin /ˌsɪlə'saɪbɪn/ n. a hallucinogenic alkaloid found in Mexican mushrooms of the genus Psilocybe.

psittacosis /ˌsɪtə'koːsɪs/ n. a contagious viral disease of birds transmissible (esp. from parrots) to human beings as a form of pneumonia.

psoriasis /sə'raɪəsɪs/ n. a skin disease marked by red scaly patches. ☐ **psoriatic** /ˌsɔri'ætɪk/ adj.

psst interj. (also **pst**) a whispered exclamation seeking to attract a person's attention surreptitiously.

PST abbr. **1** Cdn provincial sales tax. **2** Pacific Standard Time.

psych informal ● v.tr. **1** (usu. foll. by up; often refl.) prepare (oneself or another person) mentally for an ordeal etc. **2 a** (usu. foll. by out) analyze (a person's motivation etc.) for one's own advantage (trying to psych him out). **b** subject to psychoanalysis. **3** (often foll. by out) influence a person psychologically, esp. negatively; intimidate, frighten. ● n. N Amer. psychology (also attrib.). ● adj. N Amer. psychiatric (psych ward).

psyche /'saɪki/ n. **1** the soul; the spirit. **2** the mind.

psychedelia /ˌsaɪkə'deliə, -'diːliə/ n.pl. psychedelic articles, esp. posters, paintings, music, etc.

psychedelic /ˌsaɪkə'delɪk/ ● adj. **1 a** expanding the mind's awareness etc., esp. through the use of hallucinogenic drugs. **b** (of an experience) hallucinatory; bizarre. **c** (of a drug) producing hallucinations. **2** informal **a** producing an effect resembling that of a psychedelic drug; having vivid colours or designs etc. **b** (of colours, patterns, etc.) bright, bold and often abstract. ● n. a hallucinogenic drug. ☐ **psychedelically** adv.

psychiatry n. the study and treatment of mental disease. ☐ **psychiatric** adj. **psychiatrically** adv. **psychiatrist** n.

psychic ● adj. **1 a** (of a person) considered to have occult powers, such as telepathy, clairvoyance, etc. **b** (of a faculty, phenomenon, etc.) inexplicable by natural laws. **2** of or relating to the soul or mind. ● n. a person considered to have psychic powers; a medium. ☐ **psychical** adj. **psychically** adv.

psycho informal ● n. (pl. **-os**) a psychopath. ● adj. psychopathic.

psycho- comb. form of the mind or psychology.

psychoactive adj. (of a drug) affecting the mind.

psychoanalysis n. a therapeutic method of treating mental disorders by investigating the interaction of conscious and unconscious elements in the mind and bringing repressed fears and conflicts into the conscious mind. ☐ **psychoanalyze** v.tr. **psychoanalyst** n. **psychoanalytic** adj. **psychoanalytical** adj. **psychoanalytically** adv.

psychobabble n. informal derogatory writing or talk filled with psychiatric jargon, esp. concerning personality and relationships, esp. when used by lay people with little regard for accuracy.

psychobiography n. (pl. **-ies**) biography or a biography dealing esp. with the psychology of the subject. ☐ **psychobiographer** n.

psychobiology n. the branch of science that deals with the biological basis of behaviour and mental phenomena. ☐ **psychobiological** adj. **psychobiologist** n.

psychodrama n. **1** a form of psychotherapy in which patients act out events from their past. **2** a play or film etc. in which psychological elements are the main interest.

psychodynamics n.pl. (treated as sing.) the study of the activity of and the interrelation between various parts of an individual's personality or psyche. ☐ **psychodynamic** adj.

psychogenic adj. having a psychological origin or cause rather than a physical one.

psychohistory n. **1** the interpretation of historical events with the aid of psychological theory. **2** psychobiography; the psychological history of an individual. ☐ **psychohistorian** n. **psychohistoric** adj. **psychohistorical** adj.

psycholinguistics n.pl. (treated as sing.) the study of the psychological aspects of language and language-learning. ☐ **psycholinguist** n. **psycholinguistic** adj.

psychological adj. **1** of, relating to, affecting, or arising in the mind. **2** of or relating to psychology. **3** informal (of an ailment etc.) having a basis in the mind; imaginary. ☐ **psychologically** adv.

psychological warfare n. a campaign, esp. involving the use of propaganda, directed at reducing an opponent's morale.

psychology n. (pl. **-ies**) **1** the scientific study of the human mind and its functions, esp. those affecting behaviour in a given context. **2 a** the mental characteristics or attitude of a person or group. **b** the mental factors governing a situation or activity (the psychology of crime). ☐ **psychologist** n. **psychologize** v.tr. & intr.

psychometrics /ˌsaɪko'metrɪks/ n.pl. (treated as sing.) the science of measuring mental capacities and processes.

psychometry /saɪ'kɒmətri/ n. **1** the supposed divination of facts about events, people, etc., from inanimate objects associated with them. **2** the measurement of mental abilities. ☐ **psychometric** adj. **psychometrically** adv. **psychometrist** n.

psychomotor adj. concerning the study of movement resulting from mental activity.

psychoneurosis n. (pl. **-oses**) = NEUROSIS. ☐ **psychoneurotic** adj.

psychopath n. **1** a person suffering from chronic mental disorder esp. with abnormal or violent social behaviour. **2** a mentally or emotionally unstable person. ☐ **psychopathic** adj. **psychopathically** adv.

psychopathology n. **1** the scientific study of mental disorders. **2** a mentally or behaviourally disordered state. □ **psychopathological** adj. **psychopathologist** n.

psychopathy /sai'kɒpəθi/ n. psychopathic or psychologically abnormal behaviour.

psychopharmacology n. the branch of science that deals with the effects of drugs on the mind and behaviour. □ **psychopharmacological** adj. **psychopharmacologist** n.

psychophysics n. the branch of science that deals with the relations between mental states and physical events and processes. □ **psychophysical** adj.

psychosexual adj. of or involving the psychological aspects of the sexual instinct.

psychosis /sai'ko:sɪs/ n. (pl. **psychoses** /-si:z/) a severe mental derangement, esp. when resulting in delusions and loss of contact with external reality.

psychosocial adj. of or involving the influence of social factors or human interactive behaviour.

psychosomatic /ˌsaɪko:sə'mætɪk/ adj. **1** (of an illness etc.) caused or aggravated by mental conflict, stress, etc. **2** of the mind and body together.

psychotherapy n. (pl. **-ies**) the treatment of mental disorder by psychological means. □ **psychotherapeutic** adj. **psychotherapist** n.

psychotic /sai'kɒtɪk/ • adj. of or characterized by a psychosis. • n. a person suffering from a psychosis. □ **psychotically** adv.

psychotropic /ˌsaɪko:'trɒpɪk/ n. (of a drug) acting on the mind.

psyllium /'sɪliəm/ n. **1** a leafy-stemmed Mediterranean plantain, *Plantago afra*. **2** the seeds of this or several related plantains, used as a mild laxative.

PT abbr. **1** PACIFIC TIME. **2** PHYSICAL TRAINING.

Pt symbol the element platinum.

pt. abbr. **1** part. **2** pint. **3** point. **4** port.

PTA abbr. PARENT-TEACHER ASSOCIATION.

ptarmigan /'tɑrmɪgən/ n. (pl. same or **-s**) any of various game birds of Arctic regions of the genus *Lagopus*, resembling a grouse but with feathered toes and predominantly white plumage in winter.

Pte abbr. (also **Pte.**) PRIVATE n. 1.

pterodactyl /ˌterə'dæktɪl/ n. a large extinct flying birdlike reptile with a long slender head and neck.

PTFE abbr. POLYTETRAFLUOROETHYLENE.

PTH abbr. parathyroid hormone (see PARATHYROID).

PTO abbr. **1** POWER TAKEOFF. **2** please turn over.

Ptolemaic /ˌtɒlə'meɪɪk/ adj. **1** of or relating to the Greek astronomer Ptolemy (2nd c.) or his theories, esp. the theory that the earth is the stationary centre of the Universe. **2** of or relating to the Ptolemies, Macedonian rulers of Egypt 323–30 BC.

ptomaine /'to:mein/ n. any of various amine compounds, some toxic, in putrefying animal and vegetable matter.

ptomaine poisoning n. food poisoning.

ptooey interj. representing the noise of spitting, esp. in contempt, disgust, etc.

PTSD abbr. POST-TRAUMATIC STRESS DISORDER.

Pu symbol plutonium.

pub n. an establishment that is licensed to sell alcoholic drinks and usu. also serves light meals etc.

pubbing n. the action of going drinking in pubs.

pub-crawl • n. a drinking tour of several pubs or bars. • v.intr. make such a tour.

puberty n. the period during which adolescents reach sexual maturity and become capable of reproduction.

pubes /'pju:bi:z/ n. (pl. same) **1** the lower part of the abdomen at the front of the pelvis, covered with hair from puberty. **2** informal the pubic hair.

pubescence /pju:'besəns/ n. **1** the time when puberty begins. **2** Bot. soft down on the leaves and stems of plants. **3** Zool. soft down on various parts of animals, esp. insects. □ **pubescent** adj.

pubic adj. of or relating to the pubes or pubis (*pubic hair*).

pubis /'pju:bɪs/ n. (pl. **pubes** /-bi:z/) either of a pair of bones forming the two sides of the pelvis.

public • adj. **1** of or concerning the people as a whole (*in the public interest*). **2** open to or shared by all the people (*public meeting*). **3** done or existing openly (*made her views public*). **4 a** (of a service, funds, etc.) provided or heavily subsidized by, or concerning a government (*public money; public housing*). **b** (of a person) in government (*had a distinguished public career*). **5** devoted or directed to the promotion of the general welfare; patriotic (*public spirit*). **6** well-known; famous (*a public figure*). **7** Cdn of or relating to a public school or the public school system. • n. **1** (as *sing.* or *pl.*) the community in general, or members of the community. **2** a section of the community having a particular interest or in some special connection (*the reading public*). □ **go public 1** become a public company. **2** reveal previously unknown information etc. **in public** openly, publicly. **in the public eye** at the centre of public attention; famous or notorious. □ **publicly** adv.

public access n. (usu. attrib.) designating a type of television programming that is made available to community groups or members of the public.

public accounts committee n. Cdn & Brit. a standing committee of a legislature, responsible for reviewing government expenditure, primarily by examining the Auditor General's report.

public address system n. an electronic system used to amplify sound, used at public meetings etc.

public administration n. **1** the implementation of government policy, usu. by the civil service. **2** a branch of study preparing students for careers in this.

public affairs n.pl. = CURRENT AFFAIRS.

public assistance n. N Amer. = SOCIAL ASSISTANCE.

publication n. **1 a** the preparation and issuing of a book, newspaper, engraving, music, etc. to the public. **b** a book etc. so issued. **2** the act or an instance of making something publicly known.

public company n. a company whose shares are traded freely on a stock exchange.

public corporation n. **1** a corporation that is owned and operated by a government to serve the public. **2** N Amer. = PUBLIC COMPANY.

Public Curator n. Cdn (Que.) a provincial government official responsible for the affairs of persons legally unfit to conduct them themselves.

public debt n. debt incurred by a government.

public domain n. the legal status of a work on which copyright has expired, or which has never been copyrighted.

public enemy n. a notorious wanted criminal.

public health n. services, such as immunization, preventive medicine, etc., that are provided by a government and intended to improve the general health of citizens (also attrib.: *public health nurse*).

public holiday n. Cdn & Brit. a usu. annual holiday, often marking a historical, religious, etc. occasion, and granted to most employees.

publicist n. a person who promotes something, esp. a person employed by a company or individual to obtain publicity for products, services, etc.

publicity n. **1** the action or fact of publicizing someone or something or of being publicized. **2 a** the technique or the process of promoting or advertising a product, person, etc. **b** material or information used for this. **3** public exposure; fame, notoriety.

publicity stunt *n.* something done merely for the publicity that it will generate.

publicize *v.tr.* make publicly known; advertise.

public key *n. Computing* a publicly available cryptographic key used to convert data into a form which cannot be read by unauthorized persons (often *attrib.*: *public-key encryption*).

public law *n.* **1** the law of relations between individuals and the state. **2** a piece of legislation affecting the public as a whole.

public library *n.* a library, usu. funded by a municipal government, that lends books and other materials to the general public.

public mischief *n. Cdn* the criminal offence of making a false accusation, reporting an offence that did not occur, etc.

public opinion *n.* the prevalent view or views held by the majority of the community.

public ownership *n.* ownership by the state.

public purse *n. informal* the national treasury.

public relations *n.pl.* **1** the work of presenting a good image of an organization, person, etc., to the public, esp. by providing information (*she works in public relations*). **2** the state of the relationship between an organization and the public (*the company sponsors literacy groups, which is good for public relations*).

public relations officer *n.* a person employed by a company etc. to promote a favourable public image.

public school *n.* **1** a primary or secondary school that is supported by public funds. **2** *Cdn (Ont.)* **a** a school that is part of the public school system (*compare* SEPARATE SCHOOL 1). **b** an elementary school that is part of the public school system. **c** elementary schooling in the public school system.

public school board *n. Cdn* **1** an elected board of trustees responsible for the public schools of a particular area. **2** the administrative unit responsible for the public schools in a given area. **3** the area within which such a board has jurisdiction.

public school system *n. Cdn* a system of publicly-funded non-denominational schools.

public sector *n.* that part of the economy that is under direct control by the state.

public servant *n.* a government employee, esp. of a federal government.

public service *n.* **1** public servants collectively. **2** a service provided to the public without charge by a corporation etc.

public service announcement *n. N Amer.* **1** free air time donated by a radio or television station to a non-profit organization. **2** a message aired by a radio or television station as a service to the public.

public speaking *n.* an act or the skill of addressing an audience effectively.

public spirit *n.* a willingness to engage in community action. □ **public-spirited** *adj.* **public-spiritedly** *adv.* **public-spiritedness** *n.*

public transit *n.* (also **public transportation**, **public transport**) a system of buses, trains, etc., running on fixed routes, esp. when owned by a government agency.

Public Trustee *n. Cdn* a provincial government official who administers the estates of people who die intestate, missing persons, etc.

public utility *n.* an organization or corporation supplying water, electricity, etc. to the public.

public works *n.* building work, e.g. of roads, hospitals, etc., which is paid for by the government.

publish *v.* **1** *tr. & intr.* (of an author, publisher, etc.) prepare and issue (a book, a newspaper, computer software, etc.) for public sale. **2** *tr.* (esp. as **published** *adj.*) publish the works of (a particular writer or composer) (*a published poet*). **3** *tr.* make generally known. **4** *tr.* announce (an edict etc.) formally; read (marriage banns). **5** *tr. Law* communicate (a libel etc.) to a third party. □ **publishable** *adj.* **publishing** *n.*

publisher *n.* **1** a person or esp. a company that produces and distributes copies of a book, newspaper, etc. for sale. **2** *N Amer.* a newspaper proprietor.

PUC *abbr. N Amer.* public utilities commission, a government regulatory body for public utilities.

puce /pjuːs/ ● *n.* a dark reddish purple. ● *adj.* of this colour.

puck *n.* **1** a hard rubber disc used in hockey. **2** *Cdn* something shaped like a hockey puck, esp. a disc of chlorine used in swimming pool systems.

pucka *var. of* PUKKA.

puck bunny *n.* a young female hockey fan, esp. one motivated more by a desire to watch, meet, or become esp. sexually involved with the players than by an interest in the sport itself.

puck carrier *n. Hockey* the player in possession of the puck.

pucker ● *v.tr. & intr.* (often foll. by *up*) **1** gather or cause to gather into wrinkles, folds, or bulges. **2** contract (the lips) as when preparing to kiss. ● *n.* such a wrinkle, bulge, fold, etc. □ **puckery** *adj.*

puck-handling *n. Hockey* the ability to control the puck while deking, stickhandling, receiving passes, etc. □ **puckhandler** *n.*

puck hog *n.* a hockey player who selfishly refuses to pass the puck to his or her teammates.

puckster *n. Cdn slang* a hockey player.

pudding *n.* **1** any of various cooked desserts that are heavier and more moist than cake, esp.: **a** a steamed dessert made of flour, suet, fruit, etc. (*Christmas pudding*). **b** a cake-like dessert with a sauce on the bottom. **c** a dessert incorporating bread, rice, tapioca, etc. in a sauce made of milk, eggs, etc. (*rice pudding*). **2** *N Amer.* = MILK PUDDING. **3** an unsweetened dish containing flour, suet, etc., served with the main course of a meal (*Yorkshire pudding*).

puddle ● *n.* a small pool, esp. of rainwater or melted snow on a road etc. ● *v.intr.* **1** dabble or wallow in mud or shallow water. **2** busy oneself in an untidy way. □ **puddler** *n.* **puddly** *adj.*

puddle-jumper *n. N Amer. informal* a small, fast, highly manoeuvrable airplane, esp. used for short trips.

pudendum /pjuːˈdɛndəm/ *n.* (*pl.* **pudenda** /-də/) (usu. in *pl.*) the genitals, esp. of a woman.

pudgy *adj.* (**-ier**, **-iest**) *informal* plump, thickset. □ **pudge** *n.* **pudginess** *n.*

pueblo /ˈpwɛbloʊ/ ● *n.* (*pl.* **-os**) **1** a town or village in Latin America, esp. an Indian settlement. **2** (**Pueblo**) a member of a N American Indian people living esp. in New Mexico and Arizona. **3** a communal dwelling consisting of a number of multi-storey adobe or stone houses joined together, used by certain Indian peoples of the southwestern US. ● *adj.* (**Pueblo**) of or relating to the Pueblos or their culture.

puerile /ˈpjʊəraɪl/ *adj.* **1** trivial, childish, immature. **2** of or like a child. □ **puerility** /-ˈrɪlɪti/ *n.* (*pl.* **-ies**)

Puerto Rican /ˌpɔːrtoʊ ˈriːkən, pɔːrtə-, pwɛrtoʊ-/ ● *n.* **1 a** native of Puerto Rico, an island of the Greater Antilles. **2** a person of Puerto Rican descent. ● *adj.* of or relating to Puerto Rico or its inhabitants.

puff ● *n.* **1 a** a short quick blast of breath or wind. **b** the sound of this; a similar sound. **c** a small quantity of vapour, smoke, etc., emitted in one blast (*a puff of smoke*). **d** an inhalation or exhalation from a cigarette etc. **2** a food that is light or fluffy (*cream puff*). **3** a gathered mass of material in a dress etc. **4** a roll of hair that is cylindrical in shape. **5 a** (also **puff piece**) an extravagantly, esp. uncritically enthusiastic or favourable review, article, etc., esp. in a newspaper. **b** an advertisement for goods etc., esp. in a newspaper. **6** = POWDER-PUFF. ● *v.* **1** *intr.* emit a puff of air or breath; blow with short blasts. **2** *intr.* (often foll. by *out, away,* etc.) send out or move with puffs of vapour, smoke, etc. (*a train puffed out of the station*). **3** *tr.* (usu. in *passive*; often foll. by *out*) put out of breath (*arrived somewhat puffed*). **4** *intr.* breathe hard; pant. **5** *tr.* utter pantingly ('*No more,*' *she puffed*). **6** *intr. & tr.* (usu. foll. by *up, out*) become or cause to become inflated; swell. **7** *tr.* (usu. foll. by *out, up, away*) blow or emit (dust, smoke, a light object, etc.) with a puff. **8 a** *tr.* smoke (a pipe etc.) in puffs. **b** *intr.* (usu. foll. by *away* etc.) take puffs at a cigarette etc. **9** *tr.* advertise or promote (goods, a book, etc.) with exaggerated or false praise. □ **puffed up** proud or boastful.

puffball *n.* any of various fungi having a ball-shaped spore case.

puffer *n.* **1** a person or thing that puffs. **2** = PUFFERFISH.

pufferfish *n.* any tropical fish of the family Tetraodonitidae, ,able to inflate itself into a spherical form when threatened etc. and containing a deadly poison.

puffery *n.* exaggerated praise or commendation.

puffin *n.* any of various seabirds of the family Alcidae native to the N Atlantic and N Pacific having a large head with a brightly coloured triangular bill, and black and white plumage, esp. the Atlantic puffin, *Fratercula arctica*.

puff pastry *n.* a pastry prepared from alternating layers of fat and dough which expand on baking, creating large spaces between thin layers of pastry.

puffy *adj.* (**-ier, -iest**) **1** swollen. **2** fat. **3** gusty. □ **puffily** *adv.* **puffiness** *n.*

pug[1] *n.* (in full **pug dog**) a dwarf breed of dog with a broad flat nose and deeply wrinkled face.

pug[2] *n. slang* a boxer.

pugilist /ˈpjuːdʒɪlɪst/ *n.* a boxer, esp. a professional. □ **pugilistic** *adj.*

pugnacious /pʌgˈneɪʃəs/ *adj.* quarrelsome; disposed to fight. □ **pugnaciously** *adv.* **pugnacity** /-ˈnæsɪti/ *n.*

puh-leeze *interj.* (also **puh-lease**) please (indicating scorn or contempt at implied gullibility).

puja /ˈpuːdʒə/ *n.* a Hindu rite of worship.

puke *slang* ● *v.tr. & intr.* vomit. ● *n.* vomit. □ **pukey** *adj.*

pukka /ˈpʌkə/ *adj.* (also **pukkah**) *Anglo-Ind.* **1** genuine. **2** of good quality; perfect (*did a pukka job*).

Pulitzer Prize /ˈpʊlɪtsər, ˈpjuː-/ *n.* each of 13 annual awards for achievements in American journalism, literature, and music.

pull ● *v.* **1** *tr.* exert force on (a thing) tending to move it towards oneself or the origin of the force. **2** *tr.* cause to move in this way (*pulled me into the room*). **3** *intr.* exert a pulling force (*the engine will not pull*). **4** *tr.* extract (a cork or tooth) by pulling. **5** *tr.* damage (a muscle etc.) by abnormal strain. **6** *intr.* (of an engine etc.) work hard and use a lot of effort in order to operate (*the car pulled hard up the hill*). **7** *tr.* (often foll. by *on*) bring out (a weapon) for use against (a person). **8 a** *tr.* check the speed of (a horse), esp. so as to make it lose the race. **b** *intr.* (of a horse) strain against the bit. **9** *tr.* (often foll. by *in*) attract or secure (support, votes, etc.). **10** *tr.* draw (an esp. alcoholic beverage) from a barrel etc. **11** *intr.* (foll. by *at*) tear or pluck at. **12** *intr.* (often foll. by *on, at*) inhale deeply; draw or suck (on a pipe etc.). **13** *tr.* (often foll. by *up*) remove (a plant) by the root. **14** *tr.* **a** *Baseball* (of a batter) hit (the ball) away from one's opposite field, i.e. (of a right-handed batter) into left field or (of a left-handed batter) into right field. **b** *Golf* (of a right-handed player) hit (the ball) to the left or (of a left-handed player) to the right, esp. widely. **15** *tr. informal* **a** achieve or accomplish (something illicit, cunning, etc.) (*don't pull any more stunts*). **b** do something characteristic of (a specified person) (*pulled a Trudeau*). **16** *intr.* **a** (foll. by *up, in*) (of a vehicle) arrive at a place for stopping, refuelling, etc. (*saw them pull up*). **b** (foll. by *off*) (of a vehicle) exit from (a highway etc.). **17** *tr.* **a** withdraw, remove, take out of service or circulation (*pulled the ad*). **b** retrieve (a file). **18** *tr.* close (a curtain, blind, etc.). ● *n.* **1** the act of pulling. **2** the force exerted by this. **3** a means of exerting influence; an advantage. **4** something that attracts or draws attention. **b** allure, attraction. **5** a long drink from a glass, mug, etc. **6** a handle etc. for applying a pull. **7** a draw or suck at a cigarette. **8** a contest involving pulling (*tractor pull*). **9** an injury to a muscle caused by abnormal strain. □ **pull apart** (or **to pieces**) = PICK APART (see PICK[1]). **pull away 1** remove by pulling. **2** move away, depart. **3** (of a competitor) increase one's lead over others. **pull back** retreat or cause to retreat. **pull down 1** demolish (esp. a building). **2** *informal* earn (a sum of money) as wages etc. **pull even** (often foll. by *with*) reach the same level as (a leading competitor); catch up. **pull a face** assume a distinctive or specified expression (*pulled a glum face*). **pull for** support; desire success for. **pull in 1** (of a bus, train, etc.) arrive to take passengers. **2** (of a vehicle) arrive at a place for stopping, refuelling, etc. **3** earn or acquire. **4** *informal* arrest. **5** rein in, hold in, check. **pull one's hair out** be anxious, exasperated, frustrated, etc. **pull a person's leg** deceive a person playfully. **pull off 1** remove by pulling. **2** succeed in achieving or accomplishing. **3** remove from participation in (*pull her off the job*). **pull oneself together** recover control of oneself. **pull out 1** take out by pulling. **2** depart. **3** withdraw from an undertaking. **4** (of a bus, train, etc.) leave with its passengers. **5** (of a vehicle) move out from the side of the road, or from its normal position to overtake. **pull out all the stops** exert extreme effort. **pull over 1** move (a vehicle) to the side or off the road. **2** (of the police etc.) stop (a vehicle) for a traffic violation etc. **pull the plug** (often foll. by *on*) *informal* put an end to an enterprise etc.; destroy; cut off (supplies etc.). **pull punches** (usu. in *neg.*) **1** avoid using one's full force. **2** criticize less strongly than one might. **pull rank** take unfair advantage of one's seniority. **pull strings** exert (esp. clandestine) influence. **pull the strings** be the real actuator of what another does. **pull through 1** get through an illness, a dangerous situation, or a difficult undertaking. **2** enable (a person) to do this. **pull together** work in harmony. **pull up 1** stop or cause to stop moving. **2** pull out of the ground. **3** come or bring closer. **4** cause (a file etc.) to appear on a computer screen. **pull one's (own) weight** do one's fair share of work. □ **puller** *n.*

pullback *n.* **1** an act or instance of pulling something back or retreating. **2** a withdrawal of troops. **3** a contrivance or attachment for pulling something back.

pull-down *attrib.adj.* **1** that may be, or is designed to be, pulled down. **2** *Computing* designating a menu that need only be displayed onscreen when required.

pullet /'pʊlət/ n. a young hen, esp. one less than one year old.

pulley n. (pl. **-eys**) **1** a grooved wheel or set of wheels for a cord etc. to pass over, set in a block and used for changing the direction of a force. **2** a wheel or drum fixed on a shaft and turned by a belt, used esp. to increase speed or power.

Pullman /'pʊlmən/ n. **1** a railway car affording special comfort. **2** a sleeping car. **3** a large suitcase.

pull-off ● *attrib.adj.* that may be, or is designed to be, pulled off. ● n. **1** an act of pulling something off. **2** an area by the side of a road where vehicles may stop.

pull-on ● *attrib.adj.* designating a garment without fasteners that is pulled on. ● n. such a garment.

pullout ● *attrib.adj.* that may be, or is designed to be, pulled out (*pullout couch*). ● n. **1** something that can be pulled out, esp. a section of a magazine. **2** the act of pulling out; a withdrawal, esp. from military involvement. **3** = PULL-OFF 2.

pullover n. a knitted garment put on over the head and covering the top half of the body.

pull-up n. **1** an exercise involving raising oneself with one's arms by pulling up against a horizontal bar etc. fixed above one's head. **2** the act of pulling up; a sudden stop.

pulmonary /'pʌlmənəri/ *adj.* **1** of or relating to the lungs. **2** having lungs or lunglike organs.

pulmonary artery n. the artery conveying blood from the heart to the lungs.

pulmonary tuberculosis n. tuberculosis caused by inhaling the tubercle bacillus into the lungs.

pulmonary vein n. the vein carrying oxygenated blood from the lungs to the heart.

pulp ● n. **1** the soft fleshy part of fruit etc. **2** any soft thick wet mass. **3** a soft shapeless mass made of ground wood or other vegetable fibres, etc., used in papermaking. **4 a** (often *attrib.*) popular or sensational writing often regarded as of poor quality (*pulp fiction*). **b** a novel, magazine, etc. containing pulp writing. **5** vascular tissue filling the interior cavity and root canals of a tooth. **6** = PULPWOOD. ● v. **1** tr. reduce to pulp. **2** tr. withdraw (a publication) from the market, usu. recycling the paper. **3** tr. remove pulp from. **4** intr. become pulp. □ **beat a person to a pulp** beat a person severely. □ **pulpy** *adj.* **pulping** n.

pulp cutter n. a logger who cuts wood into short lengths for the pulping process.

pulpit /'pʌlpɪt, 'pʊl-/ n. **1** a lectern or raised usu. enclosed platform in a church etc. from which the preacher delivers a sermon. **2** (prec. by *the*) preachers or preaching collectively.

pulpwood n. timber suitable for making pulp.

pulque /'pʊlkeɪ, 'pʊlki/ n. an originally Mexican fermented drink made from the sap of the maguey.

pulsar /'pʌlsɑr/ n. *Astronomy* a celestial object, thought to be a rapidly rotating neutron star, emitting regular pulses of radio waves etc.

pulsate v.intr. **1** expand and contract rhythmically; throb. **2** vibrate, quiver, thrill. **3** vary in magnitude, intensity, brightness, etc. □ **pulsation** n.

pulse[1] ● n. **1 a** a rhythmical throbbing of the arteries as blood is propelled through them, esp. as felt in the wrists, temples, etc. **b** each successive beat of the arteries or heart. **2** a throb or thrill of life or emotion. **3** a general feeling or opinion (*the pulse of the nation*). **4 a** a single vibration of sound, electric current, light, etc., esp. as a signal. **b** (*attrib.*) designating a telephone system in which the number composed on a rotary dial or buttons is translated into electronic pulses

corresponding in number to the digit dialled. **5** a musical beat. **6** any regular or recurrent rhythm, e.g. of the stroke of oars. **7 a** a feature or button on a blender etc. allowing the operator to pulse. **b** an act or instance of pulsing food in a blender etc. ● v. **1** intr. pulsate. **2** tr. transmit etc. by rhythmical beats. **3** tr. & intr. **a** operate (a food processor, blender, etc.) in short bursts using a button that engages the mechanism only as long as the operator keeps it depressed. **b** process (food) in a blender etc. in this way.

pulse[2] n. **1** the edible seeds of various leguminous plants, e.g. chickpeas, lentils, beans, etc. **2** the plant or plants producing this.

pulverize /'pʌlvə,raɪz/ v. **1** tr. reduce to fine particles. **2** tr. & intr. crumble to dust. **3** tr. *informal* **a** demolish. **b** defeat utterly. □ **pulverization** n. **pulverizer** n.

puma /'pjuːmə/ n. a cougar.

pumice /'pʌmɪs/ ● n. (in full **pumice stone**) **1** a light porous volcanic rock often used as an abrasive in cleaning or polishing substances. **2** a piece of this used for removing hard skin etc. ● v.tr. rub or clean with a pumice.

pummel v.tr. & intr. (**pummelled**, **pummelling**) **1** pound or thump repeatedly. **2** beat with the fists. **3** defeat thoroughly. **4** criticize harshly.

pump[1] ● n. **1** a device, usu. with rotary action or the reciprocal action of a piston or plunger, or functioning by suction, for raising or moving liquids or gases, inflating tires, etc. **2** an instance of pumping; a stroke of a pump. ● v. **1** tr. (often foll. by *in, out, into, up,* etc.) raise or remove (liquid, gas, etc.) with a pump. **2** tr. **a** (usu. foll. by *up*) fill (a tire etc.) with air. **b** increase the volume, loudness, strength, etc. of. **3** tr. **a** remove (water etc.) with a pump. **b** (often foll. by *out*) remove the contents of (something) with a pump. **4** intr. work a pump. **5** tr. (often foll. by *out*) cause to move, pour forth, etc., in great quantities. **6** tr. elicit information from (a person) by persistent questioning. **7** tr. **a** move vigorously up and down. **b** shake (a person's hand) effusively. **8** tr. apply and release (brakes) quickly several times in succession, esp. to prevent skidding. **9** tr. (foll. by *into*) cause a major input of (money, effort, etc.). □ **pump iron** *informal* engage in bodybuilding with weights.

pump[2] n. a lightweight, low-cut women's shoe, with no laces or straps.

pumped *adj.* (also **pumped up**) **1** in senses of PUMP[1] v. **2** eager, excited, or emotionally prepared for an undertaking, event, etc.

pumper n. **1** in senses of PUMP[1] v. **2** a fire truck used to pump water or chemicals to douse a fire.

pumpernickel n. a dense, dark, sour rye bread.

pumphandle v.intr. *informal* shake a person's hand effusively.

pumpjack n. *N Amer.* a pumping apparatus at an oil well.

pumpkin n. **1** any of various plants of the genus *Cucurbita*, esp. *C. maxima*, with large lobed leaves and tendrils. **2** the large rounded orange fruit of this with a thick rind and edible flesh. **3** *N Amer.* a term of endearment, esp. to a child, pet, etc.

pumpkinseed n. a colourful N American sunfish, *Lepomis gibbosus*, with an orange belly.

pump-out n. the action of pumping out, esp. the removal of waste, sewage, etc. from a storage tank.

pump-priming n. **1** the introduction of fluid etc. into a pump to prepare it for working. **2** esp. *US* the stimulation of commerce etc. by investment.

pun ● n. the humorous use of a word to suggest different meanings, or of words of the same sound and different meanings. ● *v.intr.* (**punned, punning**) (foll. by *on*) make a pun or puns with (words). □ **punning** *n. & adj.* **punningly** *adv.*

punch[1] ● *v.tr.* **1** strike bluntly, esp. with a closed fist. **2** prod or poke with a blunt object. **3 a** pierce a hole in (metal, paper, a ticket, etc.) as or with a punch. **b** pierce (a hole) by punching. **4** *N Amer.* drive (a beast of burden) by prodding with a stick etc. **5** strike (a button on a keypad) with the fingertip. ● *n.* **1** a blow with a fist. **2** the ability to deliver this. **3** *informal* vigour; effective force. □ **beat someone to the punch** do something before someone else is able to; anticipate or forestall the actions of another. **punch the** (**time**) **clock** *N Amer.* **1** record the time of one's arrival at or departure from work by inserting a card into a timed puncher. **2** be employed in a conventional, esp. nine-to-five job. **punch in 1** punch the clock to record the time of one's arrival at work. **2** enter (data) into a computer, calculator, etc. using a keyboard or keypad. **3** dial (a number on a telephone) by hitting the keypads with the fingertip. **punch out 1** remove or detach by punching. **2** punch the clock to record the time of one's departure from work. **3** assault with punches; beat up. **punch up 1** enter or access (data) into or from a computer etc. using a keyboard or keypad. **2** make more punchy, vigorous, effective. **3** beat up. □ **puncher** *n.*

punch[2] *n.* **1** any of various devices or machines for punching holes in materials, e.g. paper, leather, metal, plaster. **2** a tool or machine for impressing a design or stamping a die on a material.

punch[3] *n.* a drink of mixed beverages, e.g. fruit juices, soft drinks, etc., often including alcohol.

punch[4] *n.* □ **as pleased** (or **proud**) **as punch** showing great pleasure (or pride).

punch bowl *n.* a large usu. glass bowl from which punch is served with a ladle.

punch card *n.* (also **punched card**) a card perforated according to a code, for conveying instructions or data to a data processor etc.

punch-drunk *adj.* stupefied from or as though from a series of heavy blows to the head.

punching bag *n. N Amer.* **1** a suspended stuffed bag punched for exercise. **2** *informal* the object of repeated attack, criticism, etc.

punchline *n.* the climactic final phrase of a joke etc.

punch-up *n. informal* (also **punchout**) a fist fight.

punchy *adj.* (**-ier, -iest**) **1** having punch or vigour; forceful. **2** PUNCH-DRUNK. **3** *N Amer.* in a state of nervous tension or extreme fatigue. **4** *a* (of a sentence etc.) terse, short. **b** composed of punchy segments (*a punchy news program*). □ **punchiness** *n.*

punctilious /pʌŋkˈtɪliəs/ *adj.* **1** attentive to formality or etiquette. **2** precise in behaviour. □ **punctiliously** *adv.* **punctiliousness** *n.*

punctual *adj.* **1** neither early nor late; precisely on time. **2** habitually occurring or arriving at the appointed time. □ **punctuality** *n.* **punctually** *adv.*

punctuate *v.tr.* **1** insert punctuation marks in. **2** interrupt at intervals (*punctuated his tale with heavy sighs*). **3** emphasize, accentuate; give force to.

punctuation *n.* **1** the system or arrangement of marks used in writing to separate sentences and phrases etc. and to clarify meaning. **2** the practice or skill of punctuating.

punctuation mark *n.* any of the marks, e.g. period and comma, used in writing to separate sentences and phrases etc. and to clarify meaning.

puncture ● *n.* **1** an act or instance of perforating with a sharp point, esp. the accidental piercing of a

tire. **2** a hole made in this way. ● *v.* **1** *tr.* make a puncture in. **2** *intr.* undergo puncture. **3** *tr.* prick or pierce. **4** *tr.* deflate (pomposity etc.); debunk.

pundit /ˈpʌndɪt/ *n.* **1** a Hindu learned in Sanskrit and in the philosophy, religion, and jurisprudence of India. **2** often *ironic* a learned expert or teacher, esp. one who makes authoritative pronouncements on current affairs. □ **punditry** *n.*

pungent /ˈpʌndʒənt/ *adj.* **1** having a sharp or strong taste or smell. **2** (of remarks) penetrating, biting, caustic. □ **pungency** *n.* **pungently** *adv.*

punish *v.* **1** *tr. & intr.* cause (an offender) to suffer for an offence. **2** *tr.* inflict a penalty for (an offence). **3** *tr.* *informal* inflict severe blows on (an opponent). **4** *tr. & intr.* subject (someone) to abusive, harsh, or improper treatment. □ **punishable** *adj.* **punisher** *n.* **punishing** *adj.* **punishingly** *adv.*

punishment *n.* **1** the act or an instance of punishing; the condition of being punished. **2** the loss or suffering inflicted in this. **3** *informal* severe treatment or suffering.

punitive /ˈpjuːnɪtɪv/ *adj.* inflicting or intended to inflict punishment. □ **punitively** *adv.*

punitive damages *n.pl.* *Law* damages exceeding simple compensation, awarded to punish the defendant.

Punjabi /pʊndˈʒæbi, ˈpʌn-/ ● *n.* (*pl.* **-is**) **1 a** *hist.* a native of the Punjab in India, now divided between India and Pakistan. **b** a native of the state of Punjab in India or the province Punjab in Pakistan. **2** the language spoken in these areas. ● *adj.* of or relating to these areas, their inhabitants, or their language.

punk ● *n.* **1** a young man or boy regarded as contemptible or insignificant, esp. because of rude or violent behaviour (often as a general term of abuse). **2** *N Amer.* a young hoodlum or ruffian. **3 a** (in full **punk rock**) a loud fast-moving form of angry and aggressive rock music. **b** the subculture or style associated with this, esp. that characterized by coloured spiked hair and leather clothing decorated with safety pins etc. **c** = PUNKER. **4** *N Amer.* an inexperienced person; a novice. **5** soft crumbly wood that has been attacked by fungus, used as tinder. ● *adj.* **1** worthless, rotten. **2** denoting punk rock and its associated subculture (*punk hair*). □ **punkish** *adj.* **punky** *adj.*

punker *n.* (also **punk rocker**) esp. *N Amer.* a person who enjoys or plays punk music; a member of the punk subculture.

punt[1] ● *n.* a long narrow flat-bottomed boat, square at both ends, used mainly for pleasure on rivers and propelled by a long pole. ● *v.* **1** *tr.* propel (a punt) with a pole. **2** *intr. & tr.* travel or convey in a punt. □ **punter** *n.*

punt[2] ● *v.tr.* kick (a ball, esp. in football or rugby) after it has dropped from the hands and before it reaches the ground. ● *n.* such a kick. □ **punter** *n.*

punter *n.* esp. *Brit.* a person who gambles or lays a bet.

puny *adj.* (**-ier, -iest**) **1** undersized. **2** weak, feeble. **3** petty. □ **punily** *adv.* **puniness** *n.*

pup ● *n.* **1** a young dog. **2** a young wolf, rat, seal, etc. ● *v.tr. & intr.* (**pupped, pupping**) bring forth (young).

pupa /ˈpjuːpə/ *n.* (*pl.* **pupae** /-piː/) an inactive immature form of an insect, being the resting stage between larva and adult, e.g. a chrysalis. □ **pupal** *adj.*

pupil[1] /ˈpjuːpəl/ *n.* a person who is taught by another, esp. a schoolchild or student in relation to a teacher.

pupil[2] *n.* the dark circular opening in the centre of the iris of the eye, varying in size to regulate the passage of light to the retina. □ **pupillary** *adj.*

puppet *n.* **1** a small figure representing a human being or animal and moved by various means as entertainment, e.g. by pulling strings attached to its limbs or by putting one's hand inside it. **2** a person, state, etc. whose actions are controlled by another (also *attrib.*: *puppet government*). □ **puppetry** *n.*

puppeteer *n.* (also **puppet master**) **1** a person who works puppets. **2** a person who manipulates others. □ **puppeteering** *n.*

puppy *n.* (*pl.* **-ies**) **1** a young, esp. immature dog. **2** a conceited or arrogant young man. **3** *slang* a person having a specified character (*he's one sick puppy*). □ **puppyhood** *n.* **puppyish** *adj.*

puppy love *n.* a strong, usu. temporary, feeling of love, esp. between adolescents.

pup tent *n.* *N Amer.* a small triangular tent, esp. for two people, usu. without side walls or a window.

purchase ● *v.tr.* **1** acquire by payment; buy. **2** obtain or achieve at some cost. ● *n.* **1** the act or an instance of buying. **2** something bought. **3** *Law* the acquisition of property by one's personal action and not by inheritance. **4** a firm hold on a thing to move it or to prevent it from slipping. □ **purchasable** *adj.* **purchaser** *n.*

purchase order *n.* a form issued by an organization authorizing the purchase of a good or service, often sequentially numbered.

purchasing power *n.* **1** a person's financial ability to make purchases. **2** the amount that a sum of money etc. can purchase.

purdah /'pɜːdə/ *n.* (also *attrib.*) a system in certain Muslim and Hindu societies of screening women from strangers by means of a veil or curtain. □ **in purdah** (of a woman) screened from contact with strangers.

pure *adj.* **1 a** unmixed (*a pure white sheet*; *pure alcohol*). **b** clean and not mixed with any harmful substances (*the air is pure*). **2** of unmixed origin or descent (*pure-blooded*). **3** chaste. **4** morally or sexually undefiled; not corrupt. **5** guiltless. **6** sincere. **7** mere, simple, nothing but, sheer, true (*it was pure malice*). **8** (of a sound) not discordant, perfectly in tune. **9** (of a subject of study) dealing with abstract concepts and not practical application. **10** having no complicated or unnecessary elements. □ **pure and simple** plainly, indisputably, certainly; and nothing else (*they were stolen, pure and simple*). □ **pureness** *n.*

purebred ● *adj.* (of an animal) bred from parents of the same breed or variety. ● *n.* such an animal.

purée /pjʊr'ei, 'pjʊr-/ ● *n.* a pulp of vegetables or fruit etc. reduced to a smooth thick liquid. ● *v.tr.* (**purées, puréed**) make a purée of.

pure laine /pjʊr 'len/ *Cdn* ● *adj.* **1** designating a francophone Quebecer descended from the French settlers in New France and having exclusively French ancestry. **2** of, relating to, or consisting of pure laine Quebecers (*pure laine nationalism*). ● *n.* such a person.

purely *adv.* **1** in a pure manner. **2** merely, solely, exclusively. **3** entirely, completely.

pure science *n.* a science depending on deductions from demonstrated truths, e.g. mathematics or logic, or one studied without practical applications.

purgation /pɜr'geiʃən/ *n.* **1** purification. **2** purging of the bowels. **3** spiritual cleansing, esp. (*Catholicism*) of a soul in purgatory.

purgative /'pɜrɡətɪv/ ● *adj.* **1** serving to purify. **2** strongly laxative. ● *n.* **1** a purgative thing. **2** a laxative.

purgatory /'pɜrɡə,tɔri/ ● *n.* (*pl.* **-ies**) **1** the condition or supposed place of spiritual cleansing, esp. (*Catholicism*) of those dying in the grace of God but having to expiate venial sins etc. **2** a place or state of temporary suffering or expiation. ● *adj.* purifying. □ **purgatorial** *adj.*

purge ● *v.tr.* **1** (often foll. by *of*) make physically or spiritually clean. **2** remove by a cleansing process. **3 a** rid (an organization, party, etc.) of persons regarded as undesirable. **b** remove (an unwanted person) from an organization. **4** rid (a person etc.) of an undesirable quality. **5 a** empty (the stomach or bowels) by inducing vomiting or evacuation. **b** empty the bowels of. **6** *Law* atone for or wipe out (an offence, esp. contempt of court). ● *n.* **1** the act or an instance of purging. **2** a purgative. □ **purger** *n.*

purify *v.tr.* (**-ies, -ied**) **1** (often foll. by *of*, *from*) cleanse or make pure. **2** make ceremonially clean. **3** clear of extraneous elements. □ **purification** *n.* **purifier** *n.*

Purim /'pʊrɪm, pu:'ri:m/ *n.* a Jewish spring festival commemorating the defeat of a plot to massacre the Jews in Persia in the 5th c. BC.

purine /'pʊri:n/ *n.* **1** an organic nitrogenous base forming uric acid on oxidation. **2** any of a group of compounds with a similar structure.

purist *n.* a stickler for or advocate of scrupulous correctness or authenticity, e.g. in language or art. □ **purism** *n.*

puritan ● *n.* **1** (**Puritan**) *hist.* a member of a group of English Protestants who regarded the Reformation of the Church under Elizabeth I as incomplete and sought to simplify and regulate forms of worship. **2** a purist member of any party. **3** a person practising, affecting, or advocating extreme strictness in religion or morals. ● *adj.* **1** (**Puritan**) *hist.* of or relating to the Puritans. **2** scrupulous and austere in religion or morals. □ **puritanism** *n.*

puritanical *adj.* often *derogatory* practising, affecting, or advocating strict religious or moral behaviour, esp. one opposed to pleasure. □ **puritanically** *adv.*

purity /'pjʊrɪti/ *n.* pureness, cleanness; freedom from physical or moral pollution.

purl¹ /pɜrl/ ● *n.* a knitting stitch made by putting the needle through the front of the previous stitch and passing the yarn around the back of the needle. ● *v.tr.* & *intr.* knit with a purl stitch.

purl² ● *v.intr.* **1** (of a brook etc.) flow with a swirling motion and babbling sound. **2** make a babbling sound. ● *n.* this motion or sound.

purlieu /'pɜrlju:/ *n.* (*pl.* **purlieus**) **1** (in *pl.*) the outskirts; an outlying region. **2** a person's usual haunts. **3** a person's bounds or limits.

purloin /pɜr'lɔin/ *v.tr.* *formal* or *jocular* steal, pilfer.

purple ● *n.* **1** a colour intermediate between red and blue. **2** a purple robe, esp. as the dress of royalty. **3** (prec. by *the*) a position of rank, authority, or privilege. **4 a** the scarlet official dress of a cardinal. **b** the position or office of a cardinal. ● *adj.* **1** of a purple colour. **2** (of writing, speech, etc.) excessively elaborate or ornate. ● *v.tr.* & *intr.* make or become purple. □ **purplish** *adj.* **purply** *adj.*

purple coneflower *n.* any of various eastern N American plants of the genus *Echinacea* with purplish flowers, esp. *E. purpurea*, grown as an ornamental.

purple gas *n.* *Cdn* (*Prairies*) gas sold with reduced taxes to farmers for farm machinery and vehicles, dyed purple for identification.

purple loosestrife *n.* a wetland plant, *Lythrum salicaria*, with a long spike of purple flowers.

purple martin *n.* a large, purplish-blue swallow, *Progne subis*, a voracious eater of insects.

purport ● *v.tr.* **1** profess; be intended to seem (*purports to be his signature*). **2** (of a document, speech, etc.) have as its meaning; state. ● *n.* **1** the ostensible meaning of something. **2** the sense or tenor (of a document or statement). □ **purportedly** adv.

purpose ● n. **1 a** something to be attained; a thing intended (our purpose was to delay). **b** the reason for which something is done or made, or for which it exists (for tax purposes). **2** resolution, determination. ● v.tr. have as one's purpose; design, intend. □ **on purpose** intentionally. **to no purpose** with no result or effect. **to the purpose 1** relevant. **2** useful.

purpose-built adj. (also **purpose-made, purpose-designed,** etc.) built or made for a specific purpose (purpose-built art gallery).

purposeful adj. **1** having or indicating purpose. **2** intentional. **3** resolute. □ **purposefully** adv. **purposefulness** n.

purposeless adj. having no aim or plan. □ **purposelessly** adv. **purposelessness** n.

purposely adv. on purpose; intentionally.

purr ● v. **1** intr. (of a cat) make a low vibratory sound usu. expressing contentment. **2** intr. (of a person, machinery, etc.) make a similar sound. **3** intr. (of a person) express pleasure. **4** tr. utter or express (words or contentment) in this way. ● n. a purring sound.

purse ● n. **1** N Amer. a small woman's bag of leather or fabric etc., for holding small personal articles, e.g. wallet, keys, makeup, etc.; a handbag or shoulder bag. **2** hist. a small pouch of leather etc. for carrying money, esp. coins. **3** a receptacle resembling a purse in form or purpose. **4** money, funds. **5** a sum collected as a present or given as a prize in a contest. ● v. **1** tr. pucker or contract (the lips). **2** intr. become contracted and wrinkled.

purser n. **1** an officer on a ship who keeps the accounts. **2** the head steward in a ship or airplane.

purse seine n. a fishing net or seine which may be drawn into the shape of a sack, used for catching shoal fish (also attrib.: purse seine vessels). □ **purse seiner** n. **purse seining** n.

purse strings n.pl. control of or access to funds (tighten the purse strings).

purslane /ˈpɜrsleɪn/ n. any of various plants of the genus Portulaca, esp. P. oleracea, with green or golden leaves, used as a herb and salad vegetable.

pursuant /pərˈsuːənt, -ˈsjuːənt/ adv. (foll. by to) conforming to or in accordance with.

pursue v. (**-sues, -sued, -suing**) **1** tr. follow with intent to overtake or capture or do harm to. **2** tr. continue or proceed along (a route or course of action). **3** tr. follow or engage in (study or other activity). **4** tr. proceed in compliance with (a plan etc.). **5** tr. seek after, aim at. **6** tr. continue to investigate or discuss (a topic). **7** tr. seek the attention or acquaintance of (a person) persistently. **8** tr. (of misfortune etc.) persistently assail. **9** tr. persistently attend, stick to. **10** intr. **a** go in pursuit. **b** continue. □ **pursuer** n.

pursuit n. **1** the act or an instance of pursuing. **2** an occupation or activity pursued. □ **in pursuit of** pursuing.

purulent /ˈpjʊrələnt, ˈpjɔːrjʊ-/ adj. **1** consisting of or containing pus. **2** discharging pus.

purvey v.tr. & intr. provide or supply (food, provisions, or esp. shady or dishonest information, services, etc.) esp. as one's business. □ **purveyor** n.

purview /ˈpɜrvjuː/ n. **1** the scope or range of a document etc. **2** the range of physical or mental vision.

pus n. a thick yellowish or greenish liquid produced from infected tissue, consisting of dead bacteria and white blood cells with tissue debris and serum.

push ● v. **1** tr. exert a force on (a thing) to move it away from oneself or from the origin of the force. **2** tr.

cause to move in this direction. **3** intr. exert such a force (do not push against the door). **4** intr. exert muscular pressure internally, esp. during the second stage of labour. **5** tr. press, depress (push the button). **6** intr. & tr. **a** thrust forward or upward. **b** project or cause to project (pushed out new roots). **7** intr. move forward by force or persistence. **8** tr. make (one's way) by pushing. **9** intr. exert oneself, esp. to surpass others. **10** tr. (often foll. by to, into, or to + infin.) urge or impel. **11** tr. tax the abilities or tolerance of; press (a person) hard. **12** tr. pursue (an action or operation) with vigour and insistence; press (a claim etc.). **13** tr. promote the use or sale or adoption of, e.g. by advertising. **14** intr. (foll. by for) demand persistently (pushed hard for reform). **15** tr. informal sell (a drug) illegally. **16** tr. informal approach (a certain number), esp. in years of age (he's pushing 40). ● n. **1** the act or an instance of pushing; a shove or thrust. **2** the force exerted in this. **3** a vigorous effort. **4** a military attack in force. **5** enterprise, determination to succeed. **6** the use of influence to advance a person. **7** the pressure of affairs. □ **be pushed for** informal have very little of (esp. time). **push around** informal bully. **push one's luck 1** take undue risks. **2** act presumptuously. **push off 1** push with an oar etc. to get a boat out into a river etc. **2** (often in imper.) informal go away. **push through** get (a scheme, proposal, etc.) completed or accepted quickly. **when push comes to shove** when action must be taken; when a decision, commitment, etc. must be made.

push button ● n. a button to be pushed esp. to operate an electrical device. ● adj. (**push-button**) **1** operated by pressing a push button. **2** easily obtainable, as at the push of a button; instant.

pushcart n. esp. N Amer. a small handcart, esp. one used by a street vendor.

pusher n. **1** informal a person who sells (esp. prohibited) drugs illegally. **2** a person or thing that pushes.

pushover n. informal **1** something easily done or won; an easy task or victory. **2** a person who can easily be overcome, persuaded, etc.

push-pin n. N Amer. a tack with a spool-shaped, usu. plastic head, used on bulletin boards etc.

push-pull adj. **1** Electronics consisting of two valves etc. operated alternately. **2** operated by pushing and pulling.

push-start ● n. the starting of a motor vehicle by pushing it to turn the engine. ● v.tr. start (a vehicle) in this way.

Pushtu /ˈpʌʃtuː/ n. & adj. = PASHTO.

push-up N Amer. ● n. **1** an exercise in which a person lies facing the floor and, keeping the back straight, raises the upper part of the body by pressing down on the hands to straighten the arms. **2** a muskrat's resting place, formed by pushing up vegetation through a hole in the ice. ● adj. designating a brassiere or similar garment which is underwired or padded to provide uplift for the breasts.

pushy adj. (**-ier, -iest**) informal excessively or unpleasantly forward or self-assertive. □ **pushily** adv. **pushiness** n.

puss[1] n. informal **1** a cat (esp. as a form of address). **2** a playful or coquettish girl.

puss[2] n. esp. N Amer. & Irish slang the face or mouth.

pussy n. (pl. **-ies**) **1** informal a cat. **2** coarse slang **a** the female genitals. **b** sexual intercourse with a woman. **c** offensive women considered sexually. **3** slang a weak or effeminate boy or man; a male homosexual.

pussycat n. informal **1** a cat. **2** a meek, mild-tempered, or amiable person.

pussyfoot v.intr. **1** move stealthily or warily. **2** act cautiously or noncommittally.

pussy willow n. any of various willows, esp. *Salix discolor*, with furry catkins.

pustule /'pʌstʃuːl, 'pʌstjuːl/ n. a pimple containing pus. □ **pustular** adj.

put ● v. (**putting**; past and past part. **put**) **1** tr. **a** move to or cause to be in a specified place or position (*put it in your pocket*; *put the children to bed*). **b** fit or fix (something) to something else (*put a new lock on the door*). **2** tr. bring into a specified condition, relation, or state (*puts me in an awkward position*). **3** tr. **a** (often foll. by *on*) impose or assign (*where do you put the blame?*). **b** (foll. by *on, to*) impose or enforce the existence of (*put a stop to it*). **4 a** tr. cause (a person) to go or be, habitually or temporarily (*put them at their ease*). **b** refl. imagine (oneself) in a specified situation (*put yourself in my shoes*). **5** tr. (foll. by *for*) substitute (one thing for another). **6** intr. express (a thought or idea) in a specified way. **7** tr. (foll. by *at*) estimate (a cost etc.) at a specified amount (*put the cost at $50*). **8** tr. (foll. by *into*) express or translate in (words, or another language). **9** tr. set (words) to music. **10** tr. (foll. by *into*) invest (money) in an asset, e.g. land. **11** tr. (foll. by *on*) stake (money) on (a horse etc.). **12** tr. (foll. by *to*) apply or devote to a use or purpose (*put it to good use*). **13** tr. (foll. by *to*) submit for consideration or attention (*put it to a vote*). **14** tr. (foll. by *to*) subject (a person) to (death, suffering, etc.). **15** tr. throw (esp. a shot or weight) as an athletic sport or exercise. **16** intr. (foll. by *back, off, out*, etc.) (of a ship etc.) proceed or follow a course in a specified direction. ● n. **1** a throw of the shot or weight. **2** *Stock Exch.* the option of selling stock at a fixed price at a given date. □ **put about 1** spread (information, rumour, etc.). **2** *Naut.* turn around; put (a ship) on the opposite tack. **put across 1** make acceptable or effective. **2** express in an understandable way. **put aside 1** save (esp. a sum of money) for later use. **2** reserve an item for a customer to collect later. **3** disregard; ignore or forget. **put away 1** put (a thing) back in the place where it is normally kept. **2** lay (money etc.) aside for future use. **3 a** confine or imprison. **b** commit to a home or mental institution. **4** *informal* consume (food and drink), esp. in large quantities. **5** = PUT DOWN 7. **put back 1** restore to its proper or former place. **2** change (a planned event) to a later date or time. **3** move back the hands of (a clock or watch). **4** check the advance of. **put down 1** suppress by force or authority. **2** *informal* snub or humiliate. **3** record or enter in writing. **4** enter the name of (a person) on a list, esp. as a member or subscriber. **5** (foll. by *as, for*) account or reckon. **6** (foll. by *to*) attribute (*put it down to bad planning*). **7** put (an old or sick animal) to death. **8** preserve or store (fruit, wine, etc.) for future use. **9** pay (a specified sum) as a deposit. **10** put (a baby) to bed. **11** land (an aircraft). **put forth 1** (of a plant) send out (buds or leaves). **2** *formal* submit or put into circulation. **put forward 1** suggest, propose, or nominate. **2 a** advance the hands of (a clock or watch). **b** move (an event etc.) to an earlier time or date (*put forward the date of our wedding*). **3** (often refl.) put into a prominent position; draw attention to. **put one's hands on** = LAY ONE'S HANDS ON (see LAY¹). **put in 1** enter or submit (a claim etc.). **b** (foll. by *for*) submit a claim for (a specified thing). **2** (foll. by *for*) be a candidate for an appointment, election, etc.). **3** spend (time) (*put in five hours of overtime*). **4** interpose (a remark, blow, etc.). **5** (of a ship) enter or call at a port, harbour, etc. **6** plant (a crop etc.). **put it to a person** (often foll. by *that* +

clause) present or submit a question, statement, etc. to (a person) for consideration or by way of appeal. **put one's mind to** devote all one's attention and energy to achieving something. **put off 1 a** postpone. **b** postpone an engagement with (a person). **2** (often foll. by *with*) evade (a person) with an excuse etc. **3** hinder or distract (*the sudden noise put her off her game*). **4** offend, disconcert; cause (a person) to lose interest in something. **5** (of a vehicle or its driver) stop to let a passenger get off. **put on 1** clothe oneself with. **2** apply (makeup, lotion, etc.) to the skin. **3** cause (an electrical device, light, etc.) to function. **4** stage (a play, show, etc.). **5 a** pretend to be affected by (an emotion). **b** assume, take on (a character or appearance). **c** (**put it on**) exaggerate one's feelings etc. **6** increase one's weight by (a specified amount). **7** (foll. by *to*) make aware of or put in touch with (*put us on to her*). **8** *informal* tease, play a trick on (*are you putting me on?*). **9** place (a tax etc.) on something (*put a duty on wine*). **10** bet (money) on something (*put $100 on the white horse*). **put out 1 a** (often as **put out** adj.) disconcert or annoy. **b** (often refl.) inconvenience (*don't put yourself out*). **2** extinguish (a fire or light). **3** *Baseball* cause (a player) to be out. **4** dislocate (a joint etc.) (*put my back out*). **5** exert (strength etc.). **6** *slang* (of a woman) readily offer sexual intercourse. **7** issue, publish, or broadcast (something). **8** blind (a person's eyes). **put one over** (foll. by *on*) *informal* get the better of; trick. **put over 1** make acceptable or effective. **2** express in an understandable way. **3** *N Amer.* postpone. **put through 1** carry out or complete (a task or transaction). **2** (often foll. by *to*) connect (a person) by telephone to another user. **3** subject to an ordeal or trying experience (*put me through hell*). **4** arrange or pay for (someone) to attend university etc. (*put her through college*). **put together 1** assemble (a whole) from parts. **2** combine (parts) to form a whole. **put under** render unconscious by anaesthetic etc. **put up 1** build or erect. **2 a** raise (a hand) to answer or ask a question. **b** raise (one's hands) to indicate surrender. **3** raise (a price etc.). **4** take or provide accommodation (*friends put me up for the night*). **5** engage in (a fight, struggle, etc.) as a form of resistance. **6** present (a proposal etc.). **7 a** present oneself for election. **b** propose for election. **8** provide (money) as a backer in an enterprise. **9** display (a notice). **10** preserve or can (fruit etc.). **11** offer for sale or competition. **12** arrange (long hair) in a bun or upswept hairstyle. **put upon** (usu. in *passive*; hyphenated when *attrib.*) *informal* make unfair or excessive demands on; take advantage of (a person). **put up or shut up** *informal* defend or justify oneself or remain silent. **put a person up to** (usu. foll. by verbal noun) instigate a person in (*put them up to stealing the money*). **put up with** endure, tolerate; submit to. □ **putter** n.

putative /'pjuːtətɪv/ adj. reputed, supposed (*his putative father*). □ **putatively** adv.

put-down n. *informal* a snub or humiliating remark or criticism.

put-in n. *N Amer.* a place on the banks of a river etc. from which to launch a canoe or other small craft.

put-on n. esp. *N Amer.* *informal* a deception or hoax.

put-out n. *Baseball* an instance of putting out a batter or baserunner.

put-put var. of PUTT-PUTT.

putrefy /'pjuːtrɪfaɪ/ v. (**-ies, -ied**) **1** intr. & tr. become or make putrid. **2** intr. fester. □ **putrefaction** /-'fækʃən/ n.

putrid /'pjuːtrɪd/ adj. **1** decomposed, rotten. **2** foul, noxious. **3** morally corrupt. **4** *slang* of poor quality; contemptible; very unpleasant.

putsch /potʃ/ *n.* an attempt at political revolution; a violent uprising. □ **putschist** *n. & adj.*

putt ● *v.tr.* (**putted, putting**) strike (a golf ball) gently to get it into or nearer to a hole. ● *n.* a putting stroke.

putter[1] *n.* **1** a golf club used in putting. **2** a golfer who putts.

putter[2] *n. & v.* = PUTT-PUTT.

putter[3] *v.intr.* **1 a** (often foll. by *around, about*) work or occupy oneself in a desultory but pleasant manner (*puttering in the garden*). **b** (often foll. by *at, in*) dabble in a subject or occupation. **2** go slowly, dawdle.

putting green *n. Golf* the smooth area of grass around a hole.

putt-putt ● *n.* **1** the rapid intermittent sound of a small gasoline engine. **2** a small boat, car, etc. fitted with such an engine. ● *v.intr.* (**-putted, -putting**) make this sound.

putty ● *n.* (*pl.* **-ies**) **1** a cement made from whiting and raw linseed oil, used for fixing panes of glass, filling holes in woodwork, etc. **2** a fine white mortar of lime and water, used in pointing brickwork, etc. **3** a light shade of yellowish grey. ● *v.tr.* (**-ies, -ied**) cover, fix, join, or fill up with putty. □ **putty in a person's hands** someone who is overcompliant, or easily influenced.

putty knife *n.* a knife with a blunt flexible spatulate blade for spreading putty.

put-up *adj.* fraudulently presented or devised (*a put-up job*).

putz /pʌts/ *N Amer.* ● *n.* **1** *slang* a fool; a stupid person. **2** *coarse slang* the penis. ● *v.intr.* (usu. foll. by *around*) waste time; fool around.

puzzle ● *n.* **1** a difficult or confusing problem. **2** a problem or toy designed to test knowledge or ingenuity (*jigsaw puzzle*). ● *v.* **1** *tr.* confound or disconcert mentally. **2** *intr.* (usu. foll. by *over* etc.) be perplexed (about). **3** *tr.* (usu. as **puzzling** *adj.*) require much thought to comprehend (*a puzzling situation*). **4** *tr.* (foll. by *out*) solve or understand by hard thought. □ **puzzled** *adj.* **puzzlement** *n.* **puzzlingly** *adv.*

puzzler *n.* **1** a difficult question or problem. **2** a person who is fond of solving puzzles.

PV *abbr.* PHOTOVOLTAIC.

PVA *abbr.* POLYVINYL ACETATE.

PVC *abbr.* POLYVINYL CHLORIDE.

PWA *abbr.* person with AIDS.

PWC *abbr.* PERSONAL WATERCRAFT.

pygmy /'pɪgmi/ *n.* (*pl.* **-ies**) **1** a member of any of several small-statured peoples of equatorial Africa and parts of SE Asia. **2** a very small person, animal, or thing. **3** an insignificant person. **4** (*attrib.*) **a** of or relating to pygmies. **b** (of a person, animal, etc.) dwarf.

pygmy hippopotamus *n. see* HIPPOPOTAMUS 2.

pyjama party *n.* esp. *N Amer.* = SLUMBER PARTY.

pyjamas *n.pl.* **1** a suit of loose trousers, shorts, or underpants and a top for sleeping in. **2** loose trousers tied around the waist, originally worn in some Asian countries. **3** (**pyjama**) (*attrib.*) designating parts of a suit of pyjamas (*pyjama jacket*) or loose trousers esp. worn by women (*pyjama pants*).

pylon *n.* **1** *N Amer.* a plastic, usu. orange cone used to mark areas of roads etc. **2** esp. *Brit.* a tall structure erected as a support (esp. for electric power cables). **3** a structure on the wing of an aircraft supporting an engine or weapon.

pylorus /pai'lɔːrəs/ *n.* (*pl.* **-ri** /-rai/) *Anat.* the opening from the stomach into the duodenum. □ **pyloric** *adj.*

pyramid ● *n.* **1** a monumental structure, usu. of stone, with a square base and sloping sides meeting centrally at an apex, esp. an ancient Egyptian royal tomb. **2** a polyhedron or solid figure of this type with a base of three or more sides. **3** a pyramid-shaped thing or pile of things. **4** an organization or a system seen as a structure in which the higher the level, the fewer people or things that occupy that level. **5** a system of financial growth achieved by a small initial investment, usu. in stock or in a company. ● *v.tr.* **1** arrange in the form a pyramid; pile up. **2 a** accumulate (assets). **b** build up (stock) from the proceeds of a series of advantageous sales. □ **pyramidal** *adj.*

pyramid selling *n.* (also **pyramid scheme**) a system of selling goods in which the right to sell the goods is sold to an increasing number of distributors at successively lower levels, each of whom is recompensed for recruiting other distributors.

pyre /pair/ *n.* a heap of combustible material esp. on which a corpse is burned.

pyrethrum /pai'riːθrəm/ *n.* **1** any of several aromatic chrysanthemums of the genus *Tanacetum*, esp. *T. coccineum*. **2** an insecticide made from the dried flowers of these plants, esp. *Tanacetum cinerariifolium*.

Pyrex *n. proprietary* a hard heat-resistant type of glass, often used for ovenware.

pyridine /'pɪrədiːn/ *n.* a colourless volatile odorous liquid, used as a solvent and in chemical manufacture.

pyrimidine /pɪ'rɪmɪdiːn/ *n.* **1** *Chem.* a cyclic organic nitrogenous base. **2** any of a group of compounds with a similar structure.

pyrite /'pairəit/ *n.* (also **pyrites**, **iron pyrites**) a yellow lustrous form of iron disulphide.

pyrogy (also **pyrohy** /pɪ'roːhi/) *var. of* PEROGY.

pyromania /,pairo'meiniə/ *n.* an obsessive desire to set things on fire. □ **pyromaniac** *n.*

pyrotechnic /,pairo'teknik/ *adj.* **1** of or relating to fireworks. **2** (of wit etc.) brilliant or sensational. □ **pyrotechnical** *adj.* **pyrotechnician** *n.*

pyrotechnics *n.pl.* **1** (treated as *sing.*) the art of making fireworks. **2** a display of fireworks. **3** any brilliant display.

pyrrhic /'pirik/ *adj.* (of a victory) won at too great a cost to be of use to the victor.

pysanka /'pɪsən,kʌ/ *n.* (*pl.* **pysanky** /-,kɪ/) *Cdn* a hand-painted Ukrainian Easter egg, usu. having elaborate and intricate designs.

Pythagorean /pɪ,θægə'riːən, pai-/ ● *adj.* of or relating to the Greek philosopher Pythagoras (*c.*560–480 BC) or his philosophy, esp. regarding the transmigration of souls. ● *n.* a follower of Pythagoras.

Pythagorean theorem *n.* the theorem attributed to Pythagoras that the square on the hypotenuse of a right-angled triangle is equal to the sum of the squares on the other two sides.

python *n.* any constricting snake of the family Pythonidae, esp. of the genus *Python*, found throughout the tropics in the Old World.

Qq

Q¹ *n.* (also **q**) (*pl.* **Qs** or **Q's**) the seventeenth letter of the alphabet.

Q² *abbr.* (also **Q.**) **1** Queen, Queen's. **2** question.

Qallunaaq /kæ'luːnæk/ *n.* (*pl.* **Qallunaat** /-næt/) *Cdn* (*North*) a person who is not Inuit, esp. a white person.

Q & A (also **Q and A**) ● *abbr.* question and answer. ● *n.* a question-and-answer session, column, etc.

QB *abbr.* **1** quarterback. **2** Queen's Bench.

QC *abbr.* **1** (also **Qc**) Quebec. **2** (also **Q.C.**) Queen's Counsel. **3** quality control.

qi /tʃiː/ *n.* the physical life force postulated by certain Chinese philosophers to flow through the body.

qigong /tʃiː'gɒŋ/ *n.* a system of techniques to focus and strengthen qi, including breathing exercises, meditation, and hand and arm movements, used in alternative medicine and in martial-arts training.

qiviut /'kɪviuːt/ *n. Cdn* (*North*) & *Alaska* fine, soft wool from the underbelly of a muskox.

QM *abbr.* quartermaster.

QPF *abbr. Cdn* Quebec Police Force; the SQ.

QPP *abbr. Cdn* Quebec Pension Plan.

qr. *abbr.* quarter(s).

QST *n. Cdn* Quebec Sales Tax.

qt. *abbr.* quart(s).

q.t. *n. informal* quiet (*on the q.t.*).

Q-tip *n. N Amer. proprietary* a cotton swab on a small stick, used for cleaning ears, applying medication etc.

qua /kwei, kwʌ/ *conj.* in the capacity of; as being (*Napoleon qua general*).

Quaalude /'kweiluːd/ *n. proprietary* **1** the tranquilizer methaqualone. **2** a tablet of this.

quack¹ ● *n.* the harsh sound made by ducks. ● *v.intr.* **1** utter this sound. **2** *informal* talk loudly and foolishly.

quack² *n.* **1 a** an unqualified practitioner of medicine. **b** (*attrib.*) of or characteristic of unskilled medical practice (*quack cure*). **2** a charlatan. □ **quackery** *n.*

quack grass *n. N Amer.* couch grass, *Agropyron repens*.

quad ● *n.* **1** *informal* a quadrangle. **2** *informal* = QUADRUPLET 1. **3** *informal* a quadriplegic. **4** quadraphony. **5** (usu. in *pl.*) *slang* = QUADRICEPS. **6** *Figure Skating* a quadruple jump, in which a skater completes four rotations in the air. ● *adj.* quadraphonic.

quad chair *n.* (also **quad chairlift**) a chairlift with chairs that seat four people.

quadrangle *n.* **1** a four-sided plane figure, esp. a square or rectangle. **2 a** a four-sided court, esp. enclosed by buildings, as in some colleges, schools, etc. **b** such a court with the buildings around it. □ **quadrangular** *adj.*

quadrant *n.* **1** a quarter of a circle's circumference. **2** a plane figure enclosed by two radii of a circle at right angles and the arc cut off by them. **3** a quarter of a sphere or spherical body. **4** any of four parts of a plane divided by two lines at right angles. **5 a** a thing, esp. a graduated strip of metal, shaped like a quarter-circle. **b** an instrument graduated for taking angular measurements.

quadraphonic /ˌkwɒdrə'fɒnɪk/ *adj.* (of sound reproduction) using four transmission channels. □ **quadraphonically** *adv.* **quadraphony** /-'rɒfəni/ *n.*

quadrat /'kwɒdrət/ *n. Ecology* a small area marked out for study.

quadratic /kwɒ'drætɪk/ *Math.* ● *adj.* involving the second and no higher power of an unknown quantity or variable (*quadratic equation*). ● *n.* **1** a quadratic equation. **2** (in *pl.*) the branch of algebra dealing with these.

quadriceps /'kwɒdrəˌseps/ *n. Anat.* a large four-headed muscle at the front of the thigh, the chief extensor of the knee.

quadrilateral /ˌkwɒdrə'lætərəl/ ● *adj.* having four sides. ● *n.* a four-sided figure.

quadrille /kwɒ'drɪl/ *n.* **1** a square dance usu. performed by four couples and containing five figures, each of which is a complete dance in itself. **2** the music for this.

quadrillion /kwɒ'drɪljən/ ● *n.* (*pl.* same or **-s**) **1** a thousand raised to the fifth power (10¹⁵). **2** *informal* a very large amount. ● *adj.* amounting to one quadrillion in number.

quadriplegia /ˌkwɒdrə'pliːdʒə/ *n. Med.* paralysis of all four limbs. □ **quadriplegic** *adj.* & *n.*

quadrophonic *var. of* QUADRAPHONIC.

quadruped ● *n.* a four-footed animal, esp. a mammal. ● *adj.* four-footed. □ **quadrupedal** *adj.*

quadruple ● *adj.* **1** fourfold. **2 a** having four parts. **b** involving four participants (*quadruple alliance*). **3** being four times as many or as much. **4** (of time in music) having four beats in a bar. ● *n.* a fourfold number or amount. ● *v.tr.* & *intr.* multiply by four; increase fourfold. □ **quadruply** *adv.*

quadruplet *n.* **1** each of four children born at one birth. **2** a set of four things working together. **3** *Music* a group of four notes to be performed in the time of three.

quadruplex *n. Cdn* a building divided into four self-contained residences.

quaff /kwɒf/ ● *v.tr.* & *intr.* **1** drink deeply or in long drafts. **2** drink copiously or repeatedly. ● *n.* **1** a beverage quaffed. **2** an act of quaffing. □ **quaffable** *adj.* **quaffer** *n.*

quagmire /'kwæɡˌmair, kwɒɡ-/ *n.* **1** a soft boggy or marshy area that gives way underfoot. **2** a hazardous or awkward situation.

quahog /'kwɒhɒɡ, 'kwæ-/ *n.* (also **quahaug**) the edible round clam, *Venus mercenaria*, of the Atlantic coast of N America.

quail¹ *n.* (*pl.* same or **-s**) **1** any small bird of the genus *Coturnix*, related to the partridge, esp. the migratory *C. coturnix*, raised for its flesh and eggs. **2** any of various similar birds of other genera, e.g. the bobwhite.

quail² *v.intr.* flinch; be apprehensive with fear.

quaint *adj.* attractively unusual or unfamiliar in character or appearance, esp. in an old-fashioned way. □ **quaintly** *adv.* **quaintness** *n.*

quake ● *v.intr.* **1** (of the earth) shake, tremble. **2** (of a person) shake or shudder. ● *n.* **1** an earthquake. **2** an act of quaking. □ **quaky** *adj.* (**-ier, -iest**).

Quaker ● *n.* a member of the Society of Friends, a Christian movement devoted to peaceful principles and eschewing formal doctrine, sacraments, and ordained ministers. ● *adj.* of or relating to Quakers. □ **Quakerism** *n.*

qualification *n.* **1** the act or an instance of qualifying. **2** an accomplishment fitting a person for a position or purpose. **3 a** a circumstance, condition, etc., that modifies or limits (*the statement had many qualifications*). **b** a thing that detracts from completeness or absoluteness (*their relief had one qualification*). **4** a condition that must be fulfilled before a right can be acquired etc.

qualify *v.* (**-ies, -ied**) **1** *tr.* make competent or fit for a position or purpose. **2** *tr.* make legally entitled. **3** *intr.* (foll. by *for*) (of a person) satisfy the conditions or requirements (for a position, award, competition, etc.). **4** *tr.* add reservations to; modify or make less absolute (a statement or assertion). **5** *tr.* (of a word, esp. an adjective) attribute a quality to (another word, esp. a noun). **6** *tr.* moderate, mitigate; make less severe or extreme. **7** *tr.* alter the strength or flavour of. **8** *tr.* (foll. by *as*) attribute a specified quality to, describe as (*the idea was qualified as absurd*). □ **qualifier** *n.*

qualifying *adj.* serving to determine those that qualify (*qualifying examination*).

qualitative *adj.* concerned with or depending on quality or qualities (*a qualitative difference*). □ **qualitatively** *adv.*

quality *n.* (*pl.* **-ies**) **1** the standard of something when compared to other things like it (*quality of life; wine of exceptional quality*). **2** a general excellence (*we provide quality at reasonable prices*). **b** (*attrib.*) of high quality (*a quality product*). **3** a distinctive, usu. good, attribute or characteristic. **4 a** the distinctive timbre of a voice or sound. **b** *Phonetics* the distinguishing characteristic or characteristics of a sound.

quality circle *n.* a group of employees who meet to consider ways of resolving problems and improving production in their organization.

quality control *n.* a system of maintaining standards in manufactured products by testing and inspection. □ **quality controlled** *adj.*

quality time *n.* time spent devoting one's undivided attention to a favourite activity, such as a hobby, or to a person, esp. a child, perceived as compensating in quality for what it lacks in duration or frequency.

qualm /kwɒm, kwɒlm/ *n.* **1** a misgiving; an uneasy doubt. **2** a scruple of conscience; a pang of doubt about one's own conduct.

quandary /ˈkwɒndri, -dəri/ *n.* (*pl.* **-ies**) **1** a state of perplexity concerning what to do in a difficult situation. **2** a difficult situation; a dilemma.

quantify *v.tr.* (**-ies, -ied**) **1** determine the quantity of. **2** measure or express as a quantity. **3** *Logic* define the application of (a term or proposition) by the use of *all*, *some*, etc. □ **quantifiable** *adj.* **quantification** *n.* **quantifier** *n.*

quantitative *adj.* **1 a** concerned with quantity. **b** measured or measurable by quantity. **2** pertaining to or based on vowel length. □ **quantitatively** *adv.*

quantity *n.* (*pl.* **-ies**) **1** an indefinite number or amount. **2** a specified or definite number or amount that can be measured or counted (*add the correct quantity of cream*). **3** a large amount or number; an abundance (*buys in quantity*). **4** the property of things that is measurable (*quantity is easy to measure, whereas quality is not*). **5** a person or thing viewed as having a specified value (*an unknown quantity*). **6** the length or shortness of vowel sounds or syllables. **7** *Math.* a value, component, etc. that may be expressed in numbers.

quantum /ˈkwɒntəm/ (*pl.* **quanta** /-tə/) ● *n.* **1** *Physics* **a** a discrete quantity of energy proportional in magnitude to the frequency of radiation it represents. **b** an analogous discrete amount of any other physical quantity. **2 a** a required or allowed amount. **b** a share or portion. ● *attrib.adj.* dramatic or significant (*a quantum advance*).

quantum leap *n.* (also **quantum jump**) **1** a sudden large increase or advance. **2** an abrupt transition in an atom or molecule from one quantum state to another.

quantum mechanics *n.pl.* a mathematical form of quantum theory dealing with the motion and interaction of esp. subatomic particles and incorporating the concept that these particles can also be regarded as waves. □ **quantum-mechanical** *adj.*

quantum theory *n.* *Physics* a theory of matter and energy based on the concept of quanta.

quarantine /ˈkwɒrənˌtiːn, ˌkwɒrənˈtiːn/ ● *n.* **1** isolation imposed on persons or animals that have arrived from elsewhere or been exposed to, and might spread, infectious or contagious disease. **2** the period of this isolation. **3** any comparable period, instance, or state of isolation, esp. a boycott or severance of diplomatic relations intended to isolate a nation. ● *v.tr.* impose such isolation on; put in quarantine.

quark[1] /kwɔːk, kwɑːk/ *n.* *Physics* any of a class of unobserved subatomic particles with a fractional electric charge, of which protons, neutrons, etc. are thought to be composed.

quark[2] *n.* a type of spreadable low-fat curd cheese.

quarrel ● *n.* **1** an angry argument or disagreement between individuals or with others. **2** an occasion of complaint against a person or thing. ● *v.intr.* (**quarrelled, quarrelling**) **1** have a dispute. **2** (often foll. by *with*) take exception; find fault. □ **quarreller** *n.*

quarrelsome *adj.* given to or characterized by quarrelling.

quarry[1] ● *n.* (*pl.* **-ies**) **1** an open-air excavation from which stone for building etc. is or has been obtained by cutting, blasting, etc. **2** any place from which stone etc. may be extracted. **3** a supply or source of something (*a quarry of information*). ● *v.tr.* (**-ies, -ied**) **1** extract (stone) from a quarry. **2** obtain or extract something by laborious methods. □ **quarrier** *n.*

quarry[2] *n.* (*pl.* **-ies**) **1** the object of pursuit by hounds, hunters, etc. **2** any object of chase, aim, or attack.

quarry[3] *n.* (*pl.* **-ies**) **1** a diamond-shaped pane of glass as used in lattice windows. **2** (in full **quarry tile**) an unglazed floor tile.

quart *n.* **1 a** a measure of capacity for liquids etc., equal to a quarter of an Imperial gallon (1.135 litres or 40 fl. oz.). **b** a measure of capacity for liquids etc., equal to a quarter of a US gallon (0.946 litre or 32 fl. oz.). **2** *N Amer.* a unit of dry measure, equal to one-thirty-second of a bushel (1.1 litres). **3** a container holding a quart.

quarter ● *n.* **1 a** each of four equal parts into which a thing is or might be divided. **b** one-fourth part of something. **2 a** 25 Canadian or US cents. **b** a coin of this denomination. **3** fifteen minutes before or after any hour. **4** a period of three months, esp. for accounting purposes. **5** each of four equal periods into which a game is divided in football, basketball, etc. **6** (in *pl.*) **a** lodgings. **b** the living accommodation of members of the armed forces. **7** a part of a city or town, esp. as occupied by a particular class or group (*residential quarter*). **8** the direction, district, or source of supply etc. (*help from any quarter*). **9** a point of the compass. **10 a** one fourth of a lunar month. **b** the moon's position between the first and second (**first quarter**) or third and fourth (**last quarter**) of these. **11** pity or mercy shown towards an enemy or an opponent who is in one's power (*his business rivals knew they could expect no quarter*). **12 a** each of the four parts into which an animal's or bird's carcass is divided, each including a leg or wing. **b** (in *pl.*) = HINDQUARTERS. **13** (in *pl.*) *hist.* the four parts into which a traitor etc. was cut after execution. **14** = QUARTER SECTION. **15** *Music* = QUARTER NOTE. **16** each of four divisions on a shield. ● *v.* **1** *tr.* divide into quarters. **2** *tr. hist.* divide (the body of an executed person) in this way. **3 a** *tr.* provide with lodging. **b** *intr.* (of a person) stay or lodge. **4** *tr. & intr.* (esp. of a dog) range or traverse (the ground) in every direction. ● *attrib. adj.* forming an amount equal to or roughly equal to a quarter.

quarterback ● *n.* **1** the player who directs the offence of a football team. Abbr.: **QB. 2** this position on a football team. ● *v.* **1** *intr.* play a game as a quarterback. **2** *tr.* lead (a team) in the role of quarterback. **3** *tr. N Amer.* lead, oversee.

quarterdeck *n.* part of a ship's upper deck near the stern, historically reserved for officers of the ship.

quarter-final *n.* a game or round of competition preceding the semifinal.

quarter horse *n. N Amer.* a small stocky breed of horse noted for agility and speed over short distances, often used to herd livestock.

quarter-hour *n.* **1** (also **quarter of an hour**) a period of 15 minutes. **2** = QUARTER *n.* 3.

quartering *n.* **1** a provision of lodging. **2** the act or an instance of dividing, esp. into four equal parts.

quarterly ● *adj.* produced or occurring once every quarter of a year (*a quarterly report*). ● *adv.* once every quarter of a year (*dividends are calculated quarterly*). ● *n.* (*pl.* **-ies**) a quarterly review or magazine.

quartermaster *n.* **1** a regimental officer in charge of quartering, rations, etc. **2** a naval petty officer in charge of steering, signals, etc.

quarter note *n. N Amer. Music* a note having the time value of a quarter of a whole note, drawn as a large dot with a stem.

quarter rest *n. N Amer. Music* a rest having the time value of a quarter note.

quarter section *n. N Amer.* (*West*) a quarter of a square mile of esp. agricultural land, 160 acres.

quartet *n.* **1** *Music* **a** a composition for four voices etc. **b** the performers of such a piece. **2** any group of four.

quartier /kart'jei/ *n.* in French-speaking regions, a district or area, esp. of a city.

quarto *n.* (*pl.* **-os**) *Printing* **1** the size given by folding a sheet of paper twice, yielding 4 leaves or 8 pages. **2** a book of sheets folded in this way. Abbr.: **4to.**

quartz *n.* a mineral consisting of silica, crystallizing in colourless or white hexagonal prisms, often coloured by impurities (as amethyst etc.), and found widely in igneous and metamorphic rocks.

quartz clock *n.* a clock operated by vibrations of an electrically driven quartz crystal.

quartzite *n.* a hard, metamorphic rock consisting mainly of granular quartz.

quartz lamp *n.* a quartz tube containing mercury vapour and used as a source of light for automotive headlights etc.

quasar /'kweizar, -sar/ *n. Astronomy* any of a class of starlike celestial objects, apparently of great size and

remoteness, often associated with a spectrum with a large red shift and intense radio emission.

quash /kwɒʃ/ *v.tr.* **1** suppress; crush (speculation, a plan, an uprising etc.). **2** reject something and declare it no longer valid, esp. by a legal procedure.

quasi /'kwɒzi/ *attrib.adj.* **1** resembling (*a quasi marriage*). **2** being nearly or in part (*a quasi democracy*).

quasi- /'kwɒzi/ *comb. form* **1** seemingly; apparently but not really (*quasi-scientific*). **2** being partly or almost (*quasi-independent*).

quaternary /'kwɒtɜr,neri, kwə'tɜrnɜri/ ● *adj.* **1 a** having four parts. **b** fourth in a series. **2** (**Quaternary**) *Geol.* of or relating to the most recent period in the Cenozoic era, comprising the Pleistocene and Holocene epochs and beginning about 2 million years ago. **3** (of an ammonium compound) containing a nitrogen atom bonded to four organic groups or atoms. ● *n.* (*pl.* **-ies**) **1** a set of four things. **2** (**Quaternary**) *Geol.* the Quaternary period.

quatrain /'kwɒtrein/ *n.* a stanza of four lines, usu. with alternate rhymes.

quaver /'kweivɜr/ ● *v.* **1** *intr.* **a** (esp. of a voice or sound) vibrate, shake, tremble. **b** use trills or shakes in singing. **2** *tr.* say or sing with a shaky or trembling voice. ● *n.* **1** a tremble in speech. **2** a trill in singing.

quavery *adj.* (of a voice etc.) tremulous.

quay /ki:/ *n.* a solid stationary artificial landing place lying alongside or projecting into water for loading and unloading boats, ships, etc.

quayside ● *n.* the land forming or near a quay. ● *adj.* at or by a quay.

Que. *abbr.* Quebec.

queasy *adj.* (**-ier, -iest**) **1** feeling or tending to feel sick or nauseous. **2** slightly nervous or worried about something; uneasy. **3** feeling disgust or revulsion (*his pretentiousness made me queasy*). **4** causing nausea, anxiety, or disgust. □ **queasily** *adv.* **queasiness** *n.*

Quebecer /kwə'bekɜr, kə-, kei-/ (also **Quebecker**) a native or inhabitant of Quebec.

Quebec heater /kwə'bek, kə-, kei-/ *n. Cdn* a tall, cylindrical stove using coal or wood for fuel, used esp. for heating or cooking.

Québécois /keibek'wɒ/ (also **Quebecois, Québécois**) *Cdn* ● *n.* a francophone native or inhabitant of Quebec. ● *adj.* of or relating to Quebec or the Québécois.

Québécoise /keibek'wɒz/ (also **Quebecoise, Québécoise**) *Cdn* ● *n.* a francophone woman who is a native or inhabitant of Quebec. ● *adj.* being a Québécoise.

Quechua /'ketʃwə/ ● *n.* (*pl.* same or **-s**) **1** a member of a S American Indian people of Peru and neighbouring countries. **2** the language of this people. ● *adj.* of or relating to this people or their language.

queen ● *n.* **1** (as a title usu. **Queen**) a female sovereign etc., esp. the hereditary ruler of an independent nation. **2** (in full **queen consort**) a king's wife. **3 a** a woman or thing pre-eminent or supreme in a specified area or of its kind (*tennis queen*). **b** a belle or mock sovereign on some occasion (*queen of the fair*). **4** the fertile female among ants, bees, etc. **5 a** the most powerful piece in chess. **b** (**queen's**) designating a chess piece or pieces starting on the queen's side of the board (*queen's knight*). **6** in a deck of playing cards, any of the four cards bearing a picture of a queen. **7** *slang derogatory* **a** a male homosexual, esp. an effeminate one. **b** = DRAG QUEEN. **8** (**the Queen**) (in Canada and the UK) the anthem 'God Save the Queen'. ● *v.tr.* make (a woman) queen. ● *adj.* denoting a queen-size bed, mattress, sheets, etc. □ **queen it** behave in an unpleasant and superior way. □ **queendom** n.

Queen Anne adj. **1** (of furniture) typical of the early 18th c., esp. characterized by the use of walnut, cabriole legs, curving lines, and upholstery. **2** (of architecture) typical of English architecture of the early 18th c., esp. characterized by quaintness and old-fashionedness achieved by blending diverse elements of earlier periods.

Queen Anne's lace n. any of several umbelliferous plants bearing lacy clusters of small white flowers, esp. (N. Amer.) wild carrot, Daucus carota.

queen bee n. **1** (of bees) the fertile female in a hive. **2 a** a woman who holds a superior position in an organization etc. **b** a woman who behaves in a superior or controlling manner.

queenly adj. (**-ier, -iest**) **1** fit for or appropriate to a queen. **2** majestic. □ **queenliness** n.

queen mother n. (as a title usu. **Queen Mother**) the dowager who is mother of the sovereign.

Queen's Bench n. (in full **Court of Queen's Bench**) (in Alberta, Saskatchewan, Manitoba, and New Brunswick) the superior-court trial division, which has the jurisdiction to hear the most serious indictable offences and civil cases.

Queen's Birthday n. Cdn (in BC and Newfoundland and Labrador) a holiday falling on the Monday immediately preceding 25 May; Victoria Day.

Queen's Counsel n. Cdn, Brit., Austral., & NZ an appointment bestowed on a barrister by the Attorney General in recognition of excellence as an advocate and following advice from the barrister's peers.

Queen's English n. the English language as correctly written or spoken in Britain.

queen-size adj. (also **queen-sized**) **1** designating the second-largest standard size of mattress, usu. 153 by 208 cm (60 by 80 in.), or the bed frame, sheets, etc. designed for such a mattress. **2** of an extra-large size, esp. designating women's hosiery.

Queen's Park n. **1** the grounds and building in Toronto where the Ontario legislature is situated. **2** the government of Ontario.

Queen's Plate n. a stakes race for three-year-olds run annually at Woodbine Racetrack in Toronto.

Queen's Printer n. Cdn an official printer of bills and reports, office stationery, bulletins, etc. for the federal or provincial governments.

queer ● adj. **1** unnatural; odd; eccentric. **2** slang (esp. of a man) homosexual. **b** of or pertaining to a homosexual or homosexuals. ¶Although in recent years some homosexuals have reappropriated the word queer to refer to themselves, its use by others is still often offensive. **3** shady; suspect; of questionable character. **4** slightly ill; giddy; faint. ● n. slang a homosexual. ● v.tr. slang spoil; put out of order. □ **queerly** adv. **queerness** n.

queer bashing n. = GAY BASHING. □ **queer basher** n.

quell v.tr. **1 a** put an end to (something), esp. by force; suppress (quell an uprising). **b** cause to submit; suppress (quell the protesters). **2** allay or suppress (feelings, fear, anger, etc.) (quelled the doubts of supporters).

quench v.tr. **1** satisfy (thirst) by drinking. **2** extinguish (a fire or light etc.). **3** esp. Metallurgy cool (a hot substance) in cold water, air, oil, etc. **4** stifle or suppress (desire etc.). □ **quencher** n.

quenelle /kə'nɛl/ n. a small dumpling-like ball of minced or chopped seasoned fish or meat usu. cooked by poaching.

querulous /'kwɛrʊləs/ adj. of a whining, complaining, or peevish nature or disposition. □ **querulously** adj. **querulousness** n.

query /'kwiːri, 'kweri/ ● n. (pl. **-ies**) **1** a question or inquiry. **2** a question that expresses doubt or reservation (queries about the feasibility of the project). **3** Computing **a** the action of searching a string of characters in a computer database. **b** a string or set of characters searched. **4** a question mark, or the word query spoken or written to question accuracy or as a mark of interrogation. ● v.tr. (**-ies, -ied**) **1** express in the form of a question. **2** express doubt about something (queried the coach's abilities). **3** N Amer. ask a question of (queried him about his preference).

quesadilla /ˌkeisə'diːjə/ n. a dish of vegetables and grated cheese etc., stuffed between two tortillas, usu. baked or fried and served with salsa, sour cream, etc.

quest ● n. **1** a search or the act of seeking; an expedition. **2** the thing sought. **3** (often foll. by to + infin.) a goal sought; an attempt or endeavour (his quest to win twenty games). ● v.intr. (often foll. by for) go about in search of something; go on a quest. □ **in quest of** seeking. □ **quester** n.

question ● n. **1** a sentence worded or expressed so as to seek information. **2 a** doubt or uncertainty about something. **b** the raising of such doubt etc. (his suitability is open to question). **3** a matter or issue that needs to be settled (the question is how should I invest the money). **4** (foll. by of) a matter or concern depending on conditions (a question of whether I can afford it). **5** a matter to be discussed or decided or voted on (the airport question). ● v.tr. **1** ask questions of; interrogate. **2** express or feel doubt about something (her honesty has never been questioned). **3** challenge; argue against (questioned the judge's ruling). □ **be a question of time** be certain to happen sooner or later. **beyond all question** undoubtedly. **come into question** be discussed; become of practical importance. **in question** that is being discussed or referred to (the person in question). **call into question** cast doubt on, dispute. **is not the question** is irrelevant. **no question of** no possibility of (there's no question of my giving in). **no question that** no doubt that. **out of the question** too impracticable etc. to be worth discussing; impossible. **put the question** require supporters and opponents of a proposal to record their votes. **without question 1** undoubtedly. **2** without hesitation □ **questioner** n.

questionable adj. **1** doubtful as regards truth or quality (questionable measurements). **2** not clearly in accordance with honesty, honour, wisdom, etc. (questionable business practices). **3** of dubious value. □ **questionably** adv.

questioning ● n. **1** interrogation, esp. of a suspect by police officers. **2** the action of posing a question or calling into question. ● adj. expressing or suggesting a question or doubt (a questioning look). □ **questioningly** adv.

question mark n. **1** a punctuation mark (?) indicating a question. **2** a cause for doubt or uncertainty (public support remains a question mark). **3** doubt or uncertainty (a question mark looms over my plans).

questionnaire n. a formulated series of questions, esp. for statistical study or market research.

question period n. Cdn a period of time set aside each day during parliamentary proceedings in which members may question government ministers.

queue /kjuː/ ● n. **1** a line or sequence of persons, vehicles, etc., awaiting their turn to be attended to or to proceed. **2** Computing a list of data items, commands, etc., stored so as to be retrievable in a definite

order, usu. the order of insertion. ● v. (**queues,
queued, queuing** or **queueing**) **1** *intr.* (often foll. by
up) (of persons etc.) form a queue; take one's place in a
queue. **2** *tr.* esp. *Computing* arrange in a queue.

queue-jump *v.tr. & intr.* **1** pass (others) to the front of a
line without waiting for one's turn. **2** receive attention or consideration for something before others
that have waited longer. □ **queue jumper** *n.*

quibble ● *n.* a petty objection; a trivial or unimportant point of criticism, sometimes used to avoid a
more important issue. ● *v.intr.* argue about small
differences or disagreements. □ **quibbler** *n.*
quibbling *adj.*

quiche /kiːʃ/ *n.* a pastry shell containing eggs, milk,
cream, cheese, etc., with vegetables, meat, fish, etc.

quiche lorraine /kiːʃ ləˈreɪn/ *n.* a quiche with bacon
in the filling.

Quichua /ˈkɪtʃwə/ *n.* var. of QUECHUA.

quick ● *adj.* **1** capable of doing something in a short
time (*a quick runner*). **2 a** with a short interval, rapid
(*wrote four novels in quick succession*). **b** prompt or immediate (*Earl issued a quick reply*). **3** requiring only a short
time, brief (*a quick shower*). **4 a** lively, agile (*quick
hands*). **b** acute, alert, perceptive (*has a quick ear*). **5 a**
(foll. by *to* + infin.) responding immediately or hastily
(*she's quick to criticize*). **b** (of a temper) easily provoked.
6 *archaic* living, alive (*the quick and the dead*). ● *adv.* **1** at
a rapid rate; quickly. **2** (as *interj.*) come, go, etc., quickly
(*Quick! Get your shoes and let's go!*). ● *n.* **1** the soft flesh
below the nails, or the skin, or a sore. **2** the source of
feeling or emotion (*hurt him to the quick*). □ **be quick**
act quickly. **cut to the quick** deeply offend or upset
someone, hurt a person's feelings. □ **quickly** *adv.*
quickness *n.*

quick and dirty *adj.* done hastily; makeshift.

quick bread *n.* a baked good, usu. less sweet and
rich than a cake or cookie, leavened with baking
powder or baking soda, e.g. a muffin, scone, etc.

quicken *v.* **1** *tr. & intr.* make or become quicker;
accelerate. **2** *tr. & intr.* enliven, animate, rouse, or
become lively, animated, or roused (*his memory quick-
ened when he saw her*). **3** *intr.* (of a fetus) begin to show
signs of life.

quick-fire *adj.* **1** (of jokes, repartee, etc.) rapid or
occurring in rapid succession. **2** firing shots in quick
succession.

quick fix *n.* a rapid (esp. inadequate) solution to a
problem.

quickie *informal* ● *n.* **1** a thing done or made quickly or
hastily. **2** a brief act of sexual intercourse. **3** an
alcoholic drink taken quickly. ● *adj.* made or executed
quickly (*quickie divorce*).

quicklime *n.* = LIME¹ *n.* 1.

quick one *n. informal* a drink taken quickly.

quicksand *n.* **1 a** loose wet sand, easily yielding to
pressure, that sucks in anything placed or falling in
it. **b** a bed of this. **2** a treacherous thing or situation.

quicksilver ● *n.* mercury. ● *adj.* in constant flux;
changeable, unpredictable (*a quicksilver temper*).

quickstep ● *n.* a fast foxtrot. ● *v.intr.* (**-stepped,
-stepping**) dance the quickstep.

quick study *n.* N Amer. a person who adapts easily to
new surroundings, a new job, etc.; a fast learner.

quick-witted *adj.* able to think quickly and issue an
immediate usu. clever reply; intelligent. □
quick-wittedness *n.*

quid¹ *n.* (*pl.* same) *Brit. slang* one pound sterling.

quid² *n.* a lump of tobacco for chewing.

quid pro quo *n.* **1** a thing given as compensation. **2**
return made (for a gift, favour, etc.).

quiescent /kwiˈesənt/ *adj.* **1** motionless, inert. **2**
temporarily inactive; dormant. □ **quiescence** *n.*

quiet ● *adj.* (**quieter, quietest**) **1** making little or no
sound. **2** smooth, still; not bumpy or rough (*a quiet
ride*; *quiet waters*). **3** free from disturbance or activity
(*the streets were quiet*). **4** informal; simple (*a quiet
wedding*). **5** of gentle or peaceful disposition; shy. **6**
not expressed loudly; restrained or concealed (*he kept
it quiet*; *quiet heroism*). **7** enjoyed in quiet (*a quiet bath*).
● *n.* **1** silence. **2** an undisturbed state; stillness,
tranquility. **3** a state of being free from urgent tasks
or agitation. ● *v.* **1** *tr.* soothe, make quiet. **2** *intr.* (often
foll. by *down*) become quiet or calm. □ **be quiet** (esp.
in *imper.*) cease talking etc. **keep quiet 1** refrain from
making a noise. **2** (often foll. by *about*) suppress or
refrain from disclosing information etc. **on the
quiet** unobtrusively; secretly. □ **quietly** *adv.*
quietness *n.*

quieten *v.tr. & intr.* esp. *Brit.* (often foll. by *down*) = QUIET *v.*

quietism *n.* **1** religious mysticism based on the rejection of outward forms of devotion in favour of passive
contemplation and extinction of the will. **2** any philosophy emphasizing human passivity and nonresistance. □ **quietist** *n. & adj.* **quietistic** *adj.*

Quiet Revolution *n.* Cdn in Quebec, the period
1960–66, characterized by province-wide social, economic, and educational reforms, as well as mounting
separatist sentiment.

quietude *n.* a state of quiet.

quill ● *n.* **1** (usu. in *pl.*) the spines of a porcupine. **2** (in
full **quill feather**) a large feather in a wing or tail. **3**
the hollow stem of this. **4** (in full **quill pen**) a pen
made of a quill. **5** a hollow rotating sleeve of metal
etc. ● *v.tr.* form into cylindrical quill-like folds.

quillwork *n.* art using porcupine quills to decorate
clothing, teepees, and utilitarian items, done by a
number of Aboriginal groups, esp. the Mi'kmaq.

quilt ● **1** a bed cover made of padding enclosed
between layers of cloth etc. and kept in place by cross
lines of stitching. **2** a collection of diverse elements
that together constitute a whole, resembling a patchwork quilt. ● *v.intr.* make a quilt. □ **quilter** *n.*

quilted *adj.* **1** covered or lined with padded material
held together with lines of stitching (*quilted diapers*).
2 (of padding and cloth) stitched or sewn together in
the manner of a quilt.

quilting *n.* **1** the practice of making quilts. **2 a** the
materials, such as cloth, padding, etc., used in the
production of quilts. **b** these materials having been
quilted.

quinazoline /kwəˈnæzəliːn/ *n.* a yellow basic crystalline solid which has a structure of fused benzene and
pyrimidine rings; any substituted derivative of this.

quince *n.* **1** a hard acid pear-shaped fruit used as a
preserve or flavouring. **2** any shrub or small tree of
the genus *Cydonia*, esp. *C. oblonga*, bearing this fruit.

quinella /kwɪˈnelə/ *n.* a form of betting in which the
better must select the first two place-winners in a
race, not necessarily in the correct order.

quinine /ˈkwɪnaɪn, ˈkwaɪ-, ˈkwɪniːn/ *n.* **1** an alkaloid
found esp. in cinchona bark. **2** a bitter drug containing this, used as a specific remedy for malaria and as
an additive to tonic water.

quinoa /ˈkiːnwə/ *n.* **1** any of several annual goose-
foots grown by the Indians of the Andes for their
edible starchy seeds. **2** these seeds used as food.

quinsy /ˈkwɪnzi/ *n.* an inflammation of the throat,
esp. an abscess in the region around the tonsils.

quint *n. N Amer. informal* a quintuplet.

quintal /'kwɪntəl/ *n.* **1** a hundredweight (112 lb.), used e.g. as a measure for dried salt cod. **2** a weight of about 100 lb. **3** a weight of 100 kg.

quintessence /kwɪn'tesəns/ *n.* **1** the most essential part of any substance; a refined extract. **2** (usu. foll. by *of*) the purest and most perfect, or most typical, form, manifestation, or embodiment of some quality or class. □ **quintessential** /ˌkwɪntɪ'senʃəl/ *adj.* **quintessentially** *adv.*

quintet *n.* **1** *Music* **a** a composition for five voices etc. **b** a group of five musicians. **2** any group of five.

quintuple ● *adj.* **1** fivefold; consisting of five parts. **2** involving five parties. **3** (of time in music) having five beats in a bar. ● *n.* a fivefold number or amount. ● *v.tr. & intr.* multiply by five; increase fivefold.

quintuplet *n.* **1** each of five children born at one birth. **2** a set of five things working together. **3** *Music* a group of five notes to be performed in the time of three or four.

quinzhee /'kwɪnzi/ *n.* (also **quinzie**) *N Amer.* a shelter created by piling up snow, letting it settle, and then hollowing out the interior.

quip ● *n.* a clever saying; an epigram; a sarcastic remark etc. ● *v.* (**quipped, quipping**) **1** *intr.* make quips. **2** *tr.* say (something) as a quip.

quire /'kwair/ *n.* **1** four sheets of paper etc. folded to form eight leaves, as often in medieval manuscripts. **2** any collection of leaves one within another in a manuscript or book. **3** 25 (also 24) sheets of paper.

quirk *n.* **1** a peculiarity of behaviour or character; an eccentricity. **2** a trick of fate; a freak. □ **quirkish** *adj.* **quirky** *adj.* (**-ier, -iest**). **quirkily** *adv.* **quirkiness** *n.*

quisling /'kwɪzlɪŋ/ *n.* **1** a person co-operating with an occupying enemy; a collaborator. **2** a traitor.

quit ● *v.* (**quitting**; *past* and *past part.* **quit**) **1** *tr. & intr.* give up; abandon (a task etc.). **2** *tr. N Amer.* cease; stop (*quit grumbling*; *trying to quit smoking*). **3** *tr. & intr.* give up (one's employment); resign. **4** *tr.* (*past* and *past part.* **quit** or **quitted**) leave or depart from (a place, person, etc.). ● *predic.adj.* (foll. by *of*) rid (*glad to be quit of her*).

quite *adv.* **1** completely; entirely; wholly; to the utmost extent; in the fullest sense. **2** somewhat; rather; to some extent. **3** (often foll. by *so*) said to indicate agreement. □ **quite a** a remarkable or outstanding (person or thing) (*it was quite an event*). **quite another** (or **other**) very different (*that's quite another matter*). **quite a few** *informal* a fairly large number of. **quite some 1** a large amount of (*quite some time ago*). **2** *informal* = QUITE A (*that was quite some movie*). **quite something** a remarkable thing.

quits *predic.adj.* on even terms by retaliation or repayment (*then we'll be quits*). □ **call it quits 1** acknowledge that things are now even; agree not to proceed further in a quarrel etc. **2** cease an activity; stop working etc.

quitter *n.* a person who gives up easily.

quitting time *n.* esp. *N Amer.* the time at which work is ended for the day.

quiver[1] ● *v.intr.* tremble slightly. ● *n.* a quivering motion or sound. □ **quiveringly** *adv.* **quivery** *adj.*

quiver[2] *n.* a case for holding arrows.

qui vive /ki: 'vi:v/ *n.* □ **on the qui vive** on the alert; watching for something to happen.

quixotic /kwɪk'sɒtɪk/ *adj.* **1** extravagantly and romantically chivalrous; regardless of material interests in comparison with honour or devotion. **2** visionary; pursuing lofty but unattainable ideals. □ **quixotically** *adv.* **quixotism** /'kwɪksə,tɪzəm/ *n.*

quiz ● *n.* (*pl.* **quizzes**) **1** esp. *N Amer.* a short test or

examination. **2** a test of knowledge, esp. between individuals or teams as a form of entertainment. ● *v.tr.* (**quizzed, quizzing**) **1** esp. *N Amer.* test or examine (students). **2** examine by questioning.

quizzical *adj.* **1** expressing or done with mild or amused perplexity. **2** strange; comical. □ **quizzically** *adv.*

qulliq /'kʌlɪk/ *n. Cdn* (*North*) = KUDLIK.

quoin /kɔɪn/ *n.* **1** an external angle of a building. **2** a stone or brick forming an angle; a cornerstone.

quoit /kɔɪt/ *n.* **1** (in *pl.*) a game consisting of aiming and throwing flat rings of rope or metal to encircle or land as near as possible to a peg. **2** such a ring.

Quonset /'kwɒnsət/ *n. N Amer. proprietary* (in full **Quonset hut**) a prefabricated metal building with a semicylindrical corrugated roof.

quorum /'kwɔrəm/ *n.* the fixed minimum number of members that must be present to make the proceedings of an assembly, society, or meeting valid.

quota *n.* **1** the share that an individual person or company is obliged to contribute to or entitled to take from a total. **2 a** a quantity of goods etc. which under official controls a producer is obliged or entitled to produce, export, import, etc. **b** *Cdn* authorization to produce a specified quantity of an agricultural product granted by a marketing board to a farmer. **3** the number of immigrants allowed to enter a country, students allowed to enrol for a course, etc. **4** a portion of something that one can normally expect to receive or give (*got my quota of sleep*).

quotable *adj.* worth, or suitable for, quoting. □ **quotability** *n.*

quotation *n.* **1** the act or an instance of quoting or being quoted. **2** a passage or remark quoted. **3** *Music* a short passage or tune taken from one piece of music to another. **4** *Stock Exch.* an amount stated as the current price of stocks or commodities. **5** an estimate of the cost of something.

quotation mark *n.* each of a set of punctuation marks, single (' ') or double (" "), used to mark the beginning and end of a quoted passage, a title, etc., or words regarded as slang, jargon, or unfamiliar.

quote ● *v.* **1** *tr.* cite or appeal to (an author, book, etc.) in confirmation of some view. **2** *tr.* repeat a statement by (another person) or copy out a passage from (*don't quote me*). **3** *tr. & intr.* **a** repeat or copy out (a passage) usu. with an indication that it is borrowed. **b** (foll. by *from*) cite (an author, book, etc.). **4** *tr.* (foll. by *as*) cite (an author etc.) as proof, evidence, etc. **5** *tr.* enclose (words) in quotation marks. **6** *tr.* **a** state (the price) of a job to a person (*they quoted $900 for the work*). **b** (often foll. by *at*) state the price of (a commodity, stock, etc.) (*gold was quoted at $700*). **c** (often foll. by *at*) name (a racehorse etc.) at specified odds (*quoted at 200 to 1*). **7** *tr. Stock Exch.* regularly list the price of. ● *n. informal* **1** a passage or statement quoted. **2** a price quoted. **3** (usu. in *pl.*) quotation marks. ● *adv.* (in speech, reading aloud, etc.) indicating the presence of opening quotation marks (*he said, quote, 'We shall never surrender'*).

quotidian /kwo:'tɪdiən/ *adj.* **1** daily, of every day. **2** commonplace, trivial.

quotient *n.* **1** a result obtained by dividing one quantity by another. **2** the degree or presence of a usu. specified characteristic in a thing or person.

Quran (also **Qur'an**) *var. of* KORAN.

q.v. *abbr. quod vide*, 'which see' (in cross-references).

QWERTY /'kwɜrti/ *attrib.adj.* (also **qwerty**) denoting the standard keyboard on English-language typewriters, word processors, etc.

Rr

R¹ *n.* (also **r**) (*pl.* **Rs** or **R's**) the eighteenth letter of the alphabet. □ **the three Rs** reading, writing, and arithmetic, as the fundamentals of learning.

R² *abbr.* (also **R.**) **1** *N Amer.* (of films) restricted. **2** *Regina* (*Elizabeth R*). **3** *Rex.* **4** River. **5** (also ®) registered as a trademark. **6** (in names of societies etc.) Royal. **7** *N Amer.* R-value (*R2000*). **8** Railway. **9** Regiment. **10** radius. **11** (in a liturgy) response.

R³ *symbol* **1** roentgen. **2** electrical resistance. **3** (in chemical formulas) an organic radical or group.

r. *abbr.* (also **r**) **1** right. **2** run(s). **3** radius.

Ra *symbol* radium.

rabbet /ˈræbɪt/ ● *n.* a step-shaped channel etc. cut along the edge or face or projecting angle of a length of wood etc., usu. to receive the edge or tongue of another piece. ● *v.tr.* (**rabbeted, rabbeting**) **1** join or fix with a rabbet. **2** make a rabbet in.

rabbi *n.* (*pl.* **-s**) **1** a Jewish scholar or teacher, esp. of the law. **2** a person appointed as a Jewish religious leader.

rabbinate /ˈræbɪnət/ *n.* **1** the position or office of a rabbi. **2** rabbis collectively.

rabbinical /rəˈbɪnɪkəl/ *adj.* (also **rabbinic**) of or relating to rabbis, or to Jewish law or teaching.

rabbit ● *n.* **1** any of various burrowing gregarious plant-eating mammals of the hare family, with long ears and a short tail, varying in colour from brown in the wild to black and white, and kept as a pet or for meat. **2** *N Amer.* a hare. **3** the fur of the rabbit. ● *v.intr.* (**rabbited, rabbiting**) hunt rabbits. □ **rabbity** *adj.*

rabbit ears *n.pl. N Amer.* an indoor television antenna consisting of a pair of telescoping aerials.

rabbit punch *n.* a short chop with the edge of the hand to the nape of the neck.

rabbit warren *n.* **1** an area in which rabbits have their burrows, or are kept for meat etc. **2** a building or part of a city with many narrow passages or streets.

rabble *n.* **1** a large disorderly group of people; a mob. **2** (prec. by *the*) the lower classes.

rabble-rouser *n.* a person who stirs up a crowd of people, esp. in agitation for social or political change. □ **rabble-rousing** *adj. & n.*

rabid *adj.* **1** (of a person, feelings, opinions, etc.) unreasoning; fanatical (*a rabid anarchist*). **2** of, relating to, or affected with rabies. □ **rabidly** *adv.*

rabies *n.* a contagious and fatal viral disease of dogs, cats, and other animals, transmissible through saliva to humans and causing madness and convulsions.

raccoon *n.* **1** any greyish-brown furry N American nocturnal flesh-eating mammal of the genus *Procyon*, with a ringed bushy tail and black masklike markings the eyes. **2** the fur of the raccoon.

race¹ ● *n.* **1** a contest of speed between athletes, horses, vehicles, etc. **2** (in *pl.*) a series of these for horses, dogs, etc. at a fixed time on a regular course. **3** any contest or competition (*leadership race*; *arms race*). **4** a determined or urgent effort, esp. one involving a number of people etc. (*the race to find a cure*). **5 a** a strong or rapid current flowing through a narrow channel in the sea or a river (*a tide race*). **b** the channel

of a stream etc., esp. one built to lead water to or from a mill, mine, etc. **6** each of two grooved rings in a ball bearing. ● *v.* **1** *intr.* take part in a race. **2** *tr.* have a race with. **3** *tr.* try to surpass in speed. **4** *intr.* (foll. by *with*) compete in speed with. **5** *tr.* cause (a horse, car, etc.) to race. **6** *intr.* go at full speed (*raced down the highway*). **7** *intr.* (esp. of the heart) beat very quickly. **8 a** *intr.* (of an engine, wheel, etc.) run or revolve very swiftly, without resistance, or uncontrollably. **b** *tr.* cause (an engine, wheel, etc.) to do this. **9** *tr.* move (a person or thing) very quickly (*the victim was raced to hospital*). **10** *intr.* (usu. as **racing** *adj.*) follow or take part in horse racing (*a racing man*).

race² *n.* **1** each of the major divisions of humankind, having distinct physical characteristics. **2** a tribe, nation, etc., regarded as of a distinct ethnic stock. **3** the fact or concept of division into races (*discrimination based on race*). **4** a genus, species, breed, or variety of animals, plants, or micro-organisms. **5** a group of persons, animals, or plants connected by common descent. **6** descent; kindred (*of noble race*). **7** a group of persons etc. with some common feature (*the race of poets*).

race car *n.* a car built for racing on a prepared track.

race-car driver *n.* (also **race driver**) a driver of race cars.

racecourse *n.* = RACETRACK.

racehorse *n.* a horse bred or kept for racing.

raceme /rəˈsiːm/ *n.* a flower cluster with the separate flowers attached by short equal stalks at equal distances along a central stem.

racer *n.* **1** a person or thing that races. **2** a horse, yacht, bicycle, etc., of a kind used for racing.

race relations *n.pl.* relations between members of different races within a particular area.

race riot *n.* an outbreak of violence due to racial antagonism.

racetrack *n.* **1** a ground or track for horse racing. **2** a track or course used for any race.

race walking *n.* an act or the practice or sport of walking as a contest of speed, requiring a continuous progress of steps in which one of the feet is always in contact with the ground. □ **race walker** *n.*

raceway *n.* **1** esp. *N Amer.* a racetrack, esp. one used for harness racing. **2** a track or channel along which something runs, esp.: **a** a channel for water. **b** a groove in which ball bearings run. **c** a pipe or tubing enclosing electrical wires.

racial *adj.* **1** of or concerning race (*racial diversity*). **2** on the grounds of or connected with difference in race (*racial discrimination*). **3** of or relating to racism; racist (*a racial incident*). □ **racially** *adv.*

racialism *n.* = RACISM 1. □ **racialist** *n. & adj.*

racing car *n.* = RACE CAR.

racing driver *n.* = RACE-CAR DRIVER.

racing stripe *n.* a thin horizontal stripe of paint along the body of a car.

racism *n.* **1** a belief in the superiority of a particular race. **2** prejudice based on this. **3** antagonism towards other races, esp. as a result of this prejudice.

4 the theory that human abilities etc. are determined by race. □ **racist** n. & adj.

rack¹ ● n. **1** a framework usu. with rails, bars, hooks, etc., for holding or storing things (*roof rack*; *coat rack*). **2** a cogged or toothed bar or rail engaging with a wheel or pinion etc., or using pegs to adjust the position of something. **3** *hist.* an instrument of torture stretching the victim's joints by the turning of rollers to which the wrists and ankles were tied. **4** *N Amer.* **a** a triangular frame in which the balls are arranged before the opening shot of a game of pool etc. **b** the balls positioned in this way. **5** *N Amer.* a set of antlers. **6** a frame for holding animal fodder. ● *v.tr.* **1** (of disease or pain) inflict suffering on. **2** *hist.* torture (a person) on the rack. **3** *N Amer.* = RACK UP 1. **4** place in or on a rack. **5** shake violently. **6** injure by straining. **7** oppress (tenants) by exacting excessive rent. □ **off the rack** *N Amer.* (of an article of clothing) available for immediate purchase; ready-made (*buys all his suits off the rack*). **on the rack** in distress or under strain. **rack one's brains** make a great mental effort. **rack up** *N Amer.* **1** place (the balls for a game of pool etc.) in the rack. **2** accumulate (points etc.) (*racked up 50 goals last season*). **3** run up (a bill, debt, etc.).

rack² n. destruction (*rack and ruin*).

rack³ n. a roast of lamb cut from the loin.

rack⁴ *v.tr.* (often foll. by *off*) draw off (wine, beer, etc.) from the lees.

rack⁵ ● n. driving clouds. ● *v.intr.* (of clouds) be driven before the wind.

rack-and-pinion *attrib.adj.* (esp. of a steering system) using a rack and pinion (see RACK¹ n. 2, PINION²).

racket¹ *var. of* RACQUET.

racket² ● n. **1** a loud unpleasant noise. **2** *informal* a scheme for obtaining money or attaining other ends by fraudulent and often violent means. **3** a form of organized crime. **4** *informal* an occupation or line of business (*starting up a new racket*). **5** social excitement; gaiety. ● *v.intr.* (**racketed, racketing**) (often foll. by *along, around*) make a racket, esp. by moving noisily. □ **rackety** *adj.*

racketball *var. of* RACQUETBALL.

racketeer n. a person who makes money through dishonest or illegal activities. □ **racketeering** n.

raconteur /ˌrækɒnˈtɜr/ n. a teller of anecdotes.

racoon *var. of* RACCOON.

racquet n. **1** a bat with a round or oval frame strung with catgut, nylon, etc., used in tennis, squash, etc. **2** (in *pl.*) a ball game for two or four persons played with racquets in a plain four-walled court. **3** a snowshoe resembling a racquet.

racquetball n. esp. *N Amer.* a game played with a small hard ball and a short-handled racquet in a four-walled handball court.

racy *adj.* (**-ier, -iest**) **1** lively and vigorous in style. **2** risqué, suggestive. **3** having characteristic qualities in a high degree (*a racy flavour*). □ **racily** *adv.* **raciness** n.

rad¹ n. (*pl.* same) radian.

rad² *slang* ● n. a political radical. ● *adj.* excellent.

rad³ n. *Physics* a unit of absorbed dose of ionizing radiation, corresponding to the absorption of 0.01 joule per kilogram of absorbing material.

rad⁴ n. *informal* radiator.

radar n. **1** a method for detecting the position and speed of aircraft, ships, or other objects, by sending out pulses of high-frequency electromagnetic waves. **2** the apparatus used for this.

radar trap n. = SPEED TRAP.

raddled *adj.* untidy, unkempt.

radial ● *adj.* **1** of, concerning, or in rays. **2 a** arranged like rays or radii; having the position or direction of a radius. **b** having spokes or radiating lines. **c** acting or moving along lines diverging from a centre. **3** *Anat.* relating to the radius (*radial artery*). **4** (of a vehicle tire) having the core fabric layers arranged radially at right angles to the circumference and the tread strengthened. ● n. **1** a radial tire. **2** *Anat.* the radial nerve or artery. □ **radially** *adv.*

radial arm saw n. (also **radial saw**) a type of circular saw mounted on an arm that can be adjusted to various angles.

radian /ˈreidiən/ n. *Math.* a unit of angle, equal to 57.296°.

radiant ● *adj.* **1** emitting rays of light. **2** (of a person, a look, etc.) beaming with joy or hope or love. **3** (of beauty) splendid or dazzling. **4** (of light) issuing in rays. **5** operating radially. **6** extending radially; radiating. ● n. the point or object from which light or heat radiates, esp. in an electric or gas heater. □ **radiance** n. **radiantly** *adv.*

radiant heat n. heat transmitted by radiation, not by conduction or convection. □ **radiant heater** n.

radiate ● *v.* **1** *intr.* **a** emit rays of light, heat, or other electromagnetic waves. **b** (of light or heat) be emitted in rays. **2** *tr.* emit (light, heat, or sound) from a centre. **3** *tr.* transmit or demonstrate (an emotion, feeling, etc.) (*radiates happiness*). **4** *intr.* & *tr.* diverge or cause to diverge or spread from a centre. ● *adj.* /ˈreidiət/ having divergent rays or parts radially arranged. □ **radiative** /-ətiv/ *adj.*

radiation n. **1** the act or an instance of radiating; the process of being radiated. **2 a** the emission of energy as electromagnetic waves or as moving particles. **b** the energy transmitted in this way, esp. invisibly.

radiation sickness n. sickness caused by exposure to radiation, such as X-rays or gamma rays.

radiation therapy n. = RADIOTHERAPY.

radiator /ˈreidiˌeitər, ˈræd-/ n. **1** a person or thing that radiates. **2 a** a device for heating a room etc., consisting of a metal case through which hot water or steam circulates. **b** a usu. portable, esp. electric heater resembling this. **3** a device in a motor vehicle or aircraft with a large surface for cooling circulating water from the engine.

radical ● *adj.* **1** of the root or roots; fundamental (*a radical error*). **2** far-reaching; thorough (*a radical change in policy*). **3 a** advocating thorough reform; holding extreme political views; revolutionary. **b** (of a measure etc.) advanced by or according to principles of this kind. **4** forming the basis; primary (*the radical idea*). **5** *Math.* of the root of a number or quantity. **6** *slang* excellent, outstanding. **7** (of surgery etc.) seeking to ensure the removal of all diseased tissue. **8** *Music* belonging to the root of a chord. **9** *Bot.* of, or springing direct from, the root. ● n. **1** a person holding radical views or belonging to a radical party. **2** *Chem.* **a** a free radical. **b** an element or atom or a group of these normally forming part of a compound and remaining unaltered during the compound's ordinary chemical changes. **3** the root of a word. **4** a fundamental principle; a basis. **5** *Math.* **a** a quantity forming or expressed as the root of another. **b** a radical sign. □ **radicalism** n. **radicalize** *v.tr.* & *intr.* **radicalization** n. **radically** *adv.*

radical sign n. a symbol, √, ∛, etc., indicating the square, cube, etc., root of the number following.

radicchio /rəˈdiːkiəʊ/ n. (*pl.* **-os**) a variety of chicory with dark red leaves, used esp. in salads.

radii pl. of RADIUS.

radio ● n. (pl. **-os**) **1** (often attrib.) **a** the transmission and reception of sound messages etc. by electromagnetic waves of radio frequency. **b** an apparatus for receiving, broadcasting, or transmitting radio signals. **c** a message sent or received by radio. **2** sound broadcasting in general (prefers radio to television). **3** a broadcasting station or network (CBC Radio). ● v. (**-oes**, **-oed**) **1** tr. **a** send (a message) by radio. **b** send a message to (a person) by radio. **2** intr. communicate or broadcast by radio. ● adj. **1** of, relating to, or transmitting radio signals (a radio station). **2** of or using radio frequencies. **3** (of a vehicle) equipped with a two-way radio for use in communication (radio car).

radio- comb. form **1** denoting radio or broadcasting. **2 a** connected with radioactivity. **b** denoting artificially prepared radioisotopes of elements (radiocesium). **3** connected with rays or radiation.

radioactive adj. of or exhibiting radioactivity. □ **radioactively** adv.

radioactivity n. **1** the spontaneous disintegration of atomic nuclei, with the emission of usu. penetrating radiation or particles. **2** radioactive substances, or the radiation they emit.

radio astronomy n. the branch of astronomy which uses radio frequencies rather than visible light to study the universe.

radio beacon n. = BEACON 3.

radiocarbon n. a radioactive isotope of carbon.

radiocarbon dating n. a method of estimating the age of organic archaeological specimens by determining the ratio of carbon-14 (which decays at a known rate) to another isotope which remains constant.

radio collar n. a collar equipped with a small radio transmitter, used e.g. for tracking an animal's movement in the wild. □ **radio-collar** v.tr.

radio-controlled adj. (of a model aircraft etc.) controlled from a distance by radio.

radio frequency n. (pl. **-ies**) the frequency band of telecommunication, ranging from 10^4-10^{11} or 10^{12} Hz.

radiogram n. **1** a picture obtained by X-rays, gamma rays, etc. **2** a radio-telegram.

radiograph ● n. = RADIOGRAM 1. ● v.tr. obtain a picture of by X-ray, gamma ray, etc. □ **radiographer** n. **radiographic** adj. **radiography** n.

radioisotope n. a radioactive isotope.

radiology n. the scientific study of X-rays and other high-energy radiation, esp. as used in medicine. □ **radiological** adj. **radiologist** n.

radiometer /ˌreidiˈɒmɪtər/ n. an instrument for measuring the intensity or force of radioactivity. □ **radiometric** adj. **radiometry** n.

radiometric dating n. a method of dating geological specimens by determining the relative proportions of the isotopes of a radioactive element present in a sample.

radionuclide /ˌreidioˈnuːklaɪd, -ˈnjuː-/ n. a radioactive nuclide.

radiopaque /ˌreidioˈpeɪk/ adj. (also **radio-opaque**) opaque to X-rays etc. □ **radiopacity** /-ˈpæsɪti/ n.

radio phone n. = RADIO TELEPHONE.

radio play n. **1** a play written for performance on radio. **2** broadcast time on radio.

radio-telegraphy n. telegraphy using radio transmission. □ **radio-telegram** n.

radio telephone n. a telephone that uses radio transmission.

radio telescope n. a directional aerial system for collecting and analyzing radiation in the radio frequency range from stars etc.

radiotherapy n. the treatment of cancer and other diseases by X-rays or other forms of radiation. □ **radiotherapeutic** adj. **radiotherapist** n.

radish n. **1** a cruciferous plant, Raphanus sativus, with a fleshy pungent root. **2** this root, eaten esp. raw.

radium n. a radioactive metallic element originally obtained from pitchblende etc., used esp. in luminous materials and in radiotherapy.

radium therapy n. the treatment of disease by the use of radium.

radius ● n. (pl. **radii** or **radiuses**) **1** Math. **a** a straight line from the centre to the circumference of a circle or sphere. **b** a radial line from the focus to any point of a curve. **c** the length of the radius of a circle etc. **2** a usu. specified distance from a centre in all directions (within a radius of 20 miles). **3 a** the thicker and shorter of the two bones in the human forearm (compare ULNA). **b** the corresponding bone in a vertebrate's foreleg or a bird's wing. **4** any of the five armlike structures of a starfish. **5 a** any of a set of lines diverging from a point like the radii of a circle. **b** an object of this kind, e.g. a spoke. **6 a** the outer rim of a composite flower head, e.g. a daisy. **b** a radiating branch of an umbel. ● v.tr. (as **radiused** adj.) give a rounded form to (an edge etc.).

RAdm abbr. Cdn REAR ADMIRAL.

radon /ˈreidɒn/ n. a naturally occurring gaseous inert radioactive element arising from the disintegration of radium, and used in radiotherapy.

RAF abbr. (in the UK) Royal Air Force.

raffia /ˈræfiə/ n. **1** a palm tree, Raphia ruffia, native to Madagascar, having very long leaves. **2** the fibre from its leaves used for making hats, baskets, etc.

raffish /ˈræfɪʃ/ adj. **1** disreputable, esp. in an attractive manner. **2** tawdry. □ **raffishness** n.

raffle ● n. a fundraising lottery with goods as prizes. ● v.tr. (often foll. by off) dispose of by means of a raffle.

raft[1] ● n. **1** a flat floating structure of logs, barrels, etc. tied together and used as a boat or a floating platform. **2** a lifeboat or small (often inflatable) boat, esp. for use in emergencies. **3** N Amer. Forestry a mass of squared timber or logs fastened together for transportation on water. **4** N Amer. a large floating accumulation of fallen trees, ice, etc. ● v. **1** tr. transport as or on a raft. **2** tr. N Amer. Forestry move (logs) by means of a raft. **3** tr. cross (water) on a raft. **4** tr. form into a raft. **5** intr. use a raft; travel by raft. **6** intr. engage in the sport of whitewater rafting. **7** intr. (of an ice floe) be driven on top of or underneath another floe. □ **rafting** n.

raft[2] n. (foll. by of) informal a large number or amount.

rafter[1] n. each of the usu. sloping beams forming the framework of a roof. □ **raftered** adj.

rafter[2] n. **1** a person who travels by raft, esp. to flee a country. **2** a person who engages in whitewater rafting. **3** N Amer. Forestry a person who rafts timber.

rag[1] n. **1 a** a torn, frayed, or worn piece of woven material. **b** one of the irregular scraps to which cloth etc. is reduced by wear and tear. **2 a** (in pl.) old or worn clothes. **b** informal a garment of any kind. **3** (collect.) scraps of cloth used as material for paper, stuffing, etc. **4** derogatory **a** a newspaper or magazine, esp. one regarded as inferior or worthless. **b** a flag, handkerchief, curtain, etc. **5** an odd scrap; an irregular piece. **6** a jagged projection, esp. on metal. □ **in rags 1** much torn. **2** in old torn clothes. **on the rag** N Amer. slang **1** menstruating. **2** angry or irritable.

rag[2] v.tr. (**ragged**, **ragging**) scold; reprove severely;

criticize. □ **rag on** *N Amer. slang* nag, bother, scold. **rag the puck 1** *Hockey* keep possession of the puck by skilful stickhandling so as to waste time. **2** *Cdn slang* waste time intentionally.

rag³ *n.* a ragtime composition or tune.

raga /'rɑːgə/ *n.* (in Indian music) **1** a pattern of notes used as a basis for improvisation. **2** a piece using a particular raga.

ragamuffin *n.* **1** a person in ragged dirty clothes, esp. a child. **2** = RAGGAMUFFIN.

ragbag *n.* **1** a bag in which scraps of fabric etc. are kept for use. **2** (often foll. by *of*) a miscellaneous collection. **3** *slang* a sloppily-dressed woman.

rag doll *n.* a stuffed doll made of cloth.

rage ● *n.* **1** fierce or violent anger. **2** a fit of this. **3** the violent action of a natural force (*the rage of the storm*). **4** (foll. by *for*) **a** a vehement desire or passion. **b** a widespread temporary enthusiasm or fashion. ● *v.intr.* **1** be full of anger. **2** (often foll. by *at*, *against*) speak furiously or madly; rave. **3** (of wind, battle, debate, fever, etc.) be violent; be at its height; continue unchecked. □ **all the rage** very popular, fashionable.

ragg ● *n.* **1** a strong wool fibre treated so as to retain its natural oils. **2** a greyish yarn made from a blend of ragg and nylon. ● *adj.* (of a garment, blanket, etc.) made from this yarn.

ragga *n.* a style of popular music combining elements of reggae and hip hop.

raggamuffin *n.* **1** an exponent or follower of ragga, typically dressing in ragged clothes. **2** = RAGGA.

ragged *adj.* **1** (of clothes etc.) torn; frayed. **2** rough; shaggy; hanging in tufts. **3** (of a person) in ragged clothes. **4** with a broken or jagged outline or surface. **5** *Printing* (esp. of a right margin) unjustified and so uneven. **6** faulty; imperfect. **7** lacking finish, smoothness, or uniformity (*ragged rhymes*). **8** (of a sound) harsh, discordant. **9** exhausted (*I've been run ragged*). □ **raggedly** *adv.* **raggedness** *n.* **raggedy** *adj.*

raggedy-jacket *n.* *Cdn* (*Nfld*) a young harp seal whose coat is changing from pure white to brown and white.

ragging *n.* **1** the process or technique of decorating a wall etc. by applying or smudging paint with a rag or piece of material. **2** the effect or finish so produced.

raggle-taggle *adj.* constituted of an assortment of (often disreputable) people; ragtag.

raging *adj.* extreme, very painful (*a raging headache*).

raglan /'ræglən/ ● *n.* an overcoat without shoulder seams, the sleeves running in a sloping line from the neck to under the arms. ● *adj.* cut in this design.

ragout /ræˈguː/ *n.* a stew.

rag rolling *n.* = RAGGING. □ **rag-rolled** *adj.*

rag rug *n.* a small rug made from strips of rags woven together.

rags-to-riches *attrib.adj.* denoting a person who starts out poor and ends up rich, or a story describing such a development.

ragtag ● *adj.* (also **ragtail**) esp. *N Amer.* **1** disorganized, ill-assorted, scraggly. **2** ragged or shabby; unkempt. ● *n.* *derogatory* the rabble or riff-raff.

ragtime ● *n.* a style of popular music characterized by a syncopated melodic line and regularly accented accompaniment, evolved by American black musicians in the 1890s and played esp. on the piano. ● *adj.* of or resembling ragtime.

ragtop *n.* **1** a convertible car with a top made of cloth. **2** the top of such a car.

ragweed *n.* **1** *N Amer.* any plant of the genus *Ambrosia*, with allergenic pollen. **2** = RAGWORT.

ragwort *n.* any yellow-flowered ragged-leaved plant of the genus *Senecio*.

rah *interj.* esp. *N Amer. informal* an expression of encouragement, approval, etc.

rah-rah *N Amer. slang* ● *n.* a shout of support and encouragement, as for a sports team. ● *adj.* marked by great enthusiasm or excitement.

raid ● *n.* **1** a rapid surprise attack, esp.: **a** by troops, aircraft, etc. in warfare. **b** to commit a crime or do harm. **c** *N Amer. informal* as a prank or to gain food, drink, etc. (*a raid on the kitchen*). **2** a surprise attack by police etc. to arrest suspected persons or seize illicit goods. **3** *Stock Exch.* an attempt to lower prices by the concerted selling of shares. **4** the luring away of a competitor's workers, members, etc. ● *v.tr.* **1** make a raid on (a person, place, or thing). **2** plunder, deplete. □ **raider** *n.*

rail¹ ● *n.* **1** a level or sloping bar or series of bars: **a** forming part of a fence or barrier as protection against contact, falling over, etc. **b** used to hang things on. **c** running along the top of a set of banisters; a handrail. **2** a steel bar or continuous line of bars laid on the ground, usu. as one of a pair forming a railway track. **3** (often *attrib.*) a railway (*send it by rail*; *rail fares*). **4** (in *pl.*) the inside boundary fence of a racetrack. ● *v.tr.* **1** furnish with a rail or rails. **2** (usu. foll. by *in*, *off*) enclose with rails (*a small space was railed off*). □ **off the rails** deranged.

rail² *v.intr.* (often foll. by *at*, *against*) complain vehemently; rant. □ **railer** *n.* **railing** *n. & adj.*

rail³ *n.* any bird of the family Rallidae, often inhabiting marshes, including coots and moorhens.

rail fence *n.* esp. *N Amer.* a fence made of wooden posts and rails.

railhead *n.* **1** the furthest point reached by a railway. **2** the point on a railway at which road transport of goods begins.

railing *n.* **1** esp. *N Amer.* a banister; handrail. **2 a** (often in *pl.*) a fence or barrier made of rails. **b** the material for these.

railroad ● *n.* esp. *N Amer.* = RAILWAY. ● *v.tr.* **1** (often foll. by *to*, *into*, *through*, etc.) rush or coerce (a person or thing) (*railroaded me into going*; *railroaded it through the legislature*). **2** send (a person) to prison by means of false evidence. □ **railroader** *n.*

railway *n.* esp. *Cdn & Brit.* **1** a track or set of tracks made of steel rails upon which trains run. **2** such a system operated by a single company. **3** the organization and personnel required for its working. **4** a similar set of tracks for other vehicles etc.

railway hotel *n.* a hotel built and operated by a railway company, usu. close to a railway station.

railwayman *n.* (*pl.* **-men**) esp. *Brit. & Cdn* a railway employee.

railway yard *n.* (also **rail yard**) the area where rolling stock is kept and made up into trains.

raiment /'reɪmənt/ *n.* *literary & archaic* clothing.

rain ● *n.* **1 a** the condensed moisture of the atmosphere falling visibly in separate drops. **b** the fall of such drops. **c** (*attrib.*) designating garments etc. protecting against or worn in the rain (*rain jacket*). **2** (in *pl.*) **a** (prec. by *the*) the rainy season in tropical countries. **b** rainfalls. **3 a** falling liquid or solid particles or objects. **b** the rainlike descent of these. **c** a large or overwhelming quantity (*a rain of congratulations*). ● *v.* **1** *v.intr.* (of rain) fall. **2 a** *intr.* fall like rain (*tears rained down their cheeks*). **b** *tr.* (prec. by *it* as subject) send in large quantities (*it is raining invitations*). **3** *tr.* send down like rain; lavishly bestow (*rained blows upon him*). **4** *intr.* (of the sky, clouds, etc.)

send down rain. □ **rain on someone's parade** *informal* spoil a person's good time. **rain out** (esp. in *passive*) cause (an event etc.) to be terminated or cancelled because of rain. **rain or shine** whether it rains or not. □ **rainless** *adj.*

rainbow ● *n.* **1** an arch of colours (conventionally red, orange, yellow, green, blue, indigo, violet) formed in the sky (or across a waterfall etc.) opposite the sun by reflection, twofold refraction, and dispersion of the sun's rays in falling rain or in spray or mist. **2** a similar effect formed by the moon's rays. **3** a wide variety of related things (*a rainbow of colours*). **4** = RAINBOW TROUT. ● *adj.* many-coloured. □ **chase a rainbow** pursue an illusory goal. □ **rainbowed** *adj.*

rainbow coalition *n.* a loose coalition or alliance of several different left-of-centre political groups, representing social, ethnic, and other minorities.

rainbow smelt *n.* a blue and silver smelt, *Osmerus mordax*, with iridescent colouring on its flanks, of inland lakes and eastern coastal waters of N America.

rainbow trout *n.* a large trout, *Oncorhynchus mykiss*, originally of the Pacific coast of N America, but now widespread throughout the continent.

rain check *n.* esp. *N Amer.* **1** a ticket given for later use when a sports or other outdoor event is interrupted or postponed by rain. **2** a promise that an offer will be maintained though deferred. **3** a voucher given to a customer when a sale item sells out, entitling the customer to purchase the item at the sale price when more stock arrives. □ **take a rain check on** reserve the right to take up (an offer) at a later date.

rain cloud *n.* a cloud bringing rain.

raincoat *n.* a waterproof or water-resistant coat.

rain date *n.* *N Amer.* an alternate date on which a sports event, garage sale, or other outdoor activity can be held if postponed because of rain.

raindrop *n.* a single drop of rain.

rainfall *n.* **1** a fall of rain. **2** the quantity of rain falling within a given area in a given time.

rain forest *n.* a luxuriant forest in an area of heavy rainfall with little seasonal variation.

rainmaker *n.* **1** a person who seeks to cause rain to fall, either by magic or by a technique such as seeding. **2** esp. *N Amer. slang* a person who is highly successful esp. in business. □ **rainmaking** *n.*

rainout *n.* **1** *N Amer.* the cancellation or premature ending of an event because of rain. **2** radioactive debris or other atmospheric pollution carried to the earth's surface by precipitation.

rainproof *adj.* (esp. of a building, garment, etc.) resistant to rainwater.

rain shadow *n.* an area on the leeward side of mountains or other high ground, having relatively little precipitation because clouds release their moisture on the windward side.

rainstorm *n.* a storm with heavy rain.

rainwater *n.* water obtained from collected rain, as distinct from a well etc.

rainwear *n.* clothes for wearing in the rain.

rainy *adj.* (**-ier**, **-iest**) **1** (of weather, a climate, day, region, etc.) in or on which rain is falling or much rain usually falls. **2** (of cloud, wind, etc.) laden with or bringing rain. □ **rainily** *adv.* **raininess** *n.*

rainy day *n.* a time of special need in the future.

raise ● *v.tr.* **1** put or take into a higher position. **2** (often foll. by *up*) cause to rise or stand up or be vertical; set upright. **3** increase the amount or value or strength of (*raised prices*). **4** (often foll. by *up*) construct or build up. **5** collect or bring together (*raise*

money; *raise an army*). **6** cause to be heard or considered (*raise an objection*). **7** set going or bring into being; arouse (*raise hopes*). **8 a** give a higher or nobler character to (a person, style, thoughts, etc.) **b** heighten (consciousness or sensitivity). **9 a** rouse from sleep or from a lair. **b** restore to life. **10** bring up; educate. **11** breed or grow (*raise vegetables*). **12** promote to a higher rank. **13** (foll. by *to*) *Math.* multiply (a quantity) to a specified power. **14** (often as **raised** *adj.*) leaven with yeast (*raised doughnuts*). **15** *Cards* **a** bet more than (another player). **b** increase (a stake). **16** abandon or force an enemy to abandon (a siege or blockade). **17** remove (a barrier or embargo). **18** cause (a ghost etc.) to appear. **19** establish contact with (a person etc.) by radio or telephone. **20** make a nap on (cloth). **21** *Curling* strike (a rock) with another rock to move it deeper on the sheet. ● *n.* **1** esp. *N Amer.* an increase in salary. **2** *Cards* an increase in a stake (*compare* sense 15 of *v.*). **3** the action of raising something, esp. a part of the body as a fitness exercise. **4** *Curling* the act or an instance of striking a rock with another rock to move it deeper on the sheet. □ **raise from the dead** restore to life. **raise one's glass to** drink the health of. **raise one's hand to** make as if to strike (a person). **raise one's hat** (often foll. by *to*) remove it momentarily as a gesture of courtesy or respect. **raise hell** (or **the devil**) *informal* make a disturbance. **raise a laugh** cause others to laugh. **raise a person's spirits** give him or her new courage or cheerfulness. **raise a stink** create a fuss or disturbance. **raise one's voice** speak, esp. louder. □ **raiser** *n.* (also in *comb.*).

raised bed *n.* a flower bed enclosed by walls so that the surface of the soil is above ground level.

raisin *n.* **1** a partially dried grape. **2** the dark purplish-brown colour of raisins. □ **raisiny** *adj.*

raison d'être /,reiz5 'detr/ *n.* (*pl.* **raisons d'être** *pronunc.* same) a purpose or reason that accounts for or justifies or originally caused a thing's existence.

raita /ræ'i:tə/ *n.* an Indian side dish of chopped cucumber (or other vegetables) and spices in yogourt.

Raj /rɒdʒ, rɒʒ, rædʒ/ *n.* (*prec.* by *the*) *hist.* the period of British rule in the Indian subcontinent before 1947.

raja /'rɒdʒə, 'rɒʒə, 'rædʒə/ *n.* (also **rajah**) *hist.* **1** an Indian king or prince. **2** a petty dignitary or noble in India. **3** a Malay or Javanese chief.

rake¹ ● *n.* **1 a** an implement consisting of a pole with a crossbar toothed like a comb at the end, or with several tines held together by a crosspiece, for drawing together fallen leaves etc. or smoothing loose soil or gravel. **b** a similar larger agricultural implement mounted on wheels. **2** a similar implement used for other purposes, e.g. by a croupier drawing in money at a gaming table. ● *v.* **1** *tr.* collect or gather or remove with or as with a rake. **2** *tr.* make tidy or smooth with a rake (*raked it level*). **3** *intr.* use a rake. **4** *tr. & intr.* search with or as with a rake; search thoroughly, ransack. **5** *tr.* **a** direct gunfire along (a line) from end to end. **b** sweep with the eyes. **6** *tr.* scratch or scrape. □ **rake in** *informal* amass (profits etc.). **rake up** (or **over**) revive the memory of (past quarrels etc.). □ **raker** *n.*

rake² *n.* a fashionable or stylish man of dissolute or promiscuous habits.

rake³ ● *v.* **1** *tr. & intr.* set or be set at a sloping angle. **2** *intr.* (of a mast or funnel) incline from the perpendicular towards the stern. ● *n.* **1** a raking position or build. **2** the amount by which a thing rakes. **3** the slope of the stage or the auditorium in a theatre. **4** the angle of the edge or face of a cutting tool. □ **raked** *adj.*

rakish[1] *adj.* of or like a rake (*see* RAKE[2]). □ **rakishly** *adv.* **rakishness** *n.*

rakish[2] *adj.* dashing; jaunty (*a hat at a rakish angle*).

raku /ˈrɑːkuː/ *n.* a kind of Japanese lead-glazed earthenware, primarily for use in the tea ceremony.

rallentando /ˌrælənˈtændo:/ *adv. & adj.* with a gradual decrease of speed.

rally[1] ● *v.* (**-ies, -ied**) **1** *tr. & intr.* (often foll. by *around, behind, to*) bring or come together as support or for concentrated action. **2** *tr. & intr.* bring or come together again after a rout or dispersion. **3 a** *tr.* revive (courage etc.) by an effort of will. **b** *tr.* rouse (a person or animal) to fresh energy. **c** *intr.* pull oneself together. **4** *intr.* (of a sports team, athlete, etc.) acquire or assume fresh vigour or energy, esp. by coming from behind to tie or win a game. **5** *intr.* recover after illness or prostration or fear; regain health or consciousness, revive. **6** *intr.* (of share prices etc.) increase after a fall. **7** *intr. Tennis etc.* engage in a rally. ● *n.* (*pl.* **-ies**) **1** an act of reassembling forces or renewing conflict. **2** a recovery of energy after or in the middle of exhaustion or illness. **3** a mass meeting of supporters or persons having a common interest (*protest rally*). **4** a rapid rise in share prices etc. after a fall. **5** *Baseball* the scoring of two or more runs in one inning. **6** *Tennis etc.* an extended exchange of strokes between players. **7** a competition for motor vehicles, usu. over public roads or rough terrain.

rally[2] *v.tr.* (**-ies, -ied**) subject to good-humoured ridicule.

rallying cry *n.* a slogan.

RAM *abbr. Computing* random access memory.

ram ● *n.* **1** an uncastrated male sheep. **2** *hist.* = BATTERING RAM. **3** the falling weight of a piledriver. ● *v.tr.* (**rammed, ramming**) **1** force or squeeze into place by pressure. **2** (usu. foll. by *down, in, into*) beat down or drive in by heavy blows. **3** (of a ship, vehicle, etc.) strike violently, crash against. **4** (foll. by *against, at, on, into*) dash or violently impel. **5** (foll. by *through*) push (a bill etc.) through a legislature. □ **ram home** stress forcefully (an argument, lesson, etc.). □ **rammer** *n.*

-rama *comb. form informal* or *jocular* forming nouns denoting abundance, a spectacle, extravaganza, etc., or the place containing it (*nostalgia-rama*).

Ramadan /ˈræməˌdæn/ *n.* the ninth month of the Muslim year, during which strict fasting is observed from sunrise to sunset.

ramble ● *v.intr.* **1** walk for pleasure, with or without a definite route. **2** (often foll. by *on*) wander in discourse; talk or write disconnectedly and usu. at length. **3** (esp. of buildings, paths, etc.) spread in various directions with no regular pattern. ● *n.* a walk taken for pleasure.

rambler *n.* **1** a person who rambles. **2** a straggling or climbing rose (*crimson rambler*).

rambling *adj.* **1** peripatetic, wandering. **2** disconnected, desultory, incoherent. **3** (of a house, street, etc.) irregularly arranged. **4** (of a plant) straggling, climbing. □ **ramblingly** *adv.*

Rambo *n.* (*pl.* **-os**) a man given to displays of physical violence or aggression; a macho man.

rambunctious *adj.* esp. *N Amer. informal* **1** active; full of energy (*rambunctious children*). **2** boisterous; unruly; difficult to control. □ **rambunctiously** *adv.* **rambunctiousness** *n.*

ramekin /ˈræmɪkɪn/ *n.* **1** a small, usu. round dish for baking and serving an individual portion of food. **2** food served in such a dish, esp. a small quantity of cheese baked with breadcrumbs, eggs, etc.

ramen /ˈrɒmən/ *n.pl.* quick-cooking noodles, usu. served in a broth with meat and vegetables.

ramification /ˌræməfɪˈkeɪʃən/ *n.* **1** the act or an instance of ramifying; the state of being ramified. **2** a subdivision of a complex structure or process comparable to a tree's branches. **3** a consequence, esp. when complex or unwelcome.

ramify /ˈræməˌfaɪ/ *v.* (**-ies, -ied**) **1** *intr.* form branches or subdivisions or offshoots, branch out. **2** *tr.* (usu. in *passive*) cause to branch out; arrange in a branching manner.

ramp ● *n.* **1** a slope or inclined plane, esp. for joining two levels of ground, floor, etc. (*wheelchair ramp*). **2** *N Amer.* a short sloping road leading on or off a highway. **3** movable stairs for entering or leaving an aircraft. **4** the apron of an airfield. **5** part of the handrail of a stair with a concave or upward bend, as at a landing. **6** an access point to the Internet. ● *v.* **1** *tr.* (usu. as **ramped** *adj.*) furnish or build with a ramp. **2** *intr.* **a** assume or be in a threatening posture. **b** storm, rage, rush. **3** *intr. & tr.* (often foll. by *up*) increase; gradually build.

rampage ● *v.intr.* (often foll. by *through, across*, etc.) rush wildly or violently about; rage, storm. ● *n.* an instance of uncontrolled, often prolonged, unruly or violent behaviour. □ **on the rampage** rampaging.

rampant *adj.* **1** unchecked, flourishing excessively (*rampant violence*). **2** violent or extravagant in action or opinion (*rampant theorists*). **3** rank, luxuriant. □ **rampantly** *adv.*

rampart ● *n.* **1 a** a defensive wall with a broad top and usu. a stone parapet, built around a castle, fort, etc. **b** a walkway on top of such a wall. **2** a defence or protection. **3** (in *pl.*) *Cdn* (*BC, Alta., & North*) steep rock walls, as found on either side of a river gorge. ● *v.tr.* fortify or protect with or as with a rampart.

ramrod ● *n.* **1** a rod for ramming down the charge of a muzzle-loading firearm. **2** a thing that is very straight or rigid. **3** *N Amer. informal* a foreman or boss. ● *adj.* **1** solemn, formal. **2** very straight (*ramrod posture*). ● *adv.* like a ramrod (*ramrod straight*). ● *v.tr.* (**-rodded, -rodding**) force or drive as with a ramrod (*ramrodded the bill through the legislature*).

ramshackle *adj.* **1** (of a house etc.) tumbledown, rickety. **2** (of an organization or system) poorly designed or organized.

ran *past of* RUN.

ranch ● *n.* **1 a** a cattle-breeding farm esp. in the western US and Canada. **b** a farm where other animals are bred (*mink ranch*). **2** (in full **ranch house, ranch home**, or **ranch bungalow**) *N Amer.* **a** a house on a cattle ranch, usu. of one storey and with a long, low design. **b** a similar type of house, usu. found in the suburbs. **3** *N Amer.* a type of thick, white salad dressing made with sour cream. ● *v.* **1** *intr.* run or work on a ranch. **2** *tr.* breed or rear (animals) on or as on a ranch. **3** *tr.* use (land) as a ranch. □ **ranching** *n.*

rancher *n.* **1** a person who owns or works on a ranch. **2** *N Amer.* = RANCH *n.* 2b.

ranchero /rænˈtʃero:/ *n.* (*pl.* **-os**) a rancher, esp. in Mexico and the southwestern US.

ranchland *n.* land used for or suitable for ranching.

ranch-style *adj.* (of a house) having one storey and a long, low design.

rancid *adj.* **1** (of fats, oils, or fatty meats such as bacon) smelling or tasting rank and stale as a result of oxidation. **2** nasty, disagreeable, odious. □ **rancidity** *n.*

rancour /ˈræŋkər/ *n.* (*also esp. US* **rancor**) inveterate bitterness, malignant hate, spitefulness. □ **rancorous** *adj.* **rancorously** *adv.*

rand /rænd, rænt/ *n.* the chief monetary unit of South Africa and Namibia.

R & B *abbr.* (also **r & b**) rhythm and blues.

R & D *abbr.* (also **R and D**) research and development.

random *adj.* **1** made, done, etc., without method or conscious choice (*random selection*). **2** *Statistics* **a** with equal chances for each item. **b** given by a random process (*random sample*). □ **at random** without aim or purpose or principle. □ **randomize** *v.tr.* **randomization** *n.* **randomly** *adv.* **randomness** *n.*

random access *n.* *Computing* (also *attrib.*) a process that allows information in a computer to be stored or recovered quickly without reading through items stored previously.

R and R *abbr.* (also **R & R**) **1** rest and recreation. **2** rest and relaxation. **3** rest and recuperation. **4** rescue and resuscitation.

randy *adj.* (**-ier, -iest**) **1** lustful; eager for sexual gratification. **2** bawdy, risqué. □ **randiness** *n.*

rang[1] *past of* RING[1].

rang[2] /rã/ *n.* *Cdn* (*Que.*) *hist.* Surveying a row of long lots, usu. along a road.

range ● *n.* **1 a** the region between limits of variation, esp. as representing a scope of effective operation (*a voice of astonishing range*). **b** such limits. **c** a limited scale or series (*the range of the thermometer readings*). **d** a series representing variety or choice; a selection. **2** the area included in or concerned with something. **3 a** the distance attainable by a gun or projectile (*is out of range*). **b** the distance between a gun or projectile and its objective. **4 a** a row, series, line, or tier, esp. of mountains or buildings. **b** *Cdn* a row of prison cells. **5 a** an open or enclosed area with targets for shooting. **b** a testing ground for military equipment. **6** *N Amer.* an electric or gas stove. **7** the area over which a thing, esp. a plant or animal, is distributed. **8** the distance that can be covered by a vehicle or aircraft without refuelling. **9** the distance between a camera and the subject to be photographed. **10** the extent of time covered by a forecast etc. **11 a** a large area of open land for grazing or hunting. **b** a tract over which one wanders. **12** lie, direction (*the range of the strata is east and west*). **13** *Cdn* (*Que.* & *Ont.*) a row of lots forming a concession. **14** *N Amer.* (*West*) a series of townships extending north and south parallel to the principal meridian of a survey. ● *v.* **1** *intr.* a vary or extend between limits (*prices range between $7 and $10*). **b** run in a line (*ranges north and south*). **2** *tr.* (usu. in *passive* or *refl.*) **a** place or arrange in a row or ranks or in a specified order (*flowerpots ranged in rows*). **b** place or align (oneself) with a certain group, cause, etc. (*has ranged herself with the Opposition*). **3** *intr.* rove, wander (*ranged through the woods*). **4** *tr.* traverse in all directions (*ranging the woods*). *Printing* **a** *tr.* make (type) lie flush at the ends of successive lines. **b** *intr.* (of type) lie flush. **6** *intr.* **a** (of a gun) send a projectile over a specified distance (*ranges over a mile*). **b** (of a projectile) cover a specified distance. **c** obtain the range of a target by adjustment after firing past it or short of it.

rangefinder *n.* an instrument for estimating the distance of an object, esp. one to be shot at or photographed.

rangeland *n.* an extensive area of open country used for grazing or hunting animals.

ranger *n.* **1 a** = FOREST RANGER. **b** (in full **park ranger**) = PARK WARDEN. **2** a member of a body of armed men, esp. a mounted soldier. **3** (**Ranger**) *Cdn hist.* a member of the Newfoundland Rangers (1935-49), a police

force which served those parts of Newfoundland and Labrador outside the jurisdiction of the St. John's police force. **4** *Cdn* (*North*) an Indian or Inuit who serves as a military scout or observer on a voluntary basis. **5** (**Ranger**) *Cdn & Brit.* a member of the senior branch of the Girl Guides, aged 15 or older.

rangy *adj.* (**-ier, -iest**) **1** (of a person) tall and slim. **2** (of an animal) having a long, slender form. **3** having a tendency or ability to range or wander about.

rank[1] ● *n.* **1 a** a position in a hierarchy, a grade of advancement. **b** a distinct social class (*people of all ranks*). **c** a grade of dignity or achievement (*in the top rank of performers*). **d** high social position (*persons of rank*). **e** a place in a scale. **2** a row or line. **3** a single line of soldiers drawn up abreast. **4** order, array. ● *v.* **1** *intr.* have rank or place (*ranks next to the king*). **2** *tr.* classify, give a certain grade to. **3** *tr.* arrange (esp. soldiers) in a rank or ranks. □ **break rank** (or **ranks**) **1** fail to remain in line. **2** fail to maintain solidarity. **close ranks** maintain solidarity. **the ranks 1** the common soldiers, i.e. privates and corporals. **2** a group of people of a specified type (*joined the ranks of the unemployed*). **rise from the ranks 1** (of a private or a non-commissioned officer) receive a commission. **2** (of a self-made man or woman) advance by one's own efforts.

rank[2] *adj.* **1** too luxuriant, coarse; choked with or apt to produce weeds or excessive foliage. **2 a** foul-smelling, offensive. **b** loathsome, indecent, corrupt. **3** complete, unmistakable, strongly marked (*rank amateur*). □ **rankly** *adv.* **rankness** *n.*

rank and file *n.* (usu. treated as *pl.*) **1** the ordinary soldiers who are not officers. **2** the ordinary members of any group or society as opposed to the leaders (also *attrib.*: *rank-and-file workers*).

ranking ● *n.* ordering by rank; classification. ● *adj.* *N Amer.* having a high rank or position.

rankle *v.* **1** *intr.* (of envy, disappointment, etc., or their cause) cause persistent annoyance or resentment. **2** *tr.* (of an experience, event, etc.) cause, or continue to cause, bad, esp. bitter feelings in (a person).

ransack *v.tr.* **1** pillage or plunder (a house, country, etc.). **2** thoroughly search (a place, a receptacle, a person's pockets, one's conscience, etc.).

ransom ● *n.* **1** a sum of money or other payment demanded or paid for the release of a prisoner. **2** the liberation of a prisoner in return for this. ● *v.tr.* **1** buy the freedom or restoration of; redeem. **2** hold to ransom. **3** release for a ransom.

rant ● *v.intr.* **1** (often foll. by *about, on*) speak vehemently or wildly, esp. at length. **2** use bombastic language. ● *n.* a piece of ranting; a tirade. □ **rant and rave** express anger noisily and forcefully. □ **ranter** *n.*

rap[1] ● *n.* **1** a quick sharp blow or knock. **2** *slang* **a** criticism, punishment. **b** (often foll. by *on, against*) a charge, accusation, or reputed fault (*a drunk driving rap*). **3** *slang* a conversation (*rap session*). **4 a** (in full **rap music**) a style of popular music characterized by the rhythmic and usu. rapid reciting of rhyming lyrics against an often sampled background with a pronounced beat. **b** the reciting of lyrics in rap music. **c** a rap song. ● *v.* (**rapped, rapping**) **1** *tr.* strike briskly. **2** *intr.* knock; make a sharp tapping sound (*rapped on the table*). **3** *tr.* *informal* **a** criticize adversely. **b** accuse, charge. **4** *intr.* *slang* talk. **5 a** *intr.* perform rap music, talk in the style of rap. **b** *tr.* utter in this style. □ **beat the rap** *N Amer.* escape punishment. **rap a person's knuckles** (also **rap a person on the knuckles**) **1** strike a person's knuckles sharply. **2** criticize or reprimand a person. **rap on the**

knuckles a reprimand or reproof. **rap out 1** utter (an oath, order, etc.) abruptly or on the spur of the moment. **2** express or reproduce (a rhythm, signal, etc.) by raps. **take the rap** suffer the consequences.

rap^2 n. a small amount, the least bit (*don't care a rap*).

rapacious /rəˈpeiʃəs/ adj. greedy, grasping, extortionate. □ **rapacity** /rəˈpæsiti/ n.

rape^1 ● n. **1** the action or an act of forcing a person, esp. a woman or girl, to have sexual intercourse unwillingly. **2** (often foll. by *of*) plunder, abuse, or violation (*the rape of our natural resources*). ● v.tr. **1** commit rape on (a person, usu. a woman). **2** violate, assault, pillage. **3** *literary* take by force.

rape^2 n. a plant, *Brassica napus*, the seeds of which yield oil used in cooking etc. See also CANOLA.

rape^3 n. the refuse of grapes after winemaking, used in making vinegar.

rape crisis centre n. an agency offering advice and support to victims of rape.

rapeseed n. **1** the seed of the rape plant. **2** the rape plant.

rapeseed oil n. (also **rape oil**) an oil made from rapeseed and used as a lubricant and in foodstuffs.

rape-shield n. (*attrib.*) designating legislation limiting the allowable questioning of the victim of an alleged sexual assault on matters of personal esp. sexual history.

rapid ● adj. **1** quick, swift. **2** acting or completed in a short time. **3** (of a slope) descending steeply. **4** *Photog.* fast. ● n. (usu. in *pl.*) a section of a river with a swift turbulent current. □ **rapidity** /rəˈpiditi/ n. **rapidly** adv.

rapid eye movement n. a type of jerky movement of the eyes during periods of dreaming. Abbr.: **REM**.

rapid-fire attrib.adj. fired, uttered, etc., in quick succession (*a rapid-fire exchange*).

rapid transit n. high-speed urban transportation of passengers, usu. by rail.

rapier /ˈreipiər/ ● n. a light slender sword used for thrusting. ● adj. having the sharpness or incisiveness of a rapier (*rapier wit*).

rapini /rəˈpiːni/ n.pl. the edible leaves of an immature white turnip.

rapist n. a person who commits rape.

rappel /ræˈpel/ ● v.intr. (**rappelled, rappelling**) descend a steep rock face by using a doubled rope coiled round the body and fixed at a higher point. ● n. a descent made by rappelling.

rapper n. **1** a performer of rap music. **2** a person or thing that raps.

rapport /rəˈpɔr/ n. a relationship or communication, esp. when useful and harmonious (*establish a rapport*).

rapprochement /ˌræprɒˈʃmɑ/ n. the establishment or resumption of harmonious relations, esp. between nations.

rap sheet n. N Amer. slang an official record of one's criminal activities.

rapt adj. **1** fully absorbed or intent, enraptured (*listen with rapt attention*). **2** carried away with feeling or lofty thought. □ **raptly** adv. **raptness** n.

raptor n. **1** any bird of prey. **2** informal = VELOCIRAPTOR.

rapture n. **1 a** ecstatic delight, mental transport. **b** (in *pl.*) great pleasure or enthusiasm or the expression of it. **2** (**Rapture**) (in some millenarian teaching) the transporting of believers to heaven at the Second Coming of Christ. □ **rapturous** adj. **rapturously** adv.

rare^1 adj. (**rarer, rarest**) **1** seldom done or found or occurring, uncommon. **2** of less than the usual den-

sity, with only loosely packed substance (*the rare atmosphere of the mountaintops*). □ **rareness** n.

rare^2 adj. (**rarer, rarest**) (of meat) slightly cooked. □ **rareness** n.

rare bird n. a rarity; a kind of person or thing rarely encountered.

rare earth n. **1** a lanthanide element (also *attrib.*: *rare-earth element*). **2** an oxide of such an element.

rarefied /ˈrerifaid/ adj. (also **rarified**) **1** (of air, a gas, etc.) thinner or less dense than usual. **2 a** often *ironic* refined, subtle. **b** elevated, exalted.

rarefy /ˈrerifai/ v. (also **rarify**) (**-ies, -ied**) **1** tr. & intr. make or become less dense or solid. **2** tr. purify or refine (a person's nature etc.). **3** tr. make (an idea etc.) subtle. □ **rarefaction** /-ˈfækʃən/ n.

rarely adv. **1** seldom; not often. **2** in an unusual degree; exceptionally.

raring adj. (foll. by *to* + infin.) informal enthusiastic, eager (*raring to go*).

rarity n. (pl. **-ies**) **1** rareness. **2** an uncommon thing, esp. one valued for being rare.

rascal n. often *jocular* a dishonest or mischievous person, esp. a child. □ **rascality** n. (pl. **-ies**). **rascally** adj.

rash^1 adj. reckless, hasty; acting or done without due consideration. □ **rashly** adv. **rashness** n.

rash^2 n. **1** an eruption of the skin in spots or patches. **2** (usu. foll. by *of*) a sudden widespread phenomenon, esp. of something unwelcome (*a rash of robberies*).

rasher n. a thin slice of bacon or ham.

rasp ● n. **1** a grating noise or utterance. **2** a coarse kind of file having separate teeth. ● v. **1** tr. a scrape with a rasp. **b** scrape roughly. **c** (foll. by *off, away*) remove by scraping. **2 a** intr. make a grating sound. **b** tr. say gratingly or hoarsely. **3** tr. grate upon (a person or a person's feelings), irritate. □ **raspy** adj.

raspberry ● n. (pl. **-ies**) **1 a** a bramble of the genus *Rubus*, esp. *R. idaeus*, having usu. red berries consisting of numerous drupelets on a conical receptacle. **b** this berry. **2** the red colour of a raspberry, usu. a deep red. **3** informal **a** a sputtering sound made with the lips and tongue expressing dislike, derision, or disapproval. **b** a show of strong disapproval (*got a raspberry from the audience*). ● adj. deep red.

raspberry cane n. a raspberry plant.

Rastafarian /ˌræstəˈferiən/ (also **Rasta** /ˈræstə/) ● n. a member of a sect of Jamaican origin regarding blacks as a chosen people and the former Emperor Haile Selassie of Ethiopia (d. 1975, entitled *Ras Tafari* as God. ● adj. of or relating to this sect. □ **Rastafarianism** n.

raster /ˈræstər/ n. a pattern of horizontal lines of pixels composing an image on a cathode ray tube display or for printing etc. (also *attrib.*: *raster graphics*).

rat ● n. **1 a** any of several rodents of the genus *Rattus*, usu. having a pointed snout and a long sparsely haired tail. **b** = MUSKRAT. **c** any similar rodent (*water rat*). **2** a deserter from a party, cause, difficult situation, etc.; a turncoat or informant. **3** informal an unpleasant person. **4** a worker who refuses to join a strike. **5** informal a person frequently found in a specified place (*mall rat*). ● v.intr. (**ratted, ratting**) **1** (usu. foll. by *on, out*) **a** inform on; be an informant against. **b** betray; let down. **2** (of a person, dog, etc.) hunt or kill rats. **3** informal desert a cause, party, etc. □ **not give a rat's ass** N Amer. slang not care in the least.

ratable var. of RATEABLE.

rat-a-tat-tat (also **rat-a-tat**) var. of RAT-TAT-TAT.

ratatouille /ˌrætəˈtuːi, -ˈtwiː/ n. a dish of stewed onions, zucchini, tomatoes, eggplant, and peppers.

ratchet ● n. **1** a set of teeth on the edge of a bar or wheel in which a device engages to ensure motion in one direction only. **2** a wheel with a rim so toothed. ● v. (**ratcheted, ratcheting**) **1** tr. a provide with a ratchet. **b** make into a ratchet. **2** tr. & intr. (often foll. by *up*) move as under the control of a ratchet (*ratchet interest rates up another notch*).

rate¹ ● n. **1** a stated numerical proportion between two sets of things (the second usu. expressed as unity), esp. as a measure of amount or degree (*a rate of 50 miles per hour*) or as the basis of calculating an amount or value (*rate of taxation*). **2** a fixed or appropriate charge or cost or value; a measure of this (*postal rates*). **3** rapidity of movement or change (*prices increasing at a dreadful rate*). **4** class or rank (*first-rate*). ● v. **1** tr. **a** estimate the worth or value of (*how do you rate your chances of winning?*). **b** assign a fixed value to (a coin or metal) in relation to a monetary standard. **c** assign a value to (work, the power of a machine, etc.). **2** tr. consider; regard as (*I rate them among my benefactors*). **3** intr. **a** (often foll. by *as*) rank or be rated. **b** rank highly; be of importance or esteemed (*I guess I don't rate*). **4** tr. be worthy of, deserve. **5** tr. **a** place (a film etc.) in a category relative to its suitability for viewing. **b** *Naut.* place (a sailor) in a specified class (compare RATING¹ 4). □ **at any rate** in any case, whatever happens. **at this** (or **that**) **rate** if this example is typical or this assumption is true.

rate² v.tr. scold angrily.

rateable adj. able to be rated or estimated. □ **rateability** n. **rateably** adv.

rate of return n. the annual amount of income from an investment, expressed as a percentage of the original investment.

ratepayer n. *Cdn & Brit.* a person paying local property taxes.

rater n. **1** a person or thing that rates (*bond rater*). **2** a person or thing rated (*second-rater*).

rat fink n. *N Amer. slang* = FINK n.

rather adv. **1** (often foll. by *than*) by preference; for choice (*would rather not go; would rather stay than go*). **2** (usu. foll. by *than*) more truly; as a more likely alternative (*is stupid rather than honest*). **3 a** more precisely (*a book, or rather, a pamphlet*). **b** (often foll. by *than*) on the contrary, instead (*of*) (*rescheduled for Friday rather than today*). **4** slightly; to some extent; somewhat (*rather drunk*). □ **had rather** would rather.

rathole n. *N Amer.* **1** a cramped or squalid building etc. **2** a seemingly bottomless hole, esp. one down which expenditures disappear.

ratify /ˈrætɪˌfaɪ/ v.tr. (**-ies, -ied**) confirm or accept (an agreement made in one's name) by formal consent, signature, etc. □ **ratifiable** adj. **ratification** n.

rating¹ n. **1 a** the act or an instance of placing in a rank or class or assigning a value to. **b** the class, rank, or value assigned. **2** the estimated standing of a person, organization, etc. as regards credit etc. **3** the relative popularity of a broadcast program as determined by the estimated size of the audience. **4 a** *Cdn & Brit.* a non-commissioned sailor. **b** a person's position or class on a ship's books.

rating² n. an angry reprimand.

ratio /ˈreɪʃioː, -ʃoː/ n. (pl. **-os**) **1** the quantitative relation between two similar magnitudes determined by the number of times one contains the other integrally or fractionally (*in the ratio of three to two; the ratio 1:5*). **2** a proportional relationship between things not precisely measurable.

ration ● n. **1** a fixed official allowance of food, clothing, etc., in a time of shortage. **2** (foll. by *of*) a single portion of provisions, fuel, clothing, etc. **3** (usu. in pl.) a fixed daily allowance of food, esp. in the armed forces. **4** (in pl.) provisions. ● v.tr. **1** limit (persons or provisions) to a fixed ration. **2** (usu. foll. by *out*) share out (food etc.) in fixed quantities.

rational adj. **1** of or based on reasoning or reason. **2** sensible, sane, moderate; not foolish or absurd or extreme. **3** endowed with reason, reasoning. **4** rejecting what is unreasonable or cannot be tested by reason in religion or custom. **5** *Math.* (of a quantity or ratio) expressible as a ratio of whole numbers. □ **rationality** n. **rationally** adv.

rationale /ˌræʃəˈnæl/ n. **1** (often foll. by *for, of*) the fundamental reason or logical basis of anything. **2** a reasoned exposition; a statement of reasons.

rationalism n. **1** *Philos.* the theory that reason is the foundation of certainty in knowledge (compare EMPIRICISM). **2** *Theol.* the practice of treating reason as the ultimate authority in religion. **3** a belief in reason rather than religion as a guiding principle in life. **4** the principle or practice of using reasoning and calculation as a basis for analysis, a course of action, etc. □ **rationalist** n. **rationalistic** adj.

rationalize v. **1** a tr. offer or subconsciously adopt a rational but specious explanation of (one's behaviour or attitude). **b** intr. explain one's behaviour or attitude in this way. **2** tr. make logical and consistent. **3** tr. make (a business etc.) more efficient by reorganizing it to reduce or eliminate waste of labour, time, or materials; downsize. **4** tr. (often foll. by *away*) explain or explain away rationally. **5** tr. clear of irrational numbers. **6** intr. be or act as a rationalist. □ **rationalization** n.

rat kangaroo n. any of various small rat-like marsupials of the family Potoroidae, having kangaroo-like hind limbs for jumping.

rat pack n. a group of associates, friends, etc.

rat race n. a fiercely competitive struggle for position, power, etc.

rats interj. expressing annoyance, frustration, disappointment, etc.

rat's nest n. *N Amer. informal* a muddled or confused place or situation.

rat-tail n. (also **rat's tail**) a thing shaped like the tail of a rat, i.e. long, slender, and tapering (also attrib.: *rat-tail haircut*). □ **rat-tailed** adj.

rattan /rəˈtæn/ n. any East Indian climbing palm of the genus *Calamus* etc. with long thin jointed pliable stems used for wickerwork.

rat-tat-tat n. a knocking or rapping staccato sound (also attrib.: *rat-tat-tat dialogue*).

rattle ● v. **1 a** intr. give out a rapid succession of short sharp hard sounds, usu. through being shaken or vibrating against something. **b** tr. make (a chair, window, dishes, etc.) do this. **c** intr. cause such sounds by shaking something (*rattled at the door*). **2** intr. move with a rattling noise. **3** tr. (usu. foll. by *off*) say or recite rapidly. **b** intr. (usu. foll. by *on*) talk in a lively thoughtless way. **4** tr. (also in *passive*) *informal* disconcert, alarm, fluster, frighten. ● n. **1** a rattling sound. **2** an instrument or plaything made to rattle esp. in order to amuse babies or to give an alarm. **3** the set of rings in a rattlesnake's tail. **4** a plant with seeds that rattle in their cases when ripe (*red rattle*). **5** uproar, bustle, noisy gaiety, racket. **6 a** a noisy flow of words. **b** empty chatter, trivial talk. **7** *Cdn (Nfld & NS)* rapids or fast-flowing water. □ **rattly** adj.

rattlesnake n. (also *informal* **rattler**) any of various poisonous N American snakes of the family Viperidae, esp. of the genus *Crotalus* or *Sistrurus*, with a rattling structure of rings in its tail.

rattletrap *informal* ● *n.* a rickety old vehicle etc. ● *adj.* rickety.

rattling ● *adj.* **1** that rattles. **2** brisk, vigorous (*a rattling pace*). ● *adv.* remarkably (*a rattling good story*). □ **rattlingly** *adv.*

ratty *adj.* (**-ier, -iest**) **1** relating to or infested with rats. **2** *informal* shabby, tattered, wretched. □ **rattily** *adv.* **rattiness** *n.*

raucous /'rɔːkəs/ *adj.* harsh-sounding; loud and hoarse. □ **raucously** *adv.* **raucousness** *n.*

raunch *n.* *slang* **1** earthiness, bawdiness, provocative sexuality. **2** the sound of a distorted electric guitar.

raunchy *adj.* (**-ier, -iest**) *informal* **1** coarse, earthy; sexually provocative. **2 a** (of the sound of an electric guitar) distorted. **b** (of music) featuring raunchy guitars. **3** esp. *US* slovenly, grubby. □ **raunchily** *adv.* **raunchiness** *n.*

ravage ● *v.tr. & intr.* devastate, plunder; damage. ● *n.* **1** the act or an instance of ravaging; devastation, damage. **2** (usu. in *pl.*; foll. by *of*) destructive effect (*survived the ravages of winter*).

rave ● *v.* **1** *intr.* talk wildly or furiously in or as in delirium. **2** *intr.* (usu. foll. by *about, over*) speak with rapturous admiration; go into raptures. **3** *intr.* (of the sea, wind, etc.) howl, roar. **4** *intr.* *slang* attend a rave. ● *n.* **1 a** (usu. *attrib.*) *informal* a highly enthusiastic review of a film, play, etc. (*a rave review*). **b** an enthusiastic reaction. **2** *slang* a large often illicit all-night party or event, often held in a warehouse or open field, with dancing to loud fast electronic music (also *attrib.*: *rave music*).

ravel /'rævəl/ ● *v.* (**ravelled, ravelling**) **1** *tr. & intr.* entangle or become entangled or knotted. **2** *tr.* confuse or complicate (a question or problem). **3** *intr.* fray out. **4** *tr.* (often foll. by *out*) disentangle, unravel, distinguish the separate threads or subdivisions of. ● *n.* **1** a tangle or knot. **2** a complication. **3** a frayed or loose end.

ravelling *n.* a thread from fabric which is frayed or unravelled.

raven¹ /'reivən/ ● *n.* a large glossy blue-black crow, *Corvus corax*, feeding chiefly on carrion etc., having a hoarse cry, and noted for its craftiness. ● *adj.* glossy black (*raven tresses*).

raven² *v.* **1** *intr.* **a** plunder. **b** prowl for prey (*ravening beast*). **2 a** *tr.* devour voraciously. **b** *intr.* (usu. foll. by *for*) have a ravenous appetite. **c** *intr.* (often foll. by *on*) feed voraciously.

ravenous /'rævənəs/ *adj.* **1** very hungry, famished. **2** (of hunger, eagerness, etc., or of an animal) voracious. **3** rapacious. □ **ravenously** *adv.*

raver *n.* **1** *slang* a person who attends raves. **2** a person who raves; a madman or madwoman.

ravine *n.* a narrow, steep-sided valley, esp. one formed by erosion by running water.

raving ● *n.* (usu. in *pl.*) wild or delirious talk. ● *adj.* **1** delirious, frenzied. **2** *informal* as an intensifier (*a raving beauty*). ● *adv.* *informal* as an intensifier (*raving mad*). □ **ravingly** *adv.*

ravioli *n.* small squares of pasta stuffed with minced meat, cheese, spinach, etc.

ravish *v.tr.* **1** commit rape on. **2** enrapture; fill with delight. □ **ravisher** *n.* **ravishment** *n.*

ravishing *adj.* **1** entrancing, delightful. **2** (of a person) extraordinarily beautiful. □ **ravishingly** *adv.*

raw *adj.* **1** (of food) uncooked. **2** in the natural state; not processed (*raw sewage*). **3** (of statistics, data, etc.)

not analyzed or processed. **4** (of a person) inexperienced, untrained; new to an activity (*raw recruits*). **5 a** stripped of skin; having the flesh exposed. **b** sensitive to the touch from having the flesh exposed. **c** abnormally sensitive (*touched a raw nerve*). **6** (of the atmosphere, day, etc.) chilly and damp. **7 a** crude in artistic quality; lacking finish. **b** not controlled or refined (*raw emotion*). **8** (of the edge of cloth) without hem or selvage. **9** (of liquor) undiluted. **10** (of silk) as reeled from cocoons. **11** (of milk) not pasteurized. **12** (of leather) untanned. **13** (of film or video footage etc.) unedited. □ **in the raw 1** in its natural state without mitigation (*life in the raw*). **2** naked. □ **rawly** *adv.* **rawness** *n.*

raw-boned *adj.* gaunt and bony.

raw deal *n.* harsh or unfair treatment.

rawhide *n.* **1** untanned hide. **2** a rope or whip of this.

raw material *n.* material from which products are manufactured.

ray¹ ● *n.* **1** a single line or narrow beam of light from a small or distant source. **2** a straight line in which radiation travels to a given point. **3** (in *pl.*) radiation of a specified type (*X-rays*). **4** a trace or beginning of an enlightening or cheering influence (*a ray of hope*). **5 a** any of a set of radiating lines or parts of things. **b** the part of a straight line extending from a point indefinitely in one direction. **6** the marginal portion of a composite flower, e.g. a daisy. **7 a** a radial division of a starfish. **b** each of a set of bones etc. supporting a fish's fin. ● *v.* **1** *intr.* (foll. by *out, forth*) (of light, thought etc.) issue in or as if in rays. **2** *intr. & tr.* radiate. □ **catch** (or **get, bag,** etc.) **some rays** *N Amer. informal* sunbathe. □ **rayed** *adj.*

ray² *n.* a large cartilaginous fish of the order Batoidea, with a broad flat body, wing-like pectoral fins and a long slender tail.

ray³ *var. of* RE².

ray gun *n.* (esp. in science fiction) a gun causing damage by the emission of a ray or beam of energy.

rayon *n.* any of various textile fibres or fabrics made from viscose.

raze *v.tr.* **1** completely destroy; tear down (*razed to the ground*). **2** erase; scratch out (esp. in abstract senses).

razor ● *n.* an instrument with a sharp blade or blades used in cutting hair or bristles esp. from the skin. ● *v.tr.* **1** use a razor on. **2 a** shave; cut down close. **b** slice.

razorback *n.* an animal with a sharp ridged back, esp. a semi-wild hog of the southern US.

razorbill *n.* (also **razor-billed auk**) an auk, *Alca torda*, with a sharp-edged bill, breeding along the coasts of the N Atlantic.

razor blade *n.* a blade used in a razor, esp. a flat piece of metal with a sharp edge or edges.

razor's edge *n.* (also **razor edge**) **1** a sharp edge. **2** a critical situation (*found themselves on a razor's edge*). **3** a sharp line of division. □ **razor-edged** *adj.*

razor-sharp *adj.* extremely sharp.

razor wire *n.* a type of coiled wire with extremely sharp edges or points, used as a barrier or run along the top of walls etc.

razz *N Amer. slang* ● *n.* = RASPBERRY 3. ● *v.tr.* tease, ridicule.

razzle-dazzle *n.* (also **razzle**) esp. *N Amer. informal* **1** glitter, showiness, pageantry; a flamboyant often insincere display, as of publicity (also *attrib.*: *razzle-dazzle costumes*). **2** glamorous excitement; bustle.

razzmatazz *n.* *informal* = RAZZLE-DAZZLE.

Rb *symbol* rubidium.

RBI /ɑːrbiː'ai, *informal* 'rɪbi/ *n.* (*pl.* same or **RBIs**) *Baseball*

1 run batted in (pl. **runs batted in**), a run scored because of a batter's hit, sacrifice fly, walk, etc., and counted among the batter's statistics (leads the team with 57 RBIs). **2** (attrib.) designating a hit etc. which drives a runner home to score a run (RBI double).

RC abbr. **1** Roman Catholic. **2** Red Cross.

RCAF abbr. hist. Royal Canadian Air Force.

RCL abbr. Royal Canadian Legion.

RCM abbr. Cdn (Que.) REGIONAL COUNTY MUNICIPALITY.

RCMP ● abbr. Royal Canadian Mounted Police. ● n. Cdn informal an RCMP officer.

RCN abbr. hist. Royal Canadian Navy.

RCNVR abbr. hist. Royal Canadian Naval Volunteer Reserve.

Rd. abbr. Road.

RDA abbr. recommended daily allowance (for a vitamin etc.).

RDI abbr. recommended daily intake (for a vitamin, mineral, etc.).

rDNA abbr. RECOMBINANT DNA.

Re symbol rhenium.

re¹ /ri:, rei / prep. **1** in the matter of (as the first word in a heading). **2** informal about, concerning.

re² n. Music **1** (in tonic sol-fa) the second note of a major scale. **2** the note D in the fixed-do system.

re- prefix attachable to almost any verb or its derivative, meaning: **1** once more; afresh, anew (renumber). **2** back; with return to a previous state (reassemble). ¶A hyphen is normally used when the word begins with e (re-enact), or to distinguish the compound from a one-word form (re-form = form again).

're abbr. informal (usu. after pronouns) are (you're).

reach ● v. **1** intr. & tr. (often foll. by out) stretch out; extend. **2** intr. stretch out a limb, the hand, etc.; make a reaching motion or effort. **3** tr. (often foll. by for) make a motion or effort to touch or get hold of, or to attain (reached for his mug). **4** tr. get as far as; arrive at (reached Sudbury; your letter reached me today). **5** tr. get to or attain (a specified point) on a scale (the temperature reached 40°). **6** tr. & intr. extend as far as (shorts that reached to his knees). **7** tr. succeed in achieving; attain (reach agreement). **8** tr. make contact with (could not be reached). **9** tr. (of a broadcast, broadcasting station, etc.) be received by. **10** tr. succeed in influencing or having the required effect on (could not manage to reach their audience). **11** tr. (often foll. by down) hand, pass (reach me down that can). ● n. **1** the extent to which a hand etc. can be reached out, influence exerted, motion carried out, mental powers used, etc. **2** an act of reaching out. **3 a** a continuous extent, esp. a stretch of river between two bends, or an expanse of land etc. **b** (usu. in pl.) a level or stratum (the higher reaches of the organization). **4** the number of people who watch a specified television channel or listen to a specified radio station at any time during a specified period. □ **out of reach** not able to be reached or attained. □ **reachable** adj. **reacher** n.

react v. **1** intr. (foll. by to) respond to a stimulus; undergo a change or show behaviour due to some influence (how did they react to the news?). **2** intr. (often foll. by against) be actuated by repulsion to; tend in a reverse or contrary direction. **3** intr. (often foll. by upon) produce a reciprocal or responsive effect; act upon the agent. **4** intr. (foll. by with) Chem. & Physics (of a substance or particle) be the cause of activity or interaction with another (nitrous oxide reacts with the metal). **5** tr. (foll. by with) Chem. cause (a substance) to react with another.

reactance n. a component of impedance in an AC circuit, due to capacitance or inductance or both.

reaction n. **1** the act or an instance of reacting; a responsive or reciprocal action. **2 a** a responsive feeling (what was your reaction to the news?). **b** an immediate or first impression. **3** the occurrence of a (physical or emotional) condition after a period of its opposite. **4** a bodily response to an external stimulus, e.g. a drug. **5** a tendency to oppose change or to advocate return to a former system, esp. in politics. **6** the interaction of substances undergoing chemical change. **7** Physics a force that is equal in magnitude but opposite in direction to some other force.

reactionary usu. derogatory ● adj. tending to oppose (esp. political) change and advocate return to a former system. ● n. (pl. **-ies**) a reactionary person.

reactive adj. **1** showing reaction. **2** reacting rather than taking the initiative. **3** having a tendency to react chemically. **4** of or relating to reactance. □ **reactivity** n.

reactor n. **1** a person or thing that reacts. **2** (in full **nuclear reactor**) an apparatus or structure in which a controlled nuclear chain reaction releases energy. **3** Electricity a component used to provide reactance, esp. an inductor. **4** an apparatus for the chemical reaction of substances.

read¹ ● v. (past and past part. **read**) **1** tr. & intr. look at and understand the meaning of written or printed words or symbols. **2** tr. & intr. examine or peruse printed matter for recreation or personal enjoyment. **3** tr. (often foll. by off, out, aloud) render (written or printed matter) in speech (the judge read off the charges). **4** tr. **a** interpret (letters, words, sentences) by passing fingers over engraved or embossed characters or Braille. **b** interpret (letters, words, sentences) by examining a person's hand gestures as sign language. **c** interpret speech by observing the movements of (a speaker's lips). **5** tr. interpret or assess (read her mood). **6** tr. interpret (a statement or action) in a certain sense (my silence is not to be read as consent). **7** tr. **a** (often foll. by that + clause) learn a piece of information by examining written or printed material. **b** learn a piece of information by examining other signs etc. (I read it in your eyes). **8** tr. **a** (of a meter or other recording instrument) show (a specified figure etc.) (the thermometer reads 20°). **b** inspect and record elsewhere the figure shown on such an instrument (read the meter). **9** tr. **a** receive and understand the words of a person by radio or telephone. **b** understand the meaning of a speaker (I read you loud and clear). **10** intr. give a certain impression when read (it reads like a parody). **11** Computing sense and retrieve or interpret data from a form of storage or input medium. **12** tr. **a** interpret (cards, a person's palm, etc.) as a fortune teller. **b** interpret (a map, chart, graph, etc.). **c** guess (a person's mind or thoughts). **d** interpret (the sky) as an astrologer or meteorologist. **13** tr. check the correctness of and emend (a printed text). **14** tr. **a** (of a text) have at a particular place (reads 'battery' not 'buttery'). **b** replace (a word, etc.) with a more appropriate one (for 'illitterate' read 'illiterate'; he calls himself 'financially conservative' (read 'cheap'!)). **15** tr. interpret

---

reabsorb v.tr.

reabsorption n.

reacquaint v.tr. & refl.

reacquaintance n.

reactivate v.tr.

reactivation n.

and understand (musical symbols). ● *n.* **1** a period or act of reading. **2** a book etc. as regards its readability (*is a really good read*). **3** (usu. foll. by *on*) an interpretation (*get a read on things*). □ **read between the lines** look for or find hidden meaning (in a document etc.). **read a person like a book** understand a person's motives etc. **read into** find or assume meanings in the words of a speaker or writer which are not intended (*you're reading too much into her comment*). **read my lips** *N Amer. informal* listen carefully (*read my lips: I'm going home!*). **read back** read aloud (a message just received) so that the sender can check its accuracy. **read up on** make a special study of (a subject).

read² *adj.* (often in *comb.*) educated or versed in a subject (esp. literature) by reading (*well-read*). □ **take as read** accept without reading or discussing.

readable *adj.* **1** able to be read; legible. **2** interesting or pleasant to read. **3** (usu. in *comb.*) (of data) able to be processed (by a computer, human, etc.). □ **readability** *n.*

reader *n.* **1** a person who reads or is reading. **2** a device that interprets data encoded on CD-ROMs, magnetic strips, bar codes, etc., usu. in order to display it in readable form on a monitor. **3 a** a book of written passages, exercises, etc. used in learning to read. **b** a collection of writings on a subject, used esp. as a supplement to a textbook. **4** a publisher's employee who reports on submitted manuscripts. **5** a person employed by a printer to correct proofs. **6** a person appointed to read aloud, esp. parts of a service in a church. **7** a device for producing an image that can be read from microfilm etc.

reader-friendly *adj.* **1** designating written material using a format and level of language that is manageable for the reader; pleasant to read. **2** (of a setting, library, etc.) conducive to reading.

readerly *adj.* of or pertaining to a reader or readers.

readership *n.* **1** the readers of a newspaper etc. **2** the number or extent of these.

readily *adv.* **1** without showing reluctance; willingly. **2** easily, promptly; without difficulty.

reading *n.* **1 a** the action or an instance of reading or perusing. **b** matter to be read (*have plenty of reading with me*). **2** the ability to read (*she must work on her reading*). **3** (*attrib.*) **a** used for reading (*reading glasses*). **b** of or concerning the ability to read (*reading program*). **4** an event at which a work of fiction, poetry, etc., is read aloud, often by the author (*poetry reading*). **5** the formal public recital of (a will etc.). **6 a** a figure etc. shown by a meter or other recording instrument (*an accurate reading*). **b** an instance of measuring using a recording instrument (*take a reading*). **7 a** an analysis or interpretation of a written or printed text, poem, etc. (*a feminist reading*). **b** an analysis of a situation, facts, etc. **c** an analysis of tarot cards, a person's palm, etc. in order to predict the future. **8** literary knowledge (*a person of wide reading*). **9** the interpretation (of a dramatic role, musical composition, etc.) as reflected in its performance. **10** each of the successive occasions on which a bill must be presented to a legislature for acceptance. **11** a passage of scripture etc. to be read aloud at a religious service. **12** the

version of a text, or the particular wording, conjectured or given by an editor etc.

reading room *n.* a room in a library in which patrons may read non-circulating books and other documents.

reading week *n. Cdn* a week usu. halfway through a university term during which there are no classes, intended for students to concentrate on their reading, research, etc.

read-only memory *n. Computing* a memory read at high speed but not capable of being changed by program instructions. Abbr.: **ROM**.

readout *n.* **1** the display of data by an automatic device in an understandable form. **2** a record of output produced by a computer or scientific instrument.

read/write *adj. Computing* capable of reading existing data and accepting alterations or further input.

ready ● *adj.* (**-ier, -iest**) (usu. *predic.*) **1** with preparations complete; prepared (*dinner is ready*). **2** having reached a certain state or maturity (*ready for a nap*). **3** inclined, eager, or resolved (*always ready to complain*). **4** within reach; easily secured (*a ready source of income*). **5** fit for immediate use (*always has a glib answer ready*). **6** immediate, unqualified (*found ready acceptance*). **7** prompt, quick (*has a ready wit*). **8** about to do something (*a building ready to collapse*). **9** (in *comb.*) prepared for (*oven-ready chickens*). ● *adv.* (done, prepared, etc.) beforehand (*ready assembled furniture*). ● *v.tr.* (**-ies, -ied**) make ready; prepare. □ **at the ready** ready for action. **get** (or **make**) **ready** prepare (*get ready for bed*). □ **readiness** *n.*

ready cash *n.* (also **ready money**) **1** actual coin or banknotes. **2** payment on the spot.

ready-made ● *adj.* **1** (esp. of clothes) made in a standard size, not to the measurements of a particular customer (*a ready-made suit*). **2** (esp. of food) prepared in advance (*ready-made dough*). **3** ideal or very appropriate and already available (*a ready-made solution*). ● *n.* something that is ready-made.

ready-mix ● *adj.* (also **ready-mixed**) having some or all of the constituents already mixed together (*ready-mix cookie dough*). ● *n.* concrete with some or all of the constituents mixed together.

ready-to-wear ● *n.* clothing or an article of clothing that is made in standard sizes, not tailored to a particular customer. ● *adj.* pertaining to this style of clothing; ready-made.

reagent /riːˈeɪdʒənt/ *n. Chem.* **1** a substance used to test for the presence of another substance by means of the reaction which it produces. **2** any substance used in chemical reactions.

real ● *adj.* **1** actually existing as a thing or occurring in fact; not imaginary or fictional. **2** (*attrib.*) actual or true, not just appearing so (*what's the real reason?*). **3** genuine, sincere; not feigned (*cried real tears*). **4** not artificial (*real cream*). **5** (*attrib.*) complete, utter, serious (*that's a real shame*). **6** *Law* (usu. *attrib.*) consisting of or relating to immovable property such as land or houses (*real estate*) (*compare* PERSONAL PROPERTY). **7** (usu. *attrib.*) appraised by purchasing power; adjusted for changes in the wages of money (*real value; income in real terms*). ● *adv. N Amer. & Scot. informal* really, very.

re-address *v.tr.*   **readmission** *n.*   **readopt** *v.tr.*   **reaffirm** *v.tr.*
readjust *v.tr. & intr.*   **readmit** *v.tr.*   **readoption** *n.*   **reaffirmation** *n.*
readjustment *n.*   (**readmitted, readmitting**)

¶Considered non-standard by many and should not be used in writing. ☐ **for real** *informal* **1** in earnest (*playing for real*). **2** genuine (*that's just acting, it's not for real*). **get real** *N Amer. slang* get serious. **the real thing** (of an object or emotion) genuine, not illusory or inferior (*this isn't just a crush, this is the real thing*). ☐ **realness** *n.*

real estate *n. N Amer.* **1** immovable property, such as land or houses, and the proprietary rights over these. **2** the business of buying and selling land, buildings, houses, etc. (*she's in real estate*). **3** *Computing* (esp. of memory, a disk, a screen, etc.) available space.

real estate agent *n. N Amer.* a person whose business is to represent clients in the purchase, sale, or rental of houses etc. ☐ **real estate agency** *n.*

realism *n.* **1** an interest in regarding things in their true nature and dealing with them as they are. **2** fidelity to nature in representation; the showing of life etc. as it is in fact, esp. in literature, theatre, or the visual arts. **3** (also **Realism**) a movement in esp. French art of the 19th c. characterized by a rebellion against the traditional historical, mythological, and religious subjects in favour of unidealized scenes of modern life. ☐ **realist** *n. & adj.*

realistic *adj.* **1** having or showing a sensible and practical idea of what can be done, achieved, etc. (*a realistic solution*). **2** true to real life; resembling the original (*a realistic rubber snake*). **3** (of art) depicting things in their true nature, free from enhancement or idealization. **4** of or pertaining to philosophical realism. ☐ **realistically** *adv.*

reality *n.* (*pl.* **-ies**) **1** what exists or is real; that which underlies appearances. **2** (foll. by *of*) the real nature or truth of (a thing) (*the reality of the situation*). **3** one's true personal situation and the problems that exist in one's life (*she's lost touch with reality*). **4** a real aspect or condition of something, esp. one that cannot be avoided (*snow is one of the realities of Canadian winter*). **5** resemblance to an original (*the model was impressive in its reality*). ☐ **in reality** in fact.

reality check *n. N Amer.* an occasion on which one consciously confronts reality, esp. in contrast with one's desires, expectations, beliefs, habits, etc.

realize *v.tr.* **1** (often foll. by *that* + clause) become fully aware of; accept something as fact. **2** understand clearly. **3** make (plans, dreams, ideas) happen in reality; achieve. **4 a** convert into money. **b** acquire (profit). **c** be sold for (a specified price). **5** present as real; make realistic; give apparent reality to (*the story was powerfully realized on stage*). **6** *refl.* develop one's own faculties, abilities, etc. ☐ **realizable** *adj.* **realizability** *n.* **realization** *n.* **realizer** *n.*

real life ● *n.* life lived by actual people as distinct from the world of fiction, TV, theatre, etc. ● *attrib.adj.* (usu. **real-life**) actually having occurred; not fictional or imagined (*based on real-life experiences*).

real live *attrib.adj.* often *jocular* actual; not pretended or simulated (*a real live burglar*).

really *adv.* **1** in actual fact; truly. **2** thoroughly, very (*really useful*). **3** (as a strong affirmative) seriously, I assure you. **4** (also in *interrog.*) an expression of disbelief, mild protest, or surprise.

realm /relm/ *n.* **1** *formal* a kingdom. **2** a province of some abstract conception (*the realm of possibility*). **3** a field of activity or interest (*the realm of public health*).

real money *n.* **1** current coin or banknotes; cash. **2** *informal* a large sum of money.

realpolitik /rei,ælpɒli'ti:k/ *n.* politics based on realities and material needs, rather than on morals or ideals.

real property *n.* = REAL ESTATE 1.

real time ● *n.* the actual time during which a process or event occurs. ● *attrib.adj.* (usu. **real-time**) *Computing* **1** (of a system) in which input data is processed within milliseconds so that it is available virtually immediately as feedback to the process from which it is coming, e.g. in an airline booking system. **2** (of information, an image, etc.) responding virtually immediately to changes in the state of affairs it reflects (*real-time weather forecasting*).

Realtor *n. N Amer.* **1** *proprietary* (in Canada) a member firm of the Canadian Real Estate Association. **2** (**realtor**) a real estate agent.

realty *n.* real estate.

real world ● *n.* (usu. prec. by *the*) **1** the world as it really exists as distinguished from any model of existence considered to be ideal, hypothetical, or fictitious. **2** real life as distinguished from any lifestyle considered to be sheltered or privileged. ● *adj.* (**real-world**) **1** of or pertaining to the real world, esp. consisting of harsh realities. **2** practical (*real-world knowledge*).

ream¹ *n.* **1** twenty quires or 500 (formerly 480) sheets of paper. **2** (in *pl.*) a large quantity of paper, writing, or printed matter (*wrote reams about it*).

ream² *v.tr.* **1** widen (a hole in metal etc.) with a borer. **2** *N Amer.* extract the juice from (fruit) with a reamer. ☐ **ream a person out** *N Amer. informal* reprimand a person harshly.

reamer *n.* **1** a tool for enlarging or finishing drilled holes. **2** *N Amer.* a kitchen implement with a central ridged dome on which a half fruit can be pressed down and turned to extract its juice.

reap *v.tr.* **1** cut (a crop, esp. grain) as a harvest. **2** gather or harvest the crop of (a field etc.). **3** receive as the consequence of one's own or others' actions.

reaper *n.* **1** a person who reaps. **2** esp. *hist.* a machine for reaping. **3** (**Reaper**) (prec. by *the*) = GRIM REAPER.

rear¹ ● *n.* **1** the back part of anything. **2** the space behind, or position at the back of, anything. **3** (also **rear end**) *informal* the buttocks. **4** the hindmost part of an army or fleet. ● *adj.* at the back. ☐ **bring up the rear** come last. **in the rear** behind; at the back.

rear² *v.* **1** *tr.* **a** bring up and educate (children). **b** breed and care for (animals). **2** *intr.* (usu. foll. by *up*) **a** (of a horse etc.) raise itself on its hind legs. **b** get up, rise (*she reared up from the bench*). **3** *tr.* **a** set upright. **b** build. **c** hold up. **4** *intr.* extend to a great height. ☐ **rear back** *N Amer. Baseball* (of a pitcher) lean back on one leg before lurching forward to throw a pitch. **rear** (or **raise**) **its** (**ugly**) **head** (of a situation, problem, etc.) make an (unwelcome) appearance. ☐ **rearing** *n.*

realign *v.tr.*
realignment *n.*
reallocate *v.tr.*
reallocation *n.*
reanalysis *n.*

reanalyze *v.tr.*
reanimate *v.tr.*
reanimation *n.*
reappear *v.intr.*
reappearance *n.*

reapplication *n.*
reapply *v.tr. & intr.*
(**-ies, -ied**)
reappoint *v.tr.*
reappointment *n.*

reapportion *v.tr.*
reapportionment *n.*
reappraisal *n.*
reappraise *v.tr.*

rear admiral *n.* (also **Rear Admiral**) a naval officer ranking below a vice admiral. Abbr.: **RAdm.**

rear-end *v.tr. N Amer.* (of a car, truck, etc., or its driver) crash into the back of (another vehicle).

rear-ender *n. N Amer. informal* a collision in which one vehicle rear-ends another.

rearguard *n.* **1** a body of troops detached to protect the rear, esp. in retreats. **2** a defensive or conservative element in an organization etc. **3** *Hockey slang* a defenceman.

rearguard action *n.* **1** *Military* an engagement undertaken by a rearguard. **2** a defensive stand in an argument etc., esp. when losing.

rearmost *adj.* furthest back; last.

rear-view mirror *n.* (also **rear-view**) a mirror fixed inside the windshield of a car, truck, etc. enabling the driver to see traffic etc. behind.

rearward ● *adv.* towards the rear. ● *adj.* located at or towards the rear.

rear-wheel drive *n.* a drive system in a car etc. in which engine power operates through the rear wheels alone.

reason ● *n.* **1** a motive, cause, or justification. **2** a fact adduced or serving as this (*give me one good reason why I should let you*). ¶The well-established idioms *the reason why* and *the reason is because* continue to be strongly criticized as redundant by many teachers of composition in spite of a long history of literary use by respected writers. To avoid such criticism, one can use *the reason* for the former and *the reason is that* for the latter. **3** the intellectual faculty by which conclusions are drawn from premises. **4** sanity (*has lost his reason*). **5** sense; sensible conduct; what is right or practical or practicable; moderation. **6** a faculty transcending the understanding and providing a priori principles; intuition. ● *v.* **1** *intr.* form or try to reach conclusions by connected thought. **2** *intr.* (foll. by *with*) use an argument (with a person) by way of persuasion. **3** *tr.* (foll. by *that* + clause) conclude or assert in argument. **4** *tr.* (foll. by *out*) think or work out (consequences etc.). □ **by reason of** owing to. **in** (or **within**) **reason** within the bounds of sense or moderation. **it stands to reason** (often foll. by *that* + clause) it is evident or logical. **listen to reason** be persuaded to act sensibly. **see reason** acknowledge the force of an argument. **with reason** justifiably. □ **reasoned** *adj.* **reasoner** *n.* **reasoning** *n.*

reasonable *adj.* **1** having sound judgment; moderate; ready to listen to reason. **2** in accordance with reason; not absurd. **3 a** within the limits of reason; fair, moderate (*a reasonable request*). **b** inexpensive; not extortionate. **c** fairly good, average. □ **reasonableness** *n.* **reasonably** *adv.*

reassure *v.tr.* **1** restore confidence to; dispel the apprehensions of. **2** confirm; assure again. □ **reassurance** *n.* **reassuring** *adj.* **reassuringly** *adv.*

Reb *n.* a traditional Jewish courtesy title used preceding a man's forename or surname.

rebar /ˈriːbɑr/ *n.* a steel reinforcing rod in concrete.

rebate¹ ● *n.* **1** a partial refund of money paid. **2** a deduction from a sum to be paid; a discount. ● *v.tr.* pay back as a rebate. □ **rebatable** *adj.*

rebate² *n. & v.tr.* = RABBET.

rebbe /ˈrebə/ *n.* **1** a Jewish religious leader or rabbi. **2** (**Rebbe**) a title of respect used for a Hasidic religious leader.

Rebekah /rəˈbekə/ *n.* a member of a women's social and charitable society allied with the Oddfellows.

rebel ● *n.* /ˈrebəl/ **1** a person who fights against, resists, or refuses allegiance to, the established government. **2** a person who resists authority, control, or convention. ● *adj.* /ˈrebəl/ (*attrib.*) **1** rebellious. **2** of or concerning rebels. **3** in rebellion. ● *v.intr.* /rəˈbel, rɪ-/ (**rebelled, rebelling**) (often foll. by *against*) **1** act as a rebel; revolt. **2** feel or display repugnance.

rebellion *n.* **1** open resistance to authority, esp. organized armed resistance to an established government. **2** an instance of this.

rebellious *adj.* **1** tending to rebel; insubordinate. **2** in rebellion. **3** defying lawful authority. **4** (of a thing) unmanageable, refractory. □ **rebelliously** *adv.* **rebelliousness** *n.*

rebind *v.tr.* (*past* and *past part.* **rebound**) bind (esp. a book) again or differently.

rebirth /riːˈbɜrθ, ˈriː-/ *n.* **1** a new incarnation. **2** spiritual enlightenment. **3** a revival (*the rebirth of learning*).

reboot *Computing* ● *v.tr. & intr.* boot up (a system) again. ● *n.* an act or instance of rebooting.

reborn *adj.* **1** having experienced a complete spiritual change; born-again. **2** existing or active again; brought back to life. **3** having experienced a profound transformation.

rebound¹ ● *v.* **1** *intr.* spring back after action or impact. **2** *intr.* make a recovery (*gold prices are beginning to rebound*). **3** /ˈriːbaʊnd/ *tr. & intr.* *Basketball* recover (a ball) that has bounced off the backboard or rim of the basket. **4** *intr.* (foll. by *upon*) (of an action) have an adverse effect upon (the doer). ● *n.* **1** the act or an instance of rebounding; recovery. **2** *Sport* a puck, ball, etc. which has bounced back from the goal, basket, etc. or been let loose by the goaltender. ● *attrib.adj.* (of a medical condition, illness, etc.) occurring again (*a rebound earache*). □ **on the rebound 1** while still recovering from an emotional shock, esp. rejection by a lover. **2** while bouncing back (*scored on the rebound*). □ **rebounder** *n.* **rebounding** *n.*

rebound² *past and past part. of* REBIND.

rebroadcast ● *v.tr.* (*past* **-cast** or **-casted**; *past part.* **-cast**) **1** broadcast (a program received from another station). **2** broadcast again. ● *n.* **1** the action or act of rebroadcasting a program. **2** a repeat broadcast.

rebuff ● *n.* **1** a rejection of one who makes advances, offers help or sympathy, shows interest or curiosity, makes a request, etc. **2** a repulse; a snub. ● *v.tr.* reject, disregard; give a rebuff to.

rebuild ● *v.* (*past* and *past part.* **rebuilt**) **1** *tr.* build (a car, house, etc.) again from new or previously used parts and materials. **2** *tr. & intr.* make or become successful, functional, etc. again. **3** *tr.* re-establish or revive (confidence, a country's economy, etc.). ● *n.* (esp. of a car or car part, such as an engine) something that has been or needs to be rebuilt.

rebuke ● *v.tr.* scold or reprimand harshly; subject to protest or censure. ● *n.* a stern reprimand or reproof. □ **rebuker** *n.* **rebukingly** *adv.*

---

rearm *v.tr. & intr.*
rearmament *n.*
rearrange *v.tr.*
rearrangement *n.*
rearranging *n.*

rearrest *v.tr. & n.*
reassemble *v.intr. & tr.*
reassembly *n.*
reassert *v.tr.*

reassertion *n.*
reassess *v.tr.*
reassessment *n.*
reassign *v.tr.*

reassignment *n.*
reattach *v.tr.*
reawaken *v.tr. & intr.*
reawakening *n.*

rebus /ˈriːbəs/ n. a type of puzzle or visual pun in which a word is represented by pictures etc. suggesting its parts.

rebut /rəˈbʌt, ri-/ v.tr. (**rebutted, rebutting**) **1** refute or disprove (evidence or a charge). **2** oppose, turn back (an opponent). □ **rebuttable** adj. **rebuttal** n.

rec¹ adj. N Amer. **1** recreation (rec centre). **2** recreational (rec league).

rec² abbr. record (on a button on a VCR etc.).

recalcitrant /rəˈkælsɪtrənt, ri-/ ● adj. **1** resisting discipline or authority; obstinately disobedient (a recalcitrant child). **2** difficult to manage or operate (a recalcitrant lock). ● n. a recalcitrant person. □ **recalcitrance** n.

recall ● v.tr. **1** recollect, remember. **2 a** summon a person to return (a player recalled from the minors). **b** request the return of something, esp. a manufactured product with a defect. **3** bring back to memory; serve as a reminder of (that picture recalls a funny story I once heard). **4** revoke or annul (an action or decision). ● n. **1** the act or an instance of recalling, esp. a summons to come back. **2** a request for the return of a faulty product. **3** the ability to remember. **4** N Amer. removal of an elected official from office. □ **beyond recall** that cannot be brought back to the original state or cancelled (damaged beyond recall).

recant v. **1** tr. withdraw and renounce (a former belief or statement) as erroneous or heretical. **2** intr. disavow a former opinion, esp. with a public confession of error. □ **recantation** n. **recanter** n.

recap informal ● v.tr. & intr. (**recapped, recapping**) recapitulate; give a summary. ● n. a recapitulation; a summary or review.

recapitulate v.tr. **1** go briefly through (the main points of a speech, argument, etc.) again; summarize. **2** repeat and reflect (an event).

recapitulation n. **1** the act or an instance of recapitulating. **2** Music part of a movement, esp. in sonata form, in which themes from the exposition are restated.

recapture ● v.tr. **1** capture again; recover or regain. **2** experience (a past emotion etc.) again. ● n. the act or an instance of recapturing.

recast ● v.tr. (past and past part. **recast**) **1** put into a new form. **2** change the cast of (a play etc.). ● n. **1** the act or an instance of recasting. **2** a recast form.

recede v.intr. **1** withdraw or move backwards from a previous position or away from an observer, or appear to do so. **2** fade, become remote (hopes of a settlement are receding). **3** slope backwards (a receding chin). **4** decline in force, value, or significance. **5** (foll. by from) withdraw or retreat from (an engagement, promise, etc.). **6** (of a person's hair) cease to grow at the front, sides, etc. (receding hairline).

receipt ● n. **1** the act or an instance of receiving or being received into one's possession (will pay on receipt of the goods). **2** a printed or written acknowledgement of the acceptance of goods or payment of money. **3** a printed statement issued by a cashier to a customer detailing the items purchased and the means of payment. **4** (usu. in pl.) an amount of money etc. received (gate receipts). ● v.tr. acknowledge the receipt of (a sum of money, etc.) by issuing a printed or written statement. □ **in receipt of** having received. □ **receipted** adj.

receivable ● adj. **1** capable of being received. **2** (of

bills, accounts, etc.) for which money has not yet been received. ● n. (in pl.) debts owed to a business, esp. regarded as assets.

receive v. **1** tr. acquire or accept (something offered or given). **2** tr. accept delivery of (something sent). **3** tr. be granted or have conferred upon one (received many honours; received a degree). **4** tr. experience (received an injury). **5** tr. consent to hear (a confession or oath) or consider (a petition). **6** tr. welcome or entertain as a guest, esp. formally (she received visitors in the afternoon). **7** tr. react to, esp. in a specified manner (the book was well received). **8** tr. allow a person to enter as a guest, member, etc. (was received into the priesthood). **9** tr. apprehend mentally (I received the impression he was lying). **10** tr. convert (broadcast signals) into sound or pictures. **11** tr. & intr. Tennis be the player to whom the server serves (the ball). **12** tr. & intr. N Amer. Football be the player or team to whom the offensive team kicks the ball. **13** tr. be able to hold (a specified amount) or bear (a specified weight). **14** tr. buy or accept (stolen goods) knowing that they are stolen. □ **be at** (or **on**) **the receiving end** informal bear the brunt of something unpleasant.

received adj. generally accepted as authoritative or true (received opinion).

receiver n. **1** a person or thing that receives. **2 a** the part of a machine or instrument that receives sound, signals, etc. **b** the apparatus contained within the earpiece of a telephone. **c** the handset of a telephone. **3** (in full **official receiver**) a person appointed by a court to manage the property of a bankrupt or insane person, or property under litigation. **4** an apparatus, such as a radio etc., that receives signals transmitted as electromagnetic waves. **5** N Amer. Football (in full **wide receiver**) a player on the offensive team who is eligible to catch passes from the quarterback. **6** a person who receives stolen goods.

receiver general n. (pl. **receivers general**) an official appointed to receive public revenues.

receivership n. **1** the state of being dealt with by a receiver (in receivership). **2** the position of receiver.

receiving order n. Cdn & Brit. an order of a court authorizing an official receiver (see RECEIVER 3) to act.

recent ● adj. **1** not long past; that happened, appeared, began to exist, or existed lately. **2** not long established; lately begun; modern. **3** (**Recent**) Geol. = HOLOCENE. ● n. Geol. = HOLOCENE. □ **recently** adv.

receptacle n. **1** a container in which something is stored or deposited. **2** esp. N Amer. an electrical outlet. **3** Bot. **a** the common base of floral organs. **b** the part of a leaf or thallus in some algae where the reproductive organs are situated. **4** Zool. an organ or structure which receives a secretion, eggs, sperm, etc.

reception n. **1** the act or an instance of receiving or the process of being received, esp. of a person into a place or group. **2** the manner in which a person or thing is received (got a cool reception). **3** a formal social event to which guests are invited to mark some occasion, e.g. a wedding. **4** a place where guests or clients etc. report on arrival at a hotel, office, etc. **5 a** the receiving of broadcast signals. **b** the quality of this (the reception is very good). **6** N Amer. Football a catch of a ball thrown by the quarterback.

receptionist n. a person employed in an organization to welcome and direct visitors, answer the telephone, etc.

---

recalculate v.tr.   **recalculation** n.

reception room n. **1** a room in an office or building for the reception of clients, patients, visitors, etc. **2** a large room in a restaurant, hotel, etc., where a large party or reception may be held.

receptive adj. **1** quick or able to receive impressions or ideas. **2** (often foll. by to) willing or anxious to hear, acknowledge, or accept; open (was receptive to suggestions; a receptive audience). **3** concerned with receiving stimuli etc. □ **receptivity** n.

receptor n. (often attrib.) Biol. **1** a cell or group of cells, found in the eyes, ears, nose, etc., specialized to detect a particular stimulus, such as light, heat, or a drug, and to initiate the transmission of impulses via the sensory nerves. **2** a region in a tissue or molecule in a cell (esp. in a membrane) which specifically recognizes and responds to a complimentary molecule, such as a hormone, or other substance.

recess ● n. **1** N Amer. a short break between classes, esp. in elementary school. **2** a temporary cessation from work, esp. of Parliament or a court. **3** a space set back in a wall; a niche. **4** (often in pl.) a hidden, isolated, or secret place (the innermost recesses). **5** Anat. a fold or indentation in an organ. ● v. **1** tr. make a recess in. **2** tr. place in a recess; set back. **3** intr. N Amer. take a recess; adjourn.

recessed adj. placed in such a way as to be flush or set back from the surface in which it is set.

recession n. **1** a temporary decline in economic activity or prosperity associated with lower levels of production and employment. **2** a receding or withdrawal from a place or point. **3** a receding part of an object; a recess. □ **recessionary** adj.

recessional ● adj. **1** of or pertaining to a recession or recessions. **2** (of a hymn or other piece of music) sung or played while the clergy etc. withdraw after a service. ● n. a recessional hymn.

recession-proof adj. (of a business, market, city, etc.) unaffected by economic recession.

recessive ● adj. **1** Genetics (of an inherited characteristic) appearing in offspring only when not masked by a dominant characteristic inherited from one parent. **2** tending to recede. **3** of or relating to an economic recession. ● n. **1** an individual in which a particular recessive allele or gene is expressed. **2** an allele that does not function when two different alleles are present in the cells of an organism; a recessive allele.

recharge ● v. **1** tr. put a fresh charge in; refill. **2** tr. restore an electric charge to (a battery or piece of equipment powered by batteries). **3** intr. (of a battery etc.) be recharged. **4** intr. (of a person) recover energy by resting or relaxing for a short time. ● n. a renewed charge. □ **rechargeable** adj. & n. **recharger** n.

recharger n. a device for recharging batteries or equipment powered by batteries.

recherché /rəˈʃɛrʃei/ adj. **1** carefully sought out; rare or exotic. **2** far-fetched, obscure.

recidivist /rəˈsɪdɪvɪst, ri-/ n. a person who relapses into crime. □ **recidivism** n.

recipe n. **1** a statement of the ingredients and procedure required for preparing a dish. **2** a means of achieving or attaining something (a recipe for success).

recipient ● n. a person who receives something. ● adj. **1** receiving. **2** receptive.

reciprocal /rəˈsɪprəkəl, ri-/ ● adj. **1** in return (a reciprocal greeting). **2** mutual (their feelings are reciprocal). **3** Grammar (of a pronoun) expressing mutual action or relation (as in each other). **4** inversely correspondent; complementary (natural kindness matched by a reciprocal severity). ● n. **1** a thing corresponding in some way to another; an equivalent or counterpart. **2** Math. an expression or function so related to another that their product is unity ($\frac{1}{2}$ is the reciprocal of 2). □ **reciprocally** adv.

reciprocate /rəˈsɪprəˌkeit, ri-/ v. **1** tr. return or requite (affection etc.). **2** intr. (foll. by with) offer or give something in return. **3** tr. give and receive mutually; interchange. **4 a** intr. (of a part of a machine) move backwards and forwards. **b** tr. cause to do this.

reciprocity /ˌrɛsəˈprɒsɪti/ n. (pl. -ies) **1** the act or condition of being reciprocal. **2** give and take. **3** a mutual exchange of advantages or privileges as a basis for commercial relations between two countries.

recital n. **1** the act or an instance of reciting or being recited. **2** the performance of a program of instrumental music, song, or dance, by a soloist or small group. **3** (foll. by of) a detailed account of (connected things or facts); a narrative. **4** Cdn & Brit. Law the part of a legal document that states the facts. □ **recitalist** n. (in sense 2).

recitation /ˌrɛsəˈteiʃən/ n. **1** the act or an instance of reciting, esp. the act of repeating a text from memory or of reading a text aloud before an audience. **2** a thing recited.

recitative /ˌrɛsətəˈtiːv/ n. **1** declamatory speech-like singing used esp. in opera or oratorio for advancing the plot (compare ARIA, ARIOSO). **2** a passage or part of a musical score given in this form.

recite v. **1** tr. repeat aloud or declaim (a poem or passage) from memory, esp. before an audience. **2** intr. give a recitation. **3** tr. mention in order; enumerate (she recited her accomplishments). **4** tr. give a detailed description or account of. □ **reciter** n.

reckless adj. disregarding the consequences or danger etc.; lacking caution; rash. □ **recklessly** adv. **recklessness** n.

reckon v. **1** tr. count or compute by calculation. **2** tr. **a** (often foll. by that + clause) conclude after calculation. **b** informal (foll. by to + infin.) expect (reckons to finish by Friday). **c** informal think, suppose (reckon it'll rain today?). **3** intr. (foll. by on) rely on, count on, or base plans on (didn't reckon on it being so hard). **4** tr. (usu. in passive) consider or regard (she is reckoned an authority on the subject). **5** tr. (foll. by in) count in or include in computation. **6** intr. (foll. by with) **a** take into account. **b** settle accounts with. **7** intr. make calculations; add up an account or sum. □ **to be reckoned with** (or **to reckon with**) of considerable importance; not to be ignored or taken lightly (they are a force to be reckoned with).

reckoning n. **1** the act or an instance of counting or calculating. **2** an opinion or judgment. **3 a** the settlement of an account. **b** an account. □ **day of reckoning** the time when something must be atoned for or avenged.

reclaim ● v.tr. **1** seek the return of (one's property, etc.). **2** make wasteland fit for cultivating, esp. by

---

recheck v.tr. & intr. & n.   **rechristen** v.tr.   **recirculate** v.tr. & intr.   **recirculation** n.

draining it. **3** recover raw material from waste products so that it can be used again. **4 a** win back or away from vice or error; reform. **b** tame, civilize. ● *n.* the act or an instance of reclaiming; the process of being reclaimed. □ **reclaimed** *adj.* **reclamation** *n.*

recline *vtr & intr.* lie or cause to lie backwards in a horizontal or leaning position, esp. in resting *(reclined in the chair; reclined the seat back).* □ **reclining** *adj.*

recliner *n.* a comfortable chair for reclining in, usu. with adjustable back and footrest.

recluse /rə'klu:s, ri-/ *n.* a person preferring or living in seclusion or isolation. □ **reclusive** *adj.*

recognition *n.* **1** the action or an act of recognizing a person or thing; the fact of being recognized. **2** the acknowledgement or admission of a service, achievement, ability, etc.; appreciation, acclaim. **3** formal sanction or approval. **4** the mental process whereby things are identified as having been previously apprehended or as belonging to a known category. **5** (also **diplomatic recognition**) the process by which a country declares that another political entity fulfills the conditions of statehood and acknowledges its willingness to deal with it as a member of the international community. **6** the identification of printed characters using photoelectric devices (see OPTICAL CHARACTER RECOGNITION). □ **beyond recognition** to such a degree that it cannot be recognized *(changed beyond recognition).*

recognizance /rə'kɒɡnizəns, -'kɒn-/ *n.* **1** a bond by which a person undertakes before a court or magistrate to observe some condition, e.g. to appear when summoned. **2** a sum pledged as surety for this.

recognize *vtr.* **1** identify (a person or thing) as already known; know again. **2** discover the nature of, esp. by some distinctive feature *(I can always recognize a phony).* **3** (foll. by *that*) realize or admit. **4** acknowledge the existence, validity, character, or claims of. **5** show appreciation of; reward. **6** (foll. by *as, for*) treat or acknowledge. **7** (of a chairperson etc.) allow (a person) to speak in a debate etc. **8** grant diplomatic recognition to (a country). □ **recognizable** *adj.* **recognizability** *n.* **recognizably** *adv.* **recognizer** *n.*

recoil ● *v.intr.* **1** suddenly move or spring back in fear, horror, or disgust. **2** shrink mentally in this way. **3** rebound after an impact. **4** (foll. by *on, upon*) have an adverse reactive effect on (the originator). **5** (of a gun) be driven backwards by its discharge. ● *n.* **1** the act or an instance of recoiling. **2** the sensation of recoiling. **3** the extent to which a gun etc. recoils when discharged. □ **recoilless** *adj.* (in sense 5).

recollect /,rekə'lekt/ *vtr.* **1** remember. **2** succeed in remembering; call to mind.

recollection *n.* **1** the act or power of recollecting. **2** a thing recollected. **3 a** a person's memory *(to the best of my recollection).* **b** the time over which memory extends *(happened within my recollection).*

Récollet /'rekəlei/ *n.* a member of the reformed branch of the Franciscan Observants, founded in France in the late 16th c., and active in New France.

recombinant /ri:'kɒmbənənt/ *adj. Biol.* (of a gene etc.) formed by recombination.

recombinant DNA *n.* DNA that has been recombined using constituents from different sources.

recombination *n. Biol.* the rearrangement, esp. by crossing over in chromosomes, of genes to form a combination different from that of its parents.

recombine *vtr. & intr.* combine again or differently.

recommend *vtr.* **1 a** suggest as fit for some purpose or use. **b** suggest (a person) as suitable for a particular position. **2** (often foll. by *that* + clause or *to* + infin.) advise as a course of action etc. *(I recommend that you stay where you are).* **3** (of qualities, conduct, etc.) make acceptable or desirable *(a plan with little to recommend it).* □ **recommendable** *adj.* **recommendation** *n.* **recommender** *n.*

recompense /'rekəm,pens/ ● *vtr.* **1** make amends to (a person) or for (a loss etc.); compensate. **2** make repayment to (a person) for (a thing, action, service, etc.). ● *n.* **1** a repayment, reward, or requital. **2** retribution; satisfaction given for an injury.

recon /rə'kɒn/ *n.* (often *attrib.*) esp. *US slang* military reconnaissance.

reconcile *vtr.* **1** make friendly again after an estrangement. **2** (usu. in *refl.* or *passive;* foll. by *to*) make acquiescent or contentedly submissive to (something disagreeable or unwelcome) *(was reconciled to failure).* **3** settle (a quarrel etc.). **4 a** harmonize; make compatible. **b** show the compatibility of by argument or in practice *(cannot reconcile your views with the facts).* □ **reconcilability** *n.* **reconcilable** *adj.* **reconciliatory** *adj.*

reconciliation *n.* **1** an act or an instance of reconciling. **2** = PENANCE 2a. **3** *Accounting* the action or practice of making one account consistent with another, esp. by allowing for transactions begun but not yet completed.

reconnaissance /rə'kɒnəsəns, ri-/ *n.* **1** a survey of a region, esp. a military examination to locate an enemy or ascertain strategic features. **2** a preliminary survey or inspection.

reconnoitre /,rekə'nɔitər/ (also **reconnoiter**) ● *v.* **1** *tr.* make a reconnaissance of (an area, enemy position, etc.). **2** *intr.* make a reconnaissance. ● *n.* a reconnaissance.

reconstitute *vtr.* **1** build up again from parts; reconstruct. **2** restore the previous constitution of (dried food etc.) by adding water. □ **reconstitution** *n.*

reconstruct *vtr.* **1** build or form again. **2 a** form a mental or visual impression of (past events) by assembling the evidence for them. **b** re-enact (a crime). **3** reorganize. □ **reconstructive** *adj.*

---

reclassification *n.*	**recommencement** *n.*	**recomputation** *n.*	**reconfirmation** *n.*
reclassify *v.tr.*	**recommit** *v.tr.*	**recompute** *v.tr.*	**reconnect** *v.tr.*
(-ies, -ied)	**(recommitted,**	**reconceptualization** *n.*	**reconnection** *n.*
reclothe *v.tr.*	**recommitting)**	**reconceptualize** *v.tr.*	**reconquer** *v.tr.*
recode *v.tr.*	**recommitment** *n.*	**recondition** *v.tr.*	**reconquest** *n.*
recolonization *n.*	**recommittal** *n.*	**reconfiguration** *n.*	**reconsider** *v.tr. & intr.*
recolonize *v.tr.*	**recompose** *v.tr.*	**reconfigure** *v.tr.*	**reconsideration** *n.*
recommence *v.tr. & intr.*	**recomposition** *n.*	**reconfirm** *v.tr.*	

reconstruction *n.* **1** the act or a mode of reconstructing. **2** a thing reconstructed. **3** (**Reconstruction**) *US hist.* the period (1865-77) following the Civil War. **4** the rebuilding of, and restoration of economic stability to, an area devastated by war.

reconvert *v.tr.* convert back to a former state.

record ● *n.* **1 a** a piece of evidence or information constituting an (esp. official) account of something that has occurred, been said, etc. **b** a document preserving this. **2** the state of being set down or preserved in writing or some other permanent form (*is a matter of record*). **3 a** a thin plastic disc carrying recorded sound in grooves on each surface, for reproduction by a record player. **b** a trace made on this or some other medium, e.g. magnetic tape. **4 a** an official report of the proceedings and judgment in a court of justice. **b** a copy of the pleadings etc. constituting a case to be decided by a court. **5 a** the facts known about a person's past. **b** a piece of evidence about the past or several such pieces cumulatively (*the fossil record*). **6** (in full **criminal record**) **a** a list of a person's previous criminal convictions. **b** a history of being convicted for crime (*has a record*). **7** the best performance (esp. in sport) or most remarkable event of its kind on record (often *attrib.*: *record low temperatures*). **8** an object serving as a memorial of a person or thing; a portrait. **9** *Computing* a number of related items of information which are handled as a unit. ● *v.tr.* **1** set down in writing or some other permanent form for later reference, esp. as an official record. **2** convert (sound, a broadcast, etc.) into permanent form for later reproduction. **3** establish or constitute a historical or other record of. ▢ **break** (or **beat**) **the record** outdo all previous performances etc. **for the record** as an official statement etc. **go on record** state one's opinion or judgment openly or officially, so that it is recorded. **a matter of record** a thing established as a fact by being recorded. **off the record** as an unofficial or confidential statement etc. **on record** officially recorded; publicly known. **set** (or **put** or **get**) **the record straight** correct a misapprehension. ▢ **recordability** *n.* **recordable** *adj.*

record-breaking *attrib.adj.* that breaks a record (*see* RECORD *n.* 7).

recorder *n.* **1** an apparatus for recording, esp. a tape recorder. **2 a** a keeper of records. **b** a person who makes an official record. **3** *Music* a reedless cylindrical wind instrument, played by blowing directly into one end while covering differing combinations of holes along the cylinder.

record holder *n.* a person who holds a record (*see* RECORD *n.* 7).

recording *n.* **1** the process by which audio or video signals are recorded for later reproduction. **2** material or a program recorded. **3** the compact disc, record, or tape so produced.

recording artist *n.* a musician or singer who records performances for reproduction and sale under contract to a record company.

record player *n.* an apparatus for reproducing sound from phonograph records by means of a turntable and stylus.

recount[1] /rə'kaunt, ri-/ *v.tr.* **1** narrate. **2** tell in detail.

recount[2] ● *v.tr.* /'ri:kaunt, ri:'kaunt/ count again. ● *n.* /'ri:kaunt/ a recounting, esp. of votes.

recoup *v.tr.* **1** recover or regain (a loss). **2** compensate or reimburse for a loss.

recourse /'ri:kɔrs, rɪ'kɔrs/ *n.* **1** the action or an act of turning to a possible source of help, advice, protection, etc. **2** a person or thing turned to. ▢ **have recourse to** turn to (a person or thing) for help.

recover *v.* **1** *tr.* regain possession or use or control of; reclaim. **2** *intr.* return to health or consciousness or to a normal state or position (*the country never recovered from the war*). **3** *tr.* obtain or secure (compensation etc.) by legal process. **4** *tr.* retrieve or make up for (a loss, setback, etc.). **5** *refl.* regain composure or consciousness or control of one's limbs. **6** *tr.* retrieve (reusable substances) from industrial waste. ▢ **recoverability** *n.* **recoverable** *adj.* **recovering** *adj.*

re-cover *v.tr.* **1** cover again. **2** provide (a chair etc.) with a new cover.

recovery *n.* (*pl.* **-ies**) **1** the act or an instance of recovering; the process of being recovered. **2** the process of overcoming an addiction to drugs etc.

recreate *v.tr.* create over again. ▢ **recreation** *n.*

recreation *n.* **1** the process or means of entertaining oneself. **2** an activity or pastime pursued, esp. habitually, for the pleasure or interest it gives (often *attrib.*: *recreation centre*). ▢ **recreationist** *n.*

recreational *adj.* **1** of or pertaining to recreation. **2** used for recreation (*recreational facilities*). **3** designating or relating to the taking of a drug on an occasional basis for pleasure, esp. when socializing. ▢ **recreationally** *adv.*

recreational vehicle *n.* a van or camper used for recreational purposes, such as touring and camping, esp. a large motorhome. Abbr.: **RV.**

recreation room *n.* N Amer. **1** = REC ROOM. **2** a room in a school, hospital, etc. in which people can relax, play games, etc.

recriminate *v.intr.* make mutual or counter accusations. ▢ **recrimination** *n.*

rec room *n.* N Amer. a room in a house, usu. in the basement, used for relaxation and entertainment.

recruit ● *n.* **1** a serviceman or servicewoman newly enlisted and not yet fully trained. **2** a new employee or member of a society or organization. ● *v.* **1** *tr.* enlist (a person) as a recruit. **b** attempt to hire or enrol (a person) (*recruit new members*). **2** *tr.* form (an army etc.) by enlisting recruits. **3** *intr.* get or seek recruits. **4** *tr.* N Amer. (attempt to) induce (an athlete) to sign on as a student at a college or university. ▢ **recruiter** *n.* **recruitment** *n.*

recta *pl. of* RECTUM.

rectal *adj.* of or relating to the rectum.

rectangle *n.* a plane figure with four straight sides and four right angles, esp. one with the adjacent sides unequal.

rectangular *adj.* **1 a** shaped like a rectangle. **b** having the base or sides or section shaped like a rectangle. **2 a** placed at right angles. **b** having parts or lines placed at right angles.

---

recontextualization *n.*　**reconvene** *v.tr. & intr.*　**recriminalize** *v.*　**recrystallization** *n.*
recontextualize *v.tr.*　**recriminalization** *n.*　**recross** *v.tr. & intr.*　**recrystallize** *v.tr. & intr.*

rectangular coordinate *n.* (usu. in *pl.*) each of a set of coordinates measured along axes at right angles to one another.

rectifier *n.* **1** *Electricity* an electrical device that allows a current to flow preferentially in one direction by converting an alternating current into a direct one. **2** a person or thing that rectifies.

rectify *v.tr.* (**-ies, -ied**) **1** adjust or make right; correct, amend. **2** purify or refine, esp. by repeated distillation. **3** find a straight line equal in length to (a curve). **4** convert (alternating current) to direct current. □ **rectifiable** *adj.* **rectification** *n.*

rectilinear /ˌrɛktɪˈlɪnɪər/ *adj.* (also **rectilineal** /-nɪəl/) **1** bounded or characterized by straight lines. **2** in or forming a straight line. □ **rectilinearity** /-ˈærɪti/ *n.*

rectitude *n.* **1** moral uprightness. **2** righteousness. **3** correctness.

recto *n.* (*pl.* **-os**) **1** the right-hand page of an open book. **2** the front of a printed leaf of paper or manuscript (*opp.* VERSO 1b).

rector *n.* **1 a** (in the Church of England) the incumbent of a parish where all tithes formerly passed to the incumbent (*compare* VICAR 1a). **b** (in other Anglican churches) a member of the clergy who has charge of a parish. **2** *Catholicism* a priest in charge of a church or religious institution. **3** the head of some schools, universities, and colleges.

rectory *n.* (*pl.* **-ies**) a rector's house.

rectum *n.* (*pl.* **-s** or **recta**) the final section of the large intestine, terminating at the anus.

recumbent /rəˈkʌmbənt, ri-/ *adj.* lying down.

recuperate *v.intr.* recover from illness, exhaustion, financial loss, etc. □ **recuperation** *n.* **recuperative** *adj.*

recur *v.intr.* (**recurred, recurring**) **1** occur again; be repeated. **2** (of a thought, idea, etc.) come back to one's mind. **3** (foll. by *to*) go back in thought or speech.

recurrent *adj.* **1** recurring; happening repeatedly. **2** (of a nerve, vein, branch, etc.) turning back so as to reverse direction. □ **recurrence** *n.* **recurrently** *adv.*

recurring decimal *n.* a decimal fraction in which the same figures are repeated indefinitely.

recurve ● *v.tr. & intr.* bend backwards. ● *n. Archery* **1** a backward-curving end of the limb of a bow. **2** a bow with this feature.

recycle *v.* **1 a** *tr.* return (material) to a previous stage of a cyclic process, esp. convert (waste) to reusable material. **b** *intr.* practise recycling; participate in a recycling program (*our household recycles!*). **2** *tr.* use again with little or no alteration (*recycle a speech*). **3** *tr.* convert (an object) into something new (*recycle a wine bottle into a vase*). □ **recyclability** *n.* **recyclable** *adj. & n.* **recycler** *n.* **recycling** *n.*

red ● *adj.* **1** of or near the colour seen at the least-refracted end of the visible spectrum, of shades ranging from that of blood to pink or deep orange. **2** flushed in the face with shame, anger, etc. **3** (of the eyes) bloodshot or red-rimmed with weeping. **4** (of the hair) reddish brown, orange. **5** involving or having to do with bloodshed, burning, violence, or revolution. **6** *informal* communist or socialist. **7** *Cdn* of or relating to the Liberal Party. **8** (**Red**) *hist.* Russian, Soviet (*the Red Army*). **9** (of wine) made from dark grapes and coloured by their skins. **10** (in the names

of animals) having red or reddish colouring. **11 a** (in the names of plants etc.) having red or reddish flowers, berries, bark, etc. **b** (in the names of vegetables) purple in colour (*red cabbage*). **c** (of potatoes) having a reddish skin. **d** (of wheat) designating a variety having reddish grains. **12** *Cards* belonging to hearts or diamonds. ● *n.* **1** a red colour or pigment. **2** red clothes or material (*dressed in red*). **3** *informal* a communist or socialist. **4** *Cdn informal* a Liberal. **5 a** a red ball, piece, etc., in a game etc. **b** the player using such pieces. **6** the debit side of an account (*in the red*). **7** a red light. **8** red wine. **9** *slang* a red-coloured capsule of secobarbital. **10** *N Amer. informal* a sockeye salmon. □ **reddish** *adj.* **reddy** *adj.* **redness** *n.*

red admiral *n.* a holarctic butterfly, *Vanessa atalanta*, with red bands on each pair of wings.

red alert *n.* **1** an urgent warning of imminent danger. **2** an instruction to prepare for an emergency. **3** a state of readiness for an emergency.

red alga *n.* a seaweed with red pigment found esp. in deep water of tropical seas.

Red Army *n.* **1** *hist.* originally, the army of the Bolsheviks, the Workers' and Peasants' Red Army; later, the army of the Soviet Union (1917–46). **2** the army of China or some other (esp. Communist) countries. **3** a left-wing extremist terrorist organization in Japan.

red-bait *v.tr. & intr.* harass and persecute (a person) on account of known or suspected Communist sympathies. □ **red-baiter** *n.* **red-baiting** *n.*

red-berry *n. Cdn* (esp. *Nfld*) (*pl.* **-ies**) **1** any of various plants bearing red berries, e.g. partridgeberry, cranberry. **2** the fruit of any of these plants.

red blood cell *n.* (also **red cell**) = ERYTHROCYTE.

red-blooded *adj.* full of life, spirited.

redbreast *n.* a robin.

red-breasted *adj.* (of a bird) having a red breast (*red-breasted merganser*).

red-brick *adj.* (of a building) made from bricks of a red-brown colour.

Red Brigades *n.* an extreme left-wing terrorist organization based in Italy, which from the early 1970s was responsible for carrying out kidnappings, murders, and acts of sabotage.

redbud *n.* any of several early-flowering leguminous trees of the genus *Cercis*, esp. the N American *C. canadensis*.

redcap *n. N Amer.* a railway porter.

red carpet *n.* **1** a strip of red carpet traditionally laid down on formal occasions to greet important visitors. **2** a ceremonial welcome; a lavish reception (*rolled out the red carpet*).

red cedar *n.* **1** any of various conifers with reddish wood, esp. (in full **eastern red cedar**) a tree-sized juniper of eastern N America, *Juniperus virginiana*, or (in full **western red cedar**) an arborvitae of western N America, *Thuja plicata*. **2** the wood of a red cedar.

red cent *n.* esp. *N Amer.* **1** the (originally copper) coin of the lowest value. **2** a trivial sum (frequently in negative contexts) (*not one red cent of taxpayers' money*).

Red Chamber *n. Cdn* **1** the Senate chamber of the Parliament Buildings in Ottawa. **2** the Senate itself.

red clover *n.* a Eurasian clover, *Trifolium pratense*, naturalized throughout N America and extensively cultivated for fodder.

recut *v.tr.* (**recutting;** *past* and *past part.* **recut**)

redcoat n. hist. **1** Cdn a member of the North West Mounted Police. **2** a British soldier.

redcurrant n. **1** a widely cultivated shrub, Ribes rubrum. **2** the small red edible berry of this plant.

redd n. a hollow in a riverbed made by a trout or salmon to spawn in.

red deer n. a large deer, Cervus elaphus, having a reddish-brown coat; a wapiti.

Red Delicious n. see DELICIOUS n.

redden v. **1** tr. & intr. make or become red. **2** intr. blush.

redeem v.tr. **1** buy back; recover by expenditure of effort or by a stipulated payment. **2** make a single payment to discharge (a regular charge or obligation). **3** convert (tickets, bonds, etc.) into goods or cash. **4** Theol. deliver from sin and damnation. **5** make up for; be a compensating factor in (has one redeeming feature). **6** (foll. by from) save from (a defect). **7** refl. compensate for past failings, esp. so as to regain favour. **8** save (a person's life) by ransom. **9** save or rescue or reclaim. **10** fulfill (a promise). □ **redeemable** adj.

redeemer n. **1** a person who redeems. **2** (**Redeemer**) Jesus Christ.

redemption n. **1** the act or an instance of redeeming; the process of being redeemed. **2** Christianity humankind's deliverance from sin and damnation. **3** a thing that redeems. □ **redemptive** adj.

redemption centre n. Cdn (Maritimes & Nfld) a place where consumers return beer bottles, pop cans, etc. and receive back the deposit paid at the time of purchase.

Redemptorist /rə'demptɒrɪst, ri-/ n. a member of the Congregation of the Most Holy Redeemer, a Catholic order of priests and lay brothers founded in 1732, devoted chiefly to preaching.

Red Ensign n. any of several predominantly red flags having the Union Jack in the upper corner along the hoist, esp.: **1** Cdn hist. one used as Canada's national flag until 1965, with the Canadian coat of arms in the fly. **2** Cdn one used as the provincial flag of Ontario or Manitoba, with the provincial coat of arms in the fly. **3** Cdn hist. one used as the flag of the Hudson's Bay Company, having the initials HBC in the fly. **4** the ensign of the British merchant navy.

red-eye n. **1** a red reflection from the blood vessels of a person's retina, seen on a colour photograph taken with a flash. **2** (in full **red-eye flight**) informal an overnight airline flight. **3** Cdn a drink made with tomato juice and beer. **4** any of various fish with red eyes, e.g. the rock bass or smallmouth bass.

red-eyed adj. **1** having red eyes from crying etc. **2** (of a bird) having eyes surrounded by a red ring.

red-faced adj. embarrassed, ashamed.

Red Fife n. Cdn a high-yielding variety of wheat, with superior milling and baking qualities, developed in the 1840s near Peterborough, Ont.

redfish n. any of various reddish fishes.

red flag ● n. **1** a warning of danger. **2** (in auto racing etc.) a red flag waved as a signal to stop. **3** a symbol of revolution, socialism, or Communism. ● v.tr. **1** (of an official) wave a red flag to stop (a race, participants, etc.). **2 a** warn (a person). **b** call attention to (issues etc.) of concern.

red fox n. the common fox of Eurasia and N America, Vulpes vulpes, having a characteristic red or fawn coat.

red giant n. a very large star of high luminosity and low surface temperature.

Red Guard n. any of various radical or socialist groups, in particular a militant youth movement in China (1966–76), who carried out vicious attacks on intellectuals and other disfavoured groups as part of Mao's Cultural Revolution.

red-handed adj. in or just after the act of committing a crime, doing wrong, etc. (caught red-handed).

redhead n. **1** a person with red hair. **2** a diving duck of N America, Aythya americana, with a reddish-chestnut head and grey and black body.

red-headed adj. **1** (of a person) having red hair. **2** (of birds etc.) having a red head (red-headed woodpecker).

red herring n. **1** dried smoked herring. **2** a misleading clue or distraction.

red-hot ● adj. **1 a** sufficiently hot to glow red. **b** very hot (the stove is red-hot). **2 a** highly exciting. **b** sexy; passionate (red-hot jazz). **3** intensely excited. **4** (of news) sensational; completely new. **5** (of a sports team, player, etc.) on a winning streak; performing exceptionally. ● n. N Amer. (**red hot**) a hot dog.

redial ● v.tr. & intr. (**redialed, redialing; redialled, redialling**) dial again. ● n. the facility on a telephone by which (in the event of a number being busy, etc.) the number just dialed may be automatically redialed by pressing a single button.

redid past of REDO.

Red Indian n. offensive a N American Indian.

red ink n. N Amer. fiscal deficit (drowning in red ink).

redirect v.tr. **1** use (resources etc.) in a different, more desirable way (redirect funds). **2** send (an object, person, etc.) in a different direction (redirect the ball). **3** change the address of (a letter). □ **redirection** n.

redistribution n. **1** the action or process of redistributing something, esp. of wealth by means of taxation. **2** Cdn the reapportioning, made every ten years, of the number of seats in the House of Commons to reflect changes in the size of the population. □ **redistributionist** n. & adj.

red-letter day n. a day that is pleasantly noteworthy or memorable.

red light n. **1** a signal to stop on a road, railway, etc. **2** a warning or refusal.

red-light district n. a district containing many brothels, strip clubs, etc.

red line ● n. **1** Hockey the centre line on the ice surface, midway between the two blue lines. **2** a red mark on a gauge, dial, etc., indicating the maximum safe value of speed, rate of working, or other quantity. ● v.tr. (**redline**) (of a bank etc.) refuse credit to (a business, neighbourhood, etc.), esp. arbitrarily.

red maple n. a maple of eastern N America, Acer rubrum, with red twigs, buds, and flowers.

red meat n. meat that is red when raw, e.g. beef.

red mullet n. a red or reddish-brown marine food fish, Mullus surmuletus, of the Mediterranean and NE Atlantic.

---

redecorate v.tr.
redecoration n.
rededicate v.tr.
rededication n.

redefine v.tr.
redefinition n.
redeploy v.tr.
redeployment n.

redesign v.tr. & n.
redevelop v.tr.
redeveloper n.
redevelopment n.

rediscover v.tr.
rediscovery n. (pl. **-ies**)
redistribute v.tr.
redistributive adj.

redneck esp. *N Amer. derogatory* ● *n.* **1** an uneducated working-class white in the southern US, esp. one holding reactionary political views. **2** anyone holding reactionary political views. ● *adj.* reactionary; conservative.

redo ● *v.tr.* (*3rd sing. present* **redoes**; *past* **redid**; *past part.* **redone**) **1** do again or differently. **2** redecorate or renovate. ● *n.* / ˈriːduː / (*pl.* **redos**) an act or instance of redoing.

red oak *n.* **1** a N American oak, *Quercus rubra*, with leaves with bristle-tipped lobes. **2** the hard reddish wood of this tree.

redolent / ˈredələnt / *adj.* **1** (foll. by *of*, *with*) strongly reminiscent or suggestive or mentally associated. **2** fragrant. **3** having a strong smell; odorous. □ **redolence** *n.* **redolently** *adv.*

redouble *v.tr. & intr.* make or grow greater or more intense or numerous; intensify (*redoubled their efforts*).

redoubt / rɪˈdaʊt / *n.* **1** *Military* an outwork or fieldwork, usu. square or polygonal and without flanking defences. **2** something serving as a refuge; an entrenched standpoint.

redoubtable *adj.* **1** formidable, esp. as an opponent. **2** (of a person) commanding respect.

red pepper *n.* the ripe fruit of the sweet pepper, *Capsicum annuum*, used as a vegetable.

red pine *n.* **1** any of several coniferous trees with reddish wood, esp. a N American pine, *Pinus resinosa*, found from Newfoundland to Manitoba. **2** the wood of this tree.

redpoll *n.* any of various holarctic finches, with red crests.

redraft ● *v.tr.* draft (a writing or document) again. ● *n.* a second or new draft.

redress ● *v.tr.* / rəˈdres, ri- / **1** remedy or rectify (a wrong or grievance etc.). **2** readjust; set straight again. ● *n.* / ˈriːdres, rəˈdres / **1** reparation for a wrong. **2** (foll. by *of*) the act or process of redressing (a grievance etc.). □ **redress the balance** restore equality.

re-dress *v.tr. & intr.* dress again or differently.

red ribbon ● *n.* **1 a** (in Canada) an award given for coming first in a contest. **b** (in the US) an award given for coming second in a contest. **2** a loop of red ribbon as a symbol of AIDS awareness. ● *adj.* designating a worthy but tokenistic concern with AIDS.

Red River cart *n. Cdn hist.* a sturdy two-wheeled wooden cart pulled by oxen or horses, used for transportation on the Prairies.

Red River jig *n. Cdn* **1** a Metis stepdance originating in the Red River valley of Manitoba, combining French-Canadian dance rhythms and Aboriginal powwow steps, including an element of improvisation by dancers who compete for originality and precise footwork. **2** the music for this.

Red River Rebellion *n. Cdn hist.* an uprising in 1869–70 by the Metis in the Red River valley in Manitoba under Louis Riel, in response to the takeover of their territory by the government of Canada.

Red Rome Beauty *n.* a large red eating and cooking apple with green streaks and tiny green dots.

red salmon *n.* = SOCKEYE.

red shift *n.* the shift of spectral lines toward longer wavelengths, arising when a galaxy or celestial body and its observer are moving apart. □ **red-shifted** *adj.*

redskin *n. dated offensive* a North American Indian.

red snapper *n.* an edible marine fish of the family Lutjanidae, esp. *Lutjanus campechinus* of the W Atlantic.

red spider *n.* = SPIDER MITE.

red spruce *n.* a spruce of eastern Canada and the northeastern US, *Picea rubens*.

red squirrel *n.* a small N American squirrel, *Tamiasciurus hudsonicus*, with reddish fur.

Red Star *n.* esp. *hist.* the emblem of some Communist countries.

redstart *n.* **1** any of various American warblers with red markings. **2** any European red-tailed songbird of the genus *Phoenicurus*.

red-tailed hawk *n.* a common North and Central American hawk, *Buteo jamaicensis*, with a russet-coloured tail.

red tape *n.* excessive bureaucracy or adherence to formalities esp. in public business.

red-throated loon *n.* a small Holarctic loon, *Gavia stellata*, with a grey head, red throat patch, and plain, uncheckered back.

red tide *n.* a discoloration of marine waters caused by an outbreak of toxic red dinoflagellates.

Red Tory *n. Cdn* a Progressive Conservative who holds more liberal views on certain esp. social issues than his or her fellow party members. □ **Red Toryism** *n.*

reduce *v.* **1** *tr. & intr.* make or become smaller or less. **2** *tr.* (foll. by *to*) bring by force or necessity (to some undesirable state or action) (*reduced them to tears*; *were reduced to begging*). **3** *tr.* convert to another (esp. simpler) form (*reduced it to a powder*). **4** *tr.* convert (a fraction) to the form with the lowest terms. **5** *tr.* (foll. by *to*) bring or simplify or adapt by classification or analysis (*the dispute may be reduced to three issues*). **6** *tr.* make lower in status or rank. **7** *tr.* lower the price of. **8** *intr.* lessen one's weight or size. **9** *tr.* weaken (*is in a very reduced state*). **10** *tr.* impoverish. **11** *tr.* subdue; bring back to obedience. **12** *intr. & tr. Chem.* **a** combine or cause to combine with hydrogen. **b** undergo or cause to undergo addition of electrons (*opp.* OXIDIZE 3). **13** *tr. Chem.* convert (oxide etc.) to metal. **14** *tr. Photog.* make (a negative or print) less dense. **15** *tr. Cooking* boil so as to concentrate (a liquid, sauce, etc.). □ **reduce to the ranks** demote (an NCO) to the rank of private. □ **reducer** *n.* **reducible** *adj.*

reduction *n.* **1** the act or an instance of reducing; the process of being reduced. **2** an amount by which prices etc. are reduced. **3** a reduced copy of a picture, map, etc. **4** an arrangement of an orchestral score for piano etc. □ **reductive** *adj.* **reductively** *adv.* **reductiveness** *n.*

reductionism *n.* **1** the tendency to or principle of analyzing complex things into simple constituents. **2** often *derogatory* the doctrine that a system can be fully understood in terms of its isolated parts, or an idea in terms of simple concepts (*compare* HOLISM 1). □ **reductionist** *n.* **reductionistic** *adj.*

redundant *adj.* **1** superfluous. **2** that can be omitted without any loss of significance. **3** (of a person) no longer needed at work and therefore unemployed. **4** *Engin. & Computing* (of a component) not needed but included in case of failure in another component. □ **redundancy** *n.* (*pl.* **-ies**). **redundantly** *adv.*

reduplicate *v.tr.* repeat (a letter or syllable or word) exactly or with a slight change, e.g. hurly-burly, seesaw. □ **reduplication** *n.*

redux /rɪ'dʌks/ *adj.* brought back, revived, restored (placed after noun: *romance redux*).

red willow *n.* any of several willows with reddish twigs, esp. *Salix laevigata* of western N America.

redwing *n.* any of several red-winged birds, esp. the red-winged blackbird.

red-winged blackbird *n.* a very common N and Central American blackbird, *Agelaius phoeniceus*, the male of which has a conspicuous red patch on the wings.

redwood *n.* **1** an exceptionally large Californian conifer, *Sequoia sempervirens*, yielding red wood. **2** any tree yielding red wood.

red worm *n.* an earthworm, *Lumbricus rubellus*, used as bait in fishing.

reed *n.* **1 a** any of various water or marsh plants with a firm stem, esp. of the genus *Phragmites*. **b** a tall straight stalk of this. **2** (*collect.*) reeds growing in a mass or used as material esp. for thatching. **3** a pipe of reed or straw. **4 a** the vibrating part of the mouthpiece of some wind instruments, e.g. the oboe and clarinet, made of reed or other material and producing the sound. **b** (esp. in *pl.*) a reed instrument.

reed bed *n.* a bed or growth of reeds.

reedy *adj.* (**-ier, -iest**) **1** full of reeds. **2** like a reed, esp. in weakness or slenderness. **3** (of a voice) high, thin, and harsh; not resonant.

reef¹ *n.* **1** a ridge of rock or coral etc. at or near the surface of the sea. **2 a** a lode of ore. **b** the bedrock surrounding this.

reef² *Naut.* ● *n.* each of several strips across a sail, for taking it in or rolling it up to reduce the surface area in a high wind. ● *v.tr.* **1** take in a reef or reefs of (a sail). **2** shorten (a topmast or a bowsprit).

reefer¹ *n.* **1** *slang* a marijuana cigarette. **2** a thick close-fitting double-breasted jacket.

reefer² *n.* a refrigerated truck, railway car, or ship.

reef knot *n.* a double knot made symmetrically to hold securely and cast off easily.

reek ● *v.intr.* (often foll. by *of*) **1** smell strongly and unpleasantly. **2** have unpleasant or suspicious associations (*this reeks of corruption*). **3** give off smoke or fumes. ● *n.* **1** a foul or stale smell. **2** vapour; a visible exhalation (esp. from a chimney). □ **reeky** *adj.*

reel ● *n.* **1** a cylindrical device on which film, tape, etc., are wound. **2** a quantity of thread etc. wound on a reel. **3** a device for winding and unwinding a line as required, esp. in fishing. **4** a revolving part in various machines. **5 a** lively folk or Scottish dance with two or more couples facing each other. **b** a piece of music for this. ● *v.* **1** *tr.* wind (thread, a fishing line, etc.) on a reel. **2** *tr.* (foll. by *in, up*) draw (fish etc.) in or up by the use of a reel. **3** *intr.* stand or walk or run unsteadily. **4** *intr.* be shaken mentally or physically. **5** *intr.* rock from side to side, or swing violently. **6** *intr.* dance a reel. □ **reel off** say or recite very rapidly and without apparent effort. □ **reeler** *n.*

reel-to-reel *adj.* designating a tape recorder in which the tape passes between two reels mounted separately, rather than within a cassette.

re-enact *v.tr.* act out (a past event). □ **re-enactment** *n.*

re-engineer *v.tr. & intr.* **1** design and construct again (*a re-engineered automobile*). **2** change the structure of a business or other organization, usu. by introducing improved technology and reducing staff, to improve efficiency. □ **re-engineering** *n.*

re-enter *v.* **1** *tr. & intr.* enter (a building etc.) again; go back in. **2** *tr.* participate in (a race, politics, a contest, etc.) again. □ **re-entrance** *n.*

re-entrant ● *adj.* **1** (of an angle) pointing inwards (*opp.* SALIENT *adj.* 2). **2** *Math.* (of an interior angle in a polygon) greater than 180°. ● *n.* **1** a re-entrant angle. **2** a person who re-enters (esp. the workforce).

re-entry *n.* (*pl.* **-ies**) **1** the act of entering again, esp. (of a spacecraft, missile, etc.) re-entering the earth's atmosphere. **2** *Law* an act of retaking or repossession.

reeve¹ *n. Cdn* (in Ontario and the Western provinces) the elected leader of the council of a town or other rural municipality. □ **reeveship** *n.*

reeve² *v.tr.* (*past* **rove** or **reeved**) *Naut.* **1** (usu. foll. by *through*) thread (a rope or rod etc.) through a ring or other aperture. **2** pass a rope through (a block etc.). **3** fasten (a rope or block) in this way.

ref *informal* ● *n.* a referee in hockey, basketball, football, etc. ● *v.tr. & intr.* (**reffed, reffing**) supervise (a game or match) as a referee. □ **reffing** *n.*

ref. *abbr.* **1** reference. **2** refer to. **3** (**Ref.**) *Cdn* Reform.

reface *v.tr.* repair or replace the facing on (esp. a building).

refer *v.* (**referred, referring**) (usu. foll. by *to*) **1** *intr.* allude (to) or describe (*I wasn't referring to you*). **2** *intr.* represent; pertain (to) (*the word 'doe' can be used to refer to a female rabbit*). **3** *tr.* send or direct (someone) to a person or thing for help, information, advice, etc. (*referred me to a psychiatrist*). **4** *tr.* direct (questions to be answered, matters to be dealt with, issues to be resolved, etc.) to someone (*refer all questions to me*). **5** *intr.* consult (notes, instructions, etc.) for information or advice. **6** *tr.* trace or attribute something to a person or thing as a cause or source.

referee ● *n.* **1** an official who supervises a hockey, basketball, etc. game or boxing match to ensure that the competitors obey the rules. **2** a person whose opinion or judgment is sought, esp. by mutual consent of parties in a legal dispute. **3** a person appointed to examine and assess an academic work being considered for publication. ● *v.* (**referees, refereed**) **1** *intr.* act as referee. **2** *tr.* supervise (a game etc.) as a referee. **3** *tr.* review (an academic publication) as a referee. □ **refereed** *adj.* **refereeing** *n.*

reference ● *n.* **1** (foll. by *to*) **a** an allusion (*made no reference to our problems*). **b** a relation or correspondence. **2 a** a direction of attention to a book or passage of a book, esp. one used as a source of information for a research paper, article, etc. **b** a useful source of information, such as a book, article, etc. **c** such sources of information considered collectively. **d** the act of looking up a passage etc. or looking in a book for information. **3 a** a written

re-edit *v.tr.*
(-edited, -editing)
re-edition *n.*
re-educate *v.tr.*
re-education *n.*
re-elect *v.tr.*

re-election *n.*
re-emerge *v.intr.*
re-emergence *n.*
re-emphasis *n.*
re-emphasize *v.tr.*
re-employ *v.tr.*

re-employment *n.*
re-enlist *v.intr.*
re-equip *v.tr. & intr.*
(-equipped, -equipping)
re-equipment *n.*
re-establish *v.tr.*

re-establishment *n.*
re-evaluate *v.tr.*
re-evaluation *n.*
re-examination *n.*
re-examine *v.tr.*
refashion *v.tr.*

testimonial supporting an applicant for employment etc. **b** a person giving this. **4 a** the referring of a matter for decision, settlement, or consideration to some authority. **b** a case or matter referred for consideration. ● *v.tr.* **1** cite; make mention of or a reference to. **2** provide (a book etc.) with references to authorities. □ **with** (or **in**) **reference to** regarding; as regards. **without reference to** not taking account of. □ **referential** *adj.* **referentiality** *n.*

reference book *n.* a book intended to be consulted for information on individual matters rather than read continuously.

reference library *n.* a library in which the books are for consultation, not loan. □ **reference librarian** *n.*

reference point *n.* a basis or standard for evaluation, assessment, or comparison.

referendum *n.* (*pl.* **-s** or **-da**) **1** the process of referring a political question to the electorate for a direct decision by general vote. **2** a vote taken by referendum.

referent /ˈrefərənt/ *n.* the idea or thing that a word etc. symbolizes.

referral *n.* the referring of an individual to an expert or specialist for advice, esp. the directing of a patient by a general practitioner to a medical specialist.

refill ● *v.tr. & intr.* fill or become filled again (*he refilled our glasses; the hole refilled with water*). ● *n.* **1** a replacement for something that has been used up, esp. fitting in the same container or device as the original (*lead refills for a pencil*). **2** a second serving, esp. of a beverage etc., replacing one consumed, usu. served in the same cup. □ **refillable** *adj.*

refinance *v.* **1** *tr. & intr.* finance again; arrange a new financial agreement for (*refinance a house*). **2** *tr.* repay some or all of (a loan) by obtaining fresh loans, usu. at a lower rate of interest. □ **refinancing** *n.*

refine *v.tr.* **1** free from impurities or defects; purify, clarify. **2** make or become more polished, elegant, or cultured. **3** make or become more subtle or delicate in thought, feelings, etc. **4** fine-tune, improve or perfect (*refine the mechanism*). □ **refining** *n.*

refined *adj.* **1** characterized by polish, elegance, or subtlety. **2** (esp. of sugar, oil, etc.) purified, freed from impurities or extraneous matter. **3** fine-tuned, perfected (*a refined process*).

refinement *n.* **1** the act of refining or the process of being refined. **2** polish or elegance in behaviour, manners, or taste. **3** an added development or improvement. **4** a fine distinction.

refiner *n.* a person or company whose business is to refine crude oil, sugar, etc.

refinery *n.* (*pl.* **-ies**) a place where oil etc. is refined.

refinish *v.tr.* **1** apply a new finish to (a surface). **2** remove old layers of paint or varnish from (wood, furniture, etc.) and apply new stain, varnish, etc. to.

refit ● *v.tr. & intr.* (**refitted, refitting**) restore or be restored to a serviceable condition by renewals and repairs. ● *n.* the act or an instance of refitting; the process of being refitted. □ **refitting** *n.*

reflect *v.* **1** *tr.* (of an esp. smooth or polished surface) throw back or cause to rebound (heat, light, sound, etc.). **2** *tr.* (esp. of a mirror, water, glass, etc.) reproduce or show an image of. **3** *tr.* result from; suggest or point to something as a cause or source (*his aggressive behaviour reflects a will to win*). **4** *intr.* (usu. foll. by *on, upon*) bring credit or discredit to (*this loss reflects badly on the coaching*). **5 a** *intr.* (often foll. by *on, upon*) meditate on; think about. **b** *tr.* (foll. by *that, how,* etc. + clause) consider; remind oneself. **6** *intr.* (of light, heat,

an image, etc.) be cast back; bounce back or off (*moonlight reflected off the water*). **7** *tr.* (of an action, result, etc.) show or bring (credit, discredit, etc.).

reflection *n.* **1** the act or an instance of a surface reflecting light, heat, sound, etc.; the process of being reflected. **2** a reflected light, heat, or colour. **b** a reflected image. **3** long and careful consideration. **4** (often foll. by *on, of*) an indication of something (*your clothes are a reflection of your personality*). **5** an account or representation of something; a commentary. **6** a thought.

reflective *adj.* **1** (of a surface etc.) reflecting light, images, etc. **2** (of a person or mood etc.) given to meditation. **3** (of an account) characterized by deep thought or reflection. **4** (foll. by *of*) indicative; symptomatic. □ **reflectively** *adv.*

reflector *n.* **1** a piece of glass or metal etc. for reflecting light in a required direction, e.g. a red one on the back of a bicycle. **2 a** a telescope etc. using a mirror to produce images. **b** the mirror itself. **3** any surface which reflects light, heat, etc., or something considered in terms of its reflective properties.

reflex ● *n.* **1** an involuntary or automatic response of any organ or body part to a stimulus. **2** an immediate or automatic reaction to something, esp. a habitual response (*hitting the snooze button is a reflex*). **3** (in *pl.*) the ability, usu. physical, to react quickly, esp. dexterously or with coordination (*Eric has excellent reflexes*). ● *adj.* **1** (of an action) independent of the will, as an automatic response to the stimulation of a nerve (e.g. a sneeze). **2** (of a response or reaction) automatic, immediate, unthinking. **3** (of an effect or influence) reactive; coming back upon its author or source. **4** bent backwards.

reflexed /rəˈfleksd, ri-/ *adj. Zool. & Bot.* bent, folded, or curved backwards.

reflexive *adj.* **1** triggered by, or as if by, reflex. **2 a** (of a person) focused on or concerning oneself. **b** (of a thing) concerning itself; intended more for oneself than for others. **3** *Grammar* (of a word or form) referring back to the subject of a sentence (esp. of a pronoun, e.g. *myself*). **4** *Grammar* (of a verb) having a reflexive pronoun as its object (as in *to wash oneself*). □ **reflexively** *adv.* **reflexivity** /-ˈsɪvɪti/ *n.*

reflexology /ˌriːflekˈsɒlədʒi/ *n.* **1** a technique for treating tension, alleviating symptoms by massaging points on the feet, hands, and head. **2** *Psych.* **a** the theory that all behaviour consists merely of innate or conditioned responses. **b** the branch of knowledge that deals with reflex action as it affects behaviour. □ **reflexologist** *n.*

reflux /ˈriːflʌks/ *n.* **1** a backward flow. **2** *Med.* a reverse flow, esp. of gastric fluid etc. **3** *Chem.* a method of boiling a liquid so that any vapour is liquefied and returned to the boiler.

refocus *v.tr.* (**-focused, -focusing** or **-focussed, -focussing**) **1** (of a camera lens) adjust the focus of. **2** change the scope or object of (attention, a study, goals, etc.).

reforest *v.tr.* replant (former forestland) with trees. □ **reforestation** *n.*

reform ● *v.* **1** *tr. & intr.* make or become better by the removal of faults and errors; improve. **2** *tr.* abolish or cure (an abuse or vice). **3** *tr. N Amer.* correct (a legal document). **4** *tr. Chem.* convert (a straight-chain hydrocarbon) by catalytic reaction to a branched-chain form for use as gasoline. ● *n.* **1** significant changes suggested or made to something; an overhaul (*Senate reform*). **2** the removal of faults or abuses, esp. of a moral or political or social kind (*committed to reform*).

3 (Reform) Cdn = REFORM PARTY (also attrib.: Reform member). **4 (Reform)** (attrib.) Cdn hist. designating those who opposed the Family Compact in Upper Canada or the Château Clique in Lower Canada in the movement for responsible government in the 19th c. **5** (usu. **Reform**) = REFORM JUDAISM (also attrib.: Reform synagogue). □ **reformed** adj.

re-form v.tr. & intr. form again. □ **re-formation** n.

reformat v.tr. (**reformatted, reformatting**) **1** revise or represent in another format. **2** Computing make adjustments to (a storage medium) to enable it to receive data.

reformation /ˌrefərˈmeɪʃən/ n. **1** the act of reforming or process of being reformed, esp. a radical change for the better in political or religious or social affairs. **2 (Reformation)** (prec. by the) hist. the 16th-c. movement to reform the doctrine and practices of the Catholic Church, which resulted in the establishment of the Protestant Churches.

reformatory /rəˈfɔrmətɔri, ri-/ ● n. (pl. **-ies**) N Amer. an institution to which young offenders are sent to be reformed. ● adj. tending or designed to reform.

Reformed adj. **1** designating a Church that has accepted the principles of the Reformation, esp. a Calvinist Church. **2** belonging to or falling under the influence of a Reformed Church.

reformer n. **1** a person who advocates or brings about (esp. political or social) reform. **2 (Reformer)** Cdn a supporter or member of the Reform Party. **3** (**Reformer**) Cdn hist. a person who participated in the movement for responsible government in Upper and Lower Canada in the 19th c.

reformist ● n. an advocate or supporter of social, political, or religious reform. ● adj. of or pertaining to reformists or their policies. □ **reformism** n.

Reform Judaism n. a branch of Judaism which has reformed or abandoned aspects of Orthodox Jewish worship and ritual in an attempt to adapt to modern social, political, and cultural changes.

Reform Party n. Cdn **1** an esp. Western Canadian right-wing political party favouring greater power for the provinces, deficit reduction, reduced power for government, and conservative social values. **2** hist. the party of Reformers that opposed the Tories in Upper Canada in the 19th c.

reform school n. = REFORMATORY.

refract v.tr. **1** (of water, air, glass, etc.) deflect (a ray of light, sound, etc.) at a certain angle when it enters obliquely from another medium. **2** change, distort, or influence (an idea, emotion, etc.) as it is passed through an intermediary (refracted through the language of advertising). **3** determine the refractive condition of (the eye). □ **refracted** adj.

refraction n. the process by which, or the extent to which, light, sound, etc., is refracted when passing obliquely through the interface between one medium and another or through a medium of varying density.

refractive adj. involving or capable of causing refraction.

refractive index n. the ratio of the velocity of light in a vacuum to its velocity in a specified medium.

refractor n. **1** a refracting medium or lens. **2** a telescope using a lens to produce an image.

refractory ● adj. **1** stubborn, unmanageable, rebellious. **2 a** (of a wound, disease, etc.) not yielding to treatment. **b** (of a person etc.) resistant to infection. **3** (of a substance) hard to fuse or work. **4** temporarily unresponsive to nervous or sexual stimuli (refractory period). ● n. (pl. **-ies**) a substance or building material especially resistant to heat, corrosion, etc.

refrain[1] v.intr. (usu. foll. by from) avoid doing (an action); abstain (refrain from smoking).

refrain[2] n. **1** a recurring phrase or number of lines, esp. at the ends of stanzas. **2** the music accompanying this. **3** an often repeated idea or expression.

refresh ● v.tr. **1 a** impart strength or energy to (a person etc.); invigorate (the nap refreshed her). **b** (refl.) revive with food, rest, etc. (refreshed myself with a drink). **2** revive or stimulate (the memory), esp. by consulting the source of one's information. **3** replenish. **4** Computing replenish or recharge the data stored in a memory device. **5** Computing (of a monitor or screen) repeat the display of digital information on a screen or cathode ray tube at rapid intervals in order to make an image appear continuous. ● n. Computing **1** the process of renewing the data stored in a memory device. **2** = REFRESH RATE. □ **refreshed** adj.

refresher n. **1** something that refreshes, esp. a drink. **2** an update or review of previous education (also attrib.: refresher course).

refreshing adj. **1** serving to refresh. **2** pleasantly new or different. **3** (of food or drink) cooling or thirst-quenching. □ **refreshingly** adv.

refreshment n. **1** the act of refreshing or the process of being refreshed in mind or body. **2** (usu. in pl.) food or drink, esp. provided for or sold to people in a public place or at a public event. **3** something that refreshes or stimulates the mind.

refresh rate n. Computing the rate at which a screen is filled with digital information or an image, measured in hertz.

refried beans n.pl. a Mexican dish of cooked beans which have been left to cool, then fried.

refrigerant ● n. **1** a substance used for refrigeration. **2** Med. a substance that cools or allays fever. ● adj. cooling.

refrigerate v. **1** tr. & intr. make or become cool or cold. **2** tr. subject (food etc.) to cold in order to freeze or preserve it. □ **refrigerated** adj. **refrigeration** n.

refrigerator n. **1** a cabinet or room in which food etc. is kept cold. **2** (usu. attrib.) designating a truck, railway car, etc. equipped with a refrigerator.

refuel v. (**-fuelled, -fuelling**) **1** intr. replenish a fuel supply. **2** tr. supply with more fuel.

refuge n. **1** a shelter from pursuit, danger, or trouble. **2** a person or place etc. offering this. **3** a thing or course used as a means of escape from difficulties, problems, etc. (alcohol is his refuge). **4** N Amer. a park or sanctuary in which esp. endangered animals are protected. □ **take refuge in** resort to as a means of escape or shelter.

refugee n. a person taking refuge, esp. in a foreign country, from war, persecution, or natural disaster (also attrib.: refugee status).

refugee determination n. (in full **refugee determination process**) Cdn the process by which the validity of a claim of refugee status is assessed.

---

reformulate v.tr.
reformulation n.

refreeze v.tr. & intr. (past **refroze**; past part. **refrozen**)

refund ● *v.tr.* **1** pay back (money or expenses). **2** reimburse (a person). ● *n.* **1** an act of refunding. **2** a sum refunded; a repayment. □ **refundable** *adj.*

refurbish *v.tr.* **1** brighten up, redecorate. **2** restore, repair. □ **refurbished** *adj.* **refurbishment** *n.*

refusal *n.* **1** the act or an instance of refusing; the state of being refused. **2** (in full **first refusal**) the right or privilege of deciding to take or leave a thing before it is offered to others.

refuse[1] *v.* **1** *tr.* decline to take or accept (something offered or presented). **2** *tr. & intr.* (often foll. by to + infin.) adamantly decline; be stubbornly unwilling (*the car refuses to start; I refuse!*). **3** *tr. & intr.* withhold permission or consent (*I refuse to let you stay up past your bedtime*). **4** *tr.* decline to give (to a person something requested); deny (*refused me a day off*). **5** *tr.* decline to admit (a person) to a particular position or place.

refuse[2] *n. formal* items rejected as worthless; garbage.

refusenik *n.* **1** *hist.* a Jew in the former Soviet Union who was refused permission to emigrate to Israel. **2** a person who refuses to comply with rules or regulations imposed by an establishment, esp. due to moral beliefs.

refute /rə'fju:t, ri-/ *v.tr.* **1** prove the falsity or error of (a statement etc. or the person proposing it). **2** rebut or repel by argument. **3** *disputed* reject, deny, or contradict (without argument or proof). ¶Some language commentators maintain that refutation must always be backed up by proof. □ **refutability** *n.* **refutation** /ˌrefjʊ'teɪʃən/ *n.*

reg /reg/ *n.* (usu. in *pl.*) regulation.

Reg. *abbr. Regina* (queen).

reg. *abbr.* **1** registered. **2** regular price.

regain *v.tr.* **1** obtain possession or use of after loss. **2** get back to, reach (a place, position) again.

regal *adj.* of, like, or fit for a monarch (*regal splendour; a regal gesture*). □ **regally** *adv.*

regale /rə'geil, ri-/ *v.tr.* **1** (foll. by *with*) entertain or divert with (talk etc.). **2** entertain lavishly with feasting.

regalia /rə'geiliə, -'geiljə/ *n.pl.* **1** any distinctive or elaborate clothes or accoutrements. **2** the decorations or insignia of royalty used esp. at coronations. **3** the decorations or insignia of any order.

regard ● *v.tr.* **1** (usu. foll. by *as*) look upon or view; consider (*is regarded as our best swimmer*). **2** esteem, value (*we regard your work highly*). **3** (of a thing) relate to; have some connection with (*this note is regarding our conversation of last night*). **4** gaze on steadily (usu. in a specified way) (*she regarded them with apprehension*). ● *n.* **1** (foll. by *for, to*) concern (for); proper consideration or appreciation (of) (*lived with no regard for anyone but herself*). **2** (often foll. by *for*) esteem; opinion (*she held his work in high regard*). **3** a respect (*in this regard*). **4** (in *pl.*) an expression of friendliness in a letter etc.; compliments (*give him my regards*). **5** a gaze; a steady or significant look. □ **as regards** about, concerning. **with** (or **in**) **regard to** as concerns; with respect to.

regarding *prep.* about, concerning; with respect to.

regardless ● *adj.* (usu. foll. by *of*) without regard or consideration for (*regardless of the expense*). ● *adv.* despite what might happen; anyway, nevertheless (*we must carry on regardless*).

regatta /rə'gætə, ri-/ *n.* a marine sporting event consisting of a series of races of boats, yachts, etc.

Regatta Day *n. Cdn (Nfld)* **1** a marine event held annually on usu. the first Wednesday in August on Quidi Vidi Lake in St. John's, Newfoundland, associ-

ated with a carnival. **2** (in Newfoundland) a provincial statutory holiday held on this day.

regency /'ri:dʒənsi/ *n.* (*pl.* **-ies**) **1 a** the office or jurisdiction of regent. **b** a commission acting as regent. **c** the period of office of a regent or regency commission. **2** (**Regency**) **a** the period (1811–20) during the reign of George III in Britain when George, Prince of Wales, was regent. **b** (usu. *attrib.*) designating clothing, architecture, furniture, and other decorative arts of this period, inspired by Greco-Roman models and characterized esp. by purity and simplicity of line and detail. **3** (**Regency**) **a** (in France) the period from 1715 to 1723 during the reign of Louis XV when Philip, Duke of Orleans, was regent. **b** (usu. *attrib.*) designating architecture and furniture typical of this period, characterized esp. by delicate finishes and curved lines.

regenerate ● *v.* /ri'dʒenə,reit/ **1** *tr.* reconstitute in a new and improved form; revive (*regenerate the neighbourhood*). **2** *tr. & intr.* bring or come into renewed existence, esp. of a greater spiritual or moral nature. **3** *intr. & tr.* regrow or cause (new plant or animal tissue) to regrow to replace lost or damaged tissue. **4** *tr. & intr. Chem.* restore or be restored to an initial state of reaction or process. ● *adj.* /ri'dʒenərət/ **1** spiritually born again. **2** reformed. □ **regenerative** /-rətiv/ *adj.* **regenerator** *n.*

regeneration *n.* **1** a revival; reconstitution in an improved form. **2** *Med. & Biol.* **a** the formation of new animal tissue. **b** the natural replacement of lost parts or organs. **3** the fact or process of being reborn, esp. spiritually. **4** the natural regrowth of a forest which has been felled or thinned. **5** *Chem.* the action or process of regenerating polymeric fibres.

regent /'ri:dʒənt/ ● *n.* **1** a person appointed to administer a country or state because the monarch is a minor, absent, or incapacitated. **2** *N Amer.* a member of the governing body of a university or other academic institution. ● *adj.* (placed after noun) acting as regent (*Prince Regent*).

reggae /'regei/ *n.* a W Indian style of popular music indigenous to the black culture of Jamaica, developed from an eclectic mix of African religious music, Christian black revival songs, New Orleans rhythm and blues, and Rastafarian liturgical music.

regie /rei'ʒi:/ *n. Cdn (Que.)* (also **Régie**) (usu. prec. by *the*) any of several Quebec government bodies regulating insurance, housing, language, etc.

regime /rei'ʒi:m/ *n.* **1 a** a method of government or dominance of a country or state, esp. one that is or is considered to be oppressive (*a military regime*). **b** a period in which such a government is in power (*during the Nazi regime*). **2** a system of managing or organizing something (*a tax regime*). **3** a (medical) regimen.

regimen /'redʒɪˌmen/ *n.* **1** *Med.* a prescribed course of exercise, way of life, or diet. **2** a strict routine or schedule, usu. imposed or suggested.

regiment /'redʒɪmənt/ *n.* **1** a permanent unit of an army usu. commanded by a colonel and divided into several companies, troops, or batteries and often into two battalions. **2** (usu. foll. by *of*) a large array or number. □ **regimental** *adj.*

regimentation *n.* **1** the action of imposing order; the process by which (people etc.) are integrated in a system, institution, etc. **2** strict organization, order.

regimented *adj.* **1** characterized by strict discipline or order. **2** organized, usu. strictly or oppressively, in definite groups or according to an order or system. **3** belonging to a regiment.

Regina /rəˈdʒainə, reˈdʒiːnə/ n. the reigning queen (following a name or in the titles of lawsuits).

Regina Manifesto /rəˈdʒainə/ n. Cdn hist. the declaration of principles and objectives, including the goal of establishing a welfare state, adopted by the CCF in 1933.

Reginan /rəˈdʒainən/ ● n. a native or inhabitant of Regina, Saskatchewan. ● adj. of or relating to Regina.

region n. **1** a (usu. specified) area of land or division of the earth's surface without fixed limits but having definable features such as climate, fauna, flora, etc. (wine-growing region). **2** an area of land or division of the earth's surface marked by certain boundaries (the region between the Ottawa and St. Lawrence rivers). **3 a** the area of land outside a principal city (Edmonton and surrounding regions). **b** the area of land surrounding and including a (usu. specified) place (the Great Lakes region). **c** (in pl.) esp. Cdn the areas of a country, province, etc. away from the political centre. **4** a part of the body near or including a (usu. specified) organ etc. (the lower back region). **5** a relatively large administrative division of a country or province, esp. one uniting several large municipalities. **6** an area of the world made up of neighbouring countries which are considered socially, economically, or politically interdependent (the Baltic region). **7** a sphere or realm (the region of medicine). **8** a separate part of the world or universe. ☐ **in the region of** approximately.

regional ● adj. of, pertaining to, or characteristic of a region. ● n. **1** a thing, such as a stamp, newspaper, etc., produced or used in a particular region. **2** (in pl.) N Amer. a tournament or championship involving teams, athletes, etc. from a particular region. ☐ **regionally** adv.

regional county municipality n. Cdn (Que.) one of 96 regional municipalities comprising urban and rural municipalities, but excluding urban communities.

regional district n. Cdn (BC) an administrative unit that coordinates the services of municipalities and rural areas within its boundaries, similar to a regional municipality.

regionalism n. **1** the theory or practice of regional rather than central systems of administration of economic, cultural, or political affiliation. **2** allegiance to or concern for one's region rather than one's country. **3** a linguistic feature, custom, etc. peculiar to a particular region and not found or heard elsewhere in a country. ☐ **regionalist** n. & adj.

regionalize v. **1** tr. bring under the control of a region for administrative purposes. **2** tr. & intr. divide into regions. ☐ **regionalization** n.

regional municipality n. Cdn (Ont. & Que.) a large municipality representing a federation of all the area municipalities within its borders. Abbr.: **RM**.

register ● n. **1** an official list or record of births, deaths, marriages, guests, students in attendance at school, etc. **2** a book in which such items or names are recorded for reference. **3** a device that records information automatically, esp. a cash register. **4** a device used to store information within a computer system for high-speed access. **5** an adjustable plate for widening or narrowing an opening and regulating the passage of air, heat, smoke, etc. (floor register). **6** a device that regulates the flow of air through an organ or woodwind instrument, thereby raising or lowering the pitch. **7 a** the range of tones of a voice or instrument. **b** a part of this range (lower register). **8** Linguistics each of several forms of a language (colloquial, formal, literary, etc.) usually used in particular

circumstances. ● v. **1** tr. set down or record a name, an event, a sale, etc. in a list or register for official purposes. **2** intr. **a** check into a hotel. **b** (foll. by for) enrol in a course etc. **3 a** intr. (of a couple to be married etc.) have a list of gifts compiled and kept at a store for consultation by gift buyers. **b** tr. (usu. in passive) (of a gift store) compile and maintain a list of gifts for (a couple to be married etc.) (where are you registered?). **4** tr. **a** (of an instrument) record automatically; indicate. **b** (of temperature, winds, an earthquake, etc.) be or reach a certain figure when measured. **5 a** tr. express (an emotion) facially or by gesture (registered surprise). **b** intr. (of an emotion) show in a person's face or gestures. **6** intr. make an impression; be recognized or noted mentally (did not register at all). **7** tr. entrust (a letter etc.) to a post office for transmission by registered mail. ☐ **registerable** adj.

registered adj. **1** recorded; officially set down, esp. in a register. **2** officially licensed; certified (registered firearm). **3** signed up; enrolled. **4** (of dogs etc.) registered as a purebred by an authorized breeder.

Registered Education Savings Plan n. Cdn = RESP.

Registered Home Ownership Savings Plan n. Cdn = RHOSP.

registered mail n. **1** a postal procedure with special precautions for safety and for compensation in case of loss. **2** letters or mail sent this way.

registered nurse n. esp. N Amer. a nurse who is licensed to practise and is a registered member of a nurses' association.

registered nursing assistant n. a nursing assistant who holds a certificate issued by a professional body of nurses.

registered practical nurse n. a person who is registered by a professional association of nurses as being trained to perform basic nursing tasks under the direction of a physician or registered nurse.

Registered Retirement Income Fund n. Cdn = RRIF.

Registered Retirement Savings Plan n. Cdn = RRSP.

registered trademark n. a sign, name, or logo of a manufacturer etc. which is officially recorded and protected from use by others.

registrant /ˈredʒistrənt/ n. a person who registers or has registered for something.

registrar /ˈredʒis,trar/ n. **1** an official responsible for keeping a register or official records. **2** an official at an educational institution responsible for maintaining records of students' enrolment, marks, etc. **3** Cdn & Brit. Law a judicial and administrative officer responsible for issuing and filing court documents.

Registrar General n. **1** a government official responsible for recording births, deaths, and marriages. **2** a government official responsible for keeping records of registered individuals and organizations, e.g. lobbyists.

registration n. **1** the act or an instance of registering; the process of being registered. **2** the form or certificate that verifies that something or someone has been registered. **3** the selection of a series of organ or harpsichord stops used in the performance of a piece.

registration number n. a number or series of numbers and letters used to identify a registration.

registry n. (pl. **-ies**) **1** a place or office where registers or records are kept. **2** registration. **3** a list of gifts requested e.g. by a couple to be married, and of those already purchased, kept at a store for consultation by gift buyers (*bridal registry*). **4** a ship's country of origin as indicated on its registration.

registry office *n. Cdn* **1** a government office where private property, such as vehicles, real estate, etc., may be registered and where records of ownership are kept. **2** a government office where records of births, deaths, and marriages are kept.

regress ● *v.* /rə'gres, ri-/ **1** *intr.* **a** move backwards. **b** (esp. in abstract senses) return to a previous or less advanced state. **2** *intr.* & *tr. Psych.* return or cause to return mentally to a former stage of life, esp. through hypnosis or mental illness. ● *n.* /'ri:gres/ **1** the act or an instance of going back. **2** reasoning from effect to cause.

regression *n.* **1** a backward movement, esp. a return to a former state. **2** a relapse or reversion. **3** *Psych.* a return to an earlier stage of development, esp. through hypnosis or mental illness. **4** *Statistics* a measure of the relation between the mean value of one variable (e.g. output) and corresponding values of other variables (e.g. time and cost) (also *attrib.*: *regression analysis*).

regressive *adj.* **1** regressing; characterized by regression. **2** (of a tax) proportionally greater on lower incomes. □ **regressively** *adv.*

regret ● *v.tr.* (**regretted, regretting**) (often foll. by *that* + clause) **1** feel or express sorrow or distress over (an action or loss etc.) (*we regretted your absence*). **2** express polite apologies for (an error, inability, inconvenience, etc.). **3 a** (often foll. by *to* + infin. or *that* + clause) acknowledge with sorrow or remorse. **b** (often foll. by *to* + infin.) be reluctant (to say something etc.) for fear of causing offence or disappointment. ● *n.* **1** a feeling of sorrow, repentance, disappointment, etc., over an action or loss etc. **2** (often in *pl.*) an (esp. polite or formal) expression of disappointment or sorrow at an occurrence, inability to comply, etc. (*refused with many regrets*). □ **live to regret** (of an action) eventually feel the consequences of. **give** (or **send**) **one's regrets** formally decline an invitation.

regretful *adj.* feeling or showing regret. □ **regretfully** *adv.* **regretfulness** *n.*

regrettable *adj.* (of events or conduct) unfortunate, unwelcome; deserving censure. □ **regrettably** *adv.*

regroup *v.* **1** *tr.* & *intr.* group or arrange again or differently. **2** *intr.* become organized before attempting something again.

regular ● *adj.* **1** usual, standard, customary. **2** conforming to a rule or principle; systematic. **3** acting or done uniformly or in a calculable time or manner. **4 a** habitual (*a regular contributor*). **b** constant, steady (*a regular job*). **5** *informal* absolute; genuine (*a regular hero*). **6** (of coffee) containing an average amount of cream and sugar. **7** (of merchandise) of an average size, between large and small (*a regular soft drink*). **8** (of a person) defecating or menstruating at predictable times. **9** (of forces or troops etc.) relating to or constituting a permanent professional body. **10** (of a structure or arrangement) harmonious, symmetrical (*regular features*). **11** *Math.* **a** (of a figure) having all sides and all angles equal. **b** (of a solid) bounded by a number of equal figures. **12** *Grammar* (of a noun, verb, etc.) following the normal type of inflection. **13** *Christianity* (placed before or after noun) **a** bound by

religious rule. **b** belonging to a religious or monastic order (*canon regular*). ● *n.* **1** *informal* a regular customer, visitor, participant, etc. **2 a** a coffee containing an average amount of cream and sugar. **b** a serving of a beverage etc. of a size between a small and a large. **3** *Sport* a player who starts every or nearly every game. **4** a regular soldier. □ **keep regular hours** do the same thing, esp. going to bed and getting up, at the same time each day. □ **regularity** *n.* **regularize** *v.tr.* **regularization** *n.*

regularly *adv.* **1** at regular intervals or times. **2** in a balanced or regular manner.

regular season *n. N Amer. Sport* the schedule of games that follows the exhibition season and leads up to the playoffs (also *attrib.*: *regular-season record*).

regulate *v.tr.* **1** govern or control by law; subject to esp. legal restrictions. **2** keep (a biological function etc.) regular; maintain the health of (*drugs that regulate the immune system*). **3** adapt to requirements. **4** alter the speed of (a machine or clock) so that it may work accurately. □ **regulator** *n.*

regulation *n.* **1** the act or an instance of regulating; the process of being regulated. **2 a** a prescribed rule; an authoritative direction. **b** a subordinate form of legislation that may be established without the necessity of enacting a new statute. **3** (*attrib.*) **a** in accordance with regulations; of the correct type etc. (*a regulation tie*). **b** *informal* usual (*the regulation soup*).

regulation time *n. N Amer. Sport* the time normally allotted for the completion of a game which does not result in a tie (*compare* OVERTIME).

regulatory /'regjələ,tɔri/ *adj.* **1** having to do with a regulation or regulations (*regulatory agency*). **2** in violation of a regulation (*a regulatory offence*).

regurgitate /ri'gɜrdʒɪ,teit/ *v.* **1** *tr.* bring (swallowed food) up again to the mouth. **2** *tr.* cast or pour out again (*regurgitating facts*). **3** *intr.* be brought up again; gush back. □ **regurgitation** *n.*

rehab *informal* ● *n.* rehabilitation. ● *adj.* rehabilitated, reconditioned. ● *v.tr.* & *intr.* (**rehabbed, rehabbing**) *N Amer.* rehabilitate; undergo rehabilitation.

rehabilitate /,ri:hə'bɪlɪteit/ *v.tr.* **1 a** restore (a person) to effectiveness or normal life by training etc., esp. after imprisonment, injury, or illness. **b** heal (an injury etc.). **2** recondition, overhaul. **3** restore the reputation or standing of. □ **rehabilitation** *n.* **rehabilitative** /-,teitɪv/ *adj.*

rehash ● *v.tr.* put (old material) into a new form without significant change or improvement. ● *n.* **1** material rehashed. **2** the act or an instance of rehashing.

rehearsal *n.* **1** the act or an instance of rehearsing. **2** a trial performance or practice of a play, ceremony, etc.

rehearse *v.* **1** *tr.* practise (a play, recital, ceremony, etc.) for later public performance. **2** *intr.* hold a rehearsal. **3** *tr.* train (a person) by rehearsal. **4** *tr.* recite or say over, esp. in preparation for some subsequent event. **5** *tr.* give a list of; enumerate.

rehydrate *v.* **1** *intr.* absorb water again after dehydration. **2** *tr.* cause (a person or thing) to absorb moisture or fluid. □ **rehydration** *n.*

Reich /raix, rəik/ *n.* the former German nation or Commonwealth, esp. the Third Reich.

reify /'ri:ɪ,fai/ *v.tr.* (**-ies, -ied**) convert (a concept etc.) into a thing; materialize. □ **reification** *n.*

---

regrade *v.tr.*
regrow *v.intr.* & *tr.* (*past* **regrew;** *past part* **regrown**)

regrowth *n.*
reheat *v.tr.* & *n.*

reheater *n.*
rehouse *v.tr.*

reign ● *v.intr.* **1** hold royal office; be king or queen. **2** (often in phr. **reign supreme**) prevail; hold sway (*confusion reigns*). **3** (of a winner, champion, etc.) be currently holding the title etc. ● *n.* **1** sovereignty, rule. **2** the period during which a sovereign rules. **3** a period during which a specified person, quality, etc. holds sway (*the reign of love and peace*). □ **reigning** *adj.*

reign of terror *n.* **1** a period of remorseless repression or bloodshed, during which the general population lives in constant fear of death or violence. **2** (**Reign of Terror**) *see* TERROR 4.

reiki /'reɪki/ *n.* a supposed healing technique in which a therapist channels energy into a patient by means of touch, to activate the natural healing processes of the patient's body and restore physical and emotional well-being.

reimburse *v.tr.* **1** repay (a person who has expended money). **2** repay (a person's expenses). □ **reimbursement** *n.*

rein ● *n.* (in *sing.* or *pl.*) **1** a long narrow strap with each end attached to the bit, used to guide or check a horse etc. in riding or driving. **2** a means of control (*took over the reins of government*). ● *v.tr.* **1** check or manage with reins. **2** (foll. by *up*, *back*) pull up or back with reins. **3** (foll. by *in*) hold in as with reins; restrain. **4** govern, restrain, control. □ **free** (or **full**) **rein** complete freedom of action. **keep a tight rein on** allow little freedom to.

reincarnation /ˌriːɪnkɑːˈneɪʃən/ *n.* **1** the rebirth of a soul in a new body. **2** a new embodiment or occurrence of a person, idea, etc. □ **reincarnate** /-neit/ *v.tr.* **reincarnate** /-nət/ *adj.*

reindeer *n.* (*pl.* same) a subarctic deer, *Rangifer tarandus*, of which both sexes have large antlers, domesticated in northern Eurasia.

reinforce *v.tr.* strengthen or support, esp. with additional personnel or material or by an increase of numbers or quantity or size etc. □ **reinforcer** *n.*

reinforced concrete *n.* concrete with metal bars or wire etc. embedded to increase its tensile strength.

reinforcement *n.* **1** the act or an instance of reinforcing; the process of being reinforced. **2** a thing that reinforces. **3** (in *pl.*) reinforcing personnel or equipment etc. **4** the strengthening or establishing of a response through the repetition of a stimulus or the satisfaction of a need (*positive reinforcement*).

reintegrate *v.* **1** *tr.* restore wholeness or unity to. **2** *tr.* & *intr.* integrate or be reintegrated back into society. □ **reintegration** *n.*

reintroduce *v.tr.* **1** introduce again. **2** introduce (a species) to a place it formerly inhabited. □ **reintroduction** *n.*

reinvent *v.tr.* **1** invent again. **2** change something so much that it appears to be something completely new. □ **reinvent the wheel** waste effort by doing something that has already been done and does not need redoing. □ **reinvention** *n.*

reinvest *v.tr.* invest again (esp. money made from one investment in other investments etc.). □ **reinvestment** *n.*

reject ● *v.tr.* **1** put aside or send back as not to be used or done or complied with etc. **2** refuse to accept or believe in (an idea). **3 a** fail to give (a person or an animal) due attention, care, or affection. **b** fail to accept (a person) into a group. **4** *Med.* show an immune response to (a transplanted organ or tissue) so that it fails to survive. ● *n.* a thing or person rejected as unfit or below standard. □ **rejection** *n.* **rejector** *n.*

rejig *v.tr.* (**rejigged, rejigging**) *Cdn* & *Brit.* reconfigure, rearrange; reorganize.

rejoice *v.intr.* **1** feel great joy. **2** (foll. by *that* + clause or *to* + infin.) be glad. **3** (foll. by *in*, *at*) take delight. **4** celebrate some event. □ **rejoicing** *n.*

rejoin[1] *v.* **1** *tr.* & *intr.* join together again; reunite. **2** *tr.* join (a companion etc.) again.

rejoin[2] *v.* **1** *tr.* say in answer, retort. **2** *intr.* *Law* reply to a charge or pleading in a lawsuit.

rejoinder *n.* **1** what is said in reply. **2** a retort. **3** *Law* a reply by rejoining.

rejuvenate *v.tr.* **1** make young or as if young again. **2** inject new vigour, liveliness, efficiency, etc. into (*rejuvenate the political process*). **3** make new or as if new again (*rejuvenated the old building*). □ **rejuvenation** *n.* **rejuvenator** *n.*

rekey *v.tr.* esp. *Computing* re-enter (text or other data) using a keyboard.

relapse ● *v.intr.* (often foll. by *into*) **1** experience a return of an illness after partial or apparently complete recovery. **2** fall back or sink again into any state, practice, etc. ● *n.* the act or an instance of relapsing.

relate *v.* **1** *tr.* narrate or recount (incidents, a story, etc.). **2** *tr.* (in *passive*; often foll. by *to*) be connected by blood or marriage. **3** *tr.* (usu. foll. by *to*, *with*) bring into relation (with one another); establish a connection between (*cannot relate your opinion to my own experience*). **4** *intr.* (foll. by *to*) have reference to; concern (*see only what relates to himself*). **5** *intr.* **a** (foll. by *to*) understand or have empathy for (*I can relate to that*). **b** understand, be connected to, or have empathy for a person etc. (*we just don't relate*).

related *adj.* **1** connected by blood or marriage. **2** associated or connected (also in *comb.*: *work-related stress*). **3** of the same type; in the same group, category, etc. (*related industries*). □ **relatedness** *n.*

relation *n.* **1 a** the way in which one person or thing is related to another. **b** the existence or effect of a connection, correspondence, contrast, or feeling prevailing between persons or things, esp. when qualified in some way (*bears no relation to the facts*; *enjoyed good relations for many years*). **2** a person connected by blood or marriage; a relative. **3** (in *pl.*) **a** (usu. foll. by *with*) dealings, rapport, interaction (with others). **b** sexual intercourse. **4** = RELATIONSHIP. **5** **a** narration (*his relation of the events*). **b** a narrative. **6** *Law* the laying of an information. □ **in relation to** as regards.

reinfect *v.tr.*	**reinstatement** *n.*	**reinterpretation** *n.*	**reiteration** *n.*
reinfection *n.*	**reinter** *v.tr.*	**reinvigorate** *v.tr.*	**reiterative** *adj.*
reinjure *v.tr.*	(**reinterred, reinterring**)	**reinvigoration** *n.*	**rekindle** *v.tr.* & *intr.*
reinsert *v.tr.*	**reinterment** *n.*	**reissue** *v.tr.* & *n.*	**relabel** *v.tr.*
reinsertion *n.*	**reinterpret** *v.tr.*	(**reissues, reissued,**	(**relabelled,**
reinstall *v.tr.*	(**reinterpreted,**	**reissuing**)	**relabelling**)
reinstate *v.tr.*	**reinterpreting**)	**reiterate** *v.tr.*	

relational *adj.* **1** of, belonging to, or characterized by relation. **2** having relation. **3** (of a word or grammar) expressing or characterized by relations between words.

relational database *n.* *Computing* a database structured to recognize the relation of stored items of information.

relationship *n.* **1** the fact or state of being related. **2 a** a connection or association (*a good working relationship*). **b** an emotional (esp. sexual) association between two people. **3** kinship.

relative ● *adj.* **1** considered or having significance in relation to something else; not absolute (*they live in relative comfort*). **2** (foll. by *to*) proportionate to (something else); in proportion to (*growth is relative to input*). **3 a** comparative; compared one with another (*their relative advantages*). **b** (foll. by *to*) in relation to (*move slowly relative to each other*). **4** having mutual relations; related to each other. **5** (usu. foll. by *to*) having reference; relating, relevant (*the facts relative to the issue*). **6** *Grammar* **a** (of a word, esp. a pronoun) referring to an expressed or implied antecedent and attaching a subordinate clause to it, e.g. *which*, *who*. **b** (of a clause) attached to an antecedent by a relative word. ● *n.* **1** a person connected by blood or marriage. **2** a species related to another by common origin (*the apes, humans' closest relatives*). **3** *Grammar* a relative word, esp. a pronoun. ☐ **relatively** *adv.*

relative humidity *n.* humidity expressed as the ratio of the mass of water vapour in a volume of air to the value for saturated air at the same temperature.

relativism *n.* the doctrine or belief that knowledge, truth, morality, etc., are relative and not absolute. ☐ **relativist** *n.*

relativistic *adj.* **1** of, pertaining to, or characterized by relativism. **2** *Physics* (of phenomena etc.) accurately described only by the theory of relativity.

relativity *n.* **1** the fact or state of being relative. **2** *Physics* **a** (in full **special theory of relativity**) a theory based on the principle that all motion is relative and that light has constant velocity, regarding space-time as a four-dimensional continuum, and modifying previous conceptions of geometry. **b** (in full **general theory of relativity**) a theory extending this to gravitation and accelerated motion.

relativize *v.tr.* make relative. ☐ **relativization** *n.*

relax *v.* **1 a** *tr. & intr.* make or become less stiff or rigid or tense. **b** *intr.* become at ease, unperturbed, etc. **2** *tr. & intr.* make or become less formal or strict (*rules were relaxed*). **3** *tr.* reduce or abate (one's attention, efforts, etc.). **4** *intr.* cease work or effort. ☐ **relaxed** *adj.* **relaxer** *n.* **relaxing** *ad. & n.*

relaxant ● *n.* a drug etc. that reduces tension and produces relaxation, esp. of muscles. ● *adj.* causing relaxation.

relaxation *n.* **1** the act of relaxing or state of being relaxed. **2** recreation or rest, esp. after a period of work. **3** a partial remission or relaxing of a penalty, duty, etc. **4** a lessening of severity, precision, etc.

relay ● *n.* **1** a set of people etc. appointed to relieve others or to operate in shifts (*operated in relays*). **2** = RELAY RACE. **3** a device activating changes in an electric circuit etc. in response to other changes affecting itself. **4 a** a device, installation, satellite, etc. which

receives, amplifies, and retransmits a transmission, broadcast, etc. **b** a relayed message or transmission. **5** a fresh set of people or horses substituted for tired ones. ● *v.tr.* **1** receive (a message, broadcast, etc.) and transmit it to others. **2 a** arrange in relays. **b** provide with or replace by relays.

re-lay *v.tr.* (*past* and *past part.* **re-laid**) lay again or differently.

relay race *n.* a race between teams of which each member in turn covers part of the distance.

release ● *v.tr.* **1** (often foll. by *from*) set free; liberate, unfasten. **2** allow to move from a fixed position. **3 a** make (information, a recording, etc.) publicly or generally available. **b** issue (a film etc.) for general exhibition. **4** *Law* **a** remit (a debt). **b** surrender (a right). **c** make over (property or money) to another. **d** free (a person) from the obligations of a contract. **5** give free rein to (an emotional or instinctual drive); ease (tension). ● *n.* **1** deliverance or liberation from a restriction, duty, or difficulty. **2** a handle or catch that releases part of a mechanism. **3** a document or item of information made available for publication (*press release*). **4 a** a film or CD etc. that is released. **b** the act or an instance of releasing or the process of being released in this way. **5** *Law* **a** the act of releasing (property, money, or a right) to another. **b** a document effecting this. **6** a document freeing a person from legal responsibility or obligation. ☐ **releasable** *adj.*

relegate /ˈreləˌgeit/ *v.tr.* **1** consign or dismiss to an inferior or less important position, category, etc. **2** banish or send into exile. **3** (foll. by *to*) transfer (a matter) for decision or implementation. ☐ **relegation** *n.*

relent *v.intr.* **1** decide to be less strict, harsh, or determined. **2** yield to compassion. **3** relax one's severity; become less stern.

relentless *adj.* **1** unrelenting; insistent and uncompromising. **2** continuous; oppressively constant (*the pressure was relentless*). ☐ **relentlessly** *adv.* **relentlessness** *n.*

relevant *adj.* (often foll. by *to*) bearing on or having reference to the matter in hand. ☐ **relevance** *n.* **relevancy** *n.* **relevantly** *adv.*

reliable *adj.* **1** that may be relied on. **2** of sound and consistent character or quality. ☐ **reliability** *n.* **reliably** *adv.*

reliance *n.* **1** (foll. by *on*) dependence; the act or state of relying on something. **2** trust, confidence. ☐ **reliant** *adj.*

relic *n.* **1** an object interesting because of its age or association with the past. **2** a part of a deceased holy person's body or belongings etc. kept as an object of reverence. **3 a** a surviving custom, belief, thing, etc. from a past age. **b** an old person, esp. one embodying old practices, customs, etc. **4** a memento or souvenir. **5** (in *pl.*) what has survived destruction or wasting or use. **6** (in *pl.*) the dead body or remains of a person.

relict /ˈrelikt/ *n.* a species, structure, etc., surviving from a previous age or in changed circumstances after the disappearance of related species, structures, etc.

relief *n.* **1 a** the alleviation of or deliverance from pain, distress, anxiety, etc. **b** the feeling accompanying such deliverance. **c** alleviation of some burden, esp. taxation. **d** the action of relieving pressure (also *attrib.*: *relief valve*). **2** a feature etc. that diversifies monotony or relaxes tension. **3 a** assistance given to those in special need or difficulty (*disaster relief fund*). **b** financial and other assistance given to the poor from government funds. **4 a** the replacing of a person or persons on duty by another or others. **b** a person or persons replacing others in this way. **5** (foll. by *of*) the reinforcement (esp. the raising of a siege) of a place. **6 a** a method of moulding or carving or stamping in which the design stands out from the surface, with projections proportioned to and more (**high relief**) or less (**low relief**) closely approximating those of the objects depicted. **b** a piece of sculpture etc. in relief. **c** a representation of relief given by an arrangement of line or colour or shading. **7** vividness, distinctness (*brings the facts out in sharp relief*). **8** *Baseball* the act or an instance of a pitcher entering a game already in progress to replace the current pitcher because of ineffectiveness, fatigue, etc. (*pitched three innings of relief*; *relief innings*). **9** esp. *Law* the redress of a hardship or grievance. **10** (usu. *attrib.*) designating a printing process using raised type (*relief printing*).

relief camp *n. Cdn hist.* one of a number of camps set up across Canada at the height of the Depression (1932–36) in which single, unemployed, homeless men were provided with lodging, food, medical care, work clothes, and minimal pay for work.

relief pitcher *n. Baseball* a pitcher who replaces another in mid-game.

relieve *v.tr.* **1** bring or provide aid or assistance to. **2** alleviate or reduce (pain, suffering, pressure, etc.). **3** mitigate the tedium or monotony of. **4** bring military support for (a besieged place). **5** release (a person) from a duty by acting as or providing a substitute. **6** (foll. by *of*) take (a burden or responsibility) away from (a person). **7** bring into relief; cause to appear solid or detached. □ **relieve oneself** urinate or defecate.

relieved *predic.adj.* freed from anxiety or distress (*am very relieved to hear it*). □ **relievedly** *adv.*

reliever *n.* **1** in senses of RELIEVE. **2** = RELIEF PITCHER.

religion *n.* **1** the belief in a superhuman controlling power, esp. in a personal God or gods entitled to obedience and worship. **2** the expression of this in worship. **3** a particular system of faith and worship. **4** life under monastic vows. **5** a thing that one is strongly devoted to (*football is their religion*).

religionist *n.* a religious person, esp. a follower of a specified religion.

religiosity /rɪˌlɪdʒɪˈɒsɪti/ *n.* the condition of being religious or excessively religious.

religious ● *adj.* **1** devoted to religion; pious, devout. **2** of or concerned with religion. **3** of or belonging to a religious order, e.g. of monks. **4** scrupulous, conscientious (*a religious attention to detail*). ● *n.* (*pl.* same) a person bound by religious vows, e.g. a monk, nun, etc. □ **religiously** *adv.*

relinquish /rəˈlɪŋkwɪʃ, ri-/ *v.tr.* **1** surrender or resign (a right or possession). **2** give up or cease from (a habit, plan, belief, etc.). **3** relax hold of (an object held). □ **relinquishment** *n.*

reliquary /ˈrelɪkweri/ *n.* (*pl.* **-ies**) esp. *Christianity* a receptacle for relics.

relish ● *n.* **1** great liking, enjoyment, or satisfaction (*told the story with great relish*). **2 a** an appetizing flavour. **b** an attractive quality (*fishing loses its relish in winter*). **3** a condiment eaten with plainer food to add flavour, esp. a sauce made of pickled chopped vegetables. ● *v.tr.* **1 a** get pleasure out of; enjoy greatly. **b** look forward to, anticipate with pleasure (*did not relish what lay before her*). **2** add relish to.

reload *v.tr. & intr.* **1** load (a gun, camera, etc.) again. **2** load (ammunition, film, etc.) into a gun, camera, etc.

relocate *v.* **1** *tr.* locate in a new place. **2** *tr. & intr.* move to a new place (esp. to live or work). □ **relocatable** *adj.* **relocation** *n.*

reluctant *adj.* **1** (often foll. by *to* + infin.) unwilling or disinclined (*reluctant to leave*). **2** done or produced with unwillingness or disinclination (*reluctant hospitality*). □ **reluctance** *n.* **reluctantly** *adv.*

rely *v.intr.* (**-ies**, **-ied**) (foll. by *on*, *upon*) **1** depend on with confidence or assurance (*am relying on your judgment*). **2** be dependent on (*relies on her for everything*).

REM *abbr.* RAPID EYE MOVEMENT.

rem *n.* (*pl.* same) a unit of effective absorbed dose of ionizing radiation in human tissue, equivalent to one roentgen of X-rays.

remain *v.intr.* **1** be left over after others or other parts have been removed or used or dealt with. **2** continue to exist or stay; be left behind (*remained at home*). **3** continue to be (*remained calm*; *remained friends*). □ **remain to be seen** be not yet known or certain. □ **remaining** *adj.*

remainder ● *n.* **1** a part remaining or left over. **2** remaining persons or things. **3** a number left after division or subtraction. **4** a copy of a book left unsold when it is no longer in great demand, often disposed of at a reduced price. ● *v.tr.* (esp. as **remaindered** *adj.*) dispose of (books) at a reduced price.

remains *n.pl.* **1** what remains after other parts have been removed or used etc. **2** relics of antiquity, esp. of buildings (*Roman remains*). **3** a person's body after death.

remake ● *v.tr.* (*past* and *past part.* **remade**) make again or differently. ● *n.* a thing that has been remade, esp. a film or recording.

remand /rəˈmænd/ ● *v.tr.* return (a prisoner) to custody, esp. to allow further inquiries to be made or while awaiting trial. ● *n.* **1** a recommittal to custody. **2** the state of having been remanded (also *attrib.*: *remand centre*).

remark ● *v.* **1** *tr.* (often foll. by *that* + clause) **a** say by way of comment. **b** take notice of; regard with attention. **2** *intr.* (usu. foll. by *on*, *upon*) make a comment. ● *n.* **1** a written or spoken comment; anything said. **2 a** the act of noticing or observing (*worthy of remark*). **b** the act of commenting (*let it pass without remark*).

remarkable *adj.* **1** worth notice; exceptional. **2** striking, conspicuous. □ **remarkably** *adv.*

remaster *v.tr.* (often as **remastered** *adj.*) rework or adjust the master of (a recording), esp. to improve the sound quality. □ **remastering** *n.*

remedial /rɪˈmiːdɪəl/ *adj.* **1** affording or intended as a remedy (*took remedial action*). **2** (of teaching etc.) for learners requiring special attention or aid.

---

relight *v.tr.* (*past* **relit**; *past part.* **relit or relighted**)
reline *v.tr.*

relive *v.tr.*

remarriage *n.*
remarry *v.intr. & tr.* (**-ies**, **-ied**)

rematch *n.*

remedy • n. (pl. **-ies**) (often foll. by for, against) **1** a medicine or treatment (for a disease etc.). **2** a means of counteracting or removing anything undesirable. **3** redress; legal or other reparation. • v.tr. (**-ies, -ied**) rectify; make good.

remember v. **1** tr. keep in the memory; not forget. **2 a** tr. & intr. bring back into one's thoughts, call to mind (knowledge or experience etc.). **b** tr. (often foll. by to + infin. or that + clause) have in mind (a duty, commitment, etc.) (will you remember to lock up?). **3** tr. think of or acknowledge (a person) in some connection, as in commemoration or in making a gift etc. **4** tr. (foll. by to) convey greetings from (one person) to (another) (remember me to your mother). **5** tr. mention (in prayer).

remembrance n. **1** the act of remembering or process of being remembered. **2** a memory or recollection. **3** a thing serving to remind one of another; a keepsake or souvenir. **4** a gift made in remembrance of another. **5** (in pl.) greetings conveyed through a third person.

Remembrance Day n. (in Canada) Nov. 11, the anniversary of the armistice at the end of World War I, on which the war dead are commemorated.

remind v.tr. **1** (foll. by of) cause (a person) to remember or think of. **2** (foll. by to + infin. or that + clause) cause (a person) to remember (a commitment etc.) (remind them to pay their subscriptions).

reminder n. **1** a thing that reminds, esp. a letter or bill. **2** (often foll. by of) a memento or souvenir.

reminisce /ˌremɪˈnɪs/ v.intr. (often foll. by about) indulge in remembering events from one's past.

reminiscence /ˌremɪˈnɪsəns/ n. **1** the recalling of one's past experiences or events, esp. with enjoyment. **2 a** a past fact or experience that is remembered. **b** the process of narrating this. **3** (in pl.) a collection in literary form of incidents and experiences that a person remembers. **4** a characteristic of one thing reminding or suggestive of another.

reminiscent adj. **1** (foll. by of) tending to remind one of or suggest. **2** concerned with reminiscence. **3** (of a person) given to reminiscing. □ **reminiscently** adv.

remiss /rəˈmɪs, ri-/ adj. careless of duty; negligent.

remission /rəˈmɪʃən, ri-/ n. **1 a** a diminution of force, effect, or degree (esp. of disease or pain). **b** the period or duration of this. **2** Cdn & Brit. the reduction of a prison sentence on account of good behaviour etc. **3** the remitting of a debt or penalty etc. **4** (often foll. by of) forgiveness (of sins etc.).

remit v. (**remitted, remitting**) **1** tr. cancel or refrain from exacting (a debt or punishment etc.). **2** intr. & tr. abate or slacken; cease or cause from partly or entirely. **3** tr. send (money etc.) in payment. **4** tr. send by mail. **5** tr. **a** (often foll. by to) refer (a matter for decision etc.) to some authority. **b** Law send back (a case) to a lower court. **6** tr. **a** (often foll. by to) postpone or defer. **b** (foll. by in, into) send or put back into a previous state. **7** tr. Theol. (usu. of God) pardon (sins etc.).

remittance n. **1** money sent, esp. by mail, for goods etc. or as an allowance. **2** the act of sending money.

remittance man n. hist. an emigrant who is supported or assisted by money sent from home.

remittent /rəˈmɪtənt, ri-/ adj. that abates at intervals (remittent fever).

remix • v.tr. mix (esp. a recording) again. • n. a sound recording that has been remixed to produce a new version (see MIX v. 8, 9). □ **remixer** n.

remnant • n. **1** a small remaining quantity. **2** a piece of cloth etc. left when the greater part has been used or sold. **3** (foll. by of) a surviving trace (a remnant of empire). • adj. remaining; leftover.

remodel v.tr. (**remodelled, remodelling**) **1** model again or differently. **2** change the structure or shape of (esp. a room or building); reconstruct. □ **remodeller** n.

remonstrance /rəˈmɒnstrəns/ n. **1** the act or an instance of remonstrating. **2** a protest.

remonstrate /ˈremənˌstreɪt/ v. **1** intr. (foll. by with) make a protest; argue forcibly (remonstrated with them over the delays). **2** tr. (often foll. by that + clause) urge protestingly. □ **remonstration** n.

remorse n. **1** deep regret for a wrong committed. **2** a compassionate reluctance to inflict pain. □ **remorseful** adj. **remorsefully** adv. **remorseless** adj. **remorselessly** adv.

remote (**remoter, remotest**) • adj. **1** far away in place or time. **2** out of the way; situated away from the main centres of population, society, etc. **3** distantly related (a remote ancestor). **4** slight, faint (not the remotest chance). **5** (of a person) aloof; not friendly. **6** (foll. by from) widely different; separate by nature (ideas remote from the subject). **7** situated, occurring, operating, or performed at or from a (not necessarily great) distance (remote camera). • n. = REMOTE CONTROL 2. □ **remotely** adv. **remoteness** n.

remote control n. **1** control of a machine or apparatus from a distance by means of signals transmitted from a radio or electronic device. **2** such a device, esp. a hand-held one controlling a television etc. □ **remote-controlled** adj.

remote sensing n. the scanning of the earth by satellite or high-flying aircraft in order to obtain information about it.

remount • v. **1 a** tr. mount (a horse etc.) again. **b** intr. get on horseback again. **2** tr. get on to or ascend (a ladder, hill, etc.) again. **3** tr. put (a picture, object, etc.) on a new or different mount. **4** tr. present or perform (a play, musical, exhibition, etc.) again. • n. a fresh horse for a rider.

removal n. **1** the act or an instance of removing; the process of being removed. **2** dismissal, e.g. from a job.

remove • v. **1** tr. take off or away from the place or position occupied. **2** tr. **a** move or take to another place; change the situation of. **b** get rid of; eliminate (will remove all doubts). **3** tr. cause to be no longer present or available; take away (all privileges were removed). **4** tr. (often foll. by from) dismiss (a person) from office. **5** tr. informal kill, assassinate. **6** tr. (in passive; foll. by from) distant or remote in condition (not far removed from anarchy). • n. **1** a degree or remoteness; a distance. **2** a stage in a gradation; a degree (is several removes from what I expected). □ **removable** adj. **removability** n. **remover** n.

removed adj. **1** (esp. of cousins) separated by a specified number of steps of descent (a first cousin twice removed). **2** (foll. by from) distant, remote, separated.

remunerate /rɪˈmjuːnəˌreɪt/ v.tr. **1** reward; pay for services rendered. **2** serve as or provide recompense for (toil etc.) or to (a person). □ **remuneration** n. **remunerative** /-rətɪv/ adj.

Renaissance /ˈrenəˌsɒns, -ˌsɑ̃s, rəˈneɪ-/ n. **1** the period in Western European history in the 14th–16th c. of intensified classical scholarship and humanism, marked by advances in art and literature under the influence of classical models. **2** the culture and style of art, architecture, etc. developed during this era. **3** (**renaissance**) a revival, esp. of culture.

Renaissance man n. a person with many talents or pursuits, esp. in the humanities.

renal /ˈriːnəl/ adj. of or concerning the kidneys.

rend v. (past and past part. **rent**) **1** tr. & intr. (foll. by off, from, away, etc.) tear or wrench forcibly. **2** *tr.* & *intr.* split or divide in pieces or into factions (*a country rent by civil war*). **3** *tr.* cause emotional pain to (the heart etc.). □ **rend the air** sound piercingly.

render *v.tr.* **1** cause to be or become; make (*rendered us helpless*). **2** give or pay (money, service, etc.), esp. in return or as a thing due (*render thanks*). **3** (often foll. by *to*) **a** give (assistance) (*rendered aid*). **b** show (obedience etc.). **c** do (a service etc.). **4 a** submit; send in; present (an account, reason, etc.). **b** hand down (a verdict). **5 a** represent or portray artistically, musically, etc. **b** perform (a role); represent (a character, idea, etc.) (*the dramatist's conception was well rendered*). **c** *Music* perform; execute. **6** translate (*rendered the poem into French*). **7** (often foll. by *down*) melt down (fat etc.) esp. to clarify; extract by melting. □ **renderer** *n.*

rendering *n.* **1 a** the act or an instance of performing music, drama, etc.; an interpretation or performance (*an excellent rendering of the part*). **b** a translation. **2** the process of extracting, melting, or clarifying fat. **3** the act or an instance of giving, yielding, or surrendering.

rendezvous /ˈrɒndei,vuː/ • *n.* (*pl.* same /-,vuːz/) **1** an agreed or regular meeting place. **2** a meeting by arrangement. **3** a place appointed for assembling troops etc. **4** a pre-arranged meeting between spacecraft in space. • *v.intr.* (**-vouses** /-,vuːz/; **-voused** /-,vuːd/; **-vousing** /-,vuːɪŋ/) meet at a rendezvous.

rendition *n.* (often foll. by *of*) **1** an interpretation or rendering of a dramatic role, piece of music, etc. **2** a translation. **3** a visual representation. **4** the act or an instance of rendering.

renegade /ˈrenə,geid/ • *n.* **1 a** a person who deserts a party or principles. **b** a person who changes allegiance. **2** a person living outside of or in opposition to a society; an outlaw. • *adj.* **1** traitorous, rebellious. **2** of changed allegiance.

renege /rəˈneg, ri-, -ˈneig/ *v.intr.* (**reneged, reneging**) **1** go back on one's word; change one's mind; recant. **2** (foll. by *on*) go back on (a promise or undertaking).

renew *v.* **1** *tr.* revive; regenerate; make new again; restore to the original state. **2** *tr.* reinforce; resupply; replace. **3** *tr.* repeat or re-establish; resume after an interruption (*a renewed attack*). **4** *tr.* get, begin, make, say, give, etc. anew. **5** *tr.* & *intr.* **a** grant or be granted a continuation of or continued validity of (a licence, subscription, lease, etc.). **b** extend the period of loan of (a library book). **6** *tr.* recover (one's youth, strength, etc.). □ **renewal** *n.*

renewable • *adj.* **1** able to be renewed. **2** (of a source of material or energy) not depleted by utilization. • *n.* a renewable source of material or energy. □ **renewability** *n.*

rennet /ˈrenət/ *n.* **1** curdled milk found in the stomach of an unweaned calf, used in curdling milk for cheese, junket, etc. **2** a preparation made from the stomach membrane of a calf or from certain fungi, used for the same purpose.

reno /ˈrenoː/ *n.* (*pl.* **-os**) *Cdn informal* **1** a renovated house. **2** renovation (also *attrib.*: *reno project*).

renounce *v.tr.* **1** consent formally to abandon; surrender; give up (a claim, right, possession, etc.). **2** repudiate; refuse to recognize any longer. **3 a** decline further association or disclaim relationship with (*renounced my former friends*). **b** withdraw from; discontinue; forsake. □ **renounce the world** abandon society or material affairs. □ **renouncer** *n.*

renovate *v.tr.* **1** remodel or install new fixtures etc. in (a building or part of it). **2** restore to good condition; repair. **3** refresh; reinvigorate. □ **renovation** *n.* **renovator** *n.*

renown *n.* fame; high distinction.

renowned *adj.* famous; celebrated.

rent¹ • *n.* **1** a regular payment made by a tenant to an owner or landlord for the use of land or premises. **2** payment for the use of a service, equipment, etc. • *v.* **1** *tr.* occupy or use (property, equipment, etc.) for a fixed, usu. temporary period, in return for payment. **2** *tr.* (often foll. by *out*) allow a person to use (something) in return for rent. **3** *intr.* occupy and use property in return for paying rent (*fed up with renting*). **4** *intr.* be leased or hired out at a specified rate (*the apartment rents for $850 a month*). □ **for rent** *N Amer.* available to be rented. □ **renter** *n.*

rent² *n.* **1** a large tear, opening. **2** a breach or split, e.g. in relations between people etc.

rent³ *past* and *past part.* of REND.

rent-a- *comb. form* often *jocular* denoting availability for hire (*rent-a-van*).

rentable *adj.* **1** available or suitable for renting. **2** giving an adequate ratio of profit to capital. □ **rentability** *n.*

rental • *n.* **1** the amount paid or received as rent. **2** the act of renting. **3** *N Amer.* a rented house, car, etc. • *adj.* **1** of or relating to rent. **2** available for rent; rented (*a rental car*).

rent control *n.* a system of keeping rent increases within fixed limits, supervised by a government agency. □ **rent-controlled** *adj.*

rente /rɑ̃t/ *n.* *Cdn hist.* an annual payment made (in cash or produce) by a tenant to a landowner under the seigneurial system (*compare* CENS).

rent-free *adj.* & *adv.* with exemption from rent.

rentier /ˈrɑ̃ti,ei/ *n.* a person living on dividends from property, investments, etc. (also *attrib.*: *the rentier class*).

renunciation /rə,nʌnsiˈeiʃən/ *n.* **1** the act or an instance of renouncing or giving up. **2** self-denial. **3** a document expressing renunciation. □ **renunciatory** /rəˈnʌnʃətəri/ *adj.*

re-offer *v.intr.* *Cdn* (*Maritimes*) stand as a candidate for re-election (*the Halifax MP has decided not to re-offer*).

reorganize *v.tr.* **1** organize differently. **2** restructure the management of (a corporation), esp. to solve financial difficulties. □ **reorganization** *n.* **reorganizer** *n.*

reorient *v.tr.* **1** give a new direction to (ideas etc.); redirect (a thing). **2** help (a person) find his or her bearings again. **3** change the outlook of (a person). **4** (*refl.*) adjust oneself to or come to terms with something.

reorientate *v.tr.* = REORIENT. □ **reorientation** *n.*

Rep. *abbr.* **1** *US* Representative. **2** *US* Republican. **3** Republic.

---

rename *v.tr.*
renegotiable *adj.*
renegotiate *v.tr.* & *intr.*
renegotiation *n.*

renumber *v.tr.*
reoccupation *n.*
reoccupy *v.tr.*
(-ies, -ied)

reoccur *v.intr.*
(reoccurred,
reoccurring)
reoccurrence *n.*

reoffend *v.intr.*
reopen *v.tr.* & *intr.*
reopening *n.*
reorder *v.tr.* & *intr.* & *n.*

rep¹ *n. informal* **1** a representative, esp. a sales representative. **2 a** repertory. **b** a repertory theatre or company. **3** *N Amer.* reputation. **4** (usu. in *pl.*) a repetition of a fitness exercise.

rep² *n.* a textile fabric with a corded surface, used in curtains and upholstery.

repackage *v.tr.* **1** package again or differently. **2** present in a new form. □ **repackaging** *n.*

repaid *past and past part. of* REPAY.

repair¹ ● *v.tr.* **1** restore to good condition after damage or wear. **2** renovate or mend by replacing or fixing parts or by compensating for loss or exhaustion. **3** set right or make amends for (loss, wrong, error, etc.). ● *n.* **1** (usu. in *pl.*) the act or an instance of restoring to sound condition (*in need of repairs*). **2** the result of this (*the repair is hardly visible*). **3** good or relative condition for working or using (*in good repair*). □ **repairable** *adj.* **repairer** *n.*

repair² *v.intr.* (foll. by *to*) go, make one's way (*repaired to the living room*).

repairman *n.* (*pl.* **-men**) a person who repairs vehicles, machinery, appliances, etc.

repaper *v.tr.* paper (a wall etc.) again.

reparation /ˌrɛpəˈreɪʃən/ *n.* **1** the act or an instance of making amends. **2 a** compensation. **b** (esp. in *pl.*) compensation for war damage paid by the defeated country. **3** the act or an instance of repairing or being repaired.

repartee /ˌrɛpɑrˈteɪ, -ˈtiː/ *n.* **1** the practice or faculty of making witty retorts. **2 a** a witty retort. **b** conversation that consists of quick clever comments and replies.

repass *v.tr. & intr.* **1** pass again, esp. on the way back. **2** (of a legislature) pass (a bill) again.

repast /rɪˈpæst/ *n. formal* **1** a meal, esp. of a specified kind (*a light repast*). **2** food and drink supplied for or eaten at a meal.

repatriate ● *v.* **1 a** *tr.* restore (a person) to his or her native land. **b** *intr.* return to one's own native land. **2** *tr.* bring (legislation, esp. a constitution) under the authority of the autonomous country to which it applies, used with reference to laws passed on behalf of that country by its former mother country. **3** *tr.* return (capital) from a foreign investment to investment in the country from which it came. ● *n.* a person who has been repatriated. □ **repatriation** *n.*

repay *v.* (*past and past part.* **repaid**) **1** *tr.* pay back (money). **2** *tr.* return (a visit etc.). **3** *tr.* make repayment to (a person). **4** *tr.* make return for (a service, action, etc.) (*the book repays close study*). **5** *tr.* (often foll. by *for*) give in recompense. **6** *intr.* make repayment. □ **repayable** *adj.* **repayment** *n.*

Rep by Pop *n. Cdn hist.* = REPRESENTATION BY POPULATION.

repeal ● *v.tr.* revoke, rescind, or annul (a law etc.). ● *n.* the act or an instance of repealing.

repeat ● *v.* **1** *tr.* say or do over again. **2** *tr.* recite, rehearse, report, or reproduce (something from memory) (*repeated a poem*). **3** *tr.* say or report (something heard). **4** *tr.* imitate (an action etc.). **5** *intr.* recur; appear again, perhaps several times (*a repeating pattern*). **6** *intr.* do or say something over again. **7** *tr. & intr.* take (an academic course) over again, esp. to obtain a passing grade. **8** *intr.* (of food) be tasted intermittently for some time after being swallowed as a result of belching or indigestion. **9** *intr.* (of a firearm) fire several shots without reloading. **10** *intr. N Amer.* repeat a particular success, achievement, etc., esp. win a particular championship etc. again, esp. for the second consecutive time. ● *n.* **1 a** the act or an instance of repeating. **b** a thing repeated (also *attrib.*: *repeat prescription*). **2** a repeated broadcast. **3** *Music* **a** a passage intended to be repeated. **b** a mark indicating this. **4** a pattern repeated in wallpaper etc. **5** *Commerce* **a** a consignment similar to a previous one. **b** an order given for this; a reorder. ● *adv.* indicating emphasis (*will not, repeat not, allow this to happen*). □ **repeat itself** recur in the same form. **repeat oneself** say or do the same thing over again. □ **repeatable** *adj.* **repeatability** *n.*

repeated *adj.* frequent; done or said again and again (*repeated attempts*). □ **repeatedly** *adv.*

repeater *n.* **1** a person or thing that repeats. **2** a firearm which fires several shots without reloading. **3** a device for the automatic retransmission or amplification of an electrically transmitted message.

repeating decimal *n.* a recurring decimal.

repel *v.* (**repelled, repelling**) **1** *tr.* drive back; ward off; repulse. **2** *tr.* refuse admission or approach or acceptance to (*repel an assailant*). **3** *tr. & intr.* be repulsive or distasteful to. **4** *tr.* resist mixing with or admitting (*repels moisture*). **5** *tr. & intr.* (of a magnetic pole) push away from itself (*like poles repel*). □ **repeller** *n.*

repellent ● *adj.* **1** that repels. **2** disgusting, repulsive. ● *n.* (also **repellant**) **1** a substance that repels, esp. a chemical that repels insects. **2** a substance used to treat fabric etc. so that water does not penetrate it. □ **repellency** *n.* **repellently** *adv.*

repent *v.* **1** *tr. & intr.* wish one had not done, regret (one's wrongdoing, omission, etc.); resolve not to continue (a wrongdoing etc.). **2** *intr.* (often foll. by *of*) feel deep sorrow about one's actions etc. □ **repentance** *n.* **repentant** *adj.*

repercussion /ˌriːpərˈkʌʃən, ˌrɛp-/ *n.* **1** (usu. in *pl.*; often foll. by *of*) an indirect effect or reaction following an event or action (*consider the repercussions of moving*). **2** the recoil after impact. **3** an echo or reverberation.

repertoire /ˈrɛpərˌtwɑr, ˈrɛpəˌtwɑr/ *n.* **1** a stock of pieces etc. that a company or a performer knows or is prepared to perform. **2** all of the works existing in a particular artistic genre. **3** a stock of regularly performed pieces, regularly used techniques, etc. (*went through her repertoire of excuses*).

repertory /ˈrɛpərtɔri, ˈrɛpətɔri/ *n.* (*pl.* **-ies**) **1** = REPERTOIRE. **2** the performance of various theatrical productions for short periods in rotation by one company. **3 a** a company performing repertory. **b** repertory theatres regarded collectively. **4** a store or collection, esp. of information, instances, etc.

repertory theatre *n.* **1 a** a theatre at which plays are performed for short runs in sequence by the same company. **b** such theatres collectively. **2** a movie theatre at which esp. second-run films are shown for short runs, often for one showing only.

repetition *n.* **1 a** the act or an instance of repeating or being repeated. **b** the thing repeated. **2** a copy or replica.

---

repack *v.tr.*   **repaint** *v.tr.*   **repave** *v.tr.*

repetitious *adj.* characterized by repetition, esp. when unnecessary or tiresome. □ **repetitiously** *adv.*

repetitive *adj.* = REPETITIOUS. □ **repetitively** *adv.* **repetitiveness** *n.*

repetitive strain injury *n.* injury arising from the prolonged use of particular muscles, esp. during keyboarding. Abbr.: **RSI**.

rephrase *v.tr.* express in an alternative way.

replace *v.tr.* **1** put back in place. **2** take the place of; succeed; be substituted for. **3** find or provide a substitute for. **4** (often foll. by *with*, *by*) fill up the place of. **5** (in *passive*, often foll. by *by*) be succeeded or have one's place filled by another; be superseded. □ **replaceable** *adj.* **replacer** *n.*

replacement *n.* **1** the act or an instance of replacing or being replaced. **2** a person or thing that takes the place of another.

replan *v.tr.* (**replanned, replanning**) plan again or differently.

replant *v.tr.* **1** transfer (a plant etc.) to a larger pot, a new site, etc. **2** plant (ground) again.

replay ● *v.tr.* **1** play back (a piece of film, sound recording, etc.). **2** play (a game etc.) again. ● *n.* **1** the action or an instance of replaying a piece of film, sound recording, etc. *See also* INSTANT REPLAY. **2** a replayed game or match.

replenish /rə'plenɪʃ, ri-/ *v.tr.* **1** fill up again. **2** renew (a supply etc.). □ **replenisher** *n.* **replenishment** *n.*

replete /rə'pliːt, ri-/ *adj.* (often foll. by *with*) **1** filled or well-supplied with. **2** stuffed; gorged; sated. **3** equipped with. □ **repletion** *n.*

replica /'replɪkə/ *n.* **1** a facsimile, an exact copy. **2** a copy or model, esp. on a smaller scale. **3** a duplicate of a work made by the original artist.

replicate *v.* **1** *tr.* repeat (an experiment etc.). **2** *tr.* make a replica of. **3** *intr. & refl. Biol.* (of genetic material or a living organism) reproduce or give rise to a copy of (itself). □ **replicable** /'replɪkəbəl/ *adj.* **replicability** *n.* (both in sense 1 of *v.*). **replication** *n.* **replicator** *n.*

reply ● *v.* (**-ies, -ied**) **1** *intr.* (often foll. by *to*) make an answer, respond in word or action. **2** *tr.* say in answer. ● *n.* (*pl.* **-ies**) **1** the act of replying (*what did they say in reply?*). **2** what is replied; a response. **3** *Law* the plaintiff's response to the defendant's plea.

repo /'riːpəʊ/ *n.* (*pl.* **-os**) esp. *N Amer.* an instance of repossession, e.g. of a car etc. (also *attrib.*: *repo man*).

report ● *v.* **1** *tr.* **a** bring back or give an account of. **b** state as fact or news, narrate or describe or repeat, esp. as an eyewitness or hearer etc. **c** relate as spoken by another. **2** *tr.* make an official or formal statement about. **3** *tr.* (often foll. by *to*) name or specify (an offender or offence) (*reported them to the police*). **4** *intr.* (often foll. by *to*) present oneself to a person as having returned or arrived (*report to me when you arrive*). **5** *tr. & intr.* take down word for word or summarize or write a description of for publication. **6** *intr.* **a** make or draw up or send in a report. **b** (usu. foll. by *on*) investigate as a journalist; act as a reporter. **7** *intr.* (often foll. by *to*) be responsible (to a superior, supervisor, etc.). **8** *tr. Parl.* (of a committee chairman) announce that the committee has dealt with (a bill). **9** *intr.* (often foll. by *of*) give a report to convey that one is well, badly, etc. impressed (*reports well of the prospects*). ● *n.* **1** an account given or opinion formally expressed after investigation or consideration. **2** a description, summary, or reproduction of a scene or speech or law case, esp. for newspaper publication or broadcast. **3** common talk; rumour. **4** the way a person or thing is spoken of (*I hear a good report of you*). **5** = REPORT CARD 1.

6 the sound of an explosion. □ **report back** deliver a report to the person, organization, etc. for whom one acts etc. □ **reportable** *adj.* **reportedly** *adv.*

reportage /ˌrepɔː'tɒʒ/ *n.* **1** the describing of events, esp. the reporting of news etc. for the press and for broadcasting. **2** the typical style of this. **3** reported news collectively (*reportage on prison life*).

report card *n. N Amer.* **1** a written statement of a student's marks and behaviour at school, sent home to the parent or guardian. **2** an evaluation of performance (*a report card on health care*).

reported speech *n.* the speaker's words with the changes of person, tense, etc. usual in reports, e.g. *she said that she was tired* (opp. DIRECT SPEECH).

reporter *n.* **1** a person employed to report news etc. for newspapers or broadcasts. **2** a person who reports. **3** *N Amer.* = COURT REPORTER 1.

report stage *n. Cdn & Brit.* the debate on a bill in Parliament after it is reported.

repose¹ ● *n.* **1** the cessation of activity or excitement or toil. **2** sleep. **3** a peaceful or quiescent state; stillness; tranquillity. ● *v.* **1** *intr. & refl.* lie down in rest (*reposed on a sofa*). **2** *tr.* (often foll. by *on*) lay (one's head etc.) to rest (on a pillow etc.). **3** *intr.* (often foll. by *in*, *on*) lie; be lying or laid. **4** *tr.* give rest to; refresh with rest. **5** *intr.* (foll. by *on*, *upon*) be supported or based on. **6** *intr.* (foll. by *on*) (of memory etc.) dwell on.

repose² *v.* **1** *tr.* (foll. by *in*) place (trust etc.) in. **2** *intr.* be kept in a place (*the manuscript reposes in the library*).

reposition *v.* **1** *tr.* move or place in a different position. **2** *intr.* adjust or alter one's position. **3** *tr.* change the image of (a company, product, etc.) to target a new or wider market.

repository /rɪ'pɒzəˌtɔːri, -ˌtri/ *n.* (*pl.* **-ies**) **1** a place where things are stored or may be found, esp. a warehouse or museum. **2** a receptacle. **3** (often foll. by *of*) **a** a book, person, etc. regarded as a store of information etc. **b** the recipient of confidences or secrets.

repossess *v.tr.* regain possession of (esp. property or goods on which repayment of a debt is in arrears). □ **repossession** *n.* **repossessor** *n.*

repot *v.tr.* (**repotted, repotting**) put (a plant) in another, esp. larger, pot.

repp *var.* of REP².

reprehensible /ˌreprɪ'hensɪbəl/ *adj.* deserving censure or rebuke. □ **reprehensibility** *n.* **reprehensibly** *adv.*

represent *v.tr.* **1** stand for or correspond to (*the report does not represent all our views*). **2** (often in *passive*) be a specimen or example of; exemplify (*all types of people were represented in the room*). **3** act as an embodiment of; symbolize (*numbers are represented by letters*). **4** call up in the mind by description or portrayal or imagination; place a likeness of before the mind or senses. **5** serve or be meant as a likeness of. **6 a** state by way of remonstration or persuasion (*represented the rashness of it*). **b** (foll. by *to*) try to bring (the facts influencing conduct) home to (*represented the risks to her client*). **7** (often foll. by *as*, *to be*) describe or depict as; declare or make out (*not what you represent it to be*). **8** (foll. by *that* + clause) allege. **9** show, or play the part of, on stage. **10** fill the place of; be a substitute or deputy for; be entitled to act or speak for. **11** be elected as a Member of Parliament, a legislature, etc. by (*represents a rural riding*).

representation *n.* **1** the act or an instance of representing or being represented. **2** a thing (esp. a painting etc.) that represents another. **3** (esp. in *pl.*) a statement made by way of allegation or to convey opinion.

representational *adj.* **1** (of a painting etc.) depicting an object as it actually appears to the eye (*representational art*). **2** of or relating to representation.

Representation by Population *n. Cdn hist.* the concept, esp. in the Province of Canada after 1851, that legislative representation should be based proportionally on population, rather than divided equally between Canada East and Canada West.

representative ● *adj.* **1** typical of a class or category. **2** containing typical specimens of all or many classes (*a representative sample*). **3 a** consisting of elected deputies etc. **b** based on the representation of a nation etc. by such deputies (*representative government*). **4** (foll. by *of*) serving as a portrayal or symbol of (*representative of their attitude to work*). **5** that presents or can present ideas to the mind (*imagination is a representative faculty*). **6** (of art) representational. ● *n.* **1** (foll. by *of*) a sample, specimen, or typical embodiment or analogue of. **2 a** the agent of a person or society. **b** a salesperson, esp. a travelling salesperson. **3** a delegate; a substitute. **4 a** a deputy in a representative assembly. **b (Representative)** (in the US) a member of the House of Representatives. □ **representativeness** *n.*

repress *v.tr.* **1 a** check; restrain; quell. **b** suppress; prevent from rioting etc. **2** *Psych.* **a** suppress or control (thoughts, desires, etc.) in oneself or another. **b** actively exclude (an unwelcome thought) from conscious awareness. □ **repression** *n.* **repressive** *adj.* **repressively** *adv.* **repressiveness** *n.*

repressed *adj.* affected or characterized by psychological repression.

reprieve ● *v.tr.* **1 a** relieve or rescue from impending punishment. **b** remit, commute, or postpone the execution of (a condemned person). **2** give respite to. ● *n.* **1 a** the act or an instance of reprieving or being reprieved. **b** a warrant for this. **2** respite; a respite or temporary escape.

reprimand ● *n.* (often foll. by *for*) an official or sharp rebuke (for a fault etc.). ● *v.tr.* express severe disapproval of (a person or their actions), esp. officially.

reprint ● *v.tr.* print again. ● *n.* **1** the act or an instance of reprinting a book etc. **2** a book etc. reprinted. **3** the quantity reprinted.

reprisal /rɪˈpraɪzəl/ *n.* **1** retaliation against an enemy involving the infliction of equal or greater injuries. **2** any act of retaliation.

reprise /rɪˈpraɪz, -ˈpriːz/ ● *n.* **1** a repeated passage in music. **2** a repeated item in a musical program. ● *v.tr.* repeat (a performance, song, etc.); restage, rewrite.

repro /ˈriːprəʊ/ *n.* (*pl.* **-os**) (often *attrib.*) a reproduction or copy.

reproach ● *v.tr.* **1** express disapproval to (a person) for a fault etc. **2** scold; rebuke; censure. ● *n.* **1 a** rebuke or censure. **2** blame, criticism (*her behaviour was above reproach*). **3** (often foll. by *to*) a thing that brings disgrace or discredit. □ **above** (or **beyond**) **reproach** perfect. □ **reproachable** *adj.* **reproachful** *adj.* **reproachfully** *adv.*

reprobate /ˈreprəˌbeɪt/ ● *n.* **1** an unprincipled person; a person of highly immoral character. **2** a person who is condemned by God. ● *adj.* **1** immoral. **2** hardened in sin. ● *v.tr.* express or feel disapproval of; censure. □ **reprobation** *n.*

reproduce *v.* **1** *tr.* produce a copy or representation of. **2** *tr.* cause to be seen or heard etc. again (*tried to reproduce the sound exactly*). **3** *intr.* produce further members of the same species by natural means. **4** *refl.* produce offspring (*reproduced itself several times*). **5** *intr.* give a specified quality or result when copied (*reproduces badly*). **6** *tr. Biol.* form afresh (a lost part etc. of the body). □ **reproducer** *n.* **reproducible** *adj.* **reproducibility** *n.* **reproducibly** *adv.*

reproduction *n.* **1** the act or an instance of reproducing. **2** a copy of a work of art, esp. a print or photograph of a painting. **3** (*attrib.*) (of furniture etc.) made in imitation of a certain style or of an earlier period. **4** the quality of reproduced sound. **5** the process by which a new organism is produced by or from an existing organism or organisms of the same species.

reproductive *adj.* **1** of, pertaining to, or effecting reproduction of an organism, esp. human reproduction (*reproductive technology*). **2** serving to reproduce. □ **reproductively** *adv.*

reprogram *v.tr.* (also **-gramme**) (**-grammed**, **-gramming** or **-gramed**, **-graming**) program (esp. a computer) again or differently. □ **reprogrammable** *adj.* (also **-gramable**).

reproof /rɪˈpruːf/ *n.* **1** blame (*a glance of reproof*). **2** a rebuke; words expressing blame.

reprove /rɪˈpruːv/ *v.tr.* rebuke (a person, a person's conduct, etc.). □ **reproving** *adj.* **reprovingly** *adv.*

rept. *abbr.* report.

reptile /ˈreptaɪl/ *n.* **1** any cold-blooded scaly animal of the class Reptilia, including snakes, lizards, crocodiles, turtles, tortoises, etc. **2** a grovelling or repulsive person. □ **reptilian** /-ˈtɪliən/ *adj. & n.*

republic *n.* **1 a** a state in which supreme power is held by the people or their elected representatives or by an elected or nominated president, not by a monarch etc. **b** the system of government of such a state. **c** a period during which a state has such a government. **2** a society with equality between its members (*the literary republic*).

republican ● *adj.* **1** of or constituted as a republic. **2** characteristic of a republic. **3** advocating or supporting republican government. ● *n.* **1** a person advocating or supporting republican government. **2** (**Republican**) (in the US) a member or supporter of the Republican Party. **3** (also **Republican**) an advocate of a united Ireland. □ **republicanism** *n.*

Republican Party *n.* one of the two main US political parties, favouring only a moderate degree of central power (compare DEMOCRATIC PARTY).

repudiate /rɪˈpjuːdiˌeɪt, ri-/ *v.tr.* **1 a** disown; disavow; reject. **b** refuse dealings with. **c** deny. **2** refuse to recognize or obey (authority or a treaty). **3** refuse to discharge (an obligation or debt). □ **repudiation** *n.*

repugnance /rɪˈpʌɡnəns, ri-/ *n.* **1** (usu. foll. by *to*, *against*) antipathy; aversion. **2** (usu. foll. by *of*, *between*, *to*, *with*) inconsistency or incompatibility of ideas etc.

repugnant *adj.* **1** (often foll. by *to*) extremely distasteful. **2** (often foll. by *to*) contradictory. **3** (often foll. by *with*) incompatible.

repulse ● *v.tr.* **1** drive back (an attack or attacking enemy) by force of arms. **2 a** rebuff (friendly advances or their maker). **b** refuse (a request or offer or its maker). **3** be repulsive to, repel, disgust. ● *n.* **1** the act or an instance of repulsing or being repulsed. **2** a rebuff.

---

reprocess *v.tr.* **reprocessing** *n.* **republication** *n.* **republish** *v.tr. & intr.*

repulsion n. **1** aversion; disgust. **2** esp. *Physics* the force by which bodies tend to repel each other or increase their mutual distance (*opp.* ATTRACTION). □ **repulsive** *adj.* **repulsively** *adv.* **repulsiveness** n.

reputable /ˈrɛpjʊtəbəl/ *adj.* having a good reputation; respectable. □ **reputably** *adv.*

reputation /ˌrɛpjʊˈteɪʃən/ n. **1** what is generally said or believed about a person's or thing's character or standing (*has a reputation for honesty*). **2** the state of being well thought of; distinction; respectability. **3** (foll. by *of*, *for* + verbal noun) fame, credit, or notoriety for doing something. **4** a reputation for promiscuity, drunkenness, etc. (*has a reputation*).

repute /rəˈpjuːt, ri-/ n. reputation.

reputed *adj.* **1** generally considered or reckoned (*is reputed to be the best*). **2** passing as being, but probably not being (*his reputed father*). □ **reputedly** *adv.*

request ● n. **1** the act or an instance of asking for something; a petition (*came at his request*). **2** a thing asked for. **3 a** a letter, phone call, etc. asking for a particular recording etc. to be played on a radio program, often with a personal message. **b** the recording etc. played in response to such a letter etc. ● *v.tr.* **1** ask to be given or allowed or favoured with (*requests your presence*). **2** (foll. by *to* + infin.) ask a person to do something (*requested her to go*). **3** (foll. by *that* + clause) ask that. □ **by** (or **on** or **upon**) **request** in response to an expressed wish. □ **requester** n.

requiem /ˈrɛkwiəm, -iem/ n. **1** (**Requiem**) (also *attrib.*) esp. *Catholicism* a Mass for the repose of the souls of the dead. **2** *Music* a musical setting for this. **3** (often foll. by *for*) a memorial (*his book was a fitting requiem*).

require *v.tr.* **1** need; depend on for success or fulfillment (*the work requires patience*). **2** lay down as an imperative (*did all that was required by law*). **3** command; instruct (a person etc.). **4** order; insist on (an action or measure). **5** (often foll. by *of*, *from*, or *that* + clause) demand (of or from a person) as a right. **6** wish to have (*is there anything you require?*). □ **requirement** n.

requisite /ˈrɛkwəzɪt/ ● *adj.* required by circumstances; necessary to success etc. ● n. (often in *pl.*; often foll. by *for*) a thing needed (for some purpose).

requisition /ˌrɛkwəˈzɪʃən/ ● n. **1** an official order for the use of property or materials, esp. by an army during a war. **2 a** a formal written demand that a duty etc. should be performed. **b** the form on which such a request is written (*filled out a requisition*). **3** the state or condition of being called or put into service. ● *v.tr.* demand the use or supply of, esp. by requisition order.

requite /rəˈkwaɪt, ri-/ *v.tr.* **1** make return for (a service). **2** (often foll. by *with*) reward or avenge (a favour or injury). **3** (often foll. by *for*) make return to (a person). **4** (often foll. by *for*, *with*) repay with good or evil (*requite hate with love*). □ **requital** n.

re-release ● *v.tr.* release (a record, film, etc.) again. ● n. a re-released record, film, etc.

reroute *v.tr.* (**-routing**) send or carry by a different route.

rerun ● *v.tr.* (**rerunning**; *past* **reran**; *past part.* **rerun**) **1** show a television program, film, etc. again. **2** run (a race, computer program, etc.) again. ● n. **1** the act or an instance of rerunning. **2** a television program etc. shown again.

res¹ /rɛz/ n. *informal* resolution (of a computer screen etc.).

res² n. *Cdn slang* a university or college residence.

res³ *var. of* REZ.

resale n. the sale of a thing previously bought (often *attrib.*: *resale value*). □ **resaleable** *adj.* (also **resalable**).

rescind /rəˈsɪnd, ri-/ *v.tr.* abrogate, revoke, cancel. □ **rescission** /-ˈsɪʒən/ n.

rescue ● *v.tr.* (**rescues, rescued, rescuing**) (often foll. by *from*) save or set free or bring away from attack, custody, danger, harm, or an unpleasant situation. ● n. the act or an instance of rescuing or being rescued. □ **rescuer** n.

research /ˈriːsɜːtʃ, rɪˈsɜːtʃ/ ● n. **1 a** the systematic investigation into and study of materials, sources, etc., in order to establish facts and reach new conclusions. **b** (usu. in *pl.*) an endeavour to discover new or collate old facts etc. by the scientific study of a subject or by a course of critical investigation. **2** (*attrib.*) engaged in or intended for research (*research assistant*). ● *v.* **1** *tr.* do research into or for. **2** *intr.* make researches. □ **researcher** n.

research and development n. (in industry etc.) work directed towards the innovation, introduction, and improvement of products and processes.

research station n. an establishment where scientific research and development activities in agriculture, biotechnology, etc. are conducted.

resemblance n. (often foll. by *to*, *between*, *of*) a likeness or similarity.

resemble *v.tr.* be like; have a similarity to, or features in common with, or the same appearance as.

resent *v.tr.* show or feel indignation at; be aggrieved by (a circumstance, action, or person). □ **resentful** *adj.* **resentfully** *adv.* **resentment** n.

reservation n. **1** the act or an instance of reserving or being reserved. **2** a booking (of a room, seat, etc.). **3** the thing booked, e.g. a room in a hotel. **4** (often in *pl.*) an express or tacit limitation, qualification, or exception to an agreement etc. (*had reservations about the plan*). **5** an area of land reserved for occupation by American Indians in the US, Australian Aboriginals, etc. (*compare* RESERVE n. 5). **6 a** a right or interest retained in an estate being conveyed. **b** the clause reserving this. **7** *Cdn* a constitutional power residing with the Governor General or Lieutenant-Governor of a province to withhold royal assent from a bill until it has been re-examined.

reserve ● *v.tr.* **1** postpone, put aside, or keep back for a later occasion or special use. **2** order to be specially retained or allocated for a particular person or at a particular time. **3** retain or secure, esp. by formal or legal stipulation (*reserve the right to*). **4** postpone delivery of (judgment etc.) (*reserved my comments*). **5** *Cdn* (of the Governor General or a Lieutenant-Governor)

---

repurchase *v.tr.* & n.
reread *v.tr.* (*past* and *past part.* **reread**)
rereading n.

re-record *v.tr.*
re-recording n.
reschedule *v.tr.*
reseal *v.tr.*

resealable *adj.*
reseed *v.tr.*
resell *v.tr.* (*past* and *past part.* **resold**)

reseller n.

withhold royal assent from (a bill). ● *n.* **1** a thing reserved for future use; an extra stock or amount (*a great reserve of strength*; *energy reserves*). **2** a limitation, qualification, or exception attached to something (*accept your offer without reserve*). **3 a** self-restraint; reticence; coolness or distance of manner. **b** (in artistic or literary expression) absence from exaggeration or ill-proportioned effects. **4** a place reserved for special use, esp. as a habitat for wildlife (*nature reserve*). **5** (in Canada) an area of land set aside for the use of a specific group of Aboriginal people. **6** (in *sing.* or *pl.*) assets kept readily available as cash or at a central bank, or as gold or foreign exchange (*reserve currency*). **7** (in *sing.* or *pl.*) **a** troops withheld from action to reinforce or protect others. **b** forces in addition to the regular army, navy, air force, etc., but available in an emergency. **8** a member of the military reserve. **9** an extra player chosen to be a possible substitute in a team. **10** the intentional suppression of the truth (*exercised a certain amount of reserve*). ● *adj.* **1** of or pertaining to a reserve or reserves (*reserve land*). **2** kept in reserve; constituting a reserve (*reserve Chardonnay*; *reserve fund*). □ **in reserve** unused and available if required.

reserved *adj.* **1** reticent; slow to reveal emotion or opinions; uncommunicative. **2 a** set apart, destined for some use or fate. **b** booked in advance. **c** (often foll. by *for, to*) left by fate for; falling first or only to.

reserve price *n.* the lowest acceptable price stipulated for an item sold at an auction.

reservist *n.* a member of a country's reserve forces.

reservoir /'rezər,vwɑr, 'rezə-/ *n.* **1** a large natural or artificial lake or pool used for collecting and storing water for public and industrial use, irrigation, etc. **2 a** any natural or artificial receptacle esp. for or of fluid. **b** a place where fluid etc. collects. **3** a part of a machine etc. holding fluid. **4** a body of porous rock holding a large quantity of oil or natural gas. **5** a reserve or supply (*a reservoir of information*).

reset ● *v.tr.* (**-setting**; *past* and *past part.* **-set**) **1** set (a broken bone, gems, a measuring gauge, etc.) again or differently. **2** cause (a device or appliance) to return to a former state, esp. to a condition of readiness. ● *n.* **1** the action or an act of resetting something. **2** a device for resetting an instrument etc.

reshoot ● *v.tr. & intr.* (*past* and *past part.* **reshot**) shoot (a scene in a film etc.) again. ● *n.* a scene in a film etc. shot again.

reshuffle ● *v.tr.* **1** shuffle (cards) again. **2** interchange the posts of (government ministers, employees, etc.). **3** change the position or order of; interchange. ● *n.* the act or an instance of reshuffling.

reside *v.intr.* **1** (of a person) have one's home, dwell permanently. **2** (of power, a right, etc.) rest or be vested in. **3** (of an incumbent official) be in residence. **4** (foll. by *in*) (of a quality) be present or inherent in.

residence *n.* **1** the act or an instance of residing. **2 a** the place where a person resides; an abode. **b** a house, esp. an impressive one. **3** *N Amer.* a building providing accommodation for students at a university or college. □ **in residence** dwelling at a specified place. **-in-residence** (in *comb.*) designating a practitioner of one of the arts, working in or associated with a university, organization, etc., in order to share professional knowledge (*artist-in-residence*).

residency *n.* (*pl.* **-ies**) **1** = RESIDENCE 1. **2** *N Amer.* a period of specialized medical training; the position of a resident. **3 a** *Brit. & Cdn* a regular engagement at a club, theatre, etc. for a musician, dance company, etc. **b** the position of an artist-in-residence.

resident ● *n.* **1** (often foll. by *of*) **a** a permanent inhabitant (of a city, neighbourhood, building, etc.). **b** a bird belonging to a species that does not migrate. **2** *N Amer.* a medical graduate engaged in specialized practice under supervision in a hospital. **3** an intelligence agent in a foreign country. ● *adj.* **1** residing; in residence. **2 a** having quarters on the premises of one's work etc. (*resident housekeeper*). **b** working regularly in a particular place. **c** frequenting a particular place (*the resident intellectual at our table*). **3** located; inherent (*powers of feeling are resident in the nerves*). **4** (of birds etc.) non-migratory. **5** *Computing* (of a program etc.) occupying a permanent place in memory, esp. in main memory or the memory built into a particular device, and hence rapidly accessible during processing.

residential *adj.* **1** suitable for or occupied by private houses, apartment buildings, etc. (*residential area*). **2** used as a residence (*residential complex*). **3** based on or connected with residence (*a residential course of study*).

residential school *n.* esp. *Cdn* a boarding school operated or subsidized by religious orders or the federal government to accommodate Aboriginal and Inuit students.

residual /rə'zɪdʒʊəl, ri-/ ● *adj.* **1** remaining; still left. **2** esp. *Chem.* left as a residue, esp. at the end of some process. **3** *Math.* resulting from subtraction. **4** (in calculation) still unaccounted for or not eliminated. ● *n.* **1** a quantity left over or *Math.* resulting from subtraction. **2** an error in calculation not accounted for or eliminated. **3** (in *pl.*) a royalty paid to an actor, musician, etc., for a repeat of a television commercial, song, etc. □ **residually** *adv.*

residual power *n.* a power remaining with one political group after other powers have been allocated to another group, as between a federal government and a province.

residue /'rezɪ,duː, -,djuː/ *n.* **1** what is left over or remains; a remainder; the rest. **2** *Law* what remains of an estate after the payment of charges, debts, and bequests. **3** esp. *Chem.* a substance left after combustion, evaporation, etc.; a deposit, a sediment.

resign *v.* **1** *intr.* **a** (often foll. by *from*) give up office, one's employment, etc. **b** (often foll. by *as*) retire (*resigned as chief executive*). **2** *tr.* **a** give up (office, one's employment, etc.). **b** surrender; hand over (a right, charge, task, etc.). **3** *tr.* give up (hope etc.). **4** *refl.* (usu. foll. by *to*) reconcile (oneself, one's mind, etc.) to the inevitable (*have resigned myself to the idea*).

re-sign *v.* **1** *tr.* sign (a document etc.) again. **2** *intr.* (of a sports player etc.) sign a contract for a further period.

resignation *n.* **1** the act or an instance of resigning, esp. from one's job or office. **2** the document etc. conveying this intention. **3** the uncomplaining endurance of a sorrow or difficulty.

resigned *adj.* (often foll. by *to*) having resigned oneself; acquiescent. □ **resignedly** /-nɪdli/ *adv.*

resilient /rə'zɪljənt, ri-, -ɪənt/ *adj.* **1** (of a substance etc.) recoiling; springing back; resuming its original shape after bending, stretching, compression, etc. **2** (of a person) readily recovering from shock, depression, etc. □ **resilience** *n.* **resiliently** *adv.*

resin ● *n.* **1** an adhesive inflammable substance insoluble in water, secreted by some plants, and often extracted by incision, esp. from fir and pine (*compare* GUM[1] *n.* 1a). **2** (in full **synthetic resin**) a solid or liquid organic compound made by polymerization etc. and used in plastics etc. ● *v.tr.* (**resined, resining**) rub or treat with resin. □ **resinous** *adj.*

resist *v.* **1** *tr.* withstand the action or effect of; repel. **2** *tr.* stop the course or progress of; prevent from reaching, penetrating, etc. **3** *tr.* abstain from (pleasure, temptation, etc.). **4** *tr.* strive against; try to impede; refuse to comply with (*resist arrest*). **5** *intr.* offer opposition; refuse to comply. □ **cannot** (or **could not** etc.) **resist 1** (foll. by verbal noun) feel obliged or strongly inclined to (*cannot resist teasing me*). **2** is certain to be amused, attracted, etc., by (*can't resist children's clothes*). □ **resister** *n.* **resistibility** *n.* **resistible** *adj.*

resistance *n.* **1** the act or an instance of resisting; refusal to comply. **2** the power of resisting (*showed resistance to wear and tear*). **3 a** *Biol.* the ability to withstand adverse conditions, esp. a person's capacity for withstanding common infections or a plant's capacity to withstand common diseases. **b** *Med. & Biol.* lack of sensitivity to a drug, insecticide, etc., esp. owing to continued exposure or genetic change. **4** the impeding, slowing, or stopping effect exerted by one material thing on another. **5** *Physics* **a** the property of hindering the conduction of electricity, heat, etc. **b** the measure of this in a body. Symbol: **R**. **6** a resistor. **7 a** (in full **resistance movement**) a secret organization resisting authority, esp. in an occupied country. **b** (**Resistance**) (prec. by *the*) the underground movement formed in France during World War II to fight the German occupying forces and the Vichy government. **8** *Psych.* opposition, frequently unconscious, to the emergence into consciousness of repressed memories or desires. □ **resistant** *adj.*

resistive *adj.* **1** able to resist. **2** *Electricity* of or concerning resistance.

resistivity /ˌriːzɪsˈtɪvɪti, rɪ-/ *n.* *Electricity* a measure of the resisting power of a specified material to the flow of an electric current.

resistor *n.* *Electricity* a device having resistance to the passage of an electrical current.

resize *v.tr.* alter the size of; make larger or smaller.

resolute /ˈrɛzəˌluːt/ *adj.* (of a person or a person's mind or action) determined; decided; not vacillating. □ **resolutely** *adv.* **resoluteness** *n.*

resolution *n.* **1 a** a formal expression of opinion or intention by a legislative body or meeting. **b** the formulation of this (*passed a resolution*). **2** a thing resolved on; an intention (*New Year's resolutions*). **3** a resolute temper or character; boldness and firmness of purpose. **4** (often foll. by *of*) the act or an instance of solving doubt or a problem or question (*conflict resolution*). **5 a** esp. *Chem.* separation into components; decomposition. **b** the replacing of a single force etc. by two or more jointly equivalent to it. **6** (foll. by *into*) analysis; conversion into another form. **7** *Music* the act or an instance of causing discord to pass into concord. **8** *Physics etc.* the smallest interval measurable by a scientific (esp. optical) instrument. **9 a** the degree of detail visible in a photographic or television image. **b** the amount of graphical information that can be shown on a computer screen, usu. denoted by the number of lines that can be distinguished visibly, or by the number of pixels that can be displayed in the horizontal and vertical directions of a graphics screen.

resolve ● *v.* **1** *intr.* make up one's mind; decide firmly (*resolve to do better*). **2** *tr.* (foll. by *that* + clause) (of an assembly or meeting) pass a resolution by vote. **3** *intr. & tr.* (often foll. by *into*) separate or cause to separate into constituent parts; disintegrate. **4** *tr.* (of optical or photographic equipment) separate or distinguish between closely adjacent objects. **5** *tr. & intr.* (foll. by *into*) convert or be converted. **6** *tr. & intr.* (foll. by *into*) reduce by mental analysis into. **7** *tr.* solve; explain; clear up; settle (doubt, argument, etc.). **8** *tr. & intr.* *Music* convert or be converted into concord. ● *n.* **1** a firm mental decision or intention; a resolution. **2** resoluteness; steadfastness. □ **resolvable** *adj.*

resolved *adj.* resolute, determined.

resonance /ˈrɛzənəns/ *n.* **1** the reinforcement or prolongation of sound by reflection or synchronous vibration. **2** *Mech.* a condition in which an object or system is subjected to an oscillating force having a frequency close to its own natural frequency. **3** an allusion, connotation, or feature reminiscent of another person or thing; an overtone in thought, art, language, etc. **4** a short-lived subatomic particle that is an excited state of a more stable particle.

resonant *adj.* **1** (of sound) echoing, resounding; continuing to sound; reinforced or prolonged by reflection or synchronous vibration. **2** (of a body, room, etc.) tending to reinforce or prolong sounds esp. by synchronous vibration. **3** having the power to bring images, feelings, memories, etc. to mind (*a resonant poem*). **4** (often foll. by *with*) (of a place) resounding (*resonant with the sound of bees*). **5** of or relating to resonance. □ **resonantly** *adv.*

resonate /ˈrɛzəˌneɪt/ *v.intr.* produce or show resonance; resound.

resonator *n.* **1** a device responding to a specific vibration frequency, and used for detecting it when it occurs in combination with other sounds. **2** a structure or device which reinforces or amplifies sound by resonance, esp. an acoustical chamber of a musical instrument, such as the hollow body of a stringed instrument. **3** a device which displays electrical resonance, esp. one used for the detection of radio waves.

resort ● *n.* **1** a place frequented esp. for holidays or for a specified purpose or quality (*ski resort*). **2 a** a person or thing to which one has recourse; an expedient or measure (*a taxi was our best resort*). **b** (foll. by *to*) recourse to; use of (*without resort to violence*). ● *v.intr.* (foll. by *to*) **1** turn to as an expedient (*resorted to threats*). **2** go often or in large numbers to. □ **in the** (or **as a**) **last resort** when all else has failed.

resort village *n.* *Cdn* (*Sask.*) a small urban municipality having at least 50 dwellings or businesses and 100 assessed property owners.

resound /rəˈzaʊnd, rɪ-/ *v.intr.* **1** (often foll. by *with*) (of a place) ring or echo (*the hall resounded with laughter*). **2** (of a voice, instrument, sound, etc.) produce echoes; go on sounding. **3 a** (of fame, a reputation, etc.) be much talked of. **b** (foll. by *through*) produce a sensation (*the scandal resounded through Europe*).

resounding *adj.* **1** in senses of RESOUND. **2** unmistakable; emphatic (*a resounding success*). □ **resoundingly** *adv.*

resource /ˈriːzɔːrz, rɪˈzɔːrz, -sɔːrz/ ● *n.* **1** (usu. in *pl.*) **a** the means available to achieve an end, fulfill a function, etc. **b** a stock or supply that can be drawn on. **c** *N Amer.* available assets. **2** (often in *pl.*) a material or condition occurring in nature and capable of economic exploitation (often *attrib.*: *resource development*). **3** (in *pl.*) a country's collective wealth or means of defence. **4** (often in *pl.*) a book, videotape, or other material which supplies information on a particular topic (*educational resources*). **5** an expedient or device (*escape was their only resource*). **6 a** (often in *pl.*) skill in devising expedients (*a person of great resource*). **b** practical ingenuity; quick wit (*full of resource*). ● *v.tr.* (usu. in *passive*) provide with resources. □ **one's own resources** one's own abilities, ingenuity, etc. □ **resourceful** *adj.* **resourcefully** *adv.* **resourcefulness** *n.* **resourceless** *adj.* **resourcing** *n.*

resource centre *n.* a library etc. which houses a collection of resources for educational purposes.

resource person *n.* a person with expertise in a certain area who may be called upon as necessary to perform a particular task.

resource teacher *n.* *Cdn* **1** a teacher who provides educational resources, curriculum advice, and teaching ideas to other teachers. **2** a teacher who works with special-needs or gifted children.

RESP *abbr. Cdn* Registered Educational Savings Plan, a tax-sheltered plan for saving money for a child's post-secondary education.

respect ● *n.* **1** deferential esteem felt or shown towards a person, thing, or quality. **2 a** (foll. by *of, for*) heed or regard. **b** (foll. by *to*) attention to or consideration of (*without respect to national borders*). **3** an aspect, detail, particular, etc. (*correct in this respect*). **4** reference, relation (*a morality that has no respect to religion*). **5** (in *pl.*) a person's polite messages or attentions (*give my respects to your mother*). ● *v.tr.* **1** regard with deference, esteem, or honour. **2 a** avoid interfering with, harming, degrading, insulting, injuring, or interrupting. **b** treat with consideration. **c** refrain from offending, corrupting, or tempting (a person, a person's feelings, etc.). □ **with** (or **with all due**) **respect** a mollifying formula preceding an expression of disagreement with another's views. **with respect to** (or **in respect of**) as concerns; with reference tó. □ **respecter** *n.*

respectable *adj.* **1** deserving respect (*a respectable hypothesis; a respectable person*). **2 a** of good social standing or reputation (*a respectable middle-class family*). **b** characteristic of or associated with people of such status or character (*a respectable neighbourhood*). **3 a** honest and decent in character or conduct. **b** characterized by (a sense of) convention or propriety; socially acceptable (*respectable behaviour*). **c** derogatory highly conventional; prim. **4 a** commendable, meritorious (*an entirely respectable ambition*). **b** comparatively good or competent; passable, tolerable (*a respectable effort*). **5** reasonably good in condition or appearance; presentable. **6** appreciable in number, size, amount, etc. (*earns a respectable salary*). **7** accepted or tolerated on account of prevalence (*materialism has become respectable again*). □ **respectability** *n.* **respectably** *adv.*

respectful *adj.* feeling or showing respect, deferential (*stood at a respectful distance*). □ **respectfully** *adv.* **respectfulness** *n.*

respecting *prep.* with reference or regard to.

respective *adj.* concerning or appropriate to each of several individually (*go to your respective places*).

respectively *adv.* each individually or in turn, and in the order mentioned (*she and I gave $10 and $5 respectively*).

respiration *n.* **1 a** the act or an instance of breathing. **b** a single inspiration or expiration; a breath. **2** *Biol.* in living organisms, the process involving the production of energy and release of carbon dioxide from the oxidation of complex organic substances.

respirator *n.* **1** *Med.* an apparatus for maintaining artificial respiration. **2** an apparatus worn over the face to prevent gas, air, dust particles, etc., from being inhaled.

respiratory /ˈresprəˌtɔri, ˈrespərə-/ *adj.* pertaining to, affecting, or serving for respiration.

respiratory tract *n.* the passage of the mouth, nose, throat, and lungs, through which air passes in respiration.

respire *v.* **1** *intr.* inhale and exhale air; breathe. **2** *intr.* (of living organisms) carry out respiration. **3** *tr.* breathe (air etc.). **4** *intr.* breathe again; take a breath.

respite /ˈrespoit, -pit/ ● *n.* **1** an interval of rest or relief. **2** a delay permitted before the discharge of an obligation or the suffering of a penalty. ● *v.tr.* **1** grant respite to; reprieve (a condemned person). **2** postpone the execution or exaction of (a sentence, obligation, etc.). **3** give temporary relief from (pain or care) or to (a sufferer).

respite care *n.* temporary institutional care of a dependent elderly, ill, or handicapped person, granting a respite to the usual caregiver.

resplendent /rəˈsplendənt, ri-/ *adj.* brilliant, dazzlingly or gloriously bright. □ **resplendently** *adv.*

respond *v.* **1** *intr.* answer, give a reply. **2** *intr.* act or behave in an answering or corresponding manner. **3** *intr.* (usu. foll. by *to*) **a** react favourably (*animals respond to kindness*). **b** exhibit a response; react (*cells respond to stimuli*). **4** *intr.* (of a congregation) make answers to a priest etc. **5** *tr.* say (something) in answer. □ **responder** *n.*

respondent ● *n.* **1** a person who answers questions or defends an argument etc. **2** a defendant, esp. in an appeal or divorce case. ● *adj.* **1** making answer. **2** in the position of defendant.

response *n.* **1** an answer given in word or act. **2** a feeling, movement, change, etc., caused by a stimulus or influence. **3** (often in *pl.*) *Christianity* any part of the liturgy said or sung in answer to the clergy etc.

response time *n.* **1** *Computing* the elapsed time between the issuing of a command by a user and the receipt of some form of response or feedback from the computer. **2** the elapsed time between the receipt of an emergency call and the arrival of police, paramedics, etc. at the scene of the emergency.

responsibility *n.* (*pl.* **-ies**) **1 a** (often foll. by *for, of*) the state or fact of being responsible. **b** the ability to act independently and make decisions (*a job with more responsibility*). **2** a person, duty, or thing for which one is responsible (*the food is my responsibility*). □ **on one's own responsibility** without authorization.

responsible *adj.* **1** (often foll. by *to, for*) liable to be called to account (to a person or for a thing). **2** morally accountable for one's actions; capable of rational conduct. **3** of good credit, position, or repute; respectable; evidently trustworthy. **4** (often foll. by *for*) being the primary cause. **5** involving responsibility (*a responsible job*). □ **responsibly** *adv.*

responsible government *n.* *Cdn* a form of government in which the cabinet or executive branch is held collectively responsible and accountable to an elected legislature, and may remain in power only so long as it has the support of the legislature.

respell *v.tr.* (*past and past part.* **respelled or respelt**)

responsive *adj.* **1** (often foll. by *to*) responding readily (to some influence). **2** responding with interest or enthusiasm; receptive (*a responsive class*). □ **responsively** *adv.* **responsiveness** *n.*

rest¹ ● *v.* **1** *intr.* abstain from action, exertion, or labour; be tranquil. **2** *intr.* be still or asleep, esp. to refresh oneself or recover strength. **3** *tr.* relieve or refresh by rest (*a chair to rest my legs*). **4** *intr.* (foll. by *on, upon, against*) lie on; be supported by; be propped against. **5** *intr.* (foll. by *on, upon*) (of a look) fall or alight upon; remain directed on. **6** *tr.* (foll. by *on, upon*) a place, lay, or set for support (*rested her elbows on the table*). **b** fix, settle, or direct (one's eyes, a look, etc.) (*she rested her eyes upon me*). **7** *intr.* (of a problem or subject) be left without further investigation or discussion (*let the matter rest*). **8** *intr.* (usu. foll. by *with*) be left in the hands or charge of (*the arrangements rest with you*). **9** *intr.* (foll. by *on, upon*) depend, be based, or rely on. **10** *intr.* N Amer. Law conclude the calling of witnesses in a law case (*the prosecution rests*). **11** *intr.* lie in death. ● *n.* **1** the natural relief from daily activity obtained by repose or sleep. **2** a period of resting (*take a 15-minute rest*). **3** the cessation of, or freedom from, worry, activity, etc. (*give the subject a rest*). **4** a support or prop for holding or steadying something. **5** Music **a** an interval of silence of a specified duration. **b** the sign denoting this. **6** the repose of death (*eternal rest*). □ **at rest 1** not moving. **2** lying dead. **3** not agitated or troubled. **give it a rest** N Amer. leave (a usu. contentious or perplexing issue) for the moment. **put** (or **lay**) **to rest 1** put a decisive end to (a rumour, notion, myth, etc.). **2** bury in a grave. **rest** (or **God rest**) **his** (or **her**) **soul** may God grant his (or her) soul repose. **rest one's case** conclude one's argument etc. **rest up** N Amer. rest oneself thoroughly. **set at rest** settle or relieve (a question, a person's mind, etc.).

rest² ● *n.* (prec. by *the*) the remaining part or parts; the others; the remainder of some quantity or number (*leave the rest*). ● *v.intr.* remain in a specified state (*you can rest assured that I'll get it done*). □ **rest easy** remain or become calm, relaxed.

rest area *n.* N Amer. a small park located off a highway, usu. having picnic tables and sometimes a public washroom, where motorists may stop to refresh themselves.

restaurant *n.* a commercial establishment where meals are prepared, served, and eaten.

restaurateur /ˌrɛstərəˈtɜr/ *n.* (also **restauranteur** /ˌrɛstərɒnˈtɜr/) a person who owns or manages a restaurant. ¶The spelling *restauranteur* is considered incorrect by many, though accepted by others because it is increasingly common.

rested *adj.* refreshed or reinvigorated by resting.

restful *adj.* **1** favourable to quiet or repose; soothing. **2** free from disturbing influences. **3** relaxed or refreshed by rest.

rest home *n.* a home for old or infirm people that is run privately and offers special care for its residents.

Restigouche salmon /ˌrɛstəˈguːʃ/ *n.* a variety of Atlantic salmon associated with the Restigouche River in N New Brunswick.

resting place *n.* **1** a place provided or used for resting. **2** (esp. **final resting place, last resting place**) a place in which a person is buried.

restitution /ˌrɛstɪˈtjuːʃən, -tjuː-/ *n.* **1** (often foll. by *of*) the act or an instance of restoring something lost or stolen to its proper owner. **2** compensation for an injury. **3** esp. Theol. the restoration of a thing to its original state. **4** the resumption of an original shape or position because of elasticity.

restive *adj.* **1 a** impatient, restless. **b** uneasy, nervous, anxious. **2** (of a horse) refusing to advance, stubbornly standing still or moving backwards or sideways. **3** (of a person) unmanageable; rejecting control; refractory. □ **restiveness** *n.*

restless *adj.* **1** uneasy; agitated. **2 a** (of a person) fidgeting; unable to be still. **b** (of a thing) constantly moving (*a restless camera*). **3** affording no rest. □ **restlessly** *adv.* **restlessness** *n.*

restoration /ˌrɛstərˈeɪʃən/ *n.* **1** the return of something to a former or original state (*building restoration*). **2** the act of returning something to a former owner, place, or condition. **3** a model or drawing representing the supposed original form of a ruined building etc. **4** (**Restoration**) hist. **a** (prec. by *the*) the re-establishment of Charles II as king of England in 1660. **b** the period marked by this event. **c** (often *attrib.*) the literary period following this (*Restoration comedy*).

restorative /rəˈstɔrətɪv, ri-/ ● *adj.* **1** tending or able to restore health or strength. **2** Dentistry pertaining to the use of structures provided to replace or repair dental tissue so as to restore its form and function. ● *n.* a restorative medicine, food, etc.

restore *v.tr.* **1** bring back to the original or former state by rebuilding, repairing, repainting, etc. **2** bring back to good health etc.; cure. **3** give back to the original or former owner; make restitution of. **4** bring back to dignity or right; reinstate. **5** put back; replace. **6** make a representation of the supposed original state of (a ruin, extinct animal, etc.). □ **restored** *adj.* **restorer** *n.*

restrain *v.tr.* **1** (often *refl.*) **a** (usu. foll. by *from*) prevent (someone or oneself) from doing something (*I couldn't restrain her from asking*). **b** keep (someone or oneself) under control (*tried to restrain myself*). **2** impose a limit upon; repress (*high prices restrain sales*). **3** forcibly control or confine (*restrained her dog*).

restrained *adj.* **1** repressed, confined; kept under control or within bounds. **2** not excessive or extravagant; characterized by restraint or reserve.

restraining order *n.* N Amer. & Austral. Law a temporary court order issued to prevent an individual from committing a particular action, such as seeing or talking with a person.

restraint *n.* **1** self-control; avoidance of excess or exaggeration. **2** reserve of manner. **3** a device that restrains, such as a harness, seat belt, etc. **4** restriction of liberty or freedom of action; confinement. **5** a controlling agency or influence.

restrict *v.tr.* **1** (foll. by *to*) **a** limit to a specific person or group of people (*parking is restricted to customers and employees*). **b** limit (a person or thing) according to specific guidelines (*restrict your speech to the key points*). **2** control, curtail, or reduce (*restrict the use of chemical weapons*). **3** (usu. foll. by *from*) discourage, prevent (*factors restricting men from becoming nurses*).

---

respray *v.tr.* & *n.*
restage *v.tr.*

restart *v.tr.* & *intr.* & *n.*
restate *v.tr.*

restatement *n.*

restock *v.tr.* & *intr.*

restricted ● *adj.* **1** confined, controlled, or limited in some way. **2** (of land, access, information, etc.) available or accessible only to certain authorized individuals or to a certain group. **3** *N Amer.* of or pertaining to a movie with the classification 'Restricted'. ● *n.* (**Restricted**) **1** *Cdn* a film classification designating movies that may contain scenes of graphic violence, sex, coarse language, etc. and which have been deemed unsuitable for people under the age of 18. **2** *US* a film classification designating movies that cannot be viewed by people under the age of 18 unless accompanied by an adult.

Restricted Adult *Cdn (Alta.) n.* a film classification designating movies that may contain scenes of graphic violence, sex, coarse language, etc., to which people under the age of 18 are not admitted.

Restricted designated *n. Cdn (BC)* a film classification designating movies containing a preponderance of graphic sexual scenes, which may be shown only in certain specifically designated theatres, to people 18 and over.

restricted weapon *n. Cdn* a firearm, esp. a handgun, of a category that may be used only by licensed operators under specific conditions.

restriction *n.* **1** the act or an instance of restricting; the state of being restricted. **2** a thing that restricts. **3** a limitation placed on action; a limiting condition or regulation.

restrictive *adj.* **1** tending to limit, prevent, or restrict; imposing restrictions. **2** *Grammar* (of a clause or phrase) delimiting the meaning of a reference of a modified noun phrase or element, e.g. 'that I met yesterday' in the phrase 'the woman that I met yesterday'. □ **restrictively** *adv.* **restrictiveness** *n.*

restrictive practice *n.* (also **restrictive trade practice**) an arrangement in trade or industry aimed at restricting or controlling competition or output.

restroom *n.* esp. *US* a public washroom in a restaurant, bar, store, etc.

restructure *v.* **1** *tr.* give a new structure to; rebuild. **2** *tr. & intr.* fundamentally reorganize (a business, corporation, etc.). □ **restructuring** *n.*

rest stop *n. N Amer.* = REST AREA.

restyle *v.tr.* **1** reshape; remake in a new style. **2** give a new designation to (a person or thing).

result ● *n.* **1** a consequence or outcome of something. **2** (often in *pl.*) a satisfactory outcome; a favourable result (*she doesn't just work hard, she gets results*). **3** a quantity, formula, etc., obtained by calculation. **4** (in *pl.*) **a** a list of scores or winners etc. in an exam or sporting event. **b** the findings of a research study, survey, etc. ● *v.intr.* **1** (often foll. by *from*) arise as the actual consequence or follow as a logical consequence (from conditions, causes, etc.). **2** (often foll. by *in*) have a specified end or outcome (*resulted in a large profit*). □ **as a result** consequently, therefore. **as a result of** because of; due (to). **without result** in vain; fruitless.

resultant *adj.* **1** occurring as a result; consequent (*resultant unemployment*). **2** resulting as the total outcome of more or less opposed forces.

resume *v.* **1** *tr. & intr.* begin again or continue after an interruption. **2** *tr.* recover, occupy again (*resumed my lifestyle; resume a political position*).

resumé /'rezə,mei, 'rezjʊ,mei/ *n.* **1** *N Amer.* a brief account of one's education, experience, previous employment, and interests, usu. submitted with a job application. **2** a summary.

resumption *n.* the act or an instance of resuming.

resurface *v.* **1** *intr.* rise again; turn up or appear again. **2** *tr.* lay a new surface on (a road, ice rink, etc.).

resurgence /rə'sɜrdʒəns, ri-/ *n.* **1** a renewed prominence or popularity (*the resurgence of disco*). **2** a recovery; an increase after decline (*resurgence of the economy*). □ **resurgent** *adj.*

resurrect /,rezə'rekt/ *v.tr.* **1** bring back from obscurity or disrepair; revive. **2** raise from the dead.

resurrection /,rezə'rekʃən/ *n.* **1** the act or an instance of rising from the dead. **2** (usu. **Resurrection**) **a** Christ's rising from the dead. **b** the rising of the dead at the Last Judgment. **3** a revival after disuse or neglect. **4** the return of something to prominence, vogue, or popularity.

resuscitate /rə'sʌsɪ,teit, ri-/ *v.tr. & intr.* **1** revive from unconsciousness or apparent death. **2** revive or restore (*resuscitate the ailing economy*). □ **resuscitation** *n.* **resuscitator** *n.*

ret. *abbr.* **1** retired. **2** returned.

retail ● *n.* the sale of goods in relatively small quantities to the public, and usu. not for resale. ● *adj.* **1** (usu. *attrib.*) of or pertaining to the retailing of goods (*retail industry*). **2** sold by retail (*retail price*). ● *adv.* by retail; at a retail price (*do you buy wholesale or retail?*). ● *v.* **1** *tr.* sell (goods) in retail trade. **2** *intr.* (often foll. by *at, of*) (of goods) be sold in this way (esp. for a specified price) (*retails at $4.95*). □ **retailer** *n.* **retailing** *n.*

retain *v.tr.* **1** maintain possession of; keep. **2** allow to remain or prevail; preserve (*retains its shape*). **3** (often as **retaining** *adj.*) keep in place; hold fixed (*retaining wall*). **4** secure (a hotel room etc., or professional services, esp. of a lawyer) with a preliminary payment. **5** keep in one's memory.

retainer *n.* **1** *Law* a fee for retaining a lawyer etc. **2 a** *hist.* a dependant or follower of a person of rank. **b** a long-standing family friend or servant. **3** a thing that holds something in place or retains (also *attrib.*: *retainer screws*). **4** *Dentistry* **a** a device consisting of wires cemented to the teeth or a moulded plastic plate fitting over the teeth to keep teeth aligned once they have been straightened. **b** a structure cemented to a tooth to keep a bridge in place. □ **on** (a) **retainer** with services secured by a preliminary payment (*she was available on retainer*).

retake ● *v.tr.* (*past* **-took**; *past part.* **-taken**) **1** take again. **2** recapture. **3** film (a scene) or make (a recording) again. ● *n.* **1 a** the act or an instance of retaking. **b** a thing retaken, e.g. an exam. **2 a** the act or an instance of filming a scene or recording music etc. again. **b** a scene or recording obtained in this way.

retaliate *v.intr.* respond to an injury, insult, assault, etc. in like manner; attack in return. □ **retaliation** *n.* **retaliatory** *adj.*

---

restring *v.tr.* (*past and past part.* **restrung**)

resubmit *v.tr.*

resupply *v.tr. & intr. & n.* (**-ies, -ied**)

re-survey *v.tr. & n.*

retard ● *v.tr.* **1** delay the progress, development, arrival, or accomplishment of. **2** make slow or late. ● *n. N Amer. slang offensive* **1** a mentally retarded person. **2** a stupid or foolish person. □ **retardation** *n.* **retarder** *n.*

retardant *adj. & n.* ● *adj.* (usu. in comb.) tending to slow or resist; capable of remaining unaffected by (fire-retardant paint). ● *n.* **1** an agent that slows a process (corrosion retardant). **2** an agent that remains unaffected by or resistant to something (flame-retardant).

retarded *adj.* **1** less developed, esp. mentally, than is normal for one's age. **2** slow to develop or occur; late.

retch ● *v.intr.* make an attempt to vomit, esp. involuntarily and without effect. ● *n.* such a motion or the sound of it. □ **retching** *n.*

retention *n.* **1** the act or an instance of retaining; the state of being retained. **2** the ability to retain something; the capacity for holding or keeping something. **3** the ability to retain things experienced or learned; memory. **4** *Med.* the failure to evacuate urine or another secretion.

retentive *adj.* **1** tending to retain (moisture etc.). **2** not forgetful. □ **retentiveness** *n.*

reticence /ˈretəsəns/ *n.* **1** the avoidance of saying all one knows or feels, or of saying more than is necessary. **2** reserve or restraint in speech, style, or manners. □ **reticent** *adj.*

reticulate ● *v.tr. & intr.* /rɪˈtɪkjʊˌleɪt/ **1** divide or be divided in fact or appearance into a network. **2** arrange or be arranged in small squares or with intersecting lines. ● *adj.* /rəˈtɪkjʊlət, rɪ-/ reticulated. □ **reticulation** *n.*

reticulum /rəˈtɪkjʊləm, rɪ-/ *n.* (pl. **reticula** /-lə/) **1** a netlike structure. **2 a** a fine network of membranes etc. in living organisms. **b** a fine network within the cytoplasm of a cell (endoplasmic reticulum). **3** a ruminant's second stomach. □ **reticular** *adj.*

retina /ˈretɪnə/ *n.* a light-sensitive layer at the back of the eyeball that triggers nerve impulses through the optic nerve to the brain where the visual image is formed. □ **retinal** *adj.*

Retin-A /ˌretɪnˈeɪ/ *n. proprietary* a brand of drug chemically related to vitamin A used as a topical ointment esp. in the treatment of wrinkles etc.

retinitis /ˌretɪˈnaɪtɪs/ *n.* inflammation of the retina.

retinitis pigmentosa /ˌpɪgmenˈtoːsə/ *n.* a chronic hereditary retinopathy characterized by black pigmentation and gradual degeneration of the retina.

retinol /ˈretɪˌnɒl/ *n.* a vitamin found in green and yellow vegetables, egg yolk, and fish-liver oil, essential for growth and vision in dim light.

retinopathy /ˌretənˈɒpəθi:/ *n.* any (esp. non-inflammatory) disease of the retina.

retinue /ˈretəˌnju:, -ˌnu:/ *n.* a body of attendants accompanying an important person.

retire *v.* **1 a** *intr.* leave office or employment, esp. because of age. **b** *tr.* cause (a person) to retire from work. **c** *tr.* cease to employ or use (something), or remove it from service. **2** *intr.* withdraw or retreat, esp. to another room or location. **3** *intr.* go to bed. **4** *tr.*

Baseball put out (a batter); cause (a side) to end a turn at bat. **5** *tr.* withdraw (a bill or note) from circulation or currency. **6** *tr. & intr.* retreat; withdraw (troops).

retired *adj.* **1** having retired from employment. **2** withdrawn from society or public life; secluded.

retiree *n.* esp. *N Amer.* a person who has retired from work.

retirement *n.* **1 a** the act or an instance of retiring. **b** the condition of having retired, esp. from office or employment. **2** seclusion or privacy.

retirement age *n.* the age at which most people retire from work.

retirement community *n. N Amer.* **1** a community of homes with facilities designed for people who are retired but still active. **2** a retirement home.

retirement home *n.* **1** a house, apartment, etc. to which a person moves in old age. **2** an institution for elderly people needing care.

retirement pension *n.* = OLD-AGE PENSION.

retiring *adj.* shy; fond of seclusion.

retook *past of* RETAKE.

retool *v.* **1** *tr.* equip (a factory etc.) with new tools. **2** *intr. N Amer.* equip or prepare oneself again or for a new challenge or task. **3** *tr. N Amer.* change the essential components or qualities of (retool the stories).

retort[1] ● *n.* **1** an incisive, witty, or angry reply. **2** the turning of a charge or argument against its originator. **3** an act of retaliation. ● *v.* **1** *tr.* reply angrily or wittily; say by way of a retort. **2** *intr.* make a retort.

retort[2] *n.* **1** a vessel usu. of glass with a long recurved neck used in distilling liquids. **2** a vessel for heating mercury for purification, coal to generate gas, etc.

retouch ● *v.tr.* **1** improve or repair (a painting, makeup, etc.) by fresh touches or alterations; touch up. **2** alter or restore a photograph, print, negative, etc. by making minor changes after development. ● *n.* the act or an instance of retouching. □ **retouching** *n.*

retrace *v.tr.* **1** go back over (one's steps etc.). **2** go back over (the course of an event etc.) in one's memory. **3** trace back to a source or beginning.

retract *v.tr. & intr.* **1** withdraw or revoke (a statement, accusation, proposal, etc.). **2** (of a part of the body) draw or be drawn back or in. **3 a** (of a part of a device or mechanism) draw or be drawn back. **b** draw (an undercarriage etc.) into the body of an aircraft. □ **retractable** *adj.* **retraction** *n.*

retractile /rəˈtræktaɪl, rɪ-/ *adj.* able to be retracted.

retractor *n.* **1** a muscle used for retracting. **2** a device for retracting. **3** *Med.* an instrument or appliance used in surgical operations to hold back skin, tissues, etc. from the area of the operation.

retread ● *v.tr.* **1** put a fresh tread on (a tire). **2** alter (a person or thing) so that it is superficially different but essentially the same as its predecessor. ● *n.* **1** a retreaded tire. **2** a superficial reworking or revival of a well-known song, story, idea, etc. **3** a person recalled to service or retrained for new work.

---

retell *v.tr.* (*past and past part.* **retold**)	*and past part.* **rethought**)	**retrain** *v.tr. & intr.*	**retransmit** *v.tr.*
retelling *n.*	**retie** *v.tr.* (**retying**)	**retraining** *n.*	(**retransmitted,**
rethink *v.tr. & n.* (*past*	**retitle** *v.tr.*	**retransmission** *n.*	**retransmitting**)

retreat ● *v.intr.* **1** (esp. of military forces) retire or draw back from a superior force during or following defeat; turn away from difficulty or opposition. **2** relinquish or abandon a position, stance, or view; back down. **3** become smaller in size or extent; decline, recede. **4** withdraw into privacy or security, one's own thoughts, etc.; take refuge. **5** move backwards. ● *n.* **1 a** the act or an instance of retiring or withdrawing in the face of opposition, difficulty, or danger. **b** *Military* a signal for this (*sound the retreat*). **2** a place of seclusion. **3 a** a period of seclusion for prayer and religious meditation. **b** a period during which co-workers or people sharing a common interest meet away from their home or workplace to exchange ideas. **4** *Military* **a** a bugle call at sunset. **b** a flag-lowering ceremony including this.

retrench *v.* **1 a** *tr.* reduce or eliminate (costs, employees, etc.). **b** *intr.* cut down expenses; economize. **2** *tr.* shorten or abridge. □ **retrenchment** *n.*

retrial *n.* a second or further (judicial) trial.

retribution /ˌretrəˈbjuːʃən/ *n.* **1** punishment of a crime, injury, etc.; vengeance. **2** requital or recompense in another life for one's good or bad deeds in this world. □ **retributive** /rəˈtrɪbjʊtɪv, ri-/ *adj.*

retrieval *n.* **1** the action of retrieving, recovering, or recalling something; an instance of this. **2** the obtaining or consulting of material stored in a computer system, in books, on tape, etc. (*retrieval system*).

retrieve ● *v.* **1** *tr.* regain possession of; recover and bring back. **2** *tr.* & *intr.* (of a dog) find and bring back (game, a ball, a stick, etc.); fetch. **3** *tr.* *Computing* find or extract (information stored in a computer). **4** *tr.* & *intr.* reel in (a fishing line). **5** *tr.* repair or set right (a loss or error etc.) (*retrieved the situation*). ● *n.* **1** the act or an instance of recovering and returning something. **2** the action or an act of reeling or drawing in a fishing line. □ **retrievable** *adj.*

retriever *n.* **1** a breed of dog used for retrieving game. **2** a person or thing that retrieves something.

retro /ˈretro/ ● *n.* (*pl.* **-os**) style or fashion imitating the past, esp. in dress, music, etc. ● *adj.* **1** imitative of a style or fashion from the past (also in *comb.*: *retro-chic*). **2** nostalgic for a previous time (*a retro mood*).

retro- /ˈretro:/ *comb. form* **1** denoting action back, backwards, or in return (*retroactive*). **2** *Anat.* & *Med.* denoting location behind.

retroactive *adj.* **1** (esp. of legislation) applying to the past as well as to the present or future; retrospective. **2** (often foll. by *to*) taking effect from a past date. □ **retroactively** *adv.* **retroactivity** *n.*

retrofit ● *v.tr.* (**-fitted, -fitting**) **1** modify (machinery etc.) to incorporate changes and developments introduced after manufacture. **2** provide (an older building etc.) with new fixtures, equipment, etc. that did not exist at the time of construction. ● *n.* **1** a modification made to a product to incorporate changes made in later products of the same type or model. **2** a retrofitted product.

retrograde ● *adj.* **1** directed backwards; retreating. **2** reverting to a less developed or inferior state; reactionary. **3** *Astronomy* in retrograde or showing retrograde. ● *n.* *Astronomy* **1** the apparent backward motion of a planet in the zodiac. **2** the apparent motion of a celestial body from east to west.

retrogression *n.* **1** backward or reversed movement. **2** a reversal of development or return to a less advanced state. □ **retrogressive** *adj.*

retrospect *n.* a survey of past time or events. □ **in retrospect 1** when looked back on. **2** when looking back; with hindsight.

retrospection *n.* the action or an instance of looking back on or surveying past time or events.

retrospective ● *adj.* **1** looking back on or dealing with the past. **2** (of a film series, exhibition, recital, etc.) showing an artist's development over his or her lifetime. **3** (of legislation) retroactive. ● *n.* a retrospective film series, concert, exhibition, etc. □ **retrospectively** *adv.*

retrovirus *n.* any of a group of RNA viruses which insert a DNA copy of their genome into the host cell in order to replicate, e.g. HIV. □ **retroviral** *adj.*

retry *v.* (**-ies, -ied**) **1** *tr.* *Law* try (a defendant or lawsuit) a second or further time. **2** *tr.* & *intr.* *Computing* endeavour to complete (a function) or run (a program) after a failed attempt.

retune *v.* **1** *tr.* & *intr.* tune (a musical instrument) again or differently. **2** *tr.* tune (a radio etc.) to a different frequency. **3** *tr.* alter the tuning of (an engine etc.) to improve smoothness and efficiency.

return ● *v.* **1** *intr.* come or go back (to or from a place etc.). **2** *intr.* go back (to a particular state or condition) (*things will return to normal*). **3** *tr.* bring, put, or send (something) back to the person or place etc. that it came from (*have you returned my scissors?*). **4** *tr.* feel, say, or do the same in response; reciprocate (*did not return her love; doesn't return phone calls*). **5** *tr.* yield (a profit). **6** *tr.* (esp. of a jury) render or give (a verdict, decision, etc.). **7** *tr.* (of an electorate) elect as an MP, government, etc. **8** *tr.* (in tennis etc.) hit or send (the ball) back after receiving it. **9** *tr.* & *intr.* *N Amer. Football* catch a ball that has been kicked by the opposing team and carry it back downfield. **10** *tr.* say in reply; retort. ● *n.* **1** the act or an instance of coming or going back. **2** an act of coming or going back to an earlier state or position (*a return to prominence*). **3 a** the act or an instance of giving, sending, or putting back. **b** a thing given or sent back. **4** (in *sing.* or *pl.*) **a** the proceeds or profit of an investment or undertaking. **b** the acquisition of these. **5** a formal report or statement compiled or submitted by order (*an income tax return*). **6** (in *pl.*) decision; results (*election returns*). **7 a** (in full **carriage return key**) a key pressed to return the carriage of an electric typewriter to a fixed position. **b** (in full **return key**) a key pressed on a computer keyboard to simulate this. **8** (in tennis etc.) the act of hitting a ball back in the direction of the server. **9** *N Amer. Football* the act of receiving a kicked ball and bringing it back downfield. **10** an air vent allowing cool air to return to a gas furnace. **11** (in full **return ticket**) esp. *Brit.* a ticket for a journey to a place and back to the point of origin. ● *adj.* **1** characterized by return or returning (*return fire*). **2** *Cdn* & *Brit.* providing for transportation to a destination and back (*return airfare to Regina*). **3** designating part of a journey etc. during which one returns to one's place of departure (*the return leg of our trip*). **4** occurring for a second or subsequent time (*a return engagement*). **5** facilitating the delivery of mail, a package, etc. (*return address*). ● *adv.* *Cdn* & *Brit.* (of travel) to a particular destination and back (*flying return to Edmonton*). □ **by return** (**mail**) by the next available mail delivery in the return direction. **in return** as an exchange or reciprocal action. **many happy returns** a greeting on a birthday. □ **returner** *n.*

returnable ● *adj.* **1** able or intended to be returned. **2** (esp. of bottles etc.) that may be returned for money, esp. a deposit paid at the time of purchase. ● *n.* a bottle, can, etc. that may be returned, esp. for money.

returned *adj.* **1** that has come or been brought back.

2 *Cdn*, *Austral.*, & *NZ* (of a member of the armed forces) discharged after active service, esp. abroad.

returnee *n.* **1** a person who returns to or from a place or position. **2** a person who has returned home after war or service abroad.

returning office *n.* *Cdn* an office where the returning officer and other administrative staff for an election etc. work.

returning officer *n.* *Cdn*, *Brit.*, *Austral.*, & *NZ* an official organizing and overseeing the conduct of an election, referendum, etc. in a constituency.

Reuben /ˈruːbən/ *n.* *N Amer.* (in full **Reuben sandwich**) a sandwich containing corned beef, sauerkraut, and usu. Swiss cheese, made with rye bread and served hot.

reunion *n.* **1 a** the act or an instance of reuniting. **b** the condition of being reunited. **2** a social gathering esp. of relatives, friends, or former classmates after a long period of separation.

reuse ● *v.tr.* use again or more than once. ● *n.* a second or further use. □ **reused** *adj.*

Rev. *abbr.* **1** Reverend. **2** Review.

rev *informal* ● *n.* (in *pl.*) the number of revolutions of an engine per minute (*running at 3,000 revs*). ● *v.* (**revved, revving**) (often foll. by *up*) **1** *intr.* **a** (of an internal combustion engine) revolve with increasing speed; turn over. **b** (of a vehicle) operate with increasing revolution of the engine, esp. with the clutch disengaged. **2** *tr.* & *intr.* **a** increase the speed of revolution of (an internal combustion engine). **b** increase the speed of revolution of the engine of (a vehicle), with the clutch disengaged. **3** *tr.* *N Amer.* stimulate, activate, or accelerate (*rev up your love life*). **4** *intr.* *N Amer.* **a** (of a person) become enthusiastic or excited (*revving up for the game*). **b** (of a thing) increase in activity or pace (*the industry is revving up for spring*).

revalue *v.tr.* (**revalues, revalued, revaluing**) *Econ.* **1** assess the value of something again. **2** give a different or esp. higher value to (a currency) in relation to other currencies or gold (*opp.* DEVALUE 2). □ **revaluation** *n.*

revamp ● *v.tr.* **1** repair, restore (*revamp a damaged reputation*). **2** renovate, overhaul (*completely revamp the education system*). ● *n.* **1** a revamped version; a renovation, overhaul, or revision. **2** an act of revamping something.

RevCan *n.* *Cdn slang* Revenue Canada.

reveal[1] *v.tr.* **1** display, show, or expose; allow to appear. **2** disclose, divulge, betray (*revealed her plans*). **3** (esp. of God) make known by inspiration or supernatural means. **4** *tr.* (in *refl.* or *passive*) appear or become apparent; come into view. □ **revealer** *n.*

reveal[2] *n.* an internal side surface of an opening or recess, esp. of a doorway or window frame.

revealing *adj.* **1 a** providing insight esp. into something obscure or private (*her autobiography is quite revealing*). **b** striking, shocking. **2** (of an article of dress etc.) allowing more of the body to be seen than is usual or conventional (*a revealing blouse*). □ **revealingly** *adv.*

reveille /ˈrevəli/ *n.* a signal given in the morning, usu. on a drum or bugle, to waken soldiers and indicate that it is time to rise.

réveillon /ˈreveiˌʒɔ̃/ *n.* (among francophones) a festive meal on Christmas morning after midnight Mass or on New Year's Eve.

revel ● *v.intr.* (**revelled, revelling**) **1** (foll. by *in*) take great delight in (*revelled in her new-found freedom*). **2** engage in riotous or noisy festivities. ● *n.* (in *sing.* or *pl.*) the act or an instance of revelling. □ **reveller** *n.*

revelation *n.* **1** the act or an instance of making something known (*the revelation of truth*). **2** something revealed; a striking disclosure (*revelations about her life*). **3 a** the disclosure of knowledge to humankind by a divine or supernatural agency. **b** an instance of this. **c** a thing disclosed or made known by supernatural or divine means.

revelatory /ˈrevələˌtɔri/ *adj.* serving to reveal, esp. something significant.

revelry *n.* (*pl.* **-ies**) the action of revelling or merrymaking; boisterous gaiety or mirth.

revenge ● *n.* **1** retaliation for an offence or injury. **2 a** an act of retaliation. **b** the opportunity to retaliate or avenge a loss etc. **3** the desire for this; a vindictive feeling. ● *v.* **1** *tr.* take revenge for (an offence). **2** *tr.* & *refl.* retaliate on behalf of (a person). □ **revenger** *n.*

revenge of the cradle *n.* *Cdn* (prec. by *the*) the extremely high birth rate of French Canadians from the 19th to the mid-20th c., perceived as a means of retaliation against the English.

revenue *n.* **1 a** income, esp. of a large amount, from any source. **b** (in *pl.*) items constituting this. **2 a** government's annual income from which public expenses are met. **3** the department of the civil service collecting this.

revenuer *n.* *N Amer.* a person who collects taxes or customs duties etc.

reverb /rɪˈvɜrb, ˈriːvɜrb/ *n.* *Music informal* **1** reverberation. **2** a device to produce this.

reverberate /rɪˈvɜrbəˌreit/ *v.* **1 a** *intr.* (of sound, light, or heat) be returned or echoed or reflected repeatedly. **b** *tr.* return (a sound etc.) in this way. **2** *intr.* **a** (of a story, rumour, etc.) be heard much or repeatedly. **b** (of an event) have continuing effects. □ **reverberant** *adj.* **reverberation** *n.*

revere /rəˈviːr/ *v.tr.* hold in deep and usu. affectionate or religious respect; venerate.

reverence /ˈrevərəns/ ● *n.* **1 a** the act of revering or the state of being revered (*hold in reverence; feel reverence for*). **b** the capacity for revering (*lacks reverence*). **2** (**Reverence**) a title used of or to some members of the clergy. ● *v.tr.* regard or treat with reverence.

Reverend /ˈrevrənd, ˈrevərənd/ ● *adj.* (as the title of a member of the clergy). *Abbr.*: **Rev.** ¶Some clergy prefer *The Reverend* (or *The Rev.*) to *Reverend* (or *Rev.*) on the grounds that since *Reverend* is an adjective, it needs to be preceded by an article. ● *n. informal* (also **reverend**) a clergyman.

Reverend Mother *n.* the title of the Mother Superior of a convent.

reverent /ˈrevərənt/ *adj.* feeling or showing great respect or admiration. □ **reverently** *adv.*

reverential /ˌrevəˈrenʃəl/ *adj.* of the nature of, due to, or characterized by reverence. □ **reverentially** *adv.*

---

retype *v.tr.*
reunification *n.*

reunify *v.tr.* (**-ies, -ied**)
reunite *v.tr.* & *intr.*

reupholster *v.tr.*
reupholstery *n.*

revaccinate *v.tr.*
revaccination *n.*

reverie /'revɜri/ n. **1** a state of absent-minded meditation or musing; a daydream (was lost in a reverie). **2** Music an instrumental piece suggesting a dreamy or musing state.

reverse ● v. **1** tr. turn the other way around or up or inside out. **2** tr. change to the opposite character or effect (reversed the decision). **3** intr. & tr. move backwards or in the opposite direction. **4** tr. make (an engine etc.) work in a contrary direction. **5** tr. revoke or annul (a verdict, decree, act, etc.). ● adj. **1** placed or turned in an opposite direction or position. **2** opposite or contrary in character or order; inverted. ● n. **1** the opposite or contrary (is the reverse of the truth). **2** the contrary of the usual manner. **3** an occurrence of misfortune; a disaster, esp. a defeat in battle (suffered a reverse). **4** reverse gear or motion. **5** the reverse side of something. **6** Football a play in which one offensive player hands the ball off to a player running in the opposite direction. **7 a** the side of a coin or medal etc. bearing the secondary design. **b** this design (compare OBVERSE 1). **8** the verso of a leaf. **9** a device, as on a tape player, that turns something over or backwards. □ **reverse the charges** make the recipient of a telephone call responsible for payment. □ **reversal** n. **reverser** n. **reversibility** n. **reversible** adj. **reversibly** adv.

reverse discrimination n. discrimination against men or white people that results from policies intended to end discrimination against women or racial minorities.

reverse engineering n. the reproduction of another manufacturer's product following detailed examination of its construction or composition.

reverse gear n. a gear used to make a vehicle etc. travel backwards.

reverse mortgage n. N Amer. a mortgage taken out esp. by a senior citizen against the capital investment in a home; the principal plus accrued interest is paid off only when the house is sold.

reverse osmosis n. the process by which a solvent passes through a porous membrane in the direction opposite to that for natural osmosis.

reverse psychology n. the principle or practice of suggesting to a person that he or she do the opposite of what one really wants him or her to do.

reverse video n. a mode on a computer monitor in which the colours normally used for the background and characters are reversed.

reversing falls n. Cdn a set of rapids on a tidal river, the flow of which reverses regularly due to the pressure of the incoming tide.

reversion /rə'vɜrʒən, ri-/ n. **1** a return to a previous state, habit, etc. **2** Biol. a return to ancestral type. **3 a** the legal right (esp. of the original owner, or his or her heirs) to possess or succeed to property on the death of the present possessor. **b** property to which a person has such a right. **4** a sum payable on a person's death, esp. by way of life insurance. □ **reversionary** adj.

revert v.intr. **1** (foll. by to) **a** return to a former state or condition. **b** return to a former practice or habit. **c** return to an earlier topic of conversation or thought. **2** (of property, an office, etc.) return by reversion. **3** fall back into a wild state.

review ● n. **1** a general survey or assessment of a subject or thing. **2** a retrospect or survey of the past. **3** a reconsideration or examination, with the possibility or intention of change if desirable or necessary (is under review; rent review). **4** N Amer. an act or instance of reviewing a subject or material already learned. **5** Law consideration of a judgment, sentence, etc., by some higher court or authority. **6** a display and formal inspection of troops etc. **7** an account or criticism of a book, performance, etc., esp. when published or broadcast. **8** a periodical publication with critical articles on current events, the arts, etc. **9** a second view. ● v. **1** tr. survey or look back on. **2** tr. reconsider or revise. **3** N Amer. **a** tr. go over (a lesson, or series of lessons) to reinforce a subject already learned. **b** intr. present or study material again, e.g. to prepare for a test. **4** tr. hold a review of (troops etc.). **5** tr. **a** publish or broadcast a review of (a book, performance, etc.). **b** write a review of (a scholarly article) to assess its suitability for publication. **6** tr. Law submit (a sentence, decision, etc.) to review. **7** tr. view again. □ **reviewable** adj.

reviewer n. a person who writes or broadcasts reviews of books, performances, etc.; a critic.

revile v. **1** tr. abuse; criticize abusively. **2** intr. talk abusively; rail. □ **reviling** n.

revise v. **1** tr. examine or re-examine and improve or amend (esp. written or printed matter). **2** tr. consider and alter (an opinion etc.). □ **reviser** n. **revisory** adj.

Revised Standard Version n. a revision in 1946–52 of the Authorized Version of the Bible. Abbr.: **RSV**.

Revised Version n. a revision in 1881–5 of the Authorized Version of the Bible. Abbr.: **RV**.

revision n. **1** the act or an instance of revising; the process of being revised. **2** a revised edition or form. □ **revisionary** adj.

revisionism n. often derogatory **1** a policy of revision or modification, esp. of Marxism on evolutionary socialist (rather than revolutionary) or pluralist principles. **2** the theory or practice of revising a previously accepted situation or point of view. □ **revisionist** n. & adj.

revisit v.tr. (**-visited**, **-visiting**) **1** visit again. **2** take up (a subject etc.) again; reconsider or re-examine.

revival n. **1** an improvement in the condition or strength of something; a recovery. **2** the process of bringing something back into existence, use, fashion, etc. **3 a** a reawakening of religious fervour. **b** a series of evangelistic meetings to promote this. **4** a new production of an old play etc. **5** restoration to bodily or mental vigour or to life or consciousness.

revivalism n. **1** belief in or the promotion of a revival, esp. of religious fervour. **2** a tendency or desire to revive a former custom or practice. □ **revivalist** n. & adj. **revivalistic** adj.

revive v. **1** tr. & intr. come or bring back to consciousness or life or strength. **2** tr. & intr. come or bring back to existence, use, notice, etc. **3** tr. produce (a play etc.) that has not been performed for some time.

revivify /ri'vivi,fai/ v.tr. (**-ies**, **-ied**) restore to activity, vigour, or life. □ **revivification** n.

revoke v.tr. rescind, withdraw, or cancel (a licence, decision, promise, etc.). □ **revocable** /rə'vo:kəbəl, 'revək-/ adj. **revocation** /,revə'keiʃən/ n.

revolt ● *v.* **1** *intr.* rise in rebellion against authority. **2** *tr.* (often in *passive*) affect with strong disgust; nauseate (*was revolted by the thought of it*). ● *n.* **1** an act of rebelling. **2** a state of insurrection (*in revolt*). **3** a sense of loathing. **4** a mood of protest or defiance.

revolting *adj.* disgusting, horrible. □ **revoltingly** *adv.*

revolution *n.* **1 a** the forcible overthrow of a government or social order, in favour of a new system. **b** (in Marxism) the replacement of one ruling class by another; the class struggle which is expected to lead to political change and the triumph of communism. **2** any fundamental change or reversal of conditions (*the Industrial Revolution*). **3** the act or an instance of revolving. **4 a** motion in orbit or a circular course or around an axis or centre; rotation. **b** the single completion of an orbit or rotation. **c** the time taken for this. **5** a cyclic recurrence.

revolutionary ● *adj.* **1** involving a complete or dramatic change. **2** of or causing political revolution. **3** (**Revolutionary**) of or relating to a particular revolution, esp. the American Revolution. ● *n.* (*pl.* **-ies**) an instigator or supporter of esp. political revolution.

revolutionize *v.tr.* introduce fundamental change to.

Révolution tranquille /reivɒlu:'sjɔ̃ trã'ki:l/ *n.* *Cdn* = QUIET REVOLUTION.

revolve *v.* **1** *intr. & tr.* turn or cause to turn around, esp. on an axis; rotate. **2** *intr.* move in a circular orbit. **3** *tr.* ponder (a problem etc.) in the mind. **4** *intr.* (foll. by *around*) have as its chief concern; be centred upon (*my life revolves around my job*).

revolver *n.* a pistol with revolving chambers enabling several shots to be fired without reloading.

revolving door *n.* **1** a door with usu. four partitions turning around a central axis. **2 a** a situation, organization, etc. in which new arrivals depart again almost immediately, usu. without due care or attention given them, and often return again very soon (*the revolving door of psychiatric care*). **b** (*attrib.*) (usu. **revolving-door**) designating or describing an institution etc. where people are processed quickly or through which people pass constantly.

revue /rɪ'vju:, ri-/ *n.* a theatrical entertainment of a series of short usu. satirical sketches and songs.

revulsion /rɪ'vʌlʃən, ri-/ *n.* **1** abhorrence; a sense of loathing. **2** a sudden violent change of feeling.

reward ● *n.* **1 a** a return or recompense for service or merit. **b** requital for good or evil; retribution. **2** a sum offered for the detection of a criminal, the restoration of lost property, etc. **3** a benefit provided in return for frequent use of a commercial service, as in a frequent-flyer program. ● *v.tr.* **1** give a reward to (a person) or for (a service etc.). **2** make return for (an action) (*the book rewards a close reading*). □ **go to one's reward** die.

rewarding *adj.* (of an activity etc.) well worth doing; providing satisfaction. □ **rewardingly** *adv.*

rewind ● *v.tr.* (*past* and *past part.* **-wound**) wind (a film or tape etc.) back to the beginning. ● *n.* **1** a mechanism for rewinding film, tape, etc. **2** the action or process of rewinding film, tape, etc. □ **rewinder** *n.*

reword *v.tr.* change the wording of.

rework *v.tr.* revise; refashion. □ **reworking** *n.*

rewrite ● *v.tr.* (*past* **-wrote**; *past part.* **-written**) **1** write again or differently. **2** present or depict (history or a historical event) in a new or different light, esp. to further one's own interests. ● *n.* **1** the act or an instance of rewriting. **2** a thing rewritten.

Rex *n.* the reigning king (following a name or in the titles of lawsuits).

Reye's syndrome /raiz, reiz/ *n.* a frequently fatal metabolic disorder in young children, of uncertain cause but sometimes precipitated by ASA, involving encephalitis and degeneration of the liver.

rez *n.* *N Amer. informal* an Indian reserve or reservation.

rezone *v.tr.* classify (a property, area, etc.) as belonging to a different zone or subject to a different set of zoning regulations.

Rf *symbol* rutherfordium.

r.f. *abbr.* (also **RF**) radio frequency.

RGB *abbr.* red-green-blue.

Rh¹ *symbol* rhodium.

Rh² *abbr.* **1** rhesus. **2** rhesus factor.

r.h. *abbr.* right hand.

Rhaeto-Romance /'ri:to:/ ● *n.* a group of Romance dialects spoken in SE Switzerland, W Austria, and NE Italy, including Romansh and Ladin. ● *adj.* of or relating to this group of dialects.

rhapsodize *v.intr.* **1** talk or write about a person or thing with great enthusiasm. **2** write a rhapsody or rhapsodies.

rhapsody /'ræpsədi/ *n.* (*pl.* **-ies**) **1** an exaggeratedly enthusiastic or ecstatic expression of feeling. **2** *Music* a piece of music in one extended movement, usu. emotional in character. □ **rhapsodic** /-'sɒdɪk/ *adj.*

rhea /'ri:ə/ *n.* any of several S American flightless birds of the family Rheidae, like but smaller than an ostrich.

Rhenish /'ri:nɪʃ, 'ren-/ ● *adj.* of the Rhine River in W Europe, and the regions adjoining it. ● *n.* wine from this area.

rhenium /'ri:niəm/ *n.* a rare metallic element, occurring naturally in molybdenum ores and used in the manufacture of superconducting alloys.

rheostat /'ri:ə,stæt/ *n.* *Electricity* an instrument used to control a current by varying the resistance. □ **rheostatic** *adj.*

rhesus /'ri:səs/ *n.* (in full **rhesus monkey**) a small monkey, *Macaca mulatta*, common in N India.

rhesus factor *n.* an antigen occurring on the red blood cells of most humans and some other primates.

rhesus negative *adj.* lacking the rhesus factor.

rhesus positive *adj.* having the rhesus factor.

rhetoric /'retərɪk/ *n.* **1** the art of effective or persuasive speaking or writing. **2** language designed to persuade or impress (often with an implication of insincerity or exaggeration etc.).

rhetorical /rɪ'tɒrɪkəl/ *adj.* **1** expressed with a view to persuasive or impressive effect; artificial or extravagant in language. **2** of the nature of rhetoric. **3 a** of or relating to the art of rhetoric. **b** given to rhetoric; oratorical. □ **rhetorically** *adv.*

rhetorical question *n.* a question asked not for information but to produce an effect, e.g. *who cares?*

---

rewash *v.tr.*   **rewire** *v.tr.*   **rewrap** *v.tr.* (**rewrapped, rewrapping**)

rhetorician /ˌretəˈrɪʃən/ n. **1** an orator. **2** a teacher of rhetoric. **3** a rhetorical speaker or writer.

rheum /ruːm/ n. a watery discharge from a mucous membrane, esp. of the eyes or nose. ☐ **rheumy** adj.

rheumatic /ruːˈmætɪk/ ● adj. **1** of, relating to, or suffering from rheumatism. **2** producing or produced by rheumatism. ● n. a person suffering from rheumatism. ☐ **rheumatically** adv.

rheumatic fever n. a non-infectious fever with inflammation and pain in the joints.

rheumatism /ˈruːməˌtɪzəm/ n. any disease marked by inflammation and pain in the joints, muscles, or fibrous tissue, esp. rheumatoid arthritis.

rheumatoid arthritis /ˈruːməˌtɔid/ n. a chronic progressive disease causing inflammation and stiffening of the joints.

Rh factor n. = RHESUS FACTOR.

rhinestone n. an imitation diamond.

rhino n. (pl. same or **-os**) **1** informal a rhinoceros. **2** (**Rhino**) Cdn slang a member of the Rhinoceros Party.

rhinoceros n. (pl. same or **rhinoceroses**) **1** any large thick-skinned plant-eating ungulate of the family Rhinocerotidae of Africa and S Asia, with one or two horns on the nose and plated or folded skin. **2** (**Rhinoceros**) Cdn a member of the Rhinoceros Party.

Rhinoceros Party n. Cdn a spoof political party which first ran candidates in the 1960s; the party's goal is to demonstrate the supposed shortcomings of the traditional Canadian political parties.

rhinoplasty /ˈrainoːˌplæsti/ n. plastic surgery of the nose.

rhizome /ˈraizoːm/ n. an underground rootlike stem bearing both roots and shoots. ☐ **rhizomatous** adj.

Rh-negative adj. = RHESUS NEGATIVE.

rho /roː/ n. the seventeenth letter of the Greek alphabet (P, ρ).

Rhode Islander a native or inhabitant of the US state of Rhode Island.

Rhode Island Red n. a reddish-black domestic fowl raised for meat and eggs.

Rhodes Scholarship n. any of several scholarships awarded annually and tenable at Oxford University by students from certain Commonwealth countries, South Africa, the US, and Germany. ☐ **Rhodes Scholar** n.

rhodium /ˈroːdiəm/ n. a hard white metallic element, occurring naturally in platinum ores and used in making alloys and plating jewellery.

rhododendron /ˌroːdəˈdendrən/ n. any evergreen shrub or small tree of the genus Rhododendron, with usu. large clusters of trumpet-shaped flowers.

rhomb /rɒm/ n. = RHOMBUS. ☐ **rhombic** /ˈrɒmbɪk/ adj.

rhomboid /ˈrɒmbɔid/ ● adj. (also **rhomboidal** /-ˈbɔidəl/) having or nearly having the shape of a rhombus. ● n. a quadrilateral of which only the opposite sides and angles are equal.

rhombus /ˈrɒmbəs/ n. (pl. **-buses** or **-bi** /-bai/) Math. a parallelogram with oblique angles and equal sides.

RHOSP /ˈɑːrhɒsp/ abbr. Cdn Registered Home Ownership Savings Plan, a tax-sheltered account in which a first-time homebuyer may save money for a down payment.

Rh-positive adj. = RHESUS POSITIVE.

RHR abbr. (in Canada) Royal Highland Regiment.

rhubarb n. **1 a** any of various plants of the genus Rheum, esp. R. rhaponticum, producing long fleshy dark red leaf stalks used cooked as food. **b** the leaf stalks of this. **2 a** a root of a Chinese and Tibetan plant of the genus Rheum. **b** a purgative made from this. **3** N Amer. slang a heated dispute.

rhumba var. of RUMBA.

rhyme ● n. **1** the quality shared by words or syllables that have or end with the same sound as each other, esp. when such words etc. are used at the ends of lines of poetry. **2** (in sing. or pl.) verse having rhymes. **3** a poem having rhymes. **4** a word that has the same sound as another. ● v. **1** intr. **a** (of words or lines) produce a rhyme. **b** (foll. by with) act as a rhyme (with another). **2** intr. make or write rhymes; versify. **3** tr. put or make (a story etc.) into rhyme. **4** tr. (foll. by with) treat (a word) as rhyming with another. ☐ **rhyme or reason** (usu. in negative expressions) sense or logic (there's no rhyme or reason to it). ☐ **rhymer** n.

rhyolite /ˈraiəˌlait/ n. a fine-grained volcanic rock of granitic composition. ☐ **rhyolitic** /-ˈlɪtɪk/ adj.

rhythm n. **1** a measured flow of words and phrases in verse or prose determined by various relations of long and short or accented and unaccented syllables. **2 a** the aspect of musical composition concerned with periodical accent and the duration of notes. **b** a particular type of pattern formed by this (samba rhythm). **3** movement with a regular succession of strong and weak elements. **4** a regularly recurring sequence of events. **5** a sense of rhythm. **6** Art a harmonious correlation of parts.

rhythm and blues n. (hyphenated when attrib.) popular music with a blues theme and strong rhythm.

rhythmic adj. (also **rhythmical**) **1** relating to or characterized by rhythm. **2** regularly occurring. ☐ **rhythmically** adv.

rhythm method n. birth control by avoiding sexual intercourse when ovulation is likely to occur.

rhythm section n. the part of a band etc. mainly supplying rhythm, usu. consisting of drums, bass, etc.

RI abbr. Rhode Island (also in postal use).

rib ● n. **1** each of the curved bones articulated in pairs to the spine and protecting the thoracic cavity and its organs. **2 a** a roast of meat from this part of an animal. **b** (usu. in pl.) = SPARERIBS. **3** a ridge or long raised piece often of stronger or thicker material across a surface or through a structure serving to support or strengthen it. **4** any of a ship's transverse curved timbers forming the framework of the hull. **5** Knitting a combination of plain and purl stitches producing a ribbed, somewhat elastic fabric. **6** a vein of a leaf or an insect's wing. **7** a structural member in an airfoil. ● v.tr. (**ribbed**, **ribbing**) **1** provide with ribs; act as the ribs of. **2** informal make fun of; tease. **3** mark with ridges. ☐ **ribless** adj.

ribald /ˈrɪbəld, ˈrai-/ adj. (of language or its user) referring to sexual matters in a rude but humorous way.

ribaldry /ˈrɪbəldri/ n. ribald talk or behaviour.

ribbed adj. **1** having ribs or riblike markings. **2** Knitting having ribbing.

ribbing n. **1** ribs or a riblike structure. **2** a pattern in knitting of alternate ridges and depressions. **3** informal the act or an instance of teasing.

ribbit n. N Amer. the sound made by a frog.

ribbon n. **1 a** a narrow strip or band of fabric, used esp. for trimming or decoration. **b** material in this form. **2** a ribbon of a special colour etc. worn to indicate some honour, allegiance, or membership of a sports team etc. **3** a long narrow strip of anything, e.g. impregnated material forming the inking agent in a typewriter or printer. **4** (in pl.) ragged strips (torn to ribbons). ☐ **ribboned** adj.

rib cage *n.* the wall of bones formed by the ribs around the chest.

rib-eye *n.* (in full **rib-eye steak**) a roundish steak cut from the rib.

rib-knit *n.* a knitted garment or fabric having a ribbed pattern.

riboflavin /ˌraiboːˈfleivɪn/ *n.* a vitamin of the B complex, found in liver, milk, and eggs, essential for energy production.

ribonucleic acid /ˌraibənuːˈkliːɪk, -njuː-, -kleiɪk/ *n.* a nucleic acid present in living cells, esp. in ribosomes where it is involved in protein synthesis. Abbr.: **RNA**.

ribosome /ˈraibəˌsoːm/ *n. Biochem.* each of the minute particles consisting of RNA and associated proteins found in the cytoplasm of living cells, concerned with the synthesis of proteins. □ **ribosomal** *adj.*

rib-tickler *n.* something amusing; a joke. □ **rib-tickling** *adj.*

rice ● *n.* **1** the grain of the grass *Oryza sativa*, a major world cereal. **2** the plant producing this grain, grown in warmer parts of the world, usu. in standing water. ● *v.tr. N Amer.* pass (cooked potatoes etc.) through a coarse sieve to produce long strands. □ **ricer** *n.*

rice cake *n.* a round, crisp biscuit made of puffed rice.

rice paper *n.* **1** edible paper made from the pith of an oriental tree and used for painting and in cookery. **2** paper made wholly or partly from the straw of rice.

rich *adj.* **1** having much wealth. **2** (often foll. by *in*, *with*) splendid, costly, elaborate (*rich tapestries*; *rich with lace*). **3** valuable (*rich offerings*). **4** copious, abundant, ample (*a rich harvest*). **5** (often foll. by *in*, *with*) abundantly supplied with (*rich with wildlife*). **6** (of food or diet) containing a large amount of fat, butter, eggs, sugar, etc. **7** (of the mixture in an internal combustion engine) containing a high proportion of fuel (compare LEAN[2] 6). **8** (of colour or sound or smell) mellow and deep, strong and full. **9 a** (of an incident or assertion etc.) highly ludicrous; outrageous. **b** (of humour) earthy. **10** (of soil) very fertile; abounding in nutrients. **11** (of a country, region, etc.) abounding in natural resources or means of production.

-rich *comb. form* having or containing much; abundant in (*oil-rich*; *vitamin-rich*).

Richardson's ground squirrel *n.* a ground squirrel, *Spermophilus richardsonii*, of western N America, commonly called a gopher.

riches *n.pl.* wealth; money and valuable possessions.

richly *adv.* **1** in a rich way. **2** fully, thoroughly.

Richter scale /ˈrɪktər/ *n.* a scale for representing the strength of an earthquake, beginning at near 0 for the smallest and increasing exponentially.

rick ● *n.* a stack of hay, straw, etc., built into a regular shape and usu. covered or thatched. ● *v.tr.* form into a rick or ricks.

rickets *n.* a disease of children characterized by softening of the bones (esp. the spine) and bow legs, caused by vitamin D deficiency.

rickettsia /rɪˈketsiə/ *n.* (*pl.* **-siae** or **-sias**) a parasitic micro-organism of the genus *Rickettsia* causing typhus and other febrile diseases. □ **rickettsial** *adj.*

rickety *adj.* insecure or shaky in construction; likely to collapse. □ **ricketiness** *n.*

rickey *n.* (*pl.* **-eys**) a drink of lime juice, soda water, and usu. gin.

rickrack *n.* (also **ricrac**) a zigzag braided trimming for garments.

rickshaw *n.* a light, two-wheeled, usu. hooded vehicle drawn by one or more persons.

ricochet /ˈrɪkəˌʃei/ ● *n.* the action of a projectile, esp. a shell or bullet, in rebounding off a surface. ● *v.intr.* (**ricocheted** /-ˌʃeid/; **ricocheting** /-ˌʃeiɪŋ/) rebound one or more times from a surface.

ricotta /rɪˈkɒtə/ *n.* a soft Italian cheese with a texture resembling that of fine cottage cheese, used esp. in pasta dishes and desserts.

rid *v.tr.* (**ridding**; *past* and *past part.* **rid**) (foll. by *of*) make (a person or place) free of something unwanted. □ **be** (or **get**) **rid of** be freed or relieved of (something unwanted); dispose of.

riddance *n.* the act of getting rid of something.

ridden ● *v. past part.* of RIDE. ● *adj.* (in *comb.*) infested or afflicted (*a rat-ridden cellar*).

riddle[1] ● *n.* **1** a question or statement testing ingenuity in divining its answer or meaning. **2** a puzzling fact, thing, or person. ● *v.* **1** *intr.* speak in or propound riddles. **2** *tr.* solve or explain (a riddle). □ **riddler** *n.*

riddle[2] *v.tr.* (usu. foll. by *with*) **1** make many holes in, esp. with gunshot. **2** (in *passive*) fill; spread through; permeate (*was riddled with errors*).

riddle[3] *n. Cdn* (*Nfld*) a short pliable wooden rod woven between horizontal rails in making fences (also *attrib.*: *riddle fence*).

RIDE *n. Cdn* (*Ont.*) a program to reduce impaired driving, in which police stop vehicles randomly and check drivers for signs of intoxication, esp. during the holiday season (also *attrib.*: *a RIDE checkpoint*).

ride ● *v.* (*past* **rode**; *past part.* **ridden**) **1 a** *tr.* travel or be carried on (a bicycle, motorcycle, etc.) or esp. *N Amer.* in or on (a vehicle, bus, etc.). **b** *intr.* (often foll. by *on*, *in*) travel or be conveyed (on or in a vehicle). **2 a** *tr.* sit on and control or be carried by (a horse etc.). **b** *intr.* (often foll. by *on*) be carried (on a horse etc.). **3** *tr.* **a** traverse on horseback etc.; ride over or through or along. **b** compete or take part in on horseback etc. (*rode a good race*). **4** *tr.* (of a rider) cause (a horse etc.) to move forward. **5 a** *intr.* lie at anchor; float or appear to float buoyantly. **b** *tr.* be carried or supported by (*the ship rides the waves*). **c** *tr.* be animated, stimulated, or spurred on by circumstance etc. (*riding a wave of popularity*). **6** *tr.* give a ride to; cause to ride (*rode the child on his back*). **7** *tr.* yield to (a blow) so as to reduce its impact. **8** *tr.* (in *passive*; foll. by *by*, *with*) be oppressed or dominated by; be infested with (*was ridden with guilt*). **9** *intr.* (of a thing normally level or even) project or overlap. **10** *tr. coarse slang* have sexual intercourse with. **11** *tr. N Amer.* annoy or seek to annoy. ● *n.* **1 a** an act or period of travel in a vehicle. **b** a period of riding on a horse, bicycle, person's back, etc. **c** a demonstration of (esp. horse) riding as entertainment (*musical ride*). **2** the quality of sensations when riding (*gives a bumpy ride*). **3** a roller coaster, merry-go-round, etc., ridden at an amusement park or fairground. **4** a means of transportation esp. at no cost (*do you need a ride?*). □ **come** (or **go** etc.) **along for the ride** participate disinterestedly or just for fun. **let a thing ride** leave it alone; let it take its natural course. **ride again** reappear, esp. unexpectedly and reinvigorated. **ride down** overtake or trample on horseback. **ride for a fall** act recklessly risking defeat or failure. **ride high** be elated or successful. **ride on** be dependent on or conditioned by (*so much is riding on the outcome*). **ride out** come safely through; endure, bear (a storm etc. or a danger or difficulty). **ride shotgun** esp. *N Amer.* **1** travel as a guard in the seat next to the driver of a vehicle. **2** ride in the passenger seat of a vehicle. **3** act as a protector. **ride the pine** (or **bench**) *N Amer. Sport* (of an athlete) not participate, esp. because of poor performance; be benched. **ride up** (of a garment) work or move upwards out of its proper position (*these pants ride up at the back*). **take for a ride** *informal* hoax or deceive.

ride-on *attrib.adj.* (esp. of a lawn mower) on which one rides while operating it.

rider *n.* **1** a person who rides (a horse, bus, bicycle, etc.). **2 a** an additional clause amending or supplementing a document. **b** an addition or amendment to a bill before it is passed. **c** a condition, proviso, qualification, etc. □ **riderless** *adj.*

ridership *n.* esp. *N Amer.* the number of passengers using a particular form of mass transportation.

ridge ● *n.* **1** the line of the junction of two surfaces sloping upwards towards each other (*the ridge of a roof*). **2** a long narrow hilltop, mountain range, or watershed. **3** any narrow elevation across a surface. **4** *Meteorol.* an elongated region of high barometric pressure. **5** *Agriculture* a raised strip of arable land, usu. one of a set separated by furrows. ● *v.* **1** *tr.* mark with ridges. **2** *tr. & intr.* gather into ridges.

ridged *adj.* with a surface marked by ridges.

ridgepole *n.* esp. *N Amer.* **1** the horizontal pole of a long tent. **2** a beam along the ridge of a roof.

ridgetop *n.* *N Amer.* the top or crest of a ridge.

ridicule ● *n.* derision or mockery. ● *v.tr.* make fun of; subject to ridicule; laugh at.

ridiculous *adj.* **1** unreasonable, absurd. **2** deserving or inviting ridicule. **3** outrageous, astounding. □ **ridiculously** *adv.* **ridiculousness** *n.*

riding[1] *n.* **1** in senses of RIDE *v.* **2** the practice or skill of riders of horses.

riding[2] *n.* (in Canada) a district whose voters elect a representative member to a legislative body; a constituency or electoral district.

riding association *n.* *Cdn* a unit of organization of a political party at the level of the riding, responsible for nominating a candidate for election and conducting the election campaign in the riding.

riding habit *n.* see HABIT 6b.

riding mower *n.* *N Amer.* a lawn mower on which one rides while operating it.

Riel Rebellion *n.* *Cdn* **1** = RED RIVER REBELLION. **2** = NORTHWEST REBELLION. **3** these collectively.

Riesling /ˈriːzlɪŋ, -slɪŋ/ *n.* **1** a kind of dry white wine produced in Germany, Austria, and elsewhere. **2** the variety of grape from which this is produced.

rife *predic.adj.* **1** of common occurrence; widespread (esp. of something undesirable). **2** (foll. by *with*) abounding in; teeming with (esp. something undesirable).

riff ● *n.* **1** a short repeated phrase in rock, jazz, etc., often played over changing chords or harmonies or used as a background to a solo (*a guitar riff*). **2** *informal* any commentary, improvisation, etc. on a theme (*launched into a riff on old movies*). ● *v.intr.* **1** play riffs. **2** *informal* (foll. by *on*) comment or expound.

riffle ● *v.* **1** *tr.* a turn (pages) in quick succession. **b** shuffle (playing cards) esp. by flicking up and releasing the corners or sides of two piles of cards so that they intermingle and may be slid together to form a single pile. **2** *intr.* (often foll. by *through*) leaf quickly (through pages etc.). **3** *tr.* (esp. of wind) disturb the smoothness of or cause ripples in or on; ruffle (*wind-riffled hair*). ● *n.* **1** the act or an instance of riffling. **2** *N Amer.* a shallow part of a stream where the water flows brokenly. **b** a patch of waves or ripples on water.

riff-raff *n.* (often prec. by *the*) the rabble.

rifle[1] ● *n.* **1** a gun with a long rifled barrel, esp. one fired from shoulder level. **2** (in *pl.*) infantry armed with rifles. ● *v.tr.* **1** (esp. as **rifled** *adj.*) make spiral grooves in (a gun or its barrel or bore) to make a bullet spin. **2** shoot, throw, launch, etc. forcefully in a straight line.

rifle[2] *v.* **1** *intr.* (foll. by *through*) search through. **2** *tr.* search and rob, esp. of all that can be found; ransack. **3** *tr.* carry off as booty.

rifleman *n.* (*pl.* **-men**) a soldier armed with a rifle.

rifling *n.* the arrangement of grooves on the inside of a gun's barrel.

rift ● *n.* **1 a** a crack or split in an object. **b** an opening in a cloud etc. **2** a cleft or fissure in earth or rock. **3 a** a large fault bounding a rift valley. **b** = RIFT VALLEY. **4** a disagreement; a breach in friendly relations. ● *v.* **1** *tr.* tear or burst apart. **2** *intr.* form fissures or clefts; split or move apart.

rift valley *n.* a steep-sided valley formed by subsidence of the earth's crust between nearly parallel faults.

rig ● *v.tr.* (**rigged**, **rigging**) **1 a** provide (a ship) with sails, rigging, etc. **b** prepare (a sailing ship) for sailing. **2** (often foll. by *out, up*) fit with clothes or other equipment. **3** (foll. by *up*) set up hastily, esp. by making do with what is available. **4** (often foll. by *to*) connect with ropes, wires, etc. **5** assemble and adjust the parts of (an aircraft etc.). **6** *Forestry* prepare (a spar tree) by attaching guy lines, skylines, and the mainline. **7** manage or conduct fraudulently; fix (*they rigged the election*). ● *n.* **1** the arrangement of masts, sails, rigging, etc. of a sailing ship. **2** equipment for a special purpose, e.g. a radio transmitter or fishing tackle; gear. **3** = OIL RIG, DRILLING RIG. **4** esp. *N Amer. & Austral.* a large vehicle, esp. a transport truck or tractor-trailer. **5** an outfit, uniform, or style of dress. □ **rigged** *adj.* (also in *comb.*).

rigamarole *N Amer. var. of* RIGMAROLE.

rigatoni /rɪgəˈtoːni/ *n.* pasta in the form of short broad hollow fluted tubes.

rigger *n.* **1** a person who rigs or who arranges rigging. **2** *Forestry* = HIGH RIGGER. **3** a ship rigged in a specified way. **4** a worker on an oil rig. **5** a person who manages an election etc. fraudulently.

rigging *n.* **1** a ship's spars, ropes, etc., supporting and controlling the sails. **2** an arrangement of ropes, wires, etc. in any structure or system, e.g. on an airship. **3** *Forestry* the lines, blocks, hooks, and other equipment used in yarding logs by means of cables.

rigging crew *n.* *Forestry* the work crew in charge of rigging trees.

right ● *adj.* **1** (of conduct etc.) just; morally or socially correct (*it is only right to tell you*; *do the right thing*). **2** true, correct; not mistaken (*the right time*; *you were right*). **3** more or most suitable, preferable, or helpful (*the right person for the job*; *along the right lines*). **4** in a sound or normal condition; physically or mentally healthy; satisfactory (*the engine doesn't sound right*). **5 a** on or towards the side of the human body which corresponds to the position of east if one faces north. **b** on or towards that part of an object which is analogous to a person's right side or (with opposite sense) which is nearer to a spectator's right hand. **6** (of a side of a piece of paper, fabric, etc.) meant for display or use (*turn it right side up*). **7 a** formed by or with reference to a straight line or plane perpendicular to another straight line or plane. **b** (of a solid figure) having the ends or base at right angles with the axis. **8** of or relating to the political right. ● *n.* **1 a** that which is morally or socially correct or just; justice. **b** the just, good, equitable, or correct points or aspects of something (often in *pl.*: *rights and* *wrongs*). **2** (often foll. by *to*, or *to* + infin.) a justification or fair claim (*has no right to speak like that*). **3 a** a thing one may legally or morally claim; the state of being entitled to a privilege or immunity or authority to act (*a right of reply; human rights*). **b** (in *pl.*) a title or authority to perform, publish, film, or televise a particular work, event, etc. **c** (in *pl.*) a legal claim to possession or exploitation (*mineral rights*). **4** the right-hand part or region or direction. **5 a** a street etc. on the right (*take the next right*). **b** a right turn (*make a right at the lights*). **6** *Boxing* **a** the right hand. **b** a blow with this. **7** (often **Right**) **a** a political group or section favouring conservatism. **b** such conservatives collectively. **8** = STAGE RIGHT. ● *v.tr.* **1** (often *refl.*) restore to a proper or straight or vertical position. **2 a** correct (mistakes etc.); set in order. **b** avenge (a wrong or a wronged person); make reparation for or to. **c** vindicate, justify, rehabilitate. ● *adv.* **1** straight (*go right on in*). **2** immediately; without delay (*I'll be right back*; *do it right now*). **3 a** (foll. by *to*, *around*, *through*, etc.) all the way (*right to the bottom*). **b** (foll. by *off*, *out*, etc.) completely (*am right out of butter*). **4** exactly, quite (*right in the middle*). **5** justly, properly, correctly, truly, satisfactorily (*hold it right*). **6** on or to the right side. ● *interj. informal* **1** expressing agreement or assent. **2** *ironic* expressing scorn. □ **as right as rain** perfectly sound and healthy. **by right** (or **rights**) justly, in fairness, properly. **do right by** act dutifully towards (a person). **in one's own right** on account of one's own status, effort, etc.; independently of one's relationship with others. **in the right** having justice or truth on one's side. **in one's right mind** sane; competent to think and act. **on the right side of 1** not violating (a law etc.). **2** in the favour of (a person etc.). **put** (or **set**) **right 1** restore to order, health, etc. **2** correct the mistaken impression etc. of (a person or thing). **put** (or **set**) **to rights** make correct or well ordered. **right and left** (or **right, left, and centre**) on all sides. **right away** (also **right off**) immediately. **right enough** *Cdn & Brit. informal* certainly, indeed, undeniably, sure enough. **right on** *informal* **1** an expression of strong approval or encouragement. **2** absolutely to the point (*the speech was right on*). **right you are!** *informal* an exclamation of assent. **too right** *informal* an expression of agreement. **within one's rights** not exceeding one's authority or entitlement. □ **rightness** *n.*

right angle *n.* a 90° angle. □ **at right angles (to)** placed to form a right angle (with). □ **right-angled** *adj.*

right arm *n.* one's most reliable helper.

right bank *n.* the bank of a river on one's right when one is facing downstream.

right brain *n.* the right half of the cerebrum, controlling the left side of the body, in humans often associated with spatial perception and intuition.

right-centre *n.* (in full **right-centre field**) *Baseball* the part of the outfield between centre field and right field (*a fly to deep right-centre*).

righteous /ˈrɔɪtʃəs/ *adj.* (of a person or conduct) morally right; virtuous. □ **righteously** *adv.* **righteousness** *n.*

right field *n.* *Baseball* **1** the part of the outfield to the right of the batter as he or she faces the pitcher. **2** the position of the player who covers this area. □ **right fielder** *n.*

rightful *adj.* **1 a** (of a person) having status etc. legitimately or justly (*the rightful owner*). **b** (of status, position, property, etc.) that one is entitled to (*has assumed its rightful place*). **2** (of an action etc.) equitable, fair. □ **rightfully** *adv.* **rightfulness** *n.*

right hand *n.* **1** = RIGHT-HAND MAN. **2** the most important position next to a person (*sit at God's right hand*).

right-hand *adj.* **1** on or towards the right side of a person or thing (*right-hand corner*). **2** done with the right hand (*right-hand blow*). **3** (of a screw) = RIGHT-HANDED 4b.

right-handed ● *adj.* **1 a** using the right hand by preference as more serviceable than the left. **b** using a tool etc. by preference on one's right side (*right-handed batter*). **2** (of a tool, instrument, etc.) made to be used by right-handed people (*right-handed guitar*). **3** (of a blow) struck with the right hand. **4** a turning to the right; towards the right. **b** (of a screw) advanced by turning to the right (clockwise). ● *adv.* with the right hand or to the right side (*plays right-handed*). □ **right-handedly** *adv.* **right-handedness** *n.*

right-hander *n.* **1** a right-handed person. **2** a right-handed blow etc.

right-hand man *n.* an indispensable or chief assistant.

Right Honourable *adj.* (in Canada) a title given for life to the Governor General, the prime minister, and the chief justice. Abbr.: **Rt. Hon.**

rightist ● *adj.* professing or supporting the principles or policies of the right. ● *n.* a person or thing supporting or professing such principles or policies.

rightly *adv.* justly, properly, correctly, justifiably.

right-of-centre *adj.* (of political parties, voters, etc.) having somewhat rightist views, policies, etc.

right-of-way *n.* (*pl.* **rights-of-way**) **1** a right established by usage to pass over another's ground. **2** a path subject to such a right. **3** the right of one vehicle to proceed before another. **4** *N Amer.* a strip of land reserved for a road, railway, hydro lines, etc.

Right Reverend *n.* the title of a bishop.

rightsize *v.tr. & intr.* = DOWNSIZE.

rightsizing *n.* **1** the reducing of something in size or scope, esp. of a company (by firing workers, eliminating positions, etc.); downsizing. **2** the replacing of a larger computer with a smaller one or a network of smaller ones.

right stuff *n.* (prec. by *the*) esp. *N Amer.* requisite talent, disposition, character, etc.

right-thinking *adj.* **1** having sound views and principles. **2** having views in accord with what might be expected.

right-to-life *adj.* = PRO-LIFE. □ **right-to-lifer** *n.*

rightward ● *adv.* (also **rightwards**) towards the right. ● *adj.* going towards or facing the right.

right whale *n.* each of three baleen whales of the family Balaenidae, of Arctic and temperate waters, having long baleen plates and a deeply curved jaw, esp. the widespread *Balaena glacialis*.

right wing ● *n.* **1** the conservative or reactionary section of a political party or system. **2** *Hockey* **a** the forward position to the right of centre. **b** the player at this position. **3** the right side of an army. ● *adj.* (usu. **right-wing**) conservative or reactionary. □ **right winger** *n.*

righty (*pl.* **-ies**) ● *n.* **1** a right-handed person. **2** *Polit.* a right winger. ● *adj.* **1** right-handed. **2** rightist. ● *adv.* esp. *Baseball* with the right hand or to the right side (*bats righty*).

rigid *adj.* **1** not flexible; that cannot be bent (*a rigid frame*). **2** (of a person, conduct, etc.) inflexible, unbending, strict, harsh (*a rigid disciplinarian*). □ **rigidity** *n.* **rigidly** *adv.*

rigmarole n. **1** a lengthy and complicated procedure. **2 a** a rambling or meaningless account or tale. **b** such talk.

rigor n. Med. **1** a sudden feeling of cold with shivering accompanied by a rise in temperature, preceding a fever etc. **2** rigidity of the body caused by shock or poisoning etc.

rigor mortis /ˌrɪgər 'mɔrtɪs/ n. stiffening of the body after death.

rigorous adj. **1** characterized by or showing rigour; strict. **2** strictly exact or accurate. **3** (of the weather) cold, severe. □ **rigorously** adv. **rigorousness** n.

rigour n. (also **rigor**) **1 a** severity, strictness, harshness. **b** (in pl.) harsh measures or conditions. **2** (often in pl.) severity of weather or climate; extremity of cold. **2** logical exactitude. **3** strict enforcement of rules etc. (the utmost rigour of the law). **4** austerity of life; puritanical discipline.

rig-out informal ● n. an outfit of clothes. ● v.tr. (**rig out**) (esp. as **rigged out** adj.) dress in an outfit etc. (all rigged out).

Rig-Veda /rɪg'veɪdə, -'viːdə/ n. the oldest and principal of the Hindu Vedas (see VEDA).

rile v.tr. **1** informal (often foll. by up) anger, irritate. **2** N Amer. make (water) turbulent or muddy.

rill n. **1** a small stream. **2** a shallow channel cut in the surface of soil or rocks by running water.

rim ● n. **1 a** a raised edge or border. **b** a margin or verge, esp. of something circular. **2** the part of a pair of eyeglasses surrounding the lenses. **3** the outer edge of a wheel, on which the tire is fitted. **4** a boundary line (the rim of the horizon). ● v.tr. (**rimmed**, **rimming**) **1 a** provide with a rim. **b** be a rim for or to. **2** edge, border. □ **rimless** adj. **rimmed** adj. (also in comb.).

rime ● n. **1** frost, esp. formed from cloud or fog. **2** literary hoarfrost. ● v.tr. cover with rime.

rimrock n. esp. N Amer. an outcrop of resistant rock, esp. one forming a cliff at the edge of a plateau.

rind ● n. **1** the tough outer layer or covering of fruit and vegetables, cheese, bacon, etc. **2** the bark of a tree or plant. ● v.tr. strip the bark from.

ring[1] ● n. **1** a circular band, usu. of precious metal, worn on a finger as an ornament or a token of marriage or betrothal. **2** a circular band of any material. **3** the rim of a cylindrical or circular object, or a line or band around it. **4** a mark or part having the form of a circular band (smoke rings). **5** = GROWTH RING. **6 a** an enclosure for a circus performance, bullfighting, the showing of cattle, etc. **b** a roped enclosure for boxing or wrestling. **7 a** a group of people or things arranged in a circle. **b** such an arrangement. **8 a** a combination of traders, bookmakers, spies, politicians, etc. acting together usu. illicitly for the control of operations or profit. **b** a group of people engaged in a criminal activity (drug ring). **9** a circular or spiral course. **10 a** a thin band or disc of particles etc. around a planet. **b** a halo around the moon. **11** Chem. a group of atoms each bonded to two others in a closed sequence. **12** (in pl.) a gymnastics event in which the gymnast holds on to two suspended rings. **13** a small ring, stud, or other ornament worn on the flesh, usu. by piercing (nose ring). ● v.tr. **1** make or draw a circle around. **2** (often foll. by around, about, in) encircle or hem in. **3** put a ring on (a bird etc.) or through the nose of (a pig, bull, etc.). □ **run** (or **make**) **rings around** informal outclass or outwit (another person). □ **ringed** adj. (also in comb.). **ringless** adj.

ring[2] ● v. (past **rang**; past part. **rung**) **1** intr. (often foll. by out etc.) give a clear resonant or vibrating sound of or as of a bell (a shot rang out; the doorbell rang). **2 a** tr. make (esp. a bell) ring. **b** intr. call for service or attention by ringing a bell. **3 a** intr. (of a telephone) emit a ring, buzz, beep, or other sound indicating an incoming call. **b** tr. & intr. (often foll. by up) esp. Brit. call by telephone. **4** intr. (usu. foll. by with, to) (of a place) resound or be permeated with a sound (the theatre rang with applause). **5** intr. (of the ears) be filled with a sensation of ringing. **6** tr. **a** sound (a peal etc.) on bells. **b** (of a bell) sound (the hour etc.). **7** tr. (foll. by in, out) usher in or out with bell-ringing (rang in the new year). **8** intr. (of sentiments etc.) convey a specified impression (words rang hollow). ● n. **1** a ringing sound or tone. **2 a** the act of ringing a bell. **b** the sound caused by this. **3** informal a telephone call (give me a ring). **4** a specified feeling conveyed by an utterance (had a melancholy ring). □ **ring down** (or **up**) **the curtain 1** cause the curtain to be lowered (or raised). **2** (foll. by on) mark the end (or the beginning) of (an enterprise etc.). **ring in one's ears** (or **heart** etc.) linger in the memory. **ring off** end a telephone call by replacing the receiver; hang up. **ring off the hook** (of a telephone) ring incessantly. **ring true** (or **false**) convey an impression of truth (or falsehood). **ring up 1** record (an amount spent or earned) on or as on a cash register. **2** accomplish; record (a victory etc.). □ **ringed** adj. (also in comb.). **ringer** n. **ringing** adj. **ringingly** adv.

ringbark v.tr. cut a ring in the bark of (a tree) to kill it or retard its growth and thereby improve fruit production.

ring bearer n. N Amer. the person, usu. a young boy, who ceremoniously bears the rings at a wedding.

ring-billed gull n. a small grey N American gull, Larus delawarensis, with black wing tips and a black band across a yellow bill.

ring binder n. a loose-leaf binder with ring-shaped clasps that can be opened to pass through holes in the paper.

ringed plover n. either of two small plovers, Charadrius hiaticula and C. dubius.

ringed seal n. an Arctic seal, Phoca hispida, with irregular ring-shaped markings.

ringer n. slang **1 a** esp. N Amer. a fraudulent substitute, esp. in sports. **b** a person resembling another, esp. an imposter. **2** a person or thing that rings. □ **be a ringer** (or **dead ringer**) **for** resemble (a person) exactly.

ringette n. Cdn a game resembling hockey, played (esp. by women and girls) with a straight stick and a rubber ring.

ring fence ● n. **1** a fence completely enclosing a piece of land. **2** an effective barrier. ● v.tr. **1** enclose with a ring fence. **2 a** guard securely. **b** Business protect or guarantee (funds).

ring finger n. the finger next to the little finger, esp. of the left hand, on which the wedding ring is usu. worn.

ringleader n. a leading instigator in an esp. illicit or illegal activity.

ringlet n. a curly lock of hair, esp. a long one. □ **ringleted** adj.

ringmaster n. **1** the person directing a circus performance. **2** informal a leader or director.

ring mould n. a tube pan with smooth sides and a rounded bottom.

ringneck n. any of various ring-necked birds, esp. the ring-necked pheasant, Phasianus colchicus, with a white ring around the neck.

ring-necked *adj. Zool.* having a band or bands of colour around the neck.

ring-pull *n.* a ring on a door etc. for pulling it open.

ring road *n.* a bypass encircling a town.

ringside *n.* the area immediately beside a boxing ring, circus ring, or other centre of attention (often *attrib.: a ringside seat*).

ring-tailed *adj.* **1** (of monkeys, lemurs, raccoons, etc.) having a tail ringed in alternate colours. **2** with the tail curled at the end.

ring toss *n. N Amer.* a game in which rings are tossed onto an upright peg.

ringworm *n.* any of various fungous infections of the skin causing circular inflamed patches.

rink *n.* **1** an area of natural or artificial ice for skating, playing hockey, curling, etc. **2** an area for roller skating. **3** a building containing either of these. **4** a team in curling.

rink rat *n. see* RAT *n.* 5.

rinkside *N Amer.* ● *n.* the area adjacent to the ice at a rink (often *attrib.: rinkside seats*). ● *adv.* along the edge of the ice at a rink (*sat rinkside*).

rinky-dink *adj. esp. N Amer. informal* second-rate, small-time, inferior, amateurish (*a rinky-dink production*).

rinse ● *v.* (often foll. by *out*) **1** *tr.* wash with clean water, esp. to remove soap or detergent. **2** *tr.* apply liquid to. **3** *tr.* wash lightly. **4** (also foll. by *away*) *a tr.* remove (soap, impurities, etc.) by rinsing. **b** *intr.* be removed by rinsing (*soap that rinses out easily*). ● *n.* **1** the act or an instance of rinsing (*give it a rinse*). **2** a dye for the temporary tinting of hair (*a blue rinse*).

Rioja /rɪ'o:hə/ *n.* wine produced in Rioja, a district in N Spain.

riot ● *n.* **1 a** an esp. violent disturbance of the peace by a crowd; an occurrence of serious public disorder. **b** (*attrib.*) involved in suppressing riots (*riot police*). **2** uncontrolled revelry; noisy behaviour. **3** (foll. by *of*) a lavish display (*a riot of colour*). **4** *informal* a very amusing thing or person. ● *v.intr.* make or engage in a riot. □ **run riot 1** throw off all restraint. **2** (of plants) grow or spread uncontrolled. □ **rioter** *n.*

Riot Act *n.* a proclamation in the Criminal Code of Canada which is read to order rioters to disperse. □ **read the riot act** put a firm stop to insubordination etc.; give a severe warning.

riot gear *n.* protective clothing, helmets, etc., worn by police or prison officers in situations of violence or potential violence.

riotous *adj.* **1** marked by or involving rioting. **2** characterized by wanton conduct. **3** uproarious, characterized by boisterous revelry. **4** wildly profuse. □ **riotously** *adv.* **riotousness** *n.*

RIP *abbr.* may he or she or they rest in peace.

rip¹ ● *v.* (**ripped, ripping**) **1** *tr.* tear (a thing) quickly or forcibly away or apart (*ripped the book up*). **2** *tr.* **a** make (a hole etc.) by ripping. **b** make a long tear or cut in. **c** cut (wood) along the grain. **3** *intr.* come violently apart; split. **4** *intr.* rush along. **5** *tr. informal* criticize or castigate. ● *n.* **1** a long tear or cut. **2** an act of ripping. **3** the sound of something being ripped. **4** *informal* an instance of fraud; a swindle, a rip-off (*what a rip!*). □ **let rip** *informal* **1** act or proceed without restraint. **2** speak violently. **3** not check the speed of or interfere with (a person or thing). **rip into** attack verbally. **rip off** *informal* **1 a** defraud (a person etc.). **b** steal (a thing). **2** rob (a store).

rip² *n.* a stretch of rough water in the sea or in a river, caused by the meeting of currents.

riparian /rɪ'perɪən/ *adj.* of or on a riverbank.

rip cord *n.* a cord for releasing a parachute from its pack.

rip current *n.* a strong surface current from the shore.

ripe *adj.* **1** (of grain, fruit, cheese, etc.) ready to be reaped or picked or eaten. **2** mature; fully developed (*a ripe beauty*). **3** (of a person's age) advanced. **4** (often foll. by *for*) fit or ready (*land ripe for development*). **5** (of the complexion etc.) red and full like ripe fruit. □ **ripely** *adv.* **ripeness** *n.*

ripen *v.tr. & intr.* make or become ripe.

rip-off *n. informal* **1** a fraud or swindle. **2** an act or instance of financial exploitation. **3** part of a song etc. seemingly copied from another.

riposte /rɪ'pɒst/ ● *n.* a quick sharp reply or retort. ● *v.intr.* deliver a riposte.

ripped *adj.* **1** *in senses of* RIP¹. **2** *informal* drunk, intoxicated; high.

ripper *n.* **1** a person or thing that rips. **2** a murderer who rips the victims' bodies.

ripple ● *n.* **1** a ruffling of the water's surface; a small wave or series of waves. **2** a gentle lively sound that rises and falls, e.g. of laughter or applause. **3** a wavy appearance in hair, material, etc. **4** *Electricity* a slight variation in the strength of a current etc. **5** ice cream with added syrup giving a coloured ripple effect (*raspberry ripple*). **6** *N Amer.* a riffle in a stream. **7** (usu. *attrib.*) designating potato chips having a corrugated appearance. ● *v.* **1** *a intr.* form ripples; flow in ripples. **b** *tr.* cause to do this. **2** *intr.* show or sound like ripples. □ **ripply** *adj.*

ripple effect *n.* the continuous and spreading results or consequences of an event or action.

rip-rap *esp. N Amer.* ● *n.* a collection of loose stone as a foundation for a breakwater, embankment, etc. ● *v.tr.* (**-rapped, -rapping**) fortify (the bank of a river etc.) with loose stone.

rip-roaring *adj.* **1** wildly noisy or boisterous. **2** excellent, first-rate. □ **rip-roaringly** *adv.*

ripstop ● *attrib.adj.* (of fabric, clothing, etc.) woven so that a tear will not spread. ● *n.* ripstop fabric.

riptide *n.* **1** = RIP CURRENT. **2** = RIP².

Rip Van Winkle *n.* **1** a person who has been asleep or unperceptive for a long time. **2** a person who has remained oblivious to fundamental social and political changes over an extended period.

RISC /rɪsk/ *n.* **1** a computer designed to perform a limited set of operations at high speed. **2** computing using this kind of computer.

rise ● *v.intr.* (*past* **rose**; *past part.* **risen**) **1** move from a lower position to a higher one; come or go up. **2** grow, project, expand, or incline upwards; become higher. **3** (of the sun, moon, or stars) appear above the horizon. **4 a** get up from lying or sitting or kneeling (*rose to their feet*). **b** *formal* get out of bed, esp. in the morning (*she rose early*). **5** recover a standing or vertical position; become erect (*rose to my full height*). **6** (of a meeting etc.) cease to sit for business; adjourn (*the court will rise*). **7** reach a higher position or level or amount. **8** develop greater intensity, strength, volume, or pitch (*the wind is rising; their voices rose with excitement*). **9** make progress; reach a higher social position (*rose from the ranks*). **10 a** come to the surface of liquid (*bubbles rose from the bottom*). **b** (of a person) react to provocation (*rise to the bait*). **11** become or be visible above the surroundings etc., stand prominently (*mountains rose to our right*). **12 a** (of buildings etc.) undergo construction from the foundations (*office blocks were rising all around*). **b** (of a tree etc.) grow to a (usu. specified) height. **13** come to life again (*risen from the dead*). **14** (of dough) swell by the action of yeast etc. **15** (often foll. by *up*) cease to be quiet or submissive; rebel (*rise in arms*). **16** originate; have as its source (*the river rises in the mountains*). **17** (of wind) start to blow. **18** (of a person's spirits) become cheerful or more optimistic. **19** (of a barometer) show a higher atmospheric pressure. **20** (of a bump, blister, etc.) form. ● *n.* **1** an act or manner or amount of rising. **2** an upward slope or hill or movement (*the house stood on a rise*). **3** an increase in sound or pitch. **4** an increase in amount, extent, etc. (*a rise in unemployment*). **5** an increase in status or power. **6** social, commercial, or political advancement; upward progress. **7** the movement of fish to the surface. **8** origin. **9 a** the vertical height of a step, arch, incline, etc. **b** = RISER 2. □ **get a rise out of** *informal* provoke an emotional reaction from (a person), esp. by teasing. **on the rise** on the increase. **rise above 1** be superior to (petty feelings etc.). **2** show dignity or strength in the face of (difficulty, poor conditions, etc.). **rise and shine** (usu. as *imper.*) *informal* get out of bed; wake up. **rise in the world** attain a higher position in a hierarchy. **rise to** develop powers equal to (an occasion). **rise with the sun** get up early in the morning.

riser *n.* **1** a person who rises, esp. from bed (*an early riser*). **2** a vertical section between the treads of a staircase. **3** a vertical pipe for the flow of liquid or gas. **4 a** a low platform on a stage etc. **b** one of a series of these arranged in step-like fashion, usu. for seating.

risible /ˈrɪzɪbəl/ *adj.* **1** laughable, ludicrous. **2** inclined to laugh; capable of laughter. □ **risibility** *n.*

rising ● *adj.* **1** going up; getting higher. **2** increasing (*rising costs*). **3** advancing to maturity or high standing (*a rising young lawyer*). **4** (of ground) sloping upwards. ● *n.* **1** a revolt or insurrection. **2** a piece of rising ground; a hill, a mound.

risk ● *n.* **1** a chance or possibility of danger, loss, injury, or other adverse consequences (*a health risk*). **2** a person or thing causing a risk or regarded in relation to risk (*is a poor risk*). ● *v.tr.* **1** expose to risk. **2** accept the chance of (*could not risk getting wet*). **3** venture on. □ **at risk** exposed to danger. **at one's (own) risk** accepting responsibility, agreeing to make no claims. **at the risk of** with the possibility of (an adverse consequence). **put at risk** expose to danger. **risk one's neck** put one's own life in danger. **run a** (or **the**) **risk** (often foll. by *of*) expose oneself to danger or loss etc. **take** (or **run**) **a risk** chance the possibility of danger etc.

risk-averse *adj.* averse to taking risks.

risk capital *n.* = VENTURE CAPITAL.

risk factor *n.* a circumstance or condition increasing a specified risk.

risky *adj.* (**-ier, -iest**) **1** involving risk. **2** = RISQUÉ. □ **riskily** *adv.* **riskiness** *n.*

risotto /rɪˈzɒtəʊ/ *n.* (*pl.* **-os**) an Italian dish of esp. arborio rice cooked in broth with various other ingredients, as meat, onions, etc.

risqué /rɪsˈkeɪ/ *adj.* slightly indecent.

Ritalin /ˈrɪtəlɪn/ *n. proprietary* a drug which stimulates the central nervous system, used esp. to treat attention deficit disorder.

rite *n.* **1** a religious or solemn observance or act (*burial rites*). **2** an action or procedure required or usual in this. **3** a body of customary observances characteristic of a Church or a part of it (*the Latin rite*).

rite of passage *n.* (often in *pl.*) a ritual or event

marking a stage of a person's advance through life, e.g. marriage.

ritual ● *n.* **1** a prescribed order of performing rites. **2** a procedure regularly followed. ● *adj.* of or done as a ritual or rites (*ritual dance*). □ **ritualize** *v.tr. & intr.* **ritualization** *n.* **ritually** *adv.*

ritualism *n.* the regular or excessive practice of ritual. □ **ritualist** *n.* **ritualistic** *adj.* **ritualistically** *adv.*

ritz *n.* esp. ostentatious luxury. □ **put on the ritz** behave ostentatiously.

ritzy *adj.* (**-ier, -iest**) *informal* **1** high-class, luxurious. **2** ostentatiously fashionable.

rival ● *n.* **1** a person, team, organization, etc. competing with another for the same objective. **2** a person or thing that equals another in quality etc. **3** (*attrib.*) being a rival or rivals (*a rival firm*). ● *v.tr.* (**rivalled, rivalling**) **1** be the rival of or comparable to. **2** seem or claim to be as good as.

rivalry *n.* (*pl.* **-ies**) the state or an instance of being rivals; competition. □ **rivalrous** *adj.*

rive /raɪv/ *v.* (*past* **rived**; *past part.* **riven** /ˈrɪvən/) *archaic* or *literary* (usu. in *passive*) **1** tr. split or tear apart violently. **2 a** tr. split (wood or stone). **b** *intr.* be split.

river *n.* **1** a natural stream of water flowing in a channel to the ocean or a lake etc. (often *attrib.*: *river valley*). **2** a copious flow (*rivers of blood*). **3** (*attrib.*) (in the names of animals, plants, etc.) living in or associated with the river. □ **sell down the river** *informal* betray or let down. **up the river** *informal* to or in prison.

riverbank *n.* the raised or sloping edge of a river.

riverbed *n.* the bed or channel in which a river flows.

riverboat *n.* a boat designed for use on rivers.

river bottom *n.* **1** the bottom of a river. **2** N Amer. low-lying alluvial land along the banks of a river.

river drive *n. Cdn* a log drive down a river. □ **river-drive** *v.tr.* **river driver** *n.*

riverfront ● *n.* land adjacent to a river. ● *adj.* situated or occurring beside a river.

riverine /ˈrɪvəraɪn/ *adj.* of or on a river or riverbank.

river lot *n. Cdn hist.* a long narrow farm lot extending back from a river, esp. one along the St. Lawrence River or in the Red River Settlement.

riverman *n.* **1** a person who has worked on a river for many years and possesses a great deal of knowledge about its currents, fluctuations in level, etc. **2** *hist.* (in Canada) a voyageur.

river otter *n.* an otter of N America, *Lutra canadensis*, noted for its agile swimming and playful behaviour.

river runner *n. N Amer.* a whitewater rafter. □ **river running** *n.*

riverside *n.* the ground along a riverbank (often *attrib.*: *riverside path*).

rivet ● *n.* a nail or bolt for holding together metal plates etc., its headless end being beaten out or pressed down when in place. ● *v.tr.* (**riveted, riveting**) **1 a** join or fasten with rivets. **b** beat out or press down the end of (a nail or bolt). **c** fix; make immovable. **2 a** (foll. by *on, upon*) direct intently (one's eyes or attention etc.). **b** (esp. as **riveting** *adj.*) engross (a person or the attention). □ **riveter** *n.*

rivulet /ˈrɪvjʊlət/ *n.* **1** a small stream or brook. **2** a thin stream of liquid (*rivulets of sweat*).

RM *abbr. Cdn* **1** RURAL MUNICIPALITY. **2** REGIONAL MUNICIPALITY.

rm. *abbr.* room.

RMT *abbr.* Registered Massage Therapist.

RN *abbr.* **1** Registered Nurse. **2** (in the UK) Royal Navy.

Rn *symbol* radon.

RNA *abbr.* **1** ribonucleic acid. **2** = REGISTERED NURSING ASSISTANT.

roach[1] *n.* (*pl.* same) **1** a small freshwater fish of Europe, esp. *Rutilus rutilus*, allied to the carp. **2** any of various freshwater fishes of N America.

roach[2] *n.* **1** *informal* a cockroach. **2** *slang* the butt of a marijuana cigarette.

road ● *n.* **1** a path or way with a specially prepared surface, used by motor vehicles, cyclists, etc.; a street. **2 a** one's way or route (*our road took us through unexplored territory*). **b** a method or means of accomplishing something. **3** *N Amer.* a railway. **4** (usu. in *pl.*) a partly sheltered piece of water near the shore in which ships can ride at anchor. ● *adj. N Amer.* Sport of or relating to a game or games played at an opponent's venue (*a poor road record*). □ **get out of the** (or **my** etc.) **road** *informal* cease to obstruct a person. **go down the road** *Cdn* leave one's hometown in search of employment, adventure, etc., esp. leave the Maritimes for central or western Canada. **in the** (or **my** etc.) **road** *informal* obstructing a person or thing. **one for the road** *informal* a final (esp. alcoholic) drink before departure. **on the road 1** travelling, esp. as a sales representative or a performer. **2** (of a car etc.) in working condition; able to be driven. **the road to** the way of getting to or achieving (*the road to Owen Sound*; *the road to ruin*). **take to the road** set out. □ **roadless** *adj.*

road allowance *n. Cdn* **1** a strip of land retained by government authorities for the construction of a road. **2** an area at either side of a road which remains a public right-of-way.

road apple *n. slang* (usu. in *pl.*) **1** *N Amer.* a piece of horse manure. **2** *Cdn hist.* a frozen piece of horse manure used as a hockey puck, esp. on the Prairies.

roadbed *n.* **1** the foundation structure of a railway. **2** the material laid down to form a road. **3** *N Amer.* the part of a road on which vehicles travel.

roadblock *n.* **1** a barrier or barricade on a road, esp. one set up by police or military personnel to stop and check vehicles. **2** any obstruction (*roadblocks to peace*). **3** the action of blocking a road as a protest.

road grader *n.* a vehicle with a heavy blade, used in road construction for levelling the ground.

road hockey *n. Cdn* (esp. *S Ont.*) = STREET HOCKEY.

roadholding *n.* the capacity of a moving vehicle to remain stable when cornering at high speeds etc.

roadhouse *n.* **1** a restaurant or bar located on a major road usu. on the outskirts of a town or city. **2** a theatre designed for touring companies.

roadie *n. informal* a person employed by a touring pop group etc. to set up and maintain equipment.

roadkill *n.* esp. *N Amer.* **1** the killing of an animal by a vehicle on a road. **2** an animal killed in this way.

road map *n.* **1** a folding map showing the roads of a country or area, used esp. by motorists. **2** any plan or guide (*our road map to the future*).

road movie *n.* **1** a genre of dramatic film whose central motif is a motorcycle or car journey undertaken by the main characters to elude capture by authorities, for adventure, etc. **2** a film of this type.

road racing *n.* a competitive event of racing on foot or in cars, motorcyles, or bicycles over public roads, as distinct from racing on a closed track or drag strip. □ **road race** *n.* **road racer** *n.*

road rage *n.* violent anger caused by the stress and frustration of driving.

roadrunner *n.* a bird of Mexican and US deserts, *Geococcyx californianus*, related to the cuckoo, which flies poorly but runs fast.

road salt *n.* coarse salt used to melt ice on roads etc.

road show *n.* **1 a** a performance given by a group of touring entertainers, esp. a theatre company. **b** a company giving such performances. **2** a radio or television program done on location, esp. a series of programs each from a different venue. **3** a touring political or advertising campaign.

roadside *n.* the strip of land beside a road (often *attrib.: a roadside stand*).

road sign *n.* a sign giving information or instructions to road users.

roadster *n.* **1** an open two-seater car. **2** a motorcycle for use on roads.

road test ● *n.* **1 a** a test of the performance of a vehicle on the road. **b** a test of any new product. **2** = DRIVING TEST. ● *v.tr.* (**road-test**) **1** test (a vehicle) on the road. **2** test (any new product). **3** perform a preliminary version of (a new song, play, etc.) before an audience to gauge reaction to it.

road trip ● *n.* **1** *N Amer.* Sport a series of games played away from home. **2** any journey made by car, bicycle, bus, etc. ● *v.intr.* (**road-trip**) go on a road trip.

roadway *n.* **1** a road. **2** the main or central portion of a road, esp. that part used by vehicles. **3** the part of a bridge or railway used for traffic.

roadwork *n.* **1** the construction or repair of roads, or other work involving digging up a road. **2** athletic exercise or training involving running on roads.

roadworthy *adj.* fit to be used on the road. □ **roadworthiness** *n.*

roam ● *v.* **1** *intr.* ramble, wander. **2** *tr.* travel unsystematically over, through, or about. ● *n.* an act of roaming; a ramble.

roan[1] ● *adj.* (of an animal, esp. a horse) having a coat of which the prevailing colour is interspersed with hairs of another colour, esp. bay or sorrel or chestnut mixed with white or grey. ● *n.* a roan animal.

roan[2] *n.* soft sheepskin leather used in bookbinding as a substitute for morocco.

roar ● *n.* **1** a loud deep hoarse sound, as made by a lion, a loud engine, thunder, a person in pain or rage or excitement, etc. **2** a loud laugh. ● *v.* **1** *intr.* **a** utter or make a roar. **b** utter loud laughter. **2** *intr.* travel in a vehicle at high speed, esp. with the engine roaring. **3** *tr.* (often foll. by *out*) say, sing, or utter (words, an oath, etc.) in a loud tone.

roaring *adj.* *in senses of* ROAR *v.* □ **roaring drunk** *informal* very drunk and noisy. **roaring success** *informal* a great success. **roaring trade** (or **business**) *informal* very brisk trade or business.

Roaring Twenties *n.pl. informal* the decade of the 1920s.

roast ● *v.* **1** *tr.* **a** cook (food, esp. meat) in an oven or by exposure to open heat. **b** heat (coffee beans) before grinding. **2** *tr.* criticize severely, denounce. **3** *tr.* *N Amer.* honour (a person) with a roast. **4** *intr.* undergo roasting. ● *attrib.adj.* (of meat or a potato, chestnut, etc.) roasted. ● *n.* **1 a** roast meat. **b** a dish of this. **c** a piece of meat for roasting. **2** the process of roasting. **3** *N Amer.* a party where roasted food is eaten (*pig roast*). **4** *N Amer.* a mock-serious ceremonial tribute at which friends of the guest of honour offer short speeches of praise and good-natured insult. □ **roast alive** subject to intense heat. **roast in hell** suffer damnation.

roaster *n.* **1** a person or thing that roasts. **2 a** an oven or dish for roasting food in. **b** a coffee-roasting apparatus. **3** something fit for roasting, e.g. a fowl.

roasting ● *adj.* **1** very hot. **2** used for or fit for roasting (*roasting pan*; *roasting chicken*). ● *n.* **1** *in senses of* ROAST *v.* **2** a severe criticism or denunciation.

rob v. (**robbed, robbing**) (often foll. by of) **1** tr. take unlawfully from, esp. by force or threat of force (robbed the safe; robbed her of her jewels). **2** tr. deprive of what is due or normal (was robbed of my sleep). **3** intr. commit robbery. **4** tr. informal overcharge (a customer). □ **rob Peter to pay Paul** take away from one to give to another, discharge one debt by incurring another. **robber** n. a person who commits robbery.

robbery n. (pl. **-ies**) **1 a** the act or process of robbing, esp. with force or threat of force. **b** an instance of this. **2** excessive financial demand or cost (set us back $50 — it was sheer robbery).

robe ● n. **1** a long loose outer garment. **2** esp. N Amer. a dressing gown or bathrobe. **3** (often in pl.) a long outer garment worn as an indication of the wearer's rank, office, profession, etc. **4** N Amer. a blanket or wrap of fur. ● v. **1** tr. clothe (a person) in a robe; dress. **2** intr. put on one's robes or vestments.

Robertson n. Cdn proprietary **1** a type of screw with a square notch on the head. **2** a type of screwdriver with a square tip designed to fit into this.

robin n. **1** N Amer. a red-breasted thrush, Turdus migratorius. **2** (also **robin redbreast**) a small brown European bird, Erithacus rubecula, the adult of which has a red throat and breast. **3** a bird similar in appearance etc. to either of these.

Robin Hood n. a person who acts illegally or unfavourably toward the rich for the benefit of the poor.

robin's egg blue ● n. a pale greenish-blue colour. ● adj. of this colour.

robot n. **1** a machine with a human appearance or functioning like a human. **2** a machine capable of carrying out a complex series of actions automatically. **3** a person who works mechanically and efficiently but insensitively. □ **robotic** adj. **robotically** adv. **robotize** v.tr. **robotization** n.

robotics /rəˈbɒtɪks/ n.pl. (usu. treated as sing.) the study of robots; the art or science of their design and operation. □ **roboticist** n.

robust adj. (**robuster, robustest**) **1 a** strong and sturdy, esp. in physique or construction. **b** healthy, vigorous; not readily damaged or weakened (a robust industry). **2** (of exercise, discipline, etc.) vigorous, requiring strength. **3** (of intellect or mental attitude) straightforward, not given to nor confused by subtleties. **4** (of a statement, reply, etc.) bold, firm, unyielding. **5** (of wine etc.) rich and full-bodied. □ **robustly** adv. **robustness** n.

robusta /rəˈbʌstə/ n. **1** coffee or coffee beans from a widely grown African species of coffee plant, Coffea canephora (formerly robusta). **2** the plant itself.

ROC /rɒk/ abbr. Cdn the parts of Canada outside the province of Quebec.

rock¹ n. **1 a** the hard material of the earth's crust, exposed on the surface or underlying the soil. **b** a similar material on other planets. **2** Geol. any natural material, hard or soft, e.g. clay, consisting of one or more minerals. **3** a mass of rock projecting and forming a hill, cliff, reef, etc. **4** (**the Rock**) a Cdn the island of Newfoundland. **b** Gibraltar. **5** a large detached stone. **6** N Amer. a stone of any size. **7** a large polished circular stone with a handle on top, used in the game of curling. **8** a firm and dependable support or protection. **9** (usu. in pl.) a source of danger or destruction. **10** slang a precious stone, esp. a diamond. **11** slang a solid form of cocaine. **12** (in pl.) coarse slang the testicles. □ **between a rock and a hard place** N Amer. in a dilemma. **get one's rocks off** coarse slang **1** achieve sexual satisfaction. **2** obtain

enjoyment. **on the rocks** informal **1** (esp. of a marriage) in danger of breaking up. **2** (of a drink) served undiluted with ice cubes. □ **rocklike** adj.

rock² ● v. **1** tr. move gently to and fro in or as if in a cradle; set or maintain such motion (rocked by the waves). **2** intr. be or continue in such motion (sat rocking in his chair). **3 a** intr. sway from side to side under some impact or stress; shake. **b** tr. cause to do this (an earthquake rocked the house). **4** tr. distress, perturb. **5** intr. dance to or play rock music. **6** intr. (of popular music) possess a strong beat, esp. in 2/4 or 4/4 time; exhibit the characteristics of rock music. ● n. **1** a rocking movement (gave the chair a rock). **2** a period of rocking (had a rock in his chair). **3** (often attrib.) **a** = ROCK 'N' ROLL. **b** a form of popular music which evolved from rock 'n' roll and pop music, usu. characterized by a harsher sound. □ **rock the boat** informal disturb the equilibrium of a situation.

rockabilly /ˈrɒkəˌbɪli/ n. a type of popular music combining elements of rock 'n' roll and hillbilly music.

rock and roll (also **rock & roll**) var. of ROCK 'N' ROLL.

rock bass n. a N American freshwater fish, Ambloplites rupestris, frequenting rocky shallows in weedy lakes and streams.

rock-bottom ● adj. the very lowest (rock-bottom prices). ● n. (**rock bottom**) the very lowest level.

rock climbing n. the sport of climbing rock faces, esp. with the aid of ropes etc. □ **rock climb** n. & v.intr. **rock climber** n.

Rock Cornish n. (also **Rock Cornish hen, Rock Cornish game hen**) a compact, meaty chicken, a hybrid of Cornish and White Rock chickens, slaughtered at six weeks to provide a single-serving sized bird, usu. roasted.

rock cut n. **1** a sheer rock face along a highway or road, the result of blasting through a mountain or hill to create the highway or road. **2** a tunnel for cars, trains, etc. cut through a mountain or hill.

rocker n. **1** a person or thing that rocks. **2** a curved bar or similar support, on which something can rock. **3** a rocking chair. **4 a** a person who performs, dances to, or enjoys rock music. **b** a popular song that rocks; a rock song. **5** a skate with a highly curved blade. **6** any rocking device forming part of a mechanism. □ **off one's rocker** slang crazy.

rockery n. (pl. **-ies**) = ROCK GARDEN.

rocket ● n. **1** a cylindrical projectile that can be propelled to a great height or distance by combustion of its contents, used esp. as a firework or signal. **2** (in full **rocket engine** or **rocket motor**) an engine using a similar principle but not dependent on air intake for its operation. **3** a rocket-propelled missile, spacecraft, etc. **4** anything that moves very quickly, e.g. a train, ball, etc. (hit a rocket to left field). **5** any of various fast-growing plants of the mustard family. **6** = ARUGULA. ● v. (**rocketed, rocketing**) **1** tr. bombard with rockets. **2** intr. **a** move rapidly upwards or away. **b** increase rapidly (prices rocketed). **3** tr. propel (someone or something) at speed; send by or as by rocket.

rocket launcher n. a device or structure for launching missiles or space rockets.

rocket scientist n. **1** a scientific expert in the science or practice of rocket propulsion. **2** jocular a person who is highly intelligent, esp. in scientific and mathematical matters. □ **rocket science** n.

rocket ship n. a spaceship powered by rockets.

rock face n. a vertical surface of natural rock.

rockfall n. **1** a descent of loose rocks. **2** a mass of fallen rock.

rockfish n. any of various fishes frequenting rocks or rocky bottoms, e.g. the striped bass.

rock garden n. a garden composed of large stones with plants growing between them.

rock-hard adj. extremely hard, strong, or tough.

rockhound n. esp. N Amer. informal **1** a geologist. **2** an amateur collector or student of rocks and minerals. □ **rockhounding** n.

rocking chair n. a chair mounted on rockers or springs for gently rocking in.

rocking horse n. a wooden or plastic horse mounted on rockers or springs for a child to rock on.

rock 'n' roll ● n. a type of popular music originating in the 1950s, characterized by a heavy beat and simple melodies. ● adj. informal exciting, energetic (a rock 'n' roll performance). ● v.intr. informal get down to business; make progress. □ **rock 'n' roller** n.

rock ptarmigan n. a ptarmigan, Lagopus mutus, found in extreme northern regions, distinguished by its black tail feathers in winter.

rock salt n. common salt as a solid mineral.

rock slide n. **1** the sliding down of a mass of rock from a mountain, cliff, etc. **2** the mass of rock fragments which has so fallen.

rock-solid adj. very solid or firm.

rock-steady ● adj. unlikely to collapse, be changed, etc.; rock-solid. ● n. (**rocksteady**) /rɒkˈstedi/ a style of popular music originating in Jamaica, characterized by a slow tempo and accentuated offbeat.

rockumentary n. (pl. **-ies**) a documentary about rock music and musicians.

rockwool n. a wool-like substance made from inorganic material, used esp. for insulation etc.

rocky[1] adj. (**-ier, -iest**) **1** of or like rock. **2** full of or abounding in rock or rocks. □ **rockiness** n.

rocky[2] adj. (**-ier, -iest**) informal **1** fraught with difficulties, disagreements, etc. (the marriage got off to a rocky start). **2** unsteady, tottering. □ **rockiness** n.

Rocky Mountain goat n. see MOUNTAIN GOAT 1.

rocky road n. **1** (attrib.) N Amer. designating a mixture of chocolate chips, marshmallow, and nuts used in ice cream or as a topping for brownies etc. **2** a course of action fraught with difficulties, obstacles, etc.

rococo /rəˈkoːkoː/ ● adj. **1** of a late baroque style of decoration prevalent in 18th-c. continental Europe, with asymmetrical patterns involving scroll-work, shell motifs, etc. **2** (of literature, music, architecture, and the decorative arts) highly ornamented, florid. ● n. the rococo style.

rod n. **1** a slender straight bar esp. of wood or metal. **2** this as a symbol of office. **3 a** a stick or bundle of twigs used in caning or flogging. **b** (prec. by the) the use of this. **4 a** = FISHING ROD. **b** an angler using a rod. **5 a** a slender straight round stick growing as a shoot on a tree. **b** this when cut. **6** N Amer. slang = HOT ROD. **7** = CURTAIN ROD. **8** any of numerous rod-shaped structures in the eye, detecting dim light. **9** a metal shaft in an internal combustion engine etc. (piston rod). **10** a long slender piece of fuel for a nuclear reactor. □ **ride the rods** Cdn. hist. informal ride surreptitiously and without paying on a freight train. □ **rod-like** adj.

rode[1] past of RIDE.

rode[2] n. N Amer. a rope securing an anchor or net.

rodent ● n. any mammal of the order Rodentia with strong incisors and no canine teeth, e.g. rat, mouse, squirrel, beaver, porcupine. ● adj. of the order Rodentia. □ **rodent-like** adj.

rodeo /ˈroːdioː/ ● n. (pl. **-os**) **1** a display or competition exhibiting the skills of riding broncos, roping cattle, wrestling steers, etc. **2** a similar (usu. competitive) exhibition of other skills, e.g. motorcycle riding, cycling, etc. **3** a roundup of cattle on a ranch for branding etc. ● v.intr. (**rodeoed, rodeoing**) compete in a rodeo.

rodman n. (pl. **-men**) N Amer. a surveyor's assistant.

rodney /ˈrɒdni/ n. Cdn (Nfld) a small fishing boat.

roe[1] n. **1** (also **hard roe**) the mass of eggs in a female fish's ovary. **2** (also **soft roe**) the milt of a male fish.

roe[2] n. (pl. same or **roes**) (also **roe-deer**) a small European and Asian deer, Capreolus capreolus.

roebuck n. a male roe.

roentgen /ˈrɒntgən, ˈrʌnt-/ n. a unit of ionizing radiation, the amount producing one electrostatic unit of positive or negative ionic charge in one cubic centimetre of air under standard conditions.

roger interj. **1** your message has been received and understood (used in radio communication etc.). **2** slang all right; OK.

rogue n. **1** a dishonest or unprincipled person. **2** jocular a mischievous person, esp. a child. **3** (usu. attrib.) **a** a wild animal driven away or living apart from the herd and of fierce temper. **b** a stray, irresponsible, or undisciplined person or thing.

rogues' gallery n. **1** a collection of photographs of known criminals etc., used for identification of suspects. **2** any collection of people notable for a certain shared quality or characteristic, esp. a disreputable one.

roguish adj. **1** playfully mischievous. **2** characteristic of rogues. □ **roguishly** adv. **roguishness** n.

'roid n. slang an anabolic steroid, when taken for its muscle-building properties by an athlete.

roil v. **1** tr. make (a liquid) turbid by agitating it. **2** intr. move in a confused or turbulent manner. □ **roily** adj.

roister v.intr. (esp. as **roistering** adj.) revel noisily; be uproarious. □ **roisterer** n. **roistering** n.

role n. **1** a performer's part in a play, film, etc. **2** a person's or thing's characteristic or expected function. **3** the part played or assumed by a person in society, life, etc., influenced by his or her conception of what is appropriate.

role model n. a person looked to by others as an example in a particular role or situation.

role-playing n. (also **role play**) an exercise in which participants act the part of another character, used in psychotherapy, language teaching, etc. □ **role-play** v.tr. & intr. **role player** n.

roll ● v. **1 a** intr. move or go in some direction by turning over and over on an axis (the ball rolled under the table). **b** tr. cause to do this (rolled the barrel across the yard). **2** tr. make revolve between two surfaces (rolled the clay between her palms). **3 a** intr. (foll. by along, by, etc.) move or advance on or (of time etc.) as if on wheels etc. **b** tr. cause to do this (rolled the cart down the hall). **c** intr. (of a person) be conveyed in a vehicle (rolled by on a tractor). **4 a** tr. turn over and over on itself to form a more or less cylindrical or spherical shape, or to make shorter (rolled up her sleeves). **b** tr. make by forming material into a cylinder or ball (rolled a huge snowball). **c** tr. accumulate into a mass (rolled the dough into a ball). **d** intr. (foll. by into) make a specified shape of itself (rolled into a ball). **5** tr. flatten or form by passing a roller etc. over or by passing between rollers. **6** intr. & tr. change or cause to change direction by rotatory movement (his eyes rolled; he rolled his eyes). **7** intr. **a** wallow, turn about in a fluid or a loose medium (the dog rolled in the dust). **b** (of a horse etc.) lie on its back and kick about, esp. so as to dislodge its rider. **8** intr. **a** (of a moving ship etc.) sway to and fro on an axis parallel to the direction of motion. **b** walk with an unsteady swaying gait. **9 a** *intr.* undulate, show or go with an undulating surface or motion (*rolling hills; the waves roll in*). **b** *tr.* carry or propel with such motion (*the river rolls its waters to the sea*). **10 a** *intr.* (of machinery) start functioning or moving (*the cameras rolled*). **b** *tr.* cause (machinery) to do this. **c** *intr.* set out; start moving, working, etc. (*let's roll!*). **d** *intr.* (often foll. by *along*) progress satisfactorily or speedily (*the rewriting is rolling right along*). **11 a** *tr.* display (credits for a film or television program) moving as if on a roller up the screen. **b** *intr.* (of credits) be displayed in this way. **12** *intr.* & *tr.* sound or utter with a vibratory or trilling effect (*thunder rolled in the distance; they roll their* rs). **13** *N Amer. slang* **a** *tr.* overturn (a car etc.). **b** *intr.* (of a car etc.) overturn. **14** *tr. N Amer.* throw (dice). **15** *tr. slang* rob (esp. a helpless victim). ● *n.* **1 a** a cylinder formed by turning flexible material over and over on itself without folding (*a roll of carpet*). **b** a filled item of food of similar form (*jelly roll*). **2 a** a small portion of bread individually baked; a bun. **b** this with a specified filling (*lobster roll*). **3** a more or less cylindrical or semicylindrical straight or curved mass of something (*rolls of fat*). **4 a** an official list or register (*the electoral roll*). **b** the total numbers on this (*the school's rolls have fallen*). **5** a rolling motion or gait; undulation (*the roll of the hills*). **6 a** a period of rolling (*a roll in the mud*). **b** a gymnastic exercise in which the body is rolled into a tucked position and turned in a forward or backward circle. **c** (esp. **a roll in the hay**) *informal* an act of sexual intercourse or erotic fondling. **7** the continuous rhythmic sound of thunder or a drum. **8** a complete revolution of an aircraft about its longitudinal axis. **9** a cylinder or roller, esp. to shape metal in a rolling mill. **10** *N Amer. & Austral.* money, esp. as banknotes rolled together. **11** a throw of dice. **12** *slang* a bout of success or progress. □ **be rolling** *informal* be very rich. **be rolling in** *informal* have plenty of (esp. money). **on a roll** *slang* experiencing a bout of success or progress; engaged in a period of intense activity. **roll back 1** *N Amer.* cause (esp. prices or wages) to decrease; reduce. **2** turn or force back or further away (*roll back Communism*). **3** cancel; annul (*roll back a decision*). **rolled into one** combined in one person or thing. **roll in** arrive in great numbers or quantity. **roll in the aisles** *informal* laugh uproariously. **roll on** put on or apply by rolling. **roll out 1** unveil (a new aircraft or spacecraft). **b** launch (a new product, campaign, etc.). **2** *N Amer. slang* get out of bed. **roll over 1** send (a person) sprawling or rolling. **2** *Econ.* reinvest (stocks, bonds, mutual funds, etc.). **roll up 1** *informal* arrive in a vehicle; appear on the scene. **2** make into or form a roll. **roll with the punches** *informal* adapt oneself to difficult circumstances.

rollaway ● *adj.* (of a bed etc.) that can be removed on wheels or casters. ● *n.* a rollaway bed etc.

rollback *n.* **1** a reduction or decrease in prices, wages, etc. **2** the action or an act of rolling backwards.

roll bar *n.* an overhead metal bar strengthening the frame of a vehicle (esp. in racing) and protecting the occupants if the vehicle overturns.

roll call *n.* **1** a process of calling out a list of names to establish who is present. **2** a distinguished list of persons, things, etc. (*a roll call of former champions*).

rolled oats *n.pl.* oats that have been husked and crushed.

roller *n.* **1 a** a hard revolving cylinder for smoothing the ground, spreading ink or paint, crushing or stamping, rolling up cloth on, etc., used alone or as a rotating part of a machine. **b** a cylinder for diminishing friction when moving a heavy object. **2** a small cylinder on which hair is rolled for setting. **3** a long swelling wave. **4** *Baseball* a weakly-hit ground ball which rolls rather than bouncing.

rollerball *n.* a ballpoint pen using thinner ink than other ballpoints.

Rollerblade ● *n.* proprietary an in-line skate. ● *v.intr.* (**rollerblade**) skate using in-line skates. □ **rollerblader** *n.*

roller coaster ● *n.* **1** a ride at an amusement park etc., having small open railway cars which travel in a linked line on an elevated, winding track up and down steep hills and around sharp corners. **2** any experience, time, etc. marked by sudden ups and downs or changes (*an emotional roller coaster*). ● *attrib.adj.* (**roller-coaster**) that goes up and down, or changes, suddenly and repeatedly (*a roller-coaster economy*). ● *v.intr.* (**roller-coaster**) (also **rollercoast**) go up and down or change in this way.

roller hockey *n.* N Amer. hockey played on in-line skates.

roller rink *n.* **1** a rink used for roller skating. **2** a building containing such a rink.

roller skate ● *n.* each of a pair of boots with wheels attached (or metal or plastic frames with wheels, fitted to shoes) for riding on paved surfaces etc. ● *v.intr.* move on roller skates. □ **roller skater** *n.*

rollick *v.intr.* (esp. as **rollicking** *adj.*) be jovial or exuberant; revel.

rollie *n.* Cdn informal a hand-rolled cigarette.

rolling mill *n.* a machine or factory for rolling metal into shape.

rolling pin *n.* a cylinder made of wood or plastic for rolling out pastry, dough, etc.

rolling stock *n.* the locomotives, cars, or other vehicles used on a railway.

rolling stone *n.* a person who is unwilling to settle for long in one place.

roll-on ● *attrib.adj.* (of deodorant etc.) applied by means of a rotating ball in the neck of the container. ● *n.* a roll-on deodorant, cosmetic, etc.

rollout *n.* **1 a** the official wheeling out of a new aircraft or spacecraft. **b** the official launch of a new product. **2** the part of a landing during which an aircraft travels along the runway losing speed.

rollover *n.* **1** *Econ.* the extension or transfer of a debt or other financial relationship, esp. the reinvestment of stocks, bonds, mutual funds, etc. **2** *informal* the overturning of a vehicle etc.

roll-up *adj.* that can be rolled up; made by rolling up (*roll-up awnings*).

Rolodex /ˈroːlədeks/ *n.* proprietary a desktop card index mounted on a rotating axis, used for storing addresses and telephone numbers.

roly-poly *adj.* pudgy, plump.

ROM /rɒm/ *n.* Computing read-only memory.

Rom /rɒm/ *n.* (pl. **Roma** /ˈrɒmə/) a male gypsy.

rom. *abbr.* roman (type).

Roma /ˈroːmə/ *n.* a variety of tomato with pear-shaped fruit, thick flesh, and few seeds.

romaine /roːˈmeɪn/ *n.* N Amer. a variety of lettuce with crisp narrow leaves forming a long upright head.

Roman ● *adj.* **1** of ancient Rome or its territory or people. **2** of medieval or modern Rome. **3** of papal Rome, esp. = ROMAN CATHOLIC. **4** surviving from a period of Roman rule (*Roman road*). **5** (**roman**) (of type) of a plain upright kind used in ordinary print. **6** (of the alphabet etc.) based on the ancient Roman system with letters A–Z. ● *n.* **1 a** a citizen of the ancient Roman Republic or Empire. **b** a soldier of the Roman Empire. **2** a citizen of modern Rome. **3** = ROMAN CATHOLIC. **4 (roman)** roman type.

Roman Catholic ● *adj.* of or relating to the part of the Christian Church acknowledging the Pope as its head. ● *n.* a member of this Church. □ **Roman Catholicism** *n.*

romance /'rɔ:mans, rɔ:'mans/ ● *n.* **1 a** a love affair. **b** sentimental or idealized love. **c** a prevailing sense of wonder or mystery surrounding the mutual attraction in a love affair. **2** a feeling of excitement and adventure (*the romance of travel*). **3 a** a literary genre with romantic love or highly imaginative unrealistic episodes forming the central theme. **b** a work of this genre. **4** a medieval tale, usu. in verse, of some hero of chivalry, of the kind common in the Romance languages. **5 a** a exaggeration or picturesque falsehood. **b** an instance of this. ● *adj.* **(Romance)** of any of the languages descended from Latin (French, Italian, Spanish, etc.). ● *v.* **1** *intr.* exaggerate or distort the truth, esp. fantastically. **2** *tr.* a court, woo. **b** seek the attention or custom of, esp. by flattery.

Romanesque /ˌrɔ:mə'nesk/ ● *n.* a style of architecture prevalent in Europe *c.* 900–1200, with massive vaulting and round arches (compare NORMAN *adj.* 4). ● *adj.* of the Romanesque style of architecture.

Romanian ● *n.* **1 a** a native or national of Romania in E Europe. **b** a person of Romanian descent. **2** the Romance language of Romania. ● *adj.* of or relating to Romania or its people or language.

romanize *v.tr.* **1** make Roman or Roman Catholic in character. **2** put into the Roman alphabet or into roman type. □ **romanization** *n.*

Roman law *n.* the law code developed by the ancient Romans and forming the basis of many modern codes.

Roman numeral *n.* any of the Roman letters representing numbers: I = 1, V = 5, X = 10, L = 50, C = 100, D = 500, M = 1000.

Romano /rɔ:'mæno:/ *n.* a strong-tasting hard cheese, originally made in Italy.

Romanov /'rɔ:mənɒf/ *n.* a dynasty that ruled in Russia 1613–1917.

Romansh /rɔ:'mænʃ/ ● *n.* the Rhaeto-Romance dialects, esp. as spoken in the Swiss region of Grisons. ● *adj.* of these dialects.

romantic ● *adj.* **1** inclined towards or suggestive of romance in love (*a romantic woman; romantic words*). **2** of, characterized by, or suggestive of an idealized, sentimental, or fantastic view of reality (*a romantic picture*). **3** (of a person) imaginative, visionary, idealistic. **4 a** (of style in art, music, etc.) concerned more with feeling and emotion than with form and aesthetic qualities; preferring grandeur or picturesqueness to finish and proportion. **b** (also **Romantic**) of or relating to the Romanticism of the 18th & 19th c. **5** (of a project etc.) unpractical, fantastic. ● *n.* **1** a romantic person. **2** a romanticist. □ **romantically** *adv.*

romanticism *n.* **1** (also **Romanticism**) adherence to a romantic style in art, music, etc. **2** a tendency towards romance or romantic views. **3** (**Romanticism**) a movement in the arts and literature, originating in the late 18th c., characterized by a rejection of rationalism and the order and restraint of classicism and neoclassicism, favouring instead inspiration, irrationality, subjectivity, and the primacy of the individual.

romanticist *n.* (also **Romanticist**) a writer or artist of the romantic school.

romanticize *v.* **1** *tr.* **a** make or render romantic or unreal (*a romanticized account of war*). **b** describe or portray in a romantic fashion. **2** *intr.* indulge in romantic thoughts or actions. □ **romanticization** *n.*

Romany /'rɒməni, 'rɔ:-/ ● *n.* (*pl.* **-ies**) **1** a gypsy. **2** the Indo-European language of the gypsies. ● *adj.* of or relating to gypsies or their language.

Rome Beauty *n.* see RED ROME BEAUTY.

Romeo *n.* (*pl.* **-os**) a passionate male lover or seducer.

romp ● *v.intr.* **1** play about roughly and energetically. **2** *informal* proceed easily or rapidly. **3** win a race, contest, etc. with ease. ● *n.* **1** a period of romping or boisterous play. **2** a song, play, etc. that is lively, energetic, and lighthearted. **3** a playful and lighthearted journey or excursion. **4** *Sport* an easy victory. **5** a sexual encounter that is usu. spontaneous, playful, lighthearted, and carefree.

romper *n.* **1** (also **romper suit, rompers** *n.pl.*) a young child's one-piece garment covering the legs and trunk. **2 a** a loose-fitting woman's garment combining esp. a short-sleeved or sleeveless top and wide-legged shorts. **b** a similar garment worn in bed.

rondo /'rɒndo:/ *n.* (*pl.* **-os**) *Music* a form of composition with a recurring theme, often found in the final movement of a sonata or concerto etc.

röntgen *var. of* ROENTGEN.

roof ● *n.* (*pl.* **roofs**) **1 a** the upper outside covering of a building, esp. a house, usu. supported by its walls. **b** any external covering forming a shelter or top (*the roof of the car*). **2 a** the overhead inner surface of a room, cavity, etc. (*the roof of a cave*). **b** the top inner surface of a compartment or opening (*the roof of the mouth*). **3** (of prices etc.) the upper limit or highest point. ● *v.tr.* **1** (usu. in *passive*) (often foll. by *over*) cover with or as with a roof. **2** put (something) on top of a roof, accidentally or intentionally (*roofed a tennis ball*). □ **go through the roof** *informal* (of prices etc.) reach extreme or unexpected heights. **hit** (or **go through**) **the roof** *informal* become very angry. **raise the roof** make a lot of noise inside a building, esp. by cheering or shouting. **a roof over one's head** somewhere to live. **under one roof** in the same building. **under a person's roof** in a person's home. □ **roofed** *adj.* (also in *comb.*). **roofing** *n.* **roofless** *adj.*

roofer *n.* a person who constructs or repairs roofs.

roof garden *n.* an area, usu. with plants etc., built on the flat roof of a building for outdoor eating or entertainment.

roofline *n.* the outline or silhouette of a roof or roofs.

roof of the mouth *n.* the palate.

roof rack *n.* a frame that can be mounted on the roof of a car, truck, etc. for carrying luggage, skis, etc.

rooftop *n.* the outer surface of a roof, esp. the roof of a house.

rook[1] ● *n.* a black European and Asiatic bird, *Corvus frugilegus*, of the crow family, nesting in colonies in treetops. ● *v.tr.* **1** charge (a customer) extortionately. **2** win money from (a person) at cards etc. esp. by swindling.

rook[2] *n.* in chess, each of the four pieces set in the corner squares at the beginning of a game, moving in a straight line forwards, backwards, or laterally over any number of unoccupied squares.

rook[3] *n.* *informal* = ROOKIE.

rookery *n.* (*pl.* **-ies**) **1 a** a colony of seabirds (esp. penguins) or seals. **b** a place where seabirds, sea lions, seals, etc. breed. **2 a** a colony of rooks. **b** a clump of trees having rooks' nests.

rookie n. informal **1** N Amer. an athlete who is playing his or her first full season in a particular league (also attrib.: rookie season). **2** a new recruit, esp. in an army or police force. **3** (usu. attrib.) a novice (a rookie politician).

room ● n. **1 a** space that is or might be occupied by something. **b** the ability to accommodate contents; available or required space (I can't have a dog, I don't have room). **c** available space in or on (shelf room). **d** space required or available for something specified (headroom). **2 a** a part of a building enclosed by walls or partitions, floor, and ceiling. **b** (in pl.) a set of these occupied by a person or family; apartments or lodgings. **c** a bedroom. **3** (in comb.) a room or area for a specified purpose (lunchroom). **4** (foll. by for or to + infin.) capacity to allow a particular action; opportunity (still room for improvement). **5** people present in a room (the room fell silent). ● v.intr. N Amer. rent a room or rooms; lodge, board. ☐ **make room** (often foll. by for) clear a space (for a person or thing) by removal of others. **not enough** (or **no**) **room to swing a cat** not enough space to live or work in. ☐ **-roomed** adj. (in comb.). **roomful** n. (pl. **-fuls**).

room and board n. N Amer. **1** accommodation and meals. **2** the cost of this.

roomer n. N Amer. **1** a lodger occupying a room or rooms without meals. **2** a house or apartment having a specified number of rooms (a one-roomer).

roomette n. N Amer. **1** a private single compartment in the sleeping car of a train. **2** a small bedroom that is rented out.

roomie n. N Amer. informal a roommate.

rooming house n. esp. N Amer. a house or building divided into furnished rooms or apartments for rent.

roommate n. a person who lives in the same apartment, room, etc. as another.

room service n. **1** (in a hotel etc.) drinks or a meal served in a guest's room. **2** the department that provides this service.

room temperature n. a temperature that would be considered comfortable for a normal room in a house, usu. approx. 20° C or 68° F.

roomy adj. (**-ier, -iest**) having plenty of room to contain people or things; spacious. ☐ **roominess** n.

roost ● n. **1 a** a branch, perch, etc. where birds or bats regularly settle, esp. to sleep. **b** a place where domestic fowl perch at night, esp. in a henhouse. **2** a place offering temporary rest or accommodation. ● v.intr. (of a bird) settle for rest or sleep. ☐ **come home to roost** (of a scheme etc.) recoil unfavourably upon the originator.

rooster n. esp. N Amer. a male chicken.

rooster tail n. N Amer. the spray of water, dust, or snow thrown up behind a moving vehicle etc.

root[1] ● n. **1 a** the part of a plant normally below the ground, attaching it to the earth and conveying nourishment to it from the soil. **b** (in pl.) such a part divided into branches or fibres. **c** the permanent underground stock of a plant. **2** a plant that is grown for its edible underground part to be used as food, spice, or medicine, e.g. a turnip, ginger, or ginseng. **3 a** the embedded part of a bodily organ or structure, such as a hair, tooth, nail, etc. **b** the part of a thing attaching it to a greater or more fundamental whole. **4** (in pl.) social, cultural, or ethnic origins, esp. as the reasons for one's long-standing emotional attachment to a place, community, etc. **5 a** the basic cause, source, origin, or ancestor (love of money is the root of all evil). **b** (attrib.) designating a problem, idea, etc. from which something has ensued (the root cause of the situation). **6** the essential substance or nature of

something (get to the root of things). **7** Math. **a** a number or quantity that when multiplied by itself a usu. specified number of times gives a specified number or quantity (the cube root of eight is two). **b** a square root. **c** a value of an unknown quantity satisfying a given equation. **8** Linguistics any ultimate unanalyzable element of language, not necessarily surviving as a word in itself, from which words are made by affixation or other modification. **9** Music the fundamental note of a chord. ● v. **1** intr. develop roots and become firmly established. **2** tr. a fix firmly with roots or as if with roots (fear rooted him to the spot). **b** be based in (fear is rooted in ignorance). **3** tr. (usu. foll. by out, up) dig up by the roots. ☐ **pull up by the roots 1** uproot. **2** eradicate, destroy. **put down roots 1** begin to draw nourishment from the soil. **2** become settled or established. **root and branch** thorough(ly), radical(ly). **strike at the root** (or **roots**) of set about destroying. **take root 1** begin to grow and draw nourishment from the soil. **2** become fixed or established. **root out** find and get rid of. ☐ **rootless** adj. **rootlessness** n. **rootlike** adj. **rooty** adj.

root[2] v. **1** intr. (of an animal, esp. a pig) turn up (the ground) with the snout, beak, etc., in search of food. **2 a** intr. (foll. by around, in, etc.) rummage around or look for something. **b** tr. (foll. by out or up) find or extract by rummaging. **3** intr. (foll. by for) N Amer. informal **a** Sport encourage with cheering, applause, etc. **b** offer support to. ☐ **rooter** n. (in sense 3).

root ball n. the mass formed by the roots of a plant and the soil surrounding them.

root beer n. N Amer. a carbonated drink made from an extract of roots.

root canal n. **1** the pulp-filled cavity in the root of a tooth. **2** N Amer. a procedure to replace the infected pulp of a tooth with an inert material.

root cellar n. N Amer. an underground room in a house for storing esp. vegetables and fruit.

rooted adj. **1** firmly established (her affection was deeply rooted). **2 a** having a root or roots. **b** (in comb.) having roots of a specified type, number, or quality. ☐ **rootedness** n.

rootin' tootin' adj. N Amer. informal **1** resembling or characteristic of the Wild West or an inhabitant of the Wild West. **2** boisterous, noisy, rip-roaring (a rootin' tootin' good time).

rootlet n. **1** a slender root or division of a root. **2** a thin strand of something.

root sign n. Math. = RADICAL SIGN.

rootstock n. **1** a stock onto which another variety has been grafted or budded. **2** a rhizome, esp. one from which new leaves and shoots grow annually. **3** a primary form from which offshoots have arisen.

rootsy adj. (**-ier, -iest**) informal (esp. of music) uncommercialized, full-blooded, esp. showing traditional origins. ☐ **rootsiness** n.

rope ● n. **1 a** a strong thick cord made by twisting together strands of hemp, cotton, nylon, wire, or similar material. **b** a piece of this. **2** (foll. by of) **a** a quantity of similar things held together by or as if by a string passed through the middle of each (a rope of pearls). **b** a strand of a semi-liquid substance (rope of saliva). **3** (in pl., prec. by the) **a** the rules and procedures of a business, operation, etc. (learning the ropes). **b** the ropes enclosing a boxing or wrestling ring etc. **4** (prec. by the) **a** a halter for hanging a person. **b** execution by hanging. **5** N Amer. a lasso. ● v.tr. **1** fasten, secure, or catch with rope. **2** (usu. foll. by off) enclose (a space) with rope. **3** (usu. foll. by in, into) persuade or entice someone to join or participate in an activity (*I got roped into doing the dishes*). **4** *Mountaineering* connect (a party) with a rope; attach (a person) to a rope. □ **give a person plenty of rope** (or **enough rope to hang himself**) give a person enough freedom of action to bring about his or her own downfall. **on the ropes 1** *Boxing* forced against the ropes by the opponent's attack. **2** near defeat. **rope up** (or **down**) *Mountaineering* climb up (or down) using a rope. □ **roping** *n.* **ropelike** *adj.* **ropy** *adj.*

rope burn *n.* a burn caused by the friction of rope esp. on the hands.

rope ladder *n.* two long ropes connected by short crosspieces, used as a ladder.

roper *n.* N *Amer.* a person who uses a lasso to rope cattle etc.

rope tow *n.* a type of ski lift consisting of an endless moving rope driven by a motor.

Roquefort /ˈrɒkfər, rɔːk-, -fərt/ *n. proprietary* **1** a soft blue cheese made from ewes' milk. **2** a salad dressing made of this.

rorqual /ˈrɔːkwəl/ *n.* any of various baleen whales of the family Balaenopteridae characterized by a pleated throat and small dorsal fin, esp. the finback or the minke whale.

Rorschach /ˈrɔːrʃæk, -ʃɒk/ *adj. Psych.* designating or pertaining to a type of personality test in which a standard set of ink blots is presented one by one to the subject, who is asked to describe what they suggest or resemble.

rosary /ˈrəʊzəri/ *n.* (*pl.* **-ies**) **1** *Catholicism* **a** a form of devotion accompanying the contemplation of fifteen mysteries (now usu. in groups of five) in which fifteen decades of Hail Marys are repeated, each decade preceded by an Our Father and followed by a Glory Be. **b** a string of beads divided into sets used for keeping count in the recital of this. **2** a similar string of beads or knotted cord used for counting prayers in other religions.

rose[1] ● *n.* **1** a prickly, erect or climbing shrub of the genus *Rosa*. **2** the flower of this bush or shrub, generally fragrant and of a red, pink, yellow, or white colour. **3** any flowering plant resembling this (*Christmas rose*). **4 a** a light crimson colour; pink. **b** (usu. in *pl.*) a rosy complexion (*roses in her cheeks*). **5 a** (*attrib.*) representing or designating something resembling a rose in form or appearance (*rose diamond*). **b** a rose-shaped design, e.g. on a compass. **6** a thing of beauty, perfection, or superior standing. **7** a perforated cap attached to the spout of a watering can or hose. ● *adj.* pink or pale red. □ **come up roses** develop in a very favourable way. **come up smelling of roses** emerge in a very favourable light, esp. from a difficult situation. □ **roselike** *adj.*

rose[2] *past of* RISE.

rosé /ˈrəʊzeɪ/ *n.* any pale red or pink wine, coloured by only brief contact with the skins of red grapes.

roseate /ˈrəʊziət/ *adj.* **1** having a partly pink plumage (*roseate tern*). **2** = ROSE-COLOURED.

rosebowl *n.* a bowl for displaying cut roses.

rose-breasted grosbeak *n.* a grosbeak, *Pheuctius ludovicianus*, which breeds across most of N America east of the Rockies, the male of which is black and white with a red patch on its breast.

rosebud *n.* **1** a bud of a rose. **2** (often *attrib.*) representing or designating something resembling a rosebud in nature or appearance (*rosebud mouth*).

rose bush *n.* a rose plant.

rose-coloured *adj.* **1** of the colour of a pale red rose; rose-pink. **2** optimistic, sanguine, cheerful (*a rose-coloured view of things*). □ **see through**

rose-coloured glasses regard (circumstances etc.) with unfounded optimism or naïveté.

rosehip *n.* = HIP[2].

rosemary *n.* **1** a fragrant shrub of the mint family, *Rosmarinus officinalis*, native to southern Europe, cultivated esp. for its use as a spice and in perfume. **2** the leaves of this plant used as a flavouring.

rose pink ● *n.* the colour of a pale red rose, warm pink. ● *adj.* (usu. **rose-pink**) of this colour.

rose red ● *n.* the colour of a red rose; dark red, crimson. ● *adj.* (usu. **rose-red**) of this colour.

rose-tinted *adj.* = ROSE-COLOURED.

rosette *n.* **1** an ornament or other object carved, moulded, shaped, or arranged to resemble or represent a rose (*a rosette of butter*). **2 a** a naturally occurring circular arrangement of horizontally spreading leaves, esp. about the base of a stem. **b** a similar but abnormal cluster of leaves on the stem, a symptom of disease. **3** a rose-shaped arrangement of ribbon worn esp. as a badge of membership or support, or as a symbol of a prize won in a competition. **4** markings resembling a rose, esp. on the skin of a leopard.

rosewater *n.* water distilled from roses, or scented with the essence of roses, used as a perfume and as a flavouring in cooking.

rosewood *n.* any of several fragrant woods derived esp. from tropical leguminous trees of the genus *Dalbergia* used in making furniture.

Rosh Hashanah /rɒʃ həˈʃɒnə/ *n.* the festival celebrating the Jewish New Year marked by penitence, self-reflection, and an examination of one's relationship with and responsibilities to God.

rosin /ˈrɒzɪn/ ● *n.* the solid amber residue obtained after the distillation of crude turpentine oleoresin, or of naphtha extract from pine stumps, used in adhesives, varnishes, inks, etc. or used, esp. powdered, to prevent slipping when applied to the bows of stringed instruments, the hands of baseball players, etc. ● *v.tr.* (**rosined, rosining**) treat with rosin.

roster ● *n.* **1** N *Amer. Sport* a list of players belonging or available to a team. **2** (often foll. by *of*) **a** any list of people or things belonging to a specified group (*a roster of experts*). **b** a group of people or things considered as being on a roster (*the whole roster will be performing*). **3** a list or plan showing turns of duty or leave for individuals or groups in any organization, originally a military force. ● *v.tr.* place on a roster.

rostrum /ˈrɒstrəm/ *n.* (*pl.* **rostra** /-strə/ or **-s**) **1** a platform or pulpit for public speaking. **2** *Zool. & Bot.* a beak, stiff snout, or beaklike part.

rosy *adj.* (**-ier, -iest**) **1 a** coloured like a pink or red rose. **b** (esp. of the complexion) pink as an indication of health or youth (*rosy cheeks*). **2 a** promising (*a rosy future*). **b** optimistic, unjustifiably so (*painted a rosy picture of the situation*). □ **rosily** *adv.* **rosiness** *n.*

rot ● *v.* (**rotted, rotting**) **1** *intr.* **a** (of animal or vegetable matter) lose its original form by the chemical action of bacteria, fungi, etc.; decay. **b** (foll. by *away*) decay to the point of falling apart (*the old barn was rotting away*). **c** (foll. by *off*) separate from the main body because of decay (*dead branches rotted off*). **d** (of ice on lakes etc.) disintegrate into a honeycombed structure due to thawing. **2** *intr.* (of society, institutions, etc.) deteriorate; become corrupt or degenerate due to neglect or abuse. **3** *intr.* (of a person) languish, waste away (*he was left to rot in prison*). **4** *tr.* cause to rot, make rotten (*too much candy will rot your teeth*). ● *n.* **1 a** the process or state of rotting. **b** rotten or decayed matter. **2** *Bot.* any of various diseases in plants characterized by the weakening or decay of tissue. **3** a decline or breakdown in standards or behaviour (*the rot has set in*). **4** *slang* nonsense (*her ideas were nothing but rot*).

Rotarian /roˈtɛriən/ ● *n.* a member of a Rotary Club. ● *adj.* of a Rotary Club or its members.

rotary ● *adj.* **1** acting by rotation (*a rotary blade*). **2** operating through the rotation of some part (*a rotary mower*). ● *n.* (*pl.* **-ies**) **1** *US & Cdn* (*NS, Nfld, & BC*) a traffic circle or roundabout. **2** (**Rotary**) **a** (in full **Rotary International**) a worldwide organization of charitable societies for businesspeople and professionals, founded in 1905 to promote international goodwill. **b** (in full **Rotary Club**) a local branch of this.

rotary phone *n.* (in full **rotary-dial phone**) a telephone with a numbered dial which is rotated for each digit of a number being called.

rotate *v.* **1** *intr. & tr.* move around an axis or centre; spin, revolve. **2 a** *tr.* change the position, responsibility, etc. of a person or thing in a regularly recurring order (*rotate the tires*). **b** *intr.* act or occur in turns or in a particular order (*you wash, I'll dry, and tomorrow we'll rotate*). □ **rotatable** *adj.* **rotatory** *adj.*

rotation *n.* **1** the act or an instance of rotating or being rotated. **2** a regular organized sequence of things or events. **3 a** a regular succession of members of a group through positions or duties etc. **b** (in full **starting rotation**) *Baseball* the group of usu. four or five pitchers on a team that start games in succession. **4** the movement of a celestial body on its axis. **5** a system of growing different crops in regular order to avoid exhausting the soil. □ **rotational** *adj.*

rotator /roˈteitər/ *n.* **1** a muscle that rotates a limb etc. **2** a machine or device for causing something to rotate. **3** a revolving apparatus or part.

rotator cuff *n.* the muscles associated with a capsule with fused tendons that supports the arm at the shoulder joint.

rote *n.* (usu. *attrib.*) a mechanical practice, routine, performance, etc. (*rote lectures*). □ **by rote 1** in a mechanical or repetitious manner. **2** acquired through memorization without proper understanding or reflection.

rotgut *n.* *slang* cheap adulterated usu. inferior alcoholic liquor (also *attrib.*: *rotgut whisky*).

roti /ˈroːtiˌ/ *n.* a dish of Indian origin, common in the Caribbean, consisting of a flat pancake or unleavened bread folded over usu. a spicy meat filling with chickpeas.

rotini /roˈtiːniˌ/ *n.* a variety of pasta in small spirals.

rotisserie /roˈtisəri/ ● *n.* **1** a usu. motor-driven rotating spit for roasting meat esp. over a barbecue or in an oven. **2** (in full **rotisserie league baseball**) a game in which fans draft imaginary baseball teams of usu. 23 players by bidding on actual players with a set amount of money, and collect points for each home run, RBI, stolen base, etc. their players compile. **3** (*attrib.*) designating things pertaining to rotisserie or to any similar esp. baseball fantasy league (*rotisserie player*). ● *v.tr.* barbecue or roast meat with a rotisserie.

rotor *n.* **1** a rotary part of a machine, esp. in the distributor of an internal combustion engine. **2** a hub with a set of radiating airfoils on a helicopter etc. that provides lift when rotated in an approximately horizontal plane.

Rototiller *n.* *N. Amer.* a machine with rotating blades and prongs used for breaking up or tilling the soil. □ **rototill** *v.tr. & intr.*

rotten *adj.* (**rottener**, **rottenest**) **1 a** in a state of

decomposition or decay. **b** falling to pieces or liable to break from age or use. **2** miserable, wretched, unfortunate (*I feel rotten today*). **3** despicable, vile, loathsome (*rotten scoundrel*; *what a rotten thing to do!*). **4** (also **rotting**) *Cdn* designating ice or snow which, in the course of melting, has become granular and weak; disintegrating. **5** morally, socially, or politically corrupt. □ **spoil someone rotten** spoil or indulge a person excessively. □ **rottenness** *n.*

Rottweiler /ˈrɒtˌwailər/ *n.* **1** a breed of large, stocky, powerful dog having short coarse hair with black and tan markings, a broad head with pendent ears, and usu. a docked tail. **2** a very tenacious person.

rotund /roˈtʌnd/ *adj.* **1** round, circular, spherical. **2** (of a person) large and plump; fat. □ **rotundity** *n.*

rotunda /roˈtʌndə/ *n.* **1 a** a circular hall or room. **b** the main hall of a public building. **2** a building with a circular ground plan, esp. one with a dome.

rouge /ruːʒ/ ● *n.* **1** a red powder or cream used for colouring the cheeks. **2** (**rouge**) *Cdn* esp. *hist.* a Quebec supporter of a Liberal party. **3** *Cdn Football* a single point scored when the receiving team fails to run a kick out of the end zone, such as on a punt, kickoff, or missed field goal. ● *v.* **1** *tr.* colour with rouge. **2** *intr.* apply rouge to one's cheeks.

rough ● *adj.* **1** having an uneven or irregular surface, not smooth or level or polished. **2** (of ground, country, etc.) uneven, uncultivated, rugged, wild. **3 a** (of a person) aggressive, rugged, hard; not mild or quiet or gentle. **b** disorderly, riotous, violent (*a rough sport*). **c** (usu. foll. by *on*) harsh, unreasonable, or unfair (*he is quite rough on them*). **4 a** difficult, rigorous, arduous. **b** unfortunate, unreasonable, undeserved (*rough luck*). **5** harsh, insensitive, indelicate, inconsiderate (*rough words*). **6 a** (of the sea, weather, etc.) violent, stormy, turbulent. **b** (of a flight, landing, trip, etc.) turbulent, bumpy. **7** lacking finish, elaboration, comfort, etc. (*rough lodgings*). **b** incomplete, rudimentary (*a rough copy*). **8 a** inexact, approximate, preliminary (*a rough sketch*). **b** (of paper etc.) for use in writing rough notes etc. **9 a** (of hair, a beard, etc.) shaggy, unkempt, coarse. **b** (of hands, skin, cloth, etc.) coarse in texture or feel; not soft. **10** *informal* **a** sick, unwell (*I'm feeling rough*). **b** depressed, dejected. **11 a** (of food or drink) sharp or harsh in taste (*rough wine*). **b** (of a voice, music, etc.) harsh, grating. ● *adv.* **1** in a rough manner (*he likes to play rough*). **2** (live or sleep etc.) outdoors, without a proper bed or accommodation; on the street. ● *n.* **1** (usu. prec. by *the*) a hard part or aspect of life; hardship (*take the rough with the smooth*). **2** rough or uncultivated ground. **3** *Golf* rough ground off the fairway between tee and green. **4** an unfinished, provisional, or natural state (*I've written it in rough*). ● *v.tr.* (foll. by *out*) **1** shape or plan roughly. **2** make coarse or heavy cuts in a workpiece of stone, metal, wood, etc. to produce a rough form to be detailed, finished, etc. later. □ **rough and ready** simple or crude but effective; not elaborate but adequate. **rough around the edges 1** (of a person) irritable. **2** (of a thing) having a few imperfections, unpolished. **rough in 1** install (wiring, plumbing, ductwork, etc.) for a room that is planned but is not yet built. **2** lay the groundwork or make preliminary arrangements for (a room) (*rough in a bedroom*). **rough it** live in rough accommodation without basic comforts or conveniences. **rough up** *slang* treat (a person) with violence or abuse. □ **roughness** *n.*

roughage *n.* **1** = DIETARY FIBRE. **2** coarse fodder.

rough-and-tumble ● *adj.* disregarding rules or convention; riotous, disorderly. ● *n.* **1** a scuffle or fight. **2**

rough and aggressive but often enjoyable activity, competition, etc.

roughcast *n.* plaster of lime and gravel, used on outside walls.

rough cut ● *n.* the first version of a film after preliminary editing. ● *adj. N Amer.* (usu. **rough-cut**) (of a log, lumber, etc.) having been cut with a coarse blade to an approximate size before a more precise, finished cut is made.

roughen *v.tr. & intr.* make or become rough.

rough-hew *v.tr. (past part.* **-hewed** or **-hewn**) shape out roughly; give crude form to.

rough-hewn *adj.* **1** uncouth, unrefined. **2** (of timber, stone, etc.) cut or shaped out roughly.

roughhouse *esp. N Amer.* ● *n.* boisterous or rambunctious play or wrestling, esp. indoors. ● *v.intr.* engage in rambunctious behaviour or roughhouse. □ **roughhousing** *n.*

rough ice *n. Cdn* a large bank of ice that has accumulated on the shore of a river from the freezing of successive tides.

rough-in *n. N Amer.* **1** (in a building) a preliminary installation of wiring, plumbing, ductwork, etc. for a room that will be added later. **2** the foundation or groundwork for a room that will be added later.

roughing *n. Hockey* an unnecessary or excessive use of force for which a player is given a penalty.

rough-legged hawk *n.* a hawk of boreal regions, *Buteo lagopus,* having legs covered with feathers to the base of the toes.

roughly *adv.* **1** approximately (*roughly 20*). **2** in a coarse or uneven manner (*roughly cut timbers*). **3** in a harsh manner (*she spoke roughly*). □ **roughly speaking** in an approximate sense.

roughneck *informal* ● *n.* **1** a rough or rowdy person. **2** a worker on an oil rig. ● *v.intr.* work as a roughneck on an oil-drilling operation.

rough ride *n.* a difficult time or experience.

roughrider *n.* a person who breaks in or can ride unbroken horses.

roughshod *adj.* (of a horse) having shoes with nail-heads projecting to prevent slipping. □ **ride roughshod over** domineer over; treat with disrespect or disregard.

roughy *n.* (*pl.* **-ies**) any of several rough-skinned fish of the family Trachichthyidae, esp. orange roughy.

roulette /ruːˈlet/ *n.* **1** a gambling game in which a ball is dropped onto a revolving wheel with numbered compartments in the centre of a table, players betting on the number at which the ball will come to rest. **2** a revolving toothed wheel.

round ● *adj.* **1 a** shaped like or approximately like a circle, sphere, or cylinder; having a convex or circular outline or surface; curved, not angular. **b** (esp. of a part of the body) full and curved; plump (*round cheeks*). **2** done with or involving circular motion. **3 a** entire, continuous, complete; fully expressed or developed; all together, not broken or defective or scanty (*a round dozen*). **b** (of a sum of money) considerable. **4** genuine, candid, outspoken; (of a statement etc.) categorical, unmistakable. **5** (usu. *attrib.*) (of a number) expressed for convenience or as an estimate in fewer significant numerals or with a fraction removed (*spent $297.32, or in round numbers $300*). **6 a** (of a style) flowing. **b** (of a voice) full and mellow; not harsh. ● *n.* **1** a round object or form. **2 a** a revolving motion, a circular or recurring course (*the earth in its yearly round*). **b** a regular recurring series of activities or functions (*her life is one long round of parties*). **c** a recurring succession or series of meet-

ings for discussion etc. (*a new round of talks*). **3** (often in *pl.*) a route or sequence by which people or things are regularly supervised or inspected (*a doctor's rounds*). **4** an allowance of something distributed or measured out, esp.: **a** a single provision of drinks etc. to each member of a group. **b** ammunition to fire one shot; the act of firing this. **5** each of a set or series, a sequence of actions by each member of a group in turn, esp.: **a** one spell of play in a game etc. **b** one stage in a competition. **6** a cut of beef taken from the thigh, below the rump and above the shank. **7** *Golf* the playing of all the holes in a course once. **8** *Boxing* one of a number of three-minute periods that make up a match. **9** a canon for three or more unaccompanied voices singing at the same pitch or in octaves. **10** a single distinct outburst of applause. ● *adv. & prep.* esp. *Brit.* = AROUND. ● *v.* **1 a** *tr.* give a round shape to. **b** *intr.* assume a round shape. **2** *tr.* pass around (a corner, cape, etc.). **3** *tr.* (usu. foll. by *off*) express (a number) in a less exact but more convenient form (also foll. by *down* when the number is decreased and *up* when it is increased). □ **go the rounds** (of news etc.) be passed on from person to person. **in the round 1** with all features shown; all things considered. **2** *Theatre* with the audience around at least three sides of the stage. **3** (of sculpture) with all sides shown; not in relief. **4** (of undressed timber or logs) trimmed on only two sides. **5** (of a fish) not gutted; whole. **make** (or **do**) **the rounds of** go around from place to place. **make one's rounds** take a customary route for inspection etc. **round about 1** in a ring (about); all round; on all sides (of). **2** with a change to an opposite position. **3** approximately (*cost round about $50*). **round and round** several times round. **round off 1** bring to a complete or symmetrical or well-ordered state. **2** smooth out; blunt the corners or angles of. **3** = ROUND *v.* 3. **round on a person** make a sudden verbal attack on or unexpected retort to a person. **round out 1** = ROUND OFF 1. **2** provide more detail about. **round peg in a square hole** = SQUARE PEG IN A ROUND HOLE (see PEG). **round up** collect or bring together (members of a group, suspects, cattle, etc.) (*see also* sense 3 of *v.*). □ **roundish** *adj.* **roundness** *n.*

roundabout *adj.* circuitous, indirect.

round brackets *n.pl.* brackets of the form ( ).

round dance *n.* **1** a dance in which couples move in circles around the ballroom. **2** a dance in which the dancers form one large circle. □ **round dancing** *n.*

rounded *adj.* **1** that has been rounded. **2** having a circular, spherical, or curving shape. **3** possessing a pleasing depth or wide range of characteristics etc. (*a rounded flavour*). **4** (of the voice etc.) sonorous; mellow, full. □ **roundedly** *adv.* **roundedness** *n.*

roundel /ˈraʊndəl/ *n.* **1** a small circular object, esp. a decorative medallion. **2** a circular identifying mark, usu. incorporating the colours of the national flag, painted on military aircraft. **3** a poem of eleven lines in three stanzas.

rounder *n.* **1** *N Amer. slang* a person who makes the rounds of prisons or bars; a habitual criminal or drunkard. **2** (in *comb.*) a boxing match of a specified number of rounds. **3** *Cdn (Nfld)* a small cod that is gutted, salted and dried without being split.

Roundhead *n.* a member or supporter of the party opposing Charles I in the English Civil War (1642–9).

roundhouse *n.* **1** a circular repair shed for railway locomotives, built around a turntable. **2** *slang* a punch given with a wide sweep of the arm.

roundly *adv.* **1** bluntly, in plain language, severely *(was roundly criticized).* **2** vigorously; energetically *(was roundly applauded).* **3** in a circular way.

round roast *n.* a roast cut from the round of beef.

round robin *n.* **1** *N Amer.* a tournament in which each competitor plays in turn against every other. **2** a petition esp. with signatures in a circle to conceal the order of writing. **3** any letter or petition which is passed from person to person in a group, often with written contributions added by each. **4** a sequence.

round-shouldered *adj.* with shoulders bent forward so that the back is rounded.

round steak *n.* *N Amer.* a steak from a round of beef.

round table *n.* an assembly for discussion, esp. at a conference (often *attrib.* : *round-table talks*).

round-the-clock *attrib.adj.* lasting or covering all day and usu. all night *(round-the-clock care).*

round trip *n.* a trip to a place and back to the point of origin (often *attrib.* : *round-trip airfare*).

roundup *n.* **1** a systematic rounding up of people or things, esp.: **a** the arrest of people suspected of a particular crime or crimes. **b** the rounding up of cattle etc. usu. for the purpose of registering ownership, counting, etc. **2** the people and horses engaged in the rounding up of cattle etc. **3** a summary.

roundwood *n.* timber used in the round without being squared by sawing or hewing, such as logs, posts, and pilings.

roundworm *n.* a nematode worm, esp. a parasitic one infesting the gut of a mammal or bird, as *Ascaris lumbricoides* (which infests humans).

rouse *v.* **1 a** *tr.* (often foll. by *from, out of*) bring out of sleep; wake. **b** *intr.* (often foll. by *up*) cease to sleep, wake up. **2** (often foll. by *up*) **a** *tr.* stir up, make active or excited, startle out of inactivity or confidence or carelessness *(was roused to protest).* **b** *intr.* become active. **3** *tr.* provoke to anger *(is terrible when roused).* **4** *tr.* evoke (feelings). □ **rouse oneself** overcome one's indolence; become active. □ **rouser** *n.*

rousing *adj.* exciting, stirring. □ **rousingly** *adv.*

roust *v.tr.* **1** (often foll. by *up, out*) a rouse, stir up. **b** root out. **2** *N Amer. slang* jostle, harass, rough up.

rout¹ ● *n.* **1 a** a disorderly retreat of defeated troops. **b** a decisive defeat. **2** riot, tumult, disturbance, clamour, fuss. **3** an assemblage or company esp. of revellers or rioters. ● *v.tr.* **1** cause to retreat in disorder. **2** defeat decisively. □ **put to rout** put to flight, defeat utterly.

rout² *v.* **1** *intr.* & *tr.* = ROOT² 1, 2. **2** *tr.* cut a groove, or any pattern not extending to the edges, in (a wooden or metal surface). □ **rout out** force or fetch out of bed or from a house or hiding place.

route /ruːt/ ● *n.* **1 a** a way or course taken (esp. regularly) in getting from a starting point to a destination *(drove home by the quickest route).* **b** a series of steps taken to achieve something *(the route to success).* **c** (esp. in the US) (with following numeral) a specific highway *(Route 66).* **2** *N Amer.* a round of stops regularly travelled in delivering, selling, or collecting goods *(paper route).* ● *v.tr.* (**routing**) send or forward or direct to be sent by a particular route. □ **router** *n.*

router /ˈraʊtər/ *n.* a tool for cutting grooves etc.

routine ● *n.* **1** a regular course or procedure, an unvarying performance of certain acts. **2** a set sequence in a performance, esp. a dance, comedy act, etc. **3** *informal* a hackneyed, predictable response or formula of speech *(went into her overprotective mother routine).* **4** *Computing* a sequence of instructions for performing a task. ● *adj.* **1** performed as part of a routine *(routine duties).* **2** of a customary or standard kind *(routine surgery).* □ **routinely** *adv.*

routinize *v.tr.* subject to a routine; make into a matter of routine. □ **routinization** *n.*

rove ● *v.* **1** *intr.* wander without a settled destination, roam, ramble. **2** *intr.* (of eyes) look in changing directions. **3** *tr.* wander over or through. ● *n.* an act of roving *(on the rove).*

rover *n.* **1** a roving person; a wanderer. **2** *Football* a defensive linebacker assigned to move around in anticipation of opponents' play. **3** a remote-controlled surface vehicle for extraterrestrial exploration. **4** (**Rover**) *Cdn* a member of the senior level (ages 18-26) in Scouting.

roving *adj.* **1** wandering, roaming. **2** (of a journalist etc.) required to travel to locations to deal with events as they occur. **3** characterized by roving; inclined to wander *(a roving life).*

row¹ *n.* **1** a number of persons or things in a more or less straight line. **2** a line of seats across a theatre etc. *(in the front row).* **3** a street with a continuous line of houses along one or each side. **4** a line of plants in a field or garden. **5** a horizontal line of entries in a table etc. **6** a complete line of stitches in knitting or crochet. □ **a hard** (or **long etc.**) **row to hoe** a difficult task. **in a row 1** forming a row. **2** in succession *(two Sundays in a row).*

row² ● *v.* **1** *tr.* propel (a boat) with oars. **2** *tr.* convey (a passenger) in a boat in this way. **3** *intr.* propel a boat in this way. **4** *tr.* make (a stroke) or achieve (a rate of striking) in rowing. **5** *tr.* compete in (a race) by rowing. **6** *tr.* row a race with. ● *n.* **1** a period of rowing. **2** an excursion in a rowboat. □ **rower** *n.*

row³ *informal* ● *n.* **1** a fierce quarrel or dispute. **2** esp. *Brit.* a loud noise or commotion. ● *v.intr.* make or engage in a row. □ **make** (or **kick up**) **a row** make a vigorous protest.

rowan /ˈroːən, ˈraʊ-/ *n.* **1** (in full **rowan tree**) = MOUNTAIN ASH. **2** (in full **rowanberry**) the scarlet berry of this tree.

rowboat *n.* *N Amer.* a small boat propelled by oars.

rowdy ● *adj.* (**-ier, -iest**) noisy and disorderly. ● *n.* (*pl.* **-ies**) a rowdy person. □ **rowdily** *adv.* **rowdiness** *n.* **rowdyism** *n.*

row house *n.* *N Amer.* any of a row of usu. similar houses joined by party walls.

rowing machine *n.* an exercise machine for simulating the action of rowing.

royal ● *adj.* **1** of or suited to or worthy of a king or queen. **2** in the service or under the patronage of a king or queen *(Royal Winnipeg Ballet).* **3** belonging to the king or queen *(the royal hands).* **4** of the family of a king or queen. **5** kingly, majestic, stately, splendid. **6** on a great scale, of exceptional size or quality, first-rate *(gave us a royal send-off).* **7** *informal* extreme; of the highest degree *(a royal pain).* ● *n.* *informal* a member of the royal family. □ **royal road to** way of attaining without trouble. □ **royally** *adv.*

Royal Air Force *n.* the British air force. Abbr.: **RAF**.

royal assent *n.* (in Canada, the UK, and other Commonwealth countries) the formal consent of the sovereign or his or her representative to a bill passed by Parliament.

royal blue ● *n.* a deep vivid blue. ● *adj.* of this colour.

Royal Canadian Air Force *n.* *hist.* Canada's permanent air force between 1924 and unification of the armed forces in 1968. Abbr.: **RCAF**.

Royal Canadian Legion *n.* see LEGION 2.

Royal Canadian Mounted Police *n.* Canada's national police force, which enforces federal statutes and provides policing for jurisdictions without municipal police protection in all provinces and territories except Ontario and Quebec. Abbr.: **RCMP**.

Royal Canadian Navy *n. hist.* Canada's permanent naval force between 1910 and unification of the Armed Forces in 1968. Abbr.: **RCN**.

Royal Commission *n.* (in Canada, the UK, and other Commonwealth countries) **1** a commission of inquiry appointed by the Crown at the request of the government to investigate and report on a particular matter. **2** a committee so appointed.

royal family *n.* the family to which a sovereign belongs.

royal flush *n.* a poker hand consisting of the five highest cards in one suit.

royal icing *n.* a hard white icing made from icing sugar and egg whites, used on wedding cakes.

royalist ● *n.* **1 a** a supporter of monarchy. **b** *hist.* a supporter of the King against Parliament in the English Civil War. **2** *informal* a member of a conservative or reactionary right-wing group; one who believes in the superiority of a minority over the majority (*an economic royalist*). ● *adj.* of or pertaining to royalists or royalism. □ **royalism** *n.*

royal jelly *n.* a substance secreted by honeybee workers and fed by them to future queen bees.

Royal Marine *n.* a British marine (see MARINE *n.* 2a).

Royal Navy *n.* the British navy. Abbr.: **RN**.

royalty *n.* (pl. **-ies**) **1** the office or dignity or power of a king or queen, sovereignty. **2 a** royal persons. **b** a member of a royal family. **3** a sum paid to a patentee for the use of a patent or to an author etc. for each copy of a book etc. sold or for each public performance of a work. **4 a** a royal right (now esp. over minerals) granted by the sovereign to an individual or corporation. **b** a payment made by a producer of minerals, oil, or natural gas to the owner of the site or of the mineral rights over it.

royal 'we' *n.* the use of 'we' instead of 'I' by a single person (as traditionally by a sovereign).

rpm *abbr.* revolutions per minute.

RPN *abbr.* REGISTERED PRACTICAL NURSE.

RR *abbr. N Amer.* **1** railroad. **2** RURAL ROUTE.

RRIF /rɪf/ *abbr. Cdn* Registered Retirement Income Fund, a tax-sheltered savings plan which provides retirement income.

RRSP *abbr. Cdn* Registered Retirement Savings Plan, a tax-sheltered plan for saving for retirement.

RSA *abbr.* Republic of South Africa.

R.S.C. *abbr. Cdn* Revised Statutes of Canada.

RSI *abbr.* REPETITIVE STRAIN INJURY.

RSP *abbr. Cdn* Retirement Savings Plan.

RSV *abbr.* REVISED STANDARD VERSION.

RSVP ● *n.* a reply to an invitation. ● *v.intr.* (**RSVP'd**; **RSVP'ing**) reply to an invitation.

rt. *abbr.* right.

Rte. *abbr.* route.

Rt. Hon. *abbr.* Right Honourable.

Rt. Rev. *abbr.* Right Reverend.

Ru *symbol* ruthenium.

rub ● *v.* (**rubbed, rubbing**) **1** *tr.* move one's hand or another object with firm pressure over the surface of. **2** *tr.* (usu. foll. by *against, in, on, over*) apply (one's hand etc.) in this way. **3** *tr.* clean or polish or make dry or bare by rubbing. **4** *tr.* (often foll. by *over*) apply (polish, ointment, etc.) by rubbing. **5** *tr.* (foll. by *in, into, through*) use rubbing to make (a substance) go into or through something. **6** *tr.* (often foll. by *together*) move or slide (objects) against each other. **7** *intr.* (foll. by *against, on*) move with contact or friction. **8** *tr.* chafe or make sore

by rubbing. **9** *intr.* (of cloth, skin, etc.) become frayed or worn or sore or bare with friction. **10** *tr.* reproduce the design of (a sepulchral brass or a stone) by rubbing paper laid on it with coloured chalk etc. **11** *tr.* (foll. by *to*) reduce to powder etc. by rubbing. ● *n.* **1** a period or an instance of rubbing (*give it a rub*). **2** an impediment or difficulty (*there's the rub*). **3** a substance applied by rubbing. **4** a massage. □ **not have two coins to rub together** have no money. **rub down 1** dry or smooth or clean by rubbing. **2** massage. **rub elbows** (or **shoulders**) **with** *N Amer.* associate or come into contact with (another person or thing). **rub one's hands** rub one's hands together usu. in sign of keen satisfaction, or for warmth. **rub it in** (or **rub a person's nose in it**) emphasize or repeat an embarrassing fact etc. **rub noses** (of two people) touch noses in greeting, as a sign of friendship in some societies. **rub off 1** (usu. foll. by *on*) be transferred by contact (*some of his attitudes have rubbed off on me*). **2** remove by rubbing. **rub out 1** erase. **2** esp. *N Amer. slang* kill, eliminate. **rub salt into** (or **in**) **the wound** (or **wounds**) behave or speak so as to aggravate a hurt already inflicted. **rub the wrong way** irritate or repel as by stroking a cat against the lie of its fur.

rubato /ru:'bɑːto:/ *Music* ● *n.* (pl. **-os** or **rubati** /-ti/) the temporary disregarding of strict tempo. ● *adj.* performed with a flexible tempo.

rubber[1] *n.* **1** a tough elastic polymeric substance made from the latex of plants or synthetically (often *attrib.*: *rubber boots*). **2** a piece of this or another substance for erasing pencil or ink marks. **3** *informal* a condom. **4** (in *pl.*) **a** *N Amer.* galoshes. **b** *Cdn* (*Nfld*) long, waterproof boots worn esp. by fishermen and sealers. **5** a person who rubs; a masseur or masseuse. **6** an implement used for rubbing. **7** (*prec. by the*) *Hockey slang* the puck. **8** *Baseball* an oblong piece of rubber embedded in the pitcher's mound on which the pitcher stands to deliver the ball. □ **burn** (or **lay**) **rubber** esp. *N Amer.* **1** travel very quickly in a car; speed. **2** leave tire tracks on a surface, usu. by accelerating or braking rapidly. □ **rubbery** *adj.*

rubber[2] *n.* **1** a match of three or five successive games between the same sides or persons at bridge, lawn tennis, etc. **2** (*prec. by the*) **a** the act of winning a majority of games in a rubber. **b** a deciding game when scores are even.

rubber band *n.* a loop of rubber for holding papers etc. together.

rubber cement *n.* an adhesive containing rubber in a solvent.

rubber-chicken *adj. N Amer. slang* of or relating to the round of dinner and luncheon appearances made by a speaker, politician, etc. (*rubber-chicken circuit*).

rubber-faced *adj.* having a face that is able to assume easily many esp. grotesque expressions.

rubberize *v.tr.* treat or coat with rubber.

rubberneck *informal* ● *n.* a person who stares inquisitively or stupidly. ● *v.intr.* act in this way. □ **rubbernecker** *n.*

rubber plant *n.* **1** an evergreen plant, *Ficus elastica*, with dark green shiny leaves, often cultivated as a houseplant. **2** (also **rubber tree**) any of various tropical trees yielding latex, esp. *Hevea brasiliensis*.

rubber stamp ● *n.* **1** a device for inking and imprinting on a surface. **2 a** a person who mechanically copies or agrees to others' actions. **b** an indication of such agreement. ● *v.tr.* (**rubber-stamp**) approve automatically without proper consideration.

rubbing *n.* **1** *in senses of* RUB *v.* **2** an impression or copy made by rubbing (*see* RUB *v.* 10).

rubbing alcohol *n.* denatured alcohol used in massaging, as an antiseptic, etc.

rubbish *n.* **1** *esp. Brit.* waste material; refuse. **2** worthless material or articles. **3** absurd ideas or suggestions; nonsense. □ **rubbishy** *adj.*

rubble *n.* rough fragments of stone or brick etc., esp. from demolished or decaying buildings.

rubby *n.* (*pl.* **-ies**) *Cdn slang* a person who drinks rubbing alcohol, aftershave, etc. mixed with cheap wine etc.; a derelict alcoholic.

rub-down *n.* a massage.

rube *n.* *N Amer. informal* a country bumpkin.

Rube Goldberg *adj.* *N Amer.* designating a device that is unnecessarily complicated or impracticable.

rubella /ruːˈbelə/ *n.* *Med.* German measles.

rubidium /ruːˈbɪdiəm/ *n.* a soft silvery element occurring naturally in various minerals and as the radioactive isotope rubidium-87.

ruble /ˈruːbəl/ *n.* the chief monetary unit of Russia and some other former republics of the USSR.

rubric /ˈruːbrɪk/ *n.* **1** a heading or passage in red or special lettering. **2** a direction for the conduct of divine service inserted in a liturgical book. **3** a category or designation. **4** explanatory words. **5** an established custom.

ruby ● *n.* (*pl.* **-ies**) **1** a rare precious stone consisting of corundum with a colour varying from deep crimson or purple to pale rose. **2** a glowing purplish-red colour. ● *adj.* of this colour. ● *v.tr.* (**-ies, -ied**) dye or tinge with a ruby colour.

ruby-throated hummingbird *n.* a hummingbird, *Archilochus colubris*, that has a metallic green back (the male having a bright red throat).

ruche /ruːʃ/ *n.* a frill or gathering of lace etc. as a trimming. □ **ruched** *adj.* **ruching** *n.*

ruck¹ *n.* **1** (*prec. by the*) **a** an undistinguished crowd of persons or things. **b** (in racing) the main body of competitors not likely to overtake the leaders. **2** *Rugby* a loose scrum with the ball on the ground.

ruck² ● *v.tr. & intr.* (often foll. by *up*) make or become creased or wrinkled. ● *n.* a crease or wrinkle.

rucksack *n.* a backpack.

ruckus *n.* *esp. N Amer.* a noisy disturbance; an uproar.

rudbeckia /rʌdˈbekiə/ *n.* any of various tall plants constituting the genus *Rudbeckia* of the composite family, native to N America, bearing yellow or orange flowers with a prominent conical dark-coloured disc, and including black-eyed Susan.

rudder *n.* **1 a** a flat piece hinged vertically to the stern of a vessel for steering. **b** a vertical airfoil pivoted from the tailplane of an aircraft, for controlling its horizontal movement. **2** a guiding principle etc. □ **rudderless** *adj.*

ruddy *adj.* (**-ier, -iest**) **1** (of a person or complexion) freshly or healthily red. **2** reddish. □ **ruddiness** *n.*

ruddy duck *n.* a duck, *Oxyura jamaicensis*, the male of which has deep red-brown plumage.

rude *adj.* **1** (of a person, remark, etc.) impolite or offensive. **2** roughly made or done; lacking subtlety or accuracy (*a rude plow*). **3** primitive or unsophisticated (*rude simplicity*). **4** abrupt, sudden, startling, violent (*a rude awakening*). **5** *informal* indecent, lewd (*a rude joke*). □ **rudely** *adv.* **rudeness** *n.*

rudiment /ˈruːdɪmənt/ *n.* **1** (in *pl.*) the elements or first principles of a subject. **2** (in *pl.*) an imperfect beginning of something undeveloped or yet to develop. **3** *Biol.* an undeveloped or immature part or organ, esp. a structure in an embryo or larva which will develop into a limb etc.

rudimentary /ˌruːdɪˈmentri, -təri/ *adj.* **1** involving basic principles; fundamental. **2** incompletely developed; vestigial.

rue¹ ● *v.tr.* (**rues, rued, rueing** or **ruing**) repent of; bitterly feel the consequences of; wish to be undone or non-existent (esp. *rue the day*). ● *n.* **1** repentance; dejection at some occurrence. **2** compassion or pity.

rue² *n.* a perennial evergreen shrub, *Ruta graveolens*, with bitter leaves formerly used in medicine.

rueful *adj.* expressing sorrow or regret in a genuine or humorous way. □ **ruefully** *adv.*

ruff¹ *n.* **1** a projecting starched frill worn around the neck esp. in the 16th c. **2** a projecting or conspicuously coloured ring of feathers or hair around a bird's or animal's neck. **3** *N Amer.* a fringe of fur around the hood or along the edges of a jacket.

ruff² *n.* a representation of a dog's bark.

ruffed grouse *n.* a N American woodland grouse, *Bonasa umbellus*, which has a black or reddish ruff on the sides of the neck, much prized as a game bird.

ruffian *n.* a violent lawless person. □ **ruffianly** *adv.*

ruffle ● *v.* **1** *tr.* disturb the smoothness or tranquility of. **2** *tr.* upset the calmness of (a person). **3** *tr.* gather (fabric) into a ruffle. **4** *tr.* **a** (of a bird) erect (its feathers) in anger, display, etc. **b** disorder or disarrange (hair). **5** *intr.* undergo ruffling. **6** *intr.* lose smoothness or calmness. ● *n.* **1** an ornamental frill of fabric, lace, etc. used to decorate the edge of a garment, pillowcase, etc. **2** perturbation, bustle. **3** a rippling effect on water. **4** the ruff of a bird etc. □ **ruffle feathers** (or **a person's feathers**) *informal* upset or annoy (a person). □ **ruffly** *adj.*

rufous /ˈruːfəs/ *adj.* (esp. of animals) reddish brown.

rug *n.* **1** a piece of thick material, usu. with a deep or shaggy pile or woven in a pattern of colours, or a piece of dressed animal skin, placed as a covering or decoration on part of a floor. **2** *esp. N Amer. slang* a toupée, a wig. □ **pull the rug (out) from under** deprive of support; weaken, unsettle.

rugby *n.* (in full **rugby football**) (also **Rugby**) a team game played with an oval ball that may be kicked, carried, and passed from hand to hand.

rugby pants *n.pl.* men's casual pants, usu. made of cotton, with pockets, an elastic waistband, and no fly.

rugby shirt *n.* a men's usu. cotton casual shirt with a collar and a few buttons at the neck.

rugged *adj.* **1** (of ground or terrain) having a rough uneven surface. **2** (of features) strongly marked; irregular in outline. **3 a** unpolished; lacking gentleness or refinement (*rugged grandeur*). **b** austere, unbending (*rugged honesty*). **c** involving hardship (*a rugged life*). **d** (esp. of a machine) robust, sturdy. □ **ruggedly** *adv.* **ruggedness** *n.*

ruggedized *adj.* (of a piece of computer equipment etc.) made hard-wearing or shock-resistant.

rugosa /ruːˈɡəʊsə/ *n.* a Japanese rose, *R. rugosa*, with dark green wrinkled leaves and deep pink flowers.

rug rat *n.* *esp. N Amer. slang* a small child.

ruin ● *n.* **1** a destroyed or wrecked state (*the palace fell to ruin*). **2** a person's or thing's downfall or elimination (*the ruin of my hopes*). **3** the complete loss of one's property or position (*bring to ruin*). **4** (in *sing.* or *pl.*) the remains of a building etc. that has suffered ruin (*ancient ruins*). **5** a cause of ruin; a destructive thing or influence (*will be the ruin of us*). ● *v.tr.* **1 a** bring to ruin (*your extravagance has ruined me*). **b** utterly impair or wreck (*the rain ruined my hat*). **2** (esp. as **ruined** *adj.*)

reduce to ruins. □ **in ruins 1** in a state of ruin. **2** completely wrecked (*their hopes were in ruins*).

ruination *n.* **1** the act of bringing to ruin. **2** the act of ruining or the state of being ruined.

ruinous *adj.* **1** bringing ruin; disastrous (*at ruinous expense*). **2** in ruins; dilapidated. □ **ruinously** *adv.*

rule ● *n.* **1** a principle to which an action, procedure, etc. conforms or is required to conform. **2** a prevailing custom or standard; the normal state of affairs. **3** government or dominion (*under British rule*). **4** the period of time during which a government or monarch holds power. **5** = RULER 2. **6** a code of discipline of a religious order. **7** *Law* an order made by a judge or court with reference to a particular case only. ● *v.* **1** *tr.* exercise decisive influence over; keep under control. **2** *tr. & intr.* have sovereign control of (*rules over a vast kingdom*). **3** *tr.* (often foll. by *that* + clause) pronounce authoritatively (*was ruled out of order*). **4** *tr.* **a** make parallel lines across (paper). **b** make (a straight line) with a ruler etc. **5** *intr.* be customary or prevalent (*apathy rules in this organization*). **6** *intr. slang* be superior or pre-eminent (*hockey rules!*). **7** *tr.* (in *passive*; foll. by *by*) consent to follow (advice etc.); be guided by. **8** *intr.* (of a court etc.) make a formal decision or ruling (*waiting for the Supreme Court to rule*). □ **as a rule** usually; more often than not. **by rule** in a regulation manner; mechanically. **rule out 1** exclude; pronounce irrelevant or ineligible. **2** prevent; make impossible. **rule the roost** be in control.

rule book *n.* a book containing the rules governing a particular activity, organization, etc.

rule of thumb *n.* a rule for general guidance, based on experience or practice rather than theory.

ruler *n.* **1** a person exercising government or dominion. **2** a straight usu. graduated strip or cylinder of plastic, wood, metal, etc., used to draw lines or measure distance. □ **rulership** *n.*

ruling ● *n.* an authoritative decision or announcement. ● *adj.* prevailing; currently in force.

rum *n.* a spirit distilled from sugar cane residues or molasses.

Rumanian *var. of* ROMANIAN.

rumba /ˈrʌmbə/ ● *n.* **1** an Afro-Cuban dance. **2 a** a ballroom dance imitative of this, danced on the spot with a pronounced movement of the hips. **b** the music for it. ● *v.tr.* (**rumbas, rumbaed** /-bəd/ or **rumba'd, rumbaing** /-bəɪŋ/) dance the rumba.

rum baba *n.* = BABA¹.

rumble ● *v.* **1** *intr.* make a continuous deep resonant sound as of distant thunder. **2** *intr.* (foll. by *along, by, past*, etc.) (of a person or vehicle) move with a rumbling noise. **3** *tr.* (often foll. by *out*) utter or say with a rumbling sound. **4** *intr. N Amer. slang* engage in a street fight. ● *n.* **1** a rumbling sound. **2** *N Amer. slang* a street fight between gangs.

rumblings *n.pl.* early indications of some state of affairs or incipient change (*rumblings of discontent*).

rumen /ˈruːmen/ *n.* (*pl.* **-s** or **rumina** /-mɪnə/) the first stomach of a ruminant, in which food, esp. cellulose, is partly digested by bacteria.

ruminant /ˈruːmənənt/ ● *n.* an animal that chews the cud regurgitated from its rumen. ● *adj.* **1** of or belonging to ruminants. **2** contemplative; given to or engaged in meditation.

ruminate /ˈruːmɪˌneɪt/ *v.* **1** *tr. & intr.* meditate, ponder. **2** *intr.* (of ruminants) chew the cud. □ **rumination** *n.* **ruminative** /-nətɪv/ *adj.* **ruminatively** *adv.*

rummage ● *v.* **1** *tr. & intr.* search, esp. untidily and unsystematically. **2** *tr.* (foll. by *around*) disarrange; make untidy in searching. **3** *tr.* (foll. by *out, up*) find

among other things. ● *n.* **1** an instance of rummaging. **2** things found by rummaging; a miscellaneous accumulation.

rummage sale *n.* esp. *N Amer.* a sale of miscellaneous usu. second-hand articles, esp. for charity.

rummy¹ *n.* a card game in which the players try to form sets and sequences of cards.

rummy² *n. N Amer. slang* an alcoholic or drunkard.

rumour (also **rumor**) *n.* **1** general talk or hearsay of doubtful accuracy. **2** (often foll. by *of*, or *that* + clause) a current but unverified statement or assertion (*heard a rumour that you are leaving*). ● *v.tr.* (usu. in *passive*) report by way of rumour (*it is rumoured that he is leaving; you are rumoured to be sick*). □ **rumour has it** it is rumoured (*rumour has it that she is resigning*).

rumour monger *n.* a person who spreads rumours. □ **rumour mongering** *n.*

rump *n.* **1** the hind part of a mammal, esp. the buttocks. **2** a small remnant of a parliament or similar body.

rumple *v.tr. & intr.* make or become creased or ruffled. □ **rumpled** *adj.*

rump steak *n.* a cut of beef from the rump.

rumpus *n. informal* a disturbance, brawl, row, or uproar.

rumpus room *n. N Amer., Austral., & NZ* a room, usu. in the basement of a house, for games and play.

rum-runner *n. N Amer.* a person or ship engaged in smuggling alcohol, esp. during Prohibition. □ **rum-running** *n.*

run ● *v.* (**running**; *past* **ran** /ran/; *past part.* **run**) **1** *intr.* go with quick steps on alternate feet, never having both or all feet on the ground at the same time. **2** *intr.* **a** flee, abscond. **b** (often foll. by *to*) have recourse for support, comfort, help, etc. (*she's always running to her father*). **3 a** *intr.* go or travel hurriedly, briefly, etc. **b** *tr.* pass or cause to pass quickly (*run a comb through your hair*). **4** *intr.* **a** advance by or as by rolling or on wheels, or smoothly or easily. **b** be in action or operation (*left the engine running*). **5** *intr.* be current or operative; have duration (*the lease runs for 99 years; the movie ran for three hours*). **6 a** *intr.* (of a bus, train, airplane, etc.) travel or be travelling on its route (*this train runs between Toronto and London*). **b** *tr.* cause (a bus, train, airplane, etc.) to travel a specified route (*the company runs buses from Fredericton to Saint John*). **7** *intr.* (of a play, exhibition, etc.) be staged or presented. **8** *intr.* **a** extend (*the road runs by the lakeshore*). **b** have a course or order or tendency (*prices are running high*). **c** proceed in a specified manner (*running late*). **9 a** *intr.* compete in a race. **b** *intr.* finish a race in a specified position. **c** *tr.* compete in (a race). **10 a** *intr.* (often foll. by *for*) seek election (*ran for president*). **b** *tr.* (esp. of a political party) sponsor (a candidate) in an election (*ran a candidate in almost every riding*). **11 a** *intr.* (of a liquid etc.) flow, drip profusely. **b** *tr.* flow with. **c** *intr.* (foll. by *with*) flow or be wet; drip (*his face ran with sweat*). **12** *tr.* **a** cause (water etc.) to flow. **b** fill (a bathtub etc.) with water. **c** cause water to flow over (a thing) held under a tap etc. **13** *intr.* spread or pass rapidly (*a shiver ran down my spine*). **14** *tr.* esp. *N Amer. informal* drive past or fail to stop at (a red traffic light, stop sign, etc.). **15** *tr.* traverse or make one's way through or over (a course, race, or distance). **16** *tr.* perform (an errand). **17 a** *tr.* publish (an article etc.) in a newspaper or magazine. **b** *intr.* (of an article etc.) appear in print (*the story ran in all the newspapers*). **18 a** *tr.* cause (a machine or vehicle etc.) to operate. **b** *intr.* (of a mechanism or component etc.) move or work freely. **19** *tr.* direct or manage (a business etc.). **20** *tr.* own and drive (a vehicle) regularly. **21** *tr.* take (a person) for a ride in a vehicle (*I'll run you to the bank*). **22** *tr.* cause to run or go in a specified way (*ran the car into a tree*). **23** *tr.* enter (a horse etc.) in a race. **24** *tr.* smuggle (guns etc.). **25** *tr.* be suffering from (a fever). **26** *intr.* (of salmon) go upriver from the sea. **27** *intr.* (of a colour in a fabric) spread from the dyed parts. **28** **a** *intr.* (of a thought, the eye, the memory, etc.) pass in a transitory or cursory way (*ideas ran through my mind*). **b** *tr.* cause (one's eye) to look cursorily (*ran my eye down the page*). **29** *intr.* (of a stocking etc.) develop a run. **30** *intr.* (of a rumour etc.) spread quickly. **31** *intr.* (esp. of the eyes or nose) exude liquid matter. **32** *N Amer.* **a** *tr.* (of something purchased etc.) cost (a person) a certain amount (*the repairs will run you $500*). **b** *intr.* amount or total (*the final bill will run to over ten million dollars*). **33** *tr.* perform (a test, experiment, etc.) using a particular procedure. **34** *Computing* **a** *tr.* (of a computer or computer user) execute (a program or series of commands). **b** *intr.* (often foll. by *under*) (of a computer program or system) operate within a specified environment. **35** *tr. N Amer.* navigate (rapids, a waterfall, etc.) in a boat. ● *n.* **1 a** an act, instance, or period of running. **b** a running race (*the 5 km run*). **2** a short trip or excursion, esp. for pleasure. **3** a distance travelled. **4** a general tendency of development or movement. **5** a rapid motion. **6** a regular route. **7** a continuous or long stretch or period or course (*had a run of bad luck*). **8** (often foll. by *on*) a high general demand (for a commodity, currency, etc.) (*a run on the dollar*). **b** a sudden demand for repayment by a large number of customers (of a bank). **9** a quantity produced in one period of production (*a print run*). **10** a general or average type or class (*not typical of the general run*). **11** *Baseball* a point scored usu. by the batter returning to the plate after touching the other bases. **12** (foll. by *of*) free use of or access to (*had the run of the house*). **13** a vertical strip of unravelled fabric in hosiery. **14** *Music* a rapid scale passage. **15** a class or line of goods. **16** a shoal of fish in motion. **17 a** a single journey, esp. by an aircraft. **b** (of an aircraft) a flight on a straight and even course at a constant speed before or while dropping bombs. **c** an offensive military operation. **18** (in *pl.*) (prec. by *the*) *informal* diarrhea. **19** a continuous series of performances. **20** a sequence of cards in the same suit. **21** a snow-covered slope used for skiing, tobogganing, etc. **22** *N Amer.* = BUFFALO RUN. **23** *Cdn* (*Nfld & Maritimes*) a narrow passage of water. □ **at a run** running. **on the run 1** escaping, running away. **2** hurrying about from place to place. **run across 1** happen to meet. **2** (foll. by *to*) make a brief journey or a flying visit (to a place). **run after 1** pursue with attentions; seek the society of. **2** give much time to (a pursuit etc.). **3** pursue at a run. **run along** *informal* depart. **run around 1** bustle; hurry from one place to another. **2** deceive or evade repeatedly. **3** (often foll. by *with*) *informal* engage in sexual relations (esp. casually or illicitly). **run at** attack by charging or rushing. **run away 1** get away by running; flee, abscond. **2** elope. **3** (of a child) leave the parental home. **run away with 1** carry off (a person, stolen property, etc.). **2** win (a prize) easily. **3** leave home to have a relationship with. **4** deprive of self-control or common sense (*lets her ideas run away with her*). **run down 1** knock down or collide with. **2** reduce the strength or numbers of (resources). **3** (of an unwound clock etc.) stop. **4** (of a person or a person's health) become feeble from overwork or undernourishment. **5** discover after a search. **6** disparage. **run dry** cease to flow, be exhausted. **run**

for it seek safety by fleeing. **a run** (or **a good run**) **for one's money 1** vigorous competition. **2** pleasure derived from an activity. **3** return for outlay or effort. **run afoul** (or **foul**) **of** act contrary to; go against. **run high 1** (of feelings) be strong. **2** (of the sea) have a strong current with a high tide. **run in 1** *informal* arrest. **2** incur (a debt). **run in the family** (of a trait) be common in the members of a family. **run into 1** collide with. **2** encounter. **3** reach as many as (a specified figure). **4** be continuous or coalesce with. **run into the ground** *informal* bring (a person) to exhaustion etc. **run its course** follow its natural progress; be left to itself. **run low** (or **short**) become depleted, have too little (*supplies ran low; ran short of sugar*). **run off 1** flee. **2** produce (copies etc.) on a machine. **3** decide (a race or other contest) after a series of heats or in the event of a tie. **4** flow or cause to flow away. **5** write or recite fluently. **6** digress suddenly. **run off at the mouth** esp. *N Amer. informal* talk indiscreetly or incessantly. **run off one's feet** very busy. **run on 1** (of written characters) be joined together. **2** continue in operation. **3** elapse. **4** speak volubly. **5** talk incessantly. **run out 1** come to an end; become used up. **2** (foll. by *of*) exhaust one's stock of. **3** escape from a container. **4** (of rope) pass out; be paid out. **run out on** *informal* desert (a person). **run over 1** overflow. **2** study or repeat quickly. **3** (of a vehicle or its driver) pass over; knock down or crush. **4** touch (the keys of a piano etc.) in quick succession. **5** (often foll. by *to*) go quickly by a brief journey or for a flying visit. **run ragged** exhaust (a person). **run the show** *informal* dominate in an undertaking etc. **run through 1** examine or rehearse briefly. **2** peruse. **3** deal successively with. **4** consume (an estate etc.) by reckless or quick spending. **5** pass through by running. **6** pervade. **7** pierce with a sword etc. **run to 1** have the money or ability for. **2** reach (an amount or number). **3** (of a person) show a tendency to (*runs to fat*). **4 a** be enough for (some expense or undertaking). **b** have the resources or capacity for. **5** fall into (ruin). **run to earth** (or **to ground**) **1** *Hunting* chase to its lair. **2** discover after a long search. **run up 1** accumulate (a debt etc.) quickly. **2** build or make hurriedly. **3** raise (a flag). **4** grow quickly. **run up against** meet with (a difficulty or difficulties). **run wild 1** grow unchecked or untrained. **2** act or behave without any control or restraint. **run with 1** proceed with (*if she agrees to the idea we'll run with it*). **2** associate with (*runs with a rough crowd*).

runabout *n.* **1** a light car. **2** a small pleasure boat.

run-and-shoot *n.* (in full **run-and-shoot offence**) *N Amer. Football* a style of offence featuring a speedy mobile quarterback throwing quick short passes while scrambling.

runaround *n.* deceit or evasion (*gave me the runaround*).

runaway ● *adj.* **1** (of a person) having run away (*runaway children*). **2** (of an animal or vehicle) no longer under the control of its rider or owner (*a runaway freight train*). **3** happening very rapidly; out of control (*runaway inflation*). **4** happening very easily (*a runaway victory*). ● *n.* **1** a person who has run away (*teenage runaways*). **2** an animal or vehicle that is running out of control. **3** an easy victory. **4** a fugitive.

rundown ● *n.* **1** a reduction in numbers. **2** a detailed analysis. **3** *Baseball* a play in which usu. two fielders try to tag out a runner caught between bases. ● *adj.* **1** decayed after prosperity. **2** enfeebled through overwork etc. **3** dilapidated.

rune *n.* **1** any of the letters of the earliest Germanic alphabet used by Scandinavians and Anglo-Saxons from about the 3rd c. and formed by modifying Roman or Greek characters to suit carving. **2** something mysterious or secret. □ **runic** *adj.*

rung[1] *n.* **1** each of the horizontal supports of a ladder. **2** a strengthening crosspiece in the structure of a chair etc. **3** a level or rank in society, an organization, one's career, etc. □ **runged** *adj.*

rung[2] *past part. of* RING[2].

run-in *n.* a quarrel.

runnel /ˈrʌnəl/ *n.* **1** a brook or small stream. **2** a gutter.

runner *n.* **1** a person, horse, etc., that runs, esp. in a race or for fitness. **2 a** *Baseball* = BASERUNNER. **b** *Football* the ball carrier. **3** *Cdn & Irish* = RUNNING SHOE. **4 a** a creeping plant stem that can take root. **b** a twining plant. **5** each of the long pieces on the underside of a sleigh etc. that forms the contact in sliding. **6** a rod or groove or blade on which a thing slides. **7** a long narrow ornamental cloth or rug. **8 a** a messenger, collector, or agent for a bank, stockbroker, etc. **b** a messenger or agent for a bookmaker, drug dealer, etc. **9** (in full **runner bean**) any of several cultivated climbing varieties of bean or their edible pods, esp. the scarlet runner bean *Phaseolus coccineus*, with red flowers and long green pods. **10** a roller for moving a heavy article.

runner-up *n.* (*pl.* **runners-up**) **1** the competitor or team taking second place. **2** a competitor or team that comes close to winning.

running ● *n.* **1** the action of runners in a race etc. **2** the way a race etc. proceeds. **3** management or operation. **4** an act or an instance of racing. ● *adj.* **1** continuing on an essentially continuous basis though changing in detail (*a running joke*). **2** consecutive; one after another (*three days running*). **3** done with a run (*a running jump*). □ **in** (or **out of**) **the running** (of a competitor) with a good (or poor) chance of winning. **make** (or **take up**) **the running** take the lead; set the pace. **take a running jump** (esp. as *interj.*) *slang* go away. **up and running** in operation.

running back *n. Football* a back whose main task is to run carrying the ball.

running board *n.* a footboard on either side of a motor vehicle, used as a step etc.

running commentary *n.* an oral description of events as they occur.

running dog *n. derogatory* a servile political follower.

running knot *n.* a knot that slips along the rope etc. and changes the size of a noose.

running light *n.* **1** = NAVIGATION LIGHT. **2** each of a small set of lights on a motor vehicle that remain illuminated while the vehicle is running.

running mate *n.* **1** *US* a candidate for a supporting position in an election, esp. for the vice presidency. **2** a horse entered in a race in order to set the pace for another horse from the same stable.

running shoe *n.* any of various shoes having an upper made of nylon, canvas, etc. and a rubber or synthetic sole.

running water *n.* **1** water flowing in a stream etc. **2** indoor plumbing.

runny *adj.* (**-ier, -iest**) **1** tending to run or flow. **2** excessively fluid.

runoff *n.* **1** an amount of rainfall or melted snow that is carried off an area by streams and rivers. **2** *N Amer.* the spring thaw. **3** an amount of water coming off a roof etc. **4** an additional competition, election, race, etc., after a tie.

run-of-the-mill *adj.* ordinary, undistinguished.

runt *n.* **1** a small pig, esp. the smallest in a litter. **2** a weakling; an undersized person. □ **runtish** *adj.* **runty** *adj.*

run-through *n.* **1** a rehearsal, usu. of a whole production, complete act, etc., with as few stops as possible. **2** a brief survey.

run-up *n.* **1** (often foll. by *to*) the period preceding an important event. **2** *Golf* a low approach shot.

runway *n.* **1** a specially prepared surface along which aircraft take off and land. **2** a trail to an animals' watering hole. **3** an incline down which logs are slid. **4** a long raised platform in a theatre etc.

rupee /ruːˈpiː/ *n.* the basic monetary unit of India, Pakistan, Sri Lanka, and several other countries.

rupture ● *n.* **1** the act or an instance of breaking; a breach. **2** a breach of harmonious relations; a disagreement and parting. **3** *Med.* an abdominal hernia. ● *v.* **1** *tr.* break or burst (a cell or membrane etc.). **2** *tr.* sever (a connection). **3** *intr.* undergo a rupture. **4** *tr. & intr.* affect with or suffer a hernia.

rural *adj.* **1** of, relating to, or suggesting the country (*opp.* URBAN). **2** living in the country. **3** of or concerning agriculture. □ **rurally** *adv.*

rural municipality *n. Cdn* **1** *Prairies & Que.* a usu. sparsely populated municipality outside of urban municipalities that is administered by an elected council or the provincial government. Abbr.: **RM**. **2** *NS* one of the 24 districts that contain incorporated cities and towns.

rural route *n. N Amer.* a mail delivery route in an area outside of a town or city. Abbr.: **RR**.

ruse /ruːz, ruːs/ *n.* a stratagem or trick.

rush[1] ● *v.* **1** *intr.* go, move, or act precipitately or with great speed. **2** *tr.* move or transport with great haste (*was rushed to hospital*). **3** *intr.* (foll. by *at*) **a** move suddenly and quickly towards. **b** begin impetuously. **4** *tr.* perform or deal with hurriedly (*the bill was rushed through Parliament*). **5** *tr.* force (a person) to act hastily. **6** *tr.* attack or capture by sudden assault. **7** *intr. Hockey* bring the puck up the ice, esp. into the opposing team's zone. **8** *Football* **a** *tr.* move (the ball) forward by carrying it rather than by passing etc. **b** *intr.* move the ball forward by carrying it. **c** *tr.* move the ball forward (a distance) by carrying it. **d** *tr.* attempt to force a way into the backfield in pursuit of (the back with the ball). **9** *intr.* flow, fall, spread, or roll impetuously or fast (*the blood rushed to my face*). ● *n.* **1** an act of rushing; a violent advance or attack. **2 a** a period of great activity (*the Christmas rush*). **b** = RUSH HOUR. **3** (*attrib.*) done with great haste or speed (*a rush job*). **4** *informal* a thrill or feeling of excitement; a high (*gets a rush out of performing*). **5** (foll. by *on, for*) a sudden strong demand for a commodity. **6** (in *pl.*) *informal* the first prints of a film after a period of shooting. **7** *N Amer.* (*attrib.*) designating a seat at a performance purchased at a reduced price on the day of the performance, or a ticket purchased for such a seat (*a rush ticket*). **8** *Hockey* an instance of bringing the puck up the ice. **9** *Football N Amer.* an instance of rushing the football. **10** a sudden migration of large numbers (*gold rush*). □ **rusher** *n.*

rush[2] *n.* **1** any marsh or waterside plant of the family Juncaceae, with slender stems and inconspicuous greenish or brownish flowers used for making chair seats, baskets, etc. **2** a stem of this. **3** (*collect.*) rushes as a material. □ **rushlike** *adv.*

rush hour *n.* a time of day when traffic is at its heaviest.

rusk *n.* a slice of bread baked a second time, usu. as a light biscuit.

russet ● *adj.* reddish brown. ● *n.* **1** a reddish-brown colour. **2** a kind of rough-skinned russet-coloured apple. **3** a variety of potato with a reddish skin.

Russian ● *n.* **1 a** a native or national of Russia, a country in N Asia and E Europe, or the Russian Federation. **b** a person of Russian descent. **2** *hist.* a native or national of the former USSR. **3** the official language of Russia and the former USSR. ● *adj.* **1** of or relating to Russia. **2** of or in Russian.

Russian doll *n.* a set of hollow and usu. decorated wooden doll figures of differing sizes, each one made so as to nest inside the next largest.

Russian olive *n.* = OLEASTER.

Russian Orthodox Church *n.* the national Church of Russia. □ **Russian Orthodox** *adj.*

Russian roulette *n.* **1** an act of daring in which one (usu. with others in turn) squeezes the trigger of a revolver held to one's head with one chamber loaded, having first spun the chamber. **2** a potentially dangerous enterprise.

Russian thistle *n.* N Amer. a European prickly tumbleweed, *Salsola kali*, a weed in N America.

Russify *v.tr.* (**-ies, -ied**) make Russian in character. □ **Russification** *n.*

Russki *n.* (also **Russky**) (*pl.* **-is** or **-ies**) *slang derogatory* a Russian or Soviet.

Russo- *comb. form* Russian; Russian and.

rust ● *n.* **1 a** a reddish-brown or yellowish-brown coating formed on iron or steel by oxidation, esp. as a result of moisture. **b** a similar coating on other metals. **2 a** any of various plant diseases with rust-coloured spots caused by fungi of the order Uredinales. **b** the fungus causing this. **3** an impaired state due to disuse or inactivity. **4** a reddish-brown or brownish-red colour. ● *adj.* of a reddish-brown or brownish-red colour. ● *v.* **1** *tr. & intr.* affect or be affected with rust; undergo oxidation. **2** *intr.* lose quality or efficiency by disuse or inactivity. □ **rustless** *adj.*

rust belt *n.* *informal* an area of once profitable heavy industry, esp. (**Rust Belt**) in the US Midwest and northeastern states.

rustbucket *n.* *informal* an old and rusty car, ship, etc.

rustic ● *adj.* **1** having the characteristics of or associations with the country or country life. **2** unsophisticated, simple, unrefined. **3** of rude or country workmanship. ● *n.* a person from or living in the country, esp. a simple unsophisticated one. □ **rustically** *adv.* **rusticity** *n.*

rusticate *v.* **1** *intr.* retire to or live in the country. **2** *tr.* make rural. □ **rustication** *n.*

rustle ● *v.* **1** *intr. & tr.* make or cause to make a gentle sound as of dry leaves blown in a breeze. **2** *intr.* (often foll. by *along* etc.) move with a rustling sound. **3** *tr. & intr.* steal (cattle or horses). **4** *intr.* N Amer. *informal* move or act quickly or energetically. ● *n.* a rustling sound or movement. □ **rustle up** *informal* produce quickly when needed. □ **rustler** *n.* (esp. in sense 3 of *v.*).

rustproof ● *adj.* (of a metal) not susceptible to corrosion by rust. ● *v.tr.* make rustproof.

rusty *adj.* (**-ier, -iest**) **1** rusted or affected by rust. **2** stiff with age or disuse. **3** (of knowledge etc.) faded or impaired by neglect (*my French is a bit rusty*). **4** rust-coloured. **5 a** of antiquated appearance. **b** antiquated or behind the times. **6** (of a voice) croaking or creaking. □ **rustily** *adv.* **rustiness** *n.*

rut¹ ● *n.* **1** a deep track made by the passage of wheels. **2** any groove, furrow, etc. **3** an established (esp. tedious) mode of practice or procedure. ● *v.tr.* (**rutted,**

rutting) mark with ruts. □ **in a rut** following a fixed (esp. tedious or dreary) pattern of behaviour that is difficult to change. □ **rutty** *adj.*

rut² ● *n.* **1** the periodic sexual excitement or activity of a male deer, goat, ram, etc. **2** the period during which this happens. ● *v.intr.* (**rutted, rutting**) be affected with rut.

rutabaga /ˈruːtəˌbeɪɡə/ *n.* esp. N Amer. **1** a cruciferous plant, *Brassica napus*, with a large yellow-fleshed root, originally from Sweden. **2** this root as a vegetable.

ruthenium /ruːˈθiːnɪəm/ *n.* a rare hard white metallic element, occurring naturally in platinum ores, and used as a chemical catalyst and in certain alloys.

rutherfordium /ˌrʌðərˈfɔːdɪəm/ *n.* a name variously proposed for the artificial radioactive elements of atomic number 104 and 106.

ruthless *adj.* having no pity or compassion. □ **ruthlessly** *adv.* **ruthlessness** *n.*

RV *abbr.* **1** N Amer. RECREATIONAL VEHICLE. **2** REVISED VERSION.

R-value *n.* N Amer. a measure of the insulating capability of a wall, building material, etc., with greater numbers indicating greater resistance to heat loss.

Rwandan /ruːˈɒndən/ ● *adj.* a native or inhabitant of Rwanda, a country in central Africa. ● *adj.* of or relating to Rwanda or its people.

Rx *abbr.* **1** prescription. **2** (in prescriptions) take.

rye *n.* **1 a** a cereal plant, *Secale cereale*, with spikes bearing wheatlike grains. **b** the grain of this used for bread and fodder. **2** (in full **rye whisky**) **a** a whisky blended from rye and other grains. **b** whisky distilled from fermented rye. **3** rye bread.

ryegrass *n.* any forage or lawn grass of the genus *Lolium*, esp. *L. perenne*.

Ss

S¹ *n.* (also **s**) (*pl.* **Ss** or **S's**) **1** the nineteenth letter of the alphabet. **2** an S-shaped object or curve.

S² *abbr.* (also **S.**) **1** small. **2 a** Saturday. **b** Sunday. **3** soprano. **4** South, Southern. **5** *Cdn* Senate. **6** Saint. **7** Society.

S³ *symbol Chem.* **1** the element sulphur. **2** siemens.

s *abbr.* (also **s.**) **1** second(s). **2** shilling(s). **3** singular. **4** son. **5** section.

's *abbr.* **1** is, has. **2** us. **3** *informal* does (*what's he say?*).

-'s *suffix* denoting the possessive case of singular nouns and of plural nouns not ending in *-s* (*John's book*; *the book's cover*; *the children's shoes*).

SA *abbr.* **1** Salvation Army. **2** sex appeal. **3 a** South Africa. **b** South America. **c** South Australia. **4** *hist.* Sturmabteilung (see BROWNSHIRT 1).

Saanich /ˈsænɪtʃ/ *n.* **1** a member of a division of Straits people living on the Saanich Peninsula. **2** the dialect of Songhee spoken by the Saanich.

sabayon /ˈsæbaijɒn/ *n.* = ZABAGLIONE.

Sabbath *n.* **1** a day of rest and worship kept by Jews and some Christians on Saturday. **2** a day of worship celebrated by most Christians on Sunday. **3** a period of rest.

sabbatical /səˈbætɪkəl/ ● *adj.* **1** (of leave) granted at intervals to a professor or teacher for study or travel, orig. every seventh year. **2** of or appropriate to the Sabbath. ● *n.* a period of sabbatical leave.

saber *esp. US var. of* SABRE.

Sabine's gull /ˈsæbaɪnz/ *n.* an Arctic gull with a forked tail, dark grey head, and black and yellow bill.

Sabin vaccine /ˈseɪbɪn/ *n.* an oral vaccine giving immunity against polio.

sable¹ *n.* **1** a small brown-furred flesh-eating mammal, *Martes zibellina*, of N Europe and parts of N Asia, related to the marten. **2** its skin or fur.

sable² ● *n.* **1** esp. *literary* black. **2** (in full **sable antelope**) a large African antelope with long curved horns, *Hippotragus niger*, the males of which are mostly black in old age. ● *adj.* esp. *literary* dark, gloomy. □ **sabled** *adj.*

sabotage /ˈsæbətɑʒ/ ● *n.* deliberate damage to or destruction of property, esp. in order to disrupt the production of goods or as a political or military act. ● *v.tr.* **1** commit sabotage on. **2** make useless (*sabotaged my plans*).

saboteur /ˌsæbəˈtɜr/ *n.* a person who sabotages.

sabre *n.* (also esp. *US* **saber**) **1** a cavalry sword with a curved blade. **2** a light fencing sword with a tapering blade.

sabre-rattling *n.* a display or threat of force.

sabre-toothed *adj.* designating any of various extinct mammals with long sabre-shaped upper canines.

sac *n.* **1** a bag-like cavity, enclosed by a membrane, in an animal or plant. **2** the distended membrane surrounding a hernia, cyst, tumour, etc.

saccharide /ˈsækəˌraɪd/ *n. Chem.* = SUGAR 2.

saccharin /ˈsækrɪn, ˈsækrɪn/ *n.* a very sweet substance, used as a substitute for sugar.

saccharine /ˈsækəˌrɪn, ˈsækrɪn/ ● *adj.* **1** sweet; sugary.

2 of, containing, or like sugar. **3** unpleasantly overpolite, sentimental, etc. ● *n.* something that is excessively sweet, sentimental, etc.

sachem /ˈseɪtʃəm/ *n.* the supreme chief of some N American Aboriginal peoples.

sachet /sæˈʃeɪ/ *n.* **1** a small perfumed bag. **2** a packet of potpourri etc. for laying among clothes etc.

sack¹ ● *n.* **1 a** a large strong bag, esp. one made of heavy fabric, for storing or conveying goods. **b** this with its contents (*a sack of potatoes*). **2** (prec. by *the*) *informal* dismissal, esp. from employment. **3** (prec. by *the*) *N Amer. slang* bed. **4** *Baseball* a base. **5** *Football* an act or instance of sacking. **6** a woman's short loose dress with a sacklike appearance. **7** a man's or woman's loose-hanging coat not shaped to the back. ● *v.tr.* **1** put into a sack or sacks. **2** *informal* dismiss esp. from employment. **3** *Football* tackle (the quarterback) behind the line of scrimmage before he is able to throw the ball. □ **hit the sack** *informal* go to bed. **sack out** *informal esp. N Amer.* go to bed; go to sleep. □ **sackful** *n.* (*pl.* **-fuls**) **sacklike** *adj.*

sack² ● *v.tr.* **1** plunder and destroy (a captured town etc.). **2** steal valuables from (a place). ● *n.* the sacking of a captured place.

sackcloth *n.* **1** a coarse fabric, as of flax or hemp. **2** clothes of this, formerly worn as a penance or in mourning.

sacking *n.* material for making sacks; sackcloth.

sacra *pl. of* SACRUM.

sacral /ˈseɪkrəl/ *adj.* **1** *Anat.* of or relating to the sacrum. **2** *Anthropology* of or for sacred rites.

sacrament *n.* **1** a religious ceremony or act of the Christian Churches regarded as an outward and visible sign of inward and spiritual grace. **2** a thing of mysterious and sacred significance. **3** (also **Blessed** or **Holy Sacrament**) (prec. by *the*) **a** the Eucharist. **b** the consecrated elements, esp. the bread or Host.

sacramental ● *adj.* **1** of or of the nature of a sacrament. **2** (of a doctrine etc.) attaching great importance to the sacraments. ● *n.* an observance analogous to but not reckoned among the sacraments, e.g. the use of holy water or the sign of the cross. □ **sacramentally** *adv.*

sacred *adj.* **1 a** exclusively dedicated or appropriated (to a god or to some religious purpose). **b** made holy by religious association. **c** connected with religion; used for a religious purpose (*sacred music*). **2 a** safeguarded or required by religion, reverence, or tradition. **b** sacrosanct. **3** (of writings etc.) embodying the laws or doctrines of a religion. **4** treated with utmost respect; inviolable. □ **sacredness** *n.*

sacred cow *n. informal* an idea or institution unreasonably held to be above criticism.

Sacred Heart *n. Catholicism* **1** the heart of Christ as an object of devotion. **2** an image representing this.

sacrifice ● *n.* **1 a** the act of giving up something valued for the sake of something else more important or worthy. **b** a thing given up in this way. **c** the loss entailed in this. **2 a** the slaughter of an animal or person or the surrender of a possession as an offering to a deity. **b** an animal, person, or thing offered in this way. **3** an act of prayer, thanksgiving, or penitence as propitiation. **4** *Christianity* **a** Christ's offering of himself in the Crucifixion. **b** the Eucharist as either a propitiatory offering of the body and blood of Christ or an act of thanksgiving. **5** *Baseball* a play in which a batter deliberately hits the ball solely to advance a baserunner and is himself put out (usu. *attrib.*: *sacrifice fly*). **6** (in games) a loss incurred deliberately to avoid a greater loss or to obtain a compensating advantage. ● *v.* **1** *tr. & intr.* give up or offer as a sacrifice. **2** *tr.* devote or give over to. **3** *tr. Baseball* advance (a baserunner) by hitting a sacrifice fly, bunt, etc. □ **sacrificial** /-'fɪʃəl/ *adj.* **sacrificially** *adv.*

sacrificial lamb *n.* **1** a lamb offered as a religious sacrifice. **2** a person, principle, etc. sacrificed to achieve an end.

sacrilege /'sækrɪlɪdʒ/ *n.* **1** the violation or misuse of what is regarded as sacred. **2** an act or instance of this. □ **sacrilegious** *adj.* **sacrilegiously** *adv.*

sacristy /'sækrɪsti/ *n.* (*pl.* **-ies**) a room in a church where the vestments, sacred vessels, etc., are kept.

sacrosanct /'sækro:,sæŋkt/ *adj.* (of a person, place, law, etc.) most sacred; exempt from criticism etc.

sacrum /'sækrəm, 'seikrəm/ *n.* (*pl.* **sacra** /-krə/) a triangular bone formed from fused vertebrae and situated between the two hip bones of the pelvis.

SAD *abbr.* SEASONAL AFFECTIVE DISORDER.

sad *adj.* (**sadder, saddest**) **1** unhappy; regretful. **2** causing or suggesting sorrow (*a sad story*). **3** regrettable. **4** shameful, deplorable (*is in a sad state*). **5** *slang* contemptible, pathetic, unfashionable. □ **sadly** *adv.* **sadness** *n.*

sadden *v.tr. & intr.* make or become sad.

saddhu *var. of* SADHU.

saddle ● *n.* **1** a seat of leather etc., usu. raised at front and rear, fastened on a horse etc. for riding. **2** a seat for the rider of a bicycle etc. **3** a cut of meat consisting of the two loins. **4** a ridge rising to a summit at each end. **5** a part of an animal's back resembling a saddle in shape or marking. ● *v.tr.* **1** put a saddle on (a horse etc.). **2** burden (a person) with a task, responsibility, debt, etc. **3** (of a trainer) enter (a horse) for a race. □ **in the saddle 1** mounted. **2** in office or control. **saddle up** put a saddle on (a horse) in preparation for riding.

saddleback *n.* **1** a thing, esp. a hill or ridge, with a concave upper outline. **2** any of various animals or birds with saddle-like markings on the back.

saddlebag *n.* **1** each of a pair of bags laid across a horse etc. behind the saddle. **2** a bag attached behind the saddle of a bicycle, motorcycle, snowmobile, etc. **3** (*attrib.*) *Cdn hist.* designating a preacher, doctor, etc., who travelled from place to place to work; itinerant.

saddle bronc *n. N Amer.* **1** a saddled horse ridden in rodeo competition. **2** a rodeo event in which a rider attempts to stay on a saddled bucking horse.

saddle horn *n.* a pommel on a saddle.

saddle horse *n.* a horse for riding.

saddler *n.* a maker of or dealer in saddles and other equipment for horses.

saddlery *n.* (*pl.* **-ies**) the saddles, other equipment, or business premises of a saddler.

saddle shoe *n.* esp. *N Amer.* a two-toned oxford shoe with a band of leather in the second colour across the instep, originally popular in the 1950s.

saddle stitch ● *n.* **1** a stitch of thread or a wire staple passed through the centre of a magazine or booklet. **2** a top stitch made with long stitches on the upper side alternated with short stitches on the

underside. ● *v.tr.* (**saddle-stitch**) **1** sew with a saddle stitch. **2** bind (a booklet etc.) with saddle stitches. □ **saddle-stitched** *adj.* **saddle-stitching** *n.*

Sadducee /'sædjʊ,si:/ *n.* a member of a Jewish sect or party of the time of Christ that denied the resurrection of the dead, the existence of spirits, and the obligation of the traditional oral law.

sadhu /'sɑ:du:/ *n.* (in India) a holy man, sage, or ascetic.

sadism /'seidizəm/ *n.* **1** a form of sexual perversion characterized by the enjoyment of inflicting pain or suffering on others (*compare* MASOCHISM 1). **2** *informal* the enjoyment of cruelty to others. □ **sadist** *n.* **sadistic** /sə'dɪstɪk/ *adj.* **sadistically** *adv.*

sado-masochism /,seido:'mæsə,kɪzəm/ *n.* sexual gratification achieved through inflicting and receiving pain. □ **sado-masochist** *n.* **sado-masochistic** *adj.*

sad sack *n.* esp. *N Amer. informal* a very inept person (also *attrib.*: *a sad-sack character*).

S.A.E. *abbr.* **1** self-addressed envelope. **2** stamped addressed envelope.

safari *n.* (*pl.* **-s**) **1** a hunting or scientific expedition, esp. in East Africa (*go on safari*). **2** a sightseeing trip esp. to see African animals in their natural habitat.

safe ● *adj.* **1 a** free of danger or injury. **b** out of or not exposed to danger (*safe from their enemies*). **2** affording security or not involving danger or risk (*put it in a safe place*). **3 a** reliable, certain (*a safe investment*; *a safe method*). **b** *Cdn & Brit.* (of a riding, seat in Parliament, etc.) usually won easily by a particular party. **4** prevented from escaping or doing harm (*safe behind bars*). **5** (also **safe and sound**) uninjured; with no harm done. **6 a** cautious and unenterprising; consistently moderate. **b** (of an action etc.) moderate, cautious, conservative (*a safe estimate*). **7** *Baseball* having reached a base without being put out (*safe at second*). **8** (in *comb.*) **a** resistant to damage etc. by the specified object or condition (*microwave-safe*). **b** not harmful to something specified (*child-safe*). ● *n.* **1** a strong lockable cabinet etc. for valuables. **2** a cupboard etc. for storing food (*pie safe*). **3** *N Amer.* (esp. *Cdn*) *slang* a condom. ● *adv. informal* in a safe manner (*play safe*). □ **on the safe side** with a margin of security against risks. □ **safely** *adv.*

safe bet *n.* a bet that is certain to succeed.

safe conduct *n.* **1** a privilege of immunity from arrest or harm, esp. on a particular occasion. **2** a document securing this.

safe deposit *n.* = SAFETY DEPOSIT.

safeguard ● *n.* **1** a proviso etc. that tends to prevent something undesirable. **2** a safe conduct. ● *v.tr.* guard or protect (rights etc.) by a precaution or stipulation.

safe harbour *n.* **1** a harbour offering protection to ships. **2** any place or circumstance offering protection.

safe house *n.* a place of refuge or rendezvous for spies, criminals, police informants, etc.

safekeeping *n.* preservation in a safe place.

safe sex *n.* (also **safer sex**) sexual activity in which precautions are taken to reduce the risk of spreading sexually transmitted diseases, esp. AIDS.

safety *n.* (*pl.* **-ies**) **1** the condition of being safe; freedom from danger or risks. **2 a** any of various devices for preventing injury from machinery (also *attrib.*: *safety feature*). **b** (*attrib.*) designating items of protective clothing (*safety helmet*). **3** *Football* **a** a defensive back who plays in a deep position. **b** a play in which the offensive team moves the ball into its own end zone and either downs the ball or is tackled there or moves it out of bounds, resulting in two points being awarded to the defensive team. **c** the two points so awarded. **4** *Baseball* = BASE HIT. □ **safety first** a motto advising caution.

safety belt *n.* **1** = SEAT BELT. **2** a belt or strap securing a person to prevent injury.

safety deposit *n.* (also **safe deposit**) a place in which valuables are stored (*safety deposit box*).

safety glass *n.* glass that will not splinter when broken.

safety glasses *n.pl.* eyeglasses with reinforced lenses to protect the eyes.

safety net *n.* **1** a net placed to catch an acrobat etc. in case of a fall. **2** any means of protection against difficulty or loss (*the social safety net*).

safety pin ● *n.* a pin with a point that is bent back to the head and is held in a guard when closed. ● *v.tr.* (**safety-pin**) fasten with a safety pin.

safety touch *n. Cdn Football* = SAFETY 3b.

safety valve *n.* **1** a valve opening automatically to relieve excessive pressure. **2** a means of giving harmless vent to excitement, energy, etc.

safflower *n.* an orange-flowered thistle-like plant, *Carthamus tinctorius*, whose seeds yield an edible oil.

saffron ● *n.* **1** an orange-yellow flavouring and food colouring made from the dried stigmas of the crocus, *Crocus sativus*. **2** the orange-yellow colour of this. ● *adj.* of an orange-yellow colour.

sag ● *v.intr.* (**sagged, sagging**) **1 a** sink or subside under weight or pressure, esp. unevenly. **b** droop, hang down loosely. **2** have a downward bulge or curve in the middle. **3** decline, weaken, diminish. **4** fall in price. ● *n.* **1 a** the amount that a rope etc. sags. **b** the distance from the middle of its curve to a straight line between its supports. **2** a sinking condition; subsidence. **3** a fall in price. □ **saggy** *adj.*

saga /ˈsɑːɡə, ˈsɒɡə/ *n.* **1** a long story of heroic achievement, esp. a medieval Icelandic or Norwegian prose narrative. **2** a series of connected books giving the history of a family etc. **3** a long involved story.

sagacious /səˈɡeɪʃəs/ *adj.* **1** wise, esp. on practicalities. **2** (of an animal) exceptionally intelligent; seeming to reason or deliberate. □ **sagaciously** *adv.* **sagacity** /səˈɡæsɪti/ *n.*

sagamore /ˈsæɡəˌmɔːr/ *n.* = SACHEM.

sage[1] ● *n.* **1** an aromatic herb, *Salvia officinalis*, with dull greyish-green leaves. **2** its leaves used in cooking. **3** (also **sage green**) the dull greyish-green colour of sage leaves. ● *adj.* (also **sage-green**) of this colour.

sage[2] ● *n.* **1** often *ironic* a profoundly wise person. **2** any of the ancients traditionally regarded as the wisest of their time. ● *adj.* **1** profoundly wise, esp. from experience. **2** of or indicating profound wisdom. **3** often *ironic* wise-looking; solemn-faced. □ **sagely** *adv.* **sageness** *n.*

sagebrush *n.* **1** a growth of shrubby aromatic plants of the genus *Artemisia*, esp. *A. tridentata*, found in some semi-arid regions of western N America. **2** this plant.

Sagittarius /ˌsædʒɪˈteriəs/ *n.* **1** a large constellation, said to represent a centaur carrying a bow and arrow. **2 a** the ninth sign of the zodiac. **b** a person born when the sun is in this sign, usu. between Nov. 22 and Dec. 21. □ **Sagittarian** *adj. & n.*

sago /ˈseɪɡoʊ/ *n.* (*pl.* **-os**) **1** a kind of starch, made from the powdered pith of the sago palm and used in puddings etc. **2** (in full **sago palm**) any of several tropical palms and cycads, esp. *Cycas circinalis* and *Metroxylon sagu*, from which sago is made.

Saharan *adj.* of or relating to the Sahara Desert in N Africa.

sahib /ˈsɑːhɪb, ˈsɑːɪb/ *n.* **1** (in India) a polite form of address, often placed after a person's name or title. **2** a gentleman (*pukka sahib*).

Sahtu Dene /ˌsɑːtuːˈdeneɪ/ ● *n.* **1** a member of a Dene people living near Great Bear Lake, NWT. **2** the Athapaskan language of this people. ● *adj.* of or relating to this people or their culture or language.

said ● *v.* past and past part. of SAY. ● *adj.* (prec. by *the*) the previously mentioned (*the said witness*).

sail ● *n.* **1** a piece of material extended on rigging to catch the wind and propel a boat or ship. **2** a ship's sails collectively. **3** a voyage or excursion in a sailing ship. **4** a ship, esp. as discerned from its sails. **5** (*collect.*) ships in a squadron or company (*a fleet of twenty sail*). **6** a wind-catching apparatus, usu. a set of boards, attached to the arm of a windmill. ● *v.* **1** *intr.* travel on water by the use of sails or engine power. **2** *tr.* **a** navigate (a ship etc.). **b** travel on (a sea). **3** *intr.* glide or move smoothly or in a stately manner. **4** *intr.* (often foll. by *through*) *informal* move or succeed easily (*sailed through the exams*). □ **make sail** *Naut.* **1** spread a sail or sails. **2** start a voyage. **sail close to the wind 1** sail as nearly against the wind as possible. **2** come close to indecency or dishonesty; risk overstepping the mark. **sail into** *informal* attack physically or verbally with force. **under sail** with sails set; sailing. □ **sailed** *adj.* (also in *comb.*).

sailboard *n.* a board with a mast and sail, used in windsurfing. □ **sailboarder** *n.* **sailboarding** *n.*

sailboat *n. N Amer.* a boat driven by sails.

sailcloth *n.* **1** canvas for sails. **2** a canvas-like dress material.

sailer *n.* a sailing vessel, esp. one that sails in a specified way.

sailfish *n.* any fish of the genus *Istiophorus*, with a large dorsal fin.

sailing ship *n.* (also **sailing craft, sailing vessel**, etc.) a vessel driven by sails.

sailmaker *n.* a person who makes, repairs, or alters sails. □ **sailmaking** *n.*

sailor *n.* **1** a member of a ship's crew, esp. one below the rank of officer. **2** a person who sails for recreation. **3** a person considered as liable or not to be seasick (*a good sailor*).

sailor collar *n.* a collar cut deep and square at the back, tapering to a V at the front.

sailplane *n.* a glider designed for sustained flight.

saint *n.* **1** a holy or (in some Churches) a canonized person regarded as having a place in heaven. **2** (**Saint** or **St.**) the title of a saint or archangel. **3 a** a very virtuous person; a person of great real or affected holiness. **b** a person regarded as worthy of high esteem by the followers of a movement or cause. **4** a soul in heaven (*with all the angels and saints*). **5** (*Bible, archaic*, and used by Puritans, Mormons, etc.) one of God's chosen people; a member of the Christian Church or one's own branch of it. □ **sainthood** *n.* **saintlike** *adj.*

St. Andrew's cross *n.* an X-shaped cross, esp. white on a blue background as the flag of Scotland.

St. Andrew's Day *n.* Nov. 30, the feast of St. Andrew, esp. as a celebration of Scottish heritage.

St. Bernard *n.* a breed of very large dog originally kept to rescue travellers by the monks of the Hospice on the Great St. Bernard Pass in the Alps.

St. David's Day *n.* March 1, the feast of St. David, esp. as a celebration of Welsh heritage.

sainted *adj.* sacred; of a saintly life; worthy to be regarded as a saint.

St. George's cross *n.* a +-shaped cross, red on a white background.

St. George's Day *n.* April 23, the feast day of St. George, esp. as a celebration of English heritage.

St. James Street *n. Cdn* **1** a street in Montreal where the offices of many financial institutions are located. **2** the moneyed interests of Montreal, esp. as opposed to other regions of Canada.

Saint-Jean-Baptiste Day /sæ͂ ˌʒɑ̃ bæˈtiːst/ *n. Cdn* (in Quebec) the former official name (still commonly in use) for the Fête nationale, June 24.

saintly *adj.* (**-ier, -iest**) very holy or virtuous; befitting a saint. □ **saintliness** *n.*

St. Patrick's Day *n.* March 17, the feast day of St. Patrick, on which Irish heritage is celebrated.

saint's day *n.* (*pl.* **saints' days**) a Church festival in memory of a saint.

sake¹ *n.* (esp. **for the sake of** or **for one's sake**) **1** out of consideration for; in the interest of; because of; owing to (*for my own sake as well as yours*). **2** in order to please, honour, get, or keep (*for the sake of uniformity*). □ **for Christ's** (or **God's** or **goodness'** or **Heaven's** or **Pete's** etc.) **sake** an expression of urgency, impatience, supplication, anger, etc. **for old times' sake** in memory of former times.

sake² /ˈsɒki/ *n.* (also **saké, saki**) a Japanese alcoholic drink made from fermented rice.

salaam /səˈlɒm/ ● *n.* **1** (in Muslim countries and India) the salutation 'Peace'. **2** an Indian obeisance, with or without the salutation, consisting of a low bow of the head and body with the right palm on the forehead. ● *v.* **1** *tr.* make a salaam to (a person). **2** *intr.* make a salaam.

salable esp. *US var. of* SALEABLE.

salacious /səˈleɪʃəs/ *adj.* **1** lustful; lecherous. **2** (of writings, pictures, talk, etc.) tending to cause sexual desire. □ **salaciously** *adv.* **salaciousness** *n.*

salad *n.* **1** a cold dish of various mixtures of raw or cooked vegetables, esp. lettuce, tomatoes, etc., or pasta, sometimes combined with meat or cheese, and usu. seasoned with oil and vinegar or other dressing. **2** *N Amer.* a mixture of fish, meat, etc. with mayonnaise and other seasonings, often as a sandwich filling (*egg salad*). **3** a vegetable or herb suitable for eating raw, e.g. lettuce.

salad days *n.pl.* a period of youthful inexperience.

salal /səˈlæl/ *n.* a shrub of western N America, *Gaultheria shallon*, with racemes of pink or white flowers and edible purple-black berries.

salamander /ˈsæləˌmændər/ *n.* **1** any tailed scaleless newt-like amphibian of the order Caudata. **2** a mythical lizard-like creature thought able to endure fire. **3** an elemental spirit living in fire.

salami *n.* (*pl.* **-s**) a highly-seasoned dried sausage often flavoured with garlic.

sal ammoniac /ˌsæl əˈmoːniˌæk/ *n.* ammonium chloride, a white crystalline salt.

salary ● *n.* (*pl.* **-ies**) a fixed regular payment made by an employer to an employee, esp. payment made for professional or non-manual work, usu. expressed as an annual sum (*a $35,000 salary*). ● *v.tr.* (**-ies, -ied**) (usu. as **salaried** *adj.*) pay a salary to.

salbutamol /sælˈbjuːtəmɒl/ *n.* a drug used esp. as a bronchodilator to treat asthma.

Salchow /ˈsaʊkaʊ/ *n.* Figure Skating a jump from the backward inside edge of one skate to the backward outside edge of the other, with a full turn in the air.

sale *n.* **1** the exchange of a commodity for money etc.; an act or instance of selling. **2** the amount sold (*the sales were enormous*). **3** (in *pl.*) the branch of a company etc. concerned with the selling of goods (also *attrib.*: *sales staff*). **4** an offering of goods or services at reduced prices for a period, e.g. at the end of a season etc. **5 a** an event at which goods are sold. **b** a public auction. □ **for sale** offered for purchase. **on sale** for sale, esp. at a reduced price.

saleable *adj.* fit to be sold; finding purchasers. □ **saleability** *n.*

sales clerk *n. N Amer.* a salesperson in a store.

saleslady *n.* (*pl.* **-ies**) a saleswoman.

salesman *n.* (*pl.* **-men**) a man employed to sell goods or services in a store etc. or as an agent between the producer and retailer; a sales representative.

salesmanship *n.* **1** skill in selling. **2** selling techniques.

salesperson *n.* (*pl.* **-people** or **-persons**) a salesman or saleswoman.

sales pitch *n.* an argument used to persuade someone, esp. to buy something.

sales representative *n.* (also *informal* **sales rep**) a person who represents a business to prospective customers and solicits orders.

salesroom *n.* **1** a room in which merchandise is shown for sale. **2** a room in which items are auctioned.

sales talk *n.* persuasive talk to promote the sale of goods or the acceptance of an idea etc.

sales tax *n.* a tax on sales or on the receipts from sales, added to the cost of a purchase.

saleswoman *n.* (*pl.* **-women**) a woman employed to sell goods or services in a store etc. or as an agent between the producer and retailer.

salicylate /səˈlɪsɪˌleɪt/ *n.* a salt or ester of salicylic acid.

salicylic acid /ˌsælɪˈsɪlɪk/ *n.* a bitter chemical used as a fungicide and in acetylsalicylic acid and dyes.

salient /ˈseɪliənt/ ● *adj.* **1** most important or notable. **2** (of an angle etc.) pointing outwards (*opp.* RE-ENTRANT *adj.* 1). ● *n.* **1** a salient angle or part of a work in fortification. **2** an outward bulge in a line of military attack or defence. □ **salience** *n.* **saliently** *adv.*

saline /ˈseɪliːn/ ● *adj.* **1** (of natural waters) impregnated with or containing salt or salts. **2** (of food or drink etc.) tasting of salt. **3** of chemical salts. **4** of the nature of a salt. **5** (of medicine) containing a salt or salts of alkaline metals or magnesium, esp. sodium chloride. ● *n.* (in full **saline solution**) a solution of salt in water. □ **salinity** /səˈlɪnɪti/ *n.* (*pl.* **-ies**). **salinization** *n.*

Salisbury steak /ˈsɒlzbəri/ *n. N Amer.* a patty of minced beef mixed with milk, bread crumbs, and seasoning, and cooked.

Salish /ˈsælɪʃ/ *n.* = SNE NAY MUXW.

Salishan /ˈsælɪʃən/ ● *n.* an Aboriginal language group of the west coast of N America, including Comox, Halkomelem, Lillooet, Nuxalk, Okanagan, Sechelt, Shuswap, Squamish, Straits, and Nlaka'pamux. ● *adj.* of or relating to this group.

saliva *n.* liquid secreted into the mouth by glands to provide moisture and facilitate chewing and swallowing; spittle. □ **salivary** /ˈsælɪveri/ *adj.*

salivate /ˈsælɪveɪt/ *v.intr.* secrete or discharge saliva esp. in excess or in anticipation. □ **salivation** *n.*

sallow ● *adj.* (**sallower, sallowest**) (of the skin) of a sickly yellow or pale brown. ● *v.tr. & intr.* make or become sallow. □ **sallowness** *n.*

Sally *n. informal* (usu. prec. by *the*) the Salvation Army.

sally (*pl.* **-ies**) ● *n.* **1** a sudden charge from a fortification upon its besiegers. **2** an excursion. **3** a lively remark esp. by way of attack upon a person or thing or of a diversion in argument. **4** a sudden start into activity; an outburst. ● *v.intr.* (**-ies, -ied**) **1** (usu. foll. by *out, forth*) go for a walk, set out on a journey, etc. **2** (usu. foll. by *out*) make a military sally.

Sally Ann *n. Cdn & Brit. informal* (usu. prec. by *the*) the Salvation Army.

salmon ● *n.* (*pl.* same or (esp. of types) **-s**) **1** a migratory fish of the family Salmonidae, esp. of the genus *Salmo*, much prized for its pink flesh. **2** any of various similar but unrelated fishes. **3** (also **salmon pink**) the colour of salmon flesh, usu. pink with a tinge of orange. ● *adj.* (also **salmon-pink**) of the colour of salmon.

salmonberry *n. N Amer.* **1** any of several pink- or orange-fruited N American brambles, esp. the pink-flowered *Rubus spectabilis* of the west coast. **2** the fruit of such a shrub.

salmonella /ˌsælməˈnelə/ *n.* (*pl.* **-ae** /-iː/ or **-s**) **1** a bacterium of the genus *Salmonella* comprising pathogenic rod-shaped forms, some of which cause food poisoning, typhoid, and paratyphoid in people and various diseases in animals. **2** food poisoning caused by this.

salmonellosis /ˌsælməneˈloʊsɪs/ *n.* infection with, or a disease caused by, salmonellae.

salmonid /ˈsælmənɪd, sælˈmɒnɪd/ ● *adj.* of or relating to the family Salmonidae, which includes salmon and trout. ● *n.* a fish of this family.

salmon trout *n.* a lake trout or Dolly Varden trout.

salon *n.* **1** a boutique or parlour specializing in fashionable products such as clothes, or services such as hairdressing. **2** the reception room of a mansion or large house; a drawing-room. **3 a** an exhibition of painting, sculpture, books, etc. **b** (**Salon**) an annual exhibition in Paris of the work of living artists. **4** a gathering of intellectuals etc. hosted by a celebrity or socialite.

saloon *n. N Amer.* **1** *hist.* a bar found esp. in mining, logging, and ranching communities of the Old West, often associated with heavy drinking, gambling, prostitution, and fighting. **2** a bar or tavern, esp. one modelled after a saloon of the Old West.

salsa /ˈbælsə/ *n.* **1** a Latin American spicy sauce made with tomatoes and chilies etc. and used usu. as a dip or garnish. **2 a** a kind of dance music of Latin American origin, incorporating jazz and rock elements. **b** a dance performed to this music.

salsa verde *n.* **1** an Italian sauce made with olive oil, garlic, capers, anchovies, vinegar or lemon juice, and a large quantity of chopped parsley, usu. served with fish. **2** a Mexican sauce of finely chopped onion, garlic, coriander, parsley, and hot peppers.

SALT /sɒlt/ *abbr.* Strategic Arms Limitation Talks (or Treaty).

salt ● *n.* **1 a** a substance, sodium chloride, found esp. in water or as a reddish brown mineral. **b** this substance, esp. in a white, granular form, used esp. for seasoning and preserving food. **c** = ROAD SALT. **2** a chemical compound formed from the reaction of an acid with a base, with all or part of the hydrogen of the acid replaced by a metal or metal-like radical. **3** (often in *pl.*) a substance resembling common salt, used esp. as a medicine or cosmetic (*bath salts*). **4** salt mixed with a usu. specified flavouring used as a seasoning (*garlic salt*). **5** an experienced sailor. ● *adj.* **1** containing or tasting of salt (*salt air*). **2** (of beef, fish,

etc.) treated, cured, or preserved with salt (*salt cod*). **3** (of a plant) growing in the sea or in salt marshes. ● *v.tr.* **1** cure or preserve (meat or fish etc.) with salt or brine. **2** season with salt. **3** sprinkle with salt, esp. in order to melt snow or ice. **4 a** make (a geological sample etc.) appear to be more valuable a source than it is by depositing extraneous ore etc. in it. **b** fraudulently increase the figures represented in (the books, accounts, etc.). □ **salt away** *informal* save or stash (money, information, etc.) for the future. **the salt of the earth 1** a person or people of great worthiness, reliability, honesty, etc. **2** those people whose qualities are a model for the rest. **take with a grain** (or **pinch**) **of salt** be justifiably skeptical of; believe only in part. **worth one's salt** deserving what one earns; capable.

salt and pepper *adj.* having dark and light (esp. grey) colours interspersed.

saltbox *N Amer.* (*Maritimes, Nfld, & New England*) ● *adj.* designating a house etc. with two storeys at the front and one at the back, having a steep pitched roof sloping towards the back. ● *n.* a saltbox house.

saltcellar *n.* a small container for holding salt.

saltchuck *n. N Amer.* (*BC, Alaska, & US Northwest*) *informal* the ocean, or an inlet, canal, or bay, etc. of salt water.

salt dome *n.* a mass of salt forced up into the overlying strata of sedimentary rock, sometimes forming a trap for gas and oil etc.

Salteaux *var. of* SAULTEAUX.

salted *adj.* seasoned, treated, or preserved with salt.

salter *n.* esp. *Cdn* a truck which dispenses salt on roads to melt snow and ice.

salt fish *n. N Amer. & Caribbean* preserved cod that has been split, salted, and dried.

salt hay *n. N Amer.* hay made from grasses that have grown in salt meadows.

saltie *n. Cdn informal* an ocean-going ship.

saltine /sɒlˈtiːn/ *n.* esp. *N Amer.* a salted cracker.

salting *n.* **1 a** the action of applying salt as a seasoning. **b** the process of covering meat, fish, etc. in salt or soaking it in brine in order to preserve it. **2** (esp. in *pl.*) a salt marsh.

salt lake *n.* a lake of salt water.

salt lick *n.* **1** a place where animals go to lick naturally occurring salt from the ground. **2** a block of salt or a preparation of salt given to domestic horses and cattle etc. to lick.

salt marsh *n.* (also **saltwater marsh**) a marsh that has been flooded by the tide, sometimes used as a pasture or for collecting water for making salt.

salt meadow *n. N Amer.* a meadow subject to flooding with salt water.

salt mine *n.* **1** a mine yielding rock salt. **2** *jocular* a place of gruelling labour, esp. one's workplace.

saltpetre /ˌsɒltˈpiːtər/ *n.* potassium nitrate, a white crystalline salty substance used esp. in manufacturing gunpowder and wrongly believed to curb libido.

salt pond *n.* (also **saltwater pond**) *N Amer.* an inlet or small pool of sea water barely joined to the ocean.

salt pork *n. N Amer.* cured pork fat, highly salted.

salt water ● *n.* **1** water with a high concentration of salt, esp. sea water. **2** the ocean, sea, etc. ● *adj.* (usu. **saltwater**) **1** of, pertaining to, or consisting of salt water. **2** living in or by a body of salt water.

saltwater taffy *n.* a candy made by boiling sugar or molasses and butter in sea water or salted fresh water.

salty *adj.* (**-ier, -iest**) **1** tasting of, containing, or preserved with salt. **2 a** (of humour etc.) racy, risqué.

b (of language) coarse, vulgar. **3** relating to or characteristic of a sailor or life at sea. □ **saltiness** *n.*

salubrious /sə'lu:briəs/ *adj.* **1** favourable to good health. **2** pleasant; agreeable.

salutary /'sælju,teri/ *adj.* producing good effects.

salutation /,sælju:'teiʃən/ *n.* **1** a sign or expression of greeting or recognition of another's arrival or departure. **2** the initial words of a letter used to address the person being written to. **3** the act or an instance of saluting; a gesture of respect.

salute ● *n.* **1** a gesture of respect, courteous recognition, or solidarity, esp. when arriving or departing. **2** *Military & Naut.* a prescribed or specified movement of the hand, weapons, or flags as a sign of respect or recognition. **3** the discharge of a gun or guns as a formal or ceremonial sign of respect or celebration. **4** a tribute or testimonial (to). ● *v.* **1** *tr.* make a salute to. **b** *intr.* (often foll. by *to*) perform a salute. **2** *tr.* (foll. by *with*) receive or greet with (a smile, handshake, etc.). □ **in salute** as a form of salute (*we raised our glasses in salute*).

Salvadoran (also **Salvadorean**) ● *adj.* of or relating to El Salvador, a republic in Central America. ● *n.* **1** a native or national of El Salvador. **2** a person of Salvadoran descent.

salvage ● *v.tr.* **1** save or recover (materials) from a shipwreck, fire, etc. **2** recover, save, or preserve (something) from the brink of loss or ruin (*tried to salvage their marriage*). ● *n.* **1** the rescue of a ship, its cargo, or other property from loss at sea, destruction by fire, etc. **2** the retrieval or saving of waste materials for recycling. **3** property or materials that have been salvaged. □ **salvageable** *adj.* **salvager** *n.*

salvation *n.* **1** the act of saving or being saved. **2** preservation from destruction, harm, etc. **3** the saving of the soul through deliverance from sin and its consequences. **4** a person or thing that saves (*her policies were the salvation of the country's economy*).

Salvation Army *n.* an international evangelical organization with a military structure, which assists the poor and homeless.

salvationism *n.* **1** (**Salvationism**) the principles or methods of the Salvation Army. **2** a religious teaching laying particular stress on individual salvation. □ **salvationist** *n. & adj.* (also **Salvationist**).

salve /sælv, sæv/ ● *n.* **1** a healing ointment. **2** a thing that soothes (hurt feelings, an uneasy conscience, etc.). ● *v.tr.* soothe or calm (pride, conscience, etc.).

salver /'sælvər/ *n.* a tray usu. of silver or other metal, on which drinks, letters, etc. are presented.

salvia /'sælviə/ *n.* any plant of the genus *Salvia* of the mint family, esp. *S. splendens* with red or blue flowers.

salvo /'sælvo:/ *n.* (*pl.* **-oes** or **-os**) **1** the simultaneous or concentrated discharge of artillery or other weapons in battle or as a salute. **2** a sudden vigorous or aggressive act or series of acts.

salvor /'sælvər/ *n.* a person engaged in, assisting in, or attempting salvage.

SAM *abbr.* surface-to-air missile.

samara /'sæmərə, sə'mɑr-/ *n.* a dry winged fruit, as in the maple etc.

Samaritan /sə'mærɪtən/ ● *n.* **1** (in full **good Samaritan**) a charitable or helpful person. **2** a native of Samaria in W Jordan. **3** the language of this people. ● *adj.* of Samaria or the Samaritans.

samarium /sə'meriəm/ *n.* a soft silvery metallic element, used in making alloys.

Sama-Veda /,sæmə'veidə, -vi:də/ *n.* an ancient collection of sacred Hindu hymns and incantations, traditionally called the third Veda but originating outside Vedic society.

samba /'sæmbə/ ● *n.* **1** a rhythmically complex Brazilian dance of African folk origin. **2** a related ballroom dance of moderate tempo. **3** the music for this. ● *v.intr.* (**sambas, sambaed** /-bəd/ or **samba'd, sambaing** /-bəɪŋ/) dance the samba.

sambuca /zam'buka/ *n.* an Italian aniseed-flavoured liqueur traditionally served aflame with a coffee bean floating on top.

same ● *adj.* **1** (often prec. by *the*) **a** identical in form, appearance, or number (*the same dress; they are the same age*). **b** not different (*we go to the same doctor*). **2** unchanged, unvarying, uniform (*always serves the same dish*). **3** (of a person or thing) previously alluded to (*this same child went on to become a doctor*). ● *pron.* (prec. by *the*) the same person or thing. ● *adv.* (usu. prec. by *the*) similarly; in the same way (*I hope you feel the same*). □ **all** (or **just**) **the same** nevertheless; anyway. **at the same time 1** simultaneously. **2** notwithstanding. **be all** (or **just**) **the same** to be a matter of indifference, or of little importance or interest (*if it's all the same to you, I'd rather go out*). **same difference** *informal* no difference, the same thing. **same here** *informal* the same applies to me. **the same to you!** may you do, have, find, etc., the same thing; likewise. **the very same** emphatically the same. □ **sameness** *n.*

same-day *adj.* **1** designating a service provided on the day of purchase etc. **2** occurring on the same day as another related event (*a same-day news conference*).

same-sex *adj.* designating or pertaining to a sexual relationship in which both partners are of the same sex (*same-sex couple*).

Sam Hill *n. N Amer. slang euphemism* (usu. prec. by *in* or *the*) = HELL *interj.* (*what in Sam Hill are we going to do now?*).

Sami /'sɒmi/ ● *n.* the Lapps collectively. ● *adj.* of or relating to the Lapps. ¶This is the preferred native and scholarly term.

Samoan /sə'mo:ən/ ● *adj.* of or relating to Samoa, a group of islands in Polynesia. ● *n.* **1** a native or inhabitant of Samoa. **2** a person of Samoan descent.

samosa /sə'mo:sə/ *n.* an Indian snack consisting of a triangular pastry stuffed with a spicy mixture of diced vegetables or meat, fried in ghee or oil.

samovar /'sæmə,vɑr/ *n.* a metal, usu. ornate, Russian urn for making tea, with an internal heating tube to keep water at boiling point.

Samoyed /'sæmə,jed/ *n.* a breed of white dog, once used for working in the Arctic, having a thick shaggy coat, stocky build, pricked ears, and a tail curling over the back.

sampan /'sæm,pæn/ *n.* a small boat or skiff with a flat bottom usu. propelled by a scull or oars set in the stern, used along the coasts and rivers of the Far East.

sample ● *n.* **1** a small part or quantity intended to show what the whole is like. **2** a small amount of a product given usu. free of charge to prospective customers. **3** a specimen, esp. one taken for scientific testing or analysis (*a blood sample*). **4** *Statistics* a portion selected from a population, the study of which is intended to provide statistical estimates relating to the whole. **5** a unit of sound or piece of music that has been digitalized. **6** an illustrative or typical example (*provide a writing sample*). ● *v.tr.* **1** try or examine (something) by experiencing it or taking a sample (*sample our down-home cooking*). **2 a** ascertain the momentary value of (an analog signal) many times a second so that these values may be represented digitally; convert (an analog signal) to a digital one. **b** record (sound) digitally for subsequent electronic processing. □ **sampling** n.

sampler n. **1** a piece of embroidery sewn in various stitches as a demonstration of skill, usu. containing the alphabet or mottos and often displayed on a wall. **2** an electronic device used to digitalize analog sound or music. **3** esp. N Amer. a collection of representative items etc. **4** a device for obtaining samples for scientific study.

samurai /'sæmʊˌraɪ/ n. (pl. same) **1** (in feudal Japan) a member of a military caste. **2** a Japanese army officer.

San /sɒn/ ● n. (pl. same) **1** a member of the aboriginal Bushmen of southern Africa. **2 a** the group of Khoisan languages spoken by the San. **b** any of these languages. ● adj. of or relating to the San or their languages.

sanatorium /ˌsænəˈtɔːrɪəm/ n. (pl. **-s** or **sanatoria** /-rɪə/) an establishment for the treatment of convalescents and those suffering chronic mental or physical disorders, tuberculosis, etc.

Sancerre /sɑ̃ˈsɛr/ n. a light white (occasionally red) wine, produced in central France.

sanctify v.tr. (**-ies, -ied**) **1** consecrate; make holy. **2** purify or free from sin. **3** make legitimate or binding by religious sanction. **4** make productive of or conducive to holiness. □ **sanctification** n.

sanctimonious /ˌsæŋktɪˈməʊnɪəs/ adj. affecting or pretending piety, sanctity, or holiness. □ **sanctimoniously** adv. **sanctimoniousness** n. **sanctimony** /'sæŋktɪˌməʊnɪ/ n.

sanction ● n. **1** approval or encouragement granted for a particular action. **2** the action of making something legally binding; official ratification. **3** (esp. in pl.) military or esp. economic action by a country to coerce another to conform to an international agreement or norms of conduct. **4** a penalty or reward enacted to enforce obedience to a law or rule. ● v.tr. **1** authorize, ratify, or agree to (an action etc.). **2** enforce (conduct, a legal obligation, etc.) esp. by attaching a penalty to the transgression.

sanctity n. (pl. **-ies**) **1** holiness of life; saintliness. **2** sacredness. **3** inviolability.

sanctuary n. (pl. **-ies**) **1** a holy place such as a church or temple etc. **2 a** esp. Jewish Hist. the inmost recess or holiest part of a temple etc.; the holy of holies. **b** the part of a church containing the altar. **3** a place where birds, wild animals, etc., are bred and protected. **4** a place of refuge, esp. a church or sacred building. **5** immunity from arrest; asylum. □ **take sanctuary** resort to a place of refuge.

sanctum n. (pl. **-s, sancta**) **1** a holy place. **2** informal a person's private room, study, or den.

Sanctus n. **1** the prayer beginning 'Holy, holy, holy' said or sung at the end of the Eucharistic preface in some Christian liturgies. **2** a musical setting of this.

sand ● n. **1** a loose granular substance resulting from the weathering of esp. siliceous rocks, found on beaches, deserts, etc. **2** (in pl.) an area predominantly of sand. **3** a light yellow-brown colour like that of sand. **4** N Amer. informal courage, determination. ● v.tr. **1** smooth or grind by rubbing with sandpaper. **2** sprinkle or cover with, or bury under, sand. □ **sand down** sand (a usu. painted surface) down to the bare wood etc. **sands of time** the moments or passage of time. **the sands are running out** the allotted time is nearly at an end.

sandal n. a light open shoe consisting of a sole attaching to the foot with light straps, worn esp. in warm weather.

sandalled adj. wearing sandals.

sandalwood n. the scented wood of any of several trees of the genus Santalum, esp. the white sandalwood of India, used esp. in carving and incense.

sandbag ● n. a bag filled with sand, esp.: **1** stacked with others to make temporary fortifications for the defence of a military camp against enemy fire. **2** used to protect buildings etc. against flood waters, heavy winds, etc. **3** used as a weapon to inflict a heavy blow without leaving a mark. **4** used as ballast esp. for a boat or balloon. ● v.tr. (**-bagged, -bagging**) **1 a** tr. place sandbags around or against (a building, river, etc.) in order to fortify it. **b** intr. build protective dikes with sandbags. **2** tr. knock down with a blow from a sandbag. **3** tr. N Amer. coerce by harsh means; bully. **4** tr. & intr. hinder or obstruct (a business transaction, the passage of legislation, etc.), esp. with prolonged talks or debate. **5** tr. & intr. Sport lull (an opponent) into overconfidence by downplaying one's chances or abilities. □ **sandbagger** n.

sandbank n. a deposit of sand formed in shallow water by the action of tides and currents.

sandbar n. a large bank of sand forming in a river or sea, often exposed at low tide.

sandblast v.tr. roughen, treat, or clean with a jet of sand driven by compressed air or steam. □ **sandblaster** n.

sandbox n. N Amer. **1** a shallow pile of sand enclosed on four sides for children to play in. **2** (attrib.) jocular designating juvenile behaviour or an attitude characteristic of a child at play (sandbox diplomacy).

sandcastle n. a shape like a castle made in sand, usu. by a child on a beach.

sandcherry n. (pl. **-ies**) any of several shrubby wild cherries of N America, purple-leaved varieties of which are often cultivated in gardens.

sand dollar n. esp. N Amer. any of various round flat sea urchins, esp. of the order Clypeasteroida.

sand dune n. a shifting mound or ridge of sand formed by the wind.

sand eel n. = SAND LANCE.

sander n. **1** a power tool that uses sandpaper to smooth surfaces, remove layers of paint, etc. **2 a** a vehicle that sprinkles sand on icy streets and highways etc. **b** a person operating such a vehicle.

sanderling n. a small wading bird, Calidris alba, of the sandpiper family.

sandfly n. (pl. **-ies**) **1** any midge of the genus Simulium; a blackfly. **2** any biting fly of the genus Phlebotomus transmitting leishmaniasis.

S&H abbr. shipping and handling.

sandhill n. a hill of sand, esp. a dune on a shore.

sandhill crane n. a grey N American crane, Grus canadensis, with a bare reddish patch on the forehead.

sand lance n. (also **sand launce**) N Amer. any eel-like fish of the family Ammodytidae or Hypotychidae.

sandlot n. N Amer. a small plot of unoccupied land used by children for games and sports (also attrib.: sandlot baseball). □ **sandlotter** n.

S&M abbr. sexual gratification achieved through inflicting and receiving pain; sadism and masochism or sado-masochism.

sandman n. a make-believe figure that is supposed to make children sleep by sprinkling sand or sleep in their eyes; a personification of tiredness.

sandpaper ● n. strong paper coated with sand or another abrasive, used for smoothing or roughening up a surface. ● v.tr. = SAND v. 1. □ **sandpapery** adj.

sandpiper *n.* any of various wading birds of the family Scolopacidae.

sandpit *n.* a pit from which sand is or has been excavated.

sandstone *n.* **1** any of various sedimentary rocks of consolidated grains of sand, esp. of quartz, red, yellow, brown, grey, or white in colour. **2** any clastic rock containing particles visible to the naked eye.

sandstorm *n.* a storm, esp. in a desert, of wind with clouds of sand.

sand trap *n. N Amer.* a shallow pit of fine sand serving as an obstacle or hazard on a golf course.

sandwich /'sændwɪtʃ, 'sænwɪtʃ, 'sæm-/ ● *n.* **1** two or more slices of usu. buttered bread with a filling. **2** anything resembling a sandwich in composition or appearance (*an ice cream sandwich*). ● *v.* **1** *tr.* place or insert (a thing) between two dissimilar ones **2** *tr. & intr.* squeeze in between others. **3** *tr.* (in football, hockey, etc.) trap or crush (an opposing player) between oneself and a teammate, the boards, etc.

sandwich board *n.* **1** a pair of signs, usu. bearing advertisements, joined at the top by straps and suspended from the shoulders so that one sign is displayed over the front of the wearer, the other over the back. **2** a similar pair of signs joined at the top and forming a tent so that they may be free-standing.

sandwich generation *n. N Amer.* the generation of adults in their late 20s or early 30s trying to raise children while also caring for aged parents.

sandy *adj.* (**-ier, -iest**) **1** composed of or containing a large proportion of sand. **2** having the texture of sand. **3 a** (of hair) light reddish-blond. **b** (of a person) having sandy hair. □ **sandiness** *n.*

sane /sein/ *adj.* **1** of sound mind; not mad. **2** (of views etc.) sensible, reasonable; moderate. □ **sanely** *adv.*

sang *past of* SING.

sang-froid /sæŋ'frwʌ, sã-, -fwʌ/ *n.* coolness of mind or action, esp. in the face of danger or adversity.

sangria /sæŋ'griːə/ *n.* a drink of red wine with water, sugar, fruit juice, sliced citrus fruit, and usu. soda.

sanguine /'sæŋgwɪn/ *adj.* **1** optimistic; confident. **2** *hist.* relating to the predominance of blood over the bodily humours, characterized by a ruddy complexion and a courageous, amorous disposition.

sanitarium /,sænɪ'teriəm/ *n.* (*pl.* **-s** or **sanitaria** /-riə/) *N Amer.* = SANATORIUM.

sanitary *adj.* **1** of or pertaining to the conditions affecting health, the promotion of good health, or protection against infection. **2** hygienic; free from or designed to kill or prevent germs, infection, etc.

sanitary engineer *n.* a person who works on the design, construction, or maintenance of systems needed to maintain public health, such as sewerage. □ **sanitary engineering** *n.*

sanitary landfill *n.* an area of garbage disposed of under layers of earth.

sanitary pad *n.* (also **sanitary napkin**) *N Amer.* an absorbent pad worn during menstruation.

sanitation *n.* **1** systems designed to protect or promote health. **2** the maintenance or improving of these. **3** the disposal of sewage and garbage.

sanitize *v.tr.* **1** make (something) hygienic or thoroughly free from germs; sterilize, disinfect. **2** *N Amer.* render (information etc.) more acceptable by removing indecent or disturbing material. □ **sanitization** *n.* **sanitizer** *n.*

sanitorium /,sænɪ'tɔriəm/ *n.* (*pl.* **-s** or **sanitoria** /-riə/) *N Amer.* = SANATORIUM.

sanity *n.* **1 a** the state of being sane. **b** mental health. **2** reasonableness, moderation.

sank *past of* SINK.

sans /sɒnz, sã/ *prep. jocular* without a.

sans-culotte /,sãkju:'lɒt/ *n.* **1** *hist.* a lower-class Parisian republican in the French Revolution. **2** an extreme republican or revolutionary.

Sansei /'sænsei/ *n.* (*pl.* same) a N American whose grandparents were immigrants from Japan.

Sanskrit /'sænskrɪt/ ● *n.* the ancient Indo-Aryan language of the Indian subcontinent, the principal language of religious writings and scholarship, the source of some of the modern languages of the area, and one of the languages recognized for official use in India. ● *adj.* of or in this language. □ **Sanskritic** *adj.*

sans serif ● *n.* a form of type without serifs. ● *adj.* without serifs.

Santa Claus (also **Santa**) a folk figure, usu. represented as a fat, white-bearded old man in a red suit, said to bring presents on Christmas Eve.

Santee /sæn'ti:/ *n.* **1** a member of a Dakota group originally inhabiting Minnesota, now also living in Manitoba and Saskatchewan. **2** the Siouan language of this people.

sap¹ ● *n.* **1** the fluid, chiefly water with dissolved sugars and mineral salts, that circulates in a plant and is essential to its growth. **2** the sap of the sugar maple, used for making maple syrup etc. (also *attrib.*: *sap bucket*). **3** vitality. **4** = SAPWOOD. ● *v.tr.* (**sapped, sapping**) drain or dry (wood) of sap.

sap² ● *n.* a tunnel or trench to conceal assailants' approach to a fortified place. ● *v.* (**sapped, sapping**) **1** *intr.* dig a sap or saps. **b** approach by a sap. **2** *tr.* undermine; make insecure by removing the foundations. **3** *tr.* weaken or destroy insidiously (*my energy had been sapped*).

sap³ *n. slang* a foolish person.

sapient /'seipiənt/ *adj. literary* **1** wise. **2** pretending to be wise. □ **sapience** *n.* **sapiently** *adv.*

sapling *n.* **1** a young tree. **2** a youth.

sapodilla /,sæpə'dɪlə/ *n.* **1** a large tropical American evergreen, *Manilkara zapota*, with edible fruit and durable wood, and sap from which chicle is obtained. **2** (also **sapodilla plum**) the fruit of this tree.

saponin /'sæpənɪn/ *n.* any of a group of plant glycosides that foam when shaken with water, used in detergents and fire extinguishers.

sapper *n.* **1** a person who digs saps. **2** *N Amer.* a military engineer who detects and disarms mines. **3** (also **Sapper**) *Cdn & Brit.* a soldier having the rank of private in regiments of engineers.

sapphire ● *n.* **1** a transparent blue precious stone consisting of corundum. **2** precious transparent corundum of any colour. **3** (also **sapphire blue**) an intense blue colour. ● *adj.* **1** (also **sapphire-blue**) of sapphire blue. **2** set with a sapphire or sapphires.

sappy *adj.* (**-ier, -iest**) **1** *N Amer. informal* too sentimental. **2** full of sap. □ **sappily** *adv.* **sappiness** *n.*

saprophyte /'sæprə,fʌɪt/ *n.* any plant or microorganism living on dead or decayed organic matter. □ **saprophytic** /-'fɪtɪk/ *adj.*

sapsucker *n.* a small woodpecker that pecks holes in trees and visits them for sap and insects.

sapwood *n.* the soft outer layers of recently formed wood between the heartwood and the bark.

SAR /sɑr/ *abbr.* SEARCH AND RESCUE.

Saracen /'særəsən/ *hist.* ● *n.* **1** an Arab or Muslim at the time of the Crusades. **2** a nomad of the Syrian

and Arabian desert. ● *adj.* of the Saracens. □
Saracenic /ˌsærə'senɪk/ *adj.*

Saran /sə'ræn/ *n.* (also **Saran Wrap**) *proprietary* clear thin plastic film, used to wrap foods.

sarcasm *n.* **1** the use of bitter or wounding, esp. ironic, remarks; language consisting of such remarks. **2** such a remark. □ **sarcastic** /sɑr'kæstɪk/ *adj.* **sarcastically** *adv.*

Sarcee /'sɑrsi:, -'si:/ ● *n.* **1** a member of a small Athapaskan group living on the Bow River near Calgary. **2** the language of this people. ● *adj.* of or relating to this people or their culture or language.

sarcoma /sɑr'ko:mə/ *n.* (*pl.* **-s** or **sarcomata** /-mətə/) a malignant tumour of connective or other non-epithelial tissue.

sarcophagus /sɑr'kɒfəgəs/ *n.* (*pl.* **sarcophagi** /-ˌgai, -ˌdʒai/) a stone coffin, esp. one adorned with a sculpture or inscription.

sardine *n.* **1** any of various fish of the herring family. **2** a young Atlantic or Pacific herring preserved in oil or brine and canned. **3** a young European pilchard likewise preserved. □ **like sardines** crowded close together (as sardines are in cans).

Sardinian /sɑr'dɪnɪən/ ● *n.* **1** a native or inhabitant of Sardinia, a large island in the Mediterranean Sea. **2** the Romance language of Sardinia. ● *adj.* of or relating to Sardinia or its people or language.

sardonic /sɑr'dɒnɪk/ *adj.* bitterly mocking or cynical. □ **sardonically** *adv.*

sargasso /sɑr'gæso:/ *n.* (also **sargassum** /-əm/) (*pl.* **-os** or **-oes** or **sargassa** /-ə/) any seaweed of the genus *Sargassum*, with berry-like air vessels, found floating in island-like masses, esp. in the Sargasso Sea, in the W Atlantic.

sarge *n. slang* sergeant.

sari *n.* (also **saree**) (*pl.* **-s**) a length of cotton or silk draped around the body, traditionally worn as a main garment by Indian women.

sarin /'sɑrɪn/ *n.* an organic phosphorus compound used as a nerve gas.

sarong /sə'rɒŋ/ *n.* **1** a Malay and Javanese garment, worn by both sexes, consisting of a long strip of (often striped) cloth worn tucked around the waist or under the armpits. **2** a woman's garment resembling this.

sarsaparilla /ˌsæspə'rɪlə/ *n.* **1** a preparation of the dried roots of various plants of the genus *Smilax*, used as a flavouring and formerly as a tonic. **2** any of the plants yielding this. **3** a soft drink flavoured with sarsaparilla. **4** a plant of the genus *Aralia*, used as a substitute for sarsaparilla.

SAR Tech *n. Cdn* a search and rescue technician, a non-commissioned member of the Canadian Forces specialized in performing rescue operations and highly trained in such related skills as parachuting, mountain climbing, first aid, etc.

sartorial /sɑr'tɔriəl/ *adj.* **1** of or relating to clothes or clothing. **2** of a tailor or tailoring. □ **sartorially** *adv.*

SASE *abbr. N Amer.* self-addressed stamped envelope.

sash *n.* **1** a long strip of cloth worn tied around the waist or over one shoulder. **2** a frame holding the glass in a sash window and usu. made to slide up and down in the grooves of a window aperture.

sashay *v.intr.* esp. *N Amer. informal* **1** walk or move casually or nonchalantly; saunter. **2** walk or move so as to attract attention.

sashimi /sæ'ʃiːmi/ *n.* a Japanese dish of garnished raw fish in thin slices.

sash window *n.* a window with one or two sashes.

Sask. *abbr.* Saskatchewan.

Saskatchewan Day *n. Cdn* (*Sask.*) a statutory holiday occurring on the first Monday in August.

Saskatchewanian /ˌsəˌskætʃə'wɒnɪən/ ● *adj.* of or relating to Saskatchewan. ● *n.* a native or inhabitant of Saskatchewan.

Saskatchewan Party *n.* a political party of Saskatchewan formed in 1997 by the Conservatives and some Liberals as an alternative to the NDP.

saskatoon *n. Cdn* (*Prairies*) **1** a shrub, *Amelanchier alnifolia*, of western N America. **2** (also **saskatoon berry**) the sweet purple berry of this shrub.

sasquatch /'sæskwɒtʃ/ *n.* a supposed yeti-like animal of northwestern N America.

sass *N Amer. informal* ● *n.* impudence, cheek. ● *v.tr.* be impudent to.

sassafras /'sæsəˌfræs/ *n.* **1** a small tree, *Sassafras albidum*, native to N America, with aromatic leaves and bark. **2** a preparation of oil extracted from the leaves or bark, used in medicines and perfumes.

sassy *adj.* (**-ier, -iest**) esp. *N Amer. informal* = SAUCY 1,2. □ **sassily** *adv.* **sassiness** *n.*

SAT *abbr. proprietary* SCHOLASTIC APTITUDE TEST.

Sat. *abbr.* Saturday.

sat *past and past part. of* SIT.

Satan the Devil; Lucifer.

satanic /sə'tænɪk/ *adj.* **1** of, like, or befitting Satan or Satanism. **2** diabolical, hellish. □ **satanically** *adv.*

Satanism *n.* **1** the worship of Satan. **2** a travesty of Christian forms, used in worship of Satan. **3** deliberate evil or wickedness. □ **Satanist** *n.*

satay /sæ'tei, 'sætei/ *n.* (also **saté**) an Indonesian and Malaysian dish of small pieces of meat grilled on a skewer and usu. served with spicy peanut sauce.

SATB *abbr. Music* soprano, alto, tenor, and bass.

satchel *n.* a small bag usu. of leather and hung from the shoulder with a strap, for carrying books etc. esp. to and from school.

sate *v.tr.* **1** gratify to the full. **2** weary with overabundance.

satellite ● *n.* **1** a celestial body orbiting the earth or another planet. **2** an artificial body placed in orbit round the earth or another planet, esp. for observation or remote sensing of the earth's surface, for astronomical observation, or as a relay for telecommunication. **3** a follower; a hanger-on. **4** something that is subordinate to or reliant on another place or thing (*lives in a satellite of Toronto*). ● *adj.* **1** transmitted by satellite (*satellite television*). **2** (of a region etc.) subordinate to another body etc.

satellite dish *n.* a saucer-shaped aerial for receiving broadcasting signals transmitted by satellite.

sati *var. of* SUTTEE.

satiate /'seiʃiˌeit/ *v.tr.* = SATE. □ **satiation** *n.*

satiety /sə'taiiti/ *n.* the state of feeling satiated.

satin ● *n.* **1** a fabric with a glossy surface on one side produced by a twill weave with the weft threads almost hidden. **2** a low-lustre paint. ● *adj.* **1** smooth as satin. **2** made of satin. ● *v.tr.* (**satined, satining**) give a glossy surface to (paper). □ **satiny** *adj.*

satinwood *n.* **1 a** (in full **Ceylon satinwood**) a tree, *Chloroxylon swietenia*, native to central and southern India and Ceylon. **b** a tree, *Zanthoxylum flavum*, native to the Caribbean and southern Florida. **2** the yellow glossy timber of either of these trees.

satire *n.* **1** the use of ridicule etc., to expose folly or vice or to lampoon an individual. **2** a work or composition using satire. **3** this genre of literature. □
satiric /sə'ti:rɪk/ *adj.* (also **satirical**). **satirically** *adv.*
satirist /'sætərɪst/ *n.* **satirization** *n.* **satirize** *v.tr.*

satisfaction n. **1** the act or an instance of satisfying; the state of being satisfied. **2** a thing that satisfies desire or gratifies feeling. **3** a thing that settles an obligation or pays a debt. **4** atonement; compensation (*demanded satisfaction*). □ **to one's satisfaction** so that one is satisfied.

satisfactory adj. satisfying expectations or needs; leaving no room for complaint (*a satisfactory result*). □ **satisfactorily** adv.

satisfy v. (**-ies, -ied**) **1** tr. a meet the expectations or desires of; comply with (a demand). **b** be accepted by (a person, a person's taste) as adequate; be equal to (a preconception etc.). **2** tr. put an end to (an appetite or want) by supplying what was required. **3** tr. rid (a person) of an appetite or want in a similar way. **4** intr. give satisfaction; leave nothing to be desired. **5** tr. pay (a debt or creditor). **6** tr. adequately meet, fulfil, or comply with (conditions, obligations, etc.). **7** tr. provide with adequate information or proof, convince (*satisfy the court of their innocence*). **8** tr. (in passive) **a** (foll. by with) contented or pleased with. **b** (foll. by to) demand no more than or consider it enough to do. □ **satisfy oneself** be certain in one's own mind. □ **satisfying** adj. **satisfyingly** adv.

satori /sə'tɔːri/ n. Buddhism sudden enlightenment.

satrap /'sætræp/ n. **1** a provincial governor in the ancient Persian Empire. **2** a subordinate ruler etc.

saturate v.tr. **1** fill with moisture; soak thoroughly. **2** fill to capacity. **3** cause (a substance) to absorb, hold, or combine with the greatest possible amount of another substance, or of moisture, magnetism, electricity, etc. **4** supply (a market) beyond the point at which the demand for a product is satisfied. **5** imbue with or steep in (learning, prejudice, etc.). **6** overwhelm by concentrated bombing. □ **saturation** n.

saturated adj. **1** completely wet. **2** (of a solution) containing the greatest amount of solute that it can for the temperature it is at. **3** (of fat molecules) containing the greatest number of hydrogen atoms. **4** (of colour) free from an admixture of white.

saturation point n. the stage beyond which no more can be absorbed or accepted.

Saturday ● n. the day of the week following Friday. ● adv. **1** on Saturday. **2** (**Saturdays**) on Saturdays; each Saturday.

satyr /'sætər, 'seɪt-/ n. **1** one of a class of Greek woodland gods with a horse's ears and tail, or (in Roman representations) with a goat's ears, tail, legs, and budding horns. **2** a lustful or sensual man.

sauce ● n. **1** any of various liquid or semi-liquid preparations eaten with food. **2** N Amer. stewed fruit, e.g. apples, eaten as dessert or used as a garnish. **3** something adding piquancy or excitement. **4** informal impudence, impertinence. **5** esp. N Amer. informal alcohol. ● v.tr. informal be impudent to. □ **sauceless** adj.

sauced adj. **1** served with a sauce. **2** N Amer. slang drunk.

saucepan n. a usu. metal pot, usu. round, often with a lid and long handle, used for cooking over heat.

saucer n. **1** a shallow circular dish, esp. for standing a teacup on. **2** something saucer-shaped (*flying saucer*).

saucy adj. (**-ier, -iest**) **1** impudent. **2** (of a person) perky. **3** N Amer. covered with sauce. **4** (of clothing) dashing (*a saucy hat*). □ **saucily** adv. **sauciness** n.

Saudi /'saʊdi/ (also **Saudi Arabian**) ● adj. of or relating to Saudi Arabia, a country in SW Asia occupying most of the Arabian peninsula, or its ruling dynasty. ● n. (pl. **Saudis**) **1** a person of Saudi nationality or descent. **2** a member of the ruling dynasty of Saudi Arabia.

sauerkraut /'saʊərˌkraʊt/ n. pickled cabbage.

sauger /'sɒɡər/ n. a N American fish of the perch family, *Stizoostedion canadense*, with a large mouth.

Saulteaux /'soːtoː/ (pl. same) ● n. **1** a member of an Aboriginal people formerly living on the shore of Lake Superior north of Sault Ste. Marie, now esp. in Manitoba. **2** the Ojibwa dialect of this people. ● adj. of or relating to this people or their language.

sauna n. **1** a special room filled with steam to clean and refresh the body. **2** a period spent in a sauna.

saunter ● v.intr. or go slowly; amble, stroll. ● n. a leisurely ramble. □ **saunterer** n.

saurian /'sɔːriən/ adj. of or like a lizard.

sauropod /'sɔːrəˌpɒd/ n. any of a group of plant-eating dinosaurs with a long neck and tail, and four thick limbs.

saury /'sɔːri/ n. (pl. **-ies**) any of various elongated marine fishes of the family Scomberescocidae, having narrow beaklike jaws, esp. *Scomberesox saurus* of the N Atlantic and southern hemisphere or *Cololabis saira* of the N Pacific.

sausage n. **1 a** ground meat seasoned and often mixed with other ingredients, usu. encased in cylindrical form in a skin. **b** a length of this. **2** a sausage-shaped object.

sausage meat n. minced pork used in sausages or as a stuffing etc.

sausage roll n. sausage meat enclosed in pastry and baked.

sauté /'soʊteɪ, -'teɪ, soː-/ ● v.tr. (**sautéed**) fry (food) quickly in a little hot fat. ● n. food cooked in this way.

Sauternes /soː'tɜːn/ n. a sweet white wine from Sauternes in the Bordeaux region of France.

Sauvignon /'soːviːnjɒ̃/ n. (also **Sauvignon Blanc**) **1** a variety of white grape used in winemaking. **2** a dry white wine made from these grapes.

savage ● adj. **1** fierce; cruel (*savage persecution*). **2** wild (*a savage animal*). **3** archaic offensive uncivilized; primitive. **4** informal angry; bad-tempered (*in a savage mood*). ● n. **1** archaic offensive a member of a primitive tribe. **2** a cruel or barbarous person. ● v.tr. **1** attack and bite or maul etc. **2** criticize fiercely. □ **savagely** adv. **savagery** n. (pl. **-ies**).

savannah /sə'vænə/ n. (also **savanna**) a grassy plain in the tropics and subtropics with few or no trees.

savannah sparrow n. a small sparrow, *Passerculus sandwichensis*, of the family Emberizidae, common throughout most of N America, found esp. in moist grasslands such as hayfields and meadows.

savant /sæ'vɑ̃, -'vɑ̃t/ n. a learned person, esp. a distinguished scientist etc.

save¹ ● v. **1** tr. rescue, protect, etc. from danger, discredit, etc. **2** tr. & intr. keep for future use; refrain from spending or using. **3** tr. a relieve from spending (money, time, trouble, etc.); prevent exposure to (annoyance etc.) (*saved myself $50*; *a word processor saves time*). **b** obviate the need or likelihood of (*soaking saves scrubbing*). **4** tr. preserve from damnation; convert (*saved her soul*). **5** tr. & refl. preserve (one's strength etc.) (*save your energy*). **6** tr. & intr. Computing store (data) on a hard drive etc. **7** tr. a avoid losing (a game, match, etc.). **b** prevent an opponent from scoring (a goal etc.). **c** stop (a ball etc.) from entering the goal. ● n. **1** Hockey etc. an act of preventing an opponent from scoring. **2** Baseball **a** a statistical credit given to a relief pitcher for maintaining a team's winning lead. **b** the action of maintaining such a lead. □ **save one's breath**

not waste time speaking to no effect. **save the day** (or **situation**) find or provide a solution to difficulty or disaster. **save face** preserve esteem; avoid humiliation. **save it** *N Amer. slang* shut up. **save one's neck** (or **skin** or **ass** or **bacon**) avoid loss, injury, or death; escape from danger. **save the trouble** avoid useless or pointless effort. □ **savable** *adj.* (also **saveable**). **saver** *n.*

save² *prep. & conj. archaic or literary* except.

saving ● *adj.* (often in *comb.*) making economical use of (*labour-saving*). ● *n.* **1** anything that is saved. **2** an economy. **3** (usu. in *pl.*) money saved. ● *prep.* **1** except (*all saving that one*). **2** without offence to (*saving your presence*).

saving grace *n.* a redeeming quality.

savings account *n.* an interest-paying bank account on which cheques may not usually be drawn.

savings and loan *n.* (in the US) a co-operative association which accepts savings at interest and lends money to savers for houses or other purchases.

savings bond *n.* = BOND *n.* 4.

saviour *n.* (also **savior**) **1** a person who saves or delivers from danger, destruction, etc. (*the country's saviour*). **2** (**Saviour**) *Christianity* (prec. by *the*, *our*) Christ.

savoir faire /ˌsævwɑr ˈfer/ *n.* the ability to act suitably in any situation.

savory *n.* (*pl.* **-ies**) any herb of the genus *Satureja*, esp. summer savory and winter savory, used esp. in cookery.

savour (also **savor**) ● *v.tr.* **1** appreciate and enjoy the taste of (food). **2** enjoy or appreciate (an experience etc.). ● *n.* **1** a characteristic taste, flavour, etc. **2** a quality suggestive of or containing a small amount of another.

savoury *adj.* (also **savory**) **1** having an appetizing taste or smell. **2** (of food) salty or piquant, not sweet (*a savoury omelette*). **3** pleasant; acceptable.

Savoy /ˈsævɔɪ, səˈvɔɪ/ *n.* (also **Savoy cabbage**) a hardy variety of cabbage with wrinkled leaves.

savvy *slang* ● *n.* knowingness; shrewdness. ● *adj.* (**-ier**, **-iest**) *N Amer.* knowing; shrewd.

saw¹ ● *n.* **1** a tool for cutting with a toothed blade. **2** *Zool. etc.* a serrated organ or part. ● *v.* (*past part.* **sawn** /sɒn/ or **sawed**) **1** *tr.* **a** cut with a saw. **b** make (boards etc.) with a saw. **2** *intr.* use a saw. **3** *a intr.* move to and fro with a motion as of a saw or person sawing (*sawing away on his violin*). **b** *tr.* divide (the air etc.) with gesticulations. □ **saw logs** *N Amer. slang* snore. **saw off** *Cdn* compromise by trading concessions (*they sawed off over wages and job security*). **saw up** saw into pieces. □ **sawlike** *adj.*

saw² *past of* SEE¹.

saw³ *n.* a proverb; a maxim (*that's just an old saw*).

sawbill *n.* = MERGANSER.

sawbuck *n.* *N Amer.* **1** a sawhorse. **2** *slang* a $10 bill.

sawdust *n.* powdery wood particles produced in sawing.

sawed-off *adj.* **1** (of a gun) having part of the barrel sawn off to make it easier to handle and give a wider field of fire. **2** *informal* (of a person) short.

sawhorse *n.* a rack supporting wood for sawing.

sawlog *n.* a felled tree suitable for cutting into timber.

sawmill *n.* a factory in which wood is sawn mechanically into planks, boards, etc. □ **sawmiller** *n.* **sawmilling** *attrib.adj.*

sawn *past part.* of SAW¹.

saw-off *n.* *Cdn* **1** an arrangement between political rivals in which each agrees not to contest a seat etc.

held by the other. **2** any compromise involving mutual concessions. **3** a tie, deadlock, stalemate, etc.

sawtooth *adj.* (also **sawtoothed**) (esp. of a roof, wave, etc.) shaped like the teeth of a saw, esp. with one steep and one slanting side.

saw-whet owl *n.* a small brown N American owl of the genus *Aegolius*, of coniferous and deciduous woods.

sawyer /ˈsɔɪr, ˈsɒjɪr/ *n.* **1** a person who saws timber professionally. **2** any of various longhorn beetles esp. of the genus *Monochamus*, the larvae of which bore in the wood of conifers.

sax *n.* *informal* **1** a saxophone. **2** a saxophone player. □ **saxist** *n.*

saxifrage /ˈsæksɪfreɪdʒ, -frədʒ/ *n.* any plant of the genus *Saxifraga*, growing on rocky or stony ground and usu. bearing small white, yellow, or red flowers.

Saxon ● *n.* **1** *hist.* **a** a member of a Germanic people originally of N Germany, of which a portion conquered and occupied parts of England in the 5th–6th c. **b** (usu. **Old Saxon**) the language of the Saxons. **2** = ANGLO-SAXON *n.* **3** a native of modern Saxony in N Germany. ● *adj.* **1** *hist.* of or concerning the Saxons. **2** belonging to or originating from the Saxon language or Old English. **3** of or concerning modern Saxony or Saxons.

saxophone *n.* **1** a metal woodwind reed instrument in several sizes and registers, the most recognizable form of which has an upturned bell, used esp. in jazz and popular music. **2** its player. □ **saxophonist** *n.*

say ● *v.* (*3rd sing. present* **says**; *past and past part.* **said**) **1** *tr.* **a** utter in a speaking voice; remark. **b** put into words. **2** *tr.* **a** promise or prophesy; maintain, allege (*says that there will be war*). **b** have specified wording; indicate (*says here that he was killed*; *the clock says ten to six*). **3** *tr.* (in *passive*) be asserted or described (*is said to be 93 years old*). **4** *tr.* *informal* tell a person to do something (*he said to bring the car*). **5** *tr.* convey (information) (*spoke for an hour but said little*). **6** *tr.* put forward as an argument or excuse. **7 a** *tr.* & *intr.* form and give an opinion or decision as to (*who did it I cannot say*). **b** *tr.* present as an opinion (*I say we wait a little longer*). **8** *tr.* select, assume, or take as an example or (a specified number etc.) as near enough (*shall we say this one?*). **9** *tr.* **a** speak the words of (prayers etc.). **b** repeat (a lesson etc.); recite. **10** *tr.* convey (inner meaning or intention) (*what is the director saying in this film?*). ● *interj.* esp. *US* an exclamation of surprise, to attract attention, etc. ● *n.* **1 a** an opportunity for stating one's opinion etc. **b** a stated opinion. **2** a share in a decision. ● *adv.* selecting, assuming, or taking as an example or (a specified number etc.) as near enough (*paid, say, $20*). □ **have to say for oneself** have to say by way of conversation or in explanation of one's actions etc. **I** etc. **cannot** (or **could not**) **say** I etc. do not know. **I'll say** *informal* yes indeed. **it is said** the rumour is that. **not to say** and indeed; or possibly even (*his language was rude not to say offensive*). **say again?** please repeat. **say much** (or **something**) **for** indicate the high quality of. **says you!** *informal* I disagree. **say what?** *slang* an expression of astonishment. **say when** *informal* indicate when enough drink or food has been given. **say the word 1** indicate that you agree or give permission. **2** give the order etc. **that is to say 1** in other words, more explicitly. **2** or at least. **they say** it is rumoured. **to say nothing of** = NOT TO MENTION (see MENTION). **what do** (or **would**) **you say to** would you like? **when all is said and done** after all, in the long run. **you can say that again!** (or **you said it!**) *informal* I agree emphatically. **you**

don't say *informal* an expression of amazement or disbelief. □ **sayable** *adj.* **sayer** *n.*

saying *n.* **1** the act or an instance of saying. **2** a maxim etc. □ **as the saying goes** an expression used in introducing a proverb, cliché, etc. **go without saying** be too well known or obvious to need mention. **there is no saying** it is impossible to know.

sayonara /saɪəˈnɑːrə/ *interj.* goodbye.

say-so *n.* **1** the power of decision. **2** mere assertion.

Sb *symbol* antimony.

SC *abbr.* **1** South Carolina (also in postal use). **2** *Cdn* STAR OF COURAGE. **3** *Cdn & Brit.* SPECIAL CONSTABLE.

Sc *symbol* scandium.

Sc. *abbr.* science.

scab ● *n.* **1** a dry rough crust formed over a cut, sore, etc. in healing. **2** (often *attrib.*) *informal derogatory* a person who refuses to strike or join a trade union, or who tries to break a strike by working. **3** mange or a similar skin disease esp. in animals. **4** a fungous plant disease causing scablike roughness. ● *v.intr.* (**scabbed**, **scabbing**) **1** act as a scab. **2** (of a wound etc.) form a scab; heal over. □ **scabbed** *adj.* **scabbiness** *n.* **scabby** *adj.* (**-ier**, **-iest**). **scablike** *adj.*

scabbard *n. hist.* a sheath for a sword, bayonet, etc.

scabies /ˈskeɪbiːz/ *n.* a contagious skin disease causing severe itching.

scabrous /ˈskæbrəs/ *adj.* **1** having a rough surface; bearing short stiff hairs, scales, etc. **2** (of a subject, situation, etc.) requiring tact; hard to handle with decency. **3 a** indecent, salacious; scandalous. **b** behaving licentiously. □ **scabrousness** *n.*

scad *n.* any of numerous fish of the family Carangidae, usu. having an elongated body and very large spiky scales.

scads *n.pl. N Amer. informal* large quantities.

scaffold /ˈskæfoːld, -fəld/ ● *n.* **1** = SCAFFOLDING. **2 a** *hist.* a raised wooden platform used for the execution of criminals. **b** any similar raised platform. **3** (prec. by *the*) death by execution. ● *v.tr.* attach scaffolding to (a building). □ **scaffolder** *n.*

scaffolding *n.* **1** a temporary structure formed of poles, planks, etc., used by workers while building or repairing a house etc. **2** materials used for this. **3** any supporting framework.

scag *var. of* SKAG.

scalable *adj.* **1** capable of being scaled or climbed. **2** *Computing* able to be used or produced at different ranges of size, capability, etc. □ **scalability** *n.*

scalar /ˈskeɪlər/ *Math. & Physics* ● *adj.* (of a quantity) having only magnitude, not direction. ● *n.* a scalar quantity (*compare* VECTOR).

scalawag *n.* a scamp; a rascal.

scald ● *v.tr.* **1** burn (the skin etc.) with hot liquid or steam. **2** heat (esp. milk) to near boiling point. **3** clean (a pan etc.) by rinsing with boiling water. **4** treat (food, poultry, etc.) with boiling water in preparation for cooking etc. ● *n.* a burn etc. caused by scalding.

scalding *adj.* **1** extremely hot. **2** producing an effect like that of scalding (*scalding truths*).

scale¹ ● *n.* **1** each of the small thin bony or horny overlapping plates protecting the skin of fish and reptiles. **2** something resembling a fish scale, esp.: **a** a pod or husk. **b** a flake of skin; a scab. **c** a rudimentary leaf, feather, or bract. **d** each of the structures covering the wings of butterflies and moths. **e** *Bot.* a layer of a bulb. **3 a** a flake formed on the surface of rusty iron. **b** a thick white deposit formed in a kettle,

boiler, etc. by the action of heat on water. **4** plaque formed on teeth. **5 a** = SCALE INSECT. **b** the diseased condition of plants infested with scale insects. ● *v.* **1** *tr.* remove scale or scales from. **2** *tr.* remove plaque from (teeth) by scraping. **3** *intr.* **a** form, come off in, or drop, scales. **b** (usu. foll. by *off*) (of scales) come off. □ **scales fall from a person's eyes** a person is no longer deceived. □ **scaled** *adj.* (also in *comb.*). **scaleless** /ˈskeɪlləs/ *adj.* **scaler** *n.*

scale² ● *n.* (also in *pl.*) a weighing machine or device (*bathroom scale*). ● *v.tr.* (of something weighed) show (a specified weight) in the scales. □ **tip the scales 1** weigh (*tips the scale at 200 pounds*). **2** (of a motive, circumstance, etc.) be decisive.

scale³ ● *n.* **1** a series of degrees; a graded classification system (*pay fees according to a prescribed scale*; *seven points on the Richter scale*). **2 a** (often *attrib.*) a relation between the actual size of something and a map, diagram, etc. which represents it (*on a scale of one centimetre to the kilometre*; *a scale model*). **b** relative dimensions or degree (*generosity on a grand scale*). **3 a** a set of marks on a line used in measuring, reducing, enlarging, etc. **b** a rule determining the distances between these. **c** a piece of metal, apparatus, etc. on which these are marked. **4** an arrangement of all the notes in any system of music in ascending or descending order. **5** *Math.* the ratio between units in a numerical system. **6** the minimum pay rate for a particular job, as determined by a union contract. ● *v.* **1 a** *tr. & intr.* climb (a wall, height, etc.). **b** *tr.* climb (the social scale, heights of ambition, etc.). **2** *tr.* represent in proportional dimensions; reduce to a common scale. **3** *intr.* (of quantities etc.) have a common scale; be commensurable. **4** *tr. Forestry* **a** estimate the amount of (standing timber). **b** measure (a log) to estimate how much cut timber it will yield. □ **in scale** (of drawing etc.) in proportion to the surroundings etc. **scale back** reduce the scale, scope, or size of. **scale down** make smaller in proportion; reduce in size. **scale up** make larger in proportion; increase in size. **to scale** with a uniform reduction or enlargement.

scale insect *n.* any of various insects which cling to plants and secrete a shieldlike scale as covering.

scale leaf *n.* a modified leaf resembling a scale.

scalene /ˈskeɪliːn, skeɪˈliːn/ ● *adj.* **1** (of a triangle) having three unequal sides. **2** (of a cone or cylinder) with the axis not perpendicular to the base. ● *n.* a scalene triangle.

scaler *n.* a person who scales timber or logs.

scallawag *var. of* SCALAWAG.

scallion /ˈskæljən/ *n.* a shallot or green onion; any long-necked onion with a small bulb.

scallop /ˈskæləp, ˈskɒləp/ ● *n.* **1** any of various bivalve molluscs of the family Pectinidae, used as food. **2** (in full **scallop shell**) a single valve from the shell of a scallop, with grooves and ridges radiating from the middle of the hinge and edged with small rounded lobes. **3** (in *pl.*) an ornamental edging cut in material in imitation of the edge of a scallop shell. ● *v.tr.* (**scalloped**, **scalloping**) **1** ornament (an edge or material) with scallops or scalloping. **b** cut or shape in the form of a scallop. **2** (esp. as **scalloped** *adj.*) *N Amer.* bake (food, esp. potatoes) in a cream sauce. □ **scalloping** *n.* (in sense 3 of *n.*).

scalloper *n.* (also **scallop dragger**) a boat for fishing for scallops.

scallywag *var. of* SCALAWAG.

scaloppine /ˌskæləˈpiːni/ *n.* (also **scallopini**) thin, boneless slices of meat, esp. veal, sautéed or fried.

scalp ● *n.* **1** the skin covering the top of the head, with the hair etc. attached. **2 a** *hist.* the scalp of an enemy cut or torn away as a trophy. **b** a trophy or symbol of conquest. ● *v.tr.* **1** *hist.* take the scalp of (an enemy). **2** *N Amer. informal* resell (esp. tickets) at inflated prices. □ **scalper** *n.* (in sense 2 of v.). **scalpless** *adj.*

scalpel *n.* a surgeon's small sharp knife shaped for holding like a pen.

scaly *adj.* (**-ier**, **-iest**) **1** covered in or having many scales or flakes. **2** of or like a deposit of scale. □ **scaliness** *n.*

scam ● *n. N Amer. slang* a trick or swindle. ● *v.tr.* (**scammed**, **scamming**) **1** swindle. **2** obtain in a manner not considered ethical or proper (*scammed four tickets to the game*). □ **scammer** *n.*

scamp[1] *n. informal* a rascal; a rogue. □ **scampish** *adj.*

scamp[2] *v.tr.* do (work etc.) in a perfunctory or inadequate way.

scamper ● *v.intr.* (usu. foll. by *about, through*) **1** run and skip impulsively or playfully. **2** move quickly, go hastily. ● *n.* the act or an instance of scampering.

scampi /ˈskæmpi/ *n.pl.* **1** large prawns. **2** (often treated as *sing.*) a dish of these, usu. fried.

scan ● *v.* (**scanned**, **scanning**) **1** *tr.* look at intently or quickly (*scanned the text for errors*). **2** *tr.* **a** cause (a particular region) to be traversed or swept by a radar etc. beam. **b** examine all parts of (a surface etc.) to detect radioactivity etc. **3** *tr.* **a** resolve (a picture) into its elements of light and shade in a pre-arranged pattern esp. for the purposes of television transmission. **b** use a beam or detector to convert (an image, text, etc.) into a sequence of signals for processing, transmission, etc. **4** *tr.* **a** make a scan of (the body or part of it). **b** examine (a patient etc.) with a scanner. **5** *tr.* test the metre of (a line of verse etc.) by reading with the emphasis on its rhythm. **6** *intr.* (of a verse etc.) be metrically correct; be capable of being recited etc. metrically. ● *n.* **1** the act or an instance of scanning. **2** an image obtained by scanning or with a scanner.

scandal *n.* **1** a person or circumstance etc. causing general public outrage or indignation. **2** the outrage etc. so caused, esp. as a subject of common talk. □ **scandalous** *adj.* **scandalously** *adv.*

scandalize *v.tr.* offend the moral feelings, sensibilities, etc. of; shock.

Scandinavian ● *n.* **1 a** a native or inhabitant of Scandinavia, a large peninsula in NW Europe. **b** a person of Scandinavian descent. **2** the family of languages of Scandinavia. ● *adj.* of or relating to Scandinavia or its people or languages.

scandium /ˈskændiəm/ *n.* a rare soft silver-white metallic element.

scanner *n.* **1** a device for scanning, systematically examining, reading, or monitoring something. **2** a device for converting text, an image, etc. into a sequence of signals for processing, transmission, etc. **3** a machine for measuring the intensity of radiation, ultrasound reflections, etc., from the body as a diagnostic aid. **4** a person who scans or examines critically.

scant *adj.* **1** barely sufficient; deficient (*with scant regard for the truth*; *scant of breath*). **2** barely amounting to, hardly reaching (a specified quantity) (*a scant 150 kilograms*). □ **scantly** *adv.* **scantness** *n.*

scanty *adj.* (**-ier**, **-iest**) **1** of small extent or amount. **2** barely sufficient. □ **scantily** *adv.* **scantiness** *n.*

scape *n.* a long flower stalk coming from the root.

-scape *comb. form* forming nouns denoting a view or a representation of a view (*seascape*).

scapegoat ● *n.* **1** a person bearing the blame for the

sins, shortcomings, etc. of others, esp. as an expedient. **2** *Bible* a goat sent into the wilderness after the Jewish chief priest had symbolically laid the sins of the people upon it. ● *v.tr.* make a scapegoat of. □ **scapegoater** *n.* **scapegoating** *n.*

scapegrace *n.* a rascal, esp. a young person or child.

scapula /ˈskæpjʊlə/ *n.* (*pl.* **scapulae** /-ˌliː/ or **-s**) the shoulder blade.

scapular /ˈskæpjʊlər/ ● *adj.* of or relating to the shoulder or shoulder blade. ● *n.* **1 a** a monastic cloak consisting of a piece of cloth covering the shoulders and extending in front and behind almost to the feet. **b** two small rectangles of woollen cloth joined by tapes or strings passing over the shoulders, worn under one's clothing as a symbol of affiliation to a religious order or as a form of devotion. **2** a feather growing near the insertion of a bird's wing.

scar[1] ● *n.* **1** a usu. permanent mark on the skin left after the healing of a wound etc. **2** the lasting effect of grief etc. on a person's character. **3** a mark left by damage etc. (*the table bore many scars*). **4** a mark left on the stem etc. of a plant by the fall of a leaf etc. ● *v.* (**scarred**, **scarring**) **1** *tr.* (esp. as **scarred** *adj.*) mark with a scar or scars (*was scarred for life*). **2** *intr.* heal over; form a scar. **3** *tr.* form a scar on.

scar[2] *n.* a steep craggy outcrop of a mountain or cliff.

scarab /ˈskerəb, ˈskæ-/ *n.* **1** the sacred dung beetle of ancient Egypt. **2** = SCARABAEID.

scarabaeid /ˌskærəˈbiːɪd/ *n.* any beetle of the family Scarabaeidae, e.g. the dung beetle, cockchafer, etc.

scarce ● *adj.* **1** (usu. *predic.*) (esp. of food, money, etc.) insufficient for the demand; scanty. **2** hard to find; rare. ● *adv. archaic* or *literary* scarcely. □ **make oneself scarce** *informal* keep out of the way; surreptitiously disappear. □ **scarceness** *n.*

scarcely *adv.* **1** hardly; barely; only just (*I scarcely know him*). **2** surely not (*he can scarcely have said so*). **3** a mild or apologetic or ironical substitute for 'not' (*I scarcely expected to be insulted*).

scarcity *n.* (*pl.* **-ies**) (often foll. by *of*) a lack or inadequacy.

scare ● *v.* **1** *tr.* frighten, esp. suddenly. **2** *tr.* drive away by frightening. **3** *intr.* become scared. ● *n.* **1** a sudden attack of fright or worry. **2** a general, esp. baseless, fear of war, invasion, epidemic, etc. **3** (*attrib.*) denoting an effort to influence others by highlighting or exaggerating a perceived threat (*scare tactics*). **4** a financial panic causing share selling etc. □ **scare up** (or **out**) esp. *N Amer.* **1** frighten (game etc.) out of cover. **2** *informal* manage to find (*scare up a meal*). □ **scarer** *n.*

scarecrow *n.* **1** an object, esp. a human figure dressed in old clothes, set up in a field to scare birds away. **2** *informal* a badly dressed, grotesque-looking, or very thin person.

scared *adj.* frightened; terrified.

scaredy-cat *n. informal* a timid or easily frightened person.

scaremonger /ˈskerˌmʌŋgər, -mʌŋgər/ *n.* a person who spreads frightening reports or rumours. □ **scaremongering** *n.*

scarf[1] *n.* (*pl.* **scarves** or **-s**) **1** a square, triangular, or esp. oblong strip of material worn around the neck, over the shoulders, or tied around the head, for warmth or ornament. **2** *N Amer.* a cloth or other covering for a table, dresser, etc. □ **scarfed** *adj.*

scarf[2] *v.tr. N Amer. informal* eat or drink greedily.

scarifier *n.* **1** a machine for loosening soil, esp. in reforestation. **2 a** a spiked road-breaking machine. **b** a machine or implement for roughening up the iced surface of a road. **3** an implement for cutting and removing debris from a lawn.

scarify¹ *v.tr.* (**-ies, -ied**) **1** make superficial incisions in. **2** loosen (esp. soil) with a scarifier. **3** nick or make an incision in (a hard seed) to facilitate its germination. □ **scarification** *n.*

scarify² *v.tr. & intr.* (**-ies, -ied**) *informal* scare; terrify.

scarlet ● *n.* **1** a brilliant red tinged with orange. **2** clothes or material of this colour. ● *adj.* **1** of a scarlet colour. **2** sinful, immoral; promiscuous.

scarlet fever *n.* an infectious bacterial fever, affecting esp. children, with a scarlet rash.

scarlet runner *n. see* RUNNER 9.

scarlet tanager *n.* a tanager, *Piranga olivacea*, which breeds in eastern N America, the breeding male of which is bright red with black wings and tail.

scar tissue *n.* the fibrous connective tissue of which scars are formed.

scarves *pl. of* SCARF¹.

scary *adj.* (**-ier, -iest**) scaring, frightening. □ **scarily** *adv.* **scariness** *n.*

scat¹ *informal* ● *v.intr.* (**scatted, scatting**) depart quickly. ● *interj.* go!

scat² ● *n.* improvised jazz singing using sounds imitating instruments, instead of words. ● *v.intr.* (**scatted, scatting**) sing scat.

scat³ *n.* the droppings of an animal, esp. a carnivore.

scathing *adj.* witheringly scornful; severe (*scathing sarcasm*). □ **scathingly** *adv.*

scatology /skə'tɒlədʒi/ *n.* **1 a** a morbid interest in excrement. **b** a preoccupation with obscene literature, esp. that concerned with excretion. **2** the medical or zoological study or analysis of excrement. □ **scatological** *adj.*

scatter ● *v.* **1** *tr.* **a** throw here and there. **b** cover by scattering. **2** *tr. & intr.* **a** move or cause to move in flight etc.; disperse. **b** disperse or cause (hopes, clouds, etc.) to disperse. **3** *tr.* *Physics* deflect or diffuse (light, particles, etc.). **4** *intr.* (of esp. a shotgun) fire a charge of shot diffusely. **b** *tr.* fire (a charge) in this way. ● *n.* **1** the act or an instance of scattering. **2** an esp. small amount scattered. **3** the extent of distribution of esp. shot. □ **scatterer** *n.*

scatterbrain *n.* a person given to silly or disorganized thought with lack of concentration. □ **scatterbrained** *adj.*

scatter cushion *n.* (also **scatter pillow**) = THROW CUSHION.

scattered *adj.* **1** not clustered together; wide apart; sporadic (*scattered villages*). **2** scatterbrained.

scattergun esp. *N Amer.* ● *n.* a shotgun. ● *adj.* (also **scattershot**) random, haphazard.

scattering *n.* **1** a quantity or amount scattered. **2** a small number or amount.

scatty *adj.* (**-ier, -iest**) *informal* scatterbrained; disorganized.

scaup /skɒp/ *n.* either of two diving ducks of the genus *Aythya*, the males having a dark head and breast and a white-sided body.

scavenge ● *v.* **1** *tr. & intr.* search for and collect (useful items) from among usu. discarded material. **2** *intr.* (of an animal or bird) feed on (carrion) or search for food in (garbage etc.) (*scavenging backroad dumps*). ● *n.* the action or process of scavenging. □ **scavenger** *n.*

scavenger hunt *n. N Amer.* a game in which people try to collect certain miscellaneous objects, usu. outdoors over a wide area.

SCC *abbr.* Supreme Court of Canada.

scenario /sə'nerio:, -ɑrio:/ *n.* (*pl.* **-os**) **1** an outline of

the plot of a play etc., with details of the scenes, situations, etc. **2** a postulated sequence of future events. **3** *informal* a situation or scene.

scenarist /sə'nerɪst/ *n.* a writer of film or TV scenarios.

scene *n.* **1** a place in which events in real life, drama, or fiction occur; the locality of an event etc. (*the scene of the disaster*). **2 a** an incident in real life, fiction, etc. (*distressing scenes occurred*). **b** a description or representation of an incident etc. (*scenes of clerical life*). **3 a** public incident displaying emotion, temper, etc., esp. when embarrassing to others (*made a scene in the restaurant*). **4 a** a continuous portion of a theatrical production in a fixed setting and usu. without a change of performers; a subdivision of an act. **b** a similar section of a film, book, etc. **5** a landscape or a view (*a desolate scene*). **6** *informal* **a** an area of action or interest (*not my scene*). **b** a way of life; a milieu (*the jazz scene*). □ **behind the scenes 1** among the performers, scenery, etc. offstage. **2** not known to the public; secret. **behind-the-scenes** (*attrib.*) secret, using secret information (*a behind-the-scenes investigation*). **change of scene** (or **scenery**) a move to different surroundings esp. through travel. **come on the scene** arrive. **quit the scene** depart. **set the scene 1** describe the location of events. **2** give preliminary information.

scenery *n.* **1** the general appearance of the natural features of a landscape, esp. when picturesque. **2** the painted representations of landscape, rooms, etc., used as the background in a play etc.

scenic *adj.* **1 a** (esp. of natural scenery) picturesque; impressive or beautiful. **b** of or concerning natural scenery. **2** *Theatre* of or on the stage (*the scenic art*). □ **scenically** *adv.*

scenography /si:'nɒgrəfi/ *n.* **1** the painting or design of theatrical scenery. **2** *Art* the representation of objects in perspective. □ **scenographic** *adj.* **scenographer** *n.*

scent ● *n.* **1** a distinctive, esp. pleasant, smell. **2 a** a scent trail left by an animal perceptible to hounds etc. **b** clues etc. that can be followed like a scent trail. **c** a feeling of the presence of something (*a scent of danger*). **3** esp. *Brit.* = PERFUME 2. ● *v.tr.* **1 a** discern by scent (*the dog scented game*). **b** sense the presence of; detect (*scent victory*). **2** make fragrant or foul-smelling. **3** apply the sense of smell to (*scented the air*). □ **on the scent** in possession of a useful clue in an investigation. **put** (or **throw**) **off the scent** deceive by false clues etc. □ **scentless** *adj.*

scented *adj.* having esp. a pleasant smell.

scent marking *n.* the deposition by a mammal of a secreted pheromone, esp. on prominent objects in the area. □ **scent mark** *n. & v.*

sceptic etc. *var. of* SKEPTIC.

sceptre /'septər/ *n.* (*US* **scepter**) **1** a staff borne esp. at a coronation as a symbol of sovereignty. **2** royal or imperial authority. □ **sceptred** *adj.*

schedule /'skedʒuəl, 'skedʒuːl, 'ʃedjuːl, 'ʃedʒuːl/ ● *n.* **1 a** a list or plan of intended events, times, etc.; a timetable. **b** a plan of work (*not on my schedule for next week*). **2** any list, form, classification, or tabular statement, e.g. a list of rates or prices, a tabulated inventory, etc. **3** any of a number of forms attached to a tax return, which are completed if necessary to provide details of information summarized on the return. ● *v.tr.* **1** include in a schedule; arrange (an event etc.) for a certain time. **2** make a schedule of. □ **according to** (or **on**) **schedule** as planned; on time. **behind**

schedule behind time. □ **scheduler** n. **scheduling** n.

schema /ˈskiːmə/ n. (pl. **schemata** /-mətə/ or **-s**) **1** a synopsis or diagram. **2** a proposed arrangement.

schematic /skiːˈmætɪk, skɪ-/ ● adj. **1** of or concerning a scheme or schema. **2** representing objects by symbols etc. ● n. a schematic diagram, esp. of an electronic circuit. □ **schematically** adv.

scheme ● n. **1 a** a systematic plan or arrangement for work, action, etc. **b** a proposed or operational systematic arrangement (a colour scheme). **2** an artful or deceitful plot. **3** a timetable, outline, syllabus, etc. ● v. **1** intr. plan esp. secretly or deceitfully; intrigue. **2** tr. plan to bring about, esp. artfully or deceitfully (schemed their downfall). □ **scheme of things** the way things are or are planned (has little influence in the overall scheme of things). □ **schemer** n.

scheming ● adj. artful, cunning, or deceitful. ● n. plots; intrigues. □ **schemingly** adv.

schemozzle var. of SHEMOZZLE.

scherzo /ˈskɛrtsoː/ n. (pl. **-os**) a vigorous, light, or playful composition, usu. as a movement in a symphony, sonata, etc.

schism /ˈskɪzəm/ n. **1 a** the division of a group into opposing sections or parties. **b** any of the sections so formed. **2 a** the separation of a Church into two Churches or the secession of a group owing to doctrinal, disciplinary, etc., differences. **b** the offence of causing or promoting such a separation.

schist /ʃɪst/ n. a metamorphic rock composed of layers of different minerals and splitting into thin irregular plates.

schizo /ˈskɪtso/ informal offensive ● adj. schizophrenic. ● n. (pl. **-os**) a schizophrenic.

schizoid /ˈskɪtsɔɪd/ ● adj. **1** (of a person or personality etc.) tending to or resembling schizophrenia or a schizophrenic, but usu. without delusions. **2** having inconsistent or contradictory elements. ● n. a schizoid person.

schizophrenia /skɪtsəˈfriːnɪə, -ˈfriːnjə/ n. **1** a mental disease marked by a breakdown in the relation between thoughts, feelings, and actions, frequently accompanied by delusions and retreat from social life. **2** informal a mentality or approach characterized by inconsistent or contradictory elements (political schizophrenia). □ **schizophrenic** /-ˈfrenɪk/ adj. & n.

schlemiel /ʃləˈmiːl/ n. N Amer. informal an awkward or unlucky person.

schlep /ʃlep/ (also **schlepp**) informal ● v. (**schlepped, schlepping**) **1** tr. carry (esp. something burdensome). **2** intr. go or work tediously or effortfully. ● n. N Amer. **1** a tedious journey; a trek. **2** an inept or stupid person. □ **schlepper** n. **schleppy** adj. (**-ier, -iest**).

schlock /ʃlɒk/ n. esp. N Amer. informal **1** cheap, shoddy or defective goods. **2** junk (esp. applied to inferior art or entertainment). □ **schlocky** adj. (**-ier, -iest**).

schlockey /ˈʃlɒki/ n. a children's game played on a four-foot by eight-foot framed plywood sheet stationed between two players, in which each player, using a cut-off hockey stick, attempts to score by shooting a puck past a centre barrier and through a hole in the framing board at the opposing end.

schlub /ʃlʌb/ n. N Amer. slang a clumsy, stupid, or untidy person. □ **schlubby** adj.

schlump /ʃlʌmp/ n. esp. N Amer. slang a slow or slovenly person; a slob, a fool.

schm- /ʃm/ prefix (also **shm-**) N Amer. slang used in the second element of a reduplication to express contemptuous dismissal (fancy-schmancy).

schmaltz n. esp. N Amer. informal sentimentality, esp. in music, drama, etc. □ **schmaltzy** adj. (**-ier, -iest**).

schmear /ʃmiːr, ʃəˈmiːr/ n. N Amer. informal (also **schmeer**) □ **the whole schmear** everything (possible or available); every aspect of the situation.

schmo n. N Amer. slang (pl. **-oes**) an ordinary, unremarkable person.

schmooze informal ● v. **1** intr. talk, chat, esp. at a social function. **2** tr. talk to (a person, esp. an important or influential one). ● n. conversation, esp. at a social function. □ **schmoozer** n. **schmoozy** adj. (**-ier, -iest**).

schmuck[1] n. esp. N Amer. slang an objectionable or contemptible person. □ **schmucky** adj. (**-ier, -iest**).

schmuck[2] v.tr. Cdn slang hit, flatten.

schnapps /ʃnæps, ʃnʊps/ n. any of various strong usu. colourless spirits made from grain, with added flavourings such as peppermint, peach, etc.

schnauzer /ˈʃnauzər, ˈʃnautsər/ n. a German breed of dog with a close wiry coat and heavy whiskers round the muzzle.

schnitzel /ˈʃnɪtsəl/ n. a thin cutlet, esp. of veal or pork, breaded and fried.

schnozz n. (also **schnoz, schnozzle, schnozzola**) N Amer. slang the nose.

scholar n. **1** a learned person, esp. in language, literature, etc.; an academic. **2** the holder of a scholarship (Rhodes scholar). **3 a** a person with specified academic ability. **b** a person who learns (am a scholar of life). □ **scholarly** adj.

scholarship n. **1 a** academic achievement; learning of a high level. **b** the methods and standards characteristic of a good scholar (shows great scholarship). **2** a payment to maintain a student in full-time education, awarded on the basis of scholarly achievement.

scholastic /skəˈlæstɪk/ adj. of or concerning universities, schools, education, teachers, etc. □ **scholastically** adv.

Scholastic Aptitude Test n. proprietary a standardized test of a student's verbal and mathematical skills, used for admission to American colleges.

school[1] ● n. **1 a** an institution for educating or giving instruction, esp. one for students under 19 years. **b** N Amer. a college or university. **c** an institution for teaching a particular subject (art school). **d** (attrib.) associated with or for use in school (school books). **2 a** the buildings used by such institutions. **b** the pupils, staff, etc. of a school. **c** the time during which teaching is done, or the teaching itself (no school today). **3** a department or faculty of a university concerned with a particular area of study (law school). **4** a structured program of studies (summer school). **5 a** the disciples, imitators, or followers of a philosopher, artist, etc. **b** a group of artists etc. whose works share distinctive characteristics. **c** a group of people sharing a cause, principle, method, etc. (school of thought). **6** informal instructive or disciplinary circumstances, occupation, etc. (the school of adversity). ● v.tr. send to school; provide for the education of. □ **of the old school** according to former and esp. better tradition (a gentleman of the old school). **school of hard knocks** experience gained from adversity.

school[2] ● n. a large number of fish, whales, etc. swimming together. ● v.intr. form schools.

school age n. the age range in which children normally attend school (often attrib.: school-age children). □ **school-aged** adj.

school board n. N Amer. **1** an elected board responsible for decisions and policy concerning the schools in a given area. **2** the administrative unit responsible for the schools in a given area. **3** the area under the jurisdiction of a school board.

schoolboy *n.* a boy attending school.

schoolchild *n.* (*pl.* **-children**) a child attending school.

school commission *n. Cdn (Que.)* = SCHOOL BOARD 1.

school district *n. N Amer.* **1** an administrative unit responsible for the schools in a given area. **2** the area under the jurisdiction of a school division.

school division *n. Cdn (Man.)* = SCHOOL DISTRICT.

schooler *n.* (usu. in comb.) a person attending a school (*high-schooler*).

schoolgirl *n.* a girl attending school.

schoolhouse *n.* a building used as a school, esp. a small one in a village or rural area.

schooling *n.* **1** education, esp. at school. **2** training or discipline, esp. of an animal.

school inspector *n.* (in the UK and Canada) an official appointed to inspect and report on the efficiency, teaching standards, etc. of schools.

schoolmarm *n.* **1** a prim and fussy female schoolteacher. **2** *N Amer. slang* a tree which has forked into two trunks. □ **schoolmarmish** *adj.* (in sense 1).

schoolmaster *n.* a male teacher in an esp. private school. □ **schoolmasterly** *adj.*

schoolmate *n.* a companion at school.

schoolmistress *n.* a female teacher in an esp. private school.

schoolroom *n.* a room where students are taught; a classroom.

school section *n. Cdn (Ont.)* esp. *hist.* a subdivision of a school district.

schoolteacher *n.* a person who teaches in a school. □ **school teaching** *n.*

school unit *n. Cdn (PEI)* = SCHOOL DISTRICT.

school work *n.* educational exercises done during school hours and at home as homework.

schoolyard *n.* a playing area beside a school.

school year *n.* = ACADEMIC YEAR.

schooner /'skuːnər/ *n.* **1** a fore-and-aft rigged ship with two or more masts, the foremast being smaller than the other masts. **2** *N Amer. & Austral.* a tall beer glass. **3** *N Amer. hist.* = PRAIRIE SCHOONER.

schottische /ʃɒ'tiːʃ/ *n.* **1** a kind of slow polka. **2** the music for this.

schtick *var. of* SHTICK.

schuss /ʃʊs/ ● *n.* a straight downhill run on skis. ● *v.intr.* **1** make a schuss. **2** move rapidly downwards.

schwa /ʃwɒ/ *n.* **1** the indistinct unstressed vowel sound as in *a moment ago*. **2** the symbol /ə/ representing this in the International Phonetic Alphabet.

sciatic /sai'ætɪk/ *adj.* **1** of the hip. **2** of or affecting the sciatic nerve.

sciatica /sai'ætɪkə/ *n.* neuralgia of the hip and thigh; a pain in the sciatic nerve.

sciatic nerve *n.* the largest nerve in the human body, running from the pelvis to the thigh.

science *n.* **1** a branch of knowledge conducted on objective principles involving the systematized observation of and experiments with phenomena, esp. concerned with the material and functions of the physical universe. **2** systematic and formulated knowledge, esp. of a specified type or on a specified subject (*political science*). **3** skilful technique (*has house cleaning down to a science*).

science centre *n.* an institution aiming to inform and educate the non-specialist public about the principles of science and technology.

science fair *n. N Amer.* an esp. competitive fair in

which elementary school or high school students design and exhibit science projects.

science fiction *n.* fiction based on imagined future scientific or technological advances, major social or environmental changes, etc., frequently portraying space or time travel, life on other planets, etc.

scientific *adj.* **1 a** (of an investigation etc.) according to rules laid down in science for performing observations and testing the soundness of conclusions. **b** systematic, accurate. **2** used in, engaged in, or relating to (esp. natural) science. **3** constituted of scientists. □ **scientifically** *adv.*

scientific method *n.* a method of procedure consisting of systematic observation, measurement, and experiment, and the formulation, testing, and modification of hypotheses.

scientism *n.* **1 a** a method or doctrine regarded as characteristic of scientists. **b** the use or practice of this. **2** often *derogatory* an excessive belief in or application of scientific method. □ **scientistic** *adj.*

scientist *n.* **1** a person with expert knowledge of a (usu. physical or natural) science. **2** a person using scientific methods.

Scientology *n.* *proprietary* a religious system whose adherents seek self-knowledge and spiritual fulfillment through graded courses of study and training. □ **Scientologist** *n.*

sci-fi *n.* (often *attrib.*) *informal* science fiction.

scilla /'sɪlə/ *n.* any plant of the genus *Scilla*, related to the bluebell, usu. having small blue star-shaped or bell-shaped flowers and long glossy straplike leaves.

scimitar /'sɪmɪtər/ *n.* an oriental curved sword usu. broadening towards the point.

scintillate /'sɪntɪˌleit/ *v.intr.* **1** (esp. as **scintillating** *adj.*) talk cleverly or wittily; be brilliant. **2** sparkle; twinkle; emit sparks. □ **scintillatingly** *adv.*

scintillation *n.* **1** the process or state of scintillating. **2** the twinkling of a star.

scion /'saiən/ *n.* **1** a shoot of a plant etc., esp. one cut for grafting or planting. **2** a descendant; a younger member of a (esp. distinguished) family.

scissor *v.* **1** *tr.* cut with or as with scissors. **2** *intr. & tr.* move or cause to move like scissors.

scissor kick *n. Swimming* a movement, esp. in the side stroke, in which the legs are parted slowly and brought together forcefully.

scissors *n.pl.* **1** (also **pair of scissors** *sing.*) an instrument for cutting, having two pivoted blades with finger and thumb holes in the handles, operating by closing on the material to be cut. **2** (treated as *sing.*) **a** a method of high jump with a forward and backward movement of the legs. **b** a hold in wrestling in which the opponent's body or esp. head is gripped between the legs.

sclera /'sklɪərə/ *n.* the white of the eye; a white membrane coating the eyeball. □ **scleral** *adj.*

sclerosis /sklə'rəʊsɪs/ *n.* **1** an abnormal hardening of body tissue. **2** rigidity; excessive resistance to change.

sclerotic /sklə'rɒtɪk/ ● *adj.* **1** of or having sclerosis. **2** of or relating to the sclera. **3** rigid; unchanging. ● *n.* = SCLERA.

scoff[1] ● *v.intr.* speak derisively, esp. of serious subjects; mock; be scornful. ● *n.* **1** mocking words; a taunt. **2** an object of ridicule. □ **scoffer** *n.*

scoff[2] *informal* ● *v.tr. & intr.* eat greedily. ● *n.* **1** food; a meal. **2** *Cdn (Maritimes & Nfld)* a big meal, esp. of seafood, served in conjunction with a party.

scofflaw *n. N Amer. informal* a person who flouts the

law, esp. a person not complying with various laws which are difficult to enforce effectively.

scold ● v. **1** tr. rebuke or chide (esp. a child). **2** intr. find fault noisily; complain. ● n. a nagging or grumbling person, esp. a woman. □ **scolder** n. **scolding** n. **scoldingly** adv.

sconce /skɒns/ n. **1** a semicircular or triangular lighting fixture attached to a wall. **2** a bracket to support a candle, attached to a wall.

scone /skɒn, skoːn/ n. a small quick bread often containing raisins or currants, usu. served with butter and jam.

scoop ● n. **1** any of various objects resembling a spoon, esp.: **a** a short-handled deep shovel used for transferring grain, sugar, coal, etc. **b** a short-handled implement with a roughly rectangular bowl, used for measuring or transferring dry foodstuffs. **c** an instrument with a rounded bowl used for serving portions of ice cream, mashed potato, etc. **d** a large long-handled ladle used for transferring liquids. **e** the excavating part of a digging machine etc. **2** a quantity taken up by a scoop. **3** a movement of or resembling scooping. **4** a piece of news published by a newspaper etc. in advance of its rivals. **b** informal the latest information; news (what's the scoop on why she quit?). ● v.tr. **1** hollow out with or as if with a scoop. **2** a lift with a scoop. **b** pick up rapidly in the hands or arms. **3** forestall (a rival newspaper, reporter, etc.) with a scoop. **4** (usu. foll. by up) secure (something of monetary value) esp. suddenly. □ **scooper** n.

scoop neck n. a rounded low-cut neckline on a garment. □ **scoop-necked** adj.

scoot informal ● v.tr. & intr. intr. move quickly. ● n. the act or an instance of scooting.

scooter n. **1** (in full **motor scooter**) a light motorcycle with a low seat and a curved metal shield protecting the driver's legs. **2** a motorized cart used by a disabled or elderly person. **3** a child's toy consisting of a footboard mounted on two wheels and a steering column with handles, propelled by resting one foot on the footboard and pushing the other against the ground. **4** Cdn a snowmobile.

scope¹ ● n. **1** the extent to which it is possible to range (this is beyond the scope of our research). **2** the sweep or reach of mental activity, observation, or outlook (an intellect limited in its scope). **3** space or freedom to act (doesn't leave us much scope). ● v.tr. (often foll. by out) N Amer. slang investigate or assess (a person, situation, etc.); check out, examine.

scope² n. informal a telescope, microscope, or other device designated by a word ending in -scope. □ **scoped** adj.

scorch ● v. **1** tr. **a** burn the surface of with flame or heat so as to discolour, parch, injure, or hurt. **b** affect with the sensation of burning. **2** intr. become discoloured etc. with heat. **3** intr. informal (of a motorist etc.) go at excessive speed. ● n. **1** a mark made by scorching. **2** a scorching effect.

scorched earth policy n. a military strategy of burning or destroying an area's crops and other resources that would otherwise sustain an invading enemy force.

scorcher n. informal **1** a very hot day. **2** Sport an extremely fast shot or hit. **3** a scathing or harsh rebuke, attack, glance, etc. **4** a thing, esp. a book or play, that is licentious or risqué.

scorching adj. **1** informal very hot. **2** (of criticism etc.) stringent; harsh. □ **scorchingly** adv.

score ● n. **1** a the number of points etc., made by a player etc. in some games. **b** the total number of

points etc. at the end of a game (the score was 5-0). **c** a number of marks gained on a test etc. **2** (pl. same or **scores**) twenty or a set of twenty. **3** (in pl.) a great many (scores of people arrived). **4** a a reason or motive (rejected on the score of absurdity). **b** topic, subject (no worries on that score). **5** a a usu. printed copy of a composition showing all the vocal and instrumental parts arranged one below the other. **b** the music composed for a film or play, esp. for a musical. **6** informal **a** a piece of good fortune. **b** the act or an instance of scoring off another person. **7** informal the state of affairs; the present situation (asked what the score was). **8** a notch, line, etc. cut or scratched into a surface. **9** an amount due for payment. **10** slang **a** the money or goods obtained by a successful crime. **b** the victim of a robbery or swindle. **11** slang the act or process of obtaining or consuming illegal drugs. ● v. **1** tr. a win or gain (a goal, run, points, success, etc.). **b** count for a score of (points in a game etc.) (a bull's eye scores the most points). **c** allot a score to (a competitor etc.). **d** make a record of (a point etc.). **2** intr. **a** make a score in a game (failed to score). **b** keep the tally of points, runs, etc. in a game. **3** tr. & intr. gain marks on a test or an examination. **4** tr. **a** mark with notches, incisions etc. (scored his name on the desk). **b** cut shallow grooves across (meat) to prevent curling when heated. **c** make a shallow cut in (cardboard etc.) without cutting right through. **5** a tr. secure (an advantage etc.) by luck, cunning, etc. (scored a great apartment). **b** intr. succeed. **6** tr. **a** orchestrate (a piece of music). **b** (usu. foll. by for) arrange for an instrument or instruments. **c** write the music for (a film, musical, etc.). **d** write out in a score. **7** tr. **a** (usu. foll. by up) mark (a total owed etc.) in a score (see sense 10 of n.). **b** (usu. foll. by against, to) enter (an item of debt to a customer). **8** slang **a** tr. & intr. obtain (drugs) illegally. **b** tr. & intr. steal (goods). **c** intr. make a sexual conquest. □ **keep score** register the score as it is made. **know the score** informal be aware of the essential facts. **on that score** so far as that is concerned. **settle** (or **pay off**) **a** (or **the**) **score 1** requite an obligation. **2** avenge an injury. **score off** (or **score points off**) Brit. & Cdn informal humiliate, esp. verbally in repartee etc. **score points** outdo another person; make a more favourable impression. □ **scoreless** adj. **scorer** n. **scoring** n. Music.

scoreboard n. a large board in an arena etc., for publicly displaying the score in a game etc.

scorecard n. (also **scoresheet**) a printed card on which esp. sports scores are recorded.

scorekeeper n. N Amer. an official who records the score at a game, contest, etc. □ **scorekeeping** n.

scorn ● n. **1** disdain, contempt. **2** an object of contempt etc. (the scorn of all onlookers). ● v.tr. **1** hold in contempt or disdain. **2** abstain from or refuse to do as unworthy (scorns lying; scorns to lie). □ **pour scorn on** express contempt or disdain for. □ **scorner** n.

scornful adj. (often foll. by of) full of scorn; contemptuous. □ **scornfully** adv. **scornfulness** n.

Scorpio n. (pl. **-os**) **1** (usu. **Scorpius**) a large constellation between Sagittarius and Libra, traditionally regarded as contained in the figure of a scorpion. **2 a** the eighth sign of the zodiac. **b** a person born when the sun is in this sign, usu. between Oct. 23 and Nov. 21. □ **Scorpian** adj. & n.

scorpion /ˈskɔːpiən/ n. **1** an arachnid of the order Scorpionida, with lobster-like pincers and a jointed tail that can be bent over to inflict a poisoned sting on prey held in its pincers. **2** (in full **false scorpion**) a similar arachnid of the order Pseudoscorpionida, smaller and without a tail.

Scot n. **1** a native of Scotland or person of Scottish descent. **2** hist. a member of a Gaelic people that migrated from Ireland to Scotland around the 6th c.

Scotch ● adj. var. of SCOTTISH or SCOTS. ● n. **1** var. of SCOTTISH or SCOTS. ¶The use of Scotch as an alternative to Scottish or Scots is generally regarded as offensive or old-fashioned by Scottish people. It should be avoided except to mean 'Scotch whisky' and in the compounds listed below. **2** Scotch whisky.

scotch v.tr. put an end to (injury scotched his attempt).

Scotch bonnet n. a variety of small, round, red, hot pepper.

Scotch broth n. a soup made from beef or mutton with pearl barley and vegetables etc.

Scotchgard n. proprietary a chemical added to upholstery, a carpet, etc. to make it water- and stain-resistant. □ **Scotchgarded** adj.

Scotch-Irish ● adj. of the 17th c. Scottish settlers of Ulster or their descendants. ● n. (treated as pl.) these people collectively.

Scotch pine n. esp. N Amer. a pine tree, Pinus sylvestris, native to Eurasia and much planted for timber and other products.

Scotch Tape esp. N Amer. ● n. proprietary transparent adhesive tape. ● v.tr. (**Scotch-tape**) fasten with Scotch Tape.

Scotch terrier n. = SCOTTISH TERRIER.

Scotch thistle n. any of various thistles of the genus Cirsium or Onopordum, esp. O. acanthium, naturalized in N America.

Scotch whisky n. (pl. **-ies**) whisky distilled in Scotland, esp. from malted barley.

scoter /ˈskoːtər/ n. (pl. same or **-s**) each of three northern diving ducks of the genus Melanitta, which breed in the Arctic and Subarctic and overwinter off coasts further south, esp. the surf scoter or the white-winged scoter.

scot-free adv. without being punished or harmed.

Scotland Yard n. (in the UK) **1** the headquarters of the London Metropolitan Police. **2** its Criminal Investigation Department.

Scots ● adj. **1** = SCOTTISH adj. **2** in the dialect, accent, etc., of (esp. Lowlands) Scotland. ● n. **1** = SCOTTISH n. **2** the form of English spoken in (esp. Lowlands) Scotland.

Scotsman n. (pl. **-men**) **1** a native of Scotland. **2** a person of Scottish descent.

Scotswoman n. (pl. **-women**) **1** a Scottish woman. **2** a woman of Scottish descent.

Scottish ● adj. of or relating to Scotland or its inhabitants or their descendants. ● n. (prec. by the; treated as pl.) the people of Scotland or their descendants (see also SCOTS). □ **Scottishness** n.

Scottish terrier n. (also informal **Scottie, Scottie dog**) a breed of small terrier with a rough coat and short legs.

scoundrel n. a person who shows no moral principles or conscience. □ **scoundrelly** adj.

scour ● v. **1** tr. **a** cleanse or brighten (esp. metal) by rubbing, esp. with soap, chemicals, or an abrasive substance. **b** (usu. foll. by away, off, etc.) clear (rust, stains, etc.) by rubbing. **2** tr. (of water, or a person with water) clear out (a pipe, channel, etc.) by flushing through. **3** tr. wear away, erode. **4** tr. hasten over (an area etc.) searching thoroughly (scoured the pages of the newspaper). **5** intr. range hastily esp. in search or pursuit. ● n. **1** the act or an instance of scouring; the

state of being scoured. **2** (also in pl., treated as sing.) diarrhea in livestock. **3** a substance used for scouring.

scourge /skɜːdʒ/ ● n. **1** a whip used for punishment, esp. of people. **2** a person or thing that causes trouble or suffering. ● v.tr. **1** whip. **2** punish; afflict.

scouring pad n. a pad of abrasive material, e.g. steel wool, for cleaning kitchenware etc.

scout ● n. **1** a person, esp. a soldier, sent out to get information about the enemy's position, strength, etc. **2 a** = TALENT SCOUT. **b** N Amer. esp. Baseball a scout who travels ahead of the team in order to gain information about future opponents. **c** a person employed by a mining company to find new mining opportunities or report on the activities of competitors. **3** a car, ship, aircraft, etc. designed or sent out for reconnoitring. **4** (**Scout**) a boy (usu. aged 11-14) who is a member of a Scouting organization. ● v. **1** intr. act as a scout. **2** intr. make a search. **3** tr. informal explore to get information about (territory, an organization, etc.). **4** tr. **a** look for (new talent etc.). **b** discover or examine (a prospective recruit). □ **scouter** n. **scouting** n.

Scouter n. an adult member of a Scouting organization.

Scouting n. an international movement, founded in England in 1908 by Robert Baden-Powell, aiming to develop character and promote responsible behaviour in young people, usu. through outdoor activities.

scoutmaster n. a person in charge of a group of Scouts.

scout's honour interj. professing honesty or genuineness.

scow n. esp. N Amer. a flat-bottomed boat used as a barge, lighter, etc.

scowl ● n. a severe frown producing a sullen, bad-tempered, or threatening look on a person's face. ● v.intr. make a scowl.

scrabble ● v.intr. **1** scratch or grope to find or collect or hold on to something. **2** scramble on hands and feet. ● n. **1** an act of scrabbling. **2** (**Scrabble**) proprietary a game in which players use lettered tiles to form words on a special board.

scraggly adj. sparse and irregular; ragged.

scraggy adj. (**-ier, -iest**) **1** thin and bony. **2** = SCRAGGLY.

scram v.intr. (**scrammed, scramming**) (esp. in imper.) informal go away.

scramble ● v. **1** intr. make one's way over rough ground, rocks, etc., by clambering, crawling, etc. **2** intr. struggle with competitors (for a thing or share of it). **3** intr. **a** move or act with difficulty or anxiously. **b** move hastily. **4** tr. **a** mix together indiscriminately. **b** jumble or muddle. **5** tr. cook (eggs) by breaking them into a pan, often with milk etc., and stirring the mixture over heat. **6** tr. make (a broadcast transmission, telephone conversation, etc.) unintelligible to those without a corresponding decoding device. **7** tr. informal execute (an action etc.) awkwardly and inefficiently. **8** intr. (of fighter aircraft or their pilots) take off quickly in an emergency or for action. **9** intr. (of a quarterback) move quickly to dodge or evade tacklers while waiting for an opportunity to throw the ball. **10** tr. distribute by scattering randomly to a crowd. ● n. **1** an act of scrambling. **2** a difficult climb or walk. **3** (foll. by for) an eager or disorganized struggle or competition. **4** an emergency takeoff by fighter aircraft.

scrambler n. **1** a person or thing that scrambles. **2** a device used to scramble television signals, telephone conversations, etc.

scrap[1] ● n. **1** a fragment or remnant; a small detached piece. **2** rubbish or waste, usu. of some value for the material it contains. **3** an extract or cutting from something written or printed. **4** discarded metal or paper for reuse. **5** the smallest piece or amount (*not a scrap of food left*). **6** (in *pl.*) **a** odds and ends. **b** bits of uneaten food. ● *v.tr.* (**scrapped**, **scrapping**) **1** discard, esp. as useless. **2** get rid of; cancel. **3** make scrap of.

scrap[2] *informal* ● n. a fight or rough quarrel, esp. a spontaneous one. ● *v.tr.* (**scrapped**, **scrapping**) (often foll. by *with*) have a scrap.

scrapbook n. a book of blank pages for sticking clippings, drawings, photographs, etc. in.

scrape ● v. **1** tr. **a** move a hard or sharp edge across (a surface), as to make something smooth or clean. **b** apply (a hard or sharp edge) in this way. **2** tr. remove (a stain, projection, mass, etc.) by scraping. **3** tr. **a** rub (a surface) harshly against or with another. **b** scratch or damage by scraping. **4** tr. make (a hollow) by scraping. **5 a** tr. draw or move with a sound of, or resembling, scraping. **b** intr. emit or produce such a sound. **6** intr. move or pass along while almost touching close or surrounding features, obstacles, etc. **7** tr. just manage to achieve (a living etc.). **8** intr. (often foll. by *by*, *through*) **a** barely manage. **b** pass (an examination etc.) with difficulty. **9** tr. (foll. by *together*, *up*) contrive to bring or provide; amass with difficulty. ● n. **1** the act or sound of scraping. **2** a scraped place (on the skin etc.). **3** a scrap; a fight or quarrel. **4** *informal* an awkward predicament, esp. resulting from an escapade. □ **scrape (the bottom of) the barrel** *informal* be obliged to use one's last resources.

scraper n. a tool etc. used for scraping, esp. for removing ice, paint, etc. from a surface.

scrap heap n. a collection of discarded or cancelled things.

scrapie /ˈskreɪpi/ n. a disease of sheep involving the central nervous system and characterized by lack of coordination, thought to be caused by a virus-like agent.

scraping n. **1** in senses of SCRAPE v. & n. **2** (esp. in *pl.*) a fragment produced by this.

scrapper n. **1** a person who fights; a pugnacious person. **2** a competitive or tenacious person.

scrappy adj. (**-ier**, **-iest**) **1** pugnacious or tenacious. **2** consisting of scraps. **3** incomplete; carelessly arranged or put together. □ **scrappiness** n.

scratch ● v. **1** tr. score or mark the surface of with a sharp or pointed object. **2** tr. make a long narrow superficial wound (in the skin). **3** tr. & intr. scrape (something) without marking, esp. with the hand to relieve itching. **4** tr. make or form by scratching. **5** tr. write hurriedly or awkwardly (*scratched a quick reply*). **6** tr. (often foll. by *together*, *up*, etc.) obtain or achieve (a thing, a living, etc.) by scratching or with difficulty. **7** tr. cancel or strike (out) with or as with a pencil etc. **8 a** tr. withdraw (a competitor, candidate, etc.). **b** intr. (of a competitor) withdraw from a race. **9** intr. **a** scratch the ground etc. in search. **b** look around haphazardly (*they were scratching around for evidence*). ● n. **1** a mark or wound made by scratching. **2** a sound of scratching. **3** an act of scratching oneself. **4** *informal* a superficial wound. **5** a line from which competitors in a race (esp. those not receiving a handicap) start. **6** *slang* money. **7** an athlete or competitor withdrawn from a competition etc. ● *attrib.adj.* **1** collected by chance. **2 a** collected or made from whatever is

available (*a scratch crew*). **b** made from basic or rudimentary ingredients, not from prefabricated components (*scratch cake*). **3** with no handicap given (*a scratch race*). □ **from scratch 1** from the beginning. **2** (of food) prepared from the basic ingredients, without the use of prepared mixes etc. **3** without help or advantage. **scratch along** make a living etc. with difficulty. **scratch one's head** be perplexed. **scratch my back and I will scratch yours 1** do me a favour and I will return it. **2** used in reference to mutual aid or flattery. **scratch the surface 1** understand or deal with a matter only superficially. **2** investigate further. **up to scratch** up to the required standard. □ **scratcher** n.

scratch-and-sniff n. (*attrib.*) designating a perfumed card etc. whose perfume is released when the card is scratched.

scratch-and-win n. N Amer. a lottery ticket coated with an opaque substance which is scratched away to reveal whether the ticket holder wins a prize.

scratch pad n. **1** esp. N Amer. a pad of paper for scribbling. **2** *Computing* a small fast memory for the temporary storage of data.

scratchproof adj. that cannot be marred with scratches.

scratchy adj. (**-ier**, **-iest**) **1** tending to make scratches or a scratching noise. **2** (esp. of a garment) tending to itch (*a scratchy sweater*). **3** demanding relief by or as if by scratching (*a scratchy throat*). **4** (of a drawing etc.) done in scratches. □ **scratchily** adv. **scratchiness** n.

scrawl ● *v.tr. & intr.* write in a hurried untidy way. ● n. **1** a piece of hurried writing. **2** a scrawled note. **3** a careless, illegible style of handwriting.

scrawny adj. (**-ier**, **-iest**) skinny. □ **scrawniness** n.

scream ● n. **1** a loud high-pitched piercing cry expressing fear, pain, etc. **2** a similar sound, e.g. of sirens. **3** *informal* an irresistibly funny thing, person, etc. ● v. **1** intr. emit a scream. **2** tr. speak or sing (words etc.) in a screaming tone. **3** intr. make or move with a shrill sound like a scream. **4** intr. laugh uncontrollably. **5** intr. N Amer. informal move very quickly. **6** intr. be blatantly obvious or conspicuous.

screamer n. **1** a person or thing that screams. **2** *informal* a person or thing that raises screams of laughter, excitement, fear, etc. **3** N Amer. Sport something moving very fast, esp. a powerful base hit, slapshot, etc. **4** esp. US informal a sensational headline.

screamingly adv. **1** extremely (*screamingly funny*). **2** blatantly (*screamingly obvious*).

scree n. (in *sing.* or *pl.*) **1** small loose stones. **2** a mountain slope covered with these.

screech ● n. **1** a harsh high-pitched scream etc. **2** (in Canada) a potent dark rum of Newfoundland. ● *v.tr. & intr.* utter with or make a screech. □ **screech in** Cdn (*Nfld*) (usu. in *passive*) initiate (a visitor) by means of a screech-in. □ **screecher** n. **screechy** adj. (**-ier**, **-iest**).

screech-in n. Cdn (*Nfld*) a jocular ritual by which visitors to Newfoundland are 'initiated', involving the drinking of screech and performing acts such as dipping a foot in the ocean, kissing a cod, etc.

screech owl n. **1** any of various small N American eared owls of the genus *Otus*. **2** any owl that screeches instead of hooting, esp. a barn owl.

screed n. a long usu. tiresome piece of writing or speech.

screen ● n. **1** a fixed or movable upright partition for separating, concealing, or sheltering. **2** a thing used as a shelter, esp. from observation. **3 a** a measure adopted for concealment. **b** the protection afforded by this (*under the screen of night*). **4 a** a blank usu. white or silver surface on which a photographic image is projected. **b** (prec. by *the*) the film industry. **5 a** the surface of a cathode ray tube or similar electronic device, esp. of a television, computer, etc., on which images appear. **b** the collection of images etc. displayed on a computer screen at one time (*move to the next screen*). **6** a frame with fine wire netting to keep out flies, mosquitoes, etc. **7** a system of checking for the presence or absence of a disease, ability, attribute, etc. ● *v.tr.* **1 a** afford shelter to; hide partly or completely. **b** protect from detection, censure, etc. **2** shut off or hide behind a screen. **3** *Hockey* obstruct the view of (a goalie) by being positioned in front of him or her. **4 a** show (a film etc.) on a screen. **b** broadcast (a television program). **5** prevent from causing, or protect from, electrical interference. **6 a** test (a person or group) for the presence or absence of a disease. **b** check on (a person) for the presence or absence of a quality, esp. reliability, suitability, etc. **c** find out details about (an incoming telephone call) to determine whether it should be answered. □ **screener** *n.*

screen door *n.* *N Amer.* a light outer door with a screen for keeping out insects while letting in air.

screened shot *n.* (also **screen shot**) *Hockey* a shot taken while the goalie's view is obstructed.

screening *n.* **1** the showing of a film. **2** the testing of a group of people for a disease etc.

screenplay *n.* the script of a film, with acting instructions, scene directions, etc.

screen printing *n.* a process like stencilling with ink forced through a prepared sheet of fine material. □ **screen print** *n.* **screen-print** *v.tr.* (usu. as **screen-printed** *adj.*).

screen saver *n.* *Computing* a program which, after a set time, replaces an unchanging screen display with a moving image to prevent damage to the phosphor.

screen test *n.* a filmed audition of a prospective film or television actor.

screenwriter *n.* a person who writes a screenplay. □ **screenwriting** *n.*

screw ● *n.* **1** a thin cylinder or cone with a spiral ridge or thread running around the outside, used esp. for fastening. **2** a metal screw with a blunt end on which a nut is threaded to bolt things together. Also called BOLT 2. **3** a wooden or metal straight screw used to exert pressure. **4** (in *sing.* or *pl.*) an instrument of torture acting in this way. **5** (in full **screw propeller**) a form of propeller with twisted blades acting like a screw on the water or air. **6** one turn of a screw. **7** (in full **female screw**) a shaft with a spiral ridge or thread running around the inside wall. **8** *coarse slang* **a** an act of sexual intercourse. **b** a partner in this. **9** *slang* a prison guard. ● *v.* **1** *tr.* fasten or tighten with a screw or screws. **2** *tr.* turn (a screw). **3** *intr.* twist or turn around like or as a screw (*screws in easily*). **4** *tr.* **a** *slang* (often in *passive*) cheat or take advantage of; treat unfairly. **b** (often foll. by *up*) put psychological etc. pressure on to achieve an end. **c** oppress. **5** *tr.* (foll. by *out of*) *slang* extort (consent, money, etc.) from (a person). **6** *coarse slang* **a** *tr.* & *intr.* have sexual intercourse (with). **b** *tr.* (as an exclamation) used to express frustration, anger, dismissive contempt, etc. □ **have one's head screwed on** (**straight**) *informal* have common sense. **have a screw loose** *informal* be slightly crazy. **put the screws on** *informal* exert pressure, esp. to extort or intimidate. **screw around** esp. *N Amer.* **1** be

promiscuous. **2** fool around, waste time. **3** (foll. by *with*) toy with someone psychologically. **screw up 1** *slang* **a** bungle or mismanage; handle something badly, make a mistake. **b** spoil or ruin (an event, opportunity, etc.). **2** *slang* (usu. as **screwed-up** *adj.*) disturb mentally. **3** summon up (one's courage etc.). **4** contract or contort (one's face etc.). **5** contract and crush into a tight mass (a piece of paper etc.).

screwball *N Amer.* ● *n.* **1** *Baseball* a ball pitched so that it curves towards the side from which it was thrown. **2** *slang* a crazy or eccentric person. ● *adj.* **1** *slang* crazy, eccentric. **2** designating a style of zany fast-moving comedy film with eccentric characters or ridiculous situations.

screw cap *n.* = SCREW-TOP.

screwdriver *n.* **1** a tool with a shaped tip to fit into the head of a screw to turn it. **2** a cocktail of vodka and orange juice.

screwed *adj.* **1** *slang* ruined; rendered ineffective; in a hopeless state (*now we're screwed!*). **2** twisted.

screw eye *n.* a screw with a loop for passing cord etc. through instead of a slotted head.

screw-top *n.* (also *attrib.*) a cap or lid that can be screwed on to a bottle, jar, etc.

screw-up *n.* esp. *N Amer.* *slang* a bungle, muddle, mess.

screwy *adj.* (**-ier**, **-iest**) esp. *N Amer.* *slang* **1** crazy or eccentric. **2** absurd. **3** messed up, confused. □ **screwiness** *n.*

scribble ● *v.* **1** *tr.* & *intr.* write carelessly or hurriedly. **2** *intr.* often *derogatory* be an author or writer. **3** *intr.* & *tr.* draw carelessly or meaninglessly. ● *n.* **1** a scrawl. **2** a hasty note etc. **3** careless handwriting. □ **scribblings** *n.pl.* **scribbly** *adj.*

scribbler *n.* **1** *informal* a person or thing that scribbles, esp. a professional writer. **2** *Cdn* a small, soft-covered booklet for writing in; a student's notebook.

scribe *n.* **1** a person who writes out documents, esp. an ancient or medieval copyist of manuscripts. **2** *Jewish Hist.* an ancient Jewish record-keeper or, later, professional theologian and jurist. **3** (also **scriber**) a pointed instrument for making marks on wood, bricks, etc., to guide a saw, or in sign writing. **4** *N Amer.* *informal* a writer, esp. a journalist. □ **scribal** *adj.*

scrim *n.* **1** a theatrical drop made of an open-weave fabric that looks opaque when lit from in front but becomes transparent when lit from behind. **2** the fabric of which such drops are made.

scrimmage ● *n.* **1** a rough or confused struggle. **2** *Football* **a** a sequence of play beginning with a backward pass from the centre to put the ball in play and continuing until the ball is declared dead. **b** (in full **scrimmage line**) = LINE OF SCRIMMAGE. **3** *N Amer.* *Sport* a session or informal game in which a team's various squads practise plays against each other. ● *v.intr.* engage in a scrimmage.

scrimp *v.* **1** *intr.* (often foll. by *on*) be sparing or parsimonious. **2** *tr.* use sparingly. □ **scrimp and save** practise thrift to save money or in order to pay for something else.

scrimshaw ● *v.tr.* & *intr.* adorn (whalebone, ivory, shells, etc.) with carved or coloured designs. ● *n.* work or a piece of work of this kind.

scrip[1] *n.* **1** a provisional certificate of money subscribed to a bank or company etc. entitling the holder to a formal certificate and dividends. **2** (*collect.*) such certificates. **3** an extra share or shares instead of a dividend. **4** temporary paper currency.

scrip[2] *n.* (in full **land scrip**) *N Amer.* **1** a certificate entitling the holder to acquire possession of certain portions of public land. **2** *Cdn hist.* a certificate issued to Metis entitling the bearer to 240 acres or money for the purchase of land, issued in compensation for lands lost by the Metis after the Northwest Rebellion.

script ● *n.* **1** handwriting as distinct from print; written characters. **2** type imitating handwriting. **3** an alphabet or system of writing (*the Russian script*). **4 a** the text of a play, film, or broadcast. **b** a predictable or planned series of statements, actions, etc. **5** *Computing* a file containing commands or other actions that could have been entered from the keyboard, used to replay often-used sequences of actions. ● *v.tr.* **1 a** write a script for (a film etc.). **b** write (a script, dialogue, etc.). **2** (esp. as **scripted** *adj.*) provide with or have follow a script.

scriptural *adj.* **1** of or relating to a scripture, esp. the Bible. **2** having the authority of a scripture. □ **scripturally** *adv.*

scripture *n.* writings sacred to a religion or group, esp. (as **Scripture** or **the Scriptures**) the Bible.

scriptwriter *n.* a person who writes a script for a film, broadcast, etc. □ **scriptwriting** *n.*

scritch *n.* a quiet scraping or scratching sound. □ **scritching** *n. & adj.*

scrod *n.* N Amer. a young cod or haddock, esp. as food.

scroll ● *n.* **1** a roll of parchment or paper esp. with writing on it. **2** a book in the ancient roll form. **3** an ornamental design or carving imitating a roll of parchment. ● *v.* **1** *tr.* (often foll. by *down*, *up*, etc.) *Computing* move (displayed text etc.) up, down, or across on a screen or in a window in order to display different parts of it. **2** *intr.* curl up like paper.

scroll bar *n.* a long thin section at the edge of a computer display by which material can be scrolled using a mouse.

scroll saw *n.* a narrow-bladed saw for cutting along curved lines in ornamental work.

scrollwork *n.* decoration of spiral lines, esp. as cut by a scroll saw.

Scrooge *n.* a mean or miserly person.

scrotum /ˈskroːtəm/ *n.* (*pl.* **scrota** /-tə/ or **-s**) a pouch of skin containing the testicles. □ **scrotal** *adj.*

scrounge *informal* ● *v.* **1 a** *tr.* (often foll. by *up*) N Amer. search or forage for; obtain by or as by foraging. **b** *intr.* forage. **2** *intr.* search about to find something at no cost. **3** *tr. & intr.* obtain (things) illicitly or by cadging. ● *n.* an act of scrounging. □ **scrounger** *n.*

scrub¹ ● *v.* (**scrubbed**, **scrubbing**) **1** *tr.* **a** rub (a surface) hard so as to clean, esp. with a hard brush. **b** remove (dirt etc.) in this way. **2** *intr.* use a brush in this way. **3** *intr.* (often foll. by *up*) (of a surgeon etc.) thoroughly clean the hands and arms by scrubbing, before operating. **4** *tr. informal* scrap or cancel. **5** *tr.* use water to remove impurities from (gas etc.). ● *n.* **1** the act or an instance of scrubbing; the process of being scrubbed. **2** a substance, implement, etc., used in scrubbing (*facial scrub*). □ **scrubbable** *adj.*

scrub² *n.* **1 a** vegetation consisting mainly of brush or stunted forest growth. **b** an area of land covered with this. **2** N Amer. an animal of inferior breed or physique (often *attrib.: scrub horse*). **3** a small or dwarf variety (often *attrib.: scrub pine*). **4** *Sport* **a** N Amer. *informal* a team or player not of the first class. **b** Cdn an informal match played by children, amateurs, etc. (also *attrib.: scrub baseball*). **5** a worthless, insignificant, or contemptible person. □ **scrubby** *adj.*

scrubber *n.* a person or thing that scrubs, esp. apparatus for purifying gases, removing excess pollutants from exhaust, etc.

scrubland *n.* land consisting of scrub vegetation.

scrub nurse *n.* an operating room nurse who handles sterile instruments etc. and assists the surgeon.

scruff *n.* the back of the neck as used to grasp and lift or drag an animal or person by (esp. *scruff of the neck*).

scruffy *adj.* (**-ier**, **-iest**) *informal* shabby, slovenly, untidy; ragged. □ **scruffily** *adv.* **scruffiness** *n.*

scrum ● *n.* **1** *Rugby* an arrangement of the forwards of each team in opposing groups, each with arms interlocked and heads down, with the ball thrown in between them to restart play. **2** Brit. & Cdn *informal* a disorderly crowd. **3** Cdn **a** a situation where a crowd of reporters surround and interrogate a politician in an impromptu, informal, or disorderly manner. **b** the crowd of reporters in such a situation. ● *v.* **1** *intr.* (often foll. by *down*) *Rugby* form a scrum. **2** Cdn **a** *intr.* (of a politician or reporter) engage in a scrum. **b** *tr.* surround and interrogate (a politician) in a scrum.

scrum half *n.* Rugby a halfback who puts the ball into the scrum.

scrumptious *adj. informal* **1** delicious. **2** pleasing. □ **scrumptiously** *adv.* **scrumptiousness** *n.*

scrunch ● *v.* **1 a** *tr. & intr.* make or become crushed or crumpled. **b** *intr.* N Amer. squeeze oneself into a compact shape; crouch. **2** *intr. & tr.* make or cause to make a crunching sound. **3** *tr.* style (hair) by squeezing or crushing in the hands to give a tousled look. ● *n.* the act or an instance of scrunching.

scruncheon /ˈskrʌnʃən/ *n.* Cdn (Nfld) (in *pl.*) small pieces of pork fat fried crisp and usu. eaten with fish and brewis.

scrunchy *n.* (also **scrunchie**) (*pl.* **-ies**) an elastic band covered in loose fabric, used to fasten the hair in a ponytail etc.

scruple /ˈskruːpəl/ ● *n.* (in *sing.* or *pl.*) **1** regard to the morality or propriety of an action. **2** a feeling of doubt or hesitation caused by this. ● *v.intr.* **1** be reluctant because of scruples (*did not scruple to stop their allowance*). **2** feel or be influenced by scruples.

scrupulous /ˈskruːpjʊləs/ *adj.* **1** conscientious or thorough even in small matters. **2** careful to avoid doing wrong. **3** over-attentive to details. □ **scrupulosity** /-ˈlɒsɪti/ *n.* **scrupulously** *adv.* **scrupulousness** *n.*

scrutineer /skruːtɪˈnɪːr/ *n.* esp. Cdn & Brit. a person who scrutinizes or examines something, esp. the conduct and result of a ballot.

scrutinize /ˈskruːtɪˌnaɪz/ *v.tr.* look closely at; examine with close scrutiny.

scrutiny /ˈskruːtɪni/ *n.* (*pl.* **-ies**) **1** a critical gaze. **2** a close investigation or examination of details. **3** an official examination of ballot papers to check their validity or accuracy of counting.

SCSI /ˈskʌzi/ *n.* a standard interface connecting peripheral devices, such as disk storage units, to small and medium-sized computers.

scuba *n.* (*pl.* **-s**) **1** a portable breathing apparatus for divers, consisting of cylinders of compressed air strapped on the back, feeding air automatically through a mask or mouthpiece. **2** scuba diving. □ **scuba dive** *v.intr.* **scuba diver** *n.* **scuba diving** *n.*

scud ● *v.intr.* (**scudded**, **scudding**) **1** fly or run straight, fast, and lightly; skim along. **2** (of a sailboat) run before the wind. **3** (of a cloud, foam, etc.) be driven by the wind. ● *n.* (usu. **Scud**) a type of long-range surface-to-surface guided missile originally developed in the former USSR.

scuff ● *v.* **1** *tr.* graze or brush against. **2** *tr.* mark or wear the surface off (leather, esp. of shoe uppers, a floor, etc.) by scratching or grazing with or against something. **3** *tr.* Baseball scratch or roughen up the surface of (the ball) illicitly to increase its movement when pitched (see MOVEMENT 11). **4** *intr.* **a** a walk with dragging feet. **b** drag (one's feet) across a surface. ● *n.* a mark of scuffing. □ **scuffed** *adj.*

scuffle ● *n.* **1** a confused struggle or disorderly fight at close quarters; a tussle. **2** the shuffling of feet. ● *v.* **1** *intr.* engage in a scuffle. **2** *intr.* move with a shuffling gait. **3** *tr.* scarify or stir the surface of the ground, esp. between rows of crops. □ **scuffler** *n.*

scull[1] ● *n.* **1** either of a pair of small oars used by a single rower. **2** an oar placed over the stern of a boat to propel it, usu. by a twisting motion. **3** a small boat propelled with a scull or sculls. **4** (in *pl.*) a race between boats with two oars per rower. ● *v.tr.* propel (a boat) with sculls. □ **sculler** *n.*

scull[2] *n. Cdn* (*Nfld*) the seasonal migration of caplin from the sea to inshore waters to spawn.

scullery *n.* (*pl.* **-ies**) a small kitchen or room at the back of a house for washing dishes etc.

sculpin *n.* any of numerous fish native to non-tropical regions, having large spiny heads.

sculpt *v.tr. & intr.* **1** create a sculpture. **2** carve. **3** provide with a highly contoured relief. □ **sculpting** *n.* **sculptor** *n.* **sculptress** *n.*

sculpture ● *n.* **1** the art of making forms, often representational, in the round or in relief by chiselling stone, carving wood, modelling clay, casting metal, etc. **2** a work or works of sculpture. ● *v.tr.* **1** represent in or adorn with sculpture. **2** (esp. as **sculptured** *adj.*) give a markedly contoured form to. □ **sculptural** *adj.* **sculpturally** *adv.*

scum ● *n.* **1** a layer of dirt, froth, etc. forming at the top of liquid, esp. in boiling or fermentation or on stagnant water. **2** the most worthless part of something. **3** *informal* a worthless, despicable person or group. ● *v.* (**scummed, scumming**) **1** *tr.* remove scum from. **2** *tr.* be or form a scum on. **3** *intr.* (of a liquid) develop scum. □ **scummy** *adj.* (**-ier, -iest**).

scumbag *n.* (also **scumball, scum-bucket**) *slang* a contemptible, despicable, or disgusting person.

scum of the earth *n. informal* an extremely contemptible or despicable person or group.

scup *n.* a kind of porgy, *Stenostomus chrysops*, of the Atlantic coast of N America.

scupper ● *n.* (often in *pl.*) a hole in a ship's side to carry off water from the deck. ● *v.tr. slang* **1** sink (a ship or its crew). **2** defeat or ruin (a plan etc.).

scurf *n.* **1** flakes on the skin's surface, cast off as fresh skin develops below, esp. those of the head; dandruff. **2** any scaly matter on a surface. □ **scurfy** *adj.*

scurrilous /'skʌrɪləs/ *adj.* **1** (of a person or language) grossly or indecently abusive. **2** given to or expressed with coarse humour. □ **scurrility** /-'rɪlɪti/ *n.* (*pl.* **-ies**). **scurrilously** *adv.*

scurry ● *v.intr.* (**-ies, -ied**) run or move hurriedly, esp. with short quick steps. ● *n.* (*pl.* **-ies**) a scurrying movement.

S-curve *n.* two curves in a road etc., one following the other in the opposite direction.

scurvy *n.* a disease caused by lack of vitamin C, with swollen, bleeding gums and the opening of previously healed wounds.

scutellum /skʊ'teləm/ *n.* (*pl.* **scutella** /-lə/) a scale, plate, or any shieldlike formation on a plant, insect, bird, etc., esp. one of the horny scales on a bird's foot.

scutter *v.intr. informal* scurry.

scuttle ● *v.* **1** *tr.* esp. *N Amer.* abandon, thwart, or dismiss (a plan, rumour, etc.). **2** *tr.* let water into (a ship) to sink it, esp. by opening the seacocks. **3** *intr.* run or move hurriedly with short quick steps, esp.

furtively or busily. ● *n.* **1** a hole with a lid in a ship's deck or side. **2** *N Amer.* an opening in the ceiling, floor, or wall of a building; a trap door. **3** a small bucket, usu. with a sloping lip, for pouring, carrying, and holding coal. **4** a hurried pace.

scuttlebutt *n.* **1** esp. *N Amer. informal* rumour, gossip. **2** a barrel of drinking water kept on a ship's deck.

scuzzball *n.* (also **scuzzbag**) esp. *N Amer. slang* a filthy, sleazy, or shady person.

scuzzy *adj.* (**-ier, -iest**) *slang* squalid, sleazy, abhorrent, or disgusting. □ **scuzz** *n.* **scuzziness** *n.*

scythe /saɪð/ ● *n.* an agricultural tool consisting of a pole with two short handles projecting from it and a long thin curving blade at the bottom, which is swung round the ground to cut grass, grain, etc. ● *v.tr.* cut with, or as if with, a scythe.

SD *abbr.* **1** South Dakota (in postal use). **2** *Statistics* standard deviation.

S.Dak. *abbr.* South Dakota.

SDI *abbr.* STRATEGIC DEFENCE INITIATIVE.

SE *abbr.* **1** southeast. **2** southeastern.

Se *symbol* selenium.

sea *n.* **1** the expanse of salt water that covers most of the earth's surface and surrounds its land masses. **2** any part of this as opposed to land or fresh water. **3** a particular (usu. named) tract of salt water partly or wholly enclosed by land (*the Beaufort Sea*). **4** a large inland lake (*the Sea of Galilee*). **5** (esp. in *pl.*) the state of the sea with regard to the roughness or smoothness of the waves, the presence or absence of swell, etc. (*choppy seas*). **6** a vast quantity or expanse (*a sea of faces*). **7** (*attrib.*) **a** of, related to, or designed for the sea. **b** (often prefixed to the name of an animal or plant having a superficial resemblance to what it is named after) living in or near the sea (*sea cucumber*). □ **at sea** **1** in a ship on the sea. **2** (also **all at sea**) perplexed, confused. **by sea** in a ship or ships. **go to sea** become a sailor. **on the sea** **1** in a ship at sea. **2** situated on the coast. **put** (or **put out**) **to sea** leave land or port.

sea bass *n.* any of various marine fishes like the bass, esp. *Centropristis striatus*.

seabed *n.* = SEA FLOOR.

seabird *n.* any bird that lives on or near the sea.

seaboard *n.* the coastal region or land along the sea.

seaborne *adj.* carried over or supported by the sea.

sea breeze *n.* a cool gentle breeze blowing landward from the sea.

sea cadet *n.* a volunteer youth receiving training and education in naval affairs.

sea captain *n.* the captain or commander of esp. a merchant ship.

sea change *n.* a notable or unexpected transformation; a radical change.

seacoast *n.* the border of land near the sea.

seacock *n.* a valve below a ship's waterline for letting water in or out.

sea cucumber *n.* any of several hundred species of holothurian.

sea dog *n.* **1** an old or experienced sailor. **2** *N Amer. informal* a harbour seal.

Sea-Doo /'siːduː/ *n. proprietary* = PERSONAL WATERCRAFT.

seafarer *n.* **1** a sailor. **2** a traveller by sea.

seafaring ● *adj.* **1** travelling by sea. **2** related to or involved in the occupation or business of a sailor. ● *n.* **1** travel by sea. **2** the business or occupation of a sailor.

sea floor *n.* the bottom of the sea.

seafoam ● *n.* **1** foam formed on the sea. **2** (also

seafoam green) a pastel bluish-green. ● *adj.* of the colour of seafoam green.

seafood *n.* any edible animal obtained from the sea, including fish, crustaceans, and molluscs.

seafront *n.* an area or esp. the part of a coastal town directly facing the sea.

sea-going *adj.* **1** fit for crossing the sea. **2** a travelling by sea. **b** involved in the occupation of a sailor. **3** of or related to the occupation or lifestyle of a sailor.

seagrass *n.* any of various grasslike plants growing in or by the sea, esp. eelgrass, *Zostera marina*.

sea green ● *n.* the colour of the sea, a pale bluish green. ● *adj.* (usu. **sea-green**) of this colour.

seagull *n.* a gull, esp. a herring gull.

sea horse *n.* any of various small upright marine fish esp. of the genus *Hippocampus*, having a body suggestive of the head and neck of a horse.

sea ice *n.* a large expanse of ice formed from frozen salt water, esp. occurring in the sea.

sea kayak ● *n.* a usu. fibreglass kayak with a rudder. ● *v.intr.* travel by sea kayak, esp. for recreation. □ **sea kayaker** *n.* **sea kayaking** *n.*

seal[1] ● *n.* **1** a a design, crest, etc. impressed esp. on a piece of wax or paper affixed to a document as a guarantee of authenticity. **b** an engraved stamp used to make an impression on wax or paper. **c** a piece of wax etc. bearing such an impression, often used on a folded letter so that it cannot be opened unless the seal is broken. **2** a plastic wrapper etc. that must be broken before a box or container can be opened. **3** a a material or substance used to fill a gap or crack so that air, liquid, etc. cannot enter or escape. **b** protection given by this (*caulking gives a good seal*). **4** an act etc. regarded as a confirmation or guarantee, esp. of a vow or promise. **5** a significant or prophetic mark (*has the seal of death in his face*). **6** a decorative label or stamp usu. sold for charity and placed on an envelope (*Christmas seals*). ● *v.tr.* **1** a fasten or close securely. **b** close (an envelope) by sticking the flap down. **2** a close (a jar or container etc.) so that it is airtight and watertight. **b** insulate or set a seal around (a window, pipe joint, etc.) so that it is airtight or watertight. **3** certify as correct, authentic, or approved by marking with a seal or stamp. **4** determine irrevocably (*their fate is sealed*). **5** (foll. by *off*) put barriers around (an area) to prevent entry and exit, esp. as a security measure. **6** apply a heavy non-porous coating to (new wood, a wall, etc.) to make it impervious, esp. to facilitate the application of a second, finishing coat. □ **one's lips are sealed** one promises to keep a secret. **set one's seal to** (or **on**) authorize, endorse, or confirm. □ **sealable** *adj.* **sealing** *n.*

seal[2] ● *n.* **1** any fish-eating amphibious sea mammal of the family Phocidae or Otariidae, with flippers and webbed feet. **2** sealskin. ● *v.intr.* hunt for seals.

sealant *n.* **1** = SEAL *n.* 3a. **2** a substance applied to a surface to make it impervious or resistant to water, dirt, stains, etc.

sea legs *n.* the ability to keep one's balance and avoid becoming sick while at sea.

sealer[1] *n.* **1** (in full **sealer jar**) *Cdn* (esp. *Prairies & BC*) **a** a preserving jar with a glass or metal lid secured by a metal band screwed onto the mouth of the jar. **b** the contents of a sealer. **2** an undercoat of paint etc. used to give porous building materials a surface more receptive to finishing coats. **3** a device or substance used to make something airtight or impervious to water, oil, etc.

sealer[2] *n.* **1** a person who hunts seals. **2** a ship used for hunting seals.

sealer ring *n.* *Cdn* (esp. *Prairies & BC*) a rubber ring between the lid and rim of a sealer jar ensuring an airtight seal.

sea level *n.* the average level of the sea's surface, used as an international standard in calculating altitude and as a barometric standard.

sealift *n.* esp. *N Amer.* a large-scale transportation of supplies, troops, etc. by sea.

sealing *n.* the hunting of seals.

sealing wax *n.* a mixture of shellac, rosin, turpentine, and pigment, softened by heating and used to make seals.

sea lion *n.* any of several large-eared seals having broader muzzles and sparser under-fur than the fur seals.

seal of approval *n.* **1** a seal or stamp on a product etc. indicating that it has been approved by an authority. **2** an expression of endorsement etc.

seal oil *n.* oil obtained from the fat of seals.

seal-oil lamp *n.* = KUDLIK.

sealskin *n.* **1** the skin or prepared fur of a seal. **2** (often *attrib.*) a garment made from this.

seam ● *n.* **1** a line along which two pieces of cloth etc. are stitched together. **2** a line or ridge where two parallel edges meet, e.g. of floorboards fitted edge to edge. **3** a stratum of coal etc. **4** a wrinkle or scar. ● *v.tr.* **1** join with a seam. **2** (esp. as **seamed** *adj.*) mark or score (a surface) with lines or indentations. □ **come** (or **fall**) **apart at the seams** collapse emotionally. □ **seamer** *n.*

seaman *n.* (*pl.* **-men**) **1** a person whose occupation is on the sea; a sailor. **2** an enlisted member of the navy below the rank of petty officer.

seamanship *n.* the art and skill of managing, handling, and maintaining a ship or boat.

seamless *adj.* **1** without a seam. **2** uninterrupted, smooth. □ **seamlessly** *adv.* **seamlessness** *n.*

seamstress /'si:mstrəs, 'sem-/ *n.* a woman who makes and mends clothing, esp. professionally.

seamy *adj.* (**-ier**, **-iest**) **1** marked with or showing seams. **2** disreputable, degenerate, sordid.

seance /'seɪɒns, -ɑ̃s/ *n.* a meeting at which spiritualists attempt to make contact with the dead.

sea otter *n.* a Pacific otter with thick dark fur.

seaplane *n.* an aircraft designed to take off from and land and float on water.

seaport *n.* **1** a harbour or port for seagoing ships. **2** a town or city having such a harbour or port.

sear ● *v.* **1** *tr.* burn or scorch the surface of. **2** *tr. & intr.* cause great pain or anguish (to). **3** *tr.* brown (meat) quickly at a high temperature so that it will retain its juices in cooking. **4** *tr. & intr.* leave an esp. disturbing impression etc. on or in. ● *adj.* = SERE[1].

search ● *v.* **1** *tr.* look through, examine, or go over thoroughly to find something. **2** *intr.* make a search or investigation. **3** *tr. & intr.* *Computing* locate a specified piece of information or text in a table, file, document, etc. **4** *tr.* examine or question (one's mind, conscience, etc.) thoroughly (*search your heart*). **5** *tr.* (foll. by *out*) look probingly for. ● *n.* **1** an act of searching; an investigation. **2** *Computing* the locating of a specified piece of information or text. □ **in search of** trying to find. **search me!** *informal* I don't know. □ **searchable** *adj.* **searcher** *n.*

search and replace *n.* a computer function which allows a user to find a string of characters in a text and replace it automatically or interactively with another string.

search and rescue *n.* an operation designed to

find the survivors of a disaster, people who are lost or in danger, etc. and bring them to safety.

search engine *n.* a program for the retrieval of data, files, etc. from a database or network.

searching *adj.* (of an examination etc.) thorough, penetrating. □ **searchingly** *adv.*

searchlight *n.* **1** a powerful outdoor electric light with a concentrated beam that can be turned in any direction. **2** the light or beam from this.

searchmaster *n. Cdn* an air force officer in charge of coordinating a search and rescue operation, usu. from the airfield nearest the missing person etc.

search party *n.* a group of people organized to look for a lost person or thing.

search warrant *n.* a judge's order authorizing a person to enter and search a building and to seize evidence.

searing *adj.* **1** very hot; scorching. **2** very painful; agonizing. **3 a** upsetting, disturbing. **b** vicious; fuelled by anger. □ **searingly** *adv.*

sea salt *n.* salt produced by evaporating sea water.

seascape *n.* **1** a picturesque view or prospect of the sea. **2** a representation of such a view, esp. a painting.

sea serpent *n.* **1** (also **sea snake**) a snake of the family Hydrophidae, living in the sea. **2** an enormous legendary serpent-like sea monster.

seashell *n.* the shell of a marine mollusc.

seashore *n.* land close to or bordering on the sea.

seasick *adj.* suffering from dizziness or nausea from the motion of a ship at sea. □ **seasickness** *n.*

seaside *n.* the seacoast, esp. resorted to for a holiday or pleasure.

season ● *n.* **1** each of the four periods (spring, summer, fall, and winter) into which the year is divided, associated with a type of weather and a stage of vegetation. **2** a time of year characterized by climatic features (*the dry season*). **3** a time when something is plentiful, in vogue, or regularly indulged in (*tourist season*). **4 a** *Sport* the period of competition for a league or a team measured in games (*the first ten games of the season*). **b** a schedule of shows or performances for theatrical performance, broadcast, etc. (*the fall television season*). **5** (also **Season**) the time of year surrounding a particular holiday (*Season's greetings*). **6** the time of year when a usu. specified animal breeds or is hunted or fished (*salmon season*). **7** a period of indefinite or varying length (*the season of her youth*). ● *v.* **1** *tr.* flavour (food) with salt, herbs, etc. **2** *tr. & intr.* **a** make or become suitable or conditioned, esp. by exposure to the air or weather (*seasoned hardwood*). **b** make or become mature or experienced (*a seasoned pro*). **3** *tr.* enhance with wit, excitement, etc. □ **for all seasons 1** ready for any situation or emergency. **2** welcome or appropriate at any time under any conditions (*shoes for all seasons*). **in season 1** (of food) available in quantity and in good condition. **2** (of an animal) in heat. □ **seasonless** *adj.*

seasonable *adj.* **1** (of weather) usual or appropriate for the time of year. **2** meeting the needs of the occasion. □ **seasonably** *adv.*

seasonal *adj.* **1** of, depending on, or characteristic of the seasons of the year or a particular season. **2** varying with the season. **3** (of a person) employed only during a particular season. □ **seasonality** *n.* **seasonally** *adv.*

seasonal affective disorder *n.* a depressive state associated with late fall and winter and thought to be caused by a lack of light. Abbr.: **SAD**.

seasoning *n.* **1** an ingredient added to food to

enhance its flavour. **2** the flavouring of a dish achieved by adding such ingredients.

season opener *n.* the first game of a sports season or episode of a television season.

season ticket *n.* (usu. in *pl.*) (also esp. *Cdn* **season's ticket**) tickets or a pass for esp. a schedule of sporting or cultural events during a specified period, usu. bought at a reduced rate.

sea star *n. N Amer.* = STARFISH.

seat ● *n.* **1 a** a thing made or used for sitting on. **b** the part of a chair etc. on which one actually sits. **2 a** a place for one person to sit in a theatre, vehicle, etc. **b** entitlement to a place to sit in a theatre etc.; a ticket (*do you have any seats left?*). **3 a** the right to sit as a member of a deliberative or administrative body. **b** *Cdn & Brit.* a Member of Parliament's constituency. **c** *N Amer.* = COUNTY SEAT. **4** the buttocks. **5** the part of the pants etc. covering the buttocks. **6** the part of a thing on which it rests or appears to rest; the base. **7** the manner of sitting on a horse etc. **8** a site or location of something specified (*a seat of learning*). ● *v.tr.* **1** find, and guide a person or oneself to, an available seat. **2** provide sitting accommodation for. **3** place or fit in position. □ **be seated** sit down. **by the seat of one's pants** *informal* by instinct rather than logic or knowledge. **take a** (or **one's**) **seat** sit down. □ **seatless** *adj.*

seat belt *n.* a strap or set of straps designed to secure a person in a seat of a vehicle, aircraft, etc.

seated *adj.* **1** sitting. **2** positioned.

-seater *n.* (in *comb.*) a car, aircraft, piece of furniture, auditorium, etc. having a specified seating capacity.

seating *n.* **1** seats collectively (*seating area*). **2** sitting accommodation (*seating capacity*).

seatmate *n. N Amer.* a person sitting in a nearby seat.

seat-of-the-pants *adj.* based on instinct or intuition rather than logic or knowledge.

sea trout *n.* **1** any of various migratory trout, esp. a large silvery race of the trout *Salmo trutta*. **2** any of various marine fishes that resemble trout.

seat sale *n. Cdn & Brit.* a sale of esp. airline tickets at a reduced price.

sea urchin *n.* a small marine echinoderm with a spherical or flattened spiny shell.

seawall *n.* a wall or embankment erected as a breakwater to prevent encroachment by the sea.

seaward ● *adv.* (also **seawards**) towards the sea. ● *adj.* **1** going out to sea. **2** directed or facing towards the sea; situated on the side nearest the sea. ● *n.* the direction or position in which the sea lies.

seaway *n.* an inland waterway for seagoing ships.

seaweed *n.* any of various algae growing in the sea or on the rocks on a shore. □ **seaweedy** *adj.*

seaworthy *adj.* (esp. of a ship) in a suitable condition to undergo a sea voyage. □ **seaworthiness** *n.*

sebaceous gland /sə'beiʃəs/ *n.* a small gland found in the skin of mammals, which secretes oily matter to lubricate the skin and hair.

SEC *abbr.* Securities and Exchange Commission.

sec *n. informal* an instant or moment; a second (*wait just a sec*).

sec. *abbr.* second(s).

secateurs /ˌsekə'tɜːz/ *n.pl. Cdn & Brit.* a pair of pruning shears that can be used with one hand to clip usu. thin branches and flowers etc.

secede /sə'siːd/ *v.intr.* withdraw formally from an alliance, an association, a federal union, or a political or religious organization. □ **seceder** *n.*

secession /sə'seʃən/ *n.* **1** the act or an instance of seceding. **2 (Secession)** *hist.* the withdrawal of eleven southern States from the US Union in 1860, leading to the Civil War.

secessionism /sə'seʃən,ısm/ *n.* **1** the principles of those in favour of secession. **2** *hist.* the principles and beliefs of those favouring Secession from the US Union. □ **secessionist** *n. & adj.*

Sechelt /'siːʃæʃ ● *n. (pl.* same) **1** a member of an Aboriginal people living on the coast of BC, north of Vancouver. **2** their Sne Nay Muxw language. ● *adj.* of or relating to this people or their language.

seclude *v.tr.* keep (a person) sequestered or shut up in order to prevent access or influence from outside.

secluded *adj.* **1** remote; hidden from view. **2** isolated or withdrawn from human contact.

seclusion *n.* **1** a secluded state; confinement, isolation, privacy. **2** a secluded place.

secobarbital /,seko:bɑːrbɪtɒl/ *n.* a sedative and hypnotic barbiturate, used esp. for pre-operative sedation.

Seconal /'sekənɒl/ *n. proprietary* = SECOBARBITAL.

second¹ ● *adj.* **1** coming next after the first. **2** coming next in rank, quality, or importance to a person or thing regarded as first. **3** in addition to one previously mentioned or considered (*a second helping of pie*). **4** alternate (*every second Monday*). **5** of the same quality or standard as a previous one; closely reminiscent of (*the second Industrial Revolution*). **6** *Music* performing a lower or different part (*second trumpet*). ● *n.* **1** a person or thing that is second; another person or thing in addition to one previously mentioned or considered. **2** a second-place finish in a race or competition. **3** (in *pl.*) *informal* a second helping of food at a meal. **4** a slightly flawed or inferior-quality item. **5** = SECOND GEAR. **6** an assistant or attendant, esp. in a boxing match or duel. **7** *Baseball* **a** the second inning. **b** = SECOND BASE. **8** *N Amer.* Football = SECOND DOWN. **9** *Curling* the second player on a curling rink. **10** *Cdn & Brit.* (in Scouts, Girl Guides, etc.) a boy or girl chosen by their pack to assist the Sixer and replace him or her if absent. **11 a** an interval or chord spanning two consecutive notes in the diatonic scale e.g. C to D. **b** a note separated from another by this interval. ● *adv.* in the second place; secondly. ● *v.tr.* **1** support, assist; offer backing to. **2** formally support or endorse (a nomination, resolution, motion, etc., or its proposer). □ **in the second place** as a second consideration etc. **second to none** superior; better than the rest. □ **seconder** *n.*

second² *n.* **1** a sixtieth part of a minute of time or angular measurement. **2** *informal* a brief moment or instant (*I'll be there in a second*).

second³ /sə'kɒnd/ *v.tr.* **1** remove (an officer) temporarily from a regiment or corps to work on the staff or in some other extra-regimental appointment. **2** transfer (a worker) temporarily to another position or employment. □ **secondment** *n.*

secondary ● *adj.* **1** second in rank, sequence, importance, etc. to what is primary. **2** derived from, based on, or supplementing something else that is primary; not original (*used secondary sources for her research*). **3** designating, relating to, or involved in education above primary or elementary education, below college or university, usu. for students in their mid to late teens. **4** arising after or in consequence of an earlier symptom, infection, etc. **5** (of a cell or battery) generating electricity by a reversible chemical reaction and therefore able to store applied energy. **6** (of a current) induced, not supplied directly from a source; of, pertaining to, or carrying the output of electrical power in a transformer etc. ● *n.* (*pl.* **-ies**) **1** a secondary person or thing. **2** = SECONDARY SCHOOL. **3** a secondary tumour, infection, etc. **4** *N Amer. Football* **a** the defensive backs collectively. **b** the area of the field they cover; the defensive backfield. **5** *Electricity* a secondary coil, current, etc. □ **secondarily** *adv.* **secondariness** *n.*

secondary colour *n.* a colour derived from the mixing of two primary colours.

secondary picketing *n.* **1** the picketing of a firm's premises by union members not employed there. **2** the picketing of premises of a firm doing business with an employer engaged in a labour dispute but not otherwise involved.

secondary school *n.* a school offering secondary education.

secondary sexual characteristics *n.pl.* the physical characteristics distinctive to each sex but not essential to reproduction, which typically develop, in humans, during puberty.

second ballot *n.* a deciding ballot taken between a candidate who has won a previous ballot without securing an absolute majority and the candidate with the next highest number of votes.

second banana *n.* esp. *N Amer. informal* **1** a supporting comedian in a show or vaudeville skit etc. **2** a person who plays a subordinate or secondary role.

second base *n. Baseball* **1** the second of the three bases, located directly beyond the pitcher's mound from home plate. **2** the position of the player covering this base and the area of the infield between it and first base. □ **second baseman** *n.*

second-best ● *adj.* next in quality to the best or first. ● *n.* **1** a second-best person or thing. **2** a less adequate or desirable alternative.

second chamber *n.* the upper house of a bicameral legislature, usu. having the function of revising measures prepared and passed by the lower.

second childhood *n.* a state of childishness that sometimes accompanies old age; senility.

second class ● *n.* **1** a set of persons or things grouped together as second-best. **2** the second-best accommodation in a train, ship, etc., usu. available at a lower rate. ● *adj.* (usu. **second-class**) **1** belonging to or travelling by the second class. **2** inferior in quality, standard, status, etc. ● *adv.* (usu. **second-class**) by second class.

second-class citizen *n.* **1** a person deprived of normal civic and legal rights. **2** a person treated as socially inferior.

second coming *n.* **1** (usu. **Second Coming**) the prophesied return of Christ to earth. **2** the return of a person or thing, esp. in a new incarnation.

second cousin *n.* a child of one's parent's first cousin.

second-degree *adj.* **1** *N Amer.* **a** designating the second-most serious category of crime. **b** (of murder) next in culpability to first-degree murder, committed with intent but without premeditation and with certain mitigating circumstances. **2** denoting burns severe enough to cause blistering but not permanent scarring.

second down *n. Football* the second of three attempts (four in American football) to advance the ball ten yards, thereby achieving a new first down.

Second Empire ● *n. hist.* **1** the French imperial government of Napoleon III, 1852–70. **2** this period in France. ● *adj.* designating a style of architecture prominent during this time, influenced by French

Renaissance architecture and characterized esp. by use of the mansard roof.

second floor n. N Amer. the floor above the ground floor.

second gear n. the second (and next to lowest) in a sequence of gears of a car, bicycle, etc.

second generation ● n. **1** the grandchildren of immigrants who have settled in a country; the offspring of the first generation born in a country. **2** (of technology) an advanced or refined stage of development. ● adj. (usu. **second-generation**) **1** designating the offspring of a first generation. **2** designating something in an improved stage of development.

second-growth ● n. a growth of trees etc. replacing one that has been destroyed by fire, removed by logging, etc. ● adj. **1** designating a forest, trees, etc. replacing vegetation that has been destroyed. **2** designating timber etc. that has been removed from a second-growth.

second-guess v.tr. **1** anticipate or predict by guesswork. **2** question or judge with hindsight.

second hand n. the hand on an analog clock or watch that indicates the passing of seconds.

second-hand ● adj. **1 a** previously owned or used; not new. **b** selling goods that have been previously owned or used. **2** a not heard or obtained directly from the original source, but accepted on another's authority. **b** not undergone or felt personally, but vicariously through another. ● adv. **1** through an intermediary; not from the original source. **2** after being previously owned or used; not new (she buys second-hand).

second-hand smoke n. the smoke from a smoker's cigarette etc. inhaled unwillingly by others.

second honeymoon n. a honeymoon-like holiday taken by a couple after several years of marriage.

second-in-command n. **1** the officer next in rank to the commanding or chief officer. **2** a person next in authority to the person in charge.

second language n. a language spoken or used in addition to one's native language.

second-last ● adj. immediately preceding the final or most recent. ● adv. occurring or finishing immediately before the person or thing that is last or most recent. ● n. the penultimate person or thing.

second lieutenant n. (also **Second Lieutenant**) (in the Canadian Army and Air Force) an officer holding a rank below lieutenant and above officer cadet, the lowest ranking commissioned officer.

secondly adv. **1** furthermore; in the second place. **2** as a second item.

second mortgage n. a mortgage obtained on an already mortgaged property, usu. at a higher rate of interest than that given for first mortgages, and having a secondary priority in case of default etc.

second nature n. an acquired ability or habit etc. that has become instinctive.

second opinion n. a diagnosis etc. made by another person who has been consulted because there is doubt or argument about the initial diagnosis.

second-rate adj. of mediocre quality; inferior. □ **second-rateness** n. **second rater** n.

second reading n. the second of three successive occasions on which a bill must be presented to a legislature before it becomes law.

second-run n. (attrib.) designating a movie theatre showing films after their first release.

second sight n. the ability to perceive future or distant events; clairvoyance.

second storey n. = SECOND FLOOR.

second string ● n. Sport **1** a roster of backup players available to replace players from the starting lineup if they become unable to play, esp. due to injury. **2** a backup player or substitute on this roster. ● adj. (**second-string**) **1** designating a player etc. who is a backup or substitute (second-string defenceman). **2** designating a person or thing not of the first class or rank (a second-string composer). □ **second stringer** n.

second team N Amer. Sport ● n. a lineup of second-string players. ● adj. (usu. **second-team**) belonging or relating to the second team.

second thoughts n.pl. **1** a new opinion or resolution reached after further consideration. **2** apprehension or doubt about a decision, action, etc. that has already been made.

Second Vatican Council n. see VATICAN II.

second wind n. **1** recovery of the power of normal breathing during exercise after initial breathlessness. **2** a renewed energy or vigour needed to continue an effort.

secrecy n. **1** the ability or tendency to withhold information or keep things secret. **2** a state or condition in which disclosure of facts and events is strictly limited. □ **sworn to secrecy** having been made to promise to keep a secret.

secret ● adj. **1** kept or meant to be kept private, unknown, or hidden from others (no one knew about her secret life). **2** intended to be concealed from all but a few (a secret code). **3** (of a person) **a** having a role or position unknown to others (secret agent). **b** fond of, prone to, or able to preserve secrecy. **4** (of a place) hidden, completely secluded (secret hideaway). ● n. **1** a fact, matter, or action kept private or shared only with those concerned. **2** a thing known only to a few, though not intentionally concealed (this cozy restaurant is one of the city's best kept secrets). **3** a mystery (the secrets of the universe). **4** a valid but not commonly known or recognized method of achieving or maintaining something (being concise is the secret of good writing). □ **in secret** without others knowing. **in on the secret** among the number of those who know it. **keep a secret** not reveal it. **make no secret of** make perfectly clear. □ **secretly** adv.

secret agent n. a person operating covertly or engaged on secret service; a spy.

secretariat /ˌsekrəˈteriət/ n. **1** a permanent administrative and executive department of a government or similar organization. **2** the staff of such a department, or its premises. **3** the position or office of secretary.

secretary n. (pl. **-ies**) **1** a person employed to manage or assist with files and correspondence, make appointments, etc. **2** an official appointed by an organization to conduct its correspondence, keep its records, etc. **3** Cdn & Brit. = PARLIAMENTARY SECRETARY. **4** a civil servant employed as the chief assistant to an ambassador. □ **secretarial** adj. **secretaryship** n.

Secretary-General n. the principal administrator of an organization, such as the UN.

Secretary of State n. **1** Cdn **a** hist. (until 1993) a department responsible for a variety of matters, esp. those falling outside of existing jurisdictions but not considered important enough for the creation of a new department. **b** (usu. **secretary of state** when not used as a title) a government minister responsible for a specific area within a department, such as scientific research, the status of women, etc. **2** US the chief government official responsible for foreign affairs.

secrete /sə'kri:t/ v.tr. **1** (of a cell, organ, etc.) produce by means of secretion. **2** conceal; put into hiding. □ **secretory** adj.

secretion n. **1** the production and release of a substance by a cell, gland, etc. into a cavity or vessel or into the surrounding medium either for a function in the organism or for excretion. **2** the secreted substance.

secretive adj. inclined to make or keep secrets; reticent. □ **secretively** adv. **secretiveness** n.

secret police n. a police force operating in secret for political purposes.

secret service n. **1** a government department concerned with espionage and national security. **2** (**Secret Service**) (in the US) a branch of the Treasury Department dealing with counterfeiting and providing protection for the President etc.

secret society n. an organization formed to promote a cause covertly and whose members are sworn to secrecy about its existence and proceedings.

secs. abbr. seconds.

SecState n. Cdn slang = SECRETARY OF STATE.

sect n. **1** a body of people subscribing to religious doctrines usu. different from those of a larger group from which they have separated. **2** usu. derogatory a religious faction or group regarded as heretical or as deviating from orthodox tradition. **3** the system or body of adherents of a particular philosopher or philosophy, or school of thought in politics etc.

sectarian adj. **1** of or concerning a sect. **2** pertaining to or created by differences of religion or denomination (sectarian violence). **3** bigoted or narrow-minded esp. in following the doctrines of one's sect. □ **sectarianism** n.

section ● n. **1** a part cut off or separated from something. **2 a** each of the parts into which a thing is or may be divided (actually or conceptually). **b** each of the parts out of which a structure can be fitted together. **3** a group of musicians playing similar instruments forming part of a band or orchestra. **4** a subdivision of a newspaper, book, document, statute, etc. **5** N Amer. a (West) one square mile of esp. agricultural land, 640 acres (approx. 260 hectares). **b** a particular district or community of a town (residential section). **6** a department of a store, library, etc. in which similar items may be found together (produce section). **7** one of the naturally divided segments of a citrus fruit, such as an orange. **8** Cdn = SCHOOL SECTION. **9** a subdivision of an army platoon. **10 a** the cutting of a solid along a plane. **b** the resulting figure or the area of this. **11** a representation of the internal structure of something as it would appear if cut across a vertical or horizontal plane. ● v.tr. arrange in or divide into sections.

sectional ● adj. **1** of or relating to a section. **2 a** relating to a section or sections of a country, society, community, etc. **b** concerned with local or regional matters as opposed to general ones. **3** assembled or made from several sections (sectional table). ● n. a piece of furniture, such as a couch, composed of sections which can be used separately. □ **sectionalism** n. **sectionalist** n. & adj.

section road n. N Amer. (West) a road bordering a section of land.

sector n. **1** a distinct part or branch of an economy (the tourism sector). **2** the plane figure enclosed by two radii of a circle, ellipse, etc., and the arc between them. **3** Military a subdivision of an area for military

operations, controlled by one commander or headquarters. □ **sectoral** adj.

secular /'sekjələr/ adj. **1** concerned with or belonging to the material world and the affairs of this world as opposed to the eternal or spiritual world. **2 a** (of literature, music, an artist, etc.) not concerned with religious subjects. **b** (of education etc.) excluding religious instruction; not promoting religious belief. **3** (of clergy) not bound by a religious or monastic rule. □ **secularism** n. **secularist** n. **secularity** /-'lærəti/ n. **secularize** v.tr. **secularization** n. **secularly** adv.

secular humanism n. N Amer. liberalism, esp. with regard to the belief that religion should not be taught or practised within a publicly funded education system. □ **secular humanist** n. & adj.

secure ● adj. **1** free from apprehension or anxiety; assured, confident. **2** free from risk, reliable, certain not to fail. **3** fixed or fastened so as not to give way or yield under strain (made the door secure). **4** not likely to be lost or stolen etc. **5** (of a place) **a** affording protection or safety. **b** difficult to escape from. ● v.tr. **1** make secure or safe; fortify. **2** fasten or close securely. **3** obtain or achieve. **4** ensure (a situation, outcome, result, etc.) (the final goal secured the victory). **5** guarantee against loss (a loan secured by property). **6** seize and hold (a person) in custody. □ **securely** adv.

secure custody n. Cdn custody in a correctional facility designed and designated for the detention of young offenders.

securities commission n. an agency established to supervise and regulate the selling and trading of securities.

security n. (pl. **-ies**) **1 a** the condition of being protected from or not exposed to danger; safety. **b** freedom from care etc. **2** something that provides protection or safety. **3 a** measures taken to ensure safety and prevent crime or other danger in a building, office, country, etc. **b** the department or members responsible for ensuring safety. **4** measures taken to ensure confinement of a prisoner etc. (maximum-security prison). **5** the guarantee or assurance of something (job security). **6** (often in pl.) **a** a certificate attesting the ownership of, or interest in, the capital, assets, property, profits, earnings, or royalties of any person or company. **b** a document, such as a bond, debenture, or note, acknowledging a debt. **7** property etc. deposited or pledged as a guarantee of the fulfillment of an obligation, such as an appearance in court or the payment of a debt, and liable to forfeit in the event of a default.

security blanket n. **1** a familiar blanket or other object given to or esp. clung to by a child for comfort or reassurance. **2** informal something comforting or reassuring.

Security Council n. a permanent body of the UN seeking to maintain peace and security.

security guard n. a person employed to ensure the security of a person, building, vehicles, etc.

security risk n. a person whose presence may threaten security.

Secwepemc /'ʃwepmə/ n. (pl. same) = SHUSWAP.

sedan n. **1** N Amer. a car for four or more people. **2** (in full **sedan chair**) hist. an enclosed chair for conveying one person, carried between horizontal poles by two porters.

sedate ● adj. calm and steady; full of dignity. ● v.tr. make sleepy or quiet by means of drugs; administer a sedative to. □ **sedately** adv. **sedateness** n. **sedation** n.

sedative ● *n.* a drug, influence, etc., that tends to calm or soothe. ● *adj.* calming, soothing.

sedentary /'sedən,teri/ *adj.* **1** (of work etc.) characterized by much sitting and little physical exercise. **2** (of a person) spending much time seated. □ **sedentarily** *adv.* **sedentariness** *n.*

Seder /'seidər/ *n.* a Jewish ritual service and ceremonial dinner for the first night or first two nights of the Passover.

sedge *n.* **1** any of various grasslike plants of the family Cyperaceae, usu. growing in wet areas. **2** an expanse of this plant.

sediment *n.* **1** matter that settles to the bottom of a liquid; dregs. **2** *Geol.* matter that is carried by water or wind and deposited on the surface of the land. □ **sedimentation** *n.*

sedimentary *adj.* **1** of or like sediment. **2** (esp. of rocks) formed from sediment, usu. laid down in strata which are initially horizontal or nearly so.

sedition /sə'dıʃən/ *n.* **1** conduct or speech inciting to rebellion or a breach of public order. **2** agitation against the authority of a government. □ **seditious** *adj.* **seditiously** *adv.*

seduce *v.tr.* **1** tempt or entice into sexual activity. **2 a** tempt, lure (*seduced by the smell of coffee*). **b** lead astray (*seduced into a life of crime*). **c** beguile (*seduced by outward appearances*). □ **seducible** *adj.*

seducer *n.* a person, esp. a man, who sexually seduces, esp. habitually.

seduction *n.* **1** the act or an instance of seducing; the process of being seduced. **2** something that tempts or allures. □ **seductive** *adj.* **seductively** *adv.* **seductiveness** *n.*

seductress *n.* a female seducer.

sedulous /'sedjʊləs/ *adj.* **1** persevering, assiduous. **2** (of an action etc.) deliberately and consciously continued. □ **sedulously** *adv.*

sedum /'si:dəm, 'sed-/ *n.* any plant of the genus *Sedum*, with fleshy leaves and star-shaped yellow, pink, or white flowers, e.g. stonecrop.

see¹ ● *v.* (*past* **saw**; *past part.* **seen**) **1** *tr.* discern by use of the eyes. **2** *intr.* have or use the power of discerning objects with the eyes. **3** *tr.* discern mentally; understand. **4** *tr.* watch; be a spectator of (a film, game, etc.). **5** *tr.* ascertain or establish by inquiry or research or reflection (*see if the door is open*). **6** *tr.* consider; deduce from observation. **7** *tr.* foresee mentally. **8** *tr.* look at for information (usu. in *imper.* as a direction in or to printed material: *see page 15*). **9** *tr.* meet or be near and recognize. **10** *tr.* **a** meet socially. **b** meet regularly as a boyfriend or girlfriend; date. **11** *tr.* give an interview, examination, etc. to. **12** *tr.* visit to consult. **13** *tr.* find out or learn, esp. from a visual source (*I see the game has been cancelled*). **14** *intr.* reflect; consider further; wait until one knows more. **15** *tr.* interpret or have an opinion of (*I see things differently now*). **16** *tr.* experience (*I never thought I would see this day*). **17** *tr.* recognize as acceptable (*do you see your daughter marrying this man?*). **18** *tr.* observe without interfering (*stood by and saw them squander my money*). **19** *tr.* find attractive. **20** *intr.* make provision for; ensure (*see that they get home safely*). **21** *tr.* escort or conduct (to a place etc.). **22** *tr.* be a witness of (an event etc.) (*1939 saw the outbreak of war*). **23** *tr.* supervise (an action etc.) (*will stay and see the doors locked*). **24** *tr.* **a** (in gambling, esp. poker) equal (a bet). **b** equal the bet of (a player), esp. to see the player's cards. ● *interj.* **1** ascertaining the comprehension, continued interest, agreement, etc. of the person or persons addressed (*was driving along, see, when this guy ran in front of my car*). **2** expressing triumph (*see, I told you Maggie would be here!*). □ **as far as I can see** to the best of my understanding or belief. **as I see it** in my opinion. **has seen better days** has declined from former prosperity, good condition, etc. **let me see** an appeal for time to think before speaking etc. **see about** attend to. **see after 1** take care of. **2** = SEE ABOUT. **see here!** = LOOK HERE! (*see* LOOK *interj.*). **see into** investigate. **see life** gain experience of the world, often by enjoying oneself. **see the light 1** realize one's mistakes etc. **2** suddenly see the way to proceed. **3** undergo religious conversion. **see the light of day** (usu. with *neg.*) come into existence. **see off** be present at the departure of (a person). **see out 1** accompany out of a building etc. **2** finish (a project etc.) completely. **3** remain awake, alive, etc., until the end of (a period). **4** last longer than; outlive. **see red** become suddenly enraged. **see a person right** make sure that a person is rewarded, safe, etc. **see stars** *informal* see lights before one's eyes as a result of a blow to the head, dizziness, etc. **see things** have hallucinations or false imaginings. **see through 1** not be deceived by; detect the true nature of. **2** penetrate visually. **see a person through** support a person during a difficult time. **see a thing through** persist with it until it is completed. **see to it** ensure (*see to it that I am not disturbed*). **see one's way clear to** feel able or entitled to. **see you** (or **see you later**) *informal* an expression on parting. **we shall see 1** let us await the outcome. **2** a formula for declining to act at once. **will see about it** a formula for declining to act at once. **you see 1** you understand. **2** you will understand when I explain.

see² *n.* **1** the area under the authority of a bishop or archbishop; a diocese. **2** the office or jurisdiction of a bishop or archbishop.

seed ● *n.* **1 a** a flowering plant's unit of reproduction (esp. in the form of grain) capable of developing into another such plant. **b** seeds collectively, esp. for sowing. **c** (*attrib.*) suitable or kept for seed (*seed potatoes*). **2** a prime cause or beginning (*seeds of doubt*). **3** *archaic* semen or sperm. **4** *archaic* offspring, progeny, descendants (*the seed of Abraham*). **5** *Sport* a seeded player. ● *v.* **1** *tr.* place seeds in. **b** sprinkle with or as with seed. **2** *intr.* sow seeds. **3** *intr.* produce or drop seed. **4** *tr.* remove seeds from (fruit etc.). **5** *tr.* place a crystal or crystalline substance in (a solution etc.) to cause crystallization or condensation (esp. in a cloud to produce rain). **6** *tr. Sport* **a** assign to (a strong competitor in a competition) a position in an ordered list so that strong competitors do not meet each other in early rounds (*is seeded seventh*). **b** arrange (the order of play) in this way. **7** *intr.* go to seed. ● *attrib.adj.* (of funding etc.) intended to initiate a project etc. (*seed capital*). □ **go** (or **run**) **to seed 1** cease flowering as seed develops. **2** become degenerate, unkempt, ineffective, etc. □ **seedless** *adj.*

seedbed *n.* **1** a bed of fine soil in which to sow seeds. **2** a place of development.

seeder *n.* **1** a person or thing that seeds. **2** a machine for sowing seed, esp. a drill. **3** an apparatus for seeding grapes etc.

seed head *n.* a flower head in seed.

seed house *n. N Amer.* a company that sells seeds.

seedling *n.* a young plant, esp. one raised from seed and not from a cutting etc.

seed money *n.* money allocated to initiate a project.

seed pod *n.* a long seed vessel that splits when ripe.

seedy *adj.* (**-ier, -iest**) **1** full of seed. **2** going to seed. **3** dilapidated. **4** shabby-looking; in worn clothes. **5**

disreputable. **6** *informal* unwell. ☐ **seedily** *adv.*
seediness *n.*

seeing ● *conj.* (usu. foll. by *that* + clause) considering that, inasmuch as, because. ● *n.* the sense or faculty of sight.

Seeing Eye dog *n. proprietary* a dog that is specially trained to guide a blind person.

seek *v.* (*past* and *past part.* **sought**) **1** *tr. & intr.* make a search or inquiry (for). **2** *tr.* **a** try or want to find or get. **b** ask for; request (*sought help from him*). **3** *tr.* (foll. by *to* + infin.) endeavour or try. **4** *tr.* make for or resort to (a place or person, for advice, health, etc.) (*sought her bed*). ☐ **seek out 1** search for and find. **2** single out for companionship etc. **far to seek** difficult to find (*the reason is not far to seek*). ☐ **seeker** *n.* (also in *comb.*).

seem *v.intr.* **1** give the impression or sensation of being (*seems ridiculous*). **2** appear or be perceived or ascertained (*they seem to have left*). ☐ **can't seem to** *informal* seem unable to. **it seems** (or **would seem**) it appears to be true or the fact (in a hesitant, guarded, or ironical statement).

seeming ● *adj.* apparent but not genuine. ● *n.* **1** appearance, aspect. **2** deceptive appearance. ☐ **seemingly** *adv.*

seemly *adj.* (**-ier, -iest**) conforming to propriety or good taste; decorous, suitable. ☐ **seemliness** *n.*

seen *past part.* of SEE¹.

See of Rome *n.* the Holy See.

seep ● *v.intr.* **1** ooze, filter, or percolate slowly. **2** permeate. **3** pass gradually (*her anger seeped away*). ● *n.* N Amer. a place where water, petroleum, etc. oozes out of the ground.

seepage *n.* **1** the act of seeping. **2** the quantity that seeps out.

seer *n.* **1** a person who sees. **2** a person of supposed supernatural insight esp. as regards the future.

seersucker *n.* material of linen, cotton, etc., with a puckered surface.

see-saw ● *n.* **1 a** a long plank balanced on a central support for children to sit on at each end and move up and down by pushing the ground with their feet. **b** a game played on this. **2** an up-and-down or to-and-fro motion. **3** a contest or situation with each of the opposing forces repeatedly gaining the advantage. ● *v.intr.* **1** play on a see-saw. **2** move up and down as on a see-saw. **3** vacillate in policy, emotion, etc. ● *adj.* **1** with up-and-down or backward-and-forward motion. **2** characterized by vacillation or progress alternating in two opposite directions.

seethe *v.* **1** *intr.* boil, bubble over. **2** *intr.* be very agitated, esp. with anger. ☐ **seethingly** *adv.*

see-through *adj.* (esp. of clothing) translucent.

segment ● *n.* **1** each of several parts into which a thing is or can be divided or marked off. **2** *Math.* a part of a figure cut off by a line or plane intersecting it, esp.: **a** the part of a circle enclosed between an arc and a chord. **b** the part of a line included between two points. **c** the part of a sphere cut off by any plane not passing through the centre. **3 a** a division of a day's broadcasting time; a time slot. **b** a separate item, esp. within a program. **4** each of the longitudinal sections of the body of certain animals (e.g. worms). ● *v.* **1** *intr. & tr.* divide into segments. **2** *intr.* (of a cell) undergo cleavage or divide into many cells. ☐ **segmental** /seg'mentəl/ *adj.* **segmentally** *adv.* **segmentation** *n.*

segregate /'segrə,geit/ *v.* **1** *tr.* put apart from rest; isolate. **2** *tr.* enforce racial segregation on (persons) or in (a community etc.).

segregation *n.* **1** enforced separation of racial

groups in a community etc. **2** the act or an instance of segregating; the state of being segregated. ☐ **segregationist** *n. & adj.*

segue /'segwei/ ● *v.intr.* (**segues, segued, segueing** or **seguing**) **1** *Music* (usu. foll. by *into*) go on without a pause into the next section. **2** move smoothly from one thing or topic to another. ● *n.* an uninterrupted transition from one musical section or melody to another.

sei /sei/ *n.* a small rorqual, *Balaenoptera borealis*.

seigneur /si:'njɜr/ *n.* **1** *Cdn hist.* a holder of land under the seigneurial system. **2** a feudal lord; the lord of a manor. ☐ **seigneurial** *adj.*

seigneurial system *n. Cdn hist.* a system of land tenure established in New France, based on the feudal system, under which land was owned by seigneurs who rented it to tenant farmers and provided mills, a court system, and other services.

seigneury /'si:njəri/ *n.* (*pl.* **-ies**) **1** *Cdn hist.* **a** a tract of land held by a seigneur under the seigneurial system. **b** a grant of land in the interior, esp. for the harvesting of furs, fish, etc. **2** a seigneur's domain.

seine /sein/ ● *n.* (also **seine net**) a net for encircling fish, with floats at the top and weights at the bottom edge, and usu. hauled ashore (also *attrib.*: *seine boat*). ● *v.intr. & tr.* fish or catch with a seine. ☐ **seiner** *n.* **seining** *n.*

seismic /'saizmik/ *adj.* **1** of or relating to an earthquake or earthquakes or other vibrations of the earth and its crust, produced either naturally or artificially by explosions. **2** of enormous proportions or effect (*seismic shifts in the global economy*). ☐ **seismically** *adv.*

seismicity /saiz'misiti/ *n.* seismic activity; esp. the frequency of earthquakes per unit area in a region.

seismogram /'saizmə,græm/ *n.* a record given by a seismograph.

seismograph /'saizmə,græf/ *n.* an instrument that records the force, direction, etc. of earthquakes. ☐ **seismographic** *adj.*

seismology /saiz'mɒlədʒi/ *n.* the scientific study and recording of earthquakes and related phenomena. ☐ **seismological** *adj.* **seismologically** *adv.* **seismologist** *n.*

seize *v.* **1** *tr.* take hold of forcibly or suddenly. **2** *tr.* take possession of forcibly (*seized power*). **3** *tr.* take possession of (contraband goods, documents, etc.) by warrant or legal right; confiscate. **4** *tr.* affect suddenly (*panic seized us; was seized with remorse*). **5** *tr.* take advantage of (an opportunity). **6** *tr.* comprehend quickly or clearly. **7** *intr.* (usu. foll. by *on, upon*) **a** take hold forcibly or suddenly. **b** take advantage eagerly (*seized on a pretext*). **8** *intr.* (usu. foll. by *up*) **a** (of a moving part in a machine) become stuck or jammed from undue heat, friction, etc. **b** (of part of the body etc.) become stiff. ☐ **seizer** *n.*

seizure *n.* **1** the act or an instance of seizing; the state of being seized. **2** a sudden attack of epilepsy etc.

Sekani /sə'kæni/ ● *n.* (*pl.* same or **-s**) **1** a member of an Aboriginal group living on the western slope of the Rocky Mountains in north central BC. **2** the Athapaskan language of this people. ● *adj.* of or relating to this people or their language.

seldom *adv.* rarely, not often.

select ● *v.* **1** *tr.* choose, esp. as the best or most suitable. **2** *intr.* choose or pick out something from a number. ● *adj.* **1** chosen for excellence or suitability. **2** (of a society etc.) exclusive, cautious in admitting members. ☐ **selectable** *adj.* **selector** *n.*

select committee *n.* a small parliamentary committee appointed for a special purpose.

selection *n.* **1** the act or an instance of selecting; the state of being selected. **2** a selected person or thing. **3** things from which a choice may be made. **4** *Biol.* the process in which environmental and genetic influences determine which types of organism thrive better than others, regarded as a factor in evolution.

selection committee *n.* a committee that chooses a person or thing, esp. a person for a job.

selective *adj.* **1** using or characterized by selection. **2** able to select, esp. (of a radio receiver) able to respond to a chosen frequency without interference from others. **3** (of one's memory, hearing, etc.) selecting what is convenient. **4** (of a herbicide etc.) affecting only a particular species. □ **selectively** *adv.* **selectivity** /ˌselekˈtɪvɪti, ˌsiːl-/ *n.*

selenium /səˈliːniəm/ *n.* a non-metallic element occurring naturally in various metallic sulphide ores and characterized by the variation of its electrical resistivity with intensity of illumination.

self ● *n.* (*pl.* **selves**) **1** a person's or thing's own individuality or essence (*showed his true self*). **2** a person or thing as the object of introspection or reflexive action (*the consciousness of self*). **3** one's own interests or pleasure (*cares for nothing but self*). **4** used in phrases equivalent to *myself, yourself, himself,* etc. (*his very self*). ● *pron. informal* myself, yourself, himself, herself, etc. (*ticket admitting self and guest*). □ **one's better self** one's nobler impulses. **one's former** (or **old**) **self** oneself as one formerly was.

self- *comb. form* expressing reflexive action: **1** of or directed towards oneself or itself (*self-respect; self-cleaning*). **2** by oneself or itself, esp. without external agency (*self-evident*). **3** on, in, for, or relating to oneself or itself (*self-absorbed*).

self-abnegation *n.* the abnegation of oneself, one's interests, needs, etc.; self-sacrifice.

self-absorption *n.* **1** absorption in oneself. **2** the absorption, by a body, of radiation emitted within it. □ **self-absorbed** *adj.*

self-actualization *n. Psych.* the realization of one's talents and potentialities, esp. considered as a drive or need present in everyone. □ **self-actualize** *v.intr.*

self-addressed *adj.* (of an envelope etc.) having one's own address on for return communication.

self-adhesive *adj.* (of a label, stamp, etc.) adhesive, esp. without being moistened.

self-advertisement *n.* the advertising or promotion of oneself. □ **self-advertising** *adj.*

self-aggrandizement *n.* the act or process of making oneself more important in appearance or reality. □ **self-aggrandizing** *adj.*

self-analysis *n. Psych.* the analysis of oneself, one's motives, character, etc. □ **self-analyzing** *adj.*

self-appointed *adj.* designated so by oneself, not authorized by another (*a self-appointed expert*).

self-assertion *n.* the aggressive promotion of oneself, one's views, etc. □ **self-asserting** *adj.* **self-assertive** *adj.* **self-assertiveness** *n.*

self-assessment *n.* assessment or evaluation of oneself, or one's actions, attitudes, or performance.

self-assurance *n.* confidence in one's own abilities etc. □ **self-assured** *adj.* **self-assuredly** *adv.*

self-aware *adj.* conscious of one's character, feelings, motives, etc. □ **self-awareness** *n.*

self-censorship *n.* the censoring of oneself.

self-centred *adj.* (also **self-centered**) preoccupied with one's own personality or affairs. □ **self-centredly** *adv.* **self-centredness** *n.*

self-cleaning *adj.* (of an oven) equipped with a mechanism that allows heating to sufficiently high temperatures to burn off grease, dirt, etc.

self-collected *adj.* composed, serene, self-assured.

self-confessed *adj.* openly admitting oneself to be (*a self-confessed thief*).

self-confidence *n.* = SELF-ASSURANCE. □ **self-confident** *adj.* **self-confidently** *adv.*

self-congratulation *n.* = SELF-SATISFACTION. □ **self-congratulatory** *adj.*

self-conscious *adj.* **1** nervous or awkward because one is shy or worried about what others think of one. **2** strongly aware of who one is or what one is doing. □ **self-consciously** *adv.* **self-consciousness** *n.*

self-contained *adj.* **1** independent. **2** (esp. of living accommodation) complete in itself. **3** (of a person) uncommunicative. □ **self-containment** *n.*

self-contradiction *n.* internal inconsistency. □ **self-contradicting** *adj.* **self-contradictory** *adj.*

self-control *n.* the power of controlling one's external reactions, emotions, etc. □ **self-controlled** *adj.*

self-correcting *adj.* correcting itself without external help.

self-created *adj.* created by oneself or itself. □ **self-creation** *n.*

self-critical *adj.* critical of oneself, one's abilities, etc. □ **self-criticism** *n.*

self-deception *n.* deceiving oneself esp. concerning one's true feelings etc. □ **self-deceit** *n.* **self-deceiver** *n.* **self-deceiving** *adj.* **self-deceptive** *adj.*

self-defeating *adj.* (of an attempt etc.) doomed to failure because of internal inconsistencies etc.

self-defence *n.* **1** a defence of oneself, one's rights or position. **2** an instance of aggression in such defence. □ **self-defensive** *adj.*

self-delusion *n.* the act or an instance of deluding oneself. □ **self-deluded** *adj.*

self-denial *n.* = SELF-ABNEGATION. □ **self-denying** *adj.*

self-deprecation *n.* the act of disparaging or belittling oneself. ¶See DEPRECATE. □ **self-deprecating** *adj.* **self-deprecatingly** *adv.* **self-deprecatory** *adj.*

self-depreciation *n.* = SELF-DEPRECATION. ¶See DEPRECATE. □ **self-depreciatory** *adj.*

self-destruct esp. *N Amer.* ● *v.intr.* **1** (of a spacecraft, bomb, etc.) explode or disintegrate automatically, esp. when pre-set to do so. **2** destroy oneself. ● *attrib.adj.* enabling a thing to self-destruct.

self-destruction *n.* **1** the process or an act of destroying oneself or itself. **2** esp. *N Amer.* the process or an act of self-destructing. **3** *N Amer. informal* suicide. □ **self-destructive** *adj.* **self-destructively** *adv.*

self-determination *n.* **1** the freedom of a people to decide their own allegiance or form of government. **2** the freedom to live or act as one chooses, without needing to consult others. □ **self-determining** *adj.*

self-directed *adj.* **1** designating an investment trust, such as an RSP, in which the investment instruments are selected by the trust holder. **2** exercising personal control over one's own life, career, etc. **3** (of criticism, a joke, etc.) directed towards oneself.

self-discipline *n.* the act of or ability to apply oneself, control one's feelings, etc.; self-control. □ **self-disciplined** *adj.*

self-discovery *n.* the process of acquiring insight into oneself, one's character, desires, etc.

self-doubt *n.* lack of confidence in oneself, one's abilities, etc. □ **self-doubting** *adj.*

self-educated *adj.* taught by oneself by reading etc., without formal instruction. □ **self-education** *n.*

self-effacing *adj.* retiring; modest; timid. □ **self-effacement** *n.* **self-effacingly** *adv.*

self-employed *adj.* working for oneself, as a freelancer or owner of a business etc.; not employed by an employer. □ **self-employment** *n.*

self-esteem *n.* a good opinion of one's own character and abilities.

self-evident *adj.* obvious; without the need of evidence or further explanation. □ **self-evidence** *n.* **self-evidently** *adv.*

self-examination *n.* **1** the study of one's own conduct, reasons, etc. **2** the examining of one's body or a part of one's body for signs of illness etc.

self-explanatory *adj.* easily understood; not needing explanation.

self-expression *n.* the expression of one's feelings, thoughts, etc., esp. in writing, painting, music, etc. □ **self-expressive** *adj.*

self-fertilization *n.* the fertilization of plants by their own pollen. □ **self-fertilizing** *adj.*

self-financing *adj.* that finances itself, esp. (of a project or undertaking) that pays for its own implementation or continuation. □ **self-finance** *v.tr.*

self-fulfilling *adj.* **1** (of a prophecy, forecast, etc.) bound to come true as a result of actions brought about by its being made. **2** causing or bringing about self-fulfillment.

self-fulfillment *n.* (also **-fulfilment**) the fulfillment of one's own hopes and ambitions.

self-government *n.* **1** (esp. of a former colony etc.) government by its own people. **2** = SELF-CONTROL. □ **self-governed** *adj.* **self-governing** *adj.*

self-guided *adj.* **1** (of a hike, visit to a tourist attraction, etc.) performed without the supervision of a tour guide. **2** (of a hiking trail, scenic route, etc.) equipped with informative signs, plaques, etc., so as to be suitable for a self-guided tour.

self-hatred *n.* (also **self-hate**) hatred of oneself, esp. of one's actual self when contrasted with one's imagined self.

self-help *n.* **1** the theory that individuals should provide for their own support and improvement in society. **2** the act or faculty of providing for or improving oneself (also *attrib.*: *self-help book*).

selfhood *n.* personality; separate and conscious existence.

self-image *n.* one's own idea or picture of oneself, esp. in relation to others.

self-immolation *n.* the offering of oneself as a sacrifice.

self-importance *n.* a high opinion of oneself. □ **self-important** *adj.* **self-importantly** *adv.*

self-imposed *adj.* (of a task or condition etc.) imposed on and by oneself, not externally.

self-improvement *n.* the improvement of one's own position or disposition by one's own efforts.

self-induced *adj.* induced by oneself or itself.

self-indulgent *adj.* indulging or tending to indulge in pleasure, idleness, etc. □ **self-indulgence** *n.* **self-indulgently** *adv.*

self-inflicted *adj.* (of a wound, damage, etc.) inflicted on oneself, esp. deliberately.

self-interest *n.* **1** one's personal interest or advantage. **2** concern for one's own interest or advantage. □ **self-interested** *adj.*

selfish *adj.* **1** deficient in consideration for others; concerned chiefly with one's own personal profit or pleasure. **2** (of a motive etc.) appealing to self-interest. □ **selfishly** *adv.* **selfishness** *n.*

self-justification *n.* the justification or excusing of oneself, one's actions, etc. □ **self-justifying** *adj.*

self-knowledge *n.* the understanding of oneself, one's motives, etc.

selfless *adj.* disregarding oneself or one's own interests. □ **selflessly** *adv.* **selflessness** *n.*

self-loading *adj.* (esp. of a gun) loading itself. □ **self-loader** *n.*

self-loathing *n.* = SELF-HATRED.

self-love *n.* **1** selfishness; self-indulgence. **2** regard for one's own well-being and happiness.

self-made *adj.* **1** successful or rich by one's own effort. **2** made by oneself.

self-medication *n.* the use of medication to treat oneself without seeking any medical supervision. □ **self-medicate** *v.intr.*

self-mocking *adj.* mocking oneself or itself. □ **self-mockery** *n.*

self-motivated *adj.* acting on one's own initiative without external pressure. □ **self-motivation** *n.*

self-parody *n.* the act or an instance of parodying oneself. □ **self-parodic** *adj.* **self-parodying** *adj.*

self-perpetuating *adj.* perpetuating itself or oneself without external agency. □ **self-perpetuation** *n.*

self-pity *n.* extreme sorrow for one's own troubles etc. □ **self-pitying** *adj.* **self-pityingly** *adv.*

self-portrait *n.* a portrait or description of an artist, writer, etc., by himself or herself.

self-possessed *adj.* calm and confident, esp. at times of stress or difficulty. □ **self-possession** *n.*

self-preservation *n.* the preservation of one's own life, safety, best interests, etc., esp. as a basic instinct. □ **self-preserving** *adj.*

self-proclaimed *adj.* proclaimed by oneself or itself to be such.

self-propagating *adj.* (esp. of a plant) able to propagate itself. □ **self-propagation** *n.*

self-propelled *adj.* moving or able to move without external propulsion. □ **self-propelling** *adj.*

self-protection *n.* the act of protecting oneself or itself. □ **self-protective** *adj.*

self-realization *n.* **1** the development of one's faculties, abilities, etc. **2** this as an ethical principle.

self-referential *adj.* characterized by or making reference to oneself or itself. □ **self-referentiality** *n.*

self-regard *n.* **1** a proper regard for oneself. **2 a** selfishness. **b** conceit. □ **self-regarding** *adj.*

self-regulating *adj.* regulating oneself or itself without intervention. □ **self-regulation** *n.* **self-regulatory** *adj.*

self-reliance *n.* reliance on one's own resources etc.; independence. □ **self-reliant** *adj.*

self-respect *n.* respect for oneself; a feeling that one is behaving with honour, dignity, etc. □ **self-respecting** *adj.*

self-restraint *n.* = SELF-CONTROL. □ **self-restrained** *adj.*

self-righteous *adj.* excessively confident of one's own righteousness or virtue, esp. in comparison to others. □ **self-righteously** *adv.* **self-righteousness** *n.*

self-rule *n.* = SELF-GOVERNMENT 1.

self-sacrifice *n.* the negation of one's own

interests, wishes, etc., in favour of those of others. □ **self-sacrificing** *adj.*

selfsame *attrib.adj.* the very same (*the selfsame thing*).

self-satisfaction *n.* excessive and unwarranted satisfaction with oneself, one's achievements, etc. □ **self-satisfied** *adj.* **self-satisfying** *adj.*

self-seeking *adj.* & *n.* seeking one's own welfare before that of others. □ **self-seeker** *n.*

self-selection *n.* the act of selecting oneself or itself. □ **self-selected** *adj.* **self-selecting** *adj.*

self-serve (also **self-service**) ● *adj.* (often *attrib.*) **1** (esp. of a gas station) where customers serve themselves and pay at a checkout counter etc. **2** (of a machine) serving goods after the insertion of coins. ● *n. informal* a self-serve gas station etc.

self-serving *adj.* & *n.* = SELF-SEEKING.

self-starter *n.* **1** an ambitious person who needs no external motivation. **2** = STARTER 2.

self-styled *adj.* called so by oneself (*a self-styled artist*).

self-sufficient *adj.* **1** needing nothing; independent. **2** (of a person, nation, etc.) able to supply one's needs for a commodity, esp. food, from one's own resources. □ **self-sufficiency** *n.* **self-sufficiently** *adv.*

self-supporting *adj.* **1** capable of maintaining oneself or itself financially. **2** staying up or standing without external aid. □ **self-support** *n.*

self-surrender *n.* the surrender of oneself or one's will etc. to an influence, emotion, or other person.

self-sustaining *adj.* sustaining oneself or itself. □ **self-sustained** *adj.*

self-taught *adj.* educated or trained by oneself.

self-understanding *n.* **1** the act or an instance of comprehending one's actions and reactions. **2** sympathetic tolerance or awareness of oneself.

self-willed *adj.* obstinately pursuing one's own wishes. □ **self-will** *n.*

self-worth *n.* = SELF-ESTEEM.

Selkirk settler *n. Cdn hist.* an early settler at the Red River Settlement in what is now Manitoba founded by the Earl of Selkirk (1771–1820).

sell ● *v.* (*past* and *past part.* **sold**) **1** *tr.* exchange (goods, services, etc.) for money. **2** *tr.* keep a stock of for sale or be a dealer in. **3 a** *intr.* (of goods) be purchased. **b** *tr.* (of a publication or recording) attain sales of (a specified number of copies). **4** *intr.* (foll. by *for*) have a specified price. **5** *tr.* betray for money or other reward. **6** *tr.* **a** advertise or publish the merits of. **b** give (a person) information on the value of something, inspire with a desire to buy or acquire or agree to something. **7** *tr.* cause to be sold. ● *n.* **1** a manner of selling. **2** *informal* a deception or disappointment. □ **sell off** sell the remainder of (goods) at reduced prices. **sell one's body** work as a prostitute. **sell oneself 1** promote one's own abilities. **2 a** offer one's services dishonourably for money or other reward. **b** be a prostitute. **sell out 1 a** sell all one's stock of a commodity. **b** (of a commodity) be completely or all sold. **c** (of a performance etc.) sell all its tickets. **d** dispose of the whole of (one's property, shares, etc.) by sale. **2 a** (often foll. by *to*) abandon one's principles, honourable aims, etc. for personal gain. **b** betray (a person etc.). **sell short** disparage, underestimate. □ **sellable** *adj.*

seller *n.* **1** a person who sells. **2** a commodity that sells well or badly.

seller's market *n.* (also **sellers' market**) an economic position in which goods are scarce and expensive and sellers have the advantage over buyers.

selling point *n.* a feature of something that makes it attractive, esp. to buyers or customers.

sell-off *n.* **1** the privatization of a state company by a sale of shares. **2** a sale or disposal of bonds, shares, etc., usu. causing a fall in price. **3** a sale, esp. to dispose of property.

sellout *n.* **1** a commercial success, esp. the selling of all tickets for a show. **2** a betrayal.

seltzer *n.* (in full **seltzer water**) **1** natural effervescent mineral water. **2** an artificial substitute for this; soda water.

selvage /'sɛlvɪdʒ/ *n.* (also **selvedge**) an edging that prevents cloth from unravelling (either an edge along the warp or a specially woven edging).

selves *pl.* of SELF.

semantic /sə'mæntɪk/ *adj.* **1** relating to meaning in language; relating to the denotations and connotations of words. **2** of or relating to semantics. □ **semantically** *adv.*

semantics *n.pl.* (usu. treated as *sing.*) **1** the branch of linguistics concerned with meaning. **2** the interpretation or meaning of a sentence, word, etc. (*let's not fight over semantics*). □ **semanticist** /-tɪsɪst/ *n.*

semaphore /'sɛmə.fɔr/ ● *n.* **1** a system of sending messages by holding the arms or two flags in certain positions according to an alphabetic code. **2** a signalling apparatus consisting of a post with a movable arm or arms esp. for use on railways. ● *v.intr.* & *tr.* signal or send by semaphore. □ **semaphoric** *adj.*

semblance *n.* **1** the outward or superficial appearance of something. **2** resemblance.

semen *n.* the reproductive fluid of male animals, containing spermatozoa in suspension.

semester *n.* esp. *N Amer.* an academic session occupying half of the academic year, lasting usu. for 15 to 18 weeks.

semestering *n. Cdn* an educational system in which the school year is divided into two terms having school days with a reduced number of longer periods, with the whole year's course material in any given subject concentrated into one or the other term. □ **semestered** *adj.*

semi *n.* (*pl.* **semis**) *informal* **1** *Cdn* & *Brit.* a semi-detached house. **2** a semifinal. **3** *N Amer.* a semi-trailer.

semi- /'sɛmi, -maɪ/ *prefix* **1** half (*semicircle*). **2** partly; in some degree or particular (*semi-detached*). **3** almost. **4** occurring or appearing twice in a specified period (*semi-annual*).

semi-annual *adj.* occurring, published, etc., twice a year. □ **semi-annually** *adv.*

semiaquatic *adj.* **1** (of an animal) living partly on land and partly in water. **2** (of a plant) growing in very wet ground.

semi-arid *adj.* having slightly more precipitation than an arid climate, and characterized by coarse grasses and scrub.

semi-automatic ● *adj.* **1** partially automatic. **2** (of a firearm) having a mechanism for continuous loading but not for continuous firing. ● *n.* a semi-automatic firearm.

semi-autonomous *adj.* **1** partly self-governing. **2** acting to some degree independently or having the partial freedom to do so.

semicircle *n.* **1** half of a circle or of its circumference. **2** a set of objects ranged in, or an object forming, a semicircle. □ **semicircular** *adj.*

semicircular canal *n.* one of three fluid-filled channels in the ear giving information to the brain to help maintain balance.

semicolon *n.* a punctuation mark (;) of intermediate value between a comma and a period.

semiconductor *n.* a solid substance that is a non-conductor when pure or at a low temperature but has a conductivity between that of insulators and that of metals when containing a suitable impurity or at a higher temperature, used in integrated circuits, transistors, diodes, etc. □ **semiconducting** *adj.*

semi-conscious *adj.* partly conscious. □ **semi-consciously** *adv.* **semi-consciousness** *n.*

semicylinder *n.* half of a cylinder cut longitudinally. □ **semicylindrical** *adj.*

semi-desert *n.* a semi-arid area intermediate between grassland and desert.

semi-detached ● *adj.* (of a house) joined to another by a shared wall on one side only. ● *n.* a semi-detached house.

semifinal *n.* a match or round immediately preceding the final. □ **semifinalist** *n.*

semi-formal ● *adj.* (esp. of clothing) having some formal elements. ● *n.* a dance or other social occasion to which semi-formal dress is worn.

semigloss ● *adj.* (of a paint or painted surface) having or producing such a finish. ● *n.* a paint that has or produces a moderately satiny finish.

semi-independent *adj.* **1 a** partially independent of control or authority. **b** partially self-governing. **2** partially independent of financial support from public funds.

semi-liquid ● *adj.* of a consistency between solid and liquid. ● *n.* a semi-liquid substance.

Sémillon /'semijɔ̃/ *n.* **1** a white wine grape. **2** a white wine made from these grapes.

semi-monthly ● *adj.* occurring, published, etc., twice a month. ● *adv.* twice a month.

seminal /'semənəl/ *adj.* **1 a** of or relating to semen. **b** of or relating to the seeds of plants. **2 a** (of ideas etc.) providing the basis for future development. **b** (of a person, literary work, etc.) central to the understanding of a subject; influential.

seminar *n.* a small group, esp. at a university, meeting to discuss or study a particular topic.

seminary *n.* (*pl.* **-ies**) **1** a training college for priests, rabbis, etc. **2** a place of education or development. □ **seminarian** *n.*

Seminole /'semɪnoːl/ ● *n.* (*pl.* **-s**) **1** a member of any of several groupings of N American Aboriginal peoples comprising Creek Confederacy emigrants to Florida or their descendants in Florida and Oklahoma. **2** the Muskogean language of the Seminoles. ● *adj.* of or relating to this people or their language.

semiology /,siːmiˈɒlədʒi, ,sem-/ *n.* = SEMIOTICS. □ **semiological** *adj.* **semiologist** *n.*

semi-opaque *adj.* partially transparent.

semiotics /,siːmiˈɒtɪks, ,sem-/ *n.* the study of signs and symbols in various fields, esp. language. □ **semiotic** *adj.* **semiotically** *adv.* **semiotician** /-'tɪʃən/ *n.*

semi-permanent *adj.* rather less than permanent. □ **semi-permanently** *adv.*

semi-permeable *adj.* (of a membrane etc.) allowing small molecules, but not large ones, to pass through. □ **semi-permeability** *n.*

semi-precious *adj.* (of a gem) less valuable than a precious stone.

semi-private *adj.* **1** partially or somewhat private. **2** *N Amer.* (of a hospital room) shared by two patients.

semi-professional ● *adj.* **1** receiving payment for an activity but not relying on it for a living. **2** involving semi-professionals. ● *n.* a semi-professional musician, sportsman, etc. □ **semi-professionally** *adv.*

semi-retired *adj.* (of a person) partially but not completely retired. □ **semi-retirement** *n.*

semi-skilled *adj.* (of work or a worker) having or needing some training but less than for a skilled worker.

semi-soft *adj.* (of cheese) having a consistency between firm and soft.

semi-solid *adj.* = SEMI-LIQUID.

semi-sweet *adj.* (esp. of chocolate) slightly sweetened.

semi-synthetic *adj.* *Chem.* (of a substance) that is prepared synthetically but derives from a naturally occurring material.

Semite /'semaɪt, 'siːm-/ *n.* a member of any of the peoples supposed to be descended from Shem, son of Noah, including esp. the Jews, Arabs, Assyrians, and Phoenicians. □ **Semitism** /'semə,tɪzəm/ *n.* **Semitist** *n.*

Semitic /səˈmɪtɪk/ ● *adj.* **1** of or relating to the Semites, esp. the Jews. **2** of or relating to the languages of the family including Hebrew and Arabic. ● *n.* the Semitic language family.

semitone *n.* the smallest interval used in classical European music; half a tone.

semi-trailer *n.* a trailer having wheels at the back but supported at the front by a towing vehicle.

semi-transparent *adj.* partly transparent.

semi-vowel *n.* **1** a sound intermediate between a vowel and a consonant (e.g. *w*, *y*). **2** a letter representing this.

semi-weekly ● *adj.* occurring, published, etc., twice a week. ● *adv.* twice a week.

semolina /,seməˈliːnə/ *n.* the hard grains left after the milling of flour, used esp. in making pasta.

Sen. *abbr.* **1** Senior. **2** *N Amer.* **a** Senator. **b** Senate.

senate *n.* **1** (**Senate**) **a** (in Canada) the upper chamber of Parliament, consisting of senators appointed to represent the regions of Canada. **b** (in the US) the upper, elected, house of Congress or of a state legislature. **c** a similar legislative body in other countries, e.g. France. **2** the governing body of a university or college.

senator *n.* a member of a senate. □ **senatorial** *adj.* **senatorship** *n.*

send *v.* (*past* and *past part.* **sent** /sent/) **1** *tr.* **a** order or cause to go or be conveyed (*sent me a book*). **b** propel; cause to move (*sent him flying*). **c** cause to go or become (*his dancing sends her into raptures*). **d** dismiss with or without force. **2** *intr.* send a message or letter. **3** *tr.* (of God, providence, etc.) grant or bestow or inflict; bring about; cause to be. **4** *tr.* *slang* affect emotionally, put into ecstasy. □ **send away for** send an order to a dealer for (goods). **send for 1** summon. **2** order by mail. **send in 1** cause to go in. **2** submit (an entry etc.) for a competition etc. **send off 1** get (a letter, parcel, etc.) dispatched. **2** attend the departure of (a person) as a sign of respect etc. **3** *Sport* (of a referee) order (a player) to leave the field and take no further part in the game. **send off for** = SEND AWAY FOR. **send on** transmit to a further destination or in advance of one's own arrival. **send out for** order delivery of (food). **send up 1** cause to go up. **2** transmit to a higher authority. **3** *informal* satirize or ridicule, esp. by mimicking. **send word** send a message. □ **sender** *n.*

send-off *n.* a demonstration of goodwill etc. at a person's departure, the start of a project, etc.

send-up n. informal a satire or parody.

Seneca /'senəkə/ ● n. (pl. same or **-s**) **1** a member of one of the founding peoples of the Iroquois Five Nations confederacy, now living in Ontario and New York. **2** the Iroquoian language of this people. ● adj. of or relating to this people.

Senegalese /ˌsenəgə'liːz/ ● adj. of or relating to Senegal, a country on the coast of W Africa. ● n. a native or inhabitant of Senegal.

senescence /sə'nesəns/ n. aging. □ **senescent** adj.

senile /'siːnail, 'sen-/ adj. **1** of or characteristic of old age. **2** having the weaknesses or diseases of old age. □ **senility** /sə'nɪlɪti/ n.

senile dementia n. a severe form of mental deterioration in old age, characterized by loss of memory and control of bodily functions.

senior ● adj. **1** more or most advanced in age, standing, rank, etc. **2** of high or highest position. **3** (placed after a person's name) senior to another of the same name. **4** (of a school) having students in an older age range (esp. over 11). **5** esp. US of the final year at a university, high school, etc. ● n. **1 a** = SENIOR CITIZEN. **b** a person of comparatively long service etc. **2** one's elder, or one's superior in length of service, membership, etc. **3** esp. US a student in the final year at a university, high school, etc. □ **seniority** n.

senior citizen n. an elderly person, esp. a person over 65.

senior constable n. (in the OPP) an officer ranking above provincial constable and below sergeant.

senior government n. Cdn the federal or a provincial government, or both, as opposed to a municipal government.

senior high school n. N. Amer. a secondary school comprising usu. the three highest grades.

senior management n. **1** the highest level of management in an organization, immediately below the board of directors. **2** the managers at this level.

senna /'senə/ n. **1** a cassia tree. **2** a laxative prepared from the dried pods of this.

señor /sen'jɔr/ n. (pl. **señores** /-rez/) a title used of or to a Spanish-speaking man.

señora /sen'jɔrə/ n. a title used of or to a Spanish-speaking married woman.

señorita /ˌsenjə'riːtə/ n. a title used of or to a Spanish-speaking unmarried woman.

sensation n. **1** the consciousness of perceiving or seeming to perceive some state or condition of one's body or its parts or of the senses; an instance of such consciousness (lost all sensation in my arm; the sensation of falling). **2** an awareness or impression (a sensation of being watched). **3 a** a stirring of emotions or intense interest, esp. among a large group of people (caused a sensation). **b** a person, event, etc., causing such interest. **c** the sensational use of printed material.

sensational adj. **1 a** causing a sensation (a sensational crime). **b** deliberately trying to provoke interest by including material that is exciting, shocking, salacious, etc. (sensational journalism). **2** very good (a sensational singer). **3** of or causing sensation. □ **sensationalize** v.tr. **sensationally** adv.

sensationalism n. the use of or interest in sensational material in journalism, political agitation, etc. □ **sensationalist** n. & adj. **sensationalistic** adj.

sense ● n. **1 a** any of the special bodily faculties by which sensation is roused (has keen senses; the sense of smell). **b** sensitivity of all or any of these. **2** the ability to perceive or feel or to be conscious of the presence or properties of things. **3** consciousness (sense of one's own importance). **4** (often foll. by of) **a** an appreciation,

understanding, or instinct regarding a specified matter (the moral sense; my sense is that they won't come). **b** the habit of basing one's conduct on such instinct. **5** the instinctive or acquired capacity to comprehend or appreciate a specified quality, subject, etc. (has no fashion sense). **6** practical wisdom or judgment, common sense; conformity to these. **7 a** a meaning; the way in which a word etc. is to be understood (the sense of the word is clear). **b** intelligibility or coherence or possession of a meaning. **8** the prevailing opinion among a number of people. **9** (in pl.) a person's sanity or normal state of mind. ● v.tr. **1** perceive by a sense or senses. **2** be vaguely aware of. **3** realize. **4** (of a machine etc.) detect. □ **bring a person to his** or **her senses 1** cure a person of folly. **2** restore a person to consciousness. **come to one's senses 1** regain consciousness. **2** become sensible after acting foolishly. **in a** (or **one**) **sense** if the statement is understood in a particular way (is true in a sense). **make sense** be intelligible, reasonable, or practicable. **make sense of** show or find the meaning of. **out of one's senses** in or into a state of madness (frightened him out of his senses). **take leave of one's senses** go mad.

senseless adj. **1** unconscious. **2** wildly foolish. **3** without meaning or purpose. **4** incapable of sensation. □ **senselessly** adv. **senselessness** n.

sense organ n. a bodily organ conveying external stimuli to the sensory system.

sensibility n. (pl. **-ies**) **1** openness to emotional impressions (sensibility to kindness). **2 a** (in pl.) emotional capacities or feelings (was limited in his sensibilities). **b** a person's moral, emotional, or aesthetic ideas or standards (offended the sensibilities of believers).

sensible adj. **1** having or showing wisdom or common sense (a sensible person; a sensible compromise). **2 a** perceptible by the senses (sensible phenomena). **b** great enough to be perceived; appreciable (a sensible difference). **3** (of clothing etc.) practical and functional. □ **sensibleness** n. **sensibly** adv.

sensitive adj. **1** (often foll. by to) very open to or acutely affected by external stimuli or mental impressions; having sensibility. **2** (of a person) **a** easily offended or emotionally hurt. **b** attuned to others' emotions. **c** deeply and easily affected by emotion, beauty, etc. **3** (often foll. by to) (of an instrument etc.) responsive to or recording slight changes. **4** (often foll. by to) **a** (of photographic materials) prepared so as to respond (esp. rapidly) to the action of light. **b** readily affected by or responsive to external influences (an environmentally sensitive area). **5 a** (of a topic etc.) needing careful handling to avoid causing offence, embarrassment, etc. **b** involved with or likely to affect (esp. national) security. **6** (of a market) liable to quick changes of price. □ **sensitively** adv. **sensitivity** n. (pl. **-ies**)

sensitize v.tr. **1** make sensitive. **2** Photog. make sensitive to light. **3** make (an organism etc.) abnormally sensitive to a foreign substance. □ **sensitization** n. **sensitizer** n.

sensor n. a device giving a signal for the detection or measurement of a physical property to which it responds.

sensory adj. of sensation or the senses. □ **sensorily** adv.

sensual /'senʃʊəl/ adj. **1 a** of or depending on the senses only and not on the intellect or spirit; carnal, fleshly (sensual pleasures). **b** given to the pursuit of sensual pleasures or the gratification of the appetites; self-indulgent sexually or in regard to food and drink; licentious. **c** indicative of a sensual nature (*sensual lips*). ¶*Sensual* is sometimes confused with *sensuous*. While *sensual* is used to describe things that are gratifying to the body, and has sexual overtones, *sensuous* is used to mean 'affecting or appealing to the senses' in an aesthetic sense, without the pejorative implications of *sensual*. **2** of sense or sensation, sensory. □ **sensualism** *n.* **sensualist** *n.* **sensualize** *v.tr.* **sensually** *adv.*

sensuality /ˌsɛnʃʊˈælɪti/ *n.* **1** the state or quality of being sensual. **2** gratification of the senses, self-indulgence.

sensuous /ˈsɛnʃʊəs/ *adj.* of or derived from or affecting the senses, esp. aesthetically rather than sensually. ¶See Usage Note at SENSUAL. □ **sensuously** *adv.* **sensuousness** *n.*

sent *past and past part. of* SEND.

sentence ● *n.* **1 a** a set of words complete in itself as the expression of a thought, containing or implying a subject and predicate, and conveying a statement, question, exclamation, or command. **b** a piece of writing or speech between two periods or equivalent pauses, often including several grammatical sentences, e.g. *I went; he came.* **2 a** a decision of a law court, esp. the punishment allotted to a person convicted in a criminal trial. **b** the declaration of this. **3** *Logic* a series of signs or symbols expressing a proposition in an artificial or logical language. ● *v.tr.* **1** declare the sentence of (a convicted criminal etc.). **2** (foll. by *to*) declare (such a person) to be condemned to a specified punishment. □ **under sentence of** having been condemned to. □ **sentencing** *n.*

sentient /ˈsɛnʃənt/ *adj.* having the power of perception by the senses. □ **sentience** *n.*

sentiment *n.* **1** the sum of what one feels on some subject; an opinion or point of view. **2** an opinion or feeling as distinguished from the words meant to convey it; an emotional feeling conveyed in literature, art, etc. **3 a** emotional or tender feelings collectively, esp. mawkish tenderness. **b** the display of this. **4** a mental feeling (*the sentiment of pity*).

sentimental *adj.* **1** of or characterized by sentiment. **2** showing or affected by emotion rather than reason. **3** appealing to sentiment, esp. mawkishly. □ **sentimentalism** *n.* **sentimentalist** *n.* **sentimentality** *n.* **sentimentalize** *v.intr. & tr.* **sentimentalization** *n.* **sentimentally** *adv.*

sentimental value *n.* the value of a thing to a particular person because of its associations.

sentinel ● *n.* a sentry or lookout; a guard. ● *v.tr.* (**sentinelled, sentinelling**) station sentinels at or in.

sentry *n.* (*pl.* **-ies**) a soldier etc. stationed to keep guard.

sepal /ˈsiːpəl, ˈsɛp-/ *n. Bot.* each of the divisions or leaves of the calyx.

separable *adj.* able to be separated. □ **separability** *n.* **separably** *adv.*

separate ● *adj.* **1** (often foll. by *from*) forming a unit that is or may be regarded as apart or by itself. **2** *Cdn* of or relating to a separate school or the separate school system. ● *n.* (in *pl.*) separate articles of clothing suitable for wearing together in various combinations. ● *v.* **1** *tr.* make separate; sever. **2** *tr.* **a** prevent union or contact of. **b** part by occupying an intervening space (*a river separates the two counties*). **3** *intr.* go different ways, disperse. **4** *intr.* cease to live together as a married couple. **5** *intr.* (often foll. by *from*) secede. **6** *tr.* **a** divide or sort (milk, ore, fruit, light, etc.)

into constituent parts or sizes. **b** (often foll. by *out*) extract or remove (an ingredient, waste product, etc.) by such a process for use or rejection. **7** *intr.* (of a substance) stop being combined; divide into constituent parts. □ **separately** *adv.* **separateness** *n.* **separative** *adj.*

separate school *n. Cdn* **1** (in Ontario) a publicly funded school for Catholic students (*compare* PUBLIC SCHOOL 2a). **2** (in Alberta and Saskatchewan) a publicly funded school for children belonging to the religious minority (usu. Catholics) in a given district.

separate school board *n. Cdn* **1** a board of trustees responsible for the separate schools of a particular area. **2** the administrative unit responsible for the separate schools in a given area. **3** the area within which a separate school board has jurisdiction.

separate school district *n. Cdn* (in Alberta and Saskatchewan) the area within which a separate school board has jurisdiction.

separate school system *n. Cdn* a system of publicly funded denominational (usu. Catholic) schools operated alongside a public school system.

separation *n.* **1** the act or an instance of separating; the state of being separated. **2** the place or point where two or more objects are divided from one another. **3** (in full **legal separation**) an arrangement by which a husband and wife remain married but live apart. **4** any of three or more monochrome reproductions of a coloured picture which can combine to reproduce the full colour of the original. **5 a** distinction or difference between the signals carried by the two channels of a stereophonic system. **b** a measure of this.

separation anxiety *n.* anxiety provoked in a child by the threat of separation from its parents etc.

separatist ● *n.* a person who favours separation, esp. for political or ecclesiastical independence; (in Canada) a person who favours the secession of Quebec or the Western provinces from Canada. ● *adj.* of, pertaining to, or characteristic of separatists or their views. □ **separatism** *n.*

separator *n.* a machine or device for separating, e.g. cream from milk or egg yolk from egg white.

Sephardi /səˈfɑːrdi/ *n.* (*pl.* **Sephardim** /-dɪm/) a Jew of Spanish or Portuguese descent. □ **Sephardic** *adj.*

sepia /ˈsiːpiə/ ● *n.* **1 a** a dark reddish-brown colour. **2 a** a brown pigment prepared from a black fluid secreted by cuttlefish, used in monochrome drawing and in watercolours. **b** a brown tint used in photography. **3** a drawing done in sepia. ● *adj.* of a dark reddish-brown colour.

sepsis /ˈsɛpsɪs/ *n.* **1** the state of being septic. **2** blood poisoning.

Sept. *abbr.* September.

sept *n.* a clan, esp. in Ireland.

septa *pl. of* SEPTUM.

September *n.* the ninth month of the year.

septet *n.* **1** *Music* **a** a composition for seven performers. **b** the performers of such a composition. **2** any group of seven.

septic ● *adj.* **1** contaminated with bacteria from a festering wound etc.; putrefying. **2** of or relating to a septic system. ● *n.* = SEPTIC SYSTEM.

septicemia /ˌsɛptɪˈsiːmiə/ *n.* (also *Brit.* **septicaemia**) blood poisoning. □ **septicemic** *adj.*

septic field *n.* (also **septic bed**) a bed of gravel and tile laid underneath the ground to serve as a drainage area for the effluent from a septic tank.

septic system *n.* a sewage disposal system consisting of a septic tank and septic field.

septic tank *n.* a tank in which the organic matter in sewage is decomposed through bacterial activity.

septuagenarian /ˌseptuːədʒəˈneriən, ˌseptə-, ˌseptʃuːə-/ ● *n.* a person from 70 to 79 years old. ● *adj.* of this age.

Septuagint /ˈseptuːəˌdʒɪnt, ˈsepˈtuːədʒɪnt, ˈseptʃuː-/ *n.* a Greek version of the Hebrew Scriptures including the Apocrypha, said to have been made about 270 BC.

septum *n.* (*pl.* **septa**) *Anat.*, *Bot.*, & *Zool.* a partition, such as that between the nostrils. □ **septal** *adj.*

sepulchral /sɪˈpʌlkrəl/ *adj.* **1** of a tomb or interment. **2** funereal, gloomy, dismal (*sepulchral look*).

sepulchre /ˈsepəlkər/ (*US* **sepulcher**) ● *n.* a tomb esp. cut in rock or built of stone or brick, a burial vault or cave. ● *v.tr.* lay in a sepulchre.

sequel *n.* **1** what follows after or as a result of an earlier event (*famine is the sequel to war*). **2** a novel, film, etc., that continues the story of an earlier one.

sequence ● *n.* **1** succession, coming after or next. **2** order of succession (*shall follow the sequence of events*; *historical sequence*). **3** a set of things belonging next to one another on some principle of order; a series without gaps. **4** a part of a film dealing with one scene or topic. **5** a set of poems on one theme (*sonnet sequence*). **6** a set of three or more playing cards next to one another in value. **7** *Music* repetition of a phrase or melody at a higher or lower pitch. **8** succession without implication of causality (*opp.* CONSEQUENCE 1). ● *v.tr.* arrange in a definite order.

sequencer *n.* **1** a programmable electronic device for storing sequences of musical notes, chords, rhythms, etc. and transmitting them when required to an electronic musical instrument. **2** an apparatus for performing or initiating operations in the correct sequence, esp. one forming part of the control system of a computer.

sequential /sɪˈkwenʃəl/ *adj.* **1** forming a sequence or consequence. **2** esp. *Computing* occurring or performed in a particular order. □ **sequentially** *adv.*

sequester /sɪˈkwestər/ *v.tr.* **1** seclude, isolate, set apart (*sequester the jury*). **2** = SEQUESTRATE.

sequestrate /sɪˈkwestreɪt/ *v.tr.* **1** confiscate, appropriate. **2** *Law* take temporary possession of (a debtor's estate etc.). □ **sequestration** /ˌsiːkwɪˈstreɪʃən/ *n.*

sequin *n.* a circular spangle for attaching to clothing as an ornament. □ **sequined** *adj.* (also **sequinned**).

sequoia /səˈkwɔɪə/ *n.* a Californian evergreen coniferous tree, *Sequoia sempervirens*, of very great height and breadth.

sera *pl.* of SERUM.

seraph /ˈserəf/ *n.* (*pl.* **-phim** /-fɪm/ or **-s**) **1** *Bible* a supernatural being with three pairs of wings. **2** *Christianity* a member of the highest order of the nine ranks of heavenly beings, gifted esp. with love and associated with light, ardour, and purity.

Serb ● *n.* **1** a native of Serbia, a country in the Balkans. **2** a person of Serbian descent. ● *adj.* = SERBIAN *adj.*

Serbian ● *n.* **1** the dialect of the Serbs. **2** = SERB. ● *adj.* of or relating to the Serbs or their dialect.

Serbo-Croat (also **Serbo-Croatian**) ● *n.* the Slavic language of the Serbs and Croats, written in the Cyrillic alphabet by Serbs and the Roman alphabet by Croats. ● *adj.* of or relating to this language.

sere[1] /siːr/ *adj.* *literary* (esp. of a plant etc.) withered.

sere[2] *n.* *Ecology* a natural succession of plant (or animal) communities, esp. a full series from uncolonized habitat to the appropriate climax vegetation.

serenade ● *n.* **1** a piece of music sung or played in the open air, esp. by a lover at night under the window of his beloved. **2** a suite of diverse pieces for an instrumental ensemble, esp. a string orchestra or wind ensemble. ● *v.tr.* sing or play a serenade to.

serendipity /ˌserənˈdɪpɪti/ *n.* **1** the faculty of making happy and unexpected discoveries by accident. **2** good luck; good fortune. □ **serendipitous** *adj.* **serendipitously** *adv.*

serene *adj.* (**serener**, **serenest**) **1** placid, tranquil. **2 a** (of the sky etc.) clear and calm. **b** (of the sea etc.) unruffled. □ **serenely** *adv.* **serenity** *n.*

serf *n.* **1** *hist.* (under feudalism) a labourer who was not free to move from the land on which he worked. **2** an oppressed person, a drudge. □ **serfdom** *n.*

serge *n.* a durable twilled woollen or worsted fabric used mainly for clothing.

sergeant *n.* **1** (in the Canadian Army and Air Force and other armies) a non-commissioned officer ranking above corporal. **2** (in some Canadian police forces) = STAFF SERGEANT. **3** (in the SQ) an officer ranking above corporal. **4** (in Quebec municipal police forces) an officer ranking above constable. **5** (in the Royal Newfoundland Constabulary) an officer ranking above constable.

sergeant-at-arms *n.* (*pl.* **sergeants-at-arms**) an official of a court or city or parliament, with ceremonial duties.

sergeant major *n.* **1** (in the RCMP) an officer ranking above staff sergeant major. **2** (in the OPP) an officer ranking below inspector.

serger *n.* a machine used for close-stitching or overcasting to prevent material from fraying at the edge.

Sergt. *abbr.* Sergeant.

serial ● *n.* **1** a story, play, or film which is published, broadcast, or shown in regular instalments. **2** a periodical. ● *adj.* **1** of or in or forming a series. **2** (of a story etc.) in the form of a serial. **3** (of a publication) appearing in successive parts published usu. at regular intervals, periodical. **4** *Computing* **a** performed or used in sequence, sequential. **b** (of a device) involving the transfer of data as a single sequence of bits (*serial port*). **5** (of a person, action, etc.) habitual, inveterate, given to or characterized by the repetition of certain behaviour in a sequential pattern (*serial rapist*). □ **serially** *adv.*

serialize *v.tr.* **1** publish or produce in instalments. **2** arrange in a series. □ **serialization** *n.*

serial killer *n.* a person who murders repeatedly, often with no apparent motive and usually following a characteristic, predictable pattern of behaviour. □ **serial killing** *n.*

serial number *n.* a number showing position in a series, esp. one printed on a banknote or manufactured article by which it can be individually identified.

series *n.* (*pl.* same) **1** a number of things of which each is similar to the preceding or in which each successive pair are similarly related; a sequence, succession, order, row, or set. **2** a set of successive games between the same teams. **3 a** a set of programs with the same actors etc. or on related subjects but each complete in itself. **b** a set of performances offered for purchase by subscription. **4** a set of lectures by the same speaker or on the same subject. **5 a** a set of successive issues of a periodical, of articles on one subject or by one writer, etc., esp. when numbered separately from a preceding or following set (*second* *series*). **b** a set of independent books in a common format or under a common title or supervised by a common general editor. **6 a** a set of stamps, coins, etc., of different denominations but issued at one time, in one reign, etc. **b** a set or class of aircraft, vehicles, machines, etc., developed over a period of time and sharing many features of design or assembly. **7** *Geol.* **a** a set of strata with a common characteristic. **b** the rocks deposited during a specific epoch. **8 a** a set of electrical circuits or components arranged so that the current passes through each successively. **b** a set of batteries etc. having the positive electrode of each connected with the negative electrode of the next. **9** *Chem.* a set of elements with common properties or of compounds related in composition or structure. **10** *Math.* a set of quantities constituting a progression or having the several values determined by a common relation. □ **in series 1** in ordered succession. **2** *Electricity* (of a set of circuits or components) arranged so that the current passes through each successively.

serif /ˈserɪf/ *n.* **1** a slight projection finishing off a stroke of a letter, as in T contrasted with T (*compare* SANS SERIF). **2** a form of type with serifs.

serious *adj.* **1** thoughtful, earnest, sober, sedate, responsible, not reckless or given to trifling. **2** important, demanding consideration (*this is a serious matter*). **3** not slight or negligible (*a serious injury*). **4** sincere, in earnest, not ironic or joking (*are you serious?*). **5** (of music and literature) not merely for amusement (*opp.* LIGHT² 5a). **6** not perfunctory (*serious thought*). **7** not to be trifled with (*a serious opponent*). **8** (of a relationship or the people involved in it) involving profound love, the intention to marry, etc. **9** *informal* large in size or amount (*serious money*). **10** *informal* remarkable; impressive. □ **seriousness** *n.*

seriously *adv.* **1** in a serious manner (esp. introducing a sentence, implying that irony etc. is now to cease). **2** to a serious extent. **3** *informal* very, really (*seriously rich*).

sermon *n.* **1** a spoken or written discourse on a religious or moral subject, esp. a discourse based on a text or passage of Scripture and delivered in a service by way of religious instruction or exhortation. **2** a piece of admonition or reproof. □ **sermonic** *adj.*

Sermon on the Mount *n.* the discourse of Christ recorded in Matthew 5-7, an important collection of Christian ethical teachings.

seroconversion /ˌsiːroʊkənˈvɜːrʒən/ *n.* a change from a seronegative to a seropositive state.

serology /sɪˈrɒlədʒi/ *n.* the scientific study of blood sera and their effects. □ **serologic** *adj.* **serological** *adj.* **serologically** *adv.* **serologist** *n.*

seronegative /ˌsiːroʊˈnɛɡətɪv/ *adj. Med.* giving a negative result in a test of blood serum, e.g. for presence of a virus. □ **seronegativity** *n.*

seropositive /ˌsiːroʊˈpɒzɪtɪv/ *adj. Med.* giving a positive result in a test of blood serum, e.g. for presence of a virus. □ **seropositivity** *n.*

serotonin /ˌserəˈtoʊnɪn/ *n. Biol.* a compound present in blood platelets and serum, which constricts the blood vessels and acts as a neurotransmitter.

serous /ˈsiːrəs/ *adj.* of or like or producing serum; watery. □ **serosity** /-ˈrɒsɪti/ *n.*

serous membrane *n.* (also **serous gland**) a membrane or gland with a serous secretion.

serpent *n.* **1** usu. *literary* a snake, esp. of a large kind. **2** a sly or treacherous person, esp. one who exploits a position of trust. **3** (**the Serpent**) *Bible* Satan.

serpentine /ˈsɜːrpəntaɪn, -tiːn/ ● *adj.* **1** of or like a

serpent. **2** coiling, tortuous, sinuous, meandering, writhing (*serpentine windings*). **3** cunning, subtle, treacherous. ● *v.intr.* move sinuously, meander.

serrate ● *v.tr.* /seˈreɪt/ (usu. as **serrated** *adj.*) provide with a sawlike edge (*a serrated knife*). ● *adj.* /ˈsereɪt/ notched like a saw. □ **serration** *n.*

serum /ˈsiːrəm/ *n.* (*pl.* **sera** /-rə/ or **serums**) **1** the amber-coloured protein-rich liquid in which blood cells are suspended and which separates out when blood coagulates. **2** *Med.* the blood serum of an animal used esp. to provide immunity to a pathogen or toxin by inoculation or as a diagnostic agent. **3** a watery fluid in animal bodies.

servant *n.* **1** a person hired to carry out the orders of an individual or corporate employer, esp. a person employed in a house on domestic duties or as a personal attendant. **2** a devoted follower, a person willing to serve another (*a servant of Jesus*). **3** a person employed by a government (*civil servant*). □ **servanthood** *n.* **servantless** *adj.*

serve ● *v.* **1** *tr.* do a service for (a person, community, etc.). **2 a** *tr.* be a servant to. **b** *intr.* act as a servant. **3** *intr.* carry out duties (*served on six committees*). **4** *intr.* **a** (foll. by *in*) be employed in (an organization, esp. the armed forces, or a place, esp. a foreign country). **b** be a member of the armed forces. **5 a** *tr.* be useful to or serviceable for; meet the needs of (*this program has served us well*). **b** *intr.* meet requirements; perform a function (*a sofa serving as a bed*). **c** *intr.* (foll. by *to* + infin.) avail, suffice (*served only to postpone the inevitable*). **6** *tr.* **a** go through a due period of (office, apprenticeship, a prison sentence, etc.). **b** go through (a due period) of imprisonment etc. **7** *tr.* set out or present (food) for those about to eat it (*asparagus served with butter; dinner is served*). **8** *intr.* act as a waiter. **9** *tr.* **a** attend to (a customer in a store). **b** (foll. by *with*) supply with (goods) (*served the town with gas*). **10** *tr.* treat or act towards (a person) in a specified way (*has served me well*). **11** *tr.* **a** (often foll. by *on*) deliver (a writ etc.) to the person concerned in a legally formal manner (*served a warrant on him*). **b** (foll. by *with*) deliver a writ etc. to (a person) in this way (*served her with a summons*). **12** *tr.* & *intr. Tennis etc.* **a** deliver (a ball etc.) to begin or resume play. **b** make (a fault etc.) in doing this. **13** *tr.* (of an animal, esp. a stallion etc. hired for the purpose) copulate with (a female). **14** *tr.* render obedience to (a deity, monarch, etc.). ● *n. Tennis etc.* **1** the act or an instance of serving. **2** a manner of serving. **3** a person's turn to serve. □ **serve one's needs** be adequate. **serve the purpose of** take the place of, be used as. **serve a person right** be a person's deserved punishment or misfortune. **serve** (or esp. *N Amer.* **serve out**) **one's time 1** hold office for the normal period. **2** (also **serve time**) undergo imprisonment, apprenticeship, etc. **serve up** offer for acceptance.

server *n.* **1** a person who serves or attends to the requirements of another, esp. a waiter. **2** (in tennis etc.) the player who serves the ball. **3** *Christianity* a person assisting the celebrant at a service, esp. the Eucharist. **4** *Computing* **a** a program which manages shared access to a centralized resource or service in a network. **b** a device on which such a program is run. **5** a utensil for serving food (*salad servers*).

service ● *n.* (often *attrib.*) **1** the act of helping or doing work for another or for a community etc. **2** work done in this way. **3** assistance or benefit given to someone. **4** the provision or system of supplying a public need, e.g. transport, or (often in *pl.*) the supply of water, gas, electricity, etc. **5 a** the fact or status of being a servant. **b** employment or a position as a servant. **6** a state or period of employment doing work for an individual or organization (*resigned after 15 years' service*). **7 a** a public department or organization employing officials working for the government (*secret service*). **b** employment in this. **8** (in *sing.* or *pl.*) the armed forces. **9** (*attrib.*) of the kind issued to the armed forces (*a service revolver*). **10 a** (in *pl.*) the sector of the economy that supplies the needs of the consumer but produces no tangible goods, as banking or tourism. **b** a business which provides a specified service to the public (*a taxi service*). **11 a** a ceremony of worship according to prescribed forms. **b** a form of liturgy for this. **12 a** the provision of what is necessary for the installation and maintenance of a machine etc. or operation. **b** the maintenance and repair of a vehicle, machine etc. at regular intervals. **13 a** the act or process of serving customers in a store. **b** assistance or advice given to customers after the sale of goods. **14 a** the act or process of serving food, drinks, etc. **b** an extra charge nominally made for this. **15** a set of dishes, plates, etc., used for serving meals (*a dinner service*). **16** *Tennis etc.* **a** the act or an instance of serving. **b** a person's turn to serve. **c** the manner or quality of serving. **d** (in full **service game**) a game in which a particular player serves. **17** *Law* the formal delivery of a writ, summons, etc. ● *v.tr.* **1** provide service or services for, esp. maintain. **2** maintain or repair (a car etc.). **3** pay interest on (a debt). **4** supply with a service. **5 a** (of a male animal) copulate with (a female animal). **b** *coarse slang* perform sexual favours for (a person). □ **at a person's service** ready to serve or assist a person. **be of service** be available to assist. **in service 1** employed as a servant. **2** available for use. **on active service** serving in the armed forces in wartime. **out of service** not available for use. **see service 1** have experience of service, esp. in the armed forces. **2** (of a thing) be much used.

serviceable *adj.* **1** useful or usable. **2** able to render service. **3** durable; capable of withstanding difficult conditions. **4** suited for ordinary use rather than ornament. □ **serviceability** *n.* **serviceably** *adv.*

service area *n.* **1** the area served by a broadcasting station, public utility, etc. **2** the area in a store, garage, etc. set aside for the maintenance and repair of machines, cars, etc.

service bay *n. N Amer.* a space in an auto repair shop designed to accommodate one car at a time.

serviceberry *n.* (*pl.* **-ies**) **1** any N American shrub or small tree of the genus *Amelanchier*. **2** the edible fruit of this.

service book *n.* a book of authorized forms of worship of a Church.

service centre *n.* **1** a registered commercial operation where cars, appliances, etc. can be taken for maintenance and repair. **2** *Cdn* a town or city which serves as a shopping and distribution centre for a surrounding sparsely populated area.

service club *n. N Amer.* an association of business or professional people having the aims of promoting community welfare and goodwill.

service contract *n.* **1** a contract of employment. **2** a business agreement between contractor and customer, usu. guaranteeing the maintenance and servicing of equipment over a specified period.

serviced *adj. Cdn & Brit.* hooked up to utilities such as gas, water, and hydro (*a serviced campsite*).

service industry *n.* an industry engaged in providing services rather than the manufacture of goods.

service line *n.* (in tennis etc.) a line marking the limit of the area into which the ball must be served.

serviceman *n.* (*pl.* **-men**) **1** a man serving in the armed forces. **2** a man providing service etc.

service provider *n.* a company, organization, etc. which provides a service to customers, esp. one which provides access to the Internet.

service road *n.* a road parallel to a main road, giving access to houses, stores, etc.

service station *n.* = GAS STATION.

servicewoman *n.* (*pl.* **-women**) a woman serving in the armed forces.

serviette *n. Cdn & Brit.* a napkin for use at table, esp. a paper one.

servile /'sɜrvail/ *adj.* **1** slavish, fawning; completely dependent. **2** of or being or like a slave or slaves. □ **servilely** *adv.* **servility** /-'vɪlɪti/ *n.*

serving *n.* **1** the action of SERVE¹ *v.* **2** a quantity of food served to one person. **3** (*attrib.*) used for serving food (*serving spoons*).

servitude *n.* **1** slavery. **2** subjection (esp. involuntary); bondage.

servo *n.* (*pl.* **-os**) **1** (in full **servo-mechanism**) a powered mechanism producing motion or forces at a higher level of energy than the input level, e.g. in the brakes and steering of large motor vehicles, esp. where feedback is employed to make the control automatic. **2** (in full **servo-motor**) the motive element in a servo-mechanism. **3** (in *comb.*) of or involving a servo-mechanism (*servo-assisted*).

sesame /'sesəmi/ *n.* **1** an E Indian herbaceous plant, *Sesamum indicum*, with seeds used as food and yielding an edible oil. **2** its seeds.

sesquicentennial /,seskwisen'teniəl, ,seskwə-/ ● *n.* a one-hundred-and-fiftieth anniversary. ● *adj.* of or relating to a sesquicentennial.

sessile /'sesail/ *adj.* **1** *Bot. & Zool.* (of a flower, leaf, eye, etc.) attached directly by its base without a stalk. **2** fixed in one position; immobile.

session *n.* **1** the process of assembly of a deliberative or judicial body to conduct its business. **2** a single meeting for this purpose. **3** a period during which such meetings are regularly held. **4 a** an academic year or term. **b** the period during which a school etc. has classes. **5** a period devoted to an activity. **6** the governing body of a Presbyterian or United Church congregation, composed of the minister and the elders. □ **in session** assembled for business; not on vacation. □ **sessional** *adj.*

sessional indemnity *n. Cdn* = INDEMNITY 4.

set¹ *v.* (**setting**; past and past part. **set**) **1** *tr.* put, lay, or stand (a thing) in a certain position or location. **2** *tr.* (foll. by *to*) apply (one thing) to (another) (*set pen to paper*). **3** *tr.* **a** fix ready or in position. **b** dispose suitably for use, action, or display. **4** *tr.* **a** adjust the hands of (a clock or watch) to show the right time. **b** adjust (an alarm clock) to sound at the required time. **c** adjust (a dial etc.) to a certain point. **5** *tr.* **a** fix, arrange, or mount. **b** insert (a jewel) in a ring, framework, etc. **6** *tr.* make (a device) ready to operate. **7** *tr.* arrange knives, forks, glasses, etc. on (a table) for a meal (*set the table*). **8** *tr.* arrange (the hair) while damp so that it dries in the required style. **9** *tr.* (foll. by *with*) ornament or provide (a surface, esp. a precious item) (*gold set with gems*). **10** *tr.* bring by placing or arranging or other means into a specified state; cause to be (*set it on fire*). **11** *intr. & tr.* **a** harden or solidify (*the jelly is set*). **b** (of a stain or dye etc.) make or become permanent. **12** *intr.* (of the sun, moon, etc.) appear to move towards and below the earth's horizon. **13** *tr.* represent (a story, play, scene, etc.) as happening in a certain time or place. **14** tr. **a** (foll. by to + infin.) cause or instruct (a person) to perform a specified activity (set them to work). **b** (foll. by pres. part.) start (a person or thing) doing something (set the ball rolling). **15** tr. present or impose as work to be done or a matter to be dealt with (set them an essay). **16** tr. exhibit as a type or model (set a good example). **17** tr. initiate; take the lead in (set the pace). **18** tr. establish (a record etc.). **19** tr. determine or decide (the itinerary is set). **20** tr. appoint or establish (set them in authority). **21** tr. join, attach, or fasten. **22** tr. **a** put parts of (a broken or dislocated bone, limb, etc.) into the correct position for healing. **b** deal with (a fracture or dislocation) in this way. **23** tr. (in full **set to music**) provide (words etc.) with music for singing. **24** tr. (often foll. by up) Printing **a** arrange or produce (type or film etc.) as required. **b** arrange the type or film etc. for (a book etc.). **25** intr. (of a tide, current, etc.) have a certain motion or direction. **26** intr. (of a face) assume a hard expression. **27** intr. **a** (of a hen) sit on eggs. **b** tr. cause (a hen) to sit on eggs. **c** tr. place (eggs) for a hen to sit on. **28** tr. esp. N Amer. start (a fire). **29** tr. fix or put (the price of something) at a certain amount. **30** intr. **a** (of blossom) form into fruit. **b** (of fruit) develop from blossom. **c** (of a tree) develop fruit. **31** tr. incite (esp. a dog or other animal) to make an attack. **32 a** tr. rig (a sail) so as to catch the wind. **b** intr. (of a sail) be rigged so as to catch the wind. □ **set about 1** begin or take steps towards. **2** informal attack. **set (a person or thing) against (another) 1** consider or reckon (a thing) as a counterpoise or compensation for. **2** cause to oppose. **set apart** separate, reserve, differentiate. **set back 1** place further back in place or time. **2** impede or reverse the progress of. **3** informal cost (a person) a specified amount. **set down 1** record in writing. **2** allow to alight from a vehicle. **3** (foll. by to) attribute to. **4** (foll. by as) explain or describe to oneself as. **set forth 1** begin a journey. **2** make known; expound. **set forward** begin to advance. **set free** release. **set one's heart** (or **hopes**) **on** want or hope for eagerly. **set in** (of weather, a condition, etc.) begin (and seem likely to continue), become established. **set little by** consider to be of little value. **set much by** consider to be of much value. **set off 1** begin a journey. **2** detonate (a bomb etc.). **3** initiate, stimulate. **4** cause (a person) to start laughing, talking, etc. **5** serve as an adornment or foil to; enhance. **6** (foll. by against) use as a compensating item. **set on** (or **upon**) **1** attack violently. **2** cause or urge to attack. **set out 1** begin a journey. **2** (foll. by to + infin.) aim or intend. **3** demonstrate, arrange, or exhibit. **4** mark out. **5** declare. **set sail 1** hoist the sails. **2** begin a sea voyage. **set one's teeth 1** clench them. **2** summon one's resolve. **set to** begin doing something vigorously, esp. fighting, arguing, or eating. **set up 1** place in position or view. **2** organize or start (a business etc.). **3** establish in some capacity. **4** supply the needs of. **5** cause or make arrangements for (a condition or situation). **6** prepare (a task etc.) for another. **7** informal put (a person) in a dangerous or vulnerable position. **set oneself up as** make pretensions to being.

set² n. **1** a number of things or persons that belong together or resemble one another or are usually found together. **2** a collection or group. **3** a section of society consorting together or having similar interests etc. **4** a collection of implements, vessels, etc., regarded collectively and needed for a specified purpose. **5** a piece of electric or electronic apparatus,

esp. a radio or television receiver. **6** (in tennis etc.) a group of games counting as a unit towards a match for the player or side that wins a defined number or proportion of the games. **7** Math. & Logic a collection of distinct entities, individually specified or satisfying specified conditions, forming a unit. **8** a slip, shoot, bulb, etc., for planting. **9** a habitual posture; the way the jaw etc. is carried or a dress etc. flows. **10** the way in which a machine, device, etc. is set or adjusted. **11** a condition of firmness or hardness, e.g. of glue. **12** a setting, including stage furniture etc., for a play or film etc. **13 a** a sequence of songs or pieces performed by a musical ensemble, e.g. a dance band, before or after an intermission. **b** the period during which such a sequence is played. **14** the setting of the hair when damp.

set³ adj. **1** in senses of SET¹. **2** prescribed or determined in advance. **3** fixed, unchanging, unmoving. **4** (of a phrase or speech etc.) having invariable or predetermined wording; not extempore. **5** prepared for action. **6** (foll. by on, upon) determined to acquire or achieve etc. **7** (of a book etc.) specified for reading in preparation for an examination.

set-aside n. **1** the action of setting something aside for a special purpose. **2** the policy of taking land out of production to reduce crop surpluses (often attrib.: set-aside land).

setback n. **1** a reversal or arrest of progress. **2** a relapse. **3** N Amer. the distance by which a building or a part of a building is set back from the property line.

set menu n. a limited menu of a set number of courses.

set-off n. **1** a thing set off against another. **2** a thing of which the amount or effect may be deducted from that of another or opposite tendency. **3** a counterpoise. **4** a counterclaim. **5** a thing that embellishes; an adornment to something.

set piece n. **1** a formal or elaborate arrangement, esp. in art or literature. **2** a sequence of rehearsed movements etc., as in sports or military operations.

set point n. Tennis etc. **1** the state of a game when one side needs only one point to win the set. **2** this point.

settee / se'ti: / n. a seat (usu. upholstered), with a back and usu. arms, for more than one person.

setter n. **1** a breed of large, long-haired dog trained to stand rigid when scenting game. **2** a person or thing that sets.

setting n. **1** the position or manner in which a thing is set. **2** the immediate surroundings (of a house etc.). **3** the surroundings of any object regarded as its framework; the environment of a thing. **4 a** the place and time in which a story, drama, etc. is set. **b** the scenery and stage properties etc. used in a play, film, etc. **5** a frame in which a jewel is set. **6** the music to which words of a poem, song, etc., are set. **7** a set of cutlery, dishes, etc. for one person. **8** the way in which or level at which a machine is set to operate.

settle¹ v. **1** tr. & intr. (often foll. by down) establish or become established in a more or less permanent abode or way of life. **2** intr. & tr. (often foll. by down) **a** cease or cause to cease from disturbance, movement, etc. **b** adopt a regular or secure style of life. **c** (foll. by to) apply oneself (to work, an activity, a way of life, etc.) (settled down to write). **3 a** intr. sit or come down to stay for some time. **b** tr. cause to do this. **4** tr. & intr. bring to or attain fixity, certainty, composure, or quietness. **5** tr. determine or decide or agree upon (shall we settle a date?). **6** tr. **a** resolve (a dispute etc.). **b** deal with (a matter) finally. **7** tr. & intr. terminate (a lawsuit) by mutual agreement. **8** intr. **a** (foll. by for) accept or agree to (esp. an alternative not one's first choice). **b** (foll. by *on*) decide on. **9** *tr. & intr.* pay (a debt, an account, etc.). **10** *tr.* **a** aid the digestion of (food). **b** remedy the disordered state of (nerves, the stomach, etc.). **11 a** *tr.* people (a place) with inhabitants. **b** *intr.* take up residence in a new place (*our family settled here in 1834*). **12** *intr.* fall to the bottom or on to a surface (*wait till the sediment settles*). **13** *intr.* sink down gradually, as by its own weight (*the foundations are settling*). **14** *intr.* (of the ground etc.) become firm or compact. **15** *tr.* dispose of or arrange for the disposal of (an estate, etc.). **16** *tr.* get rid of the obstruction of (a person) by argument or conflict or killing. □ **settle in 1** become established in a new home etc. **2** become accustomed to a new home, new surroundings, etc. **3** dispose oneself comfortably for remaining indoors. **settle up 1** pay (an account, debt, etc.). **2** finally arrange (a matter). **settle with 1** pay all or part of an amount due to (a creditor). **2** get revenge on.

settle² *n.* a bench with a high back and arms and often with a box fitted below the seat.

settled *adj.* **1** that has settled or been settled; fixed, unchanging, established. **2** (of a person's expression or bearing) indicating a settled mind, character, or disposition. **3** (of weather) calm and fair.

settlement *n.* **1** the act or an instance of settling; the process of being settled. **2 a** the colonization of a region. **b** a place or area occupied by settlers. **c** a small village. **3 a** a political or financial etc. agreement. **b** an arrangement ending a dispute. **4 a** the terms on which property is given to a person. **b** a deed stating these. **c** the amount of property given. **5** the process of settling an account. **6** subsidence of a wall, house, soil, etc.

settler *n.* a person who goes to settle in a new country or place.

set-to *n.* (*pl.* **-tos**) *informal* a fight or argument.

set-top box *n.* a digital decoding device used to connect a television set to a source of signals.

set-up *n.* **1** an arrangement or organization. **2** the act or an instance of setting up. **3** *informal* a conspiracy or trick whereby a person is caused to incriminate himself or herself or to look foolish, or a criminal is caught red-handed. **4** *Sport* a pass or play intended to provide an opportunity for another player to score. **5** a plan or course of action. **6** a set or collection of the equipment etc. needed for a particular activity or purpose. **7** *N Amer. informal* an event or activity with a prearranged conclusion.

set-up man *n.* *Baseball* a relief pitcher whose job is to preserve a team's lead so that the closer can enter the game in a position to earn a save.

seven ● *n.* **1** one more than six. **2** a symbol for this (7, vii, VII). **3** a size etc. denoted by seven. **4** a set or team of seven individuals. **5** seven o'clock. **6** a card with seven pips. ● *adj.* that amount to seven.

seven deadly sins *n.pl.* in Christian tradition, pride, covetousness, lust, envy, gluttony, anger, and sloth, regarded as the basic human vices.

sevenfold *adj. & adv.* **1** seven times as much or as many. **2** consisting of seven parts.

seven-minute icing *n.* (also **seven-minute frosting**) *N Amer.* a fluffy icing made of egg whites and sugar etc. beaten together over low heat.

seven seas *n.pl.* the oceans of the world.

seventeen ● *n.* **1** one more than sixteen, or seven more than ten. **2** a symbol for this (17, xvii, XVII). **3** a size etc. denoted by seventeen. ● *adj.* that amount to seventeen. □ **seventeenth** *adj., adv., & n.*

seventh ● *n.* **1** the position in a sequence corresponding to the number 7 in the sequence 1–7. **2** something occupying this position. **3** one of seven equal parts of a thing. **4** *Music* **a** an interval or chord spanning seven consecutive notes in the diatonic scale (e.g. C to B). **b** a note separated from another by this interval. **5** *Baseball* the seventh inning. ● *adj.* that is the seventh. ● *adv.* in the seventh place.

Seventh-day Adventist ● *n.* a member of a branch of the Adventists with beliefs based rigidly on faith and the Scriptures and the imminent return of Christ to earth, and observing the Sabbath on Saturday. ● *adj.* of or relating to the Seventh-day Adventists.

seventy ● *n.* (*pl.* **-ies**) **1** the product of seven and ten. **2** a symbol for this (70, lxx, LXX). **3** (in *pl.*) the numbers from 70 to 79, esp. the years of a century or of a person's life. ● *adj.* that amount to seventy. □ **seventy-first, -second,** etc. the ordinal numbers between seventieth and eightieth. **seventy-one, -two,** etc. the cardinal numbers between seventy and eighty. □ **seventieth** *adj., adv., & n.*

seventy-eight *n. hist.* a gramophone record played at 78 rpm.

sever /'sevər/ *v.* **1** *tr. & intr.* (often foll. by *from*) divide, break, or make separate, esp. by cutting. **2** *tr. & intr.* end (a relationship or connection); break off something (*sever ties*). **3** *tr.* separate (a piece of land) from a larger lot. **4** *tr.* end the employment contract of (a person).

several *adj.* **1** more than two but not many. **2** separate or respective; distinct (*all went their several ways*). **3** *Law* applied or regarded separately (opp. JOINT). □ **severally** *adv.*

severance *n.* **1** the act or an instance of severing. **2** (also **severance pay**) an amount paid to an employee who is dismissed (also *attrib.*: *severance package*). **3** the act or an instance of severing a piece of land from a larger lot. **4** a severed state.

severe *adj.* **1** rigorous, strict, and harsh in attitude or treatment (*severe discipline*). **2** serious, critical (*a severe shortage*). **3** vehement or forceful (*a severe storm*). **4** extreme (in an unpleasant quality) (*a severe winter*). **5** arduous or exacting; making great demands on energy, skill, etc. (*severe competition*). **6** unadorned; plain (*severe dress*). □ **severely** *adv.* **severity** *n.*

seviche *var. of* CEVICHE.

Seville orange *n.* a bitter orange used for marmalade.

sew *v.* (*past part.* **sewn** or **sewed**) **1** *tr. & intr.* fasten, join, attach, etc., by making stitches with a needle and thread or a sewing machine. **2** *tr.* make (a garment etc.) by sewing. □ **sew up 1** join or enclose by sewing. **2** *informal* (esp. in *passive*) bring to a desired conclusion or condition; complete satisfactorily; ensure the favourable outcome of (a thing). **3** close (a hole, wound, etc.) using stitches. **4** gain complete control of (*we've sewn up the market*). □ **sewer** *n.*

sewage *n.* waste matter, esp. excrement, conveyed in sewers.

sewer *n.* a conduit, usu. underground, for carrying off drainage water and sewage. □ **sewerage** *n.*

sewing *n.* **1** a piece of material or work to be sewn. **2** the act or an instance of sewing.

sewing machine *n.* a machine for sewing or stitching.

sex ● *n.* **1** either of the main divisions (male and female) into which living things are placed on the basis of their reproductive functions. **2** the fact of belonging to one of these. **3** males or females collectively. **4** sexual intercourse. **5** sexual instincts, desires, etc., or their manifestation (*all you ever think* *about is sex!*). ● *adj.* **1** of or relating to sex (*sex education*). **2** arising from a difference or consciousness of sex (*sex discrimination*). ● *v.tr.* determine the sex of.

sex act *n.* the (or an) act of sexual intercourse.

sexagenarian /ˌseksədʒɪˈneriən/ ● *n.* a person from 60 to 69 years old. ● *adj.* of this age.

sex appeal *n.* sexual attractiveness.

sex change *n.* an apparent change of sex by surgical means and hormone treatment.

sex chromosome *n.* a chromosome concerned in determining the sex of an organism, which in most animals are of two kinds, the X chromosome and the Y chromosome.

sexed *adj.* **1** having a sexual appetite (*highly sexed*). **2** having sexual characteristics.

sex hormone *n.* a hormone affecting sexual development or behaviour.

sexism *n.* **1** prejudice or discrimination, esp. against women, on the grounds of sex. **2** behaviour or attitudes derived from a traditional stereotype of sexual roles. □ **sexist** *adj. & n.*

sex kitten *n.* *informal* a flirtatious, sexy young woman.

sexless *adj.* **1** *Biol.* neither male nor female. **2** lacking in sexual desire or attractiveness. □ **sexlessly** *adv.* **sexlessness** *n.*

sex life *n.* a person's sexual activities viewed collectively (*has an active sex life*).

sex object *n.* a person regarded mainly in terms of sexual attractiveness.

sex offender *n.* a person who commits a sexual crime.

sexology *n.* the study of sexual life or relationships, esp. in human beings. □ **sexological** *adj.* **sexologist** *n.*

sexpot *n.* *informal* a sexy person (esp. a woman).

sex symbol *n.* a person widely noted for sex appeal.

sextant *n.* an instrument with a graduated arc of 60° used in navigation and surveying for measuring the angular distance of objects by means of mirrors.

sextet *n.* **1** a musical composition for six voices etc. **2** the performers of such a piece. **3** any group of six.

sexton *n.* a person who looks after a church and churchyard, often acting as bell-ringer etc.

sex trade *n.* = SEX WORK.

sextuple /ˈseks,tʌpəl/ ● *adj.* **1** sixfold. **2** having six parts. **3** being six times as many or much. ● *n.* a sixfold number or amount. ● *v.tr. & intr.* multiply by six.

sextuplet /ˈseks,tʌplət/ *n.* each of six children born at one birth.

sexual *adj.* **1** of or relating to sex or the desire for sex (*sexual fantasies*). **2** of or relating to the sexes or the relations between them (*sexual discrimination*). **3** *Bot.* (of classification) based on the distinction of sexes in plants. **4** *Biol.* having a sex. □ **sexually** *adv.*

sexual abuse *n.* the forcing of a person, esp. a child, to engage in sexual activity or relations; the making of unwanted sexual advances etc.

sexual assault *n.* threatened or actual sexual contact with another person without consent.

sexual harassment *n.* harassment (esp. of a woman) in a workplace etc. involving the making of unwanted sexual advances, obscene remarks, demands for sexual favours etc.

sexual intercourse *n.* genital contact between individuals, esp. involving the insertion of a man's penis into a woman's vagina.

sexual interference *n.* *Law* the act or an instance

of touching directly or indirectly any part of the body of a person under 14 years of age for sexual purposes.

sexuality *n.* **1** possession of sexual powers; capacity for sexual feelings. **2** sexual feelings, desires, etc. collectively. **3** = SEXUAL ORIENTATION.

sexualize *v.tr.* **1** make sexual. **2** attribute sex or a sexual role to. □ **sexualization** *n.*

sexually transmitted disease *n.* a disease transmitted by sexual contact, e.g. AIDS, gonorrhea.

sexual orientation *n.* (also **sexual preference**) the fact of being attracted to people of the opposite sex, of one's own sex, or both sexes.

sex work *n.* prostitution. □ **sex worker** *n.*

sexy *adj.* (**-ier, -iest**) **1** sexually attractive or stimulating. **2** sexually aroused. **3** concerned with or engrossed in sex. **4** *informal* (of a project etc.) exciting, appealing, trendy. □ **sexily** *adv.* **sexiness** *n.*

SF *abbr.* **1** science fiction. **2** San Francisco.

sforzando /sfɔrˈtsændo:/ *Music* ● *adj. & adv.* with sudden emphasis. ● *n.* (*pl.* **-os** or **sforzandi** /-di/) **1** a note or group of notes especially emphasized. **2** an increase in emphasis and loudness.

SG *abbr.* **1** *Law* Solicitor General. **2** specific gravity.

SGML *abbr. Computing* Standard Generalized Mark-up Language, a form of generic coding used for producing printed material in electronic form.

Sgt *abbr.* (also **Sgt.**) SERGEANT.

sh *interj.* calling for silence.

Shabbat /ʃɒˈbʊt/ *n.* (also **Shabbos, Shabbes** /ˈʃʊbəs/) the Jewish Sabbath.

shabby *adj.* (**-ier, -iest**) **1** in bad repair or condition; faded and worn. **2** dressed in old or worn clothes. **3** of poor quality. **4** contemptible, dishonourable (*a shabby trick*). □ **shabbily** *adv.* **shabbiness** *n.*

shack *n.* a roughly built hut or cabin. □ **shack up** *slang* live together in a sexual relationship without being married. □ **shacky** *adj.*

shackle *n.* **1** a fetter enclosing the ankle or wrist. **2** (usu. in *pl.*) a restraint or impediment. **3** a metal loop or link, closed by a bolt, to connect chains etc. **4** the U-shaped part of a padlock. ● *v.tr.* **1** fetter, impede, restrain. **2** (often foll. by *to*) fasten with a shackle.

shacktown *n.* *Cdn* a community or section of a community composed of shacks or other temporary housing.

shad *n.* (*pl.* same or **-s**) a deep-bodied edible fish of the herring family, esp. the marine fish *Alosa sapidissima*, spawning in fresh water, or the freshwater fish *Dorosoma cepedianum*, found in tributaries and distributaries of the Great Lakes.

shade ● *n.* **1** comparative darkness (and usu. coolness) caused by shelter from direct light and heat. **2** a place or area sheltered from the sun. **3** a darker part of a picture etc. **4** a colour, esp. with regard to its depth or as distinguished from one nearly like it. **5** a slight amount (*a shade better*). **6 a** = LAMPSHADE. **b** = BLIND *n.* 1. **7** something that excludes or moderates light. **8** (in *pl.*) esp. *N Amer. informal* sunglasses. **9** a slightly differing variety (*many shades of opinion*). **10** *literary* **a** a ghost. **b** (in *pl.*) the underworld. ● *v.* **1** *tr.* screen from light. **2** *tr.* cover, moderate, or exclude the light of. **3** *tr.* darken, esp. with parallel pencil lines to represent shadow etc. **4** *intr. & tr.* (often foll. by *away, off, into*) pass or change by degrees. □ **put in the shade** appear or be very superior to (a person or thing). **shades of** suggesting reminiscence or unfavourable comparison (*shades of fascism*).

shading *n.* **1** the representation of light and shade, e.g. by pencilled lines, on a map or drawing. **2** the graduation of tones from light to dark to create a sense of depth.

shadow ● *n.* **1** shade or a patch of shade. **2** a dark figure projected by a body intercepting rays of light. **3** an inseparable attendant or companion. **4** a person secretly following another. **5** the slightest trace (*a shadow of a doubt*). **6** a weak or insubstantial remnant or thing (*a shadow of my former self*). **7** (*attrib.*) Cdn & Brit. denoting members of a political party in opposition holding responsibilities parallel to those of the government (*shadow cabinet*). **8** the shaded part of a picture. **9** = EYESHADOW. **10** gloom or sadness. ● *v.tr.* **1** cast a shadow over. **2** secretly follow and watch the movements of. **3** accompany (a person) at work either as training or to obtain insight into a profession. □ **in the shadow of 1** close to; very near. **2** under the influence or power of. **3** dominated or eclipsed by the personality of. □ **shadowless** *adj.*

shadow box *n.* a case with a protective transparent front for the display of a painting, jewel, etc.

shadow boxing *n.* boxing against an imaginary opponent as a form of training. □ **shadowbox** *v.intr.*

shadowy *adj.* **1** like or having a shadow. **2** full of shadows. **3** vague, indistinct.

shady *adj.* (**-ier**, **-iest**) **1** giving shade. **2** situated in shade. **3** (of a person or behaviour) disreputable; of doubtful honesty. □ **shadily** *adv.* **shadiness** *n.*

shaft ● *n.* **1** the stem or handle of a tool, implement, etc. **2** a column, esp. between the base and capital. **3** a long narrow space, usu. vertical, for access to a mine, an elevator in a building, for ventilation, etc. **4** a long and narrow part supporting or connecting or driving a part or parts of greater thickness etc. **5** each of the pair of poles between which an animal is harnessed to a vehicle. **6 a** an arrow or spear. **b** the long slender stem of these. **7** a remark intended to hurt or provoke. **8** (foll. by *of*) **a** a ray (of light). **b** a bolt (of lightning). **9** the central stem of a feather. **10** Mech. a large axle or revolving bar transferring force by belts or cogs. **11** *slang* the penis. **12** *N Amer. informal* (prec. by *the*) harsh or unfair treatment. ● *v.tr.* *N Amer. informal* treat unfairly.

shag[1] *n.* **1** a rough growth or mass of hair etc. **2** a hairstyle in which the hair is cut in layers from the top. **3 a** (*attrib.*) (of a carpet, rug, etc.) having a long rough pile. **b** a shag carpet. **c** (*attrib.*) (of a pile) long and rough. **4** a cormorant, esp. the crested cormorant, *Phalacrocorax aristotelis*.

shag[2] *coarse slang* ● *v.tr.* (**shagged**, **shagging**) **1** have sexual intercourse with. **2** (usu. in *passive*; often foll. by *out*) tire out. ● *n.* an act of intercourse.

shag[3] *v.tr.* (**shagged**, **shagging**) **1** retrieve; go after and bring back. **2** *Baseball* retrieve and throw back (fly balls), esp. in batting practice. **3** chase or follow after.

shaganappi /ˌʃæɡəˈnæpi/ esp. Cdn (West) ● *n.* **1** thread, cord, or thong made of rawhide. **2** a rough pony. ● *adj.* of inferior quality.

shagbark hickory *n.* a hickory of eastern N America, *C. ovata*, with bark that splits into long loose strips.

shaggy *adj.* (**-ier**, **-iest**) **1** hairy, rough-haired. **2** unkempt. **3** (of the hair) coarse and abundant. **4** (of cloth) having a long and coarse nap. **5** *Biol.* having a hairlike covering. □ **shaggily** *adv.* **shagginess** *n.*

shaggy-dog story *n.* a long rambling story, more amusing to the teller than the audience or amusing only by its inconsequentiality or pointlessness.

shah *n.* a title of the former monarch of Iran.

shake ● *v.* (*past* **shook**; *past part.* **shaken**) **1** *tr. & intr.* move forcefully or quickly up and down or to and fro.

2 a *intr.* tremble or vibrate markedly. **b** *tr.* cause to do this. **3** *tr.* **a** agitate or shock. **b** upset the composure of. **4** *tr.* weaken or impair; make less convincing or firm or courageous (*shook their confidence*). **5** *intr.* (of a voice, note, etc.) make tremulous or rapidly alternating sounds (*his voice shook with emotion*). **6** *tr.* brandish; make a threatening gesture with (one's fist, a stick, etc.). **7** *intr.* shake hands. **8** *tr.* esp. *N Amer. informal* = SHAKE OFF. ● *n.* **1** the act or an instance of shaking; the process of being shaken. **2** a jerk or shock. **3** (in *pl.*; prec. by *the*) a fit of or tendency to trembling or shivering, esp. caused by fear or withdrawal from drugs or alcohol. **4** = MILKSHAKE. **5** = CEDAR SHAKE. □ **in two shakes (of a lamb's tail)** very quickly. **more than you can shake a stick at** esp. *N Amer.* more than one can count, a considerable amount or number. **no great shakes** *informal* not very good or significant. **shake a person by the hand** = SHAKE HANDS. **shake down 1** settle or cause to fall by shaking. **2** settle down. **3** become established; get into harmony with circumstances, surroundings, etc. **4** *N Amer. slang* extort money from. **shake the dust off one's feet** depart indignantly or disdainfully. **shake hands** (often foll. by *with*) clasp right hands at meeting or parting, in reconciliation or congratulation, or over a concluded bargain. **shake one's head** move one's head from side to side in refusal, denial, disapproval, incredulity, or concern. **shake in one's shoes** tremble with apprehension. **shake a leg 1** hurry. **2** begin dancing. **shake off 1** get rid of (something unwanted). **2** manage to evade (a person who is following or pestering one). **shake out 1** empty by shaking. **2** spread or open (a sail, flag, etc.) by shaking. **shake up 1** mix (ingredients) by shaking. **2** restore to shape by shaking. **3** disturb or make uncomfortable. **4** rouse from lethargy, apathy, conventionality, etc.

shakedown *n.* **1** a period or process of adjustment or change. **2** esp. *N Amer. slang* a swindle; a piece of extortion. **3** *N Amer.* a search. **4** a makeshift bed. **5** (*attrib.*) denoting a voyage, flight, etc., to test a new ship or aircraft and its crew.

shaker *n.* **1** a person or thing that shakes. **2** esp. *N Amer.* a container, usu. with a perforated top, from which something is shaken (*pepper shaker*). **3** a container for shaking together the ingredients of cocktails etc. **4** (**Shaker**) **a** a member of an American religious sect living simply, in celibate mixed communities. **b** (*attrib.*) (of furniture etc.) produced by or of a type produced by Shakers, characterized by simplicity and lack of ornamentation. **5** (*attrib.*) (also **shaker knit**) designating a style of knitting, used esp. in sweaters, having parallel rows of ribbing. □ **Shakerism** *n.* (in sense 4).

Shakespearean (also **Shakespearian**) ● *adj.* **1** of or relating to the English poet and dramatist William Shakespeare (1564–1616). **2** in the style of Shakespeare. ● *n.* a student of Shakespeare's works etc. □ **Shakespeareanism** *n.*

shakeup *n.* an upheaval or drastic reorganization.

shaking tent *n.* (among some Algonquian peoples) a tent or lodge in which a shaman consulted the spirits for advice or assistance (also *attrib.*: *shaking tent ceremony*).

shaky *adj.* (**-ier**, **-iest**) **1** unsteady; apt to shake; trembling. **2** unsound, infirm. **3** unreliable, wavering (*off to a shaky start*). □ **shakily** *adv.* **shakiness** *n.*

shale *n.* soft finely stratified rock that splits easily, consisting of consolidated mud or clay. □ **shaley** adj. (also **shaly**).

shall v.aux. (3rd sing. present **shall**; archaic 2nd sing. present **shalt**; past **should**) **1** indicating future predictions. **2** indicating will or determination. **3** indicating or offering suggestions. **4** indicating orders or instructions. ¶Despite traditional attempts to distinguish clearly between shall and will, in practice will is most commonly used today in all persons, both to form the future tense and to express a strong assertion or command.

shallot /'ʃælət, ʃə'lɒt/ n. **1** a variety of onion which forms clumps of small bulbs. **2** the bulb of this, esp. as used in cooking.

shallow ● adj. **1** of little depth. **2** superficial, trivial (a shallow mind). ● n. (often in pl.) shallow waters. □ **shallowly** adv. **shallowness** n.

shalom /ʃə'lɒ:m/ n. & interj. a Jewish salutation at meeting or parting.

sham ● n. **1 a** a person or thing pretending or pretended to be what he or she or it is not. **b** imposture, pretense. **2** N Amer. a decorative cover for a bed pillow when not in use. ● adj. pretended, counterfeit. ● v. (**shammed, shamming**) **1** intr. feign, pretend. **2** tr. a pretend to be. **b** simulate (is shamming sleep).

shaman /'ʃeɪmən/ n. a person regarded as having access to the world of good and evil spirits, esp. among some peoples of N Asia and N America. □ **shamanic** /ʃə'mænɪk/ adj. **shamanism** n. **shamanistic** adj. **shamanistically** adv.

shamble ● v.intr. walk or run with a shuffling or awkward gait. ● n. a shambling gait.

shambles n.pl. (usu. treated as sing.) **1** informal a scene or situation of complete disorder; a mess (the economy was a shambles). **2** a slaughterhouse.

shame ● n. **1** a feeling of distress or humiliation caused by consciousness of the guilt or foolishness of oneself or an associate. **2** a capacity for experiencing this feeling (has no sense of shame). **3** a state of disgrace, discredit, or intense regret. **4 a** a person or thing that brings disgrace etc. **b** a thing or action that is wrong or regrettable. ● v.tr. **1** bring shame on; make ashamed; put to shame. **2** (foll. by into, out of) force by shame (was shamed into confessing). □ **for shame!** a reproof to a person for not showing shame. **put to shame** disgrace or humiliate by revealing superior qualities etc. **shame on you!** you should be ashamed. **what a shame!** how unfortunate! □ **shameful** adj. **shamefully** adv.

shamefaced adj. **1** showing shame. **2** bashful, diffident. □ **shamefacedly** adv. **shamefacedness** n.

shameless adj. **1** having or showing no sense of shame. **2** impudent, brazen. □ **shamelessly** adv. **shamelessness** n.

shampoo ● n. **1** liquid or cream used to lather and wash the hair. **2** a similar substance for washing a car or carpet etc. **3** an act or instance of cleaning with shampoo. ● v.tr. (**shampoos, shampooed**) wash with shampoo. □ **shampooer** n.

shamrock n. any of various plants with trifoliate leaves, esp. Trifolium repens or Medicago lupulina, used as the national emblem of Ireland or the Irish.

shanghai v.tr. (**-hais, -haied, -haiing**) trick or force (a person) into doing something or going somewhere.

Shangri-La n. an imaginary paradise on earth.

shank ● n. **1 a** the leg. **b** the lower part of the leg; the leg from knee to ankle. **c** the shin bone. **2 a** the lower part of an animal's foreleg, esp. that of a horse. **b** the upper part of the foreleg or hind leg of an animal as a cut of meat. **3** a shaft or stem. **4 a** the long narrow part of a tool etc. joining the handle to the working end. **b** the stem of a key, spoon, anchor, etc. **c** the straight part of a nail or fish hook. **5** the narrow middle of the sole of a shoe. **6** N Amer. slang an improvised knife, esp. as made by a prison inmate. ● v.tr. **1** Golf mis-hit (the ball) with the heel of the club. **2** N Amer. slash with a knife. □ **shanked** adj. (also in comb.).

shan't contraction shall not.

shanty¹ n. (pl. **-ies**) **1** a crudely built shack or cabin. **2** a hut or cabin. **3** esp. Cdn hist. a lumberjack's log cabin or shack. **4** esp. Cdn hist. a logging camp.

shanty² n. (pl. **-ies**) (in full **sea shanty**) a song with alternating solo and chorus, of a kind originally sung by sailors while hauling ropes etc.

shantyman n. (pl. **-men**) Cdn hist. a lumberjack; a worker at a lumber camp.

shantytown n. a poor or depressed area of a city or town, consisting of shanties.

shape ● n. **1** the total effect produced by the outlines of a thing. **2** the external form or appearance of a person or thing. **3** a specific form or guise. **4** a description or sort or way (not tolerated in any way, shape, or form). **5** a definite or proper arrangement (must get our ideas into shape). **6 a** condition, as qualified in some way (in good shape). **b** (when unqualified) good condition (back in shape). **c** the nature, qualities, or characteristics of something (the shape of things to come). **7** a person or thing as seen, esp. indistinctly or in the imagination. **8** a mould or pattern. **9** a piece of material, paper, etc., made or cut in a particular form. ● v. **1** tr. give a certain shape or form to; fashion, create. **2** tr. (foll. by to) adapt or make conform. **3** intr. give signs of a future shape or development. **4** tr. frame mentally; imagine. **5** intr. assume or develop into a shape. **6** tr. direct (one's life, course, etc.). □ **give shape to** form, mould; provide with a distinct outline or form; express clearly. **in shape** physically fit. **lick into shape** make presentable or efficient. **out of shape** physically unfit. **shape up 1** take a (specified) form or suggest that such a form will be taken (shaping up to be a cold winter). **2** show promise; make good progress; improve (were told to shape up). **shape up or ship out** achieve a satisfactory performance or be dismissed. **take shape** assume a distinct form; develop into something definite. **whip into shape** make presentable or efficient, esp. severely. □ **shaped** adj. (also in comb.). **shaper** n.

shapeless adj. lacking definite or attractive shape. □ **shapelessness** n.

shapely adj. (**-ier, -iest**) **1** well formed or proportioned. **2** of elegant or pleasing shape or appearance. □ **shapeliness** n.

shape-shifter n. (in folklore, science fiction, etc.) any creature capable of changing its form, e.g. a werewolf. □ **shape-shifting** n.

shard n. **1** a broken piece of pottery or glass etc. **2** a fragment of something shattered, broken, etc.

share¹ ● n. **1** a portion that a person receives from or gives to a common amount. **2 a** a part that is or ought to be contributed by an individual to an enterprise or commitment. **b** a part that is or ought to be received by an individual from this (a share of the credit). **3** part-proprietorship of property held by joint owners, esp. any of the equal parts into which a company's capital is divided entitling its owner to a proportion of the profits. ● v. **1** tr. get or have or give a share of. **2** tr. use or benefit from jointly with others. **3** tr. have in common (I share your opinion). **4** intr. have a share; be a sharer (must learn to share). **5** intr. (foll. by in) participate. **6** tr. (often foll. by *out*) **a** divide and distribute. **b** give away part of. **7 a** tr. tell, recount (a story, joke, one's feelings, etc.). **b** intr. tell others an esp. personal story, one's feelings, etc. □ **share and share alike** make an equal division. □ **shareable** adj. **sharer** n.

share² n. = PLOUGHSHARE.

sharecropper n. a tenant farmer who gives a part of each crop as rent. □ **sharecrop** v.tr. & intr. **(-cropped, -cropping). sharecropping** n.

shareholder n. an owner of shares in a company. □ **shareholding** n.

shareware n. software that is available free of charge and often distributed informally for evaluation, after which a fee is requested for continued use.

shark¹ n. any of various large usu. voracious marine fish with a long body and prominent dorsal fin.

shark² n. informal a person who unscrupulously exploits or swindles others (*loan shark*).

sharkskin n. **1** the rough scaly skin of a shark. **2** a smooth slightly lustrous fabric.

sharp ● adj. **1** having an edge or point able to cut or pierce. **2** tapering to a point or edge. **3** abrupt, steep, angular (*a sharp turn*). **4** well defined, clean-cut (*in sharp contrast*). **5 a** severe or intense (*a sharp pain*). **b** (of food or its flavour) pungent, acid. **c** keen (*has a sharp ear*). **d** (of a frost) severe, hard. **6** (of a voice or sound) shrill and piercing. **7** (of words, temper, a person, etc.) harsh or acrimonious (*had a sharp tongue*). **8** (of a person) quick to perceive or comprehend. **9** derogatory quick to take advantage; artful, unscrupulous, dishonest. **10** vigorous or brisk. **11** Music **a** above the desired or true pitch. **b** (of a key) having a sharp or sharps in the signature. **c** (as **C sharp** etc.) a semitone higher than C etc. **12** informal stylish or flashy with regard to dress. ● n. **1** Music **a** a note raised a semitone above natural pitch. **b** the sign (♯) indicating this. **2** informal a swindler or cheat. **3** a fine sewing needle. ● adv. **1** punctually (*at nine o'clock sharp*). **2** suddenly, abruptly, promptly (*pulled up sharp*). **3** at a sharp angle. **4** Music above the true pitch (*sings sharp*). □ **keep a sharp eye on** (or **out for**) watch carefully (for). **sharp as a tack** N Amer. extremely quick, clever, astute, alert, etc. □ **sharply** adv. **sharpness** n.

sharp-edged adj. **1** having a sharp edge. **2** biting, caustic; sharp-tongued.

Shar-Pei /ʃɑr ˈpeɪ/ n. a compact squarely built breed of dog of Chinese origin, with a characteristic wrinkly skin and short bristly coat of a fawn, cream, black, or red colour.

sharpen v.tr. & intr. make or become sharp. □ **sharpener** n.

sharp end n. informal **1** the bow of a ship. **2** the scene of direct action or decision; the front line.

sharper n. a swindler, esp. at cards.

sharp-featured adj. (of a person) having well-defined facial features.

sharpie n. = SHARPER.

sharp-shinned hawk n. (also **sharp-shin**) a small hawk, *Accipiter striatus*, of N America.

sharpshooter n. a skilled shooter or marksman. □ **sharpshooting** n. & adj.

sharp-tailed grouse n. a medium-sized grouse of grasslands in western N America, *Tympanuchus phasianellus*, with a short pointed tail.

sharp-tongued adj. harsh or cutting in speech.

shasta /ˈʃæstə/ n. (in full **shasta daisy**) a European plant, *Chrysanthemum maximum*, with daisy-like flowers.

shat past and past part. of SHIT.

shatter v. **1** tr. & intr. break suddenly in pieces. **2** tr. severely damage or utterly destroy (*shattered hopes*; *shattered the myth*). **3** tr. greatly upset or discompose; dumbfound. □ **shattering** adj. **shatteringly** adv.

shatterproof adj. (of glass etc.) designed to resist shattering.

shave ● v. (past part. **shaved** or (as adj.) **shaven**) **1** tr. & intr. remove (bristles or hair) from the face etc. with a razor. **2** tr. & intr. remove bristles or hair with a razor from the face etc. of (a person) or from (a part of the body). **3** tr. **a** reduce by a small amount. **b** take (a small amount) away from. **4** tr. cut thin slices from the surface of (wood etc.). **5** tr. pass close to without touching; miss narrowly. **6** tr. cut (hair, grass, etc.) very short. ● n. **1** an act of shaving or the process of being shaved. **2** a close approach without contact. **3** a tool for shaving wood etc.

shaver n. **1** a person or thing that shaves. **2** an electric razor. **3** informal a young boy.

shaving n. **1** a thin, curled strip cut off the surface of wood, chocolate, etc. **2** (attrib.) used in shaving.

Shavuot /ʃəˈvuːəs, ʃʊvʊˈɒt/ n. = PENTECOST 2.

shawl n. a piece of fabric, usu. rectangular and often folded into a triangle, worn over the shoulders or head or wrapped around a baby. □ **shawled** adj.

Shawnee /ʃɒˈniː/ ● n. **1** a member of an Algonquian people formerly resident in the eastern US and now chiefly in Oklahoma. **2** the language of this people. ● adj. of or pertaining to the Shawnee.

she ● pron. (obj. **her**; poss. **her**; pl. **they**) **1** the woman or girl or female animal previously named or in question. **2** a thing regarded as female, e.g. a vehicle or ship. **3** a person etc. of unspecified sex, esp. referring to one already named or identified (*ask any doctor and she will tell you*). ● n. **1** a female; a woman. **2** (in comb.) female (*she-goat*).

s/he pron. a written representation of 'he or she' used to indicate both sexes.

sheaf ● n. (pl. **sheaves**) **1** a pile or bundle of things, esp. paper. **2** a bundle of stalks and ears of grain tied after reaping. ● v.tr. make into sheaves.

shear ● v. (past **sheared**; past part. **shorn** or **sheared**) **1** tr. clip the wool off (a sheep etc.). **2** tr. remove or take off by cutting. **3** tr. **a** cut with scissors or shears etc. **b** cut down (a tree). **4** tr. (foll. by *of*) **a** strip bare. **b** deprive. **5** tr. & intr. (often foll. by *off*) distort or be distorted, or break, from a structural strain. ● n. **1** Mech. & Geol. a strain produced by pressure in the structure of a substance, when its layers are laterally shifted in relation to each other. **2** (in pl.) (also **pair of shears** sing.) a large clipping or cutting instrument shaped like scissors for use in gardens etc. **3** a hydraulically powered cutter used in logging to fell trees. **4** = WIND SHEAR. □ **shearer** n.

shearling n. **1** a sheep that has been shorn once. **2** a fleece or wool from a shearling, esp. the tanned fleece used to make garments, with the wool to the inside.

shearwater n. **1** any of a number of seabirds of the family Procellariidae, related to petrels, which habitually skim low over the open sea with wings outstretched. **2** = SKIMMER 3.

sheath n. **1** a close-fitting cover, esp. for the blade of a knife or sword. **2** a condom. **3** Bot., Anat., & Zool. an enclosing case or tissue. **4** the protective covering round an electric cable. **5** a woman's close-fitting dress.

sheathe v.tr. **1** put into a sheath. **2** encase; protect with a sheath or sheathing.

sheathing n. **1** a protective casing or covering. **2** a layer of plywood etc. covering the frame.

shebang n. N Amer. slang □ **the whole shebang** the whole situation, thing, etc.

shed¹ n. **1** a one-storeyed structure usu. of simple construction used for storage, as shelter for animals, or as a workshop etc. **2** a large roofed structure often with one side or more sides open, for storing or maintaining machinery, vehicles, etc. (drive shed).

shed² v. (**shedding**; past and past part. **shed**) **1 a** tr. let or cause to fall off (trees shed their leaves). **b** intr. (of an animal) lose hair, feathers, etc. **2** tr. take off (clothes). **3** tr. reduce (an electrical power load) by disconnection etc. **4** tr. cause to fall or flow (shed tears). **5** tr. disperse, diffuse, radiate (shed light). **6** tr. remove or get rid of (has shed 25 pounds). □ **shedder** n.

she'd contraction **1** she had. **2** she would.

sheen n. **1** a gloss or lustre on a surface. **2** radiance, brightness.

sheep n. (pl. same) **1** any ruminant mammal of the genus Ovis with a thick woolly coat, of which domesticated varieties are kept in flocks for wool or meat. **2** a bashful, defenceless, or esp. easily-led person. □ **might as well be hanged for a sheep as a lamb** might as well attempt the bolder of two strategies if the consequences of failure are the same. **separate the sheep from the goats** divide into desirable and undesirable groups. □ **sheeplike** adj.

sheepdog n. **1** a dog trained to guard and herd sheep. **2** a dog of various breeds suitable for this.

sheepfold n. an enclosure for penning sheep.

sheep herder n. a shepherd.

sheepish adj. **1** embarrassed through shame or foolishness. **2** bashful, shy, reticent. □ **sheepishly** adv. **sheepishness** n.

sheepskin n. **1** a garment or rug of sheep's skin with the wool on. **2** leather from a sheep's skin used in bookbinding.

sheer¹ ● adj. **1** complete; nothing more than (sheer luck). **2** (of a cliff or ascent etc.) perpendicular; very steep. **3** (of a textile) very thin; diaphanous. ● adv. **1** directly, outright. **2** perpendicularly. ● n. **1** sheer fabric. **2** (in pl.) **a** curtains made of sheer fabric. **b** sheer nylon hosiery. □ **sheerly** adv.

sheer² ● v.intr. **1** esp. Naut. swerve or change course. **2** (foll. by away, off) go away, esp. from a person or topic one dislikes or fears. ● n. a deviation from a course.

sheer³ n. the upward slope of a ship's lines towards the bow and stern.

sheesh interj. N Amer. expressing mild frustration, exasperation, surprise, embarrassment, etc.

sheet¹ ● n. **1** a large rectangular piece of cotton or other fabric, used esp. in pairs as inner bedclothes. **2 a** a broad usu. thin flat piece of material, e.g. paper or metal. **b** (attrib.) made in sheets (sheet metal). **3** the long rectangular ice surface on which curling is played. **4** a wide continuous surface or expanse of water, ice, flame, falling rain, etc. **5** a set of unseparated postage stamps. **6** derogatory a newspaper, esp. a disreputable one. **7** a complete piece of paper of the size in which it was made, for printing and folding as part of a book. **8** = BAKING SHEET. ● v. **1** tr. provide or cover with sheets. **2** tr. form into sheets. **3** intr. (of rain etc.) fall in sheets. □ **between the sheets** in bed, esp. engaged in sexual activity.

sheet² n. a rope or chain attached to the lower corner of a sail for securing or controlling it. □ **three sheets to the wind** slang drunk.

sheeting n. **1** an act or instance of making or cover-

ing with sheets. **2** material for making bed linen. **3** material covering another in sheets.

sheet lightning n. a lightning flash whose bolt is unseen, observed as a sudden flash of brightness illuminating a wide area.

sheet music n. **1** printed music, as opposed to performed or recorded music and books about music. **2** music published in single or interleaved sheets, not bound.

she/he pron. a written representation of 'she or he' used to indicate both sexes.

sheik / ʃiːk, ʃeik / n. (also **sheikh**) **1** a chief or head of an Arab tribe, family, or village. **2** a Muslim leader. □ **sheikdom** n.

shekel / ˈʃekəl / n. **1** the chief monetary unit of modern Israel. **2** hist. a silver coin and unit of weight used in ancient Israel etc. **3** (in pl.) informal money; riches.

shelf n. (pl. **shelves**) **1 a** a thin flat piece of wood or metal etc. projecting from a wall, or as part of a unit, used to support books etc. **b** a flat-topped recess in a wall etc. used for supporting objects. **c** an object or objects placed on a shelf (three shelves of books). **2 a** a projecting horizontal ledge in a cliff face etc. **b** a reef or sandbank under water. **c** = CONTINENTAL SHELF. □ **off the shelf** (of goods) available immediately from a retailer's stock, as opposed to custom-made. **on the shelf 1** put away indefinitely; set aside. **2** no longer active or of use. **3** informal derogatory (of a woman) past the age when she might expect to be married. □ **shelved** adj. **shelf-like** adj.

shelf ice n. floating ice permanently attached to a land mass.

shelf life n. **1** the amount of time for which a stored item of food etc. remains usable. **2** the length of time during which an idea, practice, etc. is fashionable or practicable.

shell ● n. **1 a** the hard outer case of many marine molluscs, snails, etc. (seashell). **b** the esp. hard but fragile outer covering of a bird's, reptile's, etc. egg. **c** the usu. hard outer case of a nut kernel, seed, etc. **d** the carapace of a tortoise etc. **e** the wing-case or pupa case of many insects etc. **2 a** an explosive projectile or bomb for use in a big gun or mortar. **b** a hollow metal or paper case used as a container for fireworks, explosives, cartridges, etc. **c** N Amer. a cartridge. **3** a mere semblance or outer form without substance. **4** any of several things resembling a shell in being an outer case, esp.: **a** a light racing boat. **b** a hollow pastry case. **c** the metal framework of a vehicle body etc. **d** the walls of an unfinished or gutted building, ship, etc. **5** N Amer. a very light all-weather jacket, often with a removable lining. **6** (in full **shell program**) a program which provides an interface between the user and the operating system. **7** something resembling a seashell (pasta shells). ● v. **1** tr. remove the shell or pod from. **2** tr. bombard (a town, troops, etc.) with shells. **3** tr. provide or cover with a shell or shells. **4** intr. (of a seed etc.) be released from a shell. **5** tr. separate (grain, a seed, etc.) from its shell, husk, ear, etc. □ **come out of one's shell** cease to be shy; become communicative. **shell out** informal **1** pay (money). **2** hand over (a required sum). □ **shell-less** adj. **shell-like** adj. **shelly** adj.

she'll contraction she will; she shall.

shellac / ʃəˈlæk / ● n. **1** lac resin melted into thin flakes and used for making varnish. **2** varnish made from this. ● v.tr. (**shellacked**, **shellacking**) **1** varnish with shellac. **2** N Amer. slang defeat or thrash soundly.

shellacking n. N Amer. slang a severe defeat or beating.

shelled adj. **1** (of an animal, nut, etc.) having a shell or shells, esp. of a specific kind (*hard-shelled nuts*). **2** (of an edible animal, nut, etc.) that has had its shell removed (*shelled shrimp*).

shellfish n. **1** an aquatic shelled mollusc, e.g. an oyster, scallop, etc. **2** a crustacean, e.g. a crab etc.

shell game n. N Amer. **1** a sleight-of-hand game or trick in which a small object is concealed under a walnut shell etc., with bystanders encouraged to place bets or to guess as to which shell the object is under. **2** informal a confidence trick; a deception.

shell shock n. a nervous breakdown or other psychological disturbance resulting from exposure to battle.

shell-shocked adj. **1** suffering from shell shock. **2** informal having received stunning news etc., or having been overwhelmingly defeated.

shelter ● n. **1** a structure built to give protection, esp. from the weather or from attack (*bus shelter*; *bomb shelter*) **2 a** a place of refuge provided for the homeless, abused women, etc. **b** N Amer. an animal sanctuary. **3** a shielded condition; protection (*took shelter under a tree*). **4** = TAX SHELTER. ● v. **1** tr. **a** provide (a person or thing) with protection from the weather, danger, etc. (*sheltered them from the storm*). **b** protect (a person or thing) from unpleasantness or difficulty. **2** intr. & refl. find refuge; take cover (*sheltered under a tree*). **3** tr. protect (invested income) from taxation; invest (money) with this purpose. □ **shelterless** adj.

shelter belt n. a line of trees etc. serving to break the force of the wind.

sheltered adj. **1** (of a place) not greatly exposed to bad weather, sun, etc. **2** kept away from or not exposed to unpleasant circumstances, harmful influences, or the normal difficulties of life (*a sheltered upbringing*). **3** (of a course of study, activity, etc.) provided for people with some sort of disability.

shelve[1] v.tr. **1** put (books etc.) on a shelf. **2 a** abandon or defer (a plan etc.). **b** remove (a person) from active work etc. **3** fit (a cupboard etc.) with shelves.

shelve[2] v.intr. (of ground etc.) slope in a specified direction (*land shelved away to the horizon*).

shelves pl. of SHELF.

shelving n. **1** in senses of SHELVE[1]. **2** a set of shelves; shelves collectively.

shemozzle n. slang **1** a brawl or commotion. **2** a muddle.

shenanigan n. (esp. in pl.) informal **1** high-spirited behaviour; nonsense. **2** trickery; dubious manoeuvres.

shepherd ● n. **1** a person employed to tend sheep, esp. at pasture. **2** a person, esp. a member of the clergy etc., who guides, cares for, or watches over a group of people. **3** = GERMAN SHEPHERD. ● v.tr. **1 a** tend (sheep etc.) as a shepherd. **b** guide (followers etc.). **2** marshal, drive, or direct the movement of.

shepherdess n. a woman employed to tend sheep, esp. at pasture

shepherd's pie n. a dish of ground meat under a layer of mashed potato.

Sheraton n. (often attrib.) the style of furniture introduced in England c. 1790 by Thomas Sheraton (1751–1806), known for delicate and graceful forms.

sherbet /ˈʃɜrbət/ n. **1** N Amer. a frozen dessert, similar to ice cream, made from water, milk, and sugar, usu. fruit-flavoured. **2** a flavoured sweet powder containing bicarbonate of soda, tartaric acid, etc., eaten as a candy or used to make an effervescing drink.

sheriff n. **1** Cdn an appointed official responsible for court administration and trial preparation, the selection of jury panels, the serving of legal documents, and the seizure and sale of property to settle damage claims. **2** US an officer in a county, usu. elected, responsible for keeping the peace, administering justice, etc.

Sherlock Holmes n. (also **Sherlock**) an investigator of mysteries, esp. a remarkably astute one.

Sherpa n. (pl. same or **-s**) a member of a Himalayan people living on the border of Nepal and Tibet renowned for their skill in mountaineering.

sherry ● n. (pl. **-ies**) **1 a** a fortified wine originally from S Spain. **b** a glass of this. **2** the amber colour of common varieties of this. ● adj. of this colour.

she's contraction **1** she is. **2** she has.

Shetland ● attrib.adj. of or pertaining to the Shetland Islands off the N coast of Scotland. ● n. (in full **Shetland wool**) a fine loosely twisted wool from Shetland sheep.

Shetland pony n. a small hardy rough-coated breed of pony.

Shetland sheepdog n. a small collie-like breed of dog.

Shia /ˈʃiə/ (also **Shiah**; **Shi'a**) ● n. (pl. same or **-s**) one of the two main branches of Islam, esp. in Iran, that rejects the first three Sunni caliphs and regards Ali, the fourth caliph, as Muhammad's first successor. **2** a Shi'ite. ● adj. of or relating to Shia.

shiatsu /ʃiˈætsu/ n. a kind of therapy of Japanese origin, in which pressure is applied with the fingers or palms to certain points of the body.

shibboleth /ˈʃibə,lɛθ/ n. **1** a long-standing formula, doctrine, or phrase, etc., held to be true (esp. unreflectingly) by a party or group. **2** a word, phrase, pronunciation, usage, etc. distinguishing a particular class or group of people.

shied past and past part. of SHY[1], SHY[2].

shield ● n. **1 a** a piece of metal, wooden, acrylic, etc. armour, carried on the arm or in the hand to deflect blows from the head or body. **b** a thing serving to protect (*insurance is a shield against disaster*). **2** a thing resembling a shield, esp.: **a** a trophy in the form of a shield. **b** a protective plate or screen in machinery etc. **c** a shieldlike part of an animal, esp. a shell. **d** a similar part of a plant. **3** a piece of fabric etc. worn as a liner to protect part of a garment from staining (*dress shield*). **4** Geol. **a** a large rigid area of the earth's crust, usu. of Precambrian rock, which has been unaffected by later geological episodes. **b** (**Shield**) (in Canada) the Canadian Shield. **5** Heraldry a stylized representation of a shield, characteristically of a flat-topped heart shape, used for displaying a coat of arms etc. ● v.tr. protect, shelter, or screen with or as with a shield from attack, danger, etc., or from blame or punishment; cover or hide with a shield.

Shield country n. Cdn the area covered by the Canadian Shield, characterized by thin soil, rock outcrops, countless lakes and rivers, and, in the southern areas, vast coniferous forests.

shier comparative of SHY[1].

shiest superlative of SHY[1].

shift ● v. **1 a** intr. & tr. change or move or cause to change or move from one position or state to another. **b** intr. (of cargo) get shaken out of place. **2** N Amer. **a** tr. change (gear) in a vehicle. **b** intr. change gear. **3** intr. contrive or manage as best one can. ● n. **1 a** the act or an instance of shifting. **b** the substitution of one thing for another; a rotation. **2 a** a relay of workers, players on a hockey team, etc. (*the night shift*). **b** the time for which they work, play, etc. (*scored on his last shift*). **3 a** a device, stratagem, or expedient. **b** a dodge, trick, or evasion. **4 a** a woman's straight unwaisted dress. **b** a woman's loose-fitting undergarment; a slip. **5** a displacement of spectral lines (*see also* RED SHIFT). **6** a key on a keyboard used to switch between lower and upper case, conduct special operations, etc. **7** *N Amer.* **a** a gear lever in a motor vehicle. **b** a mechanism for this. □ **make shift** manage or contrive; get along somehow (*made shift without it*). **shift for oneself** rely on one's own efforts. **shift gears** esp. *N Amer.* change one's course of action, strategy, intensity, etc. **shift (one's) ground** take up a new position in an argument etc. □ **shifting** *n.*

shifter *n.* **1** a person or thing that shifts. **2** = GEARSHIFT.

shifting sand *n.* (also **shifting sands** or **shifting ground**) a changing or unstable state of affairs.

shiftless *adj.* lacking resourcefulness; lazy; inefficient. □ **shiftlessly** *adv.* **shiftlessness** *n.*

shift work *n.* work conducted in often variable periods independent of a standard workday, usu. at night. □ **shift worker** *n.*

shifty *adj.* (**-ier, -iest**) *informal* not straightforward; evasive; deceitful. □ **shiftily** *adv.* **shiftiness** *n.*

shiitake /ʃiːˈtɒki, -ˈtæk-, -kei/ *n.* (in full **shiitake mushroom**) an edible mushroom, *Lentinus edodes*, cultivated in Japan and China on oak logs etc.

Shiite /ˈʃiːʔait/ (also **Shi'ite**) ● *n.* an adherent of the Shia branch of Islam. ● *adj.* of or relating to Shia. □ **Shiism** /ˈʃiːɪzəm/ *n.*

shiksa /ˈʃiksə/ (also **shikse**) often *offensive* ● *n.* **1** a Gentile girl or woman. **2** a Jewish girl or woman not observing traditional Jewish behaviour. ● *adj.* (of a girl or woman) Gentile.

shill *N Amer.* ● *n.* **1** an accomplice, esp. one posing as an enthusiastic or successful customer to encourage or entice potential buyers, gamblers, etc. **2** an adherent of a party or point of view etc. posing as a disinterested advocate. ● *v.* **1** *tr. & intr.* (often foll. by *for*) promote a cause, esp. with feigned disinterest. **2** *intr.* act as an accomplice or shill in a scam.

shillelagh /ʃiˈleili, -lə/ *n.* a thick stick or club of blackthorn or oak used in Ireland esp. as a weapon.

shilling *n. hist.* **1** a former British coin and monetary unit equal to one-twentieth of a pound or twelve pence. **2** any of various coins of equal or similar value used in countries of the British Empire.

shilly-shally *v.intr.* (**-ies, -ied**) act with indecision or hesitation about a choice or decision; vacillate. □ **shilly-shallyer** *n.* **shilly-shallying** *n.*

shim ● *n.* a thin strip, wedge, or washer of metal, wood, rubber, etc. inserted in a space in machinery etc. to make parts fit or align. ● *v.tr.* (**shimmed, shimming**) wedge, raise, or fill up with a shim.

shimmer ● *v.intr.* **1** shine with a tremulous or faint diffused light. **2** quiver or tremble, or appear to do so, esp. when distorted by heat waves (*the asphalt shimmered*). ● *n.* a faint tremulous light or image. □ **shimmering** *adj.* **shimmeringly** *adv.* **shimmery** *adj.*

shimmy ● *n.* (*pl.* **-ies**) an abnormal vibration of esp. the front wheels of a car or truck etc. ● *v.intr.* (**-ies, -ied**) **1** shake or sway the body, esp. with a rolling of the hips and shaking of the shoulders and breasts. **2** (esp. of a car etc.) shake or vibrate abnormally.

shin *n.* **1** the front of the leg below the knee. **2** the front or sharp edge of the tibia. **3** a cut of beef from the lower part of an animal's foreleg.

shin bone *n.* = TIBIA 1.

shindig *n.* (also **shindy** *pl.* **-ies**) *informal* **1** a lively or festive gathering; a party. **2** a brawl, commotion, or noisy disturbance.

shine ● *v.* (*past* and *past part.* **shone** or **shined**) **1** *intr.* **a** emit or give off light. **b** (of the sun, a star, etc.) not be obscured by clouds etc.; be visible (*the sun is shining today*). **2** *intr.* **a** glow or be bright, esp. with reflected light (*the water shone*). **b** (of a person's eyes or face) be unusually bright, vibrant, or animated, esp. with excitement, joy, etc. **3** *tr.* direct (light or a source of light) in a particular direction (*shone the flashlight in my eyes*). **4** *tr.* (*past* and *past part.* **shined**) make bright; polish. **5** *intr.* be brilliant in some respect; excel. ● *n.* **1** brightness or radiance emanating from a light or source of light. **2** a lustre or glow of light reflecting off a surface, esp. the result of cleaning or polishing (*the shine of chrome*). **3** *N Amer.* the act or an instance of shining esp. shoes (*how much for a shine?*). **4** *slang* = MOONSHINE 1. □ **shine through** be clearly evident. **take the shine off** spoil the brilliance or newness of. **take a shine to** *informal* take a fancy to; like. □ **shining** *adj.*

shiner *n.* **1** *informal* a black eye. **2** any of various silvery fishes, esp. any of the N American minnows of the genus *Notropis*, or the common shiner *Luxilus cornutus*.

shingle[1] *n.* (in *sing.* or *pl.*) **1** small rounded pebbles, esp. on a seashore. **2** a beach or other stretch of land covered with loose rounded pebbles. □ **shingly** *adj.*

shingle[2] ● *n.* **1** a thin rectangular tile, usu. made of asphalt or wood, used to cover esp. walls or roofs. **2** *N Amer.* a small sign or nameplate hanging outside a store or esp. the office of a doctor or lawyer etc. ● *v.tr.* install shingles on (a roof or wall etc). □ **hang out one's shingle** set up a practice or profession. □ **shingled** *adj.*

shingles *n.pl.* (usu. treated as *sing.*) a disease caused by a herpesvirus and characterized by a rash of minute blisters on the skin, often in a band across the body, and accompanied by localized pain.

shinny[1] *v.intr.* (**-ies, -ied**) (usu. foll. by *up* or *down*) *N Amer. informal* climb up or down a tree etc. by clasping it with the arms and legs and hauling oneself up.

shinny[2] *n. Cdn* **1** (in full **shinny hockey**) *informal* pickup hockey played usu. without nets, referees, or equipment except for skates, sticks, and a ball or puck etc. **2** = STREET HOCKEY. **3** *informal* hockey.

shin pad *n.* (also **shin guard**) a piece of protective equipment used to cover the shin when playing esp. hockey, football, etc.

shin splints *n.pl.* (usu. treated as *sing.*) acute pain in the shin and lower leg caused esp. by prolonged running on hard surfaces.

Shinto /ˈʃintoʊ/ *n.* a religious system incorporating the worship of ancestors, nature spirits and other divinities, and prior to 1945 the state religion of Japan, founded on a belief in the divinity of the Japanese emperor. □ **Shintoism** *n.* **Shintoist** *n.*

shiny *adj.* (**-ier, -iest**) **1** full of brightness; having a polished or gleaming surface. **2** conspicuously or apparently new. □ **shinily** *adv.* **shininess** *n.*

ship ● *n.* **1 a** a large seagoing vessel propelled by engine or sail (*compare* BOAT). **b** a sailing vessel with a bowsprit and three, four, or five square-rigged masts. **2** an aircraft. **3** a spacecraft. ● *v.* (**shipped, shipping**) **1** *tr.* transport, deliver, or convey (goods, passengers, sailors, etc.) by or on a ship. **2** *tr.* (also foll. by *off, out*) esp. *N Amer.* **a** transport (goods) by truck, rail, or other means. **b** *informal* send (a person) away; dispatch (*shipped the kids off to school*). **3** *intr.* (often foll. by *out*) **a** (of a sailor) become employed on a ship. **b** (of a ship or passenger etc.) set out on a journey, esp. by sea. **4** *tr.* **a** take in (water or waves) over the side of a ship. **b** take or draw (an anchor, oars, etc.) into the ship or boat to which it belongs. **c** put (an oar etc.) in its correct position in readiness to function. □ **run a tight ship** *N Amer.* manage a company or organization etc. with strict authority. **when a person's ship comes in** (or **home**) when a person's fortune is made.

-ship *suffix* forming nouns denoting: **1** a quality or condition (*friendship*). **2** status, title, or office (*authorship*). **3** a skill in a certain capacity (*workmanship*). **4** the collective individuals of a group (*membership*).

shipboard *adj.* occurring or used on board a ship (*a shipboard romance*). □ **on shipboard** on board ship.

shipbuilder *n.* a person or company whose occupation or business is the design and construction of ships. □ **shipbuilding** *n.*

shiplap *n.* a type of wooden siding consisting of horizontal boards rabetted in such a way that each overlaps the one below it.

shipmate *n.* a fellow member of a ship's crew.

shipment *n.* **1** an amount of goods transported, delivered, or received. **2** the action or an instance of shipping goods.

shipowner *n.* a person owning a ship or ships.

shipper *n.* a person or company that transports or receives goods by land, sea, or air.

shipping *n.* **1** the act or an instance of shipping or transporting goods by sea, land, or air. **2** ships collectively, esp. the ships of a country, frequenting a particular port, or used for a particular purpose.

shipping and handling *n.* **1** the transportation of goods and the processing involved in transporting goods, including packaging, delivery, and carrying goods through customs etc. **2** the cost of transporting and processing goods (*it costs $20 plus shipping and handling*) (*compare* POSTAGE AND HANDLING).

ship's biscuit *n. hist.* a hard coarse kind of cracker kept and eaten on board ship.

ship's boat *n.* a small boat carried on board a ship.

shipshape *adj.* in good order; tidy and neat.

ship-to-shore ● *adj.* **1** from a ship to land. **2** (of radio telephones etc.) capable of transmitting communication from a point at sea to a point on land. ● *n.* a ship-to-shore radio telephone.

shipwreck ● *n.* **1 a** the destruction of a ship by a storm, sinking, etc. **b** the remains of a ship so destroyed. **2** (often foll. by *of*) the destruction of hopes, dreams, etc.; total loss or ruin. ● *v.* **1** *tr.* cause (a person or ship etc.) to suffer shipwreck. **2** *tr.* destroy or cause the loss of (a person's hopes, dreams, fortunes, etc.). **3** *intr.* suffer shipwreck.

shipyard *n.* a large enclosed area adjoining the sea or a major river in which ships are built or repaired.

shiraz /ʃəˈræz, ʃɪ-/ *n.* the variety of Syrah produced in Australia and South Africa.

shire /ˈʃaɪr/ *n. Brit.* a county.

shirk *v.* **1** *tr.* shrink from; avoid, evade, or attempt to get out of (duty, work, responsibility, fighting, etc.). **2** *intr.* make a habit or practice of avoiding work or responsibility etc. □ **shirker** *n.*

shirt *n.* **1** an article of clothing of a light woven fabric, designed to cover the upper body and arms, having short or long sleeves, a collar, and buttons down the front. **2** any of a number of articles of clothing designed to cover the upper body, having short or long sleeves, and which may or may not have buttons or a collar. □ **get one's shirt in a knot** *see* KNICKERS. **keep one's shirt on** *informal* refrain from

becoming excited, anxious, or impatient. **lose one's shirt** *informal* lose all one's money, esp. in a bet, investment, etc. **the shirt off one's back** *informal* one's last remaining possessions. □ **shirtless** *adj.*

shirted *adj.* **1** wearing a shirt. **2** (in *comb.*) wearing a shirt of a specified kind or colour (*red-shirted youth*).

shirt front *n.* the breast of a shirt, esp. of a stiffened dress shirt.

shirt sleeve *n.* (usu. in *pl.*) **1** the sleeve of a shirt. **2** (*attrib.*, usu. **shirt-sleeve**) **a** designating weather that is warm enough that a jacket is not required (*shirt-sleeve days*). **b** designating an environment etc. that is casual, informal, or relaxed. **c** designating a person etc. that is hard-working or working-class (*a shirt-sleeve crowd*). □ **in shirt sleeves** wearing a shirt with no jacket etc. over it. □ **shirt-sleeved** *adj.*

shirt-tail ● *n.* (also in *pl.*) the lower curved part of a shirt below the waist. ● *adj. N Amer.* designating something small and insignificant or of remote relationship (*shirt-tail cousin*).

shish kebab /ʃɪʃ/ *n.* = KEBAB.

shit *coarse slang* ● *v.tr. & intr.* (**shitting**; *past* and *past part.* **shat**, **shit**, **shitted**) **1** *tr. & intr.* defecate; expel (feces etc.) from the body. **2** *refl.* **a** defecate in one's own clothing. **b** be scared or worried. **3** *tr.* lie or exaggerate to; deceive. ● *n.* **1** feces. **2** an act of defecating. **3** a despicable or hateful person or thing. **4** nonsense, garbage. **5** serious trouble or difficulty; a hassle or grief. **6** possessions, belongings; stuff. **7** a narcotic drug or substance. **8** (in *pl.*, prec. by *the*) **a** diarrhea. **b** a bad or unfavourable situation etc. **9 a** nothing (*you know shit*). **b** (with *neg.*) anything (*he doesn't know shit*). ● *interj.* an exclamation of anger, disgust, etc. □ **beat** (or **scare** or **annoy** etc.) **the shit out of someone** beat, scare, or annoy etc. a person excessively. **get one's shit together** *N Amer.* organize oneself. **give a shit** = GIVE A CRAP (*see* CRAP[1]). **shit bricks** be anxious, scared, or worried. **shit hits the fan** a serious screw-up or mistake is revealed. **up shit creek** in an unpleasant situation, in an awkward predicament.

shit disturber *n. Cdn coarse slang* a person who enjoys causing trouble or discord. □ **shit disturbing** *n. & adj.*

shit-faced *adj. coarse slang* extremely drunk.

shit for brains *n. coarse slang* a stupid person. □ **have shit for brains** be foolish or stupid.

shithead *n. coarse slang* a contemptible or worthless person. □ **shitheaded** *adj.*

shithouse *n. coarse slang* **1** an outhouse, washroom, etc. **2** a disgusting, filthy, or messy place.

shitless *predic.adj. coarse slang* □ **scared shitless** extremely frightened, worried, or nervous.

shit list *n. esp. N Amer. coarse slang* a list of those who have angered or fallen out of favour with someone.

shitload *n. esp. N Amer. coarse slang* a considerable quantity or amount.

shitty *adj.* (**-ier**, **-iest**) *coarse slang* **1 a** ill. **b** bad-tempered. **c** awful, horrible. **2** disgusting, contemptible. **3** covered with excrement.

shiv *n. esp. N Amer. slang* a knife, switchblade, or razor.

shiva /ˈʃɪvə/ (also **shivah**) *n. Judaism* a period of seven days' mourning for the dead beginning immediately after the funeral. □ **sit shiva** mourn.

shiver[1] ● *v.intr.* **1** tremble with cold, fear, etc. **2** suffer a quick trembling movement of the body; shudder. ● *n.* **1** a momentary quivering or trembling of the body. **2** (in *pl.*) **a** an attack of shivering, esp. from fear or awe. **b** excitement, fear, or disquiet (*his appearance sent shivers through the room*). □ **shivery** *adj.*

shiver[2] ● *n.* (esp. in *pl.*) each of the small pieces into which esp. glass is shattered when broken; a splinter. ● *v.tr. & intr.* break into shivers.

shlemiel *var. of* SCHLEMIEL.

shlep *var. of* SCHLEP.

shlock *var. of* SCHLOCK.

shlub *var. of* SCHLUB.

shlump *var. of* SCHLUMP.

shm- *var. of* SCHM-.

shmaltz *var. of* SCHMALTZ.

shmooze *var. of* SCHMOOZE.

shmuck *var. of* SCHMUCK¹.

shoal¹ ● *n.* **1** a school of fish, porpoises, etc. **2** a large number; a multitude. ● *v.intr.* (of fish) gather in schools.

shoal² ● *n.* **1** an area of shallow water. **2** a submerged sandbank visible at low tide. **3** (esp. in *pl.*) hidden danger or difficulty (*the shoals of constitutional reform*). ● *v.intr.* **1** (of water) become increasingly shallow. **2** (of a ship etc.) move into shallower waters. ● *adj.* (of water) shallow.

shock¹ ● *n.* **1 a** a sudden and usu. disturbing effect on the mind, feelings, or emotions, resulting in surprise, distress, depression, etc. **b** something causing such an effect (*the news was a huge shock*). **2** the condition associated with circulatory failure and a sudden drop in blood pressure, characterized esp. by pallor, sweating, a fast but weak pulse, and occasionally fainting, usu. caused by pain, fright, disease, or an injury resulting in severe blood loss. **3** a sudden and violent collision, impact, tremor, etc. **4** = ELECTRIC SHOCK 1. **5** esp. *N. Amer.* = SHOCK ABSORBER. ● *v.* **1** *tr. & intr.* **a** arouse surprise or bewilderment etc. (in a person). **b** arouse outrage, disgust, anger, etc. (in a person) (*I'm shocked to hear you say it*). **2** *intr.* experience shock (*I don't shock easily*). **3** *tr.* (esp. in *passive*) affect with an electric or physical shock. □ **shocked** *adj.*

shock² *n.* = STOOK¹.

shock³ *n.* an unkempt or shaggy mass of hair.

shock absorber *n.* **1** a device used on a car etc. to compensate for the roughness of a road by absorbing mechanical shock and vibrations. **2** anything that absorbs shocks. □ **shock absorbency** *n.* **shock absorbent** *adj.* **shock-absorbing** *adj.*

shocker *n. informal* a revelation, rumour, news item, result, etc. that causes surprise or outrage etc.

shocking *adj.* causing indignation, scandal, or disgust. □ **shockingly** *adv.* **shockingness** *n.*

shock jock *n. N Amer. slang* a radio personality that expresses outrageous or controversial views.

shock resistant *adj.* able to withstand light abuse without breaking etc. □ **shock resistance** *n.*

shock treatment *n. Psych.* (also **shock therapy**) **1** a method of treating depressive patients by artificially inducing convulsions using anaphylactic or electric shock or by drugs. **2** sudden and harsh or drastic measures taken to improve a situation (*shock treatment economics*).

shock troops *n.pl.* troops trained for assault.

shock wave *n.* **1** a sharp change of pressure in a narrow region travelling through air etc. caused by explosion or by a body moving faster than sound. **2** a series of reactions to or repercussions of an event.

shod ● *v.* past and past part. of SHOE. ● *adj.* **1** having or wearing shoes or other footwear. **2** (in *comb.*) having or wearing shoes etc. of a specified kind.

shoddy *adj.* (**-ier, -iest**) of a poor or inferior quality. □ **shoddily** *adv.* **shoddiness** *n.*

shoe ● *n.* **1** one of a matching pair of protective coverings for the foot having a sturdy sole and made

esp. of leather ending below, at, or just above the ankle. **2** a band of iron shaped to the hard part of the hoof of an animal, esp. a horse, and secured by nails to the underside to prevent wear or injury. **3** anything resembling a shoe in shape or use. **4** = BRAKE SHOE. **5** a box from which cards are dealt in blackjack, baccarat, etc., esp. found in casinos. **6** a block attached to an electric vehicle, such as a streetcar, which slides along the conductor wire or rail and collects the current for propulsion. ● *v.tr.* (**shoes, shoeing;** *past and past part.* **shod** /ʃɒd/ or **shoed** /ʃuːd/) **1** fit (esp. a horse etc.) with a shoe or shoes. **2** cover or protect with a shoe or shoes. □ **be in a person's shoes** be in his or her situation, predicament, etc. **dead men's shoes** a position or property etc. coveted by a prospective successor, but available only upon the owner's departure or death. **fill** (or **step into**) **a person's shoes** adequately fill a person's position or role. **if the shoe fits** *N Amer.* if a criticism or description seems applicable, one should be guided by it. **the shoe is on the other foot** the situation is reversed. **wait for the other** (or **second**) **shoe to drop** *N Amer.* be prepared for a further or consequential event or complication to occur. **where the shoe pinches** where one's difficulty or trouble is. □ **-shoed** *comb. form.* **shoeless** *adj.*

shoebox *n.* **1** the oblong box in which a new pair of shoes is packaged. **2** a small or cramped room, apartment, etc.

shoehorn ● *n.* a curved piece of metal, plastic, etc., used to ease the heel into a shoe. ● *v.tr.* force into a tight, inadequate, or unsuitable space or position.

shoelace *n.* a short length of string used for tying shoes and boots etc.

shoe leather *n.* leather used to manufacture or repair shoes, esp. when worn through by walking.

shoemaker *n.* a person who makes and repairs shoes and boots. □ **shoemaking** *n.*

shoepack *n.* (also **shoepac**) *N Amer.* **1** a moccasin with an extra sole. **2** a commercially manufactured oiled leather boot, esp. with a rubber sole.

shoeshine *n.* esp. *N Amer.* an act or instance of cleaning and polishing shoes.

shoestring *n.* **1** a shoelace. **2** *informal* a small esp. inadequate amount of money (*living on a shoestring*). **3** (*attrib.*) designating a business, project, plan, etc. based on or conducted with a limited amount of money (*a shoestring budget*).

shofar /ˈʃoʊfɑr/ *n.* (*pl.* **-s** or **shofroth** /ˈʃoʊfroːt/) a trumpet made of a ram's horn used by Jews in religious ceremonies and, in Biblical times, as a war trumpet.

shogun /ˈʃoʊɡʌn/ *n.* any of a succession of hereditary commanders-in-chief in feudal Japan who were generally the real rulers of the country until 1867.

shone *past and past part. of* SHINE.

shoo ● *interj.* an exclamation used to frighten or drive away. ● *v.tr.* (**shoos, shooed**) drive or urge (a person, animal, etc.) in a desired direction.

shoofly pie *n. N Amer.* an open-faced pie with a molasses or brown sugar filling, topped with streusel.

shoo-in *n. N Amer. informal* something sure to succeed or win; a certainty.

shook ● *v.* past of SHAKE. ● *predic.adj. informal* (foll. by *up*) emotionally or physically disturbed; upset.

shoot ● *v.* (*past and past part.* **shot**) **1** *tr.* **a** cause (a gun, bow, etc.) to discharge a bullet, arrow, etc. **b** discharge (a bullet, arrow, etc.) from a gun, bow, etc. **c** kill or wound (a person, animal, etc.) with a bullet, arrow, etc. from a gun, bow, etc. **2** *intr.* discharge a gun etc.

esp. in a specified way (*shoots well*). **3 a** *tr. & intr.* discharge, propel, emit, etc., esp. violently or swiftly (*blood shot from the wound*). **b** *tr.* cast, issue (a smile, glance, etc.). **4** *intr.* come or go quickly or vigorously. **5** *intr.* **a** (of a plant etc.) put forth buds etc. **b** (of a bud etc.) appear, germinate. **6** *tr.* **a** film or photograph (a scene, subject, etc.). **b** use up or fill (a roll of film) in photographing or filming a scene etc. **7 a** *tr. & intr.* (in hockey, basketball, etc.) direct (a puck or ball) toward the net, basket, etc. **b** *tr. Basketball* successfully make or score (a basket, three-pointer, etc.) **c** *tr. Basketball* practise taking shots at (a basket). **8** *tr. N Amer.* **a** play a game or round of (pool, golf, craps, etc.). **b** *Golf* make (a specified score) for a round or hole. **c** throw (a die or dice). **9** *slang* **a** *intr.* (foll. by *up*) take a drug, esp. intravenously. **b** *tr.* (often foll. by *up*) inject (esp. oneself) with a drug. **c** *tr.* take or inject (a particular drug). **10 a** *intr.* hunt game, esp. with a gun. **b** *tr.* go hunting for (duck, deer, etc.). **11** *tr.* navigate or swiftly pass over (rapids, falls, etc.). **12** *intr.* (usu. foll. by *through, up*) (of a pain) pass suddenly and sharply with a stabbing sensation. **13** (often foll. by *out*) **a** *intr.* project abruptly (*the mountain seems to shoot out of the water*). **b** *tr.* extend or project; thrust (*he shot out his hand*). ● *n.* **1** a competition in shooting. **2** a film or photography session. **3** a young branch or new growth of a plant. **4** = CHUTE[1]. ● *interj. informal* **1** an invitation for a comment, question, etc. **2** *N Amer.* an exclamation of disappointment, anger, frustration, etc. □ **shoot down 1** kill (a person) by shooting. **2** cause (an aircraft, its pilot, etc.) to crash by shooting. **3** reject (a person, argument, proposal, etc.). **shoot from the hip** *informal* speak or act spontaneously or hastily, usu. without proper consideration. **shoot it out** *slang* engage in a decisive confrontation. **shoot a line** *slang* speak misleadingly. **shoot oneself in the foot** *informal* inadvertently make a situation worse, esp. while trying to make it better. **shoot one's mouth off** *slang* talk too much or indiscreetly. **shoot the breeze** (or **bull** or **shit**) *slang* chat idly. **shoot up 1** grow rapidly, esp. (of a person) grow taller. **2** rise suddenly. **3** terrorize (a district) by indiscriminate shooting. □ **shootist** *n.*

shoot-'em-up *n. slang* **1** a fast-moving movie, esp. a Western, which features extensive shooting and gunplay. **2** (*attrib.*) designating movies, games, etc. based on or featuring abundant use of weapons etc.

shooter *n.* **1** a person who discharges a firearm. **2 a** (in *comb.*) a gun or other device for shooting (*peashooter*). **b** *slang* a firearm. **3** a player who takes a shot or is in position to take a shot in hockey, basketball, etc. **4** a small drink of alcohol, esp. liquor. **5** *slang* a person who takes drugs intravenously.

shooting ● *n.* **1 a** the wounding or killing of esp. a person by gunfire. **b** the discharge of a firearm (*heard shooting*). **2 a** the hobby or sport of hunting game. **b** the hobby or sport of firing at targets (*skeet shooting*). **3** (in hockey and basketball etc.) the ability to shoot accurately. ● *adj.* (of a pain etc.) sharp and spreading quickly. □ **the whole shooting match** *informal* everything.

shooting gallery *n.* **1** a long room or fairground booth used for recreational shooting at usu. moving targets with real or simulated guns. **2** *N Amer. slang* a place where addictive drugs may be illicitly obtained and injected.

shooting guard *n. Basketball* **1** the second guard on a team, usu. having strong ball-handling skills and good three-point shooting. **2** the position played by this guard (*compare* POINT GUARD).

shooting range *n.* esp. *N Amer.* a field equipped with targets for practising one's accuracy in rifle shooting.

shooting star *n.* **1** a small meteor burning up upon entering the earth's atmosphere. **2** *N Amer.* a plant of the primrose family *Dodecatheon meadia* and related species, with pink, swept-back petals.

shootout *n.* **1** a decisive gunfight. **2** (in full **penalty shootout**) (in soccer, hockey, etc.) a method of deciding games ending in a tie in which each team takes a specified number of penalty shots, the team scoring the most being declared the winner. **3** esp. *Hockey* a close high-scoring game.

shop ● *n.* **1 a** a building, room, or other establishment used for the retail sale of esp. specialty goods or services (*barber shop; coffee shop*). **2 a** a building or room equipped to carry out repairs or a specific type of manufacture. **b** = BODY SHOP. **3** *N Amer.* **a** a room in a school equipped for teaching woodworking or mechanical skills etc. for use in a workshop. **b** (in full **shop class**) the study of these skills as a course. **4** one's trade, profession, or business, esp. as a subject of conversation (*talk shop*). **5** esp. *Brit. informal* an act of going shopping (*we have to do a big shop this week*). ● *v.* (**shopped, shopping**) **1** *intr.* **a** go to one or several stores or shops to buy goods. **b** visit shops to look at merchandise without the express intention of making a purchase. **2** *intr.* order and buy merchandise by mail, phone, etc. **3** *tr.* shop at (a particular store), esp. regularly. **4** *tr.* (often foll. by *around*) sell or propose (an idea, information, etc.) to several prospective buyers. □ **set up shop** establish oneself in business etc. **shop around** visit several stores, service providers, etc. in search of the best price or service. **shop till one drops** *N Amer. informal* shop excessively, esp. to the point of exhaustion.

shopaholic *n. jocular* an avid or compulsive shopper.

shop floor *n. Brit. & Cdn* **1** the working environment in a factory, esp. as distinct from a management environment. **2** the workers in a factory etc. **3** (*attrib.*) (usu. **shop-floor**) working or occurring in or pertaining to a factory etc. (*shop-floor productivity*).

shopkeeper *n.* a person who owns or manages a shop or store. □ **shopkeeping** *n.*

shoplifter *n.* a person who poses as a customer to steal merchandise from a store. □ **shoplift** *v.tr. & intr.* **shoplifting** *n.*

shoppe *n.* a shop or small store having a usu. spurious old-fashioned charm or quaintness.

shopper *n.* **1** a person who makes purchases in a shop. **2** *N Amer.* an advertising supplement; a flyer.

shopping *n.* **1** (often *attrib.*) the purchase of merchandise etc. **2** goods purchased.

shopping bag *n.* a bag made of paper, plastic, nylon, or cotton, used for carrying groceries or other items bought in a store.

shopping cart *n. N Amer.* a large and sturdy rectangular cart with four wheels used by customers in a supermarket etc. to carry groceries while shopping.

shopping centre *n.* a shopping mall (*see* MALL 1).

shopping channel *n.* a television station whose programming features items for sale that may be ordered by telephone.

shopping mall *n.* = MALL 1.

shopping plaza *n.* = PLAZA 1.

shop steward *n.* a person elected by workers in a factory etc. to represent them in dealings with management.

shop talk *n.* conversation about one's job etc.

shop window *n.* **1** esp. *Brit.* = STORE WINDOW. **2** an opportunity for displaying skills, talents, etc.

shopworn *adj. N Amer.* **1** (of an item for sale) faded or dirty from being on display in a store. **2** (of a person, idea, etc.) no longer fresh or new; hackneyed or stale.

shore[1] *n.* **1** the land at the edge of the sea or a large body of water; a coast. **2** land, as opposed to sea (*ship-to-shore*). **3** (usu. in *pl.*) a country, esp. one bounded by a coast (*travelled to foreign shores*).

shore[2] ● *v.tr.* (often foll. by *up*) **1** reinforce; strengthen or fortify (*a plan to shore up the economy*). **2** support with a shore or shores. ● *n.* a beam of timber or iron set obliquely against an unsafe wall, tree, ship, etc., as a support. □ **shoring** *n.*

shorebird *n.* a bird which frequents the shore, e.g. a plover or a sandpiper.

shore dinner *n. N Amer.* **1** a dinner served by a restaurant, community group, etc., including usu. copious quantities of shellfish. **2** = SHORE LUNCH.

shore ice *n.* (also **shorefast ice**) *N Amer.* a flat expanse of sea ice that is anchored to the shore.

shoreline *n.* the line along which a stretch of water, esp. a sea or lake, meets the shore.

shore lunch *n. Cdn* a meal cooked on a lakeshore or riverbank etc. as part of a fishing or other boating excursion, featuring freshly caught fish, pan-fried.

shorn ● *v. past part. of* SHEAR. ● *adj.* **1 a** (of a person or animal) having had all or most of the hair of the head, wool, etc. removed; bald. **b** (of hair, wool, etc.) having been cut. **2** (usu. foll. by *of*) deprived.

short ● *adj.* **1 a** measuring little; not long from end to end (*a short distance*). **b** not long in duration; brief (*had a short life*). **c** seeming less than the stated amount (*this week seemed short*). **2** of little height; not tall (*was shorter than average*). **3 a** (usu. foll. by *of*, *on*) having a partial or total lack; deficient (*short of spoons*). **b** not having the amount expected, stated, or required (*short a dollar*). **c** not reaching a great distance or the distance expected or required; not far or far enough (*the throw was short*). **4 a** concise; brief (*kept his speech short*). **b** curt, abrupt; uncivil (*was short with her*). **5** (of memory) of limited range; unable to remember distant events. **6 a** (of a vowel or syllable) having the lesser of two recognized durations; unstressed. **b** (of a vowel) categorized as short with regard to quality and length, such as the short vowel i in the word *bit* as opposed to *bite* (*compare* LONG[1] *adj.* 8c). **7** (of pastry) having a high fat content and crumbling into small flakes when broken. **8** esp. *Stock Exch.* **a** (of a stockbroker) having sold stock that has not yet been acquired in the hope that it may be bought at a lower price before the time fixed for delivery. **b** (of stocks, crops, etc.) sold before having been acquired by the seller or broker. **c** (of a bill of exchange) maturing at an early date. **9** *Baseball* (of a position in the field) near, close; shallow (*short centre field*). **10** (of betting odds) offering nearly equal stakes for a winning wager. ● *adv.* **1** before the natural or expected time or place; abruptly (*cut short the celebrations*). **2** (sell or trade etc.) without sufficient quantities of a particular commodity. ● *n.* **1** a short-circuit. **2** a short film. **3** *Baseball* **a** = SHORTSTOP 2. **b** the area of the field covered by the shortstop. ● *v.* **1** *tr. & intr.* short-circuit. **2** *tr.* esp. *N Amer. informal* cheat (a person) out of something; shortchange. □ **be caught** (or **taken**) **short 1** be put at a disadvantage, esp. by being without something one badly needs. **2** *informal* urgently need to urinate or defecate. **fall** (or **come**) **short of** fail to reach or amount to. **for short** as an abbreviation (*I'm Richard, but you can call me Rick for short*). **go short** (often foll. by *of*) not have enough. **have** (or **get**) **by the short and curlies** (or **short hairs**) *informal*

have under one's complete control. **in short** to use few words; briefly. **in short supply** scarce. **in the short term** (or **run**) over a short period of time. **make short work of** accomplish, dispose of, consume, etc. quickly. **pull up** (or **bring up**) **short** stop or pause abruptly or before the expected destination. **short and curlies** (also **short hairs**) *slang* pubic hair. **short and sweet** esp. *ironic* brief and enjoyable. **short end of the stick** the less favourable part of a deal. **short for** an abbreviation for ('Bob' is short for 'Robert'). **short of 1** see sense 3a of *adj.* **2** without going so far as; except (*did everything short of destroying it*). **3** distant from (*two miles short of home*). **short of breath** panting, out of breath. □ **shortish** *adj.* **shortness** *n.*

shortage *n.* (often foll. by *of*) a deficiency or lack of something needed (*a shortage of funds*; *oil shortage*).

shortbread *n.* a crisp rich crumbly type of cookie made with butter, flour, and sugar.

shortcake *n.* a cake with a filling of fruit and whipped cream (*strawberry shortcake*).

shortchange *v.tr.* **1** cheat (a customer), accidentally or intentionally, by giving insufficient change. **2** cheat or treat unfairly.

short-circuit ● *n.* a faulty electrical connection resulting in a condition of low resistance between two points in a circuit, often causing a flow of excess current which could damage an appliance or cause a fuse to blow. ● *v.* **1** *intr.* (of an electrical appliance or apparatus) fail or cease working as a result of a short-circuit. **2** *intr.* collapse or self-destruct. **3** *tr.* bypass or avoid (a task etc.) by taking a more direct route or course of action.

shortcoming *n.* a fault, e.g. in a person's character, a plan, or system.

shortcut ● *n.* **1** a route between two places that shortens the distance travelled or the time required to make a journey. **2** a quick or easy way of accomplishing something. ● *v.tr.* (**-cutting**; *past* and *past part.* **-cut**) reduce the amount of time or effort required to complete (a journey, job, etc.).

short-eared owl *n.* a medium-sized whitish owl with brown streaks, *Asio flammeus*, with very short ear tufts, frequenting open country.

shorten *v.* **1** *tr. & intr.* become or make shorter or short; curtail. **2** *tr. Naut.* reduce the amount of (sail spread).

shortening *n.* **1** a soft fat that produces a crisp flaky effect in baked products, such as pastry, esp. a solid white fat made from hydrogenated vegetable oils, sometimes combined with lard. **2** an act or instance of making something short or shorter. **3** an act or instance of abbreviating a word, such as *ad* is a shortening of *advertisement*.

shortfall *n.* **1** a failure to reach esp. a financial goal or expectations; a failure to meet budget. **2** an esp. financial loss or deficit below what was expected.

short fuse *n. informal* a quick temper. □ **short-fused** *adj.*

shortgrass *n. N Amer.* any of a number of short grasses especially resistant to drought (also *attrib.*: *shortgrass prairie*).

shorthair *n.* (also **shorthaired**) a short-haired domestic cat or dog.

shorthand *n.* **1** a method of writing or typing in abbreviations and symbols esp. for taking dictation quickly (also *attrib.*: *shorthand typist*). **2** (often foll. by *for*) any abbreviated or symbolic mode of expression.

short-handed ● *adj.* **1** not having the usual number of workers etc.; understaffed. **2** *Hockey* **a** (of a team) playing with fewer than six players on the ice, esp.

because one or more players is serving a penalty. **b** (of a goal) scored by a team playing with fewer players on the ice than their opponent, esp. while killing a penalty. **c** (of an opportunity or situation etc.) occurring while or because a team has fewer than six players on the ice. ● *adv.* with fewer players, workers, etc. than usual (*playing short-handed*).

short-haul *n.* the transport of goods or passengers over a short distance (also *attrib.*: *short-haul route*).

Shorthorn *n.* a breed of cattle with short horns.

shortie *n.* an article of clothing that is short in length, such as a nightdress or raincoat (also *attrib.*: *shortie pyjamas*).

short list ● *n.* a list of selected candidates for a position from which a final choice is made. ● *v.tr.* (usu. **shortlist**) add (a person) to a list of candidates for a position.

short-lived *adj.* lasting only for a short time.

short loin *n.* a cut of beef from the hindquarter starting behind the ribs.

shortly *adv.* **1** in a short time; before long; soon (*we will be arriving shortly*). **2** (foll. by *before* or *after*) a short time (before or after); not long (*they arrived shortly before noon*). **3** in a few words; briefly or curtly.

short notice *n.* an announcement or warning of an event etc. made only briefly before its occurrence (*she gave him such short notice before leaving*). □ **on** (or **at**) **short notice** with little advance warning.

short order *n.* N Amer. restaurant food that can be prepared and served quickly; fast food (also *attrib.*: *short-order cook*). □ **in short order** immediately.

short-range *adj.* **1** operating or capable of operating within a small or limited area (*short-range missile*). **2** relating to a fairly immediate future time (*short-range forecast*).

short rib *n.* **1** any of the lower ribs which are not attached to the breastbone. **2** N Amer. a piece of meat containing one or more of these ribs.

shorts *n.pl.* **1** a pair of pants extending only as far as the knees or higher. **2** N Amer. men's underpants.

short shrift *n.* brusque or dismissive treatment.

short-sighted *adj.* **1** unable to focus except on comparatively near objects. **2** lacking imagination, foresight, or proper consideration (*a short-sighted plan*). □ **short-sightedly** *adv.* **short-sightedness** *n.*

short-sleeved *adj.* (of a shirt etc.) with sleeves not reaching below the elbow.

short-staffed *adj.* having insufficient staff.

shortstop *n.* Baseball **1** the player that covers the part of the infield between second and third. **2** this position.

short story *n.* a prose narrative shorter than a novel usu. involving only a few characters and concentrating on a single event or theme.

short-tempered *adj.* quick to lose one's temper; easily irritable; irascible. □ **short temper** *n.*

short-term *adj.* **1** lasting for, occurring in, or pertaining to a relatively short period of time (*short-term solution*). **2** maturing or becoming effective after a short period (*short-term deposit*). □ **in the short term** for the near or immediate future.

short time *n.* the condition of working fewer than the regular hours per day or days per week (also *attrib.*: *short-time worker*).

short ton *n.* see TON 1.

short-track speed skating *n.* a form of speed skating competition performed on a standard-size hockey rink rather than on a speed skating oval.

short-wave *n.* **1** a radio wave with a wavelength of less than about 100 metres, a frequency of 3 to 30 MHz. **2** (*attrib.*) designating radio communication or broadcasting systems employing such waves.

shorty *n.* (*pl.* **-ies**) **1** *informal* or *derogatory* a person shorter than average. **2** *var.* of SHORTIE.

shot¹ *n.* **1** the act or an instance of firing a gun, cannon, etc. (*shots were heard*). **2** an attempt to hit by shooting or throwing etc. (*took a shot at him*). **3 a** a single non-explosive missile for a cannon, gun, etc. **b** (*pl.* same or **-s**) a small lead pellet used in quantity in a single charge or cartridge in a shotgun. **c** (treated as *pl.*) these collectively. **4** *informal* a person having a specified skill with a gun etc. (*is not a good shot*). **5 a** *Sport* a stroke, kick, throw, etc., esp. one made with the aim of scoring. **b** *informal* an attempt to guess or do something (*gave it my best shot*). **6 a** a photograph. **b** a film sequence photographed continuously by one camera. **7** a heavy ball thrown by a shot putter. **8** the launch of a space rocket (*a moon shot*). **9** the range, reach, or distance to or at which a thing will carry or act. **10** a remark aimed at a person. **11** *informal* **a** a drink of esp. spirits. **b** an injection of a drug, vaccine, etc. (*had his shots*). **12** *informal* a thing with a chance of success (frequently with specified odds). □ **have** (or **take**) **a shot at** *informal* make an attempt at; try. **give something a shot** try something. **like a shot** *informal* without hesitation; willingly. **shot in the arm** *informal* stimulus or encouragement. **shot in the dark** a mere guess.

shot² ● *v.* past and past part. of SHOOT. ● *adj.* **1** (of coloured material) woven so as to show different colours at different angles (*shot silk*). **2** *informal* **a** ruined; worn out (*the transmission's shot*). **b** exhausted. □ **shot through** permeated or suffused.

shot³ *n.* *informal* a sum of money owed or due; a bill.

shot glass *n.* N Amer. a small, often graduated, typically 2-oz. glass for measuring liquor.

shotgun ● *n.* a smoothbore gun for firing small shot at short range, used esp. for hunting. ● *adj.* **1** of, pertaining to, or resembling a shotgun. **2** made or done hastily or under pressure of necessity. **3** wideranging, but random. ● *v.tr.* **1** shoot with a shotgun. **2** force as if with a shotgun; bring about forcibly. □ **shotgunner** *n.* **shotgunning** *n.*

shotgun marriage *n.* (also **shotgun wedding**) *informal* **1** an enforced or hurried wedding, esp. because of the bride's pregnancy. **2** any enforced alliance, partnership, etc.

shot put *n.* an athletic contest in which a shot is thrown a great distance. □ **shot putter** *n.*

shot rock *n.* Curling the rock lying nearest to the centre of the rings.

should *v.aux.* (*3rd sing.* **should**) past of SHALL, used esp.: **1** esp. Brit. in reported speech, esp. with the reported element in the 1st person (*I said I should be home by evening*). **2 a** to express a duty, obligation, or likelihood (*I should tell you*). **b** (in the 1st person) to express a tentative suggestion (*I should like to say something*). **3 a** esp. Brit. expressing the conditional mood in the 1st person (compare WOULD) (*I should have been killed if I had gone*). **b** forming a conditional protasis or indefinite clause (*if you should see him*). **4** expressing purpose; = MAY, MIGHT¹ (*in order that we should not worry*).

shoulder ● *n.* **1 a** the part of the body at which the arm, foreleg, or wing is attached. **b** (in full **shoulder joint**) the end of the upper arm joining with the collarbone and blade bone. **c** either of the two projections below the neck from which the arms hang. **2** the upper foreleg and shoulder blade of a pig, lamb, etc. when butchered. **3** (often in *pl.*) **a** the upper part of the back and arms. **b** this part of the body regarded as capable of bearing a burden or blame, providing comfort, etc. (*a shoulder to cry on*). **4** a strip of ground bordering a road, where vehicles may stop in an emergency. **5** a part of a garment covering the shoulder. **6** a part of anything resembling a shoulder in form or function, as in a bottle, mountain, tool, etc. ● *v.* **1** *tr.* push with the shoulder; jostle. **b** *intr.* make one's way by jostling (*shouldered through the crowd*). **2** *tr.* take (a burden etc.) on one's shoulders (*shouldered the family's problems*). □ **put one's shoulder to the wheel** make an effort. **shoulder to shoulder 1** side by side. **2** with closed ranks or united effort. □ **shouldered** *adj.* (also in *comb.*).

shoulder bag *n.* a woman's handbag that can be hung from the shoulder.

shoulder belt *n.* a seat belt or other strap passing over one shoulder and under the opposite arm.

shoulder blade *n.* either of the large flat bones of the upper back; the scapula.

shoulder butt *n.* = BUTT³ 3 *n.*

shoulder-length *adj.* (of hair etc.) reaching to the shoulders.

shoulder pad *n.* **1** a pad sewn into a garment to bulk out the shoulder. **2** a protective pad for the shoulders, worn when playing hockey etc.

shoulder strap *n.* **1** a strip of cloth going over the shoulder from front to back of a garment. **2** a strap suspending a bag etc. from the shoulder.

shouldn't *contraction* should not.

shout ● *v.* **1** *intr.* make a loud cry or vocal sound; speak loudly. **2** *tr.* say or express loudly; call out. ● *n.* a loud cry expressing joy etc. or calling attention. □ **shout at** speak loudly to etc. **shout down** reduce to silence by shouting. **shout for** call for by shouting. **shout it from the rooftops** make a thing embarrassingly public. □ **shouter** *n.*

shouting match *n.* a loud altercation.

shove ● *v.* **1** *tr. & intr.* push vigorously; move by hard or rough pushing. **2** *intr.* (usu. foll. by *along, past, through,* etc.) make one's way by pushing (*shoved through the crowd*). **3** *tr. informal* put somewhere (*shoved it in the drawer*). ● *n.* an act of shoving or of prompting a person into action. □ **shove it** *coarse slang* used for expressing contemptuous rejection or dismissal. **shove off 1** start from the shore in a boat. **2** *slang* depart; go away (*told him to shove off*). **shove over** (usu. in *imper.*) *informal* move over.

shovel ● *n.* **1 a** a spadelike tool for shifting quantities of snow, earth, etc., esp. having the sides curved upwards. **b** a shovelful. **2** a machine or part of a machine having a similar form or function. **3** *Cdn* the wide flat part of a moose's antler. ● *v.* (**shovelled, shovelling**) **1** *tr.* shift or clear (snow etc.) with or as if with a shovel. **2** *tr.* clear (an area) of snow etc. using a shovel. **3** *intr.* use a shovel. **4** *tr. informal* move (esp. food) in large quantities or roughly (*shovelled peas into his mouth*). □ **shovelful** *n.* (pl. **-fuls**). **shoveller** *n.*

show ● *v.* (*past part.* **shown** or **showed**) **1** *intr. & tr.* be, or allow or cause to be, visible; manifest; appear. **2** *tr.* (often foll. by *to*) offer, exhibit, or produce (a thing) for scrutiny etc. **3** *tr.* (often foll. by *to, toward*) demonstrate (kindness, rudeness, etc.) to a person (*showed him no mercy*). **4** *intr.* (of feelings etc.) be manifest (*his dislike shows*). **5** *tr.* a point out; prove (*has shown it to be false*). **b** (usu. foll. by *how to* + infin.) cause (a person) to understand or be capable of doing (*showed them how to knit*). **6** *tr.* (*refl.*) **a** exhibit oneself as being (*showed herself a generous host*). **b** (foll. by *to be*) exhibit oneself to be (*showed herself to be fair*). **7** *tr. & intr.* (with reference to a

film) be presented or cause to be presented. **8** *tr.* exhibit (a picture, animal, flower, etc.) in a show. **9** *intr.* (of a house etc.) make a good, bad, etc. impression on prospective buyers or renters (*this condo shows well*). **10** *intr.* (of an artist, designer, etc.) hold an exhibition of one's work. **11** *tr.* (often foll. by *in, out, up,* etc.) conduct or lead (*showed them to their rooms*). **12** *intr.* appear (*waited but he didn't show*). **13** *intr. N Amer.* finish third, esp. in a horse race. **14** *tr.* indicate (a time, measurement, etc.) (*the clock showed midnight*). **15** *intr.* (of a woman) manifest visible signs of pregnancy (*she's beginning to show*). ● *n.* **1** the act or an instance of showing; the state of being shown. **2 a** a spectacle, display, exhibition, etc. (*a fine show of blossom*). **b** a collection of things etc. shown for public entertainment or in competition (*dog show*; also *attrib.*: *show horse*). **c** a display of new products (*car show*). **3 a** a play etc., esp. a musical. **b** a radio or television program. **c** a movie. **d** any public entertainment or performance. **4 a** an outward appearance, semblance, or display (*a show of strength*). **b** empty appearance; mere display (*that's all show*). **5** *informal* an undertaking, business, etc. (*sold the whole show*). **6** esp. *Brit. informal* an opportunity of acting, defending oneself, etc. (*made a good show of it*). **7** *Med.* a discharge of blood etc. from the vagina at the onset of childbirth. **8** *N Amer.* the third position, esp. in a horse race. **9** *Cdn* a logging operation. □ **get this show on the road** *informal* get moving; make a start. **give the show** (or **whole show**) **away** demonstrate the inadequacies or reveal the truth. **nothing to show for** no visible result of (effort etc.). **on show** being exhibited. **show around** take (a person) to places of interest; act as guide for (a person) in a building etc. **show cause** *Law* allege with justification. **show one's colours** make one's opinion clear. **show a person the door** dismiss or eject a person. **show one's face** make an appearance; let oneself be seen. **show one's hand** (or **cards**) **1** disclose one's plans. **2** reveal one's cards. **show off 1** display to advantage. **2** act pretentiously; ostentatiously display one's knowledge, talent, etc. **show oneself 1** be seen in public. **2** see sense 6 of *v.* **show through 1** be visible through a covering. **2** (of real feelings etc.) be revealed inadvertently. **show up 1** make or be conspicuous or clearly visible. **2** expose (a fraud, impostor, inferiority, etc.). **3** *informal* appear; be present; arrive. **4** *informal* embarrass or humiliate. **show the way 1** indicate what has to be done etc. by attempting it first. **2** show others which way to go etc.

show and tell *n.* esp. *N Amer.* **1** a classroom activity for young children in which each student brings an object from home and describes it to his or her classmates. **2** any informative display and discussion of assembled objects.

showbiz *n. informal* = SHOW BUSINESS. □ **showbizzy** *adj.*

showboat ● *n.* **1** a river steamer on which theatrical performances are given. **2** *informal* a show-off. ● *v. intr.* act pretentiously; show off. □ **showboater** *n.* **showboating** *n.*

show business *n. informal* the entertainment industry, esp. theatre, movies, and television.

showcase ● *n.* **1** a glass case used for exhibiting goods etc. **2** a place or medium for presenting (esp. attractively) to general attention. ● *v.tr.* exhibit or display.

showdown *n.* a final test or confrontation; a decisive situation.

shower ● *n.* **1** a brief fall of esp. rain, snow, hail, etc. **2** (often *attrib.*) **a** a cubicle, bath, etc. in which one stands under a spray of water. **b** the apparatus etc. used for this. **c** the act of washing oneself in a shower. **3 a** a brisk flurry of bullets, stones, sparks, etc. **b** a similar flurry of gifts, letters, praise, etc. **4** N Amer. a party for giving presents to a prospective bride, pregnant woman, etc. ● v. **1** tr. discharge (water, missiles, etc.) in a shower. **2** intr. use a shower. **3** tr. (usu. foll. by on, upon) lavishly bestow (gifts, praise, etc.). **4** intr. descend or come in a shower (it showered on and off all day). □ **showery** adj.

shower curtain n. a waterproof curtain hung in a shower stall or bathtub.

shower head n. a nozzle from which the water sprays out in a shower.

showgirl n. an actress who sings and dances in musicals, variety shows, etc.

show home n. (also **show house**) = MODEL HOME.

showing n. **1** the act or an instance of showing. **2** a usu. specified quality of performance (made a poor showing). **3** a presentation or broadcasting of a film or a television program. **4** the presentation of a case; evidence (on present showing it must be true). **5** a visit by a prospective buyer to a property that is for sale.

show jumping n. the sport of riding horses over a course of fences and other obstacles, with penalty points for errors. □ **show jumper** n.

showman n. (pl. **-men**) **1** a person who presents or produces an esp. theatrical show. **2** an entertainer who performs with panache and style. **3** a person skilled in self-advertisement or publicity. □ **showmanship** n.

shown past part. of SHOW.

show-off informal ● n. a person who shows off. ● adj. ostentatious, showy. □ **show-offy** adj.

show of hands n. raised hands as a means of voting, showing interest, etc.

showpiece n. **1** an item of work presented for exhibition or display. **2** an outstanding example or specimen.

showplace n. a place serving to display something to its best advantage.

show ring n. an enclosed, usu. circular area where animals, plants, etc. are exhibited in competition.

showroom n. a room in a factory, office building, etc. used to display goods for sale.

showstopper n. informal **1** a performance receiving prolonged applause. **2** anything which draws great attention and admiration. □ **show-stopping** adj.

showtime n. N Amer. the time at which a movie, concert, etc. is scheduled to begin.

show tune n. a popular tune from a musical.

showy adj. (**-ier**, **-iest**) **1** gaudy, ostentatious, esp. excessively so. **2** (of a person, quality, etc.) brilliant, striking, effective. □ **showily** adv. **showiness** n.

shrank past of SHRINK.

shrapnel n. **1** fragments of a bomb etc. thrown out by an explosion. **2** a shell containing bullets or pieces of metal timed to burst short of impact.

shred ● n. **1** a scrap, fragment, or strip of esp. cloth, paper, etc. **2** the least amount, remnant (not a shred of evidence). ● v.tr. (**shredded**, **shredding**) tear or cut into shreds. □ **tear to shreds** completely refute (an argument etc.).

shredder n. **1** a machine used to reduce documents to shreds. **2** any device used for shredding. **3** N Amer. slang a snowboarder.

shrew n. **1** any small usu. insect-eating mouselike mammal of the family Soricidae, with a long pointed snout. **2** a bad-tempered or scolding woman.

shrewd adj. **1** showing astute powers of judgment; clever and judicious. **2** (of a face etc.) shrewd-looking. □ **shrewdly** adv. **shrewdness** n.

shriek ● v. **1** intr. utter a shrill screeching sound or words esp. in pain or terror. **2** tr. **a** utter (sounds or words) by shrieking (shrieked his name). **b** indicate clearly or blatantly. ● n. a high-pitched piercing cry or sound; a scream. □ **shriek with laughter** laugh uncontrollably. □ **shrieker** n.

shrike n. any bird of the family Laniidae, with a strong hooked and toothed bill, that impales its prey of small birds and insects on thorns.

shrill ● adj. **1** piercing and high-pitched in sound. **2** (of a person, argument, etc.) sharp, unrestrained, unreasoning. ● v. **1** intr. (of a cry etc.) sound shrilly. **2** tr. (of a person etc.) utter or send out (a song, complaint, etc.) shrilly. □ **shrilly** adv. **shrillness** n.

shrimp ● n. **1** (pl. same or **-s**) any of various small (esp. marine) edible crustaceans, with ten legs, grey-green when alive and pink when cooked. **2** informal a very small slight person. ● v.intr. go catching shrimps. □ **shrimper** n. **shrimp-like** adj.

shrine n. **1** esp. Catholicism **a** a chapel, church, altar, etc., sacred to a saint, holy person, relic, etc. **b** the tomb of a saint etc. **c** a niche containing a holy statue etc. **2** a place associated with or containing memorabilia of a particular person, event, etc. **3** a Shinto place of worship.

Shriner n. a member of the Order of Nobles of the Mystic Shrine, a charitable society founded in the US in 1872.

shrink ● v. (past **shrank** or **shrunk**; past part. **shrunk**) **1** tr. & intr. **a** make or become smaller, esp. by the action of moisture, heat, or cold. **b** make or become reduced in size or number (the workforce has shrunk considerably). **2** intr. (usu. foll. by from, back) recoil (shrank from her touch). **3** intr. be averse from doing (shrinks from meeting them). ● n. **1** the act or an instance of shrinking; shrinkage. **2** informal a psychiatrist. □ **shrinkable** adj. **shrinker** n.

shrinkage n. **1 a** the process or fact of shrinking. **b** the degree or amount of shrinking. **2** a reduction in a company's budget or profits due to wastage etc.

shrinking violet n. informal a very shy person.

shrink wrap ● n. thin transparent plastic film wrapped around and then shrunk tightly on to an article as packaging etc. ● v.tr. (**shrink-wrap**) enclose (an article) in shrink wrap.

shrink-wrapped adj. **1** packaged in shrink wrap. **2** (of software) readily available commercially, and usu. standardized for a mass market.

shrivel v.tr. & intr. (**shrivelled**, **shrivelling**) contract or wither into a wrinkled, folded, rolled-up, contorted, or dried-up state.

shroom (also **'shroom**) n. slang = MAGIC MUSHROOM.

shroud ● n. **1** a sheetlike garment for wrapping a corpse for burial. **2** anything that conceals like a shroud (a shroud of mystery). **3** (in pl.) Naut. a set of ropes supporting the mast or topmast. ● v.tr. **1** clothe (a body) for burial. **2** cover, conceal, or disguise.

Shrove Tuesday n. the day before Ash Wednesday.

shrub n. a woody plant smaller than a tree and having a very short stem with branches near the ground. □ **shrubby** adj.

shrubbery n. (pl. **-ies**) **1** an area planted with shrubs. **2** shrubs collectively.

shrubby cinquefoil n. see BUCKBRUSH.

shrug ● v. (**shrugged**, **shrugging**) **1** intr. slightly and momentarily raise the shoulders to express indifference, helplessness, contempt, etc. **2** tr. **a** raise (the shoulders) in this way. **b** shrug the shoulders to express (indifference etc.) (*shrugged his consent*). ● *n.* the act or an instance of shrugging. □ **shrug off** dismiss as unimportant etc. by or as if by shrugging.

shrunk *past part. of* SHRINK.

shrunken *adj.* (esp. of a face, person, etc.) having grown smaller esp. because of age, illness, etc.

shtetl /ˈʃtetəl, ˈʃteitəl/ *n.* (*pl.* **-s, shtetlach** /-læx /) *hist.* a small Jewish town or village in E Europe.

shtick *n. slang* **1** a theatrical routine, gimmick, etc. **2** a particular area of activity or interest; a sphere etc.

shuck *N Amer.* ● *n.* **1** a husk or pod, esp. the husk of an ear of corn. **2** the shell of an oyster or clam. ● *v.tr.* **1** remove the shucks of. **2** (often foll. by *off*) **a** remove, throw or strip off (clothes etc.). **b** get rid of, abandon. □ **shucker** *n.*

shucks *interj. informal* an expression of contempt or regret or self-deprecation in response to praise.

shudder ● *v.intr.* **1** shiver esp. convulsively from fear, cold, repugnance, etc. **2** feel strong repugnance etc. (*shudder to think of it*). **3** (of a machine etc.) vibrate or quiver. ● *n.* **1** the act or an instance of shuddering. **2** (in *pl.*; prec. by *the*) *informal* a state of shuddering. □ **shudderingly** *adv.* **shuddery** *adj.*

shuffle ● *v.* **1** *tr. & intr.* move with a scraping, sliding, or dragging motion (*shuffles along; shuffling his feet*). **2 a** *tr. & intr.* rearrange (a pack of cards) by sliding them over each other quickly. **b** *tr.* rearrange; intermingle; confuse (*shuffled the documents*). **c** *tr.* redistribute posts within (a cabinet, organization, etc.). **3** *tr.* (usu. foll. by *on, off, into*) assume or remove (clothes, a burden, etc.) esp. clumsily or evasively (*shuffled off responsibility*). **4** *intr.* **a** act in a shifting or evasive manner; equivocate; prevaricate. **b** continually shift one's position; fidget. **5** *intr.* (foll. by *out of*) escape evasively (*shuffled out of the blame*). ● *n.* **1** a shuffling movement. **2** the act or an instance of shuffling cards. **3** a general change of relative positions. **4** a rearrangement of ministerial posts within a government or cabinet. **5** a piece of equivocation; an evasive trick. **6 a** a quick brushing movement of the feet in dancing. **b** a dance performed with such a step. **c** a piece of music for such a dance. □ **lost in the shuffle** overlooked in a crowd, confusion, etc. □ **shuffler** *n.*

shuffleboard *n.* a game in which competitors use a long-handled implement to push discs into numbered scoring sections.

shul /ʃuːl/ *n.* **1** a synagogue. **2** a service at a synagogue.

shun *v.tr.* (**shunned, shunning**) avoid; keep clear of.

shunt ● *v.* **1** *intr. & tr.* diverge or cause (a train) to be diverted esp. on to a siding. **2** *tr. Electricity* provide (a current) with a shunt. **3** *tr.* **a** push aside or out of the way. **b** move (a person) to a different place, often a less important one (*she was shunted off to a regional office*). **4** *tr.* pass (blood, fluid, etc.) through a shunt. ● *n.* **1** the act or an instance of shunting on to a siding. **2** *Electricity* a conductor joining two points of a circuit, through which more or less of a current may be diverted. **3** *Surgery* **a** an alternative path for the circulation of blood or other fluid. **b** the construction of such a route.

shush ● *interj.* = HUSH *interj.* ● *v.* **1** *tr.* make or attempt to make silent (*shushed the baby*). **2** *intr.* be silent. **3** *intr.* make a soft, shushing sound; move with the sound of a rush of air. ● *n.* an utterance of 'shush'.

Shuswap /ˈʃuːswɒp/ (*pl.* same or **-s**) ● *n.* **1** a member of an Aboriginal people living in the Thompson River area of BC. **2** the Salishan language of this people. ● *adj.* of or relating to this people.

shut *v.* (**shutting**; *past* and *past part.* **shut**) **1** *tr.* **a** move (a door, window, lid, etc.) into position so as to block an aperture. **b** close or seal (a box, eye, mouth, etc.). **2** *intr.* become or be capable of being closed or sealed (*the door shut with a bang*). **3** *tr.* bring (a book, hand, etc.) into a folded-up state. **4** *tr.* (usu. foll. by *in, out*) keep (a person, sound, etc.) in or out of a room etc. by shutting a door etc. (*shut out the noise; shut them in*). **5** *tr.* (usu. foll. by *in*) catch (a finger, dress, etc.) by shutting something on it (*shut her finger in the door*). **6** *tr.* bar access to (a place etc.) (*this entrance is shut*). □ **be** (or **get**) **shut of** *slang* be (or get) rid of (*were glad to get shut of him*). **shut the door on** refuse to consider; make impossible. **shut down 1** stop (a factory, nuclear reactor, etc.) from operating. **2** (of a factory etc.) stop operating. **3** turn off (an engine, machine, etc.). **4** *N Amer. Sport informal* render an opponent's offence ineffective (*shut down the Jays*). **shut one's eyes** (or **ears** or **heart** or **mind**) **to** pretend not, or refuse, to see (or hear or feel sympathy for or think about). **shut in** (of hills, houses, etc.) encircle, prevent access etc. to or escape from (*were shut in by the sea on three sides*) (see also sense 4). **shut off 1 a** stop the flow of (water, gas, etc.) by shutting a valve. **b** switch off (a machine, light, etc.). **2** separate from society etc. **shut out 1** exclude (a person, light, etc.) from a place, situation, etc. **2** screen (landscape etc.) from view. **3** prevent (a possibility etc.). **4** block (a painful memory etc.) from the mind. **5** *N Amer.* prevent (the opposing team) from scoring (see also sense 4). **shut up 1** close all doors and windows of (a house etc.); bolt and bar. **2** imprison (a person). **3** close (a box etc.) securely. **4** *informal* reduce to silence by rebuke etc. **5** put (a thing) away in a box etc. **6** (esp. in *imper.*) *informal* stop talking. **shut up shop 1** close a business, shop, etc. **2** cease business etc. permanently. **shut your face** (or **mouth** or **trap**)! *slang* an impolite request to stop talking.

shutdown *n.* **1** the closure of a factory etc. **2** the turning off of a machine, computer, etc.

shut-eye *n. informal* sleep.

shut-in *n. N Amer.* (also *attrib.*) a person who is confined indoors because of ill health.

shut-off *n.* **1** something used for stopping an operation. **2** a cessation of flow, supply, or activity.

shut-off valve *n.* a valve used to cut off the flow of water esp. to a sink, etc. when doing repairs etc.

shutout *n. N Amer.* **1** the act of preventing an opposing team from scoring. **2** any game in which one side does not score.

shutter ● *n.* **1 a** each of a pair or set of hinged panels fixed inside or outside a window for security or privacy or to keep the light in or out. **b** a structure of slats on rollers used for the same purpose. **2** a device on a camera that opens to allow light to pass through the lens. **3** a person or thing that shuts. ● *v.tr.* **1** put up the shutters of. **2** close (a business, factory, etc.) permanently. **3** provide with shutters.

shutterbug *n.* an enthusiastic photographer.

shutter speed *n.* the nominal time for which a shutter on a camera is open at a given setting.

shuttle ● *n.* **1 a** a bobbin with two pointed ends used for carrying the weft thread across between the warp threads in weaving. **b** a bobbin carrying the lower thread in a sewing machine. **2** a plane, bus, etc., going to and fro over a short route continuously (also *attrib.*: *shuttle bus*). **3** = SHUTTLECOCK. **4** = SPACE SHUTTLE. ● *v.* **1** *tr.* transport (a person) in a shuttle. **2** *intr.* (of a person, train, etc.) travel backwards and forwards between places. **3** *intr. & tr.* move or cause to move to and fro like a shuttle.

shuttlecock *n.* **1** a small piece of cork, rubber, etc. fitted with a ring of feathers, or a similar device of plastic, used instead of a ball in badminton. **2** a thing passed repeatedly back and forth.

shuttle diplomacy *n.* diplomatic negotiations conducted by a mediator travelling between disputing parties.

shy¹ ● *adj.* (**shyer, shyest** or **shier, shiest**) **1 a** diffident or uneasy in company; timid. **b** (of a thing, action, etc.) characterized by or done with reserve or timidity (*a shy smile*). **c** (of an animal, bird, etc.) easily startled; timid. **2** (foll. by *of*) avoiding; chary of (*shy of going to meetings*). **3** (in *comb.*) showing fear of or distaste for (*gun-shy; work-shy*). **4** (often foll. by *of*) *informal* short of (a stated amount, measurement, etc.). ● *v.intr.* (**shies, shied**) **1** (usu. foll. by *at*) (esp. of a horse) start suddenly aside (at an object, noise, etc.) in fright. **2** (usu. foll. by *away from, at*) avoid accepting or becoming involved in (a proposal etc.) in alarm.

shy² ● *v.tr.* (**shies, shied**) fling or throw (a stone etc.). ● *n.* (*pl.* **shies**) the act or an instance of shying. □ **shyer** *n.*

shyster *n.* esp. *N Amer. informal* a person, esp. a lawyer, who uses unscrupulous methods.

SI *abbr.* INTERNATIONAL SYSTEM OF UNITS.

Si *symbol* silicon.

si / si: / *n. Music* = TI².

Siamese ● *n.* (*pl.* same) **1 a** a native of Siam (now Thailand) in SE Asia. **b** the language of Siam. **2** (in full **Siamese cat**) a breed of cream-coloured, short-haired cat, with blue eyes and brown ears, face, paws, and tail. ● *adj.* of or concerning Siam, its people, or language.

Siamese twins *n.pl.* **1** = CONJOINED TWINS. **2** any closely associated pair.

sib *n.* **1** esp. *Genetics* a sibling. **2** a blood relative.

Siberian ● *n.* **1** a native of Siberia in the northeastern part of the Russian Federation. **2** a person of Siberian descent. ● *adj.* of or relating to Siberia.

Siberian elm *n.* an elm of northeastern Asia, *Ulmus pumila*, frequently planted as a hedge.

Siberian husky *n.* a hardy breed of husky, originally from Siberia, with stocky body and blue eyes.

Siberian tiger *n.* a very large tiger of an endangered race occurring in SE Siberia and NE China.

sibilant / ˈsɪbɪlənt / ● *adj.* **1** (of a letter or set of letters, as *s, sh*) articulated with a hissing sound. **2** hissing (*a sibilant whisper*). ● *n.* a sibilant letter or letters. □ **sibilance** *n.*

sibling *n.* each of two or more children having one or both parents in common.

sibling rivalry *n.* competition arising from jealousy between siblings.

sibyl / ˈsɪbəl / *n.* **1** any of the women in ancient times supposed to utter the oracles and prophecies of a god. **2** a prophetess, fortune teller, or witch.

sic¹ / sɪk / *adv.* (usu. in brackets) used, spelled, etc., as written (confirming, or calling attention to, the form of quoted or copied words). ¶ The word *sic* is placed in brackets after a word that appears odd or erroneous to show that the word is quoted exactly as it stands in the original.

sic² *v.tr.* (**sicced, siccing**) **1** (usu. in *imper.*) (esp. to a dog) attack (a person or animal) (*sic 'em!*). **2** (usu. foll. by *on*) **a** set (an animal) on another animal or person. **b** set (a person) to follow, harass, etc. another person.

Sicilian ● *n.* **1** a native of Sicily, an island off the S coast of Italy. **2** a person of Sicilian descent. ● *adj.* of or relating to Sicily.

sick¹ *adj.* **1** ill; affected by illness. **2** (often in *comb.*) vomiting or tending to vomit (*seasick*). **3** mentally disturbed or perverted (*a sick mind*). **4** *informal* (of humour etc.) jeering at misfortune, illness, death, etc.; morbid (*sick joke*). **5 a** (often foll. by *for,* or in *comb.*) pining; longing (*lovesick*). **b** deeply affected by disappointment, fear, sorrow, grief, etc. (*worried sick*). **6** (often foll. by *of*) *informal* **a** disgusted by too much exposure (*sick of chocolates*). **b** angry, esp. because of surfeit (*am sick of being teased*). **7** of a sickly colour; pale, wan. □ **be** (or **get**) **sick** vomit; throw up. **get** (or **fall** or **take**) **sick** be taken ill. **make a person sick** disgust a person (*his hypocrisy makes me sick*). **sick and tired of** fed up with; wearied of. **sick as a dog** extremely ill. **sick to one's stomach** *N Amer.* vomiting or nauseous. □ **sickish** *adj.* **sickishly** *adv.*

sick² *var. of* SIC².

sick bay *n.* **1** part of a ship used as a hospital. **2** any room etc. for sick people.

sickbed *n.* **1** an invalid's bed. **2** the state of being an invalid.

sick building syndrome *n.* a high incidence of illness in office workers, attributed to pollutants etc. in the immediate working surroundings.

sick day *n.* a paid day off for a worker because of illness.

sicken *v.* **1** *tr.* affect with loathing or disgust. **2** *intr.* (often foll. by *at,* or *to* + *infin.*) feel nausea or disgust (*he sickened at the sight*). **3** *intr.* fall ill.

sickening *adj.* **1** causing or liable to cause sickness or nausea. **2** loathsome, disgusting. □ **sickeningly** *adv.*

sickie *n. N Amer. informal* (also **sicky**) (*pl.* **-ies**) **1** a psychotic or perverted person. **2** a person who is unwell.

sickle *n.* **1** a short-handled farm tool with a semicircular blade, used esp. for cutting grass, grain, etc. **2** (in full **sickle bar**) the cutting mechanism of a combine, mower, etc., consisting of a heavy bar with blades. **3** anything sickle-shaped, esp. the moon.

sick leave *n.* leave of absence granted because of illness.

sickle cell *n.* a sickle-shaped blood cell, found in the blood of people with sickle-cell anemia.

sickle-cell anemia *n.* a severe hereditary form of anemia, in which a mutated form of hemoglobin distorts the red blood cells into a crescent shape.

sickly *adj.* (**-ier, -iest**) **1 a** of weak health; apt to be ill. **b** (of a person's complexion, look, etc.) languid, faint, or pale, suggesting sickness (*a sickly smile*). **c** (of light or colour) faint, pale, feeble. **2** causing ill health (*a sickly climate*). **3** (of a book etc.) sentimental or mawkish. **4** inducing or connected with nausea (*a sickly taste*). **5** (of a colour) of an unpleasant shade inducing nausea (*a sickly green*). □ **sickliness** *n.*

sickness *n.* **1** the state of being ill; disease. **2** a specified disease (*sleeping sickness*). **3** vomiting or a tendency to vomit.

sicko *n.* (*pl.* **-os**) esp. *N Amer. slang* a mentally ill or perverted person.

sickroom *n.* **1** a room occupied by a sick person. **2** a room adapted for sick people.

side ● *n.* **1 a** each of the more or less flat surfaces bounding an object (*a cube has six sides*). **b** a vertical lateral surface or plane as distinct from the top or bottom, front or back, or ends (*the side of the box*). **2** the more or less vertical slope of a hill or bank (*the side of the mountain*). **3** either surface of a thing regarded as having two surfaces. **4 a** a specified direction or position relating to a person or thing (*on the north side*). **b** (often in *comb.*) a position next to a person or thing. **5** a position nearer or farther than, or right or left of, a dividing line (*on the other side of the road*). **6 a** a specified part or region in relation to a central point (*the east side of town*). **b** (*attrib.*) a subordinate, peripheral, or detached part (*a side dish*). **7 a** either of two parts of a person's body between the left or right shoulder and the corresponding hip (*has a pain in his right side*). **b** the analogous part of an animal's body. **c** either of the lateral halves of the body of a butchered animal (*a side of bacon*). **8 a** each of two sets of opponents in a dispute, political debate, game, etc. (*whose side are you on?*). **b** a cause or philosophical position etc. regarded as being in conflict with another. **c** *Baseball* a team's batters in one inning (*he struck out the side in the fifth*). **9** any of several aspects of a question, character, etc. (*look on the bright side*). **10** either side of a phonograph record or audio cassette tape. **11** a line of hereditary descent through the father or the mother. **12** *N Amer.* = SIDE ORDER. **13** *Geom.* each of the bounding lines of a plane rectilinear figure. ● *v.intr.* (usu. foll. by *with*) share an opinion, view, stance, etc. with (a person), esp. in a particular argument or dispute (*she sided with her father*). □ **from side to side 1** across the whole width. **2** alternately each way from a central line (*staggered from side to side*). **let the side down** fail one's colleagues, esp. by frustrating their efforts or embarrassing them. **on the ... side** fairly, somewhat (*he's a little on the chubby side*). **on the side 1** in addition to one's regular work etc. **2** secretly or illicitly. **3** *N Amer.* as a side dish. **side by side 1** standing close together. **2** in collaboration or solidarity. **take sides** favour or support one party in a dispute. **to one side** aside (*she took me to one side*).

sidearm *Baseball* ● *adj.* **1** (of a pitch or throw) performed or delivered with the arm swung or extended out to the side, parallel to the ground (*compare* OVERHAND 1). **2** (of a pitcher) that throws such a pitch. ● *adv.* with the arm swung or extended out to the side (*he throws sidearm*). ● *v.tr.* throw (a pitch) sidearm.

sidebar *n.* esp. *N Amer.* **1** a short, usu. boxed, article in a newspaper, magazine, etc. placed alongside a main article and containing additional or explanatory material, data, etc. **2** a secondary, additional, or incidental issue etc.

sideboard *n.* a piece of dining room furniture used to store dishes, cutlery, table linen, etc., esp. one with a flat top, cupboards, and drawers.

sideburns *n.pl.* esp. *N Amer.* hair grown by a man down the sides of his face beginning at the top of the ear and sometimes extending down as far as the cheek.

sidecar *n.* **1** a small usu. open car with one wheel for one or more passengers attached to the side of a motorcycle. **2** a cocktail of orange liqueur, lemon juice, and brandy.

side channel *n.* *Cdn* a shallow and narrow tributary running into a river.

sided *adj.* (usu. in *comb.*) having a specified number or kind of sides (*double-sided tape; cedar-sided home; one-sided game*). □ **sidedly** *adv.* **sidedness** *n.*

side dish *n.* an extra dish accompanying the main course but usu. served on a separate plate.

side door *n.* **1** a door in or at the side of a building, vehicle, etc. **2** *informal* an indirect means of escape or resolving a problem etc. (also *attrib.*: *side-door deal*).

side effect *n.* **1** *Med.* a usu. adverse reaction caused by a drug in addition to the effect for which it is administered. **2** an unintended secondary result.

sidehill *n.* *US & Cdn* (esp. *BC*) a hillside.

side impact *n.* **1** a collision against the side of a car or truck etc. **2** (*attrib.*) (usu. **side-impact**) relating to, or esp. designed to protect in case of, a collision against the side of a vehicle (*side-impact beams*).

sidekick *n.* *informal* **1** a close companion or partner, esp. in adventure. **2** the second member of a duo, subordinate and loyal to the first.

sidelight *n.* **1** a light coming from the side, esp. used in photography. **2** a piece of incidental information on a subject; an anecdote or item serving as a companion to the full account of an event etc. (*compare* HIGHLIGHT 2). **3** a window by the side of a door or other window. □ **sidelighting** *n.*

sideline ● *n.* **1 a** a part-time job or business taken up in addition to one's main employment, esp. as a secondary source of income. **b** any activity pursued as a secondary interest, hobby, etc. **2 a** (in football, basketball, soccer, etc.) one of two lines running the length of a field or court to separate the part of the playing surface that is in bounds from that which is out of bounds. **b** (usu. in *pl.*) the part of the playing surface out of bounds where coaches, players, and occasionally spectators sit. ● *v.tr.* **1** remove (a player) from participation in a game or games, esp. through injury or a suspension. **2** remove from action or consideration etc. (*they've sidelined their plans*). □ **on** (or **from**) **the sidelines** in (or from) a position removed from the main action.

sidelock *n.* a long curly lock of hair falling from the side of the head down along the cheek, worn esp. by Orthodox Jews as a distinguishing mark.

sidelong ● *adj.* directed to one side; oblique (*a sidelong glance*). ● *adv.* toward the side; obliquely (*moved sidelong*).

sideman *n.* a supporting musician in a jazz etc. band.

side order *n.* *N Amer.* a separate serving of food supplementing a meal ordered from a menu in a restaurant etc.

side plate *n.* a plate of approximately 15-20 cm in diameter, used for bread etc.

sidereal /saiˈdiːriəl/ *adj.* **1** of or concerning the constellations or fixed stars. **2** (of a period of time) determined or measured with reference to the apparent motion of the stars.

side ribs *n.pl.* *Cdn* a cut of pork from the belly including the ribs and adhering meat.

side road *n.* **1** a minor road, esp. joining or diverging from a main road; a back road. **2** *Cdn* (esp. *Ont.*) a rural road running perpendicular to a concession road.

sidesaddle ● *n.* a saddle originally designed to allow a woman wearing a skirt to sit with both feet on one side of the horse, now usu. made with supports for the knees of the rider, who sits facing forward with the right knee raised. ● *adv.* sitting in this position on a horse.

sideshow *n.* **1** a minor show or attraction in an exhibition, circus, etc. **2** a minor attraction, incident, or issue.

sideslip ● *n.* **1** (esp. of a bicycle, car, etc.) the action or instance of slipping sideways. **2** a sideways movement of an aircraft in flight, esp. downwards towards the centre of curvature of a turn. **3** *Skiing* the action of travelling at an angle down a slope or run. ● *v.intr.* **1** skid or slip sideways. **2** (of an aircraft) move sideways, esp. while turning. **3** *Skiing* travel downwards at an angle. **4** move elusively or adroitly.

sidesplit *n.* *Cdn* a house with floors raised half a level on one side, thus having an upper and lower basement and an upper and lower main floor.

sidestep ● *v.* (**-stepped, -stepping**) **1** *tr.* evade or dodge (an issue etc.) by refusing to address or confront it. **2** *tr. Sport* avoid (another player, a tackle, etc.) by stepping sideways. **3** *intr.* move laterally by stepping to the side. ● *n.* a step taken sideways.

side street *n.* a minor street usu. leading away from a main street.

side stroke *n.* a swimming stroke in which the swimmer lies on his or her side, drawing the arms through the water in opposite directions from the chest while using a scissor kick.

side-swipe ● *n.* **1** a passing jibe or verbal attack; an indirect rebuke or criticism. **2** a glancing blow along the side of esp. a car or truck etc. ● *v.tr.* **1** strike a glancing blow on the side of (esp. a car or truck etc.) in passing. **2** affect or attack indirectly.

side table *n.* a table placed next to the wall of a room or at the side of a larger table.

sidetrack ● *v.tr.* **1 a** distract (a person) from an objective, issue, topic, etc. **b** divert (a plan etc.) from its intended purpose or aim. **2** run or shunt (a train) into a siding. ● *n.* a railway siding.

side trip *n.* a minor excursion during a voyage.

sidewalk *n.* *N Amer.* **1** a paved pedestrian path or walkway on either side of a street. **2** (*attrib.*) designating things appearing or occurring on a sidewalk, esp. on the sidewalk in front of stores and other commercial buildings (*sidewalk vendor*).

sidewalk café *n.* *N Amer.* a small restaurant or coffee shop that opens onto a sidewalk and has tables set up so that customers may eat outdoors.

side wall *n.* **1 a** a wall forming the side of a structure, room, or enclosure. **b** a wall forming the side of a squash or racquetball court. **2 a** the side of a tire, usu. untreaded and distinctively marked or coloured. **b** (in full **side wall tire**) a tire with distinctive side walls.

sideways ● *adv.* **1** to or from a side (*moved sideways*). **2** with one side facing forward (*sat sideways*). **3** in an odd or unconventional manner. ● *adj.* **1** to or from a side (*a sideways movement*). **2** odd or unconventional.

side wind *n.* a crosswind.

sidewinder *n.* **1** a desert rattlesnake, *Crotalus cerastes*, native to N America, moving with a side-to-side slithering motion. **2** a punch delivered with a winding swing of the fist across the body. **3** (**Sidewinder**) a heat-seeking air-to-air missile.

siding *n.* **1** *N Amer.* material used to cover the outside of a building, usu. made of wood, aluminum, or vinyl. **2** a short length of railway track connected to an adjacent line for storing and shunting trains and enabling trains on the same line to pass each other.

sidle /ˈsaidəl/ *v.intr.* **1** (often foll. by *up*) move in a sly, guileful, or devious manner. **2** move in a cautious, timid, or furtive manner.

SIDS /sidz/ *n.* = SUDDEN INFANT DEATH SYNDROME.

siege *n.* **1 a** a military operation in which an attacking army attempts to force the surrender of a fortified place by surrounding it and cutting off supplies and communication etc. **b** a similar operation by police etc. to force the surrender of an armed person. **2** a prolonged and determined attack. **3** *N Amer.* a long period of illness or difficulty. □ **lay siege to** esp. *Military* conduct the siege of. **under siege** the object of a fierce attack or criticism.

siemens /ˈsiːmənz/ *n.* *Electricity* the SI unit of conductance, equal to one reciprocal ohm. Abbr.: **S**.

sienna /siˈenə/ *n.* **1** a kind of iron-rich earth used as a pigment in oil and watercolour painting. **2 a** the natural colour of this earth, a yellowish brown. **b** (in full **burnt sienna**) the colour of this earth when roasted, a reddish brown.

sierra /siˈerə/ *n.* a long jagged mountain chain, esp. in Spain, the US, or Latin America.

siesta /siˈestə/ *n.* an afternoon nap or rest, esp. one taken during the hottest hours of the day in a country with a warm climate.

sieur /sjɜr/ *n.* *hist.* a title for a member of the minor nobility, e.g. a seigneur, in France or New France.

sieve ● *n.* **1** a device consisting of a meshed or perforated surface enclosed in a frame, used to separate coarse particles from finer ones or from a liquid. **2** a similar kitchen utensil consisting of a fine rounded metal or plastic mesh and a circular frame with a handle, used to strain liquids or to reduce soft solids to a pulp or purée; a strainer. **3** *slang Hockey* a goalie who lets in a large number of (esp. easily stopped) goals. ● *v.tr.* esp. *Brit.* put through or sift with a sieve. □ **memory** (or **head**) **like a sieve** *informal* a memory that retains little.

sift *v.* **1** *tr.* pass through a sieve or sifter, esp. in order to separate coarser from finer particles or to combine and aerate. **2** *tr.* (usu. foll. by *out, from*) remove selectively (*read through these articles and sift out the better ones*). **3** *tr.* subject (evidence, facts, etc.) to a close or thorough examination, esp. as part of a selection process; scrutinize. **4** *intr.* (of snow, rain, sunlight, etc.) fall as if from a sieve. □ **sift through** sort through or examine (evidence etc.) for specific details.

sifter *n.* *Cooking* **1** *N Amer.* a metal or plastic cylinder, open at the top and having a meshed or perforated bottom through which dry ingredients are forced by means of a manual rotary blade in order to combine and aerate them. **2** a container with a perforated top used to sprinkle dry ingredients onto a surface.

SIG *abbr.* SPECIAL INTEREST GROUP 2.

sigh ● *v.* **1** *intr.* emit a long deep audible breath as an expression of sadness, weariness, longing, relief, etc. **2** *tr.* utter or express with sighs (*'I give up!' he sighed*). **3** *intr.* (of the wind etc.) make a sound that resembles sighing. ● *n.* a long and audible exhalation expressing sadness, weariness, etc. □ **breathe a sigh of relief** become free of the anxiety or distress esp. caused by a particular situation.

sight ● *n.* **1** the faculty of seeing with the eyes. **2** the act or an instance of seeing (*the sight of him makes me ill*). **3 a** a thing seen, esp. one that is striking or remarkable; a spectacle (*that sunset was a beautiful sight*). **b** *informal* a person or thing having a ridiculous, repulsive, or dishevelled appearance (*after the party this house was quite a sight*). **4** (usu. in *pl.*) the noteworthy features or attractions of a city, area, etc. (*seeing the sights*). **5** a range of space within which a person etc. can see or be seen (*came into sight*). **6** a view of something; a look or glimpse (*I caught sight of her*). **7** (also in *pl.*) a device on a gun or surveying instrument used to make one's aim or observation more precise. **8** *informal* a great quantity (*she's a sight better than she was*). **9** = SECOND SIGHT. **10** (*attrib.*) designating a text previously unseen by students presented to them for commentary, translation, etc. (*sight passage*). ● *v.* **1** *tr.* note the presence of; observe, notice, or glimpse (*we have sighted the suspect*). **2** *tr.* watch or locate (an object, target, etc.), esp. by viewing it through a sight. **3 a** *tr. & intr.* aim or adjust the sight of (a gun etc.). **b** *tr.* provide (a gun etc.) with sights. □ **at first sight** on first glimpse or impression. **at** (or **on**) **sight** as soon as a person or a thing has been seen (*liked him on sight*). **catch sight of** manage to see or notice; glimpse. **in** (or **within**) **sight 1** visible. **2** within reach, attainable (*the end is in sight*). **in one's sight** in one's opinion. **in** (or **within**) **sight of** visible by (a person) or from (a location). **lose sight of 1** no longer see or know the whereabouts of. **2** cease to be aware of. **lower one's sights** become less ambitious. **out of my sight!** go at once! **out of sight out of mind** it is easy to forget what is absent. **set one's sights on** strive for. **sight for sore eyes** a welcome person or thing, esp. a visitor.

sighted *adj.* **1** capable of seeing; not blind. **2** (in *comb.*) having a specified kind of sight (*far-sighted*). □ **sightedness** *n.* (in sense 2).

sight gag *n.* a humorous effect produced by a visual action etc. as opposed to something spoken or written.

sighting *n.* **1** an act or instance of seeing something, esp. an observation reported or recorded formally (*there have been two sightings*). **2** the act or procedure of adjusting the aim or sights of a gun, bow, etc.

sightline *n.* a line of vision extending from a person's eye to what is seen, esp. one extending from the eye of a spectator in a theatre or sports venue to the stage or playing surface etc.

sight-read *v.tr. & intr.* (*past* and *past part.* **-read**) play or sing a piece of music that one has not seen or practised prior to performing. □ **sight-reading** *n.*

sightseer *n.* a person who visits places of interest, esp. in a foreign city or country etc.; a tourist. □ **sightsee** *v.intr.* **sightseeing** *n.*

sight-sing *v.tr. & intr.* sing a piece of music that one has not seen or practised prior to performing. □ **sight-singing** *n.*

sight unseen *adv.* without a chance to look at or inspect a purchase etc. beforehand (*bought it sight unseen*).

sigma /ˈsɪɡmə/ *n.* the eighteenth letter of the Greek alphabet (Σ, σ, or, when final, ς), its uncial form having the shape of English *C*.

sigmoid /ˈsɪɡmɔɪd/ ● *adj.* **1** curved like the uncial sigma (ς); crescent-shaped. **2** S-shaped. ● *n.* (in full **sigmoid colon**) *Anat.* the terminal portion of the descending colon, leading to the rectum.

sign ● *n.* **1 a** an indication or suggestion of a quality or state (*trembling is a sign of fear*). **b** an act or gesture intended to prove a quality or state (*I give you this as a sign of my love*). **2 a** evidence of the existence or occurrence of something (*no signs of forced entry; no sign of him*). **b** a miracle or event serving as evidence of a supernatural or divine authority. **3** an indication or suggestion of a future state or occurrence; a portent (*first signs of spring*). **4** a publicly displayed board or placard etc. used to give information or warning, or to identify or advertise a store etc. (*street sign*). **5 a** gesture or action used to convey an idea, order, request, etc. (*gave him a sign to leave; peace sign*). **6 a** a gesture used in a system of sign language. **b** = SIGN LANGUAGE. **7** a mark or symbol used to represent a word, phrase, idea, etc. (*dollar sign*). **8 a** a technical mark or symbol used in mathematics, algebra, etc. to indicate an operation (*minus sign*). **b** the positiveness or negativeness of a quantity. **9** *Music* a technical symbol used in music to indicate key, sharps and flats, tempo, etc. (*repeat sign*). **10** each of the twelve divisions of the zodiac, named from the constellations formerly situated in them (*what's your sign?*). **11** *N Amer.* the trace or evidence of a wild animal, such as its path or tracks. **12** a basic element of communica-

tion, either linguistic (such as a letter or word) or non-linguistic (such as an image, article of dress, etc.); anything that can be construed as having a meaning. ● *v.* **1** *tr. & intr.* **a** write (one's name or initials etc.) on a document etc. to authorize or authenticate it. **b** mark (a document etc.) with one's name or autograph etc. to authorize or authenticate it. **2** *tr. & intr.* hire or be hired by signing a contract etc. (*see also* SIGN ON, SIGN UP). **3** *tr. & intr.* **a** communicate with gestures and body language (*they signed their assent*). **b** communicate in a sign language. □ **make no sign** not react or protest. **signed, sealed, and delivered** properly settled or taken care of with all the necessary formalities having been completed. **sign for** acknowledge receipt of by signing. **sign in 1** sign a register upon arrival in a hotel etc. **2** authorize the admittance of (a person) by signing a register. **sign off** say or write one's name to mark the end of a letter, television or radio broadcast, etc. **sign on 1** agree to a contract, employment, etc. **2** begin work, broadcasting, etc., esp. by writing or announcing one's name. **sign over** (or **away**) surrender (one's right, property, etc.) by signing a document etc. **sign out 1** sign a register upon leaving a hotel etc. **2** authorize or record the release or departure of (a person or thing). **sign up 1** engage or employ (a person). **2** enlist in the armed forces. **3 a** commit (a person) to a class or activity by signing the participant's name to a list (*signed my daughter up for swimming*). **b** enrol (*signed up for evening classes*).

signage *n.* signs collectively, esp. those used commercially.

signal¹ ● *n.* **1** any sound or gesture used to convey warning, direction, or information. **2** a usu. prearranged sound or gesture acting as the prompt for a particular action (*she gave us the signal to start*). **3** *Electricity* **a** a modulation of an electric current, electromagnetic wave, etc., by means of which information is conveyed from one place to another. **b** the current or wave itself, esp. regarded as conveying information. **4 a** a device, such as a light or semaphore, used to give instructions or warnings to drivers of cars and trains at railway crossings, intersections, etc. (*traffic signal*). **b** *N Amer.* = TURN SIGNAL. **5** an immediate occasion or cause of movement, action, etc. (*her entrance was the signal for applause*). **6** *N Amer. Football* a series of letters and numbers called out by a player on offence or defence to indicate to teammates which play will be run on the next down. ● *v.* (**signalled, signalling**) **1** *intr.* make a sound or gesture as a signal (*signal if you need anything*). **2** *tr.* **a** (often foll. by *to* + infin.) make signals to (a person); direct (*she signalled me to approach*). **b** transmit (an order, information, etc.) by signal; announce (*she signalled her assent*). **3** *tr.* be a sign or indication of; mark (*their surrender signalled the end of the war*). **4** *tr. & intr.* (of a cyclist or driver) indicate (one's intention to turn) by means of a hand signal or turn signal.

signal² *adj.* remarkably good or bad; noteworthy (*a signal victory*). □ **signally** *adv.*

signal fire *n.* *Cdn* a small fire or the remnant smoke of an extinguished fire serving to inform others of one's presence at a campsite etc.

signalman *n.* (*pl.* **-men**) **1** a railway employee responsible for operating signals and switches. **2** (also **signaller**) a person employed to make or transmit signals, esp. in the army or navy.

signatory /ˈsɪɡnətɔri/ ● *n.* (*pl.* **-ies**) a person, party, or country that has signed a particular document, such as a treaty. ● *adj.* (of a country etc.) that has signed a treaty or similar document.

signature *n.* **1 a** a person's name, initials, or distinctive mark used in signing a letter, document, etc. **b** an autograph. **c** the act of signing a document etc. (*this bill is ready for signature*). **2 a** a distinctive or identifying feature or characteristic. **b** (*attrib.*) designating a characteristic or skill etc. that distinguishes or typifies a person, their work, etc. (*signature tune*). **3** *Music* **a** = KEY SIGNATURE. **b** = TIME SIGNATURE. **4** *Printing* **a** a letter or figure placed at the foot of one or more pages of each sheet of a book as a guide for binding. **b** such a sheet after folding.

signboard *n.* **1** a board displaying the name or logo of a business. **2** *N Amer.* a board mounted on a signpost to direct travellers in a particular direction.

signee /sai'ni:/ *n.* a person who has signed a contract, register, etc.

signet /'signət/ *n.* **1** a small seal, usu. set in a ring, used with or instead of a signature to authenticate a document. **2** the stamp or impression of a seal.

signet ring *n.* a ring worn on the finger usu. bearing the wearer's initials or an emblem etc.

significance *n.* **1** consequence, importance (*his opinion is of no significance*). **2** a concealed or real meaning (*what is the significance of his statement?*). **3** the state of being significant.

significant *adj.* **1** of great importance or consequence (*a significant discovery*). **2** having or conveying an unstated meaning; having information that may be gathered (*I find it significant that he cannot talk to her*). **3** noteworthy, noticeable (*a significant drop in temperature*). □ **significantly** *adv.*

significant other *n.* *N Amer.* often *jocular* a spouse, partner, or lover.

signification *n.* **1** the act of signifying. **2** (often foll. by *of*) the implication, sense, or meaning, esp. of a word or phrase.

signified *n.* *Linguistics* the idea or meaning conventionally indicated by the signifier, as distinct from the external object to which it refers.

signifier *n.* **1** *Linguistics* a physical medium (such as a sound, symbol, image, etc.) expressing meaning, as distinct from the meaning expressed. **2** a thing that signifies or conveys meaning.

signify *v.* (**-ies, -ied**) **1** *tr.* **a** be a sign or symbol of; represent, denote. **b** offer a suggestion or hint of; portend (*those clouds signify a storm*). **2** *tr.* mean; have as its meaning (*'anorexia' signifies a type of eating disorder*). **3** *tr.* communicate; announce, declare (*she signified her disappointment to me*). **4** *intr.* be of importance; matter (*it signifies little*).

signing *n.* **1 a** an act or instance of signing a contract or signing a person to a contract. **b** a person who has signed a contract, esp. to join a professional sports team. **2** an instance of using, or the ability to use, sign language. **3** a session or period of time devoted to signing autographs (*a book signing*).

signing bonus *n.* esp. *Sport* a single lump payment paid to a signee upon signing a contract.

sign language *n.* a system of communication by visual gestures, used esp. by the hearing impaired.

sign law *n.* *Cdn informal* a Quebec provincial law regulating the use of languages other than French on signs.

sign-off *n.* an act or instance of terminating a letter or broadcast etc.

sign of the cross *n.* a Christian sign made in blessing or prayer, by tracing a cross from the forehead to the chest and to each shoulder, or in the air.

sign of the times *n.* an incident, event, person, etc. that typifies or foreshadows a trend developing or likely to develop in society.

sign-on *n.* an act or instance of beginning a broadcast etc.

signor /si'njɔr/ *n.* (also **signore** /-'njɔre/) (*pl.* **signori** /-'njɔri/) **1** used as a title (preceding the surname or other designation) of, or as a respectful form of address to, an Italian or Italian-speaking man. **2** an Italian man of distinction, rank, or authority.

signora /si'njɔrə/ *n.* **1** used as a title (preceding the surname or other designation) of, or as a respectful form of address to, an Italian or Italian-speaking married woman. **2** a married Italian woman.

signpost ● *n.* **1** a post with a sign giving directions or information. **2** a means of guidance; an indication or clue. ● *v.tr.* (usu. in *passive*) **1 a** provide with a signpost or signposts. **b** convey (information) by means of a signpost. **2** indicate (a course of action etc.).

sika /'si:kə/ *n.* (in full **sika deer**) a small forest-dwelling deer, *Cervus nippon*, native to Japan.

Sikh /si:k/ ● *n.* a member of a monotheistic religion founded in Punjab in the 16th c., combining Hindu and Islamic elements. ● *adj.* of or relating to Sikhs or Sikhism. □ **Sikhism** /'si:kizəm, 'sık-/ *n.*

Siksika /sık'sıkə/ ● *n.* **1** a member of an Aboriginal people, part of the Blackfoot, living in central Alberta. **2** the Algonquian language of this people. ● *adj.* of or relating to this people.

silage /'saılədʒ/ *n.* green crops preserved by pressure esp. in a silo or occasionally in a stack.

silence ● *n.* **1** a absence of sound or noise. **b** the state or a period of this (*we sat in silence; there was an awkward silence before she spoke*). **2** abstinence from, or renunciation of, speech, esp. as a religious vow or payment of respect to a deceased person or group. **3** the avoidance of mentioning or discussing a particular topic or thing; reticence (*silence is golden*). **4** the inability to speak, esp. as a result of shock, surprise, fear, etc. (*she watched in stunned silence*). ● *v.tr.* **1** make quiet or silent (*silenced the alarm clock*). **2** defy (critics, detractors, arguments, etc.) by successfully defending one's position. **3** quell or disable (an esp. military opponent, their artillery, etc.). **4** prohibit or prevent (a person) from speaking, esp. to prevent the free expression of opinion. □ **reduce** (or **put**) **to silence** overwhelm with superior argument.

silenced *adj.* (of a gun) fitted with a silencer.

silencer *n.* **1** a device used to reduce the sound of a gun as it is fired. **2** anything used to reduce the noise or sound of something.

silent ● *adj.* **1** characterized by an absence of sound or noise. **2** characterized by an absence of speech; not talking (*a silent greeting*). **3** (of a person) taciturn; speaking little. **4** (of a speaker, writer, book, etc.) omitting mention or discussion of a particular subject; offering no account or record. **5** (of a movie or film etc.) not having a recorded soundtrack or audible dialogue, but usu. having dialogue represented in printed form onscreen. **6** *Med.* producing no detectable signs or symptoms (*silent coronary*). **7** (of a letter) written but not pronounced, e.g. *b* in *doubt*. **8** inactive, quiescent (*their guns were silent*). ● *n.* a silent movie or film. □ **silently** *adv.*

silent auction *n.* *N Amer.* an auction in which bids are submitted on cards during a specified period at the end of which all the bids are opened.

silent majority *n.* the presumed majority of people having moderate opinions but being too passive to assert them.

silent partner n. N Amer. a person who has capital in a partnership but takes no part in its activities.

silhouette /ˌsɪluːˈet/ ● n. **1** a portrait or representation of a thing showing the outline only, usu. done in solid black and placed on a white or contrasting background. **2** the dark shadow or outline of a person or thing against a lighter background. **3** the contour or outline of a garment or person's body. ● v.tr. (usu. in passive) show or represent in silhouette. □ **in silhouette** seen or placed in outline.

silica /ˈsɪləkə/ n. a hard mineral substance, silicon dioxide, occurring in many rocks, soils, and sands as flint, opal, or quartz, etc., used in the manufacture of glass and ceramics. □ **siliceous** /-ˈlɪʃəs/ adj.

silicate /ˈsɪləˌkət/ n. any of the many insoluble compounds of a metal combined with silicon and oxygen, including mica, feldspar, etc.

silicon /ˈsɪlɪkən/ n. a non-metallic element occurring abundantly in oxides and silicates, used in electronic components for its semiconducting properties, as well as in the manufacture of glass.

silicon chip n. a silicon microchip.

silicone /ˈsɪlɪˌkoːn/ n. any of the many polymeric organic compounds of silicon and oxygen used as electrical insulators, waterproofing agents, etc.

silicone implant n. = BREAST IMPLANT.

Silicon Valley n. an area with a high concentration of electronics industries, esp. the Santa Clara valley southeast of San Francisco.

silk n. **1** a fine lustrous soft strong fibre produced by silkworms in making cocoons. **2** a similar fibre spun by some spiders. **3 a** a thread or cloth made from silk fibre. **b** a thread or fabric resembling silk. **c** (attrib.) denoting articles of clothing made of silk (silk blouse). **4** (in pl.) garments made of silk, esp. a jockey's cap and jacket bearing the colours of the horse's owner. **5** the long silk-like filiform styles of an ear of corn. □ **silk-like** adj.

silken adj. **1** made of silk. **2** resembling silk, esp. in texture, softness, or lustre.

silk gland n. a gland secreting the substance produced as silk.

silk moth n. (in full **silkworm moth**) any of various large moths whose larvae spin silk cocoons, esp. of the families Saturniidae and Bombycidae, esp. Bombyx mori.

silkscreen ● n. **1** a screen of fine mesh used in screen printing. **2** the process of screen printing. **3** a print made by this process. ● v.tr. print, decorate, or reproduce using a silkscreen.

silk stocking n. **1** (often in pl.) a stocking made of silk. **2** (usu. attrib., **silk-stocking**) maintaining or suggesting a wealthy lifestyle (silk-stocking attire).

silkworm n. the caterpillar of the moth Bombyx mori, which spins its cocoon of silk.

silky adj. (**-ier**, **-iest**) **1** like silk in smoothness, softness, fineness, or lustre. **2** (of a person's manner, voice, etc.) suave, smooth. **3** Bot. (of leaves) covered with fine close-set hairs having a gloss and lustre like that of silk. □ **silkily** adv. **silkiness** n.

sill n. **1** a strong horizontal beam forming the base or foundation of esp. a house. **2** (in full **windowsill**) a horizontal shelf of wood, stone, or metal forming the bottom part of a window opening. **3** the bottom timber or lowest part of a door frame; a threshold. **4** any of the lower horizontal pieces forming the frame of a car or truck etc.

silly ● adj. (**-ier**, **-iest**) **1** displaying a lack of judgment or common sense; stupid, foolish. **2** absurd, ridiculous, laughable (she looked silly). **3** senseless, stupefied, dazed (we drank ourselves silly). ● n. (pl. **-ies**) informal a foolish person. □ **sillily** adv. **silliness** n.

silo /ˈsailo/ n. (pl. **-os**) **1** a tall cylinder or pit in which green corn or hay etc. is pressed and kept for fodder, undergoing fermentation. **2** a pit or tower for the storage of grain etc. **3** an underground chamber in which a guided missile is kept ready for firing.

silt ● n. fine sand, clay, or other soil carried by moving or running water and deposited as sediment on the bottom or on the shore of a lake or stream etc. ● v. **1** tr. & intr. (often foll. by up) fill or block, or be filled or blocked, with silt. **2** intr. flow, drift, or settle like silt; pass gradually. □ **siltation** n. **silty** adj.

Silurian /səˈlʊriən/ Geol. ● adj. of or relating to the third period of the Paleozoic era, lasting from about 438 to 408 million years BP, between the Ordovician and Devonian periods. ● n. this period.

silva var. of SYLVA.

silvan var. of SYLVAN.

silver ● n. **1** a greyish-white lustrous malleable ductile precious metallic element, occurring naturally as the element and in mineral form, and used chiefly with an admixture of harder metals for coin, plate, and ornaments, and in compounds for photography etc. **2** the colour of silver. **3** coins collectively; change. **4** utensils and vessels made of or plated with silver collectively, esp. cutlery. **5** household cutlery of any material. **6** = SILVER MEDAL. ● adj. **1** made wholly or chiefly of silver. **2** coloured like silver. **3** designating the twenty-fifth event of an esp. annual series (silver wedding anniversary). ● v.tr. **1** coat or plate with silver. **2** provide (mirror glass) with a backing of tin amalgam etc.

silverberry n. a silvery-leaved N American oleaster, Elaeagnus commutata.

silver birch n. a European birch, Betula pendula, with silver-coloured bark peeling in long strips.

silver buffalo berry n. see BUFFALO BERRY.

silver bullet n. informal a cure-all or universal remedy, esp. any usu. undiscovered highly specific and highly successful drug.

silver dollar n. = HONESTY 3.

silverfish n. (pl. same or **-fishes**) **1** any small silvery wingless insect of the order Thysanura, esp. Lepisma saccharina often found living in houses. **2** a silver-coloured fish, esp. a colourless variety of goldfish.

silver fox n. **1** a N American red fox at a time when its fur is black with white tips. **2** its fur or pelt.

silver-grey ● n. a pale or lustrous grey. ● adj. of this colour.

silvering n. **1** the act of plating or coating something with silver or an amalgam of tin etc. **2** silver plating.

silver lining n. a consolation or hopeful prospect in misfortune.

silver maple n. a maple of eastern N America, Acer saccharinum, with leaves that are silvery underneath.

silver medal n. a medal of silver, usu. awarded as second prize. □ **silver medallist** n.

silver plate n. **1** vessels or utensils made of or plated with silver or an alloy of silver. **2** the material of which these are made. □ **silver-plated** adj.

silver screen n. (usu. prec. by the) the movie industry; motion pictures collectively.

silversmith n. a person who works with silver; a manufacturer of silver articles. □ **silversmithing** n.

silver spoon n. **1** a spoon made of silver. **2** a sign of wealth or future prosperity (she was born with a silver spoon in her mouth).

silver thaw n. Cdn (Maritimes & Nfld) a slick coating of ice formed on the ground or an exposed surface, caused by freezing rain or a sudden light frost.

silvertip *n.* (in full **silvertip grizzly**) *Cdn (West)* a mature grizzly bear with white-tipped hairs esp. native to the Rocky Mountains.

silver-tongued *adj.* eloquent, persuasive.

silverware *n.* tableware, esp. utensils used for eating and serving, made of silver or an alloy of silver, or of a metal coated with silver, stainless steel, etc.

silvery *adj.* **1** like silver in colour or appearance. **2** having a clear gentle ringing sound. **3** (of the hair) white and lustrous. □ **silveriness** *n.*

silviculture *n.* the branch of forestry concerned with the growing and cultivation of trees. □ **silvicultural** *adj.* **silviculturist** *n.*

sim *n.* simulation.

simcha /'sɪmtʃə, -xə/ *n.* a Jewish party or celebration.

Simcoe Day *n. Cdn (S Ont.)* (esp. in Toronto) a civic holiday celebrated on the first Monday in August.

simian /'sɪmiən/ ● *adj.* **1** of or concerning the anthropoid apes. **2** characteristic of an ape or monkey (*a simian walk*). ● *n.* an ape or monkey.

similar *adj.* **1** of the same nature or kind; alike. **2** (often foll. by *to*) having a resemblance. **3** *Math.* (of two geometrical figures etc.) shaped alike; containing the same angles, having the same shape or proportions. □ **similarly** *adv.*

similarity *n.* (*pl.* **-ies**) **1** the state or fact of being similar; resemblance. **2** a point of resemblance.

simile /'sɪmɪli/ *n.* **1** a figure of speech involving the explicit comparison of two different things, often using the words 'like' or 'as', e.g. *as brave as a lion*. **2** the use of such comparison.

similitude /sɪ'mɪlə,tu:d; -tju:d/ *n.* **1** a comparison or the expression of a comparison. **2** the outward appearance or image of a person or thing. **3** the quality or state of being similar; similarity. **4** a person or thing resembling another; a counterpart.

Simmental /'sɪməntəl/ *n.* a breed of large red and white cattle farmed for both milk and meat.

simmer ● *v.* **1 a** *intr.* (of a liquid) be at a heat at or just below the boiling point; boil or bubble gently. **b** *tr.* cook (a liquid or foods immersed in liquid) at a temperature at or just below the boiling point. **2** *intr.* be in a state of suppressed anger or excitement. ● *n.* a simmering condition. □ **simmer down** become calm or less agitated.

simp *n. N Amer. informal* a simpleton.

simpatico /sɪm'pæti,ko/ *adj.* congenial, likeable.

simper ● *v.* **1** *intr.* smile in a silly or affected way. **2** *tr.* express by or with simpering. ● *n.* such a smile.

simple *adj.* **1** easily understood or done; presenting no difficulty (*a simple explanation; a simple task*). **2** not complicated or elaborate; without luxury or sophistication. **3 a** not compound; consisting of or involving only one element or operation etc. **b** *Grammar* (of a tense) formed without an auxiliary verb. **4** absolute, unqualified, straightforward (*the simple truth*). **5** foolish or ignorant; gullible, feeble-minded. **6** plain in appearance or manner; unsophisticated, ingenuous, artless. **7** not of high social standing; ordinary (*simple people*). **8** *Bot.* **a** consisting of one part. **b** (of fruit) formed from one pistil.

simple eye *n.* an eye of an insect, having only one lens.

simple fracture *n.* a fracture of the bone only, without a skin wound.

simple interest *n.* interest payable on a capital sum only (*compare* COMPOUND INTEREST).

simple machine *n.* any of the basic mechanical devices for applying a force, e.g. an inclined plane.

simple-minded *adj.* **1** feeble-minded, stupid, foolish. **2** ingenuous, unsophisticated. □ **simple-mindedly** *adv.* **simple-mindedness** *n.*

simple sentence *n.* a sentence with a single subject and predicate.

simpleton *n.* a foolish, gullible, or halfwitted person.

simplex /'sɪmpleks/ ● *adj.* **1** simple; not compounded. **2** *Computing* (of a circuit) allowing transmission of signals in one direction only. ● *n.* a simple or uncompounded thing, esp. a word.

simplicity *n.* the fact or condition of being simple. □ **be simplicity itself** be extremely easy.

simplify *v.tr.* (**-ies, -ied**) make simple; make easy or easier to do or understand. □ **simplification** *n.*

simplistic *adj.* **1** excessively or affectedly simple. **2** oversimplified so as to conceal or distort difficulties. □ **simplistically** *adv.*

simply *adv.* **1** in a simple manner. **2** absolutely; without doubt (*simply astonishing*). **3** merely.

simulacrum /,sɪmjo'leikrəm/ *n.* (*pl.* **-cra** /-krə/) **1** an image of something. **2 a** a shadowy likeness; a deceptive substitute. **b** mere pretense.

simulate *v.tr.* **1 a** pretend to have or feel (an attribute or feeling). **b** pretend to be. **2** imitate or counterfeit. **3 a** imitate the conditions of (a situation etc.), e.g. for training or amusement. **b** produce a computer model of (a process etc.). □ **simulated** *adj.* **simulation** *n.* **simulator** *n.*

simulcast /'saɪməl,kæst, sɪm-/ *n.* **1** a simultaneous transmission of the same program on radio and television, or on two or more channels, in two or more languages, etc. **2** *N Amer.* a live transmission of a sports event, esp. a horse race, for usu. off-track betting purposes. □ **simulcasting** *n.*

simultaneous /,saɪməl'teiniəs, ,sɪm-/ *adj.* (often foll. by *with*) occurring or operating at the same time. □ **simultaneity** /-tə'neiti/ *n.* **simultaneously** *adv.*

simultaneous translation *n.* oral translation from one language to another performed with a minimal time lapse between the original speech and the translation.

SIN /sɪn/ *abbr. Cdn* SOCIAL INSURANCE NUMBER.

sin[1] ● *n.* **1 a** the breaking of divine or moral law, esp. by a conscious act. **b** such an act. **2** the condition or state resulting from such transgression. **3** an action regarded as a serious offence or fault (*it's a sin to stay inside on a nice day like this*). ● *v.intr.* (**sinned, sinning**) **1** commit a sin. **2** (foll. by *against*) offend. □ **as sin** *informal* extremely (*ugly as sin*). **cover** (or **hide** etc.) **a multitude of sins** conceal the real, usu. unpleasant, facts or situation. **do** (or **be**) **something for one's sins** *jocular* do (or be) something as a supposed punishment for something. **live in sin** *jocular* live together in a sexual relationship without being married. □ **sinless** *adj.* **sinlessness** *n.*

sin[2] /sain/ *abbr.* sine.

sin bin *n. informal* **1** *Hockey* the penalty box. **2** a place set aside for offenders of various kinds.

since ● *prep.* throughout, or at a point in, the period between (a specified time, event, etc.) and the time present or being considered (*must have happened since yesterday; has been going on since June*). ● *conj.* **1** during or in the time after (*what have you been doing since we met?*). **2** for the reason that, because (*since you are drunk I will drive*). **3** (*ellipt.*) as being (*a more useful, since better designed, tool*). ● *adv.* **1** from that time or event until now or the time being considered (*have not seen them since*). **2** ago, before now (*long since forgotten*).

sincere *adj.* (**sincerer, sincerest**) **1** free from pretense or deceit; the same in reality as in appearance. **2** genuine, honest, frank. □ **sincerity** *n.*

sincerely *adv.* in a sincere manner. □ (**yours**) **sincerely** (also **sincerely yours**) a formula for ending a letter.

sine *n. Math.* **1** the trigonometric function that is equal to the ratio of the side opposite a given angle (in a right-angled triangle) to the hypotenuse. **2** a function of the line drawn from one end of an arc perpendicularly to the radius through the other.

sinecure /'sɪnə,kjʊr/ *n.* a position that requires little or no work but usu. yields profit or honour.

sine qua non /,sɪnei kwɒ 'nɒn, -'noːn/ *n.* an indispensable condition or qualification.

sinew /'sɪnjuː/ *n.* **1** tough fibrous tissue uniting muscle to bone; a tendon. **2** (in *pl.*) muscles; bodily strength. **3** (in *pl.*) something providing strength to an organization etc. □ **sinewy** *adj.*

sinful *adj.* **1** (of a person) committing sin, esp. habitually. **2 a** (of an act) involving or characterized by sin. **b** *informal* reprehensible. **3** *informal* self-indulgently delicious (*a sinful chocolate torte*). □ **sinfully** *adv.* **sinfulness** *n.*

sing ● *v.* (*past* **sang**; *past part.* **sung**) ¶The use of *sung* instead of *sang* for the past tense, as in *She sung three songs*, is non-standard. **1** *intr.* utter musical sounds with the voice, esp. words with a set tune. **2** *tr.* **a** utter or produce by singing. **b** perform (a role in an opera etc.). **3** *intr.* (of the wind, a kettle, etc.) make melodious, humming, buzzing, or whistling sounds. **4** *tr.* bring to a specified state by singing. **5** *intr. slang* turn informer; confess. ● *n.* an act or instance of singing (*carol sing*). □ **sing out** call out loudly; shout. □ **singable** *adj.* **singer** *n.* **singing** *n. & adj.*

sing. *abbr.* singular.

singalong *n.* an informal occasion when a group of people sing songs together (also *attrib.*).

Singaporean /,sɪŋə'pɔriən/ ● *adj.* of or relating to Singapore, a country in SE Asia. ● *n.* a native or inhabitant of Singapore.

singe ● *v.tr. & intr.* (**singeing**) burn superficially or lightly. ● *n.* a superficial burn.

singer-songwriter *n.* a person who sings and writes songs, esp. professionally.

Singh /sɪŋ/ *n.* **1** a surname adopted by male Sikhs initiated into the Khalsa. **2** a title adopted by the warrior castes of N India.

Singhalese *var. of* SINHALESE.

single ● *adj.* **1** one only, not double or multiple. **2** united or undivided. **3 a** designed or suitable for one person (*single bed*). **b** used or done by one person etc. or one set or pair. **4** one by itself; not one of several (*a single tree*). **5** regarded separately (*every single thing*). **6** not married; not involved in a romantic or sexual relationship. **7** (with *neg.* or *interrog.*) even one; not to speak of more (*did not see a single person*). **8** (of a flower) having only one circle of petals. **9** lonely, unaided. ● *n.* **1** a single thing, or item in a series. **2 a** a record, compact disc, etc., containing only one or two songs or other short pieces of music. **3** *Baseball* a one-base hit. **4** (usu. *in pl.*) a game with one player on each side. **5** an unmarried person (*young singles*). ● *v.* **1** *tr.* (foll. by *out* and often by *for, as*) select from a group as worthy of special attention, praise, etc. (*singled out for praise*). **2** *Baseball* **a** *intr.* hit a single. **b** *tr.* cause (a baserunner) to advance by hitting a single. **c** *tr.* (usu. foll. by *in*) cause (a run) to score by

hitting a single. □ **singlehood** *n.* (in sense 6 of *adj.*). **singleness** *n.* **singly** *adv.*

single-breasted *adj.* (of a coat etc.) having only one set of buttons and buttonholes, not overlapping.

single-digit *adj.* esp. *N Amer.* (of a quantity, value, or percentage) less than ten (*single-digit interest rates*).

single file ● *n.* a line of people or things arranged one behind another. ● *adv.* one behind another.

single-handed ● *adv.* **1** without help from another. **2** with one hand. ● *adj.* **1** done etc. single-handed. **2** for one hand. □ **single-handedly** *adv.*

single-issue *n.* (*attrib.*) designating a group, political platform, etc., characterized by an exclusive concern with one issue (*single-issue voters*).

single malt *n.* (often *attrib.*) a malt whisky from one distillery, not blended with any other malt.

single market *n.* an association of countries trading without restrictions, esp. in the EC.

single-minded *adj.* having or intent on only one purpose. □ **single-mindedly** *adv.* **single-mindedness** *n.*

single parent *n.* a person bringing up a child or children without a partner (also *attrib.*: *single-parent families*). □ **single parenthood** *n.*

single point *n. Cdn Football* = ROUGE *n.* 3.

singles bar *n.* a bar frequented by esp. single people seeking a sexual partner, potential spouse, etc.

single-seater *n.* a vehicle etc. with one seat.

single-sex *n.* (*attrib.*) of, for, or pertaining to males only or females only (*single-sex schools*).

single space *v.tr. & intr.* lay out or print (text) on consecutive lines. □ **single-spaced** *adj.*

singleton *n.* **1** the only card of a suit in a hand. **2 a** a single person or thing. **b** an only child. **3** a single child or animal born, not a twin etc.

single-use *attrib.adj.* designating something designed to be used only once (*a single-use camera*).

single-user *attrib.adj.* **1** having one user. **2** (of a computer system, software, etc.) designed to be used by one person at a time.

singsong ● *adj.* characterized by or uttered with a monotonous or rising and falling rhythm, cadence, or intonation. ● *n.* **1** a singsong manner. **2** *Cdn & Brit.* a singalong. □ **singsongy** *adj.*

singular ● *adj.* **1** unique; much beyond the average; extraordinary. **2** eccentric or strange. **3** *Grammar* (of a word or form) denoting or referring to a single person or thing. **4** *Math.* possessing unique properties. **5** single, individual. ● *n. Grammar* **1** a singular word or form. **2** the singular number. □ **singularly** *adv.*

singularity *n.* (*pl.* **-ies**) **1** the state or condition of being singular. **2** an odd trait or peculiarity.

Sinhalese /,sɪnhə'liːz, ,sɪnə'liːz/ ● *n.* (*pl.* same) **1** a member of a people originally from N India and now forming the majority of the population of Sri Lanka. **2** an Indic language spoken by this people. ● *adj.* of or relating to this people or language.

sinister *adj.* **1** suggestive of evil; looking malignant or villainous. **2** wicked or criminal (*a sinister motive*). **3** of evil omen. □ **sinisterly** *adv.*

sink ● *v.* (*past* **sank** or **sunk**; *past part.* **sunk**. ¶Although both *sank* and *sunk* are used as the simple past of *sink*, *sunk* is more informal and is best avoided in written text.) **1** *intr.* fall or come slowly downwards; drop. **2** *intr.* **a** go or penetrate below the surface esp. of a liquid. **b** (of a ship) go to the bottom of the sea etc. **3** *tr.* send (a ship) to the bottom of the sea etc. **4** *intr.* disappear below the horizon (*the sun is sinking*). **5** *intr.* settle down comfortably (*sank into a chair*). **6** *intr.* **a**

gradually lose strength or value or quality etc.; decline (*my heart sank*). **b** (of the voice) descend in pitch or volume. **c** (of a sick person) approach death. **d** gradually fall into a specified condition. **7** *tr.* cause or allow to sink or penetrate (*sank its teeth into my leg*). **8** *tr.* cause the failure of (a plan etc.) or the discomfiture of (a person). **9** *tr.* dig (a well) or bore (a shaft). **10** *tr.* engrave (a die) or inlay (a design). **11** *tr.* **a** invest (money). **b** lose (money) by investment. **12** *tr.* **a** cause (a ball) to enter a pocket in billiards, a hole at golf, a basket in basketball, etc. **b** achieve this by (a stroke, shot, etc.). **13** *tr.* overlook or forget; keep in the background (*sank their differences*). **14** *intr.* (of a price etc.) become lower. **15** *intr.* (of a storm or river) subside. **16** *intr.* (of ground) slope down, or reach a lower level by subsidence. **17** *intr.* (foll. by *on, upon*) (of darkness) descend (on a place). **18** *tr.* lower the level of. **19** *tr.* (usu. in *passive*; foll. by *in*) absorb; hold the attention of (*be sunk in thought*). ● *n.* **1** a fixed basin with a water supply and outflow pipe. **2** a place where foul liquid collects. **3** a place of vice or corruption. **4** a pool or marsh in which a river's water disappears by evaporation or percolation. **5** *Physics* a body or process used to absorb or dissipate heat. **6** = SINKHOLE 1. ☐ **sink in 1** penetrate or make its way in; be absorbed. **2** become gradually comprehended (*paused to let the words sink in*). **sink one's teeth into** take up (a challenge, cause, etc.) fervently or energetically. **sink or swim** fail totally or survive by one's own efforts. ☐ **sinkable** *adj.*

sinker *n.* **1** a person or thing which sinks. **2** a weight used to sink a fishing line or sounding line. **3** *Baseball* **a** = SINKERBALL. **b** a hit in which the ball drops markedly.

sinkerball *n. Baseball* a pitch in which the ball drops markedly. ☐ **sinkerballer** *n.*

sinkhole *n. esp. N Amer.* **1 a** a large circular depression in the ground, occurring e.g. as a result of the collapse of a subterranean cave. **b** a cavity in limestone etc. into which a stream etc. disappears. **2** *informal* a place of vice or corruption. **3** *informal* an enterprise etc. which seems to swallow all invested money to no effect.

sinking feeling *n.* a bodily sensation, esp. in the abdomen, caused by apprehension.

sinner *n.* a person who sins, esp. habitually.

Sinn Fein / ʃin 'fein/ *n.* an Irish movement founded in 1905, originally aiming at the independence of Ireland and a revival of Irish culture and language, now dedicated, as the political wing of the IRA, to the political unification of Northern Ireland and the Republic of Ireland. ☐ **Sinn Feiner** *n.*

Sino- / 'saino:/ *comb. form* Chinese; Chinese and (*Sino-American*).

Sino-Tibetan *n.* a language family comprising Chinese, Burmese, Tibetan, and (according to some scholars) Thai.

sin tax *n. N Amer. informal* a tax levied on cigarettes, liquor, etc.

sinuous / 'sinjʊəs / *adj.* **1** with many curves. **2** moving in a smooth, flowing way. ☐ **sinuously** *adv.*

sinus *n.* **1** a cavity of bone or tissue, esp. in the skull connecting with the nostrils. **2** *Med.* a fistula esp. to a deep abscess. **3** *Bot.* the curve between the lobes of a leaf.

Sion / 'saiən/ *var. of* ZION.

Siouan / 'su:ən/ ● *n.* an Aboriginal language family including Dakota, Sioux, and Omaha. ● *adj.* pertaining to or designating this language family.

Sioux / su:/ ● *n.* (*pl.* same) **1** a member of a group of N American Aboriginal peoples chiefly inhabiting the upper Mississippi and Missouri river basins. **2** the language of this group. ● *adj.* of or relating to these people or their language.

sip ● *v.tr. & intr.* (**sipped, sipping**) drink in one or more small amounts. ● *n.* **1** a small mouthful of liquid (*a sip of brandy*). **2** the act of taking this.

siphon / 'saifən/ ● *n.* **1** a pipe or tube used for conveying liquid from one level to a lower level, using the liquid pressure differential to force a column of the liquid up to a higher level before it falls to the outlet. **2** a bottle from which carbonated water is dispensed by allowing the gas pressure to force it out. **3** *Zool.* a tubular organ in an aquatic animal, esp. a mollusc, through which water is drawn in or expelled. ● *v.tr. & intr.* (often foll. by *off*) **1** conduct or flow through a siphon. **2** divert or set aside (funds etc.).

sipper *n.* **1** a person who sips. **2** *Cdn* a drink suitable for sipping. **3** a device, cup, etc., used for sipping.

sir *n.* **1** a polite, respectful, or formal form of address or mode of reference to a man. **2** (**Sir**) a titular prefix to the first name of a knight or baronet.

sire ● *n.* **1** the male parent of an animal, esp. of a domestic quadruped. **2** *archaic* a respectful form of address, esp. to a king. ● *v.tr.* (esp. of a male domestic quadruped) beget.

siree *interj.* (also **sirree**) *N Amer. informal* as an emphatic, esp. after *yes* or *no*.

siren ● *n.* **1 a** a device for making a loud prolonged signal or warning sound, esp. by revolving a perforated disc over a jet of compressed air or steam. **b** the sound made by this. **2** (in Greek mythology) each of a number of women or winged creatures whose singing lured unwary sailors on to rocks. **3** a sweet singer. **4 a** a dangerously fascinating woman; a temptress. **b** a tempting pursuit etc. **5** any of three eel-like aquatic N American amphibians of the family Sirenidae, with external gills, no hind limbs, and tiny forelimbs, found in the southeastern US. ● *adj.* irresistibly tempting (*the siren call of power*).

sirloin *n.* the choicer part of a loin of beef, from in front of the rump.

sirloin tip *n.* a cut of beef taken from the hip along the underside of the leg bone.

sis *n. informal* a sister.

sisal / 'saisəl/ *n.* **1** a Mexican plant, *Agave sisalana*, with large fleshy leaves. **2** the fibre made from this plant, used for ropes etc.

sis-boom-bah *N Amer.* ● *interj.* expressing support or encouragement, esp. to a sports team. ● *n.* enthusiastic or partisan support, esp. of spectator sports.

siskin *n.* any of various small streaked yellowish-green finches of the genus *Carduelis*, esp. the N American pine siskin *C. pinus*.

sissy *informal* ● *n.* (*pl.* **-ies**) an effeminate or cowardly person. ● *adj.* (**-ier, -iest**) effeminate; cowardly. ☐ **sissified** *adj.* **sissiness** *n.*

sister *n.* **1** a woman or girl in relation to sons and other daughters of her parents. **2 a** (often as a form of address) a close female friend or associate. **b** a female fellow member of a trade union, class, sect, or the human race. **3** (often as a form of address) a member of a female religious order. **4** (often *attrib.*) of the same type or design or origin etc. (*sister ship*). ☐ **sisterly** *adj.* **sisterliness** *n.*

sister city *n.* **1** a city that is twinned with another. **2** a city linked to another by proximity, common interests, etc. (*Dartmouth, Halifax's sister city*).

sisterhood *n.* **1** the relationship between sisters. **2 a** a society or association of women, esp. when bound by monastic vows or devoting themselves to religious or charitable work or the feminist cause. **b** its members collectively. **3** community of feeling and mutual support between women.

sister-in-law *n.* (*pl.* **sisters-in-law**) **1** the sister of one's wife or husband. **2** the wife of one's brother. **3** the wife of one's brother-in-law.

Sister of Charity *n.* = GREY NUN.

Sisyphean /ˌsɪsɪˈfiːən/ *adj.* endless and fruitless.

sit *v.* (**sitting**; *past* and *past part.* **sat**) **1** *intr.* adopt or be in a position in which the body is supported more or less upright by the buttocks resting on the ground or a raised seat etc., with the thighs usu. horizontal. **2** *tr.* cause to sit; place in a sitting position. **3** *intr.* **a** (of a bird) perch. **b** (of an animal) rest with the hind legs bent and the body close to the ground. **4** *intr.* (of a bird) remain on its nest to hatch its eggs. **5** *intr.* **a** be engaged in an occupation in which the sitting position is usual. **b** (of a committee, legislative body, etc.) be engaged in business. **c** (of an individual) be entitled to hold some office or position (*sat as a magistrate*). **6** *intr.* be positioned, placed, or situated (*sitting in fourth place*). **7** *intr.* (usu. foll. by *for*) pose in a sitting position (for a portrait). **8** *intr.* (foll. by *for*) be a Member of Parliament for (a constituency). **9** *intr.* be in a more or less permanent position or condition (esp. of inactivity or being out of use or out of place). **10** *intr.* (of clothes etc.) fit or hang in a certain way. **11** *tr.* keep or have one's seat on (a horse etc.). **12** *intr.* & *tr.* (esp. in *comb.*) take care of a baby, house, etc. while the parents, owners, etc. are away (*babysit*; *house-sit*). **13** *tr.* (esp. of a table) be large enough for (a designated number of seated people) (*sits six*). **14** esp. *N Amer. Sport* **a** *intr.* (often foll. by *out*) not participate in a game or games because of poor play, a suspension, etc. **b** *tr.* (of a player) not participate in (a game) or for (a specified period); not play for the duration of (a suspension) (*sat out half the season*). **c** *tr.* (often foll. by *out*) (of a coach etc.) keep (a player) from participating because of poor play etc. (*sat out the rookie*). **15** *intr.* (usu. in *neg.*) (of food) be settled in the stomach (*the chicken didn't sit right*). □ **be sitting pretty** be comfortably or advantageously placed. **make a person sit up** *informal* surprise or interest a person. **sit around** sit doing nothing, esp. while waiting. **sit at a person's feet** be a person's pupil. **sit at home** be inactive. **sit back** relax one's efforts. **sit by** look on without interfering. **sit down 1** sit after standing. **2** cause to sit. **sit heavy on the stomach** take a long time to be digested. **sit in 1** occupy a place as a protest. **2** (foll. by *for*) take the place of. **3** (foll. by *on*) be present as a guest or observer at (a meeting etc.). **sit in judgment** assume the right of judging others; be censorious. **sit on 1** be a member of (a committee etc.). **2** hold a session or inquiry concerning. **3** *informal* delay action about. **sit on one's hands** take no action. **sit out 1** take no part in (a dance etc.). **2** stay till the end of (esp. an ordeal). **sit tight** *informal* **1** remain firmly in one's place. **2** not be shaken off or move away or yield to distractions. **sit up 1** rise from a lying to a sitting position. **2** sit firmly upright. **3** stay awake and later than usual, esp. while waiting for someone (*sat up watching TV*). **4** *informal* become interested or aroused etc. **sit up and take notice** *informal* have one's interest aroused, esp. suddenly. **sit well** (often foll. by *with*; usu. in *neg.*) be acceptable or undisturbing to (*their decision did not sit well with her*). **sit well on** suit or fit.

sitar /sɪˈtɑr, ˈsɪtɑr/ *n.* a long-necked Indian lute with movable frets.

sitcom *n. informal* a situation comedy.

sit-down ● *adj.* **1** (of a meal) eaten sitting at a table. **2** (of a protest etc.) in which demonstrators occupy their workplace or sit on the ground in a public place. ● *n.* **1** a period of sitting. **2** a sit-down protest etc.

site ● *n.* **1** the ground chosen or used for a town or building. **2** a place where some activity is or has been conducted (*camping site*). **3** *Computing* a single source for files, services, etc. on the Internet (*visited several sites*). ● *v.tr.* **1** locate or place. **2** provide with a site.

site licence *n.* a licence granted by a software company to a business etc. to make and use a number of copies of a software program at a specified site.

site-specific *adj.* designed for or pertaining to a specific site (*a site-specific solution*).

sit-in *n.* a protest, strike, demonstration, etc. in which people occupy a workplace, public building, etc.

Sitka /ˈsɪtkə/ *n.* a fast-growing spruce, *Picea sitchensis*, native to western N America and yielding timber.

sitter *n.* **1** a person who sits, esp. for a portrait. **2 a** = BABYSITTER (*see* BABYSIT). **b** (esp. in *comb.*) a person who takes care of a house, pet, etc. while the owners are away (*house-sitter*).

sitting ● *n.* **1** a continuous period of being seated, esp. engaged in an activity (*finished the book in one sitting*). **2** a time during which an assembly is engaged in business. **3** a session in which a meal is served (*dinner will be served in two sittings*). **4** a period during which a law court, legislature, etc. holds sessions. ● *adj.* **1** having sat down. **2** (of a legislator, Member of Parliament, etc.) currently holding office. **3** (of an animal or bird) not running or flying. **4** (of a hen) engaged in hatching.

sitting duck *n.* (also **sitting target**) *informal* a person or thing that is very easy to attack.

sitting room *n.* a room in a house for relaxed sitting in.

situate *v.tr.* (usu. in *passive*) **1** put in a certain position or circumstances (*is situated at the top of a hill*). **2** establish or indicate the place of; put in a context.

situation *n.* **1** a place and its surroundings (*the house stands in a fine situation*). **2** a set of circumstances; a position in which one finds oneself; a state of affairs (*a difficult situation*). **3** an employee's position or job. **4** a critical point or complication in a drama. □ **situational** *adj.*

situation comedy *n.* a comedy, esp. on television, in which the humour derives from the situations the characters are placed in.

situationism *n.* the theory that human behaviour is determined by surrounding circumstances rather than by personal qualities. □ **situationist** *n.* & *adj.*

sit-up *n.* an exercise to strengthen the stomach muscles, in which a person lies with the back flat on the ground and lifts the torso into a sitting position.

sitz bath *n.* a bathtub formed like a chair for sitting in water up to the hips.

SIU *abbr.* SPECIAL INVESTIGATIONS UNIT.

Siwash /ˈsaɪwɒʃ/ *n. Cdn* (*West*) (in full **Siwash sweater**) a thick woollen sweater decorated with symbols or animals from Aboriginal mythology.

six ● *n.* **1** one more than five. **2** a symbol for this (6, vi, VI). **3** a size etc. denoted by six. **4** a set or team of six individuals. **5** six o'clock. **6** a card etc. with six pips. **7** *Cdn & Brit.* a group of six Brownies, Cubs, etc. **8** *informal* = SIX-PACK. ● *adj.* that amount to six. □ **at sixes and sevens** in confusion or disagreement. **six of one and half a dozen of the other** a situation of little real difference between the alternatives.

sixer *n. Cdn & Brit.* the leader of a group of six Brownies, Cubs, etc.

sixfold *adj. & adv.* **1** six times as much or as many. **2** consisting of six parts.

Six Nations *n.* the Iroquois confederacy after the Tuscarora joined in 1722.

six-pack *n.* a pack of six identical items, esp. cans or bottles of beer.

six-shooter *n.* (also **six-gun**) a revolver with six chambers.

sixteen ● *n.* **1** one more than fifteen. **2** a symbol for this (16, xvi, XVI). **3** a set of sixteen people or things. **4** a size etc. denoted by sixteen. ● *adj.* that amount to sixteen. □ **sixteenth** *adj., adv., & n.*

sixteenth note *n.* esp. *N Amer. Music* a note having the time value of half an eighth note and represented by a large dot with a two-hooked stem.

sixteenth rest *n. N Amer. Music* a rest having the time value of a sixteenth note.

sixth ● *n.* **1** the position in a sequence corresponding to that of the number 6 in the sequence 1-6. **2** something occupying this position. **3** any of six equal parts of a thing. **4** *Music* **a** an interval or chord spanning six consecutive notes in the diatonic scale, e.g. C to A. **b** a note separated from another by this interval. **5** *Baseball* the sixth inning. ● *adj.* that is the sixth. ● *adv.* in the sixth place; sixthly. □ **sixthly** *adv.*

sixth sense *n.* **1** a supposed faculty giving intuitive or extrasensory knowledge. **2** such knowledge.

sixty ● *n.* (*pl.* **-ies**) **1** the product of six and ten. **2** a symbol for this (60, lx, LX). **3** (in *pl.*) the numbers from 60 to 69, esp. the years of a century or of a person's life. **4** a set of sixty persons or things. **5** (**Sixty**) *Cdn* the parallel of latitude 60° north of the equator as forming the boundary between the western provinces to the south and the territories to the north (*living North of Sixty*). ● *adj.* that amount to sixty. □ **sixty-first, -second**, etc. the ordinal numbers between sixtieth and seventieth. **sixty-one, -two**, etc. the cardinal numbers between sixty and seventy. □ **sixtieth** *adj., adv., & n.*

sixty-fourth note *n. N Amer. Music* a note having the time value of half a thirty-second note and represented by a large dot with a four-hooked stem.

sixty-four thousand dollar question *n.* (also **sixty-four dollar question**) a difficult and crucial question.

sixty-fourth rest *n. N Amer. Music* a rest having the time value of a sixty-fourth note.

sixty-nine *n. slang* sexual activity between two people involving mutual oral stimulation of the genitals.

sizable *adj.* (also **sizeable**) large or fairly large. □ **sizably** *adv.*

size¹ ● *n.* **1** the relative bigness or extent of a thing; dimensions, magnitude. **2** each of the classes, usu. numbered, into which things otherwise similar, esp. garments, are divided according to size (*three sizes too big*). ● *v.tr.* sort or group in sizes or according to size. □ **of a size** having the same size. **of some size** fairly large. **the size of** as big as. **the size of it** *informal* a true account of the matter (*that is the size of it*). **size up 1** estimate the size of. **2** *informal* form a judgment of. □ **sized** *adj.* (also in *comb.*). **sizer** *n.*

size² ● *n.* a gelatinous solution used in glazing paper, stiffening textiles, etc. ● *v.tr.* glaze or stiffen with size.

sizzle ● *v.* **1** *a intr.* make a sputtering or hissing sound when or as if frying. **b** *tr.* fry or burn. **2** *intr. informal* **a** be in a state of great heat or excitement. **b** be salacious or risqué. ● *n.* **1** a sizzling sound. **2** *informal* intense heat or excitement. □ **more sizzle than steak**

N Amer. slang more flash than substance. □ **sizzler** *n.*

sizzling *adj. & adv.*

SJ *abbr.* Society of Jesus.

SK *abbr.* Saskatchewan (in postal use).

ska *n.* a style of popular music of Jamaican origin, with a fast tempo and strongly accentuated offbeat.

skag *n. slang* heroin.

skank ● *n.* **1** a steady-paced dance performed to reggae music, characterized by rhythmically bending forward, raising the knees, and extending the hands palms-downwards. **2** a piece of reggae music suitable for such dancing. ● *v.intr.* play reggae music or dance in this style.

skate¹ ● *n.* **1** each of a pair of boots with steel blades fixed to the bottom for gliding on ice. **2** = ROLLER SKATE. **3** = IN-LINE SKATE. **4** an act or period of skating. **5** a device on which a heavy object moves. ● *v.* **1** *a intr.* move on or as if on skates. **b** *tr.* perform (a specified figure, a routine, etc.) on skates. **2** *intr.* (foll. by *around*, *over*) refer fleetingly to, disregard. □ **hang up one's skates** *Cdn informal* retire from professional life. **skate on thin ice** *informal* behave rashly, risk danger, esp. by dealing with a subject needing tactful treatment. □ **skating** *n.*

skate² *n.* (*pl.* same or **-s**) any cartilaginous marine fish of the family Rajidae, with a roughly diamond-shaped body and a long thin tail.

skate³ *n. slang* a contemptible, mean, or dishonest person (*cheapskate*).

skate-a-thon *n.* esp. *Cdn* a prolonged period of skating, organized to raise money for a charity or cause.

skateboard ● *n.* a short narrow board mounted on roller skate wheels, used for riding on while standing, and propelled by one foot pushing occasionally against the ground. ● *v.intr.* ride on a skateboard. □ **skateboarder** *n.* **skateboarding** *n.*

skater *n.* **1** a person who skates. **2** *Hockey* a player other than the goalie. **3** a skateboarder.

skating rink *n.* **1** an area of ice for skating. **2** a building containing a rink for skating.

skedaddle *informal* ● *v.intr.* run away, depart quickly, flee. ● *n.* a hurried departure or flight.

skeet *n.* (also **skeet shooting**) a shooting sport in which a clay target is thrown from a trap to simulate the flight of a bird.

skeeter *n.* esp. *N Amer. & Austral. slang* a mosquito.

skeg *n.* **1** the after part of a vessel's keel or a projection from it. **2** a fin underneath the rear of a surfboard.

skein /skeɪn/ *n.* **1** a loosely coiled bundle of yarn or thread. **2** a cluster or arrangement resembling a skein. **3** a flock of wild geese etc. in flight.

skeletal *adj.* **1** of, forming, or resembling a skeleton. **2** very thin, emaciated. **3** consisting of only a bare outline or minimum. □ **skeletally** *adv.*

skeleton *n.* **1 a** a hard internal or external framework of bones, cartilage, shell, woody fibre, etc., supporting or containing the body of an animal or plant. **b** the dried bones of a human being or other animal fastened together in the same relative positions as in life. **2** the supporting framework or structure or essential part of a thing. **3** a very thin or emaciated person or animal. **4** the remaining part of anything after its life or usefulness is gone. **5** an outline sketch. **6** (*attrib.*) having only the essential or minimum number of persons, parts, etc. (*skeleton staff*). □ **skeletonic** /ˌskelə'tɒnɪk/ *adj.* **skeletonize** *v.tr.*

skeleton in the closet *n.* a discreditable or embarrassing fact kept secret.

skeptic ● *n.* **1** a person who doubts the validity of accepted beliefs in a particular subject. **2** a person who doubts the truth of Christianity and other religions. **3** a person who accepts the philosophy of skepticism. ● *adj.* = SKEPTICAL.

skeptical *adj.* **1** inclined to question the truth or soundness of accepted ideas, facts, etc. **2** *Philos.* of or accepting skepticism; denying the possibility of knowledge. □ **skeptically** *adv.*

skepticism *n.* **1** a skeptical attitude in relation to accepted ideas, facts, etc.; doubting or critical disposition. **2** *Philos.* the doctrine of the skeptics; the opinion that real knowledge is unattainable.

sketch ● *n.* **1** a rough, slight, merely outlined, or unfinished drawing or painting, often made to assist in making a more finished picture. **2** a brief account without many details conveying a general idea of something; a rough draft or general outline. **3 a** a very short play, usu. humorous and limited to one scene. **b** an item or scene in a comedy program. **4** a short descriptive piece of writing. ● *v.* **1** *tr.* make or give a sketch of. **2** *intr.* draw sketches esp. of landscape (*went out sketching*). **3** *tr.* (often foll. by *in*, *out*) indicate briefly or in outline.

sketchbook *n.* **1** (also **sketch pad**) a book or pad of drawing paper for doing sketches on. **2** a notebook containing preliminary pictorial, verbal, or musical sketches or studies. **3** (usu. as a title) a book containing narrative or descriptive essays.

sketchy *adj.* (**-ier, -iest**) **1** giving only a slight or rough outline, like a sketch. **2** unsubstantial or imperfect. □ **sketchily** *adv.* **sketchiness** *n.*

skew ● *adj.* oblique, slanting, set askew. ● *n.* a slant. ● *v.* **1** *tr.* make skew. **2** *tr.* depict or represent unfairly; distort. **3** *intr.* move obliquely; twist. □ **skewness** *n.*

skewer ● *n.* **1 a** a long metal or wooden pin for holding meat, vegetables, etc. compactly together while cooking. **b** the pieces of meat, vegetables, etc. of a kebab secured on such a pin. **2** any similar pin for fastening or securing something in place. ● *v.tr.* **1** fasten together or pierce with or as with a skewer. **2** esp. *N Amer.* criticize sharply.

ski ● *n.* (*pl.* **skis**) **1** each of a pair of long narrow pieces of wood etc., usu. pointed and turned up at the front, fastened under the feet for travelling over snow. **2** a similar device under a vehicle or aircraft. **3** = WATER SKI. **4** (*attrib.*) **a** of or pertaining to skis or skiing (*ski instructor*). **b** for wear when skiing (*ski boots*). ● *v.* (**skis, skied, skiing**) **1** *intr.* travel on skis. **2** *tr.* ski at (a place). □ **skiable** *adj.*

ski bum *n. slang* an avid skier, esp. one who spends a great deal of time skiing.

skid ● *v.* (**skidded, skidding**) **1** *intr.* (of a vehicle, wheel, or driver) slide on slippery ground, esp. sideways or obliquely. **2** *tr.* cause (a vehicle etc.) to skid. **3** *intr.* slip, slide. **4** *intr. informal* fail or decline or err. **5** *tr.* support or move or protect or check with a skid. **6** *N Amer. tr.* & *intr.* slide or haul (logs) down a prepared slide or along a skid trail or skid road. ● *n.* **1** the act or an instance of skidding. **2** a plank or roller on which a heavy object may be placed to facilitate moving. **3** a piece of wood etc. serving as a support, ship's fender, inclined plane, etc. **4** *N Amer.* each of a number of peeled and partially sunk logs or timbers forming a skid road. **b** = SKID ROAD 1. **5** a braking device, esp. a wooden or metal shoe preventing a wheel from revolving or used as a drag. **6** a runner beneath an aircraft for use when landing. **7** *N Amer. Sport informal* a losing streak. □ **grease the skids** *N Amer. informal* help make things run smoothly. **hit the skids**

informal enter a rapid decline or deterioration. **on the skids** *informal* in a steadily worsening state.

skidder *n. N Amer.* **1** a type of powerful four-wheel tractor used to haul logs from a cutting area. **2** a teamster who hauls logs from a cutting area.

skidding *n. N Amer.* the process of hauling logs from a cutting area.

Ski-Doo ● *n. proprietary* a snowmobile (also *attrib.*: *Ski-Doo trails*). ● *v.intr.* (**skidoo; -oos, -ooed**) **1** ride on a snowmobile. **2** (also **skiddoo**) *N Amer. slang* go away; depart. □ **skidooer** *n.* **skidooing** *n.*

Ski-doo suit *n.* = SNOWMOBILE SUIT.

skid road *n. N Amer.* **1** *hist.* a road formed of skids along which logs were hauled. **2** *hist.* a part of a town or city frequented by loggers. **3** = SKID ROW.

skid row *n. N Amer.* a part of a town or city frequented by vagrants, alcoholics, etc. □ **on skid row** destitute.

skid trail *n. N Amer.* a trail cut through the bush for hauling logs from a cutting area.

skidway *n. N Amer.* **1** a (usu. inclined) platform for piling logs before transportation or sawing. **2** = SKID ROAD 1. **3** an inclined ramp of planks or logs used for sliding boats etc. from a higher to a lower position or vice versa.

skier *n.* a person who skis.

skiff[1] *n.* any of various types of small light boat, esp. one adapted for rowing and sailing.

skiff[2] *n. N Amer.* a light dusting of snow.

skiing *n.* the activity or sport of moving on skis.

ski jump *n.* **1** an artificial structure consisting of a steep ramp levelling off at the end to allow a skier to leap through the air. **2** a jump executed from this. **3** a competition in which such jumps are made. □ **ski jumper** *n.* **ski jumping** *n.*

skilful *adj.* (also **skillful**) (often foll. by *at*, *in*) having or showing skill. □ **skilfully** *adv.* **skilfulness** *n.*

ski lift *n.* a device for carrying skiers up a slope, usu. on seats hung from an overhead cable.

skill *n.* **1** (often foll. by *in*) expertness, practised ability, facility in an action. **2** (usu. in *pl.*) a specific aptitude, esp. of a particular type (*management skills*).

skilled *adj.* **1** (often foll. by *in*) having or showing skill; skilful. **2** (of a person) highly trained or experienced. **3** (of work) requiring skill or special training.

skillet *n. N Amer.* a frying pan.

skim ● *v.* (**skimmed, skimming**) **1** *tr.* **a** take scum or cream or a floating layer from the surface of (a liquid). **b** take (cream etc.) from the surface of a liquid. **2** *tr.* keep touching lightly or nearly touching (a surface) in passing over. **b** *tr.* (or *intr.* foll. by *over*) deal with or treat (a subject) superficially. **3** *intr.* (often foll. by *over*, *along*) go lightly over a surface, glide along in the air. **4** *tr.* throw (a flat stone) low over water so that it bounces on the surface several times. **5 a** *tr.* read superficially, look over cursorily, gather the salient facts contained in. **b** *intr.* (usu. foll. by *through*) read or look over cursorily. **6** *tr. N Amer.* (often foll. by *off*) *slang* conceal or divert (earnings or takings, esp. from gambling) to avoid paying tax. ● *n.* **1** the act or an instance of skimming. **2** a thin covering on the surface of something, esp. a liquid (*skim of ice*). **3** = SKIM MILK. □ **skim the cream off** take the best part of.

ski mask *n.* a protective, usu. knitted covering for the head and face, with holes for the eyes, mouth, and sometimes the nose, originally worn by skiers.

skimmer *n.* **1** a device for skimming liquids. **2** a person who skims. **3** any long-winged marine bird of the genus *Rynchops* that feeds by skimming over water with its knifelike lower mandible immersed. **4** a hydroplane, hydrofoil, hovercraft, etc.

skim milk *n.* milk from which the cream has been skimmed.

skimp *v.* **1** *tr.* (often foll. by *on*) use or provide a meagre or insufficient amount of, stint (material, expenses, etc.). **2** *tr.* supply (a person etc.) meagrely with food, money, etc. **3** *tr.* do hastily or carelessly. **4** *intr.* be parsimonious.

skimpy *adj.* (**-ier, -iest**) **1** meagre; not ample or sufficient (*a skimpy budget*). **2** (of clothing) very short or revealing. ☐ **skimpily** *adv.* **skimpiness** *n.*

skin ● *n.* **1** the flexible continuous covering of a human or other animal body. **2 a** the skin of a flayed animal with or without the hair etc. **b** *esp. hist.* this used as a unit of value. **c** a material prepared from skins esp. of smaller animals (*opp.* HIDE² *n.* 1). **3** a person's skin with reference to its colour or complexion (*has a fair skin*). **4** an outer layer or covering, esp. the coating of a plant, fruit, or sausage. **5** a film on the surface of a liquid etc. **6** a container for liquid, made of an animal's whole skin. **7 a** the planking or plating of a ship or boat, inside or outside the ribs. **b** the outer covering of any craft or vehicle, esp. an aircraft or spacecraft. **8** *slang* a skinhead. **9** (usu. in *pl.*) a strip of sealskin or other material attached to the bottom of a ski to give traction when climbing slopes. **10** (usu. in *pl.*) *slang* a drum. **11** *see* SKINS GAME. ● *v.tr.* (**skinned, skinning**) **1 a** remove the skin from. **b** graze (a part of the body). **2** (often foll. by *over*) cover (a sore etc.) with or as with skin. **3** *slang* fleece or swindle. ● *adj.* of, depicting, or presenting pornographic material. ☐ **be skin and bone** be very thin. **by the skin of one's teeth** by a very narrow margin. **get under a person's skin** *informal* interest or annoy a person intensely. **have a thick** (or **thin**) **skin** be insensitive (or sensitive) to criticism etc. **no skin off one's nose** *informal* a matter of indifference or even benefit to one. **skin a person alive** used when threatening to punish someone severely. **to the skin** through all one's clothing (*soaked to the skin*). ☐ **skinless** *adj.* **skinned** *adj.* (also in *comb.*).

skin care *n.* care of the skin by use of cleansers, moisturizers, etc.

skin deep *adj.* (of an emotion, an impression, a quality, etc.) superficial, not deep or lasting.

skin diver *n.* a person who swims underwater without a diving suit, usu. in deep water with scuba equipment and flippers. ☐ **skin diving** *n.*

skinflint *n.* a miserly person.

skin graft *n.* **1** the surgical transplanting of skin. **2** a piece of skin transferred in this way.

skinhead *n.* a person, esp. a youth, with shaven or close-cropped hair worn as a symbol of anarchy, racism, or nonconformity.

skink *n.* any of numerous lizards of the family Scincidae, which have smooth elongated bodies, small heads, and limbs that are small or absent.

skinner *n.* **1** a person who skins animals or prepares skins. **2** a dealer in skins, a furrier. **3** = CATSKINNER.

skinny *adj.* (**-ier, -iest**) **1 a** (of a person) thin or emaciated. **b** (of an object) narrow, slim. **2** (of clothing) tight-fitting. **3** made of or like skin. ☐ **skinniness** *n.*

skinny-dipping *n.* esp. *N Amer. informal* swimming nude. ☐ **skinny-dip** *v.intr.* **skinny dip** *n.* **skinny dipper** *n.*

skins game *n. Sport* a form of golf, curling, bowling, etc., in which the winner of each hole, end, or frame is awarded a financial prize, or 'skin', with the value of the skin increasing as the game goes on.

skin test *n.* a test to determine whether an immune reaction is elicited when a substance is applied to or injected into the skin.

skin-tight *adj.* (of a garment) very close-fitting.

skip¹ ● *v.* (**skipped, skipping**) **1** *intr.* **a** a move along lightly, esp. by taking two steps with each foot in turn. **b** jump lightly from the ground, esp. so as to clear a skipping rope. **c** jump about, gambol, caper, frisk. **2** *intr.* (often foll. by *from, off, to*) move quickly from one point, subject, or occupation to another. **3** *tr.* omit in dealing with a series or in reading; miss (*always skips the small print; my heart skipped a beat*). **4** *tr. informal* **a** not attend or participate in (*skipped class*). **b** forgo; not have (*skipped breakfast*). **5** *tr. informal* depart quickly from; leave hurriedly (*skipped town*). **6** *intr.* (often foll. by *out, off*) *informal* make off, disappear. **7** *tr.* make (a stone) ricochet on the surface of water. **8** *intr.* (of a record or compact disc) play erratically because of a defect in the playing surface. **9** *tr.* **a** advance (a student) two or more grades. **b** (of a student) advance (two or more grades). ● *n.* **1** a skipping movement or action. **2** a defect in the playing surface of a record or compact disc which causes the needle or laser to jump forwards or backwards or to remain stuck, resulting in erratic playback. **3** *Computing* the action of passing over part of a sequence of data or instructions. **4** *N Amer. informal* a person who defaults or absconds. ☐ **skip it** *slang* abandon a topic etc. **skip off** *Cdn* (*S Ont*) play truant from school. **skip out** *Cdn* (*West*) = SKIP OFF. **skip rope** *N Amer.* play or exercise with a skipping rope.

skip² ● *n.* the captain of a curling or bowling team. ● *v.tr.* (**skipped, skipping**) be the skip of.

ski patrol *n.* a person or persons patrolling a ski area to check on the safety of skiers, monitor snow conditions, perform first aid, etc. ☐ **ski patroller** *n.*

skipjack *n.* (in full **skipjack tuna**) a small striped Pacific tuna, *Katsuwonus pelamis*, used as food.

ski pole *n.* either of two poles held by a skier to assist with balance, propulsion, and braking.

skipper¹ ● *n.* **1** the captain of a ship, esp. of a small trading or fishing vessel. **2** the captain of an aircraft. **3** the captain of a side in a game or sport. ● *v.tr.* act as captain of.

skipper² *n.* **1** a person who skips. **2** any brown thick-bodied butterfly of the family Hesperiidae, with a rapid, skipping flight.

skipping rope *n. Cdn & Brit.* a length of rope etc., usu. with handles at each end, revolved over the head and under the feet while jumping as a game or exercise.

skip rock *n. Curling* one of a rink's last two rocks of an end, usu. delivered by the skip.

skip tracer *n. N Amer.* a person or business that locates persons who are in default on payments. ☐ **skip tracing** *n.*

skirl ● *n.* the shrill sound characteristic of bagpipes. ● *v.intr.* make a skirl.

skirmish ● *n.* **1** a piece of irregular or unpremeditated fighting esp. between small or outlying parts of armies or fleets; a slight engagement. **2** a short argument or contest of wit etc. ● *v.intr.* engage in a skirmish. ☐ **skirmisher** *n.*

skirt ● *n.* **1** a woman's outer garment hanging from the waist. **2** the part of a dress, coat, etc. that hangs below the waist. **3** a piece of material fitting around the sides of a bed etc. to conceal the legs. **4** (in *sing.* or *pl.*) an edge, border, or extreme part. **5** *slang offensive* a woman regarded as an object of sexual desire. **6** a surface that conceals or protects the wheels or underside of a vehicle etc. ● v. **1** tr. go along or around or past the edge of. **2** tr. be situated along. **3** tr. avoid dealing with (an issue etc.). **4** intr. (foll. by along) go along the coast, a wall, etc. □ **skirted** adj. (also in comb.).

ski run n. a slope, trail, etc. prepared for skiing.

skit n. a light, usu. short, piece of satire or comedy.

skitter v.intr. **1 a** (usu. foll. by along, across) move lightly or hastily. **b** (usu. foll. by about, off) hurry about, dart off. **2** fish by drawing bait jerkily across the surface of the water.

skittery adj. skittish, restless.

skittish adj. **1** lively, playful. **2** (of a horse etc.) nervous, inclined to shy, fidgety. **3** fickle, changeable. □ **skittishly** adv. **skittishness** n.

skittle n. **1** a pin used in the game of skittles. **2** (in pl.; usu. treated as sing.) a game played with usu. nine wooden pins set up at the end of an alley to be bowled down usu. with wooden balls or a wooden disc.

skivvy ● n. (pl. **-ies**) **1 a** esp. Brit. informal derogatory a female domestic servant. **b** a person doing work considered menial or poorly paid. **2** (in pl.) N Amer. underwear, esp. men's underwear. ● v.intr. (**-ies, -ied**) informal work as a skivvy.

skookum /'sku:kəm/ esp. Cdn (West) ● adj. strong, brave. ● n. (esp. among Aboriginal peoples of the Northwest coast) an evil spirit.

skort n. N Amer. a pair of women's shorts for casual or semi-casual wear, with a flap of material draping the front, giving the appearance of a wraparound skirt.

skua /'skju:ə/ n. any of various large predatory seabirds of the family Stercorariinae, typically having brown or brown and white plumage and a strongly hooked bill, breeding in polar or cold regions, and with a habit of robbing other seabirds of food by forcing them to disgorge the fish they have caught.

skulduggery n. (also **skullduggery**) trickery; unscrupulous behaviour.

skulk v.intr. **1** move stealthily, lurk, or keep oneself concealed, esp. in a cowardly or sinister way. **2** stay or sneak away in time of danger. □ **skulker** n.

skull n. **1** the bony case of the brain of a vertebrate. **2 a** the part of the skeleton corresponding to the head. **b** this with the skin and soft internal parts removed. **c** a representation of this. **3** the head as the centre of thought or intelligence. □ **out of one's skull** slang **1** out of one's mind, crazy. **2** very drunk. □ **skulled** adj. (also in comb.).

skull and crossbones n.pl. a representation of a skull with two thigh bones crossed below, used formerly on the flags of pirate ships and now to warn of danger, e.g. on bottles of poison.

skullcap n. **1** a small close-fitting peakless cap. **2** the top part of the skull. **3** any plant of the genus Scutellaria, having a helmet-shaped calyx after flowering.

skunk ● n. **1 a** any of various cat-sized flesh-eating mammals of the family Mustelidae, esp. Mephitis mephitis having a distinctive black and white striped fur and able to emit a powerful stench from a liquid secreted by its anal glands as a defence. **b** its fur. **2** informal a thoroughly contemptible person. ● v.tr. N Amer. **1** slang defeat soundly. **2** (in cribbage) defeat (one's opponent) by a margin of at least 31 points.

skunk cabbage n. N Amer. either of two plants of the arum family, Lysichiton americanum of western N America or Symplocarpus foetidus of eastern N America, with an offensive-smelling spathe.

skunky adj. Cdn informal (of beer) foul-tasting, esp. as a result of exposure to light.

sky ● n. (pl. **skies**) (in sing. or pl.) **1** the region of the atmosphere and outer space seen from the earth. **2** the weather or climate evidenced by this. ● v.tr. (**skies, skied**) Baseball etc. hit (a ball) high into the air. □ **the sky is the limit** there is practically no limit. **to the skies** very highly; without reserve (praised to the skies). **under the open sky** out of doors.

sky blue ● n. a bright clear blue. ● adj. (**sky-blue**) of this colour.

skybox n. esp. N Amer. a private box situated near the top of a sports stadium or arena, from where the game or event may be viewed.

skydiving n. the sport of jumping from an aircraft and falling for as long as possible before opening one's parachute. □ **skydive** v.intr. **skydiver** n.

sky-high adv. & adj. very high (sky-high interest rates).

skyhook n. **1** Basketball a high-arcing throw, a lob. **2** a launching device for aircraft, satellites, etc. **3** Mountaineering a small flattened hook with an eye for attaching a rope etc. fixed temporarily into a rock face. **4** an imaginary or fanciful device for suspension in or attachment to the sky.

skylark ● n. a lark, Alauda arvensis of Eurasia and N Africa, that sings while hovering in flight. ● v.intr. play tricks or practical jokes; indulge in horseplay; frolic.

skylight n. an opening in a roof or ceiling, covered with glass, Plexiglas, etc., for letting in daylight. □ **skylighted** adj. **skylit** adj.

skyline n. **1** the outline of hills, buildings, etc., defined against the sky. **2** N Amer. Forestry an overhead cable for transporting logs.

skyrocket ● v.intr. (**-rocketed, -rocketing**) (esp. of prices etc.) rise very steeply or rapidly. ● n. a rocket firework exploding high in the air.

skyscraper n. a very tall building.

skyward ● adv. (also **skywards**) towards the sky. ● adj. moving skyward.

skyway n. esp. N Amer. **1** a route used by aircraft. **2** the sky as a medium of transport. **3** (also **skywalk**) a covered overhead walkway between buildings. **4** a long highly elevated section of highway, esp. one spanning water (Burlington Skyway).

skywriting n. legible smoke trails made by an airplane esp. for advertising. □ **skywriter** n.

slab ● n. **1** a flat broad fairly thick usu. square or rectangular piece of solid material, e.g. concrete or stone. **2** a large flat piece of cake, chocolate, etc. **3** an outer piece of wood sawn from a log. **4** a mortuary table. ● v.tr. (**slabbed, slabbing**) remove slabs from (a log or tree) to prepare it for sawing into planks.

slack ● adj. **1** not taut; not held tensely (slack rope; also in comb.: slack-jawed). **2** inactive or sluggish. **3** negligent or remiss. **4** (of tide etc.) neither ebbing nor flowing. **5** (of trade or business or a market) with little happening. **6** relaxed, languid. ● n. **1** the slack part of a rope etc. (haul in the slack). **2** a slack time in trade etc. **3** informal a period of inactivity or laziness. ● v. **1 a** tr. & intr. slacken. **b** tr. loosen (rope etc.). **2** intr. informal be lazy; shirk. ● adv. slackly. □ **slack off 1** loosen. **2** reduce activity, effort, speed, etc. **slack up** reduce the speed of a train etc. before stopping. **take** (or **pick**) **up the slack** use up a surplus or make up a deficiency; avoid an undesirable lull. □ **slackly** adv. **slackness** n.

slacken v.tr. & intr. make or become slack. □ **slacken off** = SLACK OFF (see SLACK).

slacker n. **1** a shirker; a lazy person. **2** such a person regarded as one of a large group or generation of (esp.

young) people who find themselves without direction in life.

slacks *n.pl.* trousers, esp. for informal wear.

slag ● *n.* **1** vitreous refuse left after ore has been smelted; dross separated in a fused state in the reduction of ore. **2** cellular lava, or fragments of it. ● *v.intr.* (**slagged, slagging**) **1** form slag. **2** cohere into a mass like slag. □ **slaggy** *adj.* (**-ier, -iest**).

slag heap *n.* a hill of refuse from a mine etc.

slain *past part. of* SLAY.

slake /sleik/ *v.tr.* **1** assuage or satisfy (thirst, revenge, etc.). **2** disintegrate (quicklime) by chemical combination with water.

slaked lime *n.* = LIME¹ *n.* 2.

slalom /ˈslɒləm/ *n.* **1** a downhill ski race on a zigzag course marked by artificial obstacles, usu. flags, and descended singly by each competitor in turn. **2** a similar obstacle race for canoeists, water skiers, skateboarders, etc. ● *v.intr.* (**slalomed, slaloming**) **1** perform or compete in a slalom. **2** make frequent sharp turns in or as in a slalom. □ **slalomer** *n.*

slam¹ ● *v.* (**slammed, slamming**) **1** *tr.* & *intr.* shut forcefully and loudly. **2** *tr.* put down (an object) with a similar sound. **3** *intr.* move violently (*he slammed out of the room*). **4** *tr.* & *intr.* put or come into sudden action (*slam the brakes on*). **5** *tr.* *slang* criticize severely. **6** *tr.* *slang* hit. **7** *tr.* *slang* gain an easy victory over. ● *n.* **1** a sound of or as of a slammed door. **2** the shutting of a door etc. with a loud bang. **3** (usu. prec. by *the*) *N Amer. slang* prison. **4** a criticism or insult. **5** = SLAM DUNK 1.

slam² *n. Cards* the winning of every trick in a game.

slam-bang ● *adv.* with the sound of a slam. ● *adj.* *informal* **1** impressive, exciting, or energetic. **2** noisy, violent.

slam-dancing *n. N Amer.* a form of dancing to rock music (originally at punk rock concerts) in which participants deliberately collide violently with one another. □ **slam-dance** *n.* & *v.intr.* **slam-dancer** *n.*

slam dunk ● *n.* **1** *Basketball* a forceful and often dramatic dunk shot. **2** a sure thing; an easy victory. ● *v.* (**slam-dunk**) **1** *Basketball* **a** *tr.* dunk (the ball) in a forceful, often dramatic manner. **b** *intr.* make a forceful, often dramatic dunk shot or shots. **2** *tr.* easily defeat (a person or thing). **3** *tr.* achieve (something) in a forceful, often dramatic way.

slammer *n.* esp. *N Amer. slang* **1** (usu. prec. by *the*) prison. **2** a slam-dancer.

slander ● *n.* **1** a malicious, false, and injurious statement spoken about a person. **2** the uttering of such statements. **3** *Law* false oral defamation (*compare* LIBEL *n.* 1). ● *v.tr.* utter slander about; defame falsely. □ **slanderer** *n.* **slanderous** *adj.* **slanderously** *adv.*

slang ● *n.* words, phrases, and uses that are regarded as very informal and are often restricted to special contexts or are peculiar to a specified profession, class, geographic area, etc. (*street slang*). ● *v.* **1** *tr.* use abusive language to. **2** *intr.* use such language (*engaged in a slanging match*).

slangy *adj.* (**-ier, -iest**) **1** of the character of slang. **2** fond of using slang. □ **slangily** *adv.* **slanginess** *n.*

slant ● *v.* **1** *intr.* slope; diverge from a line; lie or go obliquely to a vertical or horizontal line. **2** *tr.* cause to do this. **3** *tr.* (often as **slanted** *adj.*) present (information) from a particular angle esp. in a biased or unfair way. ● *n.* **1** a slope; an oblique position. **2** a way of regarding a thing; a point of view, esp. a biased one. ● *adj.* sloping, oblique. □ **slantwise** *adv.* **slanty** *adj.*

slap ● *v.* (**slapped, slapping**) **1** *tr.* & *intr.* strike with the palm of the hand or a flat object, or so as to make a similar noise. **2** *tr.* lay forcefully (*slapped the money on*

the table). **3** *tr.* put hastily or carelessly (*slap some paint on the walls*). **4** *tr.* (often foll. by *down*) *informal* reprimand or snub. **5** *tr. N Amer.* strike (the ball, puck, etc.) with a sharp slap. **6** *tr. N Amer.* punish with a fine, sentence, etc. (*slapped him with a three-game suspension*). ● *n.* **1** a blow with the palm of the hand or a flat object. **2** a slapping sound. ● *adv.* with the suddenness or effectiveness or true aim of a blow; suddenly, fully, directly (*ran slap into him*).

slapdash ● *adj.* hasty and careless. ● *adv.* in a slapdash manner.

slap-happy *adj. informal* **1** cheerfully casual or flippant. **2** punch-drunk.

slap in the face *n.* a rebuff or affront.

slap on the wrist *n.* a mild rebuke or reprimand.

slapshot *n. Hockey* a hard shot taken by raising the stick to waist height before striking the puck or ball.

slapstick *n.* **1** boisterous physical comedy, characterized by pratfalls etc. **2** a device consisting of two flexible pieces of wood joined together at one end, designed to produce a loud slapping noise, used esp. by a clown etc. to simulate the dealing of a hard blow.

slash ● *v.* **1** *intr.* make a sweeping or random cut or cuts with a knife, sword, whip, etc. **2** *tr.* make such a cut or cuts at. **3** *tr.* make a long narrow gash or gashes in. **4** *tr.* reduce (prices etc.) drastically. **5** *tr. Hockey* strike or swing at (an opponent) with the stick. **6** *tr.* censure vigorously. **7** *tr.* make (one's way) by slashing. **8** *tr.* **a** lash (a person etc.) with a whip. **b** crack (a whip). **9** *tr. N Amer.* clear (land) of vegetation; cut down (trees or undergrowth). ● *n.* **1 a** a slashing cut or stroke. **b** a wound or slit made by this. **2** an oblique stroke; a solidus. **3** *N Amer. Forestry* **a** debris resulting from the felling or destruction of trees. **b** an area in a forest strewn with such debris. **4** a severe or drastic reduction. **5** *Hockey* an act or instance of slashing.

slash-and-burn *adj.* **1** (of cultivation) in which vegetation is cut down, allowed to dry, and then burned off before seeds are planted. **2** (of a person, action, etc.) outstandingly aggressive or ruthless.

slasher *n.* **1** a person or thing that slashes. **2** (in full **slasher film, slasher movie**) a film depicting violent assault with a knife etc. **3** *Cdn* a form of circular saw with several blades, used to cut logs into predetermined lengths.

slashing ● *n. Hockey* the infraction of striking or swinging at an opponent with the stick. ● *adj.* vigorously incisive or effective.

slat *n.* **1** any thin narrow piece of wood, plastic, or metal, such as one of those found on a fence or Venetian blind. **2** (in *pl.*) *N Amer. informal* the buttocks. **3** (in *pl.*) *Cdn informal* skis. □ **slatted** *adj.*

slate ● *n.* **1** a fine-grained metamorphic sedimentary rock, typically dark grey, green, or bluish-purple in colour, characterized by splitting readily into flat smooth plates. **2** a piece of such a plate used as a tile esp. to cover a roof or pave a walkway. **3** a piece of such a plate, usu. framed in wood, formerly used for writing on. **4** a bluish-grey or bluish-purple colour. **5** *N Amer.* a list of nominees for election or appointment to an official post. **6** *Film* a board giving information about a shot, held in front of the camera so that the film can be identified later. **7** *informal* an agenda, schedule, or list (*what's on the slate for tonight?*). ● *v.tr.* **1** *N Amer.* (usu. foll. by *for, to*) make arrangements for (an event etc.); plan, schedule (*slated for demolition*). **2** *N Amer.* propose or nominate (a candidate or candidates) for a position, political office etc. **3** cover (a roof etc.) with slates. ● *adj.* **1** made of slate. **2** of the colour of slate. □ **wipe the slate clean** forgive or cancel the record of past offences. □ **slating** n.

slate-coloured adj. of a dark bluish, purplish, or greenish grey.

slather esp. N Amer. informal ● v.tr. **1** (often foll. by with) cover (a surface) with a large or excessive portion of a substance. **2** spread or smear (a substance) lavishly or excessively. ● n. (often in pl.) a large amount.

slattern n. **1** a promiscuous woman; a slut. **2** an untidy and slovenly woman. □ **slatternly** adj.

slaty adj. **1** resembling slate in colour, texture, or appearance. **2** characteristic of slate.

slaughter ● n. **1 a** the killing of an animal or animals for food. **b** (attrib.) designating animals that are intended or set aside to be killed for food (slaughter cattle). **2** the killing of a person or animal in a brutal or ruthless manner. **3** the killing of many people or animals at once or over a period of time, as in a war; massacre. ● v.tr. **1** kill (an animal) for food; butcher. **2** kill or murder (a person) in a ruthless or brutal manner. **3** kill large numbers of people at once or over a period of time. **4** informal defeat easily or by a wide margin. □ **slaughterer** n.

slaughterhouse n. a place where animals are butchered for food.

Slav ● n. a member of a group of peoples in Central and E Europe speaking Slavic languages. ● adj. of or relating to the Slavs or the Slavic languages.

slave ● n. **1** a person who is the legal property of another or others and is bound to absolute obedience. **2** a person working very hard, esp. without appropriate reward or appreciation; a drudge. **3** a person completely under the domination of or subject to a specified influence (he's a slave to his passions). **4** a willing devotee to a particular activity, cause, person, etc. (a slave to fashion). **5** a subsidiary part, esp. a device which is controlled by, or which follows the movements of, another. ● v. **1** intr. (often foll. by at, away, over) toil or work very hard. **2** tr. (foll. by to) subject (a device) to control by another.

slave-driver n. **1** a person who works others hard; a demanding and unyielding supervisor, employer, teacher, etc. **2** an overseer of slaves at work.

slaveholder n. a person who owns slaves. □ **slaveholding** n. & adj.

slave labour n. **1** arduous work assigned to slaves; forced labour. **2** slaves collectively. **3** gruelling or forced labour for which one receives little remuneration.

slaver[1] /'sleɪvər/ n. hist. **1** a ship used in the slave trade. **2** a person dealing in or owning slaves.

slaver[2] /'slævər/ ● n. **1** saliva running from the mouth. **2** drivel, nonsense. ● v.intr. **1** drool. **2** show excessive desire, eagerness, or obsequiousness.

slavery n. **1** the practice or institution of keeping slaves. **2** the condition or fact of being a slave. **3** any condition or practice similar to slavery, esp. involving rigorous service or labour with little reward.

slave trade n. hist. the business of procuring, transporting, and selling humans as slaves, esp. the transporting of African blacks to the US to be sold into slavery. □ **slave trader** n.

Slavey /'sleɪvi/ ● n. a member of a number of Dene Aboriginal groups living between Lake Athabasca and Great Slave Lake. **2** any of the Athapaskan languages spoken by the Slavey. ● adj. of or relating to this people.

Slavic (also **Slavonic**) ● adj. **1** of, pertaining to, or designating the branch of Indo-European languages including Russian, Polish, Ukrainian, and Czech. **2** pertaining to, characteristic of, or designating the Slavs. ● n. one of the Slavic languages or the Slavic languages collectively.

slavish adj. **1** befitting or characteristic of a slave; servile. **2** showing no attempt at originality or development (a slavish reproduction). **3** abject, base. □ **slavishly** adv.

slaw n. coleslaw.

slay v.tr. (past **slew**; past part. **slain**) **1** literary or jocular kill; fell; strike down (slay a dragon). **2** (in passive) esp. N Amer. murder; kill (a person) in a ruthless or violent manner (the victim was slain in the parking lot). **3** slang overwhelm with amusement (this joke will slay you). **4** jocular defeat or overthrow (esp. a person or institution characterized as evil).

slayer n. (usu. in comb.) **1** literary a person who kills or has killed mythological creatures, monsters, dragons, etc. **2** jocular a nemesis or conqueror, esp. of a person, institution, or thing portrayed as being evil.

slaying n. esp. N Amer. an act or instance of killing.

SLBM abbr. submarine-launched ballistic missile.

SLE abbr. systemic lupus erythematosus.

sleaze informal ● n. **1** sleazy material, conditions, or behaviour (the city's growing reputation for sleaze). **2** a person who behaves in a sleazy way. ● v.intr. move or prowl in a sleazy fashion, esp. with shady or indecent intentions.

sleazebag n. (also **sleazeball**) slang a sordid, despicable, or shady person.

sleazoid N Amer. slang ● n. a corrupt or vulgar person; a sleaze. ● adj. of a disreputable quality or nature.

sleazy adj. (**-ier, -iest**) **1** disreputable or corrupt. **2** sexually immoral or promiscuous. **3** filthy, grimy; dilapidated. **4 a** (of clothes, materials, etc.) thin or flimsy. **b** (of clothing) sexually revealing. □ **sleazily** adv. **sleaziness** n.

sled N Amer. ● n. **1** a low vehicle mounted on runners for conveying heavy loads or passengers over snow or ice, usu. drawn by horses, dogs, or people. **2** a similar but usu. smaller vehicle, or any of various devices made of moulded plastic, used esp. by children to coast down hills. **3** a snowmobile. **4** Cdn (North) a covered vehicle mounted on runners used to carry freight or crew as part of a cat train. ● v. (**sledded, sledding**) **1** intr. ride or race on a sled. **2** tr. convey or carry by sled.

sledder n. N Amer. a person who races or rides a sled or snowmobile.

sledding n. N Amer. **1** the activity or action of racing or riding a sled or snowmobile. **2** progress in any sphere of action (tough sledding).

sled dog n. N Amer. a dog trained to pull a sled, esp. as part of a team.

sledge[1] ● n. a sled. ● v.intr. & tr. travel or convey by sledge.

sledge[2] n. a sledgehammer.

sledgehammer ● n. **1** a large heavy hammer with a long handle used to break stone etc. **2** (attrib.) heavy-handed, unwieldy, excessive (a sledgehammer approach). ● v.tr. hit or break with or as if with a sledgehammer.

sleek adj. **1 a** (of hair, fur, or skin) having a smooth and shiny appearance. **b** (of a person or animal) having a shiny coat or hair. **c** having a well-groomed and healthy appearance. **2** smooth and polished in manners and behaviour; suave. **3 a** streamlined, smooth, aerodynamic (a sleek car). **b** contemporary, stylish (a sleek interior). □ **sleekly** adv. **sleekness** n.

sleep ● n. **1** the naturally recurring condition of rest and inactivity assumed by people and many animals, in which consciousness, response to external stimuli, and voluntary muscular action are largely suspended. **2** a period of sleep (*I need a sleep*). **3** *euphemism* a state resembling sleep, esp. death. **4** the prolonged inert condition of hibernating animals. **5** a condition assumed by many plants, esp. at night, marked by the closing of petals or folding of leaves. **6** a gummy secretion found in the corners of the eyes after sleep. **7** a function of some radios that allows them to remain on for a specified period of time before shutting off automatically. • *v.* (*past and past part.* **slept**) **1** *intr.* **a** be in a state of sleep. **b** achieve a state of sleep; fall asleep. **2** *intr.* (foll. by *with, together*) **a** have or share a sexual encounter. **b** have or share a sexual relationship. **3** *intr.* (foll. by *on*) postpone a decision on (a matter or question) until the next day. **4** *tr.* provide sleeping accommodation for (*sleeps six*). **5** *tr.* **a** (foll. by *off*) cure by sleeping (*slept off her hangover*). **b** (foll. by *away*) lose, waste, or spend in sleeping (*sleep the hours away*). **6** *intr.* be inactive or dormant (*trouble never sleeps*). **7** *intr.* (of a plant) have its flowers or leaves folded over in sleep. **8** *intr. euphemism* be at peace in death; lie buried. □ **get to sleep** manage to fall asleep. **go to sleep 1** achieve a state of sleep. **2** (of a limb) become numb as a result of prolonged pressure. **in one's sleep** while asleep. **let sleeping dogs lie** avoid stirring up trouble. **lose sleep over something** lie awake worrying about something. **put to sleep 1** kill (an animal) in a humane manner. **2** anaesthetize. **sleep around** *informal* be sexually promiscuous. **sleep in 1** remain asleep later than usual in the morning. **2** (esp. of domestic help) sleep on the premises where one is employed. **sleep like a log** (or **a baby** or **the dead**) sleep soundly. **the sleep of the just** sound sleep. **sleep out 1** sleep out of doors. **2** sleep away from the premises where one is employed. **sleep over** *N Amer.* spend the night at another's house. **sleep through 1** (esp. of a baby) sleep uninterruptedly through a period of time, usu. the night. **2** fail to be woken by (*slept through my alarm*). **sleep tight!** sleep well.

sleep apnea *n.* an interruption or cessation of breathing during sleep.

sleeper *n.* **1** a person that sleeps, esp. in a specified way. **2** a thing that is produced or introduced with little attention, fanfare, or promotion, but which turns out to be successful or popular (also *attrib.*: *sleeper hit*). **3** a sleeping car. **4** a berth in the cab of a truck or the sleeping car of a train etc. **5** (usu. in *pl.*) one-piece pyjamas for infants or children. **6** a strong usu. horizontal beam or timber used to support a wall or floorboards. **7** *N Amer.* a couch or chair that turns into a bed. **8** a spy or saboteur etc. who remains inactive while establishing a secure position.

sleeping bag *n.* a warm lined or padded body-length bag, usu. having a zipper down one side and the bottom, designed for sleeping in esp. outdoors or when camping etc.

sleeping car *n.* a railway car provided with beds or berths for passengers to sleep in on overnight trips.

sleeping pill *n.* a sedative taken to induce sleep.

sleeping platform *n.* *Cdn* (*North*) the bench or ledge for sleeping left around the inside of an igloo.

sleeping sickness *n.* **1** a tropical African disease caused by the protozoans *Trypanosoma gambiense* and *T. rhodesiense*, which are transmitted by tsetse flies and proliferate in the blood vessels, ultimately affecting the central nervous system and leading to lethargy and death. **2** = ENCEPHALITIS LETHARGICA.

sleepless *adj.* **1** without sleep (*many sleepless nights*).

2 unable to sleep. **3** continually active or moving. □ **sleeplessly** *adv.* **sleeplessness** *n.*

sleepover *n.* esp. *N Amer.* an occasion of spending the night away from home, esp. (of children) at a friend's house or party.

sleepwalk *v.intr.* walk or perform other actions in one's sleep, as if one were awake. □ **sleepwalker** *n.*

sleepwear *n.* clothing worn to bed.

sleepy *adj.* (**-ier, -iest**) **1** drowsy; ready for sleep; about to fall asleep. **2** given to sleep; lazy, indolent. **3** lacking activity or bustle; quiet, tranquil (*a sleepy little town*). **4** suggestive of or conducive to sleep (*her soft sleepy voice*). □ **sleepily** *adv.* **sleepiness** *n.*

sleepyhead *n.* (esp. as a form of address) a sleepy or inattentive person.

sleet *n.* precipitation in the form of melting snow, freezing rain, or a mixture of these. □ **sleety** *adj.*

sleeve *n.* **1** the part of a shirt or jacket etc. that wholly or partly covers the arm. **2** the paper or cardboard envelope used to protect a record. **3** any tubular piece of plastic or metal etc. resembling a sleeve, used esp. to cover or protect a rod or shaft etc. of a similar shape and size. □ **roll up one's sleeves** prepare to fight or work. **up one's sleeve** concealed but ready for use; in reserve. □ **sleeved** *adj.* (also in *comb.*). **sleeveless** *adj.*

sleigh esp. *N Amer.* • *n.* a sled, esp. a large one drawn by horses and used to convey passengers over snow and ice. • *v.intr.* travel on a sleigh. □ **sleighing** *n.*

sleigh bell *n.* any of a number of small bells attached to a sleigh or to the harness of a horse drawing a sleigh.

sleight of hand / sloit / *n.* **1** manual dexterity, esp. in performing a trick or magic. **2** a particular display of this, esp. a magic trick. **3** a cunning manoeuvre, scheme, or deception.

slender *adj.* (**slenderer, slenderest**) **1** (of a person, a person's body, etc.) gracefully thin (*a slender waist*). **2** of small girth or width in proportion to length or height (*a slender post*). **3** relatively small; slight, meagre, inadequate (*slender resources*). □ **slenderly** *adv.* **slenderness** *n.*

slept *past and past part.* of SLEEP.

sleuth *informal* • *n.* a detective or investigator. • *v.* **1** *intr.* act as a detective. **2** *tr.* investigate, research.

slew[1] *v.* **1** *intr.* (often foll. by *around*) turn or swing around, esp. without moving from a position. **2** *intr.* skid or slide uncontrollably. **3** *tr.* turn or swing (a thing) around; send toppling or spinning.

slew[2] *past of* SLAY.

slew[3] *n.* esp. *N Amer. informal* (usu. foll. by *of*) a large number or quantity.

slew[4] *N Amer. var. of* SLOUGH[1].

slice • *n.* **1** a thin broad piece or wedge cut off or out of an item of food. **2** a share; a part taken, allotted, or gained (*a slice of the profits*). **3** *Baseball, Golf, & Tennis* **a** the flight of a ball that has been struck from underneath producing a spin that causes it to drift or curve forward and away from the person hitting it. **b** a swing or stroke producing such an effect. **c** a ball hit in this way. **4** a dessert that is cut into small squares for serving. **5** a cut or incision (*the blade left a deep slice in my hand*). • *v.* **1** *tr.* (often foll. by *up*) cut into slices. **2** *tr.* (foll. by *off*) cut (a piece) off. **3** *intr.* (foll. by *into, through*) **a** make a cut or incision with a knife or other sharp object. **b** penetrate or cut through as if with something sharp; move quickly and effortlessly through (*the boat sliced through the water*). **4** *tr. Baseball, Golf, & Tennis* **a** strike (the ball) so that it deviates away from the person hitting it or (in baseball) into the opposite field. **b** *intr.* (of a ball) drift or deviate away from the hitter. □ **slicer** *n.* (also in *comb.*).

sliced *adj.* **1** cut cleanly into slices. **2** (of food) sold already cut into slices. □ **the best** (or **greatest**) **thing since sliced bread** *informal* the most wonderful thing to happen, be discovered, etc., in a long time.

slice of life ● *n.* a movie, play, incident, etc. that offers a realistic representation of everyday life. ● *adj.* (usu. **slice-of-life**) realistic, unembellished.

slick ● *adj.* **1 a** (of a person) clever, artful, skilful, crafty. **b** (of an action) deftly or skilfully executed (*a slick performance*). **2 a** (of a person) superficially smooth or suave; flattering and insincere. **b** shallow in spite of its appearance; plausible but insincere. **3 a** smooth and glossy; sleek (*slick photo*). **b** (often foll. by *with*) slippery (*the road was slick with ice*). ● *n.* **1 a** a patch or stretch of oil or ice etc., esp. floating on a body of water. **b** a smooth patch on the surface of a fast-moving body of water. **2** a smooth tire having little or no tread, used for racing. **3** *N Amer.* a magazine with a glossy finish. **4** *N Amer. slang* a slick person, esp. a cheat or swindler. ● *v.tr. informal* **1** (often foll. by *up*) smarten or tidy up; make sleek. **2** (usu. foll. by *back, down*) flatten (one's hair etc.). □ **slickly** *adv.* **slickness** *n.*

slicker *n.* esp. *N Amer.* **1** a raincoat of oilskin, rubber, plastic, etc., usu. in a bright colour. **2** *informal* = CITY SLICKER.

slide ● *v.* (*past* and *past part.* **slid**) **1** *intr.* move along a smooth surface while in continuous contact with it through the same part. **2** *tr.* cause (a person or thing) to move across or down a surface while maintaining continuous contact with it. **3** *intr.* move or pass smoothly, quietly, easily, etc. (*she slid into the room*). **4** *tr.* (often foll. by *into*) slip or move (a thing) dexterously, quietly, or unobtrusively (*slid his hand into mine*). **5** *intr.* *Baseball* dive headfirst or throw one's body feet first across the field, esp. in order to reach a base or make a catch. **6** *intr.* decline or decrease (*the dollar slid half a cent today*). **7** *intr.* pass or fall gradually into a particular state (*began to slide into depression*). **8** *intr. informal* take its own course (*let it slide*). ● *n.* **1** an act or instance of sliding. **2** a structure with a smooth sloping surface down which people, esp. children, may slide for amusement, e.g. at a playground, swimming pool, etc. **3** a rapid decline or deterioration. **4** a photographic negative or transparency mounted on a thin plastic or cardboard frame, usu. placed in a projector to be shown on a screen. **5** *Baseball* an instance of sliding to reach a base or make a catch. **6** esp. *N Amer.* **a** the falling of mud, snow, ice, etc. down the side of a slope or mountain; a landslide or avalanche. **b** the material that has fallen in this way. **7 a** a steel or glass tube worn by a guitarist and placed across the frets of a guitar in order to achieve a bluesy effect (*compare* BOTTLENECK 3). **b** (also **slide guitar**) a style of blues guitar playing in which a slide or bottleneck is moved across the strings, producing a glissando effect. **8** *Cdn* a track or slope prepared with snow or ice for tobogganing. **9** a slip of glass on which an object is mounted or placed for examination under a microscope. **10** (in full **timber slide**) *Cdn* an artificial sluice way made to assist the passage of logs downstream past obstructions such as rapids or falls. **11** a part of a machine or mechanism that slides, esp. on a firearm. **12** a bed, track, or groove etc. on or in which something may slide. **13** *Music* a curved sliding part on a brass wind instrument used to alter the length of the air column and thus change the pitch. □ **let things slide** be negligent; allow deterioration.

slide projector *n.* a projector used to display photographic slides on a screen.

slider *n.* **1** a part or device that slides. **2** *Baseball* a fast pitch that breaks sharply over the plate in front of the batter, curving away from the direction in which it was thrown.

slide rule *n.* a device consisting of two rulers, one of which slides along the length of the other, both graduated logarithmically and used to make fast calculations, esp. multiplication and division.

slide show *n.* a presentation supplemented by or based on a series of photographic slides.

sliding door *n.* a door that is drawn on a track across an opening instead of swinging on hinges.

sliding scale *n.* a scale of fees, taxes, etc., that varies in accordance with variation of some standard.

slight ● *adj.* **1** small in quantity or degree; barely perceptible (*a slight increase*). **2** of little significance, importance, or value (*a slight acquaintance*). **3** slender (*slight of build*). **4** insubstantial, weak (*slight fabric*). **5** (in *superlative*, with *neg.* or *interrog.*) any whatever (*wasn't the slightest bit interested*). ● *v.tr.* treat or speak of (a person etc.) with disrespect or a lack of courtesy; snub. ● *n.* a marked display of disregard or disrespect. □ **slightingly** *adv.* **slightly** *adv.*

slim ● *adj.* (**slimmer, slimmest**) **1** of small girth or thickness; of long narrow shape. **2** (of a person) of thin or slender build; not fat. **3** poor, meagre (*a slim chance; slim pickings*). **4** (of clothing) cut on slender lines (*a slim skirt*). **5** reduced to an economical or efficient size, level, etc. (*a slim budget*). ● *v.tr. & intr.* (**slimmed, slimming**) (often foll. by *down*) make or become slim or slimmer; reduce in size or extent. □ **slimly** *adv.* **slimness** *n.*

slime ● *n.* **1** thick slippery mud or any soft substance of a similar consistency, esp. when considered noxious or unpleasant. **2** a viscous mucous secretion exuded by fish, snails, slugs, etc. **3** *N Amer. slang* = SLIMEBALL. ● *v.tr.* cover with or as if with slime.

slimeball *n.* *slang* a filthy, corrupt, morally degenerate, or despicable person; a sleaze.

slime mould *n.* a slime-like aggregate of small simple organisms that reproduce by means of spores, found esp. in damp habitats on land.

slim jim *n.* a long flat bar with a hooked end used to unlock a car door without using a key.

slimline *adj.* of sleek and slender design.

slimy *adj.* (**-ier, -iest**) **1** of the consistency of slime. **2** covered, smeared with, or full of slime. **3** disgustingly or offensively foul or dishonest. **4** slippery; hard to hold. □ **slimily** *adv.* **sliminess** *n.*

sling ● *n.* **1** a strap, rope, etc., in the form of a loop, in which an object may be raised, lowered, or suspended. **2** a bandage looped around the neck to support an injured arm. **3** a simple weapon for throwing stones etc. consisting of a loop of leather or other material in which a missile is whirled and then released. **4** a rope or net used to raise and lower cargo, esp. to or from a ship. **5** a pouch or frame supported by a strap around the neck or shoulders for carrying a young child. **6** a drink consisting usu. of gin diluted with water or soda and lemon juice and usu. sweetened. ● *v.tr.* (*past* and *past part.* **slung**) **1** hurl or cast from, or as if from, a sling. **2** *informal* speak or utter (insults, criticism, etc.). **3** hang or allow to hang, esp. loosely or sloppily; carry (*a bag slung over her shoulder*). **4** hoist or transfer (cargo etc.) with a sling. □ **have one's ass in a sling** *N Amer.* be in trouble. **sling beer** *slang* work as a bartender. **sling hash** (or

plates) *N Amer. slang* work as a chef or server in a restaurant.

slingback *n.* a woman's shoe with an open back held in place by a strap above the heel.

slinger *n.* **1** *N Amer. informal* a person who serves food or drinks in a bar or restaurant. **2** a person who operates a sling to hoist cargo. **3** (usu. in *comb.*) a person who uses or carries etc. a specified thing (*gunslinger*).

slingshot *n.* *N Amer.* a Y-shaped frame supporting an elastic used to launch a small rock or projectile.

slink *v.intr.* (*past* and *past part.* **slunk**) (often foll. by *off*, *away*, *by*) **1** move or sneak away inconspicuously as if ashamed, embarrassed, timid, or guilty. **2** walk or move in a provocative, seductive, or alluring manner.

slinky *adj.* (**-ier, -iest**) **1** attempting to be inconspicuous, esp. in a sly or cowardly manner. **2** moving in an alluring or seductive manner. **3** (of clothes) close-fitting; provocative. □ **slinkily** *adv.* **slinkiness** *n.*

slip¹ ● *v.* (**slipped, slipping**) **1** *intr.* **a** slide unintentionally (*her finger slipped on the trigger*). **b** lose one's footing or balance by sliding inadvertently. **2** *intr.* go or move easily with a sliding motion (*the bolt slipped into place*). **3** *intr.* **a** fall from one's hand or through one's fingers by being slippery or hard to hold. **b** escape restraint or capture by sneaking or running away. **c** pass or elapse quickly, fleetingly, or without notice (*the years slip by*). **4** *intr.* (often foll. by *out*) **a** make a brief or unnoticed exit. **b** be expressed or revealed inadvertently (*the truth slipped out*). **5 a** *intr.* (usu. foll. by *up*) make a careless or casual mistake. **b** *intr.* fall below the normal standard, deteriorate, lapse (*her marks are slipping*). **c** *tr.* lose or fall behind by (a number of points, positions, etc.) in a standing or total (*the stock exchange slipped 26 points today*). **6** *tr.* insert or transfer stealthily or casually (*she slipped him a note*). **7** *tr.* **a** detach, release from restraint (*slipped the dog from the leash*). **b** release (the clutch of a car or truck etc.) for a moment. **8 a** *tr.* (foll. by *on*, *off*) pull (an article of clothing) on or off quickly. **b** *intr.* (foll. by *into*) change into (an article of clothing). **9** *tr.* escape from (*it slipped my mind*). **10** *tr. Med.* suffer the dislocation of (a joint) or the herniation of (an intervertebral disc). **11** *tr.* move (a stitch) to the other needle without knitting it. ● *n.* **1** the act or an instance of slipping. **2** an accidental or slight error. **3 a** an article of lingerie usu. made of a slippery material, suspended by straps over the shoulder and extending to the hemline of a dress or skirt. **b** = HALF-SLIP. **4 a** an artificial slope of stone etc. on which boats are landed. **b** *N Amer.* a space at a dock or between two piers where a boat may be kept. **c** an inclined structure on which ships are built or repaired. **5** a pillowcase. □ **give a person the slip** escape from or evade a person. **let slip 1** accidentally utter or reveal or disclose (information, a secret, the truth, etc.). **2** allow (an opportunity) to pass without taking advantage of it. **let slip through one's fingers 1** drop; lose hold of. **2** miss the opportunity of having. **slip away** (or **off**) depart without leave-taking etc. **slip of the tongue** (or **pen**) a small mistake in which something is said (or written) unintentionally.

slip² ● *n.* **1 a** a small piece of paper esp. for writing on. **b** a small piece of paper with information printed on it (*sales slip*; *withdrawal slip*). **2** a long and narrow piece; a strip (*a slip of land*). **3** an esp. young person of a small or slender build (*a slip of a girl*). **4** a cutting taken from a plant for grafting or planting. ● *v.tr.* take (a cutting or slip) from a plant.

slip³ *n.* a mixture of clay and water used to attach decorations etc. to pottery or to coat ceramics.

slipcase *n.* a close-fitting case for a book or set of books that allows the spine or spines to remain visible. □ **slipcased** *adj.*

slipcover *N Amer.* ● *n.* a removable cover for a chair, couch, etc. or for a furniture cushion. ● *v.tr.* cover (furniture) with a slipcover.

slip-knot *n.* **1** a knot that can be undone by pulling one end. **2** a running knot.

slip-on ● *adj.* (of shoes or clothes) that can be easily slipped on and off. ● *n.* a shoe without laces or straps etc.

slippage *n.* **1 a** the act or an instance of slipping. **b** the amount or extent of this. **2** a falling away from a standard; a decline. **3** the difference between expected and actual output of a mechanical system.

slipped disc *n.* = HERNIATED DISC.

slipper *n.* **1** a light loose comfortable shoe meant to be worn indoors. **2** a light, slip-on, heelless shoe for dancing etc. □ **slippered** *adj.*

slippery *adj.* **1** difficult to hold firmly because of smoothness, wetness, sliminess, or elusive motion. **2** (of a horizontal surface) difficult to stand on or move on without slipping due to its smoothness, wetness, muddiness, etc. **3** (of a subject) requiring tactful handling. **4** (of a concept etc.) difficult to grasp or comprehend due to its complexity. **5** unreliable, unscrupulous, shifty. □ **slipperiness** *n.*

slippery elm *n.* **1** the N American red elm, *U. rubra*. **2** (also **slippery elm bark**) the inner bark of this.

slippery slope *n.* an irreversible course leading to disaster.

slippy *adj.* (**-ier, -iest**) *informal* slippery. □ **slippiness** *n.*

slipshod *adj.* **1** careless, unsystematic, esp. in working or in handling ideas or words. **2** shabby, untidy.

slipstream *n.* **1** a current of air or water driven back by a revolving propeller or a moving vehicle. **2** an assisting force regarded as drawing something along with or behind something else.

slip-up *n. informal* a mistake or blunder.

slipway *n.* a slip for building ships or landing boats.

slit ● *n.* **1** a long straight narrow incision. **2** a long narrow opening comparable to a cut. ● *v.tr.* (**slitting**; *past* and *past part.* **slit**) **1** make a slit in. **2** cut into strips. □ **slit one's eyes** squint. □ **slit-like** *adj.* **slitted slitty** *adj.* (**-ier, -iest**)

slither ● *v.intr.* **1** slide or slip with an unsteady movement, esp. from side to side or in different directions. **2** move along in a way similar to this, esp. with the body close to the ground. **3** move or go stealthily; sneak. ● *n.* a slithering movement. □ **slithery** *adj.*

sliver ● *n.* **1** a usu. long thin piece that has been split, broken, or sliced off a larger one. **2** a sharp fragment of wood, glass, metal, etc. **3** (foll. by *of*) a small amount (*a sliver of reality*). ● *v.tr. & intr.* **1** break off as a sliver. **2** break up into slivers. □ **slivered** *adj.*

slivovitz /ˈslɪvəvɪts/ *n.* a dry slightly bitter colourless plum brandy made esp. in Romania and Serbia.

slob *n.* **1** *informal* an untidy, lazy, or fat person. **2** (in full **slob ice**) *Cdn* sludgy masses of densely packed sea ice. □ **slobbish** *adj.* **slobby** *adj.*

slobber ● *v.intr.* **1** let saliva or food run from the mouth, esp. while eating. **2** (foll. by *over*) **a** be too attentive or overaffectionate towards a person. **b** be excessively sentimental or enthusiastic about a thing. ● *n.* saliva running from the mouth. □ **slobbery** *adj.*

sloe *n.* **1** the fruit of the blackthorn, a small blue-black drupe with a sharp sour taste. **2** the black-thorn, *Prunus spinosa*.

slog ● *v.* (**slogged**, **slogging**) **1** *intr.* (often foll. by *away*, *on*) work hard or steadily at something. **2** *intr.* walk or move steadily with great effort or toil. **3** *tr.* & *intr.* hit hard. ● *n.* **1 a** hard, steady work or effort. **b** a period of this. **2** a long, tiring walk or march. **3** a vigorous blow. □ **slog it out** fight or struggle until a conclusion is reached.

slogan *n.* a word or phrase that is easy to remember, used by a political party or in advertising etc. to attract people's attention or suggest an idea quickly.

sloganeer ● *v.intr.* devise or use slogans. ● *n.* one who devises or uses slogans. □ **sloganeering** *n.*

slo-mo *n. informal* = SLOW MOTION.

sloop *n.* a small, one-masted, fore-and-aft-rigged ves-sel with mainsail and jib.

slop ● *v.* (**slopped**, **slopping**) **1** (often foll. by *over*) **a** *intr.* (of a liquid) run, flow, or spill over the edge of a container, vessel, etc. **b** *tr.* splash or spill (a liquid etc.). **2** *tr.* spill or splash liquid on (clothes, the floor, etc.). **3** *intr.* walk or wander through a wet or muddy place. ● *n.* **1** a puddle or mess of spilled or splashed liquid. **2** unappetizing or poorly cooked food. **3** (in *sing.* or *pl.*) semi-liquid food for pigs, esp. the remains of food intended for people. **4** (in *pl.*) liquid household waste matter, such as the contents of a chamber pot or dirty dishwater. **5** *informal* weakly sentimental language. □ **slop about** move about in a slovenly manner.

slop bucket *n.* (also **slop pail**) a bucket for remov-ing waste from a kitchen etc.

slope ● *n.* **1** a piece of rising or falling ground. **2** a place for skiing on the side of a hill or mountain. **3** an upward or downward inclination; an inclined posi-tion or direction. **4 a** a difference in level between the two ends or sides of a thing (*a slope of 5 metres*). **b** the rate at which this increases with distance etc. ● *v.* **1** *intr.* lie obliquely, esp. downwards; have or follow a slope; slant. **2** *tr.* place or arrange or make in a sloping position. □ **hit the slopes** go skiing. □ **sloped** *adj.*

slo-pitch *n.* N *Amer.* a modified form of baseball in which the batter has three chances to hit a softball that is lobbed by the pitcher and must land within a circle encompassing the plate.

sloppy *adj.* (**-ier**, **-iest**) **1** careless, slipshod. **2** splashed with liquid. **3** untidy. **4** (of the ground, sidewalk, etc.) wet with rain or slush. **5** (of clothes) loose; baggy. **6** (of a substance) in a semi-liquid state, having a muddy consistency. **7** (of a thought or com-ment etc.) overly sentimental or emotional. □ **sloppily** *adv.* **sloppiness** *n.*

sloppy joe *n.* N *Amer.* a sandwich consisting of a thick filling made with ground beef and tomato or barbe-cue sauce served on a bun.

slosh ● *v.* **1** *intr.* (often foll. by *around*, *about*, etc.) move with a splashing sound. **2** *tr. informal* **a** pour (liquid) clumsily. **b** pour or spill liquid on. **3** *tr.* splash (liquid) onto or over a surface. ● *n.* **1 a** an instance of splash-ing or sloshing. **b** the sound of this. **2** slush, sludge. □ **sloshy** *adj.*

sloshed *adj. slang* drunk.

slot ● *n.* **1** a slit, groove, channel, or long opening into which something fits. **2** a slit or other opening in a machine for a coin or credit card etc. to be inserted. **3 a** a position to be filled in a schedule, order, or timetable. **b** an allotted place in a broadcasting schedule. **4** *Hockey* an unmarked area in front of the net considered an excellent shooting position for an offensive player. **5** (often *attrib.*) designating a screw-driver with a straight flat blade used for inserting

and removing slotted screws. **6** *informal* = SLOT MACHINE. **7** *Computing* = EXPANSION SLOT. ● *v.* (**slotted**, **slotting**) **1** *tr.* & *intr.* place or be placed into or as if into a slot. **2** *tr.* provide with a slot or slots.

slotback *n.* N *Amer. Football* **1** either of two offensive players lining up in the backfield between the offen-sive linemen and wide receivers, usu. to catch short passes. **2** this position.

sloth / slɒθ / *n.* **1** laziness or indolence; reluctance to make an effort. **2** any slow-moving nocturnal mam-mal of the family Bradypodidae or Megalonychidae of S America, having long limbs and hooked claws for hanging upside down from branches of trees. **3** *informal* a lazy or indolent person.

slot machine *n.* a coin-operated gambling machine, activated by a lever, that produces random combina-tions of symbols which must match for the player to win.

slotted *adj.* **1** having a slot or slots. **2** (of a screw) having a narrow slot on the head so that it may be turned with a slot screwdriver.

slotted spoon *n.* a large serving spoon with holes or slots in its bowl, used for draining liquid from food.

slouch ● *v.* **1** *intr.* stand or sit with the back, shoul-ders, and neck bent or drooping forwards. **2** *intr.* walk or move with a shuffling gait and slouching posture. **3** *tr.* bend one side of the brim of (a hat) downwards (*opp.* COCK 3). **4** *intr.* droop or hang down loosely. ● *n.* **1** (usu. with *neg.*) *informal* a useless or incompetent per-son or performer esp. of a particular task or pursuit (*she's no slouch at golf*). **2** a slouching posture or move-ment; a stoop. **3** a downward bend of a hat brim. □ **slouchy** *adj.* (**-ier**, **-iest**).

slough[1] / slu:, slaʊ / *n.* **1** an area of soft miry ground; a swamp or quagmire. **2** / slu: / *Cdn* (*West*) & *US Northwest* a small marshy pool or lake produced by rain or melt-ing snow flooding a depression in the soil. **3** *Cdn* (*BC*) a shallow inlet or estuary lined with grass. □ **sloughy** *adj.*

slough[2] / slʌf / ● *n.* **1** a part that an animal sheds, esp. a snake's skin. **2** a layer of dead tissue, such as a scab, that will fall away from the skin. **3** a thing that is cast off, abandoned, or discarded. ● *v.* **1** *tr.* (often foll. by *off*) shed, remove, or cast off (skin, tissue, etc.). **2** *tr.* (often foll. by *off*) (of skin, tissue, etc.) come away; drop or fall off. **3** *intr.* (of a snake etc.) cast off or shed the skin. **4** *intr.* (foll. by *off*) get rid of or abandon something (*sloughed off his complaints*). □ **sloughy** *adj.*

Slovak / ˈsloːvæk / ● *n.* **1** (also **Slovakian**) an inhabitant of Slovakia, a country in central Europe. **2** the official language of Slovakia. ● *adj.* (also **Slovakian**) of or relating to Slovakia or Slovakians.

sloven / ˈslʌvən, ˈslʌv- / *n.* **1** a person who is habitually untidy or careless. **2** *Cdn* (*Maritimes* & *Nfld*) a long low wagon esp. drawn by horses.

Slovenian / sləˈviːniːən / (also **Slovene** / ˈsloːviːn /) ● *n.* **1** an inhabitant of Slovenia, a country in SE Europe. **2** the official language of Slovenia. ● *adj.* of or relat-ing to Slovenia, its language, or people.

slovenly *adj.* **1** (of a person, the appearance, habits, etc.) careless, untidy, negligent. **2** (of an action etc.) characterized by a lack of care or precision; unmethodical. □ **slovenliness** *n.*

slow ● *adj.* **1 a** taking a relatively long time to do a thing or cover a distance (also foll. by *of*: *slow of speech*). **b** not quick; acting or moving or done without speed. **2** gradual; obtained over a length of time (*slow growth*). **3** not producing, allowing, or conducive to speed (*in the slow lane*). **4** (of a clock etc.) showing a time earlier than is the case. **5** (of a person) not understanding readily; not learning easily. **6** dull; uninteresting; tedious. **7** slack or sluggish (business is slow). **8** (of a fire or oven) not giving relatively much or the required heat. **9** Photog. **a** (of a film) needing long exposure. **b** (of a lens) having a small aperture. **10 a** reluctant; tardy (not slow to defend himself). **b** not hasty or easily moved (slow to take offence). **11** (of a sports field, racetrack, ice surface, etc.) not allowing quick movement of players, the ball, puck, etc. (the field was slow after the rain). ● adv. **1** at a slow pace; slowly. **2** (in comb.) (slow-moving traffic). ¶The use of slow as an adverb is standard in compounds such as slow-acting, slow-burning. It is also established in short imperative expressions such as go slow, but in sentences such as he drives too slow and go as slow as you can, slowly is preferable in formal contexts. ● v. (usu. foll. by down, up) **1** intr. & tr. reduce one's speed or the speed of (a vehicle etc.). **2** intr. reduce one's pace of life. **3** intr. & tr. become or cause to be slow (business is slowing down). □ **slow but** (or **and**) **sure** (or **steady**) achieving the required result eventually. □ **slowish** adj. **slowly** adv. **slowness** n.

slow burn n. (often hyphenated when attrib.) slowly mounting intensity, esp. of anger or annoyance. □ **slow-burning** adj.

slow cooker n. a large electric pot used for cooking stews etc. very slowly.

slow dance v.intr. N Amer. dance to soft music in the embrace of a partner.

slowdown n. **1** the action of slowing down. **2** a form of industrial action in which employees deliberately work slowly.

slow motion n. (often hyphenated when attrib.) **1** the technique of making or playing a film or video recording so that actions and movements appear to be slower than in real life. **2** the simulation of this in real action; motion of slower speed than normal.

slow-pitch n. N Amer. = SLO-PITCH.

slowpoke n. N Amer. a slow or lazy person, driver, etc.

slow-release attrib.adj. designating a drug, fertilizer, etc. that releases a substance slowly or intermittently so as to maintain a steady concentration.

slow-witted adj. slow to understand, learn, etc.; unintelligent. □ **slow-wittedness** n.

SLt abbr. Cdn SUB-LIEUTENANT.

sludge n. **1** thick greasy mud, mire, ooze, etc. **2** muddy or slimy sediment, as in the bed of a river etc. **3** a precipitate in a sewage tank. **4** Mech. an accumulation of dirty oil, esp. formed as waste in any of various industrial and mechanical processes. **5** Geol. sea ice newly formed in small pieces. **6** (usu. attrib.) a muddy colour (sludge green). □ **sludgy** adj.

slue var. of SLEW¹.

sluff N Amer. var. of SLOUGH².

slug¹ ● n. **1 a** a small shell-less mollusc of the class Gastropoda often destructive to plants. **b** informal a slow or lazy person or thing. **2 a** a bullet esp. of irregular shape. **b** a missile for an air gun. **3** a drink, esp. of liquor; a swig. **4** a thick piece or lump of something. **5** N Amer. a small circular piece of metal used as a counterfeit coin, esp. in machines. ● v. **1** intr. (usu. foll. by around, along) move slowly or sluggishly; trudge. **2** tr. drink (esp. alcohol) quickly.

slug² ● n. N Amer. ● v.tr. (**slugged, slugging**) **1** strike with a hard blow. **2** Baseball hit (esp. a home run). ● n. a hard blow. □ **slug it out 1** fight it out. **2** stick it out.

slugfest n. esp. N Amer. informal **1** a violent or intense fight or quarrel. **2 a** a boxing match in which the boxers throw many punches. **b** a baseball game in which many runs are scored, esp. many home runs.

sluggard n. a lazy sluggish person.

slugger n. **1** a person who delivers heavy blows, esp. a boxer. **2** a baseball player noted for hitting powerful home runs.

sluggish adj. slow-moving; lacking energy (feel sluggish). □ **sluggishly** adv. **sluggishness** n.

sluice ● n. **1** (also **sluice gate**) a sliding gate or other contrivance for controlling the volume or flow of water. **2** (also **sluiceway**) a channel or waterway controlled by means of a sluice or sluices. **3** (also **sluice box**) N Amer. & Austral. an artificial water channel fitted with grooves esp. for washing ore. **4** the act or an instance of rinsing. **5** the water above or below or issuing through a floodgate. ● v. **1** tr. provide or wash with a sluice or sluices. **2** tr. rinse, pour or throw water freely upon. **3** tr. (foll. by out, away) wash out or away with a flow of water. **4** tr. flood with water from a sluice. **5** intr. (of water) rush out from a sluice, or as if from a sluice.

slum ● n. **1** an overcrowded and squalid district etc., usu. in a city and inhabited by very poor people. **2** a house or building unfit for human habitation. ● v.intr. (**slummed, slumming**) **1** put up with less comfortable conditions, associate with persons of a lower social class, or frequent venues of a lower status etc. than one is used to. **2** live in slumlike conditions. **3** go about the slums through curiosity, to examine or experience the condition of the inhabitants. □ **slummy** adj. (**-ier, -iest**).

slumber ● v.intr. **1** sleep, esp. in a specified manner. **2** be idle, drowsy, or inactive. ● n. a sleep, esp. of a specified kind (fell into a fitful slumber). □ **slumberous** adj. **slumbrous** adj.

slumber party n. N Amer. a party for youngsters (esp. girls) who stay and sleep overnight.

slum clearance n. the demolition of slums and rehousing of their inhabitants.

slumlord n. N Amer. a landlord who rents slum property to tenants.

slump ● n. **1** a sudden severe or prolonged fall in prices or values of commodities or securities. **2** a sharp or sudden decline in trade or business usu. bringing widespread unemployment. **3** a reduction in performance; a state of lessened productivity etc. (the team has been in a slump). ● v.intr. **1** undergo a slump; fail; fall in price. **2** (often foll. by back, down) sit or fall heavily or limply (slumped into a chair). **3** lean or subside.

slumped adj. hunched or slouched.

slung past and past part. of SLING.

slunk past and past part. of SLINK.

slur ● v. (**slurred, slurring**) **1** tr. & intr. pronounce or write indistinctly so that the sounds or letters run into one another. **2** tr. Music **a** perform (a group of two or more notes) legato. **b** mark (notes) with a slur. **3** tr. (usu. foll. by over) pass over (a fact, fault, etc.) lightly. ● n. **1** an insult, aspersion, or disparaging remark; an imputation of wrongdoing (a slur on my reputation). **2** the act or an instance of slurring in pronunciation, singing, or writing. **3** Music a curved line to show that two or more notes are to be sung to one syllable or played or sung legato.

slurp ● v.tr. & intr. drink or eat noisily, esp. producing a sucking or lapping noise. ● n. **1** the sound of this. **2** a slurping gulp. □ **slurpy** adj.

slurry n. (pl. **-ies**) **1** a semi-liquid mixture of fine particles and water; thin mud. **2** thin liquid cement.

slush n. **1** partially melted snow or ice. **2** watery mud. **3** silly sentiment. **4** N Amer. a confection consisting of flavoured slushy ice. **5** *slang* unsolicited manuscripts received by a publisher.

slush fund *n.* reserve funding esp. as used for political bribery.

slushy ● *adj.* (**-ier, -iest**) **1** like slush; watery. **2** *informal* sentimental; mawkish. ● *n.* (*pl.* **-ies**) *N Amer.* = SLUSH 4. □ **slushiness** *n.*

slut *n.* *derogatory* a promiscuous woman. □ **sluttish** *adj.*

sly *adj.* (**slyer, slyest**) **1** cunning; crafty; wily. **2 a** (of a person) practising secrecy or stealth. **b** (of an action etc.) done etc. in secret. **3** hypocritical; ironical. **4** playfully mischievous; roguish. **5** knowing; arch; bantering; insinuating. □ **on the sly** privately; covertly. □ **slyly** *adv.* **slyness** *n.*

SM *abbr.* Sergeant Major.

Sm *symbol* samarium.

S/M *abbr.* = S&M.

smack ● *n.* **1** a sharp slap or blow esp. with the palm of the hand or a flat object. **2** a hard hit in baseball etc. **3** a loud kiss. **4** a loud sharp sound. **5** a noisy parting of the lips in eager anticipation or enjoyment. **6** (foll. by *of*) **a** a flavour; a taste that suggests the presence of something. **b** (in a person's character etc.) a barely discernible quality (*just a smack of greed*). **c** (in food etc.) a very small amount (*a smack of ginger*). **7** a single-masted sailboat for coasting or fishing. **8** *slang* a hard drug, esp. heroin, sold or used illegally. ● *v.* **1** *tr.* strike sharply, as with an open hand, a bat, etc. **2** *tr.* part (one's lips) noisily in eager anticipation or enjoyment of food or another delight. **3** *tr. & intr.* hit, move, propel, etc., with a smack. **4** *intr.* (foll. by *of*) **a** have a flavour of; taste of (*smacked of garlic*). **b** suggest the presence or effects of (usu. something undesirable) (*it smacks of nepotism*). ● *adv. informal* **1** with a smack. **2** suddenly; directly; violently (*landed smack on my desk*). **3** exactly (*smack in the centre*).

smacker *n.* (also **smackeroo**) *slang* **1** a loud kiss. **2** *N Amer.* one dollar.

small ● *adj.* **1 a** not large or big. **b** not large in comparison with others of the same kind (*a small city*). **2** slender; thin. **3** not great in importance, amount, number, strength, or power. **4** not much; trifling (*a small token*). **5** insignificant; unimportant (*a small matter*). **6** consisting of small particles (*small gravel*). **7** doing something on a small scale (*small businesses*). **8** socially undistinguished; poor or humble. **9** petty; mean; ungenerous; paltry (*a small spiteful nature*). **10** young; not fully grown or developed (*a small child*). **11** lower case. ● *n.* **1** the slenderest part of something. **2 a** a garment etc. of a size suited for people smaller than average. **b** a small serving of a beverage or food that is sold in more than one size. ● *adv.* into small pieces (*chop it small*). □ **be small potatoes** be insignificant. **feel** (or **look**) **small** be humiliated; appear mean or humiliated. **in a small way** unambitiously; on a small scale. **no small** considerable; a good deal of (*no small excitement about it*). **small-a** (or **b, c,** etc.) designating a common noun or general term rather than a proper name (*small-l liberal*). □ **smallish** *adj.* **smallness** *n.*

small arms *n.pl.* portable firearms, esp. rifles, pistols, light machine guns, submachine guns, etc.

small-bore *adj.* (esp. *attrib.*) **1** (of a firearm) with a narrow bore, in international and Olympic shooting usu. .22 inch calibre (5.6 millimetre bore). **2** *informal* petty, insignificant, small-time.

small calorie *n.* *see* CALORIE 2.

small cap[1] *n.* (in full **small capital**) (esp. in *pl.*) a capital letter which is of the same dimensions as the lower case letters in the same typeface, as THIS.

small cap[2] *n.* a company with a relatively small market capitalization (usu. *attrib.*: *small-cap stocks*).

small change *n.* **1** money in the form of coins as opposed to bills. **2** a relatively insignificant amount of money. **3** a trivial thing.

small claims court *n.* a general name given to a court with jurisdiction over civil claims involving relatively small amounts of money, with trials conducted by judges alone.

small forward *n.* *Basketball* **1** a versatile forward who is effective outside the key as well as near the net. **2** the position played by such a forward.

small fry *n.pl.* **1** young children or the young of various species. **2** small or insignificant things or people.

small game *n.* small animals hunted for sport (also *attrib.*: *small-game hunter*).

small hours *n.pl.* the early hours of the morning after midnight.

small intestine *n.* the duodenum, jejunum, and ileum collectively.

small letter *n.* (in printed material) a lower case letter.

small-minded *adj.* petty; of rigid opinions or narrow outlook. □ **small-mindedly** *adv.* **small-mindedness** *n.*

smallmouth *n.* (*pl.* same or **-s**) (in full **smallmouth bass**) a N American freshwater bass with a small mouth, *Micropterus dolomieu*.

small of the back *n.* the part of the back below the waist.

smallpox *n.* an acute contagious viral disease, with fever and pustules usu. leaving permanent scars, effectively eradicated through vaccination by 1979.

small press *n.* (esp. *attrib.*) an independent, relatively small publisher (*small press publishing*).

small print *n.* **1** printed matter in small type. **2** = FINE PRINT.

small-scale *adj.* made or occurring in small amounts, to a lesser degree, on a small scale, etc.

small screen *n.* (prec. by *the*) *informal* television.

small talk *n.* light social conversation. □ **small-talk** *v.intr.*

small-time *attrib.adj.* *informal* unimportant or petty.

small-town *attrib.adj.* esp. *N Amer.* relating to or characteristic of a small town; unsophisticated.

smarm *informal* ● *v.intr.* behave in a fulsomely flattering or toadying manner. ● *n.* obsequiousness.

smarmy *adj.* (**-ier, -iest**) *informal* flattering; obsequious. □ **smarmily** *adv.* **smarminess** *n.*

smart ● *adj.* **1 a** esp. *N Amer.* intelligent, keen, bright. **b** clever, witty; impudent (*don't be smart*). **c** keen in bargaining; quick to take advantage; shrewd. **2** well-groomed; neat; bright and fresh in appearance (*a smart suit*). **3** in good repair; showing bright colours, new paint, etc. (*a smart red bicycle*). **4** stylish; fashionable; prominent in society (*a smart restaurant*). **5** quick; brisk (*a smart pace*). **6** painfully severe; sharp; vigorous (*a smart blow*). **7 a** (of a device) capable of independent and seemingly intelligent action. **b** (of a powered missile, bomb, etc.) guided to a target by an optical system. ● *v.intr.* **1** (of a person or a part of the body) feel or give acute pain or distress (*smarting from the insult*). **2** (of an insult, grievance, etc.) rankle; cause bad or bitter feelings. **3** (foll. by *for*) suffer the consequences of (*you will smart for this*). ● *n.* **1** a bodily or mental sharp pain; a stinging sensation. **2** (in *pl.*)

esp. *N Amer.* intelligence, esp. of a specified kind (*street smarts*). ● *adv.* smartly; in a smart manner. □ **smartly** *adv.* **smartness** *n.*

smart aleck *n.* (also **smart alec**) (also, with hyphen, *attrib.*) *informal* a person displaying impudent or smug cleverness. □ **smart-alecky** *adj.*

smartass *n. slang* = SMART ALECK. □ **smart-ass** *attrib.adj.* **smart-assed** *adj.*

smart card *n.* a plastic card with a built-in microprocessor, esp. as a credit or other bank card for the instant transfer of funds etc.

smart cookie *n. N Amer. informal* a smart or shrewd person.

smart drug *n.* a drug which supposedly improves memory and mental acuteness.

smarten *v.tr. & intr.* (usu. foll. by *up*) make or become smart or smarter.

smart-mouth *v.tr. & intr.* esp. *N Amer. informal* give a cheeky retort to someone.

smarty *n.* (*pl.* **-ies**) (also **smarty-pants**) *informal* a know-it-all.

smash ● *v.* **1** *tr. & intr.* (often foll. by *up*) **a** break into pieces; shatter. **b** bring or come to sudden or complete destruction, defeat, or disaster. **2** *tr.* (foll. by *into, through*) (of a vehicle etc.) move with great force and impact. **3** *tr. & intr.* (foll. by *in*) break in with a crushing blow (*smashed in the window*). **4** *tr.* **a** (in tennis, squash, etc.) hit (a ball etc.) with great force, esp. downwards (*smashed it back over the net*). **b** (in baseball, golf, etc.) hit (the ball) powerfully. ● *n.* **1** the act or an instance of smashing; a violent fall, collision, or disaster. **2** the sound of this. **3** (also **smash hit**) a very successful movie, song, performer, etc. **4 a** a stroke in tennis, squash, etc., in which the ball is hit esp. downwards with great force. **b** *Baseball* a powerful hit. **5** a violent blow with a fist etc. **6** bankruptcy; a series of commercial failures.

smash-and-grab *n.* (usu. *attrib.*) a robbery in which the thief smashes a window and seizes goods quickly.

smashed *adj.* **1** broken into pieces. **2** *slang* intoxicated.

smasher *n.* **1** a person or thing that smashes. **2** *informal* a very beautiful or pleasing person or thing.

smashing *adj. informal* superlative; excellent; wonderful; beautiful. □ **smashingly** *adv.*

smash-up *n.* a violent collision; a complete smash.

smattering *n.* **1** a slight superficial knowledge of a language or subject. **2** a small amount.

smear ● *v.tr.* **1 a** daub or mark with a greasy or sticky substance or with something that stains. **b** spread a layer of (a greasy, sticky, or staining substance) on something. **2** blot; smudge; obscure the outline of (writing, artwork, etc.). **3** defame the character of; slander; attempt to or succeed in discrediting (a person or his or her name) publicly. ● *n.* **1** the act or an instance of smearing. **2** *Med.* **a** material smeared on a microscopic slide etc. for examination. **b** a specimen of this. **c** a procedure involving the removal of material to be examined in this way. **3** a substance smeared on another; a smeared stain. □ **smeary** *adj.*

smear campaign *n.* a planned effort to slander and so discredit a public figure.

smell ● *n.* **1** the faculty of perceiving odours or scents (*has a fine sense of smell*). **2** the quality in substances that is perceived by this (*the smell of oranges*). **3** an unpleasant odour. **4** the act of inhaling to ascertain smell. **5** a trace or suggestion of something; the special character of something (*the smell of success*). ● *v.* (*past and past part.* **smelled**) **1** *tr.* perceive the smell of;

examine by smell. **2** *intr.* emit odour. **3** *intr.* seem by smell to be (*this milk smells sour*). **4** *intr.* (foll. by *of*) **a** be redolent of (*smells of fish*). **b** be suggestive of (*smells of dishonesty*). **5** *intr.* stink; be rank. **6** *tr.* perceive as if by smell; detect, discern, suspect (*smell a bargain*). **7** *intr.* have or use a sense of smell. **8** *intr.* (foll. by *around, about*) sniff or search about. **9** *tr.* (foll. by *up*) fill or affect with an esp. offensive odour. □ **smell blood** (of an attacker or aggressor) be encouraged by the discernment of another's vulnerability. **smell a rat** begin to suspect trickery etc. **smell the roses** enjoy or appreciate what is often ignored. □ **smeller** *n.*

smelling salts *n.pl.* ammonium carbonate mixed with scent, sniffed as a restorative in faintness etc.

smelly *adj.* (**-ier, -iest**) having a strong or unpleasant smell. □ **smelliness** *n.*

smelt¹ *v.tr.* **1** extract metal from (ore) by melting. **2** extract (metal) from ore by melting. □ **smelting** *n.*

smelt² *n.* (*pl.* same or **-s**) any of various small silvery carnivorous fish of the family Osmeridae, of coastal sea waters and fresh waters near the coasts of the northern hemisphere, including the caplin etc.

smelter *n.* **1** a person engaged in smelting. **2** a place where ores are smelted. □ **smeltery** *n.* (*pl.* **-ies**).

smidgen *n.* (also **smidgeon, smidgin**; also **smidge**) *informal* a small bit or amount.

smile ● *v.* **1** *intr.* relax the features into a pleased or kind or gently skeptical expression or a forced imitation of these, usu. with the corners of the mouth turned up. **2** *tr.* express by smiling (*smiled their consent*). **3** *tr.* give (a smile) of a specified kind (*smiled a sardonic smile*). **4** *intr.* (foll. by *on, upon*) adopt a favourable attitude towards; encourage (*fortune smiled on me*). ● *n.* **1** the act or an instance of smiling. **2** a smiling expression or aspect. □ **smiler** *n.* **smiling** *adj.* **smilingly** *adv.*

smiley ● *adj.* displaying a smile or characterized by smiling. ● *n.* **1** = EMOTICON. **2** (in full **smiley face**) a schematic drawing of a face with two dots for eyes and an upturned curve for a mouth, usu. enclosed in a circle.

smirk ● *n.* a conceited, smug, scornful, or silly smile. ● *v.intr.* put on or wear a smirk. □ **smirky** *adj.*

smite *v.tr.* (*past* **smote**; *past part.* **smitten**) **1** strike or hit forcefully. **2** chastise; defeat. **3** (in *passive*) **a** have a sudden strong effect on (*was smitten by his conscience*). **b** infatuate, fascinate (*was smitten by her beauty*).

smith *n.* **1** (esp. in *comb.*) a worker in metal (*goldsmith*). **2** a blacksmith. □ **smithing** *n.*

smithereens /smɪðəˈriːnz/ *n.pl.* small fragments (*smashed to smithereens*).

smithy /ˈsmɪθi, ˈsmɪði/ *n.* (*pl.* **-ies**) a blacksmith's workshop; a forge.

smitten ● *v.* *past part.* of SMITE. ● *adj.* **1** struck, hit. **2** (often foll. by *with*) affected with or by something specified. **3** in love; infatuated.

smock ● *n.* **1** a loose garment, esp. as worn by artists etc. to protect their clothes. **2** a loose shirt-like garment for women and girls, with the upper part closely gathered in smocking. ● *v.tr.* (usu. as **smocked** *adj.*) adorn with smocking.

smocking *n.* an ornamental effect on cloth made by gathering the material tightly into pleats, often with stitches in a honeycomb pattern.

smog *n.* fog intensified by atmospheric pollutants. □ **smogless** *adj.* **smoggy** *adj.* (**-ier, -iest**).

smoke ● *n.* **1 a** a visible suspension of carbon etc. in air, emitted from a burning substance. **b** vapour etc. resembling smoke. **2** an act or period of smoking tobacco (*had a quiet smoke*). **3** *informal* a cigarette or cigar. **4** *Baseball informal* a very effective fastball; a pitcher's arsenal of unhittable fastballs (*throws smoke*). **5** a clouding or obscuring medium or influence, esp. false information intended as a distraction. **6** a colour like that of smoke, esp. a bluish or brownish grey. ● *v.* **1** *intr.* **a** emit smoke or visible vapour (*the ruins continued to smoke*). **b** (of an oil lamp etc.) burn badly with the emission of smoke. **c** (of a chimney or fire) discharge smoke into the room. **2 a** *intr.* inhale and exhale the smoke of a cigarette, cigar, etc. **b** *intr.* do this habitually. **c** *tr.* use (a cigarette etc.) in this way. **3** *tr.* cure or darken by the action of smoke (*smoked salmon*). **4** *tr.* **a** rid of insects etc. by the action of smoke. **b** subdue (insects, esp. bees) in this way. **5** *tr. N Amer. informal* **a** shoot with a firearm. **b** defeat overwhelmingly. **6** *tr. N Amer.* esp. *Sport* hit and propel (a ball etc.) with great speed and force; make (a powerful shot, stroke, hit, etc.). □ **go up in smoke** *informal* **1** be destroyed by fire. **2** (of a plan etc.) come to nothing. **where there's smoke there's fire** rumours are not entirely baseless. **smoke out 1** drive out by means of smoke. **2** drive out of hiding or secrecy etc. **smoke up** *Cdn* smoke a drug, esp. marijuana. □ **smokable** *adj.* (also **smokeable**). **smoking** *n. & adj.*

smoke and mirrors *n.pl. N Amer.* a thing or things intended to deceive or confuse; deceit (also, with hyphens, *attrib.*: *smoke-and-mirrors campaign*).

smoke bomb *n.* **1** a bomb or other projectile that emits dense smoke on exploding. **2** a similar device used as a special effect in concerts etc.

smoke detector *n.* a device which warns of the presence of smoke.

smoked meat *n.* **1** meat that has been cured by smoking. **2** *Cdn* (esp. *Que.* & *Ont.*) cured beef similar to pastrami but more heavily smoked.

smoke-free *adj.* **1** free from smoke. **2** where smoking is not permitted.

smokehouse *n.* esp. *N Amer.* a house or room for curing meat, fish, etc. by exposure to smoke.

smoke jumper *n. N Amer.* a firefighter who arrives by parachute to fight a forest fire. □ **smoke jump** *v.intr.*

smokeless *adj.* having or producing little or no smoke.

smoker *n.* **1** a person or thing that smokes, esp. a person who habitually smokes tobacco. **2** esp. *N Amer.* a small box used for smoking fish or other meat.

smoker's cough *n.* a persistent cough caused by excessive smoking.

smokescreen *n.* **1** a cloud of smoke diffused to conceal (esp. military) operations. **2** a device or ruse for disguising one's activities.

smoke shop *n. N Amer.* **1** a store selling tobacco products. **2** a convenience store.

smoke signal *n.* a column of smoke used as a signal.

smokestack *n.* **1** a tall chimney, esp. of a factory. **2** a chimney or funnel for discharging the smoke of a locomotive or steamer. **3** (*attrib.*) designating heavy industry, typically associated with high pollution levels and outmoded technology (*smokestack economy*).

smokey ● *adj.* var. of SMOKY. ● *n.* (pl. **-s** or **-ies**) esp. *N Amer.* a police officer or car, esp. patrolling a highway.

smokie *n. Cdn* a sausage or hot dog.

smoking gun *n.* a piece of incontrovertible incriminating evidence.

smoky *adj.* (**-ier, -iest**) **1** emitting, veiled or filled with, or obscured by, smoke (*smoky fire*; *smoky room*). **2 a** stained with smoke (*smoky glass*). **b** (of a colour etc.) resembling smoke; of a bluish-grey tinge (*smoky grey*).

3 having the taste or flavour of smoked food (*smoky bacon*). **4** (of a voice) having the slightly hoarse overtones characteristic of a heavy smoker. □ **smokily** *adv.* **smokiness** *n.*

smolder *var. of* SMOULDER.

smolt *n.* a young salmon migrating to the sea for the first time.

smooch *informal* ● *v.intr.* **1** kiss. **2** cuddle and caress. ● *n.* a kiss. □ **smoocher** *n.* **smoochy** *adj.* (**-ier, -iest**).

smooth ● *adj.* **1** having a relatively even and regular surface; free from perceptible projections, lumps, indentations, and roughness. **2** (of the skin, a complexion, etc.) not wrinkled, pitted, scored, or hairy. **3** that can be traversed without check. **4** (of liquids) of even consistency; without lumps. **5** (of the sea etc.) without waves or undulations. **6** (of a journey, passage, progress, etc.) untroubled by difficulties or adverse conditions. **7** having an easy flow or correct rhythm (*a smooth metre*). **8 a** not harsh in sound or taste. **b** (of wine etc.) not astringent. **9** often *derogatory* (of a person, his or her manner, etc.) suave, conciliatory, flattering, unruffled, or polite (*he's very smooth*). **10** (of movement etc.) not suddenly varying; not jerky. ● *v.* (also **smoothe**) **1** *tr. & intr.* (often foll. by *out*, *down*) make or become smooth. **2** (often foll. by *out*, *down*, *over*, *away*) **a** *tr.* reduce or get rid of (differences, faults, difficulties, etc.) in fact or appearance. **b** *intr.* (of difficulties etc.) diminish, become less obtrusive (*it will all smooth over*). **3** *tr.* modify (a graph, curve, etc.) so as to lessen irregularities. **4** *tr.* free from impediments or discomfort (*smooth the way*). ● *n.* **1** a smoothing touch or stroke. **2** the easy part of life (*take the rough with the smooth*). ● *adv.* smoothly (*goes down smooth*). □ **smoothly** *adv.* **smoothness** *n.*

smoothbore *n.* a gun with an unrifled barrel (also *attrib.*: *smoothbore gun*).

smoothie *n.* *informal* **1** a person who is smooth (*see* SMOOTH *adj.* 9). **2** (also **smoothy**) esp. *N Amer.*, *Austral.*, & *NZ* a thick smooth drink of fresh fruit puréed with milk, yogourt, or ice cream.

smooth muscle *n.* a muscle without striations, usu. occurring in hollow organs and performing involuntary functions.

smooth sailing *n.* easy progress.

smooth talk *informal* ● *n.* bland specious language. ● *v.tr. & intr.* (**smooth-talk**) address or persuade with this. □ **smooth talker** *n.* **smooth-talking** *adj.*

s'more *n. N Amer.* a dessert made of a graham cracker topped with melted chocolate and marshmallow.

smorgasbord /'smɔrgəsbɔrd/ *n.* **1** a buffet offering a wide variety of dishes. **2** open sandwiches served with delicacies as hors d'oeuvres or a buffet. **3** a medley; a miscellany; a variety.

smote *past of* SMITE.

smother *v.* **1** *tr.* suffocate; stifle; kill by stopping the breath of or excluding air from. **2** *tr.* (foll. by *with*) overwhelm with (kisses, gifts, kindness, etc.) (*smothered with affection*). **3** *tr.* (foll. by *in*, *with*) cover entirely in or with (*chicken smothered in mayonnaise*). **4** *tr.* extinguish or deaden (a fire or flame) by covering it or heaping it with ashes etc. **5** *intr.* **a** die of suffocation. **b** have difficulty breathing. **6** *tr.* **a** suppress or conceal; prevent from developing. **b** repress or refrain from displaying (feeling etc.) by self-control. **c** make (words etc.) indistinct or inaudible. **7** *tr. Hockey* immobilize (the puck) on the ice by falling on top of it, covering it with a glove, etc.

smoulder ● *v.intr.* **1** burn slowly with smoke but without a flame; slowly burn internally or invisibly. **2** (of emotions etc.) exist in a suppressed or concealed state. **3** (of a person) show silent or suppressed anger, hatred, passion, etc. ● *n.* a smouldering or slow-burning fire. □ **smouldering** *adj.*

smudge[1] ● *n.* a blurred or smeared line or mark; a blot; a smear of dirt. ● *v.* **1** *tr.* make a smudge on. **2** *intr.* become smeared or blurred (*smudges easily*). **3** *tr.* smear or blur the lines of (writing, drawing, etc.) (*smudge the outline*). **4** *tr.* defile, sully, stain, or disgrace. □ **smudgy** *adj.* (**-ier, -iest**).

smudge[2] *n.* *N Amer.* **1** (in full **smudge fire**) an outdoor fire with dense smoke made to keep off insects, protect plants against frost, etc. **2** dense smoke as produced by such a fire.

smug *adj.* (**smugger, smuggest**) self-satisfied; complacent. □ **smugly** *adv.* **smugness** *n.*

smuggle *v.* **1** *tr. & intr.* convey (goods) in contravention of legal prohibition or without payment of customs duties; import or export illegally. **2** *tr.* (foll. by *in, out*) convey secretly. **3** *tr.* (foll. by *away*) put into concealment. □ **smuggler** *n.* **smuggling** *n.*

smush *v.tr.* esp. *N Amer.* *informal* mash, crush, smash.

smut *n.* **1** obscene or lascivious talk, pictures, or stories. **2 a** a fungous disease of cereals in which parts of the ear change to black powder. **b** any fungus of the order Ustilaginales causing this. **3** a small flake of soot etc. **4** a spot or smudge made by this. □ **smutty** *adj.* (**-ier, -iest**) (esp. in sense 1).

Sn *symbol* the element tin.

snack ● *n.* **1** a light, casual, or hurried meal. **2** a small amount or item of food eaten between meals. ● *v.intr.* (often foll. by *on*) eat a snack. □ **snacker** *n.* **snacky** *adj.*

snack bar *n.* a usu. small store, kiosk, counter, etc. where snacks are sold.

snaffle ● *n.* (in full **snaffle bit**) (on a bridle) a simple bit without a curb and usu. with a single rein. ● *v.tr.* **1** put a snaffle on. **2** *informal* steal; seize; appropriate.

snafu /snæ'fuː, 'snæfuː/ *slang* ● *n.* (*pl.* **-s**) **1** a confused, muddled, or messed-up condition or state. **2** a mistake or blunder. ● *adj.* in utter confusion or chaos; messed up. ● *v.* (**-ed, -ing**) **1** *tr.* mess up, bungle, play havoc with. **2** *intr.* go wrong; mess up.

snag ● *n.* **1** an unexpected or hidden obstacle, drawback, or problem. **2 a** a jagged or projecting point. **b** a standing dead tree; a broken stump or branch. **c** a tree trunk or branch embedded under water, forming an obstruction to navigation. **3** a tear in material etc. **4** an act or instance of snagging. ● *v.* (**snagged, snagging**) **1 a** *tr.* catch or tear on a snag. **b** *tr.* (of a projecting point) catch or tear (something) (*something snagged my sleeve*). **c** *tr.* catch onto (a projecting point) (*the fishing line snagged a branch*). **2** *intr.* catch onto a projecting point (*the line snagged*). **2** *tr.* *N Amer.* catch, seize, or obtain, esp. by quick action (*snagged a passing waiter*). **3** *tr.* clear (land, a waterway, a tree trunk, etc.) of snags. □ **snagged** *adj.*

snaggle-toothed *adj.* having irregular or projecting teeth. □ **snaggletooth** *n.* (*pl.* **snaggleteeth**).

snail *n.* any slow-moving gastropod mollusc with a spiral shell able to enclose the whole body.

snail mail *n.* *slang* **1** the ordinary postal system as opposed to the electronic mail system. **2** correspondence sent using this.

snail's pace *n.* a very slow movement.

snake ● *n.* **1 a** any long limbless reptile of the suborder Ophidia. **b** a limbless lizard or amphibian. **2** (also **snake in the grass**) a treacherous person or secret enemy. **3** = PLUMBER'S SNAKE. ● *v.* **1** *tr. & intr.* move or twist or cause to move or twist like a snake. **2** *tr.* make (one's way) by snaking. □ **snakelike** *adj.*

snakebite *n.* a wound or condition resulting from being bitten by an esp. poisonous snake.

snake fence *n.* (also **snake-rail fence**) *Cdn* a fence of stacked roughly-split logs laid in a zigzag pattern with ends overlapping at an angle.

snakehead *n.* a member of an organized crime ring smuggling emigrants illegally from China.

snake oil *n.* *informal* **1** a quack medicine. **2** a fraudulent product. **3** nonsense.

snakeskin ● *n.* the skin of a snake. ● *adj.* made of or resembling snakeskin.

snaky *adj.* (also **snakey**) (**snakier, snakiest**) **1** of or like a snake. **2** winding; sinuous. **3** showing coldness, ingratitude, venom, or guile. **4** infested with or composed of snakes. □ **go** (or **drive someone**) **snaky** *Cdn* lose (or cause to lose) self-control.

snap ● *v.* (**snapped, snapping**) **1** *intr. & tr.* break suddenly or with a snap. **2** *intr. & tr.* emit or cause to emit a sudden sharp sound or crack. **3** *intr. & tr.* open or close, turn off or on, etc. with a snapping sound (*the bag snapped shut*). **4 a** *intr.* (often foll. by *at*) speak irritably or spitefully (to a person). **b** *tr.* say irritably or spitefully. **5** *intr.* (often foll. by *at*) (esp. of a dog etc.) make a sudden audible bite. **6** *tr. & intr.* move quickly (*snapped into action; snap to it*). **7** *tr.* take a snapshot of. **8** *tr.* *Football* put (the ball) into play on the ground by a quick backward movement. **9** *tr.* bring an end to (an esp. undecided condition, state of affairs, etc.) (*snapped their losing streak*). **10** *intr.* lose one's composure suddenly after having resisted increasing tension or pressure. ● *n.* **1** an act or sound of snapping. **2** *N. Amer. slang* an easy task (*it was a snap*). **3** a crisp biscuit or cake (*gingersnap*). **4** a snapshot. **5** (in full **cold snap**) a sudden brief spell of cold weather. **6** a card game in which players call 'snap' when two similar cards are exposed. **7** crispness of style; fresh vigour or liveliness in action; zest; dash; spring. **8** *Football* an act or instance of snapping the ball. ● *attrib.adj.* done or taken on the spur of the moment, unexpectedly, or without notice (*snap decision*). □ **in a snap** with no hesitation or difficulty. **snap at** accept (bait, a chance, etc.) eagerly. **snap off** break off or bite off. **snap one's fingers** suddenly release a finger which has been bent and checked by another finger or thumb, producing an audible snap as the finger strikes the hand. **snap out** utter forcefully. **snap out of** *informal* get rid of (a mood, habit, etc.) by a sudden effort. **snap up 1** accept (an offer, a bargain) quickly or eagerly. **2** pick up or catch hastily.

snap bean *n.* *N Amer.* a bean with edible pods.

snapdragon *n.* any of several plants of the genus *Antirrhinum* and of related genera, with a bag-shaped flower, esp. *A. majus*, cultivated in gardens.

snapper *n.* **1** a person or thing that snaps. **2** any of several fish of the family Lutjanidae, used as food. **3** = BLUEFISH. **4** a snapping turtle.

snapping turtle *n.* either of two large aggressive Central and N American freshwater turtles of the family Chelydridae, having large heads and long tails, and seizing prey with a snap of the jaws, *Chelydra serpentina* (also **common** or **Florida snapping turtle**), and *Macroclemys temminckii* (also **alligator snapping turtle**).

snappish *adj.* **1** (of a person's manner or a remark) curt; ill-tempered; sharp. **2** (of a dog etc.) inclined to snap. □ **snappishly** *adv.* **snappishness** *n.*

snappy *adj.* (**-ier, -iest**) *informal* **1** brisk, full of zest. **2** fashionable, up-to-date (*a snappy red convertible*). **3** snappish. □ **make it snappy** be quick about it. □ **snappily** *adv.* **snappiness** *n.*

snapshot *n.* **1** a casual photograph taken quickly with a small camera. **2** a description or profile of a thing or of one stage of a process etc. **3** (**snap shot**) a quick shot on goal, esp. (*Hockey*) a shot taken by lifting the stick a short distance off the ice before striking the puck quickly with a hard flicking motion.

snare ● *n.* **1** a trap for catching birds or animals, esp. with a noose of wire or cord. **2** a thing that acts as a temptation. **3** a device for tempting an enemy etc. to expose himself or herself to danger, failure, loss, capture, defeat, etc. **4** (in *sing.* or *pl.*) twisted strings of gut, hide, or wire stretched across the lower head of a drum to produce a rattling sound. **5** (in full **snare drum**) a drum fitted with snares. ● *v.tr.* **1** catch (a bird etc.) in a snare. **2** ensnare; lure or trap (a person) with a snare. **3** grab; catch (*snared the ball*).

snarf *v.tr. & intr.* esp. *N Amer. slang* eat or drink greedily.

snarky *adj.* (**-ier, -iest**) *informal* irritable; short-tempered.

snarl ● *v.* **1** *intr.* (of a dog) make an angry growl with bared teeth. **2** *intr.* (of a person) make bad-tempered complaints or criticisms. **3** *tr.* (often foll. by *out*) **a** utter in a snarling tone. **b** express (discontent etc.) by snarling. **4** *tr.* (often foll. by *up*) twist; entangle; confuse and hamper the movement of (traffic etc.). **5** *intr.* (often foll. by *up*) become entangled, congested, or confused. ● *n.* **1** the act or sound of snarling. **2** a knot or tangle. □ **snarler** *n.* **snarly** *adj.* (**-ier, -iest**).

snarl-up *n. Cdn & Brit. informal* a traffic jam.

snatch ● *v.tr.* **1** take or seize something quickly or roughly. **2 a** steal (a wallet, purse, etc.). **b** kidnap (esp. a child). **3** take or get something quickly, esp. when a chance to do so occurs (*snatched a bite to eat*). **4** (foll. by *away*, *from*) take away or from esp. suddenly (*snatched away my hand*). **5** (foll. by *from*) rescue narrowly (*snatched from the jaws of death*). **6** (foll. by *at*) **a** try to take something with the hands. **b** take (an offer, opportunity, etc.) eagerly. ● *n.* **1** an act of snatching (*made a snatch at it*). **2** a fragment of a song or talk etc. (*caught a snatch of their conversation*). **3** esp. *N Amer. slang* a kidnapping. **4** (in weightlifting) a movement in which a barbell is raised rapidly from the floor to above the head, followed by a straightening of the knees. **5** a short period of doing something (*slept in snatches*). **6** *coarse slang* the female genitals. □ **snatcher** *n.* (esp. in sense 2b of *v.*). **snatchy** *adj.*

snazzy *adj.* (**-ier, -iest**) *slang* smart or fashionable. □ **snazzily** *adv.* **snazziness** *n.*

sneak ● *v.* (*past* and *past part.* **snuck** or **sneaked**) **1** *intr. & tr.* (foll. by *in*, *out*, *past*, *away*, etc.) go quietly and secretly in the direction specified. **2** *tr. informal* take or do something secretly, often without permission (*snuck a chocolate from the box*). ¶There is a long tradition of objection to *snuck*, though it is more common than *sneaked* in speech, fiction, and journalism, and is for many people the only form used. It may, however, be safer to use *sneaked* in formal writing. ● *n.* a cowardly deceitful person, esp. one who informs on others. ● *adj.* acting or done without warning; secret (*a sneak attack*). □ **sneak up** approach a person or thing quietly and stealthily.

sneaker *n.* = RUNNING SHOE. □ **sneakered** *adj.*

sneaking *adj.* **1** furtive; undisclosed (*have a sneaking affection for her*). **2** = SNEAKY 2.

sneak preview *n.* a special showing of a new film, exhibition, etc. before it is shown to the public.

sneaky *adj.* (**-ier, -iest**) **1** given to or characterized by sneaking; furtive. **2** persistent in one's mind; nagging (*a sneaky feeling*). □ **sneakily** *adv.* **sneakiness** *n.*

sneer ● *n.* a derisive smile or remark. ● *v.* **1** *intr.* (often foll. by *at*) smile derisively. **2** *tr.* say sneeringly. **3** *intr.* (often foll. by *at*) speak derisively esp. covertly or ironically (*sneered at her attempts*). □ **sneerer** *n.* **sneering** *adj.* **sneeringly** *adv.*

sneeze ● *n.* **1** a sudden involuntary expulsion of air from the nose and mouth caused by irritation of the nostrils. **2** the sound of this. ● *v.intr.* make a sneeze. □ **sneeze at** (usu. with *neg.*) regard as of little value, note, or importance; despise, disregard, underrate. □ **sneezer** *n.* **sneezy** *adj.*

Sne Nay Muxw /snəˈnaimo:/ ● *n.* **1** a member of an Aboriginal people inhabiting lower Vancouver Island and the mainland north of Vancouver and around the Fraser River delta. **2** the Salishan language of this people. ● *adj.* of or relating to this people.

snicker ● *n.* **1** a half-suppressed secretive laugh. **2** a whinny, a neigh. ● *v.intr.* **1** make such a laugh. **2** whinny, neigh. □ **snickeringly** *adv.*

snide *adj.* (of a person, remark, etc.) sneering; slyly derogatory; insinuating. □ **snidely** *adv.*

sniff ● *v.* **1** *intr.* draw up air audibly through the nose. **2** *intr.* clear one's nose by sniffing. **3** *intr.* express disdain, contempt, etc. by sniffing. **4** *intr.* smell by sniffing. **5** *tr.* draw in the scent of (food, drink, flowers, etc.) through the nose. **6** *tr. informal* take (a drug etc.) by breathing it in through the nose. **7** *tr.* (often foll. by *up*) draw in (a scent etc.) through the nose. **8** *tr.* perceive as if by smell; discover, suspect. **9** *tr.* **a** say (something) in a complaining way. **b** say (something) in a proud or disdainful way. ● *n.* **1** an act or sound of sniffing. **2** the amount of air etc. sniffed up. **3** a hint or intimation (*left at the first sniff of danger*). □ **sniff around** search around, esp. in an underhanded way. **sniff at 1** try the smell of; show interest in. **2** show contempt for or discontent with. **sniff out** detect; discover by investigation.

sniffer *n.* **1** a person who sniffs esp. a drug or toxic substance (*glue sniffer*). **2** *informal* the nose. **3** *informal* any device for detecting gas, radiation, etc.

sniffle ● *v.intr.* sniff slightly or repeatedly, esp. as a result of weeping. ● *n.* **1** the act of sniffling. **2** (in *sing.* or *pl.*) a cold in the head causing a running nose and sniffling. □ **sniffly** *adj.*

sniffy *adj.* (**-ier, -iest**) *informal* **1** disdainful; contemptuous. **2** inclined to sniff. □ **sniffily** *adv.*

snifter *n.* **1** esp. *N Amer.* a short-stemmed glass with a large bowl tapering towards the top, used for drinking brandy. **2** *slang* a small drink of alcohol.

snigger ● *n.* = SNICKER *n.* 1. ● *v.intr.* = SNICKER *v.* 1.

snip ● *v.* (**snipped, snipping**) **1** *tr. & intr.* cut (cloth, a hole, etc.) with scissors or shears, esp. in small quick strokes. **2** *tr.* cut off or remove (something) in this way. ● *n.* **1** an act of snipping. **2** a piece of material etc. snipped off. **3** (in *pl.*) hand shears for metal cutting. **4** *N Amer. informal* **a** an insignificant person. **b** an irritating or impertinent person. □ **snip at** make snipping strokes at. □ **snipping** *n.*

snipe ● *n.* **1** (*pl.* same or **-s**) any of various wading birds, esp. of the genus *Gallinago*, with a long straight bill and frequenting marshes. **2** (*pl.* **-s**) the act or an instance of sniping. ● *v.intr.* **1** fire shots from hiding usu. at long range. **2** (foll. by *at*) make a sly critical attack. □ **sniper** *n.* **sniping** *n.*

snippet *n.* a small fragment or bit. □ **snippety** *adj.*

snippy *adj.* (**-ier, -iest**) *informal* impertinently brusque. □ **snippily** *adv.*

snit *n. N Amer.* a state of agitation, irritation, pique, etc. (*she's always in a snit*).

snitch ● *v. slang* **1** *tr.* steal. **2** *intr.* (often foll. by *on*) inform on a person. ● *n.* an informer.

snivel *v.intr.* (**snivelled, snivelling**) **1** cry and sniff in a miserable way. **2** complain, esp. in a miserable, crying voice. **3 a** have a runny nose. **b** make a repeated sniffing sound. □ **sniveller** *n.* **snivelling** *adj.*

snob *n.* **1 a** a person with an exaggerated respect for social position or wealth. **b** a person who seeks to cultivate people considered socially superior. **c** (*attrib.*) related to or characteristic of these attitudes. **2** a person who is condescending to others whose (usu. specified) tastes or attainments are considered inferior (*a wine snob*). □ **snobbery** *n.* (*pl.* **-ies**). **snobbish** *adj.* **snobbishly** *adv.* **snobbishness** *n.* **snobbism** *n.* **snobby** *adj.* (**-ier, -iest**).

sno-cone *var. of* SNOW CONE.

snook /snuːk/ *n. slang* □ **cock a snook** (often foll. by *at*) **1** make a contemptuous gesture with the thumb to the nose and the fingers spread out. **2** register one's contempt (for a person, establishment, etc.).

snooker /'snʊkər, 'snuːk-/ ● *n.* **1** a game played with cues on a rectangular table in which the players use a cue ball to pocket the other balls in a set order. **2** a position in this game in which a direct shot at a permitted ball is impossible. ● *v.tr.* **1** (also *refl.*) subject (oneself or another player) to a snooker. **2** *slang* (usu. in *passive*) **a** defeat; thwart. **b** trick; dupe.

snoop *informal* ● *v.intr.* look around a place secretly in order to find something, obtain information, etc. ● *n.* **1** an act of snooping. **2 a** a person who snoops. **b** a detective. □ **snooper** *n.* **snoopy** *adj.*

snoot *n. slang* the nose.

snooty *adj.* (**-ier, -iest**) *informal* snobbish; conceited; contemptuous. □ **snootily** *adv.* **snootiness** *n.*

snooze *informal* ● *n.* **1** a short sleep, esp. in the daytime. **2** *N Amer. informal* something boring or tedious (*that meeting was a real snooze!*). **3** (*attrib.*) designating a function, button, etc. on an alarm clock or clock radio which turns off the alarm or radio for a short, fixed period of time, and then reactivates it. ● *v.intr.* take a snooze. □ **snoozy** *adj.* (**-ier, -iest**).

snoozer *n.* **1** a person who snoozes. **2** *N Amer. informal* something boring or tedious.

snore ● *n.* a snorting or grunting sound in breathing during sleep. ● *v.intr.* make this sound. □ **snorer** *n.*

snorkel ● *n.* **1** a breathing tube for an underwater swimmer. **2** a device for supplying air to a submerged submarine. ● *v.intr.* (**snorkelled, snorkelling**) use a snorkel. □ **snorkeller** *n.*

snort ● *n.* **1** an explosive sound made by the sudden forcing of breath through the nose, esp. expressing indignation or incredulity. **2** a similar sound made by an engine etc. **3** *informal* a small drink of liquor. **4** *slang* an inhaled dose of a (usu. illegal) powdered drug. ● *v.* **1** *intr.* make a snort. **2** *intr.* (of an engine etc.) make a sound resembling this. **3** *tr. & intr. slang* inhale (a usu. illegal narcotic drug). **4** *tr.* utter (words) or express (defiance etc.) by snorting. □ **snorter** *n.*

snot *n. slang* **1** nasal mucus. **2** a contemptible person.

snot-nosed *adj.* **1** (of a person) snotty. **2** conceited.

snotty *adj.* (**-ier, -iest**) *slang* **1** producing or covered with snot. **2** showing a superior attitude toward others; conceited. **3** contemptible. □ **snottiness** *n.*

snout *n.* **1** the projecting nose and mouth of an animal. **2** *derogatory* a person's nose. **3** the pointed front of a thing; a nozzle. □ **snouted** *adj.* (also in *comb.*).

snow ● *n.* **1** atmospheric vapour frozen into ice crystals and falling to earth in light white flakes. **2** a fall of this, or a layer of it on the ground. **3** a thing resembling snow in whiteness or texture etc. **4** a mass of flickering white spots on a television or radar screen, caused by interference or a poor signal. **5** *slang* cocaine. **6** a dessert or other dish resembling snow. **7** frozen carbon dioxide. ● *v.* **1** *intr.* (of snow) fall. **2** *tr.* (foll. by *in, over, up*, etc.) confine or block with large quantities of snow. **3** *tr. & intr.* sprinkle or scatter or fall as or like snow. **4** *tr. N Amer. slang* deceive or charm with plausible words. □ **be snowed under** be overwhelmed, esp. with work.

snow angel *n. N Amer.* the outline of an angel made by a person lying on his or her back in the snow and moving the arms and legs.

snowball ● *n.* **1** snow packed together or rolled into a ball, esp. for throwing. **2** any of various plants, esp. of the honeysuckle family, bearing rounded clusters of white flowers. ● *v.intr.* grow or increase rapidly (*the idea snowballed from there*). □ **not a snowball's chance in hell** *informal* no chance at all.

snowbank *n.* a heap or mound of snow, esp. one caused by plowing or drifting.

snowbelt *n. N Amer.* a region subject to heavy snowfalls.

snowbird *n.* **1** *N Amer. informal* a person from Canada or the northern US who moves to a southern state in the winter. **2** any of various small birds resembling the finch, esp. the snow bunting or junco.

snow-blind *adj.* temporarily blinded by the glare of light reflected by large expanses of snow. □ **snow-blinded** *adj.* **snow blindness** *n.*

snow blower *n.* a machine that clears snow by blowing it to one side.

snowboard *n.* a wide board like a ski, ridden in a standing position, used for sliding downhill on snow. □ **snowboarder** *n.* **snowboarding** *n.*

snow boot *n.* a usu. insulated boot for wearing in the winter.

snowbound *adj.* prevented by snow from going out or travelling.

snow bunting *n.* a mainly white finch, *Plectrophenax nivalis*, which breeds in the Arctic and migrates further south in autumn.

snowcap *n.* the tip of a mountain when covered with snow. □ **snow-capped** *adj.*

snow cone *n. N Amer.* a paper cone filled with crushed ice flavoured with fruit syrup.

snow crab *n.* an edible spider crab, *Chionoecetes opilio*, found off the eastern coast of Canada.

snowdrift *n.* a bank of snow heaped up by the wind.

snowdrop *n.* a bulbous plant, *Galanthus nivalis*, with white drooping flowers in the early spring.

snowfall *n.* **1** a fall of snow. **2** the amount of snow that falls on one occasion or on a given area within a given time.

snow fence *n.* a usu. portable fence erected on the windward side of a road, building, etc., serving as a barrier to drifting snow. □ **snow fencing** *n.*

snowfield *n.* a permanent wide expanse of snow in mountainous or polar regions.

snowflake *n.* each of the small collections of crystals in which snow falls.

snow flurry *n.* (*pl.* **-ies**) = FLURRY *n.* 1a.

snow goggles *n.pl.* (also **snow glasses**) *N Amer.* slotted goggles of wood, bone, etc., worn as a protection against snow blindness.

snow golf *n.* a form of golf played on packed snow.

snow goose *n.* an Arctic goose, *Chen* (or *Anser*) *caerulescens*, usu. white with black-tipped wings.

snow house *n. N Amer.* a structure made of blocks of snow, e.g. an igloo.

snow job n. esp. N Amer. an attempt to deceive or persuade (a person), esp. through flattery.

snow leopard n. an Asian wild cat, *Panthera uncia*, with leopard-like markings on a cream coat.

snow line n. the level, e.g. on a mountain, above which snow never melts entirely.

snow machine n. N Amer. a motor vehicle designed to travel over snow.

snow-making n. the production of artificial snow (often *attrib.*: *snow-making machine*).

snowman n. (pl. **-men**) a figure resembling a person, made of packed snow.

snowmelt n. **1** the melting of fallen snow, esp. in the spring. **2** the water that results from this.

snowmobile n. a motor vehicle equipped with runners and Caterpillar tracks for travelling over snow. □ **snowmobiler** n. **snowmobiling** n.

snowmobile boot n. Cdn a high, heavy snow boot worn esp. when snowmobiling.

snowmobile suit n. N Amer. a one-piece winter outer garment combining both coat and pants.

snowpack n. N Amer. the accumulation of winter snow, compressed and hardened by its own weight.

snow-packed adj. N Amer. (of a road etc.) covered with a layer of hard packed snow.

snow pea n. esp. N Amer. a variety of pea eaten whole including the pod.

snowplow (also **snowplough**) ● n. **1** a device, or a vehicle equipped with one, for clearing roads etc. of snow by pushing it to one side. **2** *Skiing* a technique for slowing down or stopping in which the points of the skis are turned inwards. ● v. **1** tr. & intr. clear (a road etc.) of snow using a snowplow. **2** intr. *Skiing* execute a snowplow.

snow route n. N Amer. a major arterial road in a city which is designated for priority snow clearing.

snowshoe ● n. a flat device like a racquet attached to a boot for walking on snow without sinking in. ● v.intr. (**snowshoed**, **snowshoeing**) travel on snowshoes. □ **snowshoer** n.

snowshoe hare n. (also **snowshoe rabbit**) a N American hare, *Lepus americanus*, with large hind feet and a white coat in winter.

snowstorm n. a heavy fall of snow, esp. with a high wind.

snowsuit n. N Amer. a one- or two-piece winter outer garment combining both coat and pants.

snowthrower n. N Amer. = SNOW BLOWER.

snow tire n. a tire equipped with deep treads etc. to give increased traction on snow or ice.

snow-white adj. pure white.

snowy adj. (**-ier**, **-iest**) **1 a** of or like snow. **b** pure white. **2** (of the weather etc.) with much snow. **3** covered with snow (*snowy fields*). □ **snowily** adv. **snowiness** n.

snowy owl n. a large white owl, *Nyctea scandiaca*, native to the Arctic.

snub ● v.tr. (**snubbed**, **snubbing**) rebuff or humiliate with sharp words or a marked lack of cordiality. ● n. an act of snubbing; a rebuff. ● adj. short and blunt in shape. □ **snubber** n. **snubbingly** adv.

snub nose n. a short turned-up nose. □ **snub-nosed** adj.

snuck past and past part. of SNEAK.

snuff[1] ● n. the charred part of a candle wick. ● v.tr. **1** smother the flame of (a candle). **2** trim the snuff from (a candle). **3** slang kill (a person). □ **snuff out 1** extinguish by snuffing. **2** kill; put an end to.

snuff[2] ● n. powdered tobacco taken by sniffing it up the nostrils. ● v.intr. take snuff. □ **up to snuff** informal up to standard.

snuffer n. **1** a small hollow cone with a handle used to extinguish a candle. **2** (in pl.) an implement like scissors used to extinguish a candle or trim its wick.

snuff film n. (also **snuff video** etc.) slang a pornographic film depicting an actual murder.

snuffle ● v. **1** intr. make sniffing sounds. **2 a** intr. speak nasally, whiningly, or like one with a cold. **b** tr. say in this way. **3** intr. breathe noisily as through a partially blocked nose. **4** intr. sniff. ● n. **1** a snuffling sound or tone. **2** (in pl.) a partial blockage of the nose causing snuffling. **3** a sniff. □ **snuffly** adj.

snug ● adj. (**snugger**, **snuggest**) **1** comfortably warm and cozy. **2** secure and sheltered (*a snug harbour*). **3** compact and well-organized. **4** (of clothing etc.) close-fitting. **5** fitting exactly (*make sure that the nuts are snug but not too tight*). **6** (of an income etc.) allowing comfort and comparative ease. ● v.tr. make snug. □ **snugly** adv. **snugness** n.

snuggle v.intr. & tr. **1** (often foll. by *up*, *down*, etc.) lie or get close to a person or thing for warmth, comfort, or affection. **2** place something into a warm comfortable position.

snuggly /'snʌgəli/ adj. comfortably warm, cosy (*a snuggly blanket*).

Snugli n. N Amer. proprietary a pouch for carrying a baby.

snye /snai/ n. Cdn **1** (E Ont.) a side channel, esp. one that bypasses a falls or rapids and rejoins the main river downstream, creating an island. **2 a** a narrow or meandering side channel, esp. one that comes to a dead end. **b** such a channel used by bush pilots for landing aircraft.

SO abbr. N Amer. SIGNIFICANT OTHER.

So. abbr. South.

so[1] ● adv. **1** (often foll. by *that* + clause) to such an extent, or to the extent implied (*why are you so angry?*). **2** (with *neg.*; often foll. by *as* + clause) to the extent to which ... is or does etc., or to the extent implied (*was not so late as I expected*). **3** (foll. by *that* or *as* + clause) to the degree or in the manner implied (*so expensive that few can afford it*; *am not so foolish as to agree*). **4** (adding emphasis) to that extent; in that or a similar manner (*I want to leave and so does she*; *you said it was good, and so it is*). **5** to a great or notable degree (*I am so glad*). **6** in the way described (*am not very fond of it but may become so*). **7** (with verb of saying or thinking etc.) as previously mentioned or described (*I think so*; *so they said*). **8** informal very; extremely (*things are so expensive these days*). ¶This use occurs mostly in informal speech, and should be avoided in formal speech or writing. ● conj. (often foll. by *that* + clause) **1** with the result that (*there was none left, so we had to go without*). **2** in order that (*came home early so that I could see you*). **3** and then; as the next step (*so then the car broke down*). **4 a** (introducing a question) then; after that (*so what did you tell them?*). **b** = SO WHAT? ● adj. in conformity with reality; true as reported (*please say it isn't so*). ● pron. **1** something that is near or approximate to the number in question (*only six or so*). **2** used as a substitute for a clause of sentence (*you'll do it because I said so*). ● interj. expressing shock, surprise, indifference, inquiry, etc. □ **and so on** (also **and so forth**) **1** and others of the same kind. **2** and in other similar ways. **so as** (foll. by *to* + infin.) in order to (*so as to get it finished*). **so be it** an expression of acceptance or resignation. **so long** informal goodbye till we meet again. **so much 1** a certain amount (of). **2** a great deal of (*is so much nonsense*). **3** (with *neg.*) **a** less than; to a lesser extent (*not so much forgotten as ignored*). **b** not even (*didn't give me so much as a penny*). **so much for** that is all that need be done or said about. **so to speak** (or **say**) an expression of reserve or apology for an exaggeration or neologism etc. **so what?** *informal* why should that be considered significant?

so² *n. Music* **1** (in tonic sol-fa) the fifth note of a major scale. **2** the note G in the fixed-do system.

soak ● *v.* **1** *tr. & intr.* make or become thoroughly wet through saturation with or in liquid. **2** *tr.* (of rain etc.) drench. **3** *refl.* (often foll. by *in*) immerse (oneself) in a subject of study etc. **4** *intr.* (foll. by *in*, *into*, *through*) **a** (of liquid) make its way or penetrate by saturation. **b** (of sunlight) penetrate thoroughly. **5** *tr.* (foll. by *out*, *out of*, *off*, etc.) remove by soaking in water etc. (*soaked the label off the jar*). **6** *tr. informal* extract money from by an extortionate charge, taxation, etc. (*soak the rich*). **7** *intr. informal* drink persistently, booze. ● *n.* **1** the act of soaking or the state of being soaked. **2** *informal* a hard drinker. □ **soak up 1** absorb (liquid). **2** acquire (knowledge, experiences, etc.) copiously. **3** expose oneself to (the sun, heat, etc.) so as to absorb the maximum possible. □ **soaker** *n.*

soaked *adj.* **1** thoroughly wet; drenched. **2** very drunk.

soaking ● *adj.* (in full **soaking wet**) very wet; wet through. ● *n.* the act of soaking; an instance of being soaked.

so-and-so *n.* (*pl.* **so-and-sos**) **1** a particular person or thing not needing to be specified (*told me to do so-and-so*). **2** *informal* a person disliked or regarded with disfavour (*the so-and-so left me behind*).

soap ● *n.* **1** a cleansing agent that is a compound of fatty acid with soda or potash which, when rubbed in water, yields a lather used in washing. **2** *informal* = SOAP OPERA (also *attrib.*: *soap fan*). ● *v.tr.* **1** apply soap to. **2** scrub or rub with soap.

soapberry *n.* (*pl.* **-ies**) **1** = BUFFALO BERRY. **2** any of various tropical American shrubs, esp. of the genus *Sapindus*, with fruits yielding saponin.

soapbox *n.* **1** a makeshift stand for a public speaker. **2** something that provides an outlet for a person's opinions etc. (*her column is nothing but a soapbox*). **3** a child's homemade cart consisting of a wooden box mounted on wheels, and steerable at the front.

soap opera *n.* a television or radio drama with continuous episodes about the events and problems in the daily lives of the same group of characters.

soapstone *n.* a soft metamorphic rock with a smooth greasy feel, readily sawn into slabs or carved.

soapsuds *n.pl.* = SUDS 1.

soapy *adj.* (**-ier, -iest**) **1** of or like soap. **2** containing or smeared with soap. **3** of or like a soap opera. **4** (of a person or manner) unctuous or flattering.

soar *v.intr.* **1** fly or rise high. **2** reach a high level or standard (*prices soared*). **3** maintain height in the air without flapping the wings or using power. **4** sing or play esp. in the higher ranges in a particularly impressive or moving manner. □ **soarer** *n.* **soaring** *adj.* **soaringly** *adv.*

SOB *abbr. esp. N Amer. slang* SON OF A BITCH.

sob ● *v.* (**sobbed, sobbing**) **1** *intr.* **a** draw breath in convulsive gasps usu. with weeping under mental distress or physical exhaustion. **b** weep in this way. **2** *tr.* (usu. foll. by *out*) utter with sobs. ● *n.* a convulsive drawing of breath, esp. in weeping. □ **sobbingly** *adv.*

soba /'soːbə/ *n.* (treated as *sing.* or *pl.*) Japanese noodles made from buckwheat flour.

sober ● *adj.* (**soberer, soberest**) **1** not affected by alcohol. **2** not given to excessive drinking of alcohol. **3** moderate, well-balanced, tranquil, sedate. **4** not fanciful or exaggerated (*the sober truth*). **5** (of a colour etc.) quiet and inconspicuous. ● *v.tr. & intr.* (often foll. by *down*, *up*) make or become sober or less wild, reckless, enthusiastic, visionary, etc. (*a sobering thought*). □ **sober as a judge** completely sober. □ **soberly** *adv.*

sober sides *n.* a sedate, serious person. □ **sober-sided** *adj.*

sobriety /sə'braɪəti/ *n.* **1** the state of being sober. **2** moderation, esp. in the use of alcohol. **3** seriousness or sedateness.

sobriquet /ˌsoːbrɪ'keɪ, 'soːbrɪˌkeɪ, -'ket/ *n.* **1** a nickname. **2** an assumed name.

sob story *n. informal* a story or explanation intended to make the listener or reader feel sympathy or sadness, esp. one that fails to do so.

Soc. *abbr.* **1** Socialist. **2** Society.

soc /soːʃ/ *n. N Amer. informal* sociology (also *attrib.*: *soc prof*).

soca /'soːkə/ *n.* a kind of calypso music with elements of soul, originally from Trinidad.

so-called *adj.* commonly designated or known as, often incorrectly.

soccer *n.* a form of football played by two teams of 11, in which a round ball may be kicked or bounced off any part of the body except the arms and hands.

sociable *adj.* **1** fitted for or liking the society of other people; ready and willing to talk and act with others. **2** (of a person's manner or behaviour etc.) friendly. **3** (of a meeting etc.) marked by friendliness, not stiff or formal. □ **sociability** *n.* **sociably** *adv.*

social ● *adj.* **1** of or relating to society or its organization. **2** concerned with the mutual relations of human beings or classes of human beings. **3** living in organized communities; unfitted for a solitary life (*humans are social animals*). **4 a** needing companionship; gregarious, interdependent. **b** co-operative; practising the division of labour. **5** existing only as a member of a compound organism. **6 a** (of insects) living together in organized communities. **b** (of birds) nesting near each other in communities. **7** (of plants) growing thickly together and monopolizing the ground they grow on. ● *n.* **1** a social gathering, esp. one organized by a club etc. **2** *Cdn* (*Prairies*) a public social gathering held before a wedding to raise money for the couple that is to be married. □ **sociality** *n.* **socially** *adv.*

social assistance *n. Cdn* = SOCIAL SECURITY.

social climber *n. derogatory* a person anxious to gain a higher social status. □ **social climbing** *n.* **social-climbing** *adj.*

social conscience *n.* a sense of responsibility or concern for the problems and injustices of society.

social contract *n.* (also **social compact**) a notional agreement between individuals and the state to co-operate for social benefits, e.g. by sacrificing some individual freedom for state protection.

social credit ● *n.* **1** the economic theory that the purchasing power of consumers should be increased either by subsidizing producers so that they can reduce prices or by distributing the profits of industry to the general public. **2** (**Social Credit**) *Cdn* the Social Credit party, its supporters, etc. ● *adj.* (**Social Credit**) *Cdn* of or relating to the Social Credit Party.

Social Crediter *n. Cdn* a member of the Social Credit Party.

Social Credit Party *n. Cdn* a political party formed in the 1930s espousing the economic theories of social credit, but soon evolving into a mainstream party with conservative financial and social policies.

social Darwinism *n.* a late 19th-c. theory that

individuals, groups, and peoples are subject to the same laws of natural selection as plants and animals, and that superior individuals or groups survived and succeeded while the weaker disappeared, to the benefit of society. □ **social Darwinist** n.

social democracy n. a socialist system achieved by democratic means. □ **social democrat** n.

social engineering n. the use of sociological principles in approaching social problems.

social gospel n. N Amer. hist. the gospel interpreted as having a social application, esp. as used to advocate social reform. □ **social gospeller** n.

social housing n. Cdn & Brit. public housing.

social insurance number n. Cdn a nine-digit number by which the federal government identifies individuals for the purposes of taxation, employment insurance, pensions, etc. Abbr.: **SIN**.

socialism n. **1** a political and economic theory of social organization which advocates that the community as a whole should own and control the means of production, distribution, and exchange. **2** policy or practice based on this theory. **3** (in Marxist theory) a transitional social state between the overthrow of capitalism and the realization of communism. □ **socialist** n. & adj. **socialistic** adj.

socialite n. a person who is well-known in fashionable society and goes to a lot of fashionable parties.

socialize v. **1** intr. act in a sociable manner. **2** tr. prepare for life in society. **3** tr. organize on socialistic principles. □ **socialization** n.

social justice n. the notion that society should be organized in a way that allows equal opportunity for all its members (also attrib.: social justice issues).

social life n. leisure activities in which one associates with one's friends and acquaintances.

social order n. the network of human relationships in society.

social realism n. the realistic depiction of social conditions or political views in art and literature. □ **social realist** n.

social science n. **1** the scientific study of human society and social relationships. **2** a branch of this (e.g. politics or economics). □ **social scientist** n.

social security n. state assistance to those lacking in economic security and welfare, e.g. the aged.

social service n. (usu. in pl.) a service provided by the state or a charitable organization for the community, esp. education, health, and housing (also attrib.: social service agency).

social studies n.pl. (treated as sing.) a school course encompassing such subjects as geography, history, anthropology, sociology, etc.

social work n. work done to help people in the community with special needs. □ **social worker** n.

society n. (pl. **-ies**) **1** the sum of human conditions and activity regarded as a whole functioning interdependently. **2** a social community (all societies must have firm laws). **3 a** a social mode of life. **b** the customs and organization of an ordered community. **4** Ecology a plant community. **5 a** the socially advantaged or prominent members of a community. **b** this, or a part of it, qualified in some way (in polite society). **6** participation in hospitality; other people's homes or company (avoids society). **7** companionship, company (avoids the society of such people). **8** an association of persons united by a common aim or interest or principle. □ **societal** adj. (esp. in sense 1).

Society of Friends n. see QUAKER.

Society of Jesus n. see JESUIT.

socio- /ˈsəʊsɪəʊ:, -ʃɪə:/ comb. form **1** of society (and). **2** of or relating to sociology (and).

sociobiology n. the scientific study of the biological aspects of social behaviour. □ **sociobiological** adj. **sociobiologist** n.

socio-cultural adj. combining social and cultural factors or elements. □ **socio-culturally** adv.

socio-economic adj. relating to or concerned with the interaction of social and economic factors. □ **socio-economically** adv.

sociolinguistics n. the study of language in relation to social factors. □ **sociolinguist** n. **sociolinguistic** adj.

sociology /ˌsəʊsɪˈɒlədʒɪ, ˌsəʊʃɪ-/ n. **1** the study of the development, structure, and functioning of human society. **2** the study of social problems. □ **sociological** adj. **sociologically** adv. **sociologist** n.

sociopath /ˈsəʊsɪəˌpæθ, ˈsəʊsɪəʊ:-, ˈsəʊʃɪ-/ n. a person with a personality disorder manifesting itself in extreme anti-social attitudes and behaviour, particularly a lack of moral responsibility or social conscience. □ **sociopathic** adj. **sociopathy** n.

socio-political adj. combining social and political factors.

sock[1] n. (pl. **-s** or informal **sox**) **1** a short knitted covering for the foot, usu. not reaching the knee. **2** a removable inner sole put into a shoe for warmth etc. **3** = WINDSOCK. □ **in one's sock feet** N Amer. = IN ONE'S STOCKING FEET (see STOCKING). **knock** (or **blow**) **one's socks off** astound, amaze. **pull up one's socks** informal make an effort to improve. **put a sock in it** informal be quiet.

sock[2] informal ● v.tr. hit (esp. a person) forcefully. ● n. **1** a hard blow. **2** N Amer. the power to deliver a blow. □ **sock it to** attack or address (a person) vigorously.

socked in adj. N Amer. **1** (of an airport) closed because of snow, fog, etc. **2** (of an aircraft) grounded by adverse weather conditions.

socket n. **1** a natural or artificial hollow for something to fit into or stand firm or revolve in. **2** Electricity a device receiving a plug, light bulb, etc., to make a connection.

sockeye n. a blue-backed salmon of the N American Pacific coast, Oncorhynchus nerka.

sock hop n. N Amer. a social dance at which participants dance in their stocking feet.

Socratic /səˈkrætɪk/ ● adj. of or relating to the Greek philosopher Socrates (469–399 BC) or his philosophy, esp. the method associated with him of seeking the truth by a series of questions and answers. ● n. a follower of Socrates. □ **Socratically** adv.

Socred /ˈsəʊkrɛd/ Cdn ● adj. = SOCIAL CREDIT adj. ● n. = SOCIAL CREDITER.

sod ● n. **1** turf or a piece of turf. **2** the surface of the ground. ● v.tr. (**sodded, sodding**) cover (the ground) with sod.

soda n. **1** any of various compounds of sodium in common use (baking soda). **2** (in full **soda water**) water made effervescent by impregnation with carbon dioxide under pressure (originally made with sodium bicarbonate), and used alone or with an alcoholic beverage etc. as a drink. **3** (in full **soda pop**) esp. US = POP[1] n. 2. **4** N Amer. a sweet fizzy drink made with soda water, fruit juice and sometimes ice cream.

soda biscuit n. **1** N Amer. = SODA CRACKER. **2** a tea biscuit leavened with baking soda.

soda cracker n. N Amer. a thin crisp cracker made with baking soda.

soda fountain *n.* esp. *N Amer.* **1** a shop or counter serving soft drinks, ice cream, etc. **2** a device dispensing soda water or soft drinks.

sodbuster *n.* *N Amer. informal* a farmer who raises crops rather than livestock, esp. one of the early homesteaders on the Prairies.

sodden *adj.* **1** saturated with liquid; soaked through. **2** rendered stupid or dull, esp. through drunkenness.

sod house *n.* (also **sod hut**) *N Amer.* a house with walls of sod and a canvas or sod roof supported by wooden rafters, built esp. by settlers on the Prairies.

sodium *n.* a soft silver-white reactive metallic element, occurring naturally in soda, salt, etc., which is an essential element in living organisms.

sodium carbonate *n.* a white powder with many commercial applications including the manufacture of soap and glass.

sodium chloride *n.* a colourless crystalline compound occurring naturally in sea water and rock salt.

sodium light *n.* (also **sodium vapour light**, **sodium lamp**) a street light using an electrical discharge in sodium vapour and giving a yellow light.

sodium nitrate *n.* a white powdery compound used mainly in the manufacture of fertilizers.

Sodom /'sɒdəm/ *n.* a depraved or corrupt place.

sodomite /'sɒdə,maɪt/ *n.* a person who engages in sodomy.

sodomy /'sɒdəmɪ/ *n.* anal intercourse performed between two males or a male and a female. □ **sodomize** *v.tr.*

sod shack *n.* = SOD HOUSE.

sod-turning *n.* *Cdn* = GROUNDBREAKING *n.*

sofa *n.* a long upholstered seat with a back and arms, for two or more people.

sofa bed *n.* a sofa that can be folded out to form a bed, usu. for occasional use.

soffit *n.* the undersurface of an arch, a balcony, overhanging eaves, etc.

soft ● *adj.* **1** lacking hardness or firmness; yielding to pressure; easily cut, moulded or compressed. **2** (of cloth, skin, etc.) having a smooth surface or texture; not rough or coarse. **3** (of a light or colour etc.) not brilliant or glaring. **4** (of a voice or sounds) gentle and pleasing; not loud. **5** (of air etc.) mellow, mild, balmy; not noticeably cold or hot. **6** (of water) free from mineral salts and therefore good for lathering. **7 a** (of a consonant) sibilant or palatal (as *c* in *ice*, *g* in *age*). **b** voiced or unaspirated. **8** (of an outline etc.) not sharply defined. **9** (of an action or manner etc.) gentle, conciliatory, complimentary, amorous. **10** (of the heart or feelings etc.) compassionate, sympathetic, esp. to too great an extent. **11 a** lacking in determination, courage, etc.; weak or sentimental. **b** foolish, silly (*soft in the head*). **12** *informal* (of a job etc.) easy, undemanding. **13** (of drugs) mild; not likely to cause addiction. **14** (also **soft-core**) (of pornography) suggestive or erotic but not explicit. **15 a** (of currency) likely to fall in value; not readily exchangeable into other currencies. **b** (of a market, prices, etc.) declining; weak. **16** (of a statistic, fact, etc.) insubstantial, imprecise. **17** (of support for a political candidate, platform, etc.) not solid; liable to shift. **18** *Politics* moderate; willing to compromise (*the soft left*). **19** (of wheat) having a soft kernel rich in starch, used to make pastry flour (*compare* HARD *adj.* 16). **20 a** *Sport* (of a ball, puck, etc.) weakly or lightly hit. **b** *Hockey* (of a goal) not outstanding; that the goalie should have been able to stop. ● *adv.* softly (*play soft*). ● *n.* a soft or yielding thing; the soft part of something. □ **be soft on** *informal* **1** be lenient towards. **2** be infatuated with.

have a soft spot for be fond of or affectionate towards (a person). □ **softly** *adv.* **softness** *n.*

softball *n.* **1** a modified form of baseball played on a smaller diamond using a larger and softer ball that is pitched underarm. **2** the ball used in this sport.

soft-boiled *adj.* **1** (of an egg) lightly boiled leaving the yolk semi-liquid. **2** *informal* (of a person) mild, easygoing.

softcover *adj. & n.* = PAPERBACK *adj. & n.*

soft drink *n.* a carbonated, non-alcoholic drink.

soften *v.* **1** *tr. & intr.* make or become soft or softer. **2** *tr. & intr.* make or become less severe (*his face softened and he almost smiled*). **3** *tr.* modify, tone down; make less pronounced or prominent. **4** *tr.* reduce the force of something (*soften the blow*). **5** *tr.* (often foll. by *up*) **a** reduce the strength of (defences) by bombing or some other preliminary attack. **b** reduce the resistance of (a person). □ **softener** *n.*

soft-focus ● *adj.* **1** characterized by or producing a deliberate slight blurring or lack of definition in a photograph (*soft-focus filter*). **2** deliberately diffuse, unclear, or imprecise. ● *n.* (**soft focus**) **1** a deliberate slight blurring or lack of definition in a photograph. **2** deliberate diffuseness or imprecision.

soft-headed *adj.* foolish, feeble-minded.

soft-hearted *adj.* tender, compassionate.

softie *n.* (*pl.* **-ies**) *informal* **1** a kind, sympathetic, or sentimental person. **2** a weak or silly person. **3** *Hockey slang* a goal scored on a weak shot.

soft landing *n.* **1** a landing by a spacecraft during which no serious damage is incurred. **2** a slowing down of economic growth at an acceptable degree relative to inflation and unemployment. □ **soft-land** *v.tr. & intr.*

soft maple *n.* any of several maples with less durable wood, esp. red maple and silver maple.

soft news *n.* news that focuses on personalities, provides background for hard news, or is not immediately topical, e.g. entertainment and lifestyle reporting.

soft palate *n.* the rear part of the palate.

soft pedal ● *n.* a pedal on a piano that makes the tone softer. ● *v.tr. & intr.* (**soft-pedal**) (**-pedalled**, **-pedalling**) **1** refrain from emphasizing; be restrained (about). **2** play with the soft pedal down.

soft porn *n.* *informal* soft-core pornography (often *attrib.*: *soft-porn movie*).

soft return *n.* a carriage return inserted automatically by a word processor at the end of a line of text.

soft rock *n.* a type of rock music originating in the 1970s characterized by a pleasant, melodic sound and usu. romantic lyrics.

soft sell ● *n.* restrained or subtly persuasive salesmanship. ● *v.tr.* (**soft-sell**) (*past* and *past part.* **-sold**) sell by this method.

soft-shoe ● *n.* a kind of tap dance performed in soft-soled shoes. ● *v.intr.* **1** perform this dance. **2** move quietly or lightly.

soft soap ● *n.* **1** a semi-liquid soap, esp. one made with potassium not sodium salts. **2** *informal* persuasive flattery. ● *v.tr.* (**soft-soap**) *informal* persuade (a person) with flattery.

soft-spoken *adj.* speaking with a gentle quiet voice.

soft tissue *n.* body tissue other than bone or cartilage.

soft touch *n.* *slang* a person easily manipulated, esp. one easily induced to part with money.

software *n.* **1** the programs and other operating information used by a computer. **2** storage media such as video cassettes, audio tapes, etc. requiring playback on electronic equipment.

software engineering *n.* the professional development, production, and management of system software. □ **software engineer** *n.*

software package *n.* a set of computer programs directed at some application in general, e.g. computer graphics, word processing, etc.

softwood ● *n.* **1** the wood of pine, spruce, or other conifers, easily sawn. **2** a tree producing such wood. ● *adj.* **1** made of softwood (*softwood lumber*). **2** containing softwoods (*softwood forest*).

softy *var. of* SOFTIE.

soggy *adj.* (**-ier, -iest**) **1** sodden, saturated. **2** (of weather) rainy, dank. **3** dull, boring, lifeless. □ **sogginess** *n.*

soh *var. of* SO².

SOHC *abbr.* single overhead camshaft.

soil¹ *n.* **1** the upper layer of earth in which plants grow, consisting of disintegrated rock usu. with an admixture of organic remains. **2** the ground, the earth (*a tiller of the soil*). **3** ground belonging to a nation; territory (*on Canadian soil*). **4** any environment encouraging growth. □ **soilless** *adj.*

soil² *n.* ● *v.tr.* **1** make dirty; smear or stain with dirt. **2** dirty (diapers, clothes etc.) by involuntary defecation. **3** tarnish, defile; bring discredit to (*would not soil my hands with it*). ● *n.* **1** a dirty mark; a stain, smear, or defilement. **2** filth; refuse matter.

soil amendment *n.* (also **soil conditioner**) a substance added to the soil to improve its properties.

soil conservation *n.* protection of soil against erosion, loss of fertility, and damage.

soiree /'swɑr'ei, 'swar-/ *n.* **1** a party in the evening. **2** *Cdn (Nfld)* **a** a social gathering held by an organization or service club. **b** a large party or community social with singing, dancing, and eating.

sojourn /'so:dʒɜrn/ ● *n.* a temporary stay. ● *v.intr.* (also /so:'dʒɜrn/) stay temporarily. □ **sojourner** *n.*

sol¹ *var. of* SO².

sol² *n. hist.* a former coin and monetary unit of France and New France etc., notionally equivalent to one-twentieth of a livre but varying in actual value.

sola /'so:lə/ *n.* a pithy-stemmed E Indian swamp plant of the genus *Aeschynomene*.

solace /'sɒləs/ ● *n.* comfort in distress, disappointment, or tedium. ● *v.tr.* give solace to.

solar ● *adj.* of, relating to, or reckoned by the sun (*solar eclipse; solar time*). ● *n.* a solarium.

solar cell *n.* a photoelectric device converting solar radiation into electricity.

solar eclipse *n.* an eclipse in which the sun is obscured by the moon.

solar energy *n.* **1** radiant energy emitted by the sun. **2** = SOLAR POWER.

solar flare *n.* a short-lived, cataclysmic outburst of solar material, driven by magnetic forces, from a relatively small area of the solar surface.

solarium /sə'leriəm/ *n.* (*pl.* **-s** or **solaria** /-riə/) a room, balcony, etc. fitted with extensive areas of glass.

solar panel *n.* (also **solar collector**) a panel that harnesses the energy in the sun's radiation, either to generate electricity using solar cells or to heat water.

solar plexus *n.* **1** a complex of radiating nerves at the pit of the stomach. **2** the region of the torso in front of this, esp. as regarded as vulnerable to a blow.

solar power *n.* power obtained by harnessing the energy of the sun's rays. □ **solar-powered** *adj.*

solar radiation *n.* electromagnetic radiated energy from the sun.

solar system *n.* the collection of nine planets and their moons in orbit around the sun, together with asteroids, meteoroids, and comets.

solar wind *n.* the continuous flow of charged particles from the sun into surrounding space.

solar year *n.* the time taken for the earth to travel once around the sun, measured from equinox to equinox.

sold *past and past part. of* SELL. □ **sold on** *informal* enthusiastic about.

solder /'sɒdər/ ● *n.* **1** a fusible alloy used to join less fusible metals or wires etc. **2** a cementing or joining agency. ● *v.tr.* join with solder. □ **solderless** *adj.*

soldering iron *n.* a tool used for applying solder.

soldier ● *n.* **1** a person serving in or having served in an army. **2** a private or NCO in an army. **3** a military commander of specified ability (*a great soldier*). **4** a person who fights for a cause. **5** (in full **soldier ant**) a wingless ant or termite with a large head and jaws for fighting in defence of its colony. **6** (in full **soldier beetle**) a carnivorous beetle of the family Cantharidae, with soft reddish wing-cases. **7** each of an orderly series of upright bricks, timbers, etc., suggestive of a line of soldiers on parade. ● *v.intr.* serve as a soldier (*was off soldiering*). □ **soldier on** *informal* persevere doggedly. □ **soldierly** *adj.*

soldier of fortune *n.* an adventurous person ready to take service under any state or person.

sold-out *attrib.adj.* having all tickets sold (*sold-out show*).

sole¹ ● *n.* **1** the undersurface of the foot. **2** the part of a shoe, sock, etc., corresponding to this (esp. excluding the heel). **3** the lower surface or base of an implement, e.g. a plow. ● *v.tr.* provide (a shoe etc.) with a sole; replace the sole of. □ **-soled** *adj.* (in *comb.*).

sole² *n.* **1** any of various flatfish of the family Pleuronectidae or Soleidae, used as food. **2** the flesh of any flatfish prepared as food.

sole³ *adj.* (*attrib.*) one and only; single, exclusive (*the sole reason*). □ **solely** *adv.*

solecism /'sɒlə,sizəm/ *n.* **1** a mistake of grammar or idiom; a blunder in the manner of speaking or writing. **2** a piece of bad manners or incorrect behaviour.

solemn *adj.* **1** serious and dignified (*a solemn occasion*). **2** formal; accompanied by ceremony, esp. for religious purposes. **3** serious or cheerless in manner (*looks rather solemn*). **4** mysteriously impressive. **5** full of importance; weighty (*a solemn warning*). **6** grave, sober, deliberate; slow in movement or action (*solemn music*). □ **solemnly** *adv.*

solemnity /sə'lemnɪti/ *n.* (*pl.* **-ies**) **1** the state of being solemn; a solemn character or feeling; solemn behaviour. **2** a rite or celebration.

solemnize /'sɒləm,naiz/ *v.tr.* **1** duly perform (a ceremony esp. of marriage). **2** celebrate or commemorate (an occasion etc.) by special observances or with special formality. **3** make solemn. □ **solemnization** *n.*

solenoid /'so:lə,nɔid, 'sɒl-/ *n.* a cylindrical coil of wire acting as a magnet when carrying current.

sole practitioner *n. Cdn* a lawyer, accountant, etc. who is the sole member of a firm, rather than one who works in partnership with others.

soli *pl. of* SOLO 1a.

solicit /sə'lɪsɪt/ *v.* (**solicited, soliciting**) **1** *tr. & intr.* ask repeatedly or earnestly for or seek or invite (business etc.). **2** *tr.* (often foll. by *for*) make a request or petition to (a person). **3** *tr. & intr.* accost (a person) and offer one's services as a prostitute. □ **solicitation** *n.*

solicitor *n.* **1** *Cdn* a lawyer. **2** a person who solicits. **3** *N Amer.* a canvasser. **4** *N Amer.* the chief law officer of a city etc.

Solicitor General *n.* (*pl.* **Solicitors General**) (in Canada) a federal or provincial cabinet member who is responsible for correctional services, law enforcement, and some forms of licensing.

solicitous /səˈlɪsɪtəs/ *adj.* **1** (often foll. by *of, about,* etc.) showing interest or concern. **2** eager, anxious. □ **solicitously** *adv.*

solicitude /səˈlɪsɪˌtuːd, -ˌtjuːd/ *n.* **1** the state of being solicitous; solicitous behaviour. **2** anxiety or concern.

solid ● *adj.* **1** firm and stable in shape; not liquid or fluid (*solid food*). **2 a** of such material throughout, not hollow or containing cavities (*a solid sphere*). **b** (of a wall etc.) having no opening or window. **c** (of a line, row, etc.) continuous, unbroken. **3** of the same substance or colour throughout (*solid silver; a solid green sweater*). **4** of strong material or construction or build, not flimsy or slender etc. **5** (of a cloud etc.) having the appearance of an unbroken mass; dense, thick, compact. **6 a** having three dimensions. **b** concerned with solids (*solid geometry*). **7 a** sound and reliable; genuine (*solid arguments*). **b** staunch and dependable (*a solid worker*). **8** sound but without any special flair etc. (*a solid piece of work*). **9** financially sound. **10** (of time) uninterrupted, continuous (*four solid hours*). **11** unanimous, undivided (*support has been pretty solid so far*). ● *n.* **1** a solid substance or body. **2** (in *pl.*) solid food. **3** a solidly coloured garment or fabric (*mix stripes with solids*). **4** *Math.* a body or magnitude having three dimensions. ● *adv.* so as to become solid; solidly (*booked solid; frozen solid*). □ **solidity** *n.* **solidly** *adv.*

solidarity *n.* **1** unity or agreement of feeling or action, esp. among individuals with a common interest. **2** mutual support or cohesiveness within a group. **3** (**Solidarity**) an independent trade union movement formed in Poland in 1980 which developed into a mass campaign for political change.

solid colour *n.* colour covering the whole of an object, without a pattern etc. □ **solid-coloured** *adj.*

solidify *v.tr. & intr.* (**-ies, -ied**) make or become solid. □ **solidification** *n.*

solid state ● *n.* the state of matter that retains its boundaries without support. ● *adj.* using the electronic properties of solids, e.g. a semiconductor, to replace those of valves.

solidus /ˈsɒlɪdəs/ *n.* (*pl.* **solidi** /-ˌdaɪ/) an oblique stroke (/) used in writing fractions ($^3/_4$) etc.

soliloquy /səˈlɪləkwi/ *n.* (*pl.* **-ies**) **1** the act of talking when alone or regardless of any hearers, esp. in drama. **2** part of a play involving this. □ **soliloquize** *v.intr.*

solipsism /ˈsɒlɪpˌsɪzəm/ *n.* **1** *Philos.* the view that the self is all that exists, or is all that can be known. **2** self-centredness. □ **solipsist** *n.* **solipsistic** *adj.*

solitaire /ˈsɒlɪˌter/ *n.* **1** a diamond or other gem set by itself. **2** a ring having a single gem. **3** *N Amer.* a game for one player in which cards taken in random order have to be arranged in certain groups or sequences. **4** a game for one player played by removing pegs etc. one at a time from a board by jumping others over them until only one is left.

solitary ● *adj.* **1** living alone; not gregarious; without companions; lonely (*a solitary existence*). **2** performed alone (*a solitary expedition*). **3** (of a place) secluded or unfrequented. **4** single or sole (*a solitary instance*). **5** (of an insect) not living in communities. **6** *Bot.* growing singly, not in a cluster. ● *n.* (*pl.* **-ies**) **1** a recluse or hermit. **2** *informal* = SOLITARY CONFINEMENT. □ **solitarily** *adv.* **solitariness** *n.*

solitary confinement *n.* isolation of a prisoner in a separate cell as a punishment.

solitude *n.* **1** the state of being or living alone; solitariness. **2** a lonely or unfrequented place.

solo ● *n.* (*pl.* **-os**) **1 a** (*pl.* **-os** or **soli**) a vocal or instrumental piece or passage performed by one person with or without accompaniment. **b** a dance performed by one person. **c** (*attrib.*) performed or performing as a solo (*solo passage; solo violin*). **2 a** an unaccompanied flight by a pilot in an aircraft. **b** anything done by one person unaccompanied. **c** (*attrib.*) unaccompanied, alone. **3** (*attrib.*) *Baseball* designating a home run hit with no one on base. ● *v.intr.* (**-oes, -oed**) perform a solo, esp. a musical solo or a solo flight. ● *adv.* unaccompanied, alone (*flew solo for the first time*).

soloist *n.* **1** a performer of a solo, esp. in music or dance. **2** a dancer of a rank between corps de ballet and principal dancer, who performs some solo roles.

Solomon *n.* a very wise person.

Solomon Gundy /ˈɡʌndi/ *n.* (also **Solomon Grundy** /ˈɡrʌndi/) *Cdn* (*NS*) a dish of salted herring marinated in vinegar, spices, sugar, and onions.

Solomon's seal *n.* **1** a figure like the Star of David. **2** any plant of the genus *Polygonatum*, with arching stems and drooping green and white flowers.

solstice /ˈsɒlstɪs, ˈsɒl-/ *n.* **1** either of the two times in the year when the sun reaches its highest or lowest point in the sky at noon, marked by the longest and shortest days. **2** the point in the ecliptic reached by the sun at a solstice.

soluble /ˈsɒljʊbəl/ *adj.* **1** that can be dissolved, esp. in water. **2** that can be solved. □ **solubility** *n.*

solute /ˈsɒljuːt/ *n.* a dissolved substance.

solution *n.* **1 a** the act or a means of solving a problem or difficulty. **b** an explanation, answer, or decision. **c** *Math.* the value of an unknown or variable that satisfies an equation or set of equations. **2 a** the conversion of a solid or gas into a liquid by mixture with a liquid solvent. **b** the state resulting from this (*held in solution*). **c** a homogeneous liquid, semi-liquid, or solid mixture produced by this process. **3** the act of dissolving or the state of being dissolved. **4** the act of separating or breaking.

solve *v.tr.* find an answer to, or an action or course that removes or effectively deals with (a problem or difficulty). □ **solvability** *n.* **solvable** *adj.* **solver** *n.*

solvent ● *adj.* **1** having enough money to meet one's liabilities. **2** able to dissolve or form a solution with something. ● *n.* **1** a solvent liquid etc. **2** a dissolving or weakening agent. □ **solvency** *n.* (in sense 1 of *adj.*).

solvent abuse *n.* the use of volatile organic solvents as intoxicants by inhalation, e.g. glue sniffing.

Somali /səˈmɒli, -ˈmɑːli/ *n.* **1** (*pl.* same or **-s**) **a** a member of a Hamitic Muslim people of Somalia, a country in NE Africa. **b** a native or national of Somalia. **2** the language of this people, which belongs to the Cushitic branch of the Afro-Asiatic family of languages. ● *adj.* of or relating to Somalia, the Somalis, or their language. □ **Somalian** *adj. & n.*

somatic /səˈmætɪk/ *adj.* of or relating to the body, esp. as distinct from the mind.

somatic cell *n.* any cell of a living organism except the reproductive cells.

somatotropin /ˌsoʊmətoʊˈtroʊpɪn/ *n.* (also **-trophin**

/-fin/) a growth hormone secreted by the pituitary gland.

sombre *adj.* (also esp. *US* **somber**) **1** gloomy, shadowy (*a sombre sky*). **2** dark in colour. **3** oppressively solemn or sober. **4** dismal, foreboding (*a sombre prospect*). □ **sombrely** *adv.* **sombreness** *n.*

sombrero /sɒmˈbreːoː/ *n.* (*pl.* **-os**) a broad-brimmed felt or straw hat worn esp. in Mexico and the southwestern US.

some ● *adj.* **1** an unspecified amount or number of (*some water*; *some of them*). **2** that is unknown or unnamed (*some fool has locked the door*; *to some extent*). **3** denoting an approximate number (*waited some twenty minutes*). **4** a considerable amount or number of (*went to some trouble*). **5** (usu. stressed) **a** at least a small amount of (*do have some consideration*). **b** such to a certain extent (*that is some help*). **c** *informal* notably such (*that was some game*). **d** (used at the beginning of a sentence for expressing negative opinions) no; no kind of (*some chance!*). ● *pron.* some people or things, some number or amount (*I have some already*). ● *adv. informal* **1** to some extent (*we talked some*). **2** *N Amer.* very; to a high degree (*we were some proud*). □ **and then some** *informal* and plenty more than that.

-some *suffix* forming nouns from numerals, meaning 'a group of (so many)' (*foursome*).

somebody (also **someone**) ● *pron.* some person. ● *n.* (*pl.* **-ies**) a person of importance (*I'm a somebody*).

someday *adv.* at some time in the future.

somehow *adv.* **1** in some way; by some means (*must finish it somehow*). **2** for some reason or other (*somehow I never liked them*). **3** in some unspecified or unknown way (*he somehow dropped behind*).

someplace *adv. N Amer.* = SOMEWHERE.

somersault /ˈsʌməsɒlt/ ● *n.* **1** an acrobatic movement in which a person turns head over heels in the air or on the ground, making a complete revolution. **2 a** a complete overturn or upset. **b** a reversal of opinion, policy, etc. ● *v.intr.* perform a somersault.

something ● *n.* & *pron.* **1 a** some unspecified or unknown thing (*have something to tell you*). **b** (in full **something or other**) as a substitute for an unknown or forgotten description (*she's a professor of something or other*). **2** a known or understood but unexpressed quantity, quality, or extent (*there's something in what she says*). **3** *informal* an important or notable person or thing (*the party was quite something*). **4** (in *comb.*) used to denote a person's approximate age, esp. as being suggestive of the characteristic tastes and outlook of a particular generation (*thirtysomething*). ● *adv.* **1** somewhat; in some degree. **2** *informal* to a high degree (*hurts something terrible*). □ **or something** or some unspecified alternative possibility (*must have run away or something*). **see something of** encounter (a person) briefly or occasionally. **something like 1** an amount in the region of (*something like a million dollars*). **2** somewhat like. **3** *informal* impressive; a fine specimen of. **something of** to some extent; in some sense (*something of an expert*).

something else *n.* **1** something different. **2** *informal* something exceptional.

sometime ● *adv.* at some unspecified time. ● *adj.* **1** former (*the sometime mayor*). **2** occasional (*a sometime contributor*).

sometimes *adv.* at some times; occasionally.

somewhat ● *adv.* to some extent (*somewhat strange*). ● *n.* & *pron.* something (*loses somewhat of its force*).

somewhere ● *adv.* (also *N Amer.* dialect **somewheres**) in or to some place. ● *pron.* some unspecified place. □ **get somewhere** *informal*

achieve success. **somewhere around** approximately.

sommelier /ˌsɒməlˈjei/ *n.* a wine waiter.

somnambulism /sɒmˈnæmbjʊˌlɪzəm/ *n.* **1** sleepwalking. **2** a condition of the brain inducing this. □ **somnambulant** *adj.* **somnambulate** *v.intr.* **somnambulist** *n.* **somnambulistic** *adj.*

somnolent /ˈsɒmnələnt/ *adj.* **1** sleepy, drowsy. **2** inducing drowsiness. □ **somnolence** *n.*

son *n.* **1** a boy or man in relation to either or both of his parents. **2 a** a male descendant. **b** (foll. by *of*) a male member of a family, nation, etc. **3** a person regarded as inheriting an occupation, quality, etc., or associated with a particular attribute (*sons of freedom*). **4** (also **my son**) a form of address esp. to a boy. **5** (**the Son**) (in Christian belief) Jesus Christ. □ **sonship** *n.*

sonar /ˈsoːnɑː/ *n.* **1** a system for the underwater detection of objects by reflected or emitted sound. **2** an apparatus for this.

sonata /səˈnɒtə, -ˈnætə/ *n.* a composition for one instrument or two (one usu. being a piano accompaniment), usu. in several movements with one (esp. the first) or more in sonata form.

sonata form *n.* a type of composition in three sections, in which two themes (or subjects) are explored according to set key relationships.

song *n.* **1** a musical composition comprising a short poem or other set of words set to music; a set of words meant to be sung. **2** singing or vocal music (*burst into song*). **3** a musical composition suggestive of a song. **4** a sound suggestive of singing. **5** the usu. repeated musical call of some birds. **6** a short poem in rhymed stanzas. □ **for a song** *informal* very cheaply. □ **song-like** *adj.*

song and dance *n. informal* a fuss or commotion.

songbird *n.* **1** a bird with a musical call. **2** a perching bird of the group Oscines. **3** *informal* a superb female singer.

songbook *n.* a collection of songs with music.

song sparrow *n.* a N American sparrow, *Melospiza melodia*, with a characteristic musical song.

songwriter *n.* a writer of songs or the music for them. □ **songwriting** *n.*

sonic /ˈsɒnɪk/ *adj.* of or relating to or using sound or sound waves. □ **sonically** *adv.*

sonic boom *n.* a loud explosive noise caused by the shock wave from an aircraft when it passes the speed of sound.

son-in-law *n.* (*pl.* **sons-in-law**) the husband of one's daughter.

sonnet /ˈsɒnɪt/ *n.* a lyric poem of 14 lines, usu. written in iambic pentameter, using any of a number of formal rhyme schemes and usu. having a single theme.

sonny /ˈsʌni/ *n. informal* often derogatory a familiar form of address to a young boy or man who is one's junior.

son of a bitch *slang* ● *n.* (*pl.* **sons of bitches**) **1** a general term of contempt or abuse. **2** a despicable or pathetic person. ● *interj.* an exclamation of anger.

sonofabitching /ˌsʌnʌfəˈbɪtʃɪŋ/ *attrib.adj. slang* used as an intensifier, esp. expressing hatred or disgust.

son of a gun *informal* ● *n.* **1** a jocular or affectionate form of address or reference. **2** a rascal or rogue. ● *interj.* an exclamation of shock or amazement.

son of God *n.* **1** (**Son of God**) Jesus Christ. **2** a divine being. **3** a person spiritually attached to God.

son of man *n.* **1** (**Son of Man**) Jesus Christ. **2** a member of the human race; a mortal.

sonogram /ˈsɒnəˌɡræm/ *n. Med.* the visual image

produced by reflected sound waves in a diagnostic ultrasound examination.

sonorous /ˈsɒnərəs, ˈsɔːn-, səˈnɔːrəs/ *adj.* **1** having a loud, full, or deep sound; resonant. **2** (of speech, style, etc.) imposing, grand. ☐ **sonority** /səˈnɒrɪti/ *n.* (*pl.* **-ies**). **sonorously** *adv.*

sook /sʊk/ *n.* Austral., NZ, & Cdn (*Maritimes & Nfld*) *derogatory* a person acting childishly; a wimp or sissy.

sooky baby *n.* Cdn (*Maritimes & Nfld*) = SOOK.

soon /suːn/ *adv.* **1** within a short period of time (*we shall soon know the result*). **2** relatively early (*must you go so soon?*). **3** readily or willingly (in expressing choice or preference: *I would as soon stay behind*). ☐ **as** (or **so**) **soon as** at the moment that; not later than (*I came as soon as I heard about it*). **how soon?** in what period of time; how early (*how soon will it be ready?*). **no sooner ... than** at the very moment that (*no sooner had we arrived than the rain stopped*). **sooner or later** at some time in the future; eventually.

soopollalie /ˈsoːpəˌlæli/ *n.* Cdn (*BC*) **1** = BUFFALO BERRY. **2** a thick drink made from crushed buffalo berries.

soot /sʊt/ *n.* a black carbonaceous substance rising in fine flakes in the smoke of wood, coal, oil, etc., and deposited on the sides of a chimney etc.

soothe /suːð/ *v.* **1** *tr.* bring or restore (a person or feelings etc.) to a peaceful or tranquil state; calm. **2** *tr.* reduce the intensity of; soften, allay, or relieve (pain, an emotion, etc.). **3** *intr.* provide relief or tranquility. ☐ **soothing** *adj.* **soothingly** *adv.*

soother *n.* **1** Cdn & Brit. a ring or nipple made of rubber or plastic given to a baby to suck. **2** a thing that calms or comforts.

soothsayer /ˈsuːθˌseɪər/ *n.* a person who predicts future events; a prophet. ☐ **soothsaying** *n.*

sooty *adj.* (**-ier, -iest**) **1** covered with or full of soot. **2** (esp. of an animal or bird) of a dusky black or brownish black colour. ☐ **sootiness** *n.*

sop /sɒp/ ● *n.* **1** a thing given or done to pacify or appease a person; a concession or bribe. **2** a piece of bread etc. dipped in gravy or wine etc. ● *v.tr.* (**sopped, sopping**) **1** (foll. by *up*) absorb (liquid) in a sponge or towel etc. **2** soak or drench with liquid.

sophist /ˈsɒfɪst/ *n.* **1** a person who reasons with clever but fallacious arguments. **2** (usu. **Sophist**) Gk Hist. a paid teacher of philosophy and rhetoric, esp. one associated with moral skepticism and specious reasoning. ☐ **sophistic** *adj.*

sophisticate ● *v.tr.* /səˈfɪstɪˌkeɪt/ **1** deprive (a person) of natural simplicity or innocence, esp. through education or experience. **2** make (a theory, piece of equipment, etc.) highly developed or complex; refine. **3** falsify or corrupt (a text, argument, etc.). ● *n.* /səˈfɪstəkət/ a sophisticated person. ☐ **sophistication** *n.*

sophisticated *adj.* **1 a** (of a person) worldly, cultured, and refined; discriminating in taste and judgment. **b** showing awareness of the complexities of a subject; knowledgeable, experienced. **2** appealing to sophisticated people or sophisticated tastes. **3 a** (of a theory or idea etc.) based on or involving advanced concepts; complex, not plain or straightforward. **b** (of a piece of equipment etc.) highly developed.

sophistry /ˈsɒfəstri/ *n.* (*pl.* **-ies**) **1** the use of intentionally deceptive or specious arguments or reasoning, esp. as a dialectic exercise. **2** an instance of this.

sophomore /ˈsɒfmɔr, ˈsɒfəˌmɔr/ *n.* N Amer. **1** (esp. in the US) a student in his or her second year of high school, college, or university (also *attrib.*: *sophomore year*). **2** Sport an athlete in his or her second year at a

particular level or in a particular league (also *attrib.*: *sophomore season*). **3** (*attrib.*) designating the second work etc. of an artist or performer (*sophomore album*).

sophomoric /sɒfˈmɒrɪk/ *adj.* esp. N Amer. **1** of, relating to, or befitting a sophomore. **2** maintaining a pretentious demeanour of intellectual sophistication and maturity while immature, juvenile, or shallow.

soporific /ˌsɒpəˈrɪfɪk/ ● *adj.* **1 a** tending to induce or produce sleep. **b** tedious, boring. **2** (of a person) sleepy, drowsy. ● *n.* a soporific drug or influence.

sopping *adj.* (also **sopping wet**) soaked with liquid.

soppy *adj.* (**-ier, -iest**) **1** *informal* mawkishly sentimental; sappy, mushy. **2** soaked with water. ☐ **soppily** *adv.* **soppiness** *n.*

soprano /səˈprænoʊ/ *n.* (*pl.* **-os** or **soprani** /-niː/) **1 a** the highest singing voice. **b** a female or boy singer with this voice. **c** a part written for it. **2 a** an instrument of a high or the highest pitch in its family. **b** its player.

sorbet /sɔrˈbeɪ, ˈsɔrbət/ *n.* a soft water ice made with fruit juice or fruit purée served esp. between main courses to cleanse the palate and reinvigorate the appetite, or as a dessert.

sorbitol /ˈsɔrbɪtɒl/ *n.* a sweet crystalline alcohol found in some fruit, used as a substitute for sugar.

sorcerer /ˈsɔrsərər/ *n.* a person who claims to use magic powers; a wizard. ☐ **sorcery** *n.* (*pl.* **-ies**).

sorceress /ˈsɔrsərəs/ *n.* a woman who claims to use magic powers.

sordid /ˈsɔrdɪd/ *adj.* **1** immoral, base. **2** characterized by or proceeding from self-interest; mercenary. **3** dirty, filthy, squalid. ☐ **sordidly** *adv.* **sordidness** *n.*

sore /sɔr/ ● *adj.* **1** (of a part of the body) painful from injury or disease. **2** (of a person) suffering bodily pain. **3** esp. N Amer. angry, irritated, or vexed. ● *n.* **1** a raw or tender place on the body, such as a cut or wound. **2** a source of distress or annoyance (*reopen old sores*). ☐ **soreness** *n.*

sore loser *n.* a person who cannot accept losing a game etc. graciously.

sorely *adv.* extremely, greatly, desperately (*Michael will be sorely missed*).

sore point *n.* (also **sore spot**) a subject causing distress or annoyance; a contentious issue.

sorghum /ˈsɔrɡəm/ *n.* any tropical cereal grass of the genus *Sorghum*, e.g. durra.

sorority /səˈrɒrɪti/ *n.* (*pl.* **-ies**) N Amer. a society for female students in a university or college.

sorrel¹ /ˈsɔrəl/ *n.* any of several plants of the genus *Rumex* having acid leaves, esp. *R. acetosa*, a plant of meadows with triangular leaves sometimes used in salads and for flavouring. *See also* WOOD SORREL.

sorrel² ● *adj.* of a light reddish-brown or chestnut colour. ● *n.* **1** this colour. **2** an animal of this colour, esp. a horse.

sorrow /ˈsɔroː, ˈsɒ-/ ● *n.* **1** mental distress caused by bereavement, suffering, or disappointment; grief. **2** a cause of grief or sadness. **3** the outward expression of grief; lamentation, mourning. ● *v.intr.* feel or express sorrow or sadness; grieve, mourn. ☐ **sorrowing** *adj.*

sorrowful *adj.* **1** feeling sorrow or grief; unhappy, sad. **2** characterized by or causing sorrow; distressing, lamentable. **3** expressing sorrow (*a sorrowful expression*). ☐ **sorrowfully** *adv.* **sorrowfulness** *n.*

sorry /ˈsɔri, ˈsɒ-/ ● *adj.* (**-ier, -iest**) **1** (*predic.*) feeling sadness or regret (*we were sorry to hear of your mother's illness*). **2** (*predic.*) full of shame, guilt, and remorse, esp. about a past action (*I'm sorry I spilled coffee*). **3** used to express mild regret, disagreement, or refusal, and for making apologies and excuses (*I'm sorry we won't be able to come*). **4** wretched, pitiful, pathetic (*the sorry state of our finances*). ● *interj.* **1** used to express apology or regret (*did I kick you? Sorry.*). **2** (in *interrog.*) (as a request for something to be repeated) I beg your pardon; what did you say? □ **feel** (or **be**) **sorry for someone** feel sympathy or pity for. **feel** (or **be**) **sorry for oneself** bewail one's problems or plight; be self-indulgently depressed.

sort /sɔːt/ ● *n.* **1** a group of things or people determined on the basis of common attributes; a type or kind. **2** (foll. by *of*) an unusual or uncertain example of a specified thing (*she is some sort of writer*). **3** *informal* a person of a specified character or kind (*a good sort*). **4** *Computing* the arrangement of data in a prescribed sequence. ● *v.tr.* (often foll. by *out*, *through*) arrange systematically or according to type, class, etc.; separate and put into a different order or different groups. □ **of sorts** (or **of a sort**) *informal* of an unusual kind; not fully deserving the name (*a holiday of sorts*). **out of sorts 1** slightly irritable or grumpy. **2** slightly unwell. **sort of** *informal* to some extent (*I sort of expected it*). **sort out 1** separate and arrange into groups according to kind or type. **2** separate (things of one type) from a miscellaneous group. **3** resolve (a problem or difficulty). **4** *informal* deal with or reprimand (a person). □ **sorter** *n.* **sorting** *n.*

sorta /'sɔːtə/ *adv. informal* = SORT OF (see SORT).

sortie /'sɔːti/ ● *n.* **1** a sudden emergence, dash, or attack made by troops from a besieged garrison. **2** an operational flight by a single military aircraft. **3** *informal* a jaunt or excursion. ● *v.intr.* (**sorties, sortied, sortieing**) make or go on a sortie.

SOS /ˌesəʊˈes/ *n.* (*pl.* **SOSs**) **1** an international code signal of extreme distress, used esp. by ships at sea. **2** an urgent appeal for help.

so-so ● *adj.* (usu. *predic.*) indifferent; mediocre; neither very good nor very bad. ● *adv.* indifferently.

sot /sɒt/ *n.* a habitual drunk. □ **sottish** *adj.*

sotto voce /ˌsɒtəʊ ˈvəʊtʃi/ ● *adv.* in a low voice so as not to be heard. ● *adj.* (of a remark, comment, etc.) uttered or spoken etc. in a soft voice or undertone.

soubriquet *var. of* SOBRIQUET.

soufflé /'suːfleɪ/ ● *n.* a light spongy dish usu. made by adding egg yolks and a sweet or savoury filling to stiffly beaten egg whites then baked until puffy. ● *adj.* (of ceramics) decorated with small spots of colour applied by blowing. □ **souffléd** *adj.*

sough /saʊ, sʌf/ ● *v.intr.* make a moaning, whistling, or rushing sound as of the wind in trees etc. ● *n.* a gentle rushing or murmuring sound.

sought *past and past part. of* SEEK.

sought-after *adj.* in high demand; generally desired.

souk /suːk/ *n.* an open marketplace or bazaar in Muslim countries.

soul /səʊl/ *n.* **1** the spiritual or immaterial component or nature of a human being or animal, regarded as the seat of the emotions or intellect. **2 a** the spiritual part of a human being considered in its moral aspect or in relation to God, esp. regarded as immortal and being capable of redemption or damnation in a future state. **b** the disembodied spirit of a dead person, regarded as invested with some degree of personality and form. **3 a** (usu. foll. by *of*) a person regarded as the personification of a certain quality (*the very soul of discretion*). **b** a person regarded as embodying moral or intellectual qualities (*meaner souls*). **4** (usu. with *neg.*) an individual (*not a soul in sight*). **5** a person regarded with familiarity, affection,

pity, etc. (*the poor soul was utterly confused*). **6** (usu. foll. by *of*) **a** a person regarded as the inspirer or animating spirit of an activity or cause etc. (*she is the life and soul of the party*). **b** the essential quality or animating element of something (*honesty is the soul of this relationship*). **7** emotional or intellectual energy or intensity, esp. as revealed in a work of art. **8** (also *attrib.*) the emotional or spiritual quality of black American life and culture, manifested in art, music, etc. **9** = SOUL MUSIC. □ **upon my soul!** an exclamation of surprise. □ **-souled** *adj.* (in *comb.*).

soul brother *n. informal* **1** a black man or boy, esp. as regarded by other blacks. **2** a spiritual brother.

soul food *n.* food traditionally eaten by American blacks, esp. those dishes originating in the rural southern US.

soulful *adj.* **1** full of soul or feeling; of a highly emotional or spiritual nature. **2** *ironic* excessively or artificially sentimental or emotional. □ **soulfully** *adv.* **soulfulness** *n.*

soulless *adj.* **1** lacking sensitivity; cruel, ruthless. **2** having no soul (*the soulless machine*). **3** lacking ambition or passion; dull, uninteresting. **4** (of a thing) made or done without imagination; lacking human or distinguishing characteristics (*a soulless stretch of houses*). □ **soullessly** *adv.* **soullessness** *n.*

soulmate *n.* a person with whom one shares an interest, passion, or bond, esp. a friend or spouse.

soul music *n.* a type of black American pop music which combines rhythm and blues with the emotional intensity and expressiveness of gospel, characterized by its emphasis on vocals.

soul-searching ● *n.* a penetrating or critical examination of one's actions, beliefs, motives, or emotions. ● *adj.* characterized by such analysis or scrutiny.

soul sister *n. informal* **1** a black woman or girl, esp. as regarded by other blacks. **2** a spiritual sister.

sound¹ /saʊnd/ ● *n.* **1** a sensation caused in the ear by vibrations of longitudinal waves of pressure passing through the surrounding air or other medium. **2 a** vibrations causing this sensation. **b** similar vibrations whether audible or not. **3** anything that can be heard; a noise. **4** a pleasant or harmonious effect produced by a continuous and regular series of audible vibrations (*opp.* NOISE *n.* 3a). **5** a particular sound or series of sounds associated with a specific source (*the sound of a drum*). **6** an idea or impression conveyed by words (*don't like the sound of that*). **7** a distinctive or readily identifiable style of esp. pop music. **8** speech or music etc. accompanying a movie, TV show, computer multimedia package, or other visual presentation. **9 a** (in full **sound crew**) the department of engineers responsible for producing or recording sound for a movie or concert etc. **b** = SOUND SYSTEM. **10** (in full **speech sound**) any of a series of articulate utterances (*vowel and consonant sounds*). **11** (often *attrib.*) broadcasting by radio as distinct from television. ● *v.* **1** *intr.* convey a specific impression when heard (*you sound like you know what you're doing*). **2** *tr.* cause (an instrument etc.) to make a sound. **3** *tr.* give an audible signal for (an alarm etc.) (*sound the retreat*). **4** *intr.* produce or emit sound (*the alarm clock sounded*). **5** *tr.* (often foll. by *out*) pronounce or articulate (words) sound by sound. □ **sound and fury 1** talk or words without substance. **2** a noisy disturbance, activity, excitement, etc. **sound off** talk loudly or express one's opinions vehemently; complain. □ **soundless** *adj.* **soundlessly** *adv.* **soundlessness** *n.*

sound² ● *adj.* **1** healthy, well; free from disease or injury. **2** (of a building, structure, etc.) free from any decay or defect; undamaged, unbroken, in good condition. **3** (of advice, judgment, a policy, etc.) in full accordance with fact or reason, based on well-grounded principles; sensible, fair, correct. **4 a** financially secure (*a sound investment*). **b** (of currency) having a fixed or stable value, esp. based on gold (*sound money*). **5 a** (of sleep) deep, unbroken, undisturbed. **b** (of a person sleeping) tending to sleep deeply without being easily woken. **6** severe, hard, thorough (*a sound thrashing*). **7** (of theology) orthodox. **8** (of a person, character, etc.) honourable, honest, trustworthy. ● *adv.* in a sound manner; soundly (*sound asleep*). □ **soundly** *adv.* **soundness** *n.*

sound[3] *v.* **1** *tr.* **a** test the depth or quality of the bottom of (the sea or a river etc.). **b** measure (depth). **2** *tr.* **a** (often foll. by *out*) inquire (esp. cautiously or discreetly) into the opinions or feelings of (a person). **b** investigate, attempt to ascertain (a matter, a person's opinions, etc.). **3** *intr.* (of a whale or fish) dive to the bottom. **4** *tr.* get records of temperature, humidity, pressure, etc. from (the upper atmosphere). □ **sounder** *n.*

sound[4] *n.* **1** a narrow channel or stretch of water, esp. one between the mainland and an island or connecting two large bodies of water. **2** an arm of the sea.

sound-alike *n.* a person or thing closely resembling another in sound.

sound barrier *n.* **1** the increased drag, reduced controllability, etc. which occurs when an aircraft approaches the speed of sound. **2** a wall erected or insulated to prevent the passage of sound, as from one room to another. □ **break the sound barrier** travel faster than or accelerate past the speed of sound.

sound bite *n.* a short extract from a recorded interview, speech, etc., chosen for its pungency or appropriateness and edited into a news broadcast.

soundboard *n.* **1** a thin resonating sheet of wood in a piano or sound box of a stringed instrument, such as a violin or cello, over which the strings pass to increase the sound produced. **2** a sound card.

sound box *n.* the hollow chamber providing resonance and forming the body of a stringed instrument.

sound card *n.* a device capable of converting digitized audio signals into an analog audio signal, inserted in a computer to allow the use of audio components for multimedia applications.

sound check *n.* a test of sound equipment before a concert or recording session to ensure that the desired sound is being produced.

sound effect *n.* a sound other than speech or music made artificially to evoke a particular atmosphere or produce a realistic effect in a movie or play etc.

sounding[1] *n.* (usu. in *pl.*) **1 a** the action or process of measuring the depth of water, now usu. by means of echo. **b** (in *pl.*) the determination of any physical property at a depth in the sea or at a height in the atmosphere. **c** an instance of this. **2** cautious investigation. **3** measurements taken by sounding.

sounding[2] *adj.* **1** (in *comb.*) **a** having a specified sound. **b** giving a mental impression of a specified kind (*a funny-sounding idea*). **2** producing or capable of producing esp. loud or resonant sound (*sounding brass*). **3** having a resonant or imposing sound with little substance; boastful (*sounding promises*).

sounding board *n.* **1** a canopy, screen, or board placed above or behind a stage or pulpit to direct sound towards the audience or congregation. **2** a

means of making one's opinions, beliefs, etc. more widely known. **3** a person whose feedback will serve as an accurate assessment of how well a plan, idea, theory, etc. will succeed or be received. **4** = SOUNDBOARD 1.

sounding line *n.* a graduated line weighted at one end, used to sound the depth of water.

soundman *n.* (*pl.* **-men**) *N Amer.* an engineer responsible for producing sound for a concert, movie, etc.

soundproof ● *adj.* impervious to sound. ● *v.tr.* make soundproof. □ **soundproofing** *n.*

soundscape *n.* **1** a musical composition consisting of a texture of sounds. **2** the sounds which form an auditory environment.

sound stage *n.* an enclosed soundproof stage or studio with excellent acoustic properties, suitable for filming and recording concerts, movies, etc.

sound system *n.* a set of equipment used for the reproduction and amplification of sound, such as a stereo or public address system.

soundtrack ● *n.* **1 a** the sound element of a film recorded optically, digitally, or magnetically. **b** a narrow band on the edge of a strip of film containing this recording. **2** such a recording, or excerpts from it, made available for sale. **3** any constituent single track in a multi-track recording. ● *v.tr.* **1** provide with a soundtrack. **2** serve as a soundtrack for.

sound wave *n.* a longitudinal pressure wave in an elastic medium, such as air, esp. one that propagates audible sound.

soup /suːp/ ● *n.* **1** a usu. savoury liquid dish made by boiling meat, fish, or vegetables etc. with seasoning in stock or water, and often served as a first course. **2** *informal* anything jumbled, blended, or mixed, or having a consistency resembling that of soup, esp. a dense fog. ● *v.tr.* (usu. foll. by *up*) *informal* **1** modify (an engine, car, etc.) so as to increase its power or efficiency. **2** revise (writing, music, etc.) so as to increase its power or impact; enhance. □ **from soup to nuts** *N Amer. informal* from beginning to end, completely. **in the soup** *informal* in trouble. □ **souplike** *adj.*

soupçon /ˈsuːpsɒ̃/ *n.* a very small amount; a dash.

soup du jour *n.* the soup featured by a restaurant on a particular day.

soup kitchen *n.* a place where warm meals, usu. soup, are served to the needy for little or no charge.

soupy *adj.* (**-ier, -iest**) **1** of the consistency of soup. **2** *N Amer. informal* sentimental; mawkish. **3 a** (of fog, mist, etc.) thick, dense. **b** (of the weather) foggy.

sour /ˈsaʊr/ ● *adj.* **1** having a tart or acid taste like that of lemon, vinegar, or unripe fruit. **2 a** (of food, esp. milk or cream) having gone bad because of fermentation. **b** smelling or tasting rancid or unpleasant. **3 a** (of a person, temper, etc.) angry, resentful, bitter, cranky. **b** (of a comment, facial expression, etc.) expressing discontent or irritation. **4** (of a thing) unpleasant; disagreeable (*a sour experience*). **5** (of a musical note) out of tune. **6** (of oil or gas etc.) containing a relatively high proportion of sulphur. ● *n. N Amer.* an alcoholic drink with lemon or lime juice and ice (*whisky sour*). ● *v.tr. & intr.* **1** make or become sour. **2** make or become unpleasant or strained. □ **go** (or **turn**) **sour 1** (of food etc.) become bad because of fermentation. **2** turn out badly. □ **sourly** *adv.* **sourness** *n.*

source /sɔːrs/ ● *n.* **1 a** a place, person, or thing from which something originates or may be obtained. **b** (foll. by *of*) a cause of or reason for (*my marks were a source of concern*). **2 a** a document from which original information or evidence in support of some fact or event may be obtained (also *attrib.*: *source material*). **b** a person who supplies information or gives esp. unattributable statements to the media. **3** the beginning or origin of a river or stream. **4** *Computing* (*attrib.*) denoting files, programs, software, etc. written using a source code rather than machine code. ● *v.tr.* **1** contract a particular manufacturer or company to supply (a product, part, or materials). **2** have, cite, or identify (a book etc.) as a source of information. □ **at source** at the point of origin or issue. □ **sourceless** *adj.* **sourcing** *n.*

sourcebook *n.* **1** a collection of writings, articles, etc. on a particular subject used as a basic introduction to that subject. **2** a comprehensive directory or catalogue of a particular subject.

source code *n.* *Computing* the complex series of instructions supplied to a computer by a programmer using a compiler or interpreter which translates it into machine code.

sour cherry *n.* **1** the acid fruit of the cherry *Prunus cerasus*, used in cooking. **2** the small bushy tree which bears this fruit.

sour cream *n.* cream soured by lactic acid bacteria, used esp. in dips, salads, and as a garnish.

sourdough *n.* *N. Amer.* **1** a leaven for making bread etc. consisting of fermenting dough. **2** bread made from sourdough (also *attrib.*: *sourdough rolls*). **3** *N Amer.* (*Yukon & Alaska*) **a** *hist.* an experienced prospector or miner. **b** an old-timer.

sour grapes *n.pl.* (treated as *sing.*) resentful disparagement of something one envies or covets but cannot achieve or acquire personally.

sourpuss *n.* *informal* an irritable or sullen person.

souse /saʊs/ *n.* **1 a** a liquid, esp. made with salt, used in pickling. **b** *N Amer.* pickled meat, esp. a pig's feet and ears. **2** *informal* **a** a drinking bout. **b** a drunkard. **soused** *adj.* *informal* drunk.

south /saʊθ/ ● *n.* **1** the point of the horizon 90° clockwise from east. **2** the compass point corresponding to this. **3** the direction in which this lies. **4** (usu. **the South**) **a** the part of the world or a country or a town lying to the south. **b** *Cdn* the ten provinces south of the Yukon, Nunavut, and the Northwest Territories. **c** the Southern States of the US, bounded on the north by Maryland, the Ohio River, and Missouri. **d** *hist.* the Confederate slaveholding States of the US south of the Mason-Dixon line. ● *adj.* **1** toward, at, near, or facing the south. **2** coming from the south (*south wind*). ● *adv.* **1** toward, at, or near the south (*they travelled south*). **2** (foll. by *of*) further south than. **3** *informal* into a sharp decline (*house prices went south this month*). □ **south by east** (or **west**) between south and south-southeast (or south-southwest). **to the south** (often foll. by *of*) in a southerly direction.

South African ● *adj.* of or relating to the republic of South Africa. ● *n.* **1** a native or national of South Africa. **2** a person of South African descent.

South American ● *adj.* of or relating to S America. ● *n.* a native or citizen of S America.

South Asian ● *n.* **1** a native or inhabitant of the Indian subcontinent, including India, Pakistan, Bangladesh, and Sri Lanka. **2** a South Asian emigrant or a descendant of a South Asian living outside of the Indian subcontinent. ● *adj.* of or relating to the Indian subcontinent, South Asians, or their culture.

southbound *adj.* & *adv.* travelling or leading in a southward direction.

South Carolinian ● *adj.* of or relating to the US state of S Carolina. ● *n.* a resident or native of S Carolina.

South Dakotan /dəˈkoːtən/ ● *adj.* of or relating to the US state of S Dakota. ● *n.* a resident or native of S Dakota.

southeast ● *n.* **1** the point of the horizon midway between south and east. **2** the point on a compass corresponding to this. **3** the direction in which this lies. **4** (**Southeast**) the part of a country or city lying to the southeast. ● *adj.* of, toward, or coming from the southeast. ● *adv.* toward, at, or near the southeast. □ **southeastern** *adj.* **southeasterner** *n.*

Southeast Asian ● *n.* a native or inhabitant of Southeast Asia, a region including Brunei, Burma, Cambodia, Indonesia, Laos, Malaysia, the Philippines, Singapore, Thailand, and Vietnam. ● *adj.* of or relating to Southeast Asia.

southeasterly ● *adj.* & *adv.* = SOUTHEAST. ● *n.* (*pl.* **-ies**) (also **southeaster**) a southeast wind or storm.

southeastward *adj.* & *adv.* (also **southeastwards**) toward the southeast.

southerly /ˈsʌðərli/ ● *adj.* & *adv.* **1** in a southern position or direction. **2** (of a wind) blowing from the south. ● *n.* (*pl.* **-ies**) a southerly wind.

southern /ˈsʌðərn/ ● *adj.* **1 a** of or in the south; inhabiting the south. **b** (also **Southern**) of, relating to, or inhabiting the States of the US South. **2** lying or directed toward the south. **3** (of a wind) blowing from the south. ● *n.* the dialect of English spoken in the southern US. □ **southernmost** *adj.*

Southern Baptist *n.* **1** (in full **Southern Baptist Convention**) a body of Baptist churches in the US, established in 1845. **2** a member of any of these.

southerner *n.* **1** a native or inhabitant of the south. **2** (also **Southerner**) **a** *Cdn* an inhabitant of any of the provinces. **b** an inhabitant of the southern US.

southern hemisphere *n.* the half of the earth below the equator.

southern lights *n.pl.* the aurora australis.

South Korean ● *adj.* of or relating to South Korea (the Republic of Korea), a country in the Far East, occupying the southern part of the peninsula of Korea. ● *n.* a native or inhabitant of South Korea.

south of 60 *n.* (also **south of sixty**) *Cdn* the areas of Canada south of 60 degrees latitude, esp. the ten provinces south of the Yukon, Nunavut, and the Northwest Territories.

southpaw *n.* *informal* **1** *Baseball* a pitcher who throws with his or her left hand. **2** *Boxing* a fighter who punches or leads with the left hand. **3** a left-handed person.

South Pole *n.* see POLE² 1.

south-southeast ● *n.* the point or direction midway between south and southeast. ● *adj.* & *adv.* from, toward, in, or facing this direction.

south-southwest ● *n.* the point or direction midway between south and southwest. ● *adj.* & *adv.* from, toward, in, or facing this direction.

southward ● *adj.* & *adv.* (also **southwards**) toward the south. ● *n.* a southward direction or region.

southwest ● *n.* **1** the point of the horizon midway between south and west. **2** the point on a compass corresponding to this. **3** the direction in which this lies. **4** (**Southwest**) the part of a country etc. lying to the southwest. ● *adj.* of, toward, or coming from the southwest. ● *adv.* toward, at, or near the southwest. □ **southwestern** *adj.* **southwesterner** *n.*

southwesterly ● *adj.* & *adv.* = SOUTHWEST. ● *n.* (also **southwester**) a southwest wind or storm.

southwestward *adj. & adv.* (also **southwestwards**) toward the southwest.

souvenir /ˌsuːvəˈniːr/ *n.* a usu. inexpensive article given or purchased as a reminder of a place visited or an event witnessed etc.; a memento or keepsake (also *attrib.: souvenir postcard*).

souvlaki /suːˈvlæki/ *n.* a Greek dish of pieces of marinated meat, esp. lamb or pork, grilled on a skewer.

sou'wester /sauˈwestər/ *n.* **1** a waterproof hat, usu. made of oilskin, with a broad flap covering the neck and flaps tied under the chin, worn esp. at sea. **2** = SOUTHWESTERLY *n.*

sovereign /ˈsɒvrən/ ● *n.* **1** the recognized supreme ruler of a people or country under monarchical government; a monarch. **2** a person or body of people that has supremacy or authority over another or others. ● *adj.* **1 a** (of a thing, quality, power, etc.) supreme, greatest. **b** unmitigated (*sovereign contempt*). **2 a** characterized by independence or autonomy, esp. having the rights and responsibilities of self-government (*a sovereign state*). **b** concerned with or pertaining to independence or autonomy (*sovereign ambitions*). **3 a** (of a person) having superior or supreme rank or power, esp. holding the position of ruler or monarch. **b** of or related to a monarch; royal. **4** excellent; effective (*a sovereign remedy*). □ **sovereignly** *adv.*

sovereignist /ˈsɒvrən,ɪst/ (also **sovereigntist** /-,tɪst/) *Cdn* ● *n.* a supporter of Quebec's right to self-government; an adherent to the principle of sovereignty-association. ● *adj.* concerned with or relating to the movement for Quebec independence.

sovereignty /ˈsɒvrənti/ *n.* (*pl.* **-ies**) **1** the absolute and independent authority of a community, nation, etc.; the right to autonomy or self-government. **2** (often foll. by *over*) supremacy with respect to power and rank; supreme authority. **3** a territory or community existing as a self-governing state.

sovereignty-association *n. Cdn* a proposal introduced in 1967 which would grant Quebec political independence while maintaining a formal esp. economic association with the rest of Canada.

Soviet /ˈsoːviət/ *hist.* ● *n.* **1** a citizen of the USSR, a former federation of Communist republics occupying N Asia and part of E Europe. **2** (**soviet**) an elected local, district, or national council in the former USSR with legislative and executive functions. **3** (**soviet**) a revolutionary council of workers, peasants, etc. before 1917. ● *adj.* of or concerning the former USSR or its people. □ **Sovietism** *n.*

sow[1] /soː/ *v.* (*past* **sowed** /soːd/; *past part.* **sown** /soːn/ or **sowed**) **1** *tr. & intr.* **a** scatter, sprinkle, or deposit (seed) on or in the earth. **b** (often foll. by *with*) plant (a field etc.) with seed. **2** *tr.* initiate; arouse or spread (*sowed doubt in her mind*). **3** *tr.* (foll. by *with*) cover thickly with. □ **sow the seed** (or **seeds**) **of** instigate, introduce; plant (an idea etc.). □ **sower** *n.* **sowing** *n.*

sow[2] /sau/ *n.* **1** a female adult pig, esp. a domestic one after farrowing. **2** the full-grown female of certain other animals, e.g. the bear and guinea pig.

sowbelly *n. N Amer. informal* salt pork, esp. from the belly.

sowbug /ˈsaubʌg/ *n. N Amer.* a small terrestrial crustacean of the genus *Oniscus* feeding on rotten wood in esp. damp habitats, often able to roll into a ball.

sow thistle /sau/ *n.* any plant of the genus *Sonchus* with thistle-like leaves and milky juice.

sox *informal* pl. of SOCK[1].

soy /sɔi/ *n.* (also **soya** /ˈsɔijə/) **1** *see* SOY SAUCE. **2** *see* SOYBEAN.

soya burger *n.* (also **soyburger**) a vegetarian hamburger made with tofu instead of ground beef.

soybean *n.* (also *esp. Brit.* **soya bean**) **1** a leguminous plant, *Glycine soja*, originally of SE Asia, cultivated for the edible oil and flour it yields, and used as a replacement for animal protein in certain foods. **2** the seed of this.

soybean milk *n.* (also **soy milk**) a fat-free substitute for milk made by suspending soybean flour in water.

soy sauce *n.* (also **soya sauce**) a dark brown salty sauce made from pickled soybeans.

SP *abbr.* standard play, a setting on a VCR allowing two hours of material to be recorded on a standard tape.

sp. *abbr.* **1** *Biol.* species. **2** speed. **3 a** spelled. **b** spelling. **4** (**Sp.**) **a** Spanish. **b** Spain.

spa /spɒ/ *n.* **1** a curative or medicinal mineral spring. **2** a commercial establishment offering health and beauty treatment through steam baths, exercise equipment, etc. **3** (in full **spa bath**) = HOT TUB.

space /speis/ ● *n.* **1 a** a continuous unlimited area or expanse which may or may not contain objects. **b** an interval between one, two, or three-dimensional points or objects (*a space of 10 metres*). **c** an empty area; room. **2 a** area sufficient, required, or available for some purpose or thing (*parking space*; *cargo space*). **b** any of a number of places or positions for a person or thing (*spaces are limited*). **3 a** the immense expanse of the physical universe beyond the earth's atmosphere. **b** the near vacuum occupying the regions between the planets and stars, containing small amounts of gas and dust. **4** an interval of time (*in the space of an hour*). **5 a** time spent alone and used to think, reflect, or relax (*give me some space*). **b** = PERSONAL SPACE. **6** a usu. designated place in a book, letter, form, etc. available for or occupied by written or printed matter (*sign your name in the space below*). **7 a** an interval or blank space between printed or written words or lines. **b** the width occupied by a single typed character. **c** *Printing* any of certain small pieces of cast metal shorter than a type, used to separate words or letters in a word and to justify the line. **8** (in full **commercial space**) an area rented or sold as business premises. **9** *Math.* an instance of any of various mathematical concepts, usu. regarded as a set of points having some specified structure. ● *v.tr.* **1** set, place, or arrange at determinate intervals. **2 a** separate (words, letters, or lines) by means of a space or spaces. **b** make or insert more or wider spaces between (esp. words, letters, lines, etc.). □ **space out 1** spread out with more or wider spaces or intervals between. **2** experience an esp. drug-induced stupor or daze. □ **spacer** *n.*

space age ● *n.* (also **Space Age**) the present period, in which human exploration of space has become possible. ● *attrib.adj.* (**space-age**) **1** characteristic of the space age. **2** designed with the most sophisticated or advanced technology; extremely modern.

space bar *n.* **1** a long horizontal key on a typewriter used to make a space between characters or words etc. **2** a similar key on a computer keyboard which also moves the cursor and advances the text.

space cadet *n.* **1** *slang* a drug addict. **2** *informal* a person who seems out of touch with reality. **3** a trainee astronaut.

spacecraft *n.* any of various manned or unmanned vehicles designed to travel in outer space.

spaced *adj. slang* (also **spaced out**) in a dazed,

disoriented, or confused state, esp. from taking drugs.

space flight n. **1** a journey through outer space. **2** = SPACE TRAVEL.

space heater n. a small portable esp. electrical appliance used to heat a contained space or room. □ **space heating** n.

spaceman n. (pl. **-men**) dated **1** = ASTRONAUT 1. **2** a visitor from outer space.

space opera n. a work of science fiction, esp. a TV show or movie, set in outer space.

space probe n. = PROBE n. 4.

space program n. a program designed for the exploration of outer space and development of space technology.

space rocket n. a rocket used to launch a spacecraft.

space-saving adj. **1** designed to occupy little space. **2** that saves space.

spaceship n. a manned spacecraft.

space shuttle n. a spacecraft that is designed and built for repeated use carrying equipment and astronauts into orbit or to a space station.

space station n. a manned artificial satellite used as a long-term base for operations in space.

spacesuit n. a sealed and pressurized protective suit that allows an astronaut to survive in space.

space-time n. (in full **space-time continuum**) **1** time and three-dimensional space regarded as fused in a four-dimensional continuum containing all events. **2** (attrib.) pertaining to or situated in both space and time (space-time model).

space travel n. travel through outer space. □ **space traveller** n.

spacewalk n. any operation or activity performed by an astronaut in space outside of a spacecraft. □ **spacewalker** n. **spacewalking** n.

spacey adj. (also **spacy**) (**spacier**, **spaciest**) **1** esp. N. Amer. slang absent-minded or out of touch with reality. **2** (esp. of music) relating to or characteristic of supposed conditions in outer space.

spacial var. of SPATIAL.

spacing n. **1** the arrangement of typed or written text, esp. the precise amount of space inserted between each character, word, or line, used to make text legible. **2** the arrangement of objects at particular intervals.

spacious /'speiʃəs/ adj. **1** having ample space; roomy (a spacious room). **2** (of land etc.) of vast or indefinite extent; covering a wide area, extensive (spacious gardens). □ **spaciously** adv. **spaciousness** n.

spade /speid/ ● n. **1** a tool resembling a shovel used for digging or cutting the ground, consisting of a long handle with a grip or crossbar at the top attached to a sharp-edged square metal blade that may be driven into the ground with the foot. **2** any tool resembling this in shape or function. **3** a black inverted heart-shaped figure with a small stalk used to denote a playing card of a particular suit. **4** (in pl.) the suit denoted by this figure. **5** a playing card of this suit. ● v.tr. dig up, work, or remove with or as if with a spade. □ **call a spade a spade** speak plainly or bluntly. **in spades** informal with great or excessive force or persistence. □ **spadeful** n. (pl. **-fuls**).

spadix /'speidiks/ n. (pl. **spadices** /-,si:z/) Bot. a spike of flowers closely arranged around a fleshy axis and usu. enclosed in a spathe.

spaghetti n. **1** pasta made in solid thin strings, thicker than vermicelli. **2** a dish of this with a sauce.

spaghettini /spæge'ti:ni/ n. very thin spaghetti.

spaghetti strap n. a thin stringlike shoulder strap on a dress etc.

spaghetti western n. a western film made cheaply in Italy.

spall ● n. a splinter or chip, esp. of rock. ● v.intr. & tr. **1** (of concrete, brick, etc.) flake away. **2** break up or cause (ore) to break up in preparation for sorting. □ **spalling** n.

spam ● n. **1** (**Spam**) proprietary a tinned meat product made mainly from ham. **2** Computing slang **a** an esp. advertising message sent indiscriminately to a large number of newsgroups, mailing lists, etc. **b** such messages collectively. ● v. Computing slang **1** intr. send spam. **2** tr. send spam to (a person, newsgroup, etc.). □ **spammer** n. **spamming** n.

span ● n. **1** the full extent from end to end in space or time (the whole span of history). **2** the length of time for which attention, concentration, etc. can be maintained. **3** each arch or part of a bridge between piers or supports. **4** the maximum lateral extent of an airplane, its wing, a bird's wing, etc. **5 a** the maximum distance between the tips of the thumb and little finger. **b** this as a measurement, equal to 23 cm (9 inches). **6** a short distance or time (our life is but a span). ● v.tr. (**spanned**, **spanning**) **1 a** (of a bridge, arch, etc.) stretch from side to side of; extend across (the bridge spanned the river). **b** (of a builder etc.) bridge (a river etc.). **2** extend across (space or a period of time etc.). **3** measure or cover the extent of (a thing) with one's hand with the fingers stretched.

spanakopita /,spænəkə'pi:tə/ n. an originally Greek phyllo pastry stuffed with spinach, feta cheese, etc.

spandex n. an elastic polyurethane fabric used in foundation garments, tights, bathing suits, and other tight-fitting, stretchy garments.

spangle ● n. **1** a small thin piece of glittering material esp. used in quantity to ornament a dress etc.; a sequin. **2** a small sparkling object. ● v.tr. (esp. as **spangled** adj.) cover with or as with spangles (starspangled). □ **spangly** adj.

Spaniard n. a native or national of Spain.

spaniel n. a dog of any of various breeds with a long silky coat and drooping ears.

Spanish ● adj. of or relating to Spain, a country in SW Europe, or its people or language. ● n. **1** the principal language of Spain and Spanish America. **2** (prec. by the; treated as pl.) the people of Spain.

Spanish coffee n. coffee with brandy and coffee liqueur, served topped with whipped cream.

Spanish Inquisition n. see INQUISITION 3b.

Spanish moss n. a tropical American plant, Tillandsia usneoides, an epiphyte that grows as silvery festoons on trees.

Spanish onion n. a large, mild variety of onion.

spank ● v.tr. slap esp. on the buttocks with the open hand, a slipper, etc. ● n. a slap esp. with the open hand on the buttocks.

spanking ● adv. informal very, exceedingly (spanking new). ● n. the act or an instance of slapping, esp. on the buttocks as a punishment for children.

spanner n. esp. Brit. a wrench.

spar¹ n. **1** a stout pole esp. used for the mast, yard, etc. of a ship. **2** the main longitudinal beam of an airplane wing.

spar² ● v.intr. (**sparred**, **sparring**) **1** (often foll. by at) make the motions of boxing without landing heavy blows. **2** engage in argument. ● n. **1 a** a sparring motion. **b** a boxing match. **2** an argument or dispute.

spar[3] *n.* any crystalline, easily cleavable and nonlustrous mineral, e.g. calcite.

spare ● *adj.* **1 a** not required for ordinary use; extra, available (*spare cash*). **b** reserved for emergency or occasional use (*the spare room*). **2** lean; thin. **3** scanty; frugal; not copious (*a spare prose style*). **4** *informal* not wanted or used by others (*a spare seat*). ● *n.* **1** a spare part, esp. a spare tire. **2** *Bowling* the knocking down of all the pins with the first two balls. **3** *Cdn* a period in one's school day schedule in which one is not required to be in class. ● *v.* **1** *tr.* afford to give or do without; dispense with (*cannot spare him*). **2** *tr.* **a** abstain from killing, hurting, wounding, etc. (*spared his feelings*). **b** abstain from inflicting or causing; relieve from; refrain from troubling with (*spare me the details*). **3** *tr.* be frugal or grudging of (*no expense spared*). □ **not spare oneself** exert one's utmost efforts. **to spare** left over; additional, more than necessary. □ **sparely** *adv.* **spareness** *n.*

spareribs *n.pl.* a cut of meat, esp. pork, consisting of closely-trimmed ribs.

spare tire *n.* **1** an extra tire carried in a vehicle for emergencies. **2** *informal* a roll of fat around the waist.

sparing *adj.* **1** inclined to save; economical. **2** restrained; limited. □ **sparingly** *adv.*

spark ● *n.* **1** a fiery particle thrown off from a fire, or alight in ashes, or produced by a match etc. **2** (often foll. by *of*) a particle of a quality etc. (*a spark of interest*). **3** *Electricity* **a** a light produced by a sudden disruptive discharge through the air etc. **b** such a discharge serving to ignite the explosive mixture in an internal combustion engine. **4 a** anything acting as an incitement or inspiration to action, or which excites emotions; a catalyst. **b** energy or enthusiasm. **5** a small bright object or point, e.g. in a gem. **6 (Spark)** *Cdn* a member of the branch of Girl Guides for 5- or 6-year-olds. ● *v.* **1** *intr.* emit sparks of fire or electricity. **2** *tr.* (often foll. by *off*) stir into activity; initiate (a process) suddenly. **3** *intr. Electricity* produce sparks at the point where a circuit is interrupted. □ **sparks flew** (or **will fly** etc.) there was (or will be etc.) a heated confrontation, friction, etc. □ **sparky** *adj.*

sparkle ● *v.intr.* **1 a** emit or seem to emit sparks; glitter; glisten (*her eyes sparkled*). **b** be witty; scintillate (*sparkling repartee*). **c** perform conspicuously well. **2** (of wine etc.) effervesce (*compare* STILL[1] *adj.* 4). ● *n.* **1** a flash of light; a gleam, spark. **2** a glittering particle. **3** **a** glittering or flashing appearance or quality. **b** vivacity, liveliness of spirit. □ **sparkling** *adj.* **sparklingly** *adv.* **sparkly** *adj.*

sparkler *n.* **1** a person or thing that sparkles. **2** a hand-held firework that produces showers of sparks when lit. **3** *informal* a diamond or other gem. **4** a sparkling wine, mineral water, etc.

spark plug *n.* **1** a device fitted to the cylinder head of an internal combustion engine, used to ignite the explosive mixture by the discharge of a spark between two electrodes at its end. **2** (usu. **sparkplug**) esp. *N Amer. informal* a person or thing which initiates, inspires, or encourages an activity or undertaking.

sparrow *n.* **1** any small brownish-grey bird of the genus *Passer*, esp. the house sparrow or tree sparrow. **2** any of various small New World birds of the family Emberezidae of similar appearance.

sparrow hawk *n.* the American kestrel, *Falco sparverius*.

sparse *adj.* **1** thinly dispersed or scattered; not dense (*sparse population*; *sparse hair*). **2** scanty, meagre. □ **sparsely** *adv.* **sparseness** *n.* **sparsity** *n.*

Spartan ● *adj.* **1** of or relating to the city of Sparta in ancient Greece. **2 a** possessing the qualities of courage, endurance, stern frugality, etc., associated with Sparta. **b** (**spartan**) (of a regime, conditions, etc.) lacking comfort; austere. ● *n.* **1** a citizen of Sparta. **2** *Cdn* a medium- or large-sized red eating or cooking apple with tiny white dots, bred to withstand relatively cold winters.

spar tree *n.* esp. *Cdn* a tree or other tall structure to which cables are attached for hauling logs.

spasm *n.* **1** a sudden involuntary muscular contraction. **2 a** a sudden convulsive movement or emotion etc. (*a spasm of coughing*). **b** a condition or state characterized by a spasm or spasms. **3** (usu. foll. by *of*) *informal* a brief or sudden spell of an activity, condition, etc.

spasmodic /spæz'mɒdɪk/ *adj.* **1** of, caused by, or subject to, a spasm or spasms (*spasmodic asthma*). **2** occurring or done by fits and starts (*spasmodic efforts*). □ **spasmodically** *adv.*

spastic ● *adj.* **1** *Med.* affected by or pertaining to a spasm or sudden involuntary movements. **2** *offensive* uncoordinated, incompetent, stupid. ● *n. offensive* a spastic person. □ **spastically** *adv.* **spasticity** *n.*

spat[1] *past and past part. of* SPIT[1].

spat[2] *n.* **1** (usu. in *pl.*) *hist.* a short cloth gaiter protecting the shoe from mud etc. **2** a cover for an aircraft wheel.

spat[3] *N Amer. informal* ● *n.* a petty quarrel. ● *v.intr.* (**spatted**, **spatting**) quarrel pettily.

spat[4] *n.* the spawn of shellfish, esp. the oyster.

spate *n.* **1** a situation in which the volume of water flowing through a river is much higher than normal, usu. temporarily as a result of heavy rains or melting snow. **2** a sudden outburst; a large or excessive amount (*a spate of inquiries*). □ **in (full) spate 1** (of a river) flowing strongly at a much higher level than normal. **2** completely involved in something and likely to continue for some time.

spathe /speɪð/ *n. Bot.* a large bract or pair of bracts enveloping a spadix or flower cluster.

spatial *adj.* **1** of or concerning space (*spatial extent*). **2** having extension in space; occupying space. □ **spatiality** *n.* **spatialize** *v.tr.* **spatially** *adv.*

spatter ● *v.* **1** *tr.* **a** (often foll. by *with*) splash or stain (a person etc.) with spots of liquid etc. (*spattered him with mud*). **b** scatter or splash (liquid, mud, etc.), esp. in drops or small particles. **2** *intr.* (of rain etc.) fall here and there. ● *n.* **1** (usu. foll. by *of*) a splash (*a spatter of mud*). **2** a quick pattering sound.

spatula *n.* **1** any of various cooking utensils, esp.: **a** an implement with a broad flexible rubber blade, used to scrape the sides of a bowl etc. **b** a knifelike implement with a blunt blade, used to spread icing etc. **c** an implement with a rigid usu. square blade set at an angle, used to lift or flip pancakes, hamburgers, eggs, etc. **2** any of various broad-bladed implements for stirring, spreading, or technical uses.

spatulate /'spætʃʊlət/ *adj.* **1** having a broad rounded end. **2** (of a leaf) broad at the apex and tapering at the base.

spawn ● *v.* **1 a** *tr. & intr.* (of a fish, frog, mollusc, or crustacean) produce or fertilize (eggs). **b** *intr.* be produced as eggs or young. **2** *tr. & intr. derogatory* (of people) produce (offspring). **3** *tr.* produce or generate, esp. in large numbers. ● *n.* **1** the eggs of fish, frogs, etc. **2** *derogatory* human offspring. **3** a product, result, or effect of something. **4** a white fibrous matter from which fungi are produced; mycelium. □ **spawner** *n.*

spay *v.tr.* sterilize (a female animal) by removing the ovaries. □ **spayed** *adj.*

spaz *n.* (*pl.* **spazzes**) *N Amer. slang* an uncoordinated, awkward, or disturbed person. □ **spaz out** (**spazzed, spazzing**) lose control; become frenetic, overly excited, emotional, etc.; freak out. **take** (or **have**) **a spaz** = SPAZ OUT.

SPCA *abbr. N Amer.* Society for the Prevention of Cruelty to Animals.

speak *v.* (*past* **spoke**; *past part.* **spoken**) **1** *intr.* make articulate verbal utterances in an ordinary (not singing) voice. **2** *tr.* **a** utter (words). **b** make known or communicate (one's opinion, the truth, etc.) in this way (*never speaks sense*). **3** *intr.* **a** (foll. by *to, with*) hold a conversation (*spoke to him about his work*). **b** (foll. by *of*) mention in writing etc. (*speaks of it in his novel*). **c** (foll. by *for*) articulate the feelings of (another person etc.) in speech or writing. **4** *intr.* (foll. by *to*) **a** address; converse with (a person etc.). **b** speak in confirmation of or with reference to (*spoke to the resolution*). **c** *informal* reprove (*spoke to them about their lateness*). **d** attest; give an indication of. **5** *intr.* make a speech before an audience etc. (*spoke for an hour on the topic*). **6** *tr.* use or be able to use (a specified language) (*cannot speak French*). **7** *intr.* (usu. foll. by *to*) *literary* communicate feeling etc., affect, touch (*the sunset spoke to her*). □ **nothing to speak of** nothing worth mentioning; practically nothing. **not to speak of** = NOT TO MENTION (see MENTION). **speak for itself** need no supporting evidence. **speak for oneself 1** give one's own opinions. **2** not presume to speak for others. **speaking of** used to introduce a statement etc. on a topic recently alluded to. **speak in tongues** *Christianity* speak or be able to speak in a language one does not know, identified as a gift of the Holy Spirit. **speak one's mind** speak bluntly or frankly. **speak out** speak loudly or freely, give one's opinion. **speak up** = SPEAK OUT. **speak volumes** (of a fact etc.) be very significant. **speak volumes** (or **well** etc.) **about** (or **for**) **1** be abundant evidence of. **2** place in a favourable light.

-speak *comb. form* forming nouns denoting a particular variety of language or mode of speaking.

speakeasy *n.* (*pl.* **-ies**) *N Amer. esp. hist. slang* a bar etc. selling liquor illicitly.

speaker *n.* **1** a person who speaks, esp. in public. **2** a person who speaks a specified language (esp. in *comb.*: *a French-speaker*). **3** (**Speaker**) the presiding officer in a legislative assembly. **4** = LOUDSPEAKER. □ **speakership** *n.*

speakerphone *n.* esp. *N Amer.* a telephone with a loudspeaker and microphone, which does not need to be held in the hand.

speaking ● *n.* the act or an instance of uttering words etc. ● *adj.* **1** that speaks; capable of articulate speech. **2** (in *comb.*) speaking or capable of speaking a specified language (*French-speaking*). **3** with a reference or from a point of view specified (*roughly speaking*). □ **on speaking terms** (foll. by *with*) **1** slightly acquainted. **2** on friendly terms.

spear ● *n.* **1** a thrusting or throwing weapon with a pointed tip and a long shaft. **2** a similar barbed instrument used for catching fish etc. **3** a pointed stem of asparagus etc. ● *v.tr.* **1** pierce or strike with or as if with a spear (*speared an olive*). **2** *Hockey* jab or poke (a player) with the blade of the stick.

spearfishing *n.* fishing using a spear.

spearhead ● *n.* **1** (also **spear point**) the point of a spear; a piece of stone or metal forming this. **2** an

individual or group leading a campaign, attack, initiative, etc. ● *v.tr.* act as the spearhead of (an attack etc.).

spearing *n.* **1** *in senses of* SPEAR *v.* **2** *Hockey* the illegal jabbing or poking of an opponent with the blade of one's stick.

spearmint *n.* a common garden mint, *M. spicata*, used in cooking and to flavour chewing gum etc.

spec[1] *n. informal* □ **on spec** without the assurance of success or reward; as a gamble.

spec[2] *n.* (usu. in *pl.*) a detailed working description; a specification or specifications.

special ● *adj.* **1 a** particularly good; exceptional; out of the ordinary (*bought them a special present*). **b** peculiar; specific; not general (*lacks the special qualities required*). **2** for a particular purpose (*sent on a special assignment*). **3** in which a person specializes (*statistics is her special field*). **4** denoting education for children with particular needs, e.g. the handicapped. ● *n.* **1** a special person or thing, e.g. a special train, constable, dish on a menu, etc. **2** *N Amer.* the offering of a product or service at a temporarily reduced price (*this week's specials*). **3** esp. *N Amer.* a program scheduled and aired in place of regular programming, usu. to mark an occasion, season, holiday, etc. **4** a newspaper article by a writer who is not a regular member of the newspaper's staff. □ **on special** *N Amer.* available for purchase at a temporarily reduced price. □ **specially** *adv.* **specialness** *n.*

special area *n.* *Cdn* (*Alta.*) a large, sparsely populated area administered by the provincial government.

special branch *n.* a police department or unit dealing with political security.

special case *n.* **1** a written statement of fact presented by litigants to a court, raising a matter to be tried separately from the main action. **2** an exceptional or unusual case.

special committee *n.* a committee, e.g. of a legislature, formed to examine one particular issue or piece of proposed legislation.

special constable *n.* *Cdn & Brit.* a police officer sworn in to assist in times of emergency etc. or having a limited range of responsibilities.

special edition *n.* **1** an extra edition of a newspaper etc. including later news than the ordinary edition. **2** (often *attrib.*) a specially-modified version of a product, esp. available in limited quantities (*special edition coupe*).

special education *n.* (also *N Amer. informal* **special ed**) **1** the education of children with special needs arising from physical or mental disabilities. **2** a program providing such education.

special effects *n.pl.* scenic or optical illusions for films, television, or the stage, created by computers, props, camera work, etc.

special interest group *n.* **1** (also **special interest**) a group of people or a corporation with a common political interest or purpose. **2** a computerized discussion group on a specific topic etc.

special investigations unit *n.* an independent police unit responsible for investigating the conduct of police officers of other forces. *Abbr.:* **SIU.**

specialist *n.* **1** a person who is trained in a particular branch of a profession, esp. medicine. **2** a person who especially or exclusively studies a subject or a particular branch of a subject.

speciality (*pl.* **-ies**) *var. of* SPECIALTY 1, 2.

specialize *v.* **1** *intr.* (often foll. by *in*) **a** be or become a specialist (*specializes in optics*). **b** devote oneself to an area of interest, skill, etc. (*specializes in insulting people*). **2** *Biol.* **a** *tr.* (esp. in *passive*) adapt or set apart (an organ etc.) for a particular purpose. **b** *intr.* (of an organ etc.) become adapted etc. in this way. **3** *tr.* make specific or individual. **4** *tr.* modify or limit (an idea, statement, etc.). □ **specialization** *n.*

specialized municipality *n. Cdn (Alta.)* a municipality with a unique form of local government established to encourage its development into a village, town, or city.

special needs *n.pl.* **1** the special esp. educational requirements of people with disabilities. **2** *(attrib.)* designating such people or their education *(special-needs children).*

Special Olympics *n.pl.* an international multi-event sporting competition for people with mental disabilities, similar to the Olympic Games.

special prosecutor *n.* a lawyer not otherwise in the employ of an Attorney General's department or Ministry of Justice hired to prosecute a special case or series of cases.

special relativity *n. see* RELATIVITY 2a.

special team *n.* (also **specialty team**) *N Amer.* a group of players on a team used especially or exclusively in certain well-defined circumstances, e.g. when killing penalties in hockey.

specialty *n.* *(pl.* **-ies**) **1** esp. *N Amer.* a special pursuit, product, operation, etc., to which a company or a person gives special attention. **2** esp. *N Amer.* a special feature, characteristic, or skill. **3** *N Amer. (attrib.)* designating a product, store, etc. pertaining or devoted to a very specific interest *(a specialty bookstore).*

specie /'spiːʃi/ *n.* coin money as opposed to paper money.

species /'spiːsiːz, 'spiːʃ-/ *n.* *(pl.* same) **1** a class of things having some common characteristics. **2** a group of living organisms consisting of related similar individuals capable of exchanging genes or interbreeding, classified as a taxonomic rank below a genus and denoted by a Latin binomial. **3** a kind or sort.

specific ● *adj.* **1** clearly defined; definite, precise *(has no specific name).* **2** relating to one particular subject or thing; peculiar, particular *(music specific to the region; culture-specific).* **3 a** of or concerning a species *(the specific name for a plant).* **b** possessing, or concerned with, the properties that characterize a species *(the specific forms of animals).* ● *n.* (esp. in *pl.*) a specific aspect or factor *(shall we discuss specifics?).* □ **specifically** *adv.* **specificity** /spesɪ'fɪsɪti/ *n.*

specification /ˌspesɪfɪ'keɪʃən/ *n.* **1** the act or an instance of specifying; the state of being specified. **2 a** (esp. in *pl.*) a detailed description of the construction, workmanship, materials, etc., of work done or to be done, prepared by an architect, engineer, etc. **b** (in *pl.*) a detailed description of the components of an electronic system, e.g. a computer. **c** a specified standard of workmanship, materials, etc., to be achieved *(built to a high specification).* **3** a description by an applicant for a patent of the construction and use of his invention.

specific disease *n.* a disease caused by one identifiable agent.

specific gravity *n. Chem.* the ratio of the density of a substance to the density of a standard.

specific land claim *n. Cdn* a land claim made against the federal government when specific treaty terms have not been met.

specify *v.* **(-ies, -ied)** **1** *tr. & intr.* name or mention expressly *(specified the type).* **2** *tr.* (usu. foll. by *that* + clause) name as a condition *(specified that he must be

paid).* **3** *tr.* include in specifications *(a French window was not specified).* □ **specifiable** *adj.* **specifier** *n.*

specimen *n.* **1** an individual or part taken as an example of a class or whole, esp. when used for investigation or scientific examination *(a specimen of your handwriting).* **2** *Med.* a sample of urine, blood, tissue, etc. for testing. **3** *informal* usu. *derogatory* a person of a specified sort.

specious /'spiːʃəs/ *adj.* **1** superficially plausible or genuine but actually wrong or false *(a specious argument).* **2** misleadingly attractive in appearance. □ **speciously** *adv.*

speck ● *n.* **1** a small spot, dot, or stain. **2** (foll. by *of*) a particle *(speck of dirt).* **3** a rotten spot in fruit. ● *v.tr.* (esp. as **specked** *adj.*) marked with specks. □ **specky** *adj.*

speckle ● *n.* a small spot, mark, or stain, esp. in quantity on the skin, a bird's egg, etc. ● *v.tr.* (esp. as **speckled** *adj.*) mark with speckles or patches.

speckled trout *n.* = BROOK TROUT.

specs *n.pl. informal* a pair of eyeglasses.

spec sheet *n.* a list of an item's specifications.

spectacle *n.* **1** a public show, ceremony, etc. **2** anything attracting public attention *(a disgusting spectacle).* **3** a ridiculous person or thing. □ **make a spectacle of oneself** make oneself an object of ridicule.

spectacles *n.pl.* (also **pair of spectacles** *sing.*) a pair of eyeglasses.

spectacular ● *adj.* **1** of or like a public show; striking, amazing, lavish. **2** strikingly large or obvious *(a spectacular increase).* ● *n.* a spectacular thing or event, esp. a musical. □ **spectacularly** *adv.*

spectate *v.intr.* be a spectator, esp. at a sporting event.

spectator *n.* a person who looks on at a show, game, incident, etc. □ **spectatorship** *n.*

spectator sport *n.* a sport providing popular entertainment for spectators.

spectra *pl. of* SPECTRUM.

spectral *adj.* **1 a** of or relating to spectres or ghosts. **b** ghostlike. **2** of or concerning spectra or the spectrum *(spectral colours).* □ **spectrally** *adv.*

spectral line *n.* a line in a spectrum due to the emission or absorption of radiation, occurring at discrete wavelengths characteristic of the material producing them.

spectre *n.* (*US* **specter**) **1** a ghost. **2** a haunting presentiment or preoccupation *(the spectre of war).* **3** (esp. in *comb.*) used in the names of some animals because of their thinness, transparency, etc.

spectrograph *n.* an apparatus for photographing or otherwise recording spectra. □ **spectrogram** *n.* **spectrographic** *adj.* **spectrography** *n.*

spectrometer /spek'trɒmətər/ *n.* an instrument used for the measurement of observed spectra. □ **spectrometric** *adj.* **spectrometry** *n.*

spectroscope /'spektrə,skoːp/ *n.* an instrument for producing and recording spectra for examination. □ **spectroscopic** *adj.* **spectroscopy** /-'trɒskəpi/ *n.*

spectrum *n.* (*pl.* **spectra** or **-s**) **1** a band of colours, as seen in a rainbow etc., produced by separation of the components of light by their different degrees of refraction according to wavelength. **2** the entire range of wavelengths of electromagnetic radiation. **3 a** an image or distribution of components of any electromagnetic radiation arranged in a progressive series according to wavelength. **b** this as characteristic of a body or substance when emitting or absorbing radiation. **4** a similar image or distribution of components of sound, particles, etc., arranged according to frequency, charge, energy, etc. **5** the entire range or a wide range of anything arranged by degree or quality etc. (*political spectrum*).

speculate *v.* **1** *intr.* (usu. foll. by *on*, *upon*, *about*) form a theory or conjecture, esp. without a firm factual basis; meditate (*speculated on their prospects*). **2** *tr.* (foll. by *that*, *how*, etc. + clause) conjecture, consider (*speculated how he might achieve it*). **3** *intr.* **a** invest in stocks etc. in the hope of gain but with the possibility of loss. **b** gamble recklessly. □ **speculation** *n.* **speculator** *n.*

speculative *adj.* **1** of, based on, engaged in, or inclined to speculation. **2** (of a business investment) involving the risk of loss (*a speculative builder*). □ **speculatively** *adv.*

speculum /'spekjʊləm/ *n.* (*pl.* **specula** /-lə/ or **-s**) **1** an instrument to hold open or dilate a part of the body, esp. the vagina, for examination. **2** a mirror, usu. of polished metal. **3** a lustrous coloured area on the wing of some birds, esp. ducks.

sped past and past part. of SPEED.

speech *n.* **1** the faculty or act of speaking. **2** a usu. formal address or discourse delivered to an audience or assembly. **3** a manner of speaking (*a man of blunt speech*). **4** a remark (*after this speech he was silent*). **5** the language of a nation, group, etc. **6** = SOUND[1] *n.* 10.

Speech from the Throne *n.* Cdn a statement summarizing the government's proposed measures, read by the sovereign, Governor General, or Lieutenant-Governor at the opening of a session of Parliament or a legislature.

speechify *v.intr.* (**-ies**, **-ied**) *jocular* or *derogatory* make esp. boring or long speeches. □ **speechifier** *n.*

speech-language pathology *n.* N Amer., Austral., NZ, & South Africa (also **speech pathology**) the treatment of disorders of speech and communication. □ **speech-language pathologist** *n.*

speechless *adj.* **1** unable to speak, esp. temporarily because of emotion etc. (*speechless with rage*). **2** (of an emotion etc.) tending to deprive one temporarily of speech. □ **speechlessly** *adv.* **speechlessness** *n.*

speech recognition *n.* the identification and interpretation or response by a computer to the sounds produced in human speech.

speech therapy *n.* esp. Brit. = SPEECH-LANGUAGE PATHOLOGY. □ **speech therapist** *n.*

speechwriter *n.* a person employed to write speeches for a politician etc. to deliver. □ **speech writing** *n.*

speed ● *n.* **1** rapidity of movement (*at full speed*). **2** a rate of progress or motion over a distance in time (*attains a high speed*). **3** a gear ratio in a motor vehicle, bicycle, etc. **4** Photog. **a** the sensitivity of film to light. **b** the light gathering power of a lens. **c** the duration of an exposure. **5** slang an amphetamine drug, esp. methamphetamine. **6** esp. N Amer. informal a person, activity, etc. that suits one's abilities or personality (*robbing banks is hardly his speed*). ● *v.* (past and past part. **sped** or **speeded**) **1** *intr.* go fast (*sped down the street*). **2 a** *intr.* (of a motorist etc.) travel at an illegal or dangerous speed. **b** *tr.* regulate the speed of (an engine etc.). **c** *tr.* cause (an engine etc.) to go at a fixed speed. **3** *tr.* send fast or on its way. □ **at speed** moving quickly. **speed up** move or work at greater speed. **up to speed 1** operating at full speed. **2** operating or functioning at an anticipated level (*trying to get the company up to speed*). **3** fully informed. □ **speeder** *n.*

speed bag *n.* N Amer. a small punching bag for practising quick punches.

speedball *n.* slang a mixture of cocaine with heroin or morphine.

speedboat *n.* a motorboat designed for high speed. □ **speedboater** *n.* **speedboating** *n.*

speed bump *n.* a transverse ridge in a roadway requiring drivers to slow down to pass over it.

speed-dial *n.* a function on some telephones which allows frequently-called numbers to be entered into a memory for faster dialing. □ **speed-dialing** *n.*

speeding *n.* the traffic offence of driving at an illegal or dangerous speed.

speed limit *n.* the maximum speed at which a road vehicle may legally be driven in a particular area etc.

speed metal *n.* a variety of heavy metal music with a very fast tempo.

speedometer *n.* an instrument displaying the speed of motor vehicle etc.

speed-read *v.tr.* & *intr.* read rapidly, e.g. by assimilating several phrases or sentences at once. □ **speed-reader** *n.*

speed skating *n.* racing performed on skates around a usu. oval track against other skaters or the clock. □ **speed skater** *n.*

speedster *n.* **1** a fast motor vehicle, esp. a sports car. **2** a person or animal that runs etc. quickly. **3** a person who drives too quickly.

speed trap *n.* a part of a highway etc. where police, usu. concealed, check the speed of passing vehicles.

speed-up *n.* an increase in the speed or rate of working.

speedway *n.* **1** N Amer. a road or track used for motor racing. **2** US a highway for fast motor traffic. **3 a** motorcycle racing. **b** a stadium or track used for this.

speedy *adj.* (**-ier**, **-iest**) **1** moving quickly; rapid. **2** done without delay; prompt (*a speedy answer*). □ **speedily** *adv.* **speediness** *n.*

spell[1] *v.* (past and past part. **spelled** or **spelt**) **1** *tr.* & *intr.* write or name the letters that form (a word etc.) in correct sequence. **2** *tr.* (of letters) make up or form (a word etc.). **3** *tr.* (of circumstances, a scheme, etc.) result in; involve (*this decision spells ruin for the project*). □ **spell out 1** make out (words, writing, etc.) letter by letter. **2** explain in detail.

spell[2] *n.* **1 a** words which when spoken are thought to have magical power. **b** a state or condition caused by a person speaking such words (*put a spell on her*). **2** a fascinating or very attractive influence that a person or thing has. □ **under a spell** mastered by or as if by a spell.

spell[3] ● *n.* **1** a period of time during which something lasts. **2** a period of a specified type of weather (*a hot spell*). **3** a bout or fit of something (*had a crying spell*). **4** a period of activity or duty, esp. one which two or more people share (*take a spell at the wheel*). ● *v.tr.* (often foll. by *off*) **1** relieve or take the place of (a person) in work etc. **2** allow to rest briefly.

spellbind *v.tr.* (past and past part. **spellbound**) bind with or as if with a spell; entrance. □ **spellbinder** *n.* **spellbinding** *adj.*

spellbound *adj.* entranced, fascinated, esp. by a speaker, activity, quality, etc.

spell-check Computing ● *n.* a check of the spelling in a file of text using a spell checker. ● *v.tr.* check the spelling in (a text) using a spell checker.

spell checker *n.* (also **spelling checker**) a computer program which checks the spelling of words in files of text.

speller *n.* **1** a person who spells esp. in a specified way (*is a poor speller*). **2** a book for teaching spelling. **3** N Amer. = SPELL CHECKER.

spelling n. **1** the process or activity of writing or naming the letters of a word etc. **2** the way a word is spelled. **3** the ability to spell (*her spelling is poor*).

spelling bee n. a spelling competition in which competitors spell words orally and are eliminated for misspellings, until the competitor who spells the most words correctly is named the winner.

spelt[1] past and past part. of SPELL[1].

spelt[2] n. a species of wheat, *Triticum aestivum*.

spelunker /spɪˈlʌŋkər/ n. N Amer. a person who explores caves, esp. as a hobby. □ **spelunking** n.

spend v. (past and past part. **spent**) **1** (usu. foll. by *on*) **a** tr. & intr. pay out (money) in making a purchase etc. (*spent $50 on a new sweater*). **b** tr. pay out (money) for a particular person's benefit or for the improvement of a thing (*had to spend $200 on the car*). **2** tr. **a** use or consume (time or energy) (*spent three hours fixing it*). **b** (also refl.) use up; exhaust; wear out (*his anger was soon spent*). **3** tr. pass (time, one's life, etc.) (*spent all our summers in Goderich*). □ **spendable** adj. **spender** n.

spending money n. pocket money.

spendthrift ● n. a person who spends money too freely or wastes money. ● adj. extravagant.

spent ● v. past and past part. of SPEND. ● adj. having lost its original force or strength.

sperm n. (pl. same or **sperms**) **1** = SPERMATOZOON. **2** semen. **3** = SPERM WHALE. **4** = SPERMACETI.

spermaceti /ˌspɜːməˈseti/ n. a white waxy substance produced by the sperm whale to aid buoyancy, and formerly used in the manufacture of candles etc.

spermatic /spɜːrˈmætɪk/ adj. of or relating to a sperm.

spermatozoon /ˌspɜːrˌmætoˈzoʊɒn/ n. (pl. **-zoa** /-ˈzoʊə/) the mature motile male sex cell of an animal, by which the ovum is fertilized.

sperm bank n. a place where semen is stored for use in artificial insemination.

spermicide n. a substance able to kill spermatozoa. □ **spermicidal** adj.

sperm whale n. a large whale, *Physeter macrocephalus*, formerly hunted for the spermaceti and oil contained in its bulbous head, and for the ambergris found in its intestines.

spew ● v. **1** tr. & intr. vomit. **2** (often foll. by *out*) **a** tr. expel (contents) rapidly and forcibly. **b** intr. (of contents) be expelled in this way. **3** tr. (often foll. by *out, forth*) utter (language, esp. abusive or objectionable language) (*was always spewing lies about us*). ● n. **1** vomited food etc. **2** something spewed out.

SPF abbr. sun protection factor (indicating the effectiveness of sunscreens etc.).

sphagnum /ˈsfægnəm, ˈspæg-/ n. (in full **sphagnum moss**) any moss of the genus *Sphagnum*, growing in bogs, with spongy, absorbent leaves and stems, used as packing esp. for plants, as a soil conditioner, etc.

sphere n. **1** a solid figure, or its surface, with every point on its surface equidistant from its centre. **2** an object having this shape; a ball or globe. **3 a** any celestial body. **b** a globe representing the earth. **c** literary the heavens; the sky. **d** the sky perceived as a vault upon or in which celestial bodies are represented as lying. **4 a** a field of action, influence, or existence (*have done much within their own sphere*). **b** a (usu. specified) stratum of society or social class (*moves in quite another sphere*). □ **sphere of influence** the claimed or recognized area of a state's interests, an individual's control, etc.

spherical /ˈsfɪːrɪkəl, ˈsfer-/ adj. **1** shaped like a

sphere; globular. **2 a** of or relating to the properties of spheres (*spherical geometry*). **b** formed inside or on the surface of a sphere (*spherical triangle*). □ **spherically** adv.

spheroid /ˈsfiːrɔɪd/ n. a body resembling or approximating to a sphere in shape, esp. one formed by the revolution of an ellipse about one of its axes. □ **spheroidal** adj.

sphincter /ˈsfɪŋktər/ n. Anat. a ring of muscle surrounding and serving to guard or close an opening or tube, esp. the anus.

sphinx /sfɪŋks/ n. **1** (**Sphinx**) (in Greek mythology) the winged monster of Thebes, having a woman's head and a lion's body, whose riddle Oedipus guessed and who consequently killed herself. **2 a** any of several ancient Egyptian stone figures having a lion's body and a human or animal head. **b** (**the Sphinx**) the huge sphinx near the Pyramids at Giza. **3** a mysterious or inscrutable person. **4** (in full **sphinx moth**) a hawk moth.

spic n. US slang offensive a Spanish-speaking person from Central or S America or the Caribbean, esp. a Mexican.

spic and span adj. (also **spick-and-span**) **1** smart and new. **2** neat and clean.

spice ● n. **1** an aromatic or pungent vegetable substance used to flavour food, e.g. ginger, pepper, or cinnamon. **2** spices collectively. **3** an interesting or piquant quality. ● v.tr. **1** flavour with spice. **2** add an interesting or piquant quality to (*spiced with humour*).

spicule /ˈspɪkjuːl/ n. **1** any small sharp-pointed body. **2** Zool. a small hard calcareous or siliceous body, esp. in the framework of a sponge. **3** Bot. a small or secondary spike.

spicy adj. (**-ier, -iest**) **1** of, flavoured with, or fragrant with spice. **2** piquant, pungent; sensational or improper (*a spicy story*). □ **spiciness** n.

spider n. **1 a** any eight-legged arthropod of the order Araneae with a round unsegmented body, many of which spin webs for the capture of insects as food. **b** any of various similar or related arachnids, e.g. a red spider. **2** any object comparable to a spider, esp. as having numerous or prominent legs or spokes.

spider crab n. any of various crabs of the family Majidae with a pear-shaped body and long thin legs.

spider mite n. (in full **red spider mite**) a plant-feeding mite of the family Tetranychidae, esp. *Tetranychus urticae*, a garden and hothouse pest.

spider monkey n. any of several monkeys of the central and S America, of the genera *Ateles* and *Brachyteles*, having long slender limbs and a prehensile tail.

spider plant n. a southern African plant, *Chlorophytum comosum*, which spreads by producing plantlets and is grown as a houseplant.

spiderweb n. **1** a web spun by a spider. **2** something resembling this.

spidery adj. elongated and thin (*spidery handwriting*).

spiel[1] /ʃpiːl, spiːl/ slang ● n. a long or prepared speech or story, esp. a sales pitch. ● v. **1** intr. speak in this style; hold forth. **2** tr. reel off (a sales pitch etc.). □ **spieler** n.

spiel[2] /spiːl/ n. informal a bonspiel.

spiff v.tr. (foll. by *up*) N Amer. informal make attractive or smart.

spiffy adj. (**-ier, -iest**) esp. N Amer. informal **1** excellent. **2** well-dressed. **3** elegant, fashionable. □ **spiffily** adv.

spigot /ˈspɪgət/ n. **1** a small peg or plug, esp. for insertion into the vent of a cask. **2 a** US a tap. **b** a device for controlling the flow of liquid in a tap.

spike[1] ● *n.* **1 a** a sharp point. **b** a pointed piece of metal, esp. the top of an iron railing etc. **c** an upstanding pointed object. **2** a large nail, e.g. one used for railways or in eavestroughing. **3 a** any of several metal points set into the sole of a running shoe to prevent slipping. **b** (in *pl.*) a pair of running shoes with spikes. **c** (in *pl.*) spike heels. **4 a** a sharp increase. **b** *Electronics* a pulse of very short duration in which a rapid increase in voltage is followed by a rapid decrease. **5** (in volleyball) the act or an instance of spiking the ball. **6** = SPINDLE 5. **7** *slang* a hypodermic needle. ● *v.* **1** *tr.* **a** fasten or provide with spikes. **b** fix on or pierce with spikes. **c** form into spikes. **2** *tr.* *informal* lace (a drink) with alcohol, a drug, etc. **b** contaminate (a substance) with something added. **c** flavour (a dish) with a strong herb, spice, condiment, etc. **3** *tr.* (in volleyball) hit (the ball) forcefully from a position near the net so that it moves downward into the opposite court. **4** *tr.* *Football* fling (the ball) forcefully to the ground, esp. in celebration of a touchdown or victory. **5** *tr.* make useless, put an end to, thwart (an idea etc.). **6** *tr.* *hist.* plug up the vent of (a gun) with a spike. **7** *tr.* drive a long nail into (a tree) so as to make it dangerous to cut down the tree with a chainsaw. **8 a** *tr.* experience (a rapidly rising fever). **b** *intr.* (of a fever) rapidly rise to a high level. □ **spike a person's guns** spoil his or her plans.

spike[2] *n.* **1** a flower cluster formed of many flower heads attached closely on a long stem. **2** a separate sprig of any plant in which flowers form a spikelike cluster. □ **spikelet** *n.*

spike heel *n.* **1** a high tapering heel of a shoe. **2** a shoe having this type of heel.

spiky *adj.* **(-ier, -iest) 1** resembling a spike. **2** having a spike or spikes. **3** *informal* easily offended; prickly. □ **spikily** *adv.* **spikiness** *n.*

spile *n.* **1** *N Amer.* a small spout for tapping sap from a sugar maple. **2** a wooden peg or spigot. **3** a large timber or pile for driving into the ground.

spill[1] ● *v.* (*past and past part.* **spilled** or **spilt**) **1** *intr. & tr.* **a** fall or run or cause (a liquid, powder, etc.) to fall or run out of a container, esp. unintentionally. **b** cast (light) or (of light) be cast into a darker area. **2** *intr.* (esp. of a crowd) move out quickly from a place etc., esp. in great numbers (*spilled into the street*). **3** *tr.* *slang* disclose (information etc.). **4** *tr. & intr.* throw (a person etc.) from a vehicle, saddle, etc. ● *n.* **1 a** the act or an instance of spilling or being spilled. **b** a quantity spilled. **2 a** tumble or fall, esp. from a horse etc. (*had a nasty spill*). □ **spill the beans** *informal* divulge information etc., esp. unintentionally or indiscreetly. **spill blood** be guilty of bloodshed. **spill one's guts** reveal one's thoughts or feelings without restraint; confess. **spill over 1** overflow. **2** (of a surplus population) encroach upon an area (*compare* OVERSPILL 2). □ **spillage** *n.*

spillover *n.* **1 a** the process or an instance of spilling over. **b** a thing that spills over. **2** a consequence, repercussion, or by-product.

spillway *n.* a passage for surplus water from a dam, reservoir, etc.

spin ● *v.* (**spinning**; *past and past part.* **spun** / spʌn /) **1** *intr. & tr.* turn or cause (a person or thing) to turn or whirl round quickly. **2** *tr. & intr.* **a** draw out and twist (wool, cotton, etc.) into threads. **b** make (yarn) in this way. **c** make a similar type of thread from (a synthetic substance etc.). **3** *tr.* (of a spider, silkworm, etc.) make (a web, gossamer, a cocoon, etc.) by extruding a fine viscous thread. **4** *tr.* tell or write (a story etc.) (*spins a good tale*). **5** *tr.* impart spin to (a ball). **6** *intr.* (of a person's head etc.) be dizzy through sickness, excite-

ment, astonishment, etc. **7** *intr.* (of a wheel or wheels) revolve rapidly without providing traction. **8** *intr.* (of a ball) move through the air with spin. **9** *tr.* fish in (a stream, pool, etc.) with a spinner. **10** *tr. & intr.* *informal* play (records); act as a disc jockey (*she spins at a local dance club*). **11** *intr.* (of a washing machine) rotate wet clothing rapidly to remove excess water. ● *n.* **1** a spinning motion; a whirl. **2** = TAILSPIN *n.* 3. **3** a revolving motion through the air, esp. in a rifle bullet or ball. **4** *informal* **a** a brief excursion in a motor vehicle, airplane, etc., esp. for pleasure. **b** a rapid perusal (*a quick spin through her memoirs*). **5** esp. *N Amer.* a bias in information to give a favourable impression. **6** the cycle on a washing machine during which the clothing is spun (also *attrib.*: *spin cycle*). **7** *Figure Skating* any of a number of movements involving rotating rapidly in one spot. □ **spin off 1** *N Amer.* produce as a spinoff. **2 a** distribute (stock of a new company) to shareholders of a parent company. **b** create (a company) in this way. **3** throw off by centrifugal force in spinning. **spin out 1** prolong (a discussion etc.). **2** make (a story, money, etc.) last as long as possible. **3** spend or consume (time, one's life, etc., by discussion or in an occupation etc.). **4** *N Amer.* (esp. of a driver or car) lose or go out of control, esp. in a skid. **spin one's wheels** *N Amer.* waste one's time or efforts. □ **spinning** *n.*

spina bifida / ˌspainə ˈbɪfɪdə / *n.* a congenital defect of the spine, in which part of the spinal cord and meninges are exposed through a gap in the backbone.

spinach *n.* **1** a green garden vegetable, *Spinacia oleracea*, with succulent leaves. **2** the leaves of this plant used as food.

spinal ● *adj.* of or relating to the spine (*spinal disease*). ● *n.* *N Amer.* *informal* = EPIDURAL *n.* □ **spinally** *adv.*

spinal column *n.* the spine.

spinal cord *n.* a cylindrical structure of the central nervous system enclosed in the spine, connecting all parts of the body with the brain.

spinal fluid *n.* = CEREBROSPINAL FLUID.

spinal tap *n.* the insertion of a needle into the spine, usu. in the lumbar region, so that cerebrospinal fluid may be withdrawn or something (such as an anesthetic) may be introduced.

spinarama *n.* *Cdn* an evasive move, esp. in hockey, consisting of an abrupt 360-degree turn.

spincaster *n.* esp. *N Amer.* a fishing reel mounted on top of the rod, with an enclosed spool and thumb trigger.

spin control *n.* *N Amer.* *slang* an attempt to give a particular slant to esp. political news coverage.

spindle ● *n.* **1 a** a pin in a spinning wheel used for twisting and winding the thread. **b** a small bar with tapered ends used for the same purpose in hand spinning. **c** a pin bearing the bobbin of a spinning machine. **2** a pin or axis that revolves or on which something revolves. **3** a turned piece of wood used as a banister, chair leg, etc. **4** *Biol.* a spindle-shaped mass of microtubules formed when a cell divides. **5 a** pointed metal rod standing on a base and used for holding bills, order forms, memos, etc. ● *v.* **1** *tr. & intr.* impale (a piece of paper) on a spindle. **2** *intr.* have, or grow into, a long slender form.

spindle-shaped *adj.* having a circular cross-section and tapering towards each end.

spindly *adj.* **(-ier, -iest)** long or tall and thin; thin and weak.

spin doctor *n.* *informal* a political or corporate

spokesperson employed to give a favourable interpretation of events to the media.

spindrift *n.* spray blown along the surface of the sea.

spine *n.* **1** a series of vertebrae extending from the skull to the tailbone, enclosing the spinal cord and providing support for the thorax and abdomen; the backbone. **2** *Zool. & Bot.* any hard, pointed process or structure, e.g. a sharp-pointed ray on the fin of a fish. **3** a sharp ridge or projection, esp. of a mountain range or slope. **4** resolution, firmness of character (*he has no spine whatsoever*). **5** the part of a book's jacket or cover that encloses the part where the pages are stitched or glued. **6** a central feature, main support, or source of strength. ☐ **spined** *adj.*

spine-chiller *n.* a frightening story, film, etc. ☐ **spine-chilling** *adj.*

spinel /spɪˈnɛl/ *n.* **1** any of a group of hard crystalline minerals of various colours, consisting chiefly of oxides of magnesium and aluminum. **2** any substance of similar composition or properties.

spineless *adj.* **1** (of a person or action etc.) lacking energy or resolution; weak and purposeless. **2 a** having no spine; invertebrate. **b** (of a fish) having fins without spines. ☐ **spinelessly** *adv.* **spinelessness** *n.*

spinet /ˈspɪnət, -ˈnɛt/ *n. hist.* a small harpsichord with oblique strings.

spine-tingling *adj.* thrilling or pleasurably frightening. ☐ **spine tingler** *n.*

spinnaker /ˈspɪnəkər/ *n.* a large triangular sail carried opposite the mainsail of a racing yacht running before the wind.

spinner *n.* **1** a person or thing that spins. **2** (also **spinnerbait**) a fishing bait or lure fixed so as to revolve when pulled through the water.

spinneret /ˈspɪnəˌrɛt/ *n.* **1** any of various organs through which the silk, gossamer, or thread of spiders, silkworms, etc. is produced. **2** a device for forming filaments of synthetic fibre.

spinning machine *n.* a machine that spins fibres continuously.

spinning reel *n.* esp. *N Amer.* a fishing reel mounted under the rod, with a fixed open spool.

spinning top *n.* = TOP².

spinning wheel *n.* a device formerly used for spinning yarn or thread with a spindle driven by a wheel attached to a crank or treadle.

spinny *adj.* *Cdn* crazy, foolish.

spinoff *n.* **1** an incidental result or results. **2** something, e.g. a television program, book, etc., derived from another product of a similar type. **3** an incidental benefit arising from industrial or military technology. **4** a distribution of stock in a new company to shareholders of the parent company.

spinster *n.* **1** a woman, esp. an older one, thought unlikely to marry. **2** *Law* an unmarried woman. ☐ **spinsterhood** *n.*

spin the bottle *n.* a party game in which a bottle is spun and the person towards whom it points upon ceasing to spin kisses the spinner.

spiny *adj.* (**-ier, -iest**) **1** full of spines; prickly. **2** perplexing, troublesome, thorny. **3** having the form of a spine; sharp-pointed. ☐ **spininess** *n.*

spiny lobster *n.* any of various large edible crustaceans of the family Palinuridae, with a spiny shell and no large anterior claws.

spiraea *var. of* SPIREA.

spiral ● *adj.* **1** winding about a centre in an enlarging or decreasing continuous circular motion, either on a flat plane or rising in a cone; coiled. **2** winding continuously along or as if along a cylinder, like the thread of a screw. **3** spiral-bound (*a spiral workbook*). ● *n.* **1** a plane or three-dimensional spiral curve. **2** a spiral spring. **3** a spiral formation in a shell etc. **4** a progressive increase or deterioration, esp. one seen as being out of control (*a spiral of rising prices and wages*). **5** a continuous banking turn accompanying a descent or (rarely) ascent. ● *v.* (**spiralled, spiralling**) **1** *intr.* move in a spiral course, esp. upwards or downwards. **2** *tr.* make spiral. **3** *intr.* increase rapidly. ☐ **spiralling** *adj.* **spirally** *adv.*

spiral binding *n.* a type of binding used esp. for notebooks in which the pages are held together by a spiral of wire that coils through holes punched into the side of each page. ☐ **spiral-bound** *adj.*

spiral staircase *n.* a staircase rising in a spiral around a central axis.

spire¹ ● *n.* **1** a tapering cone- or pyramid-shaped structure built esp. on a church tower (*compare* STEEPLE). **2** any conical, pointed, or tapering thing, e.g. the spike of a flower. **3** the highest point of something. ● *v.tr.* provide with a spire.

spire² *n.* **1 a** a spiral; a coil. **b** a single twist of this. **2** the upper part of a spiral shell.

spirea /spaɪˈriːə/ *n.* any shrub of the genus *Spiraea*, with clusters of small white or pink flowers.

spirit ● *n.* **1 a** the vital animating essence of a person or animal (*was sadly broken in spirit*). **b** the intelligent non-physical part of a person; the soul. **2 a** a rational or intelligent being without a material body. **b** a supernatural being such as a ghost, fairy, etc. (*haunted by spirits*). **c** (**the Spirit**) = HOLY SPIRIT. **3 a** a prevailing mental or moral condition or attitude; a mood; a tendency (*Christmas spirit*). **4 a** (usu. in *pl.*) strong distilled liquor, e.g. brandy, whisky, gin, rum. **b** a distilled volatile liquid. **c** purified alcohol (*methylated spirits*). **d** a solution in alcohol of a specified substance (*spirit of ammonia*). **5 a** a person's mental or moral nature or qualities, usu. specified (*has an unbending spirit*). **b** a person viewed as possessing these (*is an ardent spirit*). **c** energy, vivacity, dash (*played with spirit*). **d** courage; assertiveness, determination (*argued her case with spirit*). **6** the general intent or true meaning of a statement etc. as opposed to its strict verbal interpretation (*the spirit of the law*). **7** feelings of loyalty to a team, group, organization, etc. (*team spirit*). **8** (in *pl.*) a person's feelings or state of mind. ● *v.tr.* (**spirited, spiriting**) (usu. foll. by *away, off*, etc.) convey rapidly and secretly by or as if by spirits. ● *adj.* **1** of or relating to supernatural spirits (*the spirit world*). **2** (of a fuel-burning appliance) powered by alcoholic spirits (*spirit lamp*). ☐ **in spirit** in one's thoughts (*shall be with you in spirit*). **keep a person's spirits up** cheer a person up. **the spirit moves a person** he or she feels inclined (*to do something*). **the spirit is willing (but the flesh is weak)** one's intentions and wishes are good but weakness, love of pleasure, etc. prevent one from acting according to them.

spirit bear *n.* *Cdn* a white kermode bear.

spirited *adj.* **1** full of spirit; animated, lively, brisk, or courageous. **2** having a spirit or spirits of a specified kind (*mean-spirited*). ☐ **spiritedly** *adv.* **spiritedness** *n.*

spiritless *adj.* lacking courage, vigour, or vivacity.

spirit level *n.* a device containing a bent glass tube nearly filled with alcohol, used to test horizontality by the position of an air bubble.

spiritual ● *adj.* **1** of or relating to the human spirit or soul; not of physical things. **2** concerned with sacred or religious things; holy; divine; inspired (*the spiritual life*). **3** of or relating to the Church. **4** (of the mind etc.) refined, sensitive; not concerned with the material. **5** (of a relationship etc.) concerned with the soul or spirit etc., not with external reality (*his spiritual home*). ● *n.* an emotional Christian song derived from the musical traditions of Blacks in the southern US. □ **spirituality** *n.* **spiritually** *adv.*

spiritualism *n.* **1 a** the belief that the spirits of the dead can communicate with the living, esp. through mediums. **b** the practices associated with this. **2** *Philos.* the doctrine that the spirit exists as distinct from matter, or that spirit is the only reality (compare MATERIALISM 2a). □ **spiritualist** *n. & adj.* **spiritualistic** *adj.*

spiritualize *v.tr.* **1** make (a person or a person's character, thoughts, etc.) spiritual; elevate. **2** attach a spiritual as opposed to a literal meaning to. □ **spiritualization** *n.*

spirochete /'spaɪroʊˌkiːt/ *n.* any of various flexible spirally twisted bacteria of the order Spirochaetales, esp. one that causes syphilis.

spit¹ ● *v.* (**spitting**; *past* and *past part.* **spat** or **spit**) **1** *intr.* **a** eject saliva from the mouth. **b** do this as a sign of hatred or contempt (*spat at him*). **2** *tr.* (usu. foll. by *out*) **a** eject (saliva, blood, food, etc.) from the mouth (*spat the meat out*). **b** emit or throw forcefully in a manner resembling spitting. **c** utter (oaths, threats, etc.) vehemently ('*Damn you!*' *he spat*). **3** *intr.* (of a fire, pan, etc.) send out sparks, hot fat, etc. **4** *intr.* (of rain) fall lightly (*it's only spitting*). **5** *intr.* (esp. of a cat) make a spitting or hissing noise in anger or hostility. ● *n.* **1** spittle. **2** the act or an instance of spitting. **3** the foamy liquid secretion of some insects used to protect their young. **4** (usu. in *pl.*) *Cdn* (*West*) *informal* a sunflower seed. □ **spit it out** *informal* say what is on one's mind. **spit up** *N Amer.* (esp. of a baby) vomit. □ **spitter** *n.* **spitty** *adj.*

spit² ● *n.* **1** a slender rod on which meat is skewered before being roasted on a fire etc. **2 a** a small point of land projecting into the water. **b** a long narrow underwater bank. ● *v.tr.* (**spitted, spitting**) **1** thrust a spit through (meat etc.). **2** pierce or transfix with a sword etc.

spit and polish *n.* **1** thorough cleaning and polishing of equipment, esp. by a soldier etc. **2** exaggerated neatness and cleanliness.

spitball *n.* *N Amer.* **1** a ball of chewed paper etc. usu. blown through a straw at a person as a prank. **2** *Baseball* an illegal swerving pitch made with a ball moistened with saliva or sweat. □ **spitballer** *n.*

spite ● *n.* **1** ill will, malice towards a person (*did it from spite*). **2** a grudge. ● *v.tr.* thwart, mortify, annoy (*does it to spite me*). □ **in spite of** notwithstanding. **in spite of oneself** etc. though one would rather have done otherwise (*found himself smiling in spite of himself*).

spiteful *adj.* motivated by spite; malevolent. □ **spitefully** *adv.* **spitefulness** *n.*

spitting distance *n.* a very short distance.

spitting image *n.* (foll. by *of*) *informal* the exact likeness of (another person or thing).

spittle *n.* **1** saliva, esp. as ejected from the mouth. **2** = SPIT¹ *n.* 3.

spittoon /spɪˈtuːn/ *n.* a metal or earthenware pot with esp. a funnel-shaped top, used for spitting into.

spitz *n.* a small breed of dog with a pointed muzzle, esp. a Pomeranian.

splake *n.* a hybrid trout produced by crossing the N American lake trout and the brook trout.

splash ● *v.* **1 a** *tr.* dash (liquid) against (deliberately or inadvertently) in an irregular or spasmodic way. **b** *tr.* make (something) wet or dirty by this action (*splashed her face*). **2 a** *tr. & intr.* cause (liquid) to spill, scatter, or fly about, esp. by sudden movement or agitation. **b** *intr.* (of a liquid) scatter or fly about in some quantity, esp. because of sudden movement or agitation. **3 a** *intr.* (usu. foll. by *across, along*, etc.) progress while scattering liquid etc. (*splashed across the river*). **b** *tr. & intr.* step, fall, or plunge etc. into a liquid etc. so as to cause a splash (*splashed into the lake*). **4** *tr.* display (news) prominently. **5** *tr.* decorate with scattered colour. ● *n.* **1** the act or an instance of splashing. **2 a** a quantity of liquid splashed. **b** the resulting noise (*heard a splash*). **3** a spot of dirt etc. splashed on to a thing. **4** a striking or ostentatious display or effect. **5** a prominent news feature etc. **6** a daub or patch of colour, sunlight, etc. **7** *informal* a small quantity of liquid, esp. of soda water etc. to dilute liquor. □ **make a splash** attract much attention, esp. by extravagance.

splashguard *n.* **1** = MUD FLAP. **2** any protective guard against splashes, e.g. on a nozzle of a gas pump.

splashy *adj.* (**-ier, -iest**) **1** attracting attention; ostentatious, sensational. **2** involving splashing.

splat *informal* ● *n.* a slapping sound, as of something wet hitting a surface. ● *adv.* with a splat (*the omelette fell splat on the floor*). ● *v.intr. & tr.* (**splatted, splatting**) fall or hit with a splat.

splatter ● *v.* **1** *tr.* (often foll. by *with*) make wet or dirty by splashing, esp. in droplets. **2** *tr. & intr.* splash, esp. with a continuous noisy action. **3** *tr.* (often foll. by *over*) publicize or spread (news etc.) (*the story was splattered over the front page*). ● *n.* **1** a noisy splashing sound. **2** a quantity splattered. **3** a rough patch of colour etc., esp. splashed on a surface. **4** (*attrib.*) *slang* designating or relating to films involving the depiction of many violent deaths.

splay ● *v.* **1** *tr.* (usu. foll. by *out*) spread (the fingers, legs, etc.) apart. **2** *intr.* (of an opening or its sides) diverge in shape or position. **3** *tr.* construct (a window, doorway, opening, etc.) so that it diverges or is wider at one side of the wall than the other. ● *adj.* **1** wide and flat. **2** turned outward.

spleen *n.* **1** an abdominal organ involved in the production and removal of red blood cells in most vertebrates, forming part of the immune system. **2** lowness of spirits; moroseness, ill temper, spite (*a fit of spleen*).

splendid *adj.* **1** magnificent, gorgeous, brilliant, sumptuous (*a splendid palace*). **2** dignified; impressive (*splendid isolation*). **3** excellent; fine (*a splendid chance*). □ **splendidly** *adv.* **splendidness** *n.*

splendour *n.* (also **splendor**) **1** magnificence; grandeur. **2** great or dazzling brightness.

splice ● *v.tr.* **1** join the ends of (ropes) by interweaving strands. **2** join (pieces of film etc.) by sticking together the ends. **3** join (girders, beams, etc.) by partly overlapping the ends and fastening them together. **4** unite, join. **5** (esp. as **spliced** *adj.*) *informal* join in marriage. ● *n.* a place in a film, tape, rope, etc. where it has been joined. □ **splicer** *n.*

spliff *n.* *slang* a marijuana cigarette.

spline *n.* **1** a rectangular key fitting into grooves in the hub and shaft of a wheel and allowing longitudinal play. **2** a slat. **3** a flexible wood or rubber strip used esp. in drawing large curves. ● *v.tr.* fit with a spline (sense 1).

splint ● *n.* **1 a** a strip of rigid material used for holding a broken bone etc. when set. **b** a rigid device for maintaining a part of the body, e.g. the teeth, in a fixed position. **c** a rigid or flexible strip of esp. wood used in basketwork etc. **2** a tumour or bony excrescence on the inside of a horse's leg. **3** a thin strip of wood etc. used to light a fire, pipe, etc. ● *v.tr.* secure (a broken limb etc.) with a splint or splints.

splinter ● *n.* **1** a small thin sharp piece broken off from wood, glass, stone, etc. **2** (in full **splinter group**, **splinter party**) a group or party that has broken away from a larger one. ● *v.tr. & intr.* break into fragments or factions. □ **splintery** *adj.*

split ● *v.* (**splitting**; *past* and *past part.* **split**) **1 a** *intr. & tr.* break or cause to break forcibly into parts, esp. into halves or (of a log) along the grain. **b** *intr. & tr.* (often foll. by *up*) divide into parts (*split into groups*). **c** *tr.* share between two or more people. **2** *tr. & intr.* (often foll. by *off*, *away*) remove or be removed by breaking, separating, or dividing (*split away from the main group*). **3** *intr. & tr.* **a** (usu. foll. by *up*) *informal* separate, esp. through discord (*split up after ten years*). **b** (foll. by *with*) *informal* quarrel or cease association with (another person etc.). **c** (often as **split** *adj.*) (usu. foll. by *on*, *over*) separate or divide as a result of opposing views (*the government is split over cuts to education*). **4** *tr.* cause the fission of (an atom). **5** *intr. & tr.* *slang* leave, esp. suddenly. **6** *tr.* *N Amer.* (of a team) win half of the games in (a match or series) (*split a doubleheader*). **7** *tr.* (often foll. by *up*) divide (a stock) into two or more stocks of the same total value. ● *n.* **1** the act or an instance of splitting; the state of being split. **2** a fissure, vent, crack, cleft, etc. **3 a** a separation into parties; a schism. **b** an incompatibility. **4** (in *pl.*) the feat of leaping in the air or sitting down with the legs at right angles to the body in front and behind, or at the sides with the trunk facing forwards. **5** a formation of bowling pins left standing after the first bowl in which there is a large gap between two pins or two groups of pins, making a spare difficult. **6** the time taken to complete a portion of a race, esp. recorded by a split-second watch and used as a comparative measure of performance. **7** *N Amer.* a match or series that ends with both teams having won an equal number of games. **8** a half-bottle of wine. ● *adj.* **1** that has split or been split (*split logs*). **2** divided in opinion etc. □ **split the difference** take the average of two proposed amounts. **split a gut** *N Amer.* *informal* be convulsed with laughter. **split hairs** make small and insignificant distinctions. **split one's sides** be convulsed with laughter. **split the vote** *Cdn & Brit.* (of a candidate or minority party) attract votes from another so that both are defeated by a third.

split decision *n.* **1** a decision in a boxing match in which the judges and referee are not unanimous in their choice of a winner. **2** a court ruling etc. which is not unanimous.

split end *n.* **1** (usu. in *pl.*) a hair which has split at the end from dryness etc. **2** *Football* a player at the end of and some distance from a line of players in formation.

split-finger *adj.* (also **split-fingered**) *Baseball* designating a pitch thrown with the motion of a fastball, but with the index and middle fingers spread wide apart along the seams, so that it has little backspin and dips sharply and deceptively as it approaches the plate.

split infinitive *n.* a phrase consisting of an infinitive with an adverb etc. inserted between *to* and the verb, e.g. *seems to really like it*. ¶The supposed 'rule' that an infinitive should never be split is an artificial one. In many cases a split infinitive sounds more natural than its avoidance, e.g. *What is it like to actually live in*

France? On other occasions, it is better to place the adverb after the infinitive, e.g. *He wanted to completely give up his business* is better as *He wanted to give up his business completely*, which more effectively places the emphasis on *completely*.

split-level ● *adj.* (of a room or a building, esp. a house) having the floor level of one part about half a storey above or below the floor level of an adjacent part. ● *n.* a split-level building.

split pea *n.* a pea dried and split in half for cooking.

split personality *n.* **1** the coexistence within one person, institution, etc. of seemingly contradictory or conflicting characteristics. **2** *informal* schizophrenia or multiple personality disorder.

split pin *n.* a metal cotter pin passed through a hole and held in place by its gaping split end.

split-rail *adj.* designating a type of fence, corral, etc. made from split logs.

split-run *n.* a Canadian edition of a foreign magazine, with advertising directed at the Canadian market but with little or no Canadian editorial content.

split-screen *n.* a screen on a computer etc. on which two or more separate images are displayed.

split second ● *n.* a very brief moment. ● *attrib.adj.* (**split-second**) **1** very rapid. **2** (of timing) very precise.

splitter *n.* **1** a person who splits, esp. someone employed in splitting fish. **2** a person (esp. a taxonomist) who attaches importance to differences rather than similarities in classification or analysis (compare LUMPER 2). **3** any of various devices that send electrical current, a received or transmitted signal, etc. along two or more routes.

splitting *adj.* **1** (esp. of a headache) very painful; acute. **2** (of the head) suffering great pain from a headache, noise, etc.

split-up *n.* **1** the act of splitting or dividing. **2** the termination of a relationship. **3** the division of a stock into two or more stocks of the same total value.

splotch esp. *N Amer.* ● *n.* a daub, blot, or smear. ● *v.tr.* make a large, esp. irregular, spot or patch on. □ **splotchy** *adj.*

splurge *informal* ● *n.* **1** an ostentatious display or effort. **2** an instance of sudden great extravagance. ● *v.* **1** *intr.* (usu. foll. by *on*) spend effort or esp. large sums of money (*splurged on new furniture*). **2** *tr.* spend (money etc.) extravagantly.

splutter ● *v.* **1** *intr.* **a** speak in a hurried, vehement, or choking manner. **b** make a series of spitting or choking sounds. **2** *tr.* **a** speak or utter (words, threats, a language, etc.) rapidly or incoherently. **b** emit (food, sparks, hot oil, etc.) with a spitting sound. ● *n.* spluttering speech or sound.

spoil ● *v.* (*past* and *past part.* **spoiled** or esp. *Brit.* **spoilt**) **1** *tr.* **a** damage, ruin; diminish the value of (*will spoil all the fun*). **b** reduce a person's enjoyment etc. of (*the news spoiled his dinner*). **2** *tr.* **a** harm the character of (esp. a child, pet, etc.) by excessive indulgence. **b** (also *refl.*) pamper; pay attention to the comfort and wishes of (a person). **c** accustom (a person etc.) to ease, favourable conditions, etc. so as to be unsuited to adversity (*we have been spoiled by so much fine weather*). **3** *intr.* (of food) go bad, decay; become unfit for eating. **4** *tr.* render (a ballot) invalid by improper marking. ● *n.* **1** (usu. in *pl.*) **a** plunder taken from an enemy in war, or seized by force. **b** esp. *jocular* profit or advantages gained by succeeding to public office, high position, etc. **2** earth etc. thrown up in excavating, dredging, etc. □ **be spoiling for** aggressively seek (a fight etc.).

spoilage n. **1** the deterioration or decay of food etc. **2** the amount of material that is spoiled.

spoiler n. **1 a** a person or thing that spoils something. **b** a person who obstructs or prevents an opponent's success while not being a potential winner. **2 a** a flap able to be projected from the upper surface of an aircraft wing to break up a smooth airflow and so reduce speed. **b** a similar device on a vehicle intended to reduce lift and so improve road-holding at high speed.

spoilsport n. a person who spoils others' pleasure or enjoyment.

spoke[1] ● n. **1** each of the wire rods or bars running from the hub to the rim of a wheel. **2** a rung of a ladder. **3** each radial handle of the wheel of a ship etc. ● v.tr. provide with spokes. □ **spoked** adj.

spoke[2] past of SPEAK.

spoken ● v. past part. of SPEAK. ● adj. **1** (in comb.) speaking in a specified way (soft-spoken). **2** (of language, words, etc.) uttered in speech; oral as opposed to written. □ **spoken for** claimed, requisitioned (this seat is spoken for).

spokes- comb.form informal or jocular forming nouns denoting a person or animal appearing in advertising for a particular product (spokesmodel).

spokesman n. (pl. **-men**) **1** a person who speaks on behalf of others, esp. in public relations. **2** a person deputed to express the views of a group etc.

spokesperson n. (pl. **-s** or **-people**) a spokesman or spokeswoman.

spokeswoman n. (pl. **-women**) **1** a woman who speaks on behalf of others, esp. in public relations. **2** a woman deputed to express the views of a group etc.

sponge ● n. **1** any sessile aquatic animal of the phylum Porifera, with a porous bag-like body structure and a rigid or elastic internal skeleton. **2 a** the skeleton of a sponge, esp. the soft light elastic absorbent kind used in bathing, cleansing surfaces, etc. **b** a piece of porous rubber or plastic etc. used similarly. **c** a piece of sponge or similar material (esp. one impregnated with spermicide) inserted in the vagina as a contraceptive. **3 a** a thing of spongelike absorbency or consistency, e.g. sponge cake, porous metal, etc. (lemon sponge). **b** soft fermenting bread dough. **4** = SPONGER. **5** informal a person who drinks heavily. ● v. (**sponging** or **spongeing**) **1** tr. wipe or cleanse with a sponge. **2** tr. (often foll. by down, over) sluice water over (the body, a car, etc.). **3** tr. (often foll. by out, away, etc.) wipe off or efface (writing, a memory, etc.) with or as with a sponge. **4** tr. (often foll. by up) absorb with or as with a sponge. **5** intr. (often foll. by on, off) live at the expense of (another person) with no intention of reimbursement etc. **6** tr. obtain (drink etc.) by sponging. **7** tr. **a** apply paint with a sponge to (walls, furniture, pottery, etc.) to achieve a mottled effect. **b** apply (paint) in this manner. □ **spongelike** adj.

sponge cake n. a very light cake with a spongelike consistency, made from beaten eggs, sugar, and flour, with little or no fat.

sponge hockey n. Cdn a form of hockey played on ice with rubber-soled boots and a sponge puck.

sponge puck n. Cdn a hockey puck made of hard sponge, used in recreational play or with young children.

sponger n. a person who contrives to live at another's expense.

sponge rubber n. liquid rubber latex processed into a spongelike substance.

spongiform encephalopathy /'spʌndʒɪˌfɔrm/ n. any of various degenerative diseases of the central nervous system characterized by histological change in brain tissue, which assumes a spongelike appearance.

spongy adj. (**-ier, -iest**) like a sponge, esp. in being porous, compressible, elastic, or absorbent. □ **spongily** adv. **sponginess** n.

sponsor ● n. **1** a person who supports an activity done for charity by pledging money in advance. **2 a** a person or organization that promotes or supports an artistic or sporting activity etc. **b** esp. N Amer. a business organization that promotes a broadcast program in return for advertising time. **3** an organization lending support to an election candidate. **4** a person who introduces a proposal for legislation. **5 a** a godparent at baptism. **b** esp. Catholicism a person who presents a candidate for confirmation. **6** a person who makes himself or herself responsible for another. ● v.tr. be a sponsor for. □ **sponsorship** n.

spontaneous /spɒn'teɪnɪəs/ adj. **1** acting or done or occurring because of a sudden impulse from within; not planned or caused or suggested by external forces (spontaneous applause). **2** voluntary, without external incitement (a spontaneous offer). **3** (of structural changes in plants and muscular activity esp. in young animals) instinctive, automatic, prompted by no motive. **4** (of bodily movement, literary style, etc.) gracefully natural and unconstrained. **5** (of sudden movement etc.) involuntary, not due to conscious volition. **6** growing naturally without cultivation. □ **spontaneity** /ˌspɒntə'neɪɪti/ n. **spontaneously** adv.

spontaneous combustion n. the ignition of a mineral or vegetable substance, e.g. a heap of rags soaked with oil, a mass of wet coal, etc., from heat engendered within itself, usu. by rapid oxidation.

spoof informal ● n. **1** a parody. **2** a hoax or swindle. ● v.tr. **1** parody. **2** hoax, swindle.

spook ● n. **1** informal a ghost. **2** esp. N Amer. slang a spy. ● v. esp. N Amer. slang **1** tr. frighten, unnerve, alarm. **2** intr. take fright, become alarmed.

spooky adj. (**-ier, -iest**) **1** informal ghostly, eerie. **2** N Amer. slang (of a person or animal) nervous; easily frightened. □ **spookily** adv. **spookiness** n.

spool[1] ● n. **1 a** a reel for winding thread, yarn, or wire on. **b** a reel for winding magnetic tape, photographic film, etc., on. **c** a quantity of thread, tape, etc., wound on a spool. **2** the revolving cylinder of an angler's reel. ● v.tr. wind on a spool.

spool[2] v.tr. Computing print out, read in, or otherwise process (data) on a peripheral device at the same time that an operating system is carrying out other processes. □ **spooler** n. **spooling** n.

spoon ● n. **1 a** a utensil consisting of an oval or round bowl and a handle for conveying food (esp. liquid) to the mouth, or for stirring, mixing, etc. **b** a spoonful, esp. of sugar. **c** (in pl.) Music a pair of spoons held in the hand and beaten together rhythmically as a percussion instrument. **2** a spoon-shaped thing, esp. (in full **spoon bait**) a bright revolving piece of metal used as a lure in fishing. ● v. **1** tr. (often foll. by up, out) lift and move (food, liquid etc.) with a spoon. **2** tr. hit (a ball) feebly upwards. **3** informal intr. behave in an amorous way, esp. foolishly. **4** intr. fish with a spoon bait. **5** intr. lie close together or fit into each other in the manner of spoons. □ **born with a silver spoon in one's mouth** born in affluence. □ **spooner** n. (in sense 3 of v.). **spoonful** n. (pl. **-fuls**).

spoonbill n. any of various wading birds which have a long spatulate or spoon-shaped bill for feeding in water.

spoon-feed v.tr. (past and past part. **-fed**) **1** feed (a baby etc.) with a spoon. **2** provide help etc. to (a person etc.) without requiring any effort on the recipient's part.

spoor ● *n.* the track or scent of a person or animal, esp. the footprints of a wild animal hunted as game. ● *v.tr. & intr.* follow by the spoor.

sporadic *adj.* occurring only here and there or occasionally, separate, scattered. □ **sporadically** *adv.*

sporangium / spə'rændʒɪəm/ *n.* (*pl.* **-gia** /-dʒɪə/) *Bot.* a receptacle in which spores are found.

spore *n.* **1** a specialized reproductive cell of many plants and micro-organisms. **2** these collectively.

sport ● *n.* **1 a** a game or competitive activity, esp. one involving physical exertion, e.g. hockey. **b** (usu. in *pl.*; often *attrib.*) such activities collectively. **2** (often *attrib.*) recreation, amusement, diversion, fun (*sport hunting*). **3** *informal* **a** a fair, cheerful, or generous person (*be a sport and lend me your bike*). **b** a person behaving in a specified way, esp. regarding games, rules, etc. (*a bad sport*). **4** *Biol.* an animal or plant deviating suddenly or strikingly from the normal type. **5** (*attrib.*) a sports car; a sports model of a car (*sport coupe*). ● *v.* **1** *tr.* wear, exhibit, or produce, esp. ostentatiously (*sported a pink tie*). **2** *intr.* frolic, gambol. □ **make sport of** make fun of, ridicule. □ **sporter** *n.*

sportcoat *n.* = SPORTS JACKET.

sport fish *n.* a kind of fish caught for sport. □ **sport fisherman** *n.* **sport fishery** *n.*

sport fishing *n.* fishing with a rod and line for sport or recreation.

sporting *adj.* **1** connected with or interested in sports. **2** fair, generous (*a sporting offer*).

sporting chance *n.* a reasonable chance of success.

sports bar *n.* *N Amer.* a bar where televised sports events are shown continuously.

sports car *n.* a low, fast car designed for superior acceleration and performance at high speed.

sportscast *n.* *N Amer.* a broadcast of a sports event or information about sport. □ **sportscaster** *n.*

sports coat *n.* = SPORTS JACKET.

sports day *n.* *Cdn & Brit.* a day on which schoolchildren participate in games, races, etc.

sports jacket *n.* (also **sport jacket**) a man's jacket for informal wear, not part of a suit.

sportsman *n.* (*pl.* **-men**) **1** a person who takes part in sports, esp. professionally. **2** a person who behaves fairly and generously. □ **sportsmanlike** *adj.* **sportsmanship** *n.*

sports medicine *n.* the branch of medicine that deals with injuries etc. sustained in athletics.

sportsperson *n.* (*pl.* **-persons** or **-people**) a sportsman or sportswoman.

sportsplex *n.* *Cdn* a building offering different sports facilities under one roof, e.g. a rink, pool, etc.

sports shirt *n.* (also **sport shirt**) a men's casual shirt with a squared-off shirt-tail.

sportswear *n.* **1** clothes worn for playing sports. **2** clothing of a somewhat informal type.

sportswoman *n.* (*pl.* **-women**) **1** a woman who takes part in sports, esp. professionally. **2** a woman who behaves fairly and generously.

sportswriter *n.* a journalist who writes on sports.

sport-utility *n.* (in full **sport-utility vehicle**) (also *informal* **sport ute**) *N Amer.* a hybrid between a Jeep and a minivan, used for everyday driving as well as driving over rough terrain.

sporty *adj.* (**-ier, -iest**) *informal* **1 a** fond of sports. **b** (esp. of clothes) suitable for informal wear; designed in a casual style. **2** rakish, showy. **3** (of a car) resem-

bling a sports car in appearance or performance. □ **sportily** *adv.* **sportiness** *n.*

spot ● *n.* **1 a** a small part of the surface of a thing distinguished by colour, texture, etc., usu. round or less elongated than a streak or stripe. **b** a small mark or stain. **c** a pimple or other mark on the skin. **d** a small circle or other shape used in various numbers to distinguish faces of dice, playing cards in a suit, etc. **e** a moral blemish. **f** any of various plant diseases producing small round areas of discoloration on the leaves or fruit. **2 a** a particular place; a definite locality (*settled on this spot*). **b** a place in a class, group, etc. (*phone early to reserve a spot*). **3** a particular part of one's body or aspect of one's character (*bald spot; soft spot*). **4 a** *informal* one's (esp. regular) position in an organization, program of events, etc. **b** a place or position in a performance or show (*a ten-minute guest spot*). **5** an awkward or difficult situation (*in a tight spot*). **6** = SPOTLIGHT *n.* 1, 2. **7** (usu. *attrib.*) money paid or goods delivered immediately after a sale (*spot cash*). **8** *Billiards* etc. **a** a small round black patch to mark the position where a ball is placed at certain times. **b** (in full **spot-ball**) the white ball distinguished from the other by two black spots. ● *v.* (**spotted, spotting**) **1 a** *tr. & intr.* mark or become marked with spots. **b** *tr.* stain, soil (a person's character etc.). **2** *tr.* **a** catch sight of; notice, perceive. **b** *informal* single out beforehand (the winner of a race etc.). **c** watch for and take note of (trains, talent, etc.). **d** *Military* locate (an enemy's position), esp. from the air. **3** *tr. Billiards* place (a ball) on a spot. **4** *tr. N Amer. informal* loan (*can you spot me ten bucks?*). **5** *tr.* provide safety assistance to (a gymnast etc.). □ **hit the spot** *informal* be exactly what is required. **on the spot 1** at the scene of an action or event. **2** *informal* in a position such that response or action is required. **3** without delay or change of place, then and there. **put on the spot** *informal* force to make a difficult decision, answer an awkward question, etc. **running on the spot** *Cdn & Brit.* raising the feet alternately as in running but without moving forwards or backwards.

spot check ● *n.* a test made on the spot or on a randomly selected subject. ● *v.tr.* (**spot-check**) subject to a spot check.

spotless *adj.* immaculate; absolutely clean or pure. □ **spotlessly** *adv.* **spotlessness** *n.*

spotlight ● *n.* **1** a beam of light directed on a small area, esp. on a particular part of a stage. **2** a lamp projecting this. **3** full attention or publicity. ● *v.tr.* (*past* and *past part.* **-lighted** or **-lit**) **1** direct a spotlight on. **2** draw attention to.

spot market *n.* a market in which commodities etc. are traded for delivery within two days.

spotted *adj.* marked or decorated with spots.

spotted fever *n.* **1** cerebrospinal meningitis. **2** typhus. **3** (in full **Rocky Mountain spotted fever**) a rickettsial disease transmitted by ticks.

spotted owl *n.* a large, dark brown hornless owl, *Strix occidentalis*, of the west coast of N America.

spotter *n.* **1** (often in *comb.*) a person who spots people or things (*trend spotter*). **2** an aviator or aircraft employed in locating enemy positions etc. **3** (in gymnastics etc.) a person stationed to prevent possible accident or otherwise to provide safety assistance to the performer.

spotting *n.* **1** in senses of SPOT *v.* **2 a** a slight discharge of blood from the vagina. **b** light staining due to this.

spotty *adj.* (**-ier, -iest**) **1** marked with spots. **2** patchy, irregular. □ **spottily** *adv.* **spottiness** *n.*

spousal *adj.* of or relating to marriage or a spouse.

spouse *n.* a husband or wife.

Spouse's Allowance *n. Cdn* a federal benefit paid to low-income 60–64-year-old spouses of Old Age Security pensioners.

spout ● *n.* **1** a projecting tube or lip through which a liquid etc. is poured from a teapot, kettle, etc., or issues from a fountain, pump, etc. **2** a jet or column of liquid, grain, etc. **3** a whale's blowhole. ● *v.tr. & intr.* **1** discharge or issue forcibly in a jet. **2** utter (verses etc.) or speak in a declamatory manner.

sprain ● *v.tr.* wrench (an ankle, wrist, etc.) violently so as to cause pain and swelling but not dislocation. ● *n.* **1** such a wrench. **2** the resulting inflammation and swelling.

sprang *past of* SPRING.

sprawl ● *v.* **1 a** *intr.* sit or lie or fall with limbs flung out or in an ungainly way. **b** *tr.* spread (one's limbs) in this way. **2** *intr.* **a** (of a building complex, a town, etc.) spread out irregularly to cover a large area. **b** (of a plant) be of irregular or straggling form. ● *n.* **1** a sprawling movement or attitude. **2** a straggling group or mass. **3** the straggling expansion of an urban or industrial area. □ **sprawling** *adj.*

spray[1] ● *n.* **1 a** water or other liquid flying in small drops from the force of the wind, the dashing of waves, or the action of an atomizer etc. **b** a quantity of small objects flying or propelled through the air. **2** a liquid preparation to be applied in this form, e.g. for cosmetic or medical purposes (*hairspray*). **3** an instrument or apparatus for such application. ● *v.* **1** *tr. & intr.* throw (liquid) in the form of spray. **2** *tr. & intr.* sprinkle (an object) with small drops or particles, esp. (a plant) with an insecticide. **3** *intr.* (of a male animal, esp. a cat) mark its environment with the smell of its urine, as an attraction to females. □ **sprayer** *n.*

spray[2] *n.* **1** a sprig of flowers or leaves, or a branch of a tree with branchlets or flowers, esp. a slender or graceful one. **2** a bunch of flowers decoratively arranged. **3** an ornament in a similar form.

spray can *n.* an aerosol can for applying paint etc. as a fine spray.

spray-on *adj.* (of a product, esp. a liquid) applied in the form of a spray.

spray paint ● *n.* paint packaged in an aerosol can for spraying upon a surface. ● *v.tr.* (**spray-paint**) paint (a surface) using spray paint.

spread ● *v.* (*past and past part.* **spread**) **1** *tr.* (often foll. by *out*) **a** open up or unfold (a map, blanket, etc.) so that it is laid out flat and to its fullest width. **b** lay (a collection of items, such as cards) out on a flat surface, esp. so that they may be properly displayed or viewed. **c** display fully to the eye or the mind (*the landscape was spread out before us*). **2 a** *tr.* apply (a substance, etc.) to a surface and distribute it in an even layer (*spread butter on her toast*). **b** *tr.* cover the surface of (*spread the cake with icing*). **c** *intr.* be capable of being spread (*warm butter spreads easily*). **3** *intr.* become distributed over a wider space or area; grow or increase in extent (*the fire is spreading*). **4 a** *tr.* make better known or felt etc.; disseminate, diffuse. **b** *intr.* (of an immaterial thing such as information or an emotion) become known or felt (*rumours are spreading*). **5** *tr.* separate, open, or stretch out (legs, wings, etc.) so that they are divergent or set a greater distance apart. **6** *tr.* (often foll. by *out*) distribute over a period of time (*spread the payments out over 5 months*). **7** *tr.* scatter, distribute, or disperse over a certain area (*spread the seed over the lawn*). **8 a** *intr. & refl.* (often foll. by *out*) (of a group of people etc.) separate or disperse in order to cover a wider area. **b** *refl.* (often foll. by *around*)

make (oneself) available to others. ● *n.* **1** the act or an instance of spreading. **2 a** the degree or extent of spreading; breadth, width. **b** the wingspan of an aircraft or bird. **3** diffusion or expansion (*the spread of knowledge*). **4** the distance between two points in space or time. **5** *Stock Exch.* the difference between the buying and selling price of a commodity. **6** a garnish or topping, such as jam, peanut butter, or margarine, that is put on bread or toast etc. **7** an article or advertisement displayed prominently in a newspaper or magazine, esp. on two facing pages or across more than one column. **8** *informal* an elaborate meal. **9** = POINT SPREAD. **10** *N Amer.* a farm or ranch with extensive land. **11** a cover, such as a bedspread or tablecloth. □ **spread oneself too thin** attempt to undertake too many projects at once so that none can be done properly. □ **spreadable** *adj.*

spread-eagle ● *n.* **1** a representation of an eagle with legs and wings extended, used as an emblem. **2** *Figure Skating* a straight glide made with the feet a short distance apart and turned outwards in a straight line and the arms held out to either side. ● *v.* **1 a** *tr. & refl.* place (a person or oneself) in a position with arms and legs spread out. **b** *intr.* assume the position of a spread-eagle. **2** *intr. Figure Skating* perform a spread-eagle. ● *adj. & adv.* in the position of a spread-eagle. □ **spread-eagled** *adj.*

spreader *n.* **1** a person or thing that spreads. **2** an implement used to spread manure, fertilizer, seed, etc. over a field or lawn. **3** *Naut.* a bar attached to the mast of a yacht in order to spread the angle of the upper shrouds. **4** *Fishing* a lure consisting of a weight with three baited hooks radiating from it. **5** a bar for stretching something out or keeping things apart.

spreadsheet *n.* a computer program allowing manipulation and flexible retrieval of esp. tabulated numerical data.

spree *n.* **1** a period or bout of extravagant indulgence; a frenzy (*a shopping spree*). **2** a lively outing or revelry; a romp. **3** a period or outburst of a (usu. specified) activity (*a shooting spree*).

sprig *n.* **1** a small branch or shoot. **2** a representation of this used as an esp. fabric ornament.

sprightly *adj.* (**-ier, -iest**) characterized by animation or cheerful vitality; brisk, lively, spirited. □ **sprightliness** *n.*

spring ● *v.* (*past* **sprang** or *N Amer.* **sprung**; *past part.* **sprung**) **1** *intr.* jump suddenly or quickly in a single movement; move suddenly upwards or forwards. **2** *intr.* move rapidly as from a constrained position or by the action of a spring; recoil. **3** *intr.* (usu. foll. by *from*) **a** originate or arise. **b** originate through birth or descent; be descended. **4** *intr.* (usu. foll. by *up*) come into being; appear, develop, esp. suddenly. **5** *tr.* operate or cause (a device etc.) to operate suddenly, esp. by means of a mechanism (*spring a trap*). **6** *tr.* (often foll. by *on*) reveal, introduce, or make known suddenly or unexpectedly (*sprang a surprise on him*). **7** *tr. slang* contrive or effect the escape or release of (a prisoner etc.). **8** *N Amer. & Austral. informal* **a** *intr.* (usu. foll. by *for*) pay or offer to pay for something; indulge in a purchase (*sprang for dinner*). **b** *tr.* spend (money). **9 a** *intr.* become warped or split. **b** *tr.* split or crack (wood or a wooden implement). ● *n.* **1 a** (also **Spring**) the first season of the year, in which vegetation begins to appear after winter. **b** the period from the vernal equinox to the summer solstice. **c** (often foll. by *of*) an early period or the initial stage. **d** = SPRING TIDE. **2** an act of springing; a bound, jump, or leap. **3** a resilient device usu. of bent or coiled metal having the ability to return to its original shape with the removal of force or pressure, used esp. to drive clockwork or for cushioning in furniture, automobiles, etc. **4** a recoil, rebound, or backward movement of something bent or forced out of its normal position or form. **5** elasticity; ability to bounce back strongly (*a mattress with plenty of spring*). **6** liveliness in a person or of a person's mind, faculties, etc. (*a spring in her step*). **7 a** a flow of water etc. rising or welling naturally from the earth. **b** such a flow of water having special esp. medicinal or curative properties. **c** (usu. in *pl.*) a community or locality having such springs. **8** the motive, source, or origin of an action, custom, etc. **9** *slang* an escape or release from prison. **10** the splitting or yielding of a plank etc. under strain. □ **hope springs eternal** even in the worst situations, one tends to hope for improvement. **spring a leak** develop a leak. □ **springless** *adj.* **springlike** *adj.*

springboard *n.* **1** a starting point or impetus for an activity, discussion, etc. **2** a springy board used in gymnastics to gain height or momentum in vaulting etc. **3** *Cdn & Austral.* a platform inserted into a notch cut in the side of a tree on which a lumberjack stands to chop at some height from the ground.

spring break *n. N Amer.* an esp. college or university holiday of one or two weeks in February or March.

spring breakup *n. Cdn* = BREAKUP 4.

spring chicken *n.* **1** a young chicken for eating. **2** (usu. with *neg.*) a young person (*I'm no spring chicken*).

spring cleaning *n.* a thorough cleaning of a house or room, esp. in spring. □ **spring clean** *v.tr. & intr.*

spring equinox *n.* the date on which the sun crosses the celestial equator in a southerly direction (approx. Mar. 21) or, in the southern hemisphere, in a northerly direction (approx. Sept. 22).

springer spaniel *n.* (also **Springer Spaniel**) either of two breeds of sturdy dog of medium height used esp. in hunting to rouse game, including the English springer spaniel and the Welsh springer spaniel.

spring-fed *adj. N Amer.* (of a river, pond, etc.) having a spring as its source.

spring fever *n.* a restless or lethargic feeling sometimes associated with spring.

springform pan *n. N Amer.* a round metal cake pan with sides that may be released from the bottom, allowing the cake to be easily removed when done.

spring-loaded *adj.* (of a device etc.) containing a spring that presses one part against another.

spring peeper *n.* a small brown tree frog, *Hyla crucifer*, that occurs throughout much of eastern N America and has a high-pitched piping call.

spring roll *n.* a deep-fried Oriental appetizer or snack, consisting of a very thin wrapper rolled around a mixture of chopped vegetables, usu. including bean sprouts, and sometimes meat.

spring salmon *n. Cdn* = CHINOOK 2.

springtail *n.* any wingless insect of the order Collembola, leaping by means of a springlike tail.

spring tide *n.* a tide occurring just after the new and full moon, in which there is the greatest difference between high and low water.

springtime *n.* **1** the season of spring. **2** (often foll. by *of*) the earliest and usu. most pleasant stage or period of something (*the springtime of their youth*).

spring training *n. Baseball* a period before the regular season during which players practise and participate in pre-season games.

spring water *n.* water from a spring, often bottled and sold.

spring wheat *n.* wheat that is planted in the spring (compare WINTER WHEAT).

springy *adj.* (**-ier, -iest**) **1** springing back when compressed, squeezed, or stretched; elastic, resilient. **2** (of movement, music, etc.) buoyant and vigorous; bouncing. □ **springily** *adv.* **springiness** *n.*

sprinkle ● *v.* **1** *tr.* scatter (liquid, powder, etc.) in small drops or particles; strew thinly or lightly. **2** *tr.* (often foll. by *with*) cover (a surface) with scattered drops or grains; powder or dust lightly. **3** *tr.* (usu. in *pass.*) distribute in small amounts. **4** *intr.* (of precipitation, esp. rain) fall in a fine mist. ● *n.* (usu. foll. by *of*) **1** the action or an act of sprinkling. **2** a dusting or light shower. **3** a small thinly distributed number or amount. **4** *N Amer.* (usu. in *pl.*) each of an assortment of tiny usu. multicoloured bits of candy used to decorate cookies, cupcakes, etc.

sprinkler *n.* **1** a device, machine, vehicle, etc. used to sprinkle esp. water. **2** an attachment for a garden hose used for watering flowers, a lawn, etc. **3** an overhead plumbing fixture for extinguishing fires.

sprinkling *n.* (usu. foll. by *of*) **1** a thinly distributed amount of a liquid or powder. **2** a relatively small number of things scattered over a broad area.

sprint ● *v.* **1** *intr.* run a short distance at full speed. **2** *intr.* cycle or drive etc. at full speed over a short distance, esp. in a race. **3** *tr.* cover or traverse (a certain distance) by sprinting. ● *n.* **1** a fast race in which the participants run, cycle, ride, etc. at full speed over a short distance. **2** a short burst of speed esp. to finish a longer race. □ **sprinter** *n.*

sprite *n.* **1** an elf or fairy, esp. a small mischievous or playful one. **2** a dainty or lively person.

spritz esp. *N Amer.* ● *v.tr.* **1** sprinkle, squirt, or spray (something) with a liquid (*spritzed her neck with perfume*). **2** apply (a liquid) by spraying. ● *n.* a small spray; a splash or squirt. □ **spritzy** *adj.*

spritzer *n.* a mixture of wine and soda water.

sprocket *n.* **1** each of several teeth on a wheel engaging with links of a chain on a bicycle or with holes in film etc. **2** a wheel with sprockets.

sprout ● *v.* **1** *tr.* put forth, produce, or develop (shoots, hair, etc.) (*he's sprouted a moustache*). **2** *intr.* begin to grow, put forth shoots. **3** *intr.* spring up or emerge, esp. suddenly (*new houses are sprouting up all over town*). **4** *tr.* cause, produce, or seem to cause or produce; give rise to. ● *n.* **1** a new growth developing from a bud, seed, or other part of a plant; a shoot. **2** (usu. in *pl.*) a young tender shoot of a plant, esp. a bean or alfalfa, eaten as a vegetable. **3** (usu. in *pl.*) = BRUSSELS SPROUTS. **4** *N Amer.* a young person or child.

spruce¹ ● *adj.* neat in dress and appearance; trim, smart. ● *v.tr., intr., & refl.* (usu. foll. by *up*) make or become trim, neat, or smart.

spruce² *n.* **1** any of various pyramidal evergreen coniferous trees constituting the genus *Picea*, of the pine family, with pendulous cones and with needles inserted in peglike projections. **2** the wood of this tree used as timber.

spruce beer *n. N Amer.* **1** a drink made by adding sugar or molasses to the water of boiled spruce twigs and needles, which is then fermented with yeast. **2** a similar non-alcoholic carbonated drink flavoured, usu. artificially, with spruce.

spruce budworm *n.* the brown larva of a N American moth, *Choristoneura fumiferana*, which is a serious pest of spruce and other conifers.

spruce grouse *n.* a grouse, *Dendragapus canadensis*, of N American coniferous forests.

sprung ● *v.* past and past part. of SPRING. ● *adj.* **1** fitted with springs. **2** that has been sprung.

spry *adj.* (**spryer**, **spryest**) nimble, active, lively. □ **spryly** *adv.*

spud ● *n.* **1** *slang* a potato. **2** a tool resembling a small spade with a narrow chisel-shaped blade, sometimes used for cutting the roots of weeds. **3** *derogatory* **a** a person with a stout or stocky build. **b** a lazy or dull-witted person. **4** a short length of pipe used to connect two plumbing fixtures. ● *v.tr.* (**spudded**, **spudding**) **1** make the initial drilling for (an oil well). **2** cut or remove (weeds etc.) with a spud.

Spud Island *Cdn informal* Prince Edward Island. □ **Spud Islander** *n.*

spumante /spuːˈmænti, -ˈmɒnteɪ/ *n.* any of a number of Italian sparkling white wines, esp. Asti.

spume /spjuːm/ ● *n.* foam or froth on or from a liquid. ● *v.intr.* froth, foam.

spumoni /spəˈmoːniː/ *n.* *N Amer.* a kind of rich layered ice cream with candied fruit and nuts.

spun ● *v.* past and past part. of SPIN. ● *adj.* converted into threads (*spun glass*).

spunk *n.* *informal* energy, courage.

spunky *adj.* (**-ier**, **-iest**) *informal* full of energy, courage; spirited. □ **spunkily** *adv.* **spunkiness** *n.*

spun sugar *n.* hardened sugar syrup drawn out into filaments eaten as candy floss or used as a decoration.

spur ● *n.* **1** a device with a small spike or a spiked wheel worn on a rider's heel for urging a horse forward. **2** a stimulus, incentive, or encouragement. **3** (in full **spur line**) a short stretch of track branching off a railway line, esp. one making a connection to another line. **4** a mountain or hill etc., or a ridge that projects from a mountain or hill. **5** an abnormal growth or calcareous deposit occurring esp. in the heel or elbow. **6** a sharp hard claw on the back foot or lower hind leg of a bird or animal, esp. a rooster. **7** *Bot.* **a** a slender hollow projection from part of a flower. **b** a short lateral branch or shoot, esp. one bearing fruit. **8** a pair of spikes that may be attached to a boot to facilitate climbing. ● *v.* (**spurred**, **spurring**) **1** *tr.* prick (a horse) with spurs. **2** *tr.* **a** (often foll. by *on*) encourage or incite (a person). **b** be the cause of; stimulate (interest etc.). □ **earn** (or **win**) **one's spurs 1** gain knighthood by an act of valour. **2** attain distinction, earn a high honour. **on the spur of the moment** on a sudden whim or impulse; without prior consideration or planning. **put** (or **set**) **spurs to 1** impel or urge (a horse or person). **2** stimulate (a resolution etc.).

spurge *n.* any plant of the genus *Euphorbia*, exuding an acrid milky juice once used as a purgative.

spurious *adj.* **1** not proceeding from the reputed origin, source, or author; not genuine or authentic. **2** based on false reasoning; not true or accurate (*a spurious argument*). **3** superficially resembling or simulating something, but lacking its genuine character or qualities (*spurious charm*). □ **spuriously** *adv.*

spurn *v.tr.* reject or refuse (a person or thing) in a way that indicates contempt.

spur-of-the-moment *adj.* impromptu, sudden; unplanned or unpremeditated.

spurred *adj.* (of a person, boots, etc.) fitted or provided with spurs.

spurt ● *v.* **1** *a intr.* gush out in a jet or stream. **b** *tr.* send out or expel (liquid, smoke, dust, etc.) in a jet or rapid stream; squirt. **2** *intr.* move or act with a greater speed or exertion for a short time. **3** *intr.* (of a stock, price, etc.) rise suddenly in price or value. ● *n.* **1** a short

stream of liquid etc. ejected or thrown up with some force and suddenness. **2** a marked or sudden increase of speed or exertion. **3** a sudden unsustained period of activity, growth, effort, or exertion. **4** a marked increase or improvement, esp. in business, prices, etc. **5** *Cdn* (*Nfld*) a short period of time or activity (*a spurt of fishing*).

Sputnik /ˈspʌtnɪk, ˈspʊt-/ *n.* (also **sputnik**) an unmanned Russian earth satellite, esp. each of a series of such satellites launched by the Soviet Union between 1957 and 1961.

sputter ● *v.* **1** *intr.* **a** (esp. of a machine) emit a spitting, sizzling, or slight explosive sound or series of such sounds, often suggesting a struggling operation. **b** proceed with difficulty, struggle; show signs of fatigue or failure. **2** *tr. & intr.* say or speak in a hurried, confused, or incoherent manner, esp. in anger or excitement. **3** *tr. & intr.* emit (liquid, food, smoke, sparks, etc.) in small particles or puffs with a spitting sound. ● *n.* **1** the action or an act of stammering or producing a slight explosive sound or series of sounds, esp. with the emission of small particles. **2** such a sound, esp. while speaking.

sputum /ˈspjuːtəm/ *n.* (*pl.* **sputa** /-tə/) **1** saliva, spittle. **2** a mixture of saliva and mucus coughed up from the respiratory tract, usu. a sign of certain diseases of the lungs, chest, or throat.

spy ● *n.* (*pl.* **spies**) **1** a person employed by a country or organization to collect and report secret information on esp. the military activities of an enemy or hostile foreign state, or on the activities of a rival organization. **2** a person who keeps watch on others, esp. furtively. **3** (**Spy**) = NORTHERN SPY. ● *v.* (**spies**, **spied**) **1** *tr.* catch sight of, discern, or make out, esp. by careful observation (*spied a house in the distance*). **2** *intr.* work as a spy; be on the watch or lookout. □ **spy on** maintain a close and secret observation of a person or group.

spyglass *n.* a small telescope.

spymaster *n.* *informal* the head of a spy organization.

SQ *abbr. Cdn* (in Quebec) Sûreté du Québec (see SÛRETÉ).

sq. *abbr.* square.

SQL *abbr. Computing* structured query language.

squab /skwɒb/ *n.* a newly hatched or very young bird, esp. an unfledged pigeon.

squabble ● *n.* a petty or noisy quarrel; a dispute. ● *v.intr.* engage in a petty quarrel or argument. □ **squabbler** *n.*

squad *n.* **1** a small group of people sharing a task etc. **2** *Military* a small number of soldiers assembled for drill or assigned to some special task. **3** *Sport informal* a team. **4** (often in *comb.*) a specialized unit or division within a police force (*drug squad*). **5** a group or class of people of a specified kind.

squad car *n.* a police car having a radio link with headquarters.

squadron *n.* **1** a principal division of an armoured or cavalry regiment consisting of two or more troops. **2** the basic administrative unit of an air force, usu. consisting of two or more flights. **3** a formal unit in a navy consisting of a number of ships. **4** often *jocular* an organized body of people or things.

squalid /ˈskwɒlɪd/ *adj.* **1** rundown, degenerate, unsanitary, esp. through neglect or poverty. **2** covered with filth or grime; repulsively dirty. **3** morally degraded (*a squalid lifestyle*).

squall ● *n.* **1** a sudden and short-lived violent storm or gust of wind, esp. with rain, snow, or sleet. **2** a shrill cry or scream, as of a baby. **3** a disturbance or commotion; a quarrel. ● *v.intr.* scream, cry out violently as in fear or pain. □ **squally** *adj.*

squalor /'skwɒlər/ *n.* a filthy or squalid state.

Squamish /'skwɒmɪʃ/ ● *n.* **1** a member of an Aboriginal people living in southwestern BC. **2** the Salishan language of the Squamish. ● *adj.* of or relating to this people.

squamous /'skweiməs/ *adj. Med.* & *Anat.* **1** (of a substance) covered with or composed of scales. **2 a** (of the skin) characterized by the development of scales. **b** (of a disease) accompanied by such scales.

squander /'skwɒndər/ *v.tr.* **1** spend (time, money, etc.) recklessly or lavishly; use or consume in a wasteful manner. **2** allow (an opportunity) to pass or be lost.

square ● *n.* **1 a** a plane figure with four right angles and four equal straight sides. **b** any object of this shape or approximately so. **2 a** an open usu. four-sided area enclosed by buildings in a town or city, esp. one containing a small park or laid out with trees. **b** an open space resembling this, esp. an area within army barracks used for drill. **3** an L-shaped or T-shaped instrument used esp. by a carpenter or architect to draw, obtain, or verify right angles. **4** the product of a number multiplied by itself (*81 is the square of 9*). **5** *slang* a conventional or old-fashioned person, esp. one ignorant of or opposed to current trends. **6** *N Amer. slang* a square meal (*three squares a day*). **7** *N Amer.* **a** a dessert served cut into square pieces. **b** one of these pieces. ● *adj.* **1 a** having the shape of a square; bounded by four equal straight sides at right angles to each other. **b** having a cross-section in the form of a square. **2** having or in the form of a right angle (*square corners*). **3 a** (of a person, animal, or body) having a width more nearly equal to the height or length than is usual; solid, stocky. **b** (of a feature, such as the jaw) having a square outline; not round. **4 a** (*attrib.*) designating a unit of measure equal to the area of a square whose side is one of the unit specified (*one square metre*). **b** (*predic.*) (of an area) being a square having four sides of the same specified length (*5 metres square*). **5 a** even, straight, level. **b** perpendicular; at right angles. **6** (also **all square**) **a** with all accounts settled, with no money owed; not in debt. **b** (of teams or scores) equal, tied. **7** fair and honest (*a square deal*). **8** uncompromising, direct, thorough (*a square refusal*). **9** *slang* out of touch with the ideas and conventions of a current trend; conservative, old-fashioned. **10** properly arranged; in good order, settled. **11** *Music* (of rhythm) simple, straightforward. ● *adv.* **1** *N Amer. informal* exactly, directly (*hit him square on the nose*). **2** in a rectangular form or position; upright, straight. **3** in a straightforward manner; fairly, honestly (*won fair and square*). ● *v.* **1** *tr.* **a** make square or rectangular. **b** give a rectangular cross-section to (timber etc.). **2** *tr.* multiply (a number) by itself (*3 squared is 9*). **3** (usu. foll. by *to, with*) **a** *intr.* correspond, harmonize, be consistent (*her conclusion doesn't square with her observations*). **b** *tr.* make consistent, harmonize, reconcile (*how do we square these solutions to our problem?*). **4** *tr.* & *intr.* (usu. foll. by *up*) settle (an account, debt, etc.) by means of payment. **5 a** *tr.* place (one's shoulders) squarely facing forwards, esp. in a defensive position. **b** *intr.* (often foll. by *up, around*) *Baseball* (of a batter) turn to face the pitcher with the bat held parallel to the ground while preparing to bunt. **6** *tr.* (usu. in *passive*) mark out in squares (*squared paper*). **7** *tr. informal* satisfy or secure the compliance of (a person), esp. by bribery. **8** *tr.* tie (a game or series); make scores square. □ **back to square one** *informal* back to the starting point with no prog-

ress made. **out of square** not at right angles. **squared away** *N Amer.* taken care of, dealt with, put in proper order. **square the circle 1** construct a square equal in area to a given circle (a problem incapable of a purely geometrical solution). **2** do what is impossible. **square off 1** *N Amer.* assume the stance or crouch of a boxer. **2** *N Amer.* meet in competition or opposition. **3** mark out in squares. **square up to 1** move towards (a person) in a fighting attitude. **2** face or tackle (a difficulty etc.) resolutely. □ **squarely** *adv.* **squareness** *n.* **squarish** *adj.*

square brackets *n.pl.* brackets of the form [ ].

square dance esp. *N Amer.* ● *n.* a type of dance which starts with four couples facing one another in a square, with steps shouted out by a caller. ● *v.intr.* participate in a square dance. □ **square dancer** *n.*

square-flipper seal *n. Cdn (Nfld)* = BEARDED SEAL.

square knot *n.* = REEF KNOT.

square meal *n. N Amer.* a hearty and satisfying meal.

square-rigged *adj. Naut.* with the principal sails at right angles to the length of the ship and extended by horizontal yards slung to the mast by the middle.

square root *n.* the number which produces a specified quantity when multiplied by itself.

square sail *n.* a four-cornered sail extended on a yard slung to the mast by the middle.

square timber *n. Cdn hist.* logs cut into lengths with the round sides cut flat, ready to be rafted or shipped.

squash[1] ● *v.* **1** *tr.* crush or squeeze into a pulp, flat mass, or distorted shape. **2** *tr.* pack tightly, crowd together. **3** *tr.* reject, dismiss, silence, or suppress. **4** *intr.* flatten or be crushed under pressure. ● *n.* **1** a game for two or four players with racquets and a small fairly soft ball that is struck against the walls of a closed court. **2 a** a substance, mass, etc. that is or has been squashed. **b** a sound of or as of something being squashed. □ **squashy** *adj.* (**-ier, -iest**). **squashily** *adv.*

squash[2] *n.* (*pl.* same or **squashes**) **1** the fruit of any of several kinds of gourd, cooked and eaten as a vegetable esp. in N America, esp. that of *Cucurbita melo* (in full **summer squash**), eaten before the seeds and rinds have hardened, and that of *C. maxima* or *C. moschata* (in full **winter squash**), stored and eaten when matured. **2** any of the various trailing plants producing this fruit.

squat ● *v.* (**squatted, squatting**) **1** *intr.* **a** crouch on the balls of one's feet with the hams resting on the backs of the heels. **b** sit on the ground etc. with the knees drawn up and the heels close to or touching the buttocks. **2** *intr.* settle on new, uncultivated, or unoccupied land without any legal title and without the payment of rent. **b** *intr.* live without legal right on land or in premises otherwise unoccupied. **c** *tr.* occupy (a property or building) as a squatter. **3** *Weightlifting* **a** *intr.* perform a squat. **b** *tr.* lift (a certain weight) while performing a squat. **4** *intr.* (of an animal) crouch close to the ground. ● *adj.* (**squatter, squattest**) **1** disproportionately broad or wide; short and fat. **2** in a squatting posture. ● *n.* **1** *N Amer. slang* = DIDDLY-SQUAT. **2** a property occupied by a squatter or squatters. **3** *Weightlifting* an exercise or lift in which a person squats down and rises again while carrying a barbell behind the neck. **4** a squatting posture. □ **squatty** *adj.* (**-ier, -iest**)

squatter *n.* **1** an unauthorized or illegal occupant of otherwise unoccupied land or premises. **2** *hist.* **a** a settler with no legal title to the land occupied, esp. one on land not yet allocated by a government. **b** a person who has obtained a tract of land from the

government on easy terms (also *attrib.*: *squatter settlement*).

squaw *n. offensive* **1** a N American Indian woman or wife. **2** *slang* any woman or girl, esp. one who is a wife.

squawfish *n.* (*pl.* same or **-fishes**) either of two large freshwater fish-eating fishes, *Ptychocheilus oregonensis* and *P. lucius* of NW Canada and the US, formerly important food fishes for Aboriginal peoples.

squawk ● *n.* **1** a loud harsh cry esp. of a bird. **2** a loud complaint or protest. ● *v.* **1** *intr.* utter a squawk. **2** *tr.* utter with a squawk. **3** *intr.* complain or protest loudly or vehemently. **4** *tr.* (of an aircraft) transmit (a signal) as identification.

squawk box *n. informal* **1** an intercom. **2** the loud-speaker of a public address system.

squeak ● *n.* **1** a sharp, shrill, high-pitched sound or cry. **2** = NARROW SQUEAK. ● *v.* **1** *intr.* make or emit a thin high-pitched cry or squeak. **2** *tr.* utter or sing in a shrill voice. **3** *intr.* (usu. foll. by *by*, *through*) *informal* manage, succeed, or pass by only a narrow margin. **4** *intr. slang* turn informer.

squeaker *n.* **1** esp. *N Amer.* a game etc. won by a narrow margin. **2** a person or thing that squeaks.

squeaky *adj.* (**-ier**, **-iest**) tending to squeak. □ **squeakiness** *n.*

squeaky clean *adj.* **1** above reproach; respectable, upstanding. **2** completely clean.

squeal ● *n.* a long shrill sound, such as the cry of a pig or an exclamation of delight. ● *v.* **1** *intr.* make a squeal. **2** *tr.* utter (words) with a squeal. **3** *intr.* (often foll. by *on*) *slang* reveal confidential information about a person; turn informer against. **4** *intr. slang* protest loudly or excitedly. □ **squealer** *n.*

squeamish *adj.* **1** easily turned sick, disgusted, or faint. **2** fastidious in questions of propriety, honesty, etc. □ **squeamishly** *adv.* **squeamishness** *n.*

squeegee ● *n.* **1** an implement with a handle joined to a wide rubber blade used to remove the excess liquid from glass when cleaning windows. **2** a rubber strip, pad, etc., used for squeezing or wiping mois-ture from a print, pressing a film against its mount, etc. ● *v.tr.* (**squeegees**, **squeegeed**) clean or treat (glass, photographic film, etc.) with a squeegee.

squeegee kid *n. N Amer. informal* a youth who offers to clean the windows of stopped cars, esp. for money.

squeeze ● *v.* **1** *tr.* **a** exert pressure on from opposite or all sides. **b** compress with one's hand or between two bodies. **c** reduce the size of or alter the shape of by squeezing. **2** *tr.* **a** extract (moisture) by squeezing. **b** produce with effort (*squeezed a tear out*). **3** **a** *tr.* force or cram (a person or thing) into or through a small or narrow space. **b** *tr.* (often foll. by *in*) fit (a person or activity) into a busy schedule, day, etc. **c** *tr. & intr.* make (one's way) by squeezing. **4** *tr.* **a** exert financial pres-sure on; impose financial hardship on. **b** put pres-sure on (a person). **c** obtain or extort (money etc.) from a person by force, pressure, etc. **5** *tr.* **a** press (a person's arm, hand, etc.) with one's hand as a sign of sympathy, affection, etc. **b** hug or embrace (a person) firmly. **6** *tr.* **a** (often foll. by *off*) *informal* fire (a shot, round, etc.) from a gun. **b** pull or depress (the trigger of a gun). ● *n.* **1** an instance of squeezing; the state of being squeezed. **2** a state of being forced into a small, restricted, or crowded space (*a tight squeeze*). **3** **a** *Econ.* a strong financial demand or pressure, esp. a restric-tion on borrowing, investment, etc., in a financial crisis. **b** mental or emotional pressure, a constrain-ing influence; coercion. **4** **a** a hug or close embrace. **b** strong or firm pressure of the hand on the arm etc. of another as a sign of friendship or affection. **5** *N Amer.*

slang = MAIN SQUEEZE. **6** **a** a small quantity squeezed out of something (*a squeeze of lemon*). **b** a sum of money extorted or exacted, esp. an illicit commission. **7** *Baseball* **a** (in full **squeeze play**) a play in which the batter attempts to bring a player home from third on a sacrifice bunt. **b** (in full **suicide squeeze**) a similar play in which the baserunner breaks towards the plate just as the pitch has left the pitcher's hand, before a successful bunt has been made. **8** a difficult situation; a bind. □ **put the squeeze on** *informal* coerce or pressure (a person). □ **squeezable** *adj.* **squeezer** *n.*

squeezebox *n. informal* an accordion or concertina.

squeeze bunt *n. Baseball* a sacrifice bunt attempted while executing a squeeze play.

squelch ● *v.* **1** *intr.* **a** walk or tread heavily in mud, on wet ground, or with water in the shoes, so as to make a sucking sound. **b** make a sucking sound. **2** *tr.* crush, silence, suppress; put an end to (an idea, plan, rally, etc.). ● *n.* a sucking sound as made by walking on wet muddy ground. □ **squelchy** *adj.*

squib ● *n.* **1** a small firework burning with a hissing sound and usu. a final slight explosion. **2** **a** a short piece of writing or written information, esp. a brief news item used as a filler in a newspaper. **b** a short satirical composition. **3** (also **squibber**) (esp. in baseball and football) a weakly hit or kicked ball. **4** *derogatory* a meek or cowardly person, esp. a child. ● *v.* (**squibbed**, **squibbing**) **1** *tr.* (esp. in baseball or foot-ball) hit or kick (the ball) weakly so that it travels only a short distance. **2** *intr.* (of a ball) travel a short distance after being hit or kicked weakly.

squid *n.* any of various marine cephalopods of the order Teuthoidea, having an elongated body with two stabilizing fins at the back, eight arms in a ring around two longer tentacles at the front, and a reduced internal horny shell, esp. any of the common edible squid of the genera *Loligo* and *Illex*.

squidgy *adj.* (**-ier**, **-iest**) *informal* soft, soggy, or moist.

squid jigger *n. Cdn* (*Nfld*) a weighted line with several tiny esp. unbaited hooks, used to catch small squid for bait. □ **squid jigging** *n.*

squiggle ● *n.* a short curly or wavy line, esp. in handwriting or doodling. ● *v.* **1** *tr.* write in squiggles; scrawl. **2** *intr.* wriggle, squirm. □ **squiggly** *adj.*

squinch *v.* esp. *N Amer.* **1** (usu. foll. by *up*) **a** *tr.* screw up one's eyes, face, etc. **b** *intr.* (of the eyes etc.) screw up, squint. **2** *tr. & intr.* (often foll. by *up*, *down*) squeeze or squash compactly.

squint ● *v.* **1** *intr.* look obliquely or with the eyes partly closed, esp. in order to see something better or because of very bright light. **2** *tr.* close (one's eyes) quickly; hold (one's eyes) half-shut. **3** *intr.* suffer from a disorder of the eye muscles which causes each eye to look in a different direction. ● *n.* **1** a permanent deviation or defective alignment of one or both eyes. **2** a stealthy or sidelong glance through half-closed eyes. **3** *informal* a glance or look. **4** an inclination towards a particular object or aim. □ **squinty** *adj.*

squire ● *n. hist.* a young nobleman serving as a knight's attendant. ● *v.tr.* (of a man) attend upon (a woman).

squirm *v.intr.* **1** wriggle, writhe. **2** show embarrass-ment or discomfiture. □ **squirmy** *adj.* (**-ier**, **-iest**).

squirrel ● *n.* **1** **a** any of various slender agile arboreal rodents having a long bushy tail, a furry coat, and pointy ears, esp. of the genus *Sciurus* and related genera. **b** any of various arboreal or ground-dwelling rodents, esp. of the family Sciuridae. **2** *N Amer.* the meat of the squirrel. **3** the fur of the squirrel. **4** a person who hoards objects, food, etc. ● *v.* (**squirrelled, squirrelling**) **1** *tr.* (usu. foll. by *away*) store or save; hoard (objects, food, time, etc.). **2** *intr.* (often foll. by *around*) move about in an active or industrious manner; bustle, scurry.

squirrelly *adj.* **1** restless, fidgety, anxious. **2** eccentric, crazy.

squirt ● *v.* **1** *tr.* eject or propel (a liquid or semi-liquid substance) in a jet-like stream, esp. from a small opening. **2** *intr.* (of liquid or a semi-liquid substance) be discharged in this way. **3** *tr.* splash with liquid ejected by squirting. **4** *intr.* (often foll. by *free* or *loose*) be lost or dropped; slip or fall, esp. from one's hand. ● *n.* **1 a** a jet or stream of liquid. **b** a small quantity produced by squirting. **2** *informal* **a** a young person, esp. a meddlesome child. **b** an insignificant but presumptuous person. **3 a** an initiation level of sports for young children. **b** a player at this level.

squirt gun *n. N Amer.* a water pistol.

squish esp. *N Amer.* ● *v.* **1** *intr.* yield easily to pressure when walked upon, squeezed, or squashed, esp. making a gushing or squelching sound. **2** *tr.* crush, squash, or squeeze. **3** *tr. & intr.* force or be forced into a small space; pack or be packed tightly (*squished into the car*). **4** *intr.* move with a squishing sound. ● *n.* **1** the sound of something as it is crushed or squashed. **2** the feel of something as it is squished.

squishy *adj.* (**-ier, -iest**) **1** of a soft wet texture that yields easily to pressure. **2 a** lacking strength or substance. **b** feebly sentimental; mushy.

SR *abbr.* **1** side road. **2** *Psych.* stimulus-response.

Sr *symbol* strontium.

Sr. *abbr.* **1** Senior. **2** Señor. **3** Signor. **4** *Christianity* Sister.

Sra. *abbr.* Señora.

SRAM /ˈɛsræm/ *abbr. Computing* static random access memory.

Sri /ʃri, sri/ *n.* (in the Indian subcontinent) a title of respect preceding the name of a deity or distinguished person, or the title of a sacred book.

Sri Lankan /ʃri ˈlæŋkən, sri/ ● *n.* **1** a native or national of Sri Lanka (formerly Ceylon), an island in the Indian Ocean. **2** a person of Sri Lankan descent. ● *adj.* of or relating to Sri Lanka or its people.

SRO *abbr.* **1** standing room only. **2** single-room occupancy.

SRP *abbr.* standard retail price.

SRS *abbr.* supplemental restraint system.

SS *abbr.* **1** Saints. **2** steamship. **3** secondary school. **4** *Cdn* SCHOOL SECTION. **5** shortstop.

SSE *abbr.* south-southeast.

S/Sgt. *abbr.* STAFF SERGEANT.

SSHRC /ʃɑrk/ *abbr.* Social Sciences and Humanities Research Council (of Canada).

SSR *abbr. hist.* Soviet Socialist Republic.

SSW *abbr.* south-southwest.

St. *abbr.* **1** Street. **2** Saint.

stab ● *v.* **1** (**stabbed, stabbing**) **1** *tr.* pierce or wound with a (usu. short) pointed tool or weapon, e.g. a knife or dagger. **2** *intr.* (often foll. by *at*) aim a blow with such a weapon. **3** *intr.* cause a sensation like being stabbed (*stabbing pain*). **4** *tr.* hurt or distress (a person, feelings, etc.). **5** *intr.* (foll. by *at*) aim a blow at a person's reputation, etc. **6** *tr.* pierce (a hole) in something. **7** *tr.* thrust (a pointed object) into or through something. **8 a** *tr.* direct (the hand, finger, etc.) in a jabbing lunge or gesture. **b** *intr.* (of the hand, finger, etc.) make such a gesture. ● *n.* **1 a** an instance of stabbing. **b** a blow or thrust with a knife etc. **2** a wound made in this way. **3** a sharply painful physical or mental sensation. **4** *informal* (usu. foll. by *at*) an attempt, a try. **5** a vigorous thrust; a jabbing lunge or gesture. □ **stab in the back 1** a treacherous or slanderous attack. **2** slander or betray. **stab in the dark** a blind attempt; an effort made without adequate information. □ **stabber** *n.* **stabbing** *n.*

stability *n.* the quality or state of being stable.

stabilization *n.* an act or instance of stabilizing.

stabilization payment *n. Cdn* a payment made esp. by the federal government to a region or sector in order to stabilize a faltering economy.

stabilize *v.tr. & intr.* make or become stable.

stabilizer *n.* a device or substance used to keep something stable, esp.: **1** *N Amer.* the horizontal tail-plane of an aircraft. **2** a gyroscopic device to prevent rolling of a ship. **3** a substance which prevents the breakdown of emulsions, esp. as a food additive maintaining texture.

stable¹ *adj.* (**stabler, stablest**) **1** firmly fixed or established; not easily adjusted, destroyed, disturbed or altered. **2 a** firm, resolute; not wavering or fickle. **b** mentally and emotionally sound; sane and sensible. **3** *Chem.* (of a compound) not readily decomposing. **4** *Physics* (of an isotope) not subject to radioactive decay. **5** in a stable medical condition after an injury, operation, etc. □ **stably** *adv.*

stable² ● *n.* **1** a building for keeping horses. **2** an establishment where racehorses are kept and trained. **3** the racehorses of a particular stable. **4 a** persons, products, etc., having a common origin or affiliation. **b** such an origin or affiliation. ● *v.tr.* keep (a horse) in a stable.

stablemate *n.* **1** a horse of the same stable. **2** a person, product, etc. from the same source; a member of the same organization etc.

stabling *n.* accommodation for horses.

staccato /stəˈkætoː, -ˈkɒtoː/ ● *adv. & adj.* **1** *Music* with each note sharply detached or separated from the others. **2** with short and sharp sounds (*a staccato burst of gunfire*). ● *n.* (*pl.* **-os**) **1** a staccato passage in music etc. **2** staccato delivery.

stack ● *n.* **1** a pile or heap, esp. in orderly arrangement. **2** a circular or rectangular pile of hay etc. **3** *informal* a large quantity. **4** = SMOKESTACK. **5** a stacked group of aircraft. **6** (in *pl.*) a part of a library where most of the books are stored on shelving. **7** *Computing* a set of storage locations which store data in such a way that the most recently stored item is the first to be retrieved. **8** a vertical arrangement of stereo components, speakers, etc. **9** a vertical vent pipe or waste pipe. ● *v.tr.* **1** pile in a stack or stacks. **2** arrange (cards) secretly for cheating. **3** cause (aircraft) to fly around the same point at different levels while waiting to land at an airport. **4** create a disproportion in the representation on (a committee etc.) so that it will act in one's interests. □ **stack the deck** (or **cards**) cause (circumstances etc.) to favour one person, group, etc. over another. **stack up** *N Amer. informal* present oneself, measure up. □ **stackable** *adj.* **stacker** *n.*

stacked *adj.* **1 a** put into a stack or stacks. **b** piled with goods etc. **2** (of odds, circumstances, etc.) biased. **3** (of a woman) having large breasts. **4** (of an aircraft) being one of a number of aircraft flying around the same point at different levels while waiting to land.

stadium *n.* (*pl.* **-s**) an athletic or sports ground with tiers of seats for spectators.

stadium seating *n.* an arrangement of seats, esp. in a movie theatre, in which each row of seats is on a tier one step higher than the one in front of it.

staff ● n. (pl. **-s**) **1** (pl. also **staves**) **a** a stick or pole for use in walking or climbing or as a weapon. **b** a stick or pole as a sign of office or authority. **c** a person or thing that supports or sustains. **d** a flagpole. **e** Surveying a rod for measuring distances, heights, etc. **2 a** a body of persons employed in a business etc. **b** those in authority within an organization, esp. the teachers in a school. **c** Military etc. a body of officers assisting an officer in high command and concerned with an army, regiment, fleet, or air force as a whole. **d** (in full **pitching staff**) Baseball all of a team's pitchers. **3** (pl. also **staves**) Music a set of usu. five parallel lines on which a note is placed to indicate its pitch. ● v.tr. **1** provide (an institution etc.) with staff. **2** work as a member of staff in (an institution etc.). □ **on staff** serving as a member of an organization's staff. □ **staffed** adj. (also in comb.). **staffing** n.

staffer n. esp. N Amer. a member of a staff, esp. of a newspaper.

staff inspector n. (in some Canadian municipal police forces) an officer ranking above inspector.

staff officer n. an officer serving on the staff of an army etc.

staff room n. esp. Cdn & Brit. **1** a common room for staff, esp. in a school. **2** the staff themselves.

staff sergeant n. **1** (in some Canadian police forces) an officer ranking next above sergeant. **2** hist. (in the Canadian Army) a non-commissioned officer of a rank above sergeant.

staff sergeant major n. (in the RCMP) an officer ranking between staff sergeant and sergeant major.

staff superintendent n. (in some Canadian municipal police forces) an officer ranking above superintendent and below deputy chief.

stag ● n. **1** an adult male deer, esp. one with a set of antlers. **2** N Amer. = STAG PARTY. **3** a man who attends a social gathering unaccompanied by a woman. ● attrib.adj. **1** of, for, or composed of men only. **2** pornographic. ● adv. without a date, unaccompanied (went stag).

stag and doe n. (in full **stag and doe party**) Cdn (Ont.) a dance held in honour of an engaged couple, to whom the money raised from ticket sales is given.

stage ● n. **1** a point or period in a process or development. **2 a** a raised floor or platform, esp. one on which plays etc. are performed before an audience. **b** (prec. by the) the acting or theatrical profession, esp. live theatre as opposed to film or television. **c** the art of writing or presenting plays. **d** the scene of action (the stage of politics). **e** = LANDING STAGE. **3** Cdn (Nfld) = FISHING STAGE. **4 a** a regular stopping place on a route. **b** the distance between two stopping places. **5** a section of a rocket with a separate engine, jettisoned when its propellant is exhausted. **6** Geol. a range of strata forming a subdivision of a series. **7** = STAGECOACH. ● v. **1** tr. present (a theatrical production) on stage. **2** tr. arrange the occurrence of (staged a comeback). **3** tr. (esp. as **staged** adj.) present or arrange a contrived, spurious, or mock version of (an event). **4** intr. (esp. of migrating animals) stop at a regular place on a route. □ **by easy stages** gradually; without sudden changes. **go on the stage** become an actor. **hold the stage** dominate a conversation etc. **on (the) stage** performing as an actor, dancer, singer, etc. **set the stage** (usu. foll. by for) prepare the way or conditions for (an event etc.).

stagecoach n. hist. a large closed horse-drawn coach running regularly by stages between two places.

stagecraft n. skill in mounting theatrical performances and creating theatrical effect.

stage direction n. an instruction in the text of a play as to the movement, position, tone, etc., of an actor, or sound effects etc.

stage door n. an entrance from the street to a theatre behind the stage, usu. reserved for performers and stage crew etc.

stage fright n. nervousness on facing an audience.

stagehand n. a person handling scenery etc. during a performance on stage.

stagehead n. Cdn (Nfld) the part of a fishing stage which extends over the water.

stage left n. the part of a stage which is to the left of a person facing the audience.

stage-manage v.tr. **1** be the stage manager of. **2** arrange and control for effect.

stage manager n. the person responsible for overseeing the details of a performance, giving cues to performers, stage hands, lighting crew, etc. □ **stage management**.

stage play n. a play performed on stage rather than broadcast etc.

stage right n. the part of a stage which is to the right of a person facing the audience.

stage whisper ● n. **1** a loud whisper addressed by one actor to another, meant to be heard by the audience. **2** any loud whisper meant to be heard by people other than the person addressed. ● v.tr. (**stage-whisper**) utter in a loud whisper.

stagey var. of STAGY.

stagflation n. a state of inflation without a corresponding increase of demand and employment.

stagger ● v. **1 a** intr. walk unsteadily, totter. **b** tr. cause to totter. **2 a** tr. shock, confuse; cause to hesitate or waver. **b** intr. hesitate; waver in purpose. **3** tr. arrange (events, hours of work, etc.) so that they do not coincide. **4** tr. arrange (objects, people, etc.) so that they are not in line. ● n. **1** a tottering movement. **2** (in pl.) **a** any of various parasitic or other diseases of farm animals marked by staggering or loss of balance. **b** giddiness. **3** an overhanging or slantwise or zigzag arrangement of like parts in a structure etc.

staggering adj. **1** astonishing, bewildering. **2** that staggers. □ **staggeringly** adv.

staghorn n. (also **stag's horn**) **1** the horn of a stag, used to make knife handles etc. **2** any of various ferns, esp. of the genus Platycerium, having fronds like antlers. **3** a sumac of eastern N America with twigs covered with velvety hairs.

staging n. **1** the presentation of a play etc. **2** a platform or support, esp. temporary. **3** (attrib.) referring to a stop or assembly en route to an esp. military or migratory destination (staging area).

stagnant adj. **1** (of liquid) motionless, having no current. **2** (of the mind, business, a person, etc.) showing no activity, dull, sluggish. **3** stale or foul due to lack of motion or activity. □ **stagnancy** n.

stagnate v.intr. be or become stagnant. □ **stagnation** n.

stag party n. an all-male celebration in honour of a man about to marry.

stagy adj. (**-ier**, **-iest**) theatrical; artificial; exaggerated. □ **stagily** adv. **staginess** n.

staid adj. usu. derogatory **1** serious and dull; sedate. **2** fixed, permanent, unchanging. □ **staidly** adv. **staidness** n.

stain ● v. **1** tr. & intr. discolour or be discoloured by the action of liquid sinking in. **2** tr. sully, blemish, spoil, damage (a reputation, character, etc.). **3** tr. colour (wood, glass, etc.) by a process other than painting or covering the surface. **4** *tr.* impregnate (a specimen) with colouring for microscopic examination. ● *n.* **1 a** discoloration, a spot or mark caused esp. by contact with foreign matter and not easily removed. **2 a a** blot or blemish. **b** damage to a reputation etc. **3** a substance used in staining. □ **stainable** *adj.*

stained glass *n.* dyed or coloured glass, esp. in a lead framework in a window.

stainless *adj.* **1** (esp. of a reputation) without stains. **2** not liable to stain.

stainless steel *n.* an iron alloy containing chromium and resistant to rust, used for cutlery etc.

stair *n.* **1** each of a set of fixed steps, esp. in a building. **2** (esp. in *pl.*) a set of such steps.

staircase *n.* a flight or flights of stairs and the supporting structure.

stairway *n.* a flight of stairs, a staircase; a passageway with stairs.

stairwell *n.* the shaft in which a staircase is built.

stake¹ ● *n.* **1** a stout stick or post sharpened at one end and driven into the ground as a support, boundary mark, etc. **2** *hist.* **a** the post to which a person was tied to be burned alive. **b** (prec. by *the*) death by burning as a punishment. ● *v.* **1** *tr.* fasten, secure, or support with a stake or stakes. **2** *tr. & intr.* (usu. foll. by *out*) mark off (an area) with stakes, esp. to claim a site for prospecting. **3** *tr.* state or establish (a claim). □ **pull** (or **pull up**) **stakes** depart; go to live elsewhere. **stake a** (or **one's**) **claim to** declare a special interest in; claim a right to. **stake out** *informal* **1** place under surveillance. **2** place (a person) to maintain surveillance. **3** declare a special interest in or right to e.g. a place or an area of study.

stake² ● *n.* **1** a sum of money etc. wagered on an event. **2 a** (often foll. by *in*) an interest or concern, esp. financial. **b** (in *pl.*) what is being risked; potential losses or consequences. **3** (in *pl.*) **a** money offered as a prize esp. in a horse race. **b** a horse race in which all the owners of the horses contribute to the prize money. ● *v.tr.* **1 a** a wager. **b** risk (*staked everything on convincing him*). **2** *N Amer.* *informal* give financial or other support to. □ **at stake 1** risked, to be won or lost. **2** at issue, in question.

stakeholder *n.* **1** an independent party with whom each of those who make a wager deposits the money etc. wagered. **2** a person with an interest or concern in something.

stakeout *n.* esp. *N Amer.* *informal* a continuous secret watch by the police.

stalactite /stə'læk,taɪt/ *n.* a tapering deposit of calcite hanging down like an icicle from the roof of a cave, cliff overhang, etc., formed by dripping water.

stalagmite /stə'læg,maɪt, 'stæ-/ *n.* a mound or tapering column of calcite rising from the floor of a cave etc., deposited by dripping water.

stale ● *adj.* (**staler, stalest**) **1 a** not fresh, not quite new. **b** musty, insipid, or otherwise the worse for age or use. **2** lacking novelty or interest; trite or unoriginal. **3** (of an athlete or other performer) having ability impaired by excessive exertion or practice. ● *v.tr. & intr.* make or become stale. □ **staleness** *n.*

stalemate ● *n.* **1** *Chess* a position counting as a draw, in which a player is not in check but cannot move except into check. **2** a deadlock or drawn contest. ● *v.tr.* **1** *Chess* bring (a player) to a stalemate. **2** bring to a standstill.

Stalinism /'stælɪ,nɪzəm/ *n.* **1** the policies followed by the Soviet dictator Joseph Stalin (1879–1953), esp. centralization, totalitarianism, and the pursuit of Communism. **2** any rigid centralized authoritarian form of socialism. □ **Stalinist** *n.*

stalk¹ *n.* **1** the main stem of a herbaceous plant. **2** the slender attachment or support of a leaf, flower, fruit, etc. **3** a similar support for an organ etc. in an animal. **4** a slender support or linking shaft in a machine, object, etc., e.g. the stem of a wineglass. □ **stalked** *adj.* (also in *comb.*). **stalkless** *adj.* **stalklike** *adj.* **stalky** *adj.*

stalk² ● *v.* **1 a** *tr.* pursue or approach (game, prey, an enemy, etc.) stealthily. **b** *intr.* steal up to game under cover. **2** *intr.* stride, walk in a stately or haughty manner. **3** *tr.* *formal* or *literary* move silently or threateningly through (a place) (*fear stalked the streets*). **4** *tr.* harass or persecute (a person) with unwanted and obsessive attention. ● *n.* **1** the stalking of game. **2** an imposing gait. □ **stalking** *n.*

stalker *n.* **1** a person who stalks, hounds, or follows a particular person, esp. stealthily or obsessively. **2** a person who stalks game.

stall¹ ● *n.* **1 a** a trader's stand or booth in a market etc. **b** a compartment in a building for the sale of goods. **c** a table in this on which goods are displayed. **2 a** a stable. **b** a compartment for one animal in this. **c** a compartment for one horse at the start of a race. **3** a compartment or cubicle with a single shower or toilet, esp. in a public washroom. **4** a fixed seat in the choir or chancel of a church, more or less enclosed at the back and sides. **5** *N Amer.* (*West*) an area marked off for a single vehicle in a parking lot etc.; a parking space. **6 a** the stalling of an engine or aircraft. **b** the condition resulting from this. ● *v.* **1 a** *intr.* (of a motor vehicle or its engine) stop because of an overload on the engine or an inadequate supply of fuel to it. **b** *intr.* (of an aircraft or its pilot) reach a condition where the speed is too low to allow effective operation of the controls. **c** *tr.* cause (an engine or vehicle or aircraft) to stall. **2** *intr.* **a** (of a vehicle) stick fast as in mud or snow. **b** (of a process etc.) stop moving or progressing. **3** *tr.* put or keep (cattle etc.) in a stall or stalls esp. for fattening.

stall² ● *v.* **1** *intr.* play for time when being questioned etc. **2** *tr.* delay, obstruct. ● *n.* an instance of stalling.

stalling speed *n.* (also **stall speed**) the minimum airspeed at which an aircraft can maintain straight and level flight.

stallion *n.* an uncastrated adult male horse.

stalwart /'stɒlwərt/ ● *adj.* **1** strongly built, sturdy. **2** courageous, resolute, determined. ● *n.* a stalwart person, esp. a loyal uncompromising partisan.

stamen /'steɪmən/ *n.* the male fertilizing organ of a flowering plant.

stamina *n.* the ability to endure prolonged physical or mental strain; staying power, power of endurance.

stammer ● *v.* **1** *intr.* speak with halting articulation, esp. with pauses or rapid repetitions of the same syllable. **2** *tr.* (often foll. by *out*) utter (words) in this way. ● *n.* **1** a tendency to stammer. **2** an instance of stammering.

stamp ● *v.* **1 a** *tr. & intr.* bring down (one's foot) heavily on the ground etc. **b** *tr.* crush, flatten, or bring into a specified state in this way (*stamped down the dirt*). **2** *tr.* **a** impress (a pattern, mark, etc.) on metal, paper, etc., with a die or similar instrument of metal, wood, rubber, etc. **b** impress (a surface) with a pattern etc. in this way. **3** *tr.* affix a postage or other stamp to. **4** *tr.* **a** assign a specific character to; characterize; mark out (*this latest novel stamps her as a genius*). **b** (usu. in *passive*) mark or effect with a particular feeling or attitude. **5** *tr.* crush or pulverize (ore etc.). ● *n.* **1** an instrument for stamping a pattern or mark. **2 a** a mark or pattern made by this. **b** an official mark impressed on deeds, bills of exchange, etc., as evidence of payment of tax. **3 a** = POSTAGE STAMP 1. **b** a small adhesive piece of paper indicating that a price, fee, or tax has been paid. **4** *Cdn* (*Maritimes & Nfld*) **a** *hist.* an adhesive piece of paper affixed by an employer to an employee's record of employment, collected by the employee to prove eligibility for employment insurance. **b** (in *pl.*) *slang* employment insurance benefits. **5** a mark impressed on or label etc. affixed to a commodity as evidence of quality etc. **6 a** a heavy downward blow with the foot. **b** the sound of this. **7 a** a characteristic mark or impress. **b** character, kind (*avoid people of that stamp*). **c** a mark of authoritative approval. **8** an audio or digital mark made on a recorded message, data file, etc., e.g. to indicate the time the information was recorded. □ **stamp out 1** produce by cutting out with a die etc. **2** put an end to, crush, destroy. □ **stamper** *n.*

stampede ● *n.* **1** a sudden flight and scattering of a number of horses, cattle, etc. **2** a sudden flight or hurried movement of people due to interest or panic. **3** *N Amer.* the spontaneous and simultaneous response of many persons to a common impulse. **4** *N Amer. hist.* a rush of prospectors to a newly-discovered deposit of esp. gold. **5** *Cdn & US West* an exhibition or fair involving rodeo events and other contests and entertainment. ● *v.* **1** *intr.* take part in a stampede. **2** *tr.* cause to do this. **3** *tr.* cause to act hurriedly or unreasoningly. □ **stampeder** *n.*

stamp of approval *n.* = SEAL OF APPROVAL.

stamp pad *n.* an ink-soaked pad, usu. in a box, used for inking a rubber stamp etc.

stance *n.* **1** an attitude or position of the body, esp. in sports. **2** a moral or intellectual attitude to something, esp. one that is expressed publicly.

stanch /stɑːntʃ/ *var. of* STAUNCH[2].

stanchion /ˈstɑːnʃən/ *n.* **1** a post or pillar, an upright support, a vertical strut. **2** an upright bar, pair of bars, or frame, for confining cattle in a stall.

stand ● *v.* (*past* and *past part.* **stood**) **1** *intr.* have or take or maintain an upright position, esp. on the feet or a base. **2** *intr.* be situated or located. **3** *intr.* be of a specified height. **4** *intr.* be in a specified condition. **5** *tr.* place or set in an upright or specified position (*stood it against the wall*). **6** *intr.* **a** move to and remain in a specified position (*stand aside*). **b** take a specified attitude (*stand aloof*). **7** *intr.* maintain a position; avoid falling or moving or being moved. **8** *intr.* assume a stationary position; cease to move. **9** *intr.* remain valid or unaltered; hold good. **10** *intr. Naut.* hold a specified course. **11** *tr.* endure without yielding or complaining; tolerate (*how can you stand him?*). **12** *tr.* provide for another or others at one's own expense (*stood me a drink*). **13** *intr.* (often foll. by *for*) be a candidate (for an office) (*stood for Parliament*). **14** *intr.* act in a specified capacity (*stood proxy*). **15** *tr.* undergo (trial). ● *n.* **1** a cessation from motion or progress, a stoppage. **2 a** a halt made, or a stationary condition assumed, for the purpose of resistance. **b** resistance to attack or compulsion. **3 a** a position taken up. **b** an attitude adopted. **4** a declared opinion or view; a stance (*what is your stand?*). **5** a rack, set of shelves, table, etc., on or in which things may be placed (*music stand*). **6 a** a small open-fronted structure for a vendor outdoors or in a market etc. **b** a structure occupied by a participating organization at an exhibition. **7** a standing place for vehicles (*taxi stand*). **8 a** (esp. in *pl.*) a raised structure for spectators to sit or stand on at a

performance, sports event, etc. **b** a raised structure for performers etc. **9** *N Amer.* a witness box. **10** each halt made on a tour to give one or more performances, play one or more games, etc. (*a long home stand*). **11** a group of tall growing plants (*stand of trees*). □ **as it stands 1** in its present condition, unaltered. **2** (also **as things stand**) in the present circumstances. **stand alone** be unequalled; be without peers. **stand back 1** withdraw; take up a position further from the front. **2** withdraw emotionally in order to take an objective view. **stand by 1** stand nearby; look on without interfering (*will not stand by and see a cat ill-treated*). **2** uphold, support, side with (a person). **3** adhere to, abide by (terms or promises). **4 a** *Naut.* stand ready to take hold of or operate (an anchor etc.). **b** be ready to act or assist. **stand corrected** accept correction. **stand down 1** withdraw from a team, election, etc. **2** leave the witness box. **3** *Military* go off duty; relax after a state of alert. **stand firm** (or **fast**) be steadfast or unfaltering. **stand for 1** represent, signify, imply ('*BC' stands for 'British Columbia'*). **2** (often with *neg.*) *informal* endure, tolerate, acquiesce in. **3** espouse the cause of. **stand one's ground** maintain one's position, not yield. **stand high** be high in status, price, etc. **stand in** (usu. foll. by *for*) act in place of another. **stand off** move or keep away, keep one's distance. **stand on** insist on, observe scrupulously (*stand on ceremony*). **stand on one's own** not depend on an associated or related thing or person for legitimacy; be recognized for one's own merits (*the second movement stands on its own*). **stand on one's own two feet** (or **own feet**) be self-reliant or independent. **stand out 1** be prominent or conspicuous or outstanding. **2** (usu. foll. by *against*, *for*) hold out; persist in opposition or support or endurance. **stand over 1** stand close to (a person) to watch, control, threaten, etc. **2** be postponed, be left for later settlement etc. **stand to 1** *Military* stand ready for an attack (esp. before dawn or after dark). **2** abide by, adhere to (terms or promises). **3** be likely or certain to (*stands to lose everything*). **stand up 1 a** rise to one's feet from a sitting or other position. **b** come to or remain in or place in a standing position. **2** (of an argument etc.) be valid. **3** *informal* fail to keep an appointment with. **stand up for 1** support, side with, maintain, defend (a person or cause). **2** *N Amer.* (also **stand up with**) act as best man or maid or matron of honour for (a bride or groom or both). **stand up to 1** meet or face (an opponent) courageously. **2** be resistant to the harmful effects of (wear, use, etc.). **stand well** (usu. foll. by *with*) be on good terms or in good repute. **take a** (or **one's**) **stand** commit to or declare a position in a debate etc. **where one stands 1** where one positions oneself in a debate, controversy, etc. (*where do you stand?*). **2** what one's situation, status, or condition is in a relationship etc. (*where do we stand?*). □ **stander** *n.*

stand-alone *attrib.adj.* **1** (of a computer) operating independently of a network or other system. **2** designed or intended not to rely on an external structure or system (*stand-alone copiers*).

standard ● *n.* **1** an object or quality or measure serving as an example or principle to which others conform or should conform or by which the accuracy or quality of others is judged. **2 a** the degree of excellence etc. required for a particular purpose (*not up to standard*). **b** average quality (*of a low standard*). **3** the ordinary procedure, or quality or design of a product, without added or novel features. **4 a** a ceremonial or distinctive flag, esp. one associated with a particular person or group of people. **b** the flag of a cavalry regiment. **5** an upright support. **6 a** a tree or shrub that grows on an erect stem of full height and stands alone without support. **b** a shrub grafted on an upright stem and trained in tree form. **7** a document specifying nationally or internationally agreed properties for manufactured goods etc. **8** a thing recognized as a model for imitation etc. **9** a tune or song of established popularity. **10 a** a system by which the value of a currency is defined in terms of gold or silver or both. **b** the prescribed proportion of the weight of fine metal in gold or silver coins. ● *adj.* **1** serving or used as a standard (*a standard size*). **2** of a normal or prescribed quality or size etc. **3** having recognized and permanent value; authoritative. **4** (of language) conforming to established educated usage (*standard English*). ● *adv. N Amer.* in its standard or normal state, form, etc. (*comes standard with racing stripes*). □ **set the standard** reach a level of excellence which others must try to match.

standard-bearer *n.* **1** a soldier who carries a standard. **2** a prominent leader in a cause.

standardbred *n. N Amer.* a horse of a breed able to attain a specified speed, developed esp. for harness racing.

standard deviation *n. Statistics* a quantity indicating the extent of deviation for a group.

standard issue *n.* **1** that which is issued or supplied as a matter of course, esp. to military personnel. **2** (*attrib.*) ordinary, undistinguished.

standardize *v.* **1** *tr.* cause to conform to a standard. **2** *tr.* determine the properties of by comparison with a standard. **3** *intr.* (foll. by *on*) adopt as one's standard or model. □ **standardization** *n.*

standard of living *n.* the degree of material comfort available to a person or class or community.

standard time *n.* a uniform time officially adopted for a country or region.

standby ● *n.* (*pl.* **-bys**) **1** a person or thing ready if needed in an emergency etc. **2** esp. *N Amer.* a thing which has proven to be reliable; a trusted or long-used resource etc. (*that old standby*). **3** (in full **standby time**) the maximum length of time the battery of a cellular telephone will remain charged while awaiting incoming calls (*compare* TALK TIME). ● *attrib.adj.* **1** ready for immediate use, as in an emergency etc. **2** designating or pertaining to a system of air travel whereby seats are not booked in advance but allocated on the basis of availability just before departure. **3** *Cdn & Brit.* designating theatre tickets sold on the basis of availability on the day of performance, often at a reduced price. ● *adv.* without having booked seats in advance (*fly standby*). □ **on standby** prepared for immediate use or activity and awaiting instructions etc.

stand-in *n.* a substitute, esp. for an actor when the latter's acting ability is not needed.

standing ● *n.* **1** esteem or repute, esp. high; status, position (*of high standing*). **2** duration (*of long standing*). **3** length of service, membership, etc. **4** *Law* the right to prosecute a claim or seek legal redress. **5** (in *pl.*) esp. *N Amer.* **a** a ranking of teams or competitors in a league etc. esp. according to total points. **b** a table etc. indicating this. **6** one's position in a classification or ranking. ● *adj.* **1** that stands, upright. **2 a** established, permanent (*a standing rule*). **b** not made, raised, etc., for the occasion (*a standing army*). **3** (of a jump, start, etc.) performed from rest or from a standing position. **4** (of water) stagnant. **5** (of wheat

etc.) unreaped. □ **in good standing 1** fully paid-up as a member etc. **2** in favour.

standing committee *n.* a committee that is permanent during the existence of the appointing body.

standing joke *n.* = RUNNING JOKE (*see* RUNNING *adj.* 1).

standing order *n.* **1** (in *pl.*) the rules governing the conduct of all business in a parliament, council, etc. **2** an esp. military order that remains valid and does not have to be repeated. **3** an order with a supplier to supply a product whenever it is available.

standing ovation *n.* prolonged applause during which the crowd or audience rises to its feet.

standing room *n.* **1** space to stand in. **2** accommodation in a theatre, arena, etc. where people must stand. **3** (**standing-room**; also **standing-room-only**) (*attrib.*) designating an audience etc. filling all available seats and overflowing into standing room.

standoff *n.* **1** *N Amer.* **a** a deadlock. **b** a confrontation in which each side is entrenched and threatening. **2** (**stand-off**; in full **stand-off half**) *Rugby* a halfback who forms a link between the scrum half and the three-quarters.

standoffish *adj.* cold or distant in manner. □ **standoffishly** *adv.* **standoffishness** *n.*

standout *n. informal* (often *attrib.*) a remarkable, notable, or outstanding person or thing.

standpoint *n.* **1** the position from which a thing is viewed. **2** a mental attitude.

standstill *n.* a stoppage; an inability to proceed.

stand-up ● *attrib.adj.* **1** denoting a brand of comedy performed by standing before an audience and telling jokes. **2** that stands or is used upright, not turned down or on its side (*a stand-up collar*). **3** designating a bar, reception, meal, etc., at which people stand rather than sit. **4** *Baseball* designating a double or triple in which the batter reaches base standing up, i.e. easily, not needing to slide. **5** (of a fight) violent, thorough, or fair and square. ● *n.* **1** a stand-up comedian. **2** stand-up comedy.

Stanfields *n.pl. Cdn proprietary* men's underwear, esp. long underwear.

stank *past of* STINK.

Stanley Cup *n.* a trophy awarded annually to the hockey team that wins the NHL championships.

stanza *n.* the basic metrical unit in a poem or verse, consisting of a recurring group of lines which may or may not rhyme. □ **stanzaic** /-'zeɪɪk/ *adj.*

stapes /'steɪpiːz/ *n.* (*pl.* same) a small stirrup-shaped bone in the ears of mammals.

staph /stæf/ *n. informal* = STAPHYLOCOCCUS.

staphylococcus /ˌstæfɪlə'kɒkəs/ *n.* (*pl.* **staphylococci** /-kaɪ/) any bacterium of the genus *Staphylococcus*, occurring in grapelike clusters, and sometimes causing pus formation usu. in the skin and mucous membranes of animals. □ **staphylococcal** *adj.*

staple[1] ● *n.* a small thin piece of U-shaped wire that is punched into wood, sheets of paper, etc., for fastening etc. ● *v.tr.* fasten or attach with a staple or staples.

staple[2] ● *n.* **1** the principal or an important article of commerce. **2** the chief element or a main component, e.g. of a diet. **3** a raw material. **4** the fibre of cotton or wool etc. as determining its quality (*long-staple cotton*). ● *adj.* **1** main or principal (*staple commodities*). **2** important as a product or an export.

stapler *n.* a small device for forcing staples into paper etc. or for stapling papers etc. together.

star ● *n.* **1** a celestial body appearing as a luminous point in the night sky. **2** (in full **fixed star**) such a body so far from the earth as to appear motionless. **3** a large naturally luminous gaseous body, e.g. the sun. **4** a celestial body regarded as influencing a person's fortunes etc. (*born under a lucky star*). **5** a thing resembling a star in shape or appearance. **6** a small white mark between a horse's eyes. **7** a figure or object with radiating points esp. as the insignia of an order, as a decoration or mark of rank, or showing a category of excellence (*a five-star hotel; won a gold star*). **8 a** a famous person; a celebrity. **b** the principal or most prominent performer in a play, film, etc. (*the star of the show*). **c** an outstanding or particularly brilliant person (*our star pupil*). **d** one of three players judged to have made the most valuable contribution to a hockey game. ● *v.* (**starred, starring**) **1 a** *tr.* (of a film etc.) feature as a principal performer. **b** *intr.* (of a performer) be featured in a film etc. **2** (esp. as **starred** *adj.*) **a** mark, set, or adorn with a star or stars. **b** put an asterisk or star beside (a name, an item in a list, etc.). □ **my stars!** *informal* an expression of surprise. □ **stardom** *n.* **starless** *adj.* **starlike** *adj.*

star anise *n. see* ANISE 2.

starboard ● *n.* the right-hand side (looking forward) of a ship, boat, or aircraft (*compare* PORT³). ● *adj.* situated on or turned towards the starboard side.

starburst *n.* **1** a pattern of radiating lines or rays around a central object, light source, etc. **2** an explosion producing this effect.

starch ● *n.* **1** an odourless tasteless polysaccharide occurring widely in plants and obtained chiefly from cereals and potatoes, forming an important constituent of the human diet. **2** a preparation of this for stiffening fabric before ironing. **3** (in *pl.*) foods containing much starch, e.g. potatoes, rice, pasta, etc. **4** stiffness of manner; formality. **5** strength, backbone; vigour. ● *v.tr.* stiffen (clothing) with starch. □ **starchy** *adj.* (**-ier, -iest**) **starchily** *adv.* **starchiness** *n.*

star cluster *n. Astronomy* a group of stars forming a relatively close association.

stardust *n.* a romantic mystical look or sensation.

stare ● *v.intr.* **1** look fixedly, esp. as the result of curiosity, surprise, bewilderment, admiration, horror, etc. **2** (of eyes) be wide open and fixed. **3** be unpleasantly prominent or striking. ● *n.* a staring gaze. □ **stare down** outstare. **stare one in the face** be evident or imminent.

starfish *n.* an echinoderm of the class Asteroidea with five or more radiating arms.

star fruit *n.* = CARAMBOLA.

stargazer *n. informal* **1** an astronomer or astrologer. **2** a daydreamer. □ **stargaze** *v.intr.*

stark ● *adj.* **1** desolate, bare. **2** sharply evident (*in stark contrast*). **3** downright, sheer. **4** devoid of any elaboration or adornment; brutally simple. **5** completely naked. ● *adv.* completely, wholly (*stark naked*). □ **starkly** *adv.* **starkness** *n.*

starlet *n.* a promising young female performer.

starlight *n.* **1** the light of the stars. **2** (*attrib.*) = STARLIT.

starling *n.* **1** a small gregarious partly migratory bird, *Sturnus vulgaris*, with blackish-brown speckled lustrous plumage, chiefly inhabiting cultivated areas. **2** any similar bird of the family Sturnidae.

starlit *adj.* **1** lighted by stars. **2** with stars visible.

Star of Courage *n.* Canada's second-highest award for bravery, given to civilians and military personnel.

Star of David *n.* a figure consisting of two interlaced triangles, used as a Jewish and Israeli symbol.

starry *adj.* (**-ier, -iest**) **1** covered with stars. **2** resembling a star. □ **starriness** *n.*

starry-eyed *adj. informal* **1** visionary; enthusiastic but impractical. **2** euphoric.

starship *n.* (in science fiction) a large usu. manned spacecraft for interstellar space travel.

star-spangled *adj.* **1** covered or glittering with stars. **2** = STAR-STUDDED.

star-struck *adj.* fascinated or greatly impressed by celebrities or stardom.

star-studded *n.* **1** containing or covered with many stars. **2** featuring many famous performers.

START *abbr.* Strategic Arms Reduction Treaty (or Talks).

start ● *v.* **1** *tr. & intr.* begin; commence. **2** *tr.* set (proceedings, an event, etc.) in motion (*started a fire*). **3** *intr.* (often foll. by *on*) make a beginning. **4** *intr.* (often foll. by *after, for*) set oneself in motion or action. **5** *intr.* set out; begin a journey etc. (*we start at 6 a.m.*). **6** (often foll. by *up*) **a** *intr.* (of a machine) begin operating. **b** *tr.* cause (a machine etc.) to begin operating. **7 a** *tr.* cause or enable (a person) to make a beginning (with something) (*started me in business with $50,000*). **b** *tr.* (foll. by pres. part.) cause (a person) to begin (doing something) (*the smoke started me coughing*). **c** *intr. informal* complain or be critical (*don't you start*). **8** *tr.* (often foll. by *up*) found or establish; originate. **9** *intr.* (foll. by *at, with*) have as the first of a series of items, e.g. in a meal. **10** *tr.* give a signal to (competitors) to start in a race. **11** *intr.* (often foll. by *up, from,* etc.) make a sudden movement from surprise, pain, etc. **12** *intr.* (foll. by *out, up, from,* etc.) spring out, up, etc. **13** *tr. & intr.* **a** *Sport* be one of the players chosen to play at the outset of (a game). **b** *Baseball* be the starting pitcher of (a game). **14** *intr.* (foll. by *out, to,* etc.) (of a thing) move or appear suddenly (*tears started to his eyes*). **15** *intr.* (foll. by *from*) (of eyes, usu. with exaggeration) burst forward (from their sockets etc.). ● *n.* **1** a beginning of an event, action, journey, etc. **2** the place from which a race etc. begins. **3** = HEAD START. **4** an advantageous initial position in life, business, etc. (*a good start in life*). **5** a sudden movement of surprise, pain, etc. **6** an intermittent or spasmodic effort or movement (*by fits and starts*). □ **for a start** *informal* as a beginning; in the first place. **start in** *informal* **1** begin. **2** (foll. by *on*) *N Amer.* make a beginning on. **start off 1** begin; commence. **2** begin to move. **start out 1** begin a journey. **2** *informal* (foll. by *to* + infin.) proceed as intending (to do something). **start over** *N Amer.* begin again. **start something** *informal* cause trouble. **start up** arise; occur. **to start with 1** in the first place; before anything else is considered. **2** at the beginning.

starter ● *n.* **1** a person or thing that starts. **2** an esp. automatic device for starting the engine of a motor vehicle etc. **3 a** *N Amer.* a player who plays at the beginning of a game. **b** *Baseball* = STARTING PITCHER. **4** a person giving the signal for the start of a race. **5** a horse or competitor starting in a race. **6** the first course of a meal. **7** a culture used to initiate souring or fermentation in making yogourt, cheese, dough, etc. **8** the initial action etc. ● *adj.* relating to or suitable for a start or beginning (*a starter home*). □ **for starters** *informal* to start with.

starting block *n.* a shaped rigid block for bracing the feet of a runner at the start of a race.

starting gate *n.* a movable barrier for securing a fair start in horse races.

starting lineup *n. Sport* a list of players chosen from a team's roster to start a game.

starting pitcher *n. Baseball* a pitcher who pitches the initial innings of a game.

starting point *n.* the point from which a journey, process, argument, etc. begins.

starting rotation *n. Baseball* = ROTATION 3b.

startle ● *v.tr.* give a shock or surprise to; cause (a person etc.) to start with surprise or sudden alarm. ● *n.* a sudden start or shock of surprise, alarm, etc. □ **startled** *adj.* **startlement** *n.* **startling** *adj.* **startlingly** *adv.*

start-up *n.* the action or an instance of starting up, esp. the starting up of a business, machine, or series of operations (often *attrib.*: *start-up costs*).

star turn *n.* the principal item in an entertainment or performance.

starvation ● *n.* **1** the action of starving or depriving a person or animal of food. **2** the condition of having too little food to sustain life or health. ● *adj.* **1** liable to cause starvation (*a starvation diet*). **2** seeming to cause starvation (*starvation wages*).

starve *v.* **1** *tr. & intr.* (cause to) die of hunger or suffer from lack of food. **2** *intr.* suffer from extreme poverty. **3** *intr.* feel very hungry. **4** *intr.* **a** suffer from mental or spiritual want. **b** (foll. by *for*) feel a strong craving for (sympathy, amusement, knowledge, etc.). **5** *tr.* **a** (foll. by *of*) deprive of; keep scantily supplied with. **b** cause to suffer from mental or spiritual want. **6** *tr.* **a** (foll. by *into*) compel by starving (*starved into submission*). **b** (foll. by *out*) compel to surrender etc. by starving (*starved them out*). □ **-starved** *comb. form.*

Star Wars *n. informal* = STRATEGIC DEFENCE INITIATIVE.

stash *informal* ● *v.tr.* (often foll. by *away*) **1** conceal; put in a safe or hidden place. **2** hoard, stow, store. ● *n.* **1** a hiding place or hideout. **2** a thing hidden; a cache. **3** a cache or quantity of an illegal drug.

stasis /ˈsteɪsɪs, ˈstæsɪs/ *n.* (*pl.* **stases** /-siːz/) **1** a state of inactivity or equilibrium. **2** a stoppage of circulation of any of the body fluids.

stat[1] *n. informal* esp. *N Amer.* a statistic.

stat[2] *adv.* esp. *Med.* immediately.

stat[3] *n. Cdn informal* a statutory holiday.

state ● *n.* **1** the existing condition or position of a person or thing. **2** *informal* **a** an excited, anxious, or agitated mental condition (*was in a state*). **b** an untidy condition. **3 a** an organized political community under one government; a nation. **b** a political unit forming part of a federation, as in the US. **c** (**the States**) the US. **4** (*attrib.*) **a** of, for, or concerned with the state. **b** reserved for or done on occasions of ceremony (*state visit*). **c** involving ceremony (*state opening of Parliament*). **5** (usu. **State**) civil government (*Church and State*). ● *v.tr.* express, esp. fully or clearly, in speech or writing. □ **of state** concerning politics or government. □ **statable** *adj.* **statehood** *n.*

statecraft *n.* the art of diplomacy and government.

stated *adj.* **1** fixed, established; regular (*at stated intervals*). **2** explicitly set forth.

State Department *n.* (in the US) the department of foreign affairs.

stateless *adj.* **1** (of a person) having no nationality or citizenship. **2** without a state or states.

state line *n.* the boundary between two US states.

stately *adj.* (**-ier, -iest**) dignified; imposing; grand. □ **stateliness** *n.*

statement *n.* **1** the act or an instance of stating or being stated; expression in words. **2** a thing stated; a declaration. **3** a formal account of facts, esp. to the police or in a court of law. **4** a record of transactions in a bank account etc. **5** an account containing a list of bills, invoices, or payments, and showing the total amount due or the balance owing. **6** the communica-

tion of a mood, idea, etc., through something other than words, e.g. clothing.

statement of claim *n. Cdn Law* a legal document served in a civil suit which sets out the relief applied for by the plaintiff and the reasons for such relief.

state of affairs *n.* circumstances.

state of emergency *n.* a condition of danger or disaster affecting a country, esp. with normal constitutional procedures suspended.

state of the art *n.* **1** the current stage of development of a practical or technological subject. **2** (usu. **state-of-the-art**) (*attrib.*) using the latest techniques or equipment (*state-of-the-art computers*).

state of war *n.* the situation when war has been declared or is in progress.

stateroom *n.* a private compartment in a passenger ship, train, etc.

stateside esp. *US informal* ● *adj.* of, in, or relating to the US. ● *adv.* in or towards the continental US.

statesman *n.* (*pl.* **-men**) **1** a person skilled in affairs of state, esp. one taking an active part in politics. **2** a distinguished politician. *See also* ELDER STATESMAN. □ **statesmanlike** *adj.* **statesmanship** *n.*

statesperson *n.* a statesman or stateswoman.

stateswoman *n.* (*pl.* **-women**) **1** a woman skilled in affairs of state, esp. one taking an active part in politics. **2** a distinguished female politician.

state trooper *n. US* a member of a state police force.

state university *n. US* a university managed by the public authorities of a state.

statewide *US* ● *adj.* extending over or affecting an entire state. ● *adv.* so as to extend over or affect an entire state.

static ● *adj.* **1** stationary; not acting or changing; passive. **2** of or relating to static electricity. **3** *Physics* **a** concerned with bodies at rest or forces in equilibrium (*opp.* DYNAMIC 2a). **b** acting as weight but not moving (*static pressure*). **c** of statics. ● *n.* **1** static electricity. **2** electrical disturbances producing interference with the reception of telecommunications and broadcasts. **3** esp. *N Amer.* (in full **static cling**) the adhering of clothing to a person's body or to other clothing etc., caused by a buildup of static electricity. **4** *slang* aggravation; interference; criticism. □ **statically** *adv.* **staticky** *adj.* (in sense 2 of *n.*).

static electricity *n.* a stationary electric charge, usu. produced by friction, which causes sparks or cracking, or the attraction of dust, hair, fabric, etc.

statics *n.pl.* (usu. treated as *sing.*) the science of bodies at rest or of forces in equilibrium (*opp.* DYNAMICS 1).

station ● *n.* **1 a** a regular stopping place on a railway or subway line, with a platform and usu. administrative buildings or offices. **b** = BUS STATION. **c** these buildings (*go into the station*). **2** a place or building etc. where a person or thing stands or is placed. **3 a** a designated point or establishment where a particular service or activity is based or organized (*police station*). **b** *N Amer.* a subsidiary post office. **4 a** a studio or building used in making television or radio broadcasts. **b** an organization or establishment involved in radio or television broadcasting. **c** a specific frequency or band of frequencies assigned to a broadcaster. **5** a plant for generating electricity, esp. of a specified kind (*hydro station*). **6 a** a small military base. **b** the inhabitants of this. **7** position in life; rank or status. **8** *Cdn* (*Nfld*) a cove or harbour with space on the foreshore for the erection of facilities to support the fishery in nearby waters. ● *v.tr.* **1** assign a station to. **2** put in position.

stationary *adj.* **1** remaining in one place, not moving. **2** not meant to be moved; not portable. **3** not changing in magnitude, number, quality, etc.

stationer *n.* a person who sells writing materials etc.

stationery *n.* **1** writing paper. **2** writing materials, such as paper, envelopes, office supplies, etc.

station of the cross *n.* **1** each of a series of usu. 14 images representing the events in Christ's passion, before which devotions are performed in some churches. **2** (**Stations of the Cross**) the act of performing such devotions.

station wagon *n. N Amer., Austral., & NZ* a car with the passenger area extended and combined with space for luggage, usu. with an extra door at the rear.

statism /ˈsteɪtɪzəm/ *n.* centralized state administration and control of social and economic affairs. □ **statist** *n. & adj.*

statistic ● *n.* a statistical fact or item. ● *adj.* = STATISTICAL.

statistical *adj.* of or relating to statistics. □ **statistically** *adv.*

statistics *n.pl.* **1** (usu. treated as *sing.*) the science of collecting and analyzing numerical data, esp. in or for large quantities, and usu. inferring proportions in a whole from proportions in a representative sample. **2** any systematic collection or presentation of such facts. □ **statistician** *n.*

StatsCan *n. Cdn informal* Statistics Canada.

statuary ● *adj.* of or for statues. ● *n.* (*pl.* **-ies**) **1** statues collectively. **2** the art of making statues.

statue *n.* a sculptured, cast, carved, or moulded figure of a person or animal, esp. life-size or larger.

statuesque *adj.* **1** like a statue in size, dignity, or lack of movement. **2** (esp. of a woman) tall and graceful.

statuette *n.* a small statue.

stature *n.* **1** the natural height of the body (*small in stature*). **2** importance and reputation gained by ability or achievement (*her growing political stature*). □ **statured** *adj.* (also in *comb.*).

status /ˈstætəs, ˈsteɪt-/ *n.* **1** the social or professional position of a person or thing in relation to others; relative importance. **2** high rank or social position. **3** *Law* a person's legal standing which determines his or her rights and duties, e.g. citizen, civilian, refugee, etc. (*see also* MARITAL STATUS). **4** *Cdn* (*attrib.*) (of an Aboriginal person) registered as an Indian under the Indian Act. **5** the state of affairs.

status quo /ˈkwoʊ/ *n.* the existing state of affairs.

status symbol *n.* a possession that is thought to show a person's high social rank, wealth, etc.

statute *n.* **1 a** a decree or enactment passed by a legislative body, and expressed in a formal document. **b** the document containing such an enactment. **2** any of the rules of an organization or institution. **3** divine law.

statute book *n.* **1** a book or books containing the statute law. **2** the body of a country's statutes.

statute law *n.* **1** (*collect.*) the body of principles and rules of law laid down in statutes as distinct from rules formulated in practical application (*compare* COMMON LAW 1, CASE LAW). **2** a statute.

statute of limitations *n.* (*pl.* **statutes of limitations**) a law that fixes the time within which criminal charges must be laid or legal action taken.

statutory /ˈstatʃətəri, ˈstatʃuːtɔːri/ *adj.* **1** required, permitted, or enacted by statute. **2** (of an offence) punishable under a statute. **3** of, relating to, or of the nature of a statute. □ **statutorily** *adv.*

statutory holiday *n. Cdn* a public holiday established by federal or provincial statute.

statutory release *n. Cdn Law* parole as required by statute.

staunch[1] *adj.* **1** trustworthy, loyal. **2** (of a ship, joint, etc.) strong, watertight, etc. □ **staunchly** *adv.*

staunch[2] *v.tr.* **1** restrain the flow of (esp. blood). **2** restrain the flow from (esp. a wound).

stave ● *n.* **1** each of the curved pieces of wood forming the sides of a cask, pail, etc. **2** = STAFF *n.* 3. ● *v.tr.* (*past* and *past part.* **stove** or **staved**) **1** break a hole in. **2** crush or knock out of shape. □ **stave in** crush by forcing inwards. **stave off** (*past* and *past part.* **staved**) avert or defer (esp. danger or misfortune).

staves *pl.* of STAFF *n.* 1,3.

stay[1] ● *v.* **1** *intr.* continue to be in the same place or condition; not depart or change. **2** *intr.* (often foll. by *at, in, with*) have temporary residence as a visitor etc. **3** *archaic* or *literary tr.* stop or check (progress, the inroads of a disease, etc.). **4** *tr.* postpone (judgment, decision, etc.). **5** *tr.* assuage (hunger etc.) esp. for a short time. **6 a** *intr.* show endurance. **b** *tr.* show endurance to the end of (a race etc.). **7** *tr.* (often foll. by *up*) *literary* support, prop up (as or with a buttress etc.). **8** *intr.* (foll. by *for, to*) wait long enough to share or join in an activity etc. (*stay for the film*). **9** *intr.* (often foll. by *with*) (of an image etc.) remain in the mind or memory (*the sound of Dad's voice will stay with me forever*). **10** *N Amer. intr.* (foll. by *with*) (of food) give lasting satisfaction to hunger. **11** *intr.* (in poker) raise one's ante sufficiently to remain in a round. **12** *intr.* (foll. by *with*) **a** keep up with (a competitor etc.). **b** apply oneself to, continue with. ● *n.* **1 a** the act or an instance of staying or dwelling in one place. **b** the duration of this. **2** a suspension or postponement of a sentence, judgment, etc. **3** endurance, staying power. **4** a prop or support. **5** (in *pl.*) *hist.* a corset esp. with whalebone etc. stiffening, and laced. □ **has come** (or **is here**) **to stay** *informal* must be regarded as permanent. **stay the course** pursue a course of action or endure a struggle etc. to the end. **stay in** remain indoors, esp. at home or in school after hours as a punishment. **stay the night** remain until the next day. **stay on** remain in a place or position. **stay put** remain where it is placed or where one is. **stay up** not go to bed (until late at night). □ **stayer** *n.*

stay[2] ● *n.* **1** *Naut.* a rope supporting a mast. **2** a guy or rope supporting a flagpole or other pole. ● *v.tr.* **1** support by stays. **2** put (a ship) on another tack.

stay-at-home ● *adj.* **1** remaining habitually at home. **2** (esp. of a parent) choosing to remain at home, esp. to care for children, rather than seeking outside employment. **3** *Hockey* (of a defenceman) conservative; unlikely to take risks or be caught out of position. ● *n.* a person who does this.

staying power *n.* endurance, stamina.

staysail /ˈsteɪseɪl, ˈsteɪsəl/ *n.* a triangular fore-and-aft sail extended on a stay.

STD *abbr.* **1** SEXUALLY TRANSMITTED DISEASE. **2** Doctor of Sacred Theology.

stead *n.* □ **in a person's** (or **thing's**) **stead** as a substitute; instead of him or her or it. **stand a person in good stead** be advantageous or serviceable to him or her.

steadfast /ˈstɛdfæst, ˈstɛdfəst/ *adj.* **1** constant, firm, unwavering. **2** (of a person's gaze etc.) fixed in intensity; steadily directed. □ **steadfastly** *adv.* **steadfastness** *n.*

steady ● *adj.* (**-ier, -iest**) **1** firmly in place; not tottering, rocking, or wavering. **2** done or occurring in a uniform and regular manner (*a steady pace*). **3** constant, persistent; not changeable or changing (*steady boyfriend*; *a steady job*). **4** serious; cautious and dependable in behaviour. **5** not faltering (*a steady hand*). ● *v.tr. & intr.* (**-ies, -ied**) make or become steady (*steady the boat*). ● *adv.* steadily (*hold it steady*). ● *interj.* as a command or warning to take care. ● *n.* (*pl.* **-ies**) **1** *informal* a regular boyfriend or girlfriend. **2** *Cdn* (*Nfld*) **a** a stretch of still water in a river or pond; a pool. **b** a small freshwater pond. □ **go steady** (often foll. by *with*) *informal* have as a regular boyfriend or girlfriend. □ **steadily** *adv.* **steadiness** *n.*

steady state *n.* an unvarying condition, esp. in a physical process, e.g. of the universe theoretically having no beginning and no end.

steak *n.* **1** a slice of meat or fish, cut for frying or barbecuing. **2** beef cut for stewing or braising.

steakette *n. Cdn* a thin patty of ground beef.

steak house *n.* a restaurant specializing in steaks.

steak tartare *n.* (also **steak tartar**) a dish of raw chopped steak mixed with raw egg, onion, and seasonings, shaped into small cakes or patties.

steal ● *v.* (*past* **stole**; *past part.* **stolen**) **1** *tr. & intr.* take illegally without right or permission. **2** *tr.* obtain surreptitiously or by surprise (*stole a kiss*). **3** *tr.* win or gain possession of, esp. insidiously or artfully (*stole her heart away*; *stole the puck off the goalie*). **4** *intr.* (foll. by *in*, *out*, *away*, *up*, etc.) **a** move, esp. silently or stealthily (*stole out of the room*). **b** (of a sound etc.) become gradually perceptible. **5** *tr. Baseball* advance to (a base) while the ball is being pitched. ● *n.* **1** *informal* an unexpectedly easy task or good bargain. **2** *Baseball* the act of advancing a base by stealing. □ **steal a march on** get an advantage over by surreptitious means; anticipate. **steal the show** outshine other performers. **steal a person's thunder 1** use another person's idea, policy, etc., and spoil the effect the originator hoped to achieve by expressing it or acting upon it first. **2** take the limelight or attention from another person. □ **stealer** *n.* (also in *comb.*).

stealth *n.* **1** secrecy. **2** (*attrib.*) designed in accordance with or designating the technology which makes detection by radar or sonar difficult (*stealth bomber*).

stealthy *adj.* (**-ier, -iest**) **1** (of an action) done with stealth. **2** (of a person or thing) moving with stealth. □ **stealthily** *adv.* **stealthiness** *n.*

steam ● *n.* **1 a** the gas into which water is changed by boiling. **b** a mist of liquid particles of water produced by the condensation of this gas. **2** any similar vapour. **3 a** energy or power provided by a steam engine or other machine. **b** *informal* power or energy generally. ● *v.* **1** *tr.* **a** cook (food) in steam. **b** treat with steam, e.g. to remove wrinkles from garments or make timber pliable. **2** *intr.* give off steam or other vapour. **3** *intr.* **a** move under steam power (*steamed down the river*). **b** (foll. by *along*, *ahead*, etc.) *informal* proceed with speed or vigour. **4** *tr. & intr.* cover or become covered with condensed water vapour. **5** *tr. & intr. informal* be or cause to be angry or upset. **6** *tr.* (foll. by *open* etc.) apply steam to the gum of (a sealed envelope) to open it. □ **blow** (or **let**) **off steam** release one's pent up feelings or energy. **full steam ahead** with as much speed and vigour as possible. **get up steam 1** generate enough power to work a steam engine. **2** work oneself into an energetic or angry state. **lose steam** slow down. **pick up steam** speed up. **run out of steam** = RUN OUT OF GAS (see GAS). **under one's own steam** without assistance. □ **steamed** *adj.*

steam bath *n.* **1** a room etc. filled with steam for

cleaning or refreshing oneself by sweating. **2** a bath taken in such a room.

steamboat *n.* a boat propelled by a steam engine.

steamed up *adj.* **1** (of a surface) covered with condensed vapour. **2** agitated or upset; angry.

steam engine *n.* **1** an engine using the expansion or condensation of steam to generate power. **2** a locomotive powered by such an engine.

steamer *n.* **1** a thing that steams. **2** a ship etc. propelled by steam. **3** a usu. perforated container in which food is cooked by steam. **4** (also **steamer clam**) the edible longneck clam, *Mya arenaria*.

steamie *n. Cdn* (*Que.*) a steamed hot dog.

steam iron *n.* an electric iron that emits steam from its flat surface, to improve its pressing ability.

steam power *n.* the force of steam applied to machinery etc. □ **steam-powered** *adj.*

steamroller ● *n.* **1** a heavy slow-moving vehicle with a roller, used for levelling roads. **2** a crushing power or force. ● *v.tr.* (also esp. *N Amer.* **steamroll**) **1** crush forcibly or indiscriminately. **2** (foll. by *through*) force (a measure etc.) through a legislature by overriding opposition.

steam room *n.* a room that may be filled with steam for taking steam baths.

steamship *n.* a ship propelled by a steam engine.

steamy *adj.* (**-ier, -iest**) **1** like or full of steam. **2** *informal* erotic, passionate. **3** hot and humid (*a steamy July night*). □ **steamily** *adv.* **steaminess** *n.*

steed *n. archaic* or *literary* a fast powerful horse.

steel ● *n.* **1** a durable alloy of iron with carbon and usu. other elements, used as a structural and fabricating material. **2** toughness, strength (*nerves of steel*). **3 a** a steel rod for sharpening knives. **b** a piece of steel used with a flint to produce sparks. **4** *Cdn* a railway track or line. ● *adj.* **1** made of steel. **2** like steel. ● *v.tr. & refl.* harden or make resolute (*steeled myself for a shock*).

steel band *n.* a group of musicians who play (chiefly calypso-style) music on steel drums.

steel blue ● *n.* a dark bluish-grey colour. ● *adj.* (**steel-blue**) of this colour.

steel drum *n.* a percussion instrument made out of an oil drum with one end beaten down and divided into grooved sections to give different notes.

steel grey ● *n.* a dark metallic grey colour. ● *adj.* (**steel-grey**) of this colour.

steel guitar *n.* **1** a type of hand-held acoustic guitar with steel resonating discs inside the body under the bridge. **2** = HAWAIIAN GUITAR.

steelhead *n.* a large silvery N American rainbow trout, esp. after returning from the sea or when found in the Great Lakes and tributaries.

steelie *n. informal* **1** a steel ball bearing used as a marble. **2** *N Amer.* a steelhead.

steelmaker *n.* a business that manufactures steel. □ **steelmaking** *n. & adj.*

steel wool *n.* an abrasive substance consisting of a mass of fine steel threads, used for cleaning metal, making a surface smooth, etc.

steelworks *n.pl.* (usu. treated as *sing.*) (also **steel mill**) a plant where steel is manufactured. □ **steelworker** *n.*

steely *adj.* (**-ier, -iest**) **1** of, or hard as, steel. **2** inflexibly severe; cold; ruthless (*steely composure*; *steely-eyed*). □ **steeliness** *n.*

steep[1] *adj.* **1** sloping sharply (*a steep hill*). **2** (of a rise or fall) rapid (*a steep drop in prices*). **3** (*predic.*) *informal* (of a price etc.) exorbitant; unreasonable. □ **steepen** *v.intr. & tr.* **steeply** *adv.* **steepness** *n.*

steep² v. **1** tr. & intr. soak in liquid (*the tea is steeping*). **2** tr. (foll. by *in*; usu. in *passive*) **a** pervade or imbue with (*steeped in misery*). **b** make deeply acquainted with (a subject) (*steeped in the classics*).

steeple n. a tall tower, esp. one surmounted by a spire, above the roof of a church. □ **steepled** adj.

steeplechase n. **1** a horse race across the country-side or on a racecourse with ditches, hedges, etc., to jump. **2** a cross-country foot race. □ **steeplechaser** n. **steeplechasing** n.

steer¹ ● v. **1** tr. & intr. direct the course of (a boat, vehicle, aircraft, etc.). **2** intr. (of a vehicle or vessel) move in a particular direction as a result of being steered (*the boat steered around the rocks*). **3** tr. & intr. direct (one's course), esp. in a specified direction (*steered for shore*). **4** tr. guide (a person, action, etc.) by advice or instruction etc. **5** tr. guide the movement or trend of (*steered the conversation away from that subject*). ● n. esp. N Amer. a piece of advice or information. □ **steer clear of** take care to avoid. □ **steerable** adj. **steerer** n. **steering** n. (esp. in sense 1 of v.).

steer² n. a castrated male of domestic cattle, esp. one raised for beef.

steerage n. esp. hist. the part of a ship allotted to passengers travelling at the cheapest rate.

steering column n. the shaft or column which connects the steering wheel, handlebars, etc. of a vehicle to the rest of the steering gear.

steering committee n. (also **steering group**) a committee that decides the order of certain business activities and guides their general course.

steering wheel n. a wheel by which a vehicle etc. is steered.

steer wrestling n. N Amer. a rodeo event in which a contestant on a horse chases a steer, dismounts, and wrestles the steer to the ground. □ **steer wrestler** n.

stegosaurus n. (also **stegosaur**) a plant-eating dinosaur of the suborder Stegosauria, with a double row of large bony plates along the back.

stein /stʌɪn/ n. **1** a large (usu. earthenware) mug, esp. for beer. **2** the quantity contained in such a mug.

stellar adj. **1** of or relating to a star or stars. **2** esp. N Amer. **a** having star performers (*stellar cast*). **b** informal outstanding (*a stellar performance*).

Steller's jay n. a blue jay, *Cyanocitta stelleri*, found in central and western N America.

Steller's sea lion n. a large red-brown sea lion, *Eumetopias jubatus*, of the northern Pacific.

stem¹ ● n. **1** the main body or stalk of a plant or shrub. **2 a** the stalk supporting a fruit, flower, or leaf, and attaching it to a larger branch, twig, or stalk. **b** a stalk supporting or forming part of an organ or structure (*brain stem*). **3** a stem-shaped part of an object: **a** the slender part of a wineglass between the body and the base. **b** the tube of a tobacco pipe. **c** a vertical stroke in a letter or musical note. **d** the winding shaft of a watch. **4** Grammar the root or main part of a noun, verb, etc., to which inflections are added. **5** Naut. the main upright timber or metal piece at the bow of a ship to which the ship's sides are joined at the fore end. ● v. (**stemmed, stemming**) **1** intr. (foll. by *from*) spring or originate from. **2** tr. remove the stem or stems from (fruit, tobacco, etc.). □ **stemless** adj. **stemlike** adj. **stemmed** adj. (also in comb.). **stemmy** adj.

stem² ● v. (**stemmed, stemming**) **1** tr. check or stop. **2** tr. dam up (a stream etc.). **3** intr. slide the tail of one ski or both skis outwards usu. in order to turn or slow down. ● n. an act of stemming on skis.

stem cell n. an undifferentiated cell from which specialized cells develop.

stemware n. esp. N Amer. crystal or glass vessels with rounded bowls on stems, used esp. for wine.

stench n. a foul smell.

stencil ● n. **1** a thin sheet of plastic etc., in which a pattern or lettering is cut, used to produce a corresponding pattern on the surface beneath it by applying ink, paint, etc. to the cut-out areas. **2** the pattern, lettering, etc., produced by a stencil. ● v.tr. (**-cilled, -cilling**) produce (a pattern) or decorate (a surface) with a stencil.

stenography /stəˈnɒɡrəfi/ n. the art of writing shorthand. □ **stenographer** n. **stenographic** adj.

stenosis /stɪˈnoːsɪs/ n. Med. the abnormal narrowing of a passage in the body. □ **stenotic** /-ˈnɒtɪk/ adj.

stentorian /stenˈtɔːrɪən/ adj. (of a voice, sound, etc.) very loud and powerful.

step ● n. **1 a** the complete movement of one leg in walking or running. **b** the distance covered by this. **c** (in pl.) the course followed by a person in walking etc. (*retraced her steps*). **2** a unit of movement in dancing. **3** a measure taken, esp. one of several in a course of action, advancement, etc. **4** a flat-topped structure used singly or as one of a series, for passing from one level to another. **5** a short distance (*only a step from my door*). **6** the sound or mark made by a foot in walking etc. (*heard a step on the stairs*). ● v. (**stepped, stepping**) **1** intr. lift and set down one's foot in walking. **2** intr. come or go in a specified direction by stepping. **3** intr. make progress in a specified way (*stepped into a new job*). **4** tr. perform (a dance). □ **in step** (often foll. by *with*) **1** stepping in time with music or other marchers. **2** conforming with others. **in a person's steps** following a person's example. **keep step** remain in step. **out of step** (often foll. by *with*) not in step. **step by step** gradually; cautiously; by stages or degrees. **step down 1** (also **step aside**) resign from a position etc. **2** Electricity decrease (voltage) by using a transformer. **step forward** offer one's help, services, etc. **step in 1** enter a room, house, etc. **2 a** intervene to help or hinder. **b** act as a substitute for an indisposed colleague etc. **step into a person's shoes** take control of a task or job from another person. **step on it** (or **on the gas**) informal **1** accelerate a motor vehicle. **2** hurry up. **step out 1** leave temporarily. **2** be active socially. **step out of line** behave inappropriately or disobediently. **step up 1** increase, intensify (*must step up production*). **2** come forward for some purpose. **watch one's step** be careful. □ **stepless** adj. **step-like** adj. **stepped** adj.

stepbrother n. a son of one's stepmother or step-father by an earlier marriage.

step-by-step attrib.adj. (of an approach, guide, etc.) that proceeds through or involves a series of distinct stages or operations.

stepchild n. a child of one's husband or wife by a previous marriage.

step dance ● n. a dance intended to display special steps by an individual performer, esp. popular in Celtic cultures. ● v.intr. (**step-dance**) perform a step dance. □ **step dancer** n. **step-dancing** n.

stepdaughter n. a female stepchild.

stepfather n. a male step-parent.

step-in ● n. a garment or shoe put on by stepping into it. ● attrib.adj. (of a garment or shoe) put on by being stepped into without unfastening.

stepladder n. a short folding ladder, used without being leaned against a surface.

stepmother *n.* a female step-parent.

step-parent *n.* a mother's or father's later spouse.

steppe /step/ *n.* a level grassy unforested plain, esp. in SE Europe and Siberia.

stepped-up *attrib.adj.* raised by degrees to a higher level; increased, intensified.

stepper *n.* **1** an exercise machine used to simulate the activity of climbing stairs. **2** *informal* a person who steps, esp. a dancer.

stepping stone *n.* **1** a raised stone, usu. one of a series, to facilitate crossing a stream, muddy ground, etc. on foot. **2** something used as a means of advancement in a career etc.

stepsister *n.* a daughter of one's stepmother or stepfather by an earlier marriage.

stepson *n.* a male stepchild.

-ster *suffix* denoting a person engaged in or associated with a particular activity or thing (*gangster*; *youngster*).

stereo ● *n.* (*pl.* **-os**) **1** a stereophonic CD player, tape deck, etc. **2** stereophony (*broadcast in stereo*). ● *adj.* **1** = stereophonic. **2** stereoscopic.

stereophonic *adj.* (of sound reproduction) using two or more channels so that the sound has the effect of being distributed and of coming from more than one source. □ **stereophony** *n.*

stereoscope *n.* a device by which two photographs of the same object taken at slightly different angles are viewed together, giving an impression of depth. □ **stereoscopic** *adj.* **stereoscopically** *adv.*

stereotype ● *n.* **1 a** a widely held but fixed and oversimplified image of a particular type of person or thing. **b** a person or thing appearing to conform to such an image. **2** a printing plate cast from a mould of composed type. ● *v.tr.* **1** (esp. as **stereotyped** *adj.*) view or represent as a stereotype. **2 a** print from a stereotype. **b** make a stereotype of. □ **stereotypic** /-'tɪpɪk/ *adj.* **stereotypical** *adj.* **stereotypically** *adv.*

sterile /'sterail, 'sterɪl/ *adj.* **1** not able to produce children or young; infertile. **2** free from bacteria etc. (*sterile bandages*). **3** unfruitful, unproductive (*sterile discussions*). **4** lacking originality or emotive force (*the room felt cold and sterile*). **5** (of plants) not producing fruit or seeds. □ **sterility** /stə'rɪlɪti/ *n.*

sterilize *v.tr.* **1** make sterile. **2** deprive of the ability to produce offspring. □ **sterilizable** *adj.* **sterilization** *n.* **sterilizer** *n.*

sterling ● *adj.* **1** of or in British money (*pound sterling*). **2** denoting silver of 92^1/$_4$% purity. **3** made of sterling silver. **4** (of a person or their work or qualities) excellent, valuable. ● *n.* **1** British money. **2** sterling silver. **3** articles of sterling silver, esp. tableware.

stern[1] *adj.* strict, serious, severe, strict (*a stern expression*; *stern treatment*). □ **sternly** *adv.* **sternness** *n.*

stern[2] *n.* the rear part, esp. of a boat. □ **sterned** *adj.*

sternum *n.* (*pl.* **-s** or **sterna**) the breastbone. □ **sternal** *adj.*

sternwheeler *n.* a steamer propelled by a paddlewheel positioned at the stern.

steroid /'steroid, 'sti:roid/ *n.* any of a group of organic compounds with a structure of four rings of carbon atoms, including many hormones, alkaloids, and vitamins, used to treat various diseases and to increase muscle size. □ **steroidal** /-'rɔidəl/ *adj.*

sterol /'sterɒl/ *n. Chem.* any of a group of naturally occurring steroid alcohols.

stethoscope *n.* an instrument used to listen to the action of the heart, lungs, etc., usu. consisting of a circular piece placed against the chest, with flexible tubes leading to earpieces.

Stetson *n. proprietary* a soft hat with a very wide brim and a high crown, associated with cowboys.

stevedore /'sti:və,dɔr/ ● *n.* a person employed in loading and unloading ships. ● *v.tr.* load or unload the cargo of (a ship). □ **stevedoring** *n. & adj.*

stew ● *v.* **1** *tr. & intr.* simmer in a pot, slow cooker, etc. **2** *intr. informal* be oppressed by heat or humidity, esp. in a confined space. **3** *intr. informal* **a** suffer prolonged embarrassment, anxiety, etc. **b** (foll. by *about, over*) fret or be anxious. ● *n.* **1** a dish of stewed meat, fish, vegetables, etc. **2** *informal* an agitated or angry state. **3** a mixture (*a stew of different sounds*). □ **stew in one's own juice** (or **juices**) be left to suffer the consequences of one's actions.

steward ● *n.* **1** a passengers' attendant on an aircraft, ship, or train. **2** an official appointed to keep order or supervise arrangements at a large public event. **3** = SHOP STEWARD. **4** a person responsible for supplies of food etc. for a college or club etc. **5 a** a person employed to manage another's property, esp. a large house or land. **b** (esp. in the United Church) a layperson appointed to manage the financial affairs of a congregation or circuit. ● *v.tr.* act as a steward of. □ **stewardship** *n.*

stewardess *n.* a female flight attendant. ¶*Flight attendant* is now usu. preferred.

stewed *adj.* **1** cooked by stewing. **2** *informal* drunk.

stewing beef *n.* beef cut up into chunks suitable for making stew.

stewpot *n.* **1** a pot for cooking stew. **2** a mixture.

stick[1] *n.* **1 a** slender branch broken or cut from a tree. **2** a thin wooden rod or branch for a particular purpose (*Popsicle stick*; *hockey stick*; *walking stick*). **3** something resembling a stick (*stick of gum*). **4 a** = STICK SHIFT. **b** = JOYSTICK. **5** (in *pl.*; prec. by *the*) *informal* remote rural areas. □ **stick-like** *adj.*

stick[2] *v.* (*past* and *past part.* **stuck**) **1** *tr.* insert or thrust (a thing or its point) (*stuck a finger in my eye*; *stick a pin through it*). **2** *tr.* insert a pointed thing into; stab. **3** *tr. & intr.* (foll. by *in, into, on,* etc.) **a** fix or be fixed on a pointed thing. **b** fix or be fixed by or as by a pointed end. **4** *tr. & intr.* fix or become or remain fixed by or as by adhesive (*the label won't stick*). **5** *intr.* endure; make a continued impression (*the scene stuck in my mind*; *the name stuck*). **6** *intr.* lose or be deprived of the power of motion or action through adhesion or jamming or other impediment. **7** *informal* **a** *tr.* put in a specified position or place, esp. quickly or haphazardly (*stick it in your pocket*). **b** *intr.* remain or be confined in a place (*stuck indoors*). **8** *informal* **a** *intr.* (of an accusation etc.) be convincing or regarded as valid (*could not make the charges stick*). **b** *tr.* (foll. by *on*) place the blame for (a thing) on (a person). **9** *tr.* (foll. by *at*) *informal* persevere with. □ **stick around** *informal* linger; remain at the same place. **stick by** (or **with** or **to**) stay loyal or close to. **stick 'em up!** *informal* hands up! **stick fast** adhere or become firmly fixed or trapped in a position or place. **stick in one's throat** be against one's principles. **stick it out** *informal* persevere. **stick it to (a person)** *N Amer. informal* **1** treat unfairly; cheat or take advantage of. **2** get even with; achieve revenge. **stick one's chin out** show firmness or fortitude. **stick one's neck** (or **chin**) **out** expose oneself to censure etc. by acting or speaking boldly. **stick out** protrude or cause to protrude or project (*stuck his tongue out*). **stick out like a sore thumb** *informal* be very obvious or incongruous. **stick to 1** remain close to or fixed on or to. **2** remain faithful to. **3** keep to (a subject etc.) (*stick to the point*). **stick together** *informal* remain united or mutually loyal. **stick to it** persevere. **stick to the ribs** (of food) be hearty and filling. **stick up 1** be or make erect or protruding upwards. **2** fasten to an upright surface. **3** *informal* rob or threaten with a gun. **stick up for** support or defend (a person or cause). **stick up to** be assertive in the face of; offer resistance to. **stick with** *informal* remain in touch with or faithful to; persevere with.

stickball *n.* a form of baseball using a rubber ball and a broomstick etc., usu. played by children.

sticker ● *n.* **1** an adhesive label, price tag, picture, etc. **2** a person or thing that sticks. **3** a thin strip of wood placed between stacked logs or pieces of timber to separate them and allow for ventilation. ● *v.tr. N Amer.* attach a sticker to (a CD, tape, etc.) warning that the lyrics may be offensive.

sticker price *n.* the full asking price for an item, esp. a car, from which a discount may be deducted.

sticker shock *n. N Amer. informal* shock experienced on discovering the high, or increased, price of a product, esp. a big-ticket item such as a car.

stick figure *n.* a figure drawn in thin simple lines.

stickhandle *v.* **1** *intr. Hockey* skilfully control the puck with the stick. **2** *intr. & tr. Cdn* manoeuvre skilfully around (an issue etc.) □ **stickhandler** *n.* **stickhandling** *n.*

sticking point *n.* the limit of progress, agreement, etc.

stick-in-the-mud *n. informal* an unprogressive or old-fashioned person.

stickleback *n.* a small fish of the family Gasterosteidae, with sharp spines along the back.

stickler *n.* **1** a person who insists on something (*a stickler for detail*). **2** a difficult problem or puzzle.

stick-on *adj.* adhesive (*stick-on address labels*).

stick shift *n. N Amer.* **1** a manual transmission for a motor vehicle. **2** a motor vehicle having a manual transmission. **3** = GEARSHIFT.

stickup *n. informal* a robbery using a gun.

stickwork *n. Hockey* interference with the stick, e.g. butt-ending, slashing, etc.

sticky (**-ier, -iest**) ● *adj.* **1** tending or intended to stick. **2** glutinous, viscous. **3 a** (of the weather) humid. **b** damp with sweat. **4** *informal* awkward, uncooperative, difficult (*a sticky problem*). ● *n.* (*pl.* **-ies**) *informal* = POST-IT. □ **stickily** *adv.* **stickiness** *n.*

sticky bun *n.* a sweet bread roll covered with a sticky glaze or icing or with a syrup-coated bottom.

sticky tape *n.* clear adhesive tape.

stiff ● *adj.* **1** rigid; not flexible. **2** hard to move or turn etc.; not working freely. **3** thick; capable of retaining a definite shape (*beat egg whites until stiff*). **4** demanding strength or effort (*a stiff climb*). **5** severe or strong (*a stiff breeze; stiff opposition; a stiff drink*). **6** (of a person or manner) formal, constrained; not relaxed. **7** aching due to previous exertion, injury, etc. (*stiff shoulder*). **8** (of a price, demand, etc.) exorbitant. **9** (foll. by *with*) *informal* full of (*stiff with tourists*). ● *adv. informal* to an extreme degree (*bored stiff*). ● *n. slang* **1 a** corpse. **2 a** a foolish or useless person. **b** an ordinary person (*a working stiff*). **3** a commercial venture (esp. in the entertainment business) which merits or meets with public indifference. ● *v. esp. N Amer. slang* **1** *tr.* cheat; refuse to pay or tip. **2** *tr.* kill, murder. **3** *intr.* fail to sell well or be popular (*his last album stiffed*). □ **stiffish** *adj.* **stiffly** *adv.* **stiffness** *n.*

stiffen *v.tr. & intr.* make or become stiff. □ **stiffener** *n.* **stiffening** *n.*

stiff-necked *adj.* obstinate or haughty.

stiff upper lip *n.* fortitude; stoicism in adversity.

stifle /ˈstʌɪfəl/ *v.* **1** prevent or constrain (an activity or idea) (*high taxes were stifling small businesses*). **2** *tr.* smother, suppress (*stifled a yawn*). **3** *tr. & intr.* suffocate; stop or cause to stop breathing.

stifling *adj.* **1** unbearably hot. **2** oppressive. □ **stiflingly** *adv.*

stigma *n.* (*pl.* **-mata** or **-mas**) **1 a** a mark or sign of disgrace or discredit. **b** an unfavourable reputation. **2** the part of a pistil that receives the pollen in pollination. **3** (usu. as **stigmata** *pl.*) (in Christian belief) marks corresponding to those left on Christ's body by the Crucifixion, said to have been impressed by divine favour on the bodies of others. **4** a mark or spot on the skin or on a butterfly's wing. **5** *Med.* a visible sign or characteristic of a disease.

stigmatic /stɪɡˈmætɪk/ ● *adj.* of a stigma or stigmata. ● *n. Christianity* a person bearing stigmata.

stigmatize /ˈstɪɡmə,tʌɪz/ *v.tr.* **1** (often foll. by **as**) describe as discreditable or undesirable. **2** *Christianity* produce stigmata on. □ **stigmatization** *n.*

stile *n.* an arrangement of steps allowing people but not farm animals to climb over a fence or wall.

stiletto /stɪˈlɛtoː/ *n.* (*pl.* **-os**) **1** a short dagger with a thick blade. **2** (in full **stiletto heel**) **a** a high heel on a women's shoe. **b** a shoe with such a heel.

still¹ ● *adj.* **1** not or hardly moving. **2** quiet; calm and tranquil (*a still evening*). ● *n.* **1** deep silence and calm (*in the still of the night*). **2** an ordinary static photograph (as opposed to a motion picture), esp. a single shot from a cinema film. ● *adv.* **1** without moving (*stand still*). **2** even now or at a particular time. **3** nevertheless; all the same. **4** (with *comparative* etc.) even, yet, increasingly (*still greater efforts*). ● *v.tr. & intr.* make or become still; quieten. □ **still and all** *informal* nevertheless. **still waters run deep** a quiet manner conceals depths of feeling or knowledge or cunning. □ **stillness** *n.*

still² *n.* an apparatus for distilling alcoholic drinks.

stillbirth *n.* the birth of a dead child.

stillborn *adj.* **1** (of a child) born dead. **2** (of an idea, plan, etc.) abortive; not able to succeed.

still life *n.* (*pl.* **still lifes**) **1** a painting, drawing, or photograph of inanimate objects such as fruit or flowers. **2** this genre of art.

stilt *n.* **1** either of a pair of poles with supports for the feet enabling the user to walk at a distance above the ground. **2** each of a set of piles or posts supporting a building etc. **3** any wading bird of the genus *Himantopus*, with long slender legs.

stilted *adj.* **1** (of a literary style etc.) stiff and unnatural. **2** standing on stilts. □ **stiltedly** *adv.*

Stilton *n. proprietary* a kind of strong rich cheese, often with blue veins, originally made in S England.

stimulant ● *n.* **1** an agent that stimulates, esp. a drug or alcohol. **2** a stimulating influence. ● *adj.* that stimulates, esp. bodily or mental activity.

stimulate *v.tr.* **1** apply or act as a stimulus to. **2** animate, excite, arouse. **3** be a stimulant to. □ **stimulating** *adj.* **stimulatingly** *adv.* **stimulation** *n.* **stimulator** *n.* **stimulatory** *adj.*

stimulus *n.* (*pl.* **stimuli**) **1** a thing that rouses to activity or energy. **2** a stimulating or rousing effect. **3** a thing that evokes a specific functional reaction in an organ or tissue.

sting ● *n.* **1** a sharp painful wound inflicted by any of a number of insects, animals, and plants. **2** a sharp physical pain like that of a bee or wasp sting. **3** (often foll. by *of*) the painful or hurtful quality or effect of something (*the sting of poverty; the sting of her satire*). **4**

(in full **sting operation**) esp. *N Amer.* an undercover operation in which police officers, attempting to implicate a presumed criminal, pose as buyers or sellers in an ostensibly illegal transaction. **5** *slang* a swindle or robbery. **6** = STINGER[1] 1a. ● *v.* (*past and past part.* **stung**) **1 a** *tr. & intr.* (of an insect etc.) prick or pierce with a sting. **b** *intr.* be capable of stinging. **2** *tr. & intr.* cause or be capable of causing a sharp physical or emotional pain or irritation, or emotional pain (in a person). **3** *intr.* feel such pain (*my fingers are stinging from the cold*). **4** *tr. informal* **a** cause to suffer a financial loss or hardship (*small businesses were stung by the recession*). **b** cheat, swindle. □ **stinging** *adj.* **stingingly** *adv.* **stingless** *adj.*

stinger[1] *n.* **1** *N Amer.* **a** a sharp organ in various insects and other animals capable of inflicting a dangerous and painful wound, esp. by injecting poison. **b** (in plants) a stiff sharp hair which emits an irritating fluid when touched. **c** a stinging insect, nettle, etc. **2** a sharp painful blow or comment.

stinger[2] *n.* *N Amer.* a drink made with brandy and crème de menthe.

stinging nettle *n.* a nettle, *Urtica dioica*, with stinging hairs, small green flowers, and strongly toothed oval leaves.

stingray *n.* any of various broad flatfish esp. of the family Dasyatidae, having a flattened, roughly diamond-shaped body tapering to a tail with a long poisonous serrated stine at its base.

stingy *adj.* (**-ier, -iest**) **1** unwilling to give, spend, or use resources. **2** (of a portion, supply, etc.) given sparingly or grudgingly; meagre. **3** *Sport* (of a team, goaltender, etc.) giving up few goals, points, or scoring opportunities. □ **stingily** *adv.* **stinginess** *n.*

stink ● *v.* (*past* **stank** or **stunk**; *past part.* **stunk**) **1** *intr.* emit a strong offensive smell. **2** *intr. informal* **a** be abhorrently or offensively bad or inept (*this team stinks*). **b** be unbearably unpleasant (*her job stinks*). **3** *tr. & intr.* (foll. by *up*) fill (a place) with an offensive odour. **4** *intr. informal* have or be surrounded by an offensive amount of something (*the affair stinks of scandal*). ● *n.* **1** a strong or offensive smell; a stench. **2** *informal* a fuss. **3** *informal* a scandal. □ **like stink** *informal* extremely hard or fast etc. (*working like stink*).

stinker *n.* *slang* **1** a difficult or unpleasant person or thing. **2** something of inferior quality. **3** any person or thing that gives off a foul or offensive odour.

stinking ● *adj.* **1** that gives off a foul or offensive odour. **2** *slang* (*a stinking liar*). ● *adv. slang* extremely and usu. to an objectionable degree (*stinking rich*). □ **stinkingly** *adv.*

stinko *adj. slang* drunk.

stinky *adj.* (**-ier, -iest**) *informal* having a strong or unpleasant smell.

stint ● *v.* **1** *tr.* use, spend, offer, or distribute grudgingly or in small amounts (*she never stinted her praise for him*). **2** *intr.* (often foll. by *on*) be sparing or cheap; economize. ● *n.* **1** a short period of time. **2** a limitation of supply or effort (*without stint*).

stipe *n. Bot. & Zool.* a stalk or stem, such as that which supports the cap of a mushroom or toadstool.

stipend /ˈstaɪpɛnd/ *n.* **1** a salary or fixed regular sum paid for the services of a teacher, public official, or clergyman. **2** any fixed regular payment, such as an allowance or scholarship.

stipple ● *v.* **1** *tr. & intr.* mark (a surface) with small spots or flecks. **2** *tr.* produce a roughened or gritty texture on (paint or cement etc.). ● *n.* **1** (also **stippling**) the process or technique of providing a surface etc. with

a dotted or textured appearance. **2** work that has been produced using this technique.

stipulate /ˈstɪpjʊˌleɪt/ *v.tr.* **1** demand or specify as an essential part or condition of an agreement or contract etc. **2** promise or guarantee. □ **stipulation** *n.*

stipulated /ˈstɪpjʊˌleɪtəd/ *adj.* specified or set out in the terms of a contract or agreement.

stir[1] ● *v.* (**stirred, stirring**) **1** *tr. & intr.* move a spoon or other utensil around and around in (a liquid or soft mass) in order to mix the ingredients. **2** *tr.* cause to move or be disturbed, esp. slightly (*a breeze stirred the lake*). **3** *intr.* **a** move or begin to move slightly (*not a creature was stirring*). **b** rise from sleep. **4 a** *tr.* arouse, inspire, or provoke (the emotions etc., or a person as regards these) (*was stirred to anger*). **b** *intr.* (of the emotions etc.) become active or excited (*anger stirred within my breast*). ● *n.* **1** commotion or excitement (*caused quite a stir*). **2** an act of stirring (*give it a stir*). **3** the slightest movement. □ **not stir a finger** make no effort to help. **stir in** add (an ingredient) to a substance or mixture while stirring. **stir up 1** cause, start, or instigate (trouble etc.). **2** provoke, excite, arouse (a person or emotion etc.). □ **stirrer** *n.*

stir[2] *n. slang* prison (*in stir*).

stir-crazy *adj.* **1** restless, antsy, or fidgety, esp. from prolonged confinement indoors. **2** deranged from long imprisonment.

stir-fry ● *n.* (*pl.* **-ies**) a dish of assorted vegetables and sometimes meat fried rapidly at a high temperature, esp. in a wok. ● *v.tr.* (**-ies, -ied**) fry rapidly at high heat while stirring and tossing, esp. in a wok.

stirring ● *adj.* inspiring, exciting. ● *n.* (usu. in *pl.*) **1** initial stages of a particular activity (*stirrings of revolt*). **2** initial feelings (*stirrings of sympathy*). □ **stirringly** *adv.*

stirrup *n.* **1** either of a pair of supports for the foot of a person riding a horse, consisting of a flat-based metal loop attached by a leather strap to each side of a saddle. **2** a thing shaped like a stirrup. **3** either of a pair of stirrup-shaped supports at the end of an examination table, on which patients place their heels during a gynecological exam. **4 a** a loop attached to the bottom of a pant leg meant to pass beneath the foot in order to keep the pants from rising above the ankle. **b** (*attrib.*) designating an article of clothing having such straps (*stirrup pants*). **5** (in full **stirrup bone**) = STAPES.

stitch ● *n.* **1 a** (in sewing) a single pass of a threaded needle in and out of a fabric. **b** the resulting loop of thread left in the fabric between two successive needle holes. **c** (usu. with *neg.*) the least bit of fabric of an article of clothing (*hadn't a stitch on*). **2 a** a single complete movement of the needle used in knitting, crochet, embroidery, etc. **b** a particular method of knitting or crochet etc. **3** (usu. in *pl.*) *Surgery* each of the loops of material used in sewing up a wound. **4** a painful cramp in the side of the body often resulting from vigorous exercise. ● *v.tr.* **1** (usu. foll. by *up*) **a** join (one or more pieces of fabric) with a line or series of stitches. **b** make or mend (clothing etc.) by sewing. **2** (usu. foll. by *on*) fasten or attach by sewing. **3** decorate with stitches; embroider. □ **in stitches** *informal* laughing uncontrollably. **stitch in time** a timely or preventative remedy. □ **stitcher** *n.* **stitching** *n.*

Stl'atl'imx /ˈstætliːəm/ ● *n.* **1** a member of an Aboriginal people living northeast of Vancouver. **2** the Salishan language of this people. ● *adj.* of or relating to this people.

stn. *abbr.* **1** station. **2** (**Stn.**) *Cdn* Postal Station.

stochastic /stəˈkæstɪk/ *adj.* randomly determined;

having a random probability distribution or pattern that may be analyzed statistically but may not be predicted precisely.

stock ● n. **1** a supply of merchandise etc. available for sale or distribution. **2** a supply of anything, esp. acquired or allowed to accumulate for future use (*cod stocks*). **3** the raw materials or equipment used in the manufacture of a particular product. **4** = LIVESTOCK. **5 a** capital raised by a business etc. through the issue and subscription of shares. **b** a quantity of shares represented by a certificate, the holder of which is considered a part owner of the company, entitled to receive dividends of its profits. **c** a quantity of shares in a commodity or industry etc. (*gold stock*). **d** a security issued by the government or a company in fixed units with a fixed rate of interest. **6** one's reputation or popularity (*his stock is rising*). **7** liquid made by stewing bones, vegetables, etc., used as a basis for soup, gravy, etc. **8 a** one's ancestry or line of descent (*she is of Prairie stock*). **b** a family (of human beings, animals, plants, or languages). **9 a** a roll of film that has not been exposed or processed. **b** a selection of esp. outdoor scenes and cityscapes used to lend verisimilitude to a production shot on a set (also *attrib.: stock footage*). **10 a** the trunk or stem of a tree or shrub, esp. one into which a graft is inserted. **b** a plant from which cuttings are taken. **11** any plant of the cruciferous genus *Matthiola* or related genera, esp. Virginia stock, *Malcolmia maritima*. **12** (in *pl.*) *hist.* a wooden structure with holes for securing a person's feet and hands, used for punishing criminals, usu. in public. **13 a** = STOCK COMPANY 2. **b** the repertory of a stock company. **14** the handle, support, or base of a tool or machine. **15 a** the usu. wooden part of a rifle to which the barrel is attached. **b** an analogous part of an automatic or semi-automatic weapon. **16** = ROLLING STOCK. ● *adj.* **1** kept regularly in stock for sale, distribution, or use. **2 a** common or conventional (*a stock character*). **b** (of a theme, phrase, etc.) hackneyed, trite. ● *v.tr.* **1** have or keep (merchandise) available for sale or use. **2 a** furnish (a store or farm etc.) with goods, equipment, or livestock. **b** fill (a shelf) with merchandise. **c** fill (a pond etc.) with fish. **3** fit (a gun) with a stock. □ **in stock** on the premises of a store or warehouse etc. and available for immediate sale. **out of stock** not available for immediate sale. **stock up 1** obtain or purchase stocks or supplies. **2** (foll. by *on* or *with*) obtain or purchase a supply of (food, fuel, etc.). **take stock 1** make an inventory of one's stock. **2** (often foll. by *of*) assess or review (a situation etc.). **3** (foll. by *in*) concern oneself with; attach importance to. □ **stocked** *adj.*

stockade ● n. **1** a barrier of upright stakes, erected for defensive purposes. **2** esp. *N Amer.* a prison, esp. a military one. ● *v.tr.* fortify with a stockade.

stockbroker n. = BROKER 2. □ **stockbrokerage** n. **stockbroking** n.

stock car n. **1** a car with the basic chassis of a commercially produced vehicle, modified for a form of racing in which collisions often occur. **2** *N Amer.* a boxcar used to transport livestock.

stock company n. *N Amer.* **1** a company the capital of which is divided into shares represented by stock. **2** a repertory company performing esp. at a particular theatre.

stocker n. esp. *N Amer.* an animal, esp. a young steer or heifer, destined for butchering but kept until matured or fattened (also *attrib.: stocker cattle*).

stock exchange n. **1** (also **Stock Exchange**) a building where stocks and shares are traded publicly.

2 the body of dealers working there. **3** the composite index of share prices or trading activity at a particular stock exchange.

stockholder n. an owner of stocks or shares. □ **stockholding** n.

stock index n. = COMPOSITE INDEX.

stocking n. **1 a** either of a pair of separate, close-fitting coverings for the feet and part or all of the leg worn by women, esp. one of diaphanous silk or nylon reaching the thigh and held up by a garter. **b** (in *pl.*) = PANTYHOSE. **c** esp. *N Amer.* = SOCK[1] 1. **2** any close-fitting article of clothing resembling a stocking (*body stocking*). **3** = CHRISTMAS STOCKING. **4** a cylindrical bandage for the leg, esp. one worn as a remedial support, such as for a leg affected with varicose veins. □ **in one's stocking** (or **stockinged**) **feet** wearing socks but no shoes. □ **stockinged** *adj.*

stocking cap n. a knitted toque with a long tapered end which hangs down.

stocking stuffer n. *N Amer.* a small usu. inexpensive present suitable for putting in a Christmas stocking.

stock-in-trade n. **1 a** the equipment required for a particular business. **b** merchandise, esp. kept in sufficient supply by a dealer or shopkeeper to maintain business. **2** a collection of attitudes, phrases, etc. characteristic of a person or group (*flippant remarks are part of his stock-in-trade*).

stockman n. (*pl.* **-men**) **1** a person employed to look after livestock on a farm. **2** an owner of livestock.

stock market n. **1** a stock exchange. **2** the level of transactions or prices in the national or international market for stocks.

stock option n. *N Amer. see* OPTION n. 3a.

stockpile ● n. an accumulated stock of goods, materials, weapons, etc., held in reserve and available for use esp. during a shortage or emergency. ● *v.tr.* accumulate a stockpile of.

stockpot n. a large pot with handles, used for making soup, stews, sauces, etc. in large quantities.

stock-still *adv.* completely motionless.

stock-taking n. **1** the process of making an inventory of goods or merchandise in a store or factory etc. **2** an evaluation, assessment, or review of one's situation, prospects, and resources.

stocky *adj.* (**-ier, -iest**) short and strongly built; thickset. □ **stockily** *adv.* **stockiness** n.

stockyard n. an enclosure with pens and sheds where livestock is temporarily confined and sorted, esp. prior to being sold, shipped, or slaughtered.

stodgy *adj.* (**-ier, -iest**) **1** (of food) heavy and filling. **2** tediously slow. **3** excessively conventional or traditional. **4** (of a person) clumsy or awkward, esp. due to obesity. □ **stodgily** *adv.* **stodginess** n.

stogie /ˈstoʊɡi/ n. (also **stogy**) (*pl.* **-ies**) *N Amer.* a cigar.

Stoic /ˈstoʊɪk/ ● n. **1** a member of the ancient Greek school of philosophy, which sought virtue as the greatest good and taught control of one's feelings and passions and indifference to the vicissitudes of fortune and pleasure and pain. **2** (**stoic**) a person who practises repression of emotion, indifference to pleasure and pain, and patient endurance in adversity. ● *adj.* **1** (**stoic**; also **stoical**) (of a person or behaviour) characterized by an austere impassivity or resignation characteristic of a Stoic. **2** of the school of the Stoics or its system of philosophy. □ **Stoically** *adv.* (also **stoically**). **Stoicism** /-əˌsɪzəm/ n. (also **stoicism**).

stoke v. (often foll. by *up*) **1** *tr.* feed or tend (a fire, furnace, etc.) to maintain or increase the heat. **2** *tr.* encourage, fuel (*her laughter stoked his anger*).

stoked *adj.* (often foll. by *up*) exhilarated, ecstatic.

stoker *n.* **1** a person who tends the furnace on a steamship. **2** a tool or esp. mechanical device used to feed or tend a fire.

STOL /stɒl/ *n.* (usu. *attrib.*) **1** designating aircraft designed to take off and land on a short runway. **2** designating an airport or runway etc. designed to accommodate such aircraft.

stole[1] *n.* **1** a woman's long scarf or shawl made esp. of fur or wool and worn loosely over the shoulders. **2** an ecclesiastical vestment consisting of a narrow strip of silk or linen, worn over one or both shoulders and hanging down to the knee or lower.

stole[2] *past of* STEAL.

stolen ● *v. past part. of* STEAL. ● *adj.* **1** obtained by theft (*stolen cars*). **2** accomplished or enjoyed by stealth or in secret (*enjoyed their stolen hours together*).

stolen base *n. Baseball* an instance of advancing to the next base while a pitch is being thrown.

stolid *adj.* **1** failing or unlikely to feel or express emotion. **2** failing or unlikely to excite emotion; dull, uninspired. □ **stolidly** *adv.* **stolidness** *n.*

Sto:lo /ˈstɒloː, ˈstoːloː/ ● *n.* **1** a member of an Aboriginal people living along the lower Fraser River, BC. **2** the Halkomelem language of this people. ● *adj.* of or relating to this people or language.

stomach ● *n.* **1 a** the internal organ in which the first part of digestion occurs, in humans a pear-shaped enlargement of the alimentary canal linking the esophagus to the small intestine. **b** any of several such organs in animals, esp. ruminants, in which there are four. **2 a** the belly or abdomen (*punched me in the stomach*). **b** a protuberant belly (*you're getting quite a stomach!*). **3 a** (usu. foll. by *for*) an appetite. **b** the ability to digest food without becoming sick (*has a weak stomach*). **4 a** courage, inclination (*you haven't got the stomach to fight*). **b** tolerance, appreciation (*I have no stomach for bickering politicians*). ● *v.tr.* **1** (usu. with *neg.*) tolerate, endure. **2 a** find sufficiently palatable to swallow or keep down (*can't stomach seafood*). **b** have sufficient appetite for (*couldn't stomach another bite*).

stomach ache *n.* a pain in the belly or abdominal region, esp. from indigestion.

stomach-churning *adj.* causing or tending to cause nausea (*a stomach-churning ride*).

stomach upset *n.* indigestion or nausea.

stomp ● *v.* **1** *intr.* walk with loud, heavy, deliberate steps, often as a sign of anger. **2** *tr.* Amer. stamp or trample on. **3** *intr.* dance or play a stomp. ● *n.* **1** any lively dance involving a heavy stamping step. **2** (also **stomper**) a tune or song with a percussive rhythm and upbeat tempo suitable for such a dance. **3** a heavy stamping step to the beat of such a dance. □ **stomp one's foot** beat out a rhythm with one's foot. □ **stomper** *n.*

stomping ground *n.* (usu. in *pl.*) a favourite or familiar haunt or place of action.

stone ● *n.* **1 a** solid non-metallic mineral matter, of which rock is made. **b** a piece of this. **2 a** (often in *comb.*) a piece of stone, usu. artificially shaped, used for some special purpose, such as building or paving. **b** = TOMBSTONE. **3** *Archit.* **a** = FIELDSTONE. **b** = LIMESTONE. **c** = SANDSTONE. **2. 4** a precious or semi-precious mineral or gemstone. **5** *Med.* (often in *pl.*) a hard abnormal concretion in the body, esp. in the kidney, the urinary bladder, or the gallbladder. **6** a stony endocarp enclosing the kernel of certain fruits, such as a peach, plum, or olive; a pit. **7** a shaped piece of stone used for grinding or sharpening something. **8** a brownish-grey colour. **9** (in full **curling stone**) =

ROCK[1] 7. ● *adj.* **1** made of stone. **2** of a brownish-grey colour. ● *adv.* completely, totally (*stone cold*). ● *v.tr.* **1** pelt with stones. **2** remove the stones from (fruit). **3** pave, line, or build up with stones. **4** *Hockey informal* (esp. of a goaltender) thwart (an opponent). □ **throw** (or **cast**) **stones** cast aspersions on a person's character etc. **throw** (or **cast**) **the first stone** be the first to make an accusation, esp. though guilty oneself. **leave no stone unturned** explore every possibility. **a stone's throw** a short distance.

Stone Age *n.* **1** a prehistoric period characterized by the use of weapons and tools made of stone. **2** (*attrib.*) (also **stone-age**) primitive, outmoded, obsolete.

stoneboat *n. N Amer.* a flat-bottomed sled used esp. for removing stones from fields.

stone circle *n. Archaeology* a group of (usu. large embedded) stones arranged in a circle.

stonecrop *n.* any succulent plant of the genus *Sedum*, usu. having yellow or white flowers and growing among rocks or in walls.

stonecut *n.* **1** an esp. Inuit printing technique in which an image engraved on the flat face of a stone that has been cut in half is impressed on paper with coloured inks. **2** a print made using this technique.

stonecutter *n.* a person or machine that cuts, shapes, or carves building or ornamental stone.

stoned *adj. slang* intoxicated.

stonefly *n.* (*pl.* **-flies**) **1** any insect of the order Plecoptera, whose larvae are found under stones in streams. **2** *Angling* a lure tied to resemble this.

stone fruit *n.* a fruit with pulp enclosing a stone.

stone-ground *adj.* **1** (of flour) ground using millstones rather than metal rollers. **2** (esp. of bread) made with stone-ground flour.

stonemason *n.* a person who cuts, prepares, and builds with stone.

Stone sheep *n.* (also **Stone's sheep**) a thinhorn sheep, *Ovis dalli stonei*, of the south central Yukon and northern Rockies of BC.

stonewall *v.* **1** *tr. & intr.* hold up (a discussion or interrogation etc.) by making lengthy speeches and vague or evasive answers. **2** *tr.* hinder or prevent (a person or thing) (*she stonewalled their attempt to pass the legislation*). **3** *tr. Sport* thwart (an opponent) with strong defence. □ **stonewalling** *n.*

stoneware *n.* a kind of dense, impermeable, usu. opaque pottery made from clay containing a high proportion of silica and partly vitrified during firing.

stonewash ● *n.* a worn or faded appearance given to denim by washing it with abrasives (also *attrib.*: *stonewash jeans*). ● *v.tr.* wash (denim etc.) with abrasives. □ **stonewashed** *adj.*

stonework *n.* **1** masonry. **2** the parts of a building made of stone. **3** the art of working with stone.

Stoney ● *n.* **1** a member of an Aboriginal people now living in southern Alberta, and formerly living in southern Manitoba and southern Saskatchewan. **2** any of the languages spoken by this people. ● *adj.* of this people or their languages.

stony *adj.* (also **stoney**) (**-ier, -iest**) **1** full of or covered with stones (*stony soil*). **2** lacking sensitivity or feeling; hardened. **3** (also **stony-faced**) cold, expressionless (*a stony gaze*). **4** (of silence, grief, fear, etc.) cold and harsh, grim, unrelenting. **5** having the hardness of stone; rigid. □ **stonily** *adv.*

stood *past and past part. of* STAND.

stooge *n.* **1** an unquestioningly loyal or obsequious assistant; a puppet. **2** a person of subordinate rank who performs esp. routine or unpleasant labour. **3** an entertainer who feeds lines to another comedian and serves as a butt of the other's jokes.

stook¹ /stʊk, stuːk/ *Cdn & Brit.* ● *n.* a small stack of bales of hay or straw, or sheaves of grain, collected in a field, esp. to hasten drying. ● *v.tr.* arrange (bales or sheaves) in stooks. □ **stooking** *n.*

stook² *n. Cdn (West)* a card game similar to blackjack but which may be played by several players.

stool *n.* **1** a seat without a back or arms. **2** a short low bench on which to step or kneel, or for resting the foot. **3** (often in *pl.*) = FECES. □ **fall between two stools** fail because of vacillation.

stool pigeon *n.* **1** a police informer. **2** a person acting as a decoy.

stoop¹ ● *v.* **1** *tr. & intr.* lower one's body by bending (the head and shoulders or trunk) forwards and downwards. **2** *intr.* carry one's head and shoulders habitually bowed forward. **3** *intr.* (foll. by *to*) lower oneself to conduct or a course of action considered morally reprehensible or beneath oneself. ● *n.* a stooping posture. □ **stoop and scoop** *Cdn* pick up the excrement of one's pet in parks and on streets etc. (also *attrib.*: *stoop and scoop law*). □ **stooped** *adj.*

stoop² *n. N Amer.* a small raised platform or set of steps at the entrance of a house.

stop ● *v.* (**stopped, stopping**) **1** *tr.* **a** check or impede the operation or onward movement of (a person or thing). **b** (often foll. by *from*) cause (a person or thing) to desist from or pause in a course of action; prevent (*stopped them from fighting*). **2** *tr.* suspend (an action) or desist from (an activity) (*it stopped raining; stopped smoking*). **3** *intr.* **a** leave off or pause momentarily in an activity (*she stopped in mid sentence*). **b** (of a thing, process, etc.) cease from motion, action, or operation (*my watch has stopped*). **4 a** *tr.* not permit or supply as usual; discontinue or withhold (*shall stop their wages*). **b** *intr.* come to an end; cease to occur as usual (*her weekly sessions have stopped*). **5** *intr.* cease from forward movement; come to a state of rest. **6** *tr. Sport* **a** defeat (an opponent). **b** block (a puck, ball, or shot). **c** *Boxing* defeat (an opponent) by a knockout or technical knockout. **7** *tr.* (often foll. by *up*) **a** fill or close up (a hole, leak, etc.). **b** plug or clog (a drain etc.). **8** *tr.* (in full **stop payment on** or **of**) instruct a bank to withhold payment on (a cheque). **9** *tr. Music* **a** obtain the required pitch from (the string of a guitar or violin etc.) by pressing it at the appropriate point. **b** close (a finger hole of a wind instrument) in order to alter the pitch. **10** *tr.* plug the upper end of (an organ pipe), giving a note an octave lower. ● *n.* **1** the act or an instance of stopping; the state of being stopped. **2 a** a place designated for a bus or subway etc. to stop for passengers to get on and off. **b** a stay of considerable duration at a place, esp. during the course of a journey. **3** an order stopping payment, esp. of a cheque. **4** a part of a mechanism, such as a pin, bolt, or block of wood, used to check the motion or thrust of something, keep another part in place, or determine the position of something. **5** *Sport* a save or tackle made on an opponent. **6 a** the effective diameter of a lens as indicated by an f-number. **b** a plate or diaphragm with a central hole used to reduce this. **c** a unit of change of relative aperture (or exposure or film speed), a reduction of one stop being equivalent to a halving of the value. **d** = DIAPHRAGM 3. **7** a change of pitch effected by stopping a string of a violin etc. or by blocking the finger hole of a wind instrument. **8 a** (in an organ) a graduated row of pipes producing tones of the same character. **b** the handle or knob by which air is admitted to or excluded from a set of organ pipes. **9** (in telegrams etc.) a period. □ **put a stop to** cause to end, esp. abruptly. **stop at nothing** do everything required to complete a task without being deterred by setbacks; be ruthless. **stop by** *N Amer.* visit. **stop dead** (or **short**) cease abruptly. **stop in** *N Amer.* = *stop by.* **stop over** rest or make a break in one's journey.

stop-and-go *adj.* alternately stopping and starting (*traffic is stop-and-go*).

stop-gap *n.* a temporary substitute or solution (also *attrib.*: *stop-gap measures*).

stoplight *n.* **1** a *N Amer.* a traffic light. **b** a red traffic light. **2** = BRAKE LIGHT.

stopover *n.* (also **stopoff**) **1** a brief stop in a journey. **2** such a stop made with the ability to proceed on the original ticket at a later time. **3** a city, hotel, etc. where one stops during a journey.

stoppage *n.* **1** an interruption of service, labour, a game, etc. (*a work stoppage*). **2** the condition of being blocked or plugged up.

stop-payment *n.* = STOP N. 3.

stopper ● *n.* **1** a plug for closing a bottle. **2** a plug used to close the drain of a bathtub or sink. **3** *Baseball* a relief pitcher who enters the game in the late stages to preserve a lead. **4** a thing that attracts and holds attention. ● *v.tr.* close or plug with a stopper.

stopping house *n. Cdn hist.* a modest house or inn offering accommodation to travellers.

stopping place *n.* **1** *Cdn hist.* **a** a settlement where groups of travellers customarily stop for food and lodging. **b** a stopping house. **2** a place at which a person, animal, or thing may stop.

stop sign *n.* a red octagonal sign at an intersection indicating that traffic should stop before proceeding.

stopwatch *n.* a watch with a mechanism for recording elapsed time, used to time races etc.

storage *n.* **1 a** the action of storing or keeping a thing or things in reserve; the condition of being stored. **b** space available or used for storing (also *attrib.*: *storage box*). **2** the cost of storing something. **3** *Computing* **a** the electronic retention of data in a device from which they can be retrieved. **b** (in full **storage device**) = MEMORY 4b.

store ● *n.* **1 a** *N Amer.* a building or establishment where merchandise and services are available for sale at retail prices. **b** a chain of retail outlets operating under one name. **2** a quantity of something available for future use; a supply (*a store of wit*). **3** (in *pl.*) articles such as food, clothing, weapons, etc., accumulated for a particular purpose, esp. to supply an army. **4** *Cdn (Nfld & Maritimes)* = FISH STORE 2. ● *v.tr.* **1 a** accumulate a supply of (goods etc.), esp. for future use. **b** place or keep (possessions, merchandise, etc.) in a storage facility or warehouse. **2** retain (data) in some physical form that enables subsequent retrieval; transfer into a memory or storage device. **3** (of a receptacle) hold, keep, contain. **4** stock or provide with something useful (*a mind stored with facts*). □ **in store 1** kept in readiness. **2** coming in the future; about to happen. **set** (or **put**) **store by** consider to be of importance, worth, or value. □ **storable** *adj.* **storer** *n.*

store-bought *adj. N Amer.* commercially manufactured and purchased in a store; not homemade.

storefront *n.* esp. *N Amer.* **1** the side of a store that faces onto the street. **2** a commercial property that has a store window or that faces onto the street. **3** a room or rooms at the front of a commercial property or store, esp. as used for some other purpose, such as a small business, a centre for religious worship, etc. (also *attrib.*: *storefront café*).

storehouse *n.* **1** a place where things are stored. **2** (often foll. by *of*) a person or thing considered to be a treasury or repository of something (*he is a storehouse of useful information*).

storekeeper *n.* **1** *N Amer.* a store manager. **2** a store owner. **3** a person who looks after stored goods.

storeroom *n.* a room in a house or office etc. in which supplies and other items may be kept.

store window *n.* *N Amer.* **1** a large window in a storefront. **2** a space inside a store in front of a window in which merchandise is displayed.

storey *n.* (*pl.* **-eys**) **1 a** a single level of a house or building; a floor. **b** (*attrib.*; in *comb.*) designating a house or building consisting of a specified number of levels (*a ten-storey building*). **2** each of a number of rows of windows, columns, panels, etc. arranged horizontally on the facade of a building and dividing it into levels. **3** a rough estimate of height based on the approximate height of one storey of a building. □ **-storeyed** *adj.* (in *comb.*) (also **-storied**).

storied *adj.* celebrated; legendary.

stork *n.* any of various large wading birds of the family Ciconiidae, with long legs and a long heavy bill, sometimes portrayed as delivering new babies.

storm ● *n.* **1** a violent weather disturbance with high winds, heavy rain or snow, thunder and lightning, etc. **2** *Meteorol.* a wind classed as force 10 or 11 on the Beaufort scale (between a gale and a hurricane), having an average velocity of 48–63 knots (55–72 mph). **3** (foll. by *of*) **a** a violent outburst (of protest, controversy, etc.). **b** a violent shower of projectiles or blows. **4** *N Amer. informal* a storm window. **5** a violent reaction; an uproar or controversy. **6** a direct assault by troops on a stronghold. ● *v.* **1 a** *intr.* move violently or angrily (*stormed out of the meeting*). **b** *tr.* say or shout in an angry or violent manner. **2** *tr.* rush, attack; attempt to overwhelm or enter by force. **3** *intr.* (of wind, rain, etc.) be violent or tempestuous. □ **take by storm 1** capture by direct assault. **2** achieve sudden or overwhelming success with (an audience, city, etc.). **up a storm** *N Amer.* with great enthusiasm and energy (*cook up a storm*).

storm cloud *n.* **1** a dark heavy cloud. **2** a threatening state of affairs.

storm petrel *n.* any of various small seabirds of the family Hydrobatidae, which fly close to the surface of the ocean.

storm sewer *n.* *N Amer.* a drain built to carry away excess rainwater etc.

storm-stayed *adj.* *Cdn (Maritimes & Ont.)* stranded due to severe or inclement weather conditions.

storm trooper *n.* **1** *hist.* a member of the Nazi political militia. **2** a militant activist or member of any group of vigilantes or shock troops.

storm window *n.* *N Amer.* a detachable outer window put up in winter as insulation and to protect an inner window from the effects of storms.

stormy *adj.* (**-ier, -iest**) **1** (of the weather, sky, sea, etc.) disturbed by a storm; tempestuous. **2** (of a region) subject to or affected by storms. **3 a** (of an event, period, etc.) turbulent, tempestuous (*a stormy meeting*; *a stormy relationship*). **b** (of a person or their looks) angry. □ **stormily** *adv.* **storminess** *n.*

story[1] *n.* (*pl.* **-ies**) **1** an account of imaginary or real events told for entertainment. **2** an account of the life of a person or institution etc. **3** = STORYLINE. **4** a representation of facts, esp. given as evidence. **5** *informal* a fib or lie. **6 a** an item of news in a newspaper etc. **b** a subject or event that is suitable for such an article. □ **another story** a matter requiring separate treatment. **the same old story** the familiar or predictable course of events. **the story goes** it is said. **to make a long story short** a formula excusing the omission of details. **the story of my** (or **your, his, her** etc.) **life** an event, statement, or situation that supposedly epitomizes a person's life or experience.

story[2] (*pl.* **-ies**) *var. of* STOREY.

storyboard *n.* a sequence of pictures etc. outlining the plan of a movie, TV commercial, etc.

storybook ● *n.* a book of stories for children. ● *attrib.adj.* unreal, romantic (*a storybook ending*).

storyline *n.* the plot of a novel, movie, etc.

storyteller *n.* **1** a person who tells stories. **2** *informal* a liar. □ **storytelling** *n. & adj.*

stout ● *adj.* **1** rather fat. **2** of considerable thickness or strength (*a stout stick*). **3** brave, resolute, vigorous (*put up stout resistance*). ● *n.* a strong dark beer brewed with roasted malt or barley. □ **stoutly** *adv.*

stove[1] *n.* an apparatus burning fuel or using electricity for heating or cooking.

stove[2] *past and past part. of* STAVE *v.*

stovepipe *n.* a pipe conducting smoke and gases from a stove to a chimney.

stovetop ● *n.* the top surface of a stove, esp. the cooking elements. ● *adj.* located on or cooked on a stovetop (*unsuitable for stovetop use*).

stow *v.tr.* **1** pack (goods etc.) tidily and compactly. **2** place (a cargo or luggage) in its proper place. □ **stow away 1** place (a thing) where it will not cause an obstruction. **2** be a stowaway on a ship etc.

stowage *n.* **1** the act of stowing. **2** a place for this.

stowaway *n.* a person who hides on board a ship or aircraft etc. to get free passage.

straddle ● *v.* **1** *tr. & intr.* **a** sit or stand with the legs one on either side of (a thing, person, horse, etc.). **b** be situated across or on both sides of (*the town straddles the border*). **2** *intr.* **a** (of the legs) be wide apart. **b** *tr.* part (one's legs) widely. **3** *tr.* vacillate between two policies etc. regarding (an issue). **4** *tr.* participate in (two opposing or vastly different cultures etc.). ● *n.* **1** the act of straddling. **2** *Stock Exch.* a simultaneous purchase of options to buy and to sell a security or commodity at a fixed price.

strafe ● *v.tr.* attack repeatedly with bullets or bombs from low-flying aircraft. ● *n.* an act of strafing.

straggle ● *v.intr.* **1** trail behind others in a march or race etc. **2** grow, spread, or be laid out in an irregular, untidy way. ● *n.* a group of straggling people or things. □ **straggler** *n.* **straggly** *adj.* (**-ier, -iest**).

straight ● *adj.* **1 a** extending uniformly in the same direction; without a curve or bend etc. **b** *Math.* (of a line) lying on the shortest path between any two of its points. **2** successive, uninterrupted (*three straight wins*). **3** arranged in proper order; level, symmetrical. **4** honest, candid; not evasive (*a straight answer*). **5** (of thinking etc.) logical, unemotional. **6** (of drama etc.) serious, as opposed to popular or comic. **7** unmodified, undiluted. **8** *informal* **a** heterosexual. **b** (of a person etc.) conventional or respectable. **9** (of a person's back) not bowed. **10** (of the hair) not curly or wavy. **11** (of a garment) not flared. **12** coming direct from its source. ● *n.* **1** the straight part of something, esp. the concluding stretch of a racecourse. **2** a straight condition. **3** a sequence of five cards in poker. **4** *informal* **a** a heterosexual. **b** a conventional person. ● *adv.* **1** in a straight line; directly; without deviation, hesitation, or circumlocution. **2** continuously, without a break (*have been working for 16 hours straight*). **3** correctly (*can't see straight*). **4** honestly and directly; in a straightforward manner. **5** upright; in an erect posture (*stand straight!*). **6** clearly and logically (*think straight*). □ **go straight** live an honest life after being a criminal. **set** (or **put**) **a person straight** make sure that someone knows the correct facts etc. when they have the wrong idea or impression. **the straight and narrow** morally correct behaviour. **straight away** at once; immediately. **straight from the shoulder 1** (of a blow) well delivered. **2** (of a verbal attack) frank or direct. **straight off** *informal* without hesitation, deliberation, etc. (*cannot tell you straight off*). **straight up** *informal* **1** esp. *N Amer.* unmixed, undiluted. **2** truthfully, honestly. □ **straightness** *n.*

straight-ahead *adj.* **1** simple, straightforward. **2** (esp. of music) unembellished; unadorned.

straight-arm ● *v.tr.* push away or deflect (an opponent or obstacle) with the arm outstretched. ● *n.* an act of straight-arming an opponent or obstacle.

straight arrow *n. N Amer. informal* a person who lives an honest, sober life. □ **straight-arrow** *adj.*

straightaway ● *adv.* = STRAIGHT AWAY (*see* STRAIGHT). ● *n.* esp. *N Amer.* a straight course or section.

straight-backed *adj.* **1** (of a chair) having a straight rather than a sloping back. **2** (of a person) not bowed or stooping.

straightedge *n.* a bar with one edge accurately straight, used for testing.

straighten *v.* **1** *tr. & intr.* (often foll. by *out*) make or become straight. **2** *tr.* (often foll. by *up*) make (something) neat, tidy, or orderly. □ **straighten out 1** clear up (something that is confused or in disorder) (*straighten out our finances*). **2** settle or resolve (a dispute etc.). **3** (of a person) improve in character or conduct. **straighten up 1** stand erect after bending. **2** *N Amer.* reform or become reformed in character or conduct. □ **straightener** *n.*

straight face *n.* an intentionally expressionless face, esp. one that conceals an impulse to laugh or smile (*keep a straight face*). □ **straight-faced** *adj.*

straight flush *n. Cards* a flush that is a numerical sequence.

straightforward *adj.* **1** honest or frank. **2** (of a task etc.) uncomplicated. □ **straightforwardly** *adv.* **straightforwardness** *n.*

straightjacket *var. of* STRAITJACKET.

straightlaced *var. of* STRAITLACED.

straight man *n.* a member of a comedy team who makes remarks or creates situations for the main performer to make jokes about.

straight razor *n.* esp. *N Amer.* a razor having a long blade set in a handle and usu. folding like a penknife.

straight shooter *n.* esp. *N Amer. slang* a person who states bluntly what they think. □ **straight-shooting** *adj.*

straight-up *adj. informal* **1** true; trustworthy. **2** esp. *N Amer.* undiluted; unmodified.

strain[1] ● *v.* **1** *tr.* force (one's body, one's senses, or oneself) to make a strenuous or unusually great effort. **2** *intr.* make a strenuous and continuous effort. **3** *intr.* (foll. by *at*) tug, pull (*the dog strained at the leash*). **4** *tr. & intr.* stretch tightly. **5** *tr.* make severe or excessive demands on (*strained her patience*). **6** *tr.* injure (a muscle etc.) by overexerting it. **7** *tr.* **a** clear (a liquid) of solid matter by passing it through a sieve etc. **b** (foll. by *out*) filter (solids) out from a liquid. ● *n.* **1 a** force tending to pull or stretch something to an extreme or damaging degree. **2** an injury caused by straining a muscle etc. **3 a** a severe demand on physical or mental strength or resources. **b** a state of tension or

exhaustion resulting from this (*suffering from strain*). **4** (in *sing.* or *pl.*) a short musical phrase. **5** a tone or tendency in speech or writing (*more in the same strain*). **6** *Physics* **a** the condition of a body subjected to stress. **b** a quantity measuring this. □ **strain oneself 1** injure oneself by effort. **2** make undue efforts. □ **strainer** *n.*

strain[2] *n.* **1** a breed or stock of animals, plants, etc. **2** a tendency, quality, or feature of a person's character (*a strain of aggression*). **3** a distinct (natural or cultured) variety of a micro-organism.

strained *adj.* **1** constrained, forced, artificial. **2** (of a relationship) mutually distrustful or tense. **3** (of an interpretation) far-fetched, laboured. **4** (of a liquid or semi-liquid, esp. a food) that has been passed through a strainer.

strait *n.* **1** (in *sing.* or *pl.*) a narrow passage of water connecting two seas or large bodies of water. **2** (usu. in *pl.*) difficulty, trouble, or distress (*in dire straits*).

straitened *adj.* of or marked by poverty.

straitjacket ● *n.* **1** a strong garment with long sleeves which are tied in the back to prevent the person wearing it from acting violently. **2** restrictive measures. ● *v.tr.* (**-jacketed**, **-jacketing**) **1** restrain with a straitjacket. **2** severely restrict.

straitlaced *adj.* having strict moral attitudes.

Straits *n.* a N American Aboriginal language of BC, part of the Salishan language group.

strand[1] ● *v.* **1** *tr.* (esp. as **stranded** *adj.*) leave (a person) in a place where they are helpless or in a difficult situation. **2** *tr. & intr.* run aground. ● *n. literary* the margin of a sea, lake, or river, esp. the foreshore.

strand[2] ● *n.* **1** each of the threads or wires twisted round each other to make a rope or cable. **2 a** a single thread or strip of fibre. **b** a constituent filament. **c** a single linear polymer of a long-chain molecule, esp. DNA. **3** a lock of hair. **4** an element or strain in any composite whole. ● *v.tr.* **1** break a strand in (a rope). **2** arrange in strands.

strange *adj.* **1** unusual, surprising; difficult to understand. **2** (often foll. by *to*) not previously visited, seen, or met; not familiar. **3** having unpleasant feelings; not well (*felt strange, so went to lie down*). **4** not at ease or comfortable in a situation; feeling that one does not fit in (*felt strange in such company*). **5** (foll. by *to*) unaccustomed. □ **make strange** *Cdn* (of a baby or child) fuss or be shy in company. **strange to say** it is surprising or unusual (that). □ **strangely** *adv.* **strangeness** *n.*

stranger *n.* **1** a person who does not know or is not known in a particular place or company. **2** (often foll. by *to*) a person one does not know (*was a complete stranger to me*). **3** (foll. by *to*) a person entirely unaccustomed to (a feeling, experience, etc.) (*no stranger to controversy*). **4** *Parl.* a person who is not a member or official of the House of Commons.

strangle *v.tr.* **1** kill (a person or animal) by squeezing or gripping their throat tightly. **2** restrict or prevent the proper growth, operation, or development of. **3** suppress (an utterance). □ **strangler** *n.*

stranglehold *n.* **1** a wrestling hold that throttles an opponent. **2** a deadly grip. **3** complete and exclusive control.

strangulate *v.tr.* **1** *Med.* constrict or compress (an organ, duct, hernia, etc.) so as to prevent circulation or the passage of a fluid. **2** strangle. □ **strangulation** *n.*

strap ● *n.* **1** a strip of cloth, leather, or other flexible material, often with a buckle or other fastening, for keeping something in place or for fastening, carrying, or holding onto something. **2** a loop for grasping to steady oneself while standing in a moving vehicle. **3** (prec. *by the*) punishment by beating with a leather strap. **4** a strip of metal used to secure or connect. ● *v.tr.* (**strapped, strapping**) **1** (often foll. by *down, on*, etc.) secure or bind with a strap. **2** beat with a strap. ☐ **strapper** *n.*

strapless *adj.* (of a garment) without straps, esp. shoulder straps.

strapped *adj.* subject to a shortage (esp. of money) (*I'm a bit strapped for cash*).

strapping ● *adj.* (esp. of a person) large and sturdy. ● *n.* **1** material for making straps. **2** a punishment by beating with a strap.

strata /ˈstrɑːtə/ *n.* **1** pl. of STRATUM. **2** a dish made of alternating layers of foods, esp. of layers of bread with cheese etc., soaked in eggs and milk and baked.

stratagem /ˈstrætədʒəm/ *n.* a cunning plan or scheme, esp. for deceiving an enemy.

strategic /strəˈtiːdʒɪk/ *adj.* **1** of or serving the ends of strategy (*strategic considerations*). **2** (of materials) essential in fighting a war. **3** (of bombing or weapons) done or for use against an enemy's home territory as a longer-term military objective (opp. TACTICAL 2). ☐ **strategical** *adj.* **strategically** *adv.*

Strategic Defence Initiative *n.* a projected US system of defence against nuclear weapons using satellites.

strategy /ˈstrætədʒi/ *n.* (*pl.* **-ies**) **1** an esp. long-range policy designed for a particular purpose. **2** the process of planning something or carrying out a plan in a skilful way. **3** a plan or stratagem. **4 a** the art of planning and directing military activity in a battle or war (*compare* TACTICS 1). **b** an instance of this. ☐ **strategist** *n.* **strategize** *v.intr.*

stratify /ˈstrætɪˌfaɪ/ *v.* (**-ies, -ied**) **1 a** *tr.* (esp. as **stratified** *adj.*) arrange in strata. **b** *intr.* become arranged in strata. **2** *tr.* **a** construct or devise in layers. **b** arrange in a hierarchical way. ☐ **stratification** *n.*

stratigraphy /strəˈtɪɡrəfi/ *n. Geol. & Archaeology* **1** the order and relative position of strata. **2** the study of this as a means of historical interpretation. ☐ **stratigraphic** *adj.* **stratigraphical** *adj.* **stratigraphically** *adv.*

stratosphere /ˈstrætəˌsfɪːr/ *n.* **1** a layer of atmospheric air above the troposphere extending to about 50 km above the earth's surface. **2** a very high or the highest level on or as if on a stratified scale (*costs have hit the stratosphere*). ☐ **stratospheric** /-ˈsfɪːrɪk, -ˈsferɪk/ *adj.*

stratum /ˈstrætəm/ *n.* (*pl.* **strata** /-tə/) **1** esp. *Geol.* a layer or set of successive layers of any deposited substance. **2** an atmospheric layer. **3** a layer of tissue etc. **4 a** a social grade, class, etc. (*the various strata of society*). **b** *Statistics* each of the groups into which a population is divided in stratified sampling.

straw ● *n.* **1** dry cut stalks of grain, used esp. as bedding for animals. **2** a single stalk or piece of straw. **3** material made from straw and used for weaving hats, baskets, etc. **4** a hollow plastic or paper tube for sucking drink from a glass etc. **5** an insignificant thing (*not worth a straw*). **6** the pale yellow colour of straw. ● *adj.* **1** made of straw. **2** pale yellow. ☐ **draw the short straw** be chosen by lot, esp. for some disagreeable task. **grasp** (or **clutch**) **at straws** resort to an utterly inadequate expedient in desperation. **the last** (or **final**) **straw** a slight addition to a burden or difficulty that makes it finally unbearable. **straw in the wind** a slight hint of future developments.

strawberry ● *n.* (*pl.* **-ies**) **1 a** any plant of the genus *Fragaria*, esp. any of various cultivated varieties, with white flowers, trifoliate leaves, and runners. **b** the pulpy red edible fruit of this, having a seed-studded surface. **2** a deep pinkish-red colour. ● *adj.* of a deep pinkish-red colour.

strawberry blond ● *n.* **1** pinkish-blond hair. **2** a woman with such hair. ● *adj.* (hyphenated when *attrib.*) of a pinkish-blond colour.

strawberry social *n. N Amer.* a public event sponsored by a church or community group as a fundraiser, where desserts featuring strawberries are served.

straw boss *n. N Amer.* an assistant foreman.

straw-colour *n.* pale yellow. ☐ **straw-coloured** *adj.*

straw man *n.* a person or issue etc. set up as the object of an argument in order to be defeated.

straw poll *n.* (also **straw vote**) an unofficial ballot as a test of opinion.

stray ● *v.intr.* **1** wander from the right place; become separated from one's companions etc. **2** leave the subject one is supposed to be thinking about or discussing (*we seem to have strayed from the point*). **3** deviate morally, esp. be sexually unfaithful. **4** wander or roam around aimlessly. ● *n.* **1** a domestic animal that has strayed or wandered away from its home, owner, etc. **2** a homeless or friendless person or animal. ● *adj.* **1** strayed or lost. **2** isolated; found or occurring occasionally (*a stray bullet*). **3** that is not in the normal or right place (*a few stray hairs*).

streak ● *n.* **1** a long thin usu. irregular line or band, esp. distinguished by colour. **2** a strain or element in a person's character (*has a streak of mischief*). **3 a** a run or spell (*a streak of good luck*). **b** a continuous or uninterrupted series (*a 12-game losing streak*). **4** a flash of lightning. ● *v.* **1** *tr.* mark with streaks. **2** *intr.* move very rapidly, esp. in a straight line. **3** *intr.* form streaks. **4** *intr. informal* run naked in a public place as a stunt. **5** *tr.* tint (the hair) with streaks. ☐ **streaker** *n.* (esp. in sense 4 of *v.*). **streaking** *n.*

streaky *adj.* (**-ier, -iest**) **1** full of streaks. **2** changeable or variable; of uneven quality. ☐ **streakily** *adv.* **streakiness** *n.*

stream ● *n.* **1** a flowing body of water, esp. a small river. **2 a** the flow of a fluid (*a stream of lava*). **b** (in *sing.* or *pl.*) a large quantity of something that flows or moves along. **c** an unbroken mass of people or things moving constantly in the same direction. **d** a continuous flow or series of words, time, events, etc. (*a stream of obscenities*). **e** *Computing* a continuous flow of data or instructions, esp. one having a constant or predictable rate. **3** a current or direction in which things are moving or tending (*against the stream*). **4** *Cdn & Brit.* a group of schoolchildren taught together as being of similar ability for a given age. ● *v.* **1** *intr.* flow or move as a stream. **2** *intr.* run with liquid (*my eyes were streaming*). **3** *intr.* (of a banner or hair etc.) float or wave in the wind. **4** *tr.* emit a stream of (blood etc.). **5** *intr.* (foll. by *in, out, down*, etc.) (of people or animals) move together continuously in an unbroken mass. **6** *intr.* extend in rays or beams (*sunlight streaming through the windows*). **7** *tr. Cdn & Brit.* arrange (schoolchildren) in streams. ☐ **on stream** into operation or effect or participation. ☐ **streamlet** *n.*

stream bank *n.* the raised or sloping edge or border of a stream.

stream bed *n.* a channel in which a stream flows or once flowed.

streamer *n.* **1** a long narrow flag. **2** a long narrow strip of ribbon or paper, esp. in a coil that unrolls when thrown. **3** esp. *N Amer.* a fishing fly with feathers attached, resembling a small fish. **4** a banner headline. **5** (in *pl.*) the aurora borealis or australis. **6** *Cdn* an elongated band of clouds formed by convection around the Great Lakes, and generating large amounts of localized snow.

streamline ● *v.tr.* **1** give (a vehicle etc.) the form which presents the least resistance to motion. **2** make (an organization, process, etc.) simple or more efficient or better organized. ● *n.* **1** the natural course of water or air currents. **2** (often *attrib.*) the shape of an aircraft, car, etc., calculated to cause the least air resistance. □ **streamlined** *adj.*

stream of consciousness *n.* **1** *Psych.* a person's thoughts and conscious reactions to events perceived as a continuous flow. **2** a literary style depicting events in such a flow in the mind of a character. □ **stream-of-consciousness** *adj.*

streamside *n.* the ground along a stream bank (often *attrib.*: *streamside trail*).

street ● *n.* **1 a** a public road in a city, town, or village. **b** this including sidewalks. **c** this with the houses or other buildings on each side. **d** (in many N American cities) a road running perpendicular to an avenue, esp. north-south. **2** the persons who live or work on a particular street. **3 (the Street)** a *Cdn* = BAY STREET. **b** *US* = WALL STREET. ● *attrib.adj.* **1** of or adjoining the street (*use the street door*). **2** (of clothes etc.) suitable for everyday wear or use in public (*street clothes*). **3** occurring on a street (*a street party*). **4** appearing or performing on a street (*street performers*). **5** esp. *N Amer.* (of a person) homeless (*street people*). □ **on the street** (or **streets**) **1** homeless. **2** *N Amer.* out of prison; released from custody. **take to the streets** (of people) gather outdoors in a town or city in order to protest, celebrate, etc.

street address *n.* the address designating the location of a residence, office, etc. on a street in a city or town, esp. if different from the mailing address.

streetcar *n.* *N Amer.* an electrically-powered passenger vehicle running on rails laid in an urban street.

street credibility *n.* (also **street cred**) *slang* popularity with or acceptability to people involved in fashionable street culture.

street culture *n.* the outlook, values, lifestyle, etc., of esp. young people living in an urban environment, regarded as a fashionable subculture.

street drug *n.* an illegal drug sold on the streets.

street hockey *n.* *Cdn* a version of hockey played on a street usu. by children using hockey sticks and a ball in place of a puck.

street legal *adj.* **1** (of a vehicle) legally roadworthy. **2** *informal* legitimate; above-board.

street light *n.* (also **street lamp**) a light or lamp esp. on a lamppost, serving to illuminate a road etc. □ **street lighting** *n.*

street price *n.* the retail price, esp. of a piece of computer equipment.

streetproof *v.tr.* *N Amer.* train (children) to be wary of dangers outside the home or school.

streetscape *n.* a view or prospect provided by the design of a city street or streets.

street smarts *n.pl.* *N Amer. informal* **1** shrewd or cunning awareness of how to survive in an urban society or environment. **2** common sense. □ **street-smart** *adj.*

street value *n.* the price for which something illegal or illegally obtained can be sold.

streetwalker *n.* a prostitute seeking customers in the street. □ **streetwalking** *n. & adj.*

streetwise *adj.* esp. *N Amer.* familiar with the ways of modern urban life.

strength /strenθ, strenθ/ *n.* **1** the state of being strong; the degree to which or respect in which a person or thing is strong. **2** the ability to resist force or support heavy objects without breaking or being damaged. **3 a** a person or thing affording strength or support. **b** an attribute making for strength of character (*patience is your great strength*). **4** a positive quality or attribute (*identified my strengths and weaknesses*). **5** the extent to which a feeling or opinion is strong (*the strength of public opinion*). **6** the potency or intensity of a drug, drink, active ingredient, etc. **7** *Commerce* firmness of prices. **8** the number of persons present or available. **9** a full complement (*below strength*). □ **from strength** from a strong position. **from strength to strength** with ever-increasing success. **in strength** in large numbers. **on the strength of** on the basis of. **the strength of** the essence or main features of. □ **strengthless** *adj.*

strengthen *v.tr. & intr.* make or become stronger. □ **strengthen a person's hand** enable a person to act with greater effect or vigour.

strenuous /'strenjoos/ *adj.* **1** requiring or using great effort. **2** energetic; vigorously active. □ **strenuously** *adv.* **strenuousness** *n.*

strep *informal* ● *n.* **1** = STREPTOCOCCUS. **2** *N Amer.* = STREP THROAT. ● *adj.* streptococcal.

strep throat *n.* *N Amer.* an acute sore throat with fever caused by streptococcal infection.

streptococcus /,strepto'kɒkəs/ *n.* (*pl.* **-cocci** /-'kɒkai/) any bacterium of the genus *Streptococcus*, some of which cause infectious diseases. □ **streptococcal** *adj.*

streptomycin /,strepto'maisin/ *n.* an antibiotic produced by the bacterium *Streptomyces griseus*, effective against many disease-producing bacteria.

stress /stres/ ● *n.* **1 a** pressure or tension exerted on a material object. **b** a quantity measuring this. **2 a** demand on physical or mental energy. **b** a condition or adverse circumstance that disturbs, or is likely to disturb, the normal physiological or psychological functioning of an individual. **c** distress caused by this (*suffering from stress*). **3 a** emphasis (*the stress was on the need for success*). **b** emphasis laid on a syllable or word. **c** an accent, esp. the principal one in a word. **4** *Mech.* force per unit area exerted between contiguous bodies or parts of a body. ● *v.tr.* **1** lay stress on; emphasize. **2** subject to mechanical or physical or mental stress. **3** give extra force to (a word or syllable) when pronouncing it. **4** (usu. in *passive*) cause stress to. □ **lay stress on** indicate as important. **stress out** cause (a person) mental stress. □ **stressed** *adj.* **stressless** *adj.*

stressed out *adj.* *informal* debilitated or exhausted as a result of stress.

stress fracture *n.* a fracture of a bone caused by the repeated application of a high load.

stressful *adj.* causing stress; mentally tiring. □ **stressfully** *adv.* **stressfulness** *n.*

stressor *n.* a situation, experience, event, or other stimulus that causes stress.

stretch ● *v.* **1** *tr. & intr.* draw or be drawn or admit of being drawn out into greater length or size. **2** *tr. & intr.* make or become taut. **3** *tr. & intr.* place or lie at full length or spread out. **4 a** *tr.* extend (an arm, leg, etc.). **b** *intr. & refl.* thrust out one's limbs and tighten one's muscles after being relaxed. **c** *tr. & intr.* perform exercises to lengthen the muscles and improve flexibility, esp. before vigorous exercise. **5** *intr.* have a specified length or extension; extend (*farmland stretches for many miles*). **6** *tr.* strain or exert extremely or excessively; exaggerate (*stretch the truth*). **7** *tr.* increase the quantity or amount of (food, a beverage, paint, etc.) by dilution or the addition of something else. ● *n.* **1 a** a continuous extent or expanse or period (*a stretch of open road*). **2 a** the act or an instance of stretching; the state of being stretched. **b** a stretching exercise. **3** (*attrib.*) able to stretch; elastic (*stretch fabric*). **4 a** *informal* a period of imprisonment. **b** a period of time or service. **5** *N Amer.* the straight side of a racetrack. **6** (*usu. attrib.*) *informal* an aircraft or motor vehicle modified so as to have extra seating or storage capacity (*stretch limousine*). **7 a** the act or an instance of extending oneself or one's abilities or resources beyond normal limits (*it'll be a stretch*). **b** *informal* an exaggeration or distortion (*well, that's a bit of a stretch*). □ **at a stretch 1** in one continuous period (*slept for two hours at a stretch*). **2** with much effort. **stretch one's legs** exercise oneself by walking, esp. after prolonged sitting. **stretch out 1** extend (a hand or foot etc.). **2** last for a longer period; prolong. **3** make (money etc.) last for a sufficient time. **4** relax by lying at full length. **stretch a point** agree to something not normally allowed. □ **stretchable** *adj.* **stretchability** *n.* **stretchy** *adj.*

stretcher ● *n.* **1** a framework of two poles with canvas etc. between, for carrying a sick, injured, or dead person in a lying position. **2** a brick or stone laid with its long side along the face of a wall (*compare* HEADER 4). ● *v.tr.* (often foll. by *off*) convey (a sick or injured person) on a stretcher.

stretch marks *n.pl.* marks on the skin resulting from weight gain, or on the abdomen after pregnancy.

streusel /'struːzəl, 'struːsəl/ *n.* esp. *N Amer.* a crumbly mixture of flour, butter, sugar, and usu. cinnamon, used as a topping or filling for cakes etc. (also *attrib.: a cherry streusel cake*).

strew *v.tr.* (*past part.* **strewn** or **strewed**) **1** scatter or spread or be scattered or spread over a surface. **2** (usu. foll. by *with*) spread (a surface) with scattered things.

striate ● *adj.* /'straɪət/ (also **striated** /-eɪtəd/) marked with linear marks or furrows. ● *v.tr.* /'straɪeɪt/ mark with linear marks or furrows. □ **striation** *n.*

stricken *adj.* affected or overcome with illness or misfortune etc. (*stricken with measles*; *grief-stricken*).

strict *adj.* **1** (of a person) demanding that rules, esp. those concerning behaviour, are obeyed or observed. **2** following rules or beliefs exactly (*a strict Catholic*). **3** precisely limited or defined. **4** without exception or deviation (*lives in strict seclusion*). **5** requiring complete compliance or exact performance; enforced rigidly (*gave strict orders*). **6** complete or absolute. □ **strictly** *adv.* **strictness** *n.*

stricture *n.* **1** (usu. in *pl.*) a critical or censorious remark. **2** (usu. in *pl.*) rules that restrict behaviour or action. **3** *Med.* an abnormal narrowing of a canal or duct in the body.

stride ● *v.* (*past* **strode** /strəʊd/; *past part.* **stridden** /'strɪdən/) **1** *intr.* & *tr.* walk with long firm steps. **2** *tr.* cross with one step. **3** *tr.* bestride; straddle. ● *n.* **1 a** a single long step. **b** the length of this. **2** a person's gait as determined by the length of stride. **3** (usu. in *pl.*) progress (*has made great strides*). **4** the distance between the feet parted either laterally or as in walking. □ **break stride** 1 change one's gait. **2** slow down. **hit** (or **get into**) **one's stride** reach a settled or steady rate of progress or level of performance. **take in one's stride 1** manage without difficulty. **2**

clear (an obstacle) without changing one's gait to jump. □ **strider** *n.*

strident /'straɪdənt/ *adj.* **1** loud and harsh. **2** urgent and aggressive (*strident demands*). □ **stridency** *n.* **stridently** *adv.*

strife *n.* **1** conflict or struggle. **2** enmity or rivalry, esp. of a bitter kind.

strike ● *v.* (*past* **struck**; *past part.* **struck**) **1** *tr.* **a** subject to an impact. **b** deliver (a blow) or inflict a blow on. **2** *tr.* come or bring sharply into contact with (*the car struck a tree*). **3** *tr.* propel or divert with a blow (*struck the ball into the pond*). **4** *intr.* (foll. by *at*) try to hit. **5** *tr.* penetrate or cause to penetrate (*struck terror into her*). **6** *tr.* ignite (a match) or produce (sparks etc.) by rubbing. **7** *tr.* make (a coin) by stamping. **8** *tr.* produce (a musical note) by striking. **9 a** *tr.* & *intr.* (of a clock) indicate (the time) by the sounding of a chime etc. **b** *intr.* (of time) be indicated in this way. **10** *tr.* **a** attack suddenly (*was struck with sudden terror*). **b** (of a disease) afflict. **11** *tr.* cause to become suddenly (*was struck dumb*). **12** *tr.* reach or achieve (*strike a balance*). **13** *tr.* agree on (a bargain). **14** *tr.* assume (an attitude) suddenly and dramatically (*strike a pose*). **15** *tr.* **a** discover or come across. **b** find (oil etc.) by drilling. **c** encounter (an unusual thing etc.). **16** *tr.* come to the attention of or appear to (*it strikes me as silly*). **17 a** *intr.* (of employees) engage in a strike; cease work as a protest. **b** *tr.* *N Amer.* act in this way against (an employer). **18 a** *tr.* lower or take down (a flag or tent etc.). **b** *intr.* signify surrender by striking a flag; surrender. **19** *intr.* take a specified direction (*struck east*). **20** *tr.* & *intr.* secure a hook in the mouth of (a fish) by jerking the tackle. **21** *tr.* (of a snake) wound with its fangs. **22** *tr.* **a** ascertain (a balance) by deducting credit or debit from the other. **b** arrive at (an average, state of balance) by equalizing all items. **23** *tr.* compose (a jury) esp. by allowing both sides to reject the same number. **24** *tr.* *Cdn* create (a committee). ● *n.* **1** the act or an instance of striking. **2 a** the organized refusal by employees to work until some grievance is remedied. **b** a similar refusal to participate in some other expected activity. **3 a** a discovery of oil, ore, etc. by drilling, mining, etc. **b** a sudden find or success (*a lucky strike*). **4** an attack, esp. from the air. **5** *Baseball* a batter's unsuccessful attempt to hit a pitched ball, or another event counting equivalently against a batter. **6** the act of knocking down all the pins with the first ball in bowling. **7 a** a jerk by which an angler secures a hooked fish. **b** a pull on a fishing line indicating that a fish has taken the bait. **8** *N Amer.* a thing to one's discredit (*several strikes against him*). □ **on strike** taking part in an industrial etc. strike. **strike down 1** knock down. **2** bring low; afflict (*struck down by a virus*). **strike home 1** deal an effective blow. **2** have an intended effect (*my words struck home*). **strike in 1** intervene in a conversation etc. **2** (of a disease) attack the interior of the body from the surface. **strike it rich** *informal* find a source of abundance or success. **strike a light** produce a light by striking a match. **strike it lucky** have a lucky success. **strike off 1** remove with a stroke. **2** delete (a name etc.) from a list. **strike oil 1** find petroleum by sinking a shaft. **2** attain prosperity or success. **strike out 1** hit out. **2** act vigorously. **3** delete (an item or name etc.). **4** set off or begin (*struck out eastwards*). **5** use the arms and legs in swimming. **6** forge or devise (a plan etc.). **7** *Baseball* **a** dismiss (a batter) by means of three strikes. **b** be dismissed in this way. **8** be unsuccessful. **strike through** delete (a word etc.) with a stroke of one's pen. **strike up 1** start (an acquaintance, conversation, etc.) esp.

casually. **2** begin playing (a tune etc.). **strike upon 1** have (an idea etc.). luckily occur to one. **2** (of light) illuminate. **strike while the iron is hot** act promptly at a good opportunity.

strikebound *adj.* immobilized or closed by a strike.

strikebreaker *n.* one working or employed in place of others on strike. □ **strikebreaking** *n. & adj.*

strike force *n.* **1** a military or police force ready for rapid effective action. **2** a similar group, e.g. of activists etc., organized to act quickly in a specific way.

strikeout *n. Baseball* an out called when a batter has had three strikes.

strike pay *n.* an allowance paid to strikers by a union.

striker *n.* **1** a person or thing that strikes. **2** an employee on strike. **3** *Soccer* an attacking player positioned well forward in order to score goals.

strike zone *n. Baseball* an imaginary rectangle above home plate extending from the armpits to the knees of a batter.

striking ● *adj.* **1** impressive; attracting attention. **2** conspicuous (*a striking lack of effort*). **3** (of a person) on strike (*striking workers*). ● *n.* the act or an instance of striking. □ **within striking distance** near enough to hit or achieve. □ **strikingly** *adv.* **strikingness** *n.*

string ● *n.* **1** twine or narrow cord. **2** a piece of this or of similar material used for tying or holding together, pulling, etc. **3** a length of catgut or wire etc. on a musical instrument, producing a note by vibration. **4 a** (in *pl.*) stringed instruments (i.e. violin, cello, etc.) forming a section of an orchestra, group, etc. **b** (*attrib.*) relating to or consisting of stringed instruments (*string quartet*). **5** (in *pl.*) an awkward associated or consequent condition or complication (*no strings attached*). **6 a** a set of things strung together; a series or line of persons or things (*a string of beads; a string of boyfriends*). **b** *Sport* a roster of players in order of selection or skill (*second string*). **7** a group of racehorses trained at one stable. **8** a tough piece connecting the two halves of a bean pod etc. **9** a piece of catgut etc. interwoven with others to form the head of a tennis etc. racquet. **10** = STRINGER 4. **11** *Computing* a linear sequence of characters, records, or data. **12** esp. *N Amer.* a continuous series of successes or failures; a continuous sequence of games, turns at play, etc. ● *adj.* **1** made of or consisting of string (*a string bag*). **2** light greyish-brown. ● *v. (past and past part.* **strung**) **1** *tr.* supply with a string or strings. **2** *tr.* **a** arrange in or as a string (*strung lights on the Christmas tree*). **b** put (esp. words, ideas, etc.) together in a connected sequence. **3** *tr.* provide, equip, or adorn with something suspended or slung (*the backyard was strung with lanterns*). **4** *tr.* thread (beads etc.) on a string. **5** *tr.* tie with string. **6** *tr.* place a string ready for use on (a musical instrument, racquet, bow, etc.). **7** *tr.* esp. *N Amer. slang* deceive. **8** *intr. Billiards* make the preliminary strokes that decide which player begins. **9** *intr.* (often foll. by *out*) extend, stretch out. □ **on a string** under one's control or influence. **string a person a line** purposely mislead a person. **string along** *informal* deceive, mislead (a person) about one's own intentions or beliefs. **string out** extend; prolong (esp. unduly). **string up 1** hang up on strings etc. **2** *informal* kill by hanging. □ **stringlike** *adj.*

string bass *n. Music* a double bass.

string bean *n.* **1** any of various beans eaten in their fibrous pods, esp. runner or French beans. **2** *informal* a tall thin person.

stringed *adj.* (of musical instruments) having strings (also in *comb.: twelve-stringed guitar*).

stringent /ˈstrɪndʒənt/ *adj.* **1** (of rules etc.) strict, precise; requiring exact performance. **2** (of a money market etc.) hampered by scarcity; hard to operate in. □ **stringency** *n.* **stringently** *adv.*

stringer *n.* **1** a horizontal member connecting uprights in a framework, supporting a floor, etc. **2** a longitudinal structural member in a framework, esp. of a ship or aircraft. **3** *informal* a newspaper correspondent not on the regular staff, esp. one retained on a freelance basis to report on events in a particular place. **4** a supporting timber or skirting in which the ends of a staircase steps are set. **5** *N Amer.* a chain with hooks on which caught fish are strung. **6** (usu. in *comb.*) an athlete, performer, etc. ranked according to ability (*first-stringer*).

stringy *adj.* (**-ier**, **-iest**) **1** (of food etc.) fibrous, tough. **2** of or like string. **3** tall, wiry, and thin. **4** (of a liquid) viscous; forming strings. □ **stringiness** *n.*

strip¹ ● *v.* (**stripped**, **stripping**) **1** *tr.* **a** (often foll. by *of*) remove the clothes or covering from (a person or thing). **b** (often foll. by *from, away*) pull off or remove (a covering or property etc.) (*strip away the pretense*). **2** *intr.* (often foll. by *off, down*) undress oneself. **3** *tr.* (often foll. by *of*) deprive (a person) of property, titles, etc. **4** *tr.* leave bare of accessories or fittings. **5** *tr.* remove bark and branches from (a tree). **6** *tr.* (often foll. by *down*) remove the accessory fittings of or take apart (a machine etc.) to inspect or adjust it. **7** *tr.* sell off (the assets of a company) for profit. **8** *tr.* remove (paint, wax, etc.) or remove paint, wax, etc. from (a surface) (*strip a floor*). **9 a** *tr.* tear the thread from (a screw). **b** *intr.* (of a screw) lose its thread. **10** *tr.* tear the teeth from (a gearwheel). ● *n.* an act of stripping, esp. of performing a striptease.

strip² *n.* **1** a long narrow piece (*a strip of land*). **2** a narrow flat bar of iron or steel. **3** (in full **strip cartoon**) = COMIC STRIP. **4** *N Amer.* **a** an area of commercial development along a road in a town or city. **b** a part of a city street frequented by prostitutes, drug addicts, etc. **5** = AIRSTRIP. **6** = DRAG STRIP. □ **tear a strip off a person** *informal* angrily rebuke a person.

strip club *n.* (also **strip joint**) a club at which striptease performances are given.

stripe ● *n.* **1** a long narrow band or strip differing in colour or texture from the surface on either side of it. **2** *Military* a chevron etc. denoting military rank. **3** esp. *N Amer.* a category of character, opinion, etc. (*politicians of all stripes*). ● *v.tr.* mark with stripes. □ **striped** *adj.* (also in *comb.*). **stripy** *adj.*

striped bass *n.* a large bass of N American coastal waters, *Morone saxatilis*, with dark horizontal stripes along the upper sides.

striper *n.* **1** *N Amer.* = STRIPED BASS. **2** (with specifying numeral) a member of the navy, army, etc. whose uniform carries a number of stripes denoting rank.

strip loin *n. N Amer.* a long strip of beef from the loin.

strip mall *n.* a shopping mall on a street, with the stores arranged in a row and accessed from outside.

strip mine *N Amer.* ● *n.* a mine worked by removing surface material in successive parallel strips to expose the ore etc. ● *v.tr.* (**strip-mine**) obtain or work by strip mining. □ **strip mining** *n.*

stripped-down *adj.* **1** (of a car, machine, etc.) that has had all superfluous or extraneous parts removed. **2** reduced to essentials; bare, lean (*a stripped-down musical style*).

stripper *n.* **1** a person who performs striptease. **2** a device or solvent for removing paint etc. **3** a person or thing that strips something.

striptease *n.* a form of erotic entertainment in which a performer removes his or her clothes in front of an audience, usu. to musical accompaniment.

strive *v.intr.* (*past* **strove** *or* **strived**; *past part.* **striven**) **1** (often foll. by *for*, or *to* + infin.) try hard, make efforts (*strive to succeed*). **2** (often foll. by *with*, *against*) struggle or contend. □ **striver** *n.*

strobe ● *n.* (in full **strobe light**) **1** a bright light that flashes on and off, e.g. in a discotheque. **2** a stroboscopic lamp. ● *v.* **1** *tr.* light as if with a strobe. **2** *intr.* flash intermittently.

stroboscope /ˈstroʊbəˌskoʊp/ *n.* **1** *Physics* an instrument for determining speeds of rotation etc. by shining a bright light at intervals so that a rotating object appears stationary. **2** = STROBE *n.* 1 □ **stroboscopic** *adj.*

strode *past of* STRIDE.

stroganoff /ˈstroʊgəˌnɒf/ *n.* (in full **beef stroganoff**) a dish of strips of beef cooked in a sauce containing mushrooms and sour cream.

stroke ● *n.* **1** the act or an instance of striking; a blow or hit. **2** a sudden disabling attack or loss of consciousness caused by an interruption in the flow of blood to the brain, esp. through thrombosis. **3 a** an action or movement esp. as one of a series. **b** the time or way in which such movements are done. **c** the slightest such action (*has not done a stroke of work*). **4** the whole of the motion (of a wing, oar, etc.) until the starting position is regained. **5** (in rowing) the mode or action of moving the oar (*a fast stroke*). **6** the whole motion (of a piston) in either direction. **7** *Golf* the action of hitting (or hitting at) a ball with a club, as a unit of scoring. **8 a** a mode of moving the arms and legs in swimming. **b** a single movement of the legs in walking or running. **c** a pushing off movement of the legs in skating. **9** a method of striking with the bat etc. in games etc. **10 a** a specially successful or effective action or event (*a stroke of diplomacy*). **b** a feat, an achievement (*a stroke of genius*). **c** an unexpected piece of luck or misfortune. **11 a** a mark made by the movement in one direction of a pen or pencil or paintbrush. **b** a similar mark printed. **12** a detail contributing to the general effect in a description. **13** the sound made by a striking clock. **14** the act or a period of stroking. ● *v.* **1** *tr.* pass one's hand gently along the surface of (hair or fur etc.); caress lightly. **2** *tr.* *N Amer. informal* manipulate (a person) by means of flattery, persuasion, etc. **3** *tr.* **a** (foll. by *on*) apply (a cosmetic, paint, etc.) to a surface. **b** brush (a thing) gently over a surface. **4** *tr.* act as the stroke of (a boat or crew). **5** *intr.* execute swimming, skating, or rowing strokes (*stroked to victory*). **6** *tr.* hit (a ball) with a smooth, controlled movement. □ **at a stroke** by a single action. **off one's stroke** not performing as well as usual. **on** (or **at**) **the stroke of one** etc. with the clock about to strike one etc. □ **stroker** *n.* (also in comb.).

stroll ● *v.* **1** *intr.* saunter or walk in a leisurely way. **2** *tr.* walk in a leisurely fashion along (a street etc.). **3** *intr.* achieve something easily, without effort. ● *n.* **1** a short leisurely walk (*go for a stroll*). **2** something easily achieved.

stroller *n.* **1** esp. *N Amer.* a folding chair on wheels in which a baby or small child can be pushed along from place to place. **2** a person who strolls.

strolling *adj.* itinerant (*strolling players*).

strong ● *adj.* (**stronger**; **strongest**) **1** having the power of resistance; able to withstand great force or opposition; not easily damaged or overcome. **2** capable of exerting great physical force or of doing much. **3** forceful or powerful in effect (*a strong wind*). **4** (of a person's constitution) able to overcome, or not liable to, disease. **5** (of a person's nerves) resistant to fright, irritation, etc. **6** (of a patient) restored to health. **7** (of an economy) stable and prosperous; (of a market) having steadily high or rising prices. **8** decided or firmly held (*strong views*). **9** (of an argument etc.) convincing or striking. **10** powerfully affecting the senses or emotions (*a strong light*). **11** (of a person) effective; skilful; competent in a certain sphere (*she's strong in physics but weak in English*). **12** powerful in terms of size or numbers or quality. **13** capable of doing much when united (*a strong combination*). **14 a** formidable; likely to succeed (*a strong candidate*). **b** tending to assert or dominate (*a strong personality*). **15** (of a solution or drink etc.) concentrated. **16** (of a group) having a specified number (*200 strong*). **17** (of a voice) loud or penetrating. **18** (of food or its flavour) pungent. **19** (of a colour) bright, intense. **20** (of a person's breath) ill-smelling. **21** (of a literary style) vivid and terse. **22** (of a measure) drastic. **23** *Cdn* slightly more than the stated measurement (*a strong quarter of an inch*). ● *adv.* strongly. □ **come on strong** behave aggressively or assertively. **going strong** *informal* continuing action vigorously; continuing to flourish; in good health or trim. □ **strongly** *adv.*

strong-arm ● *adj.* using threats or force (*strong-arm tactics*). ● *v.tr.* threaten, intimidate; treat aggressively.

strongbox *n.* a strongly made, usu. metal chest for safeguarding valuables.

strong drink *n.* alcohol, esp. hard liquor.

stronghold *n.* **1** a fortified place. **2** a secure refuge. **3** a centre of support for a cause etc.

strongman *n.* (pl. **-men**) **1** *Politics* a forceful leader who exercises firm control over a state, group, etc. **2** a performer (at a fair etc.) of feats of strength.

strong point *n.* **1 a** a thing at which one excels. **b** a feature of something that makes it attractive. **2** (**strongpoint**) a specially fortified defensive position.

strongroom *n.* a room designed to protect valuables against fire and theft.

strong stomach *n.* a stomach not easily affected by nausea.

strong suit *n.* **1** a suit at cards in which one can take tricks. **2** a thing at which one excels.

strong-willed *adj.* **1** determined, resolute. **2** stubborn, headstrong.

strontium /ˈstrɒntɪəm, -ʃəm, -tɪəm/ *n.* a soft silver-white metallic element found in various minerals.

strop ● *n.* a device, esp. a strip of leather, for sharpening razors. ● *v.tr.* (**stropped**, **stropping**) sharpen on or with a strop.

stroud *n.* *Cdn* a coarse woollen cloth used esp. in the North to make blankets, leggings, etc.

strove *past of* STRIVE.

struck ● *v.* *past and past part. of* STRIKE. ● *adj.* *N Amer.* pertaining to or affected by an industrial strike (*a struck factory*).

structuralism *n.* a method of analyzing and organizing concepts in anthropology, linguistics, and other cognitive and social sciences in terms of contrasting relations among sets of items within conceptual systems. □ **structuralist** *n. & adj.*

structure *n.* **1 a** a whole constructed unit, esp. a building. **b** the way in which a building etc. is constructed (*has a flimsy structure*). **c** the state of being well planned or organized (*your essay lacks structure*). **2**

a set of interconnecting parts of any complex thing; a framework (*the structure of a sentence*). ● *v.tr.* give structure to; organize; frame. □ **structural** *adj.* **structurally** *adv.* **structured** *adj.* (also in *comb.*). **structureless** *adj.*

strudel /ˈstruːdəl/ *n.* a dessert of thin pastry rolled up around a usu. fruit filling and baked (*apple strudel*).

struggle ● *v.intr.* **1** make forceful or violent efforts to get free of restraint or constriction. **2** (often foll. by *for*, or to + infin.) make violent or determined efforts under difficulties; strive hard (*struggled to speak*). **3** (foll. by *with*, *against*) contend; fight strenuously (*struggled with the disease*). **4** (foll. by *along*, *up*, etc.) make one's way with difficulty (*struggled to my feet*). **5** (esp. as **struggling** *adj.*) have difficulty in gaining recognition or a living (*a struggling artist*). ● *n.* **1** the act or a period of struggling. **2** a hard or confused contest. **3** a determined effort under difficulties. □ **the struggle for existence** (or **life**) the competition between organisms esp. as an element in natural selection, or between persons seeking a livelihood.

strum ● *v.* (**strummed**, **strumming**) **1** *tr. & intr.* play (a stringed musical instrument, esp. a guitar or banjo) by sweeping the thumb or a plectrum up or down the strings. **2** *tr.* play (a tune etc.) in this way. ● *n.* **1** the sound made by strumming. **2** an instance or period of strumming. □ **strummer** *n.*

strung *past and past part.* of STRING.

strung out *adj.* **1** addicted to, using, or high on drugs. **2** in a state of extreme nervous tension.

strut ● *n.* **1** a bar forming part of a framework and designed to resist compression. **2** a strutting gait. ● *v.* (**strutted**, **strutting**) **1** *intr.* walk in a proud upright way. **2** *tr.* brace with a strut or struts. □ **strut one's stuff** *informal* display one's ability. □ **strutter** *n.*

strychnine /ˈstrɪknaɪn, -niːn, -nɪn/ *n.* a bitter and highly poisonous vegetable alkaloid obtained from plants of the genus *Strychnos* (esp. *S. nux-vomica*).

Sts. *abbr.* **1** Saints. **2** Streets.

stub ● *n.* **1** the remnant of a pencil or cigarette etc. after use. **2** the small part of a cheque, receipt, ticket etc. that remains, to be kept as a record, after the main part has been detached and given to someone. **3** a stunted tail etc. **4** the stump of a tree, tooth, etc. ● *v.tr.* (**stubbed**, **stubbing**) **1** strike (one's toe) against something. **2** (usu. foll. by *out*) extinguish (a lighted cigarette) by pressing the lighted end against something.

stubble *n.* **1** the cut stalks of cereal plants left sticking up after the harvest. **2** a short bristly growth of unshaven hair, esp. on a man's face. □ **stubbled** *adj.* **stubbly** *adj.*

stubble field *n.* a harvested, unplowed field.

stubble-jumper *n.* Cdn *slang* a prairie farmer.

stubborn *adj.* **1** unreasonably obstinate. **2** unyielding, obdurate, inflexible (*stubborn resistance*). **3** that will not respond to treatment (*a stubborn cough*). □ **stubbornly** *adj.* **stubbornness** *n.*

stubby ● *adj.* (**-ier**, **-iest**) short and thick. ● *n.* (*pl.* **-ies**) Cdn *hist.* & *Austral. informal* a small squat bottle of beer.

stucco ● *n.* (*pl.* **-oes**) plaster or cement used for coating wall surfaces or moulding into architectural decorations. ● *v.tr.* (**-oes**, **-oed**) coat with stucco.

stuck ● *v.* *past and past part.* of STICK². ● *adj.* **1** unable to progress. **2** confined in a place (*was stuck in the house*). **3** (of an animal) butchered by having its throat cut (*screaming like a stuck pig*). □ **be stuck for** be at a loss for or in need of. **be stuck on** *informal* be infatuated with. **be stuck with** *informal* be unable to get rid of or escape from; be permanently involved with.

stuck-up *adj. informal* snobbish.

stud¹ ● *n.* **1** a large-headed nail, boss, or knob, projecting from a surface esp. for ornament. **2** a small piece of jewellery for wearing in pierced ears or nostrils. **3** a small object like a button with two heads, used esp. formerly to fasten a collar or the front of a shirt. **4** a small object projecting slightly from a road surface as a marker etc. **5** a two-by-four to which drywall etc. is nailed. **6** N Amer. any of a number of metal pieces set into the tire of a motor vehicle to improve roadholding in slippery conditions. ● *v.tr.* (**studded**, **studding**) **1** set with or as with studs. **2** be scattered over or about (a surface).

stud² *n.* **1 a** a number of horses kept for breeding etc. **b** a place where these are kept. **2** (also **stud horse**) a stallion. **3** *informal* a young man, esp. one noted for sexual prowess. **4** (in full **stud poker**) a form of poker with betting after the dealing of successive rounds of cards face up. □ **at stud** (of a male horse) publicly available for breeding on payment of a fee.

studded *adj.* thickly set or strewn (*diamond-studded*).

studding *n.* the wood framing of a wall in a house etc.

student *n.* **1 a** a person who is studying, esp. at university, college, etc. **b** N Amer. a school pupil. **2** (*attrib.*) studying in order to become (*a student teacher*). **3** a person who observes or has a particular interest in something (*a student of current affairs*).

student-at-law *n.* Cdn an articling student.

student loan *n.* a usu. government loan available to university and college students.

studied *adj.* deliberate, intentional (*with studied politeness*). □ **studiedly** *adv.*

studio *n.* (*pl.* **-os**) **1** a place where films or recordings are made or where television or radio programs are made or produced. **2** a company which produces films (*works for a major studio*). **3** the workroom of a painter or photographer etc. **4** a large room where dancers rehearse. **5** (in full **studio apartment**) an apartment with only one main room.

studious *adj.* **1** devoted to or assiduous in study or reading. **2** studied, deliberate, painstaking (*studious care*). **3** (foll. by *to* + infin. or *in* + verbal noun) showing care or attention. □ **studiously** *adv.* **studiousness** *n.*

study ● *n.* (*pl.* **-ies**) **1 a** the devotion of time and attention to acquiring information or knowledge, esp. of a specified subject. **b** consideration, examination (*the proposals deserve study*). **2** (in *pl.*) the pursuit of academic knowledge (*continued their studies abroad*; *Native Studies*). **3** a detailed consideration or investigation into a specified subject, phenomenon, etc. (*a study of child poverty*). **4** a report, essay, book, etc., devoted to such an investigation. **5** a room used for reading, writing, etc. ● *v.* (**-ies**, **-ied**) **1** *tr.* make a study of; investigate or examine (a subject) (*study law*). **2** *intr.* (often foll. by *for*) apply oneself to study. **3** *tr.* scrutinize or earnestly contemplate (a visible object) (*studied their faces*). **4** *tr.* try to learn (the words of one's role etc.). **5** *tr.* take pains to achieve (a result) or pay regard to (a subject or principle etc.). **6** *tr.* read (a book) attentively. □ **make a study of** investigate carefully.

study group *n.* a group of people meeting from time to time to study a particular subject or topic.

stuff ● *n.* **1** the material that a thing is made of; material that may be used for some purpose. **2** a substance or things or belongings of an indeterminate kind or a quality not needing to be specified (*leave your stuff in the hall*). **3** a particular knowledge or activity (*knows her stuff*). **4 a** what a person is perceived to be made of; a person's capabilities or inward character. **b** the makings of future attainment or excellence (*it was the stuff of legend*). **5** valueless matter, trash, nonsense (*take that stuff away*). **6** (*prec. by the*) **a** *informal* an available supply of something, esp. drink or drugs. **b** *slang* money. **7** *N Amer. informal* **a** (in baseball) a pitcher's repertoire of pitches and his or her skill in using it. **b** (in baseball, tennis, etc.) the spin given to a ball in order to make it vary its course. ● *v.* **1** *tr.* **a** pack (a receptacle) tightly. **b** fill (a quantity of envelopes) with the same printed matter, as for a mass mailing. **2** *tr.* (foll. by *in*, *into*) force or cram (a thing) (*stuffed the socks in the drawer*). **3** *tr.* fill out the skin of (an animal or bird etc.) with material to restore the original shape. **4** *tr.* fill (poultry, vegetables, etc.) with a savoury or sweet mixture, esp. before cooking. **5 a** *tr. & refl.* fill (a person or oneself) with food. **b** *tr. & intr.* eat greedily. **6** *tr.* push, esp. hastily or clumsily (*stuffed the note behind the cushion*). **7** *tr.* (usu. in *passive*; foll. by *up*) block up (a person's nose etc.). **8** *tr.* *slang* (esp. as an expression of contemptuous dismissal) dispose of as unwanted (*you can stuff the job*). **9** *tr.* *N Amer.* place bogus votes in (a ballot box). □ **do one's stuff** *informal* do what one has to. **get stuffed** *slang* an exclamation of dismissal, contempt, etc. **stuff it** *slang* an expression of rejection or disdain. **stuff one's face** eat a great deal or to excess. □ **stuffer** *n.* (also in *comb.*).

stuffed animal *n.* **1** *N Amer.* a soft plush toy animal, such as a teddy bear. **2** an animal that has been stuffed as part of a taxidermic process.

stuffed shirt *n.* *informal* a pompous or prim person.

stuffing *n.* **1** padding used to stuff cushions etc. **2** a savoury mixture put inside a chicken, turkey, etc. before it is cooked. **3** a mixture of seasoned crumbled bread served with meat. □ **knock** (or **take**) **the stuffing out of** *informal* make feeble or weak; defeat.

stuffy *adj.* (**-ier**, **-iest**) **1** lacking fresh air or ventilation; close. **2** dull or uninteresting. **3** (of a person's nose etc.) stuffed up. **4** (of a person) dull and conventional. □ **stuffily** *adv.* **stuffiness** *n.*

stultify /'stʌltə,faɪ/ *v.tr.* (**-ies**, **-ied**) **1** make ineffective, useless, or futile, esp. as a result of tedious routine. **2** cause to appear foolish or absurd. **3** negate or neutralize. □ **stultification** *n.*

stultifying *adj.* extremely tedious or boring. □ **stultifyingly** *adv.*

stumble ● *v.intr.* **1** lurch forward or have a partial fall from catching or striking or misplacing one's foot. **2** (often foll. by *along*) walk unsteadily with repeated stumbles. **3** act in a blundering or hesitating manner, esp. make a mistake or repeated mistakes in speaking etc. **4** (foll. by *on*, *upon*, *across*) find or encounter by chance. ● *n.* an act of stumbling. □ **stumbler** *n.*

stumblebum *n.* *N Amer.* *informal* a clumsy or inept person.

stumbling block *n.* an obstacle or circumstance causing difficulty or hesitation.

stump ● *n.* **1** the projecting portion of the trunk of a cut or fallen tree that remains fixed in the ground. **2** the part remaining when a limb or other part of the body is amputated or severed. **3** the part of a broken tooth left in the gum. **4** a thing, e.g. a pencil or a candle, that has been worn down or reduced to a small part of its original length. **5** (in *pl.*) *jocular* the legs. **6** the stump of a tree, or other place, used by an orator to address a meeting. ● *v.* **1** *tr.* (of a question etc.) be too hard for; puzzle. **2** *intr.* walk stiffly or noisily as if on a wooden leg. **3** *tr. & intr.* *N Amer.* traverse (a district) making speeches esp. for an election

campaign. **4** *tr.* remove the stumps from (land). □ **on the stump** *informal* engaged in political speech making and campaigning. **up a** (or **the**) **stump** *N Amer. slang* **1** in difficulties. **2** pregnant.

stumpage *n.* **1** standing timber considered with reference to its quantity or marketable value. **2** (in full **stumpage fee**) a tax charged for the privilege of cutting timber on government-owned land.

stumped *adj.* at a loss; baffled.

stumpy *adj.* (**-ier**, **-iest**) short and thick.

stun *v.tr.* (**stunned**, **stunning**) **1** knock senseless. **2** bewilder or astound due to something shocking, unbelievable, or unexpected. **3** (of a sound) deafen temporarily.

stung past and past part. of STING.

stun gun *n.* a gun which stuns a person or animal by means of an electric shock etc.

stunk past and past part. of STINK.

stunned *adj.* *Cdn informal* stupid; foolish.

stunner *n.* *informal* **1** a thing that stuns or dazes someone or something; an amazing or astounding thing. **2** a very attractive woman or girl.

stunning *adj.* *informal* **1** very impressive or attractive. **2** surprising or shocking. □ **stunningly** *adv.*

stunt[1] *v.tr.* retard the growth or development of. □ **stuntedness** *n.*

stunt[2] ● *n.* **1** something unusual done to attract attention (*publicity stunt*). **2** an act notable or impressive on account of the skill, strength, or daring etc. required to perform it. ● *v.intr.* perform stunts, esp. aerobatics.

stuntman *n.* (*pl.* **-men**) a man employed to take an actor's place in performing dangerous stunts.

stupefy /'stju:pəfaɪ, 'stju:-/ *v.tr.* (**-ies**, **-ied**) **1** make stupid (*stupefied with drink*). **2** stun with astonishment (*the news was stupefying*). □ **stupefaction** /-'fækʃən/ *n.* **stupefying** *adj.* **stupefyingly** *adv.*

stupendous /stu:'pendəs, 'stju:-/ *adj.* amazing or prodigious, esp. in terms of size or degree (*a stupendous achievement*). □ **stupendously** *adv.*

stupid *adj.* (**stupider**, **stupidest**) **1** unintelligent (*a stupid man*). **2** showing lack of good judgment; foolish (*a stupid idea*). **3** uninteresting or boring. **4** in a state of stupor or lethargy. **5** obtuse; lacking in sensibility. **6** *informal* a general term of disparagement (*your stupid jokes*). □ **stupidity** *n.* (*pl.* **-ies**). **stupidly** *adv.*

stupor /'stu:pər, 'stju:-/ *n.* **1** *Med.* a condition of near-unconsciousness characterized by great reduction in mental activity and responsiveness, caused by disease, narcotics, alcohol, etc. **2** a dazed, stunned, or torpid state. □ **stuporous** *adj.*

sturdy *adj.* (**-ier**, **-iest**) **1** robust; strongly built. **2** vigorous and determined (*sturdy resistance*). □ **sturdily** *adv.* **sturdiness** *n.*

sturgeon *n.* any large mailed sharklike fish of the family Acipenseridae etc. swimming upriver to spawn, used as food and a source of caviar.

stutter ● *v.* **1** *intr.* stammer, esp. by involuntarily repeating the first consonants of words. **2** *tr.* (often foll. by *out*) utter (words) in this way. **3** *intr.* (esp. of a vehicle or engine) move or start with difficulty, making short sharp noises or movements. ● *n.* **1** the act or habit of stuttering. **2** an instance of stuttering. □ **stutterer** *n.*

sty[1] *n.* (*pl.* **sties**) **1** a pen or enclosure for pigs. **2** a filthy room or dwelling. **3** a place of debauchery.

sty[2] *n.* (*pl.* **sties** or **styes**) an inflamed swelling on the edge of an eyelid.

style ● *n.* **1** a kind or sort, esp. in regard to appearance and form. **2** a manner of writing or speaking or performing (*a florid style*). **3** the distinctive manner of a person or school or period, esp. in relation to painting, architecture, furniture, dress, etc. **4 a** correct or conventional use of a language (often *attrib.*: *style guide*). **b** the correct way of designating a person or thing (*the correct style when addressing an archbishop is 'Your Grace'*). **5 a** a superior quality or manner (*do it in style*). **b** = FORM *n.* 8. **c** fashionableness or attractiveness of appearance or bearing (*she dresses with such style*). **6** a particular make, shape, or pattern (*in all sizes and styles*). **7** a method of reckoning dates (*Old Style*). **8** = STYLUS 1, 4. **9** *Bot.* the narrow extension of the ovary supporting the stigma. **10** *Zool.* a small slender pointed appendage. ● *v.tr.* **1** design or make etc. in a particular (esp. fashionable) style. **2** designate in a specified way. □ **styler** *n.*

-style *comb. form* forming adjectives and adverbs with the sense 'in a manner characteristic of'.

style book *n.* a manual of house style.

stylish *adj.* **1** fashionable, chic. **2** having a superior quality, manner, etc. □ **stylishly** *adv.* **stylishness** *n.*

stylist *n.* **1 a** a person employed by a firm to create, coordinate, or promote new styles or designs, esp. of clothes or cars. **b** a hairdresser. **2 a** a writer noted for or aspiring to good literary style. **b** (in sports or music) a person who performs with style.

stylistic *adj.* of or concerning esp. literary or artistic style. □ **stylistically** *adv.*

stylistics *n.* the study of literary or linguistic style.

stylize *v.tr.* (esp. as **stylized** *adj.*) paint, draw, etc. (a subject) in a fixed, conventional, or artificial style. □ **stylization** *n.*

stylus /ˈstailəs/ *n.* (*pl.* **styli** /-lai/ or **styluses**) **1** any sharp instrument or point for engraving, tracing, etc., esp. an ancient implement for writing on wax. **2** *Computing* an electrical device shaped like a pen, used esp. to design graphical images on a computer screen. **3 a** a hard, esp. diamond or sapphire, point on the arm of a turntable that follows a groove in a record and transmits recorded sound for reproduction. **b** a similar point used to produce such a groove when recording sound. **4** a pointer for indicating a time, position, etc., esp. the gnomon of a sundial. **5** a tracing point used to produce a written record in a seismograph, telegraph receiver, etc.

stymie /ˈstaimi/ ● *v.tr.* (**stymies**, **stymied**, **stymying** or **stymieing**) **1** obstruct or thwart (a person, project, process, etc.). **2 a** puzzle or perplex (a person). **b** place (a person) in a difficult situation. **3** *Golf* block (an opponent, an opponent's ball, or oneself) with a stymie. ● *n.* (*pl.* **-ies**) *Golf* a situation on a green in which the path of a putt to the hole is obstructed by an opponent's ball.

styrene /ˈstairiːn/ *n. Chem.* a liquid hydrocarbon, easily polymerized and used in making plastics etc.

Styrofoam *n.* esp. *N Amer. proprietary* a variety of expanded polystyrene often used in the manufacture of insulation, disposable food containers, etc.

suasion /ˈsweiʒən/ *n. formal* persuasion as opposed to force (*moral suasion*). □ **suasive** *adj.*

suave /swɑːv/ *adj.* charming, smooth; polite; sophisticated. □ **suavely** *adv.* **suavity** /-viti/ *n.* (*pl.* **-ies**)

sub *informal* ● *n.* **1** a submarine. **2** a sandwich made with a long roll or small loaf and filled with a variety of meats, cheeses, etc. **3 a** a substitute. **b** *N Amer.* a substitute teacher. **4** a subscription. ● *v.intr.* (**subbed**,

subbing) (usu. foll. by *for*) act or work as a substitute for a person.

subalpine *adj.* **1** pertaining to or situated in the higher mountain slopes just below the timberline. **2** of or pertaining to the area at the foot of the Alps.

subarctic ● *n.* (usu. **Subarctic**) the region immediately south of the Arctic Circle. ● *adj.* characteristic of, pertaining to, or inhabiting this region.

subatomic *adj.* **1 a** (of a particle) existing in an atom. **b** (of a process etc.) occurring within an atom. **2 a** smaller than an atom. **b** *informal* extremely small.

sub-basement *n.* a basement below a main basement.

subcategory *n.* (*pl.* **-ies**) a secondary category.

subclass *n.* **1 a** a secondary or inferior class. **b** each of the groups or categories that constitute a class. **2** *Biol.* a taxonomic category below a class.

subcommittee *n.* a body of people appointed by a committee, usu. composed of a selection of its own members, esp. to study or deal with a specific issue or an aspect of a larger matter.

subcompact *N Amer.* ● *adj.* designating a car that is smaller than a compact, usu. having a wheelbase of less than 85 inches, and a 1 litre engine. ● *n.* a subcompact car.

subconscious ● *n.* the part of the mind which influences actions etc. without one's full awareness. ● *adj.* **1** of, pertaining to, or existing in the subconscious. **2** operating or existing without one's full awareness (*subconscious impulses*). □ **subconsciously** *adv.*

subcontinent *n.* **1** a large section of a continent having a certain geographical or political identity or independence. **2** a large land mass, smaller than a continent, e.g. Greenland. □ **subcontinental** *adj.*

subcontract ● *v.* **1** *tr.* hire a person, company, etc. to do (work) as part of a larger contract or project. **2** *intr.* make or carry out a subcontract. ● *n.* an agreement in which an individual or firm agrees to perform all or a portion of a previous contract, esp. to supply materials, labour, etc.

subcontractor *n.* an individual or company etc. to whom a principal contractor has sublet all or a portion of a contract.

subculture *n.* **1 a** a cultural group within a larger or predominant culture but distinguished from it by factors such as class, ethnic background, religion, or residence, unified by shared beliefs or interests which may be at variance with those of the larger culture. **b** the system of beliefs, customs, and behaviour etc. typical of such a group. **2** a culture of micro-organisms started from another culture. □ **subcultural** *adj.*

subcutaneous /ˌsʌbkjuːˈteiniəs/ *adj.* situated or introduced just under the skin. □ **subcutaneously** *adv.*

subdirectory *n.* (*pl.* **-ies**) *Computing* a directory that is itself contained in another directory.

subdivide *v.* **1** *tr.* **a** divide (a thing) into smaller parts or portions. **b** divide (a thing that has been divided) into smaller parts or portions. **2** *intr.* divide into smaller parts, esp. after a previous division. **3** *tr. N Amer. & Austral.* divide (a tract of land) into plots for sale or development.

subdivision *n.* **1** *N Amer. & Austral.* an area of land divided into plots for sale or development. **2** *N Amer.* a housing development that has been built on such an area. **3** each of the parts into which a thing, esp. a previous division, is or may be divided; a secondary division. **4** the act or an instance of subdividing.

subdue v.tr. (**subdues, subdued, subduing**) **1** overcome or overpower (a person or animal etc.) by physical force or violence. **2** bring (a person etc.) under one's control by intimidation, persuasion, manipulation, etc. **3** check or restrain (an impulse, emotion, thought, etc.). **4** conquer and bring into subjection (an army, people, or country).

subdued adj. **1** (of a colour, light, or sound, etc.) reduced in or lacking intensity or force. **2** (of a person) not showing much excitement or activity.

subfamily n. (pl. **-ies**) **1** Biol. a taxonomic category below a family. **2** any analogous subdivision of a family in a classification, such as in linguistics.

subfloor n. a rough floor serving as a foundation for a finished floor in a building. □ **subflooring** n.

subfreezing adj. below the freezing point.

sub-genre n. a secondary or subordinate style of esp. literature or art.

subgroup n. **1** a subordinate group; a subdivision of a group. **2** Math. **a** a series of operations forming part of a larger group. **b** any group all of whose elements are elements of a larger group.

subheading n. (also **subhead**) **1** a subordinate heading, headline, caption, or title in a chapter, article, etc. **2** a subordinate division in a classification.

subhuman ● adj. **1** (of an animal) closely related to, but of a lower order of being than, a human. **2** (of a person or behaviour) uncivilized, bestial; less than human. ● n. a subhuman person or creature.

subject ● n. **1 a** a topic or the theme of a discussion, investigation, or consideration. **b** a figure, incident, scene, etc. represented by an artist in a work of fiction, painting, photograph, etc. **c** (foll. by of) a target or focus of attention, thought, dispute, etc. (her comments have been the subject of debate). **2** a particular department of art, history, science, etc. that is studied or taught in an academic institution (math is her best subject). **3** Grammar a word or phrase in a sentence indicating who or what performs the action of a verb or upon whom or which a verb is predicated, e.g. 'we' in the sentence we ate ice cream or 'my dog' in my dog is clever. **4 a** a person owing allegiance to and under the protection of a monarch or government. **b** any person under the control of or owing obedience to another. **5** a person or corpse upon whom a medical treatment, study, or experiment is being performed. **6** Philos. **a** a thinking or feeling entity; the conscious mind; the ego, esp. as opposed to anything external to the mind. **b** the central substance or core of a thing as opposed to its attributes. **7** Logic the part of a proposition about which a statement is made. ● adj. (usu. foll. by to) **1** (foll. by to) susceptible to some esp. harmful or medical condition, occurrence, etc. **2** liable (prices are subject to change). **3** dependent or conditional upon; resting on the assumption of (subject to your approval). **4** bound by law or regulation (subject to sales tax). **5** under the rule or domination of an individual or group, sovereign, country, etc. (a subject nation). ● adv. (foll. by to) conditionally upon (subject to your consent). ● v.tr. (usu. foll. by to) **1** cause (a person or thing) to experience, undergo, or endure a specified treatment. **2** expose or make vulnerable to (subjects herself to ridicule). **3** subdue (a nation, person, etc.) to one's sway etc. □ **on the subject of** concerning, about. □ **subjection** n.

subjective ● adj. **1 a** (of art, written history, a person's views, etc.) proceeding from, or influenced by, an individual's personal thoughts and opinions. **b** (of a person) tending to emphasize or be influenced by one's own feelings or opinions. **2** esp. Philos. proceeding from or belonging to the individual consciousness or perception; partial, misconceived, or distorted. **3** (of a case or word) constructed as appropriate to the subject of a sentence or verb. **4** (of a symptom etc.) that is felt or is experienced only by a patient, and may not be diagnosed by someone else, e.g. a doctor. ● n. **1** the subjective case. **2** a word or form in this case. □ **subjectively** adv. **subjectivity** n.

subjectivism n. Philos. **1** the doctrine that knowledge, perception, morality, etc., are merely subjective and relative and that there is no external or objective truth. **2** a theory or method based exclusively on subjective facts. **3** the quality or condition of being subjective. □ **subjectivist** n.

subjugate /ˈsʌbdʒʊˌgeɪt/ v.tr. **1** bring (a country, people, etc.) into subjection; conquer. **2** bring under domination or control; make subservient or dependent. □ **subjugation** n.

subjunctive /səbˈdʒʌŋktɪv/ Grammar ● n. **1** (in full **subjunctive mood**) a mood of verbs used to express a condition, wish, fear, possibility, command, suggestion or uncertainty, e.g. if I were rich or I wish I were beautiful. **2** a verb in this mood. ● adj. (of a verb or phrase) expressed in the subjunctive.

subkingdom n. a taxonomic category below a kingdom.

sublease ● n. a transaction in which the lessee or tenant of a property leases it to another. ● v.tr. = SUBLET.

sublet ● v.tr. (**subletting**; past and past part. **sublet**) **1** acquire a lease on (an apartment etc.) from a person who is leasing it from its owner. **2** rent out (an apartment etc.) that one is leasing from its owner. ● n. an apartment etc. that is being sublet.

sub-lieutenant n. Cdn & Brit. a naval officer ranking next below lieutenant. Abbr.: **SLt**.

sublimate ● v. /ˈsʌbləˌmeɪt/ **1** tr. divert or channel the energy of (a primitive esp. sexual impulse) into a more highly valued or acceptable activity. **2** Chem. **a** tr. subject (a substance) to the action of heat to convert it into a vapour which, on cooling, is deposited in solid form. **b** intr. (of a substance) pass from a solid state to a vapour, or from a gaseous state to a solid, without liquefaction. **3** tr. elevate or refine to a high degree of purity or excellence; idealize. ● n. /ˈsʌbləmət/ Chem. a refined or concentrated product; a product of sublimation. □ **sublimation** n.

sublime /səˈblaɪm/ ● adj. (**sublimer, sublimest**) **1** of the most exalted, grand, or noble kind; of a high intellectual, moral, or spiritual level (sublime genius). **2** (of nature, art, etc.) producing an overwhelming sense of awe, reverence, or high emotion, by reason of great beauty, vastness, or grandeur. **3** usu. ironic of the most extreme kind; supreme (sublime indifference). ● n. a quality in art or nature etc. arousing or inspiring awe, reverence, terror, or high emotion in the person experiencing it. □ **from the sublime to the ridiculous** moving or ranging from what is serious or important to what is trivial or laughable. □ **sublimely** adv. **sublimity** /-ˈlɪmətɪ/ n.

subliminal /səbˈlɪmənəl/ Psych. ● adj. **1** (of a stimulus, message, advertisement, etc.) operating below the threshold of sensation or consciousness; having an influence upon the mind without one being aware of it. **2** (of recognition, perception, etc.) occurring as a result of a process or stimulus of which one is unaware. ● n. something that is subliminal, esp. a subliminal message. □ **subliminally** adv.

submachine gun *n.* a hand-held lightweight automatic or semi-automatic weapon designed to shoot small-calibre ammunition.

submarine ● *n.* **1** a vessel capable of operating under water. **2** (in full **submarine sandwich**) = SUB *n.* 2. ● *adj.* living, occurring, or used under the surface of the sea. ● *v.* **1** *tr. & intr. Baseball* deliver (a pitch or the ball) sidearm or underhand. **2** *intr.* voyage in or operate a submarine.

submariner *n.* **1** /ˌsʌbˈmerənɜr/ a person who travels in or operates a submarine. **2** /ˌsʌbməˈriːnɜr/ *Baseball* a pitcher who throws with the arm at or below shoulder level; a sidearm or underhand pitcher.

submenu *n. Computing* a secondary list of available commands, options, etc. displayed under a general heading listed in a menu.

submerge *v.* **1** *tr.* immerse, dip, or place in a liquid. **2** *tr.* overwhelm or inundate (a person) with work, problems, etc. **3** *tr.* conceal or suppress (an emotion etc.). **4** *intr.* (of a submarine, its crew, a diver, etc.) dive below the surface of water. □ **submergence** *n.*

submerged *adj.* **1** immersed, inundated, or buried in or beneath a liquid or substance. **2** suppressed, concealed, hidden. **3** growing entirely under water.

submerse *v.tr.* (esp. as **submersed** *adj.*) submerge. □ **submersion** *n.*

submersible ● *n.* a submarine operating under water for short periods, used esp. for exploration. ● *adj.* **1** capable of being submerged. **2** intended or designed to operate or be used under water.

submicroscopic *adj.* too small to be seen by an ordinary microscope.

submission *n.* **1** a thing that has been submitted for consideration, evaluation, or judgment. **2** submissiveness (*showed great submission of spirit*). **3** *Law* **a** a contract in which parties in a dispute agree to submit to arbitration. **b** a matter referred to a third party, esp. a judge or jury, for arbitration. **4 a** the action or an instance of yielding to the authority or will of another. **b** (in wrestling) the surrender of a participant yielding to the pain of a hold.

submissive *adj.* **1** obedient, subservient, meek. **2** willing to yield or back down. **3** (of an action, etc.) indicating subservience or a willingness to submit. □ **submissively** *adv.* **submissiveness** *n.*

submit *v.* (**-mitted, -mitting**) **1** (usu. foll. by *to*) **a** *intr.* cease resistance; give way; yield. **b** *refl.* consent to undergo a certain treatment or abide by a certain condition or limitation etc.; surrender (oneself) to. **2** *tr.* present (an application, essay, contest entry, etc.) for consideration or decision. **3** *tr.* (usu. foll. by *to*) subject (a person or thing) to an operation, process, treatment, etc. (*submitted it to the flames*). **4** *tr.* esp. *Law* propose, suggest, or contend, esp. deferentially.

subnormal *adj.* **1** less than or below the normal level. **2** of a level of intelligence and general ability which is below a given standard of normality.

subnotebook *n.* a computer that is smaller than a notebook but larger than a palmtop or personal digital assistant.

suborder *n.* a taxonomic category below an order.

subordinate ● *adj.* /səˈbɔrdənət/ (often. foll. by *to*) **1** (of a person, position, etc.) of inferior rank; dependent upon the authority or power of another. **2** secondary, minor. **3** (of a thing) dependent upon or subservient to a chief or principal thing of the same kind. ● *n.* /səˈbɔrdənət/ a subordinate person or thing, esp. a person working under another's control or orders. ● *v.tr.* /səˈbɔrdəˌneit/ (usu. foll. by *to*) **1** make inferior or secondary; treat or consider as less impor-

tant or valuable. **2** bring into a subordinate position; make dependent or subservient. □ **subordination** *n.*

subordinate clause *n.* a clause, usu. introduced by a conjunction, that does not constitute a sentence itself but which depends on the principal clause that it modifies or in which it serves as a noun, e.g. 'that she has come' in *I hope that she has come*.

subordinating conjunction *n.* a conjunction that joins a subordinate clause to a main clause, e.g. 'because' in *I am happy because it is sunny*.

suborn /səˈbɔrn/ *v.tr.* **1** induce or procure (a person) to commit an unlawful act by bribery or other means. **2** bribe or induce (a person) to give false testimony or commit perjury. **3** procure (false testimony) by bribery or other unlawful means.

subphylum *n.* (*pl.* **subphyla**) a taxonomic category below a phylum.

subplot *n.* a secondary plot in a novel, play, etc.

subpoena /səˈpiːnə/ ● *n.* a writ issued by a court or other authorized body requiring the attendance of a person at a stated time and place, usu. to testify or present evidence, subject to penalty for noncompliance. ● *v.tr.* (*past* and *past part.* **subpoenaed**) **1** summon (a person) to appear in court as a witness. **2** require (evidence etc.) to be brought by a witness so that it may be presented in court.

sub-post office *n.* **1** *Cdn* & *Brit.* a small local post office offering fewer services than a main post office. **2** *Cdn* a postal outlet located within a drugstore, convenience store, etc., usu. offering limited postal services.

sub-region *n.* esp. *Ecology* a subdivision of a geographical region, usu. considered in terms of the plant and animal life it sustains. □ **sub-regional** *adj.*

subroutine *n. Computing* (also **subprogram**) a routine designed to perform a frequently used operation within a program.

sub-Saharan *attrib.adj.* from or forming part of the African regions south of the Sahara desert.

subscribe *v.* **1** *intr.* (often foll. by *to*) arrange to receive a periodical, service, or series of tickets in exchange for payment. **2** *intr.* (usu. foll. by *to*) express or feel agreement with an idea or resolution etc.; hold as a belief or opinion. **3** *tr.* write or sign (one's name) at the bottom of esp. a document as a witness or consenting party. **4** *tr. & intr.* **a** (often foll. by *for*) pay or guarantee (a specified sum of money) for an issue of shares. **b** pledge or contribute (a specified sum of money) to a fund or charity etc.

subscriber *n.* **1** a person who pays a fee to receive regular issues of a periodical etc. **2** a person who pays a fee in order to receive a particular service, such as telephone or cable television service. **3** a person who purchases advance tickets to a series of theatrical productions etc. **4** a person contributing money to a charity or toward the purchase of stock etc.

subscript ● *n.* a character, number, or symbol written or printed below the line or below and usu. to the right of another symbol (*compare* SUPERSCRIPT *n.*). ● *adj.* written or printed below the line or below and to the right of another symbol.

subscription *n.* **1 a** an agreement to pay in advance for a specified number of consecutive issues of a periodical. **b** an agreement to purchase, in advance, tickets for a series of events (also *attrib.*: *subscription series*). **c** an agreement to pay for and receive service from a cable television or telephone company etc. **2** an offer or agreement to purchase shares in a company. **3** a fee paid usu. in advance to purchase tickets for a series of events, a number of issues of a periodical, etc. **4** a sum of money donated to or raised by a charity, fund, etc.

subsea adj. & adv. beneath the surface of the sea.

subsection n. a division of a section, esp. within a document or book.

subsequent adj. (usu. foll. by to) following a specified event etc. in time, esp. as a consequence. □ **subsequently** adv.

subservient / səb'sɜrviənt / adj. **1** slavishly submissive, servile, obsequious. **2** (usu. foll. by to) serving as a means; instrumental. **3** (usu. foll. by to) subordinate. □ **subservience** n. **subserviently** adv.

subset n. **1** a secondary part of a set. **2** Math. a set consisting of elements all of which are contained in another set.

subside v.intr. **1** become calm or tranquil; die down; abate (the excitement subsided). **2** (of water) be reduced to a lower level. **3** (of the ground) cave in. **4** (of a building, ship, etc.) sink into the ground or water. **5** (of swelling etc.) be reduced, become less prominent. **6** (of a person) settle into a comfortable position. □ **subsidence** / -'saidəns, 'sʌbsədəns / n.

subsidiary / səb'sɪdieri, səb'sɪdʒəri / ● adj. **1** serving to assist or supplement; auxiliary. **2** subordinate, secondary. ● n. (pl. **-ies**) a company whose controlling interest is owned by a parent company.

subsidize v.tr. **1** reduce the cost of (a commodity or service) by subsidy (government-subsidized housing). **2** support (an organization, activity, person, etc.) by grants of money. **3** support financially in an indirect way (our customers pay more to subsidize the high cost of rent here). **4** pay money to secure the assistance or co-operation of (a person, organization, country, etc.). □ **subsidization** n. **subsidized** adj. **subsidizer** n.

subsidy n. (pl. **-ies**) **1** money granted by the government to producers of certain goods to enable them to sell the goods to the public at a low price, to compete with foreign competition, or to avoid laying off employees. **2** money granted by the government to keep down the price of a service or commodity considered to be essential. **3** money granted to a charity, arts group, or other undertaking held to be in the public interest. **4** any grant or contribution of money. **5** money paid by one country to another in return for military, naval, or other aid.

subsist v.intr. **1** (often foll. by on) maintain or support oneself; be sustained or kept alive. **2** remain in being; continue to exist. **3** (foll. by in) reside or exist in; be attributable to. □ **subsistent** adj.

subsistence n. **1** the means of supporting life. **2** the production of a sufficient quantity of goods required to sustain one's own existence or to support one's household, without producing a sufficient surplus for trade. **3** a a minimal standard of living. **b** the income required to provide a minimal level of existence. **4** the state or an instance of subsisting.

subsoil n. the layer of soil lying immediately under the topsoil.

subsonic adj. pertaining to, capable of, or designating speeds less than that of sound. □ **subsonically** adv.

subspecialty n. (pl. **-ies**) a secondary specialty within a branch of esp. science or medicine. □ **subspecialize** v.intr. **subspecialist** n.

subspecies n. (pl. same) a distinct subdivision of a species, esp. one geographically or ecologically isolated from other such subdivisions.

substance n. **1** the essential esp. solid matter of which a physical thing consists. **2** a particular kind of material having a definite chemical composition and

usu. uniform properties. **3** esp. N Amer. an intoxicating or narcotic chemical or drug, esp. an illegal one (substance abuse). **4 a** the content or inward nature of a thing as opposed to its superficial appearance or form. **b** steadiness or strength of character (a man of substance). **5 a** the essential point or theme conveyed. **b** concrete evidence. **6** wealth and possessions. □ **in substance 1** in reality. **2** generally; apart from details.

substandard adj. of less than the required or normal quality or size; inadequate, inferior.

substantial adj. **1** of real importance or value (a substantial contribution). **2 a** of ample or considerable size or amount (a substantial price increase). **b** (of a meal or portion of food) ample and filling. **3** of solid structure or build (a substantial house). **4** having substance or truth; essential, real (substantial evidence). □ **substantiality** / -ʃi'æliti / n. **substantially** adv.

substantiate / səb'stænʃi,eit / v.tr. prove the truth of (a charge, statement, claim, etc.). □ **substantiation** n.

substantive / 'sʌbstəntɪv, səb'stæn- / adj. **1 a** having a firm or solid basis; important, significant. **b** of substantial extent or amount; considerable. **2** Law relating to rights and duties as opposed to forms of procedure. □ **substantively** adv.

substation n. **1** an outlet or establishment subordinate to a principal station (postal substation). **2** a station at which the high voltage of an electrical current from a generating station is reduced so that it is suitable for supply to consumers.

substituent / sʌb'stɪtjuənt / ● adj. (of a group of atoms) replacing another atom or group in a compound, esp. replacing hydrogen in an organic compound. ● n. such a group.

substitute ● n. **1 a** a thing that is or may be used in place of another, often to serve the same function but with a slightly different effect. **b** an artificial substance used as an alternative to a natural substance. **2 a** a person who is available or is used to perform the duties of another, esp. temporarily, such as during a holiday or illness. **b** (in full **substitute teacher**) N Amer. a teacher who replaces another who is unable to teach because of illness etc. ● v. **1 a** tr. (often foll. by for) use or insert (a person or thing) in place of another. **b** intr. act as a substitute. **2** tr. disputed (usu. foll. by with, by) replace (a person or thing) with another. ¶Use with the prepositions by or with should be avoided in standard English. The example substitute dairy milk with soy milk can be reworded as substitute soy milk for dairy milk. □ **substitutable** adj. **substitutability** n. **substitution** n. **substitutive** adj.

substrate / 'sʌbstreit / n. **1** a layer of soil, earth, clay, or rock beneath the surface. **2 a** the surface or material on which any particular organism grows. **b** the substance upon which an enzyme acts. **3** an underlying surface or foundation of a structure or development.

substratum n. (pl. **-strata**) **1** a foundation or basis (the substratum of truth). **2** = SUBSTRATE 1, 2.

substructure n. an underlying or supporting structure. □ **substructural** adj.

subsume v.tr. (often foll. by in or under) **1** include (a thing) in a larger group, class, or category. **2** bring (a term, idea, category, etc.) into or under the heading of a broader one. □ **subsumption** n.

subsurface ● n. that which lies immediately below the surface of something, esp. the stratum or strata below the earth's surface. ● adj. existing, lying, or operating beneath the surface of earth, water, etc.

subsystem *n.* a self-contained system within a larger system.

subtend *v.tr.* **1 a** (of a line, arc, figure, etc.) form (an angle) at a particular point when its extremities are joined at that point. **b** (of an angle or chord) have bounding lines or points that meet or coincide with those of (a line or arc). **2** *Bot.* (of a bract etc.) extend under so as to embrace, support, or enfold.

subterfuge /ˈsʌbtərˌfjuːdʒ/ *n.* **1** a deceitful statement or action resorted to in an attempt to avoid blame, justify an argument, conceal something, etc. **2** the practice or policy of employing subterfuges.

subterranean /ˌsʌbtəˈreɪniən/ *adj.* **1** existing, occurring, or done under the earth's surface. **2** existing or kept out of sight; secret, concealed.

subtext *n.* **1** an underlying, often distinct, theme in a text, conversation, etc. **2** the underlying theme of an event or period in history (*the sociological subtext of the Cold War*). □ **subtextual** *adj.*

subtitle ● *n.* **1** a secondary or additional title. **2** a translation or transcription of the dialogue of a movie etc. printed at the bottom of the screen. ● *v.tr.* provide (a book, movie, etc.) with a subtitle or subtitles. □ **subtitled** *adj.*

subtle /ˈsʌtəl/ *adj.* (**subtler, subtlest**) **1 a** difficult to perceive or detect; not easily grasped or understood (*a subtle distinction*). **b** operating or performed imperceptibly or secretly (*we must try a subtle approach*). **2** (of scent, colour, etc.) faint (*subtle perfume*). **3 a** capable of making fine distinctions (*a subtle mind*). **b** cleverly or skilfully designed. **4** cunning or clever. □ **subtlety** *n.* **subtly** *adv.*

subtotal *n.* the total of one part of a group of figures to be added.

subtract *v.* **1** *tr.* deduct (a quantity or number) from another. **2** *intr.* perform the arithmetical operation of subtraction (*learn to add and subtract*). **3** *tr.* remove (a portion or thing) from another. □ **subtraction** *n.* **subtractive** *adj.*

subtropics *n.pl.* the regions adjacent to or bordering on the tropics. □ **subtropical** *adj.*

subtype *n.* a subordinate type, esp. a type included within a broader or more general type.

subunit *n.* a distinct component, esp. each of two or more polypeptide chains in a large protein.

suburb *n.* **1** a residential district lying originally just beyond or now usu. within the boundaries of a city or town. **2** (in *pl.*) the outlying part of a city or town composed of such districts.

suburban *adj.* **1** of, belonging to, situated in, or carried on in the suburbs. **2** *derogatory* having characteristics regarded as typical of the residents, architecture, or life of the suburbs; perceived as lacking the excitement, diversity, culture, or sophistication of residents or life in the city. □ **suburbanite** *n.* **suburbanize** *v.tr.* **suburbanization** *n.*

suburban sprawl *n. N Amer.* the rapid and uncontrolled expansion of suburban areas.

suburbia *n.* **1** suburbs collectively. **2** *derogatory* the social and cultural aspects of suburban life or residents.

subversive /səbˈvɜːrsɪv/ ● *adj.* seeking to subvert (esp. a government). ● *n.* a subversive person; revolutionary. □ **subversively** *adv.* **subversiveness** *n.*

subvert /səbˈvɜːrt/ *v.tr.* overthrow or upset (religion, government, morality, etc.). □ **subversion** *n.*

subway *n.* **1** esp. *N Amer.* an esp. urban railway most parts of which are underground. **2** a subway train or car. **3** a station on a subway line.

subwoofer *n.* a loudspeaker component designed to reproduce very low bass frequencies.

sub-zero *adj.* (esp. of temperature) lower than zero.

succeed *v.* **1** *intr.* **a** accomplish one's purpose. **b** (of a plan etc.) be successful. **2 a** *tr.* come next after. **b** *intr.* come next, be subsequent. **3** *intr.* (often foll. by to) become the rightful or subsequent holder of an inheritance etc. (*succeeded to the throne*). **4** *tr.* take over an office, property, inheritance, etc. from (*succeeded his father*). □ **nothing succeeds like success** one success leads to others.

success *n.* **1** the accomplishment of an aim. **2** the attainment of wealth, fame, or position. **3** a thing or person that turns out well.

successful *adj.* **1** having or resulting in success. **2** having wealth or status. □ **successfully** *adv.* **successfulness** *n.*

succession *n.* **1 a** the process of following in order. **b** a series of things or people in succession. **2 a** the right of succeeding to an office, inheritance, the throne, etc. **b** the act or process of so succeeding. **c** those having such a right. **3** the process by which a plant or animal community successively gives way to another until a stable climax community is reached. **4 a** the rotation of crops. **b** the continuous cultivation of a crop throughout a season by successive sowings or plantings. □ **in quick succession** following one another at short intervals. **in succession** one after another, without intervention. **in succession to** as the successor of. □ **successional** *adj.*

successive *adj.* following one after another. □ **successively** *adv.* **successiveness** *n.*

successor *n.* a person who or thing which succeeds another in an office, function, or position.

success story *n.* **1** a rise from poverty, insignificance, etc. to success. **2** such a successful person etc.

succinct /səˈsɪŋkt, sʌkˈsɪŋkt/ *adj.* briefly expressed; terse, concise. ¶Though objected to by some, the pronunciation /səˈsɪŋkt/ is much more frequent in Canada. □ **succinctly** *adv.* **succinctness** *n.*

succotash /ˈsʌkəˌtæʃ/ *n. US* a dish of corn and lima beans boiled together.

Succoth *var. of* SUKKOT.

succour /ˈsʌkər/ ● *n.* assistance, esp. in time of need. ● *v.tr.* assist (esp. a person in danger or distress).

succulent /ˈsʌkjələnt/ ● *adj.* **1** juicy; palatable. **2** *informal* desirable. **3** (of a plant, its leaves, or stems) thick and fleshy. ● *n.* a succulent plant, esp. a cactus. □ **succulence** *n.* **succulently** *adv.*

succumb *v.intr.* **1** be overcome (by temptation etc.). **2** die as the result of a disease, wound, etc.

such ● *adj.* **1** of the kind or degree in question (*such a person; people such as these*). **2** so great; in such high degree (*had such a fright that he fainted*). **3** of a more than normal kind or degree (*such foul language*). **4** of the kind or degree already indicated, or implied by the context (*there are no such things; such is life*). ● *pron.* **1** the thing or action in question or referred to (*such were his words*). **2 a** *Commerce* or *informal* the aforesaid thing or things; it, they, or them (*those without tickets should purchase such*). **b** similar things; suchlike (*sandwiches and such*). □ **as such** as being what has been indicated or named (*there is no theatre as such*). **such as 1** of a kind that; like (*a person such as we all admire*). **2** for example (*insects, such as moths and bees*). **3** those who (*such as don't need help*). **such as it is** despite its shortcomings. **such a one** such a person or such a thing. **such that** in such a manner that. **such-and-such** ● *adj.* (often foll by *a*) of a particular kind but not needing to be specified (*on such-and-such a day*). ● *n.* a person or thing of this kind.

suchlike *informal* ● *adj.* of such a kind. ● *n.* things, people, etc. of such a kind.

suck ● *v.* **1** *tr. & intr.* draw (a fluid) into the mouth by contracting the lip muscles etc. to make a partial vacuum. **2 a** *tr.* apply the lips and mouth to and perform a sucking action on (the thumb etc.). **b** *tr. & intr.* hold (a candy etc.) in the mouth. **3** *intr. N Amer. slang* be very bad, disagreeable, or disgusting. **4** *intr.* make a sucking action or sound (*sucking at his pipe*). **5** *intr.* (of a pump etc.) make a gurgling or drawing sound. **6** *tr.* (usu. foll. by *down*, *in*) engulf, smother, or drown in a sucking movement. **7** *tr. & intr.* draw in some direction, esp. by producing a vacuum. **8** *tr. coarse slang* perform cunnilingus or esp. fellatio on. ● *n.* **1** the act or an instance of sucking, esp. the breast. **2** *Cdn* a crybaby or sore loser; a person who refuses to participate or go along, esp. out of spite; a feeble, self-pitying person. **3** *Cdn* a person who behaves obsequiously to those in authority, esp. a child. □ **suck dry 1** exhaust the contents of (a bottle etc.) by sucking. **2** exhaust (a person's sympathy, resources, etc.) as if by sucking. **suck in 1** absorb. **2** = sense 6 of *v.* **3** draw in (the cheeks, the abdomen, etc.). **4** take in; cheat or deceive. **5** involve (a person) in an activity etc., esp. against his or her will. **suck up 1** (often foll. by *to*) *informal* behave obsequiously esp. for one's own advantage. **2** absorb. **suck wind** (or **air**) *N Amer.* gasp for air loudly after strenuous physical exertion. □ **sucky** *adj.*

sucker ● *n.* **1** a person or thing that sucks. **2** *informal* **a** a gullible or easily deceived person. **b** (foll. by *for*) a person especially susceptible to. **3** esp. *N Amer. informal* a thing not specified by name (*I can't fix the sucker!*). **4** *N Amer. informal* a usu. round, flat hard candy on a small stick, held in the hand and sucked. **5 a** a rubber cup etc. that adheres to a surface by suction. **b** an organ enabling an organism to cling to a surface by suction. **6** *Bot.* a shoot springing from the rooted part of a stem, from the root at a distance from the main stem, from an axil, or from a branch. **7** any of various chiefly N American freshwater fishes related to carp, having a conformation of the lips which suggest that they feed by suction. ● *v.tr.* esp. *N Amer. informal* fool, trick. □ **there's a sucker born every minute** gullible people are not difficult to find.

sucker punch *n. N Amer.* an unexpected punch or blow. □ **sucker-punch** *v.tr.*

suckhole esp. *Cdn & Austral. coarse slang* ● *n.* = SUCK-UP. ● *v.intr.* (**-holed**, **-holing**) behave obsequiously.

suckle *v.* **1** *tr.* feed (young) from the breast or udder. **2** *intr.* feed by sucking the breast etc. □ **suckler** *n.*

suckling *n.* an unweaned child or animal.

suck-up *n. N Amer. informal* a person who sucks up to a person in authority etc.

sucrose /'suːkrəʊs/ *n.* common sugar, a disaccharide obtained from sugar cane, sugar beet, etc.

suction ● *n.* **1** the act or an instance of sucking. **2 a** the production of a partial vacuum by the removal of air etc. in order to force in liquid etc. or procure adhesion. **b** the force produced by this process. ● *v.tr.* draw etc. using suction; suck.

suction cup *n.* a usu. rubber concave disc which can be made to adhere to a smooth surface by suction.

Sudanese /ˌsuːdəˈniːz/ ● *adj.* of or relating to Sudan, a republic in NE Africa, or the Sudan region south of the Sahara. ● *n.* (*pl.* same) **1** a native, national, or inhabitant of Sudan. **2** a person of Sudanese descent.

sudden *adj.* occurring or done unexpectedly or with-out warning. □ **all of a sudden** unexpectedly; suddenly. □ **suddenly** *adv.* **suddenness** *n.*

sudden death *n.* an extra period or session of play to break a tie, in which the winner is the first to take the lead (often *attrib.*: *sudden-death overtime*).

sudden infant death syndrome *n.* the un-explained death of a baby while sleeping.

suds *n.pl.* **1** froth of soap and water. **2** *N Amer. informal* beer. □ **sudsy** *adj.*

sue *v.* (**sues**, **sued**, **suing**) **1** *tr. & intr.* institute legal proceedings against. **2** *intr.* make application to a law court for redress. **3** *intr.* (often foll. by *for*) make entreaty for (*sued for peace*).

suede /sweɪd/ *n.* **1** leather with the flesh side rubbed to make a velvety nap. **2** a woven fabric resembling suede.

suet /'suːət/ *n.* the hard white fat on the kidneys or loins of oxen, sheep, etc., used to make dough etc.

suet pudding *n.* a pudding of flour, sugar, etc., and suet, usu. boiled or steamed.

suffer *v.* **1** *tr & intr.* undergo (pain, grief, damage, etc.). **2** *tr.* put up with; tolerate. □ **not suffer fools gladly** refuse to be patient with people one considers fool-ish, stupid, etc. □ **sufferer** *n.* **suffering** *n.*

sufferance *n.* □ **on sufferance** with toleration implied by lack of consent or objection.

suffice /səˈfaɪs/ *v.intr.* be enough or adequate. □ **suffice (it) to say** I shall content myself with saying.

sufficiency /səˈfɪʃənsi/ *n.* (*pl.* **-ies**) **1** (often foll. by *of*) an adequate amount or adequate resources. **2** the condition or quality of being sufficient; adequacy.

sufficient *adj.* adequate. □ **sufficiently** *adv.*

suffix ● *n.* a verbal element added at the end of a word, e.g. *-ation*, *-fy*, *-ing*. ● *v.tr.* append, esp. as a suffix.

suffocate *v.* **1** *tr.* choke or kill by stopping breathing, esp. by pressure, fumes, etc. **2** *tr.* produce a choking or breathless sensation in, esp. by excitement, terror, etc. **3** *intr.* be or feel suffocated or breathless. **4** *tr. informal* restrict, stifle. □ **suffocating** *adj.* **suffocatingly** *adv.* **suffocation** *n.*

suffrage /'sʌfrɪdʒ/ *n.* **1** the right of voting in political elections (*full adult suffrage*). **2** a view expressed by voting; a vote. **3** opinion in support of a proposal etc.

suffragette /ˌsʌfrəˈdʒet/ *n. hist.* a woman engaged in esp. militant activity in favour of women's suffrage, esp. in the early 20th c.

suffragist /'sʌfrədʒɪst/ *n.* esp. *hist.* a person who advo-cates the extension of the suffrage, esp. to women. □ **suffragism** *n.*

suffuse /səˈfjuːz/ *v.tr.* **1** (of colour, moisture, etc.) spread from within to colour or moisten. **2** cover with colour etc. **3** spread throughout; fill. □ **suffusion** /-ˈfjuːʒən/ *n.*

Sufi /'suːfi/ *n.* (*pl.* **Sufis**) a member of any of various spiritual orders within Islam characterized by asceti-cism and mysticism. □ **Sufic** *adj.* **Sufism** *n.*

sugar ● *n.* **1 a** a sweet crystalline substance obtained from various plants, esp. the sugar cane and sugar beet, used in cooking, confectionery, etc.; sucrose. **b** foods containing esp. refined sugar. **2** any of a group of soluble usu. sweet-tasting crystalline carbo-hydrates found esp. in plants, e.g. glucose, and also in milk and blood. **3** esp. *N Amer. informal* darling, dear. **4** sweet words; flattery. **5** anything comparable to sugar encasing a pill in reconciling a person to what is unpalatable. **6** *slang* a narcotic drug, esp. heroin or LSD (taken on a lump of sugar). **7** *N Amer.* = MAPLE SUGAR. ● *interj.* expressing exasperation etc. ● *v.* **1** *tr.* sweeten with sugar. **2** *tr.* make (one's words, meaning, etc.) more pleasant or welcome. **3** *tr.* coat with sugar (*sugared almond*). **4** *intr.* (in full **sugar off**) *N Amer.* make maple syrup or maple sugar by collecting and boiling maple sap. □ **sugarless** *adj.*

sugar beet *n.* a beet, *Beta vulgaris*, from which sugar is extracted.

sugar bush *n. N Amer.* a grove of sugar maples.

sugar cane *n.* any perennial tropical grass of the genus *Saccharum*, esp. *S. officinarum*, with tall stout jointed stems from which sugar is extracted.

sugar-coat *v.tr.* (often as **sugar-coated** *adj.*) **1** cover or enclose (food) in sugar. **2** make superficially attractive. □ **sugar-coating** *n.*

sugar cookie *n. N Amer.* a sweet and rich plain cookie made from flour, sugar, butter, etc.

sugar daddy *n. slang* an elderly man who lavishes gifts on a young person esp. in return for sex.

sugaring *n.* **1** (also **sugaring off**) *N Amer.* the making of maple syrup or maple sugar by collecting and boiling the sap from esp. the sugar maple. **2** a method of removing unwanted hair by applying to the skin a sticky sugar mixture, which is then peeled off together with the hair.

sugar maple *n.* a N American maple, *Acer saccharum*, from the sap of which maple sugar and maple syrup are made.

sugar-pea *n.* (also **sugar snap pea**) a variety of pea eaten whole including the pod.

sugar pie *n. Cdn* esp. (*Que.*) an open-faced or lattice-topped pie with a filling of brown or maple sugar mixed with cream and baked.

sugar plum *n. archaic* a small round hard candy.

sugar shack *n. Cdn* **1** a building in which maple sap is boiled in making maple syrup or sugar. **2** esp. *Que.* a usu. small establishment in a sugar bush serving maple-flavoured dishes and other traditional fare.

sugary *adj.* **1** a containing esp. a high proportion of sugar. **b** resembling sugar. **2** excessively sweet or esp. sentimental. **3** falsely sweet or pleasant (*sugary compliments*). □ **sugariness** *n.*

suggest /səˈdʒest, səg-/ *v.tr.* **1** propose. **2** a cause (an idea, memory, association, etc.) to present itself. **b** hint at (*his behaviour suggests guilt*). □ **suggest itself** (of an idea etc.) come into the mind.

suggestible *adj.* **1** capable of being suggested. **2** open to suggestion. □ **suggestibility** *n.*

suggestion *n.* **1** the act or an instance of suggesting; the state of being suggested. **2** a theory, plan, etc., suggested (*made a helpful suggestion*). **3** a slight hint (*a suggestion of garlic*). **4** a the insinuation of a belief etc. into the mind. **b** such a belief etc.

suggestive *adj.* **1** conveying a suggestion; evocative. **2** (esp. of a remark, joke, etc.) lewd; suggesting sex. □ **suggestively** *adv.* **suggestiveness** *n.*

suicidal *adj.* **1** inclined to commit suicide. **2** of or concerning suicide. **3** self-destructive; fatally or disastrously rash. □ **suicidally** *adv.*

suicide *n.* **1** a the intentional killing of oneself. **b** a person who commits suicide. **2** a self-destructive action or course (*political suicide*). **3** (*attrib.*) *Military* designating a highly dangerous or deliberately suicidal operation etc. (*a suicide mission*).

suicide squeeze *n. see* SQUEEZE *n.* 7b.

sui generis /ˈsuːiː ˈdʒenərɪs/ *adj.* of its own kind; unique.

suit ● *n.* **1** a a set of outer clothes of matching material for men, consisting usu. of a jacket, pants, and sometimes a waistcoat. **b** a similar set of clothes for women usu. having a skirt instead of pants. **c** (esp.

in *comb.*) a set of clothes for a special occasion, occupation, etc. (*playsuit*; *bathing suit*). **2** a any of the four sets (esp. spades, hearts, diamonds, clubs) into which a pack of cards is divided. **b** a player's holding in a suit (*his strong suit was clubs*). **3** a lawsuit. **4** a a petition esp. to a person in authority. **b** the process of courting a woman (*paid suit to her*). **5** (usu. foll. by *of*) a set of armour, sails, etc. **6** *slang* a business executive. ● *v.* **1** *tr.* go well with (a person's figure, features, character, etc.); become. **2** *tr. & intr.* meet the demands or requirements of; satisfy; agree with (*can change the date if it doesn't suit*). **3** *tr.* make fitting or appropriate; adapt (*suited her style to her audience*). □ **suit the action to the word** carry out a promise or threat at once. **suit oneself** **1** do as one chooses. **2** find something that satisfies one. **suit up** *N Amer.* dress in clothing designed for a particular activity.

suitable *adj.* (usu. foll. by *to, for*) well fitted for the purpose; appropriate. □ **suitability** *n.* **suitably** *adv.*

suitcase *n.* a usu. oblong case for carrying clothes etc., having a handle and a flat lid. □ **live out of a suitcase** live temporarily with one's belongings still packed, esp. when travelling.

suite /swiːt/ *n.* **1** a set of things belonging together, esp.: **a** a set of rooms in a hotel etc. for use by one person or group of people. **b** a set of furniture, usu. a sofa and armchairs etc., or table and chairs of the same design. **2** = APARTMENT 1a. **3** a a set of instrumental compositions to be played in succession. **b** a set of selected pieces from an opera, musical, ballet, etc., arranged to be played as one instrumental work. **4** a set of people in attendance.

suited *adj.* appropriate; well fitted.

suitor *n.* **1** a man seeking to marry a specified woman. **2** a plaintiff or petitioner in a lawsuit. **3** a prospective buyer of a business or corporation.

suk (also **sukh**) *var. of* SOUK.

sukiyaki /ˌsʊkiˈjɒki/ *n.* a Japanese dish of sliced meat simmered with vegetables and sauce.

Sukkot /sʊˈkoːt, ˈsʌkəθ/ *n.* the Jewish autumn harvest and thanksgiving festival commemorating the sheltering of the Israelites in the wilderness.

sulfa *var. of* SULPHA.

sulfanilamide *var. of* SULPHANILAMIDE.

sulfate *var. of* SULPHATE.

sulfur etc. *var. of* SULPHUR etc.

sulk ● *v.intr.* indulge in a period of sullen esp. resentful silence or aloofness from others. ● *n.* a period of sulking (*has been in a sulk*; *got the sulks*).

sulky ● *adj.* (**-ier, -iest**) sullen, morose, or silent, esp. from resentment or ill temper. ● *n.* (*pl.* **-ies**) a light two-wheeled horse-drawn vehicle for one, esp. used in harness racing. □ **sulkily** *adv.*

sullen *adj.* **1** morose, resentful, sulky. **2** a (of a thing) slow-moving. **b** dismal, melancholy (*a sullen sky*). □ **sullenly** *adv.* **sullenness** *n.*

sully *v.tr.* (**-ies, -ied**) **1** disgrace or tarnish (a person's reputation or character, a victory, etc.). **2** *literary* dirty.

sulpha /ˈsʌlfə/ *n.* any drug derived from sulphanilamide (often *attrib.*: *sulpha drug*).

sulphamethoxazole /ˌsʌlfəˈmeˈθɒksəzoːl/ *n.* a sulphonamide used to treat respiratory and urinary tract infections.

sulphanilamide /ˌsʌlfəˈnɪləmaɪd/ *n.* a colourless sulphonamide drug with anti-bacterial properties.

sulphate *n.* a salt or ester of sulphuric acid.

sulphide *n.* a binary compound of sulphur.

sulphite *n.* a salt or ester of sulphurous acid.

sulphonamide /sʌlˈfɒnəmaɪd/ *n.* a substance

derived from an amide of a sulphonic acid, able to prevent the multiplication of some pathogenic bacteria.

sulphone /ˈsʌlfoːn/ n. an organic compound containing the SO₂ group united directly to two carbon atoms. □ **sulphonic** /-ˈfɒnɪk/ adj.

sulphur n. **1 a** a pale yellow non-metallic element having crystalline and amorphous forms, burning with a blue flame and a suffocating smell, and used in making gunpowder, matches, and sulphuric acid, and in the treatment of skin diseases. **b** (attrib.) like or containing sulphur. **2** the material of which hellfire and lightning were believed to consist. **3** any yellow butterfly of the family Pieridae.

sulphur dioxide n. a colourless pungent gas formed by burning sulphur in air, used in manufacturing sulphuric acid and as a food preservative.

sulphuric /sʌlˈfjʊrɪk/ adj. containing hexavalent sulphur.

sulphuric acid n. a dense oily colourless highly acid and corrosive fluid much used in the chemical industry.

sulphurous /ˈsʌlfərəs/ adj. **1 a** relating to or suggestive of sulphur, esp. in colour. **b** suggestive of burning sulphur, hellfire, etc.; fiery. **2** Chem. containing tetravalent sulphur.

sulphurous acid n. an unstable weak acid used as a reducing and bleaching acid.

sulphur spring n. a spring impregnated with sulphur or its compounds.

Sulpician /sʌlˈpɪʃən/ n. a member of a Roman Catholic society of diocesan priests founded in Paris in 1641 and established in New France in 1657, concerned esp. with the training of priests.

sultan n. **1 a** a Muslim sovereign. **b** (**the Sultan**) hist. the sultan of Turkey. **2** an absolute ruler. □ **sultanate** /-ˌneit/ n.

sultana /sʌlˈtænə/ n. **1 a** a seedless raisin used in puddings, cakes, etc. **b** the small pale yellow grape producing this. **2** the mother, wife, concubine, or daughter of a sultan.

sultry adj. (**-ier, -iest**) **1** (of the atmosphere or the weather) hot or oppressive; close. **2** (of a person, character, etc.) passionate; sensual.

sum n. **1** the total amount resulting from the addition of two or more items, facts, ideas, feelings, etc. (the sum of two and three is five; the sum of their objections is this). **2** a particular amount of money (paid a large sum for it). **3** an arithmetical problem. □ **in sum** in brief. **sum up** (**summed up, summing up**) **1** (esp. of a judge) recapitulate or review the evidence in a case etc. **2** form or express an idea of the character of (a person, situation, etc.). **3** collect into or express as a total or whole.

sumac /ˈsuːmæk/ n. (also **sumach**) **1** any of various shrubs or trees of the genus Rhus, having cone-shaped clusters of reddish fruits. **2** the dried and ground leaves of this used in tanning and dyeing.

Sumatran /səˈmɒtrən/ ● adj. of or relating to Sumatra, its people, or its language. ● n. **1 a** a native or inhabitant of Sumatra in Indonesia. **b** a person of Sumatran descent. **2** the language of Sumatra.

Sumerian /suːˈmɪərɪən/ ● adj. of or relating to the early and non-Semitic element in ancient Babylonian civilization. ● n. **1** a member of the early non-Semitic people of ancient Babylonia. **2** this language.

summa cum laude /ˌsʊmə kʊm ˈlaʊdeɪ/ adv. & adj. esp. N Amer. (of a degree, diploma, etc.) of the highest standard; with the highest distinction.

summarize v.tr. make or be a summary of; sum up. □ **summarization** n.

summary ● n. (pl. **-ies**) a brief account. ● adj. **1** dispensing with needless details or formalities; brief. **2** (of a trial etc.) without the customary legal formalities (summary justice). □ **summarily** /səˈmerɪli/ adv. **summariness** n.

summary conviction n. a conviction made by a judge or magistrates without a jury.

summary conviction offence n. (also **summary offence**) Cdn a relatively minor criminal offence tried by a magistrate and without a jury or preliminary hearing (compare INDICTABLE OFFENCE).

summary jurisdiction n. a court's authority to use summary proceedings and arrive at a judgment.

summation /sʌˈmeɪʃən/ n. **1** the finding of a total or sum. **2** a summing-up. □ **summative** adj.

summer ● n. **1** the warmest season of the year, in the northern hemisphere from June to August and in the southern hemisphere from December to February. **2** the period from the summer solstice to the autumnal equinox. **3** the hot weather typical of summer. **4** (often foll. by of) the mature stage of life; the height of achievement, powers, etc. **5** (attrib.) characteristic of or suitable for summer (summer clothes). ● v. intr. (usu. foll. by at, in) pass the summer. □ **summerless** adj. **summery** adj.

summer camp n. esp. N Amer. a camp providing esp. outdoor recreational and sporting facilities during the summer, esp. for children.

summerfallow esp. Cdn ● n. agricultural land left fallow in the summer to allow moisture and nutrient levels to recover. ● v.tr. & intr. lay (agricultural land) fallow during the summer.

summer house n. **1** a light building in a garden, park, etc. used for sitting in in fine weather. **2** a secondary residence occupied during the summer.

summer kitchen n. N Amer. an extra kitchen adjoining or separate from a house, used for cooking in hot weather.

summer sausage n. N Amer. a dry or semi-dry sausage containing beef or pork, fermented and/or cooked and smoked to ensure good keeping qualities.

summer savory n. see SAVORY.

summer school n. **1** esp. N Amer. a course of remedial or accelerating classes held in the summer. **2** a course of classes etc. held during the summer.

summer solstice n. the solstice at midsummer, at the time of the longest day, about June 21 in the northern hemisphere and Dec. 22 in the southern hemisphere.

summer squash n. see SQUASH² 1.

summer student n. Cdn an esp. university student working at a job for the summer.

summer theatre n. N Amer. **1** (also called **summer stock**) theatrical productions by a repertory company organized for the summer season, esp. at holiday resorts. **2** a theatre where such productions are put on.

summertime n. the season or period of summer.

summing-up n. **1** a review of evidence and a direction given by a judge to a jury. **2** a recapitulation of the main points of an argument, case, etc.

summit n. **1** the highest point, esp. of a mountain; the apex. **2** the highest degree of power, ambition, success, etc. **3** (in full **summit meeting, talks**, etc.) a discussion esp. between heads of government.

summiteer n. a participant in a summit meeting.

summon v.tr. **1** call upon to appear, esp. as a defendant or witness in a law court. **2** call upon (*summoned her to assist*). **3** call together for a meeting or some other purpose (*summoned the members to attend*). **4** (often foll. by *up*) gather (courage, strength, energy, etc.). ☐ **summoner** *n.*

summons ● *n.* (*pl.* **summonses**) **1** an authoritative or urgent call to attend on some occasion or do something. **2 a** a call to appear before a judge or magistrate. **b** the writ containing such a summons. ● *v.tr. esp. Law* serve with a summons.

sumo /'su:məʊ/ *n.* a Japanese form of heavyweight wrestling in which a large wrestler wins a bout by forcing his opponent outside a circle or making him touch the ground with any part of the body except the soles of the feet (also *attrib.*: *sumo wrestler*).

sump *n.* **1** a pit etc. in which superfluous liquid collects in a basement, mine, machine, etc. **2** a cesspool.

sump pump *n.* a pump for removing waste water etc. from a sump.

sumptuous *adj.* rich, lavish, magnificent. ☐ **sumptuously** *adv.* **sumptuousness** *n.*

sum total *n.* = SUM *n.* 1.

Sun. *abbr.* Sunday.

sun ● *n.* **1 a** the star around which the earth orbits and from which it receives light and warmth. **b** any similar star in the universe with or without planets. **2** the light or warmth received from the sun. **3** *literary* a person or thing regarded as a source of glory, radiance, etc. ● *v.* (**sunned**, **sunning**) **1** *refl.* bask in the sun. **2** *tr.* expose to the sun. **3** *intr.* sun oneself. ☐ **beneath** (or **under**) **the sun** anywhere in the world. **in the sun** exposed to the sun's rays. ☐ **sunless** *adj.* **sunlike** *adj.* **sunward** *adj. & adv.* **sunwards** *adv.*

sun-baked *adj.* dried or hardened or baked from the heat of the sun.

sunbathe *v.intr.* bask in the sun, esp. to tan the body. ☐ **sunbather** *n.*

sunbeam *n.* a ray of sunlight.

sunbelt *n.* a strip of territory receiving a high amount of sunshine, esp. (**the Sunbelt**), the region stretching from California to Florida.

sunblock *n.* a cream or lotion for protecting the skin from the sun.

sunburn ● *n.* inflammation of the skin caused by overexposure to the sun. ● *v.intr.* suffer from sunburn. ☐ **sunburned** *adj.* (also **sunburnt**).

sunburst ● *n.* **1** something resembling the sun and its rays, e.g. an ornament, brooch, etc. **2** a sudden burst of sunshine, as from the sun appearing suddenly from behind clouds. **3** *Cdn* a trimming of fur around the hood of a parka. ● *adj.* **1** *Cdn* (of a parka or parka hood) trimmed with a sunburst. **2** resembling a sunburst in design, colour, etc.

suncatcher *n. N Amer.* an object made esp. of stained glass or coloured plastic hung in a window to sparkle in or reflect incoming sunlight.

sundae *n.* a dish of ice cream topped with sauce, fruit, whipped cream, nuts, etc.

sun dance *n.* an annual ceremony held at midsummer by some Plains Aboriginal peoples, marked by several days of fasting, dancing, and induced visions.

Sunday ● *n.* the first day of the week, a Christian holiday and day of worship. ● *adv.* **1** on Sunday. **2** (**Sundays**) on Sundays; each Sunday.

Sunday best *n.* a person's best clothes, kept for use on Sundays and special occasions.

Sunday school *n.* **1** a school for the religious instruction of children on Sundays. **2** the members of such a school.

sundeck *n. N Amer.* a terrace or balcony positioned to catch the sun.

sunder *v.tr. & intr. archaic* or *literary* separate, sever.

sundew *n.* any small insect-consuming bog plant of the family Droseraceae, esp. of the genus *Drosera* with hairs secreting drops of moisture.

sundial *n.* an instrument showing time by the shadow of a pointer cast by the sun on to a graduated disc.

sun dog *n.* a bright spot, usu. one of two, on either side of the sun and prismatically coloured, caused by reflection of light by atmospheric ice crystals.

sundown *n.* sunset.

sun-drenched *adj.* **1** illuminated by sunshine. **2** (of a place) having very sunny weather.

sundress *n.* a sleeveless dress with a low neck and back, worn in hot weather.

sun-dried *adj.* dried by the sun, not by artificial heat.

sundry ● *adj.* various; several (*sundry items*). ● *n.* (*pl.* **-ies**) (in *pl.*) items or oddments not mentioned individually. ☐ **all and sundry** everyone.

sunfish *n.* **1** any of various almost spherical fish, esp. a large ocean fish, *Mola mola*. **2** any of various small deep-bodied freshwater fishes of the family Centrarchidae, abundant in N America, and including the largemouth and smallmouth bass and the crappies.

sunflower *n.* any very tall plant of the genus *Helianthus*, esp. *H. annus* with very large showy golden-rayed flowers, grown also for its seeds which yield an edible oil.

sung *past part. of* SING.

sunglasses *n.pl.* glasses tinted to protect the eyes from sunlight or glare.

sun god *n.* the sun worshipped as a deity.

sunk *past and past part. of* SINK.

sunken *adj.* **1** that has been sunk. **2** beneath the surface. **3** (of the eyes, cheeks, etc.) hollow. **4** placed on a lower level than the surrounding area (*a sunken living room*).

sunker *n. Cdn* (*Nfld*) a reef or rocky shoal.

sun-kissed *adj.* warmed or affected by the sun.

sun lamp *n.* a lamp giving ultraviolet rays for an artificial suntan, therapy, etc.

sunlight *n.* light from the sun. ☐ **sunlit** *adj.*

Sunna /'sʌnə/ *n.* a traditional portion of Muslim law based on Muhammad's words or acts, accepted with the Koran) as authoritative by Muslims.

Sunni /'sʌni/ ● *n.* **1** one of the two main branches of Islam, commonly described as orthodox, differing from the Shia in its understanding of the Sunna and in its rejection of Ali as Muhammad's first successor. **2** (*pl.* same or **-s**) an adherent of this branch of Islam. ● *adj.* of or relating to Sunni.

sunny *adj.* (**-ier**, **-iest**) **1 a** bright with sunlight. **b** exposed to or warmed by the sun. **2** cheery and bright in temperament. ☐ **sunnily** *adv.* **sunniness** *n.*

sun porch *n.* an enclosed porch with more windows than exterior walls, designed to receive sunlight.

sun protection factor *n. see* SPF.

sunrise *n.* **1** the sun's rising at dawn. **2** the coloured sky associated with this. **3** the time at which sunrise occurs.

sunroof *n.* a sliding part of the roof of a car that can be opened to let in air and sunlight.

sunroom *n.* a room with large windows, designed to receive sunlight.

sunscreen n. a cream or lotion rubbed on to the skin to protect it from the sun.

sunset n. **1** the sun's setting in the evening. **2** the coloured sky associated with this. **3** the time at which sunset occurs. **4** the declining period of something. **5** (attrib.) designating a provision under which an agency or program is to be disbanded or terminated at the end of a fixed period unless formally renewed (sunset clause).

sunshade n. something that provides shade, as an awning or parasol.

sunshine n. **1 a** the light of the sun. **b** an area lit by the sun. **c** the warmth of the sun. **2** fine weather. **3** cheerfulness; joy. **4** informal a form of address. ☐ **sunshiny** adj.

sunspot n. one of the dark patches, changing in shape and size and lasting for varying periods, observed on the sun's surface.

sunstroke n. acute prostration or collapse from the excessive heat of the sun.

suntan n. a brown colour of the skin caused by exposure to the sun (also attrib.: suntan lotion). ☐ **suntanned** adj. **suntanning** n.

sun-up n. esp. N Amer. sunrise.

sup v. (**supped, supping**) **1** tr. take (soup, tea, etc.) by sips or spoonfuls. **2** (usu. foll. by off, on) archaic eat supper. ● n. a sip of liquid.

super ● adj. **1** informal exceptional; splendid. **2** of or to an extreme or the highest degree, power, etc. ● n. informal **1** a superintendent. **2** a supernumerary actor. ● interj. informal expressing enthusiastic approval or assent. ● adv. informal extremely; excessively.

super- comb. form forming nouns, adjectives, and verbs, meaning: **1** above, beyond, or over in place or time or conceptually (superstructure; superimpose). **2** to a great or extreme degree (superhuman). **3** extra good or large of its kind (supertanker). **4** of a higher kind, esp. in names of classificatory divisions (superfamily).

super-absorbent adj. extremely absorbent.

superannuate /ˌsuːpərˈænjoˌeit/ v.tr. **1** retire (a person) with a pension. **2** dismiss or discard as too old for use, work, etc. ☐ **superannuated** adj.

superannuation n. **1** a pension paid to a retired person. **2** a regular payment made towards this by an employed person. **3** the process or an instance of superannuating.

superb /suːˈpɜːrb/ adj. **1** excellent; fine. **2** of the most impressive or majestic kind. ☐ **superbly** adv.

Super Bowl n. proprietary the annual deciding game between the champions of the National Football Conference and of the American Football Conference.

supercharge v.tr. **1** charge (the atmosphere etc.) with energy, emotion, etc. **2** use a supercharger on (an engine). ☐ **supercharged** adj.

supercharger n. a device supplying air or fuel to an internal combustion engine at above normal pressure to increase efficiency.

supercilious /ˌsuːpərˈsɪliəs/ adj. assuming an air of contemptuous indifference or superiority. ☐ **superciliously** adv. **superciliousness** n.

supercomputer n. a powerful computer which can deal with complex problems. ☐ **supercomputing** n.

superconductivity n. the property of zero electrical resistance in some substances at very low temperatures. ☐ **superconducting** adj. **superconductor** n.

supercontinent n. each of several large land masses thought to have divided to form the present continents in the geological past.

supercool ● v. **1** tr. cool (a liquid) below its freezing point without solidification or crystallization. **2** intr. (of a liquid) be cooled in this way. ● adj. slang very cool, relaxed, fine, etc.

supercritical adj. **1** highly critical. **2** of or relating to a mass of radioactive material in which the rate of a chain reaction increases over time.

super-duper adj. informal exceptional, super.

superego n. (pl. **-os**) Psych. the part of the mind that acts as a conscience and responds to social rules.

superfamily n. (pl. **-ies**) a taxonomic category between family and order.

superficial adj. **1** of or on the surface; lacking depth. **2** swift or cursory (a superficial examination). **3** apparent but not real (a superficial resemblance). **4** (esp. of a person) having no depth of character or knowledge. **5** lacking substance or profundity (the show had a very superficial plot). **6** not involving a profound or serious issue (superficial differences). ☐ **superficiality** /-ʃiˈælɪti/ n. (pl. **-ies**). **superficially** adv.

superfine adj. **1** in very small granules etc. (superfine sugar). **2** Commerce of extra quality.

superfluous /suːˈpɜːrfluəs/ adj. more than enough.

supergiant n. a very large and bright star.

super giant slalom n. Skiing (also informal **super G**) a downhill event with a longer course and wider turns than a giant slalom.

superglue ● n. any of various adhesives with an exceptional bonding capability. ● v.tr. (**-glues, -glued, -gluing** or **-glueing**) stick with superglue.

supergroup n. **1** a group made up of several related groups. **2 a** an exceptionally talented or successful rock group. **b** a rock group formed by star musicians from different groups.

superheat v.tr. **1** heat (a liquid) above its boiling point without vaporization. **2** heat (a vapour) above its boiling point (superheated steam). **3** heat to a very high temperature. ☐ **superheater** n.

superhero n. (pl. **-oes**) a person or fictional character with extraordinary heroic attributes.

superhighway n. N Amer. a divided highway with two or more lanes in each direction.

superhuman adj. **1** beyond normal human capability (required a superhuman effort). **2** higher than human (a superhuman being). ☐ **superhumanly** adv.

superimpose v.tr. lay (a thing) on something else. ☐ **superimposition** n.

superintend v.tr. & intr. **1** be responsible for the management or arrangement of (an activity etc.). **2** supervise (an institution, district, etc.). ☐ **superintendence** n. **superintendency** n.

superintendent ● n. **1 a** a person who superintends. **b** a director of an institution etc. **2** (on some Canadian municipal police forces) an officer ranking above staff inspector. **3** (in the OPP) an officer ranking above inspector. **4** (in the Royal Newfoundland Constabulary) an officer ranking above inspector. **5** (in the RCMP) an officer ranking above inspector. **6** N Amer. a caretaker, esp. of an apartment building. **7** the chief administrator of a school division. ● adj. superintending.

superior ● adj. **1** in a higher position; of higher rank. **2 a** above the average in quality etc. **b** having or showing a high opinion of oneself. **3** better or greater in some respect. **4** Printing (of figures or letters) placed above the line. ● n. **1** a person superior to another in rank, character, etc. **2** the head of a monastery or other religious institution (Mother Superior).

superior court n. (in Canada) the supreme court or courts of a province.

superiority n. the state of being superior.

superiority complex n. an undue conviction of one's own superiority to others.

superlative ● adj. **1** of the highest quality or degree (*superlative wisdom*). **2** (of an adjective or adverb) expressing the highest or a very high degree of a quality (e.g. *bravest*, *most fiercely*). ● n. **1** *Grammar* **a** the superlative expression or form of an adjective or adverb. **b** a word in the superlative. **2** something embodying excellence; the highest form of a thing. **3** (usu. in *pl.*) an expression of abundant praise. □ **superlatively** adv.

superman n. (*pl.* **-men**) **1** (esp. in Nietzschean philosophy) an ideal superior man of the future who achieves domination through integrity and creativity. **2** informal a man of exceptional strength or ability.

supermarket n. a large store selling foods, household goods, etc.

supermarket tabloid n. a tabloid newspaper sold in supermarkets, typically sensationalist and focusing on the lives of celebrities.

superminister n. *Cdn* a cabinet minister with responsibility for an important portfolio or a number of related portfolios.

supermodel n. a highly-paid model employed in high-profile glamour modelling.

supermom n. *N Amer. informal* a mother who fulfills all the duties of motherhood superlatively, esp. one who is also employed outside of the home.

supernatural ● adj. attributed to or thought to reveal some force above the laws of nature. ● n. supernatural, occult, or magical forces, effects, etc. □ **supernaturalism** n. **supernaturalist** n. **supernaturally** adv.

supernova n. (*pl.* **-novas** or **-novae** /-viː/) a star that suddenly increases very greatly in brightness because of an explosion ejecting most of its mass.

supernumerary /ˌsuːpərˈnuːmərˌeri, -njuː-/ ● adj. **1** in excess of the normal number. **2** (of a person) engaged for extra work. **3** (of an actor) appearing on stage but not speaking. ● n. (*pl.* **-ies**) **1** an extra or unwanted person or thing. **2** a supernumerary actor. **3** a person engaged for extra work.

superpose v.tr. esp. *Math.* place (a thing or a geometric figure) on or above something else, esp. so as to coincide. □ **superposition** /-pəˈzɪʃən/ n.

superpower n. a state with supreme power and influence, esp. the US and, formerly, the USSR.

supersaturate v.tr. add to (esp. a solution) beyond saturation point. □ **supersaturation** n.

superscript ● n. a character, number, or symbol written or printed above the line and usu. to the right of another character (*compare* SUBSCRIPT n.). ● adj. written or printed above the line, esp. *Math.* (of a symbol) written above and to the right of another.

supersede v.tr. **1 a** adopt or appoint another person or thing in place of. **b** cease to employ. **2** (of a person or thing) take the place of. □ **supersession** n.

supersonic adj. designating or having a speed greater than that of sound. □ **supersonically** adv.

supersonics n.pl. (treated as *sing.*) = ULTRASONICS.

superstar n. an extremely famous or renowned actor, film star, musician, etc. □ **superstardom** n.

superstation n. a television station using satellite technology to broadcast over a very large area.

superstition n. **1** irrational belief, esp. as based on fear of or reverence for the supernatural. **2** an irrational fear of the unknown or mysterious. **3** a practice, opinion, or religion based on these tendencies. **4** a widely held but unjustified idea of the effects or nature of a thing. □ **superstitious** adj. **superstitiously** adv. **superstitiousness** n.

superstore n. **1** a large supermarket selling a wide range of goods. **2** a very large store selling a particular type of merchandise (*appliance superstore*).

superstructure n. **1** the part of a building above its foundations. **2** a structure built on top of something else. **3** a concept or idea based on others. **4** the constructions above the upper deck of a ship.

supertanker n. a very large tanker ship.

supertwist adj. designating varieties of liquid crystal display used in portable computers, in which to change state the plane of polarized light passing through the display is rotated by at least 180 degrees.

supervene v.intr. **1** occur as an interruption in or a change from some state. **2** ensue; follow closely on. □ **supervention** n.

super VGA abbr. see SVGA.

supervise v.tr. **1** superintend, oversee the execution of. **2** oversee the actions or work of. □ **supervision** n. **supervisor** n. **supervisory** adj.

superwoman n. (*pl.* **-women**) informal a woman of exceptional strength or ability.

supine /ˈsuːpaɪn/ adj. **1** lying face upwards (*compare* PRONE 1a). **2** having the front or ventral part upwards; (of the hand) with the palm upwards. □ **supinely** adv.

supper n. **1** the evening meal, often the main meal of the day. **2** a light evening meal. **3** an evening social event, esp. one intended to raise money, at which a meal is served. □ **sing for one's supper** do something in return for a benefit.

suppertime n. the time of day at which supper is, or is customarily, served.

supplant /səˈplænt/ v.tr. dispossess and take the place of, esp. by underhand means. □ **supplanter** n.

supple adj. (**suppler, supplest**) **1** flexible, easily bent. **2** avoiding overt resistance. **3** capable of or demonstrating easy or graceful movement. □ **suppleness** n.

supplely var. of SUPPLY².

supplement ● n. **1** a thing or part added to remedy deficiencies (*dietary supplement*). **2** a part added to a book etc. to provide further information. **3** a separate section, esp. a colour magazine, added to a newspaper or periodical. **4** an additional charge payable for an extra service or facility. **5** *Math.* the amount by which an angle is less than 180° (*compare* COMPLEMENT n. 4). ● v.tr. provide a supplement for. □ **supplemental** adj. **supplementally** adv. **supplementation** n.

supplementary adj. forming or serving as a supplement; additional. □ **supplementarily** adv.

supplicate /ˈsʌplɪˌkeɪt/ v.tr. & intr. ask humbly. □ **supplicant** adj. & n. **supplication** n. **supplicatory** adj.

supply¹ ● v. (**-ies, -ied**) **1** tr. provide or furnish. **2** tr. (often foll. by *with*) provide (a person etc. with a thing needed). **3** tr. meet or make up for (a deficiency or need etc.). **4** tr. fill (a vacancy, place, etc.) as a substitute. ● n. (*pl.* **-ies**) **1** the act or an instance of providing what is needed. **2** a stock, store, amount, etc., of something provided or obtainable. **3** (in *pl.*) **a** food or other materials necessary for maintenance or for a specific activity. **b** the collected provisions and equipment for an army, expedition, etc. **c** a grant of money by Parliament for the costs of government (also attrib.: *supply bill*). **4** (often attrib.) a person, esp. a teacher or member of the clergy, acting as a temporary substitute for another. **5** (*attrib.*) providing supplies or a supply (*supply officer*). □ **in short supply** available in limited quantity. **on supply** (of a teacher etc.) acting as a supply. □ **supplier** *n.*

supply² *adv.* (also **supplely**) in a supple manner.

supply and demand *n.* the amount of a product available and needed, as factors regulating its price.

supply line *n.* **1** a transportation or communication line along which necessary supplies are delivered. **2** a conduit etc. through which something is supplied.

supply-side *adj.* denoting a policy of low taxation and other incentives to produce goods and invest (*supply-side economics*). □ **supply-sider** *n.*

supply teacher *n. Cdn & Brit.* a substitute teacher.

support ● *v.tr.* **1** carry all or part of the weight of. **2** keep from falling or sinking or failing. **3 a** provide with a home and the necessities of life. **b** provide enough food and water to keep someone or something alive. **4** enable to last out; give strength to; encourage. **5** tend to substantiate or corroborate. **6 a** give help to, back up. **b** speak in favour of. **7** help by giving one's approval, encouragement, etc. **8** be actively interested in (a particular political candidate, sports team, etc.). **9** (usu. as **supporting** *adj.*) take a part that is secondary to (a principal actor etc.). **10** occupy a position by the side of (a person) in order to give assistance or encouragement; assist by one's presence or attendance. **11** endure, tolerate (*can no longer support the noise*). **12** maintain or represent (a part or character) adequately. **13** contribute to the funds of (an institution). **14** (of a computer, operating system, etc.) allow the use or operation of (a program, device, etc.). **15** provide ongoing technical assistance for (a computer system etc.) once it is installed. ● *n.* **1** the act or an instance of supporting; the process of being supported. **2** a person or thing that supports. **3** encouragement or sympathy etc. given esp. to a person undergoing difficulties. **4** money paid by a divorced or separated person to his or her former spouse and/or their children. ● *adj.* (of hosiery) reinforced with elastic fibres in order to support the leg muscles and veins. □ **in support of** in order to support. □ **supportable** *adj.* **supporting** *adj.*

supporter *n.* **1** a person or thing that supports. **2** *Cdn* a person who pays education taxes to a usu. specified school system (*a separate school supporter*). **3** = ATHLETIC SUPPORTER.

support group *n.* a group of people who meet on a regular basis to provide mutual support by discussing a shared problem or experience.

supportive *adj.* providing support or encouragement. □ **supportively** *adv.* **supportiveness** *n.*

support staff *n.* employees providing esp. clerical and administrative assistance.

suppose *v.tr.* **1** assume, esp. in default of knowledge (*I suppose they will return*). **2** take as a possibility or hypothesis (*let's suppose you are right*). **3** (in *imper.*) as a formula of proposal (*suppose we go to the party*). **4** (of a theory or result etc.) require as a condition (*design in creation supposes a creator*). **5** (in *imper.* or *pres. part.* forming a question) in the circumstances that; if (*supposing we stay*). **6** (in *passive*; foll. by *to* + infin.) be generally accepted or believed to be so (*is generally supposed to be wealthy*). **7** (in *passive*; foll. by *to* + infin.) **a** be expected or required (*was supposed to write to you*). **b** (with *neg.*) not be allowed to (*you are not supposed to go in there*). **c** (with *neg.*) not be intended to (*we're not supposed to understand*). **8** (in *passive*; foll. by *to* + infin.)

be intended (*what is that supposed to mean?*). □ **I suppose so** an expression of hesitant agreement.

supposed *attrib.adj.* generally accepted as being so (*his supposed brother*). □ **supposedly** *adv.*

supposition /ˌsʌpəˈzɪʃən/ *n.* **1** a fact or idea etc. supposed. **2** the act or an instance of supposing.

suppository /səˈpɒzɪtəri, -tri/ *n.* (*pl.* **-ies**) a medical preparation in the form of a cone, cylinder, etc., to be inserted into the rectum or vagina to melt.

suppress *v.tr.* **1** end the activity or existence of, esp. forcibly. **2** prevent (information, etc.) from being seen, heard, or known. **3** stop (a cough, sneeze, etc.). **4** prevent (a feeling, reaction, etc.) from being expressed. **5** *Psych.* keep out of one's consciousness. □ **suppression** *n.* **suppressive** *adj.* **suppressor** *n.*

suppressant *n.* a suppressing or restraining agent (*cough suppressant*).

suppurate /ˈsʌpjəˌreit/ *v.intr.* form pus; fester. □ **suppuration** *n.* **suppurative** /-rətɪv/ *adj.*

supra /ˈsuːprə/ *adv.* above or earlier on (in a text).

supranational *adj.* transcending national limits.

supremacist /səˈpreməsɪst, su-/ *n.* a person who believes in or advocates the supremacy of a particular group, esp. determined by race or sex (also *attrib.*: *supremacist group*). □ **supremacism** *n.*

supremacy /səˈpreməsi, su-/ *n.* (*pl.* **-ies**) **1** the state of being supreme in authority, rank, or power. **2** ultimate power or authority.

supreme *adj.* **1** highest in authority, rank, or power. **2** of the highest quality or importance (*supreme achievement*). **3** greatest in amount or degree (*supreme stupidity*). **4** (of a penalty or sacrifice etc.) ultimate; resulting in death. □ **reign** (or **rule**) **supreme 1** be dominant; hold supreme power, authority, or popularity. **2** be widespread or pervasive; be a prevalent feature. □ **supremely** *adv.*

Supreme Being *n.* a name given to an omnipotent deity; God.

Supreme Court *n.* the highest judicial court of appeal in a country, province, etc. hearing civil, criminal, and constitutional cases.

Supt. *abbr.* Superintendent.

suq *var. of* SOUK.

sura /ˈsɔːrə/ *n.* a chapter or section of the Koran.

surcharge ● *n.* **1** a fee charged in addition to the normal cost of something. **2** an excessive amount charged. **3** an overwhelming or excessive load or burden. ● *v.tr.* **1** exact a surcharge from (a person, company, etc.). **2** exact (a sum) as a surcharge.

sure ● *adj.* **1** having or seeming to have adequate reason for a belief or assertion. **2** convinced (*he's guilty, I'm sure of it*). **3** having a confident anticipation or satisfactory knowledge of (*she's sure of the answer*). **4 a** reliable or unfailing (*a sure cure*). **b** steady, secure (*a sure footing*). **5 a** certain (*it's sure to rain*). **b** inevitable (*a sure win*). **6** undoubtedly true or truthful (*one thing is sure: I'll never do that again*). ● *adv. informal* certainly, truly (*I'm sure glad*). ● *interj.* yes; of course. □ **be sure** do not fail, neglect, or forget to (*be sure to turn the lights out*). **for sure** *informal* without doubt. **make sure** (often foll. by *that*) make or become certain; ensure. **make sure of** establish the truth or ensure the existence or happening of. **sure enough** *informal* **1** in fact; certainly (*I asked him to leave and, sure enough, he did*). **2** almost certainly (*they will come sure enough*). **sure of oneself** self-confident; self-assured. **to be sure 1** it is undeniable or admitted. **2** it must be admitted. □ **sureness** *n.*

surefire *adj. informal* reliable, guaranteed, assured.

sure-footed *adj.* **1** treading safely without slipping or stumbling. **2** not likely to fail or make a mistake. □ **sure-footedly** adv. **sure-footedness** n.

surely adv. **1** indeed. **2** used to express a strong belief in the statement qualified, esp. in the face of possible dissent (*surely you don't believe it*). **3** inevitably, without fail (*improving slowly but surely*).

Sûreté /ˌsuːrəˈteɪ/ n. (in full **Sûreté du Québec**) Cdn the provincial police force of Quebec.

sure thing esp. N Amer. informal ● n. a person or thing whose success is considered certain or guaranteed. ● interj. expressing consent to a proposal, request, etc.

surety /ˈʃʊrti/ n. (pl. **-ies**) **1** a person who assumes responsibility for the obligation of another, such as the payment of a debt or an appearance in court. **2 a** (in full **surety bond**) money given as a guarantee. **b** a guarantee or assurance. **3** certainty. □ **stand surety** become a surety (for).

surf ● n. **1** the swell of the sea breaking on the esp. shallow shore of a beach or a reef. **2** the foam produced by this. ● v. **1** intr. ride the crest of a wave towards the shore, esp. on a surfboard or windsurfer. **2** tr. ride (a wave, swell, etc.) on a surfboard or windsurfer. **3** tr. & intr. **a** N Amer. flip from one television channel to another in rapid succession using a remote control. **b** search or scan (the Internet) in order to sample a selection of sites. □ **surflike** adj. **surfy** adj.

surface ● n. **1 a** the outside part of something (*the earth's surface*). **b** the area of this. **2** any of the sides or faces of an object. **3** the top or outside layer of something (*the surface of the road*). **4** the upper layer or top of the ground, a body of water, or any liquid. **5 a** the superficial level or appearance of a person or thing as opposed to feelings, qualities, etc. which may not be apparent on a casual view or consideration (*seems quite happy on the surface*). **b** (attrib.) superficial (*surface politeness*). **6** a relatively flat horizontal space or area used for some particular purpose or activity (*playing surface*). **7** Geom. a continuous extent having only two dimensions, length and width without thickness, whether plane or curved, finite or infinite. **8** (attrib.) of or on the surface (*surface area; surface route*). ● v. **1** tr. cover (a road etc.) with a particular type of surface. **2** intr. **a** rise to the surface of esp. water. **b** become visible, known, or apparent. □ **come to the surface** become perceptible after being hidden.

surfaced adj. (often in comb.) having or having been furnished with a surface of a specified kind.

surface mail n. mail carried over land or sea.

surface temperature n. the temperature of a body of water or planet etc. taken at its surface.

surface tension n. the property causing the surface of a liquid to behave as if it were covered with a weak elastic skin, caused by the tendency of the exposed surface to contract to the smallest possible area.

surface-to-air attrib.adj. (of a missile) designed to be fired from the ground or sea towards a target in the air, such as an aircraft.

surface-to-surface attrib.adj. (of a missile) designed to be fired from a point on the ground or at sea and directed at a target elsewhere on the earth's surface.

surface water n. **1** water that collects on the surface of the ground. **2** the top layer of a body of water.

surfactant /sərˈfæktənt/ n. a substance which reduces surface tension of a liquid.

surf and turf n. N Amer. a restaurant meal combining seafood (esp. lobster) and steak.

surfboard n. a long narrow fibreglass board with a

small fin on the underside, on which a surfer stands or lies while being carried on the crest of a breaking wave towards the shore.

surfeit /ˈsɜːrfət/ ● n. a large or excessive amount. ● v. (**surfeited**, **surfeiting**) **1** tr. fill, supply, or feed to excess. **2** tr. & intr. be or cause to be wearied through excess. □ **surfeited** adj.

surfer n. **1 a** a person who participates in the sport of surfing. **b** (attrib.) designating aspects or elements typical of the lifestyle, culture, language, etc. of a surfer (*surfer shorts*). **2** a person who surfs the Internet.

surfing n. **1** the sport or activity of riding waves on a surfboard or windsurfer etc. **2** an instance or the hobby of surfing the Internet. **3** N Amer. = CHANNEL SURFING.

surge ● n. **1** a sudden or violent rush, onset, or burst. **2** a high rolling swell of water, esp. on the sea. **3** a rapid increase in price, activity, etc. over a short period. **4** a heavy forward or upward motion of a large or growing mass, volume, etc. **5** = POWER SURGE. ● v.intr. **1** (of the sea etc.) rise and move forward in great waves; swell or heave with great force. **2** move forward suddenly or powerfully. **3** show a large, sudden, usu. brief increase in magnitude, power, growth, etc. **4** (of a feeling, activity, etc.) increase suddenly and dramatically.

surgeon n. a medical practitioner qualified to practise surgery.

Surgeon General n. (pl. **Surgeons General**) **1** (in the US) the senior medical officer of the Bureau of Public Health or (in some states) a similar state authority. **2** the senior officer in medical service of the armed forces.

surgery n. (pl. **-ies**) **1** the branch of medicine concerned with treatment of injuries or disorders of the body by incision, manipulation, or alteration of organs etc. **2** surgical treatment. **3** esp. N Amer. the part of or a room in a hospital where surgery is performed. **4** a detailed or extensive series of repairs, changes, or modifications made to something.

surge suppressor n. (also **surge protector**) a device used to protect an electrical appliance etc. from damage in the event of a power surge. □ **surge suppression** n. (also **surge protection**).

surgical adj. **1** of, relating to, or performed by surgeons or surgery. **2** used or worn by surgeons or during surgery (*surgical gloves*). **3** designating a swift and precise military attack, esp. from the air (*surgical strike*). □ **surgically** adv.

surimi /suːˈriːmi/ n. a white relatively tasteless and odourless paste made from minced fish, used esp. to produce imitation crab and lobster.

surly adj. (**-ier, -iest**) **1** rude, unfriendly; gruff. **2** hostile, belligerent. □ **surlily** adv. **surliness** n.

surmise ● v.tr. form an opinion that something may be true without sufficient evidence to be certain. ● n. conjecture.

surmount v.tr. **1** overcome (an obstacle, difficulty, etc.). **2** (usu. in passive) rest on top of; or be situated on or above (*a ring surmounted by a beautiful diamond*). □ **surmountable** adj.

surname n. a hereditary name common to all members of a family, as distinct from a given name.

surpass v.tr. **1** be greater, better than, or superior to. **2** outdo (another person or thing) in degree or prominence (*crime has surpassed unemployment as the key concern*). **3** go beyond, exceed (a certain limit etc.). **4** be beyond the range or capacity of; transcend (*surpasses description*).

surpassing *adj.* that surpasses what is ordinary; exceptional, matchless. □ **surpassingly** *adv.*

surplice /'sɜːplɪs, -pləs/ *n. Christianity* a loose white vestment with wide sleeves, worn usu. over a cassock by some clergy and choristers.

surplus ● *n.* **1** an amount left over when requirements have been met. **2 a** an excess of revenue over expenditure in a given period (*opp.* DEFICIT 2). **b** the excess value of a company's assets over the face value of its stock. **3 a** military supplies, such as clothing and camping gear, exceeding the requirements of the forces and sold to the public. **b** (*attrib.*) designating a store or outlet etc. selling such goods. ● *adj.* exceeding what is needed or used; excess.

surplus value *n.* the difference between the value of work done and the cost of the labour that has produced it.

surprise ● *n.* **1** an unexpected or astonishing event etc. **2** astonishment, shock, or amazement. **3** a gift. **4** a person or thing that achieves unexpected success. **5** an attack or approach made upon an unsuspecting victim. **6** (*attrib.*) unexpected; made or done etc. without warning (*a surprise visit*). **7** often *jocular* or *informal* a dish, esp. a casserole, prepared with ingredients not made known to those to whom it is served (*tuna surprise*). ● *v.tr.* **1** cause to feel astonishment, shock, or amazement. **2 a** startle with a sudden or unexpected approach. **b** capture or attack by surprise. ● *interj.* used as an exclamation of triumph as a surprise is successfully revealed. □ **should come as no surprise** (a piece of information) should have been anticipated, guessed, or previously known. **surprise, surprise** *ironic* just as one might expect. **take** (or **catch**) **by surprise** startle or astonish esp. with an unexpected encounter or statement. □ **surprising** *adj.* **surprisingly** *adv.*

surprised *adj.* **1** filled with mild astonishment or amazement. **2** shocked, scandalized.

surreal /sə'riːl/ *adj.* **1** having some of the qualities of surrealism; bizarre. **2** = SURREALISTIC. □ **surreality** *n.* **surreally** *adv.*

surrealism *n.* **1** (**Surrealism**) a 20th-c. movement in art and literature to explore and express the subconscious and to move beyond the accepted conventions of reality by representing the irrational imagery of dreams using such techniques as automatism, the irrational juxtaposition of images, and the creation of mysterious symbols. **2** art or literature produced by or reminiscent of this movement. □ **surrealist** *n. & adj.* (also **Surrealist**).

surrealistic *adj.* **1** based on, influenced by, or pertaining to Surrealism or the Surrealists. **2** characteristic or suggestive of Surrealism. □ **surrealistically** *adv.*

surrender ● *v.* **1** *tr.* **a** give up possession or control of (something) to another, esp. on compulsion or demand. **b** abandon (hope etc.). **2** *intr.* offer or give oneself up as a prisoner to esp. an enemy or the police. **3** *intr. & refl.* submit or abandon oneself entirely to some influence, emotion, course of action, etc. **4** *tr. Sport* give up or allow one or a number of (goals, points, etc.). ● *n.* the act or an instance of surrendering.

surreptitious /ˌsɜrəp'tɪʃəs/ *adj.* **1** obtained, done, etc. in secret or by stealth or illicit means. **2** acting stealthily or secretly; crafty, sly. □ **surreptitiously** *adv.*

surrogacy /'sɜrəgəsi/ *n.* the practice of surrogate motherhood.

surrogate /'sʌrəgət/ *n.* **1** a person or thing taking the

place of another. **2** a person appointed by authority to act in place of another, esp. in a specific role or office. **3 a** a surrogate mother. **b** (*attrib.*) relating to or involving surrogate motherhood (*surrogate parent*). **4** a person who fills the role of an absent or estranged relative, esp. a parent, in a child's upbringing.

surrogate court *n. N Amer.* a court with jurisdiction over wills and estates of deceased persons.

surrogate mother *n.* **1** a woman who bears a child for another woman, either from her own egg fertilized by the other woman's partner or from the implantation in her uterus of a fertilized egg from the other woman. **2** a person or animal acting the role of mother. □ **surrogate motherhood** *n.* **surrogate mothering** *n.*

surround ● *v.tr.* **1** stand or be situated around. **2 a** place a thing or things on all sides of or all around. **b** (*refl.*) place people or things around (oneself); situate (oneself) among. **3** form the entourage of (a person). **4** exist as a predominant aspect of (*a mystery surrounds her disappearance*). ● *n.* **1** a structure or border placed around something. **2** the area around a place or thing; surroundings. **3** = SURROUND SOUND.

surrounding ● *adj.* located or situated around. ● *n.* (in *pl.*) all the objects, conditions, etc. that are around and may affect a person or thing.

surround sound *n.* a system of sound reproduction in which three or more speakers create a sense of space and depth, and thus a more realistic effect.

surtax ● *n.* **1** a higher rate of tax levied on personal incomes above a certain level. **2** any additional tax charged on something already taxed. ● *v.tr.* impose a surtax on.

surveillance *n.* **1** close observation or supervision, esp. of an enemy or suspected person. **2** a security device or system used to monitor premises and detect trespassers, thieves, etc.

survey ● *n.* **1 a** a general and comprehensive discussion, treatment, etc. **b** (in full **survey course**) *N Amer.* an introductory academic course which gives a broad esp. historical overview of one subject. **2** a systematic collection and analysis of data relating to the opinions, habits, etc. of a population, usu. taken from a representative sample. **3 a** the process or an act of surveying land or property. **b** a summary or report of the results or findings of this. **c** a map or plan based on the results obtained by surveying land. **d** a department carrying out the surveying of land. **4** a close inspection, investigation, or examination. ● *v.tr.* **1** make or present a general and comprehensive examination or assessment of. **2 a** record the views and opinions of (a person or group) in an opinion poll. **b** ascertain (the opinions etc.) of a person or group. **3** explore, measure, or determine the boundaries, extent, and ownership of (land etc.) in order to construct a map or detailed description.

surveying *n.* **1** the business or occupation of a surveyor. **2** the act or an instance of exploring or measuring land, inspecting a building, etc.

surveyor *n.* **1** a person whose occupation is the surveying of land and property. **2** a person who conducts opinion polls or surveys.

survivable *adj.* **1** not fatal; able to be survived. **2** capable of surviving. □ **survivability** *n.*

survival *n.* **1** the process or an instance of continuing to live, esp. after some tragic or disastrous event. **2** the practice of coping with harsh or warlike conditions, as a leisure activity or training exercise. **3** a person, thing, or practice that has remained from a former time. □ **survival of the fittest** the continued existence of organisms which are best adapted to their environment, with the extinction of others, as a concept in the Darwinian theory of evolution.

survivalism *n.* **1** a policy of trying to ensure survival, esp. in the face of competition or a natural disaster, catastrophic event, or foreign invasion. **2** the practising of outdoor survival skills as a sport or hobby. □ **survivalist** *n. & adj.*

survival kit *n.* a small pack filled with first aid supplies, emergency rations, and supplies for use when stranded or lost.

survive *v.* **1** *intr.* continue to live or exist, esp. after some event. **2** *tr.* live or exist longer than (*she survived her husband*). **3** *tr.* remain alive after going through, or continue to exist in spite of (a danger, accident, etc.) (*he has survived two strokes*). **4** *intr.* remain in use or existence. **5** *tr. & intr. informal* or *jocular* endure a difficult situation.

survivor *n.* **1** a person who survives or has survived, esp. one remaining alive after an event in which others die (*the blaze left only four survivors*). **2** *informal* one who has a knack for overcoming difficulties or surviving afflictions unscathed. □ **survivorship** *n.*

sus *var. of* SUSS.

susceptible /sə'septəbl/ *adj.* **1 a** (*predic.*; usu. foll. by *to*) likely to be affected by; prone or vulnerable to (*susceptible to pain*). **b** vulnerable, esp. deficient in defences against a disease (*the virus attacks susceptible children*). **2** impressionable, sensitive; easily moved by emotion. □ **susceptibility** *n.* **susceptibly** *adv.*

sushi /'su:ʃi/ *n.* a Japanese snack of cold boiled rice flavoured with vinegar, salt, and sugar, and garnished with a variety of toppings, often raw fish or seaweed.

suspect ● *v.tr.* **1 a** imagine (something) to be possible or likely. **b** be inclined to think. **2** believe to be guilty with insufficient proof or knowledge; doubt the innocence of. **3** believe tentatively, without clear ground. **4** doubt the genuineness or truth of; mistrust. ● *n.* a person suspected of an offence, evil intention, etc. ● *adj.* subject to or deserving of suspicion or distrust; questionable. □ **the usual suspects** *jocular* a group of people who are frequently and predictably present at events, called upon for comment, etc.

suspected *n.* **1** imagined to be. **2** that one suspects of something which is not certain. **3** (of an injury, ailment, etc.) believed to have been suffered although not yet diagnosed or confirmed.

suspend *v.tr.* **1** attach (an object) to something above so that it hangs, usu. with free movement. **2** cause to remain in a floating or elevated position without attachment. **3** refrain from making, forming, or announcing (a judgment, opinion, etc.) until a later time. **4** cancel or halt, esp. temporarily (*the police suspended her driver's licence*). **5** forbid (a person) from performing a usual duty or participating in a usual activity for a temporary or indefinite period, esp. as a penalty. □ **suspend disbelief** refrain from being skeptical about the believability of a work of fiction or its characters.

suspended animation *n.* a temporary cessation of the vital functions without death.

suspended sentence *n.* a sentence imposed but unenforced as long as the offender commits no further offence within a specified period.

suspender *n.* (in *pl.*) *N Amer.* a pair of straps of usu. elastic material worn over the shoulder and fastened to the waistband of a pair of pants to prevent them from falling down.

suspense *n.* **1** a state of uncertainty or expectation, accompanied by anxiety or excitement, about an awaited outcome, decision, etc. **2 a** a quality in a work of fiction that arouses excited expectation about the outcome, culprit, etc. in the mind of the viewer or reader. **b** works having this quality. **3** the condition of something that is in doubt or undecided. □ **keep in suspense** delay informing (a person) of important or useful information, thus heightening their excitement or anxiety. □ **suspenseful** *adj.*

suspension *n.* **1** the action of suspending or the condition of being suspended, esp. a temporary cessation or postponement. **2 a** a period during which one is prohibited from attending school or work, playing for a team, participating in an activity, etc. **b** a temporary revocation of a licence, contract, etc. **3** (in full **suspension system**) the system of springs and shocks that supports a vehicle on its axles. **4** a mixture in which small particles are distributed throughout a less dense liquid or gas.

suspension bridge *n.* a bridge having a deck suspended from cables supported by towers at each end.

suspicion *n.* **1** the feeling or state of mind of a person who suspects (*viewed him with suspicion*). **2 a** the act or an instance of suspecting (*his actions raised suspicions*). **b** the state of being suspected (*no longer under suspicion*). **3** a faint belief (*a suspicion she's lying*). **4** a presumption of guilt based on evidence sufficient for arrest but not conviction (*arrested on suspicion of murder*). □ **above suspicion** too obviously good etc. to be suspected. **under suspicion** suspected.

suspicious *adj.* **1 a** prone to suspicion; mistrustful, esp. of something or someone in particular. **b** feeling suspicion; having one's suspicion aroused. **2** indicating suspicion (*a suspicious glance*). **3** inviting or justifying suspicion (*suspicious behaviour*). □ **suspiciously** *adv.* **suspiciousness** *n.*

suss *v.tr.* (**sussed, sussing**) (usu. foll. by *out*) **1** investigate, check out (*I'll suss out restaurants*). **2** figure out.

sustain *v.tr.* **1** provide with the basic necessities required to support or preserve life, livelihood, or existence; provide for the needs of. **2** endure, stand; bear up against. **3** undergo or suffer (defeat or injury etc.). **4** maintain or keep (an action or process) going continuously. **5** (of a court etc.) uphold or decide in favour of (an objection etc.). **6** give strength to; encourage, support. **7** substantiate or corroborate (a statement or charge). **8** hold up or support the weight of, esp. for a long period. **9** *Music* hold (a note or chord) for an extended period. □ **sustained** *adj.* **sustainer** *n.* **sustaining** *adj.* **sustainment** *n.*

sustainable *adj.* **1** (esp. of development) that conserves an ecological balance by avoiding depletion of natural resources. **2** that may be maintained, esp. at a particular level. □ **sustainably** *adv.* **sustainability** *n.*

sustained yield *n.* the quantity of a crop that can be periodically harvested without long-term depletion (also *attrib.*: *sustained-yield forestry*).

sustenance *n.* **1** a means of sustaining life; nourishment. **2** a livelihood. **3** the action or process of sustaining esp. life.

Sutra /'su:trə/ *n.* **1** an aphorism or set of aphorisms in Hindu literature. **2** a narrative part of Buddhist literature. **3** Jainist scripture.

suttee /sʌ'ti:, 'sʌti/ *n.* (*pl.* **-s**) esp. *hist.* **1** the Hindu practice of a widow immolating herself on her husband's funeral pyre. **2** a widow who undergoes or has undergone this.

suture /ˈsuːtʃər/ ● n. **1 a** the joining of the edges of a wound or incision by stitching. **b** a seam or stitch made during this procedure. **c** the material used to make surgical stitches. **2** the junction of two bones forming an immovable articulation, esp. each of the serrated borders between the bones of the skull. ● v.tr. stitch up (a wound or incision) with a suture. □ **sutured** adj.

SUV abbr. = SPORT-UTILITY VEHICLE.

Suzuki /səˈzuːki/ adj. designating, pertaining to, or using a method of teaching the violin (esp. to young children), characterized by exercises involving large groups and parental participation.

svelte /svelt/ adj. slender.

Svengali /svenˈɡɑːli/ n. (pl. **-s**) a person who exercises a controlling or mesmeric influence on another, esp. for a sinister purpose.

SVGA abbr. Computing a colour graphics adapter that is an upgrade of the VGA standard.

SW abbr. **1** southwest. **2** southwestern. **3** short-wave.

swab ● n. **1 a** an absorbent pad used in surgery for cleaning or applying medication to wounds. **b** a wad of cotton or other absorbent material fixed to the end of a rod and used for cleaning or applying medication. **c** a specimen of a possibly morbid secretion collected with a swab for examination. **2** a mop or other absorbent device for cleaning or mopping up. ● v.tr. (**swabbed, swabbing**) **1** wipe or clean (a wound, ship's deck, etc.) with a swab. **2** absorb or apply (a substance) with a swab.

swaddle v.tr. **1** wrap (oneself or another or part of the body) in bandages, clothes, a blanket, etc. **2** wrap (a newborn child) in a blanket or swaddling clothes. **3** surround (a person or thing) with. □ **swaddled** adj.

swaddling clothes n.pl. hist. narrow lengths of bandage wrapped around a newborn child to restrict its movements and quieten it.

swag n. **1** slang **a** the stolen goods carried off by a thief or burglar. **b** illicit gains. **2** a length of fabric or drapery fastened in such a way that it hangs loosely over a window, sagging in the middle. **3** an ornamental arrangement of flowers, leaves, or fruit.

swagger ● v.intr. **1** walk or behave with an air of confidence or toughness. **2** talk boastfully. ● n. **1 a** an air or attitude of cockiness or toughness. **b** an air or attitude of smartness or flamboyance. **2** a swaggering gait or manner. **3** confident, boastful, or brash behaviour. □ **swaggering** adj. **swaggeringly** adv.

Swahili /swəˈhiːli, swɒ-/ ● n. (pl. same) **1** a member of a Bantu-speaking people of Zanzibar and adjacent coasts. **2** their language, used widely as a lingua franca in E Africa. ● adj. of or relating to the Swahili or their language.

swain n. literary or jocular a young lover or suitor.

swale n. esp. N Amer. a low or hollow place, esp. a marshy depression or hollow between ridges.

swallow[1] ● v. **1** tr. & intr. cause or allow (food etc.) to pass down the throat. **2** intr. perform the muscular movement of the esophagus required to do this. **3** tr. accept meekly, gullibly or unquestioningly. **4** tr. repress; resist the expression of (a feeling etc.) (had to swallow my anger). **5** tr. (often foll. by up) engulf, absorb, or consume; cause to disappear. ● n. **1** the act of swallowing. **2** an amount swallowed in one action. □ **swallow one's pride** humble oneself in order to admit guilt or error or to ask for a favour. □ **swallower** n.

swallow[2] n. any of various migratory swift-flying insect-eating birds with a forked tail and long pointed wings.

swallowtail n. **1** anything resembling the shape of a swallow's deeply forked tail. **2** any butterfly of the family Papilionidae with wings extended at the back to this shape. □ **swallow-tailed** adj.

swam past of SWIM.

swami /ˈswɒmi/ n. (pl. **-s**) **1** a Hindu male religious teacher. **2** informal an adviser or mentor.

swamp ● n. **1** a tract of low-lying ground in which water collects; a bog or marsh. **2** a difficult or messy situation. ● v. **1 a** tr. overwhelm, flood, or soak with water. **b** intr. (of a boat) become filled with water and sink. **2** tr. overwhelm with a large amount of something. **3** tr. & intr. N Amer. clear (a road) in a forest by felling trees, removing undergrowth, etc., esp. for hauling logs. □ **swampy** adj. (**-ier, -iest**).

swamped adj. overwhelmed with work.

swamper n. **1** Cdn a person who swamps logging roads. **2** Cdn (BC) an assistant to a truck driver.

swampland n. land consisting of swamps.

Swampy Cree n. **1** a member of a Cree people living in northern Manitoba and in the area of western James Bay and Hudson Bay. **2** the Cree dialect spoken by this people.

swan n. any of several large web-footed swimming birds, characterized by a long and gracefully curved neck with all white (or, in the case of Cygnus atratus, black) plumage and black feet. □ **swanlike** adj. & adv.

swan dive n. N Amer. **1** a forward dive with the arms extended sideways until the diver is close to the surface of the water, at which point the arms are brought together over the head. **2** jocular a dramatic or spectacular fall, plunge, or dive.

swank informal ● n. **1** style, elegance. **2** ostentation, flashiness, swagger. ● v.intr. boast, show off. ● adj. esp. N Amer. **1** posh, stylish. **2** pretentious, boastful. □ **swanky** adj. (**-ier, -iest**).

swan song n. the final work or performance of a writer, artist, etc. before retirement or death.

swap /swɒp/ ● v.tr. & intr. (**swapped, swapping**) exchange or trade (one thing for another). ● n. **1** an act of swapping one thing for another. **2** = SWAP MEET 1. □ **swappable** adj. **swapper** n.

swap meet n. esp. N Amer. **1** a gathering at which enthusiasts or collectors trade or exchange items of a particular kind. **2** a flea market.

swarm ● n. **1** a cluster of bees leaving the hive with the queen to establish a new colony. **2** a large number of insects or birds moving in a cluster. **3** a large or dense group, esp. when active or moving. ● v. **1** intr. gather or procede in a swarm or crowd. **2** intr. (foll. by with) (of a place) be overrun, crowded, or infested (the city swarms with tourists). **3** tr. (of a large group of people or things) fill (an area or space) (students swarmed the halls). **4** tr. gather around (a person), esp. in an aggressive or hostile manner. **5** tr. & intr. climb up (a rope or tree etc.), esp. in a rush, by clasping or clinging with the hands and knees.

swarming n. an attack on an individual by a group of attackers who taunt, shove, etc. until the victim is too intimidated or confused to resist theft or assault.

swarthy adj. (**-ier, -iest**) of a dark colour or complexion. □ **swarthiness** n.

swashbuckler n. **1** a swaggering adventurer or blustering ruffian. **2** a film etc. portraying swashbuckling characters. □ **swashbuckling** adj. & n.

swastika /ˈswɒstɪkə, ˈswɒstɪkɑː/ n. **1** an ancient symbol in the form of a cross with each of its four arms of equal length bent at right angles at the end, all in the same direction and usu. clockwise. **2** this symbol with clockwise continuations used as the emblem of

Nazi Germany and adopted subsequently as the emblem of anti-Semitic and other racially motivated hate groups.

SWAT /swɒt/ n. (in full **SWAT team**) a special detachment of some US police forces trained to deal with terrorism and other dangerous situations such as hostage-takings.

swat ● v. (**swatted, swatting**) **1** tr. crush (a fly etc.) with a sharp blow. **2** tr. hit hard and abruptly; slap, smack. **3** intr. direct a blow at a target, esp. without hitting it. ● n. a sharp slap or hit.

swatch n. **1 a** a sample, esp. of cloth, fabric, or paint colours. **b** a collection of samples. **2** a portion or section (*he appeals to a swatch of our listeners*).

swath /swɒθ/ n. (also **swathe** /sweɪð/) (pl. **swaths** /swɒθs, swɒðs/ or **swathes** /sweɪðs/) **1** a strip in a field or lawn that has been left clear after the passage of a mower etc. **2** a row or line of grass, wheat, etc. as it falls or lies when mown or reaped. **3** a broad strip or long stretch of something. □ **cut a wide swath 1** be effective in destruction. **2** make a grand or pompous display.

swathe /swɒθ, sweɪð/ v.tr. **1** wrap (a person etc.) in bandages or clothes. **2** cover in or under; envelop.

swatter n. = FLY SWATTER.

sway ● v. **1** intr. **a** move slowly and rhythmically back and forth or from side to side. **b** rock awkwardly or unsteadily as if about to fall. **2** intr. waver between two options or opinions. **3** tr. **a** influence or direct the decision or opinion of. **b** control or direct the outcome of (an event). **4** tr. cause to move or swing from side to side. **5** intr. bend, lean, or incline to one side. ● n. **1** a position of power, authority, or influence. **2** a to-and-fro movement. □ **hold sway** be supreme in power, influence, or popularity.

Swazi /'swɒzi/ ● n. **1** (pl. same or **Swazis**) **a** a member of a people inhabiting Swaziland and parts of Eastern Transvaal in South Africa. **b** a native or national of Swaziland. **2** the Nguni language of this people. ● adj. of or relating to Swaziland, the Swazi, or their language.

swear v. (past **swore**; past part. **sworn**) **1** tr. **a** state or promise solemnly or on oath. **b** take (an oath). **2** tr. informal state emphatically; insist. **3** tr. cause to take an oath (*sworn to secrecy*). **4** intr. use profane or indecent language. **5** intr. informal have or express great confidence or faith in (*I swear by my old typewriter*). **6** intr. appeal to a sacred person or thing in confirmation of the truth of a solemn declaration (*I swear to God*). **7** intr. admit the certainty of (*could not swear to it*). □ **swear in** induct into office etc. by administering an oath. **swear off** informal promise or vow to abstain from (drink etc.). **swear out** N Amer. obtain the issue of (a warrant for arrest) by making a charge on oath. □ **swearer** n.

swearing-in n. a ceremony at which a person formally accepts the conditions of an office, tenure, assignment, etc., by swearing an oath.

swear word n. a profanity.

sweat ● n. **1** moisture exuded through the pores of the skin. **2** a state or period of sweating. **3** informal a state of anxiety **4** informal **a** drudgery, effort. **b** a laborious task or undertaking. **5** condensed moisture on a surface. **6** (in pl.) esp. N Amer. informal **a** = SWEATSUIT. **b** = SWEATPANTS. **c** = SWEATSHIRT. **7** = SWEAT BATH. ● v. (past and past part. **sweated** or **sweat**) **1** intr. exude sweat; perspire. **2** intr. be terrified, suffering, etc. **3** intr. (of a wall etc.) exhibit surface moisture. **4** intr. drudge, toil. **5** tr. N Amer. informal worry about (something) (*don't sweat the details*). □ **by the sweat of one's brow** by

one's own hard work. **no sweat** informal **1** there is no need to worry. **2** without any difficulty. **sweat blood** informal **1** work strenuously. **2** be extremely anxious. **sweat one's guts out** informal work extremely hard, esp. excessively in comparison to the reward or to other people's expectations. **sweat it out** informal endure a difficult experience to the end.

sweatband n. **1** a band of absorbent material worn around the head or wrist to soak up sweat. **2** a band of absorbent material lining a hat.

sweat bath n. **1** a structure filled with hot humid air to induce sweating. **2** the action of spending time in this with the intention of sweating profusely.

sweated adj. (of goods, workers, or labour) produced by or subjected to long hours under poor conditions.

sweater n. **1** a knitted or crocheted garment covering the upper half of the body. **2** a sports jersey. □ **sweatered** adj. (also in comb.).

sweat lodge n. a structure heated by pouring water over hot stones, used by some Aboriginal groups to induce sweating, as for religious or medical purposes.

sweatpants n.pl. loose fleece pants with a drawstring or elasticized waist and often with elasticized cuffs, worn as casual attire or for sports.

sweatshirt n. a loosely fitting long-sleeved fleece top, worn as casual attire or for sports.

sweatshop n. a factory etc., esp. in the garment industry, where workers work long hours in unpleasant conditions for low pay.

sweatsuit n. a suit of a sweatshirt and sweatpants, worn as casual attire or for sports.

sweaty adj. (**-ier, -iest**) **1** covered, damp with, or smelling of sweat. **2** causing sweat. □ **sweatily** adv. **sweatiness** n.

Swede n. **1** a native or national of Sweden. **2** a person of Swedish descent.

swede saw n. Cdn a type of hand saw with a bow-like tubular frame and many cutting teeth.

Swedish ● adj. of or relating to Sweden, a country in Scandinavia, or its people or language. ● n. the language of Sweden.

sweep ● v. (past and past part. **swept**) **1** tr. clean or clear with or as with a broom. **2** intr. clean a room etc. in this way. **3** tr. collect or remove (dirt or litter etc.) by sweeping. **4** tr. (foll. by aside, away, etc.) **a** push with or as with a broom. **b** dismiss or reject abruptly (*their objections were swept aside*). **5** tr. (foll. by along, down, etc.) carry or drive along with force. **6** tr. (foll. by off, away, etc.) remove or clear forcefully. **7** tr. cross swiftly or lightly (*the wind swept the hillside*). **8** tr. impart a sweeping motion to (*swept his hand across*). **9** tr. swiftly cover or affect. **10** intr. **a** glide swiftly; speed along with unchecked motion. **b** go majestically. **c** move suddenly and with force over an area (*fire swept through the building*). **11** intr. (of geographical features etc.) have continuous extent. **12** tr. **a** pass over (something) in order to examine it or search for something (*searchlights swept the sky*). **b** drag (a river bottom etc.) to search for something. **c** examine (a building, telephone line, etc.) for electronic listening or recording devices. **13** tr. (of artillery etc.) include in the line of fire; cover the whole of. **14** tr. N Amer. win every event, award, or place in (a contest). ● n. **1** the act or motion or an instance of sweeping. **2** a curve in the road, a sweeping line of a hill, etc. **3** range or scope (*the long sweep of history*). **4** (in pl.) informal = SWEEPSTAKES 1, 2. **5** a long oar worked from a barge etc. **6** N Amer. victory in all the games in a contest etc. by one team or competitor, or the winning of all the places in a single event.

7 a a surprise raid by police through a neighbourhood, building, etc., to arrest suspected persons or seize illicit goods. **b** a comprehensive search for electronic listening or recording devices. **8** a survey of an area, esp. the night sky, made in an arc or circle. **9** *Football* = END RUN 1. **10** = CHIMNEY SWEEP. **11** a piece of rubber affixed to the bottom of an exterior door to keep out drafts. □ **make a clean sweep of 1** completely abolish or expel. **2** win all the prizes etc. in (a competition etc.). **sweep away 1** abolish swiftly. **2** (usu. in *passive*) powerfully affect, esp. emotionally. **sweep a person off his** (or **her**) **feet** affect a person with powerful emotion, esp. love.

sweeper *n.* **1** a person who cleans by sweeping. **2** a device for sweeping. **3** a person who or a vessel which sweeps for something under water. **4** *Cdn* **a** a tree overhanging a stream etc. **b** a drifting tree or log in a stream etc. **5** *Curling* a player who sweeps in front of a moving rock with a broom or brush.

sweeping ● *adj.* **1** wide in range or effect. **2** taking no account of particular cases or exceptions. **3** complete, overwhelming. **4** passing over a wide area. ● *n.* (in *pl.*) dirt etc. collected by sweeping. □ **sweepingly** *adv.*

sweepstakes *n.* (also **sweepstake**) **1** a form of gambling in which all the money bet on the result of a contest is paid to the winner or winners. **2** a race with betting of this kind. **3** a prize or prizes won in a sweepstakes.

sweet ● *adj.* **1 a** having the pleasant taste characteristic of sugar. **b** (in the names of baked goods) sweet-tasting, esp. *Cdn* (*Nfld*) containing molasses and raisins, and prepared chiefly at Christmas (*sweet bread*; *sweet loaf*). **2 a** smelling pleasant like roses or perfume etc. **b** (in the names of flowers, fruit, and vegetables) sweet-smelling or sweet-tasting (*sweet potato*). **3** (of sound etc.) melodious or harmonious. **4 a** not salty, sour, or bitter. **b** fresh and pure (*the sweet air of the countryside*). **c** (of food) fresh, with flavour unimpaired by rottenness. **d** (of water) fresh and readily drinkable. **5** (of wine) having a sweet taste (opp. DRY *adj.* 2). **6** highly gratifying or attractive (*the sweet feeling of success*). **7** amiable, pleasant (*has a sweet nature*). **8** *informal* (of a person or thing) pretty, charming, endearing. **9** (foll. by on) *informal* fond of; in love with. **10** esp. *ironic* one's own; particular, individual (*takes his own sweet time*). **11** *slang* as an intensifier in phrases meaning 'nothing at all'. **12** *informal* (of a deal etc.) with terms that are more lenient than deserved. ● *n.* **1** (in *pl.*) **a** *N Amer.* sweet foods, such as pie, cake, chocolate, etc. (*doesn't like sweets*). **b** *Cdn* (*NB*) = DAINTY *n.* 2. **2 a** sweet part of something; sweetness. **3** (in *pl.*) delights, gratification. **4** (esp. as a form of address) sweetheart etc. □ **sweetish** *adj.* **sweetly** *adv.*

sweet alyssum *n.* see ALYSSUM 1.

sweet-and-sour *attrib.adj.* cooked in a sauce containing sugar and vinegar or lemon juice etc.

sweet basil *n.* see BASIL.

sweet bay *n.* = BAY² 1.

sweetbread *n.* the pancreas or thymus of an animal, used for food.

sweet cassava *n.* see CASSAVA.

sweet chestnut *n.* see CHESTNUT 1b.

sweet corn *n.* **1** a kind of corn with kernels having a high sugar content. **2** these kernels, eaten as a vegetable when young.

sweeten *v.* **1** *tr.* & *intr.* make or become sweet or sweeter in smell, taste, or sound. **2** *tr.* make fresh or wholesome; purify (*use mouthwash to sweeten your breath*). **3** *tr.* make agreeable or less painful. **4** *tr.*

increase the attractiveness or value of (a deal, proposal, etc.). **5** *tr. Cards informal* increase the stakes (in a pot). □ **sweetening** *n.*

sweetener *n.* **1** a substance used to sweeten food or drink, esp. any of various low-calorie sugar substitutes. **2** a thing that makes something more pleasant, agreeable, or tolerable. **3** *informal* a bribe or inducement.

sweet grass *n.* *N Amer.* **1** any of several fragrant grasses, esp. *Hierochloe odorata*, used in basket making. **2** any of various grasses or other plants relished by cattle for their sweet succulent foliage.

sweetheart *n.* **1** a person with whom one is in love. **2** a term of endearment. **3** a lovable, amiable, or obliging person.

sweetheart deal *n.* (also **sweetheart contract**) *informal* an industrial agreement reached privately by employers and union leaders in their own interests.

sweetie *n.* *informal* **1** (also **sweetie pie**) a term of endearment (esp. as a form of address). **2** = SWEETHEART 3.

sweet marjoram *n.* see MARJORAM.

sweetmeat *n.* **1** a confectionery item, e.g. a preserved or candied fruit, a sugared nut, etc. **2** a small fancy cake.

sweetness *n.* the quality of being sweet. □ **sweetness and light** a display of (esp. uncharacteristic) mildness and reason.

sweet pea *n.* any climbing plant of the genus *Lathyrus*, esp. with fragrant flowers in many colours.

sweet pepper *n.* a relatively mild-tasting pepper.

sweet potato *n.* **1** a tropical climbing plant, *Ipomoea batatas*, with sweet tuberous roots used for food. **2** the root of this.

sweet spot *n.* the point on a bat, racquet, etc. at which it makes most effective contact with the ball.

sweet talk *informal* ● *n.* flattery. ● *v.tr.* (**sweet-talk**) flatter in order to persuade. □ **sweet-talking** *adj.*

sweet tooth *n.* a liking for sweet-tasting things.

sweet violet *n.* a sweet-scented violet, *Viola odorata.*

swell ● *v.* (*past part.* **swollen** or **swelled**) **1** *intr.* & *tr.* grow or cause to grow bigger or louder or more intense. **2** *intr.* & *tr.* rise or raise up from the surrounding surface. **3** *intr.* (foll. by out) bulge. **4** *intr.* (of the heart as the seat of emotion) feel full of joy, pride, etc. **5** *intr.* be hardly able to restrain (pride etc.). ● *n.* **1** an act or the state of swelling. **2** the heaving of the sea with waves that do not break. **3 a** a crescendo. **b** a mechanism in an organ etc. for obtaining a crescendo or diminuendo. **4** *informal* a person of distinction or of dashing or fashionable appearance. ● *adj.* **1** esp. *N Amer. informal* fine, splendid, excellent. **2** *informal* smart, fashionable.

swelled head *n.* *informal* excessive pride or vanity.

swelling *n.* **1** a swollen or protuberant part of something, esp. a part of the body enlarged as a result of disease or injury. **2** the process or an instance of swelling, becoming distended, or rising in intensity etc.

swelter ● *v.intr.* (usu. as **sweltering** *adj.*) be uncomfortably hot. ● *n.* a sweltering atmosphere or condition. □ **swelteringly** *adv.*

swept *past and past part.* of SWEEP.

swerve ● *v.intr.* & *tr.* change or cause to change direction, esp. abruptly. ● *n.* **1** a swerving movement. **2** divergence from a course.

swift ● *adj.* **1** soon coming or passing. **2** speedy, prompt. **3** *informal* smart, clever. ● *adv.* (*archaic* except in *comb.*) swiftly (*swift-moving*). ● *n.* **1** any swift-flying insect-eating bird of the family Apodidae, with long wings and resembling a swallow. **2** *Cdn* an area of rapidly flowing current in a river. □ **swiftly** *adv.* **swiftness** *n.*

swift fox *n.* a small fox, *Vulpes velox*, of N American prairies.

swig ● *v.tr. & intr.* (**swigged**, **swigging**) *informal* drink in large drafts. ● *n.* a large swallow of a beverage, esp. of liquor. □ **swigger** *n.*

swill ● *v. tr. & intr.* drink greedily. ● *n.* **1** scraps of waste food, usu. mixed with water, for feeding pigs. **2** inferior liquor. **3** worthless matter; rubbish.

swim ● *v.* (**swimming**; *past* **swam**; *past part.* **swum**) **1** *intr.* propel the body through water by working the arms and legs, or (of a fish) the fins and tail. **2** *tr.* a traverse by swimming. **b** compete in (a race) by swimming. **c** use (a particular stroke) in swimming. **3** *tr.* convey or propel by swimming. **4** *intr.* float on or at the surface of a liquid. **5** *intr.* appear to undulate or reel or whirl. **6** *intr.* have a dizzy effect or sensation (*my head swam*). **7** *intr.* be flooded with liquid. **8** *intr.* glide along, through, etc. ● *n.* a period of or the act of swimming. □ **in the swim** involved in or acquainted with what is going on. **swim against the tide** act against prevailing opinion or tendency. □ **swimmer** *n.* **swimming** *n.*

swim bladder *n.* a gas-filled sac in fish used to maintain buoyancy.

swimmingly *adv.* with easy and unobstructed progress.

swimsuit *n.* an esp. one-piece bathing suit worn by women. □ **swimsuited** *adj.*

swim trunks *n.pl.* (also **swimming trunks**) *see* TRUNK 6.

swimwear *n.* clothing worn for swimming.

swindle ● *v.tr.* cheat a person of money, possessions, etc. ● *n.* **1** an act of swindling. **2** a person or thing represented as what it is not. **3** a fraudulent scheme. □ **swindler** *n.*

swine *n.* **1** (*pl.* same) a pig. **2** (*pl.* same or **-s**) *informal* **a** a term of contempt for a person. **b** a very unpleasant or difficult thing. □ **swinish** *adj.* (esp. in sense 2).

swing ● *v.* (*past* and *past part.* **swung**) **1** *intr. & tr.* move or cause to move with a to-and-fro or curving motion. **2** *intr. & tr.* **a** sway. **b** hang so as to be free to sway. **c** oscillate or cause to oscillate. **3** *intr. & tr.* revolve or cause to revolve. **4** *intr.* move by gripping something and leaping etc. **5** *intr.* go with a swinging gait. **6** *intr.* (foll. by *around*) move around to the opposite direction. **7** *intr.* change from one opinion or mood to another. **8** **a** *intr.* attempt to hit or punch. **b** *tr.* throw (a punch). **9** *intr. informal* **a** be lively, modern, or trendy. **b** be promiscuous. **10** *intr. informal* (of a party etc.) be lively, successful, etc. **11** *tr.* have a decisive influence on (esp. voting etc.). **12** *tr. informal* deal with or achieve. **13** *intr. informal* be executed by hanging. ● *n.* **1** the act or an instance of swinging. **2** the motion of swinging. **3** the extent of swinging. **4** a swinging or smooth gait or rhythm or action. **5 a** a seat slung by ropes or chains etc. for swinging on or in. **b** a period of swinging on this. **6** an easy but vigorous continued action. **7** jazz or dance music with an easy flowing but vigorous rhythm. **b** dance performed to this, esp. originally that popular in the late 1930s and early 1940s. **c** the rhythmic feeling or drive of this music. **8** a discernible change in opinion, esp. the amount by which votes or points scored etc. change from one side to another (often *attrib.*: *swing riding*; *swing voter*). **9** an attempted punch. □ **swing the lead** *Brit. & Cdn*

informal malinger; shirk one's duty. □ **swinger** *n.* (esp. in sense 9 of *v.*).

swing bridge *n.* a bridge that can be swung to one side to allow the passage of ships.

swinging *adj.* **1** (of gait, melody, etc.) vigorously rhythmical. **2** *informal* **a** lively. **b** promiscuous.

swinging bridge *n.* a footbridge suspended from cables, which swings from side to side when walked on.

swinging door *n.* a door able to open in either direction and close itself when released.

swingman *n.* (*pl.* **-men**) *N Amer.* a versatile player who can play effectively in different positions, esp. both guard and forward in basketball.

swing set *n.* a fixture in a park, yard, etc. having one or more swings and sometimes a slide.

swingy *adj.* (**-ier**, **-iest**) **1** (of music) characterized by swing. **2** (of a dress etc.) designed to swing with body movement. **3** *Curling* (of ice) on which the lateral movement of a rock is greater than normal.

swipe ● *v.* **1** *tr. & intr.* hit hard and recklessly with a sweeping motion. **2** *tr. informal* steal. **3** *tr.* pass (a card) through an electronic device in order to read and process data magnetically encoded on it. ● *n.* **1** a quick swinging blow, or an attempt at this. **2** a sharp, antagonistic criticism, esp. made casually or in passing. □ **swiper** *n.*

swirl ● *v.* **1** *intr. & tr.* move or flow or carry along with or as with a whirling motion. **2** *tr.* give a twisted form to. ● *n.* **1** a swirling motion of or in water, air, etc. **2** the act of swirling. **3** a twist or curl, esp. as part of a pattern or design. **4** commotion, disorder. □ **swirly** *adj.*

swish ● *v.* **1** *intr.* move with or make a rustling or hissing sound. **2** *tr.* cause to make such a sound. **3** *tr.* swing (a stick etc.) audibly through the air, grass, etc. **4** *tr. Basketball* sink (a shot) without the ball touching the backboard or rim. ● *n.* **1** a swishing action or sound. **2** *Basketball informal* a shot that goes through the basket without touching the backboard or rim. **3** *Cdn* (Nfld & Maritimes) liquor made by filling a recently emptied rum barrel with boiling water and rotating it every few days for a couple of weeks. ● *adj. N Amer. slang* = SWISHY 2.

swishy *adj.* **1** making a swishing sound. **2** *N Amer. slang* effeminate.

Swiss ● *adj.* of or relating to Switzerland, a country in central Europe, or its people. ● *n.* (*pl.* same) **1** a native or national of Switzerland. **2** a person of Swiss descent.

Swiss Army knife *n.* a pocket knife incorporating multiple blades and other tools, such as a screwdriver, can opener, pair of scissors, etc.

Swiss chard *n.* = CHARD.

Swiss cheese ● *n.* a mild hard yellow cheese with many large holes in it, originally made in Switzerland. ● *adj.* (**Swiss-cheese**) characterized by large holes or spaces.

switch ● *n.* **1** a device for making and breaking the connection in an electric circuit. **2 a** a transfer, changeover, or deviation. **b** an exchange. **3** a slender flexible shoot cut from a tree. **4** a light tapering rod. **5** *N Amer.* a device at the junction of railway tracks for transferring a train from one track to another. ● *v.* **1** *tr.* **a** turn (an electrical device) on or off. **b** start or stop the flow or operation of (water, electricity, etc.) by means of a tap, switch, etc. **c** display or cease to display (a quality or emotion). **2** *intr.* change or transfer position, subject, etc. **3** *tr.* (often foll. by *over*) change or transfer. **4** *tr.* reverse the positions of;

exchange. **5 a** tr. divert (a train etc.) on to another track by means of a switch. **b** intr. (of a train) be diverted in this way. **6** tr. beat or flick with a switch. **7** tr. & intr. move rapidly back and forth. □ **switch off** informal cease to pay attention. □ **switchable** adj. **switcher** n.

switchback ● n. (often attrib.) a railway or road with alternate sharp ascents and descents. ● v.intr. **1** (of a road, trail, etc.) rise and fall in a number of sharp ascents and descents. **2** (of a person or animal) climb a steeply ascending and descending road, trail, etc.

switchblade n. a pocket knife with the blade released by a spring.

switchboard n. a central panel in an office etc. for the manual control of telephone connections.

switcheroo n. N Amer. slang a change, reversal, or exchange, esp. a surprising or deceptive one.

switchgear n. **1** the switching equipment used in the transmission of electricity. **2** the switches or electrical controls in a motor vehicle.

switch hitter n. N Amer. **1** Baseball a hitter who can bat either right- or left-handed. **2** slang a bisexual. □ **switch-hit** v.intr. **switch-hitting** adj.

switchover n. a change or exchange.

swivel /'swɪvl/ ● n. (often attrib.) a fastening or coupling device between two parts enabling one to revolve without turning the other. ● v.tr. & intr. (**swivelled, swivelling**) turn on or as on a swivel.

swivel chair n. a chair with a seat able to be turned horizontally.

swizzle stick n. a stick used for stirring and frothing or flattening drinks.

swollen ● v. past part. of SWELL. ● adj. enlarged, expanded, or increased by or as if by swelling (a swollen ankle; the swollen river).

swollen head var. of SWELLED HEAD.

swoon ● v.intr. **1** literary faint. **2** enter a state of rapture or ecstasy. ● n. a faint. □ **swoony** adj.

swoop ● v. **1** intr. descend rapidly like a bird of prey. **2** intr. make a sudden attack from a distance. **3** tr. informal snatch the whole of at one swoop. ● n. **1** a swooping or snatching movement or action. **2** a sudden and unexpected attack.

swoosh ● n. the noise of a sudden rush of liquid, air, etc. ● v.intr. & tr. move or cause to move with this noise.

swop var. of SWAP.

sword n. **1** a weapon usu. of metal with a long blade and hilt with a hand guard, used esp. for thrusting or striking. **2** (prec. by the) **a** slaughter, warfare. **b** the sword regarded as a symbol of military power, penal justice, etc. □ **put to the sword** kill, esp. in war. □ **sword-like** adj.

sword dance n. a dance in which the dancers wave swords or step nimbly between and over swords on the ground. □ **sword dancer** n. **sword dancing** n.

swordfish n. a large marine fish, Xiphias gladius, with an extended sword-like upper jaw.

swordplay n. **1** fencing. **2** repartee.

swordsman n. (pl. **-men**) a person of (usu. specified) skill with a sword. □ **swordsmanship** n.

swore past of SWEAR.

sworn ● v. past part. of SWEAR. ● adj. bound by or as by an oath (sworn enemies).

swum past part. of SWIM.

swung past and past part. of SWING.

sybarite /'sɪbəˌraɪt/ n. a person who is self-indulgent or devoted to sensuous luxury. □ **sybaritic** /-'rɪtɪk/ adj. **sybaritism** n.

sycamore /'sɪkəˌmɔr/ n. **1** an eastern N American

plane tree, Platanus occidentalis, having greyish-brown peeling bark. **2** (in full **sycamore maple**) a large maple of Eurasia, Acer pseudoplatanus, with winged seeds, grown for its shade and timber. **3** Bible a fig tree, Ficus sycomorus, growing in the Middle East.

sycophant /'sɪkəˌfænt, 'saɪk-, -fənt/ n. a servile flatterer. □ **sycophancy** n. **sycophantic** adj. **sycophantically** adv.

syllabary /'sɪləˌberi/ n. (pl. **-ies**) a list of characters representing syllables and (in some languages or stages of writing) serving the purpose of an alphabet.

syllabi pl. of SYLLABUS.

syllabic /sɪ'læbɪk/ ● adj. **1** of, relating to, or based on syllables. **2** based on the number of syllables. **3** (of a symbol) representing a whole syllable. **4** articulated with distinct separation of syllables. ● n. **1** a syllabic symbol. **2** (in pl.) = SYLLABARY. **3** a unit of sound capable by itself of forming a syllable. □ **syllabically** adv.

syllabication /ˌsɪlæbɪ'keɪʃən/ n. (also **syllabification**) division into or articulation by syllables. □ **syllabify** v.tr. (**-ies, -ied**).

syllable n. **1** a unit of pronunciation uttered without interruption, forming the whole or a part of a word and usu. having one vowel sound often with a consonant or consonants before or after. **2** a character or characters representing a syllable. **3** (usu. with neg.) the least amount of speech or writing (did not utter a syllable). □ **in words of one syllable** expressed plainly or bluntly. □ **syllabled** adj. (also in comb.).

syllabus /'sɪləbəs/ n. (pl. **syllabuses** or **syllabi** /-ˌbaɪ/) the program or outline of a course of study, teaching, etc.

syllogism /'sɪləˌdʒɪzəm/ n. **1** a form of reasoning in which a conclusion is drawn from two propositions (premises). **2** deductive reasoning as distinct from induction. □ **syllogistic** adj.

sylph /sɪlf/ n. **1** an elemental spirit of the air. **2** a slender graceful woman or girl. □ **sylphlike** adj.

sylva /'sɪlvə/ n. (pl. **sylvae** /-viː/ or **sylvas**) the trees of a region, epoch, or environment.

sylvan /'sɪlvən/ adj. esp. literary **1 a** of the woods. **b** having woods; wooded. **2** rural.

symbiosis /ˌsɪmbaɪ'oːsɪs, ˌsɪmbi-/ n. (pl. **symbioses** /-siːz/) **1 a** an interaction between two different organisms living in close physical association, usu. to the advantage of both. **b** an instance of this. **2 a** a mutually advantageous association or relationship between persons. **b** an instance of this. □ **symbiotic** /-'ɒtɪk/ adj. **symbiotically** adv.

symbol ● n. **1** a thing conventionally regarded as typifying, representing, or recalling something. **2** a mark or character taken as the conventional sign of some object, idea, function, or process. ● v.tr. (**symbolled, symbolling**) symbolize. □ **symbolic** adj. (also **symbolical**). **symbolically** adv.

symbolism n. **1 a** the use of symbols to represent ideas. **b** symbols collectively. **2** an artistic and poetic style using symbols and indirect suggestion rather than direct description to express ideas, emotions, etc. □ **symbolist** n. **symbolistic** adj.

symbolize v.tr. **1** be a symbol of. **2** represent by means of symbols. □ **symbolization** n.

symbology /sɪm'bɒlədʒi/ n. (pl. **-ies**) **1** the use of symbols. **2** the branch of knowledge dealing with this. **3** symbols collectively. □ **symbological** adj.

symmetry n. (pl. **-ies**) **1 a** a correct proportion of the parts of a thing. **b** beauty resulting from this. **2 a** a structure that allows an object to be divided into parts of an equal shape and size and similar position to the point or line or plane of division. **b** the possession of such a structure. **c** approximation to such a structure. **3** the repetition of exactly similar parts facing each other or a centre. □ **symmetric** *adj.* **symmetrical** *adj.* **symmetrically** *adv.*

sympathetic *adj.* **1** of, showing, or expressing sympathy. **2** due to sympathy. **3** likeable or capable of evoking sympathy. **4** (of a person) friendly and co-operative. **5** inclined to favour. **6** (of a pain etc.) caused by a pain or injury to someone else or in another part of the body. **7** sounding by a vibration communicated from another vibrating object. **8** designating the part of the autonomic nervous system consisting of nerves arising from ganglia near the middle of the spinal cord that supply the internal organs, blood vessels, and glands, and balance the action of the parasympathetic nerves. □ **sympathetically** *adv.*

sympathize *v.intr.* (often foll. by *with*) **1** feel or express sympathy; share a feeling or opinion. **2** agree with a sentiment or opinion. □ **sympathizer** *n.*

sympathy *n.* (*pl.* **-ies**) **1 a** the act of sharing or tendency to share in an emotion or sensation or condition of another person or thing. **b** compassion; condolences. **2** a favourable attitude; approval. **3** agreement (with a person etc.) in opinion or desire. **4** (*attrib.*) in support of another cause (*sympathy strike*). □ **in sympathy** (often foll. by *with*) **1** having or showing or resulting from sympathy (with another). **2** by way of sympathetic action (*working to rule in sympathy*).

sympatico *var. of* SIMPATICO.

symphonic /sɪmˈfɒnɪk/ *adj.* of or having the form or character of a symphony. □ **symphonically** *adv.*

symphony *n.* (*pl.* **-ies**) **1** an elaborate composition usu. for full orchestra, and in several movements. **2** an interlude for orchestra alone in a large-scale vocal work. **3** = SYMPHONY ORCHESTRA. **4** a harmoniously pleasing arrangement of colours, shapes, sounds, etc.

symphony orchestra *n.* a large orchestra suitable for playing symphonies etc.

symposium /sɪmˈpoːziəm/ *n.* (*pl.* **symposia** /-ziə/) **1** a conference or meeting to discuss a particular subject. **2** a collection of essays or papers for this purpose.

symptom *n.* **1** a change in the physical or mental condition of a person, regarded as evidence of a disorder. **2** a sign of the existence of something. □ **symptomatic** *adj.* **symptomatically** *adv.* **symptomless** *adj.*

symptomatology /ˌsɪmptəməˈtɒlədʒi/ *n.* the branch of medicine concerned with the study and interpretation of symptoms.

synagogue /ˈsɪnəgɒg/ *n.* **1** the building where a Jewish assembly or congregation meets for religious observance and instruction. **2** the assembly itself.

synapse /ˈsɪnæps, -ˈnæps, ˈsaɪn-/ *n.* **1** a junction of two nerve cells, consisting of a minute gap across which impulses pass by diffusion of a neurotransmitter. **2** (in *pl.*) the synapses in the brain, considered as an indicator of mental activity. □ **synaptic** *adj.*

sync /sɪŋk/ (also **synch**) *informal* ● *n.* synchronization. ● *v.tr. & intr.* (often foll. by *up*) synchronize. □ **in** (or **out of**) **sync** (often foll. by *with*) according or agreeing well (or badly).

synchro /ˈsɪnkroː/ *n.* **1** a synchronizing device. **2** synchronized swimming.

synchronic /sɪŋˈkrɒnɪk/ *adj.* describing a subject (esp. a language) as it exists at one point in time.

synchronicity /ˌsɪŋkrəˈnɪsɪti/ *n.* **1** the simultaneous occurrence of events which appear significantly related but have no discernible connection. **2** = SYNCHRONY 1.

synchronize *v.* **1 a** *tr.* cause to occur at the same time. **b** *intr.* occur at the same time. **2** *tr.* coordinate, combine (*we must synchronize our efforts*). **3 a** *tr.* cause (clocks etc.) to show a standard or uniform time. **b** *intr.* (of clocks etc.) be synchronized. **4** *intr.* operate in unison. □ **synchronization** *n.* **synchronizer** *n.*

synchronized swimming *n.* a form of swimming in which participants perform coordinated dance-like leg and arm movements to music. □ **synchronized swimmer** *n.*

synchronous /ˈsɪŋkrənəs/ *adj.* **1** existing or occurring at the same time. **2** going at the same rate and exactly together. **3** (of a motor or machine) having a speed exactly proportional to the current frequency. □ **synchronously** *adv.*

synchrony /ˈsɪŋkrəni/ *n.* **1** the state of being synchronic or synchronous. **2** the treatment of events etc. as being synchronous.

syncopate /ˈsɪŋkəpeɪt/ *v.tr.* (often as **syncopated** *adj.*) **1** displace the beats or accents so that strong beats become weak and vice versa. **2** accent (a note) on a weak beat. □ **syncopation** *n.*

syncretism /ˈsɪŋkrəˌtɪzəm/ *n.* the process or an instance of attempting to unify or reconcile differing schools of thought, religions, etc. □ **syncretic** /-ˈkretɪk/ *adj.* **syncretist** *n.* **syncretistic** *adj.*

syndicate ● *n.* **1** a combination of individuals or commercial firms to promote some common interest. **2** an association or agency supplying material simultaneously to a number of newspapers, periodicals, etc. **3** a group of people who combine to buy or rent property, gamble, organize crime, etc. ● *v.tr.* **1** form into a syndicate. **2 a** publish through a syndicate. **b** (esp. as **syndicated** *adj.*) publish the work of (a columnist, cartoonist, etc.) through a syndicate. **3** (esp. as **syndicated** *adj.*) make (a television or radio program) available to independent broadcasters. □ **syndication** *n.* **syndicator** *n.*

syndrome *n.* **1 a** a group of symptoms or pathological signs which consistently occur together. **b** a condition characterized by such a set of associated symptoms. **2** a characteristic combination of opinions, emotions, behaviour, etc.

synecdoche /sɪˈnekdəki/ *n.* a figure of speech in which a part is made to represent the whole or vice versa, e.g. *new faces at the meeting*; *Italy won by two goals*.

synergy /ˈsɪnərdʒi/ *n.* (also **synergism** /-ˌdʒɪzəm/) **1** the interaction or co-operation of two or more drugs, agents, organizations, etc., to produce an effect that exceeds or enhances the sum of their individual effects. **2** increased effectiveness, achievement, etc. produced by combined action, co-operation, etc. **3** an instance of this. □ **synergistic** *adj.* **synergistically** *adv.*

synod /ˈsɪnəd/ *n.* **1** a church council attended by delegated clergy and sometimes laity (*see also* GENERAL SYNOD). **2** a group of churches whose representatives meet regularly. **3** a Presbyterian church court above the presbyteries and subject to General Assembly. □ **synodical** /sɪˈnɒdɪkəl/ *adj.*

synonym *n.* a word or phrase that means exactly or nearly the same as another in the same language, e.g. *shut* and *close*.

synonymous /sɪˈnɒnəməs/ *adj.* **1** having the same meaning. **2** (of a thing etc.) suggestive of or associated

with another (*blackflies are synonymous with summer*). □
synonymously *adv.* **synonymousness** *n.*

synopsis /sɪˈnɒpsɪs/ *n.* (*pl.* **synopses** /-siːz/) **1 a**
summary or outline. **2** a brief general survey. □
synopsize *v.tr.*

synoptic /sɪˈnɒptɪk/ ● *adj.* **1** of, forming, or giving a
synopsis. **2** taking or affording a comprehensive mental view. **3** of the Synoptic Gospels. **4** giving a general
view of weather conditions. ● *n.* **1** (**Synoptic**) designating any of the Gospels of Matthew, Mark, and
Luke, which describe events from a similar point of
view. **2** the writer of a Synoptic Gospel. □ **synoptical**
adj. **synoptically** *adv.*

synovial /saɪˈnoʊviəl, sɪ-/ *adj.* denoting or relating to a
viscous fluid lubricating joints and tendon sheaths.

syntactic /sɪnˈtæktɪk/ *adj.* of or according to syntax.
□ **syntactical** *adj.* **syntactically** *adv.*

syntax *n.* **1** the order of words in which they convey
meaning collectively by their connection and
relation. **2** a set of rules for or an analysis of this.

synth /sɪnθ/ *n. informal* = SYNTHESIZER.

synthase /ˈsɪnθeɪz, -eɪs/ *n.* an enzyme which
catalyzes the linking together of two molecules, esp.
without the direct involvement of ATP.

synthesis /ˈsɪnθəsɪs/ *n.* (*pl.* **syntheses** /-siːz/) **1** the
process or result of building up separate elements,
esp. ideas, into a connected whole, esp. into a theory
or system. **2** a combination or composition. **3** *Chem.*
the formation of a compound by combination of its
elements or constituents, esp. the artificial production of compounds from their constituents as distinct from extraction from plants etc. □ **synthesist**
n.

synthesize *v.tr.* **1** make a synthesis of. **2** combine
into a coherent whole. **3** (esp. as **synthesized** *adj.*)
produce or imitate electronically using a synthesizer.
□ **synthesist** *n.*

synthesizer *n.* an electronic musical instrument,
esp. operated by a music keyboard, producing a wide
variety of sounds by generating and combining signals of different frequencies.

synthetic ● *adj.* **1 a** made by chemical synthesis, esp.
to imitate a natural product (*synthetic rubber*). **b** artificial, imitation, invented. **2** (of emotions etc.) affected,
insincere. **3** of, pertaining to, involving, or using
synthesis, or combination of parts into a whole. ● *n. a*
synthetic substance. □ **synthetical** *adj.*
synthetically *adv.*

synthetic resin *n. Chem. see* RESIN *n.* 2.

syph /sɪf/ *n. informal* syphilis.

syphilis /ˈsɪfɪlɪs/ *n.* a contagious venereal disease
progressing from infection of the genitals via the
skin and mucous membrane to the bones, muscles,
and brain. □ **syphilitic** /-ˈlɪtɪk/ *adj. & n.*

Syrah /ˈsiːrɑː/ *n.* **1 a** a variety of black grape used in
winemaking, grown originally in the Rhone valley of
France, now also esp. in Australia and South Africa. **b**
the vine that bears this grape. **2** a red wine produced
from these grapes.

Syrian /ˈsiːriən/ ● *n.* **1** a native or national of the
modern state of Syria in the Middle East; a person of
Syrian descent. **2** a native or inhabitant of the region
of Syria in antiquity or later. ● *adj.* of or relating to the
region or state of Syria.

syringe /sɪˈrɪndʒ, ˈsɪr-/ ● *n.* **1** a tube with a nozzle and
piston or bulb for sucking in and ejecting liquid in a
fine stream. **2** (in full **hypodermic syringe**) a
similar device with a hollow needle for insertion
under the skin. ● *v.tr.* (**syringing**) sluice or spray (the
ear, a plant, etc.) with a syringe.

syrup *n.* **1** any of various very sweet liquids used e.g.
as a topping, to flavour a drink, to preserve canned
fruit, as a form of medicine, etc. **2** excessive sweetness of style or manner. **3** *Cdn* (*Nfld*) a fruit-flavoured
drink of water and syrup. □ **syrupy** *adj.*

sysadmin /ˈsɪsədˌmɪn/ *n.* system administrator.

sysop /ˈsɪsɒp/ *n.* system operator.

system *n.* **1 a** a complex whole; a set of connected
things, parts, institutions, etc.; an organized body of
material or immaterial things (*school system*). **2** a set
of devices functioning together. **3 a** a set of organs in
the body with a common structure or function (*the
digestive system*). **b** the human or animal body as a
whole. **4 a** a method; considered principles of procedure or classification. **b** a classification. **5 a** a body of
theory or practice relating to or prescribing a particular form of government, religion, etc. **b** (prec. by *the*)
the prevailing political or social order, esp. regarded
as oppressive and intransigent. **6** a method of choosing one's procedure in gambling etc. **7** *Computing* a
group of related hardware units or programs or both,
esp. when dedicated to a single application. **8** a major
group of geological strata (*the Devonian system*). **9**
Physics a group of associated bodies moving under
mutual gravitation etc. □ **get a thing out of one's
system** *informal* be rid of a preoccupation or anxiety.
□ **systemless** *adj.*

system administrator *n.* a person who administers a computer system or network.

systematic *adj.* **1 a** done or conceived according to
a plan or system. **b** (of a person etc.) acting according
to a system; methodical. **2** regular, deliberate (*a systematic liar*). □ **systematically** *adv.*

systematize /ˈsɪstəməˌtaɪz/ *v.tr.* **1** make systematic. **2**
devise a system for. □ **systematization** *n.*
systematizer *n.*

systemic /sɪˈstemɪk/ *adj.* **1 a** of or concerning the
whole body, not confined to a particular part. **b** (of
blood circulation) other than pulmonary. **2** (of an
insecticide, fungicide, etc.) entering the plant via the
roots or shoots and passing through the tissues. **3** of
or pertaining to a system, esp. in its entirety. □
systemically *adv.*

system operator *n.* a person who manages the
operation of an electronic bulletin board.

systems analysis *n.* the analysis of a complex
process or operation in order to improve its efficiency, esp. by applying a computer system. □
systems analyst *n.*

systems operator *n.* a person who controls or
monitors the operation of complex esp. electronic
systems.

systems theory *n.* the study of systems, esp. to find
characteristics common to all systems or to classes of
systems.

Szechuan /ˈsetʃwɒn, ˈseʃ-, -ˈwɒn/ *n.* (also **Szechwan**)
(*attrib.*) designating food cooked in the distinctively
spicy style of cuisine originating in Sichuan, a province of west central China.

Tt

T¹ *n.* (also **t**) (*pl.* **Ts** or **T's**) **1** the twentieth letter of the alphabet. **2** a T-shaped thing (esp. *attrib.*: *T-joint*). **3** = T-SHIRT. □ **to a T** exactly; to a nicety.

T² *symbol* **1** *Chem.* the isotope tritium. **2** tesla. **3** temperature. **4** tenor. **5** thiamine. **6** the time at which an event, esp. the launch of a spacecraft, is scheduled to occur (*T minus three minutes*).

t. *abbr.* **1** ton(s). **2** tonne(s).

T4 *n.* (in full **T4 slip**) *Cdn* an official statement issued by an employer, indicating one's employment income for the year, the amount paid in employment insurance premiums and contributions to the Canada Pension Plan etc., used to calculate the amount of taxes owed and submitted with one's tax return.

TA *N Amer. informal* • *n.* **1** TEACHING ASSISTANT. **2** teaching assistantship. • *v.intr.* (**TA'd**, **TA'ing**) work as a TA.

Ta *symbol* tantalum.

tab¹ • *n.* **1 a** a small flap or strip of material attached for grasping, fastening, or hanging up, or for identification. **b** a similar object as a decorative part of a garment etc. **2** *N Amer. informal* a bill or price (*picked up the tab*). • *v.tr.* (**tabbed, tabbing**) **1** provide with a tab or tabs. **2** *N Amer.* designate, name, label (*was tabbed as her successor*). □ **keep tabs on** *informal* **1** keep account of. **2** have under observation or in check.

tab² *n.* **1** a function on a typewriter or computer keyboard allowing the movement of the carriage, cursor, etc. to be pre-set. **2** the key used to advance the carriage or cursor this predetermined distance. □ **tabbing** *n.*

tab³ *n. slang* a tablet, esp. containing an illicit drug.

tab⁴ *n.* tabloid.

Tabasco /tə'bæsko:/ *n. proprietary* a spicy sauce made from the fruit of *Capsicum frutescens*.

tabbouleh /tə'bu:lei/ *n.* a Syrian and Lebanese salad made with bulgur, parsley, mint, lemon juice, etc.

tabby *n.* (*pl.* **-ies**) (also **tabby cat**) **1** a grey or brownish cat mottled or streaked with dark stripes. **2** any domestic cat, esp. female.

tabernacle *n.* **1** *hist.* a tent used as a sanctuary for the Ark by the Israelites during the Exodus. **2** *Christianity* a niche or receptacle esp. for the consecrated Eucharistic elements. **3** a place of worship.

tabla /'tæblə, 'tʊ-/ *n.* (in Indian music) a pair of small drums played with the hands.

table • *n.* **1 a** a piece of furniture with a flat top and one or more legs, providing a level surface for eating, writing, or working at, playing games on, etc. **b** (*attrib.*) designating an object designed to sit or be used on a table (*table clock*). **2** a flat surface serving a specified purpose (*communion table*). **3** a group seated at table for dinner etc. **4 a** a set of facts or figures systematically displayed, esp. in columns (*a table of contents*). **b** matter contained in this. **5** a flat surface for working on or for machinery to operate on. **6 a** a slab of wood or stone etc. for bearing an inscription. **b** matter inscribed on this. **7** = TABLELAND. **8** (*prec. by the*) = BARGAINING TABLE (*sought to draw them back to the table*). **9** any plane or level area (*water table*). • *v.tr.* **1** *Cdn & Brit.* bring forward for discussion or consideration at a meeting. **2** esp. *US* postpone consideration of (a matter). ¶Because both of these contradictory meanings are in use in Canada, confusion may arise if the verb *table* is used outside of the strictly parliamentary context, where the first sense should be understood. □ **at table** taking a meal at a table. **lay on the table 1** submit for discussion. **2** esp. *US* postpone indefinitely. **on the table** offered for discussion. **turn the tables** (often foll. by *on*) reverse one's relations (with), esp. by turning an inferior into a superior position (originally in backgammon). **under the table** *informal* **1** (of a transaction etc., esp. payment) done surreptitiously esp. to avoid taxes or duties. **2** very drunk after a meal or drinking bout. □ **tableful** *n.* (*pl.* **-fuls**). **tabling** *n.*

tableau /'tæblo:/ *n.* (*pl.* **-leaux** /-lo:z/) **1** a picturesque presentation. **2** = TABLEAU VIVANT. **3** a dramatic or effective situation suddenly brought about.

tableau vivant /'vi:vã/ *n.* (*pl.* **tableaux vivants** *pronunc.* same) *Theatre* a silent and motionless group of people arranged to represent a scene.

tablecloth *n.* a cloth spread over the top of a table.

table cream *n.* cream used in coffee, for pouring over desserts, etc.

table d'hôte /,tæblə 'do:t/ *n.* a meal consisting of a set menu at a fixed price (*compare* À LA CARTE).

table hockey *n.* = TABLE-TOP HOCKEY.

table knife *n.* a knife for use at meals, esp. in eating a main course.

table lamp *n.* a small usu. decorative lamp designed to stand on a table etc.

tableland *n.* a plateau.

table linen *n.* tablecloths, napkins, etc.

table manners *n.pl.* decorum or correct behaviour while eating at table.

table saw *n.* esp. *N Amer.* a power tool consisting of a fixed circular saw mounted beneath a metal table with the blade projecting up through a slot.

tablespoon *n.* **1** a large spoon used for eating soup, cereal, etc. or for serving food. **2** a measuring spoon used in cooking, equal to ¹/₂ fluid ounce (approx. 15 ml). Abbr.: **tbsp. 3** the amount held by either of these. □ **tablespoonful** *n.* (*pl.* **-fuls**).

tablet *n.* **1** a small measured and compressed amount of a substance, esp. of a medicine or drug. **2** a flat slab of stone or wood, esp. for display or an inscription. **3** *N Amer.* a writing pad.

table talk *n.* miscellaneous informal talk at table.

table tennis *n.* an indoor game based on lawn tennis, played with small bats and a ball bounced on a table divided by a net.

tabletop *n.* **1** the top or surface of a table. **2** (*attrib.*) that can be placed or used on a tabletop.

table-top hockey *n.* *N Amer.* a game played using a board or table resembling a miniature hockey rink, with players which can be made to move and shoot using connected rods running beneath the 'ice' surface and projecting at either end.

tableware *n.* dishes, plates, etc., for use at meals.

table wine *n.* ordinary wine for a meal.

tabloid n. **1 a** a newspaper, usu. popular in style with bold headlines and large photographs, having pages half the size of those of the average broadsheet. **b** (attrib.) designating highly sensational or lurid journalism etc. (tabloid TV). **2** anything in a compressed or concentrated form.

taboo /tə'bu:, tæ-/ • n. (pl. **-s**) **1** (also **tabu**) a system or the act of setting a person or thing apart as sacred or accursed. **2** a prohibition or restriction imposed by social custom. **3** a thing, activity, word, etc. so prohibited (is considered a taboo). • adj. **1** avoided or prohibited, esp. by social custom (taboo words). **2** (also **tabu**) designated as sacred and prohibited. • v.tr. (**taboos, tabooed**) **1** put (a thing, practice, etc.) under taboo. **2** exclude or prohibit by authority or social custom.

tabular adj. **1** of or arranged in tables or lists. **2** broad and flat like a table. **3** (of a crystal) having two broad flat faces. **4** formed in thin plates.

tabula rasa /ˌtæbjʊlə 'ræzə/ n. (pl. **tabulae rasae** /ˌtæbjʊli: 'ræzi:/) **1** a tablet with the writing erased; a clean slate. **2** the human mind (esp. at birth) viewed as having no innate ideas.

tabulate v.tr. arrange (figures or facts) in tabular form. □ **tabulation** n.

tach /tæk/ n. N Amer. informal = TACHOMETER.

tachometer /tə'kɒmətər/ n. an instrument for measuring the rate of rotation of a shaft and hence the speed or velocity of a vehicle.

tachycardia /ˌtæki'kɑrdiə/ n. an abnormally rapid heart rate.

tacit /'tæsɪt/ adj. understood or implied without being stated (tacit consent). □ **tacitly** adv.

taciturn /'tæsɪˌtɜrn/ adj. reserved in speech; saying little; uncommunicative. □ **taciturnity** n.

tack¹ • n. **1 a** a small broad-headed sharp nail. **b** = THUMBTACK. **2** a long stitch used in fastening fabrics etc. lightly or temporarily together. **3 a** the direction in which a ship moves as determined by the position of its sails and regarded in terms of the direction of the wind (starboard tack). **b** a temporary change of direction in sailing made by turning the ship's head to the wind. **c** one of a consecutive series of such movements to port and starboard alternately, tracing a zigzag course, and made by a ship in order to reach a point to windward. **4** a course of action or policy (try another tack). **5** a sticky condition of varnish etc. • v. **1** tr. fasten with or as if with tacks. **2** tr. stitch (pieces of cloth etc.) lightly together. **3** tr. (foll. by to, on) annex, append (a thing). **4** intr. **a** change a ship's course by turning its head to the wind. **b** make a series of tacks in order to progress to windward. **5** intr. change one's conduct or policy etc. □ **tacker** n.

tack² • n. the saddle, bridle, etc., of a horse. • v.tr. (often foll. by up) put tack on (a horse).

tackle • n. **1** equipment for a task or sport (fishing tackle). **2** a mechanism, esp. of ropes, pulleys, blocks, hooks, etc., for lifting weights, managing sails, etc. (block and tackle). **3** a windlass with its ropes and hooks. **4** an act of tackling in football etc. **5** Football **a** the position next to the end of either the offensive or defensive line. **b** the player in this position. • v.tr. **1** try to deal with (a problem or difficulty). **2 a** (esp. in football) apprehend forcefully or throw one's body at in order to stop or take down. **b** (in soccer etc.) obstruct, intercept, or stop (a player running with the ball). **3** (often foll. by on, about) initiate discussion with (a person), esp. with regard to a disputed issue. **4** secure or lift by means of tackle. □ **tackler** n. **tackling** n.

tackle box n. esp. N Amer. a box with many compartments for storing and carrying fishing tackle.

tack room n. (also **tack shed** etc.) a room etc. in a stable where the saddles, bridles, etc. are kept.

tacky¹ adj. (**-ier, -iest**) (of glue or paint etc.) still slightly sticky after application. □ **tackiness** n.

tacky² adj. (**-ier, -iest**) esp. N Amer. informal **1** showing poor taste or style. **2** tawdry or seedy. □ **tackily** adv. **tackiness** n.

taco /'tɒko:, 'tæko:/ n. (pl. **-os**) a fried corn tortilla folded over and filled with ground meat, tomatoes, lettuce, shredded cheese, guacamole, etc.

taco shell n. a usu. crisp folded tortilla for tacos.

tact n. **1** adroitness in dealing with others or with difficulties arising from personal feeling. **2** intuitive perception of the right thing to do or say. □ **tactful** adj. **tactfully** adv. **tactfulness** n. **tactless** adj. **tactlessly** adv. **tactlessness** n.

tactic n. **1** a plan or method used to achieve something, esp. against an opponent. **2** = TACTICS.

tactical adj. **1** of, relating to, or constituting tactics (a tactical retreat). **2** (of bombing or weapons) done or for use in immediate support of military or naval operations (opp. STRATEGIC). **3** adroitly planning or planned. **4** (of voting) aimed at preventing the strongest candidate from winning by supporting the next strongest. □ **tactically** adv.

tactical team n. (also **tactical squad**) N Amer. a unit in a police force trained to handle especially volatile situations.

tactics n.pl. **1** (also treated as sing.) the art of disposing armed forces esp. in contact with an enemy (compare STRATEGY 4a). **2 a** the esp. immediate or short-range plans and means adopted in carrying out a scheme or achieving some end. **b** a skilful device or devices. □ **tactician** /tæk'tɪʃən/ n.

tactile /'tæktaɪl/ adj. **1** of the sense of touch. **2** perceived by touch. **3** tangible. □ **tactility** /-'tɪlɪti/ n.

tad n. N Amer. informal a small amount (often used adverbially: a tad too salty).

ta-dah interj. (also **ta-da**) expressing triumph, a dramatic revelation, etc.

tadpole n. the tailed aquatic larva of a frog, toad, or other amphibian from the time it leaves the egg until it loses its gills or tail and acquires legs.

Tadzhik var. of TAJIK.

tae kwon do /tai kwɒn 'do:/ n. a modern Korean martial art similar to karate.

taffeta n. a fine lustrous silk or silk-like fabric.

taffy /'tæfi/ n. (pl. **-ies**) N Amer. **1** a chewy confection similar to toffee made from brown sugar or molasses boiled with butter and pulled until glossy. **2** Cdn a similar confection made by pouring hot maple syrup onto packed snow.

tag¹ • n. **1 a** a label attached to or worn by a person or thing, esp. to indicate price, ownership, identity, etc. **b** a metal clip used to identify an animal or bird, esp. in order to trace its migratory patterns etc. **c** an electronic device that can be attached to a person or thing for monitoring purposes, e.g. to track offenders or to deter shoplifters. **d** a tag that authorizes a hunter to kill a certain type of animal (a grizzly tag). **2** informal an epithet or popular designation. **3** Theatre **a** a closing speech addressed to the audience. **b** a trite quotation or stock phrase esp. used as a motto or slogan. **4** a metal or plastic point at the end of a shoelace to facilitate threading it through an eyelet. **5** Computing a set of characters or symbols placed before or after a unit of data to make it readable in another form. **6 a** the refrain of a song. **b** a musical phrase added to the end of a piece. ● *v.tr.* (**tagged, tagging**) **1** provide with a tag or tags. **2** (often foll. by *on*, *on to*) add, esp. as an afterthought; tack on. **3** *informal* follow closely or trail behind. **4** *Computing* label (an item of data) in order to identify it for subsequent processing or retrieval. **5** attach an identifying label to (an animal). **6** label radioactively. □ **tag along** (often foll. by *with*) accompany. □ **tagged** *adj.*

tag² ● *n.* **1** a children's game in which one player chases the others, and anyone who is caught then becomes 'it' and inherits the role of the pursuer. **2** = TELEPHONE TAG. **3** *Baseball* the act of tagging a runner. ● *v.* (**tagged**, **tagging**) **1** *tr.* touch (a player) in a game of tag. **2** *Baseball* **a** *tr.* touch (a runner) with the ball or a gloved hand holding the ball. **b** *tr.* (foll. by *out*) put (a runner) out by doing this. **c** *intr.* (usu. foll. by *up*) (of a runner) return to and touch a base before attempting to advance after a fly ball is caught. **d** *tr.* score a hit or run off (a pitcher). **3** *tr. informal* strike (a person) with a powerful punch or blow.

tagalong *N Amer.* ● *n.* a follower or companion, esp. one who is uninvited or unwelcome. ● *adj.* **1** that is towed or trailed behind something else. **2** (of a follower or companion) uninvited or unwelcome.

tag end *n.* **1** a loose end of something, esp. a strand of tinsel etc. serving as the tail of an angler's fly. **2** esp. *N Amer.* = TAIL END.

tagine *var. of* TAJINE.

Tagish /ˈtægɪʃ/ ● *n.* (*pl.* same) **1** a member of an Aboriginal people living esp. in the southern Yukon Territory. **2** the Athapaskan language of this people. ● *adj.* of or relating to this people or their culture.

tagliatelle /ˌtæljəˈteli/ *n.* **1** a type of pasta made in narrow ribbons. **2** a dish consisting of this pasta served with sauce etc.

tag line *n.* = TAG¹ 3.

tag team *n.* **1** a pair of wrestlers who fight as a team by alternately competing in the ring against one of another paired team of opponents (also *attrib.*: *tag-team wrestling*). **2** two people completing a single task as a team (also *attrib.*: *tag-team approach*).

tahini /təˈhiːni/ *n.* a paste or sauce made from ground sesame seeds.

Tahitian /təˈhiːʃən, -tiən/ ● *n.* **1** a native or inhabitant of Tahiti, an island in the central S Pacific. **2** the Polynesian language of Tahiti. ● *adj.* of or relating to Tahiti, its people, or language.

Tahltan /ˈtɒltæn/ ● *n.* (*pl.* same or **-s**) **1** a member of an Aboriginal people living in the area of the Stikine River, BC. **2** the Athapaskan language of this people. ● *adj.* of or relating to this people.

Tai Chi /taɪ ˈtʃiː/ *n.* (in full **Tai Chi Chuan** /tʃwɒn/) a Chinese martial art and system of calisthenics consisting of very slow controlled movements.

taiga /ˈtaɪɡə/ *n.* any of the swampy coniferous forests of subarctic N America, Europe, and Asia, usu. lying between Arctic tundra to the north and boreal forest or steppe to the south.

taiko /ˈtaɪkoː/ *n.* any of a variety of Japanese two-headed drums made of a hollow wooden shell the opening of which is covered with cowhide.

tail ● *n.* **1** the rear part of an animal, esp. an elongation of the vertebral column forming a flexible appendage that extends beyond the rest of the body. **2 a** a thing resembling an animal's tail in shape or position. **b** the rear end of anything, e.g. of a procession of people or vehicles. **c** the inferior or weaker part of anything, esp. in a sequence. **3** the rear part of an airplane, car, missile, etc. **4 a** a luminous trail of dust extending from the head of a comet and curving

away from the sun. **b** a nearly straight trail of ionized atoms lying in the plane of a comet's orbit and blown away from the nucleus. **5 a** the hanging part of the back of a coat. **b** = SHIRT-TAIL. **6** (in *pl.*) *informal* **a** a tailcoat. **b** a man's formal attire including tailcoat. **7** a twisted or braided tress of hair, such as a pigtail. **8 a** the image on the reverse of a coin. **b** (in *pl.*) this side as a choice when tossing a coin (opp. HEAD 12). **9** an extra strip attached to the end of a kite. **10** *Cdn* the southeast portion of the Grand Banks of Newfoundland, lying outside Canada's 320-km (200-mile) fishing zone (compare NOSE 6). **11** *informal* a person who secretly watches or follows another, esp. as a detective or spy. **12 a** *slang* the buttocks (*had to work my tail off*). **b** *coarse slang* the female genitals. **c** *coarse slang* women collectively regarded as a means of male sexual gratification; sexual intercourse. **13 a** the part of a letter, e.g. *y*, that extends below the line. **b** *Music* the stem of a note. **14** the slender backward prolongation of a butterfly's wing. **15** a feathery spray of strands of tinsel, hair, etc. on a fishing fly. ● *v.* **1** *tr. & intr. informal* follow closely and secretly; spy on. **2** *intr.* (often foll. by *away*) (of an object in flight) deviate; drift, carry, or curve away from a target. **3** *tr.* provide with a tail. **4** *tr.* dock the tail of (a lamb etc.). □ **on a person's tail** closely following a person. **tail off** (or **away**) diminish gradually; decrease in intensity, output, production, etc. **with one's tail between one's legs** in a state of dejection or humiliation. □ **tailless** *adj.*

tailback *n.* *Football* the running back who lines up furthest from the line of scrimmage.

tailbone *n.* **1** each of the caudal vertebrae in an animal. **2** the small triangular bone at the base of the spinal column in humans and some apes.

tailcoat *n.* a man's morning or evening coat with long tails at the back, worn as part of formal dress.

tailed *adj.* **1** (in *comb.*) having a tail of a specified type, shape, colour, size, etc. **2** having a tail.

tail end *n.* **1** the conclusion or final part (*the tail end of the movie*). **2** the back end of a thing; the part at the rear (*the tail end of the procession*).

tail feather *n.* a strong flight feather of a bird's tail.

tail fin *n.* **1** the caudal fin of a fish. **2** an upswept projection on the rear of a car. **3** a small projecting surface on the tail of an aircraft to provide stability.

tailgate ● *n.* the hinged door at the back of a pickup truck, station wagon, or hatchback, esp. one which drops down forming a shelf to facilitate loading and unloading. ● *v.tr. & intr.* *N Amer. informal* follow (another vehicle) too closely. □ **tailgater** *n.*

tailing *n.* (usu. in *pl.*) crushed stone and other waste produced in drilling, mining, or smelting ore.

tailings pond *n.* (also **tailing pond**) a large pool into which the tailings produced by mining and drilling etc. are drained.

tail light *n.* (also **tail lamp**) *N Amer.* a usu. red light on the back or at the rear of esp. a motor vehicle.

tailor ● *n.* a person who alters men's clothing and makes suits and jackets etc. to measure. ● *v.* **1** *tr.* design and make (clothing) esp. to meet the size requirements of a particular customer. **2** *tr.* design or adapt (something) to suit a specific need or purpose (*homes tailored to meet our needs*). **3** *intr.* work as a tailor.

tailored *adj.* **1** (also in *comb.*) made by a tailor, esp. in a specified way or style (*hand-tailored*). **2** (of clothing) well cut and closely fitted; having the appearance of custom-made or tailor-made clothes. **3** having a neat design or appearance; trim, sleek (*a tailored look*). **4** made to suit a specific purpose or need.

tailoring n. **1** the business or occupation of a tailor. **2** the skill or workmanship of a tailor.

tailor-made ● adj. **1** (of clothing) made by a tailor to suit the needs of a particular customer. **2** altered or designed to meet a specific need, purpose, or requirement. **3** (of a person, situation, etc.) ideally suited; perfect. **4** (of a cigarette) made in a factory, not rolled by the smoker. ● n. **1** a tailor-made article of clothing. **2** a tailor-made cigarette.

tailpiece n. **1** an appendage attached to a thing to extend or conclude it. **2** a tube that extends from the drain of a sink to a trap.

tailpipe n. the rear section of the exhaust pipe of a motor vehicle.

tailplane n. a horizontal airfoil at the tail of an aircraft.

tailrace n. a watercourse leading away from the turbine of a power station, a water wheel, a dam, etc.

tailspin ● n. **1** a state of chaos, panic, or loss of control. **2 a** a sharp or rapid decline. **b** Sport a slump. **3** a nose-first spiralling descent of an aircraft. ● v.intr. (**-spinning**; past and past part. **-spun**) perform or fall into a tailspin.

tailwind n. a wind blowing in the direction of travel of an aircraft or vehicle.

taint ● n. **1** a trace, suggestion, or connotation of some bad or undesirable quality. **2** a corrupting influence; a cause of corruption or decay (the taint of racism). **3** a trace of rot, decay, or putrefaction, esp. an unpleasant scent or smell. ● v. **1** tr. contaminate, putrefy; cause to turn foul or rotten (toxins have tainted the lake). **2** tr. ruin, spoil (tainted love). **3** tr. (foll. by with) affect, esp. to a slight degree; imbue slightly with some bad or undesirable quality. **4** intr. (of food) become putrid or rotten; spoil. □ **tainted** adj.

Taiwanese /ˌtaɪwɒˈniːz/ ● n. **1** a native or inhabitant of Taiwan (officially called the Republic of China), an island country off the SE coast of China. **2** a person of Taiwanese descent. ● adj. of or relating to Taiwan or its people or culture.

Tajik /tɒˈdʒiːk/ ● n. **1** a native or inhabitant of the republic of Tajikistan, a mountainous republic in central Asia. **2** the Iranian language of the Tajiks. ● adj. of or relating to Tajikistan or its people.

tajine /tæˈʒiːn/ n. **1** a traditional shallow earthenware Moroccan cooking pot with a conical lid. **2** any of a variety of stews that may be cooked in this pot.

take ● v.tr. (past **took**; past part. **taken**) **1** gather into one's hands or possession. **2** pick out (an individual person or thing) from a group. **3** deprive or rid a person of (a thing). **4** capture by force (have taken a hostage). **5** carry or bring with one (you should take a jacket). **6** deliver or convey (a thing) to a person. **7** receive or accept (something offered). **8** gain use of or acquire by purchase or agreement. **9** receive (food, drink, a drug, etc.) voluntarily into one's body. **10** add (milk, cream, sugar, etc.) to tea or coffee or drink (tea or coffee) with specified ingredients, esp. regularly. **11** make use of (an opportunity, chance, advice, etc.). **12** exercise, exert (take caution). **13** own, assume, or accept (responsibility, blame, control, etc.). **14** require or use up (will only take a minute). **15 a** experience or be affected by (a feeling or emotion) (she took offence). **b** (usu. foll. by from or in) feel or experience (comfort, consolation, etc.) as a result of (I take comfort from knowing that she is safe). **16** react to (something) in a specified way (how did he take the news?). **17** put up with, tolerate, endure (I've had just about all I can take). **18** indulge in, esp. for exercise or leisure (take a walk; take a nap). **19** use as a means of

transport (take the bus). **20** (of a road etc.) lead (a person) to a specified place or in a specified direction. **21** cause (a person or animal) to accompany one (took the dog for a walk). **22** proceed to follow (a road etc.) or make (a turn) (take the next left). **23** approach and attempt to pass or succeed in passing, clearing, or getting around (an obstruction) (he took the corner too fast). **24** perform, make, or undertake (take a guess). **25** venture upon (a gamble, risk, etc.). **26** measure and record (a person's pulse, temperature, etc.). **27** require (a particular size of shoes or clothing) for a correct fit (she takes a size six). **28** write down (a name, address, notes, etc.). **29** derive (esp. a name or attribute) from a particular source (takes its name from the inventor). **30** grasp mentally; understand (I take your point; took it as a compliment). **31** (foll. by for or to be) suppose to be; consider or regard as. **32** receive instruction in (a subject) in a school etc. **33 a** make (a photograph) with a camera. **b** have (a photograph of oneself) taken with a specified degree of success (she takes a good picture). **34** bind oneself to an obligation etc. by the terms of (an oath, vow, etc.). **35** bring or receive (a person) into a specified condition or relation to oneself, as of marriage, employment, or custody. **36** obtain after fulfilling the required conditions (take a degree). **37** win (took first prize). **38** answer (a phone call). **39** informal trick, cheat, or take advantage of (a person). **40** terminate (a person's life). **41** Baseball (of a batter) refrain from swinging at (a pitch). **42** Sport attempt (a shot or swing etc.). **43** proceed to occupy (take a seat). **44** seek shelter or protection afforded by (refuge, cover, sanctuary, etc.). **45** (foll. by from) subtract (take 3 from 9). **46** hold, accommodate (this jug takes two litres). **47** use or refer to as an example. **48** Grammar have or require as part of the appropriate construction (this verb takes an object). **49** have sexual intercourse with. **50** (in passive; foll. by by, with) be attracted, charmed, or intrigued by. **51** (in passive) informal or jocular be involved in a relationship (she's taken). ● n. **1 a** a money taken or received in payment for or as the proceeds of a business transaction. **b** N Amer. the profits or earnings of business conducted esp. during a specific period (the day's take). **c** informal money acquired by theft or fraud. **2** the quantity of fish etc. caught at one time. **3 a** a scene or sequence of film photographed continuously at one time. **b** an act of shooting a scene (take one). **4** informal an interpretation or assessment (what's your take on the situation?). □ **be taken ill** become ill, esp. suddenly. **have what it takes** informal have the necessary qualities etc. for success. **on the take** slang receiving bribes. **take after** resemble (a parent or relative etc.), esp. in behaviour or attitudes. **take apart 1** dismantle. **2** informal beat or defeat conclusively. **take away 1** (foll. by from) diminish; weaken; detract from. **2** subtract. **3** remove or carry elsewhere. **take back 1** retract (a statement). **2** convey (a person or thing) to his or her or its original position. **3** help (a person) recall or imagine an earlier time or incident. **4 a** return (merchandise) to a store. **b** (of a store) accept such merchandise for return. **5** accept (a person) back into one's affections, into employment, etc. **take the cake** (or **biscuit**) informal be the most remarkable, outrageous, amusing, annoying, etc. **take down 1** write down or record (spoken words, information, etc.). **2 a** disassemble (a structure) by dismantling. **b** remove (a fixture, decoration, etc.) from a hanging position. **3** (also **take down a peg**) humiliate. **4** informal **a** seize and wrestle to the ground; tackle. **b** defeat, subdue. **5** lower (one's pants or a similar article of clothing worn below the waist). **take heart** be encouraged. **take ill** (or **sick**) *informal* become ill or sick. **take in 1** draw or receive in (esp. air or moisture); absorb, swallow, inhale. **2** understand (*did you take that in?*). **3** *informal* go out to see (a movie etc.). **4** offer hospitality or shelter to (a person or animal). **5** make (an article of clothing) smaller. **6** cheat (*take them all in*). **7** include or comprise. **take in hand 1** undertake; start doing or dealing with. **2** undertake the control or reform of (a person). **take it 1** (often foll. by *that* + clause) assume. **2** *informal* put up with or endure a difficult situation. **take it from me** (or **take my word for it**) I can assure you. **take it upon oneself** (foll. by *to* + infin.) venture or presume. **take it or leave it** (esp. in *imper.*) an expression of indifference or impatience about another's decision after making an offer. **take it out on** relieve one's frustration or anger by attacking or treating harshly. **take a lot** (or **it**) **out of** exhaust the strength of. **take off 1 a** remove (clothing) from one's or another's body. **b** lose (weight). **2** remove. **3** deduct (part of an amount). **4** *informal* depart, esp. hastily (*took off in a fast car*). **5** *informal* mimic humorously. **6** jump from the ground. **7** become airborne. **8** (of a scheme, enterprise, etc.) become successful or popular. **9** have (a period) away from work. **take on 1** undertake (work etc.). **2** hire (an employee). **3** challenge or confront (an opponent or adversary). **4** acquire (a new meaning etc.). **take out 1** escort on a date or outing. **2** *N Amer.* buy (food etc.) at a restaurant for eating elsewhere. **3 a** remove from within a place; extract. **b** carry (something) outside. **4** get (a licence or summons etc.) issued. **5** apply for and receive (a loan) from a bank. **6** borrow (a book etc.) from a library. **7** *slang* a *Sport* remove (a player) from play with a check, block, or tackle. **b** assassinate, murder. **take over 1** succeed to the management or ownership of. **2** take control (of). **take some** (or **a lot of**) **doing** be hard to do. **take that!** an exclamation accompanying a blow etc. **take one's time** not hurry. **take to 1** adopt as a habit, practice, pastime, hobby, etc. **2** form a liking for. **3** have recourse to (*took to drinking*). **4** escape to; seek refuge in. **take up 1** become interested or engaged in (an interest, pursuit, hobby, etc.). **2** adopt as a protégé. **3** occupy (time or space). **4** begin (residence etc.). **5** resume after an interruption. **6** join in (a song, chorus, etc.). **7** accept (an offer etc.). **8** shorten (a garment). **9** go over the correct answers to (homework, an assignment, a test, etc.). **10** lift up. **11** absorb (*sponges take up water*). **12** pursue (a matter etc.) further. **take a person up on** accept (a person's offer etc.). **take up the gauntlet** accept a challenge. **take up with** begin to associate with. □ **taker** *n.*

take-away *n.* *Football* an interception made or fumble forced by the defence (*compare* GIVEAWAY 4).

take-charge *attrib.adj.* esp. *N Amer.* characterized by leadership or authority (*a take-charge attitude*).

takedown *n.* **1** a wrestling manoeuvre in which an opponent is swiftly brought to the mat from a standing position. **2** *informal* a police raid or arrest.

take-home *adj.* **1** that may be taken home. **2** (of pay etc.) remaining after taxes etc. have been deducted. **3** (of a test etc.) distributed to students to be written outside of class within a specified period of time.

take-it-or-leave-it *attrib.adj.* characterized by or involving indifference (*a take-it-or-leave-it attitude*).

take-no-prisoners *attrib.adj.* very aggressive or persistent; forceful (*a take-no-prisoners approach*).

takeoff *n.* **1 a** the action or an instance of an aircraft becoming airborne. **b** the period during which this takes place. **2 a** an act of mimicking, esp. a caricature or parody. **b** an imitation. **3 a** the moment of springing from the ground during a leap or jump. **b** a place from which one jumps. **4** the beginning of a new phase of accelerated or increased growth etc.

takeout *n.* **1** esp. *N. Amer.* **a** food or a meal bought at a restaurant to be eaten off the premises (also *attrib.*: *takeout food*). **b** a restaurant preparing food that may be bought and eaten elsewhere. **2** *Curling* a shot which removes an opponent's rock from play. **3** a pullout article in a newspaper or magazine.

takeover *n.* **1** the assumption of control or ownership of a business concern, esp. the buying out of one company by another. **2** a usu. hostile assumption of power or government; a military coup. **3** the act or an instance of taking over.

takeover bid *n.* an offer made to the shareholders of a company to buy their shares at a specified price in order to gain control of that company.

take-up *n.* an apparatus for gathering up film after exposure in a projector or camera.

taking ● *adj.* **1** attractive or captivating. **2** catching or infectious. ● *n.* **1** the action or process of TAKE *v.* (*mine for the taking*). **2** (in *pl.*) = TAKE *n.* 1.

talc *n.* **1** a hydrated silicate of magnesium occurring as white, grey, or pale green masses or translucent laminae that are very soft and have a greasy feel, used esp. as a lubricant. **2** talcum. □ **talcy** *adj.*

talcum ● *n.* (in full **talcum powder**) a preparation of powdered talc, usu. scented or medicated for general cosmetic use. ● *v.tr.* (**talcumed, talcuming**) dust or treat with or as if with talcum.

tale *n.* **1 a** a story or narrative, true or fictitious, told for interest or entertainment. **b** a literary composition cast in narrative form. **2 a** a report of an alleged fact, often malicious or in breach of confidence. **b** (often in *pl.*) a false or fanciful statement; a lie. **3 a** true account of improbable or extraordinary events. □ **live to tell the tale** survive an unpleasant or catastrophic event.

talent *n.* **1** a special aptitude or faculty. **2 a** a person possessing exceptional skill or ability. **b** people of talent or ability collectively (*this team is loaded with talent*). **3** an ancient unit of weight and currency, esp. among the Greeks. □ **talented** *adj.* **talentless** *adj.*

talent scout *n.* a person looking for talented performers, in sport and entertainment.

talent show *n.* a show consisting of performances by promising amateur entertainers, esp. ones hoping to enter show business professionally.

talisman /ˈtælɪzmən, ˈtælɪs-/ *n.* (*pl.* **-s**) **1** an object, esp. an inscribed ring or stone, supposed to be endowed with magic powers esp. of averting evil from or bringing good luck to its holder. **2** a thing supposed capable of working wonders. □ **talismanic** /-ˈmænɪk/ *adj.*

talk ● *v.* **1** *intr.* (often foll. by *to, with*) **a** converse or communicate ideas, information, or feelings by spoken words. **b** refer to a person for advice or information; consult. **c** *informal* negotiate, do business (*show me an offer, then we'll talk*). **2** *intr.* have the power of speech. **3** *intr.* (foll. by *about*) **a** have as the subject of discussion. **b** (in *imper.*) *informal* used to reinforce or emphasize as a clear or extreme example of (a thing) (*talk about dense!*). **4** *tr.* discuss (*talking hockey*). **5** *tr.* (often foll. by *to*) bring (a person) into a specified condition by talking (*talked himself hoarse*). **6** *tr.* (foll. by *into, out of*) persuade (a person) to agree to do or not to do something (*he talked me into it*). **7** *tr.* express or utter in words (*you're talking nonsense*). **8** *tr.* *informal* have in mind, think in terms of, envisage (*I'm talking six figures*). **9** *intr.* reveal esp. secret information; betray secrets. **10** *intr.* gossip (*people are starting to talk*). **11** *intr.* **a** communicate without speaking, such as by writing, sign language, eye contact, etc. **b** have influence (*money talks*). **12** *tr.* use (a language) in speech. ● *n.* **1** conversation or talking. **2** a particular mode of speech (*baby talk*). **3** an informal address or lecture. **4 a** rumour or gossip (*there is talk of a merger*). **b** the subject of rumour or gossip. **5** (often in *pl.*) formal discussions or negotiations between conflicting parties etc. **6** empty promises or boasting. □ **know what one is talking about** have a thorough knowledge or understanding of a subject being discussed. **look who's talking** *informal* an expression of indignation or amusement at a person open to a criticism he or she has made of another. **now you're talking** *informal* now or at last you are saying, suggesting, etc. something that I agree with or approve of. **talk at** talk incessantly without consideration or concern for the thoughts and opinions of the person being addressed. **talk away 1** spend or consume (time etc.) in talking. **2** begin or carry on talking (*talk away! I'm listening*). **talk back** reply defiantly or with impudence. **talk big** *informal* talk boastfully. **talk is cheap** *informal* it is easier to announce one's intentions than to carry through with them. **talk down to** speak patronizingly or condescendingly to. **talk a person down 1** silence a person by greater loudness or persistence. **2** bring (a pilot or aircraft) to landing by radio instructions from the ground. **talk a person's ear off** *N Amer. informal* talk incessantly. **talk a good game** *N Amer. informal* talk convincingly yet fail to act effectively. **talk the hind leg off a donkey** *informal* talk incessantly. **talk of 1** discuss or mention. **2** (often foll. by verbal noun) express some intention of (*talked of moving*). **talk of the town** a prominent topic of local interest and popular discussion. **talk out 1** *Cdn & Brit.* prevent the passage of (a bill in Parliament) by prolonging discussion until the time of adjournment. **2** attempt to resolve by discussing. **talk over** discuss at length. **talk shop** talk, esp. tediously, about one's occupation, business, etc. **talk the talk** say things and make promises that will please or impress others and not offend (compare WALK THE WALK, see WALK). **talk through** discuss thoroughly until a decision or resolution is reached. **talk a person through** guide a person in (a task) with continuous instructions. **talk through one's hat** *informal* **1** exaggerate, bluff. **2** talk wildly or nonsensically. **talk to oneself** articulate one's thoughts to no one in particular and regardless of anyone present or listening. **talk tough** (often foll. by on or about) speak in a brash, boastful, or menacing manner. **talk trash** = TRASH TALK. **talk up** discuss (a subject) in order to arouse interest in it. **you should talk** *ironic* = LOOK WHO'S TALKING.

talkathon *n. informal* a prolonged conversation or discussion.

talkative *adj.* fond of or given to talking; chatty. □ **talkatively** *adv.* **talkativeness** *n.*

talked-about *adj.* widely discussed.

talker *n.* **1** a person who talks. **2** a chatty or talkative person. **3** one who gives talks or lectures; a speaker.

talkfest *n.* = GABFEST.

talkie *n. informal* = TALKING PICTURE.

talking ● *adj.* **1** that talks or is capable of talking (*a talking doll*). **2** (in comb.) using a specified style or manner of speaking (*smooth-talking*). **3** expressive (*talking eyes*). ● *n.* in senses of TALK *v.*

talking book *n.* a recorded reading of a book, esp. for the blind.

talking drum *n.* each of a set of drums of different pitch which are beaten to transmit words in a tonal language, originating in W Africa.

talking head *n. informal* **1** a close-up shot on a television news broadcast or documentary etc. in which a reporter or newscaster is shown only from the shoulders up. **2** a person featured in such a shot.

talking picture *n.* (also **talking film**) a film with a soundtrack, as distinct from a silent film.

talking point *n.* **1** a topic suitable for or inviting discussion. **2** a fact supporting a decision, stance, or side in esp. a political debate.

talking stick *n.* a carved staff used in native gatherings, entitling the holder to speak to the group.

talking-to *n. informal* a reproof, reprimand, or lecture.

talk radio *n.* a radio format that features interviews, listener phone-ins, and discussions.

talk show *n.* esp. *N Amer.* a TV or radio show in which people, esp. celebrities, are invited to talk informally about various topics (also *attrib.*: *talk-show host*).

talk time *n.* the length of time a cellular phone may be used before the battery will need to be recharged.

talky *adj.* **1** (of a book or theatrical production etc.) wordy or long-winded. **2** talkative.

tall ● *adj.* **1** (of a person or animal) of greater than average height. **2** of a specified height (*two metres tall*). **3** high relative to width or surrounding objects (*tall mountains*). **4** *informal* (of a statement or story) exaggerated, extravagant, unlikely. ● *adv.* straight and erect (*stand tall*). □ **tallish** *adj.* **tallness** *n.*

tall grass prairie *n. N Amer.* a prairie region characterized by certain tall moisture-favouring grasses.

tallis /ˈtælɪs/ *n.* (also **tallit**, **tallith** /tæˈliθ/, *pl.* **tallitim, tallithim** /tæliˈtiːm/) a shawl worn by Jewish men, esp. at prayer.

tall order *n.* an exorbitant or unreasonable demand.

tallow /ˈtæloʊ/ *n.* the harder kinds of esp. animal fat melted down for use in making candles, soap, etc. □ **tallowy** *adj.*

tall ship *n.* a sailing ship with a high mast.

tally ● *n.* (*pl.* **-ies**) **1 a** a total score or amount. **b** the record of an amount, debt, score, etc. **2** *Sport* a goal or run scored. **3 a** a mark or number of marks used to represent a fixed number of things, e.g. a series of four vertical lines crossed by a diagonal line used to represent the number five. **b** a particular number, such as five, taken as a group or unit to facilitate counting. **4** *hist.* **a** a piece of wood scored across with notches for the items of an account and then split into halves, each party keeping one. **b** an account kept in this way. **5** a corresponding thing, counterpart, or duplicate. ● *v.* (**-ies, -ied**) **1** *tr.* **a** set down or record (a number etc.); register. **b** (often foll. by *up*) calculate the total of. **2** *tr.* amass, accumulate; achieve a total of. **3** *intr.* agree or correspond; match. **4** *tr. & intr. Sport* score (a run or goal etc.).

tallyho /ˌtæliˈhoʊ/ *interj.* a hunter's cry to the hounds upon sighting a fox.

Talmud /ˈtælmʊd, -məd/ *n.* **1** the body of Jewish civil and ceremonial law and legend comprising the Mishnah and the Gemara. **2** either of two versions of the Gemara, containing the commentary of scholars and jurists on the administration of Jewish law, compiled AD c.200–500. □ **Talmudic** *adj.* **Talmudist** *n.*

talon *n.* **1** a claw of an animal, esp. a bird. **2 a** anything resembling this in form or appearance. **b** (often in *pl.*) a grasping human finger or hand. **3** the cards left after the deal in a card game. **4** a printed form attached to a bearer security that enables the holder to apply for a new sheet of coupons when the existing coupons have been used up. □ **taloned** *adj.*

talus /ˈteɪləs/ *n.* (*pl.* **taluses**) **1** a scree slope at the base of a mountain etc. consisting of material which has fallen from the face of the cliff above. **2** the sloping side of a wall or earthwork.

tam *n.* a round knitted or cloth Scottish cap fitting closely around the brows but large and full above.

tamale /təˈmɒli, -ˈmæli/ *n.* a Mexican food of seasoned ground meat wrapped in cornmeal dough and steamed or baked in corn husks.

tamarack /ˈtæməˌræk/ *n.* **1** any of several N American larches, esp. *Larix laricina*, found in wet places across most of Canada. **2** the wood from this.

tamari /təˈmɑri/ *n.* a rich Japanese wheat-free soy sauce.

tamarin /ˈtæmərɪn/ *n.* any of numerous small neotropical monkeys with fine silky coats and long bushy tails, of the genera *Saguinus* and *Leontopithecus*.

tamarind /ˈtæmərɪnd/ *n.* **1** the fruit of the tree *Tamarindus indica*, a brown pod containing one to twelve seeds embedded in a soft brown sticky acid pulp, valued for its laxative qualities and also used to make esp. chutney and cold drinks. **2** the leguminous tree bearing this fruit, widely grown as a shade tree in tropical countries.

tamarisk /ˈtæmərɪsk/ *n.* any shrub of the genus *Tamarix*, usu. with long slender branches and small pink or white flowers, that thrives by the sea.

tambour /ˈtæmbɔr/ *n.* **1** a flexible sliding shutter or door on a desk, cabinet, etc., made of strips of wood attached to a canvas backing (also *attrib.*: *tambour cabinet*). **2 a** a circular frame consisting of one hoop fitting inside another, used to hold fabric taut while it is being embroidered. **b** material embroidered in this way. **3** a drum, esp. a small one with a deep tone.

tambourine *n.* a musical instrument consisting of a hoop with a skin stretched over one side and pairs of small jingling discs in slots around the circumference, played by shaking, striking, etc.

tame ● *adj.* **1** reclaimed by human management from a naturally wild condition to a tractable or domesticated state. **2** (of an animal) gentle, accustomed to people; not showing the natural shyness, fear, or fierceness of a wild animal. **3 a** unlikely to harm, frighten, or offend (*a tame ski run*). **b** lacking zest or vigour (*this sauce is pretty tame*). **4** *N Amer.* **a** (of land) cultivated. **b** (of a plant) produced by cultivation. **5** (of a person) co-operative, compliant, or servile. ● *v.tr.* **1** bring (a wild animal) under the control or into the service of humans. **2** reduce the intensity of (a person, emotion, etc.); calm, temper. **3** control, subdue (a person etc.). **4** *N Amer.* cultivate (land). □ **tamely** *adv.* **tameness** *n.* **tamer** *n.* (also in *comb.*).

Tamil /ˈtæmɪl/ ● *n.* **1** a member of a Dravidian people inhabiting the southern Indian subcontinent and parts of Sri Lanka. **2** the language of this people. ● *adj.* of this people or their language.

tam-o'-shanter /ˈtæməˌʃæntər/ *n.* = TAM.

tamoxifen /təˈmɒksɪfen/ *n.* a drug which acts as an estrogen antagonist, used to treat breast cancer and infertility in women.

tamp *v.tr.* (often foll. by *down*) **1** pound down or pack (earth, gravel, asphalt, etc.) in order to produce a firm base or level surface. **2 a** stuff or consolidate (tobacco) in a pipe. **b** pack (a pipe) with tobacco. **3** pack (a blasthole) full of clay, sand, etc., to concentrate the force of the explosion. **4** quash or suppress

(a movement, speculation, etc.), esp. by forceful means. □ **tamper** *n.* **tamping** *n.* (in sense 1).

tamper *v.intr.* (foll. by *with*) **1** meddle or interfere with, esp. so as to cause alteration or harm. **2** make unauthorized alterations in (a document or file etc.). **3** contaminate with a foreign substance. **4** exert a secret or corrupt influence upon; bribe. **5** *Sport* negotiate with a player who is under contract to another team. □ **tamperer** *n.* **tampering** *n.*

tamper-proof *adj.* (also **tamper-resistant**) not readily susceptible to tampering.

tampon *n.* a soft plug of cotton or other material used to absorb secretions and stop the flow of blood etc. from an orifice or wound, esp. one inserted into the vagina during menstruation.

tan[1] ● *n.* **1** a brown skin colour resulting from exposure to the sun or another source of ultraviolet light. **2** a yellowish-brown colour. ● *adj.* **1** of a yellowish-brown colour. **2** (of a person, their body, or a part of the body) brown in colour due to exposure to ultraviolet light. ● *v.* (**tanned**, **tanning**) **1** *tr. & intr.* make or become brown by exposure to ultraviolet light. **2** *tr.* convert (rawhide) into leather by soaking in a liquid containing tannic acid or by the use of mineral salts etc. **3** *tr. slang* beat, thrash. □ **tanned** *adj.* **tanning** *n.* **tannish** *adj.*

tan[2] *abbr.* tangent.

tanager /ˈtænədʒər/ *n.* any small New World bird of the subfamily Thraupinae, the male usu. having brightly-coloured plumage.

tandem ● *n.* **1** a team of two people or arrangement of two machines working together in conjunction. **2** a bicycle or tricycle equipped with seats and pedals for two riders, one in front of the other. ● *adj.* **1** co-operative, joint, dual; involving two people, organizations, etc. **2** involving two similar things, one behind the other. **3** (of an articulated truck or trailer) supported at the rear by two axles. ● *adv.* together, one behind or after the other (*riding tandem*). □ **in tandem 1** one behind another. **2** alongside each other, together, in conjunction.

tandoor /ˈtændɔr/ *n.* **1** a clay oven of a kind used originally in N India and Pakistan. **2** (*attrib.*) designating food cooked in such an oven.

tandoori /tænˈdʊri/ *n.* **1** a style of Indian cooking based on the use of a tandoor. **2** food or a dish cooked in a tandoor (often *attrib.*: *tandoori chicken*).

tang *n.* **1** a sharp or penetrating taste, flavour, or smell. **2** a pointed projection on the blade of a knife etc., by which the blade is held in the handle. **3** a characteristic quality. □ **tanged** *adj.* (in sense 2).

tangent ● *n. Math.* **1** a straight line touching a curve or curved surface so that it meets it at a point but does not intersect it at that point. **2** the ratio of the sides opposite and adjacent to an angle in a right-angled triangle. ● *adj.* **1** *Math.* (of a line or surface) touching, but not normally intersecting, another line or surface; that is a tangent. **2** touching. □ **on** (or **at**) **a tangent** diverging from a previous course of action or thought etc.

tangential /tænˈdʒenʃəl/ *adj.* **1** *Math.* **a** of, pertaining to, or of the nature of a tangent. **b** acting or lying etc. in the direction of or along a tangent. **2** going off on a tangent; digressive, divergent (*tangential comments*). **3** peripheral (*tangential evidence*). □ **tangentially** *adv.*

tangerine *n.* **1 a** a mandarin orange, esp. one with a sweeter or tangier flavour and darker peel. **b** the tree bearing this fruit. **2** the colour of the peel of this fruit, a deep reddish orange. ● *adj.* of this colour.

tangible ● *adj.* **1** perceptible by touch; having material form (*tangible evidence*). **2** clearly intelligible; that can be grasped by the mind, not elusive or visionary (*tangible goals for the future*). **3** substantial, definite; that may be clearly viewed, evaluated, or calculated (*tangible results*). ● *n.* (usu. in *pl.*) a tangible thing, esp. an asset. □ **tangibility** *n.* **tangibly** *adv.*

tangle ● *v.* **1 a** *tr.* (often foll. by *up*) twist, intertwine, or jumble (several strands of thread or string etc.) so that all the pieces are joined in a confused mass from which they may not be easily freed. **b** *intr.* become twisted, intertwined, or jumbled. **2** *tr.* (in *passive*; often foll. by *up*) **a** become caught in a mess or tangle of rope, wires, etc. (*my foot is tangled in the cord*). **b** become embroiled in a difficult situation, controversy, affair, etc. **3** *intr.* (foll. by *with*) *informal* become involved with (a person, organization, etc.), esp. in conflict or disagreement. **4** *tr.* complicate (*a tangled affair*). ● *n.* **1** a confused mass of twisted or intertwined hairs, threads, etc. that may not be easily separated. **2** a single long thread, cord, etc. coiled or knotted in a confusing manner; a snarl. **3** a confused or complicated state; a dilemma, predicament, mess, etc. □ **tangled** *adj.* **tangly** *adj.* (**-ier, -iest**).

tango ● *n.* (*pl.* **-os**) **1** a syncopated ballroom dance of Argentinian origin, performed with long dramatic gliding movements and abrupt pauses and changes in direction in 2/4 or 4/4 time. **2** a piece of music in the rhythm of this dance and usu. used as an accompaniment. ● *v.intr.* (**-oes, -oed**) dance the tango. □ **it takes two to tango** both participants in a situation, esp. a dispute, must be held responsible.

tangram /ˈtæŋɡræm/ *n.* a Chinese geometrical puzzle consisting of a square cut into seven pieces, usu. five triangles, a rhomboid, and a square, which can be combined to make various shapes and figures.

tangy *adj.* (**-ier, -iest**) having a strong, sharp flavour or scent; pungent. □ **tanginess** *n.*

tank ● *n.* **1** a large receptacle or storage chamber usu. for liquid or gas. **2** a heavy armoured fighting vehicle carrying guns and moving on a tracked carriage. **3** a container for the fuel supply in a motor vehicle, aircraft, etc. **4** (in full **tank top**) a sleeveless upper garment with a scoop neck. **5** a pond or reservoir. **6** esp. *N Amer.* **a** a prison cell, esp. one for the temporary detention of more than one person (*drunk tank*). **b** *slang* prison (*was in the tank for 3 years*). ● *v.* **1** *tr.* (usu. foll. by *up*) fill the tank of (a vehicle etc.) with fuel. **2** *informal* **a** *intr.* (foll. by *up*) drink heavily; become drunk. **b** *tr. & refl.* (often as **tanked up** *adj.*) inebriate oneself with alcoholic drink or drugs. **3** *tr.* defeat utterly or completely. **4** *tr. & intr. Sport* lose or fail to finish (a game or match) deliberately. **5** *intr.* (of prices etc.) decline or decrease. □ **tankful** *n.* (*pl.* **-fuls**). **tankless** *adj.*

tankard *n.* **1** a tall mug with a handle and sometimes a hinged lid, esp. of silver or pewter for beer. **2** the contents of or an amount held by a tankard.

tanker *n.* a ship, aircraft, or road vehicle for carrying liquids or gases in bulk.

tank farm *n.* an area of oil or gas storage tanks.

tanner *n.* **1** a person who tans hides. **2** a person who suntans.

tannery *n.* (*pl.* **-ies**) a place where hides are tanned.

tannic /ˈtænɪk/ *adj.* **1** of or produced from the crushed bark of esp. oak trees. **2** (of wine) having an astringent flavour due to the presence of tannin.

tannin /ˈtænɪn/ *n.* (also **tannic acid**) any of a group of complex organic compounds found in tea and certain tree barks, used in leather production and as a mordant and astringent.

tansy /ˈtænzɪ/ *n.* (*pl.* **-ies**) any plant of the genus

Tanacetum, esp. *T. vulgare* with yellow button-like flowers and aromatic leaves.

tantalize *v.tr.* **1** torment or tease by the sight or promise of what is unobtainable. **2** raise and then dash the hopes of. □ **tantalization** *n.* **tantalizer** *n.* **tantalizing** *adj.* **tantalizingly** *adv.*

tantalum /ˈtæntələm/ *n.* a rare naturally-occurring hard white metallic element, resistant to heat and the action of acids, used in surgery etc.

tantamount /ˈtæntə‚maunt/ *predic.adj.* (foll. by *to*) equivalent to (*was tantamount to a denial*).

Tantra /ˈtæntrə/ *n.* any of a class of Hindu or Buddhist mystical and magical writings. □ **Tantric** *adj.* **Tantrism** *n.*

tantrum *n.* an outburst of bad temper or petulance.

Tanzanian /‚tænzəˈniːən/ ● *n.* a native or inhabitant of Tanzania, a country on the coast of E Africa. ● *adj.* of or relating to Tanzania or Tanzanians.

Tao /tau, dau/ *n.* **1** (in Taoism) the absolute being or principle underlying the universe; ultimate reality. **2** (in Confucianism) the way, method, or norm to be followed, esp. in conduct.

Taoism *n.* a Chinese philosophy based on the writings of Lao-tzu, advocating humility and religious piety. □ **Taoist** *n.* **Taoistic** *adj.*

tap¹ ● *n.* **1** a device by which a flow of liquid or gas from a pipe or vessel can be controlled. **2** an act of tapping a telephone etc. **3** a tool for cutting the thread of a female screw. **4** the surgical withdrawal of fluid from a cavity etc. (*spinal tap*). ● *v.tr.* (**tapped, tapping**) **1 a** provide (a cask) with a tap. **b** let out (a liquid) by means of, or as if by means of, a tap. **2** draw sap from (a tree) by cutting or drilling into it. **3 a** obtain information or supplies or resources from. **b** extract or obtain; discover and exploit (*tapping the skills of young people*). **4** connect a listening device to (a telephone or telegraph line etc.) to listen to a call or transmission. **5** cut a female screw thread in. **6** *Med.* drain (a cavity) of accumulated fluid. □ **on tap 1** (of beer etc.) ready to be drawn from a keg; not bottled or canned. **2** *informal* ready for immediate use; freely available. **tap into** obtain something from.

tap² ● *v.* (**tapped, tapping**) **1** *intr.* (foll. by *at, on*) strike a gentle but audible blow. **2** *tr.* strike lightly (*tapped me on the shoulder*). **3** *tr.* (foll. by *against* etc.) cause (a thing) to strike lightly (*tapped a stick against the window*). **4** *intr.* = TAP DANCE *v.* **5** *tr.* (often foll. by *out*) **a** make a tap or taps (*tapped out the rhythm*). **b** write using a typewriter or computer keyboard. **6** *intr.* walk with a tapping sound (*she tapped across the tiled floor*). ● *n.* **1 a** a light blow; a rap. **b** the sound of this (*heard a tap at the door*). **2 a** = TAP DANCE *n.* (also *attrib.*: *tap classes*). **b** a piece of metal attached to the toe and heel of a tap dancer's shoe to make the tapping sound. **3** (in *pl.*, usu. treated as *sing.*) *US* **a** a bugle call for lights to be put out in army quarters. **b** a similar signal at a military funeral. □ **tapper** *n.*

tapas /ˈtæpæs/ *n.pl.* (often *attrib.*) small savoury Spanish appetizers, esp. served with wine or beer.

tap dance ● *n.* a form of display dance performed wearing shoes fitted with metal taps, with rhythmical tapping of the toes and heels. ● *v.intr.* perform a tap dance. □ **tap dancer** *n.* **tap dancing** *n.*

tape ● *n.* **1** a narrow strip of woven material for tying up, fastening, etc. **2 a** a strip of material stretched across the finishing line of a race. **b** a similar strip for marking off an area or forming a notional barrier. **3** (in full **adhesive tape**) a strip of opaque or transparent paper or plastic etc., esp. coated with adhesive for fastening, sticking, masking, insulating, etc. **4 a** = MAGNETIC TAPE. **b** a tape recording or tape cassette. **5** (in full **tape measure**) a strip of tape or thin flexible metal marked for measuring lengths. ● *v.tr.* **1 a** tie up or join etc. with tape. **b** apply tape to. **2** (foll. by *off*) seal or mark off an area or thing with tape. **3** record on magnetic tape. **4** wrap (a joint etc.) firmly with a bandage or tape to provide support. □ **on tape** recorded on magnetic tape.

tape deck *n.* a piece of equipment for playing audio tapes, esp. as part of a stereo system.

tape machine *n.* **1** = TAPE RECORDER. **2** = TICKER 2.

tapenade /ˈtæpəˈnæd/ *n.* a Provençal dish, usu. served as an hors d'oeuvre, made mainly from puréed black olives, capers, and anchovies.

tape player *n.* a tape recorder or tape deck.

taper ● *n.* **1** a wick coated with wax etc. for conveying a flame. **2** a slender candle. **3** gradual diminution in width or thickness. ● *v. tr. & intr.* (often foll. by *off*) **1** diminish or reduce in thickness towards one end. **2** make or become gradually less. □ **tapering** *adj.*

tape recorder *n.* a machine for recording sounds on magnetic tape and playing back the recording. □ **tape-record** *v.tr.* **tape recording** *n.*

tapestry *n.* (*pl.* **-ies**) **1 a** a thick textile fabric in which coloured weft threads are woven to form pictures or designs. **b** embroidery imitating this, usu. in wools on canvas. **c** a piece of such embroidery. **2** events or circumstances etc. compared with a tapestry in being intricate, interwoven, etc. (*life's rich tapestry*). □ **tapestried** *adj.*

tapeworm *n.* any flatworm of the class Cestoda, with a body like segmented tape, living as a parasite in the intestines.

tap-in *n.* a close-range shot requiring little force, esp. into the goal in hockey.

taping *n.* **1** the act or an instance of recording something on magnetic tape, esp. a session where an item is taped for later broadcast. **2** the act of applying tape or bandages etc.

tapioca /ˌtæpiˈoːkə/ *n.* a starchy substance in hard white grains obtained from cassava and used for puddings etc.

tapir /ˈteɪpər, -piːr/ *n.* any nocturnal hoofed mammal of the genus *Tapirus*, native to Central and South America and Malaysia, having a short flexible protruding snout used for feeding on vegetation.

taproom *n.* a room in which alcoholic drinks are available, esp. in a hotel.

taproot *n.* a tapering root growing vertically.

tap water *n.* water from a piped supply, esp. as opposed to bottled water.

tar¹ ● *n.* **1** a dark thick inflammable liquid distilled from wood or coal etc. and used as a preservative of wood and iron, in making roads, as an antiseptic, etc. **2** a similar substance formed in the combustion of tobacco etc. ● *v.tr.* (**tarred, tarring**) **1** cover with tar. **2** mark or stain as with tar (*tarred the image of legitimate refugees*). □ **beat** (or **kick** or **whale** etc.) **the tar out of** *N Amer. slang* beat or thrash severely. **tar and feather** smear with tar and then cover with feathers as a punishment. **tarred with the same brush** having the same faults.

tar² *n. informal* a sailor.

tarabish /ˈtɑrbɪʃ/ *n. Cdn (Cape Breton)* a card game based on bridge.

tarantula /təˈræntʃʊlə/ *n.* any large hairy tropical spider of the family Theraphosidae, some of which are venomous.

tar baby *n.* (*pl.* **-ies**) *N Amer. informal* a difficult problem, esp. one worsened by attempts to solve it.

tardy *adj.* (**-ier, -iest**) **1** late; unpunctual, esp. consistently. **2** slow to act or come or happen. **3** delaying or delayed beyond the right or expected time. □ **tardily** *adv.* **tardiness** *n.*

tare¹ /ter/ *n.* **1** any of various vetches. **2** (in *pl.*) *New Testament* an injurious weed, probably darnel.

tare² *n.* **1** the weight of a wrapping, container, or receptacle in which goods are packed. **2** an allowance made for this. **3** the weight of a motor vehicle without its fuel or load.

target ● *n.* **1 a** a mark or point fired or aimed at, esp. a round or rectangular object marked with concentric circles. **2 a** a person or thing aimed at, or exposed to gunfire etc. (*they were an easy target*). **b** a person, group, etc. which is the object of attention, a campaign, etc. (also *attrib.*: *target audience*). **3** an objective or result aimed at (also *attrib.*: *target date*). **4** a person or thing against whom criticism, abuse, etc., is or may be directed. ● *v.tr.* (**targeted, targeting**) **1** identify or single out as an object of attention or attack. **2** aim or direct. □ **on target 1** on the correct course to meet an objective. **2** accurate; exactly right.

target language *n.* the language into which a text or speech is translated.

tariff /ˈterɪf, ˈtærɪf/ ● *n.* **1 a** a duty on a particular class of imports or exports. **b** a list of duties or customs to be paid. **2** a table of fixed charges (*a hotel tariff*). ● *v.tr.* subject (goods) to a tariff.

Tarmac /ˈtɑrmæk/ ● *n.* **1** *proprietary* = TARMACADAM. **2** a surface made of this, e.g. a runway. ● *v.tr.* (**tarmac**) (**-macked, -macking**) apply tarmacadam to.

tarmacadam /ˌtɑrməˈkædəm/ *n.* a material of stone or slag bound with tar, used in paving roads etc.

tarn *n.* a small mountain lake.

tarnation /tɑrˈneɪʃən/ *interj. N Amer.* expressing exasperation. □ **in tarnation** used as an intensifier.

tarnish ● *v.* **1** *tr.* lessen or destroy the lustre of (metal etc.). **2** *tr.* impair (one's reputation etc.). **3** *intr.* (of metal etc.) lose lustre. ● *n.* **1 a** a loss of lustre. **b** a film of colour formed on an exposed surface of a mineral or metal. **2** a blemish; a stain.

taro /ˈtɑroː/ *n.* (*pl.* **-os**) a tropical plant, *Colocasia esculenta*, with tuberous roots used as food.

tarot /ˈtæroː/ *n.* **1** (in *sing.* or *pl.*) **a** any of several games played with a pack of cards having five suits, the last of which is a set of permanent trumps. **b** a similar pack used in fortune-telling. **2 a** any of the trump cards. **b** any of the cards from a fortune-telling pack.

tarp *n. N Amer. & Austral. informal* a tarpaulin.

tarpaper *n.* esp. *N Amer.* paper impregnated with tar, often used as a building material (also *attrib.*: *tarpaper shack*). □ **tarpapered** *adj.*

tarpaulin /tɑrˈpɒlən/ *n.* **1** heavy-duty waterproof cloth. **2** a sheet or covering of this.

tar pit *n.* a seepage of natural tar, esp. one in which animals have become trapped and their remains preserved. **2** something in which one becomes bogged down.

tarpon /ˈtɑrpɒn/ *n.* **1** a large silvery fish, *Megalops atlanticus*, common in the tropical Atlantic. **2** a similar fish, *Megalops cyprinoides*, of the Pacific Ocean.

tarragon /ˈterəgən, ˈtæ-/ *n.* a bushy herb, *Artemisia dracunculus*, with leaves used to flavour salads etc.

tarry¹ /ˈtɑri/ *adj.* (**-ier, -iest**) of or like or smeared with tar. □ **tarriness** *n.*

tarry² /ˈteri, ˈtæri/ *v.intr.* (**-ies, -ied**) *archaic* or *literary* **1** defer coming or going. **2** linger, stay, wait. **3** be tardy. □ **tarrier** *n.*

tarsal /'tɑrsəl/ ● *adj.* of or relating to the bones in the ankle. ● *n.* a tarsal bone.

tar sand *n.* a deposit of sand impregnated with bitumen.

tarsus /'tɑrsəs/ *n.* (*pl.* **tarsi** /-saɪ/) **1 a** the group of bones forming the ankle and upper foot. **b** the shank of a bird's leg. **c** the terminal segment of a limb in insects. **2** the fibrous connective tissue of the eyelid.

tart[1] *n.* a small, usu. open pie containing a fruit or sweet filling. □ **tartlet** *n.*

tart[2] ● *n. slang* a prostitute or promiscuous woman. ● *v.* (foll. by *up*) *informal* **1** *tr.* (usu. *refl.*) smarten (oneself or a thing) up, esp. gaudily. **2** *intr.* dress up gaudily.

tart[3] *adj.* **1** sharp or acid in taste. **2** (of a remark etc.) cutting, bitter. □ **tartly** *adv.* **tartness** *n.*

tartan *n.* **1** a pattern of coloured stripes crossing at right angles, esp. a distinctive plaid of a sort orig. worn by the Scottish Highlanders to denote their clan. **2** woollen cloth woven in this pattern (often *attrib.*: *a tartan scarf*).

Tartar (also **Tatar** except in sense 3 of *n.*) ● *n.* **1 a** a member of a group of Turkic peoples inhabiting parts of European and Asiatic Russia. **b** *hist.* a member of the combined forces of central Asian peoples, including Mongols and Turks, who overran and devasted much of Asia and eastern Europe in the early 13th c., and established a large empire in central Europe in the 14th c. **2** the Turkic language of these peoples. **3** (**tartar**) a violent-tempered or intractable person. ● *adj.* **1** of or relating to the Tartars. **2** of or relating to Central Asia east of the Caspian Sea.

tartar *n.* **1** a hard deposit of saliva, calcium phosphate, etc., that forms on the teeth. **2** a deposit of acid potassium tartrate that forms a hard crust on the inside of a cask during the fermentation of wine.

tartaric acid /tɑr'tɑrɪk/ *n.* a natural carboxylic acid used in baking powders and as a food additive.

tartar sauce *n.* a sauce of mayonnaise and chopped pickles, capers, etc.

tartrate /'tɑrtreɪt/ *n.* any salt or ester of tartaric acid.

tartufo /tɑr'tu:fo:/ *n.* (*pl.* **-os**) a ball of ice cream with one flavour in the centre surrounded by another flavour, the whole often coated in cocoa etc.

tarty *adj.* (**-ier, -iest**) *informal* **1** (esp. of a woman) promiscuous; sleazy. **2** (of clothing, makeup, etc.) typical of that worn by prostitutes; immodest. □ **tartily** *adv.* **tartiness** *n.*

task ● *n.* **1** a piece of work to be done or undertaken. **2** a difficult or unpleasant piece of work. ● *v.tr.* **1** make great demands on (a person's powers etc.). **2** assign a task to. □ **take to task** rebuke, scold.

task force *n.* (also **task group**) **1** *Military* an armed force organized for a special operation. **2** a unit specially organized for a task.

taskmaster *n.* a person who imposes a task or burden, esp. regularly or severely.

Tasmanian /tæz'meɪniən/ ● *n.* **1** a native of Tasmania, an island state of Australia. **2** a person of Tasmanian descent. ● *adj.* of or relating to Tasmania.

Tasmanian devil *n.* a bearlike nocturnal flesh-eating marsupial, *Sarcophilus harrisii*, of Tasmania.

tassel *n.* **1** a tuft of loosely hanging threads or cords etc. attached for decoration to a cushion, scarf, cap, etc. **2** a tassel-like head of some plants, esp. a flower head with prominent stamens at the top of a corn stalk. ● *v.* (**tasselled, tasselling**) **1** *tr.* provide with a tassel or tassels. **2** *intr. N Amer.* (of corn) form tassels. □ **tasselled** *adj.*

taste ● *n.* **1** a the flavour of something, causing a particular sensation when it comes into contact with the tongue. **b** the sense by which a flavour is recognized (*was bitter to the taste*). **2** a small portion of food or drink taken as a sample. **3** a slight experience (*a taste of success*). **4** a liking or predilection (*has expensive tastes*). **5** aesthetic discernment in art, literature, fashion, etc., esp. of a specified kind (*dresses in poor taste*). **6** a sense of what is tactful or polite etc. in a given situation. ● *v.* **1** *tr.* sample or test the flavour of (food etc.) by taking it into the mouth. **2** *tr. & intr.* perceive the flavour of (*could taste the lemon*). **3** *tr.* (esp. with *neg.*) eat or drink a small portion of (*had not tasted food for days*). **4** *tr.* have experience of (*tasted failure*). **5** *intr.* (often foll. by *of*) have a specified flavour. □ **a bad** (or **bitter** etc.) **taste** *informal* a strong feeling of regret or unease. **to taste** in the amount needed for a pleasing result (*add salt to taste*). □ **tasteable** *adj.* (also **tastable**).

taste bud *n.* any of the cells or nerve endings on the surface of the tongue by which things are tasted.

tasteful *adj.* having, or done in, good taste. □ **tastefully** *adv.* **tastefulness** *n.*

tasteless *adj.* **1** lacking flavour. **2** having, or done in, bad taste. □ **tastelessly** *adv.* **tastelessness** *n.*

tastemaker *n. N Amer.* a person or institution that determines or influences what is or will become stylish or fashionable.

taster *n.* **1** a person employed to test food or drink by tasting it, esp. for quality. **2** an instrument etc. used in sampling or tasting. **3** a sample or foretaste.

taste test *n.* a usu. blind comparison of the flavours of two or more similar products. □ **taste-test** *v.tr.*

tasting *n.* a gathering at which food or drink (esp. wine) is tasted and evaluated.

tasty *adj.* (**-ier, -iest**) (of food) pleasing in flavour; appetizing. □ **tastily** *adv.* **tastiness** *n.*

tat *v.* (**tatted, tatting**) **1** *intr.* do tatting. **2** *tr.* make by tatting.

tatami /tə'tɒmi/ *n.* (*pl.* **-is** or same) a rush-covered straw mat, a traditional Japanese floor covering.

Tatar *n. & adj. see* TARTAR.

tater *n. slang* = POTATO.

tatter *n.* (usu. in *pl.*) a rag; an irregularly torn piece of cloth or paper etc. □ **in tatters** *informal* **1** torn to shreds. **2** (of a negotiation, argument, etc.) ruined, demolished. □ **tattered** *adj.* **tattery** *adj.*

tatting *n.* **1** a kind of knotted lace made by hand with a small shuttle and used for trimming etc. **2** the process of making this.

tattle ● *v.* **1** *intr.* esp. *N Amer.* (often foll. by *on*) inform against a person; tell tales (*she's always tattling*). **2 a** *intr.* prattle, chatter; gossip idly. **b** *tr.* utter (words) idly. ● *n.* gossip. □ **tattler** *n.*

tattle-tale *n. N Amer.* a person, esp. a child, who tattles on another.

tattoo[1] /tæ'tu:/ *n.* (*pl.* **-s**) **1** an evening drum or bugle signal recalling soldiers to their quarters. **2** an elaboration of this with music and marching, presented as an entertainment. **3** a rhythmic tapping or drumming.

tattoo[2] ● *v.tr.* (**tattoos, tattooed**) **1** mark (the skin) with an indelible design by puncturing it and inserting pigment. **2** make (a design) in this way. ● *n.* (*pl.* **-s**) a design made by tattooing. □ **tattooist** *n.*

tatty *adj.* (**-ier, -iest**) *informal* **1** tattered; worn. **2** inferior. **3** tawdry. □ **tattily** *adv.* **tattiness** *n.*

tau /tau, tɒ/ *n.* the nineteenth letter of the Greek alphabet (T, τ).

taught *past and past part. of* TEACH.

taunt ● *n.* a thing said in order to anger or wound a

person. ● *v.tr.* **1** assail with taunts. **2** reproach contemptuously. ☐ **taunter** *n.* **tauntingly** *adv.*

taupe /toːp/ ● *n.* a grey with a tinge of another colour, usu. brown. ● *adj.* of this colour.

Taurus /ˈtɔrəs/ *n.* **1** a constellation between Gemini and Aries, traditionally regarded as contained in the figure of a bull. **2 a** the second sign of the zodiac. **b** a person born when the sun is in this sign, usu. between Apr. 20 and May 20. ☐ **Taurean** *adj. & n.*

taut /tɔt/ *adj.* **1** (of a rope, muscles, etc.) tight; not slack. **2** (of nerves) tense. ☐ **tauten** *v.tr. & intr.* **tautly** *adv.* **tautness** *n.*

tautog /tɒˈtɒɡ/ *n.* a fish, *Tautoga onitis*, found off the Atlantic coast of N America, used as food.

tautology /tɒˈtɒlədʒi/ *n.* (*pl.* **-ies**) **1** the saying of the same thing twice over in different words, esp. as a fault of style, e.g. *arrived one after the other in succession*. **2** a statement that is necessarily true. ☐ **tautological** *adj.* **tautologically** *adv.* **tautologous** /-ləɡəs/ *adj.*

tavern *n.* **1** a drinking establishment, esp. one serving beer and wine but not hard liquor. **2** *hist.* an inn.

taverna /təˈvɜrnə/ *n.* a Greek café or restaurant.

tawdry *adj.* (**-ier**, **-iest**) **1** showy but worthless. **2** over-ornamented, gaudy, vulgar. **3** base; despicable. ☐ **tawdriness** *n.*

tawny ● *adj.* (**-ier**, **-iest**) of an orange- or yellow-brown colour. ● *n.* this colour.

tawny owl *n.* **1** a reddish-brown European owl, *Strix aluco*. **2** (**Tawny Owl**) *Cdn* an assistant adult leader of a Brownie pack.

tax ● *n.* **1** a contribution to government revenue compulsorily levied on individuals, property, or businesses. **2** (usu. foll. by *on*, *upon*) a strain or heavy demand; an oppressive or burdensome obligation. ● *v.tr.* **1** impose a tax on (persons or goods etc.). **2** deduct tax from (income etc.). **3** make heavy demands on a person's powers or resources etc.) (*you tax my patience*). **4** (foll. by *with*) confront (a person) with a wrongdoing etc. ☐ **taxable** *adj.*

taxa *pl. of* TAXON.

tax-and-spend *n.* (*attrib.*) (of a government policy or its proponents) advocating high taxes and government expenditure on programs beyond the basic responsibilities of government, esp. as an impetus to the economy.

taxation *n.* **1** the fact or condition of being taxed. **2** the act of taxing. **3** revenue raised by taxes.

tax avoidance *n.* the arrangement of financial affairs to minimize payment of tax.

tax bracket *n.* a range of incomes taxed at a given rate.

tax break *n.* *informal* a tax concession or advantage allowed by government.

Tax Court of Canada *n.* *Cdn* a federal court with jurisdiction to hear appeals on matters involving esp. income taxes, employment insurance, the CPP, etc.

tax credit *n.* a sum that may be deducted from the amount of tax owing. ☐ **tax-creditable** *adj. Cdn.*

tax-deductible *adj.* (of expenses) that may be deducted from income before the amount of tax to be paid is calculated.

tax dollar *n.* *N Amer.* a dollar paid as tax.

tax evasion *n.* the illegal nonpayment or underpayment of income tax. ☐ **tax evader** *n.*

tax-exempt *adj.* esp. *N Amer.* **1** (of income) not subject to taxation. **2** (of a security etc.) earning income that is not subject to taxation.

tax-free *adj.* exempt from taxes.

tax grab *n.* an excessive or unjustified tax demand by a government, esp. when disguised as other forms of payment, e.g. licence fees etc.

tax haven *n.* a country etc. where income tax is low.

taxi ● *n.* (*pl.* **taxis**) **1** (also **taxicab**) a car with a driver that may be hired for journeys, esp. one with a meter that records the fare to be paid. **2** a boat, airplane, etc. similarly used. ● *v.* (**taxis**, **taxied**, **taxiing**) **1 a** *intr.* (of an aircraft or pilot) move along the ground under the machine's own power before takeoff or after landing. **b** *tr.* cause (an aircraft) to taxi. **2** *intr.* go in a taxi.

taxidermy /ˈtæksɪˌdɜrmi/ *n.* the art of preparing, stuffing, and mounting the skins of animals etc. in lifelike poses. ☐ **taxidermic** *adj.* **taxidermist** *n.*

taxing *adj.* tiring or demanding; requiring great physical or mental effort.

taxis /ˈtæksɪs/ *n.* **1** *Surgery* the restoration of displaced bones or organs by manual pressure. **2** *Biol.* the movement of a cell or organism in response to an external stimulus.

taxiway *n.* a route along which an aircraft can taxi when moving to or from a runway.

taxman *n.* (*pl.* **-men**) *informal* **1** an inspector or collector of taxes. **2** the personification of the government department dealing with taxes.

Taxol /ˈtæksɒl/ *n.* *proprietary* a compound obtained from the bark of certain yews, which inhibits the growth of some tumours.

taxon /ˈtæksən/ *n.* (*pl.* **taxa**) any taxonomic group.

taxonomy /tækˈsɒnəmi/ *n.* **1** the science of the classification of living and extinct organisms. **2** the practice of this. ☐ **taxonomic** *adj.* **taxonomical** *adj.* **taxonomically** *adv.* **taxonomist** *n.*

taxpayer *n.* a person who pays taxes. ☐ **taxpaying** *adj.*

tax relief *n.* remission of a proportion of income tax.

tax return *n.* a declaration of income for taxation purposes.

tax revolt *n.* a widespread refusal to pay a tax.

tax shelter *n.* a financial arrangement, such as an investment, intended to minimize payment of tax. ☐ **tax-sheltered** *adj.*

tax year *n.* = FISCAL YEAR.

Tay–Sachs disease /teiˈsæks/ *n.* an inherited metabolic disorder in which certain lipids accumulate in the brain, causing spasticity and death in childhood.

TB *abbr.* **1 a** tubercle bacillus. **b** tuberculosis. **2** torpedo boat.

Tb *symbol* terbium.

t.b.a. *abbr.* to be announced.

T-ball *n.* *N Amer.* a form of baseball for young children, in which the ball is placed on a stand in front of the batter instead of being thrown by the pitcher.

T-bar *n.* **1** (in full **T-bar lift**) a type of ski lift in the form of a series of inverted T-shaped metal bars for towing skiers. **2** a metal bar with a T-shaped cross section. **3** a T-shaped fastening on a shoe etc.

T-bill *n.* TREASURY BILL.

T-bone ● *n.* a T-shaped bone, esp. in steak from the thin end of a loin. ● *v.tr.* (usu. in *passive*) *N Amer. informal* (of a car or truck) run into or collide with (another vehicle) on the side.

tbsp *abbr.* = TABLESPOON 2.

Tc *symbol* technetium.

T-cell *n.* = T-LYMPHOCYTE.

tchotchke /ˈtʃɒtʃki/ *n.* *N Amer. informal* a knickknack.

TCP *abbr. proprietary* a disinfectant and germicide.

TCP/IP *abbr.* *proprietary* Transmission Control Protocol/Internet Protocol, the obligatory standard to be used by any system connecting to the Internet.

TD *abbr.* touchdown.

TDD *abbr.* *N Amer.* Telephone Device for the Deaf.

Te *symbol* tellurium.

te *var. of* TI^2.

tea *n.* **1 a** an evergreen shrub or small tree, *Camellia sinensis*, of India, China, etc. **b** its dried leaves. **2 a** a drink made by infusing tea leaves in boiling water. **b** a cup of this. **3** a similar drink made from the leaves of other plants or from another substance (*camomile tea*; *beef tea*). **4 a** esp. *Brit.* a light afternoon meal consisting of tea, bread, cakes, etc. **b** esp. *Brit.* a cooked (esp. early) evening meal. **c** esp. *N Amer.* an afternoon reception at which tea is served. **d** *Cdn* (*Nfld*) an afternoon or early evening social gathering in a church hall etc. at which a light meal is sold.

tea bag *n.* a small perforated paper or cloth bag containing tea leaves for infusion.

tea biscuit *n.* *Cdn* a small baked food, leavened with baking powder or soda, often containing raisins etc.

tea caddy *n.* = CADDY^1 2.

tea ceremony *n.* an elaborate Japanese ritual of serving and drinking tea, as an expression of Zen Buddhist philosophy.

teach *v.* (*past and past part.* **taught**) **1 a** *tr.* give systematic information to (a person) or about (a subject or skill). **b** *intr.* practise this professionally. **c** *tr.* enable (a person) to do something by instruction and training (*taught me to swim*). **2 a** advocate as a moral etc. principle. **b** communicate, instruct in (*suffering taught me patience*). **3** *tr.* (foll. by *to* + infin.) **a** induce (a person) by example or punishment to do or not to do a thing (*that will teach you not to laugh*). **b** *informal* make (a person) disinclined to do a thing (*I'll teach you to interfere*). □ (**one can't**) **teach an old dog new tricks** (one cannot) successfully make old people change their ideas, methods of work, etc. **teach school** *N Amer.* be a teacher in a school.

teachable *adj.* **1** (of a subject) that can be taught or imparted by instruction, training, etc. **2** apt at learning.

teacher *n.* a person who teaches, esp. in a school. □ **teacherish** *adj.* **teacherly** *adj.*

teachers' college *n.* *N Amer.* (also **teachers college**) **1** a faculty of education within a university. **2** a college for training teachers.

teacher's pet *n.* the favoured student of a teacher.

teach-in *n.* **1** an informal debate on a matter of public, usu. political interest, originally between the staff and students of a university. **2** a conference attended by members of a profession on topics of common concern. **3** an informal teaching lecture or discussion. **4** a series of these.

teaching *n.* **1** the profession of a teacher. **2** (often in *pl.*) what is taught; a doctrine.

teaching assistant *n.* a graduate student hired to assist a professor, esp. by marking assignments and teaching seminars. □ **teaching assistantship** *n.*

teaching hospital *n.* a hospital associated with a university, where medical students receive practical training.

tea cozy *n.* a cover placed over a teapot to keep the contents hot.

teacup *n.* a cup from which tea is drunk, usu. with a matching saucer.

tea dance *n.* an afternoon tea with dancing.

tea house *n.* a restaurant, esp. in China or Japan, where tea and other refreshments are served.

teak *n.* **1** a large deciduous tree, *Tectona grandis*, native to India and SE Asia. **2** (in full **teakwood**) its hard durable timber, used esp. in shipbuilding and furniture.

teakettle *n.* = KETTLE 1. □ **ass** (or **tail**) **over teakettle** *N Amer.* *slang* head over heels.

teal ● *n.* (*pl.* same or **teals**) **1** any of various small freshwater ducks of the genus *Anas*, esp. the green-winged teal, *A. crecca*, the male of which has a chestnut head and a green stripe, and the blue-winged teal, *A. discors*, which has a chalky blue forewing and a green speculum. **2** a dark greenish-blue colour. ● *adj.* (in full **teal blue**; hyphenated when *attrib.*) of this colour.

tea leaf *n.* **1** a dried leaf of tea. **2** (esp. in *pl.*) these after infusion or as dregs, the patterns formed by which are interpreted by fortune tellers.

tea light *n.* a small candle in a shallow round metal case, used in an ornamental holder for decoration or in a stand for a teapot to keep tea warm.

team ● *n.* **1** a set of players forming one side in a game or contest (*a hockey team*; also *attrib.*: *team jacket*). **2** two or more persons working together. **3 a** a set of draft animals. **b** one animal or more in harness with a vehicle. ● *v.* **1** *intr.* & *tr.* (usu. foll. by *up*) join in a team or in common action (*decided to team up with them*). **2** *tr.* harness (horses etc.) in a team. **3** *tr.* *N Amer.* convey or transport (goods etc.) by means of a team. **4** *tr.* (foll. by *with*) match or coordinate (clothes).

teammate *n.* a fellow member of a team or group.

team player *n.* a person who plays or works well as a member of a team. □ **team play** *n.*

team spirit *n.* willingness to act as a member of a group rather than as an individual.

teamster *n.* **1** *N Amer.* (also **Teamster**) a truck driver, esp. a member of the Teamsters Union. **2** a driver of a team of animals.

teamwork *n.* the combined action of a team, group, etc., esp. when effective and efficient.

tea party *n.* a social occasion at which tea is served, esp. in the late afternoon.

tea plant *n.* = TEA n. 1a.

teapot *n.* a pot with a handle, spout, and lid, in which tea is brewed and from which it is poured.

tear^1 ● *v.* (*past* **tore**; *past part.* **torn**) **1** *tr.* (often foll. by *up*) pull apart or to pieces with some force (*tear it in half*; *tore up the letter*). **2** *tr.* **a** make a hole or rent in by tearing (*have torn my coat*). **b** make (a hole or rent). **3** *tr.* (foll. by *away*, *off*, etc.) pull violently or with some force (*tore a page out*). **4** *tr.* violently disrupt or divide (*the country was torn by civil war*; *torn by conflicting emotions*). **5** *intr.* *informal* go or travel hurriedly or impetuously (*tore across the road*). **6** *intr.* undergo tearing (*the curtain tore down the middle*). **7** *intr.* (foll. by *at* etc.) pull violently or with some force. ● *n.* **1** a hole or other damage caused by tearing. **2** a torn part of cloth etc. **3** *N Amer.* **a** a spree. **b** *Sport* a winning streak; a successful run (*on a tear*). □ **be torn between** have difficulty in choosing between. **tear apart 1** destroy, divide utterly. **2** search (a place) exhaustively. **3** criticize forcefully. **4** distress greatly. **tear down** demolish. **tear one's hair out** behave with extreme desperation or anger. **tear into 1** attack verbally; reprimand. **2** make a vigorous start on (an activity). **tear oneself away** leave despite a strong desire to stay. **tear to shreds** *informal* refute or criticize thoroughly.

tear^2 ● *n.* **1** a drop of clear salty liquid appearing in or flowing from the eyes, as a result of emotion, physical irritation, pain, etc. **2** a drop. ● *v.intr. N Amer.* (of the eyes) fill with tears. ▢ **in tears** crying; shedding tears. **without tears** presented so as to be learned or done easily. ▢ **teary** *adj.*

teardrop *n.* **1** a single tear. **2** a thing resembling a teardrop in shape, esp. a jewel.

tearful *adj.* **1** crying or inclined to cry. **2** causing or accompanied with tears; sad (*a tearful goodbye*). ▢ **tearfully** *adv.* **tearfulness** *n.*

tear gas ● *n.* a gas that causes severe irritation to the eyes, used in warfare or riot control to disable opponents or make crowds disperse (often *attrib.*: *tear-gas canister*). ● *v.tr.* (**tear-gas**) (**-gases, -gassed, -gassing**) attack with tear gas.

tearing /ˈteriŋ/ *adj.* extreme, overwhelming, violent (*in a tearing hurry*).

tearjerker *n. informal* a sentimental story, film, etc., calculated to evoke sadness or sympathy. ▢ **tear-jerking** *n. & attrib.adj.*

tear-off *attrib.adj.* (of a sheet of paper etc.) that can be removed by tearing off usu. along a perforated line.

tea room *n.* **1** a small restaurant or café where tea and other refreshments are served. **2** *N Amer. slang* a public washroom used as a meeting place by homosexuals.

tea rose *n.* a hybrid rose bush bearing flowers with a scent resembling that of tea.

tease ● *v.* **1** *tr.* **a** make fun of playfully or unkindly or annoyingly. **b** tempt or allure while refusing to satisfy the desire aroused. **2** *intr.* tease a person or animal. **3** *tr.* esp. *N Amer.* comb (the hair) from the ends towards the scalp to make it look thicker. **4** *tr.* pick (wool etc.) into separate fibres. ● *n.* **1** *informal* a person fond of teasing. **2** an instance of teasing (*it was only a tease*). **tease out 1** separate by disentangling. **2** extract, obtain or ascertain, esp. by painstaking effort (*to tease out the truth*). ▢ **teasingly** *adv.*

teasel *n.* any plant of the genus *Dipsacus*, with large prickly heads.

teaser *n.* **1** *informal* a hard question or task. **2** a teasing person. **3** esp. *N Amer.* a short introductory advertisement, esp. an excerpt or sample designed to stimulate interest or curiosity.

tea service *n.* (also **tea set**) a matching teapot, milk jug, and sugar bowl (often also including a matching coffee pot and tray), for serving tea.

tea shop *n.* = TEA ROOM 1.

teaspoon *n.* **1** a small spoon for stirring coffee, tea, etc. **2** an amount held by this, esp. as a unit of measure in cooking, equal to $1/3$ tablespoon (approx. 5 ml). Abbr.: **tsp.** ▢ **teaspoonful** *n.* (*pl.* **-fuls**).

teat /tiːt, tɪt/ *n.* a mammary nipple, esp. of an animal.

tea time *n.* the time in the afternoon when tea is served.

tea towel *n.* a thin linen or cotton towel for drying washed dishes etc.

tech *informal* ● *n.* **1** (esp. in phr. **high-tech**) technology. **2** a technician. **3** a technical college or school. ● *adj.* technical. ▢ **techy** *adj.*

techie *n.* (*pl.* **-ies**) *informal* an expert in or enthusiast for technology, esp. computers.

technetium /tekˈniːʃiəm, -ʃəm/ *n.* an artificially produced radioactive metallic element.

technic /ˈteknɪk/ *n.* **1** (usu. in *pl.*) **a** technology. **b** technical terms, details, methods, etc. **2** /tekˈniːk/ technique.

technical *adj.* **1** of or involving or concerned with the mechanical arts and applied sciences (*a technical

school*). **2** of or relating to a particular subject or craft etc. (*technical terms*). **3** (of a book or discourse etc.) requiring special knowledge to be understood. **4** due to mechanical failure (*technical difficulties*). **5** legally such; such in strict interpretation (*technical assault*). **6** of or relating to the technique of an art form, esp. as contrasted to the emotional, lyrical etc. aspects. **7** of or relating to technological equipment.

technicality *n.* (*pl.* **-ies**) **1** the state of being technical. **2** a technical expression. **3** a technical point or detail (*was acquitted on a technicality*).

technical knockout *n. Boxing* a termination of a fight by the referee on the grounds of a contestant's inability to continue, the opponent being declared the winner. Abbr.: **TKO.**

technically *adv.* **1** with reference to the technique displayed. **2** according to the facts of a case, the exact meaning of words, etc.; strictly.

technician *n.* **1** a person employed to look after technical equipment and do practical work in a laboratory etc. **2** an expert in the practical application of a science. **3** a person skilled in the technique of an art or craft.

Technicolor /ˈteknɪˌkʌlər/ *n.* (often *attrib.*) **1** *proprietary* a process of colour cinematography using synchronized monochrome films, each of a different colour, to produce a colour print. **2** (usu. **technicolor** or **technicolour**) *informal* **a** vivid colour. **b** artificial brilliance. ▢ **technicolored** *adj.*

technique *n.* **1 a** a manner of esp. artistic execution or performance in relation to mechanical or formal details. **b** skill or ability in this area. **2** a means or method of doing or achieving something.

techno ● *n.* a style of popular dance music making extensive use of electronic instruments and synthesized sound (also in *comb.*: *techno-rock*). ● *adj.* of, pertaining to, or characterized by technology; technologically advanced (*techno trends*).

techno- *comb. form* relating to or using technology.

technobabble *n. informal* incomprehensible technical jargon.

technocracy /tekˈnɒkrəsi/ *n.* (*pl.* **-ies**) **1** the government or control of society or industry by technical experts. **2** an instance or application of this.

technocrat /ˈteknəˌkræt/ *n.* an exponent or advocate of technocracy. ▢ **technocratic** *adj.*

technology *n.* (*pl.* **-ies**) **1** the study or use of the mechanical arts and applied sciences. **2** the application of this to practical tasks in industry. **3** a tool etc. used for this. ▢ **technological** *adj.* **technologically** *adv.* **technologist** *n.* **technologize** *v.tr.*

technology transfer *n.* the transfer of new technology or advanced technological information from developed to underdeveloped countries.

technophile /ˈteknəfaɪl/ ● *n.* an enthusiast about new technology. ● *adj.* **1** of or relating to a technophile. **2** compatible with new technology. ▢ **technophilia** /-ˈfɪliə/ *n.* **technophilic** *adj.*

technophobe /ˈteknəfoːb/ *n.* a person who fears, dislikes, or avoids new technology. ▢ **technophobia** *n.* **technophobic** *adj.*

tectonic /tekˈtɒnɪk/ *adj.* relating to the deformation of the earth's crust or to the structural changes caused by this. ▢ **tectonically** *adv.*

tectonics *n.pl.* (usu. treated as *sing.*) *Geol.* the study of large-scale structural features (*plate tectonics*).

teddy *n.* (*pl.* **-ies**) **1** (in full **teddy bear**) a soft toy bear. **2** a woman's undergarment combining camisole and panties.

tedious *adj.* tiresomely long or boring. □ **tediously** *adv.* **tediousness** *n.*

tedium *n.* the state of being tedious; boredom.

tee¹ *n.* = T¹.

tee² ● *n.* **1 a** a cleared space from which a golf ball is struck at the beginning of play for each hole. **b** a small support of wood or plastic from which a ball is struck at a tee. **2** a mark aimed at in curling etc. **3** *Football* a stand on which the ball is placed for a kickoff. ● *v.tr.* (**tees, teed**) (often foll. by *up*) place (a ball) on a tee ready to strike it. □ **tee off 1** play a ball from a tee. **2** *informal* start, begin. **3** *informal* make angry; annoy.

tee-hee ● *n.* **1** a titter. **2** a restrained or contemptuous laugh. ● *v.intr.* (**-hees, -heed**) titter or laugh in this way.

teem¹ *v.intr.* **1** be abundant (*fish teem in these waters*). **2** (foll. by *with*) be full of or swarming with (*teeming with ideas*). □ **teeming** *adj.*

teem² *v.intr.* (of water etc.) flow copiously; pour (*it was teeming with rain*).

teen ● *adj.* = TEENAGE. ● *n.* = TEENAGER.

teenage *adj.* relating to or characteristic of teenagers. □ **teenaged** *adj.*

teenager *n.* a person from 13 to 19 years of age.

teens *n.pl.* the years of one's life, the years of a century, or the units of a scale of temperature from 13 to 19.

teeny *adj.* (**-ier, -iest**) (also **teensy**) *informal* tiny.

teenybopper *n.* *informal* a young teenager, usu. a girl, who keenly follows the latest fashions in clothes, pop music, etc.

teeny-weeny *adj.* (also **teensy-weensy**) very tiny.

teepee *n.* a conical tent used by Plains Aboriginal peoples, made of skins, cloth, etc. on a frame of poles.

teepee ring *n.* a circle of stones used to anchor the covering of a teepee.

tee-shirt *var. of* T-SHIRT.

teeter *v.intr.* **1** totter; stand or move unsteadily. **2** hesitate; be indecisive. □ **teeter on the brink** (or **edge**) be in imminent danger (of disaster etc.).

teeter-totter *n.* *N Amer.* = SEE-SAW.

teeth *pl. of* TOOTH.

teethe /tiːð/ *v.intr.* grow baby teeth. □ **teething** *n.*

teetotal /tiːˈtoːtəl/ ● *adj.* advocating or characterized by total abstinence from alcoholic drink. ● *v.intr.* (**teetotalled, teetotalling**) practise or advocate teetotalism. □ **teetotaller** *n.* **teetotalism** *n.*

tefillin /təˈfɪlɪn/ *n.pl.* Jewish phylacteries.

TEFL /ˈtefəl/ *abbr.* teaching of English as a foreign language.

Teflon /ˈteflɒn/ *n.* **1** *proprietary* polytetrafluoroethylene, esp. used as a non-stick coating for kitchen utensils. **2** (*attrib.*) (of a politician etc.) having an undamaged reputation, in spite of scandal or misjudgment; able to deflect criticism on to others.

te-hee *var. of* TEE-HEE.

Tejano /təˈhænoː/ *n.* (*pl.* **-os**) a native or inhabitant of Texas who is of Mexican origin or ancestry (often *attrib.*: *Tejano music*).

tekkie *var. of* TECHIE.

tel. *abbr.* (also **Tel.**) telephone.

telco /ˈtelkoː/ *n.* (*pl.* **-os**) esp. *US* a telecommunications company.

telebanking *n.* a method of banking in which the customer conducts transactions by telephone, esp. by means of a computerized system using touch-tone dialling or voice-recognition technology.

telecast ● *n.* a television broadcast. ● *v.tr.* transmit by television. □ **telecaster** *n.*

telecine /ˈteləˌsɪni/ *n.* **1** the broadcasting of cinema film on television. **2** equipment for doing this.

telecom *n.* (*attrib.*) telecommunications.

telecommunication *n.* **1** communication over a distance by telephone, radio, television, etc. **2** (usu. in *pl.*) the branch of technology concerned with this.

telecommute *v.intr.* work from home, communicating by modem, telephone, fax, etc. □ **telecommuter** *n.* **telecommuting** *n.*

teleconference *n.* a conference with participants in different locations linked by telecommunication devices. □ **teleconferencing** *n.*

telefilm *n.* = TELECINE.

telegenic /ˌteləˈdʒenɪk/ *adj.* having an appearance or manner that looks pleasing on television.

telegram *n.* a message sent by telegraph and then usu. delivered in written or printed form.

telegraph ● *n.* **1** a system of or device for transmitting messages or signals to a distant place esp. by making and breaking an electrical connection. **2** (*attrib.*) used in this system (*telegraph wire*). ● *v.* **1** *tr.* send a message by telegraph to. **2** *tr.* send by telegraph. **3** *tr.* give an advance indication of. **4** *intr.* make signals (*telegraphed to me to come up*). □ **telegrapher** /ˈteləˌgræfər, tɪˈlegrəfər/ *n.*

telegraphic *adj.* **1** of or by telegraphs or telegrams. **2** economically worded. □ **telegraphically** *adv.*

telegraphy /tɪˈlegrəfi/ *n.* the science or practice of using or constructing telegraphs.

telekinesis /ˌteləkɪˈniːsɪs/ *n.* *Psych.* movement of objects at a distance supposedly by paranormal means. □ **telekinetic** /-ˈnetɪk/ *adj.*

telemark *Skiing* ● *n.* a swing turn with one ski advanced and the knee bent, used to change direction or stop short. ● *v.intr.* perform this turn.

telemarketing *n.* the marketing of goods etc. by means of usu. unsolicited telephone calls. □ **telemarketer** *n.*

telemedicine *n.* the practice of remote medical diagnosis and treatment of patients by means of the transmission of information by telecommunications.

telemeter /ˈteləˌmiːtər, təˈlemɪtər/ ● *n.* an apparatus for recording the readings of an instrument and transmitting them by radio. ● *v.* **1** *intr.* record readings in this way. **2** *tr.* transmit (readings etc.) to a distant receiving set or station. □ **telemetric** /-ˈmetrɪk/ *adj.* **telemetry** /tɪˈlemətri/ *n.*

teleology /ˌteliˈɒlədʒi, ˌtiː-/ *n.* (*pl.* **-ies**) *Philos.* **1** the explanation of phenomena by the purpose they serve rather than by postulated causes. **2** (in Christian theology) the doctrine of design and purpose in the material world. □ **teleologic** *adj.* **teleological** *adj.*

telepath /ˈteləˌpæθ/ *n.* a telepathic person.

telepathy /təˈlepəθi/ *n.* the supposed communication or perception of thoughts or ideas by extrasensory means. □ **telepathic** /ˌteləˈpæθɪk/ *adj.* **telepathically** *adv.*

telephone ● *n.* **1** an apparatus for transmitting sound (esp. speech) over a distance, esp. by converting acoustic vibrations to electrical signals. **2** a transmitting and receiving instrument used in this. **3** a system of communication using a network of telephones. ● *v.tr. & intr.* = PHONE. □ **on** (or **over**) **the telephone** by use of or using the telephone. □ **telephoner** *n.* **telephonic** *adj.* **telephonically** *adv.*

telephone book *n.* (also **telephone directory**) a book listing telephone subscribers and numbers.

telephone booth *n.* a public booth or enclosure from which telephone calls can be made.

telephone number *n.* a number assigned to a particular phone, used in connecting to it.

telephone pole *n.* a pole supporting phone wires.

telephone tag *n.* a situation in which two people try repeatedly to return each other's telephone calls but fail to make contact.

telephony /tɪˈlefəni/ *n.* the use or a system of telephones.

telephoto ● *n.* (*pl.* **-os**) (in full **telephoto lens**) a lens with a longer focal length than standard, giving a narrow field of view and a magnified image. ● *adj.* of or using such a lens (*a telephoto shot*).

teleport *v.tr. Psych.* move by telekinesis. □ **teleportation** *n.*

telepresence *n.* **1** the use of virtual reality technology esp. for remote control of machinery or for apparent participation in distant events. **2** a sensation of being elsewhere created in this way.

teleprinter *n.* a device for transmitting telegraph messages as they are keyed, and for printing messages received.

teleprompter *n. N Amer.* a device, unseen by the audience, displaying a magnified television script to a speaker or performer.

telesales *n.pl.* selling by means of the telephone.

telescope ● *n.* **1** an optical instrument using lenses or mirrors or both to make distant objects appear nearer and larger. **2** = RADIO TELESCOPE. ● *v.* **1** *tr.* press or drive (sections of a tube, colliding vehicles, etc.) together so that one slides into another like the sections of a folding telescope. **2** *intr.* close or be driven or be capable of closing in this way. **3** *tr.* compress so as to occupy less space or time.

telescopic /ˌteləˈskɒpɪk/ *adj.* **1 a** of, relating to, or made with a telescope. **b** visible only through a telescope (*telescopic stars*). **2** (esp. of a lens) able to focus on and magnify distant objects. **3** consisting of sections that telescope. □ **telescopically** *adv.*

teletext *n.* a news and information service, in the form of text and graphics, from a computer source transmitted to televisions with appropriate receivers.

teletheatre *n. N Amer.* an off-track betting facility where horse races are shown on television.

telethon /ˈteləˌθɒn/ *n.* an exceptionally long television program, esp. one featuring live performers, broadcast to raise money for a charity.

Teletype ● *n. proprietary* a kind of teleprinter. ● *v.* (**teletype**) **1** *intr.* operate a teleprinter. **2** *tr.* send by means of a teleprinter.

teletypewriter *n.* esp. *US* = TELEPRINTER.

televangelist /teləˈvændʒəlɪst/ *n.* esp. *N Amer.* an evangelical preacher who appears regularly on television. □ **televangelism** *n.*

televise *v.tr.* transmit by television.

television *n.* **1** a system for reproducing on a screen visual images converted (usu. with sound) into electrical signals and transmitted esp. by radio waves. **2** (in full **television set**) a device with a screen for receiving these signals. **3** the medium, art form, or occupation of broadcasting on television. **4** the programs broadcast on television (*watched television*).

televisual *adj.* relating to or suitable for television. □ **televisually** *adv.*

telework *v.intr.* = TELECOMMUTE. □ **teleworker** *n.* **teleworking** *n.*

telex (also **Telex**) ● *n.* **1** an international system of telegraphy with printed messages transmitted and received by teleprinters using the public telecommunications network. **2** a message sent this way. ● *v.tr.* send or communicate with by telex.

tell¹ *v.* (*past* and *past part.* **told**) **1** *tr.* relate or narrate in speech or writing; give an account of (*tell me a story*). **2** *tr.* make known; express in words; divulge (*tell me your name*). **3** *tr.* reveal or signify to (a person) (*your face tells me everything*). **4** *tr.* **a** utter (*don't tell lies*). **b** warn (*I told you so*). **5** *intr.* **a** (often foll. by *of, about*) divulge information or a description; reveal a secret (*promise you won't tell*). **b** (foll. by *on*) *informal* inform against (a person). **6** *tr.* (foll. by *to* + infin.) give (a person) a direction or order (*tell them to wait*). **7** *tr.* assure (*it's true, I tell you*). **8** *tr.* explain in writing; instruct (*this book tells you how to cook*). **9** *tr.* decide, determine, distinguish (*cannot tell which button to press*). **10** *intr.* **a** (often foll. by *on*) produce a noticeable effect (*the strain was beginning to tell on me*). **b** reveal the truth (*time will tell*). **c** have an influence (*the evidence tells against you*). **11** *tr.* count (votes) at a meeting, election, etc. □ **as far as one can tell** judging from the available information. **tell apart** distinguish between (usu. with *neg.* or *interrog.*: *could not tell them apart*). **tell it like it is** *informal* relate the facts of a matter realistically or honestly, holding nothing back. **tell me another** *informal* an expression of incredulity. **tell off 1** *informal* reprimand, scold. **2** count off or detach for duty. **tell on** tattle on; reveal a person's activities, esp. to a person in authority. **tell a tale** be significant or revealing. **tell tales** report a discreditable fact about another. **tell (the) time** determine the time from the face of a clock or watch. **there is no telling** it is impossible to know. **you're telling me** *informal* I agree wholeheartedly. □ **tellable** *adj.*

tell² *n. Archaeology* an artificial mound in the Middle East etc. formed by the accumulated remains of ancient settlements.

tell-all *adj.* designating books etc. in which a person reveals the esp. most sordid details of their life.

teller *n.* **1** a person employed to receive and pay out money in a bank etc. **2** a person who tells esp. stories (*a teller of tales*). **3** a person who counts (votes).

telling *adj.* **1** having a marked effect; striking. **2** significant. □ **tellingly** *adv.*

telltale *adj.* that reveals or betrays (*a telltale smile*).

tellurium /teˈlʊəriəm/ *n.* a rare brittle lustrous silver-white element occurring naturally in ores of gold and silver, used in semiconductors.

telnet /ˈtelnet/ ● *n.* **1** a network protocol that allows a user on one computer to log in to another computer that is part of the same network. **2** a program that establishes a connection from one computer to another by means of such a protocol. **3** a link thus established. ● *v.intr.* log in or connect to a remote computer using a telnet program.

temerity /təˈmerɪti/ *n.* **1** rashness. **2** audacity.

temp. *abbr.* temperature.

temp *informal* ● *n.* **1** a temporary employee, esp. a secretary. **2** a temperature. ● *v.intr.* work as a temp.

tempeh /ˈtempə/ *n.* a fermented soybean product, usu. eaten fried.

temper ● *n.* **1** habitual or temporary disposition of mind esp. as regards composure. **2** irritation or anger (*in a fit of temper*). **3** a tendency to have fits of anger (*have a temper*). **4** composure or calmness (*lose one's temper*). **5** the condition of metal as regards hardness and elasticity. ● *v.tr.* **1** bring (metal or clay) to a proper hardness or consistency. **2** (foll. by *with*) moderate or mitigate (*temper justice with mercy*). **3** tune or modulate (a piano etc.) so as to distance intervals correctly. □ **tempered** *adj.*

tempera /'tempərə/ *n.* **1** a method of painting using an emulsion of powdered pigment typically held together with egg yolk and water. **2** this emulsion.

temperament /'tempərəmənt, -pərmənt/ *n.* **1** a person's distinct nature and character, esp. as permanently affecting behaviour; natural disposition, personality (*a nervous temperament*). **2** a creative or spirited personality (*was full of temperament*). **3** an adjustment of intervals in tuning a piano etc. so as to fit the scale for use in all keys, esp. (**equal temperament**) an adjustment in which the 12 semitones are at equal intervals.

temperamental *adj.* **1** of or having temperament (*a temperamental aversion to hard work*). **2 a** (of a person) liable to erratic or moody behaviour. **b** (of a thing, e.g. a machine) working unpredictably; unreliable. □ **temperamentally** *adv.*

temperance /'temprəns, -pərəns/ *n.* **1** moderation or self-restraint esp. in eating and drinking. **2 a** total or partial abstinence from alcoholic drink. **b** (*attrib.*) advocating or concerned with abstinence.

temperate *adj.* **1** avoiding excess; self-restrained. **2** moderate. **3 a** (of a region or climate) characterized by mild temperatures. **b** (of a plant, tree, etc.) growing in a region characterized by mild temperatures. □ **temperately** *adv.* **temperateness** *n.*

temperate zone *n.* the belt of the earth between the frigid and the torrid zones.

temperature *n.* **1** the degree or intensity of heat of a substance, the air, etc. in relation to others, esp. as shown by a thermometer or perceived by touch etc. **2** *Med.* the degree of internal heat of the body. **3** *informal* a body temperature above the normal (*have a temperature*). □ **take a person's temperature** ascertain a person's body temperature.

-tempered *comb. form* having a specified temper or disposition. □ **-temperedly** *adv.* **-temperedness** *n.*

tempest *n.* **1** a violent windy storm. **2** violent agitation or tumult. □ **tempest in a teapot** *N Amer.* great agitation over a trivial matter.

tempestuous /tem'pestʃʊəs/ *adj.* **1** stormy. **2** (of a person, relationship, etc.) turbulent, violent, passionate. □ **tempestuously** *adv.* **tempestuousness** *n.*

template /'templeit, -plət/ *n.* **1 a** a pattern or gauge, usu. a piece of thin board or metal plate, used as a guide in cutting or drilling metal, stone, wood, etc. **b** a flat card or plastic pattern esp. for cutting cloth for patchwork etc. **2** a timber or plate used to distribute the weight in a wall or under a beam etc. **3** *Computing* a stored pattern for a document or part of a document from which new documents or parts of documents may be made.

temple¹ *n.* **1** a building devoted to the worship of a god or gods or other objects of religious reverence. **2** (**Temple**) *hist.* any of three successive religious buildings of the Jews in Jerusalem. **3** *N Amer.* a synagogue. **4** a place of Christian public worship, esp. a Mormon church. **5** a place in which God is regarded as residing, esp. a Christian's person or body. **6** any large imposing building devoted to a particular interest etc. (*a temple of the arts*).

temple² *n.* **1** the flat part of either side of the head between the forehead and the ear. **2** either of the two side pieces on a pair of glasses extending from the frame toward the ear (*compare* ARM¹ 4e).

tempo *n.* (*pl.* **-os** or **tempi**) **1** *Music* the speed at which music is or should be played, esp. as characteristic

(*waltz tempo*). **2** the rate of motion or activity (*the tempo of the war is quickening*).

temporal¹ *adj.* **1** of worldly as opposed to spiritual affairs; of this life; secular as opposed to ecclesiastical. **2** of or relating to time. □ **temporally** *adv.*

temporal² *adj. Anat.* of the temples of the head.

temporal bone *n.* either of two bones forming part of the side of the skull on each side and enclosing the middle and inner ear.

temporality *n.* (*pl.* **-ies**) temporariness.

temporal lobe *n.* each of the paired lobes of the brain lying beneath the temples, including areas concerned with the understanding of speech.

temporary ● *adj.* lasting or meant to last only for a limited time. ● *n.* (*pl.* **-ies**) a person employed temporarily. □ **temporarily** *adv.* **temporariness** *n.*

temporize /'tempə,raiz/ *v.intr.* **1** avoid committing oneself so as to gain time. **2** comply temporarily with the requirements of the occasion.

temporomandibular /,tempəro:mæn'dibjʊlər/ *adj.* of or pertaining to the hinge joint between the temporal bone and the lower jaw.

temporomandibular joint syndrome *n.* a condition caused by poor alignment of the temporomandibular joint, accompanied by limitation of jaw movement, clicking of the joint, and often headaches in the temples.

tempt *v.tr.* **1** entice or incite (a person) to do a wrong or forbidden thing. **2** allure, attract. **3** risk provoking (esp. an abstract force or power) (*would be tempting fate to try it*). □ **be tempted to** be strongly disposed to (*I am tempted to go*). □ **temptable** *adj.*

temptation *n.* **1 a** the act or an instance of tempting; the state of being tempted; incitement esp. to wrongdoing. **b** (**the Temptation**) the tempting of Christ by the Devil. **2** an attractive or tempting thing.

tempter *n.* **1** a person who tempts. **2** (**the Tempter**) the Devil.

tempting *adj.* **1** attractive, inviting. **2** enticing to evil, wrongdoing, etc. □ **temptingly** *adv.*

temptress *n.* a woman who tempts.

tempura /'tempʊrə/ *n.* (in Japanese cuisine) fish, shellfish, or vegetables, fried in batter.

ten ● *n.* **1** one more than nine. **2** a symbol for this (10, x, X). **3** a size etc. denoted by ten. **4** ten o'clock. **5** a card with ten pips. **6** a set of ten. **7** a ten-dollar bill etc. **8** (in *pl.*) the digit second from the right of a whole number in decimal notation, representing a multiple of ten less than a hundred (*numbered in the tens of thousands*). ● *adj.* **1** that amount to ten. **2** (as a round number) several (*ten times as easy*).

tenable /'tenəbəl/ *adj.* **1** that can be maintained or defended against attack or objection (*a tenable position; a tenable theory*). **2** (foll. by *for, by*) (of an office etc.) that can be held for (a specified period) or by (a specified class of person).

tenacious /tə'neiʃəs/ *adj.* **1** holding fast. **2** persistent, stubborn. **3** strongly cohesive. **4** adhesive, sticky. **5** (of memory) retentive. **6** (often foll. by *of*) keeping a firm hold of property, principles, life, etc. □ **tenaciously** *adv.* **tenacity** /tə'næsiti/ *n.*

tenancy *n.* (*pl.* **-ies**) **1** the status of a tenant; possession as a tenant. **2** the duration or period of this. **3** occupation of any position, condition, etc.

tenant ● *n.* **1** a person, business, etc. who rents a residence, premises, etc. from the owner. **2** (often foll. by *of*) the occupant of a place. **3** *Law* a person holding real property by private ownership. ● *v.tr.* occupy as a tenant.

tenant farmer *n.* a person who farms rented land.

Ten Commandments *n.pl.* (usu. prec. by *the*) *Bible* the divine rules of conduct given by God to Moses.

tend[1] *v.intr.* **1 a** (usu. foll. by *to*) be apt or inclined. **b** (usu. foll. by *toward*) suggest or exhibit a tendency towards (a quality etc.). **2** (foll. by *to*) lead (to). **3** be moving; be directed (*tends to the same conclusion*).

tend[2] *v.* **1** *tr.* take care of, look after, be responsible for. **2** *intr.* (foll. by *to*) esp. *N Amer.* give attention to.

tendency *n.* (*pl.* **-ies**) **1** (often foll. by *to*, *toward*) a leaning or inclination; a way in which a person or thing is likely to behave. **2** a group within a larger political party or movement. **3** a direction in which something moves or changes.

tendentious /tenˈdenʃəs/ *adj.* derogatory (of writing etc.) calculated to promote a particular cause or viewpoint; having an underlying purpose. □ **tendentiously** *adv.* **tendentiousness** *n.*

tender[1] *adj.* (**tenderer, tenderest**) **1** easily cut or chewed, not tough (*tender steak*). **2** easily touched or wounded, susceptible to pain or grief (*a tender heart*). **3** easily hurt, sensitive (*tender skin*). **4** delicate, fragile (*a tender reputation*). **5** loving, affectionate, fond (*wrote tender verses*). **6** requiring tact or careful handling, ticklish (*a tender subject*). **7** (of age) early, immature (*of tender years*). □ **tenderly** *adv.* **tenderness** *n.*

tender[2] ● *v.* **1** *tr.* **a** offer, present (one's services, apologies, resignation, etc.). **b** offer (money etc.) as payment. **2** *intr.* (often foll. by *for*) make a tender for the supply of a thing or the execution of work. **3** *tr.* invite bids for (a contract). ● *n.* **1** an offer, esp. an offer in writing to execute work or supply goods at a fixed price. **2** the auctioning of an item of value, e.g. a contract, to bidders. **3** money or other commodities that may be legally tendered or offered in payment (*see* LEGAL TENDER). □ **put out to tender** seek tenders with respect to (work etc.). □ **tenderer** *n.*

tender[3] *n.* **1** a person who looks after people or things. **2** a ship attending a larger one to supply stores, convey passengers or orders, etc. **3** a special railway car closely coupled to a steam locomotive to carry fuel, water, etc.

tenderfoot *n.* (*pl.* **-s** or **-feet**) a newcomer or novice, esp. in the bush or in the Scouts or Guides.

tender-hearted *adj.* having a tender heart, easily moved by pity etc. □ **tender-heartedness** *n.*

tenderize *v.tr.* make tender, esp. make (meat) tender by pounding, marinating, etc. □ **tenderizer** *n.*

tenderloin *n.* **1** a tender cut of meat from the inside of a loin of beef or pork. **2** *N Amer. slang* a district of a city where vice and corruption are prominent.

tendon *n.* **1** a cord or strand of strong fibrous tissue attaching a muscle to a bone etc. **2** (in a quadruped) = HAMSTRING *n.* 2. □ **tendinitis** /tendəˈnaɪtɪs/ *n.* (also **tendonitis**). **tendinous** /-dənəs/ *adj.*

tendril *n.* **1** each of the slender leafless shoots, often growing in a spiral form, by which some climbing plants cling for support. **2 a** a slender curl, e.g. of hair. **b** something which entwines itself pervasively or clings like a plant tendril (*tendrils of smoke*).

tenement *n.* **1** a building with apartments or rooms rented cheaply, esp. in a poor area of a city. **2** a dwelling place. **3 a** a piece of land held by an owner. **b** *Law* any kind of permanent property, e.g. lands or buildings, held from a superior.

tenet /ˈtenət/ *n.* a doctrine, dogma, or principle held by a group or person.

tenfold *adj.* & *adv.* **1** ten times as much or as many. **2** consisting of ten parts.

ten-four *interj.* your message has been received and understood (used in radio communication etc.).

10-gallon hat *n.* = COWBOY HAT.

Tenn. *abbr.* Tennessee.

tenner *n. informal* a ten-dollar bill or ten-pound note.

Tennessean /ˌtenəˈsiːən/ *n.* a native or inhabitant of the US state of Tennessee.

tennis *n.* either of two games in which two or four players strike a ball with racquets over a net stretched across a court (also *attrib.*: *tennis court*; *tennis racquet*).

tennis ball *n.* a ball used in playing tennis, esp. a hollow rubber ball with a felt or felt-like covering used in lawn tennis.

tennis elbow *n.* a painful inflammation of the tendons in the elbow caused by playing tennis or engaging in other activities involving repetitious movement of the elbow joint.

tennis shoe *n.* **1** a light canvas or leather soft-soled shoe used in tennis. **2** esp. *US* a running shoe.

tenon /ˈtenən/ ● *n.* a projecting piece of wood made for insertion into a corresponding cavity (esp. a mortise) in another piece. ● *v.tr.* **1** cut as a tenon. **2** join by means of a tenon.

tenor *n.* **1 a** a singing voice between baritone and alto, the highest of the ordinary adult male range. **b** a singer with this voice. **c** a part written for it. **2** an instrument, esp. a saxophone or viola, of which the range is roughly that of a tenor voice. **3** (usu. foll. by *of*) the general purport or drift of a document etc. **4** (usu. foll. by *of*) a settled or prevailing course or direction, esp. the course of a person's life or habits. **5** *Law* the actual wording of a document.

tenorman *n.* (*pl.* **-men**) a person who plays tenor saxophone.

tenpin *n.* **1** a pin used in 10-pin bowling. **2** (often in *pl.*) *N Amer.* = 10-PIN BOWLING. □ **tenpinner** *n.*

10-pin bowling *n.* a variety of bowling in which players have two chances to knock down sets of ten pins using a large hard rubber ball.

tense[1] ● *adj.* **1** stretched tight, strained (*tense muscles*). **2** in a state of, causing, or characterized by nervous strain or tension (*tense nerves*; *a tense moment*). ● *v.tr.* & *intr.* make or become tense. □ **tense up** become tense. □ **tensely** *adv.* **tenseness** *n.*

tense[2] *n.* *Grammar* **1** a form taken by a verb to indicate the time (also the continuance or completeness) of the action etc. (*present tense*; *imperfect tense*). **2** a set of such forms for the various persons and numbers.

tensile /ˈtensail, -səl/ *adj.* **1** of or relating to tension. **2** capable of being drawn out or stretched.

tensile strength *n.* resistance to breaking under tension.

tension ● *n.* **1** the act or an instance of stretching; the state of being stretched. **2** mental strain or excitement. **3** a strained (political, social, etc.) state or relationship. **4** *Mech.* the strained condition resulting from forces acting in opposite directions away from each other. **5** electromagnetic force. ● *v.tr.* subject to tension. □ **tensional** *adj.*

tensioner *n.* a device for applying tension to a seat belt, cable, pipeline, etc.

tensor *n.* **1** a muscle that tightens or stretches a part of the body. **2** *Math.* a generalized form of vector involving an arbitrary number of indices.

Tensor bandage *n.* *Cdn proprietary* a wide elasticized bandage used to provide support to injured joints.

ten-spot *n.* *informal* **1** a ten-dollar bill or ten-pound note. **2** a playing card with ten pips.

tent ● *n.* **1** a portable shelter or dwelling of canvas, cloth, etc., supported by a pole or poles and stretched by cords or loops attached to pegs driven into the ground. **2** (*attrib.*) composed of or occurring in or under a tent or tents. **3** *Med.* = OXYGEN TENT. ● *v.* **1** *tr.* **a** cover with or as with a tent. **b** cover (a dish) with a tent-like lid of foil etc. **2** *intr.* **a** encamp in a tent. **b** dwell temporarily. **3** *tr. & intr.* form into a tent-like shape, esp. with sides etc. meeting at a top point or ridge. □ **tented** *adj.* **tenting** *n.* **tent-like** *adj.*

tentacle *n.* **1** a long slender flexible appendage of an (esp. invertebrate) animal, used for feeling, grasping, or moving. **2** a thing used like a tentacle as a feeler etc. **3** *Bot.* a sensitive hair or filament. **4** (usu. in *pl.*) a strong esp. insidious binding force. □ **tentacled** *adj.* (also in *comb.*). **tentacular** *adj.*

tentative ● *adj.* **1** done by way of trial, experimental, provisional. **2** hesitant, not definite (*a tentative suggestion*). ● *n.* an experimental proposal or theory. □ **tentatively** *adv.* **tentativeness** *n.*

tent caterpillar *n.* the gregarious larva of any of several moths of the family Lasiocampidae, esp. of the genus *Malacosoma*, which spins a tent-like web.

tent city *n.* a very large collection of tents, esp. erected in an emergency or in protest.

tenterhook *n.* □ **on tenterhooks** in a state of suspense or mental agitation due to uncertainty.

tenth ● *n.* **1** the position in a sequence corresponding to the number 10 in the sequence 1-10. **2** something occupying this position. **3** one of ten equal parts of a thing. **4** *Music* **a** an interval or chord spanning an octave and a third in the diatonic scale. **b** a note separated from another by this interval. ● *adj.* that is the tenth. ● *adv.* in the tenth place. □ **tenthly** *adv.*

tent peg *n.* (also **tent stake**) any of the pegs to which the cords of a tent are attached.

tent pole *n.* a pole supporting a tent.

tent ring *n.* *Cdn* a ring of stones for holding down a tent, teepee, etc., esp. as indicating a past campsite.

tent trailer *n.* *N Amer.* a trailer consisting of a wheeled frame and a collapsible tent.

tenuous /ˈtɛnjʊəs/ *adj.* **1** slight, of little substance; insignificant, meagre (*tenuous connection*). **2** (of a distinction etc.) oversubtle. **3** thin, slender, small. **4** rarefied. □ **tenuously** *adv.* **tenuousness** *n.*

tenure /ˈtɛnjər/ *n.* **1** a condition, or form of right or title, under which (esp. real) property is held. **2 a** the holding or possession of an office or property. **b** the period of this (*during his tenure of office*). **3** guaranteed permanent employment, esp. as a teacher or lecturer after a probationary period.

tenured *adj.* **1** (of an official position) carrying a guarantee of permanent employment. **2** (of a teacher etc.) having guaranteed tenure of office.

tenure-track *adj.* (also **tenure-stream**) designating an employment structure whereby the holder of a (usu. academic) post is guaranteed consideration of eventual tenure (*tenure-track appointment*).

tepee *var. of* TEEPEE.

tepid /ˈtɛpɪd/ *adj.* **1** slightly warm. **2** unenthusiastic. □ **tepidly** *adv.*

tequila /təˈkiːlə/ *n.* a Mexican spirit made by distilling the fermented sap of an agave.

terbium /ˈtɜːbiəm/ *n.* a silvery metallic element.

tercentenary /ˌtɜːrsɛnˈtɛnəri, -ˈtiːnəri/ ● *n.* (*pl.* **-ies**) **1** a tercentennial. **2** a celebration of this. ● *adj.* of or relating to a tercentenary.

tercentennial /ˌtɜːrsɛnˈtɛniəl/ ● *n.* a three-hundredth anniversary. ● *adj.* **1** lasting three hundred years or occurring every three hundred years. **2** of or concerning a tercentennial.

teriyaki /ˌtɛriˈjæki, -ˈjɒki/ *n.* **1** (in Japanese cuisine) fish or meat marinated in soy sauce etc. and grilled. **2** this sauce.

term ● *n.* **1** a word used to express a definite concept, esp. in a particular branch of study etc. **2** (in *pl.*) mode of expression (*answered in no uncertain terms*). **3** (in *pl.*) a relation or footing (*we are on familiar terms*). **4** (in *pl.*) **a** conditions or stipulations (*do it on your own terms*). **b** financial charges (*my terms are very reasonable*). **5 a** a limited period of some state or activity (*for a term of five years*). **b** a period over which operations are conducted or results contemplated (*in the short term*). **c** a period of some weeks, alternating with holiday or vacation, during which instruction is given in a school etc. or during which a law court holds sessions. **d** a period of imprisonment. **e** a period of tenure. **6** *Logic* a word or words that may be the subject or predicate of a proposition. **7** *Math.* **a** each of the two quantities in a ratio. **b** each quantity in a series. **c** a part of an expression joined to the rest by + or −, e.g. *a*, *b*, *c* in $a + b - c$. **8** the completion of a normal length of pregnancy. **9** an appointed day, esp. for payment of money due. **10** (*attrib.*) designating a life insurance policy which provides a payment on death within a specified period, and which has no value once this term has expired. ● *v. tr.* denominate, call; assign a term to (*the music termed classical*). □ **bring to terms** cause to accept conditions. **come to terms** agree on conditions; come to an agreement. **come to terms with 1** reconcile oneself to (a difficulty etc.). **2** conclude an agreement with. **in terms of 1** in the language peculiar to, using as a basis of expression or thought. **2** as regards, with reference to. **make terms** conclude an agreement. **be on good** (or **friendly** etc.) **terms with** have a good relationship with. □ **termer** *n.* (esp. in *comb.*).

term deposit *n.* *Cdn* an amount of money, usu. between $1,000 and $5,000, deposited with a financial institution for a fixed term, usu. between 30 days and a year, at a fixed interest rate, which can be withdrawn before term on payment of a penalty.

terminal ● *adj.* **1 a** (of a disease) ending in death, fatal. **b** (of a patient) in the last stage of a fatal disease. **c** (of a morbid condition) forming the last stage of a fatal disease. **d** *informal* very great; irreparable (*terminal laziness*). **2** of or forming a limit or terminus (*terminal station*). **3 a** *Zool. etc.* ending a series (*terminal joints*). **b** *Bot.* borne at the end of a stem etc. ● *n.* **1** a terminating thing; an extremity. **2** a terminus for trains or long-distance buses. **3** a departure and arrival building for air passengers at an airport. **4** a point of connection for closing an electric circuit. **5** a device for entering data in to a computer or receiving its output, esp. one that can be used by a person as a means of two-way communication with a computer, e.g. a keyboard and monitor. **6** an installation where grain, oil, etc. is stored at the end of a rail line or pipeline, or at a port. □ **terminally** *adv.*

terminal elevator *n.* a large grain elevator to which grain is shipped from country elevators for storing before onward shipment, usu. by water.

terminate *v.* **1** *tr. & intr.* bring or come to an end. **2** *tr.* end (a pregnancy) by artificial means before the fetus is viable. **3** *tr.* bound, limit. **4** *tr.* fire (an employee). □ **terminator** *n.*

termination *n.* **1** the act or an instance of terminating; the state of being terminated. **2** *Med.* an induced abortion. **3** an ending or result of a specified kind (*a happy termination*). **4** dismissal from employment. **5**

the point or part in which something ends. □ **bring to a termination** make an end of.

terminology n. (pl. **-ies**) **1** the system of terms used in a particular subject. **2** the science of the proper use of terms. □ **terminological** adj. **terminologically** adv. **terminologist** n.

terminus /'tɜːmɪnəs/ n. (pl. **termini** /-naɪ/ or **terminuses**) **1 a** the end of a railway, bus route, etc. **b** a station at this point. **2** a point at the end of a pipeline etc. **3** a final point, a goal. **4** Math. the end point of a vector etc.

termite n. a small antlike social insect of the order Isoptera, destructive to timber.

term of endearment n. a pet name or other term used to convey love or fondness.

term paper n. N Amer. an essay or dissertation representative of the work done during a term.

terms of reference n. points referred to an individual or body of persons for decision or report; the scope of an inquiry etc.; a definition of this.

terms of trade n. the ratio between prices paid for imports and those received for exports.

tern n. a bird of the subfamily Sterninae, like a gull but usu. smaller and with a long forked tail, esp. the common tern *Sterna hirundo* or the Arctic tern.

terrace ● n. **1 a** each of a series of flat areas formed on a slope and used for cultivation. **b** a similar levelled top of a natural slope. **2** a level paved area next to a house. **3** the flat roof of a house, esp. in warm climates, where the roof is used as a cool resting area. **4** a row of houses on a raised level or along the top or face of a slope. **5** Geol. a horizontal shelf or bench on a slope leading to a river, sea, etc. ● v.tr. (esp. as **terraced** adj.) form into or provide with a terrace or terraces. □ **terracing** n.

terra cotta ● n. **1 a** unglazed usu. brownish-red earthenware used chiefly as an ornamental building material, in flowerpots etc., and in modelling. **b** a statuette of this. **2** the brownish-red colour of terra cotta. ● adj. of a brownish-red colour.

terraform v.tr. (esp. in science fiction) transform (a planet) so as to resemble the earth.

terrain n. **1** ground, a tract of land, esp. with regard to its physical characteristics or their capacity for use by a military tactician, traveller, etc. **2** a particular area of knowledge; a sphere of influence or action.

terrapin /'terəpɪn/ n. any of various N American edible freshwater turtles of the family Emydidae.

terrarium /tə'reəriəm/ n. (pl. **-s** or **terraria** /-riə/) **1** a vivarium for small land animals. **2** a sealed transparent globe etc. containing growing plants.

terrazzo /te'rætsoː, -'ræzoː/ n. (pl. **-os**) a flooring material of stone chips set in concrete and given a smooth surface.

terrestrial ● adj. **1** of or on or relating to the earth; earthly. **2 a** of or on dry land. **b** Zool. living on or in the ground. **3** Bot. growing in the soil. **3** Astronomy (of a planet) similar in size or composition to the earth. **4** of this world, worldly. ● n. an inhabitant of the earth. □ **terrestrially** adv.

terrible adj. **1** informal **a** dreadful, awful (*the accident was terrible*). **b** very bad (*terrible cigars*; also as an intensifier: *a terrible bore*). **2** informal very incompetent (*terrible at tennis*). **3** (predic.) informal ill (*he ate too much and feels terrible*). **4** (predic.; often foll. by *about*) informal full of remorse (*I feel terrible about it*). **5** causing or fit to cause terror. □ **terribleness** n.

terrible two n. N Amer. informal **1** a two-year-old child regarded as typically troublesome. **2** (in pl.) this age.

terribly adv. **1** informal very, extremely (*terribly nice*). **2** in a terrible manner.

terrier n. **1** any of various breeds of dog originally used for turning out foxes etc. from their earths. **2** an eager or tenacious person or animal.

terrific adj. **1** informal **a** excellent (*did a terrific job*). **b** of great size or intensity. **c** excessive (*a terrific noise*). **2** causing terror. □ **terrifically** adv.

terrify v.tr. (**-ies**, **-ied**) fill with terror; frighten severely. □ **terrifying** adj. **terrifyingly** adv.

terrine /tə'riːn/ n. **1** a kind of pâté, usu. coarse textured. **2** a usu. oval earthenware vessel, esp. one in which pâté is cooked, served, or sold.

territorial adj. **1** of land (*territorial conquests*). **2** limited to a district (*the right was strictly territorial*). **3** (of a person or animal etc.) inclined to claim and become especially defensive of an area. **4** (usu. **Territorial**) of or relating to any of the Territories of Canada or other countries. □ **territoriality** n.

Territorial Court n. Cdn a court established in a Territory by territorial legislation, usu. having both criminal and civil divisions, which conducts hearings by judge alone on relatively minor offences.

territorial waters n.pl. the waters under the jurisdiction of a country, esp. the part of the sea within a stated distance of the shore, traditionally three miles from low-water mark.

territory n. (pl. **-ies**) **1** the extent of the land under the jurisdiction of a ruler, country, city, etc. **2** (**Territory**) **a** (in Canada) a region which has not been admitted as a province and which is governed by a federally-appointed commissioner and an elected legislative assembly. **b** a region administered by the US federal government without the full rights of a state. **c** any similar division of other countries. **3 a** a conceptual subdivision of a subject or area; a sphere or domain. **b** an area of responsibility, knowledge, or concern. **4** the district over which a sales representative or agent operates. **5** Zool. **a** an area defended by an animal or group of animals against others of the same species. **b** the part of a city a person or group of people is associated with. **6** Sport an area of a playing surface, esp. one defended by a team or player. **7** a large tract of land.

terror n. **1** extreme fear or dread. **2 a** a person or thing that causes terror. **b** informal or jocular an exasperating or troublesome person, esp. a child (*the twins are holy terrors*). **c** Sport a dreaded or formidable opponent. **3** the use of organized intimidation; terrorism. **4** (**the Terror**; also **the Reign of Terror**) the period (1793–4) of the French Revolution when the ruling Jacobin faction attempted to eliminate domestic and foreign opposition to the radical Revolution through a series of extreme political, economic, and military reforms.

terrorism n. **1** the systematic employment of violence and intimidation to coerce a government or community, esp. into acceding to specific political demands. **2** an act of terrorizing, esp. continued over an extended period. □ **terrorist** n. **terroristic** adj.

terrorize v.tr. **1** fill with terror. **2** coerce by terror; use terrorism against. **3** bully, harass, persecute.

terry cloth n. N Amer. (also **terry**) an absorbent cotton pile fabric with the loops uncut, used for making towels etc. (also attrib.: *terry-cloth bathrobe*).

terse adj. (**terser**, **tersest**) **1** (of language) brief, concise, to the point. **2** (of a person's manner or speech) brusque, curt, abrupt. □ **tersely** adv. **terseness** n.

tertiary /'tɜːʃəri/ ● adj. **1** third in order or rank etc. **2**

(**Tertiary**) of or relating to the first period in the Cenozoic era, lasting from about 65 to 2 million years ago, during which mammals evolved rapidly. **3** designating the sector of the economy or workforce concerned with services, such as transportation and leisure etc. ● *n.* the Tertiary period.

TESL /ˈtesəl/ *abbr.* teaching of English as a second language.

tesla /ˈteslə/ *n.* the SI unit of magnetic flux density, equal to one weber per square metre or 10,000 gauss.

TESOL /ˈtesɒl/ *abbr.* teaching (or teachers) of English to speakers of other languages.

tessellated /ˈtesə,leitəd/ *adj.* **1** (of a floor etc.) composed of or decorated with small blocks of variously coloured material arranged in a pattern or mosaic. **2** composed or arranged in or as if in a mosaic. **3** *Bot.* & *Zool.* having colours or surface divisions in regularly arranged squares or patches. □ **tessellate** *v.tr.*

tessellation *n.* **1 a** an arrangement of shapes, colours, minute parts, etc., closely fitted together. **b** *Geom.* an arrangement of esp. identical polygons in a pattern without gaps or overlapping. **2** a piece of tessellated work; a mosaic. **3** an act or instance of tessellating; the state of being tessellated.

test ● *n.* **1 a** a critical examination or trial of the qualities, genuineness, or suitability of a person or thing (*carrying out tests*). **b** the method by which such qualities are tested (*we're using a beta test on the new software*). **c** (*attrib.*) designating equipment or materials etc. used in a test (*test facilities*). **2 a** a procedure for assessing a person's aptitude, competence, skill, or intelligence. **b** a set of questions on an academic subject to be answered without assistance (*spelling test*). **3** a procedure performed in order to determine a person's physical or psychological condition (*pregnancy test*). **4** (often foll. by *of*) a situation requiring a person to demonstrate a particular ability or strength (*talking to her is a real test of your patience*). **5** a standard for comparison or trial (*it does not stand up to our test*). **6** *Chem.* **a** a procedure for examining a substance under known conditions or with a specific reagent to determine its identity or the presence or absence of some constituent, activity, etc. **b** a substance by means of which this may be done. **7** (*attrib.*) designating esp. fishing line having a strength or capacity of a specified weight (*20-pound test line*). ● *v.* **1** *tr.* subject (a person or thing) to a close or critical examination; evaluate by experiment. **2** *tr.* (often foll. by *for*) subject (a substance) to a chemical test (*tested his blood for alcohol*). **3** (usu. foll. by *for*) **a** *tr.* & *intr.* apply or carry out a test on a person or thing (*they're testing for HIV*). **b** *tr.* achieve or receive a specific result (*tested positive for banned substances*). **4** *tr.* try the patience or endurance of (a person). □ **put to the test** cause to undergo a test. **stand** (or **withstand**) **the test of time** remain popular after a long period of time. **test out** subject to a practical test; try out. **test whether** perform a test to see; check. □ **testable** *adj.* **testability** *n.* **tested** *adj.* **testing** *n.*

testament *n.* **1** *Bible* **a** (**Testament**) either of the main divisions of the Christian Bible. **b** (**Testament**) a copy of the New Testament. **c** = COVENANT 3. **2** (usu. foll. by *to*) evidence, proof; a tribute (*it is a testament to your loyalty*). **3 a** a will (*last will and testament*). **b** a legacy; something bequeathed.

testate /ˈtesteit/ ● *adj.* having left a valid will at death. ● *n.* a testate person.

testator *n.* a person who has made a will, esp. one who dies testate.

test ban *n.* an agreement among several countries to discontinue the testing of nuclear weapons.

test bed *n.* **1** a testing site. **2** equipment for testing machines before acceptance for general use.

test case *n.* **1** *Law* an action brought to ascertain the law, thereby setting a precedent for other cases involving the same principle. **2** a person, thing, or set of circumstances used to test something.

test drive ● *v.tr.* **1** drive (a car or truck etc.) in order to assess its quality and performance before buying it. **2** run (software) to sample its features and assess its suitability. **3** *informal* sample (a product) prior to purchase. ● *n.* **1** a drive taken to assess the performance of a car or truck etc. one is thinking of buying. **2** an act or instance of trying out any product, such as computer software, prior to purchase.

tester *n.* **1** a device or instrument used to test something (*circuit tester*). **2** a person who conducts a test of esp. a product. **3 a** a small amount of a perfume or cosmetic for a customer to sample before purchase. **b** the bottle from which this is dispensed.

testes *pl.* of TESTIS.

test flight *n.* a flight during which the performance of an aircraft is tested. □ **test-fly** *v.tr.* (**-flies**; *past* **-flew**; *past part.* **-flown**).

testicle *n.* either of the two glandular organs in male humans and other mammals, which contain the sperm-producing cells and are usu. enclosed in the scrotum. □ **testicular** *adj.*

testify *v.* (**-ies**, **-ied**) **1** *Law* **a** *intr.* appear as a witness to give evidence in a court of law. **b** *tr.* (often foll. by *that*) state under oath in a court of law. **2** *tr.* (usu. foll. by *that*) affirm or declare, esp. based on first-hand knowledge or prior experience. **3** *intr.* (often foll. by *to*) bear witness; attest (*I can testify to the quality of her work*). **4** *tr.* & *intr.* (of a thing) serve as proof or evidence of (*his poetry testifies to his torment*). □ **testify against** give testimony that may help to convict (a defendant).

testimonial *n.* **1 a** a written or oral statement attesting to the quality of esp. a product or service and recommending it to others. **b** a certificate of a person's character, conduct, or qualifications. **2** a gift presented to a person, esp. in public, as a mark of esteem, in acknowledgement of services, etc.; a tribute (also *attrib.*: *testimonial dinner*).

testimony *n.* (*pl.* **-ies**) **1** *Law* **a** evidence or the body of evidence presented under oath in a court of law by one or more witnesses. **b** an act of presenting evidence; a statement given under oath. **2** a declaration or statement of fact. **3** (usu. foll. by *to*) evidence, proof; a demonstration (*the pyramids are testimony to the engineering skills of the ancient Egyptians*).

testing ground *n.* a place or situation where something may be tried out to assess its suitability or acceptability before being used, implemented, or adopted on a larger scale.

testis /ˈtestɪs/ *n.* (*pl.* **testes** /-tiːz/) a testicle.

test-market ● *v.tr.* introduce (a new product or service) in a limited region in order to assess consumer response. ● *n.* (usu. **test market**) a limited area that serves as the market for a new product.

testosterone /teˈstɒstə,rəʊn/ *n.* **1** a steroid hormone that stimulates the development of male secondary sexual characteristics, produced in the testicles and, in much smaller quantities, in the ovaries and adrenal cortex. **2** *informal* (also in *comb.*) stereotypical machismo (*testosterone-charged lyrics*).

test pilot *n.* a pilot who test-flies aircraft. □ **test-pilot** *v.tr.*

test spin *n. informal* = TEST DRIVE *n.*

test tube n. **1** a cylindrical vessel of thin transparent glass, having a closed rounded bottom at one end, used in laboratories etc. to hold small amounts of liquid for analysis and experimentation. **2** (attrib., usu. **test-tube**) designating procedures and operations carried out artificially or under laboratory conditions (test-tube fertilization).

test-tube baby n. informal a baby conceived by in vitro fertilization.

testy adj. (**-ier, -iest**) irritable, touchy. □ **testily** adv. **testiness** n.

tetanus /ˈtetnəs, ˈtetənəs/ n. **1** a disease caused by the bacterium Clostridium tetani, marked by rigidity and spasms of the voluntary muscles. **2** the prolonged contraction of a muscle caused by rapidly repeated stimuli.

tetchy adj. (**-ier, -iest**) easily angered or annoyed; peevish, irritable. □ **tetchily** adv. **tetchiness** n.

tête-à-tête /ˌtetæˈtet/ ● n. a conversation between two people. ● adv. **1** together in private (they spoke tête-à-tête). **2** face to face (we were seated tête-à-tête). ● adj. involving or attended by only two people; private.

tether ● n. **1** a rope etc. by which an animal is tied to confine it to the spot. **2** anything that attaches, binds, or confines. ● v.tr. **1** tie or confine with a tether. **2** bind by circumstances or conditions.

tetra /ˈtetrə/ n. (pl. same or **-s**) any of various small, often brightly coloured tropical fish of the family Characidae, frequently kept in aquariums.

tetrachloride /ˌtetrəˈklɔːraɪd/ n. a compound of four atoms of chlorine with some other element or radical.

tetracycline /ˌtetrəˈsaɪklɪn, -liːn/ n. **1** a compound which is a broad spectrum antibiotic. **2** any of several antibiotics structurally related to this compound, used to treat various kinds of infection.

tetrad /ˈtetræd/ n. **1** a group of four. **2** a square block of four 1-km squares within a 10-km square, used as a unit in biological recording.

tetraethyl lead /ˌtetrəˈeθəl/ n. a oily toxic liquid formerly added to gasoline as an anti-knock agent.

Tetragrammaton /ˌtetrəˈɡræmə,tɒn/ n. the Hebrew name of God transliterated in four letters as YHVH or JHVH, often regarded as ineffable and treated as a mysterious symbol of God (compare YAHWEH, JEHOVAH).

tetrahedron /ˌtetrəˈhiːdrən, -ˈhedrən/ n. (pl. **-hedrons** or **-hedra** /-drə/) a solid figure or object with four plane faces, esp. (in full **regular tetrahedron**) one with four equal equilateral triangular faces. □ **tetrahedral** adj.

tetrahydrocannabinol /ˌtetrə,haɪdrəkəˈnæbɪnɒl/ n. see THC.

Tetra Pak n. proprietary a kind of plasticized cardboard carton for packaging milk and other drinks, folded from a single sheet into a box shape, originally tetrahedral, now usu. rectangular.

tetrapod /ˈtetrə,pɒd/ n. **1** an animal with four feet or limbs. **2** a member of the group Tetrapoda, which includes amphibians, reptiles, birds, and mammals.

tetravalent /ˌtetrəˈveɪlənt/ adj. Chem. having a valence of four.

Teuton /ˈtuːtən, ˈtjuː-/ n. a member of a Teutonic nation, esp. a German.

Teutonic /tuːˈtɒnɪk, tjuː-/ adj. **1** German. **2** displaying characteristics stereotypically attributed to Germans.

Tex. abbr. Texas.

Texan ● adj. of or relating to the US state of Texas. ● n. a native or inhabitant of Texas.

Texas gate n. Cdn (West) = CATTLE GUARD.

Texas leaguer n. Baseball a shallow fly ball or pop-up that falls between the infield and outfield.

Texas mickey n. Cdn informal a 130-ounce bottle of rye whisky.

Tex-Mex ● n. **1** a Texan style of cooking characterized by the adaptation of Mexican ingredients and influences, such as tacos, enchiladas, ground beef, etc., with more moderate use of hot flavourings such as chilies. **2** a style of dance music originated by the Tejanos and characterized esp. by the use of accordion. **3** the variety of Mexican Spanish spoken in Texas. ● adj. of or relating to the blend of Texan and Mexican cooking, music, language, or culture, existing or originating in the southwestern US.

text n. **1 a** the wording of something written or printed; the actual words, phrases, and sentences as written. **b** the wording adopted by an editor as the most faithful representation of the author's original work. **2** the main written or printed part of a book as distinct from notes, illustrations, appendices, etc. **3** the original words of an author or document, esp. in the original language, form, and order as opposed to a translation, revision, paraphrase, or commentary. **4** data in textual form, esp. as stored, processed, or displayed in a word processor or text editor. **5 a** a textbook. **b** (in pl.) books prescribed for study. **6** a short passage from the Scriptures, esp. one quoted as illustrative of a belief, doctrine, or moral, or chosen as the subject or starting point for a sermon. **7** a subject or theme.

textbook ● n. a book giving instruction in a particular, esp. academic, subject. ● attrib.adj. typical of a textbook; exemplary, classic (a textbook case).

text file n. Computing a file used to store data in textual form.

textile ● n. **1** any woven fabric. **2** any of various fabrics which do not require weaving. **3** natural or synthetic fibres or yarns suitable for being spun and woven or manufactured into cloth etc. **4** (in pl.) the manufacture or production of woven or unwoven fabrics. ● adj. **1** used in or relating to the production of textiles (textile mill). **2** suitable for weaving (textile materials). **3** woven.

textual adj. **1** of, concerning, or contained in a text (textual errors). **2** based on, following, or conforming to the text of a work (textual analysis). □ **textually** adv.

textual criticism n. the study of the content and message of esp. Biblical writings.

texture ● n. **1 a** the surface of a thing assessed in terms of its roughness, smoothness, softness, etc. by the senses of esp. sight and touch. **b** the feel of food or wine in the mouth (a light creamy texture). **2** a discernible roughness or bumpiness on a surface. **3** the physical or perceived structure and composition of the constituent parts or formative elements of something, such as soil or rock. **4** the representation of the tactile quality and nature of a surface in a photograph, painting, etc. **5** Music the quality of sound created by the combination of the different elements of a work or passage. **6** the quality of a piece of writing, esp. with reference to imagery, alliteration, etc. **7** the character, appearance, or tactile quality of textile fabric as determined by its weave or arrangement of threads. **8** one's life, society, etc. seen in terms of a particular arrangement and assortment of events and individuals etc. ● v.tr. provide with a texture. □ **textural** adj. **texturally** adv.

textured adj. **1** having a discernible texture; not smooth or flat. **2** (in comb.) having a specified kind of texture (*coarse-textured*). **3** having a distinctive or characteristic texture (*textured harmonies*).

textured vegetable protein *n.* spun or extruded vegetable protein, usu. made to simulate the texture, taste, and appearance of meat. Abbr.: **TVP.**

TGIF *abbr. informal* thank God (or goodness) it's Friday.

TGV *n.* a type of high-speed French passenger train.

Th *symbol* thorium.

Th. *abbr.* Thursday.

Thai /taɪ/ ● *n.* (*pl.* same or **Thais**) **1 a** a native or inhabitant of Thailand, a kingdom in SE Asia. **b** a member of the people forming the largest ethnic group in Thailand and also inhabiting neighbouring regions. **2** the language of Thailand. ● *adj.* of or relating to Thailand or its people or language.

thalamus /ˈθæləməs/ *n.* (*pl.* **thalami** /-ˌmaɪ/) either of two masses of grey matter lying between the cerebral hemispheres on either side of the third ventricle, which relay sensory information and act as a centre for pain perception. □ **thalamic** /θəˈlæmɪk, ˈθæləmɪk/ *adj.*

thalassemia /ˌθæləˈsiːmiə/ *n.* (also **thalassaemia**) any of a group of hereditary hemolytic diseases caused by faulty hemoglobin synthesis and widespread in Mediterranean, African, and Asian countries.

thali /ˈtæli/ *n.* **1** a metal platter or flat dish on which Indian food is served. **2** an Indian meal consisting of a selection of assorted dishes, esp. served on such a platter.

thalidomide /θəˈlɪdəˌmaɪd/ *n.* **1** a drug formerly used as a sedative but found in 1961 to cause fetal malformation when taken by a mother early in pregnancy. **2** (*attrib.*) designating a baby or child etc. born with a congenital abnormality due to the effects of thalidomide.

thallium /ˈθæliəm/ *n.* a rare soft white metallic element, occurring naturally.

thallus /ˈθæləs/ *n.* (*pl.* **thalli** /-laɪ/) a plant body, such as in algae, fungi, etc., without vascular tissue and not differentiated into root, stem, and leaves.

than *conj.* **1** introducing the second element in a comparison (*you are older than he is*; *you are older than he*). ¶It is also possible to say *you are older than him*, with *than* treated as a preposition, esp. in less formal contexts. **2** introducing the second element in a statement of difference (*anyone other than me*). **3** (foll. by *to* + infin.) in a statement expressing hypothesis or consequence (*would be better to proceed than to stop*). **4** when (*we had no sooner arrived than it started to rain*).

Thanatos /ˌθəˈnætoːs/ *n.* (in Freudian psychology) the urge for destruction or self-destruction (opp. EROS 2b).

thank ● *v.tr.* **1** express gratitude to (*thanked her for the present*). **2** hold responsible (*you can thank yourself for that*). ● *n.* (in *pl.*) **1** gratitude. ● *interj.* (in *pl.*) (also **thanks a lot**) **1** used as an expression of gratitude; thank you (*thanks for your help*). **2** *ironic* used to express disappointment, anger, etc. at the action of another. □ **give thanks** say grace at a meal. **I will thank you to** *ironic* (implying reproach) I'd rather you would; I would ask you to (*I'll thank you to mind your own business!*). **no thanks to** despite. **thank goodness** (or **God** or **heavens** etc.) **1** *informal* an expression of relief or pleasure. **2** an expression of pious gratitude. **thanks to** as a (good or bad) result of (*thanks to my quick thinking; thanks to your stupid idea*).

thankful *adj.* **1** grateful, appreciative, pleased, relieved. **2** (of words or acts) expressive of thanks. □ **thankfulness** *n.*

thankfully *adv.* **1** in a thankful manner. **2** *disputed* let us be thankful; fortunately (*thankfully, nobody was hurt*). ¶See HOPEFULLY.

thankless *adj.* **1** not expressing or feeling gratitude. **2** (of a task etc.) giving no pleasure or profit; not likely to win or receive thanks. □ **thanklessly** *adv.*

Thanksgiving *n.* **1** *Cdn* **a** (in full **Thanksgiving Day**) an annual holiday, originally for giving thanks to God for the success of the harvest, celebrated on the second Monday in October. **b** (in full **Thanksgiving weekend**) the long weekend ending with Thanksgiving Day. **2** *US* **a** (in full **Thanksgiving Day**) a similar holiday observed annually on the fourth Thursday in November. **b** (in full **Thanksgiving weekend**) the long weekend beginning with Thanksgiving Day and usu. lasting until Sunday. **3** (**thanksgiving**) **a** the expression of thanks or gratitude, esp. to God. **b** a form of words used for this. **4** (**thanksgiving**) a public celebration, marked with religious services, held as an expression of gratitude for divine favour.

thank you ● *interj.* **1** a polite formula acknowledging and expressing gratitude for a gift, service, inquiry into one's health, etc. **2** used to emphasize a preceding statement, esp. one implying refusal or denial (*I said no, thank you*). ● *n. informal* **1** an instance of expressing gratitude or appreciation. **2** (*attrib.*) (usu. **thank-you**) designating a gesture etc. intended as a way of expressing appreciation or gratitude (*thank-you gift*).

that ● *demonstrative pron.* (*pl.* **those**) **1** the person or thing indicated, named, or understood, esp. when observed by the speaker or when familiar to the person addressed (*I heard that; who is that over there?; that's not fair*). **2** (contrasted with *this*) the further or less immediate or obvious etc. of two (*this bag is much heavier than that*). **3** the action, behaviour, or circumstances just observed or mentioned (*don't do that again*). **4** (esp. in relative constructions) the one, the person, etc., described or specified in some way (*those who have cars can take the luggage; a table like that described above*). **5** (*pl.* **that**) used instead of *which* or *whom* to introduce a defining clause, esp. one essential to identification (*the book that you sent me; there is nothing here that matters*). **6** (on the telephone etc.) the person spoken to (*who is that?*). ● *demonstrative adj.* (*pl.* **those**) **1** designating the person or thing indicated, named, understood, etc. (*compare sense 1 of pron.*) (*look at that dog; things were easier in those days*). **2** contrasted with *this* (*compare sense 2 of pron.*) (*this bag is heavier than that one*). **3** expressing strong feeling (*I will not soon forget that day*). ● *adv.* **1** to such a degree; so (*I won't go that far*). **2** *informal* very (*not that good*). **3** at which, on which, etc. (*the day that I first met her*). ● *conj.* introducing a subordinate clause indicating: **1** a statement or hypothesis (*they say that he is better; there is no doubt that he meant it*). **2** a purpose (*we live that we may eat*). **3** a result (*I am so sleepy that I cannot keep my eyes open*). **4** a reason or cause (*is it that she's busy?*). **5** a wish (*Oh, that summer were here!*). □ **all that** very (*I'm not all that tired*). **and all that** (or **and that**) *informal* and all or various things associated with or similar to what has been mentioned. **like that 1** of that kind (*is fond of books like that*). **2** in that manner, as you are doing, as he has been doing, etc. (*wish they would not talk like that*). **3** *informal* without effort (*did the job like that*). **4** of that character (*he's like that about money*). **that is** (or **that is to say**) a formula introducing or following an explanation of a preceding word or words. **that's** *informal* you are (by virtue of present or future obedience etc.) (*that's a good boy*). **that's more like it** an acknowledgement of improvement. **that's right** an expression of approval or assent. **that's that** a formula concluding a narrative or discussion or indicating completion of a task. **that there** *slang* = sense 1 of *adj*. **that will do** no more is needed or desirable.

thataway *adv. esp. N Amer. informal or jocular* **1** (esp. with reference to the route taken by an object of pursuit) in that direction (*he went thataway*). **2** in that manner.

thatch ● *n*. **1 a** a covering for a roof made of straw, reeds, palm leaves, or similar material. **b** the material used to make such a covering. **c** (*attrib.*) designating a hut, cottage, roof, etc. having such a covering. **2 a** a matted layer of plant debris etc. on a lawn. **b** material forming such a layer. **3** *informal* a covering of some material, such as the hair of the head. **4** any of several palms used for thatching, e.g. the palmetto thatch, *Thrinax parviflora*. ● *v.tr.* **1** cover (a roof or a building) with thatch. **2** remove (thatch) from a lawn. □ **thatcher** *n.* **thatching** *n.*

thatched *adj*. **1** made of, covered, or roofed with thatch (*thatched hut*). **2 a** covered with something resembling thatch. **b** arranged in a manner similar to thatch (*thatched hair*).

Thatcherism *n*. the conservative political and economic policies advocated by Margaret Thatcher (b.1925), prime minister of the UK 1979–90. □ **Thatcherite** *n. & adj.*

thaw ● *v*. **1** *intr.* (often foll. by *out*) **a** (of ice, snow, or something that is frozen) pass into a liquid or unfrozen state. **b** (of a person or part of the body) warm up after being very cold. **2** *intr.* (of the weather) become warm enough to melt snow and ice etc. (*it began to thaw*). **3** *tr.* (often foll. by *out*) cause (something frozen or very cold) to melt or warm up; defrost. **4** *tr. & intr.* make or become animated or amicable after a period of hostility or animosity. ● *n*. **1** the act or an instance of thawing. **2** a period of warmer weather marked by the rise of temperature above the freezing point and the melting of snow and ice. **3** *Politics* a reduction in the hostility or formality of relations; an increase in friendliness or cordiality.

THC *abbr.* tetrahydrocannabinol, the active principle of cannabis.

the ● *definite article* **1** denoting one or more people or things already mentioned, under discussion, implied, or familiar. **2** serving to describe as unique (*the Queen*; *the St. Lawrence*). **3 a** (foll. by defining adj.) which is, who are, etc. (*the embarrassed Mr. Smith*; *Edward the Seventh*). **b** (foll. by adj. used *absol.*) denoting a class described (*from the sublime to the ridiculous*). **4** best known or best entitled to the name (with the stressed: *no relation to the Kipling*; *this is the book on this subject*). **5** used to indicate a following defining clause or phrase (*the book that you borrowed*). **6 a** used to indicate that a singular noun represents a species, class, etc. (*is there a future for the novel?*). **b** used with a noun which figuratively represents an occupation, pursuit, etc. (*too fond of the bottle*). **c** (foll. by the name of a unit) a per (*20 km to the litre*). **d** designating a disease, affliction, etc. (*the measles*). **7** (foll. by a unit of time) the present, the past (*book of the month*). ● *adv*. (preceding comparatives in expressions of proportional variation) in or by that (or such a) degree; on that account (*the more he gets the more he wants*). □ **all the** in the full degree to be expected (*that makes it all the worse*). **so much the** (tautologically) so much, in that degree (*so much the worse for him*).

theatre *n*. (also **theater**) **1 a** a building or facility in which plays etc. are performed in front of an audience. **b** a movie theatre. **2 a** forms of entertainment performed in theatres, such as plays, opera, dance, or music. **b** theatrical or dramatic entertainment of a specified quality (*makes good theatre*). **c** in names of theatrical companies (*Toronto Dance Theatre*). **3 a** the writing, production, and performance of plays. **b** the drama of a particular author, period, or place (*Restoration theatre*). **4 a** a place where action takes place in public view; a scene or field of action (*the theatre of war*). **b** (*attrib.*) designating weapons intermediate between tactical and strategic (*theatre missiles*). **5** (in full **operating theatre**) = OPERATING ROOM. **6** a room or hall for lectures etc. with seats in tiers.

theatre-goer *n*. a person who often attends theatres. □ **theatre-going** *n. & adj.*

theatre of the absurd *n*. drama portraying the futility and anguish of human struggle in a senseless and inexplicable world.

theatrical ● *adj*. **1** of or for the theatre; of acting or actors. **2 a** (of a manner, speech, or gesture) calculated for effect; showy, histrionic. **b** (of a person) artificial, affected. ● *n*. **1** (usu. in *pl.*) a dramatic performance (*amateur theatricals*). **2** (in *pl.*) theatrics. □ **theatricality** *n*. **theatrically** *adv.*

theatrics *n.pl.* **1** showy dramatic gestures, exaggerated behaviour and display of emotion; histrionics (*courtroom theatrics*). **2** the art of staging or performing plays.

thee *pron. objective case of* THOU[1].

theft *n*. **1** the act or an instance of stealing. **2** *Law* dishonest appropriation of another's property with intent to deprive him or her of it permanently.

their *possess.adj.* (*attrib.*) **1** of or belonging to them or themselves (*their house*; *their own business*). **2** (**Their**) (in titles) that they are (*Their Majesties*). **3** disputed as a third person sing. indefinite meaning 'his or her' (*has anyone lost their keys?*). ¶See THEY.

theirs *possess.pron.* **1** the one or ones belonging to or associated with them (*it is theirs*; *theirs are over here*). **2** disputed the one or ones belonging to an indefinite singular antecedent (*each of them brought theirs*). □ **of theirs** of or belonging to them (*a friend of theirs*).

theism /ˈθiːɪzəm/ *n*. belief in the existence of gods or a god, esp. one God supernaturally revealed to man (*compare* DEISM), who created and intervenes in the universe. □ **theist** *n*. **theistic** *adj.*

them ● *pron*. **1** objective case of THEY (*I saw them*). **2** *informal* they (*it's them again*). **3** *disputed* him or her; used in relation to a singular noun or pronoun of undetermined gender (*if anyone comes, ask them to wait*). ¶See THEY. ● *adj. slang or dialect* those (*them bones*).

thematic /θiˈmætɪk/ *adj*. **1** of or relating to subjects or topics. **2** *Music* of melodic subjects (*thematic treatment*). □ **thematically** *adv.*

thematize /ˈθiːmətaiz/ *v.tr.* make thematic; present or select as a theme or topic of discourse. □ **thematization** *n.*

theme ● *n*. **1 a** a subject or topic on which a person speaks, writes, or thinks; a topic of discussion etc. **b** a dominant subject or motif in work of art; a topic of composition. **2** a prominent or frequently recurring melody or group of notes in a composition. **3** = THEME SONG 1. ● *v.tr.* (esp. as **themed** *adj.*) design (an event, leisure park, restaurant, etc.) around a theme to unify ambience, decor, etc.

theme park *n*. an amusement park organized around a unifying idea.

theme song n. **1** esp. N Amer. a distinctive tune used to introduce a particular program or performer on TV or radio. **2** a recurrent melody in a musical.

themselves pron. **1 a** emphatic form of THEY or THEM. **b** refl. form of THEM (compare HERSELF). **2** in their normal state of body or mind (are quite themselves again). **3** (also **themself**) disputed (referring back to an indefinite pronoun) himself, herself; himself or herself (everyone kept it to themselves). ¶This use is considered erroneous by some people. See THEY. □ **be themselves** act in their normal, unconstrained manner.

then ● adv. **1** at that time; at the time in question (was then too busy; then comes the trouble). **2 a** next, afterwards; after that (then he told me to come in). **b** and also (then, there are the children). **c** after all (it is a problem, but then that is what we are here for). **3 a** in that case; therefore; it follows that (then you should have said so). **b** if what you say is true (then why did you take it?). **c** (implying grudging or impatient concession) if you must have it so (all right then, have it your own way). **d** used parenthetically to resume a narrative etc. (the policeman, then, knocked on the door). ● attrib.adj. (often in comb.) that or who was such at the time in question (the then artistic director). ● n. that time (until then). □ **but then** but, that being so; but on the other hand. **then again** on the other hand. **then and there** immediately and on the spot.

thence adv. (also **from thence**) archaic or literary **1** from that place or source. **2** for that reason. **3** = THENCEFORTH.

thenceforth adv. (also **from thenceforth**) archaic or literary from that time onward.

theocracy /θiːˈɒkrəsɪ/ n. (pl. **-ies**) **1** a form of government by God or a god directly or by a priestly order etc. claiming divine commission. **2** a state so governed. □ **theocrat** /ˈθiːəˌkræt/ n. **theocratic** adj.

theology /θɪˈɒlədʒɪ/ n. (pl. **-ies**) **1 a** the branch of knowledge dealing with esp. theistic religion; the study of the nature, attributes, and governance of God. **b** a particular system or theory of (esp. Christian) religion. **c** the rational analysis of a religious faith. **2** a system of theoretical principles, esp. an impractical or rigid ideology. □ **theologian** n. **theological** adj. **theologically** adv. **theologist** n. **theologize** v.tr. & intr.

theorem /ˈθɪərəm, ˈθiːərəm/ n. esp. Math. **1** a general proposition not self-evident but proved by a chain of reasoning; a truth established by means of accepted truths (compare PROBLEM 4b). **2** a rule in algebra etc., esp. one expressed by symbols or formulas.

theoretical /θɪəˈrɛtɪkəl/ adj. (also **theoretic**) **1** concerned with knowledge but not with its practical application. **2** based on theory rather than experience or practice. **3** existing only in theory; ideal, hypothetical. □ **theoretically** adv.

theoretician /ˌθɪərəˈtɪʃən/ n. a person concerned with the theoretical aspects of a subject.

theorist /ˈθɪərɪst, ˈθiːrɪst/ n. a holder or inventor of a theory or theories.

theorize /ˈθɪəraɪz, ˈθiːraɪz/ v. **1** intr. form or construct theories; indulge in theories. **2** tr. consider or devise in theory. □ **theorization** n.

theory /ˈθɪərɪ, ˈθiːərɪ/ n. (pl. **-ies**) **1** a supposition or system of ideas explaining something, esp. one based on general principles independent of the particular things to be explained (opp. HYPOTHESIS 2) (atomic theory; theory of evolution). **2** a speculative (esp. fanciful) view (one of my pet theories). **3** (the sphere of) abstract knowledge or speculative thought (this is all very well in theory; has been studying theory). **4** the principles on which a subject of study is based (music theory). **5** Math. a collection of propositions to illustrate the principles of a subject (probability theory).

theosophy /θɪˈɒsəfɪ/ n. (pl. **-ies**) any of various philosophies professing to achieve a knowledge of God by spiritual ecstasy, direct intuition, or special individual relations, esp. a modern movement following Hindu and Buddhist teachings and seeking universal fellowship. □ **theosophic** /θɪəˈsɒfɪk/ adj. **theosophical** adj. **theosophist** n.

therapeutic /ˌθɛrəˈpjuːtɪk/ adj. **1** of, for, or contributing to the cure of disease. **2** contributing to general, esp. mental, well-being (finds walking therapeutic). □ **therapeutical** adj. **therapeutically** adv.

therapeutic abortion n. an abortion performed for the physical or mental health of the woman.

therapeutics n.pl. (usu. treated as sing.) the branch of medicine concerned with the treatment of disease and the action of remedial agents.

therapist n. a person who practises or administers therapy, esp. a psychotherapist.

therapy n. (pl. **-ies**) **1** the treatment of physical or mental disorders, other than by surgery. **2** a particular type of such treatment.

there ● adv. **1** in, at, or to that place or position (lived there for years; goes there every day). **2** at that point (in speech, performance, writing, etc.) (there he stopped). **3** in that respect (I agree with you there). **4** used for emphasis in calling attention (hello there!; there goes the bell). **5** used to indicate the fact or existence of something (there is a house on the corner). ● n. that place (lives somewhere near there). ● interj. **1** expressing confirmation, triumph, satisfaction, etc. (there! what did I tell you?). **2** used to soothe a child etc. (there, there, never mind). □ **be there for someone** be ready to give support etc. **have been there before** slang know all about it. **so there** informal expressing defiance or defiant triumph. **there and then** immediately and on the spot. **there it is** that is the situation; nothing can be done about it. **there you are** (or **go**) informal **1** this is what you wanted etc. **2** expressing confirmation, triumph, resignation, etc.

thereabouts adv. (also **thereabout**) **1** near that place (ought to be somewhere thereabouts). **2** near that number, quantity, etc. (two litres or thereabouts).

thereafter adv. formal after that.

thereby adv. by that means, as a result of that. □ **thereby hangs a tale** much could be said about that.

therefor adv. formal for that object or purpose.

therefore adv. for that reason; accordingly.

therein adv. formal **1** in or into that place etc. **2** in that respect; in that matter.

thereof adv. formal of that or it.

thereon adv. on that or it (of motion or position).

there's contraction there is.

thereto adv. formal that or to it.

thereupon adv. **1** in consequence of that. **2** soon or immediately after that.

thermal ● adj. **1** of, for, or producing heat. **2** promoting the retention of heat (thermal underwear). ● n. **1** a rising current of heated air. **2** (in pl.) thermal underwear. □ **thermally** adv.

thermidor see LOBSTER THERMIDOR.

thermion /ˈθɜːmɪˌɒn/ n. an ion or electron emitted by a substance at high temperature. □ **thermionic** adj.

thermionic valve n. a device giving a flow of thermionic electrons in one direction, used esp. in the rectification of a current and in radio reception.

thermodynamics *n.pl.* (usu. treated as *sing.*) the science of the relations between heat and other (mechanical, electrical, etc.) forms of energy. □ **thermodynamic** *adj.* **thermodynamically** *adv.*

thermometer *n.* an instrument for measuring temperature, esp. a graduated thin glass tube containing mercury or alcohol which expands when heated.

thermonuclear *adj.* **1** relating to or using nuclear reactions that occur only at very high temperatures. **2** relating to or characterized by weapons using thermonuclear reactions.

Thermopane *n.* *proprietary* an insulating double-glazed windowpane.

thermoplastic ● *adj.* (of a substance) that becomes soft and plastic on heating and hard and rigid on cooling, and is able to repeat these processes. ● *n.* a thermoplastic substance.

thermoregulation *n.* the regulation of temperature, esp. of body temperature. □ **thermoregulate** *v.intr.* **thermoregulatory** *n.*

Thermos *n.* (in full **Thermos bottle**) *proprietary* an insulated flask for keeping a liquid hot or cold, esp. with a double lining enclosing a vacuum.

thermosetting *adj.* (of plastics) setting permanently when heated. □ **thermoset** *adj.*

thermostat *n.* a device that automatically regulates temperature, or that activates a device when the temperature reaches a certain point. □ **thermostatic** *adj.* **thermostatically** *adv.*

thesaurus /θəˈsɔːrəs/ *n.* (*pl.* **thesauruses** or **thesauri** /-raɪ/) a book that lists words in groups of synonyms and related concepts. **3** a treasury.

these *pl.* of THIS.

thesis /ˈθiːsɪs/ *n.* (*pl.* **theses** /-siːz/) **1** a proposition to be maintained or proved. **2** a dissertation, esp. by a candidate for a degree.

thespian ● *adj.* of or relating to tragedy or drama. ● *n.* an actor or actress.

theta /ˈθiːtə/ *n.* the eighth letter of the Greek alphabet (Θ, θ).

they *pron.* (*obj.* **them**; *possess.* **their, theirs**) **1** the people, animals, or things previously named or in question (*pl.* of HE, SHE, IT). **2** people in general (*they say we are wrong*). **3** those in authority (*they have raised the fees*). **4** *disputed* as a third person sing. indefinite pronoun meaning 'he or she' (*anyone can come if they want to*). ¶The use of *they* instead of 'he or she' is common in spoken English and increasingly so in written English, although deplored by some people. It is particularly useful when the sex of the person is unspecified or unknown and the writer wishes to avoid the accusation of sexism that can arise from the use of *he*. Similarly, *their* can replace 'his' or 'his or her' and *themselves* 'himself or herself'.

they'd *contraction* **1** they had. **2** they would.

they'll *contraction* **1** they will. **2** they shall.

they're *contraction* they are.

they've *contraction* they have.

thiamine /ˈθaɪəmɪn/ *n.* a vitamin of the B complex, found in unrefined cereals, beans, and liver, a deficiency of which causes beriberi.

thick ● *adj.* **1 a** of great or specified extent between opposite surfaces (*a thick wall; a wall two metres thick*). **b** of large diameter (*a thick rope*). **2 a** (of a line etc.) broad; not fine. **b** (of script or type etc.) consisting of thick lines. **3 a** arranged closely; crowded together; dense. **b** numerous. **4** (usu. foll. by *with*) densely cov-

ered or filled (*air thick with snow*). **5 a** firm in consistency; containing much solid matter; viscous (*thick soup*). **b** made of thick material (*a thick coat*). **6** muddy, cloudy; impenetrable by sight (*thick darkness*). **7** *informal* (of a person) stupid, dull. **8** (of an accent) very marked. **9** *informal* intimate or very friendly (*thick as thieves*). **10** (of one's head) suffering from a headache, hangover, etc. ● *n.* a thick or dense part of anything. ● *adv.* thickly (*snow was falling thick*). □ **in the thick of** at the busiest or most intense part of. **2** heavily occupied with. **lay it** (or **something**) **on thick** exaggerate. **thick and fast** in great quantity or large numbers, and rapidly or in quick succession (*plaudits arrived thick and fast*). **thick on the ground** abundant; in great quantity. **through thick and thin** under all conditions; in spite of all difficulties. □ **thickish** *adj.* **thickly** *adv.*

thicken *v.* **1** *tr. & intr.* make or become thick or thicker. **2** *intr.* become more complicated (*the plot thickens*). □ **thickener** *n.*

thickening *n.* **1** the process of becoming thick or thicker. **2** a substance used to thicken liquid. **3** a thickened part.

thicket *n.* a tangle of shrubs or trees.

thickhead *n.* *informal* a stupid person. □ **thick-headed** *adj.* **thick-headedness** *n.*

thickness *n.* **1** the state of being thick. **2** the extent to which a thing is thick. **3** a layer of material of a certain thickness. **4** a part that is thick or lies between opposite surfaces (*steps cut in the thickness of the wall*).

thickset *adj.* **1** heavily or solidly built. **2** set or growing close together.

thick skin *n.* **1** a thick or hard skin or outer layer. **2** *informal* insensitivity to reproach or criticism; callousness. □ **thick-skinned** *adj.*

thief *n.* (*pl.* **thieves**) a person who steals esp. secretly and without violence.

thieve *v.* **1** *intr.* (esp. as **thieving** *adj.*) be a thief. **2** *tr.* steal (a thing).

thievery *n.* the act or practice of stealing; theft.

thievish *adj.* **1** given to stealing. **2** of, pertaining to, or characteristic of a thief or thieves. □ **thievishly** *adv.* **thievishness** *n.*

thigh *n.* **1** the part of the human leg between the hip and the knee. **2** a corresponding part in other animals. □ **-thighed** *adj.* (in *comb.*).

thigh bone *n.* = FEMUR.

thigh-high ● *adj.* reaching to the thighs (*thigh-high boots*). ● *n.* (in *pl.*) thigh-high stockings etc.

thimble *n.* **1 a** a metal or plastic cap, usu. with a closed end, worn to protect the finger and push the needle in sewing. **b** = THIMBLEFUL. **2** *Mech.* a short metal tube or ferrule etc.

thimbleberry *n.* (*pl.* **-ies**) any of several N American raspberries with thimble-shaped fruit.

thimbleful *n.* (*pl.* **-fuls**) a small quantity, esp. of liquid to drink.

thin ● *adj.* (**thinner, thinnest**) **1** having the opposite surfaces close together; of small thickness or diameter. **2 a** (of a line) narrow or fine. **b** (of a script or type etc.) consisting of thin lines. **3** made of thin material (*a thin dress*). **4** lean; not plump. **5 a** not dense or copious (*thin hair*). **b** not full or closely packed (*a thin audience*). **6** of slight consistency (*a thin paste*). **7** weak; lacking an important ingredient (*thin blood; a thin voice*). **8** (of an excuse, argument, disguise, etc.) flimsy or transparent. **9** (of a business, market, etc.) not very active or busy. ● *adv.* thinly. ● *v.* (**thinned, thinning**) **1** *tr. & intr.* make or become thin or thinner. **2** *tr. & intr.* (often foll. by *out*) reduce; make or become less dense or crowded or numerous. **3** *tr.* (often foll. by *out*) remove some of a crop of (seedlings, saplings, etc.) or some young fruit from (a vine or tree) to improve the growth of the rest. □ **thin on top** balding. □ **thinly** *adv.* **thinness** *n.* **thinning** *adj.*

thin air *n.* a state of invisibility or non-existence (*vanished into thin air*).

thin blue line *n.* the police or military seen as the only defence against lawlessness, invasion, etc.

thine *possess.pron. archaic* **1** the one or ones belonging to thee. **2** (*attrib.* before a vowel) = THY.

thing *n.* **1** a material or non-material entity, idea, action, etc., that is or may be thought about or perceived. **2** an inanimate material object (*take that thing away*). **3** an unspecified object or item (*have a few things to buy*). **4** an act, idea, or utterance (*a silly thing to do*). **5** an event (*an unfortunate thing to happen*). **6** a quality (*patience is a useful thing*). **7** (with reference to a person) expressing pity, contempt, or affection (*poor thing!*). **8** a specimen or type of something (*the latest thing in hats*). **9** *informal* one's special interest or concern (*not my thing at all*). **10** a thought, point for consideration, etc. (*and another thing...*). **11** *informal* a matter of or concerning (a preceding word) (*it's a pride thing*). **12** (prec. by *the*) *informal* **a** what is conventionally proper or fashionable (*the latest thing*). **b** what is needed or required (*was just the thing*). **c** (often foll. by *about*, *with*) what is important or to be considered (*the thing with them is they're always late; the thing is, shall we go or not?*). **13** (in *pl.*) personal belongings or clothing (*where have I left my things?*). **14** (in *pl.*) equipment (*painting things*). **15** (in *pl.*) affairs in general (*in the nature of things*). **16** (in *pl.*) circumstances or conditions (*things look good*). □ **do one's own thing** *informal* pursue one's own interests or inclinations. **do things to** *informal* affect remarkably. **have a thing about** (or **for**, **with**) *informal* be obsessed about; be peculiarly interested in, repulsed by, etc. **make a thing of** *informal* **1** regard as essential. **2** cause a fuss about. **one** (or **just one**) **of those things** *informal* something unavoidable or to be accepted.

thingy *n.* (also **thingamajig** /ˈθɪŋəməˌdʒɪg/, **thingamabob** /ˈθɪŋəməˌbɒb/, **thinguma-**; **thingummy** /ˈθɪŋəmi/) a person or thing whose name one has forgotten or does not know or does not wish or care to mention.

thinhorn sheep *n.* a mountain sheep, *Ovis dalli*, with long, slender, pointed horns flaring away from the head.

think *v.* (*past* and *past part.* **thought**) **1** *tr.* (often foll. by *that* + clause) be of the opinion. **2** *tr.* (foll. by *that* + clause or *to* + infin.) judge or consider (*is thought to be a fraud*). **3** *intr.* **a** exercise the mind positively with one's ideas etc.; meditate (*let me think*). **b** have the capacity to do this. **4** *intr.* (foll. by *of* or *about*) **a** consider; be or become mentally aware of (*think of Liz constantly*). **b** form or entertain the idea of; imagine to oneself (*couldn't think of such a thing*). **c** choose mentally; hit upon (*think of a number*). **5** *tr.* have a half-formed intention (*I think I'll stay*). **6** *tr.* form a conception of (*cannot think how you do it*). **7** *tr.* bring into or out of a specified condition by thinking (*cannot think away a toothache*). **8** *tr.* recognize the presence or existence of (*the child thought no harm*). **9** *tr.* (foll. by *to* + infin.) intend or expect (*thinks to deceive us*). **10** *tr.* (foll. by *to* + infin.) remember (*did not think to lock the door*). **11** *intr. informal* (of a computer) process data. ● *n. informal* an act of thinking (*must have a think*). □ **have another think coming** be greatly mistaken. **think again**

revise one's plans or opinions. **think aloud** utter one's thoughts as soon as they occur. **think back to** recall (a past event or time). **think better of** change one's mind about (an intention) after reconsideration. **think for oneself** have an independent mind or attitude. **think little** (or **nothing**) **of** consider to be insignificant or unremarkable. **think much** (or **highly**) **of** have a high opinion of. **think out 1** consider carefully. **2** produce (an idea etc.) by thinking. **think over** reflect upon in order to reach a decision. **think through** reflect fully upon (a problem etc.). **think twice** use careful consideration, avoid hasty action, etc. **think up** *informal* devise.

thinkable *adj.* conceivable.

thinker *n.* **1** a person who thinks, esp. in a specified way. **2** a person with a skilled or powerful mind.

thinking ● *adj.* **1** using thought or rational judgment. **2** thoughtful, reflective, intellectual. ● *n.* opinion or judgment. □ **a thinking person's** (or **man's**, **woman's**) designed for intelligent people; designating an intellectual version of a designated thing etc. (*a thinking person's sitcom*). **put on one's thinking cap** *informal* meditate on a problem.

think piece *n.* an article containing discussion, analysis, opinion, etc., rather than facts or news.

think-tank *n.* a body of experts, as a research organization, providing advice and ideas on specific national or commercial problems.

thinner *n.* a volatile liquid used to dilute paint etc.

thinnings *n.pl.* plants, trees, etc. which have been removed to improve the growth of those remaining.

thin red line *n.* = THIN BLUE LINE.

thin-skinned *adj.* **1** (esp. of fruit) having a thin skin or outer layer. **2** sensitive to reproach or criticism.

Thinsulate *n. proprietary* a thin batting made from very fine propylene fibres trapping tiny pockets of air to provide high insulation with little bulk or weight.

thiopental sodium /ˌθaɪoʊˈpɛntəl/ *n.* a barbiturate drug used as a general anaesthetic and a hypnotic, and (reputedly) as a truth drug.

third ● *n.* **1** the position in a sequence corresponding to that of the number 3 in the sequence 1–3. **2** something occupying this position. **3** each of three equal parts of a thing. **4** = THIRD GEAR. **5** *Music* **a** an interval or chord spanning three consecutive notes in the diatonic scale, e.g. C to E. **b** a note separated from another by this interval. **6** *Baseball* **a** the third inning. **b** = THIRD BASE. **7** *Football* = THIRD DOWN. **8** *Curling* = VICE-SKIP. ● *adj.* that is the third. ● *adv.* in the third place; thirdly. □ **thirdly** *adv.*

third base *n. Baseball* **1** the third of the bases that must be touched to score a run. **2** the position of the player covering this base and the area of the infield surrounding it. □ **third baseman** *n.*

third-best ● *adj.* of third quality. ● *n.* a thing in this category.

third class ● *n.* **1** a set of persons or things grouped together as third-best. **2** the third-best accommodation in a train, ship, etc. ● *adj.* (often hyphenated when *attrib.*) **1** belonging to, travelling by, etc. the third class. **2** of lower quality; inferior.

third degree ● *n.* long and severe questioning esp. by police to obtain information or a confession. ● *adj.* (**third-degree**) denoting burns of the most severe kind, affecting lower layers of tissue.

third down *n. Football* the third of three attempts (four in American football) to advance the ball ten yards in order to achieve a new first down.

third eye *n.* **1** *Hinduism & Buddhism* the 'eye of insight' in the forehead of an image of a deity, esp. the god

Siva. **2** the faculty of intuitive insight or prescience. **3** the pineal gland in certain vertebrates.

third force *n.* a group, as a political party, acting as a check on conflict between two opposing groups.

third gear *n.* the third (and in cars often next to highest) in a sequence of gears.

third-generation *adj.* designating computer technology distinguished by the introduction of integrated circuits and operating systems and belonging essentially to the period 1960 – 70.

third party ● *n.* **1** a party or person besides the two primarily concerned. **2** a person involved incidentally. **3** a political party other than the two (or more) most important. **4** *Law* a person against whom a defendant commences a claim for all or part of the plaintiff's claim (also *attrib.*: *third party claim*). ● *adj. Cdn & Brit.* (of insurance) covering damage or injury suffered by a person other than the insured.

third-rate *adj.* inferior; very poor in quality.

third reading *n.* a third presentation of a bill to a legislative assembly, in Canada to debate it for the last time in the House of Commons.

Third Reich *n.* the Nazi regime, 1933–45.

third-string *attrib.adj. N Amer.* (esp. of an athlete) inferior. □ **third-stringer** *n.*

Third Wave *n.* the current phase of economic, social, and cultural change (following the agrarian and industrial waves), in which knowledge is the primary productive force.

third way *n.* any option regarded as an alternative to two extremes.

Third World *n.* (usu. prec. by *the*) the developing countries of Asia, Africa, and Latin America.

thirst ● *n.* **1** an intense physical need or craving to drink something, associated with dehydration and a dryness of the throat and mouth. **2** a strong desire or craving (*a thirst for power*). ● *v.intr.* (usu. foll. by *for*) **1** feel thirst. **2** have a strong desire.

thirst-quenching *adj.* that satisfies or is capable of satisfying thirst. □ **thirst-quencher** *n.*

thirsty *adj.* (**-ier**, **-iest**) **1** having a need or desire to drink. **2** (of land, a crop, etc.) dry; needing moisture. **3** (often foll. by *for*) eager. **4** *informal* causing thirst (*thirsty work*). □ **thirstily** *adv.*

thirteen ● *n.* **1** one more than twelve. **2** a symbol for this (13, xiii, XIII). **3** a size etc. denoted by thirteen. **4** a a group of thirteen people or things. **b** the thirteenth person or thing of a set or series. ● *adj.* that amount to thirteen. □ **thirteenth** *adj., n. & adv.*

thirty ● *n.* (*pl.* **-ies**) **1** the product of three and ten. **2** a symbol for this (30, xxx, XXX). **3** (in *pl.*) the numbers from 30 to 39, esp. the years of a century or of a person's life. **4 a** a group of thirty people or things. **b** the thirtieth person or thing of a set or series. **5** (in *comb.*) thirty minutes past (a specified hour) (*four-thirty*). ● *adj.* that amount to thirty. □ **thirty-first, -second**, etc. the ordinal numbers between thirtieth and fortieth. **thirty-one, -two**, etc. the cardinal numbers between thirty and forty. □ **thirtieth** *adj., adv., & n.*

thirtyish *adj. informal* about thirty, esp. in age.

thirty-second note *n. N Amer. Music* a note having the time value of half a sixteenth note and represented by a large dot with a three-hooked stem.

thirty-second rest *n. N Amer. Music* a rest having the time value of a thirty-second note.

thirtysomething *informal* ● *n.* **1** an undetermined age between thirty and forty, esp. applied to members of the 'baby boom' generation entering their thirties in the mid-1980s. **2** a person of this age.

● *adj.* **1** characteristic of the tastes and lifestyle of this group. **2** between thirty and forty years of age.

this ● *demonstrative pron.* (*pl.* **these**) **1** the person or thing indicated, close by, already named, or understood. **2** (contrasted with *that*) the person or thing that is closer or more immediately in mind. **3 a** the action, behaviour, or circumstances, under consideration (*this just won't do*). **b** what is about to be demonstrated or announced (*listen to this*). **4** (on the telephone) **a** the person speaking. **b** the person spoken to. ● *demonstrative adj.* (*pl.* **these**) **1** designating the person or thing close by etc. **2** (of time) **a** the present or current (*I'm busy all this week*). **b** relating to today (*this morning*). **c** just past or to come (*this Tuesday*). **3** *informal* (in narrative) designating a person or thing previously unspecified (*so this guy comes and grabs me*). ● *adv.* to this degree or extent; to a height or extent indicated by a gesture of the hand or hands (*knew Kyle when he was this high*). □ **these days** = NOWADAYS. **this and that** *informal* various unspecified things. **this here** *slang* this particular (person or thing). **this much** the amount or extent about to be stated (*I know this much, she's not here*).

thistle *n.* **1** any of various prickly plants of the genera *Carduus*, *Cirsium*, and *Carlina*, which have tubular, chiefly purple flowers in globular heads, esp. any of those occurring as weeds. **2** any of several prickly plants of other families. **3** one of these plants as the national emblem of Scotland.

thistledown *n.* **1** the light feathery down of a thistle seed. **2** thistle seeds collectively, esp. as carried along by the wind.

this world *n.* the present world or state of existence as opposed to an imagined or future existence, esp. mortal life as opposed to life after death. □ **this-worldliness** *n.* **this-worldly** *attrib.adj.*

thither /'ðɪðər/ *adv. archaic or formal* to or towards that place.

tho' *archaic or informal var. of* THOUGH.

Thomism /'toːmɪzəm/ *n.* the philosophical or theological doctrine developed by St. Thomas Aquinas (1225–74). □ **Thomist** *n.* **Thomistic** /-'mɪstɪk/ *adj.*

Thompson /'tɒmsən/ *n.* = NLAKA'PAMUX.

-thon *comb. form* = -ATHON.

thong *n.* **1** a narrow strip of hide or leather used esp. as a lace, cord, strap, rein, or as the lash of a whip. **2** *N Amer., Austral.,* & *NZ* = FLIP-FLOP 2. **3 a** a skimpy garment for the lower body, consisting of narrow strips of cloth or leather attached to a piece of material that covers the genitals but not the buttocks. **b** (*attrib.*) designating articles of clothing that resemble this (*thong bikini*). □ **thonged** *adj.*

thorax /'θɔːræks/ *n.* (*pl.* **-es** or **thoraces** /'θɔːrə,siːz/) **1 a** the part of the body of a mammal between the neck and the abdomen, including the cavity enclosed by the ribs, breastbone, and dorsal vertebrae, and containing the chief organs of circulation and respiration. **b** the corresponding part of a bird, reptile, amphibian, or fish. **2** the middle section of the body of an arthropod, between the head and abdomen. □ **thoracic** /θɔːˈræsɪk/ *adj.*

thorium /'θɔːriəm/ *n.* a radioactive metallic element occurring naturally and used in electronic equipment and as a source of nuclear energy.

thorn *n.* **1** a stiff sharp-pointed projection on a plant. **2** a thorn-bearing bush, shrub, or tree, such as the hawthorn. **3** a cause of pain, grief, irritation, or trouble. □ **a thorn in one's side** (or **flesh**) a constant annoyance. □ **thornless** *adj.*

thornapple *n.* a plant of the nightshade family,

Datura stramonium, native to N America, bearing large funnel-shaped white or mauve flowers.

thorny *adj.* (**-ier, -iest**) **1** having many thorns. **2** (of a subject, issue, problem, etc.) difficult to handle or resolve; delicate. ☐ **thornily** *adv.* **thorniness** *n.*

thorough /ˈθʌrəʊ, ˈθʌrə, ˈθʌrə/ *adj.* **1** applied to or affecting every part or detail; not superficial (*a thorough understanding*). **2** done with great care and completeness (*a thorough job*). **3** (of a person) taking pains to do something carefully and completely (*she's very thorough*). **4** absolute, utter (*a thorough nuisance*). ☐ **thoroughly** *adv.* **thoroughness** *n.*

thoroughbred ● *n.* **1** a purebred animal, esp. a horse (also *attrib.*: *thoroughbred racing*). **2** (**Thoroughbred**) a racehorse of a breed originating from English mares and Arab stallions, whose ancestry for several generations is fully documented. ● *adj.* **1** of pure breed. **2** of outstanding quality; remarkable.

thoroughfare *n.* **1 a** a road or path open at both ends through which esp. traffic may pass. **b** a main road or highway. **2** *N Amer.* a navigable waterway, esp. a channel for shipping.

thoroughgoing *adj.* **1** extremely thorough; not superficial (*a thoroughgoing attack*). **2** (*attrib.*) absolute; out-and-out (*a thoroughgoing idiot*).

those *pl. of* THAT.

thou[1] /ðaʊ/ *pron.* (*obj.* **thee** /ðiː/; *possess.* **thy** or **thine**; *pl.* **ye** or **you**) second person singular pronoun, now replaced by *you* except in some formal, liturgical, dialect, and poetic uses.

thou[2] /θaʊ/ *n.* (*pl.* same or **thous**) *informal* a thousand, esp. a thousand dollars (*she makes 50 thou a year*).

though ● *conj.* **1** (often prec. by *even*) despite the fact that (*even though it was early we went to bed*). **2** (introducing a possibility) even if (*ask him though he may well refuse*). **3** and yet; but still; however; nevertheless (*she read on, though not to the very end*). **4** in spite of being (*the portions were small though expensive*). ● *adv. informal* **1** however; all the same (*I wish you had told me, though*). **2** (used as an intensifier after a question or emphatic statement) indeed, truly (*'She's awfully smart.' 'Isn't she, though?'*). ☐ **as though** = AS IF (*see* AS).

thought ● *n.* **1** the process or power of thinking; the faculty of reason. **2** the intellectual activity or way of thinking characteristic of or associated with a particular time, people, group, etc. (*medieval thought*; *school of thought*). **3 a** sober reflection or consideration (*a lot of thought went into this*). **b** deep meditation or contemplation (*was lost in thought*). **4 a** a piece of reasoning produced by thinking; an idea. **b** (usu. in *pl.*) what one is thinking; an opinion or assessment of a person or thing (*what are your thoughts on the subject?*). **5** (often in *pl.*) attention (*turn our thoughts to summer*). **6 a** regard, concern, consideration (*did it without any thought of the consequences*). **b** (in *pl.*) sympathy (*our thoughts are with you*). **7** (foll. by *of* + verbal noun or *to* + infin.) a hope, intention, or expectation; a notion (*gave up all thoughts of winning*). **8** the mere contemplation (*the thought of it makes me nervous*). **9** the subject of one's thinking (*my one thought was to get away*). ● *v. past and past part. of* THINK. ☐ **give thought to** consider. **on second thought** contrary to what one originally decided or announced. **without a second thought** without giving a matter full or proper consideration.

thoughtful *adj.* **1** (often foll. by *of*) showing thought or consideration for others; considerate, kind. **2** showing signs of careful thought or consideration (*thoughtful gifts*). **3 a** absorbed in meditation; deep in

thought. **b** given to contemplation; prudent, reflective. ☐ **thoughtfully** *adv.* **thoughtfulness** *n.*

thoughtless *adj.* **1** lacking in consideration for others; inconsiderate. **2** showing a lack of concern for the possible consequences of one's actions; careless. **3** resulting from a lack of thought. ☐ **thoughtlessly** *adv.* **thoughtlessness** *n.*

thought out *adj.* produced by mental effort (usu. hyphenated when *attrib.*: *a carefully thought-out plan*).

thought police *n.* *informal* an authoritarian special interest group that monitors others for signs of behaviour or views it considers deviant, inappropriate, or politically incorrect.

thought-provoking *adj.* (of an article, question, etc.) that prompts others to further contemplation of matters or issues raised.

thousand ● *n.* (*pl.* **-s** or (in sense 1) **thousand**) (in *sing.* prec. by *a* or *one*) **1** the product of a hundred and ten. **2** a symbol for this (1,000, m, M). **3** a set of a thousand things. **4 a** (in *pl.*) the numbers usu. between 1000 and 10,000, esp. referring to dollars (*the cost will be in the thousands*). **b** (in *sing.* or *pl.*) *informal* a large number. ● *adj.* that amount to a thousand. ☐ **thousandfold** *adj.* & *adv.* **thousandth** *adj.*, *adv.*, & *n.*

Thousand Island *n.* designating a piquant mayonnaise salad dressing made with tomatoes, chili sauce, finely chopped boiled egg, onion, green pepper, and occasionally celery or pickle.

thrall /θrɔːl/ *n.* *literary* **1** (often foll. by *to*) a condition or state of or like slavery or servitude; subjection to a person, power, or influence (*in thrall to the needs of her aging mother*). **2** (often foll. by *of*) power, influence, or control (*the thrall of alcohol*). **3** one who is controlled by or dependent upon a person, power, or influence; a slave. ☐ **thralldom** *n.* (also **thraldom**).

thrash ● *v.* **1** *tr.* beat severely with a stick or whip, esp. as a punishment. **2** *tr.* **a** *Sport informal* defeat (an opponent) convincingly. **b** criticize or scold severely (*was thrashed by the critics*). **3** *intr.* (foll. by *around, about*) move or fling the body, limbs, etc., about violently, esp. in panic or helplessness; flail. **4** *intr.* lash about like a flail or whip (*the branches thrashed in the wind*). **5** *tr.* = THRESH 1. ● *n.* **1** (in full **thrash metal**) a style of fast loud heavy metal rock music similar to speed metal but with a greater presence of punk elements (also *attrib.*: *thrash band*). **2** an act of thrashing. **3** *informal* a party, esp. a lavish one. ☐ **thrash out 1** discuss (a matter etc.) at length in order to reach a solution or consensus. **2** establish (a plan, solution, etc.) after discussing a matter thoroughly. ☐ **thrashing** *n.* **thrashy** *adj.* (in sense 1 of *n.*).

thrasher *n.* **1** a person that plays or listens to thrash music. **2** a person or thing that thrashes. **3** any of several N American songbirds of the family Mimidae, with greyish or brownish plumage and a slightly down-curved bill, esp. the brown thrasher, *Toxostoma rufum*. **4** = THRESHER 2.

thread ● *n.* **1 a** a fine strand made by drawing out and twisting the fibres of flax, cotton, wool, silk, etc. **b** a length of this. **2** a length of thin cord composed of two or more strands twisted together, used esp. in sewing and weaving. **3** anything resembling thread in fineness and length, such as a thin stream of liquid or a filament of a spider's web. **4 a** anything regarded as threadlike with reference to its continuity or connectedness, such as the sequence of events or ideas continuing through the whole course of a narrative, argument, one's life, etc. **b** a continuous or persistent feature of something, esp. one combining with other features to form a pattern or texture (*a* *common thread running throughout her works*). **5** the spiral ridge running along the outside of a screw or inside of a nut. **6 a** a single fibre of material in an article of clothing (*a loose thread*). **b** (in *pl.*) *informal* clothes. ● *v.* **1** *tr.* **a** pass a thread through the eye of (a needle). **b** (often foll. by *through*) pass (string etc.) through a hole or series of holes. **2** *tr.* put (beads) on a string. **3 a** *tr. & intr.* (often foll. by *through*) make (one's way) through a crowd etc. **b** *tr.* make one's way through (a narrow or obstructed passage, a crowd, etc.). **4** *tr.* form a screw thread on. **5** *tr. Sport* (esp. in hockey and football) complete (a pass) to a teammate through a crowd of players. **6** *tr.* feed (a strip of material) through a piece of machinery, such as film through a projector. □ **hang by a thread** be in a precarious state, position, etc. □ **threaded** *adj.* **threader** *n.* **threadlike** *adj.*

threadbare *adj.* **1** (of fabric, clothing, carpeting, etc.) so worn that the nap is lost and the thread visible. **2 a** having lost effect, freshness, or force through overuse (*a threadbare plot*). **b** weak or insubstantial (*a threadbare excuse*). **3** (of a person) wearing threadbare clothing.

thready *adj.* (**-ier, -iest**) **1** (of a person's pulse) barely perceptible. **2** (of a voice or sound) feeble, faint. **3** of or like a thread.

threat *n.* **1** a declaration of an intention to take some hostile action, esp. an expression of an intention to inflict pain, injury, damage, etc. unless a particular demand or set of demands is met. **2** an indication of the approach or imminent occurrence of something unwelcome or undesirable (*the threat of rain*). **3** a person or thing regarded as a likely cause of harm or damage etc. (*she's a security threat*).

threaten *v.* **1** *tr. & intr.* (often foll. by *with*) make a threat or threats against (a person) (*threatened him with a knife*). **2** *tr.* **a** declare one's intention of inflicting (punishment, injury, etc.), esp. in retaliation for something done or not done (*she is threatening legal action*). **b** (foll. by *to* + infin.) express an intention or promise (*they threatened to quit*). **3** *tr.* appear likely or certain to cause or do (something undesirable) (*the epidemic threatens to kill thousands*). **4** *tr.* jeopardize or endanger (*pollution is threatening the water supply*). **5** *tr. & intr.* be a sign or indication of the approach or imminent occurrence of (something undesirable) (*those clouds threaten rain*). **6** *tr.* intimidate or frighten.

threatened *adj.* **1** (of a species etc.) in danger of becoming rare or extinct; at risk of becoming endangered. **2** intimidated. **3** having been vowed or portended. **4** in jeopardy or danger.

threatening *adj.* **1** designed or tending to menace or intimidate (*a threatening letter*). **2** foreboding (*threatening clouds*). □ **threateningly** *adv.*

three /θriː/ ● *n.* **1 a** one more than two. **b** a symbol for this (3, iii, III). **2** a size etc. denoted by three. **3** three o'clock. **4 a** a group of three people or things. **b** the third person or thing of a set or series (*I'm on book three*). **5** a card with three pips. **6** *Basketball* a three-point field goal. ● *adj.* that amount to three.

three-and-a-half *n. Cdn* (*Que.*) an apartment having a kitchen, living room, bedroom, and bathroom.

three-card monte *n. see* MONTE 2.

three-card trick *n.* a game in which players bet on which of three cards lying face down is the queen.

three-colour *adj.* **1** having, using, or consisting of three colours. **2** designating or relating to a process of reproducing natural colours by combining or superimposing photographic images in the three primary colours. □ **three-coloured** *adj.*

three-cornered *adj.* **1** having three corners; triangular. **2** relating to or involving three individuals or groups etc.

3-D ● *adj.* **1** having or presenting a three-dimensional image or appearance (*a 3-D movie*). **2** used to produce a three-dimensional image or appearance (*3-D glasses*). ● *n.* a format that presents three-dimensional images (*the movie is in 3-D*).

three-dimensional *adj.* **1 a** having or appearing to have length, width, and depth. **b** producing the appearance of having length, width, and depth (*three-dimensional effects*). **2** (of literature etc.) vivid, realistic. □ **three-dimensionality** *n.* **three-dimensionalize** *v.tr.* **three-dimensionally** *adv.*

threefold ● *adj.* **1** three times as much or as many. **2** consisting of three parts. ● *adv.* to or by three times the number.

three-in-one *attrib.adj.* designating a single device or unit that performs three separate functions or consists of three parts that can be used separately.

three-legged *adj.* having or supported by three legs.

three-on-one *n.* (*pl.* **-ones**) **1** *Hockey* a rush led by three players against one defender and a goalie (often *attrib.: a three-on-one break*). **2** *Basketball* a rush led by three players against one defender.

three-on-three *n.* a scaled-down game of basketball involving two teams of three players playing on a schoolyard court or half court and usu. shooting at only one basket.

three-peat *N Amer. Sport informal* ● *n.* a third consecutive win of a particular championship by one player or team. ● *v.intr.* win a particular championship for a third consecutive time.

three-piece ● *adj.* **1** consisting of three matching or related parts (*a three-piece band; a three-piece furniture suite*). **2** (of a suit) consisting of matching pants, jacket, and vest. ● *n.* (also **three-piecer**) an ensemble or group consisting of three matching or related components, members, etc.

three-pitch *n. Cdn* a variety of softball in which the batter cannot draw a walk, having only three chances to hit a ball delivered underhand by a teammate.

three-ply *adj.* consisting of three layers, strands, or thicknesses.

three-point *adj. Basketball* **1** worth three points (*three-point basket*). **2** relating to the shooting of three-point field goals (*a shot from three-point range*).

three-pointer *n. Basketball* a three-point basket.

three-point turn *n.* a method of turning a vehicle around in a narrow space by moving in three arcs, forwards, backwards, and forwards again.

three-prong *adj. Electricity* **1** (of an outlet) that has been grounded and is thus capable of receiving a plug with three pins or prongs. **2** (of a plug) that has three pins or prongs and is designed to fit in a grounded outlet.

three-pronged *adj.* having three aspects, stages, aims, or lines of attack (*three-pronged attack*).

three-quarter ● *n.* **1** (in *pl.*) three of the four equal parts into which something is or may be divided (*three-quarters of an hour*). **2** (in full **three-quarter back**) *Rugby* each of three or four players playing behind the halfbacks. ● *adj.* **1** consisting of or measuring three-quarters of something (*a three-quarter length coat*). **2** (of a portrait or view etc.) **a** showing the figure as far as the hips. **b** showing three-quarters of the face; between full face and profile. ● *adv.* (**three-quarters**) to the extent of three-quarters (*the tank is three-quarters full*).

three-ring binder *n.* a ring binder with three rings.

three-ring circus n. N Amer. **1** a circus with three rings for simultaneous performances. **2 a** a showy or extravagant display. **b** a scene of confusion or disorder.

three-sixty n. (pl. **-ies**) informal a spin of 360°; a complete turn or revolution.

threesome n. **1** a group of three people. **2** an activity or game in which three people participate.

three-star adj. **1** (of a hotel, restaurant, etc.) given three stars in a grading in which this denotes a high quality, usu. one or two grades below the highest. **2** having or designating a military rank distinguished by three stars on the epaulette of the uniform.

three-way adj. **1** involving three participants (a three-way tie). **2** designating or relating to a trilight bulb (three-way bulb). **3** (of a loudspeaker) having three separate drive units for different frequency ranges.

three-wheeler n. a vehicle with three wheels, esp. a kind of small all-terrain vehicle.

thresh /θreʃ, θræʃ/ v.tr. & intr. **1** shake, beat, or mechanically treat (wheat etc.) to separate the grain from the husk and straw, esp. with a flail or by a revolving mechanism. **2** = THRASH v. 1, 3. □ **threshing** n.

thresher n. **1 a** a person that threshes grain. **b** a threshing machine. **2** (in full **thresher shark**) a shark, Alopias vulpinus, with a long upper lobe to its tail with which it lashes the water to direct its prey.

thresherman n. (pl. **-men**) N Amer. hist. a person who participates in the annual threshing of grain.

threshing machine n. hist. a machine for separating grain from the straw or husk.

threshold /'θreʃo:ld, -ho:ld/ n. **1 a** a strip of wood or stone forming the bottom of a doorway and crossed upon entering a house or room. **b** the entrance to a house or building etc. **c** the boundary of a region. **2** the point just before a new situation, period of life, etc. begins (on the threshold of victory). **3** Physiol. & Psych. a limit below which a stimulus causes no reaction (pain threshold). **4** the magnitude that must be exceeded for a certain reaction, phenomenon, result, or condition to occur or be manifested. **5** a step in a scale of wages or taxation at which increases become due or mandatory, usu. operative in specified conditions, such as a rise in the cost of living.

threw past of THROW.

thrice adv. archaic or literary **1** three times. **2** (esp. in comb.) highly (thrice-blessed).

thrift n. **1** prudent financial management; the habit of saving money and spending it carefully; frugality. **2** a European plant, Armeria maritima, having dense heads of small pink flowers, leafless stems, and dense rosettes of linear leaves. □ **thriftily** adv. **thriftiness** n. **thrifty** adj. (**-ier**, **-iest**).

thrift shop n. (also **thrift store**) a store that sells second-hand merchandise, esp. clothing, with proceeds often going to charity (also attrib.: thrift-shop dresses).

thrill ● n. **1** a powerful and often sudden feeling of excitement, exhilaration, or emotion. **2 a** a thing that causes such a feeling of excitement or exhilaration (his new book was a real thrill). **b** an exciting or exhilarating event or experience (it was a thrill to meet her). **3** intense excitement (the thrill has gone out of our marriage). ● v. **1** tr. cause (a person) to feel intense excitement. **2** tr. thoroughly please or delight. **3** intr. (usu. foll. by at or to) feel or become excited. **4** intr. quiver or throb with or as if with emotion. □ **thrilled** adj. **thrilling** adj. **thrillingly** adv.

thriller n. **1** an exciting or sensational movie or novel etc., esp. a suspenseful one involving mystery, crime,

or espionage. **2** a person or thing that thrills or excites.

thrill-seeker n. **1** a person who enjoys the excitement of participating in dangerous activities. **2** usu. derogatory a person seeking thrills. □ **thrill-seeking** adj. & n.

thrips n. (pl. same) a member of the order Thysanoptera, of minute dark-coloured insects, typically having slender bodies and four fringed wings, many of which are pests of various plants.

thrive v.intr. (past **thrived** or **throve** /θro:v/; past part. **thrived** or **thriven** /'θrɪvən/) **1** grow vigorously, flourish. **2** be or become successful or prosperous (the tourist industry thrives during the summer). □ **thrive on 1** (of an animal etc.) depend upon for growth or sustenance. **2** (of a person) be driven or encouraged by (thrives on pressure). □ **thriving** adj.

thro' var. of THROUGH.

throat n. **1** the front part of the neck beneath the chin and above the collarbone. **2** the windpipe or gullet. **3** anything resembling or compared to a throat, such as a narrow passage or entranceway. **4** the part of a chimney or furnace etc. immediately above the fireplace, which narrows down to the neck. **5** = BARREL n. 7. □ **be at each other's** (or **one another's**) **throats** quarrel violently. **cut one's own throat** bring about one's own downfall. **ram** (or **thrust** etc.) **down a person's throat** force a person to accept (a thing). □ **-throated** adj. (in comb.).

throaty adj. (**-ier**, **-iest**) **1** (of a voice) rough, husky. **2** produced or modified in the throat; deep, guttural (a throaty laugh). □ **throatily** adv. **throatiness** n.

throb ● v.intr. (**throbbed**, **throbbing**) **1** (of the heart or pulse) beat or palpitate, esp. with more than usual force or rapidity. **2** pulsate or vibrate, esp. with a deep audible rhythm. **3** ache with a recurrent or pulsating pain (my head is throbbing). ● n. **1** a palpitation or (esp. violent) pulsation. **2** a rhythmic esp. audible beat or vibration.

throe /θro:/ n. (usu. in pl.) **1** a violent pang, esp. of childbirth or death. **2** anguish, torment. □ **in the throes of 1** struggling with the task of. **2** in the midst of (esp. a volatile or emotional situation).

thrombin /'θrɒmbɪn/ n. a plasma protein which acts as an enzyme to convert fibrinogen to fibrin and so promote the clotting of blood.

thrombosis /θrɒm'bo:sɪs/ n. (pl. **thromboses** /-si:z/) a local coagulation or clotting of the blood in a part of the circulatory system. □ **thrombose** /-'bo:z/ v.tr. & intr. **thrombotic** /-'bɒtɪk/ adj.

thrombus /'θrɒmbəs/ n. (pl. **thrombi** /-bai/) a blood clot that forms on the wall of a blood vessel or a chamber of the heart, esp. in such a way that it impedes or obstructs the flow of blood.

throne ● n. **1** an ornate, elaborate, and usu. raised chair occupied by a deity, monarch, etc., esp. on ceremonial occasions. **2 a** the position, office, power, or dignity of a sovereign (a claim to the throne). **b** the occupant of a throne; a monarch or ruler. **3** informal a toilet. ● v.tr. place on or as if on a throne.

throne room n. **1** a room containing a throne, esp. one used for audiences with a monarch. **2** informal a bathroom.

Throne Speech n. Cdn = SPEECH FROM THE THRONE.

throng ● n. (often foll. by of) a crowd or multitude of esp. people. ● v. **1** tr. & intr. gather or assemble in or around (crowds thronged the streets). **2** intr. travel in large numbers (thronged to the malls).

throttle ● n. **1** (in full **throttle valve**) a valve controlling the flow of fuel or steam etc. in an engine. **2** (in full **throttle control** or **throttle lever**) a lever or pedal operating this valve. ● *v.* **1** *tr.* choke or strangle. **2** *tr.* stifle or suppress (words, a rumour, etc.). **3** *tr. & intr.* control the flow of gas or steam to (an engine etc.). □ **throttle back** (or **down**) close the throttle of (an engine or vehicle) in order to slow down or stop.

through ● *prep.* **1 a** from one end to the other of (*drove through Saskatoon*). **b** going in one side or end and out the other of (*through the tunnel*). **c** beyond; past (*drove through a stop sign*). **2** between or among (*ran through the trees*). **3 a** from beginning to end of; over each one or part of (*read through the letter*). **b** during the whole temporal extent of (*work through lunch*). **4 a** by means of (*through an ad in the paper*). **b** due to; because of (*through carelessness*). **5** *N Amer.* up to and including (*Monday through Friday*). ● *adv.* **1 a** from side to side, end to end, or beginning to end of a body or space (*I read the letter through*; *may I pass through?*). **b** all the way; to the end of a journey (*we walked through to the garden*). **2** past or across a barrier or space (*the guard let us through*). **3** successfully past a particular stage or test (*made it through to the finals*). **4** so as to be connected by telephone (*the operator will put you through*). ● *attrib.adj.* **1** (of a flight etc.) that travels the whole distance or journey without interruption or change. **2** (of traffic) going through a place to a destination. **3** (of a road, route, etc.) open at both ends, allowing a continuous journey. □ **be through** *informal* **1** (often foll. by *with*) have finished (*I'm through with the newspaper*). **2** (often foll. by *with*) cease to have dealings (*he and his girlfriend are through*). **3** have no further prospects (*is through as a politician*). **through and through 1** thoroughly; in every respect. **2** repeatedly through; through again and again.

throughout ● *prep.* **1** through all of; in or to every part of; everywhere in. **2** during the whole time, extent, or length of; from beginning to end. ● *adv.* **1** in every part or respect. **2** during the whole time.

throughput *n.* **1** the amount of material put through a process, esp. in manufacturing or computing. **2** processing or handling capacity.

throve *past of* THRIVE.

throw ● *v.* (*past* **threw**; *past part.* **thrown**) **1** *tr.* project (something) with force from the hand or arm through the air, esp. in a particular direction; cast, hurl, fling. **2** *tr.* force violently, esp. in a particular direction or into a particular position; cause to be thrust or shot through the air. **3** *tr.* cause to pass into or out of a particular state or condition, esp. suddenly or unexpectedly (*it threw her life into turmoil*). **4** *tr.* turn or move (part of the body) quickly or suddenly (*threw his arms around her*). **5** *tr.* **a** emit or project (a beam, ray, or light). **b** cast (a shadow). **6** *tr.* (of a ventriloquist) project (the voice) so that it seems to be coming from a source other than the speaker. **7** *tr.* direct (a kiss, look, insult, etc.) at a person. **8** *tr.* **a** give, deliver, or aim (a punch). **b** *Hockey* (often foll. by *on*) deliver (a hit or bodycheck) on an opponent. **9** *tr.* **a** *Sport* (often foll. by *down*) (esp. in wrestling or football) bring (an opponent) to the ground; tackle. **b** (of a horse) cause (its rider) to fall off. **10** *tr. informal* (often foll. by *off*) baffle, confuse, disconcert (*the question really threw me*). **11** *tr.* have (a tantrum or fit etc.). **12** *tr.* host (a party etc.). **13** *tr.* (foll. by *on* or *off*) put on or remove (clothes or an article of clothing) hastily. **14** *Baseball & Football* **a** *intr. & tr.* start or participate in a game as a pitcher or quarterback. **b** *tr.* (of a pitcher) earn or achieve (a strikeout, complete game, etc.). **15** *tr. informal* lose (a game or race etc.) deliberately. **16** *tr.*

move (a switch or lever) in order to turn something on. **17** *tr.* put (a vehicle) into a particular gear (*threw the car into third*). **18** *tr.* **a** cause (a die or dice) to fall on a surface, esp. by releasing or propelling them from the hand. **b** obtain (a specified number) by throwing a die or dice. ● *n.* **1** an act of throwing. **2** the distance a thing is or may be thrown (*a stone's throw*). **3** *N Amer.* **a** a light rug or piece of decorative fabric used as a casual covering for furniture. **b** a light shawl or afghan. **4** the act of throwing an opponent or being thrown in wrestling. **5** (*prec. by a*) *informal* each; per item or turn (*$20 a throw*). □ **throw around** (or **about**) **1** throw in various directions. **2** spend (one's money) in a reckless or ostentatious manner. **throw away 1** dispose of or discard (something no longer wanted), esp. by putting it in the garbage. **2 a** waste or fail to make use of (an opportunity etc.). **b** (often foll. by *on*) waste (money, one's life, etc.) in foolish ventures, on undeserving people, etc. **3** discard (a card). **4** *Theatre* speak (lines) with deliberate underemphasis. **throw back 1** (usu. in *passive*; foll. by *on*) force (a person) to rely on something (*was thrown back on his savings*). **2** pull aside (curtains, bedclothes, etc.), esp. with a sharp movement. **3** swallow (a drink) quickly and in one gulp. **throw a person a curve** confuse someone by doing or saying something unexpected. **throw down** fling, hurl, or bring to the ground or floor. **throw down the gauntlet** (or **glove**) issue a challenge. **throw for** *N Amer. Football* (of a quarterback) amass (a specified number of yards, interceptions, etc.) by passing the ball. **throw good money after bad** incur further loss in a hopeless attempt to recoup a previous loss. **throw one's hand in 1** *Cards* give up. **2** give up; withdraw from a contest. **throw in 1** include at no extra cost. **2** add or make (a remark) casually. **3 a** (in basketball or soccer) throw (the ball) in bounds. **b** (in baseball) return (the ball) from the outfield. **throw in the towel** (or **sponge**) **1** admit defeat. **2** (of a boxer or a boxer's attendant) throw the towel etc. used between rounds into the air as a token of defeat. **throw off 1** confuse or distract (a person speaking, thinking, or acting) from the matter in hand. **2** discard; contrive to get rid of. **3** write or utter in an offhand manner. **throw oneself at** make eager or overt advances upon (someone) regarded as a potential romantic partner or spouse. **throw oneself into** engage vigorously in. **throw oneself on** (or **upon**) **1** rely completely on. **2** attack. **throw open** open (a window or door etc.) wide and usu. suddenly. **2** (often foll. by *to*) make vulnerable or accessible. **throw out 1** discard or dispose of (something no longer wanted), esp. by putting it in the garbage. **2 a** force (a troublemaker, trespasser, etc.) to leave the premises. **b** evict (a tenant etc.) from a house or apartment. **c** *Sport* (of an official) eject (a player, manager, or coach) from a game as a disciplinary measure. **3** wrench or dislocate (one's back, shoulder, hip, etc.). **4** put forward tentatively. **5 a** reject (a proposal or bill) in Parliament. **b** dismiss (a case or charges) in a court of law. **6** *Baseball* put (a runner) out by throwing the ball to the base before he or she reaches it. **throw over** desert or abandon. **throw together 1** prepare or assemble hastily. **2** introduce; cause to meet. **throw up 1** vomit. **2** abandon; resign from. **4** erect hastily. **5** bring to notice. **6** lift (a sash window) quickly. **throw one's weight around** (or **about**) *informal* act with unpleasant self-assertiveness. □ **thrower** *n.* (also in *comb.*).

throwaway ● *adj.* **1** disposable (*throwaway diapers*). **2**

(of a line, word, etc.) deliberately underemphasized for effect. **3** disposed to throwing things away; wasteful (*throwaway society*). ● *n.* **1** something that is meant to be discarded after esp. one use. **2** *N Amer.* printed material meant to be discarded once read, such as a flyer or advertising supplement. **3** *N Amer.* a child or youth who has been cast out or rejected by family or society (also *attrib.: throwaway children*).

throwback *n.* (often foll. by *to*) **1** a person who embodies the principles, views, and characteristics of an earlier era. **2** a thing, such as a song, that recalls a similar thing of a previous era. **3** reversion to ancestral character.

throw cushion *n. N Amer.* (also **throw pillow**) one of usu. several small cushions placed on a chair.

throw-in *n.* (in basketball and soccer) the act of throwing the ball in bounds from the sidelines during play.

throw rug *n.* = THROW *n.* 3a.

thru *prep. & adv. N Amer. informal* through.

thrum¹ ● *v.* (**thrummed, thrumming**) **1** *tr. & intr.* play (a stringed instrument) monotonously or unskilfully. **2** *intr.* (often foll. by *on*) drum idly (*rain thrummed on the roof*). **3** *intr.* produce or emit a low hum or thrumming sound, esp. monotonously or continuously. ● *n.* **1** a low monotonous hum or drone, such as that of a car or machinery operating. **2 a** music consisting of the unskilled or monotonous playing of a guitar or other stringed instrument. **b** the sound of a guitar being thrummed.

thrum² ● *n.* loose strands or wisps of unspun wool or raw fleece etc. twisted and knitted into a toque or mitten etc. ● *v.tr.* (**thrummed, thrumming**) knit thrums into a mitten or toque etc. at regular intervals. □ **thrummed** *adj.* **thrumming** *n.*

thrush¹ *n.* any small or medium-sized songbird of the family Turdidae.

thrush² *n.* **1** a fungal disease, candidiasis, characterized by white patches on the inside of the mouth and throat and on the tongue. **2** this disease affecting any other part of the body, esp. the vagina, and characterized by pain and severe itching.

thrust ● *v.* (*past and past part.* **thrust**) **1** *tr.* push or shove with a sudden force or impulse. **2** *tr.* **a** (foll. by *on*) impose (a thing) forcibly on a person; enforce acceptance of (a thing) (*had this task thrust on me at the last minute*). **b** (usu. foll. by *into*) force (a person) into some condition or course of action (*the scandal has thrust him into the limelight*). **3 a** *tr. & intr.* (often foll. by *through or past*) make (one's way) forcibly; advance through a crowd or past an obstacle etc. (*she thrust past me abruptly*). **b** *intr.* make a sudden lunge forward. **c** *intr.* (foll. by *at or through*) lunge forward with a pointed weapon; stab. ● *n.* **1** a sudden or forcible push or lunge. **2** the propulsive force exerted by the propeller of a ship or aircraft, or developed by a jet or rocket engine. **3** (often foll. by *of*) **a** the principal theme or gist of remarks, an argument, etc. **b** the aim or underlying principle of an undertaking, movement, etc. **4** a caustic, critical, or witty remark aimed at a person. **5 a** a lunge or attack with a pointed weapon. **b** a strong attempt to penetrate an enemy's line or territory. **6** the lateral pressure exerted by an arch or other structure against an abutment or support. □ **thrust oneself in** interfere.

thruster *n.* **1** a small rocket engine on a spacecraft, used to make alterations in its flight path or altitude. **2 a** (in full **bow thruster**) a propeller located on the bow of a ship, used esp. when docking. **b** each of

several jets or propellers on an offshore rig etc. for accurate manoeuvring and maintenance of position.

thud ● *n.* a dull low sound like that of a blow on something soft. ● *v.intr.* (**thudded, thudding**) produce or fall with a thud. □ **thuddingly** *adv.*

thug *n.* **1** a vicious ruffian; a violent criminal or gangster. **2** *derogatory* a person regarded as a threat or menace; a punk or bully. □ **thuggery** *n.* **thuggish** *adj.*

thulium /ˈθuːlɪəm, ˈθjuː-/ *n.* a soft metallic element occurring naturally in apatite.

thumb ● *n.* **1 a** the short thick first digit of the human hand, opposable to the fingers. **b** a corresponding digit of the hand or foot of other animals. **2** the part of a glove meant for a thumb. ● *v.* **1** *intr.* turn the pages of a book with or as if with a thumb. **2** *tr.* make (a book or its pages etc.) dirty or worn by or as if by repeated handling with the thumb (*a well-thumbed book*). **3** *tr.* solicit or obtain (a ride etc.) by signalling with a closed fist and raised thumb to passing vehicles while standing at the side of a road or highway. □ **be all thumbs** be clumsy; lack manual dexterity. **thumb one's nose** (usu. foll. by *at*) **1** hold one's thumb to the bottom of the nose with the hand open and fingers spread out as a gesture of derision or contempt. **2** mock, deride, or scorn. **thumbs-down** an indication of rejection or failure. **thumbs-up** an indication of success or approval. **under a person's thumb** completely under a person's influence or sway. □ **thumbed** *adj.* (also in *comb.*).

thumb index ● *n.* a set of labelled notches cut into the side of a dictionary etc. for easy reference. ● *v.tr.* provide (a book) with these. □ **thumb-indexed** *adj.*

thumbnail *n.* **1** the nail of a thumb. **2 a** a concise descriptive account. **b** (*attrib.*) designating a description etc. that is short and concise (*a thumbnail sketch*).

thumbprint *n.* **1** an impression of a thumb used esp. for identification. **2** a distinguishing trait etc.

thumbscrew *n.* **1** an instrument of torture for crushing the thumbs. **2** a screw with a flattened head for turning with the thumb and forefinger.

thumb-sucker *n.* **1** a child that habitually sucks his or her thumb. **2** *informal* a serious article in a newspaper or periodical. □ **thumb-sucking** *n. & adj.*

thumbtack *N Amer.* ● *n.* a pin with a flat head that may be pushed into a bulletin board for fastening a notice or message etc. ● *v.tr.* fasten (a note, message, artwork, etc.) to a wall or bulletin board etc. using a thumbtack or thumbtacks.

thump ● *v.* **1** *tr.* beat or strike heavily, esp. with the fist. **2** *intr.* throb or pulsate strongly (*my heart was thumping*). **3** *intr.* step or tread heavily; stomp. **4** *intr.* (usu. foll. by *on*) pound with the hand, esp. to attract attention. **5** *tr. informal* achieve a resounding victory over. **6** *tr. & intr.* play (a tune etc.) with a heavy touch. ● *n.* **1** a dull heavy blow, as with the fist or a blunt instrument. **2** the sound of this. □ **thumper** *n.*

thumping ● *adj.* **1** *informal* exceptionally large (*a thumping lie*). **2** that thumps. ● *n.* **1** a series of repeated thumps or the sound of this. **2** *informal* a thorough beating. □ **thumpingly** *adv.*

thunder ● *n.* **1** a loud rumbling or crashing noise accompanying a flash of lightning, caused by the sudden heating and expansion of gases along the channel of the discharge. **2** a resounding loud deep noise (*the thunder of applause*). **3** powerful, vehement, or terrifying speech. ● *v.* **1** *intr.* (of thunder) sound (*it thundered all night*). **2** *intr.* make or proceed with a noise suggestive of thunder (*bison thundered across the* prairie). **3** *tr.* utter or communicate in a loud voice or forceful manner; shout, roar. **4** *intr.* **a** rant. **b** (usu. foll. by *against*) criticize or denounce loudly or vehemently. □ **steal a person's thunder** spoil the effect of another's idea, action, etc. by expressing or doing it first. □ **thunderer** *n.* **thundery** *adj.*

thunderbird *n.* a mythical bird which, according to the legends of many N American Aboriginal peoples, created the thunder with its beating wings and the lightning with its flashing eyes.

thunderbolt *n.* **1** a flash of lightning with a simultaneous crash of thunder. **2 a** a bolt of lightning believed to be used as an agent of divine punishment or destruction. **b** the representation of a bolt or shaft of lightning wielded by various gods. **3** a sudden and unexpected occurrence or item of news.

thunderclap *n.* **1** a crash of thunder. **2** a very loud, sudden noise (also *attrib.*: *thunderclap voice*). **3** something startling or unexpected.

thundercloud *n.* **1** a cumulonimbus cloud with a towering or spreading top, which is charged with electricity and produces thunder and lightning. **2** something threatening or dreadful.

thunderhead *n.* esp. *N Amer.* a tall cumulonimbus cloud with an anvil-shaped top extending horizontally, usu. portending a thunderstorm.

thundering *adj. informal* **1** very great or excessive; immense (*a thundering nuisance*). **2** as loud as thunder. □ **thunderingly** *adv.*

thunderous *adj.* **1** powerful, violent, very hard or heavy (*a thunderous collision*). **2** very loud; rumbling or resounding like thunder. □ **thunderously** *adv.*

thundershower *n.* esp. *N Amer.* a rain shower accompanied by thunder and lightning.

thunderstorm *n.* a storm with thunder and lightning, and usu. heavy rain or hail.

thunderstruck *adj.* amazed, astonished.

thunk¹ *n. & v. informal* = THUD.

thunk² *informal* esp. *jocular past and past part. of* THINK.

Thurs. *abbr.* (also **Thur.**) Thursday.

Thursday ● *n.* the fifth day of the week, following Wednesday. ● *adv.* **1** on Thursday. **2** (**Thursdays**) on Thursdays; each Thursday.

thus *adv. formal* **1 a** in this way; in the manner that has been shown or indicated. **b** as follows; in the manner about to be shown or indicated. **2** therefore, consequently; as a result. **3** so; to the degree or extent indicated (*thus far*).

thusly *adv.* thus. ¶Generally regarded as a superfluous synonym for *thus* except in those cases where it is used with deliberate irony or humour.

thwack ● *n.* **1** a sharp resonant sound as produced esp. by one flat surface striking another. **2** a heavy blow producing such a sound. ● *v.tr.* lash, slap, or whack (a person or thing), esp. with something flat, such as the palm of one's hand.

thwart ● *v.tr.* successfully oppose (a person or thing); foil, frustrate, block. ● *n.* a structural member extending across a boat, esp. a seat in a canoe etc.

thy *possess.pron.* (*attrib.*) (also **thine** before a vowel) of or belonging to thee: now replaced by *your* except in some formal, liturgical, dialect, and poetic uses.

thyme /taim/ *n.* any herb or shrub of the genus *Thymus* with aromatic leaves, esp. *T. vulgare*.

thymine /'θaimi:n/ *n.* a pyrimidine found in all living tissue as a component base of DNA.

thymus /'θaiməs/ *n.* (*pl.* **thymuses** or **thymi** /-mai/) (in full **thymus gland**) a lymphoid organ situated near the base of the neck of vertebrates which is the site of maturation of T-lymphocytes, in humans becoming much smaller at the approach of puberty.

thyroid /'θairɔid/ ● *n.* **1 a** (in full **thyroid gland**) a large ductless gland in the neck of vertebrates which secretes hormones regulating growth and development through control of the rate of metabolism. **b** an extract prepared from the thyroid gland of animals and used to treat hypothyroid conditions, such as goitre and cretinism. **2** (in full **thyroid cartilage**) the largest of the cartilages of the larynx, consisting of two broad four-sided plates joined in front at an angle, enclosing the vocal cords and, in men, forming the Adam's apple. ● *adj.* of, pertaining to, or connected with the thyroid (*thyroid artery*).

thyself *pron. archaic emphatic & refl. form of* THOU¹, THEE.

Ti *symbol* titanium.

ti¹ /ti:/ (also **ti tree**) *n.* any woody plant of the genus *Cordyline* and related genera, esp. *C. terminalis* with edible roots, cultivars of which are frequently grown as houseplants.

ti² *n.* **1** (in tonic sol-fa) the seventh note of a major scale. **2** the note B in the fixed-do system.

tiara /ti'erə, -'ɑrə/ *n.* a woman's jewelled ornamental coronet or headband worn on the front of the hair.

Tibetan /tɪ'betən/ ● *n.* **1 a** a native or inhabitant of Tibet, a mountainous country in Asia forming an autonomous region of China. **b** a person of Tibetan descent. **2** the language of Tibet. ● *adj.* of or relating to Tibet or its language.

Tibetan Buddhism *n.* the religion of Tibet, a form of Mahayana Buddhism.

tibia /'tɪbiə/ *n.* (*pl.* **tibiae** /-bi,i:/ or **-s**) **1** the inner and larger of the two bones of the lower leg extending from the knee to the ankle, articulating at its upper end with the fibula. **2** the corresponding part in other tetrapod animals. **3** the fourth segment of the leg in insects. □ **tibial** *adj.*

tibiotarsus /,tɪbio:'tɑrsəs/ *n.* (*pl.* **tibiotarsi** /-sai/) the bone in a bird corresponding to the tibia, fused at the lower end with the proximal bones of the tarsus.

tic *n.* **1** a disorder characterized by a repeated habitual spasmodic twitching of one or more muscles, esp. of the face, largely involuntary and accentuated under stress. **2** a habitual mannerism or idiosyncrasy; a habit or quirk.

tick¹ ● *n.* **1 a** the regular slight click made by a watch or clock. **b** the short soft metallic sound of two things clicking together. **2** a mark (√) made with a pen etc. to check off items on a list, indicate the correctness of an answer, etc. **3** *Stock Exch.* the smallest recognized amount by which the price of a commodity or stock etc. may fluctuate. ● *v.* **1** *intr.* **a** (of a clock etc.) operate with or make a tick. **b** (foll. by *away, down*) (of time) pass. **2** *intr.* (of a mechanism) operate, function, work. **3** *tr.* (often foll. by *off*) mark (an item on a list, a box or option on an application form, a written answer, etc.) with a tick. □ **tick off** *informal N Amer.* annoy, irritate. **tick over** (of a person, project, etc.) be working or functioning at a basic or minimum level. **what makes a person tick** *informal* what makes a person behave in a certain way; a person's motivation.

tick² *n.* **1** any of various bloodsucking acarids of the families Argasidae and Ixodidae, which attach themselves to the skin of dogs, cattle, and other mammals, and may transmit disease to humans. **2** any of various parasitic flies of the families Hippoboscidae, infesting birds and sheep etc., and Nycteribiidae.

tick³ *n.* *Cdn & Brit. informal* credit (*buy it on tick*).

tick[4] n. **1** a case or cover filled with feathers etc. to form a mattress or pillow. **2** = TICKING.

tick-borne adj. (of a disease) transmitted by ticks.

ticked adj. (in full **ticked off**) informal angry.

ticker n. **1** informal **a** the heart. **b** a watch. **2** N Amer. an electronic instrument for receiving and recording telegraph messages, esp. one that prints out stock prices or news stories.

tickertape n. **1** a long narrow strip of paper on which a ticker prints esp. stock prices. **2** this or similar material, such as streamers, ribbon, or confetti, thrown from windows to greet a celebrity in a motorcade (also attrib.: tickertape parade).

ticket • n. **1 a** a written or printed piece of paper or card entitling the holder to enter a place, watch or participate in an event, travel by public transport, etc. **b** a similar printed card making the bearer eligible for a raffle, draw, etc. **c** a receipt for an item left temporarily for safe keeping, such as at a coat check. **2** an official notification of a traffic violation (speeding ticket). **3** esp. N Amer. **a** a list of candidates for election nominated by a political party or group. **b** the declared principles or policies of a political party or group. **4** a tag or label attached to an item and giving its name, price, or other details. **5** Cdn a negotiable cash receipt issued to a farmer by the manager of a grain elevator for grain received. **6 a** (foll. by to) a means of reaching or achieving (this promotion is my ticket to upper management). **b** (foll. by out) something enabling a person to leave an unfavourable location or situation (his ticket out of unemployment). **7** (prec. by the) informal the ideal, correct, or required thing (that's just the ticket). **8** a person or thing, esp. a performer or performance, the popularity of which is judged according to its availablility or accessibility (this band's the hottest ticket in town!). **9** a certificate of qualification as a ship's officer, pilot, etc. **10** Cdn hist. = LOCATION TICKET. • v. (**ticketed, ticketing**) **1 a** tr. issue a ticket to (the driver of a vehicle). **b** tr. & intr. place a parking ticket on the windshield of (a car). **2** tr. attach a ticket to; label. **3** tr. **a** issue (a person) with a ticket for a trip. **b** informal (usu. in passive) designate (a person) for a particular role or destiny (is ticketed to be the starting goalie). □ **write one's own ticket** dictate one's own terms. □ **ticketed** adj. **ticketless** adj.

ticket agent n. a person who sells tickets to esp. theatrical or sporting events. □ **ticket agency** n. (pl. -ies).

ticket holder n. a person who has purchased a ticket for a sporting or theatrical event, concert, etc.

ticking n. a strong durable usu. striped linen or cotton fabric used esp. to cover mattresses etc.

tickle[1] • v. **1 a** tr. lightly touch, stroke, or poke (a person or part of a person's body) in such a way that the nerves are excited, producing a reflex spasmodic movement and usu. laughter. **b** intr. (of a part of the body) be affected by this sensation (my throat tickles). **c** intr. cause this sensation (this sweater tickles). **2** tr. amuse, delight, or excite (a person, curiosity, a sense of humour, etc.) (I was tickled by the thought of it). • n. **1** an act of tickling. **2** a tickling sensation (a tickle in my throat). □ **tickled pink** (or **to death**) informal extremely amused or pleased. □ **tickler** n. **tickly** adj.

tickle[2] n. Cdn (Nfld & Maritimes) **1** a narrow strait or channel between islands or between an island and the mainland, esp. one that is difficult to navigate. **2** an entrance to a harbour that is narrow and difficult to navigate.

ticklish /ˈtɪkəlɪʃ, ˈtɪklɪʃ/ adj. **1** sensitive to tickling. **2** (of a matter to be dealt with etc.) requiring careful treatment or handling; tricky, delicate. **3** (of a person) touchy; easily offended, irritated, or upset. □ **ticklishly** adv. **ticklishness** n.

tick-tock n. the ticking sound of esp. a large clock.

tic-tac-toe n. (also **tick-tack-toe**) **1** N Amer. a children's game in which players attempt to complete a row of three Xs or three Os marked alternately on a square grid of nine squares drawn on paper etc. **2** Hockey a swift three-way passing play that results in a scoring opportunity and often a goal. **b** (attrib.) designating a skilful style of play involving quick accurate passes.

tidal adj. of, related to, or affected by the tides; ebbing and flowing periodically (tidal basin). □ **tidally** adv.

tidal pool n. (also **tide pool**) N Amer. a usu. large pool of water that remains on a shore or beach etc. after the tide has receded.

tidal wave n. **1** the undulation of the surface of the sea which passes around the earth and causes high tide as its highest point reaches each successive place. **2** (not in technical use) an exceptionally large ocean wave, esp. one caused by an underwater earthquake or volcanic eruption. **3 a** a widespread manifestation of feeling, opinion, etc. **b** a large or overwhelming quantity or amount of something.

tidbit n. N Amer. **1** a small piece of food; a dainty morsel or delicacy. **2** an interesting or piquant item of news or information.

tiddlywink n. **1** a small plastic counter flicked into a cup by being pressed on its edge by a larger one. **2** (in pl.) this game.

tide n. **1 a** the alternate rising and falling of the sea, usu. twice each lunar day in a given place, due to the attraction of the moon and sun. **b** the alternate inflow and outflow of water on a shore or coast produced by this (see EBB n. 1, FLOOD n. 3). **c** the water as affected by this. **2** the course or trend of opinion, luck, or events (turned the tide in our favour). **3** the flow or movement of a large amount of something (the tide of illegal drugs). **4** (archaic except in comb.) a particular time or season (Eastertide). □ **tide over** enable or help (a person) to get through esp. a difficult period (the money will tide me over). □ **tideless** adj.

tide line n. **1** the level reached by the sea water at high tide. **2** a mark left on the shore by the water at this level.

tidewater n. **1** water carried or affected by tides. **2** N Amer. a region situated on tidewater (also attrib.: tidewater port).

tidings n.pl. literary news, information.

tidy • adj. (-**ier**, -**iest**) **1** neat, orderly; methodically arranged. **2** (of a person) **a** having a clean and neat appearance. **b** inclined to keep things neat. **3** free of complications; convenient (a tidy ending). **4** informal considerable (it cost a tidy sum). • v.tr. (-**ies**, -**ied**) (often foll. by up) **1** make (a room, oneself, etc.) neat; put or arrange in good order. **2** (also foll. by away) put (things) away for the sake of tidiness (tidy up the mess on the floor). • n. (pl. -**ies**) an act or period of tidying (give the place a quick tidy). □ **tidily** adv. **tidiness** n.

tie • v. (**tied, tying**) **1** tr. **a** (often foll. by together) bind or fasten (two things) with rope or string etc. **b** (often foll. by to, on) fasten or secure (a person or thing) to another with rope or string etc. **c** (often foll. by up) confine or restrict the movement of (a person or thing) with rope or string etc. **2** tr. **a** form (a string, ribbon, shoelace, etc.) into a knot or bow. **b** make (a knot or bow) in a piece of rope or string etc. **c** secure (an article of clothing, esp. a shoe or boot) by tying a lace, belt, etc. **3** tr. (usu. in passive) **a** be closely or inextricably linked to (a person or thing). **b** bind or restrict (a person) with an obligation or responsibility etc. **4 a** *tr. & intr.* (often foll. by *for, at*) finish a game, event, or competition with the same score or standing as (an opponent or opponents) (*the teams tied at three; we tied them for first place*). **b** *tr.* make (a game or score) even (*the goal tied the game*). **c** *tr.* match or equal (a record). **5** *tr. Fishing* make (an artificial fly) by dressing a hook with strands of silk and feathers etc. **6** *tr. Music* **a** connect (written notes) with a tie or ligature. **b** perform (two notes) as one unbroken note. ● *n.* **1 a** rope, cord, or chain, etc. used for fastening or tying something (*a twist-tie*). **2** a strip of material worn around the neck under the collar and tied with a knot in front. **3** (often in *pl.*) something uniting or restricting people or things; a link or connection, esp. a bond or obligation (*all economic ties have been severed*). **4 a** a game or competition etc. in which two or more opponents have or finish with the same score. **b** the condition of having the same score as an opponent (*the game ended in a tie*). **5** *N Amer.* a wooden or concrete beam laid horizontally to support the rails of a train track. **6** *Music* a curved line above or below two notes of the same pitch indicating that they are to be played for the combined duration of their time values. □ **fit to be tied** *informal* very angry. **tie down 1** fasten or secure with rope to a fixed point. **2** limit or restrict (a person), esp. with responsibility or commitment. **tie in** (foll. by *with*) make or be relevant to or consistent with; fit. **tie one on** esp. *N Amer.* get drunk. **tie up 1** bind or fasten securely with cord etc. **2** (usu. in *passive*) fully occupy or engage (a person), esp. in business or a meeting etc. **3** hinder or obstruct; prevent from acting freely. **4 a** complete (an undertaking etc.). **b** take care of (loose ends). **5** invest or reserve (capital etc.) so that it is not immediately available for use. **6** moor (a boat). **7** secure or tether (an animal). □ **tied** *adj.* **tieless** *adj.*

tie-back *n.* a decorative strip of fabric or cord for holding a curtain back from the window.

tiebreaker *n.* (also **tiebreak**) esp. *Sport* **1** a means of determining the winner when two competitors are tied. **2** a goal or point etc. that gives a person or team the lead in a tie game. □ **tiebreaking** *adj.*

tie-down *n.* a device, esp. a cord or strap, used to secure or fasten something (also *attrib.: tie-down chain*).

tie-dye ● *n.* **1** a method of producing coloured patterns on fabric or a garment by tying parts of it so that they receive less dye than other parts when the fabric is dyed. **2** a garment etc. dyed in this way (also *attrib.: tie-dye T-shirt*). ● *v.tr.* dye (fabric or a garment) using this method. □ **tie-dyed** *adj.*

tie-in *n.* **1** a connection or association; a link. **2 a** a joint promotion of related items esp. featuring promotional merchandise produced to take advantage of the success of a movie or television series etc. **b** (also *attrib.*) an item marketed in such a promotion.

tier¹ /ti:r/ *n.* **1** each of a series of rows or horizontal units placed one above another in a structure, such as in theatre seating. **2** a rank, grade, or stratum. □ **tiered** *adj.* (also in *comb.*).

tier² /tair/ *n.* a person who ties something, esp. a person who ties artificial flies for fishing.

tie-up *n.* **1 a** a connection, a link. **b** a business partnership, merger, or takeover, etc. **2** *N Amer.* **a** a stoppage, esp. of labour or business. **b** a traffic jam.

TIFF *n.* a file format used widely in desktop publishing for representing colour or grey-scale images.

tiff *n.* a petty quarrel; a minor disagreement or rift.

tiffany /'tɪfəni/ *n.* (in full **tiffany lamp**) any of various lamps with stained-glass shades, esp. a suspended ceiling lamp with a polygonal shade scalloped around the bottom edge.

tiger *n.* **1** a large powerful carnivorous feline, *Panthera tigris*, tawny yellow in colour with blackish transverse stripes and a white belly, found in several races in parts of Asia. **2** a person of great energy, strength, or courage. □ **have a tiger by the tail** be engaged in an undertaking etc. which proves unexpectedly difficult but cannot easily or safely be abandoned. □ **tigerish** *adj.*

tiger cat *n.* any moderate-sized feline resembling the tiger, e.g. the ocelot or margay.

tiger lily *n.* a tall E Asian lily, *Lilium tigrinum*, with flowers of dull orange spotted with black or purple, naturalized in N America.

tiger shrimp *n.* a large shrimp marked with dark bands, of the genus *Penaeus*.

tight ● *adj.* **1** set or fastened securely in place so as not to move or to move only with difficulty. **2** (of a rope, surface, muscle, etc.) drawn or stretched so as to be tense; not loose, slack, or relaxed. **3** (of clothing etc.) fitting very closely or too closely. **4 a** (of money etc.) scarce; not easily obtainable. **b** (of a money market) in which money is scarce. **5** dense, compact (*a tight ball*). **6 a** (of control etc.) strictly imposed. **b** (of a deadline, budget, etc.) allowing no leeway. **c** (of a schedule) having no free time. **7** difficult to deal with or manage; resolved or achieved by a narrow margin (*a tight situation*). **8** (usu. in *comb.*) of such close texture as to be impervious to a specified thing (*airtight*). **9** (of a corner or curve) having a short radius. **10** (of a game, competition, etc.) close. **11** *informal* on terms of close friendship; intimate. **12** *informal* drunk. **13** *informal* (of a person) cheap, stingy. ● *adv.* tightly (*hold on tight!*). □ **run a tight ship** *N Amer.* maintain the efficiency of an organization etc. with strict management. **sit tight 1** remain in one's seat. **2** do nothing, either as a safeguard against making a mistake or so as to wait for an opportunity to get what one wants. □ **tightly** *adv.* **tightness** *n.*

tight-assed *adj.* esp. *N Amer. slang* **1** rigidly conventional and uptight; straightlaced. **2** stingy, cheap. □ **tight-ass** *n.* (also *attrib.*).

tighten *v.tr. & intr.* (often foll. by *up*) make or become tight or tighter.

tight end *n. Football* **1** an offensive end who lines up next to the tackle and may be used either as a blocker or to receive passes. **2** this position.

tight-fisted *adj.* stingy. □ **tight-fistedness** *n.*

tight-fitting *adj.* **1** (of clothing) fitting very close to the body. **2** that fits snugly or securely (*tight-fitting lid*).

tight-lipped *adj.* **1** refusing to discuss esp. a particular matter; secretive. **2** with the lips pursed, esp. in anger.

tightly knit *adj.* (also **tight-knit**) = CLOSE-KNIT.

tightrope *n.* **1** a rope or wire stretched tightly high above the ground, on which acrobats perform. **2** a delicate or risky situation.

tightrope walker *n.* one who performs on a tightrope. □ **tightrope walk** *n.* **tightrope walking** *n.*

tights *n.pl.* a one-piece article of clothing made usu. of knitted nylon, designed to cover the hips and each of the legs and feet, worn by women, dancers, etc.

tightwad *n.* esp. *N. Amer. slang* a cheap or miserly person.

tigress *n.* **1** a female tiger. **2** a fierce or passionate woman.

tikka /ˈtɪkə, ˈtiːkə/ n. (usu. in comb.) an Indian dish of marinated meat, esp. chicken or lamb, threaded on skewers and grilled.

'til prep. & conj. (also **til**) informal = UNTIL.

tilde /ˈtɪldə/ n. a mark (˜), placed over a letter, e.g. over a Spanish n when pronounced ny (as in señor) or a Portuguese nasal a or o (as in São Paulo).

tile ● n. **1** a thin slab of baked clay, usu. of a regular shape, used in series for paving a floor, lining a wall or fireplace, covering a roof, etc. **2** a piece of glazed ceramic, cork, linoleum, slate, etc., used for similar purposes. **3** tiles collectively. **4** a hollow, usu. cylindrical pipe used for draining land, roads, etc. **5** a thin flat piece used in a game, such as in Scrabble or mahjong. ● v.tr. **1** cover with tiles. **2** lay drainage tile in. □ **on the tiles** informal enjoying a night out in a wild or reckless manner, esp. drinking. □ **tiled** adj. **tiler** n.

tiling n. **1** the profession or an instance of covering a surface with tiles. **2 a** work consisting of tiles. **b** tiles collectively. **3** the occupation or an instance of laying drainage tiles.

till[1] prep. & conj. = UNTIL. ¶Till is an accepted variant of until and may be used interchangeably with it except at the beginning of a sentence.

till[2] n. a drawer for money in a store etc., esp. with a device recording the amount of each purchase.

till[3] v.tr. **1** prepare and use (land, soil, etc.) for growing crops. **2** plow (land, a field, etc.). □ **tillable** adj.

till[4] n. stiff clay containing boulders, sand, etc. deposited by melting glaciers and ice sheets.

tillage n. **1** the action or process of tilling land. **2** tilled land.

tiller[1] n. a horizontal bar fitted to the head of a boat's rudder to turn it in steering.

tiller[2] n. **1** a machine or implement used for breaking up or cultivating soil. **2** a person who tills soil or cultivates a crop.

tilt[1] ● v. **1 a** intr. lean from the vertical or incline from the horizontal. **b** tr. cause to lean, slant, or slope. **2** intr. (often foll. by towards) incline towards a particular opinion. **3** tr. **a** bias or influence (a decision, verdict, etc.) in favour of a particular person or thing. **b** aim or direct (something) towards a particular audience or objective (their advertising is tilted at middle-aged men). **4** intr. **a** challenge; take on. **b** hist. rush or charge at in a joust. **5** tr. Film move (a camera) in a vertical plane. ● n. **1** a slanting or sloping position; a lean. **2** an inclination or bias. **3 a** an encounter between opponents (an entertaining tilt). **b** hist. a joust between two knights on horseback with lances, each attempting to throw the other from the saddle. **4** a function of some cars and trucks etc. that enables the height and angle of the steering wheel to be adjusted. **5** Film the upward or downward pivoting movement of a camera across the screen. **6** (in full **pelvic tilt**) an exercise designed to relieve back ailments by flattening the small of the back. □ **full** (or **at full**) **tilt 1** at full speed. **2** with the utmost force or energy.

tilt[2] n. Cdn (Nfld) **1** a small shack, cabin, or hut characterized by a sloping roof, used seasonally by fishermen and trappers. **2** a rudimentary tent or shelter consisting of a sealskin or canvas covering.

tilth n. **1** the condition of cultivated soil (a fine tilth). **2** tillage.

timbale n. **1** /tɑˈbɛl/ **a** a dish consisting of meat, fish, or vegetables in a creamy sauce, or fruit etc. served in a drum-shaped china or copper mould, a pastry shell, or a similar crust made of rice or pasta. **b** the mould, shell, or crust in which this is served. **2** /tæmˈbæli/ (usu. in pl.) each of a pair of single-headed drums played with drumsticks, used esp. in Latin American dance music.

timber ● n. **1** wood that has been prepared for use as building material, in carpentry, etc. **2 a** a beam or piece of wood forming or capable of forming part of a building or structure. **b** (usu. in pl.) the pieces of wood forming the ribs, bends, or frames of a ship's hull. **3 a** large standing trees suitable for timber. **b** trees in their natural state not considered as building material. **c** an area of woodland or forest. ● interj. a warning that a tree is about to fall. □ **timbering** n.

timbered adj. **1** (esp. of a building) made wholly or partly of timber. **2** (of land, a region, etc.) covered with trees; wooded (timbered mountains).

timber frame ● n. **1** a usu. factory-prepared section of timber framework used in the construction of houses and barns etc. **2** a house etc. built using a timber framework. ● adj. **1** (usu. **timber-framed**) (usu. attrib.) having a frame of esp. large timbers. **2** (attrib.) (of a house) built using usu. factory-prepared sections of timber framework. □ **timber framer** n.

timberland n. N Amer. land covered with forest yielding timber.

timber licence n. Cdn Forestry a licence to cut timber from a berth conditional upon payment of dues to the government.

timberline n. N Amer. **1** the altitudinal level on a mountain above which no trees grow. **2** = TREELINE 1.

timber rights n.pl. Cdn Forestry the rights to cut timber of a certain diameter in a specified region, which are controlled by the provincial government and may be obtained in exchange for payment.

timber wolf n. = WOLF 1.

timbre /ˈtæmbər, ˈtæbrə/ n. the distinctive character or quality of a sound, esp. that of a musical voice or instrument, apart from its pitch and intensity. □ **timbral** adj.

Timbuktu /ˌtɪmbʌkˈtuː/ (also **Timbuctoo**) any remote or outlandish place in a faraway country.

time ● n. **1** the indefinite and continuous duration of existence seen as a series of events progressing from the past through the present into the future. **2 a** the passage of time regarded as affecting people or things (time will tell). **b** (**Time**) the personification of time, esp. as an old man with a scythe and hourglass. **3** (in sing. or pl.) **a** a more or less definite portion of time in history, esp. belonging to particular events or circumstances (the time of Confederation; prehistoric times). **b** the period contemporary with a specified person (in Laurier's time). **c** (prec. by the) the era being considered (scientists of the time). **d** the prevailing conditions of a period or era (hard times; times have changed). **4** (prec. by a) an indefinite period (waited for a time). **5 a** a portion of time available to do something; free time (have some time this afternoon). **b** the amount of time required to do something (we don't have time for a walk). **6 a** (usu. in comb.) a recognizable part of a day or year (lunchtime; springtime). **b** a point in the course of a day expressed by hours and minutes past midnight or noon. **7** time or an amount of time as measured or determined by a conventional standard (eight o'clock Eastern Daylight Time). **8 a** an occasion (last time I saw you). **b** an event or occasion qualified in some way (we had a good time). **9** a suitable moment or occasion (now is the time to strike). **10** Cdn (Maritimes & Nfld) a festive gathering of friends and relatives, esp. in celebration of an event, such as a wedding. **11** a lifetime. **12 a** informal a prison sentence (is doing time). **b** an apprenticeship (served my time). **13 a** the date or expected date of death or of childbirth *(my time is drawing near).* **b** a period of gestation. **14** measured time spent at work. **15 a** the rhythm of a piece of music, as shown by division into bars and expressed by a time signature. **b** the tempo characteristic of a type of music, esp. used as the tempo for a particular piece *(in waltz time).* **c** the duration of a note. **16** *Sport* a time out. ● *interj.* (also **time out**) *Sport* used by a player or coach to ask an official for a time out during a game. ● *v.tr.* **1** measure and record the amount of time taken by (a process or activity, or a person doing it). **2** choose or establish a suitable occasion for *(I timed my vacation to coincide with hers).* **3** esp. *Sport* execute (a jump, shot, etc.) at a calculated instant. **4** regulate the duration or interval of; establish times of operation for. **5** arrange the time of arrival of (a train etc.) *(trains are timed to arrive on the hour).* □ **against time** with utmost speed, in order to finish by a certain time *(working against time).* **ahead of one's time** having ideas too enlightened or advanced to be accepted by one's contemporaries. **ahead of time** in advance of an event or occurrence; earlier, beforehand. **all the time 1** constantly *(nags all the time).* **2** at all times *(leaves a light on all the time).* **3** during the whole of the time referred to (often despite some contrary expectation etc.) *(he was there all the time).* **at one time 1** in or during a known but unspecified past period. **2** simultaneously. **at the same time 1** simultaneously; at a time that is the same for all. **2** nevertheless. **at a time** separately or in successive groups of a specified number each *(one at a time).* **at times** occasionally, periodically. **before one's time 1** prematurely *(old before her time).* **2** before one was born or present etc. *(that was before my time).* **call time** *Sport* ask an official for a time out. **find the time** make arrangements to one's schedule so that there is enough time for a particular activity. **for the time being** for the present; until some other arrangement is made. **give a person the time of day 1** tell a person what time it is. **2** (with *neg.*) *slang* refuse to help or talk or pay attention to a person; snub, ignore. **half the time** *informal* **1** very often, esp. too often *(I couldn't tell if he was being serious half the time).* **2** in a relatively short period *(she did the job in half the time).* **have no time for 1** be unable or unwilling to spend time on. **2** dislike. **have the time 1** be able to spend the time needed. **2** know what time it is. **have a time of it** undergo trouble or difficulty. **in no** (or **less than no**) **time 1** very soon. **2** very quickly. **in one's own good** (or **sweet**) **time** at a pace decided by oneself. **in one's own time** outside working hours. **in time 1** not late, punctual. **2** eventually *(in time you may agree).* **in one's time** in one's heyday. **keep good** (or **bad**) **time 1** (of a clock etc.) record time accurately (or inaccurately). **2** be habitually punctual (or not punctual). **keep time** move or sing etc. in time. **know the time of day** be well informed. **lose no time** (often foll. by *in* + verbal noun) act immediately *(lost no time in cashing the cheque).* **make time** (usu. foll. by *for* or *to* + infin.) find an opportunity to spend time with a person or participate in some activity, esp. while one is already very busy. **no time** *informal* a very short time *(came in no time).* **pass the time of day** *informal* exchange a greeting or casual remarks. **time after time 1** repeatedly, on many occasions. **2** in many instances. **time and** (or **time and time**) **again** on many occasions. **time and motion** (usu. *attrib.*) concerned with measuring the efficiency of industrial and other operations. **the time of day** the hour by the clock. **the time of one's life** a thrilling, exciting, or extremely enjoyable occasion or moment. **time of the month** *informal* or *euphemism* a woman's menstrual period. **time was** there was a time.

time and a half *n.* an increased amount of money paid to an employee for overtime work, equal to one and a half times the pay the employee would normally earn for working the same number of hours.

time bomb *n.* **1** a bomb designed to explode at a preset time. **2 a** a situation on the verge of becoming a crisis or disaster if not defused in time. **b** an unpredictable or moody person, esp. one whose psychological stability is questioned.

time capsule *n.* a sealed box etc. containing objects chosen as representative of life at a particular time, buried for discovery in the future.

time clock *n.* **1** a clock with a mechanism that records an employee's hours of arrival and departure. **2** *Sport* the clock on a scoreboard indicating the amount of time remaining to be played.

time code *n.* a coded signal on videotape or film giving information about the frame number, time of recording or exposure, scene, camera, etc.

time-consuming *adj.* (of a process, activity, etc.) that requires a large or inconvenient amount of time.

time exposure *n.* **1** a method of taking a photograph in which the film is exposed for longer than the maximum normal shutter setting. **2** a picture taken using this method.

time frame *n.* a specific period in which something occurs, has occurred, or is planned to occur.

time-honoured *adj.* (also **time-honored**) (of a custom, tradition, etc.) that is revered as a result of having been observed etc. for many years.

time immemorial *n.* a longer time than anyone can remember or trace.

timekeeper *n.* **1** an official responsible for recording time, esp. at a competition or game. **2 a** a device that records time, such as a watch or clock, esp. in terms of its accuracy *(a good timekeeper).* **b** a person regarded in terms of punctuality. □ **timekeeping** *n.*

time lag *n.* an interval of time between related events, esp. a cause and its effect.

time-lapse *adj.* pertaining to a method of taking a sequence of photographs at long intervals to photograph a slow process, and showing them at a faster speed.

timeless *adj.* not affected by the passage of time; remaining popular, effective, significant, etc., over time. □ **timelessly** *adv.* **timelessness** *n.*

time limit *n.* the period of time within which a task must be accomplished or completed.

timeline *n.* **1** a line graduated in years on which esp. historical events are marked, used to teach or learn the dates and order of important events in history. **2** a schedule for a project etc. showing the dates by which certain stages must be completed in order for the project to be ready on time.

timely /ˈtaɪmli/ *adj.* (**-ier**, **-iest**) opportune; occurring, done, or made at a suitable or appropriate time. □ **timeliness** *n.*

time machine *n.* an imaginary machine capable of transporting a person backwards or forwards in time.

time off *n.* a period of time spent away from work, esp. taken for rest or recreation.

time out *n.* esp. N Amer. **1** *Sport* a short stoppage in play requested so that a team can consider or discuss strategy, attend to an injured player, etc. **2** a short break or period away from an activity.

timepiece *n.* an instrument, such as a clock or watch, for measuring the passage of time.

timer *n.* **1** a device that measures elapsed time, esp. one that sounds to indicate that a certain amount of time has passed. **2** a device that can be set to turn an appliance etc. on or off at a pre-set time. **3** a person responsible for keeping track of time.

times ● *n.* used following a number to express multiplication of what follows (*two times six is twelve; ten times better*). ● *adv.* multiplied by (*the party will cost $10 times the number of people coming*).

time saver *n.* an activity, method, tool, etc., that reduces the amount of time required to do something. □ **time-saving** *adj.*

time scale *n.* the time allowed for or taken by a sequence of events.

time-sensitive *adj.* that must be completed, performed, arranged, etc. at or by a certain time.

time-share *n.* **1** (also *attrib.*) a property that is owned jointly by several people under a time-sharing arrangement. **2** a share in a property owned jointly under a time-sharing arrangement.

time-sharing *n.* **1** an arrangement in which a vacation home is jointly owned or rented by several people, each of whom is entitled to use it for a fixed limited period of time each year. **2** the simultaneous use of a single computer system by several users stationed at different terminals and performing different operations.

time signature *n. Music* an indication of tempo, expressed as a fraction with the numerator giving the number of beats in each bar and the denominator giving the basic note value of each beat.

time slot *n.* = SLOT *n.* 3b.

time span *n.* a period of time, usu. of a specified length (*during a five-week time span*).

times table *n. Math.* **1** a chart showing the products of a number when multiplied by each of the numbers from one to twelve, learned and often memorized by children in school. **2** (in *pl.*) the times tables for each of a range of numbers, esp. those from one to twelve (*do you know your times tables?*).

timetable ● *n.* **1** a list or plan of the times or dates when successive things are to occur or be done; a schedule or timeline. **2 a** a student's schedule indicating the days and times of classes. **b** a schedule of departure and arrival times of buses, trains, airplanes, etc. ● *v.tr.* outline or arrange (events etc.) in a timetable; schedule.

time-tested *adj.* that has, over time, been proven or shown to be effective, useful, or accurate; reliable.

time travel *n.* travel through time into the past or the future, esp. as a feature of science fiction. □ **time traveller** *n.*

time trial *n.* a race in which participants are individually timed, often used to determine qualifiers and their starting positions for a later race.

time warp *n.* **1** (in science fiction) an imaginary or hypothetical distortion of space in relation to time that causes or enables a person to remain stationary in time or to travel backwards or forwards in time. **2** a state in which the styles, attitudes, etc. of a past period are retained (*stuck in a 1950s time warp*).

time-worn *adj.* **1** antiquated. **2** adversely affected by age or time. **3** trite; hackneyed.

time zone *n.* each of the longitudinal divisions of the globe throughout which a standard time is used.

timid *adj.* **1** easily frightened; meek, shy. **2** characterized by or indicating a fear or shyness (*a timid handshake*). □ **timidity** *n.* **timidly** *adv.*

timing *n.* **1** the ability to act or speak at the right time in order to achieve the greatest effect. **2** the time or period of time chosen for an event etc. **3** the act of recording time. **4** the regulation of the opening and closing of valves in an internal combustion engine.

Timorese /ˌtiːmɔːˈriːz/ ● *n.* a member of the indigenous people of Timor, a large island in the S Malay Archipelago. ● *adj.* of or pertaining to this island or these people.

timorous /ˈtɪmərəs/ *adj.* **1** timid; easily alarmed. **2** frightened. □ **timorously** *adv.* **timorousness** *n.*

timothy *n.* a fodder grass, *Phleum pratense*.

timpani /ˈtɪmpəni/ *n.pl.* kettledrums. □ **timpanist** *n.*

tin *n.* **1 a** a silvery-white metallic element resisting corrosion, used esp. in alloys and for plating thin iron or steel sheets to form tin plate. **2 a** a container made of tin (*a cookie tin*). **b** esp. *Brit.* a hermetically sealed container made of tin, tin plate, or aluminum, in which food is preserved and sold; a can. **3** = TIN PLATE. ● *v.tr.* (**tinned, tinning**) **1** seal (food) in an airtight tin for preservation. **2** cover or coat with tin. □ **tinned** *adj.*

tin can *n.* a metal can used to preserve food.

tincture /ˈtɪŋktʃər/ ● *n.* **1** (often foll. by *of*) a tinge, trace, or hint. **2** a medicinal solution, usu. in alcohol, of the active constituents of a natural substance, esp. one of plant origin. ● *v.tr.* (often foll. by *with*) imbue or affect slightly with (a quality, colour, etc.).

tinder /ˈtɪndər/ *n.* a dry substance, such as bits of wood, that readily catches fire, used to start a fire from a spark struck with a flint. □ **tindery** *adj.*

tinderbox *n.* **1** *hist.* a box containing tinder, flint, and steel, formerly used for kindling fires. **2** a volatile or explosive person, thing, or situation.

tine *n.* any of a series of projecting points or prongs, such as on a fork, comb, cultivating tool, the antler of a deer, etc. □ **tined** *adj.* (also in *comb.*).

tinfoil *n.* = FOIL² 1c.

ting ● *n.* a thin clear high-pitched sound made by a small bell or glass etc. when struck. ● *v.intr. & tr.* emit or cause to emit this sound.

tinge ● *v.tr.* (**tinged, tingeing** or **tinging**) (usu. in *passive*; often foll. by *with*) **1** give a slight shade of a usu. specified colour to. **2** modify or affect slightly with the addition of a small amount of a characteristic or quality. ● *n.* **1** a trace of some colour. **2** a touch or trace of something.

tingle ● *n.* **1** a slight prickling or stinging sensation, usu. felt in a limb that has been exposed to cold or which has fallen asleep. **2** a slight tickling sensation or goosebumps as a result of stimulation or excitement. ● *v.tr. & intr.* experience or cause this sensation. □ **tingly** *adj.* (**-ier, -iest**).

tinker ● *v.intr.* **1** (foll. by *with, at*) **a** work in an amateurish or desultory way, esp. to adjust or mend machinery etc. **b** meddle; tamper. **2** (usu. foll. by *with*) make minor adjustments to; refine. **3** work as a tinker. ● *n.* **1** an itinerant mender of kettles and pans etc. **2** a period of tinkering. **3** a clumsy or unskilful worker. **not give a tinker's damn** not care at all. □ **tinkerer** *n.* **tinkering** *n.*

Tinkertoy *n. proprietary* **1** a type of building toy consisting of short coloured dowels that may be inserted into round connecting blocks. **2** (*attrib.*) jocular designating anything resembling a Tinkertoy model, esp. in appearance or simplicity.

tinkle ● *v.* **1** *intr. & tr.* make or cause to make a succession of short light ringing sounds. **2** *intr. informal* urinate. ● *n.* **1** a tinkling sound. **2** *informal* or *euphemism* an act of urinating. □ **tinkly** *adj.*

tinnitus /tɪˈnaɪtəs/ n. Med. a ringing in the ears.

tinny adj. (**-ier, -iest**) **1 a** having a sound like that of tin being struck. **b** (of music, esp. on a recording) thin and metallic, missing the lower frequencies. **2** (of a metal object) flimsy, insubstantial. □ **tinnily** adv. **tinniness** n.

tin plate n. sheet iron or sheet steel coated with tin.

tin-plated adj. coated with tin. □ **tin-plate** v.tr.

tinpot adj. crude, second-rate, inferior (a tinpot navy).

tinsel ● n. **1** glittering metallic strands or threads used for decoration, esp. on a Christmas tree. **2** cheap or superficial brilliance or splendour; showiness, glitz. ● v.tr. (**tinselled, tinselling**) **1** adorn with tinsel. **2** give a speciously attractive or showy appearance to. □ **tinselled** adj. **tinselly** adj.

tinsmith n. a person who manufactures or repairs items of tin and tin plate. □ **tinsmithing** n.

tinsnips n. a pair of hand-held shears used to cut sheet metal.

tint ● n. **1 a** a shade, colour, or hue. **b** (in painting) a particular colour obtained by adding a pigment to a base. **2** a faint colour spread over the surface of something to give a specified tone to a different colour. **3** a semi-permanent hair dye. ● v.tr. **1** apply a tint to (hair, paint, a picture, etc.); colour. **2** give (glass) a darker tone or colour in order to decrease the strength of light passing through.

tiny adj. (**-ier, -iest**) very small; minuscule, minute. □ **tinily** adv. **tininess** n.

tip[1] ● n. **1** an extremity or end, esp. of a small or tapering thing (the northern tip of the island). **2** a small piece or part attached to or over the end of something. **3** (usu. in pl.) a leaf bud of tea. ● v.tr. (**tipped, tipping**) **1** provide or adorn with a tip. **2** colour or mark the tip of. □ **on the tip of one's tongue** about to be remembered. **the tip of the iceberg** a small evident part of something much larger or more significant. □ **tipped** adj. (also in comb.).

tip[2] ● v. (**tipped, tipping**) **1** (often foll. by up) tr. & intr. (cause to) assume a slanting position. **2** (usu. foll. by over) **a** intr. become overturned; fall or turn over. **b** tr. cause (something) to be overturned. **3** tr. **a** tilt (a container) in order to empty its contents. **b** (usu. foll. by into) pour out or spill (contents). **4** tr. strike or touch lightly. **5** tr. **a** Hockey deflect (a shot or the puck) toward the net in an attempt to score. **b** Baseball (of a batter) barely hit (a pitch or the ball) foul or into the catcher's glove. **c** Basketball tap (a rebound) lightly toward the basket in an attempt to score. ● n. **1** a gentle push or slight tilt. **2** Hockey an act of deflecting the puck. **3** Baseball an act of tipping a pitch or ball. **4** Basketball **a** the act of tapping a ball towards the basket. **b** = TIPOFF 3. □ **tip the balance** settle a matter that was previously undetermined. **tip one's hand** unintentionally reveal one's intentions. **tip one's hat** (or **cap**) **1** raise or touch one's hat or cap in greeting or acknowledgement. **2** (usu. foll. by to) acknowledge or thank. **tip off** Basketball (of two teams) begin a game with a jump ball.

tip[3] ● n. **1** a small sum of money given in appreciation for a service done. **2** a useful suggestion or piece of advice. **3** a piece of private or special information, esp. regarding an investment or bet. ● v.tr. (**tipped, tipping**) give a small sum of money to (a person) in appreciation for a service given. □ **tip off** informal give advance warning or confidential information, esp. discreetly or covertly. □ **tipper** n.

tipi var. of TEEPEE.

tip-in n. Hockey & Basketball a shot that is tipped in.

tipoff n. **1** a warning or piece of information etc. given discreetly or confidentially. **2** something that serves as a warning; a sign or indication. **3** Basketball a jump ball at the start of a game.

tippet /ˈtɪpət/ n. Fishing a length of twisted nylon or hair to which a hook is attached.

tipple ● v. **1** intr. drink liquor habitually. **2** tr. drink (liquor) repeatedly in small amounts. ● n. informal an alcoholic drink. □ **tippler** n.

tippy adj. (**-ier, -iest**) N Amer. informal unstable; liable to tip over.

tippytoe n., v., adj., & adv. N Amer. informal = TIPTOE.

tipsheet n. a publication offering readers information, advice, and predictions, esp. on wagering or the stock market.

tipster n. a person who provides tips or confidential information, esp. about betting at horse races.

tipsy adj. (**-ier, -iest**) **1** slightly drunk. **2** caused by or showing intoxication (a tipsy grin). **3** = TIPPY. □ **tipsily** adv. **tipsiness** n.

tiptoe ● n. the tips of the toes. ● v.intr. (**tiptoes, tiptoed, tiptoeing**) **1** walk gently with the heels raised and one's weight supported by the toes and balls of the feet. **2** (usu. foll. by around) cautiously avoid. ● adj. **1** characterized by standing or walking on tiptoe. **2** extremely cautious or careful. ● adv. (also **on tiptoe**) (stand etc.) on the toes and balls of the feet with the heels raised.

tip-top adj. excellent.

tip-up ● n. N Amer. (in ice fishing) a rod or arm that supports the line and tilts up when a fish has been hooked. ● adj. that may be tipped or folded up (tip-up seats).

tirade /ˈtaɪreɪd/ n. a long vehement rant or outburst, esp. in denunciation of a particular thing.

tiramisù /ˌtiːrəmɪˈsuː, -ˈmiːsuː/ n. an Italian dessert consisting of layers of sponge cake or biscuit soaked in coffee and brandy or liqueur, filled with mascarpone cheese and topped with cocoa powder.

tire[1] v. **1 a** tr. (often foll. by out) make weak or exhausted through exertion. **b** intr. become weak or exhausted from exertion. **2** (usu. foll. by of) **a** tr. (in passive) exhaust the patience or interest of; bore (I am tired of their excuses). **b** intr. have one's interest or patience exhausted by. □ **tiring** adj.

tire[2] n. a rubber covering, either solid or hollow and inflated, placed around each of the wheels of a vehicle to give a soft contact with the road.

tired adj. **1** (often foll. by out) weak, exhausted, or fatigued from exercise or exertion. **2** (of an idea etc.) overused; trite. **3** (of vegetables, flowers, etc.) limp, no longer fresh. □ **tiredly** adv. **tiredness** n.

tireless adj. showing or characterized by inexhaustible energy; indefatigable. □ **tirelessly** adv.

tiresome adj. **1** wearisome, tedious. **2** informal annoying (you are becoming awfully tiresome). □ **tiresomely** adv. **tiresomeness** n.

'tis /tɪz/ archaic it is.

tissue n. **1** the material of which an animal or plant body, or any of its parts or organs, is composed, consisting of an aggregation of specialized cells. **2 a** (in full **facial tissue**) a disposable piece of thin soft absorbent paper for blowing one's nose, drying one's eyes, etc. **b** (in full **toilet tissue**) = TOILET PAPER. **3** (in full **tissue paper**) thin translucent paper, often coloured, used esp. for wrapping fragile articles or gifts. **4** (foll. by of) an intricate mass, series, or network of things (a tissue of lies). **5** any of various rich or fine materials of a delicate or gauzy texture. □ **tissuey** adj.

tissue culture *n. Biol. & Med.* **1** the growth in an artificial medium of cells derived from living tissue. **2** a culture of this kind.

tit¹ *n.* any small bird esp. of the family Paridae.

tit² *n.* **1** *informal* a nipple; a teat. **2** *coarse slang* a woman's breast.

Titan /'tʌɪtən/ *n.* **1** (often **titan**) a person or organization of very great power, importance, or strength. **2** *Gk Myth* a member of a family of early gigantic gods, the offspring of Heaven and Earth.

titanic¹ /tʌɪ'tænɪk/ *adj.* **1** huge, gigantic, colossal. **2** of or like the Titans. □ **titanically** *adv.*

titanic² *adj.* of titanium, esp. in tetravalent form.

titanium /tʌɪ'teɪnɪəm/ *n.* a grey metallic element occurring in many clays etc., and used to make strong light alloys that are resistant to corrosion.

titanium dioxide *n.* (also **titanium oxide**) the oxide TiO_2, a naturally-occurring inert compound, used esp. as a white pigment in the production of paints and plastics.

titch *n. informal N Amer.* a small amount.

titer *var. of* TITRE.

tit-for-tat *n.* a situation in which a blow, injury, insult, etc. is given in retaliation for one received (also *attrib.*: tit-for-tat insults).

tithe /tʌɪð/ ● *n.* **1** *hist.* one-tenth of the annual produce of agriculture, formerly taken as a tax for the support of the Church and clergy. **2 a** a tenth of an individual's income, pledged or donated to a church. **b** any tax or donation, usu. of one-tenth of a person's income. **3** a tenth part or very small amount of anything. ● *v.* **1** *tr. & intr.* (often foll. by *to*) pay one-tenth of (one's earnings etc.), esp. towards the support of a church and clergy. **2** *tr.* impose the payment of a tithe on (a person). □ **tithing** *n.*

titian /'tɪʃən/ *adj.* (also **Titian**) (of hair) bright golden auburn.

titillate /'tɪtɪleɪt/ *v.tr.* **1** excite, arouse, or stimulate, esp. sexually. **2** delight, amuse. **3** touch lightly, tickle. □ **titillating** *adj.* **titillation** *n.*

title ● *n.* **1** the name given to a book, work of art, piece of music, etc. **2** the formal heading of each section of a legal document, statute, book, etc. **3 a** the title page of a book or its contents. **b** a publication (*published 20 new titles*). **4** a caption or credit in a movie etc. **5 a** a form of nomenclature indicating a person's status or rank, either appended to a person's name, e.g. *Dr.*, *Mrs.*, or used as a form of address or reference, e.g. *Your Majesty.* **b** a description indicating a person's role, job, or function, e.g. *Queen*, *Editor-in-Chief*, *Assistant Coach.* **6** *Sport* a championship. **7** *Law* **a** the right to the possession of land or property. **b** the evidence of such a right. **c** (foll. by *to*) a just or recognized claim. **8** (*attrib.*) **a** designating a song featured on an album of the same name. **b** designating the role or part in a play etc. from which the title of the piece is taken. ● *v.tr.* give a title to.

titled *adj.* having a title of nobility or rank.

title page *n.* a page at the beginning of a book giving the title, author, and usu. the publisher.

titmouse *n.* (*pl.* **titmice**) any of various small birds of the family Paridae, esp. of the genus *Parus.*

titrate /'tʌɪtreɪt/ *v.tr. Chem.* ascertain the amount of a constituent in (a solution) by slowly adding measured volumes of a suitable reagent of known concentration until the point when the reaction just begins or ceases to occur. □ **titration** *n.*

titre /'tʌɪtər/ *n.* (also **titer**) **1** *Chem.* the concentration of a solution as determined by titration. **2** *Med.* the

concentration of an antibody, as determined by finding the highest dilution at which it is still active.

titter ● *v.intr.* laugh or giggle, esp. nervously. ● *n.* a restrained or nervous giggle.

tittle *n.* **1** the smallest part of something; a minute and insignificant amount; a whit. **2** a small written or printed stroke or dot.

tittle-tattle *n.* petty gossip.

titty *n.* (*pl.* **-ies**) *slang* = TIT².

titular /'tɪtjʊlər/ *adj.* **1** being what is specified in name or title only without having the attributes or exercising the functions implied by it (*titular ruler*). **2** from whom or which a title or name is taken (*the book's titular hero*). **3** of or relating to a title.

tizzy *n.* (*pl.* **-ies**) (also **tiz**, **tizz**; *pl.* **-es**) *informal* a flustered, agitated, or hysterical state; a panic of excitement or nervousness.

TKO ● *n. Boxing* a technical knockout. ● *v.tr.* (**TKO's**, **TKO'd**, **TKO'ing**) **1** *Boxing* defeat (an opponent) by technical knockout. **2** *informal* thwart (a person), esp. at the last minute to prevent completion of a task (*I got TKO'd by a subway delay*).

Tl *symbol* thallium.

TLC *abbr. informal* tender loving care.

Tlingit /'tlɪŋɡɪt/ ● *n.* (*pl.* same or **-s**) **1** a member of an Aboriginal people living on the islands and coast of SE Alaska and northern BC. **2** the language of this people. ● *adj.* of or relating to this people or their culture or language.

T-lymphocyte *n. Physiol.* a lymphocyte of a type produced by the thymus gland and active in the immune response.

TM *abbr.* **1** trademark. **2** transcendental meditation.

Tm *symbol* thulium.

TMJ *abbr.* **1** the temporomandibular joint. **2** = TEMPOROMANDIBULAR JOINT SYNDROME.

TN *abbr.* Tennessee (in postal use).

TNT *abbr.* trinitrotoluene, a high explosive that is relatively insensitive to shock.

to ● *prep.* **1** introducing a noun: **a** expressing what is reached, approached, or touched (*fell to the ground*; *drove to Alberta*; *five minutes to six*). **b** expressing what is aimed at: often introducing the indirect object of a verb (*throw it to me*; *explained the problem to them*). **c** as far as; until (*went on to the end*; *stayed from Tuesday to Friday*). **d** to the extent of (*were all drunk to a man*; *was starved to death*). **e** expressing what is followed (*according to instructions*; *dance to the music*). **f** expressing what is considered or affected (*am used to that*; *that is nothing to me*). **g** expressing what is caused or produced (*turn to stone*; *tear to shreds*). **h** expressing what is compared (*comparable to any other*; *equal to the occasion*; *a score of three to two*). **i** expressing what is increased (*add it to mine*). **j** expressing what is involved or composed as specified (*there is nothing to it*; *more to him than meets the eye*). **2** introducing the infinitive: **a** as a verbal noun (*to get there is the priority*). **b** expressing purpose, consequence, or cause (*we eat to live*; *left him to starve*; *am sorry to hear that*). **c** as a substitute for *to* + infinitive (*wanted to come but was unable to*). ● *adv.* **1** in the normal or required position or condition (*come to*; *heave to*). **2** in a nearly closed position (*close the door to*).

toad *n.* **1** any frog-like amphibian of the family Bufonidae, esp. of the genus *Bufo*, breeding in water but living chiefly on land, esp. any of those that have a dry warty skin and walk rather than leap. **2** any of various similar amphibians including the Suriname toad. **3** a repulsive or loathsome person.

toadstool *n.* a non-technical name for the spore-bearing structure of various fungi, usu. poisonous or inedible, consisting of a round flat cap that surmounts a slender stalk or stipe.

toady ● *n.* (*pl.* **-ies**) a person who behaves servilely towards another; a sycophant. ● *v.intr.* (**-ies, -ied**) (often foll. by *to, up to*) behave servilely or obsequiously towards a person; fawn upon. □ **toadying** *adj.*

to and fro ● *adv.* **1** backwards and forwards. **2** repeatedly between the same points. ● *n.* (usu. **to-and-fro**; *pl.* **tos-and-fros**) **1** movement to and fro. **2** vacillation, indecision, or debate on an issue. □ **toing and froing** constant bustling movement or travelling back and forth or here and there.

toast ● *n.* **1** sliced bread browned on both sides by exposure to dry heat. **2 a** a very brief speech or tribute offered in honour of a person, occasion, institution, etc., before drinking, esp. at a formal dinner or celebration. **b** a call by the speaker to other guests to endorse this tribute by raising their glasses before drinking. **3 a** a person, institution, etc. in whose honour a company is asked to drink. **b** (foll. by *of*) a person or thing that is extremely popular or celebrated among a specified group of people or in a specified place etc. (*the toast of the town*). **4** *N Amer. informal* a person or thing that is or is about to be in severe difficulty (*if I don't get this done on time I'm toast*). ● *v.* **1** *tr.* cook or brown (bread, almonds, marshmallows, etc.) by exposure to a source of radiant heat. **2** *intr.* (of bread etc.) become brown in this way. **3** *tr.* warm (one's feet, oneself, etc.) at a fire etc. **4** *tr.* drink to the health or in honour of (a person or thing).

toaster *n.* a device used to toast bread etc., esp. an electrical appliance that automatically shuts off when the toast is ready.

toaster oven *n.* a tabletop electrical appliance used as a toaster and as a small oven.

toasty *adj.* (**-ier, -iest**) **1** comfortably warm. **2** like or resembling toast. □ **toastiness** *n.*

tobacco *n.* (*pl.* **-os**) **1** a narcotic and addictive preparation of the dried leaves esp. of the plant *Nicotiana tabacum* and hybrids, which is smoked or chewed for pleasure, and used for ceremonial and religious purposes among some N American Aboriginal groups. **2** (in full **tobacco plant**) any of several plants of the genus *Nicotiana* of the nightshade family, esp. *N. tabacum* and its cultivars.

Tobacco Nation *n.* = PETUN.

tobacconist /təˈbækənɪst/ *n.* a person who deals in tobacco, esp. the owner of a store selling tobacco, pipes, cigars, cigarettes, and other assorted items.

tobacco pipe *n.* see PIPE *n.* 2a.

Tobagonian /ˌtoːbəˈɡoːniːən/ ● *n.* a native or inhabitant of Tobago, an island in the W Indies, part of the country of Trinidad and Tobago. ● *adj.* of or relating to Tobago.

to-be *adj.* (usu. in *comb.*) that will soon become what is specified; future (*bride-to-be*).

toboggan *esp. N Amer.* ● *n.* a long narrow sled without runners, bent or curled upwards at the front, which may be drawn by a rope over compacted snow or ice or used to coast down hills. ● *v.intr.* coast down hills or ride on a toboggan. □ **tobogganing** *n.*

toboggan slide *n. Cdn* **1** = SLIDE *n.* 8. **2** *informal* a rapid and usu. irreversible decline.

toccata /təˈkɑːtə/ *n.* a brisk musical composition for a keyboard instrument, having the air of an improvisation and designed to demonstrate the performer's touch and technique.

tock ● *n.* a short, hollow sound, deeper and more resonant than a tick. ● *v.intr.* make this sound.

tocopherol /ˌtoːˈkɒfərɒl/ *n.* any of several closely related alcohols occurring in plant oils, wheat germ, egg yolk, and leafy vegetables, and which are antioxidants essential in the diets of animals and humans.

today ● *adv.* **1** on or in the course of this present day. **2** nowadays, in modern times. ● *n.* **1** this present day. **2** modern times. □ **a week today** one week from today.

toddle /ˈtɒdl/ *v.intr.* **1** walk with short unsteady steps like those of a small child. **2** *informal* **a** take a casual or leisurely walk. **b** (usu. foll. by *off, along*) depart.

toddler *n.* a child who has just recently learned to walk, usu. between the ages of a year and a half and three years. □ **toddlerhood** *n.*

toddy *n.* (*pl.* **-ies**) an alcoholic drink made with esp. rum or whisky and hot water, usu. flavoured with lemon juice and sweetened with sugar or honey.

to-do *n.* a commotion or fuss.

to-do list *n.* a list of chores, projects, assignments, etc. that one must or hopes to complete.

toe ● *n.* **1** any of the five terminal projections of the foot. **2** the corresponding part of an animal. **3** the part of an item of footwear that covers the toes. **4** *Figure Skating* **a** = TOE PICK. **b** = TOE LOOP. **5** a part resembling a toe or the toes in shape or position, esp. the lower end, tip, or point of something. ● *v.* (**toes, toed, toeing**) **1** *tr.* touch (esp. a line or mark) with the toe of one's shoe. **2** *tr.* strike or direct (an object) with the toe. **3** (foll. by *in, out*) **a** *intr.* walk with the toes pointed in or out. **b** *tr.* cause (a pair of objects, such as wheels, speakers, etc.) to converge or diverge slightly at the front. □ **make a person's toes curl** excite or thrill a person. **on one's toes** alert, ready. **step** (or **tread**) **on a person's toes** offend or threaten a person by encroaching upon their privileges or responsibilities, esp. unintentionally. **toe the line** conform to a general policy or principle, esp. unwillingly or under pressure. **toe to toe 1** directly in front of and facing (another or each other). **2** (of adversaries, rivals, etc.) in competition or conflict.

toecap *n.* the reinforced outer covering of the toe of a boot or shoe.

toed *adj.* (in *comb.*) **1** (of an animal) having toes of a specified number or kind. **2** (of a shoe, boot, etc.) having a toe of a specified kind (*steel-toed boots*).

toehold *n.* **1** a small foothold. **2** a favourable position from which a minor advantage may be gained or influence or support increased minimally. **3** *Wrestling* a hold in which the opponent's toe is seized and the leg forced backwards.

toe loop *n. Figure Skating* a loop jump in which the toe of the free skate is dug into the ice to assist the takeoff from the opposite foot.

toenail ● *n.* **1** the nail at the tip of each toe. **2** a nail driven obliquely through the end of a board or beam etc. ● *v.tr.* fasten (a board etc.) with a toenail.

toe pick *n. Figure Skating* a jagged toothed edge on the front tip of a blade, used to dig into the ice when completing various technical manoeuvres, esp. jumps.

toffee *n.* a hard and often brittle candy that softens in the mouth, made by boiling sugar and butter.

tofu /ˈtoːfuː/ *n.* a pale curd of varying consistency made from soybean milk and used as a source of protein esp. in vegetarian recipes and Asian cuisine.

tog *informal* ● *n.* (in *pl.*) clothes, esp. several articles of clothing constituting a single outfit (*ski togs*). ● *v.tr. & intr.* (**togged, togging**) (foll. by *out, up*) dress up, esp. elaborately or stylishly.

toga *n.* **1** *Rom. Hist.* a loose flowing outer garment made of a single piece of cloth and covering the whole body apart from the right arm. **2** a robe or gown of office.

together ● *adv.* **1** in company or conjunction (*we built it together*). **2** simultaneously; at the same time (*let's all sing together*). **3** in notional combination; collectively (*makes more than all of us put together*). **4** with coherence or combination of parts or elements belonging to single body or thing; so as to form a connected, united, or coherent whole (*I hope this mixture holds together*). **5** (of two or more people, parts, etc.) into association, proximity, contact, or union; so as to unite (*tied them together*; *put two and two together*). **6** into one gathering, company, or body (*called all the employees together*). **7** (of two people) one with another, esp. in a relationship (*we're getting back together*). **8** *informal* **a** into an organized state (*get your things together*). **b** into a rational state of mind (*pull yourself together*). ● *adj. informal* composed, self-assured; free of emotional difficulties or inhibitions. □ **together with** as well as; in addition to.

togetherness *n.* **1** a feeling of comfort proceeding from a close and harmonious association with others. **2** the condition of being together.

toggle ● *n.* **1** a short decorative crosspiece sewn on one side of esp. a coat or other garment, fastened by being pushed through a loop or hole on the other side. **2** *Computing* a key or command that is always operated in the same way but has opposite effects on successive occasions. **3** a pin or other crosspiece put through the eye of a rope, a link of a chain, etc., to keep it in place. ● *v.* **1** *Computing* **a** *intr.* (often foll. by *between*) switch from one function or state of operation to another by using a toggle. **b** *tr.* & *intr.* (usu. foll. by *on* or *off*) activate or deactivate (a feature or function etc.) using a toggle. **2** *tr.* provide or fasten with a toggle.

toggle switch *n.* **1** an electric switch operated by means of a short projecting lever that is moved usu. up and down. **2** *Computing* = TOGGLE *n.* 2.

toil ● *v.intr.* **1** work laboriously or incessantly. **2** make slow painful progress (*toiled along the path*). ● *n.* prolonged or intensive labour. □ **toiler** *n.*

toilet *n.* **1 a** a bathroom fixture for defecation and urination, consisting of a large basin usu. with a hinged lid and seat and a flushing mechanism. **b** a room containing such a fixture. **2** (also **toilette** /twɒˈlet/) the process of washing, dressing, arranging one's hair, etc. (*make one's toilet*). □ **go into** (or **down**) **the toilet** *N Amer.* **1** go into sharp decline, esp. in quality. **2** become irrecoverably lost.

toilet paper *n.* (also **toilet tissue**) soft absorbent paper, usu. in a long continuous perforated sheet wound around a cardboard roll, used for cleaning oneself after defecating or urinating.

toiletry *n.* (*pl.* **-ies**) (usu. in *pl.*) any of various articles or cosmetics used in washing and dressing, such as soap, shampoo, deodorant, etc.

toilet training *n.* the process of teaching a young child to use the toilet. □ **toilet train** *v.tr.*

Tokay /təˈkeɪ/ *n.* **1** a sweet aromatic wine made near Tokaj in Hungary. **2** a similar wine produced elsewhere, esp. in California and Australia.

toke *N Amer. slang* ● *n.* **1** a drag on a cigarette containing a narcotic substance, esp. marijuana. **2** a marijuana cigarette. ● *v.intr.* (often foll. by *up*) smoke or take a drag on a marijuana cigarette.

token ● *n.* **1 a** a visible or tangible representation of something abstract or immaterial. **b** a thing given as an expression of affection, or to be kept as a

memento. **2** a coin-like object, used as a limited medium of exchange, such as on public transit, in a casino, etc. **3** a person chosen as a nominal representative of an under-represented group, usu. in order to pre-empt charges of discrimination. **4** *Computing* **a** the smallest meaningful unit of information in a sequence of data. **b** a unique sequence of bits granting permission to transmit information in a token ring. **5** a thing serving as evidence of authenticity or as a guarantee. ● *attrib.adj.* **1** chosen out of tokenism as a nominal representative of a minority group (*the token woman*). **2** done or made as a matter of form; nominal (*token effort*). **3** conducted briefly to demonstrate strength of feeling (*token resistance*). **4** serving to acknowledge a principle only (*a token payment*). □ **by the same token 1** in the same way; similarly. **2** moreover. □ **in token of** as a symbol of.

tokenism *n.* esp. *Politics* the principle or practice of granting minimum concessions, esp. to minority or under-represented groups, as a token gesture to appease public pressure, comply with legal requirements, etc. □ **tokenistic** *adj.*

token ring *n.* *Computing* a network architecture configured in such a way that each node must receive a token from an adjacent node before it can transmit information to another.

told past and past part. of TELL[1].

tolerable /ˈtɒlərəbəl/ *adj.* **1** able to be endured; bearable. **2** reasonably good; passable, mediocre. □ **tolerability** *n.* **tolerably** *adv.*

tolerance /ˈtɒlərəns/ *n.* **1** a willingness or ability to accept or allow without protest or irritation. **2** the disposition to adopt a liberal attitude towards the opinions or acts of others, esp. those of other religions or ethnic backgrounds. **3** the capacity to withstand or endure. **4 a** the ability of an organism to withstand some particular environmental condition. **b** the ability to endure large doses of active drugs, or to resist the action of a toxin etc.

tolerant *adj.* **1** disposed to adopt a liberal attitude towards the beliefs and opinions of others. **2** (usu. foll. by *of*) patient, forgiving; willing to allow or put up with. **3** able to withstand the action of a drug, toxin, etc. **4** able to withstand a (usu. specified) environmental condition. □ **tolerantly** *adv.*

tolerate /ˈtɒləˌreɪt/ *v.tr.* **1** allow the existence, practice, or occurrence of. **2** endure or allow with patience, leniency, or understanding. **3** sustain or endure (pain, suffering, etc.). **4** be capable of continued subjection to (a drug, radiation, etc.) without harm.

toleration *n.* **1** sanction for the practice of forms of religion at variance with those officially accepted or recognized by a country or state. **2** = TOLERANCE.

toll[1] *n.* **1** a sum of money charged for permission to travel along a road or highway etc. (also *attrib.*: *toll bridge*). **2** the loss or damage caused by a disaster etc. (*death toll*). **3** *N Amer.* a charge for a long-distance telephone call. □ **take its toll** cause or be accompanied by loss, damage, injury, etc.

toll[2] ● *v.* **1** *tr.* ring (a bell) with a slow succession of uniform strokes. **2** (of a bell) **a** sound with a slow succession of uniform strokes. **b** *tr.* announce or mark (a death etc.) in this way. **c** *tr.* strike (the hour). ● *n.* the action or sound of a bell as it tolls or is struck.

toll booth *n.* a booth at a bridge or highway etc. where tolls are collected.

toll-free ● *adj.* (esp. of a telephone call, number, or service) that can be made, used, or accessed without charge. ● *adv.* without charge.

tollgate ● *n.* **1** a gate preventing passage until a toll is paid. **2** *Cdn* a barrier imposed illegally on business or trade etc. pending payment of a bribe or tribute. ● *v.tr. & intr. Cdn* block or hinder (a business contract etc.) pending payment of a bribe or tribute.

tollgating *n. Cdn* the illegal practice of paying or extorting a bribe or tribute for the right to do business with or within a province, country, etc.

toluene /ˈtɒljuˌiːn/ *n.* (also **toluol** /ˈtɒljuːɒl/) a colourless liquid hydrocarbon obtained from coal tar and petroleum, and used esp. as a solvent as well as in the manufacture of explosives.

tom¹ *n.* **1** = TOMCAT *n.* **2** a male of various other animals, such as a turkey.

tom² *n.* = TOM-TOM 2.

tomahawk *n.* a tool or weapon with a handle and a sharp stone or iron cutting head, formerly used by some N American Indians.

tomatillo /tɒməˈtiːloʊ/ *n.* (*pl.* **-os**) esp. *US* **1** a purplish edible fruit. **2** a Mexican plant, *Physalis philadelphica*, bearing this.

tomato /təˈmeɪtoʊ, -ˈmætoʊ/ *n.* (*pl.* **-oes**) **1** a glossy, usu. bright red and pulpy edible fruit, eaten raw or cooked as a vegetable. **2** a plant, *Lycopersicon esculentum*, bearing this. □ **tomatoey** *adj.*

tomato clam cocktail *n.* a drink consisting of tomato juice mixed with clam juice.

tomb *n.* **1** a large usu. underground vault for the burial of the dead. **2** an excavation in the earth etc. to receive a corpse. **3** a monument erected over a person's grave. **4** (prec. by *the*) *literary* the state of death.

tomboy *n.* a girl whose behaviour, pastimes, and style of dress are considered typical of those of a young boy. □ **tomboyish** *adj.* **tomboyishly** *adv.* **tomboyishness** *n.*

tombstone *n.* a usu. engraved stone slab placed upright or laid flat over a person's grave as a memorial.

tomcat ● *n.* a male cat. ● *v.intr.* (**-catted, -catting**) *slang* (of a man) pursue women promiscuously.

Tom, Dick, and Harry *n.* (usu. prec. by *any, every*) usu. *derogatory* ordinary people taken at random (*every Tom, Dick, and Harry was there!*).

tome *n.* **1** a large, heavy, learned book or volume of a work. **2** *informal* or *jocular* a book, esp. one that is excessively long or dull.

tomfool *n.* **1** a foolish or silly person; a buffoon. **2** (*attrib.*) foolish, stupid. □ **tomfoolery** *n.* (*pl.* **-ies**).

tommycod *n.* (*pl.* same) (also **tomcod**) *N Amer.* any of various small marine fishes, now esp. *Microgadus tomcod* of the W Atlantic, *M. proximus* of the E Pacific, and the related *Urophycis floridana*.

tomography /təˈmɒgrəfi/ *n.* any of various techniques which provide images of successive plane sections of the human body or other solid objects using X-rays or ultrasound, now usu. processed by computer to give a three-dimensional image.

tomorrow ● *n.* **1** the day after today. **2** the future, esp. the near future. ● *adv.* **1** on the day after today. **2** at some future time. □ **like** (or **as if**) **there is no tomorrow** with no regard for the future; recklessly.

tom-tom *n.* **1** a simple hand-beaten drum associated with N American Aboriginal, African, or Eastern cultures. **2** a small to medium-sized drum used esp. as part of a drum kit.

ton ● *n.* **1** (in full **short ton**) esp. *N Amer.* a unit of weight equal to 2,000 lb. avoirdupois (907.19 kg). **2** (in full **long ton**) *Brit.* a unit of weight equal to 2,240 lb. avoirdupois (1016.05 kg). **3** = METRIC TON. **4 a** (in full **displacement ton**) a unit of measurement of a ship's weight or volume in terms of its displacement of water with the load line just immersed, equal to 2,240 lb. (1016.05 kg) or 35 cu. ft. (0.99 cubic metres). **b** (in full **freight ton**) a unit of weight or volume of cargo, equal to a metric ton (1 000 kg) or 40 cu. ft. **5 a** (in full **gross ton**) a unit of gross internal capacity, equal to 100 cu. ft. (2.83 cubic metres). **b** (in full **net** or **register ton**) an equivalent unit of net internal capacity. **6** a measure of capacity for various materials, esp. 40 cu. ft. of timber. **7** (usu. in *pl.*) *informal* a large number or amount (*tons of things to do; has a ton of stuff to learn*). ● *adv.* (usu. in *pl.*) *informal* much, a lot (*feel tons better*). □ **weigh a ton** *informal* be very heavy.

tonal *adj.* **1 a** of or relating to tone or tonality. **b** designating or pertaining to music written in a definite key or keys. **2** (of a fugue etc.) having repetitions of the subject at different pitches in the same key. □ **tonally** *adv.*

tonality /toʊˈnælɪti/ *n.* (*pl.* **-ies**) **1** *Music* **a** the relationship between the tones of a musical scale. **b** the observance of a single tonic key as the basis of a composition. **2** the colour scheme of a picture.

tone ● *n.* **1** a musical or vocal sound, esp. with reference to its pitch, quality, and strength. **2** (often in *pl.*) modulation of the voice expressing a particular feeling or mood (*a cheerful tone; suspicious tones*). **3** a manner of expression in writing. **4** *Music* an interval of a major second, e.g. C–D. **5 a** the general effect of colour or of light and shade in a photograph, painting, etc. **b** the tint or shade of a colour. **6 a** the general spirit or character of something. **b** an attitude or sentiment expressed in a letter, speech, etc. **7** (of the body) the state of being firm and strong. **8** a state of good or specified health or quality. ● *v.* **1** *tr.* give the desired tone to. **2** *tr.* modify the tone of. **3** *tr.* strengthen, firm (*tone the skin*). **4** *intr.* (often foll. by *to*) attune. **5** *tr. Photog.* give (a monochrome picture) an altered colour in finishing by means of a chemical solution. **6** *intr.* undergo a change in colour by toning. □ **tone down 1** make or become softer in tone of sound or colour. **2** make less strong or extreme. **tone up 1** make or become stronger in tone of sound or colour. **2** strengthen (muscles etc.). **3** make (a statement etc.) more emphatic. □ **toneless** *adj.*

tone-deaf *adj.* unable to perceive differences of musical pitch accurately. □ **tone-deafness** *n.*

tone poem *n.* = SYMPHONIC POEM.

toner *n.* **1** a chemical bath for toning a photographic print. **2** a powder used in xerographic copying processes, laser printers, etc. **3** an astringent applied to the face to control oiliness and tighten pores.

tong *n.* a Chinese guild, association, or secret society.

Tongan /ˈtɒŋən/ ● *adj.* of or relating to the island group of Tonga in the S Pacific or its people or language. ● *n.* **1** a native or national of Tonga. **2** the Polynesian language spoken in Tonga.

tongs *n.pl.* (also **pair of tongs** *sing.*) an instrument with two hinged or sprung arms for grasping etc.

tongue ● *n.* **1** the fleshy muscular organ in the mouth used in tasting, licking, and swallowing, and (in humans) for speech. **2** the tongue of an ox etc. as food. **3** the faculty of or a tendency in speech (*a sharp tongue*). **4** a particular language. **5** a thing like a tongue in shape or position, esp.: **a** a long low promontory. **b** a strip of leather etc., attached at one end only, under the laces in a shoe. **c** the clapper of a bell. **d** the pin of a buckle. **e** the projecting strip on a wooden etc. board fitting into the groove of another. **f** a vibrating slip in the reed of some musical instruments. **g** a jet of flame. ● *v.* (**tongues,**

tongued, tonguing) **1** *tr.* produce staccato etc. effects with (a flute etc.) by means of tonguing. **2** *intr.* use the tongue in this way. **3** *tr.* kiss with the tongue. **4** *tr.* touch or move with the tongue; lick up. □ **find** (or **lose**) **one's tongue** be able (or unable) to express oneself after a shock etc. **the gift of tongues** the power of speaking in unknown languages, regarded as one of the gifts of the Holy Spirit. **give tongue** speak one's thoughts. **with one's tongue hanging out** eagerly or expectantly. **with one's tongue in one's cheek** insincerely or ironically. □ **tongued** *adj.* (also in *comb.*). **tongueless** *adj.*

tongue-and-groove *n.* (usu. *attrib.*) panelling etc. with a projecting strip down one side and a groove down the other.

tongue depressor *n.* a flat wooden stick for pressing down the tongue, esp. to allow inspection of the mouth or throat.

tongue-in-cheek ● *adj.* ironic; slyly humorous. ● *adv.* insincerely or ironically.

tongue-lashing *n.* a severe scolding or reprimand.

tongue-tied *adj.* too shy or embarrassed to speak.

tongue trooper *n. Cdn slang* (in Quebec) a member of the language police.

tongue twister *n.* a sequence of words difficult to pronounce quickly and correctly.

tonguing *n.* the technique of playing a wind instrument using the tongue to articulate notes.

tonic ● *n.* **1** an invigorating medicine or medicinal agent. **2** anything serving to invigorate. **3** = TONIC WATER. **4** *Music* the first degree of a scale, forming the keynote of a piece (see KEYNOTE 3). ● *adj.* **1** serving as a tonic; invigorating. **2** *Music* denoting the first degree of a scale. **3 a** designating or involving continuous muscular contraction without relaxation. **b** restoring normal tone to organs.

tonic sol-fa *n. Music* a system of notation used esp. in teaching singing, with do as the keynote of all major keys and la as the keynote of all minor keys.

tonic water *n.* a carbonated drink containing quinine, often used as a mix with gin.

tonight ● *n.* the evening or night of the present day. ● *adv.* on the present or approaching evening or night.

tonnage *n.* **1** a ship's internal cubic capacity or freight-carrying capacity measured in tons. **2** the total carrying capacity esp. of a country's mercantile marine. **3** a charge per ton on freight or cargo.

tonne /tʌn/ *n.* = METRIC TON.

tonsil *n.* either of two small masses of lymphoid tissue on each side of the root of the tongue.

tonsillectomy /ˌtɒnsəˈlektəmi/ *n.* (pl. **-ies**) the surgical removal of the tonsils.

tonsillitis /ˌtɒnsəˈlaɪtɪs/ *n.* tonsil inflammation.

tonsure /ˈtɒnʃər/ ● *n.* **1** the shaving of the crown of the head or the entire head, esp. of a person entering a monastic order etc. **2** a bare patch made in this way. ● *v.tr.* give a tonsure to. □ **tonsured** *adj.*

Tony *n.* (pl. **-ys**) any of the awards given annually in the US for excellence in some aspect of theatre.

tony *adj.* (**-ier, -iest**) *N Amer. informal* stylish, fashionable, high-class (*a tony neighbourhood*).

too *adv.* **1** to a greater extent than is desirable, permissible, or possible for a specified or understood purpose (*too large*). **2** in addition, also (*them too?*). **3** *informal* very; extremely (*you're too kind*). **4** moreover (*we must consider, too, the time of year*). □ **none too 1** rather less than (*feeling none too good*). **2** barely.

toodle *N Amer.* var of. TOOTLE.

toodle-oo *interj. informal* goodbye.

took *past of* TAKE.

tool ● *n.* **1 a** any device or implement used to carry out mechanical functions whether manually or by a machine. **b** an item of software for interactive applications. **2** a thing used in an occupation or pursuit (*reference tools*). **3** a person used as a mere instrument by another. **4** *coarse slang* the penis. ● *v.* **1** *tr.* work or shape (stone, wood, etc.) with a tool. **2** *tr.* impress a design on (leather). **3** *intr.* (foll. by *along, around,* etc.) *slang* drive or ride, esp. in a casual or leisurely manner. **4** *tr. & intr.* (often foll. by *up*) equip with tools. □ **tooler** *n.*

toolbar *n.* a row of icons which can be clicked on to execute frequently used commands.

tool box *n.* **1** (also **tool chest**) a box or container for keeping tools in. **2 a** a set of software tools. **b** the set of programs or functions accessible from a single menu.

tooling *n.* **1** the process of dressing stone or wood with a chisel etc. **2** the impressing of ornamental designs on leather with heated tools. **3** the designs so formed.

tool kit *n.* **1** a set of tools. **2** a set of software tools, usu. designed for a specific application. **3** a repertoire of techniques used to solve problems, make decisions, etc.

toolmaker *n.* a person who makes and maintains precision tools. □ **toolmaking** *n.*

tool shed *n.* a shed in which tools etc. are stored.

toon *n. informal* **1** = CARTOON *n.* 1, 2, 3. **2** a cartoon character.

toonie *n. Cdn informal* the Canadian two-dollar coin.

toot ● *n.* **1** a short sharp sound as made by a horn. **2** *slang* cocaine or a snort of cocaine. **3** *N Amer. slang* a drinking spree. ● *v.* **1** *tr.* sound (a horn etc.) with a short sharp sound. **2** *intr.* give out such a sound. **3** *intr. slang* break wind. □ **toot one's own horn** praise oneself; boast. □ **tooter** *n.*

tooth *n.* (pl. **teeth**) **1** each of a set of hard bony enamel-coated structures in the jaws of most vertebrates, used for biting and chewing. **2** a toothlike part or projection, e.g. the cog of a gearwheel, the point of a saw or comb, etc. **3** (in *pl.*) force or effectiveness (*the penalties give the contract teeth*). □ **armed to the teeth** completely and elaborately armed or equipped. **fight tooth and nail** fight very fiercely. **get one's teeth into** devote oneself seriously to. **in the teeth of 1** in spite of (opposition or difficulty etc.). **2** contrary to (instructions etc.). □ **toothed** *adj.* (also in *comb.*). **toothlike** *adj.*

toothache *n.* a (usu. prolonged) pain in a tooth.

toothbrush *n.* a small brush with a long narrow handle, for cleaning the teeth.

toothed whale *n.* a whale of the suborder Odonticeti, having teeth rather than baleen plates, including sperm whales, killer whales, dolphins, porpoises, etc.

tooth fairy *n.* (in folk legend) a fairy who leaves a small amount of money for a child in exchange for a baby tooth placed under the child's pillow at night.

toothless *adj.* **1** having no teeth. **2** lacking the means of compulsion or enforcement; ineffectual.

toothpaste *n.* a usu. minty-tasting paste for cleaning the teeth, applied with a toothbrush.

toothpick *n.* a small pointed stick, usu. of wood or plastic, for removing bits of food stuck between the teeth.

toothsome *adj.* **1** (of food) delicious, appetizing. **2** alluring; sexy.

toothy *adj.* (**-ier, -iest**) having or showing large, numerous, or prominent teeth. □ **toothily** *adv.*

tootle ● *v.* **1** *intr. informal* move casually or aimlessly. **2** *intr.* toot gently or repeatedly. **3** *tr.* play (a wind instrument). ● *n.* an act of tootling.

too-too *adj. & adv. informal* extreme, excessive(ly).

toots /toots/ *n. N Amer. slang* used as a familiar form of address, esp. to a woman or girl. ¶Often *offensive* if used to a stranger.

tootsie *n.* (*pl.* **-ies**) **1** (usu. in *pl.*) *informal* usu. *jocular* a foot; a toe. **2** *esp. N Amer. slang* **a** a woman; a female lover. **b** a prostitute.

top¹ ● *n.* **1** the highest point or part. **2** the highest rank or place (*at the top of her profession*). **3** the upper surface of a thing. **4** the upper part of a thing, esp.: **a** a garment covering the upper part of the body. **b** the upper part of a shoe or boot. **c** the stopper of a bottle. **d** the lid of a jar, pot, or other container. **e** the folding roof of a car, baby carriage, etc. **5** the utmost degree; height (*shouted at the top of his voice*). **6** *Baseball* the first half of an inning, in which the visiting team bats. **7** the beginning (of a piece of music, scene in a play, etc.) (*start again from the top*). **8** (in *pl.*) *informal* a person or thing of the best quality (*he's tops at golf*). **9** (esp. in *pl.*) the leaves etc. of a plant grown esp. for its root (*turnip tops*). **10** = TOPSPIN. ● *adj.* **1** highest in position. **2** highest in degree, importance, or skill. ● *v.tr.* (**topped, topping**) **1** provide with a top, cap, etc. **2** remove the top of (a tree, plant, fruit, etc.). **3 a** be higher or better than; surpass. **b** be at the top of (*topped the list*). **4** reach the top of (a hill etc.). □ **at the top** in the highest rank of a profession etc. (**at**) **tops** esp. *N Amer.* at the most. **come to the top** win distinction. **from top to toe** from head to foot; completely. **on top 1** in a superior position; above. **2** on the upper part of the head. **on top of 1** fully in command of. **2** in close proximity to. **3** in addition to. **on top of the world** *informal* exuberant. **over the top 1** esp. *hist.* over the parapet of a trench (and into battle); into action. **2** (hyphenated when *attrib.*) to excess, beyond reasonable limits (*that joke was over the top*). **top off 1** put an end or the finishing touch to (a thing). **2** = TOP UP 1b. **top out 1** reach a peak; stop rising (*prices topped out at around $200*). **2** put the highest stone on (a building). **top up 1 a** add to; bring up to a certain level (*topped up EI benefits*). **b** fill up (a glass or other partly full container). **2** top up something for (a person) (*your glass is empty — may I top you up?*). □ **topmost** *adj.*

top² *n.* a toy spinning on a point when set in motion.

Top 40 *n.* (also **Top Forty**) the forty most popular songs in the music charts at a given time.

topaz /ˈtoːpæz/ *n.* a transparent or translucent aluminum silicate mineral, usu. yellow, used as a gem.

top banana *n. slang* **1** *N Amer.* a leader of an organization etc. **2** a comedian topping the bill.

top brass *n. see* BRASS *n.* 4.

top-class *adj.* of the best quality or highest order.

topcoat *n.* **1** an overcoat. **2** an outer coat of paint, nail polish, etc.

top dog *n. informal* a victor or master.

top dollar *n.* esp. *N Amer.* a high or the highest price.

top-down *attrib.adj.* **1** proceeding from general to particular, or from the top downwards. **2** hierarchical.

top drawer ● *n.* **1** the uppermost drawer in a chest etc. **2** *informal* high social position or origin. ● *attrib.adj.* (**top-drawer**) *informal* of the highest quality or esp. social level.

top dressing *n.* **1** the application of manure or

fertilizer to the top of the earth. **2** manure so applied. **3** a superficial show. □ **top-dress** *v.tr.*

tope *v.intr. archaic or literary* drink alcohol to excess, esp. habitually. □ **toper** *n.*

top-end *adj.* = HIGH-END.

top-flight *adj.* in the highest rank of achievement.

top-grade *adj.* of the best quality or highest order.

top gun *n.* esp. *N Amer. informal* **1** an ace fighter pilot. **2** an important person, company, etc.

top hat *n.* a man's tall hat, worn esp. on formal occasions. □ **top-hatted** *adj.*

top-heavy *adj.* **1** disproportionately heavy at the top so as to be in danger of toppling. **2 a** (of an organization etc.) having a disproportionately large number of people in senior administrative positions. **b** overcapitalized. **3** *informal* (of a woman) having a disproportionately large bust. □ **top-heavily** *adv.* **top-heaviness** *n.*

topiary /ˈtoːpiˌeri/ ● *adj.* concerned with or formed by clipping shrubs, trees, etc. into ornamental or animal forms. ● *n.* (*pl.* **-ies**) **1** topiary art. **2** a piece or example of topiary work.

topic *n.* **1** a theme for a book, discourse, etc. **2** the subject of a conversation or argument.

topical *adj.* **1** of or pertaining to current affairs or a subject in the news etc. **2** dealing with a place. **3** (of an ailment, medicine, etc.) affecting or applied externally to a part of the body. **4** of or concerning topics. □ **topicality** *n.* **topically** *adv.*

topknot *n.* **1** a bun or tuft of hair worn on the crown of the head. **2** a tuft or crest growing on the head.

topless *adj.* **1** without or seeming to be without a top. **2 a** (of clothes) having no upper part. **b** (of a person) bare-breasted. **c** (of a place, esp. a beach) where women go topless. □ **toplessness** *n.*

top-level *adj.* of the highest level of importance, prestige, etc.

top-line *attrib.adj.* **1** of the highest quality. **2** (esp. of an entertainment act) considered worthy of top billing.

topmast *n.* the mast next above the lower mast on a sailing ship.

topmost *adj.* uppermost.

top-notch *adj. informal* first-rate. □ **top-notcher** *n.*

topo /ˈtoːpo/ ● *n.* **1** topography. **2** a topographical map. ● *adj.* topographical.

top-of-the-line *adj.* the most expensive (and usu. highest quality) of a group of similar products.

topography /təˈpɒɡrəfi/ *n.* **1** a detailed description, representation on a map, etc., of the natural and artificial features of an area. **2** such features. □ **topographer** *n.* **topographic** *adj.* **topographical** *adj.* **topographically** *adv.*

topology /təˈpɒlədʒi/ *n. Math.* **1** the study of geometrical properties and spatial relations unaffected by the continuous change of shape or size of figures. **2** the way in which constituent parts are interrelated or arranged. □ **topological** *adj.* **topologically** *adv.*

toponym /ˈtɒpənɪm/ *n.* **1** a place name. **2** a descriptive place name, usu. derived from a topographical feature of the place.

toponymy /təˈpɒnɪmi/ *n.* the study of the place names of a region. □ **toponymic** *adj.*

topos /ˈtɒpɒs, ˈtoːpoːs, -pɒs/ *n.* (*pl.* **topoi** /ˈtɒpɔɪ/) a stock theme in literature etc.

topper *n.* **1** a thing that tops. **2** *informal* = TOP HAT. **3** esp. *N Amer.* a woman's short loose jacket or coat. **4** *Cdn* a short curtain, often ruffled or gathered, hung at the top of a window.

topping *n.* a garnish, sauce, etc. put on top of food.

topple *v.intr. & tr.* **1** totter and fall (over), or cause to do so. **2** overthrow or be overthrown.

topsail /ˈtɒpseil, -səl/ *n.* **1** the square sail, or each of two such sails, next above the lowest on a sailing ship. **2** a fore-and-aft sail above the gaff.

top secret *adj.* of the highest secrecy.

top seed *n.* the top-ranked competitor or team in a tournament etc. □ **top-seeded** *adj.*

top shelf *Hockey informal* ● *n.* the highest part of the net, just beneath the crossbar. ● *adv.* at or into this part of the net.

topside ● *n.* the side of a ship above the waterline. ● *adv.* on or to the upper deck of a ship.

Topsider *n.* (usu. in *pl.*) *proprietary* a casual shoe, usu. made of canvas with a rubber sole.

topsoil *n.* the surface layer of soil (opp. SUBSOIL).

topspin *n.* a fast forward spin imparted to a ball in tennis etc. by hitting it forward and upward.

topstitch *v.tr.* make a row of neat, esp. decorative, stitches on the right side of (fabric). □ **topstitching** *n.*

topsy-turvy ● *adv. & adj.* **1** upside down. **2** in utter confusion. ● *n.* utter confusion. □ **topsy-turvily** *adv.* **topsy-turviness** *n.*

topwater *adj. N Amer.* (of a bait) that floats on top of the water.

toque *n.* **1** /tuːk/ *Cdn* **a** a close-fitting knitted hat, often with a tassel or pompom on the crown. **b** a long knitted stocking cap. **2** /toːk/ a tall white hat with a full pouched crown, worn by chefs.

Torah /ˈtɔːrə/ *n.* **1 a** the Pentateuch. **b** a scroll containing this. **2** the will of God as revealed in Mosaic law.

torch ● *n.* **1 a** a piece of wood, cloth, etc., soaked in a flammable substance and lighted. **b** any similar lamp, e.g. an oil lamp on a pole. **2** a source of heat, illumination, or enlightenment. **3** esp. *N Amer.* a blowtorch. ● *v.tr. N Amer. slang* set fire to, esp. as an act of arson. □ **carry a torch for** suffer from unrequited love for. **put to the torch** destroy by burning.

torchbearer *n.* **1** a person who leads the way in an attempt to reform, inspire, etc. **2** a person who carries a usu. ceremonial torch.

torchlight ● *n.* the light of a torch or torches. ● *adj.* done or accompanied by torchlight. □ **torchlit** *adj.*

torch song *n.* a melancholy or sentimental romantic song with a slow tempo. □ **torch singer** *n.*

tore *past of* TEAR[1].

tori *pl. of* TORUS.

torment ● *n.* **1** severe physical or mental suffering. **2** a cause of this (*public speaking was a torment*). ● *v.tr.* **1** subject to torment. **2** tease or worry excessively. □ **tormentingly** *adv.* **tormentor** *n.*

torn ● *v. past part. of* TEAR[1]. ● *adj.* **1** that has been torn or violently pulled apart. **2** anxious because having to make a painful choice between two options.

tornado *n.* (pl. **-oes**) **1** a violent storm with very strong circular winds over a small area, often accompanied by a funnel-shaped cloud. **2** a violent or destructive person or thing.

Torontonian *n.* a native or inhabitant of Toronto.

torpedo ● *n.* (pl. **-oes**) **1 a** a self-propelled underwater missile, usu. cylindrical with a pointed or tapered nose, fired at a ship and exploding on impact. **b** (in full **aerial torpedo**) a similar device dropped from an aircraft. **2** = ELECTRIC RAY. ● *v.tr.* (**-oes, -oed**) **1** destroy or attack with a torpedo. **2** make ineffective or inoperative. □ **damn the torpedoes** *N Amer. slang* let us proceed aggressively without fear of the danger or concern for consequences. □ **torpedo-like** *adj.*

torpedo boat *n.* a small fast lightly armed warship for carrying or discharging torpedoes.

torpid *adj.* **1 a** sluggish, inactive. **b** dull, apathetic. **2** (of a part of the body etc.) numb. **3** (of a hibernating animal) dormant. □ **torpidity** *n.* **torpidly** *adv.*

torpor *n.* a torpid state.

torque /tɔːk/ ● *n.* **1** a twisting or rotating force, esp. in a mechanism. **2** the moment of a system of forces producing rotation. ● *v.tr.* **1** apply torque or a twisting force to. **2** (often foll. by *up*) *N Amer. informal* heighten; increase (sound, intensity, etc.). □ **torquey** *adj.*

torrent *n.* **1** a rushing stream of water, lava, etc. **2** (in *pl.*) a great downpour of rain. **3** a violent or copious flow. □ **torrential** *adj.* **torrentially** *adv.*

torrid /ˈtɒrɪd/ *adj.* **1 a** (of the weather) very hot and dry. **b** (of land etc.) parched by such weather. **2** (of language etc.) emotionally charged; passionate. **3** hard to contain or stop (*a torrid economy*).

torrid zone *n.* the central belt of the earth between the Tropics of Cancer and Capricorn.

torsion /ˈtɔːʃən/ *n.* **1** twisting, esp. of one end of a body while the other is held fixed. **2** the extent to which a curve departs from being planar. **3** the state of being twisted into a spiral. □ **torsional** *adj.* **torsionally** *adv.*

torsion bar *n.* a bar forming part of a vehicle suspension, twisting in response to the motion of the wheels, and absorbing their vertical movement.

torso *n.* (pl. **-os**) **1 a** the trunk of the human body. **b** the part of the human body between the pelvis or waist and the shoulders. **2** a statue of a human consisting of the trunk alone, without head or limbs.

tort *n.* *Law* a breach of duty (other than under contract) for which damages can be obtained in a civil court by the person wronged.

torte *n.* an elaborate rich cake, esp. one with ground nuts as an ingredient and having multiple layers.

tortellini /tɔːtəˈliːni/ *n.* small crescent-shaped pasta poouches stuffed with meat, cheese, etc.

tortilla /tɔːˈtiːə/ *n.* (esp. in Mexican cooking) a thin round bread made with either cornmeal or wheat flour and usu. filled with meat, cheese, beans, etc.

tortilla chip *n.* (usu. in *pl.*) a fried segment of a corn tortilla, often covered with a cheesy or spicy powdered coating, eaten cold like a potato chip.

tortious /ˈtɔːʃəs/ *adj.* constituting a tort; wrongful.

tortoise /ˈtɔːtəs/ *n.* **1** any slow-moving land or freshwater reptile encased in a scaly or leathery domed shell and having a retractile head and elephantine legs. **2** a slow-moving person or thing. **3** tortoiseshell; tortoiseshell colour. □ **tortoise-like** *adj. & adv.*

tortoiseshell ● *n.* **1** the yellowish-brown mottled or clouded outer shell of some turtles, used for decorative combs, jewellery, etc. **2 a** (in full **tortoiseshell cat**) a domestic cat with a mottled black, orange, and cream or white coat. **b** (in full **tortoiseshell butterfly**) any of various butterflies, esp. of the genus *Aglais* or *Nymphalis*, with wings mottled like tortoiseshell. ● *adj.* **1** having the colouring or appearance of tortoiseshell. **2** made of tortoiseshell or a synthetic substitute.

tortuous /ˈtɔːtʃuːəs/ *adj.* **1** full of twists and turns. **2** not direct or straightforward; unnecessarily complex. □ **tortuosity** /-ˈɒsɪtɪ/ *n.* (pl. **-ies**). **tortuously** *adv.*

torture ● *n.* **1** the infliction of severe bodily pain esp. as a punishment or a means of interrogation or intimidation. **2** severe physical or mental suffering. ● *v.tr.* subject to physical or mental torture. □ **torturer** *n.* **torturous** *adj.*

torus /'tɔrəs/ n. (pl. **tori** /-rai/ or **toruses**) **1** Geom. a surface or solid formed by rotating a closed curve, esp. a circle, about a line in its plane but not intersecting it, e.g. like a ring doughnut. **2** a thing of this shape, esp. a large ring-shaped chamber used in physical research. **3** Bot. the receptacle of a flower.

Tory informal ● n. (pl. **-ies**) a member or supporter of a Conservative party, esp. (in Canada) the Progressive Conservative Party. ● adj. of or relating to a Conservative party. □ **Toryism** n.

toss ● v. **1** tr. throw lightly or carelessly or easily. **2** tr. & intr. roll about, throw, or be thrown, restlessly or from side to side. **3 a** tr. throw (a coin) into the air to decide a choice etc. by the side on which it lands. **b** intr. settle a question or dispute in this way. **c** tr. settle a dispute with (a person) in this way (will toss you for it). **4** tr. **a** (of a horse etc.) throw (a rider) off its back. **b** (of a bull etc.) throw (a person etc.) up with the horns. **c** throw (a pancake) up so that it flips on to the other side in the frying pan. **5** tr. coat (food) with dressing etc. by stirring with a light up-and-down motion. **6** tr. debate; discuss (tossed the question back and forth). ● n. **1** the act or an instance of tossing (a coin, the head, etc.). **2** N Amer. a game or competition in which something is tossed (ring toss). □ **toss in** N Amer. add (an ingredient or element) to a mixture, concoction, etc., esp. casually. **toss off 1** dispatch (work) rapidly or without effort. **2** drink in one gulp. **3** utter in an offhand manner. □ **tosser** n.

toss-up n. **1** a situation in which either of two alternatives is equally possible. **2** the tossing of a coin.

tostada /tə'stɒdə/ n. (also **tostado** /tə'stɒdo:/ pl. **-os**) a corn tortilla topped with a seasoned mixture of beans, ground meat, and vegetables.

tot[1] n. **1** a small child (a tiny tot). **2** a dram of liquor.

tot[2] v. (**totted**, **totting**) **1** tr. (usu. foll. by up) add (figures etc.). **2** intr. (foll. by up) (of items) mount up.

total ● adj. **1** complete, comprising the whole or all. **2** absolute, unqualified. **3** (of an eclipse) in which the whole disc (of the sun, moon, etc.) is obscured. ● n. a total number or amount. ● v. (**totalled, totalling**) **1** tr. amount in number to. **b** find the total of (things, a set of figures, etc.). **2** intr. amount to, mount up to. **3** tr. N Amer. slang wreck (a car etc.) completely. ● adv. in total. □ **totally** adv.

totalitarian /toː,tælɪ'teriən/ ● adj. **1** of or relating to a centralized dictatorial form of government requiring complete subservience to the state. **2** demanding strict obedience in all matters. ● n. a person advocating such a system. □ **totalitarianism** n.

totality /toː'tælɪti/ n. **1** the complete amount or sum. **2** the quality of being total; entirety.

totalize v. **1** tr. collect into a total; find the total of. **2** tr. & intr. (of a corporation or societal institution) subsume (other institutions) in establishing an all-pervading influence. □ **totalization** n.

totalizer n. **1** a device showing the number and amount of bets staked on a race, to facilitate the division of the total among those backing the winner. **2** a person or thing which totalizes.

total recall n. the ability to remember every detail of one's experience clearly.

total war n. a war in which all available weapons and resources are employed.

tote informal ● v. tr. esp. N Amer. **1** carry (toting a gun). **2** find the total of (things, a set of figures, etc.) (toted up the cost). ● n. **1** (in full **tote bag**) esp. N Amer. a large open bag with handles, usu. made of fabric, esp. canvas. **2** Cdn any large container for storage etc. **3** slang (in full **tote board**) a totalizer. □ **toter** n. (also in comb.). **-toting** adj. (in comb.).

totem n. **1 a** (among some N American Aboriginal peoples) the emblem or symbol of a clan or family, usually the animal or plant that the family claims as its mythical ancestor. **b** an image of this. **2** an emblem or symbol. □ **totemic** /-'temɪk/ adj. **totemism** n. **totemistic** adj.

totem pole n. **1** a pole on which family crests or totems are carved or hung. **2** a hierarchy.

tote road n. N Amer. a rough temporary road used esp. to convey provisions to a work camp.

totter ● v. intr. **1** stand or walk unsteadily or feebly. **2 a** shake or rock as if about to collapse. **b** (of an institution, government, etc.) be about to fall. ● n. an unsteady or shaky movement or gait. □ **tottering** adj. **tottery** adj.

toucan /'tuːkæn/ n. a brightly coloured tropical American fruit-eating bird, with a huge beak.

touch ● v. **1** tr. come into or be in physical contact with at one or more points. **2 a** tr. bring the hand etc. into contact with. **b** intr. bring esp. the hand into contact with something; handle. **3 a** intr. (of two things etc.) be in or come into contact with one another. **b** tr. bring (two things) into mutual contact. **4** tr. rouse tender or painful feelings in. **5** tr. strike lightly. **6** tr. (usu. with neg.) **a** disturb or interfere with. **b** have any dealings with. **c** consume; use up; make use of. **7** tr. **a** deal with (a subject) lightly or in passing. **b** concern. **8** tr. **a** reach or rise as far as, esp. momentarily. **b** (usu. with neg.) approach in excellence etc. **9** tr. affect slightly; modify (pity touched with fear). **10** tr. affect in a way specified or implied by the context; transform (has touched many lives). **11** tr. strike (the keys, strings, etc. of a musical instrument). **12** tr. (usu. foll. by for) slang ask for and get money etc. from (a person) as a loan or gift (touched him for $5). ● n. **1** the act or an instance of touching, esp. with the body or hand. **2 a** the faculty of perception through physical contact, esp. with the fingers. **b** the qualities of an object etc. as perceived in this way. **3** a small amount; a slight trace. **4 a** a musician's manner of playing keys or strings. **b** the manner in which the keys or strings respond to touch. **c** an artist's or writer's style of workmanship, writing, etc. **5 a** a distinguishing quality or trait. **b** a special skill or proficiency. **6** (esp. in pl.) **a** a light stroke with a pen, pencil, etc. **b** a slight alteration or improvement. **7** (prec. by a) slightly. **8** slang **a** the act of asking for and getting money etc. from a person. **b** a person from whom money etc. is so obtained. **9** Soccer & Rugby the part of the field outside the sidelines. □ **get** (or **put**) **in** (or **into**) **touch with** come or cause to come into communication with; contact. **in touch** (often foll. by with) **1** in communication (still in touch after all these years). **2** up to date, esp. regarding news etc. **3** aware, conscious, empathetic (not in touch with her own feelings). **lose touch** (often foll. by with) **1** cease to be informed. **2** cease to correspond with or be in contact with another person. **lose one's touch** not show one's customary skill. **out of touch 1** not in correspondence. **2** not up to date or modern. **3** lacking in awareness or sympathy (out of touch with her son's beliefs). **touch bottom 1** reach the bottom of water with one's feet. **2** be at the lowest or worst point. **touch down 1** (of an aircraft or spacecraft) make contact with the ground in landing. **2** Rugby touch the ground with the ball behind one's own or esp. the opponent's goal line. **touch off 1** explode by touching with a match etc. **2** initiate (a process, incident, etc.) suddenly. **touch on** (or **upon**) **1** treat (a subject) briefly, refer to or mention casually. **2** verge on. **touch the spot** *informal* find out or do exactly what was needed. **touch up 1** give finishing touches to or retouch (a picture, writing, etc.). **2** *slang* **a** caress so as to excite sexually. **b** sexually molest. **touch wood** touch something wooden with the hand to avert bad luck. **would not touch with a 10-foot** (or **barge**) **pole** refuse to be associated or concerned with (a person or thing). □ **touchable** *adj.* **touchably** *adv.* **toucher** *n.* **touchless** *adj.*

touch and go *adj.* (hyphenated when *attrib.*) uncertain regarding the outcome.

touchdown *n.* **1 a** *Football* the act or an instance of scoring six points by being in possession of the ball in the opposing side's end zone. **b** *Rugby* an act of touching the ground behind the opposing side's goal with the ball held in the hands, to score points. **2** the act or an instance of an aircraft making contact with the ground during landing.

touché /tuːˈʃei/ *interj.* **1** the acknowledgement of a hit by a fencing opponent. **2** the acknowledgement of a justified accusation, a witticism, or a point made in reply to one's own.

touched *adj.* **1** *in senses of* TOUCH *v.* **2** (also in phr. **touched in the head**) *informal* slightly mad.

touch football *n. N Amer.* a form of football in which the ball carrier need only be touched to be stopped.

touching *adj.* exciting tender feeling or sympathy; moving. □ **touchingly** *adv.* **touchingness** *n.*

touchline *n. Soccer & Rugby* either of the lines marking the side boundaries of the field.

touchpad *n.* **1** a usu. square area on a flat panel that needs only to be touched to activate an electrical device. **2** a panel including these.

touch screen *n.* a computer screen that responds to the touch of a finger or stylus by transmitting the coordinates of the touched area to the computer.

touch-sensitive *adj.* **1** operated by the touch of a finger, stylus, etc. **2** designating an electronic musical keyboard which responds dynamically to the varying force of a player's touch.

touchstone *n.* **1** a fine-grained dark schist or jasper used for testing alloys of gold etc. by observing the colour of the mark which they make on it. **2** a thing which serves to test the genuineness or value of anything; a standard or criterion.

Touch-Tone *n.* (*attrib.*) *proprietary* designating a telephone system in which a different single tone is generated by each of the numbered buttons pushed to make a call.

touch type *v.tr. & intr.* type without looking at the keys. □ **touch typing** *n.* **touch typist** *n.*

touch-up *n.* a quick restoration or improvement (of paintwork, a piece of writing, etc.).

touchy *adj.* (**-ier**, **-iest**) **1** apt to take offence; oversensitive. **2** delicate; requiring careful handling (*a touchy subject*). □ **touchily** *adv.* **touchiness** *n.*

touchy-feely *adj.* displaying, encouraging, or relating to an uninhibited sharing of thoughts and emotions, often associated with physical touching, hugging, etc., as the basis of relationships.

tough ● *adj.* 1 hard to break, cut, tear, or chew; durable. **2** (of a person) able to endure hardship. **3** unyielding, stubborn; difficult. **4** *informal* **a** acting sternly. **b** (of circumstances, luck, etc.) severe, unpleasant, unjust. **5** (of a law, policy, etc.) demanding; strictly enforced. **6** *informal* rough, aggressive, or violent. ● *n.* a tough person, esp. a ruffian or criminal. ● *interj. ironic* that is unfortunate (used

unsympathetically or defiantly to underscore an unfortunate condition or circumstance which another must face). □ **be a tough sell** *N Amer.* be difficult to convince others about. **have it tough** be hard-pressed or in difficulty. **tough as nails** *N Amer.* extremely tough (also *attrib.*: *a tough-as-nails competitor*). **tough** (**it**) **out** *informal* endure or withstand (difficult conditions). □ **toughish** *adj.* **toughly** *adv.* **toughness** *n.*

toughen *v.tr. & intr.* make or become tough.

tough guy *n. informal* a hard, aggressive, or unyielding person (hyphenated when *attrib.*: *his tough-guy swagger*).

toughie *n.* (also **toughy** *pl.* **-ies**) *informal* a tough person or problem.

tough love *n.* esp. *N Amer.* the protection of another's welfare by enforcing certain constraints on them.

tough luck *informal* ● *n.* bad luck, misfortune. ● *interj.* (also esp. *N Amer. coarse slang* **tough shit, tough titty**) often *ironic* that is unfortunate.

tough-minded *adj.* **1** realistic, not sentimental. **2** determined. □ **tough-mindedness** *n.*

tough nut *n.* = HARD NUT.

toupée /tuːˈpei/ *n.* a wig or artificial hairpiece to cover a bald spot.

tour ● *n.* 1 a a journey from place to place as a holiday. **b** an excursion, ramble, or walk (*made a tour of the garden*). **c** an organized and guided trip, excursion, or visit. **2 a** a period of duty on military or diplomatic service. **b** the time to be spent at a particular post. **3** a series of performances, matches, etc., at different places on a route through a country etc. ● *v.* **1** *intr.* make a tour. **2** *tr.* make a tour of (a country etc.). □ **on tour** (esp. of a performer, team, etc.) touring.

tour de force /tor də ˈfɔrs/ *n.* (*pl.* **tours de force** *pronunc.* same) a feat of skill or strength; an impressive performance, achievement, or creation.

Tourette's syndrome /toˈrets/ *n.* (also **Tourette Syndrome**) a neurological disorder characterized by involuntary tics and vocalizations and the compulsive utterance of obscenities.

tourism *n.* the business or industry of attracting and providing accommodation and services for visitors and travellers on holiday.

tourist *n.* a person making a visit or tour as a holiday; a person travelling for pleasure. □ **touristic** *adj.*

tourist trap *n.* a place where tourists are exploited, e.g. where everything is excessively expensive.

touristy *adj.* usu. *derogatory* appealing to or visited by many tourists.

tourmaline /ˈtɔːrməliːn/ *n.* a boron aluminum silicate mineral of various colours, possessing unusual electrical properties, and used in electrical and optical instruments and as a gemstone.

tournament *n.* **1** any contest of skill or series of contests involving a number of competitors (*tennis tournament*). **2** *hist.* **a** a pageant in which jousting with blunted weapons took place. **b** a meeting for jousting between single knights for a prize etc.

tournedos /ˈtɔːrnədoʊ/ *n.* (*pl.* same /-ˌdoʊz/) a small round thick cut from a fillet of beef.

tourney *n.* (*pl.* **-eys**) a tournament.

tourniquet /ˈtɜːrnəkət, ˈtɔːr-, -ˌkei, -ˌkiː/ *n.* a device for stopping the flow of blood through an artery by twisting a bar etc. in a ligature or bandage so as to tighten it.

tour of duty *n.* = TOUR *n.* 2.

tourtière /tɔːrˈtjer/ *n.* a French-Canadian meat pie consisting esp. of ground pork and spices with a flaky double crust, traditionally served at Christmas.

tousle /ˈtʌusəl, ˈtauzəl/ ● v.tr. **1** make (esp. the hair) untidy; rumple. **2** handle roughly or rudely. ● n. a tousled mass of hair etc.

tousle-haired adj. having untidy hair.

tout ● v. **1** tr. extol, recommend. **2** intr. solicit patronage persistently. **3** tr. (of a vendor etc.) **a** try to sell (goods or services), esp. persistently. **b** solicit the patronage of (a customer, passersby, etc.) persistently. **4** intr. N Amer. offer racing tips for a share of the resulting profit. ● n. a person employed in touting. □ **touted** adj.

touton /ˈtuːtɒn/ n. Cdn (Nfld) a deep-fried flat round of bread dough, eaten with molasses.

tow ● v.tr. **1** pull (a boat, motor vehicle, etc.) along by a rope, chain, etc. **2** pull (a person or thing) along behind one. **3** remove (a motor vehicle) to a pound, garage, etc. ● n. **1** the act or an instance of towing; the state of being towed. **2** N Amer. Forestry a set of boomed logs gathered to be towed. **3** N Amer. a mechanism for pulling skiers up a hill. □ **in tow 1** (also **under tow**) being towed. **2** accompanying, often as a charge or as an admirer etc. □ **towable** adj.

toward prep. (also **towards**) **1** in the direction of. **2** as regards; in relation to. **3** as a contribution to. **4** near. ¶*toward* and *towards* are equally common in Canada; the fact that this dictionary lists *toward* first should not discourage the use of *towards*.

towboat n. a boat used to tow other boats etc.

towel ● n. **1** a piece of rough-surfaced absorbent, usu. terry cloth, used for drying oneself or a thing after washing. **2** absorbent paper used for this. ● v. (**towelled, towelling**) (N Amer. also foll. by *off*) **1** tr. (often refl.) wipe or dry with a towel. **2** intr. wipe or dry oneself with a towel.

towelette n. a small moistened tissue for wiping esp. the hands or face, often individually wrapped.

towelling n. **1** in senses of TOWEL v. **2** absorbent cloth, esp. cotton with uncut loops, used as material for towels.

tower ● n. **1 a** a tall narrow building or structure, either standing alone or forming part of a castle, church, etc. **b** a fortress etc. comprising or including a tower. **c** a tall structure housing machinery, apparatus, operators, etc. (*control tower*). **d** a tall building containing offices or apartments. **2** a lofty pile or mass. **3** a casing for computer components which stands upright, either alone or on a desk etc. **4** a place of defence; a protection. ● v.intr. reach or be high or above; be superior. □ **towered** adj.

towering adj. **1** high, lofty. **2** extremely eminent, exalted. **3** violent (*towering rage*).

tow-headed adj. having very light-coloured or unkempt hair. □ **towhead** n.

towhee /ˈtauhiː, toː-/ n. any of several buntings of the genus *Pipilo*, of brush and woodland in N America, esp. *P. erythrophthalmus*, having a black back, rust sides, and a white breast.

town n. **1 a** an urban area with a name, defined by boundaries, and local government, usu. larger than a village and smaller than a city. **b** any densely populated area, esp. as opposed to the country or suburbs. **c** the people of a town. **d** the government, administration, or employees of a town. **2** the central business or shopping area in a neighbourhood. □ **go to town** informal act or work with energy or enthusiasm. **on the town** informal enjoying the entertainments, esp. the nightlife, of a town; celebrating.

town council n. the elective governing body in a town. □ **town councillor** n.

town hall n. **1** a building for the administration of local government, having public meeting rooms etc. **2** (also **town hall meeting**) N Amer. a meeting or television broadcast allowing people to express their opinions on political issues to political leaders.

townhouse n. **1** (N Amer. also **townhome**) any of a row of usu. similar joined houses, two or three storeys high; a row house. **2** an urban residence, esp. of a person with a house in the country.

townie n. (also **townee**) derogatory a person living in a town, esp. as opposed to those living in the country or (in a university town) a student etc.

town line n. Cdn (Ont.) a road separating two municipalities, esp. townships.

town meeting n. N Amer. a general assembly of the inhabitants of a town.

town planner n. an urban planner. □ **town planning** n.

townscape n. **1** the visual appearance of a town or towns. **2** a picture of a town.

townsfolk n. the inhabitants of a particular town.

township n. **1** N Amer. a division of a county with some corporate powers. **2** N Amer. (in areas of W Canada and the US surveyed into ranges and townships) a district six miles square, containing thirty-six sections. **3** hist. an urban area in South Africa set aside for black occupation.

Townshipper /ˈtaunˌʃɪpər/ n. Cdn a resident of the Eastern Townships.

townsite n. N Amer. (esp. Cdn) **1** the site of a town, esp. a tract of land set apart by legal authority to be occupied by a town, and usu. surveyed and laid out with streets etc. **2** an unincorporated town in a national park etc.

townsman n. (pl. **-men**) an inhabitant of a town.

townspeople n.pl. the people of a town.

towpath n. a path beside a river or canal, originally used for towing barges by horse.

tow truck n. N Amer. a truck used to tow away motor vehicles.

toxemia /tɒkˈsiːmiə/ n. (also esp. Brit. **toxaemia**) **1** blood poisoning. **2** a condition in pregnancy characterized by increased blood pressure. □ **toxemic** adj.

toxic /ˈtɒksɪk/ adj. **1** of or relating to poison (*toxic symptoms*). **2** poisonous (*toxic gas*). **3** caused by poison (*toxic anemia*). □ **toxically** adv. **toxicity** n.

toxicology /ˌtɒksɪˈkɒlədʒi/ n. the scientific study of poisons. □ **toxicological** adj. **toxicologist** n.

toxic shock syndrome n. acute septicemia in women, typically caused by bacterial infection from a retained tampon, IUD, etc. Abbr.: **TSS**.

toxin n. a poison produced by a living organism, esp. one formed in the body and stimulating the production of antibodies.

toxoplasmosis /ˌtɒksoˈplæzˈmoːsɪs/ n. a disease caused by infection with the protozoan *Toxoplasma gondii*, transmitted esp. through poorly prepared food or in cat feces and dangerous in unborn children.

toy ● n. **1 a** a plaything, esp. for a child. **b** a model or miniature replica of a thing, esp. as a plaything (*toy boat*). **2 a** a thing, esp. a gadget or instrument, regarded as providing amusement or pleasure. **b** a task or undertaking regarded in an unserious way. **3** (usu. attrib.) a small breed or variety of dog etc. ● v.intr. (usu. foll. by *with*) **1 a** consider something casually or without serious intent. **b** deal with something or someone thoughtlessly. **2 a** move an object idly. **b** nibble at food etc. unenthusiastically. □ **toylike** adj.

toy boy n. informal a much younger male lover.

Tpr *abbr.* (also **Tpr.**) TROOPER 1.

trace¹ ● *v.tr.* **1 a** observe, discover, or find vestiges or signs of by investigation. **b** follow or mark the track or position of. **c** follow to its origins. **2** copy (a drawing etc.) by drawing over its lines on a superimposed piece of translucent paper, or by using carbon paper. **3** mark out, sketch, or write esp. laboriously. **4** pursue one's way along (a path etc.). ● *n.* **1 a** a sign or mark or other indication of something having existed. **b** a very small quantity. **2 a** track or footprint left by a person or animal. **3** a track left by the moving pen of an instrument etc. **4** a line on the screen of a cathode ray tube showing the path of a moving spot. **5** a curve's projection on or intersection with a plane etc. **6** *N Amer.* the track made by the passage of a person or thing. □ **traceable** *adj.* **traceability** *n.* **traceless** *adj.*

trace² *n.* each of the two side straps, chains, or ropes by which a horse draws a vehicle. □ **kick over the traces** become insubordinate or reckless.

trace element *n.* **1** a chemical element occurring in minute amounts. **2** (also **trace mineral**) a chemical element needed only in minute amounts by living organisms for normal growth.

tracer *n.* **1** a person or thing that traces. **2** a bullet etc. visible in flight because of flames etc. emitted. **3** an artificially produced radioactive isotope capable of being followed through the body by the radiation it produces. **4** a person whose business is the tracing of missing persons, property, etc.

tracery *n.* (*pl.* **-ies**) **1** ornamental stone openwork esp. in the upper part of a Gothic window. **2** a fine or delicate decorative pattern.

trachea /ˈtreɪkɪə, trəˈkiːə/ *n.* (*pl.* **tracheae** /-ˈkiːiː/) the passage reinforced by rings of cartilage, through which air reaches the bronchial tubes from the larynx; the windpipe. □ **tracheal** *adj.*

tracheotomy /ˌtreɪkiˈɒtəmi, ˌtræki-/ *n.* (also **tracheostomy** /-ˈɒstəmi/) (*pl.* **-ies**) a surgical operation to make an opening in the trachea, esp. so that the patient can breathe through it via a curved tube.

trachoma /trəˈkoːmə/ *n.* a contagious eye disease with inflamed granulation on the lids' inner surface.

tracing *n.* **1** a copy of a drawing etc. made by tracing. **2** = TRACE¹ *n.* 3. **3** the act or an instance of tracing.

tracing paper *n.* translucent paper used for making tracings.

track ● *n.* **1** a mark or marks left by a person, animal, or thing in passing. **2** a rough path, esp. one beaten by use. **3** a continuous railway line. **4 a** a racecourse for horses etc. **b** *Sport* a prepared course for runners etc. **c** esp. *N Amer. Sport* the athletic events, esp. running, which take place on a track. **d** = WARNING TRACK. **5 a** a section of a phonograph record, cassette tape, compact disc, etc., containing one song etc. **b** one of several lengthwise divisions of a strip of magnetic tape, containing one sequence of signals; a channel. **c** that which is recorded on such a strip (*laugh track*). **6 a** a line of travel, passage, or motion. **b** the path travelled by a ship, aircraft, etc. **7** a continuous band around the wheels of a tank, tractor, etc. **8 a** a course of action or conduct; a way of proceeding. **b** a line of reasoning or thought (*this track proved fruitless*). **9** = CAREER PATH (*tenure-track*). **10** (in full **track mark**) (usu. in *pl.*) *slang* a line on the skin made by repeated injections of an addictive drug. ● *v.* **1** *tr.* **a** follow the track of (an animal, person, spacecraft, etc.). **b** trace the movements of. **2** *tr.* **a** follow (a course, development, etc.). **b** follow the course or development of. **3** *intr.* (of a film or TV camera) move in relation to the

subject being filmed. **4** *tr. N Amer.* make a track with (dirt etc.) from the feet. □ **in one's tracks** *informal* where one stands, there and then (*stopped him in his tracks*). **keep** (or **lose**) **track of** follow (or fail to follow) the course or development of. **make tracks** *informal* go or run away. **make tracks for** *informal* go in pursuit of or toward. **off the track** away from the subject. **on a person's track 1** in pursuit of him or her. **2** in possession of a clue to a person's conduct, plans, etc. **on the right** (or **wrong**) **track** following the right (or wrong) line of inquiry. **on** (or **off**) **track** following (or deviating from) the desired direction or goal. **on the wrong side of the tracks** *informal* in a poor or less prestigious part of town. **track down** reach or capture by tracking.

track and field *n.* esp. *N Amer.* athletic events comprising track events (such as sprints, hurdles, etc.) and field events (such as throwing and jumping).

trackball *n. Computing* a small ball that is rotated in a holder to move a cursor on a screen.

tracked *adj.* (of a wheeled vehicle) equipped with tracks (see TRACK *n.* 7).

tracker *n.* **1** a person or thing that tracks. **2** a police dog tracking by scent.

tracking *n.* **1** *in senses of* TRACK *v.* **2** the formation of a conducting path over the surface of an insulating material. **3** in a VCR, the alignment of the tape with the tape head, which may need to be adjusted for tapes recorded on another machine.

trackless *adj.* **1** without a track or tracks. **2** leaving no track or trace. **3** (esp. of a vehicle) not running on a track. □ **tracklessness** *n.*

track light *n.* (usu. in *pl.*) one of a line of lights fitted on a metal or plastic strip, each of which can be positioned individually. □ **track lighting** *n.*

track pants *n.pl.* loose pants, usu. with elasticated cuffs, worn casually or by an athlete etc. for exercising or jogging.

track record *n.* the past achievements of a person or an organization.

track shoe *n.* a shoe with a flat rubber sole, worn by runners or as casual footwear.

trackside *n.* (often *attrib.*) the area beside a railway line or racetrack.

track suit *n.* a loose warm two-piece suit worn by an athlete etc. for exercising or jogging.

tract *n.* **1** a region or area of indefinite, esp. large, extent. **2** an area of an organ or system (*respiratory tract*). **3** a short treatise in pamphlet form esp. on a religious or political subject. **4** an anthem replacing the alleluia in some Masses.

tractable *adj.* **1** (of a person) easily handled; docile. **2** (of material etc.) malleable. □ **tractability** *n.* **tractably** *adv.*

tract house *n.* (also **tract home**) *N Amer.* one of a number of similar houses built as part of a real estate development. □ **tract housing** *n.*

traction *n.* **1** the grip of a tire, footwear, etc. on the ground. **2** the act of drawing or pulling a thing over a surface, esp. a road or track. **3 a** a sustained pulling on a limb, muscle, etc., by means of pulleys, weights, etc. to maintain the positions of fractured bones, correct deformity, etc. **b** the state of being subjected to such a pull. **c** contraction, e.g. of a muscle. □ **tractive** *adj.*

tractor *n.* a powerful motor vehicle used for hauling etc., esp. one with large treaded rear wheels used to haul farm machinery.

tractor pull *n. N Amer.* a competition in which tractors pull increasingly heavy loads.

tractor-trailer *n. N Amer.* an articulated truck consisting of a powerful cab pulling a large detachable trailer.

tractor train *n. Cdn (North)* a train of sleds pulled by a tractor etc.

trad *adj. informal* traditional.

trade ● *n.* **1 a** buying and selling. **b** buying and selling conducted between nations etc.; the exchange of goods between peoples. **c** business conducted for profit (esp. as distinct from a profession). **d** business of a specified nature or time (*tourist trade*). **2** a skilled handicraft esp. requiring an apprenticeship. **3** (usu. prec. by *the*) the people engaged in a specific trade. **4** *N Amer.* **a** a transaction, esp. a swap. **b** *Sport* an exchange of players between two or more franchises or teams. ● *v.* **1** *intr.* (often foll. by *in*, *with*) buy and sell. **2** *tr.* **a** exchange in commerce; barter (goods). **b** exchange (insults, blows, etc.). **c** esp. *N Amer.* (foll. by *for*) swap, exchange. **d** *N Amer.* exchange products or commodities with (a person). **e** *N Amer. Sport* (of a franchise or team) relinquish the rights to (a player) to another team in exchange for the rights to one or more of theirs or for other considerations. **3** *intr.* have a transaction with a person for a thing. **4** *intr.* (of shares, currency, etc.) be bought and sold. □ **trade in** exchange (esp. a used car etc.) in part payment for another. **trade off** exchange, esp. as a compromise. **trade on** take advantage of (a person's credulity, one's reputation, etc.). **trade up** sell something in order to buy a better or more expensive replacement. □ **tradable** *adj.* (also **tradeable**).

trade balance *n.* = BALANCE OF TRADE.

trade barrier *n.* a policy or regulation that restricts trade between countries, provinces, etc.

tradecraft *n.* **1** skill or art in connection with a trade or calling. **2** skill in espionage and intelligence.

trade deficit *n.* (also **trade gap**) the extent by which a country's imports exceed its exports.

trade fair *n.* = TRADE SHOW.

trade goods *n.pl.* goods exchanged between countries, peoples, etc.

trade-in *n.* a thing, esp. a car, exchanged in part payment for another.

trade journal *n.* (also **trade paper**) a periodical containing news etc. concerning a particular trade.

trademark ● *n.* **1** a logo, word, or words, secured by legal registration or established by use as representing a company, product, etc. **2** a distinctive characteristic etc. ● *adj.* characteristic or distinctive (*wearing his trademark cap*) ● *v.tr.* (usu. as **trademarked** *adj.*) **1** provide with a trademark. **2** register as a trademark.

trade name *n.* **1** a name by which a thing is called in a trade. **2** a name given to a product; a brand name. **3** a name under which a business operates.

trade-off *n.* a balance achieved between two desirable but incompatible features; a compromise.

trader *n.* **1** a person engaged in trading. **2** a person who trades stocks.

trade show *n.* a gathering of members of a trade or industry for the exhibition of the latest technology, products, developments, etc.

tradesman *n.* (*pl.* **-men**) a person engaged in a trade, esp. a skilled craftsman.

tradespeople *n.pl.* people engaged in trade.

tradeswoman *n.* (*pl.* **-women**) a woman engaged in a trade, esp. a skilled craftswoman.

trade union *n.* an organized association of workers formed to protect and further their rights and interests and to bargain collectively with employers. □ **trade unionism** *n.* **trade unionist** *n.*

trade war *n.* a situation in which governments act aggressively in international markets to promote their own countries' trading interests.

trade wind *n.* a wind blowing continually towards the equator and deflected westward.

trading *n.* the act of engaging in trade.

trading card *n. N Amer.* a small card depicting a figure or figures from popular culture, esp. sports, for collecting or trading.

trading post *n.* a store or other place for conducting trade, usu. in remote areas, esp. originally established by colonial powers to trade with Aboriginal peoples.

tradition *n.* **1 a** a custom, opinion, or belief handed down to posterity esp. orally or by practice. **b** this process of handing down. **2** an established practice or custom. □ **traditional** *adj.* **traditionally** *adv.*

traditionalism *n.* **1** respect or support for tradition, esp. in contrast with modern practices or styles. **2** a philosophical system referring all religious knowledge to divine revelation and tradition. □ **traditionalist** *n.*

traffic ● *n.* **1** (often *attrib.*) **a** vehicles moving on a public road or highway, esp. of a specified kind, density, etc. **b** such movement in the air, at sea, or by rail. **c** people moving, esp. on foot. **2** trade, esp. illegal. **3 a** the transportation of goods, the coming and going of people or goods by road, rail, air, sea, etc. **b** the persons or goods so transported. **4** dealings or communication between people etc. **5** the messages, signals, etc., transmitted through a communications system; the flow or volume of such signals. ● *v.* (**trafficked**, **trafficking**) **1** *intr.* **a** deal in something, esp. illegally. **b** engage in (*traffics in half-truths*). **2** *tr.* deal in; barter. □ **trafficker** *n.*

traffic calming *n.* (often *attrib.*) the deliberate slowing of traffic, esp. along residential streets, by building speed bumps, obstructions, etc.

traffic circle *n. N Amer.* a road junction at which traffic moves in one direction around a central island.

traffic island *n.* a paved or grassed area in a road to divert traffic, provide a refuge for pedestrians, etc.

traffic jam *n.* traffic at a standstill because of volume, construction, an accident, etc.

trafficked *adj.* (of a roadway, route, etc.) used by an esp. specified amount of traffic.

traffic light *n.* (usu. in *pl.*) each of a set of automatic lights, usu. red, amber, and green, for controlling road traffic, esp. at intersections.

traffic sign *n.* a sign conveying information, a warning, etc., to road traffic.

tragedy *n.* (*pl.* **-ies**) **1** a serious accident, crime, or natural catastrophe. **2 a** a sad event; a calamity. **b** a tragic element; tragic circumstances. **3 a** a dramatic representation dealing with tragic events and with an unhappy ending, esp. concerning the downfall of the protagonist. **b** the tragic genre.

tragic *adj.* **1** greatly distressing (*a tragic tale*). **2** of, or in the style of, tragedy (*a tragic actor*). □ **tragically** *adv.*

tragicomedy *n.* (*pl.* **-ies**) **1 a** a play having a mixture of comedy and tragedy. **b** plays of this kind as a genre. **2** an event etc. having tragic and comic elements. □ **tragicomic** *adj.*

trail ● *n.* **1 a** a track left by a thing, person, etc., moving over a surface. **b** a track, scent, or other trace followed in hunting, seeking, etc. **2 a** a beaten or maintained path or track, esp. through a park, wild region, etc., often for a specified traffic (*ski trail*). **b** a route into or through wild territory, followed by a wave of migrants, prospectors, etc. **c** *N Amer.* a highway route designated for its interest to tourists (*the Cabot Trail*). **d** *Cdn* (in Alberta) a major arterial road through a city. **e** a tour or series of performances, shows, etc. (*on the festival trail*). **3** a part dragging behind a thing or person (*a trail of smoke*). ● v. **1** *tr. & intr.* draw, be drawn, or appear to draw along behind. **2** *intr.* (often foll. by *behind*) walk wearily. **3** *tr.* follow the trail of. **4 a** *intr.* be losing in a game or other contest. **b** *tr.* have fewer points in a game, series, etc. than (one's opponent). **5** *intr.* (usu. foll. by *away, off*) peter out. **6** *intr.* **a** (of a plant etc.) grow or hang over a wall, along the ground etc. **b** (of a garment etc.) hang loosely.

trail bike *n.* = DIRT BIKE.

trailblazer *n.* **1** a person who marks a new track through wild country. **2** an innovator. □ **trail-blazing** *n. & attrib.adj.*

trail-breaker *n.* a person who clears a path through rough terrain, deep snow, etc. □ **trail-breaking** *n.*

trailer ● *n.* **1** a vehicle towed by another, esp.: **a** the rear section of a tractor-trailer. **b** an open cart. **c** a platform for transporting a boat etc. **d** *N Amer.* a camper, mobile home, house trailer, or other towed vehicle with living accommodations. **2** a series of brief extracts from a film etc., used to advertise it in advance; a preview. **3** a person or thing that trails. **4** a trailing plant. ● *v.tr. & intr.* transport or travel by trailer.

trailer park *n. N Amer.* (also **trailer court**) a place where mobile homes or other trailers may be parked for holiday or more permanent accommodation.

trailhead *n. N Amer.* the starting point of a trail.

trailing arbutus *n. N Amer.* the mayflower.

trailing edge *n.* the rear edge of an aircraft's wing etc.

trail mix *n. esp. N Amer.* a mixture of nuts, dried fruit, chocolate chips, etc., esp. as a snack eaten by hikers.

trail ride *n. N Amer.* a ride on horseback along a trail esp. through rugged country. □ **trail riding** *n.*

train ● *v.* **1 a** *tr.* teach (a person, animal, oneself, etc.) a specified skill esp. by practice. **b** *intr.* undergo this process. **2** *tr. & intr.* bring or come into a state of physical efficiency by exercise, diet, etc.; undergo physical exercise, esp. for a specific purpose (*trains every day*). **3** *tr.* cause (a plant) to grow in a required shape. **4** *tr.* (usu. as **trained** *adj.*) improve the abilities of (the mind, eye, voice, etc.) as a result of instruction, practice, etc. **5** *tr.* point or aim (a gun, camera, etc.) at an object etc. ● *n.* **1 a** a series of railway cars drawn by a locomotive. **b** *Cdn (North)* = TRACTOR TRAIN. **2** something dragged along behind or forming the back part of a dress, robe, etc. **3** a succession or series of people, things, events, etc. (*train of thought*). **4** a body of followers. **5** a succession of military vehicles etc., including artillery, supplies, etc. (*baggage train*). **6** a series of connected wheels or parts in machinery. □ **in train** properly arranged or directed. **in a person's train** following behind a person. □ **trainable** *adj.* **trainability** *n.*

trainee *n.* (often *attrib.*) a person undergoing training. □ **traineeship** *n.*

trainer *n.* **1** a person who trains. **2 a** a person who trains athletes, horses, etc., as a profession. **b** a person who attends to the medical and physical wellbeing of athletes, esp. on a team. **3** an aircraft or device simulating it used to train pilots. **4** a piece of equipment used for training; an exercise machine.

training *n.* **1** the act or process of teaching or learning a skill, discipline, etc. **2** the process of developing physical fitness and efficiency by diet and exercise. **3**

(*attrib.*) designating a thing designed or modified to facilitate the learning of a skill etc. (*training pants*).

training camp *n.* **1** the gathering of members of a sports team for organized training before the start of a season. **2** any camp where training occurs.

training ground *n.* any setting where one learns or develops specific skills, attributes, etc.

training school *n.* **1** (also **training college**) a college or school where students are trained in a particular profession or occupation. **2** *N Amer.* a vocational institution for juvenile delinquents.

training wheel *n. N Amer.* a small wheel fitted to each side of the rear wheel of a bicycle to stabilize it for a child learning to ride.

trainload *n.* a number of people, or quantity of goods etc., transported by train.

trainman *n.* (*pl.* **-men**) a railway employee working on trains.

trainspotter *n. Brit. slang* a derogatory term for an obsessive follower of any specialized hobby. □ **trainspotting** *n.*

traipse /treips/ *informal* ● *v.intr.* **1** tramp or trudge wearily. **2** walk aimlessly or carelessly. **3** (often foll. by *around*) go on errands. ● *n.* a tedious journey on foot.

trait /treit/ *n.* **1** a distinguishing feature or characteristic esp. of a person. **2** an inherited or inheritable characteristic.

traitor *n.* a person who is treacherous or disloyal, esp. to his or her country. □ **traitorous** *adj.* **traitorously** *adv.*

trajectory /trə'dʒektəri/ *n.* (*pl.* **-ies**) the path described by a projectile flying or an object moving under the action of given forces.

tram *n.* **1** *esp. Brit.* = STREETCAR. **2** *N Amer.* = GONDOLA 3. **3** a four-wheeled vehicle used in coal mines.

trammel ● *v.tr.* (**trammelled, trammelling**) impede the free action of; hinder, constrain. ● *n.* **1** (usu. in *pl.*) an impediment to free movement. **2** a triple dragnet for fish, which are trapped in a pocket formed when they attempt to swim through.

tramp ● *v.* **1** *intr.* **a** walk heavily and firmly. **b** go on foot, esp. a distance. **2** *tr.* **a** cross on foot, esp. wearily or reluctantly. **b** cover (a distance) in this way. **3** *tr.* tread on; trample. ● *n.* **1** an itinerant vagrant or beggar. **2** *esp. N Amer. slang derogatory* a promiscuous woman. **3** the sound of a person, or esp. people, walking, marching, etc., or of horses' hooves. **4** a journey on foot, esp. protracted. **5** a merchant ship running on no regular line or route. □ **trampy** *adj.*

trample ● *v.tr.* **1** tread under foot. **2** press down or crush in this way. **3** disregard with contempt; put down. ● *n.* the sound or act of trampling. □ **trample on** (or **over**) **1** tread heavily on. **2** treat roughly or with contempt; disregard (a person's feelings etc.).

trampoline ● *n.* a strong fabric sheet connected by springs to a horizontal frame, used by gymnasts etc. for somersaults, as a springboard, etc. ● *v.intr.* use a trampoline.

tramway *n.* **1** a crude road with wooden, stone, or metal tracks for wheels, used in mining etc. **2 a** rails for a streetcar. **b** a streetcar system.

trance *n.* **1 a** a sleeplike or half-conscious state without response to stimuli. **b** a hypnotic or cataleptic state. **2** such a state as entered into by a medium. **3** a state of extreme exaltation or rapture; ecstasy. **4** a stunned or dazed state. **5** a state of mental absorption or abstraction from external things. □ **trancelike** *adj.*

tranche /trænʃ/ *n.* a portion, esp. of income, or of a block of shares.

trank *slang* ● *n.* (usu. in *pl.*) a tranquilizer. ● *v.tr.* (esp. as **tranked** *adj.*) tranquilize.

tranny *n.* (*pl.* **-ies**) *N Amer. Mech. slang* a transmission.

tranquil *adj.* calm, serene. □ **tranquility** *n.* **tranquilly** *adv.*

tranquilize *v.tr.* make tranquil, esp. by a drug etc. □ **tranquilizing** *adj.*

tranquilizer *n.* a person or thing which tranquilizes, esp. a drug used to diminish tension or anxiety.

trans- *prefix* across (*transcontinental*).

transact *v.tr.* perform or carry through (business).

transaction *n.* **1 a** a piece of esp. commercial business done. **b** *N Amer.* = TRADE 4b. **c** the management of business etc. **2** (in *pl.*) published reports of discussions, papers read, etc., at the meetings of a learned society.

transactional *adj.* **1** *in senses of* TRANSACTION. **2** *Psych.* of, pertaining to, or involving interpersonal communication viewed as transactions of attitude between participants. □ **transactionally** *adv.*

transatlantic *adj.* **1** crossing or spanning the Atlantic. **2** beyond the Atlantic, esp. (*N Amer.*) European. □ **transatlantically** *adv.*

transaxle *n.* an integral driving axle and differential gear in a motor vehicle.

transborder *adj.* that crosses, is situated on, or pertains to both sides of a border.

trans-Canada ● *adj.* spanning, including, or involving all of Canada. ● *n.* (**Trans-Canada**) (prec. by *the*) (in full **Trans-Canada Highway**) a highway spanning Canada from St. John's to Victoria.

transceiver /træn'si:vər/ *n.* any device which is both a transmitter and receiver of signals.

transcend /træn'send/ *v.tr.* **1** be beyond the range or grasp of (human experience, reason, belief, etc.). **2** excel; surpass. **3** be above or independent of; go beyond or exceed the limits of.

transcendent *adj.* **1** excelling, surpassing. **2** transcending human experience. **3** (esp. of the supreme being) existing apart from, not subject to the limitations of, the material universe. □ **transcendence** *n.* **transcendently** *adv.*

transcendental /ˌtrænsen'dentəl/ *adj.* **1** = TRANSCENDENT. **2 a** visionary, abstract. **b** vague, obscure. □ **transcendentally** *adv.*

transcendental meditation *n.* a method of detaching oneself from problems, anxiety, etc., by silent meditation and repetition of a mantra.

transcontinental ● *adj.* extending across a continent. ● *n.* a transcontinental railway or train.

transcribe *v.tr.* **1** make a copy of, esp. in writing. **2** transliterate. **3** write out (shorthand, notes, etc.) in ordinary characters or continuous prose. **4 a** record for subsequent reproduction. **b** broadcast in this form. **5** arrange (music) for a different instrument etc. **6** represent (a speech sound or spoken word) in a written form using phonetic characters. □ **transcriber** *n.*

transcript *n.* **1 a** a written or recorded copy. **b** something transcribed. **2** any copy. **3** a written record of public proceedings etc. **4** *N Amer.* an official record of a student's grades etc.

transcription *n.* **1 a** the action or process of transcribing something. **b** an instance of this. **2** a transcript or copy. □ **transcriptional** *adj.* **transcriptionally** *adv.* **transcriptionist** *n.*

transcultural *adj.* pertaining to or involving more than one culture; cross-cultural.

transduce *v.tr.* convert (energy, esp. in the form of a signal) into a different medium or form of energy. □ **transduction** *n.*

transducer *n.* any device for converting a signal from one medium of transmission to another, esp. a non-electrical signal into an electrical one, e.g. pressure into voltage.

transect ● *v.tr.* cut across or transversely. ● *n.* a line or strip across the earth's surface or through any object, along which a survey or observations are made. □ **transection** *n.*

transept /'trænsept/ *n.* **1** either arm of the part of a cross-shaped church at right angles to the nave (*north transept; south transept*). **2** this part as a whole.

transexual *var. of* TRANSSEXUAL.

trans fat *n.* (in full **trans fatty acid**) any unsaturated fatty acid with the same atoms on opposite sides of its double bonds, found frequently in margarines and cooking oils as a result of hydrogenation.

transfer ● *v.* (**transferred, transferring**) **1** *tr.* (often foll. by *to*) **a** move from one place to another. **b** hand over the possession of to a person. **2** *tr.* & *intr.* move or change to another department, school, group, etc. **3** *intr.* change from one route, airport, station, etc., to another on a journey. **4** *tr.* **a** reroute (a telephone connection) to another line, department, etc. **b** reroute the telephone connection of (a caller) to another line, department, etc. **5** *tr.* convey or apply (a drawing or design) from one surface to another, esp. from a prepared sheet. **6** *tr.* change (the sense of a word etc.) by extension or metaphor. ● *n.* **1** the act or an instance of transferring or being transferred. **2** *N Amer.* a ticket allowing a journey to be continued on another route etc. **3 a** a design etc. conveyed or to be conveyed from one surface to another. **b** a small usu. coloured picture or design on paper, which is transferable to another surface. **4** a person who is or is to be transferred. **5 a** the conveyance of property, a right, etc. **b** a document effecting this. **6** = TRANSFER PAYMENT. □ **transferee** *n.* **transferor** *n.* esp. *Law*.

transferable *adj.* that can be transferred. □ **transferability** *n.*

transference /'trænsfərəns/ *n.* **1** the act or an instance of transferring; the state of being transferred. **2** *Psych.* the redirection of childhood emotions to a new object, esp. to a psychoanalyst.

transfer payment *n.* a direct payment from a government not made in exchange for goods or services, e.g. to an individual or family in the form of an employment insurance payment or family allowance, or (in Canada) esp. to another level of government.

transferral *n.* = TRANSFER *n.* 1.

transfer RNA *n.* RNA conveying an amino acid molecule from the cytoplasm to a ribosome for use in protein synthesis etc. Abbr.: **tRNA**.

transfer station *n.* a facility where garbage is collected for compression etc. before being trucked to a landfill.

transfiguration *n.* **1** a change of form or appearance. **2 a** Christ's appearance in radiant glory to three of his disciples. **b** (**Transfiguration**) the festival of Christ's transfiguration.

transfigure *v.tr.* change in form or appearance, esp. so as to elevate or idealize.

transfix *v.tr.* **1** pierce with a sharp implement or weapon. **2** root (a person) to the spot with fascination, astonishment, fear, etc.

transform *v.* **1 a** *tr.* make a thorough or dramatic change in the form, outward appearance, character, etc., of. **b** *intr.* (often foll. by *into, to*) undergo such a

change. **2** *tr.* change the voltage etc. of (a current). □
transformable *adj.* **transformative** *adj.*

transformation *n.* **1** the act or an instance of
transforming; the state of being transformed. **2** a
complete change of form at metamorphosis, esp. of
insects, amphibians, etc. □ **transformational** *adj.*
transformationally *adv.*

transformer *n.* **1** an apparatus for reducing or
increasing the voltage of an alternating current. **2** a
person or thing that transforms.

transfuse *v.tr.* **1** permeate. **2 a** transfer (blood) from
one person or animal to another. **b** inject (liquid) into
a blood vessel to replace lost fluid. **c** treat (a person)
with a blood transfusion. □ **transfusion** *n.*

transgenic /trænz'dʒenɪk/ *adj.* having genetic material introduced from another species.

transgress *v. tr. & intr.* contravene or go beyond the
bounds or limits set by (a commandment, law, etc.). □
transgressive *adj.* **transgressor** *n.*

transgression *n.* **1** an act or instance of
transgressing. **2** a violation of law, duty or command.

tranship *var. of* TRANSSHIP.

transient /'trænziənt/ ● *adj.* of short duration;
momentary; passing; impermanent. ● *n.* **1 a** a temporary visitor, worker, etc. **b** a vagrant; a tramp. **2**
Electricity a brief current etc. □ **transience** *n.*
transiency *n.* **transiently** *adv.*

transistor /træn'zɪstər/ *n.* **1** a semiconductor device
with three connections, capable of amplification in
addition to rectification. **2** (in full **transistor radio**)
a portable radio with transistors.

transit ● *n.* **1** the act or process of going, conveying,
or being conveyed, esp. over a distance. **2** a passage or
route. **3** *N Amer.* the local conveyance of passengers on
public routes. **4 a** the apparent passage of a celestial
body across the meridian of a place. **b** the passage of
an inferior planet across the face of the sun, or of a
moon etc. across the face of a planet. **5** a surveying
instrument for measuring horizontal angles. ● *v.*
(**transited, transiting**) **1** *tr.* make a transit across. **2**
intr. make a transit. □ **in transit** while going or being
conveyed.

transition /træn'zɪʃən/ *n.* **1 a** a passing or change
from one place, condition, etc., to another. **b** passage
from one subject to another. **2** *Music* a momentary
modulation. □ **transitional** *adj.*

transition house *n.* (also **transition home**) *Cdn* a
home operated by a social service agency, esp. for
abused women.

transitive /'trænzɪtɪv/ *Grammar* ● *adj.* (of a verb or
sense of a verb) that takes a direct object (whether
expressed or implied). ● *n.* a transitive verb. □
transitively *adv.* **transitivity** *n.*

transitory /'trænzɪ,tɔri/ *adj.* not permanent, brief,
transient. □ **transitorily** *adv.* **transitoriness** *n.*

translate *v.* **1** *tr. & intr.* express the sense of in another
language. **2** *intr.* (of a literary work etc.) be
translatable. **3** *tr.* express (an idea, book, etc.) in
another, esp. simpler, form. **4** *tr.* interpret the significance of. **5** *intr.* (foll. by *into*) express something or be
expressed in a different, esp. a more practical form
(*it's time to translate our ideas into action*). **6** *tr. Christianity*
a remove (a bishop) to another see. **b** remove (a saint's
relics etc.) to another place. **7** *tr. Bible* convey to heaven
without death; transform. □ **translatability** *n.*
translatable *adj.*

translation *n.* **1** the act or an instance of
translating. **2** a written or spoken rendering of the
meaning of a text in another language. □
translational *adj.*

translator *n.* **1** a person who translates from one
language into another. **2** a program that translates
from one (esp. programming) language into another.

transliterate /trænz'lɪtə,reit/ *v.tr.* represent (a word
etc.) in the closest corresponding letters of a different
alphabet or language. □ **transliteration** *n.*

translocate *v.tr.* move from one place to another. □
translocation *n.*

translucent /trænz'lu:sənt/ *adj.* allowing light to
pass through diffusely. □ **translucence** *n.*
translucency *n.* **translucently** *adv.*

transmigrate /,trænzmai'greit/ *v.intr.* **1** (of the soul)
pass into a different body. **2** migrate. □
transmigration *n.*

transmission *n.* **1** the act or an instance of
transmitting; the state of being transmitted. **2** a
broadcast radio or television program. **3** the mechanism by which power is transmitted from an engine
to the axle in a motor vehicle.

transmission line *n.* a conductor or conductors,
esp. a cable, carrying electricity over large distances.

transmit *v.tr.* (**transmitted, transmitting**) **1 a** pass
or hand on; transfer. **b** communicate (ideas, emotions, etc.). **2 a** allow (heat, light, sound, electricity,
etc.) to pass through; be a medium for. **b** be a medium
for (ideas, emotions, etc.) (*his message transmits hope*). **3**
broadcast (a radio or TV signal, message, etc.). □
transmissibility *n.* **transmissible** *adj.*
transmittable *adj.* **transmittal** *n.*

transmitter *n.* **1** a person or thing that transmits. **2**
a set of equipment used to generate and transmit
electromagnetic waves carrying messages, signals,
etc., esp. those of radio or TV. **=** NEUROTRANSMITTER.

transmogrify /trænz'mɒgrɪ,fai/ *v.tr.* (**-ies, -ied**) *jocular*
transform, esp. in a magical or surprising manner. □
transmogrification *n.*

transmutation *n.* **1** the act or an instance of
transmuting or changing into another form etc. **2**
the supposed process of changing base metals into
gold. **3** the changing of one element into another by
nuclear bombardment etc. □ **transmutational** *adj.*

transmute *v.tr.* **1** change the form, nature, or substance of. **2** subject (base metals) to transmutation. □
transmutability *n.* **transmutable** *adj.*

transnational ● *adj.* extending beyond national
boundaries. ● *n.* a transnational company. □
transnationally *adv.*

transoceanic *adj.* **1** situated beyond the ocean. **2**
concerned with crossing the ocean (*transoceanic
flight*).

transom *n.* **1** a horizontal bar of wood or stone
across a window or the top of a door (*compare* MULLION).
2 a strengthening crossbar. **3** *N Amer.* = TRANSOM
WINDOW. □ **over the transom** *N Amer.* offered or sent
without the prior agreement of the recipient; (esp. of
a manuscript etc.) unsolicited. □ **transomed** *adj.*

transom window *n.* **1** a window divided by a
transom. **2** a window placed above the transom of a
door or larger window.

trans-Pacific *adj.* **1** on the other side of the Pacific
Ocean. **2** crossing the Pacific Ocean.

transparency *n.* (*pl.* **-ies**) **1** (also **transparence**)
the condition of being transparent. **2** a positive transparent photograph mounted between glass plates or
in a frame to be viewed using a slide projector. **3** a
clear plastic page containing usu. written information, projected on a wall or screen using an overhead
projector. **4** a picture, inscription, etc., made visible
by a light behind it.

transparent *adj.* **1** allowing light to pass through so that bodies can be distinctly seen (*compare* TRANSLUCENT). **2 a** (of a disguise, pretext, etc.) easily seen through. **b** (of a motive, quality, meaning, etc.) easily discerned; evident; obvious. **3** (of a person etc.) easily understood; frank; open. **4** *Computing* (of a program, process, etc.) operating in a manner which the general user does not perceive, or such that other software does not need to take account of it. □ **transparently** *adv.*

transpire *v.* **1** *intr.* **a** (prec. by *it* as subject) turn out; prove to be the case (*it transpired he knew nothing about it*). **b** (of a secret or something unknown) leak out; come to be known. **2** *intr. disputed* occur; happen (*nobody knows what transpired between them*). ¶This use is considered incorrect by some people, but the objection is unjustified and the word is well established in standard English in this sense. **3** *tr. & intr.* emit (vapour, sweat, etc.), or be emitted, through the skin or lungs; perspire. **4** *intr.* (of a plant or leaf) release water vapour. □ **transpiration** *n.*

transplant ● *v.tr.* **1 a** plant in another place. **b** move to another place (*a Winnipegger transplanted to Toronto*). **2** transfer (living tissue or an organ) and implant in another part of the body or in another body. ● *n.* **1 a** the transplanting of an organ or tissue. **b** such an organ etc. **2** a thing, esp. a plant, transplanted. **3** *N Amer. informal* a person not native to his or her place of residence. □ **transplantable** *adj.* **transplantation** *n.* **transplanter** *n.*

transponder *n.* a device for receiving a radio signal and automatically transmitting a different signal.

transport ● *v.tr.* **1** take or carry (a person, goods, etc.) from one place to another. **2** *hist.* take (a criminal) to a penal colony. ● *n.* **1** an act or instance of transporting or carrying; conveyance. **2** a system of conveying people, goods, etc., from place to place. **3 a** a ship, aircraft, etc. used to carry soldiers, supplies, etc. **b** = TRANSPORT TRUCK. **4** (esp. in *pl.*) vehement emotion (*transports of joy*). □ **transportable** *adj.*

transportation *n.* **1** the act or process of transporting something; conveyance of people, goods, etc. **2 a** a system of conveying. **b** esp. *N Amer.* the means of this. **3** *hist.* removal to a penal colony.

transported *adj.* (usu. foll. by *with*) affected with strong emotion.

transporter *n.* **1** a person or device that transports. **2** a vehicle used to transport other vehicles or large pieces of machinery etc. by road.

transport truck *n. N Amer.* a large, long truck, used esp. for conveying goods long distances.

transpose *v.tr.* **1 a** cause (two or more things) to change places. **b** change the position of (a thing) in a series. **2** change the order or position of (words or a word) in a sentence. **3** (often foll. by *up*, *down*) *Music* write or perform in a different key from the original. **4** *Algebra* transfer (a term) with a changed sign to the other side of an equation. □ **transposable** *adj.* **transposer** *n.* **transposition** *n.*

transsexual ● *adj.* having the physical characteristics of one sex and the supposed psychological characteristics of the other. ● *n.* **1** a transsexual person. **2** a person whose sex has been changed by surgery. □ **transsexualism** *n.* **transsexuality** *n.*

transship *v.tr. intr.* (**-shipped**, **-shipping**) transfer from one ship or form of transport to another. □ **transshipment** *n.*

transubstantiation /ˌtrænsəbˌstænʃiˈeiʃən/ *n.* (in Catholic and Orthodox belief) the conversion in the Eucharist of the whole substance of the bread and wine into the body and blood of Christ, only the appearances of bread and wine remaining.

transverse *adj.* situated, arranged, or acting in a crosswise direction. □ **transversely** *adv.*

transverse wave *n.* a wave in which the medium vibrates at right angles to the direction of its propagation.

transvestite /trænzˈvestəit/ *n.* a person, esp. a man, who dresses in the clothes of the opposite sex, esp. as a sexual stimulus. □ **transvestism** *n.*

trap¹ ● *n.* **1 a** an enclosure or device, often baited, for catching animals, usu. by affording a way in but not a way out. **b** *Cdn* (*Nfld*) a large box-shaped fishing net used in inshore waters to catch migrating cod and salmon. **c** a device with bait for killing vermin, esp. mice. **2 a** a trick betraying a person into speech or an act (*is this question a trap?*). **b** an unpleasant situation from which escape is difficult. **3** an arrangement to catch an unsuspecting person, e.g. a speeding motorist. **4** a device for hurling an object such as a clay pigeon into the air to be shot at. **5 a** a curve in a drainpipe etc. that fills with liquid and forms a seal against the upward passage of gases. **b** a device for preventing the passage of steam etc. **6** *slang* the mouth (*shut your trap!*). **7** *Golf* a bunker. **8** = NEUTRAL-ZONE TRAP. **9** *Football* a tactical play in which an attacking team permits a defensive player to cross the line of scrimmage in order to block him from the side, so enabling the ball carrier to move unopposed through the gap created. **10** a two-wheeled carriage. **11** = TRAP DOOR. **12** (esp. in *pl.*) *informal* a percussion instrument esp. in a jazz band. **13** (usu. in *pl.*) *slang* a trapezius muscle. ● *v.* (**trapped**, **trapping**) **1** *tr.* catch (an animal or fish) in a trap. **2** *intr.* **a** catch wild animals in traps for their fur. **b** set traps for game. **3** *tr.* catch or catch out (a person) by means of a trick, plan, etc. **4** *tr.* **a** stop and retain in a trap. **b** cause a person to be unable to leave a location (*trapped on the ice*). **5** *tr.* provide (a place) with traps. **6** keep (something) in a particular place and prevent it from escaping (*trapped the puck*). **7** *tr. Baseball* catch (a ball) just after it has hit the ground. □ **trap out** deplete the supply of fur-bearing animals in a region through trapping.

trap² *v.tr.* (**trapped**, **trapping**) (often foll. by *out*) **1** provide with trappings. **2** adorn.

trap door *n.* a door or hatch in a floor, ceiling, or roof, usu. made flush with the surface.

trapeze /trəˈpiːz/ *n.* a crossbar or set of crossbars suspended by ropes used as a swing for acrobatics etc.

trapezium /trəˈpiːziəm/ *n.* (*pl.* **trapezia** /-ziə/ or **-s**) *N Amer.* a quadrilateral with no two sides parallel.

trapezius /trəˈpiːziəs/ *n.* (*pl.* **trapezii** /-ziaɪ/) either of a pair of large triangular muscles extending over the back of the neck and shoulders.

trapezoid /ˈtræpəˌzɔid/ *n. N Amer.* a quadrilateral with only one pair of sides parallel. □ **trapezoidal** *adj.*

trapline *n. N Amer.* **1** a series of traps set outdoors for catching animals. **2** the trail along which a trapper walks to check his or her traplines. **3** the general area in which a trapper has traplines set up.

trapper *n.* **1** a person who traps wild animals esp. to obtain furs. **2** *Hockey* a goalie's catching glove.

trappings *n.pl.* **1** outward signs, objects, ceremonies, etc. esp. as an indication of status (*the trappings of office*). **2** the harness of a horse esp. when ornamental.

Trappist ● *n.* a member of a branch of the Cistercian order founded in 1664 and noted for an austere rule including a vow of silence. ● *adj.* of or relating to this order.

trap shooting n. the sport of shooting at clay pigeons launched into the air from a trap. □ **trap shooter** n.

trash ● n. **1** esp. N Amer. garbage, refuse. **2 a** things of poor workmanship, quality, or material; worthless stuff. **b** literary or artistic work of an inferior quality. **3** nonsense; foolish talk. **4** a worthless person or persons. ● v.tr. esp. N Amer. informal **1** wreck, destroy. **2** expose the worthless nature of; disparage.

trash can n. esp. N Amer. a garbage can.

trashed adj. **1** informal very drunk. **2** destroyed.

trash fish n. a fish sold for animal feed etc. rather than human consumption.

trash talk esp. US informal ● n. **1** Sport ostentatiously insulting or boastful rhetoric delivered with the intention of demoralizing, intimidating, or humiliating an opponent. **2** any derisory or boastful statement. ● v. (**trash-talk**) **1** intr. deliver trash talk; bad-mouth an opponent. **2** tr. demoralize or attempt to demoralize (an opponent) with trash talk. □ **trash-talker** n. **trash-talking** n. & adj.

trashy adj. (**-ier, -iest**) **1** of poor quality; cheap, inferior. **2** (of a person) worthless, disreputable. □ **trashily** adv. **trashiness** n.

trattoria /ˌtrætəˈriːə/ n. an Italian restaurant.

trauma n. (pl. **-s**) **1 a** Psych. emotional shock following a stressful event, sometimes leading to long-term neurosis. **b** (in general use) a distressing or emotionally disturbing experience etc. **2** any physical wound or injury. **3** physical shock following this, characterized by a drop in body temperature, mental confusion, etc. □ **traumatize** v.tr. **traumatization** n.

traumatic /trəˈmætɪk/ adj. **1** of or causing trauma. **2** (in general use) distressing; emotionally disturbing.

travail /trəˈveɪl, ˈtræveɪl/ literary ● n. **1** painful or laborious effort. **2** the pangs of childbirth. ● v.intr. undergo a painful effort, esp. in childbirth.

travel ● v.intr. & tr. (**travelled, travelling**) **1** intr. go from one place to another; make a journey esp. of some length or abroad. **2** tr. **a** journey along or through (a country). **b** cover (a distance) in travelling. **3** intr. withstand a long journey (not all wines travel). **4** intr. go from place to place as a salesperson. **5** intr. move or proceed in a specified manner or at a specified rate (light travels faster than sound). **6** intr. informal move quickly. **7** intr. pass esp. in a deliberate or systematic manner from point to point (his eye travelled over the scene). **8** intr. Basketball make two or more steps' progress in any direction while carrying (esp. instead of dribbling) the ball, in violation of the rules. **9** intr. (of a machine or part) move or operate in a specified way. ● n. **1 a** the act of travelling, esp. in foreign countries. **b** (often in pl.) a period of this. **2** (attrib.) suitable for use when travelling because of size, portability, dual voltage, etc. (travel alarm). □ **travelling** n.

travel agency n. a company which makes transportation, accommodation, etc. arrangements for travellers. □ **travel agent** n.

travelled adj. experienced in travelling (also in comb.: much-travelled).

traveller n. **1** a person who travels or is travelling. **2** (also **New Age traveller**) a person who embraces New Age values and leads an itinerant and unconventional lifestyle.

traveller's cheque n. a cheque for a fixed amount that may be cashed on signature, usu. internationally.

travelling salesman n. a male sales representative who travels about to sell his wares.

travelogue /ˈtrævəˌlɒg/ n. a film, book, or illustrated lecture about travel.

traverse /trəˈvɜrs, ˈtrævɜrs/ ● v.tr. **1** travel or lie across (traversed the country). **2** consider or discuss the whole extent of (a subject). ● n. **1** a sideways movement. **2** an act of traversing. **3** a thing, esp. part of a structure, that crosses another. □ **traversal** n.

travertine /ˈtrævərˌtiːn/ n. a white or light-coloured calcareous rock deposited from springs.

travesty /ˈtrævəsti/ ● n. (pl. **-ies**) a grotesque misrepresentation or imitation (a travesty of justice). ● v.tr. (**-ies, -ied**) make or be a travesty of.

travois /trəˈvɔɪ/ n. (pl. same /-ˈvɔɪz/) hist. a V-shaped frame of teepee poles pulled by dogs or horses, used by Plains Aboriginal peoples to carry teepee covers and other possessions.

trawl ● v. **1** intr. (often foll. by through, for) **a** fish with a trawl or seine. **b** search thoroughly. **2** tr. **a** catch by trawling. **b** search thoroughly through (trawled the schools for new trainees). ● n. **1** an act of trawling. **2** (in full **trawl net**) a large wide-mouthed fishing net dragged by a boat along the sea floor. **3** (in full **trawl line**) N Amer. a long buoyed sea-fishing line supporting short lines with baited hooks.

trawler n. **1** a boat used for trawling. **2** a person who trawls.

tray n. **1 a** a flat shallow vessel usu. with a raised rim for carrying, storing, or collecting items. **b** something carried on a tray (a tray of drinks; cheese tray). **2 a** shallow lidless box forming a compartment of a cabinet, trunk, etc.

treacherous /ˈtretʃərəs/ adj. **1** guilty of or involving treachery; disloyal. **2** deceptive, unreliable. **3** (of ice, conditions, etc.) dangerous, hazardous. □ **treacherously** adv. **treacherousness** n.

treachery /ˈtretʃəri/ n. (pl. **-ies**) **1** violation of faith or trust; betrayal. **2** an instance of this.

treacle /ˈtriːkəl/ n. **1** esp. Brit. **a** a syrup produced in refining sugar. **b** molasses. **2** cloying sentimentality or flattery. □ **treacly** adj.

tread ● v. (**trod; trodden** or **trod**) **1** intr. (often foll. by on) **a** set down one's foot; walk or step. **b** (of the foot) be set down. **2** tr. **a** walk on. **b** (often foll. by down) press or crush with the feet. **3** tr. perform (steps etc.) by walking (trod a few paces). **4** tr. make (a hole etc.) by treading. **5** intr. (foll. by on) suppress; subdue mercilessly. **6** tr. make a track with (dirt etc.) from the feet. **7** tr. (often foll. by in, into) press down into the ground with the feet (trod dirt into the carpet). ● n. **1** a manner or sound of walking (recognized the heavy tread). **2** the top surface of a step or stair. **3** the thick moulded part of a vehicle tire for gripping the road. **4 a** the part of a wheel that touches the ground or rail. **b** the part of a rail that the wheels touch. **5** the part of the sole of a shoe that rests on the ground. □ **tread water 1** maintain an upright position in the water by moving the feet with a walking movement and the hands with a sideways circular motion. **2** fail to advance. □ **treader** n.

treadle ● n. a lever worked by the foot and imparting motion to a machine. ● v.intr. work a treadle.

treadmill n. **1** a device for producing motion by the weight of persons or animals stepping on steps on the inner surface of a revolving upright wheel. **2** an exercise machine consisting of a continuous moving belt on which a person walks or jogs. **3** monotonous routine work.

treason n. **1** (in full **high treason**) violation by a subject of allegiance to the sovereign or to the state, esp. by attempting to kill or overthrow the sovereign or to overthrow the government. **2** any betrayal of trust; treachery. □ **treasonous** adj.

treasonable adj. involving or guilty of treason.

treasure ● n. **1 a** wealth or riches stored or accumulated, esp. in the form of gems, precious metals, etc. **b** a hoard of such wealth. **2** a thing valued for its rarity, workmanship, associations, etc. (art treasures). **3** informal a much loved or highly valued person. ● v.tr. **1** value highly; cherish, prize. **2** store (something valuable) for preservation or future use.

treasure chest n. **1** a chest for holding or storing treasure. **2** a collection of valuable or delightful things.

treasure house n. **1** a building or room in which treasure is kept. **2** an abundant source of something valuable (a treasure house of information).

treasure hunt n. **1** a search for treasure. **2** a game in which players seek a hidden object from a series of clues.

treasurer n. **1** a person appointed to administer the funds of a society, corporation, etc. **2** an officer authorized to receive and disburse public revenues.

treasure trove n. **1** Law treasure of unknown ownership which is found hidden in the ground etc. and is declared the property of the Crown. **2** a collection of valuable or delightful things.

treasury n. (pl. **-ies**) **1** a place or building where treasure is stored. **2** the funds or revenue of a state, institution, or society. **3** (**Treasury**) **a** the department managing the public revenue of a country. **b** the offices and officers of this. **c** the place where the public revenues are kept. **4** = TREASURY BILL.

treasury bill n. a bill of exchange issued by the government to raise money for temporary needs.

Treasury Board n. Cdn a committee of the Privy Council responsible for reviewing and prioritizing planned government expenditures, programs, etc.

treasury bond n. a government bond issued by the Treasury.

Treasury Branch n. Cdn (in Alberta) one of a network of savings banks operated by the government of Alberta.

treat ● v. **1** tr. act or behave towards or deal with (a person or thing) in a certain way (treated me kindly; treat it as a joke). **2** tr. deal with or apply a process to (treat it with acid). **3** tr. apply medical care or attention to. **4** tr. present or deal with (a subject) in literature or art. **5** tr. (often foll. by to) **a** provide with food or drink or entertainment at one's own expense (treated us to dinner). **b** provide with a special gift or indulgence. **6** intr. (often foll. by with) negotiate terms (with a person). **7** intr. (often foll. by of) give a spoken or written exposition. ● n. **1** an event or circumstance (esp. when unexpected or unusual) that gives great pleasure. **2** a meal, entertainment, etc., provided by one person for the enjoyment of another or others. **3** N Amer. a candy, cookie, or other small sweet food item. □ **treatable** adj. **treater** n. **treating** n.

treatise /ˈtriːtɪs/ n. a written work dealing formally and systematically with a subject.

treatment n. **1** a process or manner of behaving towards or dealing with a person or thing. **2** the application of medical care or attention to a patient. **3 a** a manner of treating a subject in literature or art. **b** a preparatory version of a screenplay, including descriptions of sets and of the camera work required. **4** subjection to the action of a chemical, physical, or biological agent. **5** (prec. by the) informal the customary way of dealing with a person, situation, etc. (got the full treatment).

treaty n. (pl. **-ies**) **1 a** a formally concluded and ratified agreement between states. **b** the document embodying such an agreement. **2** an agreement between individuals or parties, esp. for the purchase of property.

treaty band n. Cdn an Aboriginal band that has signed a treaty with the federal government.

treaty Indian n. Cdn a status Indian who is a member of a treaty band.

treaty rights n.pl. Cdn the rights, e.g. that of holding land on a reserve, granted to a group of Aboriginal people under the terms of a treaty.

treble /ˈtrɛbl/ ● adj. **1** (of a voice) high-pitched. **2** Music = SOPRANO (esp. of an instrument or boy's voice). **3** esp. Brit. **a** threefold. **b** triple. **c** three times as much or many (treble the amount). ● n. **1 a** Music = SOPRANO (esp. a boy's voice or part, or an instrument). **b** a high-pitched voice. **2** the high-frequency output of a radio, record player, etc., corresponding to the treble in music. **3** a treble quantity or thing.

treble clef n. Music a sign that indicates that the second lowest line of the staff represents the G above middle C.

tree ● n. **1 a** a perennial plant with a woody self-supporting main stem or trunk when mature and usu. unbranched for some distance above the ground (compare SHRUB). **b** any similar plant having a tall erect usu. single stem, e.g. palm tree. **2** a piece or frame of wood etc. for various purposes. **3** archaic or literary a cross, esp. the one used for Christ's crucifixion. **4** (in full **tree diagram**) Math., Computing, etc. a branching figure or graph in which processes, relationships, etc., are represented by points or nodes joined by lines. **5** = FAMILY TREE. **6** = CHRISTMAS TREE. ● v.tr. force to take refuge in a tree. □ **grow on trees** (usu. with neg.) be plentiful. **out of one's tree** informal crazy. □ **treed** adj. **treeless** adj. **treelike** adj.

tree farm n. an area of land where trees are grown for commercial purposes.

tree fern n. a large fern, esp. of the family Cyatheaceae, with an upright trunklike stem.

tree frog n. any arboreal tailless amphibian, esp. of the family Hylidae, climbing by means of adhesive discs on its digits.

tree house n. a structure built in the branches of a tree for children to play in.

tree hugger n. esp. N Amer. informal a person who cares for trees or the environment; an environmentalist.

treeline n. **1** (in the N hemisphere) the latitudinal limit north of which no trees grow. **2** = TIMBERLINE 1.

tree ring n. a ring in a cross-section of a tree, produced by one year's growth.

tree sparrow n. a N American finch, Spizella arborea, inhabiting grassland areas.

tree surgeon n. a person who treats decayed trees in order to preserve them. □ **tree surgery** n.

tree swallow n. a N American swallow Tachycineta bicolor, with a steel-blue back and white underparts, frequenting marshes and bodies of water, and nesting in cavities in trees or in bird boxes.

treetop n. the topmost part of a tree.

tree trunk n. the trunk of a tree.

trefoil /ˈtrɛfɔɪl, ˈtriː-/ ● n. **1** any plant of the genus Trifolium, with leaves of three leaflets and flowers of various colours, esp. clover. **2** any plant with similar leaves. **3** a thing arranged in or with three lobes. ● adj. of or concerning a three-lobed plant etc.

trek ● v.intr. (**trekked**, **trekking**) travel or make one's way arduously. ● n. **1 a** a journey or walk made by trekking (it was a trek to the nearest laundromat). **b** each stage of such a journey. **2** an organized migration of a body of persons. □ **trekker** n.

Trekkie n. (also **Trekker**) slang a fan of Star Trek, a TV science fiction drama series created by US TV producer Gene Roddenberry (1921–91).

trellis ● n. a lattice or grating of light wooden or metal bars used esp. as a support for fruit trees or creepers and often fastened against a wall. ● v.tr. (**trellised, trellising**) **1** provide with a trellis. **2** support (a vine etc.) with a trellis.

tremble ● v.intr. **1** shake involuntarily from fear, excitement, weakness, etc. **2** be in a state of extreme apprehension (trembled at the very thought of it). **3** move in a quivering manner (leaves trembled in the breeze). ● n. a trembling state or movement; a quiver (couldn't speak without a tremble). □ **tremblingly** adv.

trembling aspen n. (also **trembling poplar**) a poplar found across Canada, Populus tremuloides, with leaves that tremble in a slight breeze.

trembly adj. (**-ier, -iest**) informal trembling; agitated.

tremendous adj. **1** awe-inspiring, fearful, overpowering. **2** remarkable, considerable, excellent. □ **tremendously** adv. **tremendousness** n.

tremolo /'tremələ/ n. (pl. **-s**) **1** a tremulous effect produced on musical instruments or in singing: **a** by rapid reiteration of a note, esp. on bowed stringed instruments or on an organ. **b** by rapid alternation between two notes. **c** by rapid repeated slight variation in the pitch of a note, e.g. on an electric guitar. **2** a device in an organ producing a tremolo.

tremor /'tremər/ ● n. **1** a shaking or quivering. **2** a thrill (of fear or exultation etc.). **3** a slight earthquake. ● v.intr. undergo a tremor or tremors.

tremulous /'tremjuləs/ adj. **1** trembling or quivering (spoke in a tremulous voice). **2** (of a line etc.) drawn by a tremulous hand. **3** timid or vacillating. □ **tremulously** adv. **tremulousness** n.

trench ● n. **1** a long narrow usu. deep depression or ditch. **2** Military **a** this dug by troops to stand in and be sheltered from enemy fire. **b** (in pl.) a defensive system of these, as used in World War I. **3** a long narrow deep depression in the ocean bed. **4** informal = TRENCH COAT 2. ● v. **1** tr. dig a trench or trenches in (the ground). **2** tr. turn over the earth of (a field, garden, etc.) by digging a succession of adjoining ditches. □ **in the trenches** actively involved in the practical details or hard work connected with a project.

trenchant /'trentʃənt/ adj. (of a style or language etc.) incisive, terse, vigorous. □ **trenchancy** n. **trenchantly** adv.

trench coat n. **1** a soldier's lined or padded waterproof coat. **2** a loose belted double-breasted raincoat.

trencher n. a machine, usu. self-propelled, used in digging trenches.

trench warfare n. **1** hostilities carried on from more or less permanent trenches. **2** a protracted dispute in which the parties maintain entrenched positions while persistently attacking their opponents.

trend ● n. a general direction and tendency (esp. of events, fashion, or opinion etc.). ● v.intr. **1** bend or turn away in a specified direction. **2** be chiefly directed; have a general and continued tendency.

trendoid informal often derogatory ● adj. trendy; self-consciously or extravagantly fashionable. ● n. a person who sets or follows fashions; a trendy.

trend-setter n. a person who leads the way in fashion etc. □ **trend-setting** adj.

trendy informal ● adj. (**-ier, -iest**) often derogatory fashionable; following fashionable trends. ● n. (pl. **-ies**) a fashionable person. □ **trendily** adv. **trendiness** n.

trepidation /ˌtrepɪ'deɪʃən/ n. **1** a feeling of fear or alarm; perturbation of the mind. **2** tremulous agitation. **3** the trembling of limbs, e.g. in paralysis.

très /trei/ adv. very.

trespass ● v.intr. **1** (usu. foll. by on, upon) make an unlawful or unwarrantable intrusion (esp. on land or property). **2** (foll. by on) make unwarrantable claims (shall not trespass on your hospitality). **3** (foll. by against) literary or archaic offend. ● n. **1** Law a voluntary wrongful act against the person or property of another, esp. unlawful entry to a person's land or property. **2** archaic a sin or offence. □ **trespasser** n.

tress ● n. **1** a long lock of human (esp. female) hair. **2** (in pl.) a woman's or girl's head of hair. ● v.tr. arrange (hair) in tresses. □ **tressed** adj. (also in comb.).

trestle n. **1** a supporting structure for a table etc., consisting of two frames fixed at an angle or hinged or of a bar supported by two divergent pairs of legs. **2** (in full **trestle table**) a table consisting of a board or boards laid on trestles or other supports. **3** (in full **trestlework**) an open braced framework to support a bridge etc. **4** (in full **trestle bridge**) a bridge supported on trestles.

T. Rex n. Tyrannosaurus rex (see TYRANNOSAUR).

trey /trei/ n. (pl. **-s**) **1** Basketball informal a three-point field goal. **2** a three in dice or cards.

tri- comb. form **1** forming nouns and adjectives meaning three or three times. **2** Chem. containing three atoms or groups of a specified kind.

triable adj. (of a case or person etc.) that may be tried in court; liable to a judicial trial.

triactor /'trai.æktər/ n. Cdn a bet on the first three finishers in a horse race, specifying order of finish.

triad n. **1** a group of three people or things. **2** Music a chord of three notes, consisting of a given note with the third and fifth above it. **3** (usu. **Triad**) any of several Chinese secret societies in various countries, usu. involved in criminal activities. □ **triadic** adj.

triage /'triːæʒ, -ɒʒ, -'æʒ, -'ɒʒ/ n. **1** the process of determining the order in which a large number of injured or ill patients will receive medical treatment, with priority usu. given to those patients with the most severe ailments or the greatest chance of survival. **2** the process of prioritizing a large number of people or things requiring attention.

trial ● n. **1** a judicial examination and determination of issues between parties by a judge with or without a jury. **2 a** the process or an instance of testing the ability, quality, performance, etc. of a thing, esp. before reaching a final decision about it. **b** the state or condition of a person or thing being tested or tried out. **3 a** a frustrating or exasperating experience, thing, or person. **b** (in pl.; usu. foll. by of) the frustrating aspects of something (the trials of being an artist). **4** any of various races or competitions to evaluate the speed and overall abilities of athletes, vehicles, or animals (sheepdog trials). ● v.tr. & intr. (**trialled, trialling**) subject to or undergo a test to assess performance. □ **on trial 1** being tried in a court of law. **2** being tested; to be chosen or retained only if found suitable or satisfactory.

trial and error n. a method of finding the most effective way of completing a task, resolving a situation, etc., by experimenting with various unsuccessful approaches until a suitable one is found.

trial balloon n. an announcement or experiment made in order to see how a new policy will be received.

trial court n. a court of first instance.

Trial Division n. Cdn (in Newfoundland and PEI) a division of the Supreme Court, with judges appointed federally, which has jurisdiction over a wide range of civil and criminal cases, and hears appeals from lower provincial courts.

trial lawyer n. N Amer. a lawyer practising in a trial court.

trial run n. **1** a preliminary test of the performance of a new procedure etc. **2** = TEST DRIVE n. 1.

triangle n. **1** a plane closed figure with three sides and angles. **2** a three-sided object, area, etc. having this shape (fold the napkins into triangles). **3** any three things not in a straight line, with imaginary lines joining them (the Toronto-Ottawa-Montreal triangle). **4** a percussion instrument consisting of a steel rod bent into the shape of a triangle and sounded by striking it with a small thin rod. **5** a situation or relationship involving three people (love triangle). **6** a flat wooden or plastic instrument in the form of a right-angled triangle used for drawing lines and square angles.

triangular adj. **1** arranged in the form or shape of a triangle; having three corners or sides. **2** (of a pyramid) having a three-sided base. **3** involving three people or parties (a triangular relationship).

triangulate v. **1 a** tr. arrange in the shape of a triangle. **b** intr. adopt a triangular shape. **2** tr. divide (an area) into triangles for surveying purposes. **3** tr. **a** measure and map (an area) by the use of triangles with a known base length and base angles. **b** determine (a height etc.) in this way. □ **triangulation** n.

Triassic /traiˈæsɪk/ ● adj. of or relating to the earliest period of the Mesozoic era, which lasted from about 248 to 213 million years ago. ● n. this period.

triathlon /traiˈæθlɒn/ n. an athletic contest in which competitors engage in three different events, usu. swimming, cycling, and long-distance running. □ **triathlete** n.

tribal adj. of, relating to, or characteristic of a tribe or tribes. □ **tribally** adv.

tribal council n. N Amer. an organization encompassing a number of Aboriginal communities that have grouped together for social, political, and sometimes economic strength.

tribalism n. **1** the condition of existing as a separate tribe or tribes; tribal organization. **2** loyalty to one's tribe or social group. □ **tribalist** n. **tribalistic** adj.

tribe n. **1 a** a group of families claiming descent from a common ancestor, sharing a common culture, religion, dialect, etc., and usu. occupying a specific geographical area and having a recognized leader. **b** a group of Aboriginal peoples sharing a common ancestry, language, culture and name. **2** Jewish Hist. each of the twelve divisions of the Israelites claiming descent from the twelve sons of Jacob. **3 a** a group or community of people united by a shared profession or hobby etc. (the whole tribe of actors). **b** a large family. **4** Biol. a group of related animals or plants, esp. one ranking between genus and the subfamily.

tribesman n. (pl. **-men**) a member of a tribe or of one's own tribe, esp. one who is male.

tribesperson n. (pl. **-people**) a member of a tribe.

tribeswoman n. (pl. **-women**) a female member of a tribe.

tribulation /ˌtrɪbjʊˈleɪʃən/ n. great trouble or suffering.

tribunal /traɪˈbjuːnəl, trɪ-/ n. **1** a board appointed to adjudicate in some matter, esp. one appointed by a government to investigate a matter of public concern. **2** a court of justice. **3** a seat or bench for a judge or judges. **4 a** a place of judgment. **b** judicial authority (the tribunal of public opinion).

tribune /ˈtrɪbjuːn, -ˈbjuːn/ n. **1** a popular leader who attempts to protect the rights and interests of the people, often by demagogic means. **2** Rom. Hist. **a** (in full **tribune of the people**) an official appointed to protect the rights and interests of the plebeians. **b** (in full **military tribune**) a legionary officer.

tributary /ˈtrɪbjuːˌteri/ ● n. (pl. **-ies**) **1** a stream etc. flowing into a larger river or lake. **2** hist. a person or nation required to pay a tax or tribute to another. ● adj. **1** (of a river etc.) that flows into a larger river or lake. **2** hist. required to pay or paying a tribute or tax.

tribute n. **1 a** an act, statement, or gift made or given as a gesture of respect, admiration, or affection for a person (paid tribute to her achievements; a floral tribute). **b** a show, concert, album, etc., produced to honour the life, career, or work of esp. an artist or entertainer (also attrib.: tribute album). **2** (foll. by to) a thing attributable to or indicative of a praiseworthy quality or act (his recovery is a tribute to the skill of his doctors). **3** hist. **a** a payment made periodically by one nation or ruler to another as a sign of dependence or submission or to ensure peace and protection. **b** an obligation to pay this (was laid under tribute). **4** any donation of esp. money exacted or extorted.

trice n. □ **in a trice** in a moment; instantly.

tricep /ˈtraɪsep/ n. informal a triceps muscle. ¶Although tricep is becoming common in informal use, triceps remains standard as the singular noun.

triceps /ˈtraɪseps/ n. (pl. same) any muscle having three heads or points of attachment at one end, esp. the large extensor muscle at the back of the upper arm.

triceratops /ˌtraɪˈserəˌtɒps/ n. a plant-eating dinosaur of the Cretaceous genus Triceratops, having a bony horn on the snout, two longer ones above the eyes, and a bony frill around the neck.

trichina /trɪˈkiːnə/ n. (pl. **trichinae** /-niː/) a minute parasitic nematode worm of the genus Trichinella.

tricity n. (pl. **-ies**) a metropolitan area consisting of three adjoining but independent cities (also attrib.: tricity area).

trick ● n. **1** an action or scheme undertaken to fool, outwit, or deceive. **2** an optical illusion or figment of the imagination (a trick of the light). **3** a special technique; a knack or special way of doing something. **4 a** a feat of skill or dexterity (the magician performed several tricks). **b** an unusual action learned by an animal, e.g. shaking a paw or rolling over and playing dead. **5** a mischievous or underhanded act; a prank, a practical joke. **6** a peculiar or characteristic habit or mannerism (has a trick of repeating himself). **7** (attrib.) done to deceive, mystify, or to create an illusion (trick photography; trick question). **8** slang **a** a prostitute's client. **b** a prostitute's session with a client. **9 a** the cards played in a single round of a card game, usu. one from each player. **b** such a round of play. **c** a point gained as a result of this. **10** (attrib.) designating a limb or joint that is unsound and liable to weaken suddenly and without warning (a trick knee). ● v.tr. **1** deceive by a trick; outwit. **2 a** (usu. foll. by into + verbal noun) lure or induce by trickery; fool. **b** (foll. by out of) cheat, defraud; cause (a person) to relinquish or lose something by deceitful means. □ **up to one's old tricks** informal involved in a former bad habit or reprehensible pattern of behaviour. **do the trick** informal accomplish one's purpose; achieve the required result. **how's tricks?** informal how are you? **try every trick in the book** attempt every method or technique that can be used to achieve what one wants. **turn a trick** *slang* (of a prostitute) have a session with a client. **up to a person's tricks** aware of the mischief a person is likely to attempt.

trickery *n.* (*pl.* **-ies**) the use of tricks or deception.

trickle ● *v.intr.* **1** (esp. of a liquid) flow in a thin stream or drops; seep. **2** come, go, or pass gradually (*the news has trickled out*). **3** (foll. by *down*) (esp. of wealth or information) be dispersed or distributed among recipients at various levels in diminishing amounts. ● *n.* **1** a thin or dripping stream of liquid. **2** a slow passage or flow (*traffic slows to a trickle*).

trickle-down *n.* **1** the spread or dissemination of wealth, information, etc., from concentrated levels at a limited number of sources through or among many recipients in diminishing amounts. **2** (*attrib.*) relating to the economic theory that government benefits favouring large companies will result in increased profits for smaller companies and their suppliers etc., and improvements in the economy at all levels.

trick of the trade *n.* a clever way of doing a job, known and used by experienced members of a particular industry or profession.

trick-or-treat *esp. N Amer.* ● *n.* a Halloween custom in which children, dressed in costumes, knock on the doors of neighbours soliciting a treat of esp. candy, threatening to commit a prank if denied. ● *v.intr.* (of children) call on neighbours on Halloween, asking for candy or other treats. ● *interj.* (usu. **trick or treat!**) shouted by children while trick-or-treating. □ **trick-or-treater** *n.*

trickster *n.* **1** a person who enjoys playing pranks and practical jokes on others; a joker. **2** a person who deceives others for esp. financial or political gain.

tricky *adj.* (**-ier, -iest**) **1** difficult, challenging; requiring care and adroitness (*the driving was tricky*). **2** awkward; difficult to manage or operate (*this lock is quite tricky*). **3** crafty, adroit, or deceitful. □ **trickily** *adv.* **trickiness** *n.*

tricolour /ˈtraɪˌkʌlər/ ● *n.* (also /ˈtrɪkələr/) a flag of three colours, esp. the French national flag. ● *adj.* (also **tricoloured**) having three colours.

tricycle ● *n.* a vehicle, esp. ridden by children, having three wheels, two on an axle at the back and one at the front, driven by pedals in the same way as a bicycle. ● *v.intr.* ride a tricycle.

tricyclic /traɪˈsaɪklɪk, -ˈsɪk-/ ● *adj.* having three rings or circles. ● *n.* any of a number of antidepressant drugs having molecules with three fused rings.

trident *n.* **1** a three-pronged spear. **2** (**Trident**) **a** any of a class of US nuclear-powered submarines designed to carry ballistic missiles. **b** a ballistic missile designed to be carried by such a submarine.

tried ● *v.* past and past part. of TRY. ● *adj.* proven or tested by experience or examination.

tried-and-true *adj.* proven reliable by experience.

trier *n.* a person who tests something.

trifecta /traɪˈfektə/ *n.* **1** *N Amer., Austral., & NZ Racing* = TRIACTOR. **2** a group of three related events or people.

trifle ● *n.* **1** a dessert consisting of sponge cake soaked in liquor, esp. sherry, covered with custard, jam, whipped cream, and fruit, and served from a large bowl. **2 a** a small amount of money (*it sold for a trifle*). **b** (prec. by *a*) somewhat (*she was a trifle annoyed*). **3** a thing of little value or importance. ● *v.intr.* **1** (foll. by *with*) treat someone or something with a lack of seriousness or respect; dally, fool around. **2** talk or act frivolously. □ **trifler** *n.*

trifling *adj.* **1** of little importance or significance; petty, trivial. **2** frivolous, not serious. □ **triflingly** *adv.*

trifocal ● *n.* (in *pl.*) a pair of eyeglasses having lenses with three parts, each with a different focal length. ● *adj.* having three focuses.

trifoliate /traɪˈfoʊliət/ *adj.* (of a compound leaf) having three leaflets.

trig *n.* trigonometry.

trigger ● *n.* **1 a** a movable lever for releasing a spring or catch and so setting off a mechanism. **b** a catch that may be depressed by the finger in order to release the hammer of a gunlock. **2** an event or occurrence etc. that sets off a reaction or chain reaction. ● *v.tr.* **1** set (an action or process) in motion; initiate, precipitate. **2** fire (a gun) by the use of a trigger. □ **quick on the trigger** quick to react or respond. □ **triggered** *adj.*

trigger finger *n.* the finger with which one pulls the trigger of a gun, usu. the forefinger of the right hand.

trigger-happy *adj.* **1** apt to shoot with little or no provocation. **2** liable to act or react rashly and heedless of possible consequences.

triglyceride /traɪˈɡlɪsəraɪd/ *n. Chem.* any ester formed from glycerol and three acid radicals, including the main constituents of fats and oils.

trigonometry /ˌtrɪɡəˈnɒmətri/ *n.* the branch of mathematics dealing with the relations between the sides and angles of triangles, esp. as expressed by trigonometric functions, and including the theory of triangles, of angles, and of elementary periodic functions. □ **trigonometric** *adj.*

trike *n. informal* a tricycle.

trilateral *adj.* **1** of, on, or with three sides. **2** involving or shared by three countries, esp. as parties to an agreement concerning trade and finance.

tri-level *adj.* having three levels, storeys, or floors.

trilight *n. Cdn* **1** a light bulb that can be adjusted to shine at any of three degrees of brightness. **2** (*attrib.*) designating a lamp, socket, switch, etc., used with or using such a bulb.

trilingual /traɪˈlɪŋɡwəl, -juːəl/ *adj.* **1** able to speak three languages, esp. fluently. **2** spoken or written in three languages.

trill ● *n.* **1** a musical effect produced with the voice or an instrument, in which a tremulous sound is produced by a rapid alternation of two notes a tone or semitone apart. **2** a usu. high-pitched sound resembling this, such as the warbling song of a bird. **3** the pronunciation of r with a vibration of the tongue. ● *v.* **1** *intr.* produce a trill. **2** *tr.* **a** sing or play (a song etc.) with a trill. **b** pronounce (the letter *r*) with a trill.

trillion *n.* (*pl.* same or (in sense 2) **-s**) **1** a million million (1,000,000,000,000 or 10^{12}). **2** (in *pl.*) *informal* a very large number. □ **trillionth** *adj. & n.*

trillium *n.* any of various esp. N American plants of the genus *Trillium*, of the lily family, bearing a whorl of three leaves at the summit of the stem and in the middle a solitary flower with three white or brightly coloured petals; the floral emblem of Ontario.

trilobite /ˈtraɪləˌbaɪt/ *n.* any of numerous extinct marine arthropods of the subphylum Trilobita, which had a body divided into an anterior solid head, a segmented thorax or trunk, and a posterior tail, and which are found abundantly as fossils.

trilogy /ˈtrɪlədʒi/ *n.* (*pl.* **-ies**) a group or series of three related novels, theatrical works, etc., often produced by a single author and unified by a common theme or set of characters.

trim ● *v.* (**trimmed, trimming**) **1** *tr.* make (something) neat or of regular size or shape, esp. by cutting away irregular or unwanted parts. **2** *tr.* (foll. by *off*, *away*) remove or cut away (irregular, uneven, or unwanted parts). **3** tr. **a** reduce the size, amount, or number of (a budget, payroll, costs, etc.). **b** eliminate (superfluous costs, jobs, etc.) (*they trimmed six jobs*). **4** tr. **a** decorate, finish, or adorn with ornaments etc. (*trim the Christmas tree*). **b** (often foll. by *up*) make (a person) neat in dress and appearance. **5** tr. adjust the balance of (a ship or aircraft) by distributing its cargo evenly. **6** tr. arrange (a ship's sails) to suit the wind. ● *n.* **1** a haircut to shorten a person's hair without changing the hairstyle. **2** decorative material or other ornamentation, usu. of a contrasting design or colour, added to clothing or upholstery. **3** decorative wood mouldings used esp. as a border around the windows, doorways, and walls of a house. **4** ornamental finishing pieces mounted on the outside of a car or truck etc. **5** a person's clothing or outfit (*jogging trim*). **6** the balance or inclination of an aircraft. ● *adj.* **1** neat, tidy, spruce. **2** in proper order; well arranged or equipped. **3** slender, slim, esp. as a sign of physical fitness. □ **in trim** having a neat or healthy appearance. □ **trimly** *adv.* **trimness** *n.*

trimer /'traɪmər/ *n.* a compound whose molecule is composed of three molecules of a monomer.

trimester /traɪ,mɛstər, -'mɛs-/ *n.* **1** a period of three months. **2** one third of the length of human pregnancy. **3** N Amer. each of three terms of an academic year at some universities and high schools.

trimethoprim /traɪ'mɛθəprɪm/ *n.* an antibiotic often used in conjunction with sulphamethoxazole to treat respiratory and urinary tract infections.

trimmer *n.* **1** a device or instrument, esp. an electric one, for trimming (esp. hair, grass, hedges, etc.). **2** a person who trims something.

trimming *n.* **1** ornamentation or decoration, esp. for a hat or other articles of clothing. **2** (in *pl.*) *informal* accessories, the usual accompaniments, esp. the garnishes and side dishes traditionally served with the main course of a particular meal. **3** (in *pl.*) pieces cut off in trimming.

Trinidadian /trɪnɪ'dadiən, -'deidiən/ ● *n.* a native or inhabitant of Trinidad, an island in the W Indies. ● *adj.* of or relating to Trinidad or its people.

Trinitarian /,trɪnɪ'tɛriən/ ● *n.* a person who believes in the doctrine of the Trinity. ● *adj.* **1** of or believing in the doctrine of the Trinity. **2** (**trinitarian**) composed or consisting of three parts.

trinitrotoluene /traɪ,nɒɪtrə'tɒlju:,iːn/ *n.* = TNT.

Trinity *n.* (*pl.* **-ies**) **1** *Theol.* **a** the three modes of being of the Christian Godhead as conceived in orthodox Christian belief; the Father, Son, and Holy Spirit as one God. **b** the existence of God in three persons. **2** (often foll. by *of*) a group of three people or things.

Trinity Sunday *n.* Christianity the first Sunday after Pentecost, observed in honour of the Trinity.

trinket *n.* a small ornament or piece of jewellery etc., esp. one having little worth or value.

trio *n.* (*pl.* **-os**) **1** a set or group of three. **2** *Music* **a** a composition for three performers. **b** a group of three performers. **c** the alternative section in a minuet, scherzo, march, etc., usu. in a different key or style from the preceding and following passages.

trioxide /traɪ'ɒksaɪd/ *n. Chem.* an oxide containing three oxygen atoms.

trip ● *v.* (**tripped**, **tripping**) **1 a** tr. (often foll. by *up*) cause (a person) to stumble or fall by entangling the feet. **b** intr. (often foll. by *over*) stumble or fall, esp. by suddenly catching the foot against an obstacle. **2** tr. (usu. foll. by *up*) **a** cause (a person) to make a mistake or blunder. **b** expose the error of (a person), esp. by detecting an inconsistency in their facts or

calculations. **3** intr. make an error, esp. in calculation or articulation. **4** intr. **a** run or dance with quick light steps. **b** (of a rhythm, words, etc.) flow lightly and gracefully. **5** intr. **a** esp. Cdn make a journey or expedition through rough country, esp. in a canoe (*we went canoe tripping in Algonquin Park*). **b** make an excursion to a place. **6** tr. **a** release or depress (a catch or lever etc.) in order to activate a mechanism. **b** activate (a mechanism) in this way (*she tripped the lights*). **7** intr. (often foll. by *out*) *informal* undergo a hallucinatory experience induced by drugs. ● *n.* **1** a journey or excursion, either one made repeatedly on a particular usu. short route or one taken for pleasure. **2 a** an act of causing a person to stumble or blunder. **b** a stumble or blunder. **3** an illusory or self-indulgent activity or attitude; an intense and usu. temporary enthusiasm or preoccupation (*guilt trip*). **4** *informal* a hallucinatory experience caused by a drug. **5 a** an intense or exhilarating experience. **b** an exciting or stimulating person. **6** a contrivance for a tripping mechanism etc. □ **trip the light fantastic** *jocular* dance.

tripartite /traɪ'pɑːtaɪt/ *adj.* **1** divided into or consisting of three parts. **2** shared by or involving three parties.

tripe *n.* **1** the first or second stomach of a ruminant, esp. an ox or cow, prepared as food. **2** *informal* something considered worthless or foolish.

triple ● *adj.* **1** consisting of three usu. equal parts or things; threefold. **2** involving three parties. **3** three times as much or many (*triple the amount*; *triple thickness*). **4** *Figure Skating, Dance, etc.* (of a jump, pirouette, etc.) involving three revolutions (*triple lutz*). ● *adv.* to three times the amount or extent (*the cars were triple parked*). ● *n.* **1** a threefold number or amount. **2** a set of three. **3** *Baseball* a hit that enables the batter to reach third base. **4** *Figure Skating, Dance, etc.* a jump, spin, etc. involving three revolutions. ● *v.* **1** tr. & intr. multiply or increase by three. **2** *Baseball* **a** intr. hit a triple. **b** tr. (foll. by *in* or *home*) drive (a baserunner) in by hitting a triple. □ **triply** *adv.*

Triple A *n.* = AAA 1, 3, 4 (also *attrib.*).

triple crown *n.* the title awarded to the winner of three important events, esp. to the horse that wins the Preakness, Belmont Stakes, and Kentucky Derby, or to the baseball player who finishes the year leading the league in batting average, home runs, and runs batted in.

triple-decker *n.* something with three decks, layers, or levels, e.g. a sandwich made with three pieces of bread and two layers of filling, or a three-storey building.

Triple-E Senate *n. Cdn* a proposed senate that would have more effective powers than the existing Senate and which would consist of elected members equally representing the provinces.

triple jump *n.* a field event in which athletes attempt to achieve the greatest distance on a jump that involves a hop followed by a long step and a leap. □ **triple jumper** *n.*

triple play *n. Baseball* a play in which three players, usu. the batter and two baserunners, are put out.

triplet *n.* **1** (usu. in *pl.*) each of three children or animals born at one birth. **2 a** a group of three equal notes played in the time of two. **b** a group of three successive lines of verse, esp. when rhyming and of the same length. **3** a set of three people or things.

triple time *n.* musical time with three beats to the bar; waltz time.

triple whammy n. (pl. **-ies**) informal a threefold blow or setback.

triplex /'traipleks, 'trɪ-/ ● n. (pl. **-es**) N Amer. a residential building divided into three apartments, esp. a three-storey dwelling with a separate apartment on each floor. ● adj. triple or threefold.

triplicate ● adj. /'trɪplɪkət/ **1** existing in three examples or copies. **2** having three corresponding parts. ● n. /'trɪplɪkət/ each of a set of three copies or corresponding parts. ● v.tr. /'trɪplɪ,keɪt/ **1** make in three copies. **2** multiply by three. □ **in triplicate** (written, printed, produced, etc.) in three identical or exactly corresponding copies.

triploid /'trɪplɔɪd/ ● n. an organism or cell having three times the haploid set of chromosomes. ● adj. of or being a triploid. □ **triploidy** n.

tripman n. (pl. **-men**) Cdn hist. a man hired for temporary duty on a fur brigade, paid by the trip.

tripod n. **1** a stand with three usu. adjustable and collapsible legs for supporting a camera or telescope etc. **2** a three-legged stool, seat, or table, etc.

tripper n. **1** esp. Cdn (North) a person who makes an expedition through rough country, esp. by canoe. **2** a person who goes on a journey or short trip, esp. for pleasure (day tripper).

tripping n. **1** esp. Cdn (North) the activity of travelling through rough country, esp. by canoe. **2** Hockey **a** an illegal act of causing an opponent to fall by obstructing him or her with one's stick, leg, or foot, etc. **b** a minor penalty assessed for this.

trippingly adv. with great ease and rapidity.

trippy adj. (**-ier**, **-iest**) informal (of music etc.) producing an effect resembling that of a psychedelic drug.

triptych /'trɪptɪk/ n. **1** a picture or relief carving on three panels, usu. hinged vertically together and often used as an altarpiece. **2** a set of three artistic works, usu. meant to be viewed or performed together.

tripwire n. a wire stretched close to the ground in order to trip up trespassers, enemies, etc., or to activate an alarm when disturbed.

trisodium phosphate n. a water-soluble compound, occurring as crystals, used esp. as a detergent for removing grease stains from asphalt, washing walls prior to painting, etc. Abbr.: **TSP**.

trite adj. **1** (of a phrase, opinion, etc.) stale through constant use or repetition; hackneyed, commonplace, worn out. **2** (of a work, novel, etc.) containing or characterized by stale or commonplace ideas, subjects, etc. □ **triteness** n.

triticale /trɪtə'keɪli/ n. a high-protein hybrid between wheat and rye.

tritium /'trɪtiəm/ n. a radioactive isotope of hydrogen with a mass about three times that of hydrogen, which occurs naturally in minute amounts and is produced artificially, esp. for use in fusion reactors.

triumph ● n. **1** a great success, achievement, or victory; a major accomplishment (a triumph of engineering). **2** the state of being successful or victorious (raised her fist in triumph). **3** the thrill, joy, or satisfaction of success or victory. ● v.intr. (often foll. by over) **1** be successful or victorious; prevail. **2** rejoice at victory or success; exult.

triumphal adj. done, used, or made to celebrate or commemorate a success or victory (triumphal arch).

triumphalism n. excessive or ostentatious pride or exultation over one's achievements or those of one's country, party, etc. □ **triumphalist** adj. & n.

triumphant adj. **1** victorious or successful. **2** exultant. □ **triumphantly** adv.

triumvirate /trai'ʌmvərət/ n. **1** a group of three people in a joint position of power or authority. **2** a group of three people. **3** a set of three things.

triune /'traiju:n/ adj. (esp. with reference to the Trinity) that is three in one; that constitutes or consists of three persons or things in unity.

trivalent /trai'veilənt/ adj. Chem. **1** having a valence of three. **2** (of a vaccine) providing immunity against three strains of an infective agent.

trivet /'trɪvət/ n. **1** a low, flat, usu. three-legged cast iron or ceramic stand placed under a hot kettle, pot, or serving dish to protect the surface of a table. **2** a similar stand with three or more legs used to keep something raised while being heated or cooked.

trivia n.pl. (treated as sing) **1** N Amer. unimportant but interesting or amusing tidbits of factual information, esp. on a particular subject, often used as the basis for quizzes or games (hockey trivia). **2** unimportant or inconsequential matters or details.

trivial adj. **1** of little importance or consequence; trifling. **2** commonplace, ordinary, trite. □ **triviality** n. (pl. **-ies**). **trivially** adv.

trivialize v.tr. diminish or downplay the importance, significance, or value of; minimize, belittle. □ **trivialization** n.

Trivial Pursuit n. proprietary a board game in which players advance by answering questions from one of six subject areas, the subject being determined by the colour of the space on which the player lands.

tRNA abbr. TRANSFER RNA.

trod past and past part. of TREAD.

trodden past part. of TREAD.

troglodyte /'trɒglə,dʌɪt/ ● n. **1** a cave dweller, esp. of prehistoric times. **2** derogatory **a** one regarded as living in wilful ignorance, esp. of current trends and subjects; a conservative or old-fashioned person. **b** a base, degenerate, or primitive person. **3** one living in seclusion; a hermit. ● adj. **1** dwelling in caves. **2** ignorant; old-fashioned, unmannerly, or uncouth. □ **troglodytic** /-'dɪtɪk/ adj. **troglodytical** adj.

troika /'trɔɪkə/ n. **1 a** a Russian carriage or sleigh drawn by a team of three horses. **b** this team of horses. **2** a group of three people working together, esp. in an administrative or managerial capacity. **3** a group of three people or things.

Trojan /'trəʊdʒən/ ● adj. of the ancient city of Troy on the coast of Turkey or its inhabitants. ● n. **1** a native or inhabitant of Troy. **2** a person of great energy, courage, or endurance (works like a Trojan).

Trojan Horse n. **1** a seemingly innocuous person or device that eludes a person's defences to bring about his or her downfall. **2** Computing a program that breaches the security of a computer system, esp. by ostensibly functioning as part of a legitimate program, in order to erase, corrupt, or remove data.

troll¹ n. Scand. Myth a member of a race of grotesque dwarfs (or, formerly, giants) usu. dwelling in caves or under bridges. □ **trollish** adj.

troll² ● v. **1** esp. N Amer. Fishing **a** intr. fish by drawing bait along in the water behind a moving boat. **b** tr. draw (a lure or baited line) behind a boat. **c** tr. practise this method of fishing in (a particular stretch of water). **2** intr. (foll. by for) **a** esp. N Amer. attempt to catch a particular type of fish using this method. **b** pursue, seek; go looking or searching. **3** intr. sing out in a carefree jovial manner. ● n. **1** an act or method of trolling for fish. **2** a baited line or lure used in this.

troller n. esp. N Amer. **1** a person who trolls for fish. **2** a fishing boat used for trolling.

trolley n. (pl. **-eys**) **1 a** a small cart on wheels or casters used for serving food. **b** a small wheeled cart for other purposes, e.g. carrying luggage. **2** a grooved metal pulley receiving current from an overhead electric wire and conveying this by a pole etc. to the motor of a trolley bus or streetcar. **3** (in full **trolley bus**) a bus powered by electricity from an overhead cable.

trombone n. **1** a large brass wind instrument with a sliding tube, analogous to the valves of other wind instruments, used to increase and decrease its length, thereby varying its tone. **2** a person who plays or is playing a trombone. □ **trombonist** n.

tromp v. esp. N Amer. informal **1** intr. march with a heavy step; trudge, stomp. **2** tr. trample.

trompe l'oeil /trɔpˈlɔi/ n. (also attrib.) an optical illusion, esp. a still-life painting designed to deceive the spectator by giving an illusion of reality.

troop ● n. **1** an assembled company of people or animals. **2 a** a detachment of police officers or soldiers etc., esp. a unit of artillery and armoured formation. **b** (in pl.) soldiers or armed forces. **3** a cavalry unit commanded by a captain. **4** a group of Scouts or Girl Guides usu. consisting of three or more patrols. ● v.intr. (foll. by in, out, off, etc.) walk, march, or proceed in large numbers, in or as if in a troop.

trooper n. **1** (also **Trooper**) a private in an armoured or cavalry unit. **2** US = STATE TROOPER. **3** informal a resilient, hard-working, reliable, or uncomplaining person. □ **like a trooper** constantly (swears like a trooper).

troopship n. a ship used for transporting troops.

trope /troːp/ n. a literary or rhetorical device consisting of the figurative use of a word or phrase.

trophic /ˈtrɒfɪk/ adj. **1** of or concerned with nutrition. **2** (of a hormone) stimulating the production or another specific hormone from an endocrine gland.

trophy n. (pl. **-ies**) **1** an ornamental commemorative object awarded as a prize for excellence or an outstanding achievement, e.g. in sports or academics. **2** an animal or part of an animal captured in hunting and displayed as a memorial, e.g. a deer's antlers. **3** an animal that is hunted and usu. kept to prove the skill of the hunter (also attrib.: trophy fish). **4** derogatory a person or thing regarded as having been obtained to enhance a person's status by association (also attrib.: trophy wife).

tropic ● n. **1** (**Tropic**) either of two terrestrial parallels of latitude 23°26′ north (**Tropic of Cancer**) or south (**Tropic of Capricorn**) of the equator, defining the torrid zone and representing, respectively, the northernmost and southernmost limits at which the sun can be directly overhead. **2** (**Tropic**) each of two corresponding circles on the celestial sphere where the sun appears to turn after reaching its greatest declination. **3** (in pl.) the torrid zone and parts immediately adjacent. ● adj. = TROPICAL 1.

tropical adj. **1** pertaining to, occurring in, or characteristic of the tropics. **2** resembling the tropics in climate; very hot and humid. **3** (esp. of clothing) suitable for wearing or using in the tropics.

tropical cyclone n. = CYCLONE 2.

tropical storm n. a tropical cyclone with winds ranging from 30 to 64 knots (63–118 km/h), often associated with heavy rain.

tropism /ˈtrəʊpɪzəm/ n. Biol. the turning of all or part of an organism in a particular direction by growth, bending, or locomotion, in response to an external stimulus.

troposphere /ˈtrɒpəˌsfiːr, ˈtrəʊ-/ n. the lowest region of the atmosphere, extending to a height of between 8 and 18 km and marked by convection and a general decrease of temperature with height. □ **tropospheric** /-ˈsfiːrɪk, -ˈsferɪk/ adj.

trot ● v. (**trotted**, **trotting**) **1** intr. (of a person) run with short strides at a moderate pace. **2** intr. (of a horse) proceed at a pace faster than a walk in which the legs move in diagonal pairs almost together. **3** intr. informal walk, go. **4** tr. cause (esp. a horse) to proceed at a trot. ● n. **1** a trotting pace or gait (proceed at a trot). **2** a run at this pace. **3** (**the trots**) slang an attack of diarrhea. □ **hot to trot 1** eager, enthusiastic. **2** sexually active or excited. **on the trot** informal continually busy (kept them on the trot). **trot out 1** lead out and show off the paces of (a horse). **2** produce or introduce (as if) for inspection and approval, esp. tediously or predictably.

troth /troːθ/ n. archaic **1** faith, loyalty. **2** truth. □ **plight** (or **pledge**) **one's troth** pledge one's word esp. in marriage or betrothal.

Trotskyism /ˈtrɒtskiˌɪzəm/ n. the political or economic principles of the Russian revolutionary Leon Trotsky (1879–1940), which called for a worldwide socialist revolution. □ **Trotskyist** n. **Trotskyite** n. derogatory.

trotter n. **1** a horse bred or trained for harness racing. **2** (usu. in pl.) **a** the foot of certain animals, esp. the pig, eaten as food. **b** jocular a human foot.

trotting n. = HARNESS RACING.

troubadour /ˈtruːbəˌdɔːr/ n. **1** any of a number of French medieval lyric poets composing and singing in Provençal esp. on the themes of chivalry and courtly love, living in S France, E Spain, and N Italy between the 11th and 13th c. **2** a singer or poet.

trouble ● n. **1 a** difficulty, problems, complications; a hard time. **b** disturbance of the mind or feelings; worry, distress. **2 a** an inconvenience, bother; unpleasant or unnecessary exertion (he went to a lot of trouble). **b** a cause of this (she was no trouble). **3** (usu. foll. by with) an annoying, disconcerting, or problematic feature or aspect (the trouble with you is your attitude). **4** a faulty condition or operation (engine trouble). **5 a** fighting, disturbance (we don't want any trouble). **b** (in pl.) political or social unrest, public disturbances. **6** disagreement, strife (he and his wife are having trouble). ● v. **1** tr. cause distress or anxiety to; disturb, worry (we were troubled by the news). **2** tr., intr., & refl. subject or be subjected to inconvenience, bother, or unpleasant exertion (sorry to trouble you). **3** tr. afflict; cause pain etc. to (she is troubled with arthritis). **4** intr. be disturbed or worried (don't trouble about it). □ **ask for trouble** informal invite danger or difficulty by rash or indiscreet behaviour. **be no trouble** cause no inconvenience or nuisance. **go to the** (or **some**) **trouble** devote one's time or energy to do something. **in trouble 1** involved in a matter likely to bring censure or punishment. **2** euphemism pregnant while unmarried. **look for trouble** informal **1** aggressively seek to cause trouble. **2** invite trouble. **take the trouble** = GO TO THE TROUBLE.

troubled adj. **1 a** feeling worry, distress, anxiety, or apprehension. **b** indicating worry or distress (a troubled look). **2** fraught with trouble, problems, unrest, turmoil, etc. (a financially troubled company). **3** physically unsettled or disturbed (troubled waters).

trouble-free adj. **1** free of problems, complications, or difficulties (a trouble-free journey). **2** that is unlikely to malfunction or require maintenance (a trouble-free car).

troublemaker n. a person who habitually causes trouble. □ **troublemaking** n. & attrib.adj.

troubleshooter n. **1** a person who detects and corrects faults in machinery, computer equipment, etc. **2** a mediator who specializes in resolving esp. industrial or diplomatic disputes. □ **troubleshoot** v.tr. & intr. (past and past part. **-shot**). **troubleshooting** n.

troublesome adj. **1** that causes problems or difficulty. **2** distressing, worrisome, disconcerting (troublesome news). **3** fraught with problems, complications, or turmoil (a troublesome period). □ **troublesomely** adv. **troublesomeness** n.

trouble spot n. a place where difficulties regularly occur.

trough n. **1 a** a long narrow open receptacle for water, animal feed, etc. **b** jocular a source of wealth or prosperity (the trough of political patronage). **2 a** a narrow channel or conduit for conveying a liquid. **b** = EAVESTROUGH. **3** Meteorol. an elongated region of low barometric pressure (compare RIDGE 4). **4** a hollow between two wave crests. **5** the lowest point of something, esp. the lowest level of economic activity or prosperity. **6 a** a broad elongated depression or valley (Labrador Trough). **b** an elongated depression of the sea floor.

trounce v.tr. **1** defeat decisively or convincingly. **2** beat, thrash. □ **trouncing** n.

troupe /tru:p/ n. a company of actors or dancers etc.

trouper n. **1** a member of esp. a theatrical troupe; a performer, esp. an experienced one. **2** = TROOPER 3.

trousers n.pl. **1** an outer garment reaching from the waist usu. to the ankles, divided into two parts to cover the legs. **2** (**trouser**) (attrib.) designating a part or parts of such a garment (trouser leg). □ **trousered** adj.

trousseau /ˈtruːsəʊ, -ˈsəʊ/ n. (pl. **-eaux** or **-s** /-səʊz/) the clothes collected by a bride for her marriage.

trout n. (pl. same or **-s**) **1** any of various freshwater fish of the genus Salmo of the northern hemisphere, valued as food. **2** a similar fish of the family Salmonidae (see also SALMON TROUT). **3** slang derogatory a woman, esp. an old or ill-tempered one. **4** Cdn (Nfld) informal a term of affectionate address (me old trout).

trove n. = TREASURE TROVE.

trowel ● n. **1** a small hand-held tool with a flat metal blade, used to apply and spread mortar, cement, plaster, etc. **2** a hand-held gardening tool resembling a small shovel, consisting of a pointed scoop-like blade attached to a handle, used for lifting plants or earth. ● v.tr. (**trowelled**, **trowelling**) **1** dig, move, or apply with a trowel. **2** apply plaster etc. to (a wall etc.) with a trowel.

troy n. (in full **troy weight**) a system of weights used for precious metals and gems, based on a pound of 12 ounces or 5,760 grains (also attrib.: troy ounce).

truant ● n. **1** a student who stays away from school without leave or explanation. **2** a person absent from work. ● adj. (of a person or behaviour etc.) idle, wandering, negligent, shirking, absent. ● v.intr. (also **play truant**) be absent or stay away from school or work. □ **truancy** n. (pl. **-ies**).

truce n. **1** a temporary suspension of hostilities, usu. for a limited period, between warring armies or factions or between individuals in a private feud or quarrel. **2** an agreement or treaty effecting this.

truck[1] ● n. **1** esp. N Amer. any of various kinds of large sturdy road vehicle used for a variety of purposes. **2 a** any of a variety of wheeled carts and platforms used to transport goods. **b** (in full **hand truck**) a sturdy upright metal frame with two wheels and a short perpendicular shelf used to move large appliances, boxes, etc. **3** a pivoted undercarriage with two or more pairs of wheels, mounted to the underside of a railway car. **4** each of two axle units on a skateboard or roller skate, to which the wheels are attached. ● v. **1** tr. deliver or convey by truck. **2** intr. N Amer. drive a truck, esp. for a living. **3** intr. N Amer. informal go or proceed at a casual pace.

truck[2] ● n. **1** the action or practice of bartering or trading by exchange of commodities. **2** informal small miscellaneous items or wares; odds and ends. **3** esp. hist. **a** the payment of wages in kind or as vouchers rather than money. **b** (in full **truck system**) the system or practice of such payment. ● v.tr. & intr. deal, barter, exchange. □ **have no truck with** avoid dealing, interacting, or associating with.

trucker n. esp. N Amer. **1** a person who drives a truck, esp. a person who drives a transport truck or tractor-trailer etc. for a living. **2** a company dealing in long-distance transportation of goods.

trucking n. N Amer. the action or business of transporting goods by truck.

truckle v.intr. (foll. by to) assume a subordinate or inferior position; submit, yield, back down.

truckload n. esp. N Amer. **1** the quantity of goods that is or can be transported in a truck. **2** (usu. foll. by of) informal a large quantity or amount. □ **by the truckload** in large quantities or amounts.

truck stop n. N. Amer. a roadside restaurant or diner, often having a gas station on the premises, catering esp. to truckers.

truculent /ˈtrʌkjʊlənt/ adj. **1** vehemently defiant. **2** aggressive, belligerent, pugnacious. **3** fierce, vicious, scathing. □ **truculence** n. **truculently** adv.

Trudeaumania n. Cdn widespread popularity of, and fascination with, Prime Minister Pierre Elliott Trudeau (b.1919) among the Canadian public, esp. during the election campaign of 1968.

trudge ● v. **1** intr. walk laboriously, or without energy or spirit, but steadily and persistently. **2** tr. travel (a road or specified distance etc.) in this way. ● n. a steady laborious walk.

true ● adj. **1** in accordance or consistent with fact or reality (a true story). **2** genuine, authentic; rightly or strictly so called; not spurious or counterfeit (a true friend). **3** (often foll. by to) loyal or faithful (true to one's word). **4** (foll. by to) closely conforming to a standard or expectation etc.) (true to form). **5** correctly positioned, fitted, balanced, or aligned; level, square. **6** exact, accurate, precise (a true copy). **7** (also **it is true**) certainly, admittedly (true, it would cost more). **8** (of a compass bearing) measured relative to true north. **9** reliable, trusty, sure (a true sign). ● adv. **1** in a sincere or genuine manner; truly (tell me true). **2** accurately (aim true). **3** conforming with the ancestral type; without variation (breed true). ● v.tr. (**trues, trued, truing** or **trueing**) (often foll. by up) bring into the correct, exact, or required form, position, alignment, shape, etc. □ **come true** actually happen or transpire; be realized. **out of true** not in the correct or exact position. **too good to be true** better than one could have hoped or imagined. **true to form** (or **type**) being or behaving as expected. **true to life** accurately representing or consistent with real life (also attrib.: true-to-life example). □ **trueness** n.

true believer n. **1** a person who trusts or sincerely believes (she is a true believer in homeopathy). **2** an ardent or fanatical supporter of esp. a political or religious movement or cause; a zealot (also attrib.: a true-believer environmentalist). □ **true-believing** adj.

true-blue *adj.* steadfastly loyal or devoted.

true-false *adj.* (also **true and false**) **1** designating a type of test question consisting of a statement designed to elicit either the response 'true' or 'false'. **2** designating a test consisting of such questions.

true life *n.* **1** reality; actual life or existence. **2** (*attrib.*; usu. **true-life**) designating things resembling or occurring in reality (*a true-life story*).

true love *n.* **1** genuine love. **2** a sweetheart.

true north *n.* **1** north according to the earth's axis, not magnetic north. **2** (**True North**, prec. by *the*) *Cdn informal* or *jocular* Canada.

truffle *n.* **1** any strong-smelling underground fungus of the order Tuberales, regarded as a great culinary delicacy and collected in France and N Italy with the help of trained dogs or pigs. **2** a round soft chocolate, often flavoured with alcohol. □ **truffled** *adj.*

truism /'truːɪzəm/ *n.* **1** a self-evident or indisputable truth, esp. a trivial or hackneyed one, e.g. *nothing lasts forever*. **2** a proposition that states nothing beyond what is implied in any of its terms. □ **truistic** *adj.*

truly *adv.* **1 a** sincerely, genuinely (*truly grieved*). **b** very, really (*truly frustrated*). **2** really, indeed (*truly, I do not know*). **3** faithfully, loyally (*served them truly*). **4** accurately, truthfully (*has been truly stated*). **5** rightly, properly (*well and truly*). **6** used in formulaic closings of letters (*yours truly*).

trump ● *n.* **1** (in *pl.*) *Cards* the suit determined, usu. by cutting or bidding, to rank above the other three during a deal or game (*hearts are trumps*). **2** (in full **trump card**) **a** a playing card of this suit. **b** a card cut or turned up to determine this suit. **3** (in full **trump card**) an important resource available to a person but held, usu. secretly, in reserve until an opportune moment when it may be used or revealed to gain a decisive advantage; a secret weapon. **4** *informal* an admirable, helpful, or reliable person. ● *v.* **1 a** *tr.* defeat (a card or its player) with a trump. **b** *intr.* play a trump card when another suit has been led. **2** *tr. informal* **a** foil or thwart (a person, proposal, etc.), esp. with an unexpected move at the last minute or by means of a previously secret resource. **b** surpass; gain an unexpected advantage over. □ **trump up** fabricate or invent (an accusation, excuse, etc.).

trumped-up *adj.* fabricated, invented.

trumpet ● *n.* **1 a** any of a family of brass wind instruments with a bright, penetrating tone, consisting of a straight or curved tube with a flared bell and most commonly three valves. **b** a person who plays or is playing a trumpet. **2** anything resembling a trumpet in shape, such as the tubular corona of a daffodil. **3** anything resembling the sound of a trumpet. ● *v.* (**trumpeted**, **trumpeting**) **1** *tr.* herald, announce, celebrate, or proclaim loudly. **2** *intr.* **a** blow or play a trumpet. **b** make a loud sound like that of a trumpet (*elephants trumpeting in the jungle*).

trumpeter *n.* **1** a person who plays a trumpet. **2** any of various birds having a loud cry resembling the sound of a trumpet.

trumpeter swan *n.* a large N American wild swan, *Cygnus buccinator*, with a black bill and a loud, trumpet-like, guttural call.

trumpet vine *n.* either of two climbing shrubs constituting the genus *Campsis*, with orange or red trumpet-shaped flowers, *C. radicans* of the eastern US, and the Chinese *C. grandiflora*.

truncate *v.tr.* /'trʌŋkeɪt, -'keɪt/ shorten or diminish by cutting off the top or end part of. □ **truncation** *n.*

truncated *adj.* **1** having been shortened or reduced by or as if by cutting or mutilation. **2** limited in depth or scope; narrow (*a truncated view*).

truncheon /'trʌntʃən/ *n.* a short club or cudgel, esp. carried by a police officer.

trundle *v.* **1** *intr.* move or roll on a wheel or wheels, esp. heavily or noisily. **2** *intr.* go or move, esp. heavily, noisily, or at a steady pace. **3** *tr.* push (a wheeled vehicle) along.

trunk *n.* **1** the main stem of a tree as distinct from its branches and roots. **2** the human body, or that of an animal, considered apart from the limbs and head. **3** the mobile elongated prehensile snout of an elephant, containing the passages to the nostrils and also used to draw in and spray water for cooling. **4** a large box with a hinged lid for transporting luggage, clothes, etc. **5** *N Amer.* a compartment at the rear of most cars, used to transport luggage etc. **6** (in *pl.*) a man's garment worn for swimming, boxing, etc., either loose-fitting shorts or close-fitting briefs. **7** the main part of any structure, esp. one that branches off into smaller parts. **8** the main body of a blood vessel, artery, or nerve etc. **9** an enclosed duct or conduit for cables, ventilation, etc. □ **trunkful** *n.* (*pl.* **-fuls**).

trunk line *n.* **1** a main railway line or route. **2** a large or main pipeline for oil or gas, esp. one from a production field to a refinery or terminal. **3** a telephone line running between exchanges.

trunk road *n.* *Cdn* an access road, esp. for logging.

truss ● *n.* **1** a metal or wooden structural framework, esp. consisting of rafters, posts, and struts, supporting a roof or bridge etc. **2** a medical device used to provide even pressure on a hernia, usu. consisting of a padded belt fitted with straps. **3** a compact terminal cluster of flowers or fruit. ● *v.tr.* **1** tie or skewer the wings and legs of (a fowl etc.) to the body for cooking. **2** (often foll. by *up*) tie up (a person) by binding the arms close to the body. **3** support (a roof or bridge etc.) with a truss or trusses.

trust ● *n.* **1 a** faith or confidence in the loyalty, veracity, reliability, strength, etc., of a person or thing. **b** the state or condition of being trusted or relied on. **2** the obligation or responsibility placed on a person who is trusted or relied on (*she is in a position of trust*). **3** reliance on the truth of a statement etc. without examination. **4** a confident expectation. **5** a person or thing upon whom one relies or depends (*God is our sole trust*). **6** a thing or person committed to one's care; a charge. **7** *Law* **a** the fiduciary obligation placed on a person by making that person the nominal owner of property to be used for the enjoyment and benefit of another. **b** the property or estate held in this way. **c** the legal relationship between the nominal owner and the property. **8 a** a body of trustees. **b** an organization managed by trustees. **9** a group of associated companies in a particular area of business, organized to reduce or defeat competition, lessen mutual expenses, etc., esp. one in which a central committee of trustees holds a majority or all of the stock and has a controlling vote in each company, prohibited by law in some jurisdictions, including the US. ● *v.* **1** *tr.* **a** have or place faith or confidence in the loyalty, veracity, reliability, honour, etc. of (a person or thing). **b** rely upon; have confidence in the ability of (a person or thing) (*I trust our dog to come when called*). **2** *tr.* (foll. by *with*) allow (a person) to have, use, or be responsible for something with confidence that it will be properly used or cared for (*would trust him with my life*). **3** *tr.* believe the veracity of (a person or statement etc.) (*I seldom trust what I read in that newspaper*). **4** *tr.* have faith, confidence, or hope that a thing is occurring or will occur (*I trust that she is recovering*). **5** *intr.* (foll. by *in*) place reliance on (*we trust in you*). **6** *intr.* (foll. by *to*) place (esp. undue) reliance on (*shall have to trust to luck*). **7** *tr.* (foll. by *for*) allow credit to (a customer) for goods. □ **in trust** *Law* held on the basis of trust (*see* sense 7 of *n.*). **on trust 1** on credit. **2** on the basis of trust or confidence. **take on trust** accept (an assertion, claim, etc.) without evidence or investigation. **not trust a person as far as one can throw him or her** not trust a person at all. **trust a person to do something!** it is characteristic or predictable for a person to act in such a way (*trust her to be late!*). □ **trustable** *adj.* **trusted** *adj.*

trust company *n.* a company formed to act as a trustee or to deal with trusts, esp. one that offers banking services.

trustee *n.* **1** *Law* a person given control or powers of administration of property held in trust with a legal obligation to administer it solely for the purposes specified. **2** any of a group of people appointed to manage the affairs of an institution etc. **3** *Cdn* an elected member of a school board. **4** a state made responsible for the government of an area. □ **trusteeship** *n.*

trustful *adj.* inclined to trust; not feeling or showing suspicion. □ **trustfully** *adv.* **trustfulness** *n.*

trust fund *n.* a fund of money etc. held in trust.

trusting *adj.* inclined to trust others, esp. characteristically. □ **trustingly** *adv.* **trustingness** *n.*

trustworthy *adj.* reliable, dependable. □ **trustworthiness** *n.*

trusty ● *adj.* (**-ier, -iest**) *archaic* or *jocular* trustworthy (*a trusty steed*). ● *n.* (*pl.* **-ies**) a prisoner who is given special privileges for good behaviour. □ **trustily** *adv.* **trustiness** *n.*

truth *n.* (*pl.* **truths** /truːðs, truːðz/) **1** the quality or a state of being true; conformity to fact or reality; genuineness, authenticity. **2 a** what is true; the matter or circumstance as it really is. **b** a true statement; a report or account consistent with fact or reality. **3** something held or accepted as true; a fixed or established principle (*fundamental truths*). **4** accuracy of delineation or representation, esp. in art or literature; lifelike quality. **5** ideal or spiritual reality as a subject of revelation or an object of esp. philosophical or religious interpretation or quest. □ **in truth** *literary* truly, really. **to tell the truth** (also **if truth be told** or **truth to tell**) to be honest; frankly.

truthful *adj.* **1** habitually speaking the truth; sincere, honest. **2** (of an artistic or literary representation etc.) accurate, realistic, true to life. **3** (of a story etc.) true. □ **truthfully** *adv.* **truthfulness** *n.*

truth serum *n.* (also **truth drug**) any drug supposedly able to induce a person to tell the truth.

try ● *v.* (**-ies, -ied**) **1** *intr.* make an effort with a view to success (often foll. by *to* + infin.; *informal* foll. by *and* + infin.; *tried to be on time*; *try and be early*). ¶Use with *and* is uncommon in the past tense and in negative contexts (except in *imper.*). **2** *tr.* make an effort to achieve (*try something easier*). **3** *tr.* **a** test (the quality of a thing) by use or experiment. **b** test the qualities of (a person or thing) (*have you tried the salad?*). **4** *tr.* make severe demands on (a person, quality, etc.) (*my patience has been sorely tried*). **5** *tr.* examine the effectiveness or usefulness of for a purpose (*have you tried kicking it?*). **6** *tr.* ascertain the state of fastening of (a door, window, etc.). **7** *tr.* **a** investigate and decide (a case or issue) judicially. **b** subject (a person) to trial (*will be tried for murder*). **8** *tr.* make an experiment in order to find out (*let us try which takes longest*). **9** *intr.* (foll. by *for*) **a** apply

or compete for. **b** seek to reach or attain (*am going to try for a gold medal*). **10** *tr.* (often foll. by *out*) **a** extract (oil) from fat by heating. **b** treat (fat) in this way. ● *n.* (*pl.* **-ies**) **1** an effort to accomplish something; an attempt (*give it a try*). **2** *Rugby* the act of touching the ball down behind the opposing goal line, scoring points and entitling the scoring side to a kick at goal. □ **try (on) for size** try out or test for suitability. **try one's hand** see how skilful one is, esp. at the first attempt. **try on** put on (clothes etc.) to see if they fit or suit the wearer. **try out 1 a** put to the test. **b** test thoroughly. **2** esp. *N Amer.* (often foll. by *for*) undergo a test in the hope of being selected for a role, a position on a sports team etc.

trying *adj.* annoying; hard to endure.

tryout *n.* esp. *N Amer.* (often in *pl.*) **1** a test of the qualities or performance of a person or thing. **2** a gathering of prospective members of a team, troupe, etc. for such testing.

trypanosome /ˈtrɪpənəˌsoːm, trɪˈpænə-/ *n.* any protozoan parasite of the genus *Trypanosoma* having a long trailing flagellum and infesting the blood etc.

trypanosomiasis /ˌtrɪpənəsəˈmaɪəsɪs, trɪˈpænə-/ *n.* any of several diseases caused by a trypanosome and usu. transmitted by insects, e.g. sleeping sickness.

trypsin /ˈtrɪpsɪn/ *n.* a digestive enzyme which hydrolyzes proteins, secreted by the pancreas.

tryst /trɪst/ ● *n.* an esp. secret meeting between lovers. ● *v.intr.* keep a tryst.

tsar *var. of* CZAR.

tsarina *var. of* CZARINA.

TSE *abbr.* Toronto Stock Exchange.

tsetse /ˈtsiːtsi, ˈtiːtsi/ *n.* any fly of the genus *Glossina* native to Africa, that feeds on human and animal blood and transmits trypanosomiasis.

T-shirt *n.* a short-sleeved casual top, usu. of a cotton knit fabric and having the form of a T when spread out. □ **T-shirted** *adj.*

Tsilhqot'in /tsɪlˈkoːtɪn/ ● *n.* **1** a member of an Athapaskan people inhabiting the basin of the Chilcotin River valley, between the Coast Mountains and the Fraser River in BC. **2** the Athapaskan language of this people. ● *adj.* of or relating to this people.

Tsimshian /ˈtsɪmʃiːən, -ʃən/ ● *n.* (*pl.* same or **-s**) **1** a member of a group of Aboriginal peoples living in coastal and interior northern BC. **2** the group of languages spoken by the Tsimshian and related Aboriginal peoples. ● *adj.* of or relating to this people.

tsk /tɪsk/ *interj., n., & v.* (also **tsk tsk**; *v.* **tsk-tsk**) = TUT (*see* TUT-TUT).

TSP *abbr.* TRISODIUM PHOSPHATE.

tsp. *abbr.* teaspoonful.

T-square *n.* a T-shaped instrument for drawing parallel lines or right angles.

TSR *n.* a program which stays in the computer's memory once it has been executed and remains ready to be reactivated instantly, without subsequently-activated programs needing to be terminated.

TSS *abbr.* TOXIC SHOCK SYNDROME.

tsunami /tsuːˈnɒmi/ *n.* (*pl.* **-is**) a long high sea wave caused by underwater earthquakes etc.

Tsuu T'ina /tsuːˈtɪnə/ *n. & adj.* = SARCEE.

TTY *abbr.* teletypewriter.

TU *abbr.* Trade Union.

Tu. *abbr.* Tuesday.

tub ● *n.* **1** an open flat-bottomed usu. round container for various purposes. **2** a bathtub. **3** a tub-shaped (usu. plastic) carton. **4** the amount a tub will hold. **5** *informal* a clumsy slow boat. **6** *informal* (usu. *derogatory*) a fat person. ● *v.tr. & intr.* (**tubbed, tubbing**) plant, place, bathe, or wash in a tub. □ **tubful** *n.* (*pl.* **-fuls**).

tuba *n.* (*pl.* **-s**) **1** a large, very low-pitched valved brass wind instrument. **2** a tuba player.

tubal *adj. Anat.* of or relating to a tube, esp. the Fallopian or bronchial tubes.

tubal ligation *n.* the ligation of the Fallopian tubes as a means of sterilization.

tubby *adj.* (**-ier, -iest**) fat. □ **tubbiness** *n.*

tube ● *n.* **1** a long hollow rigid or flexible cylinder, esp. for holding or carrying air, liquids, etc. **2** a soft metal or plastic cylinder sealed at one end and having a screw cap at the other, for holding a semi-liquid substance ready for use (*a tube of toothpaste*). **3 a** *Anat. & Zool.* a hollow cylindrical organ in the body (*Fallopian tubes*). **b** *Bot.* a hollow cylindrical structure in a plant. **4 a** a cathode ray tube esp. in a television set. **b** (*prec. by the*) esp. *N Amer. informal* television. **5** *N Amer.* a thermionic valve. **6** = INNER TUBE. **7** (*attrib.*) designating a close-fitting skirt or sleeveless cylindrical dress or top, esp. of elasticized fabric (*tube top*). **8** the cylindrical body of a wind instrument. ● *v.tr.* **1** equip with tubes. **2** enclose in a tube. □ **down the tube** (or **tubes**) esp. *N Amer.* = DOWN THE DRAIN (see DRAIN).

tube pan *n. N Amer.* a round baking pan with a vertical tube in the centre, used to bake ring-shaped cakes.

tuber *n.* **1** the short thick rounded part of a stem or rhizome, usu. found underground and covered with modified buds, e.g. in a potato. **2** the similar root of a dahlia etc.

tubercle /'tu:bərkəl, 'tju:-/ *n.* **1** a small rounded protuberance esp. on a bone. **2** a small rounded swelling on the body or in an organ, esp. a nodular lesion characteristic of tuberculosis in the lungs etc. **3** a small tuber; a wart-like growth.

tubercle bacillus *n.* a bacterium causing tuberculosis.

tubercular /tu:'bərkjələr/ ● *adj.* (also **tuberculous** /-'bərkjələs/) of or having tubercles or tuberculosis. ● *n.* a person with tuberculosis.

tuberculin /to'bərkjolin/ *n.* a sterile protein extract from cultures of tubercle bacillus, used in the diagnosis and (formerly) treatment of tuberculosis.

tuberculin test *n.* a hypodermic injection of tuberculin to detect a tubercular infection.

tuberculosis /tʊˌbərkjʊ'lo:sɪs/ *n.* an infectious disease caused by the bacillus *Mycobacterium tuberculosis*, characterized by tubercles, esp. in the lungs.

tuberose /'tu:bə,ro:s, 'tju:bə-/ *adj.* (also **tuberous** /'tu:bərəs, 'tju:-/) **1** covered with tubers; knobby. **2** of or resembling a tuber. **3** bearing tubers.

tube skate *n. Cdn* an ice skate with the blade running along a hollow metal tube.

tubing *n.* **1 a** a length of tube. **b** a quantity of tubes; tubes collectively. **2** *N Amer.* a recreational activity in which one sits in an inflated oversized inner tube and floats down a river, is pulled by a boat, or slides down a snow-covered hill.

tub-thumper *n. informal* a ranting preacher or orator. □ **tub-thumping** *adj. & n.*

tubular /'tu:bjolər, 'tju:b-/ *adj.* **1** tube-shaped. **2** having or consisting of tubes. **3** (of furniture etc.) made of tubular pieces.

tubule /'tu:bju:l, 'tju:-/ *n.* a small tube in a plant or an animal body.

tuck ● *v.* **1** *tr.* (often foll. by *in, up*) **a** draw, fold, or turn the outer or end parts of (cloth or clothes etc.) close together so as to be held; thrust in the edge of (a

thing) so as to confine it (*tucked his shirt into his pants*). **b** thrust in the edges of bedclothes around (a person) (*tuck me in*). **2** *tr.* draw together into a small space (*the bird tucked its head under its wing*). **3** *tr.* **a** stow (a thing) away in a specified place or way (*tucked it out of sight*). **b** (usu. in *passive*) hide away, seclude (*a town tucked away in the foothills*). **4** *intr.* (often foll. by *down*) bring one's knees to one's chest; curl oneself into a ball. **5** *tr.* **a** make a stitched fold in (material, a garment, etc.). **b** shorten, tighten, or ornament with stitched folds. ● *n.* **1** a flattened usu. stitched fold in material, a garment, etc., often one of several parallel folds for shortening, tightening, or ornament. **2** (in full **tuck position**) **a** (in diving, gymnastics, etc.) a position with the knees bent upwards into the chest and the hands clasped round the shins. **b** (in skiing) a tight crouched position, with the chest bent down to the knees and the arms close by the sides. **3** *informal* a cosmetic surgical operation (*tummy tuck*). □ **tuck in** *informal* eat food heartily. **tuck into** (or **away**) *informal* eat (food) heartily (*tucked into their dinner*).

tuckamore /'tʌkəmɔr/ *n. Cdn* (*Nfld*) **1** a stunted tree or bush, esp. a spruce or juniper, with creeping roots and interlacing branches. **2** dense scrub formed by such trees or bushes.

tucker ● *n.* a person or thing that tucks. ● *v.tr.* (esp. in *passive*; often foll. by *out*) *N Amer. informal* tire, exhaust.

tucking *n.* a series of usu. stitched tucks in material or a garment.

tuck shop *n. Cdn* a small store within a hospital, hotel, apartment block, etc., selling snacks and daily necessities to residents or guests.

'tude /tu:d/ *n. N Amer.* = ATTITUDE 3.

Tudor /'tu:dər, 'tju:-/ *hist.* ● *adj.* **1** of, characteristic of, or associated with the royal family of England ruling 1485–1603, or this period. **2** of or relating to the architectural style of this period, or one in imitation of it, esp. with half-timbering and elaborately decorated houses. ● *n.* **1** a member of the Tudor royal family. **2** a house with Tudor architecture.

Tues. *abbr.* (also **Tue.**) Tuesday.

Tuesday ● *n.* the third day of the week, following Monday. ● *adv.* **1** on Tuesday. **2** (**Tuesdays**) on Tuesdays; each Tuesday.

tufa /'tu:fə, 'tju:-/ *n.* **1** a porous rock composed of calcium carbonate and formed around mineral springs. **2** = TUFF.

tuff *n.* rock formed by consolidation of volcanic ash.

tuffet *n.* **1** a low seat. **2** = TUFT.

tuft ● *n.* a bunch or collection of threads, grass, hair, etc., held or growing together at the base. ● *v.* **1** *tr.* provide with a tuft or tufts. **2** *tr.* make depressions at regular intervals in (upholstery etc.) by passing a thread through. **3** *intr.* grow in tufts. □ **tufty** *adj.*

tufted *adj.* **1** having or growing in a tuft or tufts. **2** (of a bird) having a tuft of feathers on the head.

tufting *n.* **1** in senses of TUFT *v.* **2** (in N Canada) **a** a handicraft in which plucked moosehair or caribou hair is dyed, gathered in tufts, stitched in patterns on a background of fabric or leather, and contoured or sculpted with clippers. **b** a product of such handiwork.

tug ● *v.* (**tugged, tugging**) **1** *tr. & intr.* pull hard or violently; jerk. **2** *tr.* tow (a ship etc.) by means of a tugboat. **3** *intr.* toil, struggle; go laboriously. ● *n.* **1** a hard, violent, or jerky pull. **2** a sudden strong emotional feeling (*felt a tug as I watched them go*). **3** (also **tugboat**) a small powerful boat for towing larger ships. **4** an aircraft towing a glider. □ **tugger** *n.*

tug-of-war *n.* **1** a contest in which two teams pull at opposite ends of a rope until one drags the other over a central line. **2** an intense struggle between two opponents.

tuition *n.* **1** *N Amer.* a fee paid for education or instruction. **2** teaching or instruction, esp. if paid for.

tularemia /ˌtuːləˈriːmɪə/ *n.* (also **tularaemia**) a severe infectious disease of animals transmissible to humans, caused by the bacterium *Pasteurella tularense* and characterized by ulcers at the site of infection, fever, and loss of weight. □ **tularemic** *adj.*

tulip *n.* **1** any bulbous spring-flowering plant of the genus *Tulipa*, esp. one of the many cultivated forms with showy cup-shaped flowers of various colours and markings. **2** a flower of this plant.

tulip tree *n.* any of various trees, esp. *Liriodendron tulipifera* of eastern N America, with tulip-like flowers.

tulle /tuːl/ *n.* a soft fine net for veils and dresses.

tum *n. informal* the stomach.

tumble ● *v.* **1** *intr.* & *tr.* fall or cause to fall suddenly, clumsily, or headlong. **2** *intr.* **a** fall rapidly in amount etc. (*prices tumbled*). **b** fall in ruins; collapse, topple. **3** *intr.* (often foll. by *around*, *about*) roll or toss erratically or helplessly to and fro. **4** *intr.* move or rush in a headlong or blundering manner (*children tumbled out of the car*). **5** *intr.* (often foll. by *to*) *informal* grasp the meaning or hidden implication of an idea, circumstance, etc. (*they quickly tumbled to our intentions*). **6** *tr.* overturn; fling or push roughly or carelessly. **7** *intr.* perform gymnastic or acrobatic feats, esp. somersaults. **8** *tr.* rumple or disarrange; pull about; disorder. ● *n.* **1** a sudden or headlong fall. **2** a somersault or other acrobatic feat. **3** an untidy or confused state.

tumbledown *adj.* falling or fallen into ruin.

tumble dry *v.* & *intr.* (**-dries, -dried**) dry (clothing etc.) in a clothes dryer with a heated rotating drum.

tumbler *n.* **1** a drinking glass with no handle or foot, with a thick heavy base. **2** an acrobat or gymnast, esp. one performing somersaults. **3 a** a pivoted piece in a lock that holds the bolt until lifted by a key. **b** a notched pivoted plate in a gunlock. **4** (also **tumbling box, tumbling barrel**) a revolving drum or barrel containing an abrasive substance, in which castings, gemstones, etc., are cleaned by friction. □ **tumblerful** *n.* (*pl.* **-fuls**).

tumbleweed *n. N Amer.* & *Austral.* any of various plants, esp. of arid regions, that form a globular bush that breaks off in late summer and is tumbled about by the wind, e.g. *Amaranthus albus*.

tumescent /tjuːˈmesənt, tjuː-/ *adj.* **1** swelling. **2** swelling as a response to sexual stimulation. □ **tumescence** *n.*

tummy *n.* (*pl.* **-ies**) *informal* the stomach.

tummy tuck *n. informal* cosmetic surgery in which excess abdominal fat and skin is removed.

tumour *n.* (also **tumor**) an abnormal swelling or enlargement in any part of the body, esp. a permanent swelling without inflammation, caused by excessive continued growth and proliferation of cells in a tissue, which may be either benign or malignant. □ **tumorous** *adj.*

tumpline *n. N Amer.* a sling for carrying a load on the back, with a strap which passes around the forehead.

tumult /ˈtjuːmʌlt, ˈtuː-, -məlt, ˈtʌmʌlt/ *n.* **1** an uproar or din, esp. of a disorderly crowd. **2** an angry demonstration by a mob; a riot; a public disturbance. **3** a conflict of emotions in the mind. **4** commotion, agitation, disturbance.

tumultuous /təˈmʌltʃʊəs, tuː-, tjuː-, -tjʊəs/ *adj.* **1** noisily vehement; uproarious; making a tumult (*a tumul-*

tuous welcome). **2** disorderly; characterized by commotion or disturbance. **3** agitated. □ **tumultuously** *adv.* **tumultuousness** *n.*

tun *n.* **1** a large beer or wine cask. **2** a brewer's fermenting vat. **3** a measure of capacity, equal to 210 imperial (or 252 US) gallons (about 955 litres).

tuna[1] *n.* (*pl.* same or **-s**) **1** any of several large marine food and game fishes of the mackerel family, of the genera *Thunnus*, *Euthynnus*, *Katsuwonus*, and closely related genera, having a rounded body and pointed snout and found in warm seas worldwide, esp. the very large *Thunnus thynnus*. **2** (also **tuna fish**) the flesh of the tuna, often tinned in oil or water.

tuna[2] *n.* **1** a prickly pear, esp. *O. tuna*. **2** its fruit.

tundra *n.* a vast level treeless Arctic region usu. with a marshy surface and underlying permafrost.

Tundra Buggy *n.* (*pl.* **-ies**) *Cdn proprietary* a large wheeled sightseeing bus used to take tourists into polar bear country.

tundra swan *n.* a swan, *Cygnus columbianus*, breeding in Alaska and the low Arctic.

tundra tire *n. Cdn* a wide airplane tire inflated to low pressure, used to operate from rough terrain.

tundra wolf *n.* the larger of two subspecies of wolf in the Canadian Far North, with white, grey or brown fur, inhabiting the mainland.

tune ● *n.* **1** a melody with or without harmony. **2** a song. **3** the proper musical pitch or intonation; harmony (*out of tune*). ● *v.* **1** *tr.* put (a musical instrument) in tune. **2 a** *tr.* adjust (a radio receiver, television, etc.) to a particular frequency, channel, etc. **b** *intr.* (usu. foll. by *in*) adjust a radio receiver, television, etc. to the required signal or channel (*tuned in to their favourite station*). **c** *tr.* (in *passive*) cause to be interested in, watching, or listening to a broadcast etc. (*a sunbather tuned to the ball game*). **3** *tr.* adjust (an engine etc.) to run smoothly and efficiently. **4** *tr.* (foll. by *to*) adjust or adapt to a required or different purpose, situation, etc. **5** *intr.* (foll. by *with*) be in harmony with. □ **in tune 1** having the correct pitch or intonation (*sings in tune*). **2** (usu. foll. by *with*) harmonizing with one's company, surroundings, etc. **out of tune 1** not having the correct pitch or intonation. **2** (usu. foll. by *with*) clashing with one's company etc. **stay tuned 1** continue to watch or listen to a broadcast etc. **2** *informal* more news or information is forthcoming. **to the tune of** *informal* to the sum or amount of. **tune in** (often foll. by *to*) *informal* become acquainted with or aware of. **tune out 1** stop tuning in to a broadcast etc. **2** become oblivious to (something) or to one's surroundings. **tune up 1** (of a musician) bring one's instrument to the proper or uniform pitch. **2** bring to the most efficient condition.

tuneful *adj.* melodious, musical. □ **tunefully** *adv.* **tunefulness** *n.*

tuneless *adj.* **1** unmelodious, unmusical. **2** out of tune. □ **tunelessly** *adv.* **tunelessness** *n.*

tuner *n.* **1** a person who tunes musical instruments, esp. pianos. **2 a** a device for tuning a radio receiver. **b** a radio receiver. **3** an electronic device for tuning a musical instrument.

tunesmith *n. informal* a songwriter.

tune-up *n.* esp. *N Amer.* **1** an act or instance of making esp. minor adjustments to a motor vehicle etc. to ensure optimum performance. **2** *Sport* (often foll. by *for*) an event that serves as a practice for a subsequent event.

tung *n.* a tree, *Aleurites fordii*, native to China, bearing poisonous fruits containing seeds that yield oil used in paints, varnishes, etc.

tungsten /'tʌŋstən/ *n.* a steel-grey dense metallic element with a very high melting point, occurring naturally and used for the filaments of electric lamps and for alloying steel etc.

tunic *n.* **1** a close-fitting short coat of police or military etc. uniform. **2** a loose often sleeveless garment usu. reaching to about the knees, as worn in ancient Greece and Rome. **3** a loose, knitted, women's upper garment reaching to mid-thigh, usu. worn over leggings, a skirt, blouse, or pants. **4** a loose sleeveless usu. belted dress worn over a blouse, esp. as part of a girl's school uniform. **5** any of various loose, pleated dresses gathered at the waist with a belt or cord.

tuning *n.* **1** *in senses of* TUNE *v.* **2 a** the process or a system of putting a musical instrument in tune. **b** the state of being in tune.

tuning fork *n.* a two-pronged steel fork that gives a particular note when struck, used in tuning musical instruments etc.

Tunisian /tʊ'niːʒən, -'niːs-, -'niːz-, -'nɪs-, tjuː-, -'niːʒən/ ● *adj.* of or relating to the N African country of Tunisia. ● *n.* a native or inhabitant of Tunisia.

tunnel ● *n.* **1** an artificial underground passage through a hill or under a road or river etc., esp. for a railway or road to pass through, or in a mine. **2** an underground passage dug by a burrowing animal. **3** a long enclosed passageway or corridor through a building etc., e.g. from the dressing room to the playing area in a sports stadium. **4** a prolonged period of difficulty or suffering (esp. in metaphors, e.g. *a light at the end of the tunnel*). **5** a canal or hollow groove in the body (*carpal tunnel*). ● *v.* (**tunnelled**, **tunnelling**) **1** *intr.* (foll. by *into*, etc.) make a tunnel through (a hill etc.). **2** *tr.* make (one's way) by tunnelling. □ **tunneller** *n.*

tunnel vision *n.* **1** vision that is defective in not adequately including objects away from the centre of the field of view. **2** *informal* **a** concentration focused on a limited or single objective, perception, etc. (also *attrib.*: *a tunnel-vision approach*). **b** inability to be diverted or swayed from this.

tupelo /'tuːpəˌloʊ, 'tjuː-/ *n.* (*pl.* **-os**) **1** any of various Asian and N American deciduous trees of the genus *Nyssa*, with colourful foliage and growing in swampy conditions. **2** the wood of this tree.

tupik /'tuːpɪk/ *n.* a traditional skin tent used by Inuit groups during the summer.

Tupperware *n. proprietary* a range of plastic containers for storing food.

tuque *var. of* TOQUE 1.

turban *n.* **1** a man's headdress, consisting of a length of cotton or silk wound around a cap or the head, worn esp. by Muslims and Sikhs. **2** a woman's headdress or hat resembling this. □ **turbaned** *adj.*

turbid *adj.* **1** (of a liquid or colour) muddy, thick; not clear. **2** (of a style etc.) confused, disordered. □ **turbidity** *n.*

turbine *n.* a rotary motor or engine driven by a flow of water, steam, gas, wind, etc., esp. to produce electrical power.

turbo *n.* (*pl.* **-os**) **1 a** = TURBOCHARGER. **b** a motor vehicle equipped with this. **2** (also in *comb.*) = TURBINE.

turbocharge *v.tr.* (esp. as **turbocharged** *adj.*) **1** supply (a motor, a vehicle, etc.) with a turbocharger; use a turbocharger on. **2** *informal* greatly increase the efficiency, power, or speed of.

turbocharger *n.* a supercharger driven by a turbine powered by the engine's exhaust gases.

turbofan *n.* **1** a jet engine in which a turbine-driven fan provides additional thrust. **2** an aircraft powered by this.

turbojet *n.* **1** a jet engine in which the jet also operates a turbine-driven compressor for the air drawn into the engine. **2** an aircraft powered by this.

turboprop *n.* **1** a jet engine in which a turbine is used as in a turbojet and also to drive a propeller. **2** an aircraft powered by this.

turbot /'tɜːbət/ *n.* **1** a large speckled European flatfish, *Scophthalmus maximus*, having a broad scaleless diamond-shaped body covered with bony tubercules, valued for food. **2** any of various similar fishes including halibut.

turbulence *n.* **1 a** an irregularly fluctuating flow of air or fluid. **b** a disturbed state caused by this. **2** stormy conditions as a result of atmospheric disturbance. **3** a disturbance, commotion, or tumult.

turbulent *adj.* **1** disturbed; in commotion. **2** (of a flow of air etc.) varying irregularly; causing disturbance. **3** tumultuous. **4** insubordinate, riotous.

turd *n. coarse slang* **1** a lump of excrement. **2** a term of contempt for a person.

tureen /təˈriːn, tjʊ-/ *n.* a deep covered dish for serving soup etc.

turf ● *n.* (*pl.* **-s** or **turves**) **1 a** a layer of grass etc. with earth and matted roots as the surface of grassland. **b** a piece of this cut from the ground. **c** esp. *N Amer. informal* artificial turf. **2** a slab of peat for fuel. **3** (prec. by *the*) **a** horse racing generally. **b** a general term for racecourses. **4 a** an area regarded as being under the control of a particular person or group; one's personal territory. **b** one's sphere of influence or activity. ● *v.tr.* **1** (often as **turfed** *adj.*) cover (ground) with turf. **2** (esp. foll. by *out*) *informal* expel, eject (a person etc.).

turf war *n.* (also **turf battle**) a fight or struggle over spheres of influence or control.

turgid /'tɜːdʒɪd/ *adj.* **1** swollen, inflated, enlarged. **2** (of language) pompous, bombastic.

Turing test /'tjʊərɪŋ/ *n. Computing* a test for intelligence in a computer, which requires that a human should be unable to distinguish it from another human by the replies to questions put to both.

Turk *n.* **1 a** a native or national of Turkey, a country in W Asia and SE Europe. **b** a person of Turkish descent. **2** a member of a Central Asian people from whom the Ottomans derived, speaking Turkic languages.

turkey *n.* (*pl.* **-eys**) **1** a large mainly domesticated game bird, *Meleagris gallopavo*, originally of N America, having dark plumage with a green or bronze sheen, prized as food esp. on festive occasions including Christmas and Thanksgiving. **2** the flesh of the turkey as food. **3** *N Amer. slang* **a** a theatrical failure; a flop. **b** a stupid or inept person. □ **talk turkey** *N Amer. informal* talk frankly and straightforwardly; get down to business.

turkeycock *n.* **1** a male turkey. **2** a pompous or self-important person.

turkey vulture *n.* (also **turkey buzzard**) a N American vulture, *Cathartes aura*, having a white beak and legs and dark plumage.

Turkic /'tɜːkɪk/ ● *adj.* of or relating to a large group of Altaic languages including Turkish and Azerbaijani or the peoples speaking them. ● *n.* the Turkic languages collectively.

Turkish ● *adj.* of or relating to Turkey in W Asia and SE Europe, or to the Turks or their language. ● *n.* this language.

Turkish bath *n.* **1** a hot-air or steam bath followed by washing, massage, etc. **2** (in *sing.* or *pl.*) a building for this.

Turkish carpet *n.* a wool carpet with a thick pile and traditional bold design.

Turkmen ● *n.* (*pl.* same or **-s**) **1** a member of any of various Turkic peoples inhabiting the region east of the Caspian Sea and south of the Aral Sea, comprising Turkmenistan and parts of Iran and Afghanistan. **2** the Turkic language of these peoples. ● *adj.* of or relating to these peoples or their language.

turmeric /ˈtɜːmərɪk/ *n.* **1** a tropical Asian plant, *Curcuma longa*, of the ginger family, yielding aromatic rhizomes. **2** this rhizome powdered and used as a spice esp. in curry powder.

turmoil *n.* **1** violent confusion; agitation. **2** disturbance, tumult, trouble.

turn ● *v.* **1** *tr. & intr.* move around a fixed point or central axis; rotate, revolve. **2** *tr. & intr.* reverse the position of so that the back faces forward, the bottom faces up, or the inside faces out. **3 a** *intr.* take a new direction (*turn left*). **b** *intr.* (of a road) bend, curve. **4** *tr.* go around (a corner). **5** *tr.* change the course or direction of; aim, direct (*she turned her eyes away*). **6** *tr. & intr.* (usu. foll. by *to* or *from*) focus or conclude focusing (one's thoughts or attention) on a particular subject etc. **7** *intr.* (foll. by *to*) **a** apply oneself to; set about (*turned to doing the ironing*). **b** have recourse to (*turned to her for help*). **8** *tr. & intr.* (foll. by *into*) change in nature, form, or condition; transform. **9** *tr. & intr.* cause to become or become (*they have turned crazy*). **10** *tr. & intr.* (foll. by *against*) make or become hostile to (*our actions have turned them against us*). **11** *intr.* (foll. by *on*) become hostile towards; attack (*the dog turned on its owner*). **12 a** *intr.* (of hair or leaves) change colour. **b** *tr.* cause (the hair) to change colour. **13** *intr. & tr.* make or become sour (*the milk has turned*). **14 a** *intr.* (of the stomach) be nauseated. **b** *tr.* cause (the stomach) to become nauseated. **15** *tr.* reach the age of (*turned 40*). **16 a** *tr.* flip (a page of a book) in order to read or write on the other side. **b** *intr.* (foll. by *to*) go to (a particular page or passage). **17** *intr.* become an informer. **18** *intr.* (of the head) become giddy. **19** *tr.* twist or sprain (an ankle). **20** *intr.* (foll. by *on*) depend on; be determined by (*it all turns on the weather tomorrow*). **21** *tr. Baseball* execute (a double play). **22** *tr.* perform (a somersault etc.). **23** *tr.* make or earn (a profit etc.) (*she turned a quick buck*). **24** *tr.* (often foll. by *aside*) divert (a bullet). **25** *tr.* shape (an object) on a lathe. **26** *intr.* (of the tide) change from flood to ebb or vice versa. ● *n.* **1** an act of turning around on an axis; a total or partial revolution. **2 a** an act of turning or facing another way; a change of direction. **b** a point at which a turning or change occurs. **3 a** a place where a road turns off or branches onto another (*took a wrong turn*). **b** a place where a road, river, etc., changes direction; a bend. **4** a change of the tide from ebb to flow or from flow to ebb. **5** a change in circumstances or in the course of events, esp. for better or worse. **6** the transition from one period of time to the next (*the turn of the century*). **7** an opportunity or obligation etc. that comes successively to each of several people. **8** a period of work done by a group of people in succession; a shift. **9** a short walk or ride (*a turn in the garden*). **10** the halfway point in a round of golf. **11** an act or deed, esp. one that does good or harm to another (*one good turn deserves another*). **12** *informal* a momentary shock or feeling of concern (*the news gave me quite a turn*). **13** a variation or particular manner of linguistic expression, esp. for effect (*turn of phrase*). **14** a tendency or disposition (*is of a mechanical turn of mind*). □ **at every**

turn at every change of circumstance, at each new stage; continually. **by turns** one after the other in regular succession; alternately. **in turn** in succession; one by one. **in one's turn** when one's turn or opportunity comes. **not know which way** (or **where**) **to turn** be unsure how to act, whom to trust, etc.; be completely at a loss. **out of turn 1** at a time when it is not one's turn. **2** inappropriately; inadvisedly or tactlessly (*did I speak out of turn?*). **take turns** act or work alternately or in succession. **to a turn** (esp. cooked) to exactly the right degree etc. **turn around 1** (also **turn about**) turn and face the opposite direction. **2** adopt an opposite course or policy. **3** begin to show an opposite trend or movement. **4** receive, process, and send (passengers, goods, etc.) out again. **turn away 1** turn and face another direction; avert one's eyes. **2** refuse to accept or admit; reject, send away. **turn back 1** return, go back the way one has come. **2** fold back. **turn the corner 1** make a turn at an intersection onto a perpendicular street. **2** pass the critical point in an illness, difficulty, etc.; begin to make noticeable improvement. **turn a person's crank** *slang* (usu. with *neg.*) amuse, thrill, or excite a person. **turn down 1** reject (a proposal, application, etc.). **2** reduce the volume or strength of (sound, heat, etc.) by turning a knob etc. **3** fold down (bedsheets etc.). **turn an honest penny** earn money fairly. **turn in 1** hand in, submit. **2** achieve or register (a performance, score, etc.). **3** *informal* go to bed. **4** fold inwards. **5** incline inwards (*his toes turn in*). **6** hand over (a suspect etc.) to the authorities. **turn loose 1** release and set free (an animal). **2** allow (a person) to go where, or do as, he or she pleases. **turn off 1 a** stop the flow or operation of (water, electricity, etc.) by means of a tap, switch, etc. **b** operate (a tap, switch, etc.) to achieve this. **2 a** enter a side road. **b** (of a side road) lead off from another road. **3** *informal* cause to lose interest. **turn on 1 a** start the flow or operation of (water, electricity, etc.) by means of a tap, switch, etc. **b** operate (a tap, switch, etc.) to achieve this. **c** activate, begin to use (charm, genius, etc.). **2** *informal* excite, arouse; stimulate the interest of, esp. sexually. **3** *informal* introduce to or make aware of (*she turned me on to classical music*). **turn out 1** (often foll. by *to* + infin. or *that* + clause) prove to be the case; result. **2** extinguish (a light etc.). **3** *informal* assemble; attend a meeting etc. **4** expel. **5** produce (manufactured goods etc.). **6** dress or equip (*well turned out*). **7** empty (a pocket) to see the contents. **8** empty or clean out (a room etc.). **9** *informal* **a** get out of bed. **b** go out of doors. **turn over 1** turn from one side onto another; bring the reverse or underside into view. **2** upset; cause to fall over. **3 a** cause (an engine) to run. **b** (of an engine) start running. **4** consider thoroughly. **5** (foll. by *to*) **a** transfer the care or conduct of (a person or thing) to (a person). **b** = TURN IN 6. **6** *N Amer. Sport* lose possession of (the ball or puck) to the opposing team. **7** do business to the amount of (*turns over $5000 a week*). **turn round** esp. *Brit.* = TURN AROUND. **turn tail** run away from something feared; flee. **turn the tide** reverse the trend of events. **turn up 1** increase the volume or strength of (sound, heat, etc.) by turning a knob etc. **2** place upwards. **3** discover or reveal. **4** be found, esp. by chance (*it turned up in a bus depot*). **5** happen or present itself; (of a person) put in an appearance (*turned up late*).

turnabout *n.* **1** a change or reversal of direction. **2** an abrupt change of opinion or policy etc. **3** an act of repaying an injury etc. in kind (*turnabout is fair play*).

turnaround *n.* **1 a** an abrupt or unexpected reversal of a trend, attitude, opinion, fortune, etc. **b** an improvement or recovery, esp. in business. **2 a** the process of receiving, processing, and sending out again. **b** the process of unloading and reloading an airplane, ship, etc. **c** the amount of time required for such processes. **3** esp. *US* a place where vehicles can turn around, such as at the end of a street.

turncoat *n.* a person who changes sides in a conflict, dispute, etc.; a traitor.

turndown ● *n.* **1** a rejection or refusal. **2** an act of turning down the sheets of a bed, esp. as a courtesy performed in a hotel (also *attrib.*: *turndown service*). **3** a downturn. ● *attrib.adj.* (esp. of a collar) that is or may be turned down.

turner *n.* **1** a thing that turns or is used for turning, e.g. a spatula. **2** a person who turns wood on a lathe.

turning *n.* **1** the act or practice of using a lathe. **2** work or an article produced on a lathe.

turning circle *n.* the smallest circle in which a car, ship, etc., can turn without reversing.

turning point *n.* **1** a moment at which a decisive change occurs in one's life, a process, etc. **2** an incident that causes or results in decisive change.

turnip *n.* **1** *N Amer.* = RUTABAGA. **2 a** a cruciferous plant, *Brassica rapa*, with a large white globular root and sprouting leaves. **b** this root used as a vegetable. □ **fall off a turnip truck** (or **cart**) *N Amer.* (usu. with *neg.*) be foolish or simple-minded. □ **turnipy** *adj.*

turnkey *adj.* **1** (of a contract, solution, etc.) providing for a supply of equipment in a state ready for operation. **2** (of a computer system etc.) assembled ahead of time and complete with all the parts and equipment necessary for immediate use.

turnoff *n.* **1** a road that leads away from a larger or more important one. **2** *informal* something that causes disgust or a loss of interest.

turn of the century ● *n.* the period at the end of one century and beginning of the next, esp. around 1900. ● *adj.* (usu. **turn-of-the-century**) used, manufactured, or existing around 1900.

turn-on *n. informal* a thing or person that thrills, excites, or causes esp. sexual stimulation or arousal.

turnout *n.* **1** the number of people attending or participating in an event, such as a meeting or a vote (*low voter turnout*). **2** the quantity of goods produced in a given time. **3** *N Amer.* a place where animals may be turned out to graze.

turnover *n.* **1** the amount of money made in a business in a given time. **2** the rate at which a particular asset or product is sold and replaced. **3** the rate at which employees join and leave a company, tenants move into and out of housing, etc. **4** a small usu. triangular or semicircular pie, made by folding a piece of pastry over onto itself to enclose a usu. sweet filling. **5** *N Amer. Sport* a loss of possession of the ball or puck to the opposing team.

turnpike *n.* **1** *US* a toll highway. **2** a tollgate.

turn signal *n. N Amer.* each of a pair of flashing lights on either side of a motor vehicle used to indicate turns or lane changes.

turnstile *n.* a mechanical gate consisting of usu. four revolving arms fixed to a vertical post allowing people through singly, and usu. functioning in one direction only.

turnstone *n.* any wading bird of the genus *Arenaria*, related to the plover, that looks under stones for small animals to eat.

turntable *n.* **1** a circular revolving platform spinning a phonograph record that is being played. **2** the unit housing this; a record player. **3** a circular revolving platform for turning a railway locomotive or other vehicle.

turpentine ● *n.* **1** (also **oil of turpentine**) a volatile essential oil with a pungent odour, obtained by distilling gum turpentine or pine wood, used esp. as a solvent and thinner for paints and stains, and in medical liniments. **2** (in full **crude turpentine** or **gum turpentine**) any of various viscous oleoresins which exude from coniferous trees, esp. pines, and can be distilled to yield gum rosin and oil of turpentine. ● *v.tr.* apply turpentine to.

turpitude /'tɜrpɪˌtuːd, -ˌtjuːd/ *n. formal* wickedness.

turquoise /'tɜrkɔiz, -kwɔiz/ ● *n.* **1** a semi-precious stone, usu. opaque and of a sky-blue to blue-green colour, consisting of hydrated copper aluminum phosphate. **2** the colour of this mineral, usu. a greenish-blue. ● *adj.* of this colour.

turr *n. Cdn (Nfld)* = MURRE.

turret *n.* **1** a small tower, usu. projecting from the wall of a building, such as a castle. **2** a low flat usu. revolving armoured tower or enclosure for a gun and gunners in a ship, aircraft, fort, or tank. **3** an attachment for a lathe, drill, etc. that holds various tools or bits and may be rotated to access the one required to do a particular job. □ **turreted** *adj.*

turtle *n.* **1** any of various marine or freshwater reptiles of the order Testudines, encased in a shell of bony plates, and having flippers or webbed toes used in swimming. **2** the flesh of the turtle, esp. used for soup. □ **turn turtle** turn over, capsize.

turtledove *n.* any wild dove of the genus *Streptopelia*, esp. *S. turtur*, noted for its soft cooing and its affection for its mate and young.

turtleneck *n. N Amer.* **1** a high round turned-over collar, esp. on a knitted garment. **2** a garment having this type of neck.

turtle shell ● *n.* = TORTOISESHELL *n.* 1. ● *adj.* (**turtleshell**) = TORTOISESHELL *adj.*

turves *rare pl.* of TURF.

Tuscan /'tʌskən/ ● *n.* **1** an inhabitant of Tuscany in central Italy. **2** the classical Italian language of Tuscany. ● *adj.* of or relating to Tuscany or Tuscans.

Tuscarora /ˌtʌskəˌrɔrə/ ● *n.* **1** a member of an Iroquois people living in southern Ontario and western New York, the last member to join the Iroquoian confederacy. **2** the Iroquoian language of this people. ● *adj.* of or relating to this people.

tush /tʊʃ/ *n.* (also **tushie**, **tushy** (*pl.* **-ies**) esp. *N. Amer. slang* the buttocks.

tusk *n.* a long pointed tooth, esp. protruding from a closed mouth, as in the elephant etc. **2** anything resembling a tusk in appearance, such as a tusklike tooth of a human. □ **tusked** *adj.* (also in *comb.*).

tussle ● *n.* a struggle, scuffle, or conflict, esp. a minor or playful one. ● *v.intr.* engage in a tussle.

tussock *n.* a tuft or clump of grass etc. forming a small hill. □ **tussocky** *adj.*

tut *var.* of TUT-TUT.

Tutchone /tuːˈtʃoːni/ ● *n.* (*pl.* same or **-s**) **1** a member of an Aboriginal people living in the area of the Yukon River. **2** the Athapaskan language of this people. ● *adj.* of or relating to this people.

tutelage /'tuːtəlɪdʒ, 'tjuː-/ *n.* **1** instruction, teaching, education (*under her tutelage*). **2** protection, care, guardianship. **3** the condition or duration of being supervised by a tutor or guardian.

tutelary /'tuːtələri, 'tjuː-/ *adj.* **1** serving as a guardian, protector, or patron (*tutelary saint*). **2** of or relating to a guardian (*tutelary authority*).

tutor ● *n.* **1** a private teacher, either one in general charge of a person's education or employed to give a student additional instruction in a particular subject or subjects. **2** esp. *Brit.* a university teacher supervising the studies of assigned undergraduates. ● *v.* **1** *tr.* act as a tutor to; teach or assist (a student) privately, esp. in a particular subject. **2** *intr.* work as a tutor.

tutorial /tuːˈtɔːrɪəl, tjuː-/ ● *adj.* of or relating to a tutor or tuition. ● *n.* **1** a period of instruction given by a teaching assistant at a university to a small group of students. **2** a period of instruction given privately by a tutor, to either a single pupil or small group. **3** any training session or seminar. **4** *Computing* a program that enables a user to learn how to use a type of software by offering onscreen instruction interspersed with practice exercises.

Tutsi /ˈtʊtsi/ *n.* (*pl.* same or **-s**) a member of a Bantu-speaking people forming a minority of the population of Rwanda.

tutti-frutti /ˌtuːtiˈfruːti/ *n.* (*pl.* **-s**) **1** a candy or dessert, esp. ice cream, consisting of or flavoured with a mixture of chopped preserved fruits and nuts. **2** an artificial flavour combining the tastes of several fruits.

tut-tut ● *interj.* expressing rebuke, impatience, or contempt. ● *n.* an exclamation of 'tut-tut' or the sound of consecutive clicks of the tongue against the alveolar ridge. ● *v.intr.* (**-tutted, -tutting**) **1** exclaim 'tut-tut'. **2** express disapproval.

tutu *n.* a female ballet dancer's costume with a long, flowing bell-shaped skirt of layered tulle or a short, stiff skirt of layered net standing out from the hips.

tux *n.* *N Amer. informal* = TUXEDO.

tuxedo *n.* (*pl.* **-os** or **-oes**) *N Amer.* **1** a suit worn esp. by men on formal occasions, consisting of a usu. black jacket and matching pants, often trimmed in silk, traditionally worn with a black tie, cummerbund, and white dress shirt. **2** the formal coat or jacket worn as part of this suit.

TV *n.* television.

TV dinner *n.* esp. *N Amer.* a prepared frozen single-serving meal packaged in a compartmentalized tray in which it is heated.

TVP *abbr. proprietary* = TEXTURED VEGETABLE PROTEIN.

TV table *n.* (also **TV tray**) *N Amer.* one of usu. a set of small portable folding tables with a detachable tray forming the tabletop, from which a person sitting in an easy chair etc. may eat, as while watching TV.

twaddle ● *n.* useless, senseless, silly, or dull talk, ideas, or writing. ● *v.intr.* indulge in this.

twang ● *n.* **1 a** a strong ringing sound made by the plucked string of a musical instrument or bow. **b** any sound resembling this. **2 a** a nasal quality of pronunciation or intonation characteristic of the speech of an individual, area, country, etc. **b** an accent having such a quality. ● *v.* **1 a** *intr.* ring, resound, or resonate with a sound like that of a plucked string. **b** *tr.* cause (a bow, arrow, etc.) to produce this sound. **2** *tr.* usu. *derogatory* play (a tune or instrument) in this way. **3** *tr.* utter with a nasal twang. □ **twangy** *adj.*

'twas *archaic* it was.

twat *n. coarse slang* the female genitals.

tweak ● *v.tr.* **1** pinch and twist sharply; pull with a sharp jerk; twitch. **2** make fine adjustments to (a mechanism). **3** taunt; jibe at; pique; tease. ● *n.* an instance of tweaking.

twee *adj.* (**tweer; tweest**) usu. *derogatory* affectedly dainty, quaint, or sentimental.

tweed *n.* **1** a rough-surfaced woollen cloth of varying texture, usu. of mixed flecked colours. **2** (in *pl.*) clothes made of tweed.

tweedy *adj.* (**-ier, -iest**) **1** of or relating to tweed cloth. **2** often dressed in tweed cloth (usu. with connotations of dowdiness, heartiness, or professorial demeanour).

tween ● *n.* = TWEEN-AGER. ● *adj.* tween-age.

tween-ager *n.* (also **tweenie**) *N Amer.* a person who has not yet, or has only recently, become a teenager, usu. between the ages of 8 and 14. □ **tween-age** *adj.*

tweet ● *n.* the chirp of a small bird. ● *v.intr.* make a chirping noise.

tweeter *n.* a loudspeaker designed to reproduce high frequencies (compare WOOFER).

tweeze *v.tr.* esp. *N Amer.* **1** pinch or grab with or as if with tweezers. **2** pluck (the eyebrows) with tweezers.

tweezers *n.pl.* a small pair of pincers used for picking up tiny objects, plucking eyebrows, etc.

twelfth ● *n.* **1** the position in a sequence corresponding to the number 12. **2** the person or thing corresponding to the number 12 in a category, series, etc. **3** each of twelve equal parts of a thing. **4** *Music* **a** an interval or chord spanning an octave and a fifth in the diatonic scale. **b** a note separated from another by this interval. ● *adj.* that is the twelfth. ● *adv.* twelfthly. □ **twelfthly** *adv.*

twelve ● *n.* **1** one more than eleven. **2** a symbol for this (12, xii, XII). **3** twelve people or things identified contextually, such as years of age, points in a game, minutes, inches, etc. **4** a size etc. denoted by twelve. **5** twelve o'clock. **6** (**the Twelve**) the twelve apostles. ● *adj.* that amount to twelve.

twelve-pack *n.* *N Amer.* a case of twelve items sold together, esp. bottles or cans of beer.

12-step *adj.* designating or pertaining to a program designed to help addicts overcome esp. a drug or alcohol dependency, based on progressing through twelve stages towards recovery. □ **12-stepper** *n.* **12-stepping** *n.*

twenty ● *n.* (*pl.* **-ies**) **1** the product of two and ten. **2** a symbol for this (20, xx, XX). **3** twenty people or things identified contextually, such as years of age, points in a game, minutes, etc. **4** (in *pl.*) the numbers from 20 to 29, esp. the years of a century or of a person's life. **5** *informal* a large indefinite number (*have told you twenty times*). **6** a twenty-dollar bill etc. ● *adj.* that amount to twenty. □ **twenty-first, -second**, etc. the ordinal numbers between twentieth and thirtieth. **twenty-one, -two**, etc. the cardinal numbers between twenty and thirty. □ **twentieth** *adj., adv. & n.* **twentyfold** *adj. & adv.*

twenty-one *n.* *N Amer.* = BLACKJACK 1.

twenty-six *n.* *Cdn* a 26-ounce bottle of liquor.

twentysomething ● *n.* **1** an undetermined age between twenty and thirty. **2** a person of this age or generation. ● *adj.* **1** characteristic of the tastes and lifestyle of this group. **2** between twenty and thirty years of age.

20/20 *adj.* (also **twenty-twenty**) denoting vision of normal acuity. □ **hindsight is 20/20** it is much easier to understand and criticize events, decisions, etc. after the fact than while they are occurring or being made.

twenty-two *n.* a .22-calibre gun or cartridge.

twerp *n.* *slang* a foolish, pathetic, or insignificant person; a pipsqueak, a nobody. □ **twerpy** *adj.*

twice *adv.* **1** on two successive occasions; two times. **2** in double degree or quantity (*twice as good*).

twiddle *v.* **1 a** *tr.* cause to rotate lightly or delicately with the fingers; twirl; adjust. **b** *intr.* (often foll. by *with*) play idly; fiddle, tinker. **2** *intr.* move twirlingly. □ **twiddle one's thumbs 1** move one's thumbs around each other with the fingers linked together, esp. as a sign of boredom or impatience. **2** have nothing to do. □ **twiddler** *n.* **twiddly** *adj.*

twig[1] *n.* **1** a small branch or shoot of a tree or shrub. **2** *Anat.* a small branch of an artery etc. □ **twigged** *adj.* (also in *comb.*). **twiggy** *adj.*

twig[2] *v.* **(twigged, twigging)** *informal* **1 a** *tr.* understand; grasp the meaning or nature of. **b** *intr.* (often foll. by *to*) become conscious or aware of; catch on. **2** *tr.* recognize, perceive, observe.

twilight *n.* **1 a** the soft glowing light from the sky when the sun is below the horizon, esp. in the evening. **b** any faint light resembling this. **2** the period or time of day when this occurs, esp. in the evening. **3** an intermediate condition or period, esp. one of decline or destruction (also *attrib.*: *twilight years*). **4** a state of imperfect knowledge or understanding.

twilight zone *n.* any physical or conceptual area lying undefined or intermediate between two distinct fields or regions, having characteristics of both but belonging to neither.

twilit *adj.* (also **twilighted**) dimly illuminated by or as if by twilight.

twill *n.* **1** a woven fabric with a surface of diagonal parallel ridges, produced by passing the weft threads over one and under two or more threads of the warp, instead of over and under in regular succession. **2** the method of weaving this fabric.

twin ● *n.* **1** each of two children or animals born at the same time to the same mother, having developed from the same ovum (**identical twins**) or two separately fertilized ova (**fraternal twins**) (also *attrib.*: *twin sisters*). **2** either of two closely related or similar things; a counterpart (also *attrib.*: *twin houses*). **3** either of two parts, usu. identical, working in unison (also *attrib.*: *twin cylinder engine*). **4 a** (*attrib.*) denoting a twin-size mattress, bed, etc. (see TWIN-SIZE). **b** such a bed or mattress. **5** a twin-engined aircraft. ● *v.* **(twinned, twinning) 1 a** *tr.* couple, join, unite (two people or things) closely or intimately. **b** *intr.* (often foll. by *with*) be or become coupled or joined; pair. **2** *tr.* (usu. in *passive*) establish official links between (two cities or towns, esp. in different countries) for the purposes of friendship and cultural exchange. □ **twinning** *n.* **twinship** *n.*

twin bill *n.* *informal* **1** *Baseball* = DOUBLEHEADER 1. **2** = DOUBLE BILL.

twin-cam *attrib.adj.* (esp. of an engine) having two camshafts.

twin city *n.* **1** (**Twin Cities**) *N Amer.* two neighbouring cities situated close together, such as St. Paul and Minneapolis, Minnesota or (formerly) Fort William and Port Arthur, Ontario (now Thunder Bay). **2** each of a pair of usu. international cities with official ties for the purposes of friendship and cultural exchange.

twine ● *n.* a strong cord or string made of the twisted strands of hemp, cotton, sisal, etc. ● *v.* **1** *tr.* **a** join together (two or more strands etc.) by twisting (*she twined her hair into a braid*). **b** (often foll. by *with*) twist or join (one thing, strand, etc.) with another (*I twined my arm with hers*). **2** *intr.* (of two things) become joined, linked, or tangled (*their lives twined inextricably the moment they met*). **3** *tr.* (often foll. by *around*) wind or wrap (one or more strands etc.) (*twined the rope around a tree*). **4** *tr.* form (a garland or wreath etc.) by twisting or weaving flowers, leaves, etc. **5** *intr.* (of a plant) grow in a twisting or winding manner. □ **twiner** *n.*

twin-engined *adj.* (also **twin-engine**) (of an aircraft etc.) having two engines.

twinge ● *n.* **1** (often foll. by *in*) a sudden sharp physical pain (*she felt a twinge in her shoulder*). **2** (usu. foll. by *of*) a sudden emotional pang (*a twinge of guilt*). ● *v.tr. & intr.* cause or experience a twinge.

twinkie *n.* (also **twink**, **twinky** *pl.* **-ies**) esp. *US derogatory* **1** a weak or feeble person. **2** a homosexual.

twinkle ● *v.intr.* **1** (of a star or light etc.) shine with rapid alternation between brightness and faintness. **2** (of the eyes) have a bright lively expression, esp. of amusement. **3** (of the feet in dancing) move lightly and rapidly. ● *n.* **1** a sparkle or gleam of the eyes, esp. as a reflection of liveliness, youthfulness, or mischievousness. **2** a brief or intermittent flash, flicker, or gleam of light; a glimmer. **3 a** a blink or wink of the eye. **b** a brief moment; an instant. □ **twinkler** *n.* **twinkly** *adj.*

twinkling ● *n.* the action of twinkling. ● *adj.* that twinkles. □ **in a twinkling** (or **the twinkling of an eye**) in an instant.

twin-size *adj.* (also **twin-sized**) designating the smallest standard size of mattress, usu. 98 by 191 cm (38.5 by 75 in.), or of the bed frame, sheets, etc. designed for such a mattress.

twirl ● *v.* **1** *tr. & intr.* spin, turn, or rotate rapidly or quickly. **2** *tr.* roll or twist between the thumb and forefinger (*he twirled his moustache*). ● *n.* **1** a twirling motion. **2** a twirling object or shape, such as a flourish made with a pen. □ **twirler** *n.* **twirly** *adj.*

twist ● *v.* **1 a** *tr.* distort the shape of (something usu. long and thin) by turning two ends in opposite directions or by turning one end while the other remains fixed. **b** *tr.* cause (something long and thin, such as a string, wire, or strand of hair) to coil around an axis, thus imparting a spiral shape to it. **c** *intr.* assume a spiral or twisted form by being distorted in this way. **2** *tr.* **a** wind (strands of hemp etc.) together to form a rope. **b** form (a rope etc.) by winding strands of hemp or cotton etc. **3** *tr.* (often foll. by *around*) wind or coil (a thread etc.) around something. **4** *tr., intr., & refl.* turn (oneself or a part of one's body) around partly or completely in order to face another direction. **5 a** *tr.* accidentally turn (one's ankle, knee, etc.) sharply, so as to strain and injure the ligaments or tendons. **b** *tr.* deliberately turn (a person's arm etc.) around violently in order to cause pain or injury. **c** *tr.* screw up or contort (one's face or features), esp. in pain, anger, or contempt. **d** *intr.* (of the face or features) be contorted. **6** *tr.* distort or misrepresent (facts or someone's meaning, intentions, etc.). **7** *tr.* **a** apply a rotating movement to. **b** (foll. by *off*) remove by twisting (*twist the top off*). **8** *intr.* rotate or turn, or be capable of this (*falling leaves twisted in the air*). **9** *intr.* (of a road, river, person, etc.) follow a very winding path. **10** *intr.* dance the twist. ● *n.* **1** an act or an instance of twisting. **2** a thing formed by or as by twisting; a twisted form or shape, such as a spiral ornamentation in the stem of a wineglass. **3** a bend or curve in a road or path, esp. one followed immediately by a curve in the opposite direction. **4 a** a complication, esp. an unexpected or ironic development in a story or in a person's life. **b** a slight change made to an existing model, usu. to add interest or flair (*the old story with a modern twist*). **5** usu. *derogatory* an eccentric inclination or attitude, esp. a peculiar mental bent. **6 a** a curled piece of lemon peel to flavour a drink. **b** an item of food having a spiral or twisted shape (*cinnamon twists*). **7** (prec. by *the*) a dance in which the upper and lower body are swivelled back and forth in opposite directions, popular in the early 1960s. **8** a sprain or strain of a limb. **9** *Physics* **a** a twisting strain or force; torque. **b** forward motion combined with rotation about an axis, e.g. the movement of a screw. □ **twist a person's arm** *informal* apply coercion to a person to overcome their reluctance to do something. **twist of fate** an ironic reversal of fortune. **twist the knife** cause further damage or mental pain, in addition to some previously inflicted. **twist in the wind** be left in a state of painful suspense or uncertainty. □ **twisty** *adj.* (**-ier, -iest**).

twisted *adj.* **1** (of a person, their mind, etc.) morally warped; perverted. **2** (of a story) having many complications and unexpected changes of plot. **3** misshapen, mangled. **4** (of an ankle etc.) sprained. **5** entwined. **6** (of the face or features) contorted.

twister *n.* **1** *N Amer.* a tornado. **2** a person or thing that twists.

twist-tie ● *n.* a small strip of plastic-covered wire which can be looped around something, esp. the neck of a plastic bag, and fastened by twisting the two ends together. ● *v.tr.* (**-ties, -tied, -tying**) fasten with this.

twit ● *n.* *slang* a silly or foolish person. ● *v.tr.* (**twitted, twitting**) reproach or scold, esp. in a good-humoured or teasing manner.

twitch ● *v.* **1** *intr.* (of the features, muscles, etc.) move or contract spasmodically. **b** *tr.* move (part of the body) spasmodically. **2** *tr.* give a short sharp pull at; jerk, tug. ● *n.* **1 a** a sudden involuntary contraction or movement of a muscle etc. **b** a pang; a twinge (*a twitch of irritation*). **2** a sudden sharp pull or jerk.

twitchy *adj.* (**-ier, -iest**) **1** having a tendency to twitch. **2** nervous, fidgety.

twitter ● *v.* **1** *intr.* **a** (of a bird) chirp with a succession of light tremulous sounds. **b** (of a person) laugh, titter. **2 a** *intr.* talk rapidly in a tremulous voice; chatter. **b** *tr.* utter or express in this way. ● *n.* **1** a light tremulous chirping. **2** *informal* a state of excitement. **3** a giggle or titter. □ **twitterer** *n.* **twittery** *adj.*

two ● *n.* **1** one more than one. **2** a symbol for this (2, ii, II). **3** two people or things identified contextually, such as parts or divisions, years of age, points in a game, etc. **4** a size etc. denoted by two. **5** two o'clock. **6** a card with two pips. ● *adj.* that amount to two. □ **in two** in or into two pieces. **or two** denoting several (*a thing or two*). **put two and two together** make (esp. an obvious) inference from what is known or evident. **that makes two of us** *informal* I am in the same position or am of the same opinion. **two by two** in pairs. **two can play at that game** *informal* I am equally capable of using a person's strategy, to their disadvantage.

two-and-a-half *n.* *Cdn* (*Que.*) an apartment having two rooms, typically a combined kitchen/living room and a bedroom, plus a bathroom.

two-bagger *n.* *informal* (also **two-base hit**) *Baseball* = DOUBLE 4.

two-bit *adj.* *N Amer. informal* **1** cheap, worthless, minor, small-time. **2** worth twenty-five cents.

two bits *n.* *N Amer. informal* twenty-five cents.

two-by-four *n.* a length of timber that has a rectangular cross-section of $1^1/_2$ inches by $3^1/_2$ inches (3.8 cm by 8.9 cm) when trimmed, or 2 inches by 4 inches (5.1 cm by 10.2 cm) when not trimmed.

two cents *n.pl.* (in full **two cents' worth**) *N Amer. informal* an unsolicited opinion.

two-cycle *adj.* *N Amer.* = TWO-STROKE.

2-D ● *adj.* having or portraying a two-dimensional

appearance. ● *n.* a format that presents two-dimensional images.

two-dimensional *adj.* **1** having or appearing to have length and width but no depth. **2** lacking depth or substance; superficial.

two-faced *adj.* insincere, deceitful, hypocritical.

two-fisted *adj.* *N Amer.* tough, aggressive, vigorous.

twofold *adj. & adv.* **1** twice as much or as many. **2** consisting of two parts.

two-four *n.* *Cdn informal* a case of twenty-four bottles of beer.

2,4-D *n.* a partially soluble white to yellow crystalline powder, the active ingredient in many herbicides.

two-handed *adj.* using or requiring two hands.

twoonie *Cdn var. of* TOONIE.

two-on-one *n.* (*pl.* **-ones**) **1** *Hockey* a rush led by two players against one defender and a goalie (also *attrib.*: *two-on-one break*). **2** *Basketball* a rush led by two players against one defender.

two per cent *n.* (also **2 per cent, 2%**) *N Amer.* partly skimmed milk containing two per cent milk fat.

two-piece ● *adj.* (esp. of a suit, snowsuit, bathing suit, etc.) consisting of two matching items. ● *n.* (also **two-piecer**) a two-piece suit or bathing suit etc.

two-ply ● *adj.* consisting of two strands or thicknesses. ● *n.* two-ply wool or wood etc.

two-pronged *adj.* having two aspects, stages, aims, or lines of attack.

two-seater *n.* a vehicle or aircraft with two seats.

two-sided *adj.* **1** having two sides. **2** having two aspects; controversial.

two solitudes *n.pl.* *Cdn* the anglophone and francophone populations of Canada, portrayed as two cultures coexisting independent of and isolated from each other.

twosome *n.* **1** two people together. **2** a game, dance, etc., for two people.

two-step ● *n.* a ballroom dance for couples involving a sliding step in march or polka time. ● *v.intr.* dance the two-step. ● *adj.* involving two successive actions or stages.

two-stroke *adj.* **1** (of an internal combustion engine) having its power cycle completed in one up-and-down movement of the piston. **2** (of a vehicle) having a two-stroke engine.

two-time *informal* ● *v.tr.* **1** be unfaithful to (esp. a lover or spouse). **2** swindle, double-cross. ● *adj.* having achieved a specified distinction twice (*two-time champion*). □ **two-timer** *n.*

two-tone *adj.* having two colours or two shades of the same colour. □ **two-toned** *adj.*

two-way *adj.* **1** involving two participants. **2** (of a radio) capable of transmitting and receiving signals. **3** (of a loudspeaker) having two separate drive units for different frequency ranges, a woofer and a tweeter. **4** (of traffic etc.) moving in two esp. opposite directions.

two-way mirror *n.* a panel of glass that is transparent from one side but reflects light and images from the other.

two-wheeler *n.* a vehicle with two wheels. □ **two-wheeled** *adj.*

Twp. *abbr.* Township.

TX *abbr.* (in postal use) Texas.

tycoon *n.* a business magnate.

tyee /'taii:/ *n.* *Cdn* (*BC*) a chinook salmon, esp. one weighing more than 13.6 kg (30 lb.).

tying *pres. part. of* TIE.

tyke *n.* **1** *informal* a small child. **2** *Cdn* **a** an initiation level of sports competition for young children. **b** a player at this level.

Tylenol *n.* N Amer. proprietary acetaminophen.

tympani *var.* of TIMPANI.

tympanic /tɪmˈpænɪk/ *adj.* **1** of or having a tympanum. **2** resembling or acting like a drumhead.

tympanic membrane *n.* Anat. = EARDRUM.

tympanum /ˈtɪmpənəm/ *n.* (pl. **tympana** /-nə/ or **-s**) **1** Anat. **a** = MIDDLE EAR. **b** = EARDRUM. **2** the membrane covering the hearing organ on the leg of an insect.

Tyndall stone /ˈtɪndəl/ *n.* (also **Tyndall limestone**) Cdn a variety of mottled dolomitic limestone quarried near Winnipeg, noted for the presence of a large number of fossils.

type ● *n.* **1 a** a class of people or things distinguished by common essential characteristics. **b** a kind or sort (*a new type of coffee*). **2** a person, thing, or event serving as an illustration, symbol, or characteristic specimen of another, or of a class. **3** (in *comb.*) made of, resembling, or functioning as. **4 a** a person of a particular specified or contextually implied character (*she's not the type to pick a fight*). **b** (prec. by possessive) the kind of person to whom one is attracted (*he's not my type*). **5 a** the general form, structure, or character distinguishing a particular group or class of things. **b** an object, conception, or work of art serving as a model for subsequent artists. **6** Printing **a** a character for printing, originally a metal casting from a matrix, reproducing a punch on which a letter or other character was engraved. **b** such pieces collectively, esp. with reference to size or font. **c** printed characters collectively (*printed in large type*). ● *v.* **1** *tr.* & *intr.* write with a typewriter. **2** *tr.* **a** assign to a type; classify. **b** Biol. & Med. determine the type to which (blood, tissue, etc.) belongs. **3** *tr.* = TYPECAST.

Type A *n.* (pl. **Type A's**) **1** a personality type characterized by ambition, impatience, and aggressive competitiveness, thought to be particularly susceptible to stress. **2** a person of this type.

Type B *n.* (pl. **Type B's**) **1** a personality type characterized as easygoing and thought to have low susceptibility to stress. **2** a person of this type.

typecast *v.tr.* (*past* and *past part.* **-cast**) (usu. in *passive*) **1** assign (an actor) repeatedly to the same type of role which he or she has often played successfully in previous productions or which seems to fit his or her personality. **2** consider (a person) as fitting a stereotype. ☐ **typecasting** *n.*

typed *adj.* **1** classified as or having a certain character or type. **2** = TYPEWRITTEN.

typeface *n.* **1 a** the particular style, appearance, size, etc. of a type or set of types. **b** Computing the design of a particular font. **2 a** the inked part of type. **b** the impression made by this.

typescript *n.* a typewritten document.

typesetter *n.* **1** a person who composes type. **2** a machine used for setting matter in type. ☐ **typeset** *v.tr.* & *intr.* (**-setting**; *past* and *past part.* **-set**). **typesetting** *n.*

typewriter *n.* a machine for producing characters like those used in printing by means of keys which, when pressed one at a time, cause a type mounted on a bar or ball to strike a sheet of paper inserted around a roller, through an inked ribbon. ☐ **typewriting** *n.*

typewritten *adj.* produced with a typewriter.

typhoid /ˈtaɪfɔɪd/ ● *n.* (in full **typhoid fever**) a severe infectious fever caused by the bacterium *Salmonella typhi*, involving a rash, myalgia, and in some cases delirium and intestinal inflammation. ● *adj.* resembling or characteristic of typhus.

typhoon /taɪˈfuːn/ *n.* a violent storm occurring in or around the Indian subcontinent, esp. a tropical cyclone occurring in the region of the Indian or W Pacific Oceans.

typhus /ˈtaɪfəs/ *n.* any of a group of acute infectious fevers caused by rickettsiae, often transmitted by lice or fleas, and characterized by a purple rash, headaches, fever, and usu. delirium.

typical *adj.* **1** serving as a characteristic example; representative (*a typical student*). **2** characteristic of or serving to distinguish a type (*a typical feature of Maritime architecture*). **3** (often foll. by *of*) conforming to expected esp. undesirable behaviour, attitudes, etc. (*it's typical of them to forget*). ☐ **typically** *adv.*

typify /ˈtɪpɪˌfaɪ/ *v.tr.* (**-ies**, **-ied**) **1** be a representative example of; embody the characteristics of. **2** serve as an emblem or symbol of; symbolize.

typist *n.* a person who types or uses a typewriter, esp. professionally.

typo *n.* (pl. **-os**) informal an error in typed or printed material, esp. resulting from a mistake in typing.

typography /taɪˈpɒɡrəfi/ *n.* **1** the art or practice of printing. **2** the process of printing. **3** the style and appearance of printed matter. ☐ **typographic** *adj.* **typographical** *adj.* **typographically** *adv.*

typology /taɪˈpɒlədʒi/ *n.* (pl. **-ies**) **1 a** the branch of knowledge that deals with classes with common characteristics. **b** a classification of esp. human behaviour or characteristics according to type. **2** the branch of religion that deals with esp. Biblical symbolic representation. ☐ **typological** *adj.* **typologically** *adv.* **typologist** *n.*

tyrannical /tɪˈrænɪkəl, tə-/ *adj.* **1** of or pertaining to a tyrant or tyranny (*a tyrannical regime*). **2** resembling or characteristic of a tyrant or tyranny (*his upbringing was tyrannical*). ☐ **tyrannically** *adv.*

tyrannize /ˈtɪrəˌnaɪz/ *v.* **1** *tr.* rule, control, or behave oppressively or cruelly towards. **2** *intr.* (usu. foll. by *over*) exercise power or control oppressively or cruelly.

tyrannosaur /təˈrænəsɔːr, taɪ-, tɪ-/ *n.* (also **tyrannosaurus** /-ˌrænəˈsɔːrəs/) a huge bipedal carnivorous dinosaur, *Tyrannosaurus rex*, having powerful hind legs and jaws, a large well-developed tail, and small claw-like front legs.

tyranny /ˈtɪrəni/ *n.* (pl. **-ies**) **1 a** the arbitrary, cruel, and excessive exercise of power, control, or authority. **b** (often foll. by *of*) an unduly oppressive influence (*the tyranny of public opinion*). **2** cruel and oppressive government by more than one person. **3** a tyrannical act; tyrannical behaviour. **4** Gk Hist. **a** rule by a tyrant. **b** a period of this. **c** a state ruled by a tyrant. ☐ **tyrannous** *adj.* **tyrannously** *adv.*

tyrant /ˈtaɪrənt/ *n.* **1** an oppressive or cruel ruler. **2** any person exercising power oppressively or cruelly. **3** Gk Hist. an absolute ruler who seizes power without legal right.

tyrant flycatcher *n.* any of various small birds of the New World family Tyrannidae, which catch insects by a short flight from a perch.

tyro /ˈtaɪˌroː/ *n.* (pl. **-os**) a beginner or novice.

Tyrolean /tɪˈroːliən, -rəˈliːən/ *adj.* of or characteristic of the Tyrol, an Alpine province of Austria.

tzatziki /tsætˈsiːki/ *n.* a Greek side dish of yogourt with cucumber, garlic, and sometimes mint.

Uu

U¹ *n.* (also **u**) (*pl.* **Us** or **U's**) **1** the twenty-first letter of the alphabet. **2** a U-shaped object or curve (esp. in *comb.*: *U bolt*).

U² *abbr.* (also **U.**) university.

U³ *symbol* uranium.

U⁴ *pron. informal* you (*While-U-Wait; U-pick*).

u *symbol* = MICRO- 2.

UAE *abbr.* United Arab Emirates.

UAR *abbr.* United Arab Republic.

UAW *abbr.* United Auto Workers.

ubiquitous /juːˈbɪkwɪtəs/ *adj.* **1** present everywhere or in several places simultaneously. **2** often encountered. □ **ubiquitously** *adv.* **ubiquity** *n.*

U-boat *n. hist.* a German submarine.

UC *abbr.* (in Canada) United Church.

u.c. *abbr.* upper case.

udder *n.* the mammary gland of cattle, sheep, etc., hanging as a bag-like organ with several teats.

UDI *abbr.* unilateral declaration of independence.

udon /ˈuːdɒn/ *n.* (in Japanese cooking) a thick strip of pasta made from wheat flour.

UEL *abbr. Cdn* UNITED EMPIRE LOYALIST.

UFA *abbr. Cdn* United Farmers of Alberta.

UFFI /ˈʌfi/ *n. Cdn* urea formaldehyde foam insulation.

UFO *n.* (*pl.* **UFOs**) an unidentified flying object, esp. one supposed to have come from outer space.

Ugandan /juːˈɡændən/● *adj.* of or relating to Uganda, a landlocked country in E Africa. ● *n.* a native or inhabitant of Uganda.

ugh *interj.* **1** expressing disgust or horror. **2** the sound of a cough or grunt.

Ugli *n.* (*pl.* **Uglies**) *proprietary* a mottled green and yellow citrus fruit, a hybrid of a grapefruit and tangerine.

ugly ● *adj.* (**-ier, -iest**) **1** unpleasing or repulsive to see or hear (*an ugly scar*). **2** unpleasantly suggestive; discreditable (*ugly rumours*). **3** threatening, dangerous (*the sky has an ugly look*). **4** morally repulsive; vile (*ugly vices*). **5** characterized by violence or hostility (*an ugly confrontation*). ● *n.* (*pl.* **uglies**) (in *pl.*) ugly or unpleasant things. □ **ugliness** *n.*

ugly duckling *n.* a person who turns out to be beautiful or talented etc. against all expectations.

Ugric /ˈuːɡrɪk, ˈjuː-/ ● *adj.* **1** of or relating to the eastern branch of Finnic peoples, esp. the Magyars. **2** of or relating to the group of Finno-Ugric languages including Magyar. ● *n.* the Ugric group of languages.

uh *interj. esp. N Amer.* expressing the sound made by a speaker who hesitates or is uncertain what to say.

UHF *abbr.* ultra-high frequency.

uh-huh *interj. informal* expressing assent or a non-committal response to a question or remark.

uh-oh *interj. esp. N Amer.* expressing sudden concern, worry, etc.

UHT *abbr.* ultra-high-temperature sterilization (used to designate esp. dairy products sterilized at very high temperatures so that they can be kept without refrigeration).

uh-uh *interj.* expressing a negative response to a question or remark; no.

UI *abbr.* (in Canada) unemployment insurance.

UIC *abbr. Cdn* **1** *hist.* Unemployment Insurance Commission. **2** *informal* unemployment insurance (*has been living on UIC*).

uillean pipes /ˈɪljən/ *n.* a form of Irish bagpipe in which the bag is inflated by bellows worked by the elbow.

U-joint *n.* = UNIVERSAL JOINT.

UK *abbr.* United Kingdom.

Uke *n.* (also **Ukie**) *Cdn dated informal* a Ukrainian.

Ukrainian ● *n.* **1** a native of Ukraine, a country in E Europe. **2** the Slavic language of Ukraine. ● *adj.* of or relating to Ukraine or its people or language.

Ukrainian Catholic ● *adj.* of or pertaining to an Eastern Church of the Catholic communion under the jurisdiction of the Metropolitan of Lviv, including large communities in Canada and the US. ● *n.* a member of this Church.

Ukrainian Christmas *n.* Christmas as celebrated by Ukrainian Christians on 7 Jan.

Ukrainian Easter egg *n.* = PYSANKA.

Ukrainian Orthodox *adj.* (also **Ukrainian Greek Orthodox**) of or pertaining to an Eastern Orthodox Church under the Patriarch of Kiev or the Patriarch of Moscow, including large communities in Canada and the US.

ukulele /juːkəˈleɪli/ *n.* a small four-stringed Hawaiian (originally Portuguese) guitar.

ulcer *n.* **1 a** an open sore on an external or internal surface of the body, often forming pus. **b** = PEPTIC ULCER. **2 a** a moral blemish. **b** a corroding or corrupting influence etc. □ **ulcerous** *adj.*

ulcerate *v.tr. & intr.* (often as **ulcerated** *adj.*) form into or affect with an ulcer. □ **ulceration** *n.* **ulcerative** /-rətɪv/ *adj.*

ulna /ˈʌlnə/ *n.* (*pl.* **ulnae** /-niː/) **1** the thinner and longer bone in the forearm, on the side opposite to the thumb (*compare* RADIUS 3). **2** a corresponding bone in an animal's foreleg or a bird's wing. □ **ulnar** *adj.*

ulterior /ʌlˈtɪərɪər/ *adj.* **1** existing in the background, or beyond what is evident or admitted; hidden, secret (*ulterior motive*). **2** situated beyond. **3** more remote; not immediate; in the future.

ultimate ● *adj.* **1** last, final. **2** beyond which no other exists or is possible (*the ultimate analysis*). **3** fundamental, primary, unanalyzable (*ultimate truths*). **4** maximum (*ultimate tensile strength*). **5** *informal* unsurpassed, best (*the ultimate car wash*). ● *n.* **1** (prec. by *the*) the best achievable or imaginable. **2** a final or fundamental fact or principle. **3** a non-contact field sport resembling football but using a Frisbee, in which passes may be made in any direction, but running with the Frisbee is prohibited. □ **ultimacy** /-məsi/ *n.* (*pl.* **-ies**). **ultimately** *adj.*

ultimatum /ʌltɪˈmeɪtəm/ *n.* (*pl.* **-s** or **ultimata** /-tə/) a final demand or statement of terms by one party, the rejection of which by another could cause a breakdown in relations, war, or an end of co-operation etc.

ultra ● *adj.* **1** favouring extreme views or measures, esp. in religion or politics. **2** going beyond what is usual or ordinary; extreme. ● *adv.* very, extremely; excessively. ● *n.* an extremist.

ultra- *comb. form* extreme(ly), excessive(ly).

ultra-high *adj.* **1** extremely high. **2** (of a frequency) in the range 300 to 3000 megahertz.

ultralight ● *n. N Amer.* a very small, light, low-speed, one- or two-seater aircraft with an open frame. ● *adj.* extremely light.

ultramarine ● *n.* **1 a** a brilliant blue pigment originally obtained from lapis lazuli. **b** an imitation of this. **2** the colour of this. ● *adj.* of this colour.

ultramicroscope *n.* an optical microscope used to reveal very small particles by means of light scattered by them.

ultramicroscopic *adj.* **1** too small to be seen by an ordinary optical microscope. **2** of or relating to an ultramicroscope.

ultramontane /ˌʌltrəˈmɒntein/ ● *adj.* **1** situated on the other side of the Alps from the point of view of the speaker. **2 a** advocating supreme papal authority in matters of faith and discipline. **b** *Cdn hist.* (in Quebec) advocating the subordination of the state to the Catholic Church. ● *n.* **1** a person living on the other side of the Alps. **2** a person advocating ultramontane views. □ **ultramontanism** /-ˈtɒnɪzəm/ *n.* **ultramontanist** *n.*

ultrasonic *adj.* of or involving sound waves with a frequency above the upper limit of human hearing. □ **ultrasonically** *adv.*

ultrasonics *n.pl.* (usu. treated as *sing.*) the science and application of ultrasonic waves.

ultrasound *n.* **1** sound having an ultrasonic frequency. **2** ultrasonic waves. **3 a** (also **ultrasonography** /ˌʌltrəsəˈnɒgrəfi/) an esp. diagnostic procedure using echoes of ultrasonic pulses to delineate objects or areas of different density in the body. **b** an image produced by such a procedure.

ultraviolet *adj. Physics* of or using electromagnetic radiation having a wavelength shorter than that of the violet end of the visible spectrum but longer than that of X-rays.

ultra vires /ˌʌltrə ˈvaiˌriːz, ˌoltrə ˈviːreiz/ *adv. & predic.adj.* beyond one's legal power or authority.

ulu /ˈuːluː/ *n.* an Inuit knife consisting of a crescent-shaped blade and a handle centred behind the non-cutting edge, traditionally used by women.

ululate /ˈʌljʊˌleit, ˈjuːl-/ *v.intr.* howl, wail. □ **ululation** *n.*

um *interj.* expressing hesitation or a pause in speech.

umbel /ˈʌmbəl/ *n.* a flower cluster in which stalks nearly equal in length spring from a common centre and form a flat or curved surface, as in parsley.

umbellifer /ʌmˈbelifər/ *n.* any plant of the family Umbelliferae bearing umbels, including parsley and carrot. □ **umbelliferous** *adj.*

umber ● *n.* **1** a natural pigment like ochre but darker and browner. **2** the colour of this. ● *adj.* **1** of this colour. **2** dark, dusky.

umbilical /ʌmˈbɪlɪkəl/ ● *attrib.adj.* **1** of, situated near, or affecting the navel. **2** linking, connecting. **3** inseparably linked. ● *n.* a flexible supply or control line, hose, etc., esp. from a main source to a site otherwise difficult to access.

umbilical cord *n.* **1** a flexible cordlike structure containing blood vessels and attaching a fetus to the placenta. **2** a supply cable linking a missile to its launcher, or an astronaut in space to a spacecraft.

umbilicus /ʌmˈbɪlɪkəs, ˌʌmbɪˈlaikəs/ *n.* (pl. **umbilici** /-ˌsai/) **1** *Anat.* the navel. **2** *Bot. & Zool.* a navel-like formation.

umbra /ˈʌmbrə/ *n.* (pl. **-s** or **umbrae** /-briː/) **1** the fully shaded inner region of a shadow cast by an opaque object, esp. the area on the earth or moon experiencing the total phase of an eclipse (compare PENUMBRA 1). **2** the dark central part of a sunspot.

umbrage /ˈʌmbrɪdʒ/ *n.* offence; a sense of slight or injury (took umbrage at the suggestion).

umbrella *n.* **1** a light portable device for protection against rain, strong sun, etc., consisting of a usu. circular canopy of cloth mounted by means of a collapsible metal frame on a central stick. **2** protection or patronage. **3** (often *attrib.*) a coordinating or unifying agency (umbrella organization). **4** a screen of fighter aircraft or a curtain of fire put up as a protection against enemy aircraft. **5** the gelatinous disc of a jellyfish etc., which it contracts and expands to move through the water. □ **umbrellaed** *adj.* **umbrella-like** *adj.*

Umbrian /ˈʌmbriən/ ● *adj.* of or relating to Umbria, a region of central Italy. ● *n.* **1** the language of ancient Umbria, related to Latin. **2** an inhabitant of ancient Umbria.

umiak /ˈuːmiˌæk/ *n.* a large, open, flat-bottomed boat made by stretching an animal hide over a wooden frame, traditionally used by Inuit women.

umlaut /ˈʊmlaut/ *n.* a mark (¨) used over a vowel, esp. in Germanic languages, to indicate a vowel change.

ump *esp. N Amer. informal* ● *n.* an umpire, esp. in baseball. ● *v.* **1** *intr.* act as umpire. **2** *tr.* act as umpire in (a game).

umph *var. of* OOMPH 1.

umpire ● *n.* **1** a person chosen to enforce the rules and settle disputes in various sports, e.g. baseball. **2** a person chosen to arbitrate between disputants, or to ensure fair play. ● *v.* **1** *intr.* (usu. foll. by *for, in,* etc.) act as umpire. **2** *tr.* act as umpire in (a game etc.).

umpteen *slang* ● *adj.* indefinitely many; a lot of. ● *pron.* indefinitely many. □ **umpteenth** *adj.*

un- *prefix* **1** added to adjectives and participles and their derivative nouns and adverbs, meaning: **a** not: denoting the absence of a quality or state (unusable; unhappiness). **b** the reverse of, usu. with an implication of approval or disapproval, or with some other special connotation (unselfish; unsociable; unscientific). **2** (less often) added to nouns, meaning 'a lack of' (unrest; untruth). **3** added to verbs and (less often) nouns, forming verbs denoting: **a** the reversal or cancellation of an action or state (undress; unlock; unsettle). **b** deprivation or separation (unmask). **c** release from (unburden; uncage). **d** causing to be no longer (unman). ¶The number of words that can be formed with this prefix is potentially as large as the number of adjectives in use; consequently only a selection, being considered the most current or semantically noteworthy, can be given here. ¶Words meaning 'the reverse of' (see sense 1b above) often have neutral counterparts in *non-* (see NON- 6) and counterparts in *in-* (see IN-¹). ¶In the case of some

---

unabashed *adj.*   **unabatedly** *adv.*   **unaccented** *adj.*   **unacceptably** *adv.*
unabashedly *adv.*   **unable** *adj.*   **unacceptability** *n.*   **unaccommodating** *adj.*
unabated *adj.*   **unabridged** *adj.*   **unacceptable** *adj.*

words with the prefix *un-*, there is ambiguity as to which prefix is meant, e.g. *undressed* can mean either 'not dressed' or 'no longer dressed'.

'un /ən/ *pron. informal* one (*young 'uns; a good 'un*).

unaccompanied /ˌʌnəˈkʌmpəniːd/ *adj.* **1** not accompanied, alone. **2** *Music* without accompaniment.

unaccountable /ˌʌnəˈkaʊntəbəl/ *adj.* **1** unable to be explained. **2** unpredictable or strange in behaviour. **3** not responsible. □ **unaccountability** *n.* **unaccountably** *adv.*

unaccounted /ˌʌnəˈkaʊntəd/ *adj.* of which no account is given. □ **unaccounted for** unexplained; not included in an account.

unaccustomed *adj.* **1** (usu. foll. by *to*) not accustomed. **2** not customary; unusual (*his unaccustomed silence*). □ **unaccustomedly** *adv.*

unadulterated *adj.* **1** not adulterated; concentrated. **2** complete, utter (*unadulterated nonsense*).

unaffected *adj.* **1** (usu. foll. by *by*) not affected. **2** free from affectation; genuine; sincere. □ **unaffectedly** *adv.* **unaffectedness** *n.*

unalloyed *adj.* **1** not alloyed; pure. **2** complete; utter.

un-American *adj.* **1** not in accordance with American attitudes etc. **2** contrary to the interests of the US; (in the US) treasonable. □ **un-Americanism** *n.*

unanimous /juːˈnænɪməs/ *adj.* **1** all in agreement (*the committee was unanimous*). **2** (of an opinion, vote, etc.) held or given by general consent (*the unanimous choice*). □ **unanimity** *n.* **unanimously** *adv.*

unanswerable *adj.* **1** unable to be answered (*an unanswerable question*). **2** unable to be refuted (*has an unanswerable case*). □ **unanswerably** *adv.*

unapproachable *adj.* **1** not approachable; remote, inaccessible. **2** (of a person) unfriendly. □ **unapproachability** *n.* **unapproachably** *adv.*

unashamed *adj.* **1** feeling no guilt, shameless. **2** blatant; bold. □ **unashamedly** *adv.*

unasked *adj.* (often foll. by *for*) not asked, requested, or invited.

unassailable *adj.* unable to be attacked or questioned. □ **unassailability** *n.*

unassisted *adj.* **1** not assisted. **2** *Hockey* (of a goal) scored by a player who takes possession of the puck from the opposing team rather than receiving it from a teammate.

unassumed *adj. Cdn* (of a road) not taken over for maintenance by a local authority; privately owned.

unassuming *adj.* not pretentious or arrogant; modest. □ **unassumingly** *adv.*

unattached *adj.* **1** (often foll. by *to*) not attached, esp. to a particular body, organization, etc. **2** not engaged or married; not having a boyfriend or girlfriend.

unattended *adj.* **1 a** unsupervised; alone (*don't leave your child unattended*). **b** with the owner not present (*unattended cars will be towed*). **2** (usu. foll. by *to*) not made the object of one's attention, concern, etc.; not dealt with (*letters unattended to*).

unattributable *adj.* (esp. of information) that cannot or may not be attributed to a source etc. □ **unattributably** *adv.*

unauthorized *adj.* **1** not authorized. **2** (of a biography) written without the consent and co-operation of the subject.

unavailing *adj.* achieving nothing; ineffectual.

unaware ● *adj.* not aware (*unaware of her presence*). ● *adv.* = UNAWARES. □ **unawareness** *n.*

unawares *adv.* **1** unexpectedly (*met them unawares*). **2** inadvertently (*dropped it unawares*).

unbalance ● *v.tr.* upset the physical or mental balance of. ● *n.* lack of balance; instability, esp. mental.

unbalanced *adj.* **1** not balanced. **2** (of a mind or a person) unstable or deranged.

unban *v.tr.* (**unbanned, unbanning**) remove a ban or prohibition from (a publication, person, group, etc.); lift official restrictions on. □ **unbanning** *n.*

unbeatable *adj.* **1** not beatable; unable to be defeated. **2** superlative, excellent; that cannot be improved (*unbeatable prices*).

unbeaten *adj.* **1** not beaten. **2** (of a record etc.) not surpassed.

unbecoming *adj.* **1** (esp. of clothing) not flattering or suiting a person. **2** (often foll. by *to, for*) not fitting; indecorous or unsuitable. □ **unbecomingly** *adv.*

unbeknownst *adj.* (also **unbeknown**) (foll. by *to*) without the knowledge of (*was there all the time unbeknownst to us*).

unbelief *n.* lack of belief, esp. in religious matters. □ **unbeliever** *n.* **unbelieving** *adj.* **unbelievingly** *adv.*

unbend *v.* (*past* and *past part.* **unbent**) **1** *tr. & intr.* change from a bent position. **2** *intr.* relax from strain or severity; become affable. □ **unbendable** *adj.*

---

unacknowledged *adj.*	**unambitiously** *adv.*	**unapproved** *adj.*	**unauthentically** *adv.*
unadaptable *adj.*	**unanalyzable** *adj.*	**unarguable** *adj.*	**unauthenticated** *adj.*
unaddressed *adj.*	(also **unanalysable**)	**unarguably** *adv.*	**unavailability** *n.*
unadorned *adj.*	**unanalyzed** *adj.*	**unarm** *v.tr.*	**unavailable** *adj.*
unadventurous *adj.*	(also **unanalysed**)	**unarmed** *adj.*	**unavailableness** *n.*
unaffiliated *adj.*	**unannounced** *adj.*	**unarticulated** *adj.*	**unavoidability** *n.*
unaffordable *adj.*	**unanswered** *adj.*	**unascertained** *adj.*	**unavoidable** *adj.*
unafraid *adj.*	**unanticipated** *adj.*	**unassertive** *adj.*	**unavoidably** *adv.*
unaggressive *adj.*	**unapologetic** *adj.*	**unassertively** *adv.*	**unbaked** *adj.*
unaided *adj.*	**unapologetically** *adv.*	**unassertiveness** *n.*	**unbearable** *adj.*
unalterable *adj.*	**unappealing** *adj.*	**unassuageable** *adj.*	**unbearableness** *n.*
unalterableness *n.*	**unappealingly** *adv.*	**unassuaged** *adj.*	**unbearably** *adv.*
unalterably *adv.*	**unappeasable** *adj.*	**unattainable** *adj.*	**unbelievability** *n.*
unaltered *adj.*	**unappetizing** *adj.*	**unattractive** *adj.*	**unbelievable** *adj.*
unambiguous *adj.*	**unappetizingly** *adv.*	**unattractively** *adv.*	**unbelievably** *adv.*
unambiguously *adv.*	**unappreciated** *adj.*	**unattractiveness** *n.*	
unambitious *adj.*	**unappreciative** *adj.*	**unauthentic** *adj.*	

unbending *adj.* **1** not bending; inflexible. **2** firm; austere (*unbending rectitude*). □ **unbendingly** *adv.* **unbendingness** *n.*

unbidden *adj.* **1** not commanded or invited (*arrived unbidden*). **2** without conscious effort; spontaneous.

unblinking *adj.* **1** not blinking. **2** steadfast; not hesitating. **3** stolid; cool. □ **unblinkingly** *adv.*

unblock *v.tr.* remove an obstruction from (esp. a pipe, drain, etc.); open up, clear.

unbolted *adj.* **1** not bolted. **2** (of flour etc.) not sifted.

unborn *adj.* **1** not yet born (*an unborn child*). **2** never to be brought into being (*unborn hopes*).

unbound *adj.* **1** not bound or tied up. **2** unconstrained. **3 a** (of a book) not having a binding. **b** having paper covers.

unbounded *adj.* not bounded; infinite (*unbounded optimism*). □ **unboundedly** *adv.* **unboundedness** *n.*

unbowed *adj.* (usu. *predic.*) undaunted.

unbranched *adj.* not having or divided into branches.

unbridled *adj.* unconstrained (*unbridled insolence*).

unbroken *adj.* **1** not broken. **2** not tamed (*an unbroken horse*). **3** not crushed in health or spirit; not subdued or weakened. **4** (of ground) not broken up by digging etc. **5** not interrupted or disturbed (*unbroken sleep*). **6** not surpassed (*an unbroken record*).

unbuckle *v.tr.* release the buckle of (a strap etc.).

unbudgeable *adj. informal* that cannot be moved.

unbuild *v.tr.* (*past* and *past part.* **unbuilt**) demolish or destroy (a building, theory, system, etc.).

unbuilt *adj.* not yet built or (of land) not yet built on.

unbundle *v.tr.* **1** unpack; remove from a bundle. **2** market or price (goods or services) as individual items rather than as part of a package. **3** split (a company) into separate businesses.

unburden *v.tr.* **1** relieve of a burden. **2** (esp. *refl.*; often foll. by *to*) relieve (oneself, one's conscience, etc.) by confession etc. □ **unburdened** *adj.*

unburned *adj.* (also **unburnt**) **1** not consumed by fire. **2** not scorched; not damaged by fire etc.

unbutton *v.* **1** *tr.* **a** unfasten (a coat etc.) by taking the buttons out of the buttonholes. **b** unbutton the clothes of (a person). **2** *intr. informal* relax from tension or formality, become communicative.

unbuttoned *adj.* **1** not buttoned. **2** *informal* communicative, unrestrained, informal.

uncalled *adj.* not summoned or invited. □ **uncalled for** (hyphenated when *attrib.*) (of an opinion, action, etc.) impertinent or unnecessary (*an uncalled-for remark*).

un-Canadian *adj.* not in accordance with Canadian characteristics, practices, etc.

uncanny /ʌnˈkæni/ *adj.* (**-ier**, **-iest**) **1** seemingly supernatural; mysterious. **2** of an unsettling accuracy, intensity, etc. (*an uncanny resemblance*). □ **uncannily** *adv.* **uncanniness** *n.*

uncap *v.tr.* (**uncapped, uncapping**) remove the cap from (a jar, bottle, etc.).

uncaring *adj.* **1** neglectful. **2** lacking compassion.

unceasing *adj.* continuous (*unceasing effort*). □ **unceasingly** *adv.*

UNCED *abbr.* United Nations Conference on Environment and Development.

unceremonious *adj.* **1** lacking ceremony or formality. **2** abrupt; discourteous. □ **unceremoniously** *adv.* **unceremoniousness** *n.*

uncertain *adj.* **1** not certainly knowing or known (*the result is uncertain*). **2** unreliable (*his aim is uncertain*). **3** changeable, erratic (*uncertain weather*). **4** not confident; hesitant. □ **in no uncertain terms** clearly and forcefully. □ **uncertainly** *adv.*

uncertainty *n.* (*pl.* **-ies**) **1** the fact or condition of being uncertain. **2** an uncertain matter or circumstance.

uncertified *adj.* **1** not attested as certain. **2** not guaranteed by a certificate of competence etc. **3** not certified as insane.

unchallenging *adj.* not presenting a challenge or other stimulation.

uncharitable *adj.* unkind, harsh, and unsympathetic. □ **uncharitableness** *n.* **uncharitably** *adv.*

uncharted *adj.* not charted, mapped, or surveyed.

unchecked *adj.* **1** not checked. **2** freely allowed; unrestrained (*unchecked violence*).

unchristian *adj.* **1** contrary to Christian principles, esp. uncaring or selfish. **2** not Christian.

unchurch *v.tr.* excommunicate.

unchurched *adj.* not associated with a church; not churchgoing.

uncial /ˈʌnsiəl, -ʃəl/ *adj.* of or written in majuscule writing with rounded unjoined letters found in manuscripts of the 4th–8th c., from which modern capitals are derived.

uncivil *adj.* ill-mannered; impolite. □ **uncivilly** *adv.*

uncivilized *adj.* **1** not civilized. **2** rough; uncultured.

unclasp *v.tr.* **1** loosen the clasp or clasps of. **2** release the grip of (a hand etc.).

unclassified *adj.* **1** not classified. **2** (of state information) not secret.

uncle /ˈʌŋkəl/ *n.* **1 a** the brother of one's father or mother. **b** an aunt's husband. **2** *informal* a name given by children to a male family friend. **3** *Cdn* (*Nfld*) a term of respectful address to an older man. □ **cry** (or **say** or **yell**) **uncle** *N Amer. informal* surrender; admit defeat; yell for mercy.

unclean *adj.* **1** not clean. **2** unchaste. **3** unfit to be eaten; ceremonially impure. **4** *Bible* (of a spirit) wicked. □ **uncleanly** *adv.* **uncleanly** /ʌnˈklɛnli/ *adj.* **uncleanliness** *n.*

unclear *adj.* **1** not clear or easy to understand; obscure, uncertain. **2** (of a person) doubtful, uncertain (*I'm unclear as to what you mean*).

uncleared *adj.* **1** (of land) not cleared of trees etc. **2** not cleared away or up.

---

unbiased *adj.*
unbind *v.tr.* (*past* and *past part.* **unbound**)
unbleached *adj.*
unblemished *adj.*
unbothered *adj.*
unbreakable *adj.*
unbreathable *adj.*

unbridgeable *adj.*
unburied *adj.*
unbusinesslike *adj.*
uncarpeted *adj.*
uncastrated *adj.*
uncatalogued *adj.*
uncensored *adj.*
unchallengeable *adj.*

unchallengeably *adv.*
unchallenged *adj.*
unchangeable *adj.*
unchangeableness *n.*
unchangeably *adv.*
unchanged *adj.*
unchanging *adj.*
unchangingly *adv.*

uncharacteristic *adj.*
uncharacteristically *adv.*
uncharged *adj.*
unchaste *adj.*
unchastely *adv.*
unchastity *n.*
unclaimed *adj.*
unclassifiable *adj.*

unclench v. **1** tr. release (clenched hands, features, teeth, etc.). **2** intr. (of clenched hands etc.) become relaxed or open.

Uncle Sam n. informal a personification of the federal government or citizens of the US.

Uncle Tom n. derogatory a black man considered to be servile, cringing, etc.

unclip v.tr. release from being fastened or held with a clip.

unclog v.tr. (**unclogged**, **unclogging**) unblock (a drain, pipe, etc.).

unclothe v.tr. **1** remove the clothes from. **2** expose, reveal. □ **unclothed** adj.

unclouded adj. **1** not clouded; clear; bright. **2** untroubled (*unclouded serenity*).

uncoil v.tr. & intr. unwind.

uncollected adj. **1** left awaiting collection. **2** (of money) not collected or claimed. **3** (of literary work) not gathered into a collection for publication.

uncoloured adj. (also **uncolored**) **1** having no colour. **2** not having been coloured. **3** not influenced; impartial. **4** not exaggerated.

uncomfortable adj. **1** not comfortable. **2** uneasy; causing or feeling disquiet (*an uncomfortable silence*). □ **uncomfortableness** n. **uncomfortably** adv.

uncommitted adj. **1** not committed. **2** unattached to any specific political cause or group.

uncommon adj. **1** not common; unusual. **2** remarkably great etc. (*an uncommon fear of spiders*). □ **uncommonly** adv. **uncommonness** n.

uncommunicative adj. not wanting to communicate; taciturn.

uncompounded adj. not compounded; unmixed.

uncompromising adj. unwilling to compromise; stubborn; unyielding. □ **uncompromisingly** adv.

unconcern n. indifference; apathy. □ **unconcerned** adj. **unconcernedly** adv.

unconditional adj. not subject to conditions (*unconditional surrender*). □ **unconditionality** n. **unconditionally** adv.

unconnected adj. **1** not physically joined. **2** not connected or associated. **3** (of speech etc.) disconnected; not joined in order or sequence (*unconnected ideas*). □ **unconnectedly** adv.

unconscionable adj. **1 a** having no conscience. **b** contrary to conscience. **2 a** unreasonably excessive (*an unconscionable length of time*). **b** not right or reasonable. □ **unconscionably** adv.

unconscious ● adj. not conscious. ● n. that part of the mind which is inaccessible to the conscious mind but which affects behaviour, emotions, etc. (compare COLLECTIVE UNCONSCIOUS). □ **unconsciously** adv. **unconsciousness** n.

unconstitutional adj. not in accordance with the political constitution or with procedural rules. □ **unconstitutionality** n. **unconstitutionally** adv.

unconventional adj. not bound by convention or custom; unusual; unorthodox. □ **unconventionality** n. **unconventionally** adv.

uncool adj. slang not stylish or fashionable; not having street credibility.

uncoordinated adj. **1** not coordinated. **2** (of a person, a person's movements etc.) clumsy.

uncork v.tr. draw the cork from (a bottle etc.).

uncountable adj. inestimable, immense.

uncountable noun n. a noun that cannot form a plural or be used with the indefinite article, e.g. *happiness*.

uncounted adj. **1** not counted. **2** very many; innumerable.

uncouple v. **1** tr. unfasten, disconnect, detach. **2** tr. release (railway cars) from couplings. **3** intr. (of a couple) break up. □ **uncoupled** adj.

uncouth adj. (of a person, manners, appearance, etc.) lacking in ease and polish; uncultured, rough. □ **uncouthly** adv. **uncouthness** n.

uncover v.tr. **1** remove a cover or covering from. **2** make known; disclose (*uncovered the truth at last*).

uncovered adj. **1** not covered by a roof, clothing, etc. **2** not wearing a hat.

uncreated adj. existing without having been created; not created.

uncredited adj. not acknowledged as the author, actor, etc.

uncritical adj. **1** not critical; complacently accepting. **2** not in accordance with the principles of criticism. □ **uncritically** adv.

uncross v.tr. remove (the limbs, knives, etc.) from a crossed position.

unction /ˈʌŋkʃən/ n. **1 a** the act of anointing with oil etc. as a religious rite. **b** the oil etc. so used. **2 a** soothing words or thought. **b** excessive or insincere flattery. **3 a** the act of anointing for medical purposes. **b** an ointment so used. **4 a** a fervent or sympathetic quality in words or tone caused by or causing deep emotion. **b** a pretense of this.

unctuous /ˈʌŋktʃʊəs/ adj. **1** (of behaviour, speech, etc.) unpleasantly flattering. **2** oily. □ **unctuously** adv. **unctuousness** n.

uncultivated adj. (esp. of land) not cultivated.

uncultured adj. not cultured, unrefined.

uncured adj. **1** not cured. **2** (of pork etc.) not salted or smoked.

uncurl v.intr. & tr. relax from a curled position, untwist.

uncut adj. **1** not cut. **2** (of a book, film, etc.) complete; uncensored. **3** (of a stone, esp. a diamond) not shaped by cutting. **4** (of alcohol etc.) unadulterated.

---

uncluttered adj.
uncoated adj.
uncombed adj.
uncompetitive adj.
uncomplaining adj.
uncomplainingly adv.
uncompleted adj.
uncomplicated adj.
uncomplimentary adj.
uncomprehending adj.
uncomprehendingly adv.

uncomprehension n.
uncompressed adj.
unconcealed adj.
unconcluded adj.
unconfined adj.
unconfirmed adj.
uncongenial adj.
unconquerable adj.
unconquerably adv.
unconquered adj.
unconstrained adj.

uncontaminated adj.
uncontested adj.
uncontestedly adv.
uncontrollable adj.
uncontrollableness n.
uncontrollably adv.
uncontrolled adj.
uncontroversial adj.
uncontroversially adv.
unconvinced adj.
unconvincing adj.

unconvincingly adv.
uncooked adj.
uncooperative adj.
uncooperatively adv.
uncorrected adj.
uncorrupted adj.
uncreative adj.
uncrowded adj.
uncurtained adj.

undead ● *adj.* (esp. of a vampire etc. in fiction) technically dead but still animate. ● *n.* (prec. by *the*; treated as *pl.*) those who are undead.

undecidable *adj.* that cannot be established or refuted; uncertain. □ **undecidability** *n.*

undecided ● *adj.* **1** not settled or certain (*the question is undecided*). **2** hesitating; irresolute (*undecided about their relative merits*). ● *n.* a person who is undecided, esp. as regards a vote. □ **undecidedly** *adv.*

undecorated *adj.* **1** not adorned; plain. **2** not honoured with an award.

undefined *adj.* **1** not defined. **2** not clearly marked; vague. □ **undefinable** *adj.* **undefinably** *adv.*

undeniable *adj.* **1** unable to be denied or disputed; certain. **2** excellent (*was of undeniable character*). □ **undeniably** *adv.*

under ● *prep.* **1 a** in or to a position lower than; below; beneath (*fell under the table; under the left eye*). **b** within, on the inside of (a surface etc.) (*wore a vest under his shirt*). **2 a** inferior to; less than (*is under 18*). **b** at or for a lower cost than (*was under $20*). **3 a** subject or liable to; controlled or bound by (*lives under oppression; the country prospered under him*). **b** undergoing (*is under repair*). **c** classified or subsumed in (*that book goes under biology*). **4** at the foot of or sheltered by (*hid under the wall; under the cliff*). ● *adv.* **1** in or to a lower position or condition (*kept him under*). **2** *informal* in or into a state of unconsciousness (*put him under for the operation*). ● *adj.* lower (*the under jaw*). □ **under separate cover** in another envelope. **under the sun** anywhere in the world. **under water** in and covered by water. □ **undermost** *adj.*

under- *prefix in senses of* UNDER: **1** below, beneath (*undercarriage; underground*). **2** lower in status; subordinate (*undersecretary*). **3** insufficiently, incompletely (*undercook; underdeveloped*).

underachieve *v.intr.* do less well than might be expected (esp. scholastically). □ **underachievement** *n.* **underachiever** *n.*

underage *adj.* **1** not old enough, esp. not yet of adult status. **2** (of an activity) carried on by a person below the legal age for the activity (*underage drinking*).

underarm ● *adj.* **1** *Sport* = UNDERHAND *adj.* 1. **2** in, of, or for the armpit (*underarm deodorant*). ● *adv.* = UNDERHAND *adv.* ● *n.* the armpit.

underbelly *n.* (*pl.* **-ies**) **1** the undersurface of an animal etc. **2** an area etc. vulnerable to attack. **3** a hidden, unpleasant, or criminal part of society.

underbid ● *v.tr. & intr.* (**underbidding**; *past* and *past part.* **underbid**) make a lower bid than (a person). ● *n.* the act or an instance of underbidding.

underbrush *n.* N Amer. undergrowth in a forest.

undercapitalize *v.tr.* (esp. as **undercapitalized** *adj.*) provide (a business etc.) with insufficient capital to achieve a desired result.

undercarriage *n.* **1** the supporting frame of a vehicle. **2** a structure of wheels or floats beneath an aircraft to receive the impact on landing and support the aircraft on the ground, water, etc.

underclass *n.* a subordinate social class.

underclothes *n.pl.* clothes worn under others, esp. next to the skin; underwear.

underclothing *n.* underclothes collectively.

undercoat *n.* **1 a** a preliminary layer of paint under the finishing coat. **b** the paint used for this. **2** an animal's under layer of hair or down. **3** a coat worn under another. □ **undercoating** *n.*

undercook *v.tr.* cook insufficiently. □ **undercooked** *adj.*

undercover *adj.* (usu. *attrib.*) **1** surreptitious. **2** engaged in spying, esp. by working with or among those to be observed (*undercover agent*).

undercurrent *n.* **1** a current below the surface. **2** an underlying often contrary feeling, activity, or influence (*an undercurrent of protest*).

undercut ● *v.tr.* (**-cutting**; *past* and *past part.* **-cut**) **1** sell or work at a lower price or lower wages than. **2** *Golf etc.* strike (a ball) so as to make it rise high. **3** **a** cut away the part below or under (a thing). **b** cut away material to show (a carved design etc.) in relief. **4** render unstable or less firm, undermine. ● *n.* **1** N Amer. a notch cut in a tree trunk to guide its fall when felled. **2** any space formed by the removal or absence of material from the lower part of something.

underdeveloped *adj.* **1** not fully developed; immature. **2** (of a country etc.) below its potential economic level. **3** *Photog.* not developed sufficiently to give a normal image. □ **underdevelopment** *n.*

underdog *n.* **1** a person, team, etc. thought to be in a weaker position, and therefore not likely to win a competition, fight, etc. **2** a person who is in a state of inferiority or subjection.

underdress *v.tr. & intr.* dress too plainly or too lightly.

undereducated *adj.* poorly educated.

underemphasize *v.tr.* place an insufficient degree of emphasis on. □ **underemphasis** *n.* (*pl.* **-emphases**).

underemployed *adj.* **1** employed at a task that uses less than one's full talents or abilities. **2** employed less than full-time. **3** (of a facility etc.) used less than it could be. □ **underemployment** *n.*

underestimate ● *v.tr.* **1** fail to recognize the strength, skill, etc. of a person, esp. an opponent. **2** form too low an opinion or estimate of. ● *n.* an estimate that is too low. □ **underestimation** *n.*

underexpose *v.tr.* **1** use too short an exposure or too narrow an aperture with (a film) or when photographing (a subject), resulting in a darkened picture. **2** expose (a person etc.) too little to the public eye. □ **underexposure** *n.*

underfed *adj.* insufficiently fed.

underfoot *adv.* **1** beneath one's feet; on the ground. **2** sitting, lying, etc. right at or around one's feet so as to obstruct or inconvenience; in the way. **3** in a state of subjection.

underfunded *adj.* not having sufficient funding. □ **underfund** *v.tr.* **underfunding** *n.*

under-fur *n.* an inner layer of short fur or down underlying an animal's outer fur.

undergarment *n.* an article of underclothing.

undergird *v.tr.* **1** make secure underneath. **2** strengthen, support (*trust undergirds love*).

---

undamaged *adj.*	**undecipherable** *adj.*	**undefended** *adj.*	**undemocratic** *adj.*
undated *adj.*	**undeclared** *adj.*	**undefiled** *adj.*	**undemocratically** *adv.*
undaunted *adj.*	**undefeated** *adj.*	**undemanding** *adj.*	**undependable** *adj.*

undergo *v.tr.* (3rd sing. present **-goes**; past **-went**; past part. **-gone**) experience.

undergrad *n. & adj. informal* = UNDERGRADUATE.

undergraduate ● *n.* a student at a university who has not yet completed a bachelor's degree. ● *adj.* **1** of or related to an undergraduate or undergraduates. **2** of or related to the course of study of a student completing a bachelor's degree.

underground ● *adv.* **1** beneath the surface of the ground. **2** into hiding or some secret activity. ● *adj.* **1** situated beneath the surface of the ground. **2 a** secret, hidden, not open to the public. **b** designating a secret group, movement, or activity, esp. one aiming to subvert an established order or a ruling power. **3 a** of or pertaining to a subculture seeking to provide alternatives to the socially accepted or established mode. **b** unconventional, experimental (*underground press*). ● *n.* **1** a secret group or activity, esp. aiming to challenge or subvert a ruling power. **2** a subculture seeking to provide radical alternatives to the socially accepted or established mode. **3** a place below the surface of the earth.

underground economy *n.* financial transactions not officially declared or recorded.

Underground Railroad *n.* (also *Cdn* **Underground Railway**) *hist.* a secret network of safe houses and transportation established to help fugitive slaves escape from the southern US to Canada and the Free States of the American North in the years before the Civil War.

undergrowth *n.* a dense growth of shrubs etc., esp. under large trees.

underhand ● *adj.* **1** *Sport* (of a throw, pitch, serve, etc.) performed with the hand lower than the level of the shoulders. **2** = UNDERHANDED 1, 2. ● *adv.* (throw or pitch etc.) with the hand lower than the level of the shoulder. ● *v.tr.* throw (a ball etc.) with the hand below the level of the shoulder.

underhanded ● *adj.* **1** deceptive, crafty. **2** secret, clandestine, surreptitious. **3** = UNDERHAND 1. ● *adv.* = UNDERHAND.

underlay ● *v.tr.* (past and past part. **-laid**) lay something under (a thing) to support or raise it. ● *n.* a thing laid under another, esp. material laid under a carpet or mattress as protection or support.

underlie *v.tr.* (**-lying**; past **-lay**; past part. **-lain**) **1** lie or be situated under (a stratum etc.). **2** (of a principle, reason, etc.) be the basis of (a doctrine, law, conduct, etc.) **3** exist beneath the superficial aspect of.

underline ● *v.tr.* **1** draw a line under (a word etc.) to give emphasis or draw attention or indicate italic or other special type. **2** emphasize, stress. ● *n.* **1** a line drawn under a word etc. **2** a caption below an illustration. □ **underlining** *n.*

underling *n.* usu. derogatory a subordinate.

underlying ● *v. pres. part.* of UNDERLIE. ● *adj.* **1** lying under or beneath the surface. **2 a** having a visible effect though not immediately obvious or openly present (*an underlying cause*). **b** fundamental, basic (*underlying principle*).

undermanned *adj.* having too few people such as crew or staff.

undermine *v.tr.* **1** weaken, injure, destroy, ruin (a person, reputation, health, etc.) by secret or insidious means. **2** wear away the base or foundation of (*rivers undermine their banks*). **3** dig a tunnel or excavate beneath (a wall etc.). □ **underminer** *n.*

underneath ● *prep.* **1** at or to a lower place than: directly below. **2** below or behind a covering of (*she wore a shirt underneath her sweater*). ● *adv.* **1** at or to a lower place. **2** directly beneath or covered by something (*the cat was underneath the covers*). ● *n.* the lower surface or part. ● *adj.* lower.

undernourished *adj.* insufficiently nourished. □ **undernourishment** *n.*

underpad *n.* a layer of foam laid under carpeting to provide cushioning and protect the floor.

underpants *n.pl.* an article of underclothing worn to cover the hips, crotch, and sometimes the thighs.

underpart *n.* the lower part or underside of anything, esp. an animal.

underpass *n.* a section of road etc. providing a passage beneath another road, railway, etc.

underpay *v.tr.* (past and past part. **-paid**) pay (an employee etc.) too little. □ **underpaid** *adj.* **underpayment** *n.*

underperform *v.* **1** *intr.* perform less well or be less profitable than expected. **2** *tr.* perform less well or be less profitable than. □ **underperformance** *n.*

underpin *v.tr.* (**-pinned**, **-pinning**) **1** form the basis for; support, strengthen. **2** support or strengthen (a building etc.) from below, esp. by laying a solid foundation.

underpinning *n.* **1** a thing or structure that supports or strengthens. **2** (in *pl.*) a basis, foundation, or underlying principle.

underplay *v.* **1** *tr.* play down the importance of. **2** *tr. & intr. Theatre* **a** perform with deliberate restraint. **b** act a part etc. with insufficient force.

underpopulated *adj.* having an insufficient or very small population. □ **underpopulation** *n.*

underpowered *adj.* **1 a** lacking full electrical, mechanical, etc. power. **b** lacking sufficient amplification. **2** with insufficient authority.

underprice *v.tr.* **1** price lower than what is usual or appropriate. **2** undercut (a competitor) in price.

underprivileged ● *adj.* **1** less privileged than others; deprived. **2** not enjoying the normal standard of living or rights in a society. ● *n.* (prec. by *the*; treated as *pl.*) underprivileged people.

underrate *v.tr.* have too low an opinion of; underestimate. □ **underrated** *adj.*

under-report *v.tr.* fail to report fully.

under-represent *v.tr.* provide with inadequate or insufficient representation.

underscore *n. & v.* = UNDERLINE.

undersea *adj.* below the sea or the surface of the sea.

undersecretary *n.* (*pl.* **-ies**) a subordinate official, esp. a junior minister or senior civil servant.

undersell *v.tr.* (past and past part. **-sold**) **1** sell at a lower price than (another seller). **2** sell at less than the true value.

undershirt *n.* *N Amer.* a light usu. cotton knitted short-sleeved or sleeveless shirt with no collar worn as an article of underclothing.

undershorts *n.pl.* *N Amer.* men's underpants.

underside *n.* (also in *pl.*) the lower side or bottom; the surface underneath.

undersigned *adj.* whose signature is appended below (*we, the undersigned, wish to state...*).

undersized *adj.* (also **undersize**) of less than the usual size.

underskirt *n.* a skirt worn under another; a petticoat.

undersold past and past part. of UNDERSELL.

understaffed *adj.* having too few staff. □ **understaffing** *n.*

understand *v.* (past and past part. **-stood**) **1** *tr.* perceive the meaning of (words, a person, etc.). **2** *tr.* perceive the significance, explanation, or cause of (*I don't understand why he came*). **3 a** *tr.* have a sympathetic awareness of the character or nature of; know how to deal with, be sympathetic to (*nobody really understands me*). **b** *tr. & intr.* accept without anger or resentment (*if you can't come, I'll understand*). **4 a** *tr. & intr.* be conversant or familiar with, have a mastery of (a subject, skill, etc.) (*she understands hockey*). **b** *tr.* be sufficiently acquainted with (a language) to be able to interpret the meaning of the words employed. **5** *tr.* accept as true without positive knowledge or certainty; learn, gather, infer (*am I to understand that you refuse?*). **6** *tr.* supply (a word) mentally (*the verb may be either expressed or understood*). **7** *intr.* have understanding (in general or in particular) (*you don't have to explain, I understand perfectly*). □ **understand each other 1** know each other's views or feelings. **2** be in agreement or collusion.

understandable *adj.* **1** that one might expect; natural or reasonable (*it is an understandable mistake*). **2** comprehensible (*very understandable instructions*). □ **understandability** *n.* **understandably** *adv.*

understanding ● *n.* **1** the ability to reason and comprehend; intellect. **2 a** an individual's perception or interpretation of a situation etc. **b** a person's knowledge of a subject. **3** an agreement; a thing agreed upon, esp. informally (*had an understanding with the company*). **4** harmony in opinion or feeling. **5** sympathetic awareness or tolerance; empathy. ● *adj.* **1 a** sympathetic to others' feelings. **b** of a forgiving nature. **2** having understanding, insight, or good judgment. □ **understandingly** *adv.*

understate *v.tr.* **1** express in greatly or unduly restrained terms. **2** represent (a thing) as being less than it actually is.

understated *adj.* **1** (of fashion, architecture, appearance, etc.) restrained in style or colour; not showy, simple (*the decor is refreshingly understated*). **2** stated or expressed in unduly restrained terms (*understated irony*). □ **understatedly** *adv.*

understatement *n.* **1** a statement that expresses an idea etc. in mild or restrained terms. **2** the quality of being understated or restrained in style or appearance. **3** the action or practice of understating.

understeer ● *n.* a tendency of a car or truck etc. to turn less sharply than was intended. ● *v.intr.* (of a vehicle) have such a tendency.

understood ● *v.* past and past part. of UNDERSTAND. ● *adj.* **1** inferred or implied without being explicitly stated. **2** accepted or agreed upon. **3 a** properly interpreted or perceived. **b** capable of being properly interpreted or perceived (*he could not make himself understood*).

understorey *n.* (*pl.* **-ies**) (also **understory** *pl.* **-eys**) **1** a layer of vegetation beneath the main canopy of a forest. **2** the plants forming this.

understudy esp. *Theatre* ● *n.* (*pl.* **-ies**) a person who studies another's role or duties in order to perform at short notice in the absence of the other. ● *v.tr.* (**-ies**, **-ied**) **1** study (a role etc.) as an understudy. **2** act as an understudy to (a person).

undersurface *n.* the lower surface or surface underneath; the underside.

undertake *v.tr.* (past **undertook**; past part. **undertaken**) **1** take on (an obligation, task, etc.); commit oneself to perform. **2** (usu. foll. by to + infin.) accept an obligation; promise.

undertaker *n.* a person whose business is to make arrangements for funerals; a funeral director.

undertaking *n.* **1** work etc. undertaken (*a serious undertaking*). **2** a pledge or promise. **3** the management of funerals as a profession.

under-the-counter *adj.* (of merchandise) not available in stores without a licence, prescription, or special permission, and thus often purchased and sold illegally.

underthings *n.pl.* *informal* (esp. women's) underclothing.

undertone *n.* **1** a subdued tone of sound or colour. **2** an underlying quality. **3** an undercurrent of feeling.

undertook past of UNDERTAKE.

undertow *n.* a current below the surface of the sea moving in the opposite direction to the surface current.

underuse ● *v.tr.* use below the optimum level. ● *n.* insufficient use.

underutilized *adj.* underused. □ **underutilization** *n.* **underutilize** *v.tr.*

undervalue *v.tr.* (**-values, -valued, -valuing**) **1** value insufficiently. **2** underestimate. □ **undervaluation** *n.*

underwater ● *adj.* **1** living or situated below the surface of the water. **2** designed to be used or done under the surface of the water. ● *adv.* under water.

underway *predic.adj.* **1** (of a process, project, activity, etc.) having been instigated; in progress. **2** (of a person) having begun an activity etc. **3** *Naut.* (of a ship) in motion.

underwear *n.* **1** underclothing. **2** underpants.

underweight *adj.* weighing less than is normal or desirable.

underwent past of UNDERGO.

underwhelm *v.tr.* *jocular* fail to impress.

underwire *n.* N Amer. **1** a thin semicircular support of wire stitched into the underside of each cup of a bra (also *attrib.*: *underwire bra*). **2** a bra with such a support.

underworld *n.* **1** the part of society comprising those who live by organized crime and immorality. **2** the mythical abode of the dead under the earth.

underwrite *v.tr.* (past **underwrote**; past part. **underwritten**) **1 a** sign, issue, and accept liability under (an insurance policy). **b** insure (a person, property, etc.). **c** assume liability up to (a certain amount). **2 a** guarantee (an undertaking or venture etc.) by assuming responsibility for any losses or debts incurred. **b** pay for or contribute financially towards. **3** guarantee the sale of (shares in a new company) by agreeing to purchase a certain percentage of shares not bought by the public.

underwriter *n.* **1** a person who examines a risk, decides whether or not it can be insured, and if it can, works out a premium to be charged, usu. on the basis of the frequency of past claims for similar risks. **2** a financial institution that guarantees to buy a certain proportion of any unsold shares when a new investment security is offered to the public.

---

undeserved *adj.*   **undeservedly** *adv.*   **undeserving** *adj.*   **undeservingly** *adv.*

undesirable ● *adj.* not desirable; objectionable, unpleasant. ● *n.* (usu. in *pl.*) an objectionable or unpleasant person, animal, insect, etc. □ **undesirability** *n.* **undesirably** *adv.*

undetermined *adj.* = UNDECIDED *adj.*

undid *past of* UNDO.

undies *n.pl. informal* (esp. women's) underclothes.

undigested *adj.* **1** not digested. **2** (esp. of information, facts, etc.) not properly arranged or considered.

undiluted *adj.* **1** not diluted. **2** complete, utter.

undirected *adj.* aimless; lacking direction.

undiscriminating *adj.* **1** lacking taste or good judgment. **2** not selective, indiscriminate.

undisputed *adj.* **1** not disputed or called into question. **2** universally acknowledged; generally recognized as being (*the undisputed champion*).

undistinguished *adj.* **1** lacking any distinguishing characteristic or feature (*an undistinguished square building*). **2** unremarkable, mediocre (*an undistinguished author*).

undo ● *v.* (*3rd sing. present* **-does**; *past* **-did**; *past part.* **-done**) **1 a** *tr.* unfasten or untie (a coat, button, knot, etc.). **b** *intr.* become unfastened (*how does this necklace undo?*). **c** unfasten the clothing of (a person). **2** *tr.* restore to the original form or condition; annul, cancel (*cannot undo the past*). **3** *tr.* ruin the prospects, reputation, or morals of. ● *n. Computing* **1** a feature of some programs that allows the user to reverse the effect of the last action or actions, including restoring deletions. **2** the key on some keyboards that controls this feature.

undocumented *adj.* **1** *N Amer.* not having the appropriate legal document or licence. **2** not proved by or recorded in documents.

undoing *n.* **1 a** ruin, downfall, destruction. **b** the cause of this. **2** the process of reversing what has been done. **3** the action of opening or unfastening.

undone *adj.* **1** not done; incomplete (*left the job undone*). **2** not fastened or tied (*undone shoelaces*).

undoubted *adj.* certain, not questioned, not regarded as doubtful.

undoubtedly *adv.* beyond doubt; without question; certainly.

undramatic *adj.* **1** lacking a dramatic quality or effect. **2** understated; unremarkable. □ **undramatically** *adv.*

undreamed of *adj.* (also **undreamt of**) (usu. hyphenated when *attrib.*) not considered or imagined; completely unexpected and usu. very pleasing.

undress ● *v.* **1** *intr.* take off one's clothes. **2** *tr.* take the clothes off (a person). ● *n.* **1 a** *Military* a uniform or clothing worn on ordinary rather than ceremonial occasions (also *attrib.*: *undress cap*) (*opp.* FULL DRESS). **b** casual or informal clothing. **2** the state of being naked or only partially clothed.

undressed *adj.* **1** not or no longer dressed; partly or wholly naked. **2** (of leather etc.) not treated. **3** (of food) not having a dressing.

undue *adj.* **1** excessive, disproportionate; unwarranted. **2** inappropriate, improper, unjust. □ **unduly** *adv.*

undue influence *n. Law* influence that causes a person to act contrary to his or her own free will or without adequate attention to the consequences.

undulate ● *v.intr.* /ˈʌndjʊˌleɪt, -dʒʊˌleɪt/ **1** have a wavy or rippling outline or appearance. **2** have a wavelike motion; move with a smooth regular rising and falling or rippling back and forth. ● *adj.* /ˈʌndjʊlət, -dʒʊlət/ wavy, going alternately up and down or from side to side (*leaves with undulate margins*).

undulation *n.* **1** a wavy motion or form, a gentle rise and fall. **2** each wave of this. **3** a set of wavy lines.

undying *adj.* eternal, never-ending (*undying love*).

unearned *adj.* **1** not earned. **2** *Baseball* (of a run) resulting from an error or passed ball.

unearned income *n.* income from interest payments or investments etc. as opposed to salary, wages, or fees.

unearth *v.tr.* **1** discover by investigation, searching, or while rummaging; bring to light. **2** uncover by the removal of earth; dig up.

unearthly *adj.* **1 a** not of this world (*unearthly creature*). **b** eerie, supernatural, mysterious. **2** not typical of this world; rare, uncommon (*unearthly beauty*). **3** *informal* absurdly early or inconvenient (*an unearthly hour*).

unease *n.* lack of ease, anxiety, discomfort, distress.

uneasy *adj.* (**-ier, -iest**) **1** (of a person) apprehensive; uncomfortable in mind or body. **2** characterized by or causing nervousness or restlessness; disturbing (*an uneasy silence*). **3** tenuous, shaky (*an uneasy alliance*). □ **uneasily** *adv.* **uneasiness** *n.*

uneatable *adj.* that is not in a condition to be eaten (*compare* INEDIBLE).

uneconomic *adj.* not economic; incapable of being profitably operated etc.

uneconomical *adj.* not economical; wasteful.

unemployable ● *adj.* not qualified or suitable for paid employment. ● *n.* **1** (often in *pl.*) an unemployable person. **2** (prec. by *the*; treated as *pl.*) unemployable people collectively.

unemployed ● *adj.* **1** not having paid employment; out of work. **2** not in use. ● *n.* (prec. by *the*; treated as *pl.*) unemployed people.

unemployment *n.* **1** the state of being unemployed. **2** the condition or extent of this in a country or region etc., esp. the number or percentage of unemployed people (*unemployment is down*). **3** *Cdn informal* = UNEMPLOYMENT INSURANCE (*I'm on unemployment*).

unemployment benefit *n.* a regular payment made by a local government or, in the US, a trade union, to an unemployed person.

unemployment insurance *n. Cdn* = EMPLOYMENT INSURANCE. Abbr.: **UI**. ¶No longer in official use.

unencumbered *adj.* not encumbered; free of any encumbrance.

unending *adj.* having or apparently having no end. □ **unendingly** *adv.* **unendingness** *n.*

---

undesired *adj.*
undetectability *n.*
undetectable *adj.*
undetectably *adv.*
undetected *adj.*
undeterred *adj.*
undeveloped *adj.*

undiagnosed *adj.*
undifferentiated *adj.*
undignified *adj.*
undisciplined *adj.*
undisclosed *adj.*
undiscovered *adj.*
undisguised *adj.*

undisguisedly *adv.*
undisturbed *adj.*
undivided *adj.*
undrained *adj.*
undyed *adj.*
uneaten *adj.*
unedited *adj.*

uneducated *adj.*
unelected *adj.*
unembarrassed *adj.*
unembellished *adj.*
unemotional *adj.*
unemotionally *adv.*
unemphatic *adj.*

un-English *adj.* **1** not characteristic of the English language. **2** not characteristic of or derived from the culture or inhabitants of England.

unenviable *adj.* unpleasant, undesirable. □ **unenviably** *adv.*

unequal *adj.* **1** not equal in amount, size, value, etc. **2** (usu. foll. by *to*) inadequate in ability or resources etc. (*unequal to the task*). **3 a** (of a contest, conflict, treaty, etc.) not evenly balanced; favouring one side (*an unequal bargain*). **b** inconsistent; varying or variable (*unequal distribution*). □ **unequally** *adv.*

unequalled *adj.* **1** superior to all others. **2** (foll. by *by*) not matched or surpassed.

unequivocal *adj.* not ambiguous; plain, unmistakable. □ **unequivocally** *adv.*

unerring *adj.* **1** not missing the intended target; certain, sure. **2** not failing or making a mistake; true. □ **unerringly** *adv.*

UNESCO /juːˈnɛskoʊ/ *abbr.* (also **Unesco**) United Nations Educational, Scientific, and Cultural Organization.

uneven *adj.* **1** not level or smooth. **2** not consistent, regular, or uniform. **3** (of a competition) unequal. □ **unevenly** *adv.* **unevenness** *n.*

unexceptionable *adj.* to whom or to which no exception can be taken; perfectly satisfactory or adequate. ¶Note the difference in meaning between *Her new book is unexceptionable* (i.e. it contains nothing that would cause objections) and *Her new book is unexceptional* (i.e. it is mediocre).

unexceptional *adj.* not out of the ordinary; usual, normal. ¶See UNEXCEPTIONABLE.

unexhausted *adj.* not used up, spent, or brought to an end.

unexpected ● *adj.* not expected; surprising. ● *n.* (prec. by *the*; usu. treated as *sing.*) an unexpected thing or unexpected things collectively. □ **unexpectedly** *adv.* **unexpectedness** *n.*

unfailing *adj.* **1** unlimited, inexhaustible (*an unfailing source of comfort*). **2** unceasing, constant (*unfailing devotion*). **3** certain, reliable (*unfailing accuracy*). □ **unfailingly** *adv.*

unfair *adj.* **1** not just, reasonable, or objective (*unfair criticism*). **2** not according to the rules (*unfair play*). **3** dishonest (*obtained by unfair means*). □ **unfairly** *adv.* **unfairness** *n.*

unfaithful *adj.* **1** (of a person) not faithful, esp. to a sexual partner. **2** (of behaviour) disloyal. □ **unfaithfulness** *n.*

unfaltering *adj.* not faltering; steady, resolute.

unfasten *v.tr.* **1** loosen. **2** open the fastening or fastenings of. **3** detach.

unfastened *adj.* **1** that has not been fastened. **2** that has been loosened, opened, or detached.

unfavourable *adj.* (also **unfavorable**) not favourable or beneficial; adverse. □ **unfavourableness** *n.* **unfavourably** *adv.*

unfazed *adj.* *informal* untroubled; not disconcerted.

unfed *adj.* not fed; hungry.

unfeeling *adj.* **1** unsympathetic, harsh, not caring about others' feelings. **2** lacking sensation or sensitivity (*my unfeeling hands*). □ **unfeelingly** *adv.*

unfeminine *adj.* **1** not characteristically or stereotypically feminine. **2** not regarded as suitable or appropriate for a woman.

unfenced *adj.* **1** not provided with fences. **2** unprotected.

unfiltered *adj.* **1** not filtered. **2** (of a cigarette) not provided with a filter.

unfinished *adj.* **1** not finished; incomplete. **2** (of wood furniture etc.) not painted or stained etc.

unfinished business *n.* **1** a task or tasks that must be completed. **2** *Psych. informal* unresolved issues.

unfit *adj.* **1** (often foll. by *for* or *to* + infin.) **a** (of a thing) not fit, proper, or suitable. **b** (of a person) not qualified or worthy (*an unfit parent; unfit to stand trial*). **2** in poor physical shape. □ **unfitness** *n.*

unfitted *adj.* **1** not fitted or suited. **2** not provided with fittings.

unfitting *adj.* not fitting, proper, or right; unbecoming.

unflagging *adj.* tireless, persistent. □ **unflaggingly** *adv.*

unflappable *adj.* *informal* remaining calm in a crisis. □ **unflappability** *n.* **unflappably** *adv.*

unfledged *adj.* **1** (of a person) inexperienced. **2** (of a bird) not yet fledged.

unflinching *adj.* not showing reluctance, hesitation, indecision, or fear; unwavering, direct. □ **unflinchingly** *adv.*

unfold *v.* **1** *tr.* open the fold or folds of, spread out. **2** *intr.* develop, become clear (*the plot begins to unfold*). **3** *intr.* become opened out. **4** *tr.* reveal, explain, or make clear (a thought, idea, mystery, etc.).

unforced *adj.* **1** not produced by effort; easy, natural. **2** not compelled or constrained. □ **unforcedly** *adv.*

unforgettable *adj.* that cannot be forgotten; memorable, wonderful. □ **unforgettably** *adv.*

unforgivable *adj.* without any justifiable motive; inexcusable, disgraceful. □ **unforgivably** *adv.*

unformed *adj.* **1** not formed. **2** shapeless. **3** not developed.

---

unendurable *adj.*	**uneventfulness** *n.*	**unfamiliarity** *n.*	**unflatteringly** *adv.*
unendurably *adv.*	**unexamined** *adj.*	**unfashionable** *adj.*	**unflavoured** *adj.*
unenforceable *adj.*	**unexcited** *adj.*	**unfashionably** *adv.*	(also **unflavored**)
unenlightened *adj.*	**unexciting** *adj.*	**unfathomable** *adj.*	**unfocused** *adj.*
unenlightening *adj.*	**unexpired** *adj.*	**unfathomably** *adv.*	(also **unfocussed**)
unenterprising *adj.*	**unexplainable** *adj.*	**unfeasibility** *n.*	**unforeseeable** *adj.*
unenthusiastic *adj.*	**unexplainably** *adv.*	**unfeasible** *adj.*	**unforeseen** *adj.*
unenthusiastically *adv.*	**unexplained** *adj.*	**unfeasibly** *adv.*	**unforgiven** *adj.*
unequipped *adj.*	**unexploded** *adj.*	**unfelt** *adj.*	**unforgiving** *adj.*
unescorted *adj.*	**unexploited** *adj.*	**unfermented** *adj.*	**unforgivingly** *adv.*
unethical *adj.*	**unexplored** *adj.*	**unfertilized** *adj.*	
unethically *adv.*	**unexpressed** *adj.*	**unfettered** *adj.*	
uneventful *adj.*	**unexpurgated** *adj.*	**unfilled** *adj.*	
uneventfully *adv.*	**unfamiliar** *adj.*	**unflattering** *adj.*	

unfortunate ● *adj.* **1 a** having bad fortune; unlucky. **b** unhappy. **2** regrettable. **3** unsuitable, inappropriate, or inauspicious (*a most unfortunate choice of words*). ● *n.* (usu. in *pl.*) an unfortunate person.

unfortunately *adv.* **1** (qualifying a whole sentence) it is unfortunate that. **2** in an unfortunate manner.

unfounded *adj.* having no basis in fact; unsubstantiated, not valid (*the rumour was unfounded*).

unfree *adj.* deprived or devoid of liberty. □ **unfreedom** *n.*

unfreeze *v.* (*past* **unfroze**; *past part.* **unfrozen**) **1** *tr.* cause to thaw. **2** *intr.* thaw. **3** *tr.* remove restrictions from, make (assets, credits, etc.) realizable.

unfriendly *adj.* (**-ier, -iest**) **1** not friendly. **2** (in *comb.*) *informal* not helpful or beneficial to (*ozone-unfriendly*). □ **unfriendliness** *n.*

unfrozen ● *v.* *past part.* of UNFREEZE. ● *adj.* not frozen.

unfruitful *adj.* **1** not producing good results, unprofitable. **2** not producing fruit or crops. □ **unfruitfully** *adv.*

unfunny *adj.* (**-ier, -iest**) not amusing, although meant to be.

unfurl *v.* **1** *tr.* spread or open out (a sail, flag, etc.) to its greatest length or width. **2** *intr.* become spread out or fully extended.

unfurnished *adj.* **1** (of an apartment etc.) without furniture. **2** (often foll. by *with*) not provided or supplied.

ungainly *adj.* awkward, clumsy, ungraceful (*he walks in long ungainly strides*). □ **ungainliness** *n.*

unglamorous *adj.* **1** lacking glamour or appeal. **2** mundane.

unglued *adj.* **1** having no glue, unstuck. **2** *N Amer.* discomposed, confused, crazy. □ **come** (or **become**) **unglued** *N Amer.* **1 a** fall apart, lose one's composure. **b** become crazy. **2** fall into a state of chaos or disarray.

ungodly *adj.* **1** impious, wicked. **2** *informal* outrageous (*an ungodly hour to arrive*). □ **ungodliness** *n.*

ungovernable *adj.* uncontrollable, violent.

ungracious *adj.* not cordial, courteous, or polite; rude or unkind to others. □ **ungraciously** *adv.*

ungraspable *adj.* **1** that cannot be grasped or seized. **2** that cannot be comprehended.

ungrateful *adj.* **1** not feeling or showing gratitude. **2** not pleasant or acceptable. □ **ungratefully** *adv.* **ungratefulness** *n.*

ungrounded *adj.* **1** having no basis or justification. **2** *N Amer.* (of an electrical outlet etc.) not grounded. **3** (foll. by *in*) not properly instructed (in a subject etc.).

unguarded *adj.* **1 a** (of a person) not on one's guard; candid, open. **b** resulting from such candidness (*she told me so in an unguarded moment*). **2** careless, thoughtless, incautious (*an unguarded remark*). **3** not guarded; vulnerable. □ **unguardedly** *adv.*

unguent /'ʌŋgwənt/ *n.* a soft substance, such as a perfumed oil, used esp. as an ointment.

ungulate /'ʌŋgjʊlət, -ˌleɪt/ ● *adj.* hoofed. ● *n.* a hoofed mammal.

unhappy *adj.* (**-ier, -iest**) **1 a** not happy, miserable. **b** (often foll. by *with, about*) displeased, dissatisfied, upset. **2** unsuccessful, unfortunate, regrettable. **3** inauspicious (*an unhappy omen*). □ **unhappily** *adv.* **unhappiness** *n.*

UNHCR *abbr.* United Nations High Commissioner for Refugees.

unhealthy *adj.* (**-ier, -iest**) **1** not in good health. **2** not conducive to good physical, mental, or emotional health or well-being (*an unhealthy diet*). **3** not indicative of good health; unwholesome (*an unhealthy complexion*). **4** inappropriate, perverse (*he maintains an unhealthy attachment to her*). □ **unhealthily** *adv.* **unhealthiness** *n.*

unheard of *adj.* (usu. hyph. when *attrib.*) **1** unknown, unfamiliar. **2** unprecedented, not previously attempted or considered. **3** outrageous, preposterous.

unheralded *adj.* not heralded; unannounced.

unhesitating *adj.* **1** without pause, uncertainty, or hesitation (*an unhesitating reply*). **2** without interruption; relentless, constant (*her unhesitating generosity and kindness*). □ **unhesitatingly** *adv.*

unhinge *v.tr.* **1** take (a door etc.) off its hinges. **2 a** unsettle or unbalance (a person); make crazy. **b** throw (a situation etc.) into chaos or confusion. **3** detach, separate, or dislodge.

unhinged *adj.* unsettled, unbalanced, disordered, confused.

unhip *adj.* *informal* not hip; not aware of or consistent with the latest trends or styles.

unhitch *v.tr.* **1** release from a hitched state. **2** unhook, unfasten.

unhittable *adj.* (esp. of a pitched baseball) that cannot be hit.

unholy *adj.* (**-ier, -iest**) **1** evil, wicked. **2** *informal* dreadful, terrible (*this room is an unholy mess!*). **3** not holy. □ **unholiness** *n.*

unhook *v.tr.* **1** remove from a hook or hooks. **2** unfasten by releasing a hook or hooks.

unhoped for *adj.* (usu. hyph. when *attrib.*) not hoped for or expected.

unhuman *adj.* **1** not human. **2** superhuman. **3** inhuman, brutal.

uni- /'juːnɪ/ *comb. form* one; having or consisting of one.

unicameral /ˌjuːnɪˈkæmərəl/ *adj.* with a single legislative chamber.

UNICEF /'juːnəˌsef/ *abbr.* United Nations Children's Fund.

unicellular *adj.* (of an organism, organ, tissue, etc.) consisting of a single cell.

unicorn *n.* **1** a fabulous animal usually represented as a horse with a single straight horn projecting from its forehead. **2** a heraldic representation of this.

unicycle *n.* a single-wheeled cycle, esp. as used by acrobats. □ **unicyclist** *n.*

unideal *adj.* not ideal.

---

unframed *adj.*	**unfussy** *adj.*	**ungrammatically** *adv.*	**unhelpful** *adj.*
unfrequented *adj.*	**ungenerous** *adj.*	**unhampered** *adj.*	**unhelpfully** *adv.*
unfulfillable *adj.*	**ungenerously** *adv.*	**unharmed** *adj.*	**unhindered** *adj.*
unfulfilled *adj.*	**unglazed** *adj.*	**unhatched** *adj.*	**unhurried** *adj.*
unfulfilling *adj.*	**ungraceful** *adj.*	**unheard** *adj.*	**unhurriedly** *adv.*
unfulfillment *n.*	**ungracefully** *adv.*	**unheated** *adj.*	**unhurt** *adj.*
unfussily *adv.*	**ungrammatical** *adj.*	**unheeded** *adj.*	**unhyphenated** *adj.*

unidealized *adj.* not represented as perfect or ideal; unembellished.

unidirectional *adj.* having only one direction of motion, operation, etc.

unification *n.* **1** the act or an instance of unifying; the state of being unified. **2** *Cdn* the action or policy of merging the traditional army, navy, and air force into a single combined force.

Unification Church *n.* a religious organization founded in 1954 by Sun Myung Moon (b.1920).

Unified Family Court *n. Cdn* (in Newfoundland) a division of the Supreme Court which has jurisdiction over all aspects of family law, including divorce, custody, adoption, etc.

uniform ● *adj.* **1** not changing in form or character; the same, unvarying (*all of uniform size and shape*). **2** conforming to the same standard, rules, or pattern. **3** constant in the course of time (*uniform acceleration*). ● *n.* **1** uniform distinctive clothing worn by members of the same body, e.g. by soldiers, members of a sports team, etc. **2** clothing, usu. white or in pastel colours, worn by nurses and other members of medical professions. **3** a style of dress typical of a certain group. ● *v.tr.* **1** clothe in uniform (*a uniformed officer*). **2** make uniform. □ **uniformly** *adv.*

uniformity *n.* (*pl.* **-ies**) the state of being uniform; sameness, consistency.

unify *v.tr. & intr.* (**-ies, -ied**) make united or uniform. □ **unified** *adj.* **unifier** *n.* **unifying** *adj.*

unilateral /ˌjuːnɪˈlætərəl/ *adj.* **1** performed by or affecting only one person or party (*unilateral disarmament; unilateral declaration of independence*). **2** one-sided. □ **unilateralism** *n.* **unilaterally** *adv.*

unilingual *esp. Cdn* ● *adj.* **1** able to speak only one language. **2** spoken or written in or involving only one language. ● *n.* a unilingual person. □ **unilingualism** *n.* **unilingually** *adv.*

unimpeachable *adj.* giving no opportunity for censure; beyond reproach. □ **unimpeachably** *adv.*

unimportance *n.* lack of importance.

unimproved *adj.* **1** not made better or improved. **2** not made use of. **3** (of land) not used for agriculture or building; not developed.

unincorporated *adj.* **1** not formed into a corporation. **2** not incorporated or united.

uninfluenced *adj.* (often foll. by *by*) not influenced.

uninformed *adj.* **1** not informed or instructed. **2** ignorant, uneducated.

uninitiated *adj.* not initiated; not admitted or instructed.

uninspired *adj.* not imaginative or inspiring; dull.

uninterested *adj.* **1** not interested. **2** unconcerned. □ **uninterestedly** *adv.* **uninterestedness** *n.*

union *n.* **1 a** the act or an instance of uniting; the state of being united. **b** (**the Union**) *hist.* the uniting of the English and Scottish crowns in 1603, of the English and Scottish parliaments in 1707, or of Great Britain and Ireland in 1801. **2 a** a whole resulting from the combination of parts or members. **b** a political unit formed in this way, esp. the US, the UK, the USSR, or South Africa. **3 a** = LABOUR UNION. **b** a group of people united for a common cause. **4** marriage, matrimony. **5** concord, agreement (*lived together in perfect union*). **6** *Math.* the totality of the members of two or more sets. **7** (**the Union**) *US hist.* the body of northern states in the American Civil War. **8** a part of a flag with a device emblematic of union, normally occupying the upper corner next to the staff. **9** a joint or coupling for pipes etc.

union-busting *n. N Amer.* tactics undertaken by corporations to weaken or eliminate unions in the workplace. □ **union-buster** *n.*

Union Government *n. Cdn hist.* the coalition government that governed Canada 1917–1920.

unionist *n.* **1 a** a member of a labour union. **b** an advocate of labour unions. **2** (usu. **Unionist**) an advocate of union, esp.: **a** a person opposed to the rupture of the parliamentary union between Great Britain and Northern Ireland (formerly between Great Britain and Ireland). **b** a member of a party having these aims. **c** *hist.* a person who opposed secession during the US Civil War. □ **unionism** *n.*

unionize *v.tr. & intr.* bring or come under the organization or rules of a labour union. □ **unionization** *n.*

Union Jack *n.* the national ensign of the United Kingdom, formed by the union of the crosses of St. George, St. Andrew, and St. Patrick.

Union Nationale /ˌuːnjɔ̃ næsjaˈnæl/ *n. Cdn* (in Quebec) a provincial party identified with conservative French-Canadian nationalism which held power 1944–60 under Maurice Duplessis (1890–1959).

unique /juːˈniːk/ *adj.* **1** of which there is only one; unequalled; having no like, equal, or parallel. **2** *disputed* unusual, remarkable (*the most unique person I ever met*). **3** (foll. by *to*) limited in occurrence to a particular area, situation, etc. (*that species is unique to this part of Canada*). ¶In sense 1, *unique* should not be qualified by adverbs such as *absolutely*, *most*, and *quite* because it is an absolute concept. The use of *unique* in sense 2 is regarded as incorrect by some people. □ **uniquely** *adv.* **uniqueness** *n.*

unisex *adj.* (of clothing, hairstyles, etc.) designed to be suitable for both sexes.

unisexual *adj.* **1 a** of one sex. **b** *Bot.* having stamens or pistils but not both. **2** unisex.

---

unidentifiable *adj.*	**unimpressed** *adj.*	**uninspiringly** *adv.*	**uninterestingly** *adv.*
unidentified *adj.*	**unimpressive** *adj.*	**uninsulated** *adj.*	**uninterestingness** *n.*
unignorable *adj.*	**unimpressively** *adv.*	**uninsured** *adj.*	**uninterrupted** *adj.*
unimaginable *adj.*	**unimpressiveness** *n.*	**unintelligent** *adj.*	**uninterruptedly** *adv.*
unimaginably *adv.*	**uninfected** *adj.*	**unintelligently** *adv.*	**uninterruptedness** *n.*
unimaginative *adj.*	**uninhabitable** *adj.*	**unintelligibility** *n.*	**uninterruptible** *adj.*
unimaginatively *adv.*	**uninhabited** *adj.*	**unintelligible** *adj.*	**uninvestigated** *adj.*
unimagined *adj.*	**uninhibited** *adj.*	**unintelligibly** *adv.*	**uninvited** *adj.*
unimpaired *adj.*	**uninhibitedly** *adv.*	**unintended** *adj.*	**uninvitedly** *adv.*
unimpeded *adj.*	**uninhibitedness** *n.*	**unintentional** *adj.*	**uninviting** *adj.*
unimpededly *adv.*	**uninjured** *adj.*	**unintentionally** *adv.*	**uninvitingly** *adv.*
unimportant *adj.*	**uninspiring** *adj.*	**uninteresting** *adj.*	**uninvolved** *adj.*

unison /ˈjuːnɪsən/ ● *n.* **1** *Music* **a** identity in pitch of two or more sounds or notes. **b** the sounding of notes or melodies at the same pitch, or at pitches one or more octaves apart, by different voices or instruments together. **2** agreement, concord (*acted in perfect unison*). ● *adj. Music* coinciding in pitch. □ **in unison** together; as one (*read the poem in unison*).

unit *n.* **1 a** an individual thing, person, or group regarded as single and complete, esp. for purposes of calculation. **b** each of the (smallest) separate individuals or groups into which a complex whole may be analyzed (*the family as the unit of society*). **2** (also *attrib.*) a quantity chosen as a standard in terms of which other quantities may be expressed (*SI unit*). **3** *N Amer., Austral. & NZ* a private residence forming one of several in a large building or group of buildings; an apartment etc. **4** a device with a specified function forming part of a complex mechanism. **5** a piece of furniture for fitting with others like it or made of complementary parts. **6 a** a group with a special function in an organization. **b** a subdivision of a larger military grouping. **7** a group of buildings, wards, etc., in a hospital. **8** a portion of a school course centring on a particular theme. **9** *Cdn (PEI)* = SCHOOL UNIT. **10** the number 'one'.

unitard /ˈjuːnɪtɑrd/ *n.* a tight-fitting one-piece garment of stretchable fabric which covers the body from the shoulders to the toes or ankles.

Unitarian ● *n.* **1** a person who believes that God is not a Trinity but one person. **2** a member of a religious body maintaining this and advocating freedom from formal dogma or doctrine. ● *adj.* of or relating to the Unitarians. □ **Unitarianism** *n.*

unitary /ˈjuːnɪteri/ *adj.* **1** of a unit or units. **2** marked by unity or uniformity. **3** of or relating to a system of government in which the powers of the separate constituent parts are vested in a central body.

unite *v.* **1** *tr. & intr.* join together; make or become one; combine. **2** *tr. & intr.* join together for a common purpose or action (*united in their struggle for justice*). **3** *tr. & intr.* join in marriage. **4** *tr.* possess (qualities, features, etc.) in combination (*united anger with mercy*). **5** *intr. & tr.* form or cause to form a physical or chemical whole (*oil will not unite with water*).

united ● *adj.* **1** joined together for a common purpose. **2** joined politically. **3** joined together by love or sympathy. **4** in agreement. **5** (**United**) *Cdn* of, relating to, or belonging to the United Church. ● *n.* (**United**) *Cdn* a member of the United Church.

United Church *n.* (in full **United Church of Canada**) (in Canada) a Protestant denomination formed in 1925 by the merger of the Methodist and Congregationalist Churches together with the majority of Presbyterians.

United Empire Loyalist *n. Cdn* = LOYALIST 2.

United Farmers *n. Cdn* any of various political groups growing out of provincial farmers' organizations.

United Nations *n.* an international organization of countries set up in 1945, in succession to the League of Nations, to promote international peace, security, and co-operation. Abbr.: **UN**.

unity *n.* (*pl.* **-ies**) **1** oneness; being one, single, or individual; being formed of parts that constitute a whole (*the pictures lack unity; national unity*). **2** harmony or concord between persons etc. (*lived together in unity*). **3** a thing forming a complex whole (*a person regarded as a unity*). **4** *Math.* the number 'one'.

Univ. *abbr.* University.

universal ● *adj.* **1** of, belonging to, or done etc. by all persons or things in the world or in the class concerned; applicable to all cases (*the feeling was universal; universal approval*). **2** *Logic* (of a proposition) in which something is asserted of all of a class (*opp.* PARTICULAR 5). ● *n.* **1** *Logic* a universal proposition. **2** *Philos.* **a** a term or concept of general application. **b** a nature or essence signified by a general term. □ **universality** /-ˈsælɪti/ *n.* **universally** *adv.*

universalist *n.* **1** a person who is learned in many subjects or who has a wide range of interests etc. **2** a person advocating loyalty to and concern for others without regard to national allegiance. **3** *Theol.* a person who believes that all mankind will eventually be saved. **4** a member of an organized body of Christians who believe this. □ **universalism** *n.* **universalistic** *adj.*

universalize *v.tr.* **1** apply universally; give a universal character to. **2** bring into universal use; make available for all. □ **universalization** *n.*

universal joint *n.* a coupling or joint which can transmit rotary power by a shaft at any angle.

Universal Product Code *n.* a bar code printed on the packaging of many consumer goods and used esp. in retail sales and inventory control. Abbr.: **UPC**.

universe *n.* **1** all existing things; the cosmos. **2** all of humanity. **3** a sphere of activity, existence, interest, etc. (*he is the centre of her universe*).

university *n.* (*pl.* **-ies**) **1** an educational institution designed for instruction of students in many branches of advanced learning, conferring degrees in various faculties, and often embodying colleges and similar institutions. **2** the members of this collectively.

Unix /ˈjuːnɪks/ *n. Computing proprietary* a multi-user operating system.

unkempt *adj.* **1** untidy, of neglected appearance. **2** uncombed, dishevelled.

unkept *adj.* **1** (of a promise, law, etc.) not observed; disregarded. **2** not tended; neglected.

unkind *adj.* **1** not kind. **2** harsh, cruel. □ **unkindly** *adv.* **unkindness** *n.*

unknot *v.tr.* (**unknotted, unknotting**) release the knot or knots of, untie.

unknowable ● *adj.* that cannot be known. ● *n.* **1** an unknowable thing. **2** (**the Unknowable**) the postulated absolute or ultimate reality. □ **unknowability** *n.*

unknowing *adj.* (often foll. by *of*) not knowing; ignorant, unconscious. □ **unknowingly** *adv.*

unknown ● *adj.* (often foll. by *to*) not known, unfamiliar (*her purpose was unknown to me*). ● *n.* **1** an unknown thing or person. **2** an unknown quantity (*equation in two unknowns*). □ **unknown to** without the knowledge of (*did it unknown to me*).

unlace *v.tr.* **1** undo the lace or laces of. **2** unfasten or loosen in this way.

---

unjoined *adj.*	**unjustifiably** *adv.*	**unjustly** *adv.*	**unlabelled** *adj.* (also
unjust *adj.*	**unjustified** *adj.*	**unjustness** *n.*	esp. *US* **unlabeled**)
unjustifiable *adj.*			

unlatch v. **1** tr. release the latch of. **2** tr. & intr. open or be opened in this way.

unleaded ● adj. **1** (of gasoline etc.) without added lead. **2** not covered, weighted, or framed with lead. ● n. unleaded gasoline etc.

unlearn v.tr. (past and past part. **unlearned** or **unlearnt**) **1** discard from one's memory. **2** rid oneself of (a habit, false information, etc.).

unlearned¹ /ʌnˈlɜːnəd/ adj. not well educated; untaught, ignorant. □ **unlearnedly** adv.

unlearned² /ʌnˈlɜːnd/ adj. (also **unlearnt**) **1** that has not been learned (an unlearned lesson). **2** that does not need to be learned; innate (an unlearned behaviour).

unleash v.tr. **1** release (something powerful or destructive). **2** set free to engage in pursuit or attack.

unleavened adj. not leavened; made without yeast or other raising agent.

unless conj. if not; except when (shall go unless I hear from you; will make it home by 8 unless the train is late).

unlettered adj. **1** illiterate. **2** not well educated.

unlicensed adj. (also **unlicenced**) not licensed, esp. without a licence to sell alcoholic drink.

unlighted adj. **1** not provided with light. **2** not set burning.

unlike ● adj. **1** not like; different from (is unlike both his parents). **2** uncharacteristic of (such behaviour is unlike her). **3** dissimilar, different. ● prep. differently from (acts quite unlike anyone else). □ **unlikeness** n.

unlikely adj. (**-ier**, **-iest**) **1** improbable (an unlikely story). **2** not to be expected to do something (she's unlikely to be available). **3** unpromising (an unlikely candidate). □ **unlikelihood** n. **unlikeliness** n.

unlimited adj. without limit; unrestricted; very great in number or quantity. □ **unlimitedly** adv. **unlimitedness** n.

unlined adj. **1** (of paper etc.) without lines. **2** (of a face etc.) without wrinkles. **3** (of a garment etc.) without lining.

unlink v.tr. **1** undo the links of (a chain etc.). **2** detach or set free by undoing or unfastening a link or chain.

unlisted adj. **1** esp. N Amer. (of a telephone number) not listed in a telephone directory. **2** not included in a published list, esp. (of a security) not eligible for trading on an exchange.

unload v. **1** tr. & intr. remove a load from (a vehicle etc.). **2** tr. remove (a load) from a vehicle etc. **3** tr. remove the charge from (a firearm etc.). **4** tr. informal get rid of. **5** (often foll. by on) informal **a** tr. divulge (information). **b** tr. & intr. give vent to (feelings). □ **unloader** n.

unlock v. **1** tr. **a** release the lock of (a door, box, etc.). **b** release or disclose by unlocking. **2** tr. release thoughts, feelings, etc., from (one's mind etc.). **3** intr. become unlocked.

unlooked-for adj. unexpected, unforeseen.

unloose v.tr. (also **unloosen**) loose; set free.

unlucky adj. (**-ier**, **-iest**) **1** not fortunate or successful. **2** wretched. **3** bringing bad luck. **4** unwise; badly considered. □ **unluckily** adv. **unluckiness** n.

unmade adj. **1** not made. **2** destroyed, annulled.

unmake v.tr. (past and past part. **unmade**) undo the making of; destroy, depose, annul.

unman v.tr. (**unmanned**, **unmanning**) deprive of supposed manly qualities (e.g. self-control, courage); cause to weep etc.; discourage.

unmanageable adj. not (easily) managed, manipulated, or controlled. □ **unmanageably** adv.

unmanned adj. **1** not manned. **2** overcome by emotion etc.

unmannerly adj. **1** without good manners. **2** (of actions, speech, etc.) showing a lack of good manners.

unmapped adj. **1** not represented on a map. **2** unexplored.

unmarked adj. **1** not marked. **2** not noticed.

unmask v. **1** tr. **a** remove the mask from. **b** expose the true character of. **2** intr. remove one's mask.

unmatched adj. not matched or equalled.

unmediated adj. with no intervention; directly perceived.

unmentionable ● adj. that cannot (properly) be mentioned. ● n. **1** (in pl.) jocular undergarments. **2** a person or thing not to be mentioned. □ **unmentionability** n. **unmentionably** adv.

unmet adj. (of a quota, demand, goal, etc.) not achieved or fulfilled.

unmissable adj. that cannot or should not be missed.

unmitigated adj. **1** not mitigated or modified. **2** absolute, unqualified. □ **unmitigatedly** adv.

unmotivated adj. without motivation; without a motive.

unmould v.tr. (also **unmold**) remove (a dessert etc.) from a mould or pan.

unmoved adj. **1** not moved. **2** not changed in one's purpose. **3** not affected by emotion. □ **unmovable** adj. (also **unmoveable**).

unmoving adj. **1** not moving; still. **2** not emotive.

unmusical adj. **1** not pleasing to the ear. **2** unskilled in or indifferent to music. □ **unmusicality** n. **unmusically** adv. **unmusicalness** n.

unnameable adj. that cannot be named, esp. too bad to be named.

unnatural adj. **1** contrary to nature or the usual course of nature; not normal. **2 a** lacking natural feelings. **b** extremely cruel or wicked. **3** artificial. **4** affected. □ **unnaturally** adv. **unnaturalness** n.

unladen adj.
unladylike adj.
unlamented adj.
unlawful adj.
unlawfully adv.
unlawfulness n.
unliberated adj.
unlikeable adj.
(also **unlikable**)
unlit adj.
unlocked adj.
unlovability n.

unlovable adj.
unloved adj.
unloveliness n.
unlovely adj.
unloving adj.
unlovingly adv.
unlovingness n.
unmanliness n.
unmanly adj.
unmarried adj.
unmeasurable adj.
unmeasurably adv.

unmelodious adj.
unmentioned adj.
unmerciful adj.
unmercifully adv.
unmerited adj.
unmindful adj.
unmindfully adv.
unmindfulness n.
unmistakability n.
(also **unmistakeability**)
unmistakable adj.
(also **unmistakeable**)

unmistakableness n.
(also **unmistakeable-ness**)
unmistakably adv.
unmixed adj.
unmodified adj.
unmodulated adj.
unmolested adj.
unmounted adj.
unnamed adj.
unnavigable adj.

unnecessary ● *adj.* **1** not necessary. **2** more than is necessary (*with unnecessary care*). ● *n.* (*pl.* **-ies**) (usu. in *pl.*) an unnecessary thing. □ **unnecessarily** *adv.* **unnecessariness** *n.*

unnerve *v.tr.* deprive of strength or resolution. □ **unnerving** *adj.* **unnervingly** *adv.*

unnumbered *adj.* **1** not marked with a number. **2** not counted. **3** countless.

UNO /ˈjuːnoː/ *abbr.* United Nations Organization.

unofficial *adj.* **1** not officially authorized or confirmed. **2** not characteristic of officials. □ **unofficially** *adv.*

unorganized *adj.* not organized.

unpack *v.* **1** *tr. & intr.* open and remove the contents of (a package, luggage, etc.). **2** *tr.* take (a thing) out from a package etc. **3** *tr.* unload (a vehicle etc.).

unpaired *adj.* **1** not arranged in pairs. **2** not forming one of a pair.

unpalatable *adj.* **1** not pleasant to taste. **2** (of an idea, suggestion, etc.) disagreeable, distasteful.

unparliamentary *adj.* contrary to proper parliamentary usage.

unpeg *v.tr.* (**unpegged**, **unpegging**) **1** unfasten by the removal of pegs. **2** cease to maintain or stabilize (prices etc.).

unperson *n.* a person whose name or existence is denied or ignored.

unplayable *adj.* **1** *Sport* (of a ball) that cannot be struck or returned. **2** that cannot be played.

unplug *v.tr.* (**unplugged**, **unplugging**) **1 a** disconnect (an electrical device) by removing its plug from the socket. **b** disconnect (an electrical cord or plug) from a socket. **2** unclog. **3** remove a stopper or plug from.

unplugged *adj.* **1** that has been unplugged. **2** (of rock music, etc.) performed or played on instruments without electric amplification.

unpolished *adj.* **1** not polished; rough. **2** without refinement; crude.

unpolitic *adj.* impolitic, unwise.

unpolitical *adj.* not concerned with politics.

unpowered *adj.* (of a boat, vehicle, etc.) propelled other than by fuel.

unpractical *adj.* **1** not practical. **2** (of a person) not having practical skill. □ **unpractically** *adv.*

unprecedented *adj.* **1** having no precedent; unparalleled. **2** novel. □ **unprecedentedly** *adv.*

unprepared *adj.* not prepared (in advance); not ready. □ **unpreparedly** *adv.* **unpreparedness** *n.*

unpressed *adj.* not pressed, esp. (of clothing) not ironed.

unpriced *adj.* not having a price or prices fixed, marked, or stated.

unprincipled *adj.* lacking or not based on good moral principles. □ **unprincipledness** *n.*

unprintable *adj.* that cannot be printed, esp. because too indecent or libellous or blasphemous.

unprofessional *adj.* **1** contrary to professional standards of behaviour etc. **2** not belonging to a profession; amateur. □ **unprofessionally** *adv.*

UNPROFOR /ˈʌnprəfɔːr/ *abbr.* United Nations Protection Force.

unprotected *adj.* **1** not protected. **2** (of sexual intercourse) performed without a condom or other contraceptive. □ **unprotectedness** *n.*

unprovided *adj.* (usu. foll. by *with*) not furnished, supplied, or equipped.

unqualified *adj.* **1 a** not having the necessary qualifications. **b** not competent (*unqualified to give an answer*). **2** not legally or officially qualified (*an unqualified practitioner*). **3** not modified or restricted; complete (*an unqualified success*).

unquestioned *adj.* **1** not disputed or doubted; definite, certain. **2** not interrogated or investigated.

unquestioning *adj.* **1** asking no questions. **2** done without asking questions. □ **unquestioningly** *adv.*

unquiet *adj.* **1** restless, agitated, stirring. **2** perturbed, anxious. □ **unquietly** *adv.*

---

unneeded *adj.*
unnoticeable *adj.*
unnoticed *adj.*
unobjectionable *adj.*
unobjectionableness *n.*
unobjectionably *adv.*
unobservable *adj.*
unobservant *adj.*
unobservantly *adv.*
unobserved *adj.*
unobservedly *adv.*
unobstructed *adj.*
unobtainable *adj.*
unobtrusive *adj.*
unobtrusively *adv.*
unobtrusiveness *n.*
unoccupied *adj.*
unopened *adj.*
unopposed *adj.*
unoriginal *adj.*
unoriginality *n.*
unoriginally *adv.*
unornamented *adj.*
unorthodox *adj.*
unorthodoxly *adv.*
unorthodoxy *n.*

unostentatious *adj.*
unostentatiously *adv.*
unpaid *adj.*
unparalleled *adj.*
unpardonable *adj.*
unpardonably *adv.*
unpasteurized *adj.*
unpatriotic *adj.*
unpaved *adj.*
unpeeled *adj.*
unperceptive *adj.*
unpersuasive *adj.*
unpersuasively *adv.*
unperturbed *adj.*
unperturbedly *adv.*
unplanned *adj.*
unpleasant *adj.*
unpleasantly *adv.*
unpleasantness *n.*
unpleasing *adj.*
unpleasingly *adv.*
unplowed *adj.*
(also **unploughed**)
unpoetic *adj.*
(also **unpoetical**)

unpolluted *adj.*
unpopular *adj.*
unpopularity *n.*
unpopularly *adv.*
unpopulated *adj.*
unpredictability *n.*
unpredictable *adj.*
unpredictably *adv.*
unpredicted *adj.*
unprejudiced *adj.*
unpremeditated *adj.*
unpremeditatedly *adv.*
unprepossessing *adj.*
unpretentious *adj.*
unpretentiously *adv.*
unpretentiousness *n.*
unproblematic *adj.*
unproblematically *adv.*
unprocessed *adj.*
unproductive *adj.*
unproductively *adv.*
unproductiveness *n.*
unprofitable *adj.*
unprofitableness *n.*
unprofitably *adv.*
unprogressive *adj.*

unpromising *adj.*
unpromisingly *adv.*
unpronounceable *adj.*
unpropitious *adj.*
unpropitiously *adv.*
unprovability *n.*
unprovable *adj.*
unproven *adj.*
(also **unproved**)
unprovoked *adj.*
unpublishable *adj.*
unpublished *adj.*
unpunished *adj.*
unquenchable *adj.*
unquenchably *adv.*
unquestionability *n.*
unquestionable *adj.*
unquestionableness *n.*
unquestionably *adv.*

unquote *adv.* (in speech, reading aloud, etc.) indicating the presence of closing quotation marks.

unquoted *adj.* not quoted, esp. on the Stock Exchange.

unranked *adj.* (in sports etc.) that has not been ranked or considered a contender.

unravel *v.* (**unravelled, unravelling**) **1** *tr.* cause to be no longer ravelled, tangled, or intertwined. **2** *tr.* probe and solve (a mystery etc.). **3** *tr.* undo (a fabric, esp. a knitted one). **4** *intr.* become disentangled or unknitted. **5** *intr.* come apart, collapse (*our plans have unravelled*). □ **unravelment** *n.*

unreactive *adj.* (esp. of a substance) not reactive, inert.

unread *adj.* **1** not read. **2** (of a person) not well-read.

unreadable *adj.* **1** too dull or too difficult to be worth reading. **2** illegible. □ **unreadability** *n.* **unreadably** *adv.*

unready *adj.* **1** not ready. **2** not prompt in action. □ **unreadily** *adv.* **unreadiness** *n.*

unreal *adj.* **1** not real. **2** imaginary, illusory. **3** *N Amer. & Austral. slang* incredible, amazing. □ **unreality** *n.* **unreally** *adv.*

unreason *n.* lack of reasonable thought or action.

unreasonable *adj.* **1** going beyond the limits of what is reasonable or equitable (*unreasonable demands*). **2** not guided by or listening to reason. □ **unreasonableness** *n.* **unreasonably** *adv.*

unreconstructed *adj.* **1** not reconciled or converted to the current political orthodoxy. **2** not rebuilt.

unreel *v.tr. & intr.* unwind from or as if from a reel.

unreflecting *adj.* not thoughtful; not engaging in reflection or thought. □ **unreflectingly** *adv.*

unregenerate ● *adj.* not regenerate; obstinately wrong or bad. ● *n.* an unregenerate person.

unrelenting *adj.* **1** not relenting or yielding. **2** unmerciful. **3** not abating or relaxing. □ **unrelentingly** *adv.*

unrelieved *adj.* **1** lacking the relief given by contrast or variation. **2** not aided or assisted. □ **unrelievedly** *adv.*

unremarked *adj.* **1** not mentioned or remarked upon. **2** unnoticed.

unrepeatable *adj.* **1** that cannot be done, made, or said again. **2** too indecent to be said again.

unrequited *adj.* **1** (of love etc.) not reciprocated. **2** (of a yearning etc.) unsatisfied. □ **unrequitedness** *n.*

unreserved *adj.* **1** not reserved (*unreserved seats*). **2** without reservations; absolute (*unreserved confidence*). **3** free from reserve (*an unreserved nature*). □ **unreservedly** *adv.*

unresolved *adj.* **1 a** uncertain how to act, irresolute. **b** uncertain in opinion, undecided. **2** (of questions etc.) undetermined, undecided, unsolved. **3** not broken up or dissolved.

unrest *n.* a state of disturbance and dissatisfaction accompanied by angry protest, violence, etc.

unreturned *adj.* **1** not reciprocated or responded to. **2** not having returned or been returned.

unrivalled *adj.* having no equal; peerless.

unroll *v.* **1** *tr. & intr.* open out from a rolled-up state. **2** *tr.* (of a landscape) appear stretched out before the viewer. **3** *tr.* (of events) happen one after the other.

unruffled *adj.* **1** not agitated or disturbed; calm. **2** not physically ruffled or made rough.

unruly *adj.* (**-ier, -iest**) not easily controlled or disciplined, disorderly. □ **unruliness** *n.*

unsaddle *v.tr.* **1** remove the saddle from (a horse etc.). **2** dislodge from a saddle.

unsaid[1] *adj.* not said or uttered.

unsaid[2] *past and past part. of* UNSAY.

unsaturated *adj.* **1** (of a compound, esp. a fat or oil) having double or triple bonds in its molecule and therefore capable of further reaction. **2** not saturated.

unsavoury *adj.* (also **unsavory**) **1** disagreeable to the taste, smell, or feelings; disgusting. **2** disagreeable, unpleasant (*an unsavoury character*). **3** morally offensive. □ **unsavouriness** *n.*

unsay *v.tr.* (*past and past part.* **unsaid**) retract (a statement).

unscarred *adj.* not scarred or damaged.

unscathed /ʌnˈskeɪðd/ *adj.* without suffering any injury.

unschooled *adj.* **1** uneducated, untaught. **2** not sent to school. **3** untrained, undisciplined.

unscientific *adj.* **1** not in accordance with scientific principles. **2** not familiar with science. □ **unscientifically** *adv.*

---

unreachable *adj.*	**unrehearsed** *adj.*	**unresolvable** *adj.*	**unsaleability** *n.*
unreachableness *n.*	**unrelated** *adj.*	**unresponsive** *adj.*	(also **unsalability**)
unreachably *adv.*	**unreleased** *adj.*	**unresponsively** *adv.*	**unsaleable** *adj.*
unrealistic *adj.*	**unreliability** *n.*	**unresponsiveness** *n.*	(also **unsalable**)
unrealistically *adv.*	**unreliable** *adj.*	**unresting** *adj.*	**unsalted** *adj.*
unrealizable *adj.*	**unreliableness** *n.*	**unrestrained** *adj.*	**unsalvageable** *adj.*
unrealized *adj.*	**unreliably** *adv.*	**unrestrainedly** *adv.*	**unsanitary** *adj.*
unreasoned *adj.*	**unremarkable** *adj.*	**unrestricted** *adj.*	**unsatisfactorily** *adv.*
unreasoning *adj.*	**unremarkably** *adv.*	**unrestrictedly** *adv.*	**unsatisfactoriness** *n.*
unreasoningly *adv.*	**unremitting** *adj.*	**unrewarding** *adj.*	**unsatisfactory** *adj.*
unreceptive *adj.*	**unremittingly** *adv.*	**unrhymed** *adj.*	**unsatisfied** *adj.*
unrecognizable *adj.*	**unrepentant** *adj.*	**unripe** *adj.*	**unsatisfying** *adj.*
unrecognizableness *n.*	**unrepentantly** *adv.*	**unripeness** *n.*	**unsatisfyingly** *adv.*
unrecognizably *adv.*	**unreported** *adj.*	**unromantic** *adj.*	**unsaved** *adj.*
unrecognized *adj.*	**unrepresentative** *adj.*	**unromantically** *adv.*	**unscented** *adj.*
unrecorded *adj.*	**unrepresented** *adj.*	**unroofed** *adj.*	**unscheduled** *adj.*
unrefined *adj.*	**unresisting** *adj.*	**unsafe** *adj.*	
unregistered *adj.*	**unresistingly** *adv.*	**unsafely** *adv.*	
unregulated *adj.*	**unresistingness** *n.*	**unsafeness** *n.*	

unscramble *v.tr.* restore from a scrambled state, esp. interpret (a scrambled transmission etc.). □ **unscrambler** *n.*

unscrew *v.* **1** *tr. & intr.* unfasten or be unfastened by turning or removing a screw or screws or by twisting like a screw. **2** *tr.* loosen (a screw, lid, etc.).

unscrupulous *adj.* having no scruples, unprincipled. □ **unscrupulously** *adv.* **unscrupulousness** *n.*

unseasonable *adj.* **1** (esp. of weather) not appropriate to the season. **2** untimely, inopportune. □ **unseasonableness** *n.* **unseasonably** *adv.*

unseasonal *adj.* not typical of, or appropriate to, the time or season.

unseasoned *adj.* **1** not flavoured with salt, herbs, etc. **2** (esp. of timber) not matured. **3** inexperienced.

unseat *v.tr.* **1** remove from power or office, esp. in an election. **2** dislodge from a seat, esp. on horseback.

unseeable *adj.* that cannot be seen.

unseeded *adj. Sport* (of a player) not seeded.

unseeing *adj.* **1** not seeing; unobservant. **2** blind. □ **unseeingly** *adv.*

unseemly *adj.* (**-ier, -iest**) **1** indecent. **2** unbecoming. □ **unseemliness** *n.*

unseen *adj.* **1** not seen. **2** invisible. **3** (of a passage for translation) not previously read or prepared.

unserviceable *adj.* not serviceable; unfit for use. □ **unserviceability** *n.*

unserviced *adj. Cdn* (esp. of a campsite) not serviced with electricity etc.

unsettle *v.* **1** *tr.* disturb the settled state or arrangement of. **2** *tr.* derange. **3** *intr.* become unsettled. □ **unsettling** *adj.* **unsettlingly** *adv.*

unsettled *adj.* **1** not (yet) settled. **2** liable or open to change or further discussion. **3** (of a bill etc.) unpaid. **4** continually changing. □ **unsettledness** *n.*

unsex *v.tr.* **1** deprive (a person) of the qualities of her or his sex. **2** castrate or spay. □ **unsexed** *adj.*

unsexy *adj.* (**-ier, -iest**) **1** not sexually attractive or stimulating. **2** unfashionable or unexciting.

unsheathe *v.tr.* remove (a knife etc.) from a sheath.

unsightly *adj.* unpleasant to look at, ugly. □ **unsightliness** *n.*

unsigned *adj.* **1** not signed. **2** not having signed a contract.

unsized[1] *adj.* **1** not made to a size. **2** not sorted by size.

unsized[2] *adj.* not treated with size.

unskilled *adj.* lacking or not needing special skill or training.

unsocial *adj.* **1** not social; not suitable for, seeking, or conforming to society. **2** outside the normal working day (*unsocial hours*). **3** anti-social. □ **unsocially** *adv.*

unsolicited *adj.* not asked for.

unsophisticated *adj.* **1** not having or showing much experience of the world and social situations. **2** not complicated or refined; basic (*unsophisticated equipment*). **3** not adulterated or artificial.

unsought *adj.* **1** not searched out or sought for. **2** unasked; without being requested.

unsound *adj.* **1** unhealthy, diseased. **2** rotten, weak. **3 a** ill-founded, fallacious. **b** unorthodox, heretical. **4** unreliable. **5** wicked. □ **of unsound mind** insane.

unsparing *adj.* **1** giving freely and generously. **2** severe; not caring about people's feelings. □ **unsparingly** *adv.* **unsparingness** *n.*

unspeakable *adj.* **1** that cannot be expressed in words. **2** indescribably bad or objectionable. □ **unspeakableness** *n.* **unspeakably** *adv.*

unspent *adj.* **1** not expended or used. **2** not exhausted or used up.

unspoiled *adj.* **1** (also esp. *Brit.* **unspoilt**) not spoiled. **2** not plundered.

unspoken *adj.* **1** understood without being expressed verbally. **2** not uttered or as expressed in speech.

unsportsmanlike *adj.* (of behaviour, an act, etc.) dishonourable, unseemly; unfair.

unsportsmanlike conduct *n.* a penalty imposed in various sports for unprofessional or unseemly conduct, e.g. pulling the hair of one's opponent.

unspun *adj.* not formed or prepared by spinning.

unstable *adj.* **1** not stable. **2** changeable. **3** showing a tendency to sudden mental or emotional changes. **4** (of weather, an air mass, etc.) likely to produce precipitation. □ **unstabilized** *adj.* **unstably** *adv.*

unsteady *adj.* (**-ier, -iest**) **1** not steady or firm. **2** changeable, fluctuating. **3** not uniform or regular. □ **unsteadily** *adv.* **unsteadiness** *n.*

unstick *v.tr.* (*past* and *past part.* **unstuck**) separate (a thing stuck to another). □ **come unstuck** *informal* come to grief, fail.

unstinting *adj.* lavish. □ **unstintingly** *adv.*

unstressed *adj.* **1** (of a word, syllable, etc.) not pronounced with stress. **2** not subjected to stress.

unstring *v.tr.* (*past* and *past part.* **unstrung**) **1** remove or relax the string or strings of (a bow, guitar, etc.). **2** remove from a string. **3** (esp. as **unstrung** *adj.*) unnerve.

unstructured *adj.* **1** not structured. **2** informal.

unsuited *adj.* (usu. foll. by *for, to*) not suited (to); inappropriate; not fit (for).

---

unsealed *adj.*	**unshaded** *adj.*	**unskilfully** *adv.*	**unstated** *adj.*
unsecured *adj.*	**unshakeability** (also	**unskilfulness** *n.*	**unstoppable** *adj.*
unselfconscious *adj.*	**unshakable**)	**unsmiling** *adj.*	**unstoppably** *adv.*
unselfconsciously *adv.*	**unshakeable** *adj.*	**unsmilingly** *adv.*	**unsubstantial** *adj.*
unselfconsciousness *n.*	(also **unshakable**)	**unsociability** *n.*	**unsubstantiality** *n.*
unselfish *adj.*	**unshakeably** *adv.*	**unsociable** *adj.*	**unsubstantiated** *adv.*
unselfishly *adv.*	(also **unshakably**)	**unsociableness** *n.*	**unsubstantiated** *adj.*
unselfishness *n.*	**unshaven** *adj.*	**unsociably** *adv.*	**unsubtle** *adj.*
unsentimental *adj.*	**unshavenness** *n.*	**unsold** *adj.*	**unsubtly** *adv.*
unsentimentality *n.*	**unshed** *adj.*	**unsolved** *adj.*	**unsuccessful** *adj.*
unsentimentally *adv.*	**unsinkability** *n.*	**unspecific** *adj.*	**unsuccessfully** *adv.*
unseparated *adj.*	**unsinkable** *adj.*	**unspecified** *adj.*	**unsuitability** *n.*
unserious *adj.*	**unskilful** *adj.*	**unspectacular** *adj.*	**unsullied** *adj.*
unseriousness *n.*	(also **unskillful**)	**unspectacularly** *adv.*	

unsung adj. **1** unrecognized, unknown. **2** not sung.

unswerving adj. **1** steady, constant. **2** not turning aside. □ **unswervingly** adv.

untangle v.tr. **1** free from a tangled state. **2** free from entanglement.

untapped adj. not (yet) tapped (*untapped resources*).

untaught adj. **1** not instructed by teaching; ignorant. **2** not acquired by teaching; natural.

untaxed adj. not required to pay or not attracting taxes.

untenable adj. (of an argument, position, etc.) not tenable; that cannot be defended. □ **untenability** n. **untenably** adv.

untested adj. not tested or proved. □ **untestable** adj.

unthinkable adj. **1** that cannot be imagined or grasped by the mind. **2** *informal* highly unlikely or undesirable. □ **unthinkability** n. **unthinkably** adv.

unthinking adj. **1** not thinking. **2** characterized by thoughtlessness or absence of thought. □ **unthinkingly** adv.

unthrifty adj. **1** wasteful, extravagant, prodigal. **2** not thriving or flourishing. □ **unthriftily** adv. **unthriftiness** n.

untie v.tr. (*pres. part.* **untying**) **1** undo (a knot etc.). **2** unfasten the cords etc. of (a package etc.). **3** release from bonds or attachment.

untied adj. not tied.

until prep. & conj. ● prep. **1** up to or as late as (*wait until six o'clock*; *did not return until night*). **2** up to the time of (*faithful until death*). ● conj. **1** up to the time when (*wait until I return*). **2** so long that (*laughed until I cried*).

untimely adj. **1** inopportune. **2** (esp. of death) premature. □ **untimeliness** n.

untitled adj. having no title.

unto prep. archaic = TO prep. (*do unto others*).

untold adj. **1** not told. **2** not (able to be) counted or measured (*untold misery*).

untouchable ● adj. **1** that may not or cannot be touched. **2** that may not be harmed, criticized, disrupted, etc. ● n. **1** a member of a hereditary Hindu group held to defile members of higher castes on contact. ¶Use of the term, and social restrictions accompanying it, were declared illegal under the Indian constitution in 1949. **2** an untouchable person or thing. □ **untouchability** n.

untouched adj. **1** not touched. **2** not affected physically; not harmed, modified, used, or tasted. **3** not affected by emotion. **4** not discussed.

untoward adj. **1** inconvenient, unlucky. **2** awkward. **3** perverse, refractory. **4** unseemly, improper.

untracked adj. **1** not marked with tracks from skis etc. **2** having no previously-trodden track; unexplored. **3** not traced or followed.

untranslatable adj. that cannot be translated (satisfactorily). □ **untranslatability** n. **untranslatably** adv. **untranslated** adj.

untried adj. **1** not tried or tested. **2** inexperienced. **3** not yet tried by a judge.

untrue adj. **1** not true, contrary to what is the fact. **2** (often foll. by *to*) not faithful or loyal. **3** deviating from an accepted standard. □ **untruly** adv.

untruth n. **1** the state of being untrue, falsehood. **2** a false statement (*told me an untruth*).

untuck v.tr. free (a shirt, bedclothes, etc.) from being tucked in or up.

untutored adj. **1** uneducated, untaught. **2** simple, unsophisticated.

untwist v.tr. & intr. open from a twisted or spiralled state.

untying pres. part. of UNTIE.

unused adj. **1 a** not in use. **b** never having been used. **2** (foll. by *to*) not accustomed.

unusual adj. **1** not usual. **2** exceptional, remarkable, strange. □ **unusually** adv. **unusualness** n.

unutterable adj. inexpressible; beyond description. □ **unutterably** adv.

unvarnished adj. **1** not varnished. **2** (of a statement or person) plain and straightforward (*the unvarnished truth*).

unveil v.tr. **1** remove a veil from. **2** remove a covering from (a statue, plaque, etc.) as part of the ceremony of the first public display. **3** disclose, reveal, make publicly known. □ **unveiling** n.

unvoiced adj. **1** not spoken or expressed. **2** *Phonetics* not voiced.

unwarrantable adj. indefensible, unjustifiable. □ **unwarrantably** adv.

unwarranted adj. **1** unauthorized. **2** unjustified.

unwary adj. **1** not cautious. **2** (often foll. by *of*) not aware of possible danger etc. □ **unwarily** adv. **unwariness** n.

unwashed adj. **1** not washed. **2** not usually washed or clean. *See also* GREAT UNWASHED.

unwell predic. adj. not in good health; (somewhat) ill.

unwholesome adj. **1** not promoting, or detrimental to, physical or moral health; unhealthy. **2** unhealthy-looking. □ **unwholesomely** adv. **unwholesomeness** n.

---

unsupervised adj.	**unsustainably** adv.	**untidiness** n.	**untypical** adj.
unsupported adj.	**unsustained** adj.	**untidy** adj. (-ier, -iest)	**untypically** adv.
unsure adj.	**unsweetened** adj.	**untiring** adj.	**unusable** adj.
unsurely adv.	**unsymmetrical** adj.	**untiringly** adv.	**unvaccinated** adj.
unsureness n.	**unsymmetrically** adv.	**untraceable** adj.	**unvarying** adj.
unsurpassable adj.	**unsympathetic** adj.	**untraceably** adv.	**unvaryingly** adv.
unsurpassably adv.	**unsympathetically** adv.	**untraditional** adj.	**unverifiable** adj.
unsurpassed adj.	**unsystematic** adj.	**untrained** adj.	**unverified** adj.
unsurprised adj.	**unsystematically** adv.	**untrammelled** adj.	**unwanted** adj.
unsurprising adj.	**untainted** adj.	**untreated** adj.	**unwarlike** adj.
unsurprisingly adv.	**untalented** adj.	**untroubled** adj.	**unwavering** adj.
unsuspected adj.	**untamed** adj.	**untrustworthiness** n.	**unwaveringly** adv.
unsuspectedly adv.	**untanned** adj.	**untrustworthy** adj.	**unweaned** adj.
unsuspecting adj.	**untarnished** adj.	**untruthful** adj.	**unwed** adj.
unsuspectingly adv.	**untended** adj.	**untruthfully** adv.	**unwedded** adj.
unsuspectingness n.	**unthreatening** adj.	**untruthfulness** n.	**unwelcome** adj.
unsustainable adj.	**untidily** adv.	**unturned** adj.	**unwelcomely** adv.

unwieldy *adj.* **(-ier, -iest)** cumbersome, clumsy, or hard to manage, owing to size, shape, weight, etc. □ **unwieldily** *adv.* **unwieldiness** *n.*

unwind *v.* (*past* and *past part.* **unwound**) **1 a** *tr.* draw out (a thing that has been wound). **b** *intr.* become drawn out after having been wound. **2** *intr. & tr. informal* relax.

unwise *adj.* **1** (of a person etc.) foolish, imprudent. **2** injudicious. □ **unwisely** *adv.*

unwitting *adj.* **1** not knowing; unaware of the state of the case (*an unwitting offender*). **2** unintentional, inadvertent. □ **unwittingly** *adv.*

unwonted *adj.* not customary or usual. □ **unwontedly** *adv.*

unworked *adj.* **1** not wrought into shape. **2** not exploited.

unworldly *adj.* **1** spiritually-minded. **2** spiritual. □ **unworldliness** *n.*

unworthy *adj.* **(-ier, -iest) 1** (often foll. by *of*) not worthy or befitting the character of a person etc. **2** discreditable, unseemly. **3** contemptible, base. **4** having or possessing insufficient merit, excellence, or worth; not deserving. □ **unworthily** *adv.* **unworthiness** *n.*

unwound[1] *adj.* not wound or wound up.

unwound[2] *past* and *past part. of* UNWIND.

unwrap *v.* (**unwrapped, unwrapping**) **1** *tr.* remove the wrapping from. **2** *tr.* open or unfold. **3** *tr.* unfold, reveal, disclose. **4** *intr.* become unwrapped.

unwritten *adj.* **1** not written. **2** (of a law etc.) resting originally on custom or judicial decision, not on statute. **3** (of a convention etc.) not expressed in words, implicit.

unyielding *adj.* **1** not yielding to pressure etc. **2** firm, obstinate. □ **unyieldingly** *adv.* **unyieldingness** *n.*

unzip *v.* (**unzipped, unzipping**) **1** *tr.* unfasten the zipper of. **2** *intr.* unfasten a zipper (esp. in disrobing). **3** *tr. Computing* decompress (a compressed file).

up ● *adv.* **1** at, in, or towards a higher place or position (*jumped up in the air; what are they doing up there?*). **2** to or in a place regarded as higher, esp. northwards (*up in Yellowknife*). **3** *informal* ahead etc. as indicated (*went up front*). **4 a** to or in an erect position or condition (*stood it up*). **b** to or in a prepared or required position (*wound up the watch*). **c** in or into a condition of efficiency, activity, or progress (*stirred up trouble; up for sale*). **5** in a stronger or winning position or condition (*up three goals; am $10 up*). **6** (of a computer) running and available for use. **7** to the place or time in question or where the speaker etc. is (*a child came up to me; has been fine up till now*). **8** at or to a higher price or value (*costs are up*). **9 a** completely or effectually (*eat up; use up*). **b** more loudly or clearly (*speak up*). **10** in a state of completion; denoting the end of availability, supply, etc. (*time is up*). **11** into a compact, accumulated, or secure state (*pack up; save up*). **12** out of bed (*are you up yet?*). **13** (of the sun etc.) having risen. **14** happening, esp. unusually or unexpectedly (*something is up*). **15 a** *Baseball* at bat. **b** next in line or in order of business. **16** taught or informed (*is well up in French*). **17** (usu. foll. by *before*) appearing for trial etc. (*was up before the parole board*). **19** (of a jockey) in the saddle. **20** towards the source of a river. **21** inland. **22** (of the points etc. in a game):

a registered on the scoreboard. **b** forming the total score for the time being. **23** upstairs, esp. to bed (*are you going up yet?*). **24** (of a theatre curtain) raised etc. to reveal the stage. **25** (as *interj.*) get up. ● *prep.* **1** upward along, through, or into. **2** from the bottom to the top of. **3** along (*walked up the road*). **4 a** at or in a higher part of (*is situated up the street*). **b** towards the source of (a river). ● *adj.* directed upward. ● *n.* a period of good fortune (*we've had our ups and downs*). ● *v.* (**upped, upping**) **1** *intr. informal* begin abruptly to say or do something (*upped and hit him*). **2** *tr.* increase or raise, esp. abruptly (*upped all their prices*). □ **be all up with** (with *it* as subject) be disastrous or hopeless for (a person). **on the up and up** *informal* esp. *N Amer.* honest(ly); on the level. **something is up** *informal* something unusual or undesirable is afoot or happening. **up against 1** in or into contact with. **2** *informal* confronted with (*up against a problem*). **up against it** *informal* in great difficulties. **up and around** (or **about, doing**) having risen from bed; active. **up close** very close(ly). **up and down 1** back and forth (along) (*have been up and down the road*). **2** in every direction. **3** *informal* in varying health or spirits. **up for** available for or being considered for (office etc.). **up hill and down dale** up and down hills, or confronting many obstacles, on an arduous journey or in the fulfilment of an arduous task. **up on** informed about (a matter or subject). **up to 1** until (*up to the present*). **2** not more than (*you can have up to five*). **3** less than or equal to (*sums up to $100*). **4 a** incumbent on (*it is up to you to tell them*). **b** to be decided by (*I'll leave it up to you*). **5** capable of or fit for (*am not up to a long walk*). **6** occupied or busy with (*what have you been up to?*). **up with** *interj.* expressing support for a stated person or thing. **up yours** *coarse slang* expressing contemptuous defiance or rejection. **what's up?** *informal* **1** what is going on? **2** what is the matter?

upalong *Cdn* (*Nfld*) ● *adv.* to or on a location away from a person or place, esp. to or on mainland Canada. ● *n.* such a location (*from upalong*).

up-and-coming *adj. informal* (of a person) making good progress and likely to succeed. □ **up-and-comer** *n.*

up and running *adj. & adv.* functioning; in operation.

upbeat ● *n.* an unaccented beat in music. ● *adj. informal* optimistic or cheerful.

upbraid *v.tr.* (often foll. by *with, for*) chide or reproach (a person).

upbringing *n.* **1** the bringing up of a child; education. **2** the manner of this.

UPC *abbr.* UNIVERSAL PRODUCT CODE.

upchuck *v. & n. N Amer. slang* vomit.

up-close-and-personal *adj. informal* intimate, cozy.

upcoming *adj.* esp. *N Amer.* forthcoming; about to happen.

upcountry *adv. & adj.* inland.

update ● *v.tr.* **1** make more modern or up-to-date, esp. by replacing old material, methods, etc. or including new material. **2** provide (a person) with the latest information about something. ● *n.* **1** the act or an instance of updating. **2** an updated version; a set of updated information. □ **updated** *adj.*

updraft *n.* (also **updraught**) an upward draft.

upend *v.* **1** *tr. & intr.* set or become upside down or so

---

unwilling *adj.*	**unwinnable** *adj.*	**unworkability** *n.*	**unworkably** *adv.*
unwillingly *adv.*	**unwomanly** *adj.*	**unworkable** *adj.*	**unwoven** *adj.*
unwillingness *n.*			

that one end is at the top. **2** *tr.* knock over; cause to fall down. **2** *intr.* (of a duck etc.) dip the head below water and raise the tail into the air, when feeding in shallow water. **4** *tr. Sport* defeat.

upfield *adv.* = DOWNFIELD.

upfront *informal* ● *adv.* (usu. **up front**) **1** at the front; in front. **2** (of payments) in advance. ● *adj.* **1** honest, open, frank. **2** (of payments) made in advance. **3** at the front or most prominent.

upgrade ● *v.* **1** *tr.* raise in rank etc. **2** *tr.* improve (equipment etc.) esp. by replacing components. **3** *intr.* replace (components of) one's equipment, software, etc. with improved versions. **4** *tr.* & *intr.* move to a higher category in a hierarchy (*upgraded to business class*). ● *n.* **1** the act or an instance of upgrading. **2** an upgraded piece of equipment etc. □ **on the upgrade 1** improving in health etc. **2** advancing, progressing. □ **upgradeable** *adj.* (also **upgradable**) esp. *Computing.* **upgrader** *n.*

upheaval *n.* **1** a violent or sudden change or disruption. **2** *Geol.* an upward displacement of part of the earth's crust. **3** the act or instance of heaving up.

uphill ● *adv.* in an ascending direction up a hill, slope, etc. ● *adj.* **1** sloping up. **2** arduous, difficult (*an uphill struggle*). ● *n.* an upward slope.

uphold *v.tr.* (*past* and *past part.* **upheld**) **1** confirm or maintain (a decision etc., esp. of another). **2** give support or countenance to (a person, practice, etc.). **3** maintain unimpaired and intact. □ **upholder** *n.*

upholster /ʌpˈəʊlstər, ʌpˈhəʊl-/ *v.tr.* provide (furniture) with upholstery. □ **upholsterer** *n.*

upholstery *n.* **1** textile covering, padding, springs, etc., for furniture. **2** an upholsterer's work.

up ice *adv. Hockey* towards the opponent's end of the rink.

U-pick *N Amer.* ● *adj.* designating an orchard or farm where customers pick produce directly from the fields etc. ● *n.* such a farm or orchard.

up-island *adv.* & *adj. Cdn* towards or of the northern or more remote parts of Vancouver Island.

upkeep *n.* **1** maintenance in good condition. **2** the cost or means of this.

upland ● *n.* high or hilly country. ● *adj.* of or relating to this.

uplift ● *v.tr.* **1** raise; lift up. **2** elevate or stimulate morally or spiritually. ● *n.* **1** the act or an instance of being raised. **2** *Geol.* the raising of part of the earth's surface. **3** *informal* a morally or spiritually elevating influence. **4** support for the bust etc. from a garment. □ **uplifter** *n.* **uplifting** *adj.* (esp. in sense 2 of *v.*).

uplight *n.* a light placed or designed to throw illumination upward. □ **uplighting** *n.*

uplink ● *n.* a communications link to a satellite. ● *v.tr.* (esp. as **uplinked** *adj.*) provide with or send by an uplink.

upload *Computing* ● *v.tr.* & *intr.* transfer (data) to a larger storage device or to a central system. ● *n.* (usu. *attrib.*) a transfer of this type (*upload feature*).

upmarket *adj.* & *adv.* = UPSCALE.

upon *prep.* = ON. ¶*Upon* is sometimes more formal than *on*, but is the only idiomatic choice in *once upon a time* and in uses such as *row upon row of seats* and *Christmas is almost upon us.*

upper ● *adj.* **1** situated above another part (*the upper atmosphere; the upper lip*). **2** higher in position or status (*the upper class*) **3** (**Upper**) **a** situated on higher ground (*Upper Egypt*). **b** situated to the north (*Upper California*). **4** (often **Upper**) *Geol.* & *Archaeology* designating a younger, and hence usu. shallower, part of a stratigraphic division, archaeological deposit, etc., or the period in which it was formed or deposited. ● *n.* **1**

the part of a boot or shoe above the sole. **2** *slang* a stimulant drug, esp. an amphetamine.

Upper Canadian *Cdn* ● *n.* **1** *hist.* a native or inhabitant of the former British colony of Upper Canada (1791–1841), now the southern part of Ontario. **2** esp. *Maritimes* a native or inhabitant of Ontario. ● *adj.* **1** *hist.* of or relating to the colony of Upper Canada. **2** esp. *Maritimes* of or relating to Ontario.

upper case ● *adj.* designating the larger characters used in printing and writing, often differing in shape and size from the minuscule forms. ● *n.* (hyphenated when *attrib.*) an upper case letter.

upper class ● *n.* the highest class of society. ● *adj.* (**upper-class**) of the upper class.

upper crust *n.* (hyphenated when *attrib.*) *informal* the upper class.

uppercut ● *n.* an upward blow delivered with the arm bent. ● *v.tr.* hit with an uppercut.

upper hand *n.* dominance or control; an advantage.

upper house *n.* (also **upper chamber**) the usu. smaller body in a bicameral legislature, often representing regional or sectional interests, esp. (in Canada) the Senate.

upper middle class ● *n.* the class of society between the middle and upper classes. ● *adj.* (**upper-middle-class**) of the upper middle class.

uppermost ● *adj.* **1** highest in place or rank. **2** predominant. ● *adv.* at or to the highest or most prominent position.

uppish *adj. informal* self-assertive or arrogant. □ **uppishly** *adv.* **uppishness** *n.*

uppity *adj. informal* **1** impertinent; arrogant. **2** snobbish. □ **uppitiness** *n.* (also **uppityness**).

upraise *v.tr.* (esp. as **upraised** *adj.*) raise to a higher level.

upright ● *adj.* **1** erect, vertical (*an upright posture; stood upright*). **2** (of a piano) with vertical strings. **3** (of a person or behaviour) righteous; strictly honourable or honest. ● *n.* **1** a post or rod fixed upright esp. as a structural support. **2** (usu. in *pl.*) a goalpost, esp. in football. **3** an upright piano. ● *v.tr.* raise or restore to an upright or vertical position. □ **uprightly** *adv.* **uprightness** *n.*

uprising *n.* **1** a rebellion or revolt. **2** the action or an act of rising or uprising.

upriver ● *adv.* at or towards a point nearer the source of a river. ● *adj.* situated or occurring upriver.

uproar *n.* **1** a tumult; a violent disturbance. **2** a sustained protest; an expression of outrage.

uproarious /ʌpˈrɔːrɪəs/ *adj.* **1** very noisy. **2** provoking loud laughter. □ **uproariously** *adv.*

uproot *v.* **1** *tr.* pull (a plant etc.) up from the ground. **2** *tr.* displace (a person) from an accustomed location. **3** *tr.* eradicate, destroy. **4** *intr.* move away from one's accustomed location or home. □ **uprootedness** *n.*

UPS *abbr.* uninterruptible power supply.

upsadaisy *var. of* UPSY-DAISY.

upscale *adj.* & *adv. N Amer.* toward or relating to the more expensive or affluent sector of the market.

upset ● *v.* (**upsetting**; *past* and *past part.* **upset**) **1** *tr.* & *intr.* overturn or be overturned. **2** *tr.* disturb the composure of (*was very upset by the news*). **3** *tr.* disturb (the digestion) (*may upset the stomach*). **4** *tr.* disrupt (*upset all their plans*). **5** *tr.* defeat (a favoured opponent). ● *n.* **1** a condition of upsetting or being upset (*a stomach upset*). **2** a surprising victory over a favoured opponent. ● *adj.* **1** disturbed, esp. temporarily (*an upset stomach*). **2** distressed, esp. emotionally. □ **upsetter** *n.* **upsettingly** *adv.*

upshot *n.* (usu. prec. by *the*) the final or eventual outcome or conclusion.

upside ● n. **1** (often attrib.) the upper side or surface of something. **2** the positive aspect of something; an advantage. **3** an upward movement of share prices etc. ● prep. N Amer. slang on or against (slapped him upside the head).

upside down ● adv. **1** with the upper part where the lower part should be; in an inverted position. **2** in or into total disorder (everything was turned upside down). ● adj. (also **upside-down** attrib.) that is positioned upside down; inverted.

upside-down cake n. a cake baked with fruit in a syrup at the bottom, and inverted for serving.

upsilon /ˈjuːpsɪˌlɒn, ʌpˈsailən/ n. the twentieth letter of the Greek alphabet (Υ, υ).

upstage ● adj. & adv. **1** nearer the back of a theatre stage. **2** snobbish(ly). ● v.tr. **1** (of an actor) move upstage to make (another actor) face away from the audience. **2** divert attention from (a person) to oneself.

upstairs ● adv. **1** to or on an upper floor. **2** to or in a more influential position or higher authority. **3** informal mentally, in the head (doesn't have much upstairs). ● adj. situated upstairs. ● n. an upper floor.

upstanding adj. **1** standing up. **2** honest or straightforward.

upstart ● n. a person who has risen suddenly to prominence, esp. one who behaves arrogantly. ● adj. **1** that is an upstart. **2** of or like an upstart.

upstate US ● n. part of a state remote from its large cities, esp. the northern part of New York State. ● adj. of or relating to this part. ● adv. in or to this part.

upstream ● adv. against the flow of a stream etc. ● adj. moving upstream.

upsurge n. **1** an upward surge; a rise (as in feelings etc.). **2** a rapid growth in number or size.

upswept adj. **1** (of the hair) combed to the top of the head. **2** curved or sloped upward.

upswing n. an upward movement or trend.

upsy-daisy interj. expressing encouragement to a child who is being lifted or has fallen.

uptake n. **1** informal understanding; comprehension (slow on the uptake). **2** the act or an instance of taking up. **3** absorption or incorporation of something by a living system (oxygen uptake).

uptempo adj. & adv. at a fast or an increased tempo.

upthrust n. **1** upward thrust, e.g. of a fluid on an immersed body. **2** Geol. = UPHEAVAL 2.

uptick n. N Amer. an increase, esp. a small one.

uptight adj. informal **1** nervously tense or angry. **2** N Amer. rigidly conventional.

uptime n. time during which a machine, esp. a computer, is in operation.

up-to-date see DATE[1].

up-to-the-minute adj. (usu. attrib.) latest; most modern.

uptown N Amer. ● adj. of or in the esp. more affluent part of a city between downtown and the outer suburbs. ● adv. in or into this part. ● n. this part.

upturn ● n. **1** an upward trend; an improvement. **2** an upheaval. ● v.tr. turn up or upside down.

upward ● adv. (also **upwards**) towards what is higher, superior, larger in amount, more important, or earlier. ● adj. moving, extending, pointing, or leading upward. □ **upwards** of more than (found upwards of forty). □ **upwardly** adv.

upwardly mobile adj. able or aspiring to advance socially or professionally. □ **upward mobility** n.

upwelling n. **1** a welling upward, esp. the rising of cold water from the bottom of the sea, often bringing with it a renewed source of nutrients. **2** the water that has risen in this way.

upwind adj. & adv. against the direction of the wind.

Ural-Altaic /ˌjʊərəlælˈteɪɪk/ ● n. a family of Finno-Ugric, Turkic, Mongolian, and other languages of N Europe and Asia. ● adj. **1** of or relating to this family of languages. **2** of or relating to the region including the Ural and Altai Mountains in central Asia and its inhabitants.

Uralic /jʊˈrælɪk/ ● adj. **1** of, relating to, or denoting a family of languages spoken from N Scandinavia to W Siberia, including the Finno-Ugric group. **2** of or relating to the Ural Mountains in N Russia or the surrounding areas. ● n. the Uralic languages collectively.

uranium n. a heavy radioactive metallic element of the actinide series occurring naturally in pitchblende and other ores, which is capable of nuclear fission and used as a source of nuclear energy.

urban adj. of, living in, or situated in a town or city (an urban population) (opp. RURAL).

urban community n. Cdn (Que.) one of three regional municipalities consisting of the large metropolitan areas of Montreal, Quebec City, and Hull/Gatineau.

urbane /ɜːˈbeɪn/ adj. elegant and refined in manner and style; courteous, sophisticated, suave.

urbanism n. **1** the development of an urban community; urbanization. **2** the character or way of life of a city. **3** a study of the development or way of life of a city. □ **urbanist** n. (in sense 3).

urbanite n. a resident of a city.

urbanity /ɜːˈbænɪti/ n. (pl. **-ies**) **1** an urbane quality; refinement of manner. **2** the state, condition, or character of a city; urban life.

urbanize v.tr. **1** make (a mainly rural area) urban. **2** destroy the rural quality of (a community). □ **urbanization** n.

urban municipality n. any incorporated city, town, village, resort village, summer village, or township.

urban myth n. (also **urban legend**) an unverifiable, usu. apocryphal story, widely recounted as if true, which typically depicts outlandish or sensational happenings in a plausible contemporary setting.

urban planner n. a person who plans the construction, growth, and development of urban communities as a profession. □ **urban planning** n.

urban renewal n. the process of rejuvenating derelict or dilapidated districts of a city through slum clearance and redevelopment.

urban sprawl n. the uncontrolled expansion of urban areas.

urchin n. **1** a poor, dirty, and ill-clothed child, esp. in an urban area. **2** = SEA URCHIN.

Urdu /ˈʊərduː/ n. an Indo-Aryan language closely related to Hindi with an admixture of Persian and Arabic words, now the official language of Pakistan and also used in India.

urea /jʊˈriːə/ n. a soluble crystalline compound which is the main nitrogenous breakdown product of protein metabolism in mammals, is excreted in their urine, and is used esp. as a fertilizer, de-icing agent, and in the manufacture of synthetic resins.

urea formaldehyde n. a plastic, resin, or foam made by condensation of urea with formaldehyde, used esp. for insulation.

uremia /jʊˈriːmɪə/ n. a morbid condition due to the presence in the blood of urinary matter normally eliminated by the kidneys. □ **uremic** adj.

urethane /ˈjʊərə,θeɪn/ ● n. = POLYURETHANE. ● v.tr. coat with a polyurethane finish.

urethra /jʊˈriːθrə/ n. (pl. **urethrae** /-riː/ or **-s**) the tube or canal through which urine is carried out of the body from the bladder, and which in the male also conveys semen. □ **urethral** adj. **urethritis** /-rɪˈθraɪtɪs/ n.

urge ● v.tr. **1** (often foll. by on) drive, hasten, or impel with force or encouragement (she urged her teammates on). **2** encourage or entreat earnestly or persistently; exhort (urged them to go). **3** (often foll. by on, upon) advocate (an action or argument etc.) pressingly or emphatically (to a person). **4** advocate or recommend eagerly or insistently (we urge caution; we urge that they should be cautious). **5** present or state earnestly or insistently in argument, justification, or defence (I must urge the seriousness of this problem). ● n. a strong impulse, desire, or tendency. □ **urging** n.

urgency n. (pl. **-ies**) **1** the state, condition, or fact of being urgent. **2** a pressing or urgent need.

urgent adj. **1** demanding or requiring immediate action or attention; pressing (an urgent need for help). **2** expressing a need for prompt action or attention; insistent (an urgent call for help). □ **urgently** adv.

uric acid /ˈjʊərɪk/ n. a crystalline acid, which is the end product of purine metabolism in primates and carnivores, is excreted in their urine, and is the main nitrogenous excretory product in birds, reptiles, and insects.

urinal n. **1** a ceramic plumbing fixture for men to urinate into, usu. equipped with a flushing mechanism. **2** any receptacle for urination.

urinalysis /ˌjʊərɪˈnælɪsɪs/ n. (pl. **urinalyses** /-ˌsiːz/) the analysis of urine by physical, chemical, and microscopical means to test for the presence of disease or drugs etc.

urinary adj. **1** of or relating to urine. **2** affecting or occurring in the urinary system (urinary diseases).

urinate v.intr. discharge urine. □ **urination** n.

urine n. the pale yellow fluid containing waste products filtered from the blood by the kidneys, stored in the bladder, and discharged at intervals through the urethra.

URL /ɜːrl/ n. Computing the address used to specify the location of a Web site on the Internet.

urn n. **1** a large decorative vase or container with a rounded usu. egg-shaped body and a pedestal. **2** any usu. ornamental vessel, vase, or container used to store or bury the ashes of the cremated dead. **3** a large metal container with a tap, in which coffee or tea is made and kept hot.

urology /jʊˈrɒlədʒi/ n. the branch of medicine that deals with disorders of the kidney and urinary tract. □ **urologic** adj. **urological** adj. **urologist** n.

Ursuline /ˈɜːrsjʊ,lɪn, -laɪn/ ● n. a nun of an Augustinian order founded in 1535 for nursing the sick and teaching girls. ● adj. of this order.

Uruguayan /ˌjɜːrəˈgweɪən, jʊr-, ,ɜːr-/ ● n. a native or inhabitant of Uruguay, a country on the Atlantic coast of S America. ● adj. of or relating to Uruguay or its people or culture.

US abbr. **1** United States. **2** Undersecretary. **3** unserviceable.

us pron. **1** objective case of WE (they saw us). **2** informal = WE (it's us again). **3** N Amer. informal ourselves, to or for ourselves (we've got to get us one of those!). **4** informal = ME[1] (give us a kiss).

USA abbr. **1** United States of America. **2** United States Army.

usable adj. (also **useable**) that can be used. □ **usability** n.

USAF abbr. United States Air Force.

usage n. **1** the action or an instance of using something or of being used; employment, use. **2 a** habitual or customary practice, esp. as creating a right, obligation, or standard. **b** established or customary use of words, expressions, constructions, etc. in a language, esp. as opposed to what is prescribed. **3** a manner of using or treating; treatment (damaged by rough usage).

USDA abbr. United States Department of Agriculture.

use ● v.tr. **1 a** employ (something) for a particular purpose (can I use the phone?; use your discretion). **b** employ or avail oneself of (something) regularly (uses the subway to get to work). **2 a** (in past) did, was, or had in the past as a customary practice or continuous state (I used to be a dancer; it didn't use to rain so often). **b** (usu. in passive) familiar by habit; accustomed (not used to hard work). **3** exploit (a person or thing) for one's own ends (he's just using you to make his girlfriend jealous). **4** treat (a person) in a specified manner (they used him shamefully). **5** esp. N Amer. take (drugs, alcohol, etc.) regularly. ● n. **1** the act of using or the state of being used; application to a purpose (the use of force). **2** the manner or mode of using, employing, or utilizing something (she put it to good use). **3** the right or power of using (lost the use of my right arm). **4** advantage, value, usefulness (a flashlight would be of some use right now). **5** need or occasion for employing something; necessity, demand, call (would you have any use for this radio?). **6** habitual, usual, or common practice (long use has accustomed me to it). □ **could use** informal **1** would like to have; want. **2** would be in a position to benefit from; need. **have no use for 1** do not need. **2** dislike or be impatient with. **it's** (or **there's**) **no use** it would be pointless to; it will not help to (there's no use trying to talk to her when she's like this). **make use of 1** employ, apply. **2** benefit from. **use it or lose it 1** an opportunity etc., if not taken advantage of, may not be made available again. **2** something, e.g. a skill, may become lost or unusable through neglect. **use a person's name** quote a person as an authority or reference etc. **use up 1** consume completely, use all of. **2** find a use for (something remaining). **3** exhaust or wear out e.g. with overwork. □ **user** n.

used adj. having been previously owned; second-hand.

useful adj. **1** that can be used for a practical purpose; beneficial. **2** of use or value to someone (he's useful around the house). **3** informal reasonably effective or successful (their most useful player). □ **make oneself useful** be helpful. □ **usefully** adv. **usefulness** n.

useless adj. **1** failing to fulfill the intended purpose or produce the desired results (this knife is useless). **2** serving no purpose (useless information). **3** informal incompetent, ineffectual (I'm useless at swimming). □ **uselessly** adv. **uselessness** n.

Usenet /ˈjuː.znet/ n. any of a number of services designed to help users access information on a network, usu. consisting of an index of newsgroups arranged according to subject matter.

user-defined adj. Computing that has been specified or varied by a user.

user fee n. a fee charged for a service, esp. an additional amount of money or tax charged for a service that is paid for or subsidized by the government.

user-friendly adj. **1** (of a system, program, software, etc.) designed to make the user's task as easy as possible, esp. by offering onscreen instructions, prompts, and feedback. **2** *informal* or *jocular* easy to read, use, or understand. □ **user-friendliness** *n.*

user group *n. Computing* a newsgroup exchanging technical information, advice, and services.

user interface *n. Computing* the means of communication between a user and a system, referring esp. to the use of input/output devices with supporting software (compare GRAPHICAL USER INTERFACE).

usher ● *n.* **1** a person who shows people to their seats in a theatre, stadium, church, etc. **2** an attendant of the groom at a wedding, responsible for greeting guests at the church and showing them to their seats. ● *v.tr.* **1** (usu. foll. by *into*) show or guide (a person) into a room, to a seat, etc. (*ushered us into the room*). **2** (foll. by *in*) be the forerunner of (an era, age, movement, etc.). **3** act as usher to.

usherette *n.* a woman who shows people to their seats, esp. in a theatre or stadium etc.

Usher of the Black Rod *n. Cdn* = BLACK ROD 1.

USS *abbr.* United States Ship.

USSR *abbr. hist.* Union of Soviet Socialist Republics.

usu. *abbr.* usually.

usual ● *adj.* such as commonly occurs, or is observed or done; customary, habitual, regular. ● *n. informal* **1** (prec. by *the*) what is commonly said or done etc.; what is customary or habitual ('*What did you talk about?' 'Oh, the usual.'*). **2** (prec. by *the*, *my*, etc.) the drink or meal a person habitually orders in a bar or restaurant. □ **as usual** as is or was commonly the case (*they were late, as usual*). **than usual** than is or was customary or habitual (*I ate less than usual today*).

usually *adv.* **1** as a rule; generally speaking; normally. **2** in a usual or customary manner.

usurer /'juːʒɜrər/ *n.* a person who practises usury.

usurious /juːˈʒɜriəs/ *adj.* **1** of, involving, or practising usury. **2** (of interest) taken or charged by usury; exorbitant, excessive. □ **usuriously** *adv.*

usurp /jʊˈsɜːrp, -ˈzɜːrp/ *v.tr.* **1** seize or assume (another's position or authority) by force. **2** take possession of (land etc.) unlawfully. □ **usurpation** *n.* **usurper** *n.*

usury /'juːʒɜːri/ *n.* **1** the act or practice of lending money at interest, esp. at an exorbitant, excessive, or illegal rate. **2** interest on money lent at such a rate.

UT *abbr.* Utah (in postal use).

Utahan /juːˈtɔən/ ● *n.* a native or inhabitant of the US state of Utah. ● *adj.* of or relating to Utah.

utensil *n.* a tool or implement for domestic use, esp. any of those objects found in a kitchen and used for eating or preparing food (*cooking utensils*).

uterus /'juːtərəs/ *n.* (*pl.* **uteruses** or **uteri** /-ˌraɪ/) the womb. □ **uterine** /'juːtərˌɪn, -raɪn/ *adj.*

utilidor /juːˈtɪlədɔːr/ *n. Cdn* (*North*) an enclosed insulated conduit running above ground and carrying water, sewerage, and electricity between houses in settlements built on permafrost.

utilitarian ● *adj.* **1** designed to be practically useful rather than attractive; functional. **2** of or pertaining to the doctrine of utilitarianism. ● *n.* an adherent of utilitarianism.

utilitarianism *n.* the doctrine that an action is right in so far as it promotes happiness, and that the guiding principle of conduct should be to achieve the greatest benefit or happiness for the greatest number of people.

utility ● *n.* (*pl.* **-ies**) **1** the condition or quality of being useful or beneficial. **2** (usu. in *pl.*) a useful thing; a thing able to satisfy human needs. **3 a** (often in *pl.*) = PUBLIC UTILITY. **b** (in *pl.*) shares in a public utility. **c** (in *pl.*) electricity, natural gas, etc. as provided by a public utility. **4** *Computing* (also **utility program**) a program for carrying out a routine

function. ● *attrib.adj.* **1** designating things made for utility; useful, functional rather than attractive (*utility furniture*). **2** *Baseball* designating a substitute player, esp. an infielder, who is capable of playing several different positions. **3** *N Amer.* designating the lowest grade of domestic meat, e.g. of an animal that is missing a part.

utility pole *n. N Amer.* a pole used to carry wires above the ground; a telephone or hydro pole.

utility vehicle *n.* (also **utility truck**) *N Amer.* = SPORT-UTILITY.

utilize *v.tr.* make use of; use effectively for a practical purpose. □ **utilizable** *adj.* **utilization** *n.*

utmost **1** greatest in amount or degree; most extreme, ultimate (*of the utmost importance*). **2** furthest, most remote; outermost (*the utmost limits*). ● *n.* (prec. by *the*) **1** that which is greatest in degree, amount, or extent (*these shoes offer the utmost in durability*). **2** the extreme limit, the ultimate degree (*my patience was tested to the utmost*). **3** the greatest or best of one's ability or power (*we performed to our utmost*). □ **do one's utmost** do all that one can.

Uto-Aztecan /juːtoːˈæztekən/ ● *n.* a language family of Central America and western N America. ● *adj.* of or pertaining to this language

Utopia /juːˈtoːpiə/ *n.* (also **utopia**) **1** an imaginary or hypothetical place or state of affairs considered to be perfect; a condition of social or political perfection. **2** an impossibly ideal scheme, esp. for social or political improvement.

Utopian (also **utopian**) ● *adj.* **1** of or characteristic of Utopia. **2** impossibly ideal or perfect; idealistic. ● *n.* an idealistic reformer. □ **Utopianism** *n.*

utter[1] *attrib.adj.* complete, total, absolute, unqualified (*utter misery; an utter fool*). □ **utterly** *adv.*

utter[2] *v.tr.* **1** emit audibly (*uttered a startled cry*). **2** speak or say (words, a phrase, a prayer, etc.). **3** *Law* issue or circulate (a forged document, counterfeit money or cheques, etc.). □ **utterer** *n.*

utterance *n.* **1** the act or an instance of uttering. **2** a thing spoken. **3 a** the power of speaking. **b** a manner of speaking.

uttermost *adj. & n.* = UTMOST.

U-turn ● *n.* **1** an act of driving a vehicle in a U-shaped course in order to turn around and travel in the opposite direction. **2** a reversal of policy. ● *v.intr.* perform a U-turn.

UV *abbr.* **1** ultraviolet. **2** ultraviolet radiation (*UV protection*).

UVA *abbr.* ultraviolet radiation of relatively long wavelengths.

UVB *abbr.* ultraviolet radiation of relatively short wavelengths.

UVC *abbr.* ultraviolet radiation of very short wavelengths, which does not penetrate the earth's ozone layer.

UV Index *n.* an index used to represent the intensity of the sun's ultraviolet rays, ranging from 'low' (less than 4) to 'extreme' (more than 9).

uvula /'juːvjələ, ˈʌvjuːlə/ *n.* (*pl.* **uvulae** /-ˌliː/) a fleshy extension of the soft palate hanging above the throat.

Uzbek /'ʌzbek, 'ʊz-/ *n.* **1** a member of a Turkic people living mainly in Uzbekistan, an independent republic in central Asia. **2** the language of this people.

Uzi /'uːzi/ *n.* (in full **Uzi machine gun** or **Uzi machine pistol**) a type of submachine gun.

Vv

V¹ n. (also **v**) (pl. **Vs** or **V's**) **1** the twenty-second letter of the alphabet. **2** a V-shaped thing. **3** (as a Roman numeral) five.

V² symbol **1** vanadium. **2 a** volt(s). **b** voltage, potential difference. **3** volume.

v. abbr. **1** verse. **2** verso. **3** versus. **4** very. **5** vide.

V6 n. (pl. **V6's**) **1** an engine with six cylinders forming a V shape. **2** a vehicle with such an engine.

V8 n. (pl. **V8's**) **1** an engine with eight cylinders forming a V shape. **2** a vehicle with such an engine.

VA abbr. **1** Vice Admiral. **2** Virginia (in official postal use).

Va. abbr. Virginia.

vac n. informal a vacuum cleaner.

vacancy n. (pl. **-ies**) **1** the state of being vacant or empty. **2** an available room in a hotel, apartment building, etc. **3** an unoccupied position; a job opening. **4** emptiness of mind; lack of intelligence.

vacant adj. **1** containing no objects; empty. **2** (of land, a building, etc.) uninhabited (a vacant lot). **3** (of a place, room, etc.) unoccupied; not in use (a vacant seat). **4** (of a post or position) available. **5** characterized by or exhibiting a lack of attention or thought (a vacant stare). ☐ **vacantly** adv.

vacate /'veikeit, və'keit/ v.tr. **1** leave or cease to occupy (a place). **2** give up tenure of (a post etc.).

vacation ● n. **1** N Amer. a period of several days or weeks spent away from work or school etc., used esp. for recreation and travel; a holiday. **2** the act of vacating a house or position etc. ● v.intr. N Amer. take or spend a vacation. ☐ **vacationer** n.

vacation pay n. Cdn the wages which an employee is entitled, under federal law, to receive either as paid vacation, or in lieu of paid vacation, amounting to four per cent of the year's salary or six per cent for an employee who has worked for a single employer for six or more consecutive years.

vaccinate v.tr. & intr. immunize. ☐ **vaccination** n.

vaccine /'væk'si:n, 'væk-/ n. **1** an antigenic preparation used to stimulate the production of antibodies and procure immunity from one or several diseases. **2** Computing a program designed to protect a computer system from the effect of destructive software such as a virus.

vacillate /'væsɪˌleit/ v.intr. **1** waver between different opinions, options, actions, etc. **2** sway unsteadily. ☐ **vacillating** adj. **vacillation** n.

vacuity /və'kju:iti/ n. (pl. **-ies**) **1 a** absolute emptiness. **b** an empty or vacant space. **2 a** vacancy of mind or thought. **b** an empty or inane thing.

vacuole /'vækjuːˌol/ n. a small cavity or vesicle in organic tissue, esp. a tiny space within the cytoplasm of a cell containing air, fluid, food particles, etc.

vacuous /'vækjuːəs/ adj. **1** unintelligent, expressionless (a vacuous stare). **2** lacking substance or content; meaningless (a vacuous criticism). **3** empty. **4** idle, indolent. ☐ **vacuously** adv. **vacuousness** n.

vacuum ● n. (pl. **-s** or **vacua** /'vækjuə/) **1** a space entirely devoid of matter. **2** a space or vessel from which the air has been completely or partly removed

by a pump etc. **3 a** a place or situation etc., marked by an absence of the usual, former, or expected contents (the vacuum created by the death of his wife). **b** a place or situation etc. in which one is insulated from external influences; a state of isolation. **4** (pl. **-s**) a vacuum cleaner. **5** a decrease of pressure below the normal atmospheric value. ● v. informal **1** tr. & intr. clean (a room or carpet etc.) with a vacuum cleaner. **2** tr. remove (dust etc.) with or as if with a vacuum cleaner.

vacuum cleaner n. an electrical appliance for removing dust from carpets etc., by suction.

vacuum packed adj. **1** (esp. of food) sealed in an airtight package or container from which some or all of the air has been removed, usu. in order to preserve freshness. **2** (of a package or container etc.) hermetically sealed after the partial removal of air.

vacuum tube n. a sealed glass tube containing a near-vacuum for the free passage of electric current, esp. one used as a thermionic valve.

vade mecum /ˌvædi'mi:kəm, ˌveidi'meikəm/ n. a handbook or manual kept or carried with one for ready reference.

VAdm abbr. Cdn VICE ADMIRAL.

vagabond ● n. **1** a person who roams or wanders from place to place with no settled habitation and no visible means of support; a tramp or hobo, esp. an idle or dishonest one. **2** informal a disreputable, idle, or worthless person. ● adj. **1** roving or wandering. **2** resembling or pertaining to a homeless wanderer. ☐ **vagabondage** n.

vagary /'veigəri/ n. (pl. **-ies**) an outlandish or eccentric act or notion; a caprice or whim (the vagaries of Fortune).

vagina /və'dʒainə/ n. (pl. **-s** or **vaginae** /-ni:/) the canal leading from the vulva to the cervix of the uterus in women and most female mammals. ☐ **vaginal** /'vædʒənəl/ adj.

vagrant ● n. **1** a person with no settled home or regular work. **2** a person who roams or wanders. ● adj. **1** characteristic of or relating to a vagrant or vagrancy. **2** wandering or roving (a vagrant musician). ☐ **vagrancy** n.

vague adj. **1** (of a statement etc.) couched in general, indefinite, or imprecise terms; lacking in details or particulars (a vague answer). **2** (of an idea, notion, feeling, etc.) not definite, clear, or fully established. **3** lacking physical definiteness of form or outline; indistinctly seen or perceived. **4** (of a person or mind) inexact in thought, expression, or understanding. ☐ **vaguely** adv. **vagueness** n.

vain adj. **1** having an excessively high opinion of one's own appearance, abilities, worth, etc.; conceited. **2** useless, ineffectual, futile (a vain hope). **3** empty, trivial, unsubstantial (vain boasts). ☐ **in vain** without success; ineffectually, uselessly (it was in vain that we protested). **take a person's name in vain** mention a person's name (formerly esp. that of God) casually or irreverently, such as when swearing. ☐ **vainly** adv.

vainglory n. literary extreme vanity. ☐ **vainglorious** adj. **vaingloriously** adv. **vaingloriousness** n.

valance /'væləns, veil-/ n. a short ornamental curtain hung around a bedstead or above a window etc. in order to conceal the frame or supporting hardware.

vale n. archaic or literary a valley.

valedictorian /ˌvælədɪkˈtɔːrɪən/ n. N Amer. a person who gives a valedictory.

valedictory /ˌvæləˈdɪktəri/ ● n. (pl. **-ies**) **1** N Amer. a speech or address given by a student of a graduating class at a school or university as a part of the graduation exercises. **2** any statement or address made upon leaving or bidding farewell. ● adj. of, pertaining to, or performed as a valedictory (*valedictory address*).

valence /ˈveɪləns/ n. esp. N Amer. the power or capacity of an atom or group to combine with or displace other atoms or groups in the formation of compounds, equivalent to the number of hydrogen atoms that it could combine with or displace.

valentine n. **1** a note, card, or gift, traditionally sent anonymously, given as a token of love or affection on Valentine's Day. **2** a person courted as a sweetheart on Valentine's Day.

Valentine's Day n. (in full **St. Valentine's Day**) Feb. 14, celebrated with the courting of sweethearts and the exchange of valentines etc.

valerian /vəˈlɪərɪən/ n. **1** any of various flowering plants of the family Valerianaceae, esp. the common valerian, *Valerian officinalis*, with pink or white flowers. **2** a bitter-tasting drug derived from the rootstock of this plant, used as a stimulant etc.

valet /ˈvæleɪ, ˈvæ-/ n. **1** a male servant who attends to a gentleman's clothes, etc. **2** a hotel employee with similar duties for guests. **3** an attendant responsible for parking the cars of patrons of a restaurant etc. **4** N Amer. a rack on which clothing may be hung.

Valhalla /vælˈhælə/ n. Scand. Myth the hall in which the souls of those who have died in battle feast with Odin, the supreme god and creator, for eternity. **2** informal or jocular a place or state of perfect bliss.

valiant adj. (of a person or conduct) brave, courageous, heroic. □ **valiantly** adv.

valid adj. **1** (of an argument, assertion, etc.) well-founded and defensible; sound. **2 a** legally binding and acceptable (*a valid contract*). **b** not having reached its expiry date (*this credit card is no longer valid*). **3** having legitimacy, authenticity, or authority (*valid information*). □ **validity** n. **validly** adv.

validate v.tr. **1** make or declare legally valid. **2** lend force or validity to; confirm, substantiate. □ **validation** n.

valise /vəˈliːs/ n. a small piece of luggage similar to a suitcase or portmanteau.

Valium /ˈvælɪəm/ n. proprietary the drug diazepam used as a tranquilizer and relaxant.

Valkyrie /vælˈkɪːri, ˈvælkɪri/ n. Scand. Myth each of the twelve handmaidens who hovered over battlefields and conducted the fallen warriors to Valhalla.

valley n. (pl. **-eys**) **1 a** a low usu. elongated area more or less enclosed by hills and typically having a stream flowing through it. **b** the extensive tract of land drained by a single large river system. **2** any depression or hollow resembling or compared to this. **3** an internal angle formed by the junction of two sloping sides of a roof etc.

Valley girl n. esp. US informal or derogatory a fashionable and affluent teenage girl from the San Fernando Valley in S California, speaking a variety of slang characterized by the use of filler words such as *like* and *totally* and a limited group of adjectives expressing approval or disapproval.

valorize v.tr. **1** raise or fix the price or value of (a

commodity etc.) by artificial means, esp. by government intervention. **2** give validity to; make valid. □ **valorization** n.

valour n. (also **valor**) personal courage, esp. in battle. □ **valorous** adj.

valuable ● adj. **1** of material or monetary value; precious. **2** of great use or benefit; having considerable importance or worth. ● n. (usu. in pl.) a valuable thing, esp. a small article of personal property such as jewellery. □ **valuably** adv.

valuation n. **1 a** an estimation of a thing's monetary value, esp. by a professional appraiser. **b** the estimated monetary value. **2** an appraisal of something with respect to excellence or merit. □ **valuate** v.tr. **valuator** n.

value ● n. **1** the worth, usefulness, or importance of a thing. **2 a** the material or monetary worth of a thing; the amount of money, goods, etc., for which a thing can be exchanged or traded. **b** the monetary worth as estimated or appraised professionally; valuation. **3** the amount of a commodity, medium of exchange, etc., considered to be the equivalent of something (*the insurance paid us full value for our lost property*). **4** the worth or quality of something compared to the price paid for it. **5** the ability of a thing to serve a specified purpose or cause a specified effect (*shock value; R-value*). **6** (in pl.) the principles or moral standards of a person or social group. **7** Music the length or duration of a sound signified by a note. **8 a** Math. the amount represented by an algebraic term or expression. **b** Physics & Chem. the numerical measure of a quantity or a number denoting magnitude on some conventional scale (*the value of gravity at the equator*). **9** (foll. by *of*) **a** the meaning (of a word etc.). **b** the quality of a spoken sound; the sound represented by a letter. **10** the relative rank or importance of a playing card, chess piece, etc., according to the rules of the game. ● v.tr. (**values, valued, valuing**) **1** (often in passive, foll. by *at*) estimate the value of; appraise (esp. professionally) (*their house is valued at $400,000*). **2** consider of worth or importance; have a high opinion of (*I value his friendship*).

value added ● n. the amount by which the value of an article is increased at each stage of its production, exclusive of initial costs. ● adj. (**value-added**) **1** (of food, goods, etc.) having features or ingredients added to the basic line or model to justify an increase in price and thereby enhance the profit margin for the producer and retailer. **2** (of a company) offering specialized or extended services in a commercial area.

value-added tax n. a tax on the amount by which the value of an article has been increased at each stage of its production or distribution.

value-free adj. free from criteria imposed by subjective values or standards.

value judgment n. an estimate of esp. moral or artistic merit based on personal opinion rather than facts.

valueless adj. having no value. □ **valuelessness** n.

value system n. the set of connected or interdependent values of a person or social group.

valve n. **1** a device for controlling the passage of air, steam, water, etc. through a pipe, esp. an automatic device allowing movement in one direction only. **2** Anat. & Zool. a membranous fold in a hollow organ or tubular structure of the circulatory system, digestive tract, etc. which automatically closes to prevent the reflux of blood or other contents. **3** Music a device for extending the range of pitch of a brass instrument by increasing or decreasing the effective length of the tube. **4** each of the two shells of an oyster, mussel, etc. □ **valved** adj. (also in comb.).

vamoose /væˈmuːs/ v.intr. N Amer. (often in imper.) slang leave, disappear, take off.

vamp¹ ● n. **1** the part of a boot or shoe covering the front of the foot. **2** Music a short simple introductory passage or accompaniment, sometimes improvised and usu. repeated several times until otherwise instructed. ● v.tr. **1** (often foll. by up) **a** compile or piece together out of old materials. **b** restore or repair. **2** Music play (a passage or accompaniment etc.) as a vamp (the guitarist vamped the intro). **3** put a new vamp on (a boot or shoe).

vamp² informal ● n. a woman who uses sexual attraction to exploit men. ● v. **1** intr. behave as a vamp. **2** tr. act as a vamp towards (usu. a man). □ **vampish** adj. **vampy** adj.

vampire n. **1** a ghost or reanimated corpse supposed to leave its grave at night to suck the blood of sleeping people, often represented as a human figure with long pointed canine teeth. **2** a person who preys ruthlessly on others. □ **vampiric** /væmˈpiːrɪk/ adj.

vampire bat n. any of various tropical esp. S American bats of the family Desmodontidae, which have sharp incisors for piercing flesh and lap the blood of large mammals.

van¹ n. **1** any of a range of covered vehicles, usu. smaller than a truck, with space in the back for cargo and usu. enclosed with no side windows. **2** N Amer. a similar vehicle for carrying passengers.

van² n. = VANGUARD.

vanadium /vəˈneɪdiəm/ n. a hard grey metallic element occurring naturally in several ores, used in small quantities to strengthen some steels.

Vancouverite n. a resident or native of Vancouver.

vandal ● n. **1** a person who wilfully or maliciously destroys or damages property. **2** (**Vandal**) a member of a Germanic people that ravaged Gaul, Spain, N Africa, and Rome in the 4th–5th c., destroying many books and works of art. ● adj. of or relating to the Vandals. □ **vandalism** n. **vandalize** v.tr.

Van Doos /vænˈduːz/ n.pl. Cdn informal the Royal 22e Régiment (the Royal 22nd Regiment), a French-speaking Canadian infantry regiment.

Vandyke /vænˈdaɪk/ ● n. **1** each of a series of large points forming a border on lace or cloth etc. **2** a cape or collar etc. with these. **3** (in full **Vandyke beard**) a neat pointed beard. ● adj. in the style of dress, esp. with pointed borders, common in portraits by the Flemish painter Anthony Van Dyck (1599–1641).

vane n. **1** = WEATHER VANE. **2** a blade of a screw propeller or a windmill etc. **3** the sight of surveying instruments, a quadrant, etc. **4** the flat part of a bird's feather formed by the barbs. **5** a broad flat projecting surface designed to guide the motion of a projectile, e.g. an arrow. □ **vaned** adj.

vanguard /ˈvænɡɑːrd/ n. **1** the foremost part of an army or fleet advancing or ready to advance. **2** the leaders of a movement or of opinion etc. **3** the forefront of a movement, field of activity, etc.

Vanier Cup /ˈvænjeɪ/ n. Cdn a trophy awarded annually to the winner of the Canadian inter-university football championship.

vanilla ● n. **1 a** any tropical climbing orchid of the genus Vanilla, esp. V. planifolia, with fragrant flowers. **b** (in full **vanilla bean**) the fruit of these. **2** a substance obtained from the vanilla bean or synthesized and used to flavour ice cream and other foods. ● adj. = PLAIN-VANILLA.

vanish v. **1** intr. **a** disappear suddenly. **b** disappear gradually; fade away. **2** intr. cease to exist. **3** intr. go away. **4** tr. cause to disappear.

vanishing point n. **1** the point at which receding parallel lines viewed in perspective appear to meet. **2** the state of complete disappearance of something.

vanity n. (pl. **-ies**) **1 a** conceit and desire for admiration of one's personal attainments or attractions. **b** excessive concern with one's physical appearance. **c** something about which one is vain. **2 a** futility or unsubstantiality (the vanity of human achievement). **b** an unreal thing. **3** ostentatious display. **4** a unit consisting of a sink set into a flat top with cupboards beneath, esp. in a bathroom. **5** N Amer. a dressing table.

vanity plate n. (also **vanity licence plate**) N Amer. a vehicle licence plate bearing a personalized combination of letters, numbers, or both.

vanquish /ˈvæŋkwɪʃ/ v.tr. literary conquer or overcome.

vantage /ˈvæntɪdʒ/ n. (also **vantage point**) a place affording a good view or prospect.

vapid /ˈvæpɪd/ adj. insipid; lacking interest; flat, dull (vapid moralizing). □ **vapidity** /vəˈpɪdɪti/ n. (pl. **-ies**).

vaporize v.tr. & intr. convert or be converted into vapour. □ **vaporization** n.

vaporizer n. a device that vaporizes substances, esp. for medicinal inhalation.

vapour (also **vapor**) ● n. **1** moisture or another substance diffused or suspended in air, e.g. mist or smoke. **2** Physics a gaseous form of a normally liquid or solid substance (compare GAS 1). **3** a medicinal agent for inhaling. ● v.intr. **1** rise as vapour. **2** make idle boasts or empty talk. □ **vaporous** adj. **vapouring** n.

vapour barrier n. a thin layer of waterproof material, e.g. polyethylene film, used to protect insulation by blocking the passage of moisture from the interior space.

vapour trail n. = CONTRAIL.

vapourware n. Computing slang software that as yet exists only in the plans or publicity of its developers.

vaquero /vəˈkero/ n. (pl. **-os**) N Amer. (esp. in Spanish-speaking areas) a cattle driver.

var. abbr. variant.

variable ● adj. **1 a** that can be varied or adapted (a rod of variable length). **b** (of a gear) designed to give varying speeds. **2** apt to vary; not constant (variable fortunes). **3** Math. (of a quantity) indeterminate. **4** (of wind or currents) tending to change direction. **5** (of a star) periodically varying in brightness. **6** Bot. & Zool. (of a species) including individuals or groups that depart from the type. **7** Biol. (of an organism or part of it) tending to change in structure or function. ● n. **1 a** variable thing or quantity. **2** Math. **a** a variable quantity. **b** a symbol, such as x, y, or z, that represents this. □ **variability** n. **variably** adv.

variance n. **1** difference of opinion; dispute, disagreement; lack of harmony (a theory at variance with all known facts). **2** Law a discrepancy between statements or documents. **3** N Amer. Law an official dispensation, esp. from a building regulation or zoning bylaw.

variant ● adj. **1** differing in form or details from the main one (a variant spelling). **2** having different forms (forty variant types of pigeon). **3** variable or changing. ● n. a variant form, spelling, type, reading, etc.

variation n. **1** the act or an instance of varying. **2** departure from a former or normal condition, action, or amount, or from a standard or type (prices are subject to variation). **3** the extent of this. **4** a thing that varies from a type. **5** Music a repetition (usu. one of several) of a theme in a changed or elaborated form. **6** a deviation of a heavenly body from its mean orbit or motion. **7** *Math.* a change in a function etc. due to small changes in the values of constants etc. **8** a solo that is part of a full-length ballet etc.

varicoloured /'verɪ,kʌlərd/ *adj.* (also **varicolored**) **1** variegated in colour. **2** of various or different colours.

varicose /'verɪ,ko:s/ *adj.* (esp. of the veins of the legs) affected by a condition causing them to become dilated and swollen.

varied *adj.* showing variety; diverse.

variegate /'verə,geit, -rɪə,geit/ *v.tr.* **1** mark with irregular patches of different colours. **2** diversify in appearance, esp. in colour. □ **variegation** *n.*

variegated *adj.* **1** (of plants) having leaves containing two or more colours. **2** marked or characterized by variety or diversity.

varietal /və'raɪətəl/ ● *adj.* **1** esp. *Bot.* & *Zool.* of, forming, or designating a variety. **2** (of wine) made from a single, designated variety of grape. ● *n.* a wine made from a single, designated variety of grape.

variety *n.* (*pl.* **-ies**) **1** diversity; absence of uniformity; many-sidedness (*not enough variety in our lives*). **2** a quantity or collection of different things (*for a variety of reasons*). **3 a** a class of things different in some common qualities from the rest of a larger class to which they belong. **b** a specimen or member of such a class. **4** (foll. by *of*) a different form of a thing, quality, etc. **5** *Biol.* **a** a subspecies. **b** a cultivar. **c** an individual or group usually fertile within the species to which it belongs but differing from the species type in some qualities capable of perpetuation. **6** a mixed sequence of dances, songs, comedy acts, etc. (usu. *attrib.*: *a variety show*).

variety store *n. N Amer.* = CONVENIENCE STORE.

various *adj.* **1** different, diverse (*too various to form a group*). **2** more than one, several (*for various reasons*). **3** individual or separate (*the various members of the staff*). □ **variously** *adv.* **variousness** *n.*

varmint *n. N Amer. informal jocular* **1** a destructive or undesirable wild animal. **2** a troublesome or objectionable person.

varnish ● *n.* **1** a resinous solution used to give a hard shiny transparent coating to wood, metal, paintings, etc. **2** any other preparation for a similar purpose. **3** external appearance or display without an underlying reality. **4** artificial or natural glossiness. **5** a superficial polish of manner. ● *v.tr.* **1** apply varnish to. **2** gloss over (a fact).

varsity *adj.* **1** designating sports played at the university or college level. **2** *N Amer.* designating the most advanced level of athletic competition in a high school etc.

Varsol *n. Cdn proprietary* mineral spirits.

vary *v.* (**-ies, -ied**) **1** *tr.* make different; modify, diversify (*seldom varies the routine*). **2** *intr.* a undergo change; become or be different (*the temperature varies from 20°
to 30°*). **b** be of different kinds (*her mood varies*). **3** *intr.* (foll. by *as*) be in proportion to. □ **varying** *adj.*
varyingly *adv.*

varying hare *n.* = ARCTIC HARE.

vas /væs/ *n.* (*pl.* **vasa** /'veɪsə/) *Anat.* a vessel or duct.

vascular /'væskjʊlər/ *adj.* of, made up of, or containing vessels for conveying blood or sap etc. (*vascular functions*; *vascular tissue*).

vascular plant *n.* a plant with conducting tissue.

vas deferens /'defə,renz/ (*pl.* **vasa deferentia** /,defə'renʃɪə/) *Anat.* the spermatic duct from the testicle to the urethra.

vase /vɒz, veiz, veis/ *n.* a vessel, usu. tall and circular, used as an ornament or container, esp. for flowers.

vasectomy /və'sektəmi/ *n.* (*pl.* **-ies**) the surgical removal of part of each vas deferens esp. as a means of sterilization. □ **vasectomize** *v.tr.*

Vaseline ● *n. proprietary* a type of petroleum jelly used as an ointment, lubricant, etc. ● *v.tr.* (**vaseline**) treat with Vaseline.

vasoconstriction /,veizo:kən'strɪkʃən/ *n.* the constriction of blood vessels. □ **vasoconstrictor** *n.*

vasodilation /,veizo:dai'leiʃən/ *n.* the dilatation of blood vessels. □ **vasodilator** *n.*

vassal /'væsəl/ *n.* **1** *hist.* a holder of land by feudal tenure on conditions of homage and allegiance. **2** a humble dependant. □ **vassalage** *n.*

vast *adj.* **1** immense, huge; very great (*a vast expanse of water*). **2** *informal* great, considerable (*makes a vast difference*). □ **vastly** *adv.* **vastness** *n.*

vat *n.* a large tank or other vessel, esp. for holding liquids or something in liquid in the process of brewing, tanning, dyeing, etc.

Vatican /'vætɪkən/ *n.* (*prec. by the*) **1** the palace and official residence of the Pope in Rome. **2** papal government.

Vatican Council *n.* an ecumenical council of the Roman Catholic Church, esp. that held in 1869–70 or that held in 1962–65.

Vatican II *n.* the Second Vatican Council, held in 1962–65, which effected liturgical and organizational reforms in the Roman Catholic Church, promoted ecumenism, and emphasized the role of the laity.

vaudeville /'vɒdvɪl, 'vɒdə,vɪl/ *n.* **1** a form of variety entertainment popular esp. in the US from about 1880 until the early 1930s. **2** a stage play on a trivial theme with interspersed songs (also *attrib.*: *vaudeville act*). □ **vaudevillian** *adj.* & *n.*

vault ● *n.* **1 a** an arched roof. **b** a continuous arch. **c** a set or series of arches whose joints radiate from a central point or line. **2** a vaultlike covering (*the vault of heaven*). **3** an underground chamber, esp. as a place of interment beneath a church or in a cemetery etc. (*family vault*). **4** a place of storage, esp. for valuables (*bank vault*). **5** an act of vaulting. ● *v.* **1** *intr.* leap or spring, esp. while resting on one or both hands or with the help of a pole. **2** *tr.* spring over (a gate etc.) in this way. **3** *tr.* (esp. as **vaulted**) **a** make in the form of a vault. **b** provide with a vault or vaults.

vaulting ● *n.* **1** arched work in a vaulted roof or ceiling. **2** a gymnastic or athletic exercise in which participants vault over obstacles. ● *adj.* **1** excessively confident or presumptuous (*vaulting ambition*). **2** used to vault or in vaulting (*a vaulting pole*).

vaunt *literary* ● *v.* **1** *intr.* boast, brag. **2** *tr.* boast of; extol boastfully. ● *n.* a boast. □ **vaunter** *n.*

vaunted *adj.* highly praised, esp. to excess.

VC *abbr.* **1** VICTORIA CROSS. **2** Vice-Chairman. **3** Vice-Chancellor. **4** Vice-Consul. **5** Viet Cong.

v-chip *n.* a device that, when installed in a TV set or receiver, can be programmed by the user to block or scramble any TV program that contains violence, sex, or bad language (as indicated by a code inserted into the signal by the broadcaster).

VCR *n.* an electrical apparatus used in conjunction with a television for recording broadcast material onto videotape and for playing back video cassettes.

VD *abbr.* VENEREAL DISEASE.

VDT *abbr.* VIDEO DISPLAY TERMINAL.

VDU *abbr.* video (or visual) display unit.

VE *abbr.* Victory in Europe (in 1945).

've *abbr.* (chiefly after pronouns) = HAVE (*I've*; *they've*).

veal *n.* **1** calf's flesh. **2** a calf raised for veal.

vector ● *n.* **1** *Math. & Physics* a quantity having direction as well as magnitude, esp. as determining the position of one point in space relative to another. **2** a carrier of disease. **3** a course to be taken by an aircraft. ● *v.tr.* **1** direct (an aircraft in flight) to a desired point. **2** change or alter the direction of (the thrust of a jet engine) in order to steer an aircraft etc.

Veda /'veidə, 'viː-/ *n.* (in *sing.* or *pl.*) the most ancient Hindu scriptures, esp. four collections called Rig-Veda, Sāma-Veda, Yajur-Veda, and Atharva-Veda.

VE day *n.* May 8, the day marking the Allied victory in Europe in 1945.

Vedda /'vedə/ *n.* a Sri Lankan aboriginal.

Vedic /'veidik, 'viː-/ ● *adj.* of or relating to the Veda or Vedas. ● *n.* the language of the Vedas, an older form of Sanskrit.

vee *n.* **1** the letter V. **2** a thing shaped like a V.

veejay *n. informal* = VJ.

veep *n.* esp. *N Amer. informal* a vice-president.

veer ● *v.intr.* **1 a** change direction or course, esp. suddenly. **b** (of a conversation, or a person's behaviour or opinions) change suddenly. **2** (of the wind) change direction clockwise (*compare* BACK *v.* 5). ● *n.* a change of course or direction.

veg¹ *n. informal* a vegetable or vegetables.

veg² *v.intr.* (**vegges, vegged, vegging**) esp. *N Amer.* (often foll. by *out*) relax in a mindless manner.

vegan /'viːgən, 'vei-, 'vedʒən/ ● *n.* a person who does not eat or use animal products. ● *adj.* using or containing no animal products. □ **veganism** *n.*

vegetable ● *n.* **1** any plant or edible fungus whose leaves, roots, tubers, fruit, seeds, or flowers are used for food, e.g. lettuce, potatoes, carrots, tomatoes, and mushrooms. **2** *informal* **a** a person who is incapable of normal intellectual activity, esp. through brain injury etc. **b** a person lacking in animation or living a monotonous life. ● *adj.* **1** of, derived from, relating to, or comprising plants or plant life, esp. as distinct from animal life or mineral substances. **2** of or relating to vegetables as food. **3 a** unresponsive to stimulus (*vegetable behaviour*). **b** uneventful, monotonous (*a vegetable existence*).

vegetable oil *n.* an oil derived from plants, e.g. canola oil, olive oil, corn oil.

vegetable parchment *n. see* PARCHMENT 2.

vegetal /'vedʒətəl/ *adj.* **1** of or having the nature of plants (*vegetal growth*). **2** vegetative.

vegetarian ● *n.* a person who abstains from animal food, esp. that from slaughtered animals, though often not eggs and dairy products. ● *adj.* **1** of or relating to vegetarians or vegetarianism. **2 a** containing no meat. **b** containing no animal products. □ **vegetarianism** *n.*

vegetate *v.* **1** *intr.* live an uneventful or monotonous life. **2** *intr.* esp. *N Amer.* relax in a mindless or passive manner (*went home and spent the evening vegetating*). **3** *tr.* (usu. in *passive*) be covered or provided with vegetation or plant life (esp. of a specified kind). **4** *intr.* grow as plants do; fulfill vegetal functions.

vegetation *n.* **1** plants collectively; plant life (*luxuriant vegetation*). **2** the process of vegetating. □ **vegetational** *adj.*

vegetative *adj.* **1** of, relating to, or concerned with growth and development as distinct from reproduction. **2** of or relating to vegetation or plant

life. **3** (of reproduction) asexual. **4** (of a person or way of life) unthinking or inactive. □ **vegetatively** *adv.*

veggie *informal* ● *n.* **1** esp. *N Amer.* a vegetable. **2** a vegetarian. ● *adj.* made of vegetables; vegetarian (*veggie burger*).

vehement /'viːəmənt/ *adj.* showing or caused by strong feeling; forceful, ardent (*a vehement protest*). □ **vehemence** *n.* **vehemently** *adv.*

vehicle /'viːəkəl/ *n.* **1** any conveyance for transporting people, goods, etc., esp. on land. **2** a medium for thought, feeling, etc. **3** a liquid etc. as a medium for suspending pigments, drugs, etc. □ **vehicular** /vɪ'hɪkjʊlər/ *adj.*

veil ● *n.* **1** a piece of fabric worn, esp. by women, over the head or face for concealment, to protect the face from the sun, dust, etc., or traditionally as part of a bride's attire. **2** a piece of fabric as part of a nun's headdress, resting on the head and shoulders. **3** a curtain, esp. that separating the sanctuary in the Jewish Temple. **4** something that conceals, covers, or disguises (*a veil of mist*). ● *v.tr.* cover or conceal with or as if with a veil. □ **draw a veil over** avoid discussing or calling attention to. **take the veil** become a nun.

veiled *adj.* **1** (of a person) wearing a veil. **2** partially concealed or disguised (*veiled threats*).

vein ● *n.* **1 a** any of the anatomical tubes by which blood is conveyed to the heart (*compare* ARTERY 1). **b** (in general use) any blood vessel (*has German blood in her veins*). **2** a slender bundle of tissue forming a rib in the framework of a leaf. **3** a streak or stripe of a different colour in wood, marble, cheese, etc. **4** a fissure in rock filled with ore or other deposited material. **5** a source of a particular characteristic (*a rich vein of humour*). **6** a distinctive feature or quality (*a vein of humour in her work*). **7** a manner, style, or mood (*in a more serious vein*). ● *v.tr.* fill or cover with or as with veins. □ **veined** *adj.* **veinless** *n.* **veinlike** *adj.* **veiny** *adj.* (**-ier, -iest**)

veining *n.* a pattern of streaks or veins.

vela *pl. of* VELUM.

Velcro *proprietary* ● *n.* a fastener for clothes etc. consisting of two strips of nylon fabric, one looped and one burred, which adhere when pressed together. ● *v.tr.* fasten with Velcro. □ **Velcroed** *adj.*

veld /velt/ *n.* (also **veldt**) *South Africa* grassland.

vellum /'veləm/ *n.* **1 a** fine parchment originally from the skin of a calf. **b** a manuscript written on this. **2** smooth writing paper imitating vellum.

velociraptor /və,lɒsi'raptər/ *n.* a small bipedal carnivorous dinosaur of the genus *Velociraptor*, of the Cretaceous period, with an enlarged curved claw on each hind foot.

velocity /və'lɒsɪti/ *n.* (*pl.* **-ies**) **1** the measure of the rate of movement of a usu. inanimate object in a given direction. **2** speed in a given direction. **3** (in general use) speed.

velour /və'lʊr/ *n.* any of various fabrics with a velvet-like finish, used for clothing, upholstery, etc.

velouté /və'lʊːtei/ *n.* a sauce made from chicken stock and cream thickened with a mixture of butter and flour.

velum /'viːləm/ *n.* (*pl.* **vela** /-lə/) a membrane, membranous covering, or flap.

velvet ● *n.* **1** a closely woven fabric of silk, cotton, etc., with a thick short pile on one side. **2** the furry skin on a deer's growing antler. **3** anything smooth and soft like velvet. ● *adj.* of, like, or soft as velvet. □ **velvety** *adj.*

velveteen *n.* a cotton fabric with a pile like velvet but not as thick.

velvet revolution *n.* a non-violent political revolution, esp. (**Velvet Revolution**) the sequence of events in Czechoslovakia which led to the ending of Communist rule in late 1989.

Ven. *abbr.* Venerable.

venal /'vi:nəl/ *adj.* **1** (of a person) willing to act dishonestly or immorally, or to sacrifice principles, for money. **2** characterized by or associated with corruption or bribery. □ **venality** /-'nælɪti/ *n.*

vend *v.tr.* **1** offer (merchandise) for sale. **2** *Law* sell.

vendetta /ven'detə/ *n.* **1** a blood feud in which the family of a murdered person seeks vengeance on the murderer or the murderer's family. **2** a prolonged bitter quarrel.

vending machine *n.* a coin-operated machine for the sale of small items, e.g. pop, snacks, etc.

vendor *n.* **1** *Law* the seller in a sale, esp. of property. **2** a person who sells, esp. at an outdoor stand, in a stadium, etc. (*hot dog vendors*). **3** = VENDING MACHINE.

vendu /vã'du:/ *n.* (*pl.* **-s**) *Cdn derogatory* a Québécois who is viewed as having sold out or become assimilated to English-Canadian society.

veneer /və'ni:r/ ● *n.* **1 a** a thin covering of fine wood or other surface material applied to a coarser wood. **b** a layer in plywood. **2** (often foll. by *of*) a deceptive outward appearance of a good quality etc. ● *v.tr.* **1** apply a veneer to (wood, furniture, etc.). **2** disguise (an unattractive character etc.) with a more attractive manner etc.

venerable /'venərəbəl/ *adj.* **1** entitled to veneration on account of character, age, associations, etc. (*venerable relics*). **2** *Catholicism* as the title of a deceased person who has attained a certain degree of sanctity but has not been fully beatified or canonized. **3** as the title of an archdeacon in the Anglican Church. □ **venerability** *n.* **venerably** *adv.*

venerate /'venə,reɪt/ *v.tr.* **1** regard with deep respect. **2** revere on account of sanctity etc. □ **veneration** *n.*

venereal /və'ni:riəl/ *adj.* **1** of or relating to sexual desire or intercourse. **2** relating to venereal disease.

venereal disease *n.* any of various diseases contracted chiefly by sexual intercourse with a person already infected. Abbr.: **VD**.

Venetian /vɪ'ni:ʃən/ ● *n.* **1** a native or citizen of Venice in NE Italy. **2** the Italian dialect of Venice. **3** (**venetian**) (in full **venetian blind**) a window blind consisting of a number of adjustable horizontal slats to control the light. ● *adj.* of Venice. □ **venetianed** *adj.* (in sense 3 of *n.*).

Venezuelan /,venə'zweɪlən/ ● *n.* a native or inhabitant of Venezuela, a republic on the north coast of S America. ● *adj.* of or relating to Venezuela or its people or culture.

vengeance *n.* **1** punishment inflicted or retribution exacted for wrong to oneself or to a person etc. whose cause one supports. **2** the desire for revenge. □ **with a vengeance** in a higher degree than was expected or desired; in the fullest sense (*punctuality with a vengeance*).

vengeful *adj.* **1** vindictive; seeking vengeance. **2** characterized by or demonstrating a desire for revenge. □ **vengefully** *adv.* **vengefulness** *n.*

venial /'vi:niəl/ *adj.* (of a sin or fault) pardonable, excusable; not mortal.

venison /'venɪsən, -zən/ *n.* a deer's flesh as food.

venom *n.* **1** a poisonous fluid secreted by snakes, scorpions, etc., usu. transmitted by a bite or sting. **2** strong, bitter feeling or language; malice, spite.

venomous *adj.* **1 a** containing, secreting, or injecting venom. **b** (of a snake etc.) inflicting poisonous

wounds by this means. **2** (of a person etc.) virulent, spiteful, malignant. □ **venomously** *adv.*

venous /'vi:nəs/ *adj.* **1** of or full of veins. **2** (of blood) deoxygenated and of a dusky red colour (*opp.* ARTERIAL 1b).

vent ● *n.* **1** (also **vent hole**) a hole or opening allowing motion of air etc. out of or into a confined space. **2** an outlet; free passage or play (*gave vent to their indignation*). **3** the anus esp. of a lower animal, serving for both excretion and reproduction. **4** an aperture or outlet through which volcanic products are discharged at the earth's surface. **5** a slit in a garment, esp. in the lower edge of the back of a coat. **6** a flue of a chimney. ● *v.tr.* **1 a** make a vent in (a cask etc.). **b** (often as **vented** *adj.*) provide (a machine, space, etc.) with a vent. **2** give vent or free expression to (*vented my anger*). □ **vent one's spleen on** scold or ill-treat without cause.

ventilate *v.tr.* **1 a** cause air to circulate freely in (a room etc.). **b** provide with a vent or vents. **c** (of wind etc.) blow upon or through so as to purify or freshen. **2** submit (a question, grievance, etc.) to public consideration and discussion. **3** *Med.* **a** oxygenate (the blood). **b** admit or force air into (the lungs). □ **ventilation** *n.*

ventilator *n.* **1** an appliance or aperture for ventilating a room etc. **2** *Med.* = RESPIRATOR 2.

ventral /'ventrəl/ *adj.* **1** *Anat. & Zool.* of or on the abdomen (*compare* DORSAL 1). **2** *Bot.* of the front or lower surface. □ **ventrally** *adv.*

ventral fin *n.* either of the ventrally placed fins on a fish.

ventricle /'ventrɪkəl/ *n.* **1** either of the two muscular lower chambers of the heart (in some animals, a single chamber), which pump the blood to the arteries and through the body. **2** each of four fluid-filled cavities in the brain, formed by enlargements of the spinal cord. □ **ventricular** *adj.*

ventriloquism /ven'trɪlə,kwɪzəm/ *n.* the skill of speaking or uttering sounds so that they seem to come from the speaker's dummy or a source other than the speaker. □ **ventriloquist** *n.*

venture ● *n.* **1 a** an undertaking of a risk. **b** a risky enterprise. **2** a business enterprise involving risk. ● *v.* **1** *intr.* dare; not be afraid (*did not venture to stop them*). **2** *intr.* (usu. foll. by *out* etc.) dare to go somewhere dangerous or unpleasant. **3** *tr.* dare to put forward (an opinion, suggestion, etc.). **4 a** *tr.* expose to risk; stake (a bet etc.). **b** *intr.* take risks. **5** *intr.* (foll. by *on, upon*) dare to engage in etc. (*ventured on a journey*). □ **nothing ventured, nothing gained** one cannot expect to achieve anything without taking risks.

venture capital *n.* **1** money invested in a project in which there is a substantial element of risk, esp. money invested in a new venture or an expanding business in exchange for shares in the business. **2** (*attrib.*) designating a company investing in such ventures.

venture capitalist *n.* a supplier of venture capital for investment.

venturer *n.* **1** *hist.* a person who undertakes or shares in a trading venture. **2** (**Venturer**) *Cdn* a member of a level (ages 14–17) in Scouting.

venturesome *adj.* **1** disposed to take risks. **2** risky.

venturi /ven'tʃʊri/ *n.* (*pl.* **venturis**) (in full **venturi tube**) a tube with a narrower middle section for measuring flow rate or exerting suction.

venue *n.* **1 a** an appointed site or meeting place, as for a sports event, meeting, concert, etc. **b** a building for such a meeting or event (*downtown's newest venue*). **2** *Law* the location of a trial.

Venus flytrap /ˈviːnəs/ *n.* a flesh-consuming plant, *Dionaea muscipula*, with leaves that close on insects etc.

veracity /vəˈræsɪti/ *n.* **1** truthfulness, honesty. **2** accuracy (of a statement etc.).

veranda *n.* (also **verandah**) a usu. roofed porch or external gallery along one or more sides of a house.

verb *n.* a word used to indicate an action, state, or occurrence, and forming the main part of the predicate of a sentence, e.g. *hear*, *become*, *happen*.

verbal ● *adj.* **1** of or concerned with words (*made a verbal distinction*). **2** not written (*gave a verbal statement*). ¶Some reject this use as illogical, and prefer *oral*. However, *verbal* is the usual term in expressions such as *verbal communication*, *verbal contract*, and *verbal evidence*. **3** of or in the nature of a verb (*verbal inflections*). **4** literal (*a verbal translation*). **5** talkative, articulate. ● *n.* **1** a verbal noun. **2** a word or words functioning as a verb. □ **verbally** *adv.*

verbalize *v.* **1** *tr.* express in words. **2** *intr.* be verbose. **3** *tr.* make (a noun) into a verb. □ **verbalization** *n.*

verbal noun *n.* *Grammar* a noun formed as an inflection of a verb and partly sharing its constructions, e.g. *smoking* in *smoking is forbidden*.

verbatim /vərˈbeɪtɪm/ *adv. & adj.* in exactly the same words; word for word (*copied it verbatim*).

verbena /vərˈbiːnə/ *n.* any plant of the genus *Verbena*, bearing clusters of fragrant flowers.

verbiage /ˈvɜːbiədʒ/ *n.* needless accumulation of words; verbosity.

verbose /vərˈboːs/ *adj.* using or expressed in more words than are needed. □ **verbosely** *adv.* **verbosity** /-ˈbɒsɪti/ *n.*

verboten /vərˈboːtən, ver-/ *adj.* forbidden, esp. by an authority.

verdant /ˈvɜːdənt/ *adj.* **1** (of grass etc.) green, fresh-coloured. **2** (of a field etc.) covered with grass etc.

verdict *n.* **1** a decision on an issue of fact in a civil or criminal cause or an inquest. **2** a decision or an opinion given after testing, examining, or experiencing something.

verdigris /ˈvɜːdɪɡrɪs, -ˌɡriːs/ *n.* **1 a** a green crystallized substance formed on copper by the action of acetic acid. **b** this used as a medicine or pigment. **2** green rust on copper or brass.

verdure /ˈvɜːdjər, -dʒər/ *n.* **1** green vegetation. **2** the greenness of this.

verge¹ ● *n.* **1** an edge or border. **2** an extreme limit beyond which something happens (*on the verge of tears*). ● *v.intr.* (foll. by *on*) border on; approach closely (*verging on the ridiculous*).

verge² *v.intr.* incline downwards or in a specified direction.

verification *n.* **1** the process or an instance of establishing the truth or validity of something. **2** *Philos.* the establishment of the validity of a proposition empirically. **3** the process of verifying procedures laid down in weapons agreements.

verify *v.tr.* (**-ies**, **-ied**) **1** establish the truth or correctness of by examination or demonstration. **2** (of an event etc.) bear out or fulfill (a prediction or promise). **3** *Law* append an affidavit to (pleadings); support (a statement) by testimony or proofs. □ **verifiable** *adj.* **verifiably** *adv.* **verifier** *n.*

verisimilitude /ˌverɪsɪˈmɪlɪˌtuːd, -ˌtjuːd/ *n.* **1** the appearance or semblance of being true or real. **2** a statement etc. that merely seems true.

veritable /ˈverɪtəbəl/ *adj.* real; rightly so called (*a veritable feast*). □ **veritably** *adv.*

vérité /veriˈteɪ/ *n.* (esp. in *comb.*) realism or naturalism in the arts, esp. in film (*cinéma-vérité*).

verity /ˈverɪti/ *n.* (*pl.* **-ies**) **1** a true statement, esp. one of fundamental import. **2** truth.

vermicelli /ˌvɜːmɪˈtʃeli/ *n.* pasta made in long slender threads.

vermicomposting /ˈvɜːmɪˌkɒmpoʊˌstɪŋ/ *n.* composting using earthworms to convert organic waste into fertilizer. □ **vermicomposter** *n.*

vermiculite /vɜːˈmɪkjʊlaɪt/ *n.* **1** a hydrated silicate resulting from the alteration of mica etc., esp. an aluminosilicate of magnesium. **2** this material in flakes used as a medium for growing plants, for insulation, etc.

vermiform appendix /ˈvɜːmɪˌfɔːm/ *n.* = APPENDIX 1.

vermilion /vɜːˈmɪljən/ ● *n.* **1** a bright red mineral form of mercuric sulphide from which mercury is obtained. **2 a** a brilliant red pigment made by grinding this or artificially. **b** the colour of this. ● *adj.* of this colour.

vermin *n.* (usu. treated as *pl.*) **1** mammals and birds injurious to crops, etc., e.g. rodents and noxious insects. **2** parasitic worms or insects. **3 a** vile or contemptible persons. **b** a person of this type. □ **verminous** *adj.*

Vermonter /vɜːˈmɒntər/ *n.* a native or inhabitant of the US state of Vermont.

vermouth /vɜːˈmuːθ/ *n.* a fortified wine flavoured with aromatic herbs.

vernacular /vɜːˈnækjʊlər/ ● *n.* **1** the language or dialect of a particular country (*Latin gave place to the vernacular*). **2** the language of a particular clan or group. **3** informal speech. ● *adj.* (of language) of one's native country; not of foreign origin or of learned formation.

vernal /ˈvɜːnəl/ *adj.* of, in, or appropriate to spring.

vernal equinox *n.* = SPRING EQUINOX.

versatile /ˈvɜːsəˌtaɪl/ *adj.* **1** turning easily or readily from one subject or occupation to another (*a versatile mind*). **2** (of a device etc.) having many uses. □ **versatility** /-ˈtɪlɪti/ *n.*

verse ● *n.* **1** a metrical composition in general (also *attrib.*: *verse drama*). **b** a particular type of this (*English verse*). **2 a** a metrical line in accordance with the rules of prosody. **b** a group of a definite number of such lines. **c** a stanza of a poem or song with or without refrain. **d** a poem. **3** each of the short numbered divisions of a chapter in the Bible etc. **4 a** a versicle. **b** a passage (of an anthem etc.) for solo voice. ● *v.tr.* **1** express in verse. **2** (usu. *refl.*; foll. by *in*) instruct; make knowledgeable.

versed *adj.* (foll. by *in*) experienced or skilled in; knowledgeable about.

versicle /ˈvɜːsɪkəl/ *n.* each of the short sentences in a liturgy said or sung by a priest etc. and alternating with responses.

versify *v.* (**-ies**, **-ied**) **1** *tr.* turn into or express in verse. **2** *intr.* compose verses. □ **versification** *n.* **versifier** *n.*

version *n.* **1** an account of a matter from a particular person's point of view (*told them my version of the incident*). **2** a book or work etc. in a particular edition or translation (*Revised Standard Version*). **3** a form or variant of a thing as adapted, performed, etc.

verso /ˈvɜːsoʊ/ *n.* (*pl.* **-os**) **1 a** the left-hand page of an open book. **b** the back of a printed leaf of paper or manuscript (*opp.* RECTO). **2** the reverse of a coin.

versus prep. **1** against (esp. in legal and sports use). Abbr.: **v., vs. 2** as opposed to; in contrast with.

vertebra /'vɜːtəbrə/ n. (pl. **vertebrae** /-briː/) **1** each segment of the backbone. **2** (in pl.) the backbone. □ **vertebral** adj.

vertebrate /'vɜːtəˌbreɪt, -brət/ ● n. any animal of the subphylum Vertebrata, having a spinal column, including mammals, birds, reptiles, amphibians, and fishes. ● adj. of or relating to the vertebrates.

vertex /'vɜːteks/ n. (pl. **vertices** /-tɪˌsiːz/ or **vertexes**) **1** the highest point; the top or apex. **2** Math **a** each angular point of a polygon, polyhedron, etc. **b** a meeting point of two lines that form an angle. **c** the point at which an axis meets a curve or surface.

vertical ● adj. **1** at right angles to a horizontal plane, perpendicular. **2** in a direction from top to bottom of a picture etc. **3** of or at the vertex or highest point. **4** at, or passing through, the zenith. **5** involving all the levels in an organizational hierarchy or stages in the production of a class of goods (vertical integration). ● n. **1** a vertical line or plane. **2** (in pl.) (in full **vertical blinds**) a window blind consisting of a number of adjustable vertical slats to control the light. **3** (in full **vertical drop**) the difference in elevation between the top and bottom of a mountain, ski run, etc. □ **verticality** n. **vertically** adv.

vertically challenged adj. jocular short.

vertical takeoff n. the takeoff of an aircraft directly upwards.

vertiginous /vɜːˈtɪdʒɪnəs/ adj. of, causing, or affected by vertigo. □ **vertiginously** adv.

vertigo /'vɜːtɪɡəʊ/ n. a condition with a sensation of whirling and a tendency to lose balance; dizziness.

verve n. enthusiasm, vigour, spirit, esp. in artistic or literary work.

very ● adv. **1** in a high degree (did it very easily; a very bad cough). **2** in the fullest sense (at the very latest; my very own room). ● adj. real, true, actual; truly such (the very thing we need; her very words). □ **not very 1** in a low degree. **2** far from being. **very good** (or **well**) a formula of consent or approval.

very high frequency n. see VHF.

Very Reverend n. **1** (in Canada) the title of the moderator or a former moderator of the United Church. **2** the title of a dean etc.

vesicle /'vesɪkəl/ n. **1 a** Anat. & Biol. a small fluid-filled bladder, sac, or vacuole. **b** Bot. an air-filled swelling in a seaweed etc. **2** Geol. a small cavity in volcanic rock produced by gas bubbles. **3** Med. a blister. □ **vesicular** /və'sɪkjʊlər/ adj.

vespers /'vespərz/ n.pl. **1** the office of the sixth canonical hour of prayer, originally said towards evening. **2** evening prayer.

vessel n. **1** a hollow receptacle esp. for liquid, e.g. a cask, cup, pot, bottle, or dish. **2** a ship or boat, esp. a large one. **3 a** Anat. a duct or canal etc. holding or conveying blood or other fluid, esp. = BLOOD VESSEL. **b** Bot. a woody duct carrying or containing sap etc.

vest ● n. **1** N Amer. & Austral. a sleeveless and collarless, usu. V-necked garment covering the shoulders and reaching the waist or hip, often with a buttoned front, worn over a shirt. **2** any sleeveless garment worn for a specified purpose (bulletproof vest). ● v. **1** tr. (esp. in passive; foll. by with, in) bestow or confer (powers, authority, etc.) on (a person). **2** tr. (foll. by in) confer (property or power) on (a person) with an immediate fixed right of immediate or future possession. **3** intr. (foll. by in) (of property, a right, etc.) come into the possession of (a person). **4** intr. Christianity

put on vestments. □ **close to the vest** N Amer. cautious(ly), careful(ly), guarded(ly).

vested adj. **1** in senses of VEST v. **2** absolute, fixed; not contingent. **3** established by law or tradition.

vested interest n. **1** Law an interest (usu. in land or money held in trust) recognized as belonging to a person. **2 a** a personal interest in a state of affairs, usu. with an expectation of gain. **b** (usu. in pl.) a person or group with such an interest.

vestibule /'vestɪˌbjuːl/ n. **1 a** a hall, or lobby just inside the outer door of a building, e.g. where coats may be left. **b** the area between two sets of doorways at the main entrance of a church etc. **2** N Amer. an enclosed space between railway passenger cars. **3** Anat. **a** a chamber or channel connected with others. **b** the central cavity of the labyrinth of the inner ear. □ **vestibular** /-'stɪbjʊlər/ adj.

vestige /'vestɪdʒ/ n. **1** a trace or piece of evidence; a sign (vestiges of an earlier civilization). **2** a slight amount; a particle (without a vestige of clothing). **3** Biol. a part or organ of an organism that is reduced or functionless but was well developed in its ancestors.

vestigial /ve'stɪdʒɪəl, -dʒəl/ adj. **1** being a vestige or trace. **2** Biol. (of an organ) atrophied or functionless from the process of evolution (a vestigial wing).

vestment n. **1** (usu. in pl.) any of the official robes of clergy, choristers, etc., worn during a service. **2** a garment, esp. an official or state robe.

vest-pocket attrib.adj. N Amer. **1** small enough to fit into a small pocket as on a vest. **2** very small (vest-pocket parks).

vestry /'vestri/ n. (pl. **-ies**) **1** a room or building attached to a church for keeping vestments in. **2 a** esp. Anglicanism a meeting of the members of a parish. **b** a body of parishioners meeting in this way.

vet¹ ● n. informal a veterinarian. ● v.tr. (**vetted, vetting**) **1** make a careful and critical examination of (a scheme, work, candidate, etc.). **2** examine or treat (an animal).

vet² n. N Amer. informal an esp. military veteran.

vetch n. any plant of the genus Vicia, esp. V. sativa, largely used for silage or fodder.

veteran n. **1** a person who has grown old in or had long experience of esp. military service or an occupation (a veteran goalie). **2** N Amer. an ex-serviceman or servicewoman. **3** (attrib.) of or for veterans.

veterinarian /ˌvetrɪˈneərɪən, ˌvetərɪ-/ n. N Amer. a person qualified to treat diseased or injured animals.

veterinary ● adj. of or for diseases and injuries of esp. farm and domestic animals, or their treatment. ● n. (pl. **-ies**) a veterinarian.

veto /'viːtəʊ/ ● n. (pl. **-oes**) **1 a** a constitutional right to reject a legislative enactment. **b** the right of a permanent member of the UN Security Council to reject a resolution. **c** such a rejection. **d** an official message conveying this. **2** a prohibition (put one's veto on a proposal). ● v.tr. (**-oes, -oed**) **1** exercise a veto against (a measure etc.). **2** forbid authoritatively.

vex v.tr. **1** anger esp. by a slight or a petty annoyance; irritate, annoy. **2** puzzle, confound. **3** distress mentally; grieve, afflict. □ **vexing** adj. **vexingly** adv.

vexation n. **1** the act or an instance of vexing; the state of being vexed. **2** an annoying or distressing thing.

vexatious adj. **1** such as to cause vexation. **2** Law not having sufficient grounds for action and seeking only to annoy the defendant.

vexed adj. **1** irritated, angered. **2** (of a problem, issue, etc.) difficult; problematic.

V-formation *n.* a formation, esp. of flying geese, airplanes, etc., resembling the letter V.

VG *abbr.* very good.

VGA *abbr. Computing* video graphics array, a standard for graphics adapters originally capable of generating a 640 by 480 pixel 16-colour screen.

VHF *abbr.* very high frequency (designating radio waves of frequency *c.* 30–*c.* 300 MHz and wavelength *c.* 1–10 metres).

VHS *abbr. proprietary* Video Home System (one of the standard formats for video cassettes).

via /'vi:ə, 'vaɪə/ *prep.* **1** by way of; through (*Montreal to Rome via Paris; via satellite*). **2** by means of; with the aid of (*tried to improve the economy via fiscal restraint*).

viable /'vaɪəbl/ *adj.* **1** (of a plan etc.) feasible; practicable, esp. from an economic standpoint. **2 a** (of a seed or spore) able to germinate. **b** (of a plant, animal, etc.) capable of living or developing normally under particular environmental conditions. **3** *Med.* (of a fetus or unborn child) able to live after birth. □ **viability** *n.* **viably** *adv.*

viaduct /'vaɪə,dʌkt/ *n.* **1** a long bridgelike structure, esp. a series of arches, carrying a road or railway across a valley, low-lying ground, etc. **2** such a road or railway.

Viagra /vaɪ'ægrə/ *n. proprietary* the drug sidenafil citrate, taken orally as a tablet in the treatment of male impotence.

vial /'vaɪəl/ *n.* a small (usu. cylindrical glass) vessel esp. for holding liquid medicines.

vibe *n. informal* **1** (often in *pl.*) vibration, esp. in the sense of feelings or atmosphere communicated (*the house had bad vibes*). **2** (in *pl.*) = VIBRAPHONE.

vibrant *adj.* **1** full of life and energy; exciting. **2** (of colours etc.) bright and striking. **3** vibrating. **4** (often foll. by *with*) (of a person or thing) thrilling, quivering (*vibrant with emotion*). **5** (of sound) resonant. □ **vibrancy** *n.* **vibrantly** *adv.*

vibraphone /'vaɪbrə,foʊn/ *n.* a percussion instrument of tuned metal bars with motor-driven resonators and metal tubes giving a vibrato effect. □ **vibraphonist** *n.*

vibrate *v.* **1** *intr.* & *tr.* move or cause to move continuously and rapidly to and fro; oscillate. **2** *intr. Physics* move unceasingly to and fro, esp. rapidly. **3** *intr.* (of a sound) throb; continue to be heard. **4** *intr.* (foll. by *with*) quiver, thrill (*vibrating with passion*). **5** *intr.* (of a pendulum) swing to and fro.

vibration *n.* **1** the act or an instance of vibrating; a continuous rapid shaking movement or sensation. **2** *Physics* (esp. rapid) motion to and fro esp. of the parts of a fluid or an elastic solid whose equilibrium has been disturbed or of an electromagnetic wave. **3** (in *pl.*) **a** a mental (esp. occult) influence. **b** a characteristic atmosphere or feeling in a place. □ **vibrational** *adj.*

vibrato /vɪ'brɑːtoʊ/ *n.* a rapid slight variation in pitch in singing or playing a stringed or wind instrument, producing a tremulous effect (*compare* TREMOLO).

vibrator *n.* a device that vibrates or causes vibration, esp. an electric or other instrument used in massage or for sexual stimulation. □ **vibratory** *adj.*

viburnum /vaɪ'bɜːnəm/ *n.* any shrub of the genus *Viburnum*, usu. with white flowers.

vicar /'vɪkər/ *n.* **1 a** (in the Church of England) an incumbent of a parish where tithes formerly passed to a chapter or religious house or layman (*compare* RECTOR). **b** (in other Anglican churches) a member of the clergy deputizing for another. **2** *Catholicism* a representative or deputy of a bishop.

vicarage *n.* the residence or benefice of a vicar.

vicarious /vɪ'keriəs, vaɪ-/ *adj.* **1** experienced, enjoyed, or undergone second-hand by imagining one's own participation in the experiences of another (*vicarious pleasure*). **2** performed, accomplished, or undergone on behalf of another (*vicarious suffering*). **3** deputed, delegated (*vicarious authority*). □ **vicariously** *adv.* **vicariousness** *n.*

vice[1] *n.* **1 a** illegal or grossly immoral conduct; extreme corruption or depravity. **b** a particular form of this, esp. involving prostitution or drugs etc. **c** an immoral, dissolute, or illegal habit or practice. **2** a personal flaw or bad habit (*drunkenness was not among his vices*). □ **viceless** *adj.*

vice[2] *esp. Brit. var. of* VISE.

vice- *comb. form* forming nouns meaning 'next in rank or authority to' or 'acting as a substitute or deputy for' (*vice-chairperson; vice-governor*).

vice admiral *n.* (also **Vice Admiral**) a naval officer ranking below admiral and above rear admiral.

vice-chancellor *n.* **1** the deputy of a chancellor. **2** *Cdn & Brit.* the acting representative of the chancellor of a university, discharging most of the administrative duties.

vice-president *n.* **1** a government official who ranks immediately below the president and assumes the role and responsibilities of the president in the event of his or her inability to govern due to absence, illness, or death. **2** an executive officer deputizing for a president and often overseeing a division of a corporation etc. □ **vice-presidency** *n.* (*pl.* **-ies**). **vice-presidential** *adj.*

vice-principal *n.* the assistant to a principal, esp. in a school, college, or university.

viceregal *adj.* of or relating to a Governor General or viceroy. □ **viceregally** *adv.*

viceroy /'vaɪsrɔɪ/ *n.* a person who exercises authority over a colony or province etc. on behalf of a sovereign.

vice-skip *n.* the third player on a curling rink.

vice squad *n.* a special unit of a police force for the enforcement of laws related to prostitution, drug trafficking, illegal gambling, etc.

vice versa /,vais 'vɜːrsə ,vaisə-/ *adv.* with the order of the terms or conditions changed; the other way around (*I'll help you and vice versa*).

vichyssoise /,viːʃiː'swɒz, 'vɪ-/ *n.* a thick soup made of puréed leeks and potatoes with cream, usu. served chilled.

vicinity *n.* (*pl.* **-ies**) **1** the area within a limited distance of a place. **2** (foll. by *to*) the state of being near or close; proximity. □ **in the vicinity of 1** near (*in the vicinity of the park*). **2** approximately (*in the vicinity of $300,000*).

vicious *adj.* **1** malevolent, spiteful, wicked (*vicious sarcasm*). **2** savage, brutal (*a vicious dog; a vicious slaying*). **3** fierce, intense, severe (*a vicious storm*). **4** of, pertaining to, or characterized by vice or immorality. □ **viciously** *adv.* **viciousness** *n.*

vicious circle *n.* (also **vicious cycle**) = CIRCLE *n.* 8.

vicissitude /vɪ'sɪsɪ,tuːd, -,tjuːd/ *n.* (in *pl.*) changes in circumstance; uncertainties or variations of fortune or outcome.

victim *n.* **1** a person who suffers or dies as a result of an event or circumstance. **2** a person injured or destroyed as a result of their own or another's ambition, passion, pursuit of wealth, etc. (*he is a victim of his own success*). **3** a person fooled or taken advantage of; a dupe (*fell victim to a hoax*). □ **fall victim to** succumb to or suffer as a result of. □ **victimhood** *n.*

victimize *v.tr.* **1** make a victim of; cause (a person etc.)

to suffer harm, inconvenience, discomfort, etc. **2** single out (a person) for punishment or unfair treatment. □ **victimization** *n.* **victimizer** *n.*

victimology *n.* the study of the victims of crime or discrimination, the psychological effects on them of their experience, and methods of recovery.

victor *n.* a person or country etc. that succeeds in overcoming or defeating an adversary or opponent.

Victoria Cross *n.* a medal awarded to members of the Commonwealth armed forces for conspicuous acts of bravery, instituted by Queen Victoria in 1856.

Victoria Day *n.* Cdn a holiday falling on the Monday immediately preceding May 25.

Victorian ● *adj.* **1** of or characteristic of the reign of Queen Victoria of Great Britain and Ireland (reigned 1837–1901). **2** associated with attitudes attributed to this time, esp. of prudery and moral strictness. **3** resembling or typical of the architectural style of this time, characterized by lavish ornamentation set in forms of neoclassicism and Gothic revival. ● *n.* **1** a person of this time. **2** a resident of a place called Victoria. □ **Victorianism** *n.*

Victoriana /vɪk,tɔriˈænə/ *n.pl.* **1** articles, esp. collectors' items and furniture, of the Victorian period. **2** attitudes characteristic of this period.

Victorian Order of Nurses *n.* Cdn a non-profit community-based health organization that provides home care for the elderly and chronically ill.

victorious *adj.* **1** having won a victory; conquering, triumphant. **2** of or characterized by victory (*a victorious cheer*). □ **victoriously** *adv.*

victory *n.* (*pl.* **-ies**) **1 a** the state of having overcome or conquered an adversary in battle. **b** the state of having defeated an opponent in a game, competition, election, court trial, etc. **2** an instance of this; a triumph. **3** an instance of achieving success in some endeavour or of overcoming an obstacle or difficulty.

Victrola /vɪkˈtroːlə/ *n.* esp. hist. proprietary a kind of gramophone driven by clockwork.

victual /ˈvɪtəl/ ● *n.* (usu. in *pl.*) food, provisions. ● *v.* (**victualled**, **victualling**) **1** *tr.* supply or feed (a person) with victuals. **2** *tr. & intr.* eat, consume.

vid *n.* informal = VIDEO 3.

vide /ˈviːdeɪ/ *v.tr.* (as an instruction in a reference to a passage in a book etc.) see, consult.

video ● *n.* (*pl.* **-os**) **1** the process of recording, reproducing, or broadcasting visual images on magnetic tape (also *attrib.*: *video equipment*). **2** the visual element of television broadcasts. **3 a** a recording made on videotape, esp. one commercially produced and available for sale or rent on video cassette. **b** = MUSIC VIDEO. **4 a** = VIDEO CASSETTE (*available on video this fall*). **b** = VIDEOTAPE 1. ● *v.tr.* (**-oes, -oed**) = VIDEOTAPE.

video arcade *n.* = ARCADE 3.

video camera *n.* (also **videocam**) a camera used to record images on videotape or to transmit images to a monitor screen.

video card *n.* Computing the circuit board that enables a monitor to display graphics.

video cassette *n.* a length of videotape enclosed in a sealed plastic casing, suitable for use in a video camera or VCR.

video cassette recorder *n.* = VCR.

video conference *n.* an arrangement in which television sets linked by telephone lines are used to enable a group of people in different places to communicate with each other in sound and vision. □ **video conferencing** *n.*

videodisc *n.* an optical disk on which material is recorded for reproduction on a television screen.

video display terminal *n.* (also **video display unit**) Computing a device for displaying on a screen data stored in a computer, usu. incorporating a keyboard for manipulating the data.

video game *n.* any of a variety of games that can be played by using a joystick to manipulate computer-generated images displayed on a television screen, computer monitor, or the screen of an arcade game.

videography /ˌvɪdiˈɒɡrəfi/ *n.* the process or art of making videos. □ **videographer** *n.*

video jockey *n.* = VJ.

video lottery terminal *n.* a government-regulated gambling machine, operated by coin, that offers a selection of esp. card games on a video screen and rewards a winner in credit rather than coin, usu. located in a bar, restaurant, casino, or racetrack.

video-on-demand *n.* a pay-per-view television service that allows a customer to select from a list of programs, which may be accessed from a server through a telephone line at any time.

videophile /ˈvɪdioːˌfaɪl/ *n.* an enthusiast for videos or video technology.

videophone *n.* a telephone incorporating a television screen allowing communication in both sound and vision.

video recorder *n.* = VCR.

video recording *n.* **1** the action or process of recording something on videotape. **2** = VIDEO 3a.

video signal *n.* a signal that contains all the information required for producing a television image.

videotape ● *n.* **1** magnetic tape for recording television pictures and sound. **2 a** a length of this. **b** a video cassette, esp. one on which nothing has been recorded. **3** = VIDEO 3a. ● *v.tr.* make a recording of (a person, an event, etc.) on videotape.

videotape recorder *n.* **1** a device used to record images and sound onto an open spool of videotape, used esp. in television broadcasting. **2** = VCR.

vie *v.intr.* (**vying**) (often foll. by *with*) compete, contend.

Viennese /viəˈniːz/ ● *adj.* of, relating to, or associated with Vienna, Austria. ● *n.* (*pl.* same) a native or citizen of Vienna.

Viet Cong /ˌvietˈkɒŋ/ *n.* (*pl.* same) a member of the Communist guerrilla movement in Vietnam which fought the South Vietnamese government forces 1954–75 with the support of the North Vietnamese army and opposed the South Vietnam and US forces in the Vietnam War.

Vietnamese /viːˈetnəˈmiːz, ˈviːetnə-/ ● *adj.* of or relating to Vietnam, a country in SE Asia, or its inhabitants or language. ● *n.* (*pl.* same) **1** a native or national of Vietnam. **2** the language of Vietnam.

view ● *n.* **1** range of vision; extent of visibility. **2 a** what is seen from a particular point; a scene or prospect. **b** a picture etc. representing this. **3 a** an opinion or belief concerning a particular subject or thing. **b** a mental attitude; an outlook (*took a favourable view of the matter*). **c** a manner of considering a thing (*took a long-term view of the situation*). **4** a visual examination, inspection, or survey. **5** an opportunity for a formal visual inspection (*a private view of the exhibition*). **6** an instance of viewing, esp. a television program (*pay-per-view*). ● *v.* **1** *tr.* inspect or examine in a formal or official manner (*we are going to view the house*). **2** *tr.* catch sight of; spy, see. **3** *tr.* regard or approach in a particular manner; consider (*they viewed her with suspicion*). **4** *tr.* Computing read or examine (a document or the contents of a file) in a window in which changes and corrections cannot be made. **5** *tr. & intr.* watch (television or a program on television). □ **have in view 1** have as one's object. **2** bear (a circumstance) in mind in forming a judgment etc. **in view of 1** considering; on account of. **2** so as to be seen by; within the visible range of. **on view** being shown (for observation or inspection); being displayed or exhibited. **with a view to 1** with the hope or intention of. **2** with the aim of attaining or achieving. □ **viewable** *adj.*

viewer *n.* **1** a person who views, watches, or looks at something; an observer, a spectator. **2** a person watching television. **3** a device for looking at photographic slides or transparencies etc.

viewership *n.* **1** the audience for a television program or channel etc. **2** the number of viewers comprising this audience.

viewfinder *n.* a device on a camera showing the field of view of the lens, used in framing and focusing a picture.

viewing *n.* **1** an opportunity or occasion to view. **2** the activity or a period of watching television. **3** *N Amer.* an opportunity for mourners to see the body of a deceased person for a final time prior to a funeral.

viewpoint *n.* **1** a point of view; a mental standpoint from which a matter is considered. **2** a place or position from which a view or prospect may be seen.

vigil /ˈvɪdʒəl/ *n.* **1** a stationary and peaceful demonstration in support of a particular cause, usu. without speeches or other explicit advocacy of the cause, and often with some suggestion of mourning. **2** an occasion or period of keeping awake for any reason during a time usually devoted to sleep, esp. to keep watch or pray. **3** *Christianity* the eve of a festival or holy day as an occasion for religious observance.

vigilance *n.* the quality of being alert to harm or danger; watchfulness, circumspection, caution.

vigilant *adj.* extremely wary and heedful of harm or danger; attentive, alert. □ **vigilantly** *adv.*

vigilante /vɪdʒəˈlanti/ *n.* a person, often a member of a group, who undertakes law enforcement and executes summary justice in the absence or perceived inadequacy of legally constituted law enforcement bodies. □ **vigilantism** *n.*

vignette /vɪnˈjet/ *n.* **1 a** a brief descriptive account, anecdote, essay, or character sketch. **b** a short evocative usu. self-contained episode in a play, novel, movie, etc. **2** an illustration or decorative design on a blank space in a book.

vigorous *adj.* **1 a** (of a person, animal, etc.) physically strong, healthy and robust. **b** (of a plant) growing actively; flourishing. **2** characterized by, requiring, or involving physical force or energy. **3** (of language etc.) powerful, vehement, rousing. **4** full of or exhibiting operative force or vitality. □ **vigorously** *adv.* **vigorousness** *n.*

vigour *n.* (also **vigor**) **1** active physical strength or energy. **2** a flourishing physical condition. **3** intensity of effect or operation (*the storm's vigour*). **4** mental or emotional strength, intensity, or vitality as shown in thought or speech or in literary style.

Viking /ˈvaɪkɪŋ/ ● *n.* any of the Scandinavian seafaring pirates and traders who raided and settled in parts of NW Europe in the 8th–11th c. ● *adj.* of or relating to the Vikings or their time.

vile *adj.* **1** disgusting. **2** morally base; depraved, shameful. **3** *informal* abominably bad or unpleasant (*vile weather*). □ **vilely** *adv.* **vileness** *n.*

vilify /ˈvɪlə.faɪ/ *v.tr.* (**-ies, -ied**) deprecate or malign with abusive or slanderous language; disparage, defame. □ **vilification** *n.* **vilifier** *n.*

villa *n.* **1** a luxurious country residence, esp. in continental Europe. **2** *Rom. Hist.* a large country house with an estate.

village *n.* **1 a** a group of houses and associated buildings, larger than a hamlet and smaller than a town, esp. in a rural area. **b** the inhabitants of a village regarded as a community. **2** a self-contained district or community within a city or town, regarded as having features characteristic of a village. **3** *N Amer.* a small municipality with limited corporate powers. □ **villager** *n.*

villain /ˈvɪlən/ *n.* **1** a person guilty or capable of great wickedness. **2** the character in a play, novel, etc., whose evil actions or motives are important in the plot; the antagonist of the hero. **3** *informal* usu. *jocular* a rascal or rogue. □ **villain of the piece** the person responsible for mishandling or interfering with a situation, esp. in business or politics.

villainous *adj.* **1** characteristic of a villain; depraved, wicked. **2** atrocious, abominable. □ **villainously** *adv.*

villainy *n.* (*pl.* **-ies**) **1** conduct or behaviour typical of a villain. **2** a wicked act or deed; a crime.

-ville *comb. form* esp. *N Amer. informal* forming words designating a place, situation, etc. having a specified quality (*hicksville; dullsville*).

villein /ˈvɪlən/ *n. hist.* a feudal tenant entirely subject to a lord or attached to a manor.

villus /ˈvɪləs/ *n.* (*pl.* **villi** /-laɪ/) **1** *Anat.* any of numerous short slender hairlike projections on some membranes, esp. in the mucous membrane of the chorion or small intestines. **2** *Bot.* (in *pl.*) long soft hairs covering fruit and flowers etc. □ **villous** *adj.*

vim *n. informal* vigour, energy.

vinaigrette /ˌvɪnəˈɡret/ *n.* a dressing served with salads and cold meats, made with oil, vinegar, and various seasonings.

vindaloo /ˌvɪndəˈluː/ *n.* a heavily spiced Indian curry dish made with meat, fish, or poultry.

vindicate *v.tr.* **1** clear (a person, oneself, etc.) of blame, suspicion, or criticism by evidence or demonstration. **2** uphold or establish the truth or validity of (something disputed). **3** justify (one's actions etc.). □ **vindication** *n.* **vindicator** *n.*

vindictive /vɪnˈdɪktɪv/ *adj.* **1** tending to seek revenge. **2** characterized by this tendency; spiteful (*vindictive criticism*). □ **vindictively** *adv.* **vindictiveness** *n.*

vine *n.* **1** any climbing or trailing woody-stemmed plant, esp. of the genus *Vitis*, bearing grapes. **2** a slender trailing or climbing stem. □ **viny** *adj.*

vinegar *n.* **1** a sour liquid consisting mainly of dilute acetic acid, produced by the oxidation of the alcohol in wine or cider etc., and used as a condiment or food preservative. **2** sour behaviour or character. **3** energy, vitality. □ **vinegared** *adj.* **vinegary** *adj.*

vineyard /ˈvɪnjərd/ *n.* a plantation of grapevines, esp. one cultivated for winemaking. □ **vineyardist** *n.*

viniculture /ˈvɪnɪˌkʌltʃər/ *n.* the cultivation of grapes for the production of wine. □ **vinicultural** *adj.* **viniculturist** *n.*

vinifera /vaɪˈnɪfərə/ ● *adj.* of, derived from, or designating the vine *Vitis vinifera* or its grape, native to Europe and also widely cultivated in N America. ● *n.* (*pl.* same or **viniferas**) the vinifera wine or grape.

vinification /ˌvɪnɪfɪˈkeɪʃn/ *n.* the conversion of grape juice etc. into wine by fermentation. □ **vinify** *v.tr.* (**-ies, -ied**)

vino /ˈviːnoː/ *n. informal* or *jocular* wine.

vintage ● *n.* **1 a** the year in which the grapes are picked for the production of a particular wine. **b** the wine made from these grapes. **2** a wine of high quality from a single identified year and district. **3** the process of gathering grapes for winemaking. **4 a** the year or period when a thing was made or produced (*a car of pre-war vintage*). **b** a thing made in a particular year or period. ● *adj.* **1** being of high quality and earlier time (*a vintage house*). **2** characteristic of the best period of a person's work or career. **3** (of wine) produced in an exceptional year.

vintage car *n.* a car made between 1917 and 1930.

vintner *n.* a person who makes or sells wine.

vinyl *n.* **1** *Chem.* the radical $-CH:CH_2$, derived from ethylene by removal of a hydrogen atom (usu. *attrib.*: *vinyl group*). **2** any plastic made by polymerizing a compound containing the vinyl group, esp. polyvinyl chloride. **3 a** a phonograph record. **b** phonograph records collectively, esp. as opposed to audio tapes and compact discs.

viol /'vaɪəl/ *n.* a musical instrument of the Renaissance and Baroque periods, having five, six, or seven strings, often with frets, played with a bow and held vertically on the knees or between the legs.

viola[1] /vi'o:lə/ *n.* **1 a** a four-stringed musical instrument of the violin family, larger than the violin and of lower pitch. **b** a person who plays or is playing a viola. **2** a viol.

viola[2] /vai'o:lə, vi:-/ *n.* **1** any plant of the genus *Viola*, including the pansy and violet. **2** a cultivated hybrid of this genus.

viola da gamba /vi,o:lə də 'gæmbə/ *n.* a viol held between the player's legs, esp. one corresponding to the modern cello.

violate *v.tr.* **1** fail to observe or comply with (*violated the agreement*). **2 a** treat irreverently; desecrate, defile (a sanctuary etc.). **b** fail to respect; disregard (*violate tradition*). **3** break in or intrude upon, disturb (a person's privacy etc.). **4** assault sexually; rape. □ **violation** *n.* **violator** *n.*

violence *n.* **1** the esp. illegal exercise of physical force to cause injury or damage to a person or property; violent behaviour. **2** great force or strength; vehemence, severity, intensity (*the bomb exploded with violence*). **3** strength or intensity of emotion; fervour, passion. □ **do violence to 1** misinterpret, misapply, or distort. **2** cause harm or injury to.

violent *adj.* **1 a** involving or characterized by the use of great physical force, esp. in order to cause injury (*a violent game*). **b** involving an unlawful use of force (*violent crime*). **2** (of a person) tending to use aggressive physical force, esp. to injure or intimidate others. **3** operating with great and usu. destructive physical force (*a violent storm*). **4** passionate, intense, extreme (*violent dislike*). **5** (of death) resulting from external force or from poison. □ **violently** *adv.*

violet ● *n.* **1 a** any plant of the genus *Viola* with usu. purple, blue, yellow, or white flowers. **b** any of various plants resembling the sweet violet. **2** the bluish-purple colour seen at the end of the spectrum opposite red. ● *adj.* of a bluish-purple colour.

violin *n.* **1** a treble musical instrument with four strings, rested on the shoulder beneath the chin and played with a bow. **2** a violin player. □ **violinist** *n.*

violist /vi'o:ləst/ *n.* a person who plays a viola.

violoncello /,vi:ələn'tʃelo:, ,vaiə-/ *n.* (*pl.* **-os**) *formal* = CELLO. □ **violoncellist** *n.*

VIP *n.* (*pl.* **VIPs**) a very important person, esp. a high-ranking official or guest (also *attrib.*: *VIP lounge*).

viper *n.* **1** any venomous snake of the family Viperi-

dae, including the pit vipers, adders, etc. **2** a malignant or treacherous person. □ **viperish** *adj.* **viper-like** *adj.* **viperous** *adj.*

virago /vɪ'rɒgo:, -'reigo:/ *n.* (*pl.* **-os**) a domineering, abusive, or ill-tempered woman.

viral *adj.* of or caused by a virus.

vireo /'virio:/ *n.* (*pl.* **-os**) any small plain songbird of the family Vireonidae, inhabiting woodlands throughout the western hemisphere.

virgin ● *n.* **1** a person who has never had sexual intercourse. **2 a** (**the Virgin**) the Virgin Mary. **b** a picture or statue etc. representing the Virgin Mary. **3** *informal* a naive, innocent, or inexperienced person (*a political virgin*). **4** a member of any order of women under a vow of chastity. ● *adj.* (usu. *attrib.*) **1 a** being a virgin. **b** of or befitting a virgin (*virgin modesty*). **2** not yet used, explored, or exploited (*virgin prairie*). **3** undefiled, spotless. **4** (of olive oil) obtained from the first pressing of olives; unrefined. **5** (of wool) that has never, or only once, been spun or woven.

virginal *adj.* **1** that is a virgin. **2** that belongs or relates to a virgin. **3** that befits, resembles, or is characteristic of a virgin.

virginals *n.* (also **virginal**) an early keyboard instrument resembling a spinet and set in a box, played esp. in the 16th and 17th c. □ **virginalist** *n.*

virgin birth *n.* **1** the doctrine of Christ's birth from a mother who was a virgin. **2** parthenogenesis.

virgin forest *n.* a forest in its natural state.

Virginian ● *adj.* of or relating to the US state of Virginia. ● *n.* a native or inhabitant of Virginia.

Virginia creeper *n.* a N American vine, *Parthenocissus quinquefolia*, cultivated for ornament.

Virginia reel *n.* *N Amer.* a dance in which couples, arranged in a double line facing their partners, complete steps shouted by a caller or fiddler.

virginity *n.* **1** the state of being a virgin. **2** the state of being pure or untouched. **3** innocence, inexperience.

Virgin Mary[1] Mary, the mother of Jesus.

Virgin Mary[2] *n.* (*pl.* **Virgin Marys**) a drink of tomato juice without vodka (*compare* BLOODY MARY).

Virgo /'vɜrgo:/ *n.* (*pl.* **-os**) **1** a constellation on the celestial equator between Leo and Libra, containing several bright stars and a dense cluster of galaxies, traditionally regarded as representing a maiden or goddess associated with the harvest. **2 a** the sixth sign of the zodiac. **b** a person born when the sun is in this sign, usu. between Aug. 23 and Sept. 22. □ **Virgoan** *n. & adj.*

virile /'vɪraɪl, -əl/ *adj.* **1** of, belonging to, or characteristic of a man. **2** (of a person) full of the strength, vigour, or energy typically attributed to men. **3** (of a man) having a strong sexual drive or procreative ability. □ **virility** /və'rɪlɪti/ *n.*

virology /vaɪ'rɒlədʒi/ *n.* the branch of science that deals with the study of viruses. □ **virological** *adj.* **virologically** *adv.* **virologist** *n.*

virtual *adj.* **1** that is such in essence or effect, though not recognized as such in name or according to strict definition (*she married a virtual stranger*). **2** *Computing* **a** not physically existing but made by software to appear to do so from the point of view of the program or user (*virtual memory*). **b** designating or existing or experienced in an environment created by virtual reality. **3** *Physics* designating particles and processes that cannot be directly detected and occur over very short intervals of time and space with correspondingly indefinite energy and momenta. **4** *Optics* designating the apparent focus or image resulting from the effect of reflection or refraction upon rays of light. □ **virtuality** n.

virtual community n. Computing a group of users who communicate regularly in cyberspace.

virtually adv. **1** in effect; practically. **2** nearly, almost.

virtual memory n. Computing an apparent increase in the amount of available RAM, which is actually supported by data held in secondary storage, e.g. a hard disk, transfer between the two being made automatically as required.

virtual reality n. **1** a notional image or environment generated by computer, with which a user can interact realistically using gloves fitted with sensors and a helmet containing a screen. **2** the software or technology used to generate this environment.

virtue n. **1** conformity of life and conduct with moral principles; voluntary adherence to recognized laws or standards of conduct; moral excellence. **2** a particular form of moral excellence; a manifestation of the influence of moral principles in life or conduct (patience is a virtue). **3** chastity or sexual purity, traditionally esp. of women. **4** a particular beneficial quality or feature inherent in or pertaining to something (the virtues of the legislation). □ **by** (or **in**) **virtue of** on the strength or basis of; due to. **make a virtue of necessity** derive some credit or benefit from an unwelcome obligation.

virtuoso /ˌvɜːtʃuˈoːsoː, -tjuː-, -zoː/ ● n. (pl. **virtuosi** /-iː/ or **-os**) **1** a person who has mastered the technique of a fine art, esp. music. **2** a person with outstanding technical skill in any sphere. ● adj. requiring or displaying the skills of a virtuoso (a virtuoso piece). □ **virtuosic** /-ˈɒsɪk/ adj. **virtuosity** n.

virtuous adj. **1** possessing or displaying moral rectitude. **2** chaste. □ **virtuously** adv. **virtuousness** n.

virulent /ˈvɪrʊlənt, ˈvɪrjʊ-/ adj. **1** violently bitter or rancorous; full of acrimony or hostility (virulent abuse). **2 a** (of a disease) malignant or severe. **b** (of micro-organisms) capable of producing disease. **3** possessing venomous or poisonous qualities. □ **virulence** n. **virulently** adv.

virus n. **1 a** a submicroscopic organism that can multiply only inside living host cells, has a non-cellular structure lacking any intrinsic metabolism and usu. comprising a single DNA or RNA molecule inside a protein coat, and is usu. pathogenic. **b** an infection with such an organism. **2** = COMPUTER VIRUS. **3** a harmful, corrupting, or malignant influence.

visa ● n. **1** an endorsement on a passport etc. showing that it has been found correct, esp. as allowing the holder to enter or leave a country. **2** the term for which such an endorsement remains valid (overstayed their visa). ● v.tr. (**visas, visaed** or **visa'd, visaing**) mark with a visa.

visage /ˈvɪzɪdʒ/ n. literary a face, a countenance.

vis-à-vis /ˌviːzɑːˈviː/ ● prep. **1** in relation to; compared with. **2** opposite to; facing. ● adv. facing one another. ● n. (pl. same) **1** a person or thing facing another, esp. in some dances. **2** a person occupying a corresponding position in another group.

viscera /ˈvɪsərə/ n.pl. the interior organs in the great cavities of the body, e.g. the heart, liver, esp. in the abdomen, e.g. the intestines.

visceral adj. **1** of the viscera. **2** relating to inward feelings or instinct rather than conscious reasoning. □ **viscerally** adv.

viscid /ˈvɪsɪd/ adj. glutinous, sticky.

viscose /ˈvɪskoːs, -koːz/ n. **1** a form of cellulose in a highly viscous state suitable for drawing into yarn. **2** rayon made from this.

viscosity /vɪˈskɒsɪti/ n. (pl. **-ies**) **1** the quality or degree of being viscous. **2** Physics **a** (of a fluid) internal friction, the resistance to flow. **b** a quantity expressing this.

viscount /ˈvaikaunt/ n. a nobleman ranking between an earl or count and a baron.

viscountess /ˈvaikauntɛs/ n. **1** a viscount's wife or widow. **2** a woman holding the rank of viscount in her own right.

viscous /ˈvɪskəs/ adj. **1** glutinous, sticky. **2** semi-liquid. **3** Physics having a high viscosity.

vise /vais/ ● n. an instrument, esp. attached to a workbench, with two movable jaws between which an object may be clamped so as to leave the hands free to work on it. ● v.tr. secure in a vise. □ **viselike** adj.

visibility n. **1** the state of being visible; ability to be seen. **2** the range or possibility of vision as determined by the conditions of light and atmosphere (visibility was down to 50 metres). **3** the degree to which something impinges on public awareness or attracts attention (product visibility).

visible adj. **1 a** that can be seen by the eye. **b** (of light) within the range of wavelengths to which the eye is sensitive. **2** that can be perceived or ascertained; apparent, open (has no visible means of support). **3** in a position of public prominence; attracting attention. □ **visibly** adv.

visible minority n. esp. Cdn **1** an ethnic group whose members are clearly racially distinct from those of the predominant race in a society. **2** a member of such an ethnic group.

Visigoth /ˈvɪzɪˌgɒθ/ n. **1** a West Goth, a member of the branch of the Goths who settled in France and Spain in the 5th c. and ruled much of Spain until 711. **2** informal an uncivilized or barbarous person.

vision ● n. **1** the act or faculty of seeing. **2 a** a thing or person seen in a dream or trance. **b** a supernatural or prophetic apparition. **3** a thing or idea perceived vividly in the imagination (had visions of sandy beaches). **4** imaginative insight. **5** ability to plan or form policy in a far-sighted way, e.g. in politics. **6** a person etc. of unusual beauty. ● v.tr. see or present in or as in a vision. □ **visionless** adj.

visionary ● adj. **1** given to seeing visions or to indulging in fanciful theories. **2** having vision or foresight. **3** existing only in a vision or in the imagination. **4** not practicable. ● n. (pl. **-ies**) a visionary person.

vision quest n. (among some N American Aboriginal peoples) a sacred ceremony in which an individual, often a teenage boy, goes to a secluded place to fast and communicate with the spiritual world, often through visions.

visit ● v. (**visited, visiting**) **1 a** tr. & intr. go or come to see (a person, place, etc.) as an act of friendship or ceremony, on business or for a purpose, or from interest. **b** tr. go or come to see for the purpose of official inspection, supervision, consultation, or correction. **2** tr. reside temporarily with (a person) or at (a place). **3** intr. be a visitor. **4** tr. (of a disease, calamity, etc.) come upon, attack. **5** tr. Bible **a** (foll. by with) punish (a person). **b** (often foll. by upon) inflict punishment for (a sin). **6** intr. N Amer. **a** (foll. by with) go to see (a person) esp. socially. **b** (usu. foll. by with) converse, chat. ● n. **1 a** an act of visiting, a call on a person or at a place. **b** temporary residence with a person or at a place. **2** (foll. by to) an occasion of going to a doctor, dentist, etc. **3** a formal or official call for the purpose of inspection etc. **4** N Amer. a chat.

visitation *n.* **1** a visit, esp. a formal one. **2** a divorced person's visit with his or her child in the custody of a former spouse, granted as a right by a court. **3** a visit with a sick person in a hospital, a prison inmate, etc. **4** (**Visitation**) **a** the visit of the Virgin Mary to Elizabeth related in Luke 1:39-56. **b** the feast commemorating this on May 31 or July 2. **5** an official visit of inspection. **6** *informal* an unduly protracted visit or social call. **7** trouble or difficulty regarded as a divine punishment.

visiting ● *n.* paying a visit or visits. ● *attrib.adj.* **1** that visits (*visiting nurse*). **2** (of an academic etc.) having been invited from one institution to spend some time at another (*a visiting professor*). **3** pertaining to visits (*visiting hours*).

visiting hours *n.pl.* a designated time when visitors may call, esp. to see a patient in hospital etc.

visitor *n.* **1** a person who visits a person or place. **2** *Sport* a team competing in the opposing side's home stadium, rink, etc.

visitor centre *n.* a building in a tourist area in which exhibitions etc. are displayed as an introduction to the locality.

visor *n.* **1 a** a movable part of a helmet covering the face. **b** *N Amer.* the projecting front part of a cap. **c** a half-moon shaped shade on a headband, worn to protect the eyes from strong light. **2** a movable flap at the top of a windshield inside a car to protect the eyes from glare. □ **visored** *adj.*

vista *n.* **1** a long narrow view as between rows of trees. **2** a scenic wide view; a panorama. **3** a mental view of a long succession of remembered or anticipated events (*opened up new vistas to her ambition*).

visual ● *adj.* of, concerned with, or used in seeing. ● *n.* (usu. in *pl.*) **1** a visual image or display, a picture. **2** the visual element of a film or television broadcast. □ **visually** *adv.*

visual art *n.* (often in *pl.*) any art meant to be appreciated mainly or exclusively through sight, e.g. graphic art, sculpture, etc. □ **visual artist** *n.*

visual display unit *n.* esp. *Brit. Computing* = VIDEO DISPLAY TERMINAL. Abbr.: **VDU**.

visual field *n.* field of vision.

visualize *v.tr.* **1** make visible esp. to one's mind (a thing not visible to the eye). **2** make visible to the eye. □ **visualization** *n.*

vital ● *adj.* **1 a** essential to the existence or functioning of a thing or to the matter in hand; extremely important (*secrecy is vital*). **b** paramount, very great (*of vital importance*). **2** of, concerned with, or essential to organic life (*vital functions*). **3** full of life or activity; lively. ● *n.* (in *pl.*) the body's vital organs, e.g. the heart and brain. □ **vitally** *adv.*

vitality *n.* **1** liveliness, animation. **2** the ability to sustain life, vital power. **3** (of an institution etc.) the ability to endure and perform its functions.

vitalize *v.tr.* **1** endow with life. **2** infuse with vigour. □ **vitalization** *n.*

vital signs *n.pl.* clinical measurements that indicate the state of a person's essential body functions, esp. pulse rate, temperature, respiration rate, and blood pressure.

vital statistics *n.pl.* **1** the number of births, marriages, deaths, etc. **2** *jocular* the measurements of a woman's bust, waist, and hips.

vitamin *n.* **1** any of a group of organic compounds essential in small amounts for many living organisms to maintain normal health and development. **2** (often in *pl.*) a pill providing any of these as a dietary supplement.

vitamin A *n.* = RETINOL.

vitamin B₁ *n.* = THIAMINE.

vitamin B₂ *n.* = RIBOFLAVIN.

vitamin B₃ *n.* = NIACIN.

vitamin B₁₂ *n.* a vitamin of the B complex, found in foods of animal origin such as liver, fish, and eggs.

vitamin B complex *n.* a group of vitamins which, although not chemically related, are often found together in the same foods.

vitamin C *n.* = ASCORBIC ACID.

vitamin D *n.* any of a group of vitamins found in liver and fish oils and sunlight, essential for the absorption of calcium and the prevention of rickets.

vitamin D₃ *n.* = CHOLECALCIFEROL.

vitamin E *n.* = TOCOPHEROL.

vitamin H *n.* = BIOTIN.

vitamin K *n.* any of a group of vitamins found esp. in green leaves, essential for blood clotting.

vitamin K₁ *n.* = PHYLLOQUINONE.

vitamin M *n.* esp. *N Amer.* = FOLIC ACID.

vitiate /'vɪʃi,eit/ *v.tr.* **1** impair the quality or efficiency of; corrupt, debase, contaminate. **2** make invalid or ineffectual. □ **vitiation** *n.*

viticulture /'vɪtɪ,kʌltʃər/ *n.* the cultivation of grapevines; the science or study of this. □ **vitcultural** *adj.* **viticulturist** *n.*

vitreous /'vɪtriəs/ *adj.* **1** of, or of the nature of, glass. **2** like glass in hardness, brittleness, transparency, structure, etc. (*vitreous enamel*).

vitrify /'vɪtri,fai/ *v.tr. & intr.* (**-ies, -ied**) convert or be converted into glass or a glasslike substance esp. by heat. □ **vitrifiable** *adj.* **vitrification** *n.*

vitriol /'vɪtri,ɒl, 'vɪtriəl/ *n.* **1** sulphuric acid or a sulphate, originally one of glassy appearance. **2** caustic or hostile speech, criticism, or feeling.

vitriolic /,vɪtri'blɪk/ *adj.* (of speech or criticism) caustic or hostile.

vittle *informal var.* of VICTUAL *n.*

vituperate /vɪ'tu:pə,reit, -'tju:-, vai-/ *v.* **1** *tr.* revile, abuse; find fault with in strong or violent language. **2** *intr.* employ abusive language. □ **vituperation** *n.* **vituperative** /-rətiv/ *adj.*

viva /'vi:və/ ● *interj.* long live. ● *n.* a cry of this as a salute etc.

vivacious /vɪ'veiʃəs, vai-/ *adj.* lively, sprightly, animated. □ **vivaciously** *adv.* **vivacity** /vɪ'væsiti/ *n.*

vivarium /vai'veəriəm, vɪ-/ *n.* (*pl.* **-s** or **vivaria** /-riə/) a place artificially prepared for keeping animals in (nearly) their natural state; an aquarium etc.

viva voce /,vi:və 'vɒtʃei, 'vo:tʃei/ ● *adj.* spoken, oral. ● *adv.* out loud, orally.

vivid *adj.* **1 a** (of light or colour) strong, intense, glaring (*a vivid green*). **b** brilliantly coloured or lit. **2 a** (of an impression, description, etc.) clear, striking, graphic. **b** (of a mental faculty) capable of strong and distinct impressions, producing clear images; active (*has a vivid imagination*). **3** (of a person) lively, vigorous. □ **vividly** *adv.* **vividness** *n.*

vivify /'vɪvi,fai/ *v.tr.* (**-ies, -ied**) enliven, animate, make lively or living.

vivisection /,vɪvi'sekʃən/ *n.* **1** dissection or other painful treatment of living animals for purposes of scientific research. **2** unduly detailed or ruthless criticism. □ **vivisect** *v.tr.* **vivisectionist** *n.*

vixen /'vɪksən/ *n.* **1** a female fox. **2** a spiteful or quarrelsome woman. □ **vixenish** *adj.*

viz. *adv.* namely; that is to say; in other words (*came to a firm conclusion, viz. that we were right*).

VJ *abbr.* video jockey, a person who introduces music videos on television etc.

VJ day *n.* Aug. 15, 1945, the day Japan ceased fighting in WW II, or Sept. 2 of the same year, when Japan formally surrendered.

VLF *abbr.* very low frequency (designating radio waves of frequency *c.*3–30 kHz and wavelength *c.*10–100 km).

VLSI *abbr. Computing* very large-scale integration, the technology integrating over 100,000 transistors on a single chip.

VLT *abbr.* VIDEO LOTTERY TERMINAL.

V-neck *n.* (often *attrib.*) **1** (also **V-neckline**) a neck of a pullover etc. with straight sides meeting at an angle in the front to form a V. **2** a garment with this. □ **V-necked** *adj.*

vocab /ˈvoːkæb/ *n. informal* vocabulary.

vocabulary *n.* (*pl.* **-ies**) **1** the (principal) words used in a language or a particular book or branch of science etc. or by a particular author. **2** a list of these, arranged alphabetically with definitions or translations. **3** the range of words known to an individual (*his vocabulary is limited*).

vocal ● *adj.* **1** of or concerned with or uttered by the voice (*a vocal communication*). **2** expressing one's feelings freely in speech (*was very vocal about his rights*). **3** (of music) written for or produced by the voice with or without accompaniment (*compare* INSTRUMENTAL *adj.* 2). ● *n.* (in *sing.* or *pl.*) the sung part of a musical composition. □ **vocally** *adv.*

vocal cords *n.pl.* (also **vocal folds**) folds of the lining membrane of the larynx near the opening of the glottis, which vibrate in the airstream when close together to produce voiced sounds.

vocalic /voˈkælɪk/ *adj.* of or consisting of a vowel or vowels.

vocalist *n.* a singer, esp. of jazz or popular songs.

vocalize *v.* **1** *tr.* **a** form (a sound) or utter (a word) with the voice. **b** make voiced (*f is vocalized into v*). **2** *intr.* utter a vocal sound. **3** *tr.* articulate, express. **4** *intr. Music* sing with several notes to one vowel. □ **vocalization** *n.*

vocation /voˈkeɪʃən/ *n.* **1 a** a strong feeling of fitness for a particular career or occupation. **b** a divine call to the religious life. **2 a** a person's employment, esp. regarded as requiring dedication. **b** a trade or profession.

vocational *adj.* **1** of or relating to an occupation or employment. **2** (of education or training) directed at a particular esp. manual or technical occupation and its skills (*vocational school*). □ **vocationally** *adv.*

vocative /ˈvɒkətɪv/ *Grammar* ● *n.* the case of nouns, pronouns, and adjectives used in addressing or invoking a person or thing. ● *adj.* of or in this case.

vociferous /voˈsɪfərəs/ *adj.* **1** noisy, clamorous. **2** insistently and forcibly expressing one's views. □ **vociferously** *adv.* **vociferousness** *n.*

vodka *n.* **1** a colourless alcoholic spirit made by distillation of rye etc. **2** a drink of this.

vogue *n.* **1** (prec. by *the*) the prevailing fashion. **2** popular use or currency (*has had a great vogue*). □ **in vogue** in fashion, generally current. □ **voguish** *adj.*

voguing /ˈvoːgɪŋ/ *n.* solo dancing with movements reminiscent of a fashion model's posing.

voice ● *n.* **1 a** sound formed in the larynx etc. and uttered by the mouth, esp. human utterance in speaking, shouting, singing, etc. (*heard a voice*). **b** the ability to produce this (*has lost her voice*). **c** this regarded as characteristic of an individual. **2 a** the use of the voice; utterance, esp. in spoken or written

words (*give voice*). **b** an opinion so expressed; the expressed will of the people, a group, etc. **c** the right to express an opinion (*I have no voice in the matter*). **d** an agency by which an opinion is expressed. **3** *Grammar* a form or set of forms of a verb showing the relation of the subject to the action (*passive voice*). **4** *Music* **a** a vocal part in a composition. **b** a constituent part in a fugue. **5** *Phonetics* sound uttered with resonance of the vocal cords. **6** (usu. in *pl.*) the supposed utterance of an invisible guiding or directing spirit. ● *v.tr.* **1** give utterance to; express (*the letter voices our opinion*). **2** (esp. as **voiced** *adj.*) *Phonetics* utter with vibration of the vocal cords, as in the consonants *b, d, g, v, z*. □ **in voice** (or **good voice**) in proper vocal condition for singing or speaking. **with one voice** unanimously. □ **-voiced** *adj.* **voicing** *n.*

voice box *n.* the larynx.

voiceless *adj.* **1** dumb, mute, speechless. **2** *Phonetics* uttered without vibration of the vocal cords, as in the consonants *f, k, p, s, t*. □ **voicelessness** *n.*

voice mail *n.* (also **voice messaging**) a system for electronically storing, processing, and reproducing verbal messages left through the conventional telephone network.

voice-over *n.* narration in a film etc. not accompanied by a picture of the speaker.

voice print *n.* a visual record of speech, analyzed with respect to frequency, duration, and amplitude.

void ● *adj.* **1 a** empty, vacant. **b** (foll. by *of*) lacking; free from. **2** esp. *Law* (of a contract, deed, promise, etc.) invalid, not binding (*null and void*). **3** useless, ineffectual. ● *n.* **1** an empty space, a vacuum (*cannot fill the void made by his death*). **2** an unfilled space in a wall or building. ● *v.* **1** *tr.* render invalid. **2** *tr. & intr.* empty the contents of esp. the bowels or bladder; excrete. □ **voidable** *adj.* **voidness** *n.*

voila /vwɑˈlɒ/ *interj.* expressing satisfaction or ease of accomplishment.

voile /vɔɪl, vwɒl/ *n.* a thin semi-transparent material.

vol. *abbr.* volume.

volatile /ˈvɒlə.taɪl, -təl/ ● *adj.* **1** evaporating rapidly (*volatile salts*). **2** changeable; unstable. **3** lively, lighthearted. **4** apt to break out into violence. **5** transient. **6** *Computing* designating memory whose contents are destroyed on the removal of power to the memory. ● *n.* a volatile substance. □ **volatility** /-ˈtɪlɪti/ *n.*

volatile oil *n.* = ESSENTIAL OIL.

volcanic /vɒlˈkænɪk/ ● *adj.* of, like, or produced by a volcano. ● *n.* (usu. in *pl.*) a rock etc. formed by volcanic action. □ **volcanically** *adv.*

volcanism /ˈvɒlkənɪzəm/ *n.* volcanic activity.

volcano /vɒlˈkeɪnoː/ *n.* (*pl.* **-oes**) **1** a mountain or hill having an opening or openings in the earth's crust through which lava, cinders, steam, gases, etc. are or have been expelled continuously or at intervals. **2 a** a state of affairs likely to cause a violent outburst. **b** a violent esp. suppressed feeling.

volcanology /ˌvɒlkəˈnɒlədʒi/ *n.* the scientific study of volcanoes. □ **volcanologist** *n.*

vole /voːl/ *n.* any small rat-like or mouselike plant-eating rodent of the family Cricetidae.

volition /vəˈlɪʃən/ *n.* **1** the exercise of the will. **2** the power of willing. □ **of** (or **by**) **one's own volition** voluntarily. □ **volitional** *adj.*

volk /fʊlk/ *n.* **1** the Afrikaner people. **2** the German people (esp. with reference to Nazi ideology).

volley ● *n.* (*pl.* **-eys**) **1 a** the simultaneous discharge of a number of weapons. **b** the bullets etc. discharged in a volley. **2** (usu. foll. by *of*) a rapid emission of many things at once in quick succession (*a volley of insults*). **3 a** the return of a ball, shuttlecock, etc. in play in tennis etc. before it touches the ground. **b** a series of these. **4** *Soccer* the kicking of a ball in play before it touches the ground. **5** *Volleyball* a pass etc. made with the fingertips. ● *v.* (**-eys, -eyed**) **1** *tr. & intr. Sport* return or send (a ball) by a volley. **2** *tr. & intr.* discharge (bullets, abuse, etc.) in a volley. **3** *intr.* (of bullets etc.) fly in a volley. **4** *intr.* (of guns etc.) sound together. □ **volleyer** *n.*

volleyball *n.* **1** a game for two usu. six-player teams in which a large inflated ball is hit back and forth over a net with the fingers, fist, or forearm. **2** the ball used in this game.

vols. *abbr.* volumes.

volt *n.* the SI unit of electromotive force, the difference of potential that would carry one ampere of current against one ohm resistance. Abbr.: **V.**

voltage *n.* electromotive force or potential difference expressed in volts.

volte-face /vɒˈltə ˈfæs/ *n.* **1** a complete reversal of position in argument or opinion. **2** the act or an instance of turning around.

voltmeter *n.* an instrument for measuring electric potential in volts.

voluble /ˈvɒljʊbəl/ *adj.* speaking or spoken vehemently, incessantly, or fluently (*voluble excuses*). □ **volubility** *n.* **volubly** *adv.*

volume *n.* **1 a** a set of sheets of paper, usu. printed, and bound together; a book, esp. one of a matching set or series (*issued in three volumes; a library of 12,000 volumes*). **b** several consecutive issues of a magazine etc. esp. designed to be bound together as a book. **2 a** solid content, bulk. **b** the space occupied by a substance. **c** (usu. foll. by *of*) an amount or quantity (*large volume of business*). **d** the amount of space in a container. **3 a** quantity or power of sound. **b** a knob etc. controlling this, as on stereo equipment. **c** fullness of tone. **4** (foll. by *of*) **a** a moving mass of water etc. **b** (usu. in *pl.*) a wreath or coil or rounded mass of smoke etc. □ **volumed** *adj.* (also in *comb.*).

volumetric /ˌvɒljʊˈmetrɪk/ *adj.* of or relating to measurement by volume. □ **volumetrically** *adv.*

voluminous /vəˈluːmɪnəs, vəˈljuː-/ *adj.* **1** large in volume; bulky. **2** (of drapery, a skirt, etc.) loose and ample. **3** consisting of many volumes. **4** (of a writer) producing many books. □ **voluminously** *adv.*

voluntarism /ˈvɒləntəˌrɪzəm/ *n.* **1** the principle of relying on voluntary action rather than compulsion, esp. as regards social welfare. **2** *Philos.* the doctrine that the will is a fundamental or dominant factor in the individual or the universe. □ **voluntarist** *n.*

voluntary ● *adj.* **1** done, acting, or able to act of one's own free will; not constrained or compulsory, intentional (*a voluntary donation*). **2** unpaid (*voluntary work*). **3** (of an institution) **a** supported by voluntary contributions. **b** staffed by volunteers. **4** brought about, produced, etc., by voluntary action. **5** (of a movement, muscle, or limb) controlled by the will. **6** (of a confession by a criminal) not prompted by a promise or threat. **7** not accidental; intentional (*voluntary manslaughter*). ● *n.* (*pl.* **-ies**) **1** an organ solo played before, during, or after a church service. **2** the music for this. □ **voluntarily** *adv.* **voluntariness** *n.*

volunteer ● *n.* **1** a person who voluntarily takes part in an enterprise or offers to undertake a task. **2** a person who enrols voluntarily for military service. **3** a person who works for an organization voluntarily and without pay. **4** (*attrib.*) designating an organization etc. composed of volunteers (*volunteer fire*

department). ● *v.* **1** *tr.* (often foll. by *to* + infin.) undertake or offer (one's services, a remark or explanation, etc.) voluntarily. **2** *intr.* (often foll. by *for*) make a voluntary offer of one's services; be a volunteer. **3** *tr.* (usu. in passive; often foll. by *for*, or *to* + infin.) often *ironic* assign or commit (a person) to a particular esp. 'voluntary' undertaking, esp. without consultation. □ **volunteering** *n.*

volunteerism *n.* esp. *N Amer.* the involvement of volunteers, esp. in community service.

voluptuous /vəˈlʌptjʊəs, -tjʊ-/ *adj.* **1** of, tending to, occupied with, or derived from, sensuous or sensual pleasure. **2** suggestive of sensuous or sensual pleasure; sensuously or sensually pleasing. **3** (of a woman) curvaceous and sexually desirable. □ **voluptuously** *adv.* **voluptuousness** *n.*

vomit ● *v.* (**vomited, vomiting**) **1** *tr. & intr.* eject (matter) from the stomach through the mouth. **2** *tr.* (of a volcano, chimney, etc.) eject violently, belch forth. ● *n.* matter vomited from the stomach.

VON *abbr. Cdn* VICTORIAN ORDER OF NURSES.

voodoo *n.* **1** a religion practised in the W Indies and the southern US, characterized by sorcery and spirit possession, and combining elements of traditional African religious rites with Catholic ritual. **2** a person skilled in this. **3** a voodoo spell. □ **voodooist** *n.*

voodoo doll *n.* a small figure in the likeness of a real person, the tormenting or hexing of which supposedly affects the person.

voracious /vəˈreɪʃəs/ *adj.* **1** greedy in eating, ravenous. **2** insatiable (*a voracious reader*). □ **voraciously** *adv.* **voracity** /vəˈræsɪti/ *n.*

vortex /ˈvɔːteks/ *n.* (*pl.* **vortices** /-tɪˌsiːz/ or **vortexes**) **1** a mass of whirling fluid, esp. a whirlpool or whirlwind. **2** any whirling motion or mass. **3** a system, occupation, pursuit, etc., viewed as swallowing up or engrossing those who approach it (*the vortex of society*). □ **vortical** *adj.*

votary /ˈvəʊtəri/ *n.* (*pl.* **-ies**) **1** a devoted follower of a religion, deity, or cult, esp. one who is bound, by vow, to the worship of God. **2** (often foll. by *of*) a devoted follower, adherent, or advocate of a person, cause, occupation, or pursuit.

vote ● *n.* **1 a** a formal expression of choice or opinion by means of a ballot, show of hands, etc., concerning esp. a choice of candidate or approval or rejection of a motion or resolution. **b** a ballot or ticket used for recording one's choice (*still counting the votes*). **2** the collective votes that are or may be given by or for a particular group (*we hope to win the francophone vote*). **3** (usu. prec. by *the*) the right to vote, esp. in general elections. **4 a** an opinion expressed or decision reached by a majority of votes (*a vote of confidence*). **b** a resolution passed or grant of appropriation authorized by Parliament. ● *v.* **1** *intr.* **a** express a choice or preference by casting a vote. **b** (foll. by *on*) register or express one's opinion regarding (*they vote on the proposal today*). **2** *tr.* decide by a majority of votes (*striking workers have voted to accept the latest proposal*). **3** *tr.* support (a candidate, party, side, etc.) habitually or in a particular election (*I vote Liberal*). **4** *tr.* pronounce or declare by formal ballot or general consent (*he was voted the league's MVP*). **5** *tr. informal* announce one's proposal (*I vote that we all go home*). □ **put to a** (or **the**) **vote** submit to a decision by voting. **vote down** defeat (a proposal etc.) in a vote. **vote in** elect (a candidate) by votes. **vote out** dismiss (an incumbent) from office etc. by voting. **vote with one's feet** *informal* indicate an opinion by one's presence or absence.

vote-getter *n. informal* **1** a candidate in an election (*four of the top five vote-getters were women*). **2** a policy introduced prior to or during an election campaign in an attempt to sway voters. □ **vote-getting** *n.*

vote of confidence *n.* **1** a vote showing that the majority support the policy of the governing body etc. **2** an indication from a person of his or her support for or approval of another, their work, etc.

vote of non-confidence *n. Cdn* a vote indicating that the majority does not support a policy of the governing party, as a result of which the governing party is usu. forced to resign.

voter *n.* **1** a person eligible to vote in an election. **2** a person voting.

voters list *n.* a list of the names and addresses of those who are eligible to vote in an upcoming general election or referendum.

voting shares *n.pl.* (also **voting stock**) shares in a company that entitle the holder to vote at any meetings of the company.

votive /ˈvoʊtɪv/ *adj.* **1** offered or undertaken in fulfillment of a vow or as a thanksgiving (*votive offering*). **2** expressive of a vow or wish (*votive prayer*).

votive candle *n.* **1** (in some Christian denominations) a candle, often contained in a glass vase, that may be lit as a symbol of prayer, usu. in front of a religious image. **2** a type of squat household candle, usu. tapering at the top and often scented, used for decoration.

vouch *v.intr.* (foll. by *for*) **1** take responsibility for or express confidence in; guarantee the reliability of. **2** confirm or verify the truth or existence of something by providing proof or assurance.

voucher *n.* **1** a document which can be exchanged for goods or services, or which entitles the holder to a reduction in the price of something. **2** a person who vouches for a person, statement, etc.

vouchsafe *v.tr. formal* **1** give as a gift or privilege (*she would not vouchsafe me a reply*). **2** permit or agree.

vow ● *n.* **1** a solemn promise made to God, another deity, or a saint, to perform an action or adopt a particular way of life. **2 a** a solemn undertaking or resolve (*I made a vow never to speak to her again*). **b** (foll. by *of*) a solemn promise to observe a specified state or condition (*a vow of silence*). **3** (in *pl.*) **a** the promises by which a monk or nun is bound to poverty, chastity, and obedience. **b** the promises of fidelity made during a marriage ceremony. **4** (usu. as **baptismal vows**) the promises given at baptism by the baptized person or by sponsors. ● *v.tr.* **1** promise or undertake solemnly (*she vowed that she would never return*). **2** make a solemn resolve or threat to inflict (injury) or exact (revenge). **3** dedicate to a deity. □ **under a vow** bound by a vow one has made.

vowel *n.* **1** a speech sound made with vibration of the vocal cords but without audible friction, more open than a consonant and capable of forming a syllable. **2** a letter of the alphabet representing such a sound, such as *a, e, i, o, u.*

vox pop *n. informal* **1** popular opinion as represented by informal comments from members of the public. **2** statements or interviews of this kind.

voyage ● *n.* a journey, esp. a long one by water, air, or in space. ● *v.* **1** *intr.* make a voyage. **2** *tr.* traverse, esp. by water or air.

voyager *n.* **1** a person who makes a voyage; a traveller. **2** *Cdn* = VOYAGEUR.

voyageur /ˌvɔɪəˈʒɜr, ˌvwʊdjæˈʒɜr/ *n.* **1** esp. *Cdn hist.* a usu. French-speaking or Metis canoeman employed by merchants in Montreal to transport goods to and from trading posts in the interior. **2** *N Amer.* an out-

doorsman or adventurer, esp. one who goes canoe tripping through rough country. □ **voyaging** *n.*

voyageur canoe *n. Cdn* = CANOT DU NORD.

voyeur /vɔɪˈjɜr/ *n.* **1** a person who derives sexual gratification from the covert observation of others as they undress or engage in sexual activities. **2** a powerless or passive observer, esp. one who derives an inordinate amount of enjoyment from observing a situation without participating in it. □ **voyeurism** *n.*

voyeuristic *adj.* **voyeuristically** *adv.*

VP *abbr.* Vice-President.

VQA *n. Cdn* (often *attrib.*) designating a Canadian wine certified by the Vintners Quality Alliance, a body of winemakers, wine merchants, and federal government officials, as meeting certain standards of taste and conforming to statutory regulations.

VR *abbr.* virtual reality.

vroom ● *v.intr.* **1** (esp. of a car or engine) make a roaring or revving noise, suggestive of great speed. **2** (of a car or truck etc.) travel at high speed. ● *n.* the roaring sound of an engine. ● *interj.* an imitation of such a sound.

vs. *abbr.* versus.

V-shaped *adj.* having a shape or a cross-section resembling the letter V.

VT *abbr.* Vermont (in official postal use).

Vt. *abbr.* Vermont.

VTO *abbr.* vertical takeoff.

VTR *abbr.* = VIDEOTAPE RECORDER 1.

vulcanize /ˈvʌlkəˌnaɪz/ *v.tr.* treat (rubber or rubberlike material) with sulphur at a high temperature to increase its durability and elasticity.

vulcanology /ˌvʌlkəˈnɒlədʒi/ *var. of* VOLCANOLOGY.

vulgar *adj.* **1** likely to offend; indecent, rude, obscene (*a vulgar joke*). **2** displaying or proceeding from ignorance or a lack of refinement, manners, or taste. **3 a** popular, common. **b** of or characteristic of the common people, plebeian. □ **vulgarly** *adv.*

vulgar fraction *n.* a fraction expressed by numerator and denominator, not decimally.

vulgarism *n.* **1** a coarse or obscene word or expression. **2** an instance of coarse or uneducated behaviour.

vulgarity /vʌlˈɡerɪti/ *n.* (pl. **-ies**) **1** the quality of being vulgar. **2** an instance of this.

vulgarize *v.tr.* **1** make (a person, manners, etc.) vulgar. **2** make widely known or accessible to the public; popularize. □ **vulgarization** *n.*

Vulgate /ˈvʌlɡeɪt, -ɡət/ *n.* **1** the Latin version of the Bible prepared mainly by St. Jerome in the late 4th c. **2** the official Catholic Latin text of the Bible as revised in 1592.

vulnerable *adj.* **1** able to be physically or emotionally hurt. **2** liable to damage or harm, esp. from aggression or attack (*a vulnerable position*). **3** (foll. by *to*) exposed or susceptible to a destructive agent or influence etc. (*vulnerable to criticism*). □ **vulnerability** *n.* (pl. **-ies**). **vulnerably** *adv.*

vulture *n.* **1** any of various large birds of prey of the family Cathartidae or Accipitridae, most of which have a mainly bald head and neck, feeding chiefly on carrion and reputed to gather with others in anticipation of a death. **2** a ruthless or rapacious person, esp. one who preys upon those who are vulnerable or weak.

vulva /ˈvʌlvə/ *n.* (pl. **-s**) the external female genitals, consisting (in women) of the labia, clitoris, and vaginal opening. □ **vulval** *adj.*

vying *pres. part. of* VIE.

Ww

W¹ *n.* (also **w**) (*pl.* **Ws** or **W's**) the twenty-third letter of the alphabet.

W² *abbr.* (also **W.**) **1** watt(s). **2** West(ern). **3** women's (size).

W³ *symbol* tungsten.

w *abbr.* (also **w.**) **1** with. **2** wife. **3** weight. **4** width.

WA *abbr.* **1** Washington (State). **2** Western Australia.

waah *interj.* expressing wailing.

wacked *var.* of WHACKED.

wacko *N Amer. slang* ● *adj.* crazy, insane. ● *n.* (*pl.* **-os** or **-oes**) a crazy person.

wacky *adj.* (**-ier, -iest**) *informal* crazy, madcap, goofy. □ **wackily** *adv.* **wackiness** *n.*

wad ● *n.* **1 a** a small mass of soft material (*a wad of bubble gum*). **b** a compact bundle of material for stuffing or packing. **2 a** a number of banknotes or papers etc. stacked or rolled together. **b** (in *sing.* or *pl.*) a large quantity of esp. money. **3** a disc or plug of paper, cloth, or felt retaining the powder and shot in position in a gun or cartridge. ● *v.tr.* (**wadded, wadding**) **1** press, crumple, or arrange (soft material). **2** plug (the barrel of a gun) with a wad.

wadding *n.* **1** any soft, loose, or pliable material used to line, stuff, or pad garments, quilts, etc., or to pack fragile articles. **2** any material from which the wads for guns are made.

waddle ● *v.intr.* walk with short steps and a clumsy rocking or swaying motion, like a stout short-legged person or a bird with short legs set far apart. ● *n.* a waddling gait. □ **waddler** *n.*

wade ● *v.* **1** *intr.* walk through a deep liquid or soft substance that impedes motion, such as water, mud, or snow. **2** *intr.* (often foll. by *through*) go laboriously or doggedly through a tedious task, a long or uninteresting book, etc. **3** *tr.* walk through (water etc.). □ **wade in** (or **into**) *informal* involve oneself energetically.

wader *n.* **1** (in *pl.*) high waterproof boots, or a waterproof garment for the legs and body, worn esp. for fishing. **2 a** *N Amer.* any large, long-necked, long-legged wading bird, as a heron, stork, or crane. **b** a wading bird, esp. any of various birds of the order Charadriiformes. **3** a person who wades.

wading bird *n.* any usu. long-legged wader that finds its food in shallow waters or along the shore.

wading pool *n.* *N Amer.* a shallow pool for children to play in.

wafer *n.* **1** a very thin light crisp cookie. **2** a thin disc of unleavened bread used in the Eucharist. **3** *Electronics* a very thin slice of a semiconductor crystal used as the substrate for solid state circuitry. **4** a disc of red paper stuck on a legal document instead of a seal. □ **wafery** *adj.*

waferboard *n.* esp. *Cdn* a rigid sheet or panel ranging in thickness from 6.5 mm (¹/₄ inch) to 19 mm (³/₄ inch), of randomly arranged wood chips, larger than those of particleboard, bonded with resin.

wafer-thin ● *adj.* very thin. ● *adv.* very thinly.

waffle¹ ● *v.intr.* **1** waver in opinion or resolve. **2** (often foll. by *on*) indulge in rambling aimless speech or writing. ● *n.* **1** verbose but aimless talk or writing. **2** (**Waffle**) *Cdn hist.* a caucus of NDP members organized in 1969 to promote a socialist and nationalist agenda, which included the replacement of US private ownership of Canadian industry with Canadian public ownership, the establishment of an independent Canadian labour movement, the right of Quebec to self-determination, and the advancement of the feminist movement. □ **waffler** *n.* (also **Waffler** in sense 2 of *n.*). **waffly** *adj.*

waffle² *n.* esp. *N Amer.* **1** a crisp pancake with a grid-like pattern of indentations on each side. **2** (*attrib.* or in *comb.*) designating esp. fabrics with a texture resembling that of a waffle (*waffle-knit sweater*).

waffle iron *n.* an appliance used to bake waffles, consisting of two hinged metal pans with a grid pattern, which forms indentations on the waffle.

waft / wɒft, wæft / ● *v.* **1** *intr.* float or glide gently through or as if through the air or over water. **2** *tr.* carry or send gently through or as if through the air. ● *n.* (usu. foll. by *of*) a scent passing through the air or carried by a breeze; a whiff.

wag¹ ● *v.tr. & intr.* (**wagged, wagging**) shake, wave, or sway to and fro or from side to side, esp. in a rapid energetic manner (*wagged her finger at me*). ● *n.* a single wagging motion (*with a wag of his tail*). □ **the tail that wags the dog** a subordinate or unimportant person who controls the organization etc. of which he or she is a member. **tongues** (or **chins** or **jaws**) **wag** there is talk or gossip.

wag² *n.* a humorist; a joker or wit.

wage ● *n.* **1** (in *sing.* or *pl.*) **a** a payment made by an employer to an employee in exchange for work or service rendered. **b** a fixed regular payment, usu. daily or weekly, made by an employer to a manual or unskilled worker (*compare* SALARY). **2** (in *pl.*) *Econ.* the part of total production that is the return to labour as earned income as distinct from the remuneration received by capital as unearned income. **3** (in *sing.* or *pl.*) *literary* reward, recompense (*the wage of sin is death*). ● *v.tr.* conduct, carry on (a war, campaign, etc.).

wage earner *n.* a person who works for wages. □ **wage-earning** *attrib.adj.*

wage labour *n.* **1** the portion of the labour force working for wages. **2** the body of workers receiving wages from one employer. **3** work for which wages are paid. □ **wage labourer** *n.*

wager ● *v.* **1** *tr. & intr.* stake (esp. a sum of money) on the outcome of an uncertain event or on an undecided or unresolved matter. **2** *tr.* **a** make a bet that (a certain outcome, result, etc.) will occur (*I'll wager that my team beats yours*). **b** *informal* confidently assert; be certain (*I'll wager they've left by now*). ● *n.* **1** an instance of wagering; a betting transaction. **2** a thing, esp. a sum of money, laid down as a stake. □ **wagering** *n.*

waggish *adj.* amusing, witty, tongue-in-cheek. □ **waggishly** *adv.* **waggishness** *n.*

waggle *informal* ● *v.* **1** *tr. & intr.* move with short movements from side to side or up and down. **2** *intr.* *Golf* swing the head of one's club back and forth over the ball before playing a shot. ● *n.* a waggling motion. □ **waggly** *adj.*

Wagnerian /vɒgˈneriən/ ● *adj.* **1** of, relating to, or characteristic of the German composer Richard Wagner (1813–83) or his music and theories of musical and dramatic composition. **2** grandiose, highly dramatic. ● *n.* an admirer of Wagner or his music.

wagon *n.* **1** a large sturdy four-wheeled vehicle, usu. drawn by horse or tractor, for transporting heavy or bulky loads, esp. an open cart for carrying hay etc. with an elongated body and extended framework attached to the sides. **2** *hist.* a covered horse-drawn vehicle used for conveying goods and passengers by road. **3** *N Amer.* a child's small four-wheeled cart, drawn by hand and used for carrying light loads or passengers. **4** esp. *N Amer.* **a** = STATION WAGON. **b** = PADDY WAGON. **5** a cart or trolley for serving tea or meals. □ **fix a person's wagon** *N Amer. slang* get even with a person. **off the wagon** *informal* indulging in alcoholic drinks after a period of temperance. **on the wagon** *informal* abstaining from alcoholic drinks.

wagonload *n.* as much as a wagon can carry.

wagon train *n.* *N Amer.* esp. *hist.* a succession of wagons, esp. a train of covered wagons and horses used by migrating pioneers or settlers.

Wahhabi /wəˈhɒbi/ *n.* (also **Wahabi**) (*pl.* **-is**) a member of a strictly orthodox Sunni Muslim sect founded in the 18th c. by Muhammad ibn Abd al-Wahhab, who called for a return to the earliest doctrines and practices of Islam as embodied in the Koran and Sunna. □ **Wahhabism** *n.*

wahoo¹ /wæˈhuː/ *n.* a large fish, *Acanthocybium solanderi*, which is a streamlined and fast-swimming predator found in all tropical seas.

wahoo² /wəˈhuː/ *interj.* *N. Amer.* = YAHOO².

wah-wah /ˈwɒwɒ/ *n.* **1** an effect achieved on brass instruments by alternately applying and removing a mute, or on an electric guitar by using a pedal to control the output from the amplifier. **2** a device for producing this effect on an electric guitar, consisting of a pedal and circuit box.

waif *n.* **1** a homeless and helpless person, esp. a neglected, abandoned, or starved child. **2** a lost or ownerless article. □ **waifish** *adj.* **waiflike** *adj.*

wail ● *n.* **1** a long loud inarticulate high-pitched cry of pain, grief, or despair. **2** a sound resembling or suggestive of this. ● *v.intr.* **1** utter a wail or wails. **2** (of the wind, a siren, etc.) produce a sound like that of a person wailing. **3** complain or lament persistently and bitterly. **4** (often foll. by *away*) (of esp. a rock or jazz musician) play with great intensity or emotion. □ **wailer** *n.*

Wailing Wall *n.* = WESTERN WALL.

wainscot /ˈweinskɒt/ ● *n.* panelling of oak or other wood lining, esp. covering the lower part of a wall of a room. ● *v.tr.* (**wainscotted, wainscotting**; also **wainscoted, wainscoting**) line (a wall or room etc.) with wainscot.

wainscotting *n.* (also **wainscoting**) **1 a** a wainscot. **b** wainscots collectively. **2** the material used for this.

waist *n.* **1 a** the part of the human body below the ribs and above the hips, usu. of smaller circumference than these. **b** the circumference of this part of the body. **2 a** the part of a garment encircling or covering the waist. **b** the horizontal seam joining the upper and lower parts of a dress, often encircling the waist but sometimes raised to below the bust or lowered to the hips. **3** the narrow middle part of a violin, hourglass, etc. **4** the constriction between the thorax and abdomen of a wasp or ant etc. □ **waisted** *adj.* (also in *comb.*).

waistband *n.* a band of material fitting around the waist and forming the upper part of a garment.

waistcoat *n.* a man's formal vest, usu. buttoned and worn over a shirt and under a jacket.

waist-deep ● *adj.* **1** (of water, snow, etc.) so deep as to reach the waist. **2** submerged to the waist. ● *adv.* immersed up to the waist.

waist-high ● *adj.* as tall or high as one's waist. ● *adv.* at or up to the level of one's waist.

waistline *n.* **1** a person's waist, usu. with reference to its circumference (*chocolate is bad for the waistline*). **2** = WAIST 2.

wait ● *v.* **1** *intr.* remain inactive for a specified period of time or until some expected event occurs (*wait for the signal*; *wait while I put on my shoes*). **2** *intr.* (usu. foll. by *for*) remain for a time without something promised or expected (*waited for the bus*; *the chance I've been waiting for*). **3** *intr.* (foll. by *for*) stop or slow down so that a person catches up (*wait for me!*). **4** *tr.* = AWAIT (*wait your turn*). **5** *intr.* be ready or available (*exotic islands waiting to be discovered*). **6** *intr.* **a** (of a matter, work, etc.) be neglected or unresolved for some time. **b** be delayed or postponed (*our trip will have to wait until I've finished my work*). **7** *tr.* defer (a meal etc.) until a person's arrival (*waited supper for me*). ● *n.* **1** a period of waiting (*had a long wait for the train*). **2** the action or process of watching out for an enemy or lurking in ambush (*lie in wait*). □ **can't wait** is very impatient (*I can't wait to see what she bought me*). **wait a minute** (or **second**) used when one has just noticed something or had a sudden idea or inspiration. **wait and see** await the progress of events before acting (also *attrib.*: *wait-and-see approach*). **wait for it!** *informal* **1** do not begin before the proper moment. **2** used to create an interval of suspense before saying something unexpected or amusing. **waiting to happen** likely to happen imminently (*a disaster waiting to happen*). **wait on 1 a** attend to the needs of. **b** take orders from and serve meals to. **c** serve (a customer in a store). **2** remain in expectation of; wait for. **3** pay a respectful visit to. **wait out** esp. *N Amer. informal* remain inactive during; wait for the end of (*wait out the rain*). **wait tables** (or **on tables**) work in a restaurant taking orders from patrons and serving their meals. **wait up 1** (often foll. by *for*) not go to bed until a person arrives or an event happens. **2** (in *imper.*) used to urge a person to stop or slow down so that one can catch up. **you wait!** used to imply a threat, warning, or promise.

waiter *n.* **1** a person, esp. a man, who works in a restaurant waiting tables. **2** a tray or salver. **3** a person who waits for a time, event, or opportunity.

waiting list *n.* a list of people waiting for something not immediately available.

waiting period *n.* a specified period of time that must pass before one may do something.

waiting room *n.* a room where one may wait for an appointment, train, etc.

wait-list esp. *N Amer.* ● *n.* a waiting list. ● *v.tr.* (usu. in *passive*) place the name of (a person) on a waiting list.

waitperson *n.* (*pl.* **-persons** or **-people**) a waiter or waitress.

waitress ● *n.* a woman who works in a restaurant waiting tables. ● *v.intr.* work as a waitress. □ **waitressing** *n.*

wait staff *n.* *N Amer.* the waitpersons of a restaurant collectively.

wait state *n.* (of an operating system, CPU, etc.) the

condition of being unable to process further instructions due to being occupied with some other task.

waive *v.tr.* **1** decline to take advantage of (a right, claim, opportunity, etc.). **2** refrain from insisting upon (a rule, requirement, etc.). **3** refrain from charging or imposing (a penalty, cost, fee, etc.). **4** *N Amer. Sport* **a** (of a team) give up the rights to (a player) for the purposes of a trade, demotion, or unconditional release. **b** (of a team) refrain from exercising the right to sign (a player) from another team in the same league.

waiver *n.* **1** the act or an instance of waiving a right, claim, etc. **2** a formal document recording this, e.g. one guaranteeing that a party will not be held responsible for damage or injury sustained in the course of an activity. **3** *N Amer. Sport* **a** a team's waiving of the right to sign a player from another team in the same league before he or she is demoted, traded, or unconditionally released. **b** (in *pl.*) the process in which teams waive the right to sign or claim such a player (*he was picked up on waivers*).

Wakashan /ˈwɒkəˌʃæn/ *n.* an Aboriginal language family of the west coast of N America, including Haisla, Heiltsuk, Kwa-kwa-la, and Nuu-chah-nulth.

wake¹ ● *v.* (*past* **woke** or **waked**; *past part.* **woken** or **waked**) **1** (often foll. by *up*) **a** *intr.* come out of the state of sleep or unconsciousness. **b** *tr.* rouse from sleep or unconsciousness. **2** *tr. & intr.* (often foll. by *up*) become or cause to become alert, attentive, or aware. **3** *tr.* (usu. foll. by *up*) disturb (a place) with noise (*he woke up the whole house with his music*). **4** *tr.* stir or evoke (an emotion, memory, etc.). **5** *intr. & tr.* rise or raise from the dead. ● *n.* **1** a watch or vigil held by relatives and friends beside the body of a dead person before burial. **2** a gathering of friends and relatives to celebrate and remember the life of a person who has died, usu. over food and drink. □ **waker** *n.*

wake² *n.* **1** the track left on the water's surface by a moving vessel. **2** turbulent air left behind a moving aircraft. **3** the trail left by anything that has passed (*the storm left a path of destruction in its wake*). □ **in the wake of 1** behind, following. **2** in the aftermath of; as a result or consequence of.

wakeboard *n.* a surfboard-like board used in wakeboarding.

wakeboarding *n.* a water sport in which participants ride on a short, wide board resembling a surfboard, towed by a motorboat.

wakeful *adj.* **1** unable to sleep. **2** (of a night etc.) passed with little or no sleep. **3** vigilant, alert. □ **wakefulness** *n.*

waken *v.tr. & intr.* make or become awake.

wake-up call *n.* esp. *N Amer.* **1** a telephone call made to wake a person up, esp. one requested from a hotel employee by a guest. **2 a** an act of drawing attention to a problem or concern. **b** a surprising and esp. distressing incident etc. symptomatic of and drawing attention to a larger problem or concern requiring immediate action.

wakey-wakey *interj.* used to wake a person up.

waking *adj.* being or occurring while one is awake (*in her waking hours*).

Waldorf salad /ˈwɒldɔːf/ *n.* a salad of diced apples, walnuts, and usu. celery, with mayonnaise.

Waldorf school *n.* a private school based on the ideas of the Austrian philosopher Rudolf Steiner (1861–1925), such as the belief that the human consciousness can and must be trained to rise above attention to material things.

walk ● *v.* **1** *intr.* **a** move along at a slow or moderate pace by lifting up and putting down each foot in turn. **b** progress with similar movements (*walked on his hands; walked on stilts*). **2** *intr.* **a** travel or go on foot (*she walks to work*). **b** exercise in this way (*he walks for two hours each day*). **3** *tr.* travel on foot over or through (*walking the halls*). **4** *tr.* **a** escort or accompany on foot (*he walked me home*). **b** lead (a dog or horse etc.) at a walking pace. **5** *tr.* move (a large heavy object) by rocking it on alternate edges in a manner suggestive of walking. **6** *intr.* (of a ghost) roam or appear. **7** *Baseball* **a** *intr.* (of a batter) reach first base by taking four balls from the pitcher. **b** *tr.* (of a pitcher) allow (a batter) to go to first base by throwing four balls. **c** *tr.* (foll. by *in* or *home*) force in (a run) by issuing a walk to a batter with the bases loaded. **8** *intr. Basketball* take two or more steps with the ball without dribbling. **9** *intr. N Amer. slang* **a** be released from suspicion or from a charge. **b** = WALK OUT 2. ● *n.* **1** a short journey on foot for exercise or pleasure (*we went for a walk*). **2 a** the slowest gait or pace of a person or animal (*go at a walk*). **b** the particular manner of walking of a person or animal (*I recognized her by her walk*). **3** a place intended or suitable for walking. **4** *N Amer.* a sidewalk or the paved path leading from this to a house or building (*shovelled the front walk*). **5** a distance to be walked usu. defined by a specified amount of time required to traverse it on foot (*it's quite a walk to the store*). **6** a sponsored event in which participants walk a certain distance for charity. **7** *Baseball* a free pass to first base awarded to a batter who has taken four balls from a pitcher. □ **in a walk** esp. *N Amer. Sport* easily; without effort (*they won the game in a walk*). **walk around** (or **about**) stroll. **walk all over** *informal* **1** defeat easily. **2** take advantage of. **walk away (from)** **1** refuse to confront or become involved with. **2** survive (an accident etc.) without serious injury. **3** easily outdistance (an opponent) in a race. **walk away with** *informal* = WALK OFF WITH. **walk in** (often foll. by *on*) enter or arrive, esp. unexpectedly or with surprising ease. **walk in the park** (often with *neg.*) *N Amer.* a feat or accomplishment achieved with ease. **walk into** *informal* encounter through unwariness (*walked into the trap*). **walk off 1** depart (esp. abruptly). **2** ease the effects of (a meal, injury, etc.) by walking (*walked off his anger*). **walk a person off his** (or **her**) **feet** (or **legs**) exhaust a person with walking. **walk off the job** go on strike. **walk off with** *informal* **1** steal. **2** win easily. **walk out 1** depart suddenly in anger or protest. **2** go on strike. **walk out 1** desert, abandon. **walk over 1** *informal* = WALK ALL OVER. **2** traverse (a racecourse) at a walking pace to win a race with little or no opposition. **walk the streets 1** be a prostitute. **2** traverse the streets esp. in search of work etc. **walk tall** *informal* feel justifiable pride. **walk through 1** rehearse (a scene in a play or movie etc.). **2** guide (a person) carefully through each stage of a procedure. **walk the walk** carry through on promises made (*compare* TALK THE TALK, *see* TALK).

walkable *adj.* (of a distance or area) capable of being walked; not too large to be walked.

walkathon *n.* = WALK 6.

walker *n.* **1** a person who walks, esp. for exercise or recreation. **2** a wheeled framework with a sling or seat that supports a baby within reaching distance of the ground so that he or she can learn to walk. **3** a usu. tubular metal frame used by disabled or old people to help them walk.

walkie-talkie *n.* a small portable radio transmitter and receiver that provides two-way communication.

walk-in ● *attrib.adj.* **1** (of a storage area) large enough to walk into (*walk-in closet*). **2** designating a commercial establishment or medical facility etc. that serves customers and patients without appointments (*a walk-in clinic*). **3** designating the clientele of such an establishment or facility (*walk-in customers*). ● *n.* **1** a business or medical facility that serves customers without appointments. **2** a client of such an establishment or facility.

walking ● *n.* the activity or an instance of taking a walk, esp. for recreation or exercise. ● *adj.* **1** that can, does, or appears to walk. **2** used or worn for walking (*walking stick; walking boots*). **3** done on foot (*a walking tour of the city*). **4** a person regarded as embodying the qualities of a specified thing (*he's a walking disaster; she's a walking encyclopedia*).

walking wounded *n.pl.* **1** war casualties capable of walking despite their injuries. **2** *informal* a body of people suffering from illnesses, injuries, or mental or emotional difficulties.

Walkman *n.* (*pl.* **-mans**) *proprietary* a type of personal stereo consisting of a radio or cassette or compact disc player and lightweight headphones.

walk of life *n.* a person's profession or social rank.

walk-on *n.* **1** a small role with no or little speaking in a dramatic production. **2** an actor who plays such a role. **3** *N Amer.* a player who tries out for a team despite not having been drafted or officially invited.

walkout ● *n.* **1** a sudden angry departure, esp. in protest. **2** a strike called by workers (*compare* LOCKOUT). **3** *N Amer.* a doorway or passageway providing access to the outside or another room. ● *attrib.adj.* designating a room or building etc. with access to the outside (*a walkout basement*).

walkover *n.* **1** a horse race in which the eventual winner is unchallenged, having merely to walk over the finish line in order to record the victory. **2** an easy victory or achievement.

walk-through ● *n.* **1** a rough rehearsal of a theatrical production or film. **2** an unchallenging role in a theatrical production or film. **3** a perfunctory or lacklustre performance. ● *attrib.adj.* designating a building etc. permitting access from either end (*a walk-through garden*).

walk-up *n. N Amer.* (also *attrib.*) **1** a building with no elevator, in which access to the upper floors is possible only by stairs. **2** an apartment or office etc. located in such a building.

walkway *n.* any passage or path designed for or used by pedestrians.

wall ● *n.* **1** a continuous and usu. vertical structure of little thickness in proportion to its length and height, enclosing, protecting, or dividing a space or supporting a roof. **2** a vertical rock face, such as one that lies exposed on the steep side of a mountain, or one excavated in a quarry or mine. **3** *Anat.* the outermost layer or enclosing membrane etc. of an organ or hollow structure etc. (*stomach wall*). **4** *Baseball* the barrier enclosing the playing field at its outermost limit, extending along the curved perimeter of the outfield from one foul line to the other. **5** a thing or group of things serving as an obstacle or barrier (*a wall of security guards*). **6** an immaterial thing resembling a wall in terms of its imposing nature or in its ability to isolate or protect (*a wall of secrecy*). ● *v.tr.* **1** (usu. foll. by *off*, *in*) surround, fortify, or enclose with or as if with a wall or walls. **2** (usu. foll. by *off*, *up*) block, seal, or close (a space etc.) with a wall. **3** (foll. by *up*) confine or enclose within a sealed space. □ **between you and me and the wall** *informal* in strict confidence. **go to the wall** (usu. foll. by *for*) esp.

N Amer. do everything in one's power to help another, often putting oneself at risk in the process. **hit the wall 1** (of a long-distance or marathon runner) reach the point of onset of extreme fatigue at which the body's stores of energy are virtually exhausted. **2** reach a point at which one can proceed no further. **off the wall** *N Amer. informal* unorthodox, unconventional (also *attrib.*: *off-the-wall notions*). **up the wall** *informal* crazy or furious (*this song drives me up the wall*). **walls have ears** one should be cautious about what one says lest it be overheard. □ **walled** *adj.* (also in *comb.*). **walling** *n.*

wallaby /ˈwɒləbɪ/ *n.* (*pl.* **-ies**) any of various marsupials of the family Macropodidae, smaller than kangaroos, and having large hind feet and long tails.

wallboard *n.* = DRYWALL.

wallcovering *n.* any of various materials used to cover and decorate interior walls, such as a tapestry or wallpaper.

wallet *n.* **1** a flat pocket-sized folding case, usu. of leather, for keeping money, credit, identification, etc. on one's person. **2** a person's financial resources.

walleye *n.* **1** a large N American freshwater fish, *Stizostedion vitreum*, which has large prominent eyes and is valued as a food and sport fish. **2 a** an eye with a streaked, white, or parti-coloured iris. **b** an eye with an opaque cornea. **3** an eye squinting outwards.

walleyed *adj.* **1** having one or both eyes with a streaked or whitish iris or opaque cornea. **2** having a divergent squint. **3** having wide and glaring eyes, as if from anger or excitement.

wallflower *n.* **1 a** a fragrant spring garden plant, *Cheiranthus cheiri*, with esp. brown, yellow, or dark red clustered flowers. **b** any of various flowering plants of the genus *Cheiranthus* or *Erysimum*, growing wild on old walls or stony ground. **2** *informal* a shy or socially awkward person. **3** a person sitting out at a dance for lack of partners.

wall hanging *n.* a usu. large decorative tapestry etc. hung for display on an interior wall.

wall-mounted *adj.* (often *attrib.*) that is or may be attached by a bracket or other support to a wall.

Walloon /wɒˈluːn/ ● *n.* **1** a member of a French-speaking people inhabiting S and E Belgium and neighbouring parts of France (*compare* FLEMING²). **2** the French dialect spoken by this people. ● *adj.* of or concerning the Walloons or their language.

wallop *informal* ● *v.tr.* (**walloped, walloping**) **1 a** pound or strike wth great force. **b** spank; beat. **2** esp. *Sport* defeat decisively. ● *n.* **1** a heavy or resounding blow. **2 a** the ability to deliver such a blow. **b** the capacity to create a powerful impact or impression (*this film packs quite an emotional wallop*).

walloping ● *n.* **1** a sound thrashing. **2** a decisive victory. ● *adj.* **1** huge (*a walloping profit*). **2** powerful.

wallow ● *v.intr.* **1** (esp. of an animal) lie or roll around in mud, water, etc. **2** indulge in unrestrained self-pity, misery, sensuality, pleasure, etc. (*wallows in nostalgia*). ● *n.* **1** the act or an instance of wallowing. **2** a place used by buffalo, rhinoceros, etc., for wallowing. **3** a depression in the ground caused by this.

wallpaper ● *n.* **1** decorative paper printed or embossed with designs, usu. sold in a roll and cut into strips to be pasted on interior walls as decoration. **2** *Computing* an optional background pattern or picture displayed onscreen. **3** usu. *derogatory* a plain or common thing or collection of these regarded as constituting an unobtrusive atmosphere or backdrop etc. ● *v.tr.* decorate with wallpaper.

Wall Street *n.* the American money market or financial interests. □ **Wall Streeter** *n.*

wall-to-wall *attrib.adj.* **1** (of carpeting) covering the entire floor area; extending from one wall to another. **2** filling a space entirely (*wall-to-wall restaurants*). **3** exclusive of all else (*wall-to-wall sports coverage*).

walnut *n.* **1** any tree of the genus *Juglans*, having aromatic leaves and drooping catkins, e.g. the N American black walnut, *J. nigra*. **2** the nut of these trees, esp. the English walnut, consisting of an edible kernel in a ridged shell covered with a thick green husk. **3** the wood of the walnut tree.

walrus *n.* (*pl.* same or **walruses**) a large amphibious long-tusked Arctic mammal, *Odobenus rosmarus*, related to the seal and sea lion.

waltz ● *n.* **1** a dance in triple time performed by couples who rotate and progress around the floor. **2** the usu. flowing and melodious music for this. ● *v.* **1** *intr.* dance a waltz. **2** *intr.* (often foll. by *in, out, around*, etc.) *informal* move lightly, casually, with deceptive ease, etc. (*waltzed in and took first prize*). **3** *tr.* **a** move (a person) in a waltz. **b** cause a person to move rapidly or easily (*was waltzed off to Paris*).

wampum /'wɒmpəm/ *n. hist.* small, cylindrical, blue and white beads cut from a quahog shell and woven into strings or belts by Aboriginal peoples of eastern N America to be used as a medium of exchange or to record treaties.

WAN /wæn/ *n.* WIDE-AREA NETWORK.

wan /wɒn/ *adj.* **1** (of a person's complexion or appearance) pale, sickly; exhausted. **2** (of a star etc. or its light) partly obscured; faint. □ **wanly** *adv.*

wand *n.* **1 a** a supposedly magic stick used in casting spells by a fairy, magician, etc. **b** a stick used by a conjuror for effect. **2** a slender rod carried or used as a marker in the ground. **3** a small applicator for mascara etc., usu. with a brush at one end. **4** a handheld electronic device which can be passed over a bar code to read the data this represents.

wander ● *v.* **1** *intr.* (often foll. by *in, off*, etc.) go about from place to place aimlessly. **2** *intr.* **a** (of a person, river, road, etc.) wind about; meander. **b** (of esp. a person) get lost; leave home; stray from a path etc. **3** *intr.* **a** talk or think incoherently; be inattentive or delirious. **b** (of a talk, words, thoughts, etc.) be incoherent; lack focus. **4** *tr.* cover while wandering (*wanders the world*). ● *n.* the act or an instance of wandering (*went for a wander around the garden*). □ **wanderer** *n.* **wandering** *n.* (esp. in *pl.*).

wandering Jew *n.* any of various creeping or trailing plants, esp. any of several variegated varieties of the genus *Tradescantia* grown as houseplants.

wanderlust *n.* a desire to travel or wander.

wane ● *v.intr.* **1** (of the moon) decrease in apparent size after the full moon (*compare* WAX² 1). **2** decrease in power, vigour, importance, brilliance, size, etc.; decline. ● *n.* the process of waning. □ **on the wane** waning; declining.

wangle *informal* ● *v.tr.* **1** (often *refl.*) obtain (a favour etc.) by scheming etc. (*wangled himself a free trip*). **2** alter or fake (a report etc.) to appear more favourable. ● *n.* the act or an instance of wangling.

wank *v.intr.* & *tr.* *coarse slang* (often foll. by *off*) masturbate. ¶Usually considered a taboo word.

wanker *n. coarse slang* **1** a contemptible or ineffectual person. **2** a person who masturbates. ¶Usually considered a taboo word.

wanna *contraction informal* want to (*I wanna win*).

wannabe *n. slang* often *derogatory* a person who tries

to emulate a particular celebrity, follow the lifestyle of a particular group, etc. (also *attrib.*: *all those wannabe guitar heroes*).

want ● *v.* **1** *tr.* **a** desire; wish for possession of; need (*wants a bike; wanted to leave*). **b** need or desire (a person, esp. sexually). **c** require to be attended to in esp. a specified way (*the garden wants weeding*). **d** *informal* ought; should; need (*you want to pull yourself together*). **2** *intr.* (usu. foll. by *for*) lack; be deficient (*wants for nothing*). **3** *intr.* (foll. by *in, out*) *N Amer. informal* desire to be in, out, etc. (*wants in on the deal*). ● *n.* **1** (often foll. by *of*) **a** a lack, absence, or deficiency (*could not go for want of time*). **b** poverty; need (*living in great want*). **2 a** a desire for a thing etc. (*meets a long-felt want*). **b** a thing so desired (*can supply your wants*).

want ad *n. N Amer.* a classified advertisement, esp. seeking employees.

wanted *adj.* (of a suspected criminal etc.) sought by the police.

wanting *adj.* **1** lacking (in quality or quantity). **2** absent, not supplied or provided. □ **be found wanting** fail to meet requirements.

wanton /'wɒntən/ *adj.* **1** random; motiveless (*wanton destruction*). **2** sexually promiscuous. **3** luxuriant; unrestrained (*wanton profusion*). □ **wantonly** *adv.* **wantonness** *n.*

wapiti /'wɒpɪti/ *n.* (*pl.* **wapitis**) a N American deer, *Cervus canadensis*.

war ● *n.* **1 a** armed hostilities between esp. nations. **b** a specific conflict or the period of time during which such conflict exists (*was before the war*). **2** the operations by which armed hostilities are carried out; warfare as a profession or art. **3 a** hostility or contention between people, groups, etc. (*war of words*). **b** (often foll. by *on*) a sustained campaign against crime, disease, poverty, etc. **c** sustained rivalry or competition, e.g. between companies (*the cola war*). *See also* PRICE WAR. ● *v.intr.* (**warred, warring**) make war. □ **at war** (often foll. by *with*) engaged in a war. **go to war 1** declare or begin a war. **2** (of a soldier etc.) see active service.

warbird *n. informal* a fighter aircraft.

warble *v.* **1** *intr.* & *tr.* sing in a gentle trilling birdlike manner. **2** *tr.* **a** speak or utter in a warbling manner. **b** express in a song or verse (*warbled his love*).

warbler *n.* **1** a person, bird, etc. that warbles. **2** any small insect-eating bird of the family Sylviidae or, in N America, Parulidae, not always remarkable for their song.

war bonnet *n.* a headdress worn as traditional garb by some N American Indian peoples, esp. one with feathers attached to a headband and extending down the back, typical of some Plains peoples.

war chest *n.* a store of funds for a war or any other esp. political campaign.

war crime *n.* a crime violating the international laws of war. □ **war criminal** *n.*

war cry *n.* **1** a phrase or name shouted to rally one's troops. **2** a party slogan etc.

ward *n.* **1** a separate room or division of a hospital etc. **2** an esp. municipal administrative or electoral division. **3 a** a minor under the care of a guardian appointed by the parents or a court. **b** (in full **ward of the government**) a minor or mentally deficient person placed under the protection of a government or children's aid society. □ **ward off 1** parry (a blow). **2** avert, turn away (danger, poverty, etc.).

-ward *suffix* (also **-wards**) added to nouns of place or destination and to adverbs of direction and forming: **1** adverbs (usu. **-wards**) meaning 'towards the place etc.' **2** adjectives meaning 'turned or tending towards'.

war dance *n.* a dance performed before a battle, ceremonially, or to celebrate victory.

war dead *n.pl.* people killed in war.

warden *n.* **1** (usu. in *comb.*) a supervising official (*game warden*). **2** *Cdn* the head of a county council. **3 a** esp. *N Amer.* a prison governor. **b** the governor of an institution at a university or college (*warden of residences*). **4** = CHURCHWARDEN 1.

warder *n.* a guard.

ward-heeler *n.* *N Amer.* usu. *derogatory* a minor party worker in an election etc.

wardrobe *n.* **1** a large movable or built-in cupboard for storing clothes. **2** a person's entire stock of clothes. **3** the costume department or costumes of a performing arts company etc.

wardrobe mistress *n.* a woman in charge of a theatrical or film wardrobe.

wardroom *n.* **1** a room in a warship for the use of commissioned officers. **2** these officers collectively.

-wards *var.* of -WARD.

ware *n.* **1** (esp. in *comb.*) things of the same kind, esp. ceramics or cutlery (*silverware*; *hardware*). **2** (usu. in *pl.*) **a** articles for sale (*displayed his wares*). **b** a person's skills, talents, etc. **3** ceramics etc. of a specified material, factory, or kind.

warehouse ● *n.* **1** a building in which esp. retail goods are stored and from which they are distributed to retailers etc. **2** a wholesale or large retail store. ● *v.tr.* **1** deposit or store (goods) temporarily in a warehouse. **2** *N Amer. informal* shut up (esp. a person) in a prison or hospital etc. and forget about or ignore. □ **warehouseman** *n.* (*pl.* **-men**).

warfare *n.* **1** a state of war; the activity of fighting a war, esp. of a particular type (*chemical warfare*). **2** an aggressive or violent conflict or struggle.

warfarin /ˈwɔrfərɪn/ *n.* a water-soluble anticoagulant used esp. as a rat poison and treating thrombosis.

war game ● *n.* **1** a military exercise testing or improving tactical knowledge etc. **2** a battle etc. conducted with counters representing military units. ● *v.tr.* (**war-game**) examine or test (a strategy) by playing it through. □ **war-gaming** *n.*

warhead *n.* the explosive head of a missile, torpedo, or similar weapon.

warhorse *n.* **1** *hist.* a knight's or trooper's powerful horse. **2** *informal* a veteran of any activity, esp. a soldier, politician, etc.; a dependable or stalwart person or thing. **3** a frequently used or very familiar thing, esp. a work of art which is frequently performed.

warlike *adj.* **1** threatening war; hostile. **2** martial; soldierly. **3** of or for war; military.

warlock *n.* a sorcerer or wizard; a man who practises witchcraft.

warlord *n.* a military commander, esp. one with more or less independent control of an area or military group. □ **warlordism** *n.*

warm ● *adj.* **1** of or at a fairly or comfortably high temperature. **2** (of clothes etc.) providing warmth. **3 a** (of a person, action, feelings, etc.) sympathetic; friendly; loving (*a warm welcome*). **b** enthusiastic (*was warm in her praise*). **4** animated, excited (*a warm exchange of views*). **5** *informal* **a** (of a participant in esp. a children's game of seeking) close to the object etc. sought. **b** near to guessing or finding out a secret. **6** (of a colour, light, etc.) reddish, pink, or yellowish, etc., suggestive of warmth. **7** *Hunting* (of a scent) fresh and strong. ● *v.* **1** *tr.* **a** make warm. **b** excite; make cheerful (*warms the heart*). **2** *intr.* **a** (often foll. by *up*)

become warm. **b** (often foll. by *to*) become animated, enthusiastic, or sympathetic (*warmed to his subject*). ● *n.* **1** the act of warming; the state of being warmed. **2** the warmth of the atmosphere etc. □ **warm the bench** (or **pine**) *Sport* be made to sit inactively and not participate in a game etc. **warm up 1** (of an athlete, performer, etc.) prepare oneself by preliminary light exercise or practice. **2** become or cause to become warmer. **3** (often foll. by *to*) (of a person) become enthusiastic etc. (about). **4** (of an engine, electrical equipment, etc.) reach a temperature for efficient working. **5** reheat (food). □ **warmer** *n.* (also in *comb.*). **warming** *n.* **warmish** *adj.* **warmly** *adv.* **warmness** *n.*

warm-blooded *adj.* **1** having warm blood; mammalian. **2** ardent, passionate. □ **warm-bloodedness** *n.*

warmed-over *adj.* esp. *N Amer.* **1** (of food etc.) reheated or stale. **2** stale; second-hand.

war memorial *n.* a monument etc. commemorating those killed in a war.

warm front *n.* the leading edge of an advancing mass of warm air.

warm fuzzy *N Amer. informal* ● *n.* (*pl.* **-ies**) a feeling of emotional warmth or pleasant satisfaction as a visceral reaction to something (*donating to environmental causes always gave them the warm fuzzies*). ● *adj.* (also **warm and fuzzy**) pertaining to, evoking, or evoked by such a reaction (*a warm fuzzy feeling*).

warm-hearted *adj.* kind, friendly. □ **warm-heartedly** *adv.* **warm-heartedness** *n.*

warmonger /ˈwɔr,mɒŋgər, -mʌŋgər/ *n.* a person who seeks to bring about war. □ **warmongering** *n. & adj.*

warmth *n.* **1 a** the state of being warm. **b** moderate heat. **2** a friendly or loving attitude, personality, etc.

warm-up *n.* **1** a session of preparatory exercise or practice for a contest, performance, etc. **2** (*attrib.*) **a** designating clothing worn during an esp. athletic warm-up (*warm-up suit*). **b** designating an act that performs prior to the main attraction at a concert etc. (*warm-up band*). **3** (often in *pl.*) an esp. knitted or fleece garment worn over other clothing to provide warmth during warm-up exercises.

warn *v.* **1** *tr. & intr.* **a** inform of danger, unknown circumstances, etc. (*warned them of the danger*; *warned her that she was being watched*). **b** (often foll. by *against*) inform (a person etc.) about a specific danger, hostile person, etc. (*warned her against trusting him*). **2** *tr.* (usu. with *neg.*) admonish; tell forcefully (*has been warned not to go*). **3** *tr.* give (a person) cautionary notice regarding conduct etc. (*I've warned you many times*). □ **warn off** warn (a person) to keep away (from). □ **warner** *n.*

warning ● *n.* **1** in senses of WARN *v.* **2** anything that serves to warn; a hint or indication of difficulty, danger, etc. **3** an indication of any impending event (*without warning*). ● *attrib.adj.* serving to warn or indicate. □ **take warning** take heed; beware; recognize the danger. □ **warningly** *adv.*

warning track *n.* *Baseball* a strip of gravel etc. around a baseball field which warns fielders of the proximity of the wall, stands, etc., esp. that portion along the farthest perimeter of the outfield.

war of attrition *n.* a prolonged war in which military strategy is based on the calculation that the enemy's manpower and material resources will be exhausted before one's own as a result of numerous battles, usu. involving massive losses on both sides.

warp ● *v.tr. & intr.* **1** make or become bent or twisted out of shape, esp. by the action of heat, damp, etc. **2** make or become perverted, bitter, or strange (*too much TV* *warps the mind*). ● *n.* **1 a** a state of being warped, esp. of shrunken or expanded timber. **b** perversion, bitterness, etc. of the mind or character. **2** the threads stretched lengthwise in a loom to be crossed by the weft. **3** (in science fiction) an imaginary or hypothetical distortion in space in relation to time (*time warp*; *space warp*). **4** (*attrib.*) of or pertaining to warp speed (*warp drive*). □ **warpage** *n.* (esp. in sense 1a of *v.*).

war paint *n.* **1** paint used to adorn the body before battle, esp. *hist.* by some N American Aboriginal peoples. **2** *informal* elaborate makeup.

war party *n.* a band of warriors esp. seeking battle.

warpath *n.* **1** *hist.* the path or route taken on a warlike expedition by N American Indians. **2** *informal* any hostile course or attitude (*is on the warpath again*).

warped *adj.* **1** in senses of WARP *v.* **2** (of a person, mind, attitude, etc.) perverted, twisted; sick; bizarre.

warplane *n.* a military aircraft, esp. one equipped for fighting, bombing, etc.

warp speed *n.* **1** (in science fiction) travelling speed faster than that of light. **2** *informal* an extraordinarily high speed.

warrant ● *n.* **1 a** anything that authorizes a person or an action (*have no warrant for this*). **b** a person so authorizing (*I will be your warrant*). **2 a** a written authorization, money voucher, travel document, etc. (*travel warrant*). **b** a written authorization allowing police to search premises, arrest a suspect, etc. **c** a certificate entitling the holder to subscribe for shares of a company. ● *v.tr.* **1** justify; make necessary or appropriate in the circumstances (*nothing can warrant his behaviour*). **2** guarantee or attest to esp. the genuineness of an article, the worth of a person, etc. □ **warrantor** *n.*

warrant officer *n.* **1** (also **Warrant Officer**) (in the Canadian Army and Air Force) a non-commissioned officer of a rank below master warrant officer and above sergeant. Abbr.: **WO**. **2** an officer of a similar rank in other armies.

warranty *n.* (*pl.* **-ies**) **1** a manufacturer's written promise as to the extent to which defective goods will be repaired, replaced, etc. **2** an authority or justification. **3** an undertaking by an insured person of the truth of a statement or fulfillment of a condition.

warren *n.* **1 a** a network of interconnecting rabbit burrows. **b** a piece of ground occupied by this. **2** a densely populated or labyrinthine building etc.

warring *adj.* **1** fighting (*warring factions*). **2** conflicting (*warring principles*).

warrior *n.* **1** a person experienced or distinguished in fighting in an armed force, tribe, etc. **2** (*attrib.*) **a** of or relating to a warrior. **b** martial (*a warrior nation*).

Warsaw Convention *n.* an international agreement (1929) on compensation and liability in international air travel.

warship *n.* an armoured ship used in war.

war-surplus *attrib.adj.* designating items or *matériel* discarded by the military and made available to the public (*war-surplus binoculars*).

wart *n.* **1** a small benign growth on the skin, usu. hard and rounded, caused by a virus-induced abnormal growth of skin cells and thickening of the epidermis. **2** any protuberance, as on the skin of an animal, surface of a plant, etc. □ **warts and all** *informal* with no attempt to conceal blemishes or inadequacies. □ **warty** *adj.*

warthog *n.* an African wild pig of the genus *Phacochoerus*, with a large head and warty lumps on its face, and large curved tusks.

wartime *n.* the period during which a war is waged.

wartorn *adj.* racked or devastated by war.

war-weary *adj.* (esp. of a population) exhausted and dispirited by war. □ **war-weariness** *n.*

war whoop *n.* a war cry made on rushing into battle.

wary / 'weri/ *adj.* (**-ier**, **-iest**) **1** on one's guard. **2** (foll. by *of*) cautious, suspicious (*am wary of buying used cars*). **3** showing or done with caution or suspicion (*a wary expression*). □ **warily** *adv.* **wariness** *n.*

was *1st & 3rd sing. past of* BE.

wasabi / 'wɒsʌbi/ *n.* a plant, *Eutrema wasabi*, whose root (resembling horseradish) is used in Japanese cooking, usu. ground as an accompaniment to raw fish.

Wash. *abbr.* Washington.

wash ● *v.* **1** *tr.* cleanse with liquid, esp. water and usu. soap or detergent. **2** *tr.* (foll. by *out*, *off*, *away*, etc.) remove (a stain or dirt) in this way. **3** *intr.* wash oneself or esp. one's hands and face. **4** *intr.* wash clothes etc. **5** *intr.* (of fabric or dye) bear washing without damage. **6** *intr.* (foll. by *off*, *out*) (of a stain etc.) be removed by washing. **7** *tr.* (of a river, sea, etc.) touch (a country, coast, etc.) with its waters. **8 a** *tr.* (of moving liquid) carry along in a specified direction (*a wave washed him overboard*). **b** *intr.* be carried in this way (*shells wash up on the beaches*). **9** *tr.* scoop out (*the water had washed a channel*). **10** *intr.* (foll. by *over*, *along*, etc.) sweep, move, or splash. **11** *tr.* sift (ore) by the action of water. **12** *tr.* brush a thin coat of watery paint or ink over (paper in watercolour painting etc., or a wall). ● *n.* **1** the act or an instance of washing; the process of being washed. **2** a quantity of clothes for washing or just washed (*your pants are in the wash*). **3** the visible or audible motion of agitated water or air, esp. due to the passage of a ship etc. or aircraft. **4** a liquid to spread over a surface to cleanse, heal, or colour. **5** an expanse of colour appearing to have been washed on (*a wash of cool orange twilight*). **6** a situation or result which is of no net benefit to either of two opposing sides, values, etc. □ **come out in the wash** *informal* be clarified, or (of difficulties) be resolved or removed, in the course of time. **wash down 1** wash completely (esp. a large surface or object). **2** (usu. foll. by *with*) accompany or follow (food) with a drink. **wash one's hands of** renounce responsibility for. **wash out 1** clean the inside of (a thing) by washing. **2** clean (a garment etc.) by brief washing. **3 a** rain out (an event etc.). **b** *informal* cancel. **4** (of a flood, downpour, etc.) make a breach in (a road etc.). **5** fail, drop out (*washed out of med school*). **6** = sense 2 of *v.* **wash up 1** wash (dishes, cutlery, etc.) after use. **2** *N Amer.* wash one's face and hands. **won't wash** *informal* (of an argument etc.) will not be believed or accepted.

washable *adj.* that can be washed, esp. without damage. □ **washability** *n.*

wash-and-wear *adj.* **1** (of a fabric) easily washed, drying readily, and not needing ironing. **2** (of a haircut) requiring little or no styling after washing.

wash basin *n.* a basin for washing the hands, face, etc.

washboard *n.* **1 a** a board of ribbed wood or a sheet of corrugated zinc on which clothes are scrubbed in washing. **b** this used as a percussion instrument, played with the fingers. **2** *N Amer.* a dirt or gravel road whose surface has become corrugated by weather and use (also *attrib.*: *washboard road*). **3** (*attrib.*) designating any corrugated surface (*a washboard stomach*).

washcloth *n.* *N Amer.* = FACE CLOTH.

washed out *adj.* (hyphenated when *attrib.*) **1** faded by washing. **2** pale. **3** *informal* limp, enfeebled.

washed up adj. esp. N Amer. slang having failed.

washer n. **1 a** a person or thing that washes. **b** a washing machine. **2** a flat ring of rubber, metal, etc., to tighten or prevent leakage at a joint. **3** a similar ring placed under a nut or the head of a screw, etc., to disperse its pressure. □ **washerless** adj.

washerman n. (pl. **-men**) a person whose occupation is washing clothes, linen, etc.

washerwoman n. (pl. **-women**) a woman whose occupation is washing clothes, linen, etc.

washing n. **1** a quantity of clothes for washing or just washed. **2** the act of washing clothes.

washing machine n. a machine for washing clothes and linen etc.

Washingtonian /ˌwɒʃɪŋ'toːniən/ ● adj. **1** of or relating to the US state of Washington. **2** of or relating to Washington, DC. ● n. a native or inhabitant of the state of Washington or of Washington, DC.

washout n. **1** a narrow river channel that cuts into pre-existing sediments. **2** a breach in a road etc., caused by flooding. **3** informal **a** a fiasco; a complete failure. **b** a person who has failed or dropped out.

washroom n. **1** esp. Cdn a room with toilet facilities. **2** a room with facilities for washing oneself. □ **go to the washroom** esp. Cdn euphemism defecate or urinate.

washstand n. a piece of furniture to hold a basin, jug of water, soap, etc. for washing oneself with.

washtub n. a tub or vessel for washing clothes etc.

washy adj. (**-ier, -iest**) **1** (of liquid food) too watery or weak; insipid. **2** (of colour) faded-looking, thin, faint. **3** (of a style, sentiment, etc.) lacking vigour or intensity. □ **washily** adv. **washiness** n.

wasn't contraction was not.

WASP N Amer. usu. derogatory ● n. **1** a white Protestant of Anglo-Saxon descent. **2** a middle-class North American white Protestant. ● adj. of, pertaining to, being, or typical of a WASP or WASPs. □ **WASPish** adj. **WASPy** adj.

wasp n. a stinging often flesh-eating insect, esp. of the genus Vespula, with black and yellow stripes and a very thin waist. □ **wasplike** adj.

waspish adj. irritable, petulant; sharp in retort. □ **waspishly** adv. **waspishness** n.

wasp waist n. a very thin waist. □ **wasp-waisted** adj.

wassail /'wɒseɪl, 'wɒsəl/ archaic ● n. **1** a festive occasion, esp. during the Christmas season. **2** a usu. alcoholic drink consumed on such an occasion, e.g. mulled wine. ● v.intr. **1** make merry; celebrate with drinking etc. **2** go from house to house at Christmas-time singing carols and songs.

wast /wɒst, wəst/ archaic or dialect 2nd sing. past of BE.

wastage n. **1** an amount wasted. **2** loss or destruction of something, esp. something valuable that has not been used or kept carefully.

waste ● v. **1** tr. use to no purpose or for inadequate result or extravagantly (waste time). **2** tr. fail to use (esp. an opportunity). **3** tr. (often foll. by on) **a** give (advice etc.), utter (words etc.), without effect. **b** (often in passive) fail to be appreciated or used properly (I feel wasted in this job). **4** tr. & intr. (often foll. by away) wear gradually away; make or become weak; wither. **5** tr. treat as wasted or valueless. **6** intr. be expended without useful effect. **7** tr. esp. N Amer. slang **a** beat up. **b** kill, murder. ● adj. **1** superfluous; no longer serving a purpose. **2** (of a district etc.) not inhabited or cultivated (waste ground). ● n. **1** the act of an instance of wasting; extravagant or ineffectual use of an asset, of time, etc. **2 a** waste material or

food; refuse; useless remains or by-products. **b** excrement. **3** a waste region; a desert etc. **4** the state of being used up; diminution by wear and tear. □ **go to waste** be wasted. **lay waste** ravage, devastate. **waste not, want not** extravagance leads to poverty. □ **waster** n.

wastebasket n. a receptacle for waste paper.

wasted adj. **1** in sense of WASTE v. **2** esp. N Amer. slang **a** very tired. **b** intoxicated by alcohol or drugs.

waste disposal n. the disposing of waste products, garbage, etc., esp. as a public or corporate process.

wasteful adj. **1** extravagant. **2** causing or showing waste. □ **wastefully** adv. **wastefulness** n.

wasteland n. **1** an unproductive, useless, or devastated area of land. **2** a place or time considered spiritually or intellectually barren.

waste management n. the collection, disposal, treatment, or recycling of waste.

waste paper n. spoiled or valueless paper.

wastepaper basket n. = WASTEBASKET.

waste product n. (esp. in pl.) a useless by-product of manufacture or of an organism or organisms.

waste stream n. the mass of waste generated e.g. by a city for disposal etc.

waste water n. **1** water that has served an esp. industrial purpose, allowed to run away. **2** sewage.

wastrel /'weɪstrəl/ n. a wasteful or good-for-nothing person.

watch ● v. **1** tr. keep the eyes fixed on; look at. **2** tr. **a** keep under observation; follow observantly. **b** monitor or consider carefully; pay attention to (have to watch my weight). **c** be careful to prevent damage or harm to (watch your head). **3** intr. (often foll. by for) be in an alert state; be vigilant; take heed (watch for an opportunity). **4** intr. (foll. by over) look after; take care of. ● n. **1** a small timepiece worn on one's person. **2** a state of alert or constant observation or attention. **3** Naut. **a** a usu. four-hour spell of duty. **b** each of the halves into which a ship's crew is divided to take alternate watches. **4** hist. a watchman or group of watchmen, esp. patrolling the streets at night. **5** a former division of the night (the watches of the night). □ **on the watch** waiting for an expected or feared occurrence. **on watch** on lookout duty. **watch one's back** be alert to danger. **watch it** (or **oneself**) informal be careful. **watch out 1** (often foll. by for) be on one's guard. **2** as a warning of immediate danger. **watch one's step** proceed cautiously. □ **watchable** adj.

watchdog n. **1** a dog kept to guard property etc. **2** a person or body monitoring others' rights, behaviour, etc.

watcher n. a person who watches or observes or follows something closely (often in comb.: birdwatcher).

watchful adj. watching or observing closely; alert; on the watch. □ **watchfully** adv. **watchfulness** n.

watchkeeping n. keeping a lookout, esp. as a member of a ship's watch. □ **watchkeeper** n.

watchmaker n. a person who makes and repairs watches and clocks. □ **watchmaking** n.

watchman n. (pl. **-men**) a man employed to look after an empty building etc. at night.

watchtower n. a tower from which observation can be kept.

watchword n. a phrase summarizing a guiding principle; a slogan.

water ● n. **1** a colourless transparent odourless tasteless liquid compound of oxygen and hydrogen (see also HEAVY WATER). **2** a liquid consisting chiefly of this and found in seas, lakes, and rivers, in rain, and in secretions of organisms. **3** an expanse of water; a sea, lake, river, etc. **4** (in *pl.*) part of a sea or river (*in Canadian waters*). **5** (often as **the waters**) mineral water at a spa etc. **6** the state of a tide (*high water*). **7** a solution of a specified substance in water (*lavender water*). **8** (*attrib.*) **a** found in or near water. **b** of, for, or worked by water. **c** involving, using, or yielding water. **9 a** urine. **b** (usu. in *pl.*) the amniotic fluid discharged from the womb before childbirth. ● *v.* **1** *tr.* sprinkle or soak with water. **2** *tr.* give water to (an animal) to drink. **3** *intr.* (of the mouth or eyes) secrete saliva or tears. **4** *tr.* (usu. as **watered** *adj.*) (of silk etc.) having irregular wavy glossy markings. **5** *tr.* (usu. foll. by *down*) dilute. **6** *tr.* (of a river etc.) supply (a place) with water. **7** *intr.* (of an animal) go to a pool etc. to drink. □ **by water** using a ship etc. for travel or transport. **in deep water** (or **waters**) in serious trouble or difficulty. **like water** lavishly, profusely. **make one's mouth water** cause one's saliva to flow, stimulate one's appetite or anticipation. **make water 1** urinate. **2** (of a ship) take in water. **of the first water 1** (of a diamond) of the greatest brilliance and transparency. **2** of the finest quality or extreme degree. **on the water** on a ship etc. **water down 1** dilute with water. **2** (often as **watered down** *adj.*) make less vivid, forceful, or horrifying. **water under the bridge** past events accepted as past and irrevocable. □ **waterless** *adj.*

water arum *n.* a plant of the arum family, *Calla palustris*, found across Canada, with a white spathe and yellow spadix and fruit in a cluster of red berries.

water-based *adj.* (usu. *attrib.*) (of a solution, substance, etc.) having water as the main ingredient.

waterbed *n.* a bed with a mattress of rubber or plastic etc. filled with water.

water bird *n.* a bird frequenting esp. fresh water.

water bomber *n. Cdn* an aircraft used to drop water on forest fires, esp. one which takes on water by skimming the surface of a lake etc. □ **water bombing** *n.*

water-borne *adj.* **1** (of goods etc.) conveyed by or travelling on water. **2** (of a disease) communicated or propagated by contaminated water.

water boy *n. N Amer.* **1** a boy whose job it is to fetch water for or hand water to labourers, athletes, etc. **2** *informal* a person in a subservient position or role.

water buffalo *n.* a large Asiatic buffalo, *Bubalus arnee*, with large curved horns, which occurs widely as a domesticated beast of burden.

water chestnut *n.* **1** an aquatic plant, *Trapa natans*, bearing an edible seed. **2 a** a sedge, *Eleocharis tuberosa*, with rushlike leaves arising from a corm. **b** this corm used as food.

watercolour *n.* (also **watercolor**) **1** artists' paint made of pigment to be diluted with water and not oil. **2** a picture painted with this. **3** the art of painting with watercolours. □ **watercolourist** *n.*

water-cooled *adj.* cooled by circulating water.

water cooler *n.* a vessel in which water is cooled and kept cool, esp. a tank of cooled drinking water in a workplace as a setting for informal conversation or gossip (also, with hyphen, *attrib.*: *water-cooler rumours*).

watercourse *n.* **1** a brook, stream, or artificial water channel. **2** the bed along which this flows.

watercraft *n.* (*pl.* same) *N Amer.* any boat.

watercress *n.* a hardy perennial cress, *Nasturtium officinale*, growing in running water, with pungent leaves used in salad etc.

water cycle *n.* the circulation of water from the atmosphere, where water vapour condenses and falls as precipitation, to the earth where it collects as liquid or ice, and back to the atmosphere through evaporation or transpiration.

waterer *n.* a container for drinking water for animals.

waterfall *n.* a stream, river, or artificial watercourse flowing over a precipice or down a steep hillside.

waterfowl *n.* birds frequenting water, esp. swimming game birds.

waterfowling *n. N Amer.* the hunting of waterfowl for sport or food. □ **waterfowler** *n.*

waterfront *n.* esp. urban land adjoining a river, lake, harbour, etc. (also *attrib.*: *waterfront condos*).

water garden *n.* a garden with pools or a stream, for growing aquatic plants.

water hazard *n. see* HAZARD 4.

water heater *n.* a device for heating (esp. domestic) water.

water hole *n.* a shallow depression in which water collects; a pond, a pool.

water ice *n.* a confection of flavoured and frozen water and sugar etc.; a sorbet, slush, etc.

watering *n.* the act or an instance of supplying water or (of an animal) obtaining water.

watering can *n.* a portable container with a long spout usu. ending in a perforated sprinkler, for watering plants.

watering hole *n.* **1** a pool of water from which animals regularly drink; a water hole. **2** *slang* a bar.

water level *n.* **1 a** the surface of the water in a lake etc. **b** the height of this. **2** = WATER TABLE.

water lily *n.* an aquatic plant with broad flat floating leaves and large cup-shaped flowers.

waterline *n.* **1 a** the line along which the surface of water touches the side of something. **b** such a line marked on a ship for use in loading. **2** a pipe etc. used to convey water.

waterlogged *adj.* **1** saturated with water. **2** (of a boat etc.) hardly able to float from being saturated or filled with water. **3** (of ground) made useless by being saturated with water.

Waterloo /wɒtɜː'luː/ *n.* a decisive defeat; an irrevocable end (*meet his Waterloo*).

water main *n.* a water supply system's main pipe.

watermark ● *n.* a faint identifying design made in some paper during manufacture, when held against the light. ● *v.tr.* mark with this.

watermelon *n.* a large smooth green melon, *Citrullus lanatus*, with red pulp and watery juice.

water meter *n.* a device which measures and records the amount of water supplied to a house etc.

water mill *n.* a mill worked by a water wheel.

water moccasin *n. see* MOCCASIN 3.

water park *n.* a public recreation area with water slides, wave pools, swimming pools, etc.

Water Pik *n.* proprietary a device for cleaning the teeth by directing a jet of water at them.

water pipe *n.* **1** a pipe that conveys water. **2** = HOOKAH.

water pistol *n.* a toy pistol shooting a jet of water.

water polo *n.* a game played in a swimming pool, in which teams of seven swimmers attempt to throw an inflated ball into the other team's goal.

water power *n.* **1** mechanical force derived from the weight or motion of water. **2** a fall in the level of a river, as a source of this force.

waterproof ● *adj.* impervious to water. ● *v.tr.* make waterproof. □ **waterproofness** *n.*

water rat n. N Amer. = MUSKRAT.

water repellent adj. not easily penetrated by water (also, with hyphen, attrib.: water-repellent fabric).

water-resistant adj. (of a fabric, wristwatch, etc.) able to resist, but not entirely prevent, the penetration of water. □ **water resistance** n.

watershed n. **1** a line of separation between waters flowing to different rivers, basins, or seas. **2** a turning point in affairs. **3** the area drained by a single lake or river and its tributaries.

waterside n. the margin of a sea, lake, or river.

water ski ● n. each of a pair of long thin boards, or a single board, strapped to the feet to enable a person pulled by a motorboat to skim over the surface of the water. ● v.intr. (**water-ski**) (**-skis, -skied; -skiing**) be pulled along the water's surface while on a water ski or skis. □ **water skier** n. **waterskiing** n.

waterslide n. a usu. high or long slide down which water cascades, esp. into a swimming pool.

water snake n. any of various snakes frequenting fresh water, esp. harmless snakes of the genus Nerodia.

water softener n. an apparatus or substance for softening hard water.

water-soluble attrib.adj. soluble in water.

water sport n. (usu. in pl.) a sport practised on water, such as waterskiing, windsurfing, etc.

waterspout n. a gyrating column of water and spray formed by a whirlwind between sea and cloud.

water supply n. the provision and storage of water, or the amount of water stored, for a city, house, etc.

water table n. a level below which the ground is saturated with water.

water taxi n. a small boat for hire for transporting passengers, usu. over short distances.

watertight adj. **1** (of a joint, container, vessel, etc.) fastened or fitted or made so as to prevent the passage of water. **2** (of an argument etc.) unassailable.

water torture n. a form of torture in which the victim is exposed to the incessant dripping of water on the head, or the sound of dripping.

water tower n. a tower with an elevated tank to give pressure for distributing water.

waterway n. **1** a navigable channel. **2** a route for travel by water.

water wheel n. a wheel driven by water to work machinery, or to raise water.

waterworks n. **1** an establishment for managing a water supply. **2** informal the shedding of tears (turn on the waterworks). **3** informal the urinary system.

watery adj. **1** containing too much water. **2** too thin in consistency. **3** of, consisting of, or of the consistency of water. **4** (of the eyes) suffused or running with water. **5** (of conversation, style, etc.) vapid, uninteresting. **6** (of colour) pale. **7** (of the sun, moon, or sky) rainy-looking. □ **wateriness** n.

watt n. the SI unit of power, equivalent to one joule per second, corresponding to the rate of energy in an electric circuit where the potential difference is one volt and the current one ampere. Symbol: **W**.

wattage n. an amount of electrical power expressed in watts, esp. the operating power of an appliance etc.

watt-hour n. the energy used when one watt is applied for one hour.

wattle¹ /'wɒtəl/ n. **1** interlaced rods and split rods as a material for making fences, walls, etc. **2** (in sing. or pl.) rods and twigs for this use.

wattle² n. a loose fleshy appendage on the head or throat of a turkey or other birds. □ **wattled** adj.

wave ● v. **1** tr. & intr. move a hand etc. to and fro in greeting or as a signal. **2 a** intr. show a motion as of a flag, tree, or a field of wheat etc., in the wind. **b** tr. impart a waving motion to. **3** tr. brandish (a sword etc.) as an encouragement to followers etc. **4** tr. tell or direct (a person) by waving (waved them away). **5** tr. express (a greeting etc.) by waving (waved goodbye to them). **6** tr. give an undulating form to (hair, drawn lines, etc.); make wavy. **7** intr. (of hair etc.) have such a form; be wavy. ● n. **1** a moving ridge of water caused by the wind or tide. **2** a long body of water curling into an arched form and breaking on the shore. **3 a** a thing compared to this, e.g. a body of persons in one of successive advancing groups. **b** (usu. prec. by the) a wavelike effect produced by a crowd at a sporting event etc., whereby adjoining sections successively stand or raise hands momentarily. **4** a gesture of waving. **5 a** the process of waving the hair. **b** an undulating form produced in the hair by waving. **6 a** a temporary occurrence or increase of a condition, emotion, or influence (a wave of enthusiasm). **b** a specified period of widespread weather (heat wave). **7** Physics **a** a periodic disturbance of the particles of a substance which may be propagated without net movement of the particles, as in the passage of undulating motion, heat, sound, etc. **b** a single curve in the course of this motion. **8** Electricity a similar variation of an electromagnetic field in the propagation of light or other radiation through a medium or vacuum. □ **make waves** informal **1** cause trouble. **2** create a significant impression. **wave aside** dismiss as intrusive or irrelevant. **wave down** wave to (a vehicle or its driver) as a signal to stop. **wave off 1** signal an approaching person or thing to stop approaching. **2** (in hockey etc.) disallow (a goal). □ **waveless** adj. **wavelike** adj. & adv.

waveband n. a range of (esp. radio) wavelengths between certain limits.

wavelength n. **1** the distance between successive crests of a wave, esp. points in a sound wave or electromagnetic wave. **2** this as a distinctive feature of radio waves from a transmitter. **3** informal a particular mode or range of thinking and communicating (we don't seem to be on the same wavelength).

wavelet n. a small wave on water.

wave pool n. a large swimming pool with an apparatus for producing waves for recreation.

waver v.intr. **1** be or become unsteady; falter; begin to give way. **2** be undecided between different courses or opinions; be shaken in resolution or belief. **3** (of a light) flicker. □ **waverer** n. **waveringly** adv. **wavery** adj.

wavy adj. (**-ier, -iest**) (of a line or surface) having waves or alternate contrary curves (wavy hair). □ **wavily** adv. **waviness** n.

wa-wa var. of WAH-WAH.

wax¹ ● n. **1** a sticky mouldable yellowish substance secreted by bees as the material of honeycomb cells. **2** a white translucent material obtained from this and used for candles, as a basis of polishes, and for other purposes. **3** any similar substance, typically a lipid or hydrocarbon (earwax; paraffin wax). **4** a session of waxing to remove hair. ● v.tr. **1** cover, polish, or treat with wax. **2** remove unwanted hair by applying wax and peeling off the wax and hairs together. **3** informal defeat resoundingly. □ **the whole ball of wax** the full complement of related or necessary things. □ **waxer** n. **waxing** n.

wax² v.intr. **1** (of the moon) have an ever larger part of its visible surface illuminated, increasing in apparent size. **2** become larger or stronger. **3** pass into a specified state or mood (*wax lyrical*). □ **wax and wane** undergo alternate increases and decreases.

wax bean *n.* a yellow-podded bean.

waxbill *n.* any of various birds esp. of the family Estrildidae, with usu. red bills.

waxed paper *n.* (also **wax paper**) waterproof or greaseproof paper impregnated with wax.

waxen *adj.* having a smooth pale translucent surface as of wax.

waxwing *n.* any bird of the genus *Bombycilla*, with a crest and often with small tips like red sealing wax to some wing feathers.

waxwork *n.* **1 a** an object, esp. a lifelike dummy, modelled in wax. **b** the making of waxworks. **2** (in *pl.*) an exhibition of wax dummies.

waxy *adj.* (**-ier, -iest**) resembling wax in consistency or in its surface. □ **waxily** *adv.* **waxiness** *n.*

way ● *n.* **1** a road etc., for passing along. **2** a route for reaching a place, esp. the best one (*asked the way to Sherbrooke*). **3** a place of passage into a building etc. (*could not find the way out*). **4 a** a method or plan for achieving something (*that is not the way to do it*). **b** the ability to obtain one's object (*has a way with him*). **5 a** a person's desired or chosen course of action. **b** a custom or manner of behaving; a personal peculiarity (*that's just her way; things had a way of going badly*). **6** a specific manner of life or procedure (*soon got into the way of it*). **7** the normal course of events (*that is always the way*). **8** (also *N Amer. informal* **ways**) a travelling distance; a length traversed or to be traversed (*is a long way away; a good ways down the road*). **9 a** an unimpeded opportunity of advance. **b** a space free of obstacles. **10** a region or ground over which advance is desired or natural. **11** advance in some direction; impetus, progress (*pushed my way through*). **12** movement of a ship etc. (*gather way*). **13** the state of being engaged in movement from place to place; time spent in this (*on the way home*). **14** a specified direction (*step this way; one-way traffic*). **15** (in *pl.*) parts into which a thing is divided (*split it three ways*). **16** *informal* the scope or range of something (*want a few things in the stationery way*). **17** a specified condition or state (*things are in a bad way*). **18** a respect (*is useful in some ways*). ● *adv. informal* to a considerable extent; very much (*you're way off the mark*). □ **across the way** facing or opposite. **be on one's way 1** set off; depart. **2** be in the course of a journey etc. **by the way** incidentally; as a more or less irrelevant comment. **by way of 1** through; by means of. **2** as a substitute for or as a form of (*did it by way of apology*). **3** with the intention of (*asked by way of discovering the truth*). **come one's way** become available to one. **find a way** discover a means of obtaining one's object. **get** (or **have**) **one's way** (or **have it one's own way** etc.) get what one wants; ensure one's wishes are met. **give way 1 a** make concessions. **b** fail to resist; yield. **2** (often foll. by *to*) concede precedence (to). **3** (of a structure etc.) be dislodged or broken under a load; collapse. **4** (foll. by *to*) be superseded by. **5** (foll. by *to*) be overcome by (an emotion etc.). **go all the way 1** go the whole distance. **2** do something wholeheartedly or completely. **3** *informal* engage in sexual intercourse. **go out of one's way** (often foll. by *to* + infin.) make a special effort (*went out of their way to help*). **go one's own way** act independently, esp. against contrary advice. **go one's way 1** leave, depart. **2** (of events, circumstances, etc.) be favourable to one. **go a person's way** accompany a person (*are you going my way?*). **in its way** if regarded

from a particular standpoint appropriate to it. **in no way** not at all; by no means. **in a way** in a certain respect but not altogether or completely. **in the** (or **one's**) **way** forming an obstacle or hindrance. **lead the way 1** act as guide or leader. **2** show how to do something. **look the other way 1** ignore what one should notice. **2** disregard an acquaintance etc. whom one sees. **make way 1** (often foll. by *for*) allow room for others to proceed. **2** achieve progress. **make one's way** proceed. **one way or another** by some means. **on the** (or **one's**) **way 1** in the course of a journey etc. **2** having progressed (*is well on the way to completion*). **3** *informal* (of a child) conceived but not yet born. **on the way out** *informal* going down in status, estimation, or favour; going out of fashion. **the other way around** (or **about**) in an inverted or reversed position or direction. **out of the way 1** no longer an obstacle or hindrance. **2** disposed of; settled. **3** (of a person) imprisoned or killed. **4** (with *neg.*) common or unremarkable (*nothing out of the way*). **5** (of a place) remote, inaccessible. **out of one's way** not on one's intended route. **put a person in the way of** give a person the opportunity of. **way back** *informal* long ago.

waybill *n.* **1** a document on which a shipper, courier, etc. records details of the sender, recipient, weight, etc. of an item to be transported. **2** a list of passengers or parcels on a vehicle.

wayfarer *n.* a traveller, esp. on foot. □ **wayfaring** *n.*

waylay *v.tr.* (*past and past part.* **waylaid**) **1** lie in wait for. **2** stop to rob or talk to.

way of life *n.* the principles or habits governing all one's actions etc.

way of thinking *n.* one's usual opinion of matters.

way-out *adj. informal* **1** unusual, eccentric. **2** avant-garde, progressive. **3** excellent, exciting.

waypoint *n.* **1** a stopping place, esp. on a journey. **2** the computer-checked coordinates of each stage of a flight etc. (also *attrib.*: *waypoint identification*).

ways and means *n.pl.* **1** methods of achieving something. **2** methods of raising government revenue.

wayside *n.* **1** the side or margin of a road. **2** the land at the side of a road. □ **fall by the wayside 1** fail to continue in an endeavour etc. **2** be discarded.

way station *n.* **1** a minor station on a railway. **2** a point marking progress in a course of action etc.

wayward *adj.* **1** childishly self-willed or perverse; capricious. **2** erratic; unaccountable or freakish. □ **waywardly** *adv.* **waywardness** *n.*

Wb *abbr.* weber(s).

WCB *abbr. Cdn* Workers' Compensation Board.

WCC *abbr.* WORLD COUNCIL OF CHURCHES.

WCTU *abbr.* Woman's Christian Temperance Union.

we *pron.* (*obj.* **us**; *poss.* **our, ours**) **1** used by and with reference to more than one person speaking or writing, or one such person and one or more associated persons. **2** used for or by a royal person in a proclamation etc. and by a writer or editor in a formal context. **3** people in general (*compare* ONE *pron.* 2). **4** *informal* = I². **5** *informal* (often implying condescension) you (*how are we feeling today?*).

weak *adj.* **1** deficient in strength, power, or number; fragile; easily broken or bent or defeated. **2** deficient in vigour; sickly, feeble. **3 a** deficient in resolution; easily led (*a weak character*). **b** (of an action or features) indicating a lack of resolution (*a weak chin*). **4** unconvincing or logically deficient (*a weak argument*). **5** (of a mixed liquid or solution) watery (*weak tea*). **6** (of a syllable etc.) unstressed.

weaken *v.tr. & intr.* make or become weak or weaker.

weakfish *n.* (*pl.* same or **-fishes**) *N Amer.* a marine fish of the genus *Cynoscion*, used as food.

weak-kneed *n. informal* lacking resolution.

weakling *n.* a feeble person or animal.

weak link *n.* a weak or defective element which renders the whole vulnerable.

weakly ● *adv.* in a weak manner. ● *adj.* (**-ier, -iest**) sickly, not robust.

weakness *n.* **1** the state or condition of being weak. **2** a weak point; a defect. **3** the inability to resist a particular temptation. **4** a self-indulgent liking (*have a weakness for chocolate*).

weakside *n. Football* the side of an offensive line with the fewer number of players.

weak spot *n.* (also **weak point**) **1** a place where defences are assailable. **2** a flaw in an argument or character or in resistance to temptation.

weal[1] *n.* = WELT[2].

weal[2] *n. literary* welfare, prosperity; good fortune.

wealth *n.* **1** riches. **2** the state of being rich. **3** (foll. by *of*) an abundance or profusion (*a wealth of new material*).

wealthy *adj.* (**-ier, -iest**) having an abundance esp. of money. □ **wealthily** *adv.*

wean *v.tr.* **1** accustom (an infant or other young mammal) to food other than (esp. its mother's) milk. **2** disengage (from a habit etc.) esp. gradually. **3** (foll. by *on*) nourish with or expose to from an early age (*was weaned on talk shows and sitcoms*).

weanling *n.* a newly-weaned animal etc.

weapon *n.* **1** a thing designed or used or usable for inflicting bodily harm, e.g. a gun or knife. **2** a means used to gain an advantage (*irony is a double-edged weapon*; *weapons against disease*). □ **weaponless** *adj.*

weaponry *n.* weapons collectively.

weapons-grade *adj.* designating fissile material of a suitable quality for making nuclear weapons.

wear ● *v.* (*past* **wore**; *past part.* **worn**) **1** *tr.* have on one's person as clothing or an ornament etc. **2** *tr.* be dressed habitually in (*I don't wear black*). **3** *tr.* exhibit or present (a facial expression or appearance) (*wore a frown*). **4** (often foll. by *away, down*) **a** *tr.* injure the surface of, or partly obliterate or alter, by rubbing, stress, or use. **b** *intr.* undergo such injury or change. **5** *tr. & intr.* (foll. by *off, away*) rub or be rubbed off. **6** *tr.* **a** make (a hole etc.) by constant rubbing or dripping etc. **b** make (a path etc.) by repeated travel along the same route. **7** *tr. & intr.* (often foll. by *out*) exhaust, tire or be tired. **8** *tr.* (foll. by *down*) overcome by persistence. **9** *intr.* **a** remain for a specified time in working order or a presentable state; last long. **b** (foll. by *well, badly*, etc.) endure continued use or life. **10 a** *intr.* (of time) pass, esp. tediously. **b** *tr.* (usu. foll. by *on*) pass (time) gradually away. ● *n.* **1** the act of wearing or the state of being worn (*suitable for informal wear*). **2** things worn; clothing suitable for a specified purpose or part of the body (esp. in *comb.*: *sportswear*; *footwear*). **3** (also **wear and tear**) damage sustained from continuous use. **4** the capacity for resisting wear and tear (*still a great deal of wear left in it*). □ **in wear** being regularly worn. **wear off** lose effectiveness or intensity. **wear out 1** use or be used until no longer usable. **2** tire or be tired out. **wear thin 1** (of patience, excuses, etc.) begin to fail. **2** tax one's patience or interest. **wear the pants** (or **trousers**) be the dominant partner in a marriage or relationship. **wear** (or **wear one's years**) **well** *informal* remain young-looking. □ **wearable** *adj. & n.* **wearability** *n.* **wearer** *n.*

wearing *adj.* **1** tiring; stressful; frustrating. **2** tedious. □ **wearingly** *adv.*

wearisome /ˈwɪːrɪsəm/ *adj.* tedious. □ **wearisomely** *adv.* **wearisomeness** *n.*

weary ● *adj.* (**-ier, -iest**) **1** tired. **2** (foll. by *of*) no longer interested in or enthusiastic about. **3** tiring or tedious. ● *v.tr. & intr.* (**-ies, -ied**) make or grow weary. □ **wearily** *adv.* **weariness** *n.* **wearyingly** *adv.*

weasel ● *n.* **1** any of various small carnivorous mammals including ermines, minks, and ferrets, and noted for their ferocity, esp. the long-tailed weasel of N America, *Mustela frenata*, having a brown and yellow coat, or the least weasel of N America and Eurasia, *M. nivalis*, with a very short tail and brown and white coat. **2** *informal* a deceitful, sneaky, or treacherous person. ● *v.intr.* (**weaseled, weaseling**) **1** esp. *N Amer.* equivocate or quibble. **2** (foll. by *out*) default on an obligation. □ **weasel one's way into** obtain by cunning, sneakiness, etc. (*weaseled his way into their affection*). □ **weasely** *adj.*

weather ● *n.* **1** the state of the atmosphere at a place and time as regards temperature, cloudiness, dryness, sunshine, wind, precipitation, etc. **2** a news report concerning the weather (*listened to the weather*). **3** bad weather; destructive rain, frost, wind, etc. (*had not been expecting weather*). ● *v.* **1** *tr.* expose to or affect by atmospheric changes, esp. deliberately to dry, season, etc. (*weathered timber*). **2 a** *tr.* (usu. in *passive*) discolour or partly disintegrate (rock or stones) by exposure to air. **b** *intr.* be discoloured or worn in this way. **3** *tr.* **a** come safely through (a storm). **b** survive (a difficult period etc.). □ **keep a** (or **one's**) **weather eye on** (or **open**) be watchful. **make heavy weather of** *informal* exaggerate the difficulty or burden presented by (a problem, course of action, etc.). **under the weather** *informal* **1** slightly unwell. **2** in low spirits.

weather-beaten *adj.* worn, damaged, or discoloured by exposure to wind, rain, etc.

weatherboard ● *n.* **1** (also **weatherboarding**) = CLAPBOARD. **2** a sloping board attached to the bottom of an outside door to keep out the rain etc. ● *v.tr.* fit or supply with weatherboards.

weather forecast *n.* an analysis of the state of the weather with an assessment of likely developments over a certain time. □ **weather forecaster** *n.* **weather forecasting** *n.*

weathering *n.* **1** the action of the weather on materials etc. exposed to it. **2** exposure to adverse weather conditions (see WEATHER *v.* 1).

weatherize *v.tr. N Amer.* make (a building) impervious to the weather by insulation, double glazing, etc. □ **weatherization** *n.*

weatherman *n.* (*pl.* **-men**) **1** a man who broadcasts a weather forecast. **2** a meteorologist.

weatherproof ● *adj.* resistant to the effects of bad weather, esp. rain. ● *v.tr.* make weatherproof. □ **weatherproofed** *adj.* **weatherproofing** *n.*

weather side *n.* the side from which the wind is blowing (*opp.* LEE SIDE; *see* LEE 2).

weather station *n.* an observation post for recording meteorological data.

weatherstrip ● *n.* a piece of material used to make a door or window proof against rain or wind. ● *v.tr.* (**-stripped, -stripping**) apply a weatherstrip to. □ **weatherstripping** *n.*

weathertight *adj.* (of a dwelling) proof against bad weather.

weather vane *n.* a revolving pointer mounted on a spire or other high place to show wind direction.

weather-worn *adj.* weather-beaten.

weave¹ ● *v.* (*past* **wove**; *past part.* **woven** or **wove**) **1** *tr.* **a** form (fabric) by interlacing long threads in two directions. **b** form (thread) into fabric in this way. **2** *intr.* **a** make fabric in this way. **b** work at a loom. **3** *tr.* make (a basket or wreath etc.) by interlacing rods or flowers etc. **4** *tr.* **a** contrive, devise, or construct (a poem, spell, narrative, etc.), esp. skilfully. **b** intermingle or blend in closely as if by weaving; work up (separate elements) into an intricate and connected whole. ● *n.* a style of weaving.

weave² *v.intr.* (*past* **weaved** or **wove**; *past part.* **weaved** or **woven**) move repeatedly from side to side; take an intricate course to avoid obstructions.

weaver *n.* **1** a person who weaves. **2** (in full **weaver bird**) any tropical bird of the family Ploceidae, building elaborately woven nests.

weaving *n.* **1** the action of creating woven materials. **2** something woven, esp. a decorative hanging.

web *n.* **1** a network of fine threads constructed by a spider to catch its prey, from fluid secreted from its spinnerets. **2 a** a complete network or connected series (*a web of social problems*). **b** (usu. **Web**) = WORLD WIDE WEB. **c** a snare or trap (*a web of deceit*). **3** a membrane between the toes of a swimming animal or bird. □ **webby** *adj.*

webbed *adj.* **1 a** (of a bird's foot etc.) having the digits connected by a membrane or fold of skin. **b** (of fingers or toes) united by a fold of skin. **2** covered with or as if with a web.

webbing *n.* a web or woven fabric, esp. strong narrow closely-woven fabric used for supporting upholstery, for belts, etc.

Web browser *n.* a program used to locate and access hypertext documents on the World Wide Web.

weber /ˈveɪbər/ *n.* the SI unit of magnetic flux, causing the electromotive force of one volt in a circuit of one turn when generated or removed in one second.

web-footed *adj.* having the toes connected by webs.

web offset *n.* offset printing on a web of paper.

Web page *n.* a hypertext document that is accessible via the World Wide Web.

Web server *n.* **1** a program providing access to World Wide Web documents, which accepts requests from Web browsers, and delivers the required hypertext documents. **2** the computer or system on which such a program runs, and on which the documents are stored.

Web site *n.* **1** a hypertext document or a set of linked documents, usually associated with a particular person, organization, or topic, that is held on a computer system and can be accessed via the World Wide Web. **2** the computer system that holds such a hypertext document or documents.

Wed. *abbr.* Wednesday.

wed *v.* (**wedding**; *past* and *past part.* **wedded** or **wed**) **1** usu. *formal* or *literary* **a** *tr.* & *intr.* marry. **b** *tr.* join in marriage. **2** *tr.* unite (*wed efficiency to economy*).

we'd *contraction* **1** we had. **2** we should; we would.

wedded *adj.* **1** of or in marriage (*wedded bliss*). **2** obstinately attached or devoted (to a pursuit etc.).

wedding *n.* **1** a marriage ceremony (considered by itself or with the associated celebrations). **2** an act or instance of uniting or joining.

wedding cake *n.* a cake served at a wedding reception, esp. a multi-tiered fruitcake with white icing.

wedding dress *n.* a dress worn by a bride, esp. a long white one, often with a train.

wedding night *n.* the night after a wedding (esp. with reference to its consummation).

wedding party *n.* the principal figures at a wedding, including the bride, groom, maid or matron of honour, best man, and often including bridesmaids, ushers, a flower girl, ring bearer, etc.

wedding ring *n.* (also **wedding band**) a ring given during a wedding ceremony and worn afterwards to show that the person wearing it is married.

wedge ● *n.* **1** a piece of wood or metal etc. tapering to a sharp edge, that is driven between two objects or parts of an object to secure or separate them. **2** anything resembling or acting as a wedge (*a wedge of cheese*; *drove an emotional wedge between them*). **3** a golf club with a wedge-shaped head. **4 a** a women's shoe with a solid wedge-shaped sole which is higher at the heel and lower towards the front of the foot. **b** such a sole. ● *v.* **1** *tr.* tighten, secure, or fasten by means of a wedge (*wedged the door open*). **2** *tr.* force open or apart with a wedge. **3** *tr.* & *intr.* (foll. by *in, into*) pack or thrust (a thing or oneself) tightly in or into. □ **thin edge** (or **end**) **of the wedge** *informal* an action or procedure of little importance in itself, but likely to lead to more serious developments.

wedge-shaped *adj.* **1** shaped like a solid wedge. **2** V-shaped.

wedgie *n.* *informal* **1** a woman's shoe with a wedge sole. **2** *N Amer.* a practical joke in which the victim's underpants are pulled up tightly between the buttocks.

Wedgwood *n.* *proprietary* **1** ceramics made by the English potter Josiah Wedgwood (1730–95) and his successors, esp. a kind of fine stoneware with a white cameo design. **2** the characteristic blue colour of this stoneware.

wedlock *n.* the married state. □ **born in** (or **out of**) **wedlock** born of married (or unmarried) parents.

Wednesday ● *n.* the fourth day of the week, following Tuesday. ● *adv.* **1** on Wednesday. **2** (**Wednesdays**) on Wednesdays; each Wednesday.

wee¹ *adj.* (**weer** /ˈwiːər/, **weest** /ˈwiːɪst/) **1** *informal* very small in amount or extent (*a wee bit late*). **2** esp. *Scot.* small in size or stature.

wee² *v.* (**weed, weeing**) esp. *Brit.* *slang* = PEE-PEE 1.

weed ● *n.* **1** a wild plant growing where it is not wanted. **2** *slang* **a** marijuana. **b** tobacco. ● *v.* **1** *tr.* **a** clear (an area) of weeds. **b** remove unwanted parts from. **2** *tr.* (foll. by *out*) **a** sort out (inferior or unwanted parts, elements, etc.) for removal. **b** rid (a quantity or company) of inferior or unwanted members etc. **3** *intr.* cut off or uproot weeds. □ **weeder** *n.* **weedless** *adj.*

weedbed *n.* *N Amer.* an area of a lake etc. with many weeds, esp. as frequented by fish.

Weed Eater *n.* *proprietary* a hand-held motorized garden tool used to trim grass, weeds, etc.

weed killer *n.* a substance used to destroy weeds.

weedline *n.* *N Amer.* the edge of a weedbed.

weedy *adj.* (**-ier, -iest**) **1** having many weeds. **2** (esp. of a person) weak, feeble. □ **weediness** *n.*

week *n.* **1** a period of seven consecutive days starting on Sunday or Monday. **2** a period of seven days counted from or beginning with a usu. specified point (*three weeks since we were there*). **3** one week of the year devoted to a specific event, holiday, cause, or activity (*Grey Cup week*; *reading week*). **4** the period of five days from Monday through Friday. **5** the period during which one works in a week (*a 35-hour week*). **6** (in *pl.*) *informal* a long time (*I haven't seen you in weeks*).

weekday *n.* any of the days from Monday to Friday (also *attrib.*: *weekday mornings*).

weekend ● *n.* **1** the period from Friday evening to Sunday evening. **2** this period extended slightly (*a three-day weekend*). ● *adj.* **1** held on or over a weekend. **2** carrying out a specific activity or hobby, or fulfilling a particular role, only on weekends. **3** for use on weekends. ● *v.intr.* spend a weekend.

weekender *n.* a person who spends weekends away from home.

weekend warrior *n. N Amer. informal* or *jocular* a person who participates in an activity only in his or her spare time, esp. on weekends.

week-long *adj.* lasting for a week (*a week-long festival*).

weekly ● *adj.* **1** done, produced, or occurring once a week. **2** calculated or determined by the week (*a weekly salary*). ● *adv.* once a week; from week to week. ● *n.* (*pl.* **-ies**) a weekly newspaper etc.

weeknight *n.* each of the nights of a week not falling on a weekend, i.e. from Monday to Thursday.

weenie *n. N Amer.* **1** = WIENER 1. **2** *derogatory* (as a term of contempt) an objectionable, feeble, or insignificant person. **3** *slang* the penis.

weeny *adj.* (also **weensy**) (**-ier, -iest**) *informal* tiny.

weep ● *v.* (*past* and *past part.* **wept**) **1** *intr.* express grief or misery etc. by tears usu. accompanied by sobs and moans. **2** *intr.* (foll. by *for*) shed tears for; bewail. **3** *tr. & intr.* shed or exude (liquid etc.). ● *n.* a fit or period of weeping.

weeper *n.* **1** a person who weeps esp. habitually. **2** an emotional or sentimental ballad, song, movie, etc.

weepie *n.* (also **weepy**) (*pl.* **-ies**) *informal* a sentimental or emotional movie, novel, etc.; a tearjerker.

weeping ● *adj.* **1** (of a tree) having drooping branches. **2** that cries or weeps. ● *n.* the act of shedding tears. □ **weepingly** *adv.*

weeping willow *n.* any of several ornamental willows with drooping branches and slender yellowish-green leaves.

weepy *adj.* (**-ier, -iest**) *informal* **1** inclined to cry or weep. **2** (of a movie, novel, etc.) intended to evoke tears. □ **weepily** *adv.* **weepiness** *n.*

weevil *n.* **1** any destructive beetle of the family Curculionidae, with its head extended into a beak or rostrum and feeding esp. on grain. **2** any insect damaging stored grain.

wee-wee *n. informal* = PEE-PEE 1.

weft *n.* **1 a** the threads woven across a warp to make fabric. **b** yarn used for this. **2** strips of cane, straw, etc. used as filling in weaving baskets or mats etc. **3** a thing that is spun or woven.

weigh *v.* **1** *tr.* determine the heaviness of (a body or substance), esp. by placing it on a scale or balancing it against a counterpoise of known heaviness. **2** *tr.* (often foll. by *out*) **a** use scales to measure and remove a definite quantity of (a substance) from a larger supply. **b** distribute in exact amounts by weight. **3** *tr.* **a** consider the relative value, importance, or desirability of (*weighed the options*). **b** (foll. by *against, with*) compare (one consideration) with another. **4** *intr.* have or be equal to a specified degree of heaviness (*this weighs three kilograms; he weighs more than I do*). **5** *intr.* have a usu. specified degree of importance (*this issue will weigh heavily on the outcome*). **6** *intr.* (usu. foll. by *on*) be a source of worry or concern (to) (*it's been weighing on her mind for some time*). □ **weigh anchor** take the anchor up. **weigh down 1** bring or keep down by exerting weight. **2** be oppressive or burdensome to (*weighed down with worries*). **weigh in 1** (of a boxer, jockey, etc.) have one's weight checked officially. **2** (foll. by *at*) have a specified weight officially recorded at a weigh-in (*the prizewinning salmon weighed in at 39.2*

lb.). **3 a** bring one's weight or influence to bear; contribute to a discussion, undertaking, etc. **b** (foll. by *with*) introduce or contribute (something) to an undertaking etc. (*the whole family weighed in with offers of help*). **weigh into** *informal* attack (physically or verbally). **weigh up** *informal* consider carefully; evaluate (a person, situation, etc.). **weigh with** be of importance to. **weigh one's words** carefully choose a sensitive or tactful way of expressing something.

weigh-in *n.* an official weighing of a person or thing, such as a boxer prior to a bout or an angler's catch at the end of a competition.

weigh scale *n.* (also **weigh station**) *N Amer.* a large metal platform at the side of a highway where trucks are required to have their cargo weighed to ensure that it does not exceed the legal limit for that road.

weight ● *n.* **1** *Physics* **a** the force experienced by a body as a result of the earth's gravitational pull (*compare* MASS *n.* 8). **b** any similar force with which a body tends to a centre of attraction. **2** the heaviness of a body regarded as a property of it (*it's held in position by its weight*). **3 a** the quantitative expression of a body's weight (*it has a weight of three pounds*). **b** a unit or system of units used for measuring or expressing how much a body weighs (*troy weight*). **4** a body of a known weight for use in weighing. **5** a heavy body used to hold something down, to drive the mechanism of a clock, as a sinker in fishing, etc. **6 a** a heavy mass or load. **b** an emotional burden (*a weight off my mind*). **7 a** a power to persuade, convince, or impress; influence, sway (*carried weight with the public*). **b** preponderance (*the weight of evidence was against them*). **8** *Statistics* a relative value assigned to a factor or observation, esp. a multiplier associated with any of a set of numerical quantities that are added together. **9 a** (in *pl.*) heavy blocks or discs of metal, barbells, etc. designed to be used in lifting and other exercises to improve or demonstrate physical strength and fitness. **b** = SHOT[1] 7. **10** (in full **weight class**) each of a series of divisions to which an athlete in some sports, e.g. boxing, may be assigned, according to how much he or she weighs. **11** (usu. in *comb.*) the relative weight of a fabric or garment as a measure of its quality or suitability for a particular use or season (*a lightweight spring jacket*). ● *v.tr.* **1 a** supply with an additional weight. **b** (usu. foll. by *down*) hold down with a weight or weights. **2** devise or manipulate (a rule or law etc.) so that it favours a particular individual, group, or goal over others (*legislation weighted in favour of the working class*). **3** *Statistics* multiply (the components of an average) by factors reflecting their relative importance. **4** (foll. by *with*) impede or burden. **5** assign a handicap weight to (a horse). □ **worth one's** (or **its**) **weight in gold** extremely valuable, useful, or helpful. □ **weighted** *adj.*

weightless *adj.* **1** lacking or apparently lacking weight. **2** (of an orbiting satellite etc.) not apparently acted on by gravity, either due to a locally weak gravitational field, or because both the body and its surroundings are freely and equally accelerating under the influence of the field. **3** lacking substance, importance. □ **weightlessly** *adv.* **weightlessness** *n.*

weightlifting *n.* the sport or exercise of lifting heavy weights. □ **weightlifter** *n.*

weight loss *n.* **1** a decrease in body weight. **2** (*attrib.*; usu. **weight-loss**) designed to promote or achieve a reduction in body weight (*weight-loss clinic*).

weight room *n.* a room where weights and related equipment are kept and used for physical training.

weight training n. physical conditioning involving the use of weights. □ **weight train** v.intr.

weighty adj. (**-ier, -iest**) **1** of considerable weight; heavy. **2** of great importance or significance. **3** (of an argument, speech, etc.) producing a powerful effect; convincing, persuasive. **4** (of a person) having great authority; influential. □ **weightily** adv. **weightiness** n.

weir /wiːr/ n. **1** a dam built across a river to raise the level of water upstream or regulate its flow. **2** an enclosure of stakes and netting set in a stream or river etc., used for trapping fish.

weird adj. **1** strange, unusual, bizarre. **2** suggestive of fate or the supernatural. □ **weird out** slang **1** make or become uncharacteristically depressed or upset. **2** induce a sense of disbelief or alienation in (a person). □ **weirdly** adv. **weirdness** n.

weirdo n. (also **weirdy**) (pl. **-os** or **-ies**) informal a strange or abnormal person.

welch var. of WELSH.

welcome ● n. **1** a kind or hospitable reception given to a visitor or stranger upon arriving. **2** a greeting or reception of a specified (usu. friendly or unfriendly) kind (gave them a warm welcome). ● interj. used to greet a visitor or guest, esp. expressing pleasure at the arrival (welcome home!). ● v.tr. **1 a** greet or receive with pleasure; give a friendly reception to (welcomed them home). **b** (foll. by with) greet or receive with something of a specified kind (the audience welcomed him with boos). **2** be pleased at or receptive to the prospect of (something) (we welcome your comments). ● adj. **1** that one receives with pleasure (welcome news). **2** (foll. by to, to + infin.) freely allowed or cordially invited (you are welcome to anything in the fridge). □ **make welcome** receive hospitably. **wear out** (or **overstay** or **outstay**) **one's welcome** N.Amer. inconvenience one's host by staying longer than is reasonable or expected. **welcome aboard!** jocular a greeting to a person joining a particular group, starting a job, etc. **you're** (or **you are**) **welcome** a polite response to an expression of thanks, signifying that the recipient of a favour is without obligation to the giver. □ **welcomely** adv. **welcomer** n. **welcoming** adj. **welcomingly** adv.

welcome mat n. N.Amer. **1** a doormat typically bearing some message of greeting, such as Welcome. **2** anything used to invite, entice, or solicit investors, customers, etc.

welcome tax n. Cdn (Que.) a municipal tax levied on all house purchases in the Province of Quebec.

Welcome Wagon n. **1** proprietary an organization of people who welcome newcomers to a community by providing gifts, samples of local merchants' wares, etc. **2** (**welcome wagon**) informal a group of people delegated to greet a visitor, guest, or newcomer in a community.

weld ● v.tr. **1 a** hammer or press (pieces of heated iron or steel) into one piece. **b** join (pieces of metal or plastic etc.) by melting, using heat provided by an electric arc, acetylene torch, or laser. **c** form or repair by welding. **2** bring together (arguments, members of a group, etc.) into an effectual or homogeneous whole. ● n. a welded joint. □ **weldable** adj. **weldability** n.

welder n. **1** a person who welds, esp. as a profession. **2** a torch etc. used in welding.

welfare n. **1** well-being, happiness; health and prosperity of a person or a community etc. **2 a** the organized provision for the basic esp. physical and economic well-being of needy members of a commu-nity by legislation or social effort. **b** financial support given for this purpose. □ **on welfare** N.Amer. receiving financial assistance from the government for basic living needs.

welfare roll n. N.Amer. (usu. in pl.) a list of people entitled to welfare benefits.

welfare state n. **1** a system whereby the government of a country etc. undertakes to protect the health and well-being of its citizens, esp. those in financial or social need, by means of pensions, allowances, etc. **2** a country practising this system.

welfarism n. the principles or policies associated with a welfare state. □ **welfarist** n.

well[1] ● adv. (**better, best**) **1** in an acceptable or satisfactory manner. **2** with some talent or distinction. **3** in a way appropriate to the facts or circumstances (you did well to tell me). **4** in a kind way. **5** thoroughly, carefully. **6** favourably. **7** with equanimity or good nature (he took it well). **8** probably (you may well be right). **9** to a considerable extent (she is well over forty). **10** intimately; closely, in detail. **11** successfully, fortunately. **12** with a fortunate outcome; without disaster (were well rid of them). **13** profitably (did well for themselves). **14** comfortably (we live well). **15** informal used with preceding adverb to form intensive phrases (I should bloody well hope so!). ● adj. (**better, best**) **1** (usu. predic.) in good health; free or recovered from illness. **2** (predic.) **a** in a satisfactory state or position (all is well). **b** proper, advisable (it would be well to inquire). ● interj. **1** expressing surprise, insistence, resignation, etc. (well I never!; oh well, at least we tried). **2** used to resume or continue speaking, esp. after a pause (well...who was it?; well anyway, as I was saying). □ **all's well that ends well** the inconvenience of a problem or matter is negligible as long as it is resolved satisfactorily. **as well 1** also, in addition; to an equal extent. **2** (also **just as well**) with equal reason or result; with no loss of advantage or need for regret (we might as well go home). **as well as** in addition to. **leave** (or **let**) **well enough alone** refrain from trying to improve something that is already satisfactory. **well and good** expressing dispassionate acceptance of a statement or decision etc. **well and truly** decisively, completely. **well worth** certainly worth (well worth a visit). ¶A hyphen is normally used in combinations of well- when used attributively, but not when used predicatively, e.g. a well-made coat but the coat is well made.

well[2] ● n. **1** a shaft sunk into the ground to obtain water, oil, natural gas, etc. **2** a natural source or spring of water. **3 a** the open space or shaft in a building enclosing a staircase or housing an elevator. **b** a deep narrow space in the middle of a building or group of buildings, to provide light and ventilation. **4** a receptacle, reservoir, or depression designed to hold liquid, such as one in a dish for gravy or in a desk for ink. **5** a deep receptacle, compartment, or recess, such as that in the trunk of a car in which a spare tire is kept. **6** a source, esp. a copious one (a well of information). ● v.intr. **1** (foll. by up, out) gather, gush, or spring as in or from a fountain (anger welled up inside her). **2** (foll. by up) be filled with tears.

we'll contraction we shall; we will.

well-acquainted adj. (usu. foll. by with) familiar.

well-adjusted adj. **1** Psych. mentally and emotionally stable. **2** in a state of proper adjustment.

well-advised adj. **1** (of a person) prudent, wise (would be well-advised to wait). **2** (of an action etc.) carefully thought out.

well-aimed adj. **1** (of a jibe or criticism) incisive, biting. **2** precisely directed; accurate.

well-appointed adj. furnished with all of the necessary equipment, accessories, or desirable features (a well-appointed kitchen).

well-attended adj. (of a meeting etc.) attended by a large number of people.

well aware adj. certainly aware.

well-balanced adj. **1** having no constituent lacking or in excess; regulated to ensure a proper balance (a well-balanced diet). **2** sane, sensible.

well-behaved adj. having or demonstrating good manners or conduct.

well-being n. a happy, healthy, and prosperous state or condition; moral or physical welfare.

well-bred adj. **1** demonstrating qualities indicative of a good upbringing, such as refined speech, courteous behaviour, and excellent manners. **2** (of an animal) of good or pure stock.

well-built adj. **1** of solid and reliable construction. **2** (of a person) well-proportioned with a strong, sturdy, or muscular build.

well-chosen adj. (of words etc.) carefully selected for effect.

well-connected adj. having powerful or influential relatives, friends, associates, contacts, etc.

well-constructed adj. **1** (of a building, furniture, etc.) constructed in a sound or practical way. **2** (of a text) with a clear or carefully-planned structure.

well-defined adj. clearly marked, outlined, or indicated; having definite shape, structure, or guidelines.

well-deserved adj. rightfully merited or earned.

well-designed adj. **1** (of furniture, living space, etc.) designed for practical use. **2** of a good design (well-designed poster).

well-developed adj. **1** fully developed or grown; mature. **2** of generous size.

well-disposed adj. (often foll. by towards) having a good disposition or friendly feeling (for).

well-documented adj. supported or attested by much documentary evidence.

well done ● adj. **1** (of meat) thoroughly cooked. **2** (of a task etc.) performed or executed skilfully or effectively. ● interj. expressing approval of a person's actions.

well-dressed adj. wearing clothes of good quality.

well-educated adj. having received a high level of education.

well-endowed adj. **1** well provided with talent or resources. **2** euphemism **a** (of a woman) having large breasts. **b** (of a man) = WELL-HUNG.

well equipped adj. **1** having a plentiful supply of equipment. **2** having the necessary requirements or resources (well equipped to deal with the situation).

well-established adj. **1** (of a custom, rule, etc.) long-standing. **2** firmly entrenched in a profession, role, or position; proven (a well-established artist).

well-fed adj. **1** having had plenty to eat. **2** euphemism plump, overweight.

well-formed adj. correctly or attractively proportioned or shaped. □ **well-formedness** n.

well-founded adj. (of a belief, statement, etc.) having a foundation in fact or reason; based on strong evidence.

well-groomed adj. **1** (of a person) looking clean and neat with carefully tended hair, clothes, etc. **2** (of an animal) having a clean and brushed coat. **3** (of ski trails etc.) properly maintained or looked after.

well-grounded adj. **1** = WELL-FOUNDED. **2** (often foll. by in) having a good training in or knowledge of the basic principles of a subject.

wellhead n. **1** a structure built over an oil or gas well. **2** = WELLSPRING.

well-heeled adj. informal wealthy.

well-hung adj. slang (of a man) having large genitals.

well-informed adj. possessing or communicating much knowledge in general or of a specified subject.

wellington n. (in full **wellington boot**) (usu. in pl.) esp. Brit. a waterproof rubber or plastic boot usu. reaching the knee, worn in wet or muddy conditions.

well-intentioned adj. having or showing good intentions.

well-kept adj. **1** kept in good order or condition. **2** carefully preserved; not revealed (a well-kept secret).

well-knit adj. (of a person) compact; not sprawling.

well-known adj. **1** known to many; widely known, famous. **2** intimately or thoroughly known.

well-lit adj. (also (attrib.) **well-lighted**) suitably provided with light or lighting.

well-loved adj. regarded with great affection.

well-made adj. strongly or skilfully constructed, prepared, or devised.

well-maintained adj. **1** kept in good repair. **2** kept up to date (well-maintained inventory).

well-mannered adj. having or demonstrating good manners; courteous, polite.

well-marked adj. clearly defined, distinct; easy to distinguish or recognize.

well-matched adj. **1** compatible, suited; fit to be a pair. **2** (of opponents or adversaries) evenly matched; having similar or offsetting strengths and weakness.

well-meaning adj. **1** having or demonstrating good intentions, esp. despite being misguided or unhelpful. **2** (also **well-meant**) (of advice etc.) based on good intentions but usu. ineffective or ill-advised.

wellness n. the state of being well or in good health.

well-nigh adv. very nearly; almost (well-nigh impossible).

well off adj. **1** having plenty of money. **2** in a fortunate situation or position.

well-oiled adj. informal **1 a** sufficiently or generously lubricated. **b** (of an organization, operation, etc.) running smoothly. **2** drunk.

well-ordered adj. neatly, carefully, or properly composed or arranged.

well-organized adj. **1** skilfully or carefully organized; planned in detail. **2** (of a person) orderly; able to organize personal activities.

well-paid adj. **1** (of a person) amply rewarded for a job. **2** (also **well-paying**) (of a job) that pays well.

well placed adj. **1** set in a good place or position; properly, conveniently, or judiciously placed. **2** holding a position of influence, authority, or high social standing. **3** in a suitable position; easily able (you are well placed to know).

well-planned adj. **1** of careful or practical design. **2** (of an event, program, etc.) planned or structured carefully with attention to detail.

well-prepared adj. **1** prepared with care. **2** having prepared thoroughly (for an interview, exam, etc.).

well-preserved adj. **1** having remained in good condition over time (a well-preserved artifact). **2** (of an elderly person) showing little sign of aging.

well-proportioned n. having good, graceful, or correct proportions.

well-read adj. knowledgeable from much reading.

well-received adj. favourably received or reviewed.

well-rounded *adj.* **1** (of a person) having or showing a fully developed personality combined with a wide range of knowledge and interests. **2** well-balanced, full, and varied (*a well-rounded team*).

well-spent *adj.* (esp. of money or time) used profitably or judiciously.

well-spoken *adj.* (of a person) speaking articulately and grammatically or with an accent considered to be refined.

wellspring *n.* **1** the place where a spring breaks out of the ground; the source of a stream or river. **2** an esp. abundant source (*the wellspring of creativity*).

well-stocked *adj.* having an abundant supply.

well-suited *adj.* (usu. foll. by *to, for*) suitable.

well-supported *adj.* **1** attended by many. **2** supported by much evidence.

well-taken *adj.* (of an argument) accepted as valid.

well-thought-of *adj.* having a good reputation; esteemed, respected.

well-thought-out *adj.* carefully planned or devised in advance.

well-thumbed *adj.* (of a book or page etc.) bearing marks of frequent handling.

well-to-do *adj.* comfortably wealthy or prosperous.

well-travelled *adj.* **1** having travelled extensively. **2** (of a path etc.) much frequented.

well-used *adj.* **1 a** used properly or frequently. **b** worn from frequent handling or use. **2** (of a road or path etc.) frequently travelled.

well versed *adj.* very learned, experienced, or skilled in (a subject, art, etc.); knowledgeable about.

well-wisher *n.* a person conveying his or her congratulations, wishes of luck, etc. to another.

well-worn *adj.* **1** decrepit, shabby, or worn out from extensive use or handling. **2** (of a phrase or idea etc.) trite, hackneyed.

Welsh ● *adj.* of or relating to Wales, a principality of the United Kingdom, to the west of central England, or its people or language. ● *n.* **1** the Celtic language of Wales. **2** (prec. by *the*; treated as *pl.*) the people of Wales. □ **Welshman** *n.* (*pl.* **-men**). **Welshwoman** *n.* (*pl.* **-women**).

welsh *v.intr.* (usu. foll. by *on*) **1** fail or refuse to pay or repay money owed (*he welshes on gambling debts*). **2** fail or refuse to honour or fulfill a promise or obligation (*she welshed on our agreement*).

welt *n.* a ridge raised on the flesh by the impact of a rod, whip, etc., or by an allergic reaction.

welter *n.* a confused mixture of things or people.

welterweight *n.* **1** a weight class in certain sports between lightweight and middleweight, in the amateur boxing scale 63.5-67 kg but differing for professionals and wrestlers. **2** a boxer etc. of this weight.

Weltschmerz /'veltʃmerts/ *n.* pessimism; an apathetic or vaguely yearning outlook on life.

wench *n.* **1** *jocular* a girl or young woman. **2** *archaic* a prostitute or mistress.

wend *v.intr.* go. □ **wend one's way** make one's way.

Wen-Do /'wen'do:/ *n.* *Cdn proprietary* a program of self-defence for women, emphasizing awareness and avoidance of potentially dangerous situations as well as appropriate reactions, including, as a last resort, physical attacks directed against the particularly vulnerable areas of an assailant's body.

went *past of* GO[1].

wept *past of* WEEP.

were 2nd sing. past, pl. past, and past subj. of BE.

we're *contraction* we are.

were- /wer, wi:r/ *comb. form.* used to denote a person

imagined to be able to change at times into a specified animal (*were-rat; were-snake*).

weren't *contraction* were not.

werewolf *n.* (*pl.* **-wolves**) a mythical being who at times changes from a person to a wolf.

Wesleyan /'wezliən, 'wes-/ ● *adj.* of or relating to a Protestant denomination founded by the English evangelist John Wesley (1703–91) (*compare* METHODIST). ● *n.* a member of this denomination. □ **Wesleyanism** *n.*

west ● *n.* **1** the point of the horizon where the sun sets at the equinoxes (cardinal point 90° to the left of north). **2** the compass point corresponding to this. **3** the direction in which this lies. **4** (usu. **the West**) **a** Europe and the countries of the western hemisphere as distinguished from those of the regions or countries lying to the east of the Mediterranean, esp. China, Japan, and other E Asian countries. **b** *hist.* the non-Communist countries of Europe and N America. **5** (usu. **the West**) **a** the western part of a country or city etc. **b** *Cdn* the part of the country west of the Ontario-Manitoba border. **c** *US* the States lying to the west of the Mississippi. ● *adj.* **1** towards, at, near, or facing west. **2** coming from the west (*west wind*). ● *adv.* **1** towards, at, or near the west. **2** (foll. by *of*) further west than.

westbound *adj.* travelling or leading westwards.

West Country *n.* the southwestern counties of England.

West End *n.* **1** the district of London (England) lying between Charing Cross Road and Park Lane, noted for its many theatres and fashionable shops. **2** the western part of any city or town.

westerly ● *adj. & adv.* **1** in a western position or direction. **2** (of a wind) blowing from the west. ● *n.* (*pl.* **-ies**) a wind blowing from the west.

western ● *adj.* **1** of or in the west; inhabiting the west. **2** lying or directed towards the west. **3** (esp. of a wind) blowing from the west. **4** (**Western**) **a** of or relating to the Occident or (formerly) the non-Communist countries of Europe and N America. **b** of or related to the Canadian or American West (*see* WEST *n.* 5). ● *n.* **1** a film or novel of a genre depicting life in the N American West in the 19th and early 20th c., usu. featuring cowboys in heroic roles, gunfights, etc. **2** *N Amer.* **a** = WESTERN SANDWICH. **b** = WESTERN OMELETTE. ● *adv.* (ride etc.) in the manner of a cowboy, in a relaxed style with a deep-seated saddle and almost straight legs. □ **westernmost** *adj.*

Western Church *n.* the part of the Christian Church including the Catholic and Protestant Churches, as distinct from the Orthodox or Eastern Churches.

westerner *n.* (also **Westerner**) a native or inhabitant of the western part of any country or of any country of the western hemisphere.

western hemisphere *n.* the half of the earth containing North and South America and the surrounding waters.

westernize *v.tr.* (also **Westernize**) influence with or convert to Western ideas and customs etc., esp. the ideas and customs of Occidental countries. □ **westernization** *n.*

western omelette *n.* *N Amer.* an omelette made with diced onion, ham, and often green peppers.

Western provinces *n.pl.* Manitoba, Alberta, Saskatchewan, and British Columbia.

western red cedar *n.* *see* RED CEDAR.

western sandwich *n.* *N Amer.* a toasted sandwich with a western omelette as filling.

Western Wall *n.* the remaining part of the wall of Herod's temple in Jerusalem destroyed in AD 70, where Jews traditionally pray and lament on Fridays.

West Highland white terrier *n.* (also **Westie**) a small terrier with short legs, a white coat, and an erect tail and ears.

West Indian *n.* **1** a native or national of any island of the West Indies, a chain of islands extending from the Florida peninsula to the coast of Venezuela, lying between the Caribbean and the Atlantic. **2** a person of West Indian descent.

west-northwest *n.* the direction or compass point midway between west and northwest.

West Side *n.* the western part of any of several N American cities or boroughs, esp. of Manhattan.

west-southwest *n.* the direction or compass point midway between west and southwest.

West Virginian ● *adj.* of or relating to the US state of West Virginia. ● *n.* a native or inhabitant of West Virginia.

westward ● *adj. & adv.* (also **westwards**) towards the west. ● *n.* a westward direction or region.

wet ● *adj.* (**wetter, wettest**) **1** covered, dampened, or soaked with water or another liquid. **2** (of the weather etc.) rainy. **3** (of paint, ink, etc.) not yet dried. **4** used or done with water (*a wet shave*). **5** (of ingredients in a recipe) liquid, such as water, oil, eggs, etc. **6** (of a baby) having urinated; having a diaper that needs changing. **7** *informal* **a** of or pertaining to alcohol, esp. as drunk in substantial quantities (*a wet lunch*). **b** (of a country, of legislation, etc.) favouring or permitting the sale of alcohol. ● *v.tr.* (**wetting**; *past* and *past part.* **wet** or **wetted**) **1** dampen, make wet. **2 a** urinate in or on (*wet the bed*). **b** *refl.* urinate involuntarily (*I laughed so hard I nearly wet myself*). ● *n.* **1** moisture; liquid that makes something wet. **2** precipitation or a period of this (*come in out of the wet*). □ **all wet** *N Amer.* completely wrong or mistaken. **wet the baby's head** *informal* celebrate the birth of a baby with a drink. **wet behind the ears** immature, inexperienced. **wet through** (or **to the skin**) with one's clothes soaked. **wet one's whistle** *informal* drink. □ **wetly** *adv.* **wetness** *n.* **wettable** *adj.* **wetting** *n.* **wettish** *adj.*

wet bar *n. N Amer.* a bar or counter in the home equipped with a sink and running water, from which drinks are served.

wet dream *n.* an erotic dream with involuntary ejaculation of semen.

wet fly *n.* an artificial fly allowed to sink below the surface of the water.

wether /'weðər/ *n.* a castrated ram.

wetland *n.* (often in *pl.*) a marsh, swamp, or other stretch of land that is frequently saturated with water (also *attrib.*: *wetland vegetation*).

wet look ● *n.* **1** a shiny surface (given esp. to clothing materials. **2** a shiny or wet appearance achieved by applying a type of gel to the hair. ● *attrib.adj.* (**wet-look**) having or giving a shiny or wet appearance.

wet nurse *n.* a woman employed to breast-feed another's baby.

wet snow *n.* large cohesive flakes of snow that fall when the temperature is above or slightly below the freezing point, accumulating in dense heavy masses.

wetsuit *n.* a close-fitting one-piece rubber garment worn by scuba divers, surfers, etc., to protect them from the cold.

Wet'suwet'en /wət'su:wət,en/ ● *n.* **1** a member of an Aboriginal people living in north-central BC, along the Skeena River. **2** the Tsimshian language of this people. ● *adj.* of or relating to this people.

we've *contraction* we have.

whack *informal* ● *v.tr.* **1** strike or beat forcefully with a sharp slap or blow. **2** *N Amer. slang* kill. ● *n.* **1** a sharp or resounding blow. **2** *slang* a large number or amount (*a whole whack of people*). □ **have** (or **take**) **a whack at** *slang* attempt. **out of whack** esp. *N Amer. slang* **1** out of order; malfunctioning. **2** (of calculations, figures, etc.) maladjusted, skewed, awry. **whack off** *N Amer. coarse slang* masturbate. □ **whacker** *n.* **whacking** *n.*

whacked *adj.* **1** (usu. foll. by *out*) esp. *N Amer.* **a** mad, crazy, wild. **b** high or intoxicated on drugs or alcohol. **2** (sometimes foll. by *out*) tired out; exhausted.

whacko *var. of* WACKO.

whacky *var. of* WACKY.

whale¹ *n.* (*pl.* **-s** or same) any of various large marine mammals, having a streamlined fishlike body, forelimbs modified as fins, and a tail with horizontal flukes, and which breathes through a nasal opening on top of the head. □ **a whale of a** *informal* an exceptionally good or large etc.

whale² *v.tr.* esp. *N Amer. informal* beat, thrash.

whaleboat *n.* a long narrow double-bowed boat formerly used for whaling, now used esp. as a lifeboat.

whalebone *n.* **1** an elastic horny substance which grows in a series of thin parallel plates in the upper jaw of baleen whales, serving to strain plankton from the sea water. **2** a strip of this esp. used as a stiffening in stays and dresses etc.

whale-watch *N Amer.* ● *n.* an excursion made by boat to observe whales in their natural habitat. ● *v.intr.* go on an excursion to observe whales.

whaling *n.* the hunting and killing of whales, esp. for their oil, meat, or whalebone.

wham *informal* ● *n.* the sound of forcible impact. ● *interj.* expressing such a sound. ● *v.* (**whammed**, **whamming**) **1** *intr.* make such a sound or impact. **2** *tr.* strike with force.

whammy *n.* (*pl.* **-ies**) esp. *US informal* **1** an evil or unlucky influence; a hex or curse. **2** (esp. in phr. **double whammy**) a powerful or unpleasant effect or a problematic situation.

whang *informal* ● *v.* **1** *intr.* produce a loud resonating or ringing sound under or as if under a forceful blow. **2** *tr. & intr.* strike heavily and loudly. ● *n.* a loud resonating or ringing sound or blow.

whap /wɒp, wæp/ esp. *N Amer.* ● *n.* **1** a hard slap as if with a flat object or the palm of the hand. **2** the sound of this. ● *v.tr.* strike or slap forcefully, esp. with or as if with a flat object or the palm of the hand.

wharf ● *n.* (*pl.* **wharves** or **wharfs**) a level quayside structure to which a ship may be moored to load and unload. ● *v.tr.* **1** moor (a ship) at a wharf. **2** unload and store (goods) on a wharf.

what ● *interrog.adj.* used in asking the identity of a choice made from a set of alternatives (*what books have you read?*). ● *adj.* (usu. in exclamation) how great or remarkable (*what luck!*). ● *rel.adj.* the or any...that (*will give you what help I can*). ● *pron.* **1 a** used in asking the identity or name of a thing or things specified, indicated, or understood (*I don't know what you mean*). **b** used in asking the character, function, occupation, etc. of a person or persons specified, indicated, or understood (*what are you going to be when you grow up?*). **2** (asking for a remark to be repeated) = what did you say? **3** asking for repetition, clarification, or confirmation of something disputed or not completely understood (*you did what?*; *what, you want me to do it?*). **4 a** how much (*what is it going to cost?*). **b** how great (*what a save!*). **5** (*prec. by or*) *informal* representing the unknown final alternative in a set of proposed options (*I didn't know if she was scared, nervous, or what*). **6** (as *rel.pron.*) that or those which (*tell me what you think*). ● *adv.* to what extent (*what does it matter?*). ● *interj.* **1** expressing surprise or astonishment (*what, that's it?*). **2** expressing disbelief and inviting repetition or confirmation of a previous remark. □ **what about** what is your position on or opinion of (*what about me?*; *what about a game of tennis?*). **what for** *informal* **1** why? for what reason? **2** a severe reprimand (*gave her what for*). **what have you** *informal* (*prec. by or*) anything else similar. **what if? 1** what would result etc. if. **2** what would it matter if. **what is more** and as an additional point; moreover. **what next?** *informal* what more absurd, shocking, or surprising thing is possible? **what of?** what is the news concerning? **what of it?** why should that be considered significant? **what's his** (or **her**) **name** (also **what's his** (or **her**) **face**) *informal* a person whose name one cannot recall, does not know, or does not wish to specify. **what's what** *informal* what things are useful or important. **what's with** *informal* what is the matter with? what has happened to? what is the reason for? **what with** *informal* on account of; because of (*usu.* several things).

whatchamacallit (also **whatchacallit, what-d'you-call-it**) *n. informal* a thing the proper name of which one cannot recall, does not know, or does not wish to mention.

whatever ● *pron.* **1** anything or everything that (*do whatever it takes*). **2** no matter what (*whatever it is, it's coming this way*). **3** representing an unknown final alternative, usu. in a set of proposed options (*he'll drink wine, beer, whatever*). **4** what in any way (*whatever can you mean?*) ● *adj.* **1** any...that (*whatever money you can lend me will help*). **2** any; no matter what (*whatever garbage he writes sells*). **3** (used as a perfunctory designation of anything a speaker is reluctant or unable to describe specifically) denoting an unnamed person or thing (*for whatever reason, she left early*). **4** = WHATSOEVER *adj.* 1.

whatnot *n.* **1** (*usu.* prec. by *and*) other similar items (*a drawer full of paper, pens, and whatnot*). **2** an unspecified or trivial thing. **3** a stand with shelves used for keeping or displaying small objects.

what say ● *interj.* pardon? what did you say? ● *adv.* indicating a suggestion or proposition to which a reply is expected (*what say we go to a movie?*).

whatsit *n.* **1** = WHATCHAMACALLIT. **2** = WHAT'S HIS NAME (see WHAT).

whatsoever ● *adj.* **1** (*predic.*; with *neg.*) at all; of any kind (*there is no doubt whatsoever*). **2** *archaic* = WHATEVER *adj.* 1, 2. ● *pron. archaic* = WHATEVER *pron.* 1, 2.

wheat *n.* **1** any cereal plant of the genus *Triticum*, bearing dense four-sided seed spikes. **2** its grain, used in making flour etc.

Wheat Board *n. Cdn* a Crown corporation responsible for the sale of all wheat and barley produced in western Canada and destined for export or for domestic human consumption.

wheaten *adj.* **1** made of the grain or flour of wheat. **2** of the colour of ripe wheat, usu. a pale gold.

wheat germ *n.* the embryo of the wheat grain.

wheat grass *n.* any of several N American grasses of the genus *Agropyron*, grown as fodder.

wheat pool *n. Cdn* a grain farmers' co-operative in Western Canada for the sale of wheat and other cereal crops.

whee *interj.* expressing delight or excitement.

wheedle *v.* **1** *tr. & intr.* attempt to coax or persuade (a person) by flattery or endearments. **2** *tr.* (often foll. by *out*) talk or coax a person into giving up possession of (something); obtain or acquire by wheedling. □ **wheedler** *n.* **wheedling** *adj.*

wheel ● *n.* **1** a solid disc or circular frame with spokes radiating from the centre, attached or able to be attached at its centre to an axle around which it revolves, used to facilitate the motion of a vehicle or for various mechanical purposes. **2** anything resembling a wheel in function or appearance (*roulette wheel*; *a wheel of brie*). **3** a machine etc. of which a wheel is an essential part (*spinning wheel*). **4** (in *pl.*) *slang* a car. **5** = STEERING WHEEL. **6** a recurring course of actions or events; an endless cycle (*wheel of life*). **7** (in *pl.*, usu. foll. by *of*) the driving or animating force (*wheels of industry*). **8** a motion like that of a wheel, esp. the movement of a line of people with one end as a pivot. **9** *hist.* a large wheel used in various ways as an instrument of torture. ● *v.* **1** *tr. & intr.* turn or rotate on an axis or pivot. **2 a** *intr.* change direction or face another way, esp. quickly or suddenly. **b** *tr.* cause to do this. **3** *tr.* push or pull (a wheeled thing, esp. a bicycle, or stroller, or its load or occupant). **4** *intr.* move in circles or curves (*seagulls wheeled overhead*). **5** *intr.* (of a line of people) swing around in line with one end as a pivot. □ **at the wheel 1** (also **behind the wheel**) driving a car or truck etc. **2** directing a ship. **3** in control of affairs. **wheel and deal** engage in political or commercial scheming. **wheels within wheels 1** intricate machinery. **2** *informal* indirect or secret agencies. □ **wheeled** *adj.* (also in *comb.*). **wheelless** *adj.* **wheel-like** *adj.*

wheelbarrow *n.* a shallow open container for moving small loads, with a wheel at one end and two legs and two handles at the other.

wheelbase *n.* the distance between the front and rear axles of a vehicle.

wheelchair *n.* **1** a chair on wheels for an invalid or a disabled person. **2** (*attrib.*) **a** designating a sport or activity participated in by athletes in wheelchairs (*wheelchair basketball*). **b** designating an athlete participating in such an activity.

wheeler *n.* (in *comb.*) a vehicle having a specified number of wheels (*an 18-wheeler*).

wheeler-dealer *n.* a person who wheels and deals (see WHEEL). □ **wheeler-dealing** *n.*

wheelhouse *n.* **1** the structure on a ship containing the steering wheel. **2** *Baseball slang* the area over the plate where a pitch is most likely to be hit by a particular batter.

wheelie *n. slang* the stunt of riding a bicycle or motorcycle for a short distance with the front wheel off the ground. □ **pop a wheelie** perform this stunt.

wheel of Fortune *n.* the wheel which Fortune is fabled to turn in order to determine the fates of humans; a metaphor for luck and the mutability of personal circumstances.

wheeze ● *v.intr.* **1** breathe with an audible chesty whistling sound, due to dryness or obstruction of the air passages. **2** make a similar whistling or rasping sound (*the bus wheezed to a stop*). ● *n.* **1** a sound of or resembling wheezing. **2** *informal* a hackneyed running joke or comic phrase. □ **wheezer** *n.* **wheezy** *adj.* **wheezily** *adv.* **wheeziness** *n.*

whelk /welk/ *n.* any predatory marine gastropod mollusc of the family Buccinidae, esp. the edible kind of the genus *Baccinum*, having a spiral shell.

whelp ● *n.* a young dog, seal, or mink. ● *v. tr. & intr.* (of a female animal, esp. a bitch or seal) give birth to (a

whelp or **whelps**). □ **in whelp** (of a female animal) pregnant.

when ● *interrog.adv.* **1** at what time? **2** how soon? **3** how long ago? **4** on what occasion? under what circumstances? (*when is it best to ask?*). ● *adv.* *N Amer. informal* in the past (*I can say I knew her when*). ● *rel.adv.* (*prec. by time etc.*) at or on which (*there are times when I could cry*). ● *conj.* **1 a** at the time that, on the occasion that (*come when it is convenient*; *when I was your age*). **b** at any time that (*I smile when I hear her voice*). **2** although; considering that (*why stand when you could sit?*). **3** at which time; after which; but just then (*was nearly asleep when the phone rang*). **4** while on the contrary, whereas (*gave me $2.00 when she meant to give me $5.00*). ● *pron.* what time? (*till when can you stay?*; *since when have you been married?*). ● *n.* time, occasion, date (*fixed the where and when*).

whence *formal* ● *adv.* from what place? (*whence did they come?*). ● *conj.* **1** to the place from which (*return whence you came*). **2** (*often prec. by place etc.*) from which (*the source whence these errors arise*). **3** and thence (*whence it follows that*). ¶Although it is well-established, some speakers and writers of English avoid the expression *from whence* which they consider redundant on the grounds that *from* is implied in the meaning of *whence* and does not need to be repeated.

whenever *conj. & adv.* **1** at whatever time. **2** every time that. □ **or whenever** *informal* or at any similar time.

where ● *interrog.adv.* **1** in or at what place or position? **2** to what place? **3 a** in what book or passage of a book? **b** from whom? from what source? **4** in what direction or respect? (*where are you going with this argument?*). **5** in what situation or condition? (*where does that leave us?*). **6** at what point or stage? (*where did we go wrong?*). ● *rel.adv.* in or to which (*places where they meet*). ● *conj.* **1** in, at, or to the place in which (*put it where we can all see it*). **2** in the situation or circumstances in which (*give credit where credit is due*). **3** *N Amer. informal* that (*I see where the jewellery store was robbed again*). ● *pron.* what place? (*where do you come from?*). ● *n.* a place, esp. the or a place at which something happens, has happened, or will happen.

whereabouts ● *adv.* where or approximately where? ● *n.* (*treated as sing. or pl.*) the place in or near which a person or thing is; the approximate location. ¶Although it is more common for *whereabouts* to take a plural verb, it may be used correctly with a singular verb (*her whereabouts are not known*; *the whereabouts of the purse and its contents remains a mystery*).

whereas *conj.* **1** in contrast or comparison with the fact that. **2** (esp. in legal preambles) taking into consideration the fact that; since.

whereby *conj.* **1** by means of which; in which (*a process whereby public concerns may be expressed*). **2** according to which; under the terms of which (*a deal whereby she will receive a royalty*).

wherefore ● *adv. archaic* **1** for what cause, purpose, or reason? why? **2** on account of which; as a result of which. ● *n.* a reason (*the whys and wherefores*).

wherein *formal* ● *conj.* in which thing, matter, place, etc. ● *adv.* in what place or respect?

whereof *formal* ● *conj.* of which or whom (*the person whereof she writes*). ● *adv.* of what? □ **know whereof one speaks** recognize or understand what one is talking about.

whereupon *conj.* upon the occurrence of which; immediately after and as a consequence of which.

wherever ● *adv.* in or to whatever place. ● *conj.* in

every place that. □ **or wherever** *informal* or in any similar place.

wherewithal *n.* the means by which to do something.

whet /wet/ *v.tr.* (**whetted, whetting**) **1** sharpen (a tool or weapon) by grinding it on a stone. **2** stimulate (the appetite, a desire, interest, etc.).

whether *conj.* **1** introducing an indirect question or an expression of doubt or choice between alternatives, in which the final alternative is introduced by *or* or *or whether* (*I'm not sure whether it's Monday or Tuesday*). **2** introducing an indirect question, simple inquiry, or opinion, in which the second alternative is implied only (*I wonder whether we should go*; *I doubt whether it matters*). **3** introducing a statement that is applicable whichever of the possibilities given is true (*whether he likes it or not, he has to do it*).

whetstone *n.* **1** a shaped fine-grained stone used to sharpen tools and cutlery etc. by grinding. **2** a thing that sharpens the senses etc.

whew *interj.* expressing relief, surprise, or exhaustion as from heat or exertion.

whey *n.* the watery liquid that remains when milk forms curds.

which ● *interrog.adj.* used in asking the identity of a choice from a set of alternatives (*which Robert are you talking about?*; *tell me which book you prefer*). ● *rel.adj.* being the thing or things just referred to, usu. introducing a clause not essential for identification (*the newspaper comes at 6:00, by which time I am usually up*; *he might not come tonight, in which case I won't see him until tomorrow*). ● *interrog.pron.* **1** which person or persons (*which of you is responsible?*). **2** which thing or things (*tell me which you prefer*). ● *rel.pron.* (*possess.* **of which**, **whose**) **1** introducing a clause that describes or states something additional about the antecedent but which is not essential for identification (*compare* THAT *pron.* 5) (*this house, which happens to be for sale, was built in the 1880s*). **2** used in place of *that* after *in* or *that* (*there is the house in which I was born*; *that which you have just seen*). □ **which is which** a phrase used when two or more people or things are difficult to distinguish from each other.

whichever *adj. & pron.* **1** either or any of a definite set of people or things that (*take whichever one you like*). **2** no matter which (*whichever one wins, they both get a prize*).

whiff ● *n.* **1** a puff or breath of air, smoke, etc. **2** a smell or odour. **3** a trace or suggestion (*a whiff of danger*). **4** *Baseball informal* a strikeout. ● *v.* **1** *tr.* sniff, get a slight smell of. **2** *tr.* blow or puff lightly. **3** *Baseball informal* **a** *intr.* (of a batter) strike out. **b** *tr.* (of a pitcher) strike (a batter) out.

whiffle /ˈwɪf(ə)l/ ● *v.* **1** *tr. & intr.* (of the wind) blow gently. **2** *intr.* make the sound of or like wind blowing gently. **3** *tr. & intr.* flutter (*leaves whiffled in the wind*). ● *n.* a slight movement of air.

Whig /wɪg/ *n. hist.* **1** a member of the English, later British, reforming and constitutional party that after 1688 sought the supremacy of Parliament and was eventually succeeded in the 19th c. by the Liberal Party (*opp.* TORY 3). **2 a** a member of a 19th-c. US political party established in 1834 in opposition to the Democratic Party, favouring a protective tariff and strong central government, succeeded by the Republican Party. **b** a colonist who supported the American Revolution. □ **Whiggery** *n.* **Whiggish** *adj.*

while ● *n.* a period of time considered with respect to its duration, usu. a relatively short one. ● *conj.* **1** during the time that. **2** in spite of the fact that. **3**

when on the contrary; whereas. ● *v.tr.* (foll. by *away*) pass (a period of time) in a leisurely or pleasant manner. □ **all the while** during the whole time (that). **worth while** (or **one's while**) worth the time or effort spent; worth doing, beneficial, profitable, advantageous.

whilst / wailst/ *adv. & conj. esp. Brit.* while.

whim *n.* **1** a spontaneous and unaccountable idea or decision; a fanciful notion. **2** capriciousness.

whimbrel / 'wimbrəl/ *n.* a small curlew, esp. *Numenius phaeopus*, with a striped head and a trilling call.

whimper ● *v.* **1** *intr.* make feeble, or plaintive sounds expressive of fear, pain, or distress. **2** *tr.* say in a whimpering voice. ● *n.* **1** a feeble intermittent cry; a whimpering sound. **2** a dull, disappointing, or anticlimactic note or tone (*the conference ended on a whimper*).

whimsical *adj.* **1** spontaneous; inspired by whim. **2 a** imaginative or playful (*a whimsical sense of humour*). **b** unconventional, fanciful, or quaint (*a whimsical set of furnishings*). □ **whimsicality** *n.* **whimsically** *adv.*

whimsy *n.* (*pl.* **-ies**) **1** an unpredictable, fanciful, or playful quality or condition. **2** a spontaneous or capricious notion or fancy; a whim.

whine ● *n.* **1** a prolonged cry or wail suggesting pain, distress, or complaint. **2** a shrill prolonged sound resembling this. **3 a** a complaining tone of voice. **b** an instance of feeble or undignified complaining. ● *v.* **1** *intr.* emit or utter a whine. **2** *intr.* complain in a querulous tone, esp. about unimportant things. **3** *tr.* say or express in a whining tone. □ **whiner** *n.* **whiningly** *adv.* **whiny** *adj.* (**-ier, -iest**)

whinny ● *n.* (*pl.* **-ies**) **1** a gentle high-pitched neigh, usu. expressing pleasure. **2** a sound resembling this. ● *v.intr.* (**-ies, -ied**) give a whinny.

whip ● *n.* **1** a flexible switch or a rod with a leather lash attached, used for urging animals on or flogging. **2** a member of a political party appointed to monitor and control its conduct and tactics and to ensure the attendance and voting of its members in debates. **3** a light fluffy dessert made with whipped cream or beaten eggs. **4** a slender unbranched shoot. ● *v.* (**whipped, whipping**) **1** *tr.* beat or urge with a whip. **2** *tr.* (usu. foll. by *into*) bring (a person) into a usu. specified condition or state (*she whipped us into shape*). **3** *tr.* beat (cream or eggs etc.) into a froth. **4** *intr.* move suddenly or quickly. **5** *tr. informal* throw or propel with great force or speed. **6** *tr. slang* defeat convincingly. **7** *tr. Fishing* cast a line over (a stretch of water) repeatedly. **8** *tr.* wind rope or twine around (something) to bind it. □ **whip off 1** remove (an article of clothing) hurriedly. **2** produce or complete in a short amount of time. **whip on** urge into action. **whip out** draw out or remove suddenly (*whipped out a knife*). **whip up 1** prepare in a short amount of time or with ease (*whipped up a meal*). **2** excite or stir up (feeling etc.). □ **whip-like** *adj.* **whipper** *n.*

whiplash ● *n.* damage to the neck or spine caused by a severe jerk of the head, esp. as in a car accident. ● *v.* **1** *tr.* shake or jerk violently causing a whiplash effect. **2** *intr.* move suddenly and forcefully like the lash of a whip.

whipped *adj.* **1** that has been whipped. **2** *N Amer. informal* tired, exhausted.

whipped cream *n.* heavy cream beaten until stiff and used as a topping or filling for desserts.

whipped topping *n.* an artificial substitute for whipped cream.

whipper-snapper *n.* **1** a presumptuous or intrusive young person. **2** a child.

Whippersnipper *n. Cdn & Austral. proprietary* a hand-held motorized garden tool used to trim grass, weeds, etc.

whippet / 'wɪpɪt/ *n.* a dog of a breed that is a cross between a greyhound and a terrier or spaniel, used for racing.

whipping *n.* **1** a beating or flogging with a whip. **2** *Sport* a sound defeat.

whipping boy *n.* a scapegoat.

whipping cream *n.* heavy cream, usu. with 35% milk fat, often with stabilizers and thickeners added so as to be suitable for whipping.

whippoorwill / 'wɪpər,wɪl/ *n.* a N American bird, *Caprimulgus vociferus*, with a loud cry uttered repeatedly at dusk and during the night.

whippy *adj.* (**-ier, -iest**) flexible, springy.

whipsaw esp. *N Amer.* ● *n.* **1** a saw with a narrow blade usu. operated by two people pulling at either end of its frame. **2** something that is disadvantageous in two ways (*the whipsaw of inflation and recession*). ● *v.tr.* (*past part.* **-sawed** or **-sawn**) **1** *tr.* cut with a whipsaw. **2** *tr.* (usu. in *passive*) *slang* subject to two opposing and usu. harmful influences or forces. **3** *intr.* fluctuate between two extremes.

whir *var. of* WHIRR.

whirl ● *v.* **1** *tr. & intr.* turn around rapidly, esp. repeatedly. **2** *tr. & intr.* (often foll. by *away*) convey or travel swiftly, esp. in a vehicle. **3** *intr.* **a** (of the brain, senses, etc.) seem to spin; be dizzy or confused. **b** (of thoughts etc.) follow each other in bewildering succession. ● *n.* **1** a swift circling or whirling movement (*she vanished in a whirl of dust*). **2** *informal* an attempt (*give it a whirl*). **3** a state of intense activity (*the political whirl*). **4** a state of confusion (*my mind is in a whirl*). □ **whirler** *n.* **whirling** *adj.*

whirligig *n.* **1** anything having a rapid circling movement. **2** any of various toys that are whirled or spun around, such as a toy with four arms like miniature windmill sails which whirl around when it is moved through the air. **3** anything characterized by constant frantic activity or change (*the whirligig of time*). **4** (in full **whirligig beetle**) any of various freshwater beetles of the family Gyrinidae, which have paddle-like legs and are found in large numbers circling rapidly over the surface of still water.

whirling dervish *n.* a member of any of various Muslim religious fraternities who has taken vows of poverty and austerity and whose order includes the practice of dancing or howling as a spiritual exercise.

whirlpool *n.* **1 a** a powerful circular eddy in a body of water that draws or sucks objects to its centre, usu. caused by the meeting of adverse currents. **b** anything resembling this, such as a destructive or absorbing agency or a turbulent swirling mass. **2** a large bathtub with underwater jets of hot, usu. aerated, water, used for physiotherapy or relaxation.

whirlwind *n.* **1** a small rotating storm of wind in which a vertical usu. funnel-shaped column of air whirls rapidly around a core of low pressure and moves progressively over land or water. **2** (*attrib.*) very rapid or hasty (*a whirlwind romance*). **3** a confused tumultuous process. **4** an active, impetuous, or reckless person. □ **reap the whirlwind** suffer the consequences of one's own offence.

whirr ● *n.* a continuous droning, humming, or buzzing sound like that of machinery or the fluttering of a bird's wings. ● *v.intr.* (**whirred, whirring**) **1** make this sound. **2** move swiftly with such a sound (*the cyclists whirred away*).

whisk ● *v.* **1** *tr.* brush lightly with a sweeping movement (*she whisked the hair from her face*). **2** *tr.* (usu. foll. by *away, off*) **a** take, seize, or remove with a sudden sweeping motion. **b** convey quickly. **3** *tr.* **a** whip (cream, eggs, etc.) with a whisk. **b** (foll. by *in*, *together*) add or combine (ingredients) with a whisk. **4** *intr.* go quickly; rush, dart (*a car whisked past*). ● *n.* **1** a whisking action or motion. **2** a utensil consisting of wire hoops attached to a handle, used for beating eggs or cream etc. lightly. **3** (in full **whisk broom**) a bundle of straw or bristles bound at one end around a usu. short handle, used to sweep dust or debris from a surface.

whisker *n.* **1 a** any of the hairs growing on a person's face. **b** (in *pl.*) these hairs collectively growing on esp. a man's chin, upper lip, or cheek; a moustache or beard. **2** each of a number of long projecting hairs growing on the face of many mammals, such as dogs, cats, and seals. **3** *informal* a small distance or amount; a narrow margin (*won by a whisker*). □ **whiskered** *adj.* **whiskery** *adj.*

whisky *n.* (also **whiskey**) (*pl.* **-ies** or **-eys**) **1** an alcoholic liquor distilled esp. from rye, malted barley, or corn. **2** a drink of this. ¶Irish whiskey and bourbon whiskey are usually spelled *whiskey*.

whisky blanc /ˌwɪskiˈblɒŋk/ *n. Cdn (Que.)* a type of colourless whisky made from distilled grain alcohol.

whisky-jack *n. Cdn* = GREY JAY.

whisky trader *n. Cdn (West) & US Northwest hist.* a person selling whisky illegally, esp. a nomadic American outlaw trading with Aboriginal peoples north of the Montana border in the late 19th c.

whisper ● *v.* **1** *tr. & intr.* say or speak in a soft breathy voice without vibration of the vocal cords. **2 a** *intr.* speak or converse in private, esp. to conspire or to exchange rumours about a person or thing. **b** *tr.* (in *passive*) be rumoured. **3** *intr.* (of leaves, wind, water, etc.) make a soft rustling or murmuring sound that resembles whispering. ● *n.* **1** whispering speech (*talking in whispers*). **2** something whispered. **3 a** a rumour or piece of gossip. **b** (usu. with *neg.*) a suggestion or hint. **4** a soft rustling or whispering sound. □ **whisperer** *n.* **whispering** *n.*

whist /wɪst/ *n.* a card game for four players grouped into pairs, in which points are scored according to the number of tricks won and, in some forms, by the highest trumps or honours held by each pair.

whistle ● *n.* **1** a clear shrill sound made by forcing breath through the narrow opening made by contracting the lips or through a space between the teeth constricted by the tip of the tongue. **2** a similar sound made by a bird, the wind, a projectile, etc. **3 a** a small device that produces such a sound when blown, used esp. as a signal. **b** a simple musical instrument resembling a pipe or recorder. ● *v.* **1** *intr.* sound or emit a whistle. **2** *intr.* give a signal or call for attention or express surprise, approval, or derision by whistling. **3** *tr. & intr.* produce (a tune etc.) consisting of a series of whistled sounds of various pitch. **4** *tr.* summon, announce, or signal by whistling or blowing a whistle (*the referee whistled the play dead*). **5** *intr.* (of a kettle, train, etc.) emit a clear shrill sound produced by the passage of steam through a small opening. **6** *intr.* (of the wind, a projectile, etc.) move or fly past with a whistle. □ **as clean** (or **clear** or **dry**) **as a whistle** very clean or clear or dry. **blow the whistle on** *informal* **1** call attention to (a questionable or illicit activity) in order to have it brought to an end. **2** inform on (those responsible) for such an activity. **whistle Dixie** *N Amer.* be overly optimistic. **whistle in the dark** pretend to be unafraid.

whistle-blower *n.* a person who calls attention to a questionable or illicit activity in an attempt to have it brought to an end. □ **whistle-blowing** *adj. & n.*

whistler *n.* **1 a** a person who whistles. **b** a thing which makes a whistling sound. **2** any bird of the genus *Pachycephala*, with a whistling cry.

whistle stop *n.* **1** *N Amer.* **a** the train station of a small town at which trains stop only when given a particular signal indicating that a passenger is waiting to board. **b** a small or unimportant town. **2** a politician's brief stop in a town to give an electioneering speech during a campaign tour. **3** (*attrib.*) designating a journey or tour with brief stops made at many of the small towns along the way.

whit *n.* (usu. with *neg.*) the least possible amount (*not a whit better*).

white ● *adj.* **1** having a colour like that of fresh snow or milk. **2** (esp. of the skin) approaching such a colour; pale, esp. in the face. **3** (also **White**) a designating or belonging to any of various peoples having light-coloured skin, usu. of European origin. **b** of, relating to, or characteristic of white people or their culture. **c** predominantly inhabited by or consisting of white people (*a white neighbourhood*). **4 a** (of hair) having lost its colour, esp. in old age. **b** (of a person) white-haired. **5** (of wine) made from white grapes or dark grapes with the skins removed, and of an amber, golden, or pale yellow colour. **6** (of coffee) having milk or cream added. **7** (of metal or an object made of metal) silvery grey and lustrous. ● *n.* **1** a white colour. **2** the white or light-coloured part of anything. **3** the translucent viscous fluid surrounding the yolk of an egg, which turns white when cooked; albumen. **4** the visible part of the eyeball around the iris. **5 a** a white clothing or material (*dressed in white*). **b** (in *pl.*) white clothes as worn in tennis, as a naval uniform, etc. **c** (in *pl.*) white linen or clothing etc. separated from coloured laundry for washing. **6** (also **White**) a member of a light-skinned race. □ **white out 1** make or become white. **2** (often in *passive*) obliterate or conceal with whiteness, as with snow. **3** cover (a typewritten or printed error) with correction fluid. □ **whitely** *adv.* **whiteness** *n.* **whitish** *adj.* **whity** *adj.*

white birch *n.* a birch tree, *Betula papyrifera*, with white bark that peels in strips, traditionally used by some N American Aboriginal peoples for making canoes.

white blood cell *n.* (also **white cell**) any of various colourless nucleated cells found in the blood, lymph, and connective tissue, which produce antibodies and which migrate through the walls of vessels to the sites of injuries, where they surround and isolate dead tissue, foreign bodies, and bacteria.

whiteboard *n.* a board with a white surface, which can be written on with a marker and wiped clean.

white bread ● *n.* bread of a light colour, made from usu. bleached wheat flour from which the bran and germ have been removed. ● *adj.* (**white-bread**) *N Amer.* **1** of, belonging to, or representative of the white middle class; bourgeois. **2** conventional, inoffensive; bland.

whitecap *n.* (usu. in *pl.*) a wave or breaker with a foamy white crest.

white cedar *n.* any of several N American conifers, esp. the eastern white cedar, *Thuja occidentalis*.

white chocolate *n.* a mixture of cocoa butter, milk, and sugar, of a consistency like chocolate.

white Christmas *n.* Christmas with snow on the ground.

whitecoat *n.* **1** a young seal, having a coat of white fur. **2** the fur or skin of this seal. **3** a white lab coat, worn by doctors, scientists, laboratory workers, etc. □ **men in white coats** *jocular* attendants in a mental asylum. □ **white-coated** *adj.* (in sense 3).

white-collar *adj.* **1** designating, pertaining to, or performing non-manual, esp. clerical, administrative, or professional, work. **2 a** (of a crime) non-violent, esp. involving fraud, embezzlement, income tax evasion, etc. **b** (of a person) guilty of such a crime.

white elephant *n.* an item etc. that is no longer useful or wanted, esp. one that is difficult to maintain or dispose of.

white-faced *adj.* **1** (of an animal etc.) having white facial markings or a naturally white face. **2** having a face that is or has become pale, as with fear. **3** having a face that has been made white with makeup.

whitefish *n.* (*pl.* same or **-fishes**) **1** any freshwater fish of the genus *Coregonus* etc., of the trout family, and used esp. for food, esp. *Coregonus clupeaformis* of lakes and large rivers throughout northern N America. **2** (**white fish**) any fish with pale flesh, such as cod, haddock, plaice, etc.

white flag *n.* the flag traditionally used to signal surrender or a truce. □ **raise** (or **wave** or **run up**) **the white flag** admit defeat in an argument, contest, etc.

white flour *n.* fine wheat flour, usu. bleached, from which most of the bran and germ have been removed.

whitefly *n.* (*pl.* **-flies**) any small insect of the family Aleyrodidae, having wings covered with white powder and feeding on the sap of shrubs, crops, etc.

white gold *n.* any of various silver-coloured alloys of gold used in jewellery.

white goods *n.pl.* **1** household linen. **2** large domestic electrical equipment, such as refrigerators, washing machines, and other appliances.

whitehead *n.* a white or white-topped pimple.

white heat *n.* **1** the temperature at which metal radiates a white light. **2** a state of intense passion or activity.

white hope *n.* a person expected to bring success to an organization or group etc.

white-hot *adj.* **1** (of metal) at white heat. **2** in an intense emotional state, esp. one of passion or anger.

White House *n.* **1 a** the official residence of the US President in Washington, DC. **b** the US President or the executive branch of the US government. **2** the Russian parliament building.

white knight *n.* **1** a person who comes to the aid of someone. **2** a welcome company bidding for a company facing an unwelcome takeover bid.

white-knuckle *attrib.adj.* **1** (esp. of a flight or amusement park ride) causing fear or terror. **2** (of a participant) feeling fear or terror.

white lie *n.* a harmless or trivial untruth, esp. one told in order to avoid hurting someone's feelings.

white light *n.* colourless light, e.g. sunlight.

white matter *n.* the whitish tissue in the vertebrate central nervous system consisting mainly of nerve fibres, situated below the grey matter of the cortex and next to the core of the spinal cord.

white meat *n.* **1** any meat that is pale when cooked, such as veal or the white meat of poultry. **2** the breast meat of poultry.

whiten *v.tr. & intr.* make or become white. □ **whitening** *n.*

whitener *n.* **1** a thing that whitens, such as a bleaching agent for clothes or a toothpaste. **2** a soluble powder added to coffee as a substitute for cream.

white noise *n.* noise having nearly equal intensities at all the frequencies of its range.

whiteout *n.* **1 a** a weather condition in which the horizon and physical features of snow-covered country are indistinguishable due to uniform light diffusion. **b** a dense blizzard that reduces visibility. **2** = CORRECTION FLUID.

white pages *n.pl.* (usu. treated as *sing.*) a telephone directory or section of this containing the phone numbers and addresses of residential and business subscribers listed alphabetically.

whitepainting *n. Cdn* the renovation or reclamation of a house, building, or neighbourhood in a derelict part of a city's core. □ **whitepainter** *n.*

white paper *n.* **1** (also **White Paper**) an official report summarizing the results of an investigation into an issue, policy, or proposed legislation, and outlining the government's intention regarding it. **2** an authoritative report on an item of particular interest issued by any organization.

white pelican *n.* a pelican with white plumage, *Pelecanus erythrorhynchos*, breeding from the Prairie provinces south to Central America.

white perch *n.* a fish related to the basses, *Morone americana*, of eastern N America.

white picket fence *n.* see PICKET FENCE.

white pine *n.* any of several N American pines with needles in bundles of five and soft wood.

White Rock *n.* a variety of white Plymouth Rock chickens.

White Russian ● *n.* **1** a Belarussian. **2** a drink made with vodka, cream, and crème de cacao or coffee-flavoured liqueur. ● *adj.* Belarussian.

white sauce *n.* a sauce made with flour, melted butter, and milk or cream.

white shark *n.* = GREAT WHITE SHARK.

white slave *n.* a woman who is forced or sold into prostitution, usu. abroad. □ **white slavery** *n.*

white spruce *n.* any of several spruce trees of N America, esp. *Picea glauca*, found across Canada, and used for lumber and wood pulp.

white stuff *n. N Amer. informal* snow.

white sugar *n.* refined sugar from which the molasses has been removed.

white supremacy *n.* a belief that whites are innately superior to non-whites. □ **white supremacist** *n.*

white-tailed deer *n.* (also **whitetail, whitetail deer**) a deer, *Odocoileus virginianus*, which has a white underside to the tail and is found from Canada to northern S America.

white tie *n.* **1** a man's white bow tie worn as part of full evening dress. **2** full formal evening dress (also *attrib.*: *white-tie affair*).

white trash *n.* (*pl.* same) *N Amer. derogatory* **1** a member of the class of poor lower-class whites. **2** the members of this class collectively. **3** (*attrib.*; **white-trash**) belonging or pertaining to or characteristic of the white lower class.

whitewall *n.* (in full **whitewall tire**) an automotive tire with a white side wall.

whitewash ● *n.* **1** a solution of lime and water, or of whiting, size, and water, for whitening walls etc. **2** something that conceals faults or mistakes in order to clear or uphold the reputation of a person or institution. **3** a victory in which the opponent fails to score or is defeated by a lopsided margin. ● *v.tr.* **1** cover with whitewash. **2** attempt to clear or uphold the reputation of (a person, institution, etc.) by concealment of faults or mistakes. **3** *Sport* defeat convincingly, esp. in a shutout.

whitewater ● *n.* **1** a stretch of turbulent foamy water in a river caused by a steep drop or by large rocks in the riverbed. **2** the surf or a stretch of clear or frothy sea water, esp. on a beach or shoal. ● *attrib.adj.* **1** designating a river or stretch of a river where there is whitewater. **2** designating an activity or event that takes place on such a river (*whitewater rafting*). **3** designating a person who participates in such an activity or event.

white whale *n.* = BELUGA 1.

white-winged scoter *n.* a mainly black scoter, *Melanitta fusca*, with a white patch on the wing and a white circle around each eye.

whitey *n.* (also **Whitey**) (*pl.* **-eys**) *slang offensive* **1** a white person. **2** white people collectively.

white Zinfandel *n.* a pale pink, sweet, often slightly carbonated California wine made from Zinfandel grapes and other varieties.

whither *adv. & conj. archaic* **1** to what place? **2** to what result?

whiting *n.* **1** any of various fishes of the cod family with pearly-white flesh and white coloration. **2** ground chalk used to make whitewash, metal polish, putty, etc.

whittle *v.* **1** *tr. & intr.* cut or shape (wood etc.) by carving thin shavings from the surface with a knife. **2** *intr.* **a** (often foll. by *away*) make repeated reductions to (*whittled away at the deficit*). **b** (often foll. by *down*) reduce or diminish by repeated subtractions (*whittled down the waiting list*).

whiz (also **whizz**) *informal* ● *n.* **1** the humming or buzzing sound made by the friction of a body moving quickly through the air. **2** (also **wiz**) *informal* a person who is remarkable or skilful in some usu. specified respect (*is a whiz at chess*). **3** *slang* an act of urinating. ● *v.* (**whizzes, whizzed, whizzing**) **1** *intr.* make or emit a sibilant humming or buzzing sound. **2** *intr.* move with or as if with such a sound. **3** *tr.* cause to make such a sound, esp. by rotating rapidly in a blender or food processor etc. **4** *intr. slang* urinate. □ **whizzer** *n.*

whiz-bang *adj.* (also **whizz-bang**) *informal* **1** fast-paced, lively. **2** technologically innovative or advanced (*whiz-bang computer graphics*).

whiz kid *n. informal* an exceptionally bright or successful young person.

WHO *abbr.* World Health Organization.

who *pron.* (*obj.* **whom** or *informal* **who**; *possess.* **whose**) **1 a** what or which person or persons? (*who called?*; *you know who it was*; *whom or who did you see?*). ¶In the last example *whom* is correct but *who* is common in less formal contexts. **b** what sort of person or persons? (*who am I to object?*). **2** (a person) that (*anyone who wishes can come*; *the woman whom you met*; *the man who you saw*). ¶In the last two examples *whom* is correct but *who* is common in less formal contexts.

whoa /wo:/ *interj.* **1** commanding a horse etc. to stop. **2** *jocular* demanding a person to stop or slow down.

who'd *contraction* **1** who had. **2** who would.

whodunit /hu:ˈdʌnɪt/ *n.* (also **whodunnit**) *informal* a crime story or murder mystery.

whoever *pron.* (*obj.* **whomever** or *informal* **whoever**; *possess.* **whosever**) **1** the or any person or persons who (*whoever comes is welcome*). **2** (usu. foll. by *or*) *informal* any or some similar person (*give it to me or whoever*).

whole ● *adj.* **1** not less than; entire (*waited a whole year*; *the whole school knows*). **2** unbroken, intact (*swallowed it whole*). **3** containing all the proper or essential

constituents. ● *n.* **1** a thing complete in itself. **2** all there is of a thing (*spent the whole of the summer by the sea*). ● *adv.* in every way; entirely (*that's a whole different matter*). □ **as a whole** in its entirety. **on the whole** taking everything relevant into account; in general (*it was, on the whole, a good report*). **a whole new** (or **different**) **ball game** *informal* **1** a separate issue or matter very different from the one currently under discussion or consideration. **2** a new situation very different from the present one. **the whole nine yards** *slang* everything. □ **wholeness** *n.*

whole blood *n.* blood to which only an anticoagulant has been added after it is donated, used for transfusions.

whole cloth ● *n.* cloth of the full size as manufactured, as opposed to a cut piece used to make a garment. ● *adj.* (usu. **whole-cloth**) *N Amer.* not based on fact. □ **out of whole cloth** *N Amer.* with no basis in fact or reality (*he invents rumours out of whole cloth*).

whole food *n.* food that has not been unnecessarily processed or refined, such as brown rice.

whole-grain *adj.* (of cereal products) containing the whole grain, including the bran and the germ.

wholehearted *adj.* **1** (of a person) completely devoted or committed. **2** (of an action etc.) done with all possible effort, attention, or sincerity. □ **wholeheartedly** *adv.* **wholeheartedness** *n.*

whole milk *n.* milk which has not been skimmed.

whole note *n. N Amer. Music* a note having the time value of four quarter notes, represented by a hollow ring.

whole number *n.* a number without fractions.

whole rest *n. N Amer. Music* a rest having the time value of a whole note.

wholesale ● *n.* the selling of goods in large quantities to be retailed by others. ● *adj.* **1** of, pertaining to, or involved in wholesale (*a wholesale distributor*). **2** extensive (*wholesale changes*). ● *adv.* **1** at a wholesale price (*I can get it for you wholesale*). **2** on a large scale. ● *v.* **1** *tr.* sell (goods) wholesale. **2** *intr.* be sold wholesale, esp. for a specified price. □ **wholesaler** *n.*

wholesome *adj.* **1** promoting physical health or well-being (*wholesome food*). **2** promoting mental or moral health (*wholesome pursuits*). **3** indicative of good health (*wholesome appearance*). □ **wholesomely** *adv.* **wholesomeness** *n.*

whole wheat *n.* wheat with none of the bran or germ removed (also *attrib.*: *whole wheat flour*).

wholism *var. of* HOLISM.

who'll *contraction* who will; who shall.

wholly *adv.* **1** entirely, completely. **2** exclusively.

wholly owned *adj.* designating a company whose shares are all owned by another company (*wholly owned subsidiary*).

whom *objective case of* WHO.

whomever *objective case of* WHOEVER.

whomp *esp. N Amer. informal* ● *n.* a loud dull heavy sound. ● *v.* **1** *tr.* bang or strike heavily with such a sound. **2** *intr.* make such a sound.

whoop /wu:p, wɒp, hu:p/ ● *n.* **1** a loud excited cry. **2** a long rasping intake of air in whooping cough. ● *v.intr.* utter a whoop. □ **no big whoop** *N Amer. slang* no big deal. **whoop it up** *esp. N Amer. informal* engage in revelry.

whoop-de-do /ˈwu:pdəˌdu:/ (also **whoop-de-doo**) *N Amer. slang* ● *n.* **1** a fuss, a commotion. **2** a party or other festive event. ● *interj.* expressing exultation or ironic indifference.

whoopee *informal* ● *interj.* /wʊˈpi:/ expressing exuberant joy. ● n. /ˈwʊpi/ exuberant enjoyment or revelry. □ **make whoopee** informal **1** rejoice noisily or hilariously. **2** make love.

whoopee cushion n. a rubber cushion used in a practical joke, that when sat on makes a sound like the breaking of wind.

whooper /ˈwuːpər, huːpər/ n. a whooping crane or swan.

whooping cough /ˈwuːpɪŋ, ˈhuːpɪŋ/ n. an infectious bacterial disease, esp. of children, with a series of short violent coughs followed by a whoop.

whooping crane n. a large, endangered, mainly white, N American crane, *Grus americana*, which passes through the prairies in migration between N Alberta and Texas.

whooping swan n. a swan, *Cygnus cygnus*, with a characteristic whooping sound in flight.

whoops interj. informal expressing surprise or apology, esp. on making an obvious mistake.

whoop-up n. Cdn informal a noisy celebration or party.

whoosh /wuːʃ, wʊʃ/ ● v.intr. & tr. (cause to) move with a rushing sound. ● n. a sudden movement with by a rushing sound. ● interj. an exclamation imitating this.

whop var. of WHAP.

whopper n. slang **1** something big. **2** a blatant or gross lie.

whopping adj. slang very big.

whore /hɔr, hʊr/ ● n. **1** a prostitute. **2** derogatory a promiscuous woman. ● v.intr. **1** frequent whores. **2** act as a whore. □ **whoredom** n.

who're contraction who are.

whorehouse n. a brothel.

whorl /wɔrl, wɜrl/ n. **1** a ring of leaves etc. around a stem of a plant. **2** one turn of a spiral, esp. on a shell. **3** a coil. **4** a complete circle in a fingerprint. □ **whorled** adj.

who's contraction who is.

whose ● pron. of or belonging to which person (*whose is this book?*). ● adj. of whom or which (*whose book is this?; the house whose roof was damaged*).

whosever possess. of WHOEVER.

who's who n. **1** the significant people in a given field. **2** a list with facts about notable persons.

who've contraction who have.

whump ● n. a dull thudding sound, as of a body landing heavily. ● v. **1** intr. make or move or knock with such a sound. **2** tr. strike heavily or with such a sound.

whup v.tr. esp. US **1** whip, beat. **2** defeat soundly.

why ● adv. **1 a** for what reason or purpose (*why did you do it?*). **b** on what grounds (*why do you say that?*). **2** for which (*the reasons why I did it*). ● interj. expressing: **1** surprised discovery or recognition (*why, it's you!*). **2** impatience (*why, of course I do!*). **3** reflection (*why, yes, I think so*). **4** objection (*why, what is wrong with it?*). ● n. (pl. **whys**) a reason or explanation (*whys and wherefores*). □ **why so?** on what grounds?; for what reason or purpose?

WI abbr. **1** West Indies. **2** WOMEN'S INSTITUTE. **3** Wisconsin.

Wicca /ˈwɪkə/ n. modern witchcraft, a goddess-worshipping, shamanistic nature religion. □ **Wiccan** adj. & n.

wick ● n. a strip or thread of fibrous or spongy material feeding a flame with fuel in a candle, lamp, etc. ● v.tr. (often foll. by away) esp. N Amer. (esp. of fabric) absorb or draw off (moisture).

wicked adj. (**wickeder**, **wickedest**) **1** sinful; given to or involving immorality. **2** spiteful, ill-tempered;

intending or intended to give pain. **3** playfully malicious. **4** informal foul; very bad (*wicked weather*). **5** slang excellent. □ **wickedly** adv. **wickedness** n.

wicker n. braided twigs or osiers etc. as material for chairs, baskets, mats, etc.

wickerwork n. **1** wicker. **2** things made of wicker.

wicket n. **1** N Amer. a station for an employee in a ticket office, bank, etc., often closed by a window. **2** (in full **wicket door** or **wicket gate**) a small door or gate esp. beside or in a larger one or closing the lower part only of a doorway. **3** Cricket a set of three stumps with the bails in position defended by a batsman. **4** N Amer. a croquet hoop.

wickiup /ˈwɪkiˌʌp/ n. a hut used by some N American Indians, consisting of a frame covered with grass etc.

wide adj. **1 a** measuring much or more than other things of the same kind across or from side to side. **b** more than is needed (*a wide margin*). **2** (following a measurement) in width (*a metre wide*). **3** extensive (*has wide experience*). **4** not tight or close or restricted; loose. **5** not specialized. **6** open to the full extent (*wide eyes*). **7 a** (foll. by of) not within a reasonable distance of. **b** at a considerable distance from a point or mark. **8** (in comb.) extending over the whole of (*nationwide*). □ **wideness** n.

wide-angle attrib.adj. (of a lens) having a short focal length and hence a field covering a wide angle.

wide-area network n. Computing a communications network, typically between buildings or different sites. Abbr.: **WAN**.

wide awake adj. **1** fully awake. **2** informal wary.

wide-band adj. having a wide band of frequencies or wavelengths.

wide-body n. (often attrib.) a large jet with a cabin divided by two aisles. □ **wide-bodied** adj.

wide-eyed adj. surprised or naive.

widely adv. **1** far apart (*widely spaced*). **2** extensively (*widely read*). **3** by many people (*widely accepted*). **4** to a large degree (*holds a widely different view*).

widen v.tr. & intr. make or become wider.

wide open adj. **1** fully open. **2** stretching over an outdoor expanse (*wide open spaces*). **3** (esp. of a contest) having an unpredictable outcome. **4** (predic.: often foll. by to) exposed or vulnerable (esp. to attack).

wide-ranging adj. covering an extensive range.

wide receiver n. (also **wideout**) Football a player positioned on the wide side of the offensive line used mainly to receive passes.

wide-screen attrib.adj. designed with or for a screen presenting a wide field of vision relative to its height.

widespread adj. widely distributed or disseminated.

wide world n. (prec. by the) all the world great as it is.

widget n. informal any gadget or device.

widow n. **1** a woman whose husband has died and who has not remarried. **2** informal a woman whose husband is often away on a specified activity (*golf widow*). **3** the short last line of a paragraph at the top of a page or column (compare ORPHAN n. 3). □ **widowhood** n.

widowed adj. bereft by the death of a spouse (*my widowed mother*).

widower n. a man who has lost his wife by death and has not married again.

widow-maker n. N Amer. & Austral. slang **1** a dead branch caught high in a tree which may fall on a person below. **2** any dangerous thing usu. operated by people, e.g. an aircraft, piece of equipment, etc.

widow's walk n. N Amer. a railed or balustraded

platform built on the roof, orig. in New England houses, esp. for giving a good view of the sea.

width *n.* **1** measurement or distance from side to side. **2** a large extent. **3** a strip of material of a particular width (*you'll need two widths of fabric for each curtain*). **4** the distance between the long sides of a swimming pool. □ **widthways** *adv.* **widthwise** *adv.*

wield *v.tr.* **1** hold and use (a weapon or tool). **2** exert or command (power or authority etc.). □ **wielder** *n.*

wiener *n. esp. N Amer.* **1** a frankfurter. **2** = WEENIE 3.

wiener roast *n. N Amer.* an outdoor social gathering at which wieners are roasted or boiled over a fire.

Wiener schnitzel /ˈviːnər/ *n.* a breaded and fried pork or veal cutlet.

wienie *var. of* WEENIE.

wife *n.* (*pl.* **wives**) a married woman esp. in relation to her husband. □ **wifehood** *n.* **wifeless** *adj.* **wifely** *adj.*

wig *n.* **1** an artificial head of hair esp. to conceal baldness or as a disguise or part of a costume, or worn by a judge or lawyer. **2** a hairpiece. □ **wig out** (**wigged**, **wigging**) lose control of one's emotions.□ **wigged** *adj.* (also in *comb.*). **wigless** *adj.*

wiggle *informal* ● *v.intr. & tr.* move irregularly and quickly from side to side etc. ● *n.* an act of wiggling.□ **wiggler** *n.*

wiggly *adj.* (**-ier**, **-iest**) *informal* **1** moving with a wiggle. **2** having small irregular bends (*a wiggly line*).

wigwam /ˈwɪgwɒm/ *n.* (among some N American Aboriginal peoples) a dome-shaped house consisting of bent saplings stuck in the ground and covered with birch bark.

wild ● *adj.* **1** (of an animal or plant) in its original natural state; not domesticated or cultivated. **2** not civilized. **3** (of an area of land etc.) not cultivated or settled by people. **4** unrestrained, disorderly (*a wild youth*; *wild hair*). **5** tempestuous (*a wild night*). **6 a** intensely eager; excited, frantic (*wild with excitement*; *wild delight*). **b** (of looks, appearance, etc.) indicating distraction. **c** (foll. by *about*) *informal* enthusiastically devoted to. **7** *informal* infuriated, angry. **8** haphazard, ill-aimed, rash (*a wild guess*; *a wild shot*). **9** (of a horse etc.) shy; easily startled. **10** *informal* exciting, delightful. **11** *informal* amazing, incredible (*a wild story*). **12** (of a card) having any rank chosen by the player holding it (*the joker is wild*). ● *adv.* in a wild manner (*shooting wild*). ● *n.* (usu. in *pl.*) a wilderness.□ **in the wild** in an uncultivated etc. state. **in** (or **out in**) **the wilds** *informal* far from normal habitation. **run wild** grow or stray unchecked or undisciplined. **wild and woolly** uncouth; lacking refinement. □ **wildly** *adv.* **wildness** *n.*

wild card *n.* **1** a card having any rank chosen by the player holding it. **2** *Computing* a character that will match any character or sequence of characters in a file name etc. **3** an extra player or team chosen for a competition at the organizers' discretion after the regular places have been taken. **4** an unpredictable person or thing.

wild carrot *n.* = QUEEN ANNE'S LACE.

wildcat ● *n.* **1** a smallish cat of a non-domesticated kind; esp. *Felis sylvestris* of Eurasia and Africa, with a grey and black coat and bushy tail, or (*N Amer.*) a bobcat. **2** a hot-tempered or violent person. **3** an exploratory oil well. **4** a sudden and unofficial strike. ● *adj.* (*attrib.*) **1** esp. *N Amer.* reckless; financially unsound. **2** (of a strike) called at short notice, usu. without union backing.

wildcatter *n. N Amer.* **1** a prospector who sinks wild-

cat oil wells. **2** a person who promotes or engages in risky business enterprises. **3** a wildcat striker.

wild cucumber *n.* a climbing plant of the cucumber family, *Echinocystis lobata*, found east of the Rockies and bearing a prickly fleshy fruit.

wildebeest /ˈwɪldə,biːst, ˈvɪl–/ *n.* = GNU.

wilderness *n.* **1** a wild, uncultivated, and uninhabited region (often *attrib.*: *wilderness area*). **2** (foll. by *of*) a confused assemblage of things. □ **voice in the wilderness** an unheeded advocate of reform.

wildfire *n.* a destructive or uncontrollable fire, esp. in a forest. □ **spread like wildfire** spread quickly.

wildflower *n.* a flowering plant growing in a natural state without human intervention.

wildfowl *n.* (*pl.* same) a game bird, esp. an aquatic one.

wild goose chase *n.* a foolish or hopeless and unproductive quest.

wild grape *n.* any of several species of grape, *Vitis*, found esp. in eastern N America.

wild horse *n.* **1** a horse not domesticated or broken in. **2** (in *pl.*) *informal* even the most powerful influence etc. (*wild horses couldn't keep me away!*).

wilding *n. US* the activity or an instance of a gang of youths rampaging violently through the streets, parks, etc., attacking or mugging people at random along the way.

wildlife *n.* wild animals (often *attrib.*: *wildlife sanctuary*).

wild oat *n.* a European grass, *Avena fatua*, naturalized in N America, similar to the cultivated oat.

wild pitch *n. Baseball* a pitch not hit by the batter and not stopped by the catcher, enabling a baserunner to advance.

wild rice *n.* any tall grass of the genus *Zizania*, yielding edible grains.

wild rose *n.* any of several species of uncultivated rose, e.g. *Rosa acicularis*, the floral emblem of Alberta.

Wild West *n.* the western regions of the US in the 19th c., when they were lawless frontier districts.

wildwood *n.* uncultivated or unfrequented woodland.

wile *n.* a stratagem; a trick or cunning procedure.

wilful *adj.* **1** (of an action or state) intentional, deliberate (*wilful disobedience*). **2** headstrong. □ **wilfully** *adv.* **wilfulness** *n.*

will[1] *v.aux. & tr.* (*3rd sing. present* **will**; *past* **would**) **1** expressing the future tense in statements, commands, or questions (*you will regret this*). **2** expressing a wish or intention (*I will return soon*). **3** expressing desire, consent, or inclination (*will you have a sandwich?*; *will not open*). **4** expressing ability or capacity (*will hold 2 litres*). **5** expressing habitual or inevitable tendency (*accidents will happen*; *will sit there for hours*). **6** expressing probability or expectation (*that will be my wife*). □ **will do** *informal* expressing willingness to carry out a request. ¶ See SHALL.

will[2] ● *n.* **1** the faculty by which a person decides or is regarded as deciding on and initiating action. **2** (also **willpower**) control exercised by deliberate purpose over impulse; self-control. **3** a deliberate or fixed desire or intention (*a will to live*). **4** the power of effecting one's intentions or dominating others. **5** directions (usu. written) in legal form for the disposition of one's property after death (*make one's will*). **6** disposition toward others (*good will*). **7** what one desires or ordains (*thy will be done*). ● *v.* **1** *tr.* intend (*what God wills*). **2** *tr.* cause by the exercise of willpower (*will it to happen*). **3** *tr.* bequeath by the terms of a will (*shall will my money to charity*). □ **at will** whenever one pleases. **have one's will** obtain what one wants. **what is your will?** what do you wish done? **where there's a will there's a way** determination will overcome any obstacle. **a will of one's own** obstinacy; wilfulness of character. **with the best will in the world** however good one's intentions. **with a will** energetically or resolutely. □ **willed** adj. (also in comb.). **will-less** adj.

willet /ˈwɪlət/ n. (pl. same) a large grey and white N American shorebird with a loud call.

willful var. of WILFUL.

willie var. of WILLY.

willies n.pl. informal nervous discomfort (*gives me the willies*).

willing adj. **1** ready to consent or undertake (*a willing ally; am willing to help*). **2** given, done, etc. by a willing person (*willing help*). □ **willingly** adv. **willingness** n.

will-o'-the-wisp n. **1** phosphorescence seen on marshy ground, perhaps resulting from the combustion of gases. **2** an elusive person. **3** a delusory hope or plan.

willow n. a tree or shrub of the genus *Salix*, with small flowers borne on catkins, and pliant branches yielding osiers for baskets etc.

willow herb n. any plant of the genus *Epilobium*, with narrow leaves and pink or purple flowers.

willow ptarmigan n. (also **willow grouse**) a ptarmigan, *Lagopus lagopus*, with large amounts of white plumage even in summer.

willowy adj. **1** lithe, slender, and graceful. **2** having or bordered by willows.

willpower = WILL² n. 2.

willy n. (also **willie**) (pl. **-ies**) slang the penis.

willy-nilly ● adv. **1** whether one likes it or not. **2** haphazardly, at random. ● adj. existing or occurring willy-nilly.

wilt ● v. **1** intr. (of a plant etc.) wither, droop. **2** intr. (of a person) lose one's energy. **3** tr. cause to wilt. ● n. **1** the action or an act of wilting. **2** a plant disease causing wilting.

wily adj. (**-ier**, **-iest**) crafty, cunning. □ **wiliness** n.

wimp n. informal a feeble or ineffectual person. □ **wimp out** demonstrate one's feebleness by failing to act or by avoiding an undertaking; chicken out. □ **wimpish** adj. **wimpishness** n. **wimpy** adj.

wimple n. a linen or silk headdress covering the neck and the sides of the face, formerly worn by women and still worn by some nuns.

win ● v. (**winning**; past and past part. **won**) **1** tr. acquire or secure as a result of a fight, contest, bet, litigation, or some other effort (*won my admiration*). **2** tr. be victorious in (a fight, game, race, etc.). **3** intr. **a** be the victor; win a race or contest etc. **b** make one's way or become by successful effort. **4** tr. reach by effort (*win the summit*). ● n. a victory in a game or bet etc. □ **win the day** be victorious. **win out** overcome obstacles. **win over** persuade, gain the support of. **you can't win** informal there is no way to succeed. **you can't win them all** informal a resigned expression of consolation on failure. □ **winnable** adj.

wince ● v.intr. grimace, tense, or shrink away involuntarily in pain, embarrassment, or distress. ● n. a wincing movement. □ **wincingly** adv.

winch ● n. **1** a hoist etc. consisting of a horizontal drum or axle around which a rope etc. passes, turned by a crank or motor. **2** a windlass. ● v.tr. lift with a winch.

Winchester /ˈwɪntʃestər/ n. **1** proprietary a breech-loading repeating rifle. **2** (in full **Winchester disk** or **drive**) Computing a (usu. fixed) disk drive in a sealed unit containing a high-capacity hard disk and the read/write heads.

wind¹ ● n. **1 a** air in more or less rapid natural motion, esp. from an area of high pressure to one of low pressure. **b** a current of wind blowing from a specified direction or otherwise defined (*north wind; bitter wind*). **2** breath as needed in physical exertion or in speech. **3** mere empty words; meaningless rhetoric. **4** gas generated in the bowels etc. by indigestion. **5 a** an artificially produced current of air, esp. for sounding an organ or other wind instrument. **b** air stored for use or used as a current. **c** (usu. in pl.) (a player of) a wind instrument. ● v.tr. **1** cause (a person) to have difficulty breathing as a result of exertion or a blow. **2** renew the wind of by rest (*stopped to wind the horses*). **3** make breathe quickly and deeply by exercise. **4** detect the presence of by a scent. □ **before the wind** helped by the wind's force. **close to** (or **near**) **the wind 1** sailing as nearly against the wind as is consistent with using its force. **2** informal verging on indecency or dishonesty. **get wind of 1** detect by smell. **2** begin to suspect; hear a rumour of. **get** (or **have**) **the wind up** informal be alarmed or frightened. **how** (or **which way**) **the wind blows** (or **lies**) **1** what is the state of opinion. **2** what developments are likely. **in the wind** happening or about to happen. **like the wind** swiftly. **on the wind** (of a sound or scent) carried by the wind. **put the wind up** informal alarm or frighten. **take the wind out of a person's sails** frustrate a person by anticipating an action or remark etc. **to the winds** (or **four winds**) **1** in all directions. **2** into a state of abandonment or neglect. **wind and weather** exposure to the effects of the elements. **wind** (or **winds**) **of change** a force or influence for reform. □ **winded** adj. (also in comb.). **windless** adj.

wind² ● v. (past and past part. **wound**) **1** intr. go in a circular, spiral, curved, or crooked course (*the path winds up the hill*). **2** tr. make (one's way) by such a course (*wound their way into our affections*). **3** tr. wrap closely; surround with or as with a coil. **4** tr. & intr. coil. **5** tr. wind up (a clock etc.). **6** tr. hoist or draw with a windlass etc. (*wound the cable car up the mountain*). ● n. **1** a bend or turn in a course. **2** a single turn when winding. □ **wind down 1** lower by winding. **2** (of a mechanism) unwind. **3** (of a person) relax. **4** draw gradually to a close. **wind off** unwind (string, wool, etc.). **wind up 1** coil the whole of (a piece of string etc.). **2** esp. Brit. tighten the coiling or coiled spring of (esp. a clock etc.). **3 a** informal increase the tension or intensity of (*wound myself up to fever pitch*). **b** irritate or provoke (a person) to the point of anger. **4** bring to a conclusion (*wound up his speech*). **5** informal end in a specified state or circumstance (*wound up owing $100*). **6** draw back the arm in preparation for a throw, shot, etc. **wound up** adj. (of a person) excited or tense or angry. □ **winding** n. & adj.

windbag n. informal a person who talks a lot but says little of any value.

windblown adj. **1** carried or made untidy by the wind (*windblown snow*). **2** (of trees) made to grow in a certain shape by strong prevailing winds.

windbreak n. an obstacle, such as a row of trees, a fence, etc., which breaks the wind's force and shelters houses, crops, or animals.

windbreaker n. N Amer. a wind-resistant outer jacket with close-fitting neck, cuffs, and hip band.

windburn n. inflammation of the skin caused by

exposure to wind. ☐ **windburned** *adj.* (also **windburnt**).

wind chill *n.* the cooling effect of wind blowing on a person or surface.

wind chill factor *n.* a measure or scale of the combined effect of low temperature and wind speed on body temperature.

wind chimes *n.pl.* small pieces of glass, metal, etc. suspended so as to tinkle against one another in the wind.

windfall *n.* **1** an unexpected gift of money, piece of good luck, etc. **2** an apple or other fruit blown to the ground by the wind. **3** *N Amer.* **a** a branch or tree blown down by the wind. **b** timber thus blown down.

wind farm *n.* a group of energy-producing windmills or wind turbines.

wind gauge *n.* **1** an anemometer. **2** an apparatus attached to the sights of a gun enabling allowance to be made for the wind in shooting.

wind instrument *n.* a musical instrument in which sound is produced by the player blowing a current of air through or across a mouthpiece.

windjammer *n.* a merchant sailing ship.

windlass /ˈwɪndləs/ ● *n.* a machine with a horizontal axle for hauling or hoisting. ● *v.tr.* hoist or haul with a windlass.

windmill ● *n.* a mill, pump, or generator driven by the action of the wind on its rotating sails or blades. ● *v.tr. & intr.* whirl or fling (one's limbs) around in a manner suggestive of a windmill. ☐ **tilt at windmills** attack an imaginary enemy or grievance.

window *n.* **1 a** an opening in a wall, door, etc., usu. with glass, to admit light or air etc. and allow the occupants to see out. **b** the glass filling this opening (*have broken the window*). **2** a space for display behind the front window of a store. **3** an aperture in a wall etc. through which customers are served in a bank, ticket office, etc. **4** an opportunity to observe or learn. **5** an opening or transparent part in an envelope to show an address. **6** *Computing* a defined area on a display screen in which a part of a file or image can be displayed. **7 a** an interval during which atmospheric and astronomical circumstances are suitable for the launch of a spacecraft. **b** any interval or opportunity for action. ☐ **windowed** *adj.* (also in *comb.*). **windowless** *adj.*

window box *n.* a long narrow box placed on an outside windowsill, used for growing flowers.

window dressing *n.* **1** the art of arranging a display in a store window etc. **2** an adroit presentation of facts etc. to give a deceptively favourable impression. ☐ **window dresser** *n.*

windowing *n. Computing* the use of windows for the simultaneous display of parts of different files, images, etc.

window ledge *n.* = WINDOWSILL.

windowpane *n.* a pane of glass in a window.

window seat *n.* **1** a seat below a window, esp. in an alcove. **2** a seat next to a window in an aircraft etc.

window shop *v.tr.* look at goods displayed in store windows, usu. without buying. ☐ **window shopper** *n.*

windowsill *n.* a sill below a window.

window treatment *n.* a blind, curtain, or other drapery for a window.

windpipe *n.* the air passage from the throat to the lungs; the trachea.

windproof *adj.* (esp. of a garment) impervious to wind.

windrow /ˈwɪndroʊ:/ *n.* **1** a line of raked hay, sheaves, etc., laid out for drying by the wind. **2** *N Amer.* a long pile or row of leaves, dust, etc. heaped up by or as if by the wind. **3** *Cdn* a ridge of snow, gravel, etc. heaped along the side of a road by a snowplow, grader, etc.

wind shear *n.* a variation in wind velocity at right angles to the wind's direction.

windshield *n. N Amer.* a glass window across the front of a motor vehicle or aircraft.

windshield wiper *n.* a device consisting of a rubber blade on an arm, moving in an arc, for keeping a windshield clear of rain etc.

windsock *n.* a nylon cylinder or cone on a mast to show the direction of the wind at an airfield etc.

Windsor *n.* (usu. *attrib.*) denoting or relating to the British Royal Family since 1917.

windstorm *n.* a storm with very strong wind but little or no rain, snow, etc.

windsurfing *n.* the sport of riding on water on a sailboard. ☐ **windsurf** *v.intr.* **windsurfer** *n.*

windswept *adj.* exposed to or swept back by wind.

wind tunnel *n.* a tunnel-like device for producing an airstream of known velocity past models of aircraft, buildings, etc., in the study of wind flow or wind effects on the full-size object.

windup ● *n.* **1** a conclusion. **2** *Baseball & Hockey* the drawing back of the arm or stick as part of the throwing or shooting motion. **3** a device operated by being wound up, as a toy. ● *adj.* operated by being wound up.

windward ● *adj. & adv.* on the side from which the wind is blowing (*opp.* LEEWARD). ● *n.* the windward region, side, or direction (*to windward; on the windward of*).

windy[1] *adj.* (**-ier, -iest**) **1** stormy with wind. **2** exposed to the wind; windswept. **3** *informal* wordy. ☐ **windily** *adv.* **windiness** *n.*

windy[2] *adj.* that winds, winding (*a narrow windy path*).

wine *n.* **1** fermented grape juice as an alcoholic drink. **2** a fermented drink resembling this made from other fruits (*elderberry wine*). **3** the dark red colour of red wine. ☐ **wine and dine** entertain or be entertained with food and drink.

wine bar *n.* a bar or small restaurant where wine is the main drink available.

wine cellar *n.* **1** a cellar for storing wine. **2** the contents of this.

wine cooler *n.* **1** a drink of wine, soda water, and fruit flavours. **2** a usu. insulated bucket-like container for holding ice to chill a bottle of wine.

wineglass *n.* **1** a glass for wine, usu. with a stem and foot. **2** the contents of this.

wine grower *n.* a cultivator of grapes for wine. ☐ **wine-growing** *n. & adj.*

wine list *n.* a list of wines available in a restaurant.

winemaker *n.* a producer of wine; a wine grower.

winemaking *n.* (often *attrib.*) the production of wine, either commercially or as a hobby.

winepress *n.* a press in which grapes are squeezed in making wine.

winery *n.* (*pl.* **-ies**) esp. *N Amer.* an establishment where wine is made.

Winesap *n. N Amer.* a medium-sized, deep red apple with yellow patches and tiny white dots.

wine waiter *n.* a waiter responsible for serving wine.

wine tasting *n.* **1** the act of judging the quality of wine by tasting it. **2** an occasion for this.

winey *adj.* (**winier, winiest**) resembling wine in taste or appearance.

wing ● *n.* **1** each of the limbs or organs by which a bird, bat, or insect is able to fly. **2** anything resembling or analogous to a wing in form or function. **3** either of a pair of rigid horizontal structures extending on either side of an aircraft that support it in the air. **4** (in *pl.*) a badge depicting a pair of wings to symbolize that the holder is a certified pilot. **5** part of a building which projects or is extended in a certain direction from the main or central part (*lived in the north wing*). **6** a section of a political party or group holding more progressive or reactionary views than those of the more moderate centre (*see* RIGHT WING, LEFT WING). **7** esp. *Hockey & Soccer* **a** the area along the side of a playing surface (*he skated down the wing*). **b** the position of the forward player who covers this area. **c** a player at this position; a winger. **8 a** either of the flanks on the right or left side of the main body of an army or fleet in battle array. **b** an operational unit of some air forces consisting of two or more squadrons. **9** (in *pl.*) the sides of a theatre stage out of view of the audience. **10** a cut of beef from the short loin, including the thirteenth rib (also *attrib.*: *wing steak*). ● *v.* **1 a** *intr.* fly through the air, on wings or in an aircraft or as if so (*the ball came winging through the air*). **b** *tr.* make (one's way) through the air. **2** *tr.* (usu. in *passive*) equip with wings. **3** *tr.* esp. *N Amer.* cause to sail or soar through the air; throw. □ **give** (or **lend**) **wings to** speed up (a person or a thing). **on the wing** flying or in flight. **on a wing and a prayer** with only the slightest chance of success. **spread** (or **stretch**) **one's wings** test or develop one's abilities. **take under one's wing** treat as a protege. **take wing** fly away. **waiting in the wings** awaiting one's opportunity to fill a position expected to become available. **wing it** *informal* improvise; speak or act without preparation. □ **winged** *adj.* (also in *comb.*). **wingless** *adj.* **wing-like** *adj.*

wingback *n.* **1** *N Amer. Football* **a** an offensive back who lines up next to an end. **b** the position of this player. **2** (also **wingback chair, wing chair**) a high-backed armchair with side pieces projecting forward at the top of a high back.

wingbeat *n.* one complete cycle of movements made by the wing of a bird etc. in flying.

wing-case *n.* either of a pair of modified toughened forewings which cover the functional wings of certain insects, such as a beetle.

wingding *n. N Amer. informal* a wild party; a festive social gathering or celebration.

winger *n.* **1** esp. *Hockey & Soccer* a forward who plays on the wing. **2** (in *comb.*) a person affiliated with a specified political wing (*left winger*).

wingman *n.* (*pl.* **-men**) the pilot of an aircraft which is positioned behind and to one side of the leading aircraft, as in attack formation.

wing nut *n.* **1** a threaded nut with flat projections so that it may be tightened or loosened by hand with the thumb and forefinger, without the aid of a wrench. **2** *N Amer. slang* a stupid or inept person.

wingspan *n.* (also **wingspread**) the maximum lateral extent of the wings of a bird or aircraft.

wing tip *n.* **1** the tip of the wing of an aircraft, bird, bat, or insect. **2** *N Amer.* **a** a usu. perforated toecap with a backward extending point and curved sides. **b** (usu. **wingtip**, in full **wingtip shoe**) a shoe having such a toecap.

wingy /ˈwɪŋi/ *adj.* (**-ier, -iest**) *Cdn informal* crazy.

wink ● *v.intr.* **1** close and open one eye to convey a message to a person, or as a signal of friendliness. **2** (of a light etc.) twinkle; shine or flash intermittently. **3** (usu. foll. by *out*) disappear or go out suddenly. ● *n.* **1** an act of closing and opening the eye, esp. as a signal. **2** a brief moment; an instant (*was done in a wink*). **3** (usu. with *neg.*) *informal* a very brief or the shortest possible period of sleep (*I didn't sleep a wink*). □ **as easy as winking** *informal* very easy. **wink at** purposely avoid seeing (an offence, impropriety, etc.); pretend not to notice.

winkle ● *n.* any edible marine gastropod mollusc of the genus *Littorina*, abundant in the intertidal zone of rocky coasts; a periwinkle. ● *v.tr.* (foll. by *out*) extract (*winkled the information out of them*).

winless *adj.* esp. *N. Amer.* characterized by an absence of victories.

Winnebago /ˌwɪnəˈbeɪgoʊ/ *n. N Amer. proprietary* = RV 1.

winner *n.* **1** a person etc. who is victorious in a competition. **2** a goal etc. that decides the outcome of a game or competition. **3** *informal* a successful or highly promising idea, enterprise, etc.

winner-take-all *attrib.adj.* **1** denoting a conflict in which victory is outright or the winner alone is rewarded. **2** denoting the attitude of a person whose sole goal is outright victory.

winning ● *adj.* **1** victorious, successful. **2** that determines the outcome of a game or competition. **3** denoting a streak of consecutive victories uninterrupted by losses or ties (*a winning streak*). **4** attractive, persuasive (*a winning smile*). ● *n.* **1** the action of being victorious (*winning isn't everything*). **2** (in *pl.*) money won esp. in gambling. □ **winningly** *adv.*

winningest *adj. N Amer. Sport informal* that has won the most often.

Winnipegger *n.* a native or inhabitant of Winnipeg.

Winnipeg couch *n. Cdn* a couch with no arms or back that converts into a double bed.

Winnipeg General Strike *n. Cdn hist.* a general strike, 15 May–25 June 1919, in Winnipeg, involving over 30,000 labourers dissatisfied with low wages, poor conditions, and the lack of collective bargaining.

Winnipeg goldeye *n. Cdn* = GOLDEYE.

winnow *v.tr.* **1** expose (grain) to the wind or to a current of air so that unwanted lighter particles of chaff are separated or blown away. **2** (foll. by *out, from*) separate (chaff) from grain by exposing it to a current of air. **3** (often foll. by *down*) subject to a process which separates esp. the good from the bad (*winnow down the number of candidates*). **4** (often foll. by *out, from*) **a** extract or obtain (something valuable or desirable) by separating it from something undesirable (*winnow out the best players from a group of prospects*). **b** eliminate or clear away (something undesirable) by separating it from something useful (*winnow the lies from the truth*).

wino *n.* (*pl.* **-os**) *slang* a habitual excessive drinker of cheap wine; an alcoholic, esp. one who is destitute.

winsome *adj.* (of a person) winning, attractive, engaging. □ **winsomely** *adv.* **winsomeness** *n.*

winter ● *n.* **1 a** the fourth and coldest season of the year, beginning at the end of fall and lasting until the start of spring. **b** the period from the winter solstice to the spring equinox. **2** cold or wintry weather typical of this season. **3** a time or state of old age, decay, affliction, hostility, emotional coldness, etc. ● *attrib.adj.* **1** characteristic of, done or occurring in, or suitable for use in winter (*winter weather; winter sports; winter coat*). **2 a** (of plants or animals) active or flourishing in winter. **b** (of crops) sown in fall for harvesting the following year. ● v. **1** intr. (usu. foll. by in) spend the winter (her family winters in Florida). **2** (often foll. by over) **a** intr. (of animals) find or be provided with food and shelter in the winter. **b** tr. keep or maintain (animals or plants) during the winter.

winter aconite n. any plant of the genus Eranthis, with buttercup-like flowers blooming in early spring.

winterberry n. (pl. **-ies**) any of several deciduous N American hollies with non-prickly leaves and berries that last through the winter, esp. Ilex verticillata.

winter carnival n. N Amer. an organized festival featuring various winter sports and activities, such as dogsled and snowmobile races, ice sculptures, etc.

winter city n. a city which has long and harsh winters.

winter club n. Cdn an organization that offers access to various recreational facilities for activities such as skating and curling throughout the winter.

winterer n. Cdn hist. = WINTERING PARTNER.

wintergreen n. **1** any of several plants esp. of the genus Pyrola, Gaultheria, or Chimaphila, remaining green through the winter. **2** (in full **wintergreen oil**) an oil containing methyl salicylate, originally distilled from the leaves of G. procumbens but now usu. made synthetically, which is used medicinally in lotions and creams etc. and as a flavouring.

winter ice road n. Cdn = WINTER ROAD.

wintering ground n. (usu. in pl.) the region to which animals, esp. birds, migrate in the winter.

wintering partner n. Cdn hist. a stock-holding member and representative of a fur-trading company stationed year-round at a trading post in the northern interior to negotiate the acquisition of furs.

winterize v.tr. esp. N Amer. adapt or prepare (a home, cottage, car, etc.) for use in cold weather. □ **winterization** n. **winterized** adj.

winterkill N Amer. ● n. **1** the death of plants or animals by exposure to frost, snow, and extreme cold. **2** a plant, part of a plant, or animal that has died in this way. ● v. **1** tr. (usu. in passive) kill (plants or animals) by exposure to frost, snow, and extreme cold. **2** intr. (of a plant or animal) die from exposure to cold etc.

winter road n. Cdn (North) a secondary road made of compact snow or ice, often plowed over a frozen lake or ground impassable in the summer.

winter savory n. see SAVORY¹.

winter solstice n. the time of year when the sun appears at its lowest altitude above the horizon at noon and daylight is at a minimum, occurring in the northern hemisphere when the sun reaches its southernmost point in the sky on about Dec. 22, or in the southern hemisphere when it reaches its northernmost point on about June 21.

winter sports n.pl. sports performed on snow or ice, e.g. skiing, figure skating, hockey, etc.

winter squash n. N Amer. see SQUASH² 1.

wintertime n. the season of winter.

winter wheat n. wheat that is planted in the fall and harvested the following summer.

wintry adj. (also **wintery**) (**-ier**, **-iest**) **1** characteristic of or affected by winter (wintry weather; a wintry landscape). **2** (of a smile, greeting, etc.) lacking warmth or enthusiasm.

win-win adj. designating or pertaining to a situation which is beneficial to both parties involved.

winy var. of WINEY.

wipe ● v.tr. **1** clean or dry the surface of by rubbing with a cloth or towel etc. **2** spread or apply (a soft or

liquid substance) over a surface by rubbing with a soft cloth or the hand etc. **3** (often foll. by away, off) **a** clear or remove (moisture, dirt, etc.) from something. **b** remove or eliminate completely (the village was wiped off the map). **4** (often foll. by from) remove or erase (a thought, memory, etc.) from one's mind. **5 a** erase (data, a recording, etc.) from a computer disk, videotape, etc. **b** erase data from (a medium). ● n. **1** an act of wiping. **2** a disposable piece of absorbent paper or cloth, usu. treated with a cleaning agent, for wiping something clean. □ **wipe down** clean (esp. a vertical surface) by wiping. **wipe the floor with** informal inflict a humiliating defeat on. **wipe off** annul (a debt etc.). **wipe out 1 a** greatly or completely reduce the strength or significance of (the whole population was wiped out). **b** efface, obliterate (wiped it out of my memory). **2** slang murder. **3** informal **a** (of a surfer) fall or be knocked from one's surfboard. **b** fall, skid, or crash. **4** clean the inside of. **5** avenge (an insult etc.). **wipe up** clear or remove (a liquid etc.) by wiping or absorbing it with a cloth. □ **wipeable** adj.

wiped out adj. **1** destroyed. **2** esp. N Amer. financially ruined. **3** esp. N Amer. informal tired out.

wipeout n. **1** a fall, crash, or accident, esp. while surfing, skiing, skating, etc. **2** informal a dismal failure. **3** an instance of destruction or annihilation.

wiper n. **1** = WINDSHIELD WIPER. **2** Electricity a moving component that rotates or slides to make electrical contact with one or more terminals.

wire ● n. **1 a** metal drawn out into the form of a fine thread or thin flexible rod. **b** a piece of this. **2 a** single line of esp. copper wire, or several of these braided or twisted together, usu. insulated and used as a conductor of electrical current. **3** esp. N Amer. **a** dated a telegram. **b** = NEWS WIRE. **4** an electronic listening device, esp. one which can be concealed on a person. **5 a** a line or cable made of several strands of wire twisted or braided together for strength. **b** several strands of wire woven or arranged into a mesh (chicken wire). **6** N Amer. a wire stretched across and above a racetrack at the starting and finish line. **7** (attrib.) made of wire (a wire coat hanger). ● v.tr. **1** fit, fasten, strengthen, or secure with a wire (wired my jaw shut). **2** (often foll. by up) furnish (a building etc.) with electrical circuits, fibre optic cabling, telephone lines, etc. **3** fit (a person) with a concealed listening device. **4** esp. N Amer. informal arrange to have (money) sent, formerly by telegraph, now usu. by some other means. □ **by wire** by telegraph. **get one's wires crossed** become confused or misunderstood. **under the wire** N Amer. just in time. **wire-to-wire** N Amer. from start to finish.

wire brush n. **1** a brush with stiff wire bristles used for removing rust, paint, or dirt from hard surfaces, esp. metal. **2** either of a pair of thin sticks with long wire bristles for striking cymbals to produce a soft metallic sound.

wire cutters n.pl. (also **wire cutter**) a tool or pair of pliers used to cut wire.

wired adj. **1** slang hyper, strung out, or antsy, esp. due to the effects of a drug or stimulant, such as caffeine. **2 a** fitted with electrical connections or electric or fibre optic cables. **b** informal having access to the Internet. **3** supported, strengthened, or stiffened with wire. □ **wired for sound** fitted with or wearing an electronic listening device.

wire-hair n. any dog or breed of dog, esp. a terrier, having a rough coat of a stiff and wiry texture. □ **wire-haired** adj.

wireless ● adj. designating or pertaining to any of

various devices, communication systems, etc. not requiring wires, esp. employing radio transmission. ● *n.* (in full **wireless telegraphy**) = RADIO-TELEGRAPHY.

wire-rimmed *adj.* (of a pair of eyeglasses) having a frame made of wire.

wire rims *n.pl.* a pair of wire-rimmed eyeglasses.

wire service *n. N Amer.* a news agency that supplies syndicated news stories to its subscribers, e.g. media outlets, by electronic means.

wiretap ● *n.* **1** an act of tapping a telephone line, esp. as a means of surveillance. **2** a device used to do this. ● *v.tr.* **1** tap the telephone lines of (a house etc.). **2** monitor (a conversation etc.) by means of a wiretap. □ **wiretapper** *n.* **wiretapping** *n.*

wiring *n.* **1** a system of electrical wires in an apparatus or building. **2** the installation of these.

wiry *adj.* (**-ier, -iest**) **1** resembling wire in texture or appearance, esp. stiff and flexible (*wiry hair*). **2** (of a person) thin and sinewy. **3** made of wire.

Wis. *abbr.* Wisconsin.

Wisconsinite *n.* a native or inhabitant of the US state of Wisconsin.

wisdom *n.* **1** the state of being wise. **2** experience and knowledge together with the power of applying them critically or practically. **3** prudence; common sense. **4** wise sayings, thoughts, etc., regarded collectively. □ **in his** (or **her** etc.) **wisdom** usu. *ironic* in the belief that it would be best (*the committee in its wisdom decided to abandon the project*).

wisdom tooth *n.* each of four hindmost teeth on either side of the jaws, which usu. erupt around the age of 20, often removed if painful.

wise[1] *adj.* **1 a** having experience and knowledge and the ability to apply them judiciously. **b** (of an action, behaviour, etc.) demonstrating knowledge and judgment. **2** prudent, sensible. **3** having knowledge; learned. **4** suggestive of wisdom (*a wise nod*). **5** *N Amer. informal* **a** alert, crafty. **b** impudent, cocky. □ **wise to** *informal* aware of, esp. so as to know what to do or how to act. **none the** (or **no**) **wiser** knowing no more than before. **put a person wise** (often foll. by *to*) *informal* inform a person (about). **wise after the event** able to understand and assess an event or circumstance after its implications have become obvious. **wise up** become informed, aware, or enlightened. **without anyone's being the wiser** undetected. □ **wisely** *adv.*

wise[2] *n. archaic* way, manner. □ **in no wise** not at all.

-wise[1] *suffix informal* forming adverbs meaning 'in terms of, regarding' (*music-wise they're a success but they need to improve image-wise*). ¶Invented combinations of this sort are usually considered inelegant.

-wise[2] *suffix* forming adjectives meaning 'mindful and careful of, having or showing common sense regarding' (*a media-wise celebrity; a penny-wise investor*).

wiseacre *n.* **1** a foolish person with an air or affectation of wisdom. **2** = WISE GUY.

wiseass *n.* (also *attrib.*) esp. *N Amer. slang* = WISE GUY.

wisecrack *informal* ● *n.* a witty or sarcastic remark. ● *v.* **1** *intr.* make a wisecrack. **2** *tr.* say in a sarcastic manner. □ **wisecracker** *n.* **wisecracking** *n. & adj.*

wise guy *n. informal* a smug or cocky person who makes sarcastic quips or comments, esp. in order to display cleverness (also *attrib.*: *wise-guy attitude*).

wise man *n.* **1** a learned or prudent man, esp. one chosen as an adviser in political matters. **2** a man who practises magic, esp. each of the three Magi.

wise woman *n.* a learned or prudent woman, esp. one chosen as an adviser in political matters.

wish ● *v.* **1** *tr.* desire or aspire to (esp. something that cannot or is unlikely to occur) (*I wish I were you; I wish I played in the NHL*). **2** *tr.* intend or hope (*I wish to travel*). **3** *tr.* demand or request (*I wish you to go*). **4** *intr.* (often foll. by *for*) have or express a desire or yearning for (esp. something not easily or likely to be obtained) (*I wish for a million dollars*). **5** *tr.* have or express one's hopes for (the success or well-being etc. of another) (*I wish you no harm; she wished me a happy birthday*). **6** *tr.* (usu. with *neg.*, foll. by *on, upon*) foist on a person (*I wouldn't wish that on anyone*). ● *n.* **1 a** a desire, request, or aspiration. **b** an expression of this. **2** a thing desired (*got my wish*). □ **best** (or **good**) **wishes** hopes felt or expressed for another's happiness etc. **the wish is father to the thought** we believe a thing because we wish it true.

wishbone *n.* **1** a forked bone between the neck and breastbone of a bird, traditionally removed from the carcass of cooked fowl and broken between two people, the longer portion entitling the holder to make a wish. **2** an object of similar shape. **3** a wishbone-shaped element in the independent suspension of a vehicle, having two arms which are hinged to the chassis at their ends and to the wheel at their joint (compare DOUBLE-WISHBONE SUSPENSION).

wishful *adj.* full of yearning; having or expressing a wish. □ **wishfully** *adv.* **wishfulness** *n.*

wish-fulfillment *n.* a tendency for a desire to be satisfied in fantasy or dreams.

wishful thinking *n.* belief or expectation founded on wishes rather than on what one has reason to think is true.

wish list *n.* a list of wishes, desires, aspirations, or objectives.

wishy-washy *adj.* **1** (of a person) indecisive, irresolute, feeble. **2** lacking strength or substance; insipid (*a wishy-washy article*).

wisp *n.* **1** several strands of hair, pieces of grass, etc. **2** a thin faint diffuse trace or streak of smoke etc. (*wisps of cloud*). **3** a person or thing that is slender or delicate (*a wisp of a child*). **4** (usu. foll. by *of*) a hint or suggestion (*a wisp of hope*). □ **wispy** *adj.* (**-ier, -iest**).

wisteria /wɪˈstiːriə/ *n.* a climbing plant with hanging racemes of blue, purple, or white flowers.

wistful *adj.* (of a person, looks, etc.) yearningly or mournfully expectant or wishful. □ **wistfully** *adv.* **wistfulness** *n.*

wit[1] *n.* **1** the apt, clever, and funny expression of thought or juxtaposition of contrasting ideas and expressions, calculated to delight an audience (*conversation sparkling with wit*). **2** a person possessing such an ability; a cleverly humorous person. **3** (often in *pl.*) mental or intellectual power; intelligence, quick understanding (*a battle of wits*). □ **at one's wits'** (or **wit's**) **end** in a state of utter perplexity or despair. **have** (or **keep**) **one's wits about one** be vigilant or mentally alert. **live by one's wits** live by ingenious or crafty expedients, without a settled occupation. **match wits with** contend with someone intellectually. **out of one's wits** mad, insane. **scare** (or **frighten**) **the wits out of** frighten severely. **set one's wits to** argue with. □ **witted** *adj.* (in sense 3; also in *comb.*).

wit[2] *v.tr. & intr.* □ **to wit** that is to say; namely.

witch *n.* **1** a person, usu. a woman, who practises magic, esp. one supposed to consort with evil spirits and perform supernatural acts with their help. **2** a follower or practitioner of the religious cult of modern witchcraft; a Wiccan. **3** an ugly or malevolent old

woman; a hag. □ **witching** adj. & n. **witchlike** adj.
witchy adj. (**-ier, -iest**).

witchcraft n. **1 a** the practices of a witch, esp. the use of magic and sorcery. **b** the use of supernatural power supposed to be possessed by a person in league with the devil or evil spirits. **2** the practices and beliefs of the Wiccans. **3** bewitching power, charm, or influence, as exercised by eloquence or beauty.

witch doctor n. one who claims to cure disease and counteract witchcraft by magic, esp. a tribal magician.

witches' brew n. (also **witch's brew**) **1** a magic brew prepared by witches. **2** any harmful, suspicious, or disgusting concoction or mixture.

witch hazel n. **1** any N American shrub of the genus *Hamamelis*, with bark yielding an astringent lotion. **2** this lotion, esp. from the leaves of *H. virginiana*.

witch hunt n. **1** hist. a search for and persecution of people suspected of witchcraft. **2** a malicious campaign directed against a group of people with unpopular or unorthodox views or behaviour, formerly esp. communists. □ **witch-hunting** n.

witching hour n. midnight, when witches are supposedly active.

with prep. expressing: **1** an instrument or means used (*cut with a knife; can walk with assistance*). **2** association or company (*works with IBM; beef with gravy*). **3** separation or release (*break with tradition*). **4** cause or origin (*shiver with fear; in bed with measles*). **5** possession, attribution (*a vase with handles*). **6** circumstances (*a holiday with all expenses paid*). **7** manner adopted or displayed (*spoke with vehemence; handle with care*). **8** agreement (*sympathize with*). **9** antagonism, competition (*incompatible with; stop arguing with me*). **10** responsibility or care for (*the decision rests with you*). **11** material (*made with gold*). **12** addition or supply; possession of as a material, attribute, circumstance, etc. (*threaten with dismissal; spread with jam*). **13** reference or regard (*how are things with you?*). **14** relation or causative association (*keeps pace with the cost of living*). **15** an accepted circumstance or consideration (*with all your faults, we like you*). □ **away** (or **in** or **out** etc.) **with** (as *interj.*) take, send, or put (a person or thing) away, in, out, etc. **be with a person 1** agree with and support a person. **2** *informal* follow a person's meaning (*are you with me?*). **one with** part of the same whole as. **with child** (or **young**) *literary* pregnant. **with it** esp. N Amer. *informal* **1 a** up to date; conversant with modern or fashionable trends or ideas. **b** (*attrib.*; **with-it**) fashionable (*with-it clothes*). **2** alert, attentive. **with that** thereupon.

withdraw v. (*past* **withdrew**; *past part.* **withdrawn**) **1** tr. pull or draw aside or back. **2** tr. discontinue, cancel (*withdrew my support*). **3 a** tr. remove (a person etc.) from a position, situation, competition, etc. **b** intr. remove oneself from a position or situation etc. **4** tr. take (money) out of an account. **5** intr. **a** retire from a society or community, from public life, etc. **b** become reserved or uncommunicative. **6** tr. & intr. retract (an unparliamentary remark) made during a parliamentary debate.

withdrawal n. **1 a** the act or an instance of withdrawing (*the withdrawal of troops*). **b** the removal of money from a place of deposit. **2** the process of ceasing to take an addictive drug, often associated with unpleasant and sometimes life-threatening physical reactions. **3** a state of apathy, depression, or retreat from objective reality, usu. as a response to severe stress or physical danger. **4** = COITUS INTERRUPTUS.

withdrawn adj. **1** abnormally shy and unsociable; mentally detached. **2** (of a place) private, secluded.

wither v. **1** tr. & intr. (of a plant) become or cause to become dry and shrivelled. **2** tr. & intr. (often foll. by *away*) lose or deprive of vigour or freshness. **3** intr. (often foll. by *away*) cease to flourish. **4** tr. mortify (a person) with a look of extreme contempt.

withering adj. **1** scornful, scathing (*a withering glare*). **2** fading, decaying. □ **witheringly** adv.

withers n.pl. the highest part of the back of a horse, sheep, ox, etc., lying between the shoulder blades.

withhold v.tr. (*past* and *past part.* **-held**) **1** restrain or hold back from action. **2** keep back (what belongs to, is due to, or is desired by another); refuse to give (*withhold one's consent; withhold the truth*).

within prep. **1** inside; enclosed or contained by. **2 a** not beyond or exceeding (*within one's means*). **b** not transgressing (*within the law; within reason*). **3** not further off than (*within three miles of a station; within shouting distance*). **4** before the end of (a period of time). □ **within reach** (or **sight**) **of** near enough to be reached or seen.

without ● prep. **1** not having, feeling, or showing. **2** with freedom from. **3** in the absence of. **4** with neglect or avoidance of. ● adv. archaic or literary **1** outside (*seen from without*). **2** out of doors (*remained shivering without*). **3** in outward appearance (*rough without but kind within*). □ **without end** infinite, eternal.

withstand v. (*past* and *past part.* **-stood**) **1** tr. maintain one's position against; resist, oppose (*withstood the attack*). **2** tr. tolerate, endure, bear (*this plant will withstand the harsh climate*). **3** intr. offer resistance.

witless adj. **1** lacking wisdom or sense; stupid. **2** crazy, out of one's mind. □ **witlessly** adv. **witlessness** n.

witness ● n. **1** a person present at some event or occurrence and able to give information about it from observation. **2 a** a person giving testimony under oath in a court of law. **b** testimony, evidence, confirmation (*he was bribed to give false witness*). **3 a** a person selected or appointed to be present at a transaction etc. in order to testify to its having taken place. **b** a person who signs a document attesting to its proper execution. **4** a person or thing whose existence, condition, etc., attests or proves something (*this village is a witness to the ravages of war*). **5** (**Witness**) = JEHOVAH'S WITNESS. ● v. **1** tr. be a witness of (an event etc.) (*did you witness the accident?*). **2** tr. **a** sign (a document) as a witness of its authenticity. **b** formally be present as a witness of (a transaction etc.). **3** tr. (of a place, time, etc.) be associated with (a fact or event); be the scene or setting of (*Europe witnessed massive political change in the late 1980s*). **4** tr. (as *imper.*) introducing an illustration of the preceding statement (*he is an accomplished musician: witness his performance last week*). **5** intr. (foll. by *to*, *against*) give or serve as evidence. **6** intr. publicly assert one's religious convictions, esp. in an attempt to convert others. □ **bear witness to 1** attest the truth of. **2** state one's belief in. **call to witness** appeal to for confirmation etc.

witness box n. Cdn & Brit. (also esp. N Amer. **witness stand**) an enclosure in a court of law from which witnesses give evidence. ¶*Witness box* is the term in official use in Canadian courts.

witticism /'wɪtɪ,sɪzəm/ n. a witty remark.

witting adj. **1** aware. **2** intentional. □ **wittingly** adv.

witty adj. (**-ier, -iest**) **1** capable of or given to saying or writing clever and amusing things. **2** (of speech,

writing, etc.) characterized by wit or humour. □
wittily adv. **wittiness** n.

wives pl. of WIFE.

wiz var. of WHIZ n. 2.

wizard n. **1** a man who practises magic; a sorcerer. **2** a person noted for remarkable ability (*she's a financial wizard*). □ **wizardly** adj.

wizardry n. **1** the art or practice of a wizard. **2** remarkable skill in a particular field or activity.

wizened /'wɪzənd/ adj. shrivelled or wrinkled, esp. with age.

wk. abbr. **1** week. **2** work.

wks. abbr. weeks.

WNW abbr. west-northwest.

WO abbr. WARRANT OFFICER.

wo interj. = WHOA.

w/o abbr. without.

wobble ● v. **1** a intr. sway or rock erratically from side to side. **b** tr. cause to do this. **2** intr. stand or proceed unsteadily; stagger. **3** intr. (of the voice or a sound) quaver. **4** intr. hesitate or waver between different opinions or actions. ● n. **1** the action or an act of wobbling. **2** an instance of vacillation or pulsation.

wobbler n. **1** a person or thing that wobbles. **2** a fishing lure that wobbles and does not spin.

wobbly adj. (**-ier**, **-iest**) **1** wobbling or tending to wobble. **2** (of a line, handwriting, etc.) not straight or regular; shaky, wavy, undulating. **3** wavering, uncertain. □ **wobbliness** n.

woe n. **1** bitter grief. **2** (in pl.) troubles, misfortunes. □ **woe betide** (or **to**) there will be unfortunate consequences for. **woe is me** an exclamation of distress.

woebegone /'woːbəˌɡɒn/ adj. sad, miserable, or dismal in appearance.

woeful adj. **1** afflicted with sorrow or misfortune. **2** causing sorrow or affliction. **3** very bad or poor; dreadful (*woeful ignorance*). □ **woefully** adv. **woefulness** n.

wog n. slang offensive a foreigner, esp. a non-white one.

wok n. a large bowl-shaped frying pan used in esp. Chinese cooking.

woke past of WAKE[1].

woken past part. of WAKE[1].

wolf ● n. (pl. **wolves**) **1** a wild flesh-eating tawny-grey mammal related to the dog, esp. *Canis lupus*, hunting in packs. **2** the skin, hide, or fur of this animal. **3** slang **a** a ferocious or rapacious person. **b** a womanizer. ● v.tr. (often foll. by *down*) devour (food) ravenously. □ **cry wolf** raise repeated false alarms (so that a genuine one is disregarded). **keep the wolf from the door** have enough money to provide for oneself or one's family. **throw to the wolves** sacrifice (a friend or colleague) in order to avert danger or difficulties for oneself. **wolf in sheep's clothing** a person whose hostile intentions are concealed by a pretense of friendliness. □ **wolfish** adj. **wolfishly** adv. **wolflike** adj. & adv.

wolf cub n. **1** a young wolf. **2** (**Wolf Cub**) the former name for CUB 2.

wolfhound n. a dog of any of several large breeds, e.g. a borzoi, originally kept for hunting wolves.

wolf pack n. **1** any group which operates as a hunting and attacking pack, such as a group of submarines or aircraft. **2** a number of wolves naturally associating as a group, esp. for hunting.

wolf whistle ● n. a rising and falling whistle imitating the howl of a wolf, made esp. by a man to express his admiration of a woman's appearance. ● v.intr. (**wolf-whistle**) make such a whistling sound.

wolf willow n. Cdn = SILVERBERRY.

wolverine n. **1** a carnivorous animal, *Gulo gulo*, of the weasel family, resembling a small bear, with dark brown fur and a long bushy tail. **2** wolverine fur.

wolves pl. of WOLF.

woman n. (pl. **women**) **1** an adult female person (also in comb.: *businesswoman*; *Frenchwoman*). **2** (attrib.) female (*women friends*). **3** informal a wife or female sexual partner. **4** the female human person, esp. viewed as a type (*how does woman differ from man?*). **5** (prec. by *the*) the character or qualities traditionally associated with women (*brought out the woman in me*). □ **womanless** adj. **womanlike** adj.

womanhood n. **1 a** the state or condition of being a woman. **b** the state of being a grown woman; female maturity. **2** the character or qualities traditionally attributed to women. **3** women collectively.

womanish adj. **1** usu. derogatory (of a man) effeminate. **2** suitable to or characteristic of a woman.

womanize v.intr. (of a man) pursue or engage in casual sexual encounters with women. □ **womanizer** n.

womankind n. women collectively.

womanly adj. (of a woman) having or showing qualities traditionally associated with women; not masculine or girlish. □ **womanliness** n.

womb /wuːm/ n. **1** the organ in the body of a woman or female mammal in which offspring are carried, protected, and nourished before birth; the uterus. **2** a place of origin, development, or growth. □ **womblike** adj.

wombat /'wɒmbæt/ n. any burrowing plant-eating Australian marsupial of the family Vombatidae, resembling a small bear, with short legs.

women pl. of WOMAN.

womenfolk n.pl. **1** women collectively. **2** the women of a particular family, household, etc.

Women's Institute n. an organization founded to enable women in rural areas to meet regularly and engage in various cultural activities, social work, etc.

women's lib n. (also **Women's Lib**) informal = WOMEN'S LIBERATION.

women's libber n. informal a supporter of women's liberation.

women's liberation n. **1** the liberation of women from inequalities and subservient status in relation to men, and from sexist attitudes. **2** (also **Women's Liberation**, in full **Women's Liberation Movement**) = WOMEN'S MOVEMENT.

women's movement n. (also **Women's Movement**) a broad movement campaigning for women's liberation and for the recognition and extension of women's rights.

women's rights n.pl. the human rights of women, esp. those that promote or secure legal and social equality with men.

women's room n. N Amer. = LADIES' ROOM.

women's shelter n. N Amer. an establishment offering refuge and counselling to women who are victims of esp. domestic abuse, and their children.

women's studies n.pl. (usu. treated as sing.) a course of academic studies focusing on women and their role in society, as well as their history and literature.

women's suffrage n. **1** the right of women to vote. **2** a movement campaigning for this.

womenswear n. clothes for women.

won past and past part. of WIN.

wonder ● n. **1** the emotion excited by the perception

of something unexpected, unfamiliar, or inexplicable, esp. surprise or astonishment mingled with admiration, perplexity, or curiosity. **2** an amazing or remarkable person or thing. **3** (*attrib.*) having marvellous or amazing properties or qualities (*a wonder drug*). **4** a miraculous or surprising thing (*it is a wonder you were not hurt*). ● *v.* **1** *tr.* desire or be curious to know (*I wonder what time it is*). **2** *intr.* speculate with curiosity or doubt (*I wonder about him sometimes*). **3** *tr.* used to express a tentative inquiry or polite request (*I was wondering if you might be free tomorrow night?*). **4** *intr.* be filled with wonder or great surprise. □ **I shouldn't wonder** *informal* it would not surprise me. **no** (or **small**) **wonder** it is natural or hardly surprising; one might have guessed. **wonders will never cease** an exclamation of extreme (usu. delightful) surprise. **work** (or **do**) **wonders 1** perform miracles. **2** achieve remarkable success.

wonderful *adj.* **1** very remarkable or admirable (*a wonderful meal*). **2** marvellous, terrific (*I feel wonderful*). **3** that arouses wonder or astonishment. □ **wonderfully** *adv.* **wonderfulness** *n.*

wondering *adj.* filled with wonder; marvelling (*their wondering gaze*). □ **wonderingly** *adv.*

wonderland *n.* **1** an imaginary world of marvels. **2** an actual place of remarkable beauty (*a winter wonderland*).

wonderment *n.* a state of surprise or awe.

wonder-struck *adj.* reduced to silence by wonder.

wonder-worker *n.* a person who performs wonders or miracles. □ **wonder-working** *attrib.adj.*

wondrous *adj. literary* wonderful. □ **wondrously** *adv.*

wonk *n. N Amer. slang* usu. *derogatory* **1** a studious or hard-working person, esp. one obsessively devoted to academic studies at the expense of social activities. **2** (in full **policy wonk**) esp. *US* a person who takes an unnecessary interest in minor details of policy. □ **wonkery** *n.*

wonky *adj.* (**-ier, -iest**) *informal* **1** crooked, loose. **2** faulty, unreliable, askew. □ **wonkiness** *n.*

wont /wɒnt/ ● *predic.adj.* accustomed (*as we were wont to say*). ● *n.* what is customary, one's habit (*as is my wont*).

won't *contraction* will not.

wonted *attrib.adj.* habitual, accustomed, usual.

won ton /ˈwɒntɒn/ *n.* (in Chinese cooking) a small round dumpling containing a savoury filling, sometimes deep-fried and served as an accompaniment to a meal, but more commonly boiled and served in a broth.

woo *v.tr.* (**woos, wooed**) **1** court; seek the hand or love of (esp. a woman). **2** seek the favour or support of (*trying to woo voters*). **3** try to win (fame, fortune, etc.). **4** coax, entreat, or importune. □ **wooer** *n.*

wood *n.* **1 a** a hard fibrous material that forms the main substance of the trunk or branches of a tree etc. **b** this cut for timber or for fuel, or for use in crafts, manufacture, etc. **2** = WOODS. **3** (prec. by *the*) wooden storage, esp. a cask, for wine etc. (*poured straight from the wood*). **4** a wooden-headed golf club, or any club with a head relatively broad from face to back.

wood alcohol *n.* methanol.

wood bison *n.* (also **wood buffalo**) a subspecies of N American bison found in wooded parts of western Canada, somewhat larger than the plains bison.

woodblock *n.* **1** a block from which woodcuts are made. **2** each of the small pieces of wood used in making a parquet floor, often arranged in a pattern.

woodbox *n.* a large usu. wooden box built near a fireplace, stove, etc., for storing firewood.

wood-burning *adj.* using wood as fuel.

woodcarver *n.* **1** a person who carves designs in relief on wood. **2** a tool for carving wood.

woodcarving *n.* **1** (also *attrib.*) the act, process, or art of carving wood. **2** a design in wood produced by this art.

wood chip *n.* a small piece of wood, used in quantity for burning, filling in a garden, etc.

woodchuck *n.* a reddish-brown and grey N American marmot, *Marmota monax.*

woodcock *n.* (*pl.* same) any game bird of the genus *Scolopax*, inhabiting woodland.

woodcraft *n.* esp. *N Amer.* **1** skill in woodwork. **2** woodland knowledge, esp. in camping, scouting, etc.

woodcut *n.* **1** a relief cut on a block of wood sawn along the grain. **2** a print made from this, esp. as an illustration in a book. **3** the technique of making such reliefs and prints.

woodcutter *n.* **1** a person who cuts wood, esp. one who fells trees. **2** a woodcut maker. □ **woodcutting** *adj. & n.*

wood duck *n.* a N American wild duck, *Aix sponsa*, the male of which has an iridescent green and blue head with white stripes.

wooded *adj.* having woods or many trees.

wooden *adj.* **1** made of wood. **2** like wood. **3 a** stiff, clumsy, or stilted; without animation or flexibility (*a wooden performance*). **b** expressionless (*a wooden stare*). □ **woodenly** *adv.* **woodenness** *n.*

wood engraving *n.* **1** a relief cut on a block of wood sawn across the grain. **2** a print made from this. **3** the technique of making such reliefs and prints. □ **wood engraver** *n.*

wood fibre *n.* fibre obtained from wood esp. as material for paper.

wood grain *n.* **1** the grain of wood. **2** a surface or finish imitating this.

woodland *n.* wooded country, woods (often *attrib.*: *woodland scenery*). □ **woodlander** *n.*

woodland caribou *n.* a caribou found in wooded areas of Canada, larger than the barren ground caribou.

Woodland Cree *n.* **1** a member of any of the Cree peoples who live in forested areas (as opposed to the Plains). **2** the dialect of Cree spoken by this people.

woodlot *n. N Amer.* a treed plot of land, esp. on a farm, from which firewood may be obtained.

woodpecker *n.* any bird of the family Picidae that climbs and taps tree trunks in search of insects.

woodpile *n.* a pile of wood, esp. for fuel.

wood pulp *n.* wood fibre reduced chemically or mechanically to pulp as raw material for paper.

woodrat *n.* any rat of the N American genus *Neotoma*, most species of which build houses of twigs and other found materials, esp. the pack rat.

woodruff *n.* a white-flowered plant of the genus *Galium*, esp. *G. odoratum* grown for the fragrance of its whorled leaves when dried or crushed.

woods *n.pl.* trees densely occupying a tract of land. □ **out of the woods** out of danger or difficulty.

woodshed *n.* a shed where wood for fuel is stored.

woodsman *n.* (*pl.* **-men**) **1** a person who lives in or frequents the woods for hunting, camping, etc. **2** a person skilled in woodcraft. □ **woodsmanship** *n.*

woodsmoke *n.* the smoke from a wood fire.

wood sorrel *n.* any of various plants with trifoliate leaves, e.g. *Oxalis montana*, found east of the Rockies, with white flowers streaked with purple.

wood stain *n.* a commercially-produced substance for colouring wood.

wood stove n. a wood-burning stove.

woodsy adj. N Amer. like or characteristic of woods.

wood warbler n. any American warbler of the family Parulidae.

woodwind n. (often attrib.) **1** (collect.) the wind instruments of the orchestra that were (mostly) originally made of wood, e.g. the flute and clarinet. **2** (usu. in pl.) an individual instrument of this kind or its player (the woodwinds are out of tune).

woodwork n. **1** the making of things in wood. **2** things made of wood, esp. the wooden parts of a building. □ **crawl** (or **come**) **out of the woodwork** informal (of something unwelcome) emerge from obscurity into prominence. □ **woodworker** n. **woodworking** n.

woodworm n. **1** the wood-boring larva of the furniture beetle. **2** damaged wood affected by this.

woody ● adj. (-ier, -iest) **1** (of a region) abounding in woods. **2** like or of wood (a woody stem). ● n. (pl. -ies) informal a wood duck. □ **woodiness** n.

woody nightshade n. see NIGHTSHADE 1.

woof[1] ● n. the gruff bark of a dog. ● v. **1** intr. give a woof. **2** tr. (often foll. by down) informal consume ravenously.

woof[2] /wof, wu:f/ n. = WEFT.

woofer n. a loudspeaker designed to reproduce low frequencies (compare TWEETER).

wool n. **1** fine soft wavy hair from the fleece of sheep, goats, etc. **2 a** yarn produced from this hair. **b** cloth or clothing made from it. **3** any of various wool-like substances (steel wool). **4** soft short under-fur or down. **5** informal a person's hair, esp. when short and curly. □ **pull the wool over a person's eyes** deceive a person. □ **wool-like** adj.

woolgathering n. absent-mindedness; dreamy inattention. □ **woolgather** v.intr.

woollen (also **woolen**) ● adj. made wholly or partly of wool, esp. from short fibres. ● n. (in pl.) woollen garments.

woolly ● adj. (-ier, -iest) **1** bearing or naturally covered with wool or wool-like hair; downy. **2** resembling or suggesting wool (woolly clouds). **3** made of (esp. knitted) wool. **4** (of a sound) indistinct. **5** (of thought) vague or confused. **6** lacking in definition or incisiveness. ● n. (pl. -ies) informal a woollen garment, esp. a sweater. □ **woolliness** n.

woosh var. of WHOOSH.

woozy adj. (-ier, -iest) informal **1** dizzy or unsteady. **2** dazed or slightly drunk. □ **woozily** adv. **wooziness** n.

wop n. slang offensive an Italian.

Worcestershire sauce /'wʊstər‚ʃɪːr/ n. a pungent sauce containing soy, vinegar, and seasoning.

word ● n. **1** a sound or combination of sounds forming a meaningful element of speech, usu. written with a space on either side of it. **2** speech, esp. as distinct from action (bold in word only). **3** one's promise (gave us their word). **4** (in sing. or pl.) a thing said, a remark or conversation. **5** (in pl.) the text of a song or an actor's part. **6** (in pl.) angry talk (they had words). **7 a** news; a message (send word). **b** a rumour (word is she's left town). **8** a command, password, or motto (gave the word to begin). **9** (**the Word**) **a** any divine message. **b** the Gospel. **c** Jesus. **d** the Bible. ● v.tr. put into words; select words to express (how shall we word that?). □ **be as good as one's word** fulfil (or exceed) what one has promised. **break one's word** fail to do what one has promised. **have no words for** be unable to express. **have a word** (often foll. by with) speak briefly (to). **in other words** expressing the same thing differently. **in so many words** explicitly or bluntly. **in a** (or **one**) **word** briefly. **keep one's word** do what one has promised. **my** (or **upon my**) **word** an exclamation of surprise or consternation. **not the word for it** not an adequate or appropriate description. **of few words** taciturn. **of one's word** reliable in keeping promises (a woman of her word). **put into words** express in speech or writing. **take a person at his** or **her word** interpret a person's words literally or exactly. **take a person's word for it** believe a person's statement without investigation etc. **too ... for words** too ... to be adequately described (was too funny for words). **waste words** talk in vain. **word for word** in exactly the same or (of translation) corresponding words. **words fail me** an expression of disbelief, dismay, etc. **a word to the wise** a piece of advice etc. given in the hope that it will be sufficient to change a person's behaviour etc. □ **wordage** n. **wordless** adj. **wordlessly** adv. **wordlessness** n.

-word comb. form appended to a (frequently uppercase) letter of the alphabet to denote a word beginning with that letter, esp. denoting a word which is taboo slang or offensive, or one having negative connotations in a particular context (F-word).

word association n. the bringing to mind of one word in response to another, esp. as a revelation of a person's subconscious.

word game n. a game involving the making or selection etc. of words.

wording n. **1** a form of words used. **2** the way in which something is expressed.

word of mouth n. spoken communication between people as a means of transmitting information.

wordplay n. witty use of words, esp. by punning.

word processor n. a computer system for storing, manipulating, editing, and usu. displaying and printing text entered from a keyboard. □ **word-process** v.tr. **word processing** n.

wordsmith n. a skilled user or maker of words.

word wrap n. (in word processing) the automatic shifting of a word too long to fit on a line to the beginning of the next line.

wordy adj. (-ier, -iest) **1** using many or too many words. **2** consisting of words. □ **wordily** adv. **wordiness** n.

wore past of WEAR.

work ● n. **1** the application of mental or physical effort to a purpose. **2 a** a task to be undertaken. **b** the materials for this. **3** a thing done or made by work; the result of an action; an achievement; a thing made. **4** a person's employment or occupation etc., esp. as a means of earning income. **5 a** a literary or musical composition. **b** (in pl.) all such by an author or composer etc. **6** actions or experiences of a specified kind (good work!; this is thirsty work). **7** (in comb.) things or parts made of a specified material or with specified tools etc. (needlework). **8** (in pl.) the operative part of a clock or machine. **9** Physics the exertion of force overcoming resistance or producing molecular change (convert heat into work). **10** (in pl.) informal all that is available; everything needed. **11** (usu. in pl.) Theol. a meritorious act. **12** (usu. in pl. or in comb.) a defensive structure (earthworks). **13** (in comb.) **a** ornamentation of a specified kind (latticework). **b** articles having this. ● v. **1** intr. do work; be engaged in bodily or mental activity. **2** intr. be employed in certain work (works in industry; works as a secretary). **3** intr. make efforts; conduct a campaign (works for peace). **4** intr. (foll. by in) be a craftsman (in a material). **5** intr. operate or function, esp. effectively (*your idea will not work*). **6** *intr.* (of a part of a machine) run, revolve. **7** *tr.* carry on, manage, or control (*cannot work the machine*). **8** *tr.* **a** put or keep in operation or at work; cause to toil (*works the staff very hard*). **b** cultivate (land). **9** *tr.* **a** bring about (*worked miracles*). **b** *informal* arrange (matters) (*worked it so that we could go*). **10** *tr.* knead, hammer; bring to a desired shape or consistency. **11** *tr. & intr.* (cause to) progress or penetrate, or make (one's way), gradually or with difficulty in a specified way (*worked our way through the crowd*). **12** *intr.* gradually become (loose etc.) by constant movement. **13** *tr.* artificially excite (*worked themselves into a rage*). **14** *tr.* **a** purchase with one's labour instead of money (*work one's passage*). **b** obtain by labour the money for (one's way through university etc.). **15** *intr.* (foll. by *on, upon*) have influence. □ **at work** in action or engaged in work. **get worked up** become angry, excited, or tense. **give a person the works 1** *informal* give or tell a person everything. **2** *informal* treat a person harshly. **have one's work cut out** be faced with a hard task. **in the works** esp. *N Amer.* being planned, worked on, or produced. **set to work** begin or cause to begin operations. **work away** (or **on**) continue to work. **work in** find a place for. **work it** *informal* bring it about; achieve a desired result. **work off** get rid of by work or activity. **work out 1** solve or find out by calculation. **2** be calculated (*the total works out to 230*). **3** give a definite result. **4** have a specified result (*the plan worked out well*). **5** provide for the details of (*work out a scheme*). **6** accomplish or attain with difficulty. **7** exhaust with work (*the mine is worked out*). **8** engage in physical exercise or training. **work over 1** examine thoroughly. **2** *informal* treat with violence. **work a** (or **the) room** *informal* make the rounds of people in a room, in order to impress favourably. **work to rule** (esp. as a form of industrial action) follow official working rules exactly so as to reduce output and efficiency. **work up 1** bring gradually to an efficient state. **2** (foll. by *to*) advance gradually to a climax. **3** elaborate or excite by degrees. **4** learn (a subject) by study. □ **workless** *adj.*

workable *adj.* **1** that can be worked or will work. **2** practicable, feasible (*a workable scheme*). □ **workability** *n.*

workaday *adj.* **1** ordinary, everyday, practical. **2** fit for, used, or seen on workdays.

workaholic *n. informal* a person who willingly works too hard, esp. for too long. □ **workaholism** *n.*

workbench *n.* a bench for doing mechanical or practical work, esp. carpentry.

workbook *n.* **1** a student's book giving information on a subject and exercises. **2** a student's notebook.

workboot *n.* a sturdy leather boot worn esp. by people engaged in manual labour.

work camp *n.* **1** a prison camp enforcing a regime of hard labour. **2** a camp at which community work is done esp. by young volunteers.

workday *n.* **1** a day on which work is usually done. **2** the part of the day devoted to work (*a shorter workday*).

worker *n.* **1** one who works, esp. one who does a particular type of work (*factory workers; rescue worker*). **2 a** one who works in a specified way (*a slow worker*). **b** one who works hard (*she's quite the worker!*). **3** a neuter or undeveloped female of various social insects, esp. a bee or ant, that does the basic work of its colony.

workers' compensation *n.* money paid to a person to compensate for injury suffered on the job.

work ethic *n.* the principle that hard work is intrinsically virtuous or worthy of reward.

workfare *n.* a welfare system which requires some work or training from those receiving benefits.

workforce *n.* **1** the workers engaged or available in an industry etc. **2** the number of such workers.

workgroup *n.* a group of people who have simultaneous access via a network to shared software and data, enabling them to work together on projects.

workhorse *n.* **1** a horse used for heavy work, e.g. plowing, hauling, etc., rather than riding or racing. **2** a person, machine, etc. that does much work.

workhouse *n. Brit. hist.* a public institution where destitute people received board and lodging in return for work.

working ● *adj.* **1 a** having a job; employed. **b** having a job that involves physical labour. **c** spent in work or employment. **2** functioning or able to function (*a working model*). **3** that is good enough as a basis for work, argument, etc. and may be improved later (*the book's working title*). ● *n.* **1** the activity of work. **2** (often in *pl.*) the act or manner of functioning of a thing (*the workings of the human mind*). **3** (usu. in *pl.*) **a** a mine or quarry. **b** the part of this in which work is being or has been done (*disused mine workings*).

working capital *n.* capital needed and used in running a business and not invested in buildings, equipment, etc.

working class ● *n.* the class of people employed for wages, esp. in manual or industrial work. ● *adj.* (**working-class**) of or relating to this class.

working group *n.* a group appointed to study a particular problem or advise on some question.

working hours *n.pl.* hours normally spent at work.

working order *n.* the condition in which a machine works (satisfactorily or as specified).

work-in-progress *n.* work undertaken but not yet completed.

workload *n.* the amount of work to be done by an individual etc.

workman *n.* (*pl.* **-men**) **1** a man employed to do manual work. **2** a person considered with regard to skill in a job (*a good workman*).

workmanlike *adj.* characteristic of a good workman; showing practised skill.

workmanship *n.* **1** the degree of skill in doing a task or of quality in the product made. **2** a thing made or created by a specified person etc.

workmate *n.* a person with whom one works.

work of art *n.* a fine picture, poem, or building etc.

workout *n.* a session of physical exercise or training.

workpiece *n.* a thing worked with a tool or machine.

workplace *n.* a place at which a person works.

workroom *n.* a room for working in, esp. one equipped for a certain kind of work.

worksheet *n.* **1** a paper for recording work done or in progress. **2** a paper listing questions or activities for students etc. to work through.

workshop ● *n.* **1** a room or building in which goods are made. **2 a** a meeting for concerted discussion and practical work on a particular subject, in which knowledge and experience are shared (*a writing workshop*). **b** the members of such a group. ● *v.tr.* (**-shopped, -shopping**) present a workshop performance of (a dramatic work), esp. in order to explore aspects of the production before it is staged formally.

workspace *n.* **1** space in which to work. **2** an area rented or sold for commercial purposes. **3** *Computing* a memory storage facility for temporary use.

workstation *n.* **1** a computer terminal or the desk etc. where this is located. **2** a location on an assembly line at which a manufacturing operation is carried out.

work surface *n.* a flat surface for working on, e.g. a counter or table.

work-to-rule *n.* the act or an instance of working to rule.

workup *n.* a diagnostic examination of a patient.

workweek *n.* *N Amer.* the number of days or hours per week devoted or allotted to work.

world *n.* **1 a** the earth, or a planetary body like it. **b** its countries and their inhabitants. **c** the earth as known or in some particular respect. **2 a** the universe or all that exists; everything. **b** everything that exists outside oneself (*dead to the world*). **3 a** the time, state, or scene of human existence. **b** (prec. by *the, this*) mortal life. **4** secular interests and affairs. **5** active life (*how goes the world with you?*). **6** average, respectable, or fashionable people or their customs or opinions. **7** all that concerns or all who belong to a specified class, time, domain, etc. (*the medieval world*; *the sports world*). **8** a vast amount (*that makes a world of difference*). **9** (*attrib.*) affecting many nations, of all nations (*world politics*; *world record*). □ **be worlds apart** be completely different in attitudes etc. **bring into the world** give birth to or attend at the birth of. **come into the world** be born. **for all the world** precisely (*looked for all the world as if they were real*). **in the world** of all; at all (used as an intensifier in questions) (*what in the world is it?*). **man** (or **woman**) **of the world** a person experienced and practical in human affairs. **out of this world** *informal* extremely good etc. **see the world** travel widely. **think the world of** have a very high regard for. **the** (or **all the**) **world over** throughout the world. **the world to come** supposed life after death. **world without end** forever. □ **worlder** *n.* (also in *comb.*).

World Bank *n.* the International Bank for Reconstruction and Development, which administers economic aid between member nations.

world beat *n.* = WORLD MUSIC.

world-class *adj.* of a quality or standard regarded as high throughout the world.

World Council of Churches *n.* an association that promotes unity among the various Christian Churches; its members include almost all Christian traditions except Catholicism and Unitarianism.

World Court *n.* = INTERNATIONAL COURT OF JUSTICE.

World Cup *n.* any of various international sports competitions (or the trophies awarded for them), esp. a soccer competition held every fourth year between national teams.

world-famous *adj.* known throughout the world.

World Health Organization *n.* an agency of the United Nations, which promotes health and controls communicable diseases. Abbr.: **WHO**.

World Heritage Site *n.* a natural or man-made site of outstanding international importance and deserving special protection.

world language *n.* **1** a language in use throughout the world. **2** a language used in many countries.

worldly *adj.* (**-ier, -iest**) **1** earthly (*worldly goods*). **2** engrossed in temporal affairs, esp. the pursuit of wealth and pleasure. **3** experienced in life. □ **worldliness** *n.*

world music *n.* **1** traditional local or ethnic music, esp. from the developing world. **2** a style of pop music incorporating elements of such traditions.

world power *n.* a nation having power and influence in world affairs.

World Series *n.* a North American professional baseball championship played between the champions of the American League and the National League.

world's fair *n.* an international exhibition of the industrial, scientific, technological, and artistic achievements of the participating nations.

world view *n.* a comprehensive view or philosophy of life, the world, and the universe.

world war *n.* a war between many important nations.

World War III *n.* a hypothetical future world war, esp. one involving the destruction of the planet through the use of nuclear weapons.

world-weary *adj.* weary of the world and life on it. □ **world-weariness** *n.*

worldwide ● *adj.* affecting, occurring in, or known throughout the world. ● *adv.* throughout the world.

World Wide Web *n.* an international computer network incorporating multimedia and using hypertext links to access and retrieve information.

worm ● *n.* **1** any of various types of creeping or burrowing invertebrate animals with long slender bodies and no limbs, esp. segmented in rings or parasitic in the intestines or tissues. **2** the long slender larva of an insect, esp. in fruit or wood. **3** (in *pl.*) intestinal or other internal parasites. **4** a maggot supposed to eat dead bodies in the grave. **5** an insignificant or contemptible person. ● *v.* **1** *intr.* & *tr.* move with a crawling motion. **2** *intr.* & *refl.* (foll. by *into*) insinuate oneself into a person's favour etc. **3** *tr.* (foll. by *out*) obtain (a secret etc.) by cunning persistence (*managed to worm the truth out of them*). **4** *tr.* rid (a plant or dog etc.) of worms. □ **the worm turns** a meek person retaliates after being pushed too far. □ **wormer** *n.* **wormlike** *adj.*

worm casting *n.* (also **wormcast**) a convoluted mass of earth left on the surface by a burrowing earthworm.

worm-eaten *adj.* **1 a** eaten into by worms. **b** rotten, decayed. **2** old and dilapidated.

wormwood *n.* **1** any herbaceous plant or woody shrub of the genus *Artemisia*, with a bitter aromatic taste, esp. *A. absinthium*, used in vermouth, absinthe, and medicine. **2** bitter mortification or a source of this.

wormy *adj.* (**-ier, -iest**) **1** full of worms. **2** worm-eaten. □ **worminess** *n.*

worn ● *v.* *past part. of* WEAR. ● *adj.* **1** damaged by use or wear. **2** looking tired and exhausted. **3** (in full **well-worn**) (of a joke etc.) stale; often heard.

worn out *adj.* **1** exhausted. **2** worn, esp. so as to be no longer usable (often *attrib.*: *a worn-out engine*).

worried *adj.* **1** uneasy, troubled in the mind. **2** suggesting worry (*a worried look*).

worrisome *adj.* causing or apt to cause worry.

worry ● *v.* (**-ies, -ied**) **1** *intr.* give way to anxiety or unease; allow one's mind to dwell on difficulty or troubles. **2** *tr.* be a trouble or anxiety to. **3** *tr.* **a** (of a dog etc.) shake or pull repeatedly with the teeth. **b** attack repeatedly. ● *n.* (*pl.* **-ies**) **1** a thing that causes anxiety. **2** anxiety; a worried state. □ **not to worry** *informal* there is no need to worry. **worry along** (or **through**) manage to advance by persistence in spite of obstacles. **worry oneself** (usu. in *neg.*) take needless trouble. □ **worriedly** *adv.* **worrier** *n.* **worrying** *adj.* **worryingly** *adv.*

worrywart *n. informal* a person who tends to worry unduly.

worse ● *adj.* **1** bad to a greater degree or on a greater scale. **2** (*predic.*) in or into worse health or a worse condition (*is getting worse*). ● *adv.* more badly or more ill. ● *n.* **1** a worse thing or things (*you might do worse than accept*). **2** (*prec. by the*) a worse condition (*a turn for the worse*). □ **none the worse** (often foll. by *for*) not adversely affected (by). **or worse** or as an even worse alternative. **the worse for wear 1** damaged by use. **2** injured. **3** drunk. **worse off** in a worse (esp. financial) position.

worsen *v.tr. & intr.* make or become worse.

worship ● *n.* **1 a** reverence paid to a deity, esp. in a formal service. **b** the acts, rites, or ceremonies of worship. **2** quasi-religious adoration of or devotion to a person or principle (*the worship of wealth*). ● *v.* (**worshipped, worshipping**) **1** *tr.* adore as divine; honour with religious rites. **2** *tr.* idolize or regard with adoration (*worships the ground she walks on*). **3** *intr.* attend public worship. **4** *intr.* be full of adoration. □ **Your** (or **His** or **Her**) **Worship** esp. *Cdn & Brit.* a title of respect used to or of a mayor, certain magistrates, etc. □ **worshipper** *n.*

worshipful *adj.* **1** (usu. **Worshipful**) a title given to officers of certain organizations. **2** full of worship; adoring (*worshipful fans*). □ **worshipfully** *adv.*

worst ● *adj.* most bad. ● *adv.* most badly. ● *n.* the worst part, possibility, etc. (*the worst of the storm is over*; *prepare for the worst*). ● *v.tr.* get the better of. □ **at its** etc. **worst** in the worst state. **at worst** (or **the worst**) in the worst possible case. **get** (or **have**) **the worst of it** be defeated. **if** (**the**) **worst comes to** (**the**) **worst** if the worst happens. **in the worst way** to an extreme degree.

worst-case *adj.* pertaining to the worst of the possible foreseeable outcomes, scenarios, etc.

worsted /ˈwʊrstəd/ *n.* **1** a fine smooth yarn spun from combed long staple wool. **2** fabric made from this.

worth ● *predic.adj.* **1** of a value equivalent to (*is worth $50*). **2** such as to justify; deserving (*not worth the trouble*). **3** possessing or having property amounting to (*is worth a million dollars*). ● *n.* **1** what a person or thing is worth; the (usu. specified) merit of. **2** the equivalent of money in a commodity (*ten dollars' worth of gas*). □ **for all one is worth** *informal* with one's utmost efforts; without reserve. **for what it is worth** without a guarantee of its truth or value. **worth it** *informal* worth the time or effort spent.

worthless *adj.* without value or merit. □ **worthlessly** *adv.* **worthlessness** *n.*

worthwhile *adj.* that is worth the time or effort spent; of value or importance.

worthy ● *adj.* (**-ier, -iest**) **1** having some moral worth; deserving respect (*lived a worthy life*). **2** esp. *jocular* (of a person) entitled to recognition (*the worthy citizens of the town*). **3 a** deserving (*worthy of a mention*). **b** adequate or suitable to the dignity etc. of (*worthy of the occasion*). ● *n.* (*pl.* **-ies**) **1** a worthy person. **2** a person of some distinction. **3** *jocular* a person. □ **worthily** *adv.* **worthiness** *n.*

-worthy *comb. form* forming adjectives meaning: **1** deserving of (*blameworthy*; *noteworthy*). **2** suitable or fit for (*newsworthy*; *roadworthy*).

would *v.aux.* (*3rd sing.* **would**) *past of* WILL[1], used esp.: **1** (in the 2nd and 3rd persons, and often in the 1st: *see* SHOULD). **a** in reported speech (*he said he would be home by evening*). **b** to express the conditional mood (*they would have been killed if they had gone*). **2** to express

habitual action (*would wait for her every evening*). **3** to express a question or polite request (*would they like it?*; *would you come in, please?*). **4** to express probability (*I guess she would be over fifty by now*). **5** (foll. by *that* + clause) *literary* to express a wish (*would that you were here*). **6** to express consent (*they would not help*).

would-be *attrib.adj.* often *derogatory* desiring or aspiring to be (*a would-be politician*).

wouldn't *contraction* would not. □ **I wouldn't know** *informal* (as is to be expected) I do not know.

wound[1] ● *n.* **1** an injury done to living tissue by a cut or blow etc., esp. beyond the cutting or piercing of the skin. **2** an injury to a person's reputation or a pain inflicted on a person's feelings. ● *v.tr.* inflict a wound on (*wounded soldiers*; *wounded feelings*).

wound[2] *past and past part. of* WIND[2] (compare WIND[1] *v.* 6).

wounded *n.* suffering from or damaged by a wound or wounds. □ **woundedness** *n.*

wove *past of* WEAVE[1].

woven *past part. of* WEAVE[1].

wow[1] ● *interj.* expressing astonishment or admiration. ● *v.tr. slang* impress or excite greatly.

wow[2] *n.* a slow pitch-fluctuation in sound reproduction, perceptible in long notes.

WP *abbr.* word processor or processing.

Wpg. *abbr.* Winnipeg.

w.p.m. *abbr.* words per minute.

wrack[1] /ræk/ *n.* **1** seaweed cast up or growing on the shore. **2** a wreck or wreckage. **3** = RACK[2]. **4** = RACK[5] *n.*

wrack[2] *var of.* RACK[1] *v.*

wraith /reiθ/ *n.* **1** a ghost or apparition. **2** the spectral appearance of a living person supposed to portend that person's death. □ **wraithlike** *adj.*

wrangle ● *n.* a heated or prolonged dispute. ● *v.* **1** *intr.* engage in a wrangle. **2** *tr.* get (a thing) from a person by argument or persuasion. **3** *tr. N Amer.* herd (horses, cattle, etc.). □ **wrangling** *n.*

wrangler *n.* **1** *N Amer.* a cowboy. **2** a person who wrangles. **3** a person who supervises and handles animals used on a film set.

wrap ● *v.* (**wrapped, wrapping**) **1** *tr.* envelop in folded or soft encircling material. **2** *tr.* **a** arrange or draw (a pliant covering) around (a person). **b** use (oneself or a part of one's body) to embrace a person (*wrapped her arms around his neck*). **3** *tr.* (foll. by *around*) *slang* crash (a vehicle) into a stationary object. **4** *tr. & intr.* finish filming (a movie etc.). **5** *Computing* **a** *tr.* cause (a word or other unit of text) to be carried over to a new line automatically as the right margin is reached. **b** *intr.* (of a word etc.) be so carried over. ● *n.* **1** a shawl or scarf or other such addition to clothing. **2** esp. *N Amer.* material used for wrapping. **3** the completion of the filming of a movie etc. **4** a sandwich of any of a variety of fillings wrapped in a tortilla. □ **take the wraps off** disclose. **under wraps** in secrecy. **wrapped up in** engrossed or absorbed in. **wrap up 1** finish off, bring to completion (*wrapped up the deal in two days*). **2** put on warm clothes (*wrap up well*).

wraparound ● *adj.* **1** (of a garment, esp. a woman's skirt or top) designed to wrap around the body. **2** curving or extending around at the edges. ● *n.* anything that wraps around.

wrapper *n.* **1** a thing in which something is wrapped, esp. a flexible piece of paper etc. forming a protective covering for a product (*candy wrappers*). **2** a cover enclosing a newspaper or similar packet for mailing. **3** a paper cover of a book or magazine, usu. detachable.

wrapping *n.* (often in *pl.*) material used to wrap; wrappers, wrapping paper, etc.

wrapping paper *n.* strong or decorative paper for wrapping gifts etc.

wrap-up ● *n.* a summary, esp. of news; a conclusion (*a wrap-up of the day's events*). ● *adj.* that concludes or sums up a program, book, etc.

wrassle /'ræsəl/ *v.intr. & tr. N Amer. dialect* = WRESTLE *v.*

wrath /ræθ/ *n. literary* extreme anger. ☐ **wrathful** *adj.*
wrathfully *adv.* **wrathfulness** *n.*

WRCNS *abbr. Cdn hist.* Women's Royal Canadian Naval Service.

wreak /riːk/ *v.tr.* **1** give expression or vent to (vengeance, anger etc.). **2** cause (damage etc.).

wreath /riːθ/ *n.* (*pl.* **wreaths** /riːðz, riːθs/) **1** flowers or leaves fastened in a ring esp. as an ornament for a person's head or a building or for laying on a grave etc. as a mark of honour or respect. **2** (foll. by *of*) something shaped like a wreath (*wreaths of cloud*).

wreathe /riːð/ *v.tr.* encircle as, with, or like a wreath.

wreck ● *n.* **1 a** the destruction or disablement esp. of a ship. **b** a ship that has suffered a wreck (*the shores are strewn with wrecks*). **2** a greatly damaged or disabled building, vehicle, aircraft, etc. **3** a person whose health, esp. mental health, has been damaged or destroyed. **4** *N Amer.* a crash or collision on a road, railway, etc. **5** (foll. by *of*) a wretched remnant or disorganized set of remains. ● *v.tr.* **1** cause the wreck of (a ship etc.); damage or destroy. **2** *tr.* completely ruin (hopes, chances, etc.). **3** *intr.* suffer a wreck. **4** *intr. N Amer.* deal with wrecked vehicles etc.

wreckage *n.* **1** wrecked material. **2** the remnants of a wreck. **3** the action or process of wrecking.

wrecked *adj.* **1** involved in a shipwreck (*wrecked sailors*). **2** intoxicated by alcohol or drugs.

wrecker *n.* **1** a person or thing that wrecks or destroys. **2** esp. *N Amer.* a person employed in demolition, or in recovering a wrecked ship or its contents. **3** *N Amer.* a person who breaks up damaged vehicles for spare parts and scrap.

wrecking ball *n.* (also **wrecker's ball**) a heavy metal ball which may be swung from a crane into a building to demolish it.

wrecking bar *n.* a steel bar with one end chisel-shaped for prying and the other end bent and split to form a claw.

wren *n.* **1** any small usu. brown short-winged songbird of the family Troglodytidae, esp. *Troglodytes troglodytes* of N America and Eurasia, having an erect tail. **2** (**Wren**) *hist.* (in Canada) a member of the Women's Royal Canadian Naval Service.

wrench ● *n.* **1** a violent twist or oblique pull or act of tearing off. **2** a tool for gripping and turning a nut on a bolt etc. **3** an instance of painful uprooting or parting. ● *v.tr.* **1** twist or pull violently around or sideways. **2** pull off with a wrench. **3** injure (a limb, etc.) by undue twisting or stretching. **4** distort (facts) to suit a theory etc.

wrest *v.tr.* **1** force or wrench away from a person's grasp. **2** obtain by effort or with difficulty.

wrestle ● *n.* **1** a contest in which two opponents grapple and try to throw each other to the ground esp. as an athletic sport under a code of rules. **2** a hard struggle. ● *v.* **1** *intr.* take part in a wrestle. **2** *tr.* fight (a person) in a wrestle (*wrestled his opponent to the ground*). **3** *intr.* **a** struggle, contend. **b** do one's utmost to deal with (a task, difficulty, etc.). ☐ **wrestler** *n.*
wrestling *n.*

wretch *n.* **1** an unfortunate or unhappy person. **2** often *jocular* an evil or wicked person.

wretched *adj.* **1** unhappy or miserable. **2** of very poor quality. **3** ill or unwell. **4** despicable. **5** used to express annoyance (*this wretched car refuses to start*). ☐ **wretchedly** *adv.* **wretchedness** *n.*

wriggle ● *v.* **1** *intr.* twist or turn with short writhing movements. **2** *intr.* move or go in this way (*wriggled into the corner*). **3** *tr.* make (one's way) by wriggling. ● *n.* an act of wriggling. ☐ **wriggle out of** *informal* avoid on a contrived pretext. ☐ **wriggler** *n.* **wriggly** *adj.*

wring ● *v.tr.* (*past and past part.* **wrung**) **1 a** squeeze tightly. **b** (often foll. by *out*) squeeze and twist esp. to remove liquid. **2** twist forcibly; break by twisting. **3** distress or torture. **4** extract by squeezing. **5** (foll. by *out, from*) obtain by pressure or importunity; extort. ● *n.* an act of wringing; a squeeze. ☐ **wring a person's hand** clasp it forcibly or press it with emotion. **wring one's hands** clasp them as a gesture of great distress. **wring the neck of** kill (a chicken etc.) by twisting its neck.

wringer *n.* a device for wringing water from washed clothes etc. ☐ **put through the wringer** *informal* subject to a very stressful experience.

wringing *adj.* (in full **wringing wet**) very wet.

wrinkle ● *n.* **1** a slight crease or depression in the skin such as is produced by age. **2** a similar mark in another flexible surface. **3** *informal* a minor difficulty; a snag. **4** a clever innovation in technique etc. ● *v.* **1** *tr.* make wrinkles in. **2** *intr.* form wrinkles; become marked with wrinkles. ☐ **wrinkled** *adj.*

wrinkly *adj.* (**-ier, -iest**) having many wrinkles.

wrist *n.* **1** the joint connecting the hand with the forearm. **2** the part of a garment covering the wrist. ☐ **slap on the wrist** a mild rebuke or reprimand.

wristband *n.* **1** a band forming or concealing the end of a shirt sleeve; a cuff. **2** a strip of material worn around the wrist to absorb sweat. **3** a strap or band attached to a watch worn around the wrist. **4** a bracelet used for identification, e.g. while in hospital or as admission to an event etc.

wrist shot *n. Hockey* a shot taken by sweeping the puck along the ice before releasing it.

wristwatch *n.* a watch worn on a strap around the wrist.

writ[1] *n.* **1** a form of written command in the name of a sovereign, court, government, etc., to act or abstain from acting in some way. **2** a government document ordering an election. ☐ **serve a writ on** deliver a writ to (a person).

writ[2] ☐ **writ large** in magnified or emphasized form.

write *v.* (*past* **wrote**; *past part.* **written**) **1** *intr.* mark paper or some other surface by means of a pen, pencil, etc., with symbols, letters, or words. **2** *tr.* form (such symbols etc.). **3** *tr.* form the symbols that represent or constitute (a word or sentence, or a document etc.). **4** *tr.* fill or complete (a sheet, cheque, etc.) with writing. **5** *tr. & intr.* record (data) in a computer memory. **6** *tr.* (esp. in *passive*) indicate (a quality or condition) by one's or its appearance (*guilt was written on his face*). **7** *tr.* compose (a text, article, novel, etc.) for written or printed reproduction or publication; put into literary etc. form and set down in writing. **8** *intr.* be engaged in composing a text, article, etc. (*writes for the local newspaper*). **9** *intr.* **a** (foll. by *to*) write and send a letter (to a recipient). **b** communicate by writing (*she hardly ever writes*). **10** *tr.* write and send a letter to (a person) (*wrote him last week*). **11** *tr.* convey (news, information, etc.) by letter (*wrote that they would arrive next Friday*). **12** *tr. Cdn & South Africa* take (an exam or test). **13** *intr.* write in a cursive hand, as opposed to printing individual letters. **14** *tr.* state in written or printed form (*it is written that*). **15** *tr.* cause to be recorded. **16** *tr.* (foll. by *into, out of*) include or exclude (a character or episode) in a story by suitable changes of the text. □ **nothing to write home about** *informal* of little interest or value. **write down 1** record or take note of in writing. **2** write as if for those considered inferior. **3** reduce the nominal value of (stock, goods, etc.). **write in** send a suggestion, query, etc., in writing to an organization, esp. a broadcasting station. **write off 1** write and send a letter. **2** cancel the record of (a bad debt etc.); acknowledge the loss of or failure to recover (an asset). **3** damage (a vehicle etc.) so badly that it cannot be repaired. **4** dismiss as insignificant. **write out 1** write in full or in finished form. **2** exhaust (oneself) by writing. **write up 1** write a full account of. **2** praise or bring to public attention in writing (*the concert was written up in the newspapers*). □ **writable** *adj.*

writedown *n.* a reduction in the estimated or nominal value of stock, assets, etc.

write-off *n.* **1** a thing written off, esp. a vehicle too badly damaged to be repaired. **2** a person or thing that is given up as being hopeless etc. (*the entire weekend was a write-off*). **3** an act of cancelling a debt because there is no chance that it will be paid.

writer *n.* **1** one who writes or has written something. **2** one who writes professionally, esp. books or screenplays.

writer-in-residence *n.* a writer holding a usu. temporary residential post in a university etc. in order to share his or her professional insights with students and faculty.

writerly *adj.* **1** characteristic of a professional author. **2** consciously literary.

writer's block *n.* a (usu. temporary) inability to express thoughts in writing due to lack of inspiration.

writer's cramp *n.* a muscular spasm in the hands due to excessive writing.

write-up *n. informal* a written account, a review.

writhe /raɪð/ *v.* **1** *intr.* twist or roll oneself about in or as if in acute pain. **2** *intr.* suffer severe mental discomfort or embarrassment (*writhed with shame*). **3** *tr.* twist (one's body etc.) about.

writing *n.* **1** a group or sequence of letters or symbols. **2** = HANDWRITING. **3** (usu. in *pl.*) a piece of literary work done; a book, article, etc. **4** the work or profession of a writer. **5** (*attrib.*) used for writing (*writing paper*). □ **in writing** in written form (*give me your request in writing*). **the writing is on the wall** see HANDWRITING.

writing desk *n.* a desk for writing at, esp. with compartments for papers etc.

written ● *v. past part. of* WRITE. ● *adj.* that has been or is to be done in writing (*a written agreement*).

wrong ● *adj.* **1** mistaken; not true. **2** unsuitable; less or least desirable. **3** contrary to law or morality. **4** out of order, in or into a bad or abnormal condition. ● *adv.* in a wrong manner or direction; with an incorrect result (*guessed wrong*). ● *n.* **1** what is morally wrong; a wrong action. **2** injustice; unjust action or treatment (*suffer wrong*). ● *v.tr.* **1** treat unjustly; do wrong to. **2** mistakenly attribute bad motives to; discredit. □ **do wrong** commit sin; transgress, offend. **do wrong to** malign or mistreat (a person). **get in wrong with** incur the dislike or disapproval of (a person). **get off on the wrong foot** begin badly; make a bad start. **get wrong 1** misunderstand (a person, statement, etc.). **2** obtain an incorrect answer to. **get** (or **get hold of**) **the wrong end of the stick** misunder-

stand completely. **go down the wrong way** (of food) enter the windpipe instead of the gullet. **go wrong 1** take the wrong path. **2** stop functioning properly. **3** depart from virtuous or suitable behaviour. **in the wrong** responsible for a quarrel, mistake, or offence. **on the wrong side of 1** out of favour with (a person). **2** somewhat more than (a stated age). **wrong side out** inside out. **wrong way round** in the opposite or reverse of the normal or desirable orientation or sequence etc. □ **wronger** *n.* **wrongly** *adv.* **wrongness** *n.*

wrongdoer *n.* a person who behaves immorally or illegally. □ **wrongdoing** *n.*

wrongful *adj.* **1** characterized by unfairness or injustice. **2** contrary to law. **3** not entitled to the position etc. occupied. □ **wrongfully** *adv.*

wrongful dismissal *n.* unjust dismissal from employment.

wrong-headed *adj.* perverse and obstinate. □ **wrong-headedness** *n.*

wrote *past of* WRITE. □ **that's all she wrote** *N Amer. informal* that's it; that's the end.

wrought *adj.* **1** (of metals) beaten out or shaped by hammering. **2** worked or made (*well-wrought*).

wrought iron *n.* a tough malleable form of iron suitable for forging or rolling, not cast.

wrung *past and past part. of* WRING. □ **wrung out** exhausted.

wry *adj.* (**wryer, wryest** or **wrier, wriest**) **1** (of humour) dry and mocking. **2** (of a face or smile etc.) contorted in disappointment, mockery, etc. □ **wryly** *adv.* **wryness** *n.*

WSW *abbr.* west-southwest.

wt. *abbr.* weight.

WTO *abbr.* World Trade Organization.

wunderkind /ˈvʊndərkɪnt/ *n. informal* a person who achieves great success while relatively young.

wurst /vʊrst, vɜrst/ *n.* sausage, esp. of a German or Austrian type.

wuss /wʊs/ *n.* (also **wussy** *pl.* **-ies**) esp. *N Amer. slang* an inept, feeble, or cowardly person. □ **wussy** *adj.*

WV *abbr.* West Virginia (in postal use).

W.Va. *abbr.* West Virginia.

WW I *abbr. N Amer.* World War I.

WW II *abbr. N Amer.* World War II.

WWW *abbr.* World Wide Web.

WY *abbr.* Wyoming (in official postal use).

Wyandot /ˈwʌɪəndɒt/ (also **Wyandotte** esp. in sense 2 of *n.*) ● *n.* **1 a** a member of a N American Aboriginal people originally of Ontario, now living esp. in Oklahoma. **b** the Iroquoian language of this people. **2 a** a domestic fowl of a medium-sized American breed. **b** this breed. ● *adj.* of or relating to the Wyandots.

Wyo. *abbr.* Wyoming.

WYSIWYG /ˈwɪziwɪg/ *adj.* (also **wysiwyg**) *Computing* denoting the representation of text onscreen in a form looking exactly like the printout.

Xx

X *n.* (also **x**) (*pl.* **Xs** or **X's**) **1** the twenty-fourth letter of the alphabet. **2** (as a Roman numeral) ten. **3** (usu. **x**) *Algebra* the first unknown quantity. **4** *Math.* the first coordinate. **5** an unknown or unspecified number or person etc. **6** a cross-shaped symbol esp. used: **a** to indicate position (*X marks the spot*). **b** to indicate incorrectness. **c** to symbolize a kiss. **d** to symbolize a vote. **e** as the signature of a person who cannot write.

X-C *abbr.* (also **XC**, **X-country**) *N Amer.* cross-country.

X chromosome *n.* a sex chromosome of which the number in female cells is twice that in male cells.

Xe *symbol* xenon.

xeno- /ˈzenoː, ˈziːnoː/ *comb. form* **1 a** foreign. **b** a foreigner. **2** other.

xenon /ˈzenɒn/ *n.* a heavy colourless odourless inert gaseous element occurring in traces in the atmosphere and used in fluorescent lamps.

xenophobe /ˈzenəˌfoːb/ *n.* a person who dislikes foreigners. □ **xenophobia** *n.* **xenophobic** *adj.*

Xer /ˈeksər/ *n. informal* a member of Generation X.

xeriscaping /ˈzerɪskeɪpɪŋ/ *n.* a landscaping method requiring little or no irrigation or other maintenance, used in arid regions. □ **xeriscape** *n.*

xerography /zɪˈrɒgrəfi, zeˈ-/ *n.* a dry copying process in which black or coloured powder adheres to parts of a surface remaining electrically charged after exposure of the surface to light from an image of the document to be copied. □ **xerographic** *adj.*

Xerox /ˈziːrɒks/ ● *n. proprietary* **1** a machine for copying by xerography. **2** a copy made using this machine. ● *v.tr.* (**xerox**) reproduce by this process.

Xhosa /ˈkoːsə, ˈkɒ-/ ● *n.* **1** (*pl.* same or **-s**) a member of a Bantu-speaking people forming the second largest ethnic group in South Africa after the Zulus. **2** the language of this people, forming part of the Nguni language group. ● *adj.* of this people or language.

xi /saɪ, gzaɪ, zaɪ/ *n.* the fourteenth letter of the Greek alphabet (Ξ, ξ).

XL *abbr.* (esp. of clothing) extra large.

Xmas /ˈkrɪsməs, ˈeksməs/ *n. informal* = CHRISTMAS.

X-rated *adj.* (usu. *attrib.*) indecent, pornographic.

X-ray (also **x-ray**) ● *n.* **1** (in *pl.*) electromagnetic radiation of short wavelength, able to pass through opaque bodies. **2** an image made by passing X-rays through something onto a photographic plate. ● *v.tr.* photograph, examine, or treat with X-rays.

XS *abbr.* (esp. of clothing) extra small.

X's and O's *n.* = TIC-TAC-TOE.

Xwe Nal Mewx *var.* of SNE NAY MUXW.

XXL *abbr.* (esp. of clothing) extra, extra large.

xylem /ˈzaɪlem/ *n. Bot.* woody tissue (compare PHLOEM).

xylene /ˈzaɪliːn/ *n.* a volatile liquid hydrocarbon obtained from wood etc., used in fuels and solvents and in chemical synthesis.

xylophone /ˈzaɪləˌfoːn/ *n.* a musical instrument of wooden or metal bars graduated in length and struck with a small hammer. □ **xylophonist** *n.*

Yy

Y¹ /waɪ/ *n.* (also **y**) (*pl.* **Ys** or **Y's**) **1** the twenty-fifth letter of the alphabet. **2** (usu. **y**) *Algebra* the second unknown quantity. **3** *Math.* the second coordinate. **4 a** a Y-shaped thing. **b** a forked clamp or support.

Y² *abbr.* (also **Y.**) **1** yen. **2** *N Amer.* **a** = YMCA. **b** = YWCA. **c** = YMHA. **d** = YWHA.

Y³ *symbol* yttrium.

y. *abbr.* year(s).

-y¹ /i/ *suffix* (also **-ey**) forming adjectives: **1** from nouns and adjectives, meaning: **a** full of; having the quality of (*messy*; *icy*). **b** addicted to (*boozy*). **2** from verbs, meaning 'inclined to', 'apt to' (*runny*; *sticky*).

-y² /i/ *suffix* (also **-ey**, **-ie**) forming diminutive nouns, pet names, etc. (*granny*; *Sally*; *nightie*; *Mickey*).

Y2K *n.* **1** computer problems arising from the inability of certain software and firmware to deal correctly with dates of 1 January 2000 or later (usu. *attrib.*: *Y2K problem*; *Y2K policy*). **2** the year 2000.

ya *interj. informal* yes.

yacht /jɒt/ ● *n.* **1** a light sailing vessel, esp. equipped for racing. **2** a larger usu. power-driven vessel equipped for cruising. ● *v.intr.* race or cruise in a yacht. □ **yachting** *n.*

yachtsman *n.* (*pl.* **-men**) a person who sails yachts.

yack (also **yackety-yack**) *informal var. of* YAK².

yaffle *n. Cdn* (*Nfld*) an armful or small load, esp. of cod.

yahoo¹ ● *n.* (*pl.* **-s**) a coarse, brutish, or uncivilized person. ● *adj.* characteristic of a yahoo.

yahoo² *interj.* an exclamation of excitement.

Yahweh /'jɒweɪ/ *n.* (also **Yahveh** /'jɒveɪ/) a form of the Hebrew name of God used in the Bible.

Yajur-Veda /ˌjʌdʒʊr'veɪdə, -'viːdə/ one of the four Hindu Vedas, a collection of sacrificial formulas in early Sanskrit used in the Vedic religion by the priest in charge of sacrificial ritual.

yak¹ *n.* a long-haired Tibetan ox, *Bos grunniens*.

yak² *informal often derogatory* ● *n.* trivial or unduly persistent talk. ● *v.intr.* (**yakked**, **yakking**) chatter.

yakuza /jə'kuːzə/ *n.* (*pl.* same) **1** a Japanese gangster or racketeer; a member of a Japanese organized crime gang. **2** (*in pl.*) Japanese organized crime gangs.

yam *n.* **1 a** any tropical or subtropical climbing plant of the genus *Dioscorea*. **b** the edible starchy tuber of this. **2** esp. *US* a sweet potato.

yammer *v. informal* **1** *intr.* whine or complain; grumble. **2** *intr.* **a** make a loud noise; talk loudly. **b** talk incessantly with little substance. **3** *tr.* utter complainingly. **4** *intr.* (esp. of an animal) howl or wail.

yang *n.* (in Chinese philosophy) the active male principle of the universe (*compare* YIN).

Yank *n. informal often derogatory* a resident of the US.

yank *informal* ● *v.* **1** *tr. & intr.* pull sharply or with a jerk. **2** *tr. N Amer.* remove, withdraw, or cancel abruptly. ● *n.* a sudden hard pull.

Yankee *informal* ● *n.* **1** *often derogatory* = YANK. **2** *US* an inhabitant of New England or one of the northern States. **3** *hist.* a Federal soldier in the Civil War. ● *adj.* of or characteristic of a Yankee.

yap ● *v.intr.* (**yapped**, **yapping**) **1** bark shrilly or fussily. **2** *informal* talk noisily or complainingly. ● *n.* **1** a

shrill bark; a yelp. **2** idle or tiresome chatter. **3** *slang* the mouth (*shut your yap!*). □ **yapper** *n.*

yappy *adj.* (**-ier**, **-iest**) (of a dog) inclined to yap.

yard¹ *n.* **1** a unit of linear measure equal to 3 feet (0.9144 metre). **2** a square or cubic yard, esp. of sand, topsoil, etc. **3** a cylindrical spar tapering to each end slung across a mast for a sail to hang from. **4** (*in pl.*; foll. by *of*) *informal* a great length or amount (*we have yards of time to get there*).

yard² ● *n.* **1** a piece of enclosed ground, esp. attached to a building. **2** *N Amer. & Austral.* the area at the front or back of a house, usu. including a lawn and sometimes a garden. **3** an enclosed area used for a particular business or purpose (*lumberyard*). **4** = RAILWAY YARD. **5** *N Amer.* a place where deer or moose etc. congregate, esp. during the winter months. **6** *Forestry* = LANDING 3. ● *v.tr.* **1** put (cattle) into a stockyard. **2** *Forestry* move (felled trees) from the felling site to the landing.

yardage *n.* **1** a number of yards of material etc. **2** a distance measured in yards.

yardarm *n.* the outer extremity of a ship's yard.

yarder *n.* an engine or vehicle used to move logs from the bush to a yard, landing, etc.

yard sale *n. N Amer.* a sale of used household items, held in the front yard of a house.

yardstick *n.* **1** a measuring rod a yard long, usu. divided into inches etc. **2** a standard used for comparison.

yardwork *n. N Amer.* gardening and other maintenance work required in the yard of a residence.

yarmulke /'jɑrmǝlkǝ/ *n.* (also **yarmulka**) a skullcap worn by Jewish men.

yarn ● *n.* **1** any spun thread, esp. for knitting, weaving, rope making, etc. **2** *informal* a long or rambling story or discourse. ● *v.intr. informal* tell yarns.

yarrow /'jærǝʊ/ *n.* any perennial herb of the genus *Achillea*, esp. *A. millefolium*, with small white flowers.

yaw ● *v.intr.* **1** (of a ship) deviate temporarily from its course, esp. through faulty steering or adverse weather conditions. **2** (of an aircraft, missile, etc.) rotate about a vertical axis. ● *n.* the yawing of a ship etc. from its course.

yawn ● *v.* **1** *intr.* open the mouth wide and inhale esp. when sleepy or bored. **2** *intr.* (of a chasm etc.) gape, be wide open. **3** *tr.* utter or say with a yawn. ● *n.* **1** an act of yawning. **2** *informal* a boring or tedious idea, activity, etc. □ **yawningly** *adv.*

yawp *N Amer.* ● *n.* **1** a harsh or hoarse cry. **2** foolish or noisy talk. ● *v.intr.* make a yawp.

yaws *n.pl.* (usu. treated as *sing.*) a contagious tropical skin disease with large red swellings.

yay¹ *interj. slang* (also **yea**, **yeah**) expressing triumph, approval, or encouragement.

yay² *adv. N Amer. informal* (with adjectives of size, height, etc.) so, this (*about yay big*).

Yb *symbol* ytterbium.

Y chromosome *n.* a sex chromosome occurring only in male cells.

yd. *abbr.* yard (measure).

yds. *abbr.* yards (measure).

ye[1] *pron. archaic* pl. of THOU[1].

ye[2] *adj. pseudo-archaic* = THE (*Ye Olde Book Shoppe*).

yea ● *interj.* **1** yes. **2** = YAY[1]. ● *adv.* indeed, even (*ready, yea eager*). ● *n.* **1** the word 'yea'. **2** an affirmative answer or assent, esp. in voting. □ **the yeas have it** = THE AYES HAVE IT (see AYE[1]).

yeah *adv. informal* **1** yes. **2** = YAY[1]. □ **oh yeah?** expressing incredulity.

year *n.* **1** (also **solar year**) the time occupied by the earth in one revolution around the sun, 365 days, 5 hours, 48 minutes, and 46 seconds in length. **2** (also **calendar year**) the period of 365 or 366 days (see LEAP YEAR) from Jan. 1 to Dec. 31. **3 a** a period of the same length as this starting at any point (*four years ago today*). **b** such a period in terms of a particular activity etc. occupying its duration (*school year*). **4** (in pl.) age (*young for his years*). **5** (usu. in pl.) *informal* a very long time. **6** a group of students entering university etc. in the same academic year. □ **in the year of Our Lord** (foll. by the year) in a specified year AD. **year in, year out** continually over a period of years.

yearbook *n.* **1** an annual publication dealing with events or aspects of the (usu. preceding) year. **2** *N Amer.* a book published by the graduating class of a school etc., commemorating the events of the past year with stories and photographs.

year-end *n.* the end of esp. the financial year.

yearling ● *n.* **1** an animal between one and two years old. **2** a racehorse in the calendar year after the year of foaling. ● *adj.* a year old (*a yearling heifer*).

year-long *adj.* lasting a year or the whole year.

yearly ● *adj.* **1** done or occurring once a year. **2** lasting a year. ● *adv.* once a year; from year to year.

yearn /jɜrn/ *v.intr.* (usu. foll. by *for, after,* or *to* + infin.) have a strong emotional longing. □ **yearner** *n.* **yearning** *n. & adj.* **yearningly** *adv.*

year-round ● *adj.* existing etc. throughout the year. ● *adv.* throughout the year.

yeast *n.* **1** a greyish-yellow fungous substance obtained esp. from fermenting malt liquors and used to raise bread etc. **2** any of various unicellular fungi in which vegetative reproduction takes place by budding or fission. □ **yeastlike** *adj.*

yeast infection *n.* = THRUSH[2] 1.

yeasty *adj.* (**-ier, -iest**) **1** frothy or tasting like yeast. **2** in a ferment. **3** working like yeast. **4** (of talk etc.) light and superficial. □ **yeastiness** *n.*

yech *interj.* (also **yecch**) expressing disgust.

yee-haw *interj. N Amer.* expressing enthusiasm.

yeesh *interj. N Amer. informal* expressing frustration, exasperation, etc.

yell ● *n.* a loud sharp cry of pain, anger, fright, encouragement, delight, etc. ● *v.intr. & tr.* make or utter with a yell. □ **yelling** *n.*

yellow ● *adj.* **1** of the colour between green and orange in the spectrum, of lemons, egg yolks, or gold. **2** usu. *offensive* designating or pertaining to Oriental people. **3** *informal* cowardly. **4** (of newspapers etc.) unscrupulously sensational. ● *n.* **1** a yellow colour or pigment. **2** yellow clothes or material (*dressed in yellow*). **3 a** a yellow ball, piece, etc., in a game or sport. **b** the player using such pieces. **4** a yellow light as part of a set of traffic lights, indicating that the intersection should be cleared. ● *v.tr. & intr.* make or become yellow. □ **yellowish** *adj.* **yellowness** *n.* **yellowy** *adj.*

yellow-bellied sapsucker *n.* a N American sapsucker, *Sphyrapicus varius*, with black and white stripes on the head, a red crest, and a yellow belly.

yellow-belly *n.* **1** *informal* a coward. **2** any of various fish with yellow underparts. □ **yellow-bellied** *adj.*

yellow-billed loon *n.* a loon, *Gavia adamsii*, very similar in appearance to the common loon but with a whitish-yellow bill, which breeds in the Arctic.

yellow birch *n.* a birch of eastern Canada, *Betula alleghaniensis*, providing hardwood lumber for furniture and construction.

yellow fever *n.* an often fatal tropical virus disease characterized by fever and jaundice.

yellowhammer *n. N Amer.* a flicker with yellow plumage.

yellow jacket *n. N Amer.* a wasp of the genus *Vespula*, with black and yellow markings.

Yellowknife *n.* (*pl.* same or **-knives**) a member of an Aboriginal people formerly living around the Coppermine River, NWT; they are now absorbed into the Chipewyan.

Yellowknifer *n.* a native of Yellowknife, NWT.

yellowlegs *n.* (*pl.* same) either of two migratory sandpipers with yellow legs, *Tringa melanoleuca* or *T. flavipes*.

Yellow Pages *n. proprietary* a telephone directory or section of one printed on yellow paper, listing business subscribers according to the goods or services they offer.

yellow pepper *n.* the yellow ripe fruit of the sweet pepper, *Capsicum annuum*, used as a vegetable.

yellow peril *n. offensive* the political or military threat regarded as emanating from Asian peoples, esp. the Chinese.

yelp ● *n.* a sharp shrill cry of or as of a dog in pain or excitement. ● *v.intr.* utter a yelp.

Yemeni /ˈjeməni/ ● *n.* a native or inhabitant of Yemen, a country in the southern Arabian peninsula. ● *adj.* of or relating to Yemen or its people.

yen[1] *n.* (*pl.* same) the chief monetary unit of Japan.

yen[2] *informal* ● *n.* a longing or yearning. ● *v.intr.* (**yenned, yenning**) feel a longing.

yenta *n.* (also **yente**) *N Amer. slang* a gossip or busybody.

yeoman /ˈjoːmən/ *n.* (*pl.* **-men**) **1** *Brit.* esp. *hist.* a man holding and cultivating a small landed estate. **2** (**Yeoman**) (in full **Chief Yeoman of Signals**) a signaller in the Canadian Navy or the Royal Navy, responsible for transmitting both visual and radio signals.

yeoman service *n.* (also **yeoman's service**, **yeoman work**) efficient or useful help in need.

yep *adv. & n. N Amer. informal* = YES.

yes ● *adv.* **1** used to give an affirmative response. **2** (in answer to a summons or address) an acknowledgement of one's presence. ● *n.* **1** an utterance of the word *yes*. **2** an affirmation or assent. **3** a vote in favour of a proposition.

yeshiva /jəˈʃiːvə/ *n.* (also **yeshivah**) **1** an Orthodox Jewish college or seminary. **2** an Orthodox Jewish elementary school, teaching both religious and secular subjects.

yes-man *n.* (*pl.* **-men**) *informal* a weak person who always agrees with people in authority in order to gain their approval.

yesterday ● *adv.* **1** on the day before today. **2** in the recent past. **3** *informal* extremely urgently; immediately (*they want delivery yesterday!*). ● *n.* **1** the day before today. **2** the recent past.

yesteryear *n. literary* **1** last year. **2** the past.

yet ● *adv.* **1** as late as, or until, now or then (*there is yet time; your best work yet*). **2** (with *neg.* or *interrog.*) so soon as, or by, now or then (*it's not time yet; hasn't he finished yet?*). **3** again; in addition (*more and yet more*). **4** in the remaining time available; before all is over (*I will do it yet*). **5** (foll. by *comparative*) even (*a yet more difficult task*). **6** nevertheless; and in spite of that; but for all that (*it is strange, and yet it is true*). **7** (as an ironic intensive at the end of a sentence) too; what's more (*his own mother yet!*). ● *conj.* but at the same time; but nevertheless (*I won, yet what good has it done?*). □ **nor yet** and also not (*won't listen to me nor yet to you*).

yeti *n.* = ABOMINABLE SNOWMAN.

yew *n.* **1** any dark-leaved evergreen coniferous tree or shrub of the genus *Taxus*, historically planted in churchyards. **2** its wood, used in cabinetmaking.

YHVH see TETRAGRAMMATON.

Yid *n. slang offensive* a Jew.

Yiddish ● *n.* a vernacular used by Jews in or from central and eastern Europe, originally a German dialect with words from Hebrew and several modern languages, and written using Hebrew characters. ● *adj.* of or relating to this language.

yield ● *v.* **1** *tr. & intr.* produce or return as a fruit, profit, or result. **2** *tr.* give up; surrender, concede; comply with a demand for (*yielded the fortress*). **3** *intr.* (often foll. by *to*) **a** surrender; make submission. **b** give consent or change one's course of action in deference to. **4** *intr.* (foll. by *to*) be inferior or confess inferiority to (*I yield to none in understanding the problem*). **5** *intr.* (foll. by *to*) give right-of-way to other traffic. ● *n.* **1** an amount yielded or produced; an output. **2** the income produced by an investment. □ **yielder** *n.*

yielding *adj.* **1** compliant, submissive. **2** (of a substance) able to bend; not stiff or rigid.

yikes *interj. slang* an expression of surprise.

yin *n.* (in Chinese philosophy) the passive female principle of the universe (*compare* YANG).

yin-yang *n.* the harmonious interaction of the female and male forces of the universe.

yin-yang symbol *n.* a circle divided by an S-shaped line into a dark and a light segment, representing respectively yin and yang.

yip *v. & n. N Amer.* (**yipped, yipping**) = YELP.

yippee *interj.* expressing delight or excitement.

yippie *n.* (also **Yippie**) a member of a group of politically active hippies.

YMCA *abbr.* Young Men's Christian Association.

YMHA *abbr.* Young Men's Hebrew Association.

yo *interj. slang* used to greet someone or get their attention.

yod *n.* **1** the tenth and smallest letter of the Hebrew alphabet. **2** the semi-vowel /j/, which has the sound of the letter yod.

yodel /ˈjoːdəl/ ● *v.tr. & intr.* (**-delled, -delling** or **-deled, -deling**) sing with melodious inarticulate sounds and frequent changes between falsetto and the normal voice, in the manner of Swiss and Tyrolean mountaineers. ● *n.* a yodelling cry. □ **yodeller** *n.*

yoga /ˈjoːgə/ *n.* **1** a Hindu system of philosophic meditation and asceticism designed to effect reunion with the universal spirit. **2** a system of esp. posture and breathing exercises used to attain control of the body and mind. **3** = HATHA YOGA. □ **yogic** /ˈjoːgɪk/ *adj.*

yogh /jʊg/ *n.* a Middle English letter used for certain values of *g* and *y*.

yogi /ˈjoːgi/ *n.* a person proficient in yoga.

yogourt *n.* (also **yoghurt, yogurt**) a semi-solid slightly tart food prepared from milk fermented by added bacteria, usu. flavoured with fruit.

yoke ● *n.* **1** a wooden crosspiece fastened over the necks of two oxen etc. and attached to the plow or wagon to be drawn. **2** (*pl.* same or **-s**) a pair (of oxen etc.). **3** an object like a yoke in form or function, e.g. a wooden bar held across the shoulders for carrying a pair of pails. **4** a fitted part of a garment, usu. placed across the shoulders or around the hips, from which the rest hangs. **5** sway, dominion, or servitude, esp. when oppressive. **6** a bond or union, esp. that of marriage. **7** (in an airplane) a double handle somewhat resembling a steering wheel, by which the elevators are controlled. ● *v.* **1** *tr.* put a yoke on. **2** *tr.* couple or unite (a pair). **3** *tr.* (foll. by *to*) link (one thing) to (another). **4** *intr.* match or work together.

yokel /ˈjoːkəl/ *n.* a country bumpkin.

yolk *n.* **1** the yellow inner part of an egg that nourishes the young before it hatches. **2** *Biol.* the corresponding part of any animal ovum. □ **yolked** *adj.* (also in *comb.*). **yolky** *adj.*

Yom Kippur /jɒm kɪˈpʊr/ *n.* the most solemn Jewish religious holiday, eight days after the Jewish New Year, marked by fasting and repentance.

yon /jɒn/ *adj. & adv.* yonder.

yonder ● *adv.* over there; at some distance in that direction. ● *adj.* situated yonder. ● *n.* the distance; a remote place (*the wild blue yonder*).

yoof /juːf/ *n. esp. Brit. slang* youth; young people collectively.

yoo-hoo *interj.* used to attract a person's attention.

yore *n. literary* □ **of yore** formerly; in or of old days.

York boat *n. Cdn hist.* a type of large, shallow-draft inland cargo boat used esp. in the Prairies.

Yorkshire pudding *n.* a puffy baked mixture of flour, eggs, and milk, usu. eaten with roast beef.

Yoruba /ˈjɔːrʊbə/ ● *n.* **1** (*pl.* **-s** or same) a member of an African people inhabiting the west coast, esp. Nigeria. **2** the language of this people. ● *adj.* of or relating to the Yorubas or their language.

you ● *pron.* (*obj.* **you**; *possess.* **your, yours**) **1** used with reference to the person or persons addressed or one such person and one or more associated persons. **2** (with a noun) in an exclamatory statement (*you fools!*). **3** (in general statements) one, a person, anyone, or everyone (*it's hard work, but you get used to it*). ● *n.* the personality or essential nature of the person or persons being addressed (*that dress just isn't you*). □ **you and yours** you together with your family, property, etc.

you-all *pron. US informal* you; all of you.

you'd *contraction* **1** you had. **2** you would.

you-know-what *n.* (also **you-know-who**) a thing or person unspecified but understood.

you'll *contraction* you will; you shall.

young ● *adj.* (**younger, youngest**) **1** not far advanced in life, development, or existence; not yet old. **2 a** immature or inexperienced. **b** youthful; felt in or characteristic of youth (*young love*). **4** representing young people (*Young Liberals*). **5** distinguishing a son from his father (*young Jones*). **6** (**younger**) distinguishing one person from another of the same name (*the younger Pitt*). ● *n.* (*collect.*) offspring, esp. of animals before or soon after birth. □ **with young** (of an animal) pregnant. □ **youngish** *adj.*

young blood *n. see* BLOOD.

young lady *n.* **1** a young (esp. unmarried) woman. **2** a girl.

young man *n.* **1** a man who is young. **2** a boy.

young offender *n.* a young criminal, esp. (in Canada) one older than 12 and younger than 18.

young person *n. Law* a young man or young woman.

youngster *n.* a child or young person.

young thing *n. archaic* or *informal* an indulgent term for a young person.

Young Turk *n.* **1** a member of a group of reformers in the Ottoman Empire who carried out the revolution of 1908. **2** a young person eager for radical change to the established order. **3** (**young turk**) *offensive* a violent child or youth.

young 'un *n. informal* a youngster.

young woman *n.* a woman who is young.

your *possess.adj.* (*attrib.*) **1** of or belonging to you or yourself or yourselves (*your house*). **2** (**Your**) (in titles) that you are (*Your Majesty*). **3** *informal* usu. derogatory much talked of; well known (*why not ask your self-styled 'expert'*). **4** belonging to or associated with an unspecified person (*the second door on your left*).

you're *contraction* you are.

yours *possess.pron.* **1** the one or ones belonging to or associated with you (*it is yours*; *yours are over there*). **2** your letter (*yours of the 10th*). **3** introducing a formula ending a letter (*yours ever*). □ **of yours** of or belonging to you (*a friend of yours*).

yourself *pron.* (*pl.* **yourselves**) **1 a** *emphatic form of* YOU. **b** *refl. form of* YOU. **2** in your normal state of body or mind (*are quite yourself again*). □ **be yourself** act in your normal, unconstrained manner.

yours truly *n. informal* myself, me; I (*has a picture of yours truly on the cover*). □ **yours truly** used as a conventional formula preceding a signature.

youse /juːz/ *pron.* (also **yous**) *dialect* or *informal* you (usu. more than one person). ¶Generally considered unacceptable in writing or cultivated speech.

youth *n.* (*pl.* **youths** /juːðz/) **1** the state of being young; the period between childhood and adult age. **2** the vigour or enthusiasm, inexperience, or other characteristic of this period. **3** an early stage of development etc. **4** a young person. **5** (treated as *pl.*) young people collectively.

youth court *n. N Amer.* a court which has jurisdiction over all cases involving young offenders or youths.

youthful *adj.* **1** young, esp. in appearance or manner. **2** having the characteristics of youth (*youthful impatience*). **3** having the freshness of youth (*a youthful complexion*). □ **youthfully** *adv.* **youthfulness** *n.*

youth hostel *n.* a place where (esp. young) travellers can stay cheaply for the night. □ **youth hosteller** *n.*

you've *contraction* you have.

yowl ● *n.* a loud wailing cry of or as of a cat or dog in pain or distress. ● *v.intr.* utter a yowl.

yo-yo ● *n.* (*pl.* **yo-yos**) **1** a toy consisting of a pair of discs with a deep groove between them in which string is attached and wound, and which can be spun alternately downward and upward by its weight and momentum as the string unwinds and rewinds. **2** a thing that repeatedly falls and rises again. **3** *slang* a stupid or incompetent person. ● *adj.* characterized by repeated upward and downward movement, fluctuation, etc. ● *v.intr.* (**yo-yoes**, **yo-yoed**) **1** play with a yo-yo. **2** fall and rise; fluctuate.

yo-yo dieting *n.* repeatedly dieting and then regaining the weight so lost. □ **yo-yo dieter** *n.*

yr. *abbr.* **1** year(s). **2** your.

yrs. *abbr.* **1** years. **2** yours.

YST *abbr.* YUKON STANDARD TIME.

YT *abbr.* **1** Yukon Territory. **2** YUKON TIME.

YTD *abbr.* year to date.

ytterbium /ɪˈtɜːbɪəm/ *n.* a silvery metallic element occurring naturally as various isotopes.

yttrium /ˈɪtrɪəm/ *n.* a greyish metallic element resembling the lanthanides, occurring naturally in uranium ores and used in making superconductors.

yuan /juˈɒn/ *n.* (*pl.* same) the chief monetary unit of China.

yucca /ˈjʌkə/ *n.* any N American white-flowered plant of the genus *Yucca*, with sword-like leaves.

yuck¹ *slang* ● *interj.* an expression of strong distaste or disgust. ● *n.* something messy or repellent.

yuck² *var. of* YUK¹.

yucky *adj.* (**-ier, -iest**) *slang* **1** messy, repellent. **2** sickly, sentimental. **3** distasteful, contemptible.

Yugoslav /ˈjuːɡəˌslɒv, -slæv/ (also **Yugoslavian**) ● *n.* **1** a native or national of Yugoslavia, a country in SE Europe. **2** a person of Yugoslav descent. ● *adj.* of or relating to Yugoslavia or its people.

yuk¹ *informal* ● *v.tr. & intr.* **1** laugh heartily. **2** fool around (*yuk it up*). ● *n.* **1** a hearty laugh. **2** something, such as a joke, that causes hearty laughter.

yuk² *var. of* YUCK¹.

yukata /joˈkætə/ *n.* a light cotton kimono, frequently with stencil designs, worn after a bath or as a housecoat.

yukky *var. of* YUCKY.

Yukoner *n.* a native or inhabitant of the Yukon Territory.

Yukon Gold *n.* a large, yellow-fleshed, smooth-skinned, early-maturing variety of potato.

Yukon Standard Time *n.* = PACIFIC STANDARD TIME (see PACIFIC TIME).

Yukon stove *n. Cdn* (*North*) a simple stove for cooking and heating, esp. an oil drum on legs.

Yukon Time *n.* = PACIFIC TIME.

yule *n.* (in full **yuletide**) *archaic* or *literary* the Christmas festival.

yule log *n.* **1** a large log burned in the hearth on Christmas Eve. **2** a log-shaped rolled cake eaten at Christmas, usu. with icing resembling bark.

yum *interj.* (also **yum-yum**) expressing pleasure from eating or the prospect of eating.

yummy *adj.* (**-ier, -iest**) *informal* tasty, delicious.

yup¹ *var. of* YEP.

yup² *n.* = YUPPIE.

Yupik /ˈjuːpɪk/ ● *n.* **1** a member of a group of Aboriginal peoples living in coastal areas of Alaska and NE Siberia. **2** any of the languages spoken by the Yupik. ● *adj.* of or relating to this people.

yuppie *n.* (*pl.* **-ies**) *informal*, usu. *derogatory* a young, affluent, middle-class professional person, esp. one working in a city and characterized by careerism and desire for trendy status symbols. □ **yuppiedom** *n.*

yuppify *v.tr.* (**-ies, -ied**) (esp. as **yuppified** *adj.*) *informal* make characteristic of yuppies. □ **yuppification** *n.*

yurt /jɔːt, jɜːt/ *n.* **1** a circular tent of felt, skins, etc., on a collapsible framework, used by nomads in Mongolia and Siberia. **2** a semi-subterranean hut, usu. of timber covered with earth or turf.

YWCA *abbr.* Young Women's Christian Association.

YWHA *abbr.* Young Women's Hebrew Association.

Zz

Z /zed, zi:/ *n.* (also **z**) (*pl.* **Zs** or **Z's**) **1** the twenty-sixth letter of the alphabet. **2** (usu. **z**) *Algebra* the third unknown quantity. **3** *Math.* the third coordinate. **4** *Chem.* atomic number.

zabaglione /ˌzɒbɒˈljoːnei/ *n.* a dessert consisting of egg yolks, sugar, and (esp. Marsala) wine whipped to a frothy texture over low heat, served warm or cold.

zaftig /ˈzæftɪɡ/ *adj.* N Amer. informal (of a woman) plump; having a full, rounded figure.

zag ● *n.* a sharp change of direction in a zigzag course. ● *v.intr.* (**zagged, zagging**) perform a zag.

Zairean /zɒˈiːrɪən/ (also **Zairian**) ● *n.* **1** a native or inhabitant of Zaire (now Congo) in central Africa. **2** a person of Zairean descent. ● *adj.* of or relating to Zaire (now Congo) or its people.

Zambian /ˈzæmbɪən/ ● *n.* **1** a native or inhabitant of Zambia in central Africa. **2** a person of Zambian descent. ● *adj.* of or relating to Zambia or its people.

Zamboni /ˌzæmˈboːni/ *n.* proprietary a tractor-like machine for shaving the ice of a rink and spraying water on it to provide a clean smooth surface.

zany ● *adj.* (**-ier, -iest**) comically idiotic; crazily ridiculous. ● *n.* (*pl.* **-ies**) a foolish or eccentric person; a buffoon. □ **zanily** *adv.* **zaniness** *n.*

zap slang ● *v.* (**zapped, zapping**) **1** *tr.* a kill or destroy; deal a sudden blow to. **b** hit forcibly. **2** *intr. & tr.* a move quickly and vigorously. **b** *intr.* use a remote control to move rapidly between television channels. **3** *tr.* overwhelm emotionally. **4** *tr.* Computing erase or change (a file etc.). **5** a *intr.* (foll. by *through*) fast-forward or rewind a videotape to skip a section. **b** *tr.* delete or skip over (a television commercial or commercials), e.g. by fast-forwarding a videotape. **6** *tr.* N Amer. informal cook (food) in a microwave. ● *n.* **1** energy, vigour. **2** a strong emotional effect. ● *interj.* expressing the sound or impact of a bullet, ray gun, etc., or any sudden event.

zappable /ˈzæpəbəl/ *adj.* informal microwaveable.

zapper *n.* slang **1** a remote control for a television, VCR, etc. **2** a device, person, or technique that kills or does away with something, esp. insects.

zeal *n.* **1** earnestness or fervour in advancing a cause. **2** hearty and persistent endeavour.

zealot /ˈzelət/ *n.* **1** an uncompromising or extreme partisan; a fanatic. **2** (**Zealot**) hist. a member of a Jewish sect in Palestine during the 1st c. AD that advocated overthrowing the Romans. □ **zealotry** *n.*

zealous /ˈzeləs/ *adj.* full of zeal; enthusiastic. □ **zealously** *adv.* **zealousness** *n.*

zebra /ˈziːbrə, ˈzeb-/ *n.* **1** any of various African quadrupeds, esp. *Equus burchelli*, related to the ass and horse, with black and white stripes. **2** (*attrib.*) with alternate dark and pale stripes.

zebra mussel *n.* a tiny mussel of the genus *Dreissena*, which proliferates rapidly and adheres in large numbers to any surface, thus becoming a pest by clogging water intake pipes etc.

zed *n.* Cdn & Brit. the letter Z.

zeda /ˈzeidə/ *n.* (among Jewish people) grandfather.

zee *n.* N Amer. the letter Z. □ **catch** (or **bag**) **some zees** slang get some sleep.

Zeitgeist /ˈtsaɪtgaɪst/ *n.* **1** the spirit of the times. **2** the trend of thought and feeling in a period.

Zen /zen/ *n.* a form of Buddhism emphasizing the value of meditation and intuition. □ **Zenlike** *adj.*

Zend /zend/ *n.* an interpretation of the Avesta, each Zend being part of the Zend-Avesta.

Zend-Avesta *n.* the Zoroastrian sacred writings of the Avesta or text and Zend or commentary.

zenith /ˈziːnɪθ, ˈzen-/ *n.* **1** the part of the celestial sphere directly above an observer (opp. NADIR). **2** the highest or culminating point, e.g. of power.

zeolite /ˈziːəˌlaɪt/ *n.* each of a number of minerals consisting mainly of hydrous silicates of calcium, sodium, and aluminum, able to act as cation exchangers.

zephyr /ˈzefər/ *n.* literary a mild gentle wind or breeze.

Zeppelin /ˈzepəlɪn/ *n.* hist. a large dirigible airship of the early 20th c., originally for military use.

zero ● *n.* (*pl.* **-os**) **1** a the figure 0. **b** no quantity or number; nil. **2** a point on a scale from which a positive or negative quantity is reckoned. **3** (in full **zero hour**) a the hour at which a planned, esp. military, operation is timed to begin. **b** a crucial moment. **4** the lowest point; a nullity or nonentity. ● *adj.* that amounts to zero; no, not any (*zero tolerance*). ● *v.tr.* (**-oes, -oed**) **1** adjust (an instrument etc.) to zero point. **2** set the sights of (a gun) for firing. □ **zero in on 1** take aim at. **2** focus one's attention on.

zero-emission *adj.* designating a motor vehicle which does not emit pollutant gases (*zero-emission vehicles*).

zero gravity *n.* the state or condition in which there is no apparent force of gravity acting on a body.

zero-sum *adj.* (of a game, political situation, etc.) in which whatever is gained by one side is lost by the other so that the net change is always zero.

zero tolerance *n.* a policy of rigorously punishing all infractions against a law, behavioural code, etc., no matter how minor.

zest *n.* **1** piquancy; a stimulating flavour or quality. **2** a keen enjoyment or interest. **b** (often foll. by *for*) relish. **c** gusto. **3** the outer, coloured covering of the peel of a citrus fruit, grated and used as flavouring. □ **zestful** *adj.* **zestfully** *adv.* **zesty** *adj.* (**-ier, -iest**).

zester *n.* a kitchen utensil for obtaining zest from citrus fruit by scraping or peeling.

zeta /ˈziːtə/ *n.* the sixth letter of the Greek alphabet (Z, ζ).

zidovudine /zaiˈdɒvjuːˌdiːn/ *n.* = AZT.

zig ● *n.* an abrupt angled movement, esp. in a zigzag course. ● *v.intr.* (**zigged, zigging**) perform a zig.

ziggurat /ˈzɪɡəˌræt/ *n.* **1** a rectangular stepped tower in ancient Mesopotamia, surmounted by a temple. **2** something having this shape.

zigzag ● *n.* **1** a line or course having abrupt alternate right and left turns. **2** (often in *pl.*) each of these turns. ● *adj.* **1** having the form of a zigzag; alternating right and left. **2** (of sewing machine stitches) produced in a zigzag, used on unfinished edges etc. ● *adv.* with a zigzag course. ● *v.intr.* (**zigzagged, zigzagging**) move in a zigzag course.

zilch *n. esp. N Amer. slang* nothing.

zillion *n. informal* an indefinite large number. □ **zillionth** *adj. & n.*

zillionaire *n. informal* a very rich person.

Zimbabwean /zɪm'bɒbwiən, -weiən/ ● *n.* **1** a native or inhabitant of Zimbabwe, a landlocked country in SE Africa. **2** a person of Zimbabwean descent. ● *adj.* of or relating to Zimbabwe or its people.

zinc *n.* a white metallic element occurring naturally as zinc blende, and used as a component of brass, in galvanizing sheet iron, and in electric batteries.

zinc blende *n. see* BLENDE.

zinc oxide *n.* a powder used as a white pigment and in medicinal ointments.

zine /ziːn/ *n.* (also **'zine**) *informal* a magazine, esp. a fanzine.

Zinfandel /'zɪnfændəl/ *n.* **1** a red, white, or rosé wine made esp. in California. **2** the black grape from which this is made.

zing *informal* ● *n.* **1** vigour, energy. **2** a short, high-pitched buzzing or ringing sound, as of a bullet moving through the air. **3** zest, liveliness (*lemon juice adds zing to this cheesecake*). ● *v.* **1** *intr.* move swiftly or with a shrill sound. **2** *tr. N Amer.* criticize or rebuke (a person) severely. □ **zingy** *adj.* (**-ier, -iest**).

zinger *n. esp. N Amer. slang* **1** a witty or pointed remark. **2** an unexpected turn of events or piece of news. **3** an outstanding person or thing.

zinnia /'zɪnjə/ *n.* a composite plant of the chiefly Mexican genus *Zinnia*, with showy flowers.

Zion /'zaiən/ *n.* **1** Jerusalem; allegorically, the heavenly city or kingdom of heaven. **2** the Jewish religion or people. **3** the region of Palestine as the Jewish homeland and as the symbol of Judaism. **4** the Christian Church.

Zionism *n.* a movement orig. for the re-establishment and now the development of a Jewish nation in what is now Israel. □ **Zionist** *n.*

zip ● *n.* **1** a light fast sound, as of a bullet passing through air. **2** energy, vigour. **3** zest (*these chili peppers have a lot of zip!*). **4** *N Amer. informal* nothing, zero; zilch. **5** *esp. Brit.* **a** (in full **zip fastener**) = ZIPPER *n.* **b** (*attrib.*) having a zipper (*zip bag*). ● *v.* (**zipped, zipping**) **1** *tr. & intr.* (often foll. by *up*) fasten with a zipper. **2** *intr.* move with zip or at high speed. **3** *tr. Computing* compress (a file or files).

Zip code *n. US proprietary* a system of postal codes consisting of five- or nine-digit numbers.

zip gun *n. N Amer. informal* a cheap homemade or make-shift gun.

zip-lock *adj. N Amer.* designating a plastic bag with a special strip along the open edges that can be sealed shut by pressing and readily reopened or resealed.

zipper *esp. N Amer.* ● *n.* a fastening device of two flexible strips with interlocking projections closed or opened by pulling a slide along them. ● *v.tr.* **1** (often foll. by *up*) fasten with a zipper. **2** provide with a zipper. □ **zippered** *adj.*

zippo *n. N Amer. informal* = ZIP *n.* 4.

zippy *adj.* (**-ier, -iest**) *informal* **1** bright, fresh, lively. **2** fast, speedy. □ **zippily** *adv.* **zippiness** *n.*

zip-up *attrib.adj.* able to be fastened with a zip fastener.

zircon /'zɜːkɒn/ *n.* a zirconium silicate of which some translucent varieties are cut into gems.

zirconia /zɜːˈkoːniə/ *n.* zirconium dioxide, used in

ceramics, refractory coatings, etc., and in fused form as a synthetic substitute for diamonds in jewellery.

zirconium *n.* a grey metallic element occurring in zircon and used in various industrial applications.

zit *n. esp. N Amer. slang* a pimple.

zither /'zɪðər/ *n.* a musical instrument consisting of a flat wooden sound box with numerous strings stretched across it, placed horizontally.

zizz *informal* ● *n.* **1** a whizzing or buzzing sound. **2** a short sleep. ● *v.intr.* **1** make a whizzing sound. **2** doze or sleep.

zloty /'zlɒti/ *n.* (*pl.* same or **zlotys**) the chief monetary unit of Poland.

Zn *symbol* zinc.

zodiac *n.* **1 a** a belt of the heavens within about 8° of the ecliptic, including all apparent positions of the sun, moon, and most familiar planets, and divided into twelve parts (signs) named after constellations and used in astrology. **b** a diagram of these signs. **2** (**Zodiac**) *proprietary* a kind of inflatable rubber dinghy, esp. one powered by an outboard motor.

zodiacal /zə'daiəkəl/ *adj.* of or in the zodiac.

zombie *n.* **1** *informal* a dull, apathetic, or exceedingly tired person. **2** a corpse said to be revived by witchcraft. **3** *Cdn slang* (during World War II) a conscript, orig. for national defence as opposed to overseas service. **4** a drink consisting of several kinds of rum mixed with fruit juice and sugar. □ **zombielike** *adj.* **zombified** *adj.* **zombify** *v.tr.*

zone ● *n.* **1** an area having particular features, properties, purpose, or use. **2 a** an area between two exact or approximate concentric circles. **b** a part of the surface of a sphere enclosed between two parallel planes, or of a cone or cylinder etc., between such planes cutting it perpendicularly to the axis. **3** (in full **time zone**) a range of longitudes where a common standard time is used. **4** *Geol. etc.* a range between specified limits of depth, height, etc., esp. a section of strata distinguished by characteristic fossils. **5** *Geog.* any of five divisions of the earth bounded by circles parallel to the equator. **6** an encircling band or stripe distinguishable in colour, texture, or character from the rest of the object encircled. ● *v.tr.* **1** encircle as or with a zone. **2** arrange or distribute by zones. **3 a** divide (a city, land, etc.) into areas subject to particular planning restrictions. **b** designate (a specific area) for use or development in this manner. □ **zone out** *N Amer. slang* lose concentration; cease paying attention. □ **zonal** *adj.* **zoning** *n.* (in sense 3 of *v.*).

zonk *slang* ● *v.* **1** *tr.* hit or strike. **2** (foll. by *out*) **a** *tr.* overcome, knock out. **b** *intr.* fall heavily asleep. ● *n.* (often as *interj.*) the sound of heavy impact.

zoo *n.* **1** a place where wild animals are kept for exhibition to the public, breeding, study, etc. **2** any busy, noisy place (*it's a zoo in the lobby*). **3** a diverse or motley collection of people or things.

zoo- /'zuːə, 'zoːə/ *comb. form* of animals or animal life.

zoogeographical /ˌzuːədʒiəˈgræfɪkəl, ˌzoːə-/ *adj.* pertaining to the geographical distribution of animals.

zookeeper *n.* a person employed in a zoo to care for the animals.

zoology /zuːˈɒlədʒi, zoː-/ *n.* the scientific study of animals, esp. with reference to their structure, physiology, classification, and distribution. □ **zoologist** *n.* **zoological** *adj.* **zoologically** *adv.*

zoom ● *v.* **1** *intr.* move quickly, esp. with a low-pitched humming or buzzing sound. **2** *intr. & tr.* cause (an airplane) to mount at high speed and a steep angle. **3**

intr. alter the field of view of a camera by varying the focal length of a zoom lens, esp. (foll. by *in (on)*) so as to close up on a subject without losing focus. **4** *intr.* (of prices, costs, etc.) rise sharply. ● *n.* **1** a zooming camera shot. **2** (in full **zoom lens**) a lens with a variable focal length.

zooplankton /ˌzuːəˈplæŋktən, zoːə-/ *n.* the animal component of plankton, consisting of small animals and the immature stages of larger animals.

zoot suit *n. informal* a man's suit of an exaggerated style popular in the 1940s, characterized by a long draped jacket with padded shoulders and high-waisted tapering trousers. □ **zoot-suited** *adj.*

Zoroastrian /ˌzɔːroːˈæstriən/ ● *adj.* of or relating to the Persian prophet Zoroaster (or Zarathustra; *c.*628– *c.*551 BC) or the dualistic religious system taught by him or his followers in the Zend-Avesta, based on the concept of a conflict between a spirit of good and a spirit of evil. ● *n.* a follower of Zoroaster. □ **Zoroastrianism** *n.*

zouk /zuːk/ *n.* an exuberant style of popular music, originating in the Antilles, combining Caribbean and Western elements and characterized by a strong fast beat derived from Antillean drumming.

zowie *interj. N Amer.* expressing astonishment, admiration, or delight.

ZPG *abbr.* zero population growth.

Zr *symbol* zirconium.

zucchini /zuːˈkiːni/ *n.* (*pl.* same or **-s**) esp. *N Amer.* & *Austral.* a green-skinned summer squash, similar in appearance to a cucumber.

Zulu /ˈzuːluː/ ● *n.* **1** a member of a Bantu-speaking people forming the largest ethnic group in South Africa. **2** the language of this people. ● *adj.* of or relating to the Zulus or their language.

Zuni /ˈzuːni, ˈzuːnji/ (also **Zuñi** /ˈzuːnji/) ● *n.* **1** a member of a Pueblo people of New Mexico. **2** the language of this people. ● *adj.* of or relating to the Zuni or their language.

Zyban /ˈzaɪbæn/ *n. proprietary* an antidepressant drug, bupropion, used as an aid in quitting smoking.

zygote /ˈzaɪɡoːt/ *n. Biol.* a cell formed by the union of two gametes; a fertilized ovum.

zzz *interj.* imitating the sound of snoring.

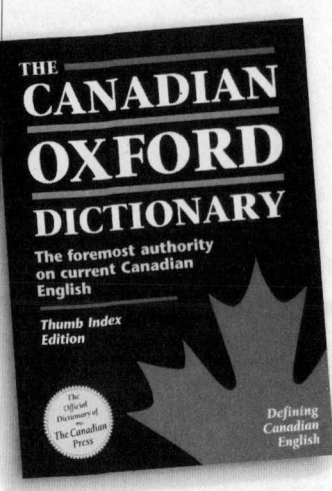

List of Abbreviations

Abbreviations in general use (such as etc., i.e.) are explained in the dictionary itself. Some abbreviations may appear in italics.

abbr.	abbreviation	hist.	with historical reference	poss.	possessive
absol.	absolute(ly)			prec.	preceded
adj.	adjective	hyph.	hyphen, hyphenated	predic.	predicative
adv.	adverb			prep.	preposition
Amer.	America(n)			pres.	present
Anat.	Anatomy	imper.	imperative	pron.	pronoun
Anglo-Ind.	Anglo-Indian	Ind.	Indian (of the Indian subcontinent)	pronunc.	pronunciation
Archit.	Architecture			Psych.	Psychology
attrib.	attributive(ly)				
attrib.adj.	attributive adjective	infin.	infinitive	ref.	reference
		interj.	interjection	refl.	reflexive
Austral.	Australia, Australian	interrog.	interrogative	rel.	related, relative
		intr.	intransitive	rel.adj.	relative adjective
aux.	auxiliary				
		masc.	masculine	rel.adv.	relative adverb
Biochem.	Biochemistry	Math.	Mathematics	rel.pron.	relative pronoun
Biol.	Biology	Mech.	Mechanics		
Bot.	Botany	Med.	Medicine	Rom.	Roman
Brit.	British, in British use	Meteorol.	Meteorology		
		Mineral.	Mineralogy	Scand.	Scandinavian
				Scot.	Scottish
c.	century	n.	noun	sing.	singular
c.	circa	N Amer.	North America(n)	Stock Exch.	Stock Exchange
Cdn	Canada, Canadian			subj.	subjunctive
		Naut.	Nautical		
Chem.	Chemistry, Chemical	neg.	negative	Theol.	Theology
		neut.	neuter	tr.	transitive
collect.	collective(ly)	n.pl.	noun plural		
comb.	combination, combining	NZ	New Zealand	US	American, in American use
compl.	complement	obj.	objective	usu.	usually
conj.	conjunction	opp.	opposite (of), (as) opposed (to)		
Crystallog.	Crystallography			v.	verb
		orig.	origin, original(ly)	var.	variant(s)
Econ.	Economics			v.aux.	auxiliary ve[rb]
ellipt.	elliptical(ly)			v.intr.	intransitive
Engin.	Engineering	Parl.	Parliament	v.refl.	reflexive ve[rb]
esp.	especial(ly)	part.	participle	v. tr.	transitive [verb]
		pers.	person(al)		
fem.	feminine	Pharm.	Pharmacology	Zool.	Zoology
foll.	followed, following	Philos.	Philosophy		
		Photog.	Photography		
		phr.	phrase		
Geog.	Geography	Physiol.	Physiology		
Geol.	Geology	pl.	plural		
Geom.	Geometry	poet.	poetical		
Gk	Greek	Polit.	Politics		